CONCORDANCE
TO THE BOOK OF CONCORD

CONCORDANCE
TO THE BOOK OF CONCORD

Editor
Kenneth E. Larson

Computer Programmer
James R. Schoech

The text of *The Book of Concord* is used for this
concordance with the permission of Fortress Press.

NORTHWESTERN PUBLISHING HOUSE
Milwaukee, Wisconsin

Library of Congress Card 89-50415

Northwestern Publishing House

1250 N. 113th St., P. O. Box 26975, Milwaukee, WI 53226-0975

© 1989 by Northwestern Publishing House.

Published 1989

Printed in the United States of America

ISBN 0-8100-0313-9

DEDICATION

In loving memory of our daughter, Renee

Errata to *Concordance to The Book of Concord*

PAGE	WORD	SYM	ART	PARA	Page (Tapp)	Number [Trig]	WORD(S) IN ERROR	CORRECTION
14	agree	AP	12	002	(182)	[0253]	confutation	Confutation
38	beheld	:	:		( )	[ ]	Word Count in error	Beheld (3), Behold (11),
39	beheld	SD	01	036	(514)	[0869]	behold	beheld
39	beheld	SD	01	036	(514)	[0869]	uniformed	unformed
39	being	:	:		( )	[ ]	missing lines	add the following

Being (29) (noun)

		SYM	ART	PARA	Page (Tapp)	Number [Trig]	
		PR	PR	024	(13)	[0021]	of the disputes which have arisen should come into **being**.
		AG	28	041	(87)	[0089]	regulations came into **being**—for example, that it is a
		AL	18	006	(40)	[0053]	through him that all these things come into **being** and are.
		AP	04	061	(115)	[0137]	knowledge, we must tell how faith comes into **being**.
		AP	04	262	(145)	[0195]	terrors of sin, a human **being** must have a very definite
		AP	07	014	(170)	[0231]	about physical well-**being**, political affairs, etc. in
		AP	18	008	(226)	[0337]	said before, it comes into **being** when terrified hearts.
		S3	03	000	(303)	[0479]	to God, for no human **being** will be justified in his sight
		LC	01	089	(377)	[0605]	regulate our whole life and **being** according to God's Word.
		LC	02	009	(412)	[0679]	than one God, it may be asked: "What kind of **being** is God?
		EP	01	000	(466)	[0779]	and best part of his **being** (that is, his rational soul in
		EP	07	012	(483)	[0811]	No other human **being**, no angel, but only Mary's Son, is so
		EP	07	014	(483)	[0811]	and knows various modes of **being** at a given place, and not
		SD	RN	009	(505)	[0855]	and that no human **being**'s writings dare be put on a par
		SD	01	023	(512)	[0865]	fall man's nature and **being** are wholly corrupted, "but
		SD	01	030	(513)	[0867]	nature of every human **being** born in the natural way from a
		SD	01	048	(517)	[0875]	corrupted nature or substance or **being** and original sin.
		SD	07	076	(583)	[0999]	No human **being**, but only Christ himself who was crucified
		SD	07	098	(586)	[1005]	modes, or all three modes, of **being** at any given place.
		SD	07	102	(587)	[1007]	be where God is and that this mode of **being** is a fiction
		SD	08	010	(593)	[1019]	hand, to be a corporeal **being** or a creature, to be flesh
		SD	08	024	(595)	[1023]	a mere, ordinary human **being**, but a human being who is
		SD	08	024	(595)	[1023]	human being, but a human **being** who is truly the Son of the
		SD	08	029	(597)	[1025]	No other human **being** can do this, since no human being is
		SD	08	029	(597)	[1025]	do this, since no human **being** is united in this manner
		SD	08	069	(604)	[1039]	majesty, which as a human **being** and according to his human
		SD	08	076	(606)	[1043]	man and no other human **being** in heaven and on earth can
		SD	08	077	(606)	[1043]	such presence only to Christ, and to no other human **being**.
		SD	08	085	(608)	[1047]	me, Jesus of Nazareth, Mary's son, born a human **being**.

PAGE	WORD	SYM	ART	PARA	Page (Tapp)	Number [Trig]	WORD(S) IN ERROR	CORRECTION
42	belongs	AP	07	035	(175)	[0239]	substances	substance
70	Christ	AP	07	035	(175)	[0239]	substances	substance
78	Christian	LC	04	081	(446)	[0751]	Church	church
159	entered	LC	04	081	(446)	[0751]	Church	church
168	examination	TR	00	051	(329)	[0519]	examinations	examination
174	eyes	SD	01	036	(514)	[0869]	behold	beheld
174	eyes	SD	01	036	(514)	[0869]	uniformed	unformed
174	Faber	TR	00	082	(335)	[0529]	Wendel	Wendal
192	first	LC	02	010	(412)	[0681]	first	First
202	formulated	SD	PR	004	(502)	[0847]	Church	church
225	God	SD	PR	004	(502)	[0847]	Church	church
242	great	SD	PR	004	(502)	[0847]	Church	church
258	holy	LC	02	034	(415)	[0687]	Church	church
294	know	:	:		( )	[ ]	Word Count in error	Know (241)
296	know	LC	06	001	(457)	[0000]	Up to now, as we all **know** from experience there has	add entire line
329	Mansfeld	TR	00	082	(335)	[0529]	Wendel	Wendal
336	mention	AP	22	010	(237)	[0359]	confutation	Confutation
374	order	AP	04	084	(119)	[0145]	. . . promise may be	remove "be"
381	participation	SD	07	054	(579)	[0991]	we bread	we break
383	pastor	TR	00	082	(335)	[0529]	Wendel	Wendal
385	pay	LC	03	121	(436)	[0731]	delusion when people pay in such a way that they dare	remove entire line
389	people	LC	03	121	(436)	[0731]	pay	pray
406	Pray	:	:		( )	[ ]	Word Count in error	Pray (123)
406	pray	LC	03	121	(436)	[0731]	delusion when people **pray** in such a way that they dare	add line
439	regeneration	SD	02	024	(525)	[0891]	In his conversion	In his own conversion
491	slavery	EP	10	006	(493)	[0829]	Gal. 5:11	Gal. 5:1
499	Spirit	LC	02	034	(415)	[0687]	Church	church
508	substance	SD	01	036	(514)	[0869]	behold	beheld
508	substance	SD	01	036	(514)	[0869]	uniformed	unformed
514	take	:	:		( )	[ ]	Word Court in error	Take (179), Taken (64),
515	taken	LC	01	270	(401)	[0657]	take	taken
547	unformed	SD	01	036	(514)	[0869]	behold	beheld
562	way	AP	12	002	(182)	[0253]	confutation	Confutation

TABLE OF CONTENTS

FOREWORD

It is a distinct privilege to write the foreword to the *Concordance to The Book of Concord*, prepared by Rev. Kenneth Larson. I remember years ago talking to my dear colleague, Arthur Carl Piepkorn, at the St. Louis Seminary, about the need for such a concordance. Both he and I taught the Confessions regularly at the St. Louis Seminary. He replied at that time that such a monumental piece of work was not possible, and he was right. But now with the tremendous advance in computer technology, the great desire of Dr. Piepkorn, and the desire of so many of the rest of us who are students of the Lutheran Confessions, has come to pass. The *Concordance to The Book of Concord* will be an invaluable aid to both professional and ordinary students of the Lutheran Confessions. I have already used it to great advantage in a book that I am scheduled to be writing on the topic of Sacred Scripture.

Members of the Lutheran Church-Missouri Synod and of the former Synodical Conference may wonder why the Tappert text was the preferred choice from which to make a concordance. The reason is quite simple. Even in Missouri Synod circles the Tappert text is the one the overwhelming number of students have been using for the last twenty years. The *Triglotta*, however, is referenced as well, which will enable older pastors and those who want to check the Latin and German the opportunity to use the concordance to great advantage as well. The reference to the Article and Paragraph, of course, make any edition of the Confessions or translation of the Confessions compatible with the concordance itself. I wish to commend Pastor Larson for the weighty undertaking and for this new and excellent contribution to confessional Lutheran studies.

Robert Preus, President
Concordia Theological Seminary
Fort Wayne, Indiana

PREFACE

Development of Concept and Brief History of Work

The idea to use a computer for word studies in the Lutheran Confessions stems from two basic sources.

The continuing interest in confessional studies at Concordia Theological Seminary, Fort Wayne, Indiana, provided the motivation. The late Dr. Harry Huth, professor of systematic theology, taught elective courses in which he assigned students to look for every occurrence of a particular word or phrase in the Confessions and determine how it was used. Each student would take a proportional share of the total text and search exhaustively and analytically for that word or phrase. The group would then collate these data into an outline on that topic or word. It was an arduous task requiring careful reading so as not to miss any of the data.

The advances in data processing technology provided the means. Beginning in 1982 the text of the Bible was made available on computer diskettes so that, with the aid of a microcomputer, exhaustive and entirely accurate searches could be made for words or phrases. In a matter of a few minutes, one could compile a list of references for any subject and print them out on paper for further study. Not long after that, the Greek and Hebrew texts were made available for study on diskettes so that one could exhaustively search for any word, phrase or grammatical construction.

The idea for this concordance was born in the office of Dr. Waldemar Degner in January 1984. While he and the editor were marveling over the possible uses of searching the Scriptures by means of a computer, the appearance of Dr. Howard Tepker turned the discussion to the advantages of having the Lutheran Confessions in a format which would allow searches and word studies of the sixteenth century documents.

This synthesis of need and technology was recognized as a project worth exploring. Could *The Book of Concord* be entered into a computer for concordance studies? This idea immediately received the encouragement of many in the academic community.

At that time we also researched similar concordances published through the aid of computer technology. We found that a complete concordance to the Latin edition of *Calvin's Institutes of the Christian Religion* was done in 1972 (Ford L. Battles, Pittsburgh Theological Seminary, 1972).

During the next two years feasibility studies were made to determine the best choices for computer formats, programs, editing and method of input. Scholars in the academic community were surveyed informally to determine needs. Parish pastors rendered their opinions.

Although the input of the English translation in the *Concordia Triglotta* (Concordia Publishing House, St. Louis, 1921) began immediately, a decision was made a year later to input the Tappert edition (*The Book of Concord*, Theodore Tappert, ed.; Fortress Press, Philadelphia, 1959) because of its wider use among English readers. Permission to do this was secured in December 1985.

We received much help from Dr. Eugene Klug, chairman of the department of systematic theology at Concordia Theological Seminary, Fort Wayne. He envisioned a three-prong approach: (1) an exhaustive, complete concordance available on microfiche; (2) an abridged, printed concordance; and (3) a computer-based concordance similar to the Bible on diskettes programs.

Later it seemed that a judicious elimination of words not deemed important for theological studies would lessen the need for an every-word concordance on microfiche.

Because the manual typing of 1,600,000 characters of the Tappert text would be error-prone and time-consuming, a search was made to find an electronic scanner capable of "reading" the Tappert pages directly into computer memory. None was found within the budget of the project. Undoubtedly scanners now coming on the market would have shortened the time for data entry and editing by almost two years.

Technical Description

Those who have in their own studies combined theology with technology may be interested in the process by which the text of *The Book of Concord* was processed to produce this concordance.

An inexpensive word processing program was used to type and edit the entire Tappert text, less footnotes and indexes, for temporary storage on computer diskettes. At first, an Osborne I was available for this process, but the gift of an IBM personal computer made input and editing a great deal more efficient and accurate. Page, article and paragraph

numbers were entered along with the text, using codes which a computer program could recognize.

The first step in editing was done by the spelling checker included in the word processing program. Words unique to *The Book of Concord* were added to the specialized dictionary of that program.

Then four teams of members of Redeemer Lutheran Church, West Palm Beach, Florida, diligently scrutinized computer printouts of the text, carefully comparing them with *The Book of Concord* text. Two complete proofreading iterations were accomplished. Other errors were discovered and corrected in the preliminary output of the actual concordance. This editing proved to be the most time-consuming portion of the project. While the aim was for 100% accuracy, it is likely that human errors remain. We quote from the Preface to *Cruden's Unabridged Concordance to the Old and New Testaments and the Apocrypha*

> [We] adopted every precaution for the attainment of the highest possible degree of accuracy. If defects should still be discovered, their existence will not arise from any deficiency of labour or expense in the execution of the work. (Alexander Cruden, Fleming H. Revell company, Old Tappen, NJ, 1953, page xii).

Feasibility studies were conducted in 1984, using small parts of *The Book of Concord*. A complete concordance to the "Treatise on the Power and Primacy of the Pope" (from the *Triglotta* text) was made available for review to some participants during the January 1985 Symposium on the Lutheran Confessions at the Fort Wayne Seminary.

Permission to use the Tappert text was received in December 1985. Input and editing of that text continued through 1986 and 1987. A computer program searched the entire 1.6 million bytes of data to find 9283 unique words with a total occurrence of 277,529. Since articles and pronouns accounted for more than half of these, it became apparent that a desk-size concordance could be produced with a reduced word list. Finally, a list of 8958 unique words was selected to produce the *Concordance to the Book of Concord*.

One of the most tedious and difficult tasks proved to be the grouping of cognate words. Since the English language has many irregular verbs, and since all forms of these verbs cannot easily be grouped by a computer program, they had to be grouped manually. Most groupings, however, were produced in rough form, using a computer program. These were then scrutinized for other irregularities and edited to the final form.

Decisions were made in some instances to index separately the cognates of certain significant theological words (e.g., justify, justified, justification, etc.) and other words where the sheer volume of entries suggested they not be grouped. In a few cases a single word was divided into two entries (e.g., "Lord" and "lord").

A computer program was written to read the list of selected words and find every occurrence of each word in the text of *The Book of Concord*. That program extracted index data (symbol, article, paragraph and page numbers) and built a context line around each "find." The algorithm used to build the context line took character size into account so that the greatest number of words possible would be provided to the user.

The total output from this program was 112,472 lines of data. Running time to produce the output was spread over several days of processing.

These data (including the necessary codes for typesetting) were scanned and edited for errors, using a computer program that simulated the typesetting process as it printed a final proof copy of 2178 pages. This "final draft" was carefully scrutinized line by line to detect other errors.

After corrections were made, the output was copied onto diskettes and delivered to General Graphics Corporation of Milwaukee, Wisconsin. Under the direction of Northwestern Publishing House, General Graphics personnel used the computer output as input to their computer typesetting equipment to produce the page proofs. This direct method eliminated hundreds of hours of tedious typesetting and proofreading work and greatly reduced the likelihood of introducing new errors. Finally, the page proofs were scanned in order to make other corrections.

Acknowledgements

We acknowledge with great thanks the kind permission of Fortress Press to use the text of *The Book of Concord* for this concordance. We are grateful to Dr. Harold Rast for his guidance in the matter of publication rights.

The editor is indebted to many in both the academic and technical communities for their words of advice and expressions of caution. It is seldom possible to recognize every contribution in a work of

this size and complexity, produced over a long period of time. Let us make these acknowledgements, with sincere apologies and thanks to any we may have inadvertently omitted.

Mr. Conrad Schaefer, Jr. encouraged us in the project and purchased a computer system and software with which the text could be entered, edited and processed.

A donor (who wishes to remain anonymous) made a generous grant making it possible to publish the work at a price considerably below the actual costs of production.

Rev. Larry Burgdorf encouraged us to publish this concordance in a form which would benefit the greatest number of people. His solicitation of the major donor made this possible.

Rev. Douglas Fountain made several suggestions and improvements, including the encouragement to include an index to the *Triglotta* edition. The dreams of using microcomputer technology to study confessional and biblical texts were actively discussed during many mornings on the racquetball court.

Proofreading of the input text demands dedication and precision. Those who scanned every word of every page deserve recognition for their careful labors: Hazel Bentz, Dorothy LaPlante, Olive Kirkman, Lyle and Laura Hilyard, Jeannie Larson, Ruth Willis and Ruth Bowman. Their only payment was to be enriched and informed by this intimate contact with the doctrinal confessions of their church. Another member, Christiana Reese, lent her typing skills to input some of the text.

When it came time to print the final output of the concordance program we were in need of a high-speed printer. Larry Casavant and the Cass Computer Company loaned this necessary piece of hardware.

There would be no concordance to the Lutheran Confessions, if my wife had not been willing to invest many hours carefully and painstakingly typing much of *The Book of Concord* into the computer. Jeannie admits to becoming quite moved by the law and comforted by the gospel which is proclaimed in the confessions of our church. Her encouraging words, and much more, her understanding and patience kept us going during times when the work seemed endless.

The editor also spent many early mornings at the keyboard, entering, correcting and editing data. Numerous utility programs were written to extract and format the text for the appendices, and to aid in the editing. Each correction found by the proof readers was double-checked with the original and entered into subsequent data disks.

One never knows whether such a project will meet with acceptance in the academic community. Those who have made the study of the Lutheran Confessions a major part of their life's work added immeasurably to this project by their unreserved endorsement and encouragement to go ahead with this concordance.

First, the editor must give many thanks to Dr. Robert Preus, president of Concordia Theological Seminary, Fort Wayne, Indiana. His contagious enthusiasm for the Confessions was caught and taught at the seminary. When his interest in the project to produce a concordance was sought, Dr. Preus gave unconditional and enthusiastic support which did not diminish. He quotes Arthur Piepkorn, one of *The Book of Concord* translators, as saying that there should be a concordance to the Concordia, but I doubt we will ever have one.

Dr. Eugene Klug lent early and continued aid to the project with much correspondence and many valuable suggestions. We adopted his proposal to print an abridged concordance of manageable size and cost which would contain all the theologically significant words. (This suggestion all but obviated any need for a microfiche edition indexing all words.)

Legal advice and counsel was provided by Richard Springer at no cost to help form the Center for Confessional-Biblical Studies, Inc. The professional assistance of Donald Pagan on tax and accounting matters was greatly appreciated.

Others who deserve mention for their suggestions and stimulation to persevere in the work include Dr. August Suelflow, director of the Concordia Historical Institute; Rev. Georg Williams, seminary classmate and parish pastor; Dr. Robert Kolb, professor of religion at Concordia College, St. Paul, Minnesota; Dr. Ralph Bohlmann, president of The Lutheran Church-Missouri Synod; Rev. Michael Heusel, parish pastor and racquetball partner; Martin Homan, former professor of theology, Concordia Teachers College, River Forest, Illinois; Ken Schurb, Steve Scheiderer, and many others who wrote to express their interest and give valuable suggestions.

We also want to salute Stephen Lawrenz and Scott Stone, two parish pastors of the Wisconsin Evangelical Lutheran Synod who had begun a similar project but had to abandon it when one of them

took a call to the foreign mission field. They were most helpful in steering us to Northwestern Publishing House where their ideas had gained some interest.

The editor-in-chief of Northwestern Publishing House also comes due for thanks. Rev. Mentor Kujath's patience and help was exactly what was needed, along with a belief that this concordance was worthy of publication. His production manager, Don Beutin, spent many hours bringing this project to completion. In the same way Mary Jean Jacobsen of General Graphics Corp. provided the technical information necessary to allow the computer output of the concordance to be input directly to typesetting equipment.

For the editor and his wife Jeannie the entire venture was a labor of love. We could not have foreseen the immensity of the project, when it was first conceived. We did not know it would involve thousands of hours of work done by dozens of people. Early on, however, we decided that this would be a non-profit venture. No remuneration other than the joy of accomplishment could cover the time invested in this concordance.

The same is true of James Schoech, who wrote the computer programs used in the production of the concordance. He took all the challenges, all the changes, and made the computer respond according to the needs of the project. He is a true servant, after the manner of his father, Rev. W.F. Schoech. When we were struggling with the task of grouping cognate words together, he came up with a program to group them semiautomatically. James also made many valuable improvements in the way the information is displayed. We owe him a debt of gratitude, but we could not ever compensate him for the thousands of dollars worth of programming he gave to the project.

TO THOSE WHO USE THIS CONCORDANCE

Location References. For each context line the users of this concordance will find a group of fourteen letters and numerals indicating the location of that line in the two most popular English editions of the *Book of Concord*.

EXAMPLE:
Adversities (1), Adversity (1)

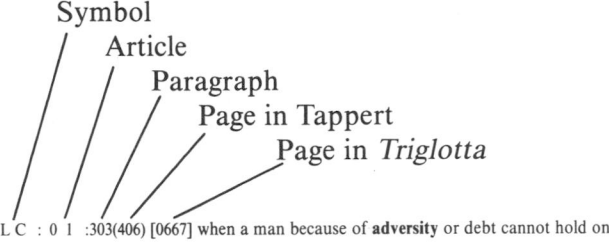

Symbol
Article
Paragraph
Page in Tappert
Page in *Triglotta*

L C : 0 1 :303(406) [0667] when a man because of **adversity** or debt cannot hold on

SYMBOL:ARTICLE:PARAGRAPH (TAPPERT PAGE) [*TRIGLOTTA* PAGE]

In the example the first line is found in the Large Catechism, Article I (that is, the Ten Commandments), in paragraph 303. In the Tappert edition this is found on page 406; or page 667 in the *Triglotta*.

Article Numeration. In all cases the numeration of the Tappert edition is followed. Thus, those making reference to the *Triglotta* may wish to note the difference, or simply use the page and paragraph to find the context line in the *Triglotta* text. However, it will be necessary in any case to note difference in the paragraph numeration (see below).

References to the Smalcald Articles are unique, owing to the division of that document into Parts. The Parts are indicated in the first element of the reference data. The second character (S1, S2, S3) indicates the Part. For example,

S 3 : 0 5 :01(310) [0491] as Augustine puts it, "The Word is **added** to the element

tells us that St. Augustine's quote regarding a sacrament is located in Smalcald Articles, Part 3, Article 5, Paragraph 1, on page 310 (Tappert) and page 491 [*Triglotta*].

The confessional documents are indicated by mnemonic and/or regularly used abbreviations as in the following table:

AG - Augsburg Confession (from the German; top of Tappert page)
AL - Augsburg Confession (from the Latin; bottom of Tappert page)
AP - Apology to the Augsburg Confession
S1 - Smalcald Articles, Part I
S2 - Smalcald Articles, Part II
S3 - Smalcald Articles, Part III
TR - Treatise on the Power and Primacy of the Pope
SC - Small Catechism of Martin Luther
LC - Large Catechism of Martin Luther
EP - Formula of Concord, Epitome
SD - Formula of Concord, Solid Declaration

Paragraph Numeration. Paragraph (section) numbers follow the approximate position of that number in the Tappert text (first full sentence or phrase). This may not always exactly correspond to the position of that paragraph number in the Latin text of the *Triglotta*.

As the Tappert edition does not number the paragraphs in the Preface to *The Book of Concord* (pages 3-16), it will be helpful for the user of this concordance to number each whole paragraph manually, ending with paragraph 27 on page 14 ("In testimony whereof we have...."). The names of those subscribing to *The Book of Concord* are included in paragraph 27.

In most places, the paragraph numbering of the Tappert and *Triglotta* texts are alike. However, where these differ, the Tappert numbering was followed. See, for example, Apology Article IX, Baptism (Tappert page 178; compare *Triglotta* page 244-45). Note also Apology Article XI, Confession (Tappert pages 180-82; compare *Triglotta* pages 246-253); Apology Article XII, Confession and Satisfaction (Tappert pages 197-211; compare *Triglotta* pages 280-309). In the latter case the Tappert includes this Article under Penitence and does not restart the paragraph numeration as does the *Triglotta*. The other large example is Apology, Article IV, Justification. Here again the user making reference to the *Triglotta* is advised to renumber the paragraphs 1-279 on pages 156-227 so that they correspond with Tappert paragraphs 122-400.

This concordance will index any future translation of *The Book of Concord*, as long as the article and

paragraph numbers conform to the Tappert system.

The paragraph numbers for the signatories of the symbols are numbered in the *Triglotta* (e.g. page 95); however, these are not numbered in the Tappert and hence are not given numerals in this concordance.

Context Line. The context line is composed of up to 65 characters showing the word indexed in bold face type. The word indexed is commonly found near the middle of the context line, unless that word is near the beginning or end of a sentence. The context lines are never longer than a sentence. In the case of headings and article titles, the context line may be a mere word or phrase, and have the first letter of each word capitalized in order to distinguish it from the text. Bracketed titles are bracketed in the context line. In most cases the titles have a zero paragraph number.

Italics indicate that the word or phrase is italicized in the Tappert text (usually a title or a Latin phrase, or a question in the Small Catechism).

When one is searching for a particular phrase, it will be helpful to look for it under one of the less common words of that phrase. For example, to find the location of the phrase "worshipping Christ," look under the word group "worship..." (which has 169 references) rather than under "Christ" (which has almost 1900 references).

Since the context lines are listed in order by symbol and article, it is easy to study how (or if) a particular word is used in a single symbol or article. For example, check the word "conversion" in Article 2 (Free Will or Human Powers) of the Formula of Concord. Then note the absence of the word "conversion" in the Large Catechism.

Of course context is the first rule. Especially because words like "not" or "reject" will not always be contained in the context line due to their distance from the indexed word, care must be taken not to quote from this concordance without checking the actual text.

The Text. The entire Tappert text is included, except for the footnotes, which were added by the translators. However, the Bible references from footnotes are included in the Index to Scripture References, Appendix II. It was not possible in a project of this size to include the German or Latin words behind the English translation. Confessional scholars would have fondly wished for such an analytical concordance. Although a few petitioned fervently that this concordance be analytical after the manner of Young's or Strong's biblical concordances to the Scriptures, this would have been too costly in terms of time and scope. Certainly one can use the *Triglotta* page and paragraph references to make an analytical study after locating the desired references with this concordance.

When the German umlaut was encountered, as in some proper names and cities, it was changed to oe, ue, etc. The user should also be aware that there are some differences between the *Triglotta* and the Tappert texts in the way a few proper names are spelled.

A few apparent errors in the Tappert translation became evident in proofreading the text and final output. In most cases, the actual text was corrected. (See, for example Tappert page 151, paragraph 290, where the sentence should read "Then it imagines that this very keeping of the law with*out* Christ, the propitiator...." (The Latin reads "*sine*.")

The apparent duplicates of some lines stem from the fact that *both* English translations of the Augsburg Confession (from the German and the Latin) are included in the text. In some cases the only difference will be the beginning two characters of the location reference (AG or AL, respectively). However, these "duplicate" references will not always be next to one another since the searches were done separately in the two translations.

The Catalog of Testimonies of 1580 (*Triglotta* pages 1105-1149) is not included in the text. Neither are the three Ecumenical Creeds. The absence of these creeds does not, of course, in any way deny their integral part of the Confessions of the Lutheran faith. We trust that these omissions will not prove to be a serious deficiency.

We did, however, include A Brief Exhortation to Confession (Tappert pages 457-461) even though this part of the Large Catechism is not found in the *Triglotta*. Also, the Brentz addition to the subscriptions (*Triglotta* page 529) was added.

Tappert titles are included in the concordance, whether they are part of the text or Dr. Tappert's additions. The fact that this concordance is based on the Tappert text means that the user may not find a particular word known to be in the *Triglotta* text. This unfortunate restriction is, of course, due to the selection of one text, or to the fact that longer Latin or German interpolations (bracketed in the *Triglotta*) were not included in the Tappert translation.

The Appendices. Appendix I provides a list of words not indexed in the *Concordance to The Book of Concord*. Most of these are articles, pronouns, adverbs and prepositions. Had these words not been eliminated, the concordance could not have been economically printed in book form. Every word *not* listed in this appendix is exhaustively searched for and found in the concordance.

Appendix II is an index to Scripture references in *The Book of Concord*. It is a complete index to every mention of a biblical book, whether in the text or in a footnote. The location reference gives both the Tappert and *Triglotta* page numbers, along with symbol, article and paragraph numbers.

FUTURE WORK

It is fondly hoped that suitable arrangements may be made to publish *The Book of Concord* on a set of computer diskettes. This would allow those interested to use a specially designed, easy-to-use program to run extensive concordance studies on the original texts (English, German or Latin). The advent of Compact Disk-Read-only-Memory (CD-ROM) technology would make word and phrase searches unbelievably quick. But even without a CD-ROM, current microcomputer equipment could be used for analytical studies of *The Book of Concord.*

Then too it would be a challenge to those familiar with the critical edition of the *Bekenntnisschriften* to put this valuable work on computer media for exhaustive study.

For those not having access to these texts on a computer of their own, another hope of this editor is to make them available in seminary, college and research libraries where confessional studies are a regularly carried on. Again, the technology exists for scanning these confessional and historical documents directly into computer media, avoiding the time-consuming and error-prone typing and proofreading of texts.

Using what God has wrought through the intelligence and ingenuity which he gives to mankind can help us study the Word and the doctrines drawn from that Word.

It is our fond hope and prayer that this concordance will serve as a useful tool for those who study the doctrines and history of the Lutheran Confessions.

The Editor

Aalen (1)
PR : PR :027(016) [0027] Mayor and Council of the City of **Aalen**.

Abandon (5), Abandoned (2), Abandonment (3)
AP : 2 3 :002(239) [0363] these men do with utter **abandon** cannot even be
AP : 2 7 :046(277) [0435] The **abandonment** of property is neither commanded nor
AP : 2 7 :046(277) [0435] not consist in the **abandonment** of property, but in the
AP : 2 7 :047(277) [0437] Since the **abandonment** of property is therefore merely a
AP : 2 7 :057(279) [0439] therefore it is proper to **abandon** a way of life so full of
S 2 : 0 3 :002(298) [0471] it would be better to **abandon** them or tear them down
TR : 0 0 :041(327) [0517] They ought rather to **abandon** and execrate the pope and
LC : 0 4 :079(446) [0751] and practice what had earlier been begun but **abandoned**.
SD : 0 1 :013(511) [0863] the devil's dominion, **abandoned** to his power, and held
SD : 1 0 :022(615) [1061] They ought rather **abandon** and execrate the pope and

Abased (1), Abasement (2)
AP : 0 7 :035(175) [0241] in promoting rigor of devotion and self-**abasement**."
S 3 : 0 3 :019(306) [0485] and the more he **abased** himself before the priest, the
S 3 : 0 3 :020(306) [0485] rest on his enumeration of sins and on his self-**abasement**.

Abate (1)
LC : 0 1 :032(369) [0589] His wrath does not **abate** until the fourth generation.

ABC (1)
LC : PR :008(359) [0569] begin learning their **ABC**'s, which they think they have

Abduct (1)
SC : 0 1 :020(344) [0543] and so we should not **abduct**, estrange, or entice away

Abel (2)
AP : 0 4 :202(134) [0175] By faith **Abel** offered a more acceptable sacrifice
AP : 2 3 :070(249) [0383] doubt that as the blood of **Abel** cried out in death

Aberrations (4)
SD : RN :004(504) [0851] or chapters against the **aberrations** of heretics, we further
SD : RN :005(504) [0851] Confession against the **aberrations** of the papacy and of
SD : RN :020(508) [0859] and faithfully against all the **aberrations** that have arisen.
SD : 0 1 :026(512) [0867] also be protected against any Manichaean **aberrations**.

Abetted (1), Abetting (1)
LC : 0 1 :182(389) [0631] or word, by signs or gestures, or by aiding and **abetting**.
LC : 0 1 :299(405) [0665] In this we are **abetted** by jurists and lawyers who twist

Abhorrent (1)
EP : 0 7 :041(486) [0817] Capernaitic, and **abhorrent** way concerning the

Abide (25), Abiding (11)
PR : PR :008(005) [0009] intention to remain and **abide** loyally by the truth once
PR : PR :008(006) [0011] their eternal welfare to **abide** by it and persist in it in a
PR : PR :025(014) [0023] of the Holy Spirit to **abide** and remain unanimously in
AP : PR :019(099) [0103] and to restore them to a godly and **abiding** harmony.
AP : 0 2 :031(104) [0113] merely actual guilt but an **abiding** deficiency in an
AP : 0 7 :009(169) [0229] The church will **abide** nevertheless; it exists despite the
LC : 0 2 :062(419) [0695] has been finished and we **abide** in it, having died to the
LC : 0 3 :070(429) [0717] of God could not **abide** on earth nor his name be
LC : 0 4 :050(443) [0745] holy Christian church will **abide** until the end of the
EP : 1 1 :014(496) [0835] Especially are we to **abide** by the revealed Word which
EP : 1 1 :022(497) [0837] in him and constantly **abide** in this Christian and
EP : 1 2 :031(500) [0843] by the grace of God to **abide** by it, we have advisedly, in
SD : PR :004(502) [0847] Confession, and we **abide** by the plain, clear, and pure
SD : PR :005(502) [0847] grace of the Almighty to **abide** until our end by this
SD : PR :006(502) [0847] true meaning or because they did not **abide** by them.
SD : RN :016(507) [0857] accord as the correct and **abiding** answer in the
SD : RN :020(508) [0859] grace we shall continue to **abide** in it loyally and faithfully
SD : 0 1 :058(519) [0879] of God will never attain **abiding** peace in this controversy
SD : 0 3 :006(540) [0917] conscience can have any **abiding** comfort or rightly
SD : 0 3 :022(543) [0923] follow in the ways of sin, **abide** and continue therein
SD : 0 3 :026(543) [0923] intention to remain and **abide** in sin, for true contrition
SD : 0 3 :035(545) [0927] to supply tempted consciences with **abiding** comfort.
SD : 0 4 :015(553) [0943] intention to continue and **abide** in sin, which is
SD : 0 7 :022(573) [0979] We shall **abide** by these words and look anyone in the eye
SD : 0 7 :029(574) [0981] I am determined to **abide** by it until my death and (so
SD : 0 7 :044(577) [0987] and which was to be an **abiding** memorial of his bitter
SD : 0 7 :050(578) [0989] and testament and of his **abiding** covenant and union, he
SD : 0 7 :059(580) [0993] We shall **abide** unanimously by this simple and
SD : 0 8 :051(600) [1033] natural, essential, and **abiding** properties, special, high,
SD : 0 8 :096(610) [1049] will be certain to find **abiding** comfort in all adversities
SD : 1 0 :018(614) [1059] by the grace of God to **abide** by this their confession.
SD : 1 1 :072(628) [1085] we may see it through and **abide** and persevere in it, we
SD : 1 1 :090(631) [1093] people the permanently **abiding** comfort of knowing that
SD : 1 1 :093(632) [1093] We shall **abide** by this simple, direct, and useful
SD : 1 2 :006(633) [1097] in all these questions we **abide** by the true, simple,
SD : 1 2 :040(636) [1103] but we intend through God's grace to **abide** by it.

Ability (20), Able (60)
PR : PR :015(007) [0013] all of us have to date been **able** to undertake such a plan
PR : PR :020(010) [0017] veracious, and hence he is **able** to accomplish what he has
AG : 2 3 :001(051) [0061] of priests who were not **able** to remain continent and who
AG : 2 3 :006(052) [0061] lies in human power and **ability** to improve or change the
AG : 2 3 :014(054) [0063] No one is **able** to alter or arrange such matters in a better
AG : 2 6 :027(068) [0073] which neither our fathers nor we have been **able** to bear?
AG : 2 7 :028(075) [0079] within human power and **ability**, and there are few,
AL : 1 8 :008(040) [0053] of nature alone, we are **able** to love God above all things,
AL : 1 8 :009(040) [0053] Although nature is **able** in some measure to perform the
AL : 2 0 :025(044) [0057] and ungodly men are not **able** to believe this article of the
AL : 2 0 :029(045) [0057] new affections as to be **able** to bring forth good works.
AL : 2 0 :033(045) [0057] live honest lives, were not **able** to do so but were defiled
AL : 2 4 :018(058) [0067] by the very men who were **able** to correct them and were
AL : 2 6 :027(068) [0073] which neither our fathers nor we have been **able** to bear?
AL : 2 7 :029(075) [0079] Before they are **able** to judge, boys and girls are
AP : 0 2 :009(102) [0107] To be **able** to love God above all things by one's own
AP : 0 2 :026(103) [0111] both elements: lack of **ability** to trust, fear, or love God;
AP : 0 2 :031(104) [0113] wise reader will easily be **able** to see that when the fear of
AP : 0 4 :087(120) [0147] matters according to the **ability** that the Lord saw fit to
AP : 0 4 :138(126) [0161] is far too weak to be **able** by its own strength to resist the
AP : 0 4 :266(146) [0197] promise so that we may be **able** to do good and that our
AP : 1 8 :004(225) [0335] as well as the liberty and **ability** to achieve civil
AP : 1 8 :007(225) [0337] free will the liberty and **ability** to do the outward works
AP : 2 3 :021(242) [0369] adds, "He who is **able** to receive this, let him receive it."
AP : 2 7 :020(272) [0425] reader will easily be **able** to conclude that we do not
AP : 2 8 :011(283) [0447] opponents will never be **able** to show that bishops have
S 1 : PR :001(288) [0455] far we were willing and **able** to yield to the papists and,
S 1 : PR :012(290) [0459] twenty diets would not be **able** to set things right again.
S 3 : 0 1 :006(302) [0477] 3. Again, that man is **able** by his natural powers to
S 3 : 0 1 :007(302) [0477] 4. Again, that man is **able** by his natural powers to love
S 3 : 0 3 :018(306) [0483] inventions, without being **able** to consider Christ and
TR : 0 0 :051(329) [0519] away, the churches are not **able** to remove impious
LC : SP :026(364) [0581] Then they will also be **able** to repeat what they have heard
LC : 0 1 :072(374) [0601] lips so that he may not be **able** to injure us as he is eager
LC : 0 1 :111(380) [0613] will share with them all he has to the best of his **ability**.
LC : 0 1 :112(380) [0613] and would have been **able** to set his conscience right
LC : 0 1 :114(380) [0613] They were **able** to ignore it and skip lightly over it, and so
LC : 0 1 :115(381) [0613] the great comfort of being **able** joyfully to boast in the
LC : 0 1 :145(385) [0623] a wonderful thing to be **able** to boast to yourself, "If I do
LC : 0 2 :002(411) [0679] a plane that all human **ability** is far too feeble and weak
LC : 0 6 :002(457) [0000] of sin that no one was **able** to confess purely enough.
EP : 0 2 :001(469) [0785] about man's will and **ability** in the second state.
EP : 0 2 :002(470) [0787] folly to him, and he is not **able** to understand them" when
EP : 0 2 :011(471) [0789] man's will is forthwith **able** by its own natural powers to
EP : 0 2 :012(471) [0789] after his conversion man is **able** to keep the law of God
EP : 0 7 :012(483) [0811] right hand of God, whence he is **able** to do these things.
EP : 0 8 :017(489) [0821] 12. Therefore he is **able** and it is easy for him to impart to
SD : 0 1 :012(510) [0863] of reason, power, and **ability**, although greatly weakened
SD : 0 1 :023(512) [0865] faculty, aptitude, skill, or **ability** to initiate and effect
SD : 0 1 :033(514) [0869] nature we are not **able** to point out and expose the nature
SD : 0 1 :042(515) [0871] is God's work that man is **able** to think, to speak, to act,
SD : 0 2 :010(522) [0883] folly to him, and he is not **able** to understand them
SD : 0 2 :012(522) [0885] aptitude, skill, and **ability** to think anything good or right
SD : 0 2 :012(523) [0885] folly to him, and he is not **able** to understand them" (I
SD : 0 2 :013(523) [0885] Much less will he be **able** truly to believe the Gospel, give
SD : 0 2 :026(526) [0891] reason and free will are **able** to lead an outwardly
SD : 0 2 :027(527) [0893] is God's work to give the **ability** to achieve something to
SD : 0 2 :032(527) [0893] ascribe to man's will any **ability** either to initiate
SD : 0 2 :043(529) [0897] and there is no power or **ability**, no cleverness or reason,
SD : 0 2 :044(529) [0897] and to the best of his **ability** against all
SD : 0 2 :046(530) [0899] means, and they are **able** actually to feel and to perceive
SD : 0 2 :048(530) [0901] new spiritual power and **ability** for good in our hearts,
SD : 0 2 :067(534) [0907] Word of God but also are **able** to assent to it and accept
SD : 0 2 :083(537) [0913] of the Holy Spirit is **able** to accept the offered grace.
SD : 0 4 :008(552) [0941] the unconverted are also **able** and require to perform, are
SD : 0 6 :011(565) [0965] does not give the power and **ability** to begin it or to do it.
SD : 0 7 :031(574) [0983] God, what will he not be **able** to do with my or someone
SD : 0 7 :043(577) [0987] he must speak, and he is **able** mightily to accomplish and
SD : 0 7 :046(577) [0989] his heart that what God promised he was also **able** to do.
SD : 0 7 :103(587) [1007] way that God's power is **able** to make a body be
SD : 0 7 :119(590) [1013] heaven that he is neither **able** nor willing to be truly and
SD : 0 7 :120(590) [1013] promised or have been **able** to achieve the true, essential
SD : 1 1 :008(617) [1065] gates of Hades" are not **able** to do anything against it
SD : 1 1 :029(621) [1073] and to give us power and **ability**, it is God's will that we
SD : 1 1 :033(621) [1073] gives grace, power, and **ability** through the Word by
SD : 1 1 :043(623) [1077] existed, before we were **able** to have done any good, God
SD : 1 2 :005(633) [1097] We wanted everyone to be **able** to see that we were not
SD : 1 2 :008(633) [1097] We have not been **able** to refrain from witnessing publicly
SD : 1 2 :012(634) [1099] the use of reason and are **able** to make their own
SD : 1 2 :033(635) [1101] the Spirit of God is **able** to keep and fulfill the law of God

Ablutions (1)
AP : 0 4 :283(150) [0201] traditions like the **ablutions** in those days, or in our own

Aboard (1)
LC : 0 4 :082(446) [0751] to it until he can climb **aboard** again and sail on in it as

Abolish (22), Abolished (12), Abolishes (1), Abolishing (3), Abolition (6)
PR : PR :011(006) [0011] were looking for could be **abolished** and taken away.
AG : 2 3 :024(055) [0065] human law can alter or **abolish** a command of God,
AG : 0 1 :001(056) [0065] We are unjustly accused of having **abolished** the Mass.
AG : 2 5 :001(061) [0069] Confession has not been **abolished** by the preachers on
AL : 0 0 :004(048) [0059] and all old ordinances are **abolished** in our churches.
AL : 2 4 :001(056) [0065] Our churches are falsely accused of **abolishing** the Mass.
AL : 2 5 :001(061) [0069] Confession has not been **abolished** in our churches, for it
AL : 2 8 :013(083) [0085] laws of civil rulers, nor **abolish** lawful obedience, nor
AP : 0 4 :110(123) [0153] this end but with the **abolition** of the promise and a
AP : 0 4 :110(123) [0153] they completely **abolish** the Gospel of the free forgiveness
AP : 0 4 :186(133) [0173] our opponents simply **abolish** this free promise.
AP : 0 4 :187(133) [0173] completely unsure and the promise would be **abolished**.
AP : 0 4 :223(138) [0181] about Christ, let them **abolish** the Gospel, if Christ is
AP : 0 4 :264(146) [0195] It would clearly be an **abolition** of the Gospel if we were
AP : 0 4 :269(147) [0197] certainly not intended to **abolish** the Gospel of Christ, the
AP : 0 4 :298(153) [0205] unless he wants utterly to **abolish** Christ and the Gospel?
AP : 0 7 :023(172) [0235] establish articles of faith, **abolish** the Scriptures by his
AP : 1 2 :048(188) [0265] new sentence is faith, **abolishing** the earlier sentence and
AP : 1 2 :075(193) [0273] of the Gospel, and the **abolition** of the promise of Christ.
AP : 1 2 :122(200) [0289] and conclude that the **abolition** of satisfactions in the
AP : 1 2 :140(204) [0295] These are supposed to **abolish** death, even when they are
AP : 1 2 :161(208) [0303] of sin he did not **abolish** it, for the sake of righteousness,
AP : 1 2 :172(209) [0305] say it is intolerable to **abolish** satisfactions contrary to the
AP : 1 4 :002(214) [0315] is the reason for the **abolition** of canonical government in
AP : 1 5 :039(220) [0325] falsely accuse us of **abolishing** good ordinances and
AP : 2 3 :007(240) [0365] regulations nor vows can **abolish** the right to contract
AP : 2 3 :009(241) [0367] into nature, and human regulations cannot **abolish** it.
AP : 2 3 :016(241) [0369] and vows cannot **abolish** either nature or lust, they
AP : 2 3 :016(241) [0369] or lust, they cannot **abolish** the statement, "It is better to
AP : 2 4 :001(249) [0383] statement that we do not **abolish** the Mass but religiously
AP : 2 4 :091(266) [0415] This is the **abolition** of the daily sacrifice in the church.
AP : 2 7 :015(271) [0425] pretend that Paul **abolished** the law of Moses and that
AP : 2 7 :017(272) [0425] — whoever does this **abolishes** the promise of Christ, has

Continued ▶

A P : 2 7 :051(278) [0437] any vows or any laws **abolish** the commandment of the
S 2 : 0 2 :007(294) [0465] and must be **abolished** because it is a direct contradiction
S 2 : 0 2 :014(295) [0467] Only when they have **abolished** their traffic in purgatorial
S 3 : 1 1 :002(314) [0499] man out of a woman or **abolish** distinctions of sex
T R : 0 0 :044(328) [0517] a firm consolation, and **abolish** true worship (that is, the
L C : 0 5 :040(451) [0761] nonsense has been **abolished** and we are freed from his
L C : 0 6 :021(459) [0000] Hereby we **abolish** the pope's tyranny, commandments,
E P : 0 8 :018(489) [0823] Nor do we deny or **abolish** the human nature in the
E P : 1 0 :012(494) [0831] indifferent things are **abolished** in a way which suggests
S D : 0 8 :061(603) [1037] we do not confuse, equalize, or **abolish** the natures in
S D : 1 0 :030(615) [1061] of indifference are **abolished** in such a way as to give the

Abominable (12), Abomination (5), Abominations (5)
A G : 2 3 :001(051) [0061] and who went so far as to engage in **abominable** vices.
A G : 2 3 :018(054) [0063] immorality and **abominable** vice that even some honest
A G : 2 3 :018(054) [0063] on account of their **abomination** and prevalence, arouse
A G : 2 4 :021(058) [0067] At the same time the **abominable** error was condemned
S 1 : P R :014(291) [0459] repent and we even try to justify all our **abominations**.
S 2 : 0 2 :001(293) [0463] and most horrible **abomination** because it runs into direct
S 2 : 0 2 :017(296) [0467] as well as to the Mass and all the other **abominations**.
S 2 : 0 4 :014(301) [0475] exalt and honor these **abominations** of his above all
S 3 : 1 1 :001(314) [0499] all sorts of horrible, **abominable**, and countless sins, in
S 3 : 1 1 :003(315) [0499] to consent to their **abominable** celibacy, nor shall we
L C : 0 1 :011(366) [0583] countless other such **abominations**, and every person
L C : 0 3 :062(428) [0715] when his lies and **abominations**, honored under the most
L C : 0 3 :104(434) [0727] atheism, blasphemy, and countless other **abominable** sins.
E P : 0 3 :007(473) [0793] are both alike an **abomination** to the Lord" (Prov. 17:15);
S D : R N :005(504) [0851] of his Word amid the **abominable** darkness of the papacy
S D : 0 1 :002(508) [0859] and that it is an **abominable**, deep, and inexpressible
S D : 0 1 :005(509) [0861] and primarily, the **abominable** and dreadful inherited
S D : 0 1 :011(510) [0863] with a deep, wicked, **abominable**, bottomless,
S D : 0 1 :045(516) [0873] it is unchristian and **abominable** to say that original sin is
S D : 0 1 :062(519) [0879] on everyone how **abominable** and dreadful this quality
S D : 0 3 :017(542) [0921] are both alike an **abomination** to the Lord" (Prov. 17:15).
S D : 0 7 :109(588) [1011] such as the **abomination** of the sacrifice of the Mass for

Abortive (1)
S 2 : 0 2 :019(296) [0467] uncommanded, **abortive**, uncertain, and even harmful

Abound (3), Abounded (2)
A P : 0 4 :103(122) [0151] sin increased, grace **abounded** all the more' (Rom. 5:20)
A P : 0 4 :149(127) [0163] Paul says that grace **abounded** more than sin
A P : 1 5 :030(219) [0323] some proofs for this, and Paul's letters **abound** in them.
A P : 2 1 :005(230) [0345] that grace does indeed **abound** more than sin
A P : 2 7 :059(279) [0441] though our monks **abound** in every delight, they claim to

Abraham (22)
A P : 0 4 :087(120) [0147] Paul also mentions **Abraham** and David, who had God's
A P : 0 4 :090(120) [0149] say that faith was reckoned to **Abraham** as righteousness."
A P : 0 4 :201(134) [0175] works when he says that **Abraham** did not receive
A P : 0 4 :209(135) [0177] The people heard that **Abraham** had offered up his son.
A P : 0 4 :209(136) [0179] But **Abraham** did not offer up his son with the idea that
A P : 0 4 :252(143) [0191] shows when he says of **Abraham**, "Faith was active along
A P : 0 4 :320(156) [0209] And of **Abraham** he says (Rom. 4:18), "In hope he
A P : 1 3 :019(213) [0313] to this, Paul denies that **Abraham** was justified by
A P : 1 6 :009(224) [0333] and held high positions, **Abraham**, David, and Daniel
A P : 2 3 :035(244) [0373] in a married man like **Abraham** or Jacob than in many
A P : 2 3 :064(248) [0381] of married men like **Abraham** and Jacob, who were
A P : 2 7 :049(277) [0437] of David to rule, or of **Abraham** to sacrifice his son, are
S C : 0 9 :007(355) [0563] husbands, as Sarah obeyed **Abraham**, calling him lord.
E P : 0 1 :005(466) [0781] he is concerned but with the descendants of **Abraham**.
S D : 0 3 :033(545) [0927] St. Paul's statement concerning **Abraham** is apposite.
S D : 0 3 :033(545) [0927] He says that **Abraham** was justified before God through
S D : 0 3 :033(545) [0927] did the righteousness of **Abraham** before God, whereby he
S D : 0 5 :023(562) [0959] likewise, of the seed of **Abraham**, but whom all nations
S D : 0 7 :046(577) [0987] **Abraham** certainly had sufficient ground for a disputation
S D : 0 7 :046(577) [0987] previous occasion when **Abraham** received the promise of
S D : 0 7 :046(577) [0989] So **Abraham** understood and believed the words and
S D : 0 7 :071(582) [0997] partook no less than **Abraham**, Paul, and others who had

Abroad (2)
T R : 0 0 :026(324) [0511] is, but is spread **abroad** through the whole world and
L C : 0 1 :332(410) [0677] for himself at home, and **abroad** among his neighbors, he

Abrogate (5), Abrogated (6), Abrogates (2), Abrogation (3)
A G : 2 7 :022(074) [0079] them, it is still impossible to **abrogate** God's command.
A G : 2 8 :059(091) [0091] Holy Scriptures have **abrogated** the Sabbath and teach
A G : 2 8 :066(092) [0093] doctrine, and this is not **abrogated** by the decree.
A G : 2 8 :075(094) [0095] persuaded to mitigate or **abrogate** human regulations
A L : 2 7 :022(074) [0079] about that a vow **abrogates** the command of God.
A L : 2 8 :013(083) [0085] of the world, nor **abrogate** the laws of civil rulers, nor
A L : 2 8 :059(091) [0091] not the church, **abrogated** the Sabbath, for after the
A P : 1 2 :077(193) [0275] we insult Christ and **abrogate** the Gospel if we believe
A P : 1 2 :089(195) [0279] doctrine of the law, an **abrogation** of the Gospel, a
A P : 1 2 :175(210) [0307] law, for human authority cannot **abrogate** divine law.
A P : 1 5 :049(221) [0329] the other hand, their **abrogation** involves its own
A P : 2 4 :027(254) [0393] Thus it **abrogates** Levitical worship.
A P : 2 4 :030(255) [0395] With the **abrogation** of Levitical worship, the New
L C : 0 1 :180(389) [0631] yet their right to take human life is not **abrogated**.
S D : 0 7 :089(585) [1003] and which are neither **abrogated** nor rendered impotent
S D : 1 0 :002(611) [1053] once more certain **abrogated** ceremonies that are in

Absence (4), Absent (11)
A G : P R :018(026) [0041] (together with the **absent** electors, princes, and
A P : 0 2 :007(101) [0107] but also the **absence** of the fear of God and of faith.
A P : 2 7 :046(277) [0435] of property, but in the **absence** of greed and of trust in
L C : 0 5 :042(451) [0763] people who abstain and **absent** themselves from the
L C : 0 5 :059(453) [0767] to be good, should not **absent** themselves, even though in
E P : 0 7 :005(482) [0809] spirit, or the power of Christ's **absent** body, or his merit.
E P : 0 7 :007(482) [0811] the bread symbolized the **absent** body and the wine the
E P : 0 7 :007(482) [0811] body and the wine the **absent** blood of Christ, but that
E P : 0 7 :031(485) [0815] and merit of the **absent** body and blood of Christ are
S D : 0 1 :010(510) [0863] is the complete lack or **absence** of the original concreated
S D : 0 1 :022(512) [0865] is not a deprivation or **absence** of man's spiritual good
S D : 0 7 :004(569) [0973] are only signs of the **absent** body of Christ, are therein
S D : 0 7 :115(589) [1011] food for our body, so the **absent** body of Christ with its
S D : 0 7 :116(589) [1011] and reminders of the **absent** body of Christ, and through
S D : 0 7 :117(589) [1013] Christ, and that in this way we partake of his **absent** body.

Absolute (4), Absolutely (5)
P R : P R :022(012) [0021] We want **absolutely** no share of the responsibility for this
A P : 0 4 :326(157) [0211] This **absolutely** denies any glory in man's righteousness,
A P : 2 1 :001(229) [0343] They **absolutely** condemn Article XXI because we do not
S 3 : 1 4 :001(315) [0501] the first chief article, they must be **absolutely** set aside.
L C : 0 1 :274(401) [0659] So you see that we are **absolutely** forbidden to speak evil
S D : 0 2 :044(529) [0897] the question of "**absolute** necessity"), indicates how he
S D : 0 7 :106(588) [1009] heart to rely on and trust in them with **absolute** certainty.
S D : 1 1 :013(618) [1067] speculate concerning the **absolute**, secret, hidden, and
S D : 1 1 :036(622) [1075] we should believe it with **absolute** certainty and not

Absolution (71)
A G : 1 1 :001(034) [0047] among us that private **absolution** should be retained and
A G : 1 2 :002(034) [0049] to repentance, and **absolution** should not be denied them
A G : 1 2 :005(034) [0049] believe the Gospel and **absolution** (namely, that sin has
A G : 1 2 :009(035) [0049] Novatians who denied **absolution** to such as had sinned
A G : 2 5 :002(061) [0069] of the Word of **absolution** so that they may esteem
A G : 2 5 :002(061) [0069] that they may esteem **absolution** as a great and precious
A G : 2 5 :004(062) [0069] us to believe this **absolution** as much as if we heard God's
A G : 2 5 :004(062) [0069] comfort ourselves with **absolution**, and that we should
A G : 2 5 :013(063) [0071] retained for the sake of **absolution** (which is its chief and
A L : 1 1 :001(034) [0047] teach that private **absolution** should be retained in the
A L : 1 2 :002(034) [0049] church ought to impart **absolution** to those who return to
A L : 1 2 :005(034) [0049] of the Gospel, or of **absolution**, believes that sins are
A L : 2 5 :002(061) [0069] in connection with **absolution**, a matter about which
A L : 2 5 :003(061) [0069] are taught to esteem **absolution** highly because it is the
A L : 2 5 :004(062) [0069] faith to believe such **absolution** as God's own voice heard
A L : 2 5 :013(063) [0071] of the great benefit of **absolution** and because it is
A P : 0 4 :271(148) [0199] so mad as to deny that **absolution** is the spoken Gospel.
A P : 0 4 :271(148) [0199] **Absolution** should be received by faith, to cheer the
A P : 1 1 :001(180) [0247] the eleventh article on retaining **absolution** in the church.
A P : 1 1 :002(180) [0249] extolled the blessing of **absolution** and the power of the
A P : 1 1 :002(180) [0249] we should believe the **absolution** and firmly believe that
A P : 1 1 :002(180) [0249] the whole power of **absolution** had been smothered by
A P : 1 1 :003(180) [0249] use the sacraments, **absolution** and the Lord's Supper,
A P : 1 2 :006(183) [0255] what is the need of **absolution** and what does the power
A P : 1 2 :012(184) [0255] very coldly about **absolution**, which really is by divine
A P : 1 2 :012(184) [0257] faith, which grasps the **absolution** and consoles the
A P : 1 2 :039(187) [0261] the Gospel through **absolution**, which is the true voice of
A P : 1 2 :039(187) [0261] we also include **absolution** since "faith comes from what
A P : 1 2 :039(187) [0261] the Gospel and hearing **absolution** strengthens and
A P : 1 2 :041(187) [0261] **Absolution** may properly be called a sacrament of
A P : 1 2 :042(187) [0263] and confirmed through **absolution**, through the hearing
A P : 1 2 :056(189) [0267] Then he hears the **absolution** (II Sam. 12:14), "The Lord
A P : 1 2 :057(189) [0267] Later she heard the **absolution** (vv. 48, 50), "Your sins are
A P : 1 2 :061(190) [0269] the reception of **absolution** is part of penitence or not.
A P : 1 2 :061(190) [0269] distinction separating **absolution** from confession, we fail
A P : 1 2 :061(190) [0269] see what value there is in confession without **absolution**.
A P : 1 2 :061(190) [0269] the reception of **absolution** from confession, then they
A P : 1 2 :061(190) [0269] of penitence since only faith can accept the **absolution**.
A P : 1 2 :061(190) [0269] faith can accept the **absolution** can be proved from Paul,
A P : 1 2 :061(190) [0269] Now, since **absolution** is the promise of the forgiveness of
A P : 1 2 :062(190) [0269] can be said to receive **absolution** unless he believes it.
A P : 1 2 :062(190) [0269] is the refusal to believe **absolution** but the accusation that
A P : 1 2 :099(197) [0281] especially because of **absolution**, which is the Word of
A P : 1 2 :100(197) [0281] be wicked to remove private **absolution** from the church.
A P : 1 2 :101(197) [0281] who despise private **absolution** understand neither the
A P : 1 2 :103(197) [0281] because the ministry of **absolution** is in the area of
A P : 1 2 :105(197) [0283] remember; therefore **absolution**, which is the voice of the
A P : 1 2 :177(210) [0307] of cases should not be an obstacle to **absolution**.
A P : 1 3 :004(211) [0309] the Lord's Supper, and **absolution** (which is the
A P : 2 1 :025(232) [0349] places this form of **absolution** is used: "The passion of
A P : 2 1 :025(232) [0349] to this declaration of **absolution**, we are reconciled and
A P : 2 8 :013(283) [0447] absolve them if they are converted and ask for **absolution**.
S 3 : 0 3 :020(306) [0485] aware of the power of **absolution**, for his consolation was
S 3 : 0 8 :001(312) [0493] Since **absolution** or the power of the keys, which was
S 3 : 0 8 :001(312) [0493] confession and **absolution** should by no means be allowed
S 3 : 0 8 :002(312) [0495] Although private **absolution** is derived from the office of
S C : 0 5 :015(349) [0553] [Confession and **Absolution**]
S C : 0 5 :016(349) [0553] other is that we receive **absolution** or forgiveness from the
L C : 0 2 :054(417) [0693] holy sacraments and **absolution** as well as through all the
L C : 0 3 :097(433) [0725] it as certain as an **absolution** pronounced by thyself."
L C : 0 5 :061(453) [0767] desires no grace and **absolution** and has no intention to
L C : 0 6 :012(458) [0000] Lord's Prayer a twofold **absolution**: our debts both to
L C : 0 6 :014(458) [0000] himself has entrusted **absolution** to his Christian church
L C : 0 6 :016(459) [0000] we were told that the **absolution** was not valid and the sin
L C : 0 6 :017(459) [0000] conscience at peace or have confidence in his **absolution**.
L C : 0 6 :021(459) [0000] and for the sake of **absolution**, let him just forget about
L C : 0 6 :022(459) [0000] The Word or **absolution**, I say, is what you should
L C : 0 6 :033(461) [0000] tremble for God's Word, **absolution**, the sacrament, etc.
S D : 1 1 :038(622) [1075] XI, we retain individual **absolution** and teach that it is
S D : 1 1 :038(622) [1075] that we "believe this **absolution** and firmly hold that when
S D : 1 1 :038(622) [1075] we believe the word of **absolution** we are as truly

Absolve (10), Absolved (15), Absolves (4), Absolving (1)
A G : 2 5 :001(061) [0069] who have not previously been examined and **absolved**.
A G : 2 5 :009(062) [0069] all, and if we were to be **absolved** only from those which
A L : 1 2 :009(035) [0049] who were unwilling to **absolve** those who had fallen after
A L : 2 5 :001(061) [0069] those who have been previously examined and **absolved**.
A P : 0 2 :036(105) [0115] because its guilt is **absolved** by the sacrament that
A P : 0 4 :305(154) [0205] judicial way to mean "to **absolve** a guilty man and
A P : 0 4 :397(167) [0227] trust that we have been **absolved**, not because of our
A P : 1 2 :040(187) [0261] the voice of the one **absolving** no less than we would
A P : 1 2 :105(197) [0283] In addition, they **absolve** us of those which we do not
A P : 1 2 :122(200) [0289] those who have been **absolved** by the priest should
A P : 1 2 :176(210) [0307] ministers of the Gospel **absolve** those who are converted,
A P : 1 3 :004(211) [0309] body, when we are **absolved**, our hearts should firmly

Continued ▶

A P : 1 5 :040(220) [0325] after they have been instructed, examined, and **absolved**.
A P : 2 4 :001(249) [0385] wish for it after they have been examined and **absolved**.
A P : 2 4 :075(263) [0411] "Go to him and be **absolved**, for he is the forgiveness of
A P : 2 8 :013(283) [0447] of public offenses or to **absolve** them if they are converted
T R : 0 0 :060(330) [0521] guilty of notorious crimes and **absolve** those who repent.
T R : 0 0 :067(331) [0523] even a layman **absolves** and becomes the minister and
T R : 0 0 :067(331) [0523] and the latter, after his Baptism, **absolved** the former.
L C : 0 3 :100(433) [0725] and have been wholly **absolved**, yet such is life that one
L C : 0 6 :014(458) [0000] and commanded us to **absolve** one another from sins.
L C : 0 6 :014(458) [0000] a man God looses and **absolves** him from his sins.
L C : 0 6 :015(459) [0000] God does, when he **absolves** me of my sins through a
E P : 0 3 :007(473) [0793] means in this article "**absolve**," that is, pronounce free
E P : 0 3 :015(475) [0795] do not mean to **absolve** or to be absolved from sin and to
E P : 0 3 :015(475) [0795] mean to absolve or to be **absolved** from sin and to obtain
S D : 0 3 :004(540) [0917] and that they are **absolved** from all their unrighteousness
S D : 0 3 :009(540) [0919] God (that is, he is **absolved** and declared utterly free from
S D : 0 3 :017(542) [0921] (Rom. 8:33), that is, **absolves** and acquits from sins.
S D : 0 3 :062(550) [0937] do not mean "to **absolve** from sins" and "to receive

Absorb (1)
L C : P R :005(359) [0567] teaching which they can **absorb** and master at one

Abstain (6), Abstained (3)
A G : 2 8 :065(092) [0093] directed that one should **abstain** from blood and from
A L : 2 8 :032(086) [0087] who commanded men to **abstain** from blood and from
A L : 2 8 :065(092) [0093] commanded that one should **abstain** from blood, etc.
A P : 2 3 :045(245) [0375] They **abstained** from wine, even in the Lord's Supper;
A P : 2 3 :045(245) [0375] the Lord's Supper; they **abstained** from the meat of all
A P : 2 3 :045(245) [0375] They also **abstained** from marriage, and this called forth
L C : 0 1 :080(375) [0603] They were to **abstain** from hard work and to rest, so that
L C : 0 1 :215(394) [0641] short, even though they **abstain** from the act, yet their
L C : 0 5 :042(451) [0763] that people who **abstain** and absent themselves from the

Abstract (1)
P R : P R :021(010) [0019] inasmuch as the word "**abstract**" has not been used

Abstruse (1)
S D : 1 1 :093(632) [1095] shall avoid and flee all **abstruse** and specious questions

Absurd (7), Absurdities (4), Absurdity (1)
A G : 2 7 :044(078) [0081] a still more indecent and **absurd** claim, namely, that they
A L : 2 7 :044(078) [0081] they invented greater **absurdities** when they claimed that
A P : 0 2 :002(100) [0105] on this point is not **absurd**, we ask them first to look at
A P : 0 4 :318(156) [0209] It is highly **absurd** when our opponents teach that good
A P : 0 4 :336(159) [0215] Though these **absurdities** do not deserve a refutation, we
A P : 0 4 :345(160) [0217] Unless it is qualified, this statement seems **absurd**.
A P : 0 4 :360(162) [0219] they draw the following **absurd** conclusion when they
A P : 1 8 :003(225) [0335] How many **absurdities** follow from these Pelagian
A P : 2 1 :023(232) [0349] books and sermons there are even greater **absurdities**.
L C : 0 4 :055(443) [0745] So you see that the objection of the sectarians is **absurd**.
L C : 0 5 :031(450) [0759] Therefore it is **absurd** to say that Christ's body and blood
S D : 0 2 :074(535) [0909] 1. The **absurdity** of the Stoics and Manichaeans in

Abundance (5), Abundant (3), Abundantly (11)
A P : 0 4 :002(107) [0121] pious consciences the **abundant** consolation that they
A P : 2 3 :028(243) [0371] and approves, as the Scriptures **abundantly** testify.
A P : 2 4 :082(264) [0411] but also causes many to thank God more **abundantly**.
A P : 2 7 :028(274) [0429] has promised this in **abundance** to those who have
A P : 2 7 :040(276) [0433] monks merit a more **abundant** eternal life, and it quotes
S 3 : 1 3 :002(315) [0499] have been poured out upon us so **abundantly** in Christ.
S C : 0 2 :002(345) [0543] provides me daily and **abundantly** with all the necessities
S C : 0 2 :006(345) [0545] church he daily and **abundantly** forgives all my sins, and
L C : 0 1 :136(383) [0619] and he will reward you **abundantly** with every blessing; on
L C : 0 1 :157(387) [0627] learn how to obtain an **abundance** of joy, happiness, and
L C : 0 1 :164(387) [0627] peace, and afterwards **abundance** and blessedness
L C : 0 1 :166(388) [0629] will give you everything **abundantly**, according to your
L C : 0 1 :290(404) [0663] most highly and bring **abundant** blessings, if only the
L C : 0 1 :328(410) [0677] confidence that he will **abundantly** reward you for all you
L C : 0 1 :330(410) [0677] and, on the contrary, **abundantly** rewards those who keep
L C : 0 2 :024(413) [0683] all his creatures, has **abundantly** provided for us in this
L C : 0 3 :056(427) [0713] of giving far more **abundantly** and liberally than anyone
L C : 0 3 :058(428) [0713] all the other things in **abundance**, as Christ teaches, "Seek
L C : 0 3 :074(430) [0719] God all good things in **abundance**, we cannot retain any

Abuse (12), Abused (6), Abuses (50), Abusing (1)
A G : P R :006(025) [0039] with reference to the said errors, dissensions, and **abuses**.
A G : 0 0 :002(048) [0059] are concerned chiefly with various traditions and **abuses**.
A G : 0 0 :002(048) [0059] why we have changed certain traditions and **abuses**.
A G : 0 0 :000(048) [0059] Account Is Given of the **Abuses** Which Have Been
A G : 0 0 :000(049) [0059] inasmuch as some **abuses** have been corrected (some of
A G : 0 0 :000(049) [0059] corrected (some of the **abuses** having crept in over the
A G : 2 4 :010(057) [0065] Such **abuses** were often condemned by learned and
A G : 2 4 :040(061) [0069] Mass, probably through **abuse**, have been discontinued,
A G : 0 0 :001(094) [0095] mentioned many more **abuses** and wrongs, to avoid
A L : 0 0 :002(047) [0059] with a certain few **abuses** which have crept into the
A L : 0 0 :005(048) [0059] complaint that certain **abuses** were connected with
A L : 0 0 :000(048) [0059] Account Is Given of the **Abuses** Which Have Been
A L : 0 0 :001(048) [0059] but only omit some few **abuses** which are new and have
A L : 0 0 :001(049) [0059] to observe these **abuses** against their conscience.
A L : 2 4 :011(057) [0065] known how widely this **abuse** extends in all the churches,
A L : 2 4 :014(057) [0065] The bishops were not ignorant of these **abuses**.
A L : 2 4 :016(057) [0067] nothing else than those **abuses** which had become so
A L : 2 4 :020(058) [0067] ever to have been so **abused** for the sake of gain as the
A L : 2 4 :040(061) [0069] of the great and manifest **abuses** it would certainly be of
A L : 0 0 :001(094) [0095] Although more **abuses** could be mentioned, to avoid
A P : P R :004(098) [0099] that we sanction certain manifest **abuses** and errors.
A P : 0 4 :010(108) [0123] monastic vows and the **abuses** of the Mass; someone has
A P : 0 4 :236(140) [0185] they even intimate their disapproval of some open **abuse**.
A P : 1 2 :016(184) [0257] satisfactions is endless, and we cannot list all the **abuses**.
A P : 1 3 :023(214) [0313] Words cannot describe the **abuses** which this fanatical
A P : 1 5 :051(222) [0329] teaching of the Gospel because of an **abuse** of liberty.
A P : 2 1 :016(231) [0347] we shall not list the **abuses** among the common people
A P : 2 1 :034(234) [0353] came invocation, with **abuses** that were enormous and
A P : 2 1 :038(235) [0355] of saints and condemn **abuses** in the worship of saints in
A P : 2 1 :039(235) [0355] duty in correcting these **abuses**; but in the Confutation
A P : 2 1 :039(235) [0355] to compel us to approve of the most notorious **abuses**.
A P : 2 1 :040(235) [0355] distinguish between their teachings and obvious **abuses**.
A P : 2 1 :040(235) [0355] pastors permitted many **abuses** to creep into the church.
A P : 2 1 :041(235) [0355] Luther was not the first to complain about public **abuses**.
A P : 2 1 :041(235) [0355] men who deplored the **abuses** of the Mass, the trust in
A P : 2 1 :042(235) [0355] our opponents to ignore **abuses** when they required us to
A P : 2 1 :042(235) [0355] take steps to correct the **abuses**, for clearly he is most
A P : 2 1 :043(235) [0357] They defend obvious **abuses** with new and illegal cruelty.
A P : 2 4 :014(251) [0389] of sacrifice among those whose **abuses** we criticize.
A P : 2 4 :089(266) [0415] This is an **abuse** of the name of God in violation of the
A P : 2 4 :091(266) [0415] be careful not to support the **abuses** of our opponents.
A P : 2 4 :098(268) [0417] Baal clings — namely, the **abuse** of the Mass, which they
A P : 2 4 :099(268) [0419] us compile all kinds of **abuses** of the Mass, we shall not
A P : 2 7 :001(268) [0419] because he had condemned certain notorious **abuses**.
A P : 2 7 :002(269) [0419] estate but had only denounced certain notorious **abuses**.
A P : 2 7 :009(270) [0423] approve and support the **abuses** of the Mass, the wicked
S 2 : 0 2 :006(293) [0463] and unspeakable **abuses** have arisen everywhere through
S 2 : 0 2 :006(293) [0463] reason than to curb such **abuses**, even if it actually
S 2 : 0 2 :006(293) [0463] forever against such **abuses** when it is so unnecessary,
S 2 : 0 2 :025(297) [0469] of saints is also one of the **abuses** of the Antichrist.
T R : 0 0 :043(328) [0517] for in addition to other **abuses** they are shamelessly
T R : 0 0 :047(328) [0517] of saints — how many **abuses** and what horrible idolatry
T R : 0 0 :075(332) [0525] And in what kinds of cases they have **abused** this power!
T R : 0 0 :076(333) [0525] and have shamefully **abused** it, there is no need, on
S C : P R :003(338) [0533] they have mastered the fine art of **abusing** liberty.
L C : 0 1 :052(371) [0595] be more grievously **abused** than for purposes of falsehood
L C : 0 1 :053(371) [0595] many ways God's name is **abused**, though it is impossible
L C : 0 1 :054(372) [0595] The greatest **abuse**, however, occurs in spiritual matters,
L C : 0 1 :097(378) [0609] we still fail to remove the **abuse** of the holy day, for we
L C : 0 1 :276(402) [0659] be carefully noted if we are to avoid this detestable **abuse**.
L C : 0 1 :317(408) [0673] get rid of the pernicious **abuse** which has become so
L C : 0 4 :055(443) [0745] on account of that **abuse** to take it again the selfsame
S D : P R :001(501) [0847] and the popish errors, **abuses**, and idolatry were
S D : 0 5 :025(563) [0961] not mean that men may **abuse** the grace of God and sin
S D : 0 7 :060(580) [0993] Such a person dishonors, **abuses**, and desecrates him who
S D : 0 7 :087(585) [1003] was against such papistic **abuses** that this rule was first
S D : 0 7 :109(588) [1011] all other papistic **abuses** of this sacrament, such as the
S D : 0 7 :110(588) [1011] These papistic **abuses** have been refuted at length in the
S D : 1 0 :012(612) [1057] circumcision and **abused** it to confirm their false doctrine

Abusus (1)
L C : 0 4 :059(444) [0747] The saying goes, "***Abusus*** *non tollit, sed confirmat*

Abyss (2)
S D : 1 1 :026(620) [1071] the secret and hidden **abyss** of divine foreknowledge.
S D : 1 1 :033(621) [1073] We should not explore the **abyss** of the hidden

Academic (2)
A P : 0 2 :044(106) [0117] did not remain purely **academic**, but moved out among
A P : 1 2 :009(183) [0255] An **academic** distinction between these two motives is

Accedat (2)
L C : 0 4 :018(438) [0737] as St. Augustine taught, "***Accedat*** *verbum ad elementum*
L C : 0 5 :010(448) [0755] It is said, "***Accedat*** *verbum ad elementum et fit*

Accept (91), Acceptable (35), Acceptance (7), Accepted (55), Accepting (2), Accepts (25)
P R : P R :016(008) [0013] due consideration they **accepted**, approved, and
P R : P R :019(009) [0017] we never understood or **accepted** the second edition in
A G : 0 9 :002(033) [0047] are committed to God and become **acceptable** to him.
A G : 1 8 :002(039) [0051] of making himself **acceptable** to God, of fearing God and
A L : 2 8 :073(093) [0093] Perhaps there were **acceptable** reasons for these
A P : P R :001(098) [0099] and he ordered our princes to **accept** this Confutation.
A P : P R :002(098) [0099] it only on terms so risky that we could not **accept** them.
A P : P R :004(098) [0099] again ordered our princes to **accept** the Confutation.
A P : P R :004(098) [0099] issue, how could they **accept** a document they had not
A P : P R :005(098) [0101] Majesty why we could not **accept** the Confutation.
A P : 0 4 :016(109) [0123] So if we **accept** this teaching of the opponents that we
A P : 0 4 :036(112) [0131] God unless faith has first **accepted** the forgiveness of sins.
A P : 0 4 :043(113) [0133] Since we can **accept** this promise only by faith, the
A P : 0 4 :044(113) [0133] sake, which we do not **accept** by works but by faith
A P : 0 4 :046(113) [0133] By freely **accepting** the forgiveness of sins, faith sets
A P : 0 4 :048(114) [0135] but the firm **acceptance** of God's offer promising
A P : 0 4 :048(114) [0135] means to want and to **accept** the promised offer of
A P : 0 4 :050(114) [0135] knowledge but is a firm **acceptance** of the promise
A P : 0 4 :050(114) [0135] For he says that only faith can **accept** the promise.
A P : 0 4 :053(114) [0137] The promise is **accepted** by faith; the fact that it is free
A P : 0 4 :055(114) [0137] this requires faith, which **accepts** the promise of mercy.
A P : 0 4 :056(114) [0137] in itself, but only because it **accepts** the promised mercy.
A P : 0 4 :060(115) [0137] and worshiped, that we **accept** his blessings and receive
A P : 0 4 :070(116) [0141] But this can be **accepted** only by faith.
A P : 0 4 :071(116) [0141] follow, by which we would become **acceptable** unto God.
A P : 0 4 :072(117) [0141] are truly accounted righteous or **acceptable** before God.
A P : 0 4 :080(118) [0143] it is only by faith that Christ is **accepted** as the mediator.
A P : 0 4 :084(119) [0145] Therefore it can be **accepted** only by faith, since a
A P : 0 4 :084(119) [0145] by faith, since a promise can be **accepted** only on faith.
A P : 0 4 :084(119) [0145] and further that the promise can be **accepted** by faith.
A P : 0 4 :102(121) [0151] of sins, and of our gracious **acceptance** for Christ's sake.
A P : 0 4 :113(123) [0155] use the word, is that which **accepts** the promise.
A P : 0 4 :116(123) [0155] of sins, renders us **acceptable** to God, and brings the Holy
A P : 0 4 :116(123) [0155] "grace that makes us **acceptable** to God" rather than love,
A P : 0 4 :154(128) [0165] law does not believe or **accept** the Messiah or seek from
A P : 0 4 :155(128) [0165] it is faith that properly **accepts** the forgiveness of sins,
A P : 0 4 :160(129) [0167] for its own sake, and it is not **acceptable** for its own sake.
A P : 0 4 :161(129) [0167] but the reconciliation by which we are later **accepted**.
A P : 0 4 :161(129) [0167] not justify, because it is **accepted** only on account of
A P : 0 4 :164(129) [0169] believe that they will be **accepted** because they have kept
A P : 0 4 :165(129) [0169] he is righteous and **acceptable** because of his own keeping
A P : 0 4 :181(132) [0171] But God **accepts** this imperfect righteousness of the law
A P : 0 4 :181(132) [0171] regenerates nor of itself makes us **acceptable** before God.
A P : 0 4 :190(133) [0175] works, true sacrifices **acceptable** to God, battles by which
A P : 0 4 :202(134) [0175] faith Abel offered a more **acceptable** sacrifice (Heb. 11:4).

Continued ▶

AP : 04 :202(134) [0175] sacrifice he made was **acceptable** to God — not to merit
AP : 04 :227(139) [0183] but rather a desire to **accept** and grasp what is offered in
AP : 04 :228(139) [0183] us to believe him and to **accept** blessings from him; this
AP : 04 :244(142) [0189] that good works are **accepted** before God because of their
AP : 04 :246(142) [0189] been reconciled and **accepted** and have obtained the
AP : 04 :264(146) [0197] Only faith can **accept** a promise.
AP : 04 :272(148) [0199] Only faith **accepts** the forgiveness of sins.
AP : 04 :278(149) [0199] of that faith which **accepts** forgiveness of sins and
AP : 04 :285(150) [0201] that not works but faith **accepts** the promised forgiveness
AP : 04 :292(152) [0203] Faith alone **accepts** the forgiveness of sins, justifies, and
AP : 04 :297(153) [0205] The promise is to be **accepted** by faith, as John says
AP : 04 :297(153) [0205] in Christ, therefore, we **accept** the promise of the
AP : 04 :303(154) [0205] truly and wholeheartedly **accepts** the promise of grace.
AP : 04 :304(154) [0205] that is, to desire and to **accept** what the promise offers —
AP : 04 :307(154) [0207] is, by it we are made **acceptable** to God because of God's
AP : 04 :309(155) [0207] is properly his; it obeys him by **accepting** his promises.
AP : 04 :368(163) [0221] please God unless we had been **accepted** because of faith.
AP : 04 :368(163) [0221] Since men are **accepted** because of faith, this incipient
AP : 04 :379(165) [0223] maintain that we are **acceptable** and righteous because of
AP : 04 :385(166) [0225] ask that everything be **accepted** because of Christ and
AP : 04 :390(166) [0225] that the church of Rome **accepts** everything that the pope
AP : 07 :016(170) [0231] are the true people who **accept** this promise of the Spirit.
AP : 07 :027(173) [0235] all religions, or if they **accept** anything, accept only what
AP : 07 :027(173) [0235] if they accept anything, **accept** only what agrees with
AP : 12 :061(190) [0269] of penitence since only faith can **accept** the absolution.
AP : 12 :061(190) [0269] That only faith can **accept** the absolution can be proved
AP : 12 :061(190) [0269] teaches in Rom. 4:16 that only faith **accepts** a promise.
AP : 12 :063(191) [0269] Then that which **accepts** the forgiveness of sins should
AP : 12 :063(191) [0269] of sins cannot be **accepted** by anything but faith alone,
AP : 12 :079(193) [0275] and he teaches us to **accept** the forgiveness of sins by
AP : 12 :080(194) [0275] Only faith **accepts** the promise.
AP : 12 :082(194) [0275] We must therefore **accept** the forgiveness of sins by faith
AP : 12 :086(194) [0277] Therefore we must **accept** the promise that by faith we
AP : 12 :110(198) [0285] many of the most generally **accepted** theologians.
AP : 12 :112(198) [0285] sinners were not **accepted** without certain satisfactions,
AP : 12 :113(199) [0285] Fathers did not want to **accept** the lapsed or the
AP : 12 :120(200) [0287] those who wanted to be **accepted** into the church; that is,
AP : 13 :019(213) [0313] these promises and **accepts** that which is promised and
AP : 13 :020(213) [0313] A promise is useless unless faith **accepts** it.
AP : 13 :020(213) [0313] He should **accept** this by faith, comfort his troubled
AP : 13 :021(214) [0313] personal faith, which **accepts** the promise as a present
AP : 14 :001(214) [0315] ordination, they **accept** Article XIV, where we say that no
AP : 15 :001(215) [0315] In Article XV they **accept** the first part, where we say
AP : 15 :010(216) [0317] Christ, provided that we **accept** it by faith; for only faith
AP : 15 :010(216) [0317] we accept it by faith; for only faith can **accept** a promise.
AP : 15 :011(216) [0317] Since it is by faith that we **accept** the forgiveness of sins
AP : 15 :012(216) [0317] we must first earn our **acceptance** and justification
AP : 15 :034(220) [0325] no one ought to create or **accept** traditions with the idea
AP : 17 :001(224) [0335] Our opponents **accept** Article XVII without exception.
AP : 18 :001(224) [0335] Our opponents **accept** Article XVIII on free will, but they
AP : 19 :001(226) [0337] Our opponents **accept** Article XIX.
AP : 21 :031(233) [0351] Therefore we cannot **accept** either their ideas about
AP : 21 :039(235) [0355] by forcing our **acceptance** of the Confutation, to compel
AP : 21 :042(235) [0355] abuses when they required us to **accept** the Confutation.
AP : 22 :017(238) [0361] immediately approves or **accepts** whatever the pontiffs
AP : 23 :024(243) [0371] synods while they want others to **accept** it as sacrosanct.
AP : 23 :032(244) [0373] faith by which a woman **accepts** the forgiveness of sins
AP : 24 :026(254) [0391] sacrifice, holy and **acceptable** to God, which is your
AP : 24 :028(254) [0393] are we to think the Jews **accepted** this declaration, which
AP : 24 :029(255) [0393] The sacrifice **acceptable** to God is a broken spirit; a
AP : 24 :032(255) [0395] of the Gospel produces faith in those who **accept** it.
AP : 24 :034(256) [0395] of the Gentiles may be **acceptable**, sanctified by the Holy
AP : 24 :034(256) [0397] may become offerings **acceptable** to God through faith.
AP : 24 :070(262) [0409] is useless unless faith **accepts** it, so the ceremony is useless
AP : 24 :072(262) [0409] blessings and the **acceptance** of them by faith, so that they
AP : 24 :090(266) [0415] The forgiveness of guilt can be **accepted** only by faith.
AP : 27 :032(274) [0431] Christ's sake to those who **accept** forgiveness by faith and
S 1 : 00 :000(287) [0453] to indicate what we could or could not **accept** or yield.
S 1 : PR :002(288) [0455] The latter **accepted** them, unanimously adopted them as
S 2 : 02 :014(295) [0467] St. Augustine are to be **accepted** when they are without
S 2 : 02 :017(295) [0467] We had to **accept** all these things as articles of faith and
S 2 : 04 :007(299) [0473] were to concede and **accept** this (which is impossible), he
S 3 : 03 :005(304) [0481] Lord and to expect and **accept** from him the forgiveness
S 3 : 08 :008(313) [0495] prayers and alms were **acceptable** to God in this faith
TR : 00 :019(323) [0509] offered to the bishop of Rome but he did not **accept** it.
SC : PR :011(339) [0535] to the sacrament, be **accepted** as sponsors in Baptism, or
SC : 03 :021(348) [0549] that such petitions are **acceptable** to our heavenly Father
LC : 01 :074(375) [0601] be more pleasing and **acceptable** to God than any
LC : 01 :140(384) [0621] and how precious and **acceptable** a work he does when he
LC : 01 :157(387) [0627] the Word and will of God and sincerely **accept** it.
LC : 01 :197(392) [0637] would be considered just as **acceptable**, and even more so.
LC : 01 :252(399) [0651] things which are heartily **acceptable** and pleasing to God.
LC : 02 :042(416) [0689] so that they grasp and **accept** it, cling to it, and persevere
LC : 02 :043(416) [0689] works and merits and made us **acceptable** to the Father.
LC : 03 :041(425) [0709] lies and make them **acceptable**; this is the worst
LC : 03 :052(427) [0711] order that we who have **accepted** it may remain faithful
LC : 03 :063(428) [0715] evil, even when we have **accepted** and believe God's
LC : 03 :065(429) [0715] God's Word is preached, **accepted** or believed, and bears
LC : 03 :088(432) [0723] here is for us to recognize and **accept** this forgiveness.
LC : 04 :036(441) [0741] beneficial to you if you **accept** it as God's command and
LC : 04 :038(441) [0741] we would still have to **accept** and observe Baptism as an
LC : 04 :050(442) [0745] Now, if God did not **accept** the Baptism of infants, he
LC : 05 :011(448) [0755] is as he says and should **accept** it with all reverence, fear,
LC : 06 :018(459) [0000] to him, but simply to **accept** and receive something from
LC : 06 :022(459) [0000] wonderful treasure to be **accepted** with all praise and
EP : RN :003(465) [0777] confessions) which were **accepted** as the unanimous,
EP : 02 :001(469) [0785] Can he or can he not **accept** the grace of God offered in
EP : 02 :011(471) [0789] itself, to apprehend and **accept** it, and to believe the
EP : 02 :019(472) [0791] give it credence and **accept** it by his own powers but
EP : 03 :004(473) [0793] righteousness we are **accepted** by God into grace and are
EP : 03 :005(473) [0793] instrument whereby we **accept** Christ and in Christ obtain
EP : 07 :017(484) [0813] as a redeemer, they must **accept** him even contrary to
EP : 07 :042(486) [0817] in other articles also, and **accept** this mystery in no other
EP : 09 :004(492) [0827] comprehend in this life but which we simply **accept**.
SD : PR :003(501) [0847] estates who had then **accepted** the pure doctrine of the
SD : PR :004(502) [0847] true Christians ought to **accept** next to the Word of God,
SD : RN :001(503) [0851] written, approved, and **accepted** in the name of those
SD : RN :002(503) [0851] shall neither prepare nor **accept** a different or a new
SD : RN :002(503) [0851] and in all places been **accepted** in all the churches of the
SD : RN :007(505) [0853] at Smalcald in 1537 and there approved and **accepted**.
SD : RN :008(505) [0853] sanctioned and **accepted** and are used publicly in the
SD : RN :009(505) [0853] publicly and generally **accepted** documents as the sum
SD : RN :010(506) [0855] doctrine they are to be **accepted** and used as helpful
SD : RN :010(506) [0855] a single, universally **accepted**, certain, and common form
SD : RN :010(506) [0855] are to be approved and **accepted**, judged and regulated.
SD : RN :011(506) [0855] and everywhere been **accepted** as the common and
SD : RN :011(506) [0855] and universally **accepted** belief of our churches, that the
SD : RN :012(506) [0855] but will gladly admit and **accept** them as witnesses to the
SD : RN :016(507) [0857] writings what he should **accept** as correct and true in each
SD : RN :016(507) [0857] our churches believe and **accept** with one accord as the
SD : RN :020(508) [0859] to the commonly **accepted** Christian meaning of the
SD : 01 :051(517) [0875] that have two or more **accepted** meanings in common
SD : 02 :002(520) [0881] himself for such grace, **accept** it and give his assent to it?
SD : 02 :007(521) [0883] way understand, believe, **accept**, imagine, will, begin,
SD : 02 :007(521) [0883] the grace of God or to **accept** the proffered grace, nor
SD : 02 :009(522) [0883] it, understand it, or believe and **accept** it as the truth.
SD : 02 :013(523) [0885] the Gospel, give his assent to it, and **accept** it as truth.
SD : 02 :044(529) [0897] not once think to turn to the holy Gospel and to **accept** it.
SD : 02 :045(530) [0899] powers to want to **accept** the Gospel and to comfort
SD : 02 :054(531) [0903] a spark of faith which **accepts** the forgiveness of sins for
SD : 02 :066(534) [0907] we entreat you not to **accept** the grace of God in vain."
SD : 02 :067(534) [0907] able to assent to it and **accept** it, even though it be in
SD : 02 :070(535) [0909] sin, to understand and **accept** the promise of grace in
SD : 02 :077(536) [0911] of God, embrace and **accept** it, believe the Gospel, and by
SD : 02 :083(537) [0913] of the Holy Spirit is able to **accept** the offered grace.
SD : 03 :010(541) [0919] we can apprehend, **accept**, apply them to ourselves, and
SD : 03 :013(541) [0919] it lays hold on and **accepts** the merit of Christ in the
SD : 03 :016(541) [0921] appropriated, and **accepted** by faith, so that thus
SD : 03 :023(543) [0923] before God (that is, **accepted** into grace) there is given the
SD : 03 :025(543) [0923] Christ, and faith which **accepts** these in the promise of the
SD : 03 :031(544) [0925] we could receive and **accept** the grace of God, the merit
SD : 03 :032(545) [0927] person is pleasing and **acceptable** to God and is adopted
SD : 03 :033(545) [0927] and was pleasing and **acceptable** to him to eternal life,
SD : 03 :038(546) [0929] which we receive, grasp, **accept**, apply to ourselves, and
SD : 03 :039(546) [0929] Gospel and received, **accepted**, applied to us, and made
SD : 03 :054(549) [0935] of sins and the gracious **acceptance** of poor sinners on
SD : 03 :055(549) [0935] the Augsburg Confession **accept** the principle that we
SD : 04 :008(552) [0941] are pleasing and **acceptable** to God, even though they are
SD : 04 :008(552) [0941] through faith, because the person is **acceptable** to God.
SD : 04 :034(556) [0949] however, mean that faith **accepts** righteousness and
SD : 05 :017(561) [0957] to be pleasing and **acceptable** to God, and threatens the
SD : 05 :025(563) [0961] sins through Christ, **accepts** them for his sake as God's
SD : 06 :012(566) [0967] what the **acceptable** will of God is (Rom. 12:2) and in
SD : 06 :022(567) [0969] spiritual sacrifices are **acceptable** to God through faith
SD : 06 :023(568) [0969] and impure, they are **acceptable** to God through Christ
SD : 07 :011(571) [0975] "Article X has been **accepted**, in which we confess that in
SD : 07 :038(576) [0985] with the bread," they still **accept** the words of Christ in
SD : 07 :045(577) [0987] our reason, but we must **accept** them in simple faith and
SD : 07 :048(578) [0989] in their usual, strict, and commonly **accepted** meaning.
SD : 07 :062(581) [0995] — namely, that we hear, **accept** with faith, and
SD : 08 :057(602) [1035] it is a unanimously **accepted** rule of the entire ancient
SD : 08 :061(602) [1035] of our own, but we **accept** and repeat the statements
SD : 11 :018(619) [1069] justify and graciously **accept** into the adoption of children
SD : 11 :018(619) [1069] all who in sincere repentance and true faith **accept** Christ.
SD : 11 :029(621) [1073] God's will that we should **accept** the Word, believe and
SD : 11 :040(623) [1077] justify and save all who **accept** Christ through true faith,
SD : 11 :041(623) [1077] few are chosen," for few **accept** the Word and obey it; the
SD : 12 :000(632) [1095] and Sects Which Never **Accepted** the Augsburg
SD : 12 :001(632) [1095] concerned which never **accepted** the Augsburg Confession
SD : 12 :008(633) [1097] papacy, unfortunately **accepted** in their innocence what

Access (20)
AP : 04 :081(118) [0143] him we have obtained **access**" to the Father, and he adds,
AP : 04 :081(118) [0143] imagine that we have **access** through our own works, by
AP : 04 :081(118) [0143] and then, through this love, have **access** to God.
AP : 04 :081(118) [0145] teaches that we have **access** (that is, reconciliation)
AP : 04 :081(118) [0145] this happens, he adds that through faith we have **access**.
AP : 04 :195(134) [0175] Through him we have obtained **access** by faith."
AP : 04 :215(137) [0179] propitiator through whom we have **access** to the Father.
AP : 04 :222(138) [0181] that by our love we have **access** to God even without
AP : 04 :223(138) [0181] death and can have **access** to God without him as
AP : 04 :246(142) [0189] by our works we have **access** to God without Christ, the
AP : 04 :256(144) [0193] through Christ we have **access** to the Father (Rom. 5:2).
AP : 04 :269(147) [0197] him we have obtained **access**" to the Father (Rom. 5:2),
AP : 04 :291(152) [0203] through him we have **access** to God through faith
AP : 04 :297(153) [0205] him we have obtained **access**" to God, adding, "through
AP : 04 :314(156) [0207] Christ we have obtained **access** to God by faith."
AP : 04 :358(162) [0219] nor the faith that has **access** to God for Christ's sake, not
AP : 04 :376(164) [0223] which believes that we have **access** to God not because of
AP : 12 :037(186) [0261] (Rom. 5:2), "Through him we have obtained **access**."
AP : 12 :063(191) [0269] him we have obtained **access** by faith to this grace," etc.
LC : 04 :077(446) [0751] we always have **access** to it so that we may again subdue

Accessory (1)
LC : 01 :309(407) [0669] neighbor, nor become **accessory** to it, nor give occasion

Accidens (2)
EP : 01 :023(469) [0785] words *substantia* and **accidens** are concerned, they are
SD : 01 :054(517) [0877] terms *substantia* and **accidens**, we maintain that the

Accident (10), Accidental (5), Accidentally (2), Accidents (2)
LC : 03 :115(435) [0731] his anger by causing **accidents** and injury to our bodies.
EP : 01 :024(469) [0785] thing and that which pertains to it only **accidentally**.
EP : 01 :025(469) [0785] permission, corrupt **accidentally** the substance which God
SD : 01 :021(512) [0865] only of certain **accidental** elements in human nature, in
SD : 01 :054(518) [0877] essence) or an **accident** (that is, an accidental thing that is

Continued ▶

SD : 01 :054(518) [0877] an accident (that is, an **accidental** thing that is not
SD : 01 :055(518) [0877] self-subsistent) but an **accident** (that is, something
SD : 01 :055(518) [0877] but an accident (that is, something **accidental**).
SD : 01 :056(518) [0877] nature itself, but an **accidental** defect and damage in the
SD : 01 :057(518) [0877] either a substance or an **accident** (that is, either a
SD : 01 :057(518) [0877] essence or something **accidental** thereto), if anyone were
SD : 01 :057(518) [0877] thing) or if it is an **accident** (that is, a thing that does not
SD : 01 :057(518) [0879] that original sin is not a substance but an **accident**.
SD : 01 :058(519) [0879] sin is a substance or an **accident** in the right and strict
SD : 01 :060(519) [0879] inquires further, What kind of **accident** is original sin?
SD : 01 :061(519) [0879] Thus the term **"accident"** does not in any way minimize
SD : 01 :062(519) [0879] used both the term **"accident"** and the term "quality" when
SD : 01 :062(519) [0879] dreadful this quality and **accident** is, which did not simply
SD : 07 :108(588) [1009] bread and wine, or their **accidents** without a subject,

Accommodate (1)
SD : 02 :011(522) [0885] powers prepare or **accommodate** himself to regain

Accompanied (2), Accompanies (2), Accompany (2)
AG : 15 :002(036) [0049] Yet we **accompany** these observances with instruction so
SC : 06 :008(352) [0557] These words, when **accompanied** by the bodily eating and
LC : 04 :033(440) [0741] in the words which **accompany** the water, they cannot be
LC : 04 :053(443) [0745] is, when the Word **accompanies** the water, Baptism is
LC : 04 :073(445) [0751] symbol, but the effect **accompanies** it; but where faith is
EP : 03 :011(474) [0795] never alone but is always **accompanied** by love and hope.

Accomplish (19), Accomplished (12), Accomplishes (3)
PR : PR :017(008) [0015] at Naumburg failed to **accomplish** the desired end of
PR : PR :020(010) [0017] and hence he is able to **accomplish** what he has ordained
AG : 18 :003(039) [0051] This is **accomplished** by the Holy Spirit, who is given
AG : 20 :010(042) [0055] imagines that he can **accomplish** this by works, or that he
AG : 20 :033(045) [0057] lives; they failed to **accomplish** this, and instead fell into
AL : 18 :004(039) [0051] begin or (much less) to **accomplish** anything in those
AL : 20 :014(043) [0055] justification, which is **accomplished** by grace, were due to
AP : 04 :101(121) [0151] that God will certainly **accomplish** what he has promised
AP : 04 :201(134) [0175] was already **accomplished**, but circumcision was added to
AP : 12 :006(183) [0255] the power of the keys **accomplish** if the sin is forgiven
AP : 13 :011(212) [0311] me empty, but it shall **accomplish** that which I purpose,
S1 : PR :006(289) [0457] However, what such persons **accomplish** is manifest.
S2 : 04 :015(301) [0475] his adversaries and will **accomplish** his purpose by his
S3 : 03 :032(308) [0489] Your repentance **accomplishes** nothing.
LC : PR :004(359) [0567] and even our utmost exertions **accomplish** but little.
LC : 02 :031(414) [0685] this redemption was **accomplished** — that is, how much it
LC : 02 :061(419) [0695] and redemption is **accomplished**, but the Holy Spirit
LC : 02 :062(419) [0695] in faith for this to be **accomplished** through the Word.
LC : 03 :031(424) [0707] What do you think has **accomplished** such great results in
LC : 03 :068(429) [0717] fury, so that they may **accomplish** nothing and we may
LC : 03 :100(433) [0725] This, however, is not **accomplished** without failures and
LC : 05 :031(450) [0759] the work was **accomplished** and forgiveness of sins was
LC : 05 :031(450) [0759] that this has been **accomplished** and offered to us if it
EP : 02 :018(472) [0791] has performed and **accomplished** this and the will of man
SD : 02 :003(520) [0881] Holy Spirit he could **accomplish** nothing with these
SD : 02 :007(521) [0883] imagine, will, begin, **accomplish**, do, effect, or cooperate,
SD : 02 :012(522) [0885] them, to do them, to **accomplish** or to cooperate in them
SD : 02 :072(535) [0909] wills to begin and **accomplish** all this, reminds us also how
SD : 02 :073(535) [0909] at all, but merely suffers what God **accomplishes** in him?
SD : 02 :089(538) [0915] Holy Spirit alone, who **accomplishes** and performs it by
SD : 07 :043(577) [0987] he is able mightily to **accomplish** and achieve what he
SD : 07 :047(578) [0989] Truth and can certainly **accomplish** and bring to pass
SD : 08 :025(596) [1023] nature could not have **accomplished** this if it had not been
SD : 11 :076(628) [1087] ordinary means or instruments to **accomplish** this end.

Accord (21), Accordance (15), Accorded (1), Accordingly (73), Accords (1)
PR : PR :013(007) [0013] **Accordingly** we, the elector of Saxony, etc., with the
PR : PR :017(008) [0015] In **accordance** therewith we have reached Christian
PR : PR :018(008) [0015] and only, in **accordance** with the pure, infallible, and
PR : PR :024(013) [0023] We are **accordingly** mindful of the obligation that we
AG : PR :007(025) [0039] **Accordingly**, after due deliberation and counsel, it was
AG : PR :011(025) [0041] All of this is in **accord** with Your Imperial Majesty's
AG : PR :023(027) [0043] Christian concord in **accordance** with Your Imperial
AG : 01 :001(027) [0043] hold and teach, in **accordance** with the decree of the
AG : 07 :002(032) [0047] be administered in **accordance** with the divine Word.
AG : 08 :003(033) [0047] **Accordingly** the Donatists and all others who hold
AG : 15 :004(037) [0049] **Accordingly** monastic vows and other traditions
AG : 16 :006(038) [0051] **Accordingly** Christians are obliged to be subject to civil
AG : 22 :011(050) [0061] **Accordingly** it is not proper to burden the consciences of
AG : 24 :025(059) [0067] **Accordingly** it is to be hoped that everyone will
AG : 24 :030(059) [0067] **Accordingly** the sacrament requires faith, and without
AG : 26 :011(065) [0071] **Accordingly** there was no end or limit to the making of
AG : 26 :021(067) [0073] **Accordingly** they should not be made into a necessary
AG : 27 :030(075) [0079] **Accordingly** it is not right to argue so rashly and
AG : 28 :070(093) [0093] is no doubt that it is in **accord** with the holy Gospel.
AG : 28 :074(093) [0093] **Accordingly** the bishops ought to be so gracious as to
AL : 20 :018(043) [0055] **Accordingly** inexperienced and profane men, who dream
AL : 20 :038(046) [0057] **Accordingly**, when there is no faith and trust in God, all
AL : 23 :025(055) [0065] **Accordingly** Cyprian advised that women who did not
AL : 24 :009(057) [0065] **Accordingly** it does not appear that the Mass is observed
AL : 24 :013(057) [0065] **Accordingly** when our priests were admonished
AL : 25 :005(062) [0069] **Accordingly** no fault is to be found with our churches on
AL : 26 :021(067) [0073] **Accordingly** our teachers have taught that we cannot
AL : 27 :013(073) [0077] serve their calling in **accordance** with God's commands.
AL : 27 :030(075) [0079] **Accordingly** it is not fair to argue so insistently about the
AL : 28 :004(081) [0085] **Accordingly** our teachers have been compelled, for the
AP : 04 :250(143) [0191] **Accordingly**, James is correct in denying that we are
AP : 07 :028(173) [0237] In **accordance** with the Scriptures, therefore, we maintain
AP : 12 :150(206) [0299] They object that it is in **accord** with God's justice to
AP : 21 :006(230) [0345] which each should imitate in **accordance** with his calling.
AP : 22 :001(236) [0357] Supper is godly and in **accord** with the institution of
AP : 24 :021(252) [0391] They were **accordingly** called propitiatory sacrifices for
S1 : PR :002(288) [0455] **Accordingly** I assembled these articles and submitted them
S2 : 02 :010(294) [0465] **Accordingly** we are and remain eternally divided and
S2 : 03 :002(298) [0471] needless effort, and **accordingly** the prophets call such
S2 : 04 :014(301) [0475] **Accordingly**, just as we cannot adore the devil himself as
S3 : 02 :002(303) [0479] **Accordingly**, in so far as they are not restrained by
S3 : 03 :010(305) [0481] will is capable of acting **accordingly**, and that God will
S3 : 03 :019(306) [0483] **Accordingly** he could never know when he had made a
S3 : 03 :032(308) [0489] **Accordingly**, if you would repent, repent rightly.
S3 : 03 :039(309) [0489] **Accordingly** the entire building, even when it is most holy
S3 : 08 :010(313) [0497] **Accordingly**, we should and must constantly maintain
S3 : 10 :003(314) [0497] **Accordingly**, as we are taught by the examples of the
S3 : 13 :003(315) [0499] **Accordingly** we cannot boast of the great merit in our
TR : 00 :008(320) [0505] **Accordingly** he said, "The kings of the Gentiles exercise
TR : 00 :016(323) [0509] recognized or acted in **accordance** with it, it is quite
TR : 00 :048(328) [0519] **Accordingly** they cannot be overlooked.
TR : 00 :057(330) [0521] **Accordingly**, even if the bishop of Rome did possess the
TR : 00 :062(330) [0521] **Accordingly** Jerome teaches clearly that in the apostolic
TR : 00 :082(334) [0529] **Accordingly** they subscribe their names.
SC : PR :022(341) [0537] preach that, of their own **accord** and without any law, the
SC : PR :023(341) [0539] hasten to it of his own **accord**, he will feel constrained to
SC : PR :024(341) [0539] **Accordingly** you are not to make a law of this, as the pope
SC : PR :024(341) [0539] will come of their own **accord** and without compulsion on
SC : 03 :005(346) [0547] as children of God, lead holy lives in **accordance** with it.
LC : 01 :020(367) [0585] **Accordingly** the heathen actually fashion their fancies and
LC : 01 :042(370) [0591] **Accordingly**, we must grasp these words, even in the face
LC : 01 :048(371) [0593] fulfillment of all the others will follow of its own **accord**.
LC : 01 :087(376) [0605] **Accordingly**, when you are asked what "You shall sanctify
LC : 01 :092(377) [0607] **Accordingly**, I constantly repeat that all our life and work
LC : 01 :118(381) [0615] a single work done in **accordance** with his commandment
LC : 01 :201(392) [0637] **Accordingly** adultery was the most common form of
LC : 01 :259(400) [0655] evidence presented, and make his decision **accordingly**.
LC : 01 :274(402) [0659] because God of his own **accord** instituted that office, and
LC : 01 :322(409) [0673] them and gladly act and live in **accordance** with them.
LC : 02 :021(413) [0683] we would also act **accordingly**, and not swagger about
LC : 03 :016(422) [0701] on account of his Word and the obedience **accorded** it.
LC : 03 :021(423) [0703] and pray not of my own **accord** or because of my own
LC : 03 :109(435) [0729] **Accordingly** we Christians must be armed and prepared
LC : 05 :043(451) [0763] will of their own **accord** urge and impel themselves to
LC : 06 :027(460) [0000] and do not come of their own **accord**, we let go their way.
EP : 01 :011(467) [0781] 1. **Accordingly** we reject and condemn the teaching that
EP : 02 :007(470) [0787] **Accordingly** we reject and condemn all the following
EP : 02 :016(472) [0791] doctrine and that **accordingly** it is well to avoid them in a
EP : 03 :004(473) [0793] 2. **Accordingly** we believe, teach, and confess that our
EP : 03 :012(474) [0795] **Accordingly** we reject and condemn all the following
EP : 04 :016(477) [0801] 1. **Accordingly** we reject and condemn spoken and written
EP : 06 :008(481) [0807] 1. **Accordingly** we condemn as dangerous and subversive
EP : 07 :009(483) [0811] and confess with one **accord** that in the celebration of the
EP : 07 :042(486) [0817] 21. **Accordingly**, we herewith condemn without any
EP : 07 :042(486) [0817] On the contrary, in **accord** with the simple words of
EP : 08 :019(490) [0823] **Accordingly** we reject and condemn as contrary to the
EP : 11 :016(497) [0837] **Accordingly** we believe and maintain that if anybody
EP : 11 :016(497) [0837] and will of God, but in **accord** with his reason and under
SD : RN :010(506) [0855] If they are in **accord** with the aforementioned pattern of
SD : RN :016(507) [0857] and accept with one **accord** as the correct and abiding
SD : 01 :030(513) [0869] from our nature and **accordingly** not coessential with us.
SD : 01 :055(518) [0877] Augustine, in **accord** with all dependable teachers,
SD : 02 :007(521) [0883] **Accordingly**, we believe that after the Fall and prior to his
SD : 02 :028(527) [0893] the Word of God and **accords** with the Augsburg
SD : 03 :009(540) [0919] confess unanimously, in **accord** with the summary
SD : 03 :017(541) [0921] **Accordingly** the word "justify" here means to declare
SD : 03 :030(544) [0925] **Accordingly** in justification before God faith trusts neither
SD : 03 :059(550) [0937] **Accordingly** we unanimously reject and condemn, in
SD : 05 :022(562) [0959] **Accordingly** every penitent sinner must believe — that is,
SD : 06 :003(564) [0963] life and behavior in **accord** with God's external and
SD : 06 :015(566) [0967] of good works that are in **accord** with the law of God —
SD : 07 :014(571) [0977] They confess, in **accordance** with the words of Irenaeus,
SD : 07 :023(573) [0979] and must, then in **accordance** with the words it is truly
SD : 07 :107(588) [1009] **Accordingly** we reject and condemn with heart and mouth
SD : 07 :108(588) [1009] **Accordingly** they assert that under the species of the
SD : 07 :117(589) [1013] **Accordingly** the term "sacramental union" is to be
SD : 08 :005(592) [1017] Word of God and in **accordance** with our plain Christian
SD : 08 :051(601) [1033] **Accordingly**, for the exercise of Christ's office, the human
SD : 10 :014(613) [1057] free and which **accordingly** are not subject either to a
SD : 11 :003(616) [1063] **Accordingly**, the net total and content of the teaching on
SD : 11 :065(626) [1083] We should **accordingly** consider God's eternal election in

Account (157)
PR : PR :009(006) [0011] on our part, that little **account** was taken by our
PR : PR :021(010) [0019] and scandal on this **account** will be removed inasmuch as
PR : PR :021(011) [0019] put it, it takes place on **account** of the personal union,
PR : PR :024(013) [0023] by divine precept, on **account** of the office we bear, over
AG : 09 :003(033) [0047] On this **account** the Anabaptists who teach that infant
AG : 12 :003(034) [0049] sorrow, or terror, on **account** of sin, and yet at the same
AG : 00 :000(048) [0059] in Dispute, in Which an **Account** Is Given of the Abuses
AG : 00 :000(049) [0059] circumstances to give an **account** of them and to indicate
AG : 23 :006(052) [0061] their deathbeds on this **account**, and many have
AG : 23 :014(053) [0063] will graciously take into **account** that fact that, in these
AG : 23 :018(054) [0063] the clergy would, on **account** of their abomination and
AG : 25 :009(063) [0069] On this **account** there is no need to compel people to give
AG : 25 :009(063) [0069] to compel people to give a detailed **account** of their sins.
AG : 26 :005(064) [0071] On this **account** St. Paul contended mightily against the
AG : 26 :013(066) [0073] fell into despair on this **account**, and some even
AG : 28 :004(081) [0085] On this **account** our teachers have been compelled, for
AG : 28 :022(084) [0087] On this **account** parish ministers and churches are bound
AL : 04 :002(030) [0045] sins are forgiven on **account** of Christ, who by his death
AL : 05 :003(031) [0045] is to say, it is not on **account** of our own merits but on
AL : 05 :003(031) [0045] of our own merits but on **account** of Christ that God
AL : 00 :002(048) [0059] as to bear with us on **account** of the confession which we
AL : 00 :000(048) [0059] Articles in Which an **Account** Is Given of the Abuses
AL : 23 :002(051) [0061] On this **account** Pope Pius is reported to have said that
AL : 23 :016(054) [0063] now and then on **account** of man's weakness, and it is
AL : 24 :040(061) [0069] is different, and on **account** of the great and manifest
AL : 25 :013(063) [0071] is retained among us on **account** of the great benefit of
AL : 26 :043(070) [0075] in Rome, and when on **account** of this difference the
AL : 27 :039(077) [0081] services and on this **account** were void, for a wicked vow,
AL : 28 :004(081) [0085] they have taught that on **account** of God's command both
AP : 04 :040(112) [0131] On this **account** the law cannot free us from sin or justify

Continued ▶

AP : 04 :086(119) [0147] children of God not on **account** of their own purity but
AP : 04 :086(119) [0147] purity but by mercy on **account** of Christ, if they grasp
AP : 04 :098(121) [0151] as the cause or price on **account** of which we are saved.
AP : 04 :109(123) [0153] attribute justification to faith except on **account** of love.
AP : 04 :110(123) [0153] forgiveness of sins on **account** of love, the forgiveness of
AP : 04 :112(123) [0155] trust in this love or on **account** of this love, just as little
AP : 04 :112(123) [0155] forgiveness of sins on **account** of the other works that
AP : 04 :145(127) [0163] sins by faith, nor that on **account** of Christ, the mediator,
AP : 04 :145(127) [0163] They think this is on **account** of our love, though they do
AP : 04 :147(127) [0163] sins through love or on **account** of love, but on account
AP : 04 :147(127) [0163] account of love, but on **account** of Christ by faith alone.
AP : 04 :151(127) [0163] virtues of the law or on **account** of them (whether
AP : 04 :151(127) [0163] forgiveness of sins on **account** of love, though it, too,
AP : 04 :154(128) [0163] And the **account** here shows what he calls "love."
AP : 04 :161(129) [0167] not justify, because it is accepted only on **account** of faith.
AP : 04 :165(129) [0169] accounted righteous on **account** of Christ, "who is at the
AP : 04 :176(131) [0171] righteous before God on **account** of our keeping of the
AP : 04 :207(135) [0177] with the notion that on **account** of them they had a
AP : 04 :234(140) [0185] the bishops take into **account** the weakness of the people.
AP : 04 :269(147) [0197] for pleasing God on **account** of faith, since they do not
AP : 04 :279(149) [0199] God is reconciled on **account** of his mercy and which
AP : 04 :280(149) [0201] single passage without taking the whole law into **account**.
AP : 04 :293(152) [0203] works please God on **account** of the justifying faith that
AP : 04 :296(152) [0205] that he was given for us to be justified on his **account**.
AP : 04 :305(154) [0205] and to do so on **account** of someone else's righteousness,
AP : 04 :321(157) [0209] are worth enough to **account** them righteous, whereas
AP : 12 :108(198) [0283] Thou dost justify us and **account** us righteous through
AP : 12 :152(206) [0299] troubles are inflicted on **account** of present sin because in
AP : 12 :154(206) [0301] and the penalties on **account** of which the satisfactions
AP : 20 :003(227) [0339] of sins itself on **account** of our works and not freely on
AP : 20 :003(227) [0339] account of our works and not freely on **account** of Christ.
AP : 20 :009(227) [0341] weighty that we shrink from no danger on **account** of it.
AP : 20 :010(228) [0341] of sins were given on **account** of our works, when would
AP : 20 :011(228) [0341] of sins not on **account** of our works but freely for Christ's
AP : 21 :001(229) [0343] this as though on this **account** the invocation of the
AP : 21 :022(232) [0349] accounted righteous on **account** of them just as we are by
AP : 21 :029(233) [0351] us or accounted us righteous or saved us on this **account**.
AP : 22 :016(238) [0361] figure out how they will **account** to God for their
AP : 23 :070(249) [0383] who will call them to **account** for breaking up marriages
AP : 27 :002(269) [0419] he became ill either on **account** of age or on account of
AP : 27 :002(269) [0419] on account of age or on **account** of the filth of the prison,
AP : 27 :015(271) [0425] of sins freely but on **account** of the works of other laws
AP : 27 :017(271) [0425] not by forgiving sins on **account** of our works but by
AP : 28 :005(282) [0445] will some day have to give **account** of your stewardship.
AP : 28 :025(285) [0451] it, will give an **account** for the schism that has been
S1 : PR :003(289) [0455] a little troubled on this **account**, for they perceive that the
S2 : 02 :004(293) [0463] wretchedness and woe on **account** of an unnecessary and
S2 : 02 :027(297) [0469] I should not on this **account** pray to you, invoke you,
S3 : 03 :003(304) [0481] hear such a judgment as this: "You are all of no **account**.
S3 : 03 :019(306) [0483] had to give an **account** of all his sins — an impossibility
S3 : 03 :036(309) [0489] On this **account** there is no uncertainty in such
S3 : 10 :002(314) [0497] must not be deprived of ministers on their **account**.
S3 : 13 :001(315) [0499] that God will and does **account** us altogether righteous
TR : 00 :024(324) [0511] of apostles, on which **account** these passages do not
TR : 00 :044(328) [0517] that sins are forgiven on **account** of the worth of our
TR : 00 :074(332) [0525] and, either on **account** of avarice or on account of other
TR : 00 :074(332) [0525] account of avarice or on **account** of other evil desires,
TR : 00 :076(333) [0525] it, there is no need, on **account** of this jurisdiction, to
TR : 00 :077(333) [0527] to obey the bishops on **account** of this jurisdiction either.
TR : 00 :078(333) [0527] and that on this **account** the magistrates ought to
SC : 03 :016(347) [0549] our sins, and on their **account** deny our prayers, for we
SC : 09 :003(355) [0561] over your souls, as men who will have to give **account**.
LC : 01 :022(367) [0585] It keeps **account** how often it has made endowments,
LC : 01 :035(369) [0589] all idolatry, and on that **account** he has destroyed both
LC : 01 :087(377) [0605] holy or unholy on your **account**, according as you spend
LC : 01 :092(377) [0607] sanctified by it, not on **account** of the external work but
LC : 01 :092(377) [0607] external work but on **account** of the Word which makes
LC : 01 :117(381) [0615] and precious, not on **account** of your worthiness but
LC : 01 :125(382) [0617] we should wish, on **account** of the commandments, that
LC : 01 :171(388) [0629] will solemnly call us to **account** and punish us for its
LC : 01 :261(400) [0655] suppressing anything on **account** of anyone's money,
LC : 01 :327(409) [0675] to them not on their own **account** but for God's sake.
LC : 02 :036(415) [0687] called Redeemer, so on **account** of his work the Holy
LC : 03 :013(422) [0701] We should think, "On my **account** this prayer would
LC : 03 :015(422) [0701] is given just as much on my **account** as on his.
LC : 03 :016(422) [0701] to his person, but not on **account** of the commandment.
LC : 03 :016(422) [0701] not regard prayer on **account** of the person, but on
LC : 03 :016(422) [0701] of the person, but on **account** of his Word and the
LC : 03 :044(425) [0709] the result that on his **account** the father suffers scorn and
LC : 03 :067(429) [0717] we must suffer on its **account**, we may patiently bear and
LC : 03 :084(431) [0721] in the world simply on **account** of false coinage, yes, on
LC : 03 :084(431) [0721] of false coinage, yes, on **account** of daily exploitation and
LC : 03 :096(433) [0725] Not on **account** of your forgiving, for God does it
LC : 04 :021(439) [0737] and exalt Baptism on **account** of the Word, since God
LC : 04 :038(441) [0741] is comprehended and on **account** of which this flesh is
LC : 04 :055(443) [0745] not be permitted on **account** of that abuse to take it again
LC : 04 :057(444) [0747] not baptize him on that **account**, but solely on the
LC : 04 :072(445) [0751] appointed not only on **account** of what it confers, but also
LC : 04 :072(445) [0751] of what it confers, but also on **account** of what it signifies.
LC : 05 :062(454) [0767] but I come not on **account** of any worthiness of mine, but
LC : 05 :062(454) [0767] of mine, but on **account** of thy Word, because Thou hast
EP : 01 :012(467) [0783] is not truly sin on **account** of which man outside of
EP : 03 :004(473) [0793] of Christ's obedience, on **account** of which righteousness
EP : 03 :015(475) [0795] in fact before God on **account** of the love and virtue that
EP : 06 :001(479) [0805] to give them on that **account** a definite rule according to
EP : 06 :002(480) [0805] they are not on that **account** without the law; on the
EP : 06 :004(480) [0805] On **account** of this Old Adam, who inheres in people's
EP : 08 :009(487) [0819] personally (that is, on **account** of the personal union), as
EP : 11 :020(497) [0837] of God's election, on **account** of which he has elected us
EP : 12 :031(500) [0843] all of us as we shall give **account** of it on the Last Day
SD : PR :019(507) [0857] Augsburg Confession on **account** of the Interim and for
SD : 01 :006(509) [0861] On **account** of this corruption and because of the fall of
SD : 01 :019(511) [0865] every person on that **account** is necessarily a child of
SD : 03 :004(540) [0917] God's children solely on **account** of the obedience of
SD : 03 :015(541) [0919] and saves us forever on **account** of this entire obedience
SD : 03 :017(542) [0921] of these sins on **account** of the righteousness of Christ
SD : 03 :022(543) [0923] for us, even though, on **account** of their corrupted
SD : 03 :023(543) [0923] up and are not reckoned to our **account** (Rom. 4:6-8).
SD : 03 :028(544) [0925] wholly pure and perfect on **account** of our corrupted flesh.
SD : 03 :030(544) [0925] Not only on this **account** but also in order to afford
SD : 03 :032(545) [0927] impure in this life on **account** of the flesh, no one can
SD : 03 :032(545) [0927] of eternal life only on **account** of Christ's obedience.
SD : 03 :043(547) [0931] associated with love, on **account** of which love the power
SD : 03 :043(547) [0931] this reason and on this **account**, that as a means and
SD : 03 :054(549) [0935] of God, on **account** of which we are declared just before
SD : 03 :054(549) [0935] of poor sinners on **account** of the obedience and merit of
SD : 03 :062(550) [0937] and truly righteous on **account** of the love and virtues
SD : 04 :032(556) [0947] "On **account** of these the wrath of God is coming upon
SD : 04 :038(557) [0951] good works are done on **account** of right causes and for
SD : 08 :018(594) [1021] On **account** of this personal union and communion, the
SD : 08 :019(595) [1021] more ineffable, since on **account** of this union and
SD : 08 :020(595) [1021] On **account** of this personal union, without which such a
SD : 08 :024(595) [1023] On **account** of this personal union and communion of the
SD : 08 :066(604) [1039] such a way that on that **account** and through this union
SD : 10 :019(614) [1059] must not be deprived of ministers on their **account**."
SD : 11 :088(631) [1093] of God's election on **account** of which God has elected us
SD : 12 :040(636) [1103] of Jesus Christ and for which we shall give an **account**.

Accountable (2), Accounted (50), Accounting (2), Accounts (2)

PR : PR :022(012) [0021] they will have to give a hard **accounting**.
AG : 20 :002(041) [0053] good and profitable **accounts** and instructions concerning
AP : 04 :018(109) [0125] of sins and are **accounted** righteous by their own keeping
AP : 04 :026(110) [0127] false, too, that men are **accounted** righteous before God
AP : 04 :048(114) [0135] because those who are **accounted** righteous before God do
AP : 04 :069(116) [0141] and believe that for his sake we are **accounted** righteous?
AP : 04 :072(117) [0141] faith itself we are truly **accounted** righteous or acceptable
AP : 04 :072(117) [0141] as well as to be pronounced or **accounted** righteous.
AP : 04 :086(119) [0147] The reconciled are **accounted** righteous and children of
AP : 04 :086(119) [0147] Scriptures testify that we are **accounted** righteous by faith.
AP : 04 :086(119) [0147] by which we are **accounted** righteous before God.
AP : 04 :089(120) [0149] clearly says that faith itself is **accounted** for righteousness.
AP : 04 :089(120) [0149] he adds that it is **accounted** freely and denies that it could
AP : 04 :089(120) [0149] denies that it could be **accounted** freely if it were a reward
AP : 04 :089(120) [0149] God, faith would not be **accounted** for righteousness
AP : 04 :097(121) [0149] Therefore we are **accounted** righteous for Christ's sake
AP : 04 :114(123) [0155] us to God, we must be **accounted** righteous by this faith
AP : 04 :161(129) [0167] not trust that we are **accounted** righteous before God by
AP : 04 :163(129) [0169] he believes that he is **accounted** righteous by faith for
AP : 04 :163(129) [0169] always hold that we are **accounted** righteous by faith for
AP : 04 :165(129) [0169] believe that we are **accounted** righteous on account of
AP : 04 :176(131) [0171] not believe that we are **accounted** righteous before God
AP : 04 :177(131) [0171] by faith we are **accounted** righteous because of Christ,
AP : 04 :179(131) [0171] for whose sake they are now **accounted** righteous.
AP : 04 :179(131) [0171] But when they are **accounted** righteous, the law cannot
AP : 04 :209(136) [0179] propitiation for which he would be **accounted** righteous.
AP : 04 :211(136) [0179] through faith they were **accounted** righteous and had a
AP : 04 :212(136) [0179] and a price because of which we are **accounted** righteous.
AP : 04 :212(136) [0179] freely by faith we are **accounted** righteous for Christ's
AP : 04 :213(136) [0179] grace and that we are **accounted** righteous before God
AP : 04 :214(136) [0179] We are **accounted** righteous before God for Christ's sake
AP : 04 :214(136) [0179] We are not **accounted** righteous because of our works
AP : 04 :221(137) [0181] the faith that we are **accounted** righteous because of
AP : 04 :230(139) [0183] the propitiator, we are **accounted** righteous when we
AP : 04 :293(152) [0203] This faith is **accounted** for righteousness before God
AP : 04 :296(152) [0205] Thus we are not **accounted** righteous because of the law
AP : 04 :362(162) [0219] will grant that we are **accounted** righteous by faith for
AP : 15 :008(216) [0317] think you deserve to be **accounted** righteous before God,
AP : 15 :012(216) [0317] justification we are not **accounted** righteous for his sake
AP : 21 :019(231) [0347] them we may be **accounted** righteous as though the
AP : 21 :019(231) [0347] we believe in him we are **accounted** righteous by our trust
AP : 21 :022(232) [0349] as though we were **accounted** righteous on account of
AP : 21 :025(232) [0349] we are reconciled and **accounted** righteous not only by
AP : 21 :029(233) [0351] were reconciled to us or **accounted** us righteous or saved
AP : 21 :031(233) [0351] Because of them we are **accounted** righteous when we
AP : 21 :031(233) [0351] not believe that we are **accounted** righteous by the merits
AP : 23 :039(244) [0375] that through faith he is **accounted** righteous before God.
AP : 27 :023(272) [0427] of which we are **accounted** righteous before God and
AP : 27 :069(281) [0443] because of them we are **accounted** righteous; that we
S3 : 03 :001(303) [0479] world may be held **accountable** to God, for no human
S3 : 03 :017(305) [0483] want to say No?) it was **accounted** as contrition and, on
S3 : 13 :002(315) [0499] of his works, shall be **accounted** and shall be righteous
LC : 01 :098(378) [0609] will require of you an **accounting** of how you have heard
LC : 01 :169(388) [0629] and injunction of God, who holds you **accountable** for it.
SD : 03 :011(541) [0919] of sins by grace, are **accounted** righteous and holy by God
SD : 03 :015(541) [0919] God forgives us our sins, **accounts** us holy and righteous,

Accurate (1), Accurately (2)

PR : PR :010(006) [0011] Word, carefully and **accurately** to explain and decide the
TR : 00 :022(323) [0511] been treated fully and **accurately** in the books of our
LC : 05 :010(448) [0755] of St. Augustine is so **accurate** and well put that it is

Accursed (13)

AG : 28 :024(084) [0087] to you, let him be **accursed**," and in II Cor. 13:8, "We
AL : 28 :024(084) [0087] other Gospel, let him be **accursed**" (Gal. 1:8), "We cannot
AP : 07 :048(177) [0245] contrary to that which you received, let him be **accursed**."
AP : 27 :040(276) [0433] Indeed, such leaving is **accursed**; for if someone leaves his
AP : 28 :020(284) [0449] "If anyone preaches another Gospel, let him be **accursed**."
S2 : 02 :014(295) [0467] shameful, blasphemous, **accursed** traffic in Masses which
TR : 00 :038(326) [0515] and such government ought to be regarded as **accursed**.
TR : 00 :038(326) [0515] which we preached to you, let him be **accursed**" (Gal. 1:8).
TR : 00 :041(328) [0517] and execrated as **accursed**, and he wrote in II Cor. 6:14,
LC : 01 :262(400) [0655] apostates, even seditious and **accursed** scoundrels.
EP : RN :001(464) [0777] to that which we preached to you, let him be **accursed**."
EP : 08 :039(491) [0827] but it opens a way for the **accursed** Arian heresy.
SD : 10 :022(615) [1061] and execrated as **accursed**, and he wrote in II Cor. 6:14,

Accusation (3), Accusations (3), Accuse (15), Accused (11), Accuses (15), Accusing (1)

AG : 2 0 :001(041) [0053] have been falsely **accused** of forbidding good works.
AG : 2 0 :035(046) [0057] faith is not to be **accused** of forbidding good works but is
AG : 0 1 :001(056) [0065] We are unjustly **accused** of having abolished the Mass.
AG : 2 5 :011(063) [0069] in public or should **accuse** yourself before others, but
AG : 2 6 :030(068) [0075] are, like Jovinian, **accused** of forbidding mortification
AL : 2 0 :001(041) [0053] Our churches are falsely **accused** of forbidding good
AL : 0 0 :005(049) [0059] from common rumors or the **accusations** of our enemies.
AL : 2 4 :001(056) [0065] Our churches are falsely **accused** of abolishing the Mass.
AL : 2 5 :011(063) [0069] in public or should **accuse** yourself before others, but I
AL : 2 6 :043(070) [0075] difference the Romans **accused** the East of schism, they
AP : 0 4 :038(112) [0131] For the law always **accuses** and terrifies consciences.
AP : 0 4 :062(115) [0139] By its **accusations**, the preaching of penitence terrifies our
AP : 0 4 :103(121) [0151] of the law all are **accused** and by the works of the law
AP : 0 4 :128(125) [0157] The law always **accuses** us, it always shows that God is
AP : 0 4 :157(129) [0165] the law does not justify so long as it can **accuse** us.
AP : 0 4 :167(130) [0169] Without this, the law always **accuses** us.
AP : 0 4 :179(131) [0171] the right of the law to **accuse** and condemn those who
AP : 0 4 :179(131) [0171] righteous, the law cannot **accuse** or condemn them, even
AP : 0 4 :204(135) [0177] The law always **accuses** them and brings forth wrath.
AP : 0 4 :239(141) [0187] when God judges and **accuses** us, but faith in Christ frees
AP : 0 4 :257(144) [0193] law works wrath; it only **accuses**; it only terrifies
AP : 0 4 :260(145) [0193] because the law works wrath and continually **accuses**.
AP : 0 4 :270(147) [0197] It always **accuses** the conscience, which does not satisfy
AP : 0 4 :285(150) [0201] The law always **accuses**.
AP : 0 4 :295(152) [0203] God; the law always **accuses** us and thus always shows us
AP : 0 4 :319(156) [0209] stilled; for the law always **accuses** us, even in good works.
AP : 0 7 :025(173) [0235] We alone are **accused**, because we preach the blessing of
AP : 1 2 :034(186) [0259] For the law only **accuses** and terrifies the conscience.
AP : 1 2 :062(190) [0269] believe absolution but the **accusation** that God is a liar?
AP : 1 2 :088(195) [0277] For the law will always **accuse** us because we never satisfy
AP : 1 5 :039(220) [0325] Our enemies falsely **accuse** us of abolishing good
AP : 2 7 :025(273) [0427] these Commandments **accuse** all the saints, "You shall
S 3 : 0 3 :005(304) [0481] That is, John was to **accuse** them all and convince them
LC : 0 1 :226(395) [0645] dares to give them a hard look or **accuse** them of theft.
LC : 0 1 :257(399) [0653] a poor, innocent man is **accused** and maligned by false
LC : 0 1 :268(401) [0657] therefore ventures to **accuse** his neighbor of such guilt
LC : 0 1 :296(405) [0665] it honorably, without **accusation** or blame for fraudulent
LC : 0 1 :310(407) [0669] rest, one that constantly **accuses** us and shows just how
LC : 0 3 :021(423) [0703] grossly dishonoring him and **accusing** him of falsehood.
LC : 0 3 :122(436) [0731] so that they despise God and **accuse** him of lying.
EP : 0 1 :018(468) [0783] the original sin which is in the nature is being **accused**.
SD : R N :014(506) [0855] correctly, but also to **accuse** the adversaries who teach
SD : 0 1 :006(509) [0861] or person is under the **accusation** and condemnation of
SD : 0 1 :030(513) [0867] God by his law does not **accuse** and condemn man's
SD : 0 1 :031(513) [0869] this corruption the law **accuses** and condemns man's
SD : 0 1 :032(513) [0869] The law, however, **accuses** and condemns our nature, not
SD : 0 3 :029(544) [0925] falsely slander and **accuse** us) but so that we may not be
SD : 0 8 :004(592) [1017] Word of God, with **accusations** of almost all the

Accustom (3), Accustomed (7)

AL : 2 4 :005(056) [0065] The people are **accustomed** to receive the sacrament
AP : 1 1 :006(181) [0251] a good practice to **accustom** the unlearned to enumerate
AP : 1 5 :051(222) [0329] be changed in the **accustomed** rites without good reason,
SC : P R :008(339) [0533] fathers, who were **accustomed** to use the same form in
LC : 0 1 :317(408) [0673] of men on earth may **accustom** themselves to look only to
LC : 0 2 :048(416) [0691] We, however, are **accustomed** to the term *Kirche*,
LC : 0 5 :085(456) [0773] them from their youth, and become **accustomed** to them.
SD : 0 7 :008(570) [0975] that they are **accustomed** to anathematize and condemn
SD : 1 1 :013(618) [1067] eternal life, we should **accustom** ourselves not to
SD : 1 1 :070(627) [1085] adversary is **accustomed** to tempt and vex pious hearts.

Achieve (18), Achieved (6), Achievements (1), Achieves (2), Achieving (1)

AL : 2 8 :064(092) [0093] moderation can never be **achieved** as long as the opinion
AP : 0 4 :137(126) [0161] own strength cannot **achieve** what they set out to do.
AP : 0 4 :203(135) [0177] the wrath of God, and **achieve** justification because of
AP : 1 2 :075(193) [0273] if the law is enough to **achieve** the forgiveness of sins,
AP : 1 2 :075(193) [0273] Christ if by our work we **achieve** the forgiveness of sins?
AP : 1 8 :004(225) [0335] To some extent it can **achieve** civil righteousness or the
AP : 1 8 :004(225) [0335] as the liberty and ability to **achieve** civil righteousness.
AP : 1 8 :004(225) [0335] that is, the reason — can **achieve** on its own without the
AP : 1 8 :005(225) [0335] seem to have wanted this righteousness did not **achieve** it.
AP : 1 8 :009(226) [0337] righteousness and that, to some extent, we can **achieve** it.
AP : 2 4 :035(256) [0397] Our opponents will really **achieve** something if we let them
LC : 0 1 :316(408) [0671] people, that no man can **achieve** such much as to keep one
LC : 0 3 :092(432) [0725] with God and cannot **achieve** such confidence, it will
LC : 0 4 :011(438) [0735] greater importance to our own **achievements** and merits.
EP : 0 8 :024(490) [0823] 5. That personal union **achieves** only common names and
EP : 1 2 :006(498) [0839] as long as they have not **achieved** the use of reason they
EP : 1 2 :007(498) [0839] baptized until they have **achieved** the use of reason and
SD : 0 2 :027(527) [0893] to give the ability to **achieve** something to those who
SD : 0 2 :052(531) [0901] to God, and to work in them both to will and to **achieve**.
SD : 0 2 :074(535) [0909] or power whatever to **achieve** a measure of external
SD : 0 6 :003(564) [0963] rule and norm for **achieving** a godly life and behavior in
SD : 0 7 :043(577) [0987] to accomplish and **achieve** what he speaks and promises,
SD : 0 7 :090(585) [1003] to our faith the power to **achieve** the presence of the body
SD : 0 7 :120(590) [1013] or have been able to **achieve** the true, essential presence
SD : 0 7 :121(590) [1013] of Christ but faith that **achieves** the presence of the body
SD : 0 8 :059(602) [1035] only to the merit that was once **achieved** on the cross.
SD : 1 0 :016(613) [1057] has not previously been **achieved**, will support the
SD : 1 2 :012(634) [1099] baptized until they have **achieved** the use of reason and

Acidia (1)

LC : 0 1 :099(378) [0609] mortal sins and was called ***acidia*** — that is, indolence or

Acknowledge (27), Acknowledged (10), Acknowledges (3), Acknowledging (2), Acknowledgment (2)

PR : P R :006(004) [0009] truth which they had once **acknowledged** and confessed.
PR : P R :025(013) [0023] and we have **acknowledged** and confessed in the past, for
AG : P R :018(026) [0041] a general council and **acknowledged** that it would be
AG : 2 3 :006(052) [0061] account, and many have themselves **acknowledged** this.
AG : 2 3 :018(054) [0063] in Rome have often **acknowledged** this and have
AG : 2 5 :006(062) [0069] opponents themselves **acknowledge** that we have written
AL : 2 8 :018(083) [0085] be held in honor and **acknowledged** as gifts and blessings
AP : 0 2 :011(102) [0109] They **acknowledge** the minor faults in human nature and
AP : 0 2 :033(104) [0113] of the grace of Christ unless we **acknowledge** our faults.
AP : 0 2 :033(104) [0113] before God unless we **acknowledge** that of itself the heart
AP : 0 4 :032(111) [0129] of God which **acknowledge** and glorify him.
AP : 0 4 :154(128) [0163] from him, she truly **acknowledged** him as the Messiah.
AP : 0 4 :154(128) [0165] the Pharisee for not **acknowledging** him as the Messiah,
AP : 0 4 :183(132) [0173] With the **acknowledgment** of the fundamentals in this
AP : 1 2 :151(206) [0299] God's help and to **acknowledge** the unbelief in their
AP : 1 4 :002(214) [0315] This keeps our priests from **acknowledging** such bishops.
AP : 2 4 :026(254) [0393] "that is, the fruit of lips that **acknowledge** his name."
AP : 2 4 :072(262) [0409] ceremony we should **acknowledge** the will and mercy of
AP : 2 4 :073(262) [0409] A faith that **acknowledges** mercy makes alive.
S 3 : 0 3 :035(309) [0489] teaches us to **acknowledge** sin — that is, to acknowledge
S 3 : 0 3 :035(309) [0489] sin — that is, to **acknowledge** that we are all utterly lost,
TR : 0 0 :004(320) [0503] These three articles we **acknowledge** and hold to be false,
TR : 0 0 :010(321) [0505] by Peter, nor does he **acknowledge** Peter as one from
TR : 0 0 :010(321) [0505] But he should have **acknowledged** Peter as his superior if
TR : 0 0 :017(323) [0509] church did not then **acknowledge** the primacy or
TR : 0 0 :021(323) [0509] ancient church had **acknowledged** the primacy of the
TR : 0 0 :024(324) [0511] it is necessary to **acknowledge** that the keys do not belong
TR : 0 0 :082(000) [0529] at Smalcald I **acknowledge** that I am of all the least, yet,
SC : P R :024(341) [0539] who do not feel and **acknowledge** their great need and
SC : 0 5 :018(350) [0553] Before God we should **acknowledge** that we are guilty of
LC : 0 1 :027(368) [0587] We must **acknowledge** everything as God's gifts and
LC : 0 1 :091(377) [0607] it is the only one we Christians **acknowledge** and have.
LC : 0 1 :108(380) [0611] obey me as your father and to **acknowledge** my authority.
LC : 0 2 :021(413) [0683] God to thank him or **acknowledge** him as Lord and
LC : 0 2 :022(413) [0683] advantage, that they **acknowledge** themselves in duty
LC : 0 4 :050(443) [0745] our adversaries must **acknowledge** that infant Baptism is
LC : 0 5 :082(456) [0773] is that we neither **acknowledge** nor believe that we are in
LC : 0 6 :009(458) [0000] Christian life, to **acknowledge** that we are sinners and to
EP : 0 1 :004(466) [0781] and God still **acknowledges** them as his handiwork, as it
EP : 0 5 :008(479) [0803] of their sin, and **acknowledgment** which Moses could
EP : 1 1 :011(496) [0835] men first to repent, to **acknowledge** their sins, to believe
EP : 1 1 :013(496) [0835] one except those who **acknowledge** his Son, Christ, and
SD : 0 2 :060(533) [0905] rebel against **acknowledged** truth, as Stephen describes
SD : 1 0 :017(614) [1059] "So everyone who **acknowledges** me before men, I also
SD : 1 0 :017(614) [1059] before men, I also will **acknowledge** before my Father

Acquainted (1)

TR : 0 0 :014(322) [0507] who are thoroughly **acquainted** with the life of each

Acquiesce (1)

S 1 : P R :014(291) [0459] were to expect God to **acquiesce** in our mummeries while

Acquire (11), Acquired (7), Acquires (3), Acquiring (4)

AP : 0 4 :321(157) [0209] — that men sometimes **acquire** the merit of congruity and
AP : 0 4 :321(157) [0209] To **acquire** the merit of condignity means to doubt and to
AP : 0 4 :351(161) [0217] his likeness"; that is, we **acquire** the true knowledge of
AP : 2 7 :036(275) [0433] but they say that it is a state for **acquiring** perfection.
AP : 2 7 :036(275) [0433] this correction, that it is a state for **acquiring** perfection.
AP : 2 7 :037(275) [0433] These, too, are states for **acquiring** perfection.
LC : 0 1 :144(385) [0623] of service and be glad to **acquire** masters and mistresses in
LC : 0 1 :184(390) [0633] devil's prompting you **acquire** many enemies who
LC : 0 1 :217(394) [0641] people may be led to **acquire** a love for married life and
LC : 0 1 :224(395) [0643] is nothing else than to **acquire** another's property by
LC : 0 1 :236(397) [0647] — which God will let you **acquire** to your undoing — there
LC : 0 1 :297(405) [0665] Everyone **acquires** all he can and lets others look out for
LC : 0 1 :300(405) [0667] honor and right when it comes to **acquiring** possessions.
LC : 0 1 :302(405) [0667] seal of the prince attesting that it was **acquired** lawfully.
LC : 0 1 :303(406) [0667] and worries him until he **acquires** a half or more of it; and
LC : 0 1 :303(406) [0667] be considered as illegally **acquired**, but rather as honestly
LC : 0 1 :304(406) [0667] how much he can **acquire** by such specious pretexts?
LC : 0 2 :038(415) [0689] completed, Christ has **acquired** and won the treasure for
LC : 0 3 :100(433) [0725] although we have **acquired** forgiveness and a good
LC : 0 4 :046(442) [0743] no other kind of life and no work on earth can **acquire**.
LC : 0 5 :031(450) [0759] forgiveness of sins was **acquired** on the cross, yet it
LC : 0 5 :079(455) [0771] see whether you will not **acquire** enemies who harm,
EP : 0 5 :007(478) [0803] of God's grace and favor **acquired** through the merits of
SD : 0 2 :071(535) [0909] in us, from where man **acquires** these things, and how he
SD : 0 7 :062(581) [0995] the benefits that he has **acquired** for us by giving his body

Acquit (1), Acquits (1), Acquittal (1), Acquitted (2)

S 3 : 0 7 :003(312) [0493] anything against myself, but I am not thereby **acquitted**."
SD : 0 3 :012(541) [0919] of righteousness leads to **acquittal** and life for all men"
SD : 0 3 :017(542) [0921] "Woe to those who **acquit** the godless for a bribe, and
SD : 0 3 :017(542) [0921] (Rom. 8:33), that is, absolves and **acquits** from sins.
SD : 0 6 :021(567) [0969] myself, but I am not thereby **acquitted**" (I Cor. 4:4).

Act (89), Acted (4), Acting (7)

AG : 1 8 :004(039) [0051] does not enable them to **act** in matters pertaining to God
AG : 0 0 :001(048) [0059] our teaching were heretical, **act** in an unkind and hasty
AG : 0 0 :002(048) [0059] should in all fairness **act** more leniently, even if there were
AG : 0 0 :000(049) [0059] perceive that we have not **acted** in an unchristian and
AG : 2 2 :011(050) [0061] or to compel them to **act** contrary to the arrangement of
AG : 2 7 :020(074) [0079] endowed with the gift of virginity by a special **act** of God.
AG : 2 8 :039(087) [0089] human ordinances also **act** contrary to God's command
AL : 1 3 :003(036) [0049] justify by the outward **act** and who do not teach that
AL : 2 4 :029(059) [0067] of the outward **act**, justification comes from the work of
AL : 2 6 :023(067) [0073] So he does not require an unprofitable **act** of worship.
AL : 2 8 :039(087) [0089] the authors of traditions **act** contrary to the command of
AP : 0 2 :008(102) [0107] commandments "according to the substance of the **act**."
AP : 0 4 :009(108) [0123] sorrow over sin elicits an **act** of love to God or does good
AP : 0 4 :036(112) [0131] of sins by an elicited **act** of love, since it is impossible to
AP : 0 4 :154(128) [0163] Christ contrasted the whole **act** of reverence of the
AP : 0 4 :155(128) [0165] he praises her entire **act** of worship, as the Scriptures
AP : 0 4 :155(128) [0165] He includes the whole **act** of worship; but meanwhile he
AP : 0 4 :222(137) [0181] the approval of a particular **act** but of the total person.
AP : 0 4 :228(139) [0183] offered promise, is no less an **act** of worship than is love.
AP : 0 4 :290(151) [0203] that we produce an **act** of love whereby we merit the
AP : 0 4 :331(158) [0211] O Lord, give heed and **act**; delay not, for thy own sake, O
AP : 0 4 :384(166) [0225] will grant that the mere **act** of confessing does not save,

Continued ▶

AP : 07 :034(175) [0239] of human traditions is an **act** of worship necessary for
AP : 07 :047(177) [0243] them, for ministers **act** in Christ's stead and do not
AP : 11 :008(181) [0251] when brothers did not **act** as brothers in their fight about
AP : 11 :008(181) [0251] human traditions, is not an **act** of worship necessary for
AP : 12 :075(193) [0273] or contrition elicits an **act** of love to God, he merits the
AP : 12 :075(193) [0273] merits the attainment of the forgiveness of sins by this **act**.
AP : 15 :040(220) [0325] rite, as if this work were an **act** of worship or at least
AP : 22 :011(238) [0361] This is the way a tyrant would **act**.
AP : 23 :005(239) [0365] will not speak, write, or **act** honestly, frankly, or openly in
AP : 23 :008(240) [0367] the nature of man without an extraordinary **act** of God.
AP : 23 :012(241) [0367] only an extraordinary **act** of God can change this right,
AP : 23 :023(242) [0369] In those times such a dismissal was an **act** of kindness.
AP : 24 :002(250) [0385] mere hearing is a beneficial **act** of worship even where
AP : 24 :017(252) [0389] common to both could be "ceremony" or "sacred **act**."
AP : 24 :018(252) [0389] is a ceremony or **act** in which God offers us the content
AP : 24 :018(252) [0389] thus Baptism is not an **act** which we offer to God but one
AP : 24 :018(252) [0389] a sacrifice is a ceremony or **act** which we render to God to
AP : 24 :052(259) [0403] among men is appointed to **act** on behalf of men in
AP : 24 :087(265) [0413] about the efficacy of the **act** *ex opere operato* and its
AP : 27 :006(269) [0421] When they **act** this way, therefore, the monks are signing
AP : 27 :040(276) [0433] or his wife in order by this **act** to merit the forgiveness of
AP : 27 :058(279) [0439] of victims would not be an **act** of worship now, so the
AP : 27 :058(279) [0439] not be proposed as an **act** of worship but should be
AP : 27 :058(279) [0439] a Word of God as an **act** of worship to merit forgiveness
AP : 27 :061(279) [0441] that this work was itself an **act** of worship that justified,
AP : 28 :004(281) [0445] punishments unless they **act** in clear opposition to God's
AP : 28 :014(283) [0447] the power of a tyrant to **act** without a definite law, nor
AP : 28 :014(283) [0447] a definite law, nor that of a king to **act** above the law.
S2 : 04 :007(299) [0473] the Council of Constance **acted** with reference to the
S3 : 02 :002(303) [0479] by punishment, they **act** against the law even more than
S3 : 03 :010(305) [0481] and the will is capable of **acting** accordingly, and that
S3 : 11 :001(314) [0499] On the contrary, they **acted** like antichristian, tyrannical,
TR : 00 :016(323) [0509] world never recognized or **acted** in accordance with it, it
TR : 00 :036(326) [0515] In this matter the **act** itself is not to be deplored so much
LC : PR :007(359) [0569] experienced as any of those who **act** so high and mighty.
LC : 01 :059(372) [0597] We prefer to **act** in secret without anyone's being aware
LC : 01 :128(382) [0617] Just so we **act** toward our parents, and there is no child
LC : 01 :142(384) [0621] in their responsibility they **act** in the capacity of fathers
LC : 01 :202(392) [0639] Not only is the external **act** forbidden, but also every kind
LC : 01 :215(394) [0641] they abstain from the **act**, yet their hearts remain so full
LC : 01 :226(395) [0645] and day-laborers who **act** high-handedly and never know
LC : 01 :237(397) [0647] They **act** as if they were lords over others' possessions and
LC : 01 :244(398) [0649] because we ignore this and **act** as if it were none of our
LC : 01 :247(398) [0651] from hand to mouth, you **act** as if everyone must live by
LC : 01 :270(401) [0657] Besides, you **act** like a knave, for no man should be
LC : 01 :283(403) [0661] If you were **acting** for your neighbor's improvement or
LC : 01 :307(406) [0669] Although you may **act** as if you have wronged no one,
LC : 01 :322(409) [0673] who prize them and gladly **act** and live in accordance with
LC : 02 :021(413) [0683] whole heart, we would also **act** accordingly, and not
LC : 03 :014(422) [0701] it was enough if the **act** was performed, whether God
LC : 03 :029(424) [0705] to pray rightly and not **act** so crudely and coldly that they
LC : 03 :040(425) [0709] on earth may be classified as word or deed, speech or **act**.
LC : 04 :010(437) [0735] by men's hands, it is nevertheless truly God's own **act**.
LC : 04 :012(438) [0735] the person performing the **act** is nobler and better.
LC : 04 :065(444) [0749] This **act** or observance consists in being dipped into the
LC : 05 :054(453) [0765] heart and conscience and **act** like a person who really
LC : 05 :063(454) [0767] Nature would like to **act** in such a way that it may rest
LC : 05 :067(454) [0769] and greatest good, we **act** so distantly toward it,
LC : 05 :068(454) [0769] Why, then, do we **act** as if the sacrament were a poison
LC : 05 :079(455) [0771] Just begin to **act** as if you want to become good and cling
LC : 06 :005(457) [0000] of their freedom, **acting** as if they will never need or
LC : 06 :015(458) [0000] The first is my work and **act**, when I lament my sin and
LC : 06 :018(459) [0000] We should not **act** as if we wanted to perform a
LC : 06 :023(459) [0000] that he would rejoice and **act** like a poor miserable
EP : 01 :021(468) [0785] were spoken, or no wicked **act** or deed took place,
EP : 03 :011(474) [0795] intention to sin and to **act** contrary to one's conscience.
SD : 01 :042(515) [0871] able to think, to speak, to **act**, and to do anything, for "in
SD : 02 :019(524) [0889] of good or evil or freely choose to **act** or not to act.
SD : 02 :019(524) [0889] of good or evil or freely choose to act or not to **act**.
SD : 02 :052(531) [0901] through which he wills to **act** efficaciously, to convert
SD : 02 :061(533) [0905] man has a mode of **acting** in the sense of a mode of doing
SD : 02 :061(533) [0905] and he cannot have a mode of **acting** in divine matters.
SD : 02 :062(533) [0905] indeed has one mode of **acting** in man as a rational
SD : 02 :062(533) [0905] conversion any mode of **acting** by which he does anything
SD : 02 :069(534) [0907] who have been baptized **act** contrary to their conscience
SD : 03 :012(541) [0919] or that "one man's **act** of righteousness leads to acquittal
SD : 04 :020(554) [0945] to do or not do them or to **act** in a contrary fashion and
SD : 08 :046(600) [1031] the person does not **act** *in, with, through,* or *according*

Action (16), Actions (11)

PR : PR :009(006) [0011] this well-intended **action** of ours was again understood
AP : PR :012(099) [0101] opponents show by their **actions** that they are after
AP : 04 :208(135) [0177] who hope that by similar **actions** they can obtain grace.
AP : 04 :208(135) [0177] zealously to copy this **action** in order thereby to merit
AP : 04 :242(141) [0187] on the more offensive **actions** of others, as the common
AP : 04 :279(149) [0199] These **actions** properly belong to the kind of faith we
AP : 24 :040(257) [0399] because we require all the **actions** that it symbolizes.
AP : 24 :074(262) [0409] also a sacrifice, since one **action** can have several
SC : 05 :023(350) [0553] set a bad example by my immodest language and **actions**.
SC : 05 :023(350) [0555] to God's commandments and to their **action** in life, etc.
LC : 01 :107(379) [0611] above all to show by our **actions**, both of heart and of
LC : 01 :111(380) [0613] to honor them by your **actions** (that is, with your body
LC : 01 :323(409) [0673] he demands that all our **actions** proceed from a heart that
LC : 04 :065(445) [0749] new man, both of which **actions** must continue in us our
EP : 02 :018(472) [0791] as referring to the **action** of divine grace in kindling new
SD : 01 :017(511) [0865] from someone else's **action** without any corruption of our
SD : 02 :062(533) [0905] and another mode of **action** to work in irrational
SD : 07 :037(576) [0985] on earth in the ordered **action** of the sacrament, though
SD : 07 :083(584) [1001] by itself, if the entire **action** of the Lord's Supper as
SD : 07 :084(584) [1001] comprehends the whole **action** or administration of this
SD : 07 :084(584) [1001] as St. Paul sets the whole **action** of the breaking of
SD : 07 :085(584) [1001] the divinely instituted **action** (that is, if one does not
SD : 07 :086(584) [1003] In this context "use" or "**action**" does not primarily mean
SD : 07 :086(584) [1003] external and visible **action** of the Supper as ordained by
SD : 07 :108(588) [1009] even apart from the **action** of the sacrament (when, for
SD : 10 :010(612) [1055] through their deeds and **actions**, the true doctrine and all
SD : 10 :029(615) [1061] is done in deed or **action** to please enemies of the holy

Activa (1)

S3 : 03 :002(304) [0479] This is not ***activa** contritio* (artificial remorse), but *passiva*

Active (18)

AP : 04 :246(142) [0189] show that it is not dead but living and **active** in the heart.
AP : 04 :252(143) [0191] of Abraham, "Faith was **active** along with his works"
AP : 04 :384(166) [0225] of faith obtains eternal life, a faith that is firm and **active**.
AP : 07 :005(169) [0227] in whom Christ is not **active** are not members of Christ.
TR : 00 :062(331) [0523] one who is known to be **active** and name him
EP : 03 :011(474) [0795] true living faith becomes "**active** through love" (Gal. 5:6).
SD : 02 :007(521) [0883] free will is mighty and **active** only in the direction of that
SD : 02 :017(524) [0887] all too mighty, alive, and **active** for everything which is
SD : 02 :024(526) [0891] unless the Holy Spirit is **active** in him and kindles and
SD : 02 :054(531) [0903] of his Word) God is **active**, breaks our hearts, and draws
SD : 02 :056(532) [0903] he assuredly is potent and **active** in our hearts
SD : 04 :010(552) [0941] Oh, faith is a living, busy, **active**, mighty thing, so that it
SD : 04 :011(553) [0941] ask, faith has already done them and is constantly **active**.
SD : 07 :075(583) [0999] cup, Christ himself is still **active** through the spoken
SD : 11 :017(619) [1069] he would be effective and **active** in us by his Holy Spirit
SD : 11 :029(621) [1073] he will be efficaciously **active** through the Word so that
SD : 11 :039(622) [1075] with and efficacious and **active** through the Word when it
SD : 11 :041(623) [1077] wills to be efficaciously **active** through the Word, as

Activities (4), Activity (8)

AG : 16 :004(037) [0051] renunciation of such **activities** as are mentioned above.
AG : 18 :002(039) [0051] the grace, help, and **activity** of the Holy Spirit man is not
AP : 21 :032(233) [0351] each saint has a special sphere of **activity** assigned to him.
LC : 01 :089(377) [0605] ourselves only to holy **activities** — that is, occupy
LC : 05 :044(451) [0763] every other Christian **activity**, hounding and driving
EP : 02 :018(472) [0791] *by God's power and **activity**,* man's new will becomes an
SD : 01 :003(509) [0861] precious merits, and the Holy Spirit's gracious **activity**.
SD : 02 :056(532) [0903] because the Holy Spirit's **activity** often is hidden, and
SD : 02 :070(534) [0909] there must be new **activities** and emotions in the intellect,
SD : 02 :083(537) [0913] when the Holy Spirit's **activity** produces no change at all
SD : 02 :083(537) [0913] the Holy Spirit's **activity** in the intellect, will, and heart of
SD : 02 :083(537) [0913] resist the Holy Spirit's **activities** and impulses, which take

Acts (62)

AG : 18 :004(040) [0051] it is only in the outward **acts** of this life that they have
AL : 18 :004(039) [0051] to God, for it is only in **acts** of this life that they have
AL : 18 :005(040) [0051] By 'good' I mean the **acts** which spring from the good in
AL : 18 :008(040) [0053] of God in so far as the substance of the **acts** is concerned.
AL : 26 :004(064) [0071] far above works and above all other **acts** of worship.
AL : 26 :006(065) [0071] by distinctions among foods and similar **acts** of worship.
AL : 26 :021(065) [0073] judged these observances to be necessary **acts** of worship.
AL : 26 :021(067) [0073] are not to be thought of as necessary **acts** of worship.
AL : 26 :029(068) [0075] righteousness cannot exist without such **acts** of worship.
AL : 26 :039(069) [0075] as if works of this sort were necessary **acts** of worship.
AL : 28 :052(089) [0091] certain observances or **acts** of worship instituted by men.
AP : 02 :003(101) [0105] we do not mean only its **acts** or fruits, but the continual
AP : 02 :012(102) [0109] more than was proper to free will and to "elicited **acts**."
AP : 04 :012(109) [0123] of sins by these elicited **acts** of ours, of what use is Christ?
AP : 04 :017(109) [0125] for they imagine that the **acts** of the will before the
AP : 04 :131(125) [0159] or at best they require only outward **acts** of worship.
AP : 04 :155(128) [0165] me with faith and with the **acts** and signs of faith.
AP : 04 :283(150) [0201] the distinctions of foods, and similar pompous **acts**.
AP : 07 :032(174) [0239] observances were really **acts** of devotion rather than
AP : 07 :034(175) [0239] human traditions are not **acts** of worship necessary for
AP : 07 :037(175) [0241] human traditions are **acts** of devotion necessary for
AP : 12 :022(185) [0257] to institute new **acts** of devotion, and to make such
AP : 12 :022(185) [0257] such satisfactions and **acts** of devotion binding upon
AP : 12 :143(204) [0297] of prayers or certain **acts** of charity are performed as acts
AP : 12 :143(204) [0297] charity are performed as **acts** of worship which *ex opere*
AP : 12 :143(204) [0297] mere performance of these **acts**, for they teach that they
AP : 12 :144(205) [0297] Christ calls these useless **acts** of worship, and so they do
AP : 12 :147(205) [0297] tradition, which Christ calls useless **acts** of worship.
AP : 15 :017(217) [0319] What if God does not approve these **acts** of worship?
AP : 15 :036(220) [0325] the Pharisees of the uselessness of these **acts** of worship.
AP : 18 :002(225) [0335] perform "the essence of the **acts**" required by his
AP : 27 :040(276) [0433] here, too, it claims perfection for artificial religious **acts**.
AP : 27 :062(280) [0441] works of monasticism are **acts** of worship and that they
AP : 27 :065(280) [0441] vows, taken for wicked **acts** of worship and with the idea
AP : 28 :007(282) [0445] traditions are useless **acts** of worship, and that therefore
AP : 28 :008(282) [0445] forgiveness of sins or were **acts** of worship that pleased
AP : 28 :009(282) [0445] Are they **acts** of worship which please God as
AP : 28 :011(283) [0447] of sins or to be **acts** of worship that please God as
AP : 28 :011(283) [0447] bishops have the power to institute such **acts** of worship.
AP : 28 :014(283) [0447] bishops may institute new **acts** of worship, for worship
AP : 28 :015(283) [0447] must not be necessary **acts** of worship but a means of
AP : 28 :015(283) [0447] though they were commanding necessary **acts** of worship.
AP : 28 :016(283) [0447] that they be not regarded as necessary **acts** of worship.
AP : 28 :016(283) [0449] the idea that human rites are necessary **acts** of worship.
AP : 28 :017(283) [0449] they are not necessary **acts** of worship, and yet we should
AP : 28 :021(284) [0449] that they are necessary **acts** of worship; that they merit
TR : 00 :038(326) [0515] And it is written in **Acts**, "We must obey God rather than
TR : 00 :048(328) [0519] How many profligate **acts** have sprung from the tradition
LC : 01 :170(388) [0629] Everybody **acts** as if God gave us children for our
LC : 02 :021(413) [0683] wretched, perverse world **acts**, drowned in its blindness,
LC : 03 :089(432) [0723] daily in word and deed, in **acts** of commission and
LC : 03 :102(434) [0727] greed and deceit, into **acts** of fraud and deception against
EP : 02 :008(471) [0789] that man always **acts** only under compulsion, even in his
EP : 02 :008(471) [0789] even in his external **acts**, and that he commits evil deeds
EP : 02 :008(471) [0789] he commits evil deeds and **acts** like fornication, robbery,
EP : 06 :004(480) [0807] self-decreed and self-chosen **acts** of serving God.
SD : 01 :010(510) [0863] faculty and the concrete **acts**, to begin and to effect
SD : 02 :074(535) [0909] as it does; that man **acts** only under coercion; that even in
SD : 02 :074(536) [0909] into doing such wicked **acts** as lechery, robbery, and
SD : 08 :046(600) [1031] to its own properties **acts** in communion with the other.

Continued ▶

SD : 08 :062(603) [1037] essential properties and **acts** of both natures are
SD : 11 :006(617) [1065] But even in wicked **acts** and works God's foreknowledge

Actual (14), Actually (33)
PR : PR :018(009) [0015] persons with the **actual** original that was submitted to the
AG : 16 :004(037) [0051] **Actually**, true perfection consists alone of proper fear of
AL : 03 :003(030) [0045] only for original guilt but also for all **actual** sins of men.
AL : 24 :001(056) [0065] **Actually**, the Mass is retained among us and is celebrated
AP : 02 :001(100) [0105] fear of God and faith is **actual** guilt, and therefore they
AP : 02 :003(101) [0105] the existence not only of **actual** fear and trust in God but
AP : 02 :003(101) [0105] trust of God, and it denies that adults **actually** produce it.
AP : 02 :031(104) [0113] this is not merely **actual** guilt but an abiding deficiency in
AP : 07 :020(171) [0233] we teach that this church **actually** exists, made up of true
AP : 12 :153(206) [0299] this sense of wrath death is **actually** no punishment at all.
AP : 13 :021(214) [0313] the forgiveness of sins is **actually** being offered, not about
AP : 15 :003(215) [0315] think that they would **actually** condemn the doctrine that
AP : 15 :049(221) [0329] and we know from **actual** experience that traditions are
AP : 21 :015(231) [0347] Thus they **actually** make them mediators of redemption.
AP : 21 :016(231) [0347] we shall prove that they **actually** make the saints not only
AP : 23 :005(240) [0365] All they are **actually** fighting for is their authority; they
AP : 24 :067(261) [0407] of the sacrament what **actually** agrees with the Fathers
AP : 27 :009(270) [0421] pretext of religion, but **actually** for the sake of appetite or
S2 : 02 :006(293) [0463] such abuses, even if it **actually** possessed some value in
S2 : 04 :011(300) [0475] This is **actually** what St. Paul calls exalting oneself over
S3 : 03 :011(305) [0481] did penance only for **actual** sins, such as wicked thoughts
S3 : 03 :028(308) [0487] think they were guilty of **actual** sins — that is, of sinful
S3 : 03 :036(309) [0489] like repentance for **actual** sins, nor is it uncertain like
LC : PR :016(361) [0573] **Actually**, he is busy teaching it from the beginning of the
LC : 01 :020(367) [0585] Accordingly the heathen **actually** fashion their fancies and
LC : 01 :085(376) [0605] **Actually**, there should be worship daily; however, since
LC : 01 :186(390) [0633] though they may not **actually** commit murder,
LC : 01 :189(390) [0635] not only when a person **actually** does evil, but also when
LC : 01 :192(391) [0635] although you have not **actually** committed all these
LC : 04 :037(441) [0741] **Actually**, we insist on faith alone as so necessary that
EP : 01 :020(468) [0783] in human nature, and the other so-called **actual** sins.
EP : 01 :021(468) [0785] the source of all other, **actual** sins, such as evil thoughts,
EP : 08 :018(489) [0823] in Christ and thus he **actually** divided the person, as
SD : 01 :002(509) [0859] inheres in his nature, all **actual** sins flow out of his heart.
SD : 01 :005(509) [0861] as sin not only the **actual** transgression of God's
SD : 01 :005(509) [0861] as the chief sin, the root and fountain of all **actual** sin.
SD : 01 :011(510) [0863] highest commands and is **actually** enmity against God,
SD : 02 :012(523) [0885] (or, as the Greek word **actually** has it, does not grasp,
SD : 02 :039(528) [0895] and delight in it (indeed, **actually** do good deeds and grow
SD : 02 :046(530) [0899] means, and they are able **actually** to feel and to perceive
SD : 02 :047(530) [0901] really elected them and **actually** purposes through his
SD : 04 :019(554) [0945] or unenthusiastic but **actually** wars against the law of his
SD : 04 :037(557) [0951] an impediment to such a person but are **actually** harmful.
SD : 07 :060(580) [0993] did the Jews when they **actually** and in deed laid violent
SD : 07 :061(581) [0995] is not only salutary but **actually** pernicious and damning.
SD : 08 :059(602) [1035] Christ but also his blood **actually** cleanses us from all
SD : 11 :095(632) [1095] to the truth and **actually** intended for its suppression.

Acumen (1)
LC : 01 :298(405) [0665] called not rascality but shrewdness and business **acumen**.

Acute (3)
PR : PR :024(013) [0021] the Holy Spirit, the most **acute** and urgent necessity
AP : 04 :033(111) [0129] that they do not need an **acute** understanding but only
SD : 09 :003(610) [1051] ourselves with exalted and **acute** speculations about how

Ad (2)
LC : 04 :018(438) [0737] taught, *"Accedat verbum* ***ad*** *elementum et fit*
LC : 05 :010(448) [0755] It is said, *"Accedat verbum* ***ad*** *elementum et fit*

Adam (44)
AG : 02 :001(029) [0043] us that since the fall of **Adam** all men who are born
AL : 02 :001(029) [0043] teach that since the fall of **Adam** all men who are
AP : 02 :002(100) [0105] that since the fall of **Adam** all men who are born
AP : 02 :005(101) [0107] to mortality that **Adam**'s descendants bear because of his
AP : 12 :053(189) [0265] first it was given to **Adam**, later to the patriarchs, then
AP : 12 :055(189) [0267] **Adam** was rebuked and terrified after his sin; this was
AP : 12 :155(207) [0301] they bring up the case of **Adam**, and of David who was
S3 : 01 :001(302) [0477] had its origin in one man, **Adam**, through whose
S3 : 01 :004(302) [0477] 1. That after the fall of **Adam** the natural powers of man
S3 : 08 :005(312) [0495] the old serpent who made enthusiasts of **Adam** and Eve.
S3 : 08 :009(313) [0497] enthusiasm clings to **Adam** and his descendants from the
S3 : 15 :005(317) [0501] Master **Adam** of Fulda, preacher in Hesse
TR : 00 :082(335) [0529] own hand both in his name and in that of **Adam** of Fulda
SC : 04 :012(349) [0551] It signifies that the old **Adam** in us, together with all sins
LC : 03 :066(429) [0717] our flesh and the old **Adam**, for it means that we must
LC : 03 :102(434) [0727] flesh and we have the old **Adam** hanging around our
LC : 04 :065(445) [0749] the slaying of the old **Adam** and the resurrection of the
LC : 04 :065(445) [0749] pertains to the old **Adam**, so that whatever belongs to the
LC : 04 :066(445) [0749] is what is born in us from **Adam**, irascible, spiteful,
LC : 04 :086(446) [0753] is, as long as we carry the old **Adam** about our necks.
EP : 01 :004(466) [0781] the body and soul of **Adam** and Eve before the Fall, but
EP : 01 :008(467) [0781] church sings, "Through **Adam**'s fall man's nature and
EP : 02 :014(471) [0789] and essence of the Old **Adam**, especially the rational soul,
EP : 06 :004(480) [0805] On account of this Old **Adam**, who inheres in people's
EP : 06 :004(480) [0807] necessary lest the Old **Adam** go his own self-willed way.
SD : 01 :001(508) [0859] as a result of the fall of **Adam**," so that ever since the Fall
SD : 01 :009(510) [0861] of the disobedience of **Adam** and Eve, are in God's
SD : 01 :011(510) [0863] one of us inherits from **Adam** a heart, sensation, and
SD : 01 :013(511) [0863] which God imposes upon **Adam**'s children and upon
SD : 01 :023(512) [0865] describes it, "Through **Adam**'s fall man's nature and being
SD : 01 :027(512) [0867] Although in the case of **Adam** and Eve man's nature was
SD : 01 :027(513) [0867] fact is, that Satan misled **Adam** and Eve through the Fall,
SD : 01 :038(515) [0871] and perverted in **Adam** and is transmitted to us in this
SD : 01 :042(515) [0873] has in this fashion corrupted God's handiwork in **Adam**.
SD : 02 :081(537) [0911] and essence of the Old **Adam**, and especially the rational
SD : 04 :010(552) [0941] from God, kills the Old **Adam**, makes us entirely different
SD : 06 :007(565) [0965] mortification of the Old **Adam** and their renewal in the
SD : 06 :007(565) [0965] nevertheless the Old **Adam** still clings to their nature and
SD : 06 :012(566) [0967] world (to which the Old **Adam** belongs) of sin and of
SD : 06 :018(567) [0967] in this life but the Old **Adam** clings to them down to the
SD : 06 :019(567) [0969] As far as the Old **Adam** who still adheres to them is
SD : 06 :023(568) [0969] continue in a constant conflict against the Old **Adam**.
SD : 06 :024(568) [0969] For the Old **Adam**, like an unmanageable and recalcitrant
SD : 11 :090(631) [1093] lose it more readily than **Adam** and Eve did in paradise —

Adamant (1)
AP : 23 :056(247) [0379] law of celibacy they are **adamant** and inexorable, though

Adapted (3)
AG : 28 :073(093) [0093] introducing them, but they are not **adapted** to our times.
AL : 28 :073(093) [0093] were introduced, but they are not **adapted** to later times.
AP : 07 :040(176) [0241] which the apostles **adapted** in modified form to the

Add (55), Added (59), Adding (4), Addition (44), Additional (8), Adds (38)
PR : PR :009(006) [0011] In **addition**, we sustained the further disadvantage that,
PR : PR :025(014) [0023] In **addition**, we have resolved and purpose to live in
AG : 20 :006(041) [0053] our works alone, but they **add** faith in Christ and say that
AG : 23 :026(055) [0065] In **addition**, all the canons show great leniency and
AG : 01 :002(056) [0065] hymns are sung in **addition** to the Latin responses for the
AG : 24 :040(061) [0069] which were held in **addition** to the parochial Mass,
AG : 26 :022(067) [0073] traditions, and he **adds**, "In vain do they worship me,
AG : 26 :028(068) [0073] of consciences with **additional** outward ceremonies,
AG : 26 :045(070) [0075] church usages and **adds** the profitable Christian
AG : 27 :003(071) [0077] In **addition** to monastic vows many other requirements
AG : 27 :012(072) [0077] What is more, they **added** that monastic life not only
AL : 13 :002(035) [0049] the promises that are set forth and offered, is **added**.
AL : 20 :027(045) [0057] Our teachers teach in **addition** that it is necessary to do
AL : 24 :002(056) [0065] These are **added** for the instruction of the people, for
AL : 24 :021(058) [0067] To all this was **added** an opinion which infinitely
AL : 26 :022(067) [0073] Our teachers **add** testimonies from the Scriptures.
AL : 27 :002(071) [0077] into decay, vows were **added** for the purpose of restoring
AL : 27 :003(071) [0077] observances were gradually **added** in addition to vows.
AL : 27 :003(071) [0077] observances were gradually added in **addition** to vows.
AL : 27 :010(072) [0077] To these evils was **added** the fact that vows had such a
AL : 27 :012(072) [0077] What is more, they **added** that monastic life merited not
AL : 27 :032(076) [0079] to human weakness, **adds** a few years and forbids making
AL : 28 :060(091) [0091] to do this for the **additional** reason that men would have
AP : PR :010(099) [0101] but as it was going through the press I **added** some things.
AP : 02 :035(104) [0115] after Baptism, and they **add** that this doctrine was
AP : 04 :014(109) [0123] on natural ethics that nothing further needs to be **added**.
AP : 04 :048(114) [0135] it is merely knowledge, we **add** that to have faith means to
AP : 04 :051(114) [0135] and was raised unless we **add** this article, the purpose of
AP : 04 :058(115) [0137] He **adds**, "There is forgiveness with thee" (v. 4).
AP : 04 :081(118) [0143] access" to the Father, and he **adds**, "through faith."
AP : 04 :081(118) [0145] how this happens, he **adds** that through faith we have
AP : 04 :082(118) [0145] as an expiation," and Paul **adds**, "to be received by faith."
AP : 04 :083(118) [0145] And he **adds**, "when we believe in him."
AP : 04 :083(119) [0145] In **addition**, he cites the consensus of all the prophets,
AP : 04 :084(119) [0145] Then he **adds** that the promise of the forgiveness of sins
AP : 04 :086(119) [0147] We shall therefore **add** clear testimonies stating that faith
AP : 04 :089(120) [0149] to be righteousness; he **adds** that it is accounted freely and
AP : 04 :100(121) [0151] God is propitious; and he **adds** that this same faith
AP : 04 :141(126) [0161] In fact, we **add** that it is impossible to separate faith from
AP : 04 :152(127) [0163] his own words when he **adds**: "Your faith has saved you"
AP : 04 :175(131) [0171] important, it must be **added** that we should realize how
AP : 04 :184(132) [0173] works, therefore, we must **add** that faith is necessary, and
AP : 04 :188(133) [0173] Later we **add** the teaching of the law.
AP : 04 :193(133) [0175] Let us **add** a word here about reward and merit.
AP : 04 :201(134) [0175] but circumcision was **added** to give him a sign written in
AP : 04 :221(137) [0181] speak of faith they always **add** the correction that they
AP : 04 :221(137) [0181] Here they do not **add** the correction: We need the faith
AP : 04 :222(137) [0181] only our opponents should not **add** their own whims to it.
AP : 04 :224(138) [0181] that our opponents **add** to it on their own, for they
AP : 04 :239(141) [0187] built upon Christ, and he **adds** (I Pet. 2:6), "He who
AP : 04 :244(142) [0189] our opponents falsely **add** their wicked opinions that by
AP : 04 :255(144) [0193] The other is a promise that is **added**.
AP : 04 :255(144) [0193] They do not **add** that sins are forgiven without faith or
AP : 04 :257(144) [0193] Therefore it is necessary to **add** the Gospel promise, that
AP : 04 :258(144) [0193] Thus the prophet urges penitence and **adds** a promise.
AP : 04 :258(144) [0193] of sins to be received by faith, and so he **adds** a promise.
AP : 04 :259(144) [0193] he says, "Forgive," and he **adds** the promise, "You will be
AP : 04 :260(145) [0193] of the Gospel must be **added**, that is, that the forgiveness
AP : 04 :263(146) [0195] The promise is therefore **added** (Dan. 4:27), "Behold,
AP : 04 :264(146) [0195] Here Jerome **adds** an extraneous particle expressing
AP : 04 :264(146) [0195] at the commandments, **adding** to them the human theory
AP : 04 :272(148) [0199] the forgiveness of sins is **added**, depending not on the
AP : 04 :280(149) [0201] Then they **add** something from their own opinions.
AP : 04 :281(149) [0201] Gospel of Christ must be **added** to the preaching of the
AP : 04 :282(149) [0201] inwardly and then **adds** concerning the outward
AP : 04 :283(149) [0201] Christ **adds** this conclusion to both clauses: all things will
AP : 04 :284(150) [0201] outward giving of alms is **added** (that is, all the works of
AP : 04 :286(150) [0201] Everywhere they **add** human opinions to what the words
AP : 04 :288(151) [0203] men are in great peril they **add** other forms of worship to
AP : 04 :297(153) [0205] obtained access" to God, **adding**, "through faith"
AP : 04 :324(157) [0209] merits in such a way as to **add** nothing about this faith
AP : 04 :335(159) [0215] Then they **add** that works are worthless to God, but that
AP : 04 :346(160) [0217] mercy is spoken of, faith in the promise must be **added**.
AP : 04 :361(162) [0219] We must **add** certain "sacraments" of this transfer, as
AP : 04 :362(162) [0219] of eternal life has been **added**, according to Rom. 8:30,
AP : 04 :376(164) [0223] of congruity or, if love is **added**, by the merit of
AP : 04 :381(165) [0223] faith should be **added**, since we take hold of God's
AP : 07 :001(168) [0227] And they have **added** a lengthy dissertation, that the
AP : 07 :003(168) [0227] That is why we **added** the eighth article, to avoid the
AP : 07 :007(169) [0229] He also **added** the outward marks, the Word and the
AP : 07 :008(169) [0229] seems to have been **added** to explain what "church"
AP : 07 :014(170) [0231] political affairs, etc. in **addition** to the promise about
AP : 07 :020(171) [0233] And we **add** its marks, the pure teaching of the Gospel
AP : 11 :001(180) [0247] But on confession they **add** the correction that the
AP : 11 :007(181) [0251] as what the summists **added** to it later, including the
AP : 11 :009(182) [0251] more tolerable if they had **added** one word on faith,
AP : 12 :014(184) [0257] They **add** further that satisfactions ought to be works of

Continued ▶

AP : 1 2 :035(186) [0261] of penitence, we therefore **add** faith in Christ, that amid
AP : 1 2 :043(187) [0263] is plain and clear, it **adds** to the honor of the power of the
AP : 1 2 :055(189) [0267] when punishment is still **added** afterwards, this
AP : 1 2 :056(189) [0267] A punishment is also **added** here, but it does not merit
AP : 1 2 :057(189) [0267] punishments always **added**, but contrition and faith there
AP : 1 2 :059(190) [0267] We shall therefore **add** a few proofs to show that the
AP : 1 2 :065(191) [0271] his name," and he **adds**: "every one who believes in him."
AP : 1 2 :068(192) [0271] Biel, and the like in **addition** to patristic statements which
AP : 1 2 :071(192) [0271] of the Holy Spirit was **added** to this statement of Peter,
AP : 1 2 :073(192) [0273] forbearance of God; but **add** further that you also believe
AP : 1 2 :074(192) [0273] by mercy, but he bids us **add** the personal faith that they
AP : 1 2 :091(196) [0279] faith, and the scholastics **add** nothing about faith in their
AP : 1 2 :105(197) [0283] In **addition**, they absolve us of those which we do not
AP : 1 2 :118(199) [0287] They **add** further that part of this temporal punishment is
AP : 1 2 :124(201) [0289] The Roman pontiff did not **add** anything to his dignity in
AP : 1 2 :145(205) [0297] and second, because they **add** human traditions, whose
AP : 1 2 :146(205) [0297] In **addition**, they obscure penitence and grace.
AP : 1 2 :154(207) [0301] they mean, why do they **add** that we must make
AP : 1 3 :003(211) [0309] promise of grace has been **added**," we can easily
AP : 1 3 :008(212) [0311] there is no need for **additional** sacrifices as though this
AP : 1 3 :016(213) [0311] command and a promise **added** to them, then why not
AP : 1 3 :017(213) [0313] themselves are signs to which God has **added** promises.
AP : 1 5 :012(216) [0317] "No one **adds** even to a man's covenant."
AP : 1 5 :012(216) [0317] Christ's sake, we dare not **add** the condition that we must
AP : 1 5 :014(217) [0319] the establishment of **additional** ceremonies without his
AP : 1 8 :001(224) [0335] XVIII on free will, but they **add** several proofs which are
AP : 1 8 :001(225) [0335] They also **add** a caution, lest too much be conceded to
AP : 1 8 :006(225) [0335] to this they **add** that such works, by the merit of
AP : 2 0 :014(228) [0343] They **add** other proofs that are no more relevant.
AP : 2 2 :010(237) [0361] use of one kind, and they **add**, "Thus our laity should be
AP : 2 3 :021(242) [0369] continence and therefore **adds**, "He who is able to receive
AP : 2 3 :032(244) [0373] Let the reader note that he **adds** faith and does not praise
AP : 2 3 :032(244) [0373] Then he **adds** a certain task of her calling, as performance
AP : 2 3 :040(245) [0375] eunuchs, but he **adds**, "for the sake of the kingdom of
AP : 2 3 :041(245) [0375] In **addition**, the Levitical laws about uncleanness do not
AP : 2 4 :014(251) [0387] stated our case, we must **add** a few things because of the
AP : 2 4 :028(254) [0393] He **adds** that God had commanded faith.
AP : 2 4 :047(258) [0401] In **addition**, they horribly profaned the Mass and
AP : 2 4 :048(258) [0401] They **add** to it the teaching of the good works which God
AP : 2 4 :053(259) [0403] The Scripture itself **adds** immediately that Christ is the
AP : 2 4 :069(262) [0409] New Testament, the Word is the **added** promise of grace.
AP : 2 4 :093(267) [0417] Then they **add**, "Yet we offer Thee this reasonable service
AP : 2 7 :012(270) [0423] And they **add** that the monks observe everything for
AP : 2 7 :017(271) [0425] sets his own merits, in **addition** to Christ's propitiation,
AP : 2 7 :024(273) [0427] To this they **add** many other false and wicked ideas.
AP : 2 7 :030(274) [0431] In **addition**, they insult Christ when they say that by a
AP : 2 7 :032(274) [0431] but at the end Bernard **adds**: "Let nobody deceive
AP : 2 7 :036(275) [0433] altogether, they **added** this correction, that it is a state for
AP : 2 7 :041(276) [0435] He **adds** the phrase "for the Gospel" (Mark 10:29) to show
AP : 2 7 :048(277) [0437] consists in that which Christ **adds**, "Follow me."
AP : 2 7 :056(278) [0439] In **addition** to all this, there is the danger that those who
AP : 2 8 :015(283) [0447] we nevertheless **added** the extent to which it is legitimate
S 1 : PR :003(289) [0455] and confession (in **addition** to the confession which I
S 3 : 0 3 :004(304) [0481] Testament immediately **adds** the consoling promise of
S 3 : 0 3 :007(304) [0481] office alone, without the **addition** of the Gospel, there is
S 3 : 0 3 :012(305) [0481] satisfaction — with the **added** consolation that a man who
S 3 : 0 3 :042(310) [0491] They **add** that if anyone sins after he has received faith
S 3 : 0 5 :001(310) [0491] puts it, "The Word is **added** to the element and it
S 3 : 1 3 :003(315) [0499] To this we must **add** that if good works do not follow,
S 3 : 1 5 :005(316) [0501] In **addition**, there are blessings of candles, palms, spices,
TR : 0 0 :002(320) [0503] Then he **adds** that by divine right he possesses both
TR : 0 0 :006(320) [0505] more horrible is that he **adds** that it is necessary to
TR : 0 0 :010(321) [0505] who were of repute **added** nothing to me" (Gal. 2:6).
TR : 0 0 :024(324) [0511] In **addition**, it is necessary to acknowledge that the keys
TR : 0 0 :038(326) [0515] third article this must be **added**: Even if the bishop of
TR : 0 0 :043(328) [0517] Masses is manifest, for in **addition** to other abuses they
TR : 0 0 :049(328) [0519] To these errors, then, two great sins must be **added**.
TR : 0 0 :060(330) [0521] the sacraments, and, in **addition**, exercise jurisdiction,
TR : 0 0 :067(331) [0523] to the church, and he **adds** that they are given for the
TR : 0 0 :071(332) [0525] on new ceremonies were **added**, many of which Dionysius
TR : 0 0 :071(332) [0525] Still more recent writers **added** the words, "I give thee the
TR : 0 0 :078(333) [0527] in their courts, there is **additional** reason why other
TR : 0 0 :079(333) [0527] of the pope; since, in **addition**, they have wrested
TR : 0 0 :082(000) [0529] that your courtesy may **add** my name, if it be necessary,
SC : PR :012(339) [0535] In **addition**, parents and employers should refuse to
SC : 0 5 :023(350) [0555] and mistresses should **add** whatever else they have done
SC : 0 5 :029(351) [0555] A confessor will know **additional** passages of the
LC : 0 1 :063(373) [0597] In **addition**, you must also know how to use the name of
LC : 0 1 :166(388) [0629] of the whole world cannot **add** an hour to our life or raise
LC : 0 1 :167(388) [0629] In **addition**, it would be well to preach to parents on the
LC : 0 1 :208(393) [0639] above all others and, in **addition**, has supplied and
LC : 0 1 :218(394) [0643] Then God will **add** his blessing and grace so that men
LC : 0 1 :293(404) [0665] God therefore **added** these two commandments to teach
LC : 0 1 :333(410) [0677] while at the same time he **adds** such glorious promises
LC : 0 3 :022(423) [0703] to pray because, in **addition** to this commandment and
LC : 0 3 :093(433) [0725] but comforting clause is **added**, "as we forgive our
LC : 0 3 :121(436) [0731] dare not whole-heartedly **add** "yes" and conclude with
LC : 0 4 :014(438) [0735] but that God's Word and commandment are **added** to it.
LC : 0 4 :017(438) [0735] substance but because here something nobler is **added**.
LC : 0 4 :018(438) [0737] that when the Word is **added** to the element or the
LC : 0 4 :020(439) [0737] the commandment is **added**, "You shall honor father and
LC : 0 4 :062(444) [0749] foot and would, in **addition**, pervert and nullify all God's
LC : 0 5 :046(452) [0763] say, "But the words are **added**, 'as often as you do it'; so
LC : 0 5 :047(452) [0763] And they are **added** because Christ wishes the sacrament
LC : 0 6 :008(458) [0000] with, I have said that in **addition** to the confession which
EP : 0 2 :011(471) [0789] its own natural powers to **add** something (though it be
EP : 1 1 :008(495) [0833] In **addition** he promises the power and operation of the
SD : RN :007(505) [0853] of God's Word, and in **addition** the grounds and reasons
SD : 0 2 :055(531) [0903] follow, if there were not **added** the power and operation
SD : 0 2 :081(537) [0913] put on the new man by **adding**, 'Therefore lay aside lies
SD : 0 3 :023(543) [0923] to us, without the **addition** of our works, so that our sins
SD : 0 3 :033(545) [0927] Mediator without the **addition** of his own works, not only
SD : 0 3 :034(545) [0927] God reckons righteousness without the **addition** of works.
SD : 0 3 :044(547) [0933] clear, namely, that in **addition** to the errors already
SD : 0 3 :059(550) [0937] reject and condemn, in **addition** to the previously
SD : 0 5 :006(559) [0953] In **addition**, however, the word "Gospel" is also used in
SD : 0 5 :009(559) [0955] to God unless there is **added** faith in Christ, whose merit
SD : 0 5 :009(559) [0955] of the Gospel must be **added** so that it becomes a
SD : 0 5 :014(560) [0957] this office it immediately **adds** the promise of God's grace
SD : 0 5 :015(561) [0957] salutary repentance; the Gospel must also be **added** to it."
SD : 0 6 :020(567) [0969] You shall not **add** to it nor take from it" (Deut. 12:8, 28,
SD : 0 7 :026(573) [0981] of these words which are **added** to the bread and wine.'
SD : 0 7 :035(575) [0983] In **addition** to the words of Christ and of St. Paul (the
SD : 0 7 :050(578) [0991] things more clearly by **adding** the words, "given for you,
SD : 0 7 :065(581) [0995] But Christ **adds** another command, and in addition to the
SD : 0 7 :065(581) [0995] command, and in **addition** to the oral eating he ordains
SD : 0 7 :128(591) [1015] **Additional** antitheses and rejected erroneous views have
SD : 0 7 :128(591) [1015] Whatever **additional** condemnable opinions or erroneous
SD : 0 8 :012(593) [1019] properties but that in **addition** thereto, through the
SD : 0 8 :049(600) [1031] nothing was **added** to or detracted from the essence
SD : 0 8 :051(600) [1033] humiliation) received, in **addition** to its natural, essential,

Address (4), Addressed (5), Addresses (1)

AP : 2 1 :018(231) [0347] to me, all who labor," which is certainly **addressed** to us.
AP : 2 1 :024(232) [0349] not want appeals to be **addressed** to him through others.
S 2 : 0 4 :002(298) [0471] customary, but must **address** him as "most gracious lord,"
TR : 0 0 :025(324) [0511] Therefore Christ **addresses** Peter as a minister and says,
LC : 0 1 :107(379) [0611] It requires us not only to **address** them affectionately and
LC : 0 1 :110(380) [0611] toward them, and not **address** them discourteously,
LC : 0 1 :300(405) [0665] commandment, then, is **addressed** not to those whom the
LC : 0 5 :035(450) [0761] lets these words be **addressed** to him and believes that
LC : 0 5 :045(452) [0763] They are words **addressed** to disciples of Christ; hence
SD : 0 2 :011(522) [0885] dead, in sin, prepare or **address** himself by his own power

Adduce (9), Adduces (2)

AG : 0 0 :005(095) [0095] it necessary to **adduce** and mention in order that it may
AP : 2 4 :009(251) [0387] and the arguments they **adduce** are silenced by the fact
AP : 2 4 :090(266) [0415] has, the reasons they **adduce** in support of the doctrine of
AP : 2 7 :010(270) [0423] arguments and what they **adduce** to support their case.
S 2 : 0 2 :013(295) [0465] The papists here **adduce** passages from Augustine and
SC : PR :018(340) [0537] Always **adduce** many examples from the Scriptures to
SD : 0 2 :081(537) [0911] on Ps. 25, where he **adduces** and explains St. Paul's
SD : 0 7 :001(568) [0971] sought forcibly to **adduce** and pervert the Augsburg
SD : 0 7 :099(586) [1005] which the enthusiasts **adduce** concerning Christ's leaving
SD : 0 8 :018(594) [1021] We could **adduce** many testimonies on this point from the
SD : 1 1 :086(631) [1091] The holy apostle **adduces** Pharaoh's example for the sole

Adequate (1), Adequately (4)

PR : PR :024(013) [0021] and have been **adequately** assured of this in our hearts
AP : 2 0 :010(228) [0341] a work that it thought **adequate** to placate the wrath of
LC : 0 1 :161(387) [0627] God will **adequately** recompense those who do so and
LC : 0 1 :208(393) [0639] this estate might be provided for richly and **adequately**.
LC : 0 1 :271(401) [0657] then, that cannot be **adequately** proved is false witness.

Adhere (9), Adhered (2), Adherence (8), Adherents (17), Adheres (3), Adhering (2)

PR : PR :009(006) [0011] in such a way by **adherents** of erroneous opinions which
PR : PR :013(007) [0013] princes, and estates **adhering** to the Augsburg Confession
PR : PR :018(008) [0015] have hitherto at all times **adhered** and appealed to, we
AG : PR :004(025) [0039] all of us embrace and **adhere** to a single, true religion and
AG : PR :023(027) [0043] declare our continuing **adherence**, and we shall not be
AG : 2 7 :009(072) [0077] matter the canons were not strictly **adhered** to.
AP : 0 4 :042(113) [0133] Rom. 4:14, "If it is the **adherents** of the law who are to be
AP : 1 2 :124(201) [0289] good men these slanders will not gain any **adherents**.
S 1 : PR :002(288) [0455] if the pope and his **adherents** ever became so bold as
S 1 : PR :003(289) [0455] Even **adherents** of that party have lost hope that the
S 1 : PR :003(289) [0455] suffer himself and his **adherents** to be reformed a little
S 1 : PR :004(289) [0455] those who profess to be **adherents** of our party — that
S 1 : PR :015(291) [0459] The pope and his **adherents** are lost.
S 2 : 0 4 :007(299) [0473] whom all others should **adhere**, in order that the unity of
S 2 : 0 4 :008(299) [0473] and would ultimately be without any **adherents** at all.
TR : 0 0 :039(327) [0515] pontiffs and their **adherents** defend godless doctrines and
TR : 0 0 :041(327) [0517] the pope and his **adherents** as the kingdom of the
TR : 0 0 :044(328) [0517] by the pope and his **adherents**, who teach that sins are
TR : 0 0 :079(333) [0527] the bishops who are **adherents** of the pope defend
SC : PR :007(339) [0533] should adopt one form, **adhere** to it, and use it repeatedly
SC : PR :008(339) [0535] that pleases you, therefore, and **adhere** to it henceforth.
SC : PR :009(339) [0535] are teaching the young, **adhere** to a fixed and unchanging
SC : PR :015(340) [0535] you may prefer, and **adhere** to them without changing a
EP : 0 0 :000(463) [0775] of the Theologians **Adhering** to this Confession, Resolved
SD : PR :003(502) [0847] in controversy between them and the pope's **adherents**.
SD : PR :006(502) [0847] benefiting from their **adherence** to the Augsburg
SD : RN :002(503) [0851] among the **adherents** of the Augsburg Confession and
SD : RN :005(504) [0851] We therefore declare our **adherence** to the first, unaltered
SD : RN :005(504) [0853] to appeal and confess **adherence** to the Nicene Creed.
SD : RN :006(504) [0853] pledge our **adherence** to this Apology also, because in it
SD : RN :008(505) [0853] declare our unanimous **adherence** to Dr. Luther's Small
SD : RN :008(505) [0853] of those churches which **adhere** to the Augsburg
SD : RN :012(506) [0855] anyone who sincerely **adheres** to the Augsburg Confession
SD : 0 3 :022(543) [0923] in essence and life **adheres** to those who have been
SD : 0 6 :019(567) [0969] the Old Adam who still **adheres** to them is concerned, he
SD : 0 7 :001(568) [0971] others who professed **adherence** to the Augsburg
SD : 0 7 :041(576) [0985] of the churches which **adhere** to the Augsburg Confession
SD : 0 7 :111(589) [1011] our churches as **adherents** of the Augsburg Confession.
SD : 0 8 :003(592) [1017] publicly profess our **adherence**, clearly demonstrate.
SD : 1 0 :022(615) [1061] the pope and his **adherents** as the kingdom of Antichrist.
SD : 1 1 :052(625) [1081] and brood, but we are to **adhere** exclusively to the

Adiaphora (10)

AP : 1 5 :052(222) [0329] willingness to observe **adiaphora** with others, even where
AP : 2 7 :027(273) [0429] observance of other things which are called "**adiaphora**."
EP : 1 0 :000(492) [0829] X. Church Usages, Called **Adiaphora** or Indifferent Things
SD : 1 0 :000(610) [1053] Rites That Are Called **Adiaphora** or Things Indifferent
SD : 1 0 :002(611) [1053] oneself to them in such **adiaphora** or matters of
SD : 1 0 :005(611) [1053] and guise of external **adiaphora** and are given a different
SD : 1 0 :005(611) [1053] among truly free **adiaphora** or things indifferent those
SD : 1 0 :007(611) [1055] in the church, true **adiaphora** or things indifferent.
SD : 1 0 :008(611) [1055] and confess that true **adiaphora** or things indifferent, as
SD : 1 0 :014(613) [1057] with the external **adiaphora** which in their nature and

Adjudge (1), Adjudged (1)

A P : 0 2 :013(102) [0109] This cannot be **adjudged** except from the Word of God,
A P : 1 2 :127(201) [0291] these questions and **adjudge** them rightly, because you do

Administer (41), Administered (17), Administering (5), Administers (1), Administration (24), Administrative (1), Administrator (2), Administrators (1)

P R : P R :027(014) [0025] of Brandenburg, **administrator** of the archdiocese of
P R : P R :027(014) [0025] bishop of Luebeck, **administrator** of the diocese of
P R : P R :027(016) [0027] The whole **administration** of the City of Hildesheim.
A G : P R :018(026) [0041] Majesty's viceroy, **administrators**, and councilors of the
A G : 0 7 :001(032) [0047] holy sacraments are **administered** according to the
A G : 0 7 :002(032) [0047] the sacraments be **administered** in accordance with the
A G : 0 8 :001(033) [0047] even if the priests who **administer** them are wicked men,
A G : 1 4 :000(036) [0049] teach or preach or **administer** the sacraments in the
A G : 2 2 :006(050) [0061] that the priests who **administered** the sacrament
A G : 2 5 :001(061) [0069] among us of not **administering** the sacrament to those
A G : 2 8 :005(081) [0085] and retain sins, and to **administer** and distribute the
A G : 2 8 :008(082) [0085] Word of God and by **administering** the sacraments (to
A G : 2 8 :009(082) [0085] of preaching and of **administering** the holy sacraments,
A G : 2 8 :012(083) [0085] to preach the Gospel and **administer** the sacraments.
A G : 2 8 :019(084) [0087] and kings for the temporal **administration** of their lands.
A G : 2 8 :029(085) [0087] they like to or not, to **administer** justice to their subjects
A G : 2 8 :070(093) [0093] Now, however, they **administer** the sacrament in one kind
A G : 2 8 :070(093) [0093] in one kind and prohibit **administration** in both kinds.
A L : 0 5 :001(031) [0045] the Gospel and **administering** the sacraments was
A L : 0 7 :001(032) [0047] purely and the sacraments are **administered** rightly.
A L : 0 7 :002(032) [0047] of the Gospel and the **administration** of the sacraments.
A L : 0 8 :001(033) [0047] even when they are **administered** by evil men, according
A L : 0 8 :002(033) [0047] of Christ even if they are **administered** by evil men.
A L : 1 4 :000(036) [0049] in the church or **administer** the sacraments unless he is
A L : 2 2 :006(050) [0061] who said, "The priests **administer** the Eucharist and
A L : 2 4 :033(060) [0067] that the sacrament is **administered** to those who have
A L : 2 4 :034(060) [0067] sacrament, it is also **administered** to those who ask for it.
A L : 2 5 :001(061) [0069] it is not customary to **administer** the body of Christ
A L : 2 7 :056(080) [0083] marriage and the **administration** of the state, withdrew
A L : 2 8 :005(081) [0085] remit and retain sins, and to **administer** the sacraments.
A L : 2 8 :008(082) [0085] the Gospel and by **administering** the sacraments either to
A L : 2 8 :012(083) [0085] to preach the Gospel and **administer** the sacraments.
A L : 2 8 :019(083) [0087] and emperors for the civil **administration** of their lands.
A L : 2 8 :029(085) [0087] against their will, to **administer** justice to their subjects
A P : 0 4 :193(133) [0175] the outward **administration** of Christ's rule among men.
A P : 0 7 :003(168) [0227] the sacraments which evil men or hypocrites **administer**.
A P : 0 7 :003(169) [0227] efficacy when they are **administered** by evil men; indeed,
A P : 0 7 :003(169) [0227] use sacraments that are **administered** by evil men.
A P : 0 7 :005(169) [0227] of the Gospel and the **administration** of the sacraments in
A P : 0 7 :019(171) [0233] are efficacious even when wicked men **administer** them.
A P : 0 7 :028(173) [0237] the sacraments are **administered** by unworthy men, this
A P : 0 7 :030(173) [0237] of the Gospel and the **administration** of the sacraments.
A P : 0 7 :047(177) [0243] even when evil men **administer** them, for ministers act in
A P : 1 2 :039(187) [0261] The power of the keys **administers** and offers the Gospel
A P : 1 2 :156(207) [0301] remits them apart from the **administration** of the keys.
A P : 1 3 :007(212) [0311] of the Word or the **administration** of the sacraments to
A P : 1 3 :009(212) [0311] preach the Gospel and **administer** the sacraments to the
A P : 1 4 :001(214) [0315] should be allowed to **administer** the Word and the
A P : 1 4 :004(215) [0315] the Word of God and rightly **administer** the sacraments.
A P : 1 5 :025(219) [0323] of one's calling, the **administration** of public affairs, the
A P : 1 5 :025(219) [0323] of public affairs, the **administration** of the household,
A P : 1 5 :026(219) [0323] have given up their **administrative** positions in the
A P : 2 1 :036(234) [0353] The saints **administered** public affairs, underwent
A P : 2 1 :036(234) [0353] about faith or fear in the **administration** of public affairs.
A P : 2 2 :007(237) [0359] was customary in some places to **administer** only one part.
A P : 2 4 :083(264) [0413] the verb means to care for or to **administer** public goods.
A P : 2 8 :003(281) [0443] proper preaching and **administration** of the sacraments in
S 2 : 0 2 :008(294) [0465] in the sacrament **administered** according to Christ's
S 3 : 0 5 :004(311) [0493] made, and the church should **administer** Baptism to them.
S 3 : 0 6 :002(311) [0493] hold that it is not to be **administered** in one form only.
S 3 : 0 6 :003(311) [0493] as under both, yet **administration** in one form is not the
S 3 : 1 0 :002(314) [0497] or teach or baptize or **administer** Communion or
T R : 0 0 :012(321) [0507] of Alexandria should **administer** the churches in the East
T R : 0 0 :012(322) [0507] bishop of Rome should **administer** the suburban
T R : 0 0 :031(325) [0513] the forgiveness of sins, **administer** the sacraments, and
T R : 0 0 :060(330) [0521] the Gospel, remit sins, **administer** the sacraments, and, in
T R : 0 0 :065(331) [0523] that ordination **administered** by a pastor in his own
T R : 0 0 :066(331) [0523] and are unwilling to **administer** ordination, the churches
T R : 0 0 :067(331) [0523] exists, the right to **administer** the Gospel also exists.
T R : 0 0 :072(332) [0525] are heretics or refuse to **administer** ordination, the
T R : 0 0 :080(334) [0527] as alms for the **administration** and profit of the churches,
S C : P R :022(341) [0537] as it were, compel us pastors to **administer** it to them.
S C : P R :023(341) [0539] to receive it, he will insist that you **administer** it to him.
L C : 0 1 :259(400) [0653] He who is to **administer** justice equitably in all cases will
L C : 0 1 :262(400) [0655] it is applied to spiritual jurisdiction or **administration**.
L C : 0 1 :266(401) [0657] and authorized to **administer** punishment by virtue of
L C : 0 5 :002(447) [0753] to the sacrament and **administer** it to those who do not
L C : 0 5 :015(448) [0757] a wicked priest can **administer** the sacrament, and like
L C : 0 5 :016(448) [0757] knave should receive or **administer** it, it is the true
L C : 0 5 :039(451) [0761] which is daily **administered** and distributed among
L C : 0 6 :031(460) [0000] we are compelled to preach and **administer** the sacrament.
E P : 0 7 :024(484) [0815] 3. The **administration** of only one kind of the sacrament
E P : 1 2 :002(498) [0839] politic and secular **administration**, or in domestic society.
E P : 1 2 :027(500) [0843] teach profitably or **administer** true and genuine
S D : 0 7 :024(573) [0979] a wicked priest can **administer** and give the sacrament,
S D : 0 7 :079(584) [1001] In the **administration** of Communion the words of
S D : 0 7 :084(584) [1001] the whole action or **administration** of this sacrament
S D : 0 7 :110(588) [1011] only one species is **administered** to the laity contrary to
S D : 0 7 :121(590) [1013] words of institution in the **administration** of the Supper.
S D : 0 7 :121(590) [1013] be omitted in the **administration** of the Supper, as shown
S D : 1 0 :019(614) [1059] or teach or baptize or **administer** Communion or
S D : 1 2 :035(635) [1101] teach profitably nor **administer** genuine and true

Admirably (1), Admiration (1)

A P : 2 3 :045(245) [0377] from marriage, and this called forth the most **admiration**.
L C : 0 1 :200(392) [0637] They are **admirably** arranged.

Admired (1), Admires (1), Admiringly (1)

A L : 2 6 :011(065) [0071] civil occupations — and **admired** the monks and others
A P : 0 4 :265(146) [0197] Human reason naturally **admires** them; because it sees
A P : 2 3 :045(245) [0375] about marriage and **admiringly** about celibacy.

Admit (26), Admits (2), Admitted (3), Admittedly (1), Admitting (1)

P R : P R :022(011) [0019] which have up to now **admittedly** not come to agreement
A G : 2 0 :008(042) [0053] so long (as all must **admit**) while nothing but works was
A G : 2 8 :070(093) [0093] clergymen to marry an **admit** no one to the ministry
A L : 2 4 :006(056) [0065] worship, for none are **admitted** unless they are first heard
A L : 2 5 :012(063) [0071] the chapter "Consideret," **admits** that such confession is
A L : 2 8 :070(093) [0093] demand celibacy and will **admit** no one to the ministry
A P : 0 2 :004(101) [0105] Our scholastic opponents **admit** that concupiscence is the
A P : 0 4 :268(147) [0197] Afterwards, as we readily **admit**, the punishments that
A P : 0 4 :301(153) [0205] at all, as our opponents **admit**, or surely they feel that it
A P : 0 4 :304(154) [0205] since even the scholastics **admit** that the will commands
A P : 0 7 :005(169) [0227] much our opponents also **admit**, that the wicked are dead
A P : 1 2 :004(183) [0253] even the theologians, **admit** that before Luther's writings
A P : 1 2 :113(199) [0285] the decree warns, and **admitting** notorious people to
A P : 1 2 :118(199) [0287] Still our opponents **admit** that satisfactions do not
A P : 1 2 :147(205) [0297] of Christ; our opponents **admit** that the works of
A P : 1 2 :150(206) [0299] Our opponents **admit** that contrition can be so great as to
A P : 1 2 :173(209) [0305] In fact, they **admit** in their schools that it is not a sin to
A P : 2 1 :040(235) [0355] with a little sense would **admit** that the teachings of the
A P : 2 2 :001(236) [0357] we suppose our opponents **admit**, all of the church uses
A P : 2 3 :028(243) [0371] our opponents must **admit** that for believers marriage is
A P : 2 8 :003(281) [0445] They **admit** all kinds of people to the priesthood quite
S C : P R :011(339) [0535] They should not be **admitted** to the sacrament, be
L C : S P :002(362) [0575] among Christians nor **admitted** to a sacrament, just as a
L C : 0 1 :224(395) [0643] they are unwilling to **admit** it, were hanged on the
L C : 0 3 :016(422) [0701] The reason is this: I freely **admit** that he is holier in
L C : 0 3 :111(435) [0729] will see the temptation cease and eventually **admit** defeat.
L C : 0 4 :054(443) [0745] faith, we should have to **admit** that his Baptism was
L C : 0 5 :002(447) [0753] For we do not intend to **admit** to the sacrament and
L C : 0 5 :074(455) [0771] neither feel their infirmities nor **admit** to being sinners.
E P : 0 1 :003(466) [0779] because the view that **admits** no distinction between our
E P : 0 7 :033(485) [0815] human nature could neither permit nor **admit** this.
S D : R N :012(506) [0855] documents but will gladly **admit** and accept them as
S D : 0 3 :029(544) [0925] of this article cannot **admit** any treatment or discussion

Admixture (1)

S D : 0 5 :001(558) [0951] purely and without **admixture**, for by it Christians can

Admonish (12), Admonished (15), Admonishes (8), Admonishing (1), Admonition (12), Admonitions (6)

P R : P R :000(001) [0004] the Instruction and **Admonition** of their Lands, Churches,
A G : 2 6 :043(070) [0075] the church, they were **admonished** by others that it was
A L : 1 5 :002(036) [0049] Nevertheless, men are **admonished** not to burden
A L : 1 5 :003(036) [0049] They are also **admonished** that human traditions which
A L : 2 0 :004(041) [0053] adversaries have been **admonished** about these things,
A L : 2 0 :023(044) [0055] Men are also **admonished** that here the term "faith" does
A L : 2 0 :026(045) [0057] Augustine, too, **admonishes** his readers in this way
A L : 2 4 :007(056) [0065] The people are also **admonished** concerning the value and
A L : 2 4 :013(057) [0065] when our priests were **admonished** concerning this sin,
A L : 2 6 :017(066) [0073] and prudently **admonishes** Januarius that he should know
A L : 2 6 :043(070) [0075] of schism, they were **admonished** by others that such
A L : 2 7 :059(080) [0083] Concerning such things it was necessary to **admonish** men.
A P : 0 4 :276(148) [0199] signs that constantly **admonish**, cheer, and confirm
A P : 0 4 :284(150) [0201] The **admonition** has many parts, some of which command
A P : 0 7 :044(177) [0243] The apostles wisely **admonished** the reader neither to
A P : 1 1 :005(181) [0249] are found never to commune, let them be **admonished**.
A P : 1 3 :003(211) [0309] though they may instruct or **admonish** the simple folk.
A P : 2 4 :005(250) [0385] that do not teach or **admonish**, simply *ex opere operato*,
A P : 2 4 :049(258) [0401] of sins and as an **admonition** to timid consciences really
S C : P R :025(341) [0539] you do not give such **admonitions**, or if you adopt odious
S C : 0 9 :001(354) [0561] *by which they may be* ***admonished*** *to do their respective*
S C : 0 9 :003(354) [0561] you in the Lord and **admonish** you, and to esteem them
L C : P R :014(360) [0571] were not enough to **admonish** us to read the Catechism
L C : 0 1 :097(378) [0609] to be preached to and **admonished** but we listen without
L C : 0 1 :220(394) [0643] St. Paul so urgently **admonishes** husbands and wives to
L C : 0 1 :276(402) [0659] your neighbor but **admonish** him privately so that he may
L C : 0 1 :319(408) [0673] the first part, both for instruction and for **admonition**.
L C : 0 1 :330(410) [0677] always to teach, **admonish**, and remind young people of
L C : 0 3 :033(424) [0707] Let this be said as an **admonition** in order that men may
L C : 0 4 :022(439) [0737] I therefore **admonish** you again that these two, the Word
L C : 0 5 :039(451) [0761] great need also of an **admonition** and entreaty that so
L C : 0 6 :007(458) [0000] confession to instruct and **admonish** the simple folk.
E P : 0 4 :004(476) [0797] that people should be **admonished** to do good works
E P : 0 5 :002(478) [0801] according to St. Paul's **admonition**, the Word of God
E P : 0 6 :004(480) [0807] will not only by the **admonitions** and threats of the law,
E P : 0 9 :003(492) [0827] questions, and **admonishes** all Christians to simplicity of
S D : 0 2 :021(525) [0889] All pleas, all appeals, all **admonitions** are in vain.
S D : 0 2 :072(535) [0909] these gifts, and **admonishes** us not to receive this grace of
S D : 0 4 :032(556) [0947] punishments and **admonitions**: "Do you not know that
S D : 0 4 :040(558) [0951] most diligently to be **admonished** and urged to apply
S D : 0 6 :006(565) [0965] any instruction, **admonition**, exhortation, or driving by
S D : 0 6 :006(565) [0965] without any **admonition**, exhortation, compulsion,
S D : 0 6 :009(565) [0965] the daily teaching and **admonition**, warning and
S D : 0 6 :012(566) [0967] He also **admonishes** them to do these, and when because
S D : 0 6 :021(567) [0969] Thus, when Paul **admonishes** those who have been born
S D : 0 6 :024(568) [0969] with the instruction, **admonition**, urging, and threatening
S D : 0 8 :096(609) [1049] break their heads, we **admonish** all Christians not to pry
S D : 1 1 :012(618) [1067] I Cor. 1:21, 30, 31), to **admonish** us to repent (II Tim.
S D : 1 1 :027(620) [1071] stead, and God is **admonishing** you through us, 'Be
S D : 1 1 :036(622) [1075] daily reminds and **admonishes** us to learn and to
S D : 1 1 :051(624) [1079] also contains mighty **admonitions** and warnings, among
S D : 1 1 :052(625) [1081] This **admonition** is eminently necessary.
S D : 1 1 :085(630) [1091] the more he was **admonished** was a punishment for his
S D : 1 1 :085(630) [1091] rebelled against all the **admonitions** and warnings, God

Adopt (5), Adopted (14), Adopting (1), Adoption (9)

P R : P R :008(005) [0009] and intention to **adopt**, to defend, or to spread a different

Continued ▶

A G : 2 7 :016(073) [0077] people gathered and **adopted** monastic life for the
A G : 2 8 :074(093) [0093] some regulations were **adopted** from want of
A L : 0 0 :001(048) [0059] are new and have been **adopted** by the fault of the times
A L : 2 2 :010(050) [0061] This custom has been **adopted** not only in defiance of the
A L : 2 8 :074(093) [0093] apparent that some were **adopted** out of
A P : 1 2 :116(199) [0287] particular, lest by their **adoption** the righteousness of faith
A P : 2 1 :013(230) [0345] should not coerce us to **adopt** something uncertain, for
A P : 2 4 :023(253) [0391] which the heathen **adopted** from their misinterpretation
S 1 : P R :002(288) [0455] them, unanimously **adopted** them as their confession, and
S 1 : P R :014(291) [0459] What is the use of **adopting** a multitude of decrees and
S 2 : 0 2 :013(295) [0467] that would constrain him to **adopt** such an opinion.
S C : P R :007(339) [0533] the contrary, he should **adopt** one form, adhere to it, and
S C : P R :025(341) [0539] admonitions, or if you **adopt** odious laws on the subject,
E P : 1 2 :023(500) [0841] the Lord God seals the **adoption** of children and effects
S D : 0 3 :004(540) [0917] and the fact that we are **adopted** as God's children solely
S D : 0 3 :009(540) [0919] damnation, and is **adopted** as a child of God and an heir
S D : 0 3 :016(541) [0921] sins, the grace of God, **adoption**, and the inheritance of
S D : 0 3 :019(542) [0921] forgiveness of sins and our **adoption** as God's children.
S D : 0 3 :025(543) [0923] with God, **adoption**, and the inheritance of eternal life.
S D : 0 3 :032(545) [0927] acceptable to God and is **adopted** to sonship and the
S D : 0 3 :053(548) [0933] simultaneously receive **adoption** and the inheritance of
S D : 0 4 :023(555) [0945] good works, and are **adopted** by the papists and used to
S D : 0 7 :012(571) [0977] concerning this article **adopted** the confession of our
S D : 0 7 :018(572) [0979] articles of agreement, **adopted** in the previous year, to
S D : 1 0 :018(614) [1059] which were drafted and **adopted** in 1537, show that this
S D : 1 1 :018(619) [1069] accept into the **adoption** of children and into the
S D : 1 1 :024(620) [1069] election of God to **adoption** and to eternal salvation.
S D : 1 2 :031(635) [1101] the Lord God seals the **adoption** of sons and works

Adoration (4), Adore (2), Adored (3)
S 2 : 0 4 :014(301) [0475] just as we cannot **adore** the devil himself as our lord or
S 3 : 1 5 :005(316) [0501] we commend for **adoration** to their god and to
E P : 0 7 :040(486) [0817] bread and wine in the holy sacrament should be **adored**.
S D : 0 7 :087(585) [1003] about, or exposed for **adoration**, just as the baptismal
S D : 0 7 :087(585) [1003] or to cure leprosy, or is otherwise exposed for **adoration**.
S D : 0 7 :108(588) [1009] or is carried about as a spectacle and for **adoration**).
S D : 0 7 :126(591) [1015] forms of the blessed bread and wine) are to be **adored**.
S D : 0 7 :126(591) [1015] is rightly used, should be **adored** in spirit and in truth in
S D : 1 0 :020(614) [1059] state: "Just as we cannot **adore** the devil himself as our

Adorn (1), Adorned (9), Adornment (2), Adorns (1)
A L : 2 3 :020(055) [0063] the heathen, have **adorned** marriage with the greatest
A P : 2 3 :002(239) [0363] as if the church were **adorned** by the public disgrace and
A P : 2 4 :051(259) [0401] The real **adornment** of the churches is godly, practical,
A P : 2 4 :051(259) [0403] but they are not the peculiar **adornment** of the church.
L C : 0 1 :209(393) [0639] of God's Word, by which it is **adorned** and sanctified.
L C : 0 1 :314(407) [0671] buildings, they are so **adorned** that everything gleams and
L C : 0 4 :020(439) [0737] I see another man, **adorned** and clothed with the majesty
L C : 0 4 :046(442) [0743] jewel, therefore, can **adorn** our body and soul than
E P : 0 1 :006(467) [0781] dead as his creation, and **adorns** it gloriously as his
E P : 1 2 :028(500) [0843] Holy Spirit, but is merely **adorned** with divine majesty
S D : 0 3 :033(545) [0927] Spirit had renewed and **adorned** him with many
S D : 0 8 :052(601) [1033] Christ is endowed and **adorned** are created gifts or finite
S D : 1 2 :036(635) [1101] God the Father, but only **adorned** with divine majesty

Adulterate (1), Adulterated (5)
P R : P R :004(004) [0007] that he might thereby **adulterate** the pure doctrine of
P R : P R :014(007) [0013] so that no **adulterated** doctrine might in the future be
P R : P R :019(009) [0017] Supper as well as other **adulterated** teaching under the
P R : P R :019(009) [0017] doctrine any false and **adulterated** teaching that might be
P R : P R :022(011) [0019] rejections of false and **adulterated** doctrine, especially in
P R : P R :024(013) [0021] and distinguished from **adulterated** doctrine and so that

Adulterers (2), Adulteries (1), Adultery (15)
A G : 2 3 :003(051) [0061] unbecoming offense, **adultery**, and other lechery, some of
A G : 2 3 :018(054) [0063] offense, so much **adultery**, and such terrible, shocking
A L : 2 3 :018(054) [0063] causes many scandals, **adulteries**, and other crimes which
A P : 1 2 :155(207) [0301] Adam, and of David who was punished for his **adultery**.
A P : 1 2 :174(210) [0307] of the flesh instead of **adultery** and fornication,
A P : 1 8 :004(225) [0335] choose to keep the hands from murder, **adultery**, or theft.
A P : 2 3 :035(244) [0373] that the law forbids, but lust, **adultery**, and promiscuity.
S 3 : 0 3 :043(310) [0491] sin (as David fell into **adultery**, murder, and blasphemy),
T R : 0 0 :075(333) [0525] persons involved in **adultery**, but in this connection they
S C : 0 1 :011(343) [0541] *"You shall not commit **adultery**."*
L C : S P :006(362) [0575] 6. You shall not commit **adultery**.
L C : 0 1 :199(392) [0637] *"You shall not commit **adultery**."*
L C : 0 1 :201(392) [0637] **Adultery** is particularly mentioned because among the
L C : 0 1 :201(392) [0637] Accordingly **adultery** was the most common form of
L C : 0 3 :042(425) [0709] and God's people are **adulterers**, drunkards, gluttons,
L C : 0 5 :075(455) [0771] of the flesh are plain: **adultery**, immorality, impurity,
E P : 0 4 :019(477) [0801] though they fall into **adultery** and other sins and persist in
S D : 0 4 :032(556) [0947] nor idolaters, nor **adulterers** will inherit the kingdom of

Adults (2)
A P : 0 2 :003(101) [0105] trust of God, and it denies that **adults** actually produce it.
S 3 : 0 8 :007(313) [0495] **Adults** who have attained the age of reason must first

Advance (9), Advanced (9), Advancement (1), Advances (1)
A P : 0 4 :087(119) [0147] In chap. 3 he **advances** this conclusion, embodying the
A P : 0 4 :390(166) [0225] or bishops or some theologians or monks **advance**.
A P : 2 0 :006(227) [0339] to suffer for Christ and the **advancement** of the church.
A P : 2 1 :044(236) [0357] you want to extol and **advance**, we implore you not to
A P : 2 3 :006(240) [0365] truth which we have **advanced**, our opponents have
T R : 0 0 :054(329) [0519] first care of kings should be to **advance** the glory of God.
L C : 0 2 :012(412) [0681] For the somewhat more **advanced** and the educated,
L C : 0 2 :052(417) [0691] Before we had **advanced** this far, we were entirely of the
L C : 0 2 :070(420) [0697] the Scriptures, and thus **advance** and grow richer in
L C : 0 3 :052(427) [0711] among other people and **advance** with power throughout
L C : 0 5 :085(456) [0773] us who are grown and **advanced** in years, but also for the
E P : 0 7 :041(486) [0817] the Sacramentarians **advance** most blasphemously and
S D : 0 4 :027(555) [0945] the Anabaptists, who **advanced** this interpretation: We
S D : 0 7 :059(580) [0993] which they formerly **advanced** against the
S D : 0 7 :091(585) [1005] The spiritualists have **advanced** no new arguments since
S D : 0 7 :093(586) [1005] ones that Dr. Luther **advanced** against the
S D : 0 7 :127(591) [1015] expressions which are **advanced** in a coarse, fleshly,
S D : 0 8 :063(603) [1037] which these people **advance**, namely, that it is all only a
S D : 1 1 :004(616) [1063] He sees and knows in **advance** all that is or shall be, all
S D : 1 1 :006(617) [1065] sees and knows in **advance** the evil as well, but not in such

Advantage (20), Advantages (2)
A L : 2 4 :040(061) [0069] it would certainly be of **advantage** to reduce the number.
A P : 0 4 :364(162) [0219] to work for their own **advantage**, since they should work
A P : 0 4 :364(163) [0219] in another; for the weak work for their own **advantage**.
A P : 1 5 :052(222) [0329] preferred to all other **advantages**, but we shall have more
A P : 2 4 :087(265) [0413] nor prayers provide an **advantage** *ex opere operato*
A P : 2 7 :021(272) [0427] them for their physical **advantage**, to have more leisure
S C : P R :017(340) [0537] benefits, dangers, **advantages**, and disadvantages, as you
S C : P R :024(341) [0539] clearly to set forth the **advantage** and disadvantage, the
S C : 0 9 :003(355) [0561] for that would be of no **advantage** to you" (Heb. 13:17).
L C : 0 1 :066(373) [0599] of the good and for the **advantage** of our neighbor we are
L C : 0 1 :224(395) [0643] this includes taking **advantage** of our neighbor in any
L C : 0 1 :224(395) [0643] but also when he takes **advantage** of his neighbor at the
L C : 0 1 :227(396) [0645] bad coins, and takes **advantage** of him by underhanded
L C : 0 1 :233(396) [0647] harm his neighbor, take **advantage** of him, or defraud him
L C : 0 1 :299(405) [0665] such affairs gets most **advantage** out of the law, for as the
L C : 0 1 :304(406) [0667] neighbor is being taken **advantage** of and forced to
L C : 0 2 :004(411) [0679] before we explain the **advantage** and necessity of the
L C : 0 2 :022(413) [0683] Yet Christians have this **advantage**, that they
L C : 0 6 :004(457) [0000] Moreover, we have the **advantage** of knowing how to use
L C : 0 6 :005(457) [0000] they please and take **advantage** of their freedom, acting
S D : 0 4 :023(555) [0945] and used to their own **advantage** against the pure
S D : 0 7 :018(572) [0979] year, to their own **advantage**, namely, that the body of

Advent (2)
P R : P R :023(012) [0021] Spirit until the glorious **advent** of our only Redeemer and
S 1 : P R :015(291) [0459] own, and by thy glorious **advent** deliver thy servants.

Adversaries (33), Adversary (3)
P R : P R :004(004) [0007] also knows how the **adversaries** of divine truth took
P R : P R :007(004) [0009] matters which our **adversaries** had been interpreting to
P R : P R :008(005) [0011] hope that thereby the **adversaries** of pure evangelical
P R : P R :009(006) [0011] was taken by our **adversaries** of this explanation and
P R : P R :010(006) [0011] way the mouths of the **adversaries** might be stopped by
P R : P R :011(006) [0011] for slander that the **adversaries** were looking for could be
P R : P R :018(008) [0015] calumny of our **adversaries** that we ourselves do not know
P R : P R :018(009) [0015] that from now on our **adversaries** will spare us and our
P R : P R :020(010) [0017] himself, were drawn by **adversaries** (although against the
P R : P R :020(010) [0017] But when the **adversaries** assail this our ingenuous faith
A L : 2 0 :004(041) [0053] Since our **adversaries** have been admonished about these
A L : 2 4 :009(057) [0065] more devotion among our **adversaries** than among us.
A L : 2 5 :006(062) [0069] point, for even our **adversaries** are forced to concede to
A L : 2 6 :030(068) [0075] Here our **adversaries** charge that our teachers, like
A L : 2 7 :027(075) [0079] place, why do our **adversaries** exaggerate the obligation
A P : 0 4 :396(167) [0225] by the crowd of **adversaries** who condemn our teaching.
S 1 : P R :004(289) [0455] — not only among our **adversaries**, but also false brethren
S 2 : 0 1 :005(292) [0463] the devil, and all our **adversaries** will gain the victory.
S 2 : 0 4 :015(301) [0475] Lord, has attacked his **adversaries** and will accomplish
T R : 0 0 :039(327) [0515] Paul calls him "an **adversary** of Christ who opposes and
T R : 0 0 :039(327) [0515] he calls that man "an **adversary** of Christ" because he will
T R : 0 0 :061(330) [0521] of all, even our **adversaries**, it is evident that this power
L C : 0 4 :050(443) [0745] end of the world, our **adversaries** must acknowledge that
S D : P R :003(502) [0847] The **adversaries** took a jaundiced view of this Confession,
S D : P R :008(502) [0849] at the present time our **adversaries**, the papists, rejoice
S D : R N :014(506) [0855] but also to accuse the **adversaries** who teach otherwise
S D : R N :020(508) [0859] We do not, as our **adversaries** charge, veer from one
S D : 0 3 :029(544) [0925] works and love (as the **adversaries** falsely slander and
S D : 0 8 :051(601) [1033] This even the **adversaries** cannot and dare not any longer
S D : 1 0 :003(611) [1053] especially when the **adversaries** are attempting either by
S D : 1 0 :010(612) [1055] we should not yield to **adversaries** even in matters of
S D : 1 0 :010(612) [1055] ceremonies on us by **adversaries** in order to undermine
S D : 1 0 :014(613) [1057] this article because the **adversaries** will forthwith publicly
S D : 1 1 :070(627) [1085] the troublesome **adversary** is accustomed to tempt and
S D : 1 2 :003(632) [1095] Our **adversaries** have had the effrontery to pretend and
S D : 1 2 :006(633) [1097] so clearly that our very **adversaries** would have to confess

Adversities (1), Adversity (1)
L C : 0 1 :303(406) [0667] when a man because of **adversity** or debt cannot hold on
S D : 0 8 :096(610) [1049] abiding comfort in all **adversities** and will be well

Adverted (1)
S D : 1 2 :001(632) [1095] we have not explicitly **adverted** in this statement of ours

Advertisement (1)
E P : 0 5 :009(479) [0803] preaching and **advertisement** of God's wrath which really

Advice (8)
A P : 0 4 :119(123) [0155] opponents give men bad **advice** when they bid them
A P : 1 2 :106(197) [0283] giving a bit of domestic **advice** to the head of a
L C : 0 1 :149(385) [0623] everyone who can take **advice** remember that God is not
L C : 0 5 :075(455) [0771] feel it, I know no better **advice** than to suggest that they
L C : 0 5 :083(456) [0773] Take others' **advice** and seek their prayers, and never give
L C : 0 6 :013(458) [0000] a brother, seeking his **advice**, comfort, and strength.
L C : 0 6 :020(459) [0000] one, has here the faithful **advice** to go and obtain this
S D : 0 4 :036(557) [0949] it is safest to follow the **advice** of St. Paul to maintain the

Advise (4), Advised (2), Advisedly (2), Advocate (5)
A G : 2 1 :002(047) [0057] the only highpriest, **advocate**, and intercessor before God
A G : 2 1 :004(047) [0059] anyone sins, we have an **advocate** with the Father, Jesus
A L : 2 1 :004(047) [0059] anyone sins, we have an **advocate** with the Father," etc.
A L : 2 3 :025(055) [0065] Accordingly Cyprian **advised** that women who did not
A P : 0 4 :381(165) [0223] Yet it is peculiar that they **advise** us to trust our love
A P : 2 7 :046(277) [0435] is neither commanded nor **advised** in the Scriptures.
L C : 0 1 :069(374) [0599] Therefore I **advise** and urge, as I have before, that by
L C : 0 1 :188(390) [0633] not use our tongue to **advocate** or advise harming
L C : 0 1 :188(390) [0633] tongue to advocate or **advise** harming anyone; again, we
L C : 0 6 :026(460) [0000] Rather we **advise**: If you are poor and miserable, then go

Continued ▶

EP : 1 2 :031(500) [0843] to abide by it, we have **advisedly**, in true fear and
SD : 1 2 :013(634) [1099] very highly and do not **advocate** it, contrary to the
SD : 1 2 :040(636) [1103] In view of this we have **advisedly**, in the fear and

Aepinus (2)
S3 : 1 5 :005(317) [0501] I, John **Aepinus**, subscribe
TR : 0 0 :082(335) [0529] John **Aepinus**, superintendent in Hamburg, subscribed

Aerius (3)
AP : 2 4 :096(267) [0417] us the condemnation of **Aerius**, who they say was
AP : 2 4 :096(267) [0417] Epiphanius testifies that **Aerius** believed that prayers for
AP : 2 4 :096(267) [0417] We do not support **Aerius** either.

Aeschines (1)
AP : 2 4 :010(251) [0387] **Aeschines** reminded the Jews that both parties in a

Affair (1), Affairs (22)
AL : 1 6 :000(037) [0051] XVI. Civil **Affairs**
AL : 2 6 :015(066) [0073] the importance of civil **affairs**, and the consolation of
AP : 0 7 :014(170) [0231] well-being, political **affairs**, etc. in addition to the promise
AP : 0 7 :023(172) [0235] of the world, and of all public and private **affairs**.
AP : 1 2 :126(201) [0289] to guide religious **affairs**, ought in such times to exercise
AP : 1 5 :025(219) [0323] administration of public **affairs**, the administration of the
AP : 1 5 :043(221) [0327] kingdom) and political **affairs**, marriage, the education
AP : 1 6 :013(224) [0333] whole matter of political **affairs** so clearly that many good
AP : 2 1 :036(234) [0353] faith and as an incentive to imitate them in public **affairs**.
AP : 2 1 :036(234) [0353] administered public **affairs**, underwent troubles and
AP : 2 1 :036(234) [0353] about faith or fear in the administration of public **affairs**.
AP : 2 1 :037(234) [0355] who know nothing about either faith or public **affairs**.
AP : 2 3 :040(245) [0375] unmarried man is anxious about the **affairs** of the Lord."
S2 : 0 4 :008(300) [0473] a complicated and confused state of **affairs** that would be!
LC : PR :017(361) [0573] In all **affairs** and circumstances he can counsel, help,
LC : 0 1 :012(366) [0583] money, help them in love **affairs**, protect their cattle,
LC : 0 1 :055(372) [0595] in ordinary worldly **affairs** or in sublime and difficult
LC : 0 1 :284(403) [0661] For when an **affair** is manifest to everybody there can be
LC : 0 1 :299(405) [0665] and shrewdest in such **affairs** gets most advantage out of
LC : 0 1 :303(405) [0667] in ordinary business **affairs**, where one cunningly slips
LC : 0 1 :332(410) [0677] circumstances, in all his **affairs** and dealings, as if they
LC : 0 3 :073(430) [0719] of our domestic and our civil or political **affairs**.
SD : 0 1 :024(512) [0865] temporal, and civil **affairs** which are subject to human

Affect (2), Affecting (3), Affection (1), Affectionately (1), Affections (3), Affects (2)
PR : PR :025(014) [0025] to his station, all **affection**, service, and friendship.
AL : 1 8 :009(040) [0053] produce the inward **affections**, such as fear of God, trust
AL : 2 0 :029(045) [0057] and endowed with new **affections** as to be able to bring
AL : 2 0 :031(045) [0057] are full of ungodly **affections** and are too weak to do
SC : 0 3 :020(348) [0549] manner of evil, whether it **affect** body or soul, property
LC : 0 1 :107(379) [0611] only to address them **affectionately** and reverently, but
LC : 0 3 :028(424) [0705] is aware of anything that **affects** him or other people
LC : 0 3 :117(436) [0731] him for everything that **affects** our bodily welfare and
LC : 0 5 :006(447) [0755] that he would permit them to **affect** his ordinance?
SD : 0 1 :030(513) [0867] part involving and **affecting** the goodness, truth, holiness,
SD : 0 2 :002(520) [0881] do in external things **affecting** this temporal life, nor
SD : 0 2 :020(524) [0889] and external matters **affecting** the nurture and needs of

Affiliation (1)
AP : 0 7 :016(171) [0231] had an outward **affiliation** with the church (that is, with

Affirm (5), Affirmation (1), Affirmative (10), Affirmed (2), Affirming (1), Affirms (3)
PR : PR :003(003) [0007] many heresies and errors, and repeatedly **affirmed**.
PR : PR :019(009) [0017] hereby to attest and **affirm** publicly that, then as now, it
AP : 0 4 :001(107) [0121] of their merits, and for **affirming** that men receive the
AP : 1 0 :002(179) [0247] only the Roman Church **affirms** the bodily presence of
AP : 1 5 :017(217) [0319] can justify since we can **affirm** nothing about the will of
AP : 2 1 :010(230) [0345] But our Confession **affirms** only this much, that Scripture
AP : 2 1 :012(230) [0345] Word of God, we cannot **affirm** that the saints are aware
AP : 2 1 :036(234) [0353] sickness and constantly **affirmed** that God hears the
LC : 0 3 :120(436) [0731] than an unquestioning **affirmation** of faith on the part of
EP : 0 1 :001(466) [0779] **Affirmative** Theses
EP : 0 2 :001(470) [0787] **Affirmative** Theses
EP : 0 3 :002(473) [0793] **Affirmative** Theses
EP : 0 4 :004(476) [0797] **Affirmative** Theses
EP : 0 4 :007(476) [0799] The Apostle **affirms** in clear terms, "So also David
EP : 0 5 :001(478) [0801] **Affirmative** Theses
EP : 0 6 :001(480) [0805] **Affirmative** Theses
EP : 0 7 :005(482) [0809] **Affirmative** Theses
EP : 0 8 :003(487) [0819] **Affirmative** Theses
EP : 1 0 :002(493) [0829] **Affirmative** Theses
EP : 1 1 :001(494) [0831] **Affirmative**
SD : 0 2 :023(525) [0889] defend free will, they **affirm** a capacity for this freedom in
SD : 0 3 :008(540) [0919] settle it by his grace, we **affirm** our teaching, belief, and

Afflicted (3), Affliction (5), Afflictions (25)
AG : 2 7 :049(079) [0083] help from him in every **affliction** connected with our
AL : 2 1 :003(047) [0057] approves, namely, that in all **afflictions** he be called upon.
AL : 2 6 :031(068) [0075] the cross that Christians are obliged to suffer **afflictions**.
AL : 2 6 :032(068) [0075] be harassed by various **afflictions** and to be crucified with
AP : PR :019(099) [0103] him to regard his **afflicted** and scattered churches and to
AP : 0 4 :008(108) [0121] the expectation of God's help in death and all **afflictions**.
AP : 0 4 :008(108) [0121] to God in death and all **afflictions**, lest we try to flee these
AP : 0 4 :045(113) [0133] be sure that he hears us, and obey him in all **afflictions**.
AP : 0 4 :060(115) [0137] consolation in all **afflictions**, and our opponents take it
AP : 0 4 :125(124) [0157] and praise him, and to submit to him in our **afflictions**.
AP : 0 4 :142(126) [0161] be strengthened in these terrors and in other **afflictions**.
AP : 0 4 :167(130) [0169] endures patiently enough the **afflictions** that God sends?
AP : 0 4 :170(130) [0171] will and runs away from **afflictions** that it ought to bear
AP : 0 4 :193(133) [0175] confession of doctrine, **afflictions**, works of charity, and
AP : 0 4 :293(152) [0203] God in the midst of **afflictions**, and practice chastity, love
AP : 0 4 :364(162) [0219] to escape despair amid **afflictions**, they should know that
AP : 0 4 :367(163) [0221] Works and **afflictions** merit not justification but other
AP : 0 4 :387(166) [0225] fullest comfort in all **afflictions** and shows us the work of
AP : 0 7 :018(171) [0233] is the same, whether now glorified or previously **afflicted**.
AP : 1 2 :158(207) [0301] explains that Job's **afflictions** were not imposed on him
AP : 1 2 :158(207) [0301] So **afflictions** are not always punishments or signs of
AP : 1 3 :017(213) [0313] be listed here, as well as **afflictions**, which in themselves
AP : 2 4 :025(253) [0391] confession, the **afflictions** of the saints, yes, all the good
AP : 2 4 :032(255) [0395] to God, they bear **afflictions** in confession, they do good
AP : 2 4 :038(257) [0399] be an offering in thanksgiving, confession, and **affliction**.
AP : 2 4 :067(261) [0407] the reconciled, just as **afflictions** do not merit
LC : 0 1 :244(398) [0649] He lays on us one **affliction** after another, or he quarters
LC : 0 3 :119(436) [0731] set before us all the **afflictions** that may ever beset us in
SD : 0 6 :009(565) [0965] good for me that I was **afflicted** that I might learn thy
SD : 1 1 :030(621) [1073] and comfort in **afflictions** (Eph. 1:11, 13; Rom. 8:25).
SD : 1 1 :048(624) [1079] in times of trial and **affliction**, that in his counsel before
SD : 1 1 :049(624) [1079] which specific cross and **affliction** he would conform each
SD : 1 1 :049(624) [1079] that in each case the **afflictions** should and must "work

Afford (3), Afforded (2), Affords (1)
AL : 2 0 :007(042) [0053] former one, and it can **afford** more consolation than their
SC : PR :023(341) [0539] in which aid is **afforded** against such evil and in which
LC : 0 1 :202(392) [0639] are to be chaste and to **afford** no occasion, aid, or
SD : 0 3 :030(544) [0925] but also in order to **afford** saddened consciences
SD : 0 8 :087(608) [1047] of their highest comfort, **afforded** them in the cited
SD : 1 1 :045(624) [1079] This doctrine also **affords** the beautiful and glorious

Afield (1)
AP : 2 4 :085(264) [0413] Why go so far **afield** for the etymology when the term

Aflame (5)
AG : 2 3 :004(051) [0061] to marry than to be **aflame** with passion" (I Cor. 7:9).
AL : 2 3 :004(051) [0061] better to marry than to be **aflame** with passion" (I Cor.
AP : 2 3 :016(241) [0369] 9), "It is better to marry than to be **aflame** with passion."
AP : 2 3 :016(241) [0369] "It is better to marry than to be **aflame** with passion."
AP : 2 3 :016(241) [0369] Thus anyone who is **aflame** retains the right to marry.

Afraid (5)
AL : 2 7 :054(079) [0083] therefore some are not **afraid** to take vengeance in their
AP : 0 2 :021(103) [0111] Peter Lombard is not **afraid** to say that original
S1 : PR :003(289) [0455] Roman court is dreadfully **afraid** of a free council and
LC : 0 1 :162(387) [0627] resists and rebels; all are **afraid** that their bellies will
LC : 0 6 :010(458) [0000] everyone's presence, no one being **afraid** of anyone else.

Agape (1)
AP : 2 4 :086(265) [0413] the Mass was called ***agape*** in some places, unless some

Age (21)
AG : 2 7 :004(071) [0077] on many before they had attained an appropriate **age**.
AG : 2 7 :031(075) [0079] annul vows that are made under the **age** of fifteen years.
AG : 2 7 :031(075) [0079] They hold that before this **age** one does not possess
AG : 2 7 :033(076) [0079] the cloister in their childhood, before attaining such **age**.
AL : 2 3 :026(056) [0065] before attaining a proper **age**, and as a rule vows used to
AL : 2 7 :004(071) [0077] to the canons, before they had attained a lawful **age**.
AL : 2 7 :031(075) [0079] vows made before the **age** of fifteen on the ground that
AL : 2 7 :031(075) [0079] ground that before that **age** a person does not seem to
AL : 2 7 :033(076) [0079] of them took vows before they reached such an **age**.
AP : 2 7 :002(269) [0419] ill either on account of **age** or on account of the filth of
AP : 2 7 :005(269) [0421] as from a golden **age** to an iron age, or as the Platonic
AP : 2 7 :005(269) [0421] a golden age to an iron **age**, or as the Platonic cube
AP : 2 7 :066(280) [0441] as a widow who is under sixty years of **age**" (I Tim. 5:9).
AP : 2 7 :066(280) [0441] Thus vows made before that **age** must be invalid.
S3 : 0 8 :007(313) [0495] who have attained the **age** of reason must first have
LC : 0 1 :201(392) [0637] Youths were married at the earliest **age** possible.
EP : 0 8 :016(489) [0821] therefore truly increase in **age**, wisdom, and favor with
EP : 1 0 :004(493) [0829] in every locality and every **age** has authority to change
SD : 0 8 :012(593) [1019] is named not only in this **age** but also in that which is to
SD : 0 8 :051(601) [1033] is named, not only in this **age** but also in that which is to
SD : 0 8 :076(606) [1043] "I am with you always even to the close of the **age**."

Agent (2)
AP : 0 4 :317(156) [0209] thereby makes Christ "an **agent** of sin" since he does not
AP : 1 5 :012(216) [0317] that Christ would be "an **agent** of sins" (Gal. 2:17) if we

Aggravated (2), Aggravates (1)
PR : PR :024(013) [0021] many intrusive errors, **aggravated** scandals, dissensions,
LC : 0 1 :056(372) [0595] sin, but it is greatly **aggravated** when we attempt to justify
EP : 0 7 :018(484) [0813] magnifies, and **aggravates** this condemnation (I Cor.

Agitated (1)
SD : 0 2 :073(535) [0909] of years have been **agitated** in the churches of the

Agnoetes (1)
SD : 0 8 :075(606) [1043] the Arians, called the **Agnoetes**, who taught that the Son,

Ago (10)
AG : PR :001(024) [0039] A short time **ago** Your Imperial Majesty graciously
AG : PR :017(026) [0041] last diet in Spires a year **ago**, the electors, princes, and
AG : 2 3 :012(052) [0063] only four hundred years **ago** that the priests in Germany
AL : 2 3 :012(052) [0063] until four hundred years **ago** were priests in Germany
AP : 2 0 :014(228) [0343] a thousand years **ago**, in the days of Augustine.
AP : 2 1 :002(229) [0343] Jerome conquered Vigilantius eleven hundred years **ago**."
AP : 2 7 :001(268) [0419] Thirty years **ago**, in the Thuringian town of Eisenach,
LC : PR :008(359) [0569] ABC's, which they think they have outgrown long **ago**.
LC : 0 1 :312(407) [0671] they were too insignificant or had been fulfilled long **ago**.
LC : 0 4 :070(445) [0749] If a year **ago** a man was proud and greedy, this year he is

Agony (1)
AP : 0 4 :037(112) [0131] But in the **agony** of conscience and in conflict, the

Agree (22), Agreeable (2), Agreed (6), Agreeing (1), Agreement (36), Agreements (1), Agrees (9)
PR : PR :000(001) [0004] by the Unanimous **Agreement** and Order of the
PR : PR :004(004) [0007] Christian charity and **agreement**, and in this way hold
PR : PR :005(004) [0009] of God's Word and in **agreeable** Christian concord and
PR : PR :007(004) [0009] basis of a memorandum **agreed** to at
PR : PR :013(007) [0013] the just cited written **agreement** composed with reference
PR : PR :016(008) [0013] which had arisen was **agreeable** and conformable first of

Continued ▶

P R : P R :016(008) [0015] Therefore this Christian **agreement** is called and also is
P R : P R :017(008) [0015] and well-intended **agreements** reached by our
P R : P R :017(008) [0015] unanimity and **agreement** among ourselves in this Book
P R : P R :019(010) [0017] in so far as they are in **agreement** with the norm
P R : P R :022(011) [0019] up to now admittedly not come to **agreement** with us.
P R : P R :022(012) [0021] by this Christian **agreement** for any molestation and
P R : P R :023(012) [0021] To this end the present **agreement** was proposed,
P R : P R :024(013) [0023] of this Christian **agreement** of ours it was never our
P R : P R :025(013) [0023] new by this work of **agreement** or to depart in any way at
P R : P R :025(013) [0023] in the past, for our **agreement** is based on the prophetic
A G : P R :002(025) [0039] us to unite the same in **agreement** on one Christian truth,
A G : 0 0 :001(047) [0059] teaching than that which **agrees** with the pure Word of
A L : 0 7 :002(032) [0047] the church it is enough to **agree** concerning the teaching
A L : 2 2 :012(051) [0061] of the sacrament does not **agree** with the institution of
A P : 0 2 :004(101) [0105] length that our definition **agrees** with the traditional one.
A P : 0 2 :012(102) [0109] righteousness, which we **agree** is subject to reason and
A P : 0 2 :022(103) [0111] with which Augustine's interpretation of the image **agrees**.
A P : 0 2 :030(104) [0113] These opinions **agree** with the Scriptures.
A P : 0 2 :051(107) [0119] is correct and in **agreement** with Christ's church catholic.
A P : 0 4 :175(131) [0171] Holy Spirit and that their impulses **agree** with God's law.
A P : 0 4 :284(150) [0201] whole passage shows its **agreement** with the rest of the
A P : 0 4 :389(166) [0225] that what we have said **agrees** with the prophetic and
A P : 0 7 :010(170) [0229] the world who **agree** on the Gospel and have the same
A P : 0 7 :019(171) [0233] Christ's parables **agree** with this.
A P : 0 7 :027(173) [0235] accept only what **agrees** with human reason and regard
A P : 0 7 :030(173) [0237] the church it is enough to **agree** concerning the teaching
A P : 1 2 :002(182) [0253] and therefore we can in no way **agree** to the confutation.
A P : 1 2 :096(196) [0281] faith just as faith obtains it from the written **agreement**."
A P : 2 0 :002(227) [0339] We would rather **agree** with this church of the prophets
A P : 2 0 :009(227) [0341] every one of you who has **agreed** to our Confession, when
A P : 2 1 :044(236) [0357] we implore you not to **agree** to the violent counsels of our
A P : 2 2 :013(238) [0361] should keep us from **agreeing** with our opponents, even
A P : 2 3 :060(247) [0379] we cannot conscientiously **agree** with our opponents in
A P : 2 4 :067(261) [0407] sacrament what actually **agrees** with the Fathers and with
A P : 2 4 :068(262) [0407] banquets are symbols of **agreement** and friendship.
A P : 2 7 :056(278) [0439] chapters are forced to **agree** with the persecutors of the
A P : 2 8 :024(285) [0451] church needs, nor can we **agree** with our opponents who
S 3 : 0 5 :002(310) [0491] Therefore we do not **agree** with Thomas and the
S 3 : 0 5 :003(311) [0491] Nor do we **agree** with Scotus and the Franciscans who
S 3 : 0 6 :005(311) [0493] is and remains there **agrees** better with the Scriptures, as
T R : 0 0 :024(324) [0511] Christ said, "If two or three of you **agree** on earth," etc.
T R : 0 0 :059(330) [0521] other hand, those who **agree** with the pope and defend his
T R : 0 0 :082(000) [0529] I judge that all these **agree** with Holy Scripture, and with
L C : 0 3 :096(433) [0725] the promise which is in **agreement** with this petition,
E P : 0 2 :016(472) [0791] these expressions do not **agree** with the form of sound
E P : 1 0 :002(493) [0829] have not come to an **agreement** with us in doctrine, may
E P : 1 0 :007(493) [0831] long as there is mutual **agreement** in doctrine and in all
E P : 1 0 :007(494) [0831] in fasting does not destroy **agreement** in faith."
S D : P R :010(503) [0849] the controverted issues **agrees** with the Word of God and
S D : R N :002(503) [0851] declared in mutual **agreement** that we shall neither
S D : R N :015(506) [0857] a basic and mutual **agreement** that we shall at all times
S D : R N :016(507) [0857] and express mutual **agreement** concerning the chief and
S D : R N :016(507) [0857] This **agreement** we have set forth as a certain and public
S D : 0 3 :041(546) [0931] "There is a beautiful **agreement** between faith and good
S D : 0 4 :008(552) [0941] We **agree** that this is so for the sake of the Lord Christ
S D : 0 7 :001(569) [0971] it appear to be in full **agreement** with the teaching of the
S D : 0 7 :012(571) [0977] articles of Christian **agreement** in Wittenberg, and Dr.
S D : 0 7 :017(572) [0979] precisely in words which **agree** in the most exact way with
S D : 0 7 :018(572) [0979] articles of **agreement**, adopted in the previous year, to
S D : 0 7 :038(576) [0985] articles of **agreement** of 1536 and elsewhere.
S D : 0 7 :058(580) [0993] of Paul in words which **agree** in the best possible way
S D : 0 7 :074(583) [0999] and unanimous **agreement** among ourselves: No man's
S D : 1 0 :002(611) [1053] have not come to an **agreement** with us in doctrine, one
S D : 1 0 :005(611) [1053] (or are demanded or **agreed** to with that intention) that
S D : 1 0 :005(611) [1053] have been brought into **agreement** and become one body,
S D : 1 0 :016(613) [1057] things, where Christian **agreement** in doctrine has not
S D : 1 0 :031(616) [1063] as they are otherwise **agreed** in doctrine and in all its
S D : 1 0 :031(616) [1063] its articles and are also **agreed** concerning the right use of
S D : 1 0 :031(616) [1063] in fasting should not destroy **agreement** in faith."
S D : 1 2 :003(633) [1095] two preachers who are **agreed** in each and every article of
S D : 1 2 :005(633) [1097] to deceive and that our **agreement** was not a mere

Agricola (3)
S 3 : 1 5 :005(317) [0501] John **Agricola**, of Eisleben, subscribed
S 3 : 1 5 :005(317) [0501] I, Stephen **Agricola**, minister in Hof, subscribe
T R : 0 0 :082(334) [0529] Stephen **Agricola**, minister in Chur, subscribed with his

Agriculture (1)
A P : 2 3 :038(244) [0373] science surpasses **agriculture**, and eloquence surpasses

Ah (1)
L C : 0 1 :270(401) [0657] **Ah**, now do you smell the roast?

Ahead (2)
L C : 0 1 :047(371) [0593] path and walk straight **ahead**, using all of God's gifts
L C : 0 1 :267(401) [0657] are not content just to know but rush **ahead** and judge.

Aid (11), Aided (2), Aiding (1), Aids (1)
A G : 2 3 :015(054) [0063] who instituted marriage to **aid** human infirmity and
A L : 1 9 :000(041) [0053] If not **aided** by God, the will of the wicked turns away
A P : 0 4 :232(139) [0185] be nurtured by mutual **aid**, for it is not possible to
S 3 : 0 3 :024(307) [0485] see in Rome came to the **aid** of the poor church and
S C : P R :020(340) [0537] when they refuse their **aid** in the training of children to
S C : P R :023(341) [0539] the sacrament in which **aid** is afforded against such evil
L C : 0 1 :182(389) [0631] or word, by signs or gestures, or by **aiding** and abetting.
L C : 0 1 :191(391) [0635] do not offer counsel and **aid** to men in need and in peril
L C : 0 1 :202(392) [0639] and to afford no occasion, **aid**, or encouragement to
L C : 0 1 :203(392) [0639] and on the contrary to **aid** and assist him so that he may
L C : 0 1 :247(398) [0651] whom you ought to give **aid**, he will go away wretched
L C : 0 1 :314(407) [0671] **Aided** by great pomp, splendor, and magnificent
L C : 0 2 :055(418) [0693] us, and we forgive, bear with, and **aid** one another.
L C : 0 5 :068(454) [0769] soothing medicine which **aids** and quickens us in both
S D : 0 2 :076(536) [0911] Holy Spirit comes to the **aid** of the good work which man

Aim (2), Aimed (1), Aimlessly (1)
A L : 2 8 :066(092) [0093] must consider what the perpetual **aim** of the Gospel is.
A P : 0 4 :245(142) [0189] life (I Tim. 1:5), "The **aim** of our charge is love that issues
L C : 0 3 :014(422) [0701] that is to stake prayer on luck and to mumble **aimlessly**.
L C : 0 5 :082(456) [0773] are at every moment **aimed** at you, you would be glad to

Air (7)
A P : 0 7 :050(178) [0245] legitimate for them to use the **air**, light, food, and drink.
A P : 1 6 :002(222) [0331] make use of medicine or architecture, food or drink or **air**.
L C : 0 2 :014(412) [0681] heavens, day and night, **air**, fire, water, the earth and all
L C : 0 3 :080(431) [0721] to destroy crops and cattle, why he poisons the **air**, etc.
S D : 0 7 :100(586) [1007] my vision penetrates **air**, light, or water and does not
S D : 0 7 :100(586) [1007] or tone passes through **air** or water or a board and a wall
S D : 0 7 :100(586) [1007] light and heat go through **air**, water, glass, or crystal and

Alarm (1)
S D : 1 1 :074(628) [1087] David, "I had said in my **alarm**, I am driven far from thy

Alas (2)
L C : 0 1 :112(380) [0613] **Alas**, it is utterly despised and brushed aside, and no one
L C : 0 5 :055(453) [0767] into consternation, saying, "**Alas**, I am not worthy!"

Albert (2)
P R : P R :027(015) [0025] **Albert**, count of Schwarzburg [-Rudolstadt]
P R : P R :027(015) [0025] **Albert** Geroge, count of Stolberg

Albs (2)
S 1 : P R :013(291) [0459] and tomfoolery with **albs**, great tonsures, broad
S 3 : 1 2 :003(315) [0499] of surplices, tonsures, **albs**, or other ceremonies of theirs

Alert (1)
L C : 0 1 :249(398) [0651] They should be **alert** and resolute enough to establish and

Alexander (1)
A P : 1 5 :034(220) [0325] When **Alexander** could not untie the Gordian knot, he

Alexandria (10)
A G : 2 4 :041(061) [0069] read and expounded in **Alexandria**, and all these services
A L : 2 4 :041(061) [0069] in Book 9, "Again, in **Alexandria**, the Scriptures are read
A P : 2 7 :038(275) [0433] in the city of **Alexandria** as a basis for comparison.
S 2 : 0 4 :009(300) [0473] writes that the priests of **Alexandria** governed the
S 3 : 1 0 :003(314) [0497] the church in **Alexandria** that it was originally governed
T R : 0 0 :012(321) [0507] that the bishop of **Alexandria** should administer the
T R : 0 0 :012(322) [0507] from him and transfer it to the bishop of **Alexandria**.
T R : 0 0 :018(323) [0509] or Rhegium or **Alexandria** — he is of the same dignity and
T R : 0 0 :019(323) [0509] to the patriarch of **Alexandria**, Gregory objected to having
T R : 0 0 :062(331) [0523] For in **Alexandria**, from the time of Mark the Evangelist

Alien (6), Alienate (1), Alienated (2)
A P : 1 2 :051(189) [0265] is his deed! and to work his work — **alien** is his work!"
A P : 1 2 :051(189) [0265] He calls it God's **alien** work to terrify because God's own
A P : 1 2 :123(201) [0289] such tricks they try to **alienate** men's minds and fan their
A P : 1 2 :158(207) [0301] that God is doing his **alien** work in order to do his proper
S 3 : 0 2 :004(303) [0479] find it, and begins to be **alienated** from God, to murmur,
E P : 0 1 :005(466) [0781] thus took on himself not **alien** flesh, but our own, and
E P : 0 1 :018(468) [0783] something extraneous and **alien** within man, and that
E P : 0 5 :010(479) [0803] and therefore it is an "**alien** work" of Christ by which he
S D : 0 2 :010(522) [0883] in their understanding, **alienated** from the life of God

Alike (11)
A G : 0 1 :002(027) [0043] this one divine essence, equal in power and **alike** eternal:
A L : 0 7 :003(032) [0047] instituted by men, should be **alike** everywhere.
A L : 2 6 :043(070) [0075] by others that such customs need not be **alike** everywhere.
A P : 0 7 :030(174) [0237] instituted by men, should be **alike** everywhere."
A P : 0 7 :034(175) [0239] of the church that human traditions be **alike** everywhere.
A P : 1 5 :018(217) [0319] necessary that rites instituted by men be everywhere **alike**.
E P : R N :001(464) [0777] all doctrines and teachers **alike** must be appraised and
E P : 0 3 :007(473) [0793] the righteous are both **alike** an abomination to the Lord"
E P : 1 1 :004(494) [0833] foreknowledge extends **alike** over good people and evil
S D : 0 3 :017(542) [0921] the righteous are both **alike** an abomination to the Lord"
S D : 0 7 :088(585) [1003] earth both the worthy and the unworthy **alike** participate.

Alive (25)
P R : P R :005(004) [0009] with God's Word, as they were while Dr. Luther was **alive**.
P R : P R :005(004) [0009] holy apostles were still **alive**, it happened that false
A P : 0 4 :249(142) [0191] works is dead, but it is **alive** when it brings forth good
A P : 0 4 :250(143) [0191] power that makes us **alive** and enables us to overcome
A P : 0 4 :352(161) [0217] of sin, your spirits are **alive** because of righteousness."
A P : 2 1 :002(229) [0343] while he was still **alive**, to pray for his brothers after his
A P : 2 4 :038(257) [0399] put to death, and made **alive** when the Gospel sprinkles
A P : 2 4 :039(257) [0399] the Holy Spirit who puts us to death and makes us **alive**.
A P : 2 4 :040(257) [0399] the Gospel, being put to death and being made **alive**.
A P : 2 4 :059(260) [0405] and the Holy Spirit and be put to death and made **alive**.
A P : 2 4 :071(262) [0409] is the spiritual motivation, dying and being made **alive**.
A P : 2 4 :072(262) [0409] acceptance of them by faith, so that they make us **alive**.
A P : 2 4 :073(262) [0409] A faith that acknowledges mercy makes **alive**.
A P : 2 8 :010(282) [0445] Do they make hearts **alive**?
S 1 : P R :004(289) [0455] I am still **alive**.
L C : 0 1 :042(370) [0591] can scarcely even keep **alive**; meanwhile, those who serve
E P : 0 2 :003(470) [0787] our trespasses, he made us **alive** together with Christ."
E P : 0 3 :008(474) [0793] and *vivificatio* (making **alive**) are used in place of
E P : 0 5 :010(479) [0803] — namely, to preach grace, to comfort, to make **alive**.
S D : 0 2 :011(522) [0885] liberated him from the death of sin and made him **alive**.
S D : 0 2 :017(524) [0887] to God, and all too mighty, **alive**, and active for everything
S D : 0 3 :020(542) [0921] that is, being made **alive**, has sometimes been used in the
S D : 0 3 :020(542) [0921] our trespasses, he made us **alive** together with Christ"
S D : 0 7 :006(570) [0973] Christ is present in his Supper truly, essentially, and **alive**.
S D : 0 8 :058(602) [1035] power to make the dead **alive** and to execute judgment

Allegation (1)
P R : P R :009(006) [0011] By this unfounded **allegation** many pious hearts were

Allege (1), Alleged (4), Allegedly (11), Alleges (1)
PR : PR :018(009) [0017] and for that reason **allegedly** make a new confession
PR : PR :021(011) [0019] the personal union it is **alleged** to have this majesty
AP : 0 7 :020(171) [0233] as has been slanderously **alleged**, but we teach that this
SD : 0 1 :001(508) [0859] is now after the Fall **allegedly** no difference whatsoever
SD : 0 1 :019(511) [0865] lack and damage **allegedly** are not really and truly such a
SD : 0 1 :029(513) [0867] way that man's nature is **allegedly** pure, holy, righteous,
SD : 0 1 :048(517) [0875] or soul, so that there is **allegedly** no distinction whatever
SD : 0 7 :004(569) [0973] In the beginning they **alleged** that the Lord's Supper was
SD : 0 7 :006(570) [0973] when they **alleged** and boasted that they hold no other
SD : 0 7 :108(588) [1009] of the bread, which they **allege** has lost its natural
SD : 0 7 :116(589) [1013] our faith in the Supper **allegedly** take place not through
SD : 0 7 :121(590) [1013] of the priest the power **allegedly** to effect a sacrament, the
SD : 0 7 :123(590) [1015] the unworthy which **alleges** that godless Epicureans and
SD : 0 8 :014(594) [1019] truth the two natures **allegedly** have no communion at all
SD : 0 8 :071(605) [1041] the human nature **allegedly** received equal majesty,
SD : 0 8 :089(609) [1047] the human nature has **allegedly** been blended with the
SD : 1 0 :005(611) [1055] has taken place or will **allegedly** result little by little from

Allegiance (1)
SD : RN :004(504) [0851] we further pledge **allegiance** to the three general Creeds,

Alleging (1)
LC : 0 3 :006(421) [0699] habit of never praying, **alleging** that since we reject false

Allegories (1), Allegory (1)
AP : 2 4 :035(256) [0397] let them defeat us with **allegories**, but it is evident that
AP : 2 4 :035(256) [0397] but it is evident that **allegory** does not prove or establish

Alleviating (1)
AP : 2 8 :004(281) [0445] Instead of **alleviating** such minds tortured by doubt, they

Alliance (1)
AP : 2 3 :059(247) [0379] not regret our lack of an **alliance** with such murderous

Allies (1)
LC : 0 3 :062(428) [0715] even enlisting the world and our own flesh as his **allies**.

Alloeosis (7)
SD : 0 8 :021(595) [1023] against the blasphemous ***alloeosis*** of Zwingli, who taught
SD : 0 8 :038(598) [1027] written about Zwingli's ***alloeosis***, we shall here quote Dr.
SD : 0 8 :039(598) [1027] "Zwingli calls that an ***alloeosis*** when something is said
SD : 0 8 :040(598) [1029] beware, I say, of this ***alloeosis***, for it is the devil's mask
SD : 0 8 :040(599) [1029] indescribable what the devil attempts with this ***alloeosis***."
SD : 0 8 :041(599) [1029] the grandmother of the ***alloeosis***, would say that the deity
SD : 0 8 :043(599) [1029] If Zwingli's ***alloeosis*** stands, then Christ will have to be

Allotted (1)
LC : 0 1 :212(394) [0641] everyone may have his **allotted** portion and be satisfied

Allow (34), Allowable (1), Allowed (15), Allowing (2), Allows (1)
PR : PR :018(008) [0015] lest anybody **allow** himself to be led astray by the
PR : PR :024(013) [0023] Christian effort and will **allow** nothing to stand in the
AG : PR :013(026) [0041] as God and conscience **allow**, that may serve the cause of
AG : PR :020(026) [0041] opportunity and to **allow** no hindrance to be put in the
AG : 1 1 :001(034) [0047] should be retained and not **allowed** to fall into disuse.
AG : 0 0 :000(049) [0059] be regarded as above all custom) to **allow** such changes.
AG : 2 3 :002(053) [0063] Pius II, often said and **allowed** himself to be quoted as
AG : 2 7 :024(074) [0079] were no reasons which **allowed** annulment of the
AL : 0 8 :001(033) [0047] with believers, it is **allowable** to use the sacraments even
AL : 2 4 :029(059) [0067] But the Scriptures do not **allow** this.
AL : 2 8 :063(092) [0093] the extent to which one is **allowed** to work on holy days.
AL : 2 8 :077(094) [0095] this one thing, that they **allow** the Gospel to be taught
AP : 1 4 :001(214) [0315] that no one should be **allowed** to administer the Word
AP : 1 5 :015(217) [0319] If men are **allowed** to establish new rites and if by such
AP : 1 6 :011(224) [0333] claiming that priests were not **allowed** to own property.
AP : 2 3 :024(243) [0371] the councils, for they do **allow** marriage under certain
S 1 : PR :003(289) [0455] be reformed a little and **allow** limitations to be placed on
S 2 : 0 2 :010(294) [0465] to ashes before I would **allow** a celebrant of the Mass and
S 2 : 0 2 :029(297) [0471] In short, we cannot **allow** but must condemn the Mass,
S 2 : 0 4 :011(300) [0475] who desire to do so they **allow** to believe in Christ, and
S 3 : 0 3 :002(304) [0479] He **allows** no one to justify himself.
S 3 : 0 8 :001(312) [0493] should by no means be **allowed** to fall into disuse in the
S 3 : 1 5 :005(316) [0501] I hold that, if he would **allow** the Gospel, we, too, may
TR : 0 0 :049(329) [0519] the church and does not **allow** ecclesiastical controversies
SC : PR :011(339) [0535] in Baptism, or be **allowed** to participate in any Christian
SC : PR :016(340) [0535] Moreover, **allow** yourself ample time, for it is not
LC : PR :006(359) [0569] into decay, and brazenly **allow** both pastors and
LC : 0 1 :047(371) [0593] to God's order, **allowing** none of these good things to be
LC : 0 1 :069(374) [0599] Where they are **allowed** to do as they please, no good will
LC : 0 1 :111(380) [0613] his parents will not **allow** them to suffer want or hunger,
LC : 0 1 :137(384) [0619] They will not **allow** themselves to be brought up in
LC : 0 1 :163(387) [0627] blessings and once again **allow** preachers of lies to arise
LC : 0 1 :193(391) [0635] intention that we should **allow** no man to suffer harm,
LC : 0 1 :209(393) [0641] humble themselves and **allow** all people to enter the estate
LC : 0 1 :260(400) [0655] He must not **allow** these rights to be thwarted or distorted
LC : 0 1 :272(401) [0657] what is secret should be **allowed** to remain secret, or at
LC : 0 3 :015(422) [0701] We **allow** ourselves to be hindered and deterred by such
LC : 0 3 :018(422) [0703] Nor will he **allow** our prayers to be frustrated or lost, for
LC : 0 3 :058(428) [0713] For how could God **allow** us to suffer want in temporal
LC : 0 3 :060(428) [0715] two things and never **allow** ourselves to be torn from
LC : 0 3 :100(433) [0727] again that he will not **allow** us to fall and yield to trials
LC : 0 3 :105(434) [0727] hour that God may not **allow** us to become faint and
LC : 0 4 :021(439) [0737] opened when Christ **allowed** himself to be baptized, that
LC : 0 4 :036(441) [0741] Just by **allowing** the water to be poured over you, you do
LC : 0 4 :063(444) [0749] and well armed and not **allow** ourselves to be turned
LC : 0 5 :032(450) [0761] Why, then, should we **allow** this treasure to be torn out
LC : 0 5 :062(454) [0767] compel himself to go and **allow** no one to deter him,
LC : 0 6 :019(459) [0000] to lament your need and **allow** yourself to be helped so
LC : 0 6 :031(460) [0000] We compel no man, but **allow** ourselves to be compelled,
SD : PR :003(501) [0847] the holy Gospel and had **allowed** their churches to be
SD : RN :015(507) [0857] edify, should never be **allowed** to disturb the church) and
SD : 0 7 :120(590) [1013] his assumed human nature neither permit nor **allow** this.
SD : 1 2 :008(633) [1097] of the holy Gospel was **allowed** neither room nor scope,

Alls (1)
LC : 0 4 :028(440) [0739] Our know-it-**alls**, the new spirits, assert that faith alone

Allure (1), Allurements (1), Alluring (1)
AP : 1 2 :168(209) [0305] punishments but to keep the flesh from **alluring** us to sin."
LC : 0 1 :322(409) [0673] to terrify and warn us but also to attract and **allure** us.
LC : 0 3 :106(434) [0727] temptations and **allurements** as long as we live in the flesh

Almighty (37)
PR : PR :002(003) [0007] of this transitory world **almighty** God in his
PR : PR :005(004) [0009] and petitioned the **Almighty**, that our churches and
PR : PR :013(007) [0013] Finally, after invoking **almighty** God to his praise and
PR : PR :016(008) [0013] with heartfelt thanks to **almighty** God testified that of
PR : PR :020(010) [0017] He is **almighty** and veracious, and hence he is able to
PR : PR :020(010) [0017] the right hand of God's **almighty** power and majesty) and
PR : PR :022(012) [0021] testify before the face of **almighty** God and the whole of
AG : PR :011(026) [0041] divine truth we invoke **almighty** God in deepest humility
AG : 1 9 :000(040) [0053] among us that although **almighty** God has created and
SC : 0 2 :001(344) [0543] *in God, the Father* ***almighty***, *maker of heaven and*
SC : 0 2 :003(345) [0545] *hand of God, the Father* ***almighty***, *whence he shall come*
LC : SP :011(363) [0577] in God, the Father **almighty**, maker of heaven and earth:
LC : SP :012(363) [0577] hand of God, the Father **almighty**, whence he shall come
LC : 0 2 :009(411) [0679] *in God, the Father* ***almighty***, *maker of heaven and*
LC : 0 2 :013(412) [0681] "I believe in God, the Father **almighty**, maker," etc.?
LC : 0 2 :018(412) [0681] two parts of this article, where we say, "Father **almighty**."
LC : 0 2 :025(413) [0685] *hand of God, the Father* ***almighty***, *whence he shall come*
EP : 0 7 :008(482) [0811] solely and alone to the **almighty** power of our Lord Jesus
EP : 0 8 :026(490) [0823] of the world or that the Son of man has become **almighty**.
EP : 1 1 :022(497) [0837] May the **almighty** God and Father of our Lord Jesus
SD : PR :001(501) [0847] grace and mercy of the **Almighty**, the teaching concerning
SD : PR :005(502) [0847] by the grace of the **Almighty** to abide until our end by this
SD : 0 3 :056(549) [0935] to the eternal and **almighty** God for the sins of all the
SD : 0 7 :043(576) [0987] the eternal truth and wisdom and the **almighty** God.
SD : 0 7 :044(577) [0987] his life, this truthful and **almighty** Lord, our Creator and
SD : 0 7 :045(577) [0987] eternal, truthful, and **almighty** Son of God, Jesus Christ,
SD : 0 7 :074(583) [0999] be ascribed only to the **almighty** power of God and the
SD : 0 7 :075(583) [0999] For the truthful and **almighty** words of Jesus Christ
SD : 0 7 :089(585) [1003] and institution of our **almighty** God and Saviour, Jesus
SD : 0 8 :009(593) [1017] and confess that to be **almighty**, to be eternal, to be
SD : 0 8 :023(595) [1023] at the right hand of the **almighty** power of God, and
SD : 0 8 :028(596) [1025] of God is precisely the **almighty** power of God which fills
SD : 0 8 :085(608) [1047] son, is and is called the **almighty** and everlasting God,
SD : 0 8 :096(610) [1049] right hand of the majesty and **almighty** power of God.
SD : 0 9 :003(610) [1051] at the right hand of the **almighty** power and majesty of
SD : 1 1 :046(624) [1079] for safekeeping into the **almighty** hand of our Saviour,
SD : 1 2 :006(633) [1097] schools in which the **almighty** God and Father of our

Alms (21), Almsgiving (7)
AP : 0 4 :155(128) [0165] like Luke 11:41, "Give **alms**; and behold, everything is
AP : 0 4 :155(128) [0165] He demands not only **alms**, but also the righteousness of
AP : 0 4 :192(133) [0175] just as the distribution of **alms** by the Corinthians was a
AP : 0 4 :261(145) [0195] that the king should give **alms**, but he includes all of
AP : 0 4 :261(145) [0195] him not only to the giving of **alms** but rather to faith.
AP : 0 4 :263(145) [0195] that follow or because of **alms**, but because of his promise
AP : 0 4 :276(148) [0199] without faith, so **almsgiving** does not justify *ex opere*
AP : 0 4 :277(148) [0199] be taken the same way, "**Alms** free from every sin and from
AP : 0 4 :278(149) [0199] God is pleased by that **almsgiving** which follows
AP : 0 4 :278(149) [0199] Therefore **almsgiving** does not free from sin and death *ex*
AP : 0 4 :278(149) [0199] we say in reference to **almsgiving** that it is the whole
AP : 0 4 :278(149) [0199] **Almsgiving** is an exercise of that faith which accepts
AP : 0 4 :278(149) [0199] We also grant that **alms** merit many divine blessings,
AP : 0 4 :279(149) [0199] faith is required before **almsgiving**: "Have God in mind
AP : 0 4 :281(149) [0201] in a garbled form: "Give **alms**; and behold, everything is
AP : 0 4 :282(149) [0201] outward cleanness, "Give **alms** from what you have left
AP : 0 4 :283(150) [0201] be clean if you are clean inwardly and if you give **alms**.
AP : 0 4 :283(150) [0201] part: "All things will be clean when you have given **alms**."
AP : 0 4 :284(150) [0201] the outward giving of **alms** is added (that is, all the works
AP : 1 3 :017(213) [0313] **Alms** could be listed here, as well as afflictions, which in
AP : 2 7 :005(269) [0421] crowd that gorges itself on the public **alms** of the church.
S 2 : 0 2 :016(295) [0467] of demanding Masses, vigils, pilgrimages, and other **alms**.
S 3 : 0 8 :008(313) [0495] God, and his prayers and **alms** were acceptable to God in
TR : 0 0 :080(334) [0527] been given to bishops as **alms** for the administration and
TR : 0 0 :080(334) [0527] they cannot possess these **alms** with a good conscience.
TR : 0 0 :082(334) [0527] who would consume the **alms** of the churches for luxuries
LC : 0 1 :126(382) [0617] Even **almsgiving** and all other works for our neighbor are
LC : 0 6 :025(460) [0000] about this wonderful, rich **alms** and this indescribable

Alone (182)
PR : PR :002(003) [0007] and of the Word that **alone** brings salvation to appear to
PR : PR :008(005) [0011] of the divine Word that **alone** gives salvation, to commit
PR : PR :023(012) [0021] and churches than that **alone** which is based on the Holy
PR : PR :024(013) [0023] of that Word of his that **alone** brings salvation, to the
AG : 0 6 :003(032) [0047] through works but through faith **alone**, without merit."
AG : 1 6 :004(037) [0051] true perfection consists **alone** of proper fear of God and
AG : 2 0 :006(041) [0053] before God by our works **alone**, but they add faith in
AG : 2 0 :009(042) [0053] for Christ's sake, who **alone** is the mediator who
AG : 2 0 :022(044) [0055] God is appropriated without merits, through faith **alone**.
AG : 2 0 :028(045) [0057] It is always faith **alone** that apprehends grace and
AG : 2 0 :034(045) [0057] and governs himself by his own human strength **alone**.
AG : 2 1 :002(047) [0057] He **alone** has promised to hear our prayers.
AG : 2 6 :011(065) [0071] the glamorous title of **alone** being holy and perfect
AG : 2 7 :020(074) [0079] It is not **alone** God's command that urges, drives, and
AG : 2 7 :020(074) [0079] that the man should be **alone**; I will make him a helper fit
AG : 2 7 :043(077) [0081] for they rob Christ, who **alone** justifies, of his honor and
AG : 2 7 :049(078) [0083] are told that monks **alone** are in a state of perfection.
AG : 2 8 :021(084) [0087] be done not by human power but by God's Word **alone**.
AG : 2 8 :047(088) [0089] on people, "Let them **alone**; they are blind guides" (Matt.
AL : 0 6 :003(032) [0047] works but through faith **alone**, and he shall receive
AL : 1 8 :008(040) [0053] by the power of nature **alone**, we are able to love God
AL : 2 0 :009(042) [0053] for Christ's sake, who **alone** has been ordained to be the
AL : 2 0 :034(045) [0057] by human strength **alone** without faith and without the
AL : 2 7 :020(074) [0079] Gen. 2:18, "It is not good that the man should be **alone**."

Continued ▶

A L : 2 8 :047(089) [0089] traditions, "Let them **alone**; they are blind and leaders of
A P : 0 2 :027(103) [0111] the ancient theologians **alone**, but even the more recent
A P : 0 4 :044(113) [0133] which we do not accept by works but by faith **alone**.
A P : 0 4 :072(117) [0141] to show first that faith **alone** makes a righteous man out
A P : 0 4 :073(117) [0141] The particle "**alone**" offends some people, even though
A P : 0 4 :073(117) [0141] the exclusive particle "**alone**," let them remove the other
A P : 0 4 :078(117) [0143] we are justified by faith **alone**, justification being
A P : 0 4 :080(118) [0143] By faith **alone**, therefore, we obtain the forgiveness of
A P : 0 4 :086(119) [0147] Faith **alone** justifies because we receive the forgiveness of
A P : 0 4 :086(119) [0147] the forgiveness of sins and the Holy Spirit by faith **alone**.
A P : 0 4 :112(123) [0155] of sins is received by faith **alone**—and we mean faith in
A P : 0 4 :116(123) [0155] And since this faith **alone** receives the forgiveness of sins,
A P : 0 4 :117(123) [0155] make clear that by faith **alone** we receive the forgiveness
A P : 0 4 :117(123) [0155] Christ's sake, and by faith **alone** are justified, that is, out
A P : 0 4 :118(123) [0155] this faith, for through it **alone** we recognize Christ's work
A P : 0 4 :118(123) [0155] his blessings and it **alone** provides a sure and firm
A P : 0 4 :147(127) [0163] account of love, but on account of Christ by faith **alone**.
A P : 0 4 :148(127) [0163] Faith **alone**, looking to the promise and believing with
A P : 0 4 :158(129) [0165] sure that we receive the forgiveness of sins by faith **alone**.
A P : 0 4 :182(132) [0171] before God by faith **alone**, since by faith alone we receive
A P : 0 4 :182(132) [0173] faith alone, since by faith **alone** we receive the forgiveness
A P : 0 4 :182(132) [0173] it is received by faith **alone**, though the keeping of the law
A P : 0 4 :214(136) [0179] the terrors of sin, but faith **alone** can overcome them.
A P : 0 4 :217(137) [0179] God except by faith **alone**, by which it is sure that God is
A P : 0 4 :217(137) [0179] therefore it is always received before God by faith **alone**.
A P : 0 4 :218(137) [0179] they say, Paul asserts that faith **alone** does not justify.
A P : 0 4 :244(141) [0189] is justified by works and not by faith **alone**" (James 2:24).
A P : 0 4 :252(143) [0191] by works and not by faith **alone**," for men who have faith
A P : 0 4 :259(145) [0193] speak of this one work **alone**, but of all of penitence, as
A P : 0 4 :267(147) [0197] remission of punishment **alone**, because it is vain to seek
A P : 0 4 :292(152) [0203] is received by faith **alone**, as Paul declares in Rom. 4:13.
A P : 0 4 :292(152) [0203] Faith **alone** accepts the forgiveness of sins, justifies, and
A P : 0 7 :005(169) [0227] This church **alone** is called the body of Christ, which
A P : 0 7 :025(173) [0235] We **alone** are accused, because we preach the blessing of
A P : 1 2 :034(186) [0261] Taken **alone**, this is the teaching of the law, not of the
A P : 1 2 :047(188) [0265] by faith, therefore faith **alone** quickens, according to the
A P : 1 2 :063(191) [0269] by anything but faith **alone**, according to Rom. 3:25,
A P : 1 2 :106(197) [0283] and leave other people's **alone**, but warning him not to be
A P : 1 9 :001(226) [0337] we confess that God **alone** has established all of nature
A P : 2 1 :014(230) [0347] it transfers to the saints honor belonging to Christ **alone**.
A P : 2 3 :051(246) [0377] and private morals; this **alone** should keep good men from
A P : 2 4 :040(257) [0399] symbolizes the ceremony **alone** and not preaching the
A P : 2 4 :054(259) [0403] but only to symbolize the future death of Christ **alone**.
S 2 : 0 1 :002(292) [0461] He **alone** is "the Lamb of God, who takes away the sin of
S 2 : 0 1 :004(292) [0461] certain that such faith **alone** justifies us, as St. Paul says
S 2 : 0 2 :001(293) [0463] done by the Lamb of God **alone**, as has been stated
S 2 : 0 2 :012(295) [0465] Christ instituted the sacrament for the living **alone**.
S 2 : 0 2 :015(295) [0465] article that Christ **alone**, and not the work of man, can
S 2 : 0 2 :015(295) [0467] That is the prerogative of God **alone**.
S 2 : 0 2 :026(297) [0469] Such honor belongs to God **alone**.
S 3 : 0 3 :007(304) [0481] the law exercises its office **alone**, without the addition of
S 3 : 0 3 :024(307) [0485] pope reserved for himself **alone** the right to remit the
S 3 : 0 7 :001(311) [0493] are subtle and secret and which God **alone** perceives.
S 3 : 0 7 :002(311) [0493] our power but in God's **alone** to judge which, how great,
T R : 0 0 :010(321) [0507] or confirmation was not to be sought from Peter **alone**.
T R : 0 0 :016(322) [0509] in remote places to seek ordination from him **alone**.
T R : 0 0 :023(324) [0511] did not question Peter **alone** but asked, "Who do you say
T R : 0 0 :069(331) [0525] church which, since it **alone** possesses the priesthood,
T R : 0 0 :074(332) [0525] reserved for themselves **alone** and have employed for
T R : 0 0 :079(333) [0527] tyrannically exercise it **alone**; and since, finally, they
S C : 0 9 :013(356) [0563] real widow, and is left all **alone**, has set her hope on God
L C : P R :011(360) [0571] For this reason **alone** you should eagerly read, recite,
L C : P R :014(360) [0571] That **alone** should be incentive enough.
L C : S P :024(364) [0579] will learn and retain this teaching from sermons **alone**.
L C : 0 1 :001(365) [0581] That is, you shall regard me **alone** as your God.
L C : 0 1 :002(365) [0581] and faith of the heart **alone** make both God and an idol.
L C : 0 1 :004(365) [0581] fly straight to the one true God and cling to him **alone**.
L C : 0 1 :004(365) [0581] "See to it that you let me **alone** be your God, and never
L C : 0 1 :013(366) [0583] confidence be placed in God **alone**, and in no one else.
L C : 0 1 :024(367) [0587] We are to trust in God **alone** and turn to him, expecting
L C : 0 1 :024(368) [0587] It is God **alone**, I have often enough repeated, from whom
L C : 0 1 :028(368) [0587] and you will find whether or not it clings to God **alone**.
L C : 0 1 :032(369) [0589] who trust and believe him **alone** with their whole heart.
L C : 0 1 :039(370) [0591] those who cling to God **alone** -- sheer goodness and
L C : 0 1 :080(375) [0603] the commandment was given to the Jews **alone**.
L C : 0 1 :147(385) [0623] makes a person holy; faith **alone** serves him, while our
L C : 0 1 :276(402) [0659] go and tell him his fault, between you and him **alone**."
L C : 0 1 :280(403) [0661] Then you do not stand **alone**.
L C : 0 1 :323(409) [0673] fears and regards God **alone** and, because of this fear,
L C : 0 1 :323(409) [0675] conversely, trusts him **alone** and for his sake does all that
L C : 0 2 :011(412) [0681] Apart from him **alone** I have no other God, for there is
L C : 0 2 :036(415) [0687] But God's Spirit **alone** is called Holy Spirit, that is, he
L C : 0 2 :067(420) [0697] the Creed; it must be taught by the Holy Spirit **alone**.
L C : 0 3 :030(424) [0705] that all our safety and protection consist in prayer **alone**.
L C : 0 3 :031(424) [0707] But by prayer **alone** we shall be a match both for them
L C : 0 3 :036(425) [0707] Father, grant that thy name **alone** may be holy."
L C : 0 3 :058(428) [0713] to satisfy the belly, let **alone** expect, without doubting,
L C : 0 4 :028(440) [0739] spirits, assert that faith **alone** saves and that works and
L C : 0 4 :033(440) [0741] be saved," that is, faith **alone** makes the person worthy to
L C : 0 4 :037(441) [0741] Actually, we insist on faith **alone** as so necessary that
L C : 0 4 :038(441) [0741] This **alone** would be enough, even though Baptism is an
L C : 0 5 :074(455) [0771] Therefore they **alone** are unworthy who neither feel their
L C : 0 6 :008(458) [0000] of confessing to God **alone** or to our neighbor alone,
L C : 0 6 :008(458) [0000] alone or to our neighbor **alone**, begging for forgiveness.
L C : 0 6 :016(459) [0000] emphasis on our work **alone**, and we were only concerned
E P : 0 1 :010(467) [0781] No one except God **alone** can separate the corruption of
E P : 0 2 :004(470) [0787] Spirit, for man's conversion is the Spirit's work **alone**.
E P : 0 3 :001(472) [0791] faith in Christ, so that Christ **alone** is our righteousness.
E P : 0 3 :003(473) [0793] to the divine nature **alone** nor according to the human
E P : 0 3 :003(473) [0793] nature alone nor according to the human nature **alone**.
E P : 0 3 :010(474) [0795] from our own works and give all glory to Christ **alone**.
E P : 0 3 :010(474) [0795] become righteous and are saved "**alone** by faith" in Christ.
E P : 0 3 :011(474) [0795] since such faith is never **alone** but is always accompanied
E P : 0 3 :016(475) [0795] That faith does not look **alone** to Christ's obedience, but
E P : 0 7 :008(482) [0811] to be ascribed solely and **alone** to the almighty power of
E P : 0 7 :020(484) [0813] is and consists solely and **alone** in the most holy
E P : 0 9 :002(492) [0827] and reason, but must be apprehended by faith **alone**.
E P : 1 1 :005(495) [0833] of their salvation, for he **alone** brings it about and
E P : 1 1 :010(495) [0833] from the Holy Gospel **alone**, which clearly testifies that
E P : 1 1 :015(496) [0835] he out of pure grace **alone**, without any merit of ours,
S D : 0 1 :043(516) [0873] made like us, his brethren, sin **alone** excepted (Heb. 2:17).
S D : 0 1 :043(516) [0873] essential attributes — sin **alone** excepted — identical with
S D : 0 1 :060(519) [0879] Holy Scripture **alone** can lead to a right understanding
S D : 0 2 :002(520) [0881] chief issue is solely and **alone** what the unregenerated
S D : 0 2 :025(526) [0891] part, but altogether and **alone** to the divine operation and
S D : 0 2 :039(528) [0895] apostle ascribes this work **alone** to God when he says,
S D : 0 2 :071(535) [0909] so that they are gifts and works of the Holy Spirit **alone**.
S D : 0 2 :087(538) [0915] death, is solely and **alone** the work of God, just as the
S D : 0 2 :087(538) [0915] is to be ascribed to God **alone**, as was thoroughly
S D : 0 2 :089(538) [0915] work of the Holy Spirit **alone**, who accomplishes and
S D : 0 2 :090(539) [0915] is the true craftsman who **alone** works these things, for
S D : 0 3 :004(540) [0917] to the divine nature **alone** or according to the human
S D : 0 3 :004(540) [0917] to the human nature **alone** but according to both natures;
S D : 0 3 :004(540) [0917] which, through faith **alone**, is reckoned by pure grace to
S D : 0 3 :007(540) [0917] as "without the law," "without works," "by grace **alone**."
S D : 0 3 :023(543) [0923] Christ, through faith **alone**, without any work or merit,
S D : 0 3 :029(544) [0925] Paul that we are justified **alone** through faith in Christ,
S D : 0 3 :033(545) [0927] before God through faith **alone** for the sake of the
S D : 0 3 :036(545) [0927] are justified before God and saved "through faith **alone**."
S D : 0 3 :041(546) [0931] nevertheless, it is faith **alone** which apprehends the
S D : 0 3 :041(546) [0931] And yet faith is at no time ever **alone**."
S D : 0 3 :042(547) [0931] Paul's doctrine that faith **alone** justifies without works
S D : 0 3 :055(549) [0935] rests solely and **alone** on the Lord Christ, it is important
S D : 0 3 :056(549) [0935] had in his human nature **alone** fulfilled all righteousness
S D : 0 3 :056(549) [0935] man, the divine nature **alone** could not have been our
S D : 0 3 :056(549) [0935] of the human nature **alone**, without the divine nature,
S D : 0 3 :056(549) [0935] Likewise, the deity **alone**, without the humanity, could
S D : 0 3 :058(550) [0937] and remitted by sheer grace for Christ's sake **alone**.
S D : 0 4 :002(551) [0939] in which we confess that faith **alone** justifies and saves.
S D : 0 4 :008(552) [0941] to God — and that **alone** for Christ's sake — before that
S D : 0 4 :009(552) [0941] Hence faith **alone** is the mother and source of the truly
S D : 0 4 :023(555) [0945] against the pure doctrine of salvation by faith **alone**.
S D : 0 4 :034(556) [0949] he attributes to faith **alone** the beginning, the middle, and
S D : 0 5 :019(561) [0957] Since the Gospel (which **alone**, strictly speaking, teaches
S D : 0 5 :019(561) [0957] Nevertheless, this Gospel **alone**, strictly speaking, teaches
S D : 0 5 :020(561) [0959] our sins, that through him **alone** we re-enter the good
S D : 0 6 :012(566) [0967] His office is not **alone** to comfort but also to rebuke, as it
S D : 0 7 :033(575) [0983] this, will please let me **alone** and expect no fellowship
S D : 0 7 :086(584) [1003] faith, or the oral eating **alone**, but the entire external and
S D : 0 7 :124(591) [1015] not consist in true faith **alone** but also in man's own
S D : 0 8 :002(592) [1017] majesty belongs to God **alone** and the body of Christ is
S D : 0 8 :050(600) [1031] essential properties **alone**, according to which it is in
S D : 0 8 :066(604) [1039] glory, which is the property of the divine nature **alone**.
S D : 0 8 :067(604) [1039] and the names in words **alone**, while in deed and in truth
S D : 0 8 :093(609) [1049] human nature of Christ **alone**, with which the Son of God
S D : 1 1 :007(617) [1065] misfortune, but in me **alone** is thy salvation" (Hos. 13:9).
S D : 1 1 :079(629) [1089] the work of God, who **alone** prepares vessels of honor,
S D : 1 2 :010(633) [1097] God does not depend **alone** on the sole obedience and

Altar (21), Altars (3)

A L : 2 4 :036(060) [0067] priest stands daily at the **altar**, inviting some to
A P : 2 4 :044(258) [0399] of the temples" and the **altars** standing unadorned,
A P : 2 4 :062(260) [0405] is daily offered on the **altar** for daily offenses so that in
A P : 2 4 :084(264) [0413] Scriptures mention an **altar**, the Mass must be a sacrifice;
A P : 2 4 :084(264) [0413] for Paul uses the figure of an **altar** only for illustration.
A P : 2 4 :085(264) [0413] is derived from *mizbeach*, the Hebrew term for **altar**.
S 2 : 0 2 :013(295) [0467] asked that she be remembered at the **altar** or sacrament.
S 2 : 0 2 :026(297) [0469] them, establish churches, **altars**, and services for them,
S 3 : 0 4 :000(310) [0491] the holy Sacrament of the **Altar**; fourth, through the
S 3 : 0 6 :000(311) [0493] VI. The Sacrament of the **Altar**
S 3 : 1 5 :004(316) [0501] of bells, the baptism of **altar** stones, the invitation to such
S C : 0 6 :000(351) [0555] The Sacrament of the **Altar** *in the plain form in which the*
S C : 0 6 :001(351) [0555] What is the Sacrament of the **Altar**?
L C : S P :005(362) [0575] and the Sacrament of the **Altar** and exercise all the rights
L C : S P :023(364) [0579] The Sacrament [of the **Altar**]
L C : 0 4 :009(437) [0733] and bulls and consecrated **altars** and churches solely by
L C : 0 4 :055(443) [0745] the Sacrament of the **Altar** is not vitiated if someone
L C : 0 4 :056(444) [0747] to the Sacrament of the **Altar** not on the strength of my
L C : 0 5 :000(447) [0753] [Fifth Part:] The Sacrament of the **Altar**
L C : 0 5 :008(447) [0755] Now, what is the Sacrament of the **Altar**?
S D : 0 7 :010(571) [0975] "The Sacrament of the **Altar**, instituted by Christ himself,
S D : 0 7 :020(573) [0979] he writes as follows: "What is the Sacrament of the **Altar**?
S D : 0 7 :030(574) [0983] as I have now defended the Sacrament of the **Altar**.
S D : 0 7 :032(574) [0983] in the Sacrament of the **Altar** the body and blood of

Altenburg (3)

P R : P R :027(014) [0025] Duke Frederick William [of Saxe-**Altenburg**] and
S 3 : 1 5 :005(316) [0501] George Spalatin, of **Altenburg**, subscribed
T R : 0 0 :082(334) [0529] George Spalatin, of **Altenburg**, subscribed

Alter (10), Altered (4)

P R : P R :009(006) [0011] of our religion and had **altered** it so much and so often
A G : 2 3 :008(052) [0061] and command cannot be **altered** by any human vows or
A G : 2 3 :014(054) [0063] No one is able to **alter** or arrange such matters in a better
A G : 2 3 :024(055) [0065] just as no human law can **alter** or abolish a command of
A G : 2 3 :024(055) [0065] of God, neither can any vow **alter** a command of God.
A G : 2 8 :033(086) [0087] has dispensed from and **altered** part of the Ten
A L : 2 3 :006(052) [0061] it is not in man's power to **alter** his creation without a
S C : P R :008(339) [0535] such a way that we do not **alter** a single syllable or recite
L C : 0 2 :050(417) [0691] uprooted, and it would be next to heresy to **alter** a word.
L C : 0 4 :060(444) [0747] and Word cannot be changed or **altered** by man.
L C : 0 5 :013(448) [0755] who dares to instruct Christ and **alter** what he has spoken.
L C : 0 5 :016(448) [0757] no one can change or **alter** the sacrament, even if it is
S D : 0 7 :024(573) [0981] Christ, so little can anyone **alter** or change the sacrament,
S D : 1 1 :010(618) [1067] etc., since I cannot hinder or **alter** God's foreknowledge."

Altogether (23)

AG : 28 :011(082) [0085] concerned with matters **altogether** different from the
AL : 26 :014(066) [0073] yet they did not **altogether** succeed in releasing them but
AP : 04 :017(109) [0125] not to by-pass Christ **altogether**, our opponents require a
AP : 04 :345(160) [0217] The judgment of God is another thing **altogether**.
AP : 27 :036(275) [0433] the claim of perfection **altogether**, they added this
S3 : 03 :035(309) [0489] that we must become **altogether** new and different men.
S3 : 03 :036(309) [0489] together and says, "We are wholly and **altogether** sinful."
S3 : 03 :037(309) [0489] who confesses that he is **altogether** sinful embraces all
S3 : 11 :002(314) [0499] distinctions of sex **altogether**, so little have they had the
S3 : 13 :001(315) [0499] and does account us **altogether** righteous and holy for the
LC : PR :004(359) [0567] people take the Gospel **altogether** too lightly, and even
LC : 01 :093(377) [0607] appear, or even if it be **altogether** covered with holy
LC : 01 :123(382) [0617] But young and old are **altogether** wayward and unruly;
LC : 03 :096(433) [0725] for God does it **altogether** freely, out of pure grace,
LC : 05 :053(453) [0765] more callous and cold, and eventually spurn it **altogether**.
EP : 02 :018(472) [0791] in conversion behaves "**altogether** passively" (that is, that
EP : 08 :039(492) [0827] and we shall lose Christ **altogether** along with our
SD : 01 :060(519) [0879] powers, but that it is **altogether** corrupted, so that
SD : 02 :007(521) [0883] his own powers, either **altogether** or half-way or in the
SD : 02 :025(526) [0891] and tiniest part, but **altogether** and alone to the divine
SD : 02 :046(530) [0899] that since everything is **altogether** the work of the Holy
SD : 06 :006(564) [0965] Of themselves and **altogether** spontaneously, without any
SD : 07 :001(569) [0971] error which is **altogether** contrary to the holy Word of

Always (109)

PR : PR :023(012) [0021] and intention has **always** been directed toward the goal
AG : 20 :028(045) [0057] It is **always** faith alone that apprehends grace and
AG : 26 :031(068) [0075] They have **always** taught concerning the holy cross that
AL : 24 :033(060) [0067] Ambrose said, "Because I **always** sin, I ought always take
AL : 24 :033(060) [0067] "Because I always sin, I ought **always** take the medicine."
AL : 26 :031(068) [0075] teachers, for they have **always** taught concerning the
AP : PR :011(099) [0101] controversies I have **always** made it a point to stick as
AP : 01 :002(100) [0103] We have **always** taught and defended this doctrine and we
AP : 02 :019(103) [0111] in the image of God in which God is not **always** present."
AP : 02 :035(105) [0115] He has **always** written that Baptism removes the guilt of
AP : 04 :010(108) [0123] the Mass; someone has **always** been making up this or
AP : 04 :020(110) [0125] Smug hypocrites **always** believe that they have the merit
AP : 04 :038(112) [0131] For the law **always** accuses and terrifies consciences.
AP : 04 :053(114) [0137] that these three elements **always** belong together: the
AP : 04 :110(123) [0153] forgiveness of sins will **always** be unsure, for we never
AP : 04 :128(125) [0157] The law **always** accuses us, it always shows that God is
AP : 04 :128(125) [0157] law always accuses us, it **always** shows that God is
AP : 04 :163(129) [0169] We must **always** be sure that for his sake we have a
AP : 04 :163(129) [0169] This forgiveness is **always** received by faith.
AP : 04 :163(129) [0169] Therefore it is **always** received by faith; we must always
AP : 04 :163(129) [0169] by faith; we must **always** hold that we are accounted
AP : 04 :164(129) [0169] Therefore we must **always** go back to the promise.
AP : 04 :167(130) [0169] Without this, the law **always** accuses us.
AP : 04 :168(130) [0169] present weakness there is **always** sin that could be
AP : 04 :180(132) [0171] or our works: this promise we must **always** keep in view.
AP : 04 :204(135) [0177] The law **always** accuses them and brings forth wrath.
AP : 04 :206(135) [0177] wicked idea about works has **always** clung to the world.
AP : 04 :217(137) [0179] Christ, and therefore it is **always** received before God by
AP : 04 :221(137) [0181] that speak of faith they **always** add the correction that
AP : 04 :256(144) [0193] law there are two things we must **always** keep in mind.
AP : 04 :260(145) [0195] We must **always** keep this important teaching in view.
AP : 04 :270(147) [0197] It **always** accuses the conscience, which does not satisfy
AP : 04 :279(149) [0199] and later, "Bless God **always**, and ask him to direct your
AP : 04 :285(150) [0201] It is **always** tormented and constantly invents other works
AP : 04 :285(150) [0201] The law **always** accuses.
AP : 04 :295(152) [0203] an angry God; the law **always** accuses us and thus always
AP : 04 :295(152) [0203] accuses us and thus **always** shows us an angry God.
AP : 04 :319(156) [0209] be stilled; for the law **always** accuses us, even in good
AP : 04 :319(156) [0209] The flesh **always** lusts against the Spirit (Gal. 5:17).
AP : 04 :394(167) [0225] So there have **always** been some in the world who taught
AP : 04 :394(167) [0225] of faith, and such teachers there will **always** be.
AP : 07 :018(171) [0233] quickens by his Spirit is **always** the same kingdom of
AP : 07 :022(172) [0233] the promise that it will **always** have the Holy Spirit, so it
AP : 12 :046(188) [0263] or renewal, he almost **always** names these two parts,
AP : 12 :057(189) [0267] are special punishments **always** added, but contrition and
AP : 12 :057(189) [0267] and faith there must **always** be in penitence, as in Luke
AP : 12 :088(195) [0277] For the law will **always** accuse us because we never satisfy
AP : 12 :089(195) [0277] nothing from faith if they **always** doubt whether they
AP : 12 :158(207) [0301] So afflictions are not **always** punishments or signs of
AP : 12 :160(207) [0301] troubles are not **always** penalties for certain past deeds,
AP : 13 :002(211) [0309] the Fathers did not **always** use the same enumeration.
AP : 20 :014(228) [0343] The church of Christ has **always** believed that the
AP : 23 :009(240) [0367] the right to contract marriage must **always** remain.
AP : 24 :004(250) [0385] This has **always** been the custom in the churches.
AP : 24 :034(256) [0397] But our opponents **always** apply the term "sacrifice" only
AP : 24 :097(268) [0417] clings to the world, and **always** will, that services and
S2 : 04 :008(299) [0473] He would not **always** have to have his residence in Rome
S3 : 03 :023(307) [0485] This is a case of **always** doing penance but never coming
TR : 00 :062(331) [0523] Dionysius, the presbyters **always** chose one of their
SC : PR :018(340) [0537] **Always** adduce many examples from the Scriptures to
LC : PR :014(360) [0571] enjoins that we should **always** meditate upon his precepts
LC : PR :016(361) [0573] better to teach, and he **always** keeps on teaching this one
LC : PR :016(361) [0573] busy learning it and have **always** remained pupils, and
LC : 01 :072(374) [0601] devil, I say, we should **always** keep the holy name on our
LC : 01 :101(379) [0609] It **always** awakens new understanding, new pleasure, and
LC : 01 :195(391) [0637] He **always** wants to remind us to think back to the First
LC : 01 :209(393) [0639] Therefore I have **always** taught that we should not
LC : 01 :219(394) [0643] such conditions chastity **always** follows spontaneously
LC : 01 :258(399) [0653] sit in judgment, we **always** find that, true to the usual
LC : 01 :289(404) [0663] fine, noble virtue **always** to put the best construction
LC : 01 :330(410) [0677] It is useful and necessary **always** to teach, admonish, and
LC : 02 :061(419) [0695] then, is the article which must **always** remain in force.
LC : 03 :010(421) [0699] desperately wicked that it **always** flees from God, thinking
LC : 03 :013(422) [0701] and mother, but should **always** reflect: "This is a work of
LC : 03 :013(422) [0701] for, everybody should **always** approach God in obedience
LC : 03 :023(423) [0703] our conscience would **always** be in doubt, saying, "I have
LC : 03 :028(424) [0705] we have said, he should **always** remind God of his
LC : 03 :087(432) [0723] so that it is not possible **always** to stand firm in such a
LC : 03 :094(433) [0725] through grace, we must **always** forgive our neighbor who
LC : 03 :109(435) [0729] weary; when one attack ceases, new ones **always** arise.
LC : 04 :041(441) [0743] He **always** has enough to do to believe firmly what
LC : 04 :060(444) [0747] be that Baptism **always** remains valid and retains its
LC : 04 :065(445) [0749] keep at it incessantly, **always** purging out whatever
LC : 04 :077(446) [0751] and sin, nevertheless we **always** have access to it so that
LC : 04 :083(446) [0751] the new man, **always** remains until we pass from this
LC : 05 :007(447) [0755] This must **always** be emphasized, for thus we can
LC : 05 :044(451) [0763] experience that the devil **always** sets himself against this
LC : 05 :063(454) [0767] This is difficult, for we **always** have this obstacle and
LC : 06 :001(457) [0000] confession, we have **always** taught that it should be
EP : 02 :008(471) [0789] otherwise, that man **always** acts only under compulsion,
EP : 03 :011(474) [0795] Thus good works **always** follow justifying faith and are
EP : 03 :011(474) [0795] faith is never alone but is **always** accompanied by love
EP : 08 :016(488) [0821] to the personal union he **always** possessed this majesty.
EP : 08 :016(488) [0821] and men, for he did not **always** disclose this majesty, but
SD : RN :001(503) [0851] the ancient church **always** had its dependable symbols.
SD : RN :011(506) [0855] doctrine is that they have **always** and everywhere been
SD : 01 :055(518) [0877] intelligent people have **always** held that whatever does
SD : 02 :060(533) [0905] to piety, for those who **always** resist the Holy Spirit and
SD : 05 :003(558) [0953] word "Gospel" does not **always** have one and the same
SD : 05 :015(561) [0957] Thus both doctrines are **always** together, and both of them
SD : 07 :034(575) [0983] meaning and intention in this article have **always** been.
SD : 07 :089(585) [1003] Jesus Christ, which **always** remain efficacious in
SD : 08 :017(594) [1021] the Christian church has **always** held in simple faith that
SD : 08 :066(604) [1039] itself fully, though **always** spontaneously, *in, with, and*
SD : 08 :070(604) [1039] of deity which he **always** has with him, dwells in
SD : 08 :076(606) [1043] likewise, "I am with you **always** even to the close of the
SD : 11 :001(616) [1063] Nor have our theologians **always** used the same terms.
SD : 11 :014(619) [1069] This means that we must **always** take as one unit the
SD : 11 :075(628) [1087] a right faith, he will **always** show the same old fatherly

Amassed (1), Amassing (1)

LC : 01 :043(370) [0591] and toil or, if they have **amassed** great treasures, that
LC : 01 :172(388) [0629] must not think only of **amassing** money and property for

Amazed (1), Amazing (1)

AP : 04 :107(122) [0153] It is surely **amazing** that our opponents are unmoved by
AP : 15 :021(218) [0321] We are **amazed** when our opponents maintain that

Ambassadors (2)

AP : 24 :080(264) [0411] II Cor. 5:20, "We are **ambassadors** for Christ, God
SD : 11 :027(620) [1071] he wrote, "We are **ambassadors** in Christ's stead, and God

Ambiguity (1), Ambiguous (1)

AP : 04 :185(132) [0173] **Ambiguous** and dangerous issues produce many and
AP : 24 :014(251) [0389] we purposely avoided this term because of its **ambiguity**.

Ambition (2)

AP : 02 :042(106) [0117] people; yielding to anger, desire, **ambition**, wealth, etc.
AP : 27 :004(269) [0421] how much hypocrisy, **ambition**, and greed there is in the

Ambrose (19)

AG : 06 :003(032) [0047] also teach thus, for **Ambrose** says, "It is ordained of God
AL : 06 :003(032) [0047] the ancient church, for **Ambrose** says, "It is ordained of
AL : 20 :014(043) [0055] **Ambrose** teaches similarly in *De vocatione gentium* and
AL : 20 :030(045) [0057] **Ambrose** says, "Faith is the mother of the good will and
AL : 24 :033(060) [0067] So **Ambrose** said, "Because I always sin, I ought always
AP : 02 :019(103) [0111] a great deal about it, **Ambrose** says, "That soul is not in
AP : 04 :103(121) [0151] to a certain Irenaeus, **Ambrose** says: "But the world was
AP : 04 :104(122) [0151] These are the words of **Ambrose**, which clearly support
AP : 04 :105(122) [0153] of Paul than this one sentence from **Ambrose**.
AP : 04 :235(140) [0185] **Ambrose** interprets the text this way: "Just as a building is
AP : 04 :340(159) [0215] Here **Ambrose** has clearly said, "Grace is to be
AP : 04 :389(166) [0225] with the holy Fathers **Ambrose**, Augustine, and many
AP : 12 :096(196) [0281] **Ambrose** makes this very clear statement about penitence:
AP : 23 :020(242) [0369] Therefore **Ambrose** correctly observes, "Virginity is
AP : 24 :075(263) [0411] **Ambrose** says about the comfort: "Go to him and be
TR : 00 :027(324) [0511] Fathers (such as Origen, **Ambrose**, Cyprian, Hilary, and
TR : 00 :082(335) [0529] **Ambrose** Blauer
EP : 07 :015(483) [0813] Cyprian, Leo I, Gregory, **Ambrose**, Augustine.
SD : 01 :054(518) [0877] as did Eusebius, **Ambrose**, and especially Augustine, as

Ambushes (1)

LC : PR :013(360) [0571] incessant attacks and **ambushes** of the devil with his

Amelioration (1)

AG : 27 :025(074) [0079] well aware that some **amelioration** ought to be exercised

Amen (23)

AG : PR :011(026) [0041] **Amen**.
S1 : PR :015(291) [0459] **Amen**.
S2 : 04 :015(301) [0475] **Amen**.
SC : PR :027(341) [0539] **Amen**.
SC : 02 :005(345) [0545] ***Amen.***"
SC : 03 :020(348) [0549] "***Amen.***"
SC : 03 :021(348) [0549] "**Amen**, amen" means "Yes, yes, it shall be so."
SC : 03 :021(348) [0549] "Amen, **amen**" means "Yes, yes, it shall be so."
SC : 05 :026(351) [0555] **Amen**."
SC : 05 :028(351) [0555] **Amen**.
SC : 07 :001(352) [0557] **Amen**."
SC : 07 :002(352) [0557] **Amen**."
SC : 07 :004(353) [0559] **Amen**."
SC : 07 :005(353) [0559] **Amen**."
SC : 08 :009(353) [0559] **Amen**."
SC : 08 :011(354) [0559] **Amen**."
LC : PR :020(361) [0573] **Amen**.
LC : SP :013(363) [0577] **Amen**.
LC : SP :014(363) [0577] **Amen**.
LC : 02 :034(415) [0687] ***Amen.***"
LC : 03 :112(435) [0729] ***Amen.***"
LC : 03 :119(436) [0731] our learning also to say "**Amen**" to it — that is, not to
EP : 11 :022(497) [0837] **Amen**.

Amend (3), Amendment (3)
AG : 1 2 :006(035) [0049] **Amendment** of life and the forsaking of sin would then
AG : 0 0 :001(047) [0059] of consciences, and the **amendment** of believers.
S 3 : 0 3 :013(305) [0483] until I make satisfaction for my sins and **amend** my life."
LC : 0 1 :276(402) [0659] but admonish him privately so that he may **amend**.
LC : 0 4 :068(445) [0749] Where this **amendment** of life does not take place but the
LC : 0 5 :061(453) [0767] and absolution and has no intention to **amend** his life.

Amicable (1), Amicably (3)
AG : PR :002(025) [0039] to employ all diligence **amicably** and charitably to hear,
AG : PR :010(025) [0041] they may be discussed **amicably** and charitably, our
AG : PR :012(026) [0041] Majesty's summons, if no **amicable** and charitable
AG : PR :023(027) [0043] are finally heard, **amicably** weighed, charitably settled,

Amount (4), Amounts (2)
AG : 2 8 :063(092) [0093] prescribe the kind and **amount** of work that may be done
S 2 : 0 4 :010(300) [0475] his own power, which **amounts** to nothing since it is
LC : 0 1 :316(408) [0671] all their boasting **amounts** to as much as if I boasted, "Of
LC : 0 3 :013(422) [0701] this prayer would **amount** to nothing; but it is important
LC : 0 3 :061(428) [0715] suffer an astonishing **amount** of attacks and assaults from
SD : 0 1 :012(510) [0863] tainted them that they **amount** to nothing in the sight of

Ample (6), Ampler (1), Amply (3)
AL : 0 0 :017(096) [0095] God willing, to present **ampler** information according to
AP : 0 4 :270(147) [0197] setting forth the most **ample** promise of the law.
AP : 1 5 :052(222) [0329] assembly we have shown **ample** evidence of our
AP : 2 0 :015(229) [0343] we have already given **ample** evidence of our conviction
AP : 2 7 :043(277) [0435] of a slender inheritance they find the most **ample** riches.
SC : PR :016(340) [0535] Moreover, allow yourself **ample** time, for it is not
LC : 0 1 :035(369) [0589] of history, as Scripture **amply** shows and as daily
LC : 0 1 :113(380) [0613] Now, he **amply** teaches what we should do if we wish to
LC : 0 1 :252(399) [0651] good works will here find **ample** opportunity to do things
LC : 0 3 :027(424) [0705] and others is quite **amply** indicated in the Lord's Prayer.

Amsdorf (2)
S 3 : 1 5 :005(316) [0501] Nicholas **Amsdorf**, of Magdeburg, subscribed
TR : 0 0 :082(334) [0529] Nicholas **Amsdorf**, of Magdeburg, subscribed

Amsterdam (2)
S 3 : 1 5 :005(317) [0501] Likewise I, John **Amsterdam**, of Bremen
TR : 0 0 :082(335) [0529] John **Amsterdam**, of Bremen, did the same

Amusement (1), Amuses (1)
LC : 0 1 :170(388) [0629] for our pleasure and **amusement**, gave us servants merely
SD : 0 7 :067(582) [0997] dung, by which the devil **amuses** himself and deceives

Anabaptists (25)
AG : 0 5 :004(031) [0045] Condemned are the **Anabaptists** and others who teach
AG : 0 9 :003(033) [0047] On this account the **Anabaptists** who teach that infant
AG : 1 6 :003(037) [0051] here are the **Anabaptists** who teach that none of the things
AG : 1 7 :004(038) [0051] therefore, are the **Anabaptists** who teach that the devil and
AL : 0 5 :004(031) [0045] churches condemn the **Anabaptists** and others who think
AL : 0 9 :003(033) [0047] churches condemn the **Anabaptists** who reject the Baptism
AL : 1 2 :007(035) [0049] churches condemn the **Anabaptists** who deny that those
AL : 1 6 :003(037) [0051] churches condemn the **Anabaptists** who forbid Christians
AL : 1 7 :004(038) [0051] churches condemn the **Anabaptists** who think that there
AP : 0 4 :066(116) [0139] Like the present-day **Anabaptists**, they deny that it is
AP : 0 9 :002(178) [0245] by God's favor, that no **Anabaptists** have arisen in our
AP : 0 9 :002(178) [0245] the many errors of the **Anabaptists** that we condemn is
AP : 0 9 :003(178) [0245] of little children, the **Anabaptists** teach wickedly when
AP : 0 9 :003(178) [0245] the ungodly and fanatical opinions of the **Anabaptists**.
AP : 1 3 :013(213) [0311] taught formerly and the **Anabaptists** teach now.
EP : 1 2 :001(498) [0839] Errors of the **Anabaptists**
EP : 1 2 :002(498) [0839] The **Anabaptists** have split into many factions, some of
EP : 1 2 :008(498) [0839] this reason, too, the **Anabaptists** neither think highly of
EP : 1 2 :011(499) [0841] and the errors of the **Anabaptists**; nor should one serve
SD : 0 4 :027(555) [0945] his writings against the **Anabaptists**, who advanced this
SD : 0 7 :029(574) [0981] Sacramentarians and **Anabaptists** are already beginning to
SD : 1 2 :001(632) [1095] of ours (such as the **Anabaptists**, the Schwenkfelders, and
SD : 1 2 :008(633) [1097] Erroneous Articles of the **Anabaptists**
SD : 1 2 :009(633) [1097] teaching of the **Anabaptists** which cannot be suffered or
SD : 1 2 :016(634) [1099] the errors of the **Anabaptists**; neither may one serve them

Analogies (2), Analogous (1), Analogy (14)
AP : 0 4 :339(159) [0215] the argument from **analogy** is unwarranted: from the
AP : 0 4 :339(159) [0215] two statements are not **analogous** since the causes and
AP : 1 2 :106(197) [0283] But if anybody wants by **analogy** to apply the
AP : 2 3 :027(243) [0371] This clumsy **analogy** is presented as a proof to force
AP : 2 3 :027(243) [0371] though in this very **analogy** marriage is permitted and
AP : 2 3 :041(245) [0375] As for the **analogy** with the Levitical priests, we have
AP : 2 4 :024(253) [0391] By **analogy** they were satisfactions since they gained the
AP : 2 4 :035(256) [0397] From the Levitical **analogy** it does not follow at all that
AP : 2 4 :036(256) [0397] This **analogy** symbolizes not only the ceremony but the
AP : 2 4 :040(257) [0399] this it is clear that the **analogy** of the daily sacrifice does
AP : 2 4 :052(259) [0403] The **analogy** deceives them, and they think that we should
AP : 2 4 :056(259) [0403] — unless by **analogy**, since they merited civil reconciliation
AP : 2 4 :057(260) [0405] before God and that by **analogy** there must be sacrifices
EP : 0 8 :009(488) [0819] of the natures by the **analogy** of incandescent iron and
SD : 0 7 :037(575) [0985] the personal union as an **analogy** to the words of Christ's
SD : 0 8 :018(594) [1021] and communion by **analogies** of the soul and the body
SD : 0 8 :064(603) [1039] and fire in glowing iron, **analogies** which the entire

Anarck (1)
PR : PR :027(015) [0025] **Anarck** Frederick, baron of Wildenfels.

Anathema (1), Anathematize (1)
TR : 0 0 :072(332) [0525] forms of worship should be regarded as **anathema**.
SD : 0 7 :008(570) [0975] are accustomed to **anathematize** and condemn as a

Ancient (82), Ancients (5)
PR : PR :003(003) [0007] in the approved **ancient** symbols, recognizing the doctrine
PR : PR :003(003) [0007] the doctrine as the **ancient** consensus which the universal
PR : PR :021(011) [0019] as the teachers of the **ancient** church put it, it takes place
AG : 2 2 :010(050) [0061] and also contrary to the **ancient** canons, is unjust.
AG : 2 4 :037(060) [0067] The **ancient** canons also indicate that one man officiated
AG : 2 4 :040(061) [0069] exist in the church from **ancient** times, and since no
AG : 2 6 :042(070) [0075] The **ancient** Fathers maintained such liberty with respect
AG : 2 8 :067(092) [0093] Scarcely any of the **ancient** canons are observed
AL : 0 1 :004(028) [0043] "person" is used, as the **ancient** Fathers employed it in
AL : 0 6 :003(032) [0047] by the Fathers of the **ancient** church, for Ambrose says,
AL : 0 0 :001(047) [0059] of Rome, in so far as the **ancient** church is known to us
AL : 0 0 :004(048) [0059] Among us the **ancient** rites are for the most part diligently
AL : 2 2 :010(050) [0061] also in contradiction to **ancient** canons and the example
AL : 2 3 :010(052) [0061] also evident that in the **ancient** church priests were
AL : 2 4 :035(060) [0067] the time of Gregory the **ancients** do not mention private
AL : 2 4 :037(060) [0067] And it appears from the **ancient** canons that some one
AL : 2 5 :010(063) [0069] The **ancient** writers also testify that such an enumeration
AP : 0 2 :022(103) [0111] cite the opinions of the **ancients**, with which Augustine's
AP : 0 2 :023(103) [0111] Thus when the **ancient** definition says that sin is lack of
AP : 0 2 :023(103) [0111] this it is evident that the **ancient** definition says just what
AP : 0 2 :027(103) [0111] Not the **ancient** theologians alone, but even the more
AP : 0 4 :185(132) [0173] For the word of the **ancient** poet is true, "Being sick in
AP : 0 4 :380(165) [0223] From **ancient** writers they have taken certain sayings,
AP : 0 4 :381(165) [0223] love God, as though the **ancients** meant to say that we
AP : 0 7 :033(175) [0239] we cherish the useful and **ancient** ordinances, especially
AP : 1 1 :004(181) [0249] this according to both the Gospel and the **ancient** canons.
AP : 1 1 :005(181) [0249] The **ancient** canons and the Fathers do not appoint a set
AP : 1 2 :116(199) [0285] of sins, just as those **ancient** exhibitions of satisfaction in
AP : 1 2 :119(200) [0287] in the Scriptures or in the **ancient** writers of the church.
AP : 1 4 :001(214) [0315] discipline in the manner described by the **ancient** canons.
AP : 1 5 :051(222) [0329] to foster harmony those **ancient** customs should be kept
AP : 2 1 :003(229) [0343] Nor do the rest of the **ancient** Fathers before Gregory
AP : 2 1 :003(229) [0343] merits, surely has no support among the **ancient** Fathers.
AP : 2 1 :013(230) [0345] The **ancient** prayers mention the saints, but they do not
AP : 2 1 :034(233) [0353] first mentioned, as in the **ancient** prayers, this was not
AP : 2 2 :007(237) [0359] They cannot produce any **ancient** examples to prove their
AP : 2 3 :003(239) [0363] whom even some of the **ancient** prophecies call the king
AP : 2 3 :023(242) [0369] The **ancient** canons do not forbid marriage, nor dissolve
AP : 2 3 :024(243) [0371] have set up since the **ancient** synods and contrary to their
AP : 2 4 :006(250) [0385] These are remnants of **ancient** practice, for the Fathers of
AP : 2 4 :054(259) [0403] to the theme that the **ancient** priesthood and the ancient
AP : 2 4 :054(259) [0403] priesthood and the **ancient** sacrifices were not instituted
AP : 2 4 :065(261) [0407] have the support of the **ancient** church and the Fathers.
AP : 2 4 :094(267) [0417] We know that the **ancients** spoke of prayer for the dead.
AP : 2 4 :094(267) [0417] The **ancients** do not support the opponents' idea of the
AP : 2 4 :096(267) [0417] They cite **ancient** heresies and by falsely comparing them
S 2 : 0 4 :001(298) [0471] and companions, as the **ancient** councils and the time of
S 3 : 0 3 :022(306) [0485] because, according to the **ancient** canons, seven years of
S 3 : 1 0 :003(314) [0497] by the examples of the **ancient** churches and Fathers, we
TR : 0 0 :017(323) [0509] 8. Many **ancient** synods were called and held in which the
TR : 0 0 :021(323) [0509] But if the **ancient** church had acknowledged the primacy
LC : SP :001(362) [0575] Hence from **ancient** times it has been called in Greek, a
LC : SP :006(362) [0575] of Christendom from **ancient** times, though they were
LC : 0 1 :025(368) [0587] why we Germans from **ancient** times have called God by a
LC : 0 1 :085(376) [0605] Since from **ancient** times Sunday has been appointed for
LC : 0 1 :142(384) [0621] So from **ancient** times the Romans and other peoples
LC : 0 1 :239(397) [0649] The **ancient** Romans, for example, promptly took such
LC : 0 1 :305(406) [0667] This was also the case in **ancient** times with respect to
LC : 0 3 :101(433) [0727] Temptation (or, as the **ancient** Saxons called it,
EP : RN :002(464) [0777] Other writings of **ancient** and modern teachers, whatever
EP : RN :003(465) [0777] Against these the **ancient** church formulated symbols
EP : 0 2 :016(472) [0789] Some **ancient** and modern teachers have used expressions
EP : 0 8 :009(488) [0819] The **ancient** Fathers have illustrated this union and
SD : PR :004(502) [0847] Word of God, just as in **ancient** times Christian symbols
SD : RN :001(503) [0851] this same purpose the **ancient** church always had its
SD : RN :004(504) [0851] 2. Since in **ancient** times the true Christian doctrine as it
SD : RN :005(504) [0853] appeal to it just as in the **ancient** church it was traditional
SD : RN :017(507) [0857] which the primitive, **ancient**, orthodox church rejected
SD : 0 1 :043(516) [0873] Hence all the **ancient** orthodox teachers held that
SD : 0 2 :004(520) [0881] On the other hand, both **ancient** and modern enthusiasts
SD : 0 5 :003(558) [0953] Scripture of God and by **ancient** and modern
SD : 0 7 :037(575) [0985] Many prominent **ancient** teachers, like Justin, Cyprian,
SD : 0 7 :060(580) [0995] The **ancient** Christian fathers and teachers of the church
SD : 0 7 :066(581) [0995] of them, all the **ancient** Christian teachers and the entire
SD : 0 7 :110(589) [1011] Word of God and the testimony of the **ancient** church.
SD : 0 8 :018(594) [1021] and communion, the **ancient** teachers of the church, both
SD : 0 8 :022(595) [1023] For this reason the **ancient** teachers of the church have
SD : 0 8 :051(600) [1031] Holy Scriptures, and the **ancient** Fathers on the basis of
SD : 0 8 :054(601) [1033] the Scriptures, and the **ancient** Fathers on the basis of
SD : 0 8 :057(602) [1035] rule of the entire **ancient** orthodox church that whatever
SD : 0 8 :059(602) [1035] noble testimonies of the **ancient** orthodox church
SD : 0 8 :061(602) [1035] the statements which the **ancient** orthodox church made
SD : 0 8 :062(603) [1037] and condemned in the **ancient** approved councils on the
SD : 0 8 :064(603) [1037] hold and teach with the **ancient** orthodox church, as it
SD : 0 8 :064(604) [1039] which the entire **ancient** church used in explaining this
SD : 0 8 :073(605) [1041] of the Spirit (as the **ancient** Fathers say) is communicated
SD : 0 9 :001(610) [1051] just as among the **ancient** teachers of the Christian

Andreae (2)
EP : 1 2 :031(501) [0843] Dr. James **Andreae** subscribed
SD : 1 2 :040(636) [1103] Dr. James **Andreae**, subscribed

Andrew (5)
S 3 : 1 5 :005(317) [0501] I, **Andrew** Osiander, minister in Nuremberg, subscribe
S 3 : 1 5 :005(318) [0501] the Rev. **Andrew** Menser (I Subscribe with my hand)
TR : 0 0 :082(334) [0529] I, **Andrew** Osiander, subscribe
EP : 1 2 :031(501) [0843] Dr. **Andrew** Musculus subscribed
SD : 1 2 :040(636) [1103] Dr. **Andrew** Musculus, subscribed

Anew (8)
LC : 0 5 :023(449) [0757] Baptism we are first born **anew**, our human flesh and
SD : 0 2 :026(526) [0891] But to be born **anew**, to receive inwardly a new heart,
SD : 0 2 :050(531) [0901] convert them, beget them **anew**, and sanctify them
SD : 0 4 :010(552) [0941] us and begets us **anew** from God, kills the Old Adam,
SD : 0 6 :001(563) [0963] who have been born **anew** through the Holy Spirit, who
SD : 0 6 :017(566) [0967] But when a person is born **anew** by the Spirit of God and
SD : 0 6 :017(566) [0967] in so far as he is born **anew**, he does everything from a
SD : 0 6 :021(567) [0969] who have been born **anew** to do good works, he holds up

Angel (16), Angelic (4), Angels (18)
A G : 2 7 :048(078) [0081] dazzled with this curious **angelic** spirituality and sham of
A G : 2 8 :024(084) [0087] 1:8, "Even if we, or an **angel** from heaven, should preach
A L : 2 7 :048(078) [0081] by these remarkable **angelic** observances and this pretense
A L : 2 8 :024(084) [0087] (Matt. 7:15), "If an **angel** from heaven should preach any
A P : 0 4 :105(122) [0153] — for some are called "**angelic**," others "subtle," and
A P : 2 1 :008(230) [0345] Besides, we grant that the **angels** pray for us.
A P : 2 1 :008(230) [0345] by Zech. 1:12, where the **angel** prays, "O Lord of hosts,
A P : 2 3 :046(246) [0377] condemns such "worship of **angels**" in Colossians (2:18).
S 1 : P R :011(290) [0457] he may cause a council of **angels** to descend on Germany
S 2 : 0 2 :015(295) [0467] articles of faith and no one else, not even an **angel**.
S 2 : 0 2 :026(297) [0469] Although **angels** in heaven pray for us (as Christ himself
S 2 : 0 2 :026(297) [0469] that we should invoke **angels** and saints, pray to them,
S 2 : 0 2 :028(297) [0469] honor is withdrawn from **angels** and dead saints, the
S 2 : 0 4 :004(299) [0473] he roars like a lion (as the **angel** in Rev. 10:3 suggests),
S 2 : 0 4 :013(300) [0475] even presumed to issue orders to the **angels** in heaven.
S 2 : 0 4 :016(301) [0477] ought rather speak as the **angel** spoke to the devil in
S 3 : 0 3 :030(308) [0487] Here the fiery **angel** St. John, the preacher of true
T R : 0 0 :038(326) [0515] Paul clearly teaches, "If an **angel** from heaven should
S C : 0 7 :002(352) [0557] Let thy holy **angel** have charge of me, that the wicked one
S C : 0 7 :005(353) [0559] Let thy holy **angels** have charge of me, that the wicked
L C : P R :016(361) [0573] wiser than all his holy **angels**, prophets, apostles, and all
L C : 0 1 :125(382) [0617] divine Majesty and all the **angels**, that it vexes all devils,
L C : 0 1 :198(392) [0637] and divine works in which he rejoices with all the **angels**.
L C : 0 1 :317(408) [0673] them is a heavenly, **angelic** man, far above all holiness on
L C : 0 3 :065(429) [0715] the devil with all his **angels** and the world as our enemies
L C : 0 5 :016(448) [0757] no saint on earth, yes, no **angel** in heaven can transform
E P : R N :001(464) [0777] in Gal. 1:8, "Even if an **angel** from heaven should preach
E P : 0 1 :005(466) [0781] For surely it is not with **angels** that he is concerned but
E P : 0 7 :012(483) [0811] No other human being, no **angel**, but only Mary's Son, is
E P : 0 8 :035(491) [0825] greater and more than all **angels** and other creatures; but
S D : 0 6 :006(565) [0965] necessity, and as the holy **angels** render God a completely
S D : 0 7 :024(573) [0981] saint on earth, or even an **angel** in heaven, can change
S D : 0 7 :043(576) [0987] is not a mere man or an **angel**; he is not only truthful,
S D : 0 7 :102(587) [1007] comprehension of all the **angels** in heaven, and is known
S D : 0 8 :024(595) [1023] truly the Son of the most high God, as the **angel** testifies.
S D : 0 8 :030(597) [1025] communion that even the **angels** marvel at it and find
S D : 0 8 :064(603) [1037] human beings or in the **angels**, but "bodily," as in its own
S D : 0 8 :070(604) [1039] creature, whether man or **angel**, can or should say, "All

Anger (22), Angered (1), Angers (1), Angry (14)
A P : 0 2 :008(101) [0107] and fleeing it, being **angry** at him, despairing of his grace,
A P : 0 2 :042(105) [0117] his grace, and his Word; **anger** at his judgments;
A P : 0 2 :042(106) [0117] good people; yielding to **anger**, desire, ambition, wealth,
A P : 0 4 :176(131) [0171] God's judgment and are **angry** at him, we are not
A P : 0 4 :204(135) [0177] of God, for in their **anger** they flee his judgment and
A P : 0 4 :262(145) [0195] to know God's will, namely, that he is no longer **angry**.
A P : 0 4 :295(152) [0203] We cannot even love an **angry** God; the law always
A P : 0 4 :295(152) [0203] accuses us and thus always shows us an **angry** God.
A P : 0 4 :300(153) [0205] wrath of God with our love or could love an **angry** God.
A P : 0 4 :301(153) [0205] Much more often they feel **angry** at the judgment of God,
A P : 1 2 :150(206) [0299] rebuke me not in thy **anger**"; and Jer. 10:24, "Correct me,
A P : 1 2 :150(206) [0299] just measure; not in thy **anger**, lest thou bring me to
A P : 2 7 :002(269) [0419] we are doing so out of **anger** or favor toward anyone.
S C : 0 1 :008(343) [0541] nor provoke them to **anger**, but honor, serve, obey, love,
S C : 0 5 :022(350) [0553] I have made my master **angry**, caused him to curse,
S C : 0 9 :008(356) [0563] provoke your children to **anger**, lest they become
L C : 0 1 :032(369) [0589] these words, then, how **angry** God is with those who rely
L C : 0 1 :034(369) [0589] away from him, and his **anger** continues to the fourth
L C : 0 1 :037(369) [0591] that he will not forget his **anger** down to their children's
L C : 0 1 :122(382) [0615] laid on their backs, they **anger** both God and their
L C : 0 1 :136(383) [0619] if you provoke him to **anger**, he will send upon you both
L C : 0 1 :140(384) [0621] perceive and believe how **angry** he makes God when he
L C : 0 1 :182(389) [0631] It forgives **anger** except, as we have said, to persons who
L C : 0 1 :182(389) [0631] **Anger**, reproof, and punishment are the prerogatives of
L C : 0 1 :187(390) [0633] we may learn to calm our **anger** and have a patient, gentle
L C : 0 1 :187(390) [0633] have given us occasion for **anger**, namely, our enemies.
L C : 0 1 :188(390) [0635] or malice toward anyone in a spirit of **anger** and hatred.
L C : 0 1 :327(410) [0675] omit that, you have an **angry** judge; otherwise, you have a
L C : 0 2 :065(419) [0695] from him we see nothing but an **angry** and terrible Judge.
L C : 0 3 :011(421) [0701] that we may not provoke his **anger** by such disobedience.
L C : 0 3 :011(421) [0701] the Scriptures that he is **angry** because those who were
L C : 0 3 :018(422) [0703] as a jest but will be **angry** and punish us if we do not
L C : 0 3 :021(423) [0703] realize once again that he **angers** God, grossly
L C : 0 3 :056(427) [0713] on the contrary, he is **angered** if we do not ask and
L C : 0 3 :103(434) [0727] by word and deed and drives us to **anger** and impatience.
L C : 0 3 :115(435) [0731] our life and vents his **anger** by causing accidents and
L C : 0 5 :075(455) [0771] enmity, strife, jealousy, **anger**, selfishness, dissension,
L C : 0 6 :011(458) [0000] has provoked another to **anger** and needs to beg his

Angles (1)
S C : P R :009(339) [0535] topics from different **angles** and in such a variety of ways

Anguish (3), Anguished (1)
P R : P R :004(003) [0007] Luther, and how in this **anguished** situation and amid the
S 3 : 0 3 :022(306) [0485] Here, too, there was nothing but **anguish** and misery.
L C : 0 6 :003(457) [0000] it was made sheer **anguish** and a hellish torture since
S D : 1 1 :049(624) [1079] neither "tribulation nor **anguish**, neither death nor life,

Anhalt (2)
A G : 0 0 :007(096) [0095] Wolfgang, prince of **Anhalt**
A L : 0 0 :017(096) [0095] Wolfgang, prince of **Anhalt**

Animal (1), Animals (2)
A P : 2 3 :045(245) [0375] from the meat of all **animals**, thus surpassing the
A P : 2 4 :034(256) [0397] The slaughter of **animals** in the Old Testament
S D : 0 2 :019(524) [0889] or to a wild, unbroken **animal** — not that man since the

Anne (1)
A P : 2 1 :032(233) [0351] Thus **Anne** grants riches, Sebastian wards off pestilence,

Annihilate (1), Annihilated (1)
A G : 1 7 :005(039) [0051] possess a worldly kingdom and **annihilate** all the godless.
E P : 0 7 :022(484) [0813] essence and are thus **annihilated**, in such a way that they

Announce (1), Announced (1), Announces (1)
A P : 0 4 :210(136) [0179] confess our faith and **announce** the blessings of Christ, as
L C : 0 4 :075(445) [0751] which not only **announces** this new life but also
S D : 0 5 :004(559) [0953] the chief parts are **announced**, namely, repentance and

Annoyance (1)
L C : 0 1 :225(395) [0645] to the vexation and **annoyance** of his master or mistress.

Annually (1)
A P : 1 1 :001(180) [0249] should be made **annually**, and that even though all sins

Annul (6), Annulled (1), Annulment (1)
A G : 2 7 :024(074) [0079] reasons which allowed **annulment** of the obligation of a
A G : 2 7 :031(075) [0079] and papal regulations **annul** vows that are made under
A G : 2 8 :013(083) [0085] depose kings, should not **annul** temporal laws or
A L : 2 7 :024(074) [0079] is not lawful for a man to **annul** an obligation which is
A L : 2 7 :031(075) [0079] Many canons **annul** vows made before the age of fifteen
A P : 2 2 :002(236) [0357] If it is illegal to **annul** a man's testament, it is much more
A P : 2 2 :002(236) [0357] man's testament, it is much more illegal to **annul** Christ's.
L C : 0 1 :216(394) [0641] are condemned and **annulled** by this commandment;

Anointed (1), Anointing (1)
A P : 0 4 :154(128) [0165] her reverence, her **anointing** and crying, all of which were
S D : 0 8 :072(605) [1041] called Messiah, or the **Anointed**) in such a way that he

Anonymously (1)
A P : P R :010(099) [0101] can complain that the book has appeared **anonymously**.

Ansbach (1)
P R : P R :027(014) [0025] margrave of Brandenburg [**Ansbach**-Bayreuth]

Answer (111), Answered (4), Answering (3), Answers (5)
A G : 2 8 :078(094) [0095] consider how they will **answer** for it in God's sight,
A L : 2 8 :078(094) [0095] see to it how they will **answer** for it before God that by
A P : P R :005(098) [0101] of our Confession, **answering** the opponents' objections
A P : 0 2 :028(104) [0113] sin is, it is correct to **answer** that it is immoderate lust.
A P : 0 2 :028(104) [0113] It is also correct to **answer** that it is the lack of proper
A P : 0 2 :028(104) [0113] And each of these **answers** includes the other."
A P : 0 4 :061(115) [0139] this means, and we shall **answer** our opponents'
A P : 0 4 :122(124) [0157] Before **answering** these, we must say what we believe
A P : 0 4 :147(127) [0163] To this we must **answer**, first of all, that we do not receive
A P : 0 4 :184(132) [0173] about the law we **answer** immediately that the law cannot
A P : 0 4 :218(137) [0179] Now we shall **answer** the texts that our opponents quote
A P : 0 4 :219(137) [0179] about love and works, it will be easy to **answer** this.
A P : 0 4 :231(139) [0183] we could give many **answers** about perfection, we shall
A P : 0 4 :244(141) [0189] our position more, but the **answer** is easy and clear.
A P : 0 4 :254(143) [0193] Then you shall call, and the Lord will **answer**."
A P : 0 4 :303(154) [0205] In **answer** to our opponents' quibble that many wicked
A P : 0 4 :304(154) [0205] The **answer** to this is easy, since even the scholastics
A P : 0 4 :312(155) [0207] To this we **answer** that these feelings cannot be divided in
A P : 0 4 :336(159) [0215] a refutation, we shall nevertheless give a brief **answer**.
A P : 0 4 :344(160) [0217] To this we must give a satisfactory **answer**.
A P : 0 4 :356(161) [0217] We shall **answer** briefly and clearly.
A P : 0 4 :399(168) [0227] to him than to give an **answer** written in blood to our
A P : 0 7 :009(170) [0229] the forgiveness of sins, **answer** to prayer, and the gift of
A P : 1 2 :008(183) [0255] should ask this, the **answer** must be in reference to faith
A P : 1 2 :088(195) [0277] This cannot be **answered** nor consciences quieted unless
A P : 1 2 :161(208) [0303] The **answer** is that the sin was forgiven so as not to
A P : 1 4 :002(214) [0315] see to it how they will **answer** to God for disrupting the
A P : 1 6 :006(223) [0331] they are very easy to **answer** if we keep certain things in
A P : 2 1 :017(231) [0347] to have mercy and to **answer** those who call upon him
A P : 2 2 :011(238) [0361] and if we wanted to **answer** them we would have enough
A P : 2 3 :041(245) [0375] priests, we have already **answered** that this does not make
A P : 2 4 :009(251) [0387] This single **answer** refutes all our opponents' objections,
A P : 2 4 :031(255) [0395] The **answer** is easy.
S 1 : P R :005(289) [0457] the wrath of God — **answer** them as they deserve.
S C : P R :004(338) [0533] How will you bishops **answer** for it before Christ that you
S C : 0 1 :002(342) [0539] **Answer**: We should fear, love, and trust in God above all
S C : 0 1 :004(342) [0539] **Answer**: We should fear and love God, and so we should
S C : 0 1 :006(342) [0541] **Answer**: We should fear and love God, and so we should
S C : 0 1 :008(343) [0541] **Answer**: We should fear and love God, and so we should
S C : 0 1 :010(343) [0541] **Answer**: We should fear and love God, and so we should
S C : 0 1 :012(343) [0541] **Answer**: We should fear and love God, and so we should
S C : 0 1 :014(343) [0541] **Answer**: We should fear and love God, and so we should
S C : 0 1 :016(343) [0541] **Answer**: We should fear and love God, and so we should
S C : 0 1 :018(343) [0541] **Answer**: We should fear and love God, and so we should
S C : 0 1 :020(344) [0543] **Answer**: We should fear and love God, and so we should
S C : 0 1 :021(344) [0543] **Answer**: He says, "I the Lord your God am a jealous God,
S C : 0 1 :022(344) [0543] **Answer**: God threatens to punish all who transgress these
S C : 0 2 :002(345) [0543] **Answer**: I believe that God has created me and all that
S C : 0 2 :004(345) [0545] **Answer**: I believe that Jesus Christ, true God, begotten of
S C : 0 2 :006(345) [0545] **Answer**: I believe that by my own reason or strength I
S C : 0 3 :002(346) [0545] **Answer**: Here God would encourage us to believe that he
S C : 0 3 :004(346) [0547] **Answer**: To be sure, God's name is holy in itself, but we
S C : 0 3 :005(346) [0547] **Answer**: When the Word of God is taught clearly and
S C : 0 3 :007(346) [0547] **Answer**: To be sure, the kingdom of God comes of itself,
S C : 0 3 :008(346) [0547] **Answer**: When the heavenly Father gives us his Holy
S C : 0 3 :010(347) [0547] **Answer**: To be sure, the good and gracious will of God is
S C : 0 3 :011(347) [0547] **Answer**: When God curbs and destroys every evil counsel
S C : 0 3 :013(347) [0547] **Answer**: To be sure, God provides daily bread, even to the
S C : 0 3 :014(347) [0547] **Answer**: Everything required to satisfy our bodily needs,
S C : 0 3 :016(347) [0549] **Answer**: We pray in this petition that our heavenly Father
S C : 0 3 :018(347) [0549] **Answer**: God tempts no one to sin, but we pray in this
S C : 0 3 :020(348) [0549] **Answer**: We pray in this petition, as in a summary, that
S C : 0 3 :021(348) [0549] **Answer**: It means that I should be assured that such
S C : 0 4 :002(348) [0551] **Answer**: Baptism is not merely water, but it is water used
S C : 0 4 :004(348) [0551] **Answer**: As recorded in Matthew 28:19, our Lord Christ
S C : 0 4 :006(348) [0551] **Answer**: It effects forgiveness of sins, delivers from death

Continued ▶

S C : 0 4 :008(349) [0551] **Answer**: As recoreded in Mark 16:16, our Lord Christ
S C : 0 4 :010(349) [0551] **Answer**: It is not the water that produces these effects, but
S C : 0 4 :012(349) [0551] **Answer**: It signifies that the old Adam in us, together with
S C : 0 4 :014(349) [0553] **Answer**: In Romans 6:4, St. Paul wrote, "We were buried
S C : 0 5 :016(349) [0553] **Answer**: Confession consists of two parts.
S C : 0 5 :018(350) [0553] **Answer**: Before God we should acknowledge that we are
S C : 0 5 :020(350) [0553] **Answer**: Reflect on your condition in the light of the Ten
S C : 0 5 :021(350) [0553] **Answer**: You should say to the confessor: "Dear Pastor,
S C : 0 5 :027(351) [0555] **Answer**: "Yes, I do."
S C : 0 6 :002(351) [0555] **Answer**: Instituted by Christ himself, it is the true body
S C : 0 6 :004(351) [0555] **Answer**: The holy evangelists Matthew, Mark, and Luke,
S C : 0 6 :006(352) [0557] **Answer**: We are told in the words "for you" and "for the
S C : 0 6 :008(352) [0557] **Answer**: The eating and drinking do not in themselves
S C : 0 6 :010(352) [0557] **Answer**: Fasting and bodily preparation are a good
L C : S P :026(364) [0581] and give a good, correct **answer** when they are
L C : 0 1 :002(365) [0581] **Answer**: A god is that to which we look for all good and
L C : 0 1 :050(371) [0593] taught above how to **answer** the question, What it is to
L C : 0 1 :051(371) [0595] God in vain?" you should **answer** briefly: "It is a misuse
L C : 0 1 :087(376) [0605] the holy day" means, **answer**: "It means to keep it holy."
L C : 0 2 :013(412) [0681] **Answer**: I hold and believe that I am a creature of God;
L C : 0 2 :027(414) [0685] Jesus Christ?" **answer** briefly, "I believe that Jesus Christ,
L C : 0 2 :037(415) [0687] **Answer**: Just as the Son obtains dominion by purchasing
L C : 0 2 :040(416) [0689] Holy Spirit"? you can **answer**, "I believe that the Holy
L C : 0 2 :041(416) [0689] **Answer**: "Through the Christian church, the forgiveness
L C : 0 3 :018(422) [0703] if he did not intend to **answer** you, he would not have
L C : 0 3 :019(423) [0703] our prayer will surely be **answered**, as he says in Ps.
L C : 0 3 :037(425) [0707] **Answer**: Yes, in itself it is holy, but not our use of it.
L C : 0 3 :039(425) [0709] The plainest **answer** is: When both our teaching and our
L C : 0 3 :051(426) [0711] **Answer**: Simply what we learned in the Creed, namely,
L C : 0 4 :014(438) [0735] can understand how to **answer** properly the question,
L C : 0 4 :028(440) [0739] We **answer**: It is true, nothing that is in us does it but
L C : 0 4 :035(441) [0741] To this you may **answer**: Yes, it is true that our works are
L C : 0 4 :046(442) [0743] and use of Baptism as **answering** the present purpose.
L C : 0 4 :048(442) [0743] But if you wish to **answer**, then say:
L C : 0 5 :008(447) [0755] **Answer**: It is the true body and blood of the Lord Christ
L C : 0 5 :015(448) [0757] Hence it is easy to **answer** all kinds of questions which
L C : 0 5 :033(450) [0761] many other places, the **answer** is: It is he who believes
L C : 0 5 :047(452) [0763] I **answer**: That is true, but it does not say that we should
L C : 0 5 :052(452) [0765] you; if you despise this, you must **answer** for it yourself.
L C : 0 5 :055(453) [0765] **Answer**: This also is my temptation, especially inherited
L C : 0 5 :075(455) [0771] **Answer**: For persons in such a state of mind that they
S D : R N :016(507) [0857] the correct and abiding **answer** in the controverted issues,
S D : 0 1 :057(518) [0879] necessity compels us to **answer** simply and roundly that
S D : 0 1 :060(519) [0879] reason, be it ever so keen, can give the right **answer**.
S D : 0 2 :041(529) [0897] Lord's Prayer Luther **answers** the question, "How does
S D : 0 2 :071(535) [0909] by them), our doctrine **answers** this way: Man's natural
S D : 0 3 :029(544) [0925] And then we **answer** with St. Paul that we are justified
S D : 0 3 :034(545) [0927] To this he **answers**: "To one who does not work, but
S D : 0 3 :042(547) [0931] gives the following **answer**: James calls that faith dead
S D : 0 3 :043(547) [0931] is false and incorrect to **answer**: Faith cannot justify
S D : 0 4 :037(557) [0949] give the following clear **answer**: If anyone draws good
S D : 0 7 :020(573) [0979] **Answer**: It is the true body and blood of Christ in and
S D : 0 7 :024(573) [0979] "Hence it is easy to **answer** all kinds of questions which
S D : 0 8 :041(599) [1029] and die, then you must **answer** and say: That is true, but
S D : 1 1 :025(620) [1071] An **answer** to the following question is necessary for the
S D : 1 1 :033(621) [1073] of God, even as Christ **answered** the question, "Lord, will
S D : 1 1 :063(626) [1083] and say, "Who are you, a man, to **answer** back to God?"

Antagonizes (1)
L C : 0 3 :044(425) [0709] bad, unruly child who **antagonizes** him in word and deed

Antecedent (1)
A L : 2 0 :014(043) [0055] by grace, were due to **antecedent** merits, for then it would

Anthanasius (1)
S D : 0 8 :022(595) [1023] Book IV, chap. 3; **Anthanasius** in his *Letter to Epictetus;*

Anthony (7)
A P : 0 4 :211(136) [0179] **Anthony**, Bernard, Dominic, Francis, and other holy
A P : 2 7 :038(275) [0433] there are stories of **Anthony** and of others which put
A P : 2 7 :038(275) [0433] It is written that when **Anthony** asked God to show him
A P : 2 7 :038(275) [0433] The next day **Anthony** went into the city and came to the
A P : 2 7 :038(276) [0433] Thus **Anthony** came to understand that justification was
S 3 : 1 5 :005(317) [0501] Master **Anthony** Corvinus
T R : 0 0 :082(335) [0529] **Anthony** Corvinus subscribes with his own hand both in

Anti- (4)
E P : 1 2 :028(500) [0843] Error of the **Anti**-Trinitarians
S D : 1 2 :001(632) [1095] and the New Arians and **Anti**-Trinitarians whose errors
S D : 1 2 :036(636) [1101] Erroneous Articles of the New **Anti**-Trinitarians
S D : 1 2 :037(636) [1101] 1. Some **Anti**-Trinitarians reject and condemn the old,

Antichrist (18), Antichrists (1)
A P : 0 7 :004(169) [0227] Paul also predicts that **Antichrist** will "take his seat in the
A P : 0 7 :048(177) [0245] longer function in the place of Christ, but are **antichrists**.
A P : 1 5 :018(217) [0319] they are simply establishing the kingdom of **Antichrist**.
A P : 1 5 :018(217) [0319] The kingdom of **Antichrist** is a new kind of worship of
A P : 1 5 :018(217) [0319] part of the kingdom of **Antichrist** if it maintains that
A P : 1 5 :019(217) [0319] very form and constitution of the kingdom of **Antichrist**.
A P : 2 3 :025(243) [0371] it is characteristic of **Antichrist's** kingdom to despise
A P : 2 4 :098(268) [0419] glory of his coming destroys the kingdom of **Antichrist**.
S 2 : 0 2 :025(297) [0469] of saints is also one of the abuses of the **Antichrist**.
S 2 : 0 4 :010(300) [0475] that the pope is the real **Antichrist** who has raised himself
S 2 : 0 4 :014(301) [0475] his apostle, the pope or **Antichrist**, to govern us as our
T R : 0 0 :038(327) [0515] [The Marks of the **Antichrist**]
T R : 0 0 :039(327) [0515] that the marks of the **Antichrist** coincide with those of the
T R : 0 0 :039(327) [0515] For in describing the **Antichrist** in his letter to the
T R : 0 0 :041(327) [0517] pope and his adherents as the kingdom of the **Antichrist**.
T R : 0 0 :042(328) [0517] errors to be doctrines of demons and of the **Antichrist**.
T R : 0 0 :057(330) [0521] On the contrary, it is necessary to resist him as **Antichrist**.
S D : 1 0 :020(614) [1059] his apostle, the pope or **Antichrist**, to govern us as our
S D : 1 0 :022(615) [1061] the pope and his adherents as the kingdom of **Antichrist**.

Antichristian (1)
S 3 : 1 1 :001(314) [0499] they acted like **antichristian**, tyrannical, and wicked

Anticipates (1)
S D : 0 2 :071(535) [0909] kindness and mercy **anticipates** us and has his holy

Antidote (2)
L C : P R :014(360) [0571] darts," and with a good **antidote** against their evil
L C : 0 5 :070(454) [0769] sacrament as a precious **antidote** against the poison in

Antinomians (1)
S D : 0 5 :015(561) [0957] we justly condemn the **Antinomians** or nomoclasts who

Antioch (1)
S D : 0 8 :016(594) [1021] had become a bishop in **Antioch** in Syria, taught godlessly

Antiquated (1)
A P : 1 2 :113(199) [0285] have long since become **antiquated**, nor need we bring

Antitheses (15), Antithesis (4)
A P : 0 4 :240(141) [0187] (10:12), where the **antithesis** clearly shows what it means:
T R : 0 0 :008(321) [0505] The **antithesis** here shows that lordship is disapproved.
E P : 0 1 :010(467) [0781] **Antitheses**
E P : 0 2 :006(470) [0787] **Antitheses**
E P : 0 3 :011(474) [0795] **Antitheses**
E P : 0 4 :015(477) [0801] False **Antitheses**
E P : 0 5 :010(479) [0805] **Antithesis**
E P : 0 6 :007(481) [0807] **Antithesis**
E P : 0 7 :021(484) [0813] **Antitheses**
E P : 0 8 :018(490) [0823] **Antitheses**
E P : 1 0 :007(494) [0831] **Antitheses**
E P : 1 1 :015(497) [0837] **Antitheses**
S D : R N :013(506) [0855] **Antitheses** in the Controverted Articles
S D : R N :019(507) [0857] in these theses and **antitheses**, opposing the true doctrine
S D : 0 1 :004(509) [0861] the true doctrine and its opposite in theses and **antitheses**.
S D : 0 1 :049(517) [0875] doctrine, the thesis and **antithesis**, as far as the chief
S D : 0 3 :005(540) [0917] set forth below in the **antitheses**, that is, in the
S D : 0 3 :044(547) [0931] these, too, the false **antitheses** become clear, namely, that
S D : 0 7 :128(591) [1015] Additional **antitheses** and rejected erroneous views have

Anxiety (7), Anxious (12), Anxiously (2)
P R : P R :024(013) [0023] and low, are sighing **anxiously** for this salutary work of
A L : 2 0 :015(043) [0055] men, God-fearing and **anxious** consciences find by
A L : 2 0 :022(044) [0055] in Christ in order that **anxious** consciences should not be
A L : 2 4 :007(056) [0065] consolation it offers to **anxious** consciences, that they
A L : 2 4 :030(059) [0067] Christ and should cheer and comfort **anxious** consciences.
A P : 1 2 :038(187) [0261] be clearly defined as an **anxiety** joined with faith, where
A P : 1 2 :038(187) [0261] and sustains the **anxious** heart, whereas in servile fear
A P : 1 2 :038(187) [0261] in servile fear faith does not sustain the **anxious** heart.
A P : 1 2 :044(187) [0263] mean contrition, **anxiety**, and the terrors of sin and
A P : 1 2 :095(196) [0281] unsure because an **anxious** conscience sees that these
A P : 1 2 :128(201) [0291] the doctrinal doubts of good men are mere petty **anxiety**.
A P : 2 1 :042(235) [0355] for clearly he is most **anxious** for the healing and
A P : 2 1 :043(235) [0357] of the church, which we are very **anxious** to maintain.
A P : 2 3 :040(245) [0375] "The unmarried man is **anxious** about the affairs of the
S 3 : 0 2 :004(303) [0479] and despairing, **anxiously** desires help but does not know
S C : 0 8 :008(353) [0559] Greed and **anxiety** about food prevent such satisfaction.)
L C : 0 5 :070(454) [0769] their weakness, who are **anxious** to be rid of it and desire
L C : 0 6 :023(459) [0000] him and make him so **anxious** that he would rejoice and
S D : 0 2 :047(530) [0901] may fall into grave **anxiety** and doubt, and wonder if God
S D : 0 2 :047(530) [0901] obedience but only weakness and **anxiety** and misery.
S D : 1 1 :010(618) [1065] false security and impenitence or **anxiety** and despair.

Apart (61)
A G : 2 0 :039(046) [0057] says in John 15:5, "**Apart** from me you can do nothing."
A L : 2 0 :017(043) [0055] nor can it be understood **apart** from that conflict.
A L : 2 0 :039(046) [0057] Wherefore Christ said, "**Apart** from me you can do
A P : 0 4 :041(113) [0133] God has been manifested **apart** from law" (Rom. 3:21),
A P : 0 4 :073(117) [0141] a man is justified by faith **apart** from works of law," and
A P : 0 4 :087(119) [0147] man is justified by faith **apart** from works of law" (Rom.
A P : 0 4 :256(144) [0193] Christ says (John 15:5), "**Apart** from me you can do
A P : 0 4 :266(146) [0197] Christ says (John 15:5), "**Apart** from me you can do
A P : 0 4 :269(147) [0197] he himself has said, "**Apart** from me you can do nothing"
A P : 0 4 :315(156) [0207] himself says (John 15:5), "**Apart** from me you can do
A P : 0 4 :372(164) [0221] and he himself says, "**Apart** from me you can do nothing"
A P : 1 2 :017(185) [0257] we merit grace by good works done **apart** from grace.
A P : 1 2 :085(194) [0277] Christ says (John 15:5), "**Apart** from me you can do
A P : 1 2 :156(207) [0301] imposes and remits them **apart** from the administration
A P : 2 3 :032(244) [0373] not praise domestic duties **apart** from faith: "if she
A P : 2 8 :008(282) [0445] right to create traditions **apart** from the Gospel as though
A P : 2 8 :020(284) [0449] not create an authority for bishops **apart** from the Gospel.
S 1 : P R :014(291) [0459] only a few articles, for, **apart** from these, God has laid so
S 2 : 0 1 :004(292) [0461] a man is justified by faith **apart** from works of law"
S 2 : 0 2 :009(294) [0465] to his own pleasure **apart** from the fellowship of the
S 2 : 0 2 :012(295) [0465] be discarded, **apart** entirely from the fact that it is error
S 3 : 0 3 :018(306) [0483] **Apart** from cases like this, such repentance surely was
S 3 : 0 8 :010(313) [0497] is attributed to the Spirit **apart** from such Word and
S 3 : 1 3 :003(315) [0499] if they are considered **apart** from God's grace and mercy,
T R : 0 0 :062(331) [0523] For, **apart** from ordination, what does a bishop do that a
L C : 0 1 :019(367) [0585] upon the one God, **apart** from whom there is truly no god
L C : 0 1 :080(375) [0603] Old Testament God set **apart** the seventh day and
L C : 0 1 :085(376) [0605] do, at least one day in the week must be set **apart** for it.
L C : 0 1 :089(377) [0605] and leisure, we must set **apart** several hours a week for
L C : 0 1 :093(377) [0607] conduct or work done **apart** from God's Word is unholy
L C : 0 1 :216(394) [0641] all vows of chastity **apart** from marriage are condemned
L C : 0 1 :311(407) [0671] **Apart** from these Ten Commandments no deed, no
L C : 0 1 :333(410) [0677] works which are taught and practiced **apart** from them.
L C : 0 2 :011(412) [0681] **Apart** from him alone I have no other God, for there is no
L C : 0 2 :065(419) [0695] **Apart** from him we see nothing but an angry and terrible
L C : 0 5 :014(448) [0755] elements or view them **apart** from the Word, you have
L C : 0 5 :032(450) [0761] Gospel or Word of God **apart** from the sacrament is of no
E P : 0 2 :006(470) [0787] Christ also states, "**Apart** from me you can do nothing."

Continued ▶

E P : 0 4 :007(476) [0799] God reckons righteousness **apart** from works, saying,
S D : 0 1 :019(511) [0865] in the sight of God that **apart** from Christ every person on
S D : 0 1 :028(513) [0867] independently within or **apart** from man's corrupted
S D : 0 2 :014(523) [0885] remains eternally true, "**Apart** from me you can do
S D : 0 2 :026(526) [0891] "**Apart** from me," says Christ, "you can do nothing (John
S D : 0 3 :027(543) [0925] "We are justified by faith **apart** from works (Rom. 3:28),
S D : 0 3 :029(544) [0925] we deal with good works **apart** from this matter of
S D : 0 3 :043(547) [0931] St. Paul employs, such as "**apart** from works," do not
S D : 0 3 :055(549) [0935] our entire righteousness **apart** from our own and all other
S D : 0 4 :024(555) [0945] God reckons righteousness **apart** from works (Rom. 4:6),
S D : 0 5 :005(559) [0953] in its broad sense and **apart** from the strict distinction of
S D : 0 7 :014(571) [0977] united with it **apart** from the use of the sacrament, they
S D : 0 7 :015(572) [0977] body of Christ is present **apart** from the use, as when the
S D : 0 7 :073(583) [0999] that there is no sacrament **apart** from the instituted use.
S D : 0 7 :085(584) [1001] character of a sacrament **apart** from the use instituted by
S D : 0 7 :085(584) [1001] instituted by Christ, or **apart** from the divinely instituted
S D : 0 7 :087(585) [1003] **Apart** from this use it is not to be deemed a sacrament, as
S D : 0 7 :108(588) [1009] of Christ is present even **apart** from the action of the
S D : 0 7 :108(588) [1009] can be a sacrament **apart** from God's command and the
S D : 0 8 :062(603) [1037] has them of itself and **apart** from the divine essence, nor
S D : 0 8 :081(607) [1045] he is a man like this — and **apart** from this man there is no
S D : 0 8 :083(607) [1045] devils had been unable to separate and tear them **apart**.
S D : 1 1 :065(627) [1083] in Christ, and not outside of or **apart** from Christ.

Aplenty (1)
L C : 0 1 :044(370) [0593] of this you will find **aplenty** in all histories and in the

Apollonia (1)
L C : 0 1 :011(366) [0583] to the honor of St. **Apollonia**; if he feared fire, he sought

Apollos (1)
T R : 0 0 :011(321) [0507] yours, whether Paul or **Apollos** or Cephas" (I Cor. 3:21,

Apologize (1)
S C : 0 1 :016(343) [0541] defame him, but should **apologize** for him, speak well of

Apology (45)
P R : P R :023(012) [0021] Confession and its **Apology**, correctly understood, and
P R : P R :025(013) [0023] kindest memory, in the **Apology** that followed it, and in
A P : P R :005(098) [0101] others to prepare an **apology** of our Confession,
A P : P R :007(098) [0101] They finally offered the **apology** to His Imperial Majesty,
A P : P R :009(098) [0101] And now, dear reader, you have our **Apology**.
A P : P R :010(099) [0101] we undertook the **Apology** in consultation with others,
A P : P R :019(100) [0103] **Apology** of the Confession
S 3 : 1 5 :005(317) [0501] the Confession, the **Apology**, and the Concord in the
T R : 0 0 :059(330) [0521] Confession and in the **Apology** we have set forth in
T R : 0 0 :082(334) [0529] Who Subscribed the Confession and **Apology**, 1537
T R : 0 0 :082(334) [0529] with the articles of the Confession and **Apology**.
T R : 0 0 :082(334) [0529] Confession, the **Apology**, and the article concerning the
T R : 0 0 :082(000) [0529] the Confession and **Apology** presented at Augsburg by the
E P : R N :004(465) [0777] 1530, together with the **Apology** thereof and the Articles
E P : 0 3 :008(474) [0793] Sometimes, as in the **Apology**, the words *regeneratio*
E P : 1 2 :030(500) [0843] Confession, the **Apology**, the Smalcald Articles, and the
S D : R N :006(504) [0853] submitted, an extensive **Apology** was prepared and
S D : R N :006(504) [0853] our adherence to this **Apology** also, because in it the cited
S D : R N :011(506) [0855] Augsburg confession, the **Apology**, the Smalcald Articles,
S D : 0 1 :003(509) [0861] errors, then (as the **Apology** declares) we are led to
S D : 0 1 :008(510) [0861] The **Apology** summarizes the matter under these heads:
S D : 0 2 :025(526) [0891] operation and the Holy Spirit, as the **Apology** declares.
S D : 0 2 :031(527) [0893] The **Apology** teaches as follows concerning free will: "We
S D : 0 2 :032(527) [0893] we see clearly that the **Apology** does not ascribe to man's
S D : 0 2 :045(530) [0899] Augsburg Confession, its **Apology**, the Smalcald Articles,
S D : 0 3 :006(540) [0917] In the words of the **Apology**, this article of justification by
S D : 0 3 :019(542) [0921] is frequently used in the **Apology**, where the statement is
S D : 0 3 :020(542) [0921] The **Apology** often uses the term in this sense.
S D : 0 3 :042(546) [0931] issues which the **Apology** discusses in connection with
S D : 0 3 :042(547) [0931] not have true faith), the **Apology** gives the following
S D : 0 3 :042(547) [0931] and the Latin text of the **Apology** states, "James teaches
S D : 0 3 :043(547) [0931] But, as the **Apology** declares, James is speaking of the
S D : 0 3 :066(550) [0937] in the Augsburg Confession and its subsequent **Apology**.
S D : 0 4 :014(553) [0943] Confession and its **Apology** often employ formulas like
S D : 0 4 :021(554) [0945] as the Augsburg Confession and the **Apology** have done.
S D : 0 4 :033(556) [0947] The **Apology** offers a fine example as to when and how,
S D : 0 4 :033(556) [0947] call and election," the **Apology** states in Article XX:
S D : 0 5 :015(561) [0957] And the **Apology** says: "The preaching of the law is not
S D : 0 5 :027(563) [0961] find occasionally in the **Apology** too, the Gospel is a
S D : 0 5 :027(563) [0961] But the **Apology** also indicates that, strictly speaking, the
S D : 0 7 :011(571) [0975] still more clearly in the **Apology**, but it is also supported
S D : 0 7 :055(579) [0991] benefits of Christ, as the **Apology** argues and concludes.
S D : 0 7 :110(589) [1011] of our churches, the **Apology**, the Smalcald Articles, and
S D : 1 1 :038(622) [1075] a voice from heaven," as the **Apology** explains this article.
S D : 1 2 :039(636) [1103] Confession and the **Apology**, to the Smalcald Articles, to

Apostasized (1), Apostasy (1), Apostate (1), Apostates (1)
A P : 0 7 :022(172) [0235] as those in lesser stations have **apostasized** from the faith.
A P : 1 6 :006(223) [0331] Julian the **Apostate**, Celsus, and many others opposed the
L C : 0 1 :262(400) [0655] world call them heretics, **apostates**, even seditious and
S D : 1 0 :005(611) [1053] to the papacy and an **apostasy** from the pure doctrine of

Apostle (23), Apostles (93)
P R : P R :005(004) [0009] just as, while the holy **apostles** were still alive, it happened
P R : P R :005(004) [0009] churches in which the **apostles** themselves had planted the
A G : 0 3 :006(030) [0045] the living and the dead, as stated in the **Apostles**' Creed.
A G : 2 3 :022(055) [0063] In I Tim. 4:1, 3 the **apostle** Paul calls the teaching that
A G : 2 6 :022(067) [0073] Christ defends the **apostles** for not observing the
A G : 2 6 :045(070) [0075] not the intention of the **apostles** to institute holy days but
A G : 2 8 :006(081) [0085] For Christ sent out the **apostles** with this command, "As
A G : 2 8 :039(087) [0089] God had commanded the **apostles** and bishops to
A G : 2 8 :061(091) [0093] Christ commanded the **apostles** and bishops to devise new
A G : 2 8 :065(092) [0093] The **apostles** directed that one should abstain from blood
A G : 2 8 :065(092) [0093] it commit no sin, for the **apostles** did not wish to burden
A L : 0 3 :006(030) [0045] and the dead, etc., according to the **Apostles**' Creed.
A L : 2 6 :022(067) [0073] Christ defends the **apostles** for not observing the
A L : 2 6 :045(070) [0075] not the intention of the **apostles** to enact binding laws
A L : 2 8 :006(082) [0085] For Christ sent out the **apostles** with this command, "As
A L : 2 8 :032(086) [0087] cite the example of the **apostles** who commanded men to
A L : 2 8 :039(087) [0089] had commissioned the **apostles** and bishops to institute
A L : 2 8 :061(091) [0093] Christ commissioned the **apostles** and bishops to devise
A L : 2 8 :065(092) [0093] The **apostles** commanded that one should abstain from
A L : 2 8 :065(092) [0093] it commit no sin, for the **apostles** did not wish to burden
A P : 0 3 :001(107) [0119] etc., according to the **Apostles**' and Nicene Creeds.
A P : 0 4 :099(121) [0151] the faith of which the **apostles** speak is not idle
A P : 0 4 :190(133) [0175] and sermons of the **apostle** Paul, Athanasius, Augustine,
A P : 0 4 :238(140) [0187] entered the mind of any **apostle** to say that our love
A P : 0 4 :243(141) [0189] without reason that the **apostles** speak so often about this
A P : 0 7 :026(173) [0235] the prophets, and the **apostles** define the church as
A P : 0 7 :038(176) [0241] are supposed to have been handed down by the **apostles**.
A P : 0 7 :039(176) [0241] those rites just as the **apostles** themselves did in their
A P : 0 7 :040(176) [0241] To determine the **apostles**' wish and intention, therefore,
A P : 0 7 :040(176) [0241] customs, which the **apostles** adapted in modified form to
A P : 0 7 :042(176) [0241] The **apostles** had commanded their churches to celebrate
A P : 0 7 :042(176) [0243] of this decree show, the **apostles** did not want to impose
A P : 0 7 :042(176) [0243] can easily judge that the **apostles** wanted to disabuse the
A P : 0 7 :043(177) [0243] way that we do; for the **apostles** did not intend it to refer
A P : 0 7 :044(177) [0243] The **apostles** wisely admonished the reader neither to
A P : 1 2 :053(189) [0265] Jews, and spread by the **apostles** throughout the world.
A P : 1 2 :073(192) [0273] the writings of the **apostles** attest that they believed the
A P : 1 2 :073(192) [0273] For thus the **apostle** concludes, that a man is justified
A P : 1 2 :122(200) [0289] Christ's command to the **apostles** (Luke 24:47) "that
A P : 1 2 :123(200) [0289] Christ says, "Be penitent"; the **apostles** preach penitence.
A P : 1 5 :032(220) [0323] But the **apostles** insisted that Christian liberty remain in
A P : 1 5 :034(220) [0325] Just so the **apostles** have freed consciences for good,
A P : 1 5 :034(220) [0325] precept and example the **apostles** compel us to oppose
A P : 1 5 :036(220) [0325] The **apostles** violated traditions, and Christ excused
A P : 1 6 :007(223) [0331] this so often lest the **apostles** think that they should usurp
A P : 2 3 :042(245) [0375] resist him as the **apostles** in Acts 15 resisted those who
A P : 2 4 :008(250) [0385] a week, and that this practice came from the **apostles**.
A P : 2 4 :008(250) [0385] were appointed by the **apostles** to be held on the fourth
A P : 2 4 :093(267) [0417] to all the blessed patriarchs, prophets, and **apostles**.
A P : 2 4 :096(267) [0417] with the prophets, **apostles**, and holy Fathers, namely,
A P : 2 8 :008(282) [0445] in Acts (15:9), where the **apostles** say that hearts are
A P : 2 8 :016(283) [0447] Thus even the **apostles** ordained many things that were
A P : 2 8 :018(284) [0449] a testimony given to the **apostles** so that we may believe
S 1 : 0 1 :000(292) [0461] and the dead, etc., as the **Apostles**' Creed, the Athanasian
S 2 : 0 4 :009(300) [0475] The **apostles** did the same, and after them all the bishops
S 2 : 0 4 :014(301) [0475] so we cannot suffer his **apostle**, the pope or Antichrist, to
S 3 : 0 8 :006(312) [0495] the spoken word of the **apostles** but must come through
T R : 0 0 :007(320) [0505] Christ expressly forbids lordship among the **apostles**.
T R : 0 0 :008(320) [0505] Christ reproved the **apostles** for this error and taught
T R : 0 0 :008(320) [0505] among them but that the **apostles** should be sent forth as
T R : 0 0 :010(321) [0507] not superior to the other **apostles**, and that ordination or
T R : 0 0 :011(321) [0507] of Cephas over against the authority of the other **apostles**.
T R : 0 0 :011(321) [0507] He is an **apostle** of superior rank.
T R : 0 0 :023(324) [0511] of the entire company of **apostles**, as is apparent from the
T R : 0 0 :023(324) [0511] given equally to all the **apostles** and that the apostles were
T R : 0 0 :023(324) [0511] the apostles and that the **apostles** were sent out as equals.
T R : 0 0 :024(324) [0511] of the entire company of **apostles**, on which account these
T R : 0 0 :026(324) [0511] God gives his gifts, **apostles**, prophets, pastors, teachers.
T R : 0 0 :030(325) [0513] Peter holds in common with the rest of the **apostles**.
T R : 0 0 :031(325) [0513] because Christ gave the **apostles** only spiritual power,
T R : 0 0 :038(327) [0515] from them, and the **apostles** dissented from Caiaphas and
S C : 0 7 :002(352) [0557] or standing, say the **Apostles**' Creed and the Lord's
S C : 0 7 :005(353) [0559] or standing, say the **Apostles**' Creed and the Lord's
L C : P R :016(361) [0573] all his holy angels, prophets, **apostles**, and all Christians!
L C : S P :019(363) [0579] for the dear fathers or **apostles**, whoever they were, have
L C : 0 3 :004(420) [0699] draw people to prayer, as Christ and the **apostles** also did.
E P : R N :002(465) [0777] of the prophets and **apostles** was preserved in
E P : R N :003(465) [0777] after the time of the **apostles** — in fact, already during
E P : R N :003(465) [0777] true church, namely, the **Apostles**' Creed, the Nicene
E P : 0 3 :010(474) [0795] those words of the holy **apostle** Paul which separate the
E P : 0 3 :010(474) [0795] Thus the holy **apostle** Paul uses such expressions as "*by*
E P : 0 3 :015(475) [0795] of the prophets and **apostles**, the words "to justify" and
E P : 0 4 :007(476) [0799] The **Apostle** affirms in clear terms, "So also David
E P : 0 4 :012(477) [0799] as our Lord and the **apostles** themselves explain it, as
E P : 0 5 :006(478) [0803] ministry and which his **apostles** also set forth (examples
E P : 0 7 :015(483) [0813] place in the case of the **apostles**, since it is written, "And
E P : 0 8 :018(489) [0823] highest mystery, as the **apostles** testifies, and the sole
E P : 1 0 :006(493) [0829] indifferent things, as the **apostle** Paul writes, "For freedom
S D : P R :007(502) [0849] very lifetime of the holy **apostles** frightful errors arose
S D : P R :007(502) [0849] The holy **apostles** were compelled vigorously to denounce
S D : R N :004(504) [0851] general Creeds, the **Apostles**'; the Nicene, and the
S D : 0 2 :039(528) [0895] (Phil. 2:13), just as the **apostle** ascribes this work alone to
S D : 0 3 :059(550) [0937] of the prophets and **apostles**, and our Christian faith:
S D : 0 3 :062(550) [0937] the prophets and the **apostles** speak of the righteousness
S D : 0 5 :001(558) [0951] of the holy prophets and **apostles** may be explained and
S D : 0 5 :004(559) [0953] commands his **apostles** to preach the Gospel in all the
S D : 0 5 :005(559) [0953] John, Christ, and the **apostles** began in their preaching
S D : 0 5 :012(560) [0955] is true and right that the **apostles** and the preachers of the
S D : 0 6 :008(565) [0965] Concerning this the **apostle** writes, "I know that nothing
S D : 0 7 :042(576) [0987] the holy evangelists and **apostles**, and by their disciples
S D : 0 7 :051(578) [0991] all that he had commanded them (that is, the **apostles**).
S D : 0 8 :026(596) [1025] womb, but, as the **apostle** testifies, he laid it aside, and as
S D : 0 8 :027(596) [1025] but, in the words of the **apostle** (Eph. 4:10), far above all
S D : 0 8 :027(596) [1025] Zech. 9:10) and as the **apostles** testify that he worked with
S D : 0 8 :034(597) [1027] must that be of which the **apostle** says that "in Christ the
S D : 0 8 :096(609) [1049] of the holy prophets and **apostles**, and our Christian
S D : 0 8 :096(609) [1049] but with the holy **apostles** simply to believe, close the eyes
S D : 1 0 :013(613) [1057] would not yield to false **apostles** who wanted to impose
S D : 1 0 :014(613) [1057] faith, so that, as the **apostle** testifies, the truth of the
S D : 1 0 :015(613) [1057] the mouth of the holy **apostle** so seriously commanded
S D : 1 0 :020(614) [1059] so we cannot suffer his **apostle**, the pope or Antichrist, to
S D : 1 1 :064(626) [1083] The great **apostle** Paul shows us that we cannot and
S D : 1 1 :069(627) [1085] of God's Word, as the **apostle** testifies, "Faith comes from
S D : 1 1 :080(629) [1089] The **apostle** says in unmistakable terms that God
S D : 1 1 :086(631) [1091] The holy **apostle** adduces Pharaoh's example for the sole
S D : 1 1 :092(632) [1093] For the **apostle** testifies that "Whatever was written in

Apostolic (21)
PR : PR :002(003) [0007] out of the divine, prophetic, and **apostolic** Scriptures.
PR : PR :024(013) [0021] divine, prophetic, and **apostolic** Scriptures and have been
PR : PR :025(013) [0023] on the prophetic and **apostolic** Scriptures and is
AG : 2 8 :075(094) [0095] are bound to follow the **apostolic** rule which commands
AL : 2 8 :075(094) [0095] are bound to follow the **apostolic** injunction which
AP : 0 4 :389(166) [0225] with the prophetic and **apostolic** Scriptures, with the holy
AP : 0 7 :038(176) [0241] **Apostolic** rites they want to keep, apostolic doctrine they
AP : 0 7 :038(176) [0241] rites they want to keep, **apostolic** doctrine they do not
AP : 0 7 :042(176) [0243] words are from an **apostolic** decree about Easter; from
AP : 0 7 :043(177) [0243] that because of this **apostolic** decree the Passover should
AP : 1 5 :031(219) [0323] In the **apostolic** statement in Acts 15:10, "Why do you
AP : 2 4 :086(265) [0413] The **apostolic** canons show that when they gathered they
TR : 0 0 :014(322) [0507] to divine tradition and **apostolic** usage, what is observed
TR : 0 0 :015(322) [0509] divine tradition and an **apostolic** usage, and he asserts
TR : 0 0 :062(330) [0521] clearly that in the **apostolic** letters all who preside over
EP : RN :001(464) [0777] that the prophetic and **apostolic** writings of the Old and
EP : RN :002(465) [0777] and apostles was preserved in post-**apostolic** times.
SD : RN :003(503) [0851] to the prophetic and **apostolic** writings of the Old and
SD : RN :016(507) [0857] to the prophetic and **apostolic** writings of God's Word,
SD : 0 8 :071(605) [1041] Creed and to the entire prophetic and **apostolic** doctrine.
SD : 0 8 :088(609) [1047] to the prophetic and **apostolic** writings, the orthodox

Apparent (13), Apparently (2)
PR : PR :019(009) [0017] is concerned, it is **apparent** to us and to everyone and is
PR : PR :024(013) [0023] It is further **apparent** to us that many good-hearted
AG : 2 8 :037(086) [0089] It is also **apparent** that because of this notion human
AL : 2 8 :074(093) [0093] It is also **apparent** that some were adopted out of
AP : 2 4 :002(249) [0385] **Apparently** they imagine that mere hearing is a beneficial
AP : 2 7 :057(279) [0439] From all this it is **apparent** that there are many
AP : 2 7 :062(280) [0441] Israelites, their father **apparently** wanted to distinguish
S 2 : 0 4 :014(301) [0475] with them, it becomes **apparent** that, at its best, the
TR : 0 0 :015(322) [0509] churches, it is quite **apparent** that the churches did not
TR : 0 0 :016(323) [0509] with it, it is quite **apparent** that it was not instituted.
TR : 0 0 :023(324) [0511] of apostles, as is **apparent** from the text itself, for Christ
LC : 0 1 :042(370) [0591] even in the face of this **apparent** contradiction, and learn
LC : 0 1 :112(380) [0613] it would have been **apparent** to all that they who lived
LC : 0 5 :084(456) [0773] your need will become **apparent**, and you will perceive
SD : RN :019(507) [0857] truth might be made **apparent** in every article and that

Appeal (10), Appealed (5), Appealing (6), Appeals (3)
PR : PR :003(003) [0007] They referred and **appealed** to it without either
PR : PR :017(008) [0015] and some even tried to **appeal** to them for the
PR : PR :018(008) [0015] at all times adhered and **appealed** to, we have in what
AG : PR :022(027) [0043] our protestations and **appeals** concerning these most
AG : 2 8 :033(086) [0087] Besides, they **appeal** to the fact that the Sabbath was
AG : 2 8 :033(086) [0087] No case is **appealed** to and urged so insistently as the
AL : 2 7 :006(071) [0077] some could have been freed by **appealing** to the canons.
AP : 1 2 :010(184) [0255] Here we **appeal** to the judgment of all good and wise
AP : 2 1 :024(232) [0349] he does not want **appeals** to be addressed to him through
AP : 2 4 :080(264) [0411] for Christ, God making his **appeal** through us.
LC : 0 1 :051(371) [0595] forbids is **appealing** to God's name falsely or taking his
LC : 0 3 :092(432) [0723] this petition is really an **appeal** to God not to regard our
LC : 0 3 :110(435) [0729] the Lord's Prayer and to **appeal** to God from your heart,
SD : RN :005(504) [0851] We **appeal** to it just as in the ancient church it was
SD : RN :005(504) [0853] bishops and teachers to **appeal** and confess adherence to
SD : RN :009(505) [0853] wish to be regarded as **appealing** to further extensive
SD : 0 2 :014(523) [0885] This **appealing** passage is of very great comfort to all
SD : 0 2 :021(525) [0889] All pleas, all **appeals**, all admonitions are in vain.
SD : 0 2 :044(529) [0897] We hereby **appeal** to these writings and refer others to
SD : 0 7 :029(574) [0981] or after my death **appeal** to me or misuse my writings to
SD : 0 7 :045(577) [0987] words, no matter how **appealing** our reason may find it.
SD : 0 7 :091(586) [1005] desire to have them considered as **appealed** to herewith.
SD : 0 7 :106(588) [1009] no matter how **appealing** and attractive they may appear
SD : 0 8 :086(608) [1047] go on record as having **appealed** to these as being clear

Appear (24), Appearance (16), Appearances (3), Appeared (3), Appearing (1), Appears (17)
PR : PR :002(003) [0007] alone brings salvation to **appear** to our beloved
PR : PR :018(009) [0015] our blessed end and to **appear** before the judgment seat
AG : 1 7 :005(039) [0051] even now making an **appearance** and which teach that,
AG : 2 7 :020(074) [0079] This **appears** from God's own words in Gen. 2:18, "It is
AG : 2 8 :045(088) [0089] These have an **appearance** of wisdom."
AL : 1 7 :001(038) [0051] of the world Christ will **appear** for judgment and will
AL : 2 2 :003(049) [0059] example from which it **appears** that a whole congregation
AL : 2 4 :009(057) [0065] Accordingly it does not **appear** that the Mass is observed
AL : 2 4 :037(060) [0067] And it **appears** from the ancient canons that some one
AL : 2 7 :014(073) [0077] things can be denied, for they **appear** in their own books.
AL : 2 7 :036(076) [0081] Although it **appears** that God's command concerning
AL : 2 8 :033(086) [0087] the Lord's Day — contrary to the Decalogue, it **appears**.
AL : 2 8 :045(088) [0089] These have an **appearance** of wisdom."
AL : 2 8 :060(091) [0091] ought to assemble, it **appears** that the church designated
AP : PR :008(098) [0101] Later there **appeared** a decree in which our opponents
AP : PR :010(099) [0101] can complain that the book has **appeared** anonymously.
AP : PR :018(099) [0103] is better than that which **appears** everywhere in our
AP : 0 2 :043(106) [0117] Yet these ideas **appear** in the scholastics, who improperly
AP : 0 2 :049(106) [0119] In others, even grosser vices **appear**.
AP : 0 4 :006(108) [0121] of the Decalogue, wherever they **appear** in the Scriptures.
AP : 0 4 :064(116) [0139] sin, but whenever it **appears** it brings forth good fruits, as
AP : 0 4 :139(126) [0161] reason the Son of God **appeared** was to destroy the
AP : 0 7 :019(171) [0233] about the outward **appearance** of the church when he
AP : 0 7 :035(175) [0241] These have indeed an **appearance** of wisdom in
AP : 0 7 :045(177) [0243] the histories in which it **appears** that a difference in
AP : 1 2 :055(189) [0265] These two parts also **appear** in the lives of the saints.
AP : 1 5 :022(218) [0321] traditions "have an **appearance** of wisdom," and indeed
AP : 1 5 :024(218) [0321] men are deceived by the **appearance** of wisdom and
AP : 1 5 :025(218) [0321] Once this **appearance** of wisdom and righteousness has
AP : 1 5 :029(219) [0323] Against this deceptive **appearance** of wisdom and
AP : 1 7 :001(224) [0335] of the world Christ will **appear** and raise all the dead,
AP : 2 3 :003(239) [0363] face, for the saying **appears** about you, "A man with a
AP : 2 4 :050(259) [0401] And as for outward **appearances**, our church attendance
S 1 : PR :001(288) [0455] might be summoned to **appear** before the council or be
S 1 : PR :006(289) [0457] if one does, the devil **appears** at once to poison and
S 2 : 0 2 :016(295) [0467] the knavery of **appearing** as spirits of the departed and,
S 3 : 0 3 :042(309) [0491] Some fanatics may **appear** (and perhaps they are already
S 3 : 0 6 :005(311) [0493] and retain only the **appearance** and shape of bread
S 3 : 0 8 :011(313) [0497] to Moses God wished to **appear** first through the burning
TR : 0 0 :077(333) [0527] not had it for long, for it **appears** from the *Codex* and
LC : 0 1 :046(371) [0593] deceive you with their **appearance**, which indeed endures
LC : 0 1 :093(377) [0607] and brilliant it may **appear**, or even if it be altogether
LC : 0 1 :192(391) [0635] How would I **appear** before all the world in any other
LC : 0 1 :258(399) [0653] This problem **appears** to concern us only a little at
LC : 0 1 :270(401) [0657] you cannot prove, even if it is true, you **appear** as a liar.
LC : 0 3 :052(427) [0711] kingdom which has now made its **appearance** among us.
LC : 0 4 :008(437) [0733] even though to all **appearances** it may not be worth a
LC : 0 4 :011(437) [0735] to blind us with false **appearances** and lead us away from
LC : 0 4 :011(438) [0735] a much more splendid **appearance** when a Carthusian
LC : 0 4 :012(438) [0735] and dazzling they might **appear**, they would not be as
LC : 0 5 :056(453) [0767] precious blessing, and it **appears** like a dark lantern in
LC : 0 6 :005(457) [0000] said, are unworthy to **appear** in the presence of the
EP : 0 7 :022(484) [0813] of Christ and that only the exterior **appearance** remains.
SD : 0 4 :015(553) [0943] tree since no good fruits **appear**, yes, even though he were
SD : 0 5 :006(559) [0953] So it **appears** shortly afterward in the first chapter of St.
SD : 0 7 :001(569) [0971] so as to make it **appear** to be in full agreement with the
SD : 0 7 :029(574) [0981] from this world and to **appear** before the judgment seat
SD : 0 7 :045(577) [0987] expressions, as they **appear** to our reason, but we must
SD : 0 7 :092(586) [1005] no matter what **appearance** or prestige they may have, to
SD : 0 7 :099(586) [1005] and, "When Christ who is our life **appears**" (Col. 3:4).
SD : 0 7 :106(588) [1009] and attractive they may **appear** to reason, and will enable
SD : 1 1 :026(620) [1071] of the law, or on the basis of some outward **appearance**.
SD : 1 2 :002(632) [1095] mention of them, although it now **appears** to be desirable.
SD : 1 2 :040(636) [1103] by God's grace we shall **appear** with intrepid hearts

Appease (6), Appeased (2), Appeases (1), Appeasing (1)
AL : 2 8 :041(087) [0089] natural is a work that **appeases** God, that it is a mortal sin
AL : 2 8 :043(088) [0089] for the purpose of **appeasing** God or as if they were
AP : 0 4 :080(118) [0143] to us, we cannot **appease** God's wrath by setting forth our
AP : 0 4 :203(135) [0177] and forgiveness of sins, **appease** the wrath of God, and
AP : 0 4 :212(136) [0179] by which God is **appeased** and a price because of which
AP : 0 4 :288(151) [0203] many other painful works to **appease** the wrath of God.
AP : 0 4 :393(167) [0225] men judge that God ought to be **appeased** by works.
AP : 1 5 :001(215) [0315] traditions instituted to **appease** God, to merit grace, and
AP : 1 5 :005(215) [0317] the forgiveness of sins and **appease** the wrath of God.
AP : 2 1 :028(233) [0351] sought through her to **appease** Christ, as though he were

Append (1), Appended (3)
PR : PR :000(001) [0004] Together with an **Appended** Declaration, Firmly Founded
AP : 2 7 :012(270) [0423] To this they **append** a horrible epilogue in the words:
LC : 0 2 :049(417) [0691] *communio*, which is **appended**, should not be translated
SD : 0 7 :029(574) [0981] Christian articles, he **appended** the following protestation

Appendix (4)
LC : 0 1 :029(368) [0589] [Explanation of the **Appendix** to the First
LC : 0 1 :321(408) [0673] as we heard above, this **appendix** was intended to apply
LC : 0 1 :321(408) [0673] This **appendix** ought to be regarded as attached to each
SD : 1 0 :021(614) [1059] which constitutes an **appendix** to the Smalcald Articles

Appetite (1)
AP : 2 7 :009(270) [0421] of religion, but actually for the sake of **appetite** or hatred?

Applaud (1)
AP : 2 1 :038(234) [0355] theologians, and monks **applaud** these monstrous and

Apple (2)
AP : 0 2 :007(101) [0107] through contact with the **apple** or through the serpent's
LC : 0 1 :023(367) [0585] into an idol — indeed, an "**apple**-god" — and setting up

Applicability (1), Applicable (1), Application (9), Applied (17), Applies (16), Apply (45), Applying (4)
PR : PR :006(004) [0009] we have not ceased to **apply** our diligence to the end that
AG : 2 0 :022(044) [0055] Christ and diligently to **apply** it in order that men may
AG : 2 2 :003(049) [0059] interpret them as if they **apply** only to priests, Paul shows
AG : 2 7 :044(078) [0081] namely, that they could **apply** their good works to others.
AL : 2 4 :010(057) [0065] shamefully profaned and **applied** to purposes of gain.
AP : 0 4 :334(158) [0215] (Luke 17:10) also **applies**, "When you have done all that
AP : 0 4 :363(162) [0219] Here Paul's words **apply**, "There is laid up for me the
AP : 0 4 :367(163) [0221] opponents immediately **apply** it not to the other rewards
AP : 0 9 :002(178) [0245] the promise of salvation also **applies** to little children.
AP : 0 9 :002(178) [0245] It does not **apply** to those who are outside of Christ's
AP : 0 9 :002(178) [0245] of salvation might be **applied** to them according to
AP : 1 2 :106(197) [0283] wants by analogy to **apply** the commandment given a
AP : 1 2 :133(202) [0293] passages of Scripture **apply** in no way to scholastic
AP : 1 2 :134(203) [0293] These passages cannot be **applied** to satisfactions that one
AP : 1 2 :135(203) [0293] a wicked distortion to **apply** these passages to canonical
AP : 1 2 :149(205) [0299] is a foolish distortion to **apply** the term "punishments" to
AP : 1 2 :149(205) [0299] satisfactions and not to **apply** them to the fearful terrors
AP : 1 2 :154(206) [0299] moreover, do not **apply** to these punishments because our
AP : 1 3 :014(213) [0311] promises, but these **apply** to physical life and not strictly
AP : 1 8 :001(224) [0335] several proofs which are hardly **applicable** in this matter.
AP : 2 1 :003(229) [0343] now hold about the **application** of merits, surely has no
AP : 2 1 :014(230) [0345] of the saints; they even **apply** the merits of the saints to
AP : 2 1 :022(232) [0349] These they **apply** to others in the same way as Christ's, as
AP : 2 1 :023(232) [0349] indulgences they claim to **apply** the merits of the saints.
AP : 2 1 :031(233) [0351] They **apply** the merits of the saints in the same way as the
AP : 2 2 :010(237) [0361] clowning when they **apply** the story of Eli's sons to the
AP : 2 3 :015(241) [0367] maintain that whatever **applies** to human nature in
AP : 2 3 :015(241) [0367] to human nature in general, **applies** to priests as well.
AP : 2 3 :018(242) [0369] Why do they not **apply** these magnificent commandments
AP : 2 3 :041(245) [0375] the Levitical laws about uncleanness do not **apply** to us.
AP : 2 3 :064(248) [0381] the Old Testament do not **apply** here because the Gospel
AP : 2 4 :031(255) [0395] this passage and **apply** it to the Mass, and for this they
AP : 2 4 :034(256) [0397] But our opponents always **apply** the term "sacrifice" only
AP : 2 4 :035(256) [0397] that merits the forgiveness of sins when **applied** to others.
AP : 2 4 :058(260) [0405] priest who sacrifices for sin, this can only **apply** to Christ.
AP : 2 4 :064(261) [0407] punishment by the **application** of the sacrament, though

Continued ▶

AP : 24 :087(265) [0413] and its supposed **applicability** to merit the forgiveness of
AP : 24 :088(265) [0413] "reasonable victim" and **apply** it to the body of Christ
AP : 24 :089(265) [0413] opponents defend the **application** of the ceremony to free
AP : 24 :089(266) [0415] of Scripture, and to **apply** to the dead the Lord's Supper
AP : 24 :089(266) [0415] be overcome by the **application** of someone else's work.
AP : 24 :093(267) [0417] The Greek canon does not **apply** the offering as a
AP : 24 :093(267) [0417] for the dead because it **applies** it equally to all the blessed
AP : 24 :093(267) [0417] a thanksgiving and do not **apply** it as a satisfaction for
AP : 24 :096(267) [0417] the wicked to whom it is **applied**, if they make no
AP : 24 :098(268) [0417] of the Mass, which they **apply** in order by it to merit the
AP : 27 :012(270) [0423] They **apply** the passage in Paul only to the law of Moses.
AP : 27 :043(276) [0435] the saying of Christ in **applying** it to monastic life, unless
AP : 27 :043(277) [0435] they will receive a hundredfold in this life **applies** here.
AP : 27 :053(278) [0437] of the Mass by its **application** to the dead for the sake of
AP : 28 :019(284) [0449] who hears you hears me" cannot be **applied** to traditions.
TR : 00 :027(325) [0511] in this way and not as **applying** to the person or
TR : 00 :068(331) [0523] Here the words of Christ **apply** which testify that the keys
TR : 00 :069(331) [0525] These words **apply** to the true church which, since it
TR : 00 :078(333) [0527] concerning marriage and **apply** them in their courts, there
LC : 01 :031(369) [0589] Although these words **apply** to all the commandments (as
LC : 01 :050(371) [0595] all the other commandments and **apply** them to yourself.
LC : 01 :158(387) [0627] those in the papacy who **applied** this title to themselves
LC : 01 :166(388) [0629] been said to those to whom this commandment **applies**.
LC : 01 :181(389) [0631] what is forbidden here **applies** to private individuals, not
LC : 01 :202(392) [0639] us, this commandment **applies** to every form of
LC : 01 :260(400) [0655] The first **application** of this commandment, then, is that
LC : 01 :261(400) [0655] its plainest meaning, **applying** to all that takes place in
LC : 01 :262(400) [0655] much further when it is **applied** to spiritual jurisdiction or
LC : 01 :263(400) [0655] This **applies** to false preachers with their corrupt teaching
LC : 01 :264(400) [0655] It **applies** particularly to the detestable, shameful vice of
LC : 01 :293(404) [0663] to the Jews; nevertheless, in part they also **apply** to us.
LC : 01 :296(405) [0665] a broader and higher **application**) to forbid anyone, even
LC : 01 :300(405) [0667] Seventh Commandment **applies**, since they are not much
LC : 01 :309(406) [0669] commandments therefore retain their general **application**.
LC : 01 :321(408) [0673] appendix was intended to **apply** to all the
LC : 02 :038(415) [0689] Holy Spirit to offer and **apply** to us this treasure of
LC : 03 :015(422) [0701] very commandment that **applied** to St. Paul applies also
LC : 03 :015(422) [0701] that applied to St. Paul **applies** also to me.
EP : 04 :009(476) [0799] and in a Christian way **applied** to the regenerated and are
EP : 04 :010(476) [0799] 5. However, when **applied** to the regenerated the words
EP : 04 :012(477) [0799] themselves explain it, as **applying** only to the liberated
EP : 06 :003(480) [0805] law is to be diligently **applied** not only to unbelievers and
SD : 01 :052(517) [0875] however, the term is **applied** in a wider sense to include
SD : 02 :007(521) [0883] by and for himself or can **apply** himself to it or prepare
SD : 02 :064(533) [0905] the words of St. Paul **apply** also to the regenerated, "For
SD : 03 :010(541) [0919] we can apprehend, accept, **apply** them to ourselves, and
SD : 03 :013(541) [0919] This merit has to be **applied** to us and to be made our
SD : 03 :016(541) [0921] in the sacraments, and is **applied**, appropriated, and
SD : 03 :038(546) [0929] we receive, grasp, accept, **apply** to ourselves, and
SD : 03 :038(546) [0929] office and property of **application** and appropriation we
SD : 03 :039(546) [0929] and received, accepted, **applied** to us, and made our own
SD : 03 :042(547) [0931] as we have said above, it **applies** to us and makes our own
SD : 03 :046(548) [0933] worthy and fit to have the merit of Christ **applied** to him.
SD : 04 :040(558) [0951] admonished and urged to **apply** themselves to good
SD : 07 :052(578) [0991] "This is my body," and **apply** them in one and the same
SD : 08 :043(599) [1029] person, since Zwingli **applies** all the texts concerning the
SD : 11 :057(625) [1081] The same **applies** when we observe that God gives his

Appoint (6), Appointed (28), Appointment (1)
AG : PR :018(026) [0041] Majesty's orator and **appointed** commissioners, that Your
AG : 20 :003(041) [0053] pilgrimages, **appointed** fasts, holy days, brotherhoods,
AG : 27 :013(073) [0077] of whom serve in their **appointed** calling according to
AG : 28 :058(091) [0091] who consider the **appointment** of Sunday in place of the
AG : 28 :060(091) [0091] it was necessary to **appoint** a certain day so that the
AG : 28 :060(091) [0091] the Christian church **appointed** Sunday for this purpose,
AL : 28 :037(086) [0089] more holy days were **appointed**, more fasts prescribed,
AL : 28 :060(091) [0091] it was necessary to **appoint** a certain day so that the
AP : 04 :040(112) [0131] the world and has been **appointed** as the mediator and
AP : 11 :005(181) [0249] ancient canons and the Fathers do not **appoint** a set time.
AP : 13 :012(212) [0311] has the command to **appoint** ministers; to this we must
AP : 15 :009(216) [0317] God has **appointed** Christ as the mediator; he wants to be
AP : 21 :024(232) [0349] But if a king has **appointed** a certain intercessor, he does
AP : 21 :024(232) [0349] Since Christ has been **appointed** as our intercessor and
AP : 24 :008(250) [0385] for Communion were **appointed** by the apostles to be held
AP : 24 :052(259) [0403] from among men is **appointed** to act on behalf of men in
AP : 24 :053(259) [0403] "every high priest is **appointed** to offer sacrifices for sins."
TR : 00 :035(326) [0513] and deprive the emperors of the right to **appoint** bishops.
TR : 00 :062(330) [0523] in Crete, that you might **appoint** presbyters in every
SC : PR :021(341) [0537] it, and no time or place should be **appointed** for it.
SC : 09 :004(355) [0561] resists what God has **appointed**, and those who resist will
LC : 01 :080(375) [0603] the seventh day and **appointed** it for rest and he
LC : 01 :085(376) [0605] times Sunday has been **appointed** for this purpose, we
LC : 01 :094(378) [0607] therefore instituted and **appointed** in order that God's
LC : 01 :095(378) [0607] to hear and learn it, especially at the times **appointed**.
LC : 01 :116(381) [0615] mother, which God has **appointed** and commanded next
LC : 01 :126(382) [0617] others; indeed, he has **appointed** it to be his
LC : 01 :141(384) [0621] and responsibility to others **appointed** for the purpose.
LC : 01 :266(401) [0657] bury it until you are **appointed** a judge and authorized to
LC : 02 :032(415) [0687] especially at the times **appointed** for dealing at length
LC : 02 :055(418) [0693] Word and through signs **appointed** to comfort and revive
LC : 02 :061(419) [0695] For this purpose he has **appointed** a community on
LC : 03 :098(433) [0725] Supper, which are **appointed** as outward signs, this sign
LC : 04 :072(445) [0751] external sign has been **appointed** not only on account of
SD : 12 :006(633) [1097] Lord Jesus Christ has **appointed** us teachers and

Apposite (1)
SD : 03 :033(545) [0927] St. Paul's statement concerning Abraham is **apposite**.

Appraised (1)
EP : RN :001(464) [0777] teachers alike must be **appraised** and judged, as it is

Appreciate (2), Appreciated (1)
AG : 27 :005(071) [0077] had not sufficiently **appreciated** or understood their
LC : PR :009(359) [0569] by day we relish and **appreciate** the Catechism more
LC : 04 :044(442) [0743] To **appreciate** and use Baptism aright, we must draw

Apprehend (3), Apprehended (5), Apprehends (4)
AG : 20 :028(045) [0057] always faith alone that **apprehends** grace and forgiveness
AL : 06 :001(032) [0045] and justification are **apprehended** by faith, as Christ
AL : 20 :022(044) [0055] forgiveness of sins are **apprehended** by faith in Christ.
AL : 20 :028(045) [0057] of sins and grace are **apprehended**, and because through
S2 : 01 :004(292) [0461] cannot be obtained or **apprehended** by any work, law, or
LC : 04 :046(442) [0743] with the soul and **apprehends** Baptism in the only way it
EP : 02 :011(471) [0789] to dispose itself, to **apprehend** and accept it, and to
EP : 09 :002(492) [0827] and reason, but must be **apprehended** by faith alone.
SD : 02 :012(523) [0885] grasp, take hold of, or **apprehend**) the gifts of the Spirit
SD : 03 :010(541) [0919] means whereby we can **apprehend**, accept, apply them to
SD : 03 :041(546) [0929] Faith **apprehends** the grace of God in Christ whereby the
SD : 03 :041(546) [0931] it is faith alone which **apprehends** the blessing without

Approach (6), Approachable (1), Approaches (1)
AG : 24 :036(060) [0067] some to Communion and forbidding others to **approach**.
AP : 21 :015(231) [0347] and the saints more **approachable**; so they trust more in
SC : 03 :002(346) [0545] in order that we may **approach** him boldly and
SC : 03 :002(346) [0545] even as beloved children **approach** their dear father.
LC : 03 :013(422) [0701] should always **approach** God in obedience to this
LC : 04 :055(443) [0745] not vitiated if someone **approaches** it with an evil
LC : 04 :079(446) [0751] else than a return and **approach** to Baptism, to resume
SD : 02 :005(521) [0881] nor does he of himself **approach** God, but he is and

Appropriate (8), Appropriated (4), Appropriately (1)
AG : 20 :022(044) [0055] the grace of God is **appropriated** without merits, through
AG : 27 :004(071) [0077] on many before they had attained an **appropriate** age.
AP : 23 :055(247) [0379] a time like this it was **appropriate** to guard marriage with
LC : 03 :060(428) [0715] salvation, in which we **appropriate** God with all his
LC : 05 :023(449) [0757] Therefore, it is **appropriately** called the food of the soul
LC : 05 :031(450) [0759] can they grasp and **appropriate** it, except by steadfastly
LC : 05 :036(450) [0761] it can be grasped and **appropriated** only by the heart.
LC : 05 :037(451) [0761] cannot be grasped and **appropriated** by the body.
SD : 03 :016(541) [0921] and is applied, **appropriated**, and accepted by faith, so
SD : 03 :038(546) [0929] apply to ourselves, and **appropriate** the grace and the
SD : 07 :050(578) [0989] language but the most **appropriate**, simple, indubitable,
SD : 07 :062(581) [0995] accept with faith, and **appropriate** to ourselves the Word
SD : 10 :009(612) [1055] but in an orderly and **appropriate** way, as at any time

Appropriation (2)
AP : 24 :075(263) [0411] and speak of the **appropriation** of the comfort, not of any
SD : 03 :038(546) [0929] of application and **appropriation** we must exclude love

Approval (5), Approve (26), Approved (20), Approves (16), Approving (2)
PR : PR :003(003) [0007] summarized in the **approved** ancient symbols, recognizing
PR : PR :016(008) [0013] they accepted, **approved**, and subscribed this Book of
AG : 22 :008(050) [0061] Cardinal Cusanus mentions when the use was **approved**.
AL : 21 :003(047) [0057] Christ especially **approves**, namely, that in all afflictions
AL : 00 :005(048) [0059] these could not be **approved** with a good conscience, they
AL : 22 :004(050) [0061] Cusanus mentions when the change was **approved**.
AL : 22 :009(050) [0061] of God is not to be **approved**, as the canons testify (Dist.
AP : PR :007(098) [0101] prevented us from **approving** the Confutation, but his
AP : PR :016(099) [0103] We trust that God **approves** our faithfulness, and we
AP : 01 :001(100) [0103] Our opponents **approve** Article I of our Confession.
AP : 02 :001(100) [0105] The opponents **approve** Article II, "Original Sin," but
AP : 03 :001(107) [0119] The opponents **approve** our third article, in which we
AP : 04 :222(137) [0181] justification is not the **approval** of a particular act but of
AP : 07 :030(174) [0237] "particular rites" they **approve** our article, but if we mean
AP : 07 :047(177) [0243] They have **approved** the entire eighth article.
AP : 09 :001(178) [0245] They **approve** the ninth article where we confess that
AP : 09 :003(178) [0245] it is evident that God **approves** the Baptism of little
AP : 09 :003(178) [0245] That God does **approve** the Baptism of little children is
AP : 10 :001(179) [0247] They **approve** the tenth article, where we confess our
AP : 11 :001(180) [0247] They **approve** the eleventh article on retaining absolution
AP : 11 :003(180) [0249] they are but honest, will undoubtedly **approve** and praise.
AP : 11 :008(181) [0251] The same viewpoint was **approved** by Panormitanus and
AP : 12 :001(182) [0253] the twelfth article they **approve** the first part, where we
AP : 12 :069(192) [0271] officials they quietly **approved** the errors of their
AP : 12 :110(198) [0285] Although we **approve** of confession and maintain that
AP : 13 :001(211) [0309] XIII our opponents **approve** the statement that the
AP : 13 :012(212) [0311] for we know that God **approves** this ministry and is
AP : 14 :003(214) [0315] clear and we dare not **approve** the cruelty of those who
AP : 15 :015(217) [0319] grace, we shall have to **approve** the religious rites of all
AP : 15 :017(217) [0319] What if God does not **approve** these acts of worship?
AP : 16 :001(222) [0329] Our opponents **approve** Article XVI without exception.
AP : 16 :005(223) [0331] or the family but rather **approves** them, and it commands
AP : 16 :006(223) [0331] It not only **approves** governments but subjects us to
AP : 16 :008(223) [0333] to hearts, while it **approves** the civil government.
AP : 16 :012(224) [0333] that if contacts have the **approval** of magistrates or of
AP : 21 :004(229) [0343] Our Confession **approves** giving honor to the saints.
AP : 21 :010(230) [0345] how do we know that God **approves** such invocation?
AP : 21 :012(230) [0345] are aware of it or, even if they are, that God **approves** it.
AP : 21 :039(235) [0355] to compel us to **approve** of the most notorious abuses.
AP : 22 :017(238) [0361] the church immediately **approves** or accepts whatever the
AP : 23 :006(240) [0365] We cannot **approve** the law of celibacy put forth by our
AP : 23 :028(243) [0371] of God permits and **approves**, as the Scriptures
AP : 23 :030(243) [0371] the conscience that God **approves**, and by prayer, that is,
AP : 23 :033(244) [0373] God's permission and **approval**, then marriages are pure
AP : 23 :033(244) [0373] are pure since they are **approved** by the Word of God.
AP : 23 :051(246) [0377] keep good men from **approving** a burden that has
AP : 24 :013(251) [0387] No sane person can **approve** this pharisaic and pagan
AP : 27 :008(269) [0421] them, and who do not **approve** of the cruelty which the
AP : 27 :009(270) [0423] orders are forced to **approve** and support the abuses of
AP : 27 :023(273) [0427] are services which God **approves** as righteousness before
AP : 27 :041(276) [0435] God; this Christ does not **approve**, for works which we
AP : 27 :041(276) [0435] clearer that he does not **approve** of this kind of flight,
AP : 27 :041(276) [0435] This kind of leaving Christ **approves**.
AP : 27 :046(277) [0435] are civil ordinances, **approved** by the Word of God in the
S2 : 02 :017(296) [0467] the pope gave his **approval** to these things as well as to
S2 : 02 :019(296) [0467] the pope to praise and **approve** of these practices in order

Continued ▶

TR : 0 0 :078(333) [0527] the law that in general **approves** all clandestine and
TR : 0 0 :082(334) [0529] also declare that they **approve** the article concerning the
LC : 0 1 :114(380) [0613] we have devised without ever asking God's **approval**.
LC : 0 6 :030(460) [0000] In short, we **approve** of no coercion.
EP : RN :004(465) [0777] the leading theologians **approved** by their subscription at
SD : PR :010(503) [0849] of God's Word and of **approved** writings in such a way
SD : RN :001(503) [0849] pattern, unanimously **approved**, in which the summarized
SD : RN :001(503) [0851] as had been written, **approved**, and accepted in the name
SD : RN :007(505) [0853] at Smalcald in 1537 and there **approved** and accepted.
SD : RN :010(506) [0855] other writings are to be **approved** and accepted, judged
SD : 0 7 :001(568) [0971] but in part openly **approved** the Sacramentarians'
SD : 0 8 :062(603) [1037] in the ancient **approved** councils on the basis of the
SD : 1 2 :037(636) [1101] and condemn the old, **approved** symbols, the Nicene and

Apt (1), Aptitude (3)
SC : 0 9 :002(354) [0561] dignified, hospitable, an **apt** teacher, no drunkard, not
SD : 0 1 :023(512) [0865] — such as the faculty, **aptitude**, skill, or ability to initiate
SD : 0 2 :012(522) [0885] man every capacity, **aptitude**, skill, and ability to think
SD : 0 2 :022(525) [0889] natural and efficient **aptitude**, capacity, or capability —

Aragon (2)
AG : 2 7 :026(075) [0079] as in the case of the king of **Aragon** and many others.
AL : 2 7 :026(075) [0079] is the case of the king of **Aragon**, who was recalled from a

Arbitrarily (1), Arbitrariness (1), Arbitrary (1)
TR : 0 0 :074(332) [0525] exercised intolerable **arbitrariness** and, either on account
TR : 0 0 :074(332) [0525] the power to ban men **arbitrarily** without due process of
EP : 1 1 :019(497) [0837] but that merely by an **arbitrary** counsel, purpose, and

Arch- (3)
LC : 0 1 :230(396) [0645] against the great, powerful **arch**-thieves who consort with
LC : 0 3 :113(435) [0729] of our prayer may be directed against our **arch**-enemy.
LC : 0 3 :116(435) [0731] on earth but to pray constantly against this **arch**-enemy.

Archbishop (2)
AG : 2 3 :012(052) [0063] resistance that an **archbishop** of Mayence who had
AL : 2 3 :012(052) [0063] resistance that the **archbishop** of Mayence, when about to

Archdeacon (1)
TR : 0 0 :062(331) [0523] one who is known to be active and name him **archdeacon**.

Archdiocese (1)
PR : PR :027(014) [0025] administrator of the **archdiocese** of Magdeburg

Architect (1), Architects (2), Architecture (2)
AP : 1 6 :002(222) [0331] make use of medicine or **architecture**, food or drink or air.
AP : 2 3 :038(244) [0373] agriculture, and eloquence surpasses **architecture**.
AP : 2 3 :039(244) [0375] than building makes an **architect**, so the virgin does not
AP : 2 7 :009(269) [0421] of doctrine which the **architects** of the Confutation are
AP : 2 7 :011(270) [0423] But listen how the **architects** of the Confutation slip away

Archives (1)
PR : PR :018(009) [0015] has been available in the **archives** of those sainted

Ardent (3), Ardently (2)
AG : 2 6 :002(064) [0071] daily, and were **ardently** and urgently promoted, as if
AP : 2 4 :051(259) [0401] godly use of the sacraments, **ardent** prayer, and the like.
LC : 0 3 :056(427) [0713] of us nothing more **ardently** than that we ask many and
SD : 0 2 :047(530) [0901] since they feel no strong, **ardent** faith and cordial
SD : 0 2 :068(534) [0907] and terrified, at one time **ardent** in love, strong in faith

Area (1), Areas (1)
AP : 1 2 :103(197) [0281] of absolution is in the **area** of blessing or grace, not of
LC : 0 1 :249(398) [0651] and maintain order in all **areas** of trade and commerce in

Argue (27), Argued (3), Argues (3), Arguing (8), Argument (22), Argumentation (2), Arguments (37)
PR : PR :020(010) [0017] theologians are not to **argue** from some other basis, but
AG : 2 7 :030(075) [0079] it is not right to **argue** so rashly and insistently about the
AG : 2 8 :063(092) [0093] Some **argue** that although Sunday must not be kept as of
AL : 0 1 :006(028) [0043] craftily and impiously **argue** that the Word and the Holy
AL : 2 7 :030(075) [0079] it is not fair to **argue** so insistently about the obligation
AL : 2 8 :017(083) [0085] worldly but have divine power to destroy **arguments**," etc.
AL : 2 8 :063(092) [0093] Some **argue** that the observance of the Lord's Day is not
AP : PR :002(098) [0099] and to refute their **arguments**, our party requested a copy
AP : PR :006(098) [0101] had taken notes on the main points of its **argumentation**.
AP : PR :015(099) [0101] assembled the main **arguments**, to testify to all nations
AP : 0 2 :007(101) [0107] They **argue** that the inclination to evil is a quality of the
AP : 0 2 :032(104) [0113] by the sophistic **arguments** of modern theologians.
AP : 0 2 :038(105) [0115] Let them **argue** with Augustine if this position displeases
AP : 0 2 :051(107) [0119] reluctant to enter upon their **arguments** at great length.
AP : 0 4 :067(116) [0139] But we have other more telling **arguments**.
AP : 0 4 :075(117) [0143] Therefore we **argue** this way:
AP : 0 4 :084(119) [0145] this is Paul's chief **argument**, which he often repeats
AP : 0 4 :084(119) [0147] one can devise or imagine will refute Paul's **argument**.
AP : 0 4 :117(123) [0155] of the Scriptures and **arguments** derived from the
AP : 0 4 :166(130) [0169] Again, what need is there for a long **argument**?
AP : 0 4 :182(132) [0173] Reply to the Opponents' **Arguments**
AP : 0 4 :231(139) [0183] From this they **argue** that love justifies since it makes men
AP : 0 4 :235(140) [0185] when our opponents **argue** on the basis of the word
AP : 0 4 :246(142) [0189] for our opponents to **argue** from this text that James
AP : 0 4 :280(149) [0201] rule it is improper in an **argument** to judge or reply to a
AP : 0 4 :286(150) [0201] quote against us in **arguing** that faith does not justify and
AP : 0 4 :298(153) [0205] What **argument** can anybody possibly bring against this
AP : 0 4 :335(159) [0215] They **argue** that if we are unworthy though we have done
AP : 0 4 :336(159) [0215] The **argument** is defective.
AP : 0 4 :337(159) [0215] have (James 2:19), their **argument** that faith is worthless
AP : 0 4 :338(159) [0215] are not bothered by the **argument**, "When you have
AP : 0 4 :339(159) [0215] Likewise, the **argument** from analogy is unwarranted:
AP : 0 4 :357(162) [0217] is mentioned, they **argue** that our works ought to be
AP : 0 4 :359(162) [0219] We are not **arguing** about the term "reward."
AP : 0 4 :361(162) [0219] By such a series of **arguments** the blessings of Christ and
AP : 0 4 :362(162) [0219] of faith, then we will not **argue** much about the term
AP : 0 4 :378(165) [0223] about which we are **arguing** here with our opponents.
AP : 0 4 :391(166) [0225] so great as to end all **argument**, when there are so many
AP : 1 0 :004(179) [0247] here, not to begin an **argument** on this subject (his
AP : 1 2 :045(188) [0263] We shall not **argue** if someone says that Christ also
AP : 1 2 :133(202) [0293] Many other **arguments** could be assembled to prove that
AP : 1 2 :137(203) [0293] words in refuting these silly **arguments** of our opponents.
AP : 2 0 :006(227) [0339] us more if we were **arguing** about dubious or trivial
AP : 2 0 :012(228) [0341] By the same **argument** we could say to a man who was
AP : 2 0 :013(228) [0341] Such **argumentation** is to make the effect the cause.
AP : 2 1 :007(230) [0345] real honors; they only **argue** about invocation, which,
AP : 2 1 :011(230) [0345] They **argue** about morning and evening knowledge,
AP : 2 1 :012(230) [0345] nothing against the **argument** that since invocation
AP : 2 2 :010(238) [0361] Our opponents **argue** that the laity has been kept from
AP : 2 3 :002(239) [0363] We shall review their **arguments** in a moment.
AP : 2 3 :008(240) [0365] reply with the silly **argument** that originally there was a
AP : 2 3 :008(240) [0365] Look at their clever **argument**!
AP : 2 3 :022(242) [0369] but now we are **arguing** about the regulation and about
AP : 2 3 :060(247) [0381] No sane man can **argue** with these cogent facts.
AP : 2 3 :062(247) [0381] In presenting our own **arguments**, we have incidentally
AP : 2 3 :062(247) [0381] and refuted the silly counter-**arguments** of our opponents.
AP : 2 3 :062(247) [0381] review their weighty **arguments** in defense of the law.
AP : 2 3 :064(248) [0381] The second **argument** of our opponents is that priests
AP : 2 3 :064(248) [0381] We have already refuted this very specious **argument**.
AP : 2 3 :067(248) [0383] Their third **argument** is horrible: the marriage of priests is
AP : 2 3 :070(249) [0383] With false **arguments** like these they defend a wicked and
AP : 2 3 :070(249) [0383] of our opponents' **arguments** and understand that in the
AP : 2 4 :009(251) [0387] the Fathers and the **arguments** they adduce are silenced
AP : 2 4 :010(251) [0387] be easy to evaluate the **arguments** both sides have
AP : 2 4 :052(259) [0403] is a very convincing **argument** for the ignorant, especially
AP : 2 4 :058(260) [0405] If anyone **argues**, therefore, that the New Testament must
AP : 2 4 :078(263) [0411] for the Mass they take **arguments** which do not deserve a
AP : 2 4 :084(264) [0413] It is silly to **argue** that since the Holy Scriptures mention
AP : 2 4 :087(265) [0413] Nevertheless, we are **arguing** here not about prayers, but
AP : 2 7 :009(269) [0421] should be kept, but we are **arguing** about other questions.
AP : 2 7 :010(270) [0423] hear how they twist our **arguments** and what they adduce
AP : 2 7 :010(270) [0423] through a few of our **arguments**, and in passing we shall
AP : 2 7 :029(274) [0431] is the way our opponents **argue** their case; that is the way
AP : 2 7 :057(279) [0439] that there are many **arguments** for the stand that
AP : 2 7 :069(280) [0443] a number of our **arguments**, and in passing we have
AP : 2 8 :002(281) [0443] this article we have been **arguing** about something
TR : 0 0 :010(321) [0505] this fact he expressly **argues** that his call did not depend
TR : 0 0 :021(323) [0509] [**Arguments** of Opponents Refuted]
TR : 0 0 :024(324) [0511] clear and powerful **arguments**, for after speaking of the
LC : 0 1 :301(405) [0667] they resort to whatever **arguments** have the least
LC : 0 4 :058(444) [0747] Likewise I might **argue**, "If I have no faith, then Christ is
LC : 0 4 :059(444) [0747] friend, rather invert the **argument** and conclude, Precisely
LC : 0 5 :019(449) [0757] words rest our whole **argument**, protection, and defense
SD : 0 2 :002(520) [0881] the issue which has been **argued** by some of the
SD : 0 2 :005(520) [0881] have taught and **argued** that through the fall of our first
SD : 0 2 :046(530) [0899] They **argue** that since they cannot convert themselves by
SD : 0 2 :046(530) [0899] Or they **argue** that since everything is altogether the work
SD : 0 4 :005(551) [0939] became a vehemently **argued** theological controversy
SD : 0 7 :026(573) [0981] words rest our whole **argument**, protection, and defense
SD : 0 7 :047(578) [0989] without any doubts or **arguments** as to how it is to be
SD : 0 7 :055(579) [0991] benefits of Christ, as the Apology **argues** and concludes.
SD : 0 7 :091(585) [1003] and futile counter-**arguments** of the Sacramentarians
SD : 0 7 :091(585) [1005] have advanced no new **arguments** since his death.
SD : 0 7 :093(586) [1005] Our basic **arguments**, on which we have stood
SD : 0 7 :106(588) [1009] These **arguments** are so strong and solid that they will
SD : 0 7 :106(588) [1009] refute all the counter-**arguments** and objections of the
SD : 0 8 :002(591) [1015] maintained with solid **arguments** the true, essential
SD : 0 8 :004(592) [1017] and use the same basic **arguments** about the person of
SD : 0 8 :052(601) [1033] However, they **argue** and contend that the gifts with
SD : 0 8 :052(601) [1033] and from their own **arguments** and demonstrations they
SD : 0 8 :053(601) [1033] simply believe it and not **argue** that the human nature in
SD : 0 8 :056(601) [1033] strong and irrefutable **arguments** which show that this

Arian (2), Arians (7)
AG : 0 1 :005(028) [0043] that of the Valentinians, **Arians**, Eunomians,
AL : 0 1 :005(028) [0043] those of the Valentinians, **Arians**, Eunomians,
EP : 0 8 :039(491) [0827] but it opens a way for the accursed **Arian** heresy.
EP : 1 2 :027(500) [0843] Errors of the New **Arians**
SD : 0 7 :126(591) [1015] course, no one except an **Arian** heretic can or will deny
SD : 0 8 :075(606) [1043] a peculiar sect among the **Arians**, called the Agnoetes,
SD : 1 2 :001(632) [1095] and the New **Arians** and Anti-Trinitarians whose errors
SD : 1 2 :035(635) [1101] Erroneous Articles of the New **Arians**
SD : 1 2 :036(635) [1101] the error of the New **Arians** who teach that Christ is not a

Aright (3)
LC : 0 1 :063(373) [0597] you must also know how to use the name of God **aright**.
LC : 0 4 :044(442) [0743] and use Baptism **aright**, we must draw strength and
EP : 0 3 :006(473) [0793] we recognize Christ **aright** as our redeemer and trust in

Arise (17), Arisen (28), Arises (3), Arose (10)
PR : PR :000(001) [0004] Disputation and Strife **Arose** after the blessed Death of
PR : PR :010(006) [0011] the difference that had **arisen** with reference to all the
PR : PR :016(008) [0013] dissensions which had **arisen** was agreeable and
PR : PR :024(013) [0021] of the disputes which have **arisen** should come into being.
PR : PR :026(014) [0025] continue or new ones **arise**, we shall see to it that they are
AG : 2 6 :019(067) [0073] errors which have **arisen** from a wrong estimation of
AG : 2 8 :061(091) [0093] all of which have **arisen** from the false and erroneous
AL : 2 4 :017(057) [0067] Great dissensions have **arisen** concerning the Mass,
AL : 2 6 :019(067) [0073] of these errors which had **arisen** from misunderstanding
AL : 2 8 :061(091) [0093] all of which have **arisen** from the false notion that there
AP : 0 4 :224(138) [0181] Then dissensions **arose** among them and, as Paul
AP : 0 4 :232(140) [0185] factions, and heresies that **arise** from such schisms.
AP : 0 4 :233(140) [0185] Dissensions also **arise** when the people judge their clergy's
AP : 0 4 :241(141) [0187] that if any dissensions **arise** they should be quieted and
AP : 0 4 :241(141) [0187] minor disagreements **arose**, which would never have
AP : 0 4 :242(141) [0187] Many heresies have **arisen** in the church simply from the
AP : 0 4 :353(161) [0217] we teach that this faith **arises** in penitence and ought to
AP : 0 9 :002(178) [0245] that no Anabaptists have **arisen** in our churches since our
AP : 1 2 :127(201) [0291] controversies that have **arisen** on the most important

Continued ▶

A P : 2 1 :043(235) [0357] fanatical spirits will **arise** whom our opponents will be
A P : 2 4 :076(263) [0411] From this term "eucharist" **arose** in the church.
A P : 2 4 :092(266) [0417] If the need ever **arises**, we shall discuss this whole issue
A P : 2 8 :022(284) [0451] commotions which have **arisen** under the pretext of our
S 2 : 0 2 :006(293) [0463] unspeakable abuses have **arisen** everywhere through the
T R : 0 0 :034(325) [0513] and afterwards great disturbances to **arise** in Europe.
T R : 0 0 :046(328) [0517] Out of these **arose** indulgences, which are nothing but lies
L C : 0 1 :054(372) [0595] when false preachers **arise** and peddle their lying nonsense
L C : 0 1 :163(387) [0627] allow preachers of lies to **arise** and lead us to the devil —
L C : 0 1 :330(410) [0677] take it to heart, there will **arise** a spontaneous impulse
L C : 0 2 :057(418) [0693] come forth gloriously and **arise** to complete and perfect
L C : 0 3 :109(435) [0729] weary; when one attack ceases, new ones always **arise**.
L C : 0 5 :019(449) [0757] and deceptions that have ever **arisen** or may yet arise.
L C : 0 5 :019(449) [0757] and deceptions that have ever arisen or may yet **arise**.
E P : 0 1 :010(467) [0781] which we now bear will **arise** and live forever, without
E P : 0 1 :021(468) [0783] evil thought would ever **arise** in the heart of corrupted
E P : 0 3 :001(472) [0791] foregoing a question has **arisen**, According to which
E P : 0 4 :001(475) [0797] Two controversies have **arisen** in some churches
E P : 0 4 :003(475) [0797] 2. The second controversy **arose** among certain
E P : 0 6 :001(480) [0805] that a controversy has **arisen** among a few theologians.
E P : 0 8 :001(486) [0817] a disagreement has **arisen** between the authentic
E P : 1 2 :014(499) [0841] 3. That as occasion **arises** no Christian, without violating
S D : P R :007(502) [0849] apostles frightful errors **arose** among those who pretended
S D : R N :004(504) [0851] which at that time had **arisen** within the Christian church
S D : R N :012(506) [0855] before the dissensions **arose** among the theologians of the
S D : R N :020(508) [0859] and faithfully against all the aberrations that have **arisen**.
S D : 0 1 :046(516) [0873] but without sin, shall **arise**, and that in eternal life we
S D : 0 3 :001(539) [0917] controversy which has **arisen** among several theologians
S D : 0 4 :001(551) [0939] good works has likewise **arisen** among the theologians of
S D : 0 4 :004(551) [0939] this latter controversy **arose** about the words "necessary"
S D : 0 4 :030(555) [0947] place, a disputation has **arisen** as to whether good works
S D : 0 4 :036(557) [0949] controversy subsequently **arose** on this point which led to
S D : 0 6 :001(564) [0963] A controversy has **arisen** among a few theologians
S D : 0 7 :026(573) [0981] and deceptions that have so far **arisen** or may yet arise."
S D : 0 7 :026(573) [0981] and deceptions that have so far arisen or may yet **arise**."
S D : 0 7 :073(582) [0999] There has also **arisen** a misunderstanding and dissension
S D : 0 8 :001(591) [1015] controversy has likewise **arisen** among theologians of the
S D : 1 1 :094(632) [1095] have erred and serious religious contentions have **arisen**.
S D : 1 2 :019(634) [1099] persons as occasion may **arise**, nor may a subject call

Aristippus (1)
A P : 2 7 :046(277) [0435] the philosophers praise **Aristippus** for throwing a great

Aristotle (3)
A P : 0 4 :014(109) [0123] aside the Gospel and expounded the ethics of **Aristotle**.
A P : 0 4 :014(109) [0123] was perfectly proper, for **Aristotle** wrote so well on
A P : 0 4 :024(110) [0127] good than this, as **Aristotle** correctly says, "Neither the

Arius (1)
E P : 0 8 :022(490) [0823] Christ is not true, natural, and eternal God, as **Arius** held.

Arm (2)
A P : 1 5 :029(219) [0323] rites, let us therefore **arm** ourselves with the Word of
L C : 0 3 :030(424) [0707] which Christians ought to **arm** themselves in order to

Armed (5), Armor (5), Arms (3), Army (1)
A P : 0 9 :002(178) [0245] our people have been **armed** by God's Word against the
A P : 1 2 :127(201) [0289] churches should be maintained only by force and **arms**.
A P : 1 2 :127(201) [0289] that we be conquered and destroyed by **armed** might?
A P : 1 2 :144(205) [0297] with one making a trip in **armor** and another going
A P : 1 2 :149(206) [0299] Who would not put on **armor** and seek out the church of
A P : 1 2 :163(208) [0303] to St. James dressed in **armor** or to perform similar
A P : 2 8 :004(281) [0445] such minds tortured by doubt, they call to **arms**.
T R : 0 0 :062(331) [0523] the same way in which an **army** might select a
L C : P R :014(360) [0571] against them with good "**armor**" against their "flaming
L C : P R :015(360) [0571] despise our weapons and **armor**, too lazy to give them a
L C : 0 3 :069(429) [0717] One or two Christians, **armed** with this single petition,
L C : 0 3 :075(430) [0719] be fitting if the coat-of-**arms** of every upright prince were
L C : 0 3 :109(435) [0729] we Christians must be **armed** and prepared for incessant
L C : 0 4 :063(444) [0749] be watchful and well **armed** and not allow ourselves to be

Around (11)
T R : 0 0 :062(330) [0523] separate followings **around** themselves, rend the church
L C : 0 1 :071(374) [0601] the devil, who is ever **around** us, lying in wait to lure us
L C : 0 1 :096(378) [0607] hear God's Word or lie **around** in taverns dead drunk like
L C : 0 1 :267(401) [0657] roll in the mud and root **around** in it with their snouts.
L C : 0 1 :281(403) [0661] in every corner and root **around** in the filth, nobody will
L C : 0 3 :028(424) [0705] him or other people **around** him, such as preachers,
L C : 0 3 :102(434) [0727] the old Adam hanging **around** our necks; he goes to work
L C : 0 5 :071(454) [0769] own need, which hangs **around** your neck and which is
L C : 0 5 :083(456) [0773] examine yourself, look **around** a little, cling to the
S D : 0 4 :011(553) [0941] man, blindly tapping **around** in search of faith and good
S D : 1 0 :016(613) [1059] great millstone fastened **around** his neck and to be

Arouse (6), Aroused (3)
A G : 2 3 :018(054) [0063] abomination and prevalence, **arouse** the wrath of God.
A P : 0 4 :021(110) [0127] are keeping the law, they **arouse** presumption, a vain
A P : 0 4 :276(148) [0199] fail to do good, do not **arouse** themselves to believe but
A P : 0 4 :350(161) [0217] How often our **aroused** conscience tempts us to despair
A P : 2 3 :068(249) [0383] that the best way to **arouse** the ignorant was to raise the
A P : 2 4 :003(250) [0385] something to learn that will **arouse** their faith and fear.
A P : 2 4 :070(262) [0409] As the Word was given to **arouse** this faith, so the
L C : 0 3 :089(432) [0723] God and is constantly **aroused** by evil desires and
L C : 0 6 :034(461) [0000] and love for it would be **aroused** that people would come

Arrange (2), Arranged (2), Arrangement (4), Arrangements (1), Arranges (1)
A G : 2 2 :011(050) [0061] to act contrary to the **arrangement** of our Lord Christ.
A G : 2 3 :014(054) [0063] No one is able to alter or **arrange** such matters in a better
A G : 2 7 :008(072) [0077] evils came from this **arrangement**, what scandals and
A G : 2 7 :031(076) [0079] to determine or **arrange** the order of one's whole future
A L : 2 7 :008(072) [0077] resulted from this **arrangement**, what scandals were
A P : 0 7 :042(176) [0241] Later on came the **arrangement** by which our Passover
L C : 0 1 :114(380) [0613] at all the **arrangements** we have devised without ever
L C : 0 1 :200(392) [0637] They are admirably **arranged**.
S D : 1 1 :075(628) [1087] and stumble, he **arranges** to recall them to repentance
S D : 1 1 :085(630) [1091] But after God **arranged** to have his Word proclaimed and

Arrayed (1)
L C : 0 3 :030(424) [0707] his might and his forces **arrayed** against us, trying to

Arrive (2)
A G : P R :005(025) [0039] without boasting that we were among the first to **arrive**.
S D : 0 4 :006(552) [0939] and by God's grace to **arrive** at a complete settlement, we

Arrogance (2), Arrogant (3), Arrogantly (2)
L C : 0 1 :027(368) [0587] disdained, nor are we **arrogantly** to seek other ways and
L C : 0 1 :059(372) [0597] Nor man is so **arrogant** as to boast before the whole
L C : 0 1 :234(397) [0647] pursues his defiant and **arrogant** course for a long time,
L C : 0 1 :240(397) [0649] own willful, conceited, **arrogant** way, as if it were his
L C : 0 1 :246(398) [0651] We shall endure your **arrogance** and show forgiveness and
L C : 0 1 :247(398) [0651] to the bone, and you **arrogantly** turn him away whom you
L C : 0 3 :103(434) [0727] reviling, slander, **arrogance**, and pride, along with

Arrogate (3), Arrogates (4), Arrogating (1)
A P : 0 4 :400(168) [0227] Although our opponents **arrogate** to themselves the name
A P : 2 2 :015(238) [0361] But the church cannot **arrogate** to itself the freedom to
A P : 2 7 :039(276) [0433] If this is not **arrogating** perfection to oneself, what is?
A P : 2 7 :053(278) [0437] of a double fault: it **arrogates** Christ's place to the saints,
T R : 0 0 :001(320) [0503] The Roman bishop **arrogates** to himself the claim that he
T R : 0 0 :006(320) [0505] Besides this, he **arrogates** to himself the authority to
T R : 0 0 :039(327) [0515] with the Gospel and will **arrogate** to himself divine
T R : 0 0 :040(327) [0515] Gospel, and the pope **arrogates** to himself a threefold

Arrows (1)
L C : 0 5 :082(456) [0773] many daggers, spears, and **arrows** are at every moment

Art (9), Artful (1), Artisan (1), Artisans (2), Artist (1), Arts (7)
A L : 1 8 :005(040) [0053] will to learn various useful **arts**, or will to do whatever
A L : 2 0 :040(046) [0057] church sings, "Where Thou **art** not, man hath naught,
A L : 2 8 :010(082) [0085] government as little as the **art** of singing interferes with
A P : 0 4 :072(117) [0141] the teachers of all the **arts** since it prepares for them, even
A P : 0 4 :072(117) [0141] even though it is his own **art** that makes everyone an
A P : 0 4 :072(117) [0141] though it is his own art that makes everyone an **artist**.
A P : 1 2 :108(198) [0283] have I sinned, so that thou **art** justified in thy sentence
A P : 2 7 :037(275) [0433] state of perfection than the life of a farmer or an **artisan**.
S C : P R :003(338) [0533] they have mastered the fine **art** of abusing liberty.
S C : 0 3 :001(346) [0545] *"Our Father who* **art** *in heaven."*
L C : P R :012(360) [0571] The devil is called the master of a thousand **arts**.
L C : P R :012(360) [0571] this master of a thousand **arts** with all his wiles and
L C : P R :012(360) [0571] indeed, be master of more than a hundred thousand **arts**.
L C : P R :013(360) [0571] attacks and ambushes of the devil with his thousand **arts**.
L C : S P :014(363) [0577] Our Father who **art** in heaven, hallowed be thy name.
L C : 0 1 :226(395) [0645] The same must be said of **artisans**, workmen, and
L C : 0 1 :237(397) [0647] So will it be with **artisans** and day-laborers, from whom
L C : 0 1 :245(398) [0649] For God is a master of this **art**; since everyone robs and
L C : 0 1 :298(405) [0665] We think up **artful** dodges and sly tricks (better and
L C : 0 3 :064(429) [0715] day and night, using all the **arts**, tricks, ways, and means
S D : 1 1 :007(617) [1065] Likewise, "Thou **art** not a God who delights in

Artern (1)
P R : P R :027(015) [0025] John Hoyer, count of Mansfeld [-**Artern**]

Article (252), Articles (140)
P R : P R :000(001) [0004] Only Norm, of Several **Articles** about which Disputation
P R : P R :003(003) [0007] of their faith in the chief **articles** in controversy over
P R : P R :010(006) [0011] with reference to all the **articles** in controversy, to expose
P R : P R :011(006) [0011] to hand the controverted **articles**, examined, evaluated,
P R : P R :013(007) [0013] with one another the **articles** in controversy and also the
P R : P R :015(007) [0013] had this document read **article** by article to each and
P R : P R :015(007) [0013] document read article by **article** to each and every
P R : P R :020(010) [0017] faith contradicted the **articles** of our Christian Creed
P R : P R :020(010) [0019] explanation of the **articles** of our Christian Creed that
P R : P R :020(010) [0019] as described above does not contradict these **articles**.
P R : P R :022(011) [0019] doctrine, especially in the **article** concerning the Lord's
P R : P R :022(011) [0019] of the controverted **articles** in order that everybody may
P R : P R :023(012) [0021] of the controverted **articles** we have made no new or
P R : P R :025(014) [0023] it, and in the Smalcald **Articles** and the Large and Small
A G : P R :024(027) [0043] it is specifically stated, **article** by article, in what follows.
A G : P R :024(027) [0043] it is specifically stated, article by **article**, in what follows.
A G : 0 0 :000(027) [0043] **Articles** of Faith and Doctrine
A G : 0 1 :005(028) [0043] the heresies which are contrary to this **article** are rejected.
A G : 2 0 :008(042) [0053] faith, which is the chief **article** in the Christian life, has
A G : 2 0 :025(044) [0057] do not believe this **article** concerning the forgiveness of
A G : 0 0 :001(047) [0059] cannot disagree with us in the **articles** set forth above.
A G : 0 0 :002(048) [0059] defective in the principal **articles** and since this our
A G : 0 0 :000(048) [0059] **Articles** about Matters in Dispute, in Which an Account
A G : 0 0 :000(048) [0059] our churches concerning **articles** of faith that is contrary
A G : 2 8 :052(089) [0091] For the chief **article** of the Gospel must be maintained,
A G : 2 8 :066(092) [0093] pay attention to the chief **article** of Christian doctrine,
A G : 0 0 :001(094) [0095] These are the chief **articles** that are regarded as
A G : 0 0 :006(095) [0095] to present the above **articles** as a declaration of our
A L : 0 0 :000(027) [0043] Chief **Articles** of Faith
A L : 0 1 :005(028) [0043] sprung up against this **article**, such as that of the
A L : 2 0 :023(044) [0055] the history, namely, this **article** of the forgiveness of sins
A L : 2 0 :025(044) [0057] not able to believe this **article** of the forgiveness of sins;
A L : 0 0 :000(048) [0059] **Articles** in Which an Account Is Given of the Abuses
A L : 0 0 :001(048) [0059] the church catholic in no **article** of faith but only omit
A L : 2 6 :005(064) [0071] greatest weight on this **article** and puts aside the law and
A L : 2 8 :052(089) [0091] to preserve the chief **article** of the Gospel, namely, that
A L : 0 0 :001(094) [0095] now reviewed the chief **articles** that are regarded as
A L : 0 0 :006(095) [0095] to present the above **articles** in order that our confession
A P : P R :002(098) [0099] that it condemned many **articles** that we could not
A P : P R :004(098) [0099] to condemn several **articles** where they could not give in
A P : P R :009(099) [0101] have condemned several **articles** in opposition to the clear
A P : P R :017(099) [0103] brought into view many **articles** of Christian doctrine

Continued ▶

A P : 0 1 :000(100) [0103] [**Article** I. God]
A P : 0 1 :001(100) [0103] Our opponents approve **Article** I of our Confession.
A P : 0 2 :000(100) [0105] [**Article** II. Original Sin]
A P : 0 2 :001(100) [0105] The opponents approve **Article** II, "Original Sin," but they
A P : 0 2 :051(107) [0119] with which our opponents have slandered our **article**.
A P : 0 3 :000(107) [0119] [**Article** III. Christ]
A P : 0 3 :001(107) [0119] approve our third **article**, in which we confess that there
A P : 0 4 :000(107) [0119] [**Article** IV. Justification]
A P : 0 4 :001(107) [0119] fourth, fifth, and sixth **articles**, and later in the twentieth,
A P : 0 4 :051(114) [0135] if we pay attention to the **article** of the Creed on the
A P : 0 4 :051(114) [0135] raised unless we add this **article**, the purpose of the
A P : 0 4 :051(114) [0135] be integrated with this **article**, namely, that for Christ's
A P : 0 4 :121(124) [0157] [Triglotta: **Article** III]
A P : 0 4 :294(152) [0203] From this fundamental **article** it is clear why we ascribe
A P : 0 7 :000(168) [0227] **Articles** VII and VIII. The Church
A P : 0 7 :001(168) [0227] condemned the seventh **article** of our Confession in which
A P : 0 7 :003(168) [0227] why we added the eighth **article**, to avoid the impression
A P : 0 7 :003(169) [0227] The eighth **article** exonerates us enough.
A P : 0 7 :023(172) [0235] He may establish **articles** of faith, abolish the Scriptures
A P : 0 7 :030(173) [0237] the part of the seventh **article** in which we said, "For the
A P : 0 7 :030(174) [0237] rites" they approve our **article**, but if we mean "universal
A P : 0 7 :032(174) [0239] for presenting this **article**, for it is clear that many foolish
A P : 0 7 :047(177) [0243] They have approved the entire eighth **article**.
A P : 0 9 :000(178) [0245] [**Article** IX. Baptism]
A P : 0 9 :001(178) [0245] They approve the ninth **article** where we confess that
A P : 1 0 :000(179) [0247] [**Article** X. The Holy Supper]
A P : 1 0 :001(179) [0247] They approve the tenth **article**, where we confess our
A P : 1 0 :004(179) [0247] does not disapprove this **article**), but to make clear to all
A P : 1 1 :000(180) [0247] [**Article** XI. Confession]
A P : 1 1 :001(180) [0247] approve the eleventh **article** on retaining absolution in the
A P : 1 2 :000(182) [0253] [**Article** XII. Penitence]
A P : 1 2 :001(182) [0253] In the twelfth **article** they approve the first part, where we
A P : 1 2 :077(193) [0275] this issue earlier, in the **article** on justification, where we
A P : 1 3 :000(211) [0309] [**Article** XIII.] The Number and Use of the Sacraments
A P : 1 3 :001(211) [0309] In **Article** XIII our opponents approve the statement that
A P : 1 4 :000(214) [0315] [**Article** XIV. Ecclesiastical Order]
A P : 1 4 :001(214) [0315] ordination, they accept **Article** XIV, where we say that no
A P : 1 5 :000(215) [0315] [**Article** XV.] Human Traditions in the Church
A P : 1 5 :001(215) [0315] In **Article** XV they accept the first part, where we say that
A P : 1 5 :002(215) [0315] traditions at length in **Article** XXVI of the Confession, we
A P : 1 5 :018(217) [0319] our statement in the **article** on the church that for the true
A P : 1 6 :000(222) [0329] [**Article** XVI. Political Order]
A P : 1 6 :001(222) [0329] Our opponents approve **Article** XVI without exception.
A P : 1 7 :000(224) [0335] [**Article** XVII. Christ's Return to Judgment]
A P : 1 7 :001(224) [0335] Our opponents accept **Article** XVII without exception.
A P : 1 8 :000(224) [0335] [**Article** XVIII. Free Will]
A P : 1 8 :001(224) [0335] Our opponents accept **Article** XVIII on free will, but they
A P : 1 8 :003(225) [0335] In the **article** on justification we quoted Augustine's
A P : 1 9 :000(226) [0337] [**Article** XIX. The Cause of Sin]
A P : 1 9 :001(226) [0337] Our opponents accept **Article** XIX.
A P : 2 0 :000(226) [0337] [**Article** XX. Good Works]
A P : 2 0 :001(226) [0337] In **Article** XX they expressly state their rejection and
A P : 2 0 :001(226) [0337] This **article** they explicitly reject and condemn.
A P : 2 0 :007(227) [0339] in the confession of the **article** that we receive the
A P : 2 0 :009(228) [0341] consolation which this **article** of ours offers to the
A P : 2 0 :012(228) [0341] have condemned our **article**, and it is worthwhile to
A P : 2 1 :000(229) [0343] [**Article** XXI. The Invocation of the Saints]
A P : 2 1 :001(229) [0343] They absolutely condemn **Article** XXI because we do not
A P : 2 2 :000(236) [0357] [**Article** XXII.] The Lord's Supper Under Both Kinds
A P : 2 3 :000(239) [0363] [**Article** XXIII. The Marriage of Priests]
A P : 2 4 :000(249) [0383] [**Article** XXIV.] The Mass
A P : 2 7 :000(268) [0419] [**Article** XXVII.] Monastic Vows
A P : 2 8 :000(281) [0443] [**Article** XXVIII.] Ecclesiastical Power
A P : 2 8 :001(281) [0443] is false that the present **article** states about the immunity
A P : 2 8 :002(281) [0443] sheer slander, for in this **article** we have been arguing
A P : 2 8 :006(282) [0445] In this **article** of the Confessions we included various
A P : 2 8 :009(282) [0445] they also condemned **Article** XV, in which we maintained
S 1 : 0 0 :027(287) [0453] The Smalcald **Articles**
S 1 : 0 0 :000(287) [0453] **Articles** of Christian doctrine which were to have been
S 1 : P R :001(288) [0455] to draft and assemble **articles** of our faith to serve as a
S 1 : P R :002(288) [0455] I assembled these **articles** and submitted them to our
S 1 : P R :002(288) [0455] and resolved that these **articles** should be presented
S 1 : P R :003(289) [0455] decided to publish these **articles** so that, if I should die
S 1 : P R :014(291) [0459] I have drafted only a few **articles**, for, apart from these,
S 1 : 0 1 :000(291) [0461] The first part of the **Articles** treats the sublime articles of
S 1 : 0 1 :000(291) [0461] Articles treats the sublime **articles** of the divine majesty,
S 1 : 0 1 :000(292) [0461] These **articles** are not matters of dispute or contention,
S 2 : 0 0 :000(292) [0461] second part treats the **articles** which pertain to the office
S 2 : 0 1 :000(292) [0461] [**Article** I. Christ and Faith]
S 2 : 0 1 :001(292) [0461] The first and chief **article** is this, that Jesus Christ, our
S 2 : 0 1 :005(292) [0461] Nothing in this **article** can be given up or compromised,
S 2 : 0 1 :005(292) [0463] On this **article** rests all that we teach and practice against
S 2 : 0 2 :000(293) [0463] **Article** II. [The Mass]
S 2 : 0 2 :001(293) [0463] direct and violent conflict with this fundamental **article**.
S 2 : 0 2 :001(293) [0463] or compromise in this **article** either, for the first article
S 2 : 0 2 :001(293) [0463] this article either, for the first **article** does not permit it.
S 2 : 0 2 :007(294) [0465] to the fundamental **article**, which asserts that it is not the
S 2 : 0 2 :010(294) [0465] This **article** concerning the Mass will be the decisive issue
S 2 : 0 2 :010(294) [0465] to us in all other **articles**, it would not be possible for them
S 2 : 0 2 :010(294) [0465] it would not be possible for them to yield on this **article**.
S 2 : 0 2 :012(295) [0465] to the fundamental **article** that Christ alone, and not the
S 2 : 0 2 :013(295) [0467] individuals and cannot establish an **article** of faith.
S 2 : 0 2 :015(295) [0467] It will not do to make **articles** of faith out of the holy
S 2 : 0 2 :015(295) [0467] would have to become **articles** of faith — as has happened
S 2 : 0 2 :015(295) [0467] of God shall establish **articles** of faith and no one else,
S 2 : 0 2 :017(295) [0467] accept all these things as **articles** of faith and had to live
S 2 : 0 2 :021(296) [0469] it is contrary to the first **article**, concerning redemption.
S 2 : 0 2 :024(296) [0469] also contrary to the first **article**, for the merits of Christ
S 2 : 0 2 :025(297) [0469] with the first, chief **article** and undermines knowledge of
S 2 : 0 3 :000(297) [0471] **Article** III. [Chapters and Monasteries]
S 2 : 0 3 :002(298) [0471] the first, fundamental **article** concerning redemption in
S 2 : 0 4 :000(298) [0471] **Article** IV. [The Papacy]
S 2 : 0 4 :003(298) [0473] the first, fundamental **article** which is concerned with
S 2 : 0 4 :015(301) [0475] In these four **articles** they will have enough to condemn in
S 2 : 0 4 :015(301) [0475] concede to us even the smallest fraction of these **articles**.
S 3 : 0 0 :000(302) [0477] The following **articles** treat matters which we may discuss
S 3 : 0 1 :003(302) [0477] taught concerning this **article** is therefore nothing but
S 3 : 1 4 :001(315) [0501] with the first chief **article**, they must be absolutely set
S 3 : 1 5 :003(316) [0501] These are the **articles** on which I must stand and on which
S 3 : 1 5 :004(316) [0501] silly and childish **articles**, such as the consecration of
S 3 : 1 5 :005(316) [0501] regard the above **articles** as right and Christian.
S 3 : 1 5 :005(317) [0501] is in Soest, subscribe the **articles** of the reverend father,
T R : 0 0 :004(320) [0503] These three **articles** we acknowledge and hold to be false,
T R : 0 0 :006(320) [0505] He wishes his **articles**, his decrees, and his laws to be
T R : 0 0 :006(320) [0505] laws to be regarded as **articles** of faith or commandments
T R : 0 0 :031(325) [0513] The second **article** is even clearer than the first because
T R : 0 0 :038(326) [0515] On the third **article** this must be added: Even if the bishop
T R : 0 0 :082(334) [0529] we have reread the **articles** of the Confession presented to
T R : 0 0 :082(334) [0529] in conformity with the **articles** of the Confession and
T R : 0 0 :082(334) [0529] that they approve the **article** concerning the primacy of
T R : 0 0 :082(334) [0529] Pomerania, subscribe the **articles** of the Augsburg
T R : 0 0 :082(334) [0529] the Apology, and the **article** concerning the papacy
T R : 0 0 :082(000) [0529] I have also read the **articles** written at the Assembly at
S C : 0 2 :001(344) [0543] The First **Article**: Creation
S C : 0 2 :003(345) [0545] The Second **Article**: Redemption
S C : 0 2 :005(345) [0545] The Third **Article**: Sanctification
L C : S P :010(363) [0577] II. The Chief **Articles** of Our Faith
L C : 0 2 :005(411) [0679] place, the Creed used to be divided into twelve **articles**.
L C : 0 2 :005(411) [0679] would be many more **articles**, nor could they all be clearly
L C : 0 2 :006(411) [0679] the entire Creed in three **articles**, according to the three
L C : 0 2 :006(411) [0679] The first **article**, of God the Father, explains creation; the
L C : 0 2 :007(411) [0679] three persons, and therefore three **articles** or confessions.
L C : 0 2 :008(411) [0679] The First **Article**
L C : 0 2 :010(412) [0679] This is taught here and in the following **articles**.
L C : 0 2 :012(412) [0681] however, all three **articles** can be treated more fully and
L C : 0 2 :012(412) [0681] as we have said, that this **article** deals with creation.
L C : 0 2 :016(412) [0681] Thus we learn from this **article** that none of us has his life
L C : 0 2 :018(412) [0681] other two parts of this **article**, where we say, "Father
L C : 0 2 :020(412) [0683] to describe in detail how few people believe this **article**.
L C : 0 2 :022(413) [0683] Therefore, this **article** would humble and terrify us all if
L C : 0 2 :023(413) [0683] ought daily to study this **article** and impress it upon our
L C : 0 2 :024(413) [0683] Such, very briefly, is the meaning of this **article**.
L C : 0 2 :024(413) [0683] The Second **Article**
L C : 0 2 :026(413) [0685] This **article** is very rich and far-reaching, but in order to
L C : 0 2 :026(413) [0685] the substance of the **article**; from it we shall learn how we
L C : 0 2 :027(414) [0685] you believe in the Second **Article**, concerning Jesus
L C : 0 2 :031(414) [0685] be the summary of this **article**, that the little word "Lord"
L C : 0 2 :031(414) [0685] remaining parts of this **article** simply serve to clarify and
L C : 0 2 :032(415) [0687] at length with such **articles** as the birth, passion,
L C : 0 2 :033(415) [0687] depends on the proper understanding of this **article**.
L C : 0 2 :033(415) [0687] The Third **Article**
L C : 0 2 :035(415) [0687] To this **article**, as I have said, I cannot give a better title
L C : 0 2 :040(416) [0689] Learn this **article**, then, as clearly as possible.
L C : 0 2 :046(416) [0689] Let this suffice concerning the substance of this **article**.
L C : 0 2 :059(418) [0695] us in it by means of the last two parts of this **article**.
L C : 0 2 :061(419) [0695] This, then, is the **article** which must always remain in
L C : 0 2 :064(419) [0695] In these three **articles** God himself has revealed and
L C : 0 2 :066(419) [0695] These **articles** of the Creed, therefore, divide and
L C : 0 3 :034(425) [0707] In seven successive **articles** or petitions are comprehended
L C : 0 4 :051(443) [0745] us or overthrow this **article**, "I believe one Holy Christian
L C : 0 5 :032(450) [0759] the whole Gospel and the **article** of the Creed, "I believe
E P : 0 0 :000(463) [0775] of a Number of **Articles** of the Augsburg Confession on
E P : 0 0 :000(464) [0777] Summary Epitome of the **Articles** in Controversy among
E P : R N :004(465) [0777] Apology thereof and the **Articles** drafted at Smalcald in
E P : R N :008(465) [0779] reference to controverted **articles**, and how contrary
E P : 0 1 :003(466) [0779] co-exist with the chief **articles** of our Christian faith,
E P : 0 2 :001(470) [0787] *Teaching concerning this **Article** on the Basis of God's*
E P : 0 3 :007(473) [0793] "justify" means in this **article** "absolve," that is, pronounce
E P : 0 3 :011(474) [0795] it do not belong in the **article** of justification before God.
E P : 0 4 :007(476) [0799] from a discussion of the **article** of man's salvation as well
E P : 0 4 :007(476) [0799] as well as from the **article** of our justification before God.
E P : 0 4 :018(477) [0801] against mingling good works in the **article** of justification.
E P : 0 7 :001(481) [0809] Doctrine and the Sacramentarian Doctrine in This **Article**
E P : 0 7 :011(483) [0811] "The first ground is this **article** of our Christian faith:
E P : 0 7 :042(486) [0817] Christ, as we do in other **articles** also, and accept this
E P : 0 8 :019(490) [0823] simple Christian Creed the following erroneous **articles**:
E P : 0 9 :000(492) [0827] Question at Issue in the Controversy about This **Article**
E P : 0 9 :001(492) [0827] of the Augsburg Confession concerning this **article** also.
E P : 0 9 :001(492) [0827] Does this **article** belong to Christ's suffering or to his
E P : 0 9 :002(492) [0827] This **article**, like the preceding one, cannot be
E P : 0 9 :002(492) [0827] concerning this **article**, but believe and teach it in all
E P : 0 9 :003(492) [0827] where he explains this **article** in a wholly Christian
E P : 1 0 :002(493) [0829] *Correct, True Doctrine and Confession about this **Article***
E P : 1 0 :007(493) [0831] in doctrine and in all its **articles** as well as in the right use
E P : 1 0 :007(494) [0831] *False Doctrine concerning this **Article***
E P : 1 1 :001(494) [0831] of the Augsburg Confession concerning this **article**.
E P : 1 1 :001(494) [0831] it is such a comforting **article** when it is correctly treated,
E P : 1 1 :001(494) [0831] *Pure and True Doctrine concerning this **Article***
E P : 1 1 :015(497) [0837] *False Doctrine concerning this **Article***
E P : 1 1 :022(497) [0837] of the various **articles** which for a time the theologians of
E P : 1 2 :001(498) [0839] merely to enumerate the **articles** in which they err and
E P : 1 2 :011(499) [0841] *Intolerable **Articles** in the Body Politic*
E P : 1 2 :030(500) [0843] All these and similar **articles**, together with their
E P : 1 2 :030(500) [0843] Apology, the Smalcald **Articles**, and the Catechisms of
S D : 0 0 :000(501) [0845] of a Number of **Articles** of the Augsburg Confession
S D : P R :001(501) [0847] concerning the chief **articles** of our Christian faith (which
S D : P R :003(502) [0847] concerning the chief **articles**, especially those which were
S D : P R :006(502) [0847] and significant **articles**, either because they failed to grasp
S D : P R :006(502) [0849] even dared to give a false interpretation to these **articles**.
S D : P R :010(503) [0849] that such controverted **articles** be explained on the basis
S D : R N :004(504) [0851] of God's Word in brief **articles** or chapters against the
S D : R N :005(504) [0851] is summarized in the **articles** and chapters of the
S D : R N :007(505) [0853] commit ourselves to the **Articles** which we prepared in the
S D : R N :007(505) [0853] In these **articles** the doctrine of the cited Augsburg
S D : R N :007(505) [0853] is repeated, several **articles** are further explained on the
S D : R N :010(506) [0855] and expositions of doctrinal **articles**, should be rejected.

Continued ▶

SD : RN :011(506) [0855] Apology, the Smalcald **Articles**, and Luther's Large and
SD : RN :013(506) [0855] in the controverted **articles** from these writings, for just as
SD : RN :013(506) [0855] Antitheses in the Controverted **Articles**
SD : RN :015(507) [0857] (dissension concerning **articles** of the Creed or the chief
SD : RN :016(507) [0857] each of the controverted **articles** of our Christian faith,
SD : RN :016(507) [0857] and most significant **articles** which were in controversy at
SD : RN :019(507) [0857] made apparent in every **article** and that every incorrect,
SD : 0 1 :007(510) [0861] established truth, as **Article** XIX of the Augsburg
SD : 0 1 :008(510) [0861] As the Smalcald **Articles** point out, it is something that
SD : 0 1 :024(512) [0865] which are subject to human reason in the next **article**.
SD : 0 1 :034(514) [0869] The chief **articles** of our Christian faith constrain and
SD : 0 1 :034(514) [0869] In the first place, in the **article** of creation Scripture
SD : 0 1 :038(514) [0871] exposition of the First **Article** of the Creed in the Small
SD : 0 1 :040(515) [0871] This **article** shows the difference irrefutably and clearly,
SD : 0 1 :041(515) [0871] are contrary to the first **article** of our Christian faith.
SD : 0 1 :043(515) [0873] Secondly, in the **article** of our redemption we have the
SD : 0 1 :045(516) [0873] Thirdly, in the **article** of sanctification we have the
SD : 0 1 :047(516) [0873] follow, contrary to this **article** of our Christian faith,
SD : 0 1 :048(517) [0875] The chief **articles** of our Christian faith show powerfully
SD : 0 1 :050(517) [0875] above-mentioned books use them in treating this **article**.
SD : 0 1 :052(517) [0875] of our nature as it is described in the Smalcald **Articles**.
SD : 0 2 :008(521) [0883] questions and issues stated at the beginning of this **article**.
SD : 0 2 :008(521) [0883] God that judgments on **articles** of faith are to be
SD : 0 2 :018(524) [0887] at greater length in the **article** on original sin (to which
SD : 0 2 :029(527) [0893] **Article** XX of the Augsburg Confession declares: "People
SD : 0 2 :029(527) [0893] And shortly afterward the **article** states that "human
SD : 0 2 :033(527) [0893] The Smalcald **Articles** reject the following errors
SD : 0 2 :034(527) [0893] The Smalcald **Articles** state further: "This repentance
SD : 0 2 :045(530) [0899] Apology, the Smalcald **Articles**, the Large and Small
SD : 0 2 :086(538) [0913] in his conversion, contrary to the **article** of God's grace.
SD : 0 3 :005(540) [0917] concerning this **article** of justification were occasioned
SD : 0 3 :006(540) [0917] of the Apology, this **article** of justification by faith is "the
SD : 0 3 :006(540) [0917] by faith is "the chief **article** of the entire Christian
SD : 0 3 :006(540) [0917] "Where this single **article** remains pure, Christendom will
SD : 0 3 :007(540) [0917] important it is that this **article**, side by side with the true
SD : 0 3 :024(543) [0923] Here, too, if the **article** of justification is to remain pure,
SD : 0 3 :024(543) [0923] or follows faith into the **article** of justification, as if it
SD : 0 3 :024(543) [0923] or component part of this **article**, since we cannot talk in
SD : 0 3 :027(543) [0925] works belong in the **article** or matter of justification by
SD : 0 3 :028(544) [0925] it does not belong to the **article** or matter of justification
SD : 0 3 :029(544) [0925] matter which does not belong in this **article** at all.
SD : 0 3 :029(544) [0925] we have to do with this **article** of justification, we reject
SD : 0 3 :029(544) [0925] the very nature of this **article** cannot admit any treatment
SD : 0 3 :032(545) [0927] simultaneously into the **article** of justification by faith
SD : 0 3 :035(545) [0927] or mingled into the **article** of justification before God, in
SD : 0 3 :036(545) [0927] intention when in this **article** he so earnestly and
SD : 0 3 :036(545) [0927] exclude works from the **article** of justification by faith) as
SD : 0 3 :036(545) [0927] are excluded from the **article** of justification so that in the
SD : 0 3 :036(545) [0929] the exclusive terms in the **article** of justification (that is,
SD : 0 3 :036(545) [0929] is, of the terms in the **article** of justification listed above)
SD : 0 3 :036(546) [0929] diligence and seriousness in the treatment of this **article**:
SD : 0 3 :037(546) [0929] completely from the **article** of justification all our own
SD : 0 3 :037(546) [0929] into consideration in this **article** or matter, or rely on
SD : 0 3 :039(546) [0929] to be mingled with the **article** of justification as pertinent
SD : 0 3 :043(547) [0931] works is necessary in the **article** of justification, or for our
SD : 0 3 :043(547) [0931] do not exclude works from the **article** of justification.
SD : 0 3 :053(548) [0933] as emphatically in the **article** of salvation as he does in
SD : 0 3 :053(548) [0933] of salvation as he does in the **article** of justification.
SD : 0 3 :067(551) [0937] this high and important **article** of justification before
SD : 0 4 :002(551) [0939] formerly, to oppose that **article** of our Christian faith in
SD : 0 4 :007(552) [0939] First of all, there is in this **article** no disagreement among
SD : 0 4 :022(554) [0945] and mingled with the **article** of justification and
SD : 0 4 :022(554) [0945] of exclusive terms in the **articles** of justification and
SD : 0 4 :022(554) [0945] merit completely from the **article** of justification and
SD : 0 4 :022(555) [0945] merit of Christ, as was explained in the preceding **article**).
SD : 0 4 :024(555) [0945] 4:6), or the statement in **Article** VI of the Augsburg
SD : 0 4 :029(555) [0947] and counterfeiting of the **article** of justification, were
SD : 0 4 :033(556) [0947] the Apology states in **Article** XX: "Peter teaches why we
SD : 0 4 :037(557) [0949] good works into the **article** of justification and rests his
SD : 0 5 :014(560) [0957] same vein, the Smalcald **Articles** state: "The New
SD : 0 7 :001(568) [0971] an explanation of this **article** should not be included in
SD : 0 7 :001(568) [0971] to deal only with those **articles** that were in controversy
SD : 0 7 :001(569) [0971] with the teaching of the Sacramentarians in this **article**.
SD : 0 7 :001(569) [0971] of Christ and of the Augsburg Confession in this **article**.
SD : 0 7 :001(569) [0971] Doctrine and That of the Sacramentarians in This **Article**
SD : 0 7 :011(571) [0975] from Cyril as follows: "**Article** X has been accepted, in
SD : 0 7 :012(571) [0977] concerning this **article** adopted the confession of our
SD : 0 7 :012(571) [0977] drafted the following **articles** of Christian agreement in
SD : 0 7 :017(572) [0979] drafted the Smalcald **Articles**, which all the theologians
SD : 0 7 :018(572) [0979] the aforementioned **articles** of agreement, adopted in the
SD : 0 7 :019(572) [0979] The Smalcald **Articles** state that "the bread and the wine
SD : 0 7 :028(574) [0981] and other Christian **articles**, he appended the following
SD : 0 7 :029(574) [0981] and hold this or that **article** differently, for he did not
SD : 0 7 :030(574) [0981] diligently traced all these **articles** through the Scriptures,
SD : 0 7 :032(574) [0983] listed among other **articles** the following: "In the same
SD : 0 7 :033(575) [0983] repeated his faith in this **article** with great fervor and
SD : 0 7 :034(575) [0983] meaning and intention in this **article** have always been.
SD : 0 7 :038(576) [0985] in the above-mentioned **articles** of agreement of 1536 and
SD : 0 7 :041(576) [0985] was comprehended in the **articles** of the aforementioned
SD : 0 7 :046(577) [0987] but also to the eminent **article** of faith concerning the
SD : 0 7 :050(578) [0989] just as he does in all the **articles** of faith and in the
SD : 0 7 :094(586) [1005] "1. The first is this **article** of our faith: that Jesus Christ is
SD : 0 7 :106(588) [1009] Thus our faith in this **article** concerning the true presence
SD : 0 7 :106(588) [1009] and fortify our faith in all tensions concerning this **article**.
SD : 0 7 :110(589) [1011] Apology, the Smalcald **Articles**, and other writings of
SD : 0 8 :033(597) [1027] Next to the **article** of the holy Trinity, the greatest
SD : 0 8 :059(602) [1035] church concerning this **article** are recorded elsewhere.
SD : 0 8 :086(608) [1047] in connection with this **article**, as well as of his covenant
SD : 0 8 :086(608) [1047] the Holy Supper in connection with the previous **article**.
SD : 0 9 :001(610) [1049] explanations of the **article** on Christ's descent into hell
SD : 0 9 :001(610) [1051] differentiated as distinct **articles**, and we simply believe
SD : 0 9 :003(610) [1051] and five senses this **article** cannot be comprehended any
SD : 0 9 :003(610) [1053] retain the heart of this **article** and derive from it the
SD : 1 0 :014(613) [1057] primarily with the chief **article** of our Christian faith, so
SD : 1 0 :014(613) [1057] darkens and perverts this **article** because the adversaries
SD : 1 0 :015(613) [1057] time this concerns the **article** of Christian liberty as well,
SD : 1 0 :015(613) [1057] liberty as well, an **article** which the Holy Spirit through
SD : 1 0 :015(613) [1057] As soon as this **article** is weakened and human
SD : 1 0 :018(614) [1059] drawn from the Smalcald **Articles**, which were drafted and
SD : 1 0 :019(614) [1059] The Smalcald **Articles** of 1537 declare on this: "We do not
SD : 1 0 :019(614) [1059] before this the Smalcald **Articles** declare: "If the bishops
SD : 1 0 :020(614) [1059] Under the **article** on the primacy or lordship of the pope,
SD : 1 0 :020(614) [1059] the pope, the Smalcald **Articles** state: "Just as we cannot
SD : 1 0 :021(614) [1059] to the Smalcald **Articles** and which all the theologians
SD : 1 0 :031(616) [1063] in doctrine and in all its **articles** and are also agreed
SD : 1 1 :001(616) [1063] Nevertheless, this **article** has become the occasion of very
SD : 1 1 :001(616) [1063] and schism in this **article** among our posterity, we have
SD : 1 1 :001(616) [1063] our explanation of this **article** in this document so that
SD : 1 1 :001(616) [1063] know what we teach, believe, and confess in this **article**.
SD : 1 1 :002(616) [1063] If the teaching of this **article** is set forth out of the divine
SD : 1 1 :002(616) [1063] Scriptures mention this **article** not only once, and as it
SD : 1 1 :003(616) [1063] of the teaching on this **article** consists of the following
SD : 1 1 :014(619) [1069] treats and explains this **article** (Rom. 8:28ff.; Eph. 1:4ff.)
SD : 1 1 :024(620) [1071] our thinking about this **article** in this light, we can by the
SD : 1 1 :038(622) [1075] Confession states in **Article** XI, we retain individual
SD : 1 1 :038(622) [1075] a voice from heaven," as the Apology explains this **article**.
SD : 1 1 :043(623) [1077] mightily substantiates the **article** that we are justified and
SD : 1 1 :050(624) [1079] This **article** also gives a glorious testimony that the church
SD : 1 1 :051(624) [1079] This **article** also contains mighty admonitions and
SD : 1 1 :051(625) [1079] use the teaching in this **article** in a profitable, comforting,
SD : 1 1 :062(626) [1083] If we go thus far in this **article** we will remain on the right
SD : 1 1 :064(626) [1083] not try to explore and explain everything in this **article**.
SD : 1 1 :064(626) [1083] lengthy discussion of this **article** on the basis of the
SD : 1 1 :094(632) [1095] the controverted **articles** which have been disputed among
SD : 1 2 :003(633) [1095] agreed in each and every **article** of the Augsburg
SD : 1 2 :004(633) [1097] exposition of all the **articles** which were in controversy
SD : 1 2 :008(633) [1097] Erroneous **Articles** of the Anabaptists
SD : 1 2 :027(635) [1101] They hold other similar **articles**.
SD : 1 2 :027(635) [1101] Erroneous **Articles** of the Schwenkfelders
SD : 1 2 :035(635) [1101] Erroneous **Articles** of the New Arians
SD : 1 2 :036(636) [1101] Erroneous **Articles** of the New Anti-Trinitarians
SD : 1 2 :039(636) [1103] All these and similar **articles**, and whatever attaches to
SD : 1 2 :039(636) [1103] Apology, to the Smalcald **Articles**, to Luther's
SD : 1 2 :040(636) [1103] foregoing controverted **articles** here explained, and none

Artificial (3)

AP : 2 7 :040(276) [0433] here, too, it claims perfection for **artificial** religious acts.
S 3 : 0 3 :002(304) [0479] is not *activa contritio* (**artificial** remorse), but *passiva*
S 3 : 0 3 :018(306) [0483] such contrition is an **artificial** and imaginary idea evolved

Asam (1)

AP : 2 4 :023(253) [0391] The word he uses here (***'asam***) means a victim sacrificed

Ascend (3), Ascendancy (1), Ascended (12), Ascends (2), Ascension (9)

PR : PR :020(010) [0017] of God's Son, his **ascension**, and his session at the right
AG : 0 3 :004(030) [0045] dead on the third day, **ascended** into heaven, and sits on
AL : 0 3 :004(030) [0045] Afterward he **ascended** into heaven to sit on the right
S 1 : PR :012(290) [0459] these have gained the **ascendancy** to such an extent that
S 1 : 0 1 :000(292) [0461] rose from the dead, and **ascended** to heaven; and he is
TR : 0 0 :067(331) [0523] when he says, "When he **ascended** on high he gave gifts to
SC : 0 2 :003(345) [0545] *rose from the dead, he **ascended** into heaven, and is*
LC : SP :012(363) [0577] rose from the dead, he **ascended** into heaven, and sits on
LC : 0 2 :025(413) [0683] *rose from the dead, he **ascended** into heaven, and is*
LC : 0 2 :031(414) [0687] death, and finally **ascended** into heaven and assumed
LC : 0 2 :032(415) [0687] the birth, passion, resurrection, and **ascension** of Christ.
EP : 0 7 :005(482) [0809] above, whither we should **ascend** with the thoughts of our
EP : 0 7 :029(485) [0815] us that when our faith **ascends** into heaven, it there
EP : 0 8 :008(487) [0819] to suffer, to die, to **ascend** and to descend, to move from
EP : 0 8 :013(488) [0821] hell, rose from the dead, **ascended** into heaven, and was
EP : 0 8 :016(489) [0821] as St. Paul states, He **ascended** "far above all the heavens
EP : 0 8 :039(491) [0827] the resurrection and his **ascension** all power in heaven and
SD : 0 7 :003(569) [0973] Word, lifts itself up and **ascends** above all heavens and
SD : 0 7 :009(571) [0975] the body of Christ has **ascended** into heaven it is not truly
SD : 0 7 :052(578) [0991] after Christ's **ascension** (I Cor. 11:25), unanimously and
SD : 0 7 :091(585) [1003] body, concerning the **ascension** of Christ, concerning his
SD : 0 7 :119(590) [1013] because of his bodily **ascension** to heaven Christ is so
SD : 0 8 :010(593) [1019] to suffer and die, to **ascend** and descend, to move from
SD : 0 8 :013(593) [1019] from the dead and his **ascension**, but when he was
SD : 0 8 :025(596) [1023] his resurrection, and **ascension** but also in the state of his
SD : 0 8 :027(596) [1025] But now since he **ascended** into heaven, not just like some
SD : 0 8 :085(608) [1047] my resurrection and **ascension**, when it was to have been

Ascertain (1), Ascertaining (1)

AG : 2 7 :027(075) [0079] be kept without first **ascertaining** whether a vow is of the
LC : SP :004(362) [0575] at least once a week and **ascertain** what they have learned

Ascribe (24), Ascribed (14), Ascribes (7), Ascribing (1)

PR : PR :021(011) [0019] divine majesty is not **ascribed** to the human nature of
AL : 2 7 :043(077) [0081] grace, for those who **ascribe** justification to their vows
AL : 2 7 :043(077) [0081] to their vows **ascribe** to their own works what properly
AP : 0 4 :017(109) [0125] however, what they **ascribe** to this disposition, for they
AP : 0 4 :104(122) [0151] to works and **ascribes** it to faith, which liberates us
AP : 0 4 :154(128) [0163] Nothing greater could she **ascribe** to him.
AP : 0 4 :188(133) [0173] see what the Scriptures **ascribe** to the law and what they
AP : 0 4 :188(133) [0173] ascribe to the law and what they **ascribe** to the promises.
AP : 0 4 :231(139) [0183] suppose that Paul would **ascribe** either justification or
AP : 0 4 :294(152) [0203] article it is clear why we **ascribe** justification to faith
AP : 0 4 :298(153) [0205] justification must necessarily be **ascribed** to faith.
AP : 0 4 :304(154) [0205] will and thus cannot be **ascribed** to faith, which is in the
AP : 0 4 :398(168) [0227] how can they **ascribe** any knowledge of Christ to those
AP : 1 2 :144(205) [0297] supererogation, and they **ascribe** to them the honor of
AP : 1 8 :007(225) [0337] of the law, we do not **ascribe** to it the spiritual capacity
AP : 2 7 :039(276) [0433] They are **ascribing** perfection to human traditions if they
TR : 0 0 :024(324) [0511] these passages do not **ascribe** to Peter any special
EP : 0 2 :006(470) [0787] all power to free will and **ascribes** everything to the grace
EP : 0 7 :008(482) [0811] Supper, but it is to be **ascribed** solely and alone to the

Continued ▶

SD : 02 :025(526) [0891] place, Holy Scriptures **ascribe** conversion, faith in Christ,
SD : 02 :032(527) [0893] the Apology does not **ascribe** to man's will any ability
SD : 02 :035(528) [0895] On the contrary, they **ascribe** everything to the gift of the
SD : 02 :038(528) [0895] of our contribution, but **ascribes** everything to the Holy
SD : 02 :039(528) [0895] 2:13), just as the apostle **ascribes** this work alone to God
SD : 02 :062(533) [0905] Nevertheless, one cannot **ascribe** to man prior to his
SD : 02 :087(538) [0915] of the flesh is to be **ascribed** to God alone, as was
SD : 03 :043(547) [0931] the power to justify is **ascribed** to faith; or, the presence
SD : 04 :022(555) [0945] and salvation and **ascribe** everything solely to the grace
SD : 04 :024(555) [0945] Scripture passage which **ascribes** the bliss of salvation
SD : 04 :034(556) [0949] very certain to us, Paul **ascribes** to faith not only our
SD : 05 :027(563) [0961] to one doctrine is **ascribed** to the other, it is necessary to
SD : 07 :074(583) [0999] This is to be **ascribed** only to the almighty power of God
SD : 07 :090(585) [1003] of this common rule **ascribe** to our faith the power to
SD : 07 :090(585) [1003] to receive it, rather than **ascribe** it to the omnipotence of
SD : 07 :105(588) [1009] the Sacramentarians **ascribe** to and force upon our
SD : 07 :121(590) [1013] consecration which **ascribes** to the word and work of the
SD : 08 :036(598) [1027] to one of the natures, is **ascribed** not only to the
SD : 08 :037(598) [1027] follow that whatever is **ascribed** to the person is
SD : 08 :037(598) [1027] the property in question is being **ascribed** to the person.
SD : 08 :038(598) [1027] which says we are *to **ascribe** to the entire person what is*
SD : 08 :041(599) [1029] in Christ, the Scriptures **ascribe** to the deity, because of
SD : 08 :043(599) [1029] and suffering are not **ascribed** to the natures but to the
SD : 08 :050(600) [1031] should or can be **ascribed** to the human nature in Christ
SD : 08 :054(601) [1033] the basis of Scriptures, **ascribe** to the assumed human
SD : 08 :067(604) [1039] the Son of God, is to be **ascribed** in the person of the Son
SD : 08 :077(606) [1043] The Scriptures **ascribe** such presence only to Christ, and

Ashamed (9)
AG : 27 :045(078) [0081] themselves are now **ashamed** of and wish had never
AL : 27 :045(078) [0081] be collected of which even the monks are now **ashamed**!
AP : 04 :230(139) [0183] But we are not **ashamed** of the foolishness of the Gospel.
S3 : 03 :019(306) [0485] the more he was **ashamed**, and the more he abased
LC : PR :005(359) [0567] book into a corner as if they are **ashamed** to read it again.
LC : PR :016(361) [0573] God himself is not **ashamed** to teach it daily, for he
LC : 01 :287(403) [0663] members, of which we are **ashamed**, we carefully conceal.
SD : 07 :067(582) [0997] Satan himself would be **ashamed**," just as they describe
SD : 07 :067(582) [0997] a pious Christian should be **ashamed** to translate them.

Ashes (1)
S2 : 02 :010(294) [0465] myself to be burned to **ashes** before I would allow a

Ashore (1)
LC : 04 :081(446) [0751] on which we must swim **ashore** after the ship founders" in

Asia (1)
AP : 24 :008(250) [0385] Epiphanius writes that in **Asia** Minor there were no daily

Aside (25)
AG : PR :003(025) [0039] one Christian truth, to put **aside** whatever may not have
AG : PR :023(027) [0043] we shall not be turned **aside** from our position by these or
AL : 26 :005(064) [0071] on this article and puts **aside** the law and human
AP : 04 :014(109) [0123] who, in their sermons, laid **aside** the Gospel and
S2 : 02 :019(296) [0467] of people may turn **aside** from Christ to their own merits
S3 : 03 :033(308) [0489] All have turned **aside**, together they have gone wrong."
S3 : 03 :043(310) [0491] that when holy people, **aside** from the fact that they still
S3 : 14 :001(315) [0501] the first chief article, they must be absolutely set **aside**.
LC : 01 :047(371) [0593] eventually to lay them **aside**) or as a traveler avails
LC : 01 :112(380) [0613] despised and brushed **aside**, and no one recognizes it as
LC : 04 :063(444) [0749] ourselves to be turned **aside** from the Word, regarding
EP : 08 :016(489) [0821] his resurrection he laid **aside** completely the form of a
EP : 08 :033(491) [0825] nature, after he laid **aside** the form of a slave, does not
EP : 08 :039(491) [0827] humiliation he had laid it **aside** and forsaken it even
SD : 02 :010(522) [0885] All have turned **aside**, together they have gone wrong; no
SD : 02 :081(537) [0911] of man must be laid **aside**, he himself explains what it
SD : 02 :081(537) [0913] by adding, 'Therefore lay **aside** lies and speak the truth.'
SD : 07 :015(572) [0977] as when the bread is laid **aside** or reserved in the
SD : 08 :008(593) [1017] eternity does not lay them **aside**, nor do the essential
SD : 08 :026(596) [1023] precisely that he has laid **aside** completely and entirely the
SD : 08 :026(596) [1023] (without, however, laying **aside** the human nature, which
SD : 08 :026(596) [1025] apostle testifies, he laid it **aside**, and as Dr. Luther
SD : 08 :051(600) [1033] the servant had been laid **aside** and after the humiliation)
SD : 08 :062(603) [1037] Christ has completely laid **aside** its natural and essential
SD : 08 :065(604) [1039] of a slave has been laid **aside**, it takes place fully,

Ask (58), Asked (17), Asking (4), Asks (9)
AG : 27 :049(079) [0083] that we may and should **ask** and pray God for those
AG : 28 :071(093) [0093] Our churches do not **ask** that the bishops should restore
AG : 28 :072(093) [0093] the case of need), but they **ask** only that the bishops relax
AL : 24 :007(056) [0065] to believe in God and **ask** for and expect whatever is good
AL : 24 :034(060) [0067] sacrament, it is also administered to those who **ask** for it.
AL : 27 :049(079) [0083] we have a gracious God, to **ask** of God, and assuredly to
AL : 28 :071(093) [0093] Our churches do not **ask** that the bishops restore concord
AL : 28 :072(093) [0093] pastors ought to do), but **ask** only that they relax unjust
AL : 28 :077(094) [0095] power to govern, but we **ask** for this one thing, that they
AP : 02 :002(100) [0105] point is not absurd, we **ask** them first to look at the
AP : 02 :007(101) [0107] in their awkward way they **ask** whether it came through
AP : 02 :028(104) [0113] "When the question is **asked** what original sin is, it is
AP : 04 :002(107) [0121] We therefore **ask** His Imperial Majesty kindly to hear us
AP : 04 :147(127) [0163] But someone may **ask**: Since we also grant that love is the
AP : 04 :230(139) [0183] glory we defend it and we **ask** Christ for the help of his
AP : 04 :236(140) [0185] laws in blood and are **asking** the emperor, this most
AP : 04 :279(149) [0199] "Bless God always, and **ask** him to direct your ways"
AP : 04 :332(158) [0211] if indeed these profane men ever **ask** God for anything!
AP : 04 :332(158) [0211] love and good works, and **ask** for grace as though they
AP : 04 :333(158) [0211] says (John 16:23), "If you **ask** anything of the Father, he
AP : 04 :385(166) [0225] the prayers of the church **ask** that everything be accepted
AP : 12 :008(183) [0255] If someone should **ask** this, the answer must be in
AP : 12 :061(190) [0269] First, we **ask** our opponents whether the reception of
AP : 12 :079(194) [0275] He **asks** us to look at this promise, which would certainly
AP : 12 :088(195) [0277] Chrysostom **asks** in connection with penitence, "How do
AP : 12 :088(195) [0277] In the *Sentences* our opponents **ask** the same question.
AP : 12 :159(207) [0301] When the disciples **asked** who had sinned in the case of
AP : 21 :002(229) [0343] Cyprian **asked** Cornelius, while he was still alive, to pray
AP : 21 :010(230) [0345] does not teach us to invoke the saints or to **ask** their help.
AP : 21 :017(231) [0347] (John 16:23), "If you **ask** anything of the Father, he will
AP : 21 :035(234) [0353] of her tortures, Barbara **asks** for a reward — that no one
AP : 21 :041(235) [0355] heard excellent theologians **ask** for limitations upon
AP : 21 :042(235) [0355] at this point, they would **ask** that our most gracious
AP : 22 :010(237) [0359] they were supposed to **ask** for the one part that belonged
AP : 22 :011(238) [0361] They should not **ask** for a reason; but whatever the
AP : 23 :003(239) [0363] They **ask** you to defend these libidos of theirs with your
AP : 24 :075(263) [0411] Do you **ask** who he is?
AP : 27 :038(275) [0433] that when Anthony **asked** God to show him what
AP : 28 :013(283) [0447] absolve them if they are converted and **ask** for absolution.
S1 : PR :010(290) [0457] true works, that we do not **ask** for a council for our own
S2 : 02 :013(295) [0467] mentions that his mother **asked** that she be remembered
S3 : 03 :017(305) [0483] like), such a person was **asked** if he did not wish or desire
TR : 00 :023(324) [0511] question Peter alone but **asked**, "Who do you say that I
TR : 00 :082(000) [0529] the end of the assembly, I **ask** you, most renowned man,
LC : 01 :041(370) [0591] What more could you **ask** or desire than God's gracious
LC : 01 :051(371) [0595] If you are **asked**, "How do you understand the Second
LC : 01 :087(376) [0605] when you are **asked** what "You shall sanctify the holy
LC : 01 :097(378) [0609] of the Gospel; no one **asked** about God's Word, and no
LC : 01 :114(380) [0613] we have devised without ever **asking** God's approval.
LC : 01 :323(409) [0675] his sake does all that he **asks** of us, because he shows
LC : 01 :327(409) [0675] Rather, **ask** what God wants of you and what he will
LC : 02 :010(411) [0679] than one God, it may be **asked**: "What kind of being is
LC : 02 :011(412) [0681] If you were to **ask** a young child, "My boy, what kind of
LC : 02 :027(414) [0685] If you are **asked**, "What do you believe in the Second
LC : 02 :040(416) [0689] If you are **asked**, What do you mean by the words, "I
LC : 03 :019(423) [0703] Christ says in Matt. 7:7, 8, "**Ask** and it will be given you,"
LC : 03 :019(423) [0703] "For every one who **asks** receives."
LC : 03 :024(423) [0705] a petition, naming and **asking** for something which he
LC : 03 :025(423) [0705] night; not one of them thinks of **asking** for the least thing.
LC : 03 :049(426) [0711] Here we **ask** that his kingdom may come.
LC : 03 :050(426) [0711] That is, we **ask** that it may prevail among us and with us,
LC : 03 :052(427) [0711] This we **ask**, both in order that we who have accepted it
LC : 03 :055(427) [0713] desire if God himself had not commanded us to **ask** for it.
LC : 03 :056(427) [0713] more ardently than that we **ask** many and great things of
LC : 03 :056(427) [0713] he is angered if we do not **ask** and demand confidently.
LC : 03 :057(427) [0713] who bade a poor beggar to **ask** for whatever he might
LC : 03 :057(427) [0713] gifts, and the fool **asked** only for a dish of beggar's broth.
LC : 03 :057(428) [0713] them and scarcely venture to **ask** for a morsel of bread.
LC : 03 :068(429) [0717] only ourselves when we **ask** that what otherwise must be
LC : 03 :076(431) [0721] For example, we might **ask** God to give us food and
LC : 03 :077(431) [0721] Again, to **ask** God to endow the emperor, kings, and all
LC : 03 :123(436) [0731] "If anyone prays, let him **ask** in faith, with no doubting,
LC : 05 :075(455) [0771] hands to their bosom and **ask** whether they are made of
LC : 05 :079(455) [0771] If you do not know, **ask** your neighbors about it.
SD : 01 :057(518) [0877] thereto), if anyone were to **ask** if original sin is a
SD : 02 :015(523) [0885] indicate that what they **ask** of God they cannot obtain by
SD : 02 :015(523) [0887] for example, David **asks** God more than ten times to
SD : 02 :071(535) [0909] But since the question is **asked** concerning the efficient
SD : 03 :042(547) [0931] however, the question is **asked**, how a Christian can
SD : 03 :043(547) [0931] But when we **ask** where faith gets the power to justify and
SD : 04 :011(553) [0941] Likewise, faith does not **ask** if good works are to be
SD : 04 :011(553) [0941] done, but before one can **ask**, faith has already done them
SD : 07 :022(573) [0979] come along and **ask**, How can bread and wine be the
SD : 07 :046(577) [0987] He could have **asked** if this command was to be
SD : 11 :047(624) [1079] For this reason, too, Paul **asks**, Since we are called
SD : 11 :072(628) [1087] among you, if his son **asks** for a fish, will instead of a fish
SD : 11 :072(628) [1087] give him a serpent; or if he **asks** for an egg, will give him a
SD : 11 :072(628) [1087] the Holy Spirit to those who **ask** him?" (Luke 11:11-13).

Aspect (3), Aspects (2)
PR : PR :013(007) [0013] zeal, consider it in all its **aspects**, have their opinions and
AP : 12 :142(204) [0295] 6:5) and condemns every **aspect** of lust in human nature.
LC : 01 :261(400) [0655] This is one **aspect** of the commandment, and its plainest
LC : 01 :263(400) [0655] The third **aspect** of this commandment concerns us all.
SD : 11 :053(625) [1081] do so — than with those **aspects** of the question which

Ass (1), Asses (4)
AP : 12 :123(201) [0289] Who ever taught these **asses** such logic?
AP : 21 :002(229) [0343] These **asses** do not see that in the controversy between
AP : 28 :019(284) [0449] Thus these **asses** take a statement that supports our
SC : 01 :019(344) [0543] *or his ox, or his **ass**, or anything that is your neighbor's."*
LC : 01 :170(388) [0629] to work like cows or **asses**, and gave us subjects to treat

Assail (1), Assails (2)
PR : PR :020(010) [0017] But when the adversaries **assail** this our ingenuous faith
AP : 12 :146(205) [0297] When death **assails** us, we must set something else against
LC : 03 :103(434) [0727] comes the world, which **assails** us by word and deed and

Assaults (3)
LC : PR :014(360) [0571] the constant and furious attacks and **assaults** of the devil.
LC : 03 :061(428) [0715] amount of attacks and **assaults** from all who venture to
LC : 05 :071(455) [0769] fear of death, and the **assaults** of the flesh and the devil.

Assemble (12), Assembled (15), Assembles (1), Assemblies (2), Assembly (30)
PR : PR :007(004) [0009] 1558) that we should **assemble** in a general convention
PR : PR :008(005) [0009] V in the great imperial **assembly** at Augsburg in the year
PR : PR :018(008) [0015] V at the great imperial **assembly** in Augsburg in the year
AG : PR :018(026) [0041] of the estates) who were **assembled** at the diet convened in
AG : 07 :001(032) [0047] This is the **assembly** of all believers among who the
AG : 08 :001(033) [0047] is nothing else than the **assembly** of all believers and
AG : 22 :003(050) [0059] that the whole **assembly** of the congregation in Corinth
AG : 24 :041(061) [0069] day that the people **assembled**, for according to the
AG : 27 :045(078) [0081] many items could be **assembled** which the monks
AG : 28 :054(090) [0091] that women should cover their heads in the **assembly**.
AG : 28 :054(090) [0091] also directed that in the **assembly** preachers should not
AG : 28 :055(090) [0091] proper for the Christian **assembly** to keep such
AG : 28 :060(091) [0091] when they ought to **assemble**, the Christian church
AL : 07 :001(032) [0047] The church is the **assembly** of saints in which the Gospel
AL : 08 :001(033) [0047] the church is the **assembly** of saints and true believers.
AL : 28 :054(090) [0091] cover their heads in the **assembly** and that interpreters in

Continued ▶

A L : 2 8 :060(091) [0091] when they ought to **assemble**, it appears that the church
A P : P R :001(098) [0099] had this read before the **assembly** of the princes, and he
A P : P R :015(099) [0101] Rather I have **assembled** the main arguments, to testify to
A P : 0 4 :171(130) [0171] But later we shall **assemble** more testimonies on this
A P : 0 4 :399(168) [0227] We have heard in this **assembly** that when opinions were
A P : 0 4 :399(168) [0227] as unworthy of being spoken in such an **assembly**.
A P : 0 7 :001(168) [0227] in which we said the church is the **assembly** of saints.
A P : 0 7 :008(169) [0229] means, namely, the **assembly** of saints who share the
A P : 0 7 :028(173) [0237] the proper sense is the **assembly** of saints who truly
A P : 0 7 :037(175) [0241] Scriptures and we have **assembled** much of it in the latter
A P : 0 7 :040(176) [0241] justification but to let the people know when to **assemble**.
A P : 0 7 :040(176) [0241] When they **assembled**, they also observed other rites and
A P : 1 2 :133(202) [0293] arguments could be **assembled** to prove that these
A P : 1 4 :001(214) [0315] testimony in the **assembly** to our deep desire to maintain
A P : 1 5 :020(218) [0321] the people a set time to **assemble**, because they provided
A P : 1 5 :052(222) [0329] In this very **assembly** we have shown ample evidence of
A P : 2 4 :008(250) [0385] He says, "**Assemblies** for Communion were appointed by
A P : 2 7 :069(280) [0443] We have **assembled** all this not only for the sake of our
S 1 : P R :001(288) [0455] instructed to draft and **assemble** articles of our faith to
S 1 : P R :002(288) [0455] Accordingly I **assembled** these articles and submitted them
S 1 : P R :010(290) [0457] to see a true council **assemble** in order that many things
S 1 : P R :015(291) [0459] Dear Lord Jesus Christ, **assemble** a council of thine own,
T R : 0 0 :000(319) [0503] by the Theologians **Assembled** in Smalcald in the Year
T R : 0 0 :014(322) [0507] same province should **assemble** with the people for whom
T R : 0 0 :014(322) [0509] of the bishops **assembled** in their presence, the episcopate
T R : 0 0 :082(334) [0529] been present in this **assembly** in Smalcald unanimously
T R : 0 0 :082(334) [0529] presented to the princes here in this **assembly** in Smalcald.
T R : 0 0 :082(000) [0529] articles written at the **Assembly** at Smalcald in the
T R : 0 0 :082(000) [0529] men who have now **assembled** at Smalcald I acknowledge
T R : 0 0 :082(000) [0529] to await the end of the **assembly**, I ask you, most
L C : 0 1 :084(376) [0605] that is, that they may **assemble** to hear and discuss God's
L C : 0 2 :047(416) [0691] The word *ecclesia* properly means an **assembly**.
L C : 0 2 :048(416) [0691] single reason that the group of people **assembles** there.
L C : 0 2 :048(416) [0691] For we who **assemble** select a special place and give the
L C : 0 2 :048(416) [0691] and give the house its name by virtue of the **assembly**.
L C : 0 2 :048(416) [0691] else than a common **assembly**; it is not of German but of
L C : 0 2 :048(417) [0691] congregation or **assembly**," or best and most clearly of
S D : R N :007(505) [0853] we prepared in the great **assembly** of theologians at
S D : 0 1 :054(517) [0877] we maintain that the **assemblies** of the uninstructed ought
S D : 0 7 :017(572) [0977] Augsburg Confession **assembled** from all parts of
S D : 0 7 :084(584) [1001] that in a Christian **assembly** we take bread and wine,
S D : 0 7 :126(591) [1015] places but especially where his community is **assembled**.
S D : 1 0 :021(614) [1059] all the theologians **assembled** in Smalcald subscribed with
S D : 1 2 :014(634) [1099] is no truly Christian **assembly** or congregation in the

Assent (8)
A P : 0 4 :304(154) [0205] will commands the intellect to **assent** to the Word of God.
S D : 0 2 :002(520) [0881] himself for such grace, accept it and give his **assent** to it?
S D : 0 2 :003(520) [0881] for grace and give his **assent** to it, though weakly, but
S D : 0 2 :013(523) [0885] the Gospel, give his **assent** to it, and accept it as truth.
S D : 0 2 :018(524) [0889] obey, believe, and give **assent** when the Holy Spirit offers
S D : 0 2 :027(527) [0891] reveals his will; but to **assent** to this Gospel when it is
S D : 0 2 :055(532) [0903] so that men believe this Word and give their **assent** to it.
S D : 0 2 :067(534) [0907] God but also are able to **assent** to it and accept it, even

Assert (17), Asserted (8), Asserting (1), Assertion (8), Asserts (10)
P R : P R :020(010) [0017] our theologians clearly **assert** in the Formula of Concord
A G : P R :023(027) [0043] summons) as we herewith publicly witness and **assert**.
A G : 0 1 :005(028) [0043] of the Manichaeans, who **assert** that there are two gods,
A G : 0 1 :006(028) [0043] person and sophistically **assert** that the other two, the
A G : 2 3 :003(051) [0061] the Scriptures clearly **assert** that the estate of marriage
A G : 2 3 :018(054) [0063] we have observed, the **assertion** that priests and
A G : 2 3 :023(055) [0063] Christ himself **asserts** that the devil is a murderer from
A G : 2 8 :005(081) [0085] Our teachers **assert** that according to the Gospel the
A G : 2 8 :034(086) [0087] this question our teachers **assert** that bishops do not have
A L : 2 7 :016(073) [0077] In fact, they **assert** that it is a state of perfection, and they
A L : 2 8 :034(086) [0087] question our teachers **assert**, as has been pointed out
A P : 0 1 :001(100) [0103] This **asserts** our faith and teaching that there is one
A P : 0 2 :010(102) [0107] scholastics confidently **assert**, then what can original sin
A P : 0 4 :124(124) [0157] and similar passages **assert** that we should begin to keep
A P : 0 4 :218(137) [0179] church, they say, Paul **asserts** that faith alone does not
A P : 0 9 :002(178) [0245] we condemn is also their **assertion** that the Baptism of
S 2 : 0 2 :007(294) [0465] article, which **asserts** that it is not the celebrant of a Mass
S 2 : 0 4 :004(299) [0473] Here it is **asserted** that no Christian can be saved unless
S 2 : 0 4 :012(300) [0475] not permit such faith but **asserts** that one must be
S 3 : 0 3 :010(305) [0481] original sin but **asserted** that the natural powers of man
S 3 : 1 5 :001(316) [0501] The **assertion** of the papists that human traditions effect
T R : 0 0 :005(320) [0503] the ground of this our **assertion** may be understood, we
T R : 0 0 :010(321) [0505] Gal. 2:2, 6 Paul plainly **asserts** that he was neither
T R : 0 0 :015(322) [0509] apostolic usage, and he **asserts** that it was observed in
T R : 0 0 :036(326) [0515] nefarious opinions by **asserting** that it is necessary for
L C : 0 1 :062(373) [0597] is either simply to lie and **assert** under his name
L C : 0 1 :272(401) [0657] No one should publicly **assert** as truth what is not
L C : 0 4 :028(440) [0739] the new spirits, **assert** that faith alone saves and that
E P : 0 1 :010(467) [0781] from it, as Job 19:26, 27 **asserts**, "I shall be covered by
E P : 0 1 :013(467) [0783] the Pelagian error which **asserts** that man's nature is
E P : 0 4 :002(475) [0797] when one party **asserted** that good works are necessary to
E P : 0 4 :002(475) [0797] The other party **asserted** that good works are detrimental
E P : 0 7 :004(482) [0809] in the Holy Supper but **assert** that this takes place
E P : 0 8 :003(487) [0817] Sacramentarians have **asserted** that in Christ the divine
E P : 0 8 :020(490) [0823] the Son of man another, as Nestorius foolishly **asserted**.
E P : 0 8 :034(491) [0825] spite of Christ's express **assertion**, "All authority in
S D : R N :009(505) [0855] Here he expressly **asserts** by way of distinction that the
S D : 0 3 :036(545) [0927] be summarized in the **assertion** that we are justified
S D : 0 4 :003(551) [0939] controversy a very few **asserted** the provocative
S D : 0 4 :039(557) [0951] too, because when **asserted** without explanation it is false
S D : 0 7 :002(569) [0973] For their own words **assert**, "We say that the body and
S D : 0 7 :108(588) [1009] Accordingly they **assert** that under the species of the
S D : 0 7 :113(589) [1011] 1. The **assertion** that the words of institution are not to be
S D : 0 7 :120(590) [1013] 9. Likewise, the **assertion** that Christ could not or would

Assign (2), Assigned (3), Assigning (2), Assignment (1)
A P : 1 2 :044(187) [0263] condemns us for **assigning** these two parts to penitence,
A P : 1 2 :124(201) [0289] over to these sophists such an important **assignment**.
A P : 2 1 :032(233) [0351] each saint has a special sphere of activity **assigned** to him.
S 2 : 0 2 :026(297) [0469] sorts of help to them, **assigning** to each of them a special
T R : 0 0 :021(323) [0509] the primacy should be **assigned** to the bishop of Rome.
L C : S P :025(364) [0579] well learned, you may **assign** them also some Psalms and
L C : 0 1 :112(380) [0613] a great, good, and holy work is here **assigned** to children.
L C : 0 1 :168(388) [0629] nor does he **assign** them this honor (that is, power and

Assist (3), Assistance (4)
P R : P R :008(005) [0009] Rather, with divine **assistance**, it was our intention to
P R : P R :023(012) [0021] through the help and **assistance** of the Holy Spirit until
S 3 : 0 5 :003(311) [0493] away sin through the **assistance** of the divine will, as if the
L C : 0 1 :203(392).[0639] on the contrary to aid and **assist** him so that he may
E P : 1 1 :008(495) [0833] Holy Spirit and divine **assistance** for steadfastness and
S D : 0 2 :089(538) [0915] do anything and cannot **assist** in any way toward his
S D : 1 1 :048(624) [1079] and decreed that he will **assist** us in all our necessities,

Associated (7), Associates (5), Association (7), Associations (3)
A G : P R :005(025) [0039] and princes and our **associates**, have been summoned for
A G : P R :010(025) [0041] with them and their **associates**, in so far as this can
A G : P R :012(026) [0041] our lords, friends, and **associates** who represent the
A G : P R :014(026) [0041] in the confession which we and our **associates** submit.
A G : P R :024(027) [0043] and that of our **associates**, and it is specifically stated,
A G : 2 7 :061(080) [0083] opinions and errors **associated** with monastic vows: that
A L : 2 7 :002(071) [0077] In Augustine's time they were voluntary **associations**.
A L : 2 7 :061(080) [0083] opinions which are **associated** with vows: that they
A P : 0 7 :003(169) [0227] to the outward **associations** of the church's marks — that
A P : 0 7 :005(169) [0227] is not merely an **association** of outward ties and rites like
A P : 0 7 :005(169) [0227] but it is mainly an **association** of faith and of the Holy
A P : 0 7 :005(169) [0227] it recognizable, this **association** has outward marks, the
A P : 0 7 :008(169) [0229] of saints who share the **association** of the same Gospel or
A P : 0 7 :012(170) [0231] and evil men are indeed **associated** with the true church
A P : 0 7 :028(173) [0237] in this life share an **association** in the outward marks, are
A P : 0 7 :028(173) [0237] according to this **association** in the outward marks, and
S 2 : 0 2 :012(295) [0465] business transactions **associated** with it are to be regarded
T R : 0 0 :042(328) [0517] us all not to be **associated** with and not to support
L C : 0 3 :073(430) [0719] daily business and in **associations** of every description
L C : 0 3 :102(434) [0727] we are incited by the **association** and example of other
S D : 0 3 :043(547) [0931] in so far as it is **associated** with love, on account of which
S D : 1 0 :023(615) [1061] us all not be be **associated** with and not to support

Assuage (1)
L C : 0 3 :011(421) [0701] not return to him and **assuage** his wrath and seek grace

Assume (12), Assumed (48), Assumes (3), Assumption (1)
A G : 2 7 :030(075) [0079] voluntary and should be **assumed** only after due
A P : P R :002(098) [0099] are involved, we **assumed** that the opponents would
A P : 0 3 :001(107) [0119] namely, that the Word **assumed** the human nature into
A P : 0 4 :390(166) [0225] We ought not **assume** immediately that the church of
A P : 0 7 :041(176) [0241] was unlawful for men to **assume** the right to change
A P : 1 2 :134(202) [0293] if a penitent refuses to **assume** the satisfactions he does
A P : 1 2 :173(210) [0305] Gospel compels us to **assume** these canonical
A P : 2 2 :017(238) [0361] Nor dare we **assume** that the church immediately
T R : 0 0 :011(321) [0507] other ministers should **assume** lordship or authority over
T R : 0 0 :040(327) [0515] First, because he **assumes** for himself the right to change
T R : 0 0 :040(327) [0517] Second, because he **assumes** for himself not only the
L C : S P :024(364) [0579] Do not **assume** that they will learn and retain this
L C : 0 1 :268(401) [0657] neighbor of such guilt **assumes** as much authority as the
L C : 0 2 :031(414) [0687] into heaven and **assumed** dominion at the right hand of
E P : 0 1 :005(466) [0781] the Son of God **assumed** into the unity of his person this
E P : 0 1 :006(467) [0781] original sin, has not **assumed** it, has not redeemed it, has
E P : 0 7 :033(485) [0815] and properties of his **assumed** human nature could
E P : 0 8 :014(488) [0821] human nature which he **assumed** into the unity of his
E P : 0 8 :015(488) [0821] of God, because he was **assumed** into God when he was
E P : 0 8 :033(491) [0825] the Son of God who **assumed** the human nature, after he
E P : 1 2 :003(498) [0839] 1. That Christ did not **assume** his body and blood from
S D : 0 1 :043(515) [0873] that God's Son **assumed** our nature, though without sin,
S D : 0 1 :043(516) [0873] that according to his **assumed** human nature Christ is of
S D : 0 1 :043(516) [0873] human nature which he **assumed** is in its essence and all
S D : 0 1 :044(516) [0873] Christ either did not **assume** our nature inasmuch as he
S D : 0 1 :044(516) [0873] inasmuch as he did not **assume** sin, or that Christ
S D : 0 1 :044(516) [0873] sin, or that Christ **assumed** sin inasmuch as he assumed
S D : 0 1 :044(516) [0873] Christ assumed sin inasmuch as he **assumed** our nature.
S D : 0 1 :044(516) [0873] however, God's Son **assumed** our nature, but not original
S D : 0 5 :020(561) [0959] Christ our Lord, himself **assumed** and bore the curse of
S D : 0 7 :120(590) [1013] and properties of his **assumed** human nature neither
S D : 0 8 :007(592) [1017] the human, which was **assumed** in time into the unity of
S D : 0 8 :011(593) [1019] both the divine and the **assumed** human nature, so that
S D : 0 8 :011(593) [1019] nature but also his **assumed** human nature belong to the
S D : 0 8 :011(593) [1019] Son of God who has **assumed** flesh and has become man,
S D : 0 8 :012(593) [1019] and confess that the **assumed** human nature in Christ not
S D : 0 8 :020(595) [1021] according to the **assumed** human nature) and, in the
S D : 0 8 :026(596) [1023] divine majesty according to the **assumed** human nature.
S D : 0 8 :050(600) [1031] As far as the **assumed** human nature in the person of
S D : 0 8 :053(601) [1033] according to his **assumed** human nature and of what his
S D : 0 8 :053(601) [1033] nature and of what his **assumed** human nature is capable
S D : 0 8 :054(601) [1033] Scriptures, ascribe to the **assumed** human nature in
S D : 0 8 :056(601) [1035] nature but also according to the **assumed** human nature.
S D : 0 8 :057(602) [1035] this in time according to the **assumed** human nature.
S D : 0 8 :059(602) [1035] expressly points to his **assumed** human nature when it
S D : 0 8 :060(602) [1035] communicated to the **assumed** human nature in Christ.
S D : 0 8 :061(602) [1035] not given to Christ's **assumed** human nature in the same
S D : 0 8 :061(602) [1035] but according to the **assumed** human nature he is below
S D : 0 8 :064(603) [1037] and efficacy in the **assumed** nature, spontaneously and
S D : 0 8 :066(604) [1039] *with, and through* the **assumed** exalted human nature of
S D : 0 8 :072(605) [1041] Son, according to the **assumed** human nature (whence he
S D : 0 8 :072(605) [1041] Lord according to his **assumed** human nature (according
S D : 0 8 :075(606) [1043] but that according to his **assumed** human nature many
S D : 0 8 :078(606) [1043] to and with this same **assumed** human nature of his,
S D : 0 8 :078(607) [1043] to and with his **assumed** human nature, according to
S D : 0 8 :084(608) [1045] and never separates the **assumed** humanity from himself."
S D : 0 8 :087(608) [1047] every tribulation in his **assumed** human nature, and who
S D : 0 8 :094(609) [1049] does not involve his **assumed** human nature in any way

Continued ▶

SD : 08 :095(609) [1049] 7. Likewise, that the **assumed** human nature in Christ
SD : 10 :021(614) [1061] "No one should **assume** lordship or authority over the
SD : 11 :039(622) [1075] is no basis for the **assumption** that those might be the
SD : 12 :025(635) [1099] 16. That Christ did not **assume** his flesh and blood from
SD : 12 :029(635) [1101] flesh or according to his **assumed** human nature Christ is
SD : 12 :029(635) [1101] exaltation Christ's flesh **assumed** all the divine properties

Assurance (19), Assure (5), Assured (9), Assuredly (6), Assures (6)
PR : PR :024(013) [0021] have been adequately **assured** of this in our hearts and
AG : PR :014(026) [0041] and sufficiently **assured** from what follows in the
AG : PR :015(026) [0041] Majesty graciously gave **assurance** to the electors,
AG : 20 :015(043) [0055] faith, that is, when it is **assured** and knows that for
AG : 20 :026(045) [0057] confidence in God, **assurance** that God is gracious to us,
AL : 25 :004(062) [0069] from heaven, and are **assured** that such faith truly obtains
AL : 27 :049(079) [0083] God, to ask of God, and **assuredly** to expect from him,
AP : 04 :148(127) [0163] and believing with full **assurance** that God forgives
AP : 04 :178(131) [0171] bestowed upon us to **assure** us that because of this
AP : 04 :205(135) [0177] But faith gives **assurance** of God's presence when it is sure
AP : 04 :292(152) [0203] Father has given the **assurance** that he wishes to forgive
AP : 04 :297(153) [0205] and eternal life are **assured** to us for Christ's sake.
AP : 04 :312(155) [0207] faith is defined as "the **assurance** of things hoped for."
AP : 15 :017(217) [0319] Finally, what **assurance** do we have that religious rites
AP : 15 :043(221) [0327] of faith, prayer and our **assurance** that it is efficacious
AP : 21 :017(231) [0347] must be a Word of God to **assure** us that God is willing to
AP : 23 :030(243) [0371] 4:5): by the Word which **assures** the conscience that God
AP : 28 :018(284) [0449] For Christ wants to **assure** us, as was necessary, that the
S3 : 03 :010(305) [0481] and that God will **assuredly** grant his grace to the man
S3 : 03 :032(308) [0489] who has given you any **assurance** that you will escape the
SC : 03 :016(347) [0549] And **assuredly** we on our part will heartily forgive and
SC : 03 :021(348) [0549] means that I should be **assured** that such petitions are
LC : 01 :039(370) [0591] in the promise that **assures** mercy to those who cling to
LC : 03 :020(423) [0703] pleasing to him and will **assuredly** be heard and granted,
LC : 03 :022(423) [0703] that our prayer pleases him and will **assuredly** be heard.
LC : 03 :093(433) [0725] God has promised us **assurance** that everything is forgiven
LC : 03 :095(433) [0725] have the comfort and **assurance** that you are forgiven in
LC : 03 :096(433) [0725] our strengthening and **assurance** as a sign along with the
EP : 07 :020(484) [0813] faith and of which we are **assured** through the sacrament.
EP : 07 :029(485) [0815] seals, and pledges to **assure** us that when our faith
EP : 07 :030(485) [0815] 9. That the **assurance** and strengthening of our faith in
EP : 11 :013(496) [0835] God **assures** us of this gracious election not only in mere
SD : 02 :056(532) [0903] Holy Spirit, whereby he **assuredly** is potent and active in
SD : 04 :037(557) [0949] his righteousness or his **assurance** of salvation on good
SD : 05 :002(558) [0953] which proclamation **assures** those who have been
SD : 05 :025(563) [0961] them with the **assurance** that if they believe the Gospel
SD : 07 :062(581) [0995] on this comforting **assurance** that we have a gracious God
SD : 07 :063(581) [0995] as a certain pledge and **assurance** that their sins are truly
SD : 07 :116(589) [1011] external pledge, we are **assured** that our faith, when it
SD : 07 :116(589) [1011] Thus the **assurance** and confirmation of our faith in the
SD : 08 :079(607) [1045] To make certainty and **assurance** doubly sure on this
SD : 11 :012(618) [1067] our faith and to **assure** us of our salvation (Eph. 1:9, 13,
SD : 11 :032(621) [1073] vein Holy Scripture also **assures** us that God who has
SD : 11 :036(622) [1075] will toward us and what **assures** and promises it to us
SD : 11 :072(628) [1085] grace, of which he has **assured** us in holy Baptism, and

Astonished (2), Astonishing (2), Astonishment (1)
AL : 00 :002(049) [0059] those who disseminate **astonishing** slanders among the
AP : 04 :298(153) [0205] and evident that we are **astonished** to see how furiously
LC : 01 :114(380) [0613] they simply gaped in **astonishment** at all the
LC : 03 :061(428) [0715] we must suffer an **astonishing** amount of attacks and
SD : 07 :059(580) [0993] We are justly **astonished** that some are so rash that they

Astray (3)
PR : PR :018(008) [0015] allow himself to be led **astray** by the unwarranted
AP : 23 :050(246) [0377] who seem to have gone **astray** through some sort of
LC : 01 :121(382) [0615] we may not again be led **astray** from the pure Word of

Asunder (1)
AP : 23 :023(242) [0371] "What God has joined together, let no man put **asunder**."

Ate (2)
S2 : 02 :015(295) [0467] Otherwise what they **ate**, how they dressed, and what kind
LC : 05 :068(454) [0769] were a poison which would kill us if we **ate** of it?

Athanasian (4)
S1 : 01 :000(292) [0461] Apostles' Creed, the **Athanasian** Creed, and the Catechism
EP : RN :003(465) [0777] Creed, the Nicene Creed, and the **Athanasian** Creed.
SD : RN :004(504) [0851] the Nicene, and the **Athanasian**, as the glorious
SD : 12 :037(636) [1101] the Nicene and **Athanasian** Creeds, both as to content and

Athanasius (1)
AP : 04 :190(133) [0175] of the apostle Paul, **Athanasius**, Augustine, and other

Atheism (1)
LC : 03 :104(434) [0727] to drive us into despair, **atheism**, blasphemy, and

Atone (1), Atoned (1)
AG : 26 :021(067) [0073] and sin cannot be **atoned** for by observing the said human
AP : 12 :146(205) [0297] of works does not **atone** for eternal death because it is

Attach (4), Attached (13), Attaches (3), Attaching (1)
AG : 28 :039(087) [0089] command when they **attach** sin to foods, days, and
AL : 28 :039(087) [0089] of God when they **attach** sin to foods, days, and similar
AP : 12 :069(192) [0271] that no great authority **attaches** to the statements of later
AP : 24 :015(252) [0389] use it out of context, **attaching** their own ideas to it as if
S2 : 04 :001(298) [0471] other churches as have **attached** themselves to him
S3 : 03 :025(307) [0485] pope invented the jubilee year and **attached** it to Rome.
TR : 00 :036(326) [0515] of Christ and that he can **attach** salvation to these
LC : 01 :029(368) [0589] watch over it, he has **attached** to it, first, a terrible threat
LC : 01 :031(369) [0589] hear later), yet they are **attached** precisely to this one
LC : 01 :057(372) [0597] Therefore God has **attached** to this commandment a
LC : 01 :131(383) [0619] is that God has **attached** to it a lovely promise, "That you
LC : 01 :321(408) [0673] Although primarily **attached** to the First Commandment,
LC : 01 :321(408) [0673] ought to be regarded as **attached** to each individual
LC : 03 :097(433) [0725] This sign is **attached** to the petition, therefore, that when
LC : 03 :124(436) [0731] importance that God **attaches** to our being certain that
LC : 04 :011(438) [0735] works, and we all **attach** greater importance to our own
LC : 04 :030(440) [0739] object to which faith is **attached** and bound on the ground
LC : 05 :064(454) [0769] place, a promise is **attached** to the commandment, as we
SD : 07 :078(584) [1001] speak and to do and has **attached** his own command and
SD : 11 :037(622) [1075] which he has **attached** as a seal of the promise and by
SD : 12 :039(636) [1103] articles, and whatever **attaches** to them or follows from

Attack (7), Attacked (5), Attacks (7)
PR : PR :017(008) [0015] if it should ever be **attacked** by any one or if at any time
AP : 07 :002(168) [0227] that there is no defense against the **attacks** of slanderers.
AP : 15 :042(221) [0327] their polemics they even **attack** this most salutary part of
AP : 27 :013(271) [0423] these insults with which our enemies **attack** thy Gospel!
S2 : 04 :007(299) [0473] be preserved against the **attacks** of sects and heresies; and
S2 : 04 :015(301) [0475] Christ, our Lord, has **attacked** his adversaries and will
LC : PR :013(360) [0571] the daily, incessant **attacks** and ambushes of the devil
LC : PR :014(360) [0571] the constant and furious **attacks** and assaults of the devil.
LC : 01 :042(370) [0591] grief and want and are opposed and **attacked** by the devil.
LC : 01 :230(396) [0645] in order to launch an **attack** against the great, powerful
LC : 03 :047(426) [0711] and against those who **attack** and persecute our Gospel
LC : 03 :061(428) [0715] astonishing amount of **attacks** and assaults from all who
LC : 03 :087(432) [0723] have heard, directing his **attacks** against all the previous
LC : 03 :105(434) [0727] vile life in which we are **attacked**, hunted, and harried on
LC : 03 :109(435) [0729] must be armed and prepared for incessant **attacks**.
LC : 03 :109(435) [0729] becomes weary; when one **attack** ceases, new ones always
LC : 04 :075(445) [0751] but an earnest **attack** on the old man and an entering
LC : 05 :026(449) [0759] that we resist him and **attack** the old man, and when he
SD : PR :002(501) [0847] Christian institutions, **attacked** it violently (although

Attain (15), Attained (7), Attaining (4), Attainment (3)
AG : PR :012(026) [0041] us, and if no results are **attained**, nevertheless we on our
AG : 27 :004(071) [0077] on many before they had **attained** an appropriate age.
AG : 27 :033(076) [0079] the cloister in their childhood, before **attaining** such age.
AG : 27 :047(078) [0081] exaltation of works as a means of **attaining** justification.
AL : 12 :008(035) [0049] contend that some may **attain** such perfection in this life
AL : 18 :001(039) [0051] has some liberty for the **attainment** of civil righteousness
AL : 18 :002(039) [0051] the Holy Spirit, to **attain** the righteousness of God — that
AL : 23 :026(056) [0065] have made vows before **attaining** a proper age, and as a
AL : 27 :004(071) [0077] to the canons, before they had **attained** a lawful age.
AP : PR :011(099) [0101] formulas in order to foster the **attainment** of harmony.
AP : 04 :106(122) [0153] his weakness one may **attain** to it, keep it, and live in it.
AP : 04 :204(135) [0177] such people never **attain** the knowledge of God, for in
AP : 12 :008(183) [0255] Judas, and men like them **attain** grace even though they
AP : 12 :075(193) [0273] to God, he merits the **attainment** of the forgiveness of
AP : 20 :010(228) [0341] we know that we had **attained** it, when would a terrified
AP : 27 :017(271) [0425] of God; whoever tries to **attain** to the forgiveness of sins
AP : 27 :019(272) [0425] is surer than that men **attain** the forgiveness of sins by
AP : 27 :020(272) [0425] of the opinion that we **attain** to the forgiveness of sins
AP : 27 :061(279) [0441] the mercy of God — they would **attain** eternal life.
AP : 27 :069(281) [0443] righteous; that we **attain** eternal life because of them
AP : 27 :070(281) [0443] by mercy they would **attain** eternal life and not for the
AP : 28 :006(282) [0445] to create laws which are useful for **attaining** eternal life.
S3 : 08 :007(313) [0495] Adults who have **attained** the age of reason must first
LC : 02 :058(418) [0693] forgiveness until we **attain** to that life where there will be
LC : 03 :053(427) [0713] and in eternal life hereafter to us who have **attained** it.
LC : 03 :090(432) [0723] themselves and be glad that they can **attain** forgiveness.
LC : 06 :019(459) [0000] helped so that you may **attain** a happy heart and
LC : 06 :035(461) [0000] to God that we have **attained** to this blessed knowledge
SD : 01 :058(519) [0879] of God will never **attain** abiding peace in this controversy

Attempt (8), Attempted (2), Attempting (1), Attempts (1)
PR : PR :019(009) [0017] no one that some have **attempted** to hide their error
AG : 27 :002(071) [0077] were invented, and the **attempt** was made to restore
LC : 01 :055(372) [0595] See, all this is an **attempt** to embellish yourself with
LC : 01 :056(372) [0595] aggravated when we **attempt** to justify and confirm it by
LC : 03 :068(429) [0717] against it in their **attempt** utterly to exterminate the
LC : 03 :111(435) [0729] Otherwise, if you **attempt** to help yourself by your own
EP : 11 :013(496) [0835] by the evil foe in an **attempt** to weaken for us or to rob us
SD : 04 :028(555) [0945] his own followers who **attempted** to explain the
SD : 08 :040(599) [1029] indescribable what the devil **attempts** with this *alloeosis*."
SD : 08 :052(601) [1033] and demonstrations they **attempt** to determine and to fix
SD : 10 :003(611) [1053] the adversaries are **attempting** either by force and
SD : 11 :006(617) [1065] wicked will of the devil and of men will **attempt** and do.

Attend (6), Attendance (1), Attended (3), Attending (1), Attention (25), Attentive (2)
AG : 27 :049(079) [0083] good works for others and diligently **attend** to our calling.
AG : 28 :066(092) [0093] One must pay **attention** to the chief article of Christian
AL : 26 :016(066) [0073] unable to devote their **attention** to a better kind of
AL : 27 :049(079) [0083] of good works for others and to **attend** to our calling.
AP : 02 :032(104) [0113] have evidently not paid **attention** to what the Fathers
AP : 04 :033(111) [0129] understanding but only **attentive** listening—to use the
AP : 04 :051(114) [0135] what faith is if we pay **attention** to the article of the Creed
AP : 12 :106(197) [0283] him to pay diligent **attention** to his own property and
AP : 12 :128(201) [0291] You do not pay enough **attention** to the importance of
AP : 20 :004(227) [0339] Confutation stand if their **attention** had been called to it.
AP : 24 :048(258) [0401] in our churches pay **attention** to the ministry of the
AP : 24 :050(259) [0401] appearances, our church **attendance** is greater than theirs.
AP : 27 :038(275) [0433] for the whole city and then paid **attention** to his business.
S1 : PR :005(289) [0457] who do not pay **attention** to what I write and who keep
S3 : 03 :019(306) [0485] At the same time his **attention** was directed to his own
S3 : 03 :027(308) [0487] and once again directed **attention** to uncertain human
S3 : 12 :002(315) [0499] Nor shall we pay any **attention** to what they command or
SC : PR :004(338) [0533] the people and paid no **attention** at all to the duties of
SC : PR :018(340) [0537] seem to require special **attention** among the people where
SC : 09 :005(355) [0561] are ministers of God, **attending** to this very thing.
LC : SP :026(364) [0579] young people should also **attend** preaching, especially at
LC : 01 :083(376) [0603] maid-servants who have **attended** to their work and
LC : 01 :140(384) [0621] them lightly, fastens his **attention** on other things, and
LC : 01 :171(388) [0629] necessary it is to devote serious **attention** to the young.

Continued ▶

LC : 0 1 :187(390) [0633] so that we may be **attentive** to his will and with hearty
LC : 0 1 :224(395) [0643] but people pay so little **attention** to it that the matter is
LC : 0 1 :318(408) [0673] will neither seek nor pay **attention** to any other works or
LC : 0 3 :014(422) [0701] that no one paid any **attention** to it, and men supposed it
LC : 0 5 :043(451) [0763] sacrament, we shall devote a little **attention** to this point.
LC : 0 5 :051(452) [0765] the papacy when we **attended** the sacrament merely from
EP : 0 3 :010(474) [0795] we must give special **attention** to the "exclusive
EP : 1 1 :012(496) [0835] Word, they cast it to the wind and pay no **attention** to it.
EP : 1 2 :010(498) [0839] should hear sermons or **attend** services in those temples
SD : 0 4 :019(554) [0945] Here again careful **attention** must be given to the
SD : 0 8 :027(596) [1025] the message by the signs that **attended** it (Mark 16:20).
SD : 1 0 :019(614) [1059] Nor shall we pay any **attention** to what they command or
SD : 1 1 :077(629) [1089] sinner must therefore **attend** on it, hear it with diligence,
SD : 1 2 :015(634) [1099] That one may not hear or **attend** on a sermon in those

Attest (5), Attested (4), Attesting (1), Attests (3)
PR : PR :016(008) [0013] Confession and publicly **attested** this with their hearts,
PR : PR :019(009) [0017] desired hereby to **attest** and affirm publicly that, then as
AP : 0 2 :036(105) [0115] Here he openly **attests** that sin is — that is, remains — even
AP : 1 2 :036(186) [0261] God, as the same passage **attests**, "We are justified by
AP : 1 2 :073(192) [0273] writings of the apostles **attest** that they believed the same
AP : 1 2 :150(206) [0299] David **attests** to this when he prays (Ps. 6:1), "O Lord,
AP : 2 1 :008(230) [0345] This is **attested** to by Zech. 1:12, where the angel prays, "O
AP : 2 2 :004(236) [0359] in the Latin church, as Cyprian and Jerome **attest**.
LC : 0 1 :275(402) [0659] evil, to prefer charges, to **attest**, examine, and witness.
LC : 0 1 :302(405) [0667] the seal of the prince **attesting** that it was acquired
LC : 0 4 :049(442) [0745] whose doctrine and life **attest** that they have the Holy
SD : 0 1 :057(518) [0877] it is irrefutably true, **attested** and demonstrated by the
SD : 0 8 :076(606) [1043] the Council of Ephesus **attested** when they stated that

Attire (1)
AL : 2 7 :050(079) [0083] things and not of celibacy, mendicancy, or humble **attire**.

Attitude (8), Attitudes (3)
PR : PR :010(006) [0011] they might know what **attitude** to take toward these
AP : 0 2 :042(105) [0117] dared to say that such **attitudes** as these are a neutral
AP : 0 4 :063(115) [0139] without the proper **attitude** in the recipient, as though the
AP : 0 7 :021(172) [0233] *operato*, without a good **attitude** in the one using them?
AP : 1 2 :012(184) [0257] *operato*, without a right **attitude** in the recipient, and they
AP : 1 2 :025(185) [0259] without the proper **attitude** in the recipient, that is,
AP : 1 2 :167(209) [0305] that distrust of God and similar **attitudes** are destroyed.
AP : 1 6 :009(224) [0333] of civil ordinances but **attitudes** of the heart, like a deep
LC : 0 1 :111(380) [0613] He who has the right **attitude** toward his parents will not
LC : 0 1 :324(409) [0675] man's heart has such an **attitude** toward God, he has
LC : 0 2 :066(419) [0697] do not know what his **attitude** is toward them.

Attract (1), Attraction (1), Attractive (2)
LC : 0 1 :219(394) [0643] the chief ways to make chastity **attractive** and desirable.
LC : 0 1 :322(409) [0673] to terrify and warn us but also to **attract** and allure us.
EP : 0 2 :017(472) [0791] conversion, through the **attraction** of the Holy Spirit,
SD : 0 7 :106(588) [1009] how appealing and **attractive** they may appear to reason,

Attribute (19), Attributed (9), Attributes (5), Attributing (3)
AG : 2 8 :031(085) [0087] Those who **attribute** such power to bishops cite Christ's
AL : 2 7 :047(078) [0081] Is not this **attributing** justification to works?
AL : 2 8 :031(085) [0087] Those who **attribute** this right to bishops cite as evidence
AP : 0 2 :008(101) [0107] They even **attribute** to human nature unimpaired power
AP : 0 2 :012(102) [0109] of nature and **attributed** more than was proper to free
AP : 0 2 :025(103) [0111] they simultaneously **attribute** to man a concupiscence
AP : 0 4 :107(122) [0153] Scriptures that clearly **attribute** justification to faith and
AP : 0 4 :109(123) [0153] that is, they do not **attribute** justification to faith except
AP : 0 4 :109(123) [0153] Indeed, they do not **attribute** justification to faith at all,
AP : 0 4 :229(139) [0183] Our opponents **attribute** justification to love because
AP : 0 4 :229(139) [0183] work of the law, and to it they **attributed** justification.
AP : 0 4 :269(147) [0197] in such a way that they **attribute** Christ's glory to works
AP : 0 4 :297(153) [0205] that justification must necessarily be **attributed** to faith.
AP : 0 4 :360(162) [0219] only do our opponents **attribute** to works a worthiness of
AP : 1 2 :060(190) [0269] To this faith we **attribute** justification and regeneration,
AP : 1 2 :143(204) [0297] They **attribute** satisfaction to the mere performance of
AP : 1 8 :009(226) [0337] spiritual righteousness, **attributing** the former to the free
AP : 2 0 :004(227) [0339] the blasphemy of **attributing** the honor of Christ to our
AP : 2 1 :011(230) [0345] Evidently some **attribute** divinity to the saints, the power
AP : 2 4 :089(266) [0415] It is horrible to **attribute** as much to the work of a priest
AP : 2 7 :038(276) [0433] was not to be **attributed** to the way he had undertaken.
AP : 2 7 :068(280) [0443] He does not **attribute** faith to people who have a mortal
S2 : 0 2 :026(297) [0469] in time of need, and **attribute** all sorts of help to them,
S3 : 0 8 :010(313) [0497] Whatever is **attributed** to the Spirit apart from such Word
TR : 0 0 :011(321) [0507] Therefore he does not **attribute** to Peter superiority or
TR : 0 0 :015(322) [0509] the churches did not **attribute** superiority and lordship to
EP : 0 8 :008(487) [0819] 4. The **attributes** of the human nature are to be a
EP : 1 2 :001(498) [0839] silence these errors be **attributed** to us, we wish here at
SD : 0 1 :018(511) [0865] but concreated and essential **attributes** of man's nature.
SD : 0 1 :030(513) [0867] error which Augustine **attributes** to the Manichaeans,
SD : 0 1 :043(516) [0873] and all its essential **attributes** — sin alone excepted —
SD : 0 4 :034(556) [0949] In other words, he **attributes** to faith alone the beginning,
SD : 0 8 :004(592) [1017] that nothing is to be **attributed** to the human nature in
SD : 0 8 :076(606) [1043] of Christ, things are **attributed** to Christ according to the
SD : 0 8 :092(609) [1049] something which ought not be **attributed** to the deity.
SD : 1 2 :007(633) [1097] as a result of our silence **attribute** to us the condemned

Attrite (1), Attrition (8)
AP : 0 4 :083(118) [0145] merits, our contrition, **attrition**, love, worship, or works.
AP : 1 2 :006(183) [0255] of sins takes place in **attrition** or in contrition.
AP : 1 2 :018(185) [0257] 2. We merit grace through **attrition**.
AP : 1 2 :054(189) [0265] in this promise, not by their own **attrition** or contrition.
AP : 1 2 :068(192) [0271] about the merits of **attrition** and works and similar ideas.
AP : 1 2 :075(193) [0273] a person who has **attrition** or contrition elicits an act of
AP : 1 2 :178(211) [0309] deal about the merit of **attrition**, the endless enumeration
S3 : 0 3 :016(305) [0483] he should at least be **attrite** (which I might call half-way
S3 : 0 3 :016(305) [0483] Nevertheless, such **attrition** was reckoned as a substitute

Audacious (1), Audacity (1)
AP : 2 3 :001(239) [0363] authority for their **audacious** defense of the pontifical
AP : 2 7 :019(272) [0425] These rascals have the **audacity** to call this statement

Audians (2)
AP : 0 7 :043(177) [0243] Jews; they were called **Audians**, from the originator of
AP : 0 7 :043(177) [0243] and he criticizes the **Audians** for misunderstanding it.

Audience (1)
AP : 2 4 :050(259) [0401] clear sermons hold an **audience**, but neither the people

Augmented (1)
SD : 0 8 :049(600) [1031] nature intrinsically diminished or **augmented** thereby.

Augsburg (128)
PR : PR :000(001) [0004] who Embrace the **Augsburg** Confession and of their
PR : PR :002(003) [0007] memory, at the Diet of **Augsburg** in the year 1530,
PR : PR :008(005) [0009] repeatedly mentioned **Augsburg** Confession, which had
PR : PR :008(005) [0009] imperial assembly at **Augsburg** in the year 1530, and again
PR : PR :008(005) [0009] and confessed at **Augsburg** in the year 1530, in the
PR : PR :009(006) [0011] the true and originally submitted **Augsburg** Confession.
PR : PR :009(006) [0011] frequently mentioned **Augsburg** Confession, the contrary
PR : PR :013(007) [0013] estates adhering to the **Augsburg** Confession with the
PR : PR :016(008) [0013] of God and then to the **Augsburg** Confession as well, the
PR : PR :016(008) [0013] interpretation of the **Augsburg** Confession and publicly
PR : PR :017(008) [0015] point to depart from the **Augsburg** Confession as
PR : PR :018(008) [0015] which is the genuine **Augsburg** Confession, and in order
PR : PR :018(008) [0015] Word of God, to that **Augsburg** Confession which was
PR : PR :018(008) [0015] imperial assembly in **Augsburg** in the year 1530, which
PR : PR :018(009) [0015] the incorporation of the **Augsburg** Confession that was
PR : PR :018(009) [0015] it was once confessed at **Augsburg** in the year 1530 by the
PR : PR :019(009) [0017] second edition of the **Augsburg** Confession, referred to in
PR : PR :019(009) [0017] confession submitted at **Augsburg** and that a very
PR : PR :019(009) [0017] than that of the first **Augsburg** Confession as it was
PR : PR :023(012) [0021] and is embodied in the **Augsburg** Confession and its
PR : PR :023(012) [0021] previously submitted at **Augsburg** in the year 1530 to
PR : PR :023(012) [0021] and then to the aforementioned **Augsburg** Confession.
PR : PR :025(013) [0023] Creeds as well as in the **Augsburg** Confession, submitted
AG : 0 0 :000(023) [0037] The **Augsburg** Confession
AG : 0 0 :000(023) [0037] of Faith Presented in **Augsburg** by certain Princes and
AG : PR :001(024) [0039] a diet of the empire to convene here in **Augsburg**.
S2 : 0 2 :010(294) [0465] is as Campegio said in **Augsburg**: he would suffer himself
S2 : 0 4 :016(301) [0475] secular authority, as at **Augsburg**, where we responded to
TR : 0 0 :082(334) [0529] emperor in the diet of **Augsburg** and, by the favor of
TR : 0 0 :082(334) [0529] the articles of the **Augsburg** Confession, the Apology, and
TR : 0 0 :082(335) [0529] Wolfart, minister of the Word in the church in **Augsburg**
TR : 0 0 :082(000) [0529] Apology presented at **Augsburg** by the Most Illustrious
EP : 0 0 :000(463) [0775] of Articles of the **Augsburg** Confession on Which for
EP : 0 0 :000(464) [0777] the theologians of the **Augsburg** Confession Expounded
EP : RN :004(465) [0777] the first and unaltered **Augsburg** Confession, which was
EP : RN :004(465) [0777] Emperor Charles V at **Augsburg** during the great Diet in
EP : 0 3 :001(472) [0791] and the content of the **Augsburg** Confession that we poor
EP : 0 7 :001(481) [0807] identified with the **Augsburg** Confession since they
EP : 0 7 :001(481) [0809] very outset when the **Augsburg** Confession was being
EP : 0 8 :001(486) [0817] theologians of the **Augsburg** Confession and the
EP : 0 9 :001(492) [0827] some theologians of the **Augsburg** Confession concerning
EP : 1 0 :001(492) [0829] theologians of the **Augsburg** Confession concerning those
EP : 1 1 :001(494) [0831] the theologians of the **Augsburg** Confession concerning
EP : 1 1 :022(497) [0837] the theologians of the **Augsburg** Confession have been
EP : 1 2 :000(498) [0839] Not Committed Themselves to the **Augsburg** Confession
EP : 1 2 :011(499) [0841] Gospel according to the **Augsburg** Confession and reprove
EP : 1 2 :030(500) [0843] the three Creeds, the **Augsburg** Confession, the Apology,
SD : 0 0 :000(501) [0845] of Articles of the **Augsburg** Confession Concerning Which
SD : PR :003(501) [0847] Emperor Charles V at the great Diet of **Augsburg** in 1530.
SD : PR :004(502) [0847] thoroughly scriptural **Augsburg** Confession, and we abide
SD : PR :006(502) [0847] their adherence to the **Augsburg** Confession, even dared to
SD : PR :010(503) [0849] God and the Christian **Augsburg** Confession, and so that
SD : RN :002(503) [0851] all the churches of the **Augsburg** Confession before the
SD : RN :002(503) [0851] the adherents of the **Augsburg** Confession and which were
SD : RN :005(504) [0851] and chapters of the **Augsburg** Confession against the
SD : RN :005(504) [0851] to the first, unaltered **Augsburg** Confession (in the form in
SD : RN :005(504) [0851] Emperor Charles V at **Augsburg** by a number of Christian
SD : RN :006(504) [0853] the repeatedly cited **Augsburg** Confession had been
SD : RN :006(504) [0853] genuine meaning of the **Augsburg** Confession, with a view
SD : RN :006(504) [0853] under the name of the **Augsburg** Confession someone
SD : RN :006(504) [0853] because in it the cited **Augsburg** Confession is clearly
SD : RN :007(505) [0853] as an explication of the **Augsburg** Confession, to which
SD : RN :007(505) [0853] the doctrine of the cited **Augsburg** Confession is repeated,
SD : RN :008(505) [0853] which adhere to the **Augsburg** Confession and since they
SD : RN :011(506) [0855] above listed — the **Augsburg** confession, the Apology, the
SD : RN :012(506) [0855] arose among the theologians of the **Augsburg** Confession.
SD : RN :012(506) [0855] sincerely adheres to the **Augsburg** Confession object to
SD : RN :019(507) [0857] of the theologians of the **Augsburg** Confession on account
SD : RN :020(508) [0859] Christian meaning of the **Augsburg** Confession as it was
SD : 0 1 :001(508) [0859] of theologians of the **Augsburg** Confession about what
SD : 0 1 :007(510) [0861] as Article XIX of the **Augsburg** Confession teaches, that
SD : 0 2 :001(520) [0881] a number of theologians of the **Augsburg** Confession.
SD : 0 2 :002(520) [0881] of the churches of the **Augsburg** Confession for quite a few
SD : 0 2 :005(520) [0881] the pure teachers of the **Augsburg** Confession have taught
SD : 0 2 :028(527) [0893] and accords with the **Augsburg** Confession and the other
SD : 0 2 :029(527) [0893] Article XX of the **Augsburg** Confession declares: "People
SD : 0 2 :030(527) [0893] indicate clearly that the **Augsburg** Confession does not in
SD : 0 2 :045(530) [0899] of God, the Christian **Augsburg** Confession, its Apology,
SD : 0 2 :073(535) [0909] in the churches of the **Augsburg** Confession: Whether man
SD : 0 3 :001(539) [0917] theologians of the **Augsburg** Confession concerns the
SD : 0 3 :004(539) [0917] other teachers of the **Augsburg** Confession held
SD : 0 3 :055(549) [0935] the theologians of the **Augsburg** Confession accept the
SD : 0 3 :066(550) [0937] God's Word in the **Augsburg** Confession and its
SD : 0 4 :001(551) [0939] arisen among the theologians of the **Augsburg** Confession.
SD : 0 4 :014(553) [0943] or free, both the **Augsburg** Confession and its Apology
SD : 0 4 :021(554) [0945] are necessary, as the **Augsburg** Confession and the
SD : 0 4 :024(555) [0945] in Article VI of the **Augsburg** Confession, "We are saved
SD : 0 5 :002(558) [0951] among some theologians of the **Augsburg** Confession.
SD : 0 7 :001(568) [0971] among the theologians of the **Augsburg** Confession.
SD : 0 7 :001(568) [0971] early as 1530, when the **Augsburg** Confession was drafted
SD : 0 7 :001(568) [0971] disavowed the **Augsburg** Confession, withdrew from it,

Continued ▶

SD : 0 7 :001(568) [0971] adherence to the **Augsburg** Confession no longer secretly
SD : 0 7 :001(569) [0971] adduce and pervert the **Augsburg** Confession so as to
SD : 0 7 :001(569) [0971] of Christ and of the **Augsburg** Confession in this article.
SD : 0 7 :001(569) [0971] Word of God and to the **Augsburg** Confession and which
SD : 0 7 :002(569) [0971] speech-patterns of the **Augsburg** Confession and of our
SD : 0 7 :009(570) [0975] The **Augsburg** Confession, on the other hand, teaches on
SD : 0 7 :009(570) [0975] their own confession at **Augsburg** to the effect that since
SD : 0 7 :012(571) [0977] Later on, those who at **Augsburg** had submitted their own
SD : 0 7 :017(572) [0977] were committed to the **Augsburg** Confession assembled
SD : 0 7 :033(575) [0983] the true intention of the **Augsburg** Confession better than
SD : 0 7 :034(575) [0983] the chief teacher of the **Augsburg** Confession, every
SD : 0 7 :034(575) [0983] all doubt what the **Augsburg** Confession's real meaning
SD : 0 7 :041(576) [0985] which adhere to the **Augsburg** Confession and as the
SD : 0 7 :041(576) [0985] of the aforementioned **Augsburg** Confession and delivered
SD : 0 7 :041(576) [0985] and intention of the **Augsburg** Confession cannot be
SD : 0 7 :058(580) [0993] pure teachers of the **Augsburg** Confession, explained this
SD : 0 7 :073(583) [0999] some teachers of the **Augsburg** Confession concerning the
SD : 0 7 :111(589) [1011] our churches as adherents of the **Augsburg** Confession.
SD : 0 8 :001(591) [1015] theologians of the **Augsburg** Confession concerning the
SD : 0 8 :004(592) [1017] a few theologians of the **Augsburg** Confession, not quite
SD : 0 8 :088(609) [1047] orthodox Creeds, and our Christian **Augsburg** confession:
SD : 1 0 :001(610) [1053] some theologians of the **Augsburg** Confession concerning
SD : 1 0 :018(614) [1059] the chief teachers of the **Augsburg** Confession concerning
SD : 1 1 :001(616) [1063] the theologians of the **Augsburg** Confession concerning
SD : 1 1 :038(622) [1075] that reason also, as the **Augsburg** Confession states in
SD : 1 1 :094(632) [1095] theologians of the **Augsburg** Confession for many years
SD : 1 2 :000(632) [1095] Sects Which Never Accepted the **Augsburg** Confession
SD : 1 2 :001(632) [1095] never accepted the **Augsburg** Confession and to which we
SD : 1 2 :002(632) [1095] all the churches of the **Augsburg** Confession have
SD : 1 2 :003(633) [1095] and every article of the **Augsburg** Confession, but are so
SD : 1 2 :003(633) [1095] longer know what the **Augsburg** Confession really is and
SD : 1 2 :004(633) [1097] among the theologians of the **Augsburg** Confession.
SD : 1 2 :006(633) [1097] natural, and proper meaning of the **Augsburg** Confession.
SD : 1 2 :006(633) [1097] contrary to the **Augsburg** Confession is imported into our
SD : 1 2 :008(633) [1097] our Christian and biblically-based **Augsburg** Confession.
SD : 1 2 :016(634) [1099] Gospel according to the **Augsburg** Confession and censure
SD : 1 2 :039(636) [1103] the three Creeds, to the **Augsburg** Confession and the

August (2)
PR : PR :027(014) [0025] **August**, duke of Saxony, elector.
PR : PR :027(015) [0025] Duke Sigismund **August** of Mecklenburg [in Ivernack]

Augustine (67)
AG : 1 8 :004(039) [0051] the clear words of **Augustine** on free will are here quoted
AG : 2 0 :012(043) [0055] from **Augustine**, who discusses this question thoroughly
AG : 2 0 :026(045) [0057] **Augustine** also reminds us that we would understand the
AG : 2 6 :017(066) [0073] In fact, **Augustine** was also displeased that consciences
AG : 2 7 :002(071) [0077] In the days of St. **Augustine** monastic life was voluntary.
AG : 2 7 :035(076) [0081] For St. **Augustine** says in his *Nuptiarum*, Question 27,
AG : 2 7 :035(076) [0081] be dissolved, and St. **Augustine** is no inconsiderable
AG : 2 8 :028(085) [0087] St. **Augustine** also writes in his reply to the letters of
AL : 1 8 :004(039) [0051] of his *Hypognosticon* **Augustine** said these things in so
AL : 2 0 :013(043) [0055] In many volumes **Augustine** defends grace and the
AL : 2 0 :026(045) [0057] **Augustine**, too, admonishes his readers in this way
AL : 2 6 :017(066) [0073] **Augustine** also forbids the burdening of consciences with
AL : 2 7 :002(071) [0077] In **Augustine**'s time they were voluntary associations.
AL : 2 7 :035(076) [0081] For **Augustine** denies that they should be dissolved in
AL : 2 8 :028(085) [0087] **Augustine** also says in reply to the letters of Petilian that
AP : 0 2 :022(103) [0111] ancients, with which **Augustine**'s interpretation of the
AP : 0 2 :024(103) [0111] the intention of **Augustine**'s definition that original sin is
AP : 0 2 :024(103) [0111] Thus **Augustine** includes both the defect and the vicious
AP : 0 2 :036(105) [0115] **Augustine** speaks the same way when he says, "Sin is
AP : 0 2 :036(105) [0115] Against Julian, **Augustine** says: "That law which is in the
AP : 0 2 :038(105) [0115] We have said earlier that **Augustine** defines original sin as
AP : 0 2 :038(105) [0115] Let them argue with **Augustine** if this position displeases
AP : 0 2 :041(105) [0115] In a lengthy discussion **Augustine** refutes the opinion that
AP : 0 4 :029(111) [0129] Against the Pelagians, **Augustine** maintains at length that
AP : 0 4 :033(111) [0129] use the words that **Augustine** uses in discussing this
AP : 0 4 :087(120) [0147] about the whole law, as **Augustine** correctly maintains in
AP : 0 4 :106(122) [0153] **Augustine** writes many things in the same vein against the
AP : 0 4 :106(122) [0153] A little later **Augustine** says: "By the law we fear God, by
AP : 0 4 :172(130) [0171] **Augustine** says very clearly, "All the commandments of
AP : 0 4 :190(133) [0175] Paul, Athanasius, **Augustine**, and other teachers of the
AP : 0 4 :322(157) [0209] after justification, **Augustine** says in *Grace and Free Will*,
AP : 0 4 :356(161) [0217] **Augustine** says, as do many later writers, "God crowns his
AP : 0 4 :389(166) [0225] holy Fathers Ambrose, **Augustine**, and many others, and
AP : 0 4 :400(168) [0227] **Augustine** says: "The question is, where is the church?
AP : 1 2 :148(205) [0299] for penitence because **Augustine** says that "penitence is
AP : 1 2 :148(205) [0299] But what punishment and revenge is **Augustine** discussing?
AP : 1 2 :167(209) [0305] So **Augustine** says that venial sins are consumed, that is,
AP : 1 2 :168(209) [0305] So **Augustine** says, "True satisfaction means cutting off
AP : 1 3 :005(212) [0309] have the same effect, as **Augustine** said so well when he
AP : 1 3 :023(214) [0313] In fact, **Augustine** says the opposite: that faith in the
AP : 1 8 :003(225) [0335] justification we quoted **Augustine**'s emphatic refutation of
AP : 1 8 :010(226) [0337] **Augustine** discusses it too, and more recently William of
AP : 2 0 :014(228) [0343] a thousand years ago, in the days of **Augustine**.
AP : 2 1 :036(234) [0353] having been a sorcerer; **Augustine** experienced the power
AP : 2 7 :017(272) [0425] or of the rule of **Augustine** or of other rules — whoever
S2 : 0 2 :013(295) [0465] adduce passages from **Augustine** and some of the Fathers
S2 : 0 2 :013(295) [0465] St. **Augustine** does not write that there is a purgatory, nor
S2 : 0 2 :014(295) [0467] They can never demonstrate these things from **Augustine**.
S2 : 0 2 :014(295) [0467] Masses (which St. **Augustine** never dreamed of) shall we
S2 : 0 2 :014(295) [0467] statements of St. **Augustine** are to be accepted when they
S3 : 0 3 :028(308) [0487] while we slept (as St. **Augustine**, St. Jerome, and others
S3 : 0 5 :001(310) [0491] the word"; or, again, as **Augustine** puts it, "The Word is
TR : 0 0 :014(322) [0507] in the Latin churches, as Cyprian and **Augustine** testify.
TR : 0 0 :067(331) [0523] like the example which **Augustine** relates of two
LC : 0 4 :018(438) [0737] as a sacrament, as St. **Augustine** taught, "*Accedat verbum*
LC : 0 5 :010(448) [0755] This saying of St. **Augustine** is so accurate and well put
EP : 0 2 :015(471) [0789] For as **Augustine** says, in conversion God makes willing
EP : 0 7 :015(483) [0813] Cyprian, Leo I, Gregory, Ambrose, **Augustine**.
SD : 0 1 :030(513) [0867] the error which **Augustine** attributes to the Manichaeans,
SD : 0 1 :054(518) [0877] Ambrose, and especially **Augustine**, as well as many other
SD : 0 1 :055(518) [0877] the Manichaeans, **Augustine**, in accord with all
SD : 0 1 :056(518) [0877] **Augustine** therefore constantly speaks in this fashion:
SD : 0 2 :023(525) [0889] **Augustine** has written in a similar vein in his second book
SD : 0 2 :027(526) [0891] particular which, by St. **Augustine**'s own statement,
SD : 0 2 :027(527) [0893] And St. **Augustine** says further on, "I have erred when I
SD : 0 2 :081(537) [0911] This error St. **Augustine** condemns in express words in his
SD : 0 7 :037(575) [0985] like Justin, Cyprian, **Augustine**, Leo, Gelasius,

Austere (1), Austerity (1)
AP : 0 4 :288(151) [0203] which competed in the **austerity** of their observances to
LC : 0 1 :145(385) [0623] better than the holiness and **austere** life of all the monks"?

Authentic (1)
EP : 0 8 :001(486) [0817] has arisen between the **authentic** theologians of the

Author (5), Authors (8)
AL : 2 8 :037(087) [0089] instituted because the **authors** of these things thought
AL : 2 8 :039(087) [0089] Again, the **authors** of traditions act contrary to the
AP : 0 2 :001(100) [0105] Majesty will see that the **authors** of the Confutation are
AP : 0 4 :398(167) [0227] this very gathering the **authors** of the Confutation have
AP : 0 7 :001(168) [0227] The **authors** of the Confutation have condemned the
AP : 0 7 :024(172) [0235] of Christ has as its **authors** not only the canonists but also
AP : 2 3 :063(248) [0381] Paul points out the real **author** of such a law when he
AP : 2 3 :063(248) [0381] The real **author** is evident in the results, the many
AP : 2 4 :083(264) [0413] who reads the Greek **authors** can find examples
S2 : 0 2 :013(295) [0465] and to what end the **authors** wrote these passages.
SD : 0 1 :007(510) [0861] that God is not the creator, **author**, or cause of sin.
SD : 0 1 :040(515) [0871] come from God, nor is God the creator or **author** of sin.
SD : 0 1 :041(515) [0871] since the devil is the **author** of sin, Satan is the creator of

Authoritatively (1), Authorities (17), Authority (129), Authorized (3)
AG : 1 6 :005(038) [0051] does not overthrow civil **authority**, the state, and
AG : 1 6 :006(038) [0051] to be subject to civil **authority** and obey its commands
AG : 1 6 :007(038) [0051] commands of the civil **authority** cannot be obeyed
AG : 2 6 :018(067) [0073] or contempt of spiritual **authority**, but dire need has
AG : 2 7 :018(073) [0079] the power, right, and **authority** to marry, for vows cannot
AG : 2 7 :035(076) [0081] is no inconsiderable **authority** in the Christian church,
AG : 2 7 :036(076) [0081] the command and **authority** of God is opposed to God
AG : 2 8 :004(081) [0085] power, sword, and **authority**, and they have taught that
AG : 2 8 :004(081) [0085] God's command both **authorities** and powers are to be
AG : 2 8 :010(082) [0085] interfere at all with government or temporal **authority**.
AG : 2 8 :011(082) [0085] Temporal **authority** is concerned with matters altogether
AG : 2 8 :012(083) [0085] Therefore, the two **authorities**, the spiritual and the
AG : 2 8 :018(083) [0085] distinguish the two **authorities** and the functions of the
AG : 2 8 :019(083) [0087] possess temporal **authority** and the sword, they possess it
AG : 2 8 :019(084) [0087] Such **authority** has nothing at all to do with the office of
AG : 2 8 :026(084) [0087] Again Paul refers to "the **authority** which the Lord has
AG : 2 8 :042(088) [0089] said in II Cor. 10:8 that **authority** was given for building
AL : 0 0 :002(047) [0059] have crept into the churches without proper **authority**.
AL : 2 7 :009(072) [0077] momentous matter the **authority** of the canons was
AL : 2 7 :035(076) [0081] Chapter I, and his **authority** is not inconsiderable,
AL : 2 8 :020(084) [0087] bishops, therefore, civil **authority** must be distinguished
AL : 2 8 :026(084) [0087] "Given to me is the **authority** for building up and not for
AL : 2 8 :041(087) [0089] forgiven except by the **authority** of the person who
AL : 2 8 :042(088) [0089] and Paul says that **authority** was given for building up
AL : 2 8 :058(091) [0091] by the church's **authority** as a necessary thing are
AP : 0 4 :083(119) [0145] which is really citing the **authority** of the church.
AP : 0 4 :264(146) [0195] maintains with even less **authority** that the forgiveness of
AP : 0 4 :390(166) [0225] the prelates their own **authority** is obviously more
AP : 0 4 :391(166) [0225] Their **authority** ought not seem so great as to end all
AP : 0 4 :400(168) [0227] Gospel, contrary to the **authority** of the holy Fathers, and
AP : 1 2 :066(191) [0271] church do we grant the **authority** to issue decrees contrary
AP : 1 2 :068(192) [0271] if we were to count **authorities**, they would be right; for
AP : 1 2 :069(192) [0271] in mind that no great **authority** attaches to the statements
AP : 1 2 :094(196) [0281] Even by themselves, the **authority** of the divine promises
AP : 1 2 :099(197) [0281] of the keys proclaims to individuals by divine **authority**.
AP : 1 2 :119(200) [0287] a recent fiction, without **authority** either in the Scriptures
AP : 1 2 :122(200) [0287] that this idea has **authority** in Scripture, though it was
AP : 1 2 :175(210) [0307] Now, if human **authority** can remit satisfactions and
AP : 1 2 :175(210) [0307] divine law, for human **authority** cannot abrogate divine
AP : 1 2 :177(210) [0307] (II Cor. 10:8), "Our **authority**, which the Lord gave for
AP : 1 3 :003(211) [0309] since men do not have the **authority** to promise grace.
AP : 1 3 :018(213) [0313] is taught with great **authority** throughout the papal
AP : 1 4 :001(214) [0315] although they were created by human **authority**.
AP : 1 4 :005(215) [0315] that we have undermined the **authority** of the bishops.
AP : 1 5 :018(217) [0319] God, devised by human **authority** in opposition to
AP : 1 5 :052(222) [0329] issue when we discuss vows and ecclesiastical **authority**.
AP : 1 6 :013(224) [0333] rather strengthens the **authority** of magistrates and the
AP : 1 8 :003(225) [0335] notions which the schools teach with great **authority**!
AP : 2 1 :019(231) [0347] His merits must be **authorized** to make satisfaction for
AP : 2 1 :035(234) [0353] which are being taught in public on the highest **authority**.
AP : 2 1 :039(235) [0355] would exert their **authority** and the preachers do their
AP : 2 2 :001(236) [0357] By divine **authority** and not by human authority, as we
AP : 2 2 :001(236) [0357] and not by human **authority**, as we suppose our
AP : 2 3 :001(239) [0363] false pretext of divine **authority** for their audacious
AP : 2 3 :005(239) [0365] to maintain their **authority**, which they think celibacy
AP : 2 3 :005(240) [0365] fighting for is their **authority**; they imagine that this is in
AP : 2 3 :016(241) [0369] Because human **authority**, regulations, and vows cannot
AP : 2 3 :024(243) [0371] since the ancient synods and contrary to their **authority**.
AP : 2 3 :024(243) [0371] show contempt for the **authority** of the synods while they
AP : 2 4 :008(250) [0385] and then quote the **authority** of the Fathers against us.
AP : 2 4 :031(255) [0395] it to the Mass, and for this they quote patristic **authority**.
AP : 2 4 :065(261) [0407] which they teach so **authoritatively** in the church; nor do
AP : 2 4 :092(266) [0417] services in the church without the **authority** of Scripture.
AP : 2 7 :029(274) [0431] they still cite the **authority** of Scripture and even say that
AP : 2 8 :006(282) [0445] us that bishops have the **authority** to create laws which
AP : 2 8 :013(283) [0447] namely, the **authority** to excommunicate those who are
AP : 2 8 :018(284) [0449] with unlimited **authority**," but rather a "caution about
AP : 2 8 :020(284) [0449] it does not create an **authority** for bishops apart from the
S2 : 0 4 :003(298) [0471] blasphemous, usurped **authority** have been and still are
S2 : 0 4 :016(301) [0475] emperor or the secular **authority**, as at Augsburg, where
S3 : 1 1 :001(314) [0499] The papists had neither **authority** nor right to prohibit
S3 : 1 4 :001(316) [0501] And on the **authority** of their St. Thomas, such people

Continued ▶

TR : 00 :002(320) [0503] both swords, that is, the **authority** to bestow and transfer
TR : 00 :006(320) [0505] arrogates to himself the **authority** to make laws
TR : 00 :010(321) [0505] that his call did not depend on the **authority** of Peter.
TR : 00 :010(321) [0507] him, he teaches that the **authority** of the ministry depends
TR : 00 :011(321) [0507] to Peter superiority or **authority** over the church or the
TR : 00 :011(321) [0507] assume lordship or **authority** over the church, nor burden
TR : 00 :011(321) [0507] nor let anybody's **authority** count for more than the
TR : 00 :011(321) [0507] the Word, nor set the **authority** of Cephas over against
TR : 00 :011(321) [0507] of Cephas over against the **authority** of the other apostles.
TR : 00 :011(321) [0507] and denies that Peter's **authority** is superior to that of the
TR : 00 :012(322) [0507] Originally, therefore, the **authority** of the Roman bishop
TR : 00 :018(323) [0509] 9. Jerome says, "If it is **authority** that you want, the world
TR : 00 :025(324) [0511] is not built on the **authority** of a man but on the ministry
TR : 00 :026(324) [0511] of any individual's **authority** but because of the Word
TR : 00 :030(325) [0513] they bestow a special **authority** on Peter, for Christ bids
TR : 00 :036(326) [0515] worldly kingdom by the **authority** of Christ and that he
TR : 00 :039(327) [0515] the Gospel and will arrogate to himself divine **authority**.
TR : 00 :040(327) [0515] on the pretext of the **authority** of the church and the
TR : 00 :040(327) [0515] pope arrogates to himself a threefold divine **authority**.
TR : 00 :040(327) [0517] and he exalts his **authority** above the decisions of
TR : 00 :042(328) [0517] But divine **authority** commands us all not to be associated
TR : 00 :054(329) [0519] of them to use their **authority** and power for the support
TR : 00 :063(331) [0523] bishop and presbyter (or pastor) is by human **authority**.
TR : 00 :067(331) [0523] church, and no human **authority** can take it away from
SC : PR :019(340) [0537] pains to urge governing **authorities** and parents to rule
SC : PR :020(340) [0537] parents and governing **authorities** sin in this respect is
SC : 09 :004(355) [0561] Governing **Authorities**
SC : 09 :004(355) [0561] "Let every person be subject to the governing **authorities**.
SC : 09 :004(355) [0561] For there is no **authority** except from God, and those
SC : 09 :004(355) [0561] He who resists the **authorities** resists what God has
SC : 09 :004(355) [0561] He who is in **authority** does not bear the sword in vain;
SC : 09 :005(355) [0561] Duties Subjects Owe to Governing **Authorities**
SC : 09 :005(355) [0561] "Let every person be subject to the governing **authorities**.
SC : 09 :005(355) [0561] also pay taxes, for the **authorities** are ministers of God,
SC : 09 :005(355) [0561] to rulers and **authorities**, to be obedient, to be ready for
LC : 01 :026(368) [0587] Our parents and all **authorities** — in short, all people
LC : 01 :108(380) [0611] obey me as your father and to acknowledge my **authority**.
LC : 01 :115(381) [0613] or to those who have parental **authority** over them.
LC : 01 :141(384) [0621] Out of the **authority** of parents all other authority is
LC : 01 :141(384) [0621] of parents all other **authority** is derived and developed.
LC : 01 :141(384) [0621] and delegates his **authority** and responsibility to others
LC : 01 :142(384) [0621] derive from them their power and **authority** to govern.
LC : 01 :151(386) [0625] or rebelliously resists **authority**, let him know that he
LC : 01 :154(386) [0625] master, be free from all **authority**, care nothing for
LC : 01 :167(388) [0629] how they should treat those committed to their **authority**.
LC : 01 :168(388) [0629] (that is, power and **authority** to govern) merely to receive
LC : 01 :177(389) [0631] no longer any civil order, peace, or respect for **authority**.
LC : 01 :180(389) [0631] that is, divine and paternal **authority** and obedience.
LC : 01 :181(389) [0631] God has delegated his **authority** of punishing evil-doers to
LC : 01 :218(394) [0643] decency and respect for **authority** and, when they are
LC : 01 :258(399) [0653] princes, or others in **authority** sit in judgment, we always
LC : 01 :265(401) [0657] unless he has been **authorized** to judge and reprove.
LC : 01 :266(401) [0657] appointed a judge and **authorized** to administer
LC : 01 :268(401) [0657] guilt assumes as much **authority** as the emperor and all
LC : 01 :270(401) [0657] before the proper **authorities**, then hold your tongue.
LC : 01 :285(403) [0661] it is done with proper **authority** or for his improvement.
LC : 01 :327(409) [0675] masters, and all in **authority**, being submissive and
LC : 03 :008(421) [0699] to obey our fathers and mothers and the civil **authorities**.
LC : 03 :074(430) [0719] is to pray for our civil **authorities** and the government,
LC : 04 :020(439) [0737] we speak about the parental estate and civil **authority**.
LC : 05 :040(451) [0763] his oppression and **authority**, let a year, or two, three, or
EP : 08 :016(489) [0821] he himself testifies, "All **authority** in heaven and on earth
EP : 08 :034(491) [0825] express assertion, "All **authority** in heaven and on earth
EP : 08 :039(491) [0827] words of Christ, "All **authority** has been given to me"
EP : 10 :004(493) [0829] and every age has **authority** to change such ceremonies
SD : 07 :043(577) [0987] away," and again, "All **authority** in heaven and on earth
SD : 08 :055(601) [1033] all judgment, to have all **authority** in heaven and on
SD : 08 :068(604) [1039] and to them all **authority** in heaven and on earth is given,
SD : 08 :070(604) [1039] can or should say, "All **authority** in heaven and on earth
SD : 08 :070(605) [1041] the human nature, "All **authority** in heaven and on earth
SD : 08 :074(606) [1043] are hid in him, all **authority** is given to him, and he is
SD : 08 :085(608) [1047] (Matt. 11:27), and 'All **authority** in heaven and on earth
SD : 08 :085(608) [1047] eternity I have this **authority** from the Father before I
SD : 10 :009(612) [1055] every time has the right, **authority**, and power to change,
SD : 10 :021(614) [1061] assume lordship or **authority** over the church, nor burden
SD : 10 :021(614) [1061] nor let anybody's **authority** count for more than the Word
SD : 10 :023(615) [1061] But divine **authority** commands us all not to be
SD : 11 :095(632) [1095] (since we have no **authority** to do so) to yield anything of

Autocratically (1)
S3 : 06 :004(311) [0493] but even go so far as **autocratically** to prohibit, condemn,

Avail (11), Available (5), Avails (7)
PR : PR :018(009) [0015] 1530, which has been **available** in the archives of those
AP : 04 :111(123) [0155] uncircumcision is of any **avail**, but faith working through
AP : 04 :290(151) [0203] It does not teach us to **avail** ourselves of Christ in our
AP : 12 :036(186) [0261] of Judas and Saul did not **avail** because it lacked the faith
AP : 12 :036(186) [0261] of David and Peter did **avail** because it had the faith that
AP : 12 :118(200) [0287] that these satisfactions **avail** even when they are
AP : 12 :132(202) [0293] the scholastics imagine **avail** as a payment for the
AP : 12 :143(204) [0297] for they teach that they **avail** even for those in mortal sin.
AP : 12 :162(208) [0303] traditions which they say **avails** *ex opere operato* so that
AP : 15 :024(218) [0321] Thomas writes, "Fasting **avails** to destroy and prevent
AP : 27 :034(275) [0431] and the promised mercy **available** in Christ and are
AP : 28 :010(282) [0447] Paul denies that traditions **avail** for eternal righteousness
S2 : 04 :004(299) [0473] a lion (as the angel in Rev. 10:3 suggests), are **available**.
S3 : 03 :016(305) [0483] had to muster in order to **avail** before God, this
LC : PR :002(358) [0567] teach and preach is now **available** to them in clear and
LC : 01 :047(371) [0593] aside) or as a traveler **avails** himself of an inn, food, and
LC : 01 :084(376) [0605] otherwise would not be **available**, to participate in public
EP : 03 :005(473) [0793] the "righteousness which **avails** before God," and that for
EP : 05 :005(478) [0803] the "righteousness that **avails** before God," and eternal
EP : 10 :012(494) [0831] not have the liberty to **avail** itself of one or more such
EP : 11 :009(495) [0833] good I do is of no **avail**; everything is in vain in that
SD : 03 :057(549) [0935] our righteousness which **avails** before God and is revealed
SD : 11 :015(619) [1069] "the righteousness which **avails** before God" and eternal

Avarice (2)
S1 : PR :012(290) [0459] Usury and **avarice** have burst in like a deluge and have
TR : 00 :074(332) [0525] and, either on account of **avarice** or on account of other

Aven (1)
S2 : 03 :002(298) [0471] the prophets call such service of God ***aven***, that is, vanity.

Avenge (4), Avenger (1)
AG : 27 :055(079) [0083] for Christians, even in the government, to **avenge** wrong.
AP : 21 :028(233) [0351] not a propitiator but only a terrible judge and **avenger**.
AP : 23 :070(249) [0383] God will **avenge** this cruelty.
AP : 27 :007(269) [0421] Without doubt, God will soon **avenge** these murders.
TR : 00 :053(329) [0519] of saints, whose blood God will undoubtedly **avenge**.

Aversion (1), Avert (3), Averted (2)
AP : 04 :168(130) [0169] Even this servant of God prays God to **avert** his judgment.
LC : 01 :072(374) [0601] great calamity was **averted** and vanished in the very
LC : 01 :077(375) [0603] Thus we have **averted** the misuse of the divine name and
LC : 01 :250(399) [0651] permit such a thing, but are rather to **avert** and prevent it.
LC : 05 :051(452) [0765] since we show such an **aversion** toward the sacrament,
SD : 11 :003(616) [1063] precisely in order to **avert** such misuse and

Avoid (45), Avoided (9), Avoids (1)
PR : PR :022(011) [0019] why condemnations cannot by any means be **avoided**.
AG : 20 :037(046) [0057] are commanded, render obedience, **avoid** evil lusts, etc.
AG : 00 :001(048) [0059] who presume to reject, **avoid**, and separate from our
AG : 23 :003(051) [0061] In order to **avoid** such unbecoming offense, adultery, and
AG : 23 :003(051) [0061] by the Lord God to **avoid** immorality, for Paul says,
AG : 23 :016(054) [0063] weakness and to prevent and **avoid** greater offense.
AG : 28 :065(092) [0093] but forbade such eating for a time to **avoid** offense.
AG : 00 :001(095) [0095] abuses and wrongs, to **avoid** prolixity and undue length
AL : 23 :003(051) [0061] among us desired to **avoid** such open scandals, they took
AL : 28 :065(092) [0093] but forbade such eating for a time to **avoid** offense.
AL : 00 :001(094) [0095] could be mentioned, to **avoid** undue length we have
AP : 04 :019(109) [0125] only playing in order to **avoid** the impression that they
AP : 04 :048(114) [0135] To **avoid** the impression that it is merely knowledge, we
AP : 07 :002(168) [0227] be said so carefully that it can **avoid** misrepresentation.
AP : 07 :003(168) [0227] the eighth article, to **avoid** the impression that we
AP : 12 :083(194) [0275] Scripture, and we want to **avoid** being lengthy in order to
AP : 22 :013(238) [0361] But to **avoid** the impression that we are minimizing the
AP : 24 :014(251) [0389] Confession we purposely **avoided** this term because of its
AP : 24 :081(264) [0411] have found an immunity and have **avoided** public duty."
AP : 28 :016(283) [0447] that offenses should be **avoided** and that they be not
AP : 28 :017(284) [0449] place and without superstition, in order to **avoid** offenses.
S3 : 03 :011(305) [0481] which man with his free will might well have **avoided**.
S3 : 09 :000(314) [0497] in the church until they mend their ways and **avoid** sin.
SC : PR :007(339) [0533] take the utmost care to **avoid** changes or variations in the
SC : 09 :005(355) [0561] be subject, not only to **avoid** God's wrath but also for the
LC : 01 :056(372) [0595] is and diligently shun and **avoid** every misuse of the holy
LC : 01 :069(374) [0599] and especially to **avoid** calling upon God's name in its
LC : 01 :212(394) [0641] make it easier for man to **avoid** unchastity in some
LC : 01 :214(394) [0641] the guise of great sanctity **avoid** marriage and either
LC : 01 :215(394) [0641] of secret passion, which can be **avoided** in married life.
LC : 01 :225(395) [0643] damage to happen when it could have been **avoided**.
LC : 01 :265(400) [0655] To **avoid** this vice, therefore, we should note that nobody
LC : 01 :276(402) [0659] be carefully noted if we are to **avoid** this detestable abuse.
LC : 01 :284(403) [0661] can without sin shun and **avoid** the person as one who
LC : 01 :323(409) [0673] and, because of this fear, **avoids** all that is contrary to his
LC : 05 :054(453) [0765] To **avoid** this, we must examine our heart and conscience
LC : 05 :080(456) [0771] our Lord Christ himself could not entirely **avoid** him.
EP : 02 :016(472) [0791] accordingly it is well to **avoid** them in a discussion of
EP : 10 :005(493) [0829] and offenses are to be **avoided**, and particularly the weak
EP : 12 :011(499) [0841] in any way, but flee and **avoid** them as perverters of
SD : RN :016(507) [0857] what he should reject, flee, and **avoid** as false and wrong.
SD : 01 :051(517) [0875] In order to **avoid** all contentions about words, it is
SD : 02 :033(527) [0893] will to do good and to **avoid** evil," and shortly thereafter,
SD : 02 :074(535) [0909] behavior and to **avoid** manifest sins and vices; or that the
SD : 02 :086(538) [0913] therefore is rightly to be **avoided** in the discussion of
SD : 04 :039(558) [0951] For one ought to **avoid** with the greatest diligence
SD : 05 :027(563) [0961] Gospel, and diligently to **avoid** anything that might give
SD : 06 :015(566) [0967] order as far as possible to **avoid** all misunderstandings, to
SD : 07 :111(589) [1011] forewarn our readers so they can **avoid** and shun these.
SD : 10 :005(611) [1053] and we should **avoid** as forbidden by God, ceremonies
SD : 10 :005(611) [1053] which give or (to **avoid** persecution) are designed to give
SD : 10 :016(613) [1057] Christian is obligated to **avoid** both, as it is written, "Woe
SD : 11 :093(632) [1095] revealed will, we shall **avoid** and flee all abstruse and
SD : 12 :016(634) [1099] all, but one is to flee and **avoid** them as people who
SD : 12 :039(636) [1103] Christians will and should **avoid** these as dearly as they

Await (3)
TR : 00 :082(000) [0529] as I am not permitted to **await** the end of the assembly, I
LC : 01 :178(389) [0631] explanation will have to **await** another occasion.
LC : 02 :057(418) [0693] and is growing daily, we **await** the time when our flesh

Awaken (4), Awakened (1), Awakening (1), Awakens (1)
AG : 13 :001(035) [0049] us for the purpose of **awakening** and strengthening our
AG : 24 :030(059) [0067] taken place — but to **awaken** our faith and comfort our
AL : 13 :001(035) [0049] toward us, intended to **awaken** and confirm faith in those
LC : 01 :101(379) [0609] It always **awakens** new understanding, new pleasure, and
LC : 02 :043(416) [0689] preached and does not **awaken** understanding in the
LC : 03 :020(423) [0703] certainly ought to **awaken** and kindle in our hearts a
SD : 07 :081(584) [1001] us in his testament) is **awakened**, strengthened, and

Award (1), Awarded (1)
AL : 16 :002(037) [0051] other existing laws, to **award** just punishments, to engage
LC : 01 :302(405) [0667] the owner and legally **awarded** to him with letters patent

Aware (19)
AG : 27 :025(074) [0079] the popes were well **aware** that some amelioration ought

Continued ▶

A P : 0 4 :163(129) [0169] (I Cor. 4:4), "I am not **aware** of anything against me, but
A P : 1 1 :006(181) [0251] us the regulation *Omnis utriusque;* we are **aware** of it.
A P : 2 1 :012(230) [0345] affirm that the saints are **aware** of it or, even if they are,
A P : 2 3 :068(249) [0383] They are well **aware** of this; hence they refuse to show us
A P : 2 4 :066(261) [0407] We are **aware** of the fact that the Fathers call the Mass a
S 2 : 0 2 :010(294) [0465] The papists are well **aware** that if the Mass falls, the
S 3 : 0 3 :020(306) [0485] A man did not become **aware** of the power of absolution,
S 3 : 0 7 :003(312) [0493] in I Cor. 4:4, "I am not **aware** of anything against myself,
S C : 0 3 :013(347) [0547] that God may make us **aware** of his gifts and enable us to
S C : 0 5 :018(350) [0553] of which we are not **aware**, as we do in the Lord's Prayer.
S C : 0 5 :024(350) [0555] simply mention one or two sins of which he is **aware**.
L C : 0 1 :059(372) [0597] prefer to act in secret without anyone's being **aware** of it.
L C : 0 1 :266(401) [0657] When you become **aware** of a sin, simply make your ears
L C : 0 1 :284(403) [0661] and the whole world are **aware** of it, you can without sin
L C : 0 3 :028(424) [0705] his needs, whenever he is **aware** of anything that affects
L C : 0 3 :029(424) [0705] his might, for he is well **aware** what damage and harm he
S D : 0 6 :021(567) [0969] with St. Paul, "I am not **aware** of anything against
S D : 1 1 :055(625) [1081] God is also **aware** and knows exactly how many there

Away (113)
P R : P R :009(006) [0011] hearts were frightened **away** and deterred from our
P R : P R :011(006) [0011] were looking for could be abolished and taken **away**.
P R : P R :024(013) [0023] concealed in darkness, **away** from everyone's eyes, or to
A G : 1 9 :000(041) [0053] his support, the will turns **away** from God to evil.
A G : 2 4 :022(058) [0067] of which sin was taken **away** and God was reconciled.
A G : 2 7 :041(077) [0081] be justified by the law; you have fallen **away** from grace."
A G : 2 7 :042(077) [0081] Christ and have fallen **away** from God's grace, for they
A L : 1 9 :000(041) [0053] will of the wicked turns **away** from God, as Christ says in
A L : 2 4 :022(058) [0067] its performance takes **away** the sins of the living and the
A L : 2 4 :029(059) [0067] Now, if the Mass takes **away** the sins of the living and the
A L : 2 4 :036(060) [0067] inviting some to Communion and keeping others **away**.
A L : 2 7 :041(077) [0081] be justified by the law; you have fallen **away** from grace."
A L : 2 7 :042(077) [0081] from Christ and fall **away** from grace, for those who
A L : 2 8 :002(081) [0085] of this world and take **away** the imperial power.
A P : 0 2 :042(106) [0117] us from trouble right **away**; fretting because bad people
A P : 0 4 :008(108) [0121] flee these things or turn **away** when God imposes them.
A P : 0 4 :030(111) [0129] the law; you have fallen **away** from grace' (Gal. 5:4); for
A P : 0 4 :060(115) [0137] and our opponents take it **away** when they despise and
A P : 0 4 :070(116) [0141] only the law and does **away** with Christ and the Gospel.
A P : 0 4 :081(118) [0145] Christ completely and do **away** with the whole teaching
A P : 0 4 :103(122) [0151] was subjected, he took **away** the sin of the whole world,
A P : 0 4 :103(122) [0151] the Lamb of God, who takes **away** the sin of the world!'
A P : 0 4 :135(125) [0159] us, and this error taken **away**, when God shows us our
A P : 0 4 :165(130) [0169] how a man can do **away** with Christ, the propitiator and
A P : 0 4 :170(130) [0171] defies God's will and runs **away** from afflictions that it
A P : 0 4 :179(131) [0171] us, the sinless Christ took **away** the right of the law to
A P : 0 4 :179(131) [0171] "Though you are still far **away** from the perfection of the
A P : 0 4 :190(133) [0175] the devil and drove him **away** from the believers.
A P : 0 4 :207(135) [0177] belief of those who did **away** with faith in the notion that
A P : 0 4 :219(137) [0181] Whoever casts **away** love will not keep his faith, be it ever
A P : 0 4 :277(148) [0199] so as not to take **away** from the glory of Christ, whose
A P : 0 4 :296(152) [0205] Far **away** from human reason, far away from Moses, we
A P : 0 4 :296(152) [0205] from human reason, far **away** from Moses, we must turn
A P : 1 2 :009(183) [0255] his own sake or is running **away** from eternal
A P : 1 2 :046(188) [0263] because in these troubles our natural lust is purged **away**.
A P : 1 2 :049(188) [0265] Ps. 119:28, "My soul melts **away** for sorrow; strengthen
A P : 1 2 :056(189) [0267] "The Lord has put **away** your sin; you shall not die."
A P : 1 2 :076(193) [0273] call men's consciences **away** from the law to the Gospel,
A P : 1 2 :076(193) [0273] the law to the Gospel, **away** from trust in their own
A P : 1 2 :079(194) [0275] Paul calls us **away** from the law to this promise.
A P : 1 2 :142(204) [0295] that we are far **away** from the perfection that the law
A P : 1 2 :162(208) [0303] satisfactions does not do **away** with the calamities
A P : 1 5 :018(217) [0319] They take honor **away** from Christ when they teach that
A P : 1 9 :001(226) [0337] devil and of men turning **away** from God, as Christ said
A P : 2 0 :009(228) [0341] to try to drive you **away** from the consolation which this
A P : 2 2 :002(236) [0357] why is one kind taken **away** from part of the church and
A P : 2 4 :022(253) [0391] that the blood of bulls and goats should take **away** sins."
A P : 2 4 :041(257) [0399] of the charge that we do **away** with the daily sacrifice.
A P : 2 7 :011(270) [0423] be justified by the law; you have fallen **away** from grace."
A P : 2 7 :011(270) [0423] by monastic works, take **away** from Christ's honor and
A P : 2 7 :011(270) [0423] how the architects of the Confutation slip **away** here!
A P : 2 7 :017(272) [0425] of Christ, has cast Christ **away**, and has fallen from
S 2 : 0 1 :002(292) [0461] Lamb of God, who takes **away** the sin of the world" (John
S 2 : 0 2 :007(294) [0465] of God and the Son of God who takes **away** our sin."
S 3 : 0 3 :038(309) [0489] Lamb of God who takes **away** the sin of the world.
S 3 : 0 5 :002(310) [0491] power which, through the water, washes **away** sin.
S 3 : 0 5 :003(311) [0493] that Baptism washes **away** sin through the assistance of
T R : 0 0 :051(329) [0519] process has been taken **away**, the churches are not able to
T R : 0 0 :067(331) [0523] no human authority can take it **away** from the church.
S C : 0 1 :020(344) [0543] abduct, estrange, or entice **away** our neighbor's wife,
L C : 0 1 :015(366) [0583] He wishes to turn us **away** from everything else, and draw
L C : 0 1 :034(369) [0589] upon men who turn **away** from him, and his anger
L C : 0 1 :057(372) [0597] the heart that turns **away** from him to go unpunished, so
L C : 0 1 :099(378) [0609] and stealthily take the Word of God **away** from us.
L C : 0 1 :141(384) [0621] neighbors; if he passes **away**, he confers and delegates his
L C : 0 1 :190(391) [0635] If you send a person **away** naked when you could clothe
L C : 0 1 :247(398) [0651] you arrogantly turn him **away** whom you ought to give
L C : 0 1 :247(398) [0651] to give aid, he will go **away** wretched and dejected, and
L C : 0 1 :270(401) [0657] I might be called a liar and sent **away** in disgrace."
L C : 0 1 :270(401) [0657] unless these have first been taken **away** from him publicly.
L C : 0 1 :273(401) [0659] good name are easily taken **away**, but not easily restored.
L C : 0 1 :296(405) [0665] to entice anything **away** from your neighbor, even though
L C : 0 1 :302(405) [0667] until the property is taken **away** from the owner and
L C : 0 1 :306(406) [0669] entice a rich bride **away** from another, for in the New
L C : 0 1 :306(406) [0669] us for a person to lure **away** another's man-servant or
L C : 0 1 :307(406) [0669] property, luring it **away** from him against his will, and
L C : 0 3 :011(421) [0701] not cast us out or drive us **away**, even though we are
L C : 0 3 :015(422) [0701] **Away** with such thoughts!
L C : 0 3 :065(429) [0715] fruit, there the blessed holy cross will not be far **away**.
L C : 0 3 :067(429) [0717] flesh may not yield or fall **away** through weakness or
L C : 0 3 :074(430) [0719] there our daily bread is taken **away**, or at least reduced.
L C : 0 3 :080(431) [0721] and desire it is to take **away** or interfere with all we have
L C : 0 3 :104(434) [0727] works of God, to tear us **away** from faith, hope, and
L C : 0 4 :011(437) [0735] appearances and lead us **away** from God's work to our
L C : 0 4 :083(446) [0751] own, overcomes and takes **away** sin and daily strengthens
L C : 0 4 :086(446) [0753] But if anybody falls **away** from his Baptism let him return
L C : 0 5 :014(448) [0755] that if you take the Word **away** from the elements or view
L C : 0 5 :053(453) [0765] case, that if a person stays **away** from the sacrament, day
L C : 0 5 :058(453) [0767] must be told to stay **away**, for they are not fit to receive
L C : 0 5 :073(455) [0771] purely and worthily, you must stay **away** from it forever.
L C : 0 6 :021(459) [0000] purity of his confession, let him just stay **away** from it.
L C : 0 6 :029(460) [0000] it and proudly stay **away** from confession, then we must
E P : 0 2 :003(470) [0787] will is not only turned **away** from God, but has also
S D : 0 2 :017(523) [0887] is not only totally turned **away** from God, but is also
S D : 0 2 :022(525) [0889] and severe judgment cast **away** forever the wicked spirits
S D : 0 4 :033(556) [0949] calling, lest you fall **away** and lose the Spirit and his gifts,
S D : 0 5 :024(563) [0961] points and leads not **away** from but toward the Christ
S D : 0 6 :001(564) [0963] of Moses has been taken **away**, learn from the law to live
S D : 0 7 :023(573) [0979] that if you take the Word **away** or look upon the
S D : 0 7 :043(577) [0987] and earth shall pass **away**, but my words will not pass
S D : 0 7 :043(577) [0987] my words will not pass **away**," and again, "All authority
S D : 0 7 :045(577) [0987] human reason, to turn us **away** from these words, no
S D : 0 7 :092(586) [1005] they may have, to lead us **away** from the simple, explicit,
S D : 0 7 :116(589) [1011] our faith, when it turns **away** from the Supper and rises
S D : 0 7 :122(590) [1013] of the Supper, but to look **away** from the bread of the
S D : 1 1 :011(618) [1067] did not persevere but fell **away** again, they may think, "If
S D : 1 1 :028(620) [1071] Christ has taken **away** the sin of the world (John 1:29); he
S D : 1 1 :032(621) [1073] we ourselves do not turn **away** from him but "hold fast
S D : 1 1 :042(623) [1077] joy," but after that "they fall **away** again" (Luke 8:13).
S D : 1 1 :042(623) [1077] is that they willfully turn **away** from the holy
S D : 1 1 :054(625) [1081] and who after falling **away** will return and who will
S D : 1 1 :068(627) [1085] Christ will not turn them **away**, "Him who comes to me I
S D : 1 1 :083(630) [1091] who deliberately turn **away** from the holy commandment

Awful (1)
S C : P R :020(340) [0537] them that God will inflict **awful** punishments on them for

Awkward (1)
A P : 0 2 :007(101) [0107] of the body; in their **awkward** way they ask whether it

Awl (1)
L C : 0 1 :047(371) [0593] a cobbler uses his needle, **awl**, and thread (for work,

Axiom (2), Axioms (1)
E P : 1 0 :007(494) [0831] according to the familiar **axiom**, "Disagreement in fasting
S D : 0 1 :055(518) [0877] and irrefutable **axioms** in theology that every substance
S D : 1 0 :031(616) [1063] to the well-known **axiom**, "Disagreement in fasting should

Baal (6)
A P : 2 4 :097(268) [0417] introduced the worship of **Baal**; in Judah they even
A P : 2 4 :097(268) [0417] against the worshipers of **Baal** but also against other
A P : 2 4 :098(268) [0417] in Israel the worship of **Baal** continued; yet the church of
A P : 2 4 :098(268) [0417] papal realm the worship of **Baal** clings — namely, the
A P : 2 4 :098(268) [0419] seems that this worship of **Baal** will endure together with
A P : 2 4 :099(268) [0419] the prophet Elijah in condemning the worship of **Baal**.

Babble (1), Babbling (5), Babblings (1)
A P : 2 7 :053(278) [0437] Virgin, which is mere **babbling**, as stupid as it is wicked,
A P : 2 7 :055(278) [0439] would be more useful than these endless **babblings**.
L C : P R :003(358) [0567] the useless, bothersome **babbling** of the Seven Hours, it
L C : 0 3 :007(421) [0699] true that the kind of **babbling** and bellowing that used to
L C : 0 3 :033(424) [0707] distinguish between vain **babbling** and praying for
L C : 0 4 :015(438) [0735] from the well, and then **babble**, "How can a handful of
L C : 0 5 :007(447) [0755] refute all the **babbling** of the seditious spirits who regard

Bacchantes (1)
A P : 2 3 :002(239) [0363] fathers "who look like Curius and live like **Bacchantes**."

Back (23), Backed (1), Backs (4)
P R : P R :004(004) [0007] and in this way hold **back** and perceptibly impede the
A P : 0 4 :164(129) [0169] Therefore we must always go **back** to the promise.
A P : 0 4 :224(138) [0181] them for this and calls them **back** to the duties of love.
A P : 0 4 :237(140) [0187] more understanding than the walls that fling **back** an echo.
A P : 0 4 :277(148) [0199] We must come **back** to the rule that without Christ the
A P : 1 2 :113(199) [0285] nor need we bring them **back** because they are not
A P : 2 4 :092(266) [0415] But let us get **back** to the issue.
A P : 2 4 :095(267) [0417] If they came **back** to life now and saw their sayings being
A P : 2 7 :062(280) [0441] countrymen, lest they fall **back** into the wickedness of
L C : 0 1 :076(375) [0603] will remain good only as long as the rod is on their **backs**.
L C : 0 1 :122(382) [0615] until a rod is laid on their **backs**, they anger both God
L C : 0 1 :123(382) [0617] one another behind their **backs** in any way they can.
L C : 0 1 :151(386) [0625] we seek and deserve, then, is paid **back** to us in retaliation.
L C : 0 1 :152(386) [0625] difficult do you think it will be for him to pay you **back**?
L C : 0 1 :195(391) [0637] to remind us to think **back** to the First Commandment,
L C : 0 1 :236(397) [0647] you have done you will have to pay **back** thirty-fold.
L C : 0 1 :264(400) [0655] shameful vice of **back**-biting or slander by which the
L C : 0 1 :279(403) [0661] with personally and not gossiped about behind his **back**.
L C : 0 2 :031(414) [0685] is, he who has brought us **back** from the devil to God,
L C : 0 3 :018(423) [0703] ordered you to pray and **backed** it up with such a strict
L C : 0 3 :087(432) [0723] Besides, Satan is at our **backs**, besieging us on every side
L C : 0 3 :105(434) [0727] and weary and to fall **back** into sin, shame, and unbelief.
L C : 0 3 :111(435) [0729] But prayer can resist him and drive him **back**.
L C : 0 5 :048(452) [0765] perverted it and turned it **back** into a Jewish feast).
L C : 0 6 :006(457) [0000] or his like bring them **back** into subjection and coerce
E P : 0 5 :008(479) [0803] Thus they are directed **back** to the law, and now they
S D : 0 6 :020(567) [0969] they will not be thrown **back** on their own holiness and
S D : 1 1 :063(626) [1083] and say, "Who are you, a man, to answer **back** to God?"

Backbiters (1)
L C : 0 1 :267(401) [0657] Those are called **backbiters** who are not content just to

Bad (14), Badly (3)
A L : 2 0 :018(043) [0055] righteousness, have **bad** judgment concerning this
A P : 0 2 :042(106) [0117] away; fretting because **bad** people are more fortunate
A P : 0 2 :043(106) [0117] we are neither good nor **bad**, neither to be praised nor
A P : 0 4 :119(123) [0155] Our opponents give men **bad** advice when they bid them

Continued ▶

A P : 0 4 :285(150) [0201] pious consciences very **badly** when they teach that works
A P : 0 7 :001(168) [0227] in which there are both good and **bad** fish (Matt. 13:47).
A P : 1 2 :149(205) [0299] Our opponents are **badly** mistaken if they think that
A P : 1 8 :006(225) [0335] they are ungodly; for "a **bad** tree cannot bear good fruit"
A P : 2 7 :005(269) [0421] cube degenerates into **bad** harmonies which, Plato says,
S 3 : 0 8 :001(312) [0493] and help against sin and a **bad** conscience, confession and
S C : 0 5 :023(350) [0553] I have set a **bad** example by my immodest language and
L C : 0 1 :144(385) [0623] indulgences, to their own hurt and with a **bad** conscience.
L C : 0 1 :151(386) [0625] his children will turn out **badly**; servants, neighbors, or
L C : 0 1 :227(396) [0645] dishonest weights, and **bad** coins, and takes advantage of
L C : 0 3 :044(425) [0709] an earthly father to have a **bad**, unruly child who
E P : 0 1 :022(469) [0785] word means the good or **bad** quality which inheres in the
S D : 0 4 :008(552) [0941] A **bad** tree cannot bear good fruit, and "Whatsoever does

Bade (1)
L C : 0 3 :057(427) [0713] and mighty emperor who **bade** a poor beggar to ask for

Baden (2)
P R : P R :027(015) [0025] Margrave Ernest [of **Baden**-Durlach] and
P R : P R :027(015) [0025] Margrave James of **Baden** [-Hachberg] the above two

Badgers (1)
L C : 0 3 :104(434) [0727] the devil, who baits and **badgers** us on all sides, but

Badges (1)
S D : 0 7 :115(589) [1011] Supper are no more than **badges** whereby Christians

Bag (1)
S 3 : 1 5 :004(316) [0501] there remains the pope's **bag** of magic tricks which

Bailiff (1)
L C : 0 6 :023(460) [0000] place; he would need no **bailiff** to drive and beat him but

Baits (1)
L C : 0 3 :104(434) [0727] Then comes the devil, who **baits** and badgers us on all

Balance (1), Balanced (1)
A P : 0 2 :017(102) [0109] to involve not only a **balanced** physical constitution, but
S D : 0 8 :044(599) [1029] that unless God is in the **balance** and throws in weight as

Bald (1)
E P : 0 4 :017(477) [0801] of Christian discipline that **bald** statement that good

Ban (3), Banish (4)
A G : 2 8 :002(081) [0083] and violent use of the **ban**, but have also presumed to set
A G : 0 0 :002(095) [0095] about indulgences, pilgrimages, and misuse of the **ban**.
A P : 2 3 :003(239) [0363] reverently spare, and **banish** deserted wives and orphaned
T R : 0 0 :074(332) [0525] to have the power to **ban** men arbitrarily without due
S C : P R :012(339) [0535] the prince is disposed to **banish** such rude people from his
L C : 0 1 :115(381) [0613] our young people to **banish** all other things from sight
E P : 1 1 :013(496) [0835] The Christian should **banish** all other opinions since they

Banquet (2), Banquets (1)
A P : 2 4 :068(262) [0407] Christians because **banquets** are symbols of agreement
A P : 2 4 :086(265) [0413] think it was called that because of the common **banquet**.
S D : 1 1 :051(624) [1079] invited shall taste my **banquet**" (Luke 14:24); likewise,

Baptism (177)
A G : 0 2 :002(029) [0043] are not born again through **Baptism** and the Holy Spirit.
A G : 0 7 :004(032) [0047] belongs to your call, one Lord, one faith, one **baptism**."
A G : 0 9 :000(033) [0047] IX. **Baptism**
A G : 0 9 :001(033) [0047] is taught among us that **Baptism** is necessary and that
A G : 0 9 :002(033) [0047] be baptized, for in **Baptism** they are committed to God
A G : 0 9 :003(033) [0047] who teach that infant **Baptism** is not right are rejected.
A G : 1 2 :001(034) [0049] that those who sin after **Baptism** receive forgiveness of sin
A G : 1 2 :009(035) [0049] denied absolution to such as had sinned after **Baptism**.
A G : 2 7 :011(072) [0077] vows were equal to **Baptism**, and that by monastic life
A G : 2 7 :013(072) [0077] so monastic vows were praised more highly than **Baptism**.
A L : 0 2 :002(029) [0043] are not born again through **Baptism** and the Holy Spirit.
A L : 0 7 :004(032) [0047] says, "One faith, one **baptism**, one God and Father of
A L : 0 9 :000(033) [0047] IX. [**Baptism**]
A L : 0 9 :001(033) [0047] Our churches teach that **Baptism** is necessary for
A L : 0 9 :001(033) [0047] God is offered through **Baptism**, and that children should
A L : 0 9 :002(033) [0047] offered to God through **Baptism** they are received into his
A L : 0 9 :003(033) [0047] who reject the **Baptism** of children and declare that
A L : 0 9 :003(033) [0047] and declare that children are saved without **Baptism**.
A L : 1 2 :001(034) [0049] who have fallen after **Baptism** can receive forgiveness of
A L : 1 2 :009(035) [0049] who had fallen after **Baptism** although they returned to
A L : 2 7 :011(072) [0077] that vows were equal to **Baptism**, and they taught that
A L : 2 7 :013(072) [0077] was far better than **Baptism**, and that monastic life was
A P : 0 2 :035(104) [0115] original sin remains after **Baptism**, and they add that this
A P : 0 2 :035(105) [0115] by this statement that original sin remains after **Baptism**.
A P : 0 2 :035(105) [0115] has always written that **Baptism** removes the guilt of
A P : 0 2 :035(105) [0115] the Holy Spirit, given in **Baptism**, begins to mortify lust
A P : 0 2 :036(105) [0115] says, "Sin is forgiven in **Baptism**, not that it no longer is,
A P : 0 4 :276(148) [0199] **Baptism** and the Lord's Supper, for example, are signs
A P : 0 9 :000(178) [0245] [Article IX. **Baptism**]
A P : 0 9 :001(178) [0245] where we confess that **Baptism** is necessary for salvation;
A P : 0 9 :001(178) [0245] are to be baptized; the **Baptism** of children is not useless
A P : 0 9 :002(178) [0245] also their assertion that the **Baptism** of children is useless.
A P : 0 9 :002(178) [0245] is offered to all, so **Baptism** is offered to all — men,
A P : 0 9 :002(178) [0245] be baptized because salvation is offered with **Baptism**.
A P : 0 9 :003(178) [0245] that God approves the **Baptism** of little children, the
A P : 0 9 :003(178) [0245] when they condemn the **Baptism** of little children.
A P : 0 9 :003(178) [0245] God does approve the **Baptism** of little children is shown
A P : 0 9 :003(178) [0245] For if this **Baptism** were useless, the Holy Spirit would be
A P : 1 2 :001(182) [0253] who have fallen after **Baptism** can obtain the forgiveness
A P : 1 3 :004(211) [0309] therefore, are **Baptism**, the Lord's Supper, and absolution
A P : 2 4 :018(252) [0389] to the ceremony; thus **Baptism** is not an act which we
A P : 2 7 :009(270) [0421] Are they equal to **Baptism**?
A P : 2 7 :020(272) [0427] says that a monastic profession is equal to **Baptism**.
S 3 : 0 4 :000(310) [0491] world; second, through **Baptism**; third, through the holy
S 3 : 0 5 :000(310) [0491] V. **Baptism**
S 3 : 0 5 :001(310) [0491] **Baptism** is nothing else than the Word of God in water,
S 3 : 0 5 :003(311) [0493] who teach that **Baptism** washes away sin through the
S 3 : 0 5 :004(311) [0493] As for infant **Baptism**, we hold that children should be
S 3 : 0 5 :004(311) [0493] made, and the church should administer **Baptism** to them.
S 3 : 0 8 :007(313) [0495] who came to faith in **Baptism** came to their faith through
S 3 : 0 8 :007(313) [0495] not receive the Spirit and **Baptism** until ten years later.
S 3 : 1 4 :001(316) [0501] people boast that a monastic vow is equal to **Baptism**.
S 3 : 1 5 :004(316) [0501] of churches, the **baptism** of bells, the baptism of altar
S 3 : 1 5 :004(316) [0501] the baptism of bells, the **baptism** of altar stones, the
S 3 : 1 5 :004(316) [0501] and mockery of holy **Baptism** which should not be
T R : 0 0 :067(331) [0523] and the latter, after his **Baptism**, absolved the former.
S C : P R :011(339) [0535] accepted as sponsors in **Baptism**, or be allowed to
S C : 0 4 :000(348) [0551] [IV] The Sacrament of Holy **Baptism**
S C : 0 4 :001(348) [0551] What is **baptism**?
S C : 0 4 :002(348) [0551] Answer: **Baptism** is not merely water, but it is water used
S C : 0 4 :005(348) [0551] What gifts or benefits does **Baptism** bestow?
S C : 0 4 :010(349) [0551] Word of God the water is merely water and no **Baptism**.
S C : 0 4 :010(349) [0551] the Word of God it is a **Baptism**, that is, a gracious water
S C : 0 4 :014(349) [0553] therefore with him by **baptism** into death, so that as
L C : S P :005(362) [0575] daily — yet they come to **Baptism** and the Sacrament of
L C : S P :020(364) [0579] **Baptism** and the holy Body and Blood of Christ,
L C : S P :021(364) [0579] ***Baptism***
L C : S P :022(364) [0579] to know this much about **Baptism** from the Scriptures.
L C : 0 3 :037(425) [0707] we became Christians at **Baptism**, and so we are called
L C : 0 3 :098(433) [0725] can be effected by **Baptism** and the Lord's Supper, which
L C : 0 4 :000(436) [0733] Fourth Part: **Baptism**
L C : 0 4 :002(436) [0733] First we shall take up **Baptism**, through which we are first
L C : 0 4 :003(437) [0733] the words upon which **Baptism** is founded and to which
L C : 0 4 :006(437) [0733] not doubt, then, that **Baptism** is of divine origin, not
L C : 0 4 :006(437) [0733] so I can also boast that **Baptism** is no human plaything
L C : 0 4 :007(437) [0733] that we regard **Baptism** as excellent, glorious, and
L C : 0 4 :007(437) [0733] sects who proclaim that **Baptism** is an external thing and
L C : 0 4 :008(437) [0733] been instituted, established, and confirmed in **Baptism**.
L C : 0 4 :009(437) [0735] then we ought to regard **Baptism** as much greater and
L C : 0 4 :013(438) [0735] forth and, because **Baptism** is not dazzling like the works
L C : 0 4 :014(438) [0735] how to answer properly the question, What is **Baptism**?
L C : 0 4 :015(438) [0735] in order to slander **Baptism**, ignore God's Word and
L C : 0 4 :017(438) [0735] the distinction, then: **Baptism** is a very different thing from
L C : 0 4 :021(439) [0737] should honor and exalt **Baptism** on account of the Word,
L C : 0 4 :022(439) [0737] with and could indeed be called a bathkeeper's **baptism**.
L C : 0 4 :022(439) [0737] to God's ordinance, **Baptism** is a sacrament, and it is
L C : 0 4 :022(439) [0737] Baptism is a sacrament, and it is called Christ's **Baptism**.
L C : 0 4 :023(439) [0737] we now know what **Baptism** is and how it is to be
L C : 0 4 :024(439) [0737] effect, benefit, fruit, and purpose of **Baptism** is to save.
L C : 0 4 :026(439) [0739] and important a thing **Baptism** should be regarded as
L C : 0 4 :027(440) [0739] for through the Word **Baptism** receives the power to
L C : 0 4 :029(440) [0739] and believes it to be **Baptism** in which there is sheer
L C : 0 4 :031(440) [0739] what do they refer but to **Baptism**, that is, the water
L C : 0 4 :031(440) [0739] that whoever rejects **Baptism** rejects God's Word, faith,
L C : 0 4 :031(440) [0739] faith, and Christ, who directs us and binds us to **Baptism**.
L C : 0 4 :032(440) [0739] benefit and power of **Baptism**, let us observe further who
L C : 0 4 :032(440) [0739] further who receives these gifts and benefits of **Baptism**.
L C : 0 4 :034(440) [0741] Without faith **Baptism** is of no use, although in itself it is
L C : 0 4 :035(441) [0741] it is often objected, "If **Baptism** is itself a work, and you
L C : 0 4 :035(441) [0741] **Baptism**, however, is not our work but God's (for, as was
L C : 0 4 :035(441) [0741] must distinguish Christ's **Baptism** quite clearly from a
L C : 0 4 :035(441) [0741] Baptism quite clearly from a bath-keeper's **baptism**).
L C : 0 4 :036(441) [0741] you, you do not receive **Baptism** in such a manner that it
L C : 0 4 :037(441) [0741] Thus you see plainly that **Baptism** is not a work which we
L C : 0 4 :038(441) [0741] be enough, even though **Baptism** is an entirely external
L C : 0 4 :038(441) [0741] to accept and observe **Baptism** as an ordinance of God.
L C : 0 4 :041(441) [0743] In **Baptism**, therefore, every Christian has enough to
L C : 0 4 :041(441) [0743] do to believe firmly what **Baptism** promises and brings —
L C : 0 4 :042(442) [0743] In short, the blessings of **Baptism** are so boundless that if
L C : 0 4 :043(442) [0743] Now, here in **Baptism** there is brought free to every man's
L C : 0 4 :044(442) [0743] To appreciate and use **Baptism** aright, we must draw
L C : 0 4 :045(442) [0743] two things are done in **Baptism**: the body has water
L C : 0 4 :046(442) [0743] together constitute one **Baptism**, body and soul shall be
L C : 0 4 :046(442) [0743] the soul and apprehends **Baptism** in the only way it can.
L C : 0 4 :046(442) [0743] our body and soul than **Baptism**, for through it we obtain
L C : 0 4 :046(442) [0743] benefits, and use of **Baptism** as answering the present
L C : 0 4 :046(442) [0743] [Infant **Baptism**]
L C : 0 4 :047(442) [0743] world through his sects, the question of infant **Baptism**.
L C : 0 4 :049(442) [0743] That the **Baptism** of infants is pleasing to Christ is
L C : 0 4 :050(442) [0745] God did not accept the **Baptism** of infants, he would not
L C : 0 4 :050(443) [0745] God has confirmed **Baptism** through the gift of His Holy
L C : 0 4 :050(443) [0745] must acknowledge that infant **Baptism** is pleasing to God.
L C : 0 4 :052(443) [0745] not, for in the latter case **Baptism** does not become
L C : 0 4 :053(443) [0745] I have already said, that **Baptism** is simply water and
L C : 0 4 :053(443) [0745] accompanies the water, **Baptism** is valid, even though
L C : 0 4 :053(443) [0745] For my faith does not constitute **Baptism** but receives it.
L C : 0 4 :053(443) [0745] **Baptism** does not become invalid even if it is wrongly
L C : 0 4 :054(443) [0745] faith, we should have to admit that his **Baptism** was valid.
L C : 0 4 :055(443) [0745] have proved — still their **Baptism** would be valid and no
L C : 0 4 :056(443) [0747] and confess, "The **Baptism** indeed was right, but
L C : 0 4 :057(444) [0747] We do the same in infant **Baptism**.
L C : 0 4 :058(444) [0747] there is no true faith, there also can be no true **Baptism**.
L C : 0 4 :059(444) [0747] Precisely because **Baptism** has been wrongly received, it
L C : 0 4 :060(444) [0747] therefore be that **Baptism** always remains valid and
L C : 0 4 :061(444) [0747] They regard **Baptism** only as water in the brook or in the
L C : 0 4 :063(444) [0749] the Word, regarding **Baptism** merely as an empty sign, as
L C : 0 4 :064(444) [0749] we must know what **Baptism** signifies and why God
L C : 0 4 :065(445) [0749] the power and effect of **Baptism**, which is simply the
L C : 0 4 :065(445) [0749] nothing else than a daily **Baptism**, once begun and ever
L C : 0 4 :068(445) [0749] This is the right use of **Baptism** among Christians,
L C : 0 4 :068(445) [0749] grows stronger, **Baptism** is not being used but resisted.
L C : 0 4 :071(445) [0749] is not restrained and suppressed by the power of **Baptism**.
L C : 0 4 :071(445) [0751] it means to plunge into **Baptism** and daily come forth
L C : 0 4 :073(445) [0751] with its fruits, there **Baptism** is no empty symbol, but the
L C : 0 4 :074(445) [0751] Here you see that **Baptism**, both by its power and by its
L C : 0 4 :074(445) [0751] called Penance, which is really nothing else than **Baptism**.
L C : 0 4 :075(445) [0751] you are walking in **Baptism**, which not only announces
L C : 0 4 :076(445) [0751] In **Baptism** we are given the grace, Spirit, and power to

Continued ▶

LC : 0 4 :077(446) [0751] Therefore **Baptism** remains forever.
LC : 0 4 :078(446) [0751] nevertheless be only one **Baptism**, and the effect and
LC : 0 4 :078(446) [0751] and signification of **Baptism** would continue and remain.
LC : 0 4 :079(446) [0751] return and approach to **Baptism**, to resume and practice
LC : 0 4 :080(446) [0751] among us, that our **Baptism** is something past which we
LC : 0 4 :080(446) [0751] because we regard **Baptism** only in the light of a work
LC : 0 4 :082(446) [0751] interpretation deprives **Baptism** of its value, making it of
LC : 0 4 :083(446) [0751] great and excellent thing **Baptism** is, which snatches us
LC : 0 4 :084(446) [0753] let everybody regard his **Baptism** as the daily garment
LC : 0 4 :086(446) [0753] anybody falls away from his **Baptism** let him return to it.
LC : 0 4 :086(446) [0753] forgiveness of sins in **Baptism**, so forgiveness remains day
LC : 0 5 :001(447) [0753] As we treated Holy **Baptism** under three headings, so we
LC : 0 5 :004(447) [0753] but as in the case of **Baptism**, we shall first learn what is
LC : 0 5 :009(447) [0755] As we said of **Baptism** that it is not mere water, so we say
LC : 0 5 :023(449) [0757] it is true that through **Baptism** we are first born anew, our
LC : 0 5 :033(450) [0761] said above concerning **Baptism** and in many other places,
EP : 1 2 :006(498) [0839] this innocence without **Baptism** (which according to this
EP : 1 2 :008(498) [0839] without and prior to **Baptism** the children of Christian
EP : 1 2 :008(498) [0839] think highly of infant **Baptism** nor encourage it, in spite
EP : 1 2 :023(500) [0841] 4. That the water of **Baptism** is not a means through
SD : 0 2 :015(523) [0887] and illuminated us through **Baptism** and the Holy Spirit.
SD : 0 2 :016(523) [0887] the Holy Spirit in **Baptism**, has kindled and wrought a
SD : 0 7 :050(578) [0989] kinds of sacrifice in the Old Testament, and holy **Baptism**.
SD : 0 7 :087(585) [1003] water is no sacrament or **Baptism** if it should be used to
SD : 1 1 :072(628) [1085] he has assured us in holy **Baptism**, and not doubt that
SD : 1 2 011(634) [1099] will be saved without **Baptism**, which they do not need.
SD : 1 2 013(634) [1099] and children of God even without and prior to **Baptism**.
SD : 1 2 013(634) [1099] do not esteem infant **Baptism** very highly and do not
SD : 1 2 31(635) [1101] 3. That the water of **Baptism** is not a means whereby the

Baptismal (1)
SD : 0 7 87(585) [1003] adoration, just as the **baptismal** water is no sacrament or

Baptist (3)
AP : 0 4 :263(146) [0195] worthy of penitence, as John the **Baptist** says (Matt. 3:8).
AP : 1 2 :159(207) [0301] were killed, and John the **Baptist**, and other saints.
S3 : 0 8 :012(313) [0497] John the **Baptist** was not conceived without the preceding

Baptize (9), Baptized (41), Baptizes (1), Baptizing (5)
AG : 0 9 02(033) [0047] Children, too, should be **baptized**, for in Baptism they are
AL : 0 9 002(033) [0047] that children should be **baptized**, for being offered to God
AP : 0 9 .001(178) [0245] children are to be **baptized**; the Baptism of children is not
AP : 0 9 :002(178) [0245] it is necessary to **baptize** children, so that the promise of
AP : 0 9 :002(178) [0245] to Christ's command (Matt. 28:19), "**Baptize** all nations."
AP : 0 9 :002(178) [0245] that infants should be **baptized** because salvation is
AP : 0 9 :003(178) [0245] gives the Holy Spirit to those who were **baptized** this way.
AP : 1 3 :004(211) [0309] When we are **baptized**, when we eat the Lord's body,
AP : 2 4 :018(252) [0389] but one in which God **baptizes** us through a minister
AP : 2 4 :018(252) [0389] 16:16), "He who believes and is **baptized** will be saved."
S3 : 0 5 :004(311) [0493] that children should be **baptized**, for they, too, are
S3 : 0 8 :007(313) [0495] faith before they were **baptized** and those who came to
S3 : 0 8 :007(313) [0495] "He who believes and is **baptized** will be saved" (Mark
S3 : 1 0 :002(314) [0497] to preach or teach or **baptize** or administer Communion
S3 : 1 5 :004(316) [0501] Such **baptizing** is a ridicule and mockery of holy Baptism
TR : 0 0 :067(331) [0523] in a ship, one of whom **baptized** the other (a
SC : PR :003(338) [0533] to be Christian, are **baptized**, and receive the holy
SC : 0 4 :004(348) [0551] disciples of all nations, **baptizing** them in the name of the
SC : 0 4 :008(349) [0551] "He who believes and is **baptized** will be saved; but he
SC : 0 4 :011(349) [0551] What does such **baptizing** with water signify?
LC : SP :021(364) [0579] teach all nations, and **baptize** them in the name of the
LC : SP :021(364) [0579] "He who believes and is **baptized** will be saved; but he
LC : 0 4 :004(437) [0733] *and teach all nations, **baptizing** them in the name of the*
LC : 0 4 :005(437) [0733] *who believes and is **baptized** will be saved; but he who*
LC : 0 4 :006(437) [0733] that we must be **baptized** or we shall not be saved.
LC : 0 4 :009(437) [0735] So the words read, "Go, **baptize**," not in your name but
LC : 0 4 :010(437) [0735] To be **baptized** in God's name is to be baptized not by
LC : 0 4 :010(437) [0735] in God's name is to be **baptized** not by men but by God
LC : 0 4 :021(439) [0737] allowed himself to be **baptized**, that the Holy Spirit
LC : 0 4 :023(439) [0737] above, "He who believes and is **baptized** shall be saved."
LC : 0 4 :024(439) [0737] No one is **baptized** in order to become a prince, but as the
LC : 0 4 :031(440) [0739] words, "He who believes and is **baptized** will be saved."
LC : 0 4 :033(440) [0741] "He who believes and is **baptized** will be saved," that is,
LC : 0 4 :036(441) [0741] and ordinance, so that, **baptized** in the name of God, you
LC : 0 4 :038(441) [0741] these words, "Go and **baptize**," we would still have to
LC : 0 4 :044(442) [0743] oppress us, and we must retort, "But I am **baptized**!
LC : 0 4 :044(442) [0743] And if I am **baptized**, I have the promise that I shall be
LC : 0 4 :047(442) [0743] Do children also believe, and is it right to **baptize** them?
LC : 0 4 :049(442) [0745] who have been thus **baptized** and has given them the
LC : 0 4 :052(443) [0745] concerned whether the **baptized** person believes or not,
LC : 0 4 :054(443) [0745] an evil purpose, and we **baptized** him in all good faith, we
LC : 0 4 :056(443) [0747] myself, and all who are **baptized**, must say before God: "I
LC : 0 4 :057(444) [0747] But we do not **baptize** him on that account, but solely on
LC : 0 4 :060(444) [0747] if only one person were **baptized** and he, moreover, did
LC : 0 4 :068(445) [0749] among Christians, signified by **baptizing** with water.
LC : 0 5 :061(453) [0767] We are not **baptized** because we are worthy and holy, nor
LC : 0 5 :087(456) [0773] Since they are **baptized** and received into the Christian
EP : 1 2 :007(498) [0839] children are not to be **baptized** until they have achieved
SD : 0 1 :014(511) [0863] great and terrible that in **baptized** believers it can be
SD : 0 1 :045(516) [0873] say that original sin is **baptized** in the name of the holy
SD : 0 2 :067(534) [0907] great difference between **baptized** people and unbaptized
SD : 0 2 :067(534) [0907] Paul, "all who have been **baptized** have put on Christ"
SD : 0 2 :069(534) [0907] if those who have been **baptized** act contrary to their
SD : 0 2 :069(534) [0907] him, they dare not be **baptized** again, though they must
SD : 1 0 :019(614) [1059] to preach or teach or **baptize** or administer Communion
SD : 1 2 :012(634) [1099] children should not be **baptized** until they have achieved

Bar (2)
LC : 0 6 :034(461) [0000] who ignore such a treasure and **bar** themselves from it.
EP : 1 1 :012(496) [0835] and their hearts, and thus **bar** the ordinary way for the

Barbara (1)
AP : 2 1 :035(234) [0353] midst of her tortures, **Barbara** asks for a reward — that no

Barbarians (1), Barbarous (2)
AP : 2 3 :003(239) [0363] priests whom even the **barbarians** reverently spare, and
AP : 2 3 :003(239) [0363] propose laws which no **barbarous** country, however
LC : 0 5 :041(451) [0763] they have become quite **barbarous**, and ultimately despise

Bare (4)
SD : 0 8 :020(595) [1021] it is not only the **bare** human nature (whose property it is
SD : 0 8 :067(604) [1039] that it merely shares the **bare** titles and the names in
SD : 0 8 :095(609) [1049] glory, but has only the **bare** title and name in common
SD : 1 2 :004(633) [1097] opinion with a few **bare** words or our signatures, but to

Barefoot (1)
AP : 1 2 :144(205) [0297] one making a trip in armor and another going **barefoot**.

Barnabas (1)
SD : 1 0 :013(613) [1057] When Peter and **Barnabas** in a similar situation yielded to

Baron (4)
PR : PR :027(015) [0025] Henry, **baron** of Limpurg [-Schmiedelfeld], Semperfrei.
PR : PR :027(015) [0025] George, **baron** of Schoenburg [-Waldenburg].
PR : PR :027(015) [0025] Wolf, **baron** of Schoenburg [-Penig-Remissa].
PR : PR :027(015) [0025] Anarck Frederick, **baron** of Wildenfels.

Barren (1)
SD : 0 4 :015(553) [0943] is and continues to be a **barren**, unfruitful tree since no

Base (4), Based (27)
PR : PR :003(003) [0007] is contained in it, that is **based** solidly on the divine
PR : PR :008(005) [0009] this Christian confession, **based** as it is on the witness of
PR : PR :011(006) [0011] in extensive writings **based** on God's Word, how the
PR : PR :023(012) [0021] than that alone which is **based** on the Holy Scriptures of
PR : PR :025(013) [0023] past, for our agreement is **based** on the prophetic and
AG : 2 3 :018(054) [0063] clergymen may marry is **based** on God's Word and
AP : 0 4 :084(119) [0145] **Based** upon the nature of a promise, this is Paul's chief
AP : 0 4 :287(150) [0203] modes of justification, one **based** upon reason, the other
AP : 0 4 :287(150) [0203] upon reason, the other **based** upon the law, neither one
AP : 0 4 :287(150) [0203] upon the law, neither one **based** upon the Gospel or the
AP : 0 4 :369(163) [0221] on the term "reward," **based** on the nature of the law, but
AP : 1 8 :003(225) [0335] emphatic refutation of these notions, **based** on Paul.
AP : 2 1 :017(231) [0347] Such an invocation, therefore, is not **based** on faith.
LC : PR :018(361) [0573] meditations and exercises **based** on the First
LC : SP :025(364) [0579] Psalms and some hymns, **based** on these subjects, to
LC : 0 1 :280(403) [0661] testimony the judge can **base** his decision and sentence.
LC : 0 2 :010(412) [0681] confession of Christians **based** on the First
LC : 0 2 :033(415) [0687] and blessedness are **based**, and it is so rich and broad
LC : 0 3 :016(422) [0703] on which all the saints **base** their prayer, I, too, base
LC : 0 3 :016(422) [0703] which all the saints base their prayer, I, too, **base** mine.
LC : 0 3 :017(422) [0703] all our prayers must be **based** on obedience to God,
LC : 0 4 :053(443) [0745] subtle point, but it is **based** upon what I have already
SD : RN :001(503) [0851] It **based** these not on mere private writings, but on such
SD : RN :004(504) [0851] succinct, Christian, and **based** upon the Word of God —
SD : RN :013(506) [0855] writings, for just as we **base** our position on the Word of
SD : 0 4 :007(552) [0941] own opinion or that are **based** on human traditions; that
SD : 0 7 :024(573) [0981] for the sacrament is not **based** on the holiness of men but
SD : 0 7 :107(588) [1009] aforementioned doctrine, **based** as it is on the Word of
SD : 0 7 :112(589) [1011] doctrine set forth above, **based** as it is on the Word of
SD : 1 1 :008(617) [1065] Our salvation is **based** on it in such a way that "the gates
SD : 1 2 :008(633) [1097] our Christian and biblically-**based** Augsburg Confession.

Basic (8), Basically (2)
AP : 0 4 :087(119) [0147] embodying the **basic** issue of the whole discussion: "We
AP : 0 4 :297(152) [0205] There are two **basic** facts: First we are not justified by the
AP : 2 4 :019(252) [0389] There are two, and only two, **basic** types of sacrifice.
EP : 1 1 :022(497) [0837] that have developed receive a **basic** settlement.
SD : RN :001(503) [0849] primary requirement for **basic** and permanent concord
SD : RN :015(506) [0857] point we have reached a **basic** and mutual agreement that
SD : 0 7 :093(586) [1005] Our **basic** arguments, on which we have stood
SD : 0 8 :004(592) [1017] with and use the same **basic** arguments about the person
SD : 1 0 :005(611) [1053] ceremonies which are **basically** contrary to the Word of
SD : 1 2 :027(635) [1101] can be characterized as **basically** nothing else than a new

Basil (2)
SD : 0 1 :054(518) [0877] This dichotomy was also used by Cyril and **Basil**.
SD : 0 8 :022(595) [1023] *On the Trinity*, Book IX; **Basil** and Gregory of Nyssa, in

Basilica (1)
AP : 1 2 :149(206) [0299] of St. James or the **basilica** of St. Peter rather than

Basis (72)
PR : PR :007(004) [0009] of us, decided (on the **basis** of a memorandum agreed to
PR : PR :010(006) [0011] passing day than, on the **basis** of God's Word, carefully
PR : PR :011(006) [0011] this way the pretext and **basis** for slander that the
PR : PR :020(010) [0017] to this and only this one **basis** and foundation, namely,
PR : PR :020(010) [0017] remain unattacked on this **basis**, theologians are not to
PR : PR :020(010) [0017] to argue from some other **basis**, but with ingenuous faith
PR : PR :022(012) [0019] teach about it on the **basis** of the words of his testament.
PR : PR :024(012) [0021] and faith on the **basis** of the divine, prophetic, and
AG : PR :008(025) [0039] in what manner, on the **basis** of the Holy Scriptures,
AG : 0 0 :001(048) [0059] do so without any solid **basis** of divine command or
AG : 2 7 :033(076) [0079] On the **basis** of this provision most monastics have excuse
AG : 0 0 :007(096) [0095] information on the **basis** of the divine Holy Scripture.
AP : 0 4 :013(109) [0123] On the **basis** of these opinions, things have come to such
AP : 0 4 :041(113) [0133] "If it is by works, it is no longer on the **basis** of grace."
AP : 0 4 :117(123) [0155] shown thus far, on the **basis** of the Scriptures and
AP : 0 4 :235(140) [0185] opponents argue on the **basis** of the word "perfection"
AP : 1 2 :017(185) [0257] 1. On the **basis** of God's covenant, we merit grace by good
AP : 2 1 :020(232) [0349] promise and Christ's merits must be the **basis** for prayer.
AP : 2 4 :021(252) [0391] God, but they did on the **basis** of the justice of the law;
AP : 2 7 :035(275) [0431] this briefly, for on the **basis** of what we said earlier about
AP : 2 7 :038(275) [0433] in the city of Alexandria as a **basis** for comparison.
AP : 2 8 :018(284) [0449] may believe them on the **basis** of another's Word rather
AP : 2 8 :018(284) [0449] of another's Word rather than on the **basis** of their own.

Continued ▶

AP : 2 8 :022(284) [0451] raise an objection on the **basis** of the public offenses and
S 1 : P R :001(288) [0455] of our faith to serve as a **basis** for possible deliberations
S 3 : 0 3 :017(305) [0483] as contrition and, on the **basis** of this good work of his,
SC : P R :007(339) [0533] must be instructed on the **basis** of a uniform, fixed text
EP : 0 2 :001(470) [0787] *concerning this Article on the **Basis** of God's Word*
EP : 0 3 :009(474) [0795] for Christ's sake, on the **basis** of the promises and the
EP : 0 4 :004(476) [0797] to do good works solely on the **basis** of the Gospel.
EP : 0 8 :017(489) [0823] as Dr. Luther says on the **basis** of our Christian faith as
EP : 0 8 :039(491) [0827] these errors on the firm **basis** of the divine Word and our
EP : 1 1 :009(495) [0833] ours to eternal life on the **basis** either of reason or God's
SD : P R :001(501) [0847] clearly set forth on the **basis** of the Word of God and
SD : P R :003(501) [0847] Confession on the **basis** of God's Word and submitted it
SD : P R :010(503) [0849] be explained on the **basis** of God's Word and of approved
SD : R N :000(503) [0849] Summary Formulation, **Basis**, Rule, and Norm,
SD : R N :007(505) [0853] further explained on the **basis** of God's Word, and in
SD : R N :008(505) [0853] Christian doctrine on the **basis** of God's Word for
SD : R N :009(505) [0853] in his writings on the **basis** of God's Word and
SD : R N :017(507) [0857] on the certain and solid **basis** of the holy and divine
SD : 0 1 :055(518) [0877] On this **basis** all scholars and intelligent people have
SD : 0 2 :033(527) [0893] there is no scriptural **basis** for the position that the Holy
SD : 0 2 :056(532) [0903] and gifts merely on the **basis** of our feeling, how and
SD : 0 2 :056(532) [0903] because of and on the **basis** of his promise, that the Word
SD : 0 2 :073(535) [0909] On the **basis** of this thorough presentation of the entire
SD : 0 3 :037(546) [0929] cause or the meritorious **basis** of our justification which
SD : 0 3 :045(547) [0933] works are a meritorious **basis** or cause of our justification
SD : 0 4 :033(556) [0947] to when and how, on the **basis** of the preceding, the
SD : 0 5 :017(561) [0957] teach, and confess on the **basis** of what we have said that,
SD : 0 6 :002(564) [0963] any way be urged on the **basis** of the law, since they have
SD : 0 7 :009(570) [0975] other hand, teaches on the **basis** of God's Word "that the
SD : 0 7 :059(580) [0993] the Sacramentarians, as a **basis** for their error that in the
SD : 0 7 :091(585) [1005] definitively refuted on the **basis** of God's Word by Dr.
SD : 0 7 :110(589) [1011] writings of ours on the **basis** of the Word of God and the
SD : 0 8 :002(591) [1015] the Lord's Supper on the **basis** of the words of
SD : 0 8 :025(596) [1023] On this **basis**, likewise, Christ performed all his miracles
SD : 0 8 :051(600) [1031] But it is so clear on the **basis** of God's Word that this
SD : 0 8 :051(600) [1031] ancient Fathers on the **basis** of the Scriptures, testify
SD : 0 8 :052(601) [1033] in the saints, and on the **basis** of their own calculations
SD : 0 8 :054(601) [1033] ancient Fathers on the **basis** of Scriptures, ascribe to the
SD : 0 8 :061(602) [1035] made herein on the **basis** of sound passages of the Holy
SD : 0 8 :062(603) [1037] ancient approved councils on the **basis** of the Scriptures.
SD : 0 8 :064(603) [1037] this doctrine on the **basis** of Scripture, that the human
SD : 0 8 :080(607) [1045] On the **basis** of this solid foundation, Dr. Luther, of
SD : 1 1 :003(616) [1063] set forth the correct meaning on the **basis** of Scripture.
SD : 1 1 :026(620) [1071] not pass judgment on the **basis** of our reason, or on the
SD : 1 1 :026(620) [1071] of our reason, or on the **basis** of the law, or on the basis
SD : 1 1 :026(620) [1071] basis of the law, or on the **basis** of some outward
SD : 1 1 :039(622) [1075] before, there is no **basis** for the assumption that those
SD : 1 1 :055(625) [1081] we are not, on the **basis** of our speculations, to make our
SD : 1 1 :064(626) [1083] of this article on the **basis** of the revealed Word of God,

Basket (2)
PR : P R :024(013) [0023] of divine truth under a **basket** or a table, we ought not
LC : 0 3 :072(430) [0717] consider the poor bread-**basket** — the needs of our body

Bath (1), Baths (1)
S 2 : 0 2 :012(295) [0465] Souls' Day, and with soul-**baths** that the Mass was used
LC : 0 4 :035(441) [0741] Baptism quite clearly from a **bath**-keeper's baptism).

Bathkeeper (1)
LC : 0 4 :022(439) [0737] with and could indeed be called a **bathkeeper**'s baptism.

Battle (3), Battled (1), Battles (4), Battling (1)
AP : 0 4 :170(130) [0171] Holy Spirit in our hearts **battles** against such feelings in
AP : 0 4 :190(133) [0175] acceptable to God, **battles** by which Christ restrained the
AP : 0 4 :191(133) [0175] works, true sacrifices, **battles** of God to defend the people
AP : 0 4 :192(133) [0175] a sacrifice, and a **battle** of Christ against the devil,
AP : 0 4 :303(154) [0205] does not come without a great **battle** in the human heart.
AP : 2 1 :002(229) [0343] and say, "On this field of **battle** Jerome conquered
AP : 2 1 :036(234) [0353] great danger, taught the Gospel, **battled** against heretics.
AP : 2 4 :097(268) [0417] therefore, they are **battling** not only against the
LC : 0 4 :007(437) [0733] of our contentions and **battles** because the world now is

Bayreuth (1)
PR : P R :027(014) [0025] margrave of Brandenburg [-Ansbach-**Bayreuth**]

Bear (62), Bearing (3), Bears (7)
PR : P R :006(004) [0009] to us and which we **bear**, we have not ceased to apply our
PR : P R :012(007) [0013] view of the office that we **bear** and that God has
PR : P R :024(013) [0023] account of the office we **bear**, over against the temporal
AG : 1 2 :006(035) [0049] repentance, as John says, "**Bear** fruit that befits
AG : 2 6 :010(065) [0071] of God, that a wife should **bear** children and care for
AG : 2 6 :027(068) [0073] which neither our fathers nor we have been able to **bear**?
AG : 2 8 :031(085) [0087] many things to say to you, but you cannot **bear** them now.
AL : 2 0 :002(041) [0053] and others of like import **bear** witness that they have
AL : 2 0 :037(046) [0057] anything of God, or **bear** the cross, but it seeks and trusts
AL : 0 0 :002(047) [0059] have been so lenient as to **bear** with us on account of the
AL : 2 6 :010(065) [0071] that a mother should **bear** children, that a prince should
AL : 2 6 :027(068) [0073] which neither our fathers nor we have been able to **bear**?
AL : 2 8 :031(085) [0087] many things to say to you, but you cannot **bear** them now.
AP : 0 2 :005(101) [0107] that Adam's descendants **bear** because of his guilt,
AP : 0 2 :050(106) [0119] Christ was given to us to **bear** both sin and penalty and to
AP : 0 4 :083(118) [0145] "To him all the prophets **bear** witness that every one who
AP : 0 4 :170(130) [0171] afflictions that it ought to **bear** because of God's
AP : 0 4 :220(137) [0181] justified, needed urging to **bear** good fruits lest they lose
AP : 0 4 :232(140) [0185] to preserve harmony, to **bear**, if need be, with the crude
AP : 0 4 :234(140) [0185] preserved when the strong **bear** with the weak, when the
AP : 0 4 :273(148) [0199] "To him all the prophets **bear** witness that every one who
AP : 1 2 :032(186) [0259] for human nature cannot **bear** it unless it is sustained by
AP : 1 2 :046(188) [0263] which nature could not **bear** without the support of faith.
AP : 1 2 :065(191) [0271] "To him all the prophets **bear** witness that every one who
AP : 1 2 :066(191) [0271] "To him all the prophets **bear** witness that every one who
AP : 1 2 :122(200) [0289] are passages they quote: "**Bear** fruit that befits penitence"
AP : 1 2 :132(202) [0291] when he says (Matt. 3:8), "**Bear** fruit that befits
AP : 1 2 :134(203) [0293] to this life: "Be penitent," "**Bear** fruit that befits
AP : 1 2 :135(203) [0293] like "Be penitent" and "**Bear** fruit that befits penitence."
AP : 1 2 :136(203) [0293] "**Bear** fruit that befits penitence" and "Be penitent" will
AP : 1 8 :006(225) [0335] for "a bad tree cannot **bear** good fruit" (Matt. 7:18) and
AP : 2 0 :002(227) [0339] "To him all the prophets **bear** witness that every one who
AP : 2 0 :006(227) [0339] of the world and bravely **bear** whatever we have to suffer
AP : 2 3 :032(243) [0373] he says, "Woman will be saved through **bearing** children."
AP : 2 3 :032(243) [0373] Paul says that woman is saved through **bearing** children.
AP : 2 3 :064(248) [0381] "Purify yourselves, you who **bear** the vessels of the Lord."
AP : 2 3 :064(248) [0381] yourselves, you who **bear** the vessels of the Lord," must
AP : 2 3 :066(248) [0381] yourselves, you who **bear** the vessels of the Lord,"
AP : 2 4 :032(255) [0395] give thanks to God, they **bear** afflictions in confession,
AP : 2 7 :002(269) [0419] and said that he was **bearing** these injuries with
AP : 2 7 :013(271) [0423] Christ, how long wilt Thou **bear** these insults with which
AP : 2 7 :041(276) [0435] the command rather to **bear** the injury, to let property,
AP : 2 7 :041(276) [0435] but about those who **bear** injury because of the confession
TR : 0 0 :063(331) [0523] The fact itself **bears** witness to this, for the power is the
TR : 0 0 :070(332) [0525] custom of the church also **bears** witness to this, for there
SC : 0 1 :015(343) [0541] *"You shall not **bear** false witness against your neighbor."*
SC : 0 9 :004(355) [0561] is in authority does not **bear** the sword in vain; he is the
LC : P R :011(360) [0571] For he cannot **bear** to hear God's Word.
LC : P R :020(361) [0573] and their experience will **bear** me out — that they will gain
LC : P R :020(361) [0573] what now they cannot **bear** to smell because they are so
LC : S P :008(362) [0575] 8. You shall not **bear** false witness against your neighbor.
LC : 0 1 :060(372) [0597] is a great mercy that the earth still **bears** and sustains us.
LC : 0 1 :075(375) [0601] take root, spring up, and **bear** fruit, and men may grow
LC : 0 1 :150(385) [0625] Therefore, since they **bear** this name and title with all
LC : 0 1 :161(387) [0627] that they who would **bear** the name of Christians owe it
LC : 0 1 :231(396) [0647] one offense must **bear** disgrace and punishment so as to
LC : 0 1 :247(398) [0651] you and all the world to **bear**, for they will reach God,
LC : 0 1 :254(399) [0653] *"You shall not **bear** false witness against your neighbor."*
LC : 0 1 :257(399) [0653] stand ("You shall not **bear** false witness"), this
LC : 0 1 :262(400) [0655] Here, too, everyone **bears** false witness against his
LC : 0 1 :264(400) [0655] Yet we cannot **bear** to hear the best spoken of others.
LC : 0 2 :042(416) [0689] mother that begets and **bears** every Christian through the
LC : 0 2 :055(418) [0693] us, and we forgive, **bear** with, and aid one another.
LC : 0 3 :062(428) [0715] He cannot **bear** to have anyone teach or believe rightly.
LC : 0 3 :065(429) [0715] accepted or believed, and **bears** fruit, there the blessed
LC : 0 3 :067(429) [0717] account, we may patiently **bear** and overcome, so that
LC : 0 3 :094(433) [0725] harm, violence, and injustice, **bears** malice toward us, etc.
LC : 0 3 :105(434) [0727] every Christian must **bear**, even if they come one by one.
EP : 0 1 :010(467) [0781] the nature which we now **bear** will arise and live forever,
SD : 0 2 :032(527) [0893] An evil tree cannot **bear** good fruit, and without faith no
SD : 0 4 :008(552) [0941] A bad tree cannot **bear** good fruit, and "Whatsoever does
SD : 0 7 :123(590) [1013] Christians, who only **bear** the name of Christ but do not

Beast (1), Beasts (5)
SC : P R :003(338) [0533] were pigs and irrational **beasts**, and now that the Gospel
SC : 0 8 :010(354) [0559] He gives to the **beasts** their food, and to the young ravens
LC : 0 1 :080(375) [0603] so that both man and **beast** might be refreshed and not be
LC : 0 1 :191(391) [0635] be torn to pieces by wild **beasts**, to rot in prison or perish
LC : 0 2 :014(412) [0681] forth, birds and fish, **beasts**, grain and all kinds of
LC : 0 3 :078(431) [0721] and bloodshed, famine, savage **beasts**, wicked men, etc.

Beat (2)
LC : 0 3 :069(429) [0717] now to repulse and **beat** down all that the devil, bishops,
LC : 0 6 :023(460) [0000] no bailiff to drive and **beat** him but would run there as

Beautiful (12), Beautifully (1), Beauty (2)
AP : 0 4 :024(110) [0127] the morning star is more **beautiful** than righteousness."
AP : 0 4 :329(158) [0211] flesh is grass, and all its **beauty** is like the flower of the
AP : 1 2 :148(205) [0299] saying of Scotus may be **beautiful**, that penitence is so
AP : 2 3 :070(249) [0383] flesh is grass, and all its **beauty** is like the flower of the
AP : 2 4 :076(263) [0411] thanksgiving, like the **beautiful** statement of Cyprian
AP : 2 7 :059(279) [0439] of the Rechabites is a **beautiful** parallel to our monks,
S 3 : 0 3 :039(309) [0489] when it is most holy and **beautiful**, is nothing but
LC : 0 1 :029(368) [0589] terrible threat and, then, a **beautiful**, comforting promise.
LC : 0 1 :059(372) [0597] nature we all have this **beautiful** virtue that whenever we
LC : 0 4 :033(440) [0739] This again is most **beautifully** and clearly expressed in
SD : 0 3 :006(540) [0917] will remain pure, in **beautiful** harmony, and without any
SD : 0 3 :028(544) [0925] In his **beautiful** and exhaustive exposition of the Epistle
SD : 0 3 :041(546) [0931] true: "There is a **beautiful** agreement between faith and
SD : 0 3 :067(551) [0937] brevity to Dr. Luther's **beautiful** and splendid exposition
SD : 1 1 :045(624) [1079] doctrine also affords the **beautiful** and glorious comfort

Bed (2), Beds (1)
S 3 : 0 3 :028(308) [0487] coarse clothing, and hard **beds** and tried earnestly and
LC : S P :016(363) [0577] their meals, and they go to **bed** at night; until they repeat
LC : 0 1 :047(371) [0593] of an inn, food, and **bed** (only for his temporal need).

Bede (1)
TR : 0 0 :027(324) [0511] Cyprian, Hilary, and **Bede**) interpret the statement "on

Beer (2)
LC : 0 1 :224(395) [0643] butcher stall, wine- and **beer**-cellar, work-shop, and, in
LC : 0 1 :242(397) [0649] grain will spoil in the garner and your **beer** in the cellar.

Befall (3), Befalls (2), Befell (1)
LC : 0 1 :024(368) [0587] evil, he who saves and delivers us when any evil **befalls**.
LC : 0 1 :072(374) [0601] shocking calamity would **befall** us if God did not preserve
LC : 0 2 :017(412) [0681] kind father who cares for us so that no evil may **befall** us.
LC : 0 3 :066(429) [0717] suffer patiently whatever **befalls** us, and let go whatever is
LC : 0 3 :115(435) [0731] all the evil that may **befall** us under the devil's kingdom:
SD : 0 1 :062(519) [0879] head, inasmuch as this **befell** a hitherto perfect nature."

Befit (1), Befits (7)
AG : 1 2 :006(035) [0049] John says, "Bear fruit that **befits** repentance" (Matt. 3:8).
AL : 2 8 :074(093) [0093] It would therefore **befit** the clemency of the bishops to
AP : 1 2 :122(200) [0289] quote: "Bear fruit that **befits** penitence" (Matt. 3:8); "Yield
AP : 1 2 :132(202) [0291] 3:8), "Bear fruit that **befits** penitence," and Paul when he
AP : 1 2 :134(203) [0293] penitent," "Bear fruit that **befits** penitence," "Yield your
AP : 1 2 :135(203) [0293] like "Be penitent" and "Bear fruit that **befits** penitence."
AP : 1 2 :136(203) [0293] "Bear fruit that **befits** penitence" and "Be penitent" will

Continued ▶

L C : 0 3 :013(422) [0701] other purpose than that it **befits** obedience and the

Befriend (1)
S C : 0 1 :010(343) [0541] any harm, but help and **befriend** him in every necessity of

Befuddles (1)
L C : 0 1 :099(378) [0609] the devil bewitches and **befuddles** the hearts of many so

Beg (7), Beggar (5), Beggars (1), Begged (1), Begging (1)
A P : 1 2 :003(182) [0253] We therefore **beg** you, most invincible Emperor Charles,
A P : 2 1 :030(233) [0351] lamps extinguished, they **begged** the wise ones to lend
S C : P R :006(338) [0533] I therefore **beg** of you for God's sake, my beloved
L C : P R :009(359) [0569] Therefore, I **beg** these lazy-bellies and presumptuous
L C : 0 1 :234(397) [0647] will remain a tramp and a **beggar** and will suffer all kinds
L C : 0 3 :014(422) [0701] We therefore urgently **beg** and exhort everyone to take
L C : 0 3 :057(427) [0713] who bade a poor **beggar** to ask for whatever he might
L C : 0 3 :057(427) [0713] gifts, and the fool asked only for a dish of **beggar**'s broth.
L C : 0 6 :008(458) [0000] alone or to our neighbor alone, **begging** for forgiveness.
L C : 0 6 :010(458) [0000] we come into God's presence to **beg** for forgiveness.
L C : 0 6 :011(458) [0000] provoked another to anger and needs to **beg** his pardon.
L C : 0 6 :023(459) [0000] act like a poor miserable **beggar** who hears that a rich
L C : 0 6 :024(460) [0000] into a command that all **beggars** should run to the place,
L C : 0 6 :024(460) [0000] How else would the **beggar** go but with repugnance, not
L C : 0 6 :028(460) [0000] will compel yourself and **beg** me for the privilege of

Began (10), Begin (35), Beginners (1), Beginning (54), Beginnings (1), Begins (6), Begun (16)
P R : P R :024(013) [0023] just as from the very **beginning** of this Christian
A G : 2 0 :009(042) [0053] We **begin** by teaching that our works cannot reconcile us
A G : 2 3 :021(055) [0063] Only in our time does one **begin** to persecute innocent
A G : 2 3 :023(055) [0063] the devil is a murderer from the **beginning** (John 8:44).
A G : 2 7 :001(070) [0075] vows it is necessary to **begin** by considering what
A L : 1 8 :004(039) [0051] them, without God, to **begin** or (much less) to accomplish
A L : 2 0 :005(041) [0053] They are even **beginning** to mention faith, about which
A L : 2 0 :009(042) [0053] We **begin** by teaching that our works cannot reconcile
A L : 2 4 :016(057) [0067] it is too late they are **beginning** to complain about the
A L : 2 4 :020(058) [0067] Since the **beginning** of the world nothing of divine
A P : 0 2 :035(105) [0115] Spirit, given in Baptism, **begins** to mortify lust and to
A P : 0 4 :071(116) [0141] think this refers to the **beginning**, as though faith were the
A P : 0 4 :072(117) [0141] is praised so highly because it is this kind of **beginning**.
A P : 0 4 :072(117) [0141] For **beginnings** are very important; or, as the common
A P : 0 4 :072(117) [0141] saying goes, "the **beginning** is half of everything."
A P : 0 4 :124(124) [0157] assert that we should **begin** to keep the law ever more and
A P : 0 4 :125(124) [0157] by faith, therefore, we **begin** to fear and love God, to pray
A P : 0 4 :125(124) [0157] Then we also **begin** to love our neighbor because our
A P : 0 4 :136(126) [0159] keeping of the law should **begin** in us and increase more
A P : 0 4 :161(129) [0167] not mean merely the **beginning** of our renewal, but the
A P : 0 4 :208(135) [0177] Therefore the people **began** zealously to copy this action
A P : 0 4 :219(137) [0181] we should be renewed and **begin** to keep the law,
A P : 0 4 :224(138) [0181] As usual, their zeal was very fervent in the **beginning**.
A P : 0 4 :224(138) [0181] as Paul indicates, they **began** to dislike good teachers.
A P : 0 4 :258(144) [0193] At the **beginning** he says, "Cease to do evil," as he
A P : 0 4 :270(147) [0197] the heart is at peace and **begins** to love God and to keep
A P : 0 4 :295(152) [0203] Later we **begin** to keep the law.
A P : 0 4 :297(153) [0205] and outside the law from the very **beginning** of the world.
A P : 0 4 :317(156) [0209] continually and not just at the **beginning** of justification.
A P : 0 4 :348(160) [0217] being righteous, we might **begin** to do good works and
A P : 0 4 :352(161) [0217] is, so to speak, the **beginning** of eternal life, as Paul says
A P : 1 0 :004(179) [0247] all of this here, not to **begin** an argument on this subject
A P : 1 1 :002(180) [0249] minds, and in the **beginning** brought Luther the highest
A P : 1 2 :004(183) [0253] Before **beginning** the defense of our position, we must say
A P : 1 2 :073(192) [0273] church have believed since the **beginning** of the world.
A P : 1 2 :082(194) [0275] the Holy Spirit and therefore **begin** to keep the law.
A P : 1 2 :127(201) [0289] in these places who have **begun** to doubt because of the
A P : 1 2 :151(206) [0299] has come for judgment to **begin** with the household of
A P : 1 2 :151(206) [0299] of God; and if it **begins** with us, what will be the end of
A P : 1 3 :014(213) [0311] but in the very **beginning**, at the creation of the human
A P : 1 5 :042(221) [0327] the better ones are now **beginning** to talk about good
A P : 1 6 :002(222) [0331] of God and faith, the **beginning** of eternal righteousness
A P : 1 6 :006(223) [0331] of sins and the **beginning** of eternal life in the hearts of
A P : 2 2 :007(237) [0359] their fiction that in the **beginning** of the church it was
A P : 2 3 :008(240) [0365] be fruitful only at the **beginning** of creation, but it still
A P : 2 3 :008(240) [0367] the earth did not **begin** to bring forth plants only at the
A P : 2 3 :008(240) [0367] forth plants only at the **beginning**, but yearly the fields
A P : 2 4 :001(249) [0383] To **begin** with, we must repeat the prefatory statement
A P : 2 4 :034(256) [0397] kill this old flesh and **begin** a new and eternal life in us.
A P : 2 4 :055(259) [0403] Since the **beginning** of the world, all the saints have had
A P : 2 7 :002(269) [0419] hatred, the guardian **began** to denounce him for his
S 3 : 0 2 :004(303) [0479] where to find it, and **begins** to be alienated from God, to
S 3 : 0 3 :003(304) [0481] This is what the **beginning** of true repentance is like.
S 3 : 0 3 :025(307) [0485] When this **began** to yield money and the bull market
S 3 : 0 8 :009(313) [0497] descendants from the **beginning** to the end of the world.
T R : 0 0 :035(326) [0513] Then the popes **began** to seize kingdoms for themselves,
S C : P R :010(339) [0535] **Begin** by teaching them the Ten Commandments, the
L C : P R :008(359) [0569] is to become children and **begin** learning their ABC's
L C : P R :016(361) [0573] teaching it from the **beginning** of the world to the end,
L C : S P :005(362) [0575] Christian doctrine than children and **beginners** at school.
L C : 0 1 :035(369) [0589] From the **beginning** he has completely rooted out all
L C : 0 1 :096(378) [0609] of the Word at the end of the year as at the **beginning**.
L C : 0 1 :326(409) [0675] binds the end to the **beginning** and holds everything
L C : 0 1 :329(410) [0677] depend, so that end and **beginning** are all linked and
L C : 0 2 :057(418) [0693] since holiness has **begun** and is growing daily, we await
L C : 0 2 :059(418) [0693] of the Holy Spirit, to **begin** and daily to increase holiness
L C : 0 3 :002(420) [0697] perfectly, even though he has **begun** to believe.
L C : 0 4 :065(445) [0749] else than a daily Baptism, once **begun** and ever continued.
L C : 0 4 :075(445) [0751] this new life but also produces, **begins**, and promotes it.
L C : 0 4 :079(446) [0751] and practice what had earlier been **begun** but abandoned.
L C : 0 5 :056(453) [0767] Then nature and reason **begin** to contrast our
L C : 0 5 :079(455) [0771] Just **begin** to act as if you want to become good and cling
L C : 0 6 :008(458) [0000] To **begin** with, I have said that in addition to the
E P : 0 1 :002(466) [0779] sin, not only in the **beginning** when God created man
E P : 0 2 :010(471) [0789] powers could make a **beginning** of his conversion but
E P : 0 2 :011(471) [0789] his free will to make a **beginning**, convert himself to God,
E P : 0 2 :011(471) [0789] Spirit has made the **beginning** through the preaching of
E P : 0 3 :019(475) [0795] because by faith there is **begun** in us the renewal which
E P : 0 6 :004(480) [0805] In fact, it has only **begun**, and in the spirit of their mind
S D : 0 1 :010(510) [0863] and the concrete acts, to **begin** and to effect anything in
S D : 0 1 :014(511) [0863] this process is only **begun** in this life, not to be completed
S D : 0 1 :030(513) [0867] in all its powers from **beginning** to end, down to the
S D : 0 2 :007(521) [0883] accept, imagine, will, **begin**, accomplish, do, effect, or
S D : 0 2 :008(521) [0883] questions and issues stated at the **beginning** of this article.
S D : 0 2 :012(522) [0885] to understand them, to **begin** them, to will them, to
S D : 0 2 :014(523) [0885] who has kindled this **beginning** of true godliness in their
S D : 0 2 :016(523) [0887] kindled and wrought a **beginning** of true knowledge of
S D : 0 2 :024(525) [0891] he can as little **begin**, effect, or cooperate in anything as a
S D : 0 2 :025(526) [0891] that belongs to its real **beginning** and completion in no
S D : 0 2 :029(527) [0893] For that reason we **begin** our teaching with faith, through
S D : 0 2 :036(528) [0895] still hear it, which is the **beginning** of my entrance into it.
S D : 0 2 :065(534) [0907] which the Holy Spirit has **begun** in us in conversion, as
S D : 0 2 :068(534) [0907] perfect but has only been **begun** in us, the conflict and
S D : 0 2 :072(535) [0909] the Holy Spirit wills to **begin** and accomplish all this,
S D : 0 2 :076(536) [0911] of the good work which man **began** by his natural powers.
S D : 0 2 :077(536) [0911] is too weak to make a **beginning** and by its own powers to
S D : 0 2 :077(536) [0911] Spirit has made the **beginning** and has called us by the
S D : 0 2 :089(538) [0915] no new impulses and **begins** no spiritual operations in us.
S D : 0 3 :035(545) [0927] believers possess the **beginning** of renewal, sanctification,
S D : 0 3 :049(548) [0933] because righteousness is **begun** in us by faith, or that faith
S D : 0 4 :031(556) [0947] Therefore we must **begin** by earnestly criticizing and
S D : 0 4 :034(556) [0949] salvation only at the **beginning**, and then delegates this
S D : 0 4 :034(556) [0949] to faith alone the **beginning**, the middle, and end of
S D : 0 5 :004(559) [0953] in Mark 1:1, "The **beginning** of the Gospel of Jesus
S D : 0 5 :005(559) [0953] Christ, and the apostles **began** in their preaching with
S D : 0 5 :012(560) [0955] of the law and **begin** with the law in the case of those who
S D : 0 5 :023(562) [0959] Since the **beginning** of the world these two proclamations
S D : 0 5 :023(562) [0959] only how man in the **beginning** was created righteous and
S D : 0 6 :007(565) [0965] the Holy Spirit has **begun** the mortification of the Old
S D : 0 6 :011(565) [0965] does not give the power and ability to **begin** it or to do it.
S D : 0 7 :004(569) [0973] In the **beginning** they alleged that the Lord's Supper was
S D : 0 7 :029(574) [0981] Anabaptists are already **beginning** to do, I desire with
S D : 0 7 :044(577) [0987] as he was about to **begin** his bitter passion and death for
S D : 0 7 :077(583) [0999] of Christ that, from the **beginning** of the first Communion
S D : 0 7 :093(586) [1005] at the very **beginning** in the following words): "My
S D : 0 8 :001(591) [1015] It did not at first **begin** among them, however, but
S D : 1 1 :021(619) [1069] good work which he has **begun**, and preserve them unto
S D : 1 1 :032(621) [1073] faithful that after "he has **begun** the good work in us" he
S D : 1 1 :032(621) [1073] until the end the substance which has been **begun**" in us.
S D : 1 1 :042(623) [1077] to those in whom he has "**begun** the good work."
S D : 1 1 :044(624) [1077] decreed before the world **began** that by the power of his
S D : 1 1 :049(624) [1079] out that before the world **began** God ordained in his
S D : 1 1 :054(625) [1081] that before the world **began** God foresaw right well and

Beget (2), Begets (2), Begotten (5)
S 1 : 0 1 :000(291) [0461] 2. That the Father was **begotten** by no one, the Son was
S 1 : 0 1 :000(291) [0461] by no one, the Son was **begotten** by the Father, and the
S C : 0 2 :004(345) [0545] Jesus Christ, true God, **begotten** of the Father from
L C : 0 1 :207(393) [0639] to each other, be fruitful, **beget** children, and support and
L C : 0 2 :042(416) [0689] It is the mother that **begets** and bears every Christian
S D : 0 2 :050(531) [0901] to himself, convert them, **beget** them anew, and sanctify
S D : 0 4 :010(552) [0941] us that transforms us and **begets** us anew from God, kills
S D : 1 1 :028(620) [1071] world" and gave to it his only **begotten** Son (John 3:16).
S D : 1 1 :067(627) [1085] Christ, "the only **begotten** Son, who is in the bosom of

Begrudge (2), Begrudges (1), Begrudging (1)
L C : 0 1 :184(390) [0633] many enemies who **begrudge** you even the least good,
L C : 0 1 :297(405) [0665] is nature that we all **begrudge** another's having as much
L C : 0 1 :307(406) [0669] him against his will, and **begrudging** what God gave him.
L C : 0 5 :081(456) [0773] A murderer who **begrudges** you every hour of your life.

Beguile (1)
A P : 1 2 :114(199) [0285] these spectacles tend to **beguile** the inexperienced into

Behalf (4)
A P : 2 4 :025(253) [0391] are not satisfactions on **behalf** of those who bring them,
A P : 2 4 :052(259) [0403] is appointed to act on **behalf** of men in relation to God, to
A P : 2 4 :080(264) [0411] We beseech you on **behalf** of Christ, be reconciled to
L C : 0 3 :068(429) [0717] simply expressed, yet we have prayed in our own **behalf**.

Behave (4), Behaves (3), Behavior (9)
A P : 0 4 :211(136) [0179] Fathers but only their **behavior** without their faith in
A P : 0 4 :232(140) [0185] need be, with the crude **behavior** of the brethren, to cover
A P : 0 4 :233(140) [0185] judge their clergy's **behavior** too strictly or despise them
A P : 1 5 :024(218) [0321] they copy their outward **behavior** without copying their
L C : P R :001(358) [0567] laziness and gluttony, **behave** in this matter as if they
L C : 0 1 :110(380) [0611] In your words you are to **behave** respectfully toward
L C : 0 1 :263(400) [0655] with their corrupt **behavior** in court and their lying and
L C : 0 3 :039(425) [0709] our duty in every way to **behave** as good children so that
L C : 0 5 :037(451) [0761] so that one's body may **behave** properly and reverently
E P : 0 2 :018(472) [0791] man's will in conversion **behaves** "altogether passively"
E P : 0 7 :039(486) [0817] because they are still imperfect in their external **behavior**.
E P : 1 2 :005(498) [0839] of Christ, but in renewal and in our own pious **behavior**.
S D : 0 2 :073(535) [0909] man in his conversion **behaves** and is like a block?
S D : 0 2 :074(535) [0909] and honorable **behavior** and to avoid manifest sins and
S D : 0 2 :089(538) [0915] Luther says that man **behaves** in a purely passive way in
S D : 0 6 :003(564) [0963] a godly life and **behavior** in accord with God's external

Beheaded (1)
L C : 0 1 :137(384) [0619] must daily be hanged, **beheaded**, or broken on the wheel

Beheld (2), Behold (12), Beholding (1)
A P : 0 4 :103(122) [0151] when he said (John 1:29), '**Behold** the Lamb of God, who
A P : 0 4 :155(128) [0165] Luke 11:41, "Give alms; and **behold**, everything is clean."
A P : 0 4 :263(146) [0195] added (Dan. 4:27), "**Behold**, there will be a healing of
A P : 0 4 :281(149) [0201] form: "Give alms; and **behold**, everything is clean for
A P : 0 4 :351(161) [0217] "in knowledge," and "**beholding** the glory of the Lord, we
S C : P R :002(338) [0533] Good God, what wretchedness I **beheld**!
L C : 0 1 :016(366) [0585] **Behold**, here you have the true honor and the true
L C : 0 1 :137(384) [0619] and grief that we **behold**, for it seldom happens that such

Continued ▶

LC : 0 3 :124(436) [0731] **Behold**, such is the importance that God attaches to our
EP : 0 1 :010(467) [0781] I shall see for myself, and mine eyes shall **behold** him."
SD : 0 1 :036(514) [0869] Thy eyes **behold** my unformed substance; in thy book
SD : 0 2 :081(537) [0913] **Behold**, this is laying off the old man and putting on the
SD : 0 8 :065(604) [1039] in yonder life we shall **behold** his glory face to face (John
SD : 1 1 :004(617) [1063] Again, "Thine eyes **beheld** my unformed substance, in thy
SD : 1 1 :060(626) [1083] But God permits us to **behold** his righteous and well

Behind (4)
AG : 2 7 :058(080) [0083] of life which does not have God's command **behind** it.
LC : 0 1 :088(377) [0605] Not when we sit **behind** the stove and refrain from
LC : 0 1 :123(382) [0617] depreciate one another **behind** their backs in any way
LC : 0 1 :279(403) [0661] with personally and not gossiped about **behind** his back.

Behoove (1)
TR : 0 0 :054(329) [0519] Especially does it **behoove** the chief members of the

Beings (4)
AG : 2 0 :032(045) [0057] the devil, who drives poor human **beings** into many sins.
AP : 2 3 :015(241) [0367] should marry — as though priests were not human **beings**.
SD : 0 1 :032(513) [0869] because we are human **beings** created by God but because
SD : 0 8 :064(603) [1037] as in other godly human **beings** or in the angels, but

Bekoerunge (1)
LC : 0 3 :101(433) [0727] Saxons called it, ***Bekoerunge***) is of three kinds: of the

Belabor (2)
AP : 0 7 :017(171) [0231] But why **belabor** the obvious?
AP : 2 4 :003(250) [0385] We do not want to **belabor** this point, but we leave it up

Belief (13), Beliefs (3)
AG : PR :002(025) [0039] judgments, opinions, and **beliefs** of the several parties
AG : PR :006(025) [0039] judgments, opinions, and **beliefs** with reference to the said
AP : 0 4 :207(135) [0177] do condemn the wicked **belief** of those who did away with
AP : 1 0 :001(179) [0247] where we confess our **belief** that in the Lord's Supper the
AP : 1 0 :001(179) [0247] and consideration of it, we firmly defend this **belief**.
AP : 2 7 :061(279) [0441] way of life out of the **belief** that they would merit
S3 : 0 1 :002(302) [0477] such as unbelief, false **belief**, idolatry, being without the
S3 : 0 3 :028(308) [0487] sold them to others in the **belief** that they were more than
TR : 0 0 :082(000) [0529] Scripture, and with the **belief** of the true and genuine
SD : RN :011(506) [0855] and universally accepted **belief** of our churches, that the
SD : 0 2 :006(521) [0883] the following as our teaching, **belief**, and confession:
SD : 0 3 :008(540) [0919] we affirm our teaching, **belief**, and confession as follows:
SD : 0 4 :006(552) [0939] we shall state our teaching, **belief**, and confession.
SD : 0 8 :005(592) [1017] our unanimous teaching, **belief**, and confession are as
SD : 1 2 :008(633) [1097] open idolatry and false **beliefs** of the papacy,
SD : 1 2 :040(636) [1103] other, is our teaching, **belief**, and confession in which by

Believable (1)
AG : 2 8 :040(087) [0089] It is quite **believable** that some bishops were misled by the

Believe (410), Believed (43), Believes (81), Believing (20)
PR : PR :003(003) [0007] church of Christ has **believed**, fought for against many
AG : 0 3 :004(030) [0045] and comfort all who **believe** in him, that he may bestow
AG : 0 4 :002(030) [0045] through faith, when we **believe** that Christ suffered for us
AG : 0 5 :003(031) [0045] merits but by the merit of Christ, when we **believe** this.
AG : 0 6 :003(032) [0047] of God that whoever **believes** in Christ shall be saved, and
AG : 1 2 :005(034) [0049] yet at the same time to **believe** the Gospel and absolution
AG : 1 8 :002(039) [0051] God, of fearing God and **believing** in God with his whole
AG : 2 0 :009(042) [0053] faith, that is, when we **believe** that our sins are forgiven
AG : 2 0 :023(044) [0055] the ungodly, who also **believe** the history of Christ's
AG : 2 0 :023(044) [0055] mean such true faith as **believes** that we receive grace and
AG : 2 0 :025(044) [0057] and the ungodly do not **believe** this article concerning the
AG : 2 5 :004(062) [0069] that God requires us to **believe** this absolution as much as
AG : 2 6 :027(068) [0073] But we **believe** that we shall be saved through the grace
AG : 2 7 :037(077) [0081] faith and trust when we **believe** that God receives us into
AL : 0 1 :001(027) [0043] is true and should be **believed** without any doubting.
AL : 0 3 :004(030) [0045] and sanctify those who **believe** in him by sending the
AL : 0 4 :002(030) [0045] through faith when they **believe** that they are received into
AL : 0 5 :003(031) [0045] God justifies those who **believe** that they are received into
AL : 0 6 :003(032) [0047] of God that whoever **believes** in Christ shall be saved, not
AL : 1 2 :005(034) [0049] Gospel, or of absolution, **believes** that sins are forgiven
AL : 1 3 :002(035) [0049] so used that faith, which **believes** the promises that are
AL : 1 3 :003(036) [0049] teach that faith, which **believes** that sins are forgiven, is
AL : 2 0 :009(042) [0053] only by faith when we **believe** that we are received into
AL : 2 0 :023(044) [0055] it signifies faith which **believes** not only the history but
AL : 2 0 :025(044) [0057] men are not able to **believe** this article of the forgiveness
AL : 0 0 :002(049) [0059] Majesty should not **believe** those who disseminate
AL : 2 4 :007(056) [0065] that they may learn to **believe** in God and ask for and
AL : 2 5 :004(062) [0069] God requires faith to **believe** such absolution as God's
AL : 2 6 :004(064) [0071] and that faith which **believes** that sins are forgiven for
AL : 2 6 :005(064) [0071] sort; it is faith which **believes** that for Christ's sake we are
AL : 2 6 :027(068) [0073] But we **believe** that we shall be saved through the grace
AL : 2 7 :013(072) [0077] Thus they made men **believe** that the monastic profession
AL : 2 7 :037(077) [0081] faith to those who **believe** that they are received by God
AP : PR :016(099) [0103] We **believe**, therefore, that we must endure difficulties and
AP : 0 1 :002(100) [0103] this doctrine and we **believe** that the Holy Scriptures
AP : 0 1 :002(100) [0103] maintain that those who **believe** otherwise do not belong
AP : 0 2 :024(103) [0111] fear and love God or **believe** in him, it seeks and loves
AP : 0 2 :037(105) [0115] that this is what Luther **believes** and teaches; and since
AP : 0 2 :041(105) [0115] This is undoubtedly what the Fathers **believe**.
AP : 0 2 :051(106) [0119] This, we **believe**, will satisfy His Imperial Majesty about
AP : 0 4 :018(109) [0125] use him as mediator and **believe** that for his sake they
AP : 0 4 :018(109) [0125] neither fears God nor truly **believes** that he cares.
AP : 0 4 :020(110) [0125] Smug hypocrites always **believe** that they have the merit
AP : 0 4 :027(111) [0127] law, truly fear him, truly **believe** that he hears prayer,
AP : 0 4 :035(112) [0131] as Epicurus did not **believe** that God cared for him or
AP : 0 4 :045(113) [0133] Therefore, when a man **believes** that his sins are forgiven
AP : 0 4 :051(114) [0135] So it is not enough to **believe** that Christ was born,
AP : 0 4 :062(115) [0139] This happens if they **believe** Christ's promise that for his
AP : 0 4 :069(116) [0141] in our justification and **believe** that for his sake we are
AP : 0 4 :069(116) [0141] But to **believe** means to trust in Christ's merits, that
AP : 0 4 :083(118) [0145] that every one who **believes** in him receives forgiveness of
AP : 0 4 :083(118) [0145] And he adds, "when we **believe** in him."
AP : 0 4 :084(119) [0145] in Jesus Christ might be given to those who **believe**."
AP : 0 4 :086(119) [0147] in Christ and because it **believes** that "God made Christ
AP : 0 4 :087(119) [0147] and states that when we **believe** that God is reconciled to
AP : 0 4 :092(120) [0149] in Rom. 10:10, "Man **believes** with his heart and so is
AP : 0 4 :093(120) [0149] Gal. 2:16, "We have **believed** in Christ Jesus, in order to
AP : 0 4 :094(120) [0149] "To all who **believed** in his name, he gave power
AP : 0 4 :095(121) [0149] lifted up, that whoever **believes** in him may have eternal
AP : 0 4 :096(121) [0149] He who **believes** in him is not condemned."
AP : 0 4 :097(121) [0149] by him every one that **believes** is justified from everything
AP : 0 4 :097(121) [0149] Christ was given for us to **believe** that we are justified
AP : 0 4 :097(121) [0149] Christ's sake when we **believe** that God is reconciled to us
AP : 0 4 :100(121) [0151] by the faith which **believes** that God is propitious; and he
AP : 0 4 :101(121) [0151] is rightly and truly to **believe** in Christ, to believe that
AP : 0 4 :101(121) [0151] to believe in Christ, to **believe** that God will certainly
AP : 0 4 :110(123) [0153] this love unless they **believe** that the forgiveness of sins is
AP : 0 4 :119(124) [0155] about this faith and who **believe** that they should doubt
AP : 0 4 :122(124) [0157] we must say what we **believe** about love and the keeping
AP : 0 4 :135(125) [0159] not fear God or truly **believe** in his providential care, but
AP : 0 4 :135(125) [0159] experience our failure to **believe** that God forgives and
AP : 0 4 :135(125) [0159] can think rightly about God, fear him, and **believe** in him.
AP : 0 4 :148(127) [0163] to the promise and **believing** with full assurance that God
AP : 0 4 :150(127) [0163] If somebody **believes** that he obtains the forgiveness of
AP : 0 4 :154(128) [0163] The woman came, **believing** that she should seek the
AP : 0 4 :154(128) [0163] Truly to **believe** means to think of Christ in this way, and
AP : 0 4 :154(128) [0165] woman should **believe** God, while a doctor of the law
AP : 0 4 :154(128) [0165] of the law does not **believe** or accept the Messiah or seek
AP : 0 4 :163(129) [0169] But he **believes** that he is accounted righteous by faith for
AP : 0 4 :164(129) [0169] are supposed later to **believe** that they will be accepted
AP : 0 4 :165(129) [0169] and we must firmly **believe** that we are accounted
AP : 0 4 :169(130) [0169] are those who do not **believe** that evil desires in the flesh
AP : 0 4 :176(131) [0171] Therefore we dare not **believe** that we are accounted
AP : 0 4 :179(131) [0171] and condemn those who **believe** in him, because he
AP : 0 4 :195(134) [0175] offered freely to all who **believe** that their sins are
AP : 0 4 :201(134) [0175] to his faith before others and induce them to **believe**.
AP : 0 4 :202(134) [0175] his faith and display it to others, inviting them to **believe**.
AP : 0 4 :203(135) [0175] by anyone who cannot **believe** and be sure in his heart
AP : 0 4 :204(135) [0177] flee his judgment and never **believe** that he hears them.
AP : 0 4 :206(135) [0177] did not keep their faith, **believing** that these works were a
AP : 0 4 :211(136) [0179] At the same time they **believed** that through faith they
AP : 0 4 :211(136) [0179] They did not **believe** that they received these freely
AP : 0 4 :212(136) [0179] It does not **believe** that Christ is the propitiator, or that
AP : 0 4 :214(136) [0179] We **believe** and teach, therefore, that good works must
AP : 0 4 :215(136) [0179] This is what we **believe** and teach.
AP : 0 4 :215(137) [0179] Anyone who **believes** otherwise does not give Christ the
AP : 0 4 :219(137) [0179] we have shown what we **believe** about love and works, it
AP : 0 4 :222(138) [0181] He does not **believe** that love justifies, for we are justified
AP : 0 4 :222(138) [0181] the propitiator, and **believe** that for his sake God is
AP : 0 4 :228(139) [0183] God wants us to **believe** him and to accept blessings from
AP : 0 4 :230(139) [0183] righteous when we **believe** that for Christ's sake God is
AP : 0 4 :238(141) [0187] and righteousness if we **believe** that for the sake of
AP : 0 4 :239(141) [0187] (I Pet. 2:6), "He who **believes** in him will not be put to
AP : 0 4 :252(143) [0191] righteous those who **believe** him from their heart and then
AP : 0 4 :260(145) [0193] sins is granted to us if we **believe** that our sins are
AP : 0 4 :263(146) [0195] of it unless they truly **believe** and by faith conquer sin and
AP : 0 4 :267(146) [0197] requires faith, which **believes** that God freely forgives
AP : 0 4 :273(148) [0199] that every one who **believes** in him receives forgiveness of
AP : 0 4 :276(148) [0199] terrified minds to **believe** more firmly that their sins are
AP : 0 4 :276(148) [0199] in good works, which thus urge us to **believe** more firmly.
AP : 0 4 :276(148) [0199] not arouse themselves to **believe** but despise these
AP : 0 4 :279(149) [0199] discussing, one which **believes** that God is reconciled on
AP : 0 4 :292(152) [0203] he takes heart and **believes** that he has a gracious God for
AP : 0 4 :296(152) [0205] our eyes to Christ, and **believe** that he was given for us to
AP : 0 4 :296(152) [0205] whose merits are conferred on us if we **believe** in him.
AP : 0 4 :297(153) [0205] "He who does not **believe** God, has made him a liar,
AP : 0 4 :297(153) [0205] liar, because he has not **believed** in the testimony that
AP : 0 4 :299(153) [0205] They are taught to **believe** and to rely on the sure fact
AP : 0 4 :301(153) [0205] If they are supposed to **believe** that they have a gracious
AP : 0 4 :303(154) [0205] people and demons also **believe** (James 2:19), we have
AP : 0 4 :303(154) [0205] see that a faith which **believes** that God cares for us,
AP : 0 4 :303(154) [0205] of itself the human mind **believes** no such thing about
AP : 0 4 :310(155) [0207] who sees the Son and **believes** in him should have eternal
AP : 0 4 :319(156) [0209] If a conscience **believes** that it ought to be pleasing to
AP : 0 4 :320(156) [0209] he says (Rom. 4:18), "In hope he **believed** against hope."
AP : 0 4 :321(157) [0209] smug hypocrites simply **believe** that their works are worth
AP : 0 4 :333(158) [0211] mercy of God when we **believe** that we are heard because
AP : 0 4 :335(159) [0215] we are unworthy though we have **believed** everything.
AP : 0 4 :337(159) [0215] say: "When you have **believed** everything, say, 'We are
AP : 0 4 :338(159) [0215] "When you have **believed** everything, say, 'We are
AP : 0 4 :339(159) [0215] "When you have **believed** everything, do not trust in the
AP : 0 4 :345(160) [0217] Gospel is the command to **believe** that we have a gracious
AP : 0 4 :345(160) [0217] He who **believes** in him is not condemned," etc. (John
AP : 0 4 :356(161) [0217] (John 3:36), "He who **believes** in the Son has eternal life."
AP : 0 4 :376(164) [0223] of faith, which **believes** that we have access to God not
AP : 0 4 :379(165) [0223] About this faith, which **believes** that the Father is
AP : 0 4 :382(165) [0225] are consoled by faith and **believe** that our sins are blotted
AP : 0 4 :383(166) [0225] (Rom. 10:10), "Man **believes** with his heart and so is
AP : 0 4 :395(167) [0225] majority of the people **believed** that they merited the
AP : 0 4 :397(167) [0227] should hold and **believe**, namely, "We ought to trust that
AP : 0 7 :007(169) [0229] this way, teaching us to **believe** that there is a holy,
AP : 0 7 :028(173) [0237] of saints who truly **believe** the Gospel of Christ and who
AP : 0 7 :029(173) [0237] and the Wycliffites, who **believed** that men sinned if they
AP : 0 7 :033(174) [0239] of the church, so we **believe** that the true unity of the
AP : 0 7 :036(175) [0241] God moves the heart to **believe** (like the divinely
AP : 0 7 :036(175) [0241] Therefore we must not **believe** that they are necessary for
AP : 0 7 :039(176) [0241] They did not want us to **believe** that we are justified by
AP : 1 1 :002(180) [0249] Gospel — that we should **believe** the absolution and firmly
AP : 1 1 :002(180) [0249] absolution and firmly **believe** that the forgiveness of sins
AP : 1 1 :010(182) [0253] despair because they **believed** that an enumeration of sins
AP : 1 2 :008(183) [0255] that Judas did not **believe** nor strengthen himself with the
AP : 1 2 :035(186) [0261] They should **believe** therefore that because of Christ their
AP : 1 2 :040(187) [0261] Therefore we must **believe** the voice of the one absolving
AP : 1 2 :040(187) [0261] no less than we would **believe** a voice coming from

Continued ▶

A P : 1 2 :044(187) [0263] come to Christ means to **believe** that for his sake sins are
A P : 1 2 :044(187) [0263] When we **believe**, the Holy Spirit quickens our hearts
A P : 1 2 :045(187) [0263] Christ says, "Repent, and **believe** in the Gospel."
A P : 1 2 :045(187) [0263] For to **believe** in the Gospel is not to have the general
A P : 1 2 :045(187) [0263] but, in the true sense, to **believe** that for Christ's sake the
A P : 1 2 :045(188) [0263] and faith, when it is said, "**Believe** in the Gospel."
A P : 1 2 :059(190) [0267] by which each individual **believes** that his sins are
A P : 1 2 :059(190) [0267] opponents and which we **believe** all Christians must
A P : 1 2 :060(190) [0267] the general faith which **believes** that God exists, that
A P : 1 2 :060(190) [0267] we require everyone to **believe** that his sins are forgiven
A P : 1 2 :060(190) [0269] The church of Christ **believes** the same, in spite of our
A P : 1 2 :062(190) [0269] can be said to receive absolution unless he **believes** it.
A P : 1 2 :062(190) [0269] What else is the refusal to **believe** absolution but the
A P : 1 2 :062(190) [0269] "He who does not **believe** God has made him a liar
A P : 1 2 :062(191) [0269] a liar because he has not **believed** in the testimony that
A P : 1 2 :064(191) [0269] Christ, the mediator, and **believes** the promises given for
A P : 1 2 :065(191) [0271] Isaiah (28:16), "He who **believes** in him will not be put to
A P : 1 2 :065(191) [0271] that every one who **believes** in him receives forgiveness of
A P : 1 2 :065(191) [0271] his name," and he adds: "every one who **believes** in him."
A P : 1 2 :065(191) [0271] this happens when we **believe** that our sins are forgiven
A P : 1 2 :066(191) [0271] that every one who **believes** in him receives forgiveness of
A P : 1 2 :072(192) [0271] God commands them to **believe** that they are freely
A P : 1 2 :073(192) [0273] in the church have **believed** since the beginning of the
A P : 1 2 :073(192) [0273] apostles attest that they **believed** the same thing; nor are
A P : 1 2 :073(192) [0273] unclear at all: "You must **believe**, first of all, that you
A P : 1 2 :073(192) [0273] add further that you also **believe** that through him your
A P : 1 2 :074(192) [0273] merely require that we **believe** in a general way that sins
A P : 1 2 :075(193) [0273] Besides, they teach us to **believe** that we obtain the
A P : 1 2 :076(193) [0273] extent, still we must **believe** that we obtain the
A P : 1 2 :077(193) [0275] abrogate the Gospel if we **believe** that we obtain the
A P : 1 2 :081(194) [0275] in Jesus Christ might be given to those who **believe**."
A P : 1 2 :094(196) [0281] the faith with which we **believe** him when he swears and
A P : 1 2 :094(196) [0281] When God says, 'As I live,' he wants to be **believed**.
A P : 1 2 :094(196) [0281] are we if we do not **believe** the Lord even when he swears
A P : 1 2 :095(196) [0281] Certainly this faith must **believe** firmly that God freely
A P : 1 2 :096(196) [0281] penitence: "We should **believe** both that we should be
A P : 1 2 :102(197) [0281] earlier that we do not **believe** that it is necessary by divine
A P : 1 2 :114(199) [0285] The Fathers did not **believe** that by such practices or such
A P : 1 2 :114(199) [0285] Whoever **believes** this has a Jewish and heathen faith, for
A P : 1 2 :116(199) [0285] About these we **believe**, as we do about the enumeration
A P : 1 2 :139(203) [0295] We **believe** that God's glory and command require
A P : 1 3 :001(211) [0309] us, through which he moves men's hearts to **believe**.
A P : 1 3 :002(211) [0309] We **believe** we have the duty not to neglect any of the
A P : 1 3 :004(211) [0309] our hearts should firmly **believe** that God really forgives
A P : 1 3 :005(211) [0309] moves the heart to **believe** and take hold of faith, as Paul
A P : 1 3 :009(212) [0311] sacrifice of Christ if they **believe** that it has redeemed
A P : 1 3 :018(213) [0313] It is sheer Judaism to **believe** that we are justified by a
A P : 1 3 :019(213) [0313] must be a faith which **believes** these promises and accepts
A P : 1 3 :020(214) [0313] troubled conscience, and **believe** that the testimonies are
A P : 1 3 :021(214) [0313] as a present reality and **believes** that the forgiveness of
A P : 1 3 :021(214) [0313] not about a faith which **believes** in a general way that
A P : 1 3 :023(214) [0313] (Rom. 10:10), "Man **believes** with his heart and so is
A P : 1 5 :008(216) [0317] anyone need Christ if he **believes** he is righteous by his
A P : 1 5 :009(216) [0317] These men **believe** that God is reconciled and gracious
A P : 1 5 :012(216) [0317] (Gal. 2:17) if we were to **believe** that after justification we
A P : 1 5 :016(217) [0319] of faith, they **believed** that by these they merited the
A P : 1 5 :021(218) [0321] the same reasons we also **believe** in keeping traditions.
A P : 1 5 :021(218) [0321] and precious stones," **believing** that he is reconciled by a
A P : 1 5 :032(220) [0325] If men **believe** that these observances merit justification
A P : 1 5 :052(222) [0329] We **believed** that the greatest possible public harmony,
A P : 1 8 :002(225) [0335] opponents, since both **believe** that without the Holy
A P : 1 8 :008(226) [0337] what their hearts **believe** about God's will, whether they
A P : 1 8 :008(226) [0337] will, whether they really **believe** that God regards and
A P : 2 0 :002(227) [0339] that every one who **believes** in him receives forgiveness of
A P : 2 0 :008(227) [0341] know that they must **believe** in the forgiveness of sins
A P : 2 0 :014(228) [0343] of Christ has always **believed** that the forgiveness of sins
A P : 2 1 :005(230) [0345] we are encouraged to **believe** that grace does indeed
A P : 2 1 :019(231) [0347] on us so that when we **believe** in him we are accounted
A P : 2 1 :029(233) [0351] of sins only by Christ's merits when we **believe** in him.
A P : 2 1 :031(233) [0351] righteous when we **believe** in him, as the text says (Rom.
A P : 2 1 :031(233) [0351] (Rom. 9:33), "He who **believes** in him will not be put to
A P : 2 1 :031(233) [0351] We must not **believe** that we are accounted righteous by
A P : 2 2 :005(236) [0359] to decide what he should **believe** about a divine
A P : 2 2 :010(237) [0361] hearts when they **believe** that Christ's flesh, given for the
A P : 2 3 :032(244) [0373] because of faith, and a **believing** woman is saved if she
A P : 2 3 :036(244) [0373] Christ's sake when we **believe** that for his sake God is
A P : 2 3 :039(244) [0375] he has been given to do, **believing** that for Christ's sake
A P : 2 3 :046(246) [0377] of Christ by making men **believe** that through such
A P : 2 3 :061(247) [0381] We **believe** that priests should have this same freedom; we
A P : 2 4 :018(252) [0389] (Mark 16:16), "He who **believes** and is baptized will be
A P : 2 4 :028(254) [0393] "Obey me," that is, "**Believe** that I am your God and that
A P : 2 4 :028(254) [0393] **Believe** that I want to be God, the one who justifies and
A P : 2 4 :029(255) [0393] and dost require me to **believe** it and thy promises of
A P : 2 4 :038(257) [0399] of the faith which truly **believes** that by the death of
A P : 2 4 :049(258) [0401] really to trust and **believe** that their sins are freely
A P : 2 4 :055(259) [0403] all the saints have had to **believe** that Christ would be the
A P : 2 4 :070(262) [0409] the faith which really **believes** that the forgiveness of sins
A P : 2 4 :070(262) [0409] to move the heart to **believe** through what it presents to
A P : 2 4 :075(263) [0411] not hunger, and he who **believes** in me shall never thirst.'"
A P : 2 4 :096(267) [0417] testifies that Aerius **believed** that prayers for the dead
A P : 2 4 :098(268) [0419] all those who truly **believe** the Gospel should reject those
A P : 2 7 :025(273) [0427] height of wickedness to **believe** that they satisfy the Ten
A P : 2 7 :025(273) [0429] do not fear him enough, they do not **believe** God enough.
A P : 2 7 :027(273) [0429] is a most wicked error to **believe** that evangelical
A P : 2 7 :032(274) [0431] "First of all, you must **believe** that you cannot have the
A P : 2 7 :039(276) [0433] praises about perfection, they really **believe** otherwise.
A P : 2 7 :039(276) [0433] Therefore they really **believe** that they have merits left
A P : 2 7 :050(277) [0437] for this young man to **believe** and obey this calling.
A P : 2 8 :018(284) [0449] apostles so that we may **believe** them on the basis of
S 2 : 0 1 :004(292) [0461] as this must be **believed** and cannot be obtained or
S 2 : 0 2 :014(295) [0467] opinions to make men **believe** their shameful,
S 2 : 0 4 :004(299) [0473] to say, "Although you **believe** in Christ, and in him have
S 2 : 0 4 :011(300) [0475] to do so they allow to **believe** in Christ, and they receive
S 3 : 0 1 :003(302) [0477] It must be **believed** because of the revelation in the
S 3 : 0 2 :004(303) [0479] that he would not have **believed** before without a
S 3 : 0 3 :004(304) [0481] This is to be **believed**, as Christ says in Mark 1:15,
S 3 : 0 3 :004(304) [0481] Mark 1:15, "Repent and **believe** in the Gospel," which is
S 3 : 0 3 :004(304) [0481] different, do otherwise, and **believe** my promise."
S 3 : 0 3 :042(310) [0491] matters not as long as you **believe**, for faith blots out all
S 3 : 0 8 :007(313) [0495] have heard, "He who **believes** and is baptized will be
S 3 : 0 8 :007(313) [0495] if they did not at once **believe** and did not receive the
S 3 : 0 8 :008(313) [0495] but he could not have **believed** and been justified if the
S 3 : 0 8 :008(313) [0495] he had previously **believed**, had already come, and his
S 3 : 1 2 :003(315) [0499] So children pray, "I **believe** in one holy Christian
S 3 : 1 4 :001(316) [0501] vows of monastic life **believes** that he is entering upon a
S 3 : 1 5 :005(317) [0501] that I have thus **believed** and am still preaching and
S 3 : 1 5 :005(317) [0501] and am still preaching and firmly **believing** as above.
S 3 : 1 5 :005(317) [0501] that I have hitherto thus **believed** and taught, and by the
S 3 : 1 5 :005(317) [0501] Spirit of Christ I will thus continue to **believe** and teach
T R : 0 0 :002(320) [0503] necessary for salvation to **believe** these things, and for
T R : 0 0 :006(320) [0505] that it is necessary to salvation to **believe** all these things.
T R : 0 0 :036(326) [0515] necessary for salvation to **believe** that such dominion
T R : 0 0 :082(334) [0529] in their churches they **believe** and teach in conformity
S C : P R :013(339) [0535] not compel anyone to **believe**, we should nevertheless
S C : P R :021(340) [0537] one is to be compelled to **believe** or to receive the
S C : P R :022(341) [0537] is no Christian who does not hear and **believe** the Gospel.
S C : P R :023(341) [0539] That is to say, he **believes** in none of these, although he is
S C : P R :023(341) [0539] For if he **believed** that he was involved in so much that is
S C : 0 2 :001(344) [0543] *"I believe in God, the Father almighty, maker of heaven*
S C : 0 2 :002(345) [0543] Answer: I **believe** that God has created me and all that
S C : 0 2 :004(345) [0545] Answer: I **believe** that Jesus Christ, true God, begotten of
S C : 0 2 :005(345) [0545] *"I believe in the Holy Spirit, the holy Christian church,*
S C : 0 2 :006(345) [0545] Answer: I **believe** that by my own reason or strength I
S C : 0 2 :006(345) [0545] or strength I cannot **believe** in Jesus Christ, my Lord, or
S C : 0 2 :006(345) [0545] grant eternal life to me and to all who **believe** in Christ.
S C : 0 3 :002(346) [0545] would encourage us to **believe** that he is truly our Father
S C : 0 3 :008(346) [0547] that by his grace we may **believe** his holy Word and live a
S C : 0 4 :006(349) [0551] salvation to all who **believe**, as the Word and promise of
S C : 0 4 :008(349) [0551] Christ said, "He who **believes** and is baptized will be
S C : 0 4 :008(349) [0551] saved; but he who does not **believe** will be condemned."
S C : 0 5 :016(350) [0553] doubting but firmly **believing** that our sins are thereby
S C : 0 5 :027(351) [0555] he shall say: "Do you **believe** that this forgiveness is the
S C : 0 5 :028(351) [0555] he shall say: "Be it done for you as you have **believed**.
S C : 0 6 :008(352) [0557] sacrament, and he who **believes** these words has what
S C : 0 6 :010(352) [0557] and well prepared who **believes** these words: "for you"
S C : 0 6 :010(352) [0557] hand, he who does not **believe** these words, or doubts
S C : 0 6 :010(352) [0557] for the words "for you" require truly **believing** hearts.
L C : S P :011(363) [0577] I **believe** in God, the Father almighty, maker of heaven
L C : S P :013(363) [0577] I **believe** in the Holy Spirit, the holy Christian church, the
L C : S P :021(364) [0579] "He who **believes** and is baptized will be saved; but he
L C : S P :021(364) [0579] but he who does not **believe** will be condemned" (Mark
L C : 0 1 :002(365) [0581] else than to trust and **believe** him with our whole heart.
L C : 0 1 :018(367) [0585] therefore, to have a god means to trust and **believe**.
L C : 0 1 :021(367) [0585] wants to help, nor does it **believe** that whatever good it
L C : 0 1 :032(369) [0589] is to those who trust and **believe** him alone with their
L C : 0 1 :036(369) [0589] of their mammon and **believe** that they can withstand his
L C : 0 1 :042(370) [0591] that the world does not **believe** this at all, and does not
L C : 0 1 :120(382) [0615] of the world that no one **believes** this; so thoroughly has
L C : 0 1 :140(384) [0621] people, for no one will **believe** how necessary is this
L C : 0 1 :140(384) [0621] and fails to perceive and **believe** how angry he makes God
L C : 0 1 :248(398) [0651] He who will not heed or **believe** this may go his own way
L C : 0 2 :006(411) [0679] of the Godhead, to whom all that we **believe** is related.
L C : 0 2 :007(411) [0679] in these few words: "I **believe** in God the Father, who
L C : 0 2 :007(411) [0679] Father, who created me; I **believe** in God the Son, who
L C : 0 2 :007(411) [0679] Son, who redeemed me; I **believe** in the Holy Spirit, who
L C : 0 2 :009(411) [0679] *"I believe in God, the Father almighty, maker of heaven*
L C : 0 2 :013(412) [0681] meant by these words, "I **believe** in God, the Father
L C : 0 2 :013(412) [0681] Answer: I hold and **believe** that I am a creature of God;
L C : 0 2 :020(412) [0681] to describe in detail how few people **believe** this article.
L C : 0 2 :021(413) [0683] For if we **believed** it with our whole heart, we would also
L C : 0 2 :022(413) [0683] article would humble and terrify us all if we **believed** it.
L C : 0 2 :027(414) [0685] are asked, "What do you **believe** in the Second Article,
L C : 0 2 :027(414) [0685] Christ?" answer briefly, "I **believe** that Jesus Christ, true
L C : 0 2 :034(415) [0687] *"I believe in the Holy Spirit, the holy Christian Church,*
L C : 0 2 :038(415) [0689] anything of Christ, or **believe** in him and take him as our
L C : 0 2 :040(416) [0689] mean by the words, "I **believe** in the Holy Spirit"? you can
L C : 0 2 :040(416) [0689] you can answer, "I **believe** that the Holy Spirit makes me
L C : 0 2 :043(416) [0689] That is, no one **believed** that Christ is our Lord in the
L C : 0 2 :051(417) [0691] of this phrase: I **believe** that there is on earth a little holy
L C : 0 2 :054(417) [0693] Further we **believe** that in this Christian church we have
L C : 0 2 :062(419) [0695] Therefore we **believe** in him who daily brings us into this
L C : 0 2 :066(419) [0697] even though they **believe** in and worship only the one,
L C : 0 3 :001(420) [0697] We have heard what we are to do and **believe**.
L C : 0 3 :002(420) [0697] perfectly, even though he has begun to **believe**.
L C : 0 3 :021(423) [0703] Whoever does not **believe** this promise should realize
L C : 0 3 :047(426) [0711] all who preach and **believe** falsely and against those who
L C : 0 3 :062(428) [0715] He cannot bear to have anyone teach or **believe** rightly.
L C : 0 3 :063(428) [0715] even when we have accepted and **believe** God's Word.
L C : 0 3 :065(429) [0715] is preached, accepted or **believed**, and bears fruit, there
L C : 0 3 :086(432) [0723] we have God's Word and **believe**, although we obey and
L C : 0 3 :089(432) [0723] that it does not trust and **believe** God and is constantly
L C : 0 4 :005(437) [0733] *"He who believes and is baptized will be saved; but he*
L C : 0 4 :005(437) [0733] *saved; but he who does not believe will be condemned."*
L C : 0 4 :023(439) [0737] quoted above, "He who **believes** and is baptized shall be
L C : 0 4 :029(440) [0739] must have something to **believe** — something to which it
L C : 0 4 :029(440) [0739] clings to the water and **believes** it to be Baptism in which
L C : 0 4 :029(440) [0739] When I **believe** this, what else is it but believing in God as
L C : 0 4 :029(440) [0739] this, what else is it but **believing** in God as the one who
L C : 0 4 :031(440) [0739] here the words, "He who **believes** and is baptized will be
L C : 0 4 :033(440) [0741] same words, "He who **believes** and is baptized will be
L C : 0 4 :033(440) [0741] be received unless we **believe** them whole-heartedly.
L C : 0 4 :034(440) [0741] expression, "He who **believes**," is so potent that it
L C : 0 4 :036(441) [0741] cannot do, nor the body, but the heart must **believe** it.
L C : 0 4 :040(441) [0743] special understanding to **believe** this, for it is not the
L C : 0 4 :041(441) [0743] has enough to do to **believe** firmly what Baptism
L C : 0 4 :046(442) [0743] the Word in which it **believes**, the body because it is

Continued ▶

L C : 0 4 :047(442) [0743] Do children also **believe**, and is it right to baptize them?
L C : 0 4 :051(443) [0745] overthrow this article, "I **believe** one Holy Christian
L C : 0 4 :052(443) [0745] the baptized person **believes** or not, for in the latter case
L C : 0 4 :054(443) [0745] the true sacrament even though they do not **believe**.
L C : 0 4 :055(443) [0745] even if infants did not **believe** — which, however is not the
L C : 0 4 :056(443) [0747] I say, if you did not **believe** before, then believe afterward
L C : 0 4 :056(443) [0747] not believe before, then **believe** afterward and confess,
L C : 0 4 :056(443) [0747] build on the fact that I **believe** and many people are
L C : 0 4 :057(444) [0747] and hope that he may **believe**, and we pray God to grant
L C : 0 5 :005(447) [0755] we never keep, pray, or **believe** them, so also does this
L C : 0 5 :017(448) [0757] does not say, "If you **believe**, or if you are worthy, you
L C : 0 5 :031(450) [0759] it, except by steadfastly **believing** the Scriptures and the
L C : 0 5 :032(450) [0759] article of the Creed, "I **believe** in the holy Christian
L C : 0 5 :033(450) [0761] answer is: It is he who **believes** what the words say and
L C : 0 5 :035(450) [0761] be addressed to him and **believes** that they are true has
L C : 0 5 :035(450) [0761] But he who does not **believe** has nothing, for he lets this
L C : 0 5 :035(450) [0761] take it and confidently **believe** that it is just as the
L C : 0 5 :041(451) [0763] of necessity, and that it is enough if they simply **believe**.
L C : 0 5 :049(452) [0765] then you need not **believe** or pray, for the one is just as
L C : 0 5 :076(455) [0771] feel the need, therefore, at least **believe** the Scriptures.
L C : 0 5 :078(455) [0771] dead in sin, at least **believe** the Scriptures, which
L C : 0 5 :082(456) [0773] neither acknowledge nor **believe** that we are in the flesh,
L C : 0 5 :087(457) [0773] they must all help us to **believe**, to love, to pray, and to
L C : 0 6 :005(457) [0000] For he who will not **believe** the Gospel, live according to
E P : R N :001(464) [0777] 1. We **believe**, teach, and confess that the prophetic and
E P : 0 1 :002(466) [0779] 1. We **believe**, teach, and confess that there is a distinction
E P : 0 1 :003(466) [0779] 2. We also **believe**, teach, and confess that we must
E P : 0 1 :008(467) [0781] 3. On the other hand, we **believe**, teach, and confess that
E P : 0 2 :003(470) [0787] 2. Likewise we **believe**, teach, and confess that man's
E P : 0 2 :009(471) [0789] convert himself to God, **believe** the Gospel,
E P : 0 2 :011(471) [0789] to apprehend and accept it, and to **believe** the Gospel.
E P : 0 3 :003(473) [0793] errors just recounted, we **believe**, teach, and confess
E P : 0 3 :004(473) [0793] 2. Accordingly we **believe**, teach, and confess that our
E P : 0 3 :005(473) [0793] 3. We **believe**, teach, and confess that faith is the only
E P : 0 3 :006(473) [0793] 4. We **believe**, teach, and confess that this faith is not a
E P : 0 3 :007(473) [0793] 5. We **believe**, teach, and confess that according to the
E P : 0 3 :009(474) [0793] 6. We also **believe**, teach, and confess that, although the
E P : 0 3 :009(474) [0793] although the genuinely **believing** and truly regenerated
E P : 0 3 :010(474) [0795] 7. We **believe**, teach, and confess that if we would
E P : 0 3 :011(474) [0795] 8. We **believe**, teach, and confess that the contrition that
E P : 0 4 :007(476) [0799] 2. We **believe**, teach, and confess that good works should
E P : 0 4 :008(476) [0799] 3. We **believe**, teach, and confess further that all men, but
E P : 0 4 :011(476) [0799] 6. Therefore we also **believe**, teach, and confess that the
E P : 0 4 :015(477) [0799] 10. We also **believe**, teach, and confess that not our
E P : 0 5 :002(478) [0801] 1. We **believe**, teach, and confess that the distinction
E P : 0 5 :003(478) [0801] 2. We **believe**, teach, and confess that, strictly speaking,
E P : 0 5 :005(478) [0803] condemned by it should **believe**, namely, that Christ has
E P : 0 5 :006(478) [0803] Therefore we **believe**, teach, and confess that when the
E P : 0 5 :007(478) [0803] of the Gospel, then we **believe**, teach, and confess that the
E P : 0 6 :002(480) [0805] 1. We **believe**, teach, and confess that although people
E P : 0 6 :002(480) [0805] people who genuinely **believe** and whom God has truly
E P : 0 6 :003(480) [0805] 2. We **believe**, teach, and confess that the preaching of the
E P : 0 6 :003(480) [0805] who are genuinely **believing**, truly converted,
E P : 0 6 :005(480) [0807] fruits of the Spirit we **believe**, teach, and confess that
E P : 0 7 :003(482) [0809] German words what they **believe** in their hearts, namely,
E P : 0 7 :004(482) [0809] plausibly and claim to **believe** a true presence of the true,
E P : 0 7 :006(482) [0809] 1. We **believe**, teach, and confess that in the Holy Supper
E P : 0 7 :007(482) [0811] 2. We **believe**, teach, and confess that the words of the
E P : 0 7 :008(482) [0811] the consecration we **believe**, teach, and confess that no
E P : 0 7 :009(482) [0811] But at the same time we **believe**, teach, and confess with
E P : 0 7 :015(483) [0811] 6. We **believe**, teach, and confess that with the bread and
E P : 0 7 :016(483) [0813] 7. We **believe**, teach, and confess that not only the
E P : 0 7 :017(484) [0813] consolation in the hearts of **believing** and worthy guests.
E P : 0 7 :018(484) [0813] 8. We **believe**, teach, and confess that there is only one
E P : 0 7 :018(484) [0813] of unworthy guest, namely, those who do not **believe**.
E P : 0 7 :018(484) [0813] "He who does not **believe** is condemned already" (John
E P : 0 7 :019(484) [0813] 9. We **believe**, teach, and confess that no genuine
E P : 0 7 :020(484) [0813] 10. We **believe**, teach, and confess that the entire
E P : 0 7 :025(484) [0815] not to be understood or **believed** in their simple sense, as
E P : 0 7 :042(486) [0817] testament, we hold and **believe** in a true, though
E P : 0 8 :004(487) [0819] Christian faith we teach, **believe**, and confess the
E P : 0 8 :006(487) [0819] 2. We **believe**, teach, and confess that the divine and the
E P : 0 8 :009(487) [0819] is, in one person) we **believe**, teach, and confess that this
E P : 0 8 :009(488) [0819] human that is said or **believed** about God and everything
E P : 0 8 :009(488) [0819] divine that is said or **believed** about Christ the man.
E P : 0 8 :010(488) [0819] 6. Therefore we **believe**, teach, and confess that God is
E P : 0 8 :012(488) [0821] 7. Therefore we **believe**, teach, and confess that Mary
E P : 0 8 :013(488) [0821] 8. Therefore we also **believe**, teach, and confess that it
E P : 0 8 :015(488) [0821] 10. Therefore we **believe**, teach, and confess that the Son
E P : 0 9 :003(492) [0827] this article, but **believe** and teach it in all simplicity, as
E P : 1 0 :003(493) [0829] settle this controversy we **believe**, teach, and confess
E P : 1 0 :004(493) [0829] 2. We **believe**, teach, and confess that the community of
E P : 1 0 :006(493) [0829] 4. We **believe**, teach, and confess that in time of
E P : 1 0 :007(493) [0831] 5. We **believe**, teach, and confess that no church should
E P : 1 1 :010(495) [0833] should repent and **believe** on the Lord Jesus Christ (I
E P : 1 1 :011(496) [0835] their sins, to **believe** in Christ, and to obey God, and only
E P : 1 1 :013(496) [0835] acknowledge his Son, Christ, and truly **believe** on him.
E P : 1 1 :016(497) [0837] Accordingly we **believe** and maintain that if anybody
E P : 1 1 :017(497) [0837] all men to come to repentance and to **believe** the Gospel.
E P : 1 2 :029(500) [0843] until now, which **believes**, teaches, and confesses that
S D : R N :016(507) [0857] that which our churches **believe** and accept with one
S D : 0 1 :008(510) [0861] has to be learned and **believed** from the revelation of the
S D : 0 1 :033(514) [0869] consider, discuss, and **believe** these two as distinct from
S D : 0 1 :038(514) [0871] Catechism we confess, "I **believe** that God has created
S D : 0 1 :038(515) [0871] Catechism, "I hold and **believe** that I am a creature of
S D : 0 2 :007(521) [0883] We **believe** that in spiritual and divine things the intellect,
S D : 0 2 :007(521) [0883] in any way understand, **believe**, accept, imagine, will,
S D : 0 2 :007(521) [0883] Accordingly, we **believe** that after the Fall and prior to
S D : 0 2 :009(522) [0883] it, understand it, or **believe** and accept it as the truth.
S D : 0 2 :009(522) [0883] less they understand or **believe**, and until the Holy Spirit
S D : 0 2 :010(522) [0883] that we preach to save those who **believe**" (I Cor. 1:21).
S D : 0 2 :013(523) [0885] will he be able truly to **believe** the Gospel, give his assent
S D : 0 2 :018(524) [0889] and cannot obey, **believe**, and give assent when the Holy
S D : 0 2 :024(526) [0891] do, yet he considers it folly and cannot **believe** it.
S D : 0 2 :026(526) [0891] you by God that you should **believe** on him" (Phil. 1:29).
S D : 0 2 :026(526) [0891] work of God, that you **believe** in him whom he has sent"
S D : 0 2 :027(527) [0893] lies within our power to **believe** and to will, but that it is
S D : 0 2 :027(527) [0893] to achieve something to those who **believe** and will."
S D : 0 2 :031(527) [0893] faith, do not trust or **believe** that God will hear them,
S D : 0 2 :040(528) [0895] Catechism we read: "I **believe** that by my own reason or
S D : 0 2 :040(528) [0895] or strength I cannot **believe** in Jesus Christ, my Lord, or
S D : 0 2 :041(529) [0897] that by his grace we may **believe** his holy Word and live a
S D : 0 2 :049(530) [0901] only Son, that whoever **believes** on him should not perish
S D : 0 2 :051(531) [0901] what we preach to save those who **believe**" (I Cor. 1:21).
S D : 0 2 :051(531) [0901] pray for those who are to **believe** in me through their
S D : 0 2 :055(532) [0903] hearts so that men **believe** this Word and give their assent
S D : 0 2 :075(536) [0911] can convert itself to God, **believe** the Gospel, and obey
S D : 0 2 :077(536) [0911] embrace and accept it, **believe** the Gospel, and by its own
S D : 0 2 :083(537) [0913] when man in no way **believes** the promise and is not
S D : 0 3 :009(540) [0919] of faith before God we **believe**, teach, and confess
S D : 0 3 :056(549) [0935] Therefore we **believe**, teach, and confess that the total
S D : 0 5 :006(559) [0953] Christ said, "Repent and **believe** in the Gospel" (Mark
S D : 0 5 :010(559) [0955] people, who **believe** that they can fulfill the law by
S D : 0 5 :012(560) [0955] the world of sin because they do not **believe** in me.'
S D : 0 5 :017(561) [0957] We unanimously **believe**, teach, and confess on the basis
S D : 0 5 :019(561) [0957] when a person does not **believe** the Word of God.
S D : 0 5 :019(561) [0957] the unbelief involved in men's failure to **believe** in Christ.
S D : 0 5 :020(561) [0959] what a man should **believe** in order to obtain the
S D : 0 5 :022(562) [0959] penitent sinner must **believe** — that is, he must put his
S D : 0 5 :024(562) [0961] We **believe** and confess that these two doctrines must be
S D : 0 5 :025(563) [0961] the assurance that if they **believe** the Gospel God forgives
S D : 0 6 :004(564) [0963] we unanimously **believe**, teach, and confess that, although
S D : 0 6 :004(564) [0963] that, although truly **believing** Christians, having been
S D : 0 6 :009(565) [0965] of the flesh the truly **believing**, elect, and reborn children
S D : 0 7 :007(570) [0975] "to eat Christ's body" as no more than "to **believe**."
S D : 0 7 :008(570) [0975] way that as certainly as **believing** and pious Christians eat
S D : 0 7 :014(571) [0977] of Christ) and do not **believe** that the body and blood of
S D : 0 7 :026(573) [0981] does not say, 'If you **believe** and are worthy, you have my
S D : 0 7 :032(574) [0983] who receive them do not **believe** or otherwise misuse the
S D : 0 7 :033(575) [0983] they are who will not **believe** that the Lord's bread in the
S D : 0 7 :033(575) [0983] Whoever, I say, will not **believe** this, will please let me
S D : 0 7 :039(576) [0985] beverage, but we **believe** that just as Jesus Christ, our
S D : 0 7 :046(577) [0989] and concluded and **believed** most certainly in his heart
S D : 0 7 :046(577) [0989] understood and **believed** the words and command of God
S D : 0 7 :047(578) [0989] the same way we are to **believe** in all humility and
S D : 0 7 :060(580) [0993] only godly, pious, and **believing** Christians receive the
S D : 0 7 :070(582) [0997] For whoever **believes** on the Son of God, be his faith
S D : 0 7 :089(585) [1003] godless hearers do not **believe** it (except that in them it
S D : 0 7 :089(585) [1003] receive the sacrament **believe** or do not believe, Christ
S D : 0 7 :089(585) [1003] believe or do not **believe**, Christ nonetheless remains
S D : 0 7 :092(586) [1005] we shall understand and **believe** them in the simple sense.
S D : 0 7 :100(587) [1007] Supper, and, as people **believe**, when he was born of his
S D : 0 7 :103(587) [1009] unable to do it, but who will **believe** their speculations?"
S D : 0 8 :006(592) [1017] 1. We **believe**, teach, and confess that although the Son
S D : 0 8 :007(592) [1017] 2. We **believe**, teach, and confess that henceforth in this
S D : 0 8 :008(593) [1017] 3. We furthermore **believe**, teach, and confess that in
S D : 0 8 :009(593) [1017] 4. We also **believe**, teach, and confess that to be
S D : 0 8 :011(593) [1019] 6. We also **believe**, teach, and confess that after the
S D : 0 8 :012(593) [1019] 7. We furthermore **believe**, teach, and confess that the
S D : 0 8 :023(595) [1023] plain Christian Creed we **believe**, teach, and confess
S D : 0 8 :040(598) [1029] But if I **believe** that only the human nature suffered for
S D : 0 8 :053(601) [1033] we shall simply **believe** it and not argue that the human
S D : 0 8 :060(602) [1035] we should and must **believe** that Christ received all this
S D : 0 8 :071(605) [1041] We do not in any way **believe**, teach, and confess an
S D : 0 8 :071(605) [1041] Nor do we **believe** that in its substance and essence the
S D : 0 8 :072(605) [1041] But we **believe**, teach, and confess that God the Father
S D : 0 8 :078(606) [1043] We **believe** that the cited passages illustrate the majesty
S D : 0 8 :089(609) [1047] 1. If anyone were to **believe** or teach that because of the
S D : 0 8 :096(609) [1049] holy apostles simply to **believe**, close the eyes of reason,
S D : 0 9 :001(610) [1051] in the year 1533, "I **believe** in the Lord Christ, God's Son,
S D : 0 9 :002(610) [1051] articles, and we simply **believe** that after the burial the
S D : 0 9 :003(610) [1051] We must only **believe** and cling to the Word.
S D : 1 0 :008(611) [1055] We **believe**, teach, and confess that true adiaphora or
S D : 1 0 :009(612) [1055] We further **believe**, teach, and confess that the
S D : 1 0 :010(612) [1055] We **believe**, teach, and confess that at a time of
S D : 1 0 :016(613) [1059] of these little ones who **believe** in me to sin, it were better
S D : 1 1 :001(616) [1063] may know what we teach, **believe**, and confess in this
S D : 1 1 :008(617) [1065] as were ordained to eternal life **believed**" (Acts 13:48).
S D : 1 1 :010(618) [1067] hold to the Word, repent, **believe**, etc., since I cannot
S D : 1 1 :028(621) [1071] faith in Christ to all and on all who **believe**" (Rom. 3:22).
S D : 1 1 :028(621) [1071] the Father, that all who **believe** on Christ should have
S D : 1 1 :029(621) [1073] will that we should accept the Word, **believe** and obey it.
S D : 1 1 :030(621) [1073] hear the Gospel, **believe** on Christ, pray and give thanks,
S D : 1 1 :036(622) [1075] us, so that we should **believe** it with absolute certainty
S D : 1 1 :038(622) [1075] God's command that we "**believe** this absolution and
S D : 1 1 :038(622) [1075] firmly hold that when we **believe** the word of absolution
S D : 1 1 :039(623) [1077] do not truly **believe** in Christ (Mark 16:16), make only
S D : 1 1 :054(625) [1081] those who are called will **believe** and who will not;
S D : 1 1 :067(627) [1085] is at hand; repent and **believe** in the Gospel" (Mark 1:15);
S D : 1 1 :067(627) [1085] who sees the Son and **believes** in him should have eternal
S D : 1 1 :071(627) [1085] desist from sin, repent, **believe** his promise, and trust in
S D : 1 1 :083(630) [1091] grace all who repent and **believe** in Christ; second, that he
S D : 1 2 :013(634) [1099] born of Christian and **believing** parents, are holy and
S D : 1 2 :029(635) [1101] king of heaven, who **believes** that according to the flesh

Believer (7), Believers (77)
P R : P R :013(007) [0013] of some of our fellow **believers** among the electors and
A G : 0 7 :001(032) [0047] is the assembly of all **believers** among who the Gospel is
A G : 0 8 :001(033) [0047] than the assembly of all **believers** and saints, yet because
A G : 1 7 :002(038) [0051] and everlasting joy to **believers** and the elect but to
A G : 0 0 :001(047) [0059] of consciences, and the amendment of **believers**.
A L : 0 8 :001(033) [0047] the church is the assembly of saints and true **believers**.
A L : 0 8 :001(033) [0047] are mingled with **believers**, it is allowable to use the
A P : 0 3 :001(107) [0119] justify, and sanctify the **believers**, etc., according to the
A P : 0 4 :086(119) [0147] to be propitious to **believers** in Christ and because it
A P : 0 4 :190(133) [0175] the devil and drove him away from the **believers**.

Continued ▶

AP : 07 :020(171) [0233] exists, made up of true **believers** and righteous men
AP : 12 :153(206) [0299] In the death of a **believer** even now, once his faith has
AP : 16 :006(223) [0331] and the beginning of eternal life in the hearts of **believers**.
AP : 21 :036(234) [0353] affirmed that God hears the prayers of **believers**.
AP : 23 :028(243) [0371] must admit that for **believers** marriage is pure because it
AP : 23 :034(244) [0373] are pure," that is, to **believers** in Christ who are righteous
AP : 24 :036(257) [0397] is, the sanctifying of **believers** throughout the world with
S3 : 03 :042(309) [0491] once they have become **believers**, they will persevere in
S3 : 12 :002(315) [0499] church is, namely, holy **believers** and sheep who hear the
SC : PR :013(339) [0535] matter whether he is a **believer** or, at heart, a scoundrel
SC : 02 :006(345) [0545] sins, and the sins of all **believers**, and on the last day he
EP : 03 :018(475) [0795] not God himself but only divine gifts dwell in **believers**.
EP : 03 :021(475) [0797] 9. That **believers** are justified before God and saved both
EP : 04 :010(476) [0799] which genuine **believers**, in so far as they are reborn,
EP : 06 :004(480) [0805] spirit of their mind the **believers** are in a constant war
EP : 06 :006(480) [0807] God, who dwells in the **believers**, works through the
EP : 06 :007(481) [0807] But the **believer** without any coercion and with a willing
EP : 06 :008(481) [0807] Christians and genuine **believers**, but only upon
EP : 07 :002(481) [0809] godly or godless, **believers** or unbelievers, the believers
EP : 07 :002(481) [0809] or unbelievers, the **believers** for life and salvation, the
EP : 07 :016(483) [0813] not only the genuine **believers** and those who are worthy
EP : 07 :019(484) [0813] confess that no genuine **believer**, no matter how weak he
EP : 07 :036(485) [0815] 15. That the **believers** should not seek the body of Christ
EP : 07 :039(486) [0817] 18. That genuine **believers**, who have a genuine and living
EP : 09 :004(492) [0827] destroyed hell for all **believers**, and has redeemed them
SD : PR :007(502) [0849] offense for both the unbelievers and the weak **believers**.
SD : 01 :014(511) [0863] terrible that in baptized **believers** it can be covered up and
SD : 02 :005(521) [0881] is converted, becomes a **believer**, is regenerated and
SD : 03 :004(540) [0917] by pure grace to all true **believers** as righteousness, and
SD : 03 :014(541) [0919] to faith or to the **believers** is the obedience, the passion,
SD : 03 :016(541) [0921] by faith, so that thus **believers** have reconciliation with
SD : 03 :030(544) [0925] and which is reckoned to the **believers** as righteousness.
SD : 03 :032(544) [0927] correct to say that **believers** who through faith in Christ
SD : 03 :035(545) [0927] converted persons and **believers** possess the beginning of
SD : 03 :036(545) [0927] fruits, or as though **believers** must or dare do nothing
SD : 03 :050(548) [0933] 6. Likewise that the **believers** are justified before God and
SD : 03 :065(550) [0937] That not God but only the gifts of God dwell in **believers**.
SD : 04 :001(551) [0939] are required of true **believers** as fruits of faith and since
SD : 04 :002(551) [0939] in order to retain for **believers** the firm and certain
SD : 04 :007(552) [0939] and command that **believers** walk in good works; that
SD : 04 :008(552) [0941] why the good works of **believers** are pleasing and
SD : 04 :020(554) [0945] good works are free to **believers** in the sense that it lies
SD : 04 :022(554) [0945] are necessary for the **believers'** salvation, or that it is
SD : 04 :038(557) [0951] works are detrimental to **believers** as far as their salvation
SD : 04 :038(557) [0951] are an indication of salvation in **believers** (Phil. 1:28).
SD : 04 :038(557) [0951] express command that **believers** should do good works
SD : 06 :003(564) [0963] that although true **believers** are indeed motivated by the
SD : 06 :003(564) [0963] and thereby even true **believers** learn to serve God not
SD : 06 :004(564) [0963] this constantly before **believers'** eyes and continually to
SD : 06 :006(564) [0963] If **believers** and the elect children of God were perfectly
SD : 06 :007(565) [0965] are not reckoned to **believers** for damnation, and
SD : 06 :010(565) [0965] the new obedience of **believers** and what function the law
SD : 06 :010(565) [0965] as far as the good works of **believers** are concerned.
SD : 06 :018(567) [0967] Since, however, **believers** are not fully renewed in this life
SD : 06 :020(567) [0969] **Believers**, furthermore, require the teaching of the law so
SD : 06 :021(567) [0969] **Believers**, furthermore, require the teaching of the law in
SD : 06 :022(567) [0969] why the good works of **believers** are pleasing to God, even
SD : 06 :026(568) [0971] Christians and true **believers** but only upon unbelievers,
SD : 07 :002(569) [0973] Supper the body of Christ is truly received by **believers**.
SD : 07 :027(574) [0981] only with reference to **believers** and worthy
SD : 07 :059(580) [0993] it is the means whereby **believers** are united with Christ,
SD : 07 :063(581) [0995] **Believers** receive it as a certain pledge and assurance that
SD : 07 :104(587) [1009] spirit through faith true **believers** are incorporated into
SD : 07 :105(588) [1009] work comfort and life in **believers** but also to wreak
SD : 07 :122(590) [1013] of Christ's institution **believers** are not directed to seek
SD : 07 :125(591) [1015] teaching that even true **believers** who have and retain a
SD : 08 :068(604) [1039] he is (especially **believers** and saints), he dwells, and since
SD : 08 :068(604) [1039] God is, but especially in **believers** in whom God dwells,
SD : 08 :070(604) [1041] has with him, dwells in **believers**, he does not do so bodily
SD : 09 :003(610) [1053] devil can take us or any **believer** in Christ captive or harm
SD : 10 :016(613) [1057] and scandalize true **believers** and weaken them in their
SD : 10 :019(614) [1059] church is, namely, holy **believers** and sheep who hear the
SD : 11 :037(622) [1075] and by which he confirms it to every **believer** individually.
SD : 11 :073(628) [1087] commandments of God, **believers** likewise should not be

Bellies (6)

LC : PR :001(358) [0567] or preachers for their **bellies'** sake and had nothing to do
LC : PR :002(358) [0567] and servants of their **bellies** would make better
LC : PR :009(359) [0569] I beg these lazy-**bellies** and presumptuous saints, for
LC : PR :018(361) [0573] a doubt that such lazy-**bellies** and presumptuous fellows
LC : 01 :036(369) [0589] powerful, and rich pot-**bellies** who, not caring whether
LC : 01 :162(387) [0627] all are afraid that their **bellies** will suffer, and therefore

Bellowing (2)

LC : 03 :007(421) [0699] kind of babbling and **bellowing** that used to pass for
LC : 05 :028(449) [0759] learning and wisdom, **bellowing** and blustering, "How can

Bells (5)

S3 : 15 :004(316) [0501] churches, the baptism of **bells**, the baptism of altar
TR : 00 :073(332) [0525] or the blessing of **bells**, which are almost the only things
LC : 01 :090(377) [0607] singing and ringing **bells**, without sanctifying the holy day
LC : 01 :314(407) [0671] singing and ringing of **bells**, lighting of tapers and candles
SD : 07 :087(585) [1003] be used to consecrate **bells**, or to cure leprosy, or is

Belly (2)

LC : 01 :235(397) [0647] which enables you to stuff your craw and your **belly**.
LC : 03 :058(428) [0713] for enough to satisfy the **belly**, let alone expect, without

Belong (33), Belonged (6), Belonging (7), Belongs (47)

PR : PR :024(013) [0023] and of the subjects that **belong** to us, to do and to
AG : 07 :004(032) [0047] to the one hope that **belongs** to your call, one Lord, one
AG : 27 :030(075) [0079] conceded that it **belongs** to the very nature and character
AG : 28 :044(088) [0089] of what is to come; but the substance **belongs** to Christ."
AG : 28 :045(088) [0089] why do you live as if you still **belonged** to the world?
AL : 27 :043(077) [0081] own works what properly **belongs** to the glory of Christ.
AL : 28 :021(084) [0087] right) no jurisdiction **belongs** to the bishops as bishops
AL : 28 :045(088) [0089] why do you live as if you still **belonged** to the world?
AP : 01 :002(100) [0103] believe otherwise do not **belong** to the church of Christ
AP : 02 :004(101) [0105] Hence it **belongs** in the definition, especially now when so
AP : 04 :053(114) [0137] three elements always **belong** together: the promise itself,
AP : 04 :058(115) [0137] Psalms and the prophets **belong** here; for example, "If
AP : 04 :130(125) [0157] the heart toward God, **belonging** to the essence of the
AP : 04 :146(127) [0163] the law, though this glory properly **belongs** to Christ.
AP : 04 :196(134) [0175] Eternal life **belongs** to the justified, according to the
AP : 04 :204(135) [0177] giving our works an honor that **belongs** only to Christ.
AP : 04 :279(149) [0199] These actions properly **belong** to the kind of faith we
AP : 04 :354(161) [0217] Just as justification **belongs** to faith, so eternal life
AP : 04 :354(161) [0217] justification belongs to faith, so eternal life **belongs** to it.
AP : 04 :365(163) [0219] displayed, and hence this **belongs** to the preaching of
AP : 04 :366(163) [0219] and eternal life **belong** to faith, still good works merit
AP : 04 :368(163) [0221] since a reward properly **belongs** to the law, still we must
AP : 07 :017(171) [0231] that since the wicked **belong** to the kingdom of the devil,
AP : 07 :029(173) [0237] It is clear that the wicked **belong** to the kingdom and
AP : 07 :035(175) [0239] of what is to come; but the substances **belongs** to Christ."
AP : 07 :035(175) [0239] why do you live as if you still **belonged** to the world?
AP : 12 :058(190) [0267] the parts that properly **belong** to it in conversion or
AP : 12 :143(204) [0297] tradition, such works **belong** to the human traditions of
AP : 15 :030(219) [0323] of what is to come; but the substance **belongs** to Christ."
AP : 21 :014(230) [0345] it transfers to the saints honor **belonging** to Christ alone.
AP : 21 :031(233) [0351] transfer to the saints the honor that **belongs** to Christ.
AP : 22 :010(237) [0359] ask for the one part that **belonged** to the priests (I Sam.
AP : 24 :075(263) [0411] praise; the first of these **belongs** to the nature of the
AP : 27 :021(272) [0427] Finally, they **belong** to the class of which Paul says (I
AP : 27 :056(278) [0439] danger that those who **belong** to these chapters are forced
AP : 28 :014(283) [0447] worship, for worship does not **belong** to their jurisdiction.
S2 : 02 :024(296) [0469] The sixth place **belongs** to the precious indulgences,
S2 : 02 :026(297) [0469] Such honor **belongs** to God alone.
S2 : 04 :001(298) [0471] Word, for this position **belongs** only to one, namely, to
TR : 00 :024(324) [0511] that the keys do not **belong** to the person of one
TR : 00 :036(326) [0515] that such dominion **belongs** to the pope by divine right.
TR : 00 :061(330) [0521] evident that this power **belongs** by divine right to all who
TR : 00 :067(331) [0523] among the gifts **belonging** exclusively to the church, and
TR : 00 :074(332) [0525] who are guilty of manifest crimes **belongs** to all pastors.
TR : 00 :077(333) [0527] cases had formerly **belonged** to the magistrate.
SC : PR :024(341) [0539] great need and God's gracious help **belong** to the devil.
LC : 01 :003(365) [0581] For these two **belong** together, faith and God.
LC : 01 :012(366) [0583] In this class **belong** those who go so far as to make a pact
LC : 01 :055(372) [0595] name unabashedly (these **belong** in the hangman's
LC : 01 :158(387) [0627] the name spiritual father **belongs** only to those who
LC : 01 :296(405) [0665] his neighbor of what **belongs** to him, such as his wife,
LC : 01 :300(405) [0667] especially claimed to **belong**, as many great nobles, lords,
LC : 01 :300(405) [0667] For the common masses **belong** much farther down in the
LC : 02 :005(411) [0679] in the Scriptures and **belonging** to the Creed were
LC : 02 :018(412) [0681] discussion of this subject **belongs** in the other two parts
LC : 03 :073(430) [0719] includes everything that **belongs** to our entire life in this
LC : 04 :065(445) [0749] Adam, so that whatever **belongs** to the new man may
LC : 05 :038(451) [0761] What may be further said **belongs** to another occasion.
EP : 03 :011(474) [0795] that follow it do not **belong** in the article of justification
EP : 03 :020(475) [0797] also renewal and love **belong** to our righteousness before
EP : 05 :004(478) [0801] condemns sin is and **belongs** to the proclamation of the
EP : 09 :001(492) [0827] Does this article **belong** to Christ's suffering or to his
EP : 11 :005(495) [0833] brings it about and ordains everything that **belongs** to it.
EP : 12 :019(499) [0841] way, and marry someone else **belonging** to the same faith.
EP : 12 :021(499) [0841] that the flesh of Christ **belongs** to the essence of the holy
EP : 12 :029(500) [0843] eternal, divine essence, **belonging** to the Father, Son, and
SD : 01 :023(512) [0865] all the goodness that **belongs** to spiritual and divine
SD : 02 :015(523) [0885] Here, too, **belong** all the petitions of the saints for divine
SD : 02 :025(526) [0891] and everything that **belongs** to its real beginning and
SD : 02 :037(528) [0895] the Christian church we **belonged** entirely to the devil and
SD : 03 :025(543) [0923] For not everything that **belongs** to conversion is
SD : 03 :027(543) [0925] nor the subsequent works **belong** in the article or matter
SD : 03 :028(544) [0925] Holy Spirit, it does not **belong** to the article or matter of
SD : 03 :029(544) [0925] matter which does not **belong** in this article at all.
SD : 03 :034(545) [0927] also says that salvation **belongs** solely to that person to
SD : 03 :043(547) [0931] and save, and what **belongs** thereto, then it is false and
SD : 03 :049(548) [0933] and love likewise **belong** to our righteousness before
SD : 03 :053(548) [0933] statement that salvation **belongs** to that man to whom
SD : 04 :008(552) [0941] For works which **belong** to the maintenance of outward
SD : 04 :019(554) [0945] and again, they who **belong** to Christ have crucified (that
SD : 05 :017(561) [0957] that rebukes sin is and **belongs** to the law, the proper
SD : 05 :027(563) [0961] confused so that what **belongs** to one doctrine is ascribed
SD : 06 :012(566) [0967] (to which the Old Adam **belongs**) of sin and of
SD : 06 :024(568) [0971] They **belong** to this imperfect life.
SD : 07 :033(575) [0983] "I reckon them all as **belonging** together (that is, as
SD : 08 :002(592) [1017] earth since such majesty **belongs** to God alone and the
SD : 08 :011(593) [1019] assumed human nature **belong** to the total person of
SD : 08 :036(598) [1027] any property, though it **belongs** only to one of the
SD : 08 :039(598) [1027] of Christ which after all **belongs** to the humanity, or vice
SD : 08 :071(605) [1041] another something that **belongs** to it without keeping it
SD : 08 :078(607) [1043] both natures, the divine and the human, **belong** is present.
SD : 11 :044(624) [1077] and effect in us everything that **belongs** to our conversion.
SD : 12 :029(635) [1101] and so that Christ's flesh **belongs** to the essence of the

Beloved (12)

PR : PR :002(003) [0007] to appear to our **beloved** fatherland, the German nation,
PR : PR :004(003) [0007] took place in our **beloved** German fatherland shortly
PR : PR :018(008) [0015] as well as our **beloved** posterity may be clearly and
AP : 04 :310(155) [0207] (Matt. 17:5), "This is my **beloved** Son, with whom I am
SC : PR :006(338) [0533] you for God's sake, my **beloved** brethren who are pastors
SC : 03 :002(346) [0545] in prayer, even as **beloved** children approach their dear
SD : 01 :039(515) [0871] order that through his **beloved** Son he might cleanse it
SD : 02 :051(531) [0901] heaven concerning his **beloved** Son and concerning all
SD : 08 :072(605) [1041] his Spirit to Christ, his **beloved** Son, according to the
SD : 11 :065(627) [1083] it is written, "He has loved us in the **Beloved**" (Eph. 1:6).
SD : 11 :065(627) [1083] Father says, "This is my **beloved** Son with whom I am
SD : 11 :087(631) [1093] he freely bestowed on us in the **Beloved**" (Eph. 1:5, 6).

Bench (1)

LC : 02 :043(416) [0689] entirely shoved under the **bench** and no one recognized

Benedict (1)
AP : 27 :017(272) [0425] Decalogue or the rule of **Benedict** or of the rule of

Benediction (1)
AP : 10 :003(179) [0247] we do not know the power of the mystical **benediction**?

Benefice (1)
TR : 00 :080(334) [0527] as the rule states, "The **benefice** is given because of the

Beneficial (9), Beneficially (1)
AP : 12 :130(202) [0291] that it is true, godly, and **beneficial** to godly consciences.
AP : 24 :002(249) [0385] that mere hearing is a **beneficial** act of worship even
AP : 24 :033(255) [0395] by itself, or *ex opere operato,* the ceremony is **beneficial**.
LC : 01 :275(402) [0659] to reprove evil where it is necessary and **beneficial**.
LC : 04 :036(441) [0741] But it becomes **beneficial** to you if you accept it as God's
LC : 06 :004(457) [0000] how to use confession **beneficially** for the comforting and
EP : 10 :012(494) [0831] and as it may be most **beneficial** to the church.
SD : 02 :016(523) [0887] anything pleasing to him and **beneficial** to us and others.
SD : 10 :009(612) [1055] to be most profitable, **beneficial**, and salutary for good
SD : 10 :030(616) [1061] may in Christian liberty be most **beneficial** to the church.

Benefit (23), Benefited (1), Benefiting (1), Benefits (30)
AG : 24 :029(059) [0067] grace and all sorts of **benefits** from God, not only for the
AL : 02 :003(029) [0045] of Christ's merit and **benefits** by contending that man can
AL : 24 :030(059) [0067] should remember what **benefits** are received through
AL : 24 :031(059) [0067] Christ is to remember his **benefits** and realize that they
AL : 25 :013(063) [0071] on account of the great **benefit** of absolution and because
AP : 04 :082(118) [0145] So this propitiator **benefits** us when by faith we receive
AP : 04 :382(165) [0225] suffering, then indeed Christ's suffering **benefits** us.
AP : 24 :002(249) [0385] of the faith of the church **benefits** from hearing a Mass
AP : 24 :005(250) [0385] or suggested that men **benefit** from hearing lessons they
AP : 24 :059(260) [0405] Therefore this ministry **benefits** people when he does
AP : 24 :064(261) [0407] without faith the Mass does not even **benefit** living people
AP : 24 :077(263) [0411] that a ceremony can **benefit** either the worshiper or
AP : 24 :093(267) [0417] they pray that it may **benefit** the communicants; they do
S1 : PR :010(290) [0457] many things and many people might derive **benefit** from
S2 : 02 :021(296) [0469] good works, etc. for the **benefit** of the living and the
S2 : 02 :028(297) [0469] spiritual and physical **benefit** and help are no longer
S3 : 03 :027(307) [0487] "Whoever wishes to **benefit** from the indulgence or jubilee
TR : 00 :045(328) [0517] of which they have further obscured the **benefit** of Christ.
SC : PR :017(340) [0537] respective obligations, **benefits**, dangers, advantages, and
SC : PR :024(341) [0539] and disadvantage, the **benefit** and loss, the blessing and
SC : 04 :005(348) [0551] What gifts or **benefits** does Baptism bestow?
SC : 06 :005(352) [0557] What is the **benefit** of such eating and drinking?
SC : 08 :011(354) [0559] our Father, for all thy **benefits**, through Jesus Christ our
LC : PR :011(360) [0571] if the only blessing and **benefit** you obtain from it is to
LC : SP :026(364) [0581] thus the preaching will not be without **benefit** and fruit.
LC : 01 :063(373) [0599] revealed and given to us precisely for our use and **benefit**.
LC : 01 :103(379) [0611] praise of God and the **benefit** and salvation of our
LC : 01 :175(388) [0631] trained who would be a **benefit** to the nation and the
LC : 04 :023(439) [0737] instituted, that is, what **benefits**, gifts, and effects it
LC : 04 :024(439) [0737] simply, the power, effect, **benefit**, fruit, and purpose of
LC : 04 :032(440) [0739] having learned the great **benefit** and power of Baptism,
LC : 04 :032(440) [0739] further who receives these gifts and **benefits** of Baptism.
LC : 04 :046(442) [0743] concerning the nature, **benefits**, and use of Baptism as
LC : 05 :001(447) [0753] what it is, what its **benefits** are, and who is to receive it.
LC : 05 :020(449) [0757] we come to its power and **benefit**, the purpose for which
LC : 05 :033(450) [0761] both of its essence and of its effect and **benefit**.
LC : 05 :033(450) [0761] to consider who it is that receives this power and **benefit**.
LC : 05 :053(453) [0765] point, especially for the **benefit** of the cold and
LC : 05 :068(454) [0769] For where the soul is healed, the body has **benefited** also.
LC : 06 :005(457) [0000] understand whatever **benefits** us, and we grasp with
LC : 06 :005(457) [0000] a Christian ought to do, should enjoy none of its **benefits**.
LC : 06 :006(457) [0000] to enjoy the Gospel's **benefits** but did nothing about it
SD : PR :006(502) [0847] while boasting of and **benefiting** from their adherence to
SD : 01 :003(509) [0861] more fully Christ's **benefits**, his precious merits, and the
SD : 05 :027(563) [0961] darken the merits and **benefits** of Christ, once more make
SD : 07 :003(569) [0973] in heaven, yes, of Christ himself and all his **benefits**).
SD : 07 :005(570) [0973] according to its power, operation, and **benefits**, by faith).
SD : 07 :018(572) [0979] together with all his **benefits**, is distributed with the bread
SD : 07 :049(578) [0989] of his body and the **benefits** which he had won for us by
SD : 07 :055(579) [0991] spirit, the virtue, and the **benefits** of Christ, as the
SD : 07 :062(581) [0995] man, together with all the **benefits** that he has acquired
SD : 07 :069(582) [0997] noble treasure and the **benefits** of Christ because of their
SD : 07 :081(584) [1001] in the essence and **benefits** of this sacrament (the presence
SD : 07 :081(584) [1001] of sins, and all the **benefits** which Christ has won for us
SD : 11 :016(619) [1069] That this merit and these **benefits** of Christ are to be

Bequeath (1)
AG : 00 :001(047) [0059] nor should we wish to **bequeath** to our children and

Bergen (1)
EP : 12 :031(501) [0843] Done at **Bergen**, May 29, 1577.

Bern (1)
LC : PR :011(360) [0571] the one about Dietrich of **Bern**, but as St. Paul says in

Bernard (8)
AP : 04 :211(136) [0179] Anthony, **Bernard**, Dominic, Francis, and other holy
AP : 12 :073(192) [0273] For **Bernard** says the same in words that are not unclear
AP : 12 :074(192) [0273] These words of **Bernard** marvelously illumine our case.
AP : 27 :021(272) [0427] without sinning, as did **Bernard**, Francis, and other holy
AP : 27 :032(274) [0431] As **Bernard** also says very powerfully, "First of all, you
AP : 27 :032(274) [0431] sentence, but at the end **Bernard** adds: "Let nobody
S3 : 03 :017(306) [0483] Here the example of St. **Bernard**, etc. was cited.
LC : 04 :050(443) [0745] the fathers, such as St. **Bernard**, Gerson, John Hus, and

Beseech (5)
AP : PR :019(099) [0103] We **beseech** him to regard his afflicted and scattered
AP : 24 :080(264) [0411] We **beseech** you on behalf of Christ, be reconciled to
SC : 07 :002(352) [0557] I **beseech** Thee to keep me this day, too, from all sin and
SC : 07 :005(353) [0559] I **beseech** Thee to forgive all my sin and the wrong which
SC : 09 :003(354) [0561] "We **beseech** you, brethren, to respect those who labor

Beset (3)
LC : 03 :034(425) [0707] the needs that continually **beset** us, each one so great that
LC : 03 :119(436) [0731] afflictions that may ever **beset** us in order that we may
LC : 04 :066(445) [0749] yes, and unbelieving; he is **beset** with all vices and by

Beside (2)
S2 : 04 :001(298) [0471] but chose to stand **beside** him as Christian brethren and
EP : 12 :028(500) [0843] majesty and is inferior to and **beside** God the Father.

Besieges (1), Besieging (1)
LC : 03 :087(432) [0723] Satan is at our backs, **besieging** us on every side and, as
LC : 05 :084(456) [0773] the devil so constantly **besieges** you and lies in wait to

Besought (1)
PR : PR :005(004) [0009] have preferred, and we **besought** and petitioned the

Best (28)
AG : PR :021(027) [0043] have with the highest and **best** motives requested in all
AP : 02 :006(101) [0107] of concupiscence; with the **best** of intentions we named it
AP : 04 :131(125) [0157] it were irrelevant, or at **best** they require only outward
AP : 04 :234(140) [0185] when the people put the **best** construction on the faults of
AP : 04 :242(141) [0187] and that it puts the **best** construction even on the more
AP : 04 :400(168) [0227] of him who is the truth and who knows his body **best**."
AP : 23 :068(249) [0383] They decided that the **best** way to arouse the ignorant
S2 : 02 :007(294) [0465] It is observed for this purpose when it is **best** observed.
S2 : 04 :014(301) [0475] apparent that, at its **best**, the teaching of the pope has
LC : 01 :076(375) [0603] come to no good end; at **best** they will remain good only
LC : 01 :088(377) [0605] and dress up in our **best** clothes, but, as has been said,
LC : 01 :111(380) [0613] will share with them all he has to the **best** of his ability.
LC : 01 :264(400) [0655] Yet we cannot bear to hear the **best** spoken of others.
LC : 01 :289(404) [0663] virtue always to put the **best** construction upon all we
LC : 01 :318(408) [0673] thoroughly, do your very **best**, and you will surely find so
LC : 02 :048(417) [0691] or assembly," or **best** and most clearly of all, "a holy
LC : 03 :001(420) [0697] The **best** and most blessed life consists of these things.
LC : 03 :025(423) [0705] They only thought, at **best**, of doing a good work as a
LC : 04 :051(443) [0745] This is the **best** and strongest proof for the simple and
EP : 01 :001(466) [0779] or indeed the principal and **best** part of his being (that is,
SD : 01 :050(517) [0875] phraseology, however, the **best** and safest procedure is to
SD : 02 :044(529) [0897] them diligently and to the **best** of his ability against all
SD : 03 :032(545) [0927] good works and leads the **best** kind of life, a person is
SD : 07 :050(578) [0989] Lord Christ himself, who **best** understands his words and
SD : 07 :050(578) [0989] heart and intention and is **best** qualified from the
SD : 07 :058(580) [0993] words which agree in the **best** possible way with the
SD : 08 :038(598) [1027] may be forearmed in the **best** possible way against this
SD : 08 :053(601) [1033] But the **best**, safest, and most certain way in this

Bestirred (1)
PR : PR :004(003) [0007] the foe of mankind **bestirred** himself to scatter his seed of

Bestow (12), Bestowal (1), Bestowed (14), Bestowing (1), Bestows (7)
AG : PR :011(026) [0041] humility and implore him to **bestow** his grace to this end.
AG : 03 :005(030) [0045] in him, that he may **bestow** on them life and every grace
AG : 27 :043(077) [0081] of his honor and **bestow** this honor upon their vows and
AG : 28 :010(082) [0085] the church or of bishops **bestows** eternal gifts and is used
AG : 28 :019(083) [0087] human, imperial right, **bestowed** by Roman emperors and
AL : 28 :010(082) [0085] the power of the church **bestows** eternal things and is
AP : 04 :051(114) [0135] own merits the forgiveness of sins is **bestowed** upon us.
AP : 04 :063(115) [0139] that the sacraments **bestow** the Holy Spirit *ex opere*
AP : 04 :178(131) [0171] satisfaction of Christ, **bestowed** upon us to assure us that
AP : 04 :342(159) [0215] God obligates himself to **bestow** his grace upon us,
AP : 04 :356(161) [0217] the righteousness **bestowed** on us for Christ's sake at the
AP : 21 :019(231) [0347] for others and to be **bestowed** on them by divine
AP : 21 :019(231) [0347] the merits of Christ are **bestowed** on us so that when we
AP : 21 :020(231) [0349] the promise and the **bestowal** of merits are therefore the
AP : 21 :029(233) [0351] that is, they cannot **bestow** their merits on one another,
AP : 23 :032(243) [0373] greater honor could he **bestow** than to say that woman is
AP : 24 :012(251) [0387] his merits and righteousness are **bestowed** upon us.
TR : 00 :002(320) [0503] that is, the authority to **bestow** and transfer kingdoms.
TR : 00 :024(324) [0511] Therefore, he **bestows** the keys especially and immediately
TR : 00 :030(325) [0513] no wise follows that they **bestow** a special authority on
SC : PR :023(341) [0539] against such evil and in which such good is **bestowed**.
SC : 04 :005(348) [0551] What gifts or benefits does Baptism **bestow**?
SC : 08 :009(353) [0559] goodness Thou hast **bestowed** on us, through Jesus
SC : 09 :006(355) [0561] with your wives, **bestowing** honor on the woman as the
LC : PR :009(359) [0569] Holy Spirit is present and **bestows** ever new and greater
LC : 01 :026(368) [0587] and means through which God **bestows** all blessings.
LC : 01 :074(374) [0601] and thanked!" "This God has **bestowed** upon me!" etc.
LC : 01 :128(382) [0617] how many blessings of body and soul he **bestows** upon us.
LC : 01 :322(409) [0673] he will reward, bless, and **bestow** all good things on those
LC : 02 :038(415) [0689] first offered to us and **bestowed** on our hearts through the
LC : 02 :064(419) [0695] Moreover, having **bestowed** upon us everything in heaven
LC : 03 :075(430) [0719] through them God may **bestow** on us still more blessings
SD : 02 :026(526) [0891] hard, stony heart and **bestows** a new and tender heart of
SD : 03 :030(544) [0925] of sins, which is **bestowed** upon us by pure grace because
SD : 11 :087(631) [1093] grace which he freely **bestowed** on us in the Beloved"

Betray (1), Betrayed (3)
SC : 01 :016(343) [0541] about our neighbor, nor **betray**, slander, or defame him,
SC : 06 :004(351) [0555] the night when he was **betrayed**, took bread, and when he
LC : SP :023(364) [0579] the night when he was **betrayed** took bread, gave thanks,
LC : 05 :003(447) [0753] *the night when he was **betrayed** took bread, gave thanks,*

Betroth (1), Betrothals (1)
TR : 00 :078(333) [0527] and underhanded **betrothals** in violation of the right of
LC : 01 :053(372) [0595] two persons secretly **betroth** themselves to each other and

Beverage (3)
SD : 07 :039(576) [0985] bread or an ordinary **beverage**, but we believe that just as
SD : 08 :019(595) [1021] either water or honey but is a blended **beverage**.
SD : 08 :076(606) [1043] blood truly a quickening **beverage**, as the two hundred

Beware (13)
A G : 2 8 :023(084) [0087] for Christ says in Matt. 7:15, "**Beware** of false prophets."
A L : 2 8 :023(084) [0087] that forbids obedience: "**Beware** of false prophets" (Matt.
A P : 0 4 :300(153) [0205] Let all good men **beware**, therefore, of yielding to their
A P : 0 7 :048(177) [0245] Christ says (Matt. 7:15), "**Beware** of false prophets"; Paul
T R : 0 0 :041(327) [0517] all Christians ought to **beware** of becoming participants
T R : 0 0 :041(327) [0517] Christ commanded, "**Beware** of false prophets" (Matt.
L C : 0 1 :246(398) [0651] But **beware** how you deal with the poor, of whom there
L C : 0 1 :247(398) [0651] **Beware** of this, I repeat, as of the devil himself.
L C : 0 3 :084(432) [0723] and oppressors **beware** lest they lose the common
S D : 0 8 :040(598) [1029] **Beware**, beware, I say, of this *alloeosis*, for it is the devil's
S D : 0 8 :040(598) [1029] Beware, **beware**, I say, of this *alloeosis*, for it is the devil's
S D : 1 0 :022(615) [1061] all Christians ought to **beware** of becoming participants
S D : 1 0 :022(615) [1061] Christ commanded, '**Beware** of false prophets' (Matt.

Bewitched (1), Bewitches (1)
L C : 0 1 :099(378) [0609] with which the devil **bewitches** and befuddles the hearts
L C : 0 1 :120(382) [0615] has the devil **bewitched** us with the false holiness and

Bible (2)
L C : P R :003(358) [0567] something else from the **Bible** and would pray the Lord's
E P : R N :005(465) [0777] They are "the layman's **Bible**" and contain everything

Biblical (1), Biblically (1)
E P : 0 1 :023(469) [0785] concerned, they are not **biblical** terms and, besides, they
S D : 1 2 :008(633) [1097] to our Christian and **biblically**-based Augsburg

Bickerings (1)
A L : 2 6 :016(066) [0073] so hindered by these **bickerings** about traditions that they

Bid (6), Bidding (1), Bids (5)
A P : 0 4 :017(109) [0125] They **bid** us merit this first disposition by our preceding
A P : 0 4 :017(109) [0125] Then they **bid** us merit an increase of this disposition and
A P : 0 4 :082(118) [0145] By **bidding** us draw near to God with trust not in our
A P : 0 4 :119(124) [0155] men bad advice when they **bid** them doubt whether they
A P : 1 2 :060(190) [0267] to the opinion that **bids** us trust not in the promise of
A P : 1 2 :074(192) [0273] forgiven by mercy, but he **bids** us add the personal faith
A P : 1 2 :076(193) [0273] This promise **bids** us trust that because of Christ we are
T R : 0 0 :030(325) [0513] on Peter, for Christ **bids** Peter to pasture the sheep, that
T R : 0 0 :044(328) [0517] Then they **bid** us to doubt whether forgiveness is
L C : 0 5 :017(448) [0757] do, what I institute, what I give you and **bid** you take.
L C : 0 5 :022(449) [0757] Christ **bids** me eat and drink in order that the sacrament
L C : 0 5 :034(450) [0761] "This is why I give it and **bid** you eat and drink, that you

Biel (3)
A P : 0 4 :210(136) [0179] in those for whom it is offered, as Gabriel **Biel** writes.
A P : 1 2 :068(192) [0271] like Duns Scotus, Gabriel **Biel**, and the like in addition to
A P : 2 1 :023(232) [0349] Gabriel **Biel**'s interpretation of the canon of the Mass

Big (2)
S 1 : P R :009(290) [0457] writings have urged such **big** lies upon the king and
L C : 0 1 :229(396) [0645] men are called gentlemen swindlers or **big** operators.

Bill (1)
L C : 0 1 :295(404) [0665] publicly by giving her a **bill** of divorce and to take

Bin (1)
L C : 0 3 :072(430) [0719] only the oven or the flour **bin**, but also the broad fields

Bind (12), Binding (5), Binds (4)
A G : 2 7 :023(074) [0079] that a vow made contrary to papal canons is not **binding**.
A G : 2 7 :039(077) [0081] Therefore they are not **binding**, for an ungodly vow,
A G : 2 8 :053(090) [0091] for sins, nor in order to **bind** men's consciences by
A L : 2 6 :045(070) [0075] of the apostles to enact **binding** laws with respect to holy
A L : 2 7 :040(077) [0081] As the canon says, no vow ought to **bind** men to iniquity.
A P : 0 4 :397(167) [0227] word of Christ, 'Whatever you **bind**,' etc. (Matt. 16:19)."
A P : 1 2 :022(185) [0257] and acts of devotion **binding** upon consciences.
A P : 1 2 :129(202) [0291] consciences, you can **bind** all nations to yourself; for men
A P : 1 2 :138(203) [0293] the words "Whatever you **bind**" refer to imposing
A P : 1 2 :176(210) [0307] keys have the power to **bind** and loose, according to the
A P : 1 2 :176(210) [0307] "Whatever you **bind** on earth shall be bound in
A P : 1 2 :176(210) [0307] to forgive sins, so "to **bind**" means not to forgive sins.
A P : 2 3 :017(242) [0369] have his own wife," **binds** all those who are not truly
S 3 : 0 7 :001(311) [0493] to the church by Christ to **bind** and loose sins, not only
T R : 0 0 :006(320) [0505] commandments of God, **binding** on the consciences of
T R : 0 0 :023(324) [0511] keys" and "whatever you **bind**") is elsewhere given in the
T R : 0 0 :023(324) [0511] elsewhere given in the plural ("Whatever you **bind**"), etc.
T R : 0 0 :040(327) [0517] the power to loose and **bind** in this life but also the
L C : 0 1 :326(409) [0675] the hoop of a wreath that **binds** the end to the beginning
L C : 0 4 :031(440) [0739] faith, and Christ, who directs us and **binds** us to Baptism.
S D : 0 4 :004(551) [0939] order which obligates and **binds** all men to be obedient to

Biography (1)
A G : 2 3 :002(053) [0063] As his **biography** shows, even one of the popes, Pius II,

Birds (1)
L C : 0 2 :014(412) [0681] all that it brings forth, **birds** and fish, beasts, grain and

Birth (15)
A P : 0 2 :029(104) [0113] He means that at **birth** we bring along an ignorance of
A P : 0 4 :374(164) [0223] that a new life and new **birth** are required, not hypocrisy.
A P : 0 4 :374(164) [0223] Such a new **birth** comes by faith amid penitence.
A P : 2 4 :059(260) [0405] when he does work to give them new **birth** and life.
L C : 0 2 :032(415) [0687] with such articles as the **birth**, passion, resurrection, and
L C : 0 2 :037(415) [0687] purchasing us through his **birth**, death, and resurrection,
E P : 0 2 :018(472) [0791] of man's will and works the new **birth** and conversion.
E P : 1 2 :008(498) [0839] of God by virtue of their **birth** from Christian and pious
S D : 0 1 :007(510) [0861] our carnal conception and **birth** out of sinful seed from
S D : 0 1 :023(512) [0865] of and from man's natural **birth** something that is good —
S D : 0 1 :052(517) [0875] Luther can say, "Your **birth**, your nature, your entire
S D : 0 2 :044(529) [0897] God himself must draw man and give him new **birth**.
S D : 0 3 :022(543) [0923] to his Father from his **birth** until his ignominious death
S D : 0 3 :058(550) [0937] obedience from his holy **birth** to his death in the stead of
S D : 0 8 :085(608) [1045] second, temporal, human **birth**, the eternal power of God

Bishop (46), Bishops (151)
P R : P R :027(014) [0025] John, **bishop** of Meissen.
P R : P R :027(014) [0025] Eberhard, **bishop** of Luebeck, administrator of the
A G : 0 0 :002(048) [0059] godly and Christian, the **bishops** should in all fairness act
A G : 2 3 :011(052) [0063] said in I Tim. 3:2, "A **bishop** must be above reproach,
A G : 2 4 :038(060) [0069] receive the sacrament in order from the **bishop** or priest."
A G : 2 7 :015(073) [0077] so that pastors and **bishops** were taken from monasteries.
A G : 2 8 :000(081) [0083] XXVIII. The Power of **Bishops**
A G : 2 8 :001(081) [0083] about the power of **bishops**, and some have improperly
A G : 2 8 :001(081) [0083] confused the power of **bishops** with the temporal sword.
A G : 2 8 :002(081) [0083] have resulted because the **bishops**, under pretext of the
A G : 2 8 :005(081) [0085] of keys or the power of **bishops** is a power and command
A G : 2 8 :008(082) [0085] This power of keys or of **bishops** is used and exercised
A G : 2 8 :010(082) [0085] of the church or of **bishops** bestows eternal gifts and is
A G : 2 8 :019(083) [0087] In cases where **bishops** possess temporal authority and
A G : 2 8 :019(083) [0087] they possess it not as **bishops** by divine right, but by
A G : 2 8 :021(084) [0087] it is the office of the **bishop** to preach the Gospel, forgive
A G : 2 8 :022(084) [0087] to be obedient to the **bishops** according to the saying of
A G : 2 8 :028(085) [0087] even regularly elected **bishops** if they err or if they teach
A G : 2 8 :029(085) [0087] power and jurisdiction **bishops** may have in various
A G : 2 8 :029(085) [0087] However, when **bishops** are negligent in the performance
A G : 2 8 :030(085) [0087] is dispute as to whether **bishops** have the power to
A G : 2 8 :031(085) [0087] attribute such power to **bishops** cite Christ's saying in
A G : 2 8 :034(086) [0087] our teachers assert that **bishops** do not have power to
A G : 2 8 :039(087) [0089] the apostles and **bishops** to institute it, as some have
A G : 2 8 :040(087) [0089] believable that some **bishops** were misled by the example
A G : 2 8 :042(088) [0089] Where did the **bishops** get the right and power to impose
A G : 2 8 :049(089) [0091] If, then, **bishops** have the power to burden the churches
A G : 2 8 :050(089) [0091] not at all proper for the **bishops** to require such services
A G : 2 8 :053(090) [0091] our teachers reply that **bishops** or pastors may make
A G : 2 8 :055(090) [0091] to be obedient to the **bishops** and parish ministers in such
A G : 2 8 :061(091) [0093] the apostles and **bishops** to devise new ceremonies which
A G : 2 8 :069(093) [0093] The **bishops** might easily retain the obedience of men if
A G : 2 8 :071(093) [0093] do not ask that the **bishops** should restore peace and
A G : 2 8 :071(093) [0093] it is incumbent on the **bishops** to do this, too, in the case
A G : 2 8 :072(093) [0093] they ask only that the **bishops** relax certain unreasonable
A G : 2 8 :074(093) [0093] Accordingly the **bishops** ought to be so gracious as to
A G : 2 8 :076(094) [0095] St. Peter forbids the **bishops** to exercise lordship as if
A G : 2 8 :077(094) [0095] ways of reducing the **bishops**' power, but we desire and
A L : 0 0 :002(047) [0059] difference in these, the **bishops** should have been so
A L : 2 3 :011(052) [0063] should be chosen to be **bishop** (I Tim. 3:2), and not until
A L : 2 4 :014(057) [0065] The **bishops** were not ignorant of these abuses.
A L : 2 4 :038(060) [0069] Holy Communion from the **bishop** or from a presbyter."
A L : 2 6 :018(067) [0073] or out of hatred for the **bishops**, as some wrongly
A L : 2 7 :015(073) [0077] church, and pastors and **bishops** were taken from them.
A L : 2 8 :001(081) [0083] about the power of **bishops**, and some have improperly
A L : 2 8 :005(081) [0085] of keys or the power of **bishops** is a power or command
A L : 2 8 :019(083) [0087] If **bishops** have any power of the sword, they have this
A L : 2 8 :019(083) [0087] they have this not as **bishops** under a commission of the
A L : 2 8 :020(084) [0087] about the jurisdiction of **bishops**, therefore, civil authority
A L : 2 8 :021(084) [0087] belongs to the **bishops** as bishops (that is, to those to
A L : 2 8 :021(084) [0087] belongs to the bishops as **bishops** (that is, to those to
A L : 2 8 :022(084) [0087] to be obedient to the **bishops** according to the text, "He
A L : 2 8 :023(084) [0087] However, when **bishops** teach or ordain anything
A L : 2 8 :028(085) [0087] that not even catholic **bishops** are to be obeyed if they
A L : 2 8 :029(085) [0087] matrimony, tithes, etc.), **bishops** have this by human
A L : 2 8 :029(085) [0087] When the **bishops** are negligent in the performance of
A L : 2 8 :030(085) [0087] it is disputed whether **bishops** or pastors have the right to
A L : 2 8 :031(085) [0087] attribute this right to **bishops** cite as evidence the
A L : 2 8 :034(086) [0087] pointed out above, that **bishops** do not have power to
A L : 2 8 :039(087) [0089] had commissioned the apostles and **bishops** to institute it.
A L : 2 8 :042(088) [0089] Where did the **bishops** get the right to impose such
A L : 2 8 :049(089) [0091] If **bishops** have the right to burden consciences with such
A L : 2 8 :050(089) [0091] that it is not lawful for **bishops** to institute such services
A L : 2 8 :053(090) [0091] reply that it is lawful for **bishops** or pastors to make
A L : 2 8 :061(091) [0093] the apostles and **bishops** to devise new ceremonies which
A L : 2 8 :069(093) [0093] The **bishops** might easily retain the lawful obedience of
A L : 2 8 :071(093) [0093] do not ask that the **bishops** restore concord at the
A L : 2 8 :074(093) [0093] befit the clemency of the **bishops** to mitigate these
A L : 2 8 :076(094) [0095] Peter forbids the **bishops** to be domineering and to coerce
A L : 2 8 :077(094) [0095] our intention that the **bishops** give up their power to
A P : 0 4 :233(140) [0185] inevitably disintegrate if **bishops** impose heavy burdens
A P : 0 4 :234(140) [0185] of their clergy, when the **bishops** take into account the
A P : 0 4 :390(166) [0225] the pope or cardinals or **bishops** or some theologians or
A P : 0 7 :041(176) [0241] why did the **bishops** later change them in so many ways?
A P : 1 2 :175(210) [0307] objection from the **bishops**, there is no point in such
A P : 1 4 :002(214) [0315] But the **bishops** either force our priests to forsake and
A P : 1 4 :002(214) [0315] This keeps our priests from acknowledging such **bishops**.
A P : 1 4 :002(214) [0315] Thus the cruelty of the **bishops** is the reason for the
A P : 1 4 :005(215) [0315] polity, provided that the **bishops** stop raging against our
A P : 1 4 :005(215) [0315] that we have undermined the authority of the **bishops**.
A P : 1 4 :005(215) [0315] the unjust cruelty of the **bishops**, we could not obtain
A P : 1 5 :031(219) [0323] Nor do **bishops** have the power to institute rites as though
A P : 2 1 :038(234) [0355] **Bishops**, theologians, and monks applaud these
A P : 2 1 :039(235) [0355] been hoping that the **bishops** would exert their authority
A P : 2 2 :017(238) [0361] prophesies about **bishops** and pastors in the words of
A P : 2 3 :059(247) [0379] from those who are regarded as the regular **bishops**.
A P : 2 8 :006(282) [0445] only reply is that **bishops** have the power to rule and to
A P : 2 8 :006(282) [0445] inform us that **bishops** have the authority to create laws
A P : 2 8 :008(282) [0445] Thus **bishops** have no right to create traditions apart from
A P : 2 8 :008(282) [0445] Nor do the **bishops** have the right to burden consciences
A P : 2 8 :011(283) [0447] be able to show that **bishops** have the power to institute
A P : 2 8 :012(283) [0447] we have said what power the Gospel grants to **bishops**.
A P : 2 8 :012(283) [0447] Those who are now **bishops** do not perform the duties of
A P : 2 8 :012(283) [0447] not perform the duties of **bishops** according to the
A P : 2 8 :012(283) [0447] though they may well be **bishops** according to canonical
A P : 2 8 :012(283) [0447] we are talking about a **bishop** according to the Gospel.
A P : 2 8 :013(283) [0447] Therefore a **bishop** has the power of the order, namely,
A P : 2 8 :014(283) [0447] A **bishops** does not have the power of a tyrant to act
A P : 2 8 :014(283) [0447] a certain jurisdiction **bishops** may institute new acts of
A P : 2 8 :020(284) [0449] not create an authority for **bishops** apart from the Gospel
A P : 2 8 :020(284) [0449] **Bishops** must not create traditions contrary to the

Continued ▶

S 1 : P R :010(290) [0457] Yet neither the **bishops** nor the canons care how the poor
S 1 : P R :013(291) [0459] broad cinctures, **bishops**' and cardinals' hats and crosiers,
S 2 : 0 4 :001(298) [0471] The pope is only the **bishop** and pastor of the churches in
S 2 : 0 4 :002(298) [0471] But now no **bishop** dares to call the pope "brother," as
S 2 : 0 4 :009(300) [0473] and by having all the **bishops** equal in office (however
S 2 : 0 4 :009(300) [0475] and after them all the **bishops** throughout Christendom,
S 3 : 0 3 :024(307) [0485] among the cardinals and **bishops** so that one could grant
S 3 : 1 0 :001(314) [0497] If the **bishops** were true bishops and were concerned
S 3 : 1 0 :001(314) [0497] If the bishops were true **bishops** and were concerned
S 3 : 1 0 :001(314) [0497] However, they neither are nor wish to be true **bishops**.
S 3 : 1 0 :003(314) [0497] governed without **bishops** by priests and preachers in
S 3 : 1 5 :005(316) [0501] that superiority over the **bishops** which he possesses by
T R : 0 0 :001(320) [0503] The Roman **bishop** arrogates to himself the claim that he
T R : 0 0 :001(320) [0503] that he is by divine right above all **bishops** and pastors.
T R : 0 0 :002(320) [0503] and for such reasons the **bishop** of Rome calls himself the
T R : 0 0 :005(320) [0503] they say that the Roman **bishop** is above all bishops by
T R : 0 0 :005(320) [0503] the Roman bishop is above all **bishops** by divine right.
T R : 0 0 :005(320) [0503] the pope is the universal **bishop** or, as they put it, the
T R : 0 0 :005(320) [0503] universal bishop or, as they put it, the ecumenical **bishop**.
T R : 0 0 :005(320) [0503] That is, all **bishops** and pastors throughout the whole
T R : 0 0 :005(320) [0505] right to elect, ordain, confirm, and depose all **bishops**.
T R : 0 0 :007(320) [0505] Gospel that the Roman **bishop** is not by divine right
T R : 0 0 :007(320) [0505] is not by divine right above all other **bishops** and pastors.
T R : 0 0 :012(321) [0507] Nicaea decided that the **bishop** of Alexandria should
T R : 0 0 :012(321) [0507] in the East and the **bishop** of Rome should administer the
T R : 0 0 :012(322) [0507] authority of the Roman **bishop** grew out of a decision of
T R : 0 0 :012(322) [0507] of human right, for if the **bishop** of Rome had his
T R : 0 0 :012(322) [0507] from him and transfer it to the **bishop** of Alexandria.
T R : 0 0 :012(322) [0507] In fact, all the Eastern **bishops** should forever have
T R : 0 0 :012(322) [0507] ordination and confirmation from the Roman **bishop**.
T R : 0 0 :013(322) [0507] of Nicaea decided that **bishops** should be elected by their
T R : 0 0 :013(322) [0507] in the presence of one or more neighboring **bishops**.
T R : 0 0 :014(322) [0507] the neighboring **bishops** of the same province should
T R : 0 0 :014(322) [0507] is to be ordained, and a **bishop** should be elected in the
T R : 0 0 :014(322) [0509] by the judgment of the **bishops** assembled in their
T R : 0 0 :015(322) [0509] were sought from the **bishop** of Rome in the greater part
T R : 0 0 :015(322) [0509] attribute superiority and lordship to the **bishop** of Rome.
T R : 0 0 :016(322) [0509] it is not possible for one **bishop** to be the overseer of all
T R : 0 0 :016(322) [0509] ordination or confirmation from the **bishop** of Rome.
T R : 0 0 :017(323) [0509] and held in which the **bishop** of Rome did not preside —
T R : 0 0 :017(323) [0509] the primacy or superiority of the **bishop** of Rome.
T R : 0 0 :018(323) [0509] Wherever there is a **bishop** — whether in Rome or
T R : 0 0 :018(323) [0509] of poverty that makes a **bishop** superior or inferior."
T R : 0 0 :019(323) [0509] objected to having himself designated as universal **bishop**.
T R : 0 0 :019(323) [0509] was offered to the **bishop** of Rome but he did not accept
T R : 0 0 :020(323) [0509] prevailed that the **bishops** of Rome were confirmed by
T R : 0 0 :021(323) [0509] disputes between the **bishops** of Rome and
T R : 0 0 :021(323) [0509] the primacy should be assigned to the **bishop** of Rome.
T R : 0 0 :035(326) [0513] to make the German **bishops** subject to their power and
T R : 0 0 :035(326) [0513] and deprive the emperors of the right to appoint **bishops**.
T R : 0 0 :038(326) [0515] be added: Even if the **bishop** of Rome should possess
T R : 0 0 :057(330) [0521] Accordingly, even if the **bishop** of Rome did possess the
T R : 0 0 :059(330) [0521] The Power and Jurisdiction of **Bishops**
T R : 0 0 :061(330) [0521] whether they are called pastors, presbyters, or **bishops**.
T R : 0 0 :062(330) [0521] over the churches are both **bishops** and presbyters.
T R : 0 0 :062(330) [0523] are followed by, "A **bishop** must be married only once"
T R : 0 0 :062(331) [0523] Evangelist to the time of **Bishops** Heracles and
T R : 0 0 :062(331) [0523] number, set him in a higher place, and called him **bishop**.
T R : 0 0 :062(331) [0523] ordination, what does a **bishop** do that a presbyter does
T R : 0 0 :063(331) [0523] between the grades of **bishop** and presbyter (or pastor) is
T R : 0 0 :064(331) [0523] a distinction between **bishops** and pastors, and this was
T R : 0 0 :064(331) [0523] it was decided that one **bishop** should ordain the
T R : 0 0 :065(331) [0523] the distinction between **bishop** and pastor is not by divine
T R : 0 0 :066(331) [0523] when the regular **bishops** become enemies of the Gospel
T R : 0 0 :070(332) [0525] was a time when the people elected pastors and **bishops**.
T R : 0 0 :070(332) [0525] Afterwards a **bishop**, either of that church or of a
T R : 0 0 :072(332) [0525] Wherefore, when the **bishops** are heretics or refuse to
T R : 0 0 :072(332) [0525] and tyranny of the **bishops** that give occasion to schism
T R : 0 0 :072(332) [0525] for Paul commands that **bishops** who teach and defend
T R : 0 0 :073(332) [0525] states) that distinguishes **bishops** from the rest of the
T R : 0 0 :073(332) [0525] for discussion of the other functions of **bishops**.
T R : 0 0 :074(332) [0525] This the **bishops** have tyrannically reserved for
T R : 0 0 :076(333) [0525] Since, therefore, the **bishops** have tyrannically reserved
T R : 0 0 :076(333) [0527] need, on account of this jurisdiction, to obey the **bishops**.
T R : 0 0 :077(333) [0527] This, too, the **bishops** have by human right only, and they
T R : 0 0 :077(333) [0527] to make these decisions if the **bishops** are negligent.
T R : 0 0 :077(333) [0527] not necessary to obey the **bishops** on account of this
T R : 0 0 :079(333) [0527] Since therefore the **bishops** who are adherents of the pope
T R : 0 0 :079(333) [0527] why the churches should not recognize them as **bishops**.
T R : 0 0 :080(334) [0527] have been given to **bishops** as alms for the administration
T R : 0 0 :082(334) [0527] there would be wicked **bishops** in the future who would
T R : 0 0 :082(334) [0529] and jurisdiction of the **bishops** which was presented to the
T R : 0 0 :082(000) [0529] the Papacy and the Power and Jurisdiction of **Bishops**.
S C : P R :004(338) [0533] How will you **bishops** answer for it before Christ that you
S C : 0 9 :002(354) [0561] **Bishops**, Pastors, and Preachers
S C : 0 9 :002(354) [0561] "A **bishop** must be above reproach, married only once,
L C : 0 1 :038(369) [0591] observe this every day in the case of **bishops** and princes.
L C : 0 1 :209(393) [0641] those of emperor, princes, **bishops**, or anyone else.
L C : 0 3 :047(426) [0711] try to suppress it, as the **bishops**, tyrants, fanatics, and
L C : 0 3 :069(429) [0717] down all that the devil, **bishops**, tyrants, and heretics can
S D : R N :005(504) [0853] synods and Christian **bishops** and teachers to appeal and
S D : 0 8 :016(594) [1021] who had become a **bishop** in Antioch in Syria, taught
S D : 1 0 :019(614) [1059] to the papists (the papist **bishops**) that they are the
S D : 1 0 :019(614) [1059] Articles declare: "If the **bishops** were true bishops and
S D : 1 0 :019(614) [1059] "If the bishops were true **bishops** and were concerned
S D : 1 0 :019(614) [1059] However, they neither are nor wish to be true **bishops**.

Bit (4)
A P : 0 4 :241(141) [0187] on civil war if either had yielded the least **bit** to the other.
A P : 1 2 :106(197) [0283] He is merely giving a **bit** of domestic advice to the head
L C : 0 1 :155(386) [0625] punishment and that we are not one **bit** improved by it.
L C : 0 1 :267(401) [0657] Learning a **bit** of gossip about someone else, they spread

Bite (1), Biting (1)
L C : 0 1 :264(400) [0655] shameful vice of back-**biting** or slander by which the
S D : 0 1 :051(517) [0875] is the serpent's nature to **bite** and poison," the term

Bitter (8), Bitterest (1), Bitterly (2), Bitterness (1)
A G : 2 6 :016(066) [0073] Gerson and others have complained **bitterly** about this.
A P : P R :016(099) [0101] extent is evident from the **bitter** hatred inflaming our
A P : 0 4 :236(140) [0185] did not insist so **bitterly** on certain traditions which have
A P : 1 2 :128(201) [0291] help producing the most **bitter** hatred against those who,
A P : 1 2 :150(206) [0299] This certainly speaks of the most **bitter** punishments.
A P : 2 4 :091(266) [0415] Indeed, the **bitterest** kind of sorrow must seize all the
L C : 0 1 :187(390) [0633] root and source of this **bitterness** toward our neighbor.
L C : 0 6 :017(459) [0000] became burdensome and **bitter**, to the manifest harm and
S D : P R :007(502) [0849] errors and the subsequent **bitter** controversies would
S D : 0 3 :009(541) [0919] of the total obedience, the **bitter** passion, the death, and
S D : 0 7 :044(577) [0987] he was about to begin his **bitter** passion and death for our
S D : 0 7 :044(577) [0987] abiding memorial of his **bitter** passion and death and all

Black (1)
A G : 2 7 :050(079) [0083] not of mendicancy or wearing a **black** or gray cowl, etc.

Blame (4), Blameless (5), Blaming (1)
A G : 2 0 :033(045) [0057] to lead honorable and **blameless** lives; they failed to
A P : 1 2 :108(198) [0283] justified in thy sentence and **blameless** in thy judgment."
A P : 1 2 :108(198) [0283] I declare Thee to be **blameless** when hypocrites judge
A P : 2 2 :016(238) [0361] We do not **blame** the church, which has suffered this
A P : 2 2 :016(238) [0361] both parts; but we do **blame** the writers who defend the
A P : 2 7 :008(269) [0421] We are not **blaming** everyone.
L C : 0 1 :188(390) [0635] Thus you should be **blameless** toward all people in body
L C : 0 1 :296(405) [0665] without accusation or **blame** for fraudulent dealing.
S D : R N :013(506) [0855] No one can **blame** us if we derive our expositions and
S D : 0 4 :034(557) [0949] present you holy and **blameless** and irreproachable before

Blankenhain (2)
P R : P R :027(015) [0025] Louis, count of Gleichen [-**Blankenhain**].
P R : P R :027(015) [0025] Charles, count of Gleichen [-**Blankenhain**].

Blaspheme (6), Blasphemed (2), Blasphemers (4), Blasphemies (3), Blasphemous (8), Blasphemously (2), Blasphemy (12)
P R : P R :022(011) [0019] and who do not **blaspheme** the truth of the divine Word,
P R : P R :022(011) [0019] and their stiff-necked proponents and **blasphemers**.
P R : P R :022(011) [0019] take no pleasure in **blasphemies** against the Holy Supper
A G : 2 8 :036(086) [0089] of Christ's merit is **blasphemed** when we presume to earn
A P : 0 1 :002(100) [0103] the church of Christ but are idolaters and **blasphemers**.
A P : 0 2 :049(106) [0119] **Blasphemy** and wicked doctrines fill the world, and by
A P : 0 4 :257(144) [0193] deserve to be regarded as **blasphemers** against Christ.
A P : 1 2 :094(196) [0281] truth; a more horrible **blasphemy** than this cannot be
A P : 2 0 :002(227) [0339] of the Confutation who so impudently **blaspheme** Christ.
A P : 2 0 :004(227) [0339] Therefore the **blasphemy** of attributing the honor of
A P : 2 7 :019(272) [0425] seen to it that such **blasphemy** was removed from the
A P : 2 7 :020(272) [0425] it is also an intolerable **blasphemy** when Thomas says
S 2 : 0 2 :014(295) [0467] believe their shameful, **blasphemous**, accursed traffic in
S 2 : 0 3 :002(298) [0471] them with their **blasphemous** services, invented by men,
S 2 : 0 4 :003(298) [0471] false, mischievous, **blasphemous**, usurped authority have
S 3 : 0 3 :043(310) [0491] adultery, murder, and **blasphemy**), faith and the Spirit
S 3 : 1 4 :001(316) [0501] This is **blasphemy**.
T R : 0 0 :041(327) [0517] the impious doctrines, **blasphemies**, and unjust cruelties
T R : 0 0 :059(330) [0521] with idolatry and **blasphemous** opinions, make
L C : 0 1 :055(372) [0595] among liars are **blasphemers**, not only the very crass ones
L C : 0 1 :262(400) [0655] persecution and **blasphemy**; it is contradicted, perverted,
L C : 0 1 :263(400) [0655] corrupt teaching and **blasphemy**, to false judges and
L C : 0 3 :042(425) [0709] name must be profaned and **blasphemed** because of us.
L C : 0 3 :104(434) [0727] into despair, atheism, **blasphemy**, and countless other
L C : 0 4 :015(438) [0735] wickedness and devilish **blasphemy** when our new spirits,
L C : 0 4 :055(443) [0747] That would be to **blaspheme** and desecrate the sacrament
L C : 0 5 :004(447) [0753] dispute with those who **blaspheme** and desecrate this
E P : 0 7 :041(486) [0817] sarcastic, and **blasphemous** questions and statements,
E P : 0 7 :041(486) [0817] advance most **blasphemously** and offensively in a coarse,
E P : 0 8 :039(491) [0827] misinterpret and **blasphemously** pervert the words of
E P : 1 1 :021(497) [0837] These are all **blasphemous** and terrible errors, for they
S D : 0 7 :008(570) [0975] anathematize and condemn as a horrendous **blasphemy**.
S D : 0 7 :127(591) [1015] scoffing, and **blasphemous** questions and expressions
S D : 0 8 :021(595) [1023] *Supper* against the **blasphemous** *alloeosis* of Zwingli, who
S D : 1 0 :022(615) [1061] the impious doctrines, **blasphemies**, and unjust cruelties
S D : 1 1 :039(622) [1075] Word and who reject, **blaspheme**, and persecute it (Matt.
S D : 1 1 :078(629) [1089] but only to despise, **blaspheme**, and ridicule it, and they

Blauer (1)
T R : 0 0 :082(335) [0529] Ambrose **Blauer**

Blemish (5), Blemishes (1)
A P : 0 7 :007(169) [0229] such thing, that it might be holy and without **blemish**."
L C : 0 1 :288(404) [0663] we should veil whatever **blemishes** and infirmities we find
L C : 0 5 :055(453) [0767] pure that God might not find the least **blemish** in us.
E P : 0 1 :014(468) [0783] insignificant spot or **blemish** that has only been sprinkled
E P : 0 1 :015(468) [0783] the view that this **blemish** may be removed as readily as a
S D : 0 1 :021(512) [0865] external spot or **blemish**, merely splashed on, or a

Blend (1), Blended (7), Blending (6), Blends (1)
S D : 0 1 :026(512) [0867] Satan infuses and **blends** original sin (as something
S D : 0 1 :026(512) [0867] into man's nature, as when poison is **blended** with water.
S D : 0 1 :027(513) [0867] essentially evil and **blended** this with their nature, as the
S D : 0 8 :007(592) [1017] never be separated, **blended** with each other, or the one
S D : 0 8 :017(594) [1021] which the natures are not **blended** into one essence but,
S D : 0 8 :019(594) [1021] thereby any sort of **blending** or equalization of the
S D : 0 8 :019(595) [1021] either water or honey but is a **blended** beverage.
S D : 0 8 :019(595) [1021] God but without thereby **blending** the natures or their
S D : 0 8 :028(596) [1025] and in truth without any **blending** or equalization of the
S D : 0 8 :031(597) [1025] each other without any **blending** or equalization of the
S D : 0 8 :060(602) [1035] a way that they are not **blended** together or the one is
S D : 0 8 :062(603) [1037] should any conversion, **blending**, or equalization of the
S D : 0 8 :063(603) [1037] transfusion which would **blend** the natures in their
S D : 0 8 :063(603) [1037] truth but without any **blending** of the natures and of their
S D : 0 8 :089(609) [1047] nature has allegedly been **blended** with the divine or has

Bless (9), Blessed (72), Blessedness (6), Blesses (1), Blessing (52), Blessings (48)

PR : PR :000(001) [0004] Strife Arose after the **blessed** Death of Martin Luther,
PR : PR :018(009) [0015] this confession until our **blessed** end and to appear before
AG : 0 3 :005(030) [0045] life and every grace and **blessing**, and that he may protect
AL : 0 3 :001(029) [0045] on man's nature in the womb of the **blessed** virgin Mary.
AL : 2 8 :018(083) [0085] in honor and acknowledged as gifts and **blessings** of God.
AP : PR :018(099) [0103] God for this great **blessing**, that on many points our
AP : 0 2 :050(106) [0119] so we cannot know his **blessings** unless we recognize our
AP : 0 4 :003(107) [0121] the glory and the **blessings** of Christ, and they rob pious
AP : 0 4 :046(113) [0133] of Christ, it uses his **blessings**, it regenerates our hearts, it
AP : 0 4 :049(114) [0135] receives God's offered **blessing**; the righteousness of the
AP : 0 4 :053(114) [0137] merits and shows that the **blessing** is offered only by
AP : 0 4 :060(115) [0137] that we accept his **blessings** and receive them because of
AP : 0 4 :076(117) [0143] according to Ps. 32:1, "**Blessed** is he whose transgression
AP : 0 4 :101(121) [0151] except to know Christ's **blessings**, the promises which by
AP : 0 4 :101(121) [0151] And to know these **blessings** is rightly and truly to believe
AP : 0 4 :103(122) [0151] the blood of Christ; for '**blessed** is he whose transgression
AP : 0 4 :118(123) [0155] work and receive his **blessings** and it alone provides a
AP : 0 4 :163(129) [0169] (Ps. 32:1; Rom. 4:7), "**Blessed** is he whose transgression is
AP : 0 4 :168(130) [0169] Again (Ps. 32:2), "**Blessed** is the man to whom the Lord
AP : 0 4 :198(134) [0175] Christ says (Matt. 5:10), "**Blessed** are those who are
AP : 0 4 :210(136) [0179] faith and announce the **blessings** of Christ, as Paul says (I
AP : 0 4 :228(139) [0183] him and to accept **blessings** from him; this he declares to
AP : 0 4 :254(143) [0193] Matt. 5:3, "**Blessed** are the poor in spirit, for theirs is the
AP : 0 4 :255(143) [0193] And again (v. 7), "**Blessed** are the merciful, for they shall
AP : 0 4 :278(149) [0199] alms merit many divine **blessings**, lighten our
AP : 0 4 :279(149) [0199] your life" (4:5), and later, "**Bless** God always, and ask him
AP : 0 4 :300(153) [0205] Such great **blessings** our opponents take from the church
AP : 0 4 :361(162) [0219] series of arguments the **blessings** of Christ and the
AP : 0 7 :015(170) [0231] things but the eternal **blessings** themselves, the Holy
AP : 0 7 :025(173) [0235] because we preach the **blessing** of Christ, that we obtain
AP : 1 1 :002(180) [0249] and extolled the **blessing** of absolution and the power of
AP : 1 2 :010(184) [0255] it obscures the **blessing** of Christ, the power of the keys,
AP : 1 2 :016(184) [0257] of faith in Christ and of the **blessing** of Christ lies buried.
AP : 1 2 :043(187) [0263] it illumines the **blessing** of Christ, and it teaches us to
AP : 1 2 :094(196) [0281] Oh, **blessed** are we for whose sake God swears an oath!
AP : 1 2 :103(197) [0281] is in the area of **blessing** or grace, not of judgment or
AP : 1 2 :141(204) [0295] penitence and quickening, and the **blessings** of Christ.
AP : 1 5 :004(215) [0315] obscures the Gospel, the **blessing** of Christ, and
AP : 2 1 :025(232) [0349] the merits of the most **blessed** virgin Mary and of all the
AP : 2 1 :027(232) [0349] Granted that **blessed** Mary prays for the church, does she
AP : 2 1 :027(232) [0349] What does Christ do if **blessed** Mary does all this?
AP : 2 1 :028(232) [0351] popular estimation the **blessed** Virgin has completely
AP : 2 1 :031(233) [0351] by the merits of the **blessed** Virgin or of the other saints.
AP : 2 1 :034(234) [0353] we saw a statue of the **blessed** Virgin which was
AP : 2 4 :019(252) [0389] for the forgiveness of sins and other **blessings** received.
AP : 2 4 :048(258) [0401] By the **blessing** of God, the priests in our churches pay
AP : 2 4 :048(258) [0401] teach the Gospel of the **blessing** of Christ, and they show
AP : 2 4 :072(262) [0409] of Christ's **blessings** and the acceptance of them by faith,
AP : 2 4 :074(263) [0409] it really gives thanks for the **blessing** of Christ's suffering.
AP : 2 4 :076(263) [0411] it gives thanks to the Giver of such a generous **blessing**."
AP : 2 4 :076(263) [0411] the greatness of God's **blessings** with the greatness of our
AP : 2 4 :091(266) [0415] who transferred the **blessed** promises of the forgiveness of
AP : 2 4 :093(267) [0417] it equally to all the **blessed** patriarchs, prophets, and
AP : 2 7 :016(271) [0425] and fanatical notion they bury the **blessing** of Christ.
AP : 2 7 :053(278) [0437] made up the rosary of the **blessed** Virgin, which is mere
S 1 : PR :015(291) [0459] Thee and the Father liveth and reigneth, **blessed** forever.
S 2 : 0 2 :004(293) [0463] in a far better and more **blessed** manner — indeed, the
S 2 : 0 2 :004(293) [0463] — indeed, the only **blessed** manner — according to the
S 2 : 0 2 :004(293) [0463] sacrament can be had in another and more **blessed** way?
S 3 : 1 5 :005(316) [0501] In addition, there are **blessings** of candles, palms, spices,
S 3 : 1 5 :005(316) [0501] These cannot be called **blessings**, and they are not, but
TR : 0 0 :073(332) [0525] confirmation or the **blessing** of bells, which are almost the
SC : PR :018(340) [0537] the Scriptures to show how God punished and **blessed**.
SC : PR :024(341) [0539] the benefit and loss, the **blessing** and danger connected
SC : 0 1 :022(344) [0543] promises grace and every **blessing** to all who keep them.
SC : 0 2 :004(345) [0545] innocence, and **blessedness**, even as he is risen from the
SC : 0 3 :020(348) [0549] comes, he may grant us a **blessed** end and graciously take
SC : 0 8 :006(353) [0559] *his household to offer **blessing** and thanksgiving at table*
SC : 0 8 :006(353) [0559] [**Blessing** before Eating]
SC : 0 8 :009(353) [0559] God, heavenly Father, **bless** us, and these thy gifts which
LC : PR :010(360) [0569] Psalm 1 calls those **blessed** who "meditate on God's law
LC : PR :011(360) [0571] even if the only **blessing** and benefit you obtain from it is
LC : PR :012(360) [0571] I were to recount all the **blessings** that flow from God's
LC : PR :013(360) [0571] despise this might, **blessing**, power, and fruit — especially
LC : 0 1 :017(367) [0585] own, to which he looked for **blessings**, help, and comfort.
LC : 0 1 :024(367) [0587] protection, peace, and all temporal and eternal **blessings**.
LC : 0 1 :026(368) [0587] So we receive our **blessings** not from them, but from God
LC : 0 1 :026(368) [0587] and means through which God bestows all **blessings**.
LC : 0 1 :027(368) [0587] be not receiving our **blessings** from God but seeking them
LC : 0 1 :039(370) [0591] — sheer goodness and **blessing**, not only for themselves
LC : 0 1 :041(370) [0591] brings you either eternal **blessing**, happiness, and
LC : 0 1 :041(370) [0591] will be yours with every **blessing** and will protect and help
LC : 0 1 :047(371) [0593] demand of us than a hearty trust in him for all **blessings**.
LC : 0 1 :071(374) [0601] This is a **blessed** and useful habit, and very effective
LC : 0 1 :114(380) [0613] and reared in true **blessedness**; they would have remained
LC : 0 1 :128(382) [0617] us and how many **blessings** of body and soul he bestows
LC : 0 1 :128(382) [0617] and forget all the **blessings** we have received throughout
LC : 0 1 :130(383) [0619] as those through whom God has given him all **blessings**.
LC : 0 1 :132(383) [0619] welfare, to lead us to a quiet, pleasant, and **blessed** life.
LC : 0 1 :136(383) [0619] abundantly with every **blessing**; on the other hand, if you
LC : 0 1 :137(384) [0621] The godly and the obedient, however, are **blessed**.
LC : 0 1 :146(385) [0623] How can you lead a more **blessed** or holy life, as far as
LC : 0 1 :151(386) [0625] know that he shall have no favor or **blessing** from God.
LC : 0 1 :152(386) [0625] overwhelmed with our **blessings** and we shall have all
LC : 0 1 :153(386) [0625] God's favor, peace, and **blessing** than you will with
LC : 0 1 :156(386) [0625] people, or else God would not grant us so many **blessings**!
LC : 0 1 :163(387) [0627] us of his Word and his **blessings** and once again allow
LC : 0 1 :164(387) [0627] peace, and afterwards abundance and **blessedness** forever.
LC : 0 1 :175(388) [0631] done, God would richly **bless** us and give us grace so that
LC : 0 1 :207(393) [0639] maintain, and cherish it as a divine and **blessed** estate.
LC : 0 1 :208(393) [0639] has therefore most richly **blessed** this estate above all
LC : 0 1 :217(394) [0641] life and know that it is a **blessed** and God-pleasing estate.
LC : 0 1 :218(394) [0643] Then God will add his **blessing** and grace so that men
LC : 0 1 :242(397) [0649] pronounce this kind of **blessing** over them: "Your grain
LC : 0 1 :252(399) [0653] upon them a wonderful **blessing**: We shall be richly
LC : 0 1 :253(399) [0653] does not desire this **blessing** will find wrath and
LC : 0 1 :290(404) [0663] and bring abundant **blessings**, if only the blind world and
LC : 0 1 :322(409) [0673] how richly he will reward, **bless**, and bestow all good
LC : 0 1 :323(409) [0675] a kind father and offers us every grace and **blessing**.
LC : 0 1 :333(410) [0677] that he will shower us with all good things and **blessings**.
LC : 0 2 :015(412) [0681] physical and temporal **blessings** — good government,
LC : 0 2 :021(413) [0683] misusing all the **blessings** and gifts of God solely for its
LC : 0 2 :023(413) [0683] we see, and every **blessing** that comes our way, should
LC : 0 2 :023(413) [0683] a desire to use all these **blessings** to his glory and praise.
LC : 0 2 :030(414) [0685] of life and righteousness and every good and **blessing**.
LC : 0 2 :030(414) [0685] his righteousness, wisdom, power, life, and **blessedness**.
LC : 0 2 :033(415) [0687] it all our salvation and **blessedness** are based, and it is so
LC : 0 2 :039(416) [0689] Christ to receive this **blessing**, which we could not obtain
LC : 0 2 :052(417) [0691] participant and co-partner in all the **blessings** it possesses.
LC : 0 2 :066(419) [0697] They cannot be confident of his love and **blessing**.
LC : 0 2 :066(419) [0697] are not illuminated and **blessed** by the gifts of the Holy
LC : 0 3 :001(420) [0697] The best and most **blessed** life consists of these things.
LC : 0 3 :044(425) [0709] and enjoy his manifold **blessings** fail to teach, speak, and
LC : 0 3 :054(427) [0713] may live forever in perfect righteousness and **blessedness**."
LC : 0 3 :055(427) [0713] a temporal, perishable **blessing**, but for an eternal,
LC : 0 3 :057(428) [0713] so many inexpressible **blessings**, despise them or lack
LC : 0 3 :058(428) [0713] expect, without doubting, eternal **blessings** from God.
LC : 0 3 :065(429) [0715] and bears fruit, there the **blessed** holy cross will not be far
LC : 0 3 :072(430) [0719] grain to grow and did not **bless** and preserve it in the
LC : 0 3 :075(430) [0719] we could not have the steady **blessing** of daily bread.
LC : 0 3 :075(430) [0719] may bestow on us still more **blessings** and good things.
LC : 0 3 :083(431) [0721] gives and provides these **blessings** bountifully, even for
LC : 0 3 :086(432) [0723] by God's gift and **blessing**, nevertheless we are not
LC : 0 4 :017(438) [0737] heavenly, holy, and **blessed** water — praise it in any other
LC : 0 4 :027(440) [0739] well described as a divine, **blessed**, fruitful, and gracious
LC : 0 4 :033(440) [0741] Since these **blessings** are offered and promised in the
LC : 0 4 :042(442) [0743] In short, the **blessings** of Baptism are so boundless that if
LC : 0 5 :005(447) [0755] them, so also does this **blessed** sacrament remain
LC : 0 5 :022(449) [0757] and may be a source of **blessing** to me as a sure pledge
LC : 0 5 :035(450) [0761] for he lets this gracious **blessing** be offered to him in vain
LC : 0 5 :039(451) [0761] themselves to receive this **blessed** sacrament frequently.
LC : 0 5 :056(453) [0767] this great and precious **blessing**, and it appears like a dark
LC : 0 6 :028(460) [0000] urge that such a precious **blessing** should not be despised,
LC : 0 6 :035(461) [0000] we have attained to this **blessed** knowledge of confession.
EP : 0 4 :007(476) [0799] from works, saying, '**Blessed** are those whose iniquities
EP : 0 7 :009(483) [0811] it is written, "the cup of **blessing** which we bless" (I Cor.
EP : 0 7 :009(483) [0811] cup of blessing which we **bless**" (I Cor. 10:16; 11:23-25).
EP : 0 7 :009(483) [0811] This **blessing** occurs through the recitation of the words
EP : 0 9 :003(492) [0827] as Dr. Luther of **blessed** memory taught in his sermon
SD : PR :001(501) [0847] by Dr. Luther, of **blessed** and holy memory, and the
SD : RN :002(503) [0851] of God as Dr. Luther of **blessed** memory had explained
SD : RN :009(505) [0853] which Dr. Luther of **blessed** memory clearly set forth in
SD : 0 3 :028(544) [0925] and sanctification are a **blessing** of Christ, the mediator,
SD : 0 3 :041(546) [0929] faith alone which apprehends the **blessing** without works.
SD : 0 4 :008(552) [0941] them with temporal **blessings** in this world, but since they
SD : 0 5 :023(562) [0959] all nations should be **blessed**; likewise, of David's son,
SD : 0 6 :004(564) [0963] Lord, as it is written, "**Blessed** is the man whose delight is
SD : 0 7 :002(569) [0973] as far distant from the **blessed** bread and wine in the
SD : 0 7 :008(570) [0975] orally received with the **blessed** bread even by hypocrites
SD : 0 7 :032(574) [0983] protestation Luther, of **blessed** memory, listed among
SD : 0 7 :039(576) [0985] and blood, so the food **blessed** by him through the Word
SD : 0 7 :044(577) [0987] and death and all of his **blessings**, a seal of the new
SD : 0 7 :044(577) [0987] Christ said of the **blessed** and proffered bread, "Take,
SD : 0 7 :046(577) [0989] the promise of the **blessed** seed of Isaac, although this
SD : 0 7 :052(578) [0991] the same matter to the **blessed** and proffered bread
SD : 0 7 :054(579) [0991] Cor. 10:16 ("The cup of **blessing** which we bless, is it not
SD : 0 7 :054(579) [0991] cup of blessing which we **bless**, is it not a participation in
SD : 0 7 :054(579) [0991] the cup which Christ **blessed** in the Last Supper and not
SD : 0 7 :054(579) [0991] that which we break and **bless** is participation in the body
SD : 0 7 :056(579) [0991] that all who receive the **blessed** bread also partake of the
SD : 0 7 :057(579) [0993] all who partake of the **blessed** and broken bread in the
SD : 0 7 :063(581) [0995] all who eat and drink the **blessed** bread and wine in the
SD : 0 7 :075(583) [0999] cup and distribute the **blessed** bread and cup, Christ
SD : 0 7 :076(583) [0999] *Passion: "Christ himself prepares this table and **blesses** it.*
SD : 0 7 :076(583) [0999] the elements set before us in the Supper are **blessed**.
SD : 0 7 :082(584) [1001] and wine are hallowed or **blessed** in this holy use, so that
SD : 0 7 :082(584) [1001] Paul says, "The cup of **blessing** which we bless," which
SD : 0 7 :082(584) [1001] cup of blessing which we **bless**," which happens precisely
SD : 0 7 :083(584) [1001] But this **blessing** or recitation of Christ's words of
SD : 0 7 :083(584) [1001] (if, for instance, the **blessed** bread is not distributed,
SD : 0 7 :086(584) [1003] or the oral eating of the **blessed** bread and wine, the body
SD : 0 7 :099(586) [1005] at the proper time by the **blessed** God" (I Tim. 6:15), and,
SD : 0 7 :108(588) [1009] that the consecrated or **blessed** bread and wine in the
SD : 0 7 :126(591) [1015] (the visible forms of the **blessed** bread and wine) are to be
SD : 0 8 :006(592) [1017] man, born of the most **blessed** virgin Mary, as it is
SD : 0 8 :006(592) [1017] Christ, who is God over all, **blessed** for ever" (Rom. 9:5).
SD : 0 8 :024(595) [1023] natures, Mary, the most **blessed** virgin, did not conceive a
SD : 0 8 :080(607) [1045] Dr. Luther, of **blessed** memory, has written about the

Blind (24), Blinded (4), Blindly (1), Blindness (10), Blinds (1)

PR : PR :022(012) [0021] them against it, lest one **blind** person let himself be misled
AG : 2 8 :047(088) [0091] "Let them alone; they are **blind** guides" (Matt. 15:14).
AL : 2 7 :048(078) [0081] when the eyes of men are **blinded** by these remarkable
AL : 2 8 :047(089) [0091] "Let them alone; they are **blind** and leaders of the blind."
AL : 2 8 :047(089) [0091] "Let them alone; they are blind and leaders of the **blind**."
AP : 0 4 :169(130) [0169] More than **blind** are those who do not believe that evil
AP : 0 4 :288(151) [0203] Being **blind** to the uncleanness of the heart, reason thinks
AP : 1 2 :159(207) [0301] sinned in the case of the **blind** man, Christ replied that
AP : 1 2 :159(207) [0301] that the reason for his **blindness** was not sin but "that the
AP : 1 6 :010(224) [0333] outward hypocrisy and **blinded** them to the essence of
S 3 : 0 1 :002(302) [0477] presumption, despair, **blindness** — in short, ignorance or
S 3 : 0 2 :003(303) [0479] Others become **blind** and presumptuous, imagining that
S 3 : 0 3 :018(306) [0483] Here we see how **blind** reason gropes about in matters
S 3 : 0 3 :032(308) [0487] you are full of unbelief, **blindness**, and ignorance of God
LC : 0 1 :011(366) [0583] what we used to do in our **blindness** under the papacy.

Continued ▶

L C : 0 1 :120(382) [0615] plight and the miserable **blindness** of the world that no
L C : 0 1 :157(386) [0627] be delivered from the **blindness** and misery in which we
L C : 0 1 :209(393) [0639] disdain marriage, as the **blind** world and the false clergy
L C : 0 1 :259(400) [0655] He must therefore be quite **blind**, shutting his eyes and
L C : 0 1 :262(400) [0655] But let this pass; it is the **blind** world's nature to condemn
L C : 0 1 :290(404) [0663] blessings, if only the **blind** world and the false saints
L C : 0 1 :316(408) [0671] to see, these miserable, **blind** people, that no man can
L C : 0 2 :021(413) [0683] acts, drowned in its **blindness**, misusing all the blessings
L C : 0 2 :027(414) [0685] condemned to death and entangled in sin and **blindness**.
L C : 0 4 :011(437) [0735] the devil sets to work to **blind** us with false appearances
L C : 0 4 :029(440) [0739] but these leaders of the **blind** are unwilling to see that
L C : 0 4 :061(444) [0747] But these fanatics are so **blinded** that they do not discern
L C : 0 5 :081(456) [0773] from God's Word and **blinds** it, making you unable to
E P : 0 2 :002(470) [0787] and reason are **blind** and that he understands nothing by
E P : 0 9 :004(492) [0827] others as well, which our **blind** reason cannot
S D : 0 1 :013(511) [0863] with other kinds of **blindness**, and drives them headlong
S D : 0 2 :005(521) [0881] salvation, he is by nature **blind** and does not and cannot
S D : 0 2 :009(521) [0883] it is so ignorant, **blind**, and perverse that when even the
S D : 0 2 :010(522) [0885] (that is, in the dark, **blind** world which neither knows nor
S D : 0 2 :044(529) [0897] contrary, he states that **blind** and captive man performs
S D : 0 4 :011(553) [0941] works is a faithless man, **blindly** tapping around in search
S D : 0 7 :046(578) [0989] of Isaac than he could comprehend with his **blind** reason.
S D : 1 1 :057(625) [1081] one becomes hardened, **blinded**, and is given over to a
S D : 1 1 :083(630) [1091] with obduracy and **blindness** those who have been
S D : 1 1 :083(630) [1091] that he would harden, **blind**, and for ever damn them if

Bliss (2)
A P : 2 8 :006(282) [0445] toward the goal of eternal **bliss**, and that the power to
S D : 0 4 :024(555) [0945] passage which ascribes the **bliss** of salvation solely to the

Blithely (1)
L C : P R :006(359) [0569] So they **blithely** let parishes fall into decay, and brazenly

Bloated (1)
L C : P R :020(361) [0573] bear to smell because they are so **bloated** and surfeited.

Block (10)
A P : 0 4 :029(111) [0129] also 'the stumbling-**block** of the cross has been removed'
A P : 0 7 :019(171) [0233] men so that this stumbling **block** may not offend the
L C : 0 1 :125(382) [0617] that God would set up a **block** or a stone which we might
S D : 0 2 :024(526) [0891] in anything as a stone, a **block**, or a lump of clay could.
S D : 0 2 :024(526) [0891] respect he is worse than a **block** because he is resistant
S D : 0 2 :059(532) [0905] case it is correct to say that man is not a stone or a **block**.
S D : 0 2 :059(532) [0905] A stone or a **block** does not resist the person who moves
S D : 0 2 :059(532) [0905] worse than a stone or **block**, for he resists the Word and
S D : 0 2 :062(533) [0905] to work in irrational creatures or in a stone or **block**.
S D : 0 2 :073(535) [0909] man in his conversion behaves and is like a **block**?

Blockheads (1)
L C : 0 1 :037(369) [0589] Just because such **blockheads** imagine, when God refrains

Blood (196)
P R : P R :009(006) [0011] of the body and the **blood** of Christ and other erroneous
A G : 1 0 :001(034) [0047] us that the true body and **blood** of Christ are really
A G : 2 2 :006(050) [0061] sacrament distributed the **blood** of Christ to the people.
A G : 2 3 :023(055) [0063] to maintain such a teaching with the shedding of **blood**.
A G : 2 4 :012(057) [0065] unworthily is guilty of the body and **blood** of Christ),
A G : 2 8 :032(086) [0087] 29, where the eating of **blood** and what is strangled was
A G : 2 8 :065(092) [0093] one should abstain from **blood** and from what is
A L : 1 0 :001(034) [0047] teach that the body and **blood** of Christ are truly present
A L : 2 0 :014(043) [0055] says: "Redemption by the **blood** of Christ would become
A L : 2 2 :005(050) [0061] places testifies that the **blood** was given to the people.
A L : 2 2 :006(050) [0061] and distribute the **blood** of Christ to the people."
A L : 2 4 :012(057) [0065] be guilty of profaning the body and **blood** of the Lord."
A L : 2 8 :032(086) [0087] men to abstain from **blood** and from what is strangled.
A L : 2 8 :065(092) [0093] commanded that one should abstain from **blood**, etc.
A P : P R :012(099) [0101] they are after neither truth no harmony, but our **blood**.
A P : 0 4 :094(120) [0149] who were born, not of **blood** nor of the will of the flesh
A P : 0 4 :103(122) [0151] and by shedding his **blood** canceled the bond that stood
A P : 0 4 :103(122) [0151] frees men through the **blood** of Christ; for 'blessed is he
A P : 0 4 :104(122) [0153] it to faith, which liberates us through the **blood** of Christ.
A P : 0 4 :236(140) [0185] They are writing laws in **blood** and are asking the
A P : 0 4 :273(148) [0199] redemption through his **blood**, the forgiveness of our
A P : 0 4 :399(168) [0227] give an answer written in **blood** to our Confession written
A P : 1 0 :001(179) [0247] Supper the body and **blood** of Christ are truly and
A P : 1 0 :004(179) [0247] Supper the body and **blood** of Christ are truly and
A P : 1 2 :002(182) [0253] what is this but to insult the **blood** and death of Christ?
A P : 1 2 :063(191) [0269] as an expiation by his **blood**, to be received by faith," and
A P : 2 2 :004(236) [0359] and distribute the **blood** of the Lord to the people."
A P : 2 3 :070(249) [0383] Have no doubt that as the **blood** of Abel cried out in
A P : 2 3 :070(249) [0383] death (Gen. 4:10), so the **blood** of the many innocent
A P : 2 4 :022(253) [0391] "It is impossible that the **blood** of bulls and goats should
A P : 2 4 :036(257) [0397] the world with the **blood** of the lamb, by the
A P : 2 4 :036(257) [0397] to Jesus Christ and for sprinkling with his **blood**."
A P : 2 4 :038(257) [0399] when the Gospel sprinkles us with the **blood** of Christ.
A P : 2 4 :069(262) [0409] new testament with my **blood**, which is poured out for
A P : 2 4 :080(264) [0411] shows forth the body and **blood** of the Lord to the
A P : 2 4 :088(265) [0413] about the body and **blood** of the Lord in particular, but
A P : 2 4 :091(266) [0415] are "guilty of the body and **blood** of the Lord."
A P : 2 4 :091(266) [0415] of guilt and the body and **blood** of the Lord for their own
A P : 2 4 :093(267) [0417] of offering the body and **blood** of the Lord, but about the
A P : 2 8 :004(281) [0445] forth an edict written in **blood**, threatening men with
S 2 : 0 1 :003(292) [0461] which is in Christ Jesus, by his **blood**" (Rom. 3:23-25).
S 3 : 0 3 :038(309) [0489] but of the sufferings and **blood** of the innocent Lamb of
S 3 : 0 6 :001(311) [0493] are the true body and **blood** of Christ and that these are
T R : 0 0 :053(329) [0519] murder of saints, whose **blood** God will undoubtedly
T R : 0 0 :059(330) [0521] themselves guilty of the **blood** of the godly whom the
S C : 0 2 :004(345) [0545] with his holy and precious **blood** and with his innocent
S C : 0 6 :002(351) [0555] it is the true body and **blood** of our Lord Jesus Christ,
S C : 0 6 :004(351) [0557] the new covenant in my **blood**, which is poured out for
L C : S P :020(364) [0579] and the holy Body and **Blood** of Christ, according to the
L C : S P :023(364) [0579] the new testament in my **blood**, which is shed for you for
L C : 0 1 :158(387) [0627] fathers by **blood**, fathers of a household, and fathers of
L C : 0 1 :163(387) [0627] the devil — and wring sweat and **blood** out of us besides.
L C : 0 1 :184(390) [0633] rage and we are ready to shed **blood** and take revenge.
L C : 0 1 :200(392) [0637] namely, his wife, who is one flesh and **blood** with him.
L C : 0 1 :212(393) [0641] of marriage; for flesh and **blood** remain flesh and blood,
L C : 0 1 :212(393) [0641] blood remain flesh and **blood**, and the natural
L C : 0 2 :031(414) [0687] not with silver and gold but with his own precious **blood**.
L C : 0 3 :031(424) [0707] devil would have destroyed all Germany in its own **blood**.
L C : 0 3 :104(434) [0727] into our hearts, not by flesh and **blood** but by the devil.
L C : 0 4 :020(439) [0737] and why I should honor this particular flesh and **blood**.
L C : 0 4 :038(441) [0741] only to human flesh and **blood**, yet we look not at the
L C : 0 4 :038(441) [0741] look not at the flesh and **blood** but at God's
L C : 0 4 :056(444) [0747] he gives me his body and **blood**; he will not lie or deceive
L C : 0 5 :003(447) [0753] *the new testament in my* ***blood****, which is poured out for*
L C : 0 5 :008(447) [0755] It is the true body and **blood** of the Lord Christ in and
L C : 0 5 :010(448) [0755] which is rightly called Christ's body and **blood**.
L C : 0 5 :012(448) [0755] 'How can bread and wine be Christ's body and **blood**?'
L C : 0 5 :013(448) [0755] of it, all of you, this is the new covenant in my **blood**,' etc.
L C : 0 5 :014(448) [0757] of them they are truly the body and **blood** of Christ.
L C : 0 5 :016(448) [0757] is, Christ's body and **blood**) just as truly as when one uses
L C : 0 5 :016(448) [0757] into Christ's body and **blood**, so likewise no one can
L C : 0 5 :017(448) [0757] you receive my body and **blood**," but, "Take, eat and
L C : 0 5 :017(448) [0757] but, "Take, eat and drink, this is my body and **blood**."
L C : 0 5 :018(448) [0757] have Christ's body and **blood** by virtue of these words
L C : 0 5 :021(449) [0757] "This is my body and **blood**, given and poured out *for*
L C : 0 5 :023(449) [0757] our human flesh and **blood** have not lost their old skin.
L C : 0 5 :028(449) [0759] are Christ's body and **blood** and with which the words are
L C : 0 5 :029(449) [0759] it is Christ's body and **blood** and that these are yours as
L C : 0 5 :031(450) [0759] that Christ's body and **blood** are not given and poured
L C : 0 5 :037(451) [0761] and reverently toward the body and **blood** of Christ.
L C : 0 5 :060(453) [0767] retain many common infirmities in his flesh and **blood**.
L C : 0 5 :064(454) [0769] *for you,*"'"This is my **blood**, poured out *for you* for the
L C : 0 5 :075(455) [0771] bosom and ask whether they are made of flesh and **blood**.
E P : 0 1 :005(466) [0781] share in flesh and **blood**, he himself likewise partook of
E P : 0 7 :002(481) [0809] are the true body and **blood** of our Lord Jesus Christ
E P : 0 7 :004(482) [0809] and living body and **blood** of Christ in the Holy Supper
E P : 0 7 :005(482) [0809] of the Holy Supper, seek the body and **blood** of Christ.
E P : 0 7 :006(482) [0809] Holy Supper the body and **blood** of Christ are truly and
E P : 0 7 :007(482) [0811] and the wine the absent **blood** of Christ, but that because
E P : 0 7 :007(482) [0811] union they are truly the body and **blood** of Christ.
E P : 0 7 :008(482) [0811] presence of the body and **blood** of Christ in the Holy
E P : 0 7 :015(483) [0811] and wine the body and **blood** of Christ are received not
E P : 0 7 :016(484) [0813] receive the true body and **blood** of Christ; but if they are
E P : 0 7 :024(484) [0815] so that they are deprived of the **blood** of Christ.
E P : 0 7 :028(485) [0815] and types of the far-distant body and **blood** of Christ.
E P : 0 7 :029(485) [0815] partakes of the body and **blood** of Christ as truly as we
E P : 0 7 :030(485) [0815] and not by the truly present body and **blood** of Christ.
E P : 0 7 :031(485) [0815] of the absent body and **blood** of Christ are distributed.
E P : 0 7 :033(485) [0815] that his body and **blood** would be essentially present in
E P : 0 7 :035(485) [0815] presence of the body and **blood** of Christ in the Holy
E P : 0 7 :037(486) [0815] not receive the body and **blood** of Christ, but only bread
E P : 0 7 :042(486) [0817] body and drinking of his **blood**, which we cannot
E P : 0 8 :008(487) [0819] creature, to be flesh and **blood**, to be finite and
E P : 0 8 :014(488) [0821] in Acts 20:28, We are purchased with God's own **blood**.
E P : 0 8 :017(489) [0823] to us his true body and **blood** which are present in the
E P : 1 2 :003(498) [0839] not assume his body and **blood** from the virgin Mary, but
E P : 1 2 :024(500) [0843] and by which Christ distributes his body and **blood**.
S D : 0 3 :057(550) [0935] (Rom. 5:19), and "the **blood** of Jesus, his Son, cleanses us
S D : 0 7 :002(569) [0973] true, essential body and **blood** of Christ are as far distant
S D : 0 7 :002(569) [0973] say that the body and **blood** of Christ are distant from
S D : 0 7 :004(569) [0973] to his divine nature, but not with his body and **blood**).
S D : 0 7 :006(570) [0973] not true of his body and **blood**, which is now in heaven
S D : 0 7 :006(570) [0975] gives us his true body and **blood** to eat spiritually by faith
S D : 0 7 :009(570) [0975] "that the true body and **blood** of Christ are really present
S D : 0 7 :010(571) [0975] is the true body and **blood** of our Lord Jesus Christ,
S D : 0 7 :011(571) [0975] Supper the body and **blood** of Christ are truly and
S D : 0 7 :013(571) [0977] sacrament of the body and **blood** of Christ, namely thus:
S D : 0 7 :014(571) [0977] and wine the body and **blood** of Christ are truly and
S D : 0 7 :014(571) [0977] wine into the body and **blood** of Christ) and do not
S D : 0 7 :014(571) [0977] believe that the body and **blood** of Christ are locally
S D : 0 7 :016(572) [0977] observed, the body and **blood** of Christ are truly
S D : 0 7 :016(572) [0977] into Christ, and are washed by the **blood** of Christ."
S D : 0 7 :019(572) [0979] are the true body and **blood** of Jesus Christ which are
S D : 0 7 :020(573) [0979] It is the true body and **blood** of Christ in and under the
S D : 0 7 :021(573) [0979] and wine but is and is called Christ's body and **blood**."
S D : 0 7 :022(573) [0979] can bread and wine be the body and **blood** of Christ?'
S D : 0 7 :022(573) [0979] of it, all of you, this is the new covenant in my **blood**,' etc.
S D : 0 7 :023(573) [0979] with the words it is truly the body and **blood** of Christ.
S D : 0 7 :024(573) [0981] is, Christ's body and **blood**) just as much as when one
S D : 0 7 :024(573) [0981] wine into the body and **blood** of Christ, so little can
S D : 0 7 :026(573) [0981] you have my body and **blood**,' but, 'Take, eat and drink,
S D : 0 7 :026(573) [0981] but, 'Take, eat and drink, this is my body and **blood**.'
S D : 0 7 :026(573) [0981] here have his body and **blood** by virtue of these words
S D : 0 7 :027(574) [0981] presence of the body and **blood** of Christ in the holy
S D : 0 7 :032(574) [0983] of the Altar the body and **blood** of Christ are truly eaten
S D : 0 7 :038(576) [0985] union of the body and **blood** of Christ with the bread and
S D : 0 7 :039(576) [0985] salvation had flesh and **blood**, so the food blessed by him
S D : 0 7 :039(576) [0985] is the true flesh and **blood** of the Lord Jesus Christ."
S D : 0 7 :044(577) [0987] or the wine, "This is my **blood** of the new covenant which
S D : 0 7 :049(578) [0989] and of his true, essential **blood**, which was shed for us on
S D : 0 7 :053(579) [0991] the new covenant in my **blood**" (Luke 22:20; I Cor.
S D : 0 7 :053(579) [0991] mouth from the cup) is my **blood** of the new covenant,
S D : 0 7 :054(579) [0991] we bless, is it not a participation in the **blood** of Christ?
S D : 0 7 :054(579) [0991] of the body and **blood** of Christ in the Communion.
S D : 0 7 :054(579) [0991] in the body and **blood** of Christ, so that all who eat this
S D : 0 7 :054(579) [0991] receive and partake of the true body and **blood** of Christ.
S D : 0 7 :057(579) [0993] the Lord and partaking of the body and **blood** of Christ.
S D : 0 7 :057(579) [0993] receiving the body and **blood** of Christ to their own
S D : 0 7 :060(580) [0993] receive the true body and **blood** of Christ orally in the
S D : 0 7 :060(580) [0993] sin grievously against the body and **blood** of Christ.
S D : 0 7 :060(580) [0993] figures of the body and **blood**, but becomes guilty of
S D : 0 7 :060(580) [0993] of profaning the body and **blood** of the Lord Jesus Christ
S D : 0 7 :062(581) [0995] death and by shedding his **blood** for us (that is to say, the
S D : 0 7 :063(581) [0995] of the true, essential body and **blood** of Christ orally.

Continued ▶

SD : 07 :064(581) [0995] called his true body and **blood**, and said therewith, "Eat
SD : 07 :068(582) [0997] punishments) and profane the body and **blood** of Christ.
SD : 07 :072(582) [0997] in the body and **blood** of Christ, the one through faith
SD : 07 :074(583) [0999] presence of the body and **blood** of Christ in the Supper.
SD : 07 :075(583) [0999] used, and the body and **blood** of Christ are truly present,
SD : 07 :076(583) [0999] and wine set before us the body and **blood** of Christ.
SD : 07 :076(583) [0999] that his true body and **blood** are present in the church's
SD : 07 :077(583) [0999] wine but his body and **blood**, as his words read, 'This is
SD : 07 :077(583) [0999] words read, 'This is my body,' etc., 'This is my **blood**,' etc.
SD : 07 :077(583) [0999] body and the wine the **blood** that are daily distributed
SD : 07 :081(584) [1001] presence of the body and **blood** of Christ, the forgiveness
SD : 07 :081(584) [1001] and the shedding of his **blood** and which he gives to us in
SD : 07 :082(584) [1001] therewith the body and **blood** of Christ are distributed to
SD : 07 :086(585) [1003] blessed bread and wine, the body and **blood** of Christ.
SD : 07 :105(588) [1009] we say that the body and **blood** of Christ in the Holy
SD : 07 :106(588) [1009] presence of the body and **blood** of Christ in the Holy
SD : 07 :108(588) [1009] of the body and **blood** of Christ, so that only the mere
SD : 07 :111(589) [1011] presence of the body and **blood** of Christ against the
SD : 07 :113(589) [1011] presence of the body and **blood** of Christ in the Supper,
SD : 07 :114(589) [1011] eating of the body and **blood** of Christ in the Supper, and
SD : 07 :116(589) [1011] up there of the body and **blood** of Christ as truly as in the
SD : 07 :116(589) [1013] the true present body and **blood** of Christ, distributed to
SD : 07 :117(590) [1013] wine have a similarity with the body and **blood** of Christ.
SD : 07 :118(590) [1013] 7. Or that the body and **blood** of Christ are only received
SD : 07 :120(590) [1013] presence of his body and **blood** in the Supper because the
SD : 07 :123(590) [1013] wine in the Supper and not the body and **blood** of Christ.
SD : 07 :123(590) [1015] and not the body and the **blood** of Christ for their
SD : 08 :002(591) [1015] presence of the body and **blood** of Jesus Christ in the
SD : 08 :004(592) [1017] true, essential presence of the body and **blood** of Christ.
SD : 08 :010(593) [1019] a creature, to be flesh and **blood**, to be finite and
SD : 08 :029(596) [1025] present with his body and **blood** in the Holy Supper
SD : 08 :044(599) [1031] said: God dead, God's passion, God's **blood**, God's death.
SD : 08 :045(600) [1031] suffered for us, died, and redeemed us with his **blood**.
SD : 08 :058(602) [1035] the Son of Man and inasmuch as he has flesh and **blood**.
SD : 08 :059(602) [1035] when it states, "The **blood** of Jesus his Son cleanses us
SD : 08 :059(602) [1035] in Christ but also his **blood** actually cleanses us from all
SD : 08 :076(606) [1043] a life-giving food and his **blood** truly a quickening
SD : 08 :079(607) [1045] nature, too, according to which he has flesh and **blood**.
SD : 08 :096(610) [1049] that our flesh and **blood** have in Christ been made to sit
SD : 11 :028(620) [1071] world" (John 6:51); his **blood** is "the propitiation for the
SD : 12 :025(635) [1099] not assume his flesh and **blood** from the virgin Mary but
SD : 12 :032(635) [1101] through which Christ distributes his body and **blood**.

Bloodhounds (1)
LC : 01 :192(391) [0635] to reproach such persons as murderers and **bloodhounds**?

Bloodless (4)
AP : 24 :08((265) [0413] and supplications and **bloodless** sacrifices for all the
AP : 24 :088(265) [0413] and supplications and **bloodless** sacrifices for the people.
AP : 24 :088(265) [0413] It calls even prayers "**bloodless** sacrifices."
AP : 24 :088(265) [0413] "We offer Thee this reasonable and **bloodless** service."

Bloodshed (2)
PR : PR :022(012) [0021] no share of the responsibility for this **bloodshed**.
LC : 03 :078(431) [0721] from war and **bloodshed**, famine, savage beasts, wicked

Blot (3), Blots (1), Blotted (1)
AP : 04 :382(165) [0225] believe that our sins are **blotted** out by Christ's death and
AP : 12 :019(185) [0257] 3. To **blot** out sin, it is enough to detest the sin.
AP : 12 :024(185) [0257] of purgatory, or they profit as a payment to **blot** out guilt.
S3 : 03 :014(305) [0483] works to overcome and **blot** out their sins before God.
S3 : 03 :042(310) [0491] not as long as you believe, for faith **blots** out all sins," etc.

Blow (1), Blows (6)
AP : 04 :329(158) [0211] the breath of the Lord **blows** upon it"; that is, the flesh
S3 : 03 :002(304) [0479] of which God with one **blow** destroys both open sinners
LC : 01 :076(375) [0603] by means of rods and **blows** will come to no good end; at
LC : 01 :123(382) [0617] until they are driven with **blows**; and they defame and
LC : 01 :184(390) [0633] Then follow cursing and **blows**, and eventually calamity
LC : 01 :330(410) [0677] brought up, not only with **blows** and compulsion, like
LC : 03 :109(435) [0729] us but shall at all times expect his **blows** and parry them.

Blush (2), Blushing (1)
AP : 23 :002(239) [0363] abandon cannot even be mentioned without **blushing**.
LC : 01 :118(381) [0615] whole world, they shall **blush** with shame before a little
LC : 01 :273(401) [0659] him straight to his face and make him **blush** for shame.

Blustering (1)
LC : 05 :028(449) [0759] wisdom, bellowing and **blustering**, "How can bread and

Board (1), Boards (2)
EP : 08 :009(487) [0819] union), as when two **boards** are glued together and
SD : 07 :100(586) [1007] through air or water or a **board** and a wall and neither
SD : 08 :014(594) [1019] with each other like two **boards** glued together, so that in

Boast (29), Boasted (3), Boasting (7), Boasts (8)
AG : PR :005(025) [0039] and can say without **boasting** that we were among the
AG : 20 :011(042) [0055] — not because of works, lest any man should **boast**," etc.
AG : 01 :009(056) [0065] Without **boasting**, it is manifest that the Mass is observed
AG : 00 :005(095) [0095] (to speak without **boasting**) that we have diligently and
AP : 04 :073(117) [0141] lest any man should **boast**," and again (Rom. 3:24), "They
AP : 04 :093(120) [0149] God—not because of works, lest any man should **boast**."
AP : 04 :326(157) [0211] When David elsewhere **boasts** of his righteousness, he is
AP : 04 :381(165) [0223] quote in a twisted way, **boasting** in the schools that good
AP : 04 :382(165) [0225] In the schools they also **boast** that our good works are
AP : 27 :025(273) [0429] is false for the monks to **boast** that the observance of a
AP : 27 :027(273) [0429] the Mohammedans could **boast** that they have
AP : 28 :027(285) [0451] opponents are right in **boasting** that they have really
S3 : 08 :003(312) [0495] from the spiritualists who **boast** that they possess the
S3 : 08 :004(312) [0495] enthusiasm, for the pope **boasts** that "all laws are in the
S3 : 08 :006(313) [0495] their writings since they **boast** that the Spirit came upon
S3 : 13 :003(315) [0499] Accordingly we cannot **boast** of the great merit in our
S3 : 13 :003(315) [0499] is written, "Let him who **boasts**, boast of the Lord"
S3 : 13 :003(315) [0499] "Let him who boasts, **boast** of the Lord" (I Cor. 1:31).
S3 : 13 :003(315) [0499] is to say, all is well if we **boast** that we have a gracious
S3 : 14 :001(316) [0501] St. Thomas, such people **boast** that a monastic vow is
LC : 01 :005(365) [0581] he trusts and of them he **boasts** so stubbornly and
LC : 01 :010(366) [0583] So, too, if anyone **boasts** of great learning, wisdom,
LC : 01 :022(367) [0585] it relies and of them it **boasts**, unwilling to receive
LC : 01 :036(369) [0589] God frowns or smiles, **boast** defiantly of their mammon
LC : 01 :059(372) [0597] man is so arrogant as to **boast** before the whole world of
LC : 01 :115(381) [0613] of being able joyfully to **boast** in the face of all who are
LC : 01 :116(381) [0615] all come forward and **boast** of their many great,
LC : 01 :145(385) [0623] thing to be able to **boast** to yourself, "If I do my daily
LC : 01 :159(387) [0627] St. Paul **boasts** that he is a father in I Cor. 4:15, where he
LC : 01 :197(392) [0637] they have shamelessly **boasted** and bragged of their
LC : 01 :213(394) [0641] and forbid marriage, and **boast** and vow that they will
LC : 01 :278(402) [0661] see if they can make the **boast** that they have gained one
LC : 01 :298(405) [0665] We brazenly dare to **boast** of it, and insist that it should
LC : 01 :312(407) [0671] how our great saints can **boast** of their spiritual orders
LC : 01 :316(408) [0671] Therefore all their **boasting** amounts to as much as if I
LC : 01 :316(408) [0671] to as much as if I **boasted**, "Of course, I haven't a single
LC : 02 :021(413) [0683] about and brag and **boast** as if we had life, riches, power,
LC : 03 :015(422) [0701] He can **boast** of no better or holier commandment than
LC : 03 :070(429) [0717] It is our solace and **boast** that the will and purpose of the
LC : 03 :090(432) [0723] that if anybody **boasts** of his goodness and despises
LC : 03 :121(436) [0731] should I be so bold as to **boast** that God hears my
LC : 04 :006(437) [0733] God himself, so I can also **boast** that Baptism is no
EP : 02 :006(470) [0787] God, so that no one might **boast** in the presence of God
EP : 04 :007(476) [0799] of works, lest any man should **boast**" (Eph. 2:8-9).
SD : PR :006(502) [0847] Some, while **boasting** of and benefiting from their
SD : 02 :026(526) [0891] received it, why do you **boast** as if it were not a gift?"
SD : 07 :006(570) [0973] when they alleged and **boasted** that they hold no other

Bodies (12)
AL : 28 :011(082) [0085] protects not souls but **bodies** and goods from manifest
AP : 04 :352(161) [0217] is in you, although your **bodies** are dead because of sin,
AP : 12 :132(202) [0291] "Present your **bodies** as a living sacrifice, holy,"
AP : 12 :160(207) [0303] the will of God that our **bodies** should be sacrifices, to
AP : 15 :045(221) [0327] says (Rom. 12:1), "Present your **bodies** as a sacrifice."
AP : 23 :018(242) [0369] and to subdue their **bodies** with labors and fasting.
AP : 24 :026(254) [0391] Rom. 12:1, "Present your **bodies** as a living sacrifice, holy
LC : 01 :287(403) [0663] same thing in our own **bodies**, as St. Paul says in I Cor.
LC : 02 :058(418) [0693] and all evil, living in new, immortal and glorified **bodies**.
LC : 03 :115(435) [0731] his anger by causing accidents and injury to our **bodies**.
EP : 01 :004(466) [0781] the Fall, but also our **bodies** and souls after the Fall, even
SD : 07 :005(570) [0973] which is everywhere, our **bodies**, in which the Spirit of

Bodily (39)
AG : 26 :033(069) [0075] with reference to such **bodily** exercise as fasting and other
AG : 26 :034(069) [0075] Such **bodily** exercise should not be limited to certain
AG : 28 :008(082) [0085] this way are imparted no **bodily** but eternal things and
AL : 26 :033(069) [0075] and curb himself with **bodily** discipline, or bodily
AL : 26 :033(069) [0075] with bodily discipline, or **bodily** exercises and labors, that
AL : 26 :034(069) [0075] Such **bodily** discipline ought to be encouraged at all
AL : 28 :008(082) [0085] For it is not **bodily** things that are thus given, but rather
AP : 04 :355(161) [0217] works merit other **bodily** and spiritual rewards because
AP : 04 :366(163) [0219] merit other rewards, both **bodily** and spiritual, in various
AP : 07 :034(175) [0239] observe them for the sake of tranquility or **bodily** profit.
AP : 10 :002(179) [0247] Church affirms the **bodily** presence of Christ, but that the
AP : 10 :003(179) [0247] teaches that Christ is offered to us **bodily** in the Supper.
AP : 10 :003(179) [0247] Christ to dwell in us **bodily** through the communication
AP : 15 :024(218) [0321] human reason interprets fasting and **bodily** discipline.
AP : 27 :021(272) [0427] Paul says (I Tim. 4:8), "**Bodily** training is of little value."
S2 : 04 :011(300) [0475] Christ, and they receive **bodily** tribute and obedience from
SC : 03 :014(347) [0547] required to satisfy our **bodily** needs, such as food and
SC : 06 :007(352) [0557] How can **bodily** eating and drinking produce such great
SC : 06 :008(352) [0557] when accompanied by the **bodily** eating and drinking, are
SC : 06 :010(352) [0557] Answer: Fasting and **bodily** preparation are a good
LC : 01 :083(376) [0603] We keep them, first, for the sake of **bodily** need.
LC : 01 :185(390) [0633] so that no one may do him **bodily** harm or injury.
LC : 01 :189(391) [0635] and save him from suffering **bodily** harm or injury.
LC : 03 :117(436) [0731] that affects our **bodily** welfare and directs us to seek and
EP : 02 :003(470) [0787] can quicken itself to **bodily**, earthly life, so little can man
EP : 08 :034(491) [0825] whole fullness of deity **bodily**" (Col. 2:9), Christ,
SD : 01 :013(511) [0863] together with other **bodily**, spiritual, temporal, and
SD : 02 :087(538) [0915] work of God, just as the **bodily** resurrection of the flesh is
SD : 07 :011(571) [0975] Church has taught the **bodily** presence of Christ in the
SD : 07 :011(571) [0975] effect that Christ dwells **bodily** in the Supper through the
SD : 07 :036(575) [0985] of the deity dwells **bodily**," or "God was with him," or
SD : 07 :099(586) [1005] as when he walked **bodily** on earth and vacated or
SD : 07 :119(590) [1013] that because of his **bodily** ascension to heaven Christ is so
SD : 08 :030(597) [1025] fullness of deity dwells **bodily** (Col. 2:9), and in this
SD : 08 :034(597) [1027] of the deity dwells **bodily**" (Col. 2:9) in such a way that
SD : 08 :064(603) [1037] beings or in the angels, but "**bodily**," as in its own body.
SD : 08 :068(604) [1039] fullness of deity dwells **bodily**, there likewise are hid all
SD : 08 :070(604) [1041] he does not do so **bodily** nor is he personally united with
SD : 08 :070(605) [1041] whole fullness of deity **bodily**" (Col. 2:9); likewise, "Thou

Bodo (1)
PR : PR :027(015) [0025] **Bodo**, count of Regenstein

Body (364)
PR : PR :009(006) [0011] the holy sacrament of the **body** and the blood of Christ
AG : 07 :004(032) [0047] Eph. 4:4, 5, "There is one **body** and one Spirit, just as you
AG : 10 :001(034) [0047] among us that the true **body** and blood of Christ are
AG : 23 :012(053) [0063] during an uprising of the entire **body** of priests.
AG : 24 :012(057) [0065] unworthily is guilty of the **body** and blood of Christ),
AG : 26 :037(069) [0075] said that he pommeled his **body** and subdued it, and by
AG : 26 :038(069) [0075] merit grace but to keep the **body** in such a condition that
AG : 28 :011(082) [0085] penalties it protects **body** and goods from the power of
AL : 10 :001(034) [0047] churches teach that the **body** and blood of Christ are
AL : 24 :012(057) [0065] be guilty of profaning the **body** and blood of the Lord."
AL : 24 :026(059) [0067] the offering of the **body** of Jesus Christ once for all," and
AL : 24 :037(060) [0067] and deacons received the **body** of the Lord from him, for
AL : 25 :001(061) [0069] to administer the **body** of Christ except to those who

Continued ▶

AL : 26 :037(069) [0075] Paul also said, "I pommel my **body** and subdue it."
AL : 26 :038(069) [0075] that he pommeled his **body** not to merit forgiveness of
AL : 26 :038(069) [0075] discipline but to keep his **body** in subjection and fit for
AP : 02 :007(101) [0107] to evil is a quality of the **body**; in their awkward way they
AP : 02 :026(103) [0111] not only the desires of the **body** but also carnal wisdom
AP : 04 :143(127) [0161] you put to death the deeds of the **body**, you will live."
AP : 04 :201(134) [0175] him a sign written in his **body** by which he might be
AP : 04 :400(168) [0227] of him who is the truth and who knows his **body** best."
AP : 07 :005(169) [0227] church alone is called the **body** of Christ, which Christ
AP : 07 :005(169) [0227] the church, which is his **body**, the fullness," that is, the
AP : 07 :012(170) [0231] that which is the living **body** of Christ and is the church in
AP : 07 :029(173) [0237] church, properly so called, is termed the **body** of Christ.
AP : 07 :029(173) [0237] to the kingdom and **body** of the devil, who drives them on
AP : 10 :001(179) [0247] in the Lord's Supper the **body** and blood of Christ are
AP : 10 :001(179) [0247] participation in the Lord's **body**," it would follow that the
AP : 10 :001(179) [0247] be a participation in the **body** of Christ but only in his
AP : 10 :001(179) [0247] only in his spirit if the Lord's **body** were not truly present.
AP : 10 :002(179) [0247] may be changed and become the very **body** of Christ.
AP : 10 :003(179) [0247] Paul say, 'We are all one **body** in Christ' Rom. 12:5); 'We
AP : 10 :003(179) [0247] who are many are one **body**, for we all partake of the
AP : 10 :004(179) [0247] in the Lord's Supper the **body** and blood of Christ are
AP : 12 :042(187) [0263] clearly state, "This is my **body** which is given for you.
AP : 12 :046(188) [0263] hands, by putting off the **body** of the sins of the flesh."
AP : 12 :046(188) [0263] The one is putting off the **body** of sins, the other is being
AP : 12 :046(188) [0263] putting off the **body** of sins, being raised — we are not to
AP : 12 :046(188) [0263] Paul calls "putting off the **body** of sins" because in these
AP : 12 :131(202) [0291] the indulgence of the **body** in lusts, and true faith is not
AP : 12 :148(205) [0299] mortification of the **body** which follows true sorrow in
AP : 12 :152(206) [0299] says (Rom. 8:10), "Your **body** is dead because of sin";
AP : 13 :004(211) [0309] when we eat the Lord's **body**, when we are absolved, our
AP : 15 :045(221) [0327] to the mortifying of the **body** and the discipline of the
AP : 15 :046(221) [0327] says (I Cor. 9:27), "I pommel my **body** and subdue it."
AP : 22 :003(236) [0359] Christ says first about the **body**; later he says the same
AP : 23 :020(242) [0369] have tried to control their **body** but without much
AP : 23 :048(246) [0377] that discipline and restraint of the **body** are necessary.
AP : 23 :049(246) [0377] for the discipline of the **body** and for public morality),
AP : 24 :022(253) [0391] the offering of the **body** of Jesus Christ once for all."
AP : 24 :062(260) [0405] when he writes, "The **body** of the Lord, once offered on
AP : 24 :069(262) [0409] the text says, "This is my **body**, which is given for you";
AP : 24 :080(264) [0411] shows forth the **body** and blood of the Lord to the
AP : 24 :088(265) [0413] it is not talking about the **body** and blood of the Lord in
AP : 24 :088(265) [0413] victim" and apply it to the **body** of Christ itself.
AP : 24 :091(266) [0415] are "guilty of the **body** and blood of the Lord."
AP : 24 :091(266) [0415] of guilt and the **body** and blood of the Lord for their own
AP : 24 :093(267) [0417] not only of offering the **body** and blood of the Lord, but
AP : 27 :042(276) [0435] We should leave our **body**, too, for the Gospel.
AP : 27 :042(276) [0435] suicide and to leave our **body** without the command of
S2 : 04 :014(301) [0475] the eternal destruction of **body** and soul are characteristic
S3 : 01 :011(303) [0479] have died only for the **body** and not for the soul inasmuch
S3 : 01 :011(303) [0479] be sound and only the **body** would be subject to death.
S3 : 06 :001(311) [0493] in the Supper are the true **body** and blood of Christ and
TR : 00 :067(331) [0523] work of ministry and for building up the **body** of Christ.
SC : 02 :002(345) [0543] me and still sustains my **body** and soul, all my limbs and
SC : 02 :005(345) [0545] *sins, the resurrection of the **body**, and the life everlasting.*
SC : 03 :020(348) [0549] of evil, whether it affect **body** or soul, property or
SC : 06 :002(351) [0555] himself, it is the true **body** and blood of our Lord Jesus
SC : 06 :004(351) [0555] said, 'Take, eat; this is my **body** which is given for you.
SC : 07 :002(352) [0557] thy hands I commend my **body** and soul and all that is
SC : 07 :005(353) [0559] thy hands I commend my **body** and soul and all that is
LC : SP :013(363) [0577] sins, the resurrection of the **body**, and the life everlasting.
LC : SP :020(364) [0579] Baptism and the holy **Body** and Blood of Christ,
LC : SP :023(364) [0579] 'Take and eat, this is my **body**, which is given for you.
LC : 01 :024(367) [0587] for it is he who gives us **body**, life, food, drink,
LC : 01 :068(374) [0599] they miserably perished, **body**, soul, and possessions.
LC : 01 :073(374) [0601] to God — our soul and **body**, wife, children, servants, and
LC : 01 :107(379) [0611] both of heart and of **body**, that we respect them very
LC : 01 :111(380) [0613] actions (that is, with your **body** and possessions), serving
LC : 01 :128(382) [0617] how many blessings of **body** and soul he bestows upon
LC : 01 :129(383) [0617] that he has received his **body** and life from them and that
LC : 01 :188(390) [0635] toward all people in **body** and soul, especially toward him
LC : 01 :191(391) [0635] and aid to men in need and in peril of **body** and life.
LC : 01 :202(392) [0639] your lips, and your whole **body** are to be chaste and to
LC : 01 :255(399) [0653] Besides our own **body**, our wife or husband, and our
LC : 01 :257(399) [0653] consequently punished in his **body**, property, or honor.
LC : 01 :287(403) [0663] "The parts of the **body** which seem to be weaker are
LC : 01 :287(403) [0663] and those parts of the **body** which we think less
LC : 01 :287(403) [0663] and eyes, even the whole **body**, must help cover and veil
LC : 01 :294(404) [0665] own choice; with their **body** and all they had they were
LC : 02 :013(412) [0681] constantly sustains my **body**, soul, and life, my members
LC : 02 :022(413) [0683] with eyes and ears, hands, **body** and soul, money and
LC : 02 :034(415) [0687] *sins, the resurrection of the **body**, and the life everlasting.*
LC : 02 :037(415) [0687] sins, the resurrection of the **body**, and the life everlasting.
LC : 02 :041(416) [0689] the resurrection of the **body**, and the life everlasting."
LC : 02 :060(418) [0695] Idiomatically we would say "resurrection of the **body**."
LC : 03 :065(429) [0717] honor, house and home, wife and children, **body** and life.
LC : 03 :072(430) [0717] — the needs of our **body** and our life on earth.
LC : 03 :073(430) [0719] other necessities for our **body**, but also peace and concord
LC : 03 :076(431) [0721] house, home, and a sound **body**; to cause the grain and
LC : 03 :078(431) [0721] all kinds of harm to our **body** and our livelihood, from
LC : 03 :111(435) [0729] which it can slip, the whole **body** will irresistibly follow.
LC : 04 :036(441) [0741] hand cannot do, nor the **body**, but the heart must believe
LC : 04 :044(442) [0743] be saved and have eternal life, both in soul and **body**."
LC : 04 :045(442) [0743] are done in Baptism: the **body** has water poured over it,
LC : 04 :046(442) [0743] constitute one Baptism, **body** and soul shall be saved and
LC : 04 :046(442) [0743] in which it believes, the **body** because it is united with the
LC : 04 :046(442) [0743] therefore, can adorn our **body** and soul than Baptism, for
LC : 04 :056(444) [0747] and that he gives me his **body** and blood; he will not lie
LC : 05 :003(447) [0753] *said, 'Take, eat; this is my **body**, which is given for you.*
LC : 05 :008(447) [0755] Answer: It is the true **body** and blood of the Lord Christ
LC : 05 :010(448) [0755] which is rightly called Christ's **body** and blood.
LC : 05 :012(448) [0755] 'How can bread and wine be Christ's **body** and blood?'
LC : 05 :013(448) [0755] Here we have Christ's word, 'Take, eat; this is my **body**.'
LC : 05 :014(448) [0757] of them they are truly the **body** and blood of Christ.
LC : 05 :016(448) [0757] (that is, Christ's **body** and blood) just as truly as when
LC : 05 :016(448) [0757] and wine into Christ's **body** and blood, so likewise no one
LC : 05 :017(448) [0757] worthy, you receive my **body** and blood," but, "Take, eat
LC : 05 :017(448) [0757] but, "Take, eat and drink, this is my **body** and blood."
LC : 05 :018(448) [0757] you here have Christ's **body** and blood by virtue of these
LC : 05 :021(449) [0757] just quoted, "This is my **body** and blood, given and
LC : 05 :028(449) [0759] wine which are Christ's **body** and blood and with which
LC : 05 :029(449) [0759] truths, that it is Christ's **body** and blood and that these
LC : 05 :030(449) [0759] Christ's **body** can never be an unfruitful, vain thing,
LC : 05 :031(450) [0759] absurd to say that Christ's **body** and blood are not given
LC : 05 :037(451) [0761] exercise so that one's **body** may behave properly and
LC : 05 :037(451) [0761] and reverently toward the **body** and blood of Christ.
LC : 05 :037(451) [0761] cannot be grasped and appropriated by the **body**.
LC : 05 :064(454) [0769] lovely words, "This is my **body**, given *for you,*" "This is
LC : 05 :068(454) [0769] which aids and quickens us in both soul and **body**.
LC : 05 :068(454) [0769] For where the soul is healed, the **body** has benefited also.
LC : 05 :084(456) [0773] and destroy you, soul and **body**, so that you cannot be
EP : 01 :001(466) [0779] nature, essence, **body**, and soul on the one hand, and
EP : 01 :004(466) [0781] God not only created the **body** and soul of Adam and
EP : 01 :008(467) [0781] has survived in man's **body** or soul, in his inward or
EP : 07 :002(481) [0809] Communion are the true **body** and blood of our Lord
EP : 07 :004(482) [0809] true, essential, and living **body** and blood of Christ in the
EP : 07 :005(482) [0809] spirit, or the power of Christ's absent **body**, or his merit.
EP : 07 :005(482) [0809] They deny that the **body** of Christ is present in any
EP : 07 :005(482) [0809] of the Holy Supper, seek the **body** and blood of Christ.
EP : 07 :006(482) [0809] in the Holy Supper the **body** and blood of Christ are truly
EP : 07 :007(482) [0811] symbolized the absent **body** and the wine the absent
EP : 07 :007(482) [0811] union they are truly the **body** and blood of Christ.
EP : 07 :008(482) [0811] effect this presence of the **body** and blood of Christ in the
EP : 07 :015(483) [0811] the bread and wine the **body** and blood of Christ are
EP : 07 :015(483) [0813] not a participation in the **body** of Christ?" (I Cor. 10:16)
EP : 07 :015(483) [0813] — that is, whoever eats this bread eats the **body** of Christ.
EP : 07 :016(484) [0813] receive the true **body** and blood of Christ; but if they are
EP : 07 :022(484) [0813] are transmuted into the **body** of Christ and that only the
EP : 07 :026(485) [0815] in the holy sacrament the **body** of Christ is not received
EP : 07 :026(485) [0815] and that we receive the **body** of Christ only spiritually by
EP : 07 :028(485) [0815] and types of the far-distant **body** and blood of Christ.
EP : 07 :029(485) [0815] it there partakes of the **body** and blood of Christ as truly
EP : 07 :030(485) [0815] and not by the truly present **body** and blood of Christ.
EP : 07 :031(485) [0815] and merit of the absent **body** and blood of Christ are
EP : 07 :032(485) [0815] 11. That the **body** of Christ is so enclosed in heaven that
EP : 07 :033(485) [0815] have promised that his **body** and blood would be
EP : 07 :034(485) [0815] statement!) to cause his **body** to be essentially present at
EP : 07 :035(485) [0815] cause this presence of the **body** and blood of Christ in the
EP : 07 :036(485) [0815] should not seek the **body** of Christ in the bread and wine
EP : 07 :036(485) [0815] the bread to heaven and there seek the **body** of Christ.
EP : 07 :037(486) [0815] do not receive the **body** and blood of Christ, but only
EP : 07 :042(486) [0817] Capernaitic eating of the **body** of Christ as though one
EP : 07 :042(486) [0817] eating of Christ's **body** and drinking of his blood, which
EP : 08 :009(488) [0819] iron and the union of **body** and soul in man.
EP : 08 :017(489) [0823] to impart to us his true **body** and blood which are present
EP : 08 :017(489) [0823] of Christ's testament declare, *"This is, is, is my **body**,"* etc.
EP : 08 :023(490) [0823] true human nature with a **body** and a soul, as Marcion
EP : 08 :030(490) [0825] place, still less to be present with his **body** everywhere.
EP : 09 :001(492) [0827] the deity, or according to **body** and soul, spiritually or
EP : 12 :002(498) [0839] in the church, or in the **body** politic and secular
EP : 12 :003(498) [0839] Christ did not assume his **body** and blood from the virgin
EP : 12 :011(499) [0841] *Intolerable Articles in the **Body** Politic*
EP : 12 :024(500) [0843] and by which Christ distributes his **body** and blood.
SD : 01 :002(508) [0859] or essence (that is, man's **body** or soul), which even after
SD : 01 :002(508) [0859] in man's nature, in his **body**, soul, and all his powers, and
SD : 01 :002(509) [0859] man (that is, between his **body** and soul, which are God's
SD : 01 :028(513) [0867] itself the proper essence, **body**, or soul of man or man
SD : 01 :030(513) [0867] by original sin in **body** and in soul, in all its powers from
SD : 01 :033(514) [0869] of corrupted man, our **body** and soul or man himself
SD : 01 :033(514) [0869] of external leprosy the **body** which is leprous and the
SD : 01 :033(514) [0869] the leprosy on or in the **body** are not one and the same
SD : 01 :038(514) [0871] God is man's creator who creates **body** and soul for him.
SD : 01 :038(515) [0871] me and still sustains my **body** and soul, eyes, ears, and all
SD : 01 :038(515) [0871] constantly sustains my **body**, soul, and life, my members
SD : 01 :041(515) [0871] nature and essence of our **body** and soul (which are
SD : 01 :041(515) [0871] creator of our nature, our **body** and soul, which would
SD : 01 :042(515) [0871] creation that man has a **body** and soul; likewise, that it is
SD : 01 :047(516) [0873] between our corrupted **body** and soul on the one hand
SD : 01 :047(516) [0875] of this essence of our **body** and soul, we should have
SD : 01 :048(517) [0875] substance, its essence, its **body** or soul, so that there is
SD : 01 :051(517) [0875] the word "nature" means man's essence, **body** and soul.
SD : 01 :052(517) [0875] is, man himself with the **body** and soul in which sin is and
SD : 02 :020(524) [0889] nurture and needs of the **body**, man is indeed very clever,
SD : 02 :024(526) [0891] direct the members of his **body**, can hear the Gospel and
SD : 04 :019(554) [0945] Paul says, "I pommel my **body** and subdue it" (I Cor.
SD : 06 :009(565) [0965] And again, "I pommel my **body** and subdue it, lest after
SD : 07 :002(569) [0973] in the Holy Supper the **body** of Christ is truly received by
SD : 07 :002(569) [0973] that the true, essential **body** and blood of Christ are as
SD : 07 :002(569) [0973] assert, "We say that the **body** and blood of Christ are
SD : 07 :003(569) [0973] this presence of the **body** of Christ not as taking place
SD : 07 :003(569) [0973] only spiritually, of the **body** of Christ which is there in
SD : 07 :003(569) [0973] not in heaven, so also the **body** of Christ is now in heaven
SD : 07 :004(569) [0973] only signs of the absent **body** of Christ, are therein
SD : 07 :004(569) [0973] to his divine nature, but not with his **body** and blood).
SD : 07 :005(570) [0973] Christ to confess that the **body** of Christ is present in the
SD : 07 :005(570) [0973] earth, are united with the **body** of Christ, which is in
SD : 07 :006(570) [0973] and is not true of his **body** and blood, which is now in
SD : 07 :006(570) [0975] Christ gives us his true **body** and blood to eat spiritually
SD : 07 :007(570) [0975] of the Supper, "This is my **body**," not strictly, the way the
SD : 07 :007(570) [0975] interpret "to eat Christ's **body**" as no more than "to
SD : 07 :007(570) [0975] For them "**body**" is the same as a "symbol" (that is, a sign
SD : 07 :007(570) [0975] is, a sign or figure of the **body** of Christ which is not in
SD : 07 :007(570) [0975] such a way that Christ's **body** is even now present on
SD : 07 :008(570) [0975] That is, the **body** of Christ is sacramentally or
SD : 07 :008(570) [0975] by faith also of the **body** of Christ which is up in heaven.
SD : 07 :008(570) [0975] But the teaching that the **body** of Christ is essentially
SD : 07 :009(570) [0975] God's Word "that the true **body** and blood of Christ are

Continued ▶

SD : 0 7 :009(571) [0975] to the effect that since the **body** of Christ has ascended
SD : 0 7 :010(571) [0975] Christ himself, is the true **body** and blood of our Lord
SD : 0 7 :011(571) [0975] in the Lord's Supper the **body** and blood of Christ are
SD : 0 7 :011(571) [0975] If the **body** of Christ were not truly present, but only the
SD : 0 7 :011(571) [0975] is a participation in the **body** of Christ, etc., it would
SD : 0 7 :011(571) [0975] a participation not in the **body** but in the spirit of Christ.
SD : 0 7 :013(571) [0977] the holy sacrament of the **body** and blood of Christ,
SD : 0 7 :014(571) [0977] the bread and wine the **body** and blood of Christ are truly
SD : 0 7 :014(571) [0977] bread and wine into the **body** and blood of Christ) and do
SD : 0 7 :014(571) [0977] do not believe that the **body** and blood of Christ are
SD : 0 7 :014(572) [0977] sacramental union the bread is the **body** of Christ, etc.
SD : 0 7 :015(572) [0977] do not maintain that the **body** of Christ is present apart
SD : 0 7 :016(572) [0977] are observed, the **body** and blood of Christ are truly
SD : 0 7 :018(572) [0979] namely, that the **body** of Christ, together with all his
SD : 0 7 :018(572) [0979] spiritual presence of the **body** of the Lord Christ through
SD : 0 7 :019(572) [0979] in the Supper are the true **body** and blood of Jesus Christ
SD : 0 7 :020(573) [0979] Answer: It is the true **body** and blood of Christ in and
SD : 0 7 :021(573) [0979] and wine but is and is called Christ's **body** and blood."
SD : 0 7 :022(573) [0979] can bread and wine be the **body** and blood of Christ?'
SD : 0 7 :022(573) [0979] Here we have Christ's word, 'Take eat, this is my **body**.
SD : 0 7 :023(573) [0979] with the words it is truly the **body** and blood of Christ.
SD : 0 7 :024(573) [0981] (that is, Christ's **body** and blood) just as much as when
SD : 0 7 :024(573) [0981] bread and wine into the **body** and blood of Christ, so
SD : 0 7 :026(573) [0981] are worthy, you have my **body** and blood,' but, 'Take, eat
SD : 0 7 :026(573) [0981] but, 'Take, eat and drink, this is my **body** and blood.'
SD : 0 7 :026(573) [0981] you here have his **body** and blood by virtue of these
SD : 0 7 :027(574) [0981] the true presence of the **body** and blood of Christ in the
SD : 0 7 :032(574) [0983] of the Altar the **body** and blood of Christ are truly eaten
SD : 0 7 :033(575) [0983] Supper is his true, natural **body**, which the godless or
SD : 0 7 :035(575) [0983] the Lord's Supper "is true **body** of Christ" or "a
SD : 0 7 :035(575) [0983] or "a participation in the **body** of Christ"), we at times
SD : 0 7 :035(575) [0985] substance of the bread and the **body** of Christ.
SD : 0 7 :037(575) [0985] to the words of Christ's testament, "This is my **body**."
SD : 0 7 :037(575) [0985] bread and the true natural **body** of Christ, are present
SD : 0 7 :038(576) [0985] though the union of the **body** and blood of Christ with
SD : 0 7 :038(576) [0985] testament), "This is my **body**," we have to do with a
SD : 0 7 :044(577) [0987] "Take, eat, this is my **body** which is given for you," and
SD : 0 7 :048(578) [0989] "bread," as though the **body** of Christ were spiritual bread
SD : 0 7 :049(578) [0989] (that is, a change in meaning) in the word "**body**."
SD : 0 7 :049(578) [0989] of a symbol of his **body**, or of a representation or of his
SD : 0 7 :049(578) [0989] a representation or of his **body** in a figurative sense, or of
SD : 0 7 :049(578) [0989] or of the virtue of his **body** and the benefits which he had
SD : 0 7 :049(578) [0989] which he had won for us by the sacrifice of his **body**.
SD : 0 7 :049(578) [0989] of his true, essential **body**, which he gave into death for
SD : 0 7 :052(578) [0991] of Christ, "This is my **body**," and apply them in one and
SD : 0 7 :054(579) [0991] not a participation in the **body** of Christ?") are to be
SD : 0 7 :054(579) [0991] and distribution of the **body** and blood of Christ in the
SD : 0 7 :054(579) [0991] is participation in the **body** and blood of Christ, so that
SD : 0 7 :054(579) [0991] receive and partake of the true **body** and blood of Christ.
SD : 0 7 :055(579) [0991] For if the **body** of Christ were not truly and essentially
SD : 0 7 :055(579) [0991] called participation in the **body** but in the spirit, the
SD : 0 7 :056(579) [0991] participation in the **body** of Christ through faith, as the
SD : 0 7 :056(579) [0991] the spirit or faith is participation in the **body** of Christ.
SD : 0 7 :056(579) [0991] is participation in the **body** of Christ, and that means
SD : 0 7 :056(579) [0991] the blessed bread also partake of the **body** of Christ.
SD : 0 7 :056(579) [0991] or oral eating of the **body** of Christ in which both the
SD : 0 7 :057(579) [0993] the Lord and partaking of the **body** and blood of Christ.
SD : 0 7 :057(579) [0993] them against receiving the **body** and blood of Christ to
SD : 0 7 :057(579) [0993] Supper participate in the **body** of Christ, St. Paul
SD : 0 7 :058(580) [0993] we break is the distributed **body** of Christ, or the common
SD : 0 7 :058(580) [0993] of Christ, or the common **body** of Christ distributed
SD : 0 7 :059(580) [0993] in the Lord's Supper the **body** of Christ is received only
SD : 0 7 :059(580) [0993] is participation in the **body** of Christ (that is, it is that
SD : 0 7 :059(580) [0993] have participation in the **body** of Christ, which is the
SD : 0 7 :059(580) [0993] are incorporated into the **body** of Christ, which is the
SD : 0 7 :060(580) [0993] Christians receive the true **body** and blood of Christ
SD : 0 7 :060(580) [0993] sin grievously against the **body** and blood of Christ.
SD : 0 7 :060(580) [0993] and figures of the **body** and blood, but becomes guilty of
SD : 0 7 :060(580) [0993] guilty of profaning the **body** and blood of the Lord Jesus
SD : 0 7 :060(580) [0995] violent hands upon the **body** of Christ and murdered
SD : 0 7 :062(581) [0995] for us by giving his **body** for us into death and by
SD : 0 7 :063(581) [0995] The other eating of the **body** of Christ is oral or
SD : 0 7 :063(581) [0995] of the true, essential **body** and blood of Christ orally.
SD : 0 7 :064(581) [0995] which he called his true **body** and blood, and said
SD : 0 7 :066(581) [0995] unanimously that the **body** of Christ is received not only
SD : 0 7 :068(582) [0997] oral eating of the **body** of Christ burden themselves with
SD : 0 7 :068(582) [0997] punishments) and profane the **body** and blood of Christ.
SD : 0 7 :072(582) [0997] participation in the **body** and blood of Christ, the one
SD : 0 7 :074(583) [0999] the true presence of the **body** and blood of Christ in the
SD : 0 7 :075(583) [0999] words are used, and the **body** and blood of Christ are
SD : 0 7 :076(583) [0999] and wine set before us the **body** and blood of Christ.
SD : 0 7 :076(583) [0999] he speaks, 'This is my **body**,' the elements set before us in
SD : 0 7 :076(583) [0999] brings about that his true **body** and blood are present in
SD : 0 7 :077(583) [0999] bread and wine but his **body** and blood, as his words
SD : 0 7 :077(583) [0999] words read, 'This is my **body**,' etc., 'This is my blood,'
SD : 0 7 :077(583) [0999] world, make the bread the **body** and the wine the blood
SD : 0 7 :078(583) [1001] bread there is, 'This is the **body** of Christ,' nothing would
SD : 0 7 :078(583) [1001] and say, 'This is my **body**,' then it is his body, not because
SD : 0 7 :078(583) [1001] is my body,' then it is his **body**, not because of our
SD : 0 7 :081(584) [1001] (the presence of the **body** and blood of Christ, the
SD : 0 7 :082(584) [1001] use, so that therewith the **body** and blood of Christ are
SD : 0 7 :086(585) [1003] blessed bread and wine, the **body** and blood of Christ.
SD : 0 7 :088(585) [1003] and the oral eating of the **body** of Christ, in which here
SD : 0 7 :088(585) [1003] that the reception of the **body** of Christ takes place only
SD : 0 7 :088(585) [1003] the presence of Christ's **body** in the Holy Supper and that
SD : 0 7 :088(585) [1003] do not receive the **body** of Christ because it is not present
SD : 0 7 :089(585) [1003] in his words when he says, "Take eat, this is my **body**."
SD : 0 7 :090(585) [1003] the presence of the **body** of Christ and to receive it, rather
SD : 0 7 :091(585) [1003] properties of the human **body**, concerning the ascension
SD : 0 7 :091(585) [1005] *These Words "This Is My **Body**" Still Stand Firm*, his
SD : 0 7 :098(586) [1005] "Furthermore, the one **body** of Christ has three different
SD : 0 7 :102(587) [1007] to prove certainly that the **body** of Christ cannot in any
SD : 0 7 :103(587) [1007] more modes whereby Christ's **body** can be anywhere.
SD : 0 7 :103(587) [1007] mode of presence to the **body** of Christ although they are
SD : 0 7 :103(587) [1007] power is able to make a **body** be simultaneously in many
SD : 0 7 :104(587) [1009] Christ and become true, spiritual members of his **body**.
SD : 0 7 :105(588) [1009] when we say that the **body** and blood of Christ in the
SD : 0 7 :106(588) [1009] the true presence of the **body** and blood of Christ in the
SD : 0 7 :108(588) [1009] into the substance of the **body** and blood of Christ, so
SD : 0 7 :108(588) [1009] is no longer bread, the **body** of Christ is present even
SD : 0 7 :111(589) [1011] the true presence of the **body** and blood of Christ against
SD : 0 7 :113(589) [1011] essential presence of the **body** and blood of Christ in the
SD : 0 7 :114(589) [1011] of an oral eating of the **body** and blood of Christ in the
SD : 0 7 :114(589) [1011] that in the Supper the **body** of Christ is partaken of only
SD : 0 7 :115(589) [1011] types of the far-distant **body** of Christ (for example, just
SD : 0 7 :115(589) [1011] are external food for our **body**, so the absent body of
SD : 0 7 :115(589) [1011] our body, so the absent **body** of Christ with its merit is
SD : 0 7 :116(589) [1011] reminders of the absent **body** of Christ, and through these
SD : 0 7 :116(589) [1011] partakes up there of the **body** and blood of Christ as truly
SD : 0 7 :116(589) [1013] through the true present **body** and blood of Christ,
SD : 0 7 :117(589) [1013] merit of the far-distant **body** of Christ, and that in this
SD : 0 7 :117(589) [1013] Christ, and that in this way we partake of his absent **body**
SD : 0 7 :117(590) [1013] wine have a similarity with the **body** and blood of Christ.
SD : 0 7 :118(590) [1013] 7. Or that the **body** and blood of Christ are only received
SD : 0 7 :120(590) [1013] essential presence of his **body** and blood in the Supper
SD : 0 7 :121(590) [1013] the presence of the **body** of Christ in the Holy Supper,
SD : 0 7 :122(590) [1013] not directed to seek the **body** of Christ in the bread and
SD : 0 7 :122(590) [1013] Christ is present with his **body** and there to partake of
SD : 0 7 :123(590) [1013] wine in the Supper and not the **body** and blood of Christ.
SD : 0 7 :123(590) [1015] Holy Supper and not the **body** and the blood of Christ
SD : 0 8 :002(591) [1015] essential presence of the **body** and blood of Jesus Christ
SD : 0 8 :002(591) [1015] by saying that the **body** of Christ could not be a true and
SD : 0 8 :002(591) [1015] a true and genuine human **body** if it were present at the
SD : 0 8 :002(592) [1017] to God alone and the **body** of Christ is incapable of it.
SD : 0 8 :004(592) [1017] true, essential presence of the **body** and blood of Christ.
SD : 0 8 :018(594) [1021] analogies of the soul and the **body** and of glowing iron.
SD : 0 8 :019(594) [1021] For the **body** and soul, as well as fire and iron, have a
SD : 0 8 :029(596) [1025] is truly present with his **body** and blood in the Holy
SD : 0 8 :064(603) [1037] beings or in the angels, but "bodily," as in its own **body**.
SD : 0 8 :064(603) [1039] as the soul does in the **body** and fire in glowing iron,
SD : 0 8 :092(609) [1049] can be present with his **body**, which he has placed at the
SD : 1 0 :005(611) [1053] and become one **body**, or that a return to the papacy and
SD : 1 0 :020(614) [1059] the eternal destruction of **body** and soul are characteristic
SD : 1 2 :009(633) [1097] in the churches or in the **body** politic or in domestic
SD : 1 2 :032(635) [1101] through which Christ distributes his **body** and blood.

Bohemia (1)
AG : PR :018(026) [0041] Majesty of Hungary and **Bohemia**, etc.) and by Your

Bold (3), Boldly (4)
AG : 2 3 :023(055) [0063] marriage and then to be so **bold** as to maintain such a
AP : 2 0 :009(227) [0341] but go on still more **boldly**," every one of you who has
S1 : PR :002(288) [0455] adherents ever became so **bold** as seriously, in good faith,
SC : 0 3 :002(346) [0545] we may approach him **boldly** and confidently in prayer,
LC : 0 1 :238(397) [0647] Just let them keep on **boldly** fleecing people as long as
LC : 0 3 :121(436) [0731] "Why should I be so **bold** as to boast that God hears my
EP : 0 8 :003(487) [0819] They declare **boldly** that the "personal union makes

Bolt (1)
LC : 0 1 :226(395) [0645] can guard with lock and **bolt**, or if we catch them we can

Bonaventure (1)
AP : 0 2 :028(104) [0113] **Bonaventure** writes: "When the question is asked what

Bond (11), Bonds (1)
PR : PR :004(004) [0007] of God's Word, sever the **bond** of Christian charity and
AP : 0 2 :049(106) [0119] the world, and by these **bonds** the devil has enthralled
AP : 0 4 :103(122) [0151] his blood canceled the **bond** that stood against us (Col.
AP : 0 4 :231(139) [0183] us Col. 3:14, "love, which is the **bond** of perfection."
AP : 0 4 :232(139) [0185] He says that love is a **bond** and unbroken chain linking
AP : 1 2 :048(188) [0265] that Christ cancels the **bond** which stood against us with
AP : 1 2 :048(188) [0265] there are two parts, the **bond** and the cancellation of the
AP : 1 2 :048(188) [0265] are two parts, the bond and the cancellation of the **bond**.
AP : 1 2 :048(188) [0265] The **bond** is the conscience denouncing and condemning
AP : 1 2 :048(188) [0265] The **bond** therefore is contrition itself, condemning us.
AP : 1 2 :048(188) [0265] The cancellation of the **bond** is the removal of the
SD : 0 7 :044(577) [0987] hearts, and a true **bond** and union of Christians with

Bondage (9)
AG : 2 8 :039(087) [0089] Christendom with the **bondage** of the law, as if in order to
AG : 2 8 :051(089) [0091] namely, that **bondage** to the law is not necessary for
AG : 2 8 :065(092) [0093] consciences with such **bondage** but forbade such eating
AL : 2 8 :039(087) [0089] the church with the **bondage** of the law, as if in order to
AL : 2 8 :051(089) [0091] churches, namely, that **bondage** to the law is not
AL : 2 8 :065(092) [0093] consciences with such **bondage** but forbade such eating
SD : 0 2 :015(523) [0887] of ignorance and the **bondage** of sin and death through
SD : 0 2 :044(529) [0897] matter in his book *The **Bondage** of the Will*, in which he
SD : 1 0 :011(612) [1057] they might bring us into **bondage**: to whom we did not

Bondservants (1)
SD : 0 6 :016(566) [0967] extorted by the law, just as in the case of **bondservants**.

Bone (3), Bones (6)
AP : 1 2 :031(186) [0259] languishing; O Lord, heal me, for my **bones** are troubled.
AP : 1 2 :031(186) [0259] help until morning; like a lion he breaks all my **bones**."
S2 : 0 2 :022(296) [0469] been invented about the **bones** of dogs and horses that
LC : 0 1 :091(377) [0607] Though we had the **bones** of all the saints or all the holy
LC : 0 1 :247(398) [0651] him right down to the **bone**, and you arrogantly turn him
LC : 0 4 :020(439) [0737] skin and hair, flesh and **bones**, they look no different from
SD : 0 1 :035(514) [0869] and flesh, and knit me together with **bones** and sinews.
SD : 0 8 :078(607) [1045] and we flesh of his flesh and **bone** of his bone (Eph. 5:30).
SD : 0 8 :078(607) [1045] and we flesh of his flesh and bone of his **bone** (Eph. 5:30).

Boniface (2)
TR : 0 0 :033(325) [0513] the constitution of **Boniface** VIII, Distinction 22 of the
TR : 0 0 :082(335) [0529] **Boniface** Wolfart, minister of the Word in the church in

Book (40), Booklet (2), Books (23)
PR : PR :000(001) [0004] Preface to the **Book** of Concord
PR : PR :000(003) [0005] Preface to the Christian **Book** of Concord
PR : PR :013(007) [0013] and is necessary for this end and put it down in one **book**.
PR : PR :016(008) [0013] and subscribed this **Book** of Concord as the correct
PR : PR :017(008) [0015] among ourselves in this **Book** of Concord and repetition
PR : PR :018(009) [0015] into our declaration and **Book** of Concord that follows
AG : 1 8 :004(039) [0051] here quoted from the third **book** of his *Hypognosticon:*
AG : 2 0 :013(043) [0055] His whole **book**, *De spiritu et litera,* proves this.
AG : 2 4 :041(061) [0069] to the Tripartite History, **Book** 9, on Wednesday and
AG : 2 6 :045(070) [0075] the Tripartite History, **Book** 9, gathers many examples of
AG : 2 7 :014(073) [0077] can be denied, for they are found in their own **books**.
AL : 1 8 :004(039) [0051] In **Book** III of his *Hypognosticon* Augustine said these
AL : 2 3 :025(055) [0065] His words in the first **book** of his letters, Epistle XI, are
AL : 2 4 :041(061) [0069] History testifies in **Book** 9, "Again, in Alexandria, the
AL : 2 6 :045(070) [0075] In the Tripartite History, **Book** 9, many examples of
AL : 2 7 :014(073) [0077] things can be denied, for they appear in their own **books**.
AP : PR :010(099) [0101] one can complain that the **book** has appeared
AP : 0 4 :015(109) [0123] We see that there are **books** in existence which compare
AP : 0 4 :235(140) [0185] All the **books** of the sages are full of these commands of
AP : 0 4 :322(157) [0209] In the ninth **book** of the *Confessions* he says, "Woe to the
AP : 0 7 :032(174) [0239] there are many foolish **books** by the summists and
AP : 1 2 :069(192) [0271] not produce their own **books** but only compiled them
AP : 1 2 :069(192) [0271] and transferred these opinions from one **book** to another.
AP : 2 1 :009(230) [0345] recorded in the Second **Book** of the Maccabees (15:14).
AP : 2 1 :023(232) [0349] there in our opponents' **books** and sermons there are even
AP : 2 4 :009(251) [0387] Confutation and in all their other **books** about the Mass.
AP : 2 4 :015(251) [0389] publishing almost endless **books** about sacrifice, but none
AP : 2 4 :020(252) [0389] If the limits of this **book** permitted, we would enumerate
AP : 2 4 :046(258) [0401] All their **books** and sermons were silent about the
AP : 2 7 :010(270) [0423] carefully and fully in his **book** called *Monastic Vows,* we
AP : 2 7 :010(270) [0423] we want to be interpreted here as reiterating that **book**.
S 2 : 0 2 :007(293) [0463] (as the cannon and all **books** on the subject declare), for
S 2 : 0 4 :004(298) [0473] All the pope's bulls and **books**, in which he roars like a
S 2 : 0 4 :014(301) [0475] government, as I have demonstrated in many **books**.
TR : 0 0 :022(323) [0511] and accurately in the **books** of our theologians, and all
SC : PR :006(338) [0533] better at least take this **booklet** and these forms and read
SC : PR :014(339) [0535] the explanations in this **booklet**, or choose any other
SC : PR :017(340) [0537] at length in the many **books** written for this purpose.
LC : PR :002(358) [0567] in the many excellent **books** which are in reality what the
LC : PR :002(358) [0567] honest as to buy these **books**, or if they have them, to
LC : PR :003(358) [0567] the Catechism, the Prayer **Book**, the New Testament, or
LC : PR :005(359) [0567] it once they toss the **book** into a corner as if they are
LC : PR :006(359) [0569] they have everything in **books** and can learn it all by
LC : 0 1 :284(403) [0661] is publicly set forth in **books** and shouted throughout the
EP : 1 1 :007(495) [0833] us to Christ, who is "the **book** of life" in which all who
EP : 1 1 :013(496) [0835] Word of God, which shows us Christ as the "**book** of life."
EP : 1 1 :013(496) [0835] opens and reveals this **book** for us, as it is written, "Those
SD : RN :001(503) [0851] writings, but on such **books** as had been written,
SD : RN :010(506) [0855] good, useful, and pure **books**, such as interpretations of
SD : RN :019(507) [0857] matter where or in what **books** it might be found or who
SD : 0 1 :036(514) [0869] substance; in thy **book** were written, every one of them,
SD : 0 1 :050(517) [0875] and the above-mentioned **books** use them in treating this
SD : 0 2 :023(525) [0889] in a similar vein in his second **book** *Against Julian.*
SD : 0 2 :044(529) [0897] this entire matter in his **book** *The Bondage of the Will,* in
SD : 0 3 :021(542) [0921] used the term in his **book** *On the Councils and the*
SD : 0 8 :022(595) [1023] the other (Irenaeus, **Book** IV, chap. 3; Anthanasius in his
SD : 0 8 :022(595) [1023] Hilary, *On the Trinity,* **Book** IX; Basil and Gregory of
SD : 0 8 :022(595) [1023] in Theodoret; John Damascene, **Book** III, chap. 19).
SD : 0 8 :086(608) [1047] writings, especially in the **book** *That These Words Still*
SD : 1 1 :004(617) [1063] substance, in thy **book** were written every one of them,
SD : 1 1 :013(619) [1067] is the genuine and true "**book** of life" as it is revealed to
SD : 1 1 :025(620) [1071] names are written in the **book** of life" will be saved, how
SD : 1 1 :066(627) [1085] all men to Christ as to the **book** of life in whom they are
SD : 1 1 :070(627) [1085] to Christ, who is the "**book** of life" and of the eternal
SD : 1 1 :089(631) [1093] in his holy Gospel as the "**book** of life," this doctrine

Bopfingen (1)
PR : PR :027(016) [0027] Mayor and Council of **Bopfingen**

Bore (3), Born (56), Borne (4)
AG : 0 2 :001(029) [0043] of Adam all men who are **born** according to the course of
AG : 0 2 :001(029) [0043] to the course of nature are conceived and **born** in sin.
AG : 0 2 :002(029) [0043] God all those who are not **born** again through Baptism
AG : 0 3 :001(029) [0045] God the Son became man, **born** of the virgin Mary, and
AG : 0 3 :002(029) [0045] true man, who was truly **born**, suffered, was crucified,
AL : 0 2 :001(029) [0043] who are propagated according to nature are **born** in sin.
AL : 0 2 :002(029) [0043] on those who are not **born** again through Baptism and
AL : 0 3 :002(030) [0045] and true man, who was **born** of the virgin Mary, truly
AL : 1 2 :005(034) [0049] the other is faith, which is **born** of the Gospel, or of
AL : 2 4 :016(057) [0067] become so manifest that they could no longer be **borne**.
AL : 2 7 :049(079) [0083] all things which are to be **borne** in connection with our
AP : 0 2 :002(100) [0105] of Adam all men who are **born** according to the course of
AP : 0 2 :002(100) [0105] to the course of nature are conceived and **born** in sin.
AP : 0 2 :003(101) [0105] that in those who are **born** according to the flesh we deny
AP : 0 2 :003(101) [0105] We say that anyone **born** in this way has concupiscence
AP : 0 2 :005(101) [0107] sin but, like a child **born** of a slave, is in this condition
AP : 0 2 :006(101) [0107] since human nature is **born** full of corruption and faults.
AP : 0 2 :011(102) [0109] hate of God, and similar faults that we are **born** with.
AP : 0 4 :031(111) [0129] is written, "Unless one is **born** of water and the Spirit,
AP : 0 4 :031(111) [0129] But if we must be **born** again through the Holy Spirit,
AP : 0 4 :051(114) [0135] to believe that Christ was **born**, suffered, and was raised
AP : 0 4 :094(120) [0149] of God; who were **born**, not of blood nor of the will of
AP : 0 4 :135(125) [0159] care, but supposes that men are **born** and die by chance.
AP : 0 4 :291(152) [0203] not promised, revealed, **born**, crucified, and raised in
AP : 0 4 :297(153) [0205] not promised, revealed, **born**, crucified, and raised in
AP : 0 4 :297(153) [0205] believed in the testimony that God has **borne** to his Son.
AP : 0 7 :014(170) [0231] Testament people, those **born** according to the flesh had
AP : 1 2 :062(191) [0269] believed in the testimony that God has **borne** to his Son."
AP : 2 3 :010(241) [0367] that formerly men were **born** with a sex and now they are
AP : 2 3 :010(241) [0367] that originally they were **born** with a natural right and
S 1 : 0 1 :000(291) [0461] of man, and was **born** of the pure, holy, and virgin Mary.
S 3 : 0 3 :028(308) [0487] hereditary evil which is **born** in us did what is its nature to
S 3 : 0 3 :045(310) [0491] St. John says, "No one **born** of God commits sin; he
SC : 0 2 :003(345) [0545] *by the Holy Spirit,* **born** *of the virgin Mary, suffered*
SC : 0 2 :004(345) [0545] and also true man, **born** of the virgin Mary, is my Lord,
LC : SP :012(363) [0577] by the Holy Spirit, **born** of the virgin Mary, suffered
LC : 0 2 :025(413) [0683] *by the Holy Spirit,* **born** *of the virgin Mary, suffered*
LC : 0 2 :031(414) [0687] man, conceived and **born** without sin, of the Holy Spirit
LC : 0 4 :066(445) [0749] He is what is **born** in us from Adam, irascible, spiteful,
LC : 0 5 :023(449) [0757] Baptism we are first **born** anew, our human flesh and
EP : 0 8 :012(488) [0821] that Mary conceived and **bore** not only a plain, ordinary,
EP : 1 2 :025(500) [0843] a Christian who is truly **born** again through the Spirit of
SD : 0 1 :027(513) [0867] all men, conceived and **born** in the natural way from a
SD : 0 1 :030(513) [0867] of every human being **born** in the natural way from a
SD : 0 2 :018(524) [0889] with which he was **born**, he defiantly resists God and his
SD : 0 2 :026(526) [0891] But to be **born** anew, to receive inwardly a new heart,
SD : 0 2 :067(534) [0907] (Gal. 3:27), are thus truly **born** again, and now have a
SD : 0 3 :056(549) [0935] without sin and had been **born** and had in his human
SD : 0 3 :058(550) [0937] under the law for us, **bore** our sin, and in his path to the
SD : 0 5 :020(561) [0959] Lord, himself assumed and **bore** the curse of the law and
SD : 0 6 :001(563) [0963] but those who have been **born** anew through the Holy
SD : 0 6 :017(566) [0967] But when a person is **born** anew by the Spirit of God and
SD : 0 6 :017(566) [0967] law and, in so far as he is **born** anew, he does everything
SD : 0 6 :021(567) [0969] those who have been **born** anew to do good works, he
SD : 0 7 :046(577) [0987] the promised seed, Christ, who was to be **born** of Isaac.
SD : 0 7 :100(587) [1007] as people believe, when he was **born** of his mother, etc.
SD : 0 8 :006(592) [1017] true eternal God, **born** of the Father from eternity, and
SD : 0 8 :006(592) [1017] and also a true man, **born** of the most blessed virgin
SD : 0 8 :024(595) [1023] womb in that he was **born** of a virgin without violating
SD : 0 8 :085(608) [1047] me, Jesus of Nazareth, Mary's son, **born** a human being.
SD : 1 1 :088(631) [1093] but even before we were **born** (in fact, "before the
SD : 1 2 :013(634) [1099] because they are **born** of Christian and believing parents,
SD : 1 2 :033(635) [1101] a Christian who is truly **born** again through the Spirit of

Bored (2)
LC : PR :016(361) [0571] Look at these **bored**, presumptuous saints who will not or
LC : 0 5 :044(451) [0763] in preaching, lest people become indifferent and **bored**.

Boredom (1)
LC : PR :005(359) [0567] plague of security and **boredom** has overtaken us.

Bosom (4)
AP : 2 7 :013(271) [0423] Thou who are in the **bosom** of the Father hast revealed to
LC : 0 2 :037(415) [0687] placing us upon the **bosom** of the church, where he
LC : 0 5 :075(455) [0771] put their hands to their **bosom** and ask whether they are
SD : 1 1 :067(627) [1085] Son, who is in the **bosom** of the Father" (John 1:18), has

Bother (2), Bothered (3), Bothersome (1)
AP : 0 4 :338(159) [0215] grounds we are not **bothered** by the argument, "When you
AP : 0 4 :400(168) [0227] of our opponents will not **bother** us since they defend
AP : 0 7 :042(176) [0243] if they have made a mistake, do not let this **bother** you."
AP : 0 7 :042(177) [0243] they tell them not to be **bothered** even if there has been a
AP : 0 7 :044(177) [0243] they tell him not to be **bothered** even if there has been a
LC : PR :003(358) [0567] free from the useless, **bothersome** babbling of the Seven

Bottom (1), Bottomless (1)
SD : 0 1 :011(510) [0863] wicked, abominable, **bottomless**, inscrutable, and
SD : 0 8 :044(599) [1029] we shall sink to the **bottom** with our scale.

Bound (33), Bounds (1)
PR : PR :012(007) [0013] also regarded ourselves **bound** to promote it with
PR : PR :024(013) [0021] who do not want to be **bound** to any certain formula of
AG : 2 8 :022(084) [0087] and churches are **bound** to be obedient to the bishops
AG : 2 8 :075(094) [0095] without sin, we are **bound** to follow the apostolic rule
AL : 0 6 :001(031) [0045] teach that this faith is **bound** to bring forth good fruits
AL : 1 2 :006(035) [0049] which are the fruits of repentance, are **bound** to follow.
AL : 1 6 :006(038) [0051] Christians are necessarily **bound** to obey their magistrates
AL : 2 6 :011(065) [0071] grieved that they were **bound** to an imperfect kind of life
AL : 2 8 :022(084) [0087] Churches are therefore **bound** by divine law to be
AL : 2 8 :029(085) [0087] their duties, princes are **bound**, even against their will, to
AL : 2 8 :053(090) [0091] nor that consciences are **bound** so as to regard these as
AL : 2 8 :075(094) [0095] kept without sin, we are **bound** to follow the apostolic
AP : 1 2 :142(204) [0295] limit which man is **bound** to observe, namely, the
AP : 1 2 :176(210) [0307] bind on earth shall be **bound** in heaven, and whatever you
S 1 : PR :002(289) [0455] free council, as indeed the pope is in duty **bound** to do.
TR : 0 0 :026(324) [0511] New Testament is not **bound** to places and persons, as the
TR : 0 0 :055(329) [0521] followers, whom he has **bound** by horrible oaths and
SC : PR :013(339) [0535] to reside in a city is **bound** to know and observe the laws
SC : 0 2 :002(345) [0543] For all of this I am **bound** to thank, praise, serve, and
LC : 0 1 :329(410) [0677] that end and beginning are all linked and **bound** together.
LC : 0 2 :019(412) [0681] that we are in duty **bound** to love, praise, and thank him
LC : 0 2 :022(413) [0683] themselves in duty **bound** to serve and obey him for all
LC : 0 4 :030(440) [0739] faith is attached and **bound** on the ground that the object
LC : 0 4 :053(443) [0745] received or used, for it is **bound** not to our faith but to
LC : 0 5 :047(452) [0763] sacrament to be free, not **bound** to a special time like the
LC : 0 5 :047(452) [0765] and need, being **bound** to no special place or time"
EP : 0 4 :003(476) [0797] regenerated persons are **bound** to render such obedience.
EP : 1 2 :015(499) [0841] conscience nor pay oath-**bound** feudal homage to his
EP : 1 2 :017(499) [0841] but is in conscience **bound** to put it into a common
SD : 0 3 :040(546) [0929] faith and good works is **bound** to be maintained and
SD : 0 4 :014(553) [0943] to indicate what we are **bound** to do because of God's
SD : 0 7 :045(577) [0987] We are therefore **bound** to interpret and explain these
SD : 0 8 :042(599) [1029] is likewise within the **bounds** of truth, for you must say
SD : 1 2 :020(634) [1099] a court or pay oath-**bound** feudal homage to his prince or

Boundary (1)
LC : 0 1 :183(389) [0633] commandments as a **boundary** between good and evil.

Boundless (3)
LC : 0 2 :023(413) [0683] them his fatherly heart and his **boundless** love toward us.
LC : 0 4 :042(442) [0743] of Baptism are so **boundless** that if timid nature considers
SD : 0 2 :050(530) [0901] To this end, in his **boundless** kindness and mercy, God

Bountiful (1), Bountifully (3)
AP : 0 4 :367(163) [0221] sparingly, he who sows **bountifully** will also reap

Continued ▶

A P : 0 4 :367(163) [0221] will also reap **bountifully**" (II Cor. 9:6); here the degree of
S C : 0 8 :009(353) [0559] thy gifts which of thy **bountiful** goodness Thou hast
L C : 0 3 :083(431) [0721] these blessings **bountifully**, even for wicked men and

Bounty (1)
A P : 2 7 :016(271) [0425] They brag about poverty amid a **bounty** of everything.

Bow (1)
L C : 0 5 :011(448) [0755] feet every knee should **bow** and confess that it is as he

Box (1)
L C : 0 1 :229(396) [0645] who loot a cash **box**, they sit in office chairs and are

Boy (2), Boys (3)
A G : 2 7 :008(072) [0077] must have seen that both **boys** and girls were thrust into
A L : 2 7 :008(072) [0077] they saw that girls and **boys** were thrust into monasteries
A L : 2 7 :029(075) [0079] they are able to judge, **boys** and girls are persuaded, and
A P : 2 3 :044(245) [0375] We all know the verse, "The **boy** who is used to being lazy
L C : 0 2 :011(412) [0681] to ask a young child, "My **boy**, what kind of God have

Brag (4), Bragged (1)
A P : P R :008(098) [0101] in which our opponents **brag** that they have refuted our
A P : 2 7 :016(271) [0425] They **brag** about poverty amid a bounty of everything.
A P : 2 7 :016(271) [0425] They **brag** about obedience though no class of men has
L C : 0 1 :197(392) [0637] shamelessly boasted and **bragged** of their hypocritical
L C : 0 2 :021(413) [0683] not swagger about and **brag** and boast as if we had life,

Branches (5)
A G : 2 7 :015(073) [0077] Holy Scripture and other **branches** of learning which are
A L : 2 7 :015(073) [0077] Scriptures and other **branches** of learning which were
A P : 1 0 :003(179) [0247] and that we are truly **branches**, deriving life from him for
A P : 1 2 :085(194) [0277] do nothing," and "I am the vine, you are the **branches**."
A P : 1 2 :086(194) [0277] reconciled to God and becoming the **branches** of Christ.

Brandenburg (5)
P R : P R :027(014) [0025] John George, margrave of **Brandenburg**, elector
P R : P R :027(014) [0025] margrave of **Brandenburg**, administrator of the
P R : P R :027(014) [0025] margrave of **Brandenburg** [-Ansbach-Bayreuth]
A G : 0 0 :007(096) [0095] George, margrave of **Brandenburg**
A L : 0 0 :017(096) [0095] George, margrave of **Brandenburg**

Brave (1), Bravely (1)
A P : 2 0 :006(227) [0339] terrors of the world and **bravely** bear whatever we have to
L C : 0 1 :259(400) [0653] but also a wise, sagacious, **brave**, and fearless man.

Brazenly (2), Brazenness (1)
A P : 2 3 :002(239) [0363] can one read of greater **brazenness** than that of our
L C : P R :006(359) [0569] fall into decay, and **brazenly** allow both pastors and
L C : 0 1 :298(405) [0665] We **brazenly** dare to boast of it, and insist that it should

Breach (1)
L C : 0 3 :062(428) [0715] out of men's hearts and a **breach** is made in his kingdom.

Bread (178)
A G : 1 0 :001(034) [0047] Lord under the form of **bread** and wine and are there
A L : 2 4 :012(057) [0065] said, "Whoever eats the **bread** or drinks the cup of the
A P : 0 4 :254(143) [0193] Isa. 58:7, 9, "Share your **bread** with the hungry.
A P : 0 4 :259(144) [0193] (Isa. 58:7) "Share your **bread** with the hungry," he
A P : 1 0 :001(179) [0247] things that are seen, the **bread** and the wine, to those who
A P : 1 0 :001(179) [0247] since Paul says that the **bread** is "a participation in the
A P : 1 0 :001(179) [0247] it would follow that the **bread** would not be a
A P : 1 0 :002(179) [0247] clearly prays that the **bread** may be changed and become
A P : 1 0 :002(179) [0247] says distinctly that "the **bread** is not merely a figure but is
A P : 1 0 :004(180) [0247] offered with those things that are seen, **bread** and wine.
A P : 2 2 :003(236) [0359] himself, and so eat of the **bread** and drink of the cup."
A P : 2 2 :007(237) [0359] passages that mention **bread**, like Luke 24:35, which says
A P : 2 2 :007(237) [0359] disciples recognized Christ in the breaking of the **bread**.
A P : 2 2 :007(237) [0359] other passages that talk about the breaking of the **bread**.
A P : 2 4 :035(256) [0397] "As often as you eat this **bread** and drink the cup, you
A P : 2 4 :075(263) [0411] (John 6:35), 'I am the **bread** of life; he who comes to me
A P : 2 4 :086(265) [0413] they gathered they brought **bread**, wine, and other things.
S 3 : 0 6 :001(311) [0493] We hold that the **bread** and the wine in the Supper are
S 3 : 0 6 :005(311) [0493] of those who teach that **bread** and wine surrender or lose
S 3 : 0 6 :005(311) [0493] appearance and shape of **bread** without any longer being
S 3 : 0 6 :005(311) [0493] any longer being real **bread**, for that bread is and remains
S 3 : 0 6 :005(311) [0493] being real bread, for that **bread** is and remains there
S 3 : 0 6 :005(311) [0493] Paul himself states, "The **bread** which we break" (I Cor.
S 3 : 0 6 :005(311) [0493] and again, "Let a man so eat of the **bread**" (I Cor. 11:28).
S C : 0 3 :012(347) [0547] *"Give us this day our daily **bread**."*
S C : 0 3 :013(347) [0547] sure, God provides daily **bread**, even to the wicked,
S C : 0 3 :013(347) [0547] enable us to receive our daily **bread** with thanksgiving.
S C : 0 3 :014(347) [0547] What is meant by daily **bread**?
S C : 0 6 :002(351) [0555] Jesus Christ, under the **bread** and wine, given to us
S C : 0 6 :004(351) [0555] he was betrayed, took **bread**, and when he had given
L C : P R :013(360) [0571] daily as we need our daily **bread**; we also must use it daily
L C : S P :014(363) [0577] Give us this day our daily **bread**; and forgive us our
L C : S P :023(364) [0579] he was betrayed took **bread**, gave thanks, and broke it
L C : 0 1 :160(387) [0627] the country and grudge them as much as a piece of **bread**.
L C : 0 1 :164(387) [0627] Not only shall they have **bread**, clothing, and money for a
L C : 0 3 :055(427) [0713] here not for a crust of **bread** or for a temporal, perishable
L C : 0 3 :057(428) [0713] them and scarcely venture to ask for a morsel of **bread**.
L C : 0 3 :071(430) [0717] *"Give us this day our daily **bread**."*
L C : 0 3 :072(430) [0717] Here we consider the poor **bread**-basket — the needs of
L C : 0 3 :072(430) [0719] When you pray for "daily **bread**" you pray for everything
L C : 0 3 :072(430) [0719] to have and enjoy daily **bread** and, on the contrary,
L C : 0 3 :072(430) [0719] provide for us our daily **bread** and all kinds of
L C : 0 3 :072(430) [0719] could never take a loaf of **bread** from the oven to set on
L C : 0 3 :073(430) [0719] in this world; only for its sake do we need daily **bread**.
L C : 0 3 :074(430) [0719] God provide us our daily **bread** and all the comforts of
L C : 0 3 :074(430) [0719] prevail, there our daily **bread** is taken away, or at least
L C : 0 3 :075(430) [0719] with a loaf of **bread** instead of a lion or a wreath of rue,
L C : 0 3 :075(430) [0719] of rue, or if a loaf of **bread** were stamped on coins, to
L C : 0 3 :075(430) [0719] we could not have the steady blessing of daily **bread**.
L C : 0 3 :081(431) [0721] receives a morsel of **bread** from God and eats it in peace.
L C : 0 3 :084(432) [0723] oppress the poor and deprive them of their daily **bread**!
L C : 0 3 :113(435) [0729] and will, our daily **bread**, a good and cheerful conscience,
L C : 0 5 :003(447) [0753] *he was betrayed took **bread**, gave thanks, broke it, and*
L C : 0 5 :008(447) [0755] Christ in and under the **bread** and wine which we
L C : 0 5 :009(447) [0755] here that the sacrament is **bread** and wine, but not mere
L C : 0 5 :009(447) [0755] and wine, but not mere **bread** or wine such as is served at
L C : 0 5 :009(447) [0755] It is **bread** and wine comprehended in God's Word and
L C : 0 5 :010(448) [0755] distinguishes it from mere **bread** and wine and constitutes
L C : 0 5 :012(448) [0755] and say, 'How can **bread** and wine be Christ's body and
L C : 0 5 :014(448) [0755] Word, you have nothing but ordinary **bread** and wine.
L C : 0 5 :016(448) [0757] in heaven can transform **bread** and wine into Christ's
L C : 0 5 :018(448) [0757] these words which are coupled with the **bread** and wine."
L C : 0 5 :028(449) [0759] and blustering, "How can **bread** and wine forgive sins or
L C : 0 5 :028(449) [0759] we do not claim this of **bread** and wine — since in itself
L C : 0 5 :028(449) [0759] and wine — since in itself **bread** is bread — but of that
L C : 0 5 :028(449) [0759] — since in itself bread is **bread** — but of that bread and
L C : 0 5 :028(449) [0759] is bread — but of that **bread** and wine which are Christ's
L C : 0 6 :032(461) [0000] They snatch at the **bread** just like a hunted hart, burning
E P : 0 7 :002(481) [0809] are distributed with the **bread** and the wine and if they
E P : 0 7 :003(482) [0809] in the Holy Supper only **bread** and wine are present,
E P : 0 7 :004(482) [0809] Holy Supper nothing but **bread** and wine are present and
E P : 0 7 :005(482) [0809] and there, but not in the **bread** and wine of the Holy
E P : 0 7 :006(482) [0809] truly distributed and received with the **bread** and wine.
E P : 0 7 :007(482) [0811] and not as though the **bread** symbolized the absent body
E P : 0 7 :015(483) [0811] and confess that with the **bread** and wine the body and
E P : 0 7 :015(483) [0813] St. Paul says, "The **bread** which we break, is it not a
E P : 0 7 :015(483) [0813] — that is, whoever eats this **bread** eats the body of Christ.
E P : 0 7 :022(484) [0813] in the papacy that the **bread** and wine in the Holy Supper
E P : 0 7 :026(485) [0815] received orally with the **bread**, but that with the mouth
E P : 0 7 :026(485) [0815] mouth we receive only **bread** and wine and that we
E P : 0 7 :027(485) [0815] 6. That **bread** and wine in the Holy Supper are no more
E P : 0 7 :028(485) [0815] 7. That the **bread** and wine are only figures, images, and
E P : 0 7 :029(485) [0815] 8. That the **bread** and wine are no more than reminders,
E P : 0 7 :029(485) [0815] truly as we eat and drink **bread** and wine in the Supper.
E P : 0 7 :030(485) [0815] by the external signs of **bread** and wine and not by the
E P : 0 7 :036(485) [0815] the body of Christ in the **bread** and wine of the Holy
E P : 0 7 :036(485) [0815] lift their eyes from the **bread** to heaven and there seek the
E P : 0 7 :037(486) [0815] the body and blood of Christ, but only **bread** and wine.
E P : 0 7 :040(486) [0817] visible elements of **bread** and wine in the holy sacrament
E P : 1 2 :024(500) [0843] 5. That **bread** and wine in the Holy Supper are not means
S D : 0 7 :002(569) [0973] distant from the blessed **bread** and wine in the Supper as
S D : 0 7 :003(569) [0973] For just as the **bread** and wine are here on earth and not
S D : 0 7 :003(569) [0973] consequently nothing but **bread** and wine are orally
S D : 0 7 :004(569) [0973] nothing more than mere **bread** and wine, which are only
S D : 0 7 :006(570) [0973] else, and that with the **bread** and wine Christ gives us his
S D : 0 7 :008(570) [0975] united with the **bread** in such a way that as certainly as
S D : 0 7 :008(570) [0975] pious Christians eat the **bread** with their mouths, just so
S D : 0 7 :008(570) [0975] received with the blessed **bread** even by hypocrites or
S D : 0 7 :009(570) [0975] under the forms of **bread** and wine and that they are
S D : 0 7 :010(571) [0975] Jesus Christ, under the **bread** and wine, given to us
S D : 0 7 :011(571) [0975] the visible elements, the **bread** and the wine, to those who
S D : 0 7 :011(571) [0975] when Paul says that the **bread** which we break is a
S D : 0 7 :011(571) [0975] it would follow that the **bread** is a participation not in the
S D : 0 7 :014(571) [0977] and teach that with the **bread** and wine the body and
S D : 0 7 :014(571) [0977] an essential change of the **bread** and wine into the body
S D : 0 7 :014(571) [0977] are locally enclosed in the **bread**, or are in some other
S D : 0 7 :014(572) [0977] sacramental union the **bread** is the body of Christ, etc.
S D : 0 7 :015(572) [0977] from the use, as when the **bread** is laid aside or reserved
S D : 0 7 :018(572) [0979] is distributed with the **bread** in precisely the same way as
S D : 0 7 :019(572) [0979] Articles state that "the **bread** and the wine in the Supper
S D : 0 7 :020(573) [0979] of Christ in and under the **bread** and wine which Christ's
S D : 0 7 :021(573) [0979] it that it is not mere **bread** and wine but is and is called
S D : 0 7 :022(573) [0979] along and ask, How can **bread** and wine be the body and
S D : 0 7 :023(573) [0979] you then have nothing but ordinary **bread** and wine.
S D : 0 7 :024(573) [0981] in heaven, can change **bread** and wine into the body and
S D : 0 7 :026(573) [0981] of these words which are added to the **bread** and wine.'
S D : 0 7 :032(574) [0983] eaten and drunk in the **bread** and wine, though the priests
S D : 0 7 :032(575) [0983] They, indeed have only **bread** and wine, for they do not
S D : 0 7 :033(575) [0983] believe that the Lord's **bread** in the Supper is his true,
S D : 0 7 :035(575) [0983] Christ and of St. Paul (the **bread** in the Lord's Supper "is
S D : 0 7 :035(575) [0983] the formulas "*under* the **bread**, *with* the bread, *in* the
S D : 0 7 :035(575) [0983] formulas "*under* the bread, *with* the **bread**, *in* the bread."
S D : 0 7 :035(575) [0983] formulas "*under* the bread, *with* the bread, *in* the **bread**."
S D : 0 7 :035(575) [0985] substance of the **bread** and the body of Christ.
S D : 0 7 :037(575) [0985] two essences, the natural **bread** and the true natural body
S D : 0 7 :038(576) [0985] blood of Christ with the **bread** and wine is not a personal
S D : 0 7 :038(576) [0985] different formulas, "in the **bread**, under the bread, with
S D : 0 7 :038(576) [0985] "in the bread, under the **bread**, with the bread," they still
S D : 0 7 :038(576) [0985] under the bread, with the **bread**," they still accept the
S D : 0 7 :039(576) [0985] this not as ordinary **bread** or an ordinary beverage, but
S D : 0 7 :044(577) [0987] the blessed and proffered **bread**, "Take, eat, this is my
S D : 0 7 :048(578) [0989] speaking of true, natural **bread** and natural wine as well
S D : 0 7 :048(578) [0989] in meaning) in the word "**bread**," as though the body of
S D : 0 7 :048(578) [0989] of Christ were spiritual **bread** or a spiritual food for the
S D : 0 7 :052(578) [0991] the blessed and proffered **bread** without any
S D : 0 7 :054(579) [0991] The **bread** which we break, is it not a participation in the
S D : 0 7 :054(579) [0991] Supper and not only the **bread** which Christ himself
S D : 0 7 :054(579) [0991] so that all who eat this **bread** and drink the cup truly
S D : 0 7 :055(579) [0991] and operation, then the **bread** could not be called
S D : 0 7 :056(579) [0991] he would not say that the **bread** but that the spirit or faith
S D : 0 7 :056(579) [0991] But he says that the **bread** is participation in the body of
S D : 0 7 :056(579) [0991] who receive the blessed **bread** also partake of the body of
S D : 0 7 :057(579) [0993] of the blessed and broken **bread** in the Supper participate
S D : 0 7 :058(580) [0993] of Christ by saying, "The **bread** which we break is the
S D : 0 7 :058(580) [0993] distributed among those who receive the broken **bread**."
S D : 0 7 :059(580) [0993] write as follows: "The **bread** is participation in the body
S D : 0 7 :060(580) [0993] Paul says, "Who eats the **bread** or drinks the cup of the
S D : 0 7 :060(580) [0993] sins not only against the **bread** and wine, not only against
S D : 0 7 :063(581) [0995] eat and drink the blessed **bread** and wine in the Lord's
S D : 0 7 :064(581) [0995] his disciples natural **bread** and natural wine, which he
S D : 0 7 :075(583) [0999] speak his words over the **bread** and cup and distribute the
S D : 0 7 :075(583) [0999] and distribute the blessed **bread** and cup, Christ himself is

Continued ▶

SD : 07 :076(583) [0999] for us, can make of the **bread** and wine set before us the
SD : 07 :077(583) [0999] and receive ordinary **bread** and wine but his body and
SD : 07 :077(583) [0999] of the world, make the **bread** the body and the wine the
SD : 07 :078(583) [1001] I were to say over all the **bread** there is, 'This is the body
SD : 07 :082(584) [1001] thereby the elements of **bread** and wine are hallowed or
SD : 07 :083(584) [1001] for instance, the blessed **bread** is not distributed,
SD : 07 :084(584) [1001] assembly we take **bread** and wine, consecrate it, distribute
SD : 07 :084(584) [1001] action of the breaking of **bread**, or of the distribution and
SD : 07 :086(584) [1003] oral eating of the blessed **bread** and wine, the body and
SD : 07 :087(585) [1003] in the papistic Mass the **bread** is not distributed but is
SD : 07 :100(586) [1007] locked doors, in the **bread** and wine in the Lord's
SD : 07 :108(588) [1009] consecrated or blessed **bread** and wine in the Holy
SD : 07 :108(588) [1009] only the mere species of **bread** and wine, or their
SD : 07 :108(588) [1009] under the species of the **bread**, which they allege has lost
SD : 07 :108(588) [1009] and is no longer **bread**, the body of Christ is present even
SD : 07 :108(588) [1009] (when, for instance, the **bread** is locked up in the
SD : 07 :114(589) [1011] in the Supper our mouth receives only **bread** and wine.
SD : 07 :115(589) [1011] the teaching that **bread** and wine in the Supper are no
SD : 07 :115(589) [1011] (for example, just as **bread** and wine are external food for
SD : 07 :117(590) [1013] — in other words, only as **bread** and wine have a
SD : 07 :122(590) [1013] the body of Christ in the **bread** and wine of the Supper,
SD : 07 :122(590) [1013] to look away from the **bread** of the Supper and by their
SD : 07 :123(590) [1013] saving faith, receive only **bread** and wine in the Supper
SD : 07 :123(590) [1015] of the church receive only **bread** and wine in the use of
SD : 07 :126(591) [1015] forms of the blessed **bread** and wine) are to be adored.
SD : 12 :032(635) [1101] 4. That the **bread** and wine in the Holy Supper are not

Break (11), Breaking (6), Breaks (5)
AG : 27 :034(076) [0079] Finally, although the **breaking** of monastic vows might be
AP : 04 :236(140) [0185] They are **breaking** up churches.
AP : 12 :031(186) [0259] help until morning; like a lion he **breaks** all my bones."
AP : 22 :007(237) [0359] disciples recognized Christ in the **breaking** of the bread.
AP : 22 :007(237) [0359] other passages that talk about the **breaking** of the bread.
AP : 23 :070(249) [0383] call them to account for **breaking** up marriages and
AP : 23 :071(249) [0383] God's will and Word to **break** up marriages and to issue
S1 : PR :010(290) [0457] everywhere that our hearts would **break** with grief.
S3 : 03 :002(304) [0479] like a hammer which **breaks** the rock in pieces?"
S3 : 06 :005(311) [0493] "The bread which we **break**" (I Cor. 10:16), and again,
S3 : 15 :002(316) [0501] that it is a mortal sin to **break** such precepts of men, this,
LC : 01 :100(379) [0609] is not heard, the devil **breaks** in and does his damage
LC : 03 :090(432) [0723] serve God's purpose to **break** our pride and keep us
LC : 03 :115(435) [0731] He **breaks** many a man's neck and drives others to
EP : 07 :015(483) [0813] "The bread which we **break**, is it not a participation in the
SD : 02 :054(531) [0903] his Word) God is active, **breaks** our hearts, and draws
SD : 07 :011(571) [0975] that the bread which we **break** is a participation in the
SD : 07 :054(579) [0991] The bread which we **break**, is it not a participation in the
SD : 07 :054(579) [0991] but also that which we **break** and bless is participation in
SD : 07 :058(580) [0993] "The bread which we **break** is the distributed body of
SD : 07 :084(584) [1001] the whole action of the **breaking** of bread, or of the
SD : 08 :096(609) [1049] over which all heretics **break** their heads, we admonish

Breasts (1)
LC : 01 :026(368) [0587] he gives to the mother **breasts** and milk for her infant,

Breath (2)
AP : 02 :007(101) [0107] or through the serpent's **breath**, and whether medicine can
AP : 04 :329(158) [0211] flower fades, when the **breath** of the Lord blows upon it";

Bremen (2)
S3 : 15 :005(317) [0501] Likewise I, John Amsterdam, of **Bremen**
TR : 00 :082(335) [0529] John Amsterdam, of **Bremen**, did the same

Brentz (1)
TR : 00 :082(000) [0529] John **Brentz**, Minister of Hall (Triglotta text only)]

Brenz (3)
PR : PR :019(009) [0017] Melanchthon or of [John] **Brenz**, Urban Rhegius, [John
S3 : 15 :005(317) [0501] the name of Master John **Brenz**, who on his departure
TR : 00 :082(335) [0529] in the name of Master John **Brenz**, as he commanded me

Brethren (21)
AP : 04 :097(121) [0149] known to you therefore, **brethren**, that through this man
AP : 04 :232(140) [0185] crude behavior of the **brethren**, to cover up minor
AP : 07 :042(176) [0241] the Passover with the **brethren** who had been converted
AP : 07 :042(176) [0243] one should mind if his **brethren** do not correctly compute
AP : 07 :042(176) [0243] but whenever your **brethren** of the circumcision do,
AP : 07 :043(177) [0243] the example of the chief **brethren** who had been converted
AP : 12 :109(198) [0283] of the reconciliation of **brethren** to each other, for it
S1 : PR :004(289) [0455] but also false **brethren** among those who profess to be
S2 : 04 :001(298) [0471] beside him as Christian **brethren** and companions, as the
S3 : 04 :000(310) [0491] the mutual conversation and consolation of **brethren**.
S3 : 15 :005(317) [0501] and in the name of my **brethren** and of the church of
S3 : 15 :005(317) [0501] I have shown to these **brethren** who have subscribed
TR : 00 :014(322) [0509] by the votes of all the **brethren** and by the judgment of
SC : PR :006(338) [0533] God's sake, my beloved **brethren** who are pastors and
SC : 09 :003(354) [0561] "We beseech you, **brethren**, to respect those who labor
EP : 01 :005(466) [0781] had to be made like his **brethren** in every respect," sin
SD : 01 :043(515) [0873] he was made like us, his **brethren**, sin alone excepted
SD : 01 :043(516) [0873] essence with us, his **brethren**, because the human nature
SD : 08 :050(600) [1031] respect made like its **brethren**, and that for this reason
SD : 08 :087(608) [1047] us as with men and his **brethren**, he wills to be with us in
SD : 10 :011(612) [1055] "But because of false **brethren** secretly brought in, who

Brevity (6)
SD : 02 :018(524) [0887] (to which for the sake of **brevity** we only refer), that the
SD : 03 :067(551) [0937] direct him for the sake of **brevity** to Dr. Luther's
SD : 07 :066(581) [0997] the interest of desirable **brevity** we direct the Christian
SD : 07 :091(586) [1005] for the sake of desirable **brevity**, merely refer the
SD : 07 :128(591) [1015] for the sake of desirable **brevity** we have not wanted to
SD : 08 :086(608) [1047] For the sake of **brevity** we here merely go on record as

Bribe (1), Bribery (1)
LC : 01 :302(405) [0667] great estate, he practices **bribery**, through friendly
SD : 03 :017(542) [0921] acquit the godless for a **bribe**, and deprive the innocent of

Bride (1)
LC : 01 :306(406) [0669] by trickery entice a rich **bride** away from another, for in

Brief (19), Briefer (2), Briefly (31)
PR : PR :003(003) [0007] and that is also **briefly** summarized in the approved
AL : 00 :003(095) [0095] points at issue, being **briefly** set forth, may more readily
AP : 04 :336(159) [0215] a refutation, we shall nevertheless give a **brief** answer.
AP : 04 :345(160) [0217] We shall therefore reply **briefly**.
AP : 04 :356(161) [0217] We shall answer **briefly** and clearly.
AP : 04 :389(166) [0225] However **brief** this discussion may be, we hope that good
AP : 12 :059(190) [0267] enough about this earlier, we shall be **briefer** at this point.
AP : 23 :062(247) [0381] Now we shall **briefly** review their weighty arguments in
AP : 24 :099(268) [0419] We have **briefly** said this about the Mass to let all good
AP : 27 :010(270) [0423] Therefore we shall **briefly** run through a few of our
AP : 27 :020(272) [0425] of sins because of our works, we shall be **briefer** here.
AP : 27 :035(275) [0431] We have discussed this **briefly**, for on the basis of what
AP : 27 :055(278) [0439] and exhort the hearers, **brief** and pointed lessons would
AP : 28 :023(284) [0451] We shall respond to this in **brief**.
TR : 00 :023(324) [0511] we shall respond **briefly** by way of interpretation.
SC : PR :001(338) [0533] me to prepare this **brief** and simple catechism or
SC : PR :014(339) [0535] or choose any other **brief** and fixed explanations which
SC : PR :017(340) [0535] you have thus taught this **brief** catechism, take up a large
SC : 05 :021(350) [0553] Please give me a **brief** form of confession.
LC : PR :018(361) [0573] the Catechism, which is a **brief** compend and summary of
LC : SP :027(364) [0581] and learned manner but **briefly** and very simply, so that it
LC : 01 :051(371) [0595] vain?" you should answer **briefly**: "It is a misuse of God's
LC : 01 :053(371) [0595] To discuss it **briefly**, misuse of the divine name occurs
LC : 01 :062(373) [0597] To repeat very **briefly**, it is either simply to lie and assert
LC : 01 :066(373) [0599] The explanation is **briefly** this: We are not to swear in
LC : 01 :185(390) [0633] **Briefly**, he wishes to have all people defended, delivered,
LC : 01 :188(390) [0633] **Briefly**, then, to impress it unmistakably upon the
LC : 02 :001(411) [0679] and receive from God; in **brief**, it teaches us to know him
LC : 02 :006(411) [0679] to children, we shall **briefly** sum up the entire Creed in
LC : 02 :007(411) [0679] Hence the Creed may be **briefly** comprised in these few
LC : 02 :008(411) [0679] Let us **briefly** comment on these words.
LC : 02 :010(411) [0679] These words give us a **brief** description of God the
LC : 02 :024(413) [0683] Such, very **briefly**, is the meaning of this article.
LC : 02 :026(413) [0685] but in order to treat it **briefly** and simply, we shall take up
LC : 02 :027(414) [0685] Jesus Christ?" answer **briefly**, "I believe that Jesus Christ,
LC : 02 :032(415) [0687] different points is not the **brief** children's sermons, but
LC : 03 :034(425) [0707] we shall treat the Lord's Prayer very **briefly** and clearly.
LC : 03 :072(430) [0717] It is a **brief** and simple word, but very comprehensive.
LC : 03 :073(430) [0719] To put it **briefly**, this petition includes everything that
LC : 03 :076(431) [0719] Let us outline very **briefly** how comprehensively this
LC : 03 :119(436) [0731] Thus God has **briefly** set before us all the afflictions that
LC : 04 :001(436) [0733] to have at least some **brief**, elementary instruction in them
LC : 04 :048(442) [0743] To this we reply **briefly**: Let the simple dismiss this
LC : 05 :020(449) [0757] We have **briefly** considered the first part, namely, the
LC : 05 :033(450) [0761] **Briefly**, as we said above concerning Baptism and in many
LC : 06 :000(457) [0000] A **Brief** Exhortation to Confession [Tappert Only]
EP : RN :003(465) [0777] symbols (that is, **brief** and explicit confessions) which
EP : 11 :015(496) [0835] 14. This **brief** exposition of the doctrine of God's eternal
EP : 11 :022(497) [0837] This is a **brief** and simple explanation of the various
SD : RN :004(504) [0851] out of God's Word in **brief** articles or chapters against the
SD : 01 :016(511) [0865] For this reason we shall **briefly** enumerate the contrary
SD : 07 :017(572) [0979] true meaning is set forth **briefly** and precisely in words

Bright (1), Brighter (1)
AP : 04 :299(153) [0205] Christ's glory becomes **brighter** when we teach men to
LC : 05 :056(453) [0767] lantern in contrast to the **bright** sun, or as dung in

Brilliant (3)
LC : 01 :093(377) [0607] matter how splendid and **brilliant** it may appear, or even
LC : 01 :102(379) [0609] pleased than by any work of hypocrisy, however **brilliant**.
SD : 05 :001(558) [0951] Gospel is an especially **brilliant** light which serves the

Bring (68), Bringing (1), Brings (49), Brought (45)
PR : PR :002(003) [0007] of the Word that alone **brings** salvation to appear to our
PR : PR :004(004) [0007] and discord and to **bring** about destructive and
PR : PR :011(006) [0011] might be settled and **brought** to a conclusion without
PR : PR :013(007) [0013] careful diligence, they **brought** together in good order, by
PR : PR :024(013) [0023] Word of his that alone **brings** salvation, to the tranquillity
AG : PR :020(026) [0041] offered to promote and **bring** about the calling of such a
AG : PR :023(027) [0043] charitably settled, and **brought** to Christian concord in
AG : 26 :010(065) [0071] his wife and children and **bring** them up in the fear of
AL : 02 :002(029) [0043] even now damns and **brings** eternal death on those who
AL : 06 :001(031) [0045] that this faith is bound to **bring** forth good fruits and that
AL : 20 :029(045) [0057] new affections as to be able to **bring** forth good works.
AL : 24 :016(057) [0067] the disturbance was **brought** about by nothing else than
AL : 25 :004(062) [0069] of the great consolation it **brings** to terrified consciences,
AL : 26 :010(065) [0071] that a father should **bring** up his children, that a mother
AL : 26 :012(065) [0071] third place, traditions **brought** great dangers to
AL : 27 :022(074) [0079] one pleases, it cannot be **brought** about that a vow
AP : PR :017(099) [0103] we have undoubtedly **brought** into view many articles of
AP : 02 :029(104) [0113] He means that at birth we **bring** along an ignorance of
AP : 02 :030(104) [0113] lust at work in our members and **bringing** forth evil fruit.
AP : 02 :032(104) [0113] we have cleansed and **brought** to light important
AP : 04 :002(107) [0121] the honor of Christ and **brings** to pious consciences the
AP : 04 :036(112) [0131] human nature cannot **bring** itself to love a wrathful,
AP : 04 :038(112) [0131] Paul says (Rom. 4:15), "The law **brings** wrath."
AP : 04 :044(113) [0133] This faith **brings** to God a trust not in our own merits,
AP : 04 :045(113) [0133] Thus it regenerates us and **brings** us the Holy Spirit, so
AP : 04 :062(115) [0139] Amid such fears this faith **brings** peace of mind, consoles
AP : 04 :064(116) [0139] but frees us from death, **brings** forth a new life in our
AP : 04 :064(116) [0139] but whenever it appears it **brings** forth good fruits, as we
AP : 04 :100(121) [0151] faith quickens because it **brings** forth peace, joy, and
AP : 04 :116(123) [0155] acceptable to God, and **brings** the Holy Spirit, it should
AP : 04 :125(124) [0157] Since faith **brings** the Holy Spirit and produces a new life
AP : 04 :132(125) [0159] and the Holy Spirit, to **bring** forth in us eternal
AP : 04 :146(127) [0163] nature continually **brings** forth evil desires, though the
AP : 04 :204(135) [0177] The law always accuses them and **brings** forth wrath.
AP : 04 :236(140) [0185] up to them, they would **bring** peace to both church and

Continued ▶

A P : 0 4 :241(141) [0187] which would never have **brought** on civil war if either had
A P : 0 4 :247(142) [0191] "Of his own will he **brought** us forth by the word of truth
A P : 0 4 :249(142) [0191] is dead, but it is alive when it **brings** forth good works.
A P : 0 4 :262(145) [0195] complete penitence and **bring** out the promise, "Redeem
A P : 0 4 :263(146) [0195] Reborn in this way, they **bring** forth fruits worthy of
A P : 0 4 :265(146) [0197] the merit of these works **brings** forgiveness of sins and
A P : 0 4 :270(147) [0197] of the law, "for the law **brings** wrath" (Rom. 4:15).
A P : 0 4 :298(153) [0205] can anybody possibly **bring** against this proof unless he
A P : 0 4 :303(154) [0205] teaching and that it will **bring** godly and wholesome
A P : 0 4 :314(156) [0207] about the whole issue and **bring** consolation to
A P : 0 4 :343(160) [0217] men can easily judge when they are **brought** to light.
A P : 0 4 :387(166) [0225] this faith, for it **brings** the fullest comfort in all afflictions
A P : 0 7 :015(170) [0231] But the Gospel **brings** not the shadow of eternal things
A P : 0 7 :025(173) [0235] pope for which no one has ever been **brought** to trial.
A P : 1 1 :002(180) [0249] and in the beginning **brought** Luther the highest praise of
A P : 1 2 :007(183) [0255] is there that will finally **bring** peace to the conscience?
A P : 1 2 :050(189) [0265] "The Lord kills and **brings** to life; he brings down to
A P : 1 2 :050(189) [0265] kills and brings to life; he **brings** down to Sheol and
A P : 1 2 :060(190) [0269] us from our terrors and **brings** forth peace, joy, and a new
A P : 1 2 :073(192) [0273] that the Holy Spirit **brings** in your heart, saying, 'Your
A P : 1 2 :084(194) [0277] that this position of ours **brings** devout consciences a firm
A P : 1 2 :088(195) [0277] As Paul says (Rom. 4:15), "The law **brings** wrath."
A P : 1 2 :113(199) [0285] antiquated, nor need we **bring** them back because they
A P : 1 2 :138(203) [0293] remission removes eternal death and **brings** eternal life.
A P : 1 2 :150(206) [0299] measure; not in thy anger, lest thou **bring** me to nothing."
A P : 1 2 :155(207) [0301] In rebuttal they **bring** up the case of Adam, and of David
A P : 1 2 :164(208) [0303] faith, and good fruits — **brings** about the mitigation of
A P : 1 5 :046(221) [0327] this mortification **brought** on by the cross, a
A P : 1 5 :049(221) [0329] as necessary, they **bring** exquisite torture to a conscience
A P : 1 6 :008(223) [0333] to see that the Gospel **brings** eternal righteousness to
A P : 2 1 :037(234) [0353] imitate the epics and **bring** only superstitious examples of
A P : 2 3 :008(240) [0367] the earth did not begin to **bring** forth plants only at the
A P : 2 4 :007(250) [0385] of the mendicant friars **brought** on the multiplication of
A P : 2 4 :013(251) [0387] and scholastics have **brought** this pharisaic notion into
A P : 2 4 :025(253) [0391] on behalf of those who **bring** them, nor can they be
A P : 2 4 :025(254) [0391] Those who **bring** them are already reconciled.
A P : 2 4 :085(265) [0413] of the Passover had to **bring** some gift as a contribution.
A P : 2 4 :086(265) [0413] when they gathered they **brought** bread, wine, and other
A P : 2 8 :023(284) [0451] of sins for Christ's sake, **brings** enough good to hide all
S 2 : 0 2 :011(294) [0465] that is, the Mass — has **brought** forth a brood of vermin
S 3 : 0 2 :005(303) [0479] by Rom. 4:15, "The law **brings** wrath," and Rom. 5:20,
T R : 0 0 :048(328) [0519] from the glory of God and **bring** destruction to souls.
T R : 0 0 :070(332) [0525] neighboring church, was **brought** in to confirm the
S C : 0 1 :014(343) [0541] money or property, nor **bring** them into our possession by
S C : 0 9 :008(356) [0563] become discouraged, but **bring** them up in the discipline
L C : 0 1 :038(369) [0591] When they are rebuked, to **bring** them to their senses and
L C : 0 1 :041(370) [0591] For it **brings** you either eternal blessing, happiness, and
L C : 0 1 :061(373) [0597] so that they may be **brought** up not merely with
L C : 0 1 :075(375) [0601] methods like these we may **bring** up our youth in the fear
L C : 0 1 :076(375) [0601] would be the right way to **bring** up children, so long as
L C : 0 1 :118(381) [0615] their religion they could **bring** before God a single work
L C : 0 1 :137(384) [0619] allow themselves to be **brought** up in kindness;
L C : 0 1 :137(384) [0619] punishment of God they **bring** upon themselves the
L C : 0 1 :138(384) [0621] some of them were **brought** up well and revered their
L C : 0 1 :141(384) [0621] is unable by himself to **bring** up his child, he calls upon a
L C : 0 1 :168(388) [0629] etc., but especially to **bring** them up to the praise and
L C : 0 1 :174(388) [0629] of losing divine grace, to **bring** up his children in the fear
L C : 0 1 :175(389) [0631] who would faithfully **bring** up their children and servants
L C : 0 1 :176(389) [0631] in this respect and fail to **bring** up your children to
L C : 0 1 :176(389) [0631] You **bring** upon yourself sin and wrath, thus earning hell
L C : 0 1 :181(389) [0631] in Moses, parents had to **bring** their own children to
L C : 0 1 :207(393) [0639] children, and support and **bring** them up to the glory of
L C : 0 1 :208(393) [0639] to him that persons be **brought** up to serve the world,
L C : 0 1 :218(394) [0643] youth that they will be **brought** up to decency and respect
L C : 0 1 :247(398) [0651] and defy this, see whom you have **brought** upon yourself.
L C : 0 1 :270(401) [0657] I reply: "Why don't you **bring** it before the regular
L C : 0 1 :273(401) [0659] one who otherwise would **bring** some poor man into
L C : 0 1 :280(403) [0661] If this does not help, then **bring** the matter before the
L C : 0 1 :284(403) [0661] person as one who has **brought** disgrace upon himself,
L C : 0 1 :290(404) [0663] God most highly and **bring** abundant blessings, if only
L C : 0 1 :330(410) [0677] this so that they may be **brought** up, not only with blows
L C : 0 2 :014(412) [0681] the earth and all that it **brings** forth, birds and fish,
L C : 0 2 :031(414) [0685] that is, he who has **brought** us back from the devil to
L C : 0 2 :031(414) [0685] in order to win us and **bring** us under his dominion.
L C : 0 2 :037(415) [0687] church, where he preaches to us and **brings** us to Christ.
L C : 0 2 :039(415) [0689] is nothing else than to **bring** us to the Lord Christ to
L C : 0 2 :052(417) [0691] I was **brought** to it by the Holy Spirit and incorporated
L C : 0 2 :062(419) [0695] believe in him who daily **brings** us into this community
L C : 0 2 :064(419) [0695] his Holy Spirit, through whom he **brings** us to himself.
L C : 0 2 :068(420) [0697] But the Creed **brings** pure grace and makes us upright
L C : 0 3 :029(424) [0705] like to see the people **brought** again to pray rightly and
L C : 0 3 :051(426) [0711] power of the devil and to **bring** us to himself and rule us
L C : 0 3 :063(428) [0715] flight, cut us down, and **bring** us once more under his
L C : 0 3 :080(431) [0721] men with his lies and **bring** them under his power, but he
L C : 0 4 :023(439) [0737] that is, what benefits, gifts, and effects it **brings**.
L C : 0 4 :030(440) [0739] by the senses and thus **brought** into the heart, just as the
L C : 0 4 :041(441) [0743] Baptism promises and **brings** — victory over death and
L C : 0 4 :043(442) [0743] here in Baptism there is **brought** free to every man's door
L C : 0 4 :057(444) [0747] We **bring** the child with the purpose and hope that he
L C : 0 5 :027(449) [0759] Lord's Supper is given to **bring** us new strength and
L C : 0 5 :066(454) [0769] us all the treasure he **brought** from heaven for us, to
L C : 0 5 :084(456) [0773] How quickly can he **bring** you into misery and distress
L C : 0 5 :085(456) [0773] people who ought to be **brought** up in Christian doctrine
L C : 0 5 :086(456) [0773] so that they in turn may **bring** up their children
L C : 0 6 :006(457) [0000] let the pope or his like **bring** them back into subjection
L C : 0 6 :032(460) [0000] If I **bring** you to this point, I have also brought you to
L C : 0 6 :032(460) [0000] you to this point, I have also **brought** you to confession.
E P : 0 3 :007(474) [0793] likewise, "Who shall **bring** any charge against God's elect?
E P : 1 1 :005(495) [0833] salvation, for he alone **brings** it about and ordains
E P : 1 2 :003(498) [0839] the virgin Mary, but **brought** them with him from
S D : R N :005(504) [0851] has in these last days **brought** to light the truth of his
S D : 0 1 :027(513) [0867] wounding which Satan **brought** about, this loss has so
S D : 0 2 :004(520) [0881] of the Word of God) and **brings** them to the saving
S D : 0 2 :006(521) [0883] and by God's grace to **bring** it to an end, we submit the
S D : 0 2 :036(528) [0895] The Holy Spirit has **brought** me thereto and has
S D : 0 2 :038(528) [0895] through the ministry he **brings** us into the church,
S D : 0 2 :042(529) [0897] enlightens, sanctifies, and **brings** us to Christ in true faith
S D : 0 2 :071(535) [0909] II Cor. 3:4-12) to **bring** it about that God in his
S D : 0 2 :073(535) [0909] Whether conversion is **brought** about through coercion,
S D : 0 3 :017(542) [0921] "Who shall **bring** any charge against God's elect?
S D : 0 3 :020(542) [0921] when the Holy Spirit has **brought** a person to faith and
S D : 0 4 :010(552) [0941] and all our powers, and **brings** the Holy Spirit with it.
S D : 0 4 :017(554) [0943] freely (Ps. 110:3), who **bring** free-will offerings (Ps. 54:6),
S D : 0 5 :024(562) [0961] of the unrepentant and **bring** them to a knowledge of
S D : 0 6 :001(563) [0963] people, (2) and to **bring** people to a knowledge of their sin
S D : 0 6 :012(566) [0967] both offices, "he kills and **brings** to life, he brings down
S D : 0 6 :012(566) [0967] kills and brings to life, he **brings** down into Sheol, and
S D : 0 7 :047(578) [0989] certainly accomplish and **bring** to pass whatever he
S D : 0 7 :076(583) [0999] and until his return it **brings** about that his true body and
S D : 0 7 :077(583) [0999] institution can and does **bring** it about that we do not
S D : 1 0 :005(611) [1053] religions have been **brought** into agreement and become
S D : 1 0 :011(612) [1055] of false brethren secretly **brought** in, who slipped in to
S D : 1 0 :011(612) [1057] Jesus, that they might **bring** us into bondage: to whom we
S D : 1 1 :023(619) [1069] and effective working to **bring** them to salvation and to
S D : 1 1 :026(620) [1071] of his will" and has **brought** it forth through Christ so
S D : 1 1 :045(624) [1079] purpose" how he would **bring** me thereto and keep me
S D : 1 1 :048(624) [1079] comfort, create hope, and **bring** everything to such an
S D : 1 2 :025(635) [1099] from the virgin Mary but **brought** it along from heaven.

Brixius (2)
S 3 : 1 5 :005(317) [0501] I, **Brixius** Northanus, minister of the church of Christ
T R : 0 0 :082(335) [0529] **Brixius** Northanus, minister in Soest

Broad (4), Broader (1)
S 1 : P R :013(291) [0459] with albs, great tonsures, **broad** cinctures, bishops' and
L C : 0 1 :296(405) [0665] (though they also have a **broader** and higher application)
L C : 0 2 :033(415) [0687] and it is so rich and **broad** that we can never learn it
L C : 0 3 :072(430) [0719] the flour bin, but also the **broad** fields and the whole land
S D : 0 5 :005(559) [0953] "Gospel" is used in its **broad** sense and apart from the

Broadcast (2)
A P : 1 2 :141(204) [0295] that the devil has **broadcast** in the church to suppress the
A P : 1 6 :004(223) [0331] because the monks had **broadcast** many dangerous ideas

Broke (8), Broken (7)
A G : 2 3 :012(053) [0063] of priests but also **broke** up the marriages which were of
A G : 2 7 :034(076) [0081] marriage of those who **broke** them should be dissolved.
A P : 2 4 :029(255) [0393] acceptable to God is a **broken** spirit; a broken and
A P : 2 4 :029(255) [0393] God is a broken spirit; a **broken** and contrite heart, O
S C : 0 6 :004(351) [0555] he had given thanks, he **broke** it, and gave it to the
L C : S P :023(364) [0579] bread, gave thanks, and **broke** it and gave it to his
L C : 0 1 :068(373) [0599] in the case of many who **broke** their promise of marriage;
L C : 0 1 :137(384) [0619] be hanged, beheaded, or **broken** on the wheel if not
L C : 0 3 :070(429) [0717] For if their will were not **broken** and frustrated, the
L C : 0 5 :003(447) [0753] *took bread, gave thanks,* ***broke*** *it, and gave it to his*
S D : P R :004(502) [0847] when great controversies **broke** out, and orthodox
S D : 0 4 :034(556) [0949] he says, "They were **broken** off because of their unbelief,
S D : 0 7 :054(579) [0991] which Christ himself **broke** and distributed, but also that
S D : 0 7 :057(579) [0993] of the blessed and **broken** bread in the Supper participate
S D : 0 7 :058(580) [0993] distributed among those who receive the **broken** bread."

Bronstedt (1)
P R : P R :027(015) [0025] Bruno, count of Mansfeld [-**Bronstedt**]

Brood (5)
S 2 : 0 2 :011(294) [0465] — has brought forth a **brood** of vermin and the poison of
S 3 : 0 3 :032(308) [0489] not need to repent, you **brood** of vipers, who has given
S D : 0 2 :058(532) [0905] as a hen gathers her **brood** under her wings, and you
S D : 1 1 :052(625) [1081] our own conclusions and **brood**, but we are to adhere
S D : 1 1 :055(625) [1081] draw conclusions, or **brood** over it, but cling solely to his

Brook (1)
L C : 0 4 :061(444) [0747] only as water in the **brook** or in the pot, and magistrates

Broth (1)
L C : 0 3 :057(427) [0713] gifts, and the fool asked only for a dish of beggar's **broth**.

Brother (12), Brotherly (2), Brothers (9)
A G : 2 3 :025(055) [0065] they do not give their **brothers** and sisters occasion for
A L : 2 3 :025(055) [0065] they should give no offense to their **brothers** and sisters."
A P : 1 1 :008(181) [0251] the proper priest, when **brothers** did not act as brothers in
A P : 1 1 :008(181) [0251] brothers did not act as **brothers** in their fight about
A P : 2 1 :002(229) [0343] was still alive, to pray for his **brothers** after his departure.
A P : 2 7 :028(274) [0429] who have forsaken home and **brothers** (Matt. 19:29)."
A P : 2 7 :040(276) [0433] parents or wife or **brothers** is a work we should do
S 2 : 0 4 :002(298) [0471] dares to call the pope **"brother,"** as was then customary,
L C : 0 1 :105(379) [0611] With respect to **brothers**, sisters, and neighbors in general
L C : 0 1 :275(402) [0659] parents, even **brothers** and sisters and other good friends
L C : 0 1 :276(402) [0659] Christ says, "If your **brother** sins against you, go and tell
L C : 0 1 :278(402) [0661] And that would be the **brotherly** thing to say, for the evil
L C : 0 1 :278(402) [0661] "If he listens to you, you have gained your **brother**."
L C : 0 1 :278(402) [0661] Do you think it is an insignificant thing to gain a **brother**?
L C : 0 1 :278(402) [0661] can make the boast that they have gained one **brother**!
L C : 0 1 :305(406) [0669] King Herod took his **brother**'s wife while the latter was
L C : 0 5 :083(456) [0773] more need to lament both to God and to your **brother**.
L C : 0 6 :013(458) [0000] which takes place privately before a single **brother**.
L C : 0 6 :013(458) [0000] our complaint before a **brother**, seeking his advice,
E P : 0 1 :005(466) [0781] and according to our flesh has truly become our **brother**.
S D : 0 8 :078(607) [1043] to which he is our **brother** and we flesh of his flesh and
S D : 0 8 :087(608) [1047] by which he is our **brother** and we are flesh of his flesh.
S D : 1 1 :073(628) [1087] patience, and **brotherly** love, and should diligently seek to

Brotherhoods (2)
A G : 2 0 :003(041) [0053] appointed fasts, holy days, **brotherhoods**, etc.
A L : 2 0 :003(041) [0053] days, prescribed fasts, **brotherhoods**, pilgrimages, services

Bruise (1), Bruised (1)
SD : 0 5 :023(562) [0959] woman's seed, who would **bruise** the serpent's head;
SD : 0 5 :023(562) [0959] our transgressions and **bruised** for our iniquities and with

Bruno (1)
PR : PR :027(015) [0025] **Bruno**, count of Mansfeld [-Bronstedt]

Brunswick (6)
PR : PR :027(014) [0025] Julius, duke of **Brunswick** [-Wolfenbuettel] and
PR : PR :027(014) [0025] Otto, duke of **Brunswick** and Lueneburg [-Harburg]
PR : PR :027(014) [0025] the Younger, duke of **Brunswick** [-Wolfenbuettel] and
PR : PR :027(014) [0025] the Younger, duke of **Brunswick** and Lueneburg
PR : PR :027(014) [0025] Wolf, duke of **Brunswick** [-Grubenhagen] and
PR : PR :027(016) [0027] The Council of the City of **Brunswick**

Brushed (1)
LC : 0 1 :112(380) [0613] it is utterly despised and **brushed** aside, and no one

Brutes (1)
LC : 0 1 :033(369) [0589] themselves to luck, like **brutes** who think that it makes no

Bucer (3)
TR : 0 0 :082(334) [0529] Martin **Bucer**
TR : 0 0 :082(000) [0529] made at Wittenberg with Dr. **Bucer** and others.
SD : 0 7 :013(571) [0977] heard how Master Martin **Bucer** has explained his

Bugenhagen (5)
PR : PR :019(009) [0017] Urban Rhegius, [John **Bugenhagen**] of Pomerania, and
S 3 : 1 5 :005(316) [0501] Dr. John **Bugenhagen**, of Pomerania, subscribed
S 3 : 1 5 :005(317) [0501] I, Dr. John **Bugenhagen** of Pomerania, again subscribe
TR : 0 0 :082(334) [0529] I, Dr. John **Bugenhagen**, of Pomerania, subscribe the
TR : 0 0 :082(000) [0529] man, Dr. John **Bugenhagen**, most revered Father in

Build (7), Builders (2), Building (10), Buildings (1), Built (9)
AG : 1 8 :005(040) [0051] or undress, whether to **build** a house, take a wife, engage
AG : 2 8 :026(084) [0087] Lord has given me for **building** up and not for tearing
AG : 2 8 :042(088) [0089] authority was given for **building** up and not for tearing
AL : 1 8 :005(040) [0051] to clothe oneself, will to **build** a house, will to marry, will
AL : 2 8 :026(084) [0087] me is the authority for **building** up and not for tearing
AL : 2 8 :042(088) [0089] authority was given for **building** up and not for tearing
AP : 0 4 :098(121) [0149] was rejected by you **builders**, but which has become the
AP : 0 4 :235(140) [0185] text this way: "Just as a **building** is said to be perfect or
AP : 0 4 :239(141) [0187] come to Christ and to be **built** upon Christ, and he adds
AP : 0 7 :020(172) [0233] weak people in it who **build** on this foundation perishing
AP : 0 7 :021(172) [0233] of the holy Fathers show that even they sometimes **built**
AP : 1 2 :177(210) [0307] authority, which the Lord gave for **building** you up."
AP : 2 3 :009(241) [0367] ordinance which God has **built** into nature, and human
AP : 2 3 :039(244) [0375] before God than **building** makes an architect, so the
S 3 : 0 3 :039(309) [0489] and everything that is **built** on our good works, for all of
S 3 : 0 3 :039(309) [0489] Accordingly the entire **building**, even when it is most holy
TR : 0 0 :022(323) [0511] and on this rock I will **build** my church" (Matt. 16:18).
TR : 0 0 :025(324) [0511] "On this rock I will **build** my church" (Matt. 16:18), it is
TR : 0 0 :025(324) [0511] that the church is not **built** on the authority of a man but
TR : 0 0 :028(325) [0511] and not "on Peter," for he **built** his church not on the man
TR : 0 0 :029(325) [0513] On this rock of confession, therefore, the church is **built**.
TR : 0 0 :067(331) [0523] work of ministry and for **building** up the body of Christ.
LC : 0 1 :314(407) [0671] and magnificent **buildings**, they are so adorned that
LC : 0 2 :048(416) [0691] a group of people but a consecrated house or **building**.
LC : 0 3 :061(428) [0715] need not only for good **builders** and rulers, but also for
LC : 0 4 :056(443) [0747] nevertheless I cannot **build** on the fact that I believe and
LC : 0 4 :056(444) [0747] On this I **build**, that it is thy Word and command."
EP : 1 2 :005(498) [0839] the most part this piety is **built** on one's own individual
SD : 0 7 :106(588) [1009] in the Holy Supper is **built** upon the truth and

Bull (3), Bulls (6)
AP : 0 4 :397(167) [0227] The **bull** of Leo X has condemned a very necessary
AP : 1 2 :067(191) [0271] forgiveness of sins in his **bull**, and our opponents
AP : 2 4 :022(253) [0391] that the blood of **bulls** and goats should take away sins."
AP : 2 4 :029(255) [0393] victims and requires prayer: "Do I eat the flesh of **bulls**?
S 2 : 0 4 :004(298) [0473] All the pope's **bulls** and books, in which he roars like a
S 3 : 0 3 :025(307) [0485] to yield money and the **bull** market became profitable,
S 3 : 0 3 :026(307) [0487] indulgences for the dead through **bulls** and jubilee years.
S 3 : 0 3 :027(307) [0487] when he declared in his **bulls**, "Whoever wishes to benefit
LC : 0 4 :009(437) [0733] with his letters and **bulls** and consecrated altars and

Bulwark (1)
LC : 0 3 :069(429) [0717] petition, shall be our **bulwark**, against which the others

Burden (31), Burdened (14), Burdening (4), Burdens (9), Burdensome (3)
PR : PR :018(009) [0017] ministers the onerous **burden** of their pretense that we are
AG : 1 5 :002(036) [0049] consciences may not be **burdened** by the notion that such
AG : 2 2 :011(050) [0061] it is not proper to **burden** the consciences of those who
AG : 2 6 :012(065) [0071] out to be a grievous **burden** to consciences, for it was not
AG : 2 6 :017(066) [0073] that consciences were **burdened** with so many traditions,
AG : 2 6 :028(068) [0073] Here Peter forbids the **burdening** of consciences with
AG : 2 6 :041(070) [0075] to be observed without **burdening** consciences, which is to
AG : 2 7 :004(071) [0077] and such fetters and **burdens** were laid on many before
AG : 2 7 :008(072) [0077] what scandals and **burdened** consciences resulted.
AG : 2 8 :002(081) [0083] forms of worship and **burdened** consciences with reserved
AG : 2 8 :039(087) [0089] and similar things and **burden** Christendom with the
AG : 2 8 :049(089) [0091] have the power to **burden** the churches with countless
AG : 2 8 :056(090) [0091] should not be **burdened** by contending that such things
AG : 2 8 :065(092) [0093] apostles did not wish to **burden** consciences with such
AG : 2 8 :072(093) [0093] certain unreasonable **burdens** which did not exist in the
AL : 1 5 :002(036) [0049] are admonished not to **burden** consciences with such
AL : 2 5 :007(062) [0069] should not be **burdened** with a scrupulous enumeration
AL : 2 6 :017(066) [0073] also forbids the **burdening** of consciences with such
AL : 2 6 :028(068) [0073] Here Peter forbids the **burdening** of consciences with
AL : 2 8 :002(081) [0083] forms of worship and **burdened** consciences with
AL : 2 8 :039(087) [0089] and similar things and **burden** the church with the
AL : 2 8 :041(087) [0089] This is the origin of such **burdens** as this, that it is a
AL : 2 8 :049(089) [0091] bishops have the right to **burden** consciences with such
AL : 2 8 :056(090) [0091] should not be **burdened** by suggesting that they are
AL : 2 8 :065(092) [0093] apostles did not wish to **burden** consciences with such
AL : 2 8 :072(093) [0093] that they relax unjust **burdens** which are new and were
AP : 0 4 :210(136) [0179] *operato* and removes the **burden** of guilt and punishment
AP : 0 4 :233(140) [0185] if bishops impose heavy **burdens** on the people or have no
AP : 0 7 :039(176) [0241] want to impose such a **burden** on consciences, nor to
AP : 1 2 :031(186) [0259] over my head; they weigh like a **burden** too heavy for me.
AP : 1 2 :175(210) [0307] of public penitence so as not to **burden** men too heavily.
AP : 1 5 :031(219) [0323] charges that to put this **burden** on the church is a great
AP : 2 1 :044(236) [0357] — ways that will not **burden** faithful consciences nor
AP : 2 3 :042(245) [0375] of celibacy in order to **burden** consciences with these
AP : 2 3 :043(245) [0375] which is often so **burdensome** to good men that domestic
AP : 2 3 :051(246) [0377] men from approving a **burden** that has destroyed so many
AP : 2 3 :052(246) [0377] complaining about this **burden** for a long time, either for
AP : 2 4 :099(268) [0419] of the Mass lest they **burden** themselves with other men's
AP : 2 8 :003(281) [0445] they impose intolerable **burdens** on them, as though they
AP : 2 8 :008(282) [0445] bishops have the right to **burden** consciences with such
AP : 2 8 :008(282) [0445] and enlarging on the sin of those who **burden** the church.
AP : 2 8 :011(283) [0447] as righteousness or to **burden** consciences so that their
S 3 : 0 3 :025(307) [0485] eager to be delivered from the heavy, unbearable **burden**.
S 3 : 1 1 :001(314) [0499] to prohibit marriage and **burden** the divine estate of
TR : 0 0 :011(321) [0507] over the church, nor **burden** the church with traditions,
SC : PR :027(341) [0539] It subjects us to greater **burdens** and labors, dangers and
SC : 0 5 :024(350) [0555] that his conscience is **burdened** by such or by greater
SC : 0 5 :029(351) [0555] consciences are heavily **burdened** or who are distressed
LC : PR :003(358) [0567] delivered from so many **burdens** and troubles, and they
LC : 0 1 :240(397) [0649] New **burdens** and high prices are imposed.
LC : 0 1 :249(398) [0651] the poor may not be **burdened** and oppressed and in
LC : 0 5 :073(455) [0771] until you are rid of your **burden** in order to come to the
LC : 0 6 :001(457) [0000] and from the intolerable **burden** he imposed upon the
LC : 0 6 :002(457) [0000] Moreover, it so greatly **burdened** and tortured
LC : 0 6 :017(459) [0000] us but it also became **burdensome** and bitter, to the
SD : 0 7 :068(582) [0997] of the body of Christ **burden** themselves with judgment
SD : 1 0 :021(614) [1061] over the church, nor **burden** the church with traditions,
SD : 1 1 :010(618) [1067] themselves with **burdensome** doubts and say: "Since God
SD : 1 1 :070(627) [1085] wants to be saved should **burden** and torture himself with
SD : 1 1 :070(627) [1085] men who are laden and **burdened** with sin to come to him
SD : 1 1 :089(631) [1093] and calls all poor, **burdened**, and heavy-laden sinners to

Burghausen (1)
PR : PR :027(015) [0025] Otto, count of Hoya [-Nienburg] and **Burghausen**

Burn (1), Burned (1), Burning (6), Burns (1), Burnt (5)
AP : 0 4 :207(135) [0177] 7:22, "I did not command concerning **burnt** offerings."
AP : 2 3 :054(246) [0379] in the flood and the **burning** of Sodom and Gomorrah
AP : 2 4 :021(253) [0391] sacrifices for sin or **burnt** offerings for trespasses.
AP : 2 4 :028(254) [0393] command them concerning **burnt** offerings and sacrifices.
AP : 2 4 :028(254) [0393] the fathers concerning **burnt** offerings and sacrifices, but
AP : 2 4 :029(255) [0393] Ps. 51:16, 17 says, "Thou hast no delight in **burnt** offering
AP : 2 4 :036(257) [0397] of this daily sacrifice, the **burning** of the lamb, the drink
AP : 2 4 :036(257) [0397] The **burning** of the lamb symbolizes the death of Christ.
S 2 : 0 2 :010(294) [0465] would suffer myself to be **burned** to ashes before I would
S 3 : 0 8 :011(313) [0497] appear first through the **burning** bush and the spoken
LC : PR :011(360) [0571] the power of God which **burns** the devil and gives us
LC : 0 1 :244(398) [0649] by way of thanks they **burn** and ravage house and home
LC : 0 1 :314(407) [0671] There is **burning** of incense, singing and ringing of bells,
LC : 0 6 :032(461) [0000] just like a hunted hart, **burning** with heat and thirst, as

Burst (1)
S 1 : PR :012(290) [0459] Usury and avarice have **burst** in like a deluge and have

Bury (4), Burial (2), Burials (2), Buried (14)
AG : 0 3 :003(030) [0045] and was **buried** in order to be a sacrifice not only for
AG : 0 0 :002(095) [0095] of confessions, about **burials**, about sermons on special
AL : 0 3 :002(030) [0045] was crucified, dead, and **buried**, that he might reconcile
AL : 0 0 :002(095) [0095] rights, confessions, **burials**, and countless other things.
AP : 0 4 :018(109) [0125] Thus they **bury** Christ; men should not use him as
AP : 0 4 :081(118) [0143] Christ were completely **buried**, they imagine that we have
AP : 0 4 :081(118) [0143] Does this not **bury** Christ completely and do away with
AP : 1 2 :016(184) [0257] of faith in Christ and of the blessing of Christ lies **buried**.
AP : 2 7 :016(271) [0425] and fanatical notion they **bury** the blessing of Christ.
S 1 : 0 1 :000(292) [0461] he suffered, died, was **buried**, descended to hell, rose from
SC : 0 2 :003(345) [0545] *was crucified, dead, and* ***buried****: he descended into hell,*
SC : 0 4 :014(349) [0553] St. Paul wrote, "We were **buried** therefore with him by
LC : SP :012(363) [0577] was crucified, dead, and **buried**: he descended into hell,
LC : 0 1 :266(401) [0657] your ears a tomb and **bury** it until you are appointed a
LC : 0 2 :025(413) [0683] *was crucified, dead, and* ***buried****: he descended into hell,*
LC : 0 2 :031(414) [0687] suffered, died, and was **buried** that he might make
LC : 0 2 :038(415) [0689] treasure might not be **buried** but put to use and enjoyed,
LC : 0 2 :057(418) [0693] be put to death, will be **buried** with all its uncleanness,
EP : 0 8 :013(488) [0821] for us suffered, died, was **buried**, descended into hell, rose
SD : 0 9 :001(610) [1051] God's Son, who died, was **buried**, and descended into
SD : 0 9 :001(610) [1051] Herein the **burial** and the descent into hell are
SD : 0 9 :002(610) [1051] believe that after the **burial** the entire person, God and

Bush (1)
S 3 : 0 8 :011(313) [0497] first through the burning **bush** and the spoken word, and

Busy (8), Business (23)
AG : 2 7 :053(079) [0083] keep his possessions and engage in **business** without sin.
AL : 2 7 :053(079) [0083] when they keep their possessions or engage in **business**.
AP : 0 4 :020(110) [0125] But this whole **business** is the invention of idle men who
AP : 0 4 :224(138) [0181] In justification our **business** is with God; his wrath must
AP : 1 2 :016(184) [0257] In short, the whole **business** of satisfactions is endless,
AP : 1 6 :013(224) [0333] in politics and in **business** have testified how they were
AP : 1 6 :013(224) [0333] the Gospel permitted such public and private **business**.
AP : 2 3 :005(240) [0365] or act honestly, frankly, or openly in this whole **business**.
AP : 2 3 :044(245) [0375] Such continence is easy for the godly and **busy**.
AP : 2 3 :044(245) [0375] boy who is used to being lazy hates those who are **busy**."
AP : 2 4 :064(261) [0407] to merchants for good **business**, to hunters for good
AP : 2 7 :038(275) [0433] for the whole city and then paid attention to his **business**.
AP : 2 7 :049(277) [0437] just as matters of **business** themselves vary with times and
S 1 : PR :005(289) [0457] and who keep themselves **busy** by shamefully twisting and
S 2 : 0 2 :012(295) [0465] the pomp, services, and **business** transactions associated

Continued ▶

LC : PR :016(361) [0573] Actually, he is **busy** teaching it from the beginning of the
LC : PR :016(361) [0573] and saints have been **busy** learning it and have always
LC : 0 1 :053(371) [0595] obviously in worldly **business** and in matters involving
LC : 0 1 :224(395) [0643] and, in short, wherever **business** is transacted and money
LC : 0 1 :227(396) [0645] market and everyday **business** the same fraud prevails in
LC : 0 1 :233(396) [0647] him by any faithless or underhanded **business** transaction.
LC : 0 1 :244(398) [0649] as if it were none of our **business**, God must punish us
LC : 0 1 :266(401) [0657] but to make him the talk of the town is not my **business**.
LC : 0 1 :277(402) [0661] That is none of our **business**.
LC : 0 1 :289(404) [0663] tongues of those who are **busy** wherever they can pry out
LC : 0 1 :298(405) [0665] called not rascality but shrewdness and **business** acumen.
LC : 0 1 :303(405) [0667] happens in ordinary **business** affairs, where one cunningly
LC : 0 3 :073(430) [0719] and concord in our daily **business** and in associations of
LC : 0 3 :084(431) [0723] and usury in public **business**, trading, and labor on the
SD : 0 2 :020(525) [0889] man is indeed very clever, intelligent, and extremely **busy**.
SD : 0 4 :010(552) [0941] Oh, faith is a living, **busy**, active, mighty thing, so that it

Businessmen (1)
AP : 2 1 :004(229) [0345] as Christ praises faithful **businessmen** (Matt. 25:21, 23).

Butcher (3)
AP : 1 4 :004(215) [0315] their edicts, who even **butcher** anyone who teaches what
LC : 0 1 :224(395) [0643] in a grocery shop, **butcher** stall, wine- and beer-cellar,
LC : 0 2 :060(418) [0695] (flesh), we think no farther than the **butcher** shop.

Buy (10), Buying (3), Bought (1)
AG : 1 6 :002(037) [0051] wars, serve as soldiers, **buy** and sell, take required oaths,
AG : 2 4 :010(057) [0065] it into a sort of fair, by **buying** and selling it, and by
AP : 0 2 :048(106) [0119] Christ's help, so we cannot **buy** our way out of the slavery
AP : 1 2 :015(184) [0257] As they **buy** off purgatory with satisfactions, so later on a
AP : 1 2 :015(184) [0257] a most profitable way of **buying** off satisfactions was
AP : 1 2 :015(184) [0257] They **buy** off the satisfactions of the dead not only by
AP : 1 2 :118(199) [0287] the keys, and the rest must be **bought** off by satisfactions.
AP : 1 2 :123(200) [0289] therefore satisfactions **buy** off the punishments of
AP : 1 2 :162(208) [0303] even those in mortal sin can **buy** off their punishments.
AP : 1 2 :173(209) [0305] Gospel commanded us to **buy** off punishment by such
AP : 1 2 :174(210) [0307] truthfulness — not to **buy** off eternal punishment but to
AP : 2 1 :030(233) [0351] of others, for everyone must **buy** oil for his own lamp."
S 2 : 0 2 :006(293) [0463] everywhere through the **buying** and selling of Masses, it
LC : PR :002(358) [0567] upright and honest as to **buy** these books, or if they have

Caelius (2)
S 3 : 1 5 :005(317) [0501] Michael **Caelius**, preacher in Mansfeld, subscribed
TR : 0 0 :082(335) [0529] Michael **Caelius**, preacher in Mansfeld

Caesar (3)
AP : 0 4 :241(141) [0187] Between Gaius **Caesar** and Pompey certain minor
SC : 0 9 :005(355) [0561] "Render therefore to **Caesar** the things that are Caesar's,
SC : 0 9 :005(355) [0561] Caesar the things that are **Caesar**'s, and to God the things

Caiaphas (1)
TR : 0 0 :038(327) [0515] apostles dissented from **Caiaphas** and were under no

Cain (1)
SD : 0 6 :016(566) [0967] Such people are saints after the order of **Cain**.

Cakes (1)
S 3 : 1 5 :005(316) [0501] are blessings of candles, palms, spices, oats, **cakes**, etc.

Calamities (4), Calamity (5)
AP : 0 4 :128(125) [0157] is overwhelming us with temporal and eternal **calamities**?
AP : 1 2 :162(208) [0303] not do away with the **calamities** common to man — that
AP : 1 2 :164(208) [0303] punishments and **calamities**, as Isa. 1:16-19 teaches:
AP : 2 4 :023(253) [0391] God when, amid great **calamities**, it seemed to be
LC : 0 1 :058(372) [0597] it is now a common **calamity** all over the world that there
LC : 0 1 :071(374) [0601] wait to lure us into sin and shame, **calamity** and trouble.
LC : 0 1 :072(374) [0601] a terrible and shocking **calamity** would befall us if God
LC : 0 1 :072(374) [0601] that often sudden, great **calamity** was averted and
LC : 0 1 :184(390) [0633] cursing and blows, and eventually **calamity** and murder.

Calculate (1)
AP : 0 7 :042(176) [0243] in Epiphanius: "Do not **calculate**, but whenever your

Calculation (2), Calculations (3)
AG : 2 8 :037(086) [0089] have multiplied beyond **calculation** while teaching
AL : 2 8 :037(086) [0089] church almost beyond **calculation**, while the teaching
AP : 0 7 :042(177) [0243] even if there has been a mistake in the **calculations**.
AP : 0 7 :044(177) [0243] even if there has been a mistake in the **calculations**.
SD : 0 8 :052(601) [1033] the basis of their own **calculations** and from their own

Calendar (1)
SD : 0 8 :085(608) [1047] but according to our **calendar** Jesus the son of Mary is

Call (112)
AG : PR :016(026) [0041] would diligently urge it upon the pope to **call** a council.
AG : PR :019(026) [0041] pope would not refuse to **call** a general council, and so
AG : 0 7 :004(032) [0047] hope that belongs to your **call**, one Lord, one faith, one
AG : 1 4 :000(036) [0049] the sacraments in the church without a regular **call**.
AG : 2 0 :025(044) [0057] enmity with God, cannot **call** upon him, and have no
AG : 2 0 :037(046) [0057] weak to do good works, **call** upon God, have patience in
AG : 2 1 :003(047) [0059] is sincerely to seek and **call** upon this same Jesus Christ in
AG : 2 8 :049(089) [0091] Why does it **call** them doctrines of the devil?
AL : 2 0 :025(044) [0057] God as an enemy, do not **call** upon him, and expect no
AL : 2 0 :037(046) [0057] Without faith it does not **call** upon God, expect anything
AL : 2 8 :049(089) [0091] Why does it **call** them doctrines of demons?
AP : 0 2 :035(105) [0115] remains — or, as they **call** it, the "material element" of sin
AP : 0 2 :040(105) [0115] For they clearly **call** lust sin, by nature worthy of death if
AP : 0 4 :017(109) [0125] disposition or, as they **call** it, "initial grace," which they
AP : 0 4 :059(115) [0137] worship, as in Ps. 50:15: "**Call** upon me in the day of
AP : 0 4 :141(126) [0161] who cares about us, we **call** upon him, give thanks to
AP : 0 4 :188(133) [0173] Therefore we **call** upon devout minds to consider the
AP : 0 4 :208(135) [0177] The examples of the saints **call** forth imitation in those
AP : 0 4 :243(141) [0189] this duty of love which the philosophers **call** "leniency."
AP : 0 4 :254(143) [0193] Then you shall **call**, and the Lord will answer."
AP : 0 4 :268(147) [0197] to you" (Zech. 1:3); "**Call** upon me in the day of trouble"
AP : 0 7 :028(173) [0237] because of the church's **call**, as Christ testifies (Luke
AP : 1 2 :028(185) [0259] If someone wants to **call** fruits worthy of penitence
AP : 1 2 :046(188) [0263] Thus what we usually **call** contrition Paul calls "putting
AP : 1 2 :063(191) [0269] or its goal — the "terminus to which," as they **call** it.
AP : 1 2 :076(193) [0273] We, on the contrary, **call** men's consciences away from
AP : 1 2 :089(195) [0277] such doubt, how can they **call** upon God, how can they
AP : 1 2 :115(199) [0285] works that are not due; we **call** them canonical
AP : 1 2 :144(205) [0297] with fancy titles; they **call** them works of supererogation,
AP : 1 3 :014(213) [0311] therefore wants to **call** it a sacrament, he should
AP : 2 0 :012(228) [0341] quote (II Pet. 1:10), "Be zealous to confirm your **call**."
AP : 2 0 :012(228) [0341] "Confirm your **call** by good works"; therefore works
AP : 2 0 :013(228) [0341] in order to confirm their **call**, that is, lest they fall from
AP : 2 0 :013(228) [0341] call, that is, lest they fall from their **call** by sinning again.
AP : 2 0 :013(228) [0341] works to persevere in your **call** and not to lose its gifts,
AP : 2 1 :017(231) [0347] and to answer those who **call** upon him through this
AP : 2 1 :018(231) [0347] we have the command to **call** upon Christ, according to
AP : 2 1 :035(234) [0353] monks taught the people to **call** on Christopher, as
AP : 2 1 :037(234) [0355] or the legends, as they **call** them, and the mirrors and the
AP : 2 2 :015(238) [0361] to itself the freedom to **call** Christ's ordinances matters of
AP : 2 3 :003(239) [0363] of the ancient prophecies **call** the king with the modest
AP : 2 3 :006(240) [0365] Our other controversies **call** for some theological
AP : 2 3 :070(249) [0383] of God, who will **call** them to account for breaking up
AP : 2 4 :016(252) [0389] Plato would really **call** our opponents "poor cooks," for
AP : 2 4 :029(255) [0393] **Call** upon me in the day of trouble; I will deliver you, and
AP : 2 4 :029(255) [0393] of thanksgiving and **call** on the name of the Lord."
AP : 2 4 :032(255) [0395] They **call** upon God, they give thanks to God, they bear
AP : 2 4 :044(258) [0399] They **call** these trifles the ornament of the churches.
AP : 2 4 :066(261) [0407] of the fact that the Fathers **call** the Mass a sacrifice; but
AP : 2 4 :066(261) [0407] talking about thanksgiving; hence they **call** it "eucharist."
AP : 2 4 :079(264) [0411] The Greeks **call** the Mass "liturgy," and this, they say,
AP : 2 7 :008(269) [0421] services, as some writers **call** them, and who do not
AP : 2 7 :019(272) [0425] rascals have the audacity to **call** this statement wicked.
AP : 2 7 :041(276) [0435] One happens without a **call**, without a command of God;
AP : 2 7 :049(277) [0437] Thus the **call** of David to rule, or of Abraham to sacrifice
AP : 2 8 :004(281) [0445] such minds tortured by doubt, they **call** to arms.
AP : 2 8 :018(284) [0449] It is not what they **call** a "commandment with unlimited
S 2 : 0 3 :002(298) [0471] accordingly the prophets **call** such service of God *aven*,
S 2 : 0 4 :002(298) [0471] now no bishop dares to **call** the pope "brother," as was
S 3 : 0 1 :002(302) [0477] name, failure to pray and **call** upon God, neglect of God's
S 3 : 0 3 :016(305) [0483] be attrite (which I might **call** half-way or partially
TR : 0 0 :010(321) [0505] he expressly argues that his **call** did not depend on the
TR : 0 0 :062(330) [0523] Again, Peter and John **call** themselves presbyters.
TR : 0 0 :077(333) [0527] courts (as they **call** them), especially matrimonial cases.
SC : 0 1 :004(342) [0539] but in every time of need **call** upon him, pray to him,
LC : PR :012(360) [0571] What, then, shall we **call** God's Word, which routs and
LC : 0 1 :051(371) [0595] misuse of God's name if we **call** upon the Lord God in
LC : 0 1 :064(373) [0599] properly; again, when we **call** on his name in time of
LC : 0 1 :064(373) [0599] command in Ps. 50:15, "**Call** upon me in the day of
LC : 0 1 :125(382) [0617] a block or a stone which we might **call** father and mother.
LC : 0 1 :171(388) [0629] Majesty, who will solemnly **call** us to account and punish
LC : 0 1 :186(390) [0633] murder, nevertheless **call** down curses and imprecations
LC : 0 1 :225(395) [0645] defiant and insolent and dare anyone to **call** him a thief!
LC : 0 1 :247(398) [0651] before all the world you may **call** God and me liars.
LC : 0 1 :262(400) [0655] endure having the world **call** them heretics, apostates,
LC : 0 2 :045(416) [0689] is no Holy Spirit to create, **call**, and gather the Christian
LC : 0 3 :002(420) [0697] is so necessary as to **call** upon God incessantly and drum
LC : 0 3 :005(420) [0699] the holy name and pray or **call** upon it in every need.
LC : 0 3 :005(420) [0699] For to **call** upon it is nothing else than to pray.
LC : 0 3 :008(421) [0699] Commandment teaches, is to **call** upon God in every need
LC : 0 3 :019(423) [0703] as he says in Ps. 50:15, "**Call** upon me in the day of
LC : 0 3 :039(425) [0709] Since in this prayer we **call** God our Father, it is our duty
LC : 0 3 :088(432) [0723] again there is great need to **call** upon God and pray,
LC : 0 5 :049(452) [0765] ever desiring the sacrament, I **call** that despising it.
LC : 0 5 :081(456) [0773] than what the Scriptures **call** him, a liar and a murderer.
EP : 0 7 :014(483) [0811] single mode which the philosophers **call** *local* or spatial."
EP : 1 1 :014(496) [0835] will of God and "to confirm our **call**," as St. Peter says.
EP : 1 2 :014(499) [0841] and that subjects may not **call** upon the government to
SD : 0 1 :062(519) [0879] he wrote, "Whether we **call** original sin a quality or a
SD : 0 2 :050(531) [0901] And it is God's will to **call** men to eternal salvation, to
SD : 0 2 :060(533) [0905] This the Scriptures **call** the creation of a new heart.
SD : 0 4 :033(556) [0947] zealous to confirm your **call** and election," the Apology
SD : 0 7 :038(576) [0985] Luther and our theologians **call** it in the above-mentioned
SD : 0 7 :067(582) [0997] entire church when they **call** oral eating and eating on the
SD : 0 7 :097(586) [1005] the one which the philosophers **call** local or spatial.
SD : 0 8 :096(609) [1049] Since the Holy Scriptures **call** Christ a mystery over
SD : 1 1 :004(616) [1063] it happens — what we **call** God's foreknowledge —
SD : 1 1 :014(619) [1069] our redemption, **call**, justification, and salvation, as Paul
SD : 1 1 :027(620) [1071] Now, God does not **call** without means but through the
SD : 1 1 :028(621) [1071] of all, rich toward all who **call** upon him" (Rom. 10:12).
SD : 1 1 :029(621) [1073] we should not regard this **call** of God which takes place
SD : 1 1 :034(622) [1075] chosen" is not that in his **call**, which takes place through
SD : 1 1 :034(622) [1075] indeed through the Word **call** all of you, to whom I give
SD : 1 1 :034(622) [1075] majority of those whom I **call** through the Word are not
SD : 1 1 :034(622) [1075] although I speak differently in my **call** to them."
SD : 1 1 :038(622) [1075] will toward us from the **call** which comes to us through
SD : 1 1 :040(623) [1077] that the Holy Spirit would **call**, enlighten, and convert the
SD : 1 1 :041(623) [1077] offers to him through the **call** and resists the Holy Spirit
SD : 1 1 :056(625) [1081] each person the time and hour of his **call** and conversion.
SD : 1 1 :073(628) [1087] seek to "confirm their **call** and election" so that the more
SD : 1 1 :088(631) [1093] of works but because of his **call**, she was told, 'The elder
SD : 1 2 :019(634) [1099] arise, nor may a subject **call** upon the government for

Called (159)
PR : PR :016(008) [0015] Christian agreement is **called** and also is the unanimous
AG : PR :019(026) [0041] that it would be profitable to have such a council **called**.
AG : 0 1 :002(027) [0043] divine essence, which is **called** and which is truly God,
AG : 0 7 :004(032) [0047] Spirit, just as you were **called** to the one hope that
AG : 2 6 :029(068) [0075] food or marriage are **called** a doctrine of the devil, for it
AG : 2 7 :016(073) [0077] In fact, it is **called** a state of perfection and is regarded as
AL : 0 1 :002(027) [0043] divine essence, which is **called** and which is God, eternal,
AL : 1 4 :000(036) [0049] or administer the sacraments unless he is regularly **called**.

Continued ▶

AL : 21 :003(047) [0057] approves, namely, that in all afflictions he be **called** upon.
AL : 23 :022(055) [0063] To prohibit marriage is **called** a doctrine of demons by
AL : 27 :057(080) [0083] They **called** this "fleeing from the world" and "seeking a
AP : 02 :004(101) [0105] concupiscence is the so-**called** "material element" of
AP : 02 :051(107) [0119] formal element of original sin or the so-**called** deficiency.
AP : 04 :105(122) [0153] titles — for some are **called** "angelic," others "subtle," and
AP : 04 :116(123) [0155] Holy Spirit, it should be **called** "grace that makes us
AP : 04 :152(127) [0163] familiar figure of speech, **called** synecdoche, by which we
AP : 04 :331(158) [0211] because thy city and thy people are **called** by thy name."
AP : 04 :356(161) [0217] reply that eternal life is **called** a reward and that therefore
AP : 04 :360(162) [0219] one word "reward": "It is **called** a reward, therefore we
AP : 07 :005(169) [0227] This church alone is **called** the body of Christ, which
AP : 07 :011(170) [0229] by any spot cannot be **called** part of the church of Christ,
AP : 07 :014(170) [0231] wicked among them were **called** the people of God
AP : 07 :020(171) [0233] This church is properly **called** "the pillar of truth" (I Tim.
AP : 07 :029(173) [0237] the church, properly so **called**, is termed the body of
AP : 07 :043(177) [0243] with the Jews; they were **called** Audians, from the
AP : 12 :012(184) [0257] This is really what is **called** "departing before the
AP : 12 :041(187) [0261] may properly be **called** a sacrament of penitence, as even
AP : 12 :148(205) [0299] that penitence is so **called** because it holds punishment.
AP : 13 :005(212) [0309] said so well when he **called** the sacrament "the visible
AP : 13 :009(212) [0311] Thus priests are not **called** to make sacrifices that merit
AP : 13 :009(212) [0311] Testament, but they are **called** to preach the Gospel and
AP : 13 :015(213) [0311] If matrimony should be **called** a sacrament because it has
AP : 13 :015(213) [0311] or offices might also be **called** sacraments because they
AP : 13 :016(213) [0311] not prayer, which can most truly be **called** a sacrament?
AP : 14 :001(214) [0315] and the sacraments in the church unless he is duly **called**.
AP : 15 :050(222) [0329] sins, and they require so-**called** "universal rites" as
AP : 16 :004(223) [0331] They **called** it an evangelical state to hold property in
AP : 16 :004(223) [0331] in common, and they **called** it an evangelical counsel not
AP : 20 :004(227) [0339] Confutation stand if their attention had been **called** to it.
AP : 23 :007(240) [0365] sinful lust but about so-**called** "natural love," the desire
AP : 23 :013(241) [0367] about the desire which is **called** "natural love," which lust
AP : 23 :045(245) [0377] from marriage, and this **called** forth the most admiration.
AP : 24 :021(252) [0389] The Old Testament **called** certain sacrifices propitiatory
AP : 24 :021(252) [0391] They were accordingly **called** propitiatory sacrifices for
AP : 24 :023(253) [0391] to be unusually severe; this they **called** a trespass offering.
AP : 24 :023(253) [0391] The Greeks **called** them either "refuse" or "offscouring."
AP : 24 :024(253) [0391] sacrifices were so **called** only as symbols of a future
AP : 24 :025(253) [0391] are eucharistic sacrifices, **called** "sacrifices of praise": the
AP : 24 :029(255) [0393] Prayer is **called** a sacrifice of thanksgiving.
AP : 24 :078(263) [0411] the fact that the Mass is **called** a sacrifice that it grants
AP : 24 :086(265) [0413] the Mass was **called** *agape* in some places, unless some
AP : 24 :086(265) [0413] one prefers to think it was **called** that because of the
AP : 24 :087(265) [0413] even though the Mass is **called** an offering, what does
AP : 24 :087(265) [0413] It can be **called** an offering, as it is called a eucharist,
AP : 24 :087(265) [0413] called an offering, as it is **called** a eucharist, because
AP : 27 :010(270) [0423] and fully in his book **called** *Monastic Vows,* we want to
AP : 27 :027(273) [0429] observance of other things which are **called** "adiaphora."
S1 : PR :001(288) [0455] Pope Paul III **called** a council to meet in Mantua last
S3 : 01 :001(302) [0477] This is **called** original sin, or the root sin.
S3 : 03 :005(304) [0481] who preceded Christ, is **called** a preacher of repentance —
S3 : 03 :025(307) [0485] This was **called** remission of all penalty and guilt, and the
S3 : 03 :039(309) [0489] foundation which is **called** good works or the law,
S3 : 03 :041(309) [0491] the Gospel, and yet it is **called** a heresy by godless saints.
S3 : 10 :002(314) [0497] condemn those who have been **called** to do these things.
S3 : 15 :005(316) [0501] These cannot be **called** blessings, and they are not, but
TR : 00 :017(323) [0509] Many ancient synods were **called** and held in which the
TR : 00 :039(327) [0515] himself against every so-**called** god or object of worship,
TR : 00 :042(328) [0517] many nations and to be **called** schismatics is a serious
TR : 00 :061(330) [0521] whether they are **called** pastors, presbyters, or bishops.
TR : 00 :062(331) [0523] number, set him in a higher place, and **called** him bishop.
TR : 00 :074(332) [0525] the officials (as they are **called**) have exercised intolerable
SC : 02 :006(345) [0545] But the Holy Spirit has **called** me through the Gospel,
LC : PR :012(360) [0571] The devil is **called** the master of a thousand arts.
LC : SP :001(362) [0575] ancient times it has been **called** in Greek, a "catechism" —
LC : 01 :025(368) [0587] from ancient times have **called** God by a name more
LC : 01 :072(374) [0601] and vanished in the very moment I **called** upon God.
LC : 01 :079(375) [0603] day" or "holiday" is so **called** from the Hebrew word
LC : 01 :090(377) [0607] Where it is not, it cannot be **called** a Christian holy day.
LC : 01 :093(377) [0607] holy relics, as are the so-**called** spiritual estates who do
LC : 01 :094(378) [0607] are not properly **called** holy work unless the doer himself
LC : 01 :099(378) [0609] the mortal sins and was **called** *acidia* — that is, indolence
LC : 01 :142(384) [0621] Thus all who are **called** masters stand in the place of
LC : 01 :142(384) [0621] the Scriptures they are all **called** fathers because in their
LC : 01 :142(384) [0621] and other peoples **called** the masters and mistresses of the
LC : 01 :142(384) [0621] and overlords were **called** *patres patriae* (that is, fathers
LC : 01 :202(392) [0639] applies to every form of unchastity, however it is **called**.
LC : 01 :229(396) [0645] These men are **called** gentlemen swindlers or big
LC : 01 :229(396) [0645] sit in office chairs and are **called** great lords and
LC : 01 :267(401) [0657] Those are **called** backbiters who are not content just to
LC : 01 :270(401) [0657] it publicly; I might be **called** a liar and sent away in
LC : 01 :281(403) [0661] Moreover, when you are **called** upon to witness, you will
LC : 01 :298(405) [0665] insist that it should be **called** not rascality but shrewdness
LC : 01 :307(406) [0669] It may not be **called** stealing or fraud, yet it is coveting —
LC : 02 :036(415) [0687] But God's Spirit alone is **called** Holy Spirit, that is, he
LC : 02 :036(415) [0687] As the Father is **called** Creator and the Son is called
LC : 02 :036(415) [0687] Creator and the Son is **called** Redeemer, so on account of
LC : 02 :036(415) [0687] the Holy Spirit must be **called** Sanctifier, the One who
LC : 02 :048(416) [0691] the house should not be **called** a church except for the
LC : 02 :048(417) [0691] therefore it ought to be **called** "a Christian congregation
LC : 02 :051(417) [0691] It is **called** together by the Holy Spirit in one faith, mind,
LC : 03 :007(421) [0699] folk; while it may be **called** singing or reading exercise, it
LC : 03 :024(423) [0705] which he desires; otherwise it cannot be **called** a prayer.
LC : 03 :037(425) [0707] at Baptism, and so we are **called** children of God and
LC : 03 :042(425) [0709] when those who are **called** Christians and God's people
LC : 03 :044(425) [0709] dishonored if we who are **called** by his name and enjoy
LC : 03 :044(426) [0709] that he must hear us **called** not children of God but
LC : 03 :101(433) [0727] as the ancient Saxons **called** it, *Bekoerunge*) is of three
LC : 03 :108(435) [0729] If we did not feel it, it could not be **called** a temptation.
LC : 04 :022(439) [0737] with and could indeed be **called** a bathkeeper's baptism.
LC : 04 :022(439) [0737] Baptism is a sacrament, and it is **called** Christ's Baptism.
LC : 04 :038(441) [0741] on account of which this flesh is **called** father and mother.
LC : 04 :074(445) [0751] third sacrament, formerly **called** Penance, which is really
LC : 05 :010(448) [0755] which is rightly **called** Christ's body and blood.
LC : 05 :023(449) [0757] it is appropriately **called** the food of the soul since it
LC : 06 :008(458) [0000] even greater right to be **called** the Christians' common
EP : 01 :020(468) [0783] in human nature, and the other so-**called** actual sins.
EP : 02 :008(470) [0787] The mad dream of the so-**called** Stoic philosophers and
EP : 06 :005(480) [0807] to the law are, and are **called**, works of the law as long as
EP : 08 :003(487) [0819] common," so that God is **called** man and a man is called
EP : 08 :003(487) [0819] called man and a man is **called** God, but that God really
EP : 08 :011(488) [0821] man, Mary's son, truly be **called** or be God, or the Son of
EP : 08 :012(488) [0821] this reason she is rightly **called**, and truly is, the mother
EP : 10 :000(492) [0829] X. Church Usages, **Called** Adiaphora or Indifferent
EP : 10 :002(492) [0829] when a confession is **called** for, and when the enemies of
EP : 11 :012(496) [0835] The passage, "Many are **called**, but few are chosen," does
EP : 11 :013(496) [0835] us, as it is written, "Those he predestined, he also **called**."
SD : 01 :001(508) [0859] sin itself, which has been **called** "nature-sin" or
SD : 02 :040(528) [0895] But the Holy Spirit has **called** me through the Gospel,
SD : 02 :077(536) [0911] the beginning and has **called** us by the Gospel and offers
SD : 03 :055(549) [0935] in what way Christ is **called** our righteousness in this
SD : 05 :011(560) [0955] this reason the latter is **called** the Paraclete, as Luther
SD : 05 :021(562) [0959] strictly speaking is, and is **called**, the Gospel, a good and
SD : 05 :027(563) [0961] of the Gospel, strictly so **called** in distinction from the
SD : 07 :021(573) [0979] and wine but is and is **called** Christ's body and blood."
SD : 07 :055(579) [0991] the bread could not be **called** participation in the body
SD : 07 :064(581) [0995] natural wine, which he **called** his true body and blood,
SD : 08 :021(595) [1023] Luther **called** this the devil's mask and damned it to the
SD : 08 :036(598) [1027] and man (whether he is **called** God or whether he is called
SD : 08 :036(598) [1027] (whether he is called God or whether he is **called** man).
SD : 08 :040(598) [1029] I would not want to be **called** a Christian, that is, a
SD : 08 :072(605) [1041] nature (whence he is **called** Messiah, or the Anointed) in
SD : 08 :075(606) [1043] sect among the Arians, **called** the Agnoetes, who taught
SD : 08 :085(608) [1047] man, Mary's son, is and is **called** the almighty and
SD : 10 :000(610) [1053] Rites That Are **Called** Adiaphora or Things Indifferent
SD : 10 :019(614) [1059] condemn those who have been **called** to do these things.
SD : 10 :023(615) [1061] many nations and to be **called** schismatics is a serious
SD : 11 :022(619) [1069] life those whom he has elected, **called**, and justified.
SD : 11 :027(620) [1071] elected, and decreed, he has also **called**" (Rom. 8:29, 30).
SD : 11 :029(621) [1073] through which we are **called** is a ministry of the Spirit —
SD : 11 :032(621) [1073] us that God who has **called** us will be so faithful that
SD : 11 :033(621) [1073] and ability through the Word by which he has **called** us.
SD : 11 :034(622) [1075] reason why "many are **called** and few are chosen" is not
SD : 11 :040(623) [1077] all who, when they are **called** through the Word, spurn
SD : 11 :041(623) [1077] In this sense "many are **called**, but few are chosen," for
SD : 11 :047(624) [1079] Paul asks, Since we are **called** according to the purpose
SD : 11 :049(624) [1079] for good" since they are "**called** according to his purpose."
SD : 11 :051(624) [1079] likewise, "Many are **called**, but few are chosen" (Matt.
SD : 11 :054(625) [1081] who of those who are **called** will believe and who will
SD : 12 :008(633) [1097] in their innocence what **called** itself evangelical and was

Calling (44)

AG : PR :020(026) [0041] and bring about the **calling** of such a general council by
AG : 16 :005(038) [0051] according to his own **calling**, manifest Christian love and
AG : 21 :001(046) [0057] are to be an example for us, each of us in his own **calling**.
AG : 26 :010(065) [0071] to do according to his **calling** — for example, that a
AG : 26 :038(069) [0075] that one can perform the duties required by one's **calling**.
AG : 27 :013(073) [0077] serve in their appointed **calling** according to God's Word
AG : 27 :049(079) [0083] with our particular **calling** and station in life; and that
AG : 27 :049(079) [0083] good works for others and diligently attend to our **calling**.
AG : 28 :008(082) [0085] persons or to individuals, depending on one's **calling**).
AL : 21 :001(046) [0057] their faith and good works according to our **calling**.
AL : 26 :038(069) [0075] and for discharging his duty according to his **calling**.
AL : 27 :013(073) [0077] observances, serve their **calling** in accordance with God's
AL : 27 :049(079) [0083] of good works for others and to attend to our **calling**.
AL : 28 :008(082) [0085] to many or to individuals, depending on one's **calling**.
AP : 04 :167(130) [0169] Who lives up to the requirements of his **calling**?
AP : 12 :174(210) [0307] faithfulness to one's **calling**, peaceable conduct instead of
AP : 13 :011(212) [0311] we have no obligation to **calling** ordination a sacrament.
AP : 13 :012(212) [0311] shall not object either to **calling** the laying on of hands a
AP : 15 :025(219) [0323] like the tasks of one's **calling**, the administration of public
AP : 15 :027(219) [0323] to be performed in one's **calling**, but only the traditions
AP : 21 :006(230) [0345] which each should imitate in accordance with his **calling.**
AP : 21 :015(231) [0347] proof from Scripture for **calling** them mediators of
AP : 23 :032(244) [0373] adds a certain task of her **calling**, as performance of the
AP : 23 :032(244) [0373] the tasks of a particular **calling** should follow everyone's
AP : 23 :032(244) [0373] saved if she serves faithfully in these duties of her **calling**.
AP : 24 :029(255) [0393] It declares that **calling** upon God is really worshiping and
AP : 27 :027(273) [0429] mercy promised in Christ, and in devotion to one's **calling**
AP : 27 :037(275) [0433] All men, whatever their **calling**, ought to seek perfection,
AP : 27 :049(277) [0437] This sets forth the example of obedience in a **calling**.
AP : 27 :049(277) [0437] Since callings vary, this **calling** is not for everyone, but
AP : 27 :050(277) [0437] for this young man to believe and obey this **calling**.
AP : 27 :050(277) [0437] for each of us with true faith to obey his own **calling**.
S1 : PR :003(289) [0455] ever permit a free council, to say nothing of **calling** one.
TR : 00 :067(331) [0523] to retain the right of **calling**, electing, and ordaining
SC : 09 :007(355) [0563] husbands, as Sarah obeyed Abraham, **calling** him lord.
LC : 01 :064(373) [0599] this is what we mean by **calling** upon his name in service
LC : 01 :069(374) [0599] and especially to avoid **calling** upon God's name in its
LC : 01 :070(374) [0601] to it for all consolation and therefore **calling** upon it.
LC : 01 :072(374) [0601] did not preserve us through our **calling** upon his name.
LC : 01 :197(392) [0637] of their hypocritical **calling** and works as "the most
LC : 01 :326(409) [0675] use his name properly by **calling** upon him in prayer,
SD : 04 :033(556) [0947] that we confirm our **calling**, that is, that we do not fall
SD : 04 :033(556) [0949] we do not fall from our **calling** by lapsing again into sin.
SD : 04 :033(556) [0949] remain in your heavenly **calling**, lest you fall away and

Callings (9)

AG : 20 :037(046) [0057] diligently engage in **callings** which are commanded,
AL : 20 :002(041) [0053] kinds of work are pleasing to God in the several **callings**.
AL : 26 :010(065) [0071] of God pertaining to **callings** were without honor — for
AL : 27 :049(079) [0083] in connection with our **callings**; meanwhile to be diligent
AP : 27 :049(277) [0437] Since **callings** vary, this calling is not for everyone, but
AP : 27 :049(277) [0437] **Callings** are personal, just as matters of business
S1 : PR :010(290) [0457] of the various **callings** of life, and with true works, that
S2 : 03 :002(298) [0471] life and to the offices and **callings** established by God.
TR : 00 :048(328) [0519] to works performed in **callings** which God requires and

Calls (65)
AG : 2 0 :024(044) [0057] God, truly knows God, **calls** upon him, and is not, like
AG : 2 3 :022(055) [0063] the apostle Paul **calls** the teaching that forbids marriage
AG : 2 6 :023(067) [0073] Since he **calls** them vain service, they must not be
AL : 2 0 :024(044) [0057] God, knows that God cares for him, and **calls** upon God.
AL : 2 6 :029(068) [0075] And in I Tim. 4:1,3 Paul **calls** the prohibition of foods a
AP : 0 4 :154(128) [0163] And the account here shows what he **calls** "love."
AP : 0 4 :224(138) [0181] scolds them for this and **calls** them back to the duties of
AP : 0 4 :356(161) [0217] Paul **calls** eternal life a "gift" (Rom. 6:23) because the
AP : 0 7 :020(171) [0233] Gospel and what Paul **calls** the "foundation" (I Cor.
AP : 0 7 :040(176) [0241] In fact, Paul **calls** such opinions "doctrines of demons."
AP : 1 2 :046(188) [0263] call contrition Paul **calls** "putting off the body of sins"
AP : 1 2 :051(189) [0265] He **calls** it God's alien work to terrify because God's own
AP : 1 2 :079(194) [0275] Paul **calls** us away from the law to this promise.
AP : 1 2 :144(205) [0297] Christ **calls** these useless acts of worship, and so they do
AP : 1 2 :147(205) [0297] tradition, which Christ **calls** useless acts of worship.
AP : 1 5 :004(215) [0315] Scripture **calls** traditions "doctrines of demons" (I Tim.
AP : 1 8 :004(225) [0335] the Holy Spirit, Scripture **calls** the righteousness of the
AP : 2 1 :035(234) [0353] reward — that no one who **calls** upon her should die
AP : 2 1 :044(236) [0357] with his own name and **calls** them gods (Ps. 82:6), "I say,
AP : 2 2 :002(236) [0357] changed, especially since he himself **calls** it his testament?
AP : 2 3 :029(243) [0371] Christ **calls** marriage a divine union when he says in
AP : 2 3 :063(248) [0381] of such a law when he **calls** it a "doctrine of demons"
AP : 2 3 :065(248) [0381] and of what Paul **calls** possessing one's vessel in holiness
AP : 2 4 :070(262) [0409] picture or "seal," as Paul **calls** it (Rom. 4:11), showing
AP : 2 4 :082(264) [0411] In Phil. 2:25 he **calls** Epaphroditus a "minister to my
AP : 2 4 :088(265) [0413] It **calls** even prayers "bloodless sacrifices."
AP : 2 7 :035(275) [0431] And since Christ **calls** traditions "useless services," they
AP : 2 7 :048(277) [0437] Yet Christ **calls** it perfection here!
AP : 2 7 :067(280) [0441] This is what he **calls** "first faith" — not a monastic vows,
S 2 : 0 4 :011(300) [0475] is actually what St. Paul **calls** exalting oneself over and
S 3 : 0 8 :008(313) [0495] to God in this faith (Luke **calls** him "devout" and
S 3 : 0 9 :000(314) [0497] as the pope **calls** it, to be merely a civil penalty which
TR : 0 0 :002(320) [0503] the bishop of Rome **calls** himself the vicar of Christ on
TR : 0 0 :015(322) [0509] Cyprian **calls** this custom a divine tradition and an
TR : 0 0 :039(327) [0515] to the Thessalonians Paul **calls** him "an adversary of
TR : 0 0 :039(327) [0515] kings of nations, and he **calls** that man "an adversary of
SC : 0 2 :006(345) [0545] me in true faith, just as he **calls**, gathers, enlightens, and
LC : PR :010(360) [0569] Psalm 1 **calls** those blessed who "meditate on God's law
LC : 0 1 :141(384) [0621] to bring up his child, he **calls** upon a schoolmaster to
LC : 0 1 :191(391) [0635] Therefore God rightly **calls** all persons murderers who do
LC : 0 2 :047(416) [0689] The Creed **calls** the holy Christian church a *communio*
LC : 0 4 :027(440) [0739] "washing of regeneration," as St. Paul **calls** it in Titus 3:5.
EP : 0 1 :020(468) [0783] Luther **calls** original sin "nature-sin," "person-sin,"
EP : 0 6 :006(481) [0807] In his epistles St. Paul **calls** it the law of Christ and the
EP : 1 1 :008(495) [0833] 7. This Christ **calls** all sinners to himself and promises
EP : 1 1 :018(497) [0837] wanting all men to come to him when he **calls** us to him.
SD : 0 1 :006(509) [0861] Dr. Luther **calls** this sin "nature-sin" or "person-sin" in
SD : 0 2 :010(522) [0885] In this way Scripture **calls** the natural man simply
SD : 0 2 :023(525) [0889] Dr. Luther **calls** this a "capacity," which he explains as
SD : 0 2 :040(528) [0895] me in true faith, just as he **calls**, gathers, enlightens, and
SD : 0 2 :051(531) [0901] the eternal Father **calls** out from heaven concerning his
SD : 0 3 :002(539) [0917] of faith, which St. Paul **calls** the righteousness of God, is
SD : 0 3 :042(547) [0931] following answer: James **calls** that faith dead where all
SD : 0 3 :054(549) [0935] Paul speaks and which he **calls** the righteousness of God,
SD : 0 4 :009(552) [0941] For this reason St. Paul **calls** them fruits of faith or of the
SD : 0 5 :004(559) [0953] Likewise, Paul **calls** his entire teaching "Gospel" (Acts
SD : 0 5 :011(560) [0955] perform what the prophet **calls** "a strange deed" (that is,
SD : 0 6 :016(566) [0967] St. Paul **calls** the works of such a man "works of the law"
SD : 0 6 :017(567) [0967] the Spirit, or, as St. Paul **calls** them, the law of the mind
SD : 0 8 :039(598) [1027] "Zwingli **calls** that an *alloeosis* when something is said
SD : 0 8 :085(608) [1047] (Rom. 1:4), and John **calls** it 'glorified' (John 7:39;
SD : 1 1 :027(620) [1071] to his son's wedding he **calls** through the messengers
SD : 1 1 :029(621) [1073] in those whom he thus **calls** he will be efficaciously active
SD : 1 1 :036(622) [1075] which he deals with us and **calls** us, so that we should
SD : 1 1 :089(631) [1093] sinner but invites and **calls** all poor, burdened, and

Callous (3), Calloused (1)
LC : 0 5 :053(453) [0765] become more and more **callous** and cold, and eventually
LC : 0 5 :059(453) [0767] others, who are not so **callous** and dissolute but would
LC : 0 5 :067(454) [0769] we grow quite cold and **callous** and lose all desire and
SD : 1 1 :085(630) [1091] became hardened and **calloused** and God executed his

Calm (1), Calmness (1)
AP : 0 4 :241(141) [0187] be quieted and settled by **calmness** and forbearance.
LC : 0 1 :187(390) [0633] Thus we may learn to **calm** our anger and have a patient,

Calumnies (2), Calumny (1)
PR : PR :009(006) [0011] thereby from the **calumnies** that had been circulated.
PR : PR :010(006) [0011] the mendacious **calumnies** and the religious controversies
PR : PR :018(008) [0015] by the unwarranted **calumny** of our adversaries that we

Calvinists (1)
EP : 0 8 :001(486) [0817] Confession and the **Calvinists** (who have misled some

Camels (1)
S 1 : PR :013(291) [0459] we are willing to swallow **camels** and strain out gnats, if

Campegio (1)
S 2 : 0 2 :010(294) [0465] It is as **Campegio** said in Augsburg: he would suffer

Campegius (2)
AP : 1 2 :125(201) [0289] It was up to you, **Campegius**, in keeping with your
AP : 1 2 :126(201) [0289] You see, **Campegius**, that these are the last times, in which

Cana (1)
SD : 0 8 :025(596) [1023] at the wedding in **Cana** of Galilee, again when he was

Cancel (1), Canceled (2), Cancellation (2), Cancels (2)
AG : 2 7 :024(074) [0079] no man has the right to **cancel** an obligation which is
AP : 0 4 :103(122) [0151] by shedding his blood **canceled** the bond that stood
AP : 1 2 :048(188) [0265] in Col. 2:14 that Christ **cancels** the bond which stood
AP : 1 2 :048(188) [0265] are two parts, the bond and the **cancellation** of the bond.
AP : 1 2 :048(188) [0265] The **cancellation** of the bond is the removal of the
AP : 2 7 :069(281) [0443] the monks, which Christ **cancels** with one declaration
S 3 : 0 3 :024(307) [0485] was remitted and **canceled**, first for seven years in a single

Candid (1)
PR : PR :021(010) [0019] declare in clear and **candid** words (so that all

Candidate (1)
TR : 0 0 :014(322) [0509] with the life of each **candidate** (as we have seen it done

Candles (4)
AP : 2 4 :044(258) [0399] altars standing unadorned, without **candles** or statues.
AP : 2 4 :051(259) [0401] **Candles**, golden vessels, and ornaments like that are
S 3 : 1 5 :005(316) [0501] there are blessings of **candles**, palms, spices, oats, cakes,
LC : 0 1 :314(407) [0671] lighting of tapers and **candles** until nothing else can be

Cannon (1)
S 2 : 0 2 :007(293) [0463] of evil scoundrels (as the **cannon** and all books on the

Canon (21), Canonical (24), Canonists (9), Canons (63)
AG : 2 2 :008(050) [0061] Not a single **canon** can be found which requires the
AG : 2 2 :010(050) [0061] and also contrary to the ancient **canons**, is unjust.
AG : 2 3 :013(053) [0063] and contrary to the **canons** which the popes had
AG : 2 3 :016(054) [0063] The old **canons** also state that it is sometimes necessary to
AG : 2 3 :021(055) [0063] contrary not only to divine law but also to **canon** law.
AG : 2 3 :026(055) [0065] In addition, all the **canons** show great leniency and
AG : 2 4 :037(060) [0067] The ancient **canons** also indicate that one man officiated
AG : 2 4 :038(060) [0067] the words of the Nicene **canon** read, "After the priests the
AG : 2 6 :014(066) [0073] of the summists and **canonists** how consciences have been
AG : 2 7 :001(071) [0077] not only to the Word of God but also to papal **canons**.
AG : 2 7 :006(071) [0077] fact that even the papal **canons** might have set many of
AG : 2 7 :009(072) [0077] a momentous matter the **canons** were not strictly adhered
AG : 2 7 :023(074) [0079] that a vow made contrary to papal **canons** is not binding.
AG : 2 7 :031(075) [0079] Several **canons** and papal regulations annul vows that are
AG : 2 7 :032(076) [0079] Another **canon** concedes still more years to human
AG : 2 7 :040(077) [0081] Even the **canons** teach that an oath should not be an
AG : 2 8 :027(085) [0087] **Canon** law requires the same in Part II, Question 7, in the
AG : 2 8 :034(086) [0089] above and as is taught by **canon** law throughout the
AG : 2 8 :041(087) [0089] in spite of the fact that **canon** law says nothing of the
AG : 2 8 :067(092) [0093] any of the ancient **canons** are observed according to the
AL : 0 0 :002(048) [0059] drawn up, for even the **canons** are not so severe as to
AL : 0 0 :001(049) [0059] to the intent of the **canons**, we pray that Your Imperial
AL : 2 2 :009(050) [0061] to be approved, as the **canons** testify (Dist. 3, chap.
AL : 2 2 :010(050) [0061] contradiction to ancient **canons** and the example of the
AL : 2 3 :013(053) [0063] and contrary even to the **canons**, both those made by the
AL : 2 3 :016(054) [0063] The **canons** themselves state that in later times the old
AL : 2 3 :021(055) [0063] to the intent of the **canons**, for no other cause than
AL : 2 3 :026(055) [0065] The **canons** show some consideration toward those who
AL : 2 4 :011(057) [0065] and how many celebrate Masses contrary to the **canons**.
AL : 2 4 :037(060) [0067] appears from the ancient **canons** that some one person or
AL : 2 4 :037(060) [0067] the words of the Nicene **canon** read, "In order, after the
AL : 2 5 :011(063) [0069] is quoted in the **canons** as saying, "I do not say that you
AL : 2 7 :001(071) [0077] monasteries every day that were contrary to the **canons**.
AL : 2 7 :004(071) [0077] on many, contrary to the **canons**, before they had attained
AL : 2 7 :006(071) [0077] some could have been freed by appealing to the **canons**.
AL : 2 7 :009(072) [0077] the authority of the **canons** was utterly ignored and
AL : 2 7 :023(074) [0079] The **canons** state that every vow is subject to the right of
AL : 2 7 :031(075) [0079] Many **canons** annul vows made before the age of fifteen
AL : 2 7 :032(076) [0079] Another **canon**, making a greater concession to human
AL : 2 7 :033(076) [0079] Whether we follow one **canon** or the other, most
AL : 2 7 :040(077) [0081] As the **canon** says, no vow ought to bind men to iniquity.
AL : 2 8 :027(084) [0087] The **canons** require the same thing (II, question 7, in
AL : 2 8 :028(085) [0087] anything contrary to the **canonical** Scriptures of God.
AL : 2 8 :034(086) [0089] The **canons** concede this throughout the whole of Dist. 9.
AL : 2 8 :038(087) [0089] So the penitential **canons** formerly increased, and we can
AL : 2 8 :041(087) [0089] a mortal sin to omit the **canonical** hours, that in a
AL : 2 8 :041(087) [0089] the case, although the **canons** themselves speak only of
AL : 2 8 :067(092) [0093] Scarcely any of the **canons** are observed according to the
AL : 2 8 :068(093) [0093] that one recognizes that **canons** are kept without holding
AL : 2 8 :074(094) [0095] with the passing of time, as the **canons** themselves show.
AP : PR :017(099) [0103] writings of the monks, **canonists**, and scholastic
AP : 0 4 :288(151) [0203] For this reason the **canonists** have twisted ecclesiastical
AP : 0 7 :023(172) [0235] from any laws, divine, **canonical**, or civil, as he wishes.
AP : 0 7 :024(172) [0235] its authors not only the **canonists** but also Dan. 11:36-39.
AP : 1 0 :002(179) [0247] Evidence for this is their **canon** of the Mass, in which the
AP : 1 1 :004(181) [0249] this according to both the Gospel and the ancient **canons**.
AP : 1 1 :005(181) [0249] The ancient **canons** and the Fathers do not appoint a set
AP : 1 1 :005(181) [0249] The **canon** says only this: "If any enter the church of God
AP : 1 1 :008(181) [0251] by Panormitanus and other learned in the **canon** law.
AP : 1 2 :003(183) [0253] of the scholastics and **canonists** had overwhelmed the
AP : 1 2 :016(184) [0257] of penitence as taught by the scholastics and **canonists**.
AP : 1 2 :024(185) [0257] 8. **Canonical** satisfactions are necessary to redeem the
AP : 1 2 :027(185) [0259] cases, not only the **canonical** punishment but also the
AP : 1 2 :112(198) [0285] Different offenses had different **canons**.
AP : 1 2 :115(199) [0285] that are not due; we call them **canonical** satisfactions.
AP : 1 2 :116(199) [0285] of sins, that **canonical** satisfactions are not necessary by
AP : 1 2 :121(200) [0287] But the gloss on the **canons** says several times that these
AP : 1 2 :122(200) [0289] from the Fathers and the **canons** and conclude that the
AP : 1 2 :131(202) [0291] nothing whatever about **canonical** satisfactions or the
AP : 1 2 :135(203) [0293] to apply these passages to **canonical** satisfactions.
AP : 1 2 :138(203) [0293] to say, therefore, that **canonical** satisfactions compensate
AP : 1 2 :139(203) [0295] punishments referred to **canonical** penalties, part of which
AP : 1 2 :139(203) [0295] of purgatory or **canonical** satisfactions can remit eternal
AP : 1 2 :147(205) [0297] may safely conclude that **canonical** satisfactions are not
AP : 1 2 :149(205) [0299] if they think that **canonical** satisfactions are more genuine
AP : 1 2 :154(206) [0299] **Canonical** satisfactions, moreover, do not apply to these
AP : 1 2 :162(208) [0303] The performance of **canonical** satisfactions does not do
AP : 1 2 :171(209) [0305] described by the **canons** dealing with satisfactions.
AP : 1 2 :171(209) [0305] they did not regard these **canons** as necessary for the
AP : 1 2 :171(209) [0305] one required in the **canons** dealing with satisfactions.
AP : 1 2 :172(209) [0305] not command that these **canonical** satisfactions or
AP : 1 2 :173(210) [0305] Gospel compels us to assume these **canonical** satisfactions
AP : 1 2 :177(210) [0307] It is the reservation of **canonical** penalties, not the

Continued ▶

AP : 14 :001(214) [0315] proviso that we employ **canonical** ordination, they accept
AP : 14 :001(214) [0315] discipline in the manner described by the ancient **canons**.
AP : 14 :002(214) [0315] for the abolition of **canonical** government in some places,
AP : 14 :004(215) [0315] and true, though the **canons** themselves are gentler with
AP : 14 :005(215) [0315] the ecclesiastical and **canonical** polity, provided that the
AP : 15 :039(220) [0325] are more faithful to the **canons** than our opponents are.
AP : 15 :041(220) [0325] at all, though even the **canons** give prescriptions about it.
AP : 15 :048(221) [0329] do not even observe the **canonical** prescriptions.
AP : 21 :023(232) [0349] Biel's interpretation of the **canon** of the Mass confidently
AP : 21 :040(235) [0355] of the scholastics and **canonists** contain many false
AP : 21 :041(235) [0355] theologians and **canonists** and was teaching things
AP : 23 :003(239) [0363] of the nations, and the **canons** of the councils, they
AP : 23 :023(242) [0369] regulation also disagrees with the **canons** of the councils.
AP : 23 :023(242) [0369] The ancient **canons** do not forbid marriage, nor dissolve
AP : 23 :023(242) [0369] These new **canons** do not represent the decision of the
AP : 23 :057(247) [0379] The **canon** commands that priests be suspended; our
AP : 23 :057(247) [0379] be suspended; our **canonists** suspend them all right — not
AP : 23 :060(247) [0379] disagrees even with the **canons**; it is superstitious and full
AP : 24 :086(265) [0413] The apostolic **canons** show that when they gathered they
AP : 24 :088(265) [0413] The Greek **canon** also says much about an offering; but it
AP : 24 :088(265) [0413] For the **canon** is talking about the whole service; and by
AP : 24 :093(267) [0417] The Greek **canon** does not apply the offering as a
AP : 27 :010(270) [0423] about such vows, which even the papal **canons** condemn.
AP : 27 :057(279) [0439] Finally, the **canons** themselves release many who took
AP : 27 :057(279) [0439] Not even the **canons** maintain that such vows are really
AP : 28 :012(283) [0447] be bishops according to **canonical** polity, to which we do
S1 : PR :010(290) [0457] the bishops nor the **canons** care how the poor people live
S1 : PR :014(291) [0459] multitude of decrees and **canons** in a council, especially
S3 : 03 :022(306) [0485] according to the ancient **canons**, seven years of penance
TR : 00 :038(326) [0515] The **canons** likewise clearly teach that a heretical pope is
TR : 00 :049(329) [0519] of councils, as the **canons** sometimes impudently declare
TR : 00 :050(329) [0519] question of the third **canon** states, "No one shall judge the
TR : 00 :077(333) [0527] cases which according to **canon** law pertain to
TR : 00 :077(333) [0527] This is conceded by the **canons**.

Canticles (1)
AG : 26 :040(069) [0075] of the Mass and various **canticles**, festivals, and the like)

Capability (2), Capable (14)
AG : 18 :002(039) [0051] Holy Spirit man is not **capable** of making himself
AG : 18 :005(040) [0051] I mean what they are **capable** of by nature: whether or
AP : 12 :130(202) [0291] but do not hear teachers **capable** of setting their
AP : 21 :043(235) [0357] They do not tolerate **capable** clergy in the churches.
S1 : PR :009(290) [0457] convert those who are **capable** of conversion and turn
S3 : 03 :010(305) [0481] that reason is **capable** of right understanding and the will
S3 : 03 :010(305) [0481] and the will is **capable** of acting accordingly, and that
SC : PR :009(339) [0535] and in such a variety of ways as you may be **capable** of.
LC : 01 :172(388) [0629] If we want qualified and **capable** men for both civil and
EP : 01 :016(468) [0783] the capacity, skill, **capability**, or power to initiate, to
SD : 02 :022(525) [0889] again become and be **capable** of and a partaker in
SD : 02 :022(525) [0889] aptitude, capacity, or **capability** — our human nature is in
SD : 08 :052(601) [1033] Christ could or should be **capable** or incapable without
SD : 08 :053(601) [1033] human nature is **capable** over and above its natural
SD : 08 :053(601) [1033] argue that the human nature in Christ is not **capable** of it.
SD : 08 :071(605) [1041] or on earth, is not **capable** of the omnipotence of God in

Capacity (13), Capacities (1)
AP : 02 :003(101) [0105] nature has the gift and **capacity** to produce the fear and
AP : 02 :025(103) [0111] inclination of man's higher **capacities** to carnal things.
AP : 04 :029(111) [0129] *Grace* he says: "If natural **capacity**, with the help of free
AP : 18 :007(225) [0337] ascribe to it the spiritual **capacity** for true fear of God,
LC : 01 :142(384) [0621] they act in the **capacity** of fathers and ought to have
EP : 01 :016(468) [0783] — for example, the **capacity**, skill, capability, or power to
SD : 02 :007(521) [0883] nor that he has any **capacity** for grace by and for himself
SD : 02 :012(522) [0885] of the natural man every **capacity**, aptitude, skill, and
SD : 02 :012(523) [0885] God (that is, he has no **capacity** for spiritual things) for
SD : 02 :022(525) [0889] and efficient aptitude, **capacity**, or capability — our
SD : 02 :023(525) [0889] Dr. Luther calls this a "**capacity**," which he explains as
SD : 02 :023(525) [0889] free will, they affirm a **capacity** for this freedom in such a
SD : 02 :078(536) [0911] above that such a **capacity** naturally to prepare oneself
SD : 08 :051(601) [1033] or only as far as their **capacity** extends, but primarily from

Capernaitic (7)
EP : 07 :015(483) [0811] — however, not in a **Capernaitic** manner, but because of
EP : 07 :041(486) [0817] in a coarse, carnal, **Capernaitic**, and abhorrent way
EP : 07 :042(486) [0817] any qualification the **Capernaitic** eating of the body of
EP : 08 :017(489) [0823] is not mundane or **Capernaitic** although it is true and
SD : 07 :064(581) [0995] in a coarse, carnal, **Capernaitic** manner, but in a
SD : 07 :105(588) [1009] Thus we reject the **Capernaitic** conception of a gross,
SD : 07 :127(591) [1015] in a coarse, fleshly, **Capernaitic** way about the

Capital (1)
EP : 12 :016(499) [0841] a clear conscience inflict **capital** punishment upon

Captiously (2)
AL : 20 :012(042) [0055] Lest anyone should **captiously** object that we have
AL : 22 :003(049) [0059] Lest anybody should **captiously** object that this refers

Captive (19), Captives (2), Captivate (1), Captivity (2), Captured (1)
AP : 02 :039(105) [0115] my mind and making me **captive** to the law of sin which
AP : 04 :139(126) [0161] (Ps. 68:18), "He led **captivity** captive and gave gifts to
AP : 04 :139(126) [0161] "He led **captivity captive** and gave gifts to men."
AP : 07 :016(171) [0231] by the devil and are his **captives**; they are not ruled by the
AP : 07 :029(173) [0237] of the devil, who drives them on and holds them **captive**.
AP : 23 :045(245) [0375] among the Encratites **captured** the imagination of the
S3 : 03 :008(304) [0481] it) from the dreadful **captivity** to sin, and this comes to us
S3 : 07 :001(311) [0493] that in his flesh he was **captive** to "the law of sin."
S3 : 08 :008(313) [0495] Messiah did not hold him **captive** with the hardened,
SC : PR :023(341) [0539] deeply immersed in them and is held **captive** by the devil.
LC : 01 :216(394) [0641] indeed, all poor, **captive** consciences deceived by their
LC : 01 :314(407) [0671] other hand, those other works **captivate** all eyes and ears.
LC : 02 :027(414) [0685] Lord and King but was **captive** under the power of the
EP : 06 :004(480) [0807] to follow the Spirit and surrender himself a **captive**.
EP : 07 :042(486) [0817] Here we take our intellect **captive** in obedience to Christ,
SD : 01 :013(511) [0863] abandoned to his power, and held **captive** in his servitude.
SD : 02 :007(521) [0883] of sin (John 8:34), the **captive** of the devil who drives him
SD : 02 :017(524) [0887] my mind and making me **captive** to the law of sin" (Rom.
SD : 02 :030(527) [0893] the contrary, it declares that man is the **captive** of Satan.
SD : 02 :043(529) [0897] remain the dupes and **captives** of sin and the property of
SD : 02 :044(529) [0897] he states that blind and **captive** man performs only the
SD : 02 :064(533) [0905] my mind and making me **captive** to the law of sin which
SD : 06 :008(565) [0965] of my mind and making me **captive** to the law of sin."
SD : 08 :096(609) [1049] take their intellect **captive** to obey Christ, comfort
SD : 09 :003(610) [1053] can take us or any believer in Christ **captive** or harm us.

Cardinal (2), Cardinals (3)
AG : 22 :008(050) [0061] was introduced, although **Cardinal** Cusanus mentions
AL : 22 :004(050) [0061] was changed, although **Cardinal** Cusanus mentions when
AP : 04 :390(166) [0225] that the pope or **cardinals** or bishops or some theologians
S1 : PR :013(291) [0459] cinctures, bishops' and **cardinals'** hats and crosiers, and
S3 : 03 :024(307) [0485] distributed among the **cardinals** and bishops so that one

Care (29), Cared (1), Careful (12), Carefully (18), Careless (2), Carelessness (1), Cares (14), Caring (2)
PR : PR :010(006) [0011] basis of God's Word, **carefully** and accurately to explain
PR : PR :013(007) [0013] mature reflection and **careful** diligence, they brought
AG : 25 :002(061) [0069] time the people are **carefully** instructed concerning the
AG : 26 :010(065) [0071] should bear children and **care** for them, that a prince and
AG : 28 :002(081) [0083] Out of this **careless** confusion many serious wars,
AL : 20 :024(044) [0055] God, knows that God **cares** for him, and calls upon God.
AL : 25 :006(062) [0069] doctrine of repentance and have treated it with great **care**.
AL : 27 :002(071) [0077] of restoring discipline, as in a **carefully** planned prison.
AP : 04 :018(109) [0125] neither fears God nor truly believes that he **cares**.
AP : 04 :035(112) [0131] did not believe that God **cared** for him or regarded or
AP : 04 :131(125) [0157] about the first table they **care** nothing, as though it were
AP : 04 :135(125) [0159] believe in his providential **care**, but supposes that men are
AP : 04 :141(126) [0161] have a gracious God who **cares** about us, we call upon
AP : 04 :303(154) [0205] which believes that God **cares** for us, forgives us, and
AP : 04 :314(156) [0207] our case very well, and a **careful** consideration of it will
AP : 04 :350(161) [0217] the conviction that God **cares** for us, forgives us, and
AP : 04 :351(161) [0217] to fear him and to trust that he **cares** for us and hears us.
AP : 07 :002(168) [0227] Nothing can be said so **carefully** that it can avoid
AP : 07 :027(173) [0235] How many of them **care** anything for the Gospel or think
AP : 10 :001(179) [0247] After **careful** examination and consideration of it, we
AP : 12 :003(182) [0253] and to consider **carefully** this most important issue,
AP : 12 :007(183) [0255] Others are more **careful** and suppose that the power of
AP : 12 :125(201) [0289] the faith, she should take **care** that men of learning and
AP : 12 :126(201) [0289] which, unless you take **care**, indicate a change in the Holy
AP : 12 :129(202) [0291] suppose that they can take **care** of this easily since they
AP : 15 :014(217) [0319] in my statutes, and be **careful** to observe my ordinances."
AP : 21 :044(236) [0357] They should take **care** to maintain and propagate divine
AP : 24 :020(252) [0389] types of sacrifice and be very **careful** not to confuse them.
AP : 24 :081(264) [0411] pay for the games, ships, **care** of the gymnasium, and
AP : 24 :083(264) [0413] thus the verb means to **care** for or to administer public
AP : 24 :091(266) [0415] consciences should be **careful** not to support the abuses
AP : 27 :010(270) [0423] this whole issue **carefully** and fully in his book called
AP : 27 :032(274) [0431] for if he considers **carefully**, he will undoubtedly discover
S1 : PR :010(290) [0457] bishops nor the canons **care** how the poor people live or
S3 : 00 :000(302) [0477] pope and his court do not **care** much about these things;
S3 : 02 :004(303) [0479] that he neither has nor **cares** for God or that he worships
TR : 00 :054(329) [0519] For the first **care** of kings should be to advance the glory
TR : 00 :080(334) [0527] of education, the **care** of the poor, and the establishment
SC : PR :006(338) [0533] who are entrusted to your **care**, and that you help me to
SC : PR :007(338) [0533] should take the utmost **care** to avoid changes or
SC : 09 :015(356) [0563] Let each his lesson learn with **care**
LC : PR :019(361) [0573] with the greatest **care** and diligence against the poisonous
LC : SP :027(364) [0581] The reason we take such **care** to preach on the Catechism
LC : 01 :005(365) [0581] so stubbornly and securely that he **cares** for no one.
LC : 01 :021(367) [0585] It neither **cares** for God nor expects good things from him
LC : 01 :028(368) [0587] Let everyone, then, take **care** to magnify and exalt this
LC : 01 :036(369) [0589] rich pot-bellies who, not **caring** whether God frowns or
LC : 01 :041(370) [0591] Therefore let everyone be **careful** not to regard this as if it
LC : 01 :043(370) [0591] men have devoted all their **care** and diligence to scraping
LC : 01 :108(380) [0611] commands you to be **careful** to obey me as your father
LC : 01 :111(380) [0613] them, helping them, and **caring** for them when they are
LC : 01 :143(385) [0623] maid-servants should take **care** not only to obey their
LC : 01 :145(385) [0623] thank God; and with her **careful** work, for which she
LC : 01 :154(386) [0625] be free from all authority, **care** nothing for anyone, and
LC : 01 :206(393) [0639] to speak of it, let us **carefully** note, first, how highly God
LC : 01 :225(395) [0645] that through laziness, **carelessness**, or malice a servant
LC : 01 :226(395) [0645] people and yet are **careless** and unreliable in their work.
LC : 01 :235(397) [0647] you servants ought to take **care** of your master's or
LC : 01 :276(402) [0659] which ought to be **carefully** noted if we are to avoid this
LC : 01 :287(403) [0663] members, of which we are ashamed, we **carefully** conceal.
LC : 02 :017(412) [0681] merit, as a kind father who **cares** for us so that no evil
LC : 03 :006(421) [0699] knows whether God heeds my prayer or **cares** to hear it?
LC : 03 :010(421) [0699] that he neither wants nor **cares** for our prayers because
LC : 03 :030(424) [0707] Therefore we must **carefully** select the weapons with
LC : 03 :082(431) [0721] wishes to show us how he **cares** for us in all our needs and
LC : 03 :084(432) [0723] church, and let them take **care** lest this petition of the
LC : 05 :006(447) [0755] Do you think God **cares** so much about our faith and
LC : 06 :018(459) [0000] We should therefore take **care** to keep the two parts
SD : 01 :003(509) [0861] honor properly when we **carefully** distinguish his work
SD : 01 :035(514) [0869] and steadfast love; and thy **care** has preserved my spirit"
SD : 01 :051(517) [0875] is necessary to explain **carefully** and distinctly all
SD : 02 :044(529) [0897] against Erasmus and **carefully** and in great detail presents
SD : 03 :055(549) [0935] is important to consider **carefully** in what way Christ is
SD : 04 :019(554) [0945] Here again **careful** attention must be given to the
SD : 04 :022(554) [0945] we must be extremely **careful** that works are not drawn
SD : 07 :044(577) [0987] with great deliberation and **care** in ordaining and
SD : 11 :004(616) [1063] the very outset we must **carefully** note the difference
SD : 11 :052(625) [1079] We must, however, **carefully** distinguish between what
SD : 11 :079(629) [1089] Hence Paul very **carefully** distinguishes between the work

Carlstadt (1)
AP : 16 :003(223) [0331] It was mad of **Carlstadt** to try to impose on us the judicial

Catastrophes (1)
LC : 0 3 :115(435) [0731] many he hounds to suicide or other dreadful **catastrophes**

Catch (1)
LC : 0 1 :226(395) [0645] lock and bolt, or if we **catch** them we can deal with them

Catechism (37), Catechisms (6), Catechization (1)
PR : PR :025(014) [0023] the Large and Small **Catechism** of that highly enlightened
AP : 1 5 :041(220) [0325] opponents there is no **catechization** of the children at all,
S 1 : 0 1 :000(292) [0461] Creed, and the **Catechism** in common use for children
SC : 0 0 :000(337) [0531] The Small **Catechism** of Dr. Martin Luther for Ordinary
SC : PR :001(338) [0533] this brief and simple **catechism** or statement of Christian
SC : PR :006(338) [0533] help me to teach the **catechism** to the people, especially
SC : PR :008(339) [0535] syllable or recite the **catechism** differently from year to
SC : PR :017(340) [0535] thus taught this brief **catechism**, take up a large catechism
SC : PR :017(340) [0535] take up a large **catechism** so that the people may have a
LC : PR :001(358) [0567] we constantly treat the **Catechism** and strongly urge
LC : PR :003(358) [0567] a page or two from the **Catechism**, the Prayer Book, the
LC : PR :005(359) [0567] Many regard the **Catechism** as a simple, silly teaching
LC : PR :007(359) [0569] Yet I do as a child who is being taught the **Catechism**.
LC : PR :008(359) [0569] still read and study the **Catechism** daily, yet I cannot
LC : PR :008(359) [0569] a child and pupil of the **Catechism**, and I do it gladly.
LC : PR :009(359) [0569] these parts of the **Catechism** perfectly, or at least
LC : PR :009(359) [0569] if their knowledge of **Catechism** were perfect (though that
LC : PR :009(359) [0569] day we relish and appreciate the **Catechism** more greatly.
LC : PR :011(360) [0571] and practice the **Catechism**, even if the only blessing and
LC : PR :014(360) [0571] us to read the **Catechism** daily, there is God's command.
LC : PR :016(361) [0571] who will not or cannot read and study the **Catechism** daily
LC : PR :018(361) [0573] know and despise the **Catechism**, which is a brief
LC : PR :019(361) [0573] themselves in the **Catechism** daily, and constantly put it
LC : PR :020(361) [0573] they work with the **Catechism**, the less they know of it
LC : SP :001(362) [0575] been called in Greek, a "**catechism**" — that is, instruction
LC : SP :003(362) [0575] the various parts of the **Catechism** or children's sermons
LC : SP :026(364) [0579] time designated for the **Catechism**, so that they may hear
LC : SP :027(364) [0581] care to preach on the **Catechism** frequently is to impress it
LC : 0 2 :070(420) [0697] these teachings of the **Catechism** all that they learn in the
EP : RN :005(465) [0777] Small and Large **Catechisms** as both of them are
EP : 1 1 :022(497) [0837] of God and the plain **Catechism**, every simple Christian
EP : 1 2 :030(500) [0843] the Smalcald Articles, and the **Catechisms** of Luther.
SD : RN :008(505) [0853] Small and Large **Catechisms**, as he prepared them and
SD : RN :011(506) [0855] Large and Small **Catechisms** — in the cited summary of
SD : 0 1 :038(514) [0871] the Creed in the Small **Catechism** we confess, "I believe
SD : 0 1 :038(515) [0871] we confess in the Large **Catechism**, "I hold and believe
SD : 0 2 :036(528) [0895] In his Large **Catechism** Dr. Luther writes: "I am also a
SD : 0 2 :038(528) [0895] In these words the **Catechism** makes no mention whatever
SD : 0 2 :040(528) [0895] In Dr. Luther's Small **Catechism** we read: "I believe that
SD : 0 2 :045(530) [0899] the Large and Small **Catechisms** of Luther, and other
SD : 0 7 :010(571) [0975] same view in the Small **Catechism** in the following words:
SD : 0 7 :020(572) [0979] of God in the Large **Catechism**, where he writes as
SD : 0 7 :027(573) [0981] from the Large **Catechism**, which establishes the true
SD : 1 2 :039(636) [1103] Apology, to the Smalcald Articles, to Luther's **Catechisms**

Catechumen (1)
TR : 0 0 :067(331) [0523] baptized the other (a **catechumen**), and the latter, after

Cathedral (1)
AG : 2 3 :018(054) [0063] honest men among the **cathedral** clergy and some of the

Catholic (13)
AL : 0 0 :001(047) [0059] the Scriptures or the **catholic** church or the church of
AL : 0 0 :001(048) [0059] dissent from the church **catholic** in no article of faith but
AL : 2 8 :028(085) [0087] of Petilian that not even **catholic** bishops are to be obeyed
AL : 2 8 :072(093) [0093] introduced contrary to the custom of the church **catholic**.
AL : 0 0 :005(095) [0095] that is contrary to Scripture or to the church **catholic**.
AP : 0 2 :032(104) [0113] Scripture or the church **catholic**, but we have cleansed
AP : 0 2 :051(107) [0119] is correct and in agreement with Christ's church **catholic**.
AP : 0 7 :007(169) [0229] us to believe that there is a holy, **catholic** church.
AP : 0 7 :010(170) [0229] It says "the church **catholic**" lest we take it to mean an
AP : 1 4 :003(214) [0315] we know that our confession is true, godly, and **catholic**.
AP : 2 4 :006(250) [0385] contrary to the church **catholic** in our having only the
TR : 0 0 :082(000) [0529] with the belief of the true and genuine **catholic** Church.
EP : RN :003(465) [0777] as the unanimous, **catholic**, Christian faith and

Cattle (14)
AL : 1 8 :005(040) [0051] will to marry, will to keep **cattle**, will to learn various
AP : 2 4 :026(254) [0391] only with the sacrifices of **cattle** but also with human
AP : 2 4 :026(254) [0391] Levitical worship, where **cattle** were slaughtered, but with
S 1 : PR :008(290) [0457] all live promiscuously like **cattle** and everybody does
SC : 0 1 :020(344) [0543] wife, servants, or **cattle**, but encourage them to remain
LC : SP :010(363) [0577] man-servant, maid-servant, **cattle**, or anything that is his.
LC : 0 1 :012(366) [0583] love affairs, protect their **cattle**, recover lost possessions,
LC : 0 1 :242(397) [0649] Your **cattle** will die in the stall.
LC : 0 1 :292(404) [0663] *man-servant, maid-servant, **cattle**, or anything that is his.*"
LC : 0 1 :294(404) [0665] property, the same as his **cattle** and other possessions.
LC : 0 1 :296(405) [0665] as his wife, servants, house, fields, meadows, or **cattle**.
LC : 0 1 :330(410) [0677] and compulsion, like **cattle**, but in the fear and reverence
LC : 0 3 :078(431) [0721] poison, pestilence, and **cattle**-plague; from war and
LC : 0 3 :080(431) [0721] hail to destroy crops and **cattle**, why he poisons the air,

Cause (61), Caused (9), Causes (17), Causing (3)
PR : PR :022(012) [0021] just as Christian charity **causes** us to have special
PR : PR :024(013) [0023] stand in the way of this **cause** and the promotion of
AG : PR :013(026) [0041] allow, that may serve the **cause** of Christian unity.
AG : 1 9 :000(040) [0053] XIX. The **Cause** of Sin
AG : 1 9 :000(040) [0053] nature, yet sin is **caused** in all wicked men and despisers
AG : 2 3 :009(052) [0061] to themselves for these and other reasons and **causes**.
AG : 2 3 :014(053) [0063] of marriage may not **cause** worse and more disgraceful
AG : 2 3 :018(054) [0063] of celibacy has been the **cause** of so much frightful and
AG : 2 6 :016(066) [0073] that such traditions **caused** so much strife in the church
AG : 2 6 :041(070) [0075] a sin to omit them if this is done without **causing** scandal.
AL : 1 9 :000(040) [0053] XIX. The **Cause** of Sin
AL : 1 9 :000(040) [0053] and preserves nature, the **cause** of sin is the will of the
AL : 2 3 :018(054) [0063] although impure celibacy **causes** many scandals,
AL : 2 3 :021(055) [0063] intent of the canons, for no other **cause** than marriage.
AP : PR :019(099) [0103] so we shall commend our **cause** to Christ, who will one
AP : 0 4 :098(121) [0151] here means that which is cited as the **cause** of salvation.
AP : 0 4 :098(121) [0151] the name of Christ as the **cause** or price on account of
AP : 0 4 :152(127) [0163] we sometimes combine **cause** and effect in the same
AP : 0 4 :185(132) [0173] "Being sick in itself, an unjust **cause** needs wise remedies."
AP : 0 4 :244(141) [0189] The words of James will **cause** no trouble if our
AP : 0 4 :326(157) [0211] he is speaking of his **cause** against the persecutors of
AP : 0 4 :326(158) [0211] for the defense of God's **cause** and his glory, as in Ps. 7:8,
AP : 0 4 :339(159) [0215] not analogous since the **causes** and objects of trust in the
AP : 1 0 :003(179) [0247] is in us, does it not also **cause** Christ to dwell in us bodily
AP : 1 2 :090(195) [0279] right for us to forsake the **cause** — not our cause but the
AP : 1 2 :090(195) [0279] the cause — not our **cause** but the cause of Christ and the
AP : 1 2 :090(195) [0279] — not our cause but the **cause** of Christ and the church.
AP : 1 2 :168(209) [0305] means cutting off the **causes** of sin, that is, mortifying and
AP : 1 9 :000(226) [0337] [Article XIX. The **Cause** of Sin]
AP : 1 9 :001(226) [0337] Nevertheless, the **cause** of sin is the will of the devil and
AP : 2 0 :013(228) [0341] Such argumentation is to make the effect the **cause**.
AP : 2 3 :068(249) [0383] the impression that our **cause** had been tried and
AP : 2 4 :072(262) [0409] (Ps. 111:4, 5), "He has **caused** his wonderful works to be
AP : 2 4 :082(264) [0411] the saints need but also **causes** many to thank God more
AP : 2 4 :099(268) [0419] This is a great **cause** and a great issue, not inferior to the
AP : 2 7 :005(269) [0421] into bad harmonies which, Plato says, **cause** destruction.
AP : 2 7 :051(278) [0437] anybody whose weakness **causes** him to defile himself
S 1 : PR :007(289) [0457] ours ever larger, and has **caused**, and still causes, them
S 1 : PR :007(289) [0457] and has caused, and still **causes**, them and their lies to be
S 1 : PR :011(290) [0457] makes me fear that he may **cause** a council of angels to
S 2 : 0 3 :002(298) [0471] Moreover, it **causes** dangerous and needless effort, and
TR : 0 0 :034(325) [0513] This notion has **caused** horrible darkness to descend over
SC : 0 1 :010(343) [0541] our neighbor's life, nor **cause** him any harm, but help and
SC : 0 5 :022(350) [0553] made my master angry, **caused** him to curse, neglected to
SC : 0 5 :022(350) [0553] neglected to do my duty, and **caused** him to suffer loss.
LC : 0 1 :038(369) [0591] them to their senses and **cause** them to mend their ways
LC : 0 1 :202(392) [0639] but also every kind of **cause**, motive, and means.
LC : 0 1 :310(407) [0669] destroy all the roots and **causes** of our injuries to our
LC : 0 2 :038(415) [0689] use and enjoyed, God has **caused** the Word to be
LC : 0 2 :043(416) [0689] Where he does not **cause** the Word to be preached and
LC : 0 2 :053(417) [0693] increases sanctification, **causing** it daily to grow and
LC : 0 3 :072(430) [0719] For if God did not **cause** grain to grow and did not bless
LC : 0 3 :076(431) [0721] and a sound body; to **cause** the grain and fruits of the
LC : 0 3 :076(431) [0721] children, and servants; to **cause** our work, craft, or
LC : 0 3 :080(431) [0721] This is why he **causes** so much contention, murder,
LC : 0 3 :115(435) [0731] and vents his anger by **causing** accidents and injury to
LC : 0 4 :007(437) [0733] It is the chief **cause** of our contentions and battles
EP : 0 2 :019(472) [0791] are only two efficient **causes**, namely, the Holy Spirit and
EP : 0 3 :020(475) [0797] as if it were the primary **cause** of our righteousness, but
EP : 0 7 :034(485) [0815] (a dreadful statement!) to **cause** his body to be essentially
EP : 0 7 :035(485) [0815] testament, effect and **cause** this presence of the body and
EP : 1 1 :004(494) [0833] But it is not a **cause** of evil or of sin which compels
EP : 1 1 :004(495) [0833] Neither is it the **cause** of man's perdition; for this man
EP : 1 1 :005(495) [0833] It is a **cause** of their salvation, for he alone brings it
EP : 1 1 :012(496) [0835] The **cause** of condemnation is that men either do not hear
EP : 1 1 :020(497) [0837] there is also within us a **cause** of God's election, on
SD : PR :007(502) [0849] This **caused** serious and dangerous schisms in the true
SD : 0 1 :006(509) [0861] of this corruption and be **cause** of the fall of the first
SD : 0 1 :007(510) [0861] that God is not the creator, author, or **cause** of sin.
SD : 0 2 :071(535) [0909] concerning the efficient **cause** (that is, who works these
SD : 0 2 :090(538) [0915] of the three efficient **causes** of unregenerated man's
SD : 0 3 :037(546) [0929] our works as either the **cause** or the meritorious basis of
SD : 0 3 :039(546) [0929] posited to be a part or a **cause** of our justification, nor
SD : 0 3 :043(547) [0931] for our justification, as a **cause** without which a person
SD : 0 3 :045(547) [0933] are a meritorious basis or **cause** of our justification before
SD : 0 3 :049(548) [0933] they are not the principal **cause** but that our justification
SD : 0 4 :001(551) [0939] is dead, although such love is not a **cause** of salvation.
SD : 0 4 :021(554) [0945] explain why and for what **causes** they are necessary, as
SD : 0 4 :038(557) [0951] done on account of right **causes** and for right ends (that
SD : 1 0 :016(613) [1057] and again, "Whoever **causes** one of these little ones who
SD : 1 1 :007(617) [1065] The source and **cause** of evil is not God's foreknowledge
SD : 1 1 :008(617) [1065] in Christ Jesus it is also a **cause** which creates, effects,
SD : 1 1 :010(618) [1065] pernicious opinions and **causes** and fortifies in people's
SD : 1 1 :012(618) [1067] will in no way **cause** or support either impenitence or
SD : 1 1 :080(629) [1089] and not God, are the **cause** of their being fitted for
SD : 1 1 :081(629) [1089] God is not the **cause** of sin, nor is he the cause of the
SD : 1 1 :081(629) [1089] cause of sin, nor is he the **cause** of the punishment, the
SD : 1 1 :081(629) [1089] The only **cause** of man's damnation is sin, for the "wages
SD : 1 1 :088(631) [1093] when men teach that the **cause** of our election is not only
SD : 1 1 :088(631) [1093] there is also within us a **cause** of God's election on

Caution (2), Cautious (1)
AP : PR :014(099) [0101] in some places it could deceive even the **cautious** reader.
AP : 1 8 :001(225) [0335] They also add a **caution**, lest too much be conceded to
AP : 2 8 :018(284) [0449] authority," but rather a "**caution** about something

Cease (6), Ceased (2), Ceaseless (1), Ceases (3), Ceasing (4)
PR : PR :006(004) [0009] we bear, we have not **ceased** to apply our diligence to the
AP : 0 4 :258(144) [0193] preaching of penitence: "**Cease** to do evil, learn to do
AP : 0 4 :258(144) [0193] At the beginning he says, "**Cease** to do evil," as he
AP : 1 2 :164(208) [0303] as Isa. 1:16-19 teaches: "**Cease** to do evil, learn to do
AP : 2 8 :024(285) [0451] "The former good will **ceases**, and mortals are forgetful,"
S 2 : 0 2 :028(297) [0469] expected, the saints will **cease** to be molested in their
LC : 0 1 :079(375) [0603] means to rest, that is, to **cease** from labor; hence our
LC : 0 1 :120(381) [0615] with fasting and pray on their knees without **ceasing**"?
LC : 0 2 :019(412) [0681] and thank him without **ceasing**, and, in short, to devote
LC : 0 3 :024(423) [0705] ought to drive and impel us to pray without **ceasing**.
LC : 0 3 :067(429) [0717] case to pray without **ceasing**: "Thy will be done, dear
LC : 0 3 :087(432) [0723] possible always to stand firm in such a **ceaseless** conflict.
LC : 0 3 :109(435) [0729] weary; when one attack **ceases**, new ones always arise.
LC : 0 3 :111(435) [0729] will see the temptation **cease** and eventually admit defeat.
SD : 0 4 :005(551) [0939] time, however, the issue **ceased** to be only a semantic
SD : 0 8 :019(594) [1021] of honey and water and **ceases** to be distinguishably

Celebrant (2), Celebrants (1)
AP : 1 5 :040(220) [0325] opponents, unwilling **celebrants** and hirelings perform
S 2 : 0 2 :007(294) [0465] asserts that it is not the **celebrant** of a Mass and what he
S 2 : 0 2 :010(294) [0465] before I would allow a **celebrant** of the Mass and what he

Celebrate (5), Celebrated (13), Celebrating (1), Celebration (6), Celebrations (1)
PR : PR :022(012) [0019] Holy Supper as it is **celebrated** in our churches according
AL : 2 3 :013(053) [0063] popes and those made by the most **celebrated** councils.
AL : 2 4 :001(056) [0065] among us and is **celebrated** with the greatest reverence.
AL : 2 4 :011(057) [0065] of men Masses are **celebrated** only for revenues or
AL : 2 4 :011(057) [0065] stipends, and how many **celebrate** Masses contrary to the
AL : 2 4 :037(060) [0067] one person or other **celebrated** Mass and the rest of the
AP : 0 4 :218(137) [0179] Here they **celebrate** a great victory.
AP : 0 7 :042(176) [0241] of Nicaea some people **celebrated** Easter at one time and
AP : 0 7 :042(176) [0241] their churches to **celebrate** the Passover with the brethren
AP : 0 7 :042(176) [0243] do not correctly compute the time in **celebrating** Easter.
AP : 0 7 :042(176) [0243] of the circumcision do, **celebrate** it at the same time with
AP : 0 7 :043(177) [0243] the Passover should be **celebrated** with the Jews; they
AP : 0 7 :043(177) [0243] when Easter should be **celebrated**, but for the sake of
AP : 2 3 :032(243) [0373] they would stage a wonderful victory **celebration**.
AP : 2 4 :001(249) [0383] our churches Mass is **celebrated** every Sunday and on
AP : 2 4 :008(250) [0385] but Communion was **celebrated** three times a week, and
AP : 2 4 :072(262) [0409] Christ is not the vain **celebration** of a show or a
AP : 2 4 :072(262) [0409] of a show or a **celebration** for the sake of example, the
AP : 2 4 :072(262) [0409] example, the way plays **celebrate** the memory of Hercules
AP : 2 4 :085(265) [0413] coming to the **celebration** of the Passover had to bring
S 2 : 0 2 :012(294) [0465] monthly, and yearly **celebrations** of requiems, with the
TR : 0 0 :014(322) [0507] that for the proper **celebration** of ordinations the
LC : 0 1 :022(367) [0585] it has made endowments, fasted, **celebrated** Mass, etc.
EP : 0 7 :009(483) [0811] one accord that in the **celebration** of the Holy Supper the
EP : 1 2 :010(498) [0839] where formerly papistic Masses were read and **celebrated**.
SD : 0 7 :119(590) [1013] in the Supper, which is **celebrated** according to Christ's

Celestial (1)
EP : 0 7 :041(486) [0817] the supernatural and **celestial** mysteries of this sacrament.

Celibacy (49), Celibate (1), Celibates (2)
AG : 2 3 :005(052) [0061] have the gift of living in **celibacy**, and he certainly knew
AG : 2 3 :012(052) [0063] were compelled by force to take the vows of **celibacy**.
AG : 2 3 :012(053) [0063] The decree concerning **celibacy** was at once enforced so
AG : 2 3 :013(053) [0063] that such enforced **celibacy** and such prohibition of
AG : 2 3 :018(054) [0063] and that the vow of **celibacy** has been the cause of so
AG : 2 7 :018(073) [0079] who are not suited for **celibacy** have the power, right, and
AG : 2 7 :051(079) [0083] hearing the state of **celibacy** praised above all measure,
AL : 2 3 :005(052) [0061] men are not suited for **celibacy** because God created man
AL : 2 3 :007(052) [0061] who are not suited for **celibacy** ought to marry, for no law
AL : 2 3 :012(052) [0063] priests in Germany compelled by force to live in **celibacy**.
AL : 2 3 :018(054) [0063] and although impure **celibacy** causes many scandals,
AL : 2 7 :018(073) [0079] who are not suited for **celibacy** to marry, for vows can
AL : 2 7 :050(079) [0083] these things and not of **celibacy**, mendicancy, or humble
AL : 2 7 :052(079) [0083] They hear **celibacy** praised above measure, and therefore
AL : 2 8 :070(093) [0093] But now they demand **celibacy** and will admit no one to
AP : 2 3 :001(239) [0363] notoriety of their defiled **celibacy**, our opponents not only
AP : 2 3 :005(239) [0365] But they are not serious in their defense of **celibacy**.
AP : 2 3 :005(239) [0365] their authority, which they think **celibacy** enhances.
AP : 2 3 :006(240) [0365] approve the law of **celibacy** put forth by our opponents
AP : 2 3 :014(241) [0367] command, directed to anyone not suited for **celibacy**.
AP : 2 3 :024(243) [0371] shriek that the councils have commanded **celibacy**.
AP : 2 3 :025(243) [0371] about perpetual **celibacy** is peculiar to this new pontifical
AP : 2 3 :026(243) [0371] claim that they require **celibacy** because it is pure, as
AP : 2 3 :026(243) [0371] and sinful or as though **celibacy** merited justification
AP : 2 3 :027(243) [0371] proof to force perpetual **celibacy** on priests, though in
AP : 2 3 :032(243) [0373] a passage like that about **celibacy**, they would stage a
AP : 2 3 :032(243) [0373] to the hypocrisy of **celibacy**, what greater honor could he
AP : 2 3 :035(244) [0373] Therefore **celibacy** is not necessarily pure.
AP : 2 3 :036(244) [0373] Finally, if they interpret **celibacy** as a purity that merits
AP : 2 3 :041(245) [0375] make it necessary to impose perpetual **celibacy** on priests.
AP : 2 3 :042(245) [0375] supports the law of **celibacy** in order to burden
AP : 2 3 :045(245) [0375] about marriage and admiringly about **celibacy**.
AP : 2 3 :047(246) [0377] is the exaggerated way the monks have praised **celibacy**.
AP : 2 3 :050(246) [0377] do not demand **celibacy** for religious reasons, for they
AP : 2 3 :051(246) [0377] many reasons for rejecting the law of perpetual **celibacy**.
AP : 2 3 :056(247) [0379] laws; on this one law of **celibacy** they are adamant and
AP : 2 3 :060(247) [0379] their defense of the pontifical law of perpetual **celibacy**.
AP : 2 3 :061(247) [0381] to force anyone into **celibacy** or to dissolve existing
AP : 2 3 :063(248) [0381] for the law of perpetual **celibacy**, though it conflicts with
AP : 2 3 :064(248) [0381] lust than that of many **celibates** who are really continent.
AP : 2 3 :066(248) [0381] who are not continent in **celibacy** should marry in order
AP : 2 3 :066(248) [0381] Lord," requires impure **celibates** to become pure
AP : 2 3 :067(248) [0383] the world still did not know the law of perpetual **celibacy**.
AP : 2 3 :069(249) [0383] on the relative value of marriage and **celibacy**.
AP : 2 7 :016(271) [0425] As for **celibacy**, we would rather not discuss it.
AP : 2 7 :021(272) [0427] obedience, poverty, and **celibacy**, provided they are not
AP : 2 7 :059(279) [0441] monks abound in every delight, they claim to be **celibate**.
AP : 2 8 :026(285) [0451] What disgrace there is in **celibacy**!
S 3 : 1 1 :001(314) [0499] burden the divine estate of priests with perpetual **celibacy**.
S 3 : 1 1 :003(315) [0499] to their abominable **celibacy**, nor shall we suffer it.
TR : 0 0 :048(328) [0519] profligate acts have sprung from the tradition of **celibacy**!
TR : 0 0 :078(333) [0527] The law concerning the **celibacy** of priests is likewise

Cellar (2)
LC : 0 1 :224(395) [0643] stall, wine- and beer-**cellar**, work-shop, and, in short,
LC : 0 1 :242(397) [0649] grain will spoil in the garner and your beer in the **cellar**.

Celsus (1)
AP : 1 6 :006(223) [0331] Julian the Apostate, **Celsus**, and many others opposed the

Censure (4), Censured (3), Censures (1), Censoriously (1)
PR : PR :022(011) [0019] to the condemnations, **censures**, and rejections of false
AG : 2 7 :034(076) [0079] monastic vows might be **censured**, it would not follow
AG : 2 7 :060(080) [0083] In former times Gerson **censured** the error of the monks
AP : 0 7 :023(172) [0235] must have unlimited power beyond question or **censure**.
TR : 0 0 :036(326) [0515] as the pretext is to be **censured** that he can transfer the
TR : 0 0 :056(330) [0521] other Christians ought to **censure** the rest of the pope's
LC : 0 1 :110(380) [0613] critically, and **censoriously**, but submit to them and hold
LC : 0 1 :284(403) [0661] For example, we now **censure** the pope and his teaching,
SD : 1 2 :016(634) [1099] Confession and **censure** the errors of the Anabaptists;

Center (1)
AP : 2 4 :051(259) [0403] If our opponents **center** their worship in such things

Centos (1)
AP : 1 2 :093(196) [0279] who have compiled these **centos** of the sentences and

Central (1)
AP : 0 4 :357(161) [0217] They also omit the **central** thought of the discussion; they

Centuries (1)
AL : 2 4 :018(058) [0067] in the church for many **centuries** by the very men who

Cephas (3)
TR : 0 0 :011(321) [0507] whether Paul or Apollos or **Cephas**" (I Cor. 3:21, 22).
TR : 0 0 :011(321) [0507] nor set the authority of **Cephas** over against the authority
TR : 0 0 :011(321) [0507] time, however, they reasoned thus: "**Cephas** observes this.

Ceremonial (6)
AP : 0 4 :006(108) [0121] nothing about the **ceremonial** and civil laws of Moses.
AP : 0 4 :134(125) [0159] both the moral and the **ceremonial**; that is, hypocrites
AP : 2 4 :024(253) [0391] righteousness of the **ceremonial** law and prevented the
AP : 2 4 :034(256) [0397] of the heart, not the **ceremonial** sacrifices for sin offered
AP : 2 7 :054(278) [0439] discussions or on **ceremonial** traditions that obscure
AP : 2 7 :055(278) [0439] not discuss their whole **ceremonial** worship — lessons,

Ceremony (28), Ceremonies (88)
AG : 0 7 :003(032) [0047] Christian church that **ceremonies**, instituted by men,
AG : 0 1 :002(056) [0065] made in the public **ceremonies** of the Mass, except that in
AG : 0 1 :003(056) [0065] the chief purpose of all **ceremonies** is to teach the people
AG : 2 4 :040(061) [0069] made in the public **ceremonies** of the Mass except that
AG : 2 6 :002(064) [0071] reason new fasts, new **ceremonies**, new orders, and the
AG : 2 6 :028(068) [0073] additional outward **ceremonies**, whether of Moses or of
AG : 2 6 :040(069) [0075] part also retain many **ceremonies** and traditions (such as
AG : 2 6 :042(070) [0075] with respect to outward **ceremonies**, for in the East they
AG : 2 8 :030(085) [0087] the power to introduce **ceremonies** in the church or
AG : 2 8 :037(087) [0089] been prescribed, new **ceremonies** and new venerations of
AG : 2 8 :053(090) [0091] and other similar church ordinances and **ceremonies**?
AG : 2 8 :059(091) [0091] of the Gospel all **ceremonies** of the old law may be
AG : 2 8 :061(091) [0093] of the law, of the **ceremonies** of the New Testament, and
AG : 2 8 :061(091) [0093] bishops to devise new **ceremonies** which would be
AG : 0 0 :005(095) [0095] either in doctrine or in **ceremonies**, that is contrary to
AL : 0 7 :003(032) [0047] traditions or rites and **ceremonies**, instituted by men,
AL : 0 0 :004(048) [0059] to charge that all **ceremonies** and all old ordinances are
AL : 0 0 :004(049) [0059] of teaching and of **ceremonies** observed among us are not
AL : 0 0 :006(049) [0059] as the proper observance of **ceremonies** in the churches.
AL : 2 4 :002(056) [0065] all the customary **ceremonies** are also retained, except
AL : 2 4 :003(056) [0065] of the people, for **ceremonies** are needed especially in
AL : 2 4 :040(061) [0069] the customary public **ceremonies** are for the most part
AL : 2 6 :002(064) [0071] from the fact that new **ceremonies**, new orders, new holy
AL : 2 8 :030(085) [0087] the right to introduce **ceremonies** in the church and make
AL : 2 8 :037(086) [0089] prescribed, and new **ceremonies** and new orders instituted
AL : 2 8 :059(091) [0091] of the Gospel all **ceremonies** of the Mosaic law can be
AL : 2 8 :061(091) [0093] of the law, concerning **ceremonies** of the new law,
AL : 2 8 :061(091) [0093] bishops to devise new **ceremonies** which would be
AL : 0 0 :005(095) [0095] us, in doctrine or in **ceremonies**, that is contrary to
AP : 0 4 :087(120) [0147] as referring to Levitical **ceremonies**, but Paul is talking
AP : 0 4 :087(120) [0147] talking about the whole law, not only about **ceremonies**.
AP : 0 4 :124(124) [0157] We are not speaking of **ceremonies**, but of Decalogue, the
AP : 0 7 :012(170) [0231] true church as far as outward **ceremonies** are concerned.
AP : 0 7 :030(174) [0237] traditions or rites and **ceremonies**, instituted by men,
AP : 0 7 :031(174) [0237] was tied to the Mosaic **ceremonies**, because this
AP : 0 7 :046(177) [0243] uniform human **ceremonies** for the unity of the church
AP : 1 3 :002(211) [0309] any of the rites and **ceremonies** instituted in Scripture,
AP : 1 3 :018(213) [0313] we are justified by a **ceremony** without a good disposition
AP : 1 5 :010(216) [0317] between our traditions and the **ceremonies** of Moses.
AP : 1 5 :010(216) [0317] Paul condemns the **ceremonies** of Moses as well as
AP : 1 5 :014(217) [0319] of additional **ceremonies** without his command?
AP : 1 5 :021(218) [0321] the Fathers kept **ceremonies**, and for the same reasons we
AP : 1 5 :023(218) [0321] expanded such **ceremonies**, just as they have been
AP : 1 5 :026(219) [0323] Compared with these **ceremonies** such tasks seem
AP : 1 5 :030(219) [0323] the divinely instituted **ceremonies** of Moses do not
AP : 1 5 :032(219) [0323] in the Old Testament **ceremonies** were necessary for the
AP : 1 5 :044(221) [0327] discipline, pious **ceremonies**, and the good customs of the
AP : 2 1 :037(234) [0355] and other profitable **ceremonies**, are clowns who know
AP : 2 1 :037(234) [0355] rosaries and similar **ceremonies**, or the legends, as they
AP : 2 3 :027(243) [0371] this they refer to the **ceremonies** of the Mosaic law which
AP : 2 3 :064(248) [0381] said that the outward **ceremonies** and purity laws of the
AP : 2 3 :064(248) [0381] purity of the heart and not **ceremonies** of the law.
AP : 2 4 :003(250) [0385] purpose of observing **ceremonies** is that men may learn
AP : 2 4 :005(250) [0385] understand, or from **ceremonies** that do not teach or
AP : 2 4 :017(252) [0389] common to both could be "**ceremony**" or "sacred act."
AP : 2 4 :018(252) [0389] A sacrament is a **ceremony** or act in which God offers us
AP : 2 4 :018(252) [0389] promise joined to the **ceremony**; thus Baptism is not an
AP : 2 4 :018(252) [0389] contrast, a sacrifice is a **ceremony** or act which we render
AP : 2 4 :023(253) [0391] for our sins, as the **ceremonies** of the law were not;
AP : 2 4 :032(255) [0395] do not refer to a **ceremony** *ex opere operato* but to all
AP : 2 4 :033(255) [0395] wants to include the **ceremony** here, we shall gladly
AP : 2 4 :033(255) [0395] by itself, or *ex opere operato*, the **ceremony** is beneficial.
AP : 2 4 :033(256) [0395] we shall explain how even a **ceremony** is a sacrifice.
AP : 2 4 :033(256) [0395] the pharisaic idea of **ceremonies** *ex opere operato;*
AP : 2 4 :034(256) [0395] not support the notion of **ceremonies** *ex opere operato*.
AP : 2 4 :034(256) [0397] always apply the term "sacrifice" only to the **ceremony**.
AP : 2 4 :034(256) [0397] though it was for these that the **ceremony** was instituted.
AP : 2 4 :035(256) [0397] the whole Mass, the **ceremony** and also the proclamation
AP : 2 4 :035(256) [0397] the New Testament; the **ceremony** was instituted because
AP : 2 4 :035(256) [0397] all that there must be a **ceremony** that justifies *ex opere*
AP : 2 4 :036(256) [0397] symbolizes not only the **ceremony** but the proclamation
AP : 2 4 :038(257) [0397] Although the **ceremony** is a memorial of the death of
AP : 2 4 :039(257) [0399] of the idea that **ceremonies** work *ex opere operato*, we
AP : 2 4 :040(257) [0399] that it symbolizes the **ceremony** alone and not preaching
AP : 2 4 :042(257) [0399] keep only the **ceremony**, which they put on in public as a
AP : 2 4 :052(259) [0403] we should have some **ceremony** or sacrifice for sins, just

Continued ▶

AP : 2 4 :070(262) [0409] of sins, while the **ceremony** is a sort of picture or "seal,"
AP : 2 4 :070(262) [0409] faith accepts it, so the **ceremony** is useless without the
AP : 2 4 :072(262) [0409] This means that in the **ceremony** we should acknowledge
AP : 2 4 :074(263) [0409] It uses the **ceremony** itself as praise to God, as a
AP : 2 4 :074(263) [0411] Thus the **ceremony** becomes a sacrifice of praise.
AP : 2 4 :077(263) [0411] The **ceremony** is not a thanksgiving that can be
AP : 2 4 :077(263) [0411] The theory that a **ceremony** can benefit either the
AP : 2 4 :087(265) [0413] But neither **ceremonies** nor prayers provide an advantage
AP : 2 4 :089(265) [0413] the application of the **ceremony** to free the souls of the
AP : 2 4 :089(266) [0415] *ex opere operato*, a **ceremony** is a sacrifice that reconciles
AP : 2 7 :053(278) [0437] by such wicked **ceremonies** as the desecration of the Mass
AP : 2 7 :055(278) [0439] imagine that these **ceremonies** are the worship of God to
AP : 2 7 :055(278) [0439] That is why they multiply these **ceremonies**.
AP : 2 7 :058(279) [0439] exercise like the other **ceremonies** of the Old Testament.
S 2 : 0 4 :014(301) [0475] given concerning the **ceremonies** of churches, vestments,
S 3 : 1 2 :003(315) [0499] albs, or other **ceremonies** of theirs which they have
S 3 : 1 5 :004(316) [0501] the invitation to such **ceremonies** of sponsors who might
TR : 0 0 :071(332) [0525] Later on new **ceremonies** were added, many of which
LC : 0 1 :313(407) [0671] places, rites, and **ceremonies**, but are common, everyday
EP : 1 0 :001(492) [0829] concerning those **ceremonies** or church usages which are
EP : 1 0 :002(493) [0829] reintroduce some **ceremonies** that have fallen into disuse
EP : 1 0 :002(493) [0829] with them in such **ceremonies** and indifferent things?
EP : 1 0 :003(493) [0829] unanimously that the **ceremonies** or church usages which
EP : 1 0 :004(493) [0829] to change such **ceremonies** according to circumstances, as
EP : 1 0 :007(493) [0831] fewer or more external **ceremonies** not commanded by
EP : 1 0 :010(494) [0831] 2. When such **ceremonies**, precepts, and institutions are
EP : 1 0 :011(494) [0831] the truth) in such indifferent things and **ceremonies**.
EP : 1 0 :012(494) [0831] 4. When such external **ceremonies** and indifferent things
EP : 1 0 :012(494) [0831] of one or more such **ceremonies** according to its
SD : 1 0 :001(610) [1053] Confession concerning **ceremonies** and church rites which
SD : 1 0 :002(611) [1053] more certain abrogated **ceremonies** that are in themselves
SD : 1 0 :005(611) [1053] as forbidden by God, **ceremonies** which are basically
SD : 1 0 :005(611) [1053] indifferent those **ceremonies** which give or (to avoid
SD : 1 0 :005(611) [1053] when these **ceremonies** are intended to create the illusion
SD : 1 0 :005(611) [1053] will allegedly result little by little from these **ceremonies**.
SD : 1 0 :009(612) [1055] reduce, or to increase **ceremonies** according to its
SD : 1 0 :010(612) [1055] the imposition of such **ceremonies** on us by adversaries in
SD : 1 0 :024(615) [1061] on how we are to treat **ceremonies** in general and matters
SD : 1 0 :030(616) [1061] to use one or more **ceremonies** at any time and place,
SD : 1 0 :031(616) [1063] of a difference in **ceremonies**, when in Christian liberty

Certain (153), Certainly (68), Certainty (9)

PR : PR :018(008) [0015] and possess final **certainty** as to which Christian
PR : PR :024(012) [0021] are, and since we are **certain** of our Christian confession
PR : PR :024(013) [0021] want to be bound to any **certain** formula of pure
AG : 0 0 :000(023) [0037] Presented in Augsburg by **certain** Princes and Cities to
AG : 1 5 :001(036) [0049] among them being **certain** holy days, festivals, and the
AG : 1 7 :005(038) [0051] Rejected, too, are **certain** Jewish opinions which are even
AG : 0 0 :001(047) [0059] **Certainly** we would not wish to put our own souls and
AG : 0 0 :002(048) [0059] why we have changed **certain** traditions and abuses.
AG : 2 3 :005(052) [0061] of living in celibacy, and he **certainly** knew man's nature.
AG : 2 3 :016(054) [0063] case relaxation would **certainly** be both Christian and
AG : 0 1 :002(056) [0065] the Mass, except that in **certain** places German hymns are
AG : 2 6 :034(069) [0075] should not be limited to **certain** specified days but should
AG : 2 7 :047(078) [0081] **Certainly** this is exaltation of works as a means of
AG : 2 8 :060(091) [0091] necessary to appoint a **certain** day so that the people
AG : 2 8 :072(093) [0093] that the bishops relax **certain** unreasonable burdens which
AL : 1 5 :001(036) [0049] Such are **certain** holy days, festivals, and the like.
AL : 0 0 :002(047) [0059] is concerned with a **certain** few abuses which have crept
AL : 0 0 :005(048) [0059] common complaint that **certain** abuses were connected
AL : 2 4 :040(061) [0069] manifest abuses it would **certainly** be of advantage to
AL : 2 6 :008(065) [0071] in the observance of **certain** holy days, rites, fasts, and
AL : 2 6 :016(066) [0073] Hence Gerson and **certain** other theologians greatly
AL : 2 6 :039(069) [0075] to conscience prescribe **certain** days and certain foods as
AL : 2 6 :039(069) [0075] certain days and **certain** foods as if works of this sort
AL : 2 7 :048(078) [0081] to the people a **certain** service invented by men without
AL : 2 8 :041(087) [0089] no offense to others, that **certain** foods defile the
AL : 2 8 :052(089) [0091] Christ and not through **certain** observances or acts of
AL : 2 8 :060(091) [0091] necessary to appoint a **certain** day so that the people may
AP : PR :004(098) [0099] insisted that we sanction **certain** manifest abuses and
AP : 0 2 :023(103) [0111] be produced without **certain** gifts and help of grace.
AP : 0 4 :015(109) [0123] existence which compare **certain** teachings of Christ with
AP : 0 4 :017(109) [0125] that he merited for us a **certain** disposition or, as they
AP : 0 4 :018(109) [0125] reason performs only **certain** external works and
AP : 0 4 :033(111) [0129] to God's law, it is **certainly** sinning even when it produces
AP : 0 4 :053(114) [0137] because there must be a **certain** propitiation for our sins.
AP : 0 4 :082(118) [0145] Second, it is **certain** that sins are forgiven because of
AP : 0 4 :085(119) [0147] by faith; here they have a **certain** and firm consolation
AP : 0 4 :101(121) [0151] to believe that God will **certainly** accomplish what he has
AP : 0 4 :103(121) [0151] In a letter to a **certain** Irenaeus, Ambrose says: "But the
AP : 0 4 :159(129) [0165] law, and obedience to the law **certainly** is righteousness.
AP : 0 4 :211(136) [0179] holy Fathers chose a **certain** kind of life for study or for
AP : 0 4 :232(139) [0185] men cover and forgive **certain** mistakes in their midst.
AP : 0 4 :236(140) [0185] not insist so bitterly on **certain** traditions which have no
AP : 0 4 :241(141) [0187] Caesar and Pompey **certain** minor disagreements arose,
AP : 0 4 :251(143) [0191] by faith and works, he **certainly** does not mean that we
AP : 0 4 :252(143) [0191] faith and good works are **certainly** pronounced righteous.
AP : 0 4 :256(144) [0193] men can at most do **certain** outward works, this universal
AP : 0 4 :259(144) [0193] but he requires a new life, which is **certainly** necessary.
AP : 0 4 :264(146) [0195] Gospel promises the forgiveness of sins with **certainty**.
AP : 0 4 :269(147) [0197] teaching of the law is **certainly** not intended to abolish the
AP : 0 4 :274(148) [0199] since a new life is **certainly** required; but here our
AP : 0 4 :289(151) [0203] are righteous through a **certain** disposition (which is love)
AP : 0 4 :306(154) [0207] own righteousness, which **certainly** resides in the will.
AP : 0 4 :308(155) [0207] technically because of **certain** carping critics: faith is truly
AP : 0 4 :345(160) [0217] a right or debt is **certain**, while mercy is uncertain.
AP : 0 4 :345(160) [0217] mercy has God's clear and **certain** promise and his
AP : 0 4 :361(162) [0219] We must add **certain** "sacraments" of this transfer, as
AP : 0 4 :367(163) [0221] here, too, the law offers a reward for a **certain** work.
AP : 0 4 :380(165) [0223] writers they have taken **certain** sayings, decrees as it
AP : 0 4 :389(166) [0225] church of Christ, which **certainly** confesses that Christ is
AP : 0 4 :398(167) [0227] of sin—is most true and **certain** and indispensable for all
AP : 0 7 :002(168) [0227] The saying is **certainly** true that there is no defense
AP : 0 7 :007(169) [0229] **Certainly** the wicked are not a holy church!
AP : 0 7 :010(170) [0229] it to mean an outward government of **certain** nations.
AP : 0 7 :013(170) [0231] the outward observance of **certain** devotions and rituals.
AP : 0 7 :014(170) [0231] from other nations by **certain** outward ordinances and
AP : 0 7 :016(171) [0231] **Certainly** the Pharisees had an outward affiliation with
AP : 0 7 :031(174) [0237] a righteousness tied to **certain** traditions, as the
AP : 0 7 :032(174) [0239] We **certainly** had weighty reasons for presenting this
AP : 0 7 :040(176) [0241] They observed **certain** days, not because such observance
AP : 0 7 :040(176) [0241] continued to observe **certain** Old Testament customs,
AP : 0 7 :042(176) [0241] the Council of Nicaea, **certain** nations held tenaciously to
AP : 0 7 :046(177) [0243] Lord's Supper, which **certainly** was previously a universal
AP : 0 9 :002(178) [0245] It is most **certain** that the promise of salvation also
AP : 1 1 :003(180) [0249] regard to the time, it is **certain** that most people in our
AP : 1 1 :006(181) [0251] unlearned to enumerate **certain** things so that they might
AP : 1 1 :008(181) [0251] It is **certain** that we neither remember nor understand
AP : 1 2 :009(183) [0255] and the prophets and **certainly** experienced by those who
AP : 1 2 :022(185) [0257] punishments, to impose **certain** satisfactions upon
AP : 1 2 :068(192) [0271] **Certainly**, if we were to count authorities, they would be
AP : 1 2 :079(194) [0275] promise, which would **certainly** be useless if we were
AP : 1 2 :088(195) [0277] We teach that such a **certainty** of faith is required in the
AP : 1 2 :090(195) [0279] in the church **certainly** give us no pleasure; therefore if we
AP : 1 2 :095(196) [0281] **Certainly** this faith must believe firmly that God freely
AP : 1 2 :112(198) [0285] not accepted without **certain** satisfactions, they made
AP : 1 2 :114(199) [0285] for even the heathen had **certain** expiations or sin by
AP : 1 2 :115(199) [0285] custom in prescribing **certain** satisfactions in confession.
AP : 1 2 :122(200) [0289] Then they quote **certain** statements from the Fathers and
AP : 1 2 :129(202) [0291] of all nations; they **certainly** demand that these issues be
AP : 1 2 :138(203) [0293] for the keys to commute **certain** punishments or to remit
AP : 1 2 :142(204) [0295] weakness God has fixed a **certain** limit which man is
AP : 1 2 :143(204) [0297] Thus **certain** fasts were instituted not to control the flesh
AP : 1 2 :143(204) [0297] number of prayers or **certain** acts of charity are
AP : 1 2 :148(205) [0299] **Certainly** true punishment and revenge, that is, contrition
AP : 1 2 :150(206) [0299] He is **certainly** punishing it when amid the terrors of
AP : 1 2 :150(206) [0299] This **certainly** speaks of the most bitter punishments.
AP : 1 2 :157(207) [0301] only by the payment of **certain** penalties over and above
AP : 1 2 :160(207) [0301] not always penalties for **certain** past deeds, but works of
AP : 1 2 :173(209) [0305] by such works, then they would **certainly** be obligatory.
AP : 1 2 :174(210) [0307] only the observance of **certain** traditions and the penalties
AP : 1 2 :178(211) [0307] on penitence; we are **certain** that it is godly and
AP : 1 3 :014(213) [0311] of God and also **certain** promises, but these apply to
AP : 1 3 :020(213) [0313] communicant should be **certain** that the free forgiveness
AP : 1 3 :020(214) [0313] are not false but as **certain** as though God, by a new
AP : 1 5 :014(216) [0319] wants to institute **certain** works to merit the forgiveness
AP : 1 5 :037(220) [0325] If our people drop **certain** useless traditions, they have
AP : 1 5 :048(221) [0327] But their prescription of **certain** foods and seasons
AP : 1 6 :006(223) [0331] are very easy to answer if we keep **certain** things in mind.
AP : 2 0 :002(227) [0339] For what is more **certain** in the church than that the
AP : 2 1 :007(230) [0345] even if it were not dangerous, is **certainly** unnecessary.
AP : 2 1 :018(231) [0347] to me, all who labor," which is **certainly** addressed to us.
AP : 2 1 :020(232) [0349] We must be completely **certain** that we are heard for
AP : 2 1 :024(232) [0349] if a king has appointed a **certain** intercessor, he does not
AP : 2 1 :026(232) [0349] Some of us have seen a **certain** monastic theologian,
AP : 2 1 :037(234) [0353] superstitious examples of **certain** prayers, fasts, and other
AP : 2 3 :024(243) [0371] do allow marriage under **certain** circumstances; but we do
AP : 2 3 :032(244) [0373] Then he adds a **certain** task of her calling, as performance
AP : 2 3 :048(246) [0377] that one should trust in **certain** observances for
AP : 2 3 :049(246) [0377] public morality), just as **certain** rites were introduced as
AP : 2 3 :059(247) [0379] these conditions are **certainly** displeasing to God, we do
AP : 2 3 :071(249) [0383] wrong in marrying, it is **certainly** contrary to God's will
AP : 2 4 :021(252) [0389] The Old Testament called **certain** sacrifices propitiatory
AP : 2 4 :067(261) [0407] **Certainly** this fiction about merit *ex opere operato* is not
AP : 2 4 :068(261) [0407] of profession, just as a **certain** type of hood is the mark
AP : 2 7 :001(268) [0419] because he had condemned **certain** notorious abuses.
AP : 2 7 :002(269) [0419] estate but had only denounced **certain** notorious abuses.
AP : 2 7 :003(269) [0419] in the commentaries he left on **certain** passages in Daniel.
AP : 2 7 :011(270) [0423] First, it **certainly** is not a legitimate vow if the one making
AP : 2 7 :038(275) [0433] pointed in a dream to a **certain** shoemaker in the city of
AP : 2 7 :062(280) [0441] to distinguish them by **certain** marks from their
AP : 2 8 :014(283) [0447] that since they have a **certain** jurisdiction bishops may
AP : 2 8 :018(284) [0449] **Certainly** the statement, "He who hears you hears me"
S 2 : 0 1 :004(292) [0461] or merit, it is clear and **certain** that such faith alone
S 2 : 0 1 :005(292) [0463] we must be quite **certain** and have no doubts about it.
S 2 : 0 2 :006(293) [0463] more useful, and more **certain** without the Mass.
S 2 : 0 2 :013(295) [0467] but a human opinion of **certain** individuals and cannot
S 2 : 0 2 :018(296) [0467] It is **certain** that we have not been commanded to make
S 2 : 0 2 :029(297) [0471] in its purity and **certainly** according to the institution of
S 2 : 0 4 :015(301) [0475] Of this we may be **certain**, and we must rely on the hope
S 3 : 0 1 :008(302) [0477] does what he can, God is **certain** to grant him his grace.
S 3 : 0 3 :028(308) [0487] This is **certainly** true, and there are seals, letters, and
TR : 0 0 :022(323) [0511] Here **certain** passages are quoted against us: "You are
TR : 0 0 :022(323) [0511] my sheep" (John 21:17), and **certain** other passages.
TR : 0 0 :025(324) [0511] (Matt. 16:18), it is **certain** that the church is not built on
TR : 0 0 :068(331) [0523] church and not merely to **certain** individuals: "Where two
TR : 0 0 :069(331) [0525] the priesthood, **certainly** has the right of electing and
TR : 0 0 :074(332) [0525] It is **certain** that the common jurisdiction of
TR : 0 0 :078(333) [0527] since they have framed **certain** unjust laws concerning
SC : 0 2 :002(345) [0543] This is most **certainly** true.
SC : 0 2 :004(345) [0545] This is most **certainly** true.
SC : 0 2 :006(345) [0545] This is most **certainly** true.
SC : 0 9 :001(354) [0561] *consisting of* ***certain*** *passages of the Scriptures, selected*
LC : PR :014(360) [0571] **Certainly** God did not require and command this so
LC : PR :017(361) [0573] This much is **certain**: anyone who knows the Ten
LC : 0 1 :040(370) [0591] **Certainly**, if we desire all good things in time and eternity,
LC : 0 1 :115(381) [0615] pleasing to my God in heaven; this I know for **certain**."
LC : 0 1 :138(384) [0621] have many children, it is **certainly** because some of them
LC : 0 1 :269(401) [0657] even though, to your **certain** knowledge, he is guilty.
LC : 0 3 :020(423) [0703] Such promises **certainly** ought to awaken and kindle in
LC : 0 3 :097(433) [0725] seal to it, making it as **certain** as an absolution
LC : 0 3 :121(436) [0731] "yes" and conclude with **certainty** that God hears their
LC : 0 3 :124(436) [0731] God attaches to our being **certain** that we do not pray in
LC : 0 4 :034(441) [0741] For it is **certain** that whatever is not faith contributes
LC : 0 5 :053(453) [0765] It is **certainly** true, as I have found in my own experience,
LC : 0 6 :023(460) [0000] is to be given out at a **certain** place; he would need no

Continued ▶

E P : 0 3 :009(474) [0795] but they must regard it as **certain** that for Christ's sake,
E P : 0 3 :011(474) [0795] justifying faith and are **certainly** to be found with it, since
E P : 0 4 :003(475) [0797] controversy arose among **certain** theologians concerning
E P : 0 4 :006(476) [0797] fruits of a good tree, **certainly** and indubitably follow
E P : 0 8 :036(491) [0825] human spirit Christ has **certain** limitations as to how
E P : 1 1 :019(497) [0837] sin, God has predestined **certain** people to damnation so
S D : R N :010(506) [0855] universally accepted, **certain**, and common form of
S D : R N :016(507) [0857] we have set forth as a **certain** and public testimony, not
S D : R N :017(507) [0857] and condemned on the **certain** and solid basis of the holy
S D : R N :019(507) [0857] there in the writings of **certain** theologians, lest anyone be
S D : 0 1 :021(512) [0865] or a corruption only of **certain** accidental elements in
S D : 0 2 :024(526) [0891] and meditate on it to a **certain** degree, and can even talk
S D : 0 2 :031(527) [0893] also declare that to a **certain** extent reason has a free will.
S D : 0 2 :055(532) [0903] Holy Spirit, but should be **certain** that, when the Word
S D : 0 2 :055(532) [0903] meditate on it, God is **certainly** present with his grace and
S D : 0 2 :056(532) [0903] weakness, we should be **certain**, because of and on the
S D : 0 2 :065(534) [0907] the holy sacraments, it is **certain** that we can and must
S D : 0 2 :069(534) [0907] again, though they must **certainly** be converted again, as
S D : 0 3 :027(543) [0923] Love is a fruit which **certainly** and necessarily follows
S D : 0 3 :027(543) [0923] not love, this indicates **certainly** that he is not justified
S D : 0 3 :029(544) [0925] "We **certainly** grant that we must teach about love and
S D : 0 3 :036(545) [0927] not follow true faith as **certain** and unquestioned fruits,
S D : 0 4 :002(551) [0939] for believers the firm and **certain** promise of salvation.
S D : 0 4 :012(553) [0941] trust in God's grace, so **certain** that it would die a
S D : 0 4 :034(556) [0949] salvation may be very **certain** to us, Paul ascribes to faith
S D : 0 6 :003(564) [0963] and Word, which is a **certain** rule and norm for achieving
S D : 0 7 :008(570) [0975] in such a way that as **certainly** as believing and pious
S D : 0 7 :008(570) [0975] their mouths, just so **certainly** do they partake spiritually
S D : 0 7 :030(574) [0983] to defend all of them as **certainly** as I have now defended
S D : 0 7 :046(577) [0987] Abraham **certainly** had sufficient ground for a disputation
S D : 0 7 :046(577) [0989] and believed most **certainly** in his heart that what God
S D : 0 7 :047(578) [0989] obedience the explicit, **certain**, clear, and earnest words
S D : 0 7 :047(578) [0989] and Truth and can **certainly** accomplish and bring to pass
S D : 0 7 :048(578) [0989] simple, clear, manifest, **certain**, and indubitable, can and
S D : 0 7 :052(578) [0991] these simple, clear, **certain**, and truthful words of Christ,
S D : 0 7 :056(579) [0991] Therefore he **certainly** cannot be speaking of a spiritual
S D : 0 7 :057(579) [0993] body of Christ, St. Paul **certainly** could not be speaking
S D : 0 7 :060(580) [0993] who is there present as **certainly** as did the Jews when
S D : 0 7 :062(581) [0995] we rest indomitably, with **certain** trust and confidence, on
S D : 0 7 :063(581) [0995] Believers receive it as a **certain** pledge and assurance that
S D : 0 7 :071(582) [0997] in the weakness or **certainty** of faith, be it greater or
S D : 0 7 :097(586) [1005] ways to be present at a **certain** place, not only, as the
S D : 0 7 :102(587) [1007] we know how to prove **certainly** that the body of Christ
S D : 0 7 :106(588) [1009] heart to rely on and trust in them with absolute **certainty**.
S D : 0 7 :119(590) [1013] and circumscribed by a **certain** space in heaven that he is
S D : 0 8 :053(601) [1033] the best, safest, and most **certain** way in this controversy
S D : 0 8 :053(601) [1033] in this case give us clear, **certain** testimony, we shall
S D : 0 8 :073(605) [1041] knows and can do only **certain** things in the way in which
S D : 0 8 :074(606) [1043] not that he knows only **certain** things and does not know
S D : 0 8 :074(606) [1043] and does not know **certain** other things, or that he can do
S D : 0 8 :074(606) [1043] things, or that he can do **certain** things and cannot do
S D : 0 8 :074(606) [1043] things and cannot do **certain** other things, but that he
S D : 0 8 :079(607) [1045] To make **certainty** and assurance doubly sure on this
S D : 0 8 :096(610) [1049] In this way they will be **certain** to find abiding comfort in
S D : 1 0 :002(611) [1053] restore once more **certain** abrogated ceremonies that are
S D : 1 0 :013(613) [1057] situation yielded to a **certain** extent, Paul criticized them
S D : 1 1 :012(618) [1067] with the following clear, **certain**, and unfailing
S D : 1 1 :029(621) [1073] but should know **certainly** that God reveals his will in this
S D : 1 1 :034(622) [1075] heart I am not thinking of all, but only of a **certain** few.
S D : 1 1 :036(622) [1075] believe it with absolute **certainty** and not doubt it in the
S D : 1 1 :039(622) [1075] Holy Spirit wills to be **certainly** present with and
S D : 1 1 :046(624) [1079] salvation so firmly and **certainly** — for due to the
S D : 1 1 :049(624) [1079] From this Paul draws the **certain** and indubitable
S D : 1 1 :054(625) [1081] right well and with utter **certainty**, and that he still
S D : 1 1 :060(626) [1083] deserved judgement over **certain** lands, nations, and
S D : 1 1 :092(632) [1093] But it is **certain** that any interpretation of the Scriptures

Certified (1)
P R : P R :018(009) [0015] very diligently by well-**certified** persons with the actual

Cesspool (1)
L C : 0 1 :202(392) [0639] is a shameful mess and **cesspool** of all kinds of vice and

Chaff (1)
A P : 0 7 :001(168) [0227] a threshing floor on which **chaff** and wheat are heaped

Chain (2)
A P : 0 4 :232(139) [0185] is a bond and unbroken **chain** linking the many members
L C : 0 4 :020(439) [0737] I say, is the golden **chain** about his neck, yes, the crown

Chairs (1)
L C : 0 1 :229(396) [0645] box, they sit in office **chairs** and are called great lords and

Chalcedon (3)
T R : 0 0 :019(323) [0509] that at the Council of **Chalcedon** the primacy was offered
S D : 0 8 :018(594) [1021] after the Council of **Chalcedon**, have often used the term
S D : 0 8 :046(600) [1031] or as the Council of **Chalcedon** declares, each nature

Chalice (1)
A G : 2 2 :002(049) [0059] Concerning the **chalice** Christ here commands with clear

Challenge (1)
L C : 0 1 :333(410) [0677] we can fling out the **challenge**: Let all wise men and saints

Chamberlain (1)
P R : P R :027(016) [0027] **Chamberlain** and Council of the City of Regensburg

Champion (1)
A P : 1 5 :050(222) [0329] Paul is our constant **champion**; everywhere he insists that

Chance (3)
A P : 0 4 :135(125) [0159] care, but supposes that men are born and die by **chance**.
A P : 0 4 :167(130) [0169] history is governed by God's counsels or by **chance**?
L C : 0 3 :120(436) [0731] not pray as a matter of **chance** but knows that God does

Change (48), Changed (28), Changeless (1), Changers (1), Changes (11), Changing (3)
A G : 0 0 :002(048) [0059] reasons why we have **changed** certain traditions and
A G : 0 0 :000(049) [0059] reasons for permitting **changes** in these cases in order
A G : 0 0 :000(049) [0059] be regarded as above all custom) to allow such **changes**.
A G : 2 3 :006(052) [0061] and ability to improve or **change** the creation of God, the
A G : 0 1 :002(056) [0065] no conspicuous **changes** have been made in the public
A G : 2 4 :040(061) [0069] and since no conspicuous **change** has been made in the
A G : 2 7 :015(073) [0077] But now the picture is **changed**.
A G : 2 8 :033(086) [0087] that the Sabbath was **changed** to Sunday — contrary, as
A G : 2 8 :033(086) [0087] so insistently as the **change** of the Sabbath, for thereby
A G : 2 8 :061(091) [0093] Testament, and of the **change** of the Sabbath, all of which
A G : 2 8 :074(094) [0093] inasmuch as such **changes** do not destroy the unity of
A L : 0 0 :001(049) [0059] hear both what has been **changed** and what our reasons
A L : 0 0 :001(049) [0059] our reasons for such **changes** are in order that the people
A L : 2 2 :004(050) [0061] when or by whom it was **changed**, although Cardinal
A L : 2 2 :004(050) [0061] Cusanus mentions when the **change** was approved.
A L : 2 7 :024(074) [0079] of vows could not be **changed** for any reason at all, the
A L : 2 8 :033(086) [0087] Besides, they cite the **change** from the Sabbath to the
A L : 2 8 :033(086) [0087] No case is made more of than this **change** of the Sabbath.
A L : 2 8 :061(091) [0093] new law, concerning the **change** of the Sabbath, all of
A L : 2 8 :068(093) [0093] even if the usage of men **changes** in such matters.
A L : 2 8 :074(093) [0093] now, for such **change** does not impair the unity of the
A L : 2 8 :074(094) [0093] traditions have been **changed** with the passing of time, as
A P : 0 4 :261(145) [0195] is, redeem your sins by **changing** your heart and works.
A P : 0 4 :351(161) [0217] of the Lord, we are **changed** into his likeness"; that is, we
A P : 0 7 :041(176) [0241] why did the bishops later **change** them in so many ways?
A P : 0 7 :041(176) [0241] was unlawful for men to assume the right to **change** them.
A P : 0 7 :046(177) [0243] they themselves have **changed** the ordinance of Christ in
A P : 0 7 :046(177) [0243] necessary, why do they **change** the ordinance of Christ's
A P : 1 0 :002(179) [0247] that the bread may be **changed** and become the very body
A P : 1 0 :002(179) [0247] is not merely a figure but is truly **changed** into flesh."
A P : 1 2 :007(183) [0255] remove guilt, but only **changes** eternal punishments into
A P : 1 2 :013(184) [0257] eternal punishments are **changed** into the punishments of
A P : 1 2 :046(188) [0263] sense as counterfeit **changes**; but mortification means
A P : 1 2 :126(201) [0289] you take care, indicate a **change** in the Holy Roman
A P : 1 2 :164(208) [0303] really happens in contrition and in a **changed** life.
A P : 1 5 :051(222) [0329] Nothing should be **changed** in the accustomed rites
A P : 1 6 :006(223) [0331] of the seasons and to the **change** of winter and summer as
A P : 1 6 :007(223) [0331] spiritual kingdom does not **change** the civil government.
A P : 2 2 :002(236) [0357] Why is Christ's ordinance **changed**, especially since he
A P : 2 2 :014(238) [0361] which are not cogent enough to **change** Christ's ordinance
A P : 2 3 :008(240) [0367] regulations cannot **change** the nature of the earth, so
A P : 2 3 :008(240) [0367] human regulations can **change** the nature of man without
A P : 2 3 :009(241) [0367] Where nature does not **change**, there must remain that
A P : 2 3 :012(241) [0367] act of God can **change** this right, the right to contract
A P : 2 3 :053(246) [0377] it has been customary to **change** other laws if the common
A P : 2 3 :053(246) [0379] many good reasons for **changing** it, especially in these
A P : 2 3 :056(247) [0379] the pontiffs dispense and **change** other good laws; on this
A P : 2 3 :071(249) [0383] princes do not delight in **change** for its own sake, but they
A P : 2 4 :007(250) [0385] Mass, reasons of piety or of profit later **changed** this.
A P : 2 4 :008(250) [0385] when it suits them, they **change** the institutions of the
A P : 2 4 :064(261) [0405] of merit, like the money-**changers** with gold or silver.
A P : 2 7 :004(269) [0421] oracles, which threaten a **change** in the monastic regime.
A P : 2 7 :027(273) [0429] Cor. 3:18) thus: "We are **changed** from glory to glory, as
A P : 2 8 :016(283) [0449] many things that were **changed** by time, and they did not
A P : 2 8 :016(283) [0449] not set them down as though they could not be **changed**.
S 2 : 0 4 :007(299) [0473] in their power and choice to **change** or depose this head.
S 3 : 1 3 :001(315) [0499] I do not know how I can **change** what I have heretofore
S 3 : 1 5 :003(316) [0501] I do not know how I can **change** or concede anything in
T R : 0 0 :006(320) [0505] worship, concerning **changes** in the sacraments, and
T R : 0 0 :040(327) [0515] for himself the right to **change** the doctrine of Christ and
S C : P R :007(339) [0533] the utmost care to avoid **changes** or variations in the text
S C : P R :015(340) [0535] adhere to them without **changing** a single syllable, as
L C : 0 1 :085(376) [0605] been appointed for this purpose, we should not **change** it.
L C : 0 4 :060(444) [0747] and Word cannot be **changed** or altered by man.
L C : 0 5 :016(448) [0757] so likewise no one can **change** or alter the sacrament, even
L C : 0 5 :086(456) [0773] For it is clearly useless to try to **change** old people.
L C : 0 6 :024(460) [0000] that the invitation were **changed** into a command that all
E P : 0 2 :017(472) [0791] of the Holy Spirit, God **changes** stubborn and unwilling
E P : 0 2 :018(472) [0791] the will of man has been **changed** and renewed *solely by*
E P : 0 5 :011(479) [0805] the Gospel is again **changed** into a teaching of the law,
E P : 0 8 :006(487) [0819] and that the one is not **changed** into the other, but that
E P : 0 8 :018(489) [0823] the person of Christ, or **change** the one nature into the
E P : 0 8 :021(490) [0823] human nature has been **changed** into the deity, as
E P : 1 0 :004(493) [0829] age has authority to **change** such ceremonies according to
S D : 0 2 :070(534) [0909] there must be a **change**, there must be new activities and
S D : 0 2 :083(537) [0913] activity produces no **change** at all for the good in the
S D : 0 2 :083(537) [0913] is that kind of **change** through the Holy Spirit's activity in
S D : 0 5 :001(558) [0951] the two doctrines and **change** the Gospel into law.
S D : 0 7 :014(571) [0977] (that is, an essential **change** of the bread and wine into
S D : 0 7 :022(573) [0979] he can correct Christ and **change** what he has spoken.
S D : 0 7 :024(573) [0981] an angel in heaven, can **change** bread and wine into the
S D : 0 7 :024(573) [0981] little can anyone alter or **change** the sacrament, even
S D : 0 7 :032(574) [0983] of God — unless they first **change** God's Word and
S D : 0 7 :032(575) [0983] but have perverted and **changed** it according to their own
S D : 0 7 :048(578) [0989] no metaphor (that is, a **change** in meaning) in the word
S D : 0 7 :049(578) [0989] a metonymy (that is, a **change** in meaning) in the word
S D : 0 7 :052(578) [0991] proffered bread without any interpretation and **change**.
S D : 0 8 :007(592) [1017] each other, or the one **changed** into the other, but in the
S D : 0 8 :060(602) [1035] together or the one is **changed** into the other, and since
S D : 1 0 :009(612) [1055] authority, and power to **change**, to reduce, or to increase
S D : 1 1 :010(618) [1067] fail and no one can ever **change** or hinder it (Isa. 14:27;
S D : 1 1 :075(628) [1087] himself because he is **changeless** in his will and essence.

Channel (1), Channels (1)
L C : 0 1 :026(368) [0587] are only the hands, **channels**, and means through which
L C : 0 1 :311(407) [0671] must spring, the true **channel** through which all good

Chant (2), Chants (2)
A P : 1 5 :040(220) [0325] When they **chant** the Psalms, it is not to learn or pray but
A P : 1 5 :040(220) [0325] The children **chant** the Psalms in order to learn; the
A P : 2 7 :055(278) [0439] worship — lessons, **chants**, and the like — which could be
A P : 2 7 :069(281) [0443] of foods, lessons, **chants**, vestments, sandals, cinctures —

Chapter (15), Chapters (12), Chap (4)
AG : 27 :035(076) [0081] Question 27, **Chapter** I, that such a marriage should not be
AG : 28 :027(085) [0087] Question 7, in the **chapters** "Sacerdotes" and "Oves."
AL : 22 :009(050) [0061] the canons testify (Dist. 3, **chap.** "Veritate" and the
AL : 22 :009(050) [0061] (Dist. 3, chap. "Veritate" and the following **chapters**).
AL : 25 :012(063) [0071] Dist. 5, in the **chapter** "Consideret," admits that such
AL : 27 :035(076) [0081] Question 27, **Chapter** I, and his authority is not
AL : 28 :027(085) [0087] thing (II, question 7, in **chapters** "Sacerdotes" and
AP : 04 :062(115) [0139] In the last **chapter** of Luke (24:47) Christ commands that
AP : 04 :087(119) [0147] In **chap.** 3 he advances this conclusion, embodying the
AP : 12 :030(186) [0259] of the Gospel in the last **chapter** of Luke (24:47), "That
AP : 12 :135(203) [0293] indulgences remit, as the **chapter** on "Penitence and
AP : 12 :158(207) [0301] teaches in a long sermon in his twenty-eighth **chapter**.
AP : 15 :019(217) [0319] In his eleventh **chapter** Daniel says that the invention of
AP : 27 :056(278) [0439] who belong to these **chapters** are forced to agree with the
AP : 27 :067(280) [0441] this way in the same **chapter** (I Tim. 5:8), "If any one
S2 : 02 :021(296) [0467] Here monasteries, **chapters**, and vicars have obligated
S2 : 03 :000(297) [0471] Article III. [**Chapters** and Monasteries]
S2 : 03 :001(297) [0471] The **chapters** and monasteries which in former times had
S3 : 03 :028(308) [0487] in monasteries and **chapters** fought against evil thoughts
TR : 00 :033(325) [0513] Distinction 22 of the **chapter** "Omnes," and other similar
SD : RN :004(504) [0851] Word in brief articles or **chapters** against the aberrations
SD : RN :005(504) [0851] in the articles and **chapters** of the Augsburg Confession
SD : 01 :004(509) [0861] to set forth in short **chapters** the true doctrine and its
SD : 02 :044(529) [0897] of Genesis, especially of **Chapter** 26, he repeats and
SD : 04 :028(555) [0947] their work (in his *Commentary on Genesis*, **Chapter** 22).
SD : 05 :006(559) [0953] afterward in the first **chapter** of St. Mark, where Christ
SD : 08 :022(595) [1023] other (Irenaeus, Book IV, **chap.** 3; Anthanasius in his
SD : 08 :022(595) [1023] in Theodoret; John Damascene, Book III, **chap.** 19).
SD : 11 :033(622) [1073] sin as Paul teaches from the first to the eighth **chapter**.
SD : 11 :033(622) [1075] when in the eighth **chapter** you are tested under the cross
SD : 11 :033(622) [1075] tenth, and eleventh **chapters** will show you how

Character (6), Characteristic (5), Characterized (1)
AG : 27 :030(075) [0079] to the very nature and **character** of a vow that it should
AG : 28 :057(091) [0091] Of like **character** is the observance of Sunday, Easter,
AP : 12 :028(185) [0259] of the whole life and **character** a third part, we shall not
AP : 12 :112(198) [0285] prescribed without knowing the **character** of the offense.
AP : 23 :025(243) [0371] Daniel says that it is **characteristic** of Antichrist's kingdom
AP : 23 :045(245) [0375] complains that this **characteristic** among the Encratites
S2 : 04 :014(301) [0475] of body and soul are **characteristic** of his papal
LC : 01 :256(399) [0653] reputation, honor, and **character** any more than of his
SD : 01 :051(517) [0875] means — as it often does — a disposition or **characteristic**
SD : 07 :085(584) [1001] Nothing has the **character** of a sacrament apart from the
SD : 10 :020(614) [1059] of body and soul are **characteristic** of his papal
SD : 12 :027(635) [1101] sect, however, can be **characterized** as basically nothing

Charge (15), Charged (4), Charges (6)
AL : 20 :035(046) [0057] this teaching is not to be **charged** with forbidding good
AL : 00 :004(048) [0059] is false and malicious to **charge** that all ceremonies and
AL : 26 :030(068) [0075] Here our adversaries **charge** that our teachers, like
AP : 02 :002(100) [0105] will exonerate us of the **charge** of innovation, for it says:
AP : 04 :154(128) [0165] He **charges** him with irreverence and reproves him with
AP : 04 :245(142) [0189] "The aim of our **charge** is love that issues from a
AP : 14 :005(215) [0315] and future, against the **charge** that we have undermined
AP : 15 :031(219) [0323] a yoke," etc., Peter **charges** that to put this burden on the
AP : 21 :022(232) [0349] We are not making false **charges** here.
AP : 23 :059(247) [0379] ourselves open to the **charge** of schism because we seem
AP : 23 :067(248) [0383] This is a new **charge**, that marriage is a heresy!
AP : 24 :041(257) [0399] see the falsity of the **charge** that we do away with the
AP : 27 :012(271) [0423] what has here been **charged** against monasticism is
AP : 27 :013(271) [0423] revealed to the world — then the **charge** against us is true.
AP : 27 :018(272) [0425] written, "What has been **charged** against monasticism
TR : 00 :075(333) [0525] this is a very serious **charge**, nobody should be
SC : 07 :002(352) [0557] Let thy holy angel have **charge** of me, that the wicked one
SC : 07 :005(353) [0559] Let thy holy angels have **charge** of me, that the wicked
LC : 01 :249(398) [0651] may not themselves be **charged** with other men's sins.
LC : 01 :270(401) [0657] yourself to make your **charges** before the proper
LC : 01 :275(402) [0659] to report evil, to prefer **charges**, to attest, examine, and
EP : 03 :007(474) [0793] "Who shall bring any **charge** against God's elect?
SD : PR :006(502) [0847] — except for the **charges** of the papists — it can
SD : RN :020(508) [0859] do not, as our adversaries **charge**, veer from one doctrine
SD : 03 :017(542) [0921] "Who shall bring any **charge** against God's elect?

Charitable (1), Charitably (4)
AG : PR :002(025) [0039] diligence amicably and **charitably** to hear, understand,
AG : PR :010(025) [0041] discussed amicably and **charitably**, our differences may be
AG : PR :012(026) [0041] if no amicable and **charitable** negotiations take place
AG : PR :023(027) [0043] amicably weighed, **charitably** settled, and brought to
SC : 01 :016(343) [0541] well of him, and interpret **charitably** all that he does.

Charity (6)
PR : PR :004(004) [0007] the bond of Christian **charity** and agreement, and in this
PR : PR :022(012) [0021] For just as Christian **charity** causes us to have special
AP : 04 :193(133) [0175] afflictions, works of **charity**, and the mortification of the
AP : 12 :139(203) [0295] like true fasting, prayer, and **charity** have his command.
AP : 12 :143(204) [0295] True prayer, **charity**, and fasting have God's command:
AP : 12 :143(204) [0297] prayers or certain acts of **charity** are performed as acts of

Charles (18)
PR : PR :002(003) [0007] to the then Emperor **Charles** V, of most praiseworthy
PR : PR :008(005) [0009] submitted to Emperor **Charles** V in the great imperial
PR : PR :018(008) [0015] submitted to Emperor **Charles** V at the great imperial
PR : PR :018(009) [0015] submitted it to Emperor **Charles** V at the said imperial
PR : PR :023(012) [0021] year 1530 to Emperor **Charles** V, of Christian memory.
PR : PR :025(013) [0023] year 1530 to Emperor **Charles** V, of kindest memory, in
PR : PR :027(015) [0025] **Charles**, count of Gleichen [-Blankenhain]
AG : 00 :000(023) [0037] Princes and Cities to His Imperial Majesty **Charles** V
AP : 12 :002(182) [0253] What shall we do here, O **Charles**, most invincible
AP : 12 :003(182) [0253] most invincible Emperor **Charles**, to hear us out patiently
AP : 21 :044(235) [0357] gracious Emperor **Charles**, for the sake of the glory of
AP : 23 :003(239) [0363] right hand, Emperor **Charles** — you whom even some of
AP : 27 :018(272) [0425] most clement Emperor **Charles**; look, princes; look, all
EP : RN :004(465) [0777] was delivered to Emperor **Charles** V at Augsburg during
SD : PR :003(501) [0847] submitted it to Emperor **Charles** V at the great Diet of
SD : PR :005(502) [0847] Confession as it was delivered to Emperor **Charles** in 1530
SD : RN :005(504) [0851] submitted to Emperor **Charles** V at Augsburg by a
SD : 07 :041(576) [0985] delivered to Emperor **Charles** V, therefore the true

Chased (1)
LC : PR :013(360) [0571] food but also to be **chased** out by dogs and pelted with

Chaste (8), Chastely (2)
AG : 23 :006(052) [0061] What honest and **chaste** manner of life, what Christian,
AP : 23 :003(239) [0363] of theirs with your **chaste** right hand, Emperor Charles —
AP : 23 :003(239) [0363] To you, our most **chaste** and excellent Emperor, they
AP : 23 :019(242) [0369] He wants men to be **chaste** by using the remedy he offers,
SC : 01 :012(343) [0541] and so we should lead a **chaste** and pure life in word and
LC : 01 :202(392) [0639] whole body are to be **chaste** and to afford no occasion,
LC : 01 :205(393) [0639] is required both to live **chastely** himself and to help his
LC : 01 :212(393) [0641] is not possible to remain **chaste** outside of marriage; for
LC : 01 :219(394) [0643] everyone not only to live **chastely** in thought, word, and
LC : 03 :109(435) [0729] Even if at present I am **chaste**, patient, kind, and firm in

Chasten (1), Chastened (1), Chastening (1), Chastised (1), Chastisement (1), Chastising (1)
AP : 04 :268(147) [0197] the punishments that **chasten** us are lightened by our
AP : 12 :049(188) [0265] "The Lord has **chastened** me sorely, but he has not given
AP : 12 :113(199) [0285] **Chastising** the lapsed served as an example, as the gloss
AP : 12 :151(206) [0299] they cry out is thy **chastening** upon them" (Isa. 26:16);
AP : 12 :174(210) [0307] needy, restraint and **chastisement** of the flesh instead of
LC : 01 :099(378) [0609] fellows should be **chastised** who, after hearing a sermon

Chastity (26)
AG : 23 :025(055) [0065] were unable to keep their vows of **chastity** should marry.
AG : 23 :025(055) [0065] or unable to keep their **chastity**, it is better for them to
AG : 27 :028(075) [0079] what an extent perpetual **chastity** lies within human
AG : 27 :048(078) [0081] spirituality and sham of poverty, humility, and **chastity**.
AL : 23 :025(055) [0065] who did not keep the **chastity** which they had promised
AL : 27 :028(075) [0079] to what an extent perpetual **chastity** lies in man's power.
AL : 27 :048(078) [0081] and this pretense of poverty, humility, and **chastity**.
AP : 04 :151(127) [0163] them (whether patience, **chastity**, or obedience to the
AP : 04 :293(152) [0203] afflictions, and practice **chastity**, love toward our
AP : 07 :031(174) [0239] the Holy Spirit, as are **chastity**, patience, the fear of God,
AP : 07 :036(175) [0241] (like love of neighbor, **chastity**, etc.), and are not means
AP : 15 :043(221) [0327] instruction of children, **chastity**, and all the works of
AP : 20 :015(229) [0343] by which love, patience, **chastity**, and other fruits of the
AP : 23 :005(239) [0365] well how few practice **chastity**, but they use religion as a
AP : 23 :050(246) [0377] for they know that **chastity** is not the usual thing.
AP : 27 :016(271) [0425] because of their poverty, **chastity**, and obedience —
AP : 27 :051(277) [0437] Third, in monastic vows **chastity** is promised.
LC : 01 :211(393) [0641] so that they can maintain **chastity** outside of marriage.
LC : 01 :213(394) [0641] will maintain perpetual **chastity** while they deceive the
LC : 01 :214(394) [0641] love and inclination for **chastity** as those who under the
LC : 01 :216(394) [0641] Therefore all vows of **chastity** apart from marriage are
LC : 01 :216(394) [0641] their power to maintain **chastity**, and if they remain they
LC : 01 :219(394) [0643] For marital **chastity** it is above all things essential that
LC : 01 :219(394) [0643] the chief ways to make **chastity** attractive and desirable.
LC : 01 :219(394) [0643] Under such conditions **chastity** always follows
LC : 01 :313(407) [0671] love toward enemies, **chastity**, kindness, etc., and all that

Chasuble (1), Chasubles (1)
S1 : PR :013(291) [0459] concerning fasts, vestments, tonsures, and **chasubles**.
LC : 01 :314(407) [0671] in a gold-embroidered **chasuble** or a layman remains on

Chattering (1), Chatters (1)
S3 : 08 :006(312) [0495] fill the world with their **chattering** and scribbling, as if the
SD : 04 :011(553) [0941] and in the meantime he **chatters** and jabbers a great deal

Cheap (1)
S3 : 03 :026(307) [0487] In time souls got to be so **cheap** that they were released at

Cheat (1), Cheated (1), Cheats (1)
LC : 01 :225(395) [0645] — a servant can **cheat** his employer out of thirty or forty
LC : 01 :227(396) [0645] One person openly **cheats** another with defective
LC : 01 :242(397) [0649] Yes, where you have **cheated** and defrauded anyone out

Checked (2), Checking (1)
PR : PR :006(004) [0009] into them might be **checked** and that our subjects might
LC : 01 :239(397) [0649] well regulated, such insolence might soon be **checked**.
LC : 03 :031(424) [0707] plots of our enemies and **checking** their murderous and

Cheer (5), Cheerful (6), Cheerfully (6)
AL : 24 :030(059) [0067] Christ and should **cheer** and comfort anxious
AP : 04 :271(148) [0199] be received by faith, to **cheer** the terrified conscience.
AP : 04 :276(148) [0199] constantly admonish, **cheer**, and confirm terrified minds
AP : 04 :314(156) [0207] than by faith, but also to **cheer** ourselves in the midst of
SC : 01 :022(344) [0543] him, trust in him, and **cheerfully** do what he has
SC : 03 :016(347) [0549] will heartily forgive and **cheerfully** do good to those who
SC : 08 :008(353) [0559] enough to eat to make them joyful and of good **cheer**.
LC : 01 :009(365) [0583] few there are who are **cheerful**, who do not fret and
LC : 01 :111(380) [0613] you should do not only **cheerfully**, but with humility and
LC : 01 :126(382) [0617] and incentive to do **cheerfully** and gladly whatever we
LC : 01 :143(385) [0623] but gladly and **cheerfully**; and they should do it for the
LC : 01 :151(386) [0625] ready to serve, and **cheerfully** gives honor where it is due,
LC : 03 :092(432) [0725] grant us a happy and **cheerful** conscience to stand before
LC : 03 :113(435) [0729] will, our daily bread, a good and **cheerful** conscience, etc.
SD : 04 :017(554) [0943] Rom. 6:7) because God loves a **cheerful** giver (II Cor. 9:7)
SD : 07 :069(582) [0997] with a stronger and more **cheerful** faith and a purer
SD : 07 :071(582) [0997] Paul, and others who had a **cheerful** and strong faith.

Cheese (1)
SD : 01 :035(514) [0869] not pour me out like milk and curdle me like **cheese**?

Chemnitz (2)
EP : 12 :031(501) [0843] Dr. Martin **Chemnitz**
SD : 12 :040(636) [1103] Dr. Martin **Chemnitz**

Cherish (4), Cherished (1), Cherishing (2)
A P : 0 7 :033(175) [0239] a very thankful spirit we **cherish** the useful and ancient
L C : 0 1 :207(393) [0639] to honor, maintain, and **cherish** it as a divine and blessed
L C : 0 1 :219(394) [0643] but also to love and **cherish** the wife or husband whom
L C : 0 1 :219(394) [0643] in love and harmony, **cherishing** each other
L C : 0 3 :048(426) [0711] his Word taught in its purity and **cherished** and treasured.
L C : 0 5 :043(451) [0763] true Christians who **cherish** and honor the sacrament will
L C : 0 6 :022(459) [0000] on, magnifying and **cherishing** it as a great and

Chest (1), Chests (1)
L C : 0 1 :013(366) [0583] him, or put him into a purse, or shut him up in a **chest**.
L C : 0 1 :244(398) [0649] hour they clean out our **chests** and purse down to the last

Chicanery (1)
S D : 1 0 :010(612) [1055] and confirm their idolatry by force or **chicanery**.

Chide (2), Chides (1)
A P : 0 4 :030(111) [0129] I will exclaim and **chide** them with a Christian's
A P : 0 4 :154(128) [0165] He **chides** the Pharisee for not acknowledging him as the
A P : 0 4 :154(128) [0165] example moved Christ to **chide** the Pharisee, this wise and

Chief (78), Chiefly (8)
P R : P R :003(003) [0007] of their faith in the **chief** articles in controversy over
P R : P R :013(007) [0013] that they and their **chief** theologians peruse it with
A G : 2 0 :008(042) [0053] about faith, which is the **chief** article in the Christian life,
A G : 0 0 :002(048) [0059] dissension are concerned **chiefly** with various traditions
A G : 0 1 :003(056) [0065] After all, the **chief** purpose of all ceremonies is to teach
A G : 2 5 :013(063) [0071] of absolution (which is its **chief** and most important
A G : 2 8 :052(089) [0091] For the **chief** article of the Gospel must be maintained,
A G : 2 8 :066(092) [0093] must pay attention to the **chief** article of Christian
A G : 0 0 :001(094) [0095] These are the **chief** articles that are regarded as
A G : 0 0 :003(095) [0095] good in order that the **chief** points at issue may better be
A L : 0 0 :000(027) [0043] **Chief** Articles of Faith
A L : 2 0 :008(042) [0053] which ought to be the **chief** teaching in the church, has so
A L : 2 6 :004(064) [0071] of faith, which is the **chief** part of the Gospel and ought
A L : 2 8 :004(081) [0085] in reverence and honor as the **chief** gifts of God on earth.
A L : 2 8 :052(089) [0091] necessary to preserve the **chief** article of the Gospel,
A L : 0 0 :001(094) [0095] We have now reviewed the **chief** articles that are regarded
A L : 0 0 :003(095) [0095] of this sort so that the **chief** points at issue, being briefly
A P : 0 2 :014(102) [0109] These are the **chief** flaws in human nature, transgressing
A P : 0 4 :005(108) [0121] be divided into these two **chief** doctrines, the law and the
A P : 0 4 :084(119) [0145] of a promise, this is Paul's **chief** argument, which he often
A P : 0 7 :013(170) [0231] understand what it is that **chiefly** makes us members, and
A P : 0 7 :043(177) [0243] follow the example of the **chief** brethren who had been
A P : 1 2 :003(182) [0253] issue, involving the **chief** doctrine of the Gospel, the true
A P : 1 2 :005(183) [0253] sum of the matter nor the **chief** requirements of penitence
A P : 1 2 :010(184) [0255] at hand is a great one, the **chief** doctrine of the Gospel,
A P : 1 2 :044(187) [0263] Scripture makes them the **chief** parts in the penitence or
A P : 1 2 :045(187) [0263] There are, then, two **chief** parts here, contrition and
A P : 1 2 :045(188) [0263] names contrition and faith as the **chief** parts of penitence.
A P : 1 2 :052(189) [0265] to teach that these are the **chief** parts of penitence,
A P : 1 2 :053(189) [0265] These are the two **chief** works of God in men, to terrify
A P : 1 2 :055(189) [0267] These are the **chief** parts.
A P : 1 2 :059(190) [0267] For this is the **chief** issue on which we clash with our
A P : 1 5 :042(221) [0327] But the **chief** worship of God is the preaching of the
A P : 2 4 :068(262) [0409] idea that ignores the **chief** use of what God has instituted.
S 2 : 0 1 :001(292) [0461] The first and **chief** article is this, that Jesus Christ, our
S 2 : 0 2 :025(297) [0469] in conflict with the first, **chief** article and undermines
S 3 : 0 2 :004(303) [0479] However, the **chief** function or power of the law is to
S 3 : 1 4 :001(315) [0501] conflict with the first **chief** article, they must be absolutely
T R : 0 0 :054(329) [0519] does it behoove the **chief** members of the church, the
S C : 0 6 :008(352) [0557] and drinking, are the **chief** thing in the sacrament, and he
L C : S P :010(363) [0577] II. The **Chief** Articles of Our Faith
L C : 0 1 :150(385) [0625] with all honor as their **chief** glory, it is our duty to honor
L C : 0 1 :174(388) [0629] know that it is his **chief** duty, on pain of losing divine
L C : 0 1 :219(394) [0643] This is one of the **chief** ways to make chastity attractive
L C : 0 1 :230(396) [0645] become of the head and **chief** protector of all thieves, the
L C : 0 1 :232(396) [0647] this not to Christians but **chiefly** to knaves and
L C : 0 1 :286(403) [0663] Our **chief** reason for doing so should be the one which
L C : 0 1 :324(409) [0675] of the first and **chief** commandment, from which all the
L C : 0 1 :329(410) [0677] First Commandment is the **chief** source and fountainhead
L C : 0 3 :074(430) [0719] and the government, for **chiefly** through them does God
L C : 0 3 :080(431) [0721] directed against our **chief** enemy, the devil, whose whole
L C : 0 3 :103(434) [0727] everyone wants to sit in the **chief** seat and be seen by all.
L C : 0 3 :107(434) [0729] for example, are tempted **chiefly** by the flesh; older
L C : 0 4 :001(436) [0733] finished with the three **chief** parts of our common
L C : 0 4 :007(437) [0733] It is the **chief** cause of our contentions and battles
L C : 0 5 :004(447) [0753] or command, which is the **chief** thing to be considered.
E P : 0 1 :003(466) [0779] cannot co-exist with the **chief** articles of our Christian
E P : 0 4 :000(475) [0797] The **Chief** Issue in the Controversy Concerning Good
E P : 0 5 :000(477) [0801] The **Chief** Question at Issue in This Controversy
E P : 0 6 :000(479) [0805] The **Chief** Question at Issue in This Controversy
E P : 0 7 :001(481) [0809] The **Chief** Question at Issue between Our Doctrine and
E P : 0 8 :001(487) [0817] The **Chief** Question at Issue in This Controversy
E P : 0 8 :002(487) [0817] The **chief** question has been, Because of personal union in
E P : 0 9 :000(492) [0827] The **Chief** Question at Issue in the Controversy about
E P : 1 0 :001(492) [0829] The **Chief** Question at Issue in this Controversy
E P : 1 0 :002(492) [0829] The **chief** question has been, In times of persecution,
S D : P R :001(501) [0847] teaching concerning the **chief** articles of our Christian
S D : P R :003(502) [0847] churches concerning the **chief** articles, especially those
S D : R N :011(506) [0855] of our churches, that the **chief** and most illustrious
S D : R N :015(507) [0857] of the Creed or the **chief** parts of our Christian doctrine,
S D : R N :016(507) [0857] agreement concerning the **chief** and most significant
S D : 0 1 :005(509) [0861] must consider this as the **chief** sin, the root and fountain
S D : 0 1 :034(514) [0869] The **chief** articles of our Christian faith constrain and
S D : 0 1 :048(517) [0875] The **chief** articles of our Christian faith show powerfully
S D : 0 1 :049(517) [0875] antithesis, as far as the **chief** points in this controversy are
S D : 0 1 :049(517) [0875] but are treating only the **chief** points in summary fashion.
S D : 0 2 :002(520) [0881] The **chief** issue is solely and alone what the unregenerated
S D : 0 3 :006(540) [0917] by faith is "the **chief** article of the entire Christian
S D : 0 4 :018(554) [0943] It was **chiefly** in this interest that many defended the
S D : 0 5 :003(558) [0953] we find that it was **chiefly** occasioned by the fact that the
S D : 0 5 :004(559) [0953] Shortly thereafter the **chief** parts are announced, namely,
S D : 0 7 :001(569) [0971] The **Chief** Issue between Our Doctrine and That of the
S D : 0 7 :034(575) [0983] of Dr. Luther, as the **chief** teacher of the Augsburg
S D : 0 7 :061(580) [0995] spiritual, of which Christ speaks **chiefly** in John 6:48-58.
S D : 1 0 :014(613) [1057] dealing primarily with the **chief** article of our Christian
S D : 1 0 :018(614) [1059] and the confession of the **chief** teachers of the Augsburg

Child (32), Children (153)
A G : 0 9 :002(033) [0047] **Children**, too, should be baptized, for in Baptism they are
A G : 1 6 :004(037) [0051] house and home, wife and **child**, and the renunciation of
A G : 0 0 :001(047) [0059] wish to bequeath to our **children** and posterity any other
A G : 2 6 :010(065) [0071] to support his wife and **children** and bring them up in the
A G : 2 6 :010(065) [0071] that a wife should bear **children** and care for them, that a
A G : 2 7 :056(080) [0083] men who forsook wife and **child**, and also their civil
A L : 0 9 :002(033) [0047] Baptism, and that **children** should be baptized, for being
A L : 0 9 :003(033) [0047] reject the Baptism of **children** and declare that children
A L : 0 9 :003(033) [0047] and declare that **children** are saved without Baptism.
A L : 2 6 :010(065) [0071] should bring up his **children**, that a mother should bear
A L : 2 6 :010(065) [0071] a mother should bear **children**, that a prince should
A P : 0 2 :005(101) [0107] of original sin but, like a **child** born of a slave, is in this
A P : 0 4 :086(119) [0147] accounted righteous and **children** of God not on account
A P : 0 4 :094(120) [0149] gave power to become **children** of God; who were born,
A P : 0 4 :354(161) [0217] that the justified are **children** of God and fellow heirs with
A P : 0 7 :034(175) [0239] can be righteous and a **child** of God even if he does not
A P : 0 7 :034(175) [0239] men can be righteous, **children** of God, and the church of
A P : 0 9 :001(178) [0245] necessary for salvation; **children** are to be baptized; the
A P : 0 9 :001(178) [0245] baptized; the Baptism of **children** is not useless but is
A P : 0 9 :002(178) [0245] also their assertion that the Baptism of **children** is useless.
A P : 0 9 :002(178) [0245] the promise of salvation also applies to little **children**.
A P : 0 9 :002(178) [0245] it is necessary to baptize **children**, so that the promise of
A P : 0 9 :002(178) [0245] is offered to all — men, women, **children**, and infants.
A P : 0 9 :003(178) [0245] the Baptism of little **children**, the Anabaptists teach
A P : 0 9 :003(178) [0245] when they condemn the Baptism of little **children**.
A P : 0 9 :003(178) [0245] the Baptism of little **children** is shown by the fact that
A P : 1 5 :025(219) [0323] of the household, married life, and the rearing of **children**
A P : 1 5 :040(220) [0325] The **children** chant the Psalms in order to learn; the
A P : 1 5 :041(220) [0325] no catechization of the **children** at all, though even the
A P : 1 5 :043(221) [0327] and instruction of **children**, chastity, and all the works of
A P : 2 3 :003(239) [0363] spare, and banish deserted wives and orphaned **children**.
A P : 2 3 :032(243) [0373] he says, "Woman will be saved through bearing **children**."
A P : 2 3 :032(243) [0373] Paul says that woman is saved through bearing **children**.
A P : 2 3 :059(247) [0379] and the exile of poor women and orphaned **children**.
A P : 2 4 :081(264) [0411] though the number of **children** does not excuse parents
A P : 2 7 :041(276) [0435] of leaving wife and **children** makes it even clearer that he
A P : 2 7 :041(276) [0435] the command of God forbids deserting wife and **children**.
A P : 2 7 :041(276) [0435] let property, wife, and **children**, even life itself, be taken
A P : 2 7 :041(276) [0435] do injury to wife and **children** but about those who bear
A P : 2 7 :042(276) [0435] friends, wife, and **children** without the command of God.
S 1 : 0 1 :000(292) [0461] and the Catechism in common use for **children** teach.
S 2 : 0 2 :018(296) [0467] of God, their wives and **children**, etc. and pursue these
S 3 : 0 5 :004(311) [0493] Baptism, we hold that **children** should be baptized, for
S 3 : 1 2 :002(315) [0499] God, a seven-year-old **child** knows what the church is,
S 3 : 1 2 :003(315) [0499] So **children** pray, "I believe in one holy Christian
T R : 0 0 :008(321) [0505] the kingdom, Christ put a **child** in the midst of the
T R : 0 0 :008(321) [0505] among ministers, just as a **child** neither seeks nor takes
S C : P R :018(340) [0537] when instructing **children** and the common people in
S C : P R :019(340) [0537] and parents to rule wisely and educate their **children**.
S C : P R :020(340) [0537] aid in the training of **children** to become pastors,
S C : 0 1 :021(344) [0543] of the fathers upon the **children** to the third and the
S C : 0 3 :002(346) [0545] and we are truly his **children** in order that we may
S C : 0 3 :002(346) [0545] prayer, even as beloved **children** approach their dear
S C : 0 3 :005(346) [0547] and purely and we, as **children** of God, lead holy lives in
S C : 0 3 :014(347) [0547] a pious spouse and good **children**, trustworthy servants,
S C : 0 5 :023(350) [0553] faithful in training my **children**, servants, and wife to the
S C : 0 8 :007(353) [0559] When **children** and the whole household gather at the
S C : 0 9 :002(354) [0561] well, keeping his **children** submissive and respectful in
S C : 0 9 :007(355) [0563] And you are now her **children** if you do right and let
S C : 0 9 :008(356) [0563] do not provoke your **children** to anger, lest they become
S C : 0 9 :009(356) [0563] ***Children***
S C : 0 9 :009(356) [0563] "**Children**, obey your parents in the Lord, for this is right.
L C : P R :007(359) [0569] Yet I do as a **child** who is being taught the Catechism.
L C : P R :008(359) [0569] I wish, but must remain a **child** and pupil of the
L C : P R :008(359) [0569] they need is to become **children** and begin learning their
L C : S P :001(362) [0575] for the instruction of **children** and uneducated people.
L C : S P :001(362) [0575] in Greek, a "catechism" — that is, instruction for **children**
L C : S P :003(362) [0575] of the Catechism or **children**'s sermons and diligently
L C : S P :004(362) [0575] to examine his **children** and servants at least once a week
L C : S P :005(362) [0575] Christian doctrine than **children** and beginners at school.
L C : S P :016(363) [0577] Our **children** should be taught the habit of reciting them
L C : 0 1 :030(368) [0589] *of the fathers upon the* ***children*** *to the third and fourth*
L C : 0 1 :037(369) [0591] will not forget his anger down to their **children**'s children.
L C : 0 1 :037(369) [0591] will not forget his anger down to their children's **children**.
L C : 0 1 :039(370) [0591] but also for their **children** to a thousand and even many
L C : 0 1 :045(370) [0593] with all that he had; not one of his **children** remained.
L C : 0 1 :060(372) [0597] wayward wives and **children** and servants, and troubles
L C : 0 1 :069(374) [0599] and punishment, **children** be trained in due time to shun
L C : 0 1 :070(374) [0601] On the other hand, **children** should be constantly urged
L C : 0 1 :073(374) [0601] our soul and body, wife, **children**, servants, and all that
L C : 0 1 :074(374) [0601] came the custom of **children** who cross themselves when
L C : 0 1 :074(374) [0601] **Children** used to be trained to fast and pray to St.
L C : 0 1 :076(375) [0601] right way to bring up **children**, so long as they can be
L C : 0 1 :077(375) [0603] for when we preach to **children**, we must also speak their
L C : 0 1 :112(380) [0613] a great, good, and holy work is here assigned to **children**.
L C : 0 1 :112(380) [0613] Every **child** would have remained faithful to this
L C : 0 1 :114(380) [0613] should have had godly **children**, properly taught, and
L C : 0 1 :114(380) [0613] lightly over it, and so **children** could not lay it to heart;
L C : 0 1 :115(381) [0613] Every **child** who knows and does this has, in the first
L C : 0 1 :118(381) [0615] with shame before a little **child** that has lived according to
L C : 0 1 :121(382) [0615] in their houses, and **children** would win their parents'
L C : 0 1 :124(382) [0617] and as they have lived, so live their **children** after them.
L C : 0 1 :128(382) [0617] devil rules in the world; **children** forget their parents, as
L C : 0 1 :128(383) [0617] parents, and there is no **child** that recognizes and
L C : 0 1 :134(383) [0619] life — health, wife and **child**, livelihood, peace, good
L C : 0 1 :137(384) [0621] They see their **children**'s children, as we said above, "to

Continued ▶

LC : 01 :137(384) [0621] They see their children's **children**, as we said above, "to
LC : 01 :138(384) [0621] prosper and have many **children**, it is certainly because
LC : 01 :141(384) [0621] by himself to bring up his **child**, he calls upon a
LC : 01 :143(385) [0621] What a **child** owes to father and mother, the entire
LC : 01 :149(385) [0623] obey him you are his dear **child**; if you despise this
LC : 01 :151(386) [0625] or famine, or his **children** will turn out badly; servants,
LC : 01 :154(386) [0625] as much wrong from your own wife, **children**, or servants.
LC : 01 :168(388) [0629] material support of their **children**, servants, subjects, etc.,
LC : 01 :170(388) [0629] acts as if God gave us **children** for our pleasure and
LC : 01 :172(388) [0629] and educating our **children** to serve God and mankind.
LC : 01 :173(388) [0629] has given and entrusted **children** to us with the command
LC : 01 :174(388) [0629] grace, to bring up his **children** in the fear and knowledge
LC : 01 :175(389) [0631] faithfully bring up their **children** and servants to be
LC : 01 :176(389) [0631] and fail to bring up your **children** to usefulness and piety.
LC : 01 :176(389) [0631] have reared your own **children**, no matter how devout
LC : 01 :181(389) [0631] had to bring their own **children** to judgment and sentence
LC : 01 :207(393) [0639] other, be fruitful, beget **children**, and support and bring
LC : 01 :243(398) [0649] that they can never enjoy it or pass it on to their **children**.
LC : 01 :244(398) [0649] house and home and outrage and kill wife and **children**.
LC : 01 :256(399) [0653] before his wife, **children**, servants, and neighbors.
LC : 01 :262(400) [0655] the truth and the **children** of God and yet consider this no
LC : 01 :314(407) [0671] a poor girl tends a little **child**, or faithfully does what she
LC : 01 :320(408) [0673] *of the fathers upon the **children** to the third and fourth*
LC : 02 :006(411) [0679] simple for teaching to **children**, we shall briefly sum up
LC : 02 :011(412) [0681] you were to ask a young **child**, "My boy, what kind of
LC : 02 :013(412) [0681] means of support, wife and **child**, servants, house and
LC : 02 :032(415) [0687] points is not the brief **children**'s sermons, but rather the
LC : 03 :007(421) [0699] as an exercise for young **children**, pupils, and simple folk;
LC : 03 :013(422) [0701] A **child** should never despise obedience to his father and
LC : 03 :032(424) [0707] from on high, "Yes, dear **child**, it shall indeed be done in
LC : 03 :037(425) [0707] and so we are called **children** of God and enjoy the
LC : 03 :038(425) [0709] and praying, as good **children**, that his name, which is
LC : 03 :039(425) [0709] way to behave as good **children** so that he may receive
LC : 03 :044(425) [0709] to have a bad, unruly **child** who antagonizes him in word
LC : 03 :044(425) [0709] as godly and heavenly **children** with the result that he
LC : 03 :044(426) [0709] must hear us called not **children** of God but children of
LC : 03 :044(426) [0709] us called not children of God but **children** of the devil.
LC : 03 :065(429) [0717] honor, house and home, wife and **children**, body and life.
LC : 03 :076(431) [0721] to us a good wife, **children**, and servants; to cause our
LC : 04 :047(442) [0743] Do **children** also believe, and is it right to baptize them?
LC : 04 :057(444) [0747] We bring the **child** with the purpose and hope that he
LC : 04 :070(445) [0749] A young **child**, who has no particular vice, becomes
LC : 05 :037(451) [0761] preparation and **children**'s exercise so that one's body
LC : 05 :086(456) [0773] that they in turn may bring up their **children** successfully.
LC : 05 :087(456) [0773] or have taught to his **children** the things they ought to
EP : 01 :005(466) [0781] "Since therefore the **children** share in flesh and blood, he
EP : 01 :012(467) [0783] of which man outside of Christ is a **child** of wrath.
EP : 04 :012(477) [0799] out of a love of righteousness, like a **child** (Rom. 8:15).
EP : 04 :013(477) [0799] 8. However, in the elect **children** of God this spontaneity
EP : 06 :006(481) [0807] In this sense the **children** of God live in the law and walk
EP : 06 :006(481) [0807] Thus God's **children** are "not under the law, but under
EP : 08 :017(489) [0823] of our Christian faith as we teach this to our **children**.
EP : 11 :005(495) [0833] only with the pious **children** of God in whom he is well
EP : 12 :006(498) [0839] sight of God unbaptized **children** are not sinners but are
EP : 12 :007(498) [0839] 5. That **children** are not to be baptized until they have
EP : 12 :008(498) [0839] and prior to Baptism the **children** of Christian parents are
EP : 12 :008(498) [0839] parents are holy and the **children** of God by virtue of
EP : 12 :023(500) [0841] God seals the adoption of **children** and effects rebirth.
SD : 01 :006(509) [0861] we are "by nature the **children** of wrath," of death, and of
SD : 01 :009(510) [0861] God's disfavor and are **children** of wrath by nature, as St.
SD : 01 :013(511) [0863] imposes upon Adam's **children** and upon original sin is
SD : 01 :019(511) [0865] account is necessarily a **child** of wrath and of damnation
SD : 02 :058(532) [0903] I have gathered your **children** together as a hen gathers
SD : 03 :004(540) [0917] we are adopted as God's **children** solely on account of the
SD : 03 :009(540) [0919] and is adopted as a **child** of God and an heir of eternal
SD : 03 :019(542) [0921] forgiveness of sins and our adoption as God's **children**.
SD : 03 :020(542) [0921] he has transformed a **child** of wrath into a child of God
SD : 03 :020(542) [0921] a child of wrath into a **child** of God and thus has
SD : 05 :025(563) [0961] for his sake as God's **children**, and out of pure grace,
SD : 06 :006(564) [0963] If believers and the elect **children** of God were perfectly
SD : 06 :009(565) [0965] elect, and reborn **children** of God require in this life not
SD : 06 :009(565) [0965] then you are illegitimate **children** and not sons" (Heb.
SD : 10 :019(614) [1059] God, a seven-year-old **child** knows what the church is,
SD : 11 :001(616) [1063] concerning the eternal election of the **children** of God.
SD : 11 :004(616) [1063] the eternal election of his **children** to eternal salvation.
SD : 11 :005(617) [1065] but only over the **children** of God, who have been elected
SD : 11 :013(618) [1067] and ordering of the **children** of God to eternal life, we
SD : 11 :018(619) [1069] into the adoption of **children** and into the inheritance of
SD : 11 :031(621) [1073] elect "that they are the **children** of God," and when they
SD : 11 :070(627) [1085] election of all God's **children** to eternal life, and who
SD : 11 :072(628) [1087] give good gifts to your **children**, how much more will the
SD : 11 :073(628) [1087] to the elect that they are "**children** of God" (Rom. 8:16).
SD : 11 :075(628) [1087] Hence when his **children** become disobedient and
SD : 11 :085(630) [1091] which he oppressed the **children** of Israel by many,
SD : 11 :087(631) [1091] election of the elect **children** of God gives God his due
SD : 12 :011(634) [1099] 2. That unbaptized **children** are not sinners before God
SD : 12 :012(634) [1099] 3. That **children** should not be baptized until they have
SD : 12 :013(634) [1099] 4. That the **children** of Christians, because they are born
SD : 12 :013(634) [1099] parents, are holy and **children** of God even without and

Childbirth (1)
AP : 23 :032(244) [0373] marital intercourse, by **childbirth**, and by her other

Childhood (1)
AG : 27 :033(076) [0079] the cloister in their **childhood**, before attaining such age.

Childish (7)
AG : 20 :003(041) [0053] were concerned with **childish** and useless works like
AL : 20 :003(041) [0053] Instead, they urged **childish** and needless works, such as
AP : 02 :051(107) [0119] Majesty about the **childish** and trivial quibbling with
AP : 04 :336(159) [0215] Look how this **childish** sophistry delights our opponents!
AP : 04 :342(159) [0215] It is obviously a **childish** quibble to interpret "unworthy
S3 : 15 :004(316) [0501] which contains silly and **childish** articles, such as the
LC : 01 :075(375) [0601] With **childish** and playful methods like these we may

Choice (11), Choices (1)
AG : 18 :001(039) [0051] life and to make **choices** among the things that reason
AG : 18 :007(040) [0053] other hand, by his own **choice** man can also undertake
AL : 18 :001(039) [0051] righteousness and for the **choice** of things subject to
AL : 26 :020(067) [0073] that they merit grace by observances of their own **choice**.
AP : 18 :004(225) [0335] grasp, it also retains a **choice** in these things, as well as
S2 : 04 :007(299) [0473] in their power and **choice** to change or depose this head.
LC : 01 :115(381) [0613] with works of their own **choice**: "See, this work is well
LC : 01 :294(404) [0665] according to their own **choice**; with their body and all
LC : 03 :008(421) [0699] This God requires of us; he has not left it to our **choice**.
LC : 03 :009(421) [0699] so, it is not left to my **choice** here whether to pray or not,
LC : 05 :046(452) [0763] it'; so he compels no one, but leaves it to our free **choice**."
EP : 04 :003(476) [0797] is not a matter of our **choice** but that regenerated persons

Choose (11), Chooses (1), Chose (5), Chosen (19)
AG : 18 :004(040) [0051] of this life that they have freedom to **choose** good or evil.
AG : 26 :020(067) [0073] supposed that grace is earned through self-**chosen** works.
AG : 27 :036(076) [0081] service of God that is **chosen** and instituted by men to
AL : 18 :004(039) [0051] of this life that they have freedom to **choose** good or evil.
AL : 23 :011(052) [0063] a married man should be **chosen** to be bishop (I Tim.
AL : 27 :027(075) [0079] ought to be voluntary and **chosen** freely and deliberately?
AL : 27 :036(076) [0081] God that is instituted and **chosen** by men to merit
AP : 04 :211(136) [0179] and other holy Fathers **chose** a certain kind of life for
AP : 04 :212(136) [0179] men constantly **choose** other works, make up new
AP : 18 :004(225) [0335] will has freedom to **choose** among the works and things
AP : 18 :004(225) [0335] Externally, it can **choose** to keep the hands from murder,
AP : 24 :052(259) [0403] (5:1), "Every high priest **chosen** from among men is
AP : 27 :041(276) [0435] for works which we have **chosen** are "vain worship"
S2 : 04 :001(298) [0471] These churches did not **choose** to be under him as under
S2 : 04 :001(298) [0471] as under an overlord but **chose** to stand beside him as
TR : 00 :062(330) [0523] observes: "One man was **chosen** over the rest to prevent
TR : 00 :062(331) [0523] the presbyters always **chose** one of their number, set him
TR : 00 :062(331) [0523] itself, the deacons may **choose** from their number one
SC : PR :008(339) [0535] **Choose** the form that pleases you, therefore, and adhere
SC : PR :014(339) [0535] in this booklet, or **choose** any other brief and fixed
LC : 01 :045(370) [0593] Saul was a great king, **chosen** by God, and an upright
LC : 01 :117(381) [0615] thank God that he has **chosen** and fitted you to perform a
LC : 01 :221(395) [0643] estates" that are **chosen** without God's Word and
LC : 02 :060(418) [0695] "resurrection of the flesh," however, is not well **chosen**.
LC : 05 :057(453) [0767] If you **choose** to fix your eye on how good and pure you
EP : 06 :004(480) [0807] self-decreed and self-**chosen** acts of serving God.
EP : 11 :007(495) [0833] as it is written, "He **chose** us in him before the foundation
EP : 11 :012(496) [0835] are called, but few are **chosen**," does not mean that God
EP : 12 :005(498) [0839] one's own individual self-**chosen** spirituality, which in
SD : 02 :019(524) [0889] of good or evil or freely **choose** to act or not to act.
SD : 02 :026(526) [0891] one to whom the Son **chooses** to reveal him" (Matt.
SD : 11 :005(617) [1065] St. Paul says, "Even as he **chose** us in him, he destined us
SD : 11 :034(622) [1075] are called and few are **chosen**" is not that in his call,
SD : 11 :041(623) [1077] are called, but few are **chosen**," for few accept the Word
SD : 11 :051(624) [1079] are called, but few are **chosen**" (Matt. 22:14); likewise,
SD : 12 :010(634) [1097] peculiar precepts and self-**chosen** spirituality as on a kind

Chores (1)
AP : 23 :040(245) [0375] and serving and is not so distracted by household **chores**.

Christ (1890)
PR : PR :003(003) [0007] and orthodox church of **Christ** has believed, fought for
PR : PR :009(006) [0011] body and the blood of **Christ** and other erroneous
PR : PR :018(009) [0015] seat of our Lord Jesus **Christ** with joyful and fearless
PR : PR :020(010) [0017] of the two natures in **Christ**, our theologians clearly assert
PR : PR :020(010) [0017] namely, the words of institution of **Christ**'s testament.
PR : PR :020(010) [0017] faith they are to stay with the plain words of **Christ**.
PR : PR :020(010) [0017] words of the testament of **Christ** and decry and condemn
PR : PR :020(010) [0019] of the words of **Christ** as described above does not
PR : PR :021(010) [0019] nature in the person of **Christ**, in that it is seated at the
PR : PR :021(011) [0019] to the human nature of **Christ** outside the personal union,
PR : PR :022(012) [0019] our churches according to **Christ**'s institution and as we
PR : PR :023(012) [0021] advent of our only Redeemer and Saviour Jesus **Christ**.
AG : PR :004(025) [0039] and church, even as we are all enlisted under one **Christ**.
AG : PR :011(025) [0041] as we are all under one **Christ** and should confess and
AG : PR :011(025) [0041] one Christ and should confess and contend for **Christ**.
AG : 02 :003(029) [0045] thus disparaging the sufferings and merit of **Christ**.
AG : 03 :002(029) [0045] person that there is one **Christ**, true God and true man,
AG : 03 :004(030) [0045] The same **Christ** also descended into hell, truly rose from
AG : 03 :006(030) [0045] The same Lord **Christ** will return openly to judge the
AG : 04 :001(030) [0045] before God by grace, for **Christ**'s sake, through faith,
AG : 04 :002(030) [0045] when we believe that **Christ** suffered for us and that for
AG : 05 :003(031) [0045] merit but by the merit of **Christ**, when we believe this.
AG : 06 :002(032) [0045] through faith in **Christ**, as Christ himself says, "So you
AG : 06 :002(032) [0047] faith in Christ, as **Christ** himself says, "So you also, when
AG : 06 :003(032) [0047] that whoever believes in **Christ** shall be saved, and he
AG : 08 :001(033) [0047] are wicked men, for as **Christ** himself indicated, "The
AG : 10 :001(034) [0047] true body and blood of **Christ** are really present in the
AG : 12 :005(035) [0049] been obtained through **Christ**), and this faith will comfort
AG : 15 :003(037) [0049] to the Gospel and the teaching about faith in **Christ**.
AG : 17 :000(038) [0051] XVII. [The Return of **Christ** to Judgment]
AG : 17 :001(038) [0051] us that our Lord Jesus **Christ** will return on the last day
AG : 19 :000(041) [0053] It is as **Christ** says in John 8:44, "When the devil lies, he
AG : 20 :006(041) [0053] but they add faith in **Christ** and say that faith and works
AG : 20 :009(042) [0053] our sins are forgiven for **Christ**'s sake, who alone is the
AG : 20 :010(042) [0055] can merit grace, despises **Christ** and seeks his own way to
AG : 20 :013(043) [0055] God through faith in **Christ** and not through works.
AG : 20 :015(043) [0055] and knows that for **Christ**'s sake it has a gracious God, as
AG : 20 :022(044) [0055] doctrine about faith in **Christ** and diligently to apply it in
AG : 20 :023(044) [0055] also believe the history of **Christ**'s suffering and his
AG : 20 :023(044) [0055] we receive grace and forgiveness of sin through **Christ**.
AG : 20 :024(044) [0055] Whoever knows that in **Christ** he has a gracious God,
AG : 20 :036(046) [0057] without faith and without **Christ** human nature and
AG : 20 :038(046) [0057] done without the help of **Christ**, as he himself says in John
AG : 21 :002(047) [0057] between God and men, **Christ** Jesus" (I Tim. 2:5), who is
AG : 21 :003(047) [0059] and call upon this same Jesus **Christ** in every time of need
AG : 21 :004(047) [0059] with the Father, Jesus **Christ** the righteous" (I John 2:1).

Continued ▶

AG : 2 2 :001(049) [0059] command and order of **Christ**, "Drink of it, all of you"
AG : 2 2 :002(049) [0059] Concerning the chalice **Christ** here commands with clear
AG : 2 2 :006(050) [0061] sacrament distributed the blood of **Christ** to the people.
AG : 2 2 :011(050) [0061] sacrament according to **Christ**'s institution or to compel
AG : 2 2 :011(050) [0061] to act contrary to the arrangement of our Lord **Christ**.
AG : 2 2 :012(051) [0061] to the institution of **Christ**, the customary carrying about
AG : 2 3 :005(051) [0061] Moreover, when **Christ** said in Matt. 19:11, "Not all men
AG : 2 3 :023(055) [0063] **Christ** himself asserts that the devil is a murderer from the
AG : 0 1 :003(056) [0065] to teach the people what they need to know about **Christ**.
AG : 2 4 :012(057) [0065] unworthily is guilty of the body and blood of **Christ**),
AG : 2 4 :021(058) [0067] was taught that our Lord **Christ** has by his death made
AG : 2 4 :023(058) [0067] Meanwhile faith in **Christ** and true service of God were
AG : 2 4 :026(058) [0067] sin, or for any other sin, except the one death of **Christ**.
AG : 2 4 :027(059) [0067] to the Hebrews that **Christ** offered himself once and by
AG : 2 4 :025(059) [0067] in church doctrine that **Christ**'s death should have made
AG : 2 4 :030(059) [0067] grace and forgiveness of sin are promised us by **Christ**.
AG : 2 6 :004(064) [0071] first place, the grace of **Christ** and the teaching concerning
AG : 2 6 :004(064) [0071] we regard the merit of **Christ** as something great and
AG : 2 6 :004(064) [0071] and know that faith in **Christ** is to be esteemed far above
AG : 2 6 :005(064) [0071] it is only through faith in **Christ** that we obtain grace for
AG : 2 6 :005(064) [0071] faith in Christ that we obtain grace for **Christ**'s sake.
AG : 2 6 :013(066) [0073] heard anything of the consolation of the grace of **Christ**.
AG : 2 6 :016(066) [0073] hindered from coming to a right knowledge of **Christ**.
AG : 2 6 :022(067) [0073] In Matt. 15:1-20 **Christ** defends the apostles for not
AG : 2 6 023(067) [0073] Thereupon **Christ** says, "Not what goes into the mouth
AG : 2 6 035(069) [0075] **Christ** speaks of this in Luke 21:34, "Take heed to
AG : 2 7)15(073) [0077] and inveigled into a monastery learned little about **Christ**.
AG : 2 7)36(076) [0081] So **Christ** himself says in Matt. 15:9, "In vain do they
AG : 2 7 37(077) [0081] us into his favor for the sake of **Christ**, his only Son.
AG : 2 7 38(077) [0081] and honor of the grace of **Christ** and deny the
AG : 2 7 41(077) [0081] "You are severed from **Christ**, you who would be justified
AG : 2 7 42(077) [0081] by vows are severed from **Christ** and have fallen away
AG : 2 7 : 43(077) [0081] God's grace, for they rob **Christ**, who alone justifies, of his
AG : 2 7 :(19(079) [0083] faith, and trust that for **Christ**'s sake we have a gracious,
AG : 2 8 :( )2(081) [0083] the power given them by **Christ**, have not only introduced
AG : 2 8 :0)6(081) [0085] For **Christ** sent out the apostles with this command, "As
AG : 2 8 :0 14(083) [0085] **Christ** himself said, "My kingship is not of this world,"
AG : 2 8 :(22(084) [0087] according to the saying of **Christ** in Luke 10:16, "He who
AG : 2 8 :(23(084) [0087] obedient in such cases, for **Christ** says in Matt. 7:15,
AG : 2 8 31(085) [0087] power to bishops cite **Christ**'s saying in John 16:12, 13, "I
AG : 2 8)36(086) [0089] grace, for the glory of **Christ**'s merit is blasphemed when
AG : 2 8 .044(088) [0089] of what is to come; but the substance belongs to **Christ**."
AG : 2 8 :045(088) [0089] in Col. 2:20-23, "If with **Christ** you died to the regulations
AG : 2 8 :047(088) [0089] **Christ** himself says concerning those who urge human
AG : 2 8 :052(089) [0091] in Gal. 5:1, "For freedom **Christ** has set us free; stand fast
AG : 2 8 :052(089) [0091] of God through faith in **Christ** without our merits; we do
AG : 2 8 :061(091) [0093] Jewish services and that **Christ** commanded the apostles
AL : 0 2 :003(029) [0045] who obscure the glory of **Christ**'s merit and benefits by
AL : 0 3 :002(029) [0045] unity of his person, one **Christ**, true God and true man,
AL : 0 3 :006(030) [0045] The same **Christ** will openly come again to judge the living
AL : 0 4 :001(030) [0045] but are freely justified for **Christ**'s sake through faith when
AL : 0 4 :002(030) [0045] forgiven on account of **Christ**, who by his death made
AL : 0 5 :003(031) [0045] merits but on account of **Christ** that God justifies those
AL : 0 5 :003(031) [0045] believe that they are received into favor for **Christ**'s sake.
AL : 0 6 :001(032) [0047] apprehended by faith, as **Christ** himself also testifies,
AL : 0 6 :003(032) [0047] that whoever believes in **Christ** shall be saved, not through
AL : 0 8 :001(033) [0047] according to the saying of **Christ**, "The scribes and
AL : 0 8 :002(033) [0047] and commandment of **Christ** even if they are administered
AL : 1 0 :001(034) [0047] the body and blood of **Christ** are truly present and are
AL : 1 2 :005(034) [0049] that sins are forgiven for **Christ**'s sake, comforts the
AL : 1 7 :000(038) [0051] XVII. [The Return of **Christ** for Judgment]
AL : 1 7 :001(038) [0051] of the world **Christ** will appear for judgment and will raise
AL : 1 9 :000(041) [0053] turns away from God, as **Christ** says in John 8:44, "When
AL : 2 0 :009(042) [0053] are received into favor for **Christ**'s sake, who alone has
AL : 2 0 :010(042) [0055] the merit and grace of **Christ** and seeks a way to God
AL : 2 0 :010(042) [0055] a way to God without **Christ**, by human strength,
AL : 2 0 :010(042) [0055] human strength, although **Christ** has said of himself, "I
AL : 2 0 :014(043) [0055] by the blood of **Christ** would become of little value and
AL : 2 0 :015(043) [0055] they are sure that for **Christ**'s sake they have a gracious
AL : 2 0 :022(044) [0055] concerning faith in **Christ** in order that anxious
AL : 2 0 :022(044) [0055] and forgiveness of sins are apprehended by faith in **Christ**
AL : 2 0 :023(044) [0055] righteousness, and forgiveness of sins through **Christ**.
AL : 2 0 :024(044) [0055] to him through **Christ** truly knows God, knows that God
AL : 2 0 :039(046) [0057] Wherefore **Christ** said, "Apart from me you can do
AL : 2 1 :002(047) [0057] intercessor whom the Scriptures set before us is **Christ**.
AL : 2 1 :003(047) [0057] Such worship **Christ** especially approves, namely, that in
AL : 2 2 :002(049) [0059] **Christ** has here manifestly commanded with reference to
AL : 2 2 :006(050) [0061] Eucharist and distribute the blood of **Christ** to the people.
AL : 2 2 :012(051) [0061] with the institution of **Christ**, the processions which were
AL : 2 3 :005(051) [0061] In the second place, **Christ** said, "Not all men can receive
AL : 2 4 :021(058) [0067] Masses, namely, that **Christ** had by his passion made
AL : 2 4 :024(058) [0067] and diminish the glory of **Christ**'s passion, for the passion
AL : 2 4 :025(058) [0067] passion, for the passion of **Christ** was an oblation and
AL : 2 4 :026(059) [0067] of the body of Jesus **Christ** once for all," and again, "By a
AL : 2 4 :028(059) [0067] that we are justified before God through faith in **Christ**.
AL : 2 4 :030(059) [0067] **Christ** commands us to do this in remembrance of him.
AL : 2 4 :030(059) [0067] are received through **Christ** and should cheer and comfort
AL : 2 4 :031(059) [0067] For to remember **Christ** is to remember his benefits and
AL : 2 5 :001(061) [0069] to administer the body of **Christ** except to those who have
AL : 2 6 :004(064) [0071] in it, so that the merit of **Christ** may be well known and
AL : 2 6 :004(064) [0071] that sins are forgiven for **Christ**'s sake may be exalted far
AL : 2 6 :005(064) [0071] which believes that for **Christ**'s sake we are received into
AL : 2 6 :022(067) [0073] In Matt. 15:1-20 **Christ** defends the apostles for not
AL : 2 6 :023(067) [0073] Shortly afterward **Christ** says, "Not what goes into the
AL : 2 6 :032(068) [0075] and to be crucified with **Christ** is true and real, rather than
AL : 2 6 :035(069) [0075] So **Christ** commands, "Take heed to yourselves lest your
AL : 2 7 :036(076) [0081] of God is wicked, for **Christ** says, "In vain do they worship
AL : 2 7 :037(077) [0081] that they are received by God into favor for **Christ**'s sake.
AL : 2 7 :038(077) [0081] detract from the glory of **Christ** and obscure and deny the
AL : 2 7 :041(077) [0081] "You are severed from **Christ**, you who would be justified
AL : 2 7 :042(077) [0081] by vows are severed from **Christ** and fall away from
AL : 2 7 :043(077) [0081] own works what properly belongs to the glory of **Christ**.
AL : 2 7 :049(079) [0083] faith and to trust that for **Christ**'s sake we have a gracious
AL : 2 8 :006(082) [0085] For **Christ** sent out the apostles with this command, "As
AL : 2 8 :014(083) [0085] **Christ** says, "My kingdom is not of this world," and
AL : 2 8 :036(086) [0089] for the glory of **Christ**'s merit is dishonored when we
AL : 2 8 :045(088) [0089] Again, "If with **Christ** you died to the elemental spirits of
AL : 2 8 :047(088) [0089] In Matt. 15 **Christ** says concerning those who require
AL : 2 8 :052(089) [0091] grace through faith in **Christ** and not through certain
AL : 2 8 :061(091) [0093] Levitical service and that **Christ** commissioned the
AP : PR :015(099) [0101] we hold to the Gospel of **Christ** correctly and faithfully.
AP : PR :016(099) [0103] dangers for the glory of **Christ** and the good of the
AP : PR :019(099) [0103] commend our cause to **Christ**, who will one day judge
AP : 0 1 :002(100) [0103] belong to the church of **Christ** but are idolaters and
AP : 0 2 :010(102) [0107] is there for the grace of **Christ** if we can become righteous
AP : 0 2 :033(104) [0113] magnitude of the grace of **Christ** unless we acknowledge
AP : 0 2 :040(105) [0115] though it is not imputed to those who are in **Christ**.
AP : 0 2 :044(106) [0117] and obscuring the knowledge of the grace of **Christ**.
AP : 0 2 :045(106) [0117] but they need the grace of **Christ** to be forgiven and the
AP : 0 2 :048(106) [0119] be conquered without **Christ**'s help, so we cannot buy our
AP : 0 2 :050(106) [0119] **Christ** was given to us to bear both sin and penalty and to
AP : 0 2 :051(107) [0119] is correct and in agreement with **Christ**'s church catholic.
AP : 0 3 :000(107) [0119] [Article III. **Christ**]
AP : 0 3 :001(107) [0119] there are two natures in **Christ**, namely, that the Word
AP : 0 3 :001(107) [0119] his person; that this same **Christ** suffered and died to
AP : 0 4 :001(107) [0121] own merits, but freely for **Christ**'s sake, by faith in him.
AP : 0 4 :001(107) [0121] of sins by faith and by faith in **Christ** are justified.
AP : 0 4 :002(107) [0121] magnifies the honor of **Christ** and brings to pious
AP : 0 4 :003(107) [0121] glory and the blessings of **Christ**, and they rob pious
AP : 0 4 :003(107) [0121] consciences of the consolation offered them in **Christ**.
AP : 0 4 :005(108) [0121] it presents the promise of **Christ**; this it does either when
AP : 0 4 :005(108) [0121] the New Testament, the **Christ** who came promises
AP : 0 4 :012(109) [0123] is there between philosophy and the teaching of **Christ**?
AP : 0 4 :012(109) [0123] of sins by these elicited acts of ours, of what use is **Christ**?
AP : 0 4 :012(109) [0123] its works, what need is there of **Christ** or of regeneration?
AP : 0 4 :015(109) [0123] certain teachings of **Christ** with the teachings of Socrates,
AP : 0 4 :015(109) [0123] and others, as though **Christ** had come to give some sort
AP : 0 4 :017(109) [0125] In order not to by-pass **Christ** altogether, our opponents
AP : 0 4 :017(109) [0125] of the history about **Christ** and claim that he merited for
AP : 0 4 :018(109) [0125] Thus they bury **Christ**; men should not use him as
AP : 0 4 :021(110) [0127] vain trust in works and a contempt for the grace of **Christ**
AP : 0 4 :024(110) [0127] it ought not be praised at the expense of **Christ**.
AP : 0 4 :028(111) [0129] too, and a reproach to **Christ**, that men who keep the
AP : 0 4 :029(111) [0129] leading a holy life, then '**Christ** died to no purpose' (Gal.
AP : 0 4 :030(111) [0129] are severed from **Christ**, you who would be justified by
AP : 0 4 :030(111) [0129] For even as **Christ** is 'the end of the law,' so likewise he is
AP : 0 4 :040(112) [0131] of sins and justification was given because of **Christ**.
AP : 0 4 :043(113) [0133] of forgiveness of sins and justification because of **Christ**.
AP : 0 4 :043(113) [0133] righteousness of faith in **Christ**, which the law does not
AP : 0 4 :044(113) [0133] offers reconciliation for **Christ**'s sake, which we do not
AP : 0 4 :044(113) [0133] own merits, but only in the promise of mercy in **Christ**.
AP : 0 4 :045(113) [0133] are forgiven because of **Christ** and that God is reconciled
AP : 0 4 :045(113) [0133] to him because of **Christ**, this personal faith obtains the
AP : 0 4 :046(113) [0133] our merits of love, but **Christ** the mediator and
AP : 0 4 :046(113) [0133] is the true knowledge of **Christ**, it uses his blessings, it
AP : 0 4 :047(113) [0133] which proclaims the righteousness of faith in **Christ**.
AP : 0 4 :051(114) [0135] not enough to believe that **Christ** was born, suffered, and
AP : 0 4 :051(114) [0135] article, namely, that for **Christ**'s sake and not because of
AP : 0 4 :052(114) [0135] For why did **Christ** have to be offered for our sins if our
AP : 0 4 :053(114) [0137] is free, and the merits of **Christ** as the price and
AP : 0 4 :053(114) [0137] by mercy; the merits of **Christ** are the price because there
AP : 0 4 :057(114) [0137] knew the promise of the **Christ**, that for his sake God
AP : 0 4 :057(114) [0137] they understood that the **Christ** would be the price for our
AP : 0 4 :060(115) [0137] Faith in **Christ** Justifies
AP : 0 4 :062(115) [0139] chapter of Luke (24:47) **Christ** commands that penitence
AP : 0 4 :062(115) [0139] For **Christ**'s sake it offers forgiveness of sins and
AP : 0 4 :062(115) [0139] happens if they believe **Christ**'s promise that for his sake
AP : 0 4 :069(116) [0141] hold to the proposition, "**Christ** is the mediator," then we
AP : 0 4 :069(116) [0141] For how will **Christ** be the mediator if we do not use him
AP : 0 4 :069(116) [0141] believe means to trust in **Christ**'s merits, that because of
AP : 0 4 :070(116) [0141] "The promise of **Christ** is necessary over and above the
AP : 0 4 :070(116) [0141] we must maintain that the promise of **Christ** is necessary.
AP : 0 4 :070(116) [0141] only the law and does away with **Christ** and the Gospel.
AP : 0 4 :072(117) [0141] but rather that because of **Christ** by faith itself we are
AP : 0 4 :074(117) [0143] We Obtain the Forgiveness of Sins Only by Faith in **Christ**
AP : 0 4 :077(117) [0143] of sins only by faith in **Christ**, not through love, or
AP : 0 4 :079(118) [0143] who gives us the victory through our Lord Jesus **Christ**."
AP : 0 4 :079(118) [0143] But we conquer through **Christ**.
AP : 0 4 :079(118) [0143] by firm trust in the mercy promised because of **Christ**.
AP : 0 4 :080(118) [0143] Since **Christ** is set forth to be the propitiator, through
AP : 0 4 :080(118) [0143] For it is only by faith that **Christ** is accepted as the
AP : 0 4 :080(118) [0143] hearts with trust in the mercy promised for **Christ**'s sake.
AP : 0 4 :081(118) [0143] by trust in the mercy promised for **Christ**'s sake.
AP : 0 4 :081(118) [0143] opponents suppose that **Christ** is the mediator and
AP : 0 4 :081(118) [0143] Instead, as though **Christ** were completely buried, they
AP : 0 4 :081(118) [0143] Does this not bury **Christ** completely and do away with
AP : 0 4 :081(118) [0145] we have access (that is, reconciliation) through **Christ**.
AP : 0 4 :081(118) [0145] By faith, therefore, for **Christ**'s sake we receive the
AP : 0 4 :082(118) [0145] are forgiven because of **Christ**, the propitiator, according
AP : 0 4 :082(118) [0145] not in our merits but in **Christ**, the high priest, this
AP : 0 4 :083(119) [0145] We cannot take hold of the name of **Christ** except by faith
AP : 0 4 :084(119) [0145] forgiveness of sins is a thing promised for **Christ**'s sake.
AP : 0 4 :084(119) [0145] promised to faith in Jesus **Christ** might be given to those
AP : 0 4 :085(119) [0147] the forgiveness of sins for **Christ**'s sake only by faith; here
AP : 0 4 :086(119) [0147] by mercy on account of **Christ**, if they grasp this mercy by
AP : 0 4 :086(119) [0147] God's promise that for **Christ**'s sake he wishes to be
AP : 0 4 :086(119) [0147] propitious to believers in **Christ** and because it believes
AP : 0 4 :086(119) [0147] believes that "God made **Christ** our wisdom, our
AP : 0 4 :087(119) [0147] God is reconciled to us for **Christ**'s sake we are justified
AP : 0 4 :087(120) [0147] would be no need for **Christ** and the promise, and
AP : 0 4 :087(120) [0147] precepts of a good life, but through faith in Jesus **Christ**."
AP : 0 4 :093(120) [0149] "We have believed in **Christ** Jesus, in order to be justified
AP : 0 4 :093(120) [0149] to be justified by faith in **Christ**, and not by works of the
AP : 0 4 :097(121) [0149] describe the work of **Christ** and justification more clearly?
AP : 0 4 :097(121) [0149] **Christ** was given for us to believe that we are justified
AP : 0 4 :097(121) [0149] accounted righteous for **Christ**'s sake when we believe that

Continued ▶

A P : 0 4 :098(121) [0149] But only faith takes hold of the name of **Christ**.
A P : 0 4 :098(121) [0151] are saved by trust in the name of **Christ**, not in our works.
A P : 0 4 :098(121) [0151] To cite the name of **Christ** is to trust in the name of Christ
A P : 0 4 :098(121) [0151] is to trust in the name of **Christ** as the cause or price on
A P : 0 4 :101(121) [0151] what is the knowledge of **Christ** except to know Christ's
A P : 0 4 :101(121) [0151] of Christ except to know **Christ**'s blessings, the promises
A P : 0 4 :101(121) [0151] and truly to believe in **Christ**, to believe that God will
A P : 0 4 :101(121) [0151] accomplish what he has promised for **Christ**'s sake.
A P : 0 4 :102(121) [0151] it teaches the promises of **Christ**, of the forgiveness of
A P : 0 4 :102(121) [0151] of sins, and of our gracious acceptance for **Christ**'s sake.
A P : 0 4 :103(122) [0151] men through the blood of **Christ**; for 'blessed is he whose
A P : 0 4 :104(122) [0153] it to faith, which liberates us through the blood of **Christ**.
A P : 0 4 :111(123) [0155] as Paul also says, "In **Christ** Jesus neither circumcision
A P : 0 4 :114(123) [0155] righteous by this faith for **Christ**'s sake before we love and
A P : 0 4 :117(123) [0155] the forgiveness of sins for **Christ**'s sake, and by faith alone
A P : 0 4 :118(123) [0155] it alone we recognize **Christ**'s work and receive his
A P : 0 4 :120(124) [0155] are forgiven freely for **Christ**'s sake) must be retained in
A P : 0 4 :121(124) [0155] free forgiveness of sins and of the righteousness of **Christ**.
A P : 0 4 :123(124) [0157] **Christ** says (Matt. 19:17), "If you would enter life, keep
A P : 0 4 :126(124) [0157] to keep the law without **Christ**; it is impossible to keep the
A P : 0 4 :130(125) [0157] works of the law, without **Christ** and the Holy Spirit, still
A P : 0 4 :132(125) [0159] But **Christ** was given so that for his sake we might receive
A P : 0 4 :135(126) [0159] it is clear that without **Christ** and without the Holy Spirit
A P : 0 4 :139(126) [0161] Nothing less than **Christ**'s power is needed for our conflict
A P : 0 4 :139(126) [0161] We know that for **Christ**'s sake we have a gracious God
A P : 0 4 :139(126) [0161] For **Christ** conquered the devil and gave us his promise
A P : 0 4 :140(126) [0161] it but because we are in **Christ**, as we shall show a little
A P : 0 4 :141(126) [0161] For through **Christ** we come to the Father; and having
A P : 0 4 :143(126) [0161] for those who are in **Christ** Jesus, who do not walk
A P : 0 4 :145(127) [0163] nor that on account of **Christ**, the mediator, we have a
A P : 0 4 :146(127) [0163] keep the law, though this glory properly belongs to **Christ**
A P : 0 4 :147(127) [0163] account of love, but on account of **Christ** by faith alone.
A P : 0 4 :148(127) [0163] God forgives because **Christ** did not die in vain, conquers
A P : 0 4 :149(127) [0163] are forgiven, he insults **Christ** because he thinks that his
A P : 0 4 :149(127) [0163] the death and promise of **Christ**, though Paul says that
A P : 0 4 :150(127) [0163] he loves, he insults **Christ** and in God's judgment he will
A P : 0 4 :152(127) [0163] **Christ** says in Luke 7:47, "Her sins, which are many, are
A P : 0 4 :152(127) [0163] Now **Christ** did not want to say that by her works of love
A P : 0 4 :154(128) [0163] that she should seek the forgiveness of sins from **Christ**.
A P : 0 4 :154(128) [0163] This is the highest way of worshiping **Christ**.
A P : 0 4 :154(128) [0163] believe means to think of **Christ** in this way, and in this
A P : 0 4 :154(128) [0163] Moreover, **Christ** used the word "love" not toward the
A P : 0 4 :154(128) [0163] the Pharisee, because **Christ** contrasted the whole act of
A P : 0 4 :154(128) [0165] she was looking for the forgiveness of sins from **Christ**.
A P : 0 4 :154(128) [0165] powerful example moved **Christ** to chide the Pharisee, this
A P : 0 4 :156(128) [0165] issue, the honor of **Christ** and the source of sure and firm
A P : 0 4 :156(128) [0165] we should put our trust in **Christ** or in our own works.
A P : 0 4 :157(128) [0165] it in our works, we rob **Christ** of his honor as mediator
A P : 0 4 :157(128) [0165] do not come freely for **Christ**'s sake, but for the sake of
A P : 0 4 :158(129) [0165] Justification is reconciliation for **Christ**'s sake.
A P : 0 4 :159(129) [0167] reconciliation by faith for **Christ**'s sake, not for the sake
A P : 0 4 :159(129) [0167] necessarily follows that we are justified by faith in **Christ**.
A P : 0 4 :161(129) [0167] and keeping of the law, but only because of **Christ**.
A P : 0 4 :162(129) [0169] is so because, first of all, **Christ** does not stop being the
A P : 0 4 :163(129) [0169] **Christ** remains the mediator.
A P : 0 4 :163(129) [0169] righteous by faith for **Christ**'s sake, according to the
A P : 0 4 :163(129) [0169] we are accounted righteous by faith for the sake of **Christ**.
A P : 0 4 :165(129) [0169] righteous on account of **Christ**, "who is at the right hand
A P : 0 4 :165(130) [0169] rather than because of **Christ**'s promise, he insults this
A P : 0 4 :165(130) [0169] a man can do away with **Christ**, the propitiator and
A P : 0 4 :166(130) [0169] God for its own sake, but for the sake of faith in **Christ**.
A P : 0 4 :172(130) [0171] requires our faith that for **Christ**'s sake we please God and
A P : 0 4 :174(131) [0171] which is sure that for **Christ**'s sake we have a gracious
A P : 0 4 :177(131) [0171] righteous because of **Christ**, not because of the law or our
A P : 0 4 :178(131) [0171] death and satisfaction of **Christ**, bestowed upon us to
A P : 0 4 :179(131) [0171] he says in Gal. 3:13, "**Christ** redeemed us from the curse
A P : 0 4 :179(131) [0171] sacrifice for us, the sinless **Christ** took away the right of
A P : 0 4 :179(131) [0171] you, because for **Christ**'s sake we have a firm and sure
A P : 0 4 :180(131) [0171] of his promise, because of **Christ**, God wishes to be
A P : 0 4 :180(132) [0171] being sure that because of **Christ** and his promise they
A P : 0 4 :182(132) [0173] and reconciliation for **Christ**'s sake, and reconciliation or
A P : 0 4 :182(132) [0173] promised because of **Christ**, not because of the law.
A P : 0 4 :184(132) [0173] cannot be kept without **Christ**, and that if civil works are
A P : 0 4 :184(132) [0173] works are done without **Christ** they do not please God.
A P : 0 4 :186(132) [0173] free promise of the forgiveness of sins for **Christ**'s sake.
A P : 0 4 :188(133) [0173] and the reconciliation that comes through faith in **Christ**.
A P : 0 4 :189(133) [0175] and the reign of **Christ**, whereby he shows his rule before
A P : 0 4 :190(133) [0175] to God, battles by which **Christ** restrained the devil and
A P : 0 4 :192(133) [0175] Through these works **Christ** shows his victory over the
A P : 0 4 :192(133) [0175] a sacrifice, and a battle of **Christ** against the devil, who is
A P : 0 4 :193(133) [0175] the outward administration of **Christ**'s rule among men.
A P : 0 4 :195(134) [0175] same and equal to all, as **Christ** is one, and it is offered
A P : 0 4 :195(134) [0175] who believe that their sins are forgiven for **Christ**'s sake.
A P : 0 4 :195(134) [0175] we have peace with God through our Lord Jesus **Christ**.
A P : 0 4 :196(134) [0175] of God, moreover, it also makes us co-heirs with **Christ**.
A P : 0 4 :196(134) [0175] of God and co-heirs with **Christ**, we do not merit eternal
A P : 0 4 :198(134) [0175] as is evident in Job, in **Christ**, and in other saints.
A P : 0 4 :198(134) [0175] And **Christ** says (Matt. 5:10), "Blessed are those who are
A P : 0 4 :203(135) [0175] sure in his heart that for **Christ**'s sake he is freely forgiven
A P : 0 4 :204(135) [0177] it obscures the glory of **Christ** when men offer these works
A P : 0 4 :204(135) [0177] giving our works an honor that belongs only to **Christ**.
A P : 0 4 :210(136) [0179] us of the promises of **Christ**, the remembrance might
A P : 0 4 :210(136) [0179] announce the blessings of **Christ**, as Paul says (I Cor.
A P : 0 4 :211(136) [0179] gracious God because of **Christ**, not because of their own
A P : 0 4 :211(136) [0179] received these freely because of **Christ**, the propitiator.
A P : 0 4 :212(136) [0179] It does not believe that **Christ** is the propitiator, or that
A P : 0 4 :212(136) [0179] by faith we are accounted righteous for **Christ**'s sake.
A P : 0 4 :213(136) [0179] rather than because of **Christ** by faith — what is this but
A P : 0 4 :213(136) [0179] — what is this but to rob **Christ** of his honor as mediator
A P : 0 4 :214(136) [0179] law must follow faith; but we still give **Christ** his honor.
A P : 0 4 :214(136) [0179] accounted righteous before God for **Christ**'s sake by faith.
A P : 0 4 :214(136) [0179] because of our works without **Christ**, the mediator.
A P : 0 4 :214(136) [0179] Only **Christ**, the mediator, can be pitted against God's
A P : 0 4 :215(137) [0179] otherwise does not give **Christ** the honor due him, for he
A P : 0 4 :217(137) [0179] God is reconciled to us for **Christ**'s sake, according to the
A P : 0 4 :217(137) [0179] freely because of **Christ**, and therefore it is always received
A P : 0 4 :221(137) [0181] are accounted righteous because of **Christ**, the propitiator
A P : 0 4 :221(137) [0181] our opponents exclude **Christ** from justification and teach
A P : 0 4 :222(138) [0181] to God even without **Christ**, the propitiator; that by our
A P : 0 4 :222(138) [0181] when we take hold of **Christ**, the propitiator, and believe
A P : 0 4 :222(138) [0181] even to be dreamed without **Christ**, the propitiator.
A P : 0 4 :223(138) [0181] the promise about **Christ**, let them abolish the Gospel, if
A P : 0 4 :223(138) [0181] abolish the Gospel, if **Christ** is unnecessary and by our
A P : 0 4 :227(138) [0183] which takes hold of **Christ**, communicating to us Christ's
A P : 0 4 :227(139) [0183] communicating to us **Christ**'s merits and, through them,
A P : 0 4 :227(139) [0183] accept and grasp what is offered in the promise of **Christ**.
A P : 0 4 :230(139) [0183] namely, that because of **Christ**, the propitiator, we are
A P : 0 4 :230(139) [0183] when we believe that for **Christ**'s sake God is gracious to
A P : 0 4 :230(139) [0183] Because of **Christ**'s glory we defend it and we ask Christ
A P : 0 4 :230(139) [0183] we defend it and we ask **Christ** for the help of his Holy
A P : 0 4 :231(139) [0183] that makes men perfect, **Christ**, the propitiator, will be
A P : 0 4 :231(139) [0183] Only faith takes hold of **Christ**, the propitiator.
A P : 0 4 :231(139) [0185] Paul would never permit **Christ**, the propitiator, to be
A P : 0 4 :238(140) [0187] death; or that in place of **Christ**, the mediator, love is the
A P : 0 4 :238(141) [0187] or that love is righteousness without **Christ**, the mediator.
A P : 0 4 :238(141) [0187] that for the sake of **Christ**, the propitiator, the Father is
A P : 0 4 :238(141) [0187] to us and that the merits of **Christ** are granted to us.
A P : 0 4 :239(141) [0187] commands us to come to **Christ** and to be built upon
A P : 0 4 :239(141) [0187] and to be built upon **Christ**, and he adds (I Pet. 2:6), "He
A P : 0 4 :239(141) [0187] accuses us, but faith in **Christ** frees us in the midst of these
A P : 0 4 :239(141) [0187] because we know that for **Christ**'s sake we are forgiven.
A P : 0 4 :242(141) [0187] to God; that in place of **Christ** the mediator it is our
A P : 0 4 :244(142) [0189] that we do not need mercy and **Christ**, the propitiator.
A P : 0 4 :245(142) [0189] the faith by which we take hold of **Christ**, the propitiator.
A P : 0 4 :245(142) [0189] to it, but keeps it, lest **Christ**, the propitiator, be excluded
A P : 0 4 :246(142) [0189] we have access to God without **Christ**, the propitiator.
A P : 0 4 :247(142) [0191] hold of the promise of **Christ** when we set it against the
A P : 0 4 :251(143) [0191] is due in part to **Christ** and in part to our works.
A P : 0 4 :253(143) [0193] works please God without **Christ**, the propitiator; that
A P : 0 4 :253(143) [0193] propitiator; that works do not need **Christ**, the propitiator
A P : 0 4 :256(144) [0193] been reborn by faith in **Christ**, as Christ says (John 15:5),
A P : 0 4 :256(144) [0193] by faith in Christ, as **Christ** says (John 15:5), "Apart from
A P : 0 4 :256(144) [0193] promise that through **Christ** we have access to the Father
A P : 0 4 :257(144) [0193] by itself, why would **Christ** and the Gospel be necessary?
A P : 0 4 :257(144) [0193] Gospel promise, that for **Christ**'s sake sins are forgiven
A P : 0 4 :257(144) [0193] and that by faith in **Christ** we obtain the forgiveness of
A P : 0 4 :257(144) [0193] exclude the Gospel of **Christ** from the preaching of
A P : 0 4 :257(144) [0193] they deserve to be regarded as blasphemers against **Christ**.
A P : 0 4 :259(144) [0193] **Christ** is preaching penitence when he says, "Forgive," and
A P : 0 4 :260(145) [0193] us if we believe that our sins are forgiven for **Christ**'s sake.
A P : 0 4 :260(145) [0193] need would there be of **Christ**, what need of the Gospel?
A P : 0 4 :260(145) [0195] oppose those who reject **Christ**, destroy the Gospel, and
A P : 0 4 :262(145) [0195] forgiveness of sins in the **Christ** was promised not only to
A P : 0 4 :266(146) [0197] the Gospel and the promise of **Christ** are presented to us.
A P : 0 4 :266(146) [0197] not reject the promise of **Christ** when the law is preached
A P : 0 4 :266(146) [0197] be pleasing to God, as **Christ** says (John 15:5), "Apart
A P : 0 4 :269(147) [0197] law is not kept without **Christ**—as he himself has said,
A P : 0 4 :269(147) [0197] intended to abolish the Gospel of **Christ**, the propitiator.
A P : 0 4 :269(147) [0197] a way that they attribute **Christ**'s glory to works and make
A P : 0 4 :269(147) [0197] they do not please him without **Christ**, the propitiator.
A P : 0 4 :269(147) [0197] (Rom. 5:2), not by works without **Christ**, the mediator.
A P : 0 4 :270(147) [0197] keep the commandments or please God without **Christ**.
A P : 0 4 :270(147) [0197] But without **Christ** this law is not kept.
A P : 0 4 :270(147) [0197] God is reconciled to us for **Christ**'s sake even though we
A P : 0 4 :270(147) [0197] When faith takes hold of **Christ**, the mediator, the heart is
A P : 0 4 :270(147) [0199] to God for the sake of **Christ**, the mediator, even though
A P : 0 4 :272(148) [0199] depending not on the work but on **Christ** through faith.
A P : 0 4 :274(148) [0199] of sins by faith because of **Christ** and not because of our
A P : 0 4 :275(148) [0199] Nevertheless, **Christ** frequently connects the promise of
A P : 0 4 :277(148) [0199] away from the glory of **Christ**, whose prerogative it is to
A P : 0 4 :277(149) [0199] to the rule that without **Christ** the teaching of the law has
A P : 0 4 :281(149) [0201] we say that the Gospel of **Christ** must be added to the
A P : 0 4 :281(149) [0201] everywhere they exclude **Christ** and teach that we merit
A P : 0 4 :282(149) [0201] **Christ** is upbraiding the Pharisees for thinking that they
A P : 0 4 :282(149) [0201] These **Christ** rejects, and in place of this false cleansing he
A P : 0 4 :283(149) [0201] **Christ** adds this conclusion to both clauses: all things will
A P : 0 4 :285(150) [0201] and illumines the glory of **Christ**, who was surely given to
A P : 0 4 :286(150) [0203] the law in such a way as to hide the Gospel of **Christ**.
A P : 0 4 :287(150) [0203] one based upon the Gospel or the promise of **Christ**.
A P : 0 4 :290(151) [0203] modes, since both exclude **Christ** and therefore both are
A P : 0 4 :290(151) [0203] teach us to avail ourselves of **Christ** in our regeneration.
A P : 0 4 :290(151) [0203] not teach that by faith in **Christ** we overcome the terrors
A P : 0 4 :290(151) [0203] keeping of the law and not through **Christ**, the propitiator
A P : 0 4 :290(151) [0203] of the law with[out] **Christ**, the propitiator, is a
A P : 0 4 :291(151) [0203] **Christ** was not promised, revealed, born, crucified, and
A P : 0 4 :291(152) [0203] It compels us to make use of **Christ** in justification.
A P : 0 4 :291(152) [0203] It teaches that by faith in **Christ** we receive the forgiveness
A P : 0 4 :292(152) [0203] he wishes to forgive and to be reconciled for **Christ**'s sake.
A P : 0 4 :292(152) [0203] and believes that he has a gracious God for **Christ**'s sake.
A P : 0 4 :293(152) [0203] justifying faith that for **Christ**'s sake we have a gracious
A P : 0 4 :294(152) [0203] come to God without **Christ**, the mediator; nor do we
A P : 0 4 :294(152) [0203] of sin because of our love but because of **Christ**.
A P : 0 4 :295(152) [0203] promise by faith, that for **Christ**'s sake the Father is
A P : 0 4 :296(152) [0205] we must turn our eyes to **Christ**, and believe that he was
A P : 0 4 :296(152) [0205] of the law but because of **Christ**, whose merits are
A P : 0 4 :297(153) [0205] and eternal life are assured to us for **Christ**'s sake.
A P : 0 4 :297(153) [0205] **Christ** was not promised, revealed, born, crucified, and
A P : 0 4 :297(153) [0205] the promise of grace in **Christ** was not given in vain,
A P : 0 4 :297(153) [0205] **Christ** says, "If the Son makes you free, you will be free
A P : 0 4 :297(153) [0205] By faith in **Christ**, therefore, we accept the promise of the
A P : 0 4 :298(153) [0205] unless he wants utterly to abolish **Christ** and the Gospel?
A P : 0 4 :299(153) [0205] **Christ**'s glory becomes brighter when we teach men to
A P : 0 4 :299(153) [0205] Father because of **Christ**, not because of our righteousness
A P : 0 4 :299(153) [0205] righteousness but because **Christ** still helps us to keep the
A P : 0 4 :300(153) [0205] mention how we must set **Christ** against the wrath of
A P : 0 4 :302(154) [0205] It transfers **Christ**'s glory to human works; it leads

Continued ▶

A P : 0 4 :303(154) [0205] are talking about faith in **Christ** and in the forgiveness of
A P : 0 4 :305(154) [0207] righteousness, namely, **Christ**'s, which is communicated to
A P : 0 4 :306(154) [0207] of your life in Jesus **Christ**, whom God made our wisdom,
A P : 0 4 :307(154) [0207] the righteousness of **Christ** is given to us through faith,
A P : 0 4 :308(155) [0207] the Gospel takes hold of **Christ**, the propitiator, and is
A P : 0 4 :308(155) [0207] satisfy the law, but for **Christ**'s sake this is forgiven us, as
A P : 0 4 :308(155) [0207] now no condemnation for those who are in **Christ** Jesus."
A P : 0 4 :310(155) [0207] About this worship **Christ** speaks in John 6:40, "This is
A P : 0 4 :313(155) [0207] do not teach us to use **Christ** as the mediator in
A P : 0 4 :314(156) [0207] (Rom. 5:2), "Through **Christ** we have obtained access to
A P : 0 4 :314(156) [0207] love and merits without **Christ**, the mediator, rather than
A P : 0 4 :315(156) [0207] that without the help of **Christ** we cannot keep the law, as
A P : 0 4 :316(156) [0209] faith or the fact that for **Christ**'s sake we please God by
A P : 0 4 :316(156) [0209] earns eternal life without needing **Christ**, the mediator.
A P : 0 4 :317(156) [0209] works and not because of **Christ**, what else is this but a
A P : 0 4 :317(156) [0209] is this but a transfer of **Christ**'s glory to our works, a
A P : 0 4 :317(156) [0209] that if a man justified in **Christ** must then seek his
A P : 0 4 :317(156) [0209] he thereby makes **Christ** "an agent of sin" since he does
A P : 0 4 :318(156) [0209] grace through a good work and not by faith in **Christ**.
A P : 0 4 :319(156) [0209] work and not because of **Christ**, how will it have peace
A P : 0 4 :320(156) [0209] and eternal life are given us freely for **Christ**'s sake.
A P : 0 4 :324(157) [0211] faith and obscures **Christ**'s glory and mediatorial work.
A P : 0 4 :332(158) [0211] the mercy of God, insults **Christ**, who intercedes for us as
A P : 0 4 :333(158) [0211] we are heard because of **Christ** the high priest, as he
A P : 0 4 :334(158) [0215] Here **Christ**'s statement (Luke 17:10) also applies, "When
A P : 0 4 :335(159) [0215] our opponents make a marvelous play on **Christ**'s words.
A P : 0 4 :339(159) [0215] **Christ** condemns trust in our own works; he does not
A P : 0 4 :342(159) [0215] **Christ** is speaking of that worthiness whereby God
A P : 0 4 :345(160) [0217] to believe that we have a gracious God because of **Christ**.
A P : 0 4 :350(161) [0217] cares for us, forgives us, and hears us for **Christ**'s sake.
A P : 0 4 :352(161) [0217] Paul says (Rom. 8:10), "If **Christ** is in you, although your
A P : 0 4 :354(161) [0217] children of God and fellow heirs with **Christ** (Rom. 8:17).
A P : 0 4 :356(161) [0217] bestowed on us for **Christ**'s sake at the same time makes
A P : 0 4 :356(161) [0217] God and fellow heirs with **Christ** (Rom. 8:17), and
A P : 0 4 :357(162) [0219] without needing mercy or the mediator **Christ** or faith.
A P : 0 4 :358(162) [0219] therefore we need neither **Christ** the mediator nor the faith
A P : 0 4 :358(162) [0219] has access to God for **Christ**'s sake, not for our works'
A P : 0 4 :359(162) [0219] of the faith that takes hold of **Christ**, the mediator.
A P : 0 4 :360(162) [0219] their own sake, not for the sake of **Christ**, the mediator.
A P : 0 4 :361(162) [0219] the blessings of **Christ** and the righteousness of faith are
A P : 0 4 :362(162) [0219] righteous by faith for **Christ**'s sake and that good works
A P : 0 4 :366(163) [0221] and made fellow heirs with **Christ** (Rom. 8:17).
A P : 0 4 :367(163) [0221] freely because of **Christ**'s merits, not ours, and Christ's
A P : 0 4 :367(163) [0221] merits, not ours, and **Christ**'s merits are communicated to
A P : 0 4 :368(163) [0221] that the Gospel offers justification freely for **Christ**'s sake.
A P : 0 4 :372(164) [0221] we must know that **Christ**, the mediator, should not be
A P : 0 4 :372(164) [0221] are led by the Spirit of **Christ**; nor can good works please
A P : 0 4 :372(164) [0221] God without the mediator **Christ** and faith, according to
A P : 0 4 :375(164) [0223] of faith and the mediator **Christ** but in themselves are not
A P : 0 4 :376(164) [0223] them the righteousness of faith and **Christ**, the mediator.
A P : 0 4 :376(165) [0223] our works but because of **Christ**, and that through his
A P : 0 4 :377(165) [0223] neglected in the church of **Christ**; without it the work of
A P : 0 4 :377(165) [0223] without it the work of **Christ** cannot be understood, and
A P : 0 4 :377(165) [0223] and the teaching of the promise given for **Christ**'s sake.
A P : 0 4 :378(165) [0223] omitting the faith that takes hold of the mediator **Christ**.
A P : 0 4 :379(165) [0223] is propitious to us for **Christ**'s sake, there is not a syllable
A P : 0 4 :382(165) [0225] our good works are valid by virtue of **Christ**'s suffering.
A P : 0 4 :382(165) [0225] **Christ** is a propitiation, as Paul says, through faith (Rom.
A P : 0 4 :382(165) [0225] sins are blotted out by **Christ**'s death and that God has
A P : 0 4 :382(165) [0225] to us because of **Christ**'s suffering, then indeed Christ's
A P : 0 4 :382(165) [0225] suffering, then indeed **Christ**'s suffering benefits us.
A P : 0 4 :382(165) [0225] our works are valid by virtue of the suffering of **Christ**.
A P : 0 4 :385(166) [0225] be accepted because of **Christ** and request everything
A P : 0 4 :385(166) [0225] of Christ and request everything because of **Christ**.
A P : 0 4 :385(166) [0225] prayer closes with this phrase: "through **Christ** our Lord."
A P : 0 4 :386(166) [0225] God is reconciled and propitious to us because of **Christ**.
A P : 0 4 :387(166) [0225] comfort in all afflictions and shows us the work of **Christ**.
A P : 0 4 :387(166) [0225] by faith deny that **Christ** is the mediator and propitiator,
A P : 0 4 :388(166) [0225] cannot be kept without **Christ**, and that we are not
A P : 0 4 :388(166) [0225] but by the Gospel, the promise of grace offered in **Christ**.
A P : 0 4 :389(166) [0225] with the whole church of **Christ**, which certainly confesses
A P : 0 4 :389(166) [0225] certainly confesses that **Christ** is the propitiator and the
A P : 0 4 :390(166) [0225] than the Gospel of **Christ**, and everybody knows that
A P : 0 4 :392(167) [0225] the knowledge of **Christ** has remained with some faithful
A P : 0 4 :392(167) [0225] obscuring the work of **Christ** and making of him not the
A P : 0 4 :393(167) [0225] own works and devotions, not by faith for **Christ**'s sake.
A P : 0 4 :397(167) [0227] because of the word of **Christ**, 'Whatever you bind,' etc.
A P : 0 4 :398(168) [0227] ascribe any knowledge of **Christ** to those who condemned
A P : 0 4 :400(168) [0227] know that the church of **Christ** is among those who teach
A P : 0 4 :400(168) [0227] who teach the Gospel of **Christ**, not among those who
A P : 0 4 :400(168) [0227] words or in the words of its head, our Lord Jesus **Christ**?
A P : 0 7 :001(168) [0227] together (Matt. 3:12) and **Christ** compared it to a net in
A P : 0 7 :005(169) [0227] of the sacraments in harmony with the Gospel of **Christ**.
A P : 0 7 :005(169) [0227] alone is called the body of **Christ**, which Christ renews,
A P : 0 7 :005(169) [0227] the body of Christ, which **Christ** renews, consecrates, and
A P : 0 7 :005(169) [0227] Thus those in whom **Christ** is not active are not members
A P : 0 7 :005(169) [0227] in whom Christ is not active are not members of **Christ**.
A P : 0 7 :007(169) [0229] He says, "**Christ** loved the church and gave himself up for
A P : 0 7 :009(169) [0229] of the wicked, and **Christ** supplies it with the gifts he has
A P : 0 7 :010(170) [0229] Gospel and have the same **Christ**, the same Holy Spirit,
A P : 0 7 :011(170) [0229] part of the church of **Christ**, nor can he be said to be
A P : 0 7 :011(170) [0229] of Christ, nor can he be said to be subject to **Christ**."
A P : 0 7 :012(170) [0231] which is the living body of **Christ** and is the church in fact
A P : 0 7 :013(170) [0231] that the kingdom of **Christ** is the righteousness of the
A P : 0 7 :014(170) [0231] affairs, etc. in addition to the promise about **Christ**.
A P : 0 7 :016(170) [0231] church is the kingdom of **Christ**, the opposite of the
A P : 0 7 :016(171) [0231] To them **Christ** says (John 8:44), "You are of your father
A P : 0 7 :016(171) [0231] is truly the kingdom of **Christ**, is, precisely speaking, the
A P : 0 7 :016(171) [0231] are his captives; they are not ruled by the Spirit of **Christ**.
A P : 0 7 :017(171) [0231] is truly the kingdom of **Christ**, is distinguished from the
A P : 0 7 :017(171) [0233] because the kingdom of **Christ** has not yet been revealed,
A P : 0 7 :018(171) [0233] come does not make the wicked the kingdom of **Christ**.
A P : 0 7 :018(171) [0233] the same kingdom of **Christ**, whether it be revealed or
A P : 0 7 :018(171) [0233] under the cross, just as **Christ** is the same, whether now

A P : 0 7 :019(171) [0233] **Christ**'s parables agree with this.
A P : 0 7 :019(171) [0233] **Christ** is talking about the outward appearance of the
A P : 0 7 :019(171) [0233] not the true kingdom of **Christ** and members of Christ,
A P : 0 7 :019(171) [0233] of Christ and members of **Christ**, for they are members of
A P : 0 7 :020(171) [0233] that is, the true knowledge of **Christ** and faith.
A P : 0 7 :021(172) [0233] This, too, means to remove **Christ** as the foundation.
A P : 0 7 :022(172) [0235] they are not, properly speaking, the kingdom of **Christ**.
A P : 0 7 :023(172) [0235] right to rule, and this at **Christ**'s command; for as the
A P : 0 7 :024(172) [0235] than of the church of **Christ** has as its authors not only the
A P : 0 7 :025(173) [0235] we preach the blessing of **Christ**, that we obtain
A P : 0 7 :026(173) [0235] **Christ**, the prophets, and the apostles define the church as
A P : 0 7 :028(173) [0237] believe the Gospel of **Christ** and who have the Holy
A P : 0 7 :028(173) [0237] persons but the person of **Christ**, because of the church's
A P : 0 7 :028(173) [0237] of the church's call, as **Christ** testifies (Luke 10:16), "He
A P : 0 7 :028(173) [0237] they offer the Word of **Christ** or the sacraments, they do
A P : 0 7 :028(173) [0237] or the sacraments, they do so in **Christ**'s place and stead.
A P : 0 7 :028(173) [0237] **Christ**'s statement teaches us this in order that we may not
A P : 0 7 :029(173) [0237] church, properly so called, is termed the body of **Christ**.
A P : 0 7 :034(175) [0237] of God, and the church of **Christ** even though they dress
A P : 0 7 :035(175) [0239] of what is to come; but the substances belongs to **Christ**."
A P : 0 7 :035(175) [0239] again (vv. 20-23): "If with **Christ** you died to the elemental
A P : 0 7 :046(177) [0243] changed the ordinance of **Christ** in the use of the Lord's
A P : 0 7 :046(177) [0243] change the ordinance of **Christ**'s Supper, which is not
A P : 0 7 :047(177) [0243] them, for ministers act in **Christ**'s stead and do not
A P : 0 7 :048(177) [0245] longer function in the place of **Christ**, but are antichrists.
A P : 0 7 :048(177) [0245] **Christ** says (Matt. 7:15), "Beware of false prophets"; Paul
A P : 0 7 :049(178) [0245] **Christ** has also warned us in his parables on the church
A P : 0 9 :002(178) [0245] those who are outside of **Christ**'s church, where there is
A P : 0 9 :002(178) [0245] nor sacrament, because **Christ** regenerates through Word
A P : 0 9 :002(178) [0245] to them according to **Christ**'s command (Matt. 28:19),
A P : 1 0 :001(179) [0247] the body and blood of **Christ** are truly and substantially
A P : 1 0 :001(179) [0247] in the body of **Christ** but only in his spirit if the Lord's
A P : 1 0 :002(179) [0247] the bodily presence of **Christ**, but that the Greek Church
A P : 1 0 :002(179) [0247] may be changed and become the very body of **Christ**.
A P : 1 0 :003(179) [0247] Cyril which teaches that **Christ** is offered to us bodily in
A P : 1 0 :003(179) [0247] deny that we are joined to **Christ** spiritually by true faith
A P : 1 0 :003(179) [0247] Who has ever doubted that **Christ** is a vine in this way
A P : 1 0 :003(179) [0247] 'We are all one body in **Christ**' Rom. 12:5); 'We who are
A P : 1 0 :003(179) [0247] us, does it not also cause **Christ** to dwell in us bodily
A P : 1 0 :003(179) [0247] bodily through the communication of the flesh of **Christ**?"
A P : 1 0 :003(179) [0247] we must consider that **Christ** is in us, not only according
A P : 1 0 :004(179) [0247] the body and blood of **Christ** are truly and substantially
A P : 1 0 :004(180) [0247] the presence of the living **Christ**, knowing that "death no
A P : 1 1 :002(180) [0249] is granted to us freely for **Christ**'s sake and that we should
A P : 1 1 :005(181) [0251] **Christ** says (I Cor. 11:29) that those who receive in an
A P : 1 1 :009(182) [0251] They say nothing about **Christ**.
A P : 1 2 :002(182) [0253] what is this but to insult the blood and death of **Christ**?
A P : 1 2 :003(182) [0253] the true knowledge of **Christ**, and the true worship of
A P : 1 2 :003(182) [0253] salutary, and necessary for the universal church of **Christ**.
A P : 1 2 :008(183) [0255] himself with the Gospel and the promise of **Christ**.
A P : 1 2 :010(184) [0255] it obscures the blessing of **Christ**, the power of the keys,
A P : 1 2 :016(184) [0257] righteousness of faith in **Christ** and of the blessing of
A P : 1 2 :016(184) [0257] of faith in Christ and of the blessing of **Christ** lies buried.
A P : 1 2 :020(185) [0257] of sins because of contrition, not by faith in **Christ**.
A P : 1 2 :025(185) [0259] attitude in the recipient, that is, without faith in **Christ**.
A P : 1 2 :029(186) [0259] sins and righteousness for **Christ**'s sake, to grant the Holy
A P : 1 2 :030(186) [0259] **Christ** gives this summary of the Gospel in the last chapter
A P : 1 2 :035(186) [0261] we therefore add faith in **Christ**, that amid these terrors
A P : 1 2 :035(186) [0261] terrors the Gospel of **Christ** ought to be set forth to
A P : 1 2 :035(186) [0261] freely promises the forgiveness of sins through **Christ**.
A P : 1 2 :035(186) [0261] therefore that because of **Christ** their sins are freely
A P : 1 2 :036(186) [0261] grasps the forgiveness of sins granted for **Christ**'s sake.
A P : 1 2 :036(186) [0261] grasps the forgiveness of sins granted for **Christ**'s sake.
A P : 1 2 :037(186) [0261] law is not kept without **Christ**, according to the passage
A P : 1 2 :043(187) [0263] illumines the blessing of **Christ**, and it teaches us to make
A P : 1 2 :043(187) [0263] teaches us to make use of **Christ** as our mediator and
A P : 1 2 :044(187) [0263] **Christ** says in Matt. 11:28, "Come to me, all who labor
A P : 1 2 :044(187) [0263] To come to **Christ** means to believe that for his sake sins
A P : 1 2 :044(187) [0263] Spirit quickens our hearts through the Word of **Christ**.
A P : 1 2 :045(187) [0263] In Mark 1:15 **Christ** says, "Repent, and believe in the
A P : 1 2 :045(187) [0263] sense, to believe that for **Christ**'s sake the forgiveness of
A P : 1 2 :045(188) [0263] if someone says that **Christ** also includes the fruits of
A P : 1 2 :048(188) [0265] Paul says in Col. 2:14 that **Christ** cancels the bond which
A P : 1 2 :053(189) [0265] the Gospel, that is, the promise of grace granted in **Christ**.
A P : 1 2 :053(189) [0265] and revealed by **Christ** among the Jews, and spread by the
A P : 1 2 :057(189) [0267] who was a sinner came to **Christ** in tears, which showed
A P : 1 2 :060(190) [0269] not in the promise of **Christ** but in contrition, confession,
A P : 1 2 :060(190) [0269] The church of **Christ** believes the same, in spite of our
A P : 1 2 :064(191) [0269] only when it takes hold of **Christ**, the mediator, and
A P : 1 2 :064(191) [0269] peace without faith in **Christ** do not understand what the
A P : 1 2 :065(191) [0271] own works and not in **Christ** to receive the forgiveness of
A P : 1 2 :065(191) [0271] only through the name of **Christ**, that is, because of him
A P : 1 2 :065(191) [0271] we believe that our sins are forgiven because of **Christ**.
A P : 1 2 :067(191) [0271] of sins by faith for **Christ**'s sake and not for the sake of
A P : 1 2 :072(192) [0271] freely forgiven because of **Christ**, not because of our
A P : 1 2 :075(193) [0273] of the Gospel, and the abolition of the promise of **Christ**.
A P : 1 2 :075(193) [0273] rather than in God's Word and the promise of **Christ**?
A P : 1 2 :075(193) [0273] What need is there of **Christ** if by our work we achieve the
A P : 1 2 :076(193) [0273] in the promise and in **Christ**; for the Gospel shows us
A P : 1 2 :076(193) [0273] for the Gospel shows us **Christ** and promises the
A P : 1 2 :076(193) [0273] us trust that because of **Christ** we are reconciled to the
A P : 1 2 :076(193) [0273] for there is no other mediator or propitiator but **Christ**.
A P : 1 2 :076(193) [0273] the law before we have been reconciled through **Christ**.
A P : 1 2 :076(193) [0275] works but because of **Christ**, the mediator and
A P : 1 2 :077(193) [0275] Truly, we insult **Christ** and abrogate the Gospel if we
A P : 1 2 :077(193) [0275] of the law or in any other way except by faith in **Christ**.
A P : 1 2 :078(193) [0275] Nor should the honor of **Christ** be transferred to our
A P : 1 2 :079(193) [0275] of sins granted for **Christ**'s sake, and he teaches us to
A P : 1 2 :079(194) [0275] the forgiveness of sins by faith, freely for **Christ**'s sake.
A P : 1 2 :080(194) [0275] promise was given and **Christ** revealed to us precisely
A P : 1 2 :080(194) [0275] of sins granted for **Christ**'s sake, and to be sure that freely
A P : 1 2 :080(194) [0275] to be sure that freely for **Christ**'s sake they have a gracious

Continued ▶

A P : 1 2 :081(194) [0275] promised to faith in Jesus **Christ** might be given to those
A P : 1 2 :084(194) [0277] the forgiveness of sins for **Christ**'s sake, by faith we ought
A P : 1 2 :084(194) [0277] the wrath of God not our works but **Christ**, the mediator.
A P : 1 2 :085(194) [0277] to God through **Christ**, though Christ says (John 15:5),
A P : 1 2 :085(194) [0277] through Christ, though **Christ** says (John 15:5), "Apart
A P : 1 2 :086(194) [0277] that we are members of Moses rather than of **Christ**.
A P : 1 2 :086(194) [0277] reconciled to God and becoming the branches of **Christ**.
A P : 1 2 :086(194) [0277] contends that we cannot keep the law without **Christ**.
A P : 1 2 :087(195) [0277] in our love or works, but only in **Christ**, the mediator.
A P : 1 2 :088(195) [0277] are forgiven freely for **Christ**'s sake, not doubting that
A P : 1 2 :090(195) [0279] — not our cause but the cause of **Christ** and the church.
A P : 1 2 :095(196) [0281] forgives us because of **Christ** and because of his promise,
A P : 1 2 :116(199) [0287] of sins because of **Christ**, not because of our works, either
A P : 1 2 :122(200) [0289] (Rom. 6:19); **Christ**'s preaching of penitence (Matt. 4:17),
A P : 1 2 :122(200) [0289] "Be penitent"; **Christ**'s command to the apostles
A P : 1 2 :123(200) [0289] **Christ** says, "Be penitent"; the apostles preach penitence.
A P : 1 2 :126(201) [0289] the last times, in which **Christ** predicted there would be
A P : 1 2 :132(202) [0291] When **Christ** says (Matt. 4:17), "Be penitent," he is surely
A P : 1 2 :133(202) [0293] For this word of **Christ** is a word of command, "Be
A P : 1 2 :138(203) [0293] **Christ** is talking about the remission of sins when he says
A P : 1 2 :140(204) [0295] The death of **Christ**, furthermore, is a satisfaction not only
A P : 1 2 :140(204) [0295] it is, then, to say that **Christ**'s satisfaction redeems our
A P : 1 2 :140(204) [0295] be taken to mean not **Christ** but our works — and not
A P : 1 2 :141(204) [0295] penitence and quickening, and the blessings of **Christ**.
A P : 1 2 :143(204) [0297] traditions of which **Christ** says (Matt. 15:9), "In vain do
A P : 1 2 :144(205) [0297] **Christ** calls these useless acts of worship, and so they do
A P : 1 2 :146(205) [0297] Faith in **Christ** overcomes death, just as it overcomes the
A P : 1 2 :146(205) [0297] who gives us the victory through our Lord Jesus **Christ**."
A P : 1 2 :147(205) [0297] death is the death of **Christ**; our opponents admit that the
A P : 1 2 :147(205) [0297] of human tradition, which **Christ** calls useless acts of
A P : 1 2 :157(207) [0301] of sins freely because of **Christ**, who is the victor over sin
A P : 1 2 :159(207) [0301] the case of the blind man, **Christ** replied that the reason
A P : 1 2 :176(210) [0307] It is of a spiritual kingdom that **Christ** is speaking.
A P : 1 3 :004(211) [0309] firmly believe that God really forgives us for **Christ**'s sake.
A P : 1 3 :008(212) [0311] the sacrificial death of **Christ** on the cross was sufficient
A P : 1 3 :009(212) [0311] of this one sacrifice of **Christ** if they believe that it has
A P : 1 3 :020(213) [0313] of the New Testament, as **Christ** clearly says (I Cor.
A P : 1 5 :004(215) [0315] Gospel, the blessing of **Christ**, and righteousness of faith.
A P : 1 5 :005(215) [0317] teaches that by faith, for **Christ**'s sake, we freely receive
A P : 1 5 :005(215) [0317] But **Christ** clearly says (Matt. 15:9), "In vain do they
A P : 1 5 :006(215) [0317] God not because of works but freely for **Christ**'s sake.
A P : 1 5 :007(216) [0317] to set up another justifier and mediator instead of **Christ**?
A P : 1 5 :008(216) [0317] "You are severed from **Christ**, you who would be justified
A P : 1 5 :008(216) [0317] before God, then **Christ** is of no use to you, for why does
A P : 1 5 :008(216) [0317] why does anyone need **Christ** if he believes he is righteous
A P : 1 5 :009(216) [0317] God has appointed **Christ** as the mediator; he wants to be
A P : 1 5 :009(216) [0317] because of the traditions and not because of **Christ**.
A P : 1 5 :009(216) [0317] Thus they rob **Christ** of his honor as the mediator.
A P : 1 5 :010(216) [0317] obscured the work of **Christ** and the righteousness of
A P : 1 5 :010(216) [0317] but freely because of **Christ**, provided that we accept it by
A P : 1 5 :011(216) [0317] have a gracious God for **Christ**'s sake, it is an ungodly
A P : 1 5 :012(216) [0317] To this Paul replies that **Christ** would be "an agent of
A P : 1 5 :012(216) [0317] will be gracious to us for **Christ**'s sake, we dare not add
A P : 1 5 :018(217) [0319] God, devised by human authority in opposition to **Christ**.
A P : 1 5 :018(217) [0319] are freely justified before God by faith for **Christ**'s sake.
A P : 1 5 :018(217) [0319] take honor away from **Christ** when they teach that we are
A P : 1 5 :020(218) [0321] the glory or work of **Christ** but taught that we are justified
A P : 1 5 :020(218) [0321] are justified by faith for **Christ**'s sake, not for the sake of
A P : 1 5 :025(218) [0321] righteousness of faith in **Christ** is obscured and replaced
A P : 1 5 :027(219) [0323] a single syllable about **Christ** or faith in him or the good
A P : 1 5 :030(219) [0323] of what is to come; but the substance belongs to **Christ**."
A P : 1 5 :036(220) [0325] violated traditions, and **Christ** excused them, for this was
A P : 1 5 :042(221) [0327] of faith or about faith in **Christ** or about comfort for the
A P : 1 5 :043(221) [0327] the fear of God, faith in **Christ**, the righteousness of faith,
A P : 1 5 :043(221) [0327] between the kingdom of **Christ** (or the spiritual kingdom)
A P : 1 5 :046(221) [0327] Of this **Christ** says (Luke 21:34), "Take heed to yourselves
A P : 1 6 :002(222) [0329] of the distinction between **Christ**'s kingdom and a
A P : 1 6 :002(222) [0331] **Christ**'s kingdom is spiritual; it is the knowledge of God in
A P : 1 6 :007(223) [0331] private revenge, and **Christ** stresses this so often lest the
A P : 1 7 :000(224) [0335] [Article XVII. **Christ**'s Return to Judgment]
A P : 1 7 :001(224) [0335] of the world **Christ** will appear and raise all the dead,
A P : 1 9 :001(226) [0337] away from God, as **Christ** said about the devil (John
A P : 2 0 :002(227) [0339] of sins is freely given for **Christ**'s sake, that not our works
A P : 2 0 :002(227) [0339] that not our works but **Christ** is the propitiation for sin?
A P : 2 0 :002(227) [0339] of the Confutation who so impudently blaspheme **Christ**.
A P : 2 0 :003(227) [0339] account of our works and not freely on account of **Christ**.
A P : 2 0 :004(227) [0339] attributing the honor of **Christ** to our works is
A P : 2 0 :005(227) [0339] anyone who knows that **Christ** was given to us to be a
A P : 2 0 :005(227) [0339] has laid our iniquities on our works and not on **Christ**.
A P : 2 0 :006(227) [0339] increases the glory of **Christ** — we can easily ignore the
A P : 2 0 :006(227) [0339] we have to suffer for **Christ** and the advancement of the
A P : 2 0 :007(227) [0339] of sins freely for **Christ**'s sake and that our works do not
A P : 2 0 :008(227) [0341] in the forgiveness of sins freely given for **Christ**'s sake.
A P : 2 0 :010(228) [0341] as it were, that sins are freely forgiven for **Christ**'s sake.
A P : 2 0 :011(228) [0341] not on account of our works but freely for **Christ**'s sake.
A P : 2 0 :014(228) [0343] The church of **Christ** has always believed that the
A P : 2 1 :004(229) [0343] using these gifts, just as **Christ** praises faithful businessmen
A P : 2 1 :014(230) [0347] it transfers to the saints honor belonging to **Christ** alone.
A P : 2 1 :015(231) [0347] this obscures the work of **Christ** and transfers to the saints
A P : 2 1 :015(231) [0347] to the saints the trust we should have in **Christ**'s mercy.
A P : 2 1 :015(231) [0347] Men suppose that **Christ** is more severe and the saints
A P : 2 1 :015(231) [0347] than in the mercy of **Christ** and they flee from Christ and
A P : 2 1 :015(231) [0347] of Christ and they flee from **Christ** and turn to the saints.
A P : 2 1 :017(231) [0347] For **Christ** there is such a promise (John 16:23), "If you
A P : 2 1 :018(231) [0347] command to call upon **Christ**, according to Matt. 11:28,
A P : 2 1 :018(231) [0347] In John 5:23 **Christ** says, "That all may honor the Son,
A P : 2 1 :018(231) [0347] "May our Lord Jesus **Christ** himself, and God our Father
A P : 2 1 :019(231) [0347] Thus the merits of **Christ** are bestowed on us so that when
A P : 2 1 :019(231) [0347] righteous by our trust in **Christ**'s merits as though we had
A P : 2 1 :020(232) [0349] in God's promise and **Christ**'s merits must be the basis for
A P : 2 1 :020(232) [0349] that we are heard for **Christ**'s sake and that by his merits
A P : 2 1 :021(232) [0349] than in the mercy of **Christ**, though Christ commanded us
A P : 2 1 :021(232) [0349] mercy of Christ, though **Christ** commanded us to come to
A P : 2 1 :022(232) [0349] others in the same way as **Christ**'s, as though we were
A P : 2 1 :022(232) [0349] on account of them just as we are by **Christ**'s merits.
A P : 2 1 :023(232) [0349] salvation, they are being put on the same level as **Christ**.
A P : 2 1 :024(232) [0349] Since **Christ** has been appointed as our intercessor and
A P : 2 1 :025(232) [0349] passion of our Lord Jesus **Christ** and the merits of the
A P : 2 1 :025(232) [0349] righteous not only by **Christ**'s merits but also by the
A P : 2 1 :027(232) [0349] What does **Christ** do if blessed Mary does all this?
A P : 2 1 :027(232) [0349] put on the same level as **Christ** but to have her example
A P : 2 1 :028(233) [0351] the blessed Virgin has completely replaced **Christ**.
A P : 2 1 :028(233) [0351] through her to appease **Christ**, as though he were not a
A P : 2 1 :029(233) [0351] of sins only by **Christ**'s merits when we believe in him.
A P : 2 1 :031(233) [0351] same way as the merits of **Christ** and thus transfer to the
A P : 2 1 :031(233) [0351] transfer to the saints the honor that belongs to **Christ**.
A P : 2 1 :031(233) [0351] in the intercession of **Christ** because only this has God's
A P : 2 1 :031(233) [0351] know that the merits of **Christ** are our only propitiation.
A P : 2 1 :034(233) [0351] our whole knowledge of **Christ** disappears if we seek out
A P : 2 1 :034(233) [0351] other mediators besides **Christ** and put our trust in them.
A P : 2 1 :035(234) [0353] those who would carry **Christ**, that is, those who would
A P : 2 1 :036(234) [0353] was forgiven for denying **Christ**; Cyprian was forgiven for
A P : 2 1 :038(235) [0355] in order to emphasize the honor and the work of **Christ**.
A P : 2 1 :044(236) [0357] the sake of the glory of **Christ**, which we know you want
A P : 2 1 :044(236) [0357] that is, the Gospel of **Christ**, and as vicars of God they
A P : 2 2 :001(236) [0357] with the institution of **Christ** and the words of Paul.
A P : 2 2 :001(236) [0357] For **Christ** instituted both kinds, and he did not do so
A P : 2 2 :002(236) [0357] If **Christ** instituted it for all of the church, why is one kind
A P : 2 2 :002(236) [0357] Why is **Christ**'s ordinance changed, especially since he
A P : 2 2 :002(236) [0357] man's testament, it is much more illegal to annul **Christ**'s.
A P : 2 2 :003(236) [0359] "Do this," **Christ** says first about the body; later he says
A P : 2 2 :007(237) [0359] the disciples recognized **Christ** in the breaking of the
A P : 2 2 :010(237) [0361] when they believe that **Christ**'s flesh, given for the life of
A P : 2 2 :010(238) [0361] food and that they come to life by being joined to **Christ**.
A P : 2 2 :014(238) [0361] which are not cogent enough to change **Christ**'s ordinance
A P : 2 2 :015(238) [0361] itself the freedom to call **Christ**'s ordinances matters of
A P : 2 3 :016(241) [0369] And **Christ** clearly said (Matt. 19:11), "Not all men can
A P : 2 3 :019(242) [0369] **Christ** shows that it does require a special gift; therefore,
A P : 2 3 :021(242) [0369] the objection here that **Christ** commends those "who have
A P : 2 3 :021(242) [0369] let him remember that **Christ** is praising those who have
A P : 2 3 :022(242) [0369] Impure continence does not please **Christ**.
A P : 2 3 :023(242) [0371] this in open defiance of **Christ**'s command (Matt. 19:6),
A P : 2 3 :029(243) [0371] **Christ** calls marriage a divine union when he says in Matt.
A P : 2 3 :031(243) [0373] and holy through faith in **Christ** just as the use of food,
A P : 2 3 :034(244) [0373] that is, to believers in **Christ** who are righteous by faith.
A P : 2 3 :036(244) [0373] we justified, but freely for **Christ**'s sake when we believe
A P : 2 3 :039(244) [0375] to do, believing that for **Christ**'s sake he obtains the
A P : 2 3 :040(244) [0375] Neither **Christ** nor Paul commends virginity because it
A P : 2 3 :040(245) [0375] Thus **Christ** does not simply commend those who make
A P : 2 3 :046(246) [0377] the knowledge of **Christ** by making men believe that
A P : 2 4 :012(251) [0387] with the knowledge of **Christ**; for his sake we are
A P : 2 4 :022(253) [0391] in the world, the death of **Christ**, as the Epistle to the
A P : 2 4 :022(253) [0391] it says about the will of **Christ** (v. 10), "By that will we
A P : 2 4 :022(253) [0391] the offering of the body of Jesus **Christ** once for all."
A P : 2 4 :023(253) [0391] to mean that the death of **Christ** is a real satisfaction or
A P : 2 4 :023(253) [0391] of another (namely, of **Christ**) to reconcile him to us.
A P : 2 4 :023(253) [0391] and Paul mean that **Christ** became a sacrificial victim or
A P : 2 4 :023(253) [0391] then, that the death of **Christ** is the only real propitiatory
A P : 2 4 :026(254) [0393] him let us offer," namely, through faith in **Christ**.
A P : 2 4 :027(254) [0393] **Christ** says in John 4:23, 24, "The true worshipers will
A P : 2 4 :032(255) [0395] makes known the name of **Christ** and the Father's mercy
A P : 2 4 :032(255) [0395] name of Christ and the Father's mercy promised in **Christ**
A P : 2 4 :032(255) [0395] in confession, they do good works for the glory of **Christ**.
A P : 2 4 :034(256) [0397] both the death of **Christ** and the proclamation of the
A P : 2 4 :036(257) [0397] come; thus this depicted **Christ** and the whole worship of
A P : 2 4 :036(257) [0397] The burning of the lamb symbolizes the death of **Christ**.
A P : 2 4 :036(257) [0397] for obedience to Jesus **Christ** and for sprinkling with his
A P : 2 4 :038(257) [0397] memorial of the death of **Christ**, therefore, it is not the
A P : 2 4 :038(257) [0399] that by the death of **Christ** God has been reconciled.
A P : 2 4 :038(257) [0399] when the Gospel sprinkles us with the blood of **Christ**.
A P : 2 4 :043(257) [0399] or point out that sins are freely forgiven for **Christ**'s sake.
A P : 2 4 :046(258) [0401] and about the free forgiveness of sins for **Christ**'s sake.
A P : 2 4 :048(258) [0401] Gospel of the blessing of **Christ**, and they show that the
A P : 2 4 :048(258) [0401] that the forgiveness of sins comes freely for **Christ**'s sake.
A P : 2 4 :053(259) [0403] itself adds immediately that **Christ** is the high priest.
A P : 2 4 :053(259) [0403] and say that it was a picture of **Christ**'s priesthood.
A P : 2 4 :053(259) [0403] picture of the sacrifice of **Christ** which was to be the one
A P : 2 4 :054(259) [0403] but only to symbolize the future death of **Christ** alone.
A P : 2 4 :055(259) [0403] promise of the forgiveness of sins given for **Christ**'s sake.
A P : 2 4 :055(259) [0403] have had to believe that **Christ** would be the offering and
A P : 2 4 :056(260) [0405] only the sacrifice of **Christ** can be valid for the sins of
A P : 2 4 :056(260) [0405] Testament except the one sacrifice of **Christ** on the cross.
A P : 2 4 :057(260) [0405] besides the death of **Christ** that are valid for the sins of
A P : 2 4 :057(260) [0405] negates the merit of **Christ**'s suffering and the
A P : 2 4 :057(260) [0405] Testament, and it replaces **Christ** as our mediator and
A P : 2 4 :058(260) [0405] priest who sacrifices for sin, this can only apply to **Christ**.
A P : 2 4 :058(260) [0405] other mediators besides **Christ** if we were to look for some
A P : 2 4 :059(260) [0405] it has for the sins of others is the sacrifice of **Christ**.
A P : 2 4 :060(260) [0405] anything else but faith in **Christ**, as we read (Rom. 5:1),
A P : 2 4 :063(261) [0405] they destroy the glory of **Christ**'s suffering and the
A P : 2 4 :068(261) [0407] In the second place, **Christ** was supposed to be very
A P : 2 4 :071(262) [0409] For such use **Christ** instituted it, as he commanded
A P : 2 4 :072(262) [0409] The remembrance of **Christ** is not the vain celebration of
A P : 2 4 :072(262) [0409] the remembrance of **Christ**'s blessings and the acceptance
A P : 2 4 :074(263) [0409] it really gives thanks for the blessing of **Christ**'s suffering.
A P : 2 4 :080(264) [0411] regard us, as ministers of **Christ** and dispensers of the
A P : 2 4 :080(264) [0411] "We are ambassadors for **Christ**, God making his appeal
A P : 2 4 :080(264) [0411] We beseech you on behalf of **Christ**, be reconciled to God
A P : 2 4 :088(265) [0413] victim" and apply it to the body of **Christ** itself.
A P : 2 4 :089(266) [0415] as much to the work of a priest as to the death of **Christ**.
A P : 2 4 :089(266) [0415] except by faith in **Christ**, as Paul teaches (Rom. 5:1),
A P : 2 4 :090(266) [0415] the Mass would be on a par with the death of **Christ**.
A P : 2 4 :096(267) [0417] wicked errors which rob **Christ**'s suffering of its glory and
A P : 2 4 :097(268) [0417] when only the sacrifice of **Christ** is honored as a
A P : 2 4 :098(268) [0419] with the papal realm until **Christ** comes to judge and by
A P : 2 4 :098(268) [0419] to obscure the glory of **Christ** and the righteousness of

Continued ▶

A P : 2 7 :002(269) [0419] with equanimity for **Christ**'s sake inasmuch as he had
A P : 2 7 :006(269) [0421] But **Christ** warns that tasteless salt is usually "thrown out
A P : 2 7 :011(270) [0423] sins is given us freely for **Christ**'s sake, as we have said at
A P : 2 7 :011(270) [0423] "You are severed from **Christ**, you who would be justified
A P : 2 7 :011(270) [0423] of sins not by faith in **Christ**, but by monastic works, take
A P : 2 7 :011(270) [0423] works, take away from **Christ**'s honor and crucify him
A P : 2 7 :012(270) [0423] observe everything for **Christ**'s sake and try to live more
A P : 2 7 :013(271) [0423] O **Christ**, how long wilt Thou bear these insults with
A P : 2 7 :013(271) [0423] of sins is received freely for **Christ**'s sake, through faith.
A P : 2 7 :015(271) [0425] law of Moses and that **Christ** took its place, so that he
A P : 2 7 :016(271) [0425] and fanatical notion they bury the blessing of **Christ**.
A P : 2 7 :016(271) [0425] who observe this law of **Christ**, the monks come closer in
A P : 2 7 :017(271) [0425] **Christ** takes Moses' place, not by forgiving sins on
A P : 2 7 :017(271) [0425] own merits, in addition to **Christ**'s propitiation, against
A P : 2 7 :017(272) [0425] abolishes the promise of **Christ**, has cast Christ away, and
A P : 2 7 :017(272) [0425] of Christ, has cast **Christ** away, and has fallen from
A P : 2 7 :017(272) [0425] of Christ, has cast Christ away, and has fallen from **Christ**
A P : 2 7 :019(272) [0425] men attain the forgiveness of sins by faith for **Christ**'s sake
A P : 2 7 :020(272) [0427] with an ordinance of **Christ** which has both a command
A P : 2 7 :023(272) [0427] which teaches that for **Christ**'s sake righteousness and
A P : 2 7 :023(273) [0427] It also conflicts with **Christ**'s statement (Matt. 15:9), "In
A P : 2 7 :027(273) [0429] in the mercy promised in **Christ**, and in devotion to one's
A P : 2 7 :027(274) [0429] and of the kingdom of **Christ**, which is eternal life, in
A P : 2 7 :028(274) [0429] Indeed, **Christ** has promised this in abundance to those
A P : 2 7 :030(274) [0431] In addition, they insult **Christ** when they say that by a
A P : 2 7 :032(274) [0431] life is given by mercy for **Christ**'s sake to those who accept
A P : 2 7 :033(275) [0431] the mercy promised in **Christ**, much less do monastic
A P : 2 7 :034(275) [0431] mercy available in **Christ** and are transferring to their own
A P : 2 7 :034(275) [0431] their own foolish observances the trust that is due **Christ**.
A P : 2 7 :034(275) [0431] Instead of **Christ** they worship their own cowls and their
A P : 2 7 :035(275) [0431] And since **Christ** calls traditions "useless services," they
A P : 2 7 :040(276) [0433] **Christ** does not mean to say that leaving parents or wife
A P : 2 7 :040(276) [0435] forgiveness of sins or eternal life, he is insulting **Christ**.
A P : 2 7 :041(276) [0435] a command of God; this **Christ** does not approve, for
A P : 2 7 :041(276) [0435] The fact that **Christ** speaks of leaving wife and children
A P : 2 7 :041(276) [0435] This kind of leaving **Christ** approves.
A P : 2 7 :043(276) [0435] twist the saying of **Christ** in applying it to monastic life,
A P : 2 7 :048(277) [0437] Yet **Christ** calls it perfection here!
A P : 2 7 :048(277) [0437] Perfection consists in that which **Christ** adds, "Follow me
A P : 2 7 :049(277) [0437] but only for the person with whom **Christ** is talking here.
A P : 2 7 :052(278) [0437] undaunted by the voice of **Christ** upbraiding the Pharisees
A P : 2 7 :053(278) [0437] double fault: it arrogates **Christ**'s place to the saints, and
A P : 2 7 :054(278) [0437] forgiveness of sins for **Christ**'s sake, about the
A P : 2 7 :054(278) [0439] or on ceremonial traditions that obscure **Christ**.
A P : 2 7 :065(280) [0441] secure eternal life for us instead of mercy for **Christ**'s sake
A P : 2 7 :069(281) [0443] of the monks, which **Christ** cancels with one declaration
A P : 2 7 :069(281) [0443] of them rather than because of **Christ** through mercy.
A P : 2 7 :070(281) [0443] of sins freely for **Christ**'s sake, that for Christ's sake by
A P : 2 7 :070(281) [0443] for Christ's sake, that for **Christ**'s sake by mercy they
A P : 2 8 :007(282) [0445] receive forgiveness of sins freely for **Christ**'s sake by faith.
A P : 2 8 :007(282) [0445] **Christ** wanted to leave their use free when he said (Matt.
A P : 2 8 :014(283) [0447] to that Word which they have received from **Christ**.
A P : 2 8 :015(283) [0447] in the freedom with which **Christ** has set you free, and do
A P : 2 8 :018(284) [0449] For **Christ** wants to assure us, as was necessary, that the
A P : 2 8 :019(284) [0449] For **Christ** requires them to teach in such a way that he
A P : 2 8 :023(284) [0451] the forgiveness of sins for **Christ**'s sake, brings enough
S 1 : P R :009(290) [0457] the judgment seat of **Christ**, who in their writings have
S 1 : P R :009(290) [0457] **Christ**, the lord and judge of us all, knows very well that
S 1 : P R :010(290) [0457] poor people live or die, although **Christ** died for them too
S 1 : P R :010(290) [0457] Those people cannot hear **Christ** speak to them as the true
S 1 : P R :015(291) [0459] Dear Lord Jesus **Christ**, assemble a council of thine own,
S 2 : 0 0 :000(292) [0461] the office and work of Jesus **Christ**, or to our redemption.
S 2 : 0 1 :000(292) [0461] [Article I. **Christ** and Faith]
S 2 : 0 1 :001(292) [0461] article is this, that Jesus **Christ**, our God and Lord, "was
S 2 : 0 1 :003(292) [0461] redemption which is in **Christ** Jesus, by his blood" (Rom.
S 2 : 0 2 :002(293) [0463] all human inventions, for **Christ** says, 'In vain do they
S 2 : 0 2 :004(293) [0463] blessed manner — according to the institution of **Christ**.
S 2 : 0 2 :008(294) [0465] sacrament administered according to **Christ**'s institution.
S 2 : 0 2 :010(294) [0465] considered equal or superior to my Saviour, Jesus **Christ**.
S 2 : 0 2 :012(295) [0465] for the dead although **Christ** instituted the sacrament for
S 2 : 0 2 :012(295) [0465] fundamental article that **Christ** alone, and not the work of
S 2 : 0 2 :019(296) [0467] may turn aside from **Christ** to their own merits and (what
S 2 : 0 2 :024(296) [0469] pope sells the merits of **Christ** together with the
S 2 : 0 2 :024(296) [0469] article, for the merits of **Christ** are obtained by grace,
S 2 : 0 2 :025(297) [0469] first, chief article and undermines knowledge of **Christ**.
S 2 : 0 2 :025(297) [0469] not), we have everything a thousandfold better in **Christ**.
S 2 : 0 2 :026(297) [0469] in heaven pray for us (as **Christ** himself also does), and
S 2 : 0 2 :027(297) [0469] ways in which I can honor, love, and thank you in **Christ**.
S 2 : 0 2 :029(297) [0471] to the institution of **Christ** and may use and receive it in
S 2 : 0 3 :002(298) [0471] article concerning redemption in Jesus **Christ**.
S 2 : 0 4 :001(298) [0471] this position belongs only to one, namely, to Jesus **Christ**.
S 2 : 0 4 :003(298) [0473] which is concerned with redemption in Jesus **Christ**.
S 2 : 0 4 :004(299) [0473] "Although you believe in **Christ**, and in him have
S 2 : 0 4 :009(300) [0473] of us live under one head, **Christ**, and by having all the
S 2 : 0 4 :010(300) [0475] and set himself against **Christ**, for the pope will not
S 2 : 0 4 :011(300) [0475] so they allow to believe in **Christ**, and they receive bodily
S 2 : 0 4 :013(300) [0475] up as equal to and above **Christ** and to proclaim himself
S 2 : 0 4 :014(301) [0475] so much as a mention of **Christ**, faith, and God's
S 2 : 0 4 :015(301) [0475] must rely on the hope that **Christ**, our Lord, has attacked
S 3 : 0 1 :011(303) [0479] concerning sin and concerning **Christ**, our Saviour.
S 3 : 0 1 :011(303) [0479] such teachings were true, **Christ** would have died in vain,
S 3 : 0 3 :001(303) [0479] **Christ** also says in John 16:8, "The Holy Spirit will
S 3 : 0 3 :004(304) [0481] This is to be believed, as **Christ** says in Mark 1:15,
S 3 : 0 3 :005(304) [0481] John, who preceded **Christ**, is called a preacher of
S 3 : 0 3 :006(304) [0481] **Christ** himself says this in Luke 24:47, "Repentance and
S 3 : 0 3 :014(305) [0483] There was no mention here of **Christ** or of faith.
S 3 : 0 3 :018(306) [0483] without being able to consider **Christ** and faith.
S 3 : 0 3 :018(306) [0483] powers without faith and without knowledge of **Christ**.
S 3 : 0 3 :019(306) [0485] Here, again, there was neither faith nor **Christ**.
S 3 : 0 3 :023(306) [0485] it, and neither faith nor **Christ** would have been of any
S 3 : 0 3 :029(308) [0487] scribes and Pharisees in **Christ**'s time were just such
S 3 : 0 3 :039(309) [0489] John preaches, which **Christ** subsequently preaches in the
S 3 : 0 3 :039(309) [0489] no one keeps the law (as **Christ** says in John 7:19) but all
S 3 : 0 5 :001(310) [0491] by the institution of **Christ**; or as Paul says, "the washing
S 3 : 0 5 :004(311) [0493] of redemption which **Christ** made, and the church should
S 3 : 0 6 :001(311) [0493] true body and blood of **Christ** and that these are given
S 3 : 0 6 :003(311) [0493] as it was established and commanded by **Christ**.
S 3 : 0 6 :004(311) [0493] against and over **Christ**, our Lord and God, etc.
S 3 : 0 7 :001(311) [0493] given to the church by **Christ** to bind and loose sins, not
S 3 : 0 8 :001(312) [0493] which was instituted by **Christ** in the Gospel, is a
S 3 : 1 3 :001(315) [0499] righteous and holy for the sake of **Christ**, our mediator.
S 3 : 1 3 :002(315) [0499] reckoned as sin or defect for the sake of the same **Christ**.
S 3 : 1 3 :002(315) [0499] have been poured out upon us so abundantly in **Christ**.
S 3 : 1 4 :001(315) [0501] It is of these that **Christ** says in Matt. 24:5, "I am the
S 3 : 1 4 :001(315) [0501] these that Christ says in Matt. 24:5, "I am the **Christ**," etc.
S 3 : 1 4 :001(316) [0501] This is to deny **Christ**, etc.
S 3 : 1 5 :001(316) [0501] As **Christ** says, "In vain do they worship me, teaching as
S 3 : 1 5 :005(317) [0501] minister of the church of **Christ** which is in Soest,
S 3 : 1 5 :005(317) [0501] and by the Spirit of **Christ** I will thus continue to believe
T R : 0 0 :002(320) [0503] bishop of Rome calls himself the vicar of **Christ** on earth.
T R : 0 0 :007(320) [0505] In Luke 22:24-27 **Christ** expressly forbids lordship among
T R : 0 0 :008(320) [0505] were disputing when **Christ** spoke of his passion: Who
T R : 0 0 :008(320) [0505] and, as it were, the vicar of **Christ** after his departure?
T R : 0 0 :008(320) [0505] **Christ** reproved the apostles for this error and taught
T R : 0 0 :008(321) [0505] concerning the kingdom, **Christ** put a child in the midst of
T R : 0 0 :009(321) [0505] According to John 20:21 **Christ** sent his disciples out as
T R : 0 0 :016(322) [0509] that the kingdom of **Christ** is scattered over all the earth
T R : 0 0 :023(324) [0511] from the text itself, for **Christ** did not question Peter alone
T R : 0 0 :024(324) [0511] of the keys in Matt. 18:19, **Christ** said, "If two or three of
T R : 0 0 :025(324) [0511] when he declared Jesus to be the **Christ**, the Son of God.
T R : 0 0 :025(324) [0511] Therefore **Christ** addresses Peter as a minister and says,
T R : 0 0 :026(324) [0511] authority but because of the Word given by **Christ**.
T R : 0 0 :028(325) [0511] Chrysostom declares that **Christ** says "on this rock" and
T R : 0 0 :028(325) [0511] other than "You are the **Christ**, the Son of the living
T R : 0 0 :030(325) [0513] authority on Peter, for **Christ** bids Peter to pasture the
T R : 0 0 :031(325) [0513] than the first because **Christ** gave the apostles only
T R : 0 0 :031(325) [0513] For **Christ** said, "Go therefore and teach them to observe
T R : 0 0 :031(325) [0513] it is manifest that **Christ** was not sent to wield a sword or
T R : 0 0 :032(325) [0513] That **Christ** in his passion was crowned with thorns and
T R : 0 0 :036(326) [0515] to the command of **Christ**, but he even exalted himself
T R : 0 0 :036(326) [0515] by the authority of **Christ** and that he can attach salvation
T R : 0 0 :037(326) [0515] faith and the kingdom of **Christ**, they are under no
T R : 0 0 :039(327) [0515] calls him "an adversary of **Christ** who opposes and exalts
T R : 0 0 :039(327) [0515] man "an adversary of **Christ**" because he will devise
T R : 0 0 :040(327) [0515] to change the doctrine of **Christ** and the worship instituted
T R : 0 0 :041(327) [0517] **Christ** commanded, "Beware of false prophets" (Matt.
T R : 0 0 :044(328) [0517] are forgiven freely for **Christ**'s sake and that by this faith
T R : 0 0 :044(328) [0517] they obscure the glory of **Christ**, deprive consciences of a
T R : 0 0 :045(328) [0517] of which they have further obscured the benefit of **Christ**.
T R : 0 0 :048(328) [0519] transferred merit from **Christ** to human traditions and
T R : 0 0 :062(331) [0523] followings around themselves, rend the church of **Christ**.
T R : 0 0 :067(331) [0523] work of ministry and for building up the body of **Christ**.
T R : 0 0 :068(331) [0523] Here the words of **Christ** apply which testify that the keys
T R : 0 0 :082(000) [0529] most revered Father in **Christ**, that your courtesy may add
T R : 0 0 :082(000) [0529] and constantly will teach, through Jesus **Christ**, our Lord.
S C : P R :000(338) [0533] mercy, and peace in Jesus **Christ**, our Lord, from Martin
S C : P R :004(338) [0533] answer for it before **Christ** that you have so shamefully
S C : P R :011(339) [0535] tell them that they deny **Christ** and are no Christians.
S C : P R :022(341) [0537] **Christ** did not say, "Omit this," or "Despise this," but he
S C : P R :023(341) [0539] paradise, no heaven, no **Christ**, no God, nothing good at
S C : P R :027(341) [0539] But **Christ** himself will be our reward if we labor
S C : P R :027(341) [0539] be praise and thanks forever, through **Christ**, our Lord.
S C : 0 2 :003(345) [0545] *"And in Jesus **Christ**, his only son, our Lord: who was*
S C : 0 2 :004(345) [0545] I believe that Jesus **Christ**, true God, begotten of the
S C : 0 2 :006(345) [0545] I cannot believe in Jesus **Christ**, my Lord, or come to
S C : 0 2 :006(345) [0545] it in union with Jesus **Christ** in the one true faith.
S C : 0 2 :006(345) [0545] grant eternal life to me and to all who believe in **Christ**.
S C : 0 4 :004(348) [0551] Matthew 28:19, our Lord **Christ** said, "Go therefore and
S C : 0 4 :008(349) [0551] in Mark 16:16, our Lord **Christ** said, "He who believes
S C : 0 4 :010(349) [0551] us richly through Jesus **Christ** our Saviour, so that we
S C : 0 4 :014(349) [0553] into death, so that as **Christ** was raised from the dead by
S C : 0 5 :028(351) [0555] of our Lord Jesus **Christ**, I forgive you your sins in the
S C : 0 6 :002(351) [0555] Answer: Instituted by **Christ** himself, it is the true body
S C : 0 6 :002(351) [0555] blood of our Lord Jesus **Christ**, under the bread and
S C : 0 6 :004(351) [0555] thus: "Our Lord Jesus **Christ**, on the night when he was
S C : 0 7 :002(352) [0557] thy dear Son Jesus **Christ**, that Thou hast protected me
S C : 0 7 :005(353) [0559] thy dear Son Jesus **Christ**, that Thou hast this day
S C : 0 8 :009(353) [0559] Thou hast bestowed on us, through Jesus **Christ** our Lord
S C : 0 8 :011(354) [0559] benefits, through Jesus **Christ** our Lord, who lives and
S C : 0 9 :010(356) [0563] singleness of heart, as to **Christ**; not in the way of
S C : 0 9 :010(356) [0563] but as servants of **Christ**, doing the will of God from the
L C : P R :019(359) [0569] This is according to **Christ**'s promise in Matt. 18:20,
L C : S P :012(363) [0577] And in Jesus **Christ**, his only Son, our Lord: who was
L C : S P :013(363) [0577] III. The Prayer, or Our Father, Which **Christ** Taught
L C : S P :020(364) [0579] say about the sacraments which **Christ** himself instituted.
L C : S P :020(364) [0579] holy Body and Blood of **Christ**, according to the texts of
L C : S P :020(364) [0579] where they describe how **Christ** said farewell to his
L C : S P :023(364) [0579] "Our Lord Jesus **Christ** on the night when he was betrayed
L C : 0 1 :065(373) [0599] in the Gospel, and yet **Christ**, St. Paul, and other saints
L C : 0 1 :074(374) [0601] "Help, dear Lord **Christ**!" etc.
L C : 0 1 :081(375) [0603] They slandered **Christ** and would not permit him to do
L C : 0 1 :082(376) [0603] from all of which we are now set free through **Christ**.
L C : 0 1 :159(387) [0627] "I became your father in **Christ** Jesus through the
L C : 0 1 :182(389) [0631] Gospel, Matthew 5, where **Christ** himself explains and
L C : 0 1 :191(391) [0635] them in the day of judgment, as **Christ** himself declares.
L C : 0 1 :194(391) [0635] heathen virtue, as **Christ** says in Matthew 5:46, 47.
L C : 0 1 :276(402) [0659] Matthew 19, where **Christ** says, "If your brother sins
L C : 0 1 :278(402) [0661] As **Christ** himself says in the same passage, "If he listens
L C : 0 1 :279(402) [0661] **Christ** teaches further: "If he does not listen, take one or
L C : 0 1 :286(403) [0663] should be the one which **Christ** indicates in the Gospel,
L C : 0 2 :025(413) [0683] *"And in Jesus **Christ**, his only Son, our Lord: who was*
L C : 0 2 :026(414) [0685] concentrate on these words, "in Jesus **Christ**, our Lord."
L C : 0 2 :027(414) [0685] Article, concerning Jesus **Christ**?" answer briefly, "I
L C : 0 2 :027(414) [0685] "I believe that Jesus **Christ**, true Son of God, has become
L C : 0 2 :030(414) [0685] has been taken by Jesus **Christ**, the Lord of life and
L C : 0 2 :031(414) [0685] that is, how much it cost **Christ** and what he paid and

Continued ▶

LC : 0 2 :032(415) [0687] as the birth, passion, resurrection, and ascension of **Christ**
LC : 0 2 :037(415) [0687] church, where he preaches to us and brings us to **Christ**.
LC : 0 2 :038(415) [0689] ever know anything of **Christ**, or believe in him and take
LC : 0 2 :038(415) [0689] finished and completed, **Christ** has acquired and won the
LC : 0 2 :039(416) [0689] to bring us to the Lord **Christ** to receive this blessing,
LC : 0 2 :043(416) [0689] and no one recognized **Christ** as the Lord, or the Holy
LC : 0 2 :043(416) [0689] is, no one believed that **Christ** is our Lord in the sense
LC : 0 2 :045(416) [0689] For where **Christ** is not preached, there is no Holy Spirit
LC : 0 2 :045(416) [0689] and outside it no one can come to the Lord **Christ**.
LC : 0 2 :051(417) [0691] flock or community of pure saints under one head, **Christ**.
LC : 0 2 :052(417) [0691] of the devil, knowing nothing of God and of **Christ**.
LC : 0 2 :054(417) [0693] grace has been won by **Christ**, and holiness has been
LC : 0 2 :065(419) [0695] were it not for the Lord **Christ**, who is a mirror of the
LC : 0 2 :065(419) [0695] we know anything of **Christ**, had it not been revealed by
LC : 0 2 :066(419) [0697] do not have the Lord **Christ**, and, besides, they are not
LC : 0 2 :069(420) [0697] gives us all creation, **Christ** all his works, the Holy Spirit
LC : 0 3 :003(420) [0697] how to pray, our Lord **Christ** himself has taught us both
LC : 0 3 :004(420) [0699] draw people to prayer, as **Christ** and the apostles also did.
LC : 0 3 :019(423) [0703] I will deliver you," and **Christ** says in Matt. 7:7, 8, "Ask
LC : 0 3 :033(424) [0707] howling and growling, as **Christ** himself rejects and
LC : 0 3 :051(426) [0711] that God sent his Son, **Christ** our Lord, into the world to
LC : 0 3 :058(428) [0713] things in abundance, as **Christ** teaches, "Seek first the
LC : 0 3 :096(433) [0725] Therefore **Christ** repeats it immediately after the Lord's
LC : 0 4 :001(436) [0733] us to speak of our two sacraments, instituted by **Christ**.
LC : 0 4 :003(437) [0733] namely, where the Lord **Christ** says in Matt. 28:19,
LC : 0 4 :021(439) [0737] the heavens opened when **Christ** allowed himself to be
LC : 0 4 :022(439) [0737] Baptism is a sacrament, and it is called **Christ**'s Baptism.
LC : 0 4 :023(439) [0737] than from the words of **Christ** quoted above, "He who
LC : 0 4 :025(439) [0739] enter into the kingdom of **Christ** and live with him
LC : 0 4 :031(440) [0739] God's Word, faith, and **Christ**, who directs us and binds
LC : 0 4 :035(441) [0741] you must distinguish **Christ**'s Baptism quite clearly from a
LC : 0 4 :037(441) [0741] grasps, just as the Lord **Christ** upon the cross is not a
LC : 0 4 :041(442) [0743] God's grace, the entire **Christ**, and the Holy Spirit with his
LC : 0 4 :049(442) [0743] of infants is pleasing to **Christ** is sufficiently proved from
LC : 0 4 :049(442) [0745] Scriptures and to know **Christ**, which is impossible
LC : 0 4 :056(444) [0747] of my own faith, but on the strength of **Christ**'s Word.
LC : 0 4 :058(444) [0747] I might argue, "If I have no faith, then **Christ** is nothing."
LC : 0 4 :067(445) [0749] Now, when we enter **Christ**'s kingdom, this corruption
LC : 0 4 :069(445) [0749] Those who are outside of **Christ** can only grow worse day
LC : 0 4 :086(446) [0753] As **Christ**, the mercy-seat, does not recede from us or
LC : 0 5 :001(447) [0753] established from the words by which **Christ** instituted it.
LC : 0 5 :003(447) [0753] *"Our Lord Jesus* ***Christ*** *on the night when he was betrayed*
LC : 0 5 :004(447) [0755] It was instituted by **Christ** without man's counsel or
LC : 0 5 :008(447) [0755] and blood of the Lord **Christ** in and under the bread and
LC : 0 5 :008(447) [0755] are commanded by **Christ**'s word to eat and drink.
LC : 0 5 :010(448) [0755] sacrament which is rightly called **Christ**'s body and blood.
LC : 0 5 :012(448) [0755] 'How can bread and wine be **Christ**'s body and blood?'
LC : 0 5 :013(448) [0755] Here we have **Christ**'s word, 'Take, eat; this is my body.'
LC : 0 5 :013(448) [0755] see who dares to instruct **Christ** and alter what he has
LC : 0 5 :014(448) [0757] virtue of them they are truly the body and blood of **Christ**
LC : 0 5 :014(448) [0757] we have it from the lips of **Christ**, so it is; he cannot lie or
LC : 0 5 :016(448) [0757] true sacrament (that is, **Christ**'s body and blood) just as
LC : 0 5 :016(448) [0757] bread and wine into **Christ**'s body and blood, so likewise
LC : 0 5 :017(448) [0757] **Christ** does not say, "If you believe, or if you are worthy,
LC : 0 5 :018(448) [0757] or worthy, you here have **Christ**'s body and blood by
LC : 0 5 :022(449) [0757] **Christ** bids me eat and drink in order that the sacrament
LC : 0 5 :028(449) [0759] bread and wine which are **Christ**'s body and blood and
LC : 0 5 :029(449) [0759] have both truths, that it is **Christ**'s body and blood and
LC : 0 5 :030(449) [0759] **Christ**'s body can never be an unfruitful, vain thing,
LC : 0 5 :031(450) [0759] it is absurd to say that **Christ**'s body and blood are not
LC : 0 5 :033(450) [0761] hear them, those to whom **Christ** says, "Take and eat,"
LC : 0 5 :037(451) [0761] and reverently toward the body and blood of **Christ**.
LC : 0 5 :042(451) [0763] **Christ** did not institute it to be treated merely as a
LC : 0 5 :045(451) [0763] clear text in the words of **Christ**, *"Do this* in remembrance
LC : 0 5 :045(452) [0763] addressed to disciples of **Christ**; hence whoever would be
LC : 0 5 :045(452) [0763] coerced by men, but to obey and please the Lord **Christ**.
LC : 0 5 :047(452) [0763] they are added because **Christ** wishes the sacrament to be
LC : 0 5 :047(452) [0765] **Christ** means to say: "I institute a Passover or Supper for
LC : 0 5 :049(452) [0765] the one is just as much **Christ**'s commandment as the
LC : 0 5 :051(452) [0765] love and even without regard for **Christ**'s commandment.
LC : 0 5 :052(452) [0765] impel you is the fact that **Christ** desires it, and it pleases
LC : 0 5 :063(454) [0767] than upon the words that proceed from **Christ**'s lips.
LC : 0 5 :065(454) [0769] to you and me; otherwise **Christ** might just as well have
LC : 0 5 :070(454) [0769] you receive from **Christ**'s lips the forgiveness of sins, which
LC : 0 5 :071(454) [0769] the commandment and the promise of the Lord **Christ**.
LC : 0 5 :071(455) [0769] **Christ** himself says, "Those who are well have no need of
LC : 0 5 :074(455) [0771] In such a case **Christ** pronounces the judgment, "If you
LC : 0 5 :080(456) [0771] foot because our Lord **Christ** himself could not entirely
LC : 0 5 :081(456) [0773] making you unable to feel your needs or come to **Christ**.
LC : 0 6 :014(458) [0000] Thus by divine ordinance **Christ** himself has entrusted
EP : 0 1 :006(466) [0781] Thus **Christ** has redeemed our nature as his creation,
EP : 0 1 :012(467) [0783] of which man outside of **Christ** is a child of wrath.
EP : 0 2 :003(470) [0787] our trespasses, he made us alive together with **Christ**."
EP : 0 2 :006(470) [0787] **Christ** also states, "Apart from me you can do nothing."
EP : 0 3 :001(472) [0791] saved solely by faith in **Christ**, so that Christ alone is our
EP : 0 3 :001(472) [0791] by faith in Christ, so that **Christ** alone is our
EP : 0 3 :001(473) [0791] According to which nature is **Christ** our righteousness?
EP : 0 3 :002(473) [0791] One party has held that **Christ** is our righteousness only
EP : 0 3 :002(473) [0793] Others, however, held that **Christ** is our righteousness
EP : 0 3 :003(473) [0793] confess unanimously that **Christ** is our righteousness
EP : 0 3 :003(473) [0793] On the contrary, the entire **Christ** according to both
EP : 0 3 :004(473) [0793] to us the righteousness of **Christ**'s obedience, on account
EP : 0 3 :005(473) [0793] whereby we accept **Christ** and in Christ obtain the
EP : 0 3 :005(473) [0793] we accept Christ and in **Christ** obtain the "righteousness
EP : 0 3 :005(473) [0793] before God," and that for **Christ**'s sake such faith is
EP : 0 3 :006(473) [0793] of the stories about **Christ**, but the kind of gift of God by
EP : 0 3 :006(473) [0793] the Gospel we recognize **Christ** aright as our redeemer and
EP : 0 3 :009(474) [0795] it as certain that for **Christ**'s sake, on the basis of the
EP : 0 3 :010(474) [0795] separate the merit of **Christ** completely from our own
EP : 0 3 :010(474) [0795] from our own works and give all glory to **Christ** alone.
EP : 0 3 :010(474) [0795] become righteous and are saved "alone by faith" in **Christ**.
EP : 0 3 :013(474) [0795] 1. That **Christ** is our righteousness only according to the
EP : 0 3 :014(474) [0795] 2. That **Christ** is our righteousness only according to the
EP : 0 3 :016(475) [0795] does not look alone to **Christ**'s obedience, but also to his
EP : 0 3 :017(475) [0795] trust in the obedience of **Christ** that can exist and remain
EP : 0 3 :021(475) [0797] by the righteousness of **Christ** reckoned to them and by
EP : 0 3 :021(475) [0797] the reckoning to them of **Christ**'s righteousness and in
EP : 0 4 :014(477) [0799] 9. Nevertheless, for **Christ**'s sake the Lord does not reckon
EP : 0 4 :014(477) [0799] for those who are in **Christ** Jesus" (Rom. 8:1).
EP : 0 5 :005(478) [0803] believe, namely, that **Christ** has satisfied and paid for all
EP : 0 5 :006(478) [0803] the entire doctrine of **Christ** which he proclaimed
EP : 0 5 :007(478) [0803] of the law in contrast to **Christ** as a preacher of the
EP : 0 5 :007(478) [0803] solely to the merit of **Christ**, and raises them up again by
EP : 0 5 :007(478) [0803] grace and favor acquired through the merits of **Christ**.
EP : 0 5 :008(478) [0803] and hear nothing about **Christ**, the veil of Moses covers
EP : 0 5 :008(479) [0803] Therefore **Christ** takes the law into his own hands and
EP : 0 5 :009(479) [0803] the suffering and death of **Christ**, the Son of God, is an
EP : 0 5 :009(479) [0803] that we should now seek all our righteousness in **Christ**.
EP : 0 5 :010(479) [0803] the passion and death of **Christ** — proclaims God's wrath
EP : 0 5 :010(479) [0803] it is an "alien work" of **Christ** by which he comes to his
EP : 0 5 :011(479) [0805] of the law, the merit of **Christ** and the Holy Scriptures are
EP : 0 6 :002(480) [0805] are freed through **Christ** from the curse and coercion of
EP : 0 6 :006(481) [0807] St. Paul calls it the law of **Christ** and the law of the mind.
EP : 0 7 :000(481) [0807] VII. The Holy Supper of **Christ**
EP : 0 7 :002(481) [0809] blood of our Lord Jesus **Christ** truly and essentially
EP : 0 7 :004(482) [0809] living body and blood of **Christ** in the Holy Supper but
EP : 0 7 :005(482) [0809] more than the presence of **Christ**'s spirit, or the power of
EP : 0 7 :005(482) [0809] spirit, or the power of **Christ**'s absent body, or his merit.
EP : 0 7 :005(482) [0809] deny that the body of **Christ** is present in any manner or
EP : 0 7 :005(482) [0809] of the Holy Supper, seek the body and blood of **Christ**.
EP : 0 7 :006(482) [0809] the body and blood of **Christ** are truly and essentially
EP : 0 7 :007(482) [0811] words of the testament of **Christ** are to be understood in
EP : 0 7 :007(482) [0811] wine the absent blood of **Christ**, but that because of the
EP : 0 7 :007(482) [0811] union they are truly the body and blood of **Christ**.
EP : 0 7 :008(482) [0811] of the body and blood of **Christ** in the Holy Supper, but
EP : 0 7 :008(482) [0811] and alone to the almighty power of our Lord Jesus **Christ**
EP : 0 7 :009(483) [0811] Holy Supper the words of **Christ**'s institution should
EP : 0 7 :009(483) [0811] occurs through the recitation of the words of **Christ**.
EP : 0 7 :011(483) [0811] our Christian faith: Jesus **Christ** is true, essential, natural,
EP : 0 7 :012(483) [0811] **Christ**, really and truly set at this right hand of God
EP : 0 7 :015(483) [0811] the body and blood of **Christ** are received not only
EP : 0 7 :015(483) [0811] The words of **Christ** teach this clearly when they direct us
EP : 0 7 :015(483) [0813] in the body of **Christ**?" (I Cor. 10:16) — that is, whoever
EP : 0 7 :015(483) [0813] — that is, whoever eats this bread eats the body of **Christ**.
EP : 0 7 :016(484) [0813] true body and blood of **Christ**; but if they are not
EP : 0 7 :017(484) [0813] For although they reject **Christ** as a redeemer, they must
EP : 0 7 :019(484) [0813] to his condemnation, for **Christ** instituted this Supper
EP : 0 7 :020(484) [0813] and complete merit of **Christ**, which we make our own
EP : 0 7 :021(484) [0813] to our simple faith and confession about **Christ**'s Supper:
EP : 0 7 :022(484) [0813] into the body of **Christ** and that only the exterior
EP : 0 7 :024(484) [0815] to the clear Word of **Christ**'s testament, so that they are
EP : 0 7 :024(484) [0815] so that they are deprived of the blood of **Christ**.
EP : 0 7 :025(484) [0815] that the words of **Christ**'s testament are not to be
EP : 0 7 :026(485) [0815] sacrament the body of **Christ** is not received orally with
EP : 0 7 :026(485) [0815] we receive the body of **Christ** only spiritually by faith.
EP : 0 7 :028(485) [0815] and types of the far-distant body and blood of **Christ**.
EP : 0 7 :029(485) [0815] of the body and blood of **Christ** as truly as we eat and
EP : 0 7 :030(485) [0815] and not by the truly present body and blood of **Christ**.
EP : 0 7 :031(485) [0815] of the absent body and blood of **Christ** are distributed.
EP : 0 7 :032(485) [0815] 11. That the body of **Christ** is so enclosed in heaven that
EP : 0 7 :033(485) [0815] 12. That **Christ** could not have promised that his body
EP : 0 7 :035(485) [0815] the omnipotent words of **Christ**'s testament, effect and
EP : 0 7 :035(485) [0815] of the body and blood of **Christ** in the Holy Supper.
EP : 0 7 :036(485) [0815] not seek the body of **Christ** in the bread and wine of the
EP : 0 7 :036(485) [0815] the bread to heaven and there seek the body of **Christ**.
EP : 0 7 :037(486) [0815] the body and blood of **Christ**, but only bread and wine.
EP : 0 7 :038(486) [0817] only in true faith in **Christ**, but also depends on people's
EP : 0 7 :039(486) [0817] genuine and living faith in **Christ**, can also receive this
EP : 0 7 :042(486) [0817] eating of the body of **Christ** as though one rent Christ's
EP : 0 7 :042(486) [0817] Christ as though one rent **Christ**'s flesh with one's teeth
EP : 0 7 :042(486) [0817] with the simple words of **Christ**'s testament, we hold and
EP : 0 7 :042(486) [0817] supernatural, eating of **Christ**'s body and drinking of his
EP : 0 7 :042(486) [0817] captive in obedience to **Christ**, as we do in other articles
EP : 0 8 :000(486) [0817] VIII. The Person of **Christ**
EP : 0 8 :001(486) [0817] concerning the person of **Christ**, the two natures in
EP : 0 8 :001(486) [0817] of Christ, the two natures in **Christ**, and their properties.
EP : 0 8 :002(487) [0817] union in the person of **Christ**, do the divine and human
EP : 0 8 :003(487) [0817] have asserted that in **Christ** the divine and human natures
EP : 0 8 :003(487) [0819] *of the Christian Church concerning the Person of* ***Christ***
EP : 0 8 :005(487) [0819] are personally united in **Christ** in such a way that there
EP : 0 8 :009(488) [0819] divine that is said or believed about **Christ** the man.
EP : 0 8 :017(489) [0823] essential, as the words of **Christ**'s testament declare, *"This*
EP : 0 8 :018(489) [0823] do not divide the person of **Christ**, as Nestorius did.
EP : 0 8 :018(489) [0823] of the two natures in **Christ** and thus he actually divided
EP : 0 8 :018(489) [0823] nature in the person of **Christ**, or change the one nature
EP : 0 8 :018(489) [0823] **Christ** is, and remains to all eternity, God and man in one
EP : 0 8 :018(490) [0823] *Contrary False Doctrine concerning the Person of* ***Christ***
EP : 0 8 :020(490) [0823] 1. That in **Christ** God and man are not one person, but
EP : 0 8 :022(490) [0823] 3. That **Christ** is not true, natural, and eternal God, as
EP : 0 8 :023(490) [0823] 4. That **Christ** did not have a true human nature with a
EP : 0 8 :027(490) [0823] 8. That **Christ**'s human nature has become an infinite
EP : 0 8 :029(490) [0825] That the human nature of **Christ** is locally extended to
EP : 0 8 :030(490) [0825] nature it is impossible for **Christ** to be present at the same
EP : 0 8 :032(491) [0825] 13. That **Christ** is present with us on earth in the Word, in
EP : 0 8 :032(491) [0825] nature; and that after **Christ** had redeemed us by his
EP : 0 8 :034(491) [0825] 15. That in spite of **Christ**'s express assertion, "All
EP : 0 8 :034(491) [0825] of deity bodily" (Col. 2:9), **Christ**, according to the human
EP : 0 8 :035(491) [0825] to his human nature **Christ** has indeed been given greater
EP : 0 8 :035(491) [0825] the human nature of **Christ** received a power which is less
EP : 0 8 :036(491) [0825] to his human spirit **Christ** has certain limitations as to
EP : 0 8 :037(491) [0825] 18. That **Christ** does not as yet have a perfect knowledge
EP : 0 8 :038(491) [0825] to his human spirit **Christ** cannot know what has existed
EP : 0 8 :039(491) [0827] pervert the words of **Christ**, "All authority has been given
EP : 0 8 :039(491) [0827] or again returned to **Christ** according to the divine nature,
EP : 0 8 :039(491) [0827] only perverts the words of **Christ**'s testament, but it opens
EP : 0 8 :039(492) [0827] we shall finally have **Christ**'s eternal deity denied and we

Continued ▶

E P : 0 8 :039(492) [0827] denied and we shall lose **Christ** altogether along with our
E P : 0 9 :000(492) [0827] IX. **Christ**'s Descent into Hell
E P : 0 9 :001(492) [0827] to our simple Christian Creed, did **Christ** go to hell?
E P : 0 9 :001(492) [0827] Does this article belong to **Christ**'s suffering or to his
E P : 0 9 :004(492) [0827] It is enough to know that **Christ** went to hell, destroyed
E P : 1 0 :006(493) [0829] Paul writes, "For freedom **Christ** has set us free; stand fast
E P : 1 1 :007(495) [0833] God, however, leads us to **Christ**, who is "the book of life"
E P : 1 1 :008(495) [0833] 7. This **Christ** calls all sinners to himself and promises
E P : 1 1 :010(495) [0833] 9. We must learn about **Christ** from the Holy Gospel
E P : 1 1 :010(495) [0833] believe on the Lord Jesus **Christ** (I Tim. 2:6; I John 2:2).
E P : 1 1 :011(496) [0835] their sins, to believe in **Christ**, and to obey God, and only
E P : 1 1 :013(496) [0835] Word of God, which shows us **Christ** as the "book of life."
E P : 1 1 :013(496) [0835] of the Holy Gospel, **Christ** opens and reveals this book for
E P : 1 1 :013(496) [0835] In **Christ** we should seek the eternal election of the
E P : 1 1 :013(496) [0835] who acknowledge his Son, **Christ**, and truly believe on
E P : 1 1 :013(496) [0835] life out of pure grace in **Christ** without any merit of our
E P : 1 1 :020(497) [0837] the most holy merit of **Christ**, but that there is also within
E P : 1 1 :022(497) [0837] Father of our Lord Jesus **Christ** grant us the grace of his
E P : 1 2 :003(498) [0839] 1. That **Christ** did not assume his body and blood from
E P : 1 2 :004(498) [0839] 2. That **Christ** is not true God but that he only has more
E P : 1 2 :005(498) [0839] in the unique merit of **Christ**, but in renewal and in our
E P : 1 2 :020(499) [0841] 1. That all who say that **Christ** according to the flesh is a
E P : 1 2 :020(499) [0841] a right understanding of **Christ** as the reigning king of
E P : 1 2 :021(499) [0841] 2. That in **Christ**'s glorification his flesh received all the
E P : 1 2 :021(499) [0841] in such a way that **Christ** as man is fully equal in rank and
E P : 1 2 :021(499) [0841] that now both natures in **Christ** possess only one divine
E P : 1 2 :021(499) [0841] glory and that the flesh of **Christ** belongs to the essence of
E P : 1 2 :022(499) [0841] the saving knowledge of **Christ**, conversion, repentance,
E P : 1 2 :024(500) [0843] through and by which **Christ** distributes his body and
E P : 1 2 :028(500) [0843] That **Christ** is not a true, essential, natural God, of one
E P : 1 2 :031(500) [0843] judge, our Lord Jesus **Christ**, and that we shall neither
S D : P R :007(502) [0849] to be Christians and gloried in the doctrine of **Christ**.
S D : P R :007(502) [0849] others even denied that **Christ** was eternal and true God.
S D : 0 1 :003(509) [0861] and to magnify more fully **Christ**'s benefits, his precious
S D : 0 1 :006(509) [0861] we are redeemed from this state through **Christ**'s merit.
S D : 0 1 :014(511) [0863] and forgiven before God only for the Lord **Christ**'s sake.
S D : 0 1 :019(511) [0865] of God that apart from **Christ** every person on that
S D : 0 1 :031(513) [0869] nature unless the sin is forgiven for **Christ**'s sake.
S D : 0 1 :043(516) [0873] assumed human nature **Christ** is of one and the same
S D : 0 1 :044(516) [0873] would have to follow that **Christ** either did not assume
S D : 0 1 :044(516) [0873] not assume sin, or that **Christ** assumed sin inasmuch as he
S D : 0 1 :045(516) [0873] sanctifies him and that **Christ** has saved his people from
S D : 0 1 :045(516) [0873] God receives man for **Christ**'s sake into his grace but
S D : 0 2 :004(520) [0881] and brings them to the saving understanding of **Christ**.
S D : 0 2 :025(526) [0891] conversion, faith in **Christ**, regeneration, renewal, and
S D : 0 2 :026(526) [0891] Ps. 51:12); creates us in **Christ** Jesus for good works (Eph.
S D : 0 2 :026(526) [0891] No one can come to **Christ** unless the Father draws him
S D : 0 2 :026(526) [0891] "Apart from me," says **Christ**, "you can do nothing (John
S D : 0 2 :029(527) [0893] "People outside of **Christ** and without faith and the Holy
S D : 0 2 :029(527) [0893] and by pointing out that **Christ** helps us and protects us
S D : 0 2 :029(527) [0893] and power without **Christ** is much too weak for Satan,
S D : 0 2 :030(527) [0893] man by his own powers turn to the Gospel or to **Christ**?
S D : 0 2 :037(528) [0895] the devil and were completely ignorant of God and **Christ**.
S D : 0 2 :039(528) [0895] workmanship, created in **Christ** Jesus for good works,
S D : 0 2 :040(528) [0895] I cannot believe in Jesus **Christ**, my Lord, or come to
S D : 0 2 :040(528) [0895] it in union with Jesus **Christ** in the one true faith."
S D : 0 2 :042(529) [0897] our own powers come to **Christ**, but that God must give
S D : 0 2 :042(529) [0897] and brings us to **Christ** in true faith and keeps us with
S D : 0 2 :043(529) [0897] contrary to the help and grace of our Lord Jesus **Christ**.
S D : 0 2 :043(529) [0897] Outside of **Christ** death and sin are our masters and the
S D : 0 2 :050(530) [0901] Son, our only Saviour and Redeemer, Jesus **Christ**.
S D : 0 2 :050(531) [0901] of their sins and true faith in the Son of God, Jesus **Christ**
S D : 0 2 :051(531) [0901] is heard comes by the preaching of **Christ**" (Rom. 10:17).
S D : 0 2 :054(531) [0903] forgiveness of sins in **Christ** there is kindled in him a spark
S D : 0 2 :054(531) [0903] the forgiveness of sins for **Christ**'s sake and comforts itself
S D : 0 2 :057(532) [0903] For **Christ**, in whom we are elected, offers his grace to all
S D : 0 2 :067(534) [0907] been baptized have put on **Christ**" (Gal. 3:27), are thus
S D : 0 2 :067(534) [0907] liberated will — that is, as **Christ** says, they have again
S D : 0 2 :070(535) [0909] the promise of grace in **Christ**, to have good spiritual
S D : 0 3 :001(539) [0917] the righteousness of **Christ** or of faith which God by grace
S D : 0 3 :002(539) [0917] of God (namely, **Christ** himself as the true, natural,
S D : 0 3 :003(539) [0917] have held and taught that **Christ** is our righteousness only
S D : 0 3 :004(539) [0917] held unanimously that **Christ** is our righteousness, not
S D : 0 3 :004(540) [0917] of the obedience of **Christ**, which, through faith alone, is
S D : 0 3 :006(540) [0917] or rightly understand the riches of the grace of **Christ**."
S D : 0 3 :009(541) [0919] and the resurrection of **Christ**, our Lord, whose obedience
S D : 0 3 :011(541) [0919] we rightly learn to know **Christ** as our redeemer in the
S D : 0 3 :012(541) [0919] by the obedience of **Christ**, our only mediator, or that
S D : 0 3 :013(541) [0919] and accepts the merit of **Christ** in the promise of the holy
S D : 0 3 :014(541) [0919] and the resurrection of **Christ** when he satisfied the law
S D : 0 3 :015(541) [0919] Since **Christ** is not only man, but God and man in one
S D : 0 3 :015(541) [0919] in life and in death, **Christ** rendered for us to his heavenly
S D : 0 3 :017(542) [0921] of the righteousness of **Christ** which God reckons to faith
S D : 0 3 :019(542) [0921] of sins solely for **Christ**'s sake and the subsequent renewal
S D : 0 3 :020(542) [0921] he made us alive together with **Christ**" (Eph. 2:5).
S D : 0 3 :022(543) [0923] but we hold that **Christ** with his perfect obedience covers
S D : 0 3 :022(543) [0923] faith and for the sake of **Christ**'s obedience, which Christ
S D : 0 3 :022(543) [0923] Christ's obedience, which **Christ** rendered to his Father
S D : 0 3 :023(543) [0923] of the only mediator, **Christ**, through faith alone, without
S D : 0 3 :023(543) [0923] the gracious reckoning of **Christ**'s righteousness to us,
S D : 0 3 :025(543) [0923] grace of God, the merit of **Christ**, and faith which accepts
S D : 0 3 :025(543) [0923] the righteousness of **Christ** is reckoned to us and by which
S D : 0 3 :028(544) [0925] are a blessing of **Christ**, the mediator, and a work of the
S D : 0 3 :029(544) [0925] alone through faith in **Christ**, and not through the works
S D : 0 3 :030(544) [0925] due honor to the merit of **Christ** and the grace of God,
S D : 0 3 :030(544) [0925] of the unique merit of **Christ**, the mediator, and which we
S D : 0 3 :030(544) [0925] other virtues, but solely in **Christ** and (in him) in his
S D : 0 3 :031(544) [0925] grace of God, the merit of **Christ**, and the forgiveness of
S D : 0 3 :032(544) [0927] who through faith in **Christ** have been justified possess in
S D : 0 3 :032(545) [0927] passion, and death of **Christ** which is reckoned to faith
S D : 0 3 :032(545) [0927] of eternal life only on account of **Christ**'s obedience.
S D : 0 3 :035(545) [0927] preserve the glory due to **Christ**, the redeemer, and,
S D : 0 3 :038(546) [0929] the grace and the merit of **Christ** in the promise of the
S D : 0 3 :039(546) [0929] entirely for the sake of **Christ**'s merit, which treasures are
S D : 0 3 :041(546) [0929] the grace of God in **Christ** whereby the person is justified.
S D : 0 3 :042(547) [0931] it applies to us and makes our own the merits of **Christ**.
S D : 0 3 :043(547) [0931] already justified through **Christ**, who are reconciled with
S D : 0 3 :043(547) [0931] and who have obtained forgiveness of sins through **Christ**.
S D : 0 3 :043(547) [0931] grace and the merit of **Christ** in the promise of the
S D : 0 3 :046(548) [0933] worthy and fit to have the merit of **Christ** applied to him.
S D : 0 3 :050(548) [0933] reckoned righteousness of **Christ** and through their own
S D : 0 3 :050(548) [0933] part by the reckoning of **Christ**'s righteousness and in part
S D : 0 3 :054(548) [0935] been justified through **Christ** and reconciled with God,
S D : 0 3 :054(549) [0935] sinners on account of the obedience and merit of **Christ**.
S D : 0 3 :055(549) [0935] and alone on the Lord **Christ**, it is important to consider
S D : 0 3 :055(549) [0935] carefully in what way **Christ** is called our righteousness in
S D : 0 3 :055(549) [0935] upon the entire person of **Christ**, who as God and man in
S D : 0 3 :056(549) [0935] For even though **Christ** had been conceived by the Holy
S D : 0 3 :056(549) [0935] the total obedience of **Christ**'s total person, which he
S D : 0 3 :058(550) [0937] nor the human nature of **Christ** by itself is reckoned to us
S D : 0 3 :058(550) [0937] looks at the person of **Christ**, how this person was placed
S D : 0 3 :058(550) [0937] and remitted by sheer grace for **Christ**'s sake alone.
S D : 0 3 :060(550) [0937] 1. The doctrine that **Christ** is our righteousness before
S D : 0 3 :061(550) [0937] 2. That **Christ** is our righteousness only according to his
S D : 0 3 :063(550) [0937] solely to the obedience of **Christ**, but also to his divine
S D : 0 3 :064(550) [0937] trust in the obedience of **Christ** that it can be and remain
S D : 0 4 :002(551) [0939] church, lest the merit of **Christ**, our redeemer, be
S D : 0 4 :007(552) [0941] says, "has been created in **Christ** Jesus for good works."
S D : 0 4 :008(552) [0941] for the sake of the Lord **Christ** through faith, because the
S D : 0 4 :008(552) [0941] God — and that alone for **Christ**'s sake — before that
S D : 0 4 :019(554) [0945] again, they who belong to **Christ** have crucified (that is,
S D : 0 4 :022(555) [0945] of God and the merit of **Christ**, as was explained in the
S D : 0 4 :030(555) [0947] and "We share in **Christ** only if we hold our first
S D : 0 4 :033(556) [0949] to you by grace through **Christ** and which you retain
S D : 0 4 :038(557) [0951] be pleased with them for **Christ**'s sake and he promises to
S D : 0 5 :001(558) [0951] would darken the merit of **Christ** and rob disturbed
S D : 0 5 :002(558) [0953] and mercy of God for **Christ**'s sake, which proclamation
S D : 0 5 :002(558) [0953] have been converted to **Christ** that their unbelief, in which
S D : 0 5 :004(558) [0953] by it the entire teaching of **Christ**, our Lord, which in his
S D : 0 5 :004(559) [0953] beginning of the Gospel of Jesus **Christ**, the Son of God."
S D : 0 5 :004(559) [0953] Similarly when **Christ** after his resurrection commands his
S D : 0 5 :004(559) [0953] it is written, that the **Christ** should suffer and on the third
S D : 0 5 :004(559) [0953] under these heads: repentance to God and faith in **Christ**.
S D : 0 5 :005(559) [0953] For John, **Christ**, and the apostles began in their
S D : 0 5 :006(559) [0953] of St. Mark, where **Christ** said, "Repent and believe in the
S D : 0 5 :008(559) [0953] repentance and faith in **Christ** (Acts 20:21) or repentance
S D : 0 5 :009(559) [0955] there is added faith in **Christ**, whose merit the comforting
S D : 0 5 :010(559) [0955] of the law without **Christ** either produces presumptuous
S D : 0 5 :010(559) [0955] Therefore **Christ** takes the law into his hands and explains
S D : 0 5 :011(560) [0955] Therefore the Spirit of **Christ** must not only comfort but,
S D : 0 5 :011(560) [0955] To this end **Christ** has obtained and sent us the Spirit, and
S D : 0 5 :012(560) [0955] and gives nothing but grace and forgiveness in **Christ**.
S D : 0 5 :012(560) [0955] of the Gospel, just as **Christ** himself did, confirm the
S D : 0 5 :012(560) [0955] sin than the passion and death of **Christ**, his own Son?
S D : 0 5 :012(560) [0955] is not yet the Gospel nor **Christ**'s own proclamation, but
S D : 0 5 :012(560) [0957] For the Gospel and **Christ** are not ordained and given us
S D : 0 5 :013(560) [0957] And again: "**Christ** says, 'The Holy Spirit will convince
S D : 0 5 :019(561) [0957] and commands faith in **Christ**) is the Word of God, the
S D : 0 5 :019(561) [0957] the unbelief involved in men's failure to believe in **Christ**.
S D : 0 5 :019(561) [0957] strictly speaking, teaches about saving faith in **Christ**.
S D : 0 5 :020(561) [0959] this, that the Son of God, **Christ** our Lord, himself
S D : 0 5 :021(562) [0959] not to punish sins but to forgive them for **Christ**'s sake.
S D : 0 5 :022(562) [0959] solely on the Lord Jesus **Christ**, "who was put to death for
S D : 0 5 :024(563) [0961] was our custodian until **Christ** came, that we might be
S D : 0 5 :024(563) [0961] away from but toward the **Christ** who is the end of the
S D : 0 5 :025(563) [0961] of the Gospel of our Lord **Christ** will once more comfort
S D : 0 5 :025(563) [0961] all their sins through **Christ**, accepts them for his sake as
S D : 0 5 :027(563) [0961] the merits and benefits of **Christ**, once more make the
S D : 0 5 :027(563) [0961] and justification through **Christ**, whereas the law is a
S D : 0 6 :005(564) [0963] upon those who through **Christ** have been reconciled with
S D : 0 6 :007(565) [0965] the perfect obedience of **Christ**, so that they are not
S D : 0 6 :017(566) [0967] is driven by the Spirit of **Christ**), he lives according to the
S D : 0 6 :017(567) [0967] Paul calls them, the law of the mind and the law of **Christ**
S D : 0 6 :022(567) [0969] to God through faith for **Christ**'s sake (I Pet. 2:5; Heb.
S D : 0 6 :023(568) [0969] and condemnation of the law through faith in **Christ**.
S D : 0 6 :023(568) [0969] to God through **Christ** because according to their inmost
S D : 0 6 :024(568) [0969] into the obedience of **Christ**, not only with the
S D : 0 7 :001(569) [0971] of the words of **Christ** and of the Augsburg Confession in
S D : 0 7 :002(569) [0973] Holy Supper the body of **Christ** is truly received by
S D : 0 7 :002(569) [0973] body and blood of **Christ** are as far distant from the
S D : 0 7 :002(569) [0973] the body and blood of **Christ** are distant from the signs by
S D : 0 7 :003(569) [0973] presence of the body of **Christ** not as taking place here on
S D : 0 7 :003(569) [0973] spiritually, of the body of **Christ** which is there in heaven,
S D : 0 7 :003(569) [0973] is there in heaven, yes, of **Christ** himself and all his
S D : 0 7 :003(569) [0973] so also the body of **Christ** is now in heaven and not on
S D : 0 7 :004(569) [0973] signs of the absent body of **Christ**, are therein distributed.
S D : 0 7 :004(569) [0973] confessed that the Lord **Christ** is truly present in the
S D : 0 7 :005(570) [0973] by the words of **Christ** to confess that the body of Christ
S D : 0 7 :005(570) [0973] confess that the body of **Christ** is present in the Supper,
S D : 0 7 :005(570) [0973] that through the Spirit of **Christ**, which is everywhere, our
S D : 0 7 :005(570) [0973] in which the Spirit of **Christ** dwells here upon earth, are
S D : 0 7 :005(570) [0973] are united with the body of **Christ**, which is in heaven.
S D : 0 7 :006(570) [0973] than that the Lord **Christ** is present in his Supper truly,
S D : 0 7 :006(570) [0973] with the bread and wine **Christ** gives us his true body and
S D : 0 7 :007(570) [0975] They interpret "to eat **Christ**'s body" as no more than "to
S D : 0 7 :007(570) [0975] or figure of the body of **Christ** which is not in the
S D : 0 7 :007(570) [0975] in such a way that **Christ**'s body is even now present on
S D : 0 7 :008(570) [0975] That is, the body of **Christ** is sacramentally or
S D : 0 7 :008(570) [0975] by faith also of the body of **Christ** which is up in heaven.
S D : 0 7 :008(570) [0975] teaching that the body of **Christ** is essentially present here
S D : 0 7 :009(570) [0975] true body and blood of **Christ** are really present in the
S D : 0 7 :009(571) [0975] that since the body of **Christ** has ascended into heaven it
S D : 0 7 :010(571) [0975] of the Altar, instituted by **Christ** himself, is the true body
S D : 0 7 :010(571) [0975] blood of our Lord Jesus **Christ**, under the bread and
S D : 0 7 :011(571) [0975] the body and blood of **Christ** are truly and essentially
S D : 0 7 :011(571) [0975] If the body of **Christ** were not truly present, but only the

Continued ▶

SD : 0 7 :011(571) [0975] in the body of **Christ**, etc., it would follow that the bread
SD : 0 7 :011(571) [0975] a participation not in the body but in the spirit of **Christ**.
SD : 0 7 :011(571) [0975] the bodily presence of **Christ** in the Holy Communion."
SD : 0 7 :011(571) [0975] quoted to the effect that **Christ** dwells bodily in the
SD : 0 7 :013(571) [0977] sacrament of the body and blood of **Christ**, namely thus:
SD : 0 7 :014(571) [0977] the body and blood of **Christ** are truly and essentially
SD : 0 7 :014(571) [0977] the body and blood of **Christ**) and do not believe that the
SD : 0 7 :014(571) [0977] the body and blood of **Christ** are locally enclosed in the
SD : 0 7 :014(572) [0977] sacramental union the bread is the body of **Christ**, etc.
SD : 0 7 :015(572) [0977] maintain that the body of **Christ** is present apart from the
SD : 0 7 :016(572) [0977] sacrament, performed by **Christ**, that makes it valid in
SD : 0 7 :016(572) [0977] they hold that, where **Christ**'s institution and command
SD : 0 7 :016(572) [0977] the body and blood of **Christ** are truly distributed to the
SD : 0 7 :016(572) [0977] through faith in **Christ** there receive the grace and merits
SD : 0 7 :016(572) [0977] the grace and merits of **Christ**, are incorporated into
SD : 0 7 :016(572) [0977] are incorporated into **Christ**, and are washed by the blood
SD : 0 7 :016(572) [0977] into Christ, and are washed by the blood of **Christ**."
SD : 0 7 :017(572) [0979] agree in the most exact way with the words of **Christ**.
SD : 0 7 :018(572) [0979] namely, that the body of **Christ**, together with all his
SD : 0 7 :018(572) [0979] presence of the body of the Lord **Christ** through faith.
SD : 0 7 :019(572) [0979] body and blood of Jesus **Christ** which are given and
SD : 0 7 :020(573) [0979] true body and blood of **Christ** in and under the bread and
SD : 0 7 :020(573) [0979] the bread and wine which **Christ**'s word commands us
SD : 0 7 :021(573) [0979] and wine but is and is called **Christ**'s body and blood."
SD : 0 7 :022(573) [0979] How can bread and wine be the body and blood of **Christ**
SD : 0 7 :022(573) [0979] Here we have **Christ**'s word, 'Take eat, this is my body.
SD : 0 7 :022(573) [0979] thinks that he can correct **Christ** and change what he has
SD : 0 7 :023(573) [0979] with the words it is truly the body and blood of **Christ**.
SD : 0 7 :023(573) [0979] For it must be as **Christ**'s lips speak and declare, since he
SD : 0 7 :024(573) [0979] true sacrament (that is, **Christ**'s body and blood) just as
SD : 0 7 :024(573) [0981] the body and blood of **Christ**, so little can anyone alter or
SD : 0 7 :026(573) [0981] **Christ** does not say, 'If you believe and are worthy, you
SD : 0 7 :027(574) [0981] of the body and blood of **Christ** in the holy Supper from
SD : 0 7 :029(574) [0981] appear before the judgment seat of our Lord Jesus **Christ**.
SD : 0 7 :031(574) [0983] the Last Judgment at the coming of the Lord **Christ**.
SD : 0 7 :032(574) [0983] the body and blood of **Christ** are truly eaten and drunk in
SD : 0 7 :035(575) [0983] addition to the words of **Christ** and of St. Paul (the bread
SD : 0 7 :035(575) [0983] Supper "is true body of **Christ**" or "a participation in the
SD : 0 7 :035(575) [0983] in the body of **Christ**"), we at times also use the formulas
SD : 0 7 :035(575) [0985] substance of the bread and the body of **Christ**.
SD : 0 7 :036(575) [0985] Word dwelt in us," or "In **Christ** the whole fullness of the
SD : 0 7 :036(575) [0985] with him," or "God was in **Christ**," and similar
SD : 0 7 :037(575) [0985] analogy to the words of **Christ**'s testament, "This is my
SD : 0 7 :037(575) [0985] For as in **Christ** two distinct and untransformed natures
SD : 0 7 :037(575) [0985] the true natural body of **Christ**, are present together here
SD : 0 7 :038(576) [0985] of the body and blood of **Christ** with the bread and wine
SD : 0 7 :038(576) [0985] that of the two natures in **Christ**, but a sacramental
SD : 0 7 :038(576) [0985] still accept the words of **Christ** in their strict sense and as
SD : 0 7 :038(576) [0985] (that is, the words of **Christ**'s testament), "This is my
SD : 0 7 :039(576) [0985] believe that just as Jesus **Christ**, our Saviour, was
SD : 0 7 :039(576) [0985] is the true flesh and blood of the Lord Jesus **Christ**."
SD : 0 7 :040(576) [0985] the formula which **Christ** employed in the Last Supper.
SD : 0 7 :043(576) [0987] Lord and Saviour Jesus **Christ** concerning whom, as our
SD : 0 7 :044(577) [0987] and Redeemer Jesus **Christ**, selected his words with great
SD : 0 7 :044(577) [0987] union of Christians with **Christ** their head and with one
SD : 0 7 :044(577) [0987] Under these circumstances **Christ** said of the blessed and
SD : 0 7 :045(577) [0987] Son of God, Jesus **Christ**, our Lord, Creator, and
SD : 0 7 :046(577) [0987] the promised seed, **Christ**, who was to be born of Isaac.
SD : 0 7 :048(578) [0989] Lord and Saviour Jesus **Christ**, which in themselves are
SD : 0 7 :048(578) [0989] For since **Christ** gave this command at table and during
SD : 0 7 :048(578) [0989] as though the body of **Christ** were spiritual bread or a
SD : 0 7 :049(578) [0989] **Christ** himself likewise precluded a metonymy (that is, a
SD : 0 7 :050(578) [0989] of the words of Jesus **Christ** than the Lord Christ himself,
SD : 0 7 :050(578) [0989] Christ than the Lord **Christ** himself, who best understands
SD : 0 7 :052(578) [0991] same information after **Christ**'s ascension (I Cor. 11:25),
SD : 0 7 :052(578) [0991] and truthful words of **Christ**, "This is my body," and apply
SD : 0 7 :054(579) [0991] of the words of **Christ** which St. Paul gives us in I Cor.
SD : 0 7 :054(579) [0991] we bless, is it not a participation in the blood of **Christ**?
SD : 0 7 :054(579) [0991] in the body of **Christ**?") are to be regarded diligently and
SD : 0 7 :054(579) [0991] of the body and blood of **Christ** in the Communion.
SD : 0 7 :054(579) [0991] not only the cup which **Christ** blessed in the Last Supper
SD : 0 7 :054(579) [0991] not only the bread which **Christ** himself broke and
SD : 0 7 :054(579) [0991] in the body and blood of **Christ**, so that all who eat this
SD : 0 7 :054(579) [0991] receive and partake of the true body and blood of **Christ**.
SD : 0 7 :055(579) [0991] For if the body of **Christ** were not truly and essentially
SD : 0 7 :055(579) [0991] virtue, and the benefits of **Christ**, as the Apology argues
SD : 0 7 :056(579) [0991] in the body of **Christ** through faith, as the
SD : 0 7 :056(579) [0991] the spirit or faith is participation in the body of **Christ**.
SD : 0 7 :056(579) [0991] in the body of **Christ**, and that means that all who receive
SD : 0 7 :056(579) [0991] the blessed bread also partake of the body of **Christ**.
SD : 0 7 :056(579) [0991] oral eating of the body of **Christ** in which both the godly
SD : 0 7 :057(579) [0993] the Lord and partaking of the body and blood of **Christ**.
SD : 0 7 :057(579) [0993] the body and blood of **Christ** to their own judgment and
SD : 0 7 :057(579) [0993] participate in the body of **Christ**, St. Paul certainly could
SD : 0 7 :057(579) [0993] a spiritual fellowship with **Christ**, which no one could
SD : 0 7 :058(580) [0993] way with the words of **Christ** by saying, "The bread which
SD : 0 7 :058(580) [0993] is the distributed body of **Christ**, or the common body of
SD : 0 7 :058(580) [0993] or the common body of **Christ** distributed among those
SD : 0 7 :059(580) [0993] Lord's Supper the body of **Christ** is received only
SD : 0 7 :059(580) [0993] in the body of **Christ** (that is, it is that whereby we have
SD : 0 7 :059(580) [0993] in the body of **Christ**, which is the church), or it is the
SD : 0 7 :059(580) [0993] believers are united with **Christ**, just as the Word of the
SD : 0 7 :059(580) [0993] are spiritually united with **Christ** and are incorporated
SD : 0 7 :059(580) [0993] into the body of **Christ**, which is the church."
SD : 0 7 :060(580) [0993] true body and blood of **Christ** orally in the sacrament, but
SD : 0 7 :060(580) [0993] have no fellowship with **Christ**, who come to the Lord's
SD : 0 7 :060(580) [0993] sin grievously against the body and blood of **Christ**.
SD : 0 7 :060(580) [0993] of profaning the body and blood of the Lord Jesus **Christ**.
SD : 0 7 :060(580) [0995] violent hands upon the body of **Christ** and murdered him.
SD : 0 7 :061(580) [0995] There is therefore a twofold eating of the flesh of **Christ**.
SD : 0 7 :061(580) [0995] one is spiritual, of which **Christ** speaks chiefly in John
SD : 0 7 :062(581) [0995] Word of God, in which **Christ**, true God and man,
SD : 0 7 :062(581) [0995] for the sake of Jesus **Christ**, and hold to it in all difficulty
SD : 0 7 :063(581) [0995] eating of the body of **Christ** is oral or sacramental, when
SD : 0 7 :063(581) [0995] of the true, essential body and blood of **Christ** orally.
SD : 0 7 :063(581) [0995] are truly forgiven, that **Christ** dwells and is efficacious in
SD : 0 7 :064(581) [0995] This is what **Christ**'s words of institution say, when at
SD : 0 7 :065(581) [0995] But **Christ** adds another command, and in addition to the
SD : 0 7 :066(581) [0995] with these words of **Christ**'s institution and St. Paul's
SD : 0 7 :066(581) [0997] that the body of **Christ** is received not only spiritually
SD : 0 7 :067(582) [0997] ridicule the Lord **Christ**, St. Paul, and the entire church
SD : 0 7 :067(582) [0997] describe the majesty of **Christ** as "Satan's dung, by which
SD : 0 7 :068(582) [0997] oral eating of the body of **Christ** burden themselves with
SD : 0 7 :068(582) [0997] punishments) and profane the body and blood of **Christ**.
SD : 0 7 :069(582) [0997] and the benefits of **Christ** because of their great impurity,
SD : 0 7 :070(582) [0997] like this, as **Christ** says, "Come unto me, all who labor
SD : 0 7 :071(582) [0997] but solely in the merits of **Christ**, of which the distressed
SD : 0 7 :072(582) [0997] in the body and blood of **Christ**, the one through faith
SD : 0 7 :074(583) [0999] presence of the body and blood of **Christ** in the Supper.
SD : 0 7 :074(583) [0999] Word, institution, and ordinance of our Lord Jesus **Christ**
SD : 0 7 :075(583) [0999] almighty words of Jesus **Christ** which he spoke in the first
SD : 0 7 :075(583) [0999] is observed according to **Christ**'s institution and where his
SD : 0 7 :075(583) [0999] the body and blood of **Christ** are truly present,
SD : 0 7 :075(583) [0999] of the same words which **Christ** spoke in the first Supper.
SD : 0 7 :075(583) [0999] blessed bread and cup, **Christ** himself is still active through
SD : 0 7 :076(583) [0999] *Sermon on the Passion*: "**Christ** himself prepares this table
SD : 0 7 :076(583) [0999] No human being, but only **Christ** himself who was
SD : 0 7 :076(583) [0999] bread and wine set before us the body and blood of **Christ**
SD : 0 7 :077(583) [0999] and ordinance of **Christ** that, from the beginning of the
SD : 0 7 :078(583) [1001] is, 'This is the body of **Christ**,' nothing would happen, but
SD : 0 7 :080(584) [1001] we render obedience to the command of **Christ**, 'This do.'
SD : 0 7 :081(584) [1001] of the body and blood of **Christ**, the forgiveness of sins,
SD : 0 7 :081(584) [1001] and all the benefits which **Christ** has won for us by his
SD : 0 7 :082(584) [1001] the body and blood of **Christ** are distributed to us to eat
SD : 0 7 :083(584) [1001] blessing or recitation of **Christ**'s words of institution by
SD : 0 7 :083(584) [1001] of the Lord's Supper as **Christ** ordained it is not observed
SD : 0 7 :084(584) [1001] But the command of **Christ**, "Do this," which
SD : 0 7 :085(584) [1001] from the use instituted by **Christ**, or apart from the
SD : 0 7 :085(584) [1001] if one does not observe **Christ**'s institution as he ordained
SD : 0 7 :086(584) [1003] Supper as ordained by **Christ**: the consecration or words
SD : 0 7 :086(585) [1003] the blessed bread and wine, the body and blood of **Christ**.
SD : 0 7 :088(585) [1003] oral eating of the body of **Christ**, in which here on earth
SD : 0 7 :088(585) [1003] reception of the body of **Christ** takes place only spiritually
SD : 0 7 :088(585) [1003] effects the presence of **Christ**'s body in the Holy Supper
SD : 0 7 :088(585) [1003] do not receive the body of **Christ** because it is not present
SD : 0 7 :089(585) [1003] God and Saviour, Jesus **Christ**, which always remain
SD : 0 7 :089(585) [1003] believe or do not believe, **Christ** nonetheless remains
SD : 0 7 :090(585) [1003] presence of the body of **Christ** and to receive it, rather
SD : 0 7 :090(585) [1003] the omnipotence of our Lord and Saviour, Jesus **Christ**.
SD : 0 7 :091(585) [1003] the ascension of **Christ**, concerning his withdrawal from
SD : 0 7 :092(586) [1005] clear understanding of **Christ**'s word and testament to a
SD : 0 7 :094(586) [1005] of our faith: that Jesus **Christ** is essential, natural, true,
SD : 0 7 :098(586) [1005] the one body of **Christ** has three different modes, or all
SD : 0 7 :099(586) [1005] (I Tim. 6:15), and, "When **Christ** who is our life appears"
SD : 0 7 :099(586) [1005] adduce concerning **Christ**'s leaving the world and going to
SD : 0 7 :101(587) [1007] must posit this essence of **Christ** since he is one person
SD : 0 7 :102(587) [1007] certainly that the body of **Christ** cannot in any
SD : 0 7 :103(587) [1007] more modes whereby **Christ**'s body can be anywhere.
SD : 0 7 :103(587) [1007] of presence to the body of **Christ** although they are unable
SD : 0 7 :104(587) [1009] are incorporated into **Christ** and become true, spiritual
SD : 0 7 :105(588) [1009] mode according to which **Christ** is present in the Holy
SD : 0 7 :105(588) [1009] the body and blood of **Christ** in the Holy Supper are
SD : 0 7 :106(588) [1009] of the body and blood of **Christ** in the Holy Supper is
SD : 0 7 :106(588) [1009] true and eternal God, our Lord and Saviour Jesus **Christ**.
SD : 0 7 :108(588) [1009] of the body and blood of **Christ**, so that only the mere
SD : 0 7 :108(588) [1009] longer bread, the body of **Christ** is present even apart
SD : 0 7 :110(588) [1011] to the explicit command and institution of **Christ**, etc.
SD : 0 7 :111(589) [1011] of the body and blood of **Christ** against the
SD : 0 7 :113(589) [1011] of the body and blood of **Christ** in the Supper, but
SD : 0 7 :114(589) [1011] of the body and blood of **Christ** in the Supper, and the
SD : 0 7 :114(589) [1011] in the Supper the body of **Christ** is partaken of only
SD : 0 7 :115(589) [1011] of the far-distant body of **Christ** (for example, just as
SD : 0 7 :115(589) [1011] so the absent body of **Christ** with its merit is spiritual food
SD : 0 7 :116(589) [1011] of the absent body of **Christ**, and through these signs, as
SD : 0 7 :116(589) [1011] of the body and blood of **Christ** as truly as in the Supper
SD : 0 7 :116(589) [1013] body and blood of **Christ**, distributed to us, but through
SD : 0 7 :117(589) [1013] of the far-distant body of **Christ**, and that in this way we
SD : 0 7 :117(590) [1013] wine have a similarity with the body and blood of **Christ**.
SD : 0 7 :118(590) [1013] the body and blood of **Christ** are only received and
SD : 0 7 :119(590) [1013] ascension to heaven **Christ** is so confined and
SD : 0 7 :119(590) [1013] is celebrated according to **Christ**'s institution on earth, but
SD : 0 7 :119(590) [1013] the words in Acts 3:21, "**Christ** must take possession of
SD : 0 7 :119(590) [1013] of heaven," to read "**Christ** must be received by heaven"
SD : 0 7 :119(590) [1013] by heaven" — that is, **Christ** must be so taken in or
SD : 0 7 :120(590) [1013] the assertion that **Christ** could not or would not have
SD : 0 7 :121(590) [1013] and the omnipotence of **Christ** but faith that achieves the
SD : 0 7 :121(590) [1013] presence of the body of **Christ** in the Holy Supper, whence
SD : 0 7 :122(590) [1013] according to the words of **Christ**'s institution believers are
SD : 0 7 :122(590) [1013] to seek the body of **Christ** in the bread and wine of the
SD : 0 7 :122(590) [1013] place in heaven where **Christ** is present with his body and
SD : 0 7 :123(590) [1013] only bear the name of **Christ** but do not have a right,
SD : 0 7 :123(590) [1015] wine in the Supper and not the body and blood of **Christ**.
SD : 0 7 :123(590) [1015] not the body and the blood of **Christ** for their judgment.
SD : 0 7 :126(591) [1015] heretic can or will deny **Christ** himself, true God and
SD : 0 8 :000(591) [1015] VIII. The Person of **Christ**
SD : 0 8 :001(591) [1015] the Augsburg Confession concerning the person of **Christ**.
SD : 0 8 :002(591) [1015] body and blood of Jesus **Christ** in the Lord's Supper on
SD : 0 8 :002(591) [1015] by saying that the body of **Christ** could not be a true and
SD : 0 8 :002(592) [1017] to God alone and the body of **Christ** is incapable of it.
SD : 0 8 :004(592) [1017] about the person of **Christ** with which the
SD : 0 8 :004(592) [1017] true, essential presence of the body and blood of **Christ**.
SD : 0 8 :004(592) [1017] nature in the person of **Christ** that transcends or
SD : 0 8 :006(592) [1017] but in such a way that **Christ** Jesus is henceforth in *one*
SD : 0 8 :006(592) [1017] to the flesh, is the **Christ**, who is God over all, blessed for
SD : 0 8 :007(592) [1017] natures in the person of **Christ** will henceforth never be
SD : 0 8 :007(592) [1017] other, but in the person of **Christ** each remains in its

Continued ▶

SD : 08 :011(593) [1019] neither nature in **Christ** henceforth subsists for itself so as
SD : 08 :011(593) [1019] to the total person of **Christ**; and that without his
SD : 08 :011(593) [1019] his deity the person of **Christ**, or the Son of God who has
SD : 08 :011(593) [1019] Therefore **Christ** is not two different persons, but one
SD : 08 :012(593) [1019] assumed human nature in **Christ** not only possesses and
SD : 08 :013(593) [1019] 8. But **Christ** did not receive this majesty, to which he was
SD : 08 :015(594) [1019] make two Christs, so that **Christ** is one person and God
SD : 08 :015(594) [1019] person and God the Word who dwells in **Christ** is another
SD : 08 :016(594) [1021] godlessly that the Lord **Christ** was a mere man in whom
SD : 08 :016(594) [1021] each other and that in **Christ** they have no communion at
SD : 08 :016(594) [1021] at all, just as if **Christ** were one individual and God the
SD : 08 :017(594) [1021] natures in the person of **Christ** are united in such a way
SD : 08 :019(595) [1021] natures in the person of **Christ** is far different from this.
SD : 08 :019(595) [1021] nature in the person of **Christ** is far different, much
SD : 08 :023(595) [1023] and human natures in **Christ**, according to our plain
SD : 08 :023(595) [1023] said about the majesty of **Christ** according to his human
SD : 08 :023(595) [1023] natures in the person of **Christ** did not exist in deed and
SD : 08 :025(596) [1023] On this basis, likewise, **Christ** performed all his miracles
SD : 08 :028(596) [1025] and earth, in which **Christ** has been installed according to
SD : 08 :029(597) [1025] union of both natures in **Christ**, the way Jesus, the son of
SD : 08 :030(597) [1025] in such a way that in **Christ** the whole fullness of deity
SD : 08 :032(597) [1027] of natures in the person of **Christ** did not truly exist.
SD : 08 :034(597) [1027] that even we, in whom **Christ** dwells only by grace, have
SD : 08 :034(597) [1027] only by grace, have in **Christ**, because of this exalted
SD : 08 :034(597) [1027] the apostle says that "in **Christ** the whole fullness of the
SD : 08 :035(597) [1027] make about the person of **Christ**, its natures, and their
SD : 08 :036(598) [1027] In the first place, since in **Christ** two distinct natures are
SD : 08 :037(598) [1027] flesh" (Rom. 1:3), and "**Christ** was put to death in the
SD : 08 :039(598) [1027] is said about the deity of **Christ** which after all belongs to
SD : 08 :039(598) [1027] it not necessary that the **Christ** should suffer these things
SD : 08 :039(598) [1029] trick and substitutes the human nature for **Christ**.
SD : 08 :040(598) [1029] construct a kind of **Christ** after whom I would not want
SD : 08 :040(598) [1029] a Christian, that is, a **Christ** who is and does no more in
SD : 08 :040(599) [1029] suffered for me, then **Christ** would be a poor Saviour for
SD : 08 :041(599) [1029] are one person in **Christ**, the Scriptures ascribe to the
SD : 08 :042(599) [1029] must say that the person (pointing to **Christ**) suffers, dies.
SD : 08 :043(599) [1029] *alloeosis* stands, then **Christ** will have to be two persons,
SD : 08 :043(599) [1029] we regard our Lord **Christ** as God and man in one
SD : 08 :046(600) [1031] as far as the discharge of **Christ**'s office is concerned, the
SD : 08 :047(600) [1031] Thus **Christ** is our mediator, redeemer, king, high priest,
SD : 08 :049(600) [1031] of the divine nature in **Christ** through the incarnation, nor
SD : 08 :050(600) [1031] nature in the person of **Christ** is concerned, some wanted
SD : 08 :050(600) [1031] to the human nature in **Christ** which transcends or
SD : 08 :051(600) [1031] the human nature in **Christ** is personally united with the
SD : 08 :051(600) [1031] with the divine nature in **Christ**, the former (when it was
SD : 08 :051(601) [1033] for the exercise of **Christ**'s office, the human nature in
SD : 08 :051(601) [1033] the human nature in **Christ** is employed after its own
SD : 08 :052(601) [1033] the human nature in **Christ** is endowed and adorned are
SD : 08 :052(601) [1033] what the human nature in **Christ** could or should be
SD : 08 :053(601) [1033] thoroughly than the Lord **Christ** himself what Christ has
SD : 08 :053(601) [1033] Lord Christ himself what **Christ** has received through the
SD : 08 :053(601) [1033] argue that the human nature in **Christ** is not capable of it.
SD : 08 :054(601) [1033] correct and true that **Christ**'s human nature in and by
SD : 08 :054(601) [1033] Scriptures, ascribe to the assumed human nature in **Christ**
SD : 08 :055(601) [1033] to the man **Christ** (John 5:21, 27; 6:39, 40; Matt. 28:18;
SD : 08 :057(602) [1035] the Scriptures testify that **Christ** received in time he
SD : 08 :058(602) [1035] has been given to **Christ** because he is the Son of Man and
SD : 08 :059(602) [1035] only the divine nature in **Christ** but also his blood actually
SD : 08 :059(602) [1035] John 6:48-58 says that **Christ**'s flesh is a life-giving food,
SD : 08 :059(602) [1035] decreed that the flesh of **Christ** has the power to give life.
SD : 08 :060(602) [1035] and must believe that **Christ** received all this according to
SD : 08 :060(602) [1035] communicated to the assumed human nature in **Christ**.
SD : 08 :060(602) [1035] since both natures in **Christ** are united in such a way that
SD : 08 :061(602) [1035] glory were not given to **Christ**'s assumed human nature in
SD : 08 :061(602) [1035] to the divine nature is **Christ** equal with the Father, but
SD : 08 :061(603) [1037] not confuse, equalize, or abolish the natures in **Christ**.
SD : 08 :061(603) [1037] life is not in the flesh of **Christ** the way it is in his divine
SD : 08 :062(603) [1037] way that the humanity of **Christ** has them of itself and
SD : 08 :062(603) [1037] that the human nature in **Christ** has completely laid aside
SD : 08 :062(603) [1037] of the natures in **Christ** or of their essential properties be
SD : 08 :063(603) [1037] correctly the majesty of **Christ** by way of contrast, we
SD : 08 :064(603) [1037] that the human nature in **Christ** has received this majesty
SD : 08 :064(603) [1037] of the deity dwells in **Christ** (Col. 2:9), not as in other
SD : 08 :066(604) [1039] there is and remains in **Christ** only a single divine
SD : 08 :066(604) [1039] *and through* the assumed exalted human nature of **Christ**.
SD : 08 :067(604) [1039] the human nature of **Christ** has been exalted either as if
SD : 08 :067(604) [1039] or as if this majesty is in **Christ**'s human nature only in
SD : 08 :069(604) [1039] would be made between **Christ** according to his human
SD : 08 :069(604) [1039] holy people, and thus **Christ** would be robbed of his
SD : 08 :070(604) [1041] is he personally united with them as in the case of **Christ**.
SD : 08 :070(605) [1041] of the personal union that **Christ** says, also according to
SD : 08 :071(605) [1041] into the human nature of **Christ** of such a kind that
SD : 08 :071(605) [1041] Thereby **Christ**'s human nature would be denied and
SD : 08 :072(605) [1041] Father gave his Spirit to **Christ**, his beloved Son,
SD : 08 :072(605) [1041] does not rest upon **Christ** the Lord according to his
SD : 08 :073(605) [1041] Rather, since **Christ** according to the Godhead is the
SD : 08 :073(605) [1041] say) is communicated to **Christ** according to the flesh that
SD : 08 :076(606) [1043] and truth in the person of **Christ**, things are attributed to
SD : 08 :076(606) [1043] things are attributed to **Christ** according to the flesh that
SD : 08 :076(606) [1043] when they stated that **Christ**'s flesh is a life-giving flesh,
SD : 08 :077(606) [1043] that only the deity of **Christ** is present with us in the
SD : 08 :077(606) [1043] and that this presence of **Christ** in no way involves his
SD : 08 :077(606) [1043] such presence only to **Christ**, and to no other human
SD : 08 :078(606) [1043] the majesty of the man **Christ**, which Christ received
SD : 08 :078(606) [1043] of the man Christ, which **Christ** received according to his
SD : 08 :078(606) [1043] human nature of his, **Christ** can be and is present
SD : 08 :078(607) [1043] one-half of the person of **Christ**, but the entire person to
SD : 08 :080(607) [1045] about the majesty of **Christ** according to the human
SD : 08 :081(607) [1045] writes about the person of **Christ**: "Since he is a man like
SD : 08 :081(607) [1045] that everything is full of **Christ** through and through, also
SD : 08 :082(607) [1045] and say that wherever **Christ** is according to his deity, he
SD : 08 :082(607) [1045] then you must also say, '**Christ** the man is present too.'
SD : 08 :084(607) [1045] he would remain a poor **Christ** for me if he were present
SD : 08 :085(608) [1045] For the humanity of **Christ** has not, like the deity, existed
SD : 08 :086(608) [1047] of the majesty of **Christ** at the right hand of God in
SD : 08 :087(608) [1047] error to deprive **Christ** according to his humanity of this
SD : 08 :090(609) [1047] that the human nature in **Christ** is everywhere present in
SD : 08 :091(609) [1049] that the human nature in **Christ** has been equalized with
SD : 08 :092(609) [1049] that the humanity of **Christ** is locally extended into every
SD : 08 :092(609) [1049] his true human nature, **Christ**'s omnipotence and wisdom
SD : 08 :092(609) [1049] his divine omnipotence **Christ** can be present with his
SD : 08 :093(609) [1049] mere human nature of **Christ** alone, with which the Son
SD : 08 :094(609) [1049] of the holy sacraments **Christ** is present with us on earth
SD : 08 :095(609) [1049] assumed human nature in **Christ** does not share in deed
SD : 08 :096(609) [1049] the Holy Scriptures call **Christ** a mystery over which all
SD : 08 :096(609) [1049] intellect captive to obey **Christ**, comfort themselves
SD : 08 :096(610) [1049] flesh and blood have in **Christ** been made to sit so high at
SD : 09 :000(610) [1049] IX. **Christ**'s Descent into Hell
SD : 09 :001(610) [1049] of the article on **Christ**'s descent into hell have been
SD : 09 :001(610) [1051] "I believe in the Lord **Christ**, God's Son, who died, was
SD : 09 :003(610) [1051] the preceding one, how **Christ** has been made to sit at the
SD : 09 :003(610) [1053] can take us or any believer in **Christ** captive or harm us.
SD : 10 :011(612) [1055] is written, "For freedom **Christ** has set us free; stand fast
SD : 10 :011(612) [1055] which we have in **Christ** Jesus, that they might bring us
SD : 10 :017(614) [1059] particularly mindful that **Christ** says, "So everyone who
SD : 10 :022(615) [1061] **Christ** commanded, 'Beware of false prophets' (Matt.
SD : 11 :005(617) [1065] in love to be his sons through Jesus **Christ**" (Eph. 1:4, 5).
SD : 11 :008(617) [1065] will and pleasure in **Christ** Jesus it is also a cause which
SD : 11 :013(619) [1067] and ordinance of God in **Christ** Jesus, who is the genuine
SD : 11 :014(619) [1069] Eph. 1:4ff.) and as **Christ** likewise does in the
SD : 11 :015(619) [1069] 1. That through **Christ** the human race has truly been
SD : 11 :015(619) [1069] suffering, and death **Christ** has earned for us "the
SD : 11 :016(619) [1069] merit and these benefits of **Christ** are to be offered, given,
SD : 11 :018(619) [1069] all who in sincere repentance and true faith accept **Christ**.
SD : 11 :023(619) [1069] are to be saved through **Christ**, and also ordained that in
SD : 11 :026(620) [1071] brought it forth through **Christ** so that it should be
SD : 11 :027(620) [1071] "We are ambassadors in **Christ**'s stead, and God is
SD : 11 :028(620) [1071] Therefore **Christ** has commanded to preach "repentance
SD : 11 :028(620) [1071] **Christ** has taken away the sin of the world (John 1:29); he
SD : 11 :028(620) [1071] **Christ** declares, "Come unto me, all who are heavy-laden,
SD : 11 :028(621) [1071] "comes through faith in **Christ** to all and on all who
SD : 11 :028(621) [1071] that all who believe on **Christ** should have eternal life"
SD : 11 :028(621) [1073] It is **Christ**'s command that all in common to whom
SD : 11 :030(621) [1073] the Gospel, believe on **Christ**, pray and give thanks, are
SD : 11 :033(621) [1073] of God, even as **Christ** answered the question, "Lord, will
SD : 11 :033(621) [1073] yourself first with **Christ** and his Gospel so that you learn
SD : 11 :037(622) [1075] For this reason **Christ** has the promises of the Gospel
SD : 11 :039(623) [1077] do not truly believe in **Christ** (Mark 16:16), make only an
SD : 11 :039(623) [1077] righteousness and salvation outside of **Christ** (Rom. 9:31).
SD : 11 :040(623) [1077] and save all who accept **Christ** through true faith, so he
SD : 11 :041(623) [1077] through the Word, as **Christ** says, "How often would I
SD : 11 :043(623) [1077] and merit, purely by grace and solely for **Christ**'s sake.
SD : 11 :043(623) [1077] his purpose" by grace in **Christ** (Rom. 9:11; II Tim. 1:9).
SD : 11 :046(624) [1079] of our Saviour, Jesus **Christ**, out of which no one can
SD : 11 :047(624) [1079] separate us from the love of God in **Christ**?" (Rom. 8:35).
SD : 11 :049(624) [1079] from the love of God in **Christ** Jesus" (Rom. 8:28, 29, 35,
SD : 11 :052(625) [1081] have been revealed in **Christ** and of which we have spoken
SD : 11 :065(626) [1083] God's eternal election in **Christ**, and not outside of or
SD : 11 :065(627) [1083] election in Christ, and not outside of or apart from **Christ**
SD : 11 :065(627) [1083] we have been elected in **Christ** "before the foundation of
SD : 11 :065(627) [1083] And **Christ** says, "Come to me, all who are heavy-laden,
SD : 11 :065(627) [1085] And of the Holy Spirit **Christ** says, "He will glorify me"
SD : 11 :066(627) [1085] Spirit, directs all men to **Christ** as to the book of life in
SD : 11 :066(627) [1085] he would save through **Christ**, as Christ himself says, "No
SD : 11 :066(627) [1085] save through Christ, as **Christ** himself says, "No one
SD : 11 :067(627) [1085] **Christ**, "the only begotten Son, who is in the bosom of the
SD : 11 :068(627) [1085] and come to **Christ**, and according to his own word Christ
SD : 11 :068(627) [1085] to his own word **Christ** will not turn them away, "Him
SD : 11 :069(627) [1085] that we may come to **Christ**, the Holy Spirit creates true
SD : 11 :070(627) [1085] they should listen to **Christ**, who is the "book of life" and
SD : 11 :071(627) [1085] According to **Christ**'s teaching they are to desist from sin,
SD : 11 :075(628) [1087] but solely on the merit of **Christ** and the gracious will of
SD : 11 :076(628) [1087] that no one comes to **Christ** unless the Father draw him.
SD : 11 :078(629) [1089] with the Pharisees and their party at the time of **Christ**.
SD : 11 :083(630) [1091] who repent and believe in **Christ**; second, that he would
SD : 11 :087(631) [1093] through sheer mercy in **Christ** without our merit and good
SD : 11 :087(631) [1093] be his son through Jesus **Christ**, according to the purpose
SD : 11 :088(631) [1093] the most holy merit of **Christ**, but that there is also within
SD : 11 :088(631) [1093] laid") God elected us in **Christ** — "in order that God's
SD : 11 :089(631) [1093] their eternal election in **Christ** and in his holy Gospel as
SD : 11 :089(631) [1093] their sins, and to faith in **Christ** and promises them the
SD : 11 :090(631) [1093] he has revealed to us in **Christ**, out of whose hand "no one
SD : 11 :096(632) [1095] him for ever through the sole merit of **Christ**, and so forth
SD : 12 :006(633) [1097] Father of our Lord Jesus **Christ** has appointed us teachers
SD : 12 :010(633) [1097] obedience and merit of **Christ** but in renewal and in our
SD : 12 :025(635) [1099] 16. That **Christ** did not assume his flesh and blood from
SD : 12 :026(635) [1099] 17. That **Christ** is not truly and essentially God but only
SD : 12 :029(635) [1101] has a true knowledge of **Christ**, the reigning king of
SD : 12 :029(635) [1101] to his assumed human nature **Christ** is a creature.
SD : 12 :029(635) [1101] through the exaltation **Christ**'s flesh assumed all the divine
SD : 12 :029(635) [1101] so that the two natures of **Christ** have but one kind of
SD : 12 :029(635) [1101] will, and glory and so that **Christ**'s flesh belongs to the
SD : 12 :030(635) [1101] the saving knowledge of **Christ**, conversion, repentance,
SD : 12 :032(635) [1101] not means through which **Christ** distributes his body and
SD : 12 :036(635) [1101] Arians who teach that **Christ** is not a true, essential, and
SD : 12 :040(636) [1103] judgment seat of Jesus **Christ** and for which we shall give

Christs (3)

EP : 08 :005(487) [0819] that there are not two **Christs**, one the Son of God and
SD : 08 :006(592) [1017] now two persons or two **Christs**, but in such a way that
SD : 08 :015(594) [1019] other and thus make two **Christs**, so that Christ is one

Christendom (23)

PR : PR :002(003) [0007] proclaimed in all of **Christendom** throughout the wide
PR : PR :022(012) [0021] God and the whole of **Christendom** that it is in no way
AG : 26 :044(070) [0075] is not in conflict with the unity of **Christendom**.

Continued ▶

AG : 2 8 :003(081) [0085] condemned by learned and devout people in **Christendom**
AG : 2 8 :039(087) [0089] things and burden **Christendom** with the bondage of the
AG : 2 8 :042(088) [0089] such requirements on **Christendom** to ensnare men's
AG : 2 8 :051(089) [0091] of Christian liberty in **Christendom**, namely, that bondage
AG : 2 8 :061(091) [0093] opinion that in **Christendom** one must have services of
AG : 2 8 :062(091) [0093] were introduced into **Christendom** when the righteousness
S 1 : P R :003(289) [0455] pope prefers to see all **Christendom** lost and all souls
S 2 : 0 4 :001(298) [0471] is not the head of all **Christendom** by divine right or
S 2 : 0 4 :007(299) [0473] order that the unity of **Christendom** might better be
S 2 : 0 4 :007(299) [0473] Even if he could, **Christendom** would not be helped in any
S 2 : 0 4 :009(300) [0475] bishops throughout **Christendom**, until the pope raised his
L C : S P :006(362) [0575] have been heritage of **Christendom** from ancient times,
L C : 0 1 :210(393) [0641] noblest, pervading all **Christendom** and even extending
E P : 1 2 :029(500) [0843] new sect, unknown in **Christendom** until now, which
S D : 0 2 :037(528) [0895] holy community of **Christendom**, through which he heals
S D : 0 3 :006(540) [0917] article remains pure, **Christendom** will remain pure, in
S D : 0 7 :016(572) [0977] that makes it valid in **Christendom**, and that it does not
S D : 0 7 :089(585) [1003] remain efficacious in **Christendom** and which are neither
S D : 1 2 :008(633) [1097] publicly before all **Christendom** that we have no part or
S D : 1 2 :040(636) [1103] of God and of all **Christendom** among both our

Christian (371)
P R : P R :000(001) [0004] **Christian**, Reiterated, and Unanimous Confession of the
P R : P R :000(003) [0005] Preface to the **Christian** Book of Concord
P R : P R :002(003) [0007] by our pious and **Christian** predecessors to the then
P R : P R :003(003) [0007] or doubt in a **Christian** and unanimous interpretation
P R : P R :004(003) [0007] shortly after the **Christian** death of that enlightened and
P R : P R :004(004) [0007] Word, sever the bond of **Christian** charity and agreement,
P R : P R :005(004) [0009] Word and in agreeable **Christian** concord and that they
P R : P R :005(004) [0009] and carried on in a **Christian** fashion and in harmony with
P R : P R :008(005) [0009] subscribed this **Christian** confession, based as it is on the
P R : P R :008(006) [0011] it and persist in it in a **Christian** way without any further
P R : P R :009(006) [0011] of our previous **Christian** confession and that neither we
P R : P R :009(006) [0011] to us and to our **Christian** religion as if we were so
P R : P R :011(006) [0011] that had occurred were to be decided in a **Christian** way.
P R : P R :012(006) [0013] information about this **Christian** undertaking reached
P R : P R :012(007) [0013] to promote it with **Christian** earnestness and zeal in view
P R : P R :013(007) [0013] for the promotion of concord among **Christian** teachers.
P R : P R :013(007) [0013] In a **Christian** fashion they discussed with one another the
P R : P R :013(007) [0013] earnestness and **Christian** zeal, consider it in all its
P R : P R :014(007) [0013] to contain all kinds of **Christian**, necessary, and useful
P R : P R :014(007) [0013] on the way in which the **Christian** doctrine set forth in the
P R : P R :014(007) [0013] The Formula of **Christian** Concord, in the form that
P R : P R :016(008) [0013] Concord as the correct **Christian** interpretation of the
P R : P R :016(008) [0015] Therefore this **Christian** agreement is called and also is
P R : P R :017(008) [0015] the desired end of **Christian** concord, and some even tried
P R : P R :017(008) [0015] we have reached **Christian** unanimity and agreement
P R : P R :017(008) [0015] and repetition of our **Christian** faith and confession as a
P R : P R :018(008) [0015] certainty as to which **Christian** confession it is that we
P R : P R :020(010) [0017] the articles of our **Christian** Creed (especially those
P R : P R :020(010) [0019] of the articles of our **Christian** Creed that our ingenuous
P R : P R :022(012) [0021] to give occasion by this **Christian** agreement for any
P R : P R :022(012) [0021] For just as **Christian** charity causes us to have special
P R : P R :023(012) [0021] year 1530 to Emperor Charles V, of **Christian** memory.
P R : P R :024(012) [0021] we are certain of our **Christian** confession and faith on
P R : P R :024(013) [0021] of this in our hearts and **Christian** consciences through
P R : P R :024(013) [0021] long-standing schisms a **Christian** explanation and
P R : P R :024(013) [0023] and peace of **Christian** schools and churches, and to the
P R : P R :024(013) [0023] that many good-hearted **Christian** persons, of high station
P R : P R :024(013) [0023] this salutary work of **Christian** concord and have a
P R : P R :024(013) [0023] very beginning of this **Christian** agreement of ours it was
P R : P R :024(013) [0023] for divine truth and for **Christian**, God-pleasing concord
P R : P R :024(013) [0023] together with us, take **Christian** pleasure in this salutary,
P R : P R :024(013) [0023] most necessary, and **Christian** effort and will allow
P R : P R :025(014) [0023] and also with other **Christian** potentates, according to the
P R : P R :026(014) [0025] controversies about our **Christian** religion should continue
AG : P R :001(024) [0039] foe of ours and of the **Christian** religion, and how with
AG : P R :002(025) [0039] our holy faith and the **Christian** religion, and to this end it
AG : P R :002(025) [0039] in agreement on one **Christian** truth, to put aside
AG : P R :013(026) [0041] allow, that may serve the cause of **Christian** unity.
AG : P R :014(026) [0041] and every lover of the **Christian** religion who is concerned
AG : P R :019(026) [0041] toward a good, **Christian** understanding, Your Imperial
AG : P R :021(027) [0043] such a general, free, and **Christian** council as the electors,
AG : P R :023(027) [0043] settled, and brought to **Christian** concord in accordance
AG : 0 7 :001(032) [0047] among us that one holy **Christian** church will be and
AG : 0 7 :002(032) [0047] for the true unity of the **Christian** church that the Gospel
AG : 0 7 :003(032) [0047] for the true unity of the **Christian** church that ceremonies,
AG : 0 8 :001(033) [0047] Again, although the **Christian** church, properly speaking,
AG : 1 6 :003(037) [0051] teach that none of the things indicated above is **Christian**.
AG : 1 6 :004(037) [0051] are those who teach that **Christian** perfection requires the
AG : 1 6 :005(038) [0051] his own calling, manifest **Christian** love and genuine good
AG : 2 0 :002(041) [0053] instructions concerning true **Christian** estates and works.
AG : 2 0 :008(042) [0053] is the chief article in the **Christian** life, has been neglected
AG : 0 0 :001(047) [0059] our churches for proper **Christian** instruction, the
AG : 0 0 :001(047) [0059] agrees with the pure Word of God and **Christian** truth.
AG : 0 0 :001(047) [0059] to that of the universal **Christian** church, or even of the
AG : 0 0 :001(048) [0059] fashion, contrary to all **Christian** unity and love, and do
AG : 0 0 :002(048) [0059] is seen to be godly and **Christian**, the bishops should in all
AG : 0 0 :000(048) [0059] Scriptures or what is common to the **Christian** church.
AG : 2 3 :006(052) [0061] manner of life, what **Christian**, upright, and honorable
AG : 2 3 :010(052) [0061] deacons to marry in the **Christian** church of former times.
AG : 2 3 :014(053) [0063] as a most renowned **Christian** emperor, Your Majesty will
AG : 2 3 :014(053) [0063] profitable, and **Christian** to recognize this fact in order
AG : 2 3 :016(054) [0063] would certainly be both **Christian** and very necessary.
AG : 2 3 :016(054) [0063] be of disadvantage to the **Christian** church as a whole?
AG : 2 3 :018(054) [0063] deplorable that **Christian** marriage has not only been
AG : 2 4 :012(057) [0065] properly concern every **Christian** (namely, that whoever
AG : 2 5 :006(062) [0069] and treated of true **Christian** repentance in a more fitting
AG : 2 6 :009(065) [0071] also was regarded as **Christian** life: whoever observed
AG : 2 6 :009(065) [0071] in this way was said to live a spiritual and **Christian** life.
AG : 2 6 :015(066) [0073] neglected all wholesome **Christian** teachings about more
AG : 2 6 :029(068) [0075] notion that nobody is a **Christian** unless he performs such
AG : 2 6 :045(070) [0075] and adds the profitable **Christian** observation, "It was not
AG : 2 7 :015(073) [0077] are profitable to the **Christian** church, so that pastors and
AG : 2 7 :035(076) [0081] authority in the **Christian** church, even though some have
AG : 2 7 :046(078) [0081] spiritual estate of the orders was **Christian** perfection.
AG : 2 7 :048(078) [0081] no small offense in the **Christian** church that the people
AG : 2 7 :048(078) [0081] above all else in the **Christian** church, is obscured when
AG : 2 7 :049(078) [0083] For this is **Christian** perfection: that we fear God honestly
AG : 2 7 :061(080) [0083] God, that they constitute **Christian** perfection, that they
AG : 2 8 :021(084) [0087] and exclude from the **Christian** community the ungodly
AG : 2 8 :051(089) [0091] preserve the teaching of **Christian** liberty in Christendom,
AG : 2 8 :055(090) [0091] It is proper for the **Christian** assembly to keep such
AG : 2 8 :060(091) [0091] ought to assemble, the **Christian** church appointed Sunday
AG : 2 8 :060(091) [0093] have an example of **Christian** liberty and might know that
AG : 2 8 :064(092) [0093] of the righteousness of faith and **Christian** liberty.
AG : 2 8 :066(092) [0093] to the chief article of **Christian** doctrine, and this is not
AG : 2 8 :072(093) [0093] contrary to the custom of the universal **Christian** church.
AG : 2 8 :074(094) [0093] changes do not destroy the unity of **Christian** churches.
AG : 0 0 :005(095) [0095] to Holy Scripture or the universal **Christian** church.
A L : 2 0 :018(043) [0055] men, who dream that **Christian** righteousness is nothing
A L : 2 6 :005(064) [0071] the righteousness of a **Christian** is something other than
A L : 2 6 :029(068) [0075] or with the notion that **Christian** righteousness cannot
A L : 2 6 :033(069) [0075] they teach that every **Christian** ought so to control and
A L : 2 7 :046(078) [0081] invented observances were a state of **Christian** perfection.
A L : 2 7 :049(078) [0083] For this is **Christian** perfection: honestly to fear God and
A L : 2 7 :061(080) [0083] that they constitute **Christian** perfection, that the monks
A L : 2 8 :051(089) [0091] preserve the doctrine of **Christian** liberty in the churches,
A L : 2 8 :060(091) [0093] have an example of **Christian** liberty and would know
A L : 2 8 :064(092) [0093] of the righteousness of faith and **Christian** liberty.
A P : P R :017(099) [0103] view many articles of **Christian** doctrine that the church
A P : 0 2 :012(102) [0109] The scholastics mingled **Christian** doctrine with
A P : 0 4 :012(109) [0123] If this is **Christian** righteousness, what difference is there
A P : 0 4 :016(109) [0123] or Pharisaic righteousness and **Christian** righteousness.
A P : 0 4 :030(111) [0129] and chide them with a **Christian**'s sorrow—'You are
A P : 0 4 :245(142) [0189] a summary of the **Christian** life (I Tim. 1:5), "The aim of
A P : 0 4 :290(151) [0203] A **Christian** can easily evaluate both modes, since both
A P : 0 4 :353(161) [0217] Here is **Christian** and spiritual perfection, if penitence and
A P : 0 4 :390(166) [0225] more than enough philosophy with **Christian** doctrine.
A P : 1 2 :124(201) [0289] the sum total of all **Christian** doctrine, judges should have
A P : 1 5 :032(220) [0323] apostles insisted that **Christian** liberty remain in the
A P : 1 6 :001(222) [0329] we confessed that a **Christian** might legitimately hold
A P : 1 6 :001(222) [0329] ordinances in which a **Christian** may safely take part.
A P : 1 6 :009(224) [0333] also false to claim that **Christian** perfection consists in
A P : 1 6 :009(224) [0333] What makes for **Christian** perfection is not contempt of
A P : 1 6 :012(224) [0333] the rule in mind, that a **Christian** may legitimately make
A P : 2 4 :045(258) [0401] ideas and could not grasp the sum of **Christian** doctrine.
A P : 2 4 :046(258) [0401] Yet this is the principal doctrine of the **Christian** faith.
A P : 2 7 :005(269) [0421] they were schools of **Christian** instruction, they have
A P : 2 7 :046(277) [0435] examples have nothing to do with **Christian** perfection.
S 1 : 0 0 :000(287) [0453] Articles of **Christian** doctrine which were to have been
S 2 : 0 2 :005(293) [0463] but also for all godly, **Christian**, sensible, God-fearing
S 2 : 0 2 :027(297) [0469] As a **Christian** and a saint on earth, you can pray for me,
S 2 : 0 3 :002(298) [0471] superior to the ordinary **Christian** life and to the offices
S 2 : 0 4 :001(298) [0471] to stand beside him as **Christian** brethren and
S 2 : 0 4 :003(298) [0473] of the entire holy **Christian** church (in so far as this lies in
S 2 : 0 4 :004(299) [0473] it is asserted that no **Christian** can be saved unless he is
S 2 : 0 4 :005(299) [0473] The holy **Christian** church can exist very well without such
S 2 : 0 4 :006(299) [0473] use to the church because it exercises no **Christian** office.
S 2 : 0 4 :013(300) [0475] to be the head of the **Christian** church by divine right.
S 3 : 0 3 :040(309) [0489] In the case of a **Christian** such repentance continues until
S 3 : 0 8 :001(312) [0495] need to be examined and instructed in **Christian** doctrine.
S 3 : 0 8 :002(312) [0495] valued, like all other functions of the **Christian** church.
S 3 : 0 9 :000(314) [0497] lesser (that is, the truly **Christian**) excommunication
S 3 : 1 2 :003(315) [0499] So children pray, "I believe in one holy **Christian** church."
S 3 : 1 4 :001(316) [0501] that of the ordinary **Christian** and proposes by means of
S 3 : 1 5 :005(316) [0501] regard the above articles as right and **Christian**.
T R : 0 0 :034(325) [0513] **Christian** righteousness was thought to be that external
S C : P R :001(338) [0533] and simple catechism or statement of **Christian** teaching.
S C : P R :002(338) [0533] knowledge whatever of **Christian** teaching, and
S C : P R :003(338) [0533] are supposed to be **Christian**, are baptized, and receive the
S C : P R :011(339) [0535] or be allowed to participate in any **Christian** privileges.
S C : P R :022(341) [0537] the sacrament and is no **Christian**, just as he is no
S C : P R :022(341) [0537] just as he is no **Christian** who does not hear and believe
S C : 0 2 :005(345) [0545] *Holy Spirit, the holy* ***Christian*** *church, the communion of*
S C : 0 2 :006(345) [0545] and sanctifies the whole **Christian** church on earth and
S C : 0 2 :006(345) [0545] In this **Christian** church he daily and abundantly forgives
L C : S P :002(362) [0575] the minimum of knowledge required of a **Christian**.
L C : S P :005(362) [0575] understanding of all **Christian** doctrine than children and
L C : S P :013(363) [0577] Holy Spirit, the holy **Christian** church, the communion of
L C : S P :015(363) [0577] are the most necessary parts of **Christian** instruction.
L C : S P :019(363) [0579] which constitute the **Christian**'s conversation, conduct and
L C : S P :024(364) [0579] **Christian** doctrine, which we should constantly teach and
L C : 0 1 :083(376) [0603] offer ordinary people a **Christian** interpretation of what
L C : 0 1 :090(377) [0607] Where it is not, it cannot be called a **Christian** holy day.
L C : 0 1 :197(392) [0637] teaching the ordinary **Christian** life would be considered
L C : 0 2 :001(411) [0679] Thus far we have heard the first part of **Christian** doctrine
L C : 0 2 :034(415) [0687] *Holy Spirit, the holy* ***Christian*** *church, the communion*
L C : 0 2 :037(415) [0687] communion of saints or **Christian** church, the forgiveness
L C : 0 2 :041(416) [0689] Answer: "Through the **Christian** church, the forgiveness
L C : 0 2 :042(416) [0689] begets and bears every **Christian** through the Word of
L C : 0 2 :045(416) [0689] Therefore there was no **Christian** church.
L C : 0 2 :045(416) [0689] call, and gather the **Christian** church, and outside it no
L C : 0 2 :047(416) [0689] The Creed calls the holy **Christian** church a *communio*
L C : 0 2 :048(417) [0691] it ought to be called "a **Christian** congregation or
L C : 0 2 :048(417) [0691] or best and most clearly of all, "a holy **Christian** people."
L C : 0 2 :049(417) [0691] someone wished to explain what the **Christian** church is.
L C : 0 2 :053(417) [0693] remains with the holy community or **Christian** people.
L C : 0 2 :054(417) [0693] we believe that in this **Christian** church we have the
L C : 0 2 :054(418) [0693] Word in the unity of the **Christian** church, yet because we
L C : 0 2 :055(418) [0693] everything in the **Christian** church is so ordered that we
L C : 0 2 :055(418) [0693] us because we are in the **Christian** church, where there is
L C : 0 2 :056(418) [0693] But outside the **Christian** church (that is, where the
L C : 0 2 :059(418) [0695] these two means, the **Christian** church and the forgiveness
L C : 0 2 :062(419) [0695] gathered together all his **Christian** people, nor has he
L C : 0 2 :066(419) [0697] All who are outside the **Christian** church, whether

Continued ▶

LC : 0 3 :032(424) [0707] For whenever a good **Christian** prays, "Dear Father, thy
LC : 0 3 :039(425) [0709] both our teaching and our life are godly and **Christian**.
LC : 0 3 :052(427) [0711] be praised through his holy Word and our **Christian** lives.
LC : 0 3 :105(434) [0727] which every **Christian** must bear, even if they come one
LC : 0 4 :001(436) [0733] the three chief parts of our common **Christian** teaching.
LC : 0 4 :001(436) [0733] Every **Christian** ought to have at least some brief,
LC : 0 4 :001(436) [0733] these no one can be a **Christian**, although unfortunately
LC : 0 4 :002(436) [0733] which we are first received into the **Christian** community.
LC : 0 4 :041(441) [0743] therefore, every **Christian** has enough to study and to
LC : 0 4 :050(443) [0745] present day no man on earth could have been a **Christian**.
LC : 0 4 :050(443) [0745] and since the holy **Christian** church will abide until the
LC : 0 4 :051(443) [0745] "I believe one Holy **Christian** church, the communion of
LC : 0 4 :064(444) [0749] by which we are first received into the **Christian** church.
LC : 0 4 :065(445) [0749] Thus a **Christian** life is nothing else than a daily Baptism,
LC : 0 4 :081(446) [0751] we embarked when we entered the **Christian** Church.
LC : 0 5 :002(447) [0753] who wishes to be a **Christian** and go to the sacrament
LC : 0 5 :032(450) [0759] "I believe in the holy **Christian** church, the forgiveness of
LC : 0 5 :036(450) [0761] required of a **Christian** for receiving this sacrament
LC : 0 5 :044(451) [0763] this and every other **Christian** activity, hounding and
LC : 0 5 :049(452) [0765] liberty not to be a **Christian**; then you need not believe or
LC : 0 5 :049(452) [0765] But if you wish to be a **Christian**, you must from time to
LC : 0 5 :050(452) [0765] inner life and reflect: "See what sort of **Christian** I am!
LC : 0 5 :059(453) [0767] forfeited the name of **Christian** and has to be expelled
LC : 0 5 :085(456) [0773] to be brought up in **Christian** doctrine and a right
LC : 0 5 :086(456) [0773] Word of God and the **Christian** church will be preserved.
LC : 0 5 :087(456) [0773] and received into the **Christian** church, they should also
LC : 0 6 :001(457) [0000] intolerable burden he imposed upon the **Christian** church.
LC : 0 6 :005(457) [0000] to it, and do what a **Christian** ought to do, should enjoy
LC : 0 6 :009(458) [0000] essence of a genuinely **Christian** life, to acknowledge that
LC : 0 6 :010(458) [0000] confession, which each **Christian** makes toward his
LC : 0 6 :014(458) [0000] absolution to his **Christian** church and commanded us to
LC : 0 6 :019(459) [0000] If you are a **Christian**, I know this well enough anyway; if
LC : 0 6 :020(459) [0000] Rather, whoever is a **Christian**, or would like to be one,
LC : 0 6 :020(459) [0000] If you are no **Christian**, and desire no such comfort, we
LC : 0 6 :028(460) [0000] If you are a **Christian**, you need neither my compulsion
LC : 0 6 :029(460) [0000] that you are no **Christian** and that you ought not receive
LC : 0 6 :029(460) [0000] For you despise what no **Christian** ought to despise, and
LC : 0 6 :030(460) [0000] If you are a **Christian**, you should be glad to run more
LC : 0 6 :032(460) [0000] to confession, I am simply urging you to be a **Christian**.
EP : 0 0 :000(463) [0775] the Comprehensive Summary of our **Christian** Teaching
EP : 0 0 :000(464) [0777] and Settled in **Christian** Fashion in Conformity with
EP : RN :000(464) [0777] Should Be Explained and Decided in a **Christian** Way
EP : RN :003(465) [0777] unanimous, catholic, **Christian** faith and confessions of
EP : RN :004(465) [0777] and exposition of our **Christian** faith, particularly against
EP : RN :005(465) [0777] length and which a **Christian** must know for his salvation.
EP : 0 1 :003(466) [0779] the chief articles of our **Christian** faith, namely, creation,
EP : 0 3 :002(473) [0793] *Pure Doctrine of the **Christian** Church Against Both*
EP : 0 4 :004(476) [0797] *Pure Doctrine of the **Christian** Church in this*
EP : 0 4 :009(476) [0799] are correctly and in a **Christian** way applied to the
EP : 0 4 :017(477) [0801] and as subversive of **Christian** discipline that bald
EP : 0 4 :018(477) [0801] to exhort people to **Christian** discipline and good works,
EP : 0 6 :001(480) [0805] *The Correct **Christian** Teaching in this Controversy*
EP : 0 6 :008(481) [0807] and subversive of **Christian** discipline and true piety the
EP : 0 7 :001(481) [0809] under the name of this **Christian** Confession, and
EP : 0 7 :011(483) [0811] is this article of our **Christian** faith: Jesus Christ is true,
EP : 0 8 :003(487) [0819] *Pure Teaching of the **Christian** Church concerning the*
EP : 0 8 :004(487) [0819] according to our **Christian** faith we teach, believe, and
EP : 0 8 :017(489) [0823] says on the basis of our **Christian** faith as we teach this to
EP : 0 8 :019(490) [0823] of God and our simple **Christian** Creed the following
EP : 0 8 :039(491) [0827] Word and our simple **Christian** faith, we shall finally have
EP : 0 9 :001(492) [0827] according to our simple **Christian** Creed, did Christ go to
EP : 0 9 :003(492) [0827] this article in a wholly **Christian** manner, eliminates all
EP : 1 0 :006(493) [0829] the truth of the Gospel, **Christian** liberty, and the
EP : 1 0 :010(494) [0831] in violation of the **Christian** liberty which it has in
EP : 1 1 :013(496) [0835] 12. The **Christian** is to concern himself with the doctrine
EP : 1 1 :013(496) [0835] The **Christian** should banish all other opinions since they
EP : 1 1 :022(497) [0837] Catechism, every simple **Christian** can understand what is
EP : 1 1 :022(497) [0837] constantly abide in this **Christian** and God-pleasing
EP : 1 2 :001(498) [0839] our repeatedly cited **Christian** Creed and Confession.
EP : 1 2 :008(498) [0839] Baptism the children of **Christian** parents are holy and the
EP : 1 2 :008(498) [0839] by virtue of their birth from **Christian** and pious parents.
EP : 1 2 :009(498) [0839] is not truly **Christian** if sinners are still found in it.
EP : 1 2 :013(499) [0841] 2. That no **Christian** can serve or function in any civic
EP : 1 2 :014(499) [0841] as occasion arises no **Christian**, without violating his
EP : 1 2 :015(499) [0841] 4. That a **Christian** cannot swear an oath with a good
EP : 1 2 :017(499) [0841] 1. That a **Christian** cannot with a good conscience hold or
EP : 1 2 :018(499) [0841] 2. That a **Christian** cannot with a good conscience be an
EP : 1 2 :025(500) [0843] 6. That a **Christian** who is truly born again through the
EP : 1 2 :026(500) [0843] 7. That it is not true **Christian** congregation in which
SD : 0 0 :000(501) [0845] of God and the Summary Formulation of Our **Christian**
SD : PR :001(501) [0847] the chief articles of our **Christian** faith (which had been
SD : PR :002(501) [0847] the Word of God and **Christian** institutions, attacked it
SD : PR :003(501) [0847] At that time a number of **Christian** electors, princes, and
SD : PR :003(501) [0847] the preparation of a **Christian** Confession on the basis of
SD : PR :003(501) [0847] a clear and unequivocal **Christian** witness, setting forth
SD : PR :003(502) [0847] of the Evangelical **Christian** churches concerning the chief
SD : PR :004(502) [0847] subscribe this **Christian** and thoroughly scriptural
SD : PR :004(502) [0847] Confession a genuinely **Christian** symbol which all true
SD : PR :004(502) [0847] just as in ancient times **Christian** symbols and confessions
SD : PR :005(502) [0847] by this repeatedly cited **Christian** Confession as it was
SD : PR :006(502) [0847] Although the **Christian** doctrine set forth in this
SD : PR :010(503) [0849] way that anybody with **Christian** intelligence can see
SD : PR :010(503) [0849] Word of God and the **Christian** Augsburg Confession,
SD : RN :000(503) [0849] Are to Be Explained and Decided in a **Christian** Way
SD : RN :001(503) [0851] churches of the pure **Christian** religion is drawn together
SD : RN :004(504) [0851] in ancient times the true **Christian** doctrine as it was
SD : RN :004(504) [0851] of the faith — succinct, **Christian**, and based upon the
SD : RN :004(504) [0851] had arisen within the **Christian** church are clearly and
SD : RN :005(504) [0851] by a number of **Christian** electors, princes, and estates of
SD : RN :005(504) [0853] for later synods and **Christian** bishops and teachers to
SD : RN :008(505) [0853] and since they formulate **Christian** doctrine on the basis
SD : RN :009(505) [0853] but in the necessary and **Christian** terms and manner in
SD : RN :011(506) [0855] cited summary of our **Christian** doctrine is that they have
SD : RN :015(507) [0857] or the chief parts of our **Christian** doctrine, when the
SD : RN :016(507) [0857] It is true that the **Christian** reader who really delights in
SD : RN :016(507) [0857] articles of our **Christian** faith, according to the prophetic
SD : RN :020(508) [0859] the commonly accepted **Christian** meaning of the
SD : 0 1 :004(509) [0861] this controversy in a **Christian** fashion and according to
SD : 0 1 :015(511) [0865] the aforementioned Confessions of our **Christian** doctrine
SD : 0 1 :034(514) [0869] The chief articles of our **Christian** faith constrain and
SD : 0 1 :039(515) [0871] At this point all **Christian** hearts may well ponder God's
SD : 0 1 :041(515) [0871] are contrary to the first article of our **Christian** faith.
SD : 0 1 :047(516) [0873] to this article of our **Christian** faith, either that our flesh
SD : 0 1 :048(517) [0875] The chief articles of our **Christian** faith show powerfully
SD : 0 2 :006(521) [0883] this controversy in a **Christian** way according to the Word
SD : 0 2 :036(528) [0895] part and member of this **Christian** church, a shareholder
SD : 0 2 :037(528) [0895] became members of the **Christian** church we belonged
SD : 0 2 :040(528) [0895] and sanctifies the whole **Christian** church on earth and
SD : 0 2 :045(530) [0899] Scriptures of God, the **Christian** Augsburg Confession, its
SD : 0 2 :046(530) [0899] and indifferent to such **Christian** exercises as prayer,
SD : 0 2 :046(530) [0899] exercises as prayer, reading, and **Christian** meditation.
SD : 0 2 :068(534) [0907] but even the individual **Christian** in his own life discovers
SD : 0 2 :070(535) [0909] good spiritual thoughts, **Christian** intentions, and
SD : 0 3 :006(540) [0917] chief article of the entire **Christian** doctrine," "without
SD : 0 3 :008(540) [0919] this controversy in a **Christian** way according to the Word
SD : 0 3 :009(540) [0919] formulation of our **Christian** faith and confession
SD : 0 3 :042(547) [0931] question is asked, how a **Christian** can identify, either in
SD : 0 3 :059(550) [0937] of the prophets and apostles, and our **Christian** faith:
SD : 0 4 :002(551) [0939] that article of our **Christian** faith in which we confess that
SD : 0 4 :006(552) [0939] this disagreement in a **Christian** way and according to the
SD : 0 4 :015(553) [0943] used in their strict and **Christian** sense, as some have
SD : 0 4 :031(556) [0947] and that even though a **Christian** follows his evil lusts
SD : 0 5 :016(561) [0957] nicely and clearly for the **Christian** reader, we submit the
SD : 0 6 :026(568) [0971] and contrary to **Christian** discipline and true godliness,
SD : 0 7 :012(571) [0977] the following articles of **Christian** agreement in
SD : 0 7 :028(574) [0981] this doctrine and other **Christian** articles, he appended the
SD : 0 7 :060(580) [0995] The ancient **Christian** fathers and teachers of the church
SD : 0 7 :066(581) [0995] of them, all the ancient **Christian** teachers and the entire
SD : 0 7 :066(581) [0995] and the entire holy **Christian** church teach unanimously
SD : 0 7 :066(581) [0997] brevity we direct the **Christian** reader to our more
SD : 0 7 :067(582) [0997] so terrible that a pious **Christian** should be ashamed to
SD : 0 7 :084(584) [1001] (namely, that in a **Christian** assembly we take bread and
SD : 0 7 :085(584) [1001] To maintain this true **Christian** doctrine concerning the
SD : 0 7 :091(586) [1005] brevity, merely refer the **Christian** reader to these writings
SD : 0 7 :106(588) [1009] and will enable a **Christian** heart to rely on and trust in
SD : 0 8 :005(592) [1017] this controversy in a **Christian** way according to the Word
SD : 0 8 :005(592) [1017] with our plain **Christian** creed, and to settle it definitely
SD : 0 8 :017(594) [1021] condemned heresy the **Christian** church has always held
SD : 0 8 :020(595) [1021] the words of our plain **Christian** Creed, has truly died,
SD : 0 8 :023(595) [1023] according to our plain **Christian** Creed we believe, teach,
SD : 0 8 :040(598) [1029] not want to be called a **Christian**, that is, a Christ who is
SD : 0 8 :045(600) [1031] For our plain **Christian** Creed teaches us that the Son of
SD : 0 8 :071(605) [1041] This is contrary to our **Christian** Creed and to the entire
SD : 0 8 :077(606) [1043] is present with us in the **Christian** church and community
SD : 0 8 :088(609) [1047] orthodox Creeds, and our **Christian** Augsburg confession:
SD : 0 8 :096(609) [1049] and apostles, and our **Christian** Creed and Confession.
SD : 0 9 :001(610) [1051] as among the ancient teachers of the **Christian** church.
SD : 0 9 :001(610) [1051] simple statement of our **Christian** Creed, to which Dr.
SD : 1 0 :001(610) [1053] order and decorum or else to preserve **Christian** discipline
SD : 1 0 :004(611) [1053] of God, we offer the **Christian** reader the following
SD : 1 0 :007(611) [1055] neither good order, **Christian** discipline, nor evangelical
SD : 1 0 :009(612) [1055] salutary for good order, **Christian** discipline, evangelical
SD : 1 0 :010(612) [1055] yes, every individual **Christian**, and especially the
SD : 1 0 :012(612) [1057] and which in his **Christian** liberty he employed in other
SD : 1 0 :014(613) [1057] the chief article of our **Christian** faith, so that, as the
SD : 1 0 :014(613) [1057] the pure doctrine and **Christian** liberty, or they will misuse
SD : 1 0 :015(613) [1057] concerns the article of **Christian** liberty as well, an article
SD : 1 0 :016(613) [1057] external things, where **Christian** agreement in doctrine has
SD : 1 0 :016(613) [1057] and salvation, every **Christian** is obligated to avoid both,
SD : 1 0 :019(614) [1059] without pretense, humbug, and un-**Christian** ostentation.
SD : 1 0 :025(615) [1061] can learn what a **Christian** community, each individual
SD : 1 0 :025(615) [1061] each individual **Christian**, and particularly the preachers
SD : 1 0 :029(615) [1061] and in opposition to the **Christian** confession, whether in
SD : 1 0 :030(616) [1061] as may in **Christian** liberty be most beneficial to the
SD : 1 0 :031(616) [1063] in ceremonies, when in **Christian** liberty one uses fewer or
SD : 1 1 :045(624) [1079] about every individual **Christian**'s conversion,
SD : 1 1 :073(628) [1087] themselves in all **Christian** virtues, in all godliness,
SD : 1 2 :008(633) [1097] and contrary to our **Christian** and biblically-based
SD : 1 2 :013(634) [1099] because they are born of **Christian** and believing parents,
SD : 1 2 :014(634) [1099] 5. That that is no truly **Christian** assembly or congregation
SD : 1 2 :018(634) [1099] 9. That no **Christian** can hold an office in the government
SD : 1 2 :019(634) [1099] 10. That no **Christian** may with an inviolate conscience
SD : 1 2 :020(634) [1099] 11. That a **Christian** cannot with a good conscience swear
SD : 1 2 :022(634) [1099] 13. That no **Christian** can with a good conscience hold or
SD : 1 2 :023(634) [1099] 14. That no **Christian** can with a good conscience be an
SD : 1 2 :033(635) [1101] 5. That a **Christian** who is truly born again through the
SD : 1 2 :034(635) [1101] does not take place is not a true **Christian** congregation.

Christianity (4)

AL : 2 6 :008(065) [0071] **Christianity** was thought to consist wholly in the
AP : 0 4 :002(107) [0121] the main doctrine of **Christianity** is involved; when it is
AP : 2 7 :067(280) [0441] calls "first faith" — not a monastic vows, but **Christianity**.
LC : 0 2 :054(417) [0693] short, the entire Gospel and all the duties of **Christianity**.

Christians (136)

PR : PR :020(010) [0017] constant intention **Christians** are to be directed in the
PR : PR :022(012) [0021] molestation and persecution of poor, oppressed **Christians**
AG : 0 8 :001(033) [0047] in this life many false **Christians**, hypocrites, and even
AG : 1 3 :001(035) [0049] identified outwardly as **Christians**, but that they are signs
AG : 1 6 :002(037) [0051] of good order, and that **Christians** may without sin occupy
AG : 1 6 :006(038) [0051] Accordingly **Christians** are obliged to be subject to civil
AG : 2 6 :031(068) [0075] the holy cross that **Christians** are obliged to suffer, and
AG : 2 7 :055(079) [0083] it is not right at all for **Christians**, even in the
AG : 2 8 :039(087) [0089] a service of God among **Christians** like the Levitical
AL : 1 6 :002(037) [0051] and that it is right for **Christians** to hold civil office, to sit
AL : 1 6 :003(037) [0051] Anabaptists who forbid **Christians** to engage in these civil

Continued ▶

AL : 16 :006(038) [0051] Therefore **Christians** are necessarily bound to obey their
AL : 26 :031(068) [0075] the cross that **Christians** are obliged to suffer afflictions.
AL : 27 :055(079) [0083] offices are unworthy of **Christians** and in conflict with the
AL : 28 :039(087) [0089] to be a service among **Christians** similar to the Levitical,
AP : 04 :387(166) [0225] **Christians** need to understand this faith, for it brings the
AP : 04 :397(167) [0227] doctrine that all **Christians** should hold and believe,
AP : 04 :398(167) [0227] most true and certain and indispensable for all **Christians**?
AP : 07 :050(178) [0245] It is legitimate for **Christians** to use civil ordinances just
AP : 12 :059(190) [0267] and which we believe all **Christians** must understand.
AP : 16 :006(223) [0331] others opposed the **Christians** on the grounds that their
AP : 23 :042(245) [0375] and tried to impose the law of Moses on **Christians**.
AP : 24 :068(262) [0407] and friendship among **Christians** because banquets are
AP : 24 :085(265) [0413] Originally the **Christians** kept this practice.
S2 : 04 :010(300) [0475] pope will not permit **Christians** to be saved except by his
S2 : 04 :011(300) [0475] is their enmity against **Christians**, do this; those who
S2 : 04 :011(300) [0475] they receive bodily tribute and obedience from **Christians**.
S2 : 04 :014(301) [0475] slay, and plague all **Christians** who do not exalt and
S3 : 06 :001(311) [0493] received not only by godly but also by wicked **Christians**.
S3 : 15 :005(317) [0501] unity among the **Christians** who are now under him and
TR : 00 :041(327) [0517] this is the situation, all **Christians** ought to beware of
TR : 00 :056(330) [0521] And as other **Christians** ought to censure the rest of the
TR : 00 :067(331) [0523] Augustine relates of two **Christians** in a ship, one of
SC : PR :011(339) [0535] tell them that they deny Christ and are no **Christians**.
SC : 06 :002(351) [0555] bread and wine, given to us **Christians** to eat and to drink
SC : 09 :003(354) [0561] Duties **Christians** Owe Their Teachers and Pastors
SC : 09 :014(356) [0563] **Christians** in General
LC : PR :016(361) [0573] all his holy angels, prophets, apostles, and all **Christians**!
LC : PR :019(361) [0573] I once again implore all **Christians**, especially pastors and
LC : PR :019(361) [0573] Let all **Christians** exercise themselves in the Catechism
LC : SP :002(362) [0575] not be reckoned among **Christians** nor admitted to a
LC : SP :005(362) [0575] exercise all the rights of **Christians**, although those who
LC : SP :006(362) [0575] that all who wish to be **Christians** in fact as well as in
LC : 01 :082(376) [0603] sense, this commandment does not concern us **Christians**.
LC : 01 :083(376) [0603] and well informed **Christians**, for these have no need of
LC : 01 :089(377) [0605] Indeed, we **Christians** should make every day a holy day
LC : 01 :090(377) [0607] Non-**Christians** can spend a day in rest and idleness, too,
LC : 01 :091(377) [0607] it is the only one we **Christians** acknowledge and have.
LC : 01 :142(385) [0621] shame of us would-be **Christians** who do not speak of our
LC : 01 :161(387) [0627] would bear the name of **Christians** owe it to God to show
LC : 01 :232(396) [0647] must preach this not to **Christians** but chiefly to knaves
LC : 01 :262(400) [0655] are godly preachers and **Christians**, they must endure
LC : 02 :010(412) [0681] and confession of **Christians** based on the First
LC : 02 :022(413) [0683] Yet **Christians** have this advantage, that they acknowledge
LC : 02 :066(419) [0695] and distinguish us **Christians** from all other people on
LC : 02 :066(419) [0697] Turks, Jews, or false **Christians** and hypocrites, even
LC : 02 :068(420) [0697] by themselves make us **Christians**, for God's wrath and
LC : 03 :008(421) [0699] pray if we want to be **Christians**, just as it is our duty and
LC : 03 :030(424) [0707] weapons with which **Christians** ought to arm themselves
LC : 03 :037(425) [0707] to us when we became **Christians** at Baptism, and so we
LC : 03 :042(425) [0709] those who are called **Christians** and God's people are
LC : 03 :065(429) [0715] we who would be **Christians** must surely count on having
LC : 03 :069(429) [0717] One or two **Christians**, armed with this single petition,
LC : 03 :081(431) [0721] have the Word of God and would like to be **Christians**.
LC : 03 :107(434) [0729] matters (that is, strong **Christians**) are tempted by the
LC : 03 :109(435) [0729] Accordingly we **Christians** must be armed and prepared
LC : 04 :068(445) [0749] use of Baptism among **Christians**, signified by baptizing
LC : 04 :071(445) [0749] hand, when we become **Christians**, the old man daily
LC : 04 :085(446) [0753] If we wish to be **Christians**, we must practice the work
LC : 04 :085(446) [0753] we must practice the work that makes us **Christians**.
LC : 05 :008(447) [0755] and wine which we **Christians** are commanded by Christ's
LC : 05 :039(451) [0761] and distributed among **Christians**, may not be heedlessly
LC : 05 :039(451) [0761] those who claim to be **Christians** should prepare
LC : 05 :040(451) [0763] they were such strong **Christians** that they have no need
LC : 05 :042(451) [0763] a long period of time are not to be considered **Christians**.
LC : 05 :042(451) [0763] but commanded his **Christians** to eat and drink and
LC : 05 :043(451) [0763] Indeed, true **Christians** who cherish and honor the
LC : 05 :043(451) [0763] also would like to be **Christians**, may be induced to see
LC : 05 :045(452) [0763] all who would be **Christians** to partake of the sacrament.
LC : 05 :051(452) [0765] sense what sort of **Christians** we were under the papacy
LC : 06 :008(458) [0000] right to be called the **Christians**' common confession.
LC : 06 :027(460) [0000] ought to know that we do not regard them as **Christians**.
LC : 06 :032(460) [0000] really want to be good **Christians**, free from their sins,
EP : 04 :004(476) [0797] be preached at all to **Christians** but that people should be
EP : 05 :011(479) [0805] Scriptures are obscured, **Christians** are robbed of their
EP : 06 :001(480) [0805] or not the law is to be urged upon reborn **Christians**
EP : 06 :008(481) [0807] above described, upon **Christians** and genuine believers,
EP : 06 :008(481) [0807] only upon unbelievers, non-**Christians**, and the impenitent
EP : 07 :019(484) [0813] Supper particularly for **Christians** who are weak in faith
EP : 07 :027(485) [0815] than tokens whereby **Christians** recognize each one
EP : 07 :037(486) [0815] and impenitent **Christians** do not receive the body and
EP : 09 :003(492) [0827] and admonishes all **Christians** to simplicity of faith.
EP : 11 :016(497) [0837] a way that disconsolate **Christians** can find no comfort in
EP : 11 :021(497) [0837] errors, for they rob **Christians** of all the comfort that they
EP : 12 :030(500) [0843] All pious **Christians**, of high degree and low, must guard
SD : PR :004(502) [0847] symbol which all true **Christians** ought to accept next to
SD : PR :007(502) [0849] who pretended to be **Christians** and gloried in the doctrine
SD : PR :010(503) [0849] so that well-meaning **Christians** who are really concerned
SD : RN :008(505) [0853] salvation must as **Christians** know the difference between
SD : 01 :005(509) [0861] established truth that **Christians** must regard and
SD : 02 :014(523) [0885] comfort to all devout **Christians** who perceive and
SD : 02 :034(527) [0895] repentance continues in **Christians** until death, for it
SD : 02 :068(534) [0907] difference between **Christians**, one being weak and the
SD : 03 :042(547) [0931] many lazy and secure **Christians** delude themselves into
SD : 03 :054(549) [0935] with God, since all **Christians** are temples of God the
SD : 04 :032(556) [0947] and impress upon **Christians** who have been justified by
SD : 04 :040(558) [0951] But since **Christians** are not to be deterred from good
SD : 05 :001(558) [0951] admixture, for by it **Christians** can support themselves in
SD : 05 :027(563) [0961] papacy, and thus rob **Christians** of the true comfort which
SD : 06 :004(564) [0963] although truly believing **Christians**, having been genuinely
SD : 06 :007(565) [0965] But in this life **Christians** are not renewed perfectly and
SD : 06 :014(566) [0967] As often, therefore, as **Christians** trip, they are rebuked
SD : 06 :023(567) [0969] In this respect **Christians** are not under the law but under
SD : 06 :026(568) [0971] is not to be urged upon **Christians** and true believers but
SD : 06 :026(568) [0971] upon unbelievers, non-**Christians**, and the unrepentant.
SD : 07 :001(569) [0971] hearers and other pious **Christians** against this pernicious
SD : 07 :004(569) [0973] one can identify **Christians**, and that nothing more than
SD : 07 :008(570) [0975] as believing and pious **Christians** eat the bread with their
SD : 07 :008(570) [0975] or counterfeit **Christians**, is something that they are
SD : 07 :010(571) [0975] and wine, given to us **Christians** to eat and to drink."
SD : 07 :019(572) [0979] received not only by godly but also by wicked **Christians**."
SD : 07 :020(573) [0979] Christ's word commands us **Christians** to eat and drink."
SD : 07 :044(577) [0987] true bond and union of **Christians** with Christ their head
SD : 07 :060(580) [0993] pious, and believing **Christians** receive the true body and
SD : 07 :061(580) [0995] and necessary to salvation for all **Christians** at all times.
SD : 07 :066(581) [0997] false, and wicked **Christians** as well as by the godly and
SD : 07 :069(582) [0997] those timid, perturbed **Christians**, weak in faith, who are
SD : 07 :115(589) [1011] than badges whereby **Christians** recognize one another, or
SD : 07 :123(590) [1013] and wicked **Christians**, who only bear the name of Christ
SD : 08 :044(599) [1029] *and the Church:* "We **Christians** must know that unless
SD : 08 :087(608) [1047] To do so robs **Christians** of their highest comfort, afforded
SD : 08 :096(609) [1049] heads, we admonish all **Christians** not to pry
SD : 10 :022(615) [1061] this is the situation, all **Christians** ought to beware of
SD : 11 :091(631) [1093] election that sorrowing **Christians** can find no comfort in
SD : 12 :013(634) [1099] 4. That the children of **Christians**, because they are born
SD : 12 :039(636) [1103] All pious **Christians** will and should avoid these as dearly

Christopher (6)
PR : PR :027(015) [0025] Hoyer **Christopher**, count of Mansfeld [-Eisleben]
PR : PR :027(015) [0025] **Christopher**, count of Mansfeld
AP : 21 :035(234) [0353] smart person painted **Christopher** in such a way as to
AP : 21 :035(234) [0353] the people to call on **Christopher**, as though there had
EP : 12 :031(501) [0843] Dr. **Christopher** Koerner subscribed
SD : 12 :040(636) [1103] Dr. **Christopher** Koerner, subscribed

Chrysippus (1)
AP : 04 :360(162) [0219] **Chrysippus**-like, they draw the following absurd

Chrysostom (11)
AG : 24 :036(060) [0067] For **Chrysostom** reports how the priest stood every day,
AG : 25 :011(063) [0069] where these words of **Chrysostom** are quoted: "I do not
AG : 25 :011(063) [0071] be clearly seen that **Chrysostom** does not require a
AL : 24 :036(060) [0067] **Chrysostom** says that the priest stands daily at the altar,
AL : 25 :011(063) [0069] is not necessary, for **Chrysostom** is quoted in the canons
AP : 12 :088(195) [0277] **Chrysostom** asks in connection with penitence, "How do
AP : 12 :170(209) [0305] Similarly, **Chrysostom** says, "In the heart contrition, in
TR : 00 :028(325) [0511] So **Chrysostom** declares that Christ says "on this rock"
EP : 07 :015(483) [0813] Fathers, such as **Chrysostom**, Cyprian, Leo I, Gregory,
SD : 07 :037(575) [0985] Leo, Gelasius, **Chrysostom**, and others, have cited the
SD : 07 :076(583) [0999] **Chrysostom** says in his *Sermon on the Passion*: "Christ

Chur (1)
TR : 00 :082(334) [0529] Agricola, minister in **Chur**, subscribed with his own hand

Church (575)
PR : PR :003(003) [0007] universal and orthodox **church** of Christ has believed,
PR : PR :021(011) [0019] teachers of the ancient **church** put it, it takes place on
PR : PR :023(012) [0021] trained for service in the **church** and for the holy ministry
AG : PR :004(025) [0039] in one fellowship and **church**, even as we are all enlisted
AG : 07 :000(032) [0047] VII. [The **Church**]
AG : 07 :001(032) [0047] that one holy Christian **church** will be and remain
AG : 07 :002(032) [0047] unity of the Christian **church** that the Gospel be preached
AG : 07 :003(032) [0047] unity of the Christian **church** that ceremonies, instituted
AG : 08 :000(033) [0047] VIII. [What the **Church** Is]
AG : 08 :001(033) [0047] although the Christian **church**, properly speaking, is
AG : 12 :002(034) [0049] and absolution should not be denied them by the **church**.
AG : 14 :000(036) [0049] XIV. Order in the **Church**
AG : 14 :000(036) [0049] the sacraments in the **church** without a regular call.
AG : 15 :000(036) [0049] XV. **Church** Usages
AG : 15 :001(036) [0049] With regard to **church** usages that have been established
AG : 15 :001(036) [0049] and good order in the **church**, among them being certain
AG : 00 :001(047) [0059] of the universal Christian **church**, or even of the Roman
AG : 00 :001(047) [0059] or even of the Roman **church** (in so far as the latter's
AG : 00 :000(048) [0059] Scriptures or what is common to the Christian **church**.
AG : 22 :004(050) [0061] usage continued in the **church** for a long time, as can be
AG : 23 :010(052) [0061] deacons to marry in the Christian **church** of former times.
AG : 23 :016(054) [0063] who are to minister to the **church**, be of disadvantage to
AG : 23 :016(054) [0063] be of disadvantage to the Christian **church** as a whole?
AG : 24 :025(059) [0067] unprecedented novelty in **church** doctrine that Christ's
AG : 24 :035(060) [0067] formerly observed in the **church** and which can be proved
AG : 24 :040(061) [0069] which did not exist in the **church** from ancient times, and
AG : 25 :012(063) [0071] by the Scriptures, but was instituted by the **church**.
AG : 26 :003(064) [0071] Many harmful errors in the **church** have resulted from
AG : 26 :016(066) [0073] so much strife in the **church** that godly people were
AG : 26 :020(067) [0073] be emphasized in the **church**, but this teaching cannot be
AG : 26 :040(069) [0075] and the like) which serve to preserve order in the **church**.
AG : 26 :043(070) [0075] a divisive of the **church**, they were admonished by others
AG : 26 :045(070) [0075] examples of dissimilar **church** usages and adds the
AG : 27 :015(073) [0077] to the Christian **church**, so that pastors and bishops were
AG : 27 :035(076) [0081] authority in the Christian **church**, even though some have
AG : 27 :048(078) [0081] offense in the Christian **church** that the people should be
AG : 27 :048(078) [0081] all else in the Christian **church**, is obscured when man's
AG : 28 :010(082) [0085] as the power of the **church** or of bishops bestows eternal
AG : 28 :030(085) [0087] ceremonies in the **church** or establish regulations
AG : 28 :033(086) [0087] that the power of the **church** is indeed great because the
AG : 28 :033(086) [0087] indeed great because the **church** has dispensed from and
AG : 28 :053(090) [0091] Sunday and other similar **church** ordinances and
AG : 28 :055(090) [0091] may be no disorder or unbecoming conduct in the **church**.
AG : 28 :060(091) [0091] assemble, the Christian **church** appointed Sunday for this
AG : 28 :072(093) [0093] which did not exist in the **church** in former times and
AG : 28 :072(093) [0093] contrary to the custom of the universal Christian **church**.
AG : 00 :005(095) [0095] to Holy Scripture or the universal Christian **church**.
AL : 05 :000(031) [0045] V. [The Ministry of the **Church**]
AL : 06 :003(032) [0047] Fathers of the ancient **church**, for Ambrose says, "It is
AL : 07 :000(032) [0047] VII. [The **Church**]
AL : 07 :001(032) [0047] also teach that one holy **church** is to continue forever.
AL : 07 :001(032) [0047] The **church** is the assembly of saints in which the Gospel
AL : 07 :002(032) [0047] For the true unity of the **church** it is enough to agree
AL : 08 :000(033) [0047] VIII. [What Is the **Church**?]
AL : 08 :001(033) [0047] Properly speaking, the **church** is the assembly of saints

Continued ▶

A L : 0 8 :003(033) [0047] men may be used in the **church** and who have thought the
A L : 1 2 :002(034) [0049] converted, and that the **church** ought to impart
A L : 1 4 :000(036) [0049] preach publicly in the **church** or administer the
A L : 1 5 :001(036) [0049] which contribute to peace and good order in the **church**.
A L : 2 0 :008(042) [0053] the chief teaching in the **church**, has so long been
A L : 2 0 :008(042) [0053] has been treated in the **church**), our teachers have
A L : 2 0 :040(046) [0057] (John 15:5), and the **church** sings, "Where Thou art not,
A L : 0 0 :001(047) [0059] Scriptures or the catholic **church** or the church of Rome,
A L : 0 0 :001(047) [0059] catholic church or the **church** of Rome, in so far as the
A L : 0 0 :001(047) [0059] in so far as the ancient **church** is known to us from its
A L : 0 0 :001(048) [0059] dissent from the **church** catholic in no article of faith but
A L : 2 2 :004(050) [0061] This usage continued in the **church** for a long time.
A L : 2 2 :010(050) [0061] to ancient canons and the example of the **church**.
A L : 2 3 :010(052) [0061] that in the ancient **church** priests were married men.
A L : 2 3 :018(054) [0063] the custom of the **church** is well known, and although
A L : 2 4 :004(056) [0065] Paul prescribed that in **church** a language should be used
A L : 2 4 :015(057) [0067] they let many corruptions creep into the **church**.
A L : 2 4 :016(057) [0067] about the troubles of the **church**, although the
A L : 2 4 :018(058) [0067] been tolerated in the **church** for many centuries by the
A L : 2 4 :035(060) [0067] is this custom new in the **church**, for before the time of
A L : 2 4 :040(061) [0069] by the example of the **church** as seen from the Scriptures
A L : 2 6 :003(064) [0071] traditions much harm has resulted in the **church**.
A L : 2 6 :004(064) [0071] above all else to be in the **church**, and to be prominent in
A L : 2 6 :020(067) [0073] us to insist in the **church** on the teaching concerning grace
A L : 2 6 :040(069) [0075] are profitable for maintaining good order in the **church**.
A L : 2 6 :044(070) [0075] such diversity does not violate the unity of the **church**.
A L : 2 7 :015(073) [0077] were profitable to the **church**, and pastors and bishops
A L : 2 7 :048(078) [0081] is no light offense in the **church** to recommend to the
A L : 2 7 :048(078) [0081] to be taught in the **church**, is obscured when the eyes of
A L : 2 8 :001(081) [0083] the power of the **church** with the power of the sword.
A L : 2 8 :003(081) [0085] since been rebuked in the **church** by devout and learned
A L : 2 8 :004(081) [0085] between the power of the **church** and the power of the
A L : 2 8 :010(082) [0085] as the power of the **church** bestows eternal things and is
A L : 2 8 :012(083) [0085] The power of the **church** has its own commission to
A L : 2 8 :021(084) [0087] the fellowship of the **church** ungodly persons whose
A L : 2 8 :030(085) [0087] ceremonies in the **church** and make laws concerning
A L : 2 8 :033(086) [0087] say, is the power of the **church**, for it dispensed from one
A L : 2 8 :037(086) [0089] have multiplied in the **church** almost beyond calculation,
A L : 2 8 :039(087) [0089] things and burden the **church** with the bondage of the
A L : 2 8 :053(090) [0091] so that things in the **church** may be done in good order,
A L : 2 8 :054(090) [0091] that interpreters in the **church** should be heard one after
A L : 2 8 :058(091) [0091] was instituted by the **church**'s authority as a necessary
A L : 2 8 :059(091) [0091] The Scriptures, not the **church**, abrogated the Sabbath,
A L : 2 8 :060(091) [0091] it appears that the **church** designated the Lord's Day for
A L : 2 8 :060(091) [0091] and it seems that the **church** was the more pleased to do
A L : 2 8 :061(091) [0093] must be a service in the **church** like the Levitical service
A L : 2 8 :062(092) [0093] errors crept into the **church** when the righteousness of
A L : 2 8 :07: 093) [0093] introduced contrary to the custom of the **church** catholic.
A L : 2 8 :07+(093) [0093] impair the unity of the **church** inasmuch as many human
A L : 0 0 :005(095) [0095] that is contrary to Scripture or to the **church** catholic.
A P : P R :016(099) [0103] truth that is so clear and necessary for the **church**.
A P : P R :016(099) [0103] for the glory of Christ and the good of the **church**.
A P : P R :017(099) [0103] articles of Christian doctrine that the **church** sorely needs.
A P : 0 1 :002(100) [0103] do not belong to the **church** of Christ but are idolaters
A P : 0 2 :032(104) [0113] to the Scripture or the **church** catholic, but we have
A P : 0 2 :042(105) [0115] of the Scripture contradict them, but the whole **church**.
A P : 0 2 :051(107) [0119] is correct and in agreement with Christ's **church** catholic.
A P : 0 4 :010(108) [0123] types of worship in the **church**, like monastic vows and
A P : 0 4 :063(115) [0139] can grasp it, and it has the testimony of the **church**.
A P : 0 4 :083(119) [0145] which is really citing the authority of the **church**.
A P : 0 4 :119(123) [0155] be a proclamation in the **church** from which the faithful
A P : 0 4 :120(124) [0155] freely for Christ's sake) must be retained in the **church**.
A P : 0 4 :166(130) [0169] All the Scriptures and the **church** proclaim that the law
A P : 0 4 :190(133) [0175] and other teachers of the **church** are holy works, true
A P : 0 4 :210(136) [0179] was instituted in the **church** so that as this sign reminds
A P : 0 4 :218(137) [0179] Before the whole **church**, they say, Paul asserts that faith
A P : 0 4 :232(139) [0185] personal perfection but about fellowship in the **church**.
A P : 0 4 :232(139) [0185] the many members of the **church** with one another.
A P : 0 4 :232(140) [0185] that there be love in the **church** to preserve harmony, to
A P : 0 4 :232(140) [0185] minor mistakes, lest the **church** disintegrate into various
A P : 0 4 :234(140) [0185] is, the integrity of the **church**) is preserved when the
A P : 0 4 :235(140) [0185] when Paul is speaking of unity and peace in the **church**.
A P : 0 4 :236(140) [0185] them, they would bring peace to both **church** and state.
A P : 0 4 :242(141) [0187] have arisen in the **church** simply from the hatred of the
A P : 0 4 :288(151) [0203] tranquillity there should be some order in the **church**.
A P : 0 4 :300(153) [0205] opponents take from the **church** in condemning and
A P : 0 4 :322(157) [0209] Fourth, the whole **church** confesses that eternal life
A P : 0 4 :323(157) [0209] the Scriptures and in the **Church** Fathers, who declare
A P : 0 4 :325(157) [0211] in this regard when the **Church** Fathers have so clearly
A P : 0 4 :338(159) [0215] and with the whole **church** we teach that we are saved by
A P : 0 4 :344(160) [0217] us therefore hold to the **church**'s confession that we are
A P : 0 4 :377(165) [0223] not be neglected in the **church** of Christ; without it the
A P : 0 4 :385(166) [0225] as the prayers of the **church** ask that everything be
A P : 0 4 :389(166) [0225] and with the whole **church** of Christ, which certainly
A P : 0 4 :390(166) [0225] immediately that the **church** of Rome accepts everything
A P : 0 4 :392(167) [0225] and monks in the **church** have taught us to seek
A P : 0 4 :395(167) [0225] a type of what was to happen in the **church** of the future.
A P : 0 4 :400(168) [0227] the name of the **church**, therefore, we know that the
A P : 0 4 :400(168) [0227] we know that the **church** of Christ is among those who
A P : 0 4 :400(168) [0227] Augustine says: "The question is, where is the **church**?
A P : 0 7 :000(168) [0227] Articles VII and VIII. The **Church**
A P : 0 7 :001(168) [0227] in which we said the **church** is the assembly of saints.
A P : 0 7 :001(168) [0227] to be separated from the **church** since John compared the
A P : 0 7 :001(168) [0227] since John compared the **church** to a threshing floor on
A P : 0 7 :003(168) [0227] outward fellowship of the **church** or deny efficacy to the
A P : 0 7 :003(169) [0227] men are mingled with the **church** and are members of the
A P : 0 7 :003(169) [0227] and are members of the **church** according to the outward
A P : 0 7 :003(169) [0227] associations of the **church**'s marks — that is, Word,
A P : 0 7 :004(169) [0227] that is, that he will rule and hold office in the **church**.
A P : 0 7 :005(169) [0227] The **church** is not merely an association of outward ties
A P : 0 7 :005(169) [0227] This **church** alone is called the body of Christ, which
A P : 0 7 :005(169) [0227] over all things for the **church**, which is his body, the
A P : 0 7 :005(169) [0229] admit, that the wicked are dead members of the **church**.
A P : 0 7 :007(169) [0229] Paul defined the **church** in the same way in Eph. 5:25-27,
A P : 0 7 :007(169) [0229] He says, "Christ loved the **church** and gave himself up for
A P : 0 7 :007(169) [0229] with the word, that the **church** might be presented before
A P : 0 7 :007(169) [0229] Creed also defines the **church** this way, teaching us to
A P : 0 7 :007(169) [0229] us to believe that there is a holy, catholic **church**.
A P : 0 7 :007(169) [0229] Certainly the wicked are not a holy **church**!
A P : 0 7 :008(169) [0229] added to explain what "**church**" means, namely, the
A P : 0 7 :009(169) [0229] the infinite dangers that threaten the **church** with ruin.
A P : 0 7 :009(169) [0229] number of ungodly within the **church** who oppress it.
A P : 0 7 :009(169) [0229] The **church** will abide nevertheless; it exists despite the
A P : 0 7 :010(170) [0229] It says "the **church** catholic" lest we take it to mean an
A P : 0 7 :010(170) [0229] *Decrees* says that "the **church** in the larger sense includes
A P : 0 7 :010(170) [0229] wicked are part of the **church** only in name and not in
A P : 0 7 :010(170) [0229] the godly are part of the **church** in fact as well as in
A P : 0 7 :011(170) [0229] be called part of the **church** of Christ, nor can he be said
A P : 0 7 :012(170) [0231] associated with the true **church** as far as outward
A P : 0 7 :012(170) [0231] we come to define the **church**, we must define that which
A P : 0 7 :012(170) [0231] body of Christ and is the **church** in fact as well as in
A P : 0 7 :013(170) [0231] makes us members, and living members, of the **church**.
A P : 0 7 :013(170) [0231] If we were to define the **church** as only an outward
A P : 0 7 :014(170) [0231] will there be between the **church** and the Old Testament
A P : 0 7 :014(170) [0231] Yet Paul distinguishes the **church** from the Old
A P : 0 7 :014(170) [0231] by the fact that the **church** is a spiritual people, separated
A P : 0 7 :016(170) [0231] Besides the **church** is the kingdom of Christ, the opposite
A P : 0 7 :016(171) [0231] affiliation with the **church** (that is, with the saints among
A P : 0 7 :016(171) [0231] Thus the **church**, which is truly the kingdom of Christ, is,
A P : 0 7 :017(171) [0231] If the **church**, which is truly the kingdom of Christ, is
A P : 0 7 :017(171) [0231] to the kingdom of the devil, they are not the **church**.
A P : 0 7 :017(171) [0233] are mingled with the **church** and hold office in the
A P : 0 7 :017(171) [0233] are mingled with the church and hold office in the **church**.
A P : 0 7 :019(171) [0233] The field, he says, is the world, not the **church**.
A P : 0 7 :019(171) [0233] and says that the true **church** will be separated from it.
A P : 0 7 :019(171) [0233] appearance of the **church** when he says that the kingdom
A P : 0 7 :019(171) [0233] He teaches us that the **church** is hidden under a crowd of
A P : 0 7 :020(171) [0233] but we teach that this **church** actually exists, made up of
A P : 0 7 :020(171) [0233] This **church** is properly called "the pillar of truth" (I Tim.
A P : 0 7 :022(172) [0233] Just as the **church** has the promise that it will always have
A P : 0 7 :022(172) [0235] But the **church**, properly speaking, is that which has the
A P : 0 7 :022(172) [0235] may run rampant in the **church**, they are not, properly
A P : 0 7 :022(172) [0235] when he says: "The **church** is not made up of men by
A P : 0 7 :022(172) [0235] Therefore the **church** is made up of those persons in
A P : 0 7 :023(172) [0235] some such definition of the **church** as the following.
A P : 0 7 :024(172) [0235] rather than of the **church** of Christ has as its authors not
A P : 0 7 :025(172) [0235] If we defined the **church** that way, we would probably
A P : 0 7 :026(173) [0235] the apostles define the **church** as anything but such a
A P : 0 7 :027(173) [0235] prerogative of the true **church**: that they are pillars of the
A P : 0 7 :028(173) [0237] we maintain that the **church** in the proper sense is the
A P : 0 7 :028(173) [0237] are members of the **church** according to this association
A P : 0 7 :028(173) [0237] outward marks, and therefore hold office in the **church**.
A P : 0 7 :028(173) [0237] of Christ, because of the **church**'s call, as Christ testifies
A P : 0 7 :029(173) [0237] the sacraments from unworthy men in the **church**.
A P : 0 7 :029(173) [0237] defend the definition of the **church** which we had given.
A P : 0 7 :029(173) [0237] otherwise, since the **church**, properly so called, is termed
A P : 0 7 :030(173) [0237] "For the true unity of the **church** it is enough to agree
A P : 0 7 :032(174) [0239] opinions about traditions have crept into the **church**.
A P : 0 7 :033(174) [0239] not harm the unity of the **church**, so we believe that the
A P : 0 7 :033(174) [0239] that the true unity of the **church** is not harmed by
A P : 0 7 :034(175) [0239] for the true unity of the **church** that human traditions be
A P : 0 7 :034(175) [0239] children of God, and the **church** of Christ even though
A P : 0 7 :043(177) [0243] faith or the rule of the **church**, and he criticizes the
A P : 0 7 :046(177) [0243] for the unity of the **church** while they themselves have
A P : 0 7 :047(177) [0243] been mingled with the **church** and that the sacraments are
A P : 0 7 :049(178) [0245] us in his parables on the **church** that when we are
A P : 0 9 :002(178) [0245] are outside of Christ's **church**, where there is neither
A P : 0 9 :003(178) [0245] would be saved, and ultimately there would be no **church**.
A P : 1 0 :002(179) [0247] that not only the Roman **Church** affirms the bodily
A P : 1 0 :002(179) [0247] Christ, but that the Greek **Church** has taken and still
A P : 1 0 :004(179) [0247] received in the whole **church** — that in the Lord's Supper
A P : 1 1 :001(180) [0247] the eleventh article on retaining absolution in the **church**.
A P : 1 1 :005(181) [0249] this: "If any enter the **church** of God and are found never
A P : 1 1 :007(181) [0251] The whole **church** throughout Europe knows how
A P : 1 2 :003(182) [0253] salutary, and necessary for the universal **church** of Christ.
A P : 1 2 :007(183) [0255] keys forgives sins before the **church** but not before God.
A P : 1 2 :016(184) [0257] to the Holy Scriptures as well as the **Church** Fathers:
A P : 1 2 :021(185) [0257] forgiveness of sins before the **church**, but not before God.
A P : 1 2 :060(190) [0269] The **church** of Christ believes the same, in spite of our
A P : 1 2 :066(191) [0271] cry out that they are the **church** and follow the consensus
A P : 1 2 :066(191) [0271] are the church and follow the consensus of the **church**.
A P : 1 2 :066(191) [0271] cites the consensus of the **church** in support of our
A P : 1 2 :066(191) [0271] be interpreted as the consensus of the universal **church**.
A P : 1 2 :066(191) [0271] to the pope nor to the **church** do we grant the authority to
A P : 1 2 :067(192) [0271] we can judge what sort of **church** it is that is made up of
A P : 1 2 :073(192) [0273] is what the saints in the **church** have believed since the
A P : 1 2 :090(195) [0279] These dissensions in the **church** certainly give us no
A P : 1 2 :090(195) [0279] — not our cause but the cause of Christ and the **church**.
A P : 1 2 :100(197) [0281] be wicked to remove private absolution from the **church**.
A P : 1 2 :104(197) [0283] The ministers of the **church** therefore have the command
A P : 1 2 :106(197) [0283] father to the pastor of a **church**, he should surely
A P : 1 2 :112(198) [0285] The **church** writers do mention confession, but they are
A P : 1 2 :119(200) [0287] in the Scriptures or in the ancient writers of the **church**.
A P : 1 2 :120(200) [0287] were satisfactions in the **church**, but they did not notice
A P : 1 2 :120(200) [0287] to be accepted into the **church**; that is, they did not see
A P : 1 2 :120(200) [0287] not for discipline in the **church**, but for placating God.
A P : 1 2 :121(200) [0287] were instituted for the sake of **church** discipline.
A P : 1 2 :122(200) [0289] of satisfactions in the **church** would be contrary to the
A P : 1 2 :141(204) [0295] devil has broadcast in the **church** to suppress the
A P : 1 2 :149(206) [0299] armor and seek out the **church** of St. James or the
A P : 1 3 :006(212) [0309] Fathers which even the **church** does not require as
A P : 1 3 :012(212) [0311] The **church** has the command to appoint ministers; to
A P : 1 3 :023(214) [0313] in the one using them, has spawned in the **church**.
A P : 1 4 :001(214) [0315] and the sacraments in the **church** unless he is duly called.
A P : 1 4 :001(214) [0315] desire to maintain the **church** polity and various ranks of
A P : 1 4 :002(214) [0315] it how they will answer to God for disrupting the **church**.

Continued ▶

A P : 1 4 :004(214) [0315] We know that the **church** is present among those who
A P : 1 5 :000(215) [0315] [Article XV.] Human Traditions in the **Church**
A P : 1 5 :001(215) [0315] conducive to tranquillity and good order in the **church**.
A P : 1 5 :013(216) [0319] for the sake of good order and tranquility in the **church**.
A P : 1 5 :018(217) [0319] in the article on the **church** that for the true unity of the
A P : 1 5 :018(217) [0319] for the true unity of the **church** it is not necessary that
A P : 1 5 :022(218) [0321] is very becoming in the **church** and is therefore necessary.
A P : 1 5 :031(219) [0323] that to put this burden on the **church** is a great sin.
A P : 1 5 :032(220) [0323] liberty remain in the **church**, lest the observances of the
A P : 1 5 :038(220) [0325] traditions set up in the **church** because they are useful and
A P : 1 5 :039(220) [0325] us of abolishing good ordinances and **church** discipline.
A P : 1 5 :044(221) [0327] we diligently maintain **church** discipline, pious
A P : 1 5 :044(221) [0327] pious ceremonies, and the good customs of the **church**.
A P : 1 6 :004(223) [0331] had broadcast many dangerous ideas through the **church**.
A P : 2 0 :002(227) [0339] is more certain in the **church** than that the forgiveness of
A P : 2 0 :002(227) [0339] rather agree with this **church** of the prophets than with
A P : 2 0 :004(227) [0339] if they dare to smuggle such a notion into the **church**.
A P : 2 0 :006(227) [0339] truth — truth which the **church** must defend and which
A P : 2 0 :006(227) [0339] to suffer for Christ and the advancement of the **church**.
A P : 2 0 :009(228) [0341] which this article of ours offers to the universal **church**.
A P : 2 0 :014(228) [0343] The **church** of Christ has always believed that the
A P : 2 1 :004(229) [0343] men, and giving teachers and other gifts to the **church**.
A P : 2 1 :009(230) [0345] in heaven pray for the **church** in general, as they prayed
A P : 2 1 :009(230) [0345] as they prayed for the **church** universal while they were on
A P : 2 1 :010(230) [0345] do pray fervently for the **church**, it does not follow that
A P : 2 1 :013(230) [0345] to the example of the **church**, we reply that this is a novel
A P : 2 1 :013(230) [0345] church, we reply that this is a novel custom in the **church**.
A P : 2 1 :013(230) [0345] novel invocation in the **church** is not the same as the
A P : 2 1 :027(232) [0349] Mary prays for the **church**, does she receive souls in
A P : 2 1 :033(233) [0351] there is no proof for it either in the Fathers of the **church**.
A P : 2 1 :040(235) [0355] pastors permitted many abuses to creep into the **church**.
A P : 2 1 :041(235) [0355] ought to be as clear and plain as possible in the **church**.
A P : 2 1 :042(235) [0355] had the good of the **church** at heart at this point, they
A P : 2 1 :042(235) [0355] most anxious for the healing and improving of the **church**
A P : 2 1 :043(235) [0357] that the state of the **church** does not concern them very
A P : 2 1 :043(235) [0357] a summary of the doctrines of the **church** for the people.
A P : 2 1 :043(235) [0357] their position nor the **church**, and good men can easily
A P : 2 1 :043(235) [0357] They will trouble the **church** with their godless teachings
A P : 2 1 :043(235) [0357] whole organization of the **church**, which we are very
A P : 2 1 :044(236) [0357] happened before, nor crush sound doctrine in the **church**.
A P : 2 2 :001(236) [0357] do so only for part of the **church**, but for all of the
A P : 2 2 :001(236) [0357] so only for part of the church, but for all of the **church**.
A P : 2 2 :001(236) [0357] admit, all of the **church** uses the sacrament, not only the
A P : 2 2 :002(236) [0357] instituted it for all of the **church**, why is one kind taken
A P : 2 2 :002(236) [0357] taken away from part of the **church** and its use prohibited
A P : 2 2 :004(236) [0359] the entire sacrament was instituted for the whole **church**.
A P : 2 2 :004(236) [0359] it prevailed in the Latin **church**, as Cyprian and Jerome
A P : 2 2 :006(237) [0359] even try to explain to the **church** why one part of the
A P : 2 2 :006(237) [0359] should have given the **church** a valid explanation to
A P : 2 2 :007(237) [0359] in the beginning of the **church** it was customary in some
A P : 2 2 :015(238) [0361] But the **church** cannot arrogate to itself the freedom to
A P : 2 2 :016(238) [0361] We do not blame the **church**, which has suffered this
A P : 2 2 :017(238) [0361] dare we assume that the **church** immediately approves or
A P : 2 3 :002(239) [0363] the empire, as if the **church** were adorned by the public
A P : 2 3 :067(248) [0383] heresy or that the **church** condemned marriage at that
A P : 2 3 :068(249) [0383] and convicted by many previous tribunals of the **church**.
A P : 2 3 :068(249) [0383] So they often misquote these tribunals of the **church**.
A P : 2 4 :002(249) [0385] of the faith of the **church** benefits from hearing a Mass
A P : 2 4 :006(250) [0385] nothing contrary to the **church** catholic in our having
A P : 2 4 :006(250) [0385] for the Fathers of the **church** before Gregory make no
A P : 2 4 :013(251) [0387] have brought this pharisaic notion into the **church**.
A P : 2 4 :041(257) [0399] Experience shows the sort of tyrants who rule the **church**.
A P : 2 4 :041(257) [0399] and they have instituted new worship in the **church**.
A P : 2 4 :050(259) [0401] appearances, our **church** attendance is greater than
A P : 2 4 :051(259) [0403] but they are not the peculiar adornment of the **church**.
A P : 2 4 :062(260) [0405] so that in this the **church** might have a service that
A P : 2 4 :065(261) [0407] so authoritatively in the **church**; nor do they have the
A P : 2 4 :065(261) [0407] have the support of the ancient **church** and the Fathers.
A P : 2 4 :076(263) [0411] From this term "eucharist" arose in the **church**.
A P : 2 4 :089(265) [0413] such services in the **church** without the command of God
A P : 2 4 :091(266) [0415] This is the abolition of the daily sacrifice in the **church**.
A P : 2 4 :092(266) [0417] institute services in the **church** without the authority of
A P : 2 4 :098(268) [0417] Baal continued; yet the **church** of God was there,
A P : 2 7 :005(269) [0421] crowd that gorges itself on the public alms of the **church**.
A P : 2 7 :013(271) [0423] is a witness, thy whole **church** is a witness: this is truly the
A P : 2 7 :027(274) [0429] expressions in the **church**, finding the perfection of the
A P : 2 7 :064(280) [0441] widows who served the **church** and were supported from
A P : 2 7 :067(280) [0441] As a matter of fact, the **church** did not yet know about
A P : 2 8 :007(282) [0445] In the **church** we must keep this teaching, that we receive
A P : 2 8 :008(282) [0445] and enlarging on the sin of those who burden the **church**.
A P : 2 8 :011(283) [0447] not be imposed on the **church** to merit forgiveness of sins
A P : 2 8 :015(283) [0447] of preserving order in the **church**, for the sake of peace.
A P : 2 8 :016(283) [0449] worked hard to free the **church** from the idea that human
A P : 2 8 :018(284) [0449] great and learned men in the **church** have felt about it.
A P : 2 8 :024(285) [0451] the truth which the **church** needs, nor can we agree with
S 1 : P R :008(290) [0457] among us there is no **church**, no government, and no
S 1 : P R :012(290) [0459] necessary concerns of the **church**, there are countless
S 1 : P R :014(291) [0459] so many tasks upon us in **church**, state, and family that
S 2 : 0 2 :009(294) [0465] possession of the **church**, to meet his own private need
S 2 : 0 2 :009(294) [0465] his own pleasure apart from the fellowship of the **church**.
S 2 : 0 2 :024(296) [0469] merits of all the saints and the entire **church**.
S 2 : 0 3 :001(297) [0471] other ministers in the **church**, others who are necessary
S 2 : 0 4 :003(298) [0473] the entire holy Christian **church** (in so far as this lies in
S 2 : 0 4 :004(299) [0473] is manifest that the holy **church** was without a pope for
S 2 : 0 4 :005(299) [0473] The holy Christian **church** can exist very well without
S 2 : 0 4 :006(299) [0473] papacy is of no use to the **church** because it exercises no
S 2 : 0 4 :006(299) [0473] Consequently the **church** must continue to exist without
S 2 : 0 4 :007(299) [0473] that he is the head of the **church** by divine right or by
S 2 : 0 4 :008(300) [0473] and in whatever **church** God would raise up a man fitted
S 2 : 0 4 :009(300) [0473] Consequently the **church** cannot be better governed and
S 2 : 0 4 :013(300) [0475] to be the head of the Christian **church** by divine right.
S 2 : 0 4 :013(300) [0475] and then the lord of the **church**, and finally of the whole
S 3 : 0 3 :024(307) [0485] to the aid of the poor **church** and invented indulgences.
S 3 : 0 3 :025(307) [0485] into all lands until every **church** and house was reached
S 3 : 0 5 :004(311) [0493] Christ made, and the **church** should administer Baptism
S 3 : 0 7 :001(311) [0493] and power given to the **church** by Christ to bind and
S 3 : 0 8 :001(312) [0493] to fall into disuse in the **church**, especially for the sake of
S 3 : 0 8 :002(312) [0495] valued, like all other functions of the Christian **church**.
S 3 : 0 9 :000(314) [0497] which does not concern us ministers of the **church**.
S 3 : 0 9 :000(314) [0497] other fellowship in the **church** until they mend their ways
S 3 : 1 0 :001(314) [0497] were concerned about the **church** and the Gospel, they
S 3 : 1 0 :002(314) [0497] or discharge any office or work in the **church**.
S 3 : 1 0 :002(314) [0497] Yet the **church** must not be deprived of ministers on their
S 3 : 1 0 :003(314) [0497] wrote concerning the **church** in Alexandria that it was
S 3 : 1 2 :000(315) [0499] XII. The **Church**
S 3 : 1 2 :001(315) [0499] to the papists that they are the **church**, for they are not.
S 3 : 1 2 :002(315) [0499] forbid in the name of the **church**, for, thank God, a
S 3 : 1 2 :002(315) [0499] child knows what the **church** is, namely, holy believers
S 3 : 1 2 :003(315) [0499] So children pray, "I believe in one holy Christian **church**."
S 3 : 1 5 :005(317) [0501] the name of my brethren and of the **church** of Hanover
S 3 : 1 5 :005(317) [0501] Simon Schneeweiss, pastor of the **church** in Crailsheim
S 3 : 1 5 :005(317) [0501] pastor of the **church** in Koethen, subscribe
S 3 : 1 5 :005(317) [0501] Oemcken, superintendent of the **church** in Minden.
S 3 : 1 5 :005(317) [0501] minister of the **church** of Christ which is in Soest,
S 3 : 1 5 :005(317) [0501] Myconius, pastor of the **church** in Gotha, Thuringia,
S 3 : 1 5 :005(318) [0501] Lang, preacher of the **church** in Erfurt, in my own name
T R : 0 0 :004(320) [0503] be false, impious, tyrannical, and injurious to the **church**.
T R : 0 0 :011(321) [0507] and teaches that the **church** is above the ministers.
T R : 0 0 :011(321) [0507] or authority over the **church** or the other ministers.
T R : 0 0 :011(321) [0507] or authority over the **church**, nor burden the church with
T R : 0 0 :011(321) [0507] church, nor burden the **church** with traditions, nor let
T R : 0 0 :011(321) [0507] of the others and of the **church**, I Peter 5:3, "Not
T R : 0 0 :017(323) [0509] This also shows that the **church** did not then acknowledge
T R : 0 0 :020(323) [0509] pope be over the whole **church** by divine right when the
T R : 0 0 :020(323) [0509] by divine right when the **church** elects him and the custom
T R : 0 0 :021(323) [0509] But if the ancient **church** had acknowledged the primacy
T R : 0 0 :022(323) [0511] and on this rock I will build my **church**" (Matt. 16:18).
T R : 0 0 :024(324) [0511] but to the whole **church**, as is shown by many clear and
T R : 0 0 :024(324) [0511] and immediately on the **church**, and for the same reason
T R : 0 0 :024(324) [0511] for the same reason the **church** especially possesses the
T R : 0 0 :025(324) [0511] this rock I will build my **church**" (Matt. 16:18), it is
T R : 0 0 :025(324) [0511] it is certain that the **church** is not built on the authority
T R : 0 0 :028(325) [0511] Peter," for he built his **church** not on the man but on the
T R : 0 0 :029(325) [0513] On this rock of confession, therefore, the **church** is built.
T R : 0 0 :029(325) [0513] This faith is the foundation of the **church**.
T R : 0 0 :030(325) [0513] to preach the Word or govern the **church** with the Word.
T R : 0 0 :034(325) [0513] to descend over the **church**, and afterwards great
T R : 0 0 :037(326) [0515] that they have been great plagues in the **church**.
T R : 0 0 :039(327) [0515] of one who rules in the **church** and not of the kings of
T R : 0 0 :040(327) [0515] that the pope rules in the **church** and that he has set up
T R : 0 0 :040(327) [0515] of the authority of the **church** and the ministry, offering
T R : 0 0 :040(327) [0517] to be judged by the **church** or by anybody, and he exalts
T R : 0 0 :040(327) [0517] above the decisions of councils and the whole **church**.
T R : 0 0 :040(327) [0517] to be judged by the **church** or by anybody is to make
T R : 0 0 :049(328) [0519] wrests judgment from the **church** and does not allow
T R : 0 0 :054(329) [0519] the chief members of the **church**, the kings and the
T R : 0 0 :054(329) [0519] for the interests of the **church** and to see to it that errors
T R : 0 0 :055(329) [0521] hold synods, how can the **church** be purified as long as
T R : 0 0 :056(329) [0521] are decisions of the **church** and not of the pontiffs, it is
T R : 0 0 :056(329) [0521] and see to it that the **church** is not deprived of the power
T R : 0 0 :056(330) [0521] and true judgment on the part of the **church**.
T R : 0 0 :059(330) [0521] hinder the welfare of the **church** by so strengthening
T R : 0 0 :062(330) [0523] followings around themselves, rend the **church** of Christ.
T R : 0 0 :065(331) [0523] by a pastor in his own **church** is valid by divine right.
T R : 0 0 :067(331) [0523] For wherever the **church** exists, the right to administer
T R : 0 0 :067(331) [0523] it is necessary for the **church** to retain the right of calling,
T R : 0 0 :067(331) [0523] given exclusively to the **church**, and no human authority
T R : 0 0 :067(331) [0523] no human authority can take it away from the **church**.
T R : 0 0 :067(331) [0523] exclusively to the **church**, and he adds that they are given
T R : 0 0 :067(331) [0523] Where the true **church** is, therefore, the right of electing
T R : 0 0 :068(331) [0523] keys were given to the **church** and not merely to certain
T R : 0 0 :069(331) [0525] words apply to the true **church** which, since it alone
T R : 0 0 :070(332) [0525] common custom of the **church** also bears witness to this,
T R : 0 0 :070(332) [0525] a bishop, either of that **church** or of a neighboring
T R : 0 0 :070(332) [0525] or of a neighboring **church**, was brought in to confirm the
T R : 0 0 :072(332) [0525] facts it is evident that the **church** retains the right of
T R : 0 0 :080(334) [0527] they defraud the **church**, which needs these means for the
T R : 0 0 :081(334) [0527] be established without the endowments of the **church**.
T R : 0 0 :082(334) [0527] those who defraud the **church** know that God will require
T R : 0 0 :082(334) [0529] Gerard Oemcken, minister of the **church** in Minden
T R : 0 0 :082(335) [0529] Peter Geltner, preacher in the **church** in Frankfurt
T R : 0 0 :082(335) [0529] Wolfart, minister of the Word in the **church** in Augsburg
T R : 0 0 :082(000) [0529] with the belief of the true and genuine catholic **Church**.
S C : 0 2 :005(345) [0545] *Spirit, the holy Christian* ***church****, the communion of*
S C : 0 2 :006(345) [0545] the whole Christian **church** on earth and preserves it in
S C : 0 2 :006(345) [0545] In this Christian **church** he daily and abundantly forgives
L C : S P :013(363) [0577] Spirit, the holy Christian **church**, the communion of
L C : 0 1 :314(407) [0671] his knees a whole day in **church**, this is considered a
L C : 0 2 :034(415) [0687] *Spirit, the holy Christian* ***church****, the communion of*
L C : 0 2 :037(415) [0687] of saints or Christian **church**, the forgiveness of sins, the
L C : 0 2 :037(415) [0687] us upon the bosom of the **church**, where he preaches to
L C : 0 2 :041(416) [0689] "Through the Christian **church**, the forgiveness of sins,
L C : 0 2 :045(416) [0689] Therefore there was no Christian **church**.
L C : 0 2 :045(416) [0689] and gather the Christian **church**, and outside it no one
L C : 0 2 :047(416) [0689] calls the holy Christian **church** a *communio sanctorum,*
L C : 0 2 :048(416) [0691] to the term *Kirche*, **"church,"** by which simple folk
L C : 0 2 :048(416) [0691] should not be called a **church** except for the single reason
L C : 0 2 :048(416) [0691] Thus the word **"church"** *(Kirche)* really means nothing
L C : 0 2 :049(417) [0691] someone wished to explain what the Christian **church** is.
L C : 0 2 :054(417) [0693] that in this Christian **church** we have the forgiveness of
L C : 0 2 :054(418) [0693] unity of the Christian **church**, yet because we are
L C : 0 2 :055(418) [0693] in the Christian **church** is so ordered that we may daily
L C : 0 2 :055(418) [0693] we are in the Christian **church**, where there is full
L C : 0 2 :056(418) [0693] But outside the Christian **church** (that is, where the
L C : 0 2 :056(418) [0693] have expelled and separated themselves from the **church**.
L C : 0 2 :059(418) [0695] two means, the Christian **church** and the forgiveness of

Continued ▶

LC : 0 2 :066(419) [0697] are outside the Christian **church**, whether heathen,
LC : 0 3 :007(421) [0699] to pass for prayers in the **church** was not really prayer.
LC : 0 3 :045(426) [0709] name, as in the past a **church** was said to be desecrated
LC : 0 3 :084(432) [0723] intercession of the **church**, and let them take care lest this
LC : 0 4 :050(443) [0745] since the holy Christian **church** will abide until the end of
LC : 0 4 :051(443) [0745] one Holy Christian **church**, the communion of saints,"
LC : 0 4 :064(444) [0749] by which we are first received into the Christian **church**.
LC : 0 4 :081(446) [0751] we embarked when we entered the Christian **church**.
LC : 0 5 :032(450) [0759] in the holy Christian **church**, the forgiveness of sins," are
LC : 0 5 :086(456) [0773] Word of God and the Christian **church** will be preserved.
LC : 0 5 :087(456) [0773] into the Christian **church**, they should also enjoy this
LC : 0 6 :001(457) [0000] burden he imposed upon the Christian **church**.
LC : 0 6 :014(458) [0000] to his Christian **church** and commanded us to absolve
EP : RN :003(465) [0777] lifetime — false teachers and heretics invaded the **church**.
EP : RN :003(465) [0777] Against these the ancient **church** formulated symbols
EP : RN :003(465) [0777] of the orthodox and true **church**, namely, the Apostles'
EP : RN :003(465) [0777] been introduced into the **church** of God contrary to
EP : RN :008(465) [0779] by contemporaries in the **church** of God with reference to
EP : 0 1 :008(467) [0781] It is as the **church** sings, "Through Adam's fall man's
EP : 0 3 :002(473) [0793] *Doctrine of the Christian **Church** Against Both These*
EP : 0 4 :004(476) [0797] *Pure Doctrine of the Christian **Church** in this Controversy*
EP : 0 5 :002(478) [0801] with great diligence in the **church** so that, according to
EP : 0 7 :015(483) [0813] teaching of the leading **Church** Fathers, such as
EP : 0 8 :003(487) [0819] *Teaching of the Christian **Church** concerning the Person*
EP : 1 0 :000(492) [0829] X. **Church** Usages, Called Adiaphora or Indifferent
EP : 1 0 :001(492) [0829] those ceremonies or **church** usages which are neither
EP : 1 0 :001(492) [0829] been introduced into the **church** in the interest of good
EP : 1 0 :003(493) [0829] that the ceremonies or **church** usages which are neither
EP : 1 0 :007(493) [0831] and confess that no **church** should condemn another
EP : 1 0 :009(494) [0831] and institutions in the **church** are to be regarded as in
EP : 1 0 :012(494) [0831] and as it may be most beneficial to the **church**.
EP : 1 1 :001(494) [0831] concerning it might be introduced into the **church**.
EP : 1 1 :021(497) [0837] Hence they should not be tolerated in God's **church**.
EP : 1 2 :002(498) [0839] be tolerated either in the **church**, or in the body politic
EP : 1 2 :002(498) [0839] *Errors which Cannot be Tolerated in the **Church***
EP : 1 2 :022(499) [0841] That the ministry of the **church** — the Word preached
EP : 1 2 :027(500) [0843] 8. That a minister of the **church** cannot teach profitably
SD : PR :004(502) [0847] were formulated in the **church** of God when great
SD : PR :009(503) [0849] be tolerated in the **church** of God, much less be excused
SD : RN :001(503) [0849] concord within the **church** is a summary formula and
SD : RN :001(503) [0851] same purpose the ancient **church** always had its
SD : RN :004(504) [0851] within the Christian **church** are clearly and solidly
SD : RN :005(504) [0853] it just as in the ancient **church** it was traditional and
SD : RN :006(504) [0853] to insinuate into the **church** errors that had already been
SD : RN :014(506) [0855] concord within the **church**, it is essential not only to
SD : RN :015(507) [0857] be allowed to disturb the **church**) and necessary
SD : RN :017(507) [0857] ancient, orthodox **church** rejected and condemned on the
SD : 0 1 :054(518) [0877] prominent doctors of the **church**, under the necessity of
SD : 0 1 :057(518) [0877] by the testimonies of the **church**'s teachers, and never
SD : 0 2 :036(528) [0895] member of this Christian **church**, a shareholder and
SD : 0 2 :037(528) [0895] members of the Christian **church** we belonged entirely to
SD : 0 2 :038(528) [0895] he brings us into the **church**, sanctifies us therein, and
SD : 0 2 :040(528) [0895] the whole Christian **church** on earth and preserves it in
SD : 0 2 :050(531) [0901] he gathers an eternal **church** for himself out of the human
SD : 0 2 :053(531) [0903] so that he can go to **church**, listen to the sermon, or not
SD : 0 2 :080(536) [0911] in no wise tolerate in the **church** of God, the enthusiasts
SD : 0 3 :021(542) [0921] his book *On the Councils and the **Church*** and elsewhere.
SD : 0 4 :002(551) [0939] not be tolerated in the **church**, lest the merit of Christ,
SD : 0 4 :036(557) [0949] wrangling and preserve the **church** from many offenses.
SD : 0 5 :023(562) [0959] forth side by side in the **church** of God with the proper
SD : 0 5 :024(562) [0961] and diligently in the **church** of God until the end of the
SD : 0 5 :027(563) [0961] and reopen the door to the papacy in the **church** of God.
SD : 0 6 :009(565) [0965] summer portion of the **Church** Postil, on the Epistle for
SD : 0 7 :011(571) [0975] but also the Greek **Church** has taught the bodily presence
SD : 0 7 :059(580) [0993] of Christ, which is the **church**), or it is the means whereby
SD : 0 7 :059(580) [0993] into the body of Christ, which is the **church**."
SD : 0 7 :060(580) [0995] and teachers of the **church** have unanimously understood
SD : 0 7 :066(581) [0995] the entire holy Christian **church** teach unanimously that
SD : 0 7 :067(582) [0997] St. Paul, and the entire **church** when they call oral eating
SD : 0 7 :076(583) [0999] true body and blood are present in the **church**'s Supper."
SD : 0 7 :085(584) [1003] be profitably urged and retained in the **church** of God.
SD : 0 7 :110(589) [1011] Word of God and the testimony of the ancient **church**.
SD : 0 7 :123(590) [1015] community of the **church** receive only bread and wine in
SD : 0 8 :017(594) [1021] heresy the Christian **church** has always held in simple
SD : 0 8 :018(594) [1021] ancient teachers of the **church**, both before and after the
SD : 0 8 :022(595) [1023] ancient teachers of the **church** have combined both
SD : 0 8 :038(598) [1027] own words, so that the **church** of God may be forearmed
SD : 0 8 :044(599) [1029] *the Councils and the **Church**:* "We Christians must know
SD : 0 8 :057(602) [1035] entire ancient orthodox **church** that whatever the
SD : 0 8 :059(602) [1035] of the ancient orthodox **church** concerning this article are
SD : 0 8 :061(602) [1035] the ancient orthodox **church** made herein on the basis of
SD : 0 8 :064(603) [1037] with the ancient orthodox **church**, as it explained this
SD : 0 8 :064(604) [1039] which the entire ancient **church** used in explaining this
SD : 0 8 :077(606) [1043] with us in the Christian **church** and community and that
SD : 0 8 :078(607) [1043] he is present with his **church** and community on earth as
SD : 0 9 :001(610) [1051] as among the ancient teachers of the Christian **church**.
SD : 1 0 :001(610) [1053] ceremonies and **church** rites which are neither
SD : 1 0 :001(610) [1053] been introduced into the **church** with good intentions for
SD : 1 0 :007(611) [1055] decorum in the **church**, true adiaphora or things
SD : 1 0 :009(612) [1055] evangelical decorum, and the edification of the **church**.
SD : 1 0 :015(613) [1057] commanded the **church** to preserve, as we have just
SD : 1 0 :015(613) [1057] forcibly imposed on the **church** as necessary and as
SD : 1 0 :019(614) [1059] papist bishops) that they are the **church**, for they are not.
SD : 1 0 :019(614) [1059] forbid in the name of the **church**, for, thank God, a
SD : 1 0 :019(614) [1059] child knows what the **church** is, namely, holy believers
SD : 1 0 :019(614) [1059] were concerned about the **church** and the Gospel, they
SD : 1 0 :019(614) [1059] or discharge any office or work in the **church**.
SD : 1 0 :019(614) [1059] Yet the **church** must not be deprived of ministers on their
SD : 1 0 :021(614) [1061] or authority over the **church**, nor burden the church with
SD : 1 0 :021(614) [1061] church, nor burden the **church** with traditions, nor let
SD : 1 0 :024(615) [1061] exhaustively instructs the **church** of God on how we are
SD : 1 0 :030(616) [1061] may in Christian liberty be most beneficial to the **church**.
SD : 1 1 :050(624) [1079] testimony that the **church** of God shall exist and remain
SD : 1 1 :050(624) [1079] teaches us what the true **church** is, lest we be offended by
SD : 1 1 :050(624) [1079] by the outward prestige of the false **church** (Rom. 9:8ff.).
SD : 1 2 :016(634) [1099] those ministers of the **church** who preach the Gospel
SD : 1 2 :030(635) [1101] That the ministry of the **church**, the Word proclaimed
SD : 1 2 :035(635) [1101] 7. That a minister of cthe **church** who is himself not truly

Churches (206)

PR : PR :000(001) [0004] of their Lands, **Churches**, Schools, and Descendants
PR : PR :003(003) [0007] Subsequently many **churches** and schools committed
PR : PR :004(004) [0007] scandalous division in **churches** and schools so that he
PR : PR :004(004) [0007] us and our schools and **churches** so as to palliate their
PR : PR :005(004) [0009] the Almighty, that our **churches** and schools might have
PR : PR :005(004) [0009] teachings into the **churches** in which the apostles
PR : PR :005(004) [0009] also inflicted on our **churches** because of our own and the
PR : PR :007(004) [0009] of ourselves and of our **churches** and schools.
PR : PR :009(006) [0011] that neither we nor our **churches** were delivered thereby
PR : PR :009(006) [0011] and deterred from our **churches**, schools, doctrine, faith,
PR : PR :009(006) [0011] now and again introduced into our **churches** and schools.
PR : PR :018(008) [0015] it is that we and the **churches** and schools of our lands
PR : PR :018(009) [0015] doctrine in our lands, **churches**, and schools other than in
PR : PR :018(009) [0017] will spare us and our **churches** and their ministers the
PR : PR :021(011) [0019] in the schools and the **churches**): This divine majesty is
PR : PR :022(011) [0019] less do we mean entire **churches** inside or outside the
PR : PR :022(011) [0019] to tolerate in our lands, **churches**, and schools inasmuch
PR : PR :022(011) [0019] people even in those **churches** which have up to now
PR : PR :022(012) [0019] as it is celebrated in our **churches** according to Christ's
PR : PR :022(012) [0019] Word and unite with us and our **churches** and schools.
PR : PR :023(012) [0021] territories, schools, and **churches** than that alone which is
PR : PR :023(012) [0021] we have directed our **churches** and schools first of all to
PR : PR :024(013) [0023] of Christian schools and **churches**, and to the needed
PR : PR :026(014) [0025] diligent visitation of **churches** and schools, the supervision
AG : 0 0 :001(047) [0059] and taught in our **churches** for proper Christian
AG : 0 0 :001(048) [0059] and separate from our **churches** as if our teaching were
AG : 0 0 :000(048) [0059] nothing is taught in our **churches** concerning articles of
AG : 2 4 :010(057) [0065] it in almost all **churches** for a monetary consideration.
AG : 2 4 :013(057) [0065] revenues and stipends, were discontinued in our **churches**.
AG : 2 4 :041(061) [0069] times past, even in large **churches** where there were many
AG : 2 8 :022(084) [0087] parish ministers and **churches** are bound to be obedient to
AG : 2 8 :049(089) [0091] the power to burden the **churches** with countless
AG : 2 8 :053(090) [0091] so that everything in the **churches** is done in good order,
AG : 2 8 :071(093) [0093] Our **churches** do not ask that the bishops should restore
AG : 2 8 :074(094) [0093] changes do not destroy the unity of Christian **churches**.
AG : 2 8 :076(094) [0095] had power to coerce the **churches** according to their will.
AG : 0 0 :005(095) [0095] from creeping into our **churches** and gaining the upper
AL : 0 1 :001(027) [0043] Our **churches** teach with great unanimity that the decree
AL : 0 1 :005(028) [0043] Our **churches** condemn all heresies which have sprung up
AL : 0 2 :001(029) [0043] Our **churches** also teach that since the fall of Adam all
AL : 0 2 :003(029) [0045] Our **churches** condemn the Pelagians and others who
AL : 0 3 :001(029) [0045] Our **churches** also teach that the Word — that is, the Son
AL : 0 4 :001(030) [0045] Our **churches** also teach that men cannot be justified
AL : 0 5 :004(031) [0045] Our **churches** condemn the Anabaptists and others who
AL : 0 6 :001(031) [0045] Our **churches** also teach that this faith is bound to bring
AL : 0 7 :001(032) [0047] Our **churches** also teach that one holy church is to
AL : 0 8 :003(033) [0047] Our **churches** condemn the Donatists and others like them
AL : 0 9 :001(033) [0047] Our **churches** teach that Baptism is necessary for
AL : 0 9 :003(033) [0047] Our **churches** condemn the Anabaptists who reject the
AL : 1 0 :001(034) [0047] Our **churches** teach that the body and blood of Christ are
AL : 1 1 :001(034) [0047] Our **churches** teach that private absolution should be
AL : 1 1 :001(034) [0047] private absolution should be retained in the **churches**.
AL : 1 2 :001(034) [0049] Our **churches** teach that those who have fallen after
AL : 1 2 :007(035) [0049] Our **churches** condemn the Anabaptists who deny that
AL : 1 3 :001(035) [0049] Our **churches** teach that the sacraments were instituted
AL : 1 3 :003(036) [0049] [Our **churches** therefore condemn those who teach that
AL : 1 4 :000(036) [0049] Our **churches** teach that nobody should preach publicly in
AL : 1 5 :001(036) [0049] Our **churches** teach that those rites should be observed
AL : 1 6 :001(037) [0051] Our **churches** teach that lawful civil ordinances are good
AL : 1 6 :003(037) [0051] Our **churches** condemn the Anabaptists who forbid
AL : 1 7 :001(038) [0051] Our **churches** also teach that at the consummation of the
AL : 1 7 :004(038) [0051] Our **churches** condemn the Anabaptists who think that
AL : 1 8 :001(039) [0051] Our **churches** teach that man's will has some liberty for
AL : 1 8 :008(040) [0053] [Our **churches** condemn the Pelagians and others who
AL : 1 9 :000(040) [0053] Our **churches** teach that although God creates and
AL : 2 0 :001(041) [0053] Our **churches** are falsely accused of forbidding good
AL : 2 0 :008(042) [0053] have instructed our **churches** concerning faith as follows:
AL : 2 1 :001(046) [0057] Our **churches** teach that the remembrance of saints may
AL : 0 0 :002(047) [0059] have crept into the **churches** without proper authority.
AL : 0 0 :003(048) [0059] nor have the rites of all the **churches** ever been the same.
AL : 0 0 :004(048) [0059] and all old ordinances are abolished in our **churches**.
AL : 0 0 :001(048) [0059] Inasmuch as our **churches** dissent from the church
AL : 0 0 :006(049) [0059] as the proper observance of ceremonies in the **churches**.
AL : 2 3 :017(054) [0063] And it seems that the **churches** will soon be lacking in
AL : 2 4 :001(056) [0065] Our **churches** are falsely accused of abolishing the Mass.
AL : 2 4 :011(057) [0065] abuse extends in all the **churches**, by what manner of men
AL : 2 4 :041(061) [0069] In former times, even in **churches** most frequented, Mass
AL : 2 5 :001(061) [0069] been abolished in our **churches**, for it is not customary to
AL : 2 5 :005(062) [0069] is to be found with our **churches** on this point, for even
AL : 2 6 :001(063) [0071] those who teach in the **churches** that distinctions among
AL : 2 6 :002(064) [0071] the learned men in the **churches** exacted these works as a
AL : 2 6 :019(067) [0073] great need to warn the **churches** of these errors which had
AL : 2 8 :022(084) [0087] **Churches** are therefore bound by divine law to be
AL : 2 8 :023(084) [0087] contrary to the Gospel, **churches** have a command of God
AL : 2 8 :042(088) [0089] such traditions on the **churches** and thus ensnare
AL : 2 8 :051(089) [0091] Christian liberty in the **churches**, namely, that bondage to
AL : 2 8 :053(090) [0091] about Sunday and about similar rites in our **churches**?
AL : 2 8 :055(090) [0091] It is proper that the **churches** comply with such
AL : 2 8 :055(090) [0091] so that everything in the **churches** may be done in order
AL : 2 8 :071(093) [0093] Our **churches** do not ask that the bishops restore concord
AL : 2 8 :076(094) [0095] bishops to be domineering and to coerce the **churches**.
AL : 0 0 :005(095) [0095] introduction into our **churches** of any new and ungodly
AP : PR :019(099) [0103] afflicted and scattered **churches** and to restore them to a
AP : 0 4 :236(140) [0185] They are breaking up **churches**.
AP : 0 4 :243(141) [0189] unless pastors and **churches** overlook and forgive many
AP : 0 7 :032(174) [0239] Similarly, some **churches** have excommunicated others

Continued ▶

A P : 0 7 :033(174) [0239] So in our **churches** we willingly observe the order of the
A P : 0 7 :042(176) [0241] had commanded their **churches** to celebrate the Passover
A P : 0 7 :042(176) [0243] did not want to impose an ordinance on the **churches**.
A P : 0 9 :002(178) [0245] have arisen in our **churches** since our people have been
A P : 1 1 :003(180) [0249] that most people in our **churches** use the sacraments,
A P : 1 2 :127(201) [0289] if you suppose that **churches** should be maintained only
A P : 1 4 :005(215) [0315] that the bishops stop raging against our **churches**.
A P : 1 5 :020(218) [0321] and in order in the **churches**, and finally because they
A P : 1 5 :039(220) [0325] claim that in our **churches** the public liturgy is more
A P : 1 5 :041(220) [0325] and ministers of the **churches** are required to instruct and
A P : 1 5 :043(221) [0327] In our **churches**, on the other hand, all sermons deal with
A P : 1 5 :044(221) [0327] of the state of our **churches** it is evident that we diligently
A P : 2 1 :043(235) [0357] They do not tolerate capable clergy in the **churches**.
A P : 2 2 :004(236) [0359] In the Greek **churches** this practice still remains, and once
A P : 2 4 :001(249) [0383] In our **churches** Mass is celebrated every Sunday and on
A P : 2 4 :003(250) [0385] to point out that our **churches** keep the Latin lessons and
A P : 2 4 :004(250) [0385] This has always been the custom in the **churches**.
A P : 2 4 :044(258) [0399] They call these trifles the ornament of the **churches**.
A P : 2 4 :047(258) [0401] and introduced much wicked worship into the **churches**.
A P : 2 4 :048(258) [0401] God, the priests in our **churches** pay attention to the
A P : 2 4 :049(258) [0401] because in their **churches** mercenary priests use the
A P : 2 4 :049(258) [0401] In our **churches** the use is more frequent and more
A P : 2 4 :051(259) [0401] real adornment of the **churches** is godly, practical, and
A P : 2 4 :057(260) [0405] sacrificers who daily peddle their wares in the **churches**.
A P : 2 8 :001(281) [0443] article states about the immunity of **churches** and priests."
A P : 2 8 :003(281) [0443] listen to the complaints of **churches** and pious hearts!
A P : 2 8 :003(281) [0443] neglect the state of the **churches**, and they do not see to it
A P : 2 8 :003(281) [0443] and administration of the sacraments in the **churches**.
S 1 : P R :010(290) [0457] for by God's grace our **churches** have now been so
S 2 : 0 2 :026(297) [0469] to them, establish **churches**, altars, and services for them,
S 2 : 0 4 :001(298) [0471] bishop and pastor of the **churches** in Rome and of such
S 2 : 0 4 :001(298) [0471] Rome and of such other **churches** as have attached
S 2 : 0 4 :001(298) [0471] These **churches** did not choose to be under him as under
S 2 : 0 4 :004(299) [0473] at the least and that the **churches** of the Greeks and of
S 2 : 0 4 :009(300) [0475] Alexandria governed the **churches** together and in
S 2 : 0 4 :014(301) [0475] the ceremonies of **churches**, vestments, food, personnel,
S 3 : 0 8 :004(312) [0495] and commands in his **churches** is spirit and law, even
S 3 : 1 0 :003(314) [0497] examples of the ancient **churches** and Fathers, we shall
S 3 : 1 5 :004(316) [0501] as the consecration of **churches**, the baptism of bells, the
S 3 : 1 5 :005(317) [0501] superintendent of the **churches** in the Duchy of
T R : 0 0 :012(321) [0507] should administer the **churches** in the East and the bishop
T R : 0 0 :012(322) [0507] administer the suburban **churches**, that is, those that were
T R : 0 0 :013(322) [0507] be elected by their own **churches** in the presence of one or
T R : 0 0 :014(322) [0507] West and in the Latin **churches**, as Cyprian and
T R : 0 0 :015(322) [0509] in Greek or Latin **churches**, it is quite apparent that the
T R : 0 0 :015(322) [0509] quite apparent that the **churches** did not attribute
T R : 0 0 :016(322) [0509] be the overseer of all the **churches** in the world or for
T R : 0 0 :016(322) [0509] in the world or for **churches** situated in remote places to
T R : 0 0 :016(322) [0509] and that there are many **churches** in the East today which
T R : 0 0 :016(322) [0509] is impossible and the **churches** in the greater part of the
T R : 0 0 :051(329) [0519] been taken away, the **churches** are not able to remove
T R : 0 0 :060(330) [0521] who preside over the **churches** that they preach the
T R : 0 0 :061(330) [0521] all who preside over the **churches**, whether they are called
T R : 0 0 :062(330) [0521] all who preside over the **churches** are both bishops and
T R : 0 0 :064(331) [0523] should ordain the ministers in a number of **churches**.
T R : 0 0 :066(331) [0523] ordination, the **churches** retain the right to ordain for
T R : 0 0 :072(332) [0525] ordination, the **churches** are by divine right compelled to
T R : 0 0 :079(333) [0527] reasons why the **churches** should not recognize them as
T R : 0 0 :080(334) [0527] and profit of the **churches**, as the rule states, "The
T R : 0 0 :082(334) [0527] consume the alms of the **churches** for luxuries and would
T R : 0 0 :082(334) [0529] declare that in their **churches** they believe and teach in
T R : 0 0 :082(334) [0529] superintendent of the **churches** in the Duchy of
L C : 0 1 :090(377) [0607] who stand daily in the **churches**, singing and ringing
L C : 0 3 :025(423) [0705] If we gathered all the **churches** together, with all their
L C : 0 4 :009(437) [0733] consecrated altars and **churches** solely by virtue of his
E P : 0 3 :001(472) [0791] confession of our **churches** according to the Word of God
E P : 0 3 :001(473) [0791] contradictory teachings have invaded some **churches**.
E P : 0 4 :001(475) [0797] have arisen in some **churches** concerning the doctrine of
S D : P R :003(501) [0847] and had allowed their **churches** to be reformed according
S D : P R :003(502) [0847] Evangelical Christian **churches** concerning the chief
S D : P R :007(502) [0849] in the true Evangelical **churches**, just as during the very
S D : R N :001(503) [0851] confessed by the **churches** of the pure Christian religion is
S D : R N :001(503) [0851] in the name of those **churches** which confessed the same
S D : R N :002(503) [0851] been accepted in all the **churches** of the Augsburg
S D : R N :005(504) [0851] of the reformed **churches**) as our symbol in this epoch,
S D : R N :005(504) [0851] our reformed **churches** from the papacy and from other
S D : R N :008(505) [0853] are used publicly in the **churches**, the schools, and the
S D : R N :008(505) [0853] and the homes of those **churches** which adhere to the
S D : R N :009(505) [0853] The pure **churches** and schools have everywhere
S D : R N :010(506) [0855] all our Evangelical **churches** subscribe and from which
S D : R N :011(506) [0855] accepted belief of our **churches**, that the chief and most
S D : R N :011(506) [0855] and that all Evangelical **churches** and schools received
S D : R N :016(507) [0857] of that which our **churches** believe and accept with one
S D : 0 1 :016(511) [0865] which are rejected and condemned in our **churches**.
S D : 0 1 :023(512) [0865] which we sing in our **churches** describes it, "Through
S D : 0 1 :056(518) [0877] in our schools and **churches**, following the rules of logic,
S D : 0 1 :056(518) [0877] dependable teacher of our pure Evangelical **churches**.
S D : 0 1 :058(519) [0879] For this reason the **churches** of God will never attain
S D : 0 1 :059(519) [0879] controversy for our **churches** and schools therefore
S D : 0 2 :002(520) [0881] of the theologians of the **churches** of the Augsburg
S D : 0 2 :073(535) [0909] been agitated in the **churches** of the Augsburg
S D : 0 3 :055(549) [0935] Hence, since in our **churches** the theologians of the
S D : 0 4 :029(555) [0947] it is right for our **churches** to continue to insist that the
S D : 0 4 :029(555) [0947] and rejected by our **churches** as false and incorrect and as
S D : 0 4 :039(557) [0951] Hence our **churches** condemn and reject this proposition,
S D : 0 4 :040(558) [0951] this proposition, unqualifiedly stated, in our **churches**.
S D : 0 5 :015(561) [0957] of the law out of the **churches** and would have us criticize
S D : 0 7 :002(569) [0971] Confession and of our **churches** and confess that in the
S D : 0 7 :012(571) [0977] this article adopted the confession of our **churches**.
S D : 0 7 :041(576) [0985] eminent teacher of the **churches** which adhere to the
S D : 0 7 :104(587) [1009] in what sense our **churches** use the word "spiritual" in this
S D : 0 7 :105(588) [1009] to and force upon our **churches** in spite of our public and
S D : 0 7 :110(589) [1011] Confession of our **churches**, the Apology, the Smalcald
S D : 0 7 :111(589) [1011] to penetrate our **churches** as adherents of the Augsburg
S D : 1 0 :003(611) [1053] to insinuate their false doctrines into our **churches** again.
S D : 1 0 :031(616) [1063] In line with the above, **churches** will not condemn each
S D : 1 2 :002(632) [1095] whose errors all the **churches** of the Augsburg Confession
S D : 1 2 :003(633) [1095] world that among our **churches** and their teachers there
S D : 1 2 :006(633) [1097] is imported into our **churches** and schools in which the
S D : 1 2 :009(633) [1097] or tolerated in the **churches** or in the body politic or in

Chytraeus (2)
E P : 1 2 :031(501) [0843] David **Chytraeus**
S D : 1 2 :040(636) [1103] David **Chytraeus**

Cinctures (2)
A P : 2 7 :069(281) [0443] vestments, sandals, **cinctures** — all these are unprofitable
S 1 : P R :013(291) [0459] great tonsures, broad **cinctures**, bishops' and cardinals'

Circles (3)
A P : 1 5 :040(220) [0325] Lord's Day many in our **circles** use the Lord's Supper,
A P : 1 5 :041(220) [0325] In our **circles** the pastors and ministers of the churches
E P : 0 1 :024(469) [0785] In schools and learned **circles** these words can profitably

Circulated (1), Circulating (1)
P R : P R :009(006) [0011] thereby from the calumnies that had been **circulated**.
A P : 1 2 :091(195) [0279] about penitence are **circulating** which are quoted in

Circumcised (1), Circumcision (13)
A P : 0 4 :087(120) [0147] had God's command regarding **circumcision** (Rom. 4:1-6).
A P : 0 4 :111(123) [0155] Christ Jesus neither **circumcision** nor uncircumcision is
A P : 0 4 :201(134) [0175] did not receive **circumcision** in order to be justified
A P : 0 4 :201(134) [0175] accomplished, but **circumcision** was added to give him a
A P : 0 7 :042(176) [0243] your brethren of the **circumcision** do, celebrate it at the
A P : 1 2 :046(188) [0263] "In him also you were **circumcised** with a circumcision
A P : 1 2 :046(188) [0263] circumcised with a **circumcision** made without hands, by
A P : 1 3 :019(213) [0313] was justified by **circumcision**, but says that circumcision
A P : 1 3 :019(213) [0313] but says that **circumcision** was a sign given to exercise
A P : 2 3 :042(245) [0375] those who required **circumcision** and tried to impose the
A P : 2 7 :058(279) [0439] Furthermore, just as **circumcision** or the slaughter of
S D : 0 7 :050(578) [0989] or sacraments, such as **circumcision**, the many kinds of
S D : 1 0 :012(612) [1057] is here speaking of **circumcision**, which at that time was a
S D : 1 0 :012(612) [1057] prophets demanded **circumcision** and abused it to confirm

Circumscribed (4)
E P : 0 8 :008(487) [0819] to be finite and **circumscribed**, to suffer, to die, to ascend
S D : 0 7 :119(590) [1013] is so confined and **circumscribed** by a certain space in
S D : 0 7 :119(590) [1013] must be so taken in or **circumscribed** or comprehended by
S D : 0 8 :010(593) [1019] to be finite and **circumscribed**, to suffer and die, to ascend

Circumstances (25)
P R : P R :015(007) [0013] a plan because special **circumstances** interfered, as they
P R : P R :026(014) [0025] each community's **circumstances**, through diligent
A G : 0 0 :000(049) [0059] we are obliged by our **circumstances** to give an account
A G : 2 4 :024(058) [0067] the necessity of such **circumstances**, instruction was given
A P : 0 7 :032(174) [0239] vary according to the **circumstances**, one way or another.
A P : 1 1 :007(181) [0251] added to it later, including the **circumstances** of the sins.
A P : 2 3 :024(243) [0371] under certain **circumstances**; but we do object to the
S 2 : 0 2 :021(296) [0469] Therefore, it is under no **circumstances** to be tolerated.
T R : 0 0 :037(326) [0515] of Christ, they are under no **circumstances** to be ignored.
L C : P R :017(361) [0573] In all affairs and **circumstances** he can counsel, help,
L C : S P :018(363) [0577] Under no **circumstances** should a person be tolerated if
L C : 0 1 :070(374) [0601] upon their lips in all **circumstances** and experiences, for
L C : 0 1 :332(410) [0677] his daily habit in all **circumstances**, in all his affairs and
L C : 0 5 :042(451) [0763] one should under any **circumstances** be coerced or
E P : 0 7 :009(483) [0811] should under no **circumstances** be omitted, but should be
E P : 1 0 :004(493) [0829] according to **circumstances**, as it may be most profitable
E P : 1 0 :012(494) [0831] according to its **circumstances** and as it may be most
S D : 0 7 :044(577) [0987] Under these **circumstances** Christ said of the blessed and
S D : 0 7 :048(578) [0989] All **circumstances** of the institution of this Supper testify
S D : 0 7 :064(581) [0995] Under the **circumstances** this command can only be
S D : 0 7 :079(584) [1001] and are under no **circumstances** to be omitted.
S D : 0 7 :102(587) [1007] Christ cannot in any **circumstances** be where God is and
S D : 1 0 :003(611) [1053] that under no **circumstances** can this be done with a clear
S D : 1 0 :009(612) [1055] according to its **circumstances**, as long as it does so
S D : 1 0 :030(616) [1061] place, according to its **circumstances**, as may in Christian

Circumvent (1)
A P : 2 3 :010(241) [0367] thought up in order to **circumvent** the natural law.

Cite (22), Cited (19), Cites (4), Citing (3)
P R : P R :013(007) [0013] and also the just **cited** written agreement composed with
A G : 2 6 :022(067) [0073] Reasons for this shall be **cited** from the Scriptures.
A G : 2 8 :031(085) [0087] such power to bishops **cite** Christ's saying in John 16:12,
A G : 2 8 :032(085) [0087] They also **cite** the example in Acts 15:20, 29, where the
A L : 2 2 :003(049) [0059] Paul in I Cor. 11:20ff. **cites** an example from which it
A L : 2 8 :031(085) [0087] this right to bishops **cite** as evidence the passage, "I have
A L : 2 8 :032(086) [0087] They also **cite** the example of the apostles who
A L : 2 8 :033(086) [0087] Besides, they **cite** the change from the Sabbath to the
A P : 0 2 :022(103) [0111] We **cite** the opinions of the ancients, with which
A P : 0 4 :039(112) [0131] itself will compel us to **cite** further evidence; this will also
A P : 0 4 :083(119) [0145] In addition, he **cites** the consensus of all the prophets,
A P : 0 4 :083(119) [0145] prophets, which is really **citing** the authority of the
A P : 0 4 :098(121) [0151] here means that which is **cited** as the cause of salvation.
A P : 0 4 :098(121) [0151] To **cite** the name of Christ is to trust in the name of
A P : 0 4 :231(139) [0183] our opponents have also **cited** against us Col. 3:14, "love,
A P : 0 4 :373(164) [0221] "You gave me food" is **cited** as fruit and evidence of the
A P : 0 7 :037(175) [0241] But it is not necessary to **cite** a great deal of evidence
A P : 1 1 :006(181) [0251] our opponents ought not **cite** against us the regulation
A P : 1 2 :049(188) [0265] But what need is there to **cite** passages since there are so
A P : 1 2 :066(191) [0271] But here Peter **cites** the consensus of the church in
A P : 1 2 :070(192) [0271] this statement of Peter, **citing** the consensus of the
A P : 1 2 :073(192) [0273] Peter clearly **cites** the consensus of the prophets; the
A P : 1 2 :083(194) [0275] We would **cite** more passages if they were not obvious to
A P : 1 2 :173(209) [0305] non-obligatory works, why **cite** the clear teaching of the
A P : 2 1 :002(229) [0343] They **cite** this example to prove the invocation of the

Continued ▶

A P : 2 4 :096(267) [0417] They **cite** ancient heresies and by falsely comparing them
A P : 2 7 :029(274) [0431] recent invention, they still **cite** the authority of Scripture
A P : 2 7 :059(279) [0439] They also **cite** the case of the Rechabites who, as
A P : 2 7 :064(280) [0441] They also **cite** I Tim. 5:11, 12 on the widows who served
S 1 : P R :004(289) [0455] party — that they dare to **cite** my writings and teachings
S 2 : 0 2 :013(295) [0467] a purgatory, nor does he **cite** any passage of the
S 3 : 0 3 :017(306) [0483] Here the example of St. Bernard, etc. was **cited**.
L C : 0 1 :005(365) [0581] and remembered, by **citing** some common examples of
E P : 0 1 :012(467) [0783] or the teaching that the **cited** defect and damage is not
E P : 1 2 :001(498) [0839] contradict our repeatedly **cited** Christian Creed and
S D : P R :005(502) [0847] our end by this repeatedly **cited** Christian Confession as
S D : R N :006(504) [0853] 4. After the repeatedly **cited** Augsburg Confession had
S D : R N :006(504) [0853] also, because in it the **cited** Augsburg Confession is
S D : R N :007(505) [0853] articles the doctrine of the **cited** Augsburg Confession is
S D : R N :011(506) [0855] Small Catechisms — in the **cited** summary of our
S D : R N :013(506) [0855] truth, so we introduce and **cite** these writings as a witness
S D : 0 4 :015(553) [0943] to criticize and reject the **cited** propositions and formulas
S D : 0 5 :008(559) [0953] But in the **cited** passage in Mark 1:15, and in other places
S D : 0 7 :037(575) [0985] and others, have **cited** the personal union as an analogy to
S D : 0 7 :059(580) [0993] are so rash that they now **cite** this passage, which they
S D : 0 8 :045(600) [1031] to say or to write that the **cited** locutions, "God suffered,"
S D : 0 8 :078(606) [1043] We believe that the **cited** passages illustrate the majesty
S D : 0 8 :087(608) [1047] afforded them in the **cited** promises of the presence and

Citizens (3)

L C : 0 1 :150(385) [0623] many people as he has inhabitants, **citizens**, or subjects.
L C : 0 1 :175(389) [0631] have soundly instructed **citizens**, virtuous and
L C : 0 1 :229(396) [0645] and honorable, good **citizens**, and yet with a great show

City (40), Cities (7)

P R : P R :027(015) [0025] Mayor and Council of the **City** of Luebeck
P R : P R :027(015) [0027] Mayor and Council of the **City** of Landau
P R : P R :027(015) [0027] Mayor and Council of the **City** of Muenster-in-St
P R : P R :027(015) [0027] The Council of the **City** of Goslar
P R : P R :027(015) [0027] Mayor and Council of the **City** of Ulm
P R : P R :027(015) [0027] Mayor and Council of the **City** of Esslingen
P R : P R :027(015) [0027] The Council of the **City** of Reutlingen
P R : P R :027(015) [0027] Mayor and Council of the **City** of Noerdlingen
P R : P R :027(015) [0027] Mayor and Council of the **City** of Schwaebisch-Hall
P R : P R :027(016) [0027] Mayor and Council of the **City** of Heilbronn
P R : P R :027(016) [0027] Mayor and Council of the **City** of Memmingen
P R : P R :027(016) [0027] Mayor and Council of the **City** of Lindau
P R : P R :027(016) [0027] Mayor and Council of the **City** of Schweinfurt
P R : P R :027(016) [0027] The Council of the **City** of Donawerda
P R : P R :027(016) [0027] Chamberlain and Council of the **City** of Regensburg
P R : P R :027(016) [0027] Mayor and Council of the **City** of Wimpfen
P R : P R :027(016) [0027] Mayor and Council of the **City** of Giengen
P R : P R :027(016) [0027] Mayor and Council of the **City** of Aalen
P R : P R :027(016) [0027] Mayor and Council of the **City** of Kaufbeuren
P R : P R :027(016) [0027] Mayor and Council of the **City** of Isna
P R : P R :027(016) [0027] Mayor and Council of the **City** of Kempten
P R : P R :027(016) [0027] The Council of the **City** of Hamburg
P R : P R :027(016) [0027] The Council of the **City** of Goettingen
P R : P R :027(016) [0027] The Council of the **City** of Brunswick
P R : P R :027(016) [0027] Mayor and Council of the **City** of Lueneburg
P R : P R :027(016) [0027] Mayor and Council of the **City** of Leutkirch
P R : P R :027(016) [0027] The whole administration of the **City** of Hildesheim
P R : P R :027(016) [0027] Mayor and Council of the **City** of Hamelin
P R : P R :027(016) [0027] Mayor and Council of the **City** of Hanover
P R : P R :027(016) [0027] The Council of the **City** of Einbeck
P R : P R :027(016) [0027] The Council of the **City** of Northeim
A G : 0 0 :000(023) [0037] by certain Princes and **Cities** to His Imperial Majesty
A G : P R :008(025) [0039] our lands, principalities, dominions, **cities** and territories.
A P : 0 4 :331(158) [0211] O my God, because thy **city** and thy people are called by
A P : 1 2 :166(208) [0303] reconciled to God and saved their **city** from destruction.
A P : 2 3 :054(246) [0379] the fall of many other **cities**, like Sybaris and Rome.
A P : 2 7 :038(275) [0433] a certain shoemaker in the **city** of Alexandria as a basis
A P : 2 7 :038(275) [0433] day Anthony went into the **city** and came to the
A P : 2 7 :038(275) [0433] a few words for the whole **city** and then paid attention to
S 2 : 0 3 :001(298) [0471] for secular government in **cities** and states, and also well
T R : 0 0 :018(323) [0509] that you want, the world is greater than the **city**.
T R : 0 0 :035(326) [0513] in order to occupy Italian **cities** and sometimes in order to
T R : 0 0 :082(334) [0529] and of the estates and **cities** professing the doctrine of the
S C : P R :013(339) [0535] who desires to reside in a **city** is bound to know and
L C : 0 1 :230(396) [0645] daily plunder not only a **city** or two, but all Germany.
L C : 0 1 :302(405) [0667] if anyone covets a castle, **city**, county, or other great
S D : 0 7 :013(571) [0977] came with him from the **cities**, concerning the holy

Civic (4)

A P : 0 2 :012(102) [0109] God by philosophical or **civic** righteousness, which we
A P : 0 4 :394(167) [0225] righteousness of the law, understood as **civic** uprightness.
A P : 0 7 :005(169) [0227] ties and rites like other **civic** governments, however, but it
E P : 1 2 :013(499) [0841] serve or function in any **civic** office with a good and clear

Civil (80)

A G : 1 6 :000(037) [0051] XVI. **Civil** Government
A G : 1 6 :002(037) [0051] may without sin occupy **civil** offices or serve as princes
A G : 1 6 :005(038) [0051] Gospel does not overthrow **civil** authority, the state, and
A G : 1 6 :006(038) [0051] obliged to be subject to **civil** authority and obey its
A G : 1 6 :007(038) [0051] when commands of the **civil** authority cannot be obeyed
A G : 2 3 :013(053) [0063] to all divine, natural, and **civil** law, but was also utterly
A G : 2 7 :056(080) [0083] and child, and also their **civil** office, to take shelter in a
A L : 1 6 :000(037) [0051] XVI. **Civil** Affairs
A L : 1 6 :001(037) [0051] churches teach that lawful **civil** ordinances are good
A L : 1 6 :002(037) [0051] for Christians to hold **civil** office, to sit as judges, to
A L : 1 6 :003(037) [0051] who forbid Christians to engage in these **civil** functions.
A L : 1 6 :004(038) [0051] the fear of God and in faith but in forsaking **civil** duties.
A L : 1 8 :001(039) [0051] for the attainment of **civil** righteousness and for the
A L : 2 0 :018(043) [0055] is nothing else than **civil** or philosophical righteousness,
A L : 2 6 :011(065) [0071] magistracy, or in other **civil** occupations — and admired
A L : 2 6 :015(066) [0073] hope, the importance of **civil** affairs, and the consolation
A L : 2 7 :055(079) [0083] that all magistracy and all **civil** offices are unworthy of
A L : 2 8 :010(082) [0085] Word, it interferes with **civil** government as little as the
A L : 2 8 :010(082) [0085] as the art of singing interferes with **civil** government.
A L : 2 8 :011(082) [0085] For **civil** government is concerned with other things than
A L : 2 8 :012(083) [0085] ecclesiastical and **civil** power are not to be confused.
A L : 2 8 :013(083) [0085] nor abrogate the laws of **civil** rulers, nor abolish lawful
A L : 2 8 :013(083) [0085] judgments concerning any **civil** ordinances or contracts,
A L : 2 8 :013(083) [0085] contracts, nor prescribe to **civil** rulers laws about the
A L : 2 8 :019(083) [0087] kings and emperors for the **civil** administration of their
A L : 2 8 :020(084) [0087] of bishops, therefore, **civil** authority must be distinguished
A P : 0 2 :043(106) [0117] said this about the **civil** courts, not about the judgment of
A P : 0 2 :043(106) [0117] mingle philosophical and **civil** ethics with the Gospel.
A P : 0 4 :006(108) [0121] nothing about the ceremonial and **civil** laws of Moses.
A P : 0 4 :009(108) [0123] of reason—that is, **civil** works—and maintain that without
A P : 0 4 :022(110) [0127] For God wants this **civil** discipline to restrain the
A P : 0 4 :027(111) [0127] But reason can produce **civil** works.
A P : 0 4 :033(111) [0129] the flesh sins even when it performs outward **civil** works.
A P : 0 4 :034(111) [0129] table, which contain the **civil** righteousness that reason
A P : 0 4 :130(125) [0157] somewhat possible to do **civil** works, that is, the outward
A P : 0 4 :134(125) [0159] think that outward and **civil** works satisfy the law of God
A P : 0 4 :184(132) [0173] without Christ, and that if **civil** works are done without
A P : 0 4 :241(141) [0187] never have brought on **civil** war if either had yielded the
A P : 0 7 :014(170) [0231] from the heathen not by **civil** rites but by being God's
A P : 0 7 :023(172) [0235] from any laws, divine, canonical, or **civil**, as he wishes.
A P : 0 7 :050(178) [0245] The right to hold property is a **civil** ordinance.
A P : 0 7 :050(178) [0245] for Christians to use **civil** ordinances just as it is
A P : 1 2 :142(204) [0295] that God's law deals with external, **civil** righteousness.
A P : 1 2 :145(205) [0297] think that outward and **civil** works satisfy God's law; and
A P : 1 2 :169(209) [0305] **Civil** restitution is necessary, as it is written (Eph. 4:28),
A P : 1 2 :175(210) [0307] no longer refers to **civil** discipline but to payment for
A P : 1 5 :043(221) [0327] for rulers and for all **civil** ordinances, the distinction
A P : 1 6 :001(222) [0329] — in short, that lawful **civil** ordinances are God's good
A P : 1 6 :003(223) [0331] any new laws about the **civil** estate, but commands us to
A P : 1 6 :006(223) [0331] other teachings that were not suited to **civil** relationships.
A P : 1 6 :006(223) [0331] does not legislate for the **civil** estate but is the forgiveness
A P : 1 6 :007(223) [0331] spiritual kingdom does not change the **civil** government.
A P : 1 6 :008(223) [0333] to hearts, while it approves the **civil** government.
A P : 1 6 :009(224) [0333] is not contempt of **civil** ordinances but attitudes of the
A P : 1 6 :012(224) [0333] may legitimately make use of **civil** ordinances and laws.
A P : 1 6 :013(224) [0333] of magistrates and the value of **civil** ordinances generally.
A P : 1 8 :004(225) [0335] some extent it can achieve **civil** righteousness or the
A P : 1 8 :004(225) [0335] as the liberty and ability to achieve **civil** righteousness.
A P : 1 8 :005(225) [0335] For these reasons even **civil** righteousness is rare among
A P : 1 8 :009(226) [0337] distinguish between **civil** righteousness and spiritual
A P : 1 8 :009(226) [0337] that God requires this **civil** righteousness and that, to
A P : 2 4 :056(259) [0403] since they merited **civil** reconciliation — but only
A P : 2 7 :046(277) [0435] possession of property are **civil** ordinances, approved by
S 3 : 0 9 :000(314) [0497] calls it, to be merely a **civil** penalty which does not
S 3 : 0 9 :000(314) [0497] should not mingle **civil** punishments with this spiritual
T R : 0 0 :074(332) [0525] What tyranny it is for **civil** officers to have the power to
L C : 0 1 :150(385) [0623] be said of obedience to the **civil** government, which, as we
L C : 0 1 :150(385) [0623] Through **civil** rulers, as through our own parents, God
L C : 0 1 :172(388) [0629] and capable men for both **civil** and spiritual leadership,
L C : 0 1 :177(389) [0631] there is no longer any **civil** order, peace, or respect for
L C : 0 1 :180(389) [0631] both the spiritual and the **civil** government, that is, divine
L C : 0 1 :181(389) [0631] of punishing evil-doers to **civil** magistrates in place of
L C : 0 1 :209(393) [0641] as the spiritual and **civil** estates are, these must humble
L C : 0 1 :274(401) [0659] is made, however, of **civil** magistrates, preachers, and
L C : 0 1 :280(403) [0661] public, either before the **civil** or the ecclesiastical court.
L C : 0 3 :008(421) [0699] to obey our fathers and mothers and the **civil** authorities.
L C : 0 3 :073(430) [0719] of our domestic and our **civil** or political affairs.
L C : 0 3 :074(430) [0719] of all is to pray for our **civil** authorities and the
L C : 0 4 :020(439) [0737] we speak about the parental estate and **civil** authority.
S D : 0 1 :024(512) [0865] external, temporal, and **civil** affairs which are subject to

Claim (34), Claimed (8), Claiming (3), Claims (5)

A G : 2 7 :011(072) [0077] It was **claimed** that monastic vows were equal to
A G : 2 7 :013(072) [0077] They also **claimed** that more merit could be obtained by
A G : 2 7 :016(073) [0077] Scriptures, but now it is **claimed** that monastic life is of
A G : 2 7 :044(078) [0081] more indecent and absurd **claim**, namely, that they could
A G : 2 7 :045(078) [0081] to count up all these **claims** for the purpose of casting
A L : 2 6 :009(065) [0071] Such observances **claimed** for themselves the glamorous
A L : 2 7 :044(078) [0081] absurdities when they **claimed** that they could transfer
A L : 2 7 :045(078) [0081] to enlarge on these **claims**, how many things could be
A P : 0 2 :005(101) [0107] There are some who **claim** that original sin is not some
A P : 0 2 :042(105) [0115] If our opponents **claim** that the inclination to evil is a
A P : 0 4 :017(109) [0125] history about Christ and **claim** that he merited for us a
A P : 0 4 :058(115) [0137] his sins, but he does not lay **claim** to any merit of his own.
A P : 0 4 :073(117) [0141] We exclude the **claim** of merit, not the Word or the
A P : 0 4 :073(117) [0141] or the sacraments, as our opponents slanderously **claim**.
A P : 0 4 :136(126) [0159] opponents slanderously **claim** that we do not require good
A P : 0 4 :146(127) [0163] They **claim** to keep the law, though this glory properly
A P : 0 4 :210(136) [0179] But our opponents **claim** that the Mass is a work that
A P : 0 4 :213(136) [0179] a propitiation and to **claim** that they merit the forgiveness
A P : 1 2 :144(205) [0297] to placate God's displeasure, as our opponents **claim**.
A P : 1 5 :035(220) [0325] let him do so without **claiming** any value before God for
A P : 1 5 :039(220) [0325] We can truthfully **claim** that in our churches the public
A P : 1 6 :009(224) [0333] It is also false to **claim** that Christian perfection consists
A P : 1 6 :011(224) [0333] out of his mind in **claiming** that priests were not allowed
A P : 2 1 :023(232) [0349] In indulgences they **claim** to apply the merits of the
A P : 2 3 :026(243) [0371] They **claim** that they require celibacy because it is pure,
A P : 2 3 :063(248) [0381] They dare to **claim** divine revelation for the law of
A P : 2 4 :042(257) [0399] Then they make the **claim** that this work can be
A P : 2 4 :043(257) [0399] human traditions with the **claim** that these justify men
A P : 2 4 :049(258) [0401] we could lay more **claim** to observing it than our
A P : 2 7 :029(274) [0431] they make the impudent **claim** that according to the
A P : 2 7 :036(275) [0433] did not dare to deny it the **claim** of perfection altogether,
A P : 2 7 :040(276) [0433] is to say, here, too, it **claims** perfection for artificial
A P : 2 7 :059(279) [0441] monks abound in every delight, they **claim** to be celibate.
S 2 : 0 2 :023(296) [0469] of all, however, is the **claim** that relics effect indulgences
S 2 : 0 3 :002(298) [0471] invented by men, which **claim** to be superior to the
S 2 : 0 4 :007(299) [0473] pope would renounce the **claim** that he is the head of the
S 2 : 0 4 :002(300) [0475] He went so far as to **claim** to be an earthly god and even
S 3 : 0 8 :004(312) [0495] of his heart," and he **claims** that whatever he decides and
T R : 0 0 :001(320) [0503] arrogates to himself the **claim** that he is by divine right

Continued ▶

T R : 0 0 :033(325) [0513] similar statements which **claim** that the pope is by divine
L C : P R :002(358) [0567] what the old manuals **claimed** in their titles to
L C : 0 1 :231(396) [0647] unmolested by anyone, even **claiming** honor from men.
L C : 0 1 :300(405) [0667] class the Jews especially **claimed** to belong, as many great
L C : 0 3 :056(427) [0713] But because he is God, he **claims** the honor of giving far
L C : 0 5 :028(449) [0759] they know that we do not **claim** this of bread and wine —
L C : 0 5 :039(451) [0761] I mean is that those who **claim** to be Christians should
E P : 0 2 :003(470) [0787] of ourselves "sufficient to **claim** anything as coming from
E P : 0 7 :004(482) [0809] very plausibly and **claim** to believe a true presence of the
S D : 0 2 :012(522) [0885] sufficient of ourselves to **claim** anything as coming from
S D : 0 5 :002(558) [0951] The one party **claimed** that, strictly speaking, the Gospel

Clandestine (1)
T R : 0 0 :078(333) [0527] in general approves all **clandestine** and underhanded

Clarify (1)
L C : 0 2 :031(414) [0685] article simply serve to **clarify** and express how and by

Clarity (2)
A G : 2 8 :062(092) [0093] no longer taught and preached with **clarity** and purity.
A L : 2 8 :062(092) [0093] of faith was not taught with sufficient **clarity**.

Clash (1), Clashes (1)
A P : 1 2 :059(190) [0267] chief issue on which we **clash** with our opponents and
A P : 2 3 :006(240) [0365] our opponents because it **clashes** with divine and natural

Clasp (2)
L C : 0 1 :326(409) [0675] commandments, like the **clasp** or the hoop of a wreath
L C : 0 4 :016(438) [0735] it the precious jeweled **clasp** with which God has fastened

Class (5), Classed (2), Classes (2)
A P : 1 2 :004(183) [0253] All good men of all **classes**, even the theologians, admit
A P : 2 3 :032(244) [0373] is talking about the whole **class** of mothers, and above all
A P : 2 7 :016(271) [0425] obedience though no **class** of men has greater license than
A P : 2 7 :021(272) [0427] Finally, they belong to the **class** of which Paul says (I
L C : 0 1 :012(366) [0583] In this **class** belong those who go so far as to make a pact
L C : 0 1 :099(378) [0609] the sin that used to be **classed** among the mortal sins and
L C : 0 1 :150(385) [0623] as we have said, is to be **classed** with the estate of
L C : 0 1 :300(405) [0667] To this **class** the Jews especially claimed to belong, as
L C : 0 1 :317(408) [0673] every man, and that all **classes** of men on earth may

Classified (3)
A P : 2 4 :021(252) [0389] sacrifices can be **classified** under one or another of these
A P : 2 4 :051(259) [0403] they should be **classified** with those whom Daniel (11:38)
L C : 0 3 :040(425) [0709] we do on earth may be **classified** as word or deed, speech

Clause (1), Clauses (1)
A P : 0 4 :283(149) [0201] this conclusion to both **clauses**: all things will be clean if
L C : 0 3 :093(433) [0725] necessary but comforting **clause** is added, "as we forgive

Clay (2)
S D : 0 1 :035(514) [0869] that thou hast made me of **clay**, and wilt thou turn me to
S D : 0 2 :024(526) [0891] in anything as a stone, a block, or a lump of **clay** could.

Clean (11), Cleanness (3)
A P : 0 4 :155(128) [0165] Luke 11:41, "Give alms; and behold, everything is **clean**."
A P : 0 4 :281(149) [0201] "Give alms; and behold, everything is **clean** for you."
A P : 0 4 :282(149) [0201] he puts a twofold **cleanness**, one internal and the other
A P : 0 4 :282(149) [0201] concerning the outward **cleanness**, "Give alms from what
A P : 0 4 :282(149) [0201] have left over, and thus all things will be **clean** for you."
A P : 0 4 :283(149) [0201] clauses: all things will be **clean** if you are clean inwardly
A P : 0 4 :283(150) [0201] will be clean if you are **clean** inwardly and if you give
A P : 0 4 :283(150) [0201] He means that outward **cleanness** is to be sought in
A P : 0 4 :283(150) [0201] part: "All things will be **clean** when you have given alms."
A P : 0 4 :284(150) [0201] Scripture; for if hearts are **clean** and then the outward
A P : 0 4 :284(150) [0201] then men are completely **clean**, outwardly as well as
A P : 0 4 :327(158) [0211] 'I have made my heart **clean**, I am pure from my sin?"
S 3 : 1 3 :001(315) [0499] says) we get a new and **clean** heart and that God will and
L C : 0 1 :244(398) [0649] upon us; in one hour they **clean** out our chests and purse

Cleanse (4), Cleansed (7), Cleanses (8), Cleansing (2)
A P : 0 2 :032(104) [0113] catholic, but we have **cleansed** and brought to light
A P : 0 4 :099(121) [0151] Acts 15:9, "He **cleansed** their hearts by faith."
A P : 0 4 :282(149) [0201] thinking that they are **cleansed** before God and justified
A P : 0 4 :282(149) [0201] with salt "sanctifies and **cleanses** the people," and the
A P : 0 4 :282(149) [0201] and the gloss says that it **cleanses** from venial sins.
A P : 0 4 :282(149) [0201] and in place of this false **cleansing** he puts a twofold
A P : 0 4 :282(149) [0201] commands that they be **cleansed** inwardly and then adds
A P : 0 4 :327(158) [0211] myself with snow, and **cleanse** my hands with lye, yet
A P : 0 7 :007(169) [0229] might sanctify it, having **cleansed** it by the washing of
A P : 1 2 :167(209) [0305] or a satisfaction, but the **cleansing** of imperfect souls.
A P : 2 8 :008(282) [0445] say that hearts are **cleansed** by faith and then go on to
S 3 : 0 3 :040(309) [0489] This gift daily **cleanses** and expels the sins that remain
S C : 0 4 :012(349) [0551] forth daily and rise up, **cleansed** and righteous, to live
L C : 0 1 :101(379) [0609] and it constantly **cleanses** the heart and its meditations.
S D : 0 1 :039(515) [0871] his beloved Son he might **cleanse** it from sin, sanctify it,
S D : 0 1 :045(516) [0873] of Scripture that God **cleanses** man from sin, purifies
S D : 0 3 :057(550) [0935] blood of Jesus, his Son, **cleanses** us from all sin" (I John
S D : 0 8 :055(601) [1033] things under his feet, to **cleanse** from sin, and so forth are
S D : 0 8 :059(602) [1035] blood of Jesus his Son **cleanses** us from all sin" (I John
S D : 0 8 :059(602) [1035] Christ but also his blood actually **cleanses** us from all sins
S D : 1 1 :089(631) [1093] promises them the Holy Spirit to **cleanse** and renew them.

Clear (120), Clearer (5), Clearest (2), Clearly (127)
P R : P R :010(006) [0011] developments, they saw **clearly** that there was no better
P R : P R :010(006) [0011] reject false doctrine, and **clearly** to confess the divine
P R : P R :011(006) [0011] first the said theologians **clearly** and correctly described to
P R : P R :018(008) [0015] beloved posterity may be **clearly** and thoroughly informed
P R : P R :020(010) [0017] Christ, our theologians **clearly** assert in the Formula of
P R : P R :021(010) [0019] our theologians declare in **clear** and candid words (so
A G : 1 8 :004(039) [0051] teaching is no novelty, the **clear** words of Augustine on
A G : 2 0 :011(042) [0055] about faith is plainly and **clearly** treated by Paul in many
A G : 2 0 :025(045) [0057] such a way as to make it **clear** that faith is not merely a
A G : 0 0 :001(047) [0059] this teaching is grounded **clearly** on the Holy Scriptures
A G : 2 2 :001(049) [0059] reason is that there is a **clear** command and order of
A G : 2 2 :002(049) [0059] here commands with **clear** words that all should drink of
A G : 2 3 :003(051) [0061] since the Scriptures **clearly** assert that the estate of
A G : 2 5 :011(063) [0071] Here it can be **clearly** seen that Chrysostom does not
A G : 2 8 :043(088) [0089] Yet there are **clear** passages of divine Scripture which
A G : 0 0 :005(095) [0095] that it may be made very **clear** that we have introduced
A L : 2 6 :038(069) [0075] By this he **clearly** shows that he pommeled his body not
A L : 2 7 :010(072) [0077] a reputation that it was **clearly** displeasing to those
A L : 2 8 :043(088) [0089] Yet there are **clear** testimonies which prohibit the making
A P : P R :003(098) [0099] that followed, it was **clear** that our side was willing to put
A P : P R :004(098) [0099] to the opponents' point of view with a **clear** conscience?
A P : P R :009(099) [0101] in opposition to the **clear** Scripture of the Holy Spirit.
A P : P R :016(099) [0103] surrender truth that is so **clear** and necessary for the
A P : 0 2 :023(103) [0111] To make ourselves **clear**, we are naming these gifts
A P : 0 2 :031(104) [0113] our definition, but on so **clear** an issue there is no need of
A P : 0 2 :040(105) [0115] For they **clearly** call lust sin, by nature worthy of death if
A P : 0 4 :017(109) [0125] It is **clear**, however, what they ascribe to this disposition,
A P : 0 4 :033(111) [0129] These words are so **clear** that they do not need an acute
A P : 0 4 :050(114) [0135] Paul **clearly** shows that faith does not simply mean
A P : 0 4 :063(115) [0139] This is plain and **clear**, the faithful can grasp it, and it has
A P : 0 4 :065(116) [0139] we say more simply and **clearly** about the conversion of
A P : 0 4 :074(117) [0143] This we shall **clearly** show.
A P : 0 4 :086(119) [0147] We shall therefore add **clear** testimonies stating that faith
A P : 0 4 :089(120) [0149] Here he **clearly** says that faith itself is accounted for
A P : 0 4 :097(121) [0149] describe the work of Christ and justification more **clearly**?
A P : 0 4 :104(122) [0151] words of Ambrose, which **clearly** support our position; he
A P : 0 4 :106(122) [0153] Here he **clearly** says that the justifier is reconciled by faith
A P : 0 4 :107(122) [0153] in the Scriptures that **clearly** attribute justification to faith
A P : 0 4 :117(123) [0155] Scriptures, was to make **clear** that by faith alone we
A P : 0 4 :135(125) [0159] From this it is **clear** that without Christ and without the
A P : 0 4 :140(126) [0161] So it is **clear** that we require good works.
A P : 0 4 :145(127) [0163] From this it is **clear** that they teach only the law.
A P : 0 4 :153(127) [0163] Therefore he **clearly** says, "Your faith has saved you."
A P : 0 4 :158(129) [0165] Therefore it is **clear** that we are justified by faith, for it is
A P : 0 4 :161(129) [0167] what we have said it is **clear** that justification does not
A P : 0 4 :161(129) [0167] Nevertheless, it is more **clearly** evident now that this
A P : 0 4 :163(129) [0169] Paul **clearly** teaches this when he says (I Cor. 4:4), "I am
A P : 0 4 :172(130) [0171] Augustine says very **clearly**, "All the commandments of
A P : 0 4 :195(134) [0175] wrath of God, as Paul **clearly** says (Rom. 5:1), "Since we
A P : 0 4 :230(139) [0183] the help of his Holy Spirit to make it **clear** and distinct.
A P : 0 4 :240(141) [0187] where the antithesis **clearly** shows what it means: "Hatred
A P : 0 4 :244(141) [0189] our position more, but the answer is easy and **clear**.
A P : 0 4 :248(142) [0191] From this it is **clear** that James is not against us when he
A P : 0 4 :257(144) [0193] It is **clear** that we are not justified by the law.
A P : 0 4 :257(144) [0193] hear the voice of God, **clearly** promising the forgiveness
A P : 0 4 :262(145) [0195] words speak even more **clearly** about complete penitence
A P : 0 4 :264(146) [0195] It would **clearly** be an abolition of the Gospel if we were
A P : 0 4 :267(146) [0197] Secondly, because Daniel **clearly** sets forth a promise, he
A P : 0 4 :286(150) [0201] They omit the **clearest** scriptural passages on faith, select
A P : 0 4 :294(152) [0203] fundamental article it is **clear** why we ascribe justification
A P : 0 4 :298(153) [0205] These things are so **clear** and evident that we are
A P : 0 4 :304(154) [0205] We say still more **clearly**: The terrors of sin and death are
A P : 0 4 :313(155) [0207] nature of faith will be **clearly** understood, as well as the
A P : 0 4 :314(156) [0207] We stress this statement so often because it is so **clear**.
A P : 0 4 :315(156) [0207] It is also **clear** that without the help of Christ we cannot
A P : 0 4 :323(157) [0209] well known and has many **clear** testimonies in the
A P : 0 4 :325(157) [0211] Church Fathers have so **clearly** handed down the doctrine
A P : 0 4 :334(158) [0215] These words **clearly** say that God saves through mercy
A P : 0 4 :340(159) [0215] Here Ambrose has **clearly** said, "Grace is to be
A P : 0 4 :345(160) [0217] Here mercy has God's **clear** and certain promise and his
A P : 0 4 :356(161) [0217] We shall answer briefly and **clearly**.
A P : 0 4 :374(164) [0221] the fruit to make it **clearer** to the inexperienced and to
A P : 0 4 :396(167) [0225] a truth so manifest and **clear** that their ungodliness comes
A P : 0 4 :398(167) [0227] have condemned us in **clear** words for saying faith is part
A P : 0 7 :019(171) [0233] He **clearly** says in Matt. 13:38 that "the good seed means
A P : 0 7 :029(173) [0237] issue we have spoken out **clearly** enough in our
A P : 0 7 :029(173) [0237] It is **clear** that the wicked belong to the kingdom and
A P : 0 7 :029(173) [0237] All this is **clearer** than the light of noonday; if our
A P : 0 7 :032(174) [0239] this article, for it is **clear** that many foolish opinions
A P : 0 7 :035(175) [0239] Paul **clearly** teaches this in Colossians (2:16, 17): "Let no
A P : 0 9 :002(178) [0245] Therefore it **clearly** follows that infants should be
A P : 1 0 :002(179) [0247] Mass, in which the priest **clearly** prays that the bread may
A P : 1 0 :004(179) [0247] this article), but to make **clear** to all our readers that we
A P : 1 2 :016(184) [0257] following teachings are **clearly** false and foreign to the
A P : 1 2 :038(187) [0261] Filial fear can be **clearly** defined as an anxiety joined with
A P : 1 2 :042(187) [0263] in the Lord's Supper **clearly** state, "This is my body which
A P : 1 2 :043(187) [0263] of penitence is plain and **clear**, it adds to the honor of the
A P : 1 2 :052(189) [0265] of penitence could be presented more **clearly** and simply.
A P : 1 2 :065(191) [0271] not have said it any more **clearly**: "through his name,"
A P : 1 2 :073(192) [0273] Peter **clearly** cites the consensus of the prophets; the
A P : 1 2 :080(194) [0275] But **clearly** the promise was given and Christ revealed to
A P : 1 2 :087(195) [0277] We think this is **clear** enough for devout consciences, and
A P : 1 2 :090(195) [0279] penitence, which is quite **clear**, we are happy to have all
A P : 1 2 :096(196) [0281] Ambrose makes this very **clear** statement about
A P : 1 2 :135(203) [0293] So it is **clearly** a wicked distortion to apply these passages
A P : 1 2 :137(203) [0293] **Clearly** Scripture is speaking about obligatory works,
A P : 1 2 :154(206) [0301] **Clearly** the power of the keys does not remove these
A P : 1 2 :171(209) [0305] From this it is **clear** that they did not regard these canons
A P : 1 2 :172(209) [0305] satisfactions contrary to the **clear** teaching of the Gospel.
A P : 1 2 :173(209) [0305] works, why cite the **clear** teaching of the Gospel?
A P : 1 2 :173(210) [0305] **Clearly** they are falsifying the matter when they say that
A P : 1 2 :173(210) [0305] when they say that the **clear** teaching of the Gospel
A P : 1 3 :006(212) [0311] express command from God and a **clear** promise of grace.
A P : 1 3 :010(212) [0311] to the Hebrews teaches **clearly** enough, we do not have a
A P : 1 3 :020(213) [0313] The reason for this is **clear** and well founded.
A P : 1 3 :020(213) [0313] New Testament, as Christ **clearly** says (I Cor. 11:25), the
A P : 1 4 :003(214) [0315] issue our consciences are **clear** and we dare not approve
A P : 1 5 :005(215) [0317] But Christ **clearly** says (Matt. 15:9), "In vain do they
A P : 1 5 :006(216) [0317] of the Gospel, for Paul **clearly** teaches (Eph. 2:8), "By
A P : 1 5 :018(217) [0319] What need is there for words in a matter so **clear**?
A P : 1 5 :030(219) [0323] He makes it perfectly **clear** that he is talking about human
A P : 1 6 :013(224) [0333] of political affairs so **clearly** that many good men

Continued ▶

AP : 18 :010(226) [0337] not our invention but the **clear** teaching of the Scriptures.
AP : 20 :002(226) [0337] What can we say about an issue that is so **clear**?
AP : 21 :041(235) [0355] which ought to be as **clear** and plain as possible in the
AP : 21 :042(235) [0355] to correct the abuses, for **clearly** he is most anxious for
AP : 22 :003(236) [0357] delivering, but the text **clearly** shows that this was the use
AP : 23 :006(240) [0365] this one the situation is so **clear** that no discussion is
AP : 23 :006(240) [0365] In the face of the **clear** truth which we have advanced,
AP : 23 :013(241) [0367] This is so **clear** and firm as to be irrefutable.
AP : 23 :016(241) [0369] And Christ **clearly** said (Matt. 19:11), "Not all men can
AP : 23 :059(247) [0379] our opponents we would have to reject the **clear** truth.
AP : 23 :063(248) [0381] though it conflicts with **clear** passages of Scripture
AP : 23 :071(249) [0383] our princes can have a **clear** conscience on this matter.
AP : 23 :071(249) [0383] for anything else, especially when the issue is so **clear**.
AP : 24 :007(250) [0385] But is is **clear** that the prevalence of the mendicant friars
AP : 24 :010(251) [0387] issue of the controversy is **clear**, it will be easy to evaluate
AP : 24 :016(252) [0389] our enumeration of the types of sacrifice will make **clear**.
AP : 24 :027(254) [0393] This passage **clearly** condemns the notion that the
AP : 24 :028(254) [0393] **Clearly** God had commanded the fathers concerning
AP : 24 :034(256) [0395] This passage **clearly** requires the offerings of the
AP : 24 :040(257) [0399] From this it is **clear** that the analogy of the daily sacrifice
AP : 24 :050(259) [0401] Practical and **clear** sermons hold an audience, but neither
AP : 24 :051(259) [0401] is godly, practical, and **clear** teaching, the godly use of the
AP : 24 :066(261) [0407] They make **clear** that they are talking about
AP : 24 :067(261) [0407] make the whole matter as **clear** as possible, we shall say
AP : 24 :073(262) [0409] the sacrament is to make **clear** that terrified consciences
AP : 24 :075(263) [0411] others; but the Fathers **clearly** require faith and speak of
AP : 24 :088(265) [0413] about an offering; but it **clearly** shows that it is not
AP : 24 :092(266) [0417] **Clearly** this transference to the dead cannot be proved
AP : 24 :094(267) [0417] we set them against the **clearest** and surest passages of
AP : 24 :096(267) [0417] defending a heresy that **clearly** conflicts with the
AP : 27 :014(271) [0423] to human traditions, as he **clearly** shows in Col. 2:16.
AP : 27 :030(274) [0431] meriting eternal life, as he **clearly** says in Ezek. 20:25, "I
AP : 27 :035(275) [0431] traditions, it is quite **clear** that monastic vows are not a
AP : 27 :041(276) [0435] children makes it even **clearer** that he does not approve
AP : 27 :052(278) [0437] their traditions, contrary to the **clear** command of God.
AP : 27 :060(279) [0441] according to the sure and **clear** passages of Scripture, not
AP : 28 :004(281) [0445] unless they act in **clear** opposition to God's commands.
AP : 28 :011(283) [0447] The Gospel **clearly** testifies that traditions should not be
AP : 28 :021(284) [0449] **Clearly** it does not set down the universal commandment
AP : 28 :025(285) [0451] originally condemned the **clear** truth, and are now most
S2 : 01 :004(292) [0461] work, law, or merit, it is **clear** and certain that such faith
TR : 00 :010(321) [0507] Since Paul **clearly** testifies that he did not desire to seek
TR : 00 :024(324) [0511] as is shown by many **clear** and powerful arguments, for
TR : 00 :031(325) [0513] The second article is even **clearer** than the first because
TR : 00 :038(326) [0515] So Paul **clearly** teaches, "If an angel from heaven should
TR : 00 :038(326) [0515] The canons likewise **clearly** teach that a heretical pope is
TR : 00 :058(330) [0521] And it is the **clear** command of God that we should flee
TR : 00 :062(330) [0521] Jerome teaches **clearly** that in the apostolic letters all who
SC : PR :024(341) [0539] All you need to do is **clearly** to set forth the advantage
SC : 03 :005(346) [0547] Word of God is taught **clearly** and purely and we, as
LC : PR :002(358) [0567] now available to them in **clear** and simple form in the
LC : 01 :225(395) [0643] Let us make it a little **clearer** for the common people so
LC : 01 :263(400) [0655] False witness is **clearly** a work of the tongue.
LC : 01 :273(401) [0659] into disgrace, from which he could scarcely **clear** himself.
LC : 01 :304(406) [0667] From this it is **clear** that all these pretexts and shams are
LC : 02 :005(411) [0679] nor could they all be **clearly** expressed in so few words.
LC : 02 :006(411) [0679] But to make it most **clear** and simple for teaching to
LC : 02 :040(416) [0689] Learn this article, then, as **clearly** as possible.
LC : 02 :046(416) [0689] points in it are not quite **clear** to the common people, we
LC : 02 :048(417) [0691] or best and most **clearly** of all, "a holy Christian people."
LC : 02 :049(417) [0691] only of saints, or, still more **clearly**, "a holy community."
LC : 03 :011(421) [0701] he makes it **clear** that he will not cast us out or drive us
LC : 03 :033(424) [0707] precious thing and may **clearly** distinguish between vain
LC : 03 :034(425) [0707] we shall treat the Lord's Prayer very briefly and **clearly**.
LC : 03 :046(426) [0709] then, is simple and **clear** as soon as we understand the
LC : 04 :033(440) [0739] is most beautifully and **clearly** expressed in these same
LC : 04 :035(441) [0741] Christ's Baptism quite **clearly** from a bath-keeper's
LC : 05 :045(451) [0763] the first place, we have a **clear** text in the words of
LC : 05 :086(456) [0773] For it is **clearly** useless to try to change old people.
LC : 06 :018(459) [0000] therefore take care to keep the two parts **clearly** separate.
LC : 06 :023(459) [0000] If all this were **clearly** explained, and meanwhile if the
LC : 06 :023(459) [0000] us to confession were **clearly** indicated, there would be no
EP : 01 :007(467) [0781] These points **clearly** set forth the distinction between the
EP : 01 :024(469) [0785] impressions, and they **clearly** show the distinction
EP : 01 :025(469) [0785] sets forth very **clearly** the distinction between God's work
EP : 04 :007(476) [0799] The Apostle affirms in **clear** terms, "So also David
EP : 07 :003(482) [0809] who set forth in **clear** German words what they believe in
EP : 07 :015(483) [0811] words of Christ teach this **clearly** when they direct us to
EP : 07 :024(484) [0815] them, contrary to the **clear** Word of Christ's testament, so
EP : 10 :006(493) [0829] of persecution, when a **clear**-cut confession of faith is
EP : 11 :010(495) [0833] Holy Gospel alone, which **clearly** testifies that "God has
EP : 12 :013(499) [0841] in any civic office with a good and **clear** conscience.
EP : 12 :016(499) [0841] government cannot with a **clear** conscience inflict capital
SD : PR :001(501) [0847] papacy) was once more **clearly** set forth on the basis of
SD : PR :003(501) [0847] this document they gave a **clear** and unequivocal
SD : PR :004(502) [0847] and we abide by the plain, **clear**, and pure meaning of its
SD : RN :003(503) [0851] as the pure and **clear** fountain of Israel, which is the only
SD : RN :004(504) [0851] within the Christian church are **clearly** and solidly refuted
SD : RN :006(504) [0853] in 1531 to set forth **clearly** the true and genuine meaning
SD : RN :006(504) [0853] against the papacy more **clearly** and effectively and to
SD : RN :006(504) [0853] Augsburg Confession is **clearly** expounded and defended
SD : RN :006(505) [0853] it is supported with **clear** and irrefutable testimonies from
SD : RN :009(505) [0853] of blessed memory **clearly** set forth in his writings on the
SD : RN :016(507) [0857] the most distinctly and **clearly** and may be distinguished
SD : RN :016(507) [0857] and severally come to a **clear** and express mutual
SD : RN :019(507) [0857] unequivocally, **clearly**, and distinctly in these theses and
SD : RN :020(508) [0857] will show him **clearly** that there is no contradiction
SD : 01 :003(509) [0859] when it is presented **clearly** from and according to the
SD : 01 :007(510) [0861] second place, it is also a **clearly** established truth, as
SD : 01 :038(514) [0871] These passages indicate **clearly** that even after the Fall
SD : 01 :040(515) [0871] difference irrefutably and **clearly**, because original sin
SD : 02 :030(527) [0893] These statements indicate **clearly** that the Augsburg
SD : 02 :032(527) [0893] From this we see **clearly** that the Apology does not
SD : 02 :042(529) [0897] testimonies indicate **clearly** that we cannot by our own
SD : 02 :083(537) [0913] foregoing exposition it is **clear** that when the Holy
SD : 02 :085(537) [0913] in this matter thoroughly, **clearly**, and definitively.
SD : 02 :087(538) [0915] demonstrated above from **clear** passages of Holy
SD : 03 :007(540) [0919] with the true doctrine, we **clearly** segregate, expose, and
SD : 03 :044(547) [0931] false antitheses become **clear**, namely, that in addition to
SD : 03 :066(550) [0937] as contrary to the **clear** Word of God, and by God's grace
SD : 04 :013(553) [0943] explain only the controverted points simply and **clearly**.
SD : 04 :029(555) [0947] important to have a **clear** and correct confession against
SD : 04 :037(557) [0949] we give the following **clear** answer: If anyone draws good
SD : 05 :016(561) [0957] entire matter nicely and **clearly** for the Christian reader,
SD : 07 :002(569) [0973] set forth their meaning **clearly**, honestly, and explicitly,
SD : 07 :010(571) [0975] Dr. Luther **clearly** presents the same view in the Small
SD : 07 :011(571) [0975] only set forth still more **clearly** in the Apology, but it is
SD : 07 :045(577) [0987] obedience in their strict and **clear** sense, just as they read.
SD : 07 :047(578) [0989] the explicit, certain, **clear**, and earnest words and
SD : 07 :048(578) [0989] in themselves are simple, **clear**, manifest, certain, and
SD : 07 :050(578) [0989] simple, indubitable, and **clear** words, just as he does in all
SD : 07 :050(578) [0991] he explained things more **clearly** by adding the words,
SD : 07 :052(578) [0991] repeat these simple, **clear**, certain, and truthful words of
SD : 07 :054(579) [0991] these words we learn **clearly** that not only the cup which
SD : 07 :079(584) [1001] or sung distinctly and **clearly** before the congregation and
SD : 07 :092(586) [1005] the simple, explicit, and **clear** understanding of Christ's
SD : 07 :104(587) [1009] of Dr. Luther also show **clearly** in what sense our
SD : 08 :003(592) [1017] publicly profess our adherence, **clearly** demonstrate.
SD : 08 :034(597) [1027] St. Peter testifies with **clear** words that even we, in whom
SD : 08 :051(600) [1031] But it is so **clear** on the basis of God's Word that this
SD : 08 :053(601) [1033] in this case give us **clear**, certain testimony, we shall
SD : 08 :058(602) [1035] place, Scripture testifies **clearly** (John 5:21, 27; 6:39, 40)
SD : 08 :086(608) [1047] appealed to these as being **clear** expositions of the majesty
SD : 10 :002(611) [1053] one may still with a **clear** conscience, at the enemies'
SD : 10 :003(611) [1053] can this be done with a **clear** conscience and without
SD : 10 :025(615) [1061] may or may not do with a **clear** conscience in matters of
SD : 11 :012(618) [1067] with the following **clear**, certain, and unfailing
SD : 11 :082(630) [1089] And St. Paul testifies with **clear** words that God's power
SD : 11 :091(631) [1093] in their malice, then it is **clearly** evident that this teaching
SD : 11 :095(632) [1095] friends and foes may **clearly** understand that we have no
SD : 12 :004(633) [1097] but to present a **clear**, lucid, and unmistakable exposition
SD : 12 :006(633) [1097] set forth our position so **clearly** that our very adversaries

Cleaves (1)
LC : 01 :009(366) [0583] for wealth clings and **cleaves** to our nature all the way to

Clemency (1)
AL : 28 :074(093) [0093] would therefore befit the **clemency** of the bishops to

Clement (3)
AP : 04 :236(140) [0185] the emperor, this most **clement** prince, that these laws
AP : 27 :018(272) [0425] But look, most **clement** Emperor Charles; look, princes;
TR : 00 :071(332) [0525] he may be, just as the writings of **Clement** are spurious.

Clementines (1)
TR : 00 :035(326) [0513] is even written in the **Clementines**, "When the imperial

Clergy (21), Clergyman (1), Clergymen (3)
AG : 23 :009(052) [0061] our priests and other **clergy** have taken wives to
AG : 23 :002(053) [0063] the marriage of **clergymen**, there were now more
AG : 23 :016(054) [0063] of priests and the **clergy**, and especially of the pastors and
AG : 23 :018(054) [0063] that priests and **clergymen** may marry is based on God's
AG : 23 :018(054) [0063] men among the cathedral **clergy** and some of the
AG : 23 :018(054) [0063] such vices among the **clergy** would, on account of their
AG : 28 :030(085) [0087] foods, holy days, and the different orders of the **clergy**.
AG : 28 :070(093) [0093] Again, they forbid **clergymen** to marry and admit no one
AP : 04 :233(140) [0185] the people judge their **clergy**'s behavior too strictly or
AP : 04 :233(140) [0185] seek after some other kinds of doctrine and other **clergy**.
AP : 04 :234(140) [0185] on the faults of their **clergy**, when the bishops take into
AP : 04 :242(141) [0187] arisen in the church simply from the hatred of the **clergy**.
AP : 11 :003(180) [0249] Our **clergy** instruct the people about the worth and fruits
AP : 11 :008(181) [0251] secular and the regular **clergy** over the question of who
AP : 21 :043(235) [0357] They do not tolerate capable **clergy** in the churches.
AP : 21 :043(235) [0357] After the good **clergy** have been killed and sound doctrine
AP : 22 :009(237) [0359] a distinction should be made between laity and **clergy**.
AP : 22 :009(237) [0359] to elevate the position of the **clergy** by a religious rite.
AP : 24 :050(259) [0401] neither the people nor the **clergy** have ever understood
TR : 00 :011(321) [0507] church, I Peter 5:3, "Not domineering over the **clergy**."
TR : 00 :050(329) [0519] emperor, nor by all the **clergy**, nor by kings, nor by the
LC : 01 :209(393) [0639] blind world and the false **clergy** do, but view it in the
LC : 03 :025(423) [0705] together, with all their **clergy**, they would have to confess
EP : 12 :011(498) [0841] nothing to do with **clergyman** who preach the Gospel
SD : 01 :058(519) [0879] and deepened if the **clergy** are in doubt whether or not

Clerics (1)
LC : 01 :090(377) [0607] can the whole swarm of **clerics** in our day who stand daily

Clever (8), Cleverly (1), Cleverness (1)
AP : PR :014(099) [0101] realized it was written so **cleverly** and slanderously that in
AP : 04 :280(149) [0201] But our opponents, **clever** men that they are, pick out
AP : 12 :009(184) [0255] they are not so separated as these **clever** sophists imagine.
AP : 23 :008(240) [0365] Look at their **clever** argument!
AP : 24 :002(249) [0385] of Latin in the Mass, our **clever** opponents quibble about
AP : 24 :068(261) [0407] Some **clever** people imagine that the Lord's Supper was
LC : 05 :028(449) [0759] Here again our **clever** spirits comfort themselves with
SD : 02 :020(525) [0889] body, man is indeed very **clever**, intelligent, and extremely
SD : 02 :043(529) [0897] no power or ability, no **cleverness** or reason, with which
SD : 07 :092(586) [1005] should not permit any **clever** human opinions, no matter

Climb (1)
LC : 04 :082(446) [0751] cling to it until he can **climb** aboard again and sail on in

Cling (17), Clings (14), Clung (2)
AP : 04 :206(135) [0177] wicked idea about works has always **clung** to the world.
AP : 04 :265(146) [0197] This legalistic opinion **clings** by nature to the minds of
AP : 24 :097(268) [0417] But this notion **clings** to the world, and always will, that

Continued ▶

A P : 2 4 :098(268) [0417] false idea about sacrifices **clung** to the wicked priests in
A P : 2 4 :098(268) [0417] the worship of Baal **clings** — namely, the abuse of the
S 2 : 0 2 :002(293) [0463] "Why do you **cling** so tenaciously to your Masses?
S 3 : 0 8 :009(313) [0497] In short, enthusiasm **clings** to Adam and his descendants
L C : 0 1 :003(365) [0581] That to which your heart **clings** and entrusts itself is, I
L C : 0 1 :004(365) [0581] fly straight to the one true God and **cling** to him alone.
L C : 0 1 :004(365) [0581] you suffer misfortune and distress, come and **cling** to me.
L C : 0 1 :004(365) [0581] Only let your heart **cling** to no one else."
L C : 0 1 :009(366) [0583] This desire for wealth **clings** and cleaves to our nature all
L C : 0 1 :014(366) [0583] when our heart embraces him and **clings** to him.
L C : 0 1 :015(366) [0583] To **cling** to him with all our heart is nothing else than to
L C : 0 1 :028(368) [0587] and you will find whether or not it **clings** to God alone.
L C : 0 1 :028(368) [0587] contrary, does your heart **cling** to something else, from
L C : 0 1 :039(370) [0591] mercy to those who **cling** to God alone — sheer goodness
L C : 0 1 :187(390) [0633] This spirit or revenge **clings** to every one of us, and it is
L C : 0 1 :317(408) [0673] so deeply rooted and still **clings** to every man, and that
L C : 0 2 :042(416) [0689] they grasp and accept it, **cling** to it, and persevere in it.
L C : 0 3 :102(434) [0727] evil lusts which by nature **cling** to us and to which we are
L C : 0 4 :029(440) [0739] to which it may **cling** and upon which it may stand.
L C : 0 4 :029(440) [0739] Thus faith **clings** to the water and believes it to be Baptism
L C : 0 4 :082(446) [0751] head for the ship and **cling** to it until he can climb aboard
L C : 0 5 :079(455) [0771] want to become good and **cling** to the Gospel, and see
L C : 0 5 :083(456) [0773] yourself, look around a little, **cling** to the Scriptures.
E P : 0 6 :004(480) [0805] nature and kind), which **clings** to them until death.
S D : 0 6 :007(565) [0965] the Old Adam still **clings** to their nature and to all its
S D : 0 6 :018(567) [0967] life but the Old Adam **clings** to them down to the grave,
S D : 0 9 :003(610) [1051] We must only believe and **cling** to the Word.
S D : 1 1 :021(619) [1069] them unto the end, if they **cling** to God's Word, pray
S D : 1 1 :028(620) [1071] we must by all means **cling** rigidly and firmly to the fact
S D : 1 1 :055(625) [1081] or brood over it, but **cling** solely to his revealed Word, to

Cloak (8)
A P : 2 3 :026(243) [0371] being observed, still they **cloak** it with pious-sounding
L C : 0 1 :056(372) [0597] God's name and using it as a **cloak** to cover our shame.
L C : 0 1 :285(403) [0663] to overlook them, and to **cloak** and veil them with his
L C : 0 3 :027(424) [0705] desires and spread your **cloak** wide to receive many
L C : 0 3 :041(425) [0709] using his name to **cloak** lies and make them acceptable;
L C : 0 3 :042(425) [0709] the divine name as a **cloak** for their shame, by swearing,
L C : 0 3 :047(426) [0711] wear the holy name as a **cloak** and warrant for their
L C : 0 3 :049(426) [0711] his glory and name to **cloak** its lies and wickedness, but

Cloister (1), Cloisters (1)
A G : 2 7 :033(076) [0079] of them entered the **cloister** in their childhood, before
L C : 0 1 :314(407) [0671] Otherwise, why should monks and nuns go into **cloisters**?

Close (3), Closed (1), Closely (6), Closer (2), Closes (1)
A P : P R :011(099) [0101] made it a point to stick as **closely** as possible to
A P : 0 4 :385(166) [0225] known that every prayer **closes** with this phrase: "through
A P : 1 2 :059(190) [0267] and the doctrine of justification are very **closely** related.
A P : 2 1 :041(235) [0355] scholastics are usually **closer** to Scripture than the more
A P : 2 7 :012(270) [0423] sake and try to live more **closely** according to the Gospel
A P : 2 7 :016(271) [0425] Christ, the monks come **closer** in their observance than do
A P : 2 7 :017(271) [0425] monks "pattern their lives more **closely** after the Gospel"!
A P : 2 7 :039(276) [0433] try to pattern their lives more **closely** with the Gospel.
A P : 2 7 :039(276) [0433] pattern their lives more **closely** after the Gospel because
S D : 0 7 :002(569) [0971] terminology which is as **close** as possible to the formulas
S D : 0 7 :100(586) [1007] presence when he left the **closed** grave and came through
S D : 0 8 :076(606) [1043] "I am with you always even to the **close** of the age."
S D : 0 8 :096(609) [1049] apostles simply to believe, **close** the eyes of reason, take

Cloth (1)
L C : P R :019(361) [0573] Vain imaginations, like new **cloth**, suffer shrinkage!

Clothe (6), Clothed (2), Clothes (3), Clothing (12)
A L : 1 8 :005(040) [0051] to have a friend, will to **clothe** oneself, will to build a
A P : 0 7 :045(177) [0243] in food, days, **clothing**, and similar matters without
A P : 2 3 :008(240) [0367] but yearly the fields are **clothed** as long as this universe
A P : 2 7 :026(273) [0429] distinctions among **clothes** or foods, nor the surrender of
A P : 2 7 :039(276) [0433] and obey the rule in trifles like **clothing** and food.
A P : 2 8 :007(282) [0445] depends upon food, drink, **clothing**, and similar matters.
A P : 2 8 :010(282) [0447] life since food, drink, **clothing**, and the like are things
A P : 2 8 :019(284) [0449] trifles, distinction of foods and **clothing** and the like.
S 1 : P R :004(289) [0457] They try to **clothe** their venomous spirits in the garments
S 3 : 0 3 :028(308) [0487] prayers, Masses, coarse **clothing**, and hard beds and tried
S C : 0 2 :002(345) [0543] together with food and **clothing**, house and home, family
S C : 0 3 :014(347) [0547] needs, such as food and **clothing**, house and home, fields
S C : 0 9 :012(356) [0563] **Clothe** yourselves, all of you, with humility toward one
L C : 0 1 :088(377) [0605] and dress up in our best **clothes**, but, as has been said,
L C : 0 1 :164(387) [0627] shall they have bread, **clothing**, and money for a year or
L C : 0 1 :190(391) [0635] naked when you could **clothe** him, you have let him
L C : 0 1 :191(391) [0635] naked and you did not **clothe** me, I was sick and in prison
L C : 0 2 :013(412) [0681] my food and drink, **clothing**, means of support, wife and
L C : 0 3 :073(430) [0719] not only food and **clothing** and other necessities for our
L C : 0 3 :076(431) [0721] give us food and drink, **clothing**, house, home, and a
L C : 0 4 :020(439) [0737] man, adorned and **clothed** with the majesty and glory of
L C : 0 6 :023(460) [0000] a rich gift, of money or **clothes**, is to be given out at a
S D : 0 1 :035(514) [0869] Thou didst **clothe** me with skin and flesh, and knit me

Clowning (2), Clowns (1)
A P : 2 1 :037(234) [0355] ceremonies, are **clowns** who know nothing about either
A P : 2 2 :010(237) [0361] opponents are obviously **clowning** when they apply the
A P : 2 3 :018(242) [0369] our opponents are only **clowning**; they do not mean this

Club (1), Clubs (1)
L C : 0 1 :077(375) [0603] that they fear God more than they do rods and **clubs**.
S D : 0 6 :024(568) [0969] frequently also with the **club** of punishments and

Clumsy (1)
A P : 2 3 :027(243) [0371] This **clumsy** analogy is presented as a proof to force

Co- (7)
A P : 0 4 :196(134) [0175] of God, moreover, it also makes us **co**-heirs with Christ.
A P : 0 4 :196(134) [0175] makes us sons of God and **co**-heirs with Christ, we do
S 3 : 1 5 :005(318) [0501] in the names of my other **co**-workers in the Gospel,
L C : 0 2 :052(417) [0691] member, a participant and **co**-partner in all the blessings
E P : 0 1 :003(466) [0779] militates against and cannot **co**-exist with the chief
E P : 0 3 :011(474) [0795] that could coexist and **co**-persist with a wicked intention
S D : 0 8 :051(600) [1031] false, that even their own **co**-religionists now criticize and

Coarse (5)
S 3 : 0 3 :028(308) [0487] vigils, prayers, Masses, **coarse** clothing, and hard beds
E P : 0 7 :041(486) [0817] and offensively in a **coarse**, carnal, Capernaitic, and
S D : 0 2 :075(536) [0909] 2. The error of the **coarse** Pelagians, that by his own
S D : 0 7 :064(581) [0995] — not, however, in a **coarse**, carnal, Capernaitic manner,
S D : 0 7 :127(591) [1015] which are advanced in a **coarse**, fleshly, Capernaitic way

Coat (2)
L C : 0 3 :075(430) [0719] therefore be fitting if the **coat**-of-arms of every upright
L C : 0 4 :006(437) [0733] indifferent matter, then, like putting on a new red **coat**.

Cobbler (1)
L C : 0 1 :047(371) [0593] God's gifts exactly as a **cobbler** uses his needle, awl, and

Coburg (1)
P R : P R :027(014) [0025] Duke John Casimir [of Saxe-**Coburg**] and

Codex (1)
T R : 0 0 :077(333) [0527] for it appears from the ***Codex*** and *Novellae* of Justinian

Coerce (6), Coerced (7), Coercion (25)
A G : 2 8 :076(094) [0095] as if they had power to **coerce** the churches according to
A G : 2 8 :077(094) [0095] and pray that they may not **coerce** our consciences to sin.
A L : 2 8 :076(094) [0095] bishops to be domineering and to **coerce** the churches.
A P : 2 1 :013(230) [0345] our opponents should not **coerce** us to adopt something
L C : 0 5 :042(451) [0763] any circumstances be **coerced** or compelled, lest we
L C : 0 5 :045(452) [0763] not from compulsion, **coerced** by men, but to obey and
L C : 0 6 :001(457) [0000] been set free from his **coercion** and from the intolerable
L C : 0 6 :004(457) [0000] we may confess without **coercion** or fear, and we are
L C : 0 6 :006(457) [0000] back into subjection and **coerce** them like the tyrant he
L C : 0 6 :021(459) [0000] commandments, and **coercion** since we have no need of
L C : 0 6 :023(459) [0000] indicated, there would be no need of **coercion** and force.
L C : 0 6 :030(460) [0000] In short, we approve of no **coercion**.
E P : 0 4 :003(476) [0797] flow from necessity or **coercion** but from a spontaneous
E P : 0 4 :010(476) [0799] as involving not **coercion** but the due obedience which
E P : 0 4 :010(476) [0799] reborn, render not by **coercion** or compulsion of the law
E P : 0 6 :002(480) [0805] from the curse and **coercion** of the law, they are not on
E P : 0 6 :004(480) [0807] He must be **coerced** against his own will not only by the
E P : 0 6 :005(480) [0807] people only under the **coercion** of punishments and the
E P : 0 6 :007(481) [0807] of him by the law under **coercion** and unwillingly.
E P : 0 6 :007(481) [0807] the believer without any **coercion** and with a willing
S D : 0 2 :060(532) [0905] is true that God does not **coerce** anyone to piety, for
S D : 0 2 :064(533) [0905] of the Holy Spirit is no **coercion** or compulsion because
S D : 0 2 :073(535) [0909] brought about through **coercion**, so that God forcibly
S D : 0 2 :074(535) [0909] man acts only under **coercion**; that even in external
S D : 0 2 :074(536) [0909] or that the will of man is **coerced** into doing such wicked
S D : 0 4 :004(551) [0939] at times it implies the **coercion** with which the law forces
S D : 0 4 :012(553) [0941] therefore without any **coercion** a man is willing and
S D : 0 4 :017(554) [0943] against his will, by **coercion** or otherwise, so that he does
S D : 0 6 :005(564) [0963] the regenerated with its **coercion**, for according to the
S D : 0 6 :006(565) [0965] compulsion, **coercion**, or necessity, and as the holy angels
S D : 0 6 :019(567) [0969] is concerned, he must be **coerced** not only with the law
S D : 0 6 :019(567) [0969] against his will and by **coercion**, just as the unconverted
S D : 0 6 :019(567) [0969] are driven and **coerced** into obedience by the threats of
S D : 0 6 :023(568) [0969] pleasing to God not by **coercion** of the law but willingly
S D : 0 6 :024(568) [0969] of them and must be **coerced** into the obedience of
S D : 0 6 :025(568) [0971] spontaneously, without **coercion**, unhindered, perfectly,
S D : 1 0 :003(611) [1053] either by force and **coercion** or by surreptitious methods
S D : 1 0 :014(613) [1057] Any **coercion** or commandment darkens and perverts this

Coessential (1)
S D : 0 1 :030(513) [0869] from our nature and accordingly not **coessential** with us.

Coeternal (2)
A L : 0 1 :003(028) [0043] power, who are also **coeternal**: the Father, the Son, and
A P : 0 1 :001(100) [0103] three distinct and **coeternal** persons of the same divine

Coexist (4)
P R : P R :022(011) [0019] to the expressed Word of God and cannot **coexist** with it.
E P : 0 3 :011(474) [0795] connection that could **coexist** and co-persist with a
S D : P R :008(502) [0849] if the pure doctrine can **coexist** among us with such
S D : 0 3 :041(546) [0929] occasion true faith could **coexist** and survive for a while

Cogent (3)
A P : 2 2 :014(238) [0361] factors which are not **cogent** enough to change Christ's
A P : 2 3 :060(247) [0381] No sane man can argue with these **cogent** facts.
A P : 2 7 :056(278) [0439] are many serious and **cogent** reasons that release good

Coinage (1)
L C : 0 3 :084(431) [0721] on account of false **coinage**, yes, on account of daily

Coincide (1)
T R : 0 0 :039(327) [0515] marks of the Antichrist **coincide** with those of the pope's

Coins (2)
L C : 0 1 :227(396) [0645] weights, and bad **coins**, and takes advantage of him by
L C : 0 3 :075(430) [0719] of bread were stamped on **coins**, to remind both princes

Cold (7), Coldly (2)
A P : 1 2 :012(184) [0255] right, they speak very **coldly** about absolution, which
L C : 0 1 :191(391) [0635] die of hunger, thirst, and **cold**, to be torn to pieces by wild
L C : 0 3 :029(424) [0705] not act so crudely and **coldly** that they become daily more
L C : 0 5 :053(453) [0765] for the benefit of the **cold** and indifferent, that they may
L C : 0 5 :053(453) [0765] more and more callous and **cold**, and eventually spurn it
L C : 0 5 :054(453) [0765] be warmed and kindled, and it will not grow entirely **cold**.
L C : 0 5 :067(454) [0769] so long that we grow quite **cold** and callous and lose all
E P : 0 8 :008(487) [0819] to endure hunger, thirst, **cold**, heat, and the like, which
S D : 0 2 :068(534) [0907] in faith and in hope, and at another time **cold** and weak.

Collapse (1)
S 2 : 0 2 :005(293) [0463] Will the Mass not then **collapse** of itself — not only for

Collate (1), Collated (1)
P R : P R :018(009) [0015] which was afterward **collated** very diligently by
A G : 2 6 :014(066) [0073] for they undertook to **collate** the traditions and sought

Colleague (1)
T R : 0 0 :014(322) [0509] in the ordination of our **colleague** Sabinus) in order that

Collect (2), Collected (4), Collection (3), Collectively (2)
A L : 2 7 :045(078) [0081] many things could be **collected** of which even the monks
A P : 1 2 :015(184) [0257] of satisfactions, and **collect** this revenue not only from the
A P : 2 2 :004(236) [0359] it would not be hard to **collect** a great multitude of
A P : 2 4 :009(250) [0387] Our opponents have **collected** many statements to prove
A P : 2 4 :081(264) [0411] duties," like the taxes **collected** for equipping a fleet.
A P : 2 4 :082(264) [0411] In II Cor. 9:12 Paul uses this word for a **collection**.
A P : 2 4 :082(264) [0411] Taking this **collection** not only supplies what the saints
A P : 2 4 :085(265) [0413] where it means the **collection** or gifts of the people rather
S D : R N :009(505) [0853] in the Preface to the Latin edition of his **collected** works.
S D : R N :016(507) [0857] something, we have **collectively** and severally come to a
S D : 0 7 :017(572) [0979] all the theologians **collectively** and individually

Color (4)
A P : 0 2 :041(105) [0115] is a neutral thing, like the **color** of the skin or ill health.
S 1 : P R :012(290) [0459] in like a deluge and have taken on the **color** of legality.
E P : 0 1 :015(468) [0783] spot can be washed from the face or **color** from the wall.
S D : 1 0 :005(611) [1053] and are given a different **color** from their true one.

Combat (1)
L C : 0 5 :084(456) [0773] much in need of the sacrament to **combat** your misery.

Combination (1), Combine (2), Combined (3)
A P : 0 4 :152(127) [0163] by which we sometimes **combine** cause and effect in the
A P : 1 2 :045(188) [0263] too, the two parts are **combined**: contrition, when sins are
A P : 1 2 :093(196) [0279] in order to select and **combine** their opinions not only
L C : 0 1 :166(388) [0629] For the **combined** efforts of the whole world cannot add
E P : 0 8 :009(487) [0819] union is not a **combination** or connection of such a kind
S D : 0 8 :022(595) [1023] of the church have **combined** both words, "communion"

Combustion (4)
S D : 0 8 :066(604) [1039] of illumination and **combustion** — the power of
S D : 0 8 :066(604) [1039] of illumination and **combustion** is the property of fire —
S D : 0 8 :066(604) [1039] of illumination and **combustion** in and through the iron
S D : 0 8 :066(604) [1039] of illumination and **combustion** without any

Comes (64), Coming (20), Came (31)
P R : P R :001(003) [0007] whose eyes this document **comes**, we, the electors,
A G : 0 5 :004(031) [0045] that the Holy Spirit **comes** to us through our own
A G : 2 4 :010(057) [0065] time, however, the Mass **came** to be misused in many
A G : 2 6 :016(066) [0073] thereby hindered from **coming** to a right knowledge of
A G : 2 7 :008(072) [0077] also have seen what evils **came** from this arrangement,
A G : 2 7 :029(075) [0079] Before they **came** to a right understanding they were
A G : 2 8 :031(085) [0087] When the Spirit of truth **comes**, he will guide you into all
A G : 2 8 :041(087) [0089] that countless regulations **came** into being — for example,
A L : 0 5 :004(031) [0045] that the Holy Spirit **comes** to men without the external
A L : 1 2 :010(035) [0049] that remission of sins **comes** through faith but command
A L : 2 4 :029(059) [0067] outward act, justification **comes** from the work of the
A L : 2 7 :016(073) [0077] Formerly people **came** together in monasteries to learn.
A L : 2 7 :037(077) [0081] by men but that it **comes** through faith to those who
A L : 2 8 :031(086) [0087] When the Spirit of truth **comes**, he will guide you into all
A P : 0 2 :007(101) [0107] way they ask whether it **came** through contact with the
A P : 0 4 :005(108) [0121] Testament, the Christ who **came** promises forgiveness of
A P : 0 4 :030(111) [0129] of the righteousness that **comes** from God, and seeking to
A P : 0 4 :061(115) [0137] knowledge, we must tell how faith **comes** into being.
A P : 0 4 :067(116) [0139] and (Rom. 10:17), "Faith **comes** from what is heard."
A P : 0 4 :103(122) [0151] but when the Lord Jesus **came** he forgave all men the sin
A P : 0 4 :103(122) [0151] is what Paul says, 'Law **came** in, to increase the trespass.
A P : 0 4 :154(128) [0163] The woman **came**, believing that she should seek the
A P : 0 4 :188(133) [0173] and the reconciliation that **comes** through faith in Christ.
A P : 0 4 :236(140) [0185] Moreover, it **comes** in poor grace for our opponents to
A P : 0 4 :310(155) [0207] greatest possible comfort **comes** from this doctrine that
A P : 0 4 :322(157) [0209] church confesses that eternal life **comes** through mercy.
A P : 0 4 :374(164) [0223] Such a new birth **comes** by faith amid penitence.
A P : 0 4 :396(167) [0227] and clear that their ungodliness **comes** out into the open.
A P : 0 7 :042(176) [0241] Later on **came** the arrangement by which our Passover
A P : 1 2 :039(187) [0261] absolution since "faith **comes** from what is heard." as
A P : 1 2 :040(187) [0261] less than we would believe a voice **coming** from heaven.
A P : 1 2 :057(189) [0267] woman who was a sinner **came** to Christ in tears, which
A P : 1 2 :064(191) [0269] what the forgiveness of sins is nor how it **comes** to us.
A P : 1 2 :149(206) [0299] power of the grief that **comes** over even the simplest
A P : 1 3 :005(211) [0309] says (Rom. 10:17), "Faith **comes** from what is heard."
A P : 1 5 :028(219) [0323] to consciences that **comes** from this strict interpretation
A P : 1 5 :045(221) [0327] When this **comes**, we must obey God's will, as Paul says
A P : 1 8 :008(226) [0337] As we have said before, it **comes** into being when terrified
A P : 2 1 :034(234) [0353] Afterwards **came** invocation, with abuses that were
A P : 2 4 :008(250) [0383] a week, and that this practice **came** from the apostles.
A P : 2 4 :048(258) [0401] that the forgiveness of sins **comes** freely for Christ's sake.
A P : 2 4 :056(259) [0403] reconciliation — but only symbolized the **coming** sacrifice
A P : 2 4 :067(261) [0407] merit reconciliation but **comes** from the reconciled, just
A P : 2 4 :075(263) [0411] the bread of life; he who **comes** to me shall not hunger,
A P : 2 4 :085(265) [0413] Individuals **coming** to the celebration of the Passover had
A P : 2 4 :095(267) [0417] If they **came** back to life now and saw their sayings being
A P : 2 4 :098(268) [0419] papal realm until Christ **comes** to judge and by the glory
A P : 2 4 :098(268) [0419] and by the glory of his **coming** destroys the kingdom of
A P : 2 7 :032(274) [0431] up against the Lord who **comes** at him with twenty
A P : 2 7 :038(275) [0433] went into the city and **came** to the shoemaker to find out
A P : 2 7 :038(276) [0433] Thus Anthony **came** to understand that justification was
S 2 : 0 4 :015(301) [0475] will accomplish his purpose by his Spirit and his **coming**.
S 3 : 0 2 :005(303) [0479] and Rom. 5:20, "Law **came** in to increase the trespass."
S 3 : 0 3 :008(304) [0481] captivity to sin, and this **comes** to us through the Word,
S 3 : 0 3 :023(307) [0485] of always doing penance but never **coming** to repentance.
S 3 : 0 3 :024(307) [0485] Here the holy see in Rome **came** to the aid of the poor
S 3 : 0 3 :025(307) [0485] and guilt, and the people **came** running, for everyone was
S 3 : 0 8 :003(312) [0495] through or with the external Word which **comes** before.
S 3 : 0 8 :006(312) [0495] until the Spirit himself **comes** to the people without and
S 3 : 0 8 :006(313) [0495] they boast that the Spirit **came** upon them without the
S 3 : 0 8 :007(313) [0495] baptized and those who **came** to faith in Baptism came to
S 3 : 0 8 :007(313) [0495] came to faith in Baptism **came** to their faith through the
S 3 : 0 8 :008(313) [0495] from the Jews about the **coming** Messiah through whom
S 3 : 0 8 :008(313) [0495] the Messiah, in whose **coming** he had previously
S 3 : 0 8 :008(313) [0495] his faith concerning the **coming** Messiah did not hold him
S C : 0 3 :007(346) [0547] the kingdom of God **comes** of itself, without our prayer,
S C : 0 3 :011(347) [0547] his name and prevent the **coming** of his kingdom, and
S C : 0 3 :020(348) [0549] when the hour of death **comes**, he may grant us a blessed
S C : 0 7 :005(353) [0559] Graciously protect me during the **coming** night.
L C : 0 1 :021(367) [0585] it believe that whatever good it receives **comes** from God.
L C : 0 1 :026(368) [0587] much that is good **comes** to us from men, we receive it all
L C : 0 1 :040(370) [0591] since the divine Majesty **comes** to us with so gracious an
L C : 0 1 :074(374) [0601] From the same source **came** the custom of children who
L C : 0 1 :128(382) [0617] when an evil hour **comes** do we rage and grumble
L C : 0 1 :152(386) [0625] are despised, as if they **came** from some loutish peddler.
L C : 0 1 :154(386) [0625] master, another person **comes** along and treats you
L C : 0 1 :186(390) [0633] head, which, if they **came** true, would soon put an end to
L C : 0 1 :300(405) [0667] honor and right when it **comes** to acquiring possessions.
L C : 0 2 :023(413) [0683] and every blessing that **comes** our way, should remind us
L C : 0 2 :028(414) [0685] of good things, the devil **came** and led us into
L C : 0 2 :029(414) [0685] and wretchedness and **came** from heaven to help us.
L C : 0 3 :050(426) [0711] us, so also his kingdom **comes** of itself without our prayer
L C : 0 3 :053(427) [0711] God's kingdom **comes** to us in two ways: first, it comes
L C : 0 3 :053(427) [0711] to us in two ways: first, it **comes** here, in time, through
L C : 0 3 :053(427) [0711] secondly, in eternity, it **comes** through the final
L C : 0 3 :067(429) [0717] thy kingdom from **coming**; and grant that whatever we
L C : 0 3 :103(434) [0727] Next **comes** the world, which assails us by word and deed
L C : 0 3 :104(434) [0727] Then **comes** the devil, who baits and badgers us on all
L C : 0 6 :030(460) [0000] compulsion but rather **coming** and compelling us to offer
E P : 0 2 :003(470) [0787] to claim anything as **coming** from us; our sufficiency is
E P : 0 2 :004(470) [0787] likewise, that faith **comes** from the hearing of God's Word
E P : 0 5 :010(479) [0803] of Christ by which he **comes** to his proper office —
S D : 0 2 :007(521) [0883] degree, "of himself as **coming** from himself," but is a slave
S D : 0 2 :012(522) [0885] to claim anything as **coming** from us; our sufficiency is
S D : 0 2 :026(526) [0891] In short, every good gift **comes** from God (James 1:17).
S D : 0 2 :051(531) [0901] "Faith **comes** from what is heard, and what is heard
S D : 0 2 :051(531) [0901] heard, and what is heard **comes** by the preaching of
S D : 0 2 :071(535) [0909] these things, and how he **comes** by them), our doctrine
S D : 0 2 :076(536) [0911] it, the Holy Spirit **comes** to the aid of the good work
S D : 0 4 :032(556) [0947] the wrath of God is **coming** upon the sons of
S D : 0 5 :009(559) [0955] This knowledge **comes** from the law, but it is not
S D : 0 5 :011(560) [0955] is, to rebuke) until he **comes** to his own work (that is, to
S D : 0 5 :022(562) [0959] knowledge of God which **comes** from the the Gospel and
S D : 0 5 :024(563) [0961] our custodian until Christ **came**, that we might be
S D : 0 7 :013(571) [0977] the other preachers who **came** with him from the cities,
S D : 0 7 :031(574) [0983] the Last Judgment at the **coming** of the Lord Christ.
S D : 0 7 :100(586) [1007] left the closed grave and **came** through locked doors, in
S D : 1 1 :004(617) [1065] and your going out and **coming** in, and your raging
S D : 1 1 :028(621) [1071] Righteousness "**comes** through faith in Christ to all and
S D : 1 1 :038(622) [1075] us from the call which **comes** to us through the Word and
S D : 1 1 :064(626) [1083] of God, as soon as he **comes** to the point where he shows
S D : 1 1 :066(627) [1085] himself says, "No one **comes** to the Father but by me"
S D : 1 1 :068(627) [1085] them away, "Him who **comes** to me I will not cast out"
S D : 1 1 :069(627) [1085] apostle testifies, "Faith **comes** from the hearing of God's
S D : 1 1 :076(628) [1087] states, that no one **comes** to Christ unless the Father draw

Comfort (85), Comforted (2), Comforting (23), Comforts (10)
A G : 0 3 :004(030) [0045] purify, strengthen, and **comfort** all who believe in him,
A G : 1 2 :005(035) [0049] and this faith will **comfort** the heart and again set it at
A G : 2 0 :007(042) [0053] may offer a little more **comfort** than the teaching that we
A G : 2 0 :015(043) [0055] terrified consciences find it most **comforting** and salutary.
A G : 2 0 :019(043) [0055] In former times this **comfort** was not heard in preaching,
A G : 0 1 :007(056) [0065] to be used (namely, as a **comfort** for terrified consciences)
A G : 2 4 :030(059) [0067] to awaken our faith and **comfort** our consciences when
A G : 2 5 :004(062) [0069] power of keys and how **comforting** and necessary it is for
A G : 2 5 :004(062) [0069] that we should joyfully **comfort** ourselves with
A G : 2 8 :004(081) [0085] for the sake of **comforting** consciences, to point out the
A L : 0 3 :005(030) [0045] into their hearts to rule, **comfort**, and quicken them and
A L : 1 2 :005(035) [0049] for Christ's sake, **comforts** the conscience, and delivers it
A L : 2 4 :030(059) [0067] Christ and should cheer and **comfort** anxious consciences.
A P : 0 4 :058(115) [0137] Here he **comforts** himself with his trust in God's mercy.
A P : 0 4 :079(118) [0143] By faith, when we **comfort** ourselves by firm trust in the
A P : 0 4 :080(118) [0143] of sins when we **comfort** our hearts with trust in the
A P : 0 4 :081(118) [0143] of sins when we are **comforted** by trust in the mercy
A P : 0 4 :115(123) [0155] frees us from death, **comforting** and quickening terrified
A P : 0 4 :310(155) [0207] The greatest possible **comfort** comes from this doctrine
A P : 0 4 :324(157) [0209] Looking at his mercy, faith **comforts** and consoles us.
A P : 0 4 :351(161) [0217] encouragement and **comfort** in the midst of our terrors,
A P : 0 4 :387(166) [0225] for it brings the fullest **comfort** in all afflictions and
A P : 0 4 :389(166) [0225] faith and for teaching and **comforting** their conscience.
A P : 1 3 :020(214) [0313] accept this by faith, **comfort** his troubled conscience, and
A P : 1 3 :022(214) [0313] use of the sacrament **comforts** devout and troubled
A P : 1 5 :042(221) [0327] about faith in Christ or about **comfort** for the conscience.
A P : 1 5 :043(221) [0327] righteousness of faith, **comfort** for the conscience through
A P : 2 1 :018(231) [0347] and God our Father, **comfort** your hearts and establish
A P : 2 4 :012(251) [0387] of sins and death and to **comfort** our hearts with the
A P : 2 4 :075(263) [0411] a twofold effect, of the **comfort** for the conscience and of
A P : 2 4 :075(263) [0411] Ambrose says about the **comfort**: "Go to him and be
A P : 2 4 :075(263) [0411] of the appropriation of the **comfort**, not of any transfer.
A P : 2 8 :019(284) [0449] the deepest kind of **comfort** and teaching, and they
T R : 0 0 :058(330) [0521] urgent reasons are a **comfort** to the godly when, as often
S C : 0 5 :029(351) [0555] Scriptures with which to **comfort** and to strengthen the
L C : P R :011(360) [0571] and gives us immeasurable strength, **comfort**, and help.
L C : P R :017(361) [0573] he can counsel, help, **comfort**, judge, and make decisions
L C : 0 1 :017(367) [0585] own, to which he looked for blessings, help, and **comfort**.
L C : 0 1 :022(367) [0585] which seeks help, **comfort**, and salvation in its own works
L C : 0 1 :029(368) [0589] terrible threat and, then, a beautiful, **comforting** promise.
L C : 0 1 :039(370) [0591] are, much mightier is the **comfort** in the promise that
L C : 0 1 :042(370) [0591] honor, wealth, and every **comfort** in the eyes of the

Continued ▶

LC : 0 1 :115(381) [0613] the first place, the great **comfort** of being able joyfully to
LC : 0 2 :014(412) [0681] help provide the **comforts** and necessities of life — sun,
LC : 0 2 :029(414) [0685] no counsel, no help, no **comfort** for us until this only and
LC : 0 2 :054(417) [0693] well as through all the **comforting** words of the entire
LC : 0 2 :055(418) [0693] signs appointed to **comfort** and revive our consciences as
LC : 0 3 :074(430) [0719] us our daily bread and all the **comforts** of this life.
LC : 0 3 :089(432) [0723] and so it loses the **comfort** and confidence of the Gospel.
LC : 0 3 :089(432) [0723] to this petition for the **comfort** that will restore our
LC : 0 3 :093(433) [0725] a necessary but **comforting** clause is added, "as we forgive
LC : 0 3 :095(433) [0725] forgive, you have the **comfort** and assurance that you are
LC : 0 3 :110(435) [0729] times your only help or **comfort** is to take refuge in the
LC : 0 4 :039(441) [0743] in short, it is so full of **comfort** and grace that heaven and
LC : 0 4 :044(442) [0743] must draw strength and **comfort** from it when our sins or
LC : 0 5 :027(449) [0759] too sorely pressed, this **comfort** of the Lord's Supper is
LC : 0 5 :028(449) [0759] again our clever spirits **comfort** themselves with their
LC : 0 5 :072(455) [0769] and receive refreshment, **comfort**, and strength.
LC : 0 6 :003(457) [0000] what confession is and how useful and **comforting** it is.
LC : 0 6 :004(457) [0000] beneficially for the **comforting** and strengthening of our
LC : 0 6 :007(458) [0000] lose this precious and **comforting** treasure which the
LC : 0 6 :013(458) [0000] a brother, seeking his advice, **comfort**, and strength.
LC : 0 6 :015(459) [0000] my sin and desire **comfort** and restoration for my soul.
LC : 0 6 :015(459) [0000] that makes confession so wonderful and **comforting**.
LC : 0 6 :020(459) [0000] and desire no such **comfort**, we shall leave you to
LC : 0 6 :024(460) [0000] Not much joy or **comfort** would come from this, but only
LC : 0 6 :028(460) [0000] precious, and **comforting** thing confession is, and we urge
EP : 0 5 :007(478) [0803] speaking, precisely a **comforting** and joyful message
EP : 0 5 :007(478) [0803] reprove or terrify but **comforts** consciences that are
EP : 0 5 :010(479) [0803] — namely, to preach grace, to **comfort**, to make alive.
EP : 0 5 :011(479) [0805] are robbed of their true **comfort**, and the doors are again
EP : 0 7 :019(484) [0813] faith but repentant, to **comfort** them and to strengthen
EP : 0 8 :018(489) [0823] the sole foundation of our **comfort**, life, and salvation.
EP : 1 1 :001(494) [0831] But since it is such a **comforting** article when it is
EP : 1 1 :011(495) [0835] is profitable and **comforting** to the person who concerns
EP : 1 1 :013(496) [0835] entirely of the glorious **comfort** which this salutary
EP : 1 1 :013(496) [0835] and with which we can **comfort** ourselves in our greatest
EP : 1 1 :016(497) [0837] Christians can find no **comfort** in this doctrine but are
EP : 1 1 :021(497) [0837] rob Christians of all the **comfort** that they have in the
SD : 0 2 :014(523) [0885] passage is of very great **comfort** to all devout Christians
SD : 0 2 :045(530) [0899] accept the Gospel and to **comfort** himself with it, and
SD : 0 2 :054(531) [0903] for Christ's sake and **comforts** itself with the promise of
SD : 0 2 :057(532) [0903] his sins, he can neither **comfort** himself with God's
SD : 0 3 :006(540) [0917] can have any abiding **comfort** or rightly understand the
SD : 0 3 :030(544) [0925] dependable and reliable **comfort** and to give due honor to
SD : 0 3 :035(545) [0927] to supply tempted consciences with abiding **comfort**.
SD : 0 5 :001(558) [0951] consciences of the **comfort** which they would otherwise
SD : 0 5 :009(559) [0955] Christ, whose merit the **comforting** proclamation of the
SD : 0 5 :011(560) [0955] of Christ must not only **comfort** but, through the office
SD : 0 5 :011(560) [0955] his own work (that is, to **comfort** and to preach about
SD : 0 5 :012(560) [0957] or to condemn us, but to **comfort** and lift upright those
SD : 0 5 :021(562) [0959] For everything which **comforts** and which offers the
SD : 0 5 :023(562) [0959] their courage and **comforted** themselves with the
SD : 0 5 :025(563) [0961] Christ will once more **comfort** and strengthen them with
SD : 0 5 :027(563) [0961] Christians of the true **comfort** which they have in the
SD : 0 6 :012(566) [0967] His office is not alone to **comfort** but also to rebuke, as it
SD : 0 6 :014(566) [0967] them up again and **comforts** them with the preaching of
SD : 0 7 :016(572) [0977] who truly repent and **comfort** themselves through faith in
SD : 0 7 :044(577) [0987] of the new covenant, a **comfort** for all sorrowing hearts,
SD : 0 7 :062(581) [0995] and confidence, on this **comforting** assurance that we
SD : 0 7 :105(588) [1009] not only to work **comfort** and life in believers but also to
SD : 0 8 :087(608) [1047] of their highest **comfort**, afforded them in the cited
SD : 0 8 :096(609) [1049] captive to obey Christ, **comfort** themselves therewith, and
SD : 0 8 :096(610) [1049] certain to find abiding **comfort** in all adversities and will
SD : 0 9 :003(610) [1053] and derive from it the **comfort** that neither hell nor the
SD : 1 1 :020(619) [1069] when they stumble, and **comfort** and preserve them in
SD : 1 1 :025(620) [1071] and who can and should **comfort** themselves with this
SD : 1 1 :030(621) [1073] have hope, patience, and **comfort** in afflictions (Eph.
SD : 1 1 :033(622) [1075] will show you how **comforting** God's foreknowledge is."
SD : 1 1 :036(622) [1075] us the necessary and **comforting** foundation, which daily
SD : 1 1 :038(622) [1075] would be deprived of this **comfort** completely if we could
SD : 1 1 :043(623) [1077] a useful, salutary, and **comforting** doctrine, for it mightily
SD : 1 1 :045(624) [1079] beautiful and glorious **comfort** that God was so deeply
SD : 1 1 :048(624) [1079] also give us the glorious **comfort**, in times of trial and
SD : 1 1 :048(624) [1079] us patience, give us **comfort**, create hope, and bring
SD : 1 1 :049(624) [1079] presents this in a most **comforting** manner when he
SD : 1 1 :051(625) [1079] this article in a profitable, **comforting**, and salutary way.
SD : 1 1 :090(631) [1093] the permanently abiding **comfort** of knowing that their
SD : 1 1 :091(631) [1093] Christians can find no **comfort** in it but are driven to
SD : 1 1 :092(632) [1093] or even removes this **comfort** and hope is contrary to the

Command (194)

AG : PR :005(025) [0039] have complied with the **command** and can say without
AG : 0 0 :001(048) [0059] without any solid basis of divine **command** or Scripture.
AG : 0 0 :000(049) [0059] compelled by God's **command** (which is rightly to be
AG : 2 2 :001(049) [0059] is that there is a clear **command** and order of Christ,
AG : 2 2 :010(050) [0061] contrary to God's **command** and also contrary to the
AG : 2 3 :008(052) [0061] Since God's Word and **command** cannot be altered by
AG : 2 3 :018(054) [0063] may marry is based on God's Word and **command**.
AG : 2 3 :024(055) [0065] can alter or abolish a **command** of God, neither can any
AG : 2 3 :024(055) [0065] of God, neither can any vow alter a **command** of God.
AG : 2 5 :003(062) [0069] for it is spoken in God's stead and by God's **command**.
AG : 2 5 :004(062) [0069] diligence about this **command** and power of keys and how
AG : 2 7 :013(073) [0077] to God's Word and **command** without invented
AG : 2 7 :018(073) [0079] marry, for vows cannot nullify God's order and **command**
AG : 2 7 :019(073) [0079] God's **command** in I Cor. 7:2 reads, "Because of the
AG : 2 7 :020(074) [0079] It is not alone God's **command** that urges, drives, and
AG : 2 7 :022(074) [0079] them, it is still impossible to abrogate God's **command**.
AG : 2 7 :023(074) [0079] and power when they are contrary to God's **command**!
AG : 2 7 :036(076) [0081] Although God's **command** concerning marriage frees and
AG : 2 7 :036(076) [0081] God's grace without the **command** and authority of God
AG : 2 7 :036(076) [0081] and the holy Gospel and contrary to God's **command**.
AG : 2 7 :040(077) [0081] vow, made contrary to God's **command**, is null and void.
AG : 2 7 :048(078) [0081] by men without the **command** of God, and should be
AG : 2 7 :058(080) [0083] of life which has God's **command** to support it; on the
AG : 2 7 :058(080) [0083] of life which does not have God's **command** behind it.
AG : 2 8 :004(081) [0085] that because of God's **command** both authorities and
AG : 2 8 :005(081) [0085] bishops is a power and **command** of God to preach the
AG : 2 8 :006(082) [0085] the apostles with this **command**, "As the Father has sent
AG : 2 8 :023(084) [0087] Gospel, we have God's **command** not to be obedient in
AG : 2 8 :028(085) [0087] err or if they teach or **command** something contrary to
AG : 2 8 :035(086) [0089] contrary to God's **command** and Word to make laws out
AG : 2 8 :039(087) [0089] act contrary to God's **command** when they attach sin to
AL : 1 2 :010(035) [0049] through faith but **command** us to merit grace through
AL : 2 2 :001(049) [0059] this usage has the **command** of the Lord in Matt. 26:27,
AL : 2 3 :024(055) [0065] human law can nullify a **command** of God, so no vow can
AL : 2 5 :003(062) [0069] the voice of God and is pronounced by God's **command**.
AL : 2 7 :018(073) [0079] vows can not nullify the **command** and institution of
AL : 2 7 :019(074) [0079] This is the **command** of God, "Because of fornication let
AL : 2 7 :020(074) [0079] Nor is it the **command** only, but God's creation and
AL : 2 7 :021(074) [0079] those who obey this **command** and institution of God do
AL : 2 7 :022(074) [0079] about that a vow abrogates the **command** of God.
AL : 2 7 :036(076) [0081] it appears that God's **command** concerning marriage frees
AL : 2 7 :036(076) [0081] and grace without the **command** of God is wicked, for
AL : 2 7 :048(078) [0081] by men without the **command** of God and to teach that
AL : 2 7 :058(080) [0083] kind of life is one which has God's **command** in its favor.
AL : 2 8 :004(081) [0085] on account of God's **command** both are to be held in
AL : 2 8 :005(081) [0085] of bishops is a power or **command** of God to preach the
AL : 2 8 :006(082) [0085] the apostles with this **command**, "As the Father has sent
AL : 2 8 :018(083) [0085] two powers, and they **command** that both be held in
AL : 2 8 :023(084) [0087] Gospel, churches have a **command** of God that forbids
AL : 2 8 :039(087) [0089] act contrary to the **command** of God when they attach sin
AP : 0 4 :022(110) [0127] Because of God's **command**, honorable works
AP : 0 4 :087(120) [0147] David, who had God's **command** regarding circumcision
AP : 0 4 :087(120) [0147] these works, having a **command**, would have to justify.
AP : 0 4 :170(130) [0171] bear because of God's **command**; and it doubts God's
AP : 0 4 :207(135) [0177] And Jer. 7:22, "I did not **command** concerning burnt
AP : 0 4 :262(145) [0195] They **command** him to become righteous, then to do good
AP : 0 4 :284(150) [0201] many parts, some of which **command** faith, others works.
AP : 0 4 :345(160) [0217] has God's clear and certain promise and his **command**.
AP : 0 4 :345(160) [0217] the Gospel is the **command** to believe that we have a
AP : 0 7 :023(172) [0235] and this at Christ's **command**; for as the Father subjected
AP : 0 7 :045(177) [0243] clothing, and similar matters without divine **command**.
AP : 0 9 :002(178) [0245] according to Christ's **command** (Matt. 28:19), "Baptize
AP : 1 1 :002(180) [0249] have heard that it is the **command** of God — yes, the very
AP : 1 2 :011(184) [0255] they imagine that this enumeration is a divine **command**.
AP : 1 2 :014(184) [0257] or similar observances that do not have divine **command**.
AP : 1 2 :023(185) [0257] as our opponents **command** it, is necessary by divine
AP : 1 2 :072(192) [0271] themselves with this **command** of God against despair and
AP : 1 2 :088(195) [0277] we know it is God's **command** and the Gospel itself that
AP : 1 2 :104(197) [0283] therefore have the **command** to forgive sins; they do not
AP : 1 2 :104(197) [0283] they do not have the **command** to investigate secret sins.
AP : 1 2 :122(200) [0289] "Be penitent"; Christ's **command** to the apostles (Luke
AP : 1 2 :123(200) [0289] the keys have the **command** to remit part of the
AP : 1 2 :127(201) [0291] because you **command** only that we be conquered and
AP : 1 2 :133(202) [0293] this word of Christ is a word of **command**, "Be penitent."
AP : 1 2 :136(203) [0293] do these passages **command** that souls should be punished
AP : 1 2 :138(203) [0293] There is no **command** for the keys to commute certain
AP : 1 2 :139(203) [0295] that God's glory and **command** require penitence to
AP : 1 2 :139(203) [0295] like true fasting, prayer, and charity have his **command**.
AP : 1 2 :139(203) [0295] keys carries with it the **command** to commute penalties or
AP : 1 2 :143(204) [0295] and fasting have God's **command**: and where they do, it
AP : 1 2 :172(209) [0305] the Gospel does not **command** that these canonical
AP : 1 2 :174(210) [0307] and because of his **command**, and they have their reward.
AP : 1 2 :176(210) [0307] they only have the **command** to forgive the sins of those
AP : 1 2 :176(210) [0307] God's **command** is that the ministers of the Gospel
AP : 1 3 :003(211) [0309] as "rites which have the **command** of God and to which
AP : 1 3 :003(211) [0309] without God's **command** are not sure signs of grace, even
AP : 1 3 :006(212) [0311] salvation since they do not have the **command** of God.
AP : 1 3 :006(212) [0311] which have an express **command** from God and a clear
AP : 1 3 :011(212) [0311] of the Word has God's **command** and glorious promises:
AP : 1 3 :012(212) [0311] The church has the **command** to appoint ministers; to
AP : 1 3 :015(213) [0311] because it has God's **command**, then many other states or
AP : 1 3 :015(213) [0311] they have God's **command**, as, for example, government.
AP : 1 3 :016(213) [0311] things that have God's **command** and a promise added to
AP : 1 3 :016(213) [0311] It has both the **command** of God and many promises.
AP : 1 3 :017(213) [0313] are kept which have God's **command** and promises.
AP : 1 5 :014(217) [0319] of God's will without the **command** and Word of God?
AP : 1 5 :014(217) [0319] of additional ceremonies without his **command**?
AP : 1 5 :017(217) [0319] by men without God's **command** can justify since we can
AP : 1 6 :007(223) [0331] counsel but as a **command** (Matt. 5:39; Rom. 12:19).
AP : 1 6 :011(224) [0333] Scripture does not **command** holding property in
AP : 1 6 :011(224) [0333] in common, but by its **command**, "You shall not steal,"
AP : 1 6 :013(224) [0333] these have God's **command** while the Platonic commune
AP : 1 6 :013(224) [0333] the Platonic commune does not have God's **command**.
AP : 2 1 :010(230) [0345] Neither a **command** nor a promise nor an example can be
AP : 2 1 :018(231) [0347] we have the **command** to call upon Christ, according to
AP : 2 1 :021(232) [0349] God's promise nor a **command** nor an example from
AP : 2 1 :033(233) [0351] be defended if it has no **command** or proof in the Word
AP : 2 3 :008(240) [0365] originally there was a **command** to replenish the earth,
AP : 2 3 :014(241) [0367] This is an express **command**, directed to anyone not
AP : 2 3 :015(241) [0367] demand to be shown a **command** requiring that priests
AP : 2 3 :017(241) [0369] Paul's **command**, "Because of the temptation of
AP : 2 3 :023(242) [0371] defiance of Christ's **command** (Matt. 19:6), "What God
AP : 2 4 :028(254) [0393] to your fathers or **command** them concerning burnt
AP : 2 4 :028(254) [0393] But this **command** I gave them, 'Obey my voice, and I
AP : 2 4 :089(265) [0413] But for this they have no scriptural proof or **command**.
AP : 2 4 :089(265) [0413] the church without the **command** of God and the
AP : 2 4 :098(268) [0419] invented against God's **command** to obscure the glory of
AP : 2 7 :020(272) [0427] which has neither a **command** of God nor a promise, on
AP : 2 7 :020(272) [0427] Christ which has both a **command** and a promise of God,
AP : 2 7 :041(276) [0435] without a call, without a **command** of God; this Christ
AP : 2 7 :041(276) [0435] since we know that the **command** of God forbids
AP : 2 7 :041(276) [0435] which happens by a **command** of God, when a
AP : 2 7 :041(276) [0435] Here we have the **command** rather to bear the injury, to
AP : 2 7 :042(276) [0435] and to leave our body without the **command** of God.
AP : 2 7 :042(276) [0435] friends, wife, and children without the **command** of God.
AP : 2 7 :052(278) [0437] their traditions, contrary to the clear **command** of God.

Continued ▶

A P : 2 7 :052(278) [0437] setting up traditions contrary to the **command** of God.
A P : 2 7 :054(278) [0437] penitence, about works that have the **command** of God.
A P : 2 7 :061(280) [0441] because they had a **command** from their parents, they are
A P : 2 8 :014(283) [0447] But he has a definite **command**, a definite Word of God,
A P : 2 8 :014(283) [0447] Word, they have the **command** about when they should
S 2 : 0 2 :021(296) [0469] and without **command**, but it is contrary to the first
S 2 : 0 4 :007(299) [0473] divine right or by God's **command**; suppose that it were
S 2 : 0 4 :008(299) [0473] rather than on a divine **command**, he would very easily
S 3 : 1 2 :002(315) [0499] attention to what they **command** or forbid in the name of
T R : 0 0 :031(325) [0513] power, that is, the **command** to preach the Gospel,
T R : 0 0 :036(326) [0515] contrary to the **command** of Christ, but he even exalted
T R : 0 0 :058(330) [0521] And it is the clear **command** of God that we should flee
T R : 0 0 :082(334) [0529] According to the **command** of the most illustrious princes
S C : 0 4 :002(348) [0551] used according to God's **command** and connected with
S C : 0 5 :028(351) [0555] According to the **command** of our Lord Jesus Christ, I
L C : P R :014(360) [0571] us to read the Catechism daily, there is God's **command**.
L C : P R :014(360) [0571] God did not require and **command** this so solemnly
L C : 0 1 :026(368) [0587] it all from God through his **command** and ordinance.
L C : 0 1 :026(368) [0587] — have received the **command** to do us all kinds of good.
L C : 0 1 :064(373) [0599] is summarized in the **command** in Ps. 50:15, "Call upon
L C : 0 1 :112(380) [0613] recognizes it as God's **command** or as a holy, divine word
L C : 0 1 :113(380) [0613] So, if this is God's **command**, and it embodies his highest
L C : 0 1 :141(384) [0621] persons whose duty it is to **command** and to govern.
L C : 0 1 :171(388) [0629] to see that this is the **command** of the divine Majesty,
L C : 0 1 :173(388) [0629] children to us with the **command** that we train and govern
L C : 0 1 :219(394) [0643] always follows spontaneously without any **command**.
L C : 0 3 :057(427) [0713] of his imperial majesty's **command** and was unworthy to
L C : 0 4 :008(437) [0733] stand God's Word and **command** which have been
L C : 0 4 :036(441) [0741] you accept it as God's **command** and ordinance, so that,
L C : 0 4 :056(444) [0747] On this I build, that it is thy Word and **command**."
L C : 0 4 :057(444) [0747] him on that account, but solely on the **command** of God.
L C : 0 5 :004(447) [0753] Word and ordinance or **command**, which is the chief
L C : 0 5 :045(452) [0763] words of precept and **command**, enjoining all who would
L C : 0 5 :071(455) [0769] the very reason for this **command** and invitation and
L C : 0 5 :087(456) [0773] by God's injunction and **command**, to teach or have
L C : 0 6 :024(460) [0000] were changed into a **command** that all beggars should run
L C : 0 6 :024(460) [0000] from this, but only a greater hostility to the **command**.
L C : 0 6 :028(460) [0000] nor the pope's **command** at any point, but you will
L C : 0 6 :031(460) [0000] we must come under the **command** and you must come
E P : 0 6 :006(481) [0807] as if they knew of no **command**, threat, or reward.
S D : 0 2 :055(532) [0903] according to God's **command** and will, and when the
S D : 0 4 :007(552) [0939] will, ordinance, and **command** that believers walk in good
S D : 0 4 :038(557) [0951] God's will and express **command** that believers should do
S D : 0 6 :011(565) [0965] that it is God's will and **command** that we should walk in
S D : 0 6 :020(567) [0969] without his Word and **command**, as it is written, "You
S D : 0 6 :020(567) [0969] own eyes, but heed all these words which I **command** you.
S D : 0 7 :016(572) [0977] Christ's institution and **command** are observed, the body
S D : 0 7 :043(576) [0987] teacher, the earnest **command** has been given from heaven
S D : 0 7 :046(577) [0987] could have asked if this **command** was to be understood
S D : 0 7 :046(577) [0989] believed the words and **command** of God plainly and
S D : 0 7 :048(578) [0989] since Christ gave this **command** at table and during
S D : 0 7 :064(581) [0995] the circumstances this **command** can only be understood
S D : 0 7 :065(581) [0995] But Christ adds another **command**, and in addition to the
S D : 0 7 :077(583) [0999] Luther states: "This his **command** and institution can and
S D : 0 7 :077(583) [0999] or speaking but the **command** and ordinance of Christ
S D : 0 7 :078(583) [1001] his institution and **command** in the Lord's Supper and
S D : 0 7 :078(584) [1001] word, but because of his **command** in which he has told
S D : 0 7 :078(584) [1001] has attached his own **command** and deed to our
S D : 0 7 :080(584) [1001] we render obedience to the **command** of Christ, 'This do.'
S D : 0 7 :084(584) [1001] But the **command** of Christ, "Do this," which
S D : 0 7 :108(588) [1009] apart from God's **command** and the ordained use for
S D : 0 7 :110(588) [1011] contrary to the explicit **command** and institution of
S D : 1 0 :014(613) [1057] not subject either to a **command** or a prohibition,
S D : 1 0 :019(614) [1059] attention to what they **command** or forbid in the name of
S D : 1 1 :028(621) [1073] It is Christ's **command** that all in common to whom
S D : 1 1 :038(622) [1075] teach that it is God's **command** that we "believe this
S D : 1 1 :053(625) [1081] — in fact, we have no **command** to do so — than with
S D : 1 1 :056(625) [1081] to us, we must obey his **command** and operate constantly

Commanded (106)

A G : 0 6 :001(031) [0045] works as God has **commanded**, but we should do them
A G : 0 6 :002(032) [0047] have done all that is **commanded** you, say, 'We are
A G : 2 0 :037(046) [0057] in callings which are **commanded**, render obedience,
A G : 2 3 :019(054) [0063] Holy Scriptures God **commanded** that marriage be held
A G : 2 5 :012(063) [0071] such confession is not **commanded** by the Scriptures, but
A G : 2 6 :011(065) [0071] Such works, **commanded** by God, were to be regarded as
A G : 2 8 :039(087) [0089] and as if God had **commanded** the apostles and bishops
A G : 2 8 :061(091) [0093] and that Christ **commanded** the apostles and bishops to
A L : 0 6 :001(031) [0045] it is necessary to do the good works **commanded** by God.
A L : 1 6 :006(038) [0051] and laws except when **commanded** to sin, for then they
A L : 2 2 :002(049) [0059] has here manifestly **commanded** with reference to the cup
A L : 2 2 :007(050) [0061] In fact, Pope Gelasius **commanded** that the sacrament
A L : 2 3 :019(054) [0063] God has **commanded** that marriage be held in honor.
A L : 2 8 :032(086) [0087] of the apostles who **commanded** men to abstain from
A L : 2 8 :065(092) [0093] The apostles **commanded** that one should abstain from
A P : P R :005(098) [0101] They **commanded** me and several others to prepare an
A P : 0 4 :022(110) [0127] honorable works **commanded** in the Decalogue should be
A P : 0 4 :189(133) [0175] done because God has **commanded** them and in order to
A P : 0 4 :207(135) [0177] that God surely **commanded** as outward observances in
A P : 0 4 :283(150) [0201] to be sought in works **commanded** by God, not in human
A P : 0 4 :322(157) [0209] sins daily, since he is **commanded** to pray daily for his
A P : 0 4 :334(158) [0215] have done all that is **commanded** you, say, 'We are
A P : 0 7 :042(176) [0241] The apostles had **commanded** their churches to celebrate
A P : 1 2 :140(204) [0295] works that God has **commanded** but the vain works that
A P : 1 2 :143(204) [0297] But where they are not **commanded** by God's law but
A P : 1 2 :165(208) [0303] and obligatory works **commanded** by God should not be
A P : 1 2 :173(209) [0305] If the Gospel **commanded** us to buy off punishment by
A P : 1 2 :174(210) [0307] These fruits are **commanded** by God, they should be done
A P : 1 2 :175(210) [0307] cannot be a necessity **commanded** by divine law, for
A P : 1 6 :007(223) [0331] but expressly **commanded**, and it is a work of God
A P : 2 1 :021(232) [0349] Christ, though Christ **commanded** us to come to him and
A P : 2 2 :008(237) [0359] When priests were **commanded** to use lay communion,
A P : 2 3 :008(240) [0365] earth has been replenished marriage is not **commanded**.
A P : 2 3 :010(241) [0367] marriage was **commanded** but that it is no longer
A P : 2 3 :010(241) [0367] was commanded but that it is no longer **commanded**.
A P : 2 3 :020(242) [0369] but not **commanded**; it is voluntary rather than
A P : 2 3 :024(243) [0371] shriek that the councils have **commanded** celibacy.
A P : 2 4 :028(254) [0393] Clearly God had **commanded** the fathers concerning
A P : 2 4 :028(254) [0393] He adds that God had **commanded** faith.
A P : 2 4 :071(262) [0409] instituted it, as he **commanded** (I Cor. 11:24), "Do this in
A P : 2 7 :046(277) [0435] of property is neither **commanded** nor advised in the
A P : 2 7 :061(280) [0441] obedience, which God **commanded** (Ex. 20:12), "Honor
S 1 : P R :014(291) [0459] things, which are **commanded** by God, are neither
S 2 : 0 2 :002(293) [0463] They are not **commanded** by God.
S 2 : 0 2 :012(295) [0465] nothing has been **commanded** or enjoined upon us with
S 2 : 0 2 :018(296) [0467] that we have not been **commanded** to make pilgrimages,
S 2 : 0 2 :022(296) [0469] They are neither **commanded** nor commended.
S 2 : 0 2 :025(297) [0469] It is neither **commanded** nor recommended, nor does it
S 2 : 0 4 :005(299) [0473] and it is not **commanded**, it is unnecessary, and it is
S 2 : 0 4 :010(300) [0475] since it is neither established nor **commanded** by God.
S 3 : 0 5 :001(310) [0491] Word of God in water, **commanded** by the institution of
S 3 : 0 6 :003(311) [0493] as it was established and **commanded** by Christ.
T R : 0 0 :031(325) [0513] observe all that I have **commanded** you" (Matt. 28:19,
T R : 0 0 :041(327) [0517] Christ **commanded**, "Beware of false prophets" (Matt.
T R : 0 0 :041(328) [0517] Paul also **commanded** that ungodly teachers should be
T R : 0 0 :082(335) [0529] in the name of Master John Brenz, as he **commanded** me
S C : 0 1 :022(344) [0543] trust in him, and cheerfully do what he has **commanded**.
S C : 0 3 :021(348) [0549] by him, for he himself **commanded** us to pray like this
S C : 0 9 :003(354) [0561] "The Lord **commanded** that those who proclaim the
L C : 0 1 :027(368) [0587] take or give anything except as God has **commanded** it.
L C : 0 1 :027(368) [0587] means than God has **commanded**, for that would be not
L C : 0 1 :064(373) [0599] conversely that we are **commanded** to use it in the service
L C : 0 1 :080(375) [0603] it for rest and he **commanded** it to be kept holy above all
L C : 0 1 :112(380) [0613] to my parents, since God himself has **commanded** it.
L C : 0 1 :116(381) [0615] God has appointed and **commanded** next to obedience to
L C : 0 1 :120(381) [0615] work and do what is **commanded**, saying, "Lo, this is
L C : 0 1 :120(381) [0615] that God has **commanded** this; concerning the other
L C : 0 1 :120(382) [0615] the other things he has **commanded** not a word.
L C : 0 1 :198(392) [0637] that it is the works **commanded** by God's Word which are
L C : 0 1 :211(393) [0641] one, and it is solemnly **commanded** by God that in
L C : 0 1 :216(394) [0641] monastic vows are even **commanded** to forsake their
L C : 0 1 :251(399) [0651] the other hand, we are **commanded** to promote and
L C : 0 1 :309(407) [0669] We are **commanded** not to desire harm to our neighbor,
L C : 0 1 :328(410) [0675] as these things are **commanded** in that order, even though
L C : 0 3 :005(420) [0699] It is our duty to pray because God has **commanded** it.
L C : 0 3 :006(420) [0699] strictly and solemnly **commanded** as all the other
L C : 0 3 :010(421) [0699] as though prayer were **commanded** for those who are
L C : 0 3 :012(422) [0701] prayer is so urgently **commanded**, we ought to conclude
L C : 0 3 :013(422) [0701] but it is important because God has **commanded** it."
L C : 0 3 :055(427) [0713] desire if God himself had not **commanded** us to ask for it.
L C : 0 3 :110(435) [0729] Father, Thou hast **commanded** me to pray; let me not
L C : 0 4 :006(437) [0733] solemnly and strictly **commanded** that we must be
L C : 0 4 :009(437) [0735] because God has **commanded** it and, what is more, it is
L C : 0 4 :039(441) [0743] anything else God has **commanded** and ordained; in
L C : 0 4 :056(444) [0747] however, that he has **commanded** me to go, eat, and
L C : 0 5 :008(447) [0755] we Christians are **commanded** by Christ's word to eat and
L C : 0 5 :042(451) [0763] as a spectacle, but **commanded** his Christians to eat and
L C : 0 5 :050(452) [0765] longing to do what my Lord has **commanded** me to do."
L C : 0 5 :062(454) [0767] because Thou hast **commanded** it and I want to be thy
L C : 0 6 :014(458) [0000] Christian church and **commanded** us to absolve one
E P : 1 0 :001(492) [0829] which are neither **commanded** nor forbidden in the Word
E P : 1 0 :002(493) [0829] things and are neither **commanded** nor forbidden by
E P : 1 0 :003(493) [0829] which are neither **commanded** nor forbidden in the Word
E P : 1 0 :007(493) [0831] ceremonies not **commanded** by God, as long as there is
S D : 0 4 :014(553) [0943] of necessity do good works that God has **commanded**."
S D : 0 6 :016(566) [0967] because they are **commanded**, from fear of punishment or
S D : 0 7 :051(578) [0991] understanding and **commanded** them to teach all nations
S D : 0 7 :051(578) [0991] observe all that he had **commanded** them (that is, the
S D : 1 0 :001(610) [1053] rites which are neither **commanded** nor forbidden in the
S D : 1 0 :002(611) [1053] and that are neither **commanded** nor forbidden by God,
S D : 1 0 :015(613) [1057] apostle so seriously **commanded** the church to preserve,
S D : 1 0 :022(615) [1061] Christ **commanded**, 'Beware of false prophets' (Matt.
S D : 1 0 :022(615) [1061] Paul also **commanded** that ungodly teachers should be
S D : 1 1 :027(620) [1071] Word, as indeed he has **commanded** the preaching of
S D : 1 1 :028(620) [1071] Therefore Christ has **commanded** to preach "repentance
S D : 1 1 :055(625) [1081] Word, still less has **commanded** us to explore it through

Commander (1), Commanding (6)

A P : 0 2 :016(102) [0109] but also the first, **commanding** fear of God, faith and love
A P : 2 3 :016(241) [0369] Is not Paul here **commanding** those to marry who do not
A P : 2 3 :063(248) [0381] passages of Scripture **commanding** each man to have his
A P : 2 8 :015(283) [0447] as though they were **commanding** necessary acts of
T R : 0 0 :062(331) [0523] an army might select a **commander** for itself, the deacons
L C : 0 1 :113(380) [0613] good works, and by **commanding** them he shows that he
S D : 0 7 :026(573) [0981] instituting, giving you, and **commanding** you to take.

Commandment (193)

A L : 0 8 :002(033) [0047] of the institution and **commandment** of Christ even if
A L : 2 3 :008(052) [0061] no vow can nullify a **commandment** of God and an
A L : 2 3 :018(054) [0063] Although the **commandment** of God is in force, although
A P : 0 4 :103(121) [0151] the law; for by the **commandment** of the law all are
A P : 0 4 :197(134) [0175] Paul extols the **commandment** to honor our parents by
A P : 0 4 :197(134) [0175] that is connected to that **commandment** (Eph. 6:2, 3).
A P : 0 4 :208(135) [0177] thinking up new works beyond God's **commandment**.
A P : 0 4 :212(136) [0179] orders beyond God's **commandment** in the hope of
A P : 0 4 :226(138) [0183] because the great **commandment** is, "You shall love the
A P : 0 4 :238(140) [0187] this statement with the **commandment** of mutual love.
A P : 0 4 :270(147) [0197] So the First **Commandment** of the Decalogue itself states,
A P : 0 4 :346(160) [0217] hope, for it rests on the Word and **commandment** of God.
A P : 1 2 :106(197) [0283] analogy to apply the **commandment** given a father to the
A P : 1 3 :004(211) [0309] these rites have the **commandment** of God and the
A P : 1 3 :014(213) [0311] It has the **commandment** of God and also certain
A P : 2 4 :089(266) [0415] name of God in violation of the Second **Commandment**.
A P : 2 7 :046(277) [0435] Word of God in the **commandment** (Ex. 20:15), "You
A P : 2 7 :051(278) [0437] any laws abolish the **commandment** of the Holy Spirit
A P : 2 8 :018(284) [0449] not what they call a "**commandment** with unlimited

Continued ▶

A P : 2 8 :018(284) [0449] something prescribed," about a special **commandment**.
A P : 2 8 :021(284) [0449] down the universal **commandment** that we are to observe
S 2 : 0 2 :024(296) [0469] and without **commandment**, but they are also contrary to
S 2 : 0 3 :002(298) [0471] all this is without **commandment**, unnecessary, and
S C : P R :016(340) [0535] of the First **Commandment**, proceed to the Second
S C : P R :016(340) [0535] proceed to the Second **Commandment**, and so on.
S C : P R :017(340) [0535] Expound every **commandment**, petition, and part,
S C : P R :018(340) [0537] the Seventh **Commandment**, which treats of stealing,
S C : P R :018(340) [0537] So, too, the Fourth **Commandment** must be stressed when
S C : 0 9 :009(356) [0563] (this is the first **commandment** with a promise) 'that it
L C : P R :018(361) [0573] and exercises based on the First **Commandment**?
L C : 0 1 :000(365) [0581] The First **Commandment**
L C : 0 1 :004(365) [0581] The purpose of this **commandment**, therefore, is to
L C : 0 1 :005(365) [0581] examples of failure to observe this **commandment**.
L C : 0 1 :013(366) [0583] understand the nature and scope of this **commandment**.
L C : 0 1 :024(367) [0587] the meaning of this **commandment**: We are to trust in
L C : 0 1 :027(368) [0587] and thank him for them, as this **commandment** requires.
L C : 0 1 :028(368) [0587] and exalt this **commandment** above all things and not
L C : 0 1 :029(368) [0589] will not have this **commandment** taken lightly but will
L C : 0 1 :029(368) [0589] of the Appendix to the First **Commandment**]
L C : 0 1 :047(371) [0593] learn the first **commandment** well and realize that God
L C : 0 1 :048(371) [0593] Let this suffice for the First **Commandment**.
L C : 0 1 :048(371) [0593] with God and this **commandment** is kept, fulfillment of
L C : 0 1 :048(371) [0593] The Second **Commandment**
L C : 0 1 :050(371) [0593] As the First **Commandment** has inwardly instructed the
L C : 0 1 :050(371) [0593] taught faith, so this **commandment** leads us outward and
L C : 0 1 :051(371) [0593] "How do you understand the Second **Commandment**?
L C : 0 1 :051(371) [0595] Therefore what this **commandment** forbids is appealing to
L C : 0 1 :052(371) [0595] as the plain and simple meaning of this **commandment**.
L C : 0 1 :056(372) [0595] how important this **commandment** is and diligently shun
L C : 0 1 :057(372) [0597] has attached to this **commandment** a solemn threat: "for
L C : 0 1 :061(373) [0597] them with the **commandment**, and continually impress it
L C : 0 1 :065(373) [0597] have the substance of the entire **commandment** explained.
L C : 0 1 :069(374) [0601] upon such willful contempt of this **commandment**.
L C : 0 1 :077(375) [0603] The Third **Commandment**
L C : 0 1 :080(375) [0603] is concerned, the **commandment** was given to the Jews
L C : 0 1 :081(375) [0603] Jews interpreted this **commandment** too narrowly and
L C : 0 1 :081(375) [0603] Gospel — as if the **commandment** could be fulfilled by
L C : 0 1 :082(376) [0603] outward sense, this **commandment** does not concern us
L C : 0 1 :083(376) [0603] God requires in this **commandment**, we point out that we
L C : 0 1 :086(376) [0605] plain meaning of this **commandment**: Since we observe
L C : 0 1 :092(377) [0607] that happens the **commandment** is in force and is
L C : 0 1 :094(378) [0607] and force of this **commandment** consist not of the resting
L C : 0 1 :095(378) [0607] observance of this **commandment** and will punish all who
L C : 0 1 :096(378) [0607] Therefore this **commandment** is violated not only by
L C : 0 1 :098(378) [0609] It is the **commandment** of God, and he will require of you
L C : 0 1 :102(379) [0609] and put to flight, this **commandment** is fulfilled, and God
L C : 0 1 :102(379) [0609] The Fourth **Commandment**
L C : 0 1 :109(380) [0611] then, learn what this **commandment** requires concerning
L C : 0 1 :112(380) [0613] faithful to this **commandment** and would have been able
L C : 0 1 :114(380) [0613] obliged to set forth God's **commandment** in its full glory.
L C : 0 1 :115(381) [0613] from sight and give first place to this **commandment**.
L C : 0 1 :117(381) [0615] and holy treasure, the Word and **commandment** of God.
L C : 0 1 :118(381) [0615] accordance with his **commandment** and could say with a
L C : 0 1 :118(381) [0615] according to this **commandment** and confess that with the
L C : 0 1 :119(381) [0615] in trampling God's **commandment** under foot that they
L C : 0 1 :125(382) [0617] strongest reason impelling us to keep this **commandment**.
L C : 0 1 :131(383) [0619] for us to keep this **commandment** is that God has
L C : 0 1 :132(383) [0619] see how important God considers this **commandment**.
L C : 0 1 :133(383) [0619] and praises this **commandment**, saying in Eph. 6:2, 3,
L C : 0 1 :133(383) [0619] "This is the first **commandment** with a promise: that it
L C : 0 1 :134(383) [0619] whoever keeps this **commandment** will enjoy good days,
L C : 0 1 :140(384) [0621] how necessary is this **commandment**, which in the past
L C : 0 1 :140(384) [0621] when he neglects this **commandment**, and how precious
L C : 0 1 :141(384) [0621] connection with this **commandment** there is more to be
L C : 0 1 :143(385) [0623] that it is God's **commandment** and is more pleasing to
L C : 0 1 :149(385) [0623] if you despise this **commandment**, then take shame,
L C : 0 1 :152(386) [0625] But God's Word and **commandment** are despised, as if
L C : 0 1 :158(387) [0627] presented in this **commandment**: fathers by blood, fathers
L C : 0 1 :164(387) [0627] on God's will and **commandment**, however, have the
L C : 0 1 :166(388) [0629] been said to those to whom this **commandment** applies.
L C : 0 1 :167(388) [0629] to be included in this **commandment** in which he speaks
L C : 0 1 :169(388) [0629] It is a strict **commandment** and injunction of God, who
L C : 0 1 :177(389) [0629] Because this **commandment** is disregarded, God terribly
L C : 0 1 :178(389) [0631] The Fifth **Commandment**
L C : 0 1 :180(389) [0631] In this **commandment** we leave our own house and go
L C : 0 1 :180(389) [0631] is included in this **commandment**, yet their right to take
L C : 0 1 :182(389) [0631] This **commandment** is simple enough.
L C : 0 1 :183(389) [0631] and need for this **commandment** is that, as God well
L C : 0 1 :183(389) [0631] offenses against this **commandment**, as there are against
L C : 0 1 :185(390) [0633] he has set up this **commandment** as a wall, fortress, and
L C : 0 1 :186(390) [0633] What this **commandment** teaches, then, is that no one
L C : 0 1 :187(390) [0633] wants us to keep this **commandment** ever before our eyes
L C : 0 1 :188(390) [0633] the import of the **commandment** against killing is this: In
L C : 0 1 :189(390) [0635] second place, this **commandment** is violated not only
L C : 0 1 :195(391) [0637] back to the First **Commandment**, that he is our God; that
L C : 0 1 :199(392) [0637] The Sixth **Commandment**
L C : 0 1 :202(392) [0639] among us, this **commandment** applies to every form of
L C : 0 1 :205(393) [0639] Thus God by his **commandment** wants every husband or
L C : 0 1 :206(393) [0639] Inasmuch as this **commandment** is concerned specifically
L C : 0 1 :206(393) [0639] life, sanctioning and protecting it by his **commandment**.
L C : 0 1 :206(393) [0639] above in the fourth **commandment**, "You shall honor
L C : 0 1 :213(394) [0641] God's order and **commandment** when they despise and
L C : 0 1 :216(394) [0641] and annulled by this **commandment**; indeed, all poor,
L C : 0 1 :216(394) [0641] inevitably sin more and more against this **commandment**.
L C : 0 1 :219(394) [0643] conclusion that this **commandment** requires everyone not
L C : 0 1 :221(395) [0643] that are chosen without God's Word and **commandment**.
L C : 0 1 :221(395) [0643] The Seventh **Commandment**
L C : 0 1 :232(396) [0647] This **commandment** is very far-reaching, as we have
L C : 0 1 :234(397) [0647] disregards this **commandment** may indeed get by and
L C : 0 1 :238(397) [0647] God will not forget his **commandment**.
L C : 0 1 :246(398) [0649] that this is God's **commandment** and must not be treated
L C : 0 1 :248(398) [0651] fixed upon God's **commandment**, lest his wrath and
L C : 0 1 :253(399) [0653] The Eighth **Commandment**
L C : 0 1 :257(399) [0653] false witness"), this **commandment** pertains to public
L C : 0 1 :260(400) [0655] application of this **commandment**, then, is that everyone
L C : 0 1 :261(400) [0655] is one aspect of the **commandment**, and its plainest
L C : 0 1 :263(400) [0655] The third aspect of this **commandment** concerns us all.
L C : 0 1 :274(402) [0659] we must interpret this **commandment** in such a way that
L C : 0 1 :274(402) [0659] seen that the Fifth **Commandment** forbids us to injure
L C : 0 1 :274(402) [0659] not sin against God's **commandment** because God of his
L C : 0 1 :274(402) [0659] he warns in the Fifth **Commandment**, he has reserved to
L C : 0 1 :285(403) [0661] and substance of this **commandment**: No one shall harm
L C : 0 1 :290(404) [0663] This **commandment**, then, embraces a great multitude of
L C : 0 1 :296(405) [0665] Above, the seventh **commandment** prohibits seizing or
L C : 0 1 :300(405) [0665] This last **commandment**, then, is addressed not to those
L C : 0 1 :300(405) [0667] where the Seventh **Commandment** applies, since they are
L C : 0 1 :310(407) [0669] So this **commandment** remains, like all the rest, one that
L C : 0 1 :319(408) [0673] with the First **Commandment** in order to show how much
L C : 0 1 :321(408) [0673] attached to the First **Commandment**, as we heard above,
L C : 0 1 :321(408) [0673] to each individual **commandment**, penetrating and
L C : 0 1 :324(409) [0675] of the first and chief **commandment**, from which all the
L C : 0 1 :324(409) [0675] he has fulfilled this **commandment** and all the others.
L C : 0 1 :325(409) [0675] and presented this **commandment** everywhere,
L C : 0 1 :325(409) [0675] to explain the whole **commandment** in one verse, as if to
L C : 0 1 :326(409) [0675] Thus the First **Commandment** is to illuminate and impart
L C : 0 1 :326(409) [0675] in the Second **Commandment** we are told to fear God and
L C : 0 1 :326(409) [0675] love and trust which the First **Commandment** requires.
L C : 0 1 :327(409) [0675] the force of the First **Commandment**: We are to honor
L C : 0 1 :329(410) [0677] you see how the First **Commandment** is the chief source
L C : 0 2 :010(412) [0681] of Christians based on the First **Commandment**.
L C : 0 3 :005(420) [0699] told in the Second **Commandment**, "You shall not take
L C : 0 3 :008(421) [0699] pray, as the Second **Commandment** teaches, is to call
L C : 0 3 :009(421) [0699] But there stands the **commandment**, "You shall and must
L C : 0 3 :011(421) [0701] we should respect this **commandment** and turn to God so
L C : 0 3 :011(421) [0701] By this **commandment** he makes it clear that he will not
L C : 0 3 :013(422) [0701] that it befits obedience and the **commandment** of God.
L C : 0 3 :013(422) [0701] of my worthiness, but because of the **commandment**."
L C : 0 3 :013(422) [0701] always approach God in obedience to this **commandment**.
L C : 0 3 :015(422) [0701] The very **commandment** that applied to St. Paul applies
L C : 0 3 :015(422) [0701] The Second **Commandment** is given just as much on my
L C : 0 3 :015(422) [0701] He can boast of no better or holier **commandment** than I.
L C : 0 3 :016(422) [0701] to his person, but not on account of the **commandment**.
L C : 0 3 :016(422) [0703] On this **commandment**, on which all the saints base their
L C : 0 3 :018(422) [0703] will not have this **commandment** treated as a jest but will
L C : 0 3 :018(423) [0703] pray and backed it up with such a strict **commandment**.
L C : 0 3 :021(423) [0703] worthiness, but at thy **commandment** and promise, which
L C : 0 3 :022(423) [0703] in addition to this **commandment** and promise, God
L C : 0 3 :028(424) [0705] remind God of his **commandment** and promise, knowing
L C : 0 3 :045(426) [0709] in the Second **Commandment**: that his name should not
L C : 0 4 :006(437) [0733] these words contain God's **commandment** and ordinance.
L C : 0 4 :014(438) [0735] in God's Word and **commandment** and sanctified by
L C : 0 4 :014(438) [0735] but that God's Word and **commandment** are added to it.
L C : 0 4 :016(438) [0735] is God's Word or **commandment** and God's name, and
L C : 0 4 :020(439) [0737] But because the **commandment** is added, "You shall
L C : 0 4 :020(439) [0737] The **commandment**, I say, is the golden chain about his
L C : 0 4 :038(441) [0741] Similarly the **commandment**, "You shall honor your
L C : 0 4 :038(441) [0741] blood but at God's **commandment** in which it is
L C : 0 4 :039(441) [0741] have not only God's **commandment** and injunction, but
L C : 0 4 :053(443) [0745] depends upon the Word and **commandment** of God.
L C : 0 4 :061(444) [0747] that they do not discern God's Word and **commandment**.
L C : 0 5 :049(452) [0765] one is just as much Christ's **commandment** as the other.
L C : 0 5 :049(452) [0765] from time to time satisfy and obey this **commandment**.
L C : 0 5 :050(452) [0765] For this **commandment** should ever move you to examine
L C : 0 5 :051(452) [0765] love and even without regard for Christ's **commandment**.
L C : 0 5 :064(454) [0769] is attached to the **commandment**, as we heard above,
L C : 0 5 :071(454) [0769] God's part both the **commandment** and the promise of
L C : 0 6 :014(458) [0000] not included in the **commandment** like the other two but
S D : 0 2 :003(520) [0881] unable to fulfill the **commandment** of God, to trust God
S D : 0 4 :014(553) [0943] of God's ordinance, **commandment**, and will (Rom. 13:5,
S D : 0 4 :016(554) [0943] debtors we are, as his **commandment** indicates when it
S D : 1 0 :014(613) [1057] Any coercion or **commandment** darkens and perverts this
S D : 1 1 :042(623) [1077] away from the holy **commandment**, grieve and embitter
S D : 1 1 :083(630) [1091] away from the holy **commandment** and involve

Commandments (146)

A G : 2 0 :002(041) [0053] writings on the Ten **Commandments**, and other writings
A G : 2 8 :033(086) [0087] — contrary, as they say, to the Ten **Commandments**.
A G : 2 8 :033(086) [0087] from and altered part of the Ten **Commandments**.
A L : 1 8 :008(040) [0053] can also keep the **commandments** of God in so far as the
A L : 2 0 :002(041) [0053] on the Ten **Commandments** and others of like import
A L : 2 0 :036(046) [0057] do the works of the First or Second **Commandments**.
A L : 2 8 :033(086) [0087] for it dispensed from one of the Ten **Commandments**!
A P : 0 2 :008(102) [0107] and to obey his **commandments** "according to the
A P : 0 2 :009(102) [0107] and to obey his **commandments**, what else is this but to
A P : 0 2 :010(102) [0109] love God above all things and obey his **commandments**?
A P : 0 2 :046(106) [0117] man can obey the **commandments** of God by his own
A P : 0 4 :006(108) [0121] we mean the **commandments** of the Decalogue, wherever
A P : 0 4 :028(111) [0129] men who keep the **commandments** of God outside a state
A P : 0 4 :034(111) [0129] concentrate on the **commandments** of the second table,
A P : 0 4 :122(124) [0157] enter life, keep the **commandments**" (Matt. 19:17), "The
A P : 0 4 :123(124) [0157] "If you would enter life, keep the **commandments**."
A P : 0 4 :172(130) [0171] very clearly, "All the **commandments** of God are kept
A P : 0 4 :264(146) [0195] and look only at the **commandments**, adding to them the
A P : 0 4 :270(147) [0197] enter life, keep the **commandments**" (Matt. 19:17), we
A P : 0 4 :270(147) [0197] no one can keep the **commandments** or please God
A P : 0 4 :270(147) [0197] me and keep my **commandments**" (Ex. 20:6), setting forth
A P : 1 2 :131(202) [0291] to God or contemptuous of his **commandments**.
A P : 1 2 :134(203) [0293] are unquestionably **commandments** referring to this life:
A P : 1 2 :134(203) [0293] for one may not refuse the **commandments** of God.
A P : 1 2 :135(203) [0293] not release us from **commandments** like "Be penitent" and
A P : 1 2 :142(204) [0295] observe, namely, the **commandments**; over and above
A P : 1 2 :145(205) [0297] rank them above the works of God's **commandments**.
A P : 1 2 :174(210) [0307] we learn from the **commandments** — prayer,
A P : 1 5 :025(218) [0321] As a result, the **commandments** of God are obscured; for
A P : 1 8 :002(225) [0335] acts" required by his **commandments** and that without the

Continued ▶

A P : 1 8 :006(225) [0335] prescribed in the **commandments**; to this they add that
A P : 2 3 :018(242) [0369] apply these magnificent **commandments** to themselves?
A P : 2 7 :009(270) [0421] Are they the observance of **commandments** and counsels?
A P : 2 7 :025(273) [0427] they satisfy the Ten **Commandments** in such a way that
A P : 2 7 :025(273) [0427] left over, when these **Commandments** accuse all the
A P : 2 7 :025(273) [0429] life satisfies the **Commandments** and does more than the
A P : 2 7 :025(273) [0429] Commandments and does more than the **Commandments**
S 1 : P R :014(291) [0459] while we trample his solemn **commandments** underfoot.
S 2 : 0 4 :014(301) [0475] as a mention of Christ, faith, and God's **commandments**.
S 3 : 0 1 :002(302) [0477] forbidden in the Ten **Commandments**, such as unbelief,
S 3 : 0 1 :006(302) [0477] to observe and keep all the **commandments** of God.
S 3 : 0 8 :011(313) [0497] received the Spirit without the Ten **Commandments**.
T R : 0 0 :006(320) [0505] as articles of faith or **commandments** of God, binding on
T R : 0 0 :006(320) [0505] and is even to be preferred to the **commandments** of God.
S C : P R :003(338) [0533] Creed, or the Ten **Commandments**, they live as if they
S C : P R :005(338) [0533] the Creed, the Ten **Commandments**, or a single part of
S C : P R :007(339) [0533] wording of the Ten **Commandments**, the Creed, the
S C : P R :008(339) [0535] Lord's Prayer, the Creed, and the Ten **Commandments**.
S C : P R :010(339) [0535] them the Ten **Commandments**, the Creed, the Lord's
S C : P R :018(340) [0537] weight on those **commandments** or other parts which
S C : 0 1 :000(342) [0539] [I] The Ten **Commandments** *in the plain form in which*
S C : 0 1 :021(344) [0543] does God declare concerning all these **commandments**?
S C : 0 1 :021(344) [0543] of those who love me and keep my **commandments**."
S C : 0 1 :022(344) [0543] to punish all who transgress these **commandments**.
S C : 0 1 :022(344) [0543] fear his wrath and not disobey these **commandments**.
S C : 0 5 :020(350) [0553] the light of the Ten **Commandments**: whether you are a
S C : 0 5 :023(350) [0555] contrary to God's **commandments** and to their action in
S C : 0 7 :003(352) [0557] a hymn on the Ten **Commandments**) or whatever your
S C : 0 9 :014(356) [0563] "The **commandments** are summed up in this sentence:
L C : P R :007(359) [0569] Prayer, the Ten **Commandments**, the Creed, the Psalms,
L C : P R :010(360) [0571] yourself with God's **commandments** and words and to
L C : P R :017(361) [0573] who knows the Ten **Commandments** perfectly knows the
L C : S P :006(362) [0575] I. The Ten **Commandments** of God
L C : 0 1 :000(365) [0581] [First Part: The Ten **Commandments**]
L C : 0 1 :030(369) [0589] *of those who love me and keep my **commandments**."*
L C : 0 1 :031(369) [0589] apply to all the **commandments** (as we shall hear later),
L C : 0 1 :050(371) [0595] and all the other **commandments** and apply them to
L C : 0 1 :061(373) [0597] this as well as the other **commandments** in high regard.
L C : 0 1 :075(375) [0601] First and Second **commandments** may become familiar
L C : 0 1 :089(377) [0605] with the Ten **Commandments**, the Creed, and the Lord's
L C : 0 1 :100(379) [0609] and wicked thoughts against all these **commandments**.
L C : 0 1 :103(379) [0611] the first three **commandments**, which are directed toward
L C : 0 1 :116(381) [0615] not set into opposition to the preceding **commandments**.
L C : 0 1 :125(382) [0617] on account of the **commandments**, that God would set up
L C : 0 1 :125(382) [0617] worship of God described in the previous **commandments**
L C : 0 1 :129(383) [0617] By means of **commandments**, therefore, he reminds and
L C : 0 1 :133(383) [0619] Although the other **commandments** also have a promise
L C : 0 1 :167(388) [0629] stated in the Ten **Commandments**, it is frequently dealt
L C : 0 1 :182(389) [0631] those who transgress this and the other **commandments**.
L C : 0 1 :183(389) [0633] this and the other **commandments** as a boundary between
L C : 0 1 :197(392) [0637] this and the other **commandments** to the winds, regarding
L C : 0 1 :197(392) [0637] as if they were not **commandments** but mere counsels.
L C : 0 1 :200(392) [0637] The following **commandments** are easily understood from
L C : 0 1 :250(399) [0651] done in the previous **commandments**: On one hand, we
L C : 0 1 :286(403) [0663] to embrace all the **commandments** concerning our
L C : 0 1 :291(404) [0663] The Ninth and Tenth **Commandments**
L C : 0 1 :293(404) [0663] These two **commandments**, taken literally, were given
L C : 0 1 :293(404) [0663] were sufficiently forbidden in **commandments** above.
L C : 0 1 :293(404) [0663] were keeping the **commandments** when they obeyed the
L C : 0 1 :293(404) [0665] added these two **commandments** to teach them that it is
L C : 0 1 :294(404) [0665] Especially were these **commandments** needed because
L C : 0 1 :296(404) [0665] interpreted these **commandments** correctly (though they
L C : 0 1 :300(405) [0667] have not offended against the preceding **commandments**.
L C : 0 1 :309(406) [0669] Let these **commandments** therefore retain their general
L C : 0 1 :310(407) [0669] Thus these **commandments** are directed especially against
L C : 0 1 :310(407) [0669] Conclusion of the Ten **Commandments**
L C : 0 1 :311(407) [0669] we have the Ten **Commandments**, a summary of divine
L C : 0 1 :311(407) [0671] Apart from these Ten **Commandments** no deed, no
L C : 0 1 :312(407) [0671] they neglect these **commandments** as if they were too
L C : 0 1 :313(407) [0671] full to keep these **commandments**, practicing gentleness,
L C : 0 1 :315(408) [0671] and better way of life than the Ten **Commandments** teach
L C : 0 1 :316(408) [0671] keep one of the Ten **Commandments** as it ought to be
L C : 0 1 :317(408) [0673] to that of the Ten **Commandments**, for they are beyond
L C : 0 1 :319(408) [0673] how to teach and practice the Ten **Commandments**.
L C : 0 1 :320(408) [0673] *me and keep my **commandments**, I show mercy unto a*
L C : 0 1 :321(408) [0673] to apply to all the **commandments**, and all of them as a
L C : 0 1 :321(408) [0673] and compelled to keep these Ten **Commandments**.
L C : 0 1 :322(409) [0673] how important the **commandments** are to him and how
L C : 0 1 :322(409) [0673] and transgress his **commandments**; and again, how richly
L C : 0 1 :326(409) [0675] run through all the **commandments**, like the clasp or the
L C : 0 1 :327(409) [0675] the following **commandments** which concern our
L C : 0 1 :330(410) [0677] of men but the **commandments** of the most high God,
L C : 0 1 :331(410) [0677] men to write the Ten **Commandments** on every wall and
L C : 0 1 :332(410) [0677] to practice the Ten **Commandments**, and no one need
L C : 0 1 :333(410) [0677] highly these Ten **Commandments** are to be exalted and
L C : 0 1 :333(410) [0677] which God in these **commandments** so earnestly requires
L C : 0 2 :002(411) [0679] to help us do what the Ten **Commandments** require of us.
L C : 0 2 :003(411) [0679] keep the Ten **Commandments** as they ought to be kept,
L C : 0 2 :010(411) [0679] Since the Ten **Commandments** have explained that we are
L C : 0 2 :019(412) [0681] he has required and enjoined in the Ten **Commandments**.
L C : 0 2 :067(419) [0697] is a very different teaching from the Ten **Commandments**.
L C : 0 2 :067(419) [0697] The Ten **Commandments**, moreover, are inscribed in the
L C : 0 2 :068(420) [0697] Therefore the Ten **Commandments** do not by themselves
L C : 0 2 :069(420) [0697] and delight in all the **commandments** of God because we
L C : 0 2 :069(420) [0697] help us keep the Ten **Commandments**: the Father gives us
L C : 0 3 :002(420) [0697] can keep the Ten **Commandments** perfectly, even though
L C : 0 3 :002(420) [0697] obedience to the Ten **Commandments** and remove all that
L C : 0 3 :006(420) [0699] as all the other **commandments**, such as having no other
L C : 0 3 :012(422) [0701] Take an illustration from the other **commandments**.
L C : 0 4 :006(437) [0733] can say that the Ten **Commandments**, the Creed, and the
L C : 0 5 :005(447) [0755] just as the Ten **Commandments**, the Lord's Prayer, and
L C : 0 5 :051(452) [0765] and fear of men's **commandments**, without joy and love
L C : 0 5 :085(456) [0773] easily instill the Ten **Commandments**, the Creed, and the
L C : 0 6 :021(459) [0000] the pope's tyranny, **commandments**, and coercion since
S D : 0 1 :005(509) [0861] of God's **commandments** but also, and primarily, the
S D : 0 2 :026(526) [0891] we may walk in his **commandments** (Ezek. 11:19; 36:26;
S D : 0 2 :043(529) [0897] and what is contrary to God and his **commandments**."
S D : 0 6 :012(566) [0967] to them in the Ten **Commandments** what the acceptable
S D : 0 6 :021(567) [0969] precisely the Ten **Commandments** (Rom. 13:9), and he
S D : 0 6 :021(567) [0969] in the way of thy **commandments**" (Ps. 119:32), but also,
S D : 1 0 :015(613) [1057] and human **commandments** are forcibly imposed on the
S D : 1 0 :015(613) [1057] and ultimately the **commandments** of men will be
S D : 1 0 :015(613) [1057] on a par with God's **commandments**, but even above
S D : 1 0 :026(615) [1061] the view that the **commandments** of men are to be
S D : 1 0 :027(615) [1061] whereby such **commandments** are imposed by force on
S D : 1 1 :073(628) [1087] them to obey the **commandments** of God, believers

Commands (80)
A G : 1 6 :006(038) [0051] authority and obey its **commands** and laws in all that can
A G : 1 6 :007(038) [0051] But when **commands** of the civil authority cannot be
A G : 2 2 :002(049) [0059] the chalice Christ here **commands** with clear words that
A G : 2 6 :008(065) [0071] have also obscured the **commands** of God, for these
A G : 2 6 :008(065) [0071] these traditions were exalted far above God's **commands**.
A G : 2 7 :049(078) [0083] Besides, the **commands** of God and true and proper
A G : 2 7 :057(080) [0083] God by observing the **commands** God has given and not
A G : 2 7 :057(080) [0083] given and not by keeping the **commands** invented by men.
A G : 2 8 :046(088) [0089] to Jewish myths or to **commands** of men who reject the
A G : 2 8 :075(094) [0095] apostolic rule which **commands** us to obey God rather
A L : 2 2 :009(050) [0061] contrary to the **commands** of God is not to be approved,
A L : 2 4 :030(059) [0067] Christ **commands** us to do this in remembrance of him.
A L : 2 4 :039(060) [0069] Paul also **commands** concerning Communion that one
A L : 2 6 :008(065) [0071] precepts obscured the **commands** of God, for traditions
A L : 2 6 :008(065) [0071] traditions were exalted far above the **commands** of God.
A L : 2 6 :010(065) [0071] Meanwhile the **commands** of God pertaining to callings
A L : 2 6 :035(069) [0075] So Christ **commands**, "Take heed to yourselves lest your
A L : 2 7 :013(073) [0077] serve their calling in accordance with God's **commands**.
A L : 2 7 :023(074) [0079] vows valid which are made contrary to God's **commands**!
A L : 2 7 :040(077) [0081] vow, taken contrary to the **commands** of God, is invalid.
A L : 2 7 :049(078) [0083] Furthermore, the **commands** of God and true service of
A L : 2 7 :057(080) [0083] by observing the **commands** he has given and not by
A L : 2 7 :057(080) [0083] given and not by keeping the **commands** invented by men.
A L : 2 8 :046(088) [0089] to Jewish myths or to **commands** of men who reject the
A L : 2 8 :075(094) [0095] injunction which **commands** us to obey God rather than
A P : 0 4 :034(112) [0129] the first table, which **commands** us to love God, to be
A P : 0 4 :062(115) [0139] of Luke (24:47) Christ **commands** that penitence and
A P : 0 4 :106(122) [0153] the mercy of God, that he may give what he **commands**."
A P : 0 4 :232(139) [0185] In the same way Paul **commands** that there be love in the
A P : 0 4 :235(140) [0185] sages are full of these **commands** of fairness, that in
A P : 0 4 :239(141) [0187] (I Pet. 2:4, 5) Peter **commands** us to come to Christ and
A P : 0 4 :255(144) [0193] condemns wrongdoers and **commands** that they do right.
A P : 0 4 :258(144) [0193] *opere operato*, but he **commands** these works as necessary
A P : 0 4 :282(149) [0201] He **commands** that they be cleansed inwardly and then
A P : 0 4 :284(150) [0201] would not pick out the **commands** about works and skip
A P : 0 4 :304(154) [0205] admit that the will **commands** the intellect to assent to the
A P : 1 1 :008(181) [0251] This regulation **commands** the impossible, namely, that
A P : 1 2 :072(192) [0271] therefore, that God **commands** them to believe that they
A P : 1 2 :109(198) [0283] to each other, for it **commands** that the confession be
A P : 1 2 :122(200) [0289] contrary to the express **commands** of the Gospel, the
A P : 1 2 :144(204) [0297] further from God's **commands**; of these there is a great
A P : 1 5 :025(219) [0323] to the works that God **commands**, like the tasks of one's
A P : 1 5 :047(221) [0327] diligent at all times because God **commands** it at all times.
A P : 1 6 :003(223) [0331] the civil estate, but **commands** us to obey the existing
A P : 1 6 :005(223) [0331] approves them, and it **commands** us to obey them as
A P : 1 6 :011(224) [0333] right of ownership and **commands** everyone to possess his
A P : 2 0 :012(228) [0341] "The magistrate **commands** that from now on you steal
A P : 2 2 :011(238) [0361] tyrant in a play, he **commands**, "Whether they like it or
A P : 2 3 :016(241) [0369] as a remedy and **commands** it because of these flaming
A P : 2 3 :043(245) [0375] know, too, that Paul **commands** each one to possess his
A P : 2 3 :046(246) [0377] recognition of God's **commands** and gifts, which he wants
A P : 2 3 :057(247) [0379] The canon **commands** that priests be suspended; our
A P : 2 4 :026(254) [0393] He **commands** them to offer praises, that is, prayer,
A P : 2 4 :029(255) [0393] He **commands** us to trust and says that this is a right
A P : 2 4 :048(258) [0401] good works which God **commands**, and they talk about
A P : 2 7 :067(280) [0441] getting married (he **commands** the younger ones to
A P : 2 8 :004(281) [0445] unless they act in clear opposition to God's **commands**.
A P : 2 8 :021(284) [0449] (Acts 5:29) Scripture **commands** that we must obey God
S 1 : P R :013(291) [0459] first carry out God's **commands** and precepts in the
S 3 : 0 2 :002(303) [0479] they desire to do and **commands** what they are unwilling
S 3 : 0 3 :034(309) [0489] in Acts 17:30, "Now he **commands** all men everywhere to
S 3 : 0 8 :004(312) [0495] he decides and **commands** in his churches is spirit and
T R : 0 0 :042(328) [0517] But divine authority **commands** us all not to be associated
T R : 0 0 :072(332) [0525] and discord, for Paul **commands** that bishops who teach
L C : 0 1 :016(366) [0585] God and which he **commands** under penalty of eternal
L C : 0 1 :105(379) [0611] are beneath it, that he **commands** us not simply to love
L C : 0 1 :105(379) [0611] neighbors in general he **commands** nothing higher than
L C : 0 1 :108(380) [0611] God therefore **commands** you to be careful to obey me as
L C : 0 1 :113(380) [0613] What God **commands** must be much nobler than
L C : 0 1 :331(410) [0677] the Old Testament **commands** men to write the Ten
L C : 0 1 :333(410) [0677] above all orders, **commands**, and works which are taught
L C : 0 4 :008(437) [0733] What God instituted and **commands** cannot be useless.
S D : 0 1 :011(510) [0863] to God and his highest **commands** and is actually enmity
S D : 0 4 :007(552) [0939] himself prescribes and **commands** in his Word, and not
S D : 0 5 :004(559) [0953] after his resurrection **commands** his apostles to preach
S D : 0 5 :019(561) [0957] speaking, teaches and **commands** faith in Christ) is the
S D : 0 7 :020(573) [0979] which Christ's word **commands** us Christians to eat and
S D : 0 7 :047(578) [0989] and earnest words and **commands** of our Creator and
S D : 1 0 :023(615) [1061] But divine authority **commands** us all not be be
S D : 1 1 :064(626) [1083] Paul immediately **commands** silence and cuts off further

Commemorated (1), Commemoration (2)
A P : 2 4 :038(257) [0399] by itself; the **commemoration** is the real daily sacrifice,
A P : 2 4 :089(266) [0415] was instituted for **commemoration** and preaching among
S 2 : 0 2 :014(295) [0467] the dead are to be **commemorated** in the sacrament.

Commend (8), Commendations (1), Commended (7), Commending (2), Commends (4)
A L : 2 0 :035(046) [0057] it should rather be **commended** for showing how we are

Continued ▶

A L : 2 1 :001(046) [0057] of saints may be **commended** to us so that we imitate
A L : 2 7 :051(079) [0083] from such false **commendations** of monastic life.
A P : P R :019(099) [0103] And so we shall **commend** our cause to Christ, who will
A P : 0 4 :184(132) [0173] In **commending** works, therefore, we must add that faith
A P : 0 4 :184(132) [0173] and that they are **commended** because of faith as its fruit
A P : 2 3 :021(242) [0369] here that Christ **commends** those "who have made
A P : 2 3 :022(242) [0369] We, too, **commend** true continence, but now we are
A P : 2 3 :040(244) [0375] Neither Christ nor Paul **commends** virginity because it
A P : 2 3 :040(245) [0375] He **commends** virginity for the sake of mediation and
A P : 2 3 :040(245) [0375] Christ does not simply **commend** those who make
A P : 2 7 :026(273) [0429] said (I Cor. 8:8), "Food does not **commend** us to God."
S 2 : 0 2 :022(296) [0469] They are neither commanded nor **commended**.
S 3 : 0 3 :015(305) [0483] the sinner was **commended** to the grace of God.
S 3 : 1 5 :005(316) [0501] are without number, we **commend** for adoration to their
S C : 0 7 :002(352) [0557] Into thy hands I **commend** my body and soul and all that
S C : 0 7 :005(353) [0559] Into thy hands I **commend** my body and soul and all that
L C : 0 1 :073(374) [0601] to form the habit of **commending** ourselves each day to
L C : 0 1 :201(392) [0637] of virginity was not **commended**, neither were public
L C : 0 1 :300(405) [0665] people who wish to be **commended** as honest and
E P : 0 7 :041(486) [0817] By the same token we **commend** to the righteous
S D : 1 1 :061(626) [1083] and keeps them, God **commends** his pure and unmerited

Commensurate (1)
A P : 0 4 :367(163) [0221] reward is evidently **commensurate** with the degree of the

Comment (2), Commentaries (3), Commentary (5), Commentator (1), Commentators (3), Comments (1)
A P : 0 4 :065(116) [0139] let them produce one **commentary** on the *Sentences* that
A P : 0 4 :105(122) [0153] If you pile up all the **commentators** on the *Sentences* with
A P : 0 4 :264(146) [0195] doubt, and in his **commentaries** he maintains with even
A P : 0 4 :322(157) [0209] Cyprian says in his **commentary** on the Lord's Prayer:
A P : 1 2 :005(183) [0253] The **commentaries** on the *Sentences* are full of endless
A P : 1 2 :068(192) [0271] crowd of worthless **commentators** on the *Sentences* who
A P : 1 2 :070(192) [0271] to the many legions of **commentators** on the *Sentences*.
A P : 2 2 :004(236) [0359] In his **commentary** on Zephaniah, Jerome says, "The
A P : 2 4 :081(264) [0411] A **commentator** on Demosthenes says that "liturgy" is a
A P : 2 7 :003(269) [0419] down by him in the **commentaries** he left on certain
L C : 0 2 :008(411) [0679] Let us briefly **comment** on these words.
L C : 0 2 :049(417) [0691] It is nothing but a **comment** or interpretation by which
S D : 0 2 :020(524) [0889] is as Luther says in his **comments** on Ps. 91: "In secular
S D : 0 2 :081(537) [0911] express words in his **commentary** on Ps. 25, where he
S D : 0 4 :028(555) [0947] in their work (in his ***Commentary** on Genesis*, Chapter

Commerce (1)
L C : 0 1 :249(398) [0651] all areas of trade and **commerce** in order that the poor

Commission (6), Commissioned (2), Commissioners (1)
A G : P R :018(026) [0041] orator and appointed **commissioners**, that Your Imperial
A G : 2 8 :012(083) [0085] spiritual power has its **commission** to preach the Gospel
A L : 2 8 :012(083) [0085] the church has its own **commission** to preach the Gospel
A L : 2 8 :019(083) [0087] not as bishops under a **commission** of the Gospel, but by
A L : 2 8 :039(087) [0089] and as if God had **commissioned** the apostles and bishops
A L : 2 8 :061(091) [0093] and that Christ **commissioned** the apostles and bishops to
T R : 0 0 :030(325) [0513] This **commission** Peter holds in common with the rest of
L C : 0 1 :274(402) [0659] the law into their own hands without such a **commission**.
L C : 0 3 :089(432) [0723] in word and deed, in acts of **commission** and omission.

Commit (20), Commitment (1), Commits (6), Committed (22)
P R : P R :003(003) [0007] churches and schools **committed** themselves to this
P R : P R :006(004) [0009] office which God has **committed** to us and which we
P R : P R :008(005) [0011] alone gives salvation, to **commit** themselves to it, and for
P R : P R :012(007) [0013] office that we bear and that God has **committed** to us.
P R : P R :018(008) [0015] what follows purposed to **commit** ourselves exclusively
A G : P R :006(025) [0039] and estates should **commit** to writing and present, in
A G : 0 9 :002(033) [0047] for in Baptism they are **committed** to God and become
A G : 1 8 :007(040) [0053] he wills to kneel before an idol, **commit** murder, etc."
A G : 2 6 :002(064) [0071] observed and a great sin **committed** if they were omitted.
A G : 2 6 :013(066) [0073] and some even **committed** suicide, because they had not
A G : 2 8 :056(090) [0091] would say that a woman **commits** a sin if without offense
A G : 2 8 :065(092) [0093] who do not observe it **commit** no sin, for the apostles did
A L : 1 8 :007(040) [0053] as to will to worship an idol, will to **commit murder**," etc.
A L : 2 6 :041(070) [0075] God and that no sin is **committed** if they are omitted
A L : 2 8 :021(084) [0087] to whom has been **committed** the ministry of the Word
A L : 2 8 :056(090) [0091] without offense to others **commit** a sin, any more than
A L : 2 8 :065(092) [0093] who do not observe it **commit** no sin, for the apostles did
A P : 1 2 :091(195) [0279] past evils and not to **commit** again deeds that ought to be
A P : 1 2 :142(204) [0295] he can make satisfaction for the sins he **commits**.
A P : 2 7 :042(276) [0435] it is a service to God to **commit** suicide and to leave our
S 3 : 0 1 :009(302) [0477] have an evil intention to **commit** sin, for such is the
S 3 : 0 3 :015(305) [0483] sins (especially those **committed** during the course of a
S 3 : 0 3 :017(305) [0483] might have been **committed**, let us say, in whoredom,
S 3 : 0 3 :044(310) [0491] such a way that sin is **committed**, but the Holy Spirit
S 3 : 0 3 :045(310) [0491] says, "No one born of God **commits** sin; he cannot sin."
S C : 0 1 :011(343) [0541] *"You shall not **commit** adultery."*
L C : S P :006(362) [0575] 6. You shall not **commit** adultery.
L C : 0 1 :033(369) [0589] men live in security and **commit** themselves to luck, like
L C : 0 1 :056(372) [0595] name as the greatest sin that can be **committed** outwardly.
L C : 0 1 :059(372) [0597] virtue that whenever we **commit** a wrong we like to cover
L C : 0 1 :059(372) [0597] the whole world of the wickedness he has **committed**.
L C : 0 1 :167(388) [0629] how they should treat those **committed** to their authority.
L C : 0 1 :186(390) [0633] they may not actually **commit** murder, nevertheless call
L C : 0 1 :187(390) [0633] confidence and prayer **commit** to him whatever wrong we
L C : 0 1 :192(391) [0635] you have not actually **committed** all these crimes, as far
L C : 0 1 :199(392) [0637] *"You shall not **commit** adultery."*
L C : 0 1 :231(396) [0647] who have **committed** one offense must bear disgrace and
L C : 0 1 :265(401) [0657] when he has seen a sin **committed**, unless he has been
L C : 0 3 :045(426) [0709] other crime had been **committed** in it, or when a
L C : 0 5 :059(453) [0767] "Unless a man has **committed** such a sin that he has
E P : 0 1 :018(468) [0783] man himself who **commits** sin but something extraneous
E P : 0 1 :021(468) [0783] is not a sin which man **commits**; it inheres in the nature,
E P : 0 2 :008(471) [0789] acts, and that he **commits** evil deeds and acts like
E P : 1 2 :000(498) [0839] Sects Which Have Not **Committed** Themselves to the
S D : R N :007(505) [0853] the fifth place, we also **commit** ourselves to the Articles
S D : 0 7 :017(572) [0977] theologians who were **committed** to the Augsburg
S D : 0 7 :046(577) [0989] as the words read, and **committed** the entire matter to
S D : 0 8 :004(592) [1017] not quite ready to **commit** themselves publicly and
S D : 1 2 :006(633) [1097] steadfastly in our **commitment** to this Confession until we

Common (112), Commonly (4)
P R : P R :004(003) [0007] It is a matter of **common** knowledge, patent and
P R : P R :020(010) [0017] way as far as the **common** layman is concerned, for he
P R : P R :024(013) [0023] of God's glory and the **common** welfare, both eternal and
A G : 0 0 :000(048) [0059] Scriptures or what is **common** to the Christian church.
A G : 2 7 :028(075) [0079] Yet it is **commonly** known to what an extent perpetual
A G : 2 7 :051(079) [0083] However, the **common** people, hearing the state of
A G : 2 7 :053(079) [0083] When the **common** man hears that only mendicants are
A G : 0 0 :003(095) [0095] passed over for the **common** good in order that the chief
A L : 0 0 :005(048) [0059] But it has been a **common** complaint that certain abuses
A L : 0 0 :005(049) [0059] be gathered from **common** rumors or the accusations of
A L : 2 3 :001(051) [0061] There has been **common** complaint concerning priests
A L : 2 4 :022(058) [0067] From this has come the **common** opinion that the Mass is
A L : 2 4 :034(060) [0067] of the sacrament, one **common** Mass is observed among
A L : 2 4 :035(060) [0067] private Masses but speak often of the **common** Mass.
A L : 2 4 :039(060) [0069] in order that there may be a **common** participation.
A L : 2 6 :001(063) [0071] It has been the **common** opinion not only of the people
A P : 0 4 :072(117) [0141] important; or, as the **common** saying goes, "the beginning
A P : 0 4 :242(141) [0187] actions of others, as the **common** proverb says, "Know,
A P : 0 4 :280(149) [0201] because according to the **common** rule it is improper in
A P : 1 2 :151(206) [0299] to death and to all the **common** troubles, as Peter says
A P : 1 2 :154(206) [0301] does not remove these **common** troubles; but if this is
A P : 1 2 :156(207) [0301] terrors of conscience, as well as other **common** troubles.
A P : 1 2 :156(207) [0301] that over and above our **common** troubles there is a
A P : 1 2 :157(207) [0301] of certain penalties over and above our **common** troubles?
A P : 1 2 :162(208) [0303] away with the calamities **common** to man — that is, the
A P : 1 2 :165(208) [0303] to teach that our **common** evils are mitigated by our
A P : 1 5 :020(218) [0321] and finally because they helped instruct the **common** folk.
A P : 1 5 :020(218) [0321] and various rites serve as reminders for the **common** folk.
A P : 1 5 :023(218) [0321] Under this delusion the **common** people among the
A P : 1 6 :004(223) [0331] to hold property in **common**, and they called it an
A P : 1 6 :010(224) [0333] that the Gospel requires us to hold property in **common**!
A P : 1 6 :011(224) [0333] holding property in **common**, but by its command, "You
A P : 2 1 :016(231) [0347] the abuses among the **common** people but discuss only
A P : 2 3 :049(246) [0377] of discipline and the **common** weal" (that is, for the
A P : 2 3 :053(246) [0377] change other laws if the **common** good demanded it, why
A P : 2 4 :003(250) [0385] hymns to give the **common** people something to learn
A P : 2 4 :006(250) [0385] catholic in our having only the public or **common** Mass.
A P : 2 4 :007(250) [0385] be content with a single **common** daily Mass, reasons of
A P : 2 4 :017(252) [0389] The genus **common** to both could be "ceremony" or
A P : 2 4 :063(260) [0405] We also reject other **common** errors: that the Mass
A P : 2 4 :086(265) [0413] think it was called that because of the **common** banquet.
A P : 2 7 :036(275) [0433] they are modifying the **common** notion about perfection.
S 1 : 0 1 :000(292) [0461] and the Catechism in **common** use for children teach.
S 2 : 0 2 :009(294) [0465] sacrament, which is the **common** possession of the
S 2 : 0 2 :012(294) [0465] of requiems, with the **common** week, with All Souls'
S 2 : 0 4 :009(300) [0475] governed the churches together and in **common**.
S 3 : 1 0 :003(314) [0497] without bishops by priests and preachers in **common**.
T R : 0 0 :008(320) [0505] and exercise the ministry of the Gospel in **common**.
T R : 0 0 :030(325) [0513] Peter holds in **common** with the rest of the apostles.
T R : 0 0 :070(331) [0525] The most **common** custom of the church also bears
T R : 0 0 :074(332) [0525] It is certain that the **common** jurisdiction of
S C : P R :002(338) [0533] The **common** people, especially those who live in the
S C : P R :018(340) [0537] children and the **common** people in order that they may
L C : P R :004(359) [0567] As it is, the **common** people take the Gospel altogether
L C : S P :006(362) [0575] As for the **common** people, however, we should be
L C : 0 1 :005(365) [0581] by citing some **common** examples of failure to observe
L C : 0 1 :006(365) [0583] It is the most **common** idol on earth.
L C : 0 1 :053(372) [0595] This is especially **common** in marriage matters when two
L C : 0 1 :058(372) [0597] Unfortunately it is now a **common** calamity all over the
L C : 0 1 :060(372) [0597] This is the **common** course of the world.
L C : 0 1 :079(375) [0603] from labor; hence our **common** expression for "stopping
L C : 0 1 :083(376) [0603] and demands that the **common** people — man-servants
L C : 0 1 :085(376) [0605] this is more than the **common** people can do, at least one
L C : 0 1 :085(376) [0605] In this way a **common** order will prevail and no one will
L C : 0 1 :086(376) [0605] for the sake of the young and the poor **common** people.
L C : 0 1 :161(387) [0627] to impress upon the **common** people that they who
L C : 0 1 :187(390) [0633] every one of us, and it is **common** knowledge that no one
L C : 0 1 :188(390) [0633] unmistakably upon the **common** people, the import of the
L C : 0 1 :201(392) [0637] adultery was the most **common** form of unchastity among
L C : 0 1 :213(394) [0641] while they deceive the **common** people with lying words
L C : 0 1 :224(395) [0643] Stealing is a widespread, **common** vice, but people pay so
L C : 0 1 :225(395) [0643] it a little clearer for the **common** people so that we may
L C : 0 1 :228(396) [0645] thievery is the most **common** craft and the largest guild
L C : 0 1 :232(396) [0647] and explain it to the **common** people in order that they
L C : 0 1 :258(399) [0653] at present, but among the Jews it was extremely **common**.
L C : 0 1 :264(400) [0655] It is a **common** vice of human nature that everyone would
L C : 0 1 :300(405) [0667] For the **common** masses belong much farther down in the
L C : 0 1 :313(407) [0671] and ceremonies, but are **common**, everyday domestic
L C : 0 2 :046(416) [0689] not quite clear to the **common** people, we shall run
L C : 0 2 :048(416) [0691] nothing else than a **common** assembly; it is not of
L C : 0 2 :070(420) [0697] lay a foundation for the **common** people without
L C : 0 3 :079(431) [0721] to impress upon the **common** people that all these things
L C : 0 3 :084(432) [0723] beware lest they lose the **common** intercession of the
L C : 0 4 :001(436) [0733] the three chief parts of our **common** Christian teaching.
L C : 0 4 :014(438) [0735] It is not simply **common** water, but water comprehended
L C : 0 5 :043(451) [0763] in order that the **common** people and the weak, who also
L C : 0 5 :060(453) [0767] he does not retain many **common** infirmities in his flesh
L C : 0 6 :008(458) [0000] right to be called the Christians' **common** confession.
E P : 0 1 :023(469) [0785] and, besides, they are unknown to the **common** man.
E P : 0 1 :023(469) [0785] in sermons delivered to **common**, unlearned people, but
E P : 0 8 :003(487) [0817] of the other but have in **common** only the name.
E P : 0 8 :003(487) [0819] makes merely the names **common**," so that God is called
E P : 0 8 :003(487) [0819] in truth) has nothing in **common** with the humanity and
E P : 0 8 :003(487) [0819] really has nothing in **common** with the deity, its majesty,
E P : 0 8 :009(487) [0819] nature has anything in **common** with the other personally
E P : 0 8 :024(490) [0823] personal union achieves only **common** names and titles.
E P : 0 8 :025(490) [0823] the deity has nothing in **common** with the humanity, nor

Continued ▶

EP : 12 :017(499) [0841] is in conscience bound to put it into a **common** treasury.
SD : RN :001(503) [0849] summarized doctrine **commonly** confessed by the
SD : RN :002(503) [0851] well-known symbols or **common** confessions which have
SD : RN :005(504) [0851] Roman Empire as the **common** confession of the
SD : RN :010(506) [0855] accepted, certain, and **common** form of doctrine which
SD : RN :011(506) [0855] been accepted as the **common** and universally accepted
SD : RN :020(508) [0859] be found faithful to the **commonly** accepted Christian
SD : 01 :051(517) [0875] have two or more accepted meanings in **common** use.
SD : 01 :054(517) [0877] since they are not the **common** man's vocabulary.
SD : 07 :017(572) [0979] By **common** consent Dr. Luther drafted the Smalcald
SD : 07 :048(578) [0989] in their usual, strict, and **commonly** accepted meaning.
SD : 07 :058(580) [0993] body of Christ, or the **common** body of Christ distributed
SD : 07 :073(583) [0999] consecration and the **common** rule that there is no
SD : 07 :090(585) [1003] subtle perversion of this **common** rule ascribe to our faith
SD : 07 :110(588) [1011] refuted at length in the **common** Confession of our
SD : 08 :031(597) [1025] not only have names in **common** but also in deed and
SD : 08 :095(609) [1049] but has only the bare title and name in **common** with it.
SD : 11 :028(621) [1073] command that all in **common** to whom repentance is
SD : 11 :076(629) [1089] but according to his **common** ordinance he does this

Commonwealth (5)
AG : 28 :016(083) [0085] in Phil. 3:20, "Our **commonwealth** is in heaven," and in
AL : 28 :016(083) [0085] in Phil. 3:20, "Our **commonwealth** is in heaven," and in
AP : 16 :006(223) [0331] would destroy the **commonwealth** by its prohibition of
AP : 24 :021(252) [0391] did not have to be excluded from the **commonwealth**.
AP : 24 :024(253) [0391] the exclusion of the sinner from the **commonwealth**.

Commotion (1), Commotions (1)
AP : 04 :242(141) [0187] to his hatred, a major **commotion** emerged from an
AP : 28 :022(284) [0451] public offenses and **commotions** which have arisen under

Commune (7)
AP : 11 :005(181) [0249] and are found never to **commune**, let them be
AP : 11 :005(181) [0249] If they still do not **commune**, let them come to penitence.
AP : 11 :005(181) [0251] If they **commune**, let them not be permanently expelled.
AP : 11 :005(181) [0251] If they do not **commune**, let them be expelled."
AP : 16 :013(224) [0333] while the Platonic **commune** does not have God's
S2 : 02 :008(294) [0465] if he really desires to **commune**, he can do so most
S2 : 02 :008(294) [0465] To **commune** by himself is uncertain and unnecessary,

Communicant (2), Communicants (6)
AG : 24 :034(060) [0067] at other times when **communicants** are present, Mass is
AP : 13 :020(213) [0313] (I Cor. 11:25), the **communicant** should be certain that
AP : 24 :076(263) [0411] about the godly **communicant**, "Piety distinguishes
AP : 24 :093(267) [0417] it may benefit the **communicants**; they do not talk about
SD : 07 :027(574) [0981] believers and worthy **communicants** but also to the
SD : 07 :069(582) [0997] True and worthy **communicants**, on the other hand, are
SD : 07 :070(582) [0997] primarily for **communicants** like this, as Christ says,
SD : 07 :074(583) [0999] or the faith of the **communicants**, can effect the true

Communicate (2), Communicated (13), Communicating (1), Communication (6)
PR : PR :013(007) [0013] to writing, and **communicate** to us without reserve their
AG : PR :008(025) [0039] are preached, taught, **communicated**, and embraced in
AG : 24 :034(060) [0067] Mass is held and those who desire it are **communicated**.
AG : 24 :037(060) [0067] man officiated and **communicated** the other priests and
AP : 04 :227(139) [0183] takes hold of Christ, **communicating** to us Christ's merits
AP : 04 :305(154) [0207] Christ's, which is **communicated** to us through faith.
AP : 04 :367(163) [0221] ours, and Christ's merits are **communicated** to us by faith.
AP : 10 :003(179) [0247] bodily through the **communication** of the flesh of
S2 : 02 :008(294) [0465] that he wishes to **communicate** himself for the sake of his
LC : 05 :029(449) [0759] is conveyed and **communicated** to us in no other way than
EP : 08 :027(490) [0825] from God and **communicated** to and infused into the
SD : 07 :011(571) [0975] the Supper through the **communication** of his flesh in us.
SD : 08 :029(596) [1025] Because of this **communicated** power he can be and is
SD : 08 :031(597) [1025] (that is, of a true **communication** of the properties of the
SD : 08 :055(601) [1033] have been given and **communicated** to the man Christ
SD : 08 :056(601) [1033] which show that this **communication** is not merely a
SD : 08 :060(602) [1035] it was all given and **communicated** to the assumed human
SD : 08 :061(602) [1035] in which the Father **communicated** his own essence and
SD : 08 :062(603) [1037] This exchange or **communication** did not take place
SD : 08 :062(603) [1037] or by means of these **communicated** properties has
SD : 08 :063(603) [1037] "real exchange" — a **communication** or exchange that
SD : 08 :073(605) [1041] Fathers say) is **communicated** to Christ according to the

Communio (2)
LC : 02 :047(416) [0689] holy Christian church a ***communio** sanctorum,* "a
LC : 02 :049(417) [0691] Likewise the word ***communio***, which is appended, should

Communion (60)
AG : 01 :007(056) [0065] the people may be drawn to the **Communion** and Mass.
AG : 24 :034(060) [0067] dead, but should be a **Communion** in which the priest and
AG : 24 :036(060) [0067] day, inviting some to **Communion** and forbidding others
AL : 24 :036(060) [0067] altar, inviting some to **Communion** and keeping others
AL : 24 :038(060) [0069] deacons receive Holy **Communion** from the bishop or
AL : 24 :039(060) [0069] commands concerning **Communion** that one wait for
AP : 07 :008(169) [0229] following phrase, "the **communion** of saints," seems to
AP : 12 :113(199) [0285] notorious people to **communion** immediately was
AP : 22 :008(237) [0359] They also refer to "lay **communion**."
AP : 22 :008(237) [0359] commanded to use lay **communion**, this indicated that
AP : 22 :008(237) [0359] hear the phrase "lay **communion**" immediately imagine
AP : 24 :008(250) [0385] no daily Masses but **Communion** was celebrated three
AP : 24 :008(250) [0385] says, "Assemblies for **Communion** were appointed by the
AP : 24 :079(264) [0411] mention the old term "**communion**," which shows that
AP : 24 :079(264) [0411] that formerly the Mass was the **communion** of many?
S3 : 10 :002(314) [0497] baptize or administer **Communion** or discharge any office
SC : 02 :005(345) [0545] *Christian church, the **communion** of saints, the*
LC : SP :013(363) [0577] Christian church, the **communion** of saints, the
LC : 02 :034(415) [0687] *Christian church, the **communion** of saints, the*
LC : 02 :037(415) [0687] the following: the **communion** of saints or Christian
LC : 02 :047(416) [0689] church a *communio sanctorum,* "a **communion** of saints."
LC : 02 :049(417) [0691] should not be translated "**communion**" but "community."
LC : 02 :049(417) [0691] have rendered this "**communion** of saints," although no
LC : 04 :051(443) [0745] Holy Christian church, the **communion** of saints," etc.
EP : 07 :002(481) [0809] is, In the Holy **Communion** are the true body and blood
EP : 08 :009(487) [0819] here is the highest **communion** which God truly has with
EP : 08 :010(488) [0819] did not have a real and true **communion** with each other.
EP : 08 :013(488) [0821] ineffable union and **communion** with the Son of God
EP : 08 :031(491) [0825] Son of God had no **communion** with the human nature in
SD : RN :007(505) [0853] for having no **communion** with the papists, and for
SD : 07 :007(570) [0975] which is not in the **communion** on earth but only in
SD : 07 :011(571) [0975] the bodily presence of Christ in the Holy **Communion**."
SD : 07 :040(576) [0985] *Concerning the **Communion*** Dr. Luther defended with
SD : 07 :054(579) [0991] of the body and blood of Christ in the **Communion**.
SD : 07 :077(583) [0999] beginning of the first **Communion** until the end of the
SD : 07 :079(584) [1001] the administration of **Communion** the words of institution
SD : 07 :104(587) [1009] precisely that spiritual **communion** which is established
SD : 08 :014(594) [1019] allegedly have no **communion** at all with each other.
SD : 08 :015(594) [1019] two natures have no **communion** whatsoever with each
SD : 08 :016(594) [1021] in Christ they have no **communion** at all, just as if Christ
SD : 08 :017(594) [1021] way that they have true **communion** with each other, by
SD : 08 :018(594) [1021] personal union and **communion**, the ancient teachers of
SD : 08 :018(594) [1021] personal union and **communion** by analogies of the soul
SD : 08 :019(594) [1021] as fire and iron, have a **communion** with each other, not
SD : 08 :019(595) [1021] For the **communion** and union between the divine and
SD : 08 :019(595) [1021] of this union and **communion** God is man and man is
SD : 08 :020(595) [1021] which such a true **communion** of the natures is
SD : 08 :022(595) [1023] both words, "**communion**" and "union," in expounding
SD : 08 :023(595) [1023] personal union and **communion** of the divine and human
SD : 08 :023(595) [1023] personal union and **communion** of the natures in the
SD : 08 :024(595) [1023] personal union and **communion** of the natures, Mary, the
SD : 08 :025(596) [1023] united with the divine nature and had **communion** with it.
SD : 08 :030(597) [1025] and ineffable **communion** that even the angels marvel at
SD : 08 :031(597) [1025] deed and truth have **communion** between each other
SD : 08 :032(597) [1025] the personal union or **communion** of natures in the
SD : 08 :046(600) [1031] to its own properties acts in **communion** with the other.
SD : 08 :076(606) [1043] and the resultant **communion** that the divine and human
SD : 08 :092(609) [1049] his presence in his Word, as in the Holy **Communion**.
SD : 08 :093(609) [1049] Son of God had no **communion** whatever in the passion,
SD : 10 :019(614) [1059] baptize or administer **Communion** or discharge any office

Community (33), Communities (1)
PR : PR :026(014) [0025] to our own and each **community**'s circumstances, through
AG : 28 :021(084) [0087] from the Christian **community** the ungodly whose wicked
AP : 04 :232(139) [0185] in all families and **communities** harmony should be
AP : 24 :007(250) [0385] provision that each **community** should be content with a
LC : 01 :089(377) [0605] a day for the whole **community**, when we can concentrate
LC : 02 :037(415) [0687] leads us into his holy **community**, placing us upon the
LC : 02 :042(416) [0689] the first place, he has a unique **community** in the world.
LC : 02 :049(417) [0691] should not be translated "communion" but "**community**."
LC : 02 :049(417) [0691] we ought to say "a **community** of saints," that is, a
LC : 02 :049(417) [0691] of saints," that is, a **community** composed only of saints,
LC : 02 :049(417) [0691] only of saints, or, still more clearly, "a holy **community**."
LC : 02 :051(417) [0691] a little holy flock or **community** of pure saints under one
LC : 02 :052(417) [0691] Of this **community** I also am a part and member, a
LC : 02 :053(417) [0691] remains with the holy **community** or Christian people.
LC : 02 :061(419) [0695] he has appointed a **community** on earth, through which
LC : 02 :062(419) [0695] brings us into this **community** through the Word, and
LC : 04 :002(436) [0733] which we are first received into the Christian **community**.
EP : 10 :004(493) [0829] and confess that the **community** of God in every locality
EP : 10 :004(493) [0829] be most profitable and edifying to the **community** of God.
EP : 10 :010(494) [0831] imposed upon the **community** of God as necessary
EP : 10 :012(494) [0831] which suggests that the **community** of God does not have
SD : 02 :037(528) [0895] remains with the holy **community** of Christendom,
SD : 02 :057(532) [0903] the Word and the **community** of God, dies in this
SD : 07 :123(590) [1015] who are in the external **community** of the church receive
SD : 07 :126(591) [1015] places but especially where his **community** is assembled.
SD : 08 :077(606) [1043] Christian church and **community** and that this presence
SD : 08 :078(607) [1043] with his church and **community** on earth as mediator,
SD : 10 :009(612) [1055] and confess that the **community** of God in every place
SD : 10 :010(612) [1055] holy Gospel, the entire **community** of God, yes, every
SD : 10 :010(612) [1055] as the leaders of the **community** of God, are obligated to
SD : 10 :025(615) [1061] learn what a Christian **community**, each individual
SD : 10 :027(615) [1061] imposed by force on the **community** of God as necessary.
SD : 10 :030(615) [1061] impression that the **community** of God does not have the
SD : 12 :022(634) [1099] but is obliged to give his property to the **community**.

Commute (3), Commutes (1)
AP : 12 :022(185) [0257] but it was instituted to **commute** eternal to temporal
AP : 12 :118(199) [0287] to punish sin, he **commutes** the eternal punishment to a
AP : 12 :138(203) [0293] for the keys to **commute** certain punishments or to remit
AP : 12 :139(204) [0295] with it the command to **commute** penalties or to remit

Companions (1)
S2 : 04 :001(298) [0471] Christian brethren and **companions**, as the ancient

Company (3)
TR : 00 :023(324) [0511] of the entire **company** of apostles, as is apparent from the
TR : 00 :024(324) [0511] of the entire **company** of apostles, on which account these
SD : 01 :054(518) [0877] themselves or in the **company** of persons to whom these

Compare (8), Compared (5), Compares (1), Comparing (1), Comparison (4)
AP : 04 :015(109) [0123] in existence which **compare** certain teachings of Christ
AP : 07 :001(168) [0227] the church since John **compared** the church to a threshing
AP : 07 :001(168) [0227] (Matt. 3:12) and Christ **compared** it to a net in which
AP : 12 :178(211) [0307] If devout men will **compare** our teaching with the
AP : 15 :026(219) [0323] **Compared** with these ceremonies such tasks seem
AP : 21 :035(234) [0353] and pictures do not even **compare** with the fairy tales
AP : 24 :076(263) [0411] and what is forgiven; it **compares** the greatness of God's
AP : 24 :096(267) [0417] heresies and by falsely **comparing** them with our position
AP : 27 :038(275) [0433] in the city of Alexandria as a basis for **comparison**.
AP : 27 :058(279) [0439] Hence it is not right to **compare** monasticism, thought up
AP : 28 :026(285) [0451] But let us skip over the **comparison**.
S2 : 04 :014(301) [0475] Holy Scriptures, or is **compared** with them, it becomes
S3 : 03 :009(304) [0481] Now we must **compare** the false repentance of the
SD : RN :020(507) [0857] as far as is necessary, to **compare** our present position
SD : RN :020(508) [0857] Such a **comparison** will show him clearly that there is no

Continued ▶

SD : 0 2 :019(524) [0889] the Holy Scriptures **compare** the heart of unregenerated
SD : 0 3 :002(539) [0917] and that in **comparison** with this righteousness the sins of
SD : 0 3 :002(539) [0917] are like a drop of water **compared** to the mighty ocean.
SD : 1 1 :060(626) [1083] people so that, as we **compare** ourselves with them and

Compel (16), Compelled (24), Compelling (3), Compels (8)
AG : 0 0 :000(049) [0059] manner but have been **compelled** by God's command
AG : 2 2 :011(050) [0061] Christ's institution or to **compel** them to act contrary to
AG : 2 3 :012(052) [0063] in Germany were **compelled** by force to take the vows of
AG : 2 5 :007(062) [0069] that no one should be **compelled** to recount sins in detail,
AG : 2 5 :009(063) [0069] there is no need to **compel** people to give a detailed
AG : 2 6 :019(067) [0073] but dire need has **compelled** them to give instruction
AG : 2 7 :006(071) [0077] were pressed and **compelled** to remain, in spite of the fact
AG : 2 7 :020(074) [0079] that urges, drives, and **compels** us to do this, but God's
AG : 2 7 :029(075) [0079] and sometimes have been **compelled** and forced to do so.
AG : 2 8 :004(081) [0085] our teachers have been **compelled**, for the sake of
AL : 0 0 :001(049) [0059] the people may not be **compelled** to observe these abuses
AL : 2 2 :011(050) [0061] should not have been **compelled**, with offense to their
AL : 2 3 :012(052) [0063] were priests in Germany **compelled** by force to live in
AL : 2 6 :020(067) [0073] For the Gospel **compels** us to insist in the church on the
AL : 2 7 :006(071) [0077] were thus ensnared were **compelled** to remain, though
AL : 2 7 :020(074) [0079] and institution also **compel** those to marry who are not
AL : 2 7 :029(075) [0079] and sometimes even **compelled**, to take the vow.
AL : 2 8 :004(081) [0085] our teachers have been **compelled**, for the sake of
AP : 0 4 :039(112) [0131] the subject itself will **compel** us to cite further evidence;
AP : 0 4 :291(152) [0203] It **compels** us to make use of Christ in justification.
AP : 0 4 :313(155) [0207] well as the reasons that **compel** us to hold that we are
AP : 1 2 :173(210) [0305] teaching of the Gospel **compels** us to assume these
AP : 1 5 :034(220) [0325] and example the apostles **compel** us to oppose this
AP : 1 5 :034(220) [0325] They **compel** us to teach that traditions do not justify;
AP : 2 0 :011(228) [0341] treated this issue has **compelled** us to register a complaint
AP : 2 1 :039(235) [0355] of the Confutation, to **compel** us to approve of the most
TR : 0 0 :058(330) [0521] godly have weighty, **compelling**, and evident reasons for
TR : 0 0 :072(332) [0525] are by divine right **compelled** to ordain pastors and
TR : 0 0 :077(333) [0527] magistrates are **compelled** to make these decisions if the
TR : 0 0 :079(333) [0527] numerous and **compelling** reasons why the churches
SC : PR :013(339) [0535] cannot and should not **compel** anyone to believe, we
SC : PR :021(340) [0537] No one is to be **compelled** to believe or to receive the
SC : PR :022(341) [0537] and, as it were, **compel** us pastors to administer it to
SC : PR :023(341) [0539] It is not necessary to **compel** him by any law to receive
LC : 0 1 :275(402) [0659] a patient, is sometimes **compelled** to examine and handle
LC : 0 1 :321(408) [0673] we are constrained and **compelled** to keep these Ten
LC : 0 5 :042(451) [0763] be coerced or **compelled**, lest we institute a new slaughter
LC : 0 5 :046(452) [0763] often as you do it'; so he **compels** no one, but leaves it to
LC : 0 5 :052(452) [0765] But we neither force nor **compel** anyone, nor need anyone
LC : 0 5 :062(454) [0767] and consolation should **compel** himself to go and allow
LC : 0 6 :028(460) [0000] any point, but you will **compel** yourself and beg me for
LC : 0 6 :030(460) [0000] but rather coming and **compelling** us to offer it.
LC : 0 6 :031(460) [0000] We **compel** no man, but allow ourselves to be compelled,
LC : 0 6 :031(460) [0000] allow ourselves to be **compelled**, just as we are compelled
LC : 0 6 :031(460) [0000] just as we are **compelled** to preach and administer the
EP : 1 1 :004(494) [0833] of evil or of sin which **compels** anyone to do something
SD : PR :007(502) [0849] The holy apostles were **compelled** vigorously to denounce
SD : 0 1 :034(514) [0869] faith constrain and **compel** us to maintain such a
SD : 0 1 :041(515) [0871] we should be **compelled** to conclude: Either that, since
SD : 0 1 :057(518) [0879] by itself), then necessity **compels** us to answer simply and
SD : 0 2 :073(535) [0909] so that God forcibly **compels** a man to be converted

Compend (1)
LC : PR :018(361) [0573] which is a brief **compend** and summary of all the Holy

Compensate (6)
AP : 1 2 :123(200) [0289] of purgatory **compensate** for eternal punishments;
AP : 1 2 :138(203) [0293] non-obligatory works **compensate** for eternal
AP : 1 2 :138(203) [0293] canonical satisfactions **compensate** for these
AP : 1 2 :143(204) [0297] pay homage to God and to **compensate** for eternal death.
AP : 1 2 :143(204) [0297] pay homage to God and **compensate** for eternal death.
AP : 1 2 :172(209) [0305] works be done to **compensate** for punishment.

Competed (1)
AP : 0 4 :288(151) [0203] monastic orders, which **competed** in the austerity of their

Compile (1), Compiled (4)
PR : PR :002(003) [0007] a short confession was **compiled** out of the divine,
AP : 1 2 :069(192) [0271] own books but only **compiled** them from earlier ones and
AP : 1 2 :093(196) [0279] of those who have **compiled** these centos of the sentences
AP : 2 4 :099(268) [0419] our opponents make us **compile** all kinds of abuses of the
TR : 0 0 :000(319) [0503] **Compiled** by the Theologians Assembled in Smalcald in

Complacent (3)
AP : 1 5 :047(221) [0327] by satiety and become **complacent** and idle with the
SD : 0 4 :015(553) [0943] to criticize and reject a **complacent** Epicurean delusion,
SD : 0 4 :039(558) [0951] a wicked, wild, **complacent**, and Epicurean way of life.

Complain (11), Complained (4), Complaining (1), Complains (5), Complaint (7), Complaints (5)
AG : 2 3 :001(051) [0061] there has been loud **complaint** throughout the world
AG : 2 3 :018(054) [0063] this and have **complained** that such vices among the
AG : 2 6 :016(066) [0073] our time have also **complained** that such traditions caused
AG : 2 6 :016(066) [0073] Gerson and others have **complained** bitterly about this.
AG : 2 7 :009(072) [0077] Many people **complained** that in such a momentous
AG : 0 0 :002(095) [0095] there have been grave **complaints** about indulgences,
AL : 0 0 :005(048) [0059] it has been a common **complaint** that certain abuses were
AL : 2 3 :001(051) [0061] has been common **complaint** concerning priests who have
AL : 2 4 :010(057) [0065] open and very grievous **complaint** by all good men that
AL : 2 4 :016(057) [0067] they are beginning to **complain** about the troubles of the
AL : 0 0 :002(095) [0095] There have been grave **complaints** about indulgences,
AP : PR :010(099) [0101] my name, so no one can **complain** that the book has
AP : 0 2 :011(102) [0109] the prophets constantly **complain**, namely, carnal
AP : 0 4 :167(130) [0169] Who does not often **complain** because the wicked have
AP : 0 4 :393(167) [0225] So Paul often **complains** that even then there were some
AP : 2 0 :011(228) [0341] us to register a **complaint** rather than compose a
AP : 2 1 :041(235) [0355] Luther was not the first to **complain** about public abuses.
AP : 2 3 :045(245) [0375] Epiphanius **complains** that this characteristic among the
AP : 2 3 :052(246) [0377] Good men have been **complaining** about this burden for a
AP : 2 3 :052(246) [0377] but none of the popes listened to these **complaints**.
AP : 2 8 :003(281) [0443] would only listen to the **complaints** of churches and pious
AP : 2 8 :005(281) [0445] and hear the pitiful **complaints** of many good men.
S1 : PR :004(289) [0455] Why should I **complain**?
S3 : 0 7 :001(311) [0493] And Paul himself **complains** (Rom. 7:23) that in his flesh
LC : 0 1 :009(365) [0583] who do not fret and **complain**, if they do not have
LC : 0 1 :123(382) [0617] way things go in the world now, as everyone **complains**.
LC : 0 1 :155(386) [0625] and we grumble and **complain** of unfaithfulness,
LC : 0 1 :177(389) [0631] We all **complain** about this state of things, but we do not
LC : 0 1 :247(398) [0651] and because he can **complain** to no one else, he will cry to
LC : 0 1 :277(402) [0659] out on the streets to **complain** to his neighbors, he would
LC : 0 1 :301(405) [0667] to the property as to put it beyond **complaint** or dispute.
LC : 0 6 :013(458) [0000] as we wish lay our **complaint** before a brother, seeking
EP : 0 4 :013(477) [0799] weakness, as St. Paul **complains** of himself in Rom.

Complete (24), Completed (4), Completely (62), Completes (1), Completion (1)
PR : PR :014(007) [0013] follows hereafter, was **completed** with the help of such
AG : 2 6 :006(064) [0071] has been almost **completely** extinguished by those who
AP : 0 2 :042(105) [0115] Even though **complete** unanimity may be impossible, no
AP : 0 4 :081(118) [0143] as though Christ were **completely** buried, they imagine
AP : 0 4 :081(118) [0143] this not bury Christ **completely** and do away with the
AP : 0 4 :110(123) [0153] and justification, they **completely** abolish the Gospel of
AP : 0 4 :120(124) [0155] faith we are discussing **completely** destroys the Gospel.
AP : 0 4 :187(133) [0173] our works, it would be **completely** unsure and the
AP : 0 4 :237(140) [0185] But this is **completely** different from those praises of love
AP : 0 4 :262(145) [0195] even more clearly about **complete** penitence and bring
AP : 0 4 :268(147) [0197] works, indeed by our **complete** penitence, according to
AP : 0 4 :284(150) [0201] of love), then men are **completely** clean, outwardly as
AP : 0 4 :299(153) [0205] see the most **complete** consolation offered them.
AP : 0 4 :357(162) [0219] Such logic is **completely** new.
AP : 0 7 :032(174) [0239] rules of discipline, **completely** unrelated to the
AP : 0 7 :045(177) [0243] Our opponents **completely** misunderstand the meaning of
AP : 1 0 :003(179) [0247] say that this would be **completely** foreign to the sacred
AP : 1 2 :111(198) [0285] have maintained that **complete** confession is necessary for
AP : 1 2 :111(198) [0285] for salvation; this is **completely** false, as well as being
AP : 1 2 :111(198) [0285] this requirement of **complete** confession has cast upon
AP : 1 2 :111(198) [0285] will the conscience be sure that its confession is **complete**?
AP : 1 2 :153(206) [0299] this sinful flesh so that we may rise **completely** renewed.
AP : 1 2 :170(209) [0305] in the mouth confession, in the deed **complete** humility."
AP : 1 5 :001(215) [0315] They **completely** condemn the second part, where we say
AP : 2 0 :014(228) [0343] This is **completely** false.
AP : 2 1 :014(230) [0345] This is **completely** intolerable, for it transfers to the saints
AP : 2 1 :020(232) [0349] We must be **completely** certain that we are heard for
AP : 2 1 :028(233) [0351] the blessed Virgin has **completely** replaced Christ.
AP : 2 1 :039(235) [0355] our opponents **completely** ignore even the obvious
AP : 2 3 :045(245) [0377] to God, even though it was not **completely** condemned.
AP : 2 4 :057(260) [0405] It is **completely** erroneous to imagine that the Levitical
AP : 2 4 :057(260) [0405] This notion **completely** negates the merit of Christ's
AP : 2 4 :081(264) [0411] *Leptines* shows, it is **completely** taken up with public
S3 : 0 3 :019(306) [0483] had made a sufficiently **complete** or a sufficiently pure
S3 : 0 3 :019(306) [0485] was told that the more **completely** he confessed, the more
S3 : 1 3 :001(315) [0499] our flesh has not been **completely** removed or eradicated,
TR : 0 0 :044(328) [0517] of repentance has been **completely** corrupted by the pope
LC : 0 1 :010(366) [0583] to have something in which the heart trusts **completely**.
LC : 0 1 :015(366) [0583] nothing else than to entrust ourselves to him **completely**.
LC : 0 1 :035(369) [0589] the beginning he has **completely** rooted out all idolatry,
LC : 0 1 :121(382) [0615] and children would win their parents' hearts **completely**.
LC : 0 2 :026(413) [0685] — that is, how he has **completely** given himself to us,
LC : 0 2 :031(414) [0687] at the last day, he will **completely** divide and separate us
LC : 0 2 :038(415) [0689] work is finished and **completed**, Christ has acquired and
LC : 0 2 :057(418) [0693] gloriously and arise to **complete** and perfect holiness in a
LC : 0 2 :058(418) [0693] and righteousness, **completely** freed from sin, death, and
LC : 0 2 :062(419) [0695] people, nor has he **completed** the granting of forgiveness.
LC : 0 2 :069(420) [0697] that God gives himself **completely** to us, with all his gifts
LC : 0 4 :065(444) [0749] water, which covers us **completely**, and being drawn out
LC : 0 6 :016(459) [0000] made perfectly and in **complete** detail, we were told that
EP : 0 1 :010(467) [0781] without original sin and **completely** separated and
EP : 0 1 :015(468) [0783] powers and not the **complete** deprivation or loss of the
EP : 0 2 :010(471) [0789] but could not **complete** it without the grace of the Holy
EP : 0 3 :010(474) [0795] the merit of Christ **completely** from our own works and
EP : 0 4 :007(476) [0799] good works should be **completely** excluded from a
EP : 0 7 :011(483) [0811] true, essential, natural, **complete** God and man in one
EP : 0 7 :020(484) [0813] most holy obedience and **complete** merit of Christ, which
EP : 0 8 :016(489) [0821] he laid aside **completely** the form of a slave (not the
EP : 1 1 :015(496) [0835] his glory entirely and **completely**, because he out of pure
SD : 0 1 :010(510) [0863] that original sin is the **complete** lack or absence of the
SD : 0 1 :014(511) [0863] in this life, not to be **completed** until the life yonder.
SD : 0 2 :007(521) [0883] man is entirely and **completely** dead and corrupted as far
SD : 0 2 :025(526) [0891] its real beginning and **completion** in no way to the human
SD : 0 2 :035(528) [0895] pious and holy, to the **complete** exclusion of our own
SD : 0 2 :037(528) [0895] to the devil and were **completely** ignorant of God and
SD : 0 2 :076(536) [0911] man is too weak to **complete** it, the Holy Spirit comes to
SD : 0 2 :081(537) [0911] the rational soul, are **completely** destroyed and a new
SD : 0 2 :085(537) [0913] resists God entirely and is **completely** the servant of sin.
SD : 0 3 :037(546) [0929] there are excluded **completely** from the article of
SD : 0 4 :006(552) [0939] grace to arrive at a **complete** settlement, we shall state
SD : 0 4 :022(554) [0945] our works and merit **completely** from the article of
SD : 0 6 :002(564) [0963] the sun spontaneously **completes** its regular course
SD : 0 6 :006(565) [0965] angels render God a **completely** spontaneous obedience.
SD : 0 6 :007(565) [0965] life Christians are not renewed perfectly and **completely**.
SD : 0 6 :024(568) [0971] off entirely and man is **completely** renewed in the
SD : 0 6 :025(568) [0971] unhindered, perfectly, **completely**, and with sheer joy, and
SD : 0 7 :001(568) [0971] the Sacramentarians **completely** disavowed the Augsburg
SD : 0 7 :094(586) [1005] essential, natural, true, **complete** God and man in one
SD : 0 7 :108(588) [1009] in the Holy Supper **completely** lose their substance and
SD : 0 8 :006(592) [1017] a separate, distinct, and **complete** divine person and
SD : 0 8 :011(593) [1019] has assumed flesh and has become man, is not **complete**.
SD : 0 8 :026(596) [1023] that he has laid aside **completely** and entirely the form of
SD : 0 8 :026(596) [1023] has been installed in the **complete** exercise and use of the
SD : 0 8 :043(599) [1029] the human nature and **completely** excludes them from the
SD : 0 8 :062(603) [1037] nature in Christ has **completely** laid aside its natural and
SD : 0 8 :071(605) [1041] would be denied and **completely** transformed into the

Continued ▶

SD : 1 1 :032(621) [1073] it to the end and **complete** it, if we ourselves do not turn
SD : 1 1 :036(622) [1075] This would also **completely** undermine and totally destroy
SD : 1 1 :038(622) [1075] of this comfort **completely** if we could not determine
SD : 1 1 :044(623) [1077] This also **completely** refutes all false opinions and
SD : 1 1 :071(627) [1085] his promise, and trust in him **completely** and entirely.
SD : 1 1 :087(631) [1091] of God gives God his due honor fully and **completely**.

Compliant (1)
PR : PR :004(004) [0009] to make them more **compliant** in submitting to the papal

Complicated (4)
AP : 1 2 :007(183) [0255] What follows is still more **complicated**.
AP : 1 2 :178(211) [0307] our teaching with the **complicated** discussions of our
S2 : 0 4 :008(300) [0473] What a **complicated** and confused state of affairs that
S3 : 0 3 :021(306) [0485] was even more **complicated**, for nobody could know how

Compliments (1)
LC : 0 1 :264(400) [0655] us; we want the golden **compliments** of the whole world.

Comply (2), Complied (1)
AG : PR :005(025) [0039] and estates, we have **complied** with the command and can
AG : PR :012(026) [0041] of the other party do not **comply** with the procedure
AL : 2 8 :055(090) [0091] proper that the churches **comply** with such ordinances for

Component (1)
SD : 0 3 :024(543) [0923] it were a necessary or **component** part of this article, since

Compose (1), Composed (4)
PR : PR :013(007) [0013] cited written agreement **composed** with reference thereto.
PR : PR :026(014) [0025] they are settled and **composed** in timely fashion before
AP : 0 2 :027(104) [0113] that original sin is truly **composed** of the defects that I
AP : 2 0 :011(228) [0341] a complaint rather than **compose** a point-by-point
LC : 0 2 :049(417) [0691] that is, a community **composed** only of saints, or, still

Comprehend (12), Comprehended (20), Comprehending (1), Comprehends (4), Comprehensible (4), Comprehension (1), Comprehensive (5), Comprehensively (1)
PR : PR :020(010) [0017] and in the norm **comprehended** therein that according to
PR : PR :020(010) [0017] is concerned, for he cannot **comprehend** this discussion.
PR : PR :025(013) [0023] Scriptures and is **comprehended** in the three Creeds as
AG : 1 8 :001(039) [0051] make choices among the things that reason **comprehends**.
S3 : 0 3 :016(305) [0483] they are as far from **comprehending** their meaning as I
LC : SP :018(363) [0577] in Scripture is **comprehended** in short, plain, and simple
LC : 0 1 :150(385) [0623] of fatherhood, the most **comprehensive** of all relations.
LC : 0 2 :016(412) [0681] All this is **comprehended** in the word "Creator."
LC : 0 2 :067(420) [0697] No human wisdom can **comprehend** the Creed; it must be
LC : 0 3 :034(425) [0707] or petitions are **comprehended** all the needs that
LC : 0 3 :056(427) [0713] than anyone can **comprehend** — like an eternal,
LC : 0 3 :072(430) [0719] It is a brief and simple word, but very **comprehensive**.
LC : 0 3 :076(431) [0719] very briefly how **comprehensively** this petition covers all
LC : 0 4 :014(438) [0735] water, but water **comprehended** in God's Word and
LC : 0 4 :031(440) [0739] that is, the water **comprehended** in God's ordinance?
LC : 0 4 :037(441) [0741] a work but a treasure **comprehended** and offered to us in
LC : 0 4 :038(441) [0741] in which it is **comprehended** and on account of which this
LC : 0 4 :039(441) [0743] and grace that heaven and earth cannot **comprehend** it.
LC : 0 4 :074(445) [0751] by its signification, **comprehends** also the third
LC : 0 5 :009(447) [0755] It is bread and wine **comprehended** in God's Word and
LC : 0 5 :030(450) [0759] be in itself, it must be **comprehended** in the Word and
EP : 0 0 :000(463) [0775] Word of God and the **Comprehensive** Summary of our
EP : RN :000(464) [0777] The **Comprehensive** Summary, Rule, and Norm
EP : 0 1 :001(466) [0779] *to the aforesaid Standard and **Comprehensive** Exposition*
EP : 0 7 :042(486) [0817] which we cannot **comprehend** with our human sense or
EP : 0 9 :002(492) [0827] one, cannot be **comprehended** with our senses and
EP : 0 9 :004(492) [0827] blind reason cannot **comprehend** in this life but which we
SD : 0 2 :009(522) [0883] powers perceive this, **comprehend** it, understand it, or
SD : 0 2 :009(522) [0883] diligently they want to **comprehend** these spiritual things
SD : 0 2 :010(522) [0885] and the darkness has not **comprehended** it" (John 1:5).
SD : 0 2 :012(522) [0885] "The darkness **comprehended** it not" (John 1:5).
SD : 0 2 :015(523) [0887] that he might rightly **comprehend** and learn the divine
SD : 0 2 :031(527) [0893] matters which can be **comprehended** by reason we have a
SD : 0 6 :017(566) [0967] will of God as it is **comprehended** in the law and, in so
SD : 0 7 :041(576) [0985] sum and content was **comprehended** in the articles of the
SD : 0 7 :046(577) [0989] of Isaac than he could **comprehend** with his blind reason.
SD : 0 7 :084(584) [1001] "Do this," which **comprehends** the whole action or
SD : 0 7 :099(586) [1005] "1. The **comprehensible**, corporeal mode of presence, as
SD : 0 7 :101(587) [1007] touch, measure, or **comprehend** him, how much more
SD : 0 7 :101(587) [1007] cannot measure or **comprehend** him but where he has
SD : 0 7 :101(587) [1007] present to himself, measures and **comprehends** them.
SD : 0 7 :102(587) [1007] and reason, even the **comprehension** of all the angels in
SD : 0 7 :103(587) [1007] only the first, **comprehensible** mode of presence to the
SD : 0 7 :103(587) [1007] places, even in a corporeal and **comprehensible** manner.
SD : 0 7 :119(590) [1013] or circumscribed or **comprehended** by or in heaven that
SD : 0 8 :035(598) [1027] presentation it can be **comprehended** under three main
SD : 0 8 :081(607) [1045] the first, corporeal, **comprehensible** manner, but
SD : 0 9 :003(610) [1051] this article cannot be **comprehended** any more than the

Comprised (2), Comprising (1), Compromise (3), Compromised (1)
AL : 2 6 :009(065) [0071] the glamorous title of **comprising** the spiritual life and the
S2 : 0 1 :005(292) [0461] can be given up or **compromised**, even if heaven and earth
S2 : 0 2 :001(293) [0463] to be no concession or **compromise** in this article either,
S2 : 0 2 :017(296) [0467] Here, too, there can be no concession or **compromise**.
S2 : 0 2 :020(296) [0467] there may be no concession or **compromise** here either.
LC : 0 2 :007(411) [0679] Creed may be briefly **comprised** in these few words: "I
SD : 1 1 :009(617) [1065] of God, as though it **comprised** no more and that nothing

Compulsion (19)
AG : 2 4 :013(057) [0065] been held under **compulsion** for the sake of revenues and
AP : 0 4 :011(108) [0123] order, not of **compulsion**—God grants grace to those who
SC : PR :024(341) [0539] their own accord and without **compulsion** on your part.
LC : 0 1 :130(383) [0619] this light will, without **compulsion**, give all honor to his
LC : 0 1 :143(385) [0623] of them, not from **compulsion** and reluctantly but gladly
LC : 0 1 :330(410) [0677] only with blows and **compulsion**, like cattle, but in the
LC : 0 5 :045(452) [0763] sacrament, not from **compulsion**, coerced by men, but to
LC : 0 5 :051(452) [0765] merely from **compulsion** and fear of men's
LC : 0 6 :028(460) [0000] you need neither my **compulsion** nor the pope's command
LC : 0 6 :030(460) [0000] confession, not under **compulsion** but rather coming and
LC : 0 6 :031(460) [0000] For here the **compulsion** must be inverted; we must come
EP : 0 2 :008(471) [0789] always acts only under **compulsion**, even in his external
EP : 0 2 :008(471) [0789] murder, theft, and similar sins under **compulsion**.
EP : 0 4 :010(476) [0799] not by coercion or **compulsion** of the law but from a
SD : 0 2 :064(533) [0905] Spirit is no coercion or **compulsion** because the converted
SD : 0 4 :016(554) [0943] as implying **compulsion** but only as referring to the order
SD : 0 4 :017(554) [0943] reluctantly or under **compulsion** but with obedience from
SD : 0 6 :006(565) [0965] exhortation, **compulsion**, coercion, or necessity, and as
SD : 0 6 :018(567) [0969] Lord, and yet do nothing by the **compulsion** of the law.

Compute (1)
AP : 0 7 :042(176) [0243] do not correctly **compute** the time in celebrating Easter.

Comrade (1)
SD : 0 8 :084(607) [1045] No, **comrade**, wherever you put God down for me, you

Conceal (4), Concealed (5), Concealing (2)
PR : PR :019(009) [0017] and to everyone and is **concealed** from no one that some
PR : PR :019(009) [0017] teaching that might be **concealed** therein, inasmuch as we
PR : PR :024(013) [0023] concord hidden and **concealed** in darkness, away from
LC : 0 1 :261(400) [0655] right, nor perverting or **concealing** or suppressing
LC : 0 1 :287(403) [0663] members, of which we are ashamed, we carefully **conceal**.
LC : 0 1 :298(405) [0665] know how to put up a fine front to **conceal** our rascality.
EP : 0 1 :022(469) [0785] the Manichaeans to **conceal** their error and to mislead
SD : RN :016(507) [0857] may not hide and **conceal** something, we have collectively
SD : 0 5 :016(561) [0957] may see that we are **concealing** nothing in this present
SD : 0 8 :065(604) [1039] the divine majesty was **concealed** and restrained, but
SD : 0 8 :085(608) [1047] to the humanity and **concealed** it until my resurrection

Concede (17), Conceded (6), Concedes (1)
AG : 1 8 :004(039) [0051] "We **concede** that all men have a free will, for all have a
AG : 2 7 :030(075) [0079] as it is generally **conceded** that it belongs to the very
AG : 2 7 :032(076) [0079] Another canon **concedes** still more years to human
AL : 1 8 :004(039) [0051] in so many words: "We **concede** that all men have a free
AL : 2 5 :006(062) [0069] adversaries are forced to **concede** to us that our teachers
AL : 2 7 :030(075) [0079] inasmuch as it is **conceded** by all that it is contrary to the
AL : 2 8 :034(086) [0089] The canons **concede** this throughout the whole of Dist. 9.
AP : 0 4 :186(132) [0173] For we **concede** that in some places the Scripture presents
AP : 0 4 :226(138) [0183] Nevertheless, we **concede** to our opponents that the love
AP : 0 4 :366(163) [0219] We also **concede**, and have often declared, that though
AP : 0 7 :003(169) [0227] We **concede** that in this life the hypocrites and evil men
AP : 1 8 :001(225) [0335] lest too much be **conceded** to free will, as in Pelagianism,
AP : 1 8 :007(225) [0337] Although we **concede** to free will the liberty and ability to
AP : 2 4 :033(255) [0395] here, we shall gladly **concede** this, so long as he does not
S2 : 0 4 :007(299) [0473] the see of Rome were to **concede** and accept this (which is
S2 : 0 4 :015(301) [0475] they neither can nor will **concede** to us even the smallest
S3 : 1 2 :001(315) [0499] We do not **concede** to the papists that they are the
S3 : 1 5 :003(316) [0501] not know how I can change or **concede** anything in them.
S3 : 1 5 :005(316) [0501] Gospel, we, too, may **concede** to him that superiority
TR : 0 0 :077(333) [0527] This is **conceded** by the canons.
SD : 0 2 :066(534) [0907] could by no means be **conceded** without detriment to the
SD : 0 7 :103(587) [1007] are, because they **concede** only the first, comprehensible
SD : 0 8 :062(603) [1037] or of their essential properties be taught or **conceded**.
SD : 1 0 :019(614) [1059] on this: "We do not **concede** to the papists (the papist

Conceited (3)
LC : 0 1 :099(378) [0609] In the same way those **conceited** fellows should be
LC : 0 1 :240(397) [0649] in his own willful, **conceited**, arrogant way, as if it were
EP : 0 5 :008(479) [0803] thus they become either **conceited** hypocrites, like the

Conceive (2), Conceivable (1), Conceived (17)
AG : 0 2 :001(029) [0043] to the course of nature are **conceived** and born in sin.
AG : 2 7 :002(071) [0077] by means of these vows as if in a well-**conceived** prison.
AP : 0 2 :002(100) [0105] to the course of nature are **conceived** and born in sin.
AP : 0 4 :073(117) [0141] said earlier that faith is **conceived** by the Word, and we
AP : 0 4 :142(126) [0161] penitence; that is, it is **conceived** in the terrors of a
AP : 1 2 :042(187) [0263] So faith is **conceived** and confirmed through absolution,
S1 : 0 1 :000(291) [0461] in this manner: he was **conceived** by the Holy Spirit,
S3 : 0 8 :012(313) [0497] the Baptist was not **conceived** without the preceding word
SC : 0 2 :003(345) [0545] *our Lord: who was **conceived** by the Holy Spirit, born of*
LC : SP :012(363) [0577] our Lord: who was **conceived** by the Holy Spirit, born of
LC : 0 1 :073(374) [0601] have — for his protection against every **conceivable** need.
LC : 0 2 :025(413) [0683] *our Lord: who was **conceived** by the Holy Spirit, born of*
LC : 0 2 :031(414) [0687] to say, he became man, **conceived** and born without sin,
EP : 0 8 :012(488) [0821] and confess that Mary **conceived** and bore not only a
EP : 0 8 :015(488) [0821] into God when he was **conceived** by the Holy Spirit in his
SD : 0 1 :027(513) [0867] above) that all men, **conceived** and born in the natural
SD : 0 3 :056(549) [0935] though Christ had been **conceived** by the Holy Spirit
SD : 0 7 :102(587) [1007] But who can explain or even **conceive** how this occurs?
SD : 0 8 :013(593) [1019] but when he was **conceived** in his mother's womb and
SD : 0 8 :024(595) [1023] blessed virgin, did not **conceive** a mere, ordinary human

Concentrate (7), Concentrated (1)
AP : 0 4 :034(111) [0129] Our opponents **concentrate** on the commandments of the
AP : 1 2 :098(197) [0281] We have therefore **concentrated** on the explanation of
LC : 0 1 :089(377) [0605] when we can **concentrate** upon such matters and deal
LC : 0 1 :318(408) [0673] Just **concentrate** upon them and test yourself thoroughly,
LC : 0 2 :026(414) [0685] We shall **concentrate** on these words, "in Jesus Christ,
LC : 0 2 :035(415) [0687] Therefore, we must **concentrate** on the term "Holy
LC : 0 5 :063(454) [0767] contend with, that we **concentrate** more upon ourselves
LC : 0 6 :022(459) [0000] is what you should **concentrate** on, magnifying and

Concept (1)
AP : 2 4 :016(252) [0389] various members of the **concept** "sacrifice," as our

Conception (6)
SD : 0 1 :007(510) [0861] through our carnal **conception** and birth out of sinful seed
SD : 0 1 :028(513) [0867] first moment of our **conception** the seed from which man
SD : 0 2 :019(524) [0889] he cannot have a **conception** of good or evil or freely
SD : 0 7 :105(588) [1009] reject the Capernaitic **conception** of a gross, carnal
SD : 0 8 :026(596) [1023] immediately at his **conception** even in his mother's
SD : 0 8 :082(607) [1045] personally there, as his **conception** in his mother's womb

Concern (25), Concerned (45), Concerning (216), Concerns (7)

PR : PR :013(007) [0013] their considered judgment **concerning** every part of it.
PR : PR :017(008) [0015] further specifications **concerning** our confession if it
PR : PR :019(009) [0017] discussions, is **concerned**, it is apparent to us and to
PR : PR :019(009) [0017] to hide their error **concerning** the Holy Supper as well as
PR : PR :020(010) [0017] the common layman is **concerned**, for he cannot
PR : PR :022(011) [0019] especially in the article **concerning** the Lord's Supper,
AG : PR :001(024) [0039] desire to deliberate **concerning** matters pertaining to the
AG : PR :002(025) [0039] about the dissension **concerning** our holy faith and the
AG : PR :014(026) [0041] religion who is **concerned** about these questions will be
AG : PR :018(026) [0041] the proposal **concerning** a general council and
AG : PR :022(027) [0043] and appeals **concerning** these most weighty matters, and
AG : 15 :004(037) [0049] and other traditions **concerning** distinction of foods,
AG : 20 :002(041) [0053] and instructions **concerning** true Christian estates and
AG : 20 :003(041) [0053] most part sermons were **concerned** with childish and
AG : 20 :025(044) [0057] not believe this article **concerning** the forgiveness of sin,
AG : 20 :035(046) [0057] this teaching **concerning** faith is not to be accused of
AG : 00 :002(048) [0059] and dissension are **concerned** chiefly with various
AG : 00 :000(048) [0059] taught in our churches **concerning** articles of faith that is
AG : 22 :002(049) [0059] **Concerning** the chalice Christ here commands with clear
AG : 23 :001(051) [0061] throughout the world **concerning** the flagrant immorality
AG : 23 :012(053) [0063] The decree **concerning** celibacy was at once enforced
AG : 01 :007(056) [0065] with great diligence **concerning** the holy sacrament, why
AG : 01 :007(056) [0065] about other false teachings **concerning** the sacrament.
AG : 24 :012(057) [0065] which should properly **concern** every Christian (namely,
AG : 25 :002(061) [0069] are carefully instructed **concerning** the consolation of the
AG : 25 :005(062) [0069] mentioned a word **concerning** these necessary matters but
AG : 25 :007(062) [0069] **Concerning** confession we teach that no one should be
AG : 26 :004(064) [0071] Christ and the teaching **concerning** faith are thereby
AG : 26 :018(066) [0073] have not taught **concerning** these matters out of malice or
AG : 26 :031(068) [0075] have always taught **concerning** the holy cross that
AG : 27 :001(071) [0075] have hitherto been held **concerning** them, what kind of
AG : 27 :036(076) [0081] God's command **concerning** marriage frees and releases
AG : 27 :060(080) [0083] the error of the monks **concerning** perfection and
AG : 28 :011(082) [0085] Temporal authority is **concerned** with matters altogether
AG : 28 :013(083) [0085] to the temporal power laws **concerning** worldly matters.
AG : 28 :030(085) [0087] or establish regulations **concerning** foods, holy days, and
AG : 28 :034(086) [0087] **Concerning** this question our teachers assert that bishops
AG : 28 :037(086) [0089] while teaching **concerning** faith and righteousness of faith
AG : 28 :047(088) [0089] Christ himself says **concerning** those who urge human
AL : 01 :001(027) [0043] the Council of Nicaea **concerning** the unity of the divine
AL : 01 :001(027) [0043] the divine essence and **concerning** the three persons is
AL : 07 :002(032) [0047] it is enough to agree **concerning** the teaching of the
AL : 18 :008(040) [0053] of God in so far as the substance of the acts is **concerned**.
AL : 20 :003(041) [0053] **Concerning** such things preachers used to teach little.
AL : 20 :008(042) [0053] been profound silence **concerning** the righteousness of
AL : 20 :008(042) [0053] have instructed our churches **concerning** faith as follows:
AL : 20 :011(042) [0055] This teaching **concerning** faith is everywhere treated in
AL : 20 :018(043) [0055] have bad judgment **concerning** this teaching.
AL : 20 :022(044) [0055] to restore this teaching **concerning** faith in Christ in order
AL : 20 :026(045) [0057] his readers in this way **concerning** the word "faith" when
AL : 00 :002(047) [0059] The whole dissension is **concerned** with a certain few
AL : 23 :001(051) [0061] common complaint **concerning** priests who have not been
AL : 24 :007(056) [0065] are also admonished **concerning** the value and use of the
AL : 24 :013(057) [0065] were admonished **concerning** this sin, private Masses
AL : 24 :017(057) [0067] dissensions have arisen **concerning** the Mass, concerning
AL : 24 :017(057) [0067] arisen concerning the Mass, **concerning** the sacrament.
AL : 24 :024(058) [0067] **Concerning** these opinions our teachers have warned that
AL : 24 :039(060) [0069] Paul also commands **concerning** Communion that one
AL : 25 :002(061) [0069] very diligently taught **concerning** faith in connection with
AL : 25 :007(062) [0069] **Concerning** confession they teach that an enumeration of
AL : 26 :003(064) [0071] From this opinion **concerning** traditions much harm has
AL : 26 :004(064) [0071] obscured the doctrine **concerning** grace and the
AL : 26 :015(066) [0073] profitable teachings **concerning** faith, the cross, hope, the
AL : 26 :020(067) [0073] church on the teaching **concerning** grace and the
AL : 26 :031(068) [0075] have always taught **concerning** the cross that Christians
AL : 27 :001(070) [0075] is taught among us **concerning** monastic vows will be
AL : 27 :018(073) [0077] first place, we teach **concerning** those who contract
AL : 27 :027(075) [0079] while they remain silent **concerning** the nature of a vow,
AL : 27 :036(076) [0081] that God's command **concerning** marriage frees many
AL : 27 :059(080) [0083] **Concerning** such things it was necessary to admonish
AL : 27 :060(080) [0083] the error of the monks **concerning** perfection and testified
AL : 28 :011(082) [0085] For civil government is **concerned** with other things than
AL : 28 :013(083) [0085] with judgments **concerning** any civil ordinances or
AL : 28 :030(085) [0087] church and make laws **concerning** foods, holy days,
AL : 28 :034(086) [0087] **Concerning** this question our teachers assert, as has been
AL : 28 :037(086) [0089] while the teaching **concerning** faith and the righteousness
AL : 28 :047(088) [0089] In Matt. 15 Christ says **concerning** those who require
AL : 28 :061(091) [0093] monstrous discussions **concerning** the mutation of the
AL : 28 :061(091) [0093] mutation of the law, **concerning** ceremonies of the new
AL : 28 :061(091) [0093] of the new law, **concerning** the change of the Sabbath, all
AP : 02 :035(105) [0115] **Concerning** this material element, he has also said that
AP : 04 :207(135) [0177] "I did not command **concerning** burnt offerings."
AP : 04 :282(149) [0201] and then adds **concerning** the outward cleanness, "Give
AP : 04 :309(155) [0207] made him waver **concerning** the promise of God, but he
AP : 07 :012(170) [0231] true church as far as outward ceremonies are **concerned**.
AP : 07 :030(173) [0237] it is enough to agree **concerning** the teaching of the
AP : 12 :106(197) [0283] the fear of God or faith or his **concern** for God's Word.
AP : 21 :043(235) [0357] the state of the church does not **concern** them very much.
AP : 24 :028(254) [0393] or command them **concerning** burnt offerings and
AP : 24 :028(254) [0393] the fathers **concerning** burnt offerings and sacrifices, but
S1 : PR :012(290) [0459] Besides such necessary **concerns** of the church, there are
S1 : PR :013(291) [0459] reform the regulations **concerning** fasts, vestments,
S2 : 02 :010(294) [0465] This article **concerning** the Mass will be the decisive issue
S2 : 02 :021(296) [0469] it is contrary to the first article, **concerning** redemption.
S2 : 03 :002(298) [0471] fundamental article **concerning** redemption in Jesus
S2 : 04 :003(298) [0473] article which is **concerned** with redemption in Jesus
S2 : 04 :014(301) [0475] law and is a teaching **concerning** secular transactions and
S2 : 04 :014(301) [0475] instructions are given **concerning** the ceremonies of
S3 : 00 :000(302) [0477] things; they are not **concerned** about matters of
S3 : 01 :003(302) [0477] theologians taught **concerning** this article is therefore
S3 : 01 :011(303) [0479] and ignorance **concerning** sin and concerning Christ, our
S3 : 01 :011(303) [0479] concerning sin and **concerning** Christ, our Saviour.
S3 : 02 :003(303) [0479] as was just said above **concerning** the scholastic
S3 : 03 :010(305) [0481] have the right teaching **concerning** original sin but
S3 : 08 :003(312) [0495] In these matters, which **concern** the external, spoken
S3 : 08 :008(313) [0495] come, and his faith **concerning** the coming Messiah did
S3 : 09 :000(314) [0497] penalty which does not **concern** us ministers of the
S3 : 10 :001(314) [0497] true bishops and were **concerned** about the church and
S3 : 10 :003(314) [0497] St. Jerome, too, wrote **concerning** the church in
S3 : 15 :005(316) [0501] However, **concerning** the pope I hold that, if he would
TR : 00 :006(320) [0505] authority to make laws **concerning** worship, concerning
TR : 00 :006(320) [0505] concerning worship, **concerning** changes in the
TR : 00 :006(320) [0505] changes in the sacraments, and **concerning** doctrine.
TR : 00 :008(321) [0505] in a similar dispute **concerning** the kingdom, Christ put a
TR : 00 :045(328) [0517] obscured the teaching **concerning** sin and have invented a
TR : 00 :045(328) [0517] invented a tradition **concerning** the enumeration of sins
TR : 00 :048(328) [0519] have utterly extinguished the teaching **concerning** faith.
TR : 00 :078(333) [0527] certain unjust laws **concerning** marriage and apply them
TR : 00 :078(333) [0527] For the traditions **concerning** spiritual relationship are
TR : 00 :078(333) [0527] The law **concerning** the celibacy of priests is likewise
TR : 00 :082(334) [0529] approve the article **concerning** the primacy of the pope
TR : 00 :082(334) [0529] and the article **concerning** the papacy presented to the
TR : 00 :082(000) [0529] Formula of Concord **concerning** the Sacrament, made at
TR : 00 :082(000) [0529] preceptor, and the tract **concerning** the Papacy and the
SC : PR :021(340) [0537] no law is to be made **concerning** it, and no time or place
SC : 01 :021(344) [0543] What does God declare **concerning** all these
LC : SP :019(363) [0579] the Christian's conversation, conduct and **concern**.
LC : 01 :022(367) [0585] It **concerns** only that conscience which seeks help,
LC : 01 :080(375) [0603] outward observance is **concerned**, the commandment was
LC : 01 :082(376) [0603] sense, this commandment does not **concern** us Christians.
LC : 01 :097(378) [0609] to and admonished but we listen without serious **concern**.
LC : 01 :098(378) [0609] then, that you must be **concerned** not only about hearing
LC : 01 :109(380) [0611] this commandment requires **concerning** honor to parents.
LC : 01 :120(382) [0615] has commanded this; **concerning** the other things he has
LC : 01 :146(385) [0623] blessed or holy life, as far as your works are **concerned**?
LC : 01 :170(388) [0629] we please, as if it were no **concern** of ours what they learn
LC : 01 :185(390) [0633] to get the quarrel settled for the safety of all **concerned**.
LC : 01 :192(391) [0635] as far as you were **concerned** you have nevertheless
LC : 01 :204(392) [0639] wink at it as if it were no **concern** of yours, you are just
LC : 01 :206(393) [0639] this commandment is **concerned** specifically with the
LC : 01 :208(393) [0639] institution and an object of God's serious **concern**.
LC : 01 :250(398) [0651] Enough has been said **concerning** the nature of stealing.
LC : 01 :258(399) [0653] This problem appears to **concern** us only a little at
LC : 01 :263(400) [0655] The third aspect of this commandment **concerns** us all.
LC : 01 :284(403) [0661] himself, and you may testify publicly **concerning** him.
LC : 01 :286(403) [0663] all the commandments **concerning** our neighbor,
LC : 01 :300(405) [0667] they are not much **concerned** about questions of honor
LC : 01 :319(408) [0673] Let this suffice **concerning** the first part, both for
LC : 01 :327(409) [0675] commandments which **concern** our neighbor, everything
LC : 02 :027(414) [0685] in the Second Article, **concerning** Jesus Christ?" answer
LC : 02 :046(416) [0689] Let this suffice **concerning** the substance of this article.
LC : 02 :054(417) [0693] that is to be preached **concerning** the sacraments and, in
LC : 02 :070(420) [0697] present this is enough **concerning** the Creed to lay a
LC : 03 :022(423) [0703] see how sincerely he is **concerned** over our needs, and we
LC : 03 :027(424) [0705] which ought to be the **concern** of both ourselves and
LC : 03 :068(429) [0717] petitions interests which **concern** God himself have been
LC : 03 :068(429) [0717] What we pray for **concerns** only ourselves when we ask
LC : 03 :107(434) [0729] Others, who are **concerned** with spiritual matters (that is,
LC : 04 :046(442) [0743] Let this suffice **concerning** the nature, benefits, and use of
LC : 04 :052(443) [0745] we are not primarily **concerned** whether the baptized
LC : 05 :033(450) [0761] as we said above **concerning** Baptism and in many other
LC : 06 :001(457) [0000] **Concerning** confession, we have always taught that it
LC : 06 :016(459) [0000] and we were only **concerned** whether we had confessed
EP : RN :005(465) [0777] Since these matters also **concern** the laity and the
EP : 01 :005(466) [0781] with angels that he is **concerned** but with the descendants
EP : 01 :023(469) [0785] and *accidens* are **concerned**, they are not biblical terms
EP : 02 :001(470) [0787] *The Pure Teaching **concerning** this Article on the Basis*
EP : 02 :002(470) [0787] them" when he is examined **concerning** spiritual things.
EP : 03 :010(474) [0795] the pure doctrine **concerning** the righteousness of faith
EP : 04 :000(475) [0797] Chief Issue in the Controversy **Concerning** Good Works
EP : 04 :001(475) [0797] in some churches **concerning** the doctrine of good works:
EP : 04 :003(476) [0797] certain theologians **concerning** the use of the words
EP : 04 :018(477) [0801] an Epicurean dream **concerning** faith can damn people as
EP : 06 :001(480) [0805] It is **concerning** the third function of the law that a
EP : 06 :005(480) [0807] 4. **Concerning** the distinction between works of the law
EP : 06 :007(481) [0807] as far as obedience is **concerned**, rests exclusively with
EP : 07 :001(481) [0809] as far as necessary **concerning** this controversy also.
EP : 07 :008(482) [0811] 3. **Concerning** the consecration we believe, teach, and
EP : 07 :041(486) [0817] and abhorrent way **concerning** the supernatural and
EP : 08 :001(486) [0817] other theologians also) **concerning** the person of Christ,
EP : 08 :003(487) [0819] *of the Christian Church **concerning** the Person of Christ*
EP : 08 :018(490) [0823] *False Doctrine **concerning** the Person of Christ*
EP : 08 :031(491) [0825] nature in fact, as though it did not **concern** him at all.
EP : 08 :032(491) [0825] presence does not at all **concern** his human nature; and
EP : 09 :001(492) [0827] of the Augsburg Confession **concerning** this article also.
EP : 09 :002(492) [0827] engage in disputations **concerning** this article, but believe
EP : 10 :001(492) [0829] Augsburg Confession **concerning** those ceremonies or
EP : 10 :007(494) [0831] *False Doctrine **concerning** this Article*
EP : 11 :001(494) [0831] of the Augsburg Confession **concerning** this article.
EP : 11 :001(494) [0831] offensive dissension **concerning** it might be introduced
EP : 11 :001(494) [0831] *Pure and True Doctrine **concerning** this Article*
EP : 11 :005(495) [0833] of God, however, is **concerned** only with the pious
EP : 11 :011(495) [0835] to the person who **concerns** himself with the revealed will
EP : 11 :013(496) [0835] 12. The Christian is to **concern** himself with the doctrine
EP : 11 :015(497) [0837] *False Doctrine **concerning** this Article*
EP : 12 :021(499) [0841] majesty, and glory are **concerned**, and that now both
SD : 00 :000(501) [0845] Augsburg Confession **Concerning** Which There Has Been
SD : PR :001(501) [0847] Almighty, the teaching **concerning** the chief articles of
SD : PR :003(502) [0847] Christian churches **concerning** the chief articles, especially
SD : PR :010(503) [0849] who are really **concerned** about the truth may know how
SD : RN :008(505) [0853] important matters also **concern** ordinary people and
SD : RN :015(507) [0857] controversy (dissension **concerning** articles of the Creed
SD : RN :016(507) [0857] mutual agreement **concerning** the chief and most
SD : 01 :003(509) [0859] This controversy **concerning** original sin is not a useless
SD : 01 :004(509) [0861] and correct doctrine **concerning** original sin, we shall use

Continued ▶

SD : 01 :010(510) [0863] and ineptitude as far as the things of God are **concerned**.
SD : 01 :024(512) [0865] give our exposition **concerning** the external, temporal,
SD : 01 :046(516) [0873] Fourthly, **concerning** the doctrine of the resurrection
SD : 01 :049(517) [0875] far as the chief points in this controversy are **concerned**.
SD : 01 :054(517) [0877] **Concerning** the use of the Latin terms *substantia* and
SD : 02 :001(519) [0881] has been a controversy **concerning** free will, not only
SD : 02 :002(520) [0881] the question is not **concerning** the state of man's will
SD : 02 :005(521) [0881] that in divine things, **concerning** our conversion and
SD : 02 :007(521) [0883] dead and corrupted as far as anything good is **concerned**.
SD : 02 :020(525) [0889] things, however, which **concern** the salvation of his soul,
SD : 02 :027(526) [0891] it forth in his treatise ***Concerning** Predestination,* "The
SD : 02 :031(527) [0893] teaches as follows **concerning** free will: "We also declare
SD : 02 :033(527) [0893] the following errors **concerning** free will: "That man has a
SD : 02 :043(529) [0897] *Great Confession **Concerning** the Holy Supper* in which
SD : 02 :044(529) [0897] *Will,* in which he writes **concerning** the enslaved will of
SD : 02 :050(530) [0901] the wonderful counsel **concerning** our redemption,
SD : 02 :051(531) [0901] calls out from heaven **concerning** his beloved Son and
SD : 02 :051(531) [0901] his beloved Son and **concerning** all who in his name
SD : 02 :071(535) [0909] the question is asked **concerning** the efficient cause (that
SD : 03 :001(539) [0917] Augsburg Confession **concerns** the righteousness of
SD : 03 :005(540) [0917] other controversies **concerning** this article of justification
SD : 03 :009(540) [0919] confession as follows: **Concerning** the righteousness of
SD : 03 :033(545) [0927] St. Paul's statement **concerning** Abraham is apposite.
SD : 03 :054(548) [0933] correctly the discussion **concerning** the indwelling of
SD : 04 :001(551) [0939] A controversy **concerning** good works has likewise arisen
SD : 04 :007(552) [0939] disagreement among us **concerning** the following points:
SD : 04 :019(554) [0945] **Concerning** this unwilling and recalcitrant flesh, Paul
SD : 04 :037(557) [0949] In the fourth place, **concerning** the proposition that good
SD : 04 :038(557) [0951] to believers as far as their salvation is **concerned**.
SD : 06 :001(564) [0963] a few theologians **concerning** this third and last function
SD : 06 :008(565) [0965] **Concerning** this the apostle writes, "I know that nothing
SD : 06 :010(565) [0965] as far as the good works of believers are **concerned**.
SD : 06 :016(566) [0967] the individuals who are **concerned** about living according
SD : 06 :019(567) [0969] still adheres to them is **concerned**, he must be coerced not
SD : 07 :012(571) [0977] their own confession **concerning** this article adopted the
SD : 07 :013(571) [0977] him from the cities, **concerning** the holy sacrament of the
SD : 07 :040(576) [0985] in his *Last Confession **Concerning** the Communion* Dr.
SD : 07 :043(576) [0987] Saviour Jesus Christ **concerning** whom, as our unique
SD : 07 :044(577) [0987] is given for you," and **concerning** the cup or the wine,
SD : 07 :046(577) [0987] eminent article of faith **concerning** the promised seed,
SD : 07 :046(577) [0989] fulfilling the promises **concerning** the seed of Isaac than
SD : 07 :072(582) [0997] Let this suffice **concerning** the true presence and the
SD : 07 :073(583) [0999] Augsburg Confession **concerning** the consecration and
SD : 07 :085(584) [1001] true Christian doctrine **concerning** the Holy Supper and
SD : 07 :091(585) [1003] of the Sacramentarians **concerning** the essential and
SD : 07 :091(585) [1003] of the human body, **concerning** the ascension of Christ,
SD : 07 :091(585) [1003] ascension of Christ, **concerning** his withdrawal from this
SD : 07 :091(585) [1005] and *Small Confessions **concerning** the Holy Supper,* and
SD : 07 :099(586) [1005] the enthusiasts adduce **concerning** Christ's leaving the
SD : 07 :106(588) [1009] our faith in this article **concerning** the true presence of the
SD : 07 :106(588) [1009] and fortify our faith in all tensions **concerning** this article.
SD : 07 :111(589) [1011] and explanation **concerning** the true presence of the body
SD : 07 :113(589) [1011] sense, as they read, **concerning** the true essential presence
SD : 08 :001(591) [1015] Augsburg Confession **concerning** the person of Christ.
SD : 08 :003(592) [1017] and polemical writings **concerning** the Holy Supper, to
SD : 08 :021(595) [1021] his *Great Confession **concerning** the Holy Supper* against
SD : 08 :038(598) [1027] his *Great Confession **concerning** the Holy Supper* has
SD : 08 :043(599) [1029] applies all the texts **concerning** the passion only to the
SD : 08 :044(599) [1029] states in his treatise ***Concerning** the Councils and the*
SD : 08 :046(600) [1031] of Christ's office is **concerned**, the person does not act *in,*
SD : 08 :050(600) [1031] the person of Christ is **concerned**, some wanted to
SD : 08 :059(602) [1035] orthodox church **concerning** this article are recorded
SD : 08 :081(607) [1045] the *Great Confession **concerning** the Holy Supper* he
SD : 08 :085(608) [1045] In his tract ***Concerning** the Last Words of David,* which
SD : 08 :086(608) [1047] and in his *Great Confession **concerning** the Holy Supper.*
SD : 09 :003(610) [1051] We are not to **concern** ourselves with exalted and acute
SD : 10 :001(610) [1053] Augsburg Confession **concerning** ceremonies and church
SD : 10 :003(611) [1053] as things indifferent are **concerned**, in a period of
SD : 10 :013(613) [1057] far as foods, times, and days were **concerned** (Rom 14:6).
SD : 10 :015(613) [1057] At the same time this **concerns** the article of Christian
SD : 10 :018(614) [1059] Augsburg Confession **concerning** such matters of
SD : 10 :019(614) [1059] true bishops and were **concerned** about the church and
SD : 10 :031(616) [1063] and are also agreed **concerning** the right use of the holy
SD : 11 :001(616) [1063] Augsburg Confession **concerning** the eternal election of
SD : 11 :010(618) [1067] sacraments, and do not **concern** myself with repentance,
SD : 11 :013(618) [1067] not to speculate **concerning** the absolute, secret, hidden,
SD : 11 :014(619) [1069] will, and ordinance **concerning** our redemption, call,
SD : 11 :033(621) [1073] We should **concern** ourselves with this revealed will of
SD : 11 :033(621) [1073] **Concern** yourself first with Christ and his Gospel so that
SD : 11 :045(624) [1079] that God was so deeply **concerned** about every individual
SD : 11 :053(625) [1081] much greater delight in **concerning** ourselves with matters
SD : 11 :055(625) [1081] not revealed anything **concerning** it in the Word, still less
SD : 11 :070(627) [1085] himself with thoughts **concerning** the secret counsel of
SD : 11 :082(630) [1091] **Concerning** "the vessels of mercy" he says specifically that
SD : 11 :091(631) [1093] sets forth this teaching **concerning** God's gracious election
SD : 11 :094(632) [1095] This will suffice **concerning** the controverted articles
SD : 12 :001(632) [1095] sects and factions are **concerned** which never accepted the
SD : 12 :006(633) [1097] As far as our ministry is **concerned**, we do not propose to

Concession (5), Concessions (4)
AL : 27 :032(076) [0079] making a greater **concession** to human weakness, adds a
S2 : 02 :001(293) [0463] There is to be no **concession** or compromise in this article
S2 : 02 :010(294) [0465] the papists to make **concessions** to us in all other articles,
S2 : 02 :017(296) [0467] Here, too, there can be no **concession** or compromise.
S2 : 02 :020(296) [0467] there may be no **concession** or compromise here either.
S3 : 15 :003(316) [0501] wishes to make some **concessions**, let him do so at the
S3 : 15 :005(316) [0501] right, making this **concession** for the sake of peace and
EP : 10 :006(493) [0831] things we have no **concessions** to make, but we should
EP : 10 :011(494) [0831] one may make **concessions** to or come to an

Conciliar (1)
AP : 12 :167(208) [0303] patristic discussions and **conciliar** decisions about

Conclude (19), Concluded (2), Concludes (4), Concluding (1)
AG : 27 :054(079) [0083] that some should **conclude** that it is not sinful to take
AP : 04 :087(120) [0147] saw fit to grant us, we **conclude** that a man is not justified
AP : 04 :177(131) [0171] We must **conclude**, therefore, that being reconciled by
AP : 04 :226(138) [0183] How will they **conclude** from this that love justifies?
AP : 04 :285(150) [0201] He **concludes** that not works but faith accepts the
AP : 04 :386(166) [0225] Therefore we **conclude** that we are justified before God,
AP : 07 :032(174) [0239] the uninitiated have **concluded** that there can be no
AP : 12 :073(192) [0273] For thus the apostle **concludes**, that a man is justified
AP : 12 :122(200) [0289] and the canons and **conclude** that the abolition of
AP : 12 :123(201) [0289] hear this they will **conclude** that we deny all penitence.
AP : 12 :147(205) [0297] From this we may safely **conclude** that canonical
AP : 24 :052(259) [0403] From this they **conclude** that since the New Testament
AP : 27 :020(272) [0425] will easily be able to **conclude** that we do not merit the
AP : 27 :042(276) [0435] But it would be silly to **conclude** from this that it is a
AP : 28 :001(281) [0443] estate, and they **conclude** with the summary: "Everything
LC : 01 :326(409) [0675] you must let these **concluding** words run through all the
LC : 03 :012(422) [0701] we ought to **conclude** that we should by no means despise
LC : 03 :121(436) [0731] add "yes" and **conclude** with certainty that God hears
LC : 04 :010(437) [0735] fact everyone can easily **conclude** that it is of much
LC : 04 :058(444) [0747] Is it correct to **conclude** that when anybody does not do
LC : 04 :059(444) [0747] the argument and **conclude**, Precisely because Baptism
LC : 04 :061(444) [0747] nor obedience, they **conclude** that these ordinances are in
LC : 05 :076(455) [0771] Yes, and St. Paul **concludes** in Rom. 7:18, "For I know
SD : 01 :041(515) [0871] should be compelled to **conclude**: Either that, since God
SD : 07 :046(577) [0989] of truthfulness and **concluded** and believed most certainly
SD : 07 :055(579) [0991] benefits of Christ, as the Apology argues and **concludes**.

Conclusion (20), Conclusions (8)
PR : PR :011(006) [0011] and brought to a **conclusion** without violation of divine
PR : PR :025(013) [0023] In **conclusion**, we repeat once again that we are not
AG : 27 :051(079) [0083] draw many harmful **conclusions** from such false
AG : 00 :000(094) [0095] [**Conclusion**]
AL : 27 :051(079) [0083] draw many pernicious **conclusions** from such false
AL : 00 :000(094) [0095] [**Conclusion**]
AP : 04 :087(119) [0147] he advances this **conclusion**, embodying the basic issue
AP : 04 :253(143) [0193] warrant any of these **conclusions**: that works merit the
AP : 04 :283(149) [0201] Christ adds this **conclusion** to both clauses: all things will
AP : 04 :358(162) [0219] Who cannot see that this is a fallacious **conclusion**?
AP : 04 :360(162) [0219] the following absurd **conclusion** when they hear this one
SC : 01 :021(344) [0543] [**Conclusion**]
SC : 03 :020(348) [0549] [**Conclusion**]
LC : 01 :219(394) [0643] Let it be said in **conclusion** that this commandment
LC : 01 :310(407) [0669] **Conclusion** of the Ten Commandments
LC : 01 :319(408) [0673] In **conclusion**, however, we must repeat the text which we
LC : 04 :058(444) [0747] persons draw the **conclusion** that where there is no true
LC : 04 :060(444) [0747] Let the **conclusion** therefore be that Baptism always
LC : 05 :016(448) [0757] Our **conclusion** is: Even though a knave should receive or
LC : 05 :039(451) [0761] In **conclusion**, now that we have the right interpretation
LC : 06 :029(460) [0000] we must come to the **conclusion** that you are no Christian
EP : 12 :030(500) [0843] implications and **conclusions**, we reject and condemn as
SD : 01 :041(515) [0871] Both **conclusions** are contrary to the first article of our
SD : 01 :048(516) [0875] all its implications and **conclusions**, as when it is said that
SD : 07 :024(573) [0979] Our **conclusion** is that even though a rascal receives or
SD : 11 :049(624) [1079] certain and indubitable **conclusion** that neither
SD : 11 :052(625) [1081] and draw our own **conclusions** and brood, but we are to
SD : 11 :055(625) [1081] own deductions, draw **conclusions**, or brood over it, but

Conclusively (2)
SD : RN :009(505) [0853] of God's Word and **conclusively** established against the
SD : 08 :082(607) [1045] his conception in his mother's womb proves **conclusively**.

Concord (26)
PR : PR :000(001) [0004] Preface to the Book of **Concord**
PR : PR :000(003) [0005] Preface to the Christian Book of **Concord**
PR : PR :005(004) [0009] in agreeable Christian **concord** and that they might have
PR : PR :013(007) [0013] for the promotion of **concord** among Christian teachers.
PR : PR :014(007) [0013] Formula of Christian **Concord**, in the form that follows
PR : PR :016(008) [0013] subscribed this Book of **Concord** as the correct Christian
PR : PR :017(008) [0015] desired end of Christian **concord**, and some even tried to
PR : PR :017(008) [0015] ourselves in this Book of **Concord** and repetition of our
PR : PR :018(009) [0015] declaration and Book of **Concord** that follows hereunder,
PR : PR :019(010) [0017] with the norm incorporated in the [Formula of] **Concord**.
PR : PR :020(010) [0017] assert in the Formula of **Concord** itself and in the norm
PR : PR :024(013) [0023] work of Christian **concord** and have a particular longing
PR : PR :024(013) [0023] necessary effort toward **concord** hidden and concealed in
PR : PR :024(013) [0023] Christian, God-pleasing **concord** will, together with us,
PR : PR :025(014) [0023] in genuine peace and **concord** with our fellow-members,
PR : PR :026(014) [0025] of this effort at **concord** in our lands, according to our
AG : PR :023(027) [0043] brought to Christian **concord** in accordance with Your
AL : 28 :071(093) [0093] that the bishops restore **concord** at the expense of their
S3 : 15 :005(317) [0501] the Apology, and the **Concord** in the matter of the
TR : 00 :082(000) [0529] also read the Formula of **Concord** concerning the
LC : 03 :073(430) [0719] body, but also peace and **concord** in our daily business
LC : 03 :077(431) [0721] at large to live together in obedience, peace, and **concord**.
EP : 00 :000(463) [0775] Formula of **Concord**, Epitome
EP : 11 :022(497) [0837] abide in this Christian and God-pleasing **concord**.
SD : RN :001(503) [0849] for basic and permanent **concord** within the church is a
SD : RN :014(506) [0855] and God-pleasing **concord** within the church, it is

Concordant (2), Concordantly (1)
PR : PR :016(008) [0015] is the unanimous and **concordant** confession not only of a
PR : PR :019(009) [0017] or to confirm as **concordant** with Evangelical doctrine
PR : PR :022(012) [0019] institution and as we **concordantly** teach about it on the

Concordia (1)
PR : PR :000(001) [0004] ***Concordia***

Concreated (4)
EP : 01 :012(467) [0781] desires are not sin but **concreated** and essential properties
SD : 01 :010(510) [0863] absence of the original **concreated** righteousness of
SD : 01 :018(511) [0865] desires are not sin but **concreated** and essential attributes
SD : 01 :027(513) [0867] verdict man lost the **concreated** righteousness as a

Concrete (2)
SD : 0 1 :010(510) [0863] or the faculty and the **concrete** acts, to begin and to effect
SD : 0 1 :052(517) [0875] sense to include the **concrete** person or subject (that is,

Concupiscence (17), Concupiscent (1)
AL : 0 2 :001(029) [0043] of God, are without trust in God, and are **concupiscent**.
AP : 0 2 :003(101) [0105] born in this way has **concupiscence** and cannot produce
AP : 0 2 :003(101) [0105] we use the term "**concupiscence**," we do not mean only its
AP : 0 2 :004(101) [0105] opponents admit that **concupiscence** is the so-called
AP : 0 2 :006(101) [0107] we made mention of **concupiscence**; with the best of
AP : 0 2 :007(101) [0107] mentioned not only **concupiscence** but also the absence
AP : 0 2 :014(102) [0109] we also mentioned **concupiscence** and denied to man's
AP : 0 2 :024(103) [0111] Augustine's definition that original sin is **concupiscence**.
AP : 0 2 :024(103) [0111] that when righteousness is lost, **concupiscence** follows.
AP : 0 2 :025(103) [0111] **Concupiscence** is not merely a corruption of the physical
AP : 0 2 :025(103) [0111] attribute to man a **concupiscence** that has not been
AP : 0 2 :026(103) [0111] or love God; and **concupiscence**, which pursues carnal
AP : 0 2 :027(104) [0113] the defects that I have listed, as well as of **concupiscence**.
AP : 0 2 :035(105) [0115] sin, even though **concupiscence** remains — or, as they call
AP : 0 2 :038(105) [0115] they maintain that **concupiscence** is a penalty and not a
AP : 0 2 :038(105) [0115] that Augustine defines original sin as **concupiscence**.
AP : 0 2 :047(106) [0119] The deficiency and **concupiscence** are sin as well as
AP : 1 8 :005(225) [0335] great is the power of **concupiscence** that men obey their

Concur (1)
SD : 0 2 :090(539) [0915] and heard, the Holy Spirit, and man's will) **concur**.

Condemn (127), Condemned (74), Condemning (11), Condemns (29)
PR : PR :019(009) [0017] to have rejected or **condemned** any other profitable
PR : PR :020(010) [0017] of Christ and decry and **condemn** them as impiety, as if
PR : PR :022(011) [0019] we mean specifically to **condemn** only false and seductive
AG : 0 2 :002(029) [0043] sin is truly sin and **condemns** to the eternal wrath of God
AG : 0 5 :004(031) [0045] **Condemned** are the Anabaptists and others who teach
AG : 0 8 :003(033) [0047] and all others who hold contrary views are **condemned**.
AG : 1 2 :009(035) [0049] **Condemned** on the other hand are the Novatians who
AG : 1 6 :003(037) [0051] **Condemned** here are the Anabaptists who teach that none
AG : 1 6 :004(037) [0051] Also **condemned** are those who teach that Christian
AG : 1 7 :003(038) [0051] and the elect but to **condemn** ungodly men and the devil
AG : 1 7 :004(038) [0051] that the devil and **condemned** men will not suffer eternal
AG : 2 4 :010(057) [0065] Such abuses were often **condemned** by learned and
AG : 2 4 :021(058) [0067] abominable error was **condemned** according to which it
AG : 2 4 :025(059) [0067] will understand that this error is not unjustly **condemned**.
AG : 2 4 :040(061) [0069] not in fairness be **condemned** as heretical or unchristian.
AG : 2 8 :003(081) [0085] has long since been **condemned** by learned and devout
AG : 2 8 :021(084) [0087] sins, judge doctrine and **condemn** doctrine that is
AL : 0 1 :005(028) [0043] Our churches **condemn** all heresies which have sprung up
AL : 0 1 :006(028) [0043] They also **condemn** the Samosatenes, old and new, who
AL : 0 2 :003(029) [0045] Our churches **condemn** the Pelagians and others who
AL : 0 5 :004(031) [0045] Our churches **condemn** the Anabaptists and others who
AL : 0 8 :003(033) [0047] Our churches **condemn** the Donatists and others like them
AL : 0 9 :003(033) [0047] Our churches **condemn** the Anabaptists who reject the
AL : 1 2 :007(035) [0049] Our churches **condemn** the Anabaptists who deny that
AL : 1 2 :009(035) [0049] Also **condemned** are the Novatians who were unwilling to
AL : 1 3 :003(036) [0049] Our churches therefore **condemn** those who teach that
AL : 1 6 :003(037) [0051] Our churches **condemn** the Anabaptists who forbid
AL : 1 6 :004(037) [0051] They also **condemn** those who place the perfection of the
AL : 1 7 :003(038) [0051] men and devils he will **condemn** to be tormented without
AL : 1 7 :004(038) [0051] Our churches **condemn** the Anabaptists who think that
AL : 1 7 :004(038) [0051] an end to the punishments of **condemned** men and devils.
AL : 1 7 :005(038) [0051] They also **condemn** others who are now spreading Jewish
AL : 1 8 :008(040) [0053] Our churches **condemn** the Pelagians and others who
AL : 2 6 :039(069) [0075] **Condemned** therefore is not fasting in itself, but traditions
AP : PR :002(098) [0099] what our opponents **condemned** and to refute their
AP : PR :002(098) [0099] we had heard that it **condemned** many articles that we
AP : PR :004(098) [0099] that was supposed to **condemn** several articles where they
AP : PR :009(099) [0101] Scriptures, they have **condemned** several articles in
AP : 0 2 :005(101) [0107] to say that one is not **condemned** to eternal death because
AP : 0 2 :035(104) [0115] add that this doctrine was properly **condemned** by Leo X.
AP : 0 2 :043(106) [0117] good nor bad, neither to be praised nor **condemned**.
AP : 0 4 :001(107) [0119] in the twentieth, they **condemn** us for teaching that men
AP : 0 4 :001(107) [0121] They **condemn** us both for denying that men receive the
AP : 0 4 :047(113) [0133] Therefore we **condemn** our opponents for teaching the
AP : 0 4 :096(121) [0149] into the world, not to **condemn** the world, but that the
AP : 0 4 :096(121) [0149] He who believes in him is not **condemned**."
AP : 0 4 :179(131) [0171] That is, the law **condemns** all men, but by undergoing the
AP : 0 4 :179(131) [0171] of the law to accuse and **condemn** those who believe in
AP : 0 4 :179(131) [0171] law cannot accuse or **condemn** them, even though they
AP : 0 4 :179(131) [0171] of your sin do not **condemn** you, because for Christ's
AP : 0 4 :204(135) [0177] We **condemn** this wicked idea about works.
AP : 0 4 :207(135) [0177] Such passages do not **condemn** the sacrifices that God
AP : 0 4 :207(135) [0177] in the state, but they do **condemn** the wicked belief of
AP : 0 4 :245(142) [0189] Not only do they **condemn** this faith in statements and
AP : 0 4 :248(142) [0191] and living faith and **condemns** the idle and smug minds
AP : 0 4 :255(144) [0193] or of penitence, which **condemns** wrongdoers and
AP : 0 4 :300(153) [0205] from the church in **condemning** and trying to destroy the
AP : 0 4 :326(157) [0211] does not forgive but judges and **condemns** their hearts.
AP : 0 4 :339(159) [0215] Christ **condemns** trust in our own works; he does not
AP : 0 4 :339(159) [0215] our own works; he does not **condemn** trust in his promise.
AP : 0 4 :343(160) [0217] see that this passage **condemns** trust in our own works.
AP : 0 4 :345(160) [0217] into the world, not to **condemn** the world, but that the
AP : 0 4 :345(160) [0217] believes in him is not **condemned**," etc. (John 3:17, 18).
AP : 0 4 :376(164) [0223] This is what we **condemn** in our opponents' position, that
AP : 0 4 :378(165) [0223] overly subtle when we **condemn** those who teach that we
AP : 0 4 :395(167) [0225] on the contrary, **condemned** this opinion and taught the
AP : 0 4 :396(167) [0225] by the crowd of adversaries who **condemn** our teaching.
AP : 0 4 :396(167) [0225] doctrines they have **condemned** a truth so manifest and
AP : 0 4 :397(167) [0227] The bull of Leo X has **condemned** a very necessary
AP : 0 4 :398(167) [0227] the Confutation have **condemned** us in clear words for
AP : 0 4 :398(168) [0227] such a doctrine was **condemned**, how can they ascribe any
AP : 0 4 :398(168) [0227] any knowledge of Christ to those who **condemned** it?
AP : 0 7 :001(168) [0227] the Confutation have **condemned** the seventh article of
AP : 0 7 :021(172) [0233] faith, as when they **condemn** our doctrine that the
AP : 0 7 :029(173) [0237] Confession, where we **condemn** the Donatists and the
AP : 0 7 :030(173) [0237] Our opponents also **condemn** the part of the seventh
AP : 0 9 :002(178) [0245] the Anabaptists that we **condemn** is also their assertion
AP : 0 9 :003(178) [0245] wickedly when they **condemn** the Baptism of little
AP : 1 2 :001(182) [0253] They **condemn** the second part, in which we say that
AP : 1 2 :002(182) [0253] of the Confutation **condemn**, and therefore we can in no
AP : 1 2 :002(182) [0253] We cannot **condemn** the voice of the Gospel, so
AP : 1 2 :044(187) [0263] Since the Confutation **condemns** us for assigning these
AP : 1 2 :048(188) [0265] denouncing and **condemning** us; it is the voice that says
AP : 1 2 :048(188) [0265] The bond therefore is contrition itself, **condemning** us.
AP : 1 2 :048(188) [0265] declares that we are **condemned** and the substitution of
AP : 1 2 :053(189) [0265] is the law, which reveals, denounces, and **condemns** sin.
AP : 1 2 :059(190) [0267] Our opponents expressly **condemn** our statement that
AP : 1 2 :067(191) [0271] Leo quite openly **condemns** this doctrine of the
AP : 1 2 :067(191) [0271] bull, and our opponents **condemn** it in their Confutation.
AP : 1 2 :067(191) [0271] In their decrees they **condemn** this teaching that we
AP : 1 2 :090(195) [0279] But since they **condemn** the open truth, it is not right for
AP : 1 2 :108(198) [0283] Thee to be justified in **condemning** and punishing us.
AP : 1 2 :108(198) [0283] in punishing them or **condemning** those who have
AP : 1 2 :110(198) [0285] right, they will be **condemning** many of the most
AP : 1 2 :142(204) [0295] etc. (Deut. 6:5) and **condemns** every aspect of lust in
AP : 1 2 :163(208) [0303] means all of penitence; it means to "**condemn** sins."
AP : 1 3 :018(213) [0313] Here we **condemn** the whole crowd of scholastic doctors
AP : 1 4 :002(214) [0315] priests to forsake and **condemn** the sort of doctrine we
AP : 1 5 :001(215) [0315] They completely **condemn** the second part, where we say
AP : 1 5 :003(215) [0315] they would actually **condemn** the doctrine that we do not
AP : 1 5 :003(215) [0315] Now that they have **condemned** this doctrine, we have an
AP : 1 5 :010(216) [0317] Paul **condemns** the ceremonies of Moses as well as
AP : 1 5 :016(217) [0319] and the Israelites were **condemned** precisely because, in
AP : 1 5 :018(217) [0319] The Confutation **condemns** our statement in the article on
AP : 1 5 :050(222) [0329] because our opponents **condemn** us for teaching that
AP : 1 7 :001(224) [0335] joys to the godly but **condemning** the ungodly to endless
AP : 2 0 :001(226) [0337] This article they explicitly reject and **condemn**.
AP : 2 0 :006(227) [0339] our opponents are **condemning** the obvious truth — truth
AP : 2 0 :012(228) [0341] to show why they have **condemned** our article, and it is
AP : 2 0 :014(228) [0343] that our opinion was **condemned** a thousand years ago, in
AP : 2 0 :014(229) [0343] the Pelagians were **condemned** for maintaining that grace
AP : 2 1 :001(229) [0343] They absolutely **condemn** Article XXI because we do not
AP : 2 1 :038(234) [0355] of saints and **condemn** abuses in the worship of saints in
AP : 2 3 :045(245) [0377] to God, even though it was not completely **condemned**.
AP : 2 3 :046(246) [0377] Paul **condemns** such "worship of angels" in Colossians
AP : 2 3 :067(248) [0383] or that the church **condemned** marriage at that time.
AP : 2 4 :023(253) [0391] "As a sin offering he **condemned** sin," that is, through an
AP : 2 4 :027(254) [0393] This passage clearly **condemns** the notion that the
AP : 2 4 :028(254) [0393] Testament prophets also **condemn** the popular notion of
AP : 2 4 :028(254) [0393] but what Jeremiah is **condemning** is an idea of sacrifices
AP : 2 4 :029(255) [0393] Ps. 50:13, 15 also **condemns** the idea of sacrifices *ex opere*
AP : 2 4 :096(267) [0417] who they say was **condemned** because he denied that in
AP : 2 4 :097(268) [0417] When the prophets **condemn** this notion, therefore, they
AP : 2 4 :098(268) [0417] church of God was there, **condemning** wicked services.
AP : 2 4 :099(268) [0419] the prophet Elijah in **condemning** the worship of Baal.
AP : 2 7 :001(268) [0419] order because he had **condemned** certain notorious
AP : 2 7 :010(270) [0423] about such vows, which even the papal canons **condemn**.
AP : 2 7 :058(279) [0439] as we have said, we **condemn** in the vows of the monks.
AP : 2 7 :065(280) [0441] For Paul loudly **condemns** all worship, all laws, all
AP : 2 7 :067(280) [0441] Paul **condemns** the widows, not because they were getting
AP : 2 8 :009(282) [0445] Earlier they also **condemned** Article XV, in which we
AP : 2 8 :024(285) [0451] nor can we agree with our opponents who **condemn** it.
AP : 2 8 :025(285) [0451] Those who originally **condemned** the clear truth, and are
S1 : PR :001(288) [0455] the council or be **condemned** without being summoned.
S2 : 0 2 :007(294) [0465] Therefore, it should be **condemned** and must be abolished
S2 : 0 2 :022(296) [0469] in them, relics should long since have been **condemned**.
S2 : 0 2 :029(297) [0471] cannot allow but must **condemn** the Mass, its
S2 : 0 4 :015(301) [0475] will have enough to **condemn** in the council, for they
S3 : 0 6 :004(311) [0493] Especially do we **condemn** and curse in God's name those
S3 : 0 6 :004(311) [0493] to prohibit, **condemn**, and slander the use of both as
S3 : 0 8 :006(312) [0495] enthusiasts of our day **condemn** the external Word, yet
S3 : 1 0 :002(314) [0497] expel, persecute, and **condemn** those who have been
S3 : 1 5 :001(316) [0501] or merit salvation is unchristian and to be **condemned**.
TR : 0 0 :075(333) [0525] nobody should be **condemned** without due process of
SC : 0 2 :004(345) [0545] me, a lost and **condemned** creature, delivered me and
SC : 0 4 :008(349) [0551] saved; but he who does not believe will be **condemned**."
LC : SP :021(364) [0579] who does not believe will be **condemned**" (Mark 16:16).
LC : 0 1 :190(391) [0635] if you see anyone **condemned** to death or in similar peril
LC : 0 1 :216(394) [0641] from marriage are **condemned** and annulled by this
LC : 0 1 :262(400) [0655] blind world's nature to **condemn** and persecute the truth
LC : 0 1 :274(402) [0659] the right to judge and **condemn** anyone, yet if they whose
LC : 0 2 :027(414) [0685] I was **condemned** to death and entangled in sin and
LC : 0 4 :005(437) [0733] *saved; but he who does not believe will be* ***condemned***."
EP : RN :006(465) [0779] should be rejected and **condemned** as opposed to the
EP : RN :008(465) [0779] how contrary teachings were rejected and **condemned**.
EP : 0 1 :011(467) [0781] we reject and **condemn** the teaching that original sin is
EP : 0 1 :019(468) [0783] 9. We also reject and **condemn** as a Manichaean error the
EP : 0 2 :007(470) [0787] we reject and **condemn** all the following errors as being
EP : 0 2 :013(471) [0789] Likewise we reject and **condemn** the error of the
EP : 0 3 :007(473) [0793] the wicked and he who **condemns** the righteous are both
EP : 0 3 :012(474) [0795] we reject and **condemn** all the following errors:
EP : 0 4 :016(477) [0801] we reject and **condemn** spoken and written formulations
EP : 0 4 :017(477) [0801] 2. We also reject and **condemn** as offensive and as
EP : 0 4 :019(477) [0801] 3. We also reject and **condemn** the teaching that faith and
EP : 0 5 :001(478) [0801] and reproof that **condemns** unbelief, since unbelief is
EP : 0 5 :001(478) [0801] since unbelief is **condemned** not in the law but wholly
EP : 0 5 :003(478) [0801] God-pleasing and which **condemns** everything that is
EP : 0 5 :004(478) [0801] everything which **condemns** sin is and belongs to the
EP : 0 5 :005(478) [0801] not kept the law and is **condemned** by it should believe,
EP : 0 6 :008(481) [0807] 1. Accordingly we **condemn** as dangerous and subversive
EP : 0 7 :018(484) [0813] who does not believe is **condemned** already" (John 3:18).
EP : 0 7 :021(484) [0813] *The Contrary and* ***Condemned*** *Doctrine of the*
EP : 0 7 :021(484) [0813] unanimously reject and **condemn** all the following errors,
EP : 0 7 :042(486) [0817] we herewith **condemn** without any qualification the
EP : 0 8 :019(490) [0823] we reject and **condemn** as contrary to the Word of God
EP : 1 0 :007(493) [0831] that no church should **condemn** another because it has
EP : 1 0 :008(494) [0831] Therefore we reject and **condemn** as false and contrary to
EP : 1 2 :030(500) [0843] we reject and **condemn** as wrong, false, heretical, and

Continued ▶

SD : PR :001(501) [0847] the popish errors, abuses, and idolatry were **condemned**.
SD : RN :005(504) [0851] the papacy and from other **condemned** sects and heresies.
SD : RN :017(507) [0857] place, we reject and **condemn** all heresies and errors
SD : RN :017(507) [0857] church rejected and **condemned** on the certain and solid
SD : RN :018(507) [0857] place, we reject and **condemn** all the sects and heresies
SD : RN :019(507) [0857] suspicious, and **condemned** doctrine might be exposed, no
SD : 0 1 :016(511) [0865] which are rejected and **condemned** in our churches.
SD : 0 1 :017(511) [0865] and new Pelagians, we **condemn** and reject as false the
SD : 0 1 :020(511) [0865] We likewise reject and **condemn** the following and related
SD : 0 1 :023(512) [0865] we also reject and **condemn** those who teach that, though
SD : 0 1 :025(512) [0865] We **condemn** and reject these and similar false doctrines
SD : 0 1 :030(513) [0867] 2. We also **condemn** the error which Augustine attributes
SD : 0 1 :030(513) [0867] does not accuse and **condemn** man's nature, corrupted by
SD : 0 1 :031(513) [0869] the law accuses and **condemns** man's entire corrupted
SD : 0 1 :032(513) [0869] however, accuses and **condemns** our nature, not because
SD : 0 1 :055(518) [0877] and seriously **condemned** and rejected the statement,
SD : 0 2 :043(529) [0897] "I herewith reject and **condemn** as sheer error every
SD : 0 2 :073(535) [0909] expose, reject, and **condemn** such false doctrines and
SD : 0 2 :080(536) [0911] other hand, we must **condemn** with all seriousness and
SD : 0 2 :081(537) [0911] error St. Augustine **condemns** in express words in his
SD : 0 3 :007(540) [0919] segregate, expose, and **condemn** the false contrary
SD : 0 3 :017(542) [0921] the wicked and he who **condemns** the righteous are both
SD : 0 3 :029(544) [0925] we reject and **condemn** works, since the very nature of
SD : 0 3 :059(550) [0937] unanimously reject and **condemn**, in addition to the
SD : 0 4 :020(554) [0945] But we reject and **condemn** as false the view that good
SD : 0 4 :024(555) [0945] also has rejected and **condemned** these propositions:
SD : 0 4 :039(557) [0951] Hence our churches **condemn** and reject this proposition,
SD : 0 5 :010(560) [0955] severely it curses and **condemns** us because we could not
SD : 0 5 :012(560) [0957] given us to terrify or to **condemn** us, but to comfort and
SD : 0 5 :015(561) [0957] Therefore we justly **condemn** the Antinomians or
SD : 0 5 :017(561) [0957] function of which is to **condemn** sin and to lead to a
SD : 0 5 :027(563) [0961] the law is a message that rebukes and **condemns** sin.
SD : 0 6 :026(568) [0971] Hence we reject and **condemn**, as pernicious and contrary
SD : 0 7 :001(569) [0971] Confession and which has repeatedly been **condemned**.
SD : 0 7 :008(570) [0975] to anathematize and **condemn** as a horrendous
SD : 0 7 :009(570) [0975] and received," and it **condemns** the contrary doctrine
SD : 0 7 :107(588) [1009] we reject and **condemn** with heart and mouth as false,
SD : 0 7 :109(588) [1011] we also reject and **condemn** all other papistic abuses of
SD : 0 7 :112(589) [1011] Therefore we reject and **condemn** with heart and mouth
SD : 0 7 :121(590) [1013] we justly criticize and **condemn** the papistic consecration
SD : 0 7 :127(591) [1015] 16. We also reject and **condemn** all presumptuous,
SD : 0 7 :128(591) [1015] for we reject and **condemn** everything that is inconsistent
SD : 0 8 :017(594) [1021] In opposition to this **condemned** heresy the Christian
SD : 0 8 :062(603) [1037] justly rejected and **condemned** in the ancient approved
SD : 0 8 :088(609) [1047] unanimously reject and **condemn** with mouth and heart
SD : 0 8 :096(609) [1049] 8. We reject and **condemn** these errors and all others that
SD : 1 0 :019(614) [1059] expel, persecute, and **condemn** those who have been
SD : 1 0 :026(615) [1061] Therefore we reject and **condemn** as wrongful the view
SD : 1 0 :027(615) [1061] 2. We also reject and **condemn** as wrongful the procedure
SD : 1 0 :028(615) [1061] 3. We reject and **condemn** as wrongful the opinion of
SD : 1 0 :030(615) [1061] 5. We also reject and **condemn** the procedure whereby
SD : 1 0 :031(616) [1063] above, churches will not **condemn** each other because of a
SD : 1 1 :040(623) [1077] harden, reject, and **condemn** all who, when they are called
SD : 1 1 :093(632) [1095] and we reject and **condemn** all those things which are
SD : 1 1 :095(632) [1095] of true doctrine or any publicly **condemned** errors.
SD : 1 2 :002(632) [1095] have unanimously **condemned**), we had not for that
SD : 1 2 :007(633) [1097] attribute to us the **condemned** errors of the
SD : 1 2 :008(633) [1097] contrary we reject and **condemn** all these errors as
SD : 1 2 :009(633) [1097] We reject and **condemn** the erroneous and heretical
SD : 1 2 :028(635) [1101] We reject and **condemn** these errors of the
SD : 1 2 :036(635) [1101] We reject and **condemn** the error of the New Arians who
SD : 1 2 :037(636) [1101] reject and **condemn** the old, approved symbols, the
SD : 1 2 :039(636) [1103] them, we reject and **condemn** as false, erroneous,

Condemnable (1)
SD : 0 7 :128(591) [1015] Whatever additional **condemnable** opinions or erroneous

Condemnation (19), Condemnations (2)
PR : PR :022(011) [0019] With reference to the **condemnations**, censures, and
PR : PR :022(011) [0019] other reasons why **condemnations** cannot by any means
AP : 0 4 :143(126) [0161] is therefore now no **condemnation** for those who are in
AP : 0 4 :308(155) [0207] "There is now no **condemnation** for those who are in
AP : 1 2 :048(188) [0265] that we have been delivered from this **condemnation**.
AP : 1 2 :164(208) [0303] Such **condemnation** really happens in contrition and in a
AP : 2 0 :001(226) [0337] their rejection and **condemnation** of our statement that
AP : 2 4 :096(267) [0417] against us the **condemnation** of Aerius, who they say was
AP : 2 7 :064(280) [0441] and so they incur **condemnation** for having violated their
EP : 0 4 :014(477) [0799] is therefore now no **condemnation** for those who are in
EP : 0 7 :016(484) [0813] and salvation but to their judgment and **condemnation**.
EP : 0 7 :018(484) [0813] and aggravates this **condemnation** (I Cor. 11:27, 29).
EP : 0 7 :019(484) [0813] Holy Supper to his **condemnation**, for Christ instituted
EP : 0 7 :039(486) [0817] sacrament to their **condemnation** because they are still
EP : 1 1 :012(496) [0835] The cause of **condemnation** is that men either do not hear
SD : 0 1 :006(509) [0861] the accusation and **condemnation** of the law of God, so
SD : 0 5 :022(562) [0959] is a "dispensation of **condemnation**," but the Gospel is
SD : 0 6 :023(567) [0969] from the curse and **condemnation** of the law through faith
SD : 0 7 :057(579) [0993] blood of Christ to their own judgment and **condemnation**.
SD : 1 1 :034(622) [1075] be and remain under **condemnation**, although I speak
SD : 1 1 :060(626) [1083] ourselves in the same **condemnation**, we may learn the

Condescension (1)
AP : 1 2 :142(204) [0295] law they say that in **condescension** to our weakness God

Condignity (16)
AP : 0 4 :019(109) [0125] congruity and merit of **condignity**, they are only playing
AP : 0 4 :019(110) [0125] it is no longer merit of congruity but merit of **condignity**.
AP : 0 4 :019(110) [0125] can earn the merit of **condignity**, but they would have him
AP : 0 4 :019(110) [0125] one has the merit of congruity or the merit of **condignity**?
AP : 0 4 :020(110) [0125] they have the merit of **condignity**, whether or not the
AP : 0 4 :020(110) [0125] they have the merit of **condignity**, and so they run
AP : 0 4 :288(151) [0203] by the merit of congruity, then by the merit of **condignity**.
AP : 0 4 :316(156) [0209] reject our opponents' teaching on the merit of **condignity**.
AP : 0 4 :318(156) [0209] grace by the merit of **condignity**, as though when our
AP : 0 4 :321(157) [0209] can be sure of earning grace by the merit of **condignity**?
AP : 0 4 :321(157) [0209] sometimes the merit of **condignity** — was made up to
AP : 0 4 :321(157) [0209] To acquire the merit of **condignity** means to doubt and to
AP : 0 4 :324(157) [0211] doctrine of the merit of **condignity** since it teaches
AP : 0 4 :344(160) [0217] the scholastics invented the term "merit of **condignity**."
AP : 0 4 :356(161) [0217] merited by the merit of **condignity** through good works.
AP : 0 4 :376(164) [0223] added, by the merit of **condignity**; that is, that they

Condition (13), Conditions (7), Conditional (4)
AG : 2 6 :038(069) [0075] keep the body in such a **condition** that one can perform
AL : 2 7 :001(071) [0075] if it is recalled what the **condition** of monasteries was and
AP : 0 2 :005(101) [0107] of a slave, is in this **condition** because of one's mother and
AP : 0 4 :041(113) [0133] This promise is not **conditional** upon our merits but
AP : 0 4 :042(113) [0133] For if the promise were **conditional** upon our merits and
AP : 0 4 :187(133) [0173] of sins were **conditional** upon our works, it would be
AP : 1 2 :106(197) [0283] (Prov. 27:23), "Know well the **condition** of your flocks."
AP : 1 2 :106(197) [0283] to hear confessions, "**condition**" means the secrets of
AP : 1 2 :106(197) [0283] should surely interpret "**condition**" as meaning outward
AP : 1 5 :012(216) [0317] we dare not add the **condition** that we must first earn our
AP : 2 0 :010(228) [0341] is, if the promise were **conditional** on our works, it would
AP : 2 3 :059(247) [0379] Since these **conditions** are certainly displeasing to God,
S 1 : PR :010(290) [0457] or expect that a council would improve our **conditions**.
SC : PR :001(338) [0533] The deplorable **conditions** which I recently encountered
SC : 0 5 :020(350) [0553] Answer: Reflect on your **condition** in the light of the Ten
SC : 0 9 :001(354) [0561] *for various estates and **conditions** of men, by which they*
LC : 0 1 :211(393) [0641] men and women in all **conditions**, who have been created
LC : 0 1 :219(394) [0643] Under such **conditions** chastity always follows
LC : 0 1 :228(396) [0645] at mankind in all its **conditions**, it is nothing but a vast,
LC : 0 3 :093(433) [0725] pardoned, yet on the **condition** that we also forgive our
LC : 0 3 :096(433) [0725] But he has set up this **condition** for our strengthening and
SD : 0 1 :038(515) [0871] in Adam and is transmitted to us in this **condition**.
SD : 0 2 :023(525) [0889] become truly free, a **condition** for which it was originally
SD : 0 2 :057(532) [0903] of God, dies in this **condition**, and perishes in his sins, he

Condoned (2)
LC : 0 1 :057(372) [0597] no one shall a violation be **condoned** or left unpunished.
SD : 0 4 :029(555) [0947] be taught, defended, or **condoned** but are to be expelled

Conducive (4)
AP : 1 5 :001(215) [0315] sin and which are **conducive** to tranquillity and good
AP : 2 8 :006(282) [0445] what is helpful or **conducive** to the aforementioned goal.
AP : 2 8 :009(282) [0445] they also say that traditions are **conducive** to eternal life.
AP : 2 8 :010(282) [0447] explain how traditions are **conducive** to eternal life.

Conduct (18), Conducted (1)
AG : 2 3 :006(052) [0061] and honorable sort of **conduct** has resulted in many
AG : 2 6 :033(069) [0075] is under obligation to **conduct** himself, with reference to
AG : 2 7 :015(073) [0077] the monasteries had **conducted** schools of Holy Scripture
AG : 2 8 :021(084) [0087] the ungodly whose wicked **conduct** is manifest.
AG : 2 8 :055(090) [0091] may be no disorder or unbecoming **conduct** in the church.
AP : 0 7 :049(178) [0245] offended by the personal **conduct** of priests or people, we
AP : 1 2 :106(197) [0283] and not outward **conduct**, and "flocks" means men.
AP : 1 2 :106(197) [0283] surely interpret "condition" as meaning outward **conduct**.
AP : 1 2 :174(210) [0307] one's calling, peaceable **conduct** instead of murder and
AP : 2 3 :004(239) [0363] Because your **conduct** is free of disgrace and cruelty, we
LC : S P :019(363) [0579] the Christian's conversation, **conduct** and concern.
LC : 0 1 :093(377) [0607] Conversely, any **conduct** or work done apart from God's
LC : 0 1 :103(379) [0611] Word so that all our **conduct** and life may be regulated by
LC : 0 1 :180(389) [0631] to learn how we should **conduct** ourselves individually
LC : 0 1 :217(394) [0643] dissolute, disorderly **conduct** which now is so rampant
LC : 0 1 :311(407) [0671] no deed, no **conduct** can be good or pleasing to God, no
LC : 0 5 :006(447) [0755] about our faith and **conduct** that he would permit them to
SD : 0 6 :005(564) [0963] a law according to which he should **conduct** himself.
SD : 0 6 :015(566) [0967] according to which man is to **conduct** himself in this life.

Confer (2), Conferred (2), Confers (4)
AP : 0 4 :296(152) [0205] Christ, whose merits are **conferred** on us if we believe in
AP : 1 3 :018(213) [0313] obstacle, the sacraments **confer** grace *ex opere operato,*
AP : 2 4 :009(251) [0387] that the Mass does not **confer** grace *ex opere operato,*
AP : 2 4 :063(260) [0405] errors: that the Mass **confers** grace *ex opere operato* on
AP : 2 4 :066(261) [0407] not mean that the Mass **confers** grace *ex opere operato* or
TR : 0 0 :014(322) [0509] the episcopate might be **conferred** and hands imposed on
LC : 0 1 :141(384) [0621] if he passes away, he **confers** and delegates his authority
LC : 0 4 :072(445) [0751] on account of what it **confers**, but also on account of

Confess (119), Confessed (17), Confesses (8), Confessing (3)
PR : PR :006(004) [0009] truth which they had once acknowledged and **confessed**.
PR : PR :008(005) [0009] once recognized and **confessed** at Augsburg in the year
PR : PR :010(006) [0011] false doctrine, and clearly to **confess** the divine truth.
PR : PR :018(009) [0015] in which it was once **confessed** at Augsburg in the year
PR : PR :025(013) [0023] have acknowledged and **confessed** in the past, for our
AG : PR :011(025) [0041] one Christ and should **confess** and contend for Christ.
AG : 2 5 :011(063) [0071] Therefore **confess** to the Lord God, the true judge, in
AL : 2 5 :011(063) [0071] Therefore, **confess** your sins to God, the true judge, in
AP : 0 2 :043(106) [0117] Pious men have **confessed** to these things, as the Psalms
AP : 0 3 :001(107) [0119] third article, in which we **confess** that there are two
AP : 0 4 :058(115) [0137] Here the psalmist **confesses** his sins, but he does not lay
AP : 0 4 :173(131) [0171] therefore, when we **confess** that we are sinners; and our
AP : 0 4 :210(136) [0179] and we might publicly **confess** our faith and announce the
AP : 0 4 :322(157) [0209] the whole church **confesses** that eternal life comes through
AP : 0 4 :337(159) [0215] This trust in the promise **confesses** that we are unworthy
AP : 0 4 :383(166) [0225] so is justified, and he **confesses** with his lips and so is
AP : 0 4 :384(166) [0225] that the mere act of **confessing** does not save, but that it
AP : 0 4 :389(166) [0225] Christ, which certainly **confesses** that Christ is the
AP : 0 7 :047(177) [0243] There we **confess** that hypocrites and evil men have been
AP : 0 9 :001(178) [0245] ninth article where we **confess** that Baptism is necessary
AP : 1 0 :001(179) [0247] tenth article, where we **confess** our belief that in the
AP : 1 1 :007(181) [0251] of the regulation that requires all sins to be **confessed**.
AP : 1 2 :010(184) [0255] They will undoubtedly **confess** that our opponents'
AP : 1 2 :107(197) [0283] (Ps. 32:5), "I said, 'I will **confess** my transgressions to the
AP : 1 2 :107(198) [0283] feeling God's wrath, we **confess** that he is justly wrathful
AP : 1 2 :108(198) [0283] That is "I **confess** that I am a sinner worthy of eternal
AP : 1 2 :109(198) [0283] will quote James 5:16, "**Confess** your sins to one another."

Continued ▶

A P : 1 4 :002(214) [0315] of doctrine we have **confessed**, or else, in their unheard of
A P : 1 6 :001(222) [0329] There we **confessed** that a Christian might legitimately
A P : 1 7 :001(224) [0335] There we **confess** that at the consummation of the world
A P : 1 9 :001(226) [0337] There we **confess** that God alone has established all of
A P : 2 1 :035(234) [0353] who would teach or **confess** the Gospel, must be strong
S 1 : 0 1 :000(292) [0461] of dispute or contention, for both parties **confess** them.
S 3 : 0 1 :001(302) [0477] Here we must **confess** what St. Paul says in Rom. 5:12,
S 3 : 0 3 :012(305) [0481] who properly repents, **confesses**, and makes satisfaction
S 3 : 0 3 :015(305) [0483] also to be repented of, **confessed**, etc., but meanwhile the
S 3 : 0 3 :019(306) [0483] a man remembered them and thereupon **confessed** them.
S 3 : 0 3 :019(306) [0485] the more completely he **confessed**, the more he was
S 3 : 0 3 :027(307) [0487] in purgatory had truly repented and properly **confessed**.
S 3 : 0 3 :028(308) [0487] slept (as St. Augustine, St. Jerome, and others **confess**).
S 3 : 0 3 :029(308) [0487] What should they **confess** when they refrained from evil
S 3 : 0 3 :037(309) [0489] for a person who **confesses** that he is altogether sinful
S 3 : 1 5 :005(317) [0501] father, Martin Luther, **confess** that I have hitherto thus
T R : 0 0 :082(000) [0529] that I thus hold, **confess**, and constantly will teach,
S C : 0 5 :015(349) [0553] *How Plain People Are to Be Taught to* ***Confess***
S C : 0 5 :016(349) [0553] One is that we **confess** our sins.
S C : 0 5 :017(350) [0553] What sins should we **confess**?
S C : 0 5 :018(350) [0553] however, we should **confess** only those sins of which we
S C : 0 5 :022(350) [0553] "I, a poor sinner, **confess** before God that I am guilty of
S C : 0 5 :022(350) [0553] In particular I **confess** in your presence that, as a
S C : 0 5 :023(350) [0553] may say: "In particular I **confess** in your presence that I
S C : 0 5 :024(350) [0555] For example, "In particular I **confess** that I once cursed.
L C : 0 1 :118(381) [0615] this commandment and **confess** that with the merits of
L C : 0 2 :017(412) [0681] Moreover, we **confess** that God the Father not only has
L C : 0 3 :025(423) [0705] they would have to **confess** that they never prayed
L C : 0 4 :056(443) [0747] believe afterward and **confess**, "The Baptism indeed was
L C : 0 5 :011(448) [0755] knee should bow and **confess** that it is as he says and
L C : 0 5 :032(450) [0761] Our opponents must still **confess** that these are the very
L C : 0 6 :002(457) [0000] of sin that no one was able to **confess** purely enough.
L C : 0 6 :004(457) [0000] so that we may **confess** without coercion or fear, and we
L C : 0 6 :005(457) [0000] driven and tormented to **confess**, fast, etc., more than
L C : 0 6 :008(458) [0000] refer to the practice of **confessing** to God alone or to our
L C : 0 6 :010(458) [0000] We are to **confess** our guilt before one another and
L C : 0 6 :010(458) [0000] we should and we may **confess** publicly in everyone's
L C : 0 6 :016(459) [0000] only concerned whether we had **confessed** purely enough.
L C : 0 6 :017(459) [0000] inevitably despaired of **confessing** so purely (which was
L C : 0 6 :022(459) [0000] We urge you, however, to **confess** and express your
E P : R N :001(464) [0777] 1. We believe, teach, and **confess** that the prophetic and
E P : 0 1 :002(466) [0779] 1. We believe, teach, and **confess** that there is a distinction
E P : 0 1 :003(466) [0779] also believe, teach, and **confess** that we must preserve this
E P : 0 1 :008(467) [0781] we believe, teach, and **confess** that original sin is not a
E P : 0 2 :003(470) [0787] we believe, teach, and **confess** that man's unregenerated
E P : 0 3 :003(473) [0793] we believe, teach, and **confess** unanimously that Christ is
E P : 0 3 :004(473) [0793] we believe, teach, and **confess** that our righteousness
E P : 0 3 :005(473) [0793] 3. We believe, teach, and **confess** that faith is the only
E P : 0 3 :006(473) [0793] 4. We believe, teach, and **confess** that this faith is not a
E P : 0 3 :007(473) [0793] 5. We believe, teach, and **confess** that according to the
E P : 0 3 :009(474) [0793] also believe, teach, and **confess** that, although the
E P : 0 3 :010(474) [0795] 7. We believe, teach, and **confess** that if we would
E P : 0 3 :011(474) [0795] 8. We believe, teach, and **confess** that the contrition that
E P : 0 4 :007(476) [0799] 2. We believe, teach, and **confess** that good works should
E P : 0 4 :008(476) [0799] 3. We believe, teach, and **confess** further that all men, but
E P : 0 4 :011(476) [0799] also believe, teach, and **confess** that the statement, "The
E P : 0 4 :015(477) [0799] also believe, teach, and **confess** that not our works but
E P : 0 5 :002(478) [0801] 1. We believe, teach, and **confess** that the distinction
E P : 0 5 :003(478) [0801] 2. We believe, teach, and **confess** that, strictly speaking,
E P : 0 5 :006(478) [0803] we believe, teach, and **confess** that when the word
E P : 0 5 :007(478) [0803] we believe, teach, and **confess** that the Gospel is not a
E P : 0 6 :002(480) [0805] 1. We believe, teach, and **confess** that although people
E P : 0 6 :003(480) [0805] 2. We believe, teach, and **confess** that the preaching of the
E P : 0 6 :005(480) [0807] we believe, teach, and **confess** that works done according
E P : 0 7 :006(482) [0809] 1. We believe, teach, and **confess** that in the Holy Supper
E P : 0 7 :007(482) [0811] 2. We believe, teach, and **confess** that the words of the
E P : 0 7 :008(482) [0811] we believe, teach, and **confess** that no man's work nor the
E P : 0 7 :009(482) [0811] we believe, teach, and **confess** with one accord that in the
E P : 0 7 :015(483) [0811] 6. We believe, teach, and **confess** that with the bread and
E P : 0 7 :016(483) [0813] 7. We believe, teach, and **confess** that not only the
E P : 0 7 :018(484) [0813] 8. We believe, teach, and **confess** that there is only one
E P : 0 7 :019(484) [0813] 9. We believe, teach, and **confess** that no genuine
E P : 0 7 :020(484) [0813] We believe, teach, and **confess** that the entire worthiness
E P : 0 8 :004(487) [0819] faith we teach, believe, and **confess** the following:
E P : 0 8 :006(487) [0819] 2. We believe, teach, and **confess** that the divine and the
E P : 0 8 :009(487) [0819] we believe, teach, and **confess** that this personal union is
E P : 0 8 :010(488) [0819] we believe, teach, and **confess** that God is man and man
E P : 0 8 :012(488) [0821] we believe, teach, and **confess** that Mary conceived and
E P : 0 8 :013(488) [0821] also believe, teach, and **confess** that it was not a plain,
E P : 0 8 :015(488) [0821] we believe, teach, and **confess** that the Son of man
E P : 1 0 :003(493) [0829] we believe, teach, and **confess** unanimously that the
E P : 1 0 :004(493) [0829] 2. We believe, teach, and **confess** that the community of
E P : 1 0 :006(493) [0829] 4. We believe, teach, and **confess** that in time of
E P : 1 0 :007(493) [0831] 5. We believe, teach, and **confess** that no church should
E P : 1 2 :007(498) [0839] the use of reason and can **confess** their faith personally.
E P : 1 2 :029(500) [0843] believes, teaches, and **confesses** that there is not only one
S D : R N :001(503) [0849] doctrine commonly **confessed** by the churches of the pure
S D : R N :001(503) [0851] of those churches which **confessed** the same doctrine and
S D : R N :005(504) [0853] teachers to appeal and **confess** adherence to the Nicene
S D : R N :020(508) [0857] what we taught and **confessed** originally and afterward
S D : 0 1 :038(514) [0871] the Small Catechism we **confess**, "I believe that God has
S D : 0 1 :038(515) [0871] Similarly we **confess** in the Large Catechism, "I hold and
S D : 0 3 :009(540) [0919] we believe, teach, and **confess** unanimously, in accord
S D : 0 3 :056(549) [0935] we believe, teach, and **confess** that the total obedience of
S D : 0 4 :002(551) [0939] faith in which we **confess** that faith alone justifies and
S D : 0 5 :017(561) [0957] believe, teach, and **confess** on the basis of what we have
S D : 0 5 :024(562) [0961] We believe and **confess** that these two doctrines must be
S D : 0 6 :004(564) [0963] believe, teach, and **confess** that, although truly believing
S D : 0 7 :002(569) [0971] and of our churches and **confess** that in the Holy Supper
S D : 0 7 :004(569) [0973] did not hold water, they **confessed** that the Lord Christ is
S D : 0 7 :005(570) [0973] by the words of Christ to **confess** that the body of Christ
S D : 0 7 :011(571) [0975] accepted, in which we **confess** that in the Lord's Supper
S D : 0 7 :014(571) [0977] They **confess**, in accordance with the words of Irenaeus,
S D : 0 7 :029(574) [0981] with this treatise to **confess** my faith before God and all
S D : 0 7 :032(574) [0983] same way I also say and **confess** that in the Sacrament of
S D : 0 8 :006(592) [1017] 1. We believe, teach, and **confess** that although the Son
S D : 0 8 :007(592) [1017] 2. We believe, teach, and **confess** that henceforth in this
S D : 0 8 :008(593) [1017] believe, teach, and **confess** that in their nature and
S D : 0 8 :009(593) [1017] also believe, teach, and **confess** that to be almighty, to be
S D : 0 8 :011(593) [1019] also believe, teach, and **confess** that after the incarnation
S D : 0 8 :012(593) [1019] believe, teach, and **confess** that the assumed human
S D : 0 8 :023(595) [1023] we believe, teach, and **confess** everything that is said
S D : 0 8 :071(605) [1041] way believe, teach, and **confess** an outpouring of the
S D : 0 8 :072(605) [1041] we believe, teach, and **confess** that God the Father gave
S D : 1 0 :008(611) [1055] We believe, teach, and **confess** that true adiaphora or
S D : 1 0 :009(612) [1055] believe, teach, and **confess** that the community of God in
S D : 1 0 :010(612) [1055] We believe, teach, and **confess** that at a time of
S D : 1 0 :010(612) [1055] of God, are obligated to **confess** openly, not only by
S D : 1 1 :001(616) [1063] know what we teach, believe, and **confess** in this article.
S D : 1 2 :006(633) [1097] would have to **confess** that in all these questions we abide

Confession (370), Confessions (15)

P R : P R :000(001) [0004] and Unanimous **Confession** of the Doctrine and Faith of
P R : P R :000(001) [0004] Embrace the Augsburg **Confession** and of their
P R : P R :002(003) [0007] Thereupon a short **confession** was compiled out of the
P R : P R :003(003) [0007] themselves to this **confession** as the contemporary
P R : P R :008(005) [0009] mentioned Augsburg **Confession**, which had been
P R : P R :008(005) [0009] this Christian **confession**, based as it is on the witness of
P R : P R :008(005) [0011] reiterated and repeated **confession** the more seriously to
P R : P R :009(006) [0011] our previous Christian **confession** and that neither we nor
P R : P R :009(006) [0011] of our faith and of the **confession** of our religion and had
P R : P R :009(006) [0011] the true and originally submitted Augsburg **Confession**.
P R : P R :009(006) [0011] our churches, schools, doctrine, faith, and **confession**.
P R : P R :009(006) [0011] mentioned Augsburg **Confession**, the contrary doctrine
P R : P R :013(007) [0013] to the Augsburg **Confession** with the request that they
P R : P R :016(008) [0013] then to the Augsburg **Confession** as well, the persons to
P R : P R :016(008) [0013] of the Augsburg **Confession** and publicly attested this
P R : P R :016(008) [0015] and concordant **confession** not only of a few of our
P R : P R :017(008) [0015] from the Augsburg **Confession** as submitted in the year
P R : P R :017(008) [0015] concerning our **confession** if it should ever be attacked by
P R : P R :017(008) [0015] our Christian faith and **confession** as a final explanation
P R : P R :018(008) [0015] the genuine Augsburg **Confession**, and in order that our
P R : P R :018(008) [0015] as to which Christian **confession** it is that we and the
P R : P R :018(008) [0015] God, to that Augsburg **Confession** which was submitted
P R : P R :018(009) [0015] of the Augsburg **Confession** that was then submitted into
P R : P R :018(009) [0015] intend to persist in this **confession** until our blessed end
P R : P R :018(009) [0017] allegedly make a new **confession** almost every year or
P R : P R :019(009) [0017] of the Augsburg **Confession**, referred to in the Naumburg
P R : P R :019(009) [0017] rejected in the **confession** submitted at Augsburg and that
P R : P R :019(009) [0017] that of the first Augsburg **Confession** as it was submitted.
P R : P R :023(012) [0021] in the Augsburg **Confession** and its Apology, correctly
P R : P R :023(012) [0021] no new or different **confession** from the one that was
P R : P R :023(012) [0021] and then to the aforementioned Augsburg **Confession**.
P R : P R :023(012) [0021] the pure teaching and **confession** of the faith may be
P R : P R :024(012) [0021] certain of our Christian **confession** and faith on the basis
P R : P R :025(013) [0023] well as in the Augsburg **Confession**, submitted in the year
P R : P R :025(014) [0023] unanimously in this **confession** of faith and to regulate all
A G : 0 0 :000(023) [0037] The Augsburg **Confession**
A G : 0 0 :000(023) [0037] A **Confession** of Faith Presented in Augsburg by certain
A G : P R :008(025) [0039] we offer and present a **confession** of our pastors' and
A G : P R :014(026) [0041] what follows in the **confession** which we and our
A G : P R :024(027) [0043] This is our **confession** and that of our associates, and it is
A G : 1 1 :000(034) [0047] XI. **Confession**
A G : 1 1 :001(034) [0047] However, in **confession** it is not necessary to enumerate
A G : 0 0 :002(048) [0059] and since this our **confession** is seen to be godly and
A G : 2 5 :000(061) [0069] XXV. **Confession**
A G : 2 5 :001(061) [0069] **Confession** has not been abolished by the preachers on
A G : 2 5 :005(062) [0069] who taught much about **confession** never mentioned a
A G : 2 5 :007(062) [0069] Concerning **confession** we teach that no one should be
A G : 2 5 :012(063) [0071] also teaches that such **confession** is not commanded by
A G : 2 5 :013(063) [0071] diligently teach that **confession** is to be retained for the
A G : 0 0 :002(095) [0095] about the hearing of **confessions**, about burials, about
A G : 0 0 :006(095) [0095] as a declaration of our **confession** and the teaching of our
A L : 1 1 :000(034) [0047] XI. **Confession**
A L : 1 1 :001(034) [0047] However, in **confession** an enumeration of all sins is not
A L : 0 0 :002(048) [0059] us on account of the **confession** which we have now
A L : 2 5 :000(061) [0069] XXV. **Confession**
A L : 2 5 :001(061) [0069] **Confession** has not been abolished in our churches, for it
A L : 2 5 :007(062) [0069] Concerning **confession** they teach that an enumeration of
A L : 2 5 :012(063) [0071] admits that such **confession** is of human right.
A L : 2 5 :013(063) [0071] Nevertheless, **confession** is retained among us on account
A L : 0 0 :002(095) [0095] about parochial rights, **confessions**, burials, and countless
A L : 0 0 :006(095) [0095] in order that our **confession** may be exhibited in them and
A L : 0 0 :017(096) [0095] to be lacking in this **confession**, we are ready, God
A P : P R :001(098) [0099] reading of our princes' **Confession**, a number of
A P : P R :005(098) [0101] an apology of our **Confession**, answering the opponents'
A P : P R :008(098) [0101] they have refuted our **Confession** from the Scriptures.
A P : P R :018(099) [0103] on many points our **Confession**'s teaching is better than
A P : P R :019(100) [0103] Apology of the **Confession**
A P : 0 1 :001(100) [0103] Our opponents approve Article I of our **Confession**.
A P : 0 2 :002(100) [0105] them first to look at the German text of the **Confession**.
A P : 0 4 :004(108) [0121] To substantiate our **Confession** and to refute the
A P : 0 4 :154(128) [0165] which were a sign and **confession** of faith that she was
A P : 0 4 :155(128) [0165] of sins, though love, **confession**, and other good fruits
A P : 0 4 :193(133) [0175] works like the **confession** of doctrine, afflictions, works
A P : 0 4 :261(145) [0195] is the king's excellent **confession** about the God of Israel,
A P : 0 4 :322(157) [0209] the ninth book of the ***Confessions*** he says, "Woe to the
A P : 0 4 :337(159) [0215] Indeed, this **confession** that our works are worthless is the
A P : 0 4 :344(160) [0217] hold to the church's **confession** that we are saved through
A P : 0 4 :384(166) [0225] Paul says that **confession** saves in order to show what
A P : 0 4 :385(166) [0225] No faith is firm that does not show itself in **confession**.
A P : 0 4 :399(168) [0227] expressed about our **Confession**, a reverend father said
A P : 0 4 :399(168) [0227] answer written in blood to our **Confession** written in ink.
A P : 0 7 :001(168) [0227] seventh article of our **Confession** in which we said the
A P : 0 7 :003(169) [0227] marks — that is, Word, **confession**, and sacraments —
A P : 0 7 :007(169) [0229] this statement almost verbatim in our **Confession**.

Continued ▶

AP : 07 :022(172) [0235] is true knowledge and the **confession** of faith and truth."
AP : 07 :022(172) [0235] have we said in our **Confession** that is different from what
AP : 07 :029(173) [0237] clearly enough in our **Confession**, where we condemn the
AP : 07 :037(175) [0241] assembled much of it in the latter part of our **Confession**.
AP : 11 :000(180) [0247] [Article XI. **Confession**]
AP : 11 :001(180) [0247] But on **confession** they add the correction that the
AP : 11 :001(180) [0249] be observed, that **confession** should be made annually,
AP : 11 :006(181) [0251] enumeration of sins in **confession** we teach men in such a
AP : 11 :008(181) [0251] brothers in their fight about jurisdiction over **confessions**!
AP : 11 :008(181) [0251] namely, that we make **confession** of all our sins.
AP : 12 :011(184) [0255] What happens when we come to **confession**?
AP : 12 :023(185) [0257] enumeration of sins in **confession**, as our opponents
AP : 12 :060(190) [0269] Christ but in contrition, **confession**, and satisfaction *ex*
AP : 12 :061(190) [0269] absolution from **confession**, we fail to see what value
AP : 12 :061(190) [0269] see what value there is in **confession** without absolution.
AP : 12 :061(190) [0269] of absolution from **confession**, then they must maintain
AP : 12 :095(196) [0281] of our works, contrition, **confession**, or satisfactions.
AP : 12 :097(197) [0281] **Confession** and Satisfaction
AP : 12 :098(197) [0281] have written nothing about **confession** and satisfaction.
AP : 12 :099(197) [0281] For we also keep **confession**, especially because of
AP : 12 :102(197) [0281] enumeration of sins in **confession**, we have said earlier
AP : 12 :106(197) [0283] Solomon is not talking about **confession**.
AP : 12 :106(197) [0283] here means to hear **confessions**, "condition" means the
AP : 12 :107(197) [0283] The Psalms mention **confession** from time to time; for
AP : 12 :107(198) [0283] Such **confession**, made to God, is itself contrition.
AP : 12 :107(198) [0283] For when **confession** is made to God, it must come from
AP : 12 :107(198) [0283] Therefore such a **confession** is contrition; feeling God's
AP : 12 :108(198) [0283] It is the same with this **confession** (Ps. 51:4), "Against
AP : 12 :109(198) [0283] speak of the specific **confession** to be made to priests but
AP : 12 :109(198) [0283] other, for it commands that the **confession** be mutual.
AP : 12 :110(198) [0285] enumeration of sins in **confession** is necessary by divine
AP : 12 :110(198) [0285] Although we approve of **confession** and maintain that
AP : 12 :111(198) [0285] that complete **confession** is necessary for salvation; this is
AP : 12 :111(198) [0285] of complete **confession** has cast upon consciences!
AP : 12 :111(198) [0285] will the conscience be sure that its **confession** is complete?
AP : 12 :112(198) [0285] writers do mention **confession**, but they are talking about
AP : 12 :112(198) [0285] they made **confession** to the priests so that these
AP : 12 :112(198) [0285] The reason for the **confession** was not that without it
AP : 12 :115(199) [0285] custom in prescribing certain satisfactions in **confession**.
AP : 12 :124(201) [0289] For since in our **Confession** we covered almost the sum
AP : 12 :130(202) [0291] we are in doubt about **confession** that we have said this.
AP : 12 :170(209) [0305] in the mouth **confession**, in the deed complete humility."
AP : 12 :174(210) [0307] thanksgiving, the **confession** of the Gospel, the teaching
AP : 14 :003(214) [0315] for we know that our **confession** is true, godly, and
AP : 15 :002(215) [0315] in Article XXVI of the **Confession**, we must repeat a few
AP : 15 :045(221) [0327] what we said in the **Confession**, that the cross and the
AP : 20 :007(227) [0339] not gladly die in the **confession** of the article that we
AP : 20 :009(227) [0341] who has agreed to our **Confession**, when our opponents
AP : 21 :004(229) [0343] Our **Confession** approves giving honor to the saints.
AP : 21 :010(230) [0345] But our **Confession** affirms only this much, that Scripture
AP : 24 :011(251) [0387] In our **Confession** we have stated our position that the
AP : 24 :014(251) [0389] sacrifice, though in our **Confession** we purposely avoided
AP : 24 :025(253) [0391] prayer, thanksgiving, **confession**, the afflictions of the
AP : 24 :026(254) [0393] that is, prayer, thanksgiving, **confession**, and the like.
AP : 24 :030(255) [0395] prayer, thanksgiving, **confession**, and proclamation of the
AP : 24 :032(255) [0395] they bear afflictions in **confession**, they do good works
AP : 24 :032(255) [0395] faith, prayer, proclamation of the Gospel, **confession**, etc.
AP : 24 :038(257) [0399] be an offering in thanksgiving, **confession**, and affliction.
AP : 27 :010(270) [0423] In the **Confession** we said much about such vows, which
AP : 27 :013(271) [0423] In the **Confession** we said that the forgiveness of sins is
AP : 27 :041(276) [0435] who bear injury because of the **confession** of the Gospel.
AP : 28 :006(282) [0445] In this article of the **Confessions** we included various
AP : 28 :012(283) [0447] In the **Confession** we have said what power the Gospel
AP : 28 :015(283) [0447] In the **Confession** we nevertheless added the extent to
AP : 28 :027(285) [0451] have really refuted our **Confession** with the Scriptures.
S1 : PR :002(288) [0455] adopted them as their **confession**, and resolved that these
S1 : PR :002(288) [0455] publicly as the **confession** of our faith if the pope and his
S1 : PR :003(289) [0455] have my testimony and **confession** (in addition to the
S1 : PR :003(289) [0455] (in addition to the **confession** which I have previously
S3 : 03 :012(305) [0481] parts — contrition, **confession**, and satisfaction — with
S3 : 03 :013(305) [0483] pulpit when the general **confession** was recited to the
S3 : 03 :016(305) [0483] substitute for contrition when people went to **confession**.
S3 : 03 :019(306) [0483] As for **confession**, the situation was like this: Everybody
S3 : 03 :019(306) [0483] a sufficiently complete or a sufficiently pure **confession**.
S3 : 03 :020(306) [0485] and idolatry which such **confession** has produced.
S3 : 03 :027(307) [0487] year must be contrite, make **confession**, and pay money."
S3 : 03 :027(307) [0487] But the contrition and **confession** practiced by these
S3 : 03 :037(309) [0489] embraces all sins in his **confession** without omitting or
S3 : 08 :000(312) [0493] VIII. **Confession**
S3 : 08 :001(312) [0493] and a bad conscience, **confession** and absolution should
S3 : 15 :005(317) [0501] Melander, subscribe the **Confession**, the Apology, and the
TR : 00 :025(324) [0511] on the ministry of the **confession** which Peter made when
TR : 00 :029(325) [0513] On this rock of **confession**, therefore, the church is built.
TR : 00 :059(330) [0521] In the **Confession** and in the Apology we have set forth in
TR : 00 :061(330) [0521] By the **confession** of all, even our adversaries, it is evident
TR : 00 :082(334) [0529] Who Subscribed the **Confession** and Apology, 1537
TR : 00 :082(334) [0529] the articles of the **Confession** presented to the emperor in
TR : 00 :082(334) [0529] with the articles of the **Confession** and Apology.
TR : 00 :082(334) [0529] of the Augsburg **Confession**, the Apology, and the article
TR : 00 :082(000) [0529] and again reread, the **Confession** and Apology presented
SC : 05 :015(349) [0553] [**Confession** and Absolution]
SC : 05 :016(349) [0553] What is **confession**?
SC : 05 :016(349) [0553] Answer: **Confession** consists of two parts.
SC : 05 :021(350) [0553] Please give me a brief form of **confession**.
SC : 05 :021(350) [0553] Pastor, please hear my **confession** and declare that my
SC : 05 :024(350) [0555] for this would turn **confession** into torture; he should
SC : 05 :025(351) [0555] upon the general **confession** which you make to God in
SC : 05 :029(351) [0555] as an ordinary form of **confession** for plain people.
LC : PR :020(361) [0573] will make the noble **confession** that the longer they work
LC : 01 :070(374) [0601] the honor due him and then the lips do so by **confession**.
LC : 02 :007(411) [0679] three persons, and therefore three articles or **confessions**.
LC : 02 :010(412) [0681] than a response and **confession** of Christians based on the
LC : 05 :061(453) [0767] nor do we come to **confession** pure and without sin; on
LC : 05 :087(457) [0000] Here follows an exhortation to **confession**.
LC : 06 :000(457) [0000] A Brief Exhortation to **Confession** [Tappert Only]
LC : 06 :001(457) [0000] Concerning **confession**, we have always taught that it
LC : 06 :001(457) [0000] everyone to make **confession** on pain of the gravest
LC : 06 :003(457) [0000] or understood what **confession** is and how useful and
LC : 06 :003(457) [0000] people had to make **confession** even though nothing was
LC : 06 :004(457) [0000] of knowing how to use **confession** beneficially for the
LC : 06 :005(457) [0000] will never need or desire to go to **confession** any more.
LC : 06 :007(458) [0000] say something about **confession** to instruct and admonish
LC : 06 :008(458) [0000] that in addition to the **confession** which we are discussing
LC : 06 :008(458) [0000] right to be called the Christians' common **confession**.
LC : 06 :009(458) [0000] Lord's Prayer is nothing else than such a **confession**.
LC : 06 :009(458) [0000] what is our prayer but a **confession** that we neither have
LC : 06 :009(458) [0000] This kind of **confession** should and must take place
LC : 06 :010(458) [0000] Similarly the second **confession**, which each Christian
LC : 06 :013(458) [0000] daily, and necessary **confession**, there is also the secret
LC : 06 :013(458) [0000] there is also the secret **confession** which takes place
LC : 06 :014(458) [0000] This kind of **confession** is not included in the
LC : 06 :015(458) [0000] as I have often said, that **confession** consists of two parts.
LC : 06 :015(459) [0000] noble thing that makes **confession** so wonderful and
LC : 06 :016(459) [0000] it was just as if our **confession** were simply a good work
LC : 06 :016(459) [0000] Where the **confession** was not made perfectly and in
LC : 06 :017(459) [0000] Thus the precious **confession** was not only made useless
LC : 06 :021(459) [0000] anybody does not go to **confession** willingly and for the
LC : 06 :021(459) [0000] on the purity of his **confession**, let him just stay away
LC : 06 :023(459) [0000] move and induce us to **confession** were clearly indicated,
LC : 06 :025(460) [0000] Who could thus go to **confession** willingly?
LC : 06 :027(460) [0000] such a desire for **confession** that he will run toward it with
LC : 06 :028(460) [0000] and comforting thing **confession** is, and we urge that such
LC : 06 :029(460) [0000] proudly stay away from **confession**, then we must come to
LC : 06 :030(460) [0000] a hundred miles for **confession**, not under compulsion
LC : 06 :032(460) [0000] I urge you to go to **confession**, I am simply urging you to
LC : 06 :032(460) [0000] you to this point, I have also brought you to **confession**.
LC : 06 :034(461) [0000] In this way, you see, **confession** would be rightly taught,
LC : 06 :035(461) [0000] we have attained to this blessed knowledge of **confession**.
EP : 00 :000(463) [0775] of the Augsburg **Confession** on Which for Some Time
EP : 00 :000(463) [0775] Adhering to this **Confession**, Resolved and Reconciled
EP : 00 :000(464) [0777] of the Augsburg **Confession** Expounded and Settled in
EP : RN :003(465) [0777] is, brief and explicit **confessions**) which were accepted as
EP : RN :003(465) [0777] Christian faith and **confessions** of the orthodox and true
EP : RN :004(465) [0777] unaltered Augsburg **Confession**, which was delivered to
EP : 01 :001(466) [0779] *Doctrine, Faith, and **Confession** according to the*
EP : 02 :002(470) [0787] our teaching, faith, and **confession** that in spiritual
EP : 03 :001(472) [0791] It is the unanimous **confession** of our churches according
EP : 03 :001(472) [0791] of the Augsburg **Confession** that we poor sinners are
EP : 03 :022(475) [0797] in the heart and by the **confession** of the lips, along with
EP : 04 :005(476) [0797] to resolve it, this is our doctrine, faith, and **confession**:
EP : 07 :001(481) [0807] with the Augsburg **Confession** since they separated
EP : 07 :001(481) [0809] when the Augsburg **Confession** was being submitted.
EP : 07 :001(481) [0809] name of this Christian **Confession**, and therefore we have
EP : 07 :005(482) [0809] ***Confession** of the Pure Doctrine of the Holy Supper*
EP : 07 :010(483) [0811] those which Dr. Luther proposed in his *Great **Confession**.*
EP : 07 :021(484) [0813] to our simple faith and **confession** about Christ's Supper:
EP : 08 :001(486) [0817] of the Augsburg **Confession** and the Calvinists (who have
EP : 08 :018(489) [0823] Our doctrine, faith, and **confession** do not divide the
EP : 09 :001(492) [0827] of the Augsburg **Confession** concerning this article also.
EP : 10 :001(492) [0829] of the Augsburg **Confession** concerning those ceremonies
EP : 10 :002(492) [0829] of persecution, when a **confession** is called for, and when
EP : 10 :002(493) [0829] *Correct, True Doctrine and **Confession** about this Article*
EP : 10 :006(493) [0829] when a clear-cut **confession** of faith is demanded of us,
EP : 10 :006(493) [0831] witness an unequivocal **confession** and suffer in
EP : 10 :011(494) [0831] and when a public **confession** is required, one may make
EP : 11 :001(494) [0831] of the Augsburg **Confession** concerning this article.
EP : 11 :022(497) [0837] of the Augsburg **Confession** have been discussing and
EP : 12 :000(498) [0839] Not Committed Themselves to the Augsburg **Confession**
EP : 12 :001(498) [0839] our repeatedly cited Christian Creed and **Confession**.
EP : 12 :011(499) [0841] to the Augsburg **Confession** and reprove the preaching
EP : 12 :030(500) [0843] Creeds, the Augsburg **Confession**, the Apology, the
EP : 12 :031(500) [0843] the doctrine, faith and **confession** of all of us as we shall
SD : 00 :000(501) [0845] of the Augsburg **Confession** Concerning Which There
SD : PR :003(501) [0847] of a Christian **Confession** on the basis of God's Word and
SD : PR :003(502) [0847] a jaundiced view of this **Confession**, but, thank God, it
SD : PR :004(502) [0847] scriptural Augsburg **Confession**, and we abide by the
SD : PR :004(502) [0847] We consider this **Confession** a genuinely Christian symbol
SD : PR :004(502) [0847] Christian symbols and **confessions** were formulated in the
SD : PR :005(502) [0847] cited Christian **Confession** as it was delivered to Emperor
SD : PR :005(502) [0847] the aforementioned **Confession** or to set up a different
SD : PR :005(502) [0847] Confession or to set up a different and new **confession**.
SD : PR :006(502) [0847] set forth in this **Confession** has remained practically
SD : PR :006(502) [0849] to the Augsburg **Confession**, even dared to give a false
SD : PR :010(503) [0849] Christian Augsburg **Confession**, and so that well-meaning
SD : RN :002(503) [0851] nor accept a different or a new **confession** of our faith.
SD : RN :002(503) [0851] symbols or common **confessions** which have at all times
SD : RN :002(503) [0851] of the Augsburg **Confession** before the outbreak of the
SD : RN :002(503) [0851] of the Augsburg **Confession** and which were kept and
SD : RN :004(504) [0851] as the glorious **confessions** of the faith — succinct,
SD : RN :005(504) [0851] of the Augsburg **Confession** against the aberrations of the
SD : RN :005(504) [0851] unaltered Augsburg **Confession** (in the form in which it
SD : RN :005(504) [0851] Empire as the common **confession** of the reformed
SD : RN :005(504) [0851] epoch, not because this **confession** was prepared by our
SD : RN :006(504) [0853] cited Augsburg **Confession** had been submitted, an
SD : RN :006(504) [0853] of the Augsburg **Confession**, with a view both to
SD : RN :006(504) [0853] name of the Augsburg **Confession** someone might
SD : RN :006(504) [0853] it the cited Augsburg **Confession** is clearly expounded and
SD : RN :007(505) [0853] of the Augsburg **Confession**, to which the electors,
SD : RN :007(505) [0853] of the cited Augsburg **Confession** is repeated, several
SD : RN :008(505) [0853] adhere to the Augsburg **Confession** and since they
SD : RN :011(506) [0855] listed — the Augsburg **confession**, the Apology, the
SD : RN :012(506) [0855] We have included these **confessions** also because all were
SD : RN :012(506) [0855] arose among the theologians of the Augsburg **Confession**.
SD : RN :012(506) [0855] to the Augsburg **Confession** object to these documents
SD : RN :019(507) [0857] of the Augsburg **Confession** on account of the Interim
SD : RN :019(507) [0857] explain our faith and **confession** unequivocally, clearly,

Continued ▶

Continued ▶

TR : 0 0 :015(322) [0509] neither ordination nor **confirmation** were sought from the
TR : 0 0 :016(322) [0509] not seek ordination or **confirmation** from the bishop of
TR : 0 0 :020(323) [0509] the bishops of Rome were **confirmed** by the emperors?
TR : 0 0 :069(331) [0523] Finally, this is **confirmed** by the declaration of Peter,
TR : 0 0 :070(332) [0525] was ordination anything more than such **confirmation**.
TR : 0 0 :073(332) [0525] to speak about **confirmation** or the blessing of bells,
LC : 0 1 :279(402) [0661] every word may be **confirmed** by the evidence of two or
LC : 0 4 :008(437) [0733] been instituted, established, and **confirmed** in Baptism.
LC : 0 4 :021(439) [0737] and deeds and has **confirmed** it by wonders from heaven.
LC : 0 4 :050(443) [0745] Since God has **confirmed** Baptism through the gift of His
LC : 0 4 :059(444) [0747] not destroy the substance, but **confirms** its existence."
SD : 0 7 :020(572) [0979] Dr. Luther explains and **confirms** this position at greater
SD : 0 7 :027(574) [0981] from God's Word and **confirms** that it is to be understood
SD : 0 7 :054(579) [0991] too, the repetition, **confirmation**, and exposition of the
SD : 0 7 :081(584) [1001] strengthened, and **confirmed** through his Word.
SD : 0 7 :116(589) [1013] the assurance and **confirmation** of our faith in the Supper
SD : 0 8 :027(596) [1025] them everywhere and **confirmed** the message by the signs
SD : 1 1 :037(622) [1075] and by which he **confirms** it to every believer

Conflict (27), Conflicts (10)
AG : 2 6 :044(070) [0075] ordinances is not in **conflict** with the unity of
AL : 2 0 :017(043) [0055] is to be referred to that **conflict** of the terrified
AL : 2 0 :017(043) [0055] nor can it be understood apart from that **conflict**.
AL : 2 6 :029(068) [0075] of demons, for it is in **conflict** with the Gospel to institute
AL : 2 7 :055(079) [0083] of Christians and in **conflict** with the evangelical counsel.
AL : 2 8 :050(089) [0091] justification are in **conflict** with the Gospel, it follows
AP : 0 4 :037(112) [0131] of conscience and in **conflict**, the conscience experiences
AP : 0 4 :139(126) [0161] Christ's power is needed for our **conflict** with the devil.
AP : 0 4 :286(150) [0201] These passages do not **conflict** with our position.
AP : 0 4 :350(161) [0217] erased without a great **conflict** in which experience
AP : 0 4 :356(161) [0217] seem to our opponents to be in **conflict**, let them see to it.
AP : 0 4 :388(166) [0225] out the sources of this **conflict** and have explained those
AP : 2 3 :006(240) [0365] and natural law and **conflicts** with the very decrees of
AP : 2 3 :060(247) [0379] It **conflicts** with divine and natural law; it disagrees even
AP : 2 3 :063(248) [0381] celibacy, though it **conflicts** with clear passages of
AP : 2 4 :060(260) [0405] We have shown the **conflict** between the righteousness of
AP : 2 4 :077(263) [0411] else without faith **conflicts** with the righteousness of
AP : 2 4 :096(267) [0417] a heresy that clearly **conflicts** with the prophets, apostles,
AP : 2 7 :023(272) [0427] we merit eternal life **conflicts** with the Gospel of the
AP : 2 7 :023(273) [0427] It also **conflicts** with Christ's statement (Matt. 15:9), "In
AP : 2 7 :023(273) [0427] It also **conflicts** with this statement (Rom. 14:23):
AP : 2 7 :047(277) [0437] praises upon something that **conflicts** with political order.
S2 : 0 2 :001(293) [0463] into direct and violent **conflict** with this fundamental
S2 : 0 2 :025(297) [0469] It is in **conflict** with the first, chief article and undermines
S2 : 0 3 :002(298) [0471] All this, too, is in **conflict** with the first, fundamental
S2 : 0 4 :003(298) [0473] power) and come into **conflict** with the first, fundamental
S3 : 1 4 :001(315) [0501] vows are in direct **conflict** with the first chief article, they
TR : 0 0 :038(326) [0515] idolatry, and doctrines which **conflict** with the Gospel.
TR : 0 0 :039(327) [0515] devise doctrines which **conflict** with the Gospel and will
TR : 0 0 :040(327) [0515] the doctrine of the pope **conflicts** in many ways with the
TR : 0 0 :057(330) [0521] and doctrines which are in **conflict** with the Gospel.
LC : 0 3 :087(432) [0723] possible always to stand firm in such a ceaseless **conflict**.
LC : 0 4 :050(443) [0745] For he can never be in **conflict** with himself, support lies
SD : 0 2 :003(520) [0881] with these powers but would succumb in the **conflict**.
SD : 0 2 :068(534) [0907] been begun in us, the **conflict** and warfare of the flesh
SD : 0 6 :018(567) [0967] down to the grave, the **conflict** between spirit and flesh
SD : 0 6 :023(568) [0969] continue in a constant **conflict** against the Old Adam.

Conform (5), Conformable (1), Conformed (1), Conforming (1), Conformity (6)
PR : PR :016(008) [0013] was agreeable and **conformable** first of all to the Word of
AG : PR :006(025) [0039] to the faith and in **conformity** with the imperial
AG : 0 7 :002(032) [0047] Gospel be preached in **conformity** with a pure
AP : 0 4 :293(152) [0203] things are plain and in **conformity** with the Gospel, and
TR : 0 0 :082(334) [0529] believe and teach in **conformity** with the articles of the
EP : 0 0 :000(464) [0777] Christian Fashion in **Conformity** with God's Word in the
EP : RN :006(465) [0779] All doctrines should **conform** to the standards set forth
SD : RN :000(503) [0849] Should Be Judged in **Conformity** with the Word of God
SD : RN :005(504) [0851] drawn from and **conformed** to the Word of God, is
SD : 0 2 :086(538) [0913] this position does not **conform** to the form of sound
SD : 1 0 :002(611) [1053] that one may justifiably **conform** oneself to them in such
SD : 1 0 :016(613) [1057] Hence yielding or **conforming** in external things, where
SD : 1 0 :028(615) [1061] of the holy Gospel or **conform** to their practices, since
SD : 1 1 :049(624) [1079] and affliction he would **conform** each of his elect to "the

Confounded (1), Confounding (1)
SD : 0 8 :043(599) [1029] in one person, neither **confounding** the natures nor
SD : 1 1 :006(617) [1065] of his elect, and thereby the ungodly are **confounded**.

Confraternities (1)
AP : 2 3 :044(245) [0375] of lazy priests in the **confraternities**, where they can live

Confront (1)
LC : 0 1 :061(373) [0597] at once with the rod, **confront** them with the

Confuse (4), Confused (16), Confuses (2), Confusion (6), Confusions (1)
AG : 2 6 :014(066) [0073] consciences have been **confused**, for they undertook to
AG : 2 6 :039(069) [0075] and with specified foods, for this **confuses** consciences.
AG : 2 8 :001(081) [0083] some have improperly **confused** the power of bishops with
AG : 2 8 :002(081) [0083] Out of this careless **confusion** many serious wars,
AG : 2 8 :012(083) [0085] are not to be mingled or **confused**, for the spiritual power
AL : 2 8 :001(081) [0083] some have improperly **confused** the power of the church
AL : 2 8 :002(081) [0083] From this **confusion** great wars and tumults have
AL : 2 8 :012(083) [0085] ecclesiastical and civil power are not to be **confused**.
AL : 2 8 :055(090) [0091] churches may be done in order and without **confusion**.
AP : 0 4 :003(107) [0121] our opponents **confuse** this doctrine miserably, they
AP : 0 4 :302(154) [0205] How **confused** and unclear their teaching is!
AP : 0 4 :312(155) [0207] and hope seem to be **confused**, since it is hope that
AP : 1 2 :004(183) [0253] writings the doctrine of penitence was very **confused**.
AP : 1 2 :010(184) [0255] opponents' discussions are very **confused** and intricate.
AP : 1 2 :013(184) [0257] Here their discussions really become **confused**.
AP : 1 2 :120(200) [0287] as elsewhere they often **confused** the spiritual and the
AP : 2 1 :041(235) [0355] of the saints, the **confusion** in the doctrine of penitence
AP : 2 1 :041(235) [0355] from the labyrinthine **confusions** and endless disputations
AP : 2 4 :020(252) [0389] types of sacrifice and be very careful not to **confuse** them.
S2 : 0 4 :008(300) [0473] What a complicated and **confused** state of affairs that
SC : PR :007(339) [0533] They are easily **confused** if a teacher employs one form
LC : 0 4 :047(442) [0743] by which the devil **confuses** the world through his sects,
SD : 0 3 :018(542) [0921] by faith will not be **confused** with justification and so
SD : 0 3 :032(545) [0927] these two dare not be **confused** with one another or
SD : 0 5 :001(558) [0951] diligence lest we **confuse** the two doctrines and change the
SD : 0 5 :027(563) [0961] be mingled together and **confused** so that what belongs to
SD : 0 5 :027(563) [0961] give occasion for a **confusion** between them by which the
SD : 0 5 :027(563) [0961] Such a **confusion** would easily darken the merits and
SD : 0 8 :061(603) [1035] is evident that we do not **confuse**, equalize, or abolish the

Confutation (45)
AP : PR :001(098) [0099] of theologians and monks prepared a **Confutation** of it.
AP : PR :001(098) [0099] and he ordered our princes to accept this **Confutation**.
AP : PR :002(098) [0099] a copy of the **Confutation**; for we had heard that it
AP : PR :004(098) [0099] again ordered our princes to accept the **Confutation**.
AP : PR :005(098) [0101] Majesty why we could not accept the **Confutation**.
AP : PR :007(098) [0101] us from approving the **Confutation**, but his Imperial
AP : PR :013(099) [0101] monks who wrote the **Confutation**, not with the emperor
AP : PR :014(099) [0101] when I saw the **Confutation**, I realized it was written so
AP : 0 2 :001(100) [0105] that the authors of the **Confutation** are lacking not only
AP : 0 4 :231(139) [0183] In the **Confutation** our opponents have also cited against
AP : 0 4 :398(167) [0227] the authors of the **Confutation** have condemned us in
AP : 0 7 :001(168) [0227] The authors of the **Confutation** have condemned the
AP : 1 2 :002(182) [0253] these writers of the **Confutation** condemn, and therefore
AP : 1 2 :002(182) [0253] and therefore we can in no way agree to the **Confutation**.
AP : 1 2 :044(187) [0263] Since the **Confutation** condemns us for assigning these
AP : 1 2 :067(191) [0271] bull, and our opponents condemn it in their **Confutation**.
AP : 1 2 :111(198) [0285] In the **Confutation** our opponents have maintained that
AP : 1 2 :122(200) [0287] fictions of theirs in the **Confutation** that they dared to
AP : 1 2 :124(201) [0289] than in that of the sophists who wrote the **Confutation**.
AP : 1 2 :125(201) [0289] the world evaluate the **Confutation** — if it is ever
AP : 1 2 :172(209) [0305] The writers of the **Confutation** say it is intolerable to
AP : 1 5 :018(217) [0319] The **Confutation** condemns our statement in the article on
AP : 2 0 :002(227) [0337] Here the framers of the **Confutation** have shown their
AP : 2 0 :002(227) [0339] writers of the **Confutation** who so impudently blaspheme
AP : 2 0 :004(227) [0339] this statement of the **Confutation** stand if their attention
AP : 2 1 :039(235) [0355] abuses; but in the **Confutation** our opponents completely
AP : 2 1 :039(235) [0355] our acceptance of the **Confutation**, to compel us to
AP : 2 1 :040(235) [0355] everywhere else, the **Confutation** is a deceitful document.
AP : 2 1 :042(235) [0355] abuses when they required us to accept the **Confutation**.
AP : 2 2 :006(236) [0359] In the **Confutation** our opponents do not even try to
AP : 2 2 :010(237) [0359] In the **Confutation** they also mention the case of Eli's
AP : 2 3 :024(242) [0371] In the **Confutation** our opponents shriek that the councils
AP : 2 3 :068(248) [0383] show our opponents' purpose in writing the **Confutation**.
AP : 2 3 :068(249) [0383] show us a copy of the **Confutation**, lest their fraud and
AP : 2 4 :009(251) [0387] both here in the **Confutation** and in all their other books
AP : 2 4 :014(251) [0387] The **Confutation** has a great deal to say about sacrifice,
AP : 2 4 :044(258) [0399] In the **Confutation** our opponents wring their hands over
AP : 2 7 :009(269) [0421] the architects of the **Confutation** are now defending, not
AP : 2 7 :011(270) [0423] how the architects of the **Confutation** slip away here!
AP : 2 7 :019(272) [0425] that such blasphemy was removed from the **Confutation**.
AP : 2 7 :028(274) [0429] verdict our judges have rendered in the **Confutation**.
AP : 2 7 :039(276) [0433] In the **Confutation** itself they say that monks try to
AP : 2 7 :040(276) [0433] Again, the **Confutation** says that monks merit a more
AP : 2 8 :006(282) [0445] are the words of the **Confutation**, by which our opponents
AP : 2 8 :026(285) [0451] time being we have made this reply to the **Confutation**.

Congregation (12)
AG : 2 2 :003(050) [0059] whole assembly of the **congregation** in Corinth received
AL : 2 2 :003(050) [0059] it appears that a whole **congregation** used both kinds.
AP : 0 7 :005(169) [0227] that is, the whole **congregation** "of him who fills all in
AP : 0 7 :016(171) [0231] is, precisely speaking, the **congregation** of the saints.
LC : 0 2 :048(417) [0691] be called "a Christian **congregation** or assembly," or best
LC : 0 5 :059(453) [0767] be expelled from the **congregation**, he should not exclude
EP : 1 2 :009(498) [0839] 7. That a **congregation** is not truly Christian if sinners are
EP : 1 2 :026(500) [0843] it is no true Christian **congregation** in which public
SD : 0 7 :079(584) [1001] and clearly before the **congregation** and are under no
SD : 1 2 :014(634) [1099] Christian assembly or **congregation** in the midst of which
SD : 1 2 :034(635) [1101] 6. That a **congregation** in which public expulsion or
SD : 1 2 :034(635) [1101] does not take place is not a true Christian **congregation**.

Congruity (8)
AP : 0 4 :019(109) [0125] between merit of **congruity** and merit of condignity, they
AP : 0 4 :019(110) [0125] grace for the merit of **congruity**, it is no longer merit of
AP : 0 4 :019(110) [0125] it is no longer merit of **congruity** but merit of condignity.
AP : 0 4 :019(110) [0125] one has the merit of **congruity** or the merit of condignity?
AP : 0 4 :288(151) [0203] — first by the merit of **congruity**, then by the merit of
AP : 0 4 :321(157) [0209] acquire the merit of **congruity** and sometimes the merit of
AP : 0 4 :376(164) [0223] grace by the merit of **congruity** or, if love is added, by the
AP : 1 8 :006(225) [0335] works, by the merit of **congruity**, earn the forgiveness of

Conjoined (1), Conjoining (1)
AL : 0 3 :002(029) [0045] human, inseparably **conjoined** in the unity of his person,
AL : 2 0 :006(041) [0053] not by works only, but **conjoining** faith with works they

Conjunction (1)
SD : 0 3 :029(544) [0925] to the law and the works of the law in this **conjunction**."

Conjure (1), Conjuring (1)
LC : 0 1 :062(373) [0597] so, or to curse, swear, **conjure**, and, in short, to practice
LC : 0 3 :042(425) [0709] for their shame, by swearing, cursing, **conjuring**, etc.

Connected (10), Connection (31), Connections (1), Connects (3)
AG : PR :006(025) [0039] In **connection** with the matter pertaining to the faith and
AG : 0 1 :004(028) [0043] the term in this **connection**, not as a part or a property of
AG : 0 2 :003(029) [0045] Rejected in this **connection** are the Pelagians and others
AG : 2 6 :017(066) [0073] and he taught in this **connection** that they were not to be
AG : 2 7 :025(074) [0079] to be exercised in **connection** with this obligation and
AG : 2 7 :049(079) [0083] him in every affliction **connected** with our particular
AL : 0 1 :004(028) [0043] employed it in this **connection**, to signify not a part or a
AL : 0 0 :005(048) [0059] that certain abuses were **connected** with ordinary rites.

Continued ▶

A L : 2 5 :002(061) [0069] concerning faith in **connection** with absolution, a matter
A L : 2 7 :025(074) [0079] should be observed in **connection** with this obligation.
A L : 2 7 :049(079) [0083] are to be borne in **connection** with our callings;
A L : 2 8 :066(092) [0093] In **connection** with the decree one must consider what the
A P : 0 4 :050(114) [0135] He therefore correlates and **connects** promise and faith.
A P : 0 4 :197(134) [0175] to the reward that is **connected** to that commandment
A P : 0 4 :238(140) [0187] to the neighbor, for he **connects** this statement with the
A P : 0 4 :267(146) [0197] he mentions works in **connection** with penitence,
A P : 0 4 :275(148) [0199] Christ frequently **connects** the promise of forgiveness of
A P : 0 4 :369(163) [0221] take too long we shall expound it in another **connection**.
A P : 1 0 :003(179) [0247] we have no kind of **connection** with him according to the
A P : 1 2 :088(195) [0277] Chrysostom asks in **connection** with penitence, "How do
A P : 1 2 :167(209) [0305] to purgatory in this **connection** they did not mean a
A P : 1 5 :012(216) [0317] might say in this **connection** that though we do not merit
A P : 2 7 :051(277) [0437] We have said above in **connection** with the marriage of
S 2 : 0 2 :022(296) [0469] In this **connection** so many manifest lies and so much
T R : 0 0 :075(333) [0525] in adultery, but in this **connection** they often harassed
S C : P R :024(341) [0539] the blessing and danger **connected** with this sacrament.
S C : 0 4 :002(348) [0551] to God's command and **connected** with God's Word.
S C : 0 4 :010(349) [0551] but the Word of God **connected** with the water, and our
S C : 0 4 :010(349) [0551] relies on the Word of God **connected** with the water.
S C : 0 4 :010(349) [0551] But when **connected** with the Word of God it is a
L C : 0 1 :082(376) [0603] of the Old Testament **connected** with particular customs,
L C : 0 1 :141(384) [0621] In **connection** with this commandment there is more to be
L C : 0 1 :302(405) [0667] through friendly **connections** and by any other means at
L C : 0 1 :319(408) [0673] treated above in **connection** with the First
L C : 0 5 :009(447) [0755] wine comprehended in God's Word and **connected** with it.
E P : 0 3 :011(474) [0795] a kind of faith in this **connection** that could coexist and
E P : 0 8 :001(486) [0817] In **connection** with the controversy on the Holy Supper a
E P : 0 8 :009(487) [0819] not a combination or **connection** of such a kind that
S D : 0 2 :089(538) [0915] or will anything in **connection** with it, but in the way and
S D : 0 3 :042(546) [0931] the Apology discusses in **connection** with James 2:24.
S D : 0 6 :010(565) [0965] creates, and works in **connection** with the new obedience
S D : 0 6 :021(567) [0969] teaching of the law in **connection** with their good works,
S D : 0 8 :086(608) [1047] right hand of God in **connection** with this article, as well
S D : 0 8 :086(608) [1047] in the Holy Supper in **connection** with the previous
S D : 1 1 :009(617) [1065] is to be considered in **connection** with it, than that God

Conquer (8), Conquered (8), Conquers (3)

A P : 0 2 :048(106) [0119] as the devil cannot be **conquered** without Christ's help, so
A P : 0 4 :079(117) [0143] eternal death must be **conquered** in our hearts, as Paul
A P : 0 4 :079(118) [0143] But we **conquer** through Christ.
A P : 0 4 :139(126) [0161] For Christ **conquered** the devil and gave us his promise
A P : 0 4 :139(126) [0161] so that with the help of God we, too, might **conquer**.
A P : 0 4 :148(127) [0163] did not die in vain, **conquers** the terrors of sin and death.
A P : 0 4 :222(138) [0181] is not saying that love **conquers** the terrors of sin and
A P : 0 4 :223(138) [0181] and by our love we can **conquer** death and can have
A P : 0 4 :238(140) [0187] to say that our love **conquers** sin and death; or that in
A P : 0 4 :244(142) [0189] to us; that good works **conquer** the terrors of sin and
A P : 0 4 :263(146) [0195] they truly believe and by faith **conquer** sin and death.
A P : 0 4 :398(167) [0227] obtain forgiveness of sin, **conquer** the terrors of sin, and
A P : 1 2 :037(187) [0261] life it struggles with sin to **conquer** sin and death.
A P : 1 2 :127(201) [0291] only that we be **conquered** and destroyed by armed
A P : 2 1 :002(229) [0343] field of battle Jerome **conquered** Vigilantius eleven
A P : 2 4 :012(251) [0387] the necessity of faith to **conquer** the terrors of sins and
A P : 2 4 :089(266) [0415] and death cannot be **conquered** except by faith in Christ,
S D : 0 8 :025(596) [1023] by and in his death he **conquered** sin, death, the devil,
S D : 0 9 :002(610) [1051] descended into hell, **conquered** the devil, destroyed hell's

Conquest (1)

A P : 2 4 :060(260) [0405] of sins and no **conquest** of the terrors of death and sin

Conrad (4)

S 3 : 1 5 :005(317) [0501] I, **Conrad** Figenbotz, for the glory of God subscribe that I
S 3 : 1 5 :005(317) [0501] **Conrad** Oettinger, preacher of Duke Ulric of Pforzheim
T R : 0 0 :082(334) [0529] **Conrad** Figenbotz subscribes to all throughout
T R : 0 0 :082(335) [0529] **Conrad** Oettinger, of Pforzheim, preacher of Ulric, duke

Conscience (149), Consciences (163)

P R : P R :004(004) [0009] to divert poor, erring **consciences** from an understanding
P R : P R :018(009) [0015] Christ with joyful and fearless hearts and **consciences**.
P R : P R :024(013) [0021] hearts and Christian **consciences** through the grace of the
P R : P R :024(013) [0023] and instruction of poor, misguided **consciences**.
A G : P R :013(026) [0041] in so far as God and **conscience** allow, that may serve the
A G : 1 5 :002(036) [0049] with instruction so that **consciences** may not be burdened
A G : 2 0 :015(043) [0055] that weak and terrified **consciences** find it most
A G : 2 0 :015(043) [0055] The **conscience** cannot come to rest and peace through
A G : 2 0 :019(043) [0055] in preaching, but poor **consciences** were driven to rely on
A G : 2 0 :020(043) [0055] were driven by their **conscience** into monasteries in the
A G : 0 0 :001(047) [0059] the consolation of **consciences**, and the amendment of
A G : 0 0 :001(047) [0059] put our own souls and **consciences** in grave peril before
A G : 2 2 :011(050) [0061] proper to burden the **consciences** of those who desire to
A G : 2 3 :003(051) [0061] great distress of their **consciences**, especially since the
A G : 2 3 :006(052) [0061] frightful disturbance of **conscience** many have
A G : 0 1 :007(056) [0065] a comfort for terrified **consciences**) in order that the
A G : 2 4 :030(059) [0067] faith and comfort our **consciences** when we perceive that
A G : 2 5 :004(062) [0069] comforting and necessary it is for terrified **consciences**.
A G : 2 5 :005(062) [0069] but only tormented **consciences** without long
A G : 2 5 :011(063) [0071] of your sins not with your tongue but in your **conscience**."
A G : 2 5 :013(063) [0071] consolation of terrified **consciences**, and also for other
A G : 2 6 :012(065) [0071] a grievous burden to **consciences**, for it was not possible
A G : 2 6 :014(066) [0073] and canonists how **consciences** have been confused, for
A G : 2 6 :014(066) [0073] mitigations to relieve **consciences**, but they were so
A G : 2 6 :017(066) [0073] also displeased that **consciences** were burdened with so
A G : 2 6 :028(068) [0073] the burdening of **consciences** with additional outward
A G : 2 6 :039(069) [0075] and with specified foods, for this confuses **consciences**.
A G : 2 6 :041(070) [0075] without burdening **consciences**, which is to say that it is
A G : 2 7 :008(072) [0077] what scandals and burdened **consciences** resulted.
A G : 2 7 :052(079) [0083] for it follows that their **consciences** are troubled because
A G : 2 8 :002(081) [0083] worship and burdened **consciences** with reserved cases
A G : 2 8 :004(081) [0085] the sake of comforting **consciences**, to point out the
A G : 2 8 :041(087) [0089] some foods defile the **conscience**, that fasting is a work by
A G : 2 8 :042(088) [0089] on Christendom to ensnare men's **consciences**?
A G : 2 8 :049(089) [0091] and thus ensnare **consciences**, why does the divine
A G : 2 8 :053(090) [0091] in order to bind men's **consciences** by considering these
A G : 2 8 :056(090) [0091] However, **consciences** should not be burdened by
A G : 2 8 :064(092) [0093] What are such discussions but snares of **conscience**?
A G : 2 8 :065(092) [0093] did not wish to burden **consciences** with such bondage
A G : 2 8 :068(093) [0093] give counsel or help to **consciences** unless this mitigation
A G : 2 8 :068(093) [0093] and that disregard of them does not injure **consciences**.
A G : 2 8 :077(094) [0095] and pray that they may not coerce our **consciences** to sin.
A L : 1 2 :004(034) [0049] is, terror smiting the **conscience** with a knowledge of sin,
A L : 1 2 :005(035) [0049] sake, comforts the **conscience**, and delivers it from terror.
A L : 1 5 :002(036) [0049] not to burden **consciences** with such things, as if
A L : 2 0 :015(043) [0055] and anxious **consciences** find by experience that it offers
A L : 2 0 :015(043) [0055] because the **consciences** of men cannot be pacified by any
A L : 2 0 :017(043) [0055] conflict of the terrified **conscience**, nor can it be
A L : 2 0 :019(043) [0055] **Consciences** used to be plagued by the doctrine of works
A L : 2 0 :020(044) [0055] persons were by their **consciences** driven into the desert,
A L : 2 0 :022(044) [0055] in order that anxious **consciences** should not be deprived
A L : 0 0 :005(048) [0059] approved with a good **conscience**, they have to some
A L : 0 0 :001(049) [0059] to observe these abuses against their **conscience**.
A L : 2 2 :011(050) [0061] with offense to their **consciences**, to do otherwise.
A L : 2 4 :007(056) [0065] it offers to anxious **consciences**, that they may learn to
A L : 2 4 :030(059) [0067] Christ and should cheer and comfort anxious **consciences**.
A L : 2 5 :004(062) [0069] it brings to terrified **consciences**, are told that God
A L : 2 5 :007(062) [0069] not necessary and that **consciences** should not be
A L : 2 5 :009(063) [0069] are recounted, our **consciences** would never find peace,
A L : 2 5 :011(063) [0071] your tongue but with the memory of your **conscience**."
A L : 2 5 :013(063) [0071] and because it is otherwise useful to **consciences**.
A L : 2 6 :002(064) [0071] and sorely terrified the **consciences** of those who omitted
A L : 2 6 :011(065) [0071] greatly tormented the **consciences** of devout people who
A L : 2 6 :012(065) [0071] great dangers to **consciences**, for it was impossible to keep
A L : 2 6 :014(066) [0073] mitigations to relieve **consciences**; yet they did not
A L : 2 6 :014(066) [0073] them but rather entangled **consciences** even more.
A L : 2 6 :015(066) [0073] affairs, and the consolation of sorely tried **consciences**.
A L : 2 6 :017(066) [0073] the burdening of **consciences** with such observances and
A L : 2 6 :028(068) [0073] the burdening of **consciences** with numerous rites,
A L : 2 6 :039(069) [0075] which with peril to **conscience** prescribe certain days and
A L : 2 7 :008(072) [0077] were created, what snares were placed on **consciences**.
A L : 2 7 :052(079) [0083] engage in their married life with a troubled **conscience**.
A L : 2 7 :053(079) [0083] they have a troubled **conscience** when they keep their
A L : 2 8 :002(081) [0083] worship and burdened **consciences** with reservation of
A L : 2 8 :004(081) [0085] the sake of instructing **consciences**, to show the difference
A L : 2 8 :041(087) [0089] certain foods defile the **conscience**, that fasting which is
A L : 2 8 :042(088) [0089] and thus ensnare **consciences** when Peter forbids putting
A L : 2 8 :049(089) [0091] the right to burden **consciences** with such traditions, why
A L : 2 8 :053(090) [0091] for sins, nor that **consciences** are bound so as to regard
A L : 2 8 :056(090) [0091] However, **consciences** should not be burdened by
A L : 2 8 :064(092) [0093] What are discussions of this kind but snares of **conscience**
A L : 2 8 :065(092) [0093] did not wish to burden **consciences** with such bondage
A L : 2 8 :068(093) [0093] not possible to counsel **consciences** unless this mitigation
A L : 2 8 :068(093) [0093] no harm is done to **consciences** even if the usage of men
A L : 2 8 :069(093) [0093] traditions which cannot be kept with a good **conscience**.
A P : P R :002(098) [0099] Since religion and **consciences** are involved, we assumed
A P : P R :003(098) [0099] however unpleasant, that did not violate our **consciences**.
A P : P R :004(098) [0099] to the opponents' point of view with a clear **conscience**?
A P : 0 4 :002(107) [0121] and brings to pious **consciences** the abundant consolation
A P : 0 4 :003(107) [0121] and they rob pious **consciences** of the consolation offered
A P : 0 4 :020(110) [0125] God and the terrors of **conscience** drive out our trust in
A P : 0 4 :020(110) [0125] But terrified **consciences** waver and doubt and then seek
A P : 0 4 :021(110) [0127] Timid **consciences**, on the other hand, they drive to
A P : 0 4 :037(112) [0131] But in the agony of **conscience** and in conflict, the
A P : 0 4 :037(112) [0131] and in conflict, the **conscience** experiences how vain these
A P : 0 4 :038(112) [0131] For the law always accuses and terrifies **consciences**.
A P : 0 4 :038(112) [0131] not justify, because a **conscience** terrified by the law flees
A P : 0 4 :045(113) [0133] and the terrors of **conscience** it consoles and encourages
A P : 0 4 :062(115) [0139] penitence terrifies our **consciences** with real and serious
A P : 0 4 :079(118) [0143] That is, sin terrifies **consciences**; this happens through the
A P : 0 4 :084(119) [0145] Experienced **consciences** can readily understand this.
A P : 0 4 :091(120) [0149] with God," that is, our **consciences** are tranquil and
A P : 0 4 :142(126) [0161] in the terrors of a **conscience** that feels God's wrath
A P : 0 4 :157(128) [0165] trust was vain and our **consciences** will then plunge into
A P : 0 4 :164(129) [0169] the law, how can our **conscience** be sure that it pleases
A P : 0 4 :176(131) [0171] of the law; for our **conscience** to be at peace we must seek
A P : 0 4 :180(132) [0171] In this promise timid **consciences** should seek
A P : 0 4 :180(132) [0171] can never pacify the **conscience**; only the promise can do
A P : 0 4 :181(132) [0171] and peace of **conscience** elsewhere than in our love and
A P : 0 4 :195(134) [0175] is evident in terrors of **conscience**, for we cannot set any
A P : 0 4 :204(135) [0177] do not find peace of **conscience** in these works, but in
A P : 0 4 :208(135) [0177] no works can put the **conscience** at rest, they kept
A P : 0 4 :212(136) [0179] works cannot pacify the **conscience**, men constantly
A P : 0 4 :216(137) [0179] by which we take hold of grace and peace of **conscience**.
A P : 0 4 :217(137) [0179] But the **conscience** cannot find peace before God except
A P : 0 4 :224(138) [0181] must be stilled and the **conscience** find peace before him.
A P : 0 4 :245(142) [0189] a pure heart and a good **conscience** and sincere faith."
A P : 0 4 :249(143) [0191] resists the terrors of **conscience** and encourages and
A P : 0 4 :257(144) [0193] works wrath; it only accuses; it only terrifies **consciences**.
A P : 0 4 :257(144) [0193] **Consciences** cannot find peace unless they hear the voice
A P : 0 4 :270(147) [0197] It always accuses the **conscience**, which does not satisfy
A P : 0 4 :271(148) [0199] be received by faith, to cheer the terrified **conscience**.
A P : 0 4 :275(148) [0199] since a terrified **conscience** needs manifold consolations.
A P : 0 4 :285(150) [0201] counsel pious **consciences** very badly when they teach
A P : 0 4 :285(150) [0201] of sins, because a **conscience** that seeks forgiveness
A P : 0 4 :285(150) [0201] consolation to faithful **consciences** and illumines the glory
A P : 0 4 :286(150) [0203] shown all this to the satisfaction of pious **consciences**.
A P : 0 4 :288(151) [0203] forms of worship to get rid of the terrors of **conscience**.
A P : 0 4 :288(151) [0203] the terrors of **conscience** and the wrath of God.
A P : 0 4 :292(152) [0203] justified when, with his **conscience** terrified by the
A P : 0 4 :299(153) [0205] this teaching, faithful **consciences** see the most complete
A P : 0 4 :301(153) [0205] On these issues **consciences** are left in doubt.
A P : 0 4 :301(153) [0205] When will the **conscience** be at rest, therefore, and when
A P : 0 4 :302(154) [0205] human works; it leads **consciences** into either pride or
A P : 0 4 :303(154) [0205] and wholesome consolation to frightened **consciences**.
A P : 0 4 :318(156) [0209] as though when our **conscience** terrifies us after
A P : 0 4 :319(156) [0209] teaching leaves **consciences** in doubt, so that they can

Continued ▶

AP : 04 :319(156) [0209] If a **conscience** believes that it ought to be pleasing to
AP : 04 :321(156) [0209] Third, how will the **conscience** know when a work has
AP : 04 :321(157) [0209] whereas terrified **consciences** are uncertain about all their
AP : 04 :346(160) [0217] works cannot still the **conscience**, as we have often said
AP : 04 :350(161) [0217] How often our aroused **conscience** tempts us to despair
AP : 04 :382(165) [0225] When frightened **consciences** are consoled by faith and
AP : 04 :389(166) [0225] faith and for teaching and comforting their **conscience**.
AP : 04 :398(167) [0227] the terrors of sin, and receive peace for our **conscience**.
AP : 07 :039(176) [0241] such a burden on **consciences**, nor to make the
AP : 07 :044(177) [0243] a necessity upon **consciences**, since they tell him not to be
AP : 11 :002(180) [0249] that many troubled **consciences** have received consolation
AP : 11 :002(180) [0249] discloses a sure and firm consolation for the **conscience**.
AP : 11 :006(181) [0251] men in such a way as not to ensnare their **consciences**.
AP : 11 :007(181) [0251] Europe knows how **consciences** have been ensnared by
AP : 11 :008(181) [0251] on our people's **consciences** the regulation *Omnis*
AP : 11 :009(182) [0251] on faith, which consoles and encourages **consciences**.
AP : 12 :005(183) [0253] of penitence nor the source of the peace of **conscience**.
AP : 12 :007(183) [0255] is there that will finally bring peace to the **conscience**?
AP : 12 :009(183) [0255] When can a terrified **conscience** judge whether it fears
AP : 12 :012(184) [0257] which grasps the absolution and consoles the **conscience**.
AP : 12 :022(185) [0257] satisfactions upon **consciences**, to institute new acts of
AP : 12 :022(185) [0257] and acts of devotion binding upon **consciences**.
AP : 12 :028(185) [0259] order to deliver pious **consciences** from these labyrinths
AP : 12 :029(185) [0259] the genuine terror of a **conscience** that feels God's wrath
AP : 12 :032(186) [0259] In these terrors the **conscience** feels God's wrath against
AP : 12 :034(186) [0261] For the law only accuses and terrifies the **conscience**.
AP : 12 :035(186) [0261] ought to be set forth to **consciences** — the Gospel which
AP : 12 :039(187) [0261] absolution strengthens and consoles the **conscience**.
AP : 12 :047(188) [0263] is no peace for the **conscience** except by faith, therefore
AP : 12 :048(188) [0265] The bond is the **conscience** denouncing and condemning
AP : 12 :060(190) [0269] overcoming them and restoring peace to the **conscience**.
AP : 12 :064(191) [0269] For a terrified **conscience** cannot pit our works or our
AP : 12 :072(192) [0271] Let pious **consciences** know, therefore, that God
AP : 12 :076(193) [0273] contrary, call men's **consciences** away from the law to the
AP : 12 :084(194) [0277] of ours brings devout **consciences** a firm consolation
AP : 12 :087(195) [0277] enough for devout **consciences**, and from this they will
AP : 12 :088(195) [0277] Finally, when will the **conscience** find peace if we receive
AP : 12 :088(195) [0277] be answered nor **consciences** quieted unless we know it is
AP : 12 :088(195) [0277] our opponents leave **consciences** wavering and uncertain.
AP : 12 :089(195) [0277] **Consciences** do nothing from faith if they always doubt
AP : 12 :090(195) [0279] teaching is more godly and salutary for **consciences**.
AP : 12 :095(196) [0281] because an anxious **conscience** sees that these works are
AP : 12 :105(197) [0283] sins and consoling **consciences**, does not need an
AP : 12 :106(197) [0283] means the secrets of **conscience** and not outward
AP : 12 :110(198) [0285] must be controlled, lest **consciences** be ensnared; for they
AP : 12 :111(198) [0285] of complete confession has cast upon **consciences**!
AP : 12 :111(198) [0285] When will the **conscience** be sure that its confession is
AP : 12 :127(201) [0291] strengthen wavering **consciences**, because you command
AP : 12 :128(202) [0291] ought to be healing **consciences**, refuse to let the issue be
AP : 12 :129(202) [0291] kind and heal doubting **consciences**, you can bind all
AP : 12 :130(202) [0291] that it is true, godly, and beneficial to godly **consciences**.
AP : 12 :130(202) [0291] hear teachers capable of setting their **consciences** at rest.
AP : 12 :149(205) [0299] to the fearful terrors of **conscience** of which David says,
AP : 12 :156(207) [0301] contrition or terrors of **conscience**, as well as other
AP : 12 :158(207) [0301] of troubles terrified **consciences** see only God's
AP : 13 :020(214) [0313] comfort his troubled **conscience**, and believe that the
AP : 14 :003(214) [0315] In this issue our **consciences** are clear and we dare not
AP : 15 :017(217) [0319] the Word of God, the **conscience** must doubt whether
AP : 15 :026(219) [0323] so that many perform them with scruples of **conscience**.
AP : 15 :027(219) [0323] for justification, **consciences** are sorely troubled because
AP : 15 :028(219) [0323] deplores the danger to **consciences** that comes from this
AP : 15 :033(220) [0325] traditions to ease their **consciences**, yet they do not find
AP : 15 :034(220) [0325] the apostles have freed **consciences** for good, especially
AP : 15 :042(221) [0327] about faith in Christ or about comfort for the **conscience**.
AP : 15 :043(221) [0327] faith, comfort for the **conscience** through faith, the
AP : 15 :049(221) [0329] experience that traditions are real snares for **consciences**.
AP : 15 :049(221) [0329] exquisite torture to a **conscience** that has omitted some
AP : 15 :052(222) [0329] without offense to **consciences**, should be preferred to all
AP : 16 :005(223) [0331] but also "for the sake of **conscience**" (Rom. 13:5).
AP : 16 :012(224) [0333] will never satisfy good **consciences** unless they keep the
AP : 16 :012(224) [0333] This rule safeguards **consciences**, for it teaches that if
AP : 20 :006(227) [0339] Now that we see in our **conscience** that our opponents are
AP : 20 :008(227) [0339] Pious **consciences** will have no sure foundation when sin
AP : 20 :010(228) [0341] when would a terrified **conscience** find a work that it
AP : 21 :010(230) [0345] this it follows that **consciences** cannot be sure about such
AP : 21 :017(231) [0347] promise, and hence **consciences** cannot be sure that we
AP : 21 :044(236) [0357] will not burden faithful **consciences** nor persecute
AP : 23 :017(242) [0369] It is up to each man's **conscience** to decide this matter.
AP : 23 :030(243) [0371] Word which assures the **conscience** that God approves,
AP : 23 :042(245) [0375] in order to burden **consciences** with these Levitical
AP : 23 :047(246) [0377] mention cases of godly **consciences** being very troubled
AP : 23 :059(247) [0379] But our **consciences** are at ease.
AP : 23 :071(249) [0383] our princes can have a clear **conscience** on this matter.
AP : 24 :043(257) [0399] the Gospel or console **consciences** or point out that sins
AP : 24 :046(258) [0401] the enumeration of sins were a torture for **consciences**.
AP : 24 :048(258) [0401] This teaching really consoles **consciences**.
AP : 24 :049(258) [0401] admonition to timid **consciences** really to trust and
AP : 24 :073(262) [0409] clear that terrified **consciences** are the ones worthy of it,
AP : 24 :074(262) [0409] has strengthened a **conscience** to see its liberation from
AP : 24 :075(263) [0411] of the comfort for the **conscience** and of thanksgiving or
AP : 24 :091(266) [0415] we and all faithful **consciences** should be careful not to
AP : 28 :008(282) [0445] the right to burden **consciences** with such traditions so
AP : 28 :011(283) [0447] or to burden **consciences** so that their omission is judged
AP : 28 :015(283) [0447] These must not ensnare **consciences** as though they were
S2 : 04 :002(298) [0471] will nor should nor can take upon our **consciences**.
S3 : 00 :000(302) [0477] about matters of **conscience** but only about money,
S3 : 08 :001(312) [0493] against sin and a bad **conscience**, confession and
S3 : 08 :001(312) [0493] for the sake of timid **consciences** and for the sake of
S3 : 15 :003(316) [0501] let him do so at the peril of his own **conscience**.
TR : 00 :006(320) [0505] of God, binding on the **consciences** of men, because he
TR : 00 :042(328) [0517] Consequently our **consciences** are sufficiently excused.
TR : 00 :044(328) [0517] of Christ, deprive **consciences** of a firm consolation, and
TR : 00 :054(329) [0519] to it that errors are removed and **consciences** are healed.
TR : 00 :078(333) [0527] are also other snares of **conscience** in their laws, but it
TR : 00 :080(334) [0527] they cannot possess these alms with a good **conscience**.
SC : 05 :024(350) [0555] does not feel that his **conscience** is burdened by such or
SC : 05 :029(351) [0555] faith of those whose **consciences** are heavily burdened or
SC : 09 :005(355) [0561] to avoid God's wrath but also for the sake of **conscience**.
LC : 01 :022(367) [0585] It concerns only that **conscience** which seeks help,
LC : 01 :054(372) [0595] which pertain to the **conscience**, when false preachers
LC : 01 :112(380) [0613] been able to set his **conscience** right toward God, saying:
LC : 01 :122(382) [0617] this treasure and joy of **conscience** and lay up for
LC : 01 :144(385) [0623] to have such joyful **consciences** and know how to do truly
LC : 01 :144(385) [0623] indulgences, to their own hurt and with a bad **conscience**.
LC : 01 :148(385) [0623] what is more, a joyful **conscience** and a gracious God who
LC : 01 :216(394) [0641] all poor, captive **consciences** deceived by their monastic
LC : 01 :253(399) [0653] Thus with a happy **conscience** you can enjoy a hundred
LC : 02 :055(418) [0693] to comfort and revive our **consciences** as long as we live.
LC : 03 :023(423) [0703] For in the latter our **conscience** would always be in
LC : 03 :051(427) [0711] and salvation against sin, death, and an evil **conscience**.
LC : 03 :089(432) [0723] Thus our **conscience** becomes restless; it fears God's wrath
LC : 03 :089(432) [0723] petition for the comfort that will restore our **conscience**.
LC : 03 :092(432) [0725] a happy and cheerful **conscience** to stand before him in
LC : 03 :098(433) [0725] also can effect to strengthen and gladden our **conscience**.
LC : 03 :100(433) [0725] forgiveness and a good **conscience**, and have been wholly
LC : 03 :100(433) [0727] God with a good **conscience**, we must pray again that he
LC : 03 :104(434) [0727] himself where the **conscience** and spiritual matters are at
LC : 03 :113(435) [0729] will, our daily bread, a good and cheerful **conscience**, etc.
LC : 04 :044(442) [0743] it when our sins or **conscience** oppress us, and we must
LC : 05 :012(448) [0755] can strengthen your **conscience** and declare: "Let a
LC : 05 :054(453) [0765] examine our heart and **conscience** and act like a person
LC : 05 :057(453) [0767] nothing will prick your **conscience**, you will never go.
LC : 06 :002(457) [0000] burdened and tortured **consciences** with the enumeration
LC : 06 :004(457) [0000] for the comforting and strengthening of our **conscience**.
LC : 06 :009(458) [0000] we ought and a plea for grace and a happy **conscience**?
LC : 06 :017(459) [0000] nobody could feel his **conscience** at peace or have
LC : 06 :019(459) [0000] so that you may attain a happy heart and **conscience**.
LC : 06 :023(459) [0000] A man's own **conscience** would impel him and make him
LC : 06 :032(460) [0000] and happy in their **conscience**, already have the true
EP : 03 :011(474) [0795] intention to sin and to act contrary to one's **conscience**.
EP : 03 :017(475) [0795] resulting love, but continues to sin against his **conscience**.
EP : 05 :007(478) [0803] or terrify but comforts **consciences** that are frightened by
EP : 07 :042(486) [0817] witness of their own **consciences** over our many protests,
EP : 10 :002(493) [0829] we with an inviolate **conscience** yield to their pressure and
EP : 12 :013(499) [0841] in any civic office with a good and clear **conscience**.
EP : 12 :014(499) [0841] without violating his **conscience**, may use an office of the
EP : 12 :015(499) [0841] an oath with a good **conscience** nor pay oath-bound
EP : 12 :016(499) [0841] cannot with a clear **conscience** inflict capital punishment
EP : 12 :017(499) [0841] cannot with a good **conscience** hold or possess private
EP : 12 :017(499) [0841] property but is in **conscience** bound to put it into a
EP : 12 :018(499) [0841] cannot with a good **conscience** be an innkeeper, a
SD : 02 :069(534) [0907] act contrary to their **conscience** and permit sin to rule in
SD : 03 :006(540) [0917] which no poor **conscience** can have any abiding comfort
SD : 03 :030(544) [0925] to afford saddened **consciences** dependable and reliable
SD : 03 :035(545) [0927] to supply tempted **consciences** with abiding comfort.
SD : 03 :064(550) [0937] no love follows) but against his **conscience** remains in sin.
SD : 04 :015(553) [0943] persist in sins against **conscience** or embark deliberately
SD : 04 :023(555) [0945] tempted and troubled **consciences** of the consolation of
SD : 04 :031(556) [0947] to sin against his **conscience**, he can nevertheless retain
SD : 05 :001(558) [0951] and rob disturbed **consciences** of the comfort which they
SD : 07 :001(568) [0971] and against their own **consciences** sought forcibly to
SD : 07 :022(573) [0979] can strengthen your **conscience** from the Word of God
SD : 08 :063(603) [1037] against their own **conscience**, have maliciously and
SD : 10 :002(611) [1053] may still with a clear **conscience**, at the enemies' insistent
SD : 10 :003(611) [1053] be done with a clear **conscience** and without prejudice to
SD : 10 :009(612) [1055] we can with a good **conscience** give in and yield to the
SD : 10 :013(613) [1057] impose such things on **consciences** as necessary, even in
SD : 10 :025(615) [1061] may not do with a clear **conscience** in matters of
SD : 11 :085(630) [1091] inhuman devices contrary to the voice of his **conscience**.
SD : 12 :018(634) [1099] an office in the government with an inviolate **conscience**.
SD : 12 :019(634) [1099] may with an inviolate **conscience** use an office of the
SD : 12 :020(634) [1099] cannot with a good **conscience** swear an oath before a
SD : 12 :021(634) [1099] with an inviolate **conscience** impose the death penalty on
SD : 12 :022(634) [1099] can with a good **conscience** hold or possess private
SD : 12 :023(634) [1099] can with a good **conscience** be an innkeeper, a merchant,

Conscientiously (2)

AP : PR :002(098) [0099] many articles that we could not **conscientiously** surrender.
AP : 23 :060(247) [0379] why we cannot **conscientiously** agree with our opponents

Consecrate (3), Consecrated (8), Consecrates (3), Consecration (6)

AP : 07 :005(169) [0227] which Christ renews, **consecrates**, and governs by his
AP : 07 :008(169) [0229] spirit, who renews, **consecrates**, and governs their hearts.
AP : 22 :008(237) [0359] and were no longer permitted to **consecrate** the elements.
AP : 23 :030(243) [0371] and similar things are "**consecrated** by the word of God
AP : 23 :031(243) [0371] unbelieving husband is **consecrated** through his wife";
AP : 24 :080(264) [0411] that a minister who **consecrates** shows forth the body and
AP : 24 :086(265) [0413] of this was taken to be **consecrated**, the rest was
AP : 24 :093(267) [0417] For after the **consecration** they pray that it may benefit
S3 : 15 :004(316) [0501] articles, such as the **consecration** of churches, the baptism
LC : 01 :091(377) [0607] or all the holy and **consecrated** vestments gathered
LC : 02 :048(416) [0691] a group of people but a **consecrated** house or building.
LC : 04 :009(437) [0733] letters and bulls and **consecrated** altars and churches
EP : 07 :008(482) [0811] 3. Concerning the **consecration** we believe, teach, and
SD : 07 :073(583) [0999] concerning the **consecration** and the common rule that
SD : 07 :084(584) [1001] we take bread and wine, **consecrate** it, distribute it,
SD : 07 :086(584) [1003] by Christ: the **consecration** or words of institution, the
SD : 07 :087(585) [1003] if it should be used to **consecrate** bells, or to cure leprosy,
SD : 07 :108(588) [1009] they teach that the **consecrated** or blessed bread and wine
SD : 07 :121(590) [1013] condemn the papistic **consecration** which ascribes to the
SD : 11 :082(630) [1089] a vessel for noble use, **consecrated** and useful to the

Consensus (12)

PR : PR :003(003) [0007] doctrine as the ancient **consensus** which the universal and
AP : 04 :083(119) [0145] In addition, he cites the **consensus** of all the prophets,
AP : 12 :066(191) [0271] are the church and follow the **consensus** of the church.

Continued ▶

A P : 1 2 :066(191) [0271] But here Peter cites the **consensus** of the church in
A P : 1 2 :066(191) [0271] Surely the **consensus** of the prophets should be
A P : 1 2 :066(191) [0271] be interpreted as the **consensus** of the universal church.
A P : 1 2 :066(191) [0271] issue decrees contrary to this **consensus** of the prophets.
A P : 1 2 :070(192) [0271] of Peter, citing the **consensus** of the prophets, to the
A P : 1 2 :073(192) [0273] Peter clearly cites the **consensus** of the prophets; the
T R : 0 0 :042(328) [0517] To dissent from the **consensus** of so many nations and to
E P : R N :004(465) [0777] as the unanimous **consensus** and exposition of our
S D : 1 0 :023(615) [1061] To dissent from the **consensus** of so many nations and to

Consent (5), Consented (1), Consenting (1)
S 3 : 0 3 :011(305) [0481] thoughts to which they **consented** (for evil impulses, lust,
S 3 : 0 3 :029(308) [0487] to repent of when they did not **consent** to evil thoughts?
S 3 : 1 1 :003(315) [0499] therefore unwilling to **consent** to their abominable
L C : 0 1 :250(399) [0651] We are not even to **consent** to or permit such a thing, but
L C : 0 3 :107(434) [0729] quite a different thing from **consenting** and yielding to it.
L C : 0 3 :108(435) [0729] But to **consent** to it is to give it free rein and neither resist
S D : 0 7 :017(572) [0979] By common **consent** Dr. Luther drafted the Smalcald

Consequence (5), Consequences (3)
P R : P R :024(013) [0023] the only possible **consequence** of which is that finally
S 2 : 0 2 :016(295) [0467] The second is a **consequence** of this: evil spirits have
S 2 : 0 2 :029(297) [0471] implications, and its **consequences** in order that we may
S 2 : 0 4 :013(300) [0475] All this is a **consequence** of his wishing to be the head of
T R : 0 0 :037(326) [0515] The **consequences** demonstrate that they have been great
L C : 0 1 :260(400) [0655] judge or witness, let the **consequences** be what they may.
E P : 1 0 :006(493) [0831] and suffer in **consequence** what God sends us and what
S D : P R :009(503) [0849] a mere semantic problem of little or no **consequence**.

Consequent (1), Consequently (22)
P R : P R :022(012) [0019] **Consequently** the responsibility devolves upon the
A G : 2 0 :035(046) [0057] **Consequently** this teaching concerning faith is not to be
A G : 2 7 :025(074) [0079] **Consequently** the popes were well aware that some
A L : 1 3 :002(035) [0049] **Consequently** the sacraments should be so used that faith,
A L : 2 0 :010(042) [0053] **Consequently** whoever trusts that he merits grace by
A L : 2 2 :011(050) [0061] **Consequently**, if any people preferred to use both kinds in
A L : 2 4 :033(060) [0067] **Consequently** the Mass is to be used to this end, that the
A P : 0 2 :027(104) [0113] **Consequently** it is not a pure privation, but also a corrupt
S 2 : 0 2 :012(295) [0465] **Consequently** purgatory and all the pomp, services, and
S 2 : 0 2 :012(295) [0465] All this may **consequently** be discarded, apart entirely
S 2 : 0 4 :006(299) [0473] **Consequently** the church must continue to exist without
S 2 : 0 4 :009(300) [0473] **Consequently** the church cannot be better governed and
S 2 : 0 4 :016(301) [0477] **Consequently** we ought not here kiss his feet or say, "You
T R : 0 0 :016(322) [0509] **Consequently**, inasmuch as such superiority is impossible
T R : 0 0 :042(328) [0517] **Consequently** our consciences are sufficiently excused.
T R : 0 0 :066(331) [0523] **Consequently**, when the regular bishops become enemies
L C : 0 1 :029(368) [0589] **Consequently**, in order to show that God will not have
L C : 0 1 :137(384) [0619] up in kindness; **consequently**, by the punishment of God
L C : 0 1 :257(399) [0653] by false witnesses and **consequently** punished in his body,
L C : 0 1 :258(399) [0653] **Consequently**, a poor man is inevitably oppressed, loses
L C : 0 3 :002(420) [0697] **Consequently** nothing is so necessary as to call upon God
S D : 0 3 :062(550) [0937] them by the Holy Spirit and the **consequent** good works.
S D : 0 7 :003(569) [0973] and not on earth, and **consequently** nothing but bread

Consider (49), Considered (29), Considering (5), Considers (10)
P R : P R :013(007) [0013] and Christian zeal, **consider** it in all its aspects, have their
P R : P R :013(007) [0013] us without reserve their **considered** judgment concerning
P R : P R :015(007) [0013] and exhorted to **consider** diligently and earnestly the
A G : P R :018(026) [0041] in Ratisbon had **considered** the proposal concerning a
A G : 2 6 :010(065) [0071] good works were **considered** secular and unspiritual: the
A G : 2 6 :017(066) [0073] they were not to be **considered** necessary observances.
A G : 2 7 :001(070) [0075] necessary to begin by **considering** what opinions have
A G : 2 8 :053(090) [0091] men's consciences by **considering** these things necessary
A G : 2 8 :058(091) [0091] Those who **consider** the appointment of Sunday in place
A G : 2 8 :078(094) [0095] our petition, let them **consider** how they will answer for it
A G : 0 0 :005(095) [0095] matters which we have **considered** it necessary to adduce
A G : 0 0 :007(096) [0095] If anyone should **consider** that it is lacking in some
A L : 2 8 :066(092) [0093] with the decree one must **consider** what the perpetual aim
A P : 0 4 :012(108) [0123] But let the intelligent reader just **consider** this.
A P : 0 4 :039(112) [0131] errors of our opponents that we have been **considering**.
A P : 0 4 :083(119) [0145] discuss this passage later on in **considering** penitence.
A P : 0 4 :087(120) [0147] end, "Having therefore **considered** and discussed these
A P : 0 4 :188(133) [0173] upon devout minds to **consider** the promises, and we
A P : 0 4 :278(149) [0199] in penitence we must **consider** faith and fruits together, so
A P : 0 4 :280(149) [0201] It is necessary to **consider** passages in their context,
A P : 0 4 :280(149) [0201] When passages are **considered** in their own context, they
A P : 1 0 :003(179) [0247] "Therefore we must **consider** that Christ is in us, not only
A P : 1 2 :003(182) [0253] us out patiently and to **consider** carefully this most
A P : 1 2 :141(204) [0295] must enrage anyone who **considers** the demonic doctrines
A P : 1 8 :007(226) [0337] and trust that God **considers**, hears, and forgives us.
A P : 1 8 :008(226) [0337] determine this if they **consider** what their hearts believe
A P : 2 1 :027(232) [0349] Christ but to have her example **considered** and followed.
A P : 2 3 :002(239) [0363] let the intelligent reader **consider** the impudence of these
A P : 2 3 :003(239) [0363] country, however savage or cruel, would **consider**.
A P : 2 7 :032(274) [0431] deceive himself; for if he **considers** carefully, he will
S 1 : P R :013(290) [0459] of a council were to **consider** such fundamental matters
S 2 : 0 2 :010(294) [0465] and what he does to be **considered** equal or superior to
S 2 : 0 4 :004(299) [0473] all in vain unless you **consider** me your god and are
S 3 : 0 3 :011(305) [0481] they did not **consider** sin), wicked words, and wicked
S 3 : 0 3 :018(306) [0483] without being able to **consider** Christ and faith.
S 3 : 0 9 :000(314) [0497] We **consider** the greater excommunication, as the pope
S 3 : 1 3 :001(315) [0499] removed or eradicated, he will not count or **consider** it.
S 3 : 1 3 :003(315) [0499] our works if they are **considered** apart from God's grace
T R : 0 0 :052(329) [0519] Therefore, let the godly **consider** the enormous errors of
S C : 0 9 :003(354) [0561] elders who rule well be **considered** worthy of double
L C : P R :016(361) [0571] They evidently **consider** themselves much wiser than God
L C : S P :002(362) [0575] of his craft is rejected and **considered** incompetent.
L C : 0 1 :011(366) [0583] Again, **consider** what we used to do in our blindness
L C : 0 1 :116(381) [0615] nothing ought to be **considered** more important than the
L C : 0 1 :128(383) [0617] that recognizes and **considers** this, unless he is led to it by
L C : 0 1 :129(383) [0617] and impels everyone to **consider** what his parents have
L C : 0 1 :132(383) [0619] see how important God **considers** this commandment.
L C : 0 1 :139(384) [0621] how important God **considers** obedience, since he so
L C : 0 1 :168(388) [0629] Parents should **consider** that they owe obedience to God,
L C : 0 1 :197(392) [0637] Christian life would be **considered** just as acceptable, and
L C : 0 1 :262(400) [0655] and the children of God and yet **consider** this no sin.
L C : 0 1 :295(404) [0665] They **considered** this no more a sin or disgrace than it is
L C : 0 1 :300(405) [0665] those whom the world **considers** wicked rogues, but
L C : 0 1 :303(406) [0667] yet this must not be **considered** as illegally acquired, but
L C : 0 1 :304(406) [0667] The world does not **consider** this wrong, and it does not
L C : 0 1 :314(407) [0671] day in church, this is **considered** a precious work that
L C : 0 1 :330(410) [0677] Where men **consider** this and take it to heart, there will
L C : 0 2 :020(412) [0683] but we neither see nor **consider** what the words enjoin on
L C : 0 3 :057(427) [0713] He would rightly be **considered** a rogue and a scoundrel
L C : 0 3 :072(430) [0717] Here we **consider** the poor bread-basket — the needs of
L C : 0 4 :009(437) [0733] If people used to **consider** it a great thing when the pope
L C : 0 4 :015(438) [0735] Word and ordinance, **consider** nothing but the water
L C : 0 4 :038(441) [0741] Thus we have **considered** the three things that must be
L C : 0 4 :042(442) [0743] that if timid nature **considers** them, it may well doubt
L C : 0 5 :004(447) [0753] or command, which is the chief thing to be **considered**.
L C : 0 5 :020(449) [0757] We have briefly **considered** the first part, namely, the
L C : 0 5 :033(450) [0761] It remains for us to **consider** who it is that receives this
L C : 0 5 :042(451) [0763] a long period of time are not to be **considered** Christians.
L C : 0 6 :028(460) [0000] be despised, especially when we **consider** our great need.
S D : P R :004(502) [0847] We **consider** this Confession a genuinely Christian
S D : 0 1 :005(509) [0861] In fact, we must **consider** this as the chief sin, the root
S D : 0 1 :033(514) [0869] we must and can **consider**, discuss, and believe these two
S D : 0 2 :005(521) [0881] when it is preached, but **considers** it foolishness; nor does
S D : 0 2 :009(522) [0883] and teaches them they **consider** it all mere foolishness and
S D : 0 2 :024(526) [0891] hypocrites do, yet he **considers** it folly and cannot believe
S D : 0 2 :072(535) [0909] exercise ourselves in **considering** what a grievous sin it is
S D : 0 3 :012(541) [0919] of St. Paul are to be **considered** and taken as
S D : 0 3 :055(549) [0935] Christ, it is important to **consider** carefully in what way
S D : 0 7 :017(572) [0977] Germany in Smalcald to **consider** what kind of doctrinal
S D : 0 7 :029(574) [0981] for he did not **consider** it sufficiently,' etc, let me say now
S D : 0 7 :038(576) [0985] read, and they do not **consider** that in the proposition
S D : 0 7 :069(582) [0997] many and great sins, who **consider** themselves unworthy
S D : 0 7 :091(586) [1005] desire to have them **considered** as appealed to herewith.
S D : 0 8 :087(608) [1047] Hence we **consider** it a pernicious error to deprive Christ
S D : 1 0 :005(611) [1053] We should not **consider** as matters of indifference, and we
S D : 1 0 :026(615) [1061] of men are to be **considered** as of themselves worship of
S D : 1 1 :002(616) [1063] can nor should be **considered** useless and unnecessary,
S D : 1 1 :009(617) [1065] nothing more is to be **considered** in connection with it,
S D : 1 1 :013(619) [1067] the contrary, we should **consider** the counsel, purpose,
S D : 1 1 :023(619) [1069] he has also graciously **considered** and elected to salvation
S D : 1 1 :028(620) [1071] Hence if we want to **consider** our eternal election to
S D : 1 1 :065(626) [1083] We should accordingly **consider** God's eternal election in
S D : 1 1 :083(630) [1091] It is to be **considered** diligently that God punishes sin with

Considerable (2), Considerately (1), Consideration (13)
P R : P R :013(007) [0013] it was sent to a **considerable** number of electors, princes,
P R : P R :016(008) [0013] volition and with due **consideration** they accepted,
P R : P R :020(010) [0017] of the former) from a **consideration** of the Holy Supper
A G : 2 4 :010(057) [0065] it in almost all churches for a monetary **consideration**.
A G : 2 7 :007(071) [0077] seemly to show more **consideration** to women as the
A G : 2 7 :029(075) [0079] of themselves, willingly, and after due **consideration**.
A G : 2 7 :030(075) [0079] be assumed only after due **consideration** and counsel.
A L : 2 3 :026(055) [0065] canons show some **consideration** toward those who have
A L : 2 7 :007(071) [0077] men, although more **consideration** should have been given
A P : 0 4 :314(156) [0207] well, and a careful **consideration** of it will teach us much
A P : 1 0 :001(179) [0247] examination and **consideration** of it, we firmly defend
A P : 1 2 :035(186) [0261] second part of our **consideration** of penitence, we
S C : 0 9 :006(355) [0561] "You husbands, live **considerately** with your wives,
L C : 0 3 :025(423) [0705] in his promise, or out of **consideration** for his own needs.
S D : 0 2 :073(535) [0909] questions that for a **considerable** number of years have
S D : 0 3 :037(546) [0929] which God takes into **consideration** in this article or

Consideret (1)
A L : 2 5 :012(063) [0071] Dist. 5, in the chapter "**Consideret**," admits that such

Consign (1), Consigned (5)
A P : 0 4 :084(119) [0145] says (Gal. 3:22), "God **consigned** all things to sin, that
A P : 0 4 :084(119) [0145] merit, for he says that all are guilty and **consigned** to sin.
A P : 1 2 :031(186) [0259] days I must depart; I am **consigned** to the gates of Sheol.
A P : 1 2 :081(194) [0275] Gal. 3:22, "The scripture **consigned** all things to sin, that
L C : 0 1 :055(372) [0595] the truth and God's Word and **consign** it to the devil.
E P : 1 1 :010(495) [0833] testifies that "God has **consigned** all men to disobedience,

Consist (15), Consistent (1), Consistently (3), Consisting (1), Consists (27)
A G : 1 6 :004(037) [0051] Actually, true perfection **consists** alone of proper fear of
A G : 2 7 :050(079) [0083] and right service of God **consist** of these things and not
A L : 1 2 :003(034) [0049] speaking, repentance **consists** of these two parts: one is
A L : 2 6 :007(065) [0071] the whole of repentance was thought to **consist** of these.
A L : 2 6 :008(065) [0071] was thought to **consist** wholly in the observance of certain
A L : 2 7 :050(079) [0083] and true service of God **consist** of these things and not of
A P : 0 4 :173(131) [0171] righteousness does not **consist** in our own merit, but in
A P : 0 4 :392(167) [0225] judgment of all the faithful are **consistently** against them.
A P : 1 2 :014(184) [0257] and these **consist** of stupid observances like pilgrimages,
A P : 1 2 :106(197) [0283] That at least would be more **consistent**.
A P : 1 6 :009(224) [0333] Christian perfection **consists** in not holding property.
A P : 2 7 :045(277) [0435] imagined that perfection **consists** in casting off
A P : 2 7 :046(277) [0435] (Matt. 5:3) does not **consist** in the abandonment of
A P : 2 7 :048(277) [0437] Perfection **consists** in that which Christ adds, "Follow
S 3 : 0 3 :038(309) [0489] be uncertain, for it **consists** not of the dubious, sinful
S 3 : 1 2 :003(315) [0499] Its holiness does not **consist** of surplices, tonsures, albs,
S 3 : 1 2 :003(315) [0499] Holy Scriptures, but it **consists** of the Word of God and
S C : 0 5 :016(349) [0553] Answer: Confession **consists** of two parts.
S C : 0 9 :001(354) [0561] ***consisting** of certain passages of the Scriptures, selected*
L C : 0 1 :021(367) [0585] Idolatry does not **consist** merely of erecting an image and
L C : 0 1 :070(374) [0601] honor to God's name **consists** of looking to it for all
L C : 0 1 :077(375) [0603] taught that its right use **consists** not only of words but
L C : 0 1 :094(378) [0607] of this commandment **consist** not of the resting but of the
L C : 0 2 :063(419) [0695] In them **consists** all our wisdom, which surpasses all the
L C : 0 3 :001(420) [0697] The best and most blessed life **consists** of these things.
L C : 0 3 :030(424) [0705] that all our safety and protection **consist** in prayer alone.
L C : 0 3 :119(436) [0731] But the efficacy of prayer **consists** in our learning also to

Continued ▶

LC : 04 :065(444) [0749] This act or observance **consists** in being dipped into the
LC : 06 :015(458) [0000] as I have often said, that confession **consists** of two parts.
EP : 03 :004(473) [0793] before God **consists** in this, that God forgives us our sins
EP : 03 :019(475) [0795] in us the renewal which **consists** in love toward God and
EP : 07 :020(484) [0813] heavenly feast is and **consists** solely and alone in the most
EP : 07 :020(484) [0813] Worthiness **consists** not at all in our own virtues or in our
EP : 07 :038(486) [0817] heavenly meal does not **consist** only in true faith in
EP : 12 :005(498) [0839] before God does not **consist** wholly in the unique merit of
SD : 02 :027(527) [0891] "The grace of God **consists** merely in this, that God in the
SD : 03 :015(541) [0919] Therefore his obedience **consists** not only in his suffering
SD : 03 :023(543) [0923] of faith before God **consists** solely in the gracious
SD : 03 :030(544) [0925] of faith before God **consists** solely in a gracious
SD : 03 :036(545) [0929] article of justification listed above) **consists** solely therein.
SD : 03 :039(546) [0929] righteousness of faith **consists** solely in the forgiveness of
SD : 03 :048(548) [0933] by faith before God **consists** of two pieces or parts,
SD : 07 :071(582) [0997] And worthiness does not **consist** in the weakness or
SD : 07 :093(586) [1005] which we have stood **consistently** from the outbreak of
SD : 07 :124(591) [1015] that worthiness does not **consist** in true faith alone but
SD : 10 :018(614) [1059] show that this has **consistently** been the conviction and
SD : 11 :003(616) [1063] teaching on this article **consists** of the following points:

Consolation (53), Consolations (2)
PR : PR :024(013) [0023] and to the needed **consolation** and instruction of poor,
AG : 00 :001(047) [0059] instruction, the **consolation** of consciences, and the
AG : 25 :002(061) [0069] concerning the **consolation** of the Word of absolution so
AG : 25 :013(063) [0071] part), for the **consolation** of terrified consciences, and also
AG : 26 :013(066) [0073] heard anything of the **consolation** of the grace of Christ.
AG : 26 :015(066) [0073] things, such as faith, **consolation** in severe trials, and the
AL : 20 :007(042) [0053] and it can afford more **consolation** than their old
AL : 20 :015(043) [0055] it offers the greatest **consolation** because the consciences
AL : 20 :019(043) [0055] of works when **consolation** from the Gospel was not
AL : 20 :022(044) [0055] not be deprived of **consolation** but know that grace and
AL : 24 :007(056) [0065] and the great **consolation** it offers to anxious
AL : 24 :033(060) [0067] is administered to those who have need of **consolation**.
AL : 25 :004(062) [0069] reminded of the great **consolation** it brings to terrified
AL : 26 :013(066) [0073] had never heard the **consolation** of grace and of the
AL : 26 :015(066) [0073] of civil affairs, and the **consolation** of sorely tried
AP : 04 :002(107) [0121] consciences the abundant **consolation** that they need.
AP : 04 :003(107) [0121] consciences of the **consolation** offered them in Christ.
AP : 04 :060(115) [0137] This is the greatest **consolation** in all afflictions, and our
AP : 04 :062(115) [0139] For these, our hearts must again receive **consolation**.
AP : 04 :062(115) [0139] For this **consolation** is a new and spiritual life.
AP : 04 :085(119) [0147] have a certain and firm **consolation** against the terrors of
AP : 04 :106(122) [0153] by the law but receive **consolation** by faith, and that
AP : 04 :118(123) [0155] provides a sure and firm **consolation** for devout minds.
AP : 04 :156(128) [0165] of sure and firm **consolation** for pious minds — wheather
AP : 04 :275(148) [0199] since a terrified conscience needs manifold **consolations**.
AP : 04 :285(150) [0201] This offers the greatest **consolation** to faithful consciences
AP : 04 :299(153) [0205] see the most complete **consolation** offered them.
AP : 04 :303(154) [0205] godly and wholesome **consolation** to frightened
AP : 04 :314(156) [0207] whole issue and bring **consolation** to well-disposed
AP : 07 :009(170) [0229] Creed offers us these **consolations** that we may not
AP : 11 :002(180) [0249] consciences have received **consolation** from our teaching.
AP : 11 :002(180) [0249] discloses a sure and firm **consolation** for the conscience.
AP : 12 :002(182) [0253] Gospel, so exceedingly salutary and full of **consolation**.
AP : 12 :046(188) [0263] Platonic figment but as **consolation** truly sustaining a life
AP : 12 :051(189) [0265] to make room for **consolation** and quickening because
AP : 12 :051(189) [0265] not feel God's wrath in their smugness spurn **consolation**.
AP : 12 :052(189) [0265] these two, terror and **consolation**, to teach that these are
AP : 12 :084(194) [0277] consciences a firm **consolation** without which no one can
AP : 18 :008(226) [0337] terrified hearts hear the Gospel and receive **consolation**.
AP : 20 :009(228) [0341] you away from the **consolation** which this article of ours
S3 : 03 :008(304) [0481] the Gospel offers **consolation** and forgiveness in more
S3 : 03 :012(305) [0481] — with the added **consolation** that a man who properly
S3 : 03 :016(305) [0483] avail before God, this **consolation** was offered: If
S3 : 03 :018(306) [0483] to God, seeking **consolation** in its own works, according
S3 : 03 :020(306) [0485] of absolution, for his **consolation** was made to rest on his
S3 : 04 :000(310) [0491] the mutual conversation and **consolation** of brethren.
S3 : 08 :001(312) [0493] in the Gospel, is a **consolation** and help against sin and a
TR : 00 :044(328) [0517] consciences of a firm **consolation**, and abolish true
LC : 01 :016(366) [0585] should know no other **consolation** or confidence than
LC : 01 :021(367) [0585] and seeks help and **consolation** from creatures, saints, or
LC : 01 :070(374) [0601] of looking to it for all **consolation** and therefore calling
LC : 05 :062(454) [0767] desires grace and **consolation** should compel himself to go
LC : 06 :014(458) [0000] feels its sin and desires **consolation**, it has here a sure
EP : 07 :017(484) [0813] he is to work life and **consolation** in the hearts of
SD : 04 :023(555) [0945] consciences of the **consolation** of the Gospel, give

Console (6), Consoled (4), Consoles (13), Consoling (2)
AL : 20 :026(045) [0057] but as confidence which **consoles** and lifts up terrified
AP : 04 :045(113) [0133] terrors of conscience it **consoles** and encourages our
AP : 04 :062(115) [0139] brings peace of mind, **consoles** us, receives the forgiveness
AP : 04 :135(125) [0159] But when we are **consoled** by faith through hearing the
AP : 04 :198(134) [0175] teach us this as they **console** us against the good fortune
AP : 04 :249(143) [0191] conscience and encourages and **consoles** terrified hearts.
AP : 04 :324(157) [0209] Looking at his mercy, faith comforts and **consoles** us.
AP : 04 :382(165) [0225] consciences are **consoled** by faith and believe that our
AP : 11 :009(182) [0251] word on faith, which **consoles** and encourages
AP : 12 :007(183) [0255] of the keys does not **console** us before God, what is there
AP : 12 :012(184) [0257] which grasps the absolution and **consoles** the conscience.
AP : 12 :038(187) [0261] with faith, where faith **consoles** and sustains the anxious
AP : 12 :039(187) [0261] absolution strengthens and **consoles** the conscience.
AP : 12 :045(187) [0263] sins, in the latter part he **consoles** us and shows us the
AP : 12 :051(189) [0265] God's own proper work is to quicken and **console**.
AP : 12 :052(189) [0265] contrition and the faith that **consoles** and justifies.
AP : 12 :057(189) [0267] her penance, the faith that encouraged and **consoled** her.
AP : 12 :105(197) [0283] forgiving sins and **consoling** consciences, does not need an
AP : 12 :178(211) [0309] teach the faith that justifies and **consoles** faithful hearts.
AP : 21 :026(232) [0349] summoned to **console** a dying doctor of theology, do
AP : 22 :010(237) [0361] was instituted to **console** and strengthen terrified hearts
AP : 24 :043(257) [0399] not preach the Gospel or **console** consciences or point
AP : 24 :048(258) [0401] This teaching really **consoles** consciences.
S3 : 03 :004(304) [0481] immediately adds the **consoling** promise of grace in the
S3 : 03 :027(307) [0487] pope took the money, **consoled** the people with his power

Consort (1)
LC : 01 :230(396) [0645] arch-thieves who **consort** with lords and princes and daily

Conspicuous (3)
AG : 01 :002(056) [0065] Meanwhile no **conspicuous** changes have been made in
AG : 24 :040(061) [0069] times, and since no **conspicuous** change has been made in
AP : 12 :092(196) [0279] parts of penitence in order to make it more **conspicuous**.

Conspiracy (1), Conspiracies (1)
AP : 12 :068(192) [0271] who as though by a **conspiracy** defend the false notions
AP : 27 :009(270) [0423] to the saints, and the **conspiracies** against good men?

Constance (2)
S2 : 04 :007(299) [0473] in which the Council of **Constance** acted with reference to
S3 : 06 :002(311) [0493] and the Council of **Constance** that as much is included

Constancy (1)
SD : 11 :032(621) [1073] For such **constancy** he has promised his grace (I Cor. 1:8;

Constant (8), Constantly (47)
PR : PR :020(010) [0017] our and the Formula's **constant** intention Christians are
AP : 02 :011(102) [0109] these that the prophets **constantly** complain, namely,
AP : 04 :212(136) [0179] the conscience, men **constantly** choose other works, make
AP : 04 :276(148) [0199] example, are signs that **constantly** admonish, cheer, and
AP : 04 :285(150) [0201] always tormented and **constantly** invents other works and
AP : 12 :089(195) [0279] **Constantly** tossed about in such doubt, they never
AP : 12 :148(205) [0299] itself takes place by **constantly** mortifying the old life.
AP : 12 :157(207) [0301] On the contrary, it **constantly** teaches that we obtain the
AP : 15 :050(222) [0329] Here Paul is our **constant** champion; everywhere he
AP : 21 :036(234) [0353] of faith in sickness and **constantly** affirmed that God
AP : 27 :027(274) [0429] does not say, "We are **constantly** receiving another hood
S1 : PR :007(289) [0457] on their side, God has **constantly** promoted his work, has
S3 : 08 :010(313) [0497] we should and must **constantly** maintain that God will
S3 : 13 :001(315) [0499] what I have heretofore **constantly** taught on this subject,
TR : 00 :082(000) [0529] thus hold, confess, and **constantly** will teach, through
LC : PR :001(358) [0567] trivial reasons that we **constantly** treat the Catechism and
LC : PR :014(360) [0571] our eyes and in our hands as a **constant** token and sign.
LC : PR :014(360) [0571] He knows the **constant** and furious attacks and assaults
LC : PR :019(361) [0573] Catechism daily, and **constantly** put it into practice,
LC : SP :024(364) [0579] which we should **constantly** teach and require young
LC : 01 :070(374) [0601] children should be **constantly** urged and encouraged to
LC : 01 :070(374) [0601] God's name and keep it **constantly** upon their lips in all
LC : 01 :075(375) [0601] may become familiar and be **constantly** practiced.
LC : 01 :080(375) [0603] be refreshed and not be exhausted by **constant** labor.
LC : 01 :092(377) [0607] Accordingly, I **constantly** repeat that all our life and work
LC : 01 :101(379) [0609] of devotion, and it **constantly** cleanses the heart and its
LC : 01 :310(407) [0669] all the rest, one that **constantly** accuses us and shows just
LC : 01 :326(409) [0675] order that this may be **constantly** repeated and never
LC : 01 :331(410) [0677] before our eyes and **constantly** in our memory, and
LC : 02 :013(412) [0681] that he has given and **constantly** sustains my body, soul,
LC : 02 :054(417) [0693] Forgiveness is needed **constantly**, for although God's
LC : 03 :047(426) [0711] doctrine, we ought **constantly** to cry out against all who
LC : 03 :089(432) [0723] and believe God and is **constantly** aroused by evil desires
LC : 03 :089(432) [0723] Therefore it is necessary **constantly** to turn to this petition
LC : 03 :091(432) [0723] In short, unless God **constantly** forgives, we are lost.
LC : 03 :116(435) [0731] do on earth but to pray **constantly** against this
LC : 04 :019(438) [0737] Therefore, we **constantly** teach that the sacraments and
LC : 05 :084(456) [0773] because the devil so **constantly** besieges you and lies in
EP : 06 :004(480) [0805] the believers are in a **constant** war against their flesh (that
EP : 06 :004(480) [0807] for the law of God **constantly** to light their way lest in
EP : 11 :022(497) [0837] of one heart in him and **constantly** abide in this Christian
SD : RN :020(508) [0859] but that it is the same simple, unchanging, **constant** truth.
SD : 01 :038(515) [0871] that he has given and **constantly** sustains my body, soul,
SD : 01 :056(518) [0877] Augustine therefore **constantly** speaks in this fashion:
SD : 02 :060(533) [0905] Spirit and oppose and **constantly** rebel against
SD : 03 :066(550) [0937] remain steadfastly and **constantly** with the doctrine of
SD : 04 :010(553) [0941] impossible for it not to be **constantly** doing what is good.
SD : 04 :011(553) [0941] ask, faith has already done them and is **constantly** active.
SD : 05 :023(562) [0959] patriarchs themselves, **constantly** reminded themselves
SD : 05 :024(562) [0961] must be urged **constantly** and diligently in the church of
SD : 06 :004(564) [0963] necessary to hold this **constantly** before believers' eyes
SD : 06 :023(568) [0969] they continue in a **constant** conflict against the Old
SD : 07 :033(575) [0983] by it steadfastly and defended it **constantly** until he died.
SD : 08 :096(610) [1049] therewith, and rejoice **constantly** that our flesh and blood
SD : 11 :056(625) [1081] command and operate **constantly** with the Word, while

Constantinople (2)
TR : 00 :018(323) [0509] or Eugubium or **Constantinople** or Rhegium or
TR : 00 :021(323) [0509] bishops of Rome and **Constantinople** over the primacy,

Consternation (2)
AP : 02 :034(104) [0113] "I said in my **consternation**, men are all liars,"
LC : 05 :055(453) [0767] was thrown into **consternation**, saying, "Alas, I am not

Constitute (8), Constituted (1), Constitutes (3)
AG : 27 :061(080) [0083] before God, that they **constitute** Christian perfection,
AL : 27 :061(080) [0083] they justify, that they **constitute** Christian perfection, that
LC : SP :019(363) [0579] and learning which **constitute** the Christian's
LC : 04 :046(442) [0743] and the Word together **constitute** one Baptism, body and
LC : 04 :053(443) [0745] For my faith does not **constitute** Baptism but receives it.
LC : 05 :010(448) [0755] bread and wine and **constitutes** it a sacrament which is
LC : 05 :017(448) [0757] Word by which it was **constituted** a sacrament is not
EP : 02 :012(471) [0789] and that this fulfilling **constitutes** our righteousness
SD : 08 :011(593) [1019] for itself so as to be or **constitute** a distinct person, but
SD : 08 :011(593) [1019] in such a way that they **constitute** a single person in which
SD : 08 :036(598) [1027] and since both natures **constitute** only one person,
SD : 10 :021(614) [1059] of the Pope, which **constitutes** an appendix to the

Constitution (4), Constitutions (1)
AP : 02 :017(102) [0109] a balanced physical **constitution**, but these gifts as well: a
AP : 02 :025(103) [0111] of the physical **constitution**, but the evil inclination of
AP : 11 :009(182) [0251] in this heap of **constitutions**, glosses, summae, and
AP : 15 :019(217) [0319] be the very form and **constitution** of the kingdom of
TR : 00 :033(325) [0513] Wherefore the **constitution** of Boniface VIII, Distinction

Constrain (2), Constrained (6), Constrains (1)
PR : PR :008(005) [0011] doctrine would be **constrained** to desist from their
AL : 2 8 :011(082) [0085] manifest harm, and **constrains** men with the sword and
S 2 : 0 2 :013(295) [0467] Scriptures that would **constrain** him to adopt such an
SC : PR :001(338) [0533] when I was a visitor **constrained** me to prepare this brief
SC : PR :023(341) [0539] accord, he will feel **constrained** to receive it, he will insist
LC : 0 1 :321(408) [0673] we may see why we are **constrained** and compelled to
LC : 0 3 :105(434) [0727] on all sides, we are **constrained** to cry out and pray every
SD : 0 1 :034(514) [0869] of our Christian faith **constrain** and compel us to
SD : 0 7 :005(570) [0973] Later, when they were **constrained** by the words of Christ

Construct (2), Constructed (1), Construction (3)
AP : 0 4 :234(140) [0185] people put the best **construction** on the faults of their
AP : 0 4 :242(141) [0187] that it puts the best **construction** even on the more
AP : 1 2 :155(207) [0301] these instances they **construct** the universal rule that for
S 3 : 0 3 :039(309) [0489] works, for all of this is **constructed** on an unreal and
LC : 0 1 :289(404) [0663] always to put the best **construction** upon all we may hear
SD : 0 8 :040(598) [1029] mask since it will finally **construct** a kind of Christ after

Consult (1), Consultation (1), Consulting (1)
AP : PR :010(099) [0101] the Apology in **consultation** with others, but as it was
AP : 0 7 :040(176) [0241] therefore, we must **consult** their writings, not merely their
TR : 0 0 :010(321) [0505] he at once preached the Gospel without **consulting** Peter.

Consume (1), Consumed (2), Consuming (1)
AP : 1 2 :167(209) [0305] says that venial sins are **consumed**, that is, that distrust of
TR : 0 0 :082(334) [0527] the future who would **consume** the alms of the churches
LC : 0 1 :242(397) [0649] entire hoard will be **consumed** by rust so that you will
SD : 0 8 :087(608) [1047] us poor sinners is like a **consuming** fire on dry stubble,

Consummation (2)
AL : 1 7 :001(038) [0051] also teach that at the **consummation** of the world Christ
AP : 1 7 :001(224) [0335] we confess that at the **consummation** of the world Christ

Contact (2), Contacts (1)
AP : 0 2 :007(101) [0107] whether it came through **contact** with the apple or
AP : 1 6 :012(224) [0333] for it teaches that if **contacts** have the approval of
SD : 1 2 :008(633) [1097] who were forced into **contact** with the open idolatry and

Contain (13), Contained (8), Contains (14)
PR : PR :003(003) [0007] to the doctrine that is **contained** in it, that is based solidly
PR : PR :014(007) [0013] they were found to **contain** all kinds of Christian,
PR : PR :015(007) [0013] diligently and earnestly the doctrine **contained** in it.
AP : 0 2 :016(102) [0109] Scriptures righteousness **contains** not merely the second
AP : 0 4 :034(111) [0129] the second table, which **contain** the civil righteousness
AP : 0 4 :054(114) [0137] Scripture **contains** many pleas for mercy, and the holy
AP : 0 4 :252(143) [0191] the law will be justified," **contain** nothing contrary to our
AP : 0 4 :253(143) [0191] words, spoken so simply, **contain** no error, but our
AP : 0 4 :255(144) [0193] They **contain** two elements.
AP : 0 4 :261(145) [0195] Daniel's sermon **contains** two parts.
AP : 0 4 :290(151) [0203] The second **contains** much that is harmful.
AP : 0 7 :033(175) [0239] especially when they **contain** a discipline that serves to
AP : 0 7 :043(177) [0243] decree and says that it **contains** nothing contrary to the
AP : 1 2 :049(188) [0265] Here the first part **contains** contrition, while the second
AP : 1 5 :027(219) [0323] libraries, that do not **contain** a single syllable about
AP : 2 1 :034(234) [0353] these and thought they **contained** some sort of magical
AP : 2 1 :034(234) [0353] horoscopes carved at a particular time **contain** power.
AP : 2 1 :037(234) [0355] the rosaries, all of which **contain** many things that
AP : 2 1 :040(235) [0355] scholastics and canonists **contain** many false opinions and
AP : 2 7 :020(272) [0427] a promise of God, which **contains** a covenant of grace and
AP : 2 8 :019(284) [0449] our position and **contains** the deepest kind of comfort and
S 3 : 1 5 :004(316) [0501] of magic tricks which **contains** silly and childish articles,
LC : SP :018(363) [0577] in which everything **contained** in Scripture is
LC : 0 1 :293(404) [0665] the injunctions and prohibitions **contained** in them.
LC : 0 1 :322(408) [0673] said before, these words **contain** both a wrathful threat
LC : 0 2 :005(411) [0679] if all the thoughts **contained** in the Scriptures and
LC : 0 2 :026(413) [0685] up one phrase which **contains** the substance of the article;
LC : 0 4 :006(437) [0733] first, that these words **contain** God's commandment and
LC : 0 4 :017(438) [0737] sufficiently extol, for it **contains** and conveys all the
LC : 0 4 :029(440) [0739] it to us so that we may grasp the treasure it **contains**?
LC : 0 5 :070(454) [0769] of sins, which **contains** and conveys God's grace and
EP : RN :005(465) [0777] as both of them are **contained** in his printed works.
EP : RN :005(465) [0777] "the layman's Bible" and **contain** everything which Holy
SD : RN :019(507) [0857] against the errors **contained** here and there in the writings
SD : 1 1 :051(624) [1079] This article also **contains** mighty admonitions and

Container (2)
SD : 0 8 :032(597) [1025] is poured from one **container** into another, an exchange
SD : 0 8 :071(605) [1041] wine, or oil is poured from one **container** into another.

Contamination (1)
AP : 2 4 :091(266) [0415] It is a **contamination** of the Gospel, a corruption of the

Contemplating (1), Contemplation (2)
AP : 0 4 :353(161) [0217] our opponents teach about **contemplation** or perfection.
LC : 0 6 :026(460) [0000] making of you a mirror for **contemplating** themselves.
SD : 0 7 :061(580) [0995] in the preaching and **contemplation** of the Gospel as well

Contemporary (2), Contemporaries (5)
PR : PR :003(003) [0007] this confession as the **contemporary** symbol of their faith
PR : PR :018(008) [0015] and in order that our **contemporaries** as well as our
AP : PR :011(099) [0101] I could lead our **contemporaries** still further from the
EP : RN :008(465) [0779] were understood by **contemporaries** in the church of God
SD : RN :016(507) [0857] not only to our **contemporaries** but also to our posterity,
SD : 0 8 :016(594) [1021] Presbyter wrote: "A **contemporary** of the heretic Manes
SD : 1 2 :040(636) [1103] among both our **contemporaries** and our posterity, we

Contempt (16), Contemptible (2), Contemptuous (1), Contemptuously (1)
AG : 2 0 :015(043) [0055] teaching is held in great **contempt** among untried people,
AG : 2 6 :018(067) [0073] matters out of malice or **contempt** of spiritual authority,
AP : 0 2 :011(102) [0109] namely, carnal security, **contempt** of God, hate of God,
AP : 0 2 :014(102) [0109] as ignorance of God, **contempt** of God, lack of the fear of
AP : 0 2 :029(104) [0113] of God, unbelief, distrust, **contempt**, and hate of God.
AP : 0 4 :021(110) [0127] trust in works and a **contempt** for the grace of Christ.
AP : 0 4 :035(112) [0131] This **contempt** for God corrupts works that seem
AP : 1 2 :131(202) [0291] ungrateful to God or **contemptuous** of his
AP : 1 6 :009(224) [0333] perfection is not **contempt** of civil ordinances but
AP : 2 3 :024(243) [0371] The pontiffs show **contempt** for the authority of the
AP : 2 3 :045(245) [0375] they have spoken **contemptuously** about marriage and
AP : 2 3 :050(246) [0377] are therefore more **contemptible** than the Encratites, who
SC : PR :021(340) [0537] to receive the sacrament and they treat it with **contempt**.
SC : PR :025(341) [0539] own fault if the people treat the sacrament with **contempt**.
LC : 0 1 :069(374) [0601] upon such willful **contempt** of this commandment.
LC : 0 1 :117(381) [0615] seems very trivial and **contemptible**, make sure that you
LC : 0 1 :217(394) [0643] shameful vices resulting from **contempt** of married life.
LC : 0 1 :255(399) [0653] to live among men in public disgrace and **contempt**.
SD : 1 1 :041(623) [1077] The reason for such **contempt** of the Word is not God's
SD : 1 1 :058(626) [1081] a land or a people for **contempt** of his Word that the

Contend (8), Contended (10), Contending (4), Contends (7)
AG : PR :011(025) [0041] one Christ and should confess and **contend** for Christ.
AG : 2 6 :005(064) [0071] this account St. Paul **contended** mightily against the law
AG : 2 8 :056(090) [0091] not be burdened by **contending** that such things are
AL : 0 1 :006(028) [0043] old and new, who **contend** that there is only one person
AL : 0 2 :003(029) [0045] merit and benefits by **contending** that man can be justified
AL : 1 2 :008(035) [0049] and also those who **contend** that some may attain such
AP : 0 2 :038(105) [0115] and not a sin, while Luther **contends** that it is a sin.
AP : 0 4 :359(162) [0219] We do **contend** about the issue whether good works of
AP : 1 2 :060(190) [0267] We are **contending** for this personal faith, and we set it in
AP : 1 2 :079(193) [0275] For these reasons Paul **contends** that we are not justified
AP : 1 2 :086(194) [0277] Paul, on the contrary, **contends** that we cannot keep the
AP : 1 2 :110(198) [0285] If our opponents **contend** that the enumeration of sins in
AP : 1 5 :010(216) [0317] traditions, he therefore **contends** that the forgiveness of
S 3 : 0 3 :040(309) [0489] for all through life it **contends** with the sins that remain in
TR : 0 0 :049(329) [0519] In fact, he **contends** that he is above councils and can
LC : 0 5 :063(454) [0767] and hindrance to **contend** with, that we concentrate more
EP : 0 4 :003(476) [0797] The one party **contended** that we should not use the word
EP : 0 4 :004(476) [0797] The one party **contended** that the law should not be
EP : 0 8 :003(487) [0819] and his followers have **contended** for the opposite view
SD : PR :008(502) [0849] not know which of the **contending** parties they should
SD : 0 1 :001(508) [0859] One side **contended** that "man's nature and essence are
SD : 0 2 :034(527) [0895] until death, for it **contends** with the sin remaining in the
SD : 0 3 :002(539) [0917] The one party **contended** that the righteousness of faith,
SD : 0 4 :002(551) [0939] The other party **contended** on the contrary that good
SD : 0 4 :005(551) [0939] controversy when some **contended** that, because of the
SD : 0 5 :002(558) [0951] maintained and **contended** that, strictly speaking, the
SD : 0 8 :050(600) [1031] some wanted to **contend** that even in the personal union
SD : 0 8 :052(601) [1033] However, they argue and **contend** that the gifts with
SD : 1 0 :003(611) [1053] other party, however, **contended** that under no

Content (12), Contents (1)
PR : PR :025(013) [0023] any way at all, either in **content** or formulation, from the
PR : PR :025(014) [0023] according to the **content** of the ordinances of the Holy
AP : 0 4 :034(111) [0129] **Content** with this, they think they satisfy the law of God.
AP : 2 4 :007(250) [0385] community should be **content** with a single common daily
AP : 2 4 :018(252) [0389] which God offers us the **content** of the promise joined to
LC : SP :002(362) [0575] Its **contents** represent the minimum of knowledge
LC : 0 1 :187(390) [0633] Then we shall be **content** to let our enemies rave and rage
LC : 0 1 :267(401) [0657] backbiters who are not **content** just to know but rush
EP : 0 3 :001(472) [0791] Word of God and the **content** of the Augsburg
SD : 0 5 :020(561) [0959] The **content** of the Gospel is this, that the Son of God,
SD : 0 7 :041(576) [0985] doctrine in sum and **content** was comprehended in the
SD : 1 1 :003(616) [1063] the net total and **content** of the teaching on this article
SD : 1 2 :037(636) [1103] Creeds, both as to **content** and terminology, and instead

Contention (3), Contentions (6), Contentious (1)
PR : PR :024(013) [0021] and open to restless, **contentious** individuals, who do not
AP : PR :009(099) [0101] having disproved our **contentions** from the Scriptures,
S 1 : 0 1 :000(292) [0461] matters of dispute or **contention**, for both parties confess
LC : 0 3 :080(431) [0721] why he causes so much **contention**, murder, sedition, and
LC : 0 4 :007(437) [0733] the chief cause of our **contentions** and battles because the
SD : PR :009(503) [0849] misunderstandings or **contentions** about words, with one
SD : RN :015(507) [0857] and unprofitable **contentions** (which, since they destroy
SD : 0 1 :003(509) [0859] original sin is not a useless **contention** about words.
SD : 0 1 :051(517) [0875] In order to avoid all **contentions** about words, it
SD : 1 1 :094(632) [1095] have erred and serious religious **contentions** have arisen.

Context (8)
AP : 0 4 :246(142) [0189] Second, the **context** demonstrates that the works spoken
AP : 0 4 :280(149) [0201] passages in their **context**, because according to the
AP : 0 4 :280(149) [0201] considered in their own **context**, they often yield their
AP : 2 4 :015(252) [0389] Fathers and use it out of **context**, attaching their own
SD : 0 4 :016(554) [0943] is used in this **context**, it is not to be understood as
SD : 0 7 :057(579) [0993] As the purpose and **context** of St. Paul's entire discourse
SD : 0 7 :086(584) [1003] In this **context** "use" or "action" does not primarily mean
SD : 0 7 :104(587) [1009] our churches use the word "spiritual" in this **context**.

Continence (15), Continent (10)
AG : 2 3 :001(051) [0061] were not able to remain **continent** and who went so far as
AL : 2 3 :001(051) [0061] concerning priests who have not been **continent**.
AP : 2 3 :016(241) [0369] those to marry who do not have the gift of **continence**?
AP : 2 3 :017(242) [0369] his own wife," binds all those who are not truly **continent**.
AP : 2 3 :018(242) [0369] men to pray God for **continence** and to subdue their
AP : 2 3 :019(242) [0369] If **continence** were possible for everyone, it would not
AP : 2 3 :021(242) [0369] who have the gift of **continence** and therefore adds, "He
AP : 2 3 :022(242) [0369] Impure **continence** does not please Christ.
AP : 2 3 :022(242) [0369] We, too, commend true **continence**, but now we are
AP : 2 3 :022(242) [0369] and about those who do not have the gift of **continence**.
AP : 2 3 :027(243) [0371] continually, they must also preserve perpetual **continence**.
AP : 2 3 :035(244) [0373] or Jacob than in many others who are truly **continent**.
AP : 2 3 :044(245) [0375] Such **continence** is easy for the godly and busy.
AP : 2 3 :044(245) [0375] voluptuously, cannot even keep this Levitical **continence**.
AP : 2 3 :048(246) [0377] temperances or **continence**; we have said before that
AP : 2 3 :055(247) [0379] also exhort others not to despise the gift of **continence**.
AP : 2 3 :061(247) [0381] who wants to remain **continent**, as long as he is really
AP : 2 3 :061(247) [0381] to remain continent, as long as he is really **continent**.

Continued ▶

AP : 23 :064(248) [0381] lust than that of many celibates who are really **continent**.
AP : 23 :066(248) [0381] that those who are not **continent** in celibacy should marry
AP : 27 :016(271) [0425] pure this is in most of those who strive to be **continent**.
AP : 27 :016(271) [0425] And how many of them strive to be **continent**?
AP : 27 :051(278) [0437] everyone has the gift of **continence**, many fail in their
AP : 27 :051(278) [0437] many fail in their **continence** because of weakness.
AP : 27 :051(278) [0437] himself because he does not have the gift of **continence**.

Continuation (1)
SD : 02 :077(536) [0911] the Holy Spirit in the **continuation** and preservation of

Continue (26), Continued (8), Continues (12), Continual (1), Continually (20), Continuing (2)
PR : PR :024(013) [0023] to us, to do and to **continue** to do everything that is
PR : PR :026(014) [0025] Christian religion should **continue** or new ones arise, we
AG : PR :001(024) [0039] religion, and how with **continuing** help he might
AG : PR :023(027) [0043] To these we declare our **continuing** adherence, and we
AG : 22 :004(050) [0061] This usage **continued** in the church for a long time, as can
AG : 23 :017(054) [0063] of marriage is to **continue** longer, there may be a shortage
AG : 26 :034(069) [0075] certain specified days but should be practiced **continually**.
AL : 07 :001(032) [0047] also teach that one holy church is to **continue** forever.
AL : 22 :004(050) [0061] This usage **continued** in the church for a long time.
AL : 23 :017(054) [0063] lacking in pastors if marriage **continues** to be forbidden.
AL : 24 :018(058) [0067] punished for such long **continued** profanations of the
AP : 02 :003(101) [0105] its acts or fruits, but the **continual** inclination of nature.
AP : 02 :036(105) [0115] it remains because there **continue** to work those desires
AP : 04 :146(127) [0163] our unspiritual nature **continually** brings forth evil
AP : 04 :260(145) [0193] because the law works wrath and **continually** accuses.
AP : 04 :317(156) [0209] For he is the mediator **continually** and not just at the
AP : 04 :321(157) [0209] their works and therefore **continually** seek other works.
AP : 04 :353(161) [0217] in penitence and ought to grow **continually** in penitence.
AP : 07 :029(173) [0237] if our opponents still **continue** to twist it, we shall not
AP : 07 :040(176) [0241] Frequently the people **continued** to observe certain Old
AP : 12 :053(189) [0265] promise is repeated **continually** throughout Scripture;
AP : 21 :018(231) [0347] May prayer be made for him **continually**!"
AP : 23 :027(243) [0371] Testament must pray **continually**, they must also preserve
AP : 23 :032(244) [0373] apart from faith: "if she **continues**," he says, "in faith."
AP : 24 :026(254) [0391] "Through him let us **continually** offer up a sacrifice of
AP : 24 :098(268) [0417] the worship of Baal **continued**; yet the church of God was
S1 : PR :003(289) [0455] now and where, by God's grace, I will **continue** to stand.
S2 : 04 :006(299) [0473] the church must **continue** to exist without the pope.
S3 : 03 :040(309) [0489] such repentance **continues** until death, for all through life
S3 : 15 :005(317) [0501] Spirit of Christ I will thus **continue** to believe and teach
SC : 09 :013(356) [0563] her hope on God and **continues** in supplications and
LC : PR :016(361) [0573] have always remained pupils, and must **continue** to do so.
LC : PR :019(361) [0573] Let them **continue** to read and teach, to learn and
LC : 01 :034(369) [0589] him, and his anger **continues** to the fourth generation,
LC : 01 :061(373) [0597] commandment, and **continually** impress it upon them, so
LC : 01 :073(374) [0601] Thus has originated and **continued** among us the custom
LC : 01 :100(379) [0609] Therefore you must **continually** keep God's Word in your
LC : 01 :232(396) [0647] wrath of God may be **continually** and urgently kept
LC : 01 :316(408) [0671] we must seek and pray for help and receive it **continually**.
LC : 02 :058(418) [0693] The Holy Spirit must **continue** to work in us through the
LC : 03 :034(425) [0707] all the needs that **continually** beset us, each one so great
LC : 03 :056(427) [0713] gushes forth and overflows, the more it **continues** to give.
LC : 04 :065(445) [0749] of which actions must **continue** in us our whole life long.
LC : 04 :065(445) [0749] else than a daily Baptism, once begun and ever **continued**.
LC : 04 :068(445) [0749] is given free rein and **continually** grows stronger, Baptism
LC : 04 :078(446) [0751] and signification of Baptism would **continue** and remain.
LC : 05 :024(449) [0759] not weaken in the struggle but grow **continually** stronger.
LC : 05 :025(449) [0759] life should be one that **continually** develops and
EP : 03 :017(475) [0795] of resulting love, but **continues** to sin against his
SD : RN :020(508) [0859] By God's grace we shall **continue** to abide in it loyally and
SD : 02 :014(523) [0885] in their heart, wills to **continue** to support them in their
SD : 02 :021(525) [0889] over sin and death but **continues** in his carnal security —
SD : 02 :034(527) [0895] "This repentance **continues** in Christians until death, for
SD : 02 :046(530) [0899] natural powers, they will **continue** wholly to resist God or
SD : 02 :068(534) [0907] flesh against the Spirit **continues** also in the elect and
SD : 03 :022(543) [0923] ways of sin, abide and **continue** therein without
SD : 04 :015(553) [0943] a wicked intention to **continue** and abide in sin, which is
SD : 04 :015(553) [0943] though he still is and **continues** to be a barren, unfruitful
SD : 04 :029(555) [0947] for our churches to **continue** to insist that the
SD : 04 :034(557) [0949] him, provided you **continue** in the faith" (Col. 1:22).
SD : 05 :023(562) [0959] proclamations have **continually** been set forth side by side
SD : 06 :004(564) [0963] believers' eyes and **continually** to urge it upon them with
SD : 06 :018(567) [0967] the conflict between spirit and flesh **continues** in them.
SD : 06 :023(568) [0969] Nevertheless, they **continue** in a constant conflict against
SD : 08 :032(597) [1025] could not take place or **continue** if the personal union or
SD : 11 :032(621) [1073] work in us" he will also **continue** it to the end and
SD : 11 :083(630) [1091] blind, and for ever damn them if they **continue** therein.
SD : 11 :085(630) [1091] heart so that Pharaoh **continued** to sin and became the
SD : 11 :088(631) [1093] of election might **continue**, not because of works but

Contract (6), Contracted (2), Contracting (1), Contracts (4)
AL : 16 :002(037) [0051] soldiers, to make legal **contracts**, to hold property, to
AL : 23 :003(051) [0061] taught that it was lawful for them to **contract** matrimony.
AL : 27 :018(073) [0077] concerning those who **contract** matrimony that it is
AL : 28 :013(083) [0085] any civil ordinances or **contracts**, nor prescribe to civil
AP : 16 :001(222) [0329] service, enter into legal **contracts**, own property, take an
AP : 16 :001(222) [0329] requires it, or **contract** marriage — in short, that lawful
AP : 16 :012(224) [0333] discussions about **contracts** will never satisfy good
AP : 23 :007(240) [0365] nor vows can abolish the right to **contract** marriage.
AP : 23 :009(240) [0367] the right to **contract** marriage must always remain.
AP : 23 :012(241) [0367] this right, the right to **contract** marriage necessarily
AP : 23 :023(242) [0369] that have been **contracted**, though they remove those
AP : 23 :023(242) [0371] They forbid the **contracting** of marriages and dissolve
AP : 23 :023(242) [0371] once they have been **contracted**, and all this in open

Contradict (10), Contradicted (3), Contradiction (7), Contradictory (4), Contradicts (2)
PR : PR :020(010) [0017] and faith **contradicted** the articles of our Christian Creed
PR : PR :020(010) [0019] as described above does not **contradict** these articles.
AL : 22 :010(050) [0061] Scriptures but also in **contradiction** to ancient canons and
AP : 02 :008(102) [0107] And they do not see the **contradiction**.
AP : 02 :042(105) [0115] of the Scripture **contradict** them, but the whole church.
AP : 02 :051(107) [0119] They often **contradict** themselves and fail to explain
AP : 04 :244(141) [0189] passage is supposed to **contradict** our position more, but
AP : 24 :028(254) [0393] declaration, which seems to **contradict** Moses directly?
AP : 24 :059(260) [0405] ministry of the Spirit **contradicts** any such transfer *ex*
AP : 28 :016(283) [0449] For they did not **contradict** their own writings, in which
S2 : 02 :007(294) [0465] because it is a direct **contradiction** to the fundamental
S2 : 04 :014(301) [0475] of the papacy) in **contradiction** to God, and to damn,
LC : 01 :042(370) [0591] face of this apparent **contradiction**, and learn that they
LC : 01 :262(400) [0655] and blasphemy; it is **contradicted**, perverted, misused, and
EP : 03 :001(473) [0791] false and mutually **contradictory** teachings have invaded
EP : 07 :021(484) [0813] are contrary and **contradictory** to the doctrine set forth
EP : 11 :022(497) [0837] discussing and teaching in mutually **contradictory** terms.
EP : 12 :001(498) [0839] in which they err and **contradict** our repeatedly cited
SD : RN :020(508) [0857] that there is no **contradiction** between what we taught and
SD : 03 :005(540) [0917] enumeration of those who **contradict** the pure doctrine.
SD : 07 :045(577) [0987] objection or human **contradiction**, spun out of human
SD : 07 :113(589) [1011] and mutually **contradictory** views, no matter how
SD : 08 :003(592) [1017] Dr. Luther **contradicted** and mightily refuted this, as his
SD : 08 :096(609) [1049] and all others that **contradict** and contravene the above
SD : 11 :035(622) [1075] that God, who is the eternal Truth, **contradicts** himself.
SD : 11 :042(623) [1077] This would **contradict** St. Paul in Phil. 1:6.

Contrary (231)
PR : PR :008(005) [0009] that is impure, false, and **contrary** to the Word of God.
PR : PR :009(006) [0011] On the **contrary**, this well-intended action of ours was
PR : PR :009(006) [0011] Confession, the **contrary** doctrine about the holy
PR : PR :021(011) [0019] On the **contrary**, as the teachers of the ancient church put
PR : PR :022(011) [0019] On the **contrary**, we mean specifically to condemn only
PR : PR :022(011) [0019] as such teachings are **contrary** to the expressed Word of
PR : PR :023(012) [0021] doctrine be permitted entrance which is **contrary** to these.
PR : PR :023(012) [0021] On the **contrary**, we have directed our churches and
PR : PR :025(014) [0023] On the **contrary**, we are minded by the grace of the Holy
AG : 01 :005(028) [0043] the heresies which are **contrary** to this article are rejected.
AG : 08 :003(033) [0047] and all others who hold **contrary** views are condemned.
AG : 10 :002(034) [0047] The **contrary** doctrine is therefore rejected.
AG : 15 :003(036) [0049] and earning grace are **contrary** to the Gospel and the
AG : 15 :004(037) [0049] for sin, are useless and **contrary** to the Gospel.
AG : 20 :010(042) [0055] and seeks his own way to God, **contrary** to the Gospel.
AG : 00 :001(047) [0059] Scriptures and is not **contrary** or opposed to that of the
AG : 00 :001(048) [0059] and hasty fashion, **contrary** to all Christian unity and
AG : 00 :000(048) [0059] articles of faith that is **contrary** to the Holy Scriptures or
AG : 22 :010(050) [0061] a custom, introduced **contrary** to God's command and
AG : 22 :010(050) [0061] command and also **contrary** to the ancient canons, is
AG : 22 :011(050) [0061] or to compel them to act **contrary** to the arrangement of
AG : 22 :012(051) [0061] of the sacrament is **contrary** to the institution of Christ,
AG : 23 :013(053) [0063] was of course not only **contrary** to all divine, natural, and
AG : 23 :013(053) [0063] also utterly opposed and **contrary** to the canons which
AG : 23 :021(055) [0063] — although this is done **contrary** not only to divine law
AG : 24 :029(059) [0067] Manifestly **contrary** to this teaching is the misuse of the
AG : 27 :001(071) [0077] in them were **contrary** not only to the Word of God but
AG : 27 :023(074) [0079] men say that a vow made **contrary** to papal canons is not
AG : 27 :023(074) [0079] and power when they are **contrary** to God's command!
AG : 27 :036(076) [0081] and the holy Gospel and **contrary** to God's command.
AG : 27 :040(077) [0081] an ungodly vow, made **contrary** to God's command, is
AG : 28 :021(084) [0087] doctrine that is **contrary** to the Gospel, and exclude from
AG : 28 :023(084) [0087] or institute anything **contrary** to the Gospel, we have
AG : 28 :024(084) [0087] preach to you a gospel **contrary** to that which we
AG : 28 :028(085) [0087] or command something **contrary** to the divine Holy
AG : 28 :033(086) [0087] changed to Sunday — **contrary**, as they say, to the Ten
AG : 28 :034(086) [0089] or establish anything **contrary** to the Gospel, as has been
AG : 28 :035(086) [0089] It is patently **contrary** to God's command and Word to
AG : 28 :039(087) [0089] ordinances also act **contrary** to God's command when
AG : 28 :050(089) [0091] God and merit grace are **contrary** to the Gospel, it is not
AG : 28 :072(093) [0093] which were introduced **contrary** to the custom of the
AG : 00 :005(095) [0095] or in ceremonies, that is **contrary** to Holy Scripture or the
AL : 15 :004(037) [0049] for sins, are useless and **contrary** to the Gospel.
AL : 16 :005(038) [0051] On the **contrary**, it especially requires their preservation
AL : 20 :035(046) [0057] On the **contrary**, it should rather be commended for
AL : 00 :001(048) [0059] of the times although **contrary** to the intent of the
AL : 22 :009(050) [0061] a custom introduced **contrary** to the commands of God is
AL : 23 :013(053) [0063] although this was **contrary** to all laws, divine and human,
AL : 23 :013(053) [0063] divine and human, and **contrary** even to the canons, both
AL : 23 :021(055) [0063] are cruelly put to death, **contrary** to the intent of the
AL : 24 :011(057) [0065] and how many celebrate Masses **contrary** to the canons.
AL : 27 :001(071) [0077] monasteries every day that were **contrary** to the canons.
AL : 27 :004(071) [0077] were laid on many, **contrary** to the canons, before they
AL : 27 :023(074) [0079] vows valid which are made **contrary** to God's commands!
AL : 27 :030(075) [0079] conceded by all that it is **contrary** to the nature of a vow
AL : 27 :040(077) [0081] for a wicked vow, taken **contrary** to the commands of
AL : 28 :021(084) [0087] reject doctrine which is **contrary** to the Gospel, and to
AL : 28 :023(084) [0087] or ordain anything **contrary** to the Gospel, churches have
AL : 28 :028(085) [0087] to err or hold anything **contrary** to the canonical
AL : 28 :033(086) [0087] to the Lord's Day — **contrary** to the Decalogue, it
AL : 28 :034(086) [0089] have power to institute anything **contrary** to the Gospel.
AL : 28 :039(087) [0089] authors of traditions act **contrary** to the command of God
AL : 28 :072(093) [0093] and were introduced **contrary** to the custom of the church
AL : 00 :005(095) [0095] or in ceremonies, that is **contrary** to Scripture or to the
AP : 02 :008(101) [0107] evils, which are most **contrary** to the law of God, the
AP : 02 :026(103) [0111] pursues carnal ends **contrary** to the Word of God (that is,
AP : 02 :032(104) [0113] about original sin that is **contrary** to the Scripture or the
AP : 04 :252(143) [0191] contain nothing **contrary** to our position, so we maintain
AP : 04 :395(167) [0225] The prophets, on the **contrary**, condemned this opinion
AP : 04 :400(168) [0227] defend human opinions **contrary** to the Gospel, contrary
AP : 04 :400(168) [0227] contrary to the Gospel, **contrary** to the authority of the
AP : 04 :400(168) [0227] of the holy Fathers, and **contrary** to the testimony of
AP : 07 :043(177) [0243] that it contains nothing **contrary** to the faith or the rule
AP : 07 :048(177) [0245] to you a gospel **contrary** to that which you received, let
AP : 12 :060(190) [0269] the same, in spite of our opponents' cries to the **contrary**.
AP : 12 :066(191) [0271] to issue decrees **contrary** to this consensus of the
AP : 12 :076(193) [0273] We, on the **contrary**, call men's consciences away from
AP : 12 :086(194) [0277] Paul, on the **contrary**, contends that we cannot keep the
AP : 12 :122(200) [0289] in the church would be **contrary** to the express
AP : 12 :157(207) [0301] On the **contrary**, it constantly teaches that we obtain the

Continued ▶

A P : 1 2 :172(209) [0305] to abolish satisfactions **contrary** to the clear teaching of
A P : 1 5 :001(215) [0315] to make satisfaction for sin are **contrary** to the Gospel.
A P : 2 3 :024(243) [0371] since the ancient synods and **contrary** to their authority.
A P : 2 3 :041(245) [0375] Intercourse **contrary** to these laws was uncleanness; now
A P : 2 3 :070(249) [0383] to take a position **contrary** to the judgment of God, who
A P : 2 3 :071(249) [0383] marrying, it is certainly **contrary** to God's will and Word
A P : 2 4 :006(250) [0385] There is nothing **contrary** to the church catholic in our
A P : 2 7 :052(278) [0437] defend their traditions, **contrary** to the clear command of
A P : 2 7 :052(278) [0437] for setting up traditions **contrary** to the command of
A P : 2 8 :014(283) [0447] anyone does something **contrary** to that Word which they
A P : 2 8 :020(284) [0449] not create traditions **contrary** to the Gospel, nor interpret
A P : 2 8 :020(284) [0449] their traditions in a manner **contrary** to the Gospel.
S 1 : P R :013(290) [0459] secular estates as are **contrary** to God, their hands would
S 2 : 0 2 :012(295) [0465] for purgatory, too, is **contrary** to the fundamental article
S 2 : 0 2 :021(296) [0469] command, but it is **contrary** to the first article, concerning
S 2 : 0 2 :024(296) [0469] but they are also **contrary** to the first article, for the
S 3 : 0 8 :002(312) [0495] not be neglected; on the **contrary**, it should be highly
S 3 : 0 8 :004(312) [0495] when it is above and **contrary** to the Scriptures or spoken
S 3 : 1 1 :001(314) [0499] On the **contrary**, they acted like antichristian, tyrannical,
S 3 : 1 1 :003(315) [0499] On the **contrary**, we desire marriage to be free, as God
T R : 0 0 :036(326) [0515] only usurped dominion **contrary** to the command of
T R : 0 0 :038(326) [0515] On the **contrary**, such pontiffs and such government
T R : 0 0 :038(326) [0515] preach to you a gospel **contrary** to that which we
T R : 0 0 :055(329) [0521] anything to be decreed **contrary** to his will and grants
T R : 0 0 :057(330) [0521] On the **contrary**, it is necessary to resist him as
S C : P R :007(339) [0533] On the **contrary**, he should adopt one form, adhere to it,
S C : P R :011(339) [0535] On the **contrary**, they should be turned over to the pope
S C : 0 5 :023(350) [0555] else they have done **contrary** to God's commandments
L C : 0 1 :028(368) [0587] On the **contrary**, does your heart cling to something else,
L C : 0 1 :090(377) [0607] nor practice God's Word but teach and live **contrary** to it.
L C : 0 1 :203(392) [0639] or need, and on the **contrary** to aid and assist him so that
L C : 0 1 :323(409) [0673] fear, avoids all that is **contrary** to his will, lest he be
L C : 0 1 :328(410) [0677] On the **contrary**, you should do good to all men, help
L C : 0 1 :330(410) [0677] them, and, on the **contrary**, abundantly rewards those
L C : 0 3 :056(427) [0713] of him; and on the **contrary**, he is angered if we do not
L C : 0 3 :072(430) [0719] daily bread and, on the **contrary**, against everything that
L C : 0 3 :104(434) [0727] stubbornness, or, on the **contrary**, to drive us into
L C : 0 3 :108(435) [0729] as long as it is **contrary** to our will and we would prefer to
L C : 0 5 :007(447) [0755] regard the sacraments, **contrary** to the Word of God, as
L C : 0 5 :061(453) [0767] and without sin; on the **contrary**, we come as poor,
L C : 0 6 :026(460) [0000] We, on the **contrary**, do not say that men should look to
E P : R N :001(464) [0777] preach to you a gospel **contrary** to that which we
E P : R N :003(465) [0777] been introduced into the church of God **contrary** to them.
E P : R N :006(465) [0779] Whatever is **contrary** to them should be rejected and
E P : R N :008(465) [0779] articles, and how **contrary** teachings were rejected and
E P : 0 1 :006(467) [0781] On the **contrary**, in the resurrection it will be utterly
E P : 0 1 :010(467) [0781] *Rejection of the **Contrary** False Teaching*
E P : 0 2 :006(470) [0787] ***Contrary** False Doctrine*
E P : 0 2 :007(470) [0787] errors as being **contrary** to the norm of the Word of God:
E P : 0 2 :016(472) [0791] free will in conversion **contrary** to the doctrine of the
E P : 0 3 :003(473) [0793] On the **contrary**, the entire Christ according to both
E P : 0 3 :011(474) [0795] intention to sin and to act **contrary** to one's conscience.
E P : 0 3 :011(474) [0795] On the **contrary**, after a person has been justified by
E P : 0 3 :011(474) [0795] *Rejection of the **Contrary** Doctrine*
E P : 0 4 :009(476) [0799] and are in no way **contrary** to the pattern of sound words
E P : 0 5 :003(478) [0801] everything that is sinful and **contrary** to God's will.
E P : 0 5 :010(479) [0805] *Rejected **Contrary** Doctrine*
E P : 0 6 :002(480) [0805] without the law; on the **contrary**, they have been
E P : 0 7 :017(484) [0813] must accept him even **contrary** to their will as a strict
E P : 0 7 :021(484) [0813] *The **Contrary** and Condemned Doctrine of the*
E P : 0 7 :021(484) [0813] errors, which are **contrary** and contradictory to the
E P : 0 7 :024(484) [0815] of the cup from them, **contrary** to the clear Word of
E P : 0 7 :042(486) [0817] On the **contrary**, in accord with the simple words of
E P : 0 8 :009(487) [0819] On the **contrary**, here is the highest communion which
E P : 0 8 :018(490) [0823] ***Contrary** False Doctrine concerning the Person of Christ*
E P : 0 8 :019(490) [0823] reject and condemn as **contrary** to the Word of God and
E P : 1 0 :008(494) [0831] condemn as false and **contrary** to God's Word the
E P : 1 1 :022(497) [0837] pure doctrine but have also exposed the **contrary** errors.
E P : 1 2 :030(500) [0843] false, heretical, and **contrary** to the Word of God, the
E P : 1 2 :031(500) [0843] say or write anything **contrary** to it but intend by the
S D : P R :002(501) [0847] doctrine and as wholly **contrary** to the Word of God and
S D : P R :009(503) [0849] On the **contrary**, these controversies deal with weighty
S D : R N :015(507) [0857] doctrine, when the **contrary** error must be refuted in
S D : R N :020(508) [0859] On the **contrary**, we want to be found faithful to the
S D : 0 1 :002(508) [0859] party, however, took a **contrary** view and taught that
S D : 0 1 :003(509) [0859] On the **contrary**, when it is presented clearly from and
S D : 0 1 :016(511) [0865] briefly enumerate the **contrary** doctrines which are
S D : 0 1 :040(515) [0871] handiwork of God; on the **contrary**, it is the devil's work.
S D : 0 1 :041(515) [0871] Both conclusions are **contrary** to the first article of our
S D : 0 1 :043(516) [0873] they also rejected the **contrary** doctrine as patent heresy.
S D : 0 1 :044(516) [0873] Both statements are **contrary** to the Scriptures.
S D : 0 1 :047(516) [0873] then it would follow, **contrary** to this article of our
S D : 0 1 :049(517) [0875] of the doctrine and the **contrary** doctrine, the thesis and
S D : 0 1 :058(519) [0879] controversy but, on the **contrary**, the discord will only be
S D : 0 2 :007(521) [0883] of that which is displeasing and **contrary** to God.
S D : 0 2 :008(521) [0883] It is true that they are **contrary** to proud reason and
S D : 0 2 :009(522) [0883] On the **contrary**, the more zealously and diligently they
S D : 0 2 :017(524) [0887] which is displeasing to God and **contrary** to his will.
S D : 0 2 :018(524) [0889] On the **contrary**, because of the wicked and obstinate
S D : 0 2 :030(527) [0893] On the **contrary**, it declares that man is the captive of
S D : 0 2 :035(528) [0895] On the **contrary**, they ascribe everything to the gift of the
S D : 0 2 :043(529) [0897] and diametrically **contrary** to the help and grace of our
S D : 0 2 :043(529) [0897] On the **contrary**, we must remain the dupes and captives
S D : 0 2 :043(529) [0897] pleases them and what is **contrary** to God and his
S D : 0 2 :044(529) [0897] On the **contrary**, he states that blind and captive man
S D : 0 2 :044(529) [0897] only the devil's will and what is **contrary** to the Lord God.
S D : 0 2 :045(530) [0899] erroneous views are **contrary** to the Holy Scriptures of
S D : 0 2 :056(532) [0903] On the **contrary**, because the Holy Spirit's activity often
S D : 0 2 :069(534) [0907] have been baptized act **contrary** to their conscience and
S D : 0 2 :086(538) [0913] in his conversion, **contrary** to the article of God's grace.
S D : 0 2 :089(538) [0915] On the **contrary**, it is his understanding that man of
S D : 0 3 :007(540) [0919] expose, and condemn the false **contrary** doctrine.
S D : 0 3 :044(547) [0933] and similar errors as **contrary** to the preceding
S D : 0 3 :059(550) [0937] and all similar errors as **contrary** to the Word of God, the
S D : 0 3 :066(550) [0937] we reject unanimously as **contrary** to the clear Word of
S D : 0 4 :002(551) [0939] party contended on the **contrary** that good works are
S D : 0 4 :002(551) [0939] and formulas are **contrary** to the form of sound doctrine
S D : 0 4 :003(551) [0939] Another party took the **contrary** view that good works
S D : 0 4 :017(554) [0943] that is really unwilled by him or even **contrary** to his will.
S D : 0 4 :017(554) [0943] On the **contrary**, the people of the New Testament are to
S D : 0 4 :020(554) [0945] do them or to act in a **contrary** fashion and nonetheless
S D : 0 4 :022(554) [0945] propositions are directly **contrary** to the doctrine of
S D : 0 4 :024(555) [0945] Thus they are **contrary** to the pattern of sound words,
S D : 0 4 :034(556) [0949] On the **contrary**, in order that the promise that we shall
S D : 0 4 :037(557) [0951] false confidence which, **contrary** to the express Word of
S D : 0 6 :005(564) [0963] On the **contrary**, it is St. Paul's intention that the law
S D : 0 6 :013(566) [0967] Sin is everything that is **contrary** to the law of God, and
S D : 0 6 :026(568) [0971] as pernicious and **contrary** to Christian discipline and
S D : 0 7 :001(569) [0971] error which is altogether **contrary** to the holy Word of
S D : 0 7 :009(570) [0975] and it condemns the **contrary** doctrine (that is, the
S D : 0 7 :046(577) [0987] words were patently **contrary** not only to reason and to
S D : 0 7 :103(587) [1007] to prove that even this mode is **contrary** to our view.
S D : 0 7 :105(588) [1009] of our public and oft-repeated testimony to the **contrary**.
S D : 0 7 :107(588) [1009] with or opposed and **contrary** to the aforementioned
S D : 0 7 :110(588) [1011] administered to the laity **contrary** to the explicit
S D : 0 7 :112(589) [1011] with, opposed to, or **contrary** to the doctrine set forth
S D : 0 7 :114(589) [1011] in the Supper, and the **contrary** teaching that in the
S D : 0 7 :128(591) [1015] is inconsistent with, **contrary** to, or opposed to the
S D : 0 8 :019(595) [1021] their properties; on the **contrary**, each nature retains its
S D : 0 8 :037(598) [1027] On the **contrary**, it is distinctly explained according to
S D : 0 8 :071(605) [1041] This is **contrary** to our Christian Creed and to the entire
S D : 0 8 :088(609) [1047] here set forth as **contrary** to the prophetic and apostolic
S D : 0 8 :096(609) [1049] above doctrine as being **contrary** to the pure Word of
S D : 1 0 :005(611) [1053] which are basically **contrary** to the Word of God, even
S D : 1 0 :029(615) [1061] of the holy Gospel **contrary** and in opposition to the
S D : 1 1 :003(616) [1063] misunderstand it; on the **contrary**, precisely in order to
S D : 1 1 :010(618) [1067] On the **contrary**, I shall and must be saved since God's
S D : 1 1 :013(619) [1067] On the **contrary**, we should consider the counsel,
S D : 1 1 :040(623) [1077] On the **contrary**, as God has ordained in his counsel that
S D : 1 1 :059(626) [1083] to us without and **contrary** to our deserving, to whom he
S D : 1 1 :070(627) [1085] On the **contrary**, they should listen to Christ, who is the
S D : 1 1 :085(630) [1091] most inhuman devices **contrary** to the voice of his
S D : 1 1 :092(632) [1093] comfort and hope is **contrary** to the Holy Spirit's will and
S D : 1 1 :093(632) [1095] those things which are **contrary** to these true, simple, and
S D : 1 1 :095(632) [1095] because it would be **contrary** to the truth and actually
S D : 1 2 :006(633) [1097] silently while something **contrary** to the Augsburg
S D : 1 2 :008(633) [1097] many, and that on the **contrary** we reject and condemn
S D : 1 2 :008(633) [1097] as wrong, heretical, and **contrary** to our Christian and
S D : 1 2 :013(634) [1099] and do not advocate it, **contrary** to the express words of
S D : 1 2 :039(636) [1103] erroneous, heretical, **contrary** to the Word of God, to the
S D : 1 2 :040(636) [1-103] privately or publicly, **contrary** to this confession, but we

Contrast (10), Contrasted (3)

A P : 0 4 :154(128) [0163] because Christ **contrasted** the whole act of reverence of
A P : 1 2 :058(190) [0267] the Gospel when it is **contrasted** with contrition and
A P : 2 3 :032(243) [0373] In **contrast** to the hypocrisy of celibacy, what greater
A P : 2 3 :035(244) [0373] second place, the proper **contrast** is between lust and
A P : 2 4 :018(252) [0389] By way of **contrast**, a sacrifice is a ceremony or act which
A P : 2 4 :026(254) [0391] Spiritual sacrifices are **contrasted** not only with the
A P : 2 4 :026(254) [0391] Therefore the **contrast** is not only with Levitical worship,
L C : 0 1 :198(392) [0637] In **contrast** to them all human holiness is only stench and
L C : 0 5 :056(453) [0767] and reason begin to **contrast** our unworthiness with this
L C : 0 5 :056(453) [0767] like a dark lantern in **contrast** to the bright sun, or as
L C : 0 5 :056(453) [0767] to the bright sun, or as dung in **contrast** to jewels.
E P : 0 5 :007(478) [0803] as a teacher of the law in **contrast** to Christ as a preacher
S D : 0 8 :063(603) [1037] of Christ by way of **contrast**, we have spoken of a "real

Contravene (1), Contravenes (2)

S D : 0 8 :004(592) [1017] that transcends or **contravenes** its natural, essential
S D : 0 8 :050(600) [1031] which transcends or **contravenes** its natural properties,
S D : 0 8 :096(609) [1049] that contradict and **contravene** the above doctrine as

Contribute (11), Contributes (3), Contribution (2), Contributions (2)

A G : 1 5 :001(036) [0049] without sin and which **contribute** to peace and good
A L : 1 5 :001(036) [0049] without sin and which **contribute** to peace and good
A L : 0 0 :006(049) [0059] be judged that nothing **contributes** so much to the
A P : 0 4 :105(122) [0153] and reread them, they **contribute** less to an understanding
A P : 0 7 :031(174) [0237] universal or particular, **contribute** nothing; nor are they
A P : 1 2 :118(199) [0287] satisfactions do not **contribute** to the remission of guilt,
A P : 1 2 :118(199) [0287] imagine that they do **contribute** to the redemption of
A P : 1 5 :048(221) [0329] foods and seasons **contributes** nothing to the subjection
A P : 2 4 :085(265) [0413] of the Passover had to bring some gift as a **contribution**.
A P : 2 4 :086(265) [0413] kept the term "Mass" as the name for the **contributions**.
A P : 2 4 :086(265) [0413] that because of such **contributions** the Mass was called
S 2 : 0 4 :003(298) [0471] or scoundrel) which **contribute** to the destruction of the
L C : 0 1 :164(387) [0627] rewarded for all they **contribute** to their temporal and
L C : 0 1 :190(391) [0635] plead that you did not **contribute** to his death by word or
L C : 0 4 :028(440) [0739] works and external things **contribute** nothing to this end.
L C : 0 4 :034(441) [0741] whatever is not faith **contributes** nothing toward
S D : 0 2 :038(528) [0895] our free will or of our **contribution**, but ascribes
S D : 0 2 :071(535) [0909] natural powers cannot **contribute** anything or help in any

Contrite (7)

A P : 1 2 :008(183) [0255] them attain grace even though they were terribly **contrite**?
A P : 1 2 :036(186) [0261] and quickens the **contrite** according to the passage (Rom.
A P : 1 2 :080(194) [0275] it is necessary for the **contrite** by faith to take hold of the
A P : 2 4 :029(255) [0393] spirit; a broken and **contrite** heart, O God, thou wilt not
A P : 2 4 :070(262) [0409] Such a faith encourages the **contrite** mind.
S 3 : 0 3 :016(305) [0483] If anybody could not be **contrite** (that is, really
S 3 : 0 3 :027(307) [0487] or jubilee year must be **contrite**, make confession, and

Contritio (2)

S 3 : 0 3 :002(304) [0479] This is not *activa **contritio*** (artificial remorse), but *passiva*
S 3 : 0 3 :002(304) [0479] remorse), but *passiva **contritio*** (true sorrow of the heart,

Contrition (80)

AG : 1 2 :003(034) [0049] else than to have **contrition** and sorrow, or terror, on
AL : 1 2 :004(034) [0049] these two parts: one is **contrition**, that is, terror smiting
AP : 0 4 :083(118) [0145] sake of our merits, our **contrition**, attrition, love,
AP : 0 4 :397(167) [0227] not because of our **contrition** but because of the word of
AP : 1 2 :001(182) [0253] in which we say that **contrition** and faith are the parts of
AP : 1 2 :006(183) [0255] of sins takes place in attrition or in **contrition**.
AP : 1 2 :006(183) [0255] takes place because of **contrition**, what is the need of
AP : 1 2 :008(183) [0255] They teach that by **contrition** we merit grace.
AP : 1 2 :008(183) [0255] difference between the **contrition** of Judas and that of
AP : 1 2 :020(185) [0257] of sins because of **contrition**, not by faith in Christ.
AP : 1 2 :028(185) [0259] given penitence two parts, namely, **contrition** and faith.
AP : 1 2 :029(185) [0259] We eliminate from **contrition** those useless and endless
AP : 1 2 :029(185) [0259] We say that **contrition** is the genuine terror of a
AP : 1 2 :029(185) [0259] This **contrition** takes place when the Word of God
AP : 1 2 :036(186) [0261] difference between the **contrition** of Judas and Saul on
AP : 1 2 :036(186) [0261] The **contrition** of Judas and Saul did not avail because it
AP : 1 2 :036(186) [0261] The **contrition** of David and Peter did avail because it
AP : 1 2 :044(187) [0263] being heavy-laden mean **contrition**, anxiety, and the
AP : 1 2 :045(187) [0263] There are, then, two chief parts here, **contrition** and faith.
AP : 1 2 :045(188) [0263] parts are combined: **contrition**, when sins are denounced;
AP : 1 2 :045(188) [0263] enough that he names **contrition** and faith as the chief
AP : 1 2 :046(188) [0263] what we usually call **contrition** Paul calls "putting off the
AP : 1 2 :046(188) [0263] consolation truly sustaining a life that flees in **contrition**.
AP : 1 2 :047(188) [0263] There are therefore two parts here, **contrition** and faith.
AP : 1 2 :048(188) [0265] The bond therefore is **contrition** itself, condemning us.
AP : 1 2 :049(188) [0265] the first part contains **contrition**, while the second
AP : 1 2 :049(188) [0265] how we are revived in **contrition** by the Word of God
AP : 1 2 :050(189) [0265] sentences the first part means **contrition**, the second faith.
AP : 1 2 :052(189) [0265] chief parts of penitence, **contrition** and the faith that
AP : 1 2 :054(189) [0265] in this promise, not by their own attrition or **contrition**.
AP : 1 2 :055(189) [0267] was rebuked and terrified after his sin; this was **contrition**.
AP : 1 2 :056(189) [0267] This is **contrition**.
AP : 1 2 :057(189) [0267] always added, but **contrition** and faith there must always
AP : 1 2 :057(189) [0267] came to Christ in tears, which showed her **contrition**.
AP : 1 2 :058(190) [0267] when it is contrasted with **contrition** and mortification.
AP : 1 2 :059(190) [0267] *operato* because of **contrition**, but by that personal faith
AP : 1 2 :060(190) [0269] promise of Christ but in **contrition**, confession, and
AP : 1 2 :075(193) [0273] who has attrition or **contrition** elicits an act of love to
AP : 1 2 :075(193) [0273] the forgiveness of sins because of our **contrition** or love.
AP : 1 2 :076(193) [0273] not because of our **contrition** or love, for there is no
AP : 1 2 :078(193) [0275] of sins by their **contrition** and love, and should trust their
AP : 1 2 :078(193) [0275] and should trust their **contrition** and love, is simply a
AP : 1 2 :091(195) [0279] said why we set forth **contrition** and faith as the two parts
AP : 1 2 :092(196) [0279] statements, requiring **contrition** or good works and
AP : 1 2 :093(196) [0279] only about one but about both parts, **contrition** and faith.
AP : 1 2 :095(196) [0281] because of our works, **contrition**, confession, or
AP : 1 2 :097(196) [0281] Fathers not only about **contrition** and works, but also
AP : 1 2 :098(197) [0281] the true teaching about **contrition** and faith, the two parts
AP : 1 2 :107(198) [0283] Such confession, made to God, is itself **contrition**.
AP : 1 2 :107(198) [0283] such a confession is **contrition**; feeling God's wrath, we
AP : 1 2 :131(202) [0291] no true conversion or **contrition** where mortifying the
AP : 1 2 :148(205) [0299] and revenge, that is, **contrition** and true terrors.
AP : 1 2 :150(206) [0299] when amid the terrors of **contrition** he reveals his wrath.
AP : 1 2 :150(206) [0299] opponents admit that **contrition** can be so great as to
AP : 1 2 :150(206) [0299] unnecessary; thus **contrition** is a more genuine
AP : 1 2 :156(207) [0301] the work of God, like **contrition** or terrors of conscience,
AP : 1 2 :164(208) [0303] really happens in **contrition** and in a changed life.
AP : 1 2 :164(208) [0303] process of penitence — **contrition**, faith, and good fruits
AP : 1 2 :170(209) [0305] says, "In the heart **contrition**, in the mouth confession, in
S 3 : 0 3 :012(305) [0481] into three parts — **contrition**, confession, and satisfaction
S 3 : 0 3 :015(305) [0483] As for **contrition**, this was the situation: Since nobody
S 3 : 0 3 :016(305) [0483] knew how much **contrition** he had to muster in order to
S 3 : 0 3 :016(305) [0483] as a substitute for **contrition** when people went to
S 3 : 0 3 :017(305) [0483] it was accounted as **contrition** and, on the basis of this
S 3 : 0 3 :018(306) [0483] light, we see that such **contrition** is an artificial and
S 3 : 0 3 :027(307) [0487] But the **contrition** and confession practiced by these
EP : 0 3 :011(474) [0795] and confess that the **contrition** that precedes justification
EP : 0 5 :007(478) [0803] not a proclamation of **contrition** and reproof but is,
SD : 0 2 :054(531) [0903] genuine terror, **contrition**, and sorrow in his heart, and
SD : 0 3 :022(543) [0923] For genuine **contrition** must precede.
SD : 0 3 :026(543) [0923] those who live without **contrition** and sorrow and have a
SD : 0 3 :026(543) [0923] abide in sin, for true **contrition** precedes and genuine faith
SD : 0 3 :027(543) [0925] neither the preceding **contrition** nor the subsequent works
SD : 0 3 :030(544) [0925] faith trusts neither in **contrition** nor in love nor in other
SD : 0 3 :031(544) [0925] Neither is **contrition** nor love nor any other virtue the
SD : 0 3 :036(545) [0927] be true faith without **contrition**, or as though good works
SD : 0 5 :009(559) [0955] And in order that **contrition** or the terrors of the law may
SD : 0 5 :009(559) [0955] so that it becomes a "**contrition** that leads to salvation"
SD : 0 5 :015(561) [0957] criticize sin and teach **contrition** and sorrow not from the
SD : 0 7 :068(582) [0997] sacrament without true **contrition** and sorrow for their

Control (6), Controlled (1), Controls (1)

AL : 2 6 :033(069) [0075] Christian ought so to **control** and curb himself with
AP : 1 2 :110(198) [0285] better, still it must be **controlled**, lest consciences be
AP : 1 2 :143(204) [0297] were instituted not to **control** the flesh but, as Scotus
AP : 2 3 :020(242) [0369] good men have tried to **control** their body but without
AP : 2 7 :045(277) [0435] in casting off possessions and the **control** of property.
AP : 2 7 :046(277) [0435] The distribution, **control**, and possession of property are
EP : 1 1 :004(495) [0833] foreknowledge merely **controls** the evil and imposes a
SD : 0 8 :070(605) [1041] left nothing outside his **control**" (Heb. 2:7, 8), and "he is

Controversial (3), Controversies (20), Controversy (80), Controverted (13)

PR : PR :003(003) [0007] in the chief articles in **controversy** over against both the
PR : PR :003(003) [0007] to it without either **controversy** or doubt in a Christian
PR : PR :010(006) [0011] and the religious **controversies** that were expanding with
PR : PR :010(006) [0011] to all the articles in **controversy**, to expose and to reject
PR : PR :011(006) [0011] they took to hand the **controverted** articles, examined,
PR : PR :013(007) [0013] another the articles in **controversy** and also the just cited
PR : PR :022(011) [0019] settlement of the **controverted** articles in order that
PR : PR :023(012) [0021] explanation of the **controverted** articles we have made no
PR : PR :024(013) [0021] to start scandalous **controversies** at will and to introduce
PR : PR :025(014) [0023] regulate all religious **controversies** and their explanations
PR : PR :026(014) [0025] If the current **controversies** about our Christian religion
AG : 0 0 :001(094) [0095] are the chief articles that are regarded as **controversial**.
AL : 0 0 :003(049) [0059] gave occasion to this **controversy**, and now they are
AL : 2 8 :001(081) [0083] there has been great **controversy** about the power of
AL : 0 0 :001(094) [0095] the chief articles that are regarded as **controversial**.
AP : PR :011(099) [0101] In these **controversies** I have always made it a point to
AP : PR :019(099) [0103] to Christ, who will one day judge these **controversies**.
AP : 0 2 :051(107) [0119] opponents reopen the **controversy**, we shall not lack men
AP : 0 4 :002(107) [0121] In this **controversy** the main doctrine of Christianity is
AP : 0 7 :034(175) [0239] must be settled in this **controversy**, and only then can we
AP : 0 7 :037(175) [0241] fully the issue in this **controversy**, namely, the question
AP : 0 7 :046(177) [0243] But on this whole **controversy** we shall have a few things
AP : 1 2 :127(201) [0289] doubt because of the **controversies** that have arisen on the
AP : 1 5 :049(221) [0329] many difficult and **controversial** questions, and we know
AP : 2 1 :002(229) [0343] also refer to Jerome's **controversy** with Vigilantius and
AP : 2 1 :002(229) [0343] do not see that in the **controversy** between Jerome and
AP : 2 3 :006(240) [0365] Our other **controversies** call for some theological
AP : 2 3 :069(249) [0383] in the Jovinian **controversy** on the relative value of
AP : 2 4 :010(251) [0387] that both parties in a **controversy** must deal only with the
AP : 2 4 :010(251) [0387] the real issue of the **controversy** is clear, it will be easy to
AP : 2 4 :020(252) [0389] In this **controversy** as well as in many others, we must
AP : 2 8 :004(281) [0445] serious and difficult **controversies** the people desperately
AP : 2 8 :006(282) [0445] That is the issue in **controversy**.
TR : 0 0 :022(323) [0511] Since this whole **controversy** has been treated fully and
TR : 0 0 :049(329) [0519] allow ecclesiastical **controversies** to be decided in the
EP : 0 0 :000(464) [0777] of the Articles in **Controversy** among the theologians of
EP : RN :008(465) [0779] God with reference to **controverted** articles, and how
EP : 0 1 :001(466) [0779] question in this **controversy** is if, strictly and without any
EP : 0 2 :000(469) [0785] The Question at Issue in This **Controversy**
EP : 0 2 :001(469) [0785] In this **controversy** the primary question revolves
EP : 0 4 :000(475) [0797] The Chief Issue in the **Controversy** Concerning Good
EP : 0 4 :001(475) [0797] 1. Two **controversies** have arisen in some churches
EP : 0 4 :003(475) [0797] 2. The second **controversy** arose among certain
EP : 0 4 :004(476) [0797] Later on, a real **controversy** developed.
EP : 0 4 :004(476) [0797] *Pure Doctrine of the Christian Church in this* ***Controversy***
EP : 0 4 :005(476) [0797] order to explain this **controversy** from the ground up and
EP : 0 5 :000(477) [0801] The Chief Question at Issue in This **Controversy**
EP : 0 5 :006(478) [0803] and this was the original occasion of the **controversy**.
EP : 0 6 :000(479) [0805] The Chief Question at Issue in This **Controversy**
EP : 0 6 :001(480) [0805] of the law that a **controversy** has arisen among a few
EP : 0 6 :001(480) [0805] *The Correct Christian Teaching in this* ***Controversy***
EP : 0 7 :001(481) [0809] as far as necessary concerning this **controversy** also.
EP : 0 7 :003(482) [0809] order to explicate this **controversy**, it is necessary to
EP : 0 7 :010(483) [0811] which we stand in this **controversy** with the
EP : 0 8 :001(486) [0817] In connection with the **controversy** on the Holy Supper a
EP : 0 8 :001(487) [0817] The Chief Question at Issue in This **Controversy**
EP : 0 8 :004(487) [0819] and to settle this **controversy** according to our Christian
EP : 0 9 :000(492) [0827] Question at Issue in the **Controversy** about This Article
EP : 1 0 :001(492) [0829] The Chief Question at Issue in this **Controversy**
EP : 1 0 :003(493) [0829] 1. To settle this **controversy** we believe, teach, and
EP : 1 1 :022(497) [0837] this way the offensive **controversies** that have developed
SD : 0 0 :000(501) [0845] There Has Been a **Controversy** Among Some Theologians
SD : PR :003(502) [0847] those which were in **controversy** between them and the
SD : PR :004(502) [0847] of God when great **controversies** broke out, and orthodox
SD : PR :007(502) [0849] the subsequent bitter **controversies** would involve serious
SD : PR :009(503) [0849] After all, these **controversies** are not, as some may think,
SD : PR :009(503) [0849] On the contrary, these **controversies** deal with weighty
SD : PR :010(503) [0849] requires that such **controverted** articles be explained on
SD : PR :010(503) [0849] which opinion in the **controverted** issues agrees with the
SD : RN :002(503) [0851] of the several **controversies** among the adherents of the
SD : RN :012(506) [0855] parties in the various **controversies** can or should reject
SD : RN :013(506) [0855] and decisions in the **controverted** articles from these
SD : RN :013(506) [0855] Antitheses in the **Controverted** Articles
SD : RN :015(507) [0857] church) and necessary **controversy** (dissension concerning
SD : RN :016(507) [0857] and true in each of the **controverted** articles of our
SD : RN :016(507) [0857] significant articles which were in **controversy** at this time.
SD : RN :016(507) [0857] and abiding answer in the **controverted** issues, to wit:
SD : 0 1 :003(509) [0859] This **controversy** concerning original sin is not a useless
SD : 0 1 :004(509) [0861] order to explain this **controversy** in a Christian fashion
SD : 0 1 :049(517) [0875] far as the chief points in this **controversy** are concerned.
SD : 0 1 :056(518) [0877] way, prior to this **controversy**, the theologians in our
SD : 0 1 :058(519) [0879] abiding peace in this **controversy** but, on the contrary, the
SD : 0 1 :059(519) [0879] and highly detrimental **controversy** for our churches and
SD : 0 2 :001(519) [0881] There has been a **controversy** concerning free will, not
SD : 0 2 :001(520) [0881] first of all set forth the real issue in this **controversy**.
SD : 0 2 :002(520) [0881] In this **controversy** the question is not concerning the
SD : 0 2 :006(521) [0883] In order to settle this **controversy** in a Christian way
SD : 0 3 :001(539) [0917] The third **controversy** which has arisen among several
SD : 0 3 :005(540) [0917] Several other **controversies** concerning this article of
SD : 0 3 :008(540) [0919] to explain this **controversy** in a Christian way according
SD : 0 4 :001(551) [0939] A **controversy** concerning good works has likewise arisen
SD : 0 4 :003(551) [0939] In this **controversy** a very few asserted the provocative
SD : 0 4 :004(551) [0939] At first this latter **controversy** arose about the words
SD : 0 4 :005(551) [0939] argued theological **controversy** when some contended
SD : 0 4 :008(552) [0941] Neither is there a **controversy** among us as to how and
SD : 0 4 :013(553) [0943] there has been no **controversy** among us, we shall discuss
SD : 0 4 :013(553) [0943] shall explain only the **controverted** points simply and
SD : 0 4 :029(555) [0947] forth from it, and were made matters of **controversy**.
SD : 0 4 :036(557) [0949] although, prior to this **controversy**, not a few orthodox
SD : 0 4 :036(557) [0949] papists, yet, since a **controversy** subsequently arose on
SD : 0 5 :002(558) [0951] too, there has been a **controversy** among some
SD : 0 5 :003(558) [0953] rightly reflect on this **controversy**, we find that it was
SD : 0 5 :016(561) [0957] nothing in this present **controversy** but are presenting the
SD : 0 6 :001(564) [0963] A **controversy** has arisen among a few theologians
SD : 0 6 :004(564) [0963] to settle this **controversy**, we unanimously believe, teach,
SD : 0 7 :001(568) [0971] articles that were in **controversy** among the theologians
SD : 0 7 :093(586) [1005] the outbreak of this **controversy**, are these (the same ones
SD : 0 8 :001(591) [1015] A **controversy** has likewise arisen among theologians of
SD : 0 8 :005(592) [1017] order to explain this **controversy** in a Christian way
SD : 0 8 :053(601) [1033] most certain way in this **controversy** is to realize that no
SD : 1 0 :001(610) [1053] There has also been a **controversy** among some
SD : 1 0 :004(611) [1053] To explain this **controversy** and to settle it definitively by
SD : 1 1 :001(616) [1063] of very serious **controversies** at other places and has

Continued ▶

SD : 11 :094(632) [1095] suffice concerning the **controverted** articles which have
SD : 12 :004(633) [1097] articles which were in **controversy** among the theologians
SD : 12 :040(636) [1103] of all the foregoing **controverted** articles here explained,

Convene (1), Convened (2)
AG : PR :001(024) [0039] a diet of the empire to **convene** here in Augsburg.
AG : PR :018(026) [0041] assembled at the diet **convened** in Ratisbon had
S1 : 00 :000(287) [0453] was to have been **convened**, and which were to indicate

Convention (1)
PR : PR :007(004) [0009] assemble in a general **convention** and should discuss in a

Convents (2)
AG : 27 :007(071) [0077] was stricter in women's **convents** than in those of men,
AL : 27 :007(071) [0077] This was the case in **convents** of women more than in

Conversation (6)
AL : 26 :045(070) [0075] piety toward God and good **conversation** among men."
AP : 27 :038(275) [0433] In his **conversation** with the man he did not hear
S3 : 04 :000(310) [0491] through the mutual **conversation** and consolation of
LC : PR :009(359) [0569] and make it the subject of meditation and **conversation**.
LC : PR :009(359) [0569] In such reading, **conversation**, and meditation the Holy
LC : SP :019(363) [0579] the Christian's **conversation**, conduct and concern.

Conversely (3)
LC : 01 :064(373) [0599] wickedness, it follows, **conversely** that we are commanded
LC : 01 :093(377) [0607] **Conversely**, any conduct or work done apart from God's
LC : 01 :323(409) [0673] moved to wrath; and, **conversely**, trusts him alone and

Conversion (86)
AP : 04 :065(116) [0139] and clearly about the **conversion** of the wicked or the
AP : 12 :044(187) [0263] chief parts in the penitence or **conversion** of the wicked.
AP : 12 :046(188) [0263] Wherever Paul describes **conversion** or renewal, he
AP : 12 :058(190) [0267] properly belong to it in **conversion** or regeneration and
AP : 12 :131(202) [0291] after penitence (that is, **conversion** or regeneration) must
AP : 12 :131(202) [0291] There can be no true **conversion** or contrition where
S1 : PR :009(290) [0457] who are capable of **conversion** and turn them to
EP : 02 :004(470) [0787] does not effect **conversion** without means; he employs to
EP : 02 :004(470) [0787] Holy Spirit, for man's **conversion** is the Spirit's work
EP : 02 :010(471) [0789] make a beginning of his **conversion** but could not
EP : 02 :011(471) [0789] that while before his **conversion** man is indeed too weak
EP : 02 :012(471) [0789] Likewise that after his **conversion** man is able to keep the
EP : 02 :014(471) [0789] 7. Likewise that in **conversion** and rebirth God wholly
EP : 02 :014(471) [0789] soul, and that in **conversion** and rebirth he creates out of
EP : 02 :015(471) [0789] before, in, and after **conversion** resists the Holy Spirit,
EP : 02 :015(471) [0789] as Augustine says, in **conversion** God makes willing
EP : 02 :016(472) [0789] will is not idle in **conversion**, but does something."
EP : 02 :016(472) [0791] of natural free will in **conversion** contrary to the doctrine
EP : 02 :016(472) [0791] well to avoid them in a discussion of **conversion** to God.
EP : 02 :017(472) [0791] is correct to say that in **conversion**, through the attraction
EP : 02 :017(472) [0791] people, and that after **conversion**, in the daily exercise of
EP : 02 :018(472) [0791] that man's will in **conversion** behaves "altogether
EP : 02 :018(472) [0791] of man's will and works the new birth and **conversion**.
EP : 02 :019(472) [0791] Prior to man's **conversion** there are only two efficient
EP : 02 :019(472) [0791] Holy Spirit's instrument whereby he effects **conversion**.
EP : 12 :022(499) [0841] knowledge of Christ, **conversion**, repentance, faith, and
SD : 02 :002(520) [0881] Fall and prior to his **conversion** can do in external things
SD : 02 :002(520) [0881] and will can do in his **conversion** and regeneration, by
SD : 02 :003(520) [0881] powers prior to his **conversion** that he can to some extent
SD : 02 :005(521) [0881] things, concerning our **conversion** and salvation, he is by
SD : 02 :007(521) [0883] Fall and prior to his **conversion** not a spark of spiritual
SD : 02 :007(521) [0883] cooperate toward his **conversion** by his own powers,
SD : 02 :018(524) [0887] will of man prior to his **conversion** will be much more
SD : 02 :018(524) [0889] do nothing for man's **conversion**, righteousness, peace,
SD : 02 :022(525) [0889] of and a partaker in **conversion**, in the grace of God, and
SD : 02 :024(525) [0891] In his own **conversion** or regeneration he can as little
SD : 02 :025(526) [0891] Holy Scriptures ascribe **conversion**, faith in Christ,
SD : 02 :044(529) [0897] cooperation on the part of our will in man's **conversion**.
SD : 02 :045(530) [0899] it, and that thus the human will cooperates in **conversion**.
SD : 02 :046(530) [0899] as the doctrine that our **conversion** and regeneration are
SD : 02 :055(531) [0903] be in vain, and no **conversion** would follow, if there were
SD : 02 :059(532) [0905] true that prior to his **conversion** man is still a rational
SD : 02 :059(532) [0905] whatsoever toward his **conversion**, as was mentioned
SD : 02 :061(533) [0905] to say that before his **conversion** man has a mode of
SD : 02 :061(533) [0905] Prior to his **conversion** man is dead in sin (Eph. 2:5);
SD : 02 :062(533) [0905] to man prior to his **conversion** any mode of acting by
SD : 02 :065(534) [0907] has begun in us in **conversion**, as St. Paul expressly and
SD : 02 :070(534) [0909] self-evident that in true **conversion** there must be a
SD : 02 :070(535) [0909] things takes place or exists, there is no true **conversion**.
SD : 02 :071(535) [0909] wills to work such **conversion** and renewal in us, and
SD : 02 :073(535) [0909] before, in, or after his **conversion** resists the Holy Spirit,
SD : 02 :073(535) [0909] Whether man in his **conversion** behaves and is like a
SD : 02 :073(535) [0909] Whether **conversion** is brought about through coercion,
SD : 02 :076(536) [0911] and toward his own **conversion**, and that thereupon, since
SD : 02 :079(536) [0911] that man after his **conversion** can keep the law of God
SD : 02 :081(536) [0911] who imagine that in **conversion** and regeneration God
SD : 02 :082(537) [0913] before, in, and after **conversion** resists the Holy Spirit,
SD : 02 :083(537) [0913] resists the Word, **conversion** does not and cannot take
SD : 02 :083(537) [0913] For **conversion** is that kind of change through the Holy
SD : 02 :086(537) [0913] will is not idle in **conversion** but also does something,"
SD : 02 :086(538) [0913] will cooperates in his **conversion**, contrary to the article
SD : 02 :086(538) [0913] be avoided in the discussion of man's **conversion** to God.
SD : 02 :087(538) [0913] For the **conversion** of our corrupted will, which is
SD : 02 :088(538) [0915] detail above that in **conversion**, through the drawing of
SD : 02 :088(538) [0915] and that after such **conversion** man's reborn will is not
SD : 02 :089(538) [0915] passive way in his **conversion** (that is, that man does not
SD : 02 :089(538) [0915] he did not mean that **conversion** takes place without the
SD : 02 :089(538) [0915] nor did he mean that in **conversion** the Holy Spirit
SD : 02 :089(538) [0915] in any way toward his **conversion**, and that man's
SD : 02 :089(538) [0915] and that man's **conversion** is not only in part, but
SD : 02 :090(538) [0915] of unregenerated man's **conversion** to God, particularly
SD : 02 :090(539) [0915] it is evident that **conversion** to God is solely of God the
SD : 02 :090(539) [0915] in whom the Holy Spirit works **conversion** and renewal.
SD : 03 :022(543) [0923] without repentance, **conversion**, and improvement.
SD : 03 :024(543) [0923] the same way about **conversion** and about justification.
SD : 03 :025(543) [0923] that belongs to **conversion** is simultaneously also a part
SD : 03 :041(546) [0929] kindles faith in us in **conversion** through the hearing of
SD : 05 :007(559) [0953] as the entire **conversion** of man, as in Luke 13:5, "Unless
SD : 05 :009(559) [0955] sufficient for a salutary **conversion** to God unless there is
SD : 07 :060(580) [0993] true repentance and **conversion** to God, and who by their
SD : 08 :062(603) [1037] in no way should any **conversion**, blending, or
SD : 11 :044(624) [1077] and effect in us everything that belongs to our **conversion**.
SD : 11 :045(624) [1079] individual Christian's **conversion**, righteousness, and
SD : 11 :056(625) [1081] each person the time and hour of his call and **conversion**.
SD : 11 :075(628) [1087] it the Holy Spirit wills to effect their **conversion** in them.
SD : 12 :030(635) [1101] knowledge of Christ, **conversion**, repentance, and faith or

Convert (13), Converted (46), Converts (5)
AL : 12 :001(034) [0049] sins whenever they are **converted**, and that the church
AP : 04 :261(145) [0195] one God of Israel and **converted** him not only to the
AP : 04 :268(147) [0197] "If you are **converted**, I will convert you (Jer. 15:19)"
AP : 04 :268(147) [0197] you are converted, I will **convert** you" (Jer. 15:19);
AP : 07 :042(176) [0241] brethren who had been **converted** from Judaism, and so,
AP : 07 :043(177) [0243] brethren who had been **converted** from Judaism but kept
AP : 12 :001(182) [0253] of sins whenever, and as often as, they are **converted**.
AP : 12 :009(183) [0255] certainly experienced by those who are truly **converted**?
AP : 12 :027(185) [0259] be reserved in the case of someone who is truly **converted**.
AP : 12 :176(210) [0307] sins of those who are **converted** and to denounce and
AP : 12 :176(210) [0307] and excommunicate those who refuse to be **converted**.
AP : 12 :176(210) [0307] absolve those who are **converted**, according to the
AP : 12 :177(210) [0307] of guilt before God in the case of the truly **converted**.
AP : 28 :013(283) [0447] absolve them if they are **converted** and ask for
S1 : PR :009(290) [0457] God **convert** those who are capable of conversion and
SC : 09 :002(354) [0561] He must not be a recent **convert**," etc. (I Tim. 3:2-6).
EP : 02 :004(470) [0787] heed it and thus are **converted** solely through the grace
EP : 02 :009(471) [0789] Holy Spirit, man can **convert** himself to God, believe the
EP : 02 :011(471) [0789] will to make a beginning, **convert** himself to God, and
EP : 06 :002(480) [0805] whom God has truly **converted** are freed through Christ
EP : 06 :003(480) [0805] believing, truly **converted**, regenerated, and justified
EP : 07 :016(484) [0813] but if they are not **converted** and do not repent, they
SD : 02 :004(520) [0881] have taught that God **converts** man through the Holy
SD : 02 :005(521) [0881] on his part, he is **converted**, becomes a believer, is
SD : 02 :019(524) [0889] creature, or that he is **converted** to God without hearing
SD : 02 :021(525) [0889] Holy Spirit enlightens, **converts**, and regenerates man, a
SD : 02 :023(525) [0889] divine grace it can be **converted** to God and become truly
SD : 02 :024(525) [0891] man is illuminated, **converted**, reborn, renewed, and
SD : 02 :046(530) [0899] that since they cannot **convert** themselves by their own
SD : 02 :046(530) [0899] wait until God forcibly **converts** them against their will.
SD : 02 :046(530) [0899] feel and to perceive that God has truly **converted** them.
SD : 02 :048(530) [0901] of God how man is **converted** to God, how and by what
SD : 02 :050(531) [0901] to draw them to himself, **convert** them, beget them anew,
SD : 02 :052(531) [0901] to act efficaciously, to **convert** men to God, and to work
SD : 02 :053(531) [0903] person who is not yet **converted** to God and regenerated
SD : 02 :055(532) [0903] heard illuminates and **converts** hearts so that men believe
SD : 02 :059(532) [0905] with his will resists the Lord God until he is **converted**.
SD : 02 :060(533) [0905] the obstinate Jews (Acts 7:51), will not be **converted**.
SD : 02 :060(533) [0905] person whom he wills to **convert**, and draws him in such a
SD : 02 :063(533) [0905] But after a man is **converted**, and thereby enlightened,
SD : 02 :064(533) [0905] compulsion because the **converted** man spontaneously
SD : 02 :066(534) [0907] other way than that the **converted** man does good, as
SD : 02 :066(534) [0907] as though the **converted** man cooperates alongside the
SD : 02 :069(534) [0907] they must certainly be **converted** again, as we have
SD : 02 :073(535) [0909] forcibly compels a man to be **converted** against his will?
SD : 02 :075(536) [0911] Spirit, the free will can **convert** itself to God, believe the
SD : 02 :077(536) [0911] and by its own powers to **convert** itself to God and to
SD : 02 :090(539) [0915] only that which is to be **converted**, since they are the
SD : 02 :090(539) [0915] the person who is to be **converted** does nothing, but only
SD : 02 :090(539) [0915] but only lets God work in him, until he is **converted**.
SD : 03 :033(545) [0927] only when he was first **converted** from idolatry and had
SD : 03 :035(545) [0927] it follows that although **converted** persons and believers
SD : 05 :002(558) [0953] those who have been **converted** to Christ that their
SD : 06 :001(563) [0963] Spirit, who have been **converted** to the Lord and from
SD : 06 :004(564) [0963] having been genuinely **converted** to God and justified,
SD : 07 :108(588) [1009] and essence and are **converted** into the substance of the
SD : 11 :017(619) [1069] and meditated on, would **convert** hearts to true
SD : 11 :029(621) [1073] so that they may be illuminated, **converted**, and saved.
SD : 11 :034(622) [1075] not to be illuminated or **converted**, but are to be and
SD : 11 :040(623) [1077] call, enlighten, and **convert** the elect through the Word
SD : 11 :054(625) [1081] likewise, who of the **converted** will persevere and who
SD : 11 :057(625) [1081] mind while another in equal guilt is again **converted**.
SD : 11 :061(626) [1083] whereby he enlightens, **converts**, and keeps them, God
SD : 11 :083(630) [1091] obduracy and blindness those who have been **converted**.

Convey (1), Conveyed (1), Conveys (2)
LC : 04 :017(438) [0737] extol, for it contains and **conveys** all the fullness of God.
LC : 05 :029(449) [0759] This treasure is **conveyed** and communicated to us in no
LC : 05 :070(454) [0769] sins, which contains and **conveys** God's grace and Spirit
EP : 01 :024(469) [0785] they are familiar and **convey** no false impressions, and

Convict (1), Convicted (1), Conviction (7), Convicts (1)
PR : PR :017(008) [0015] and confession as a final explanation of our **conviction**.
AP : 04 :008(108) [0121] prayer to God, true **conviction** that God hears prayer, and
AP : 04 :257(144) [0193] enough to preach the law, the Word that **convicts** of sin.
AP : 04 :350(160) [0217] ever stronger in the **conviction** that God cares for us,
AP : 20 :015(229) [0343] ample evidence of our **conviction** that good works must
AP : 23 :068(249) [0383] had been tried and **convicted** by many previous tribunals
S3 : 08 :003(312) [0495] must hold firmly to the **conviction** that God gives no one
LC : 01 :280(403) [0661] through whom you can **convict** the guilty one and on
EP : 05 :011(479) [0805] is a proclamation of **conviction** and reproof and not
SD : 10 :018(614) [1059] consistently been the **conviction** and the confession of the

Convince (6), Convinced (1), Convincing (1)
AP : 04 :386(166) [0225] the fearful mind, and is **convinced** that God is reconciled
AP : 24 :052(259) [0403] This is a very **convincing** argument for the ignorant,
S3 : 03 :001(303) [0479] "The Holy Spirit will **convince** the world of sin."
S3 : 03 :005(304) [0481] to accuse them all and **convince** them that they were

Continued ▶

SD : 0 5 :011(560) [0955] the office of the law, must also **convince** the world of sin.
SD : 0 5 :012(560) [0955] 'The Holy Spirit will **convince** the world of sin because
SD : 0 5 :013(560) [0957] 'The Holy Spirit will **convince** the world of sin' (John
SD : 0 6 :012(566) [0967] Spirit shall come, he will **convince** the world (to which

Convoked (1)
PR : PR :013(007) [0013] electors and princes, **convoked** a number of prominent,

Cook (1), Cooks (2)
AP : 2 4 :016(252) [0389] lest like an unskilled **cook** he sever the member at the
AP : 2 4 :016(252) [0389] call our opponents "poor **cooks**," for they despise these
LC : 0 4 :022(439) [0737] from that which the maid **cooks** with and could indeed be

Cooperate (13), Cooperates (7), Cooperation (6)
PR : PR :013(007) [0013] with the counsel and **cooperation** of some of our fellow
PR : PR :026(014) [0025] We likewise purpose to **cooperate** with one another in the
S1 : 0 1 :000(291) [0461] Spirit, without the **cooperation** of man, and was born of
EP : 0 1 :016(468) [0783] initiate, to effect, or to **cooperate** in something spiritual.
EP : 0 2 :011(471) [0789] and feeble) to help, to **cooperate**, to prepare itself for
EP : 0 2 :017(472) [0791] of man is not idle but **cooperates** in all the works which
EP : 0 2 :018(472) [0791] hold on grace but also **cooperates** with the Holy Spirit in
SD : 0 1 :023(512) [0865] something in spiritual matters or to **cooperate** therein.
SD : 0 2 :005(521) [0881] grace and without any **cooperation** on his part, he is
SD : 0 2 :007(521) [0883] do, effect, or **cooperate**, but that man is entirely and
SD : 0 2 :007(521) [0883] or help, do, effect, or **cooperate** toward his conversion by
SD : 0 2 :012(522) [0885] to accomplish or to **cooperate** in them as of himself.
SD : 0 2 :018(524) [0889] and salvation, cannot **cooperate**, and cannot obey,
SD : 0 2 :024(525) [0891] as little begin, effect, or **cooperate** in anything as a stone,
SD : 0 2 :032(527) [0893] either to initiate something good or by itself to **cooperate**.
SD : 0 2 :042(529) [0897] make no mention whatever of our will and **cooperation**.
SD : 0 2 :044(529) [0897] There is therefore no **cooperation** on the part of our will
SD : 0 2 :045(530) [0899] it, and that thus the human will **cooperates** in conversion.
SD : 0 2 :065(534) [0907] that we can and must **cooperate** by the power of the Holy
SD : 0 2 :065(534) [0907] Such **cooperation** does not proceed from our carnal and
SD : 0 2 :066(534) [0907] the converted man **cooperates** alongside the Holy Spirit,
SD : 0 2 :077(536) [0911] a weak way — help and **cooperate** and prepare itself for
SD : 0 2 :077(536) [0911] and by its own powers **cooperate** with the Holy Spirit in
SD : 0 2 :086(538) [0913] man's naturally free will **cooperates** in his conversion,
SD : 0 2 :088(538) [0915] of repentance but **cooperates** in all the works that the
SD : 0 2 :090(539) [0915] Then he **cooperates** with the Holy Spirit in subsequent

Cope (1)
LC : 0 3 :030(424) [0707] We are far too weak to **cope** with the devil and all his

Copied (1), Copies (1), Copy (4), Copying (1)
PR : PR :018(009) [0015] German and the Latin **copies** were afterward found to be
AP : PR :002(098) [0099] our party requested a **copy** of the Confutation; for we had
AP : 0 4 :208(135) [0177] people began zealously to **copy** this action in order
AP : 0 4 :211(136) [0179] the crowd ever since has **copied** not the faith of the
AP : 1 5 :024(218) [0321] to imitate them, they **copy** their outward behavior
AP : 1 5 :024(218) [0321] copy their outward behavior without **copying** their faith.
AP : 2 3 :068(249) [0383] they refuse to show us a **copy** of the Confutation, lest

Cordial (3), Cordially (2)
PR : PR :022(012) [0021] loathing for and a **cordial** disapproval of the raging of
LC : 0 1 :040(370) [0591] so gracious an offer, so **cordial** an invitation, and so rich
SD : 0 2 :047(530) [0901] strong, ardent faith and **cordial** obedience but only
SD : 1 1 :075(628) [1087] at his Word and **cordially** return to him, as it is
SD : 1 1 :095(632) [1095] true harmony and are **cordially** inclined and determined

Corinth (1)
AG : 2 2 :003(050) [0059] of the congregation in **Corinth** received both kinds.

Corinthians (2)
AP : 0 4 :192(133) [0175] of alms by the **Corinthians** was a holy work (I Cor. 16:1),
AP : 0 4 :224(138) [0181] being justified, the **Corinthians** received many excellent

Cornelius (3)
AP : 2 1 :002(229) [0343] Cyprian asked **Cornelius**, while he was still alive, to pray
S3 : 0 8 :008(313) [0495] **Cornelius** (Acts 10:1ff.) had long since heard from the
TR : 0 0 :014(322) [0507] in his fourth letter to **Cornelius**: "Wherefore you must

Corner (6)
AP : 0 4 :098(121) [0149] builders, but which has become the head of the **corner**.
AP : 1 3 :013(213) [0311] They sit in a dark **corner** doing and saying nothing, but
LC : PR :005(359) [0567] they toss the book into a **corner** as if they are ashamed to
LC : 0 1 :267(401) [0657] they spread it into every **corner**, relishing and delighting
LC : 0 1 :281(403) [0661] about someone in every **corner** and root around in the
LC : 0 1 :331(410) [0677] on every wall and **corner**, and even on their garments.

Corporeal (6), Corporeally (1)
EP : 0 8 :008(487) [0819] nature are to be a **corporeal** creature, to be flesh and
EP : 0 9 :001(492) [0827] or according to body and soul, spiritually or **corporeally**?
SD : 0 7 :099(586) [1005] The comprehensible, **corporeal** mode of presence, as when
SD : 0 7 :099(586) [1005] spirit dreams, for God is not a **corporeal** space or place.
SD : 0 7 :103(587) [1007] many places, even in a **corporeal** and comprehensible
SD : 0 8 :010(593) [1019] the other hand, to be a **corporeal** being or a creature, to
SD : 0 8 :081(607) [1045] according to the first, **corporeal**, comprehensible manner,

Corpse (1)
EP : 0 2 :003(470) [0787] As little as a **corpse** can quicken itself to bodily, earthly

Correct (51), Corrected (9), Correcting (1), Correction (6), Correctly (29), Correctness (1)
PR : PR :010(006) [0011] by solid reasoning, and a **correct** explanation and
PR : PR :011(006) [0011] theologians clearly and **correctly** described to one
PR : PR :016(008) [0013] Book of Concord as the **correct** Christian interpretation
PR : PR :020(010) [0017] and demonstrate by a **correct** explanation of the articles
PR : PR :023(012) [0021] and its Apology, **correctly** understood, and that no
PR : PR :024(013) [0023] of which is that finally **correct** doctrine will be entirely
AG : 0 0 :000(048) [0059] Is Given of the Abuses Which Have Been **Correctef**
AG : 0 0 :000(049) [0059] some abuses have been **corrected** (some of the abuses
AL : 0 0 :005(048) [0059] conscience, they have to some extent been **corrected**.
AL : 0 0 :000(048) [0059] Is Given of the Abuses Which Have Been **Correctef**
AL : 2 4 :014(057) [0065] If they had **corrected** them in time, there would now have
AL : 2 4 :018(058) [0067] men who were able to **correct** them and were under
AP : PR :015(099) [0101] we hold to the Gospel of Christ **correctly** and faithfully.
AP : 0 2 :026(103) [0111] sin, therefore, we have **correctly** expressed both elements:
AP : 0 2 :028(104) [0113] what original sin is, it is **correct** to answer that it is
AP : 0 2 :028(104) [0113] It is also **correct** to answer that it is the lack of proper
AP : 0 2 :051(107) [0119] know that our doctrine is **correct** and in agreement with
AP : 0 2 :051(107) [0119] to explain logically and **correctly** either the formal
AP : 0 4 :014(109) [0123] the opponents' ideas are **correct**, this was perfectly
AP : 0 4 :024(110) [0127] than this, as Aristotle **correctly** says, "Neither the evening
AP : 0 4 :087(120) [0147] whole law, as Augustine **correctly** maintains in his lengthy
AP : 0 4 :132(125) [0159] Therefore we cannot **correctly** keep the law unless by faith
AP : 0 4 :185(132) [0173] from the sources, will **correct** everything that seems
AP : 0 4 :221(137) [0181] they always add the **correction** that they should be
AP : 0 4 :221(137) [0181] they do not add the **correction**: We need the faith that we
AP : 0 4 :250(143) [0191] Accordingly, James is **correct** in denying that we are
AP : 0 4 :258(144) [0193] to do good; seek justice, **correct** oppression; defend the
AP : 0 4 :258(144) [0193] only at these works: "**correct** oppression, defend the
AP : 0 4 :258(144) [0193] through these works—"**correct** oppression, defend the
AP : 0 4 :337(159) [0215] is worthless would be **correct** when they say: "When you
AP : 0 4 :381(165) [0223] this way, they would be **correct** when they say that we
AP : 0 7 :020(172) [0233] foundation, these are forgiven them or even **corrected**.
AP : 0 7 :042(176) [0243] if his brethren do not **correctly** compute the time in
AP : 1 1 :001(180) [0247] confession they add the **correction** that the regulation
AP : 1 2 :003(183) [0253] on the Gospel and have **corrected** many vicious errors
AP : 1 2 :150(206) [0299] anger"; and Jer. 10:24, "**Correct** me, O Lord, but in just
AP : 1 5 :039(220) [0325] and if you look at it **correctly** we are more faithful to the
AP : 2 1 :039(235) [0355] do their duty in **correcting** these abuses; but in the
AP : 2 1 :042(235) [0355] emperor take steps to **correct** the abuses, for clearly he is
AP : 2 3 :005(239) [0365] Now we see the **correctness** of Peter's warning (II Pet.
AP : 2 3 :009(240) [0367] have said wisely and **correctly** that the union of man and
AP : 2 3 :020(242) [0369] Therefore Ambrose **correctly** observes, "Virginity is
AP : 2 4 :069(262) [0409] will toward us; so it is **correct** to define the New
AP : 2 7 :025(273) [0429] is, they do not think **correctly** about God, they do not
AP : 2 7 :036(275) [0433] We remember that this **correction** is found in Gerson.
AP : 2 7 :036(275) [0433] they added this **correction**, that it is a state for acquiring
AP : 2 8 :006(282) [0445] the power to rule and to **correct** by force in order to guide
S3 : 0 3 :010(304) [0481] for them to teach **correctly** about repentance because they
LC : SP :006(362) [0575] taught and treated **correctly**, so that all who wish to be
LC : SP :026(364) [0581] heard and give a good, **correct** answer when they are
LC : 0 1 :278(402) [0661] for the evil would be **corrected** and the neighbor's honor
LC : 0 1 :296(405) [0665] these commandments **correctly** (though they also have a
LC : 0 4 :058(444) [0747] Is it **correct** to conclude that when anybody does not do
LC : 0 4 :080(446) [0751] I say this to **correct** the opinion, which has long prevailed
EP : 0 0 :000(463) [0775] A Thorough, Pure, **Correct**, and Final Restatement and
EP : 0 2 :017(472) [0791] On the other hand, it is **correct** to say that in conversion,
EP : 0 4 :009(476) [0799] "ought," and "must" are **correctly** and in a Christian way
EP : 0 5 :006(478) [0803] Acts 20:24), then it is **correct** to say or write that the
EP : 0 6 :001(480) [0805] *The **Correct** Christian Teaching in this Controversy*
EP : 1 0 :002(493) [0829] *The **Correct**, True Doctrine and Confession about this*
EP : 1 1 :001(494) [0831] article when it is **correctly** treated, we have included an
SD : 0 0 :000(501) [0845] A General, Pure, **Correct**, and Definitive Restatement
SD : RN :004(504) [0851] doctrine as it was **correctly** and soundly understood was
SD : RN :008(505) [0853] laymen in a most **correct** and simple, yet sufficiently
SD : RN :013(506) [0855] the unanimous and **correct** understanding of our
SD : RN :014(506) [0855] and wholesome doctrine **correctly**, but also to accuse the
SD : RN :016(507) [0857] what he should accept as **correct** and true in each of the
SD : RN :016(507) [0857] with one accord as the **correct** and abiding answer in the
SD : 0 1 :004(509) [0861] to preserve the true and **correct** doctrine concerning
SD : 0 1 :030(513) [0867] when we discussed the **correct** doctrine of original sin, the
SD : 0 1 :056(518) [0877] without ever being **corrected** either by Dr. Luther or by
SD : 0 1 :060(519) [0879] understanding and give a **correct** definition of original
SD : 0 2 :059(532) [0905] In this case it is **correct** to say that man is not a stone or a
SD : 0 2 :062(533) [0905] God operates in man, it is **correct** to say that the Lord
SD : 0 2 :085(537) [0913] explain and teach the **correct** opinion in this matter
SD : 0 3 :032(544) [0927] It is indeed **correct** to say that believers who through faith
SD : 0 3 :042(546) [0931] This **correct** distinction explains usefully and well the
SD : 0 3 :042(547) [0931] states, "James teaches **correctly** when he denies that we
SD : 0 3 :054(548) [0933] We must also explain **correctly** the discussion concerning
SD : 0 4 :022(554) [0945] Therefore we **correctly** reject the propositions that good
SD : 0 4 :029(555) [0947] to have a clear and **correct** confession against all sorts of
SD : 0 5 :001(558) [0951] and apostles may be explained and understood **correctly**.
SD : 0 5 :005(559) [0953] of law and Gospel, it is **correct** to define the word as the
SD : 0 5 :015(561) [0957] side, but in proper order and with the **correct** distinction.
SD : 0 6 :004(564) [0963] of God and what is pleasing to him is **correctly** portrayed.
SD : 0 7 :017(572) [0979] In these the **correct** and true meaning is set forth briefly
SD : 0 7 :022(573) [0979] who thinks that he can **correct** Christ and change what he
SD : 0 7 :041(576) [0985] cannot be derived more **correctly** or better from any
SD : 0 8 :042(599) [1029] God, and therefore it is **correct** to say: the Son of God
SD : 0 8 :044(599) [1031] united in one person, it is **correct** to talk about God's
SD : 0 8 :054(601) [1033] statement is, of course, **correct** and true that Christ's
SD : 0 8 :060(602) [1035] other nature, we must **correctly** explain this doctrine and
SD : 0 8 :063(603) [1037] To set forth **correctly** the majesty of Christ by way of
SD : 1 1 :003(616) [1063] we must set forth the **correct** meaning on the basis of
SD : 1 1 :012(618) [1067] but "to reproof, **correction**, and improvement" (II Tim.
SD : 1 1 :013(618) [1067] wish to think or speak **correctly** and profitably about
SD : 1 1 :076(628) [1087] It is indeed **correct** and true what Scripture states, that no

Correlates (1), Correlative (1), Correlatively (1)
AP : 0 4 :050(114) [0135] He therefore **correlates** and connects promise and faith.
AP : 0 4 :324(157) [0211] promise and faith are **correlative** and that only faith can
AP : 0 4 :324(157) [0211] the promised mercy **correlatively** requires faith and that

Correspond (1), Corresponding (2)
PR : PR :022(012) [0021] so we entertain a **corresponding** loathing for and a
AP : 1 2 :155(207) [0301] temporal punishments **corresponding** to particular sins.
SD : 0 8 :045(600) [1031] merely empty words which do not **correspond** to reality.

Corrupt (12), Corrupted (67), Corrupting (1), Corruption (27), Corruptions (3), Corrupts (5)
AG : 2 5 :008(062) [0069] "The heart is desperately **corrupt**; who can understand
AG : 2 7 :002(071) [0077] doctrine had become **corrupted**, monastic vows were
AL : 2 4 :015(057) [0065] they let many **corruptions** creep into the church.
AL : 2 5 :008(062) [0069] also says, "The heart of man is **corrupt** and inscrutable."

Continued ▶

A P : 0 2 :005(101) [0107] sin is not some vice or **corruption** in human nature, but
A P : 0 2 :006(101) [0107] since human nature is born full of **corruption** and faults.
A P : 0 2 :025(103) [0111] is not merely a **corruption** of the physical constitution,
A P : 0 2 :027(104) [0113] it is not a pure privation, but also a **corrupt** habit."
A P : 0 4 :024(110) [0127] its due credit; for our **corrupt** nature has no greater good
A P : 0 4 :030(111) [0129] is the Saviour of man's **corrupted** nature, for
A P : 0 4 :035(112) [0131] This contempt for God **corrupts** works that seem
A P : 0 4 :383(166) [0225] Therefore they **corrupt** many other statements.
A P : 2 3 :006(240) [0365] scandals, sins, and the **corruption** of public morals.
A P : 2 4 :057(260) [0405] righteousness of faith, it **corrupts** the teaching of both the
A P : 2 4 :091(266) [0415] of the Gospel, a **corruption** of the use of the sacraments.
S 1 : P R :005(289) [0457] twisting and **corrupting** my every word and letter?
S 3 : 0 1 :003(302) [0477] sin is so deep a **corruption** of nature that reason cannot
S 3 : 0 2 :004(303) [0479] his nature has fallen and how **corrupt** it has become.
T R : 0 0 :044(328) [0517] has been completely **corrupted** by the pope and his
L C : 0 1 :263(400) [0655] preachers with their **corrupt** teaching and blasphemy, to
L C : 0 1 :263(400) [0655] and witnesses with their **corrupt** behavior in court and
L C : 0 1 :326(409) [0675] and other kinds of **corruption** and wickedness, but to use
L C : 0 4 :067(445) [0749] Christ's kingdom, this **corruption** must daily decrease so
E P : 0 1 :001(466) [0779] original sin is man's **corrupted** nature, substance, and
E P : 0 1 :001(466) [0779] which inheres in the **corrupted** nature and corrupts it, is
E P : 0 1 :001(466) [0779] in the corrupted nature and **corrupts** it, is something else.
E P : 0 1 :003(466) [0779] distinction between our **corrupted** human nature and
E P : 0 1 :004(466) [0781] even though they are **corrupted**, and God still
E P : 0 1 :007(467) [0781] distinction between the **corrupted** nature itself and the
E P : 0 1 :007(467) [0781] nature itself and the **corruption** which is in the nature and
E P : 0 1 :007(467) [0781] which is in the nature and which has **corrupted** the nature
E P : 0 1 :008(467) [0781] sin is not a slight **corruption** of human nature, but that it
E P : 0 1 :008(467) [0781] but that it is so deep a **corruption** that nothing sound or
E P : 0 1 :008(467) [0781] Adam's fall man's nature and essence are all **corrupt**."
E P : 0 1 :010(467) [0781] alone can separate the **corruption** of our nature from the
E P : 0 1 :011(467) [0781] without any kind of **corruption** of our own nature.
E P : 0 1 :016(468) [0783] in man is not entirely **corrupted**, but that man still has
E P : 0 1 :019(468) [0783] without any distinction **corrupted** man's substance,
E P : 0 1 :021(468) [0783] arise in the heart of **corrupted** man, no idle word were
E P : 0 1 :021(468) [0785] man's nature is **corrupted** through original sin, innate in
E P : 0 1 :025(469) [0785] with God's permission, **corrupt** accidentally the substance
E P : 0 6 :004(480) [0805] their flesh (that is, their **corrupt** nature and kind), which
S D : P R :010(503) [0849] against the errors and **corruptions** that have invaded our
S D : 0 1 :001(508) [0859] and essence are wholly **corrupt** as a result of the fall of
S D : 0 1 :002(508) [0859] deep, and inexpressible **corruption** thereof, in the sense
S D : 0 1 :002(508) [0859] that, because of this **corruption** and this inborn sin which
S D : 0 1 :002(509) [0859] the devil by which man's nature has become **corrupted**).
S D : 0 1 :003(509) [0861] from the devil's work, the **corruption** of human nature.
S D : 0 1 :005(509) [0861] inherited disease which has **corrupted** our entire nature.
S D : 0 1 :006(509) [0861] and entirely poisoned and **corrupted** human nature.
S D : 0 1 :006(509) [0861] On account of this **corruption** and because of the fall of
S D : 0 1 :007(510) [0861] And even today, in this **corruption**, God does not create
S D : 0 1 :011(510) [0863] and inexpressible **corruption** of his entire nature in all its
S D : 0 1 :014(511) [0863] nature, which original sin has perverted and **corrupted**.
S D : 0 1 :017(511) [0865] else's action without any **corruption** of our own nature.
S D : 0 1 :021(512) [0865] merely splashed on, or a **corruption** only of certain
S D : 0 1 :023(512) [0865] greatly weakened and **corrupted** through the Fall, it has
S D : 0 1 :023(512) [0865] and being are wholly **corrupted**," but that human nature
S D : 0 1 :025(512) [0867] Word teaches that man's **corrupted** nature can of and by
S D : 0 1 :027(513) [0867] and lack, this **corruption** and wounding which Satan
S D : 0 1 :027(513) [0867] has so perverted and **corrupted** human nature (as was
S D : 0 1 :027(513) [0867] now inherit a nature with the same lack and **corruption**.
S D : 0 1 :028(513) [0867] pure and holy and is **corrupted** only subsequently through
S D : 0 1 :028(513) [0867] seed from which man is formed is sinful and **corrupted**.
S D : 0 1 :028(513) [0867] or apart from man's **corrupted** nature, just as it is not
S D : 0 1 :029(513) [0867] that has been thereby **corrupted** to be distinguished from
S D : 0 1 :030(513) [0867] that it is not the **corrupted** man himself who sins because
S D : 0 1 :030(513) [0867] condemn man's nature, **corrupted** by sin, but only the
S D : 0 1 :030(513) [0867] a father and a mother is **corrupted** and perverted by
S D : 0 1 :031(513) [0869] Because of this **corruption** the law accuses and condemns
S D : 0 1 :031(513) [0869] condemns man's entire **corrupted** nature unless the sin is
S D : 0 1 :032(513) [0869] far as our nature has been poisoned and **corrupted** by sin.
S D : 0 1 :033(514) [0869] has so poisoned and **corrupted** man's whole nature that
S D : 0 1 :033(514) [0869] nature that within the **corrupted** nature we are not able to
S D : 0 1 :033(514) [0869] things, nevertheless our **corrupted** nature or the essence
S D : 0 1 :033(514) [0869] nature or the essence of **corrupted** man, our body and
S D : 0 1 :033(514) [0869] essence, or total man is **corrupted**, dwells) are not
S D : 0 1 :033(514) [0869] (which dwells in man's nature or essence and **corrupts** it).
S D : 0 1 :038(514) [0871] Therefore the **corrupted** man cannot be identified
S D : 0 1 :038(515) [0871] God has been miserably **corrupted** by sin, for the dough
S D : 0 1 :038(515) [0871] makes man has been **corrupted** and perverted in Adam
S D : 0 1 :039(515) [0871] immediately cast this **corrupted**, perverted, and sinful
S D : 0 1 :039(515) [0871] which is so miserably **corrupted** by sin, in order that
S D : 0 1 :041(515) [0871] and soul (which are **corrupted** by original sin) and
S D : 0 1 :041(515) [0871] (by which our nature is **corrupted**), we should be
S D : 0 1 :041(515) [0871] or creature if our **corrupted** nature were unqualifiedly
S D : 0 1 :042(515) [0873] fact that our nature is **corrupted**, that our thoughts,
S D : 0 1 :042(515) [0873] sin has in this fashion **corrupted** God's handiwork in
S D : 0 1 :042(515) [0873] This **corruption** has come upon us by inheritance.
S D : 0 1 :044(516) [0873] the nature or essence of **corrupted** man and original sin,
S D : 0 1 :047(516) [0873] whatever between our **corrupted** body and soul on the
S D : 0 1 :048(516) [0875] sin is the very nature of **corrupted** man, its substance, its
S D : 0 1 :048(517) [0875] whatever between our **corrupted** nature or substance or
S D : 0 1 :048(517) [0875] of man, which is **corrupted** by sin, and the sin by and
S D : 0 1 :048(517) [0875] sin, and the sin by and through which man is **corrupted**.
S D : 0 1 :052(517) [0875] original sin is the deep **corruption** of our nature as it is
S D : 0 1 :052(517) [0875] through sin man is **corrupted**, poisoned, and sinful.
S D : 0 1 :053(517) [0877] of man is wholly **corrupted** though original sin to its very
S D : 0 1 :060(519) [0879] impairment and such a **corruption** of human nature that
S D : 0 1 :060(519) [0879] but that it is altogether **corrupted**, so that through
S D : 0 1 :061(519) [0879] in spite of its being **corrupted**, and the devil's
S D : 0 1 :061(519) [0879] profoundly and inexpressibly **corrupts** God's handiwork.
S D : 0 1 :062(519) [0879] sully human nature but **corrupts** it so deeply that
S D : 0 2 :005(521) [0881] first parents man is so **corrupted** that in divine things,
S D : 0 2 :007(521) [0883] completely dead and **corrupted** as far as anything good is
S D : 0 2 :017(524) [0887] poisoned, and **corrupted** that by disposition and nature
S D : 0 2 :022(525) [0889] our poor, fallen, and **corrupted** human nature should
S D : 0 2 :087(538) [0913] the conversion of our **corrupted** will, which is nothing
S D : 0 3 :022(543) [0923] on account of their **corrupted** nature, they are still sinners
S D : 0 3 :028(544) [0925] wholly pure and perfect on account of our **corrupted** flesh
S D : 0 4 :008(552) [0941] impure because of our **corrupted** nature and because the
S D : 0 4 :029(555) [0947] against all sorts of **corruptions** and counterfeiting of the
S D : 0 5 :020(561) [0959] has transgressed it, his **corrupted** nature, thoughts,
S D : 0 5 :023(562) [0959] laws, became a sinner, **corrupted** himself and all his
S D : 1 1 :060(626) [1083] Since our nature is **corrupted** by sin and is worthy and

Corvinus (2)
S 3 : 1 5 :005(317) [0501] Master Anthony **Corvinus**
T R : 0 0 :082(335) [0529] Anthony **Corvinus** subscribes with his own hand both in

Cost (1), Costly (1)
A P : 1 5 :019(218) [0319] with gold and silver, with precious stones and **costly** gifts."
L C : 0 2 :031(414) [0685] — that is, how much it **cost** Christ and what he paid and

Council (87), Councilors (1), Councils (17)
P R : P R :027(015) [0025] Mayor and **Council** of the City of Luebeck
P R : P R :027(015) [0027] Mayor and **Council** of the City of Landau
P R : P R :027(015) [0027] Mayor and **Council** of the City of Muenster-in-St
P R : P R :027(015) [0027] The **Council** of the City of Goslar
P R : P R :027(015) [0027] Mayor and **Council** of the City of Ulm
P R : P R :027(015) [0027] Mayor and **Council** of the City of Esslingen
P R : P R :027(015) [0027] The **Council** of the City of Reutlingen
P R : P R :027(015) [0027] Mayor and **Council** of the City of Noerdlingen
P R : P R :027(015) [0027] Mayor and **Council** of Rothenburg-on-the-Tauber
P R : P R :027(015) [0027] Mayor and **Council** of the City of Schwaebisch-Hall
P R : P R :027(016) [0027] Mayor and **Council** of the City of Heilbronn
P R : P R :027(016) [0027] Mayor and **Council** of the City of Memmingen
P R : P R :027(016) [0027] Mayor and **Council** of the City of Lindau
P R : P R :027(016) [0027] Mayor and **Council** of the City of Schweinfurt
P R : P R :027(016) [0027] The **Council** of the City of Donawerda
P R : P R :027(016) [0027] Chamberlain and **Council** of the City of Regensburg
P R : P R :027(016) [0027] Mayor and **Council** of the City of Wimpfen
P R : P R :027(016) [0027] Mayor and **Council** of the City of Giengen
P R : P R :027(016) [0027] Mayor and **Council** of Bopfingen
P R : P R :027(016) [0027] Mayor and **Council** of the City of Aalen
P R : P R :027(016) [0027] Mayor and **Council** of the City of Kaufbeuren
P R : P R :027(016) [0027] Mayor and **Council** of the City of Isna
P R : P R :027(016) [0027] Mayor and **Council** of the City of Kempten
P R : P R :027(016) [0027] The **Council** of the City of Hamburg
P R : P R :027(016) [0027] The **Council** of the City of Goettingen
P R : P R :027(016) [0027] The **Council** of the City of Brunswick
P R : P R :027(016) [0027] Mayor and **Council** of the City of Lueneburg
P R : P R :027(016) [0027] Mayor and **Council** of the City of Leutkirch
P R : P R :027(016) [0027] Mayor and **Council** of the City of Hamelin
P R : P R :027(016) [0027] Mayor and **Council** of the City of Hanover
P R : P R :027(016) [0027] The **Council** of Muehlhausen
P R : P R :027(016) [0027] The **Council** of Erfurt
P R : P R :027(016) [0027] The **Council** of the City of Einbeck
P R : P R :027(016) [0027] The **Council** of the City of Northeim
A G : P R :016(026) [0041] would diligently urge it upon the pope to call a **council**.
A G : P R :018(026) [0041] administrators, and **councilors** of the imperial
A G : P R :018(026) [0041] concerning a general **council** and acknowledged that it
A G : P R :019(026) [0041] that it would be profitable to have such a **council** called.
A G : P R :019(026) [0041] refuse to call a general **council**, and so Your Imperial
A G : P R :020(026) [0041] calling of such a general **council** by the pope, along with
A G : P R :021(027) [0043] free, and Christian **council** as the electors, princes, and
A G : 0 1 :001(027) [0043] with the decree of the **Council** of Nicaea, that there is one
A G : 2 3 :013(053) [0063] made and to the decisions of the most renowned **councils**.
A G : 0 0 :007(096) [0095] Mayor and **council** of Nuremburg
A G : 0 0 :007(096) [0095] Mayor and **council** or Reutlingen
A L : 0 1 :001(027) [0043] that the decree of the **Council** of Nicaea concerning the
A L : 2 3 :013(053) [0063] popes and those made by the most celebrated **councils**.
A P : 0 2 :002(100) [0105] from the schools, and not from the emperor's **council**.
A P : 0 7 :042(176) [0241] Before the **Council** of Nicaea some people celebrated
A P : 0 7 :042(176) [0241] and so, after the **Council** of Nicaea, certain nations held
A P : 1 2 :122(200) [0289] of the Gospel, the **councils**, and the Fathers; and that
A P : 2 2 :004(236) [0359] The **Council** of Toledo gives the same testimony, and it
A P : 2 3 :003(239) [0363] and the canons of the **councils**, they demand that you
A P : 2 3 :006(240) [0365] law and conflicts with the very decrees of **councils**.
A P : 2 3 :023(242) [0369] regulation also disagrees with the canons of the **councils**.
A P : 2 3 :024(243) [0371] shriek that the **councils** have commanded celibacy.
A P : 2 3 :024(243) [0371] We do not object to the **councils**, for they do allow
S 1 : 0 0 :000(287) [0453] by our party at the **council** in Mantua, or wherever else
S 1 : 0 0 :000(287) [0453] or wherever else the **council** was to have been convened,
S 1 : P R :001(288) [0455] Pope Paul III called a **council** to meet in Mantua last
S 1 : P R :001(288) [0455] he transferred the **council** from Mantua, and it is not yet
S 1 : P R :001(288) [0455] to appear before the **council** or be condemned without
S 1 : P R :002(289) [0455] to hold a truly free **council**, as indeed the pope is in duty
S 1 : P R :003(289) [0455] afraid of a free **council** and flees from the light in a
S 1 : P R :003(289) [0455] will ever permit a free **council**, to say nothing of calling
S 1 : P R :003(289) [0455] if I should die before a **council** meets (which I fully
S 1 : P R :003(289) [0455] postpone and prevent the **council**), those who live after
S 1 : P R :010(290) [0457] very happy to see a true **council** assemble in order that
S 1 : P R :010(290) [0457] we ourselves need such a **council**, for by God's grace our
S 1 : P R :010(290) [0457] that we do not ask for a **council** for our own sake, and we
S 1 : P R :010(290) [0457] to hope or expect that a **council** would improve our
S 1 : P R :011(290) [0457] fear that he may cause a **council** of angels to descend on
S 1 : P R :011(290) [0457] because we mock him so shamefully with the **council**.
S 1 : P R :012(290) [0459] such an extent that ten **councils** and twenty diets would
S 1 : P R :013(290) [0459] If members of a **council** were to consider such
S 1 : P R :013(291) [0459] we might just as well be satisfied with such a **council**.
S 1 : P R :014(291) [0459] decrees and canons in a **council**, especially when the
S 1 : P R :015(291) [0459] Jesus Christ, assemble a **council** of thine own, and by thy
S 2 : 0 2 :010(294) [0465] the Mass will be the decisive issue in the **council**.
S 2 : 0 4 :001(298) [0471] as the ancient **councils** and the time of Cyprian prove.
S 2 : 0 4 :007(299) [0473] the way in which the **Council** of Constance acted with
S 2 : 0 4 :015(301) [0475] to condemn in the **council**, for they neither can nor will
S 2 : 0 4 :016(301) [0475] In the **council** we shall not be standing before the
S 3 : 0 4 :000(310) [0491] the Gospel, which offers **council** and help against sin in
S 3 : 0 6 :002(311) [0493] of the sophists and the **Council** of Constance that as much

Continued ▶

TR : 0 0 :012(321) [0507] 5. The **Council** of Nicaea decided that the bishop of
TR : 0 0 :012(322) [0507] out of a decision of a **council** and is of human right, for if
TR : 0 0 :012(322) [0507] have been lawful for the **council** to withdraw any right
TR : 0 0 :013(322) [0507] 6. Again, the **Council** of Nicaea decided that bishops
TR : 0 0 :017(323) [0509] did not preside — as the **Council** of Nicaea and many
TR : 0 0 :019(323) [0509] he states that at the **Council** of Chalcedon the primacy
TR : 0 0 :040(327) [0517] above the decisions of **councils** and the whole church.
TR : 0 0 :049(329) [0519] that he is above **councils** and can rescind the decrees of
TR : 0 0 :049(329) [0519] rescind the decrees of **councils**, as the canons sometimes
EP : 0 8 :018(489) [0823] as Luther explains it in his treatise *On the **Councils**.*
SD : RN :007(505) [0853] and estates, before the **Council** in Mantua (or wherever it
SD : 0 3 :021(542) [0921] term in his book *On the **Councils** and the Church* and
SD : 0 4 :035(557) [0949] reject the decree of the **Council** of Trent and anything else
SD : 0 7 :017(572) [0979] doctrinal statement they should submit to the **council**.
SD : 0 8 :018(594) [1021] both before and after the **Council** of Chalcedon, have
SD : 0 8 :044(599) [1029] treatise *Concerning the **Councils** and the Church:* "We
SD : 0 8 :046(600) [1031] both natures, or as the **Council** of Chalcedon declares,
SD : 0 8 :059(602) [1035] and according to the **Council** of Ephesus decreed that the
SD : 0 8 :062(603) [1037] in the ancient approved **councils** on the basis of the
SD : 0 8 :076(606) [1043] hundred fathers of the **Council** of Ephesus attested when

Counsel (38), Counselors (1), Counsels (14)
PR : PR :013(007) [0013] of Saxony, etc., with the **counsel** and cooperation of
AG : PR :007(025) [0039] due deliberation and **counsel**, it was decided last
AG : 2 3 :025(055) [0065] therefore offered the **counsel** that women who were
AG : 2 7 :012(072) [0077] the precepts and the **counsels** included in the Gospel were
AG : 2 7 :030(075) [0079] be assumed only after due consideration and **counsel**.
AG : 2 7 :054(079) [0083] hear that it is only a **counsel** not to take revenge, it is
AG : 2 7 :061(080) [0083] both evangelical **counsels** and precepts, and that they
AG : 2 8 :068(093) [0093] It is impossible to give **counsel** or help to consciences
AL : 2 7 :012(072) [0077] only of the precepts but also of the **counsels** of the Gospel
AL : 2 7 :054(079) [0083] that it is an evangelical **counsel** not to take revenge, and
AL : 2 7 :054(079) [0083] that this is prohibited by a **counsel** and not by a precept.
AL : 2 7 :055(079) [0083] of Christians and in conflict with the evangelical **counsel**.
AL : 2 7 :061(080) [0083] monks observe both the **counsels** and the precepts, and
AL : 2 8 :068(093) [0093] It is not possible to **counsel** consciences unless this
AP : 0 4 :167(130) [0169] history is governed by God's **counsels** or by chance?
AP : 0 4 :285(150) [0201] that our opponents **counsel** pious consciences very badly
AP : 0 4 :300(153) [0205] beware, therefore, of yielding to their ungodly **counsels**.
AP : 1 6 :004(223) [0331] called it an evangelical **counsel** not to own property and
AP : 1 6 :007(223) [0331] not as an evangelical **counsel** but as a command (Matt.
AP : 2 1 :044(236) [0357] to agree to the violent **counsels** of our opponents but to
AP : 2 7 :009(270) [0421] Are they the observance of commandments and **counsels**?
AP : 2 7 :024(273) [0427] imagine that they observe both precepts and **counsels**.
AP : 2 7 :026(273) [0429] observances are the works of the **counsels** of the Gospel.
AP : 2 7 :026(273) [0429] For the Gospel does not **counsel** distinctions among
AP : 2 7 :039(276) [0433] the pretext that they observe both precepts and **counsels**.
SC : 0 3 :011(347) [0547] and destroys every evil **counsel** and purpose of the devil,
LC : PR :017(361) [0573] circumstances he can **counsel**, help, comfort, judge, and
LC : 0 1 :191(391) [0635] who do not offer **counsel** and aid to men in need and in
LC : 0 1 :197(392) [0637] as if they were not commandments but mere **counsels**.
LC : 0 2 :029(414) [0685] There was no **counsel**, no help, no comfort for us until
LC : 0 3 :031(424) [0707] in the past, parrying the **counsels** and plots of our
LC : 0 3 :077(431) [0721] especially our princes, **counselors**, magistrates, and
LC : 0 3 :111(435) [0729] your own thoughts and **counsels**, you will only make the
LC : 0 5 :004(447) [0755] by Christ without man's **counsel** or deliberation.
EP : 1 1 :006(495) [0833] in the secret **counsel** of God, but it is to be looked for in
EP : 1 1 :013(496) [0835] has decreed in his eternal **counsel** that he would save no
EP : 1 1 :019(497) [0837] merely by an arbitrary **counsel**, purpose, and will,
SD : 0 2 :050(530) [0901] law and the wonderful **counsel** concerning our
SD : 0 8 :072(605) [1041] and understanding, of **counsel** and might and knowledge"
SD : 1 1 :009(617) [1065] secret and inscrutable **counsel** of God, as though it
SD : 1 1 :013(619) [1067] we should consider the **counsel**, purpose, and ordinance
SD : 1 1 :014(619) [1069] of God's purpose, **counsel**, will, and ordinance concerning
SD : 1 1 :014(619) [1069] that in his purpose and **counsel** God had ordained the
SD : 1 1 :023(619) [1069] In this his eternal **counsel**, purpose, and ordinance God
SD : 1 1 :040(623) [1077] God has ordained in his **counsel** that the Holy Spirit
SD : 1 1 :040(623) [1077] has also ordained in his **counsel** that he would harden,
SD : 1 1 :044(623) [1077] natural will, for in his **counsel** God has determined and
SD : 1 1 :045(624) [1079] world was laid" he held **counsel** and ordained "according
SD : 1 1 :048(624) [1079] and affliction, that in his **counsel** before the foundation
SD : 1 1 :049(624) [1079] God ordained in his **counsel** through which specific cross
SD : 1 1 :051(624) [1079] others: They "despise the **counsel** of God against
SD : 1 1 :070(627) [1085] concerning the secret **counsel** of God, if he has been
SD : 1 1 :086(631) [1091] life, or that in his secret **counsel** God had ordained him to

Count (34), Counts (1)
PR : PR :027(014) [0025] Louis, **count** palatine on the Rhine, elector
PR : PR :027(015) [0025] George Ernest, **count** and lord of Henneberg
PR : PR :027(015) [0025] Frederick, **count** of Wuerttemberg and Montbeliard
PR : PR :027(015) [0025] John Guenther, **count** of Schwarzburg
PR : PR :027(015) [0025] William, **count** of Schwarzburg [Frankenhausen]
PR : PR :027(015) [0025] Albert, **count** of Schwarzburg [-Rudolstadt]
PR : PR :027(015) [0025] Emich, **count** of Leiningen
PR : PR :027(015) [0025] Philip, **count** of Hanau [-Lichtenburg]
PR : PR :027(015) [0025] Godfrey, **count** of Oettingen
PR : PR :027(015) [0025] George, **count** and lord of Castell [-Ruedenhausen]
PR : PR :027(015) [0025] Henry, **count** and lord of Castell [-Remlingen]
PR : PR :027(015) [0025] John Hoyer, **count** of Mansfeld [-Artern]
PR : PR :027(015) [0025] Bruno, **count** of Mansfeld [-Bronstedt]
PR : PR :027(015) [0025] Hoyer Christopher, **count** of Mansfeld [-Eisleben]
PR : PR :027(015) [0025] Peter Ernest the Younger, **count** of Mansfeld
PR : PR :027(015) [0025] Christopher, **count** of Mansfeld
PR : PR :027(015) [0025] Otto, **count** of Hoya [-Nienburg] and Burghausen
PR : PR :027(015) [0025] John, **count** of Oldenburg and Delmenhorst
PR : PR :027(015) [0025] Albert Geroge, **count** of Stolberg
PR : PR :027(015) [0025] Wolf Ernest, **count** of Stolberg
PR : PR :027(015) [0025] Louis, **count** of Gleichen [-Blankenhain]
PR : PR :027(015) [0025] Charles, **count** of Gleichen [-Blankenhain]
PR : PR :027(015) [0025] Ernest, **count** of Regenstein
PR : PR :027(015) [0025] Bodo, **count** of Regenstein
PR : PR :027(015) [0025] Louis, **count** of Loewenstein
AG : 2 7 :045(078) [0081] If one were inclined to **count** up all these claims for the
AP : 0 4 :320(156) [0209] will it find that it will **count** worthy of eternal life, if
AP : 1 2 :068(192) [0271] Certainly, if we were to **count** authorities, they would be
S 2 : 0 4 :002(298) [0471] Those who wish to do so had better not **count** on us!
S 3 : 1 3 :001(315) [0499] removed or eradicated, he will not **count** or consider it.
TR : 0 0 :011(321) [0507] let anybody's authority **count** for more than the Word,
LC : 0 1 :151(386) [0625] Where he **counts** on gaining a gulden by his
LC : 0 3 :065(429) [0715] be Christians must surely **count** on having the devil with
LC : 0 3 :065(429) [0715] as our enemies and must **count** on their inflicting every
SD : 1 0 :021(614) [1061] let anybody's authority **count** for more than the Word of

Counted (2), Counting (1), Countless (14)
AG : 2 4 :023(058) [0067] Out of this grew **countless** multiplication of Masses, by
AG : 2 8 :041(087) [0089] The result was that **countless** regulations came into being
AG : 2 8 :049(089) [0091] the churches with **countless** requirements and thus
AG : 2 8 :053(090) [0091] services of God and **counting** it a sin to omit their
AG : 0 0 :002(095) [0095] on special occasions, and about **countless** other matters.
AL : 0 0 :002(095) [0095] rights, confessions, burials, and **countless** other things.
AP : 0 4 :357(162) [0219] our works ought to be **counted** so precious that eternal
S 1 : PR :006(289) [0457] everything by wagging **countless** venomous and malicious
S 1 : PR :012(290) [0459] of the church, there are **countless** temporal matters that
S 2 : 0 2 :006(293) [0463] "4. Since such **countless** and unspeakable abuses have
S 2 : 0 4 :014(301) [0475] food, personnel, and **countless** other puerilities, fantasies,
S 3 : 1 1 :001(314) [0499] abominable, and **countless** sins, in which they are still
TR : 0 0 :051(329) [0519] forms of worship, and **countless** souls are lost generation
TR : 0 0 :054(329) [0519] support of idolatry and **countless** other crimes and for the
LC : 0 1 :011(366) [0583] There were **countless** other such abominations, and every
LC : 0 1 :055(372) [0595] Also to be **counted** among liars are blasphemers, not only
LC : 0 3 :104(434) [0727] atheism, blasphemy, and **countless** other abominable sins.

Counter (3), Countered (1)
AP : 2 3 :062(247) [0381] and refuted the silly **counter**-arguments of our
SD : 0 7 :091(585) [1003] reasons and futile **counter**-arguments of the
SD : 0 7 :106(588) [1009] and refute all the **counter**-arguments and objections of
SD : 0 8 :002(591) [1015] the Zwinglians **countered** by saying that the body of

Counteract (2)
PR : PR :010(006) [0011] was no better way to **counteract** the mendacious
AP : 0 4 :288(151) [0203] of their observances to **counteract** the terrors of

Counterbalance (1)
SD : 0 8 :044(599) [1029] in weight as a **counterbalance**, we shall sink to the bottom

Counterfeit (3), Counterfeiting (1), Counterfeits (1)
AP : 1 2 :046(188) [0263] in a Platonic sense as **counterfeit** changes; but
AP : 1 5 :045(221) [0327] us effect a genuine and not a **counterfeit** mortification.
AP : 2 7 :044(277) [0435] system is full of **counterfeits**, so they quote passages of
SD : 0 4 :029(555) [0947] of corruptions and **counterfeiting** of the article of
SD : 0 7 :008(570) [0975] even by hypocrites or **counterfeit** Christians, is something

Country (7), Countrymen (2)
AL : 2 1 :001(046) [0057] drive the Turk out of his **country**, for like David the
AL : 2 6 :010(065) [0071] bear children, that a prince should govern his **country**.
AP : 2 3 :003(239) [0363] which no barbarous **country**, however savage or cruel,
AP : 2 4 :061(260) [0405] Good men in every **country** can see this.
AP : 2 7 :062(280) [0441] marks from their **countrymen**, lest they fall back into the
AP : 2 7 :062(280) [0441] they fall back into the wickedness of their **countrymen**.
SC : PR :002(338) [0533] those who live in the **country**, have no knowledge
LC : 0 1 :142(384) [0621] (that is, fathers of the **country**) to the great shame of us
LC : 0 1 :160(387) [0627] to harry them out of the **country** and grudge them as

County (1)
LC : 0 1 :302(405) [0667] covets a castle, city, **county**, or other great estate, he

Coupled (2)
LC : 0 5 :018(448) [0757] of these words which are **coupled** with the bread and
LC : 0 5 :028(449) [0759] body and blood and with which the words are **coupled**.

Courage (1)
SD : 0 5 :023(562) [0959] but also revived their **courage** and comforted themselves

Course (35), Courses (2)
PR : PR :004(004) [0007] and perceptibly impede the **course** of the holy Gospel.
PR : PR :006(004) [0009] straying from the right **course** of divine truth which they
AG : 0 2 :001(029) [0043] are born according to the **course** of nature are conceived
AG : 2 3 :013(053) [0063] This was of **course** not only contrary to all divine,
AP : 0 2 :002(100) [0105] are born according to the **course** of nature are conceived
AP : 0 4 :348(160) [0217] Of **course**, good works are necessary.
AP : 0 7 :020(171) [0233] Of **course**, there are also many weak people in it who
AP : 1 1 :006(181) [0251] It is, of **course**, a good practice to accustom the unlearned
AP : 1 2 :129(202) [0291] hold the keys and so, of **course**, can open heaven for
AP : 2 0 :012(228) [0341] most out of their logic **courses**, for they have learned the
S 3 : 0 3 :015(305) [0483] committed during the **course** of a whole year), the
LC : 0 1 :060(372) [0597] This is the common **course** of the world.
LC : 0 1 :155(386) [0625] Of **course**, we keenly feel our misfortune, and we grumble
LC : 0 1 :234(397) [0647] his defiant and arrogant **course** for a long time, still he
LC : 0 1 :239(397) [0649] Of **course**, if our government were well regulated, such
LC : 0 1 :258(399) [0653] that, true to the usual **course** of the world, men are loathe
LC : 0 1 :316(408) [0671] much as if I boasted, "Of **course**, I haven't a single
LC : 0 2 :005(411) [0679] Of **course**, if all the thoughts contained in the Scriptures
LC : 0 3 :084(432) [0723] we must put up with, of **course**; but let exploiters and
LC : 0 4 :016(438) [0735] Of **course**, my friend!
LC : 0 5 :069(454) [0769] Of **course**, it is true that those who despise the sacrament
SD : RN :010(506) [0855] This, of **course**, does not mean that other good, useful,
SD : 0 1 :006(509) [0861] of our first parents is of **course** impossible for human
SD : 0 1 :014(511) [0863] Of **course**, this process is only begun in this life, not to be
SD : 0 1 :038(515) [0871] It is of **course** true that this creature and handiwork of
SD : 0 2 :015(523) [0887] Of **course**, such prayers and passages about our ignorance
SD : 0 2 :070(534) [0909] It is, of **course**, self-evident that in true conversion there
SD : 0 2 :084(537) [0913] Of **course**, there remains also in the regenerated a
SD : 0 4 :005(551) [0939] In the **course** of time, however, the issue ceased to be only
SD : 0 4 :030(555) [0947] This, of **course**, is a serious and important question since
SD : 0 6 :002(564) [0963] completes its regular **course** without any outside impulse,
SD : 0 6 :006(565) [0965] regularly run their **courses** according to the order which

Continued ▶

SD : 0 7 :050(578) [0989] There is, of **course**, no more faithful or trustworthy
SD : 0 7 :126(591) [1015] Of **course**, no one except an Arian heretic can or will
SD : 0 8 :044(599) [1031] Of **course**, he can also go up again or jump out of his
SD : 0 8 :054(601) [1033] The statement is, of **course**, correct and true that Christ's
SD : 0 8 :081(607) [1045] the humanity — not, of **course**, according to the first,

Court (12), Courts (12)
AP : 0 2 :043(106) [0117] said this about the civil **courts**, not about the judgment of
AP : 0 4 :345(160) [0217] In **courts** of human judgment a right or debt is certain,
AP : 1 6 :004(223) [0331] counsel not to own property and not to go to **court**.
AP : 1 6 :007(223) [0331] kinds of public redress are **court** decisions, punishments,
AP : 2 1 :024(232) [0349] from the usage at royal **courts**, where friends must be
S 1 : PR :003(289) [0455] But the Roman **court** is dreadfully afraid of a free
S 1 : PR :003(289) [0455] lost hope that the Roman **court** will ever permit a free
S 3 : 0 0 :000(302) [0477] The pope and his **court** do not care much about these
TR : 0 0 :077(333) [0527] pertain to ecclesiastical **courts** (as they call them),
TR : 0 0 :078(333) [0527] and apply them in their **courts**, there is additional reason
TR : 0 0 :078(333) [0527] additional reason why other **courts** should be established.
TR : 0 0 :078(333) [0527] account the magistrates ought to establish other **courts**.
TR : 0 0 :080(334) [0527] and the establishment of **courts**, especially courts for
TR : 0 0 :080(334) [0527] of courts, especially **courts** for matrimonial cases.
TR : 0 0 :081(334) [0527] that they require special **courts**, but these cannot be
LC : 0 1 :051(371) [0595] where men take oaths in **court** and one side lies against
LC : 0 1 :053(372) [0595] whether publicly in **court** or in the market or elsewhere,
LC : 0 1 :257(399) [0653] pertains to public **courts** of justice, where a poor,
LC : 0 1 :258(400) [0653] that men of integrity seldom preside in **courts** of justice.
LC : 0 1 :261(400) [0655] plainest meaning, applying to all that takes place in **court**.
LC : 0 1 :263(400) [0655] their corrupt behavior in **court** and their lying and
LC : 0 1 :263(400) [0655] court and their lying and malicious talk outside of **court**.
LC : 0 1 :280(403) [0661] public, either before the civil or the ecclesiastical **court**.
SD : 1 2 :020(634) [1099] swear an oath before a **court** or pay oath-bound feudal

Courtesies (1), Courtesy (1)
AP : 0 4 :154(128) [0165] show him the outward **courtesies** due a guest and a great
TR : 0 0 :082(000) [0529] Christ, that your **courtesy** may add my name, if it be

Courtiers (1)
AG : 2 3 :018(054) [0063] clergy and some of the **courtiers** in Rome have often

Covenant (19)
AP : 1 2 :017(185) [0257] 1. On the basis of God's **covenant**, we merit grace by good
AP : 1 3 :007(212) [0311] as though the new **covenant** needed a priesthood like the
AP : 1 5 :012(216) [0317] "No one adds even to a man's **covenant**."
AP : 1 5 :012(216) [0317] In other words, to the **covenant** of God, promising that
AP : 2 7 :020(272) [0427] God, which contains a **covenant** of grace and eternal life.
SC : 0 6 :004(351) [0557] This cup is the new **covenant** in my blood, which is
LC : 0 5 :013(448) [0755] of it, all of you, this is the new **covenant** in my blood,' etc.
EP : 1 2 :008(498) [0839] to those who keep his **covenant** and do not despise it
SD : 0 7 :022(573) [0979] of it, all of you, this is the new **covenant** in my blood,' etc.
SD : 0 7 :044(577) [0987] a seal of the new **covenant**, a comfort for all sorrowing
SD : 0 7 :044(577) [0987] is my blood of the new **covenant** which is shed for you
SD : 0 7 :050(578) [0989] and of his abiding **covenant** and union, he uses no
SD : 0 7 :050(578) [0989] the institution of other **covenant**-signs and signs of grace
SD : 0 7 :053(579) [0991] "This cup is the new **covenant** in my blood" (Luke 22:20;
SD : 0 7 :053(579) [0991] is my blood of the new **covenant**, whereby I establish,
SD : 0 7 :053(579) [0991] my testament and new **covenant**, namely, the forgiveness
SD : 0 8 :029(596) [1025] to the words of his **covenant**, to which he has directed us
SD : 0 8 :086(608) [1047] article, as well as of his **covenant** in the Holy Supper in
SD : 1 2 :013(634) [1099] to those who keep the **covenant** and do not despise it

Cover (11), Covered (14), Covering (1), Covers (11)
AG : 2 8 :054(090) [0091] that women should **cover** their heads in the
AL : 2 8 :054(090) [0091] that women should **cover** their heads in the assembly and
AP : 0 4 :103(122) [0151] is forgiven, whose sin is **covered**' (Ps. 32:1)."
AP : 0 4 :133(125) [0159] states that the veil that **covered** the face of Moses cannot
AP : 0 4 :232(139) [0185] tranquility unless men **cover** and forgive certain mistakes
AP : 0 4 :232(140) [0185] of the brethren, to **cover** up minor mistakes, lest the
AP : 0 4 :238(140) [0187] statement (I Pet. 4:8), "Love **covers** a multitude of sins."
AP : 0 4 :240(141) [0187] means: "Hatred stirs up strife, but love **covers** all offenses
AP : 0 4 :242(141) [0187] when it says, "Love **covers** all offenses," namely, other
AP : 0 4 :242(141) [0187] these offenses occur, love **covers** them up, forgives,
AP : 0 4 :242(141) [0187] or implacable; that it **covers** up some of the mistakes of
AP : 1 2 :078(193) [0275] as the Jews looked at Moses' face **covered** by a veil.
AP : 1 2 :096(196) [0281] Again, "It is faith that **covers** up our sins."
AP : 1 2 :124(201) [0289] in our Confession we **covered** almost the sum total of all
AP : 2 7 :026(273) [0429] are proposed under the **cover** of these titles, they are
TR : 0 0 :048(328) [0519] darkness has the teaching about vows **covered** the Gospel!
LC : SP :024(364) [0579] Thus we have, in all, five parts **covering** the whole of
LC : 0 1 :056(372) [0597] God's name and using it as a cloak to **cover** our shame.
LC : 0 1 :059(372) [0597] a wrong we like to **cover** and gloss over our disgrace so
LC : 0 1 :093(377) [0607] or even if it be altogether **covered** with holy relics, as are
LC : 0 1 :285(403) [0663] only good of everyone, to **cover** his neighbor's sins and
LC : 0 1 :287(403) [0663] No one **covers** his face, eyes, nose, and mouth; we do not
LC : 0 1 :287(403) [0663] eyes, even the whole body, must help **cover** and veil them.
LC : 0 3 :076(431) [0719] this petition **covers** all kinds of relations on earth.
LC : 0 4 :065(444) [0749] into the water, which **covers** us completely, and being
EP : 0 1 :010(467) [0781] asserts, "I shall be **covered** by this my skin, and in my
EP : 0 3 :016(475) [0795] us), and that by such indwelling our sins are **covered** up.
EP : 0 4 :007(476) [0799] are forgiven, and whose sins are **covered**'" (Rom. 4:6-8).
EP : 0 5 :008(478) [0803] Christ, the veil of Moses **covers** their eyes, as a result they
SD : 0 1 :014(511) [0863] believers it can be **covered** up and forgiven before God
SD : 0 2 :056(532) [0903] and happens under **cover** of great weakness, we should be
SD : 0 3 :022(543) [0923] with his perfect obedience **covers** all our sins which
SD : 0 3 :023(543) [0923] our sins are forgiven and **covered** up and are not
SD : 0 3 :058(550) [0937] us poor sinners, and thus **covered** up our disobedience,
SD : 0 3 :063(550) [0937] indwelling our sins are **covered** up in the sight of God.
SD : 0 6 :007(565) [0965] although their sins are **covered** up through the perfect
SD : 1 1 :095(632) [1095] minded to whitewash or **cover** up any falsification of true

Covet (12), Coveting (1), Covetousness (1), Covets (1)
AP : 0 4 :027(111) [0127] him in death and in his other visitations, and not **covet**.
AP : 0 4 :087(120) [0147] quotes the Decalogue, "You shall not **covet**" (Rom. 7:7).
AP : 2 7 :025(273) [0427] (Deut. 6:5), and again, "You shall not **covet**" (Ex. 20:17).
SC : 0 1 :017(343) [0541] *"You shall not **covet** your neighbor's house."*
SC : 0 1 :019(344) [0543] *"You shall not **covet** your neighbor's wife, or his*
LC : SP :009(363) [0577] 9. You shall not **covet** your neighbor's house.
LC : SP :010(363) [0577] 10. You shall not **covet** his wife, man-servant,
LC : 0 1 :292(404) [0663] *"You shall not **covet** your neighbor's house."*
LC : 0 1 :292(404) [0663] *"You shall not **covet** his wife, man-servant, maid-servant,*
LC : 0 1 :293(404) [0665] is sinful and forbidden to **covet** our neighbor's wife or
LC : 0 1 :296(405) [0665] with a specious pretext, to **covet** or scheme to despoil his
LC : 0 1 :302(405) [0667] Similarly, if anyone **covets** a castle, city, county, or other
LC : 0 1 :307(406) [0669] or fraud, yet it is **coveting** — that is, having designs upon
LC : 0 1 :310(407) [0669] envy and miserable **covetousness**, God's purpose being to
LC : 0 1 :310(407) [0669] he sets it forth in plain words: "You shall not **covet**," etc.

Cowl (1), Cowls (1)
AG : 2 7 :050(079) [0083] not of mendicancy or wearing a black or gray **cowl**, etc.
AP : 2 7 :034(275) [0431] Christ they worship their own **cowls** and their own filth.

Cows (1)
LC : 0 1 :170(388) [0629] to put them to work like **cows** or asses, and gave us

Craft (3), Craftily (1), Craftiness (1), Crafty (3), Craftsman (2)
AL : 0 1 :006(028) [0043] is only one person and **craftily** and impiously argue that
AP : 2 2 :013(238) [0361] we shall not say anything more about their **crafty** designs.
AP : 2 3 :010(241) [0367] fabricate anything more **crafty** than this foolishness,
SC : 0 1 :018(344) [0541] we should not seek by **craftiness** to gain possession of our
LC : SP :002(362) [0575] a sacrament, just as a **craftsman** who does not know the
LC : SP :002(362) [0575] rules and practices of his **craft** is rejected and considered
LC : 0 1 :227(396) [0645] tricks and sharp practices and **crafty** dealing.
LC : 0 1 :228(396) [0645] is the most common **craft** and the largest guild on earth.
LC : 0 3 :076(431) [0721] to cause our work, **craft**, or occupation, whatever it may
SD : 0 2 :090(539) [0915] Spirit, who is the true **craftsman** who alone works these

Crailsheim (2)
S 3 : 1 5 :005(317) [0501] Simon Schneeweiss, pastor of the church in **Crailsheim**
TR : 0 0 :082(335) [0529] Simon Schneeweiss, pastor at **Crailsheim**

Crass (5)
LC : 0 1 :055(372) [0595] not only the very **crass** ones who are well known to
EP : 0 2 :009(471) [0789] also reject the error of the **crass** Pelagians who taught
EP : 0 7 :003(482) [0809] Some are **crass** Sacramentarians who set forth in clear
EP : 0 7 :004(482) [0809] really retain the former **crass** opinion that in the Holy
SD : 0 7 :103(587) [1007] purpose was to show what **crass** fools our enthusiasts are,

Craw (1)
LC : 0 1 :235(397) [0647] which enables you to stuff your **craw** and your belly.

Crazy (1)
LC : PR :006(359) [0569] This is what one can expect of **crazy** Germans.

Create (15), Created (48), Creates (17), Creation (27)
AG : 1 9 :000(040) [0053] almighty God has **created** and still preserves nature, yet
AG : 2 3 :005(052) [0061] God **created** man as male and female according to Gen.
AG : 2 3 :006(052) [0061] improve or change the **creation** of God, the supreme
AG : 2 7 :020(074) [0079] us to do this, but God's **creation** and order also direct all
AL : 1 9 :000(040) [0053] teach that although God **creates** and preserves nature, the
AL : 2 3 :005(052) [0061] celibacy because God **created** man for procreation (Gen.
AL : 2 3 :006(052) [0061] man's power to alter his **creation** without a singular gift
AL : 2 7 :008(072) [0077] what scandals were **created**, what snares were placed on
AL : 2 7 :020(074) [0079] only, but God's **creation** and institution also compel those
AL : 2 8 :007(082) [0085] said, "Go and preach the gospel to the whole **creation**."
AP : 0 2 :018(102) [0109] it says that man was **created** in the image of God and
AP : 0 2 :035(105) [0115] begins to mortify lust and to **create** new impulses in man.
AP : 1 3 :014(213) [0311] in the very beginning, at the **creation** of the human race.
AP : 1 4 :001(214) [0315] although they were **created** by human authority.
AP : 1 5 :034(220) [0325] that no one ought to **create** or accept traditions with the
AP : 2 3 :007(240) [0365] teaches that men were **created** to be fruitful and that one
AP : 2 3 :008(240) [0365] only at the beginning of **creation**, but it still does as long
AP : 2 3 :009(240) [0367] *Second*, because this **creation** or divine ordinance in man
AP : 2 3 :012(241) [0367] otherwise, why would both sexes have been **created**?
AP : 2 8 :006(282) [0445] have the authority to **create** laws which are useful for
AP : 2 8 :008(282) [0445] bishops have no right to **create** traditions apart from the
AP : 2 8 :015(283) [0447] is legitimate for them to **create** traditions, namely, that
AP : 2 8 :020(284) [0449] to the Gospel; it does not **create** an authority for bishops
AP : 2 8 :020(284) [0449] Bishops must not **create** traditions contrary to the
S 1 : 0 1 :000(291) [0461] nature, are one God, who **created** heaven and earth, etc.
SC : 0 2 :001(344) [0543] The First Article: **Creation**
SC : 0 2 :002(345) [0543] I believe that God has **created** me and all that exists; that
LC : 0 1 :085(376) [0605] prevail and no one will **create** disorder by unnecessary
LC : 0 1 :087(377) [0605] the day needs no sanctification, for it was **created** holy.
LC : 0 1 :108(380) [0611] the will of God, who has **created** and ordained them to be
LC : 0 1 :207(393) [0639] of all institutions, and he **created** man and woman
LC : 0 1 :211(393) [0641] who have been **created** for it, shall be found in this estate.
LC : 0 2 :006(411) [0679] God the Father, explains **creation**; the second, of the
LC : 0 2 :007(411) [0679] in God the Father, who **created** me; I believe in God the
LC : 0 2 :011(412) [0681] there is no one else who could **create** heaven and earth."
LC : 0 2 :012(412) [0681] as we have said, that this article deals with **creation**.
LC : 0 2 :014(412) [0681] Besides, he makes all **creation** help provide the comforts
LC : 0 2 :028(414) [0685] When we were **created** by God the Father, and had
LC : 0 2 :045(416) [0689] there is no Holy Spirit to **create**, call, and gather the
LC : 0 2 :053(417) [0693] By it he **creates** and increases sanctification, causing it
LC : 0 2 :061(419) [0695] **Creation** is past and redemption is accomplished, but the
LC : 0 2 :064(419) [0695] He **created** us for this very purpose, to redeem and
LC : 0 2 :069(420) [0697] the Father gives us all **creation**, Christ all his works, the
LC : 0 5 :006(447) [0755] remain as God has **created** and ordered them, regardless
EP : 0 1 :002(466) [0779] the beginning when God **created** man pure and holy and
EP : 0 1 :003(466) [0779] Christian faith, namely, **creation**, redemption,
EP : 0 1 :004(466) [0781] God not only **created** the body and soul of Adam and
EP : 0 1 :006(466) [0781] our nature as his **creation**, sanctifies it as his creation,
EP : 0 1 :006(467) [0781] sanctifies it as his **creation**, quickens it from the dead as
EP : 0 1 :006(467) [0781] it from the dead as his **creation**, and adorns it gloriously
EP : 0 1 :006(467) [0781] as his creation, and adorns it gloriously as his **creation**.
EP : 0 1 :006(467) [0781] But he has not **created** original sin, has not assumed it,
EP : 0 1 :022(469) [0785] as when we say, "God has **created** human nature."
EP : 0 1 :025(469) [0785] Satan cannot **create** a substance; he can only, with God's

Continued ▶

E P : 0 1 :025(469) [0785] accidentally the substance which God has **created**.
E P : 0 2 :014(471) [0789] and rebirth he **creates** out of nothing a new essence of the
E P : 0 6 :002(480) [0805] their hearts when they were **created** in the image of God.
E P : 1 2 :022(499) [0841] Spirit teaches people and **creates** in them the saving
S D : 0 1 :002(508) [0859] Fall are and remain God's handiwork and **creation** in us.
S D : 0 1 :002(508) [0859] which he was originally **created**, that in spiritual matters
S D : 0 1 :003(509) [0861] distinguish his work and **creation** in man from the devil's
S D : 0 1 :007(510) [0861] this corruption, God does not **create** and make sin in us.
S D : 0 1 :007(510) [0861] nature which God still **creates** and makes at the present
S D : 0 1 :010(510) [0863] which man was originally **created** in truth, holiness, and
S D : 0 1 :026(512) [0867] human nature is initially **created** perfect and pure, and
S D : 0 1 :027(512) [0867] nature was originally **created** pure, good, and holy, sin
S D : 0 1 :027(512) [0867] in such a way that Satan **created** or made something
S D : 0 1 :028(513) [0867] nature is not at first **created** pure and holy and is
S D : 0 1 :030(513) [0867] imparted at **creation** to our nature in paradise.
S D : 0 1 :032(513) [0869] we are human beings **created** by God but because we are
S D : 0 1 :033(514) [0869] and soul or man himself **created** by God (within which
S D : 0 1 :033(514) [0869] (a) our nature as it is **created** and preserved by God and
S D : 0 1 :034(514) [0869] place, in the article of **creation** Scripture testifies not only
S D : 0 1 :034(514) [0869] not only that God **created** human nature before the Fall,
S D : 0 1 :038(514) [0871] God is man's creator who **creates** body and soul for him.
S D : 0 1 :038(515) [0871] "I believe that God has **created** *me* and all that exists,
S D : 0 1 :041(515) [0871] of this our nature, he has **created** and made original sin,
S D : 0 1 :042(515) [0871] that it is by God's **creation** that man has a body and soul;
S D : 0 1 :051(517) [0875] in the statement, "God **creates** man's nature," the word
S D : 0 2 :004(520) [0881] without any means or **created** instruments (that is,
S D : 0 2 :022(525) [0889] destiny for which only man, no stone or log, was **created**.
S D : 0 2 :023(525) [0889] free, a condition for which it was originally **created**."
S D : 0 2 :024(526) [0891] in him and kindles and **creates** faith and other
S D : 0 2 :026(526) [0891] Deut. 30:6; Ps. 51:12); **creates** us in Christ Jesus for good
S D : 0 2 :037(528) [0895] become strong in faith and in its fruits, which he **creates**."
S D : 0 2 :039(528) [0895] Spirit, as St. Paul says, **creates** such willing and doing
S D : 0 2 :039(528) [0895] are his workmanship, **created** in Christ Jesus for good
S D : 0 2 :060(533) [0905] This the Scriptures call the **creation** of a new heart.
S D : 0 2 :081(537) [0911] and regeneration God **creates** a new heart and a new man
S D : 0 2 :081(537) [0911] and a new substance of the soul is **created** out of nothing.
S D : 0 3 :023(543) [0923] and sanctifies them and **creates** within them love toward
S D : 0 4 :007(552) [0941] St. Paul says, "has been **created** in Christ Jesus for good
S D : 0 5 :023(562) [0959] man in the beginning was **created** righteous and holy by
S D : 0 6 :005(564) [0963] immediately after his **creation** received a law according to
S D : 0 6 :010(565) [0965] what the Gospel does, **creates**, and works in connection
S D : 0 8 :052(601) [1033] and adorned are **created** gifts or finite qualities, as in the
S D : 0 8 :054(601) [1033] by itself possesses all the **created** gifts which have been
S D : 0 8 :055(601) [1033] sin, and so forth are not **created** gifts but divine and
S D : 0 8 :073(605) [1041] the Holy Spirit who endows them only with **created** gifts.
S D : 0 8 :085(608) [1047] eternal power and has **created** and preserved everything
S D : 1 0 :005(611) [1053] are intended to **create** the illusion (or are demanded or
S D : 1 1 :007(617) [1065] (since God neither **creates** nor works evil, nor does he
S D : 1 1 :008(617) [1065] it is also a cause which **creates**, effects, helps, and furthers
S D : 1 1 :043(623) [1077] Before the **creation** of time, "before the foundation of the
S D : 1 1 :044(624) [1077] the Word he would **create** and effect in us everything that
S D : 1 1 :048(624) [1079] patience, give us comfort, **create** hope, and bring
S D : 1 1 :069(627) [1085] Christ, the Holy Spirit **creates** true faith through the

Creator (14)
A G : 0 1 :003(028) [0043] and goodness, one **creator** and preserver of all things
L C : 0 2 :016(412) [0681] All this is comprehended in the word "**Creator**."
L C : 0 2 :021(413) [0683] to thank him or acknowledge him as Lord and **Creator**.
L C : 0 2 :036(415) [0687] As the Father is called **Creator** and the Son is called
S D : 0 1 :007(510) [0861] that God is not the **creator**, author, or cause of sin.
S D : 0 1 :038(514) [0871] the Fall God is man's **creator** who creates body and soul
S D : 0 1 :038(514) [0871] sin itself, for in that case God would be the **creator** of sin.
S D : 0 1 :040(515) [0871] come from God, nor is God the **creator** or author of sin.
S D : 0 1 :041(515) [0871] that, since God is the **creator** of this our nature, he has
S D : 0 1 :041(515) [0871] of sin, Satan is the **creator** of our nature, our body and
S D : 0 4 :016(554) [0943] indicates when it enjoins the creature to obey its **Creator**.
S D : 0 7 :044(577) [0987] and almighty Lord, our **Creator** and Redeemer Jesus
S D : 0 7 :045(577) [0987] Jesus Christ, our Lord, **Creator**, and Redeemer, not as
S D : 0 7 :047(578) [0989] and commands of our **Creator** and Redeemer, without

Creature (24), Creatures (33)
A G : 0 1 :006(028) [0043] that the Holy Spirit is a movement induced in **creatures**.
A G : 0 3 :004(030) [0045] have dominion over all **creatures**, that through the Holy
A L : 0 3 :004(030) [0045] have dominion over all **creatures**, and sanctify those who
A P : 0 4 :131(125) [0159] understanding of all **creatures**: "You shall love the Lord
A P : 0 4 :247(142) [0191] that we should be a kind of first fruits of his **creatures**."
A P : 1 6 :001(222) [0329] are God's good **creatures** and divine ordinances in which
A P : 2 3 :019(242) [0369] does not want us to despise his ordinances, his **creatures**.
S 3 : 1 1 :002(314) [0499] power to separate such **creatures** of God or forbid them
S C : 0 2 :004(345) [0545] a lost and condemned **creature**, delivered me and freed
S C : 0 8 :008(353) [0559] thing" means that all **creatures** receive enough to eat to
L C : 0 1 :021(367) [0585] help and consolation from **creatures**, saints, or devils.
L C : 0 1 :026(368) [0587] **Creatures** are only the hands, channels, and means
L C : 0 1 :026(368) [0587] — things which no **creature** could produce by himself.
L C : 0 1 :027(368) [0587] good through God's **creatures** is not to be disdained, nor
L C : 0 2 :013(412) [0681] and believe that I am a **creature** of God; that is, that he
L C : 0 2 :024(413) [0683] to us, with all his **creatures**, has abundantly provided for
L C : 0 2 :030(414) [0685] snatched us, poor lost **creatures**, from the jaws of hell,
E P : 0 1 :002(466) [0779] after the fall our nature is and remains a **creature** of God.
E P : 0 8 :008(487) [0819] are to be a corporeal **creature**, to be flesh and blood, to
E P : 0 8 :016(489) [0821] things, is present to all **creatures**, and has all things in
E P : 0 8 :035(491) [0825] all angels and other **creatures**; but that he does not share
E P : 0 8 :035(491) [0825] and the power of other **creatures**) and they imagine that
E P : 0 8 :035(491) [0825] but greater than the power of other **creatures**.
E P : 1 2 :020(499) [0841] to the flesh is a **creature** do not have a right
S D : 0 1 :002(509) [0859] God's handiwork and **creatures** in us even after the Fall)
S D : 0 1 :032(513) [0869] the product, and the **creature** of God even after the Fall
S D : 0 1 :034(514) [0869] human nature is God's **creature** and handiwork (Deut.
S D : 0 1 :038(515) [0871] and believe that I am a **creature** of God; that is, that he
S D : 0 1 :038(515) [0871] of course true that this **creature** and handiwork of God
S D : 0 1 :040(515) [0871] Neither is original sin the **creature** or handiwork of God;
S D : 0 1 :041(515) [0871] his handiwork and **creature**; or that, since the devil is the
S D : 0 1 :041(515) [0871] be Satan's handiwork or **creature** if our corrupted nature
S D : 0 1 :042(515) [0871] to distinguish God's **creature** and handiwork in man from
S D : 0 1 :055(518) [0877] is either God himself or a product and **creature** of God.
S D : 0 2 :019(524) [0889] is no longer a rational **creature**, or that he is converted to
S D : 0 2 :026(526) [0891] and makes us new **creatures** (II Cor. 5:17; Gal. 6:15).
S D : 0 2 :059(532) [0905] man is still a rational **creature** with an intellect and will
S D : 0 2 :062(533) [0905] in man as a rational **creature** and another mode of action
S D : 0 2 :062(533) [0905] to work in irrational **creatures** or in a stone or block.
S D : 0 4 :012(553) [0941] mettlesome, and merry toward God and all **creatures**.
S D : 0 4 :016(554) [0943] indicates when it enjoins the **creature** to obey its Creator.
S D : 0 7 :100(586) [1005] space but penetrates every **creature**, wherever he wills.
S D : 0 7 :101(587) [1007] according to which all **creatures** are indeed much more
S D : 0 7 :101(587) [1007] be present in and with **creatures** in such a way that they
S D : 0 7 :101(587) [1007] will he be present in all **creatures** according to this exalted
S D : 0 7 :101(587) [1007] God, very far beyond **creatures**, as far as God transcends
S D : 0 7 :101(587) [1007] deep and as near in all **creatures** as God is immanent in
S D : 0 7 :102(587) [1007] he is in God beyond all **creatures** and is one person with
S D : 0 8 :010(593) [1019] be a corporeal being or a **creature**, to be flesh and blood,
S D : 0 8 :026(596) [1023] its exaltation above all **creatures** in heaven and on earth.
S D : 0 8 :068(604) [1039] present in all **creatures**, and since in whomever he is
S D : 0 8 :068(604) [1039] equal truth that in all **creatures** in whom God is, but
S D : 0 8 :069(604) [1039] to his human nature he has received above all **creatures**.
S D : 0 8 :070(604) [1039] For no other **creature**, whether man or angel, can or
S D : 0 8 :071(605) [1041] nature, like every other **creature** in heaven or on earth, is
S D : 1 1 :004(616) [1063] foreknowledge — extends to all **creatures**, good or evil.
S D : 1 2 :029(635) [1101] to his assumed human nature Christ is a **creature**.

Credence (2)
A P : 2 7 :004(269) [0419] will show how much **credence** should be given to this
E P : 0 2 :019(472) [0791] though he cannot give it **credence** and accept it by his

Credit (4), Crediting (1)
A P : 0 4 :024(110) [0127] of reason its due **credit**; for our corrupt nature has no
A P : 0 4 :213(136) [0179] To **credit** our works with being a propitiation and to claim
A P : 2 7 :014(271) [0423] even more to give this **credit** to human traditions, as he
A P : 2 7 :033(275) [0431] traditions, deserve the **credit** for meriting the forgiveness
E P : 0 7 :042(486) [0817] deliberately insist on **crediting** us with this doctrine,

Creed (59), Creeds (8)
P R : P R :020(010) [0017] articles of our Christian **Creed** (especially those pertaining
P R : P R :020(010) [0019] articles of our Christian **Creed** that our ingenuous
P R : P R :023(012) [0021] Holy Scriptures and the **Creeds**, and then to the
P R : P R :025(013) [0023] in the three **Creeds** as well as in the Augsburg Confession,
A G : 0 3 :006(030) [0045] the living and the dead, as stated in the Apostles' **Creed**.
A L : 0 3 :006(030) [0045] and the dead, etc., according to the Apostles' **Creed**.
A P : 0 3 :001(107) [0119] etc., according to the Apostles' and Nicene **Creeds**.
A P : 0 4 :051(114) [0135] to the article of the **Creed** on the forgiveness of sins.
A P : 0 7 :007(169) [0229] The **Creed** also defines the church this way, teaching us to
A P : 0 7 :009(170) [0229] The **Creed** offers us these consolations that we may not
S 1 : 0 1 :000(292) [0461] dead, etc., as the Apostles' **Creed**, the Athanasian Creed,
S 1 : 0 1 :000(292) [0461] Creed, the Athanasian **Creed**, and the Catechism in
S C : P R :003(338) [0533] the Lord's Prayer, the **Creed**, or the Ten Commandments,
S C : P R :005(338) [0533] the Lord's Prayer, the **Creed**, the Ten Commandments, or
S C : P R :007(339) [0533] Ten Commandments, the **Creed**, the Lord's Prayer, the
S C : P R :008(339) [0535] the Lord's Prayer, the **Creed**, and the Ten
S C : P R :010(339) [0535] Ten Commandments, the **Creed**, the Lord's Prayer, etc.,
S C : 0 2 :000(344) [0543] [II] The **Creed** *in the plain form in which the head of the*
S C : 0 7 :002(352) [0557] standing, say the Apostles' **Creed** and the Lord's Prayer.
S C : 0 7 :005(353) [0559] standing, say the Apostles' **Creed** and the Lord's Prayer.
L C : P R :007(359) [0569] the Ten Commandments, the **Creed**, the Psalms, etc.
L C : 0 1 :089(377) [0605] Ten Commandments, the **Creed**, and the Lord's Prayer.
L C : 0 1 :316(408) [0671] Both the **Creed** and the Lord's Prayer must help us, as we
L C : 0 2 :000(411) [0679] Second Part: The **Creed**
L C : 0 2 :001(411) [0679] The **Creed** properly follows, setting forth all that we must
L C : 0 2 :003(411) [0679] we would need neither the **Creed** nor the Lord's Prayer.
L C : 0 2 :004(411) [0679] and necessity of the **Creed**, it is sufficient, as a first step,
L C : 0 2 :004(411) [0679] simple persons to learn to understand the **Creed** itself.
L C : 0 2 :005(411) [0679] In the first place, the **Creed** used to be divided into twelve
L C : 0 2 :005(411) [0679] and belonging to the **Creed** were gathered together, there
L C : 0 2 :006(411) [0679] briefly sum up the entire **Creed** in three articles, according
L C : 0 2 :007(411) [0679] Hence the **Creed** may be briefly comprised in these few
L C : 0 2 :010(412) [0679] Thus the **Creed** is nothing else than a response and
L C : 0 2 :047(416) [0689] The **Creed** calls the holy Christian church a *communio*
L C : 0 2 :063(419) [0695] Here in the **Creed** you have the entire essence of God, his
L C : 0 2 :066(419) [0695] These articles of the **Creed**, therefore, divide and
L C : 0 2 :067(419) [0697] Now you see that the **Creed** is a very different teaching
L C : 0 2 :067(419) [0697] what we ought to do; the **Creed** tells us what God does
L C : 0 2 :067(420) [0697] can comprehend the **Creed**; it must be taught by the Holy
L C : 0 2 :068(420) [0697] But the **Creed** brings pure grace and makes us upright
L C : 0 2 :070(420) [0697] is enough concerning the **Creed** to lay a foundation for
L C : 0 3 :051(426) [0711] what we learned in the **Creed**, namely, that God sent his
L C : 0 4 :006(437) [0733] Ten Commandments, the **Creed**, and the Lord's Prayer
L C : 0 5 :005(447) [0755] Lord's Prayer, and the **Creed** retain their nature and value
L C : 0 5 :032(450) [0759] and the article of the **Creed**, "I believe in the holy
L C : 0 5 :085(456) [0773] Ten Commandments, the **Creed**, and the Lord's Prayer
E P : R N :003(465) [0777] namely, the Apostles' **Creed**, the Nicene Creed, and the
E P : R N :003(465) [0777] Creed, the Nicene **Creed**, and the Athanasian Creed.
E P : R N :003(465) [0777] Creed, the Nicene Creed, and the Athanasian **Creed**.
E P : 0 8 :019(490) [0823] and our simple Christian **Creed** the following erroneous
E P : 0 9 :001(492) [0827] to our simple Christian **Creed**, did Christ go to hell?
E P : 1 2 :001(498) [0839] our repeatedly cited Christian **Creed** and Confession.
E P : 1 2 :030(500) [0843] Word of God, the three **Creeds**, the Augsburg Confession,
S D : R N :004(504) [0851] to the three general **Creeds**, the Apostles', the Nicene, and
S D : R N :005(504) [0853] to appeal and confess adherence to the Nicene **Creed**.
S D : R N :015(507) [0857] concerning articles of the **Creed** or the chief parts of our
S D : 0 1 :038(514) [0871] of the First Article of the **Creed** in the Small Catechism
S D : 0 8 :005(592) [1017] with our plain Christian **creed**, and to settle it definitely
S D : 0 8 :020(595) [1021] of our plain Christian **Creed**, has truly died, although the
S D : 0 8 :023(595) [1023] to our plain Christian **Creed** we believe, teach, and
S D : 0 8 :045(600) [1031] For our plain Christian **Creed** teaches us that the Son of
S D : 0 8 :071(605) [1041] contrary to our Christian **Creed** and to the entire
S D : 0 8 :088(609) [1047] writings, the orthodox **Creeds**, and our Christian
S D : 0 8 :096(609) [1049] and apostles, and our Christian **Creed** and Confession.
S D : 0 9 :001(610) [1051] of our Christian **Creed**, to which Dr. Luther directs us in
S D : 1 2 :037(636) [1101] Nicene and Athanasian **Creeds**, both as to content and
S D : 1 2 :039(636) [1103] Word of God, to the three **Creeds**, to the Augsburg

Creep (3), Creeping (1), Crept (4)
AG : 0 0 :000(049) [0059] of the abuses having **crept** in over the years and others of
AG : 0 0 :005(095) [0095] godless teaching from **creeping** into our churches and
AL : 0 0 :002(047) [0059] few abuses which have **crept** into the churches without
AL : 2 4 :015(057) [0065] they let many corruptions **creep** into the church.
AL : 2 8 :062(092) [0093] These errors **crept** into the church when the righteousness
AP : 0 7 :032(174) [0239] opinions about traditions have **crept** into the church.
AP : 2 1 :040(235) [0355] pastors permitted many abuses to **creep** into the church.
SD : 0 7 :050(578) [0991] misunderstanding could **creep** in, he explained things

Crete (1)
TR : 0 0 :062(330) [0521] "This is why I left you in **Crete**, that you might appoint

Creutziger (1)
S 3 : 1 5 :005(316) [0501] Dr. Caspar **Creutziger** subscribed

Crime (5), Crimes (9), Criminally (1), Criminals (2)
AG : 2 3 :018(054) [0063] as if it were a great **crime**, in spite of that fact that in the
AL : 2 0 :032(045) [0057] to various sins, impious opinions, and manifest **crimes**.
AL : 2 0 :033(045) [0057] able to do so but were defiled by many manifest **crimes**.
AL : 2 3 :018(054) [0063] adulteries, and other **crimes** which deserve the
AP : 0 4 :023(110) [0127] weakness and by the devil, who drives it to open **crimes**.
AP : 1 2 :156(207) [0301] where the particular punishment fits the particular **crime**.
AP : 1 8 :010(226) [0337] But it has been **criminally** suppressed by those who dream
TR : 0 0 :053(329) [0519] also know how great a **crime** it is to support unjust
TR : 0 0 :054(329) [0519] and countless other **crimes** and for the murder of saints.
TR : 0 0 :059(330) [0521] errors and other **crimes** as to impose them on all
TR : 0 0 :060(330) [0521] are guilty of notorious **crimes** and absolve those who
TR : 0 0 :074(332) [0525] who are guilty of manifest **crimes** belongs to all pastors.
TR : 0 0 :082(334) [0527] know that God will require them to pay for their **crime**.
LC : 0 1 :137(384) [0619] do we have so many **criminals** who must daily be hanged,
LC : 0 1 :192(391) [0635] committed all these **crimes**, as far as you were concerned
LC : 0 3 :045(426) [0709] a murder or any other **crime** had been committed in it, or
EP : 1 2 :016(499) [0841] conscience inflict capital punishment upon **criminals**.

Critically (1), Criticism (1), Criticisms (1), Criticize (11), Criticized (2), Criticizes (1), Criticizing (1), Critics (1)
PR : PR :013(007) [0013] have their opinions and **criticisms** reduced to writing, and
AP : 0 2 :001(100) [0105] "Original Sin," but they **criticize** our definition of original
AP : 0 4 :308(155) [0207] because of certain carping **critics**: faith is truly
AP : 0 7 :006(169) [0229] We wonder why they **criticize** our description, which
AP : 0 7 :043(177) [0243] of the church, and he **criticizes** the Audians for
AP : 2 4 :014(251) [0389] of sacrifice among those whose abuses we **criticize**.
AP : 2 8 :002(281) [0443] testified that we do not **criticize** political ordinances nor
LC : 0 1 :110(380) [0611] them discourteously, **critically**, and censoriously, but
LC : 0 1 :240(397) [0649] goods as dearly as he pleases without a word of **criticism**.
LC : 0 1 :289(404) [0663] pounce on something to **criticize** in their neighbor,
SD : 0 3 :044(547) [0933] already named we must **criticize**, expose, and reject the
SD : 0 4 :015(553) [0943] It is wrong, therefore, to **criticize** and reject the cited
SD : 0 4 :015(553) [0943] be used and urged to **criticize** and reject a complacent
SD : 0 4 :031(556) [0947] must begin by earnestly **criticizing** and rejecting the false
SD : 0 5 :015(561) [0957] and would have us **criticize** sin and teach contrition and
SD : 0 7 :121(590) [1013] For while we justly **criticize** and condemn the papistic
SD : 0 7 :128(591) [1015] views have been **criticized** and rejected in the foregoing
SD : 0 8 :051(600) [1031] own co-religionists now **criticize** and reject this error.
SD : 1 0 :013(613) [1057] a certain extent, Paul **criticized** them publicly because

Crops (1)
LC : 0 3 :080(431) [0721] and hail to destroy **crops** and cattle, why he poisons the

Crosiers (1)
S 1 : PR :013(291) [0459] and cardinals' hats and **crosiers**, and similar nonsense

Cross (25)
AG : 2 6 :031(068) [0075] concerning the holy **cross** that Christians are obliged to
AL : 2 0 :037(046) [0057] of God, or bear the **cross**, but it seeks and trusts in man's
AL : 2 6 :015(066) [0073] concerning faith, the **cross**, hope, the importance of civil
AL : 2 6 :031(068) [0075] taught concerning the **cross** that Christians are obliged to
AP : 0 4 :029(111) [0129] stumbling-block of the **cross** has been removed' (Gal.
AP : 0 7 :018(171) [0233] or hidden under the **cross**, just as Christ is the same,
AP : 1 3 :008(212) [0311] death of Christ on the **cross** was sufficient for the sins of
AP : 1 5 :043(221) [0327] and is heard, the **cross**, respect for rulers and for all civil
AP : 1 5 :045(221) [0327] the Confession, that the **cross** and the troubles with which
AP : 1 5 :046(221) [0327] brought on by the **cross**, a voluntary kind of exercise
AP : 2 4 :056(260) [0405] Testament except the one sacrifice of Christ on the **cross**.
AP : 2 4 :062(260) [0405] Lord, once offered on the **cross** for the original debt, is
SC : 0 7 :001(352) [0557] rise, make the sign of the **cross** and say, "In the name of
SC : 0 7 :004(353) [0559] make the sign of the **cross** and say, "In the name of God,
LC : 0 1 :074(374) [0601] custom of children who **cross** themselves when they see or
LC : 0 1 :197(392) [0637] might live a nice, soft life without the **cross** and suffering.
LC : 0 3 :065(429) [0715] fruit, there the blessed holy **cross** will not be far away.
LC : 0 4 :037(441) [0741] the Lord Christ upon the **cross** is not a work but a
LC : 0 5 :031(450) [0759] sins was acquired on the **cross**, yet it cannot come to us in
SD : 0 3 :022(543) [0923] ignominious death on the **cross** for us, even though, on
SD : 0 3 :056(549) [0935] ignominious death of the **cross**, is reckoned to us as
SD : 0 7 :049(578) [0989] for us on the tree of the **cross** for the forgiveness of sins.
SD : 0 8 :059(602) [1035] only to the merit that was once achieved on the **cross**.
SD : 1 1 :033(622) [1075] you are tested under the **cross** and in tribulation, the
SD : 1 1 :049(624) [1079] through which specific **cross** and affliction he would

Crowd (10)
AP : 0 4 :065(116) [0139] From such a great **crowd** of writers, let them produce one
AP : 0 4 :211(136) [0179] But the **crowd** ever since has copied not the faith of the
AP : 0 4 :396(167) [0225] minds be troubled by the **crowd** of adversaries who
AP : 0 7 :019(171) [0233] church is hidden under a **crowd** of wicked men so that
AP : 1 2 :068(192) [0271] right; for there is a great **crowd** of worthless
AP : 1 3 :018(213) [0313] we condemn the whole **crowd** of scholastic doctors who
AP : 2 3 :044(245) [0375] too evident that the great **crowd** of lazy priests in the
AP : 2 7 :005(269) [0421] just feed a lazy **crowd** that gorges itself on the public alms
LC : 0 1 :248(398) [0651] follow the old, wayward **crowd**, but may keep their eyes
LC : 0 4 :043(442) [0743] Because of the pressing **crowd** of rich men no one else

Crown (6), Crowned (2), Crowns (1)
AP : 0 4 :356(161) [0217] as do many later writers, "God **crowns** his gifts in us."
AP : 0 4 :363(162) [0219] is laid up for me the **crown** of righteousness, which the
AP : 0 4 :363(162) [0219] The **crown** is owed to the justified because of the
TR : 0 0 :032(325) [0513] Christ in his passion was **crowned** with thorns and that he
LC : 0 1 :045(370) [0593] his confidence in his **crown** and power, he inevitably
LC : 0 4 :020(439) [0737] about his neck, yes, the **crown** on his head, which shows
LC : 0 4 :062(444) [0749] would like to snatch the **crown** from the rulers and
SD : 0 1 :062(519) [0879] soles of our feet to the **crown** of our head, inasmuch as
SD : 0 8 :070(605) [1041] likewise, "Thou has **crowned** him with glory and

Crucified (13), Crucify (1)
AG : 0 3 :002(029) [0045] man, who was truly born, suffered, was **crucified**, died,
AL : 0 3 :002(030) [0045] Mary, truly suffered, was **crucified**, dead, and buried,
AL : 2 6 :032(068) [0075] afflictions and to be **crucified** with Christ is true and real,
AP : 0 4 :291(152) [0203] promised, revealed, born, **crucified**, and raised in vain.
AP : 0 4 :297(153) [0205] revealed, born, **crucified**, and raised in vain; the promise
AP : 2 7 :011(270) [0423] take away from Christ's honor and **crucify** him again.
SC : 0 2 :003(345) [0545] *Pontius Pilate, was **crucified**, dead, and buried: he*
LC : SP :012(363) [0577] Pontius Pilate, was **crucified**, dead, and buried: he
LC : 0 2 :025(413) [0683] *Pontius Pilate, was **crucified**, dead, and buried: he*
EP : 0 8 :014(488) [0821] I Cor. 2:8, They have "**crucified** the Lord of glory," and in
SD : 0 4 :019(554) [0945] belong to Christ have **crucified** (that is, killed) their flesh
SD : 0 7 :076(583) [0999] Christ himself who was **crucified** for us, can make of the
SD : 0 8 :042(599) [1029] the Son of God truly is **crucified** for us — that is, this
SD : 0 8 :042(599) [1029] — this person, I say, is **crucified** according to the

Crude (1), Crudely (1)
AP : 0 4 :232(140) [0185] bear, if need be, with the **crude** behavior of the brethren,
LC : 0 3 :029(424) [0705] rightly and not act so **crudely** and coldly that they

Cruel (7), Cruelly (3), Cruelties (3), Cruelty (18)
AL : 2 3 :018(054) [0063] that nowhere is greater **cruelty** exercised than in
AL : 2 3 :021(055) [0063] men, and even priests, are **cruelly** put to death, contrary
AP : 0 4 :209(135) [0177] to death in order by this **cruel** and painful deed to placate
AP : 0 4 :399(168) [0227] from the unheard of **cruelty** which, as everyone knows,
AP : 0 4 :399(168) [0227] What would Phalaris say that was more **cruel**?
AP : 1 2 :067(192) [0271] hold this faith be put to death with all sorts of **cruelties**.
AP : 1 4 :002(214) [0315] else, in their unheard of **cruelty**, they kill the unfortunate
AP : 1 4 :002(214) [0315] Thus the **cruelty** of the bishops is the reason for the
AP : 1 4 :003(214) [0315] we dare not approve the **cruelty** of those who persecute
AP : 1 4 :005(215) [0315] protest against the unjust **cruelty** of the bishops, we could
AP : 2 1 :043(235) [0357] They defend obvious abuses with new and illegal **cruelty**.
AP : 2 3 :003(239) [0363] sentence innocent men to **cruel** punishments, slaughter
AP : 2 3 :003(239) [0363] country, however savage or **cruel**, would consider.
AP : 2 3 :004(239) [0363] is free of disgrace and **cruelty**, we hope that you will deal
AP : 2 3 :057(247) [0379] They **cruelly** kill men just because they are married.
AP : 2 3 :070(249) [0383] God will avenge this **cruelty**.
AP : 2 3 :071(249) [0383] up marriages and to issue savage and **cruel** prohibitions.
AP : 2 7 :004(269) [0421] how ignorant and **cruel** these illiterate men are; and how
AP : 2 7 :008(269) [0421] do not approve of the **cruelty** which the hypocrites among
AP : 2 8 :025(285) [0451] truth, and are now most **cruelly** persecuting it, will give an
TR : 0 0 :040(327) [0517] impiety with the greatest **cruelty** and puts to death those
TR : 0 0 :041(327) [0517] doctrines, blasphemies, and unjust **cruelties** of the pope.
TR : 0 0 :042(328) [0517] with and not to support impiety and unjust **cruelty**.
TR : 0 0 :049(328) [0519] defends these errors with savage **cruelty** and punishment.
TR : 0 0 :053(329) [0519] it is to support unjust **cruelty** in the murder of saints,
TR : 0 0 :058(330) [0521] Manifest, too, is the **cruelty** which he employs against the
TR : 0 0 :058(330) [0521] flee from idolatry, impious doctrines, and unjust **cruelty**.
TR : 0 0 :079(333) [0527] but rather support the **cruelty** of the pope; since, in
SD : 0 2 :021(525) [0889] or recognize the dreadful, **cruel** wrath of God over sin and
SD : 1 0 :022(615) [1061] doctrines, blasphemies, and unjust **cruelties** of the pope.
SD : 1 0 :023(615) [1061] with and not to support impiety and unjust **cruelty**."

Crush (5), Crushed (3), Crushing (1)
AP : 0 2 :037(105) [0115] words in order by this device to **crush** an innocent man.
AP : 1 2 :031(186) [0259] I am utterly spent and **crushed**; I groan because of the
AP : 2 1 :042(235) [0357] emperor, our opponents are doing everything to **crush** us.
AP : 2 1 :043(235) [0357] and sound doctrine **crushed**, fanatical spirits will arise
AP : 2 1 :044(236) [0357] has happened before, nor **crush** sound doctrine in the
AP : 2 4 :091(266) [0415] They have **crushed** the doctrine of faith, and under the
AP : 2 4 :096(267) [0417] comparing them with our position they try to **crush** us.
AP : 2 7 :034(275) [0431] or eternal life are simply **crushing** the Gospel about the
LC : 0 3 :031(424) [0707] the devil expected to **crush** us, and the Gospel as well,

Crust (1)
LC : 0 3 :055(427) [0713] are praying here not for a **crust** of bread or for a

Cry (16), Crying (1), Cried (2), Cries (3)
AP : 0 4 :154(128) [0165] her anointing and **crying**, all of which were a sign and
AP : 0 4 :348(160) [0217] opponents will raise the **cry** that good works are
AP : 1 2 :031(186) [0259] I **cry** for help until morning; like a lion he breaks all my
AP : 1 2 :060(190) [0269] the same, in spite of our opponents' **cries** to the contrary.
AP : 1 2 :063(191) [0269] gates of hell (Matt. 16:18) **cry** out against it, that the
AP : 1 2 :066(191) [0271] Our opponents **cry** out that they are the church and follow
AP : 1 2 :142(204) [0295] it requires, but Scripture **cries** out everywhere that we are
AP : 1 2 :151(206) [0299] "The distress in which they **cry** out is thy chastening upon
AP : 2 3 :037(244) [0373] Here they may **cry** out that we put marriage on the same
AP : 2 3 :068(249) [0383] ignorant was to raise the **cry** of heresy against us over and
AP : 2 3 :070(249) [0383] that as the blood of Abel **cried** out in death (Gen. 4:10),
AP : 2 3 :070(249) [0383] the many innocent victims of their rage will also **cry** out.
S 1 : PR :015(291) [0459] and wretched souls who **cry** unto Thee and earnestly seek
S 3 : 0 3 :042(310) [0491] They **cry** out, "Do what you will, it matters not as long as
SC : 0 8 :010(354) [0559] the beasts their food, and to the young ravens which **cry**.
LC : 0 1 :247(398) [0651] he can complain to no one else, he will **cry** to heaven.
LC : 0 1 :247(398) [0651] Such a man's sighs and **cries** will be no joking matter.
LC : 0 3 :026(424) [0705] our need, the distress that impels and drives us to **cry** out.
LC : 0 3 :047(426) [0711] we ought constantly to **cry** out against all who preach and
LC : 0 3 :105(434) [0727] we are constrained to **cry** out and pray every hour that
LC : 0 4 :037(441) [0741] they are unfair when they **cry** out against us as though we
SD : 1 1 :074(628) [1087] my supplications when I **cried** to thee for help"

Crystal (1)
SD : 0 7 :100(586) [1007] air, water, glass, or **crystal** and exist without occupying

Cube (1)
A P : 2 7 :005(269) [0421] age, or as the Platonic **cube** degenerates into bad

Culpable (2)
S D : 0 5 :017(561) [0957] and fountainhead of all **culpable** sin, the law reproves
S D : 1 0 :029(615) [1061] we hold it to be a **culpable** sin when in a period of

Culprit (1)
L C : 0 1 :204(393) [0639] of yours, you are just as guilty as the **culprit** himself.

Cult (3)
A G : 2 0 :003(041) [0053] works like rosaries, the **cult** of saints, monasticism,
A G : 2 1 :000(046) [0057] XXI. The **Cult** of Saints
A L : 2 1 :000(046) [0057] XXI. The **Cult** of Saints

Cultivation (1)
A L : 0 0 :006(049) [0059] public worship and the **cultivation** of reverence and

Cunning (1), Cunningly (1)
S 2 : 0 2 :016(295) [0467] unspeakable lies and **cunning**, of demanding Masses,
L C : 0 1 :303(405) [0667] affairs, where one **cunningly** slips something out of

Cup (29)
A G : 2 2 :005(050) [0061] Cyprian mentions that the **cup** was given to laymen in his
A L : 2 2 :002(049) [0059] with reference to the **cup** that all should drink of it.
A L : 2 4 :012(057) [0065] the bread or drinks the **cup** of the Lord in an unworthy
A P : 1 2 :042(187) [0263] This **cup** is the new testament" (Luke 22:19, 20).
A P : 1 2 :159(207) [0301] who did not deserve to drink the **cup** must drink it."
A P : 2 2 :003(236) [0359] about the body; later he says the same about the **cup**.
A P : 2 2 :003(236) [0359] himself, and so eat of the bread and drink of the **cup**."
A P : 2 4 :035(256) [0397] this bread and drink the **cup**, you proclaim the Lord's
A P : 2 4 :069(262) [0409] given for you"; "this is the **cup** of the new testament with
S C : P R :005(338) [0533] You withhold the **cup** in the Lord's Supper and insist on
S C : 0 6 :004(351) [0555] same way also he took the **cup**, after supper, and when he
S C : 0 6 :004(351) [0557] This **cup** is the new covenant in my blood, which is
L C : S P :023(364) [0579] "In the same way also the **cup**, after supper, saying, 'This
L C : S P :023(364) [0579] after supper, saying, 'This **cup** is the new testament in my
L C : 0 1 :118(381) [0615] lives they are not worthy to offer him a **cup** of water?
L C : 0 5 :003(447) [0753] *same way also he took the **cup**, after supper, gave thanks,*
L C : 0 5 :003(447) [0753] *it to them, saying, 'This **cup** is the new testament in my*
E P : 0 7 :009(483) [0811] as it is written, "the **cup** of blessing which we bless"
E P : 0 7 :024(484) [0815] and the withholding of the **cup** from them, contrary to
S D : 0 7 :044(577) [0987] you," and concerning the **cup** or the wine, "This is my
S D : 0 7 :053(579) [0991] of Luke and Paul, "This **cup** is the new covenant in my
S D : 0 7 :053(579) [0991] with your mouth from the **cup**) is my blood of the new
S D : 0 7 :054(579) [0991] us in I Cor. 10:16 ("The **cup** of blessing which we bless, is
S D : 0 7 :054(579) [0991] clearly that not only the **cup** which Christ blessed in the
S D : 0 7 :054(579) [0991] this bread and drink the **cup** truly receive and partake of
S D : 0 7 :060(580) [0993] the bread or drinks the **cup** of the Lord in an unworthy
S D : 0 7 :075(583) [0999] words over the bread and **cup** and distribute the blessed
S D : 0 7 :075(583) [0999] the blessed bread and **cup**, Christ himself is still active
S D : 0 7 :082(584) [1001] drink, as Paul says, "The **cup** of blessing which we bless,"

Curb (2), Curbs (1)
A L : 2 6 :033(069) [0075] ought so to control and **curb** himself with bodily
S 2 : 0 2 :006(293) [0463] no other reason than to **curb** such abuses, even if it
S C : 0 3 :011(347) [0547] Answer: When God **curbs** and destroys every evil counsel

Curdle (1)
S D : 0 1 :035(514) [0869] not pour me out like milk and **curdle** me like cheese?

Cure (3)
A P : 0 2 :007(101) [0107] the serpent's breath, and whether medicine can **cure** it.
L C : 0 1 :275(402) [0659] of the physician who, to **cure** a patient, is sometimes
S D : 0 7 :087(585) [1003] to consecrate bells, or to **cure** leprosy, or is otherwise

Curia (1)
L C : 0 2 :048(416) [0691] In that language the word is *kyria*, and in Latin ***curia***.

Curiosity (1), Curious (1)
A G : 2 7 :048(078) [0081] are dazzled with this **curious** angelic spirituality and sham
L C : 0 1 :208(393) [0639] no matter for jest or idle **curiosity**, but it is a glorious

Curius (1)
A P : 2 3 :002(239) [0363] fathers "who look like **Curius** and live like Bacchantes."

Current (2)
P R : P R :026(014) [0025] If the **current** controversies about our Christian religion
A P : 2 4 :014(251) [0389] already described the **current** understanding of sacrifice

Curse (11), Cursed (3), Curses (3), Cursing (5)
A P : 0 4 :179(131) [0171] redeemed us from the **curse** of the law, being made a
A P : 0 4 :179(131) [0171] us from the curse of the law, being made a **curse** for us."
A P : 0 4 :269(147) [0197] **Cursed** be our opponents, those Pharisees, who interpret
S 3 : 0 6 :004(311) [0493] do we condemn and **curse** in God's name those who not
T R : 0 0 :055(329) [0521] by horrible oaths and **curses** to defend his tyranny and
S C : 0 1 :004(342) [0539] not use his name to **curse**, swear, practice magic, lie, or
S C : 0 5 :022(350) [0553] angry, caused him to **curse**, neglected to do my duty, and
S C : 0 5 :023(350) [0553] I have **cursed**.
S C : 0 5 :024(350) [0555] For example, "In particular I confess that I once **cursed**.
L C : 0 1 :062(373) [0597] that is not so, or to **curse**, swear, conjure, and, in short, to
L C : 0 1 :184(390) [0633] Then follow **cursing** and blows, and eventually calamity
L C : 0 1 :186(390) [0633] nevertheless call down **curses** and imprecations upon
L C : 0 1 :326(409) [0675] take his name in vain by **cursing**, lying, deceiving, and
L C : 0 3 :042(425) [0709] for their shame, by swearing, **cursing**, conjuring, etc.
L C : 0 3 :045(426) [0709] in vain by swearing, **cursing**, deceiving, etc., but used
L C : 0 3 :103(434) [0727] perfidy, vengeance, **cursing**, reviling, slander, arrogance,
E P : 0 6 :002(480) [0805] through Christ from the **curse** and coercion of the law,
S D : 0 5 :010(560) [0955] of us, or how severely it **curses** and condemns us because
S D : 0 5 :020(561) [0959] assumed and bore the **curse** of the law and expiated and
S D : 0 6 :004(564) [0963] and liberated from the **curse** of the law, they should daily
S D : 0 6 :005(564) [0963] the law cannot impose its **curse** upon those who through
S D : 0 6 :023(567) [0969] have been freed from the **curse** and condemnation of the

Cusanus (2)
A G : 2 2 :008(050) [0061] although Cardinal **Cusanus** mentions when the use was
A L : 2 2 :004(050) [0061] although Cardinal **Cusanus** mentions when the change

Custodian (2), Custody (1)
P R : P R :018(009) [0015] and that remained in the **custody** of the Holy Empire, and
A P : 0 4 :022(110) [0127] Gal. 3:24, "The law is a **custodian**," and I Tim. 1:9, "The
S D : 0 5 :024(563) [0961] since "the law was our **custodian** until Christ came, that

Custom (24), Customarily (1), Customary (13), Customs (11)
A G : 0 0 :000(049) [0059] be regarded as above all **custom**) to allow such changes.
A G : 2 2 :008(050) [0061] or through whom this **custom** of receiving only one kind
A G : 2 2 :010(050) [0061] It is evident that such a **custom**, introduced contrary to
A G : 2 2 :012(051) [0061] of Christ, the **customary** carrying about of the sacrament
A G : 2 3 :010(052) [0061] the Fathers that it was **customary** for priests and deacons
A G : 2 5 :001(061) [0069] The **custom** has been retained among us of not
A G : 2 6 :022(067) [0073] for not observing the **customary** traditions, and he adds,
A G : 2 6 :043(070) [0075] was not necessary to maintain uniformity in such **customs**
A G : 2 7 :039(077) [0081] from this that the **customary** vows were an improper and
A G : 2 8 :072(093) [0093] contrary to the **custom** of the universal Christian church.
A L : 2 2 :008(050) [0061] It is only a **custom** of quite recent times that holds
A L : 2 2 :009(050) [0061] But it is evident that a **custom** introduced contrary to the
A L : 2 2 :010(050) [0061] This **custom** has been adopted not only in defiance of the
A L : 2 3 :018(054) [0063] is in force, although the **custom** of the church is well
A L : 2 4 :002(056) [0065] Almost all the **customary** ceremonies are also retained,
A L : 2 4 :035(060) [0067] Nor is this **custom** new in the church, for before the time
A L : 2 4 :040(061) [0069] especially since the **customary** public ceremonies are for
A L : 2 5 :001(061) [0069] churches, for it is not **customary** to administer the body
A L : 2 6 :022(067) [0073] for not observing the **customary** tradition, a tradition
A L : 2 6 :043(070) [0075] by others that such **customs** need not be alike
A L : 2 7 :039(077) [0081] that the vows thus **customarily** taken were wicked
A L : 2 8 :072(093) [0093] introduced contrary to the **custom** of the church catholic.
A P : 0 7 :036(175) [0241] Rather, they are **customs** that do not pertain to the heart
A P : 0 7 :040(176) [0241] certain Old Testament **customs**, which the apostles
A P : 0 7 :042(176) [0241] held tenaciously to the **custom** of using the Jewish time.
A P : 0 7 :043(177) [0243] had been converted from Judaism but kept their **customs**.
A P : 1 2 :115(199) [0285] with a remnant of the **custom** in prescribing certain
A P : 1 2 :175(210) [0307] Since the **custom** itself has now become obsolete, and
A P : 1 5 :030(219) [0323] cannot use their **customary** evasion and say that Paul is
A P : 1 5 :035(220) [0325] God in observing secular **customs**, if soldiers wear one
A P : 1 5 :041(220) [0325] the youth publicly, a **custom** that produces very good
A P : 1 5 :044(221) [0327] pious ceremonies, and the good **customs** of the church.
A P : 1 5 :051(222) [0329] harmony those ancient **customs** should be kept which can
A P : 2 1 :013(230) [0345] church, we reply that this is a novel **custom** in the church.
A P : 2 2 :007(237) [0359] of the church it was **customary** in some places to
A P : 2 2 :008(237) [0359] it means our present **custom** of giving the laity only a
A P : 2 3 :053(246) [0377] Since it has been **customary** to change other laws if the
A P : 2 4 :004(250) [0385] This has always been the **custom** in the churches.
A P : 2 4 :023(253) [0391] readily if we look at the **customs** which the heathen
A P : 2 7 :014(271) [0425] of sins, opposed as they are to the **customs** of public life?
A P : 2 7 :062(280) [0441] Then, too, the **custom** had an immediate purpose: since
S 2 : 0 4 :002(298) [0471] "brother," as was then **customary**, but must address him
T R : 0 0 :015(322) [0509] Cyprian calls this **custom** a divine tradition and an
T R : 0 0 :020(323) [0509] elects him and the **custom** gradually prevailed that the
T R : 0 0 :070(332) [0525] The most common **custom** of the church also bears
L C : 0 1 :073(374) [0601] continued among us the **custom** of saying grace and
L C : 0 1 :074(374) [0601] same source came the **custom** of children who cross
L C : 0 1 :082(376) [0603] with particular **customs**, persons, times, and places, from
S D : R N :005(504) [0853] it was traditional and **customary** for later synods and

Cut (6), Cuts (1), Cutting (2)
A P : 1 2 :168(209) [0305] "True satisfaction means **cutting** off the causes of sin,
A P : 1 5 :034(220) [0325] knot, he solved it for good by **cutting** it with his sword.
A P : 2 4 :016(252) [0389] making the distinctions to **cut** the members at the joint,
L C : 0 1 :138(384) [0621] "May his posterity be **cut** off: and may their name be cut
L C : 0 1 :138(384) [0621] cut off: and may their name be **cut** off in one generation."
L C : 0 3 :063(428) [0715] hinder us, put us to flight, **cut** us down, and bring us once
E P : 1 0 :006(493) [0829] persecution, when a clear-**cut** confession of faith is
S D : 0 3 :029(544) [0925] this reason we summarily **cut** off every reference to the
S D : 1 1 :064(626) [1083] commands silence and **cuts** off further discussion with the

Cutler (2)
E P : 1 2 :018(499) [0841] good conscience be an innkeeper, a merchant, or a **cutler**.
S D : 1 2 :023(634) [1099] good conscience be an innkeeper, a merchant, or a **cutler**.

Cyprian (16)
A G : 2 2 :005(050) [0061] In several places **Cyprian** mentions that the cup was given
A G : 2 3 :025(055) [0065] St. **Cyprian** therefore offered the counsel that women who
A L : 2 2 :005(050) [0061] **Cyprian** in several places testifies that the blood was given
A L : 2 3 :025(055) [0065] Accordingly **Cyprian** advised that women who did not
A P : 0 4 :322(157) [0209] **Cyprian** says in his commentary on the Lord's Prayer:
A P : 2 1 :002(229) [0343] **Cyprian** asked Cornelius, while he was still alive, to pray
A P : 2 1 :036(234) [0353] for denying Christ; **Cyprian** was forgiven for having been
A P : 2 2 :004(236) [0359] in the Latin church, as **Cyprian** and Jerome attest.
A P : 2 4 :076(263) [0411] beautiful statement of **Cyprian** about the godly
S 2 : 0 4 :001(298) [0471] as the ancient councils and the time of **Cyprian** prove.
T R : 0 0 :014(322) [0507] in the Latin churches, as **Cyprian** and Augustine testify.
T R : 0 0 :014(322) [0507] For **Cyprian** states in his fourth letter to Cornelius:
T R : 0 0 :015(322) [0509] **Cyprian** calls this custom a divine tradition and an
T R : 0 0 :027(324) [0511] as Origen, Ambrose, **Cyprian**, Hilary, and Bede) interpret
E P : 0 7 :015(483) [0813] such as Chrysostom, **Cyprian**, Leo I, Gregory, Ambrose,
S D : 0 7 :037(575) [0985] teachers, like Justin, **Cyprian**, Augustine, Leo, Gelasius,

Cyril (4)
A P : 1 0 :003(179) [0247] exposition of John 15 in **Cyril** which teaches that Christ is
S D : 0 1 :054(518) [0877] This dichotomy was also used by **Cyril** and Basil.
S D : 0 7 :011(571) [0975] and with a quotation from **Cyril** as follows: "Article X has
S D : 0 7 :011(571) [0975] **Cyril** is quoted to the effect that Christ dwells bodily in

Daggers (1)
L C : 0 5 :082(456) [0773] you could see how many **daggers**, spears, and arrows are

Daily (121)

AG : 2 6 :002(064) [0071] and the like were invented **daily**, and were ardently and
AG : 2 7 :001(071) [0077] and how many of the **daily** observances in them were
AL : 2 4 :021(058) [0067] oblation should be made for **daily** sins, mortal and venial.
AL : 2 4 :036(060) [0067] says that the priest stands **daily** at the altar, inviting some
AL : 2 6 :002(064) [0071] days, and new fasts were **daily** instituted, and the learned
AP : 0 4 :283(150) [0201] or in our own time the **daily** sprinkling with water, the
AP : 0 4 :322(157) [0209] and taught that he sins **daily**, since he is commanded to
AP : 0 4 :322(157) [0209] **daily**, since he is commanded to pray **daily** for his sins."
AP : 2 3 :056(247) [0379] **Daily** the pontiffs dispense and change other good laws;
AP : 2 4 :006(250) [0385] The monasteries have public, though **daily**, Mass.
AP : 2 4 :007(250) [0385] with a single common **daily** Mass, reasons of piety or of
AP : 2 4 :008(250) [0385] Asia Minor there were no **daily** Masses but Communion
AP : 2 4 :035(256) [0397] They also refer to the **daily** sacrifice: as there was a daily
AP : 2 4 :035(256) [0397] sacrifice: as there was a **daily** sacrifice in the Old
AP : 2 4 :035(256) [0397] the Mass ought to be the **daily** sacrifice of the New
AP : 2 4 :035(256) [0397] Mass to be understood as a **daily** sacrifice, provided this
AP : 2 4 :035(256) [0397] together, these are the **daily** sacrifice of the New
AP : 2 4 :036(257) [0397] lists three parts of this **daily** sacrifice, the burning of the
AP : 2 4 :038(257) [0399] therefore, it is not the **daily** sacrifice by itself; the
AP : 2 4 :038(257) [0399] is the real **daily** sacrifice, the proclamation of the faith
AP : 2 4 :039(257) [0399] spiritual worship and the **daily** sacrifice of the heart, for
AP : 2 4 :040(257) [0399] that the analogy of the **daily** sacrifice does not refute but
AP : 2 4 :041(257) [0399] of the charge that we do away with the **daily** sacrifice.
AP : 2 4 :049(258) [0401] of the sacrament were the **daily** sacrifice, we could lay
AP : 2 4 :049(258) [0401] use of the sacraments, we still have the **daily** sacrifice.
AP : 2 4 :057(260) [0405] priests and sacrificers who **daily** peddle their wares in the
AP : 2 4 :062(260) [0405] for the original debt, is **daily** offered on the altar for daily
AP : 2 4 :062(260) [0405] offered on the altar for **daily** offenses so that in this the
AP : 2 4 :091(266) [0415] This is the abolition of the **daily** sacrifice in the church.
S3 : 0 3 :040(309) [0489] This gift **daily** cleanses and expels the sins that remain
S3 : 0 3 :043(310) [0491] and feel original sin and **daily** repent and strive against it,
SC : 0 2 :002(345) [0543] that he provides me **daily** and abundantly with all the
SC : 0 2 :006(345) [0545] this Christian church he **daily** and abundantly forgives all
SC : 0 3 :012(347) [0547] *"Give us this day our **daily** bread."*
SC : 0 3 :013(347) [0547] To be sure, God provides **daily** bread, even to the
SC : 0 3 :013(347) [0547] enable us to receive our **daily** bread with thanksgiving.
SC : 0 3 :014(347) [0547] What is meant by **daily** bread?
SC : 0 3 :016(347) [0549] Although we sin **daily** and deserve nothing but
SC : 0 4 :012(349) [0551] should be drowned by **daily** sorrow and repentance and
SC : 0 4 :012(349) [0551] man should come forth **daily** and rise up, cleansed and
LC : PR :008(359) [0569] and study the Catechism **daily**, yet I cannot master it as I
LC : PR :009(359) [0569] profitable and fruitful **daily** to read it and make it the
LC : PR :013(360) [0571] do we need God's Word **daily** as we need our daily bread;
LC : PR :013(360) [0571] Word daily as we need our **daily** bread; we also must use
LC : PR :013(360) [0571] bread; we also must use it **daily** against the daily,
LC : PR :013(360) [0571] use it daily against the **daily**, incessant attacks and
LC : PR :014(360) [0571] us to read the Catechism **daily**, there is God's command.
LC : PR :016(361) [0571] will not or cannot read and study the Catechism **daily**.
LC : PR :016(361) [0573] is not ashamed to teach it **daily**, for he knows of nothing
LC : PR :019(361) [0573] in the Catechism **daily**, and constantly put it into
LC : SP :005(362) [0575] even now we find them **daily** — yet they come to Baptism
LC : SP :014(363) [0577] Give us this day our **daily** bread; and forgive us our
LC : SP :016(363) [0577] the habit of reciting them **daily** when they rise in the
LC : SP :025(364) [0579] will be led into the Scriptures so they make progress **daily**
LC : 0 1 :035(369) [0589] amply shows and as **daily** experience can still teach us.
LC : 0 1 :085(376) [0605] there should be worship **daily**; however, since this is more
LC : 0 1 :089(377) [0605] that is, occupy ourselves **daily** with God's Word and carry
LC : 0 1 :090(377) [0607] in our day who stand **daily** in the churches, singing and
LC : 0 1 :100(378) [0609] everything, still you are **daily** under the dominion of the
LC : 0 1 :137(384) [0619] many criminals who must **daily** be hanged, beheaded, or
LC : 0 1 :145(385) [0623] to yourself, "If I do my **daily** housework faithfully, that is
LC : 0 1 :173(388) [0629] make them rich without our help, as indeed he does **daily**.
LC : 0 1 :230(396) [0645] with lords and princes and **daily** plunder not only a city
LC : 0 1 :240(397) [0649] **Daily** the poor are defrauded.
LC : 0 1 :277(402) [0659] you can learn from the **daily** management of the
LC : 0 1 :298(405) [0665] ones are being devised **daily**) under the guise of justice.
LC : 0 1 :332(410) [0677] is to make them his **daily** habit in all circumstances, in all
LC : 0 2 :017(412) [0681] before our eyes, but also **daily** guards and defends us
LC : 0 2 :019(412) [0681] and on earth besides, is **daily** given and sustained by
LC : 0 2 :022(413) [0683] For we sin **daily** with eyes and ears, hands, body and
LC : 0 2 :023(413) [0683] For this reason we ought **daily** to study this article and
LC : 0 2 :053(417) [0693] sanctification, causing it **daily** to grow and become strong
LC : 0 2 :055(418) [0693] is so ordered that we may **daily** obtain full forgiveness of
LC : 0 2 :057(418) [0693] has begun and is growing **daily**, we await the time when
LC : 0 2 :058(418) [0693] in us through the Word, **daily** granting forgiveness until
LC : 0 2 :059(418) [0693] Holy Spirit, to begin and **daily** to increase holiness on
LC : 0 2 :062(419) [0695] we believe in him who **daily** brings us into this
LC : 0 3 :028(424) [0705] from his youth up to pray **daily** for all his needs,
LC : 0 3 :029(424) [0705] and coldly that they become **daily** more inept at praying.
LC : 0 3 :052(427) [0711] remain faithful and grow **daily** in it and in order that it
LC : 0 3 :053(427) [0713] and that it may come by **daily** growth here and in eternal
LC : 0 3 :071(430) [0717] *"Give us this day our **daily** bread."*
LC : 0 3 :072(430) [0719] When you pray for "**daily** bread" you pray for everything
LC : 0 3 :072(430) [0719] order to have and enjoy **daily** bread and, on the contrary,
LC : 0 3 :072(430) [0719] and provide for us our **daily** bread and all kinds of
LC : 0 3 :073(430) [0719] in this world; only for its sake do we need **daily** bread.
LC : 0 3 :073(430) [0719] peace and concord in our **daily** business and in
LC : 0 3 :074(430) [0719] does God provide us our **daily** bread and all the comforts
LC : 0 3 :074(430) [0719] and war prevail, there our **daily** bread is taken away, or
LC : 0 3 :075(430) [0719] we could not have the steady blessing of **daily** bread.
LC : 0 3 :082(431) [0721] our needs and faithfully provides for our **daily** existence.
LC : 0 3 :084(431) [0721] yes, on account of **daily** exploitation and usury in public
LC : 0 3 :084(432) [0723] oppress the poor and deprive them of their **daily** bread!
LC : 0 3 :086(432) [0723] We still stumble **daily** and transgress because we live in
LC : 0 3 :089(432) [0723] For the flesh in which we **daily** live is of such a nature
LC : 0 3 :089(432) [0723] and devices, so that we sin **daily** in word and deed, in acts
LC : 0 3 :092(432) [0725] sins and punish us as we **daily** deserve, but to deal
LC : 0 3 :102(434) [0727] goes to work and lures us **daily** into unchastity, laziness,
LC : 0 3 :113(435) [0729] kingdom and will, our **daily** bread, a good and cheerful
LC : 0 4 :065(445) [0749] life is nothing else than a **daily** Baptism, once begun and
LC : 0 4 :067(445) [0749] this corruption must **daily** decrease so that the longer we
LC : 0 4 :071(445) [0749] Christians, the old man **daily** decreases until he is finally
LC : 0 4 :071(445) [0751] means to plunge into Baptism and **daily** come forth again.
LC : 0 4 :083(446) [0751] and takes away sin and **daily** strengthens the new man,
LC : 0 4 :084(446) [0753] regard his Baptism as the **daily** garment which he is to
LC : 0 5 :024(449) [0759] Supper is given as a **daily** food and sustenance so that
LC : 0 5 :039(451) [0761] great a treasure, which is **daily** administered and
LC : 0 5 :044(451) [0763] but there must also be **daily** exhortation, so on this
LC : 0 6 :013(458) [0000] Besides this public, **daily**, and necessary confession, there
EP : 0 2 :017(472) [0791] after conversion, in the **daily** exercise of repentance, the
SD : 0 2 :016(523) [0887] Spirit and grace, through **daily** exercise in reading his
SD : 0 2 :016(523) [0887] heavenly gifts in us and strengthen us **daily** until our end.
SD : 0 2 :034(528) [0895] This gift purifies us and **daily** sweeps out the remaining
SD : 0 2 :035(528) [0895] Spirit, who purifies and **daily** makes man more pious and
SD : 0 2 :037(528) [0895] so that we grow **daily** and become strong in faith and in
SD : 0 2 :038(528) [0895] and effects in us a **daily** increase in faith and good works.
SD : 0 2 :088(538) [0915] will is not idle in the **daily** exercise of repentance but
SD : 0 6 :004(564) [0963] of the law, they should **daily** exercise themselves in the
SD : 0 6 :009(565) [0965] in this life not only the **daily** teaching and admonition,
SD : 0 7 :077(583) [0999] wine the blood that are **daily** distributed through our
SD : 1 1 :036(622) [1075] foundation, which **daily** reminds and admonishes us to

Dainty (1)

LC : PR :008(359) [0569] These **dainty**, fastidious fellows would like quickly, with

Damage (14), Damaging (1)

AP : 1 1 :007(181) [0251] has not done as much **damage** as what the summists
LC : 0 1 :100(379) [0609] devil breaks in and does his **damage** before we realize it.
LC : 0 1 :225(395) [0643] domestic duty and does **damage** or permits damage to
LC : 0 1 :225(395) [0643] does damage or permits **damage** to happen when it could
LC : 0 1 :236(397) [0647] and for every penny's **damage** you have done you will
LC : 0 1 :250(399) [0651] imaginable, whether by **damaging**, withholding, or
LC : 0 3 :029(424) [0705] he is well aware what **damage** and harm he suffers when
EP : 0 1 :009(467) [0781] This **damage** is so unspeakable that it may not be
EP : 0 1 :012(467) [0783] that the cited defect and **damage** is not truly sin on
SD : 0 1 :008(510) [0861] and understand the true nature of this inherited **damage**.
SD : 0 1 :009(510) [0861] 1. That this inherited **damage** is the reason why all of us,
SD : 0 1 :014(511) [0863] 5. This inherited **damage** is so great and terrible that in
SD : 0 1 :019(511) [0865] lack and **damage** allegedly are not really and truly such a
SD : 0 1 :056(518) [0877] itself, but an accidental defect and **damage** in the nature.
SD : 0 1 :062(519) [0879] ultimately the worst **damage** is that we shall not only

Damascene (1)

SD : 0 8 :022(595) [1023] in Theodoret; John **Damascene**, Book III, chap. 19).

Dame (1)

SD : 0 8 :041(599) [1029] states: "If the old witch, **Dame** Reason, the grandmother

Damn (4), Damnable (3), Damnation (27), Damned (10), Damning (1), Damns (1)

AL : 0 2 :002(029) [0043] sin, which even now **damns** and brings eternal death on
AP : 2 0 :002(227) [0339] than with those **damnable** writers of the Confutation who
AP : 2 7 :069(281) [0443] ideas as this are plain, **damnable** pharisaism: that these
S1 : PR :003(289) [0455] lost and all souls **damned** rather than suffer himself and
S2 : 0 2 :005(293) [0463] sin, that no one will be **damned** for not observing it, and
S2 : 0 4 :014(301) [0475] to God, and to **damn**, slay, and plague all Christians who
S2 : 0 4 :016(301) [0477] us a hearing but only to **damn**, murder, and drive us to
SC : PR :019(340) [0537] that they are guilty of **damnable** sin if they do not do so,
LC : 0 1 :198(392) [0637] and filth, and it merits nothing but wrath and **damnation**.
LC : 0 2 :028(414) [0685] doomed to eternal **damnation**, as we had deserved.
LC : 0 2 :066(419) [0697] in eternal wrath and **damnation**, for they do not have the
LC : 0 5 :069(454) [0769] unchristian lives receive it to their harm and **damnation**.
EP : 0 4 :018(477) [0801] concerning faith can **damn** people as much as a papistic
EP : 0 9 :004(492) [0827] devil, and of the eternal **damnation** of the hellish jaws.
EP : 1 1 :009(495) [0833] elected me to salvation I cannot be **damned**, do as I will."
EP : 1 1 :019(497) [0837] certain people to **damnation** so that they cannot be
SD : 0 1 :006(509) [0861] wrath," of death, and of **damnation** unless we are
SD : 0 1 :013(511) [0863] sin is death, eternal **damnation**, together with other
SD : 0 1 :019(511) [0865] a child of wrath and of **damnation** and is in the kingdom
SD : 0 2 :021(525) [0889] dangers and finally into eternal death and **damnation**.
SD : 0 2 :049(530) [0901] that anyone should be **damned** but that all men should
SD : 0 3 :009(540) [0919] verdict of well deserved **damnation**, and is adopted as a
SD : 0 3 :058(550) [0937] reckoned to us for our **damnation** but is forgiven and
SD : 0 5 :023(562) [0959] into death and eternal **damnation**, but also revived their
SD : 0 6 :007(565) [0965] to believers for **damnation**, and although the Holy Spirit
SD : 0 7 :061(581) [0995] is not only salutary but actually pernicious and **damning**.
SD : 0 7 :063(581) [0995] it orally, too, but to their judgment and **damnation**.
SD : 0 8 :021(595) [1023] this the devil's mask and **damned** it to the depths of hell.
SD : 0 8 :025(596) [1023] sin, death, the devil, hell, and eternal **damnation**.
SD : 1 1 :009(618) [1065] and how many are to be **damned**, or that he merely held a
SD : 1 1 :009(618) [1065] saved, that one shall be **damned**, this one shall persevere,
SD : 1 1 :060(626) [1083] of God's wrath and **damnation**, God owes us neither his
SD : 1 1 :078(629) [1089] receive the greater **damnation** is not that God did not
SD : 1 1 :079(629) [1089] of wrath fitted for **damnation** in order to make known
SD : 1 1 :080(629) [1089] not God, are the cause of their being fitted for **damnation**.
SD : 1 1 :081(629) [1089] and fits man for **damnation** emanates from the devil and
SD : 1 1 :081(629) [1089] not want any man to be **damned**, how could he prepare
SD : 1 1 :081(629) [1089] to be damned, how could he prepare man for **damnation**?
SD : 1 1 :081(629) [1089] sin, nor is he the cause of the punishment, the **damnation**.
SD : 1 1 :081(629) [1089] only cause of man's **damnation** is sin, for the "wages of
SD : 1 1 :081(629) [1089] death of a sinner and has no pleasure in his **damnation**.
SD : 1 1 :082(630) [1091] does not say this of the **damned**, whom God has not
SD : 1 1 :082(630) [1091] who have prepared themselves to be vessels of **damnation**.
SD : 1 1 :083(630) [1091] blind, and for ever **damn** them if they continue therein.
SD : 1 1 :084(630) [1091] God's good pleasure that he should be **damned** and lost.
SD : 1 1 :086(631) [1091] ordained him to eternal **damnation** so that he could not

Dance (1)

LC : 0 1 :145(385) [0623] a servant girl would **dance** for joy and praise and thank

Danger (23), Dangerous (20), Dangerously (1), Dangers (11)

PR : PR :022(012) [0021] and ignorantly of the **danger** to their souls and to warn
PR : PR :026(014) [0025] before they become **dangerously** widespread in order that
AG : 2 7 :058(080) [0083] other hand, that is a **dangerous** state of life which does
AL : 2 6 :012(065) [0071] traditions brought great **dangers** to consciences, for it was
AP : PR :016(099) [0101] are we indifferent to our **danger**; its extent is evident from

Continued ▶

AP : PR :016(099) [0103] endure difficulties and **dangers** for the glory of Christ and
AP : PR :017(099) [0103] under all sorts of **dangerous** opinions in the writings of
AP : 04 :185(132) [0173] Ambiguous and **dangerous** issues produce many and
AP : 04 :190(133) [0175] The **dangers**, labors, and sermons of the apostle Paul,
AP : 04 :321(157) [0209] teach on this question is full of errors and **dangers**.
AP : 04 :350(160) [0217] well as temptations and **dangers**, so that we become ever
AP : 07 :009(169) [0229] We see the infinite **dangers** that threaten the church with
AP : 12 :092(196) [0279] For there is obvious **danger** in these statements, requiring
AP : 12 :126(201) [0289] predicted there would be the greatest **danger** for religion.
AP : 15 :028(219) [0323] time he deplores the **danger** to consciences that comes
AP : 16 :004(223) [0331] had broadcast many **dangerous** ideas through the church.
AP : 16 :004(223) [0331] spiritual kingdom; they are also **dangerous** to the state.
AP : 16 :011(224) [0333] Such praise is **dangerous**, especially because it is so out of
AP : 20 :009(227) [0341] weighty that we shrink from no **danger** on account of it.
AP : 21 :007(230) [0345] even if it were not **dangerous**, is certainly unnecessary.
AP : 21 :033(233) [0351] great moderation, the precedent still would be **dangerous**.
AP : 21 :035(234) [0353] strong of soul because they have to undergo great **danger**.
AP : 21 :036(234) [0353] underwent troubles and **dangers**, helped kings in time of
AP : 21 :036(234) [0353] kings in time of great **danger**, taught the Gospel, battled
AP : 22 :014(238) [0361] They also refer to the **danger** of spilling and similar
AP : 23 :005(240) [0365] imagine that this is in **danger** and they are trying to
AP : 23 :051(246) [0377] were not unjust, it is **dangerous** to public and private
AP : 23 :052(246) [0377] those whom they saw in **danger**, but none of the popes
AP : 23 :060(247) [0381] superstitious and full of **danger**; finally, the whole thing is
AP : 27 :047(277) [0437] It is highly **dangerous** to heap such extravagant praises
AP : 27 :052(278) [0437] strange that with such **dangers** and scandals going on
AP : 27 :056(278) [0439] to all this, there is the **danger** that those who belong to
AP : 28 :008(282) [0445] of a yoke, showing how **dangerous** this is and enlarging
S2 : 02 :003(293) [0463] and so it can be omitted without sin and **danger**.
S2 : 02 :005(293) [0463] if they hear that it is a **dangerous** thing which was
S2 : 02 :006(293) [0463] useless, and **dangerous** and when we can obtain what is
S2 : 02 :018(296) [0467] way and may omit pilgrimages without sin and **danger**.
S2 : 03 :002(298) [0471] Moreover, it causes **dangerous** and needless effort, and
SC : PR :017(340) [0537] obligations, benefits, **dangers**, advantages, and
SC : PR :024(341) [0539] and loss, the blessing and **danger** connected with this
SC : PR :027(341) [0539] burdens and labors, **dangers** and temptations, with little
SC : 02 :002(345) [0543] life, protects me from all **danger**, and preserves me from
SC : 07 :002(352) [0557] protected me through the night from all harm and **danger**.
LC : PR :014(360) [0571] He knows our **danger** and need.
LC : 01 :203(392) [0639] whenever he is in **danger** or need, and on the contrary to
LC : 01 :295(404) [0665] So there was a **danger** among them that if anyone took a
LC : 02 :017(412) [0681] misfortune, warding off all sorts of **danger** and disaster.
LC : 02 :023(413) [0683] we escape distress or **danger**, we should recognize that
EP : 06 :008(481) [0807] we condemn as **dangerous** and subversive of Christian
EP : 11 :009(495) [0833] to despair and waken **dangerous** thoughts in their hearts.
SD : PR :007(502) [0849] This caused serious and **dangerous** schisms in the true
SD : 02 :021(525) [0889] runs into a thousand **dangers** and finally into eternal
SD : 04 :023(555) [0945] occasion for doubt, are **dangerous** in many ways, confirm
SD : 05 :027(563) [0961] It is therefore **dangerous** and wrong to make of the
SD : 11 :010(618) [1065] and formulate strange, **dangerous**, and pernicious

Daniel (26)
AP : 04 :261(145) [0195] Thus in **Daniel**'s sermon (4:24) faith is required.
AP : 04 :261(145) [0195] **Daniel** did not only mean to say that the king should give
AP : 04 :261(145) [0195] **Daniel** proclaimed many things to the king about the one
AP : 04 :261(145) [0195] **Daniel**'s sermon contains two parts.
AP : 04 :261(145) [0195] In the other part **Daniel** promises the king forgiveness of
AP : 04 :261(145) [0195] evangelical voice which **Daniel** surely wanted to be
AP : 04 :262(145) [0195] **Daniel** knew that the forgiveness of sins in the Christ was
AP : 04 :262(145) [0195] In his own language **Daniel**'s words speak even more
AP : 04 :266(146) [0197] If **Daniel** had said, "Redeem your sins by penitence," our
AP : 04 :266(146) [0197] of grace and faith, while **Daniel** most emphatically wants
AP : 04 :267(146) [0197] we reply to the words of **Daniel**: Since he is preaching
AP : 04 :267(146) [0197] Secondly, because **Daniel** clearly sets forth a promise, he
AP : 04 :267(146) [0197] with penitence, therefore, **Daniel** does not say that by
AP : 04 :267(147) [0197] **Daniel** is not speaking about remission of punishment
AP : 04 :268(147) [0197] opponents understand **Daniel** as referring only to
AP : 04 :331(158) [0211] Therefore **Daniel** prays (9:18, 19), "For we do not present
AP : 04 :331(158) [0211] So **Daniel** teaches us to take hold of mercy when we pray,
AP : 04 :337(159) [0215] from the example of **Daniel** referred to above, "For we do
AP : 15 :019(217) [0319] In his eleventh chapter **Daniel** says that the invention of
AP : 16 :009(224) [0333] Abraham, David, and **Daniel** were no less perfect than
AP : 23 :025(243) [0371] and with good reason: **Daniel** says that it is characteristic
AP : 24 :045(258) [0399] **Daniel** describes a vastly different desolation, ignorance
AP : 24 :047(258) [0401] This is the desolation that **Daniel** describes.
AP : 24 :051(259) [0403] with those whom **Daniel** (11:38) describes as worshiping
AP : 27 :003(269) [0419] in the commentaries he left on certain passages in **Daniel**.
EP : 11 :003(494) [0833] what will be in the latter days" (**Daniel** 2:28).

Dare (33), Dared (3), Dares (3)
AP : 02 :042(105) [0115] be impossible, no one has **dared** to say that such attitudes
AP : 04 :176(131) [0171] Therefore we **dare** not believe that we are accounted
AP : 04 :377(165) [0223] the righteousness of faith **dare** not be neglected in the
AP : 12 :074(193) [0273] Do they still **dare** to deny that we obtain the forgiveness
AP : 12 :122(200) [0287] the Confutation that they **dared** to thrust upon his
AP : 14 :003(214) [0315] are clear and we **dare** not approve the cruelty of those
AP : 15 :012(216) [0317] to us for Christ's sake, we **dare** not add the condition that
AP : 20 :004(227) [0339] all sense of shame if they **dare** to smuggle such a notion
AP : 21 :029(233) [0351] We maintain that we **dare** not trust in the transfer of the
AP : 22 :017(238) [0361] Nor **dare** we assume that the church immediately
AP : 23 :063(248) [0381] They **dare** to claim divine revelation for the law of
AP : 27 :036(275) [0433] life; but since they did not **dare** to deny it the claim of
S1 : PR :004(289) [0455] of our party — that they **dare** to cite my writings and
S2 : 04 :002(298) [0471] But now no bishop **dares** to call the pope "brother," as
LC : 01 :225(395) [0645] defiant and insolent and **dare** anyone to call him a thief!
LC : 01 :226(395) [0645] No one even **dares** to give them a hard look or accuse
LC : 01 :298(405) [0665] We brazenly **dare** to boast of it, and insist that it should
LC : 01 :315(408) [0671] those desperate saints to **dare** to find a higher and better
LC : 01 :327(409) [0675] For you **dare** not respect or fear father or mother
LC : 03 :055(427) [0713] for any human heart to **dare** to desire if God himself had
LC : 03 :092(432) [0725] cannot achieve such confidence, it will never **dare** to pray.
LC : 03 :121(436) [0731] in such a way that they **dare** not whole-heartedly add
LC : 04 :016(438) [0735] But how **dare** you tamper thus with God's ordinance and
LC : 04 :055(443) [0747] How **dare** we think that God's Word and ordinance
LC : 05 :013(448) [0755] our stand and see who **dares** to instruct Christ and alter
LC : 05 :032(450) [0761] value just as little as they **dare** say that the whole Gospel
LC : 06 :018(459) [0000] You **dare** not come and say how good or how wicked you
LC : 06 :020(459) [0000] Further, no one **dare** oppress you with requirements.
EP : 10 :006(493) [0829] is demanded of us, we **dare** not yield to the enemies in
SD : PR :006(502) [0849] Confession, even **dared** to give a false interpretation to
SD : RN :009(505) [0855] no human being's writings **dare** be put on a par with it,
SD : 02 :069(534) [0907] them and lose him, they **dare** not be baptized again,
SD : 03 :032(545) [0927] But these two **dare** not be confused with one another or
SD : 03 :036(545) [0927] works should, must, and **dare** not follow true faith as
SD : 03 :036(545) [0927] or as though believers must or **dare** do nothing good.
SD : 06 :005(564) [0963] But this **dare** not be understood without qualification, as
SD : 07 :045(577) [0987] Nor **dare** we permit any objection or human
SD : 07 :085(584) [1003] This rule **dare** not in any way be rejected, but it can and
SD : 08 :051(601) [1033] the adversaries cannot and **dare** not any longer deny.

Dark (5), Darken (2), Darkened (2), Darkening (1), Darkens (1), Darkness (17)
PR : PR :002(003) [0007] to light its way out of papistic superstition and **darkness**.
PR : PR :024(013) [0023] hidden and concealed in **darkness**, away from everyone's
AP : 12 :006(183) [0255] Good God, how great is the **darkness**!
AP : 13 :013(213) [0311] They sit in a **dark** corner doing and saying nothing, but
TR : 00 :034(325) [0513] has caused horrible **darkness** to descend over the church,
TR : 00 :041(328) [0517] unbelievers, for what fellowship has light with **darkness**?"
TR : 00 :048(328) [0519] With what **darkness** has the teaching about vows covered
LC : 01 :307(406) [0669] To do so is **dark** and underhanded wickedness, and, as we
LC : 05 :056(453) [0767] and it appears like a **dark** lantern in contrast to the bright
EP : 07 :025(485) [0815] read, but that they are **dark** sayings whose meaning must
EP : 10 :006(493) [0829] what fellowship has light with **darkness**?" (II Cor. 6:14).
SD : RN :005(504) [0851] amid the abominable **darkness** of the papacy through the
SD : 02 :010(522) [0883] of their minds; they are **darkened** in their understanding,
SD : 02 :010(522) [0885] the natural man simply "**darkness**" in spiritual and divine
SD : 02 :010(522) [0885] "The light shines in the **darkness** (that is, in the dark,
SD : 02 :010(522) [0885] darkness (that is, in the **dark**, blind world which neither
SD : 02 :010(522) [0885] regards God) and the **darkness** has not comprehended it"
SD : 02 :012(522) [0885] "The **darkness** comprehended it not" (John 1:5).
SD : 02 :015(523) [0887] liberated us from the **darkness** of ignorance and the
SD : 02 :058(532) [0903] lets him remain in the **darkness** of his unbelief and be
SD : 02 :060(533) [0905] such a way that man's **darkened** reason becomes an
SD : 04 :033(556) [0947] can be instilled without **darkening** the doctrine of faith
SD : 05 :001(558) [0951] This would **darken** the merit of Christ and rob disturbed
SD : 05 :027(563) [0961] a confusion would easily **darken** the merits and benefits
SD : 10 :006(611) [1055] and iniquity, or what fellowship has light with **darkness**?
SD : 10 :014(613) [1057] or commandment **darkens** and perverts this article
SD : 10 :022(615) [1061] unbelievers, for what fellowship has light with **darkness**?'
SD : 12 :008(633) [1097] where the profound **darkness** of the papacy still reigned,

Darts (3)
LC : PR :014(360) [0571] against their "flaming **darts**," and with a good antidote
LC : 03 :104(434) [0727] they are the real "flaming **darts**" which are venomously
EP : 11 :013(496) [0835] and thus extinguish the flaming **darts** of the devil.

Dash (1)
LC : 03 :069(429) [0717] against which the others shall **dash** themselves to pieces.

Date (3)
PR : PR :008(005) [0009] At a later **date** our sainted predecessors and some of us
PR : PR :015(007) [0013] not all of us have to **date** been able to undertake such a
EP : 11 :001(494) [0831] lest as some future **date** offensive dissension concerning it

Daughter (1)
SC : 05 :020(350) [0553] or mother, a son or **daughter**, a master or servant;

David (37)
AG : 21 :001(046) [0057] imitate the example of **David** in making war on the Turk,
AL : 21 :001(046) [0057] may follow the example of **David** in waging war to drive
AL : 21 :001(047) [0057] out of his country, for like **David** the emperor is a king.
AP : 04 :087(120) [0147] mentions Abraham and **David**, who had God's command
AP : 04 :168(130) [0169] And **David** says (Ps. 143:2), "Enter not into judgment
AP : 04 :191(133) [0175] **David**'s labors in waging war and in governing the state
AP : 04 :326(157) [0211] When **David** elsewhere boasts of his righteousness, he is
AP : 12 :036(186) [0261] on the one hand and that of Peter and **David** on the other
AP : 12 :036(186) [0261] The contrition of **David** and Peter did avail because it
AP : 12 :048(188) [0265] is the voice that says with **David** (II Sam. 12:13), "I have
AP : 12 :056(189) [0267] Thus **David** is rebuked by Nathan, and in his terror he
AP : 12 :056(189) [0267] This voice encourages **David** and by faith it sustains,
AP : 12 :149(205) [0299] of conscience of which **David** says, "The sorrows of death
AP : 12 :150(206) [0299] **David** attests to this when he prays (Ps. 6:1), "O Lord,
AP : 12 :155(207) [0301] the case of Adam, and of **David** who was punished for his
AP : 12 :156(207) [0301] penalty imposed on **David** it does not follow as a
AP : 12 :161(208) [0303] the punishment of **David** when he says: "If God had
AP : 16 :009(224) [0333] high positions, Abraham, **David**, and Daniel were no less
AP : 27 :046(277) [0435] Thus **David** was poor in a very rich kingdom.
AP : 27 :049(277) [0437] Thus the call of **David** to rule, or of Abraham to sacrifice
S3 : 03 :043(310) [0491] it, fall into open sin (as **David** fell into adultery, murder,
TR : 00 :082(335) [0529] **David** Melander, subscribed
LC : 01 :046(370) [0593] **David**, on the other hand, was a poor, despised man,
LC : 01 :325(409) [0675] The prophet **David** particularly teaches it throughout the
EP : 04 :007(476) [0799] in clear terms, "So also **David** declares that salvation
EP : 12 :031(501) [0843] **David** Chytraeus
SD : 01 :036(514) [0869] **David** says: "I will praise thee, for I am wonderfully
SD : 02 :015(523) [0887] In Ps. 119, for example, **David** asks God more than ten
SD : 02 :064(533) [0905] that which is good, as **David** says, "Your people will offer
SD : 03 :034(545) [0927] (Rom. 4:5,6), and **David** also says that salvation belongs
SD : 05 :023(562) [0959] be blessed; likewise, of **David**'s son, who should restore
SD : 06 :021(567) [0969] **David** says, "I will run in the way of thy commandments"
SD : 08 :037(598) [1027] Son was descended from **David** according to the flesh"
SD : 08 :085(608) [1045] *the Last Words of **David***, which he wrote shortly before
SD : 11 :074(628) [1087] of God and say with **David**, "I had said in my alarm, I am
SD : 11 :074(628) [1087] should nevertheless join **David** in the next words, "But
SD : 12 :040(636) [1103] **David** Chytraeus

Day (139), Days (53)
P R : P R :010(006) [0011] with each passing **day** than, on the basis of God's Word,
P R : P R :022(012) [0021] persecutors on the great **day** of the Lord before the
A G : 0 3 :004(030) [0045] from the dead on the third **day**, ascended into heaven,
A G : 1 5 :001(036) [0049] them being certain holy **days**, festivals, and the like.
A G : 1 5 :004(037) [0049] distinction of foods, **days**, etc., by which it is intended to
A G : 1 7 :001(038) [0051] will return on the last **day** for judgment and will raise up
A G : 2 0 :003(041) [0053] appointed fasts, holy **days**, brotherhoods, etc.
A G : 2 4 :034(060) [0067] On holy **days**, and at other times when communicants are
A G : 2 4 :036(060) [0067] how the priest stood every **day**, inviting some to
A G : 2 4 :041(061) [0069] Mass was not held on every **day** that the people
A G : 2 6 :034(069) [0075] to certain specified **days** but should be practiced
A G : 2 6 :039(069) [0075] of fasts on prescribed **days** and with specified foods, for
A G : 2 6 :045(070) [0075] apostles to institute holy **days** but to teach faith and
A G : 2 7 :002(071) [0077] In the **days** of St. Augustine monastic life was voluntary.
A G : 2 8 :030(085) [0087] concerning foods, holy **days**, and the different orders of
A G : 2 8 :037(086) [0089] Almost every **day** new holy days and new fasts have been
A G : 2 8 :037(086) [0089] Almost every day new holy **days** and new fasts have been
A G : 2 8 :039(087) [0089] they attach sin to foods, **days**, and similar things and
A G : 2 8 :041(087) [0089] do manual work on holy **days** (even when it does not give
A G : 2 8 :057(091) [0091] Easter, Pentecost, and similar holy **days** and usages.
A G : 2 8 :060(091) [0091] to appoint a certain **day** so that the people might know
A G : 2 8 :060(091) [0093] neither of the Sabbath nor of any other **day** is necessary.
A G : 2 8 :063(092) [0093] and amount of work that may be done on the **day** of rest.
A G : 2 8 :067(092) [0093] fall into disuse from **day** to day even among those who
A G : 2 8 :067(093) [0093] into disuse from day to **day** even among those who
A L : 0 3 :004(030) [0045] descended into hell, and on the third **day** truly rose again.
A L : 1 5 :001(036) [0049] Such are certain holy **days**, festivals, and the like.
A L : 1 5 :004(037) [0049] about foods and **days**, etc., instituted to merit grace and
A L : 2 0 :003(041) [0053] such as particular holy **days**, prescribed fasts,
A L : 2 4 :034(060) [0067] among us on every holy **day**, and on other days, if any
A L : 2 4 :034(060) [0067] holy day, and on other **days**, if any desire the sacrament,
A L : 2 4 :041(061) [0069] Mass was not held every **day**; as the Tripartite History
A L : 2 6 :002(064) [0071] new orders, new holy **days**, and new fasts were daily
A L : 2 6 :008(065) [0071] observance of certain holy **days**, rites, fasts, and
A L : 2 6 :034(069) [0075] at all times, and not merely on a few prescribed **days**.
A L : 2 6 :039(069) [0075] prescribe certain **days** and certain foods as if works of
A L : 2 6 :040(069) [0075] lessons in the Mass, holy **days**, etc.) which are profitable
A L : 2 6 :045(070) [0075] laws with respect to holy **days** but to preach piety toward
A L : 2 7 :001(071) [0077] in these monasteries every **day** that were contrary to the
A L : 2 7 :060(080) [0083] that it was a novelty in his **day** to say that monastic life is
A L : 2 8 :030(085) [0087] concerning foods, holy **days**, grades or orders of
A L : 2 8 :033(086) [0087] the Sabbath to the Lord's **Day** — contrary to the
A L : 2 8 :037(086) [0089] time to time more holy **days** were appointed, more fasts
A L : 2 8 :039(087) [0089] they attach sin to foods, **days**, and similar things and
A L : 2 8 :041(087) [0089] do manual work on holy **days**, even when it gives no
A L : 2 8 :058(091) [0091] observance of the Lord's **Day** in place of the Sabbath was
A L : 2 8 :060(091) [0091] to appoint a certain **day** so that the people may know
A L : 2 8 :060(091) [0091] designated the Lord's **Day** for this purpose, and it seems
A L : 2 8 :060(091) [0093] neither of the Sabbath nor of any other **day** is necessary.
A L : 2 8 :063(092) [0093] observance of the Lord's **Day** is not *indeed* of divine
A L : 2 8 :063(092) [0093] the extent to which one is allowed to work on holy **days**.
A L : 2 8 :067(092) [0093] become obsolete from **day** to day even among those who
A L : 2 8 :067(092) [0093] obsolete from day to **day** even among those who favor
A P : P R :019(099) [0103] to Christ, who will one **day** judge these controversies.
A P : 0 4 :059(115) [0137] "Call upon me in the **day** of trouble; I will deliver you,
A P : 0 4 :066(116) [0139] Like the present-**day** Anabaptists, they deny that it is
A P : 0 4 :133(125) [0159] what he says: "Yes, to this **day** whenever Moses is read a
A P : 0 4 :268(147) [0197] "Call upon me in the **day** of trouble" (Ps. 50:15).
A P : 0 4 :279(149) [0199] "Have God in mind all the **days** of your life" (4:5), and
A P : 0 4 :283(150) [0201] like the ablutions in those **days**, or in our own time the
A P : 0 4 :367(163) [0221] your mother, that your **days** may be long in the land"
A P : 0 7 :033(174) [0239] as the different length of **day** and night does not harm the
A P : 0 7 :033(174) [0239] of the Mass, the Lord's **day**, and the other more
A P : 0 7 :033(174) [0239] the Lord's day, and the other more important feast **days**.
A P : 0 7 :039(176) [0241] to make the observance of **days**, food, and the like a
A P : 0 7 :040(176) [0241] They observed certain **days**, not because such observance
A P : 0 7 :045(177) [0243] of observances in food, **days**, clothing, and similar
A P : 1 2 :031(186) [0259] In the noontide of my **days** I must depart; I am consigned
A P : 1 5 :040(220) [0325] Every Lord's **Day** many in our circles use the Lord's
A P : 2 0 :014(228) [0343] a thousand years ago, in the **days** of Augustine.
A P : 2 1 :018(231) [0347] says (11:10), "In that **day** the root of Jesse shall stand as
A P : 2 1 :035(234) [0353] the whole Psalter every **day** while standing on one foot.
A P : 2 4 :008(250) [0385] to be held on the fourth **day**, on Sabbath eve, and on the
A P : 2 4 :008(250) [0385] the fourth day, on Sabbath eve, and on the Lord's **day**."
A P : 2 4 :023(253) [0391] sin, he shall see his offspring, he shall prolong his **days**."
A P : 2 4 :029(255) [0393] Call upon me in the **day** of trouble; I will deliver you, and
A P : 2 4 :091(266) [0415] Some **day** they will pay the penalty for this sacrilege.
A P : 2 7 :038(275) [0433] The next **day** Anthony went into the city and came to the
A P : 2 7 :063(280) [0441] the other evils inherent in present-**day** monasticism.
A P : 2 8 :005(282) [0445] to him that you will some **day** have to give account of
S 1 : P R :003(289) [0455] the light and flee from the **day** take such wretched pains
S 1 : P R :004(289) [0455] I am still writing, preaching, and lecturing every **day**.
S 1 : P R :009(290) [0457] will face us on the last **day**, before the judgment seat of
S 2 : 0 2 :012(294) [0465] week, with All Souls' **Day**, and with soul-baths that the
S 3 : 0 3 :016(305) [0483] of these terms, and to this **day** they are as far from
S 3 : 0 3 :021(306) [0485] render, like saying five Our Fathers, fasting for a **day**, etc.
S 3 : 0 3 :024(307) [0485] another for a hundred **days**, but the pope reserved for
S 3 : 0 8 :003(312) [0495] and many still do it in our **day** who wish to distinguish
S 3 : 0 8 :006(312) [0495] so, the enthusiasts of our **day** condemn the external
S C : 0 1 :005(342) [0541] *"Remember the Sabbath* ***day****, to keep it holy."*
S C : 0 2 :003(345) [0545] *into hell, the third* ***day*** *he rose from the dead, he ascended*
S C : 0 2 :006(345) [0545] believers, and on the last **day** he will raise me and all the
S C : 0 3 :012(347) [0547] *"Give us this* ***day*** *our daily bread."*
S C : 0 7 :002(352) [0557] Thee to keep me this **day**, too, from all sin and evil, that
S C : 0 7 :005(353) [0559] Christ, that Thou hast this **day** graciously protected me.
S C : 0 9 :013(356) [0563] and prayers night and **day**; whereas she who is
L C : P R :001(358) [0567] the fat of the land all their **days**, as they used to do under
L C : P R :009(359) [0569] light and fervor, so that **day** by day we relish and
L C : P R :009(359) [0569] and fervor, so that day by **day** we relish and appreciate
L C : P R :010(360) [0569] blessed who "meditate on God's law **day** and night."
L C : S P :003(362) [0575] 3. You shall keep the Sabbath **day** holy.
L C : S P :012(363) [0577] into hell, the third **day** he rose from the dead, he ascended
L C : S P :014(363) [0577] Give us this **day** our daily bread; and forgive us our
L C : 0 1 :035(369) [0589] and Jews; just so in our **day** he overthrows all false
L C : 0 1 :038(369) [0591] We observe this every **day** in the case of bishops and
L C : 0 1 :064(373) [0599] "Call upon me in the **day** of trouble: I will deliver you and
L C : 0 1 :068(374) [0599] happy hour or a healthful **day** thereafter, and thus they
L C : 0 1 :073(374) [0601] ourselves each **day** to God — our soul and body, wife,
L C : 0 1 :078(375) [0603] *"You shall sanctify the holy* ***day****."*
L C : 0 1 :079(375) [0603] Our word "holy **day**" or "holiday" is so called from the
L C : 0 1 :079(375) [0603] work" literally means "observing a holy **day** or holiday."
L C : 0 1 :080(375) [0603] God set apart the seventh **day** and appointed it for rest
L C : 0 1 :080(375) [0603] he commanded it to be kept holy above all other **days**.
L C : 0 1 :081(375) [0603] the habit of doing on that **day**, as we read in the Gospel
L C : 0 1 :081(376) [0603] meant that we should sanctify the holy **day** or day of rest.
L C : 0 1 :081(376) [0603] meant that we should sanctify the holy day or **day** of rest.
L C : 0 1 :083(376) [0603] out that we keep holy **days** not for the sake of intelligent
L C : 0 1 :083(376) [0603] long — should retire for a **day** to rest and be refreshed.
L C : 0 1 :084(376) [0605] especially, we keep holy **days** so that people may have
L C : 0 1 :085(376) [0605] to be precisely this or that **day**, for in itself no one day is
L C : 0 1 :085(376) [0605] or that day, for in itself no one **day** is better than another.
L C : 0 1 :085(376) [0605] people can do, at least one **day** in the week must be set
L C : 0 1 :086(376) [0605] The special office of this **day**, therefore, should be the
L C : 0 1 :087(376) [0605] shall sanctify the holy **day**" means, answer: "It means to
L C : 0 1 :087(376) [0605] In itself the **day** needs no sanctification, for it was created
L C : 0 1 :087(377) [0605] according as you spend the **day** in doing holy or unholy
L C : 0 1 :089(377) [0605] should make every **day** a holy day and give ourselves only
L C : 0 1 :089(377) [0605] make every day a holy **day** and give ourselves only to
L C : 0 1 :089(377) [0605] the young, and at least a **day** for the whole community,
L C : 0 1 :090(377) [0605] Wherever this practice is in force, a holy **day** is truly kept.
L C : 0 1 :090(377) [0607] Where it is not, it cannot be called a Christian holy **day**.
L C : 0 1 :090(377) [0607] Non-Christians can spend a **day** in rest and idleness, too,
L C : 0 1 :090(377) [0607] swarm of clerics in our **day** who stand daily in the
L C : 0 1 :090(377) [0607] sanctifying the holy **day** because they neither preach nor
L C : 0 1 :092(377) [0607] there the person, the **day**, and the work are sanctified by
L C : 0 1 :094(378) [0607] sanctifying, so that this **day** should have its own
L C : 0 1 :095(378) [0607] God's Word that no holy **day** is sanctified without it, we
L C : 0 1 :096(378) [0607] and desecrate the holy **day**, like those who in their greed
L C : 0 1 :097(378) [0609] the abuse of the holy **day**, for we permit ourselves to be
L C : 0 1 :100(378) [0609] of the devil, who neither **day** nor night relaxes his effort
L C : 0 1 :103(379) [0611] love him with our whole heart all the **days** of our lives.
L C : 0 1 :103(379) [0611] Thirdly, on holy **days** or days of rest we should diligently
L C : 0 1 :103(379) [0611] Thirdly, on holy days or **days** of rest we should diligently
L C : 0 1 :134(383) [0619] will enjoy good **days**, happiness, and prosperity.
L C : 0 1 :191(391) [0635] sentence upon them in the **day** of judgment, as Christ
L C : 0 1 :226(395) [0645] of artisans, workmen, and **day**-laborers who act
L C : 0 1 :230(396) [0645] treasures of the whole world and holds them to this **day**?
L C : 0 1 :236(397) [0647] — there will come a **day** of reckoning and retribution:
L C : 0 1 :237(397) [0647] will it be with artisans and **day**-laborers, from whom we
L C : 0 1 :243(397) [0649] before our very eyes every **day** that no stolen or ill-gotten
L C : 0 1 :243(397) [0649] people scrape and scratch **day** and night and yet grow not
L C : 0 1 :283(403) [0661] not sneak about in secret, shunning the light of **day**.
L C : 0 1 :314(407) [0671] on his knees a whole **day** in church, this is considered a
L C : 0 2 :014(412) [0681] and stars in the heavens, **day** and night, air, fire, water,
L C : 0 2 :025(413) [0683] *into hell, the third* ***day*** *he rose from the dead, he ascended*
L C : 0 2 :031(414) [0687] until finally, at the last **day**, he will completely divide and
L C : 0 2 :053(417) [0691] Until the last **day** the Holy Spirit remains with the holy
L C : 0 2 :061(419) [0695] Spirit carries on his work unceasingly until the last **day**.
L C : 0 3 :019(423) [0703] "Call upon me in the **day** of trouble, and I will deliver
L C : 0 3 :025(423) [0705] howl and growl frightfully **day** and night; not one of them
L C : 0 3 :064(429) [0715] end he strives without rest **day** and night, using all the
L C : 0 3 :071(430) [0717] *"Give us this* ***day*** *our daily bread."*
L C : 0 3 :083(431) [0721] of time, as indeed we see and experience every **day**.
L C : 0 4 :050(443) [0745] time down to the present **day** no man on earth could have
L C : 0 4 :069(445) [0749] are outside of Christ can only grow worse **day** by day.
L C : 0 4 :069(445) [0749] are outside of Christ can only grow worse day by **day**.
L C : 0 4 :070(445) [0749] the real vices become more and more potent **day** by day.
L C : 0 4 :070(445) [0749] the real vices become more and more potent day by **day**.
L C : 0 4 :084(446) [0753] Every **day** he should be found in faith and amid its fruits,
L C : 0 4 :084(446) [0753] and amid its fruits, every **day** he should be suppressing
L C : 0 4 :086(446) [0753] so forgiveness remains **day** by day as long as we live, that
L C : 0 4 :086(446) [0753] remains day by **day** as long as we live, that is, as long as
L C : 0 5 :047(452) [0765] evening of the fourteenth **day** of the first full moon,
L C : 0 5 :047(452) [0765] of the first full moon, without variation of a single **day**.
L C : 0 5 :053(453) [0765] away from the sacrament, **day** by day he will become
L C : 0 5 :053(453) [0765] the sacrament, day by **day** he will become more and more
E P : 0 6 :002(480) [0805] should exercise themselves **day** and night in the law (Ps.
E P : 1 1 :003(494) [0833] what will be in the latter **days**" (Daniel 2:28).
E P : 1 2 :031(500) [0843] account of it on the Last **Day** before the righteous judge,
S D : P R :003(502) [0847] has remained unrefuted and unimpregnable until this **day**.
S D : R N :005(504) [0851] God has in these last **days** brought to light the truth of
S D : 0 1 :036(514) [0869] every one of them, the **days** that were formed for me,
S D : 0 1 :047(516) [0875] not rise on Judgment **Day** and that in eternal life, instead
S D : 0 2 :037(528) [0895] Until the Last **Day**, the Holy Spirit remains with the holy
S D : 0 2 :064(533) [0905] will offer themselves freely on the **day** you lead your host.
S D : 0 5 :004(559) [0953] suffer and on the third **day** rise from the dead, and that
S D : 0 6 :004(564) [0963] on his law he meditates **day** and night" (Ps. 1:1, 2; 119:1,
S D : 0 7 :076(583) [0999] it is efficacious until this **day**, and until his return it
S D : 0 7 :099(586) [1003] and as he will on the Last **Day**, as St. Paul says, "This will
S D : 1 0 :013(613) [1057] as far as foods, times, and **days** were concerned (Rom
S D : 1 1 :004(617) [1063] every one of them, the **days** that were formed for me,
S D : 1 1 :092(632) [1093] was written in former **days** was written for our

Dazzled (1), Dazzling (2)
A G : 2 7 :048(078) [0081] when man's eyes are **dazzled** with this curious angelic
L C : 0 4 :012(438) [0735] matter how precious and **dazzling** they might appear, they
L C : 0 4 :013(438) [0735] because Baptism is not **dazzling** like the works which we

De (6)
A G : 2 0 :013(043) [0055] His whole book, ***De*** *spiritu et litera*, proves this.
A G : 2 5 :010(063) [0069] can be seen in Dist. I, ***De*** *poenitentia*, where these words
A G : 2 5 :012(063) [0071] The marginal note in ***De*** *poenitentia*, Dist. 5, also teaches
A L : 2 0 :014(043) [0055] teaches similarly in ***De*** *vocatione gentium* and elsewhere,
A L : 2 0 :014(043) [0055] and elsewhere, for in his ***De*** *vocatione gentium* he says:
A L : 2 5 :012(063) [0071] The marginal note in ***De*** *poenitentia*, Dist. 5, in the

Deacons (6)
AG : 2 3 :010(052) [0061] for priests and **deacons** to marry in the Christian church
AG : 2 4 :037(060) [0067] and communicated the other priests and **deacons**,
AG : 2 4 :038(060) [0067] "After the priests the **deacons** shall receive the sacrament
AL : 2 4 :037(060) [0067] of the presbyters and **deacons** received the body of the
AL : 2 4 :038(060) [0067] the presbyters, let the **deacons** receive Holy Communion
TR : 0 0 :062(331) [0523] for itself, the **deacons** may choose from their number one

Dead (107), Deadly (1)
AG : 0 3 :004(030) [0045] hell, truly rose from the **dead** on the third day, ascended
AG : 0 3 :006(030) [0045] to judge the living and the **dead**, as stated in the
AG : 1 7 :001(038) [0051] and will raise up all the **dead**, to give eternal life and
AG : 1 7 :005(039) [0051] the resurrection of the **dead**, saints and godly men will
AG : 2 0 :023(044) [0055] his resurrection from the **dead**, but we mean such true
AG : 2 4 :022(058) [0067] for the living and the **dead**, a sacrifice by means of which
AG : 2 4 :029(059) [0067] for the whole world and for others, both living and **dead**.
AG : 2 4 :034(060) [0067] others, whether living or **dead**, but should be a
AL : 0 3 :002(030) [0045] suffered, was crucified, **dead**, and buried, that he might
AL : 0 3 :006(030) [0045] to judge the living and the **dead**, etc., according to the
AL : 1 7 :001(038) [0051] will appear for judgment and will raise up all the **dead**.
AL : 1 7 :005(038) [0051] the resurrection of the **dead** the godly will take possession
AL : 2 4 :022(058) [0067] takes away the sins of the living and the **dead**.
AL : 2 4 :029(059) [0067] sins of the living and the **dead** by a performance of the
AP : 0 4 :246(142) [0189] and show that it is not **dead** but living and active in the
AP : 0 4 :248(142) [0191] he distinguishes between **dead** and living faith and
AP : 0 4 :249(142) [0191] not produce good works is **dead**, but it is alive when it
AP : 0 4 :352(161) [0217] although your bodies are **dead** because of sin, your spirits
AP : 0 4 :361(162) [0219] as when a monk's hood is placed on a **dead** man.
AP : 0 7 :005(169) [0227] admit, that the wicked are **dead** members of the church.
AP : 1 2 :015(184) [0257] not only from the living but even more from the **dead**.
AP : 1 2 :015(184) [0257] off the satisfactions of the **dead** not only by indulgences
AP : 1 2 :151(206) [0299] us rely not on ourselves but on God who raises the **dead**."
AP : 1 2 :152(206) [0299] "Your body is **dead** because of sin"; that is, it is
AP : 1 7 :001(224) [0335] appear and raise all the **dead**, granting eternal life and
AP : 2 1 :002(229) [0343] cite this example to prove the invocation of the **dead**.
AP : 2 1 :009(230) [0345] in Scripture about the **dead** praying, except for the dream
AP : 2 4 :011(251) [0387] others, whether living or **dead**, forgiveness of sins or of
AP : 2 4 :013(251) [0387] whatever they need in this life, and even free the **dead**.
AP : 2 4 :064(261) [0407] even transfer it to the **dead** and free souls from
AP : 2 4 :077(263) [0411] of sins for them or to free the souls of the **dead**.
AP : 2 4 :088(265) [0413] [Mass for the **Dead**]
AP : 2 4 :089(265) [0413] to free the souls of the **dead**, from which they make
AP : 2 4 :089(266) [0415] and to apply to the **dead** the Lord's Supper which was
AP : 2 4 :091(266) [0415] been transferred to the **dead** and to satisfaction for
AP : 2 4 :092(266) [0417] faith, it follows that it is useless to transfer it to the **dead**.
AP : 2 4 :092(266) [0417] this transference to the **dead** cannot be proved from the
AP : 2 4 :093(267) [0417] as a satisfaction for the **dead** because it applies it equally
AP : 2 4 :094(267) [0417] opponents quote the Fathers on offerings for the **dead**.
AP : 2 4 :094(267) [0417] We know that the ancients spoke of prayer for the **dead**.
AP : 2 4 :094(267) [0417] of the Lord's Supper to the **dead** *ex opere operato*.
AP : 2 4 :096(267) [0417] Mass there was an offering for the living and the **dead**.
AP : 2 4 :096(267) [0417] Aerius believed that prayers for the **dead** were useless.
AP : 2 7 :053(278) [0437] Mass by its application to the **dead** for the sake of profit.
S1 : PR :004(289) [0457] Imagine what will happen after I am **dead**!
S1 : 0 1 :000(292) [0461] to hell, rose from the **dead**, and ascended to heaven; and
S1 : 0 1 :000(292) [0461] to judge the living and the **dead**, etc., as the Apostles'
S2 : 0 2 :012(295) [0465] almost exclusively for the **dead** although Christ instituted
S2 : 0 2 :012(295) [0465] or enjoined upon us with reference to the **dead**.
S2 : 0 2 :014(295) [0467] and whether the **dead** are to be commemorated in the
S2 : 0 2 :021(296) [0469] good works, etc. for the benefit of the living and the **dead**.
S2 : 0 2 :024(296) [0469] to the living and the **dead** (for money) and by which the
S2 : 0 2 :028(297) [0469] from angels and **dead** saints, the honor that remains will
S3 : 0 3 :026(307) [0487] Masses and vigils for the **dead** and afterwards by offering
S3 : 0 3 :026(307) [0487] indulgences for the **dead** through bulls and jubilee years.
TR : 0 0 :071(332) [0525] thee the power to sacrifice for the living and the **dead**."
SC : 0 2 :003(345) [0545] *Pilate, was crucified, **dead**, and buried: he descended into*
SC : 0 2 :003(345) [0545] *third day he rose from the **dead**, he ascended into*
SC : 0 2 :003(345) [0545] *whence he shall come to judge the living and the **dead**."*
SC : 0 2 :004(345) [0545] as he is risen from the **dead** and lives and reigns to all
SC : 0 2 :006(345) [0545] he will raise me and all the **dead** and will grant eternal life
SC : 0 4 :014(349) [0553] Christ was raised from the **dead** by the glory of the
SC : 0 9 :013(356) [0563] who is self-indulgent is **dead** even while she lives" (I Tim.
LC : SP :012(363) [0577] Pilate, was crucified, **dead**, and buried: he descended into
LC : SP :012(363) [0577] third day he rose from the **dead**, he ascended into
LC : SP :012(363) [0577] whence he shall come to judge the living and the **dead**.
LC : 0 1 :091(377) [0607] degree, for they are all **dead** things that can sanctify no
LC : 0 1 :096(378) [0607] or lie around in taverns **dead** drunk like swine, but also
LC : 0 1 :101(379) [0609] these words are not idle or **dead**, but effective and living.
LC : 0 1 :176(389) [0631] Think what **deadly** harm you do when you are negligent
LC : 0 2 :025(413) [0683] *Pilate, was crucified, **dead**, and buried: he descended into*
LC : 0 2 :025(413) [0683] *third day he rose from the **dead**, he ascended into*
LC : 0 2 :025(413) [0685] *whence he shall come to judge the living and the **dead**."*
LC : 0 2 :031(414) [0687] he rose again from the **dead**, swallowed up and devoured
LC : 0 5 :078(455) [0771] even if you are so utterly **dead** in sin, at least believe the
EP : 0 1 :006(467) [0781] quickens it from the **dead** as his creation, and adorns it
EP : 0 2 :003(470) [0787] through sin is spiritually **dead** raise himself to spiritual
EP : 0 2 :003(470) [0787] is written, "When we were **dead** through our trespasses,
EP : 0 4 :006(476) [0799] genuine faith — if it is a living and not a **dead** faith.
EP : 0 7 :023(484) [0815] of the Mass for the sins of the living and the **dead**.
EP : 0 8 :013(488) [0821] into hell, rose from the **dead**, ascended into heaven, and
SD : PR :007(502) [0849] the resurrection of the **dead** (I Cor. 15:12); and others
SD : 0 1 :002(508) [0859] in spiritual matters he is **dead** to that which is good and is
SD : 0 1 :060(519) [0879] and with all his powers **dead** indeed to that which is
SD : 0 2 :002(520) [0881] is going to be like after he will have risen from the **dead**.
SD : 0 2 :007(521) [0883] is entirely and completely **dead** and corrupted as far as
SD : 0 2 :010(522) [0885] that he is truly lifeless and "**dead**" (Eph. 2:1, 5; Col. 2:13).
SD : 0 2 :011(522) [0885] a person who is physically **dead** can by his own powers
SD : 0 2 :011(522) [0885] a man who is spiritually **dead**, in sin, prepare or address
SD : 0 2 :017(524) [0887] impotent, incapable, and **dead** to good, but also that by
SD : 0 2 :061(533) [0905] to his conversion man is **dead** in sin (Eph. 2:5); hence
SD : 0 2 :077(536) [0911] things man is not wholly **dead** toward that which is good,
SD : 0 2 :077(536) [0911] is good, but only grievously wounded and half-**dead**.
SD : 0 2 :090(539) [0915] of a man who is spiritually **dead**, in whom the Holy
SD : 0 3 :020(542) [0921] is written, "When we were **dead** through our trespasses,
SD : 0 3 :042(547) [0931] it from a simulated and **dead** faith (since many lazy and
SD : 0 3 :042(547) [0931] James calls that faith **dead** where all kinds of good works
SD : 0 3 :042(547) [0931] by such a faith as is without works, which is a **dead** faith."
SD : 0 4 :001(551) [0939] since faith without love is **dead**, although such love is not
SD : 0 4 :015(553) [0943] dream up for themselves a **dead** faith or superstition,
SD : 0 5 :004(559) [0953] third day rise from the **dead**, and that repentance and
SD : 0 7 :031(574) [0983] a joke or idle talk; I am in **dead** earnest, since by the
SD : 0 7 :109(588) [1011] of the sacrifice of the Mass for the living and for the **dead**.
SD : 0 8 :013(593) [1019] his resurrection from the **dead** and his ascension, but
SD : 0 8 :026(596) [1023] the resurrection from the **dead**, its exaltation above all
SD : 0 8 :044(599) [1029] if God's death and God **dead** lie in the opposite scale,
SD : 0 8 :044(599) [1031] that it could be said: God **dead**, God's passion, God's
SD : 0 8 :058(602) [1035] the power to make the **dead** alive and to execute

Deaf (1)
AP : 0 4 :281(149) [0201] Our opponents must be **deaf**.

Deal (27), Dealing (11), Dealings (1), Deals (9), Dealt (5)
AL : 2 4 :012(057) [0065] threatened those who **dealt** unworthily with the Eucharist
AP : 0 2 :019(103) [0111] And after saying a great **deal** about it, Ambrose says,
AP : 0 4 :060(115) [0137] faith and teach men to **deal** with God only by works and
AP : 0 4 :067(116) [0139] But one cannot **deal** with God or grasp him except
AP : 0 4 :087(119) [0147] Romans, especially, Paul **deals** with this subject and
AP : 0 4 :124(124) [0157] of Decalogue, the law that **deals** with the thoughts of the
AP : 0 4 :216(137) [0179] righteousness by which we **deal** with God, not with men,
AP : 0 4 :224(138) [0181] Table, through which we **deal** with men and not
AP : 0 4 :226(138) [0183] Faith and hope **deal** only with God, while love has
AP : 0 4 :262(145) [0195] These words **deal** with the total scope of penitence.
AP : 0 4 :312(155) [0207] a future event, while faith **deals** with both future and
AP : 0 4 :366(163) [0221] of the Gospel, which **deals** with the promise of grace,
AP : 0 4 :366(163) [0221] the law that follows faith **deals** with the law, in which a
AP : 0 7 :037(175) [0241] necessary to cite a great **deal** of evidence since it is
AP : 1 1 :009(182) [0253] The greater part **deals** with sins against human traditions,
AP : 1 2 :124(201) [0289] should have been found to **deal** with such important,
AP : 1 2 :142(204) [0295] imagine that God's law **deals** with external, civil
AP : 1 2 :171(209) [0305] described by the canons **dealing** with satisfactions.
AP : 1 2 :171(209) [0305] one required in the canons **dealing** with satisfactions.
AP : 1 2 :173(209) [0305] They quote passages **dealing** with obligatory works,
AP : 1 2 :178(211) [0309] have made up a great **deal** about the merit of attrition,
AP : 1 5 :043(221) [0327] other hand, all sermons **deal** with topics like these:
AP : 2 3 :004(239) [0365] we hope that you will **deal** kindly with us in this case,
AP : 2 4 :010(251) [0387] in a controversy must **deal** only with the point at issue
AP : 2 4 :014(251) [0387] Confutation has a great **deal** to say about sacrifice,
S3 : 0 8 :010(313) [0497] maintain that God will not **deal** with us except through
TR : 0 0 :075(333) [0525] real offenses, but in **dealing** with non-observance of fasts
SC : 0 1 :014(343) [0541] by dishonest trade or by **dealing** in shoddy wares, but
LC : SP :022(364) [0579] other sacrament may be **dealt** with similarly, in short,
LC : 0 1 :089(377) [0605] upon such matters and **deal** especially with the Ten
LC : 0 1 :167(388) [0629] it is frequently **dealt** with in many other passages of
LC : 0 1 :180(389) [0631] We have now **dealt** with both the spiritual and the civil
LC : 0 1 :200(392) [0637] First they **deal** with our neighbor's person.
LC : 0 1 :224(395) [0643] neighbor in any sort of **dealing** that results in loss to him.
LC : 0 1 :226(395) [0645] or if we catch them we can **deal** with them so that they
LC : 0 1 :227(396) [0645] tricks and sharp practices and crafty **dealing**.
LC : 0 1 :246(398) [0651] But beware how you **deal** with the poor, of whom there
LC : 0 1 :276(402) [0659] But the right way to **deal** with this matter would be to
LC : 0 1 :279(403) [0661] So the individual is to be **dealt** with personally and not
LC : 0 1 :296(405) [0665] without accusation or blame for fraudulent **dealing**.
LC : 0 1 :332(410) [0677] in all his affairs and **dealings**, as if they were written
LC : 0 2 :012(412) [0681] as we have said, that this article **deals** with creation.
LC : 0 2 :032(415) [0687] the times appointed for **dealing** at length with such
LC : 0 3 :092(432) [0725] as we daily deserve, but to **deal** graciously with us, forgive
LC : 0 5 :001(447) [0753] headings, so we must **deal** with the second sacrament in
SD : PR :009(503) [0849] these controversies **deal** with weighty and important
SD : 0 3 :029(544) [0925] namely, when we **deal** with good works apart from this
SD : 0 4 :011(553) [0941] and jabbers a great **deal** about faith and good works.
SD : 0 7 :001(568) [0971] in which we intend to **deal** only with those articles that
SD : 0 7 :031(574) [0983] of God I have learned to know a great **deal** about Satan.
SD : 1 0 :014(613) [1057] here we are no longer **dealing** with the external adiaphora
SD : 1 0 :014(613) [1057] Here we are **dealing** primarily with the chief article of our
SD : 1 1 :036(622) [1075] Word, through which he **deals** with us and calls us, so

Dear (22), Dearest (2), Dearly (3)
AP : PR :009(098) [0101] And now, **dear** reader, you have our Apology.
AP : 0 4 :360(162) [0219] Look out, **dear** reader, you have not yet heard the whole
AP : 2 0 :012(228) [0341] Now you see, **dear** reader, that our opponents have
S1 : PR :015(291) [0459] **Dear** Lord Jesus Christ, assemble a council of thine own,
SC : PR :025(341) [0539] So it is up to you, **dear** pastor and preacher!
SC : 0 3 :002(346) [0545] even as beloved children approach their **dear** father.
SC : 0 3 :005(346) [0547] Help us to do this, **dear** Father in heaven!
SC : 0 5 :021(350) [0553] say to the confessor: "**Dear** Pastor, please hear my
SC : 0 7 :002(352) [0557] Father, through thy **dear** Son Jesus Christ, that Thou
SC : 0 7 :005(353) [0559] Father, through thy **dear** Son Jesus Christ, that Thou
LC : SP :019(363) [0579] and simple terms, for the **dear** fathers or apostles,
LC : 0 1 :074(374) [0601] "Help, **dear** Lord Christ!" etc.
LC : 0 1 :149(385) [0623] you obey him you are his **dear** child; if you despise this
LC : 0 1 :200(392) [0637] the person nearest and **dearest** to him, namely, his wife,
LC : 0 1 :223(395) [0643] and our spouse, our temporal property is **dearest** to us.
LC : 0 1 :240(397) [0649] to sell his goods as **dearly** as he pleases without a word of
LC : 0 3 :021(423) [0703] and say, "I come to Thee, **dear** Father, and pray not of
LC : 0 3 :032(424) [0707] a good Christian prays, "**Dear** Father, thy will be done,"
LC : 0 3 :032(424) [0707] from on high, "Yes, **dear** child, it shall indeed be done in
LC : 0 3 :054(427) [0713] All this is simply to say: "**Dear** Father, we pray Thee, give
LC : 0 3 :067(429) [0717] "Thy will be done, **dear** Father, and not the will of the
LC : 0 3 :088(432) [0723] call upon God and pray, "**Dear** Father, forgive us our
LC : 0 3 :097(433) [0725] the promise and think, "**Dear** Father, I come to Thee
LC : 0 3 :110(435) [0729] to God from your heart, "**Dear** Father, Thou hast
LC : 0 3 :114(435) [0729] sum it all up by saying, "**Dear** Father, help us to get rid of
EP : 1 2 :030(500) [0843] against these if they **dearly** love their soul's eternal
SD : 1 2 :039(636) [1103] and should avoid these as **dearly** as they love their soul's

Death (231)

PR : PR :000(001) [0004] Arose after the blessed **Death** of Martin Luther, Prepared
PR : PR :004(003) [0007] shortly after the Christian **death** of that enlightened and
AG : 24 :021(058) [0067] Lord Christ has by his **death** made satisfaction only for
AG : 24 :026(058) [0067] sin, or for any other sin, except the one **death** of Christ.
AG : 24 :025(059) [0067] doctrine that Christ's **death** should have made satisfaction
AL : 02 :002(029) [0043] damns and brings eternal **death** on those who are not
AL : 04 :002(030) [0045] of Christ, who by his **death** made satisfaction for our
AL : 23 :021(055) [0063] priests, are cruelly put to **death**, contrary to the intent of
AL : 28 :011(082) [0085] protects souls from heresies, the devil, and eternal **death**.
AP : 02 :005(101) [0107] not condemned to eternal **death** because of original sin
AP : 02 :040(105) [0115] sin, by nature worthy of **death** if it is not forgiven, though
AP : 02 :046(106) [0117] is subjected not only to **death** and other physical ills, but
AP : 02 :047(106) [0119] are sin as well as penalty; **death**, other physical ills, and
AP : 02 :050(106) [0119] rule of the devil, sin, and **death**; so we cannot know his
AP : 04 :008(108) [0121] the expectation of God's help in **death** and all afflictions.
AP : 04 :008(108) [0121] obedience to God in **death** and all afflictions, lest we try
AP : 04 :027(111) [0127] willingly obey him in **death** and in his other visitations,
AP : 04 :036(112) [0131] be casting us into eternal **death**, human nature cannot
AP : 04 :040(112) [0131] are all under sin and subject to eternal wrath and **death**.
AP : 04 :044(113) [0133] us, oppressed by sin and **death**, the promise freely offers
AP : 04 :062(115) [0139] are under sin and are worthy of eternal wrath and **death**.
AP : 04 :064(116) [0139] but frees us from **death**, brings forth a new life in our
AP : 04 :079(117) [0143] of sin and of eternal **death** must be conquered in our
AP : 04 :079(118) [0143] "The sting of **death** is sin, and the power of sin
AP : 04 :085(119) [0147] of sin, against eternal **death**, and against all the gates of
AP : 04 :115(123) [0155] Spirit that frees us from **death**, comforting and
AP : 04 :119(124) [0155] For in the hour of **death**, what will sustain those who
AP : 04 :143(127) [0161] if by the Spirit you put to **death** the deeds of the body,
AP : 04 :148(127) [0163] did not die in vain, conquers the terrors of sin and **death**.
AP : 04 :149(127) [0163] and stronger than the **death** and promise of Christ,
AP : 04 :178(131) [0171] be placed the **death** and satisfaction of Christ, bestowed
AP : 04 :209(135) [0177] so they put their sons to **death** in order by this cruel and
AP : 04 :210(136) [0179] "As often as you do this, you proclaim the Lord's **death**."
AP : 04 :222(138) [0181] the terrors of sin and **death**; that we can set our love
AP : 04 :223(138) [0181] our love we can conquer **death** and can have access to
AP : 04 :238(140) [0187] our love conquers sin and **death**; or that in place of
AP : 04 :244(142) [0189] the terrors of sin and **death**; that good works are accepted
AP : 04 :247(142) [0191] Christ when we set it against the terrors of sin and **death**.
AP : 04 :250(143) [0191] us alive and enables us to overcome **death** and the devil.
AP : 04 :250(143) [0191] and overcomes **death** (Col. 2:12), "in which you were also
AP : 04 :263(146) [0195] they truly believe and by faith conquer sin and **death**.
AP : 04 :277(148) [0199] same way, "Alms free from every sin and from **death**."
AP : 04 :277(148) [0199] Christ, whose prerogative it is to free from sin and **death**.
AP : 04 :278(149) [0199] does not free from sin and **death** *ex opere operato*.
AP : 04 :278(149) [0199] of sins and overcomes **death** as it becomes ever stronger
AP : 04 :278(149) [0199] us in the perils of sin and **death**, as we said a little earlier
AP : 04 :290(151) [0203] faith in Christ we overcome the terrors of sin and **death**.
AP : 04 :291(152) [0203] and victory over the terrors of sin and **death**.
AP : 04 :304(154) [0205] The terrors of sin and **death** are not merely thoughts in
AP : 04 :314(156) [0207] the terrors of sin and **death** since we cannot set our love
AP : 04 :382(165) [0225] are blotted out by Christ's **death** and that God has been
AP : 04 :383(165) [0225] quickening the heart amid the terrors of sin and **death**.
AP : 10 :004(180) [0247] Christ, knowing that "**death** no longer has dominion over
AP : 12 :002(182) [0253] what is this but to insult the blood and **death** of Christ?
AP : 12 :037(187) [0261] life it struggles with sin to conquer sin and **death**.
AP : 12 :042(187) [0263] in its struggles against the terrors of sin and **death**.
AP : 12 :044(187) [0263] mean contrition, anxiety, and the terrors of sin and **death**.
AP : 12 :049(188) [0265] me sorely, but he has not given me over to **death**."
AP : 12 :055(189) [0267] the kingdom of the devil, **death**, and sin! this was the
AP : 12 :067(191) [0271] hold this faith be put to **death** with all sorts of cruelties.
AP : 12 :072(192) [0271] against despair and against the terrors of sin and **death**.
AP : 12 :094(196) [0281] I have no pleasure in the **death** of the wicked, but that the
AP : 12 :094(196) [0281] he has no pleasure in the **death** of the wicked, God shows
AP : 12 :128(201) [0291] many good men to whom such doubt is worse than **death**.
AP : 12 :138(203) [0293] remission removes eternal **death** and brings eternal life.
AP : 12 :140(204) [0295] The **death** of Christ, furthermore, is a satisfaction not
AP : 12 :140(204) [0295] guilt but also for eternal **death**, according to the passage
AP : 12 :140(204) [0295] the passage (Hos. 13:14), "O **Death**, I will be your death."
AP : 12 :140(204) [0295] the passage (Hos. 13:14), "O Death, I will be your **death**."
AP : 12 :140(204) [0295] our guilt but our penalties redeem us from eternal **death**!
AP : 12 :140(204) [0295] statement, "I will be your **death**," should be taken to
AP : 12 :140(204) [0295] are supposed to abolish **death**, even when they are done in
AP : 12 :143(204) [0297] pay homage to God and to compensate for eternal **death**.
AP : 12 :143(204) [0297] pay homage to God and compensate for eternal **death**.
AP : 12 :144(205) [0297] the honor of being a price paid in lieu of eternal **death**.
AP : 12 :146(205) [0297] does not atone for eternal **death** because it is useless and
AP : 12 :146(205) [0297] useless and in this life does not even get a taste of **death**.
AP : 12 :146(205) [0297] When **death** assails us, we must set something else against
AP : 12 :146(205) [0297] Faith in Christ overcomes **death**, just as it overcomes the
AP : 12 :146(205) [0297] us the victory if we set our satisfactions against **death**."
AP : 12 :147(205) [0297] frees the heart from the wrath of God and eternal **death**.
AP : 12 :147(205) [0297] satisfaction for eternal **death** is the death of Christ; our
AP : 12 :147(205) [0297] for eternal death is the **death** of Christ; our opponents
AP : 12 :149(205) [0299] says, "The sorrows of **death** encompassed me (II Sam.
AP : 12 :151(206) [0299] the saints are subject to **death** and to all the common
AP : 12 :151(206) [0299] received the sentence of **death**; but that was to make us
AP : 12 :153(206) [0299] **Death** itself serves this same purpose: to destroy this
AP : 12 :153(206) [0299] In the **death** of a believer even now, once his faith has
AP : 12 :153(206) [0299] "The sting of **death** is sin, and the power of
AP : 12 :153(206) [0299] this sense of wrath **death** is actually no punishment at all.
AP : 12 :157(207) [0301] can be freed from eternal **death** only by the payment of
AP : 12 :157(207) [0301] because of Christ, who is the victor over sin and **death**.
AP : 12 :157(207) [0301] sin, not as a payment for or a ransom from eternal **death**.
AP : 12 :160(208) [0303] but not to pay for eternal **death**; for this God has another
AP : 12 :160(208) [0303] for this God has another price, the **death** of his Son.
AP : 12 :161(208) [0303] God imposed physical **death** on man because of sin, and
AP : 12 :177(210) [0307] grant that in the hour of **death** the reservation of cases
AP : 13 :008(212) [0311] teach that the sacrificial **death** of Christ on the cross was
AP : 20 :008(227) [0341] foundation when sin and **death** terrify them and the devil
AP : 21 :026(232) [0349] us from the enemy and receive us in the hour of **death**."
AP : 21 :027(232) [0349] does she receive souls in **death**, does she overcome death,
AP : 21 :027(232) [0349] in death, does she overcome **death**, does she give life?
AP : 23 :070(249) [0383] blood of Abel cried out in **death** (Gen. 4:10), so the blood
AP : 24 :012(251) [0387] the terrors of sins and **death** and to comfort our hearts
AP : 24 :022(253) [0391] sacrifice in the world, the **death** of Christ, as the Epistle to
AP : 24 :023(253) [0391] the law to mean that the **death** of Christ is a real
AP : 24 :023(253) [0391] this issue, then, that the **death** of Christ is the only real
AP : 24 :034(256) [0397] symbolized both the **death** of Christ and the proclamation
AP : 24 :035(256) [0397] bread and drink the cup, you proclaim the Lord's **death**."
AP : 24 :036(257) [0397] The burning of the lamb symbolizes the **death** of Christ.
AP : 24 :038(257) [0397] is a memorial of the **death** of Christ, therefore, it is not
AP : 24 :038(257) [0399] truly believes that by the **death** of Christ God has been
AP : 24 :038(257) [0399] we are sanctified, put to **death**, and made alive when the
AP : 24 :039(257) [0399] the Holy Spirit who puts us to **death** and makes us alive.
AP : 24 :040(257) [0399] the Gospel, being put to **death** and being made alive.
AP : 24 :054(259) [0403] but only to symbolize the future **death** of Christ alone.
AP : 24 :057(260) [0405] Testament besides the **death** of Christ that are valid for
AP : 24 :059(260) [0405] and the Holy Spirit and be put to **death** and made alive.
AP : 24 :060(260) [0405] conquest of the terrors of **death** and sin through any work
AP : 24 :076(263) [0411] of our ills, our sin and our **death**; and it gives thanks.
AP : 24 :089(266) [0415] as much to the work of a priest as to the **death** of Christ.
AP : 24 :089(266) [0415] Then, too, sin and **death** cannot be conquered except by
AP : 24 :090(266) [0415] the Mass would be on a par with the **death** of Christ.
AP : 27 :013(271) [0423] But thy **death** is a witness, thy resurrection is a witness,
S2 : 01 :001(292) [0461] and Lord, "was put to **death** for our trespasses and raised
S2 : 02 :010(294) [0465] permit this to happen, they would put us all to **death**.
S3 : 01 :001(302) [0477] made sinners and became subject to **death** and the devil.
S3 : 01 :011(303) [0479] be sound and only the body would be subject to **death**.
S3 : 03 :002(304) [0479] (true sorrow of the heart, suffering, and pain of **death**).
S3 : 03 :007(304) [0481] the Gospel, there is only **death** and hell, and man must
S3 : 03 :040(309) [0489] continues until **death**, for all through life it contends with
S3 : 15 :003(316) [0501] and on which I will stand, God willing, until my **death**.
TR : 00 :040(327) [0517] the greatest cruelty and puts to **death** those who dissent.
SC : PR :023(341) [0537] has no sin, no flesh, no devil, no world, no **death**, no hell.
SC : 02 :004(345) [0545] me from all sins, from **death**, and from the power of the
SC : 02 :004(345) [0545] innocent sufferings and **death**, in order that I may be his,
SC : 03 :020(348) [0549] at last, when the hour of **death** comes, he may grant us a
SC : 04 :006(348) [0551] of sins, delivers from **death** and the devil, and grants
SC : 04 :012(349) [0551] repentance and be put to **death**, and that the new man
SC : 04 :014(349) [0553] with him by baptism into **death**, so that as Christ was
LC : PR :019(361) [0573] have taught the devil to **death** and have become wiser
LC : 01 :135(383) [0619] you will not obey him, then obey the grim reaper, **Death**!
LC : 01 :136(383) [0619] he will send upon you both **death** and the hangman.
LC : 01 :137(384) [0619] that such wicked people die a natural and timely **death**.
LC : 01 :181(389) [0631] own children to judgment and sentence them to **death**.
LC : 01 :190(391) [0635] you could clothe him, you have let him freeze to **death**.
LC : 01 :190(391) [0635] see anyone condemned to **death** or in similar peril and do
LC : 01 :190(391) [0635] did not contribute to his **death** by word or deed, for you
LC : 02 :027(414) [0685] me from sin, from the devil, from **death**, and from all evil.
LC : 02 :027(414) [0685] I was condemned to **death** and entangled in sin and
LC : 02 :028(414) [0685] came and led us into disobedience, sin, **death**, and all evil.
LC : 02 :031(414) [0685] the devil to God, from **death** to life, from sin to
LC : 02 :031(414) [0687] up and devoured **death**, and finally ascended into heaven
LC : 02 :031(414) [0687] us from the wicked world, the devil, **death**, sin, etc.
LC : 02 :037(415) [0687] us through his birth, **death**, and resurrection, etc., so the
LC : 02 :038(415) [0689] for us by his sufferings, **death**, and resurrection, etc.
LC : 02 :057(418) [0693] our flesh will be put to **death**, will be buried with all its
LC : 02 :058(418) [0693] freed from sin, **death**, and all evil, living in new,
LC : 03 :051(427) [0711] and salvation against sin, **death**, and an evil conscience.
LC : 03 :054(427) [0713] utterly destroyed and sin, **death**, and hell exterminated,
LC : 03 :115(435) [0731] kingdom: poverty, shame, **death**, and, in short, all the
LC : 04 :025(439) [0739] to be delivered from sin, **death** and the devil and to enter
LC : 04 :041(441) [0743] and brings — victory over **death** and the devil, forgiveness
LC : 04 :043(442) [0743] which swallows up **death** and saves the lives of all men.
LC : 05 :022(449) [0757] has provided for me against my sins, **death**, and all evils.
LC : 05 :070(454) [0769] and power against **death** and the devil and all evils.
LC : 05 :071(455) [0769] with sin, fear of **death**, and the assaults of the flesh and
EP : 01 :010(467) [0781] will take place wholly by way of **death** in the resurrection.
EP : 03 :003(473) [0793] man he rendered to his heavenly Father into **death** itself.
EP : 05 :009(479) [0803] of the suffering and **death** of Christ, the Son of God, is an
EP : 05 :010(479) [0803] namely, the passion and **death** of Christ — proclaims
EP : 06 :004(480) [0805] nature and kind), which clings to them until **death**.
EP : 08 :032(491) [0825] us by his suffering and **death** he no longer has anything to
EP : 09 :001(492) [0827] Did it happen before or after his **death**?
EP : 09 :004(492) [0827] them from the power of **death**, of the devil, and of the
SD : 01 :006(509) [0861] the children of wrath," of **death**, and of damnation unless
SD : 01 :013(511) [0863] and upon original sin is **death**, eternal damnation,
SD : 01 :062(519) [0879] God's eternal wrath and **death** but that we do not even
SD : 02 :011(522) [0885] liberated him from the **death** of sin and made him alive.
SD : 02 :015(523) [0887] the bondage of sin and **death** through his Son, and for
SD : 02 :021(525) [0889] wrath of God over sin and **death** but continues in his
SD : 02 :021(525) [0889] dangers and finally into eternal **death** and damnation.
SD : 02 :034(527) [0895] in Christians until **death**, for it contends with the sin
SD : 02 :043(529) [0897] that he will not deviate from his doctrine until his **death**.
SD : 02 :043(529) [0897] Outside of Christ **death** and sin are our masters and the
SD : 02 :049(530) [0901] I have no pleasure in the **death** of the wicked, but that the
SD : 02 :059(532) [0905] God raises him from the **death** of sin, illuminates him,
SD : 02 :087(538) [0915] the will from spiritual **death**, is solely and alone the work
SD : 03 :009(541) [0919] the bitter passion, the **death**, and the resurrection of
SD : 03 :015(541) [0919] suffering, in life and in **death**, Christ rendered for us to
SD : 03 :020(542) [0921] has translated him from **death** into life, as it is written,
SD : 03 :022(543) [0923] until his ignominious **death** on the cross for us, even
SD : 03 :027(543) [0923] not justified but is still in **death**, or that he has again lost
SD : 03 :032(545) [0927] obedience, passion, and **death** of Christ which is reckoned
SD : 03 :056(549) [0935] to the most ignominious **death** of the cross, is reckoned to
SD : 03 :058(550) [0937] from his holy birth to his **death** in the stead of us poor
SD : 05 :012(560) [0955] sin than the passion and **death** of Christ, his own Son?
SD : 05 :020(561) [0959] to the wrath of God, to **death**, to temporal miseries, and
SD : 05 :020(561) [0959] faith, are freed from **death** and all the punishments of
SD : 05 :022(562) [0959] Christ, "who was put to **death** for our trespasses and
SD : 05 :023(562) [0959] and plunged them into **death** and eternal damnation, but
SD : 07 :028(574) [0981] in the Spirit that after his **death** some would try to make
SD : 07 :029(574) [0981] my lifetime or after my **death** appeal to me or misuse my
SD : 07 :029(574) [0981] to abide by it until my **death** and (so help me God!) in
SD : 07 :029(574) [0981] any one shall say after my **death**, 'If Dr. Luther were

Continued ▶

SD : 0 7 :033(575) [0983] Shortly before his **death**, in his last confession, he
SD : 0 7 :044(577) [0987] his bitter passion and **death** for our sin, in this sad, last
SD : 0 7 :044(577) [0987] of his bitter passion and **death** and all of his blessings, a
SD : 0 7 :049(578) [0989] body, which he gave into **death** for us, and of his true,
SD : 0 7 :062(581) [0995] his body for us into **death** and by shedding his blood for
SD : 0 7 :081(584) [1001] has won for us by his **death** and the shedding of his blood
SD : 0 7 :084(584) [1001] proclaim the Lord's **death**), must be kept integrally and
SD : 0 7 :091(585) [1005] have advanced no new arguments since his **death**.
SD : 0 8 :004(592) [1017] But after his **death** a few theologians of the Augsburg
SD : 0 8 :025(596) [1023] the ground, and again in **death**, when he died not just like
SD : 0 8 :025(596) [1023] a way that by and in his **death** he conquered sin, death,
SD : 0 8 :025(596) [1023] death he conquered sin, **death**, the devil, hell, and eternal
SD : 0 8 :037(598) [1027] and "Christ was put to **death** in the flesh" and "suffered
SD : 0 8 :040(598) [1029] more in his passion and **death** than any other ordinary
SD : 0 8 :044(599) [1029] But if God's **death** and God dead lie in the opposite scale,
SD : 0 8 :044(599) [1031] said: God dead, God's passion, God's blood, God's **death**.
SD : 0 8 :044(599) [1031] to talk about God's **death** when that man dies who is one
SD : 0 8 :083(607) [1045] the person, even though **death** and all the devils had been
SD : 0 8 :085(608) [1045] wrote shortly before his **death**, Dr. Luther states:
SD : 1 1 :015(619) [1069] obedience, suffering, and **death** Christ has earned for us
SD : 1 1 :049(624) [1079] nor anguish, neither **death** nor life, etc. can separate us
SD : 1 1 :081(629) [1089] is sin, for the "wages of sin is **death**" (Rom. 6:23).
SD : 1 1 :081(629) [1089] he also does not will the **death** of a sinner and has no
SD : 1 1 :081(629) [1089] I have no pleasure in the **death** of the wicked, but that the
SD : 1 1 :084(630) [1091] he any "pleasure in the **death** of the wicked, but that the
SD : 1 2 :021(634) [1099] conscience impose the **death** penalty on evil-doers.

Deathbeds (1)
AG : 2 3 :006(052) [0061] experienced on their **deathbeds** on this account, and

Debased (1)
AP : 2 4 :091(266) [0415] satisfactions they have **debased** the forgiveness of guilt

Debate (3), Debated (1), Debating (1)
AG : 2 4 :023(058) [0067] Thereupon followed a **debate** as to whether one Mass
AL : 2 4 :023(058) [0067] Thus was introduced a **debate** on whether one Mass said
AP : 0 4 :156(128) [0165] We are **debating** about an important issue, the honor of
AP : 0 7 :032(174) [0239] Later they **debated** how it happened that they had come
S3 : 0 3 :036(309) [0489] It does not **debate** what is sin and what is not sin, but

Debt (8), Debtor (1), Debtors (8), Debts (6)
AP : 0 4 :143(126) [0161] he says, "We are **debtors**, not to the flesh, to live
AP : 0 4 :263(145) [0195] that is, the obligation or **debt** is removed because God
AP : 0 4 :264(146) [0195] that the obligation or **debt** can be removed, that the wrath
AP : 0 4 :345(160) [0217] judgment a right or **debt** is certain, while mercy is
AP : 2 1 :019(231) [0347] If one pays a **debt** for one's friend, the debtor is freed by
AP : 2 1 :019(231) [0347] debt for one's friend, the **debtor** is freed by the merit of
AP : 2 4 :062(260) [0405] the cross for the original **debt**, is daily offered on the altar
SC : 0 3 :015(347) [0549] *"And forgive us our **debts**, as we also have forgiven our*
SC : 0 3 :015(347) [0549] *us our debts, as we also have forgiven our **debtors**."*
LC : S P :014(363) [0577] bread; and forgive us our **debts**, as we also have forgiven
LC : S P :014(363) [0577] we also have forgiven our **debtors**; and lead us not into
LC : 0 1 :022(367) [0585] God were in our service or **debt** and we were his liege
LC : 0 1 :303(406) [0667] because of adversity or **debt** cannot hold on to his
LC : 0 3 :085(432) [0723] *"And forgive us our **debts**, as we forgive our debtors."*
LC : 0 3 :085(432) [0723] *"And forgive us our debts, as we forgive our **debtors**."*
LC : 0 3 :088(432) [0723] upon God and pray, "Dear Father, forgive us our **debts**."
LC : 0 3 :093(433) [0725] comforting clause is added, "as we forgive our **debtors**."
LC : 0 6 :008(458) [0000] we say, "Forgive us our **debts**, as we forgive our debtors,"
LC : 0 6 :008(458) [0000] "Forgive us our debts, as we forgive our **debtors**," etc.
LC : 0 6 :010(458) [0000] Now, all of us are **debtors** one to another, therefore we
LC : 0 6 :012(458) [0000] a twofold absolution: our **debts** both to God and to our
EP : 0 1 :011(467) [0781] that original sin is only a **debt** which we owe because of
SD : 0 4 :016(554) [0943] immutable will, whose **debtors** we are, as his

Decalogue (12)
AL : 2 4 :019(058) [0067] For in the **Decalogue** it is written, "The Lord will not hold
AL : 2 8 :033(086) [0087] the Lord's Day — contrary to the **Decalogue**, it appears.
AP : 0 2 :014(102) [0109] transgressing as they do the first table of the **Decalogue**.
AP : 0 2 :016(102) [0109] the second table of the **Decalogue**, but also the first,
AP : 0 4 :006(108) [0121] commandments of the **Decalogue**, wherever they appear
AP : 0 4 :008(108) [0121] But the **Decalogue** does not only require external works
AP : 0 4 :022(110) [0127] commanded in the **Decalogue** should be performed,
AP : 0 4 :087(120) [0147] later on he quotes the **Decalogue**, "You shall not covet"
AP : 0 4 :124(124) [0157] of ceremonies, but of **Decalogue**, the law that deals with
AP : 0 4 :270(147) [0197] Commandment of the **Decalogue** itself states, "Showing
AP : 1 6 :011(224) [0333] shall not steal," the **Decalogue** recognizes the right of
AP : 2 7 :017(272) [0425] Mosaic law or of the **Decalogue** or the rule of Benedict or

Decay (2)
AL : 2 7 :002(071) [0077] when discipline fell into **decay**, vows were added for the
LC : P R :006(359) [0569] let parishes fall into **decay**, and brazenly allow both

Deceit (5), Deceitful (4), Deceitfully (1), Deceitfulness (1), Deceive (20), Deceived (11), Deceives (2), Deceiving (5)
AP : P R :014(099) [0101] in some places it could **deceive** even the cautious reader.
AP : 0 4 :139(126) [0161] so that we may not be **deceived** and err, nor be driven to
AP : 0 4 :229(139) [0183] **Deceived** by human wisdom, they did not see the true face
AP : 0 4 :328(158) [0211] say we have no sin, we **deceive** ourselves, and the truth is
AP : 0 4 :337(159) [0215] our opponents are **deceived** with regard to the term
AP : 1 5 :024(218) [0321] So men are **deceived** by the appearance of wisdom and
AP : 1 5 :025(218) [0321] and righteousness has **deceived** men, all sorts of troubles
AP : 2 1 :040(235) [0355] everywhere else, the Confutation is a **deceitful** document.
AP : 2 3 :005(239) [0365] false prophets would **deceive** people with their fictions.
AP : 2 4 :052(259) [0403] The analogy **deceives** them, and they think that we should
AP : 2 4 :095(267) [0417] They were men and they could err and be **deceived**.
AP : 2 7 :032(274) [0431] adds: "Let nobody **deceive** himself; for if he considers
AP : 2 7 :044(277) [0435] guilty of a double sin — **deceiving** men, and doing so
AP : 2 7 :057(279) [0439] because they were **deceived** by the tricks of the monks or
S3 : 0 1 :002(302) [0477] to parents, murder, unchastity, theft, **deceit**, etc.
S3 : 0 3 :039(309) [0489] beautiful, is nothing but **deceitful** falsehood and
S3 : 0 3 :045(310) [0491] say we have no sin, we **deceive** ourselves, and the truth is
SC : 0 1 :004(342) [0539] practice magic, lie, or **deceive**, but in every time of need
SC : 0 3 :018(347) [0549] and our flesh may not **deceive** us or mislead us into
SC : 0 9 :003(354) [0561] Do not be **deceived**; God is not mocked" (Gal. 6:6, 7).
LC : 0 1 :042(370) [0591] that they neither lie nor **deceive** but will yet prove to be
LC : 0 1 :046(370) [0593] since God cannot lie or **deceive**; just leave it to the devil
LC : 0 1 :046(370) [0593] devil and the world to **deceive** you with their appearance,
LC : 0 1 :052(371) [0595] abused than for purposes of falsehood and **deceit**.
LC : 0 1 :056(372) [0595] For to lie and **deceive** is in itself a gross sin, but it is
LC : 0 1 :213(394) [0641] chastity while they **deceive** the common people with lying
LC : 0 1 :216(394) [0641] captive consciences **deceived** by their monastic vows are
LC : 0 1 :308(406) [0669] sees your wicked heart and the **deceitfulness** of the world.
LC : 0 1 :326(409) [0675] vain by cursing, lying, **deceiving**, and other kinds of
LC : 0 3 :021(423) [0703] and promise, which cannot fail or **deceive** me."
LC : 0 3 :045(426) [0709] by swearing, cursing, **deceiving**, etc., but used rightly to
LC : 0 3 :080(431) [0721] order, so that he may **deceive** men with his lies and bring
LC : 0 3 :102(434) [0727] drunkenness, greed and **deceit**, into acts of fraud and
LC : 0 4 :054(443) [0745] Jew should today come **deceitfully** and with an evil
LC : 0 4 :056(444) [0747] me his body and blood; he will not lie or **deceive** me.
LC : 0 4 :057(444) [0747] all men — may err and **deceive**, but God's Word cannot
LC : 0 5 :014(448) [0757] from the lips of Christ, so it is; he cannot lie or **deceive**."
EP : 1 1 :014(496) [0835] the revealed Word which cannot and will not **deceive** us.
SD : 0 2 :017(524) [0887] "The heart of man is **deceitful** and desperately wicked,"
SD : 0 4 :032(556) [0947] Do not be **deceived**; neither the immoral, nor idolaters,
SD : 0 5 :023(562) [0959] by God and through the **deceit** of the serpent transgressed
SD : 0 7 :006(570) [0973] important people were **deceived** by the noble and
SD : 0 7 :023(573) [0979] lips speak and declare, since he cannot lie or **deceive**.
SD : 0 7 :067(582) [0997] by which the devil amuses himself and **deceives** men."
SD : 0 7 :096(586) [1005] The third is that the Word of God is not false or **deceitful**.
SD : 0 7 :107(588) [1009] as false, erroneous, and **deceiving** every error which is
SD : 0 7 :112(589) [1011] as false, erroneous, and **deceiving** all Sacramentarian
SD : 1 1 :046(624) [1079] fingers, and through the **deceit** and power of the devil and
SD : 1 2 :005(633) [1097] anything with intent to **deceive** and that our agreement

Decent (2), Decency (4), Decently (1)
AP : 1 5 :020(218) [0321] all things could be done **decently** and in order in the
AP : 1 5 :039(220) [0325] the public liturgy is more **decent** than in theirs, and if you
S2 : 0 3 :001(297) [0471] of learned men and **decent** women should be restored to
LC : 0 1 :218(394) [0643] will be brought up to **decency** and respect for authority
EP : 0 7 :041(486) [0817] and statements, which **decency** forbids us to recite and
SD : 0 4 :039(557) [0951] weaken discipline and **decency**, and might introduce and
SD : 0 6 :001(563) [0963] external discipline and **decency** against dissolute and

Deception (5), Deceptions (2), Deceptive (2)
AP : 1 5 :029(219) [0323] Against this **deceptive** appearance of wisdom and
S1 : P R :002(288) [0455] good faith, and without **deception** or treachery to hold a
S2 : 0 4 :014(301) [0475] as our head or lord, for **deception**, murder, and the
LC : 0 3 :041(425) [0709] that is false and **deceptive**, using his name to cloak lies
LC : 0 3 :102(434) [0727] into acts of fraud and **deception** against our neighbor —
LC : 0 5 :019(449) [0757] against all errors and **deceptions** that have ever arisen or
SD : 0 7 :026(573) [0981] against all errors and **deceptions** that have so far arisen
SD : 1 0 :020(614) [1059] as our head or lord, for **deception**, murder, and the
SD : 1 1 :029(621) [1073] of the Word as a **deception**, but should know certainly

Decide (9), Decided (12), Decides (1), Decision (6), Decisions (14), Decisive (1)
PR : P R :007(004) [0009] and also some of us, **decided** (on the basis of a
PR : P R :010(006) [0011] accurately to explain and **decide** the difference that had
PR : P R :011(006) [0011] that had occurred were to be **decided** in a Christian way.
AG : P R :007(025) [0039] and counsel, it was **decided** last Wednesday that, in
AG : P R :016(026) [0041] not disposed to render **decisions** in matters pertaining to
AG : 1 6 :002(037) [0051] and judges, render **decisions** and pass sentence according
AG : 2 3 :013(053) [0063] made and to the **decisions** of the most renowned
AL : 1 6 :002(037) [0051] office, to sit as judges, to **decide** matters by the imperial
AL : 2 7 :031(076) [0079] judgment to make a **decision** involving the rest of his life.
AL : 2 8 :029(085) [0087] power or jurisdiction to **decide** legal cases (for example,
AP : 0 4 :316(156) [0209] This **decision** is easy.
AP : 0 7 :034(175) [0239] and only then can we **decide** whether it is necessary for
AP : 1 2 :090(195) [0279] all good men judge and **decide** whether our teaching or
AP : 1 2 :167(208) [0303] and conciliar **decisions** about satisfactions were a matter
AP : 1 6 :007(223) [0331] public redress are court **decisions**, punishments, wars,
AP : 2 2 :005(236) [0359] to the prudent reader to **decide** what he should believe
AP : 2 2 :016(238) [0361] out how they will account to God for their **decisions**.
AP : 2 2 :017(238) [0361] whatever the pontiffs **decide**, especially when Scripture
AP : 2 3 :017(242) [0369] It is up to each man's conscience to **decide** this matter.
AP : 2 3 :023(242) [0369] do not represent the **decision** of the synods but the
AP : 2 3 :068(248) [0383] They **decided** that the best way to arouse the ignorant
S1 : P R :003(289) [0455] Nevertheless, I have **decided** to publish these articles so
S2 : 0 2 :010(294) [0465] the Mass will be the **decisive** issue in the council.
S3 : 0 8 :004(312) [0495] claims that whatever he **decides** and commands in his
TR : 0 0 :012(321) [0507] 5. The Council of Nicaea **decided** that the bishop of
TR : 0 0 :012(322) [0507] bishop grew out of a **decision** of a council and is of
TR : 0 0 :013(322) [0507] the Council of Nicaea **decided** that bishops should be
TR : 0 0 :021(323) [0509] Phocas had finally **decided** that the primacy should be
TR : 0 0 :040(327) [0517] his authority above the **decisions** of councils and the
TR : 0 0 :049(329) [0519] controversies to be **decided** in the proper manner.
TR : 0 0 :056(329) [0521] Since **decisions** of synods are decisions of the church and
TR : 0 0 :056(329) [0521] decisions of synods are **decisions** of the church and not of
TR : 0 0 :056(329) [0521] making judgments and **decisions** according to the Word
TR : 0 0 :064(331) [0523] was ordination, for it was **decided** that one bishop should
TR : 0 0 :077(333) [0527] of Justinian that **decisions** in matrimonial cases had
TR : 0 0 :077(333) [0527] to make these **decisions** if the bishops are negligent.
LC : P R :017(361) [0573] judge, and make **decisions** in both spiritual and temporal
LC : 0 1 :259(400) [0655] evidence presented, and make his **decision** accordingly.
LC : 0 1 :280(403) [0661] testimony the judge can base his **decision** and sentence.
EP : R N :000(464) [0777] Should Be Explained and **Decided** in a Christian Way
SD : R N :000(503) [0849] Are to Be Explained and **Decided** in a Christian Way
SD : R N :013(506) [0855] our expositions and **decisions** in the controverted articles
SD : 0 2 :073(535) [0909] free will it is possible to **decide** the questions that for a

Deck (1)
LC : 0 1 :088(377) [0605] from external work, or **deck** ourselves with garlands and

Declaration (11), Declare (39), Declared (10), Declares (24), Declaring (1)
PR : P R :000(001) [0004] with an Appended **Declaration**, Firmly Founded on the
PR : P R :001(003) [0007] humble, and willing service, and hereby **declare**:

Continued ▶

PR : PR :008(005) [0009] that we might testify and **declare** to our most gracious
PR : PR :014(007) [0013] and that a pure **declaration** of the truth might be
PR : PR :018(009) [0015] submitted into our **declaration** and Book of Concord that
PR : PR :021(010) [0019] exalted, our theologians **declare** in clear and candid
AG : PR :023(027) [0043] To these we **declare** our continuing adherence, and we
AG : 0 0 :006(095) [0095] the above articles as a **declaration** of our confession and
AL : 0 9 :003(033) [0047] Baptism of children and **declare** that children are saved
AL : 2 3 :005(051) [0061] by which he **declared** that all men are not suited
AP : 0 4 :011(108) [0123] The scholastics have **declared** that by necessity—the
AP : 0 4 :062(115) [0139] The Gospel **declares** that all men are under sin and are
AP : 0 4 :085(119) [0147] be diverted from this **declaration**, that we receive the
AP : 0 4 :089(120) [0149] therefore, that God **declares** to be righteousness; he adds
AP : 0 4 :092(120) [0149] so is justified," where he **declares** that faith is the
AP : 0 4 :228(139) [0183] blessings from him; this he **declares** to be true worship.
AP : 0 4 :292(152) [0203] is received by faith alone, as Paul **declares** in Rom. 4:13.
AP : 0 4 :323(157) [0209] the Church Fathers, who **declare** unanimously that even
AP : 0 4 :332(158) [0211] If they **declare** that they are worthy because they have
AP : 0 4 :366(163) [0219] concede, and have often **declared**, that though
AP : 1 2 :048(188) [0265] of the sentence which **declares** that we are condemned and
AP : 1 2 :077(193) [0275] we gave our reasons for **declaring** that men are justified
AP : 1 2 :108(198) [0283] Therefore I **declare** Thee to be justified in condemning
AP : 1 2 :108(198) [0283] I **declare** Thee to be blameless when hypocrites judge
AP : 1 4 :005(215) [0315] we want at this point to **declare** our willingness to keep
AP : 2 1 :023(232) [0349] of the Mass confidently **declares**: "It is a divinely
AP : 2 1 :025(232) [0349] According to this **declaration** of absolution, we are
AP : 2 4 :028(254) [0393] the Jews accepted this **declaration**, which seems to
AP : 2 4 :029(255) [0393] It **declares** that calling upon God is really worshiping and
AP : 2 7 :069(281) [0443] Christ cancels with one **declaration** when he says (Matt.
S 2 : 0 2 :007(294) [0463] all books on the subject **declare**), for by means of the
S 3 : 0 3 :027(307) [0487] uncertainty when he **declared** in his bulls, "Whoever
TR : 0 0 :002(320) [0503] Finally, he **declares** that it is necessary for salvation to
TR : 0 0 :025(324) [0511] Peter made when he **declared** Jesus to be the Christ, the
TR : 0 0 :028(325) [0511] So Chrysostom **declares** that Christ says "on this rock"
TR : 0 0 :029(325) [0513] Hilary **declares**: "The Father revealed to Peter that he
TR : 0 0 :042(328) [0517] Scriptures unanimously **declare** these errors to be
TR : 0 0 :049(329) [0519] sometimes impudently **declare** — yet this was done much
TR : 0 0 :069(331) [0523] is confirmed by the **declaration** of Peter, "You are a royal
TR : 0 0 :082(334) [0529] Smalcald unanimously **declare** that in their churches they
TR : 0 0 :082(334) [0529] They also **declare** that they approve the article concerning
SC : 0 1 :021(344) [0543] What does God **declare** concerning all these
SC : 0 4 :006(349) [0551] all who believe, as the Word and promise of God **declare**.
SC : 0 5 :021(350) [0553] hear my confession and **declare** that my sins are forgiven
SC : 0 6 :008(352) [0557] has what they say and **declare**: the forgiveness of sins.
LC : PR :006(359) [0569] louts and skinflints who **declare** that we can do without
LC : 0 1 :132(383) [0619] He **declares** that it is not only an object of pleasure and
LC : 0 1 :191(391) [0635] them in the day of judgment, as Christ himself **declares**.
LC : 0 1 :268(401) [0657] can pronounce is to **declare** somebody a thief, a
LC : 0 1 :322(409) [0673] because he himself here **declares** how important the
LC : 0 5 :012(448) [0755] your conscience and **declare**: "Let a hundred thousand
LC : 0 5 :035(450) [0761] believes that they are true has what the words **declare**.
EP : RN :006(465) [0779] as opposed to the unanimous **declaration** of our faith.
EP : 0 4 :007(476) [0799] terms, "So also David **declares** that salvation pertains
EP : 0 8 :003(487) [0819] They **declare** boldly that the "personal union makes
EP : 0 8 :017(489) [0823] of Christ's testament **declare**, *"This is, is, is my body,"*
SD : 0 0 :000(501) [0845] [Part II. Solid **Declaration**]
SD : RN :002(503) [0851] and with our mouths **declared** in mutual agreement that
SD : RN :005(504) [0851] We therefore **declare** our adherence to the first, unaltered
SD : RN :008(505) [0853] and false doctrine, we **declare** our unanimous adherence
SD : 0 1 :003(509) [0861] then (as the Apology **declares**) we are led to understand
SD : 0 1 :042(515) [0871] the devil's work, we **declare** that it is by God's creation
SD : 0 2 :025(526) [0891] operation and the Holy Spirit, as the Apology **declares**.
SD : 0 2 :029(527) [0893] Augsburg Confession **declares**: "People outside of Christ
SD : 0 2 :030(527) [0893] On the contrary, it **declares** that man is the captive of
SD : 0 2 :031(527) [0893] free will: "We also **declare** that to a certain extent reason
SD : 0 2 :032(527) [0893] such external works, we **declare** that in spiritual things
SD : 0 2 :043(529) [0897] in which he solemnly **declares** that he will not deviate
SD : 0 2 :051(531) [0901] "Peter will **declare** to you a message by which you will be
SD : 0 3 :006(540) [0917] same vein Dr. Luther **declared**: "Where this single article
SD : 0 3 :009(540) [0919] is, he is absolved and **declared** utterly free from all his
SD : 0 3 :017(541) [0921] "justify" here means to **declare** righteous and free from
SD : 0 3 :043(547) [0931] But, as the Apology **declares**, James is speaking of the
SD : 0 3 :054(549) [0935] on account of which we are **declared** just before God.
SD : 0 4 :030(555) [0947] reason it is important to **declare** well and in detail how
SD : 0 4 :037(557) [0951] but Paul himself, who **declares** no less than three times in
SD : 0 7 :002(569) [0973] and explicitly, they all **declare** unanimously that the true,
SD : 0 7 :022(573) [0979] the Word of God and **declare**, 'Let a hundred thousand
SD : 0 7 :023(573) [0979] as Christ's lips speak and **declare**, since he cannot lie or
SD : 0 8 :046(600) [1031] Council of Chalcedon **declares**, each nature according to
SD : 1 0 :019(614) [1059] Smalcald Articles of 1537 **declare** on this: "We do not
SD : 1 0 :019(614) [1059] the Smalcald Articles **declare**: "If the bishops were true
SD : 1 1 :028(620) [1071] Christ **declares**, "Come unto me, all who are heavy-laden,
SD : 1 1 :084(630) [1091] so that my name may be **declared** throughout all the
SD : 1 2 :004(633) [1097] our purpose not only to **declare** our unanimous opinion

Decline (1)
AP : 2 7 :003(269) [0419] statement about the **decline** of the monastic regime and

Decorate (1)
SD : 1 1 :042(623) [1077] filth of the world, and **decorate** their hearts as a

Decorum (3)
SD : 1 0 :001(610) [1053] sake of good order and **decorum** or else to preserve
SD : 1 0 :007(611) [1055] nor evangelical **decorum** in the church,ts true adiaphora or
SD : 1 0 :009(612) [1055] discipline, evangelical **decorum**, and the edification of the

Decrease (1), Decreases (1)
LC : 0 4 :067(445) [0749] corruption must daily **decrease** so that the longer we live
LC : 0 4 :071(445) [0749] the old man daily **decreases** until he is finally destroyed.

Decree (17), Decreed (9), Decrees (10), Decretals (2)
AG : 0 1 :001(027) [0043] in accordance with the **decree** of the Council of Nicaea,
AG : 2 3 :012(052) [0063] published the new papal **decree** was almost killed during
AG : 2 3 :012(053) [0063] The **decree** concerning celibacy was at once enforced
AG : 2 8 :066(092) [0093] doctrine, and this is not abrogated by the **decree**.
AL : 0 1 :001(027) [0043] great unanimity that the **decree** of the Council of Nicaea
AL : 2 8 :066(092) [0093] In connection with the **decree** one must consider what the
AP : PR :008(098) [0101] Later there appeared a **decree** in which our opponents
AP : 0 2 :036(105) [0115] generations so much that they included it in the **decretals**.
AP : 0 4 :380(165) [0223] taken certain sayings, **decrees** as it were, and these they
AP : 0 7 :010(170) [0229] The gloss in the ***Decrees*** says that "the church in the larger
AP : 0 7 :042(176) [0243] But as the words of this **decree** show, the apostles did not
AP : 0 7 :042(176) [0243] The text of the **decree** is preserved in Epiphanius: "Do
AP : 0 7 :042(176) [0243] are from an apostolic **decree** about Easter; from them the
AP : 0 7 :043(177) [0243] because of this apostolic **decree** the Passover should be
AP : 0 7 :043(177) [0243] Epiphanius praises the **decree** and says that it contains
AP : 1 2 :066(191) [0271] the authority to issue **decrees** contrary to this consensus
AP : 1 2 :067(191) [0271] In their **decrees** they condemn this teaching that we
AP : 1 2 :068(192) [0271] statements which the **decrees** quote in garbled form.
AP : 1 2 :093(196) [0279] have compiled these centos of the sentences and **decrees**.
AP : 1 2 :113(199) [0285] as the gloss on the **decree** warns, and admitting notorious
AP : 2 0 :006(227) [0339] We see that a horrible **decree** has been drawn up against
AP : 2 3 :006(240) [0365] law and conflicts with the very **decrees** of councils.
AP : 2 7 :029(274) [0431] and even say that this **decree** of theirs is stated in the
S 1 : PR :014(291) [0459] adopting a multitude of **decrees** and canons in a council,
S 2 : 0 4 :014(301) [0475] transactions and judgments, as the papal **decretals** show.
TR : 0 0 :006(320) [0505] He wishes his articles, his **decrees**, and his laws to be
TR : 0 0 :021(323) [0509] occurred, nor would a **decree** of the emperor have been
TR : 0 0 :049(329) [0519] and can rescind the **decrees** of councils, as the canons
TR : 0 0 :055(329) [0521] permit anything to be **decreed** contrary to his will and
EP : 0 6 :004(480) [0807] they undertake self-**decreed** and self-chosen acts of
EP : 1 1 :013(496) [0835] of the Father, who has **decreed** in his eternal counsel that
SD : 0 4 :035(557) [0949] God, we rightly reject the **decree** of the Council of Trent
SD : 0 8 :059(602) [1035] the Council of Ephesus **decreed** that the flesh of Christ
SD : 1 1 :027(620) [1071] foreknown, elected, and **decreed**, he has also called"
SD : 1 1 :030(621) [1073] and they who are **decreed** "according to God's
SD : 1 1 :044(624) [1077] God has determined and **decreed** before the world began
SD : 1 1 :048(624) [1079] God has determined and **decreed** that he will assist us in
SD : 1 1 :066(627) [1085] For the Father has **decreed** from eternity that whomever

Decry (1)
PR : PR :020(010) [0017] testament of Christ and **decry** and condemn them as

Deducing (1), Deductions (1)
AP : 2 0 :012(228) [0341] have learned the trick of **deducing** from Scripture
SD : 1 1 :055(625) [1081] to make our own **deductions**, draw conclusions, or brood

Deed (42), Deeds (24)
AL : 2 0 :030(045) [0057] "Faith is the mother of the good will and the right **deed**."
AL : 2 0 :040(046) [0057] naught, Nothing good in **deed** or thought, Nothing free
AP : 0 4 :033(111) [0129] even when it produces **deeds** that are excellent and
AP : 0 4 :103(122) [0151] glory in his works since no one is justified by his **deeds**.
AP : 0 4 :143(127) [0161] you put to death the **deeds** of the body, you will live."
AP : 0 4 :208(135) [0177] forgiveness of sins by this **deed**, but because they were
AP : 0 4 :209(136) [0177] by this cruel and painful **deed** to placate the wrath of
AP : 1 2 :051(189) [0265] will be wroth, to do his **deed** — strange is his deed! and to
AP : 1 2 :051(189) [0265] his deed — strange is his **deed**! and to work his work —
AP : 1 2 :091(195) [0279] and not to commit again **deeds** that ought to be
AP : 1 2 :122(200) [0289] a people of his own who are zealous for good **deeds**."
AP : 1 2 :160(207) [0301] penalties for certain past **deeds**, but works of God,
AP : 1 2 :170(209) [0305] in the mouth confession, in the **deed** complete humility."
S 2 : 0 4 :003(298) [0471] transactions and **deeds** (except what pertains to secular
S 3 : 0 1 :002(302) [0477] are all the subsequent evil **deeds** which are forbidden in
S 3 : 0 3 :028(308) [0487] actual sins — that is, of sinful thoughts, words, and **deeds**
S 3 : 0 3 :029(308) [0487] they were innocent of evil **deeds** and could even sell their
SC : 0 1 :012(343) [0541] and pure life in word and **deed**, each one loving and
SC : 0 5 :020(350) [0553] anyone by word or **deed**; and whether you have stolen,
SC : 0 5 :022(350) [0553] I have also been immodest in word and **deed**.
SC : 0 7 :002(352) [0557] in all my thoughts, words, and **deeds** I may please Thee.
LC : 0 1 :186(390) [0633] harm another for any evil **deed**, no matter how much he
LC : 0 1 :188(390) [0633] means, first, by hand or by **deed**; next, we should not use
LC : 0 1 :190(391) [0635] to his death by word or **deed**, for you have withheld your
LC : 0 1 :195(391) [0637] us to true, noble, exalted **deeds**, such as gentleness,
LC : 0 1 :219(394) [0643] in thought, word, and **deed** in his particular situation
LC : 0 1 :252(399) [0653] lends to the Lord, and he will repay him for his **deed**."
LC : 0 1 :311(407) [0671] Ten Commandments no **deed**, no conduct can be good or
LC : 0 3 :040(425) [0709] by us either in words or in **deeds**; everything we do on
LC : 0 3 :040(425) [0709] earth may be classified as word or **deed**, speech or act.
LC : 0 3 :044(425) [0709] him in word and **deed** with the result that on his account
LC : 0 3 :046(426) [0709] our idiom "to praise, extol, and honor" in word and **deed**.
LC : 0 3 :089(432) [0723] we sin daily in word and **deed**, in acts of commission and
LC : 0 3 :103(434) [0727] assails us by word and **deed** and drives us to anger and
LC : 0 4 :021(439) [0737] honored it by words and **deeds** and has confirmed it by
EP : 0 1 :021(468) [0785] or no wicked act or **deed** took place, nevertheless man's
EP : 0 1 :021(468) [0785] evil thoughts, words, and **deeds**, as it is written, "Out of
EP : 0 2 :008(471) [0789] and that he commits evil **deeds** and acts like fornication,
EP : 0 8 :002(487) [0817] *really* (that is, in **deed** and truth) share with each other,
EP : 0 8 :003(487) [0817] the two *really* (that is, in **deed** and in truth) shares in the
EP : 0 8 :003(487) [0819] that God really (that is, in **deed** and in truth) has nothing
EP : 0 8 :011(488) [0821] hence really (that is, in **deed** and in truth) shared only the
EP : 0 8 :015(488) [0821] nature is really (that is, in **deed** and in truth) exalted to
SD : 0 1 :001(508) [0859] a thought, a word, or a **deed** but the very nature itself out
SD : 0 1 :042(515) [0873] our thoughts, words, and **deeds** are evil, is in its origin the
SD : 0 1 :053(517) [0875] only thoughts, words, and **deeds** are sin but that the
SD : 0 2 :039(528) [0895] (indeed, actually do good **deeds** and grow in
SD : 0 3 :058(550) [0937] its thoughts, words, and **deeds**, so that our disobedience
SD : 0 4 :019(554) [0945] its passions, desires, and **deeds** (Gal. 5:24; Rom. 8:13).
SD : 0 5 :011(560) [0955] prophet calls "a strange **deed**" (that is, to rebuke) until he
SD : 0 5 :017(561) [0957] thoughts, words, and **deeds** in order to be pleasing and
SD : 0 5 :020(561) [0959] thoughts, words, and **deeds** war against the law, and he is
SD : 0 7 :060(580) [0993] when they actually and in **deed** laid violent hands upon
SD : 0 7 :078(584) [1001] attached his own command and **deed** to our speaking."
SD : 0 8 :014(594) [1019] glued together, so that in **deed** and truth the two natures
SD : 0 8 :019(594) [1021] and in a strictly verbal fashion, but in **deed** and in truth.
SD : 0 8 :023(595) [1023] of Christ did not exist in **deed** and truth, all of this would
SD : 0 8 :028(596) [1025] to his humanity in **deed** and in truth without any blending
SD : 0 8 :031(597) [1025] in common but also in **deed** and truth have communion

Continued ▶

SD : 0 8 :063(603) [1037] that takes place in **deed** and in truth — to describe any
SD : 0 8 :063(603) [1037] exchange has occurred in **deed** and in truth but without
SD : 0 8 :067(604) [1039] in words alone, while in **deed** and in truth the human
SD : 0 8 :076(606) [1043] have with each other in **deed** and truth in the person of
SD : 0 8 :095(609) [1049] Christ does not share in **deed** and truth the divine power,
SD : 1 0 :010(612) [1055] but also through their **deeds** and actions, the true
SD : 1 0 :029(615) [1061] anything is done in **deed** or action to please enemies of

Deem (2), Deemed (2)
AG : 2 8 :068(093) [0093] such rules are not to be **deemed** necessary and that
SC : 0 1 :006(342) [0541] of the same, but **deem** it holy and gladly hear and learn
EP : 0 5 :011(479) [0805] 1. Hence we reject and **deem** it as false and detrimental
SD : 0 7 :087(585) [1003] this use it is not to be **deemed** a sacrament, as when in the

Deep (10), Deepened (1), Deepest (2), Deeply (8)
AG : PR :011(026) [0041] invoke almighty God in **deepest** humility and implore him
AG : 2 5 :008(062) [0069] human nature is so **deeply** submerged in sins that it is
AP : 1 4 :001(214) [0315] in the assembly to our **deep** desire to maintain the church
AP : 1 6 :009(224) [0333] of the heart, like a **deep** fear of God and a strong faith.
AP : 2 8 :019(284) [0449] position and contains the **deepest** kind of comfort and
S 1 : PR :003(289) [0455] They are **deeply** offended, as well they might be, and are
S 3 : 0 1 :003(302) [0477] This hereditary sin is so **deep** a corruption of nature that
SC : PR :023(341) [0539] of these, although he is **deeply** immersed in them and is
LC : SP :027(364) [0581] so that it may penetrate **deeply** into their minds and
LC : 0 1 :157(386) [0627] misery in which we are so **deeply** sunk and may rightly
LC : 0 1 :192(391) [0635] wearily struggling in **deep** water, or fallen into a fire, and
LC : 0 1 :317(408) [0673] which has become so **deeply** rooted and still clings to
EP : 0 1 :008(467) [0781] nature, but that it is so **deep** a corruption that nothing
SD : 0 1 :002(508) [0859] that it is an abominable, **deep**, and inexpressible
SD : 0 1 :011(510) [0863] of God in man with a **deep**, wicked, abominable,
SD : 0 1 :052(517) [0875] original sin is the **deep** corruption of our nature as it is
SD : 0 1 :058(519) [0879] only be increased and **deepened** if the clergy are in doubt
SD : 0 1 :062(519) [0879] nature but corrupted it so **deeply** that nothing in it
SD : 0 7 :101(587) [1007] you must posit it again as **deep** and as near in all
SD : 1 1 :045(624) [1079] comfort that God was so **deeply** concerned about every
SD : 1 1 :095(632) [1095] a sincere delight in and **deep** love for true harmony and

Defamation (1), Defame (2)
PR : PR :008(005) [0011] slanders and **defamation** of us and that other
SC : 0 1 :016(343) [0541] nor betray, slander, or **defame** him, but should apologize
LC : 0 1 :123(382) [0617] with blows; and they **defame** and depreciate one another

Defeat (2)
AP : 2 4 :035(256) [0397] something if we let them **defeat** us with allegories, but it
LC : 0 3 :111(435) [0729] will see the temptation cease and eventually admit **defeat**.

Defect (6), Defective (3), Defects (1)
AG : 0 0 :002(048) [0059] nothing unfounded or **defective** in the principal articles
AG : 0 0 :002(048) [0059] even if there were some **defect** among us in regard to
AP : 0 2 :024(103) [0111] includes both the **defect** and the vicious disposition that
AP : 0 2 :027(104) [0113] is truly composed of the **defects** that I have listed, as well
AP : 0 4 :336(159) [0215] The argument is **defective**.
S 3 : 0 1 :011(303) [0479] for there would be no **defect** or sin in man for which he
S 3 : 1 3 :002(315) [0499] not be reckoned as sin or **defect** for the sake of the same
LC : 0 1 :227(396) [0645] cheats another with **defective** merchandise, false
EP : 0 1 :012(467) [0783] teaching that the cited **defect** and damage is not truly sin
SD : 0 1 :056(518) [0877] itself, but an accidental **defect** and damage in the nature.

Defend (54), Defended (12), Defenders (2), Defending (5), Defends (9), Defense (18)
PR : PR :008(005) [0009] intention to adopt, to **defend**, or to spread a different or a
PR : PR :024(013) [0023] will and to introduce and **defend** monstrous errors, the
AG : 0 3 :005(030) [0045] that he may protect and **defend** them against the devil and
AG : 2 1 :001(046) [0057] office which demands the **defense** and protection of their
AG : 2 6 :022(067) [0073] In Matt. 15:1-20 Christ **defends** the apostles for not
AL : 0 3 :005(030) [0045] and quicken them and **defend** them against the devil and
AL : 2 0 :013(043) [0055] many volumes Augustine **defends** grace and the
AL : 2 6 :022(067) [0073] In Matt. 15:1-20 Christ **defends** the apostles for not
AP : 0 1 :002(100) [0103] have always taught and **defended** this doctrine and we
AP : 0 2 :051(107) [0119] not lack men to reply in **defense** of the truth, for in this
AP : 0 4 :069(116) [0141] mediator," then we must **defend** the proposition, "Faith
AP : 0 4 :070(116) [0141] the same way, if we must **defend** the proposition, "The
AP : 0 4 :070(116) [0141] the law," then we must **defend** the proposition, "Faith
AP : 0 4 :139(126) [0161] Spirit may govern and **defend** us, so that we may not be
AP : 0 4 :191(133) [0175] battles of God to **defend** the people who had God's Word
AP : 0 4 :230(139) [0183] of Christ's glory we **defend** it and we ask Christ for the
AP : 0 4 :236(140) [0185] up to even by those who most violently **defend** them.
AP : 0 4 :258(144) [0193] correct oppression; **defend** the fatherless, plead for the
AP : 0 4 :258(144) [0193] these works: "correct oppression, **defend** the fatherless."
AP : 0 4 :258(144) [0193] oppression, **defend** the fatherless"—they could merit the
AP : 0 4 :262(145) [0195] then to do good and to **defend** the poor against injustice,
AP : 0 4 :278(149) [0199] punishments, and merit a **defense** for us in the perils of
AP : 0 4 :326(158) [0211] He prays for the **defense** of God's cause and his glory, as
AP : 0 4 :400(168) [0227] not among those who **defend** wicked opinions against the
AP : 0 4 :400(168) [0227] not bother us since they **defend** human opinions contrary
AP : 0 7 :002(168) [0227] true that there is no **defense** against the attacks of
AP : 0 7 :003(168) [0227] Thus we do not need to **defend** ourselves at any length
AP : 0 7 :029(173) [0237] this seemed enough to **defend** the definition of the church
AP : 0 7 :050(178) [0245] and are preserved and **defended** by God against the devil.
AP : 1 0 :001(179) [0247] and consideration of it, we firmly **defend** this belief.
AP : 1 0 :004(179) [0247] to all our readers that we **defend** the doctrine received in
AP : 1 2 :004(183) [0253] Before beginning the **defense** of our position, we must say
AP : 1 2 :068(192) [0271] though by a conspiracy **defend** the false notions we have
AP : 1 2 :084(194) [0277] position that we are **defending**: by faith we receive the
AP : 1 2 :124(201) [0289] in making use of such **defenders** and turning over to these
AP : 1 2 :137(203) [0293] yet by these fictions they **defend** monastic orders, the sale
AP : 1 4 :005(215) [0315] willingness will be our **defense**, both before God and
AP : 1 5 :003(215) [0315] our opponents to **defend** human traditions on other
AP : 1 5 :018(217) [0319] If our opponents **defend** the notion that these human
AP : 2 0 :006(227) [0339] which the church must **defend** and which increases the
AP : 2 1 :011(230) [0345] up to honor the saints but to **defend** their religious traffic.
AP : 2 1 :033(233) [0351] Why should it be **defended** if it has no command or proof
AP : 2 1 :043(235) [0357] They **defend** obvious abuses with new and illegal cruelty.
AP : 2 1 :044(236) [0357] sound doctrine and to **defend** those who teach it.
AP : 2 1 :044(236) [0357] of God they should **defend** the life and safety of the
AP : 2 2 :009(237) [0359] the main reason for **defending** the denial of one part: to
AP : 2 2 :013(238) [0361] mystery as to why they **defend** this distinction so
AP : 2 2 :016(238) [0361] do blame the writers who **defend** the legitimacy of
AP : 2 3 :001(239) [0363] for their audacious **defense** of the pontifical law, but they
AP : 2 3 :003(239) [0363] They ask you to **defend** these libidos of theirs with your
AP : 2 3 :005(239) [0365] But they are not serious in their **defense** of celibacy.
AP : 2 3 :026(243) [0371] our opponents do not **defend** this regulation for religious
AP : 2 3 :058(247) [0379] (John 8:44), he uses these murders to **defend** his law.
AP : 2 3 :059(247) [0379] our opponents in the **defense** of this unjust law, the
AP : 2 3 :060(247) [0379] our opponents in their **defense** of the pontifical law of
AP : 2 3 :062(247) [0381] review their weighty arguments in **defense** of the law.
AP : 2 3 :070(249) [0383] arguments like these they **defend** a wicked and immoral
AP : 2 4 :001(249) [0383] not abolish the Mass but religiously keep and **defend** it.
AP : 2 4 :014(251) [0387] many passages of Scripture in **defense** of their errors.
AP : 2 4 :043(258) [0399] wickedness of some of this, they violently **defend** it.
AP : 2 4 :089(265) [0413] Our opponents **defend** the application of the ceremony to
AP : 2 4 :096(267) [0417] with you for wickedly **defending** a heresy that clearly
AP : 2 4 :099(268) [0419] help our opponents in **defending** their desecration of the
AP : 2 7 :009(269) [0421] Confutation are now **defending**, not the question whether
AP : 2 7 :052(278) [0437] our opponents should **defend** their traditions, contrary to
AP : 2 8 :003(281) [0443] Our opponents valiantly **defend** their own position and
AP : 2 8 :008(282) [0445] who vigorously **defend** their traditions and wicked
TR : 0 0 :038(326) [0515] to those pontiffs who **defend** godless forms of worship,
TR : 0 0 :039(327) [0515] and their adherents **defend** godless doctrines and godless
TR : 0 0 :040(327) [0517] Finally, he **defends** such horrible errors and such impiety
TR : 0 0 :049(328) [0519] The first is that the pope **defends** these errors with savage
TR : 0 0 :051(329) [0519] a twofold tyranny: he **defends** his errors by force and
TR : 0 0 :055(329) [0521] oaths and curses to **defend** his tyranny and wickedness
TR : 0 0 :057(330) [0521] obeyed inasmuch as he **defends** impious forms of worship
TR : 0 0 :059(330) [0521] agree with the pope and **defend** his doctrines and forms
TR : 0 0 :072(332) [0525] bishops who teach and **defend** impious doctrines and
TR : 0 0 :079(333) [0527] are adherents of the pope **defend** impious doctrines and
LC : 0 1 :185(390) [0633] wishes to have all people **defended**, delivered, and
LC : 0 1 :203(392) [0639] Moreover, you are to **defend**, protect, and rescue your
LC : 0 1 :289(404) [0663] a notorious evil, and to **defend** him against the poisonous
LC : 0 2 :017(412) [0681] but also daily guards and **defends** us against every evil
LC : 0 3 :061(428) [0715] and rulers, but also for **defenders**, protectors, and vigilant
LC : 0 3 :069(429) [0717] be our protection and **defense** now to repulse and beat
LC : 0 4 :002(437) [0733] is to be maintained and **defended** against heretics and
LC : 0 5 :019(449) [0757] protection, and **defense** against all errors and deceptions
LC : 0 5 :070(454) [0769] all his gifts, protection, **defense**, and power against death
EP : 1 2 :014(499) [0841] it has received from God for their protection and **defense**.
SD : PR :009(503) [0849] the church of God, much less be excused and **defended**.
SD : RN :006(504) [0853] clearly expounded and **defended** against errors and also
SD : 0 2 :023(525) [0889] "When the Fathers **defend** free will, they affirm a capacity
SD : 0 2 :044(529) [0897] to be understood, and **defends** them diligently and to the
SD : 0 4 :018(554) [0943] this interest that many **defended** the proposition that
SD : 0 4 :029(555) [0947] are not to be taught, **defended**, or condoned but are to be
SD : 0 4 :040(558) [0951] not tolerate, teach, or **defend** this proposition,
SD : 0 7 :026(573) [0981] protection, and **defense** against all errors and deceptions
SD : 0 7 :030(574) [0983] and have wanted to **defend** all of them as certainly as I
SD : 0 7 :030(574) [0983] certainly as I have now **defended** the Sacrament of the
SD : 0 7 :033(575) [0983] by it steadfastly and **defended** it constantly until he died.
SD : 0 7 :040(576) [0985] *Communion* Dr. Luther **defended** with great zeal and
SD : 0 8 :060(602) [1035] explain this doctrine and **defend** it against all heresies.

Deference (1)
LC : 0 1 :106(379) [0611] not only love but also **deference**, humility, and modesty,

Defy (3), Defiance (2), Defiant (2), Defiantly (2), Defies (1)
AL : 2 2 :010(050) [0061] adopted not only in **defiance** of the Scriptures but also in
AP : 0 4 :170(130) [0169] to men for help; it even **defies** God's will and runs away
AP : 2 3 :023(242) [0371] and all this in open **defiance** of Christ's command (Matt.
LC : 0 1 :036(369) [0589] frowns or smiles, boast **defiantly** of their mammon and
LC : 0 1 :072(374) [0601] To **defy** the devil, I say, we should always keep the holy
LC : 0 1 :152(386) [0625] Let us see, though, whether you are the man to **defy** him.
LC : 0 1 :225(395) [0645] may even become **defiant** and insolent and dare anyone to
LC : 0 1 :234(397) [0647] Though he pursues his **defiant** and arrogant course for a
LC : 0 1 :247(398) [0651] But if you despise and **defy** this, see whom you have
SD : 0 2 :018(524) [0889] which he was born, he **defiantly** resists God and his will

Deficiency (5)
AP : 0 2 :030(104) [0113] mentions the **deficiency**, as in I Cor. 2:14, "The
AP : 0 2 :031(104) [0113] guilt but an abiding **deficiency** in an unrenewed human
AP : 0 2 :032(104) [0113] to what the Fathers meant to say about the **deficiency**.
AP : 0 2 :047(106) [0119] The **deficiency** and concupiscence are sin as well as
AP : 0 2 :051(107) [0119] formal element of original sin or the so-called **deficiency**.

Defile (6), Defiled (3), Defiles (2)
AG : 2 6 :023(067) [0073] Christ says, "Not what goes into the mouth **defiles** a man.
AG : 2 8 :041(087) [0089] hours, that some foods **defile** the conscience, that fasting
AL : 2 0 :033(045) [0057] able to do so but were **defiled** by many manifest crimes.
AL : 2 6 :023(067) [0073] Christ says, "Not what goes into the mouth **defiles** a man.
AL : 2 8 :041(087) [0089] others, that certain foods **defile** the conscience, that
AP : 0 7 :011(170) [0229] the sinner who has been **defiled** by any spot cannot be
AP : 1 5 :014(217) [0319] their ordinances, nor **defile** yourselves with their idols.
AP : 2 3 :001(239) [0363] the notoriety of their **defiled** celibacy, our opponents not
AP : 2 7 :051(278) [0437] weakness causes him to **defile** himself because he does
AP : 2 8 :007(282) [0445] "What goes into the mouth does not **defile** a man."
TR : 0 0 :059(330) [0521] and forms of worship **defile** themselves with idolatry and

Define (10), Defined (7), Defines (2), Defining (1)
AP : 0 2 :038(105) [0115] earlier that Augustine **defines** original sin as
AP : 0 4 :312(155) [0207] In Heb. 11:1 faith is **defined** as "the assurance of things
AP : 0 7 :007(169) [0229] Paul **defined** the church in the same way in Eph. 5:25-27,
AP : 0 7 :007(169) [0229] The Creed also **defines** the church this way, teaching us to
AP : 0 7 :012(170) [0231] But when we come to **define** the church, we must define
AP : 0 7 :012(170) [0231] the church, we must **define** that which is the living body
AP : 0 7 :013(170) [0231] If we were to **define** the church as only an outward
AP : 0 7 :025(172) [0235] If we **defined** the church that way, we would probably
AP : 0 7 :026(173) [0235] and the apostles **define** the church as anything but such a
AP : 0 7 :029(173) [0237] we see how it could be **defined** otherwise, since the

Continued ▶

A P : 1 2 :038(187) [0261] Filial fear can be clearly **defined** as an anxiety joined with
A P : 1 2 :115(199) [0285] They **define** these as works that are not due; we call them
A P : 1 2 :117(199) [0287] for example, in **defining** satisfaction they say that it is
A P : 1 3 :003(211) [0309] If we **define** sacraments as "rites which have the command
A P : 2 4 :015(251) [0389] books about sacrifice, but none of them has **defined** it.
A P : 2 4 :069(262) [0409] us; so it is correct to **define** the New Testaments as signs
A P : 2 8 :006(282) [0445] the power to judge, **define**, distinguish, and establish
T R : 0 0 :005(320) [0503] we must at the outset **define** what the papists mean when
S D : 0 5 :005(559) [0953] Gospel, it is correct to **define** the word as the
S D : 1 0 :008(612) [1055] or things indifferent, as **defined** above, are in and of

Definite (8), Definitely (4)
A P : 0 4 :262(145) [0195] being must have a very **definite** Word of God to learn to
A P : 0 4 :353(161) [0217] can judge that we very **definitely** require good works,
A P : 1 5 :006(215) [0317] This is **definitely** the teaching of the Gospel, for Paul
A P : 1 5 :028(219) [0323] and cannot fix the mitigation in any **definite** degree!
A P : 2 3 :042(245) [0375] observances, we must **definitely** resist him as the apostles
A P : 2 8 :014(283) [0447] a tyrant to act without a **definite** law, nor that of a king to
A P : 2 8 :014(283) [0447] But he has a **definite** command, a definite Word of God,
A P : 2 8 :014(283) [0447] a definite command, a **definite** Word of God, which he
L C : 0 3 :033(424) [0707] vain babbling and praying for something **definite**.
E P : 0 6 :001(479) [0805] them on that account a **definite** rule according to which
S D : 0 8 :005(592) [1017] creed, and to settle it **definitely** by God's grace, our
S D : 1 1 :058(625) [1081] Paul sets a **definite** limit for us as to how far we should go

Definitive (1), Definitively (4)
S D : 0 0 :000(501) [0845] Pure, Correct, and **Definitive** Restatement and Exposition
S D : 0 2 :085(537) [0913] in this matter thoroughly, clearly, and **definitively**.
S D : 0 6 :004(564) [0963] order to explain and **definitively** to settle this
S D : 0 7 :091(585) [1005] extensively, and **definitively** refuted on the basis of God's
S D : 1 0 :004(611) [1053] and to settle it **definitively** by the grace of God, we offer

Definition (17)
A P : 0 2 :001(100) [0105] Sin," but they criticize our **definition** of original sin.
A P : 0 2 :003(101) [0105] In this sense the Latin **definition** denies that human
A P : 0 2 :004(101) [0105] show at length that our **definition** agrees with the
A P : 0 2 :004(101) [0105] Hence it belongs in the **definition**, especially now when so
A P : 0 2 :007(101) [0107] the patristic **definition** of original sin and therefore
A P : 0 2 :014(102) [0109] This was why in our **definition** of original sin we also
A P : 0 2 :015(102) [0109] understood, the old **definition** says exactly the same
A P : 0 2 :023(103) [0111] Thus when the ancient **definition** says that sin is lack of
A P : 0 2 :023(103) [0111] evident that the ancient **definition** says just what we do
A P : 0 2 :024(103) [0111] of Augustine's **definition** that original sin is
A P : 0 2 :026(103) [0111] In our **definition** of original sin, therefore, we have
A P : 0 2 :031(104) [0113] on both parts of our **definition**, but on so clear an issue
A P : 0 7 :023(172) [0235] demand some such **definition** of the church as the
A P : 0 7 :024(172) [0235] Now, this **definition** of the papal kingdom rather than of
A P : 0 7 :029(173) [0237] enough to defend the **definition** of the church which we
A P : 1 3 :003(211) [0309] By this **definition**, rites instituted by men are not
S D : 0 1 :060(519) [0879] understanding and give a correct **definition** of original sin.

Defraud (6), Defrauded (2)
T R : 0 0 :080(334) [0527] Meanwhile they **defraud** the church, which needs these
T R : 0 0 :082(334) [0527] Let those who **defraud** the church know that God will
L C : 0 1 :154(386) [0625] When you **defraud** or despise your master, another person
L C : 0 1 :226(395) [0645] whom I expect good; but they are the first to **defraud** me.
L C : 0 1 :233(396) [0647] advantage of him, or **defraud** him by any faithless or
L C : 0 1 :240(397) [0649] Daily the poor are **defrauded**.
L C : 0 1 :242(397) [0649] you have cheated and **defrauded** anyone out of a gulden,
L C : 0 1 :246(398) [0651] with those of you who despise, **defraud**, steal, and rob us.

Degenerated (2), Degenerates (1)
A P : 2 1 :041(235) [0355] recent ones, so their theology has steadily **degenerated**.
A P : 2 7 :005(269) [0421] instruction, they have **degenerated** as from a golden age
A P : 2 7 :005(269) [0421] or as the Platonic cube **degenerates** into bad harmonies

Degree (14), Degrees (2)
A G : 2 3 :001(051) [0061] both of high and of low **degree**, there has been loud
A P : 0 4 :366(163) [0219] and spiritual, in various **degrees**, according to I Cor. 3:8,
A P : 0 4 :367(163) [0221] (II Cor. 9:6); here the **degree** of the reward is evidently
A P : 0 4 :367(163) [0221] is evidently commensurate with the **degree** of the work.
A P : 1 5 :028(219) [0323] as he looks for the **degrees** and limitations of these
A P : 1 5 :028(219) [0323] and cannot fix the mitigation in any definite **degree**!
L C : 0 1 :091(377) [0607] help us in the slightest **degree**, for they are all dead things
L C : 0 3 :107(434) [0729] not all to the same **degree**; some have more frequent and
E P : 1 2 :030(500) [0843] pious Christians, of high **degree** and low, must guard
S D : 0 1 :001(508) [0859] soul in its highest **degree** and foremost powers) is original
S D : 0 1 :023(512) [0865] small, limited, and poor **degree** — such as the faculty,
S D : 0 2 :007(521) [0883] in the tiniest or smallest **degree**, "of himself as coming
S D : 0 2 :024(526) [0891] meditate on it to a certain **degree**, and can even talk
S D : 0 2 :077(536) [0911] meet God and to some **degree** — though only to a small
S D : 0 2 :090(539) [0915] God, in the manner and **degree** set forth in detail above.
S D : 0 3 :037(546) [0929] even only to the smallest **degree** factors in our

Deity (36)
E P : 0 8 :003(487) [0819] in common with the **deity**, its majesty, and its properties.
E P : 0 8 :021(490) [0823] has been changed into the **deity**, as Eutyches dreamed.
E P : 0 8 :025(490) [0823] really (that is, in fact) the **deity** has nothing in common
E P : 0 8 :025(490) [0823] with the humanity, nor the humanity with the **deity**.
E P : 0 8 :032(491) [0825] only according to his **deity**, and that this presence does
E P : 0 8 :034(491) [0825] the whole fullness of **deity** bodily" (Col. 2:9), Christ,
E P : 0 8 :039(491) [0827] laid it aside and forsaken it even according to his **deity**.
E P : 0 8 :039(492) [0827] have Christ's eternal **deity** denied and we shall lose Christ
E P : 0 9 :001(492) [0827] or only according to the **deity**, or according to body and
E P : 1 2 :029(500) [0843] essence, separate from the other persons of the **Deity**.
S D : 0 3 :056(549) [0935] Likewise, the **deity** alone, without the humanity, could
S D : 0 7 :036(575) [0985] the whole fullness of the **deity** dwells bodily," or "God
S D : 0 8 :011(593) [1019] no less than without his **deity** the person of Christ, or the
S D : 0 8 :012(593) [1019] personal union with the **deity** and afterward through the
S D : 0 8 :030(597) [1025] the whole fullness of **deity** dwells bodily (Col. 2:9), and in
S D : 0 8 :034(597) [1027] the whole fullness of the **deity** dwells bodily" (Col. 2:9) in
S D : 0 8 :039(598) [1027] is said about the **deity** of Christ which after all belongs to
S D : 0 8 :041(599) [1029] would say that the **deity** surely cannot suffer and die, then
S D : 0 8 :041(599) [1029] Scriptures ascribe to the **deity**, because of this personal
S D : 0 8 :042(599) [1029] the one part (namely, the **deity**) does not suffer,
S D : 0 8 :050(600) [1031] personal union with the **deity** the human nature has
S D : 0 8 :064(603) [1037] because the fullness of the **deity** dwells in Christ (Col.
S D : 0 8 :068(604) [1039] likewise the fullness of **deity** dwells bodily, there likewise
S D : 0 8 :070(604) [1039] with the whole fullness of **deity** which he always has with
S D : 0 8 :070(605) [1041] the whole fullness of **deity** bodily" (Col. 2:9); likewise,
S D : 0 8 :072(605) [1041] nature (according to the **deity** he is of one essence with
S D : 0 8 :077(606) [1043] to mean that only the **deity** of Christ is present with us in
S D : 0 8 :078(607) [1043] not only according to his **deity**, but also according to and
S D : 0 8 :082(607) [1045] Christ is according to his **deity**, he is there as a natural
S D : 0 8 :085(608) [1045] of Christ has not, like the **deity**, existed from eternity, but
S D : 0 8 :085(608) [1047] from the moment that the **deity** and the humanity were
S D : 0 8 :085(608) [1047] because he is one person with the **deity** and is true God.
S D : 0 8 :087(608) [1047] that not only his unveiled **deity**, which to us poor sinners
S D : 0 8 :090(609) [1047] in the same way as the **Deity**, as an infinite essence,
S D : 0 8 :092(609) [1049] something which ought not be attributed to the **deity**.
S D : 0 8 :094(609) [1049] only according to his **deity**, and that this presence does

Dejected (1)
L C : 0 1 :247(398) [0651] go away wretched and **dejected**, and because he can

Delay (1)
A P : 0 4 :331(158) [0211] O Lord, give heed and act; **delay** not, for thy own sake, O

Delegated (1), Delegates (2)
L C : 0 1 :141(384) [0621] away, he confers and **delegates** his authority and
L C : 0 1 :181(389) [0631] God has **delegated** his authority of punishing evil-doers to
S D : 0 4 :034(556) [0949] the beginning, and then **delegates** this function to works,

Deliberate (5), Deliberately (12), Deliberation (4), Deliberations (1)
A G : P R :001(024) [0039] an earnest desire to **deliberate** concerning matters
A G : P R :002(024) [0039] was also expressed for **deliberation** on what might be
A G : P R :007(025) [0039] Accordingly, after due **deliberation** and counsel, it was
A L : 2 7 :027(075) [0079] ought to be voluntary and chosen freely and **deliberately**?
A L : 2 7 :029(075) [0079] who have taken the vow spontaneously and **deliberately**!
A L : 2 7 :030(075) [0079] make a promise which is not spontaneous and **deliberate**.
S 1 : P R :001(288) [0455] as a basis for possible **deliberations** and to indicate, on
L C : 0 1 :225(395) [0645] When this is done **deliberately** — for I am not speaking of
L C : 0 1 :227(396) [0645] another in a trade and **deliberately** fleeces, skins, and
L C : 0 5 :004(447) [0755] by Christ without man's counsel or **deliberation**.
E P : 0 4 :011(477) [0799] keep his faith even if he **deliberately** were to persist in sin.
E P : 0 7 :042(486) [0817] The Sacramentarians **deliberately** insist on crediting us
S D : 0 1 :055(518) [0877] dependable teachers, **deliberately** and seriously
S D : 0 4 :012(553) [0941] Faith is a vital, **deliberate** trust in God's grace, so certain
S D : 0 4 :015(553) [0943] conscience or embark **deliberately** on such sins again,
S D : 0 4 :031(556) [0947] sin, even a wanton and **deliberate** one, or through wicked
S D : 0 4 :031(556) [0947] the Holy Spirit, and **deliberately** proceeds to sin against
S D : 0 7 :044(577) [0987] his words with great **deliberation** and care in ordaining
S D : 0 7 :119(590) [1013] Sacramentarians have **deliberately** and maliciously
S D : 1 1 :083(630) [1091] impenitence, and **deliberate** sins God punishes with
S D : 1 1 :083(630) [1091] punish those who **deliberately** turn away from the holy
S D : 1 1 :085(630) [1091] to Pharaoh, and he **deliberately** rebelled against all the

Delight (15), Delightful (1), Delighting (1), Delights (7)
A P : 0 4 :336(159) [0215] Look how this childish sophistry **delights** our opponents!
A P : 2 3 :071(249) [0383] Our princes do not **delight** in change for its own sake, but
A P : 2 4 :029(255) [0393] Ps. 51:16, 17 says, "Thou hast no **delight** in burnt offering
A P : 2 7 :059(279) [0441] monks abound in every **delight**, they claim to be celibate.
S C : 0 8 :010(354) [0559] His **delight** is not in the strength of the horse, nor his
L C : 0 1 :132(383) [0619] an object of pleasure and **delight** to himself, but also an
L C : 0 1 :139(384) [0621] exalts it, so greatly **delights** in it, so richly rewards it, and
L C : 0 1 :267(401) [0657] corner, relishing and **delighting** in it like pigs that roll in
L C : 0 2 :069(420) [0697] we come to love and **delight** in all the commandments of
E P : 0 5 :007(478) [0803] them up again by the **delightful** proclamation of God's
S D : R N :016(507) [0857] reader who really **delights** in the truth of God's Word will
S D : 0 2 :017(524) [0887] that is, in my flesh, for I **delight** in the law of God in my
S D : 0 2 :039(528) [0895] desire to do the good and **delight** in it (indeed, actually do
S D : 0 2 :063(533) [0905] or a new man, and he **delights** in the law of God
S D : 0 2 :064(533) [0905] the regenerated, "For I **delight** in the law of God in my
S D : 0 2 :085(537) [0913] But the regenerated man **delights** in the law of God
S D : 0 4 :019(554) [0945] that he is willing and **delights** in the law of God in his
S D : 0 6 :004(564) [0963] is the man whose **delight** is in the law of the Lord, and on
S D : 0 6 :005(564) [0963] to the inner man they **delight** in the law of God.
S D : 0 6 :018(567) [0967] to the inmost self they **delight** in the law of God; but the
S D : 0 8 :030(597) [1025] marvel at it and find their **delight** and joy in looking into
S D : 1 1 :007(617) [1065] art not a God who **delights** in wickedness" (Ps. 5:4).
S D : 1 1 :053(625) [1081] we take much greater **delight** in concerning ourselves with
S D : 1 1 :095(632) [1095] We have a sincere **delight** in and deep love for true

Deliver (14), Deliverance (1), Delivered (17), Delivering (1), Delivers (4)
P R : P R :009(006) [0011] nor our churches were **delivered** thereby from the
A L : 1 2 :005(035) [0049] sake, comforts the conscience, and **delivers** it from terror.
A P : 0 2 :042(106) [0117] because he does not **deliver** us from trouble right away;
A P : 0 4 :059(115) [0137] the day of trouble; I will **deliver** you, and you shall glorify
A P : 0 4 :142(126) [0161] and looks for forgiveness of sins and **deliverance** from sin.
A P : 1 2 :026(185) [0259] through indulgences, souls are **delivered** from purgatory.
A P : 1 2 :028(185) [0259] In order to **deliver** pious consciences from these
A P : 1 2 :048(188) [0265] know that we have been **delivered** from this
A P : 2 2 :003(236) [0357] the Lord what he was **delivering**, but the text clearly
A P : 2 4 :029(255) [0393] the day of trouble; I will **deliver** you, and you shall glorify
A P : 2 8 :018(284) [0449] is efficacious when it is **delivered** by men and that we
S 1 : P R :015(291) [0459] own, and by thy glorious advent **deliver** thy servants.
S 2 : 0 2 :001(293) [0463] by an evil scoundrel) **delivers** men from their sins, both
S 3 : 0 3 :025(307) [0485] was eager to be **delivered** from the heavy, unbearable
S C : 0 2 :004(345) [0545] condemned creature, **delivered** me and freed me from all
S C : 0 3 :019(348) [0549] ***"But deliver us from evil."***
S C : 0 3 :020(348) [0549] Father in heaven may **deliver** us from all manner of evil,
S C : 0 4 :006(348) [0551] forgiveness of sins, **delivers** from death and the devil, and
L C : P R :003(358) [0567] which they have been **delivered** from so many burdens
L C : S P :014(363) [0577] and lead us not into temptation, but **deliver** us from evil.
L C : 0 1 :024(368) [0587] evil, he who saves and **delivers** us when any evil befalls.
L C : 0 1 :024(368) [0587] that is good and by whom we are **delivered** from all evil.

Continued ▶

L C : 0 1 :064(373) [0599] the day of trouble: I will **deliver** you and you shall glorify
L C : 0 1 :149(385) [0623] inclined to godliness, we **deliver** to the hangman and the
L C : 0 1 :157(386) [0627] heart, so that we may be **delivered** from the blindness and
L C : 0 1 :185(390) [0633] all people defended, **delivered**, and protected from the
L C : 0 3 :019(423) [0703] day of trouble, and I will **deliver** you," and Christ says in
L C : 0 3 :051(426) [0711] the world to redeem and **deliver** us from the power of the
L C : 0 3 :112(435) [0729] *"But **deliver** us from evil.*
L C : 0 3 :113(435) [0729] Greek this petition reads, "**Deliver** or keep us from the
L C : 0 3 :118(436) [0731] are to be protected and **delivered** from all evil, his name
L C : 0 4 :025(439) [0739] nothing else than to be **delivered** from sin, death and the
E P : R N :004(465) [0777] Confession, which was **delivered** to Emperor Charles V at
E P : 0 1 :023(469) [0785] be employed in sermons **delivered** to common, unlearned
S D : P R :005(502) [0847] Confession as it was **delivered** to Emperor Charles in
S D : 0 7 :041(576) [0985] Confession and **delivered** to Emperor Charles V,
S D : 0 8 :085(608) [1047] 'All things have been **delivered** to me by my Father'

Delmenhorst (1)
P R : P R :027(015) [0025] John, count of Oldenburg and **Delmenhorst**

Delude (1), Deludes (1), Delusion (6)
A P : 0 2 :047(106) [0119] by the devil, who **deludes** it with wicked opinions and
A P : 0 4 :203(135) [0177] he imitates them in the **delusion** that by similar works he
A P : 1 5 :023(218) [0321] Under this **delusion** the common people among the
L C : 0 3 :006(421) [0699] people do who say in their **delusion**: "Why should I pray?
L C : 0 3 :121(436) [0731] is therefore a pernicious **delusion** when people pray in
S D : 0 3 :042(547) [0931] and secure Christians **delude** themselves into thinking
S D : 0 4 :015(553) [0943] a complacent Epicurean **delusion**, since many people
S D : 0 4 :031(556) [0947] the false Epicurean **delusion** which some dream up that it

Deluge (2)
S 1 : P R :012(290) [0459] have burst in like a **deluge** and have taken on the color of
L C : 0 1 :060(372) [0597] Like a great **deluge**, it has flooded all lands.

Demand (19), Demanded (9), Demanding (2), Demands (18)
P R : P R :024(013) [0021] and urgent necessity **demands** that in the presence of so
A G : 2 1 :001(046) [0057] of a royal office which **demands** the defense and
A G : 2 4 :024(058) [0067] **Demanded** without doubt by the necessity of such
A G : 2 6 :020(067) [0073] The Gospel **demands** that the teaching about faith should
A L : 0 0 :002(048) [0059] are not so severe as to **demand** that rites should be the
A L : 2 8 :070(093) [0093] But now they **demand** celibacy and will admit no one to
A P : 0 4 :155(128) [0165] He **demands** not only alms, but also the righteousness of
A P : 0 4 :272(148) [0199] of penitence not only **demands** new works but also
A P : 0 7 :023(172) [0235] Perhaps our opponents **demand** some such definition of
A P : 1 2 :012(184) [0255] While they **demand** this enumeration under the pretext
A P : 1 2 :048(188) [0265] the bond which stood against us with its legal **demands**.
A P : 1 2 :067(191) [0271] But they go further and **demand** that this teaching be
A P : 1 2 :075(193) [0273] the law and our works because the law **demands** love.
A P : 1 2 :093(196) [0279] may rightly be **demanded** of those who have compiled
A P : 1 2 :123(201) [0289] that the uninitiated may **demand** that such terrible
A P : 1 2 :127(201) [0289] Men are **demanding** instruction in religion.
A P : 1 2 :129(202) [0291] nations; they certainly **demand** that these issues be
A P : 2 1 :044(236) [0357] God **demands** this when he honors kings with his own
A P : 2 3 :003(239) [0363] of the councils, they **demand** that you dissolve marriages.
A P : 2 3 :015(241) [0367] Our opponents **demand** to be shown a command
A P : 2 3 :050(246) [0377] Our opponents do not **demand** celibacy for religious
A P : 2 3 :053(246) [0377] if the common good **demanded** it, why was not the same
A P : 2 7 :010(270) [0423] But still our opponents **demand** the rejection of
A P : 2 8 :003(281) [0445] They **demand** greater strictness in the observance of their
S 2 : 0 2 :016(295) [0467] lies and cunning, of **demanding** Masses, vigils,
L C : 0 1 :047(371) [0593] he makes no greater **demand** of us than a hearty trust in
L C : 0 1 :083(376) [0603] Nature teaches and **demands** that the common people —
L C : 0 1 :149(385) [0623] God speaks to you and **demands** obedience.
L C : 0 1 :237(397) [0647] others' possessions and entitled to whatever they **demand**.
L C : 0 1 :323(409) [0673] Thus he **demands** that all our actions proceed from a
L C : 0 1 :327(410) [0675] wants of you and what he will quite surely **demand** of you
L C : 0 2 :068(420) [0697] still remain on us because we cannot fulfill his **demands**.
L C : 0 3 :013(422) [0701] we should regard as **demanded** by God and done in
L C : 0 3 :045(426) [0709] same thing that God **demands** in the Second
L C : 0 3 :056(427) [0713] he is angered if we do not ask and **demand** confidently.
L C : 0 4 :035(441) [0741] not exclude but rather **demand** faith, for without faith
L C : 0 5 :034(450) [0761] This faith he himself **demands** in the Word when he says,
E P : 0 5 :009(479) [0803] what great things God **demands** of us in the law, none of
E P : 0 6 :007(481) [0807] flesh — does what is **demanded** of him by the law under
E P : 1 0 :002(493) [0829] to their pressure and **demands**, reintroduce some
E P : 1 0 :006(493) [0829] confession of faith is **demanded** of us, we dare not yield to
S D : R N :020(508) [0859] expounded as occasion **demanded** and what we now
S D : 0 4 :038(557) [0951] the intention that God **demands** of the regenerated), they
S D : 0 6 :022(567) [0969] The law **demands** a perfect and pure obedience if it is to
S D : 1 0 :002(611) [1053] at the enemies' insistent **demand**, restore once more
S D : 1 0 :005(611) [1053] the illusion (or are **demanded** or agreed to with that
S D : 1 0 :012(612) [1057] But when false prophets **demanded** circumcision and
S D : 1 0 :014(613) [1057] will forthwith publicly **demand** such matters of

Demon (2), Demonic (2), Demons (16)
A G : 2 6 :036(069) [0075] and again, "This kind of **demon** cannot be driven out by
A L : 2 3 :022(055) [0063] is called a doctrine of **demons** by Paul in I Tim. 4:3.
A L : 2 6 :029(068) [0075] of foods a doctrine of **demons**, for it is in conflict with the
A L : 2 6 :036(069) [0075] and again, "This kind of **demon** cannot be driven out by
A L : 2 8 :049(089) [0091] Why does it call them doctrines of **demons**?
A P : 0 4 :249(142) [0191] such as even the **demons** have, but about a faith that
A P : 0 4 :303(154) [0205] many wicked people and **demons** also believe
A P : 0 4 :303(154) [0205] wicked people nor **demons** can have the faith we are
A P : 0 4 :337(159) [0215] that the wicked and **demons** also have (James 2:19), their
A P : 0 7 :040(176) [0241] In fact, Paul calls such opinions "doctrines of **demons**."
A P : 1 2 :016(184) [0257] these scandalous and **demonic** doctrines the doctrine of
A P : 1 2 :045(187) [0263] faith that even the **demons** have (James 2:19), but, in the
A P : 1 2 :141(204) [0295] who considers the **demonic** doctrines that the devil has
A P : 1 5 :004(215) [0315] are openly replacing the Gospel with doctrines of **demons**.
A P : 1 5 :004(215) [0315] traditions "doctrines of **demons**" (I Tim. 4:1) when
A P : 2 3 :058(247) [0379] this law is a doctrine of **demons** (I Tim. 4:1-3); since the
A P : 2 3 :063(248) [0381] a law when he calls it a "doctrine of **demons**" (I Tim. 4:1).
A P : 2 7 :026(273) [0429] of these titles, they are "doctrines of **demons**" (I Tim. 4:1).
S 3 : 1 1 :003(315) [0499] for St. Paul says that to do so is a doctrine of **demons**.
T R : 0 0 :042(328) [0517] errors to be doctrines of **demons** and of the Antichrist.

Demonstrate (5), Demonstrated (9), Demonstrates (6), Demonstration (2), Demonstrations (1)
P R : P R :020(010) [0017] we should indicate and **demonstrate** by a correct
P R : P R :025(014) [0025] with them, and to **demonstrate** toward everyone,
A G : 2 0 :012(042) [0055] interpretation is here introduced can be **demonstrated**
A G : 2 2 :004(050) [0061] a long time, as can be **demonstrated** from history and
A G : 2 3 :010(052) [0061] It can be **demonstrated** from history and from the
A G : 2 3 :018(054) [0063] Besides, history **demonstrates** both that priests were
A P : 0 4 :246(142) [0189] Second, the context **demonstrates** that the works spoken
A P : 2 4 :074(263) [0411] praise to God, as a **demonstration** of its gratitude, and a
S 2 : 0 2 :014(295) [0467] They can never **demonstrate** these things from Augustine.
S 2 : 0 4 :010(300) [0475] This is a powerful **demonstration** that the pope is the real
S 2 : 0 4 :014(301) [0475] government, as I have **demonstrated** in many books.
T R : 0 0 :037(326) [0515] The consequences **demonstrate** that they have been great
S D : 0 1 :057(518) [0877] true, attested and **demonstrated** by the testimonies of the
S D : 0 2 :044(529) [0897] and in great detail presents and **demonstrates** his case.
S D : 0 2 :087(538) [0915] as was thoroughly **demonstrated** above from clear
S D : 0 3 :066(550) [0937] forth, explained, and **demonstrated** from God's Word in
S D : 0 8 :003(592) [1017] publicly profess our adherence, clearly **demonstrate**.
S D : 0 8 :024(595) [1023] He **demonstrated** his divine majesty even in his mother's
S D : 0 8 :052(601) [1033] own arguments and **demonstrations** they attempt to
S D : 0 8 :066(604) [1039] with the iron, it **demonstrates** and manifests its power of
S D : 0 8 :074(605) [1041] This fullness **demonstrates** and manifests itself
S D : 0 8 :085(608) [1047] been revealed and **demonstrated**, as St. Paul says, 'He is
S D : 1 0 :009(612) [1055] (Rom. 14) and **demonstrates** it by his own example

Demosthenes (2)
A P : 2 4 :081(264) [0411] As **Demosthenes**' oration *Leptines* shows, it is completely
A P : 2 4 :081(264) [0411] A commentator on **Demosthenes** says that "liturgy" is a

Den (1)
L C : 0 1 :240(397) [0649] free public market into a carrion-pit and a robbers' **den**.

Denial (4), Denied (19), Denies (21), Deny (46), Denying (5)
A G : 0 2 :003(029) [0045] Pelagians and others who **deny** that original sin is sin, for
A G : 1 2 :002(034) [0049] and absolution should not be **denied** them by the church.
A G : 1 2 :009(035) [0049] are the Novatians who **denied** absolution to such as had
A G : 2 7 :014(073) [0077] of these things can be **denied**, for they are found in their
A G : 2 7 :038(077) [0081] of the grace of Christ and **deny** the righteousness of faith?
A G : 2 7 :044(078) [0081] One cannot **deny** that the monks have taught and
A G : 2 8 :074(093) [0093] Nor can it be **denied** that some regulations were adopted
A L : 0 2 :003(029) [0045] Pelagians and others who **deny** that the vice of origin is
A L : 0 8 :003(033) [0047] like them who have **denied** that the ministry of evil men
A L : 1 2 :007(035) [0049] the Anabaptists who **deny** that those who have once been
A L : 2 7 :014(073) [0077] of these things can be **denied**, for they appear in their own
A L : 2 7 :035(076) [0081] For Augustine **denies** that they should be dissolved in
A L : 2 7 :038(077) [0081] of Christ and obscure and **deny** the righteousness of
A L : 2 7 :044(078) [0081] It cannot be **denied** that the monks taught that they were
A P : 0 2 :001(100) [0105] guilt, and therefore they **deny** that it is original guilt.
A P : 0 2 :003(101) [0105] according to the flesh we **deny** the existence not only of
A P : 0 2 :003(101) [0105] sense the Latin definition **denies** that human nature has
A P : 0 2 :003(101) [0105] and trust of God, and it **denies** that adults actually
A P : 0 2 :014(102) [0109] concupiscence and **denied** to man's natural powers the
A P : 0 2 :023(103) [0111] righteousness, it not only **denies** the obedience of man's
A P : 0 2 :023(103) [0111] lower powers, but also **denies** that he has knowledge of
A P : 0 2 :023(103) [0111] just what we do when we **deny** to natural man not only
A P : 0 4 :001(107) [0121] condemn us both for **denying** that men receive the
A P : 0 4 :066(116) [0139] Anabaptists, they **deny** that it is received through the
A P : 0 4 :070(116) [0141] Therefore anyone who **denies** that faith justifies teaches
A P : 0 4 :084(119) [0145] Here he **denies** us any merit, for he says that all are guilty
A P : 0 4 :089(120) [0149] it is accounted freely and **denies** that it could be
A P : 0 4 :097(121) [0149] He explicitly **denies** justification to the law.
A P : 0 4 :104(122) [0151] support our position; he **denies** justification to works and
A P : 0 4 :107(122) [0153] justification to faith and specifically **deny** it to works.
A P : 0 4 :147(127) [0163] is the keeping of the law, why do we **deny** that it justifies?
A P : 0 4 :153(128) [0163] If anybody **denies** that this is faith, he utterly
A P : 0 4 :186(132) [0173] But by their **denial** that faith justifies and by their
A P : 0 4 :229(139) [0183] We cannot **deny** that love is the highest work of the law.
A P : 0 4 :250(143) [0191] James is correct in **denying** that we are justified by a faith
A P : 0 4 :264(146) [0195] the Gospel if we were to **deny** that the forgiveness of sins
A P : 0 4 :271(148) [0199] opponents is so mad as to **deny** that absolution is the
A P : 0 4 :298(153) [0205] to see how furiously our opponents **deny** them.
A P : 0 4 :326(157) [0211] This absolutely **denies** any glory in man's righteousness,
A P : 0 4 :387(166) [0225] Those who **deny** that men are justified by faith deny that
A P : 0 4 :387(166) [0225] men are justified by faith **deny** that Christ is the mediator
A P : 0 4 :387(166) [0225] mediator and propitiator, **deny** the promise of grace and
A P : 0 7 :003(168) [0227] of the church or **deny** efficacy to the sacraments which
A P : 0 7 :050(178) [0245] schisms because they **denied** to priests the right to hold
A P : 1 0 :003(179) [0247] He says: "We do not **deny** that we are joined to Christ
A P : 1 0 :003(179) [0247] But we do **deny** that we have no kind of connection with
A P : 1 2 :001(182) [0253] of penitence, and they **deny** that faith is the second part
A P : 1 2 :002(182) [0253] If we **deny** that by faith we obtain the forgiveness of sins,
A P : 1 2 :074(193) [0273] Do they still dare to **deny** that we obtain the forgiveness
A P : 1 2 :094(196) [0281] that he is forgiven, he **denies** that God has sworn to the
A P : 1 2 :123(201) [0289] hear this they will conclude that we **deny** all penitence.
A P : 1 3 :019(213) [0313] opposition to this, Paul **denies** that Abraham was justified
A P : 1 5 :018(217) [0319] be justified before God, **denying** that men are freely
A P : 1 8 :001(225) [0335] or all liberty be **denied** it, as in Manichaeism.
A P : 1 8 :004(225) [0335] We are not **denying** freedom to the human will.
A P : 2 1 :005(229) [0345] Peter forgiven after his **denial**, we are encouraged to
A P : 2 1 :036(234) [0353] Peter was forgiven for **denying** Christ; Cyprian was
A P : 2 2 :006(237) [0359] maintain that it is right to **deny** one part, and they refuse
A P : 2 2 :009(237) [0359] reason for defending the **denial** of one part: to elevate the
A P : 2 3 :048(246) [0377] But we **deny** that one should trust in certain observances
A P : 2 4 :096(267) [0417] condemned because he **denied** that in the Mass there was
A P : 2 7 :014(271) [0423] Since Paul **denies** that by the law of Moses men merit the
A P : 2 7 :036(275) [0433] They **deny** that the monastic life is perfection, but they
A P : 2 7 :036(275) [0433] since they did not dare to **deny** it the claim of perfection
A P : 2 7 :041(276) [0435] or a tyranny forces us to leave or to **deny** the Gospel.
A P : 2 8 :010(282) [0447] Colossians (2:20-23) Paul **denies** that traditions avail for
S 3 : 0 8 :008(313) [0497] present Messiah and not **deny** or persecute him as the
S 3 : 1 4 :001(316) [0501] This is to **deny** Christ, etc.
T R : 0 0 :011(321) [0507] Peter of this pretext and **denies** that Peter's authority is

Continued ▶

SC : PR :011(339) [0535] tell them that they **deny** Christ and are no Christians.
SC : 03 :016(347) [0549] sins, and on their account **deny** our prayers, for we
LC : 01 :053(372) [0595] to each other and afterward **deny** it under oath.
LC : 01 :281(403) [0661] to witness, you will probably **deny** having said anything.
EP : 02 :006(470) [0787] In these few words he **denies** all power to free will and
EP : 04 :004(476) [0797] This the other party **denied**.
EP : 07 :005(482) [0809] They **deny** that the body of Christ is present in any
EP : 08 :018(489) [0823] He **denied** the genuine sharing of the properties of the two
EP : 08 :018(489) [0823] Nor do we **deny** or abolish the human nature in the
EP : 08 :039(492) [0827] Christ's eternal deity **denied** and we shall lose Christ
SD : PR :006(502) [0847] it can nevertheless not be **denied** that some theologians
SD : PR :007(502) [0849] some **denied** the resurrection of the dead (I Cor. 15:12);
SD : PR :007(502) [0849] and others even **denied** that Christ was eternal and
SD : 01 :010(510) [0863] description of original sin **denies** to unrenewed human
SD : 02 :012(522) [0885] Thus Scripture **denies** to the intellect, heart, and will of
SD : 03 :042(547) [0931] correctly when he **denies** that we are justified by such a
SD : 07 :014(571) [0977] And although they **deny** a transubstantiation (that is, an
SD : 07 :088(585) [1003] use of faith in order to **deny** the true, essential presence
SD : 07 :103(587) [1007] "I do not wish to have **denied** by the foregoing that God
SD : 07 :103(587) [1007] For I do not want to **deny** in any way that God's power is
SD : 07 :114(589) [1011] 2. Likewise, the **denial** of an oral eating of the body and
SD : 07 :126(591) [1015] Arian heretic can or will **deny** Christ himself, true God
SD : 08 :051(601) [1033] the adversaries cannot and dare not any longer **deny**.
SD : 08 :071(605) [1041] human nature would be **denied** and completely
SD : 11 :075(628) [1087] of the Father, who cannot **deny** himself because he is
SD : 12 :011(634) [1099] Thus they **deny** and reject the entire teaching of original

Denote (1), Denotes (1)
AP : 02 :027(104) [0113] says: "Original sin **denotes** the privation of original
AP : 12 :168(209) [0305] the public rite and use it to **denote** the real mortification.

Denounce (6), Denounced (3), Denounces (6), Denouncing (1)
AP : 04 :258(144) [0193] to do evil," as he **denounces** ungodly hearts and requires
AP : 04 :339(159) [0215] He **denounces** our works as worthless, but he does not
AP : 04 :339(159) [0215] but he does not **denounce** the promise that offers mercy
AP : 12 :029(185) [0259] takes place when the Word of God **denounces** sin.
AP : 12 :029(185) [0259] of the Gospel is to **denounce** sin, to offer the forgiveness
AP : 12 :034(186) [0261] faith, but present only the Word that **denounces** sin.
AP : 12 :045(187) [0263] In the first part he **denounces** our sins, in the latter part
AP : 12 :045(188) [0263] when sins are **denounced**; and faith, when it is said,
AP : 12 :048(188) [0265] bond is the conscience **denouncing** and condemning us; it
AP : 12 :053(189) [0265] is the law, which reveals, **denounces**, and condemns sin.
AP : 12 :176(210) [0307] are converted and to **denounce** and excommunicate those
AP : 27 :002(269) [0419] the guardian began to **denounce** him for his doctrine,
AP : 27 :002(269) [0419] estate but had only **denounced** certain notorious abuses.
LC : 01 :059(372) [0597] Then if anyone is **denounced**, God and his name have to
LC : 03 :033(424) [0707] reject prayer, but we do **denounce** the utterly useless
SD : PR :007(502) [0849] compelled vigorously to **denounce** all of these in their

Depart (10), Departed (5), Departing (1), Departs (2), Departure (3)
PR : PR :017(008) [0015] or in the least point to **depart** from the Augsburg
PR : PR :025(013) [0023] work of agreement or to **depart** in any way at all, either in
AL : 00 :001(047) [0059] is nothing here that **departs** from the Scriptures or the
AL : 24 :024(058) [0067] have warned that they **depart** from the Holy Scriptures
AP : 12 :012(184) [0257] is really what is called "**departing** before the mysteries."
AP : 12 :031(186) [0259] of my days I must **depart**; I am consigned to the gates of
AP : 12 :144(204) [0297] works, like pilgrimages, **depart** even further from God's
AP : 21 :001(229) [0343] the invocation of the **departed** saints were also necessary.
AP : 21 :002(229) [0343] was still alive, to pray for his brothers after his **departure**.
AP : 24 :093(267) [0417] for those who have **departed** in faith, forefathers, fathers,
S2 : 02 :016(295) [0467] as spirits of the **departed** and, with unspeakable lies and
S3 : 03 :043(310) [0491] faith and the Spirit have **departed** from them.
S3 : 15 :005(317) [0501] John Brenz, who on his **departure** from Smalcald directed
TR : 00 :008(320) [0505] and, as it were, the vicar of Christ after his **departure**?
LC : 01 :045(370) [0593] and he let his heart **depart** from God, placing his
LC : 01 :096(378) [0609] go to hear preaching and **depart** again with as little
LC : 01 :101(379) [0609] use, such is its power that it never **departs** without fruit.
SD : PR :005(502) [0847] doctrinal statements, to **depart** from the aforementioned
SD : PR :006(502) [0847] some theologians did **depart** from it in several important
SD : 07 :028(574) [0981] impression that he had **departed** from this doctrine and
SD : 07 :029(574) [0981] me God!) in this faith to **depart** from this world and to

Depend (10), Dependable (4), Depended (3), Depending (3), Depends (12)
AG : 28 :008(082) [0085] persons or to individuals, **depending** on one's calling).
AL : 28 :008(082) [0085] to many or to individuals, **depending** on one's calling.
AP : 04 :041(113) [0133] Reconciliation does not **depend** upon our merits.
AP : 04 :042(113) [0133] the forgiveness of sins **depended** upon our merits and if
AP : 04 :050(114) [0135] 4:16): "That is why it **depends** on faith, in order that the
AP : 04 :084(119) [0145] says, "That is why it **depends** on faith, in order that the
AP : 04 :084(119) [0145] he were to say, "If it **depended** on our merits, the promise
AP : 04 :264(146) [0195] the human theory that forgiveness **depends** upon works.
AP : 04 :272(148) [0199] of sins is added, **depending** not on the work but on Christ
AP : 04 :285(150) [0201] of righteousness does not **depend** upon our works
AP : 12 :081(194) [0275] 4:16, "That is why it **depends** on faith, in order that the
AP : 28 :007(282) [0445] sin nor righteousness **depends** upon food, drink, clothing,
S2 : 04 :008(299) [0473] to such a head would **depend** on the good pleasure of men
TR : 00 :010(321) [0505] that his call did not **depend** on the authority of Peter.
TR : 00 :010(321) [0507] authority of the ministry **depends** on the Word of God,
LC : 01 :095(378) [0607] Since so much **depends** on God's Word that no holy day
LC : 01 :156(386) [0625] If it **depended** on our merits, we would not have a penny
LC : 01 :245(398) [0649] however much you steal, **depend** on it that just as much
LC : 01 :329(410) [0677] return and upon it they **depend**, so that end and
LC : 02 :033(415) [0687] Gospel that we preach **depends** on the proper
LC : 03 :013(422) [0701] On this I can rely and **depend**, and I can revere it highly,
LC : 04 :053(443) [0745] Everything **depends** upon the Word and commandment
LC : 05 :061(453) [0767] this sacrament does not **depend** upon our worthiness.
EP : 07 :038(486) [0817] faith in Christ, but also **depends** on people's outward
SD : RN :001(503) [0851] the ancient church always had its **dependable** symbols.
SD : 01 :055(518) [0877] in accord with all **dependable** teachers, deliberately and
SD : 01 :056(518) [0877] Luther or by any other **dependable** teacher of our pure
SD : 03 :030(544) [0925] saddened consciences **dependable** and reliable comfort
SD : 03 :057(549) [0935] Gospel, upon which faith **depends** before God and which
SD : 03 :067(551) [0937] salvation of our souls **depends**, we direct him for the sake
SD : 07 :016(572) [0977] and that it does not **depend** on the worthiness or
SD : 12 :010(633) [1097] before God does not **depend** alone on the sole obedience

Depicted (2)
AP : 24 :036(257) [0397] was to come; thus this **depicted** Christ and the whole
LC : 02 :063(419) [0695] and his work exquisitely **depicted** in very short but rich

Deplore (1), Deplored (2), Deplores (1), Deplorable (2)
AG : 23 :018(054) [0063] It is therefore **deplorable** that Christian marriage has not
AP : 15 :028(219) [0323] Yet at the same time he **deplores** the danger to
AP : 21 :041(235) [0355] outstanding men who **deplored** the abuses of the Mass,
TR : 00 :036(326) [0515] the act itself is not to be **deplored** so much as the pretext
SC : PR :001(338) [0533] The **deplorable** conditions which I recently encountered
SD : 07 :069(582) [0997] their weakness in faith, **deplore** it, and heartily wish that

Depose (4), Deposed (1)
AG : 28 :002(081) [0083] presumed to set up and **depose** kings and emperors
AG : 28 :013(083) [0085] should not set up and **depose** kings, should not annul
S2 : 04 :007(299) [0473] in their power and choice to change or **depose** this head.
S2 : 04 :007(299) [0473] to the popes when it **deposed** three and elected a fourth.
TR : 00 :005(320) [0505] right to elect, ordain, confirm, and **depose** all bishops.

Depreciate (1)
LC : 01 :123(382) [0617] and they defame and **depreciate** one another behind their

Deprivation (3)
EP : 01 :015(468) [0783] and not the complete **deprivation** or loss of the same, just
SD : 01 :022(512) [0865] original sin is not a **deprivation** or absence of man's
SD : 01 :027(513) [0867] This **deprivation** and lack, this corruption and wounding

Deprive (10), Deprived (10), Deprives (2)
AL : 20 :022(044) [0055] should not be **deprived** of consolation but know that
S3 : 10 :002(314) [0497] the church must not be **deprived** of ministers on their
TR : 00 :011(321) [0507] Paul **deprives** Peter of this pretext and denies that Peter's
TR : 00 :035(326) [0513] to their power and **deprive** the emperors of the right to
TR : 00 :044(328) [0517] the glory of Christ, **deprive** consciences of a firm
TR : 00 :056(329) [0521] it that the church is not **deprived** of the power of making
LC : 01 :010(366) [0583] despondent when they lack them or are **deprived** of them.
LC : 01 :108(379) [0611] They are not to be **deprived** of their honor because of
LC : 01 :122(382) [0617] Thus they **deprive** themselves of this treasure and joy of
LC : 01 :163(387) [0627] we deserve to have God **deprive** us of his Word and his
LC : 01 :256(399) [0653] not have our neighbor **deprived** of his reputation, honor,
LC : 01 :270(401) [0657] for no man should be **deprived** of his honor and good
LC : 01 :307(406) [0669] God does not wish you to **deprive** your neighbor of
LC : 03 :084(431) [0723] oppress the poor and **deprive** them of their daily bread!
LC : 04 :082(446) [0751] This interpretation **deprives** Baptism of its value, making
LC : 05 :059(453) [0767] from the sacrament," lest he **deprive** himself of life.
EP : 07 :024(484) [0815] so that they are **deprived** of the blood of Christ.
SD : 03 :017(542) [0921] godless for a bribe, and **deprive** the innocent of his right"
SD : 04 :023(555) [0945] these propositions **deprive** tempted and troubled
SD : 08 :087(608) [1047] it a pernicious error to **deprive** Christ according to his
SD : 10 :019(614) [1059] the church must not be **deprived** of ministers on their
SD : 11 :038(622) [1075] We would be **deprived** of this comfort completely if we

Depth (2), Depths (4)
S3 : 02 :004(303) [0479] show man to what utter **depths** his nature has fallen and
LC : 02 :064(419) [0695] to us the most profound **depths** of his fatherly heart, his
SD : 01 :036(514) [0869] in secret, intricately wrought in the **depths** of the earth.
SD : 08 :021(595) [1023] this the devil's mask and damned it to the **depths** of hell.
SD : 10 :016(613) [1059] his neck and to be drowned in the **depth** of the sea."
SD : 11 :064(626) [1083] following words: "O the **depth** of the riches and wisdom

Derive (7), Derived (12), Derives (1), Deriving (2)
AG : 27 :024(074) [0079] to cancel an obligation which is **derived** from divine law.
AL : 27 :024(074) [0079] an obligation which is plainly **derived** from divine law.
AP : 04 :117(123) [0155] and arguments **derived** from the Scriptures, was to make
AP : 04 :224(138) [0181] into them instead of **deriving** the meaning from the texts
AP : 04 :287(150) [0203] whole system is **derived** either from human reason or from
AP : 04 :387(166) [0225] a doctrine of justification **derived** either from reason or
AP : 10 :003(179) [0247] we are truly branches, **deriving** life from him for
AP : 12 :143(204) [0297] law but have a set form **derived** from human tradition,
AP : 21 :024(232) [0349] Perhaps they **derive** this "order" from the usage at royal
AP : 24 :083(264) [0413] philologists do not **derive** it from *lite*, which means
AP : 24 :085(264) [0413] imagine that "Mass" is **derived** from *mizbeach*, the
S1 : PR :010(290) [0457] many things and many people might **derive** benefit from it
S3 : 08 :002(312) [0495] private absolution is **derived** from the office of the keys,
LC : 01 :025(368) [0587] other languages, a name **derived** from the word "good"
LC : 01 :141(384) [0621] of parents all other authority is **derived** and developed.
LC : 01 :142(384) [0621] the place of parents and **derive** from them their power
LC : 04 :012(438) [0735] to the person, from whom they must **derive** their worth.
LC : 04 :018(438) [0737] From the Word it **derives** its nature as a sacrament, as
SD : RN :013(506) [0855] No one can blame us if we **derive** our expositions and
SD : 07 :041(576) [0985] Confession cannot be **derived** more correctly or better
SD : 07 :085(584) [1001] rule and norm has been **derived** from the words of
SD : 09 :003(610) [1053] heart of this article and **derive** from it the comfort that

Descend (4), Descendants (8), Descended (11), Descends (1), Descent (4)
PR : PR :000(001) [0004] of their Lands, Churches, Schools, and **Descendants**
AG : 03 :004(030) [0045] The same Christ also **descended** into hell, truly rose from
AL : 03 :004(030) [0045] He also **descended** into hell, and on the third day truly
AP : 02 :005(101) [0107] mortality that Adam's **descendants** bear because of his
AP : 07 :014(170) [0231] these physical **descendants** from other nations by certain
S1 : PR :011(290) [0457] a council of angels to **descend** on Germany and destroy
S1 : 01 :000(292) [0461] died, was buried, **descended** to hell, rose from the dead,
S3 : 08 :009(313) [0497] to Adam and his **descendants** from the beginning to the
TR : 00 :034(325) [0513] horrible darkness to **descend** over the church, and
SC : 02 :003(345) [0545] *dead, and buried: he* ***descended*** *into hell, the third day he*
LC : SP :012(363) [0577] dead, and buried: he **descended** into hell, the third day he
LC : 01 :038(369) [0591] ways before punishment **descends**, they become so mad
LC : 02 :025(413) [0683] *dead, and buried: he* ***descended*** *into hell, the third day he*
LC : 04 :021(439) [0737] that the Holy Spirit **descended** visibly, and that the divine
EP : 01 :005(466) [0781] he is concerned but with the **descendants** of Abraham.
EP : 08 :008(487) [0819] to die, to ascend and to **descend**, to move from place to

Continued ▶

E P : 0 8 :013(488) [0821] died, was buried, **descended** into hell, rose from the dead,
E P : 0 9 :000(492) [0827] IX. Christ's **Descent** into Hell
S D : 0 5 :023(562) [0959] The **descendants** of the holy patriarchs, like the
S D : 0 5 :023(562) [0959] himself and all his **descendants**, and plunged them into
S D : 0 7 :001(569) [0971] to preserve it for our **descendants** also, and faithfully to
S D : 0 8 :010(593) [1019] and die, to ascend and **descend**, to move from one place
S D : 0 8 :037(598) [1027] example, "the Son was **descended** from David according
S D : 0 9 :000(610) [1049] IX. Christ's **Descent** into Hell
S D : 0 9 :001(610) [1049] of the article on Christ's **descent** into hell have been
S D : 0 9 :001(610) [1051] Son, who died, was buried, and **descended** into hell."
S D : 0 9 :001(610) [1051] Herein the burial and the **descent** into hell are
S D : 0 9 :002(610) [1051] person, God and man, **descended** into hell, conquered the

Describe (12), Described (13), Describes (11), Describing (3), Description (5)
P R : P R :011(006) [0011] clearly and correctly **described** to one another, in
P R : P R :020(010) [0019] the words of Christ as **described** above does not
A P : P R :017(099) [0103] We need not **describe** here how they lay hidden under all
A P : 0 2 :001(100) [0105] we wanted simply to **describe** what original sin includes,
A P : 0 2 :046(106) [0117] his own powers, Genesis **describes** another penalty for
A P : 0 4 :097(121) [0149] What could **describe** the work of Christ and justification
A P : 0 4 :251(143) [0191] Nor does he **describe** the manner of justification, but only
A P : 0 4 :285(150) [0201] **Describing** this process in Rom. 4:5 ff., Paul proves that
A P : 0 4 :302(153) [0205] opponents come forth to **describe** the love with which he
A P : 0 7 :006(169) [0229] why they criticize our **description**, which speaks of living
A P : 1 2 :009(183) [0255] true, and great terrors **described** in the Psalms and the
A P : 1 2 :046(188) [0263] Wherever Paul **describes** conversion or renewal, he
A P : 1 2 :049(188) [0265] while the second **describes** how we are revived in
A P : 1 2 :171(209) [0305] or formal penitence **described** by the canons dealing with
A P : 1 3 :023(214) [0313] Words cannot **describe** the abuses which this fanatical
A P : 1 4 :001(214) [0315] discipline in the manner **described** by the ancient canons.
A P : 1 5 :019(218) [0319] Here he is **describing** the invention of rites, for he says
A P : 1 5 :044(221) [0327] From this **description** of the state of our churches it is
A P : 2 2 :010(237) [0361] The story **describes** Eli's punishment.
A P : 2 4 :014(251) [0389] We have already **described** the current understanding of
A P : 2 4 :045(258) [0399] Daniel **describes** a vastly different desolation, ignorance
A P : 2 4 :047(258) [0401] This is the desolation that Daniel **describes**.
A P : 2 4 :051(259) [0403] whom Daniel (11:38) **describes** as worshiping their God
A P : 2 7 :027(273) [0429] Paul also **describes** perfection (II Cor. 3:18) thus: "We are
A P : 2 7 :058(279) [0439] be said about other vows **described** in the Old Testament.
T R : 0 0 :039(327) [0515] For in **describing** the Antichrist in his letter to the
T R : 0 0 :071(332) [0525] of which Dionysius **describes**; but he is a late and
L C : S P :020(364) [0579] Gospels where they **describe** how Christ said farewell to
L C : 0 1 :125(382) [0617] worship of God **described** in the previous
L C : 0 1 :227(396) [0645] Who can even **describe** or imagine it all?
L C : 0 2 :010(411) [0679] words give us a brief **description** of God the Father, his
L C : 0 2 :010(412) [0679] we praise or portray or **describe** him in such a way as to
L C : 0 2 :020(412) [0681] be said if we were to **describe** in detail how few people
L C : 0 3 :073(430) [0719] associations of every **description** with the people among
L C : 0 4 :027(440) [0739] Hence it is well **described** as a divine, blessed, fruitful, and
E P : 0 6 :008(481) [0807] and measure above **described**, upon Christians and
S D : 0 1 :010(510) [0863] words put it, "The **description** of original sin denies to
S D : 0 1 :023(512) [0865] we sing in our churches **describes** it, "Through Adam's
S D : 0 1 :052(517) [0875] of our nature as it is **described** in the Smalcald Articles.
S D : 0 2 :060(533) [0905] truth, as Stephen **describes** the obstinate Jews (Acts
S D : 0 3 :009(540) [0919] faith and confession **described** above, that a poor sinner
S D : 0 7 :067(582) [0997] ashamed," just as they **describe** the majesty of Christ as
S D : 0 8 :063(603) [1037] deed and in truth — to **describe** any essential, natural
S D : 1 1 :030(621) [1073] The elect are therefore **described** as follows: "My sheep

Desecrate (3), Desecrated (1), Desecrates (2), Desecration (4)
A P : 1 3 :023(214) [0313] has come the endless **desecration** of Masses, which we
A P : 2 4 :099(268) [0419] in defending their **desecration** of the Mass lest they
A P : 2 7 :053(278) [0437] ceremonies as the **desecration** of the Mass by its
A P : 2 8 :026(285) [0451] is in the sacrilegious **desecration** of the Mass for profit!
L C : 0 1 :096(378) [0607] who grossly misuse and **desecrate** the holy day, like those
L C : 0 3 :045(426) [0709] of wrong profanes and **desecrates** this holy name, as in
L C : 0 3 :045(426) [0709] a church was said to be **desecrated** when a murder or any
L C : 0 4 :055(443) [0747] be to blaspheme and **desecrate** the sacrament in the worst
L C : 0 5 :004(447) [0753] who blaspheme and **desecrate** this sacrament; but as in
S D : 0 7 :060(580) [0993] dishonors, abuses, and **desecrates** him who is there

Desert (1), Deserted (1), Deserting (1)
A L : 2 0 :020(044) [0055] driven into the **desert**, into monasteries, in the hope that
A P : 2 3 :003(239) [0363] spare, and banish **deserted** wives and orphaned children.
A P : 2 7 :041(276) [0435] the command of God forbids **deserting** wife and children.

Deserve (18), Deserved (7), Deserves (3), Deserving (2)
A L : 2 3 :018(054) [0063] and other crimes which **deserve** the punishments of just
A P : 0 4 :257(144) [0193] of penitence, they **deserve** to be regarded as blasphemers
A P : 0 4 :336(159) [0215] these absurdities do not **deserve** a refutation, we shall
A P : 1 2 :108(198) [0283] them or condemning those who have **deserved** it.
A P : 1 2 :159(207) [0301] said, "Those who did not **deserve** to drink the cup must
A P : 1 5 :008(216) [0317] of the law you think you **deserve** to be accounted
A P : 2 4 :078(263) [0411] arguments which do not **deserve** a lengthy discussion.
A P : 2 7 :033(275) [0431] mere human traditions, **deserve** the credit for meriting the
S 1 : P R :005(289) [0457] the wrath of God — answer them as they **deserve**.
S C : 0 3 :016(347) [0549] for we neither merit nor **deserve** those things for which
S C : 0 3 :016(347) [0549] we sin daily and **deserve** nothing but punishment, we
S C : 0 9 :003(354) [0561] provide, for the laborer **deserves** his wages" (Luke 10:7).
S C : 0 9 :003(354) [0561] grain,' and 'The laborer **deserves** his wages'" (I Tim. 5:17,
L C : P R :013(360) [0571] If so, we **deserve** not only to be refused food but also to
L C : 0 1 :060(372) [0597] Hence we get what we **deserve**: plague, war, famine, fire,
L C : 0 1 :151(386) [0625] What we seek and **deserve**, then, is paid back to us in
L C : 0 1 :155(386) [0625] who have roundly **deserved** punishment and that we are
L C : 0 1 :163(387) [0627] For this we **deserve** to have God deprive us of his Word
L C : 0 1 :186(390) [0633] for any evil deed, no matter how much he **deserves** it.
L C : 0 1 :231(396) [0647] thieves, and that he will punish them as they **deserve**.
L C : 0 1 :238(397) [0647] He will pay them what they **deserve**.
L C : 0 2 :028(414) [0685] doomed to eternal damnation, as we had **deserved**.
L C : 0 3 :092(432) [0725] punish us as we daily **deserve**, but to deal graciously with
L C : 0 6 :006(457) [0000] will not obey the Gospel **deserve** just such a jailer as
S D : 0 3 :009(540) [0919] from the verdict of well **deserved** damnation, and is
S D : 1 1 :058(625) [1081] It is indeed a well **deserved** punishment for sin when God
S D : 1 1 :059(626) [1081] us would rightfully have **deserved**, earned, and merited
S D : 1 1 :059(626) [1083] and contrary to our **deserving**, to whom he gives and
S D : 1 1 :060(626) [1083] sin and is worthy and **deserving** of God's wrath and
S D : 1 1 :060(626) [1083] his righteous and well **deserved** judgement over certain

Designated (4)
A L : 2 8 :060(091) [0091] appears that the church **designated** the Lord's Day for
T R : 0 0 :019(323) [0509] objected to having himself **designated** as universal bishop.
L C : S P :026(364) [0579] especially at the time **designated** for the Catechism, so
S D : 0 8 :085(608) [1047] as St. Paul says, 'He is **designated** the Son of God in

Designed (1), Designs (4)
A P : 2 2 :013(238) [0361] we shall not say anything more about their crafty **designs**.
L C : 0 1 :293(404) [0665] wife or property, or to have any **designs** on them.
L C : 0 1 :307(406) [0669] — that is, having **designs** upon your neighbor's property,
L C : 0 3 :031(424) [0707] murderous and seditious **designs** by which the devil
S D : 1 0 :005(611) [1053] avoid persecution) are **designed** to give the impression

Desire (65), Desired (6), Desires (40), Desiring (2), Desirous (1), Desirable (5)
P R : P R :017(008) [0015] failed to accomplish the **desired** end of Christian
P R : P R :019(009) [0017] We have therefore **desired** hereby to attest and affirm
P R : P R :022(012) [0021] For this reason we **desire** to testify before the face of
P R : P R :023(012) [0021] and undertaken, and we **desire** once more to have
P R : P R :023(012) [0021] We **desire** particularly that the young men who are being
A G : P R :001(024) [0039] indicated an earnest **desire** to deliberate concerning
A G : P R :002(024) [0039] The **desire** was also expressed for deliberation on what
A G : 2 2 :011(050) [0061] consciences of those who **desire** to observe the sacrament
A G : 2 4 :034(060) [0067] Mass is held and those who **desire** it are communicated.
A G : 2 7 :018(073) [0077] with regard to those who **desire** to marry that all those
A G : 2 8 :077(094) [0095] bishops' power, but we **desire** and pray that they may not
A G : 0 0 :006(095) [0095] the summons, we have **desired** to present the above
A L : 2 3 :003(051) [0061] Since priests among us **desired** to avoid such open
A L : 2 3 :016(054) [0063] and it is devoutly to be **desired** that this be done in the
A L : 2 4 :034(060) [0067] and on other days, if any **desire** the sacrament, it is also
A L : 0 0 :006(095) [0095] Majesty, we have **desired** to present the above articles in
A P : 0 2 :026(103) [0111] God (that is, not only the **desires** of the body but also
A P : 0 2 :036(105) [0115] continue to work those **desires** against which the faithful
A P : 0 2 :042(106) [0117] people; yielding to anger, **desire**, ambition, wealth, etc.
A P : 0 4 :146(127) [0163] brings forth evil **desires**, though the Spirit in us resists
A P : 0 4 :169(130) [0169] do not believe that evil **desires** in the flesh are sins, about
A P : 0 4 :169(130) [0169] says (Gal. 5:17), "The **desires** of the flesh are against the
A P : 0 4 :169(130) [0169] the Spirit, and the **desires** of the Spirit are against the
A P : 0 4 :227(139) [0183] knowledge but rather a **desire** to accept and grasp what is
A P : 0 4 :228(139) [0183] toward God, this **desire** to receive the offered promise, is
A P : 0 4 :304(154) [0205] in the will, that is, to **desire** and to accept what the
A P : 0 4 :310(155) [0207] in the Gospel is the **desire** to receive forgiveness of sins,
A P : 1 2 :129(202) [0291] of men and the silent **desires** of all nations; they certainly
A P : 1 4 :001(214) [0315] the assembly to our deep **desire** to maintain the church
A P : 1 4 :002(214) [0315] in some places, despite our earnest **desire** to keep it.
A P : 1 5 :047(221) [0327] that we indulge and pamper the **desires** of our flesh.
A P : 2 1 :042(235) [0357] most honorable and holy **desire** of the emperor, our
A P : 2 3 :007(240) [0365] that one sex should have a proper **desire** for the other.
A P : 2 3 :007(240) [0365] "natural love," the **desire** which was meant to be in
A P : 2 3 :012(241) [0367] For the natural **desire** of one sex for the other is an
A P : 2 3 :013(241) [0367] sinful lust but about the **desire** which is called "natural
A P : 2 3 :016(241) [0369] since man sinned, natural **desire** and the lust that
A P : 2 3 :059(247) [0379] Despite our most earnest **desire** to establish harmony, we
A P : 2 4 :029(255) [0393] offering thou dost not **desire**; but thou hast given me an
A P : 2 7 :064(280) [0441] from public funds, "They **desire** to marry, and so they
S 2 : 0 2 :008(294) [0465] honest, for if he really **desires** to commune, he can do so
S 2 : 0 4 :004(299) [0473] and submits to him in all that he **desires**, says, and does.
S 2 : 0 4 :011(300) [0475] do this; those who **desire** to do so they allow to believe in
S 3 : 0 2 :002(303) [0479] it forbids what they **desire** to do and commands what
S 3 : 0 2 :004(303) [0479] despairing, anxiously **desires** help but does not know
S 3 : 0 3 :017(305) [0483] was asked if he did not wish or **desire** to be repentant.
S 3 : 1 1 :003(315) [0499] On the contrary, we **desire** marriage to be free, as God
T R : 0 0 :010(321) [0507] testifies that he did not **desire** to seek confirmation from
T R : 0 0 :074(332) [0525] on account of other evil **desires**, have tormented men and
S C : P R :013(339) [0535] For anyone who **desires** to reside in a city is bound to
S C : P R :022(341) [0537] any law, the people will **desire** the sacrament and, as it
S C : P R :022(341) [0537] anyone who does not **desire** to receive the sacrament at
S C : 0 8 :007(353) [0559] thy hand; Thou satisfiest the **desire** of every living thing."
S C : 0 8 :008(353) [0559] that "satisfying the **desire** of every living thing" means
L C : 0 1 :009(366) [0583] This **desire** for wealth clings and cleaves to our nature all
L C : 0 1 :022(367) [0585] as a gift from God, but **desiring** by itself to earn or merit
L C : 0 1 :040(370) [0591] Certainly, if we **desire** all good things in time and
L C : 0 1 :041(370) [0591] more could you ask or **desire** than God's gracious
L C : 0 1 :152(386) [0625] our blessings and we shall have all that our hearts **desire**.
L C : 0 1 :166(388) [0629] everything abundantly, according to your heart's **desire**.
L C : 0 1 :188(390) [0635] do evil to somebody who **desires** and does you good is
L C : 0 1 :195(391) [0637] protect us, so that he may subdue our **desire** for revenge.
L C : 0 1 :215(394) [0641] thoughts and evil **desires** that they suffer incessant
L C : 0 1 :219(394) [0643] the chief ways to make chastity attractive and **desirable**.
L C : 0 1 :252(399) [0651] Anyone who seeks and **desires** good works will here find
L C : 0 1 :253(399) [0653] Whoever does not **desire** this blessing will find wrath and
L C : 0 1 :309(407) [0669] We are commanded not to **desire** harm to our neighbor,
L C : 0 1 :330(410) [0677] a spontaneous impulse and **desire** gladly to do God's will.
L C : 0 2 :023(413) [0683] gratitude to God and a **desire** to use all these blessings to
L C : 0 3 :020(423) [0703] awaken and kindle in our hearts a **desire** and love to pray.
L C : 0 3 :024(423) [0705] for something which he **desires**; otherwise it cannot be
L C : 0 3 :027(424) [0705] to stronger and greater **desires** and spread your cloak
L C : 0 3 :055(427) [0713] human heart to dare to **desire** if God himself had not
L C : 0 3 :056(427) [0713] He **desires** of us nothing more ardently than that we ask
L C : 0 3 :057(427) [0713] ask for whatever he might **desire** and was prepared to
L C : 0 3 :064(428) [0715] This is his only purpose, his **desire** and thought.
L C : 0 3 :080(431) [0721] whose whole purpose and **desire** it is to take away or
L C : 0 3 :089(432) [0723] aroused by evil **desires** and devices, so that we sin daily in
L C : 0 5 :037(451) [0761] faith of the heart which discerns and **desires** this treasure.
L C : 0 5 :049(452) [0765] time elapse without ever **desiring** the sacrament, I call
L C : 0 5 :052(452) [0765] you is the fact that Christ **desires** it, and it pleases him.
L C : 0 5 :054(453) [0765] act like a person who really **desires** to be right with God.
L C : 0 5 :058(453) [0767] of sins since they do not **desire** it and do not want to be
L C : 0 5 :061(453) [0767] is the person who **desires** no grace and absolution and

Continued ▶

LC : 05 :062(454) [0767] He who earnestly **desires** grace and consolation should
LC : 05 :067(454) [0769] quite cold and callous and lose all **desire** and love for it.
LC : 05 :070(454) [0769] to be rid of it and **desire** help, should regard and use the
LC : 06 :005(457) [0000] if they will never need or **desire** to go to confession any
LC : 06 :014(458) [0000] heart that feels its sin and **desires** consolation, it has here
LC : 06 :015(459) [0000] when I lament my sin and **desire** comfort and restoration
LC : 06 :020(459) [0000] you are no Christian, and **desire** no such comfort, we
LC : 06 :027(460) [0000] need will develop such a **desire** for confession that he will
LC : 06 :034(461) [0000] rightly taught, and such a **desire** and love for it would be
EP : 01 :012(467) [0781] the teaching that evil **desires** are not sin but concreated
EP : 02 :003(470) [0787] enemy of God, so that he **desires** and wills only that
EP : 11 :008(495) [0833] He earnestly **desires** that all men should come to him and
EP : 11 :012(496) [0835] does not mean that God does not **desire** to save everyone.
SD : 01 :011(510) [0863] uncleanness of the heart and evil **desires** and inclinations.
SD : 01 :018(511) [0865] that the sinful wicked **desires** are not sin but concreated
SD : 02 :017(524) [0887] 8:7), and again, "The **desires** of the flesh are against the
SD : 02 :039(528) [0895] the point where they **desire** to do the good and delight in
SD : 02 :064(533) [0907] And again, "For the **desires** of the flesh are against the
SD : 02 :064(533) [0907] the Spirit, and the **desires** of the Spirit are against the
SD : 02 :084(537) [0913] Scriptures say that the **desires** of the flesh are against the
SD : 04 :012(553) [0941] a man is willing and **desirous** to do good to everyone, to
SD : 04 :019(554) [0945] flesh with its passions, **desires**, and deeds (Gal. 5:24;
SD : 06 :008(565) [0965] Likewise, "The **desires** of the flesh are against the spirit
SD : 06 :008(565) [0965] against the spirit and the **desires** of the spirit are against
SD : 06 :009(565) [0965] Hence, because of the **desires** of the flesh the truly
SD : 07 :029(574) [0981] already beginning to do, I **desire** with this treatise to
SD : 07 :066(581) [0997] here, in the interest of **desirable** brevity we direct the
SD : 07 :091(586) [1005] for the sake of **desirable** brevity, merely refer the
SD : 07 :091(586) [1005] to these writings and **desire** to have them considered as
SD : 07 :128(591) [1015] for the sake of **desirable** brevity we have not wanted to
SD : 08 :092(609) [1049] of God, wherever he **desires** and especially where he has
SD : 10 :010(612) [1055] of the Word of God **desire** to suppress the pure doctrine
SD : 11 :096(632) [1095] We **desire** such harmony as will not violate God's honor,
SD : 12 :002(632) [1095] mention of them, although it now appears to be **desirable**.
SD : 12 :006(633) [1097] And we **desire** by God's grace to remain steadfastly in our

Desist (3)
PR : PR :008(005) [0011] would be constrained to **desist** from their fabricated
SD : 05 :008(559) [0953] to feel heartily sorry for them, and to **desist** from them.
SD : 11 :071(627) [1085] teaching they are to **desist** from sin, repent, believe his

Desolate (1), Desolation (3)
AP : 24 :044(258) [0399] their hands over "the **desolation** of the temples" and the
AP : 24 :045(258) [0399] a vastly different **desolation**, ignorance of the Gospel.
AP : 24 :047(258) [0401] This is the **desolation** that Daniel describes.
S1 : PR :010(290) [0457] see so many vacant and **desolate** parishes everywhere that

Despair (40), Despaired (1), Despairing (2), Despairs (2), Desperate (1), Desperately (4)
AG : 25 :008(062) [0069] also says, "The heart is **desperately** corrupt; who can
AG : 26 :013(066) [0073] writes that many fell into **despair** on this account, and
AL : 26 :013(066) [0073] writes that many fell into **despair**, and some even took
AP : 02 :008(101) [0107] it, being angry at him, **despairing** of his grace, trusting in
AP : 04 :020(110) [0125] they run headlong into **despair**, unless they hear, beyond
AP : 04 :021(110) [0127] other hand, they drive to **despair** because in their doubt
AP : 04 :021(110) [0127] And at last they **despair** utterly.
AP : 04 :157(128) [0165] vain and our consciences will then plunge into **despair**.
AP : 04 :204(135) [0177] up works and ultimately **despair** because they cannot find
AP : 04 :285(150) [0201] invents other works and services until it **despairs** utterly.
AP : 04 :301(153) [0205] What is this doctrine of the law but a doctrine of **despair**?
AP : 04 :302(154) [0205] works; it leads consciences into either pride or **despair**.
AP : 04 :321(157) [0209] to doubt and to work without faith until **despair** ensues.
AP : 04 :339(159) [0215] He does not want us to **despair** of God's grace and
AP : 04 :350(161) [0217] conscience tempts us to **despair** when it shows our old or
AP : 04 :364(162) [0219] But to escape **despair** amid afflictions, they should know
AP : 07 :009(170) [0229] that we may not **despair** but may know all this.
AP : 11 :010(182) [0253] devout minds to hopeless **despair** because they believed
AP : 12 :034(186) [0261] What do they teach but **despair**, when amid such terrors
AP : 12 :072(192) [0271] of God against **despair** and against the terrors of sin and
AP : 12 :089(195) [0279] faith is, and so it is that at last they rush into **despair**.
AP : 12 :089(195) [0279] law, an abrogation of the Gospel, a doctrine of **despair**.
AP : 20 :008(227) [0341] the devil tempts them to **despair** unless they know that
AP : 20 :008(227) [0341] and life to the heart in its hardest struggle against **despair**.
AP : 24 :046(258) [0401] faith in its struggle with **despair** and about the free
AP : 28 :004(281) [0445] the people **desperately** want instruction in order to have a
S3 : 01 :002(302) [0477] of God, presumption, **despair**, blindness — in short,
S3 : 02 :004(303) [0479] despondent and **despairing**, anxiously desires help but
S3 : 03 :002(304) [0479] He drives all together into terror and **despair**.
S3 : 03 :007(304) [0481] and hell, and man must **despair** like Saul and Judas.
TR : 00 :044(328) [0517] (that is, the exercise of faith struggling against **despair**).
TR : 00 :045(328) [0517] which has produced many errors and introduced **despair**.
SC : 03 :018(347) [0549] mislead us into unbelief, **despair**, and other great and
LC : 01 :008(365) [0583] has nothing doubts and **despairs** as if he never heard of
LC : 01 :315(408) [0671] on the part of those **desperate** saints to dare to find a
LC : 03 :010(421) [0699] heart is by nature so **desperately** wicked that it always
LC : 03 :104(434) [0727] contrary, to drive us into **despair**, atheism, blasphemy,
LC : 06 :017(459) [0000] everyone inevitably **despaired** of confessing so purely
EP : 05 :008(479) [0803] like the Pharisees, or they **despair**, as Judas did, etc.
EP : 11 :009(495) [0833] life, or drive men to **despair** and waken dangerous
EP : 11 :015(496) [0835] occasion either to **despair** or to lead a reckless and
EP : 11 :016(497) [0837] are driven to doubt and **despair**, or in such a way that the
SD : 02 :017(524) [0887] of man is deceitful and **desperately** wicked," that is, is so
SD : 05 :009(559) [0955] the law may not end in **despair**, the proclamation of the
SD : 05 :010(559) [0955] law by external works, or drives man utterly to **despair**.
SD : 05 :024(563) [0961] a way that they become despondent and **despair** therein.
SD : 11 :010(618) [1067] false security and impenitence or anxiety and **despair**.
SD : 11 :012(618) [1067] of thereby driving us to **despair** but in order that "by
SD : 11 :012(618) [1067] in no way cause or support either impenitence or **despair**.
SD : 11 :091(631) [1093] in it but are driven to **despair**, or when impenitent sinners

Despise (58), Despised (12), Despisers (3), Despises (11), Despising (2)
AG : 19 :000(040) [0053] in all wicked men and **despisers** of God by the perverted
AG : 20 :010(042) [0055] that he can merit grace, **despises** Christ and seeks his own
AL : 20 :010(042) [0055] he merits grace by works **despises** the merit and grace of
AL : 20 :015(043) [0055] Although this teaching is **despised** by inexperienced men,
AL : 27 :009(072) [0077] authority of the canons was utterly ignored and **despised**.
AP : 02 :008(101) [0107] namely, ignoring God, **despising** him, lacking fear and
AP : 02 :024(103) [0111] carnal things; either it **despises** the judgment of God in its
AP : 02 :026(103) [0111] righteousness in which it trusts while it **despises** God).
AP : 04 :034(112) [0129] the human heart either **despises** the judgment of God in
AP : 04 :035(112) [0131] It is inherent in man to **despise** God and to doubt his
AP : 04 :035(112) [0131] Such people **despise** God when they do these things, as
AP : 04 :060(115) [0137] take it away when they **despise** and disparage faith and
AP : 04 :233(140) [0185] behavior too strictly or **despise** them because of some
AP : 04 :276(148) [0199] arouse themselves to believe but **despise** these promises.
AP : 11 :004(180) [0249] openly wicked and the **despisers** of the sacraments are
AP : 12 :101(197) [0281] And those who **despise** private absolution understand
AP : 12 :106(197) [0283] is a neat one, worthy of these men who **despise** grammar.
AP : 15 :042(221) [0327] This the people rightly **despise** and walk out on them
AP : 23 :019(242) [0369] he does not want us to **despise** his ordinances, his
AP : 23 :025(243) [0371] of Antichrist's kingdom to **despise** women (11:37).
AP : 23 :053(246) [0377] against those who **despise** his gift and ordinance and
AP : 23 :055(247) [0379] also exhort others not to **despise** the gift of continence.
AP : 24 :016(252) [0389] "poor cooks," for they **despise** these instructions and
AP : 24 :029(255) [0393] broken and contrite heart, O God, thou wilt not **despise**."
S2 : 04 :008(299) [0473] easily and quickly be **despised** and would ultimately be
TR : 00 :032(325) [0513] spiritual kingdom was **despised** (that is, after the Gospel
SC : PR :022(341) [0537] or four times a year **despises** the sacrament and is no
SC : PR :022(341) [0537] not say, "Omit this," or "**Despise** this," but he said, "Do
SC : PR :022(341) [0537] that this be done and not that it be omitted and **despised**.
SC : 01 :006(342) [0541] and so we should not **despise** his Word and the preaching
SC : 01 :008(343) [0541] and so we should not **despise** our parents and superiors,
LC : PR :001(358) [0567] in this respect and **despise** both their office and this
LC : PR :008(359) [0569] is a sure sign that they **despise** both their office and the
LC : PR :013(360) [0571] Shall we frivolously **despise** this might, blessing, power,
LC : PR :015(360) [0571] as the devils, and yet we **despise** our weapons and armor,
LC : PR :018(361) [0573] pretend to know and **despise** the Catechism, which is a
LC : 01 :034(369) [0589] Therefore he wills to be feared and not to be **despised**.
LC : 01 :046(370) [0593] other hand, was a poor, **despised** man, hunted down and
LC : 01 :095(378) [0607] and will punish all who **despise** his Word and refuse to
LC : 01 :112(380) [0613] Alas, it is utterly **despised** and brushed aside, and no one
LC : 01 :144(385) [0623] have been neglected and **despised**; instead, everybody ran
LC : 01 :149(385) [0623] are his dear child; if you **despise** this commandment, then
LC : 01 :151(386) [0625] not do so in love, but **despises** or rebelliously resists
LC : 01 :152(386) [0625] and commandment are **despised**, as if they came from
LC : 01 :154(386) [0625] When you defraud or **despise** your master, another person
LC : 01 :166(388) [0629] He who **despises** and disdains this is not worthy to hear a
LC : 01 :209(393) [0639] that we should not **despise** or disdain marriage, as the
LC : 01 :213(394) [0641] when they **despise** and forbid marriage, and boast and
LC : 01 :246(398) [0651] up with those of you who **despise**, defraud, steal, and rob
LC : 01 :247(398) [0651] But if you **despise** and defy this, see whom you have
LC : 01 :322(409) [0673] punishing all who **despise** and transgress his
LC : 01 :326(409) [0675] should impel us not to **despise** his Word, but learn it,
LC : 01 :330(410) [0677] wrath upon those who **despise** them, and, on the
LC : 03 :012(422) [0701] we should by no means **despise** our prayers, but rather
LC : 03 :013(422) [0701] A child should never **despise** obedience to his father and
LC : 03 :014(422) [0701] these words to heart and in no case to **despise** prayer.
LC : 03 :020(423) [0703] so that we may not **despise** or disdain it or pray
LC : 03 :028(424) [0705] promise, knowing that he will not have them **despised**.
LC : 03 :057(428) [0713] inexpressible blessings, **despise** them or lack confidence
LC : 03 :090(432) [0723] of his goodness and **despises** others he should examine
LC : 03 :104(434) [0727] is to make us scorn and **despise** both the Word and the
LC : 03 :122(436) [0731] worthiness, so that they **despise** God and accuse him of
LC : 03 :124(436) [0731] vain and that we must not in any way **despise** our prayers.
LC : 05 :041(451) [0763] and ultimately **despise** both the sacrament and the Word
LC : 05 :049(452) [0765] that we are not granted liberty to **despise** the sacrament.
LC : 05 :049(452) [0765] ever desiring the sacrament, I call that **despising** it.
LC : 05 :052(452) [0765] and incites you; if you **despise** this, you must answer for
LC : 05 :069(454) [0769] it is true that those who **despise** the sacrament and lead
LC : 06 :028(460) [0000] blessing should not be **despised**, especially when we
LC : 06 :029(460) [0000] However, if you **despise** it and proudly stay away from
LC : 06 :029(460) [0000] For you **despise** what no Christian ought to despise, and
LC : 06 :029(460) [0000] no Christian ought to **despise**, and you show thereby that
LC : 06 :029(460) [0000] And this is a sure sign that you also **despise** the Gospel.
EP : 11 :008(495) [0833] hear the Word and do not stop their ears or **despise** it.
EP : 11 :012(496) [0835] of God at all but willfully **despise** it, harden their ears and
EP : 12 :008(498) [0839] his covenant and do not **despise** it (Gen. 17:4-8; 19-21).
SD : 02 :057(532) [0903] the Word of God, but **despises** the Word and the
SD : 02 :058(532) [0903] But if such a person **despises** the instruments of the Holy
SD : 11 :010(618) [1067] vice without repentance, **despise** Word and sacraments,
SD : 11 :039(622) [1075] might be the elect who **despise** God's Word and who
SD : 11 :041(623) [1077] and obey it; the majority **despise** the Word and refuse to
SD : 11 :051(624) [1079] among others: They "**despise** the counsel of God against
SD : 11 :076(629) [1087] refuse to hear or should **despise** the preaching of his
SD : 11 :078(629) [1089] not to learn but only to **despise**, blaspheme, and ridicule
SD : 11 :086(631) [1091] the impenitent and **despisers** of his Word, and in no way
SD : 12 :013(634) [1099] the covenant and do not **despise** it (Gen. 17:4-8, 19-21).

Despite (7)
AP : 04 :391(167) [0225] **Despite** its obvious falsehood, this teaching has spawned
AP : 07 :009(169) [0229] nevertheless; it exists **despite** the great multitude of the
AP : 14 :002(214) [0315] in some places, **despite** our earnest desire to keep it.
AP : 14 :005(215) [0315] Thus men may read that, **despite** our protest against the
AP : 23 :001(239) [0363] **Despite** the notoriety of their defiled celibacy, our
AP : 23 :059(247) [0379] **Despite** our most earnest desire to establish harmony, we
AP : 24 :043(258) [0399] **Despite** the obvious wickedness of some of this, they

Despoil (1)
LC : 01 :296(405) [0665] to covet or scheme to **despoil** his neighbor of what

Despondency (1), Despondent (4)
S3 : 02 :004(303) [0479] and humbled, becomes **despondent** and despairing,
LC : 01 :010(366) [0583] possessions, and how **despondent** when they lack them or
SD : 02 :047(530) [0901] On the other hand, **despondent** hearts may fall into grave
SD : 05 :024(563) [0961] a way that they become **despondent** and despair therein.
SD : 11 :089(631) [1093] never occasions either **despondency** or a riotous and

Destined (2), Destiny (1)
SD : 0 2 :022(525) [0889] and regenerates man, a **destiny** for which only man, no
SD : 1 1 :005(617) [1065] as he chose us in him, he **destined** us in love to be his
SD : 1 1 :087(631) [1093] as it is written, "He **destined** us in love to be his son

Destroy (35), Destroyed (16), Destroying (2), Destroys (8), Destruction (11), Destructive (1)
PR : PR :004(004) [0007] and to bring about **destructive** and scandalous division in
AG : 2 6 :044(070) [0075] in fasting does not **destroy** unity in faith," and there is a
AG : 2 8 :017(083) [0085] but have divine power to **destroy** strongholds and every
AG : 2 8 :074(094) [0093] as such changes do not **destroy** the unity of Christian
AL : 1 6 :004(038) [0051] the heart, but it does not **destroy** the state or the family.
AL : 2 6 :044(070) [0075] about fasting does not **destroy** unity in faith," and Pope
AL : 2 8 :017(083) [0085] worldly but have divine power to **destroy** arguments," etc.
AP : 0 2 :050(106) [0119] sin and penalty and to **destroy** the rule of the devil, sin,
AP : 0 4 :120(124) [0155] faith we are discussing completely **destroys** the Gospel.
AP : 0 4 :121(124) [0155] to see that thereby they **destroy** the entire promise of the
AP : 0 4 :139(126) [0161] of God appeared was to **destroy** the works of the devil."
AP : 0 4 :170(130) [0171] in order to suppress and **destroy** them and to give us new
AP : 0 4 :260(145) [0195] those who reject Christ, **destroy** the Gospel, and
AP : 0 4 :300(153) [0205] and trying to **destroy** the doctrine of righteousness by
AP : 0 4 :317(156) [0209] glory to our works, a **destruction** of his glory as
AP : 0 4 :376(164) [0223] This error obviously **destroys** the righteousness of faith,
AP : 0 7 :044(177) [0243] the reader neither to **destroy** evangelical liberty nor to
AP : 1 2 :055(189) [0267] be a seed that would **destroy** the kingdom of the devil,
AP : 1 2 :123(200) [0289] May God **destroy** these wicked sophists who so sinfully
AP : 1 2 :127(201) [0291] that we be conquered and **destroyed** by armed might?
AP : 1 2 :153(206) [0299] this same purpose: to **destroy** this sinful flesh so that we
AP : 1 2 :166(208) [0303] reconciled to God and saved their city from **destruction**.
AP : 1 2 :167(209) [0305] that distrust of God and similar attitudes are **destroyed**.
AP : 1 4 :004(215) [0315] among those who seek to **destroy** the Word of God with
AP : 1 5 :024(218) [0321] writes, "Fasting avails to **destroy** and prevent guilt."
AP : 1 6 :005(223) [0331] For the Gospel does not **destroy** the state or the family
AP : 1 6 :006(223) [0331] that their Gospel would **destroy** the commonwealth by its
AP : 2 3 :051(246) [0377] approving a burden that has **destroyed** so many souls.
AP : 2 3 :054(246) [0379] The **destruction** in the flood and the burning of Sodom
AP : 2 4 :063(261) [0405] ignorant monks; they **destroy** the glory of Christ's
AP : 2 4 :096(268) [0417] of its glory and utterly **destroy** the doctrine of
AP : 2 4 :098(268) [0419] the glory of his coming **destroys** the kingdom of
AP : 2 7 :003(269) [0419] He will **destroy** you, and you will be unable to resist
AP : 2 7 :005(269) [0421] into bad harmonies which, Plato says, cause **destruction**.
AP : 2 8 :003(281) [0445] they took pleasure in the **destruction** of their fellowmen.
S 1 : PR :006(289) [0457] and malicious tongues and thus **destroying** the fruit.
S 1 : PR :011(290) [0457] descend on Germany and **destroy** us utterly, like Sodom
S 2 : 0 1 :005(292) [0461] and earth and things temporal should be **destroyed**.
S 2 : 0 4 :003(298) [0471] which contribute to the **destruction** of the entire holy
S 2 : 0 4 :007(299) [0473] the overthrow and **destruction** of his whole rule and
S 2 : 0 4 :014(301) [0475] murder, and the eternal **destruction** of body and soul are
S 3 : 0 3 :002(304) [0479] God with one blow **destroys** both open sinners and false
S 3 : 0 3 :030(308) [0487] With a single thunderbolt he strikes and **destroys** both.
TR : 0 0 :048(328) [0519] from the glory of God and bring **destruction** to souls.
SC : 0 3 :011(347) [0547] When God curbs and **destroys** every evil counsel and
LC : PR :012(360) [0571] Word, which routs and **destroys** this master of a thousand
LC : 0 1 :035(369) [0589] on that account he has **destroyed** both heathen and Jews;
LC : 0 1 :310(407) [0669] God's purpose being to **destroy** all the roots and causes
LC : 0 3 :031(424) [0707] the devil would have **destroyed** all Germany in its own
LC : 0 3 :054(427) [0713] shall be utterly **destroyed** and sin, death, and hell
LC : 0 3 :080(431) [0721] tempest and hail to **destroy** crops and cattle, why he
LC : 0 4 :059(444) [0747] that is, "Misuse does not **destroy** the substance, but
LC : 0 4 :071(445) [0749] the old man daily decreases until he is finally **destroyed**.
LC : 0 5 :084(456) [0773] lies in wait to trap and **destroy** you, soul and body, so
LC : 0 6 :017(459) [0000] and bitter, to the manifest harm and **destruction** of souls.
EP : 0 1 :006(467) [0781] contrary, in the resurrection it will be utterly **destroyed**.
EP : 0 2 :014(471) [0789] and rebirth God wholly **destroys** the substance and
EP : 0 9 :004(492) [0827] Christ went to hell, **destroyed** hell for all believers, and
EP : 1 0 :007(494) [0831] in fasting does not **destroy** agreement in faith."
SD : RN :015(507) [0857] (which, since they **destroy** rather than edify, should never
SD : 0 1 :022(512) [0865] on a magnet does not **destroy** the magnet's natural power
SD : 0 1 :030(513) [0867] nature has been totally **destroyed**, or has been
SD : 0 1 :035(514) [0869] made me together round about, and thou dost **destroy** me
SD : 0 2 :081(537) [0911] soul, are completely **destroyed** and a new substance of the
SD : 0 8 :052(601) [1033] should be capable or incapable without being **destroyed**.
SD : 0 8 :053(601) [1033] and above its natural properties without being **destroyed**.
SD : 0 8 :092(609) [1049] Without transforming or **destroying** his true human
SD : 0 9 :002(610) [1051] conquered the devil, **destroyed** hell's power, and took
SD : 1 0 :020(614) [1059] murder, and the eternal **destruction** of body and soul are
SD : 1 0 :031(616) [1063] in fasting should not **destroy** agreement in faith."
SD : 1 1 :036(622) [1075] undermine and totally **destroy** for us the necessary and
SD : 1 1 :039(622) [1075] would also overturn and **destroy** for us the foundation,
SD : 1 1 :062(626) [1083] own fault that you are **destroyed**, but that there is help

Detail (14), Detailed (4), Details (1)
AG : 2 5 :007(062) [0069] compelled to recount sins in **detail**, for this is impossible.
AG : 2 5 :009(063) [0069] to compel people to give a **detailed** account of their sins.
AG : 2 5 :011(063) [0071] does not require a **detailed** enumeration of sins.
AP : 1 5 :027(219) [0323] because they cannot keep the requirements in every **detail**.
TR : 0 0 :022(323) [0511] theologians, and all the **details** cannot be reviewed here
LC : 0 2 :020(412) [0681] if we were to describe in **detail** how few people believe
LC : 0 6 :004(457) [0000] released from the torture of enumerating all sins in **detail**.
LC : 0 6 :016(459) [0000] perfectly and in complete **detail**, we were told that the
SD : 0 1 :015(511) [0865] are explained in greater **detail** in the aforementioned
SD : 0 2 :044(529) [0897] and carefully and in great **detail** presents and
SD : 0 2 :088(538) [0915] explained in sufficient **detail** above that in conversion,
SD : 0 2 :090(539) [0915] God, in the manner and degree set forth in **detail** above.
SD : 0 3 :044(547) [0931] has been set forth in **detail** in the previously mentioned
SD : 0 3 :067(551) [0937] as necessary by way of a **detailed** explanation of this high
SD : 0 4 :030(556) [0947] to declare well and in **detail** how righteousness and
SD : 0 5 :022(562) [0959] writings and showed in **detail** that there is a vast
SD : 0 8 :030(597) [1025] This we shall discuss in greater **detail** below.
SD : 1 1 :002(616) [1063] but discuss and present it in **detail** in many places.
SD : 1 2 :002(632) [1095] to make special and **detailed** mention of them, although

Detection (1)
LC : 0 1 :307(406) [0669] it is all done "under the hat" so as to escape **detection**.

Deter (3), Determine (10), Determined (8), Deterred (4)
PR : PR :009(006) [0011] frightened away and **deterred** from our churches, schools,
AG : 2 7 :031(076) [0079] understanding to **determine** or arrange the order of one's
AP : 0 4 :049(114) [0135] It is easy to **determine** the difference between this faith
AP : 0 4 :051(114) [0135] It will be easy to **determine** what faith is if we pay
AP : 0 4 :084(119) [0145] as we could never **determine** whether we had merited
AP : 0 4 :192(133) [0175] the devil, who is **determined** that nothing happen to the
AP : 0 7 :040(176) [0241] To **determine** the apostles' wish and intention, therefore,
AP : 1 3 :003(211) [0309] added," we can easily **determine** which are sacraments in
AP : 1 8 :008(226) [0337] Men can easily **determine** this if they consider what their
LC : 0 3 :008(421) [0699] thoughts that would prevent or **deter** us from praying.
LC : 0 3 :010(421) [0699] which would prevent or **deter** us from praying, as though
LC : 0 3 :015(422) [0701] to be hindered and **deterred** by such thoughts as these: "I
LC : 0 5 :041(451) [0763] themselves be kept and **deterred** from it because we have
LC : 0 5 :062(454) [0767] to go and allow no one to **deter** him, saying, "I would
SD : PR :005(502) [0847] Similarly we are **determined** by the grace of the Almighty
SD : 0 4 :040(558) [0951] Christians are not to be **deterred** from good works, but
SD : 0 7 :029(574) [0981] I am **determined** to abide by it until my death and (so
SD : 0 8 :052(601) [1033] they attempt to **determine** and to fix the limit of what the
SD : 1 1 :001(616) [1063] our posterity, we have **determined** to set forth our
SD : 1 1 :036(622) [1075] us to learn and to **determine** God's will toward us and
SD : 1 1 :038(622) [1075] if we could not **determine** God's will toward us from the
SD : 1 1 :044(623) [1077] in his counsel God has **determined** and decreed before the
SD : 1 1 :048(624) [1079] of the world God has **determined** and decreed that he will
SD : 1 1 :056(625) [1081] also knows and has **determined** for each person the time
SD : 1 1 :095(632) [1095] cordially inclined and **determined** on our part to do

Detest (1), Detestable (2)
AP : 1 2 :019(185) [0257] 3. To blot out sin, it is enough to **detest** the sin.
LC : 0 1 :264(400) [0655] particularly to the **detestable**, shameful vice of back-biting
LC : 0 1 :276(402) [0659] be carefully noted if we are to avoid this **detestable** abuse.

Detract (4), Detracted (1)
AL : 2 7 :038(077) [0081] What is this but to **detract** from the glory of Christ and
TR : 0 0 :048(328) [0519] be taken lightly, for they **detract** from the glory of God
TR : 0 0 :059(330) [0521] the pope persecutes, **detract** from the glory of God, and
SD : 0 8 :049(600) [1031] nothing was added to or **detracted** from the essence and
SD : 1 1 :096(632) [1095] God's honor, that will not **detract** anything from the

Detriment (1), Detrimental (9)
EP : 0 4 :002(475) [0797] asserted that good works are **detrimental** to salvation.
EP : 0 4 :017(477) [0801] statement that good works are **detrimental** to salvation.
EP : 0 5 :011(479) [0805] deem it as false and **detrimental** when men teach that the
SD : 0 1 :059(519) [0879] offensive and highly **detrimental** controversy for our
SD : 0 2 :066(534) [0907] means be conceded without **detriment** to the divine truth.
SD : 0 4 :003(551) [0939] principle "that good works are **detrimental** to salvation."
SD : 0 4 :037(557) [0949] are supposed to be **detrimental** to salvation, we give the
SD : 0 4 :038(557) [0951] that good works are **detrimental** to believers as far as
SD : 0 4 :039(558) [0951] diligence whatever is **detrimental** to one's salvation.
SD : 1 1 :002(616) [1063] still less offensive and **detrimental**, because the Holy

Develop (1), Developed (5), Developments (1), Develops (1)
PR : PR :010(006) [0011] noted these **developments**, they saw clearly that there was
LC : 0 1 :141(384) [0621] of parents all other authority is derived and **developed**.
LC : 0 5 :025(449) [0759] should be one that continually **develops** and progresses.
LC : 0 6 :027(460) [0000] his misery and need will **develop** such a desire for
EP : 0 4 :004(476) [0797] Later on, a real controversy **developed**.
EP : 1 1 :001(494) [0831] public dissension has **developed** among the theologians of
EP : 1 1 :022(497) [0837] controversies that have **developed** receive a basic
SD : 0 8 :061(602) [1035] this matter we have not **developed** a new doctrine of our

Deviate (1)
SD : 0 2 :043(529) [0897] declares that he will not **deviate** from his doctrine until

Device (2), Devices (3)
AL : 2 0 :038(046) [0057] all manner of lusts and human **devices** rule in the heart.
AP : 0 2 :037(105) [0115] his words in order by this **device** to crush an innocent
AP : 2 2 :009(237) [0359] possible, this is a human **device** and its purpose is quite
LC : 0 3 :089(432) [0723] by evil desires and **devices**, so that we sin daily in word
SD : 1 1 :085(630) [1091] and most inhuman **devices** contrary to the voice of his

Devil (214)
AG : 0 3 :005(030) [0045] protect and defend them against the **devil** and against sin.
AG : 1 7 :003(038) [0051] ungodly men and the **devil** to hell and eternal
AG : 1 7 :004(038) [0051] who teach that the **devil** and condemned men will not
AG : 1 9 :000(041) [0053] This is the will of the **devil** and of all ungodly men; as
AG : 1 9 :000(041) [0053] in John 8:44, "When the **devil** lies, he speaks according to
AG : 2 0 :023(044) [0055] not that possessed by the **devil** and the ungodly, who also
AG : 2 0 :025(044) [0057] For the **devil** and the ungodly do not believe this article
AG : 2 0 :025(044) [0057] it such knowledge as the **devil** and ungodly men possess.
AG : 2 0 :026(045) [0057] knowledge of historical events as the **devil** also possesses.
AG : 2 0 :032(045) [0057] it is in the power of the **devil**, who drives poor human
AG : 2 3 :022(055) [0063] the teaching that forbids marriage a doctrine of the **devil**.
AG : 2 3 :023(055) [0063] himself asserts that the **devil** is a murderer from the
AG : 2 3 :023(055) [0063] must be a doctrine of the **devil** to forbid marriage and
AG : 2 6 :029(068) [0075] called a doctrine of the **devil**, for it is diametrically
AG : 2 8 :049(089) [0091] Why does it call them doctrines of the **devil**?
AL : 0 3 :005(030) [0045] and defend them against the **devil** and the power of sin.
AL : 1 9 :000(040) [0053] will of the wicked, that is, of the **devil** and ungodly men.
AL : 1 9 :000(041) [0053] in John 8:44, "When the **devil** lies, he speaks according to
AL : 2 0 :023(044) [0055] is in the ungodly and the **devil**), but it signifies faith which
AL : 2 0 :032(045) [0057] are in the power of the **devil**, who impels men to various
AL : 2 8 :011(082) [0085] protects souls from heresies, the **devil**, and eternal death.
AP : 0 2 :046(106) [0117] and other physical ills, but also to the rule of the **devil**.
AP : 0 2 :047(106) [0119] and the tyranny of the **devil** are, in the precise sense,
AP : 0 2 :047(106) [0119] and held prisoner by the **devil**, who deludes it with wicked
AP : 0 2 :048(106) [0119] Just as the **devil** cannot be conquered without Christ's
AP : 0 2 :049(106) [0119] history itself shows the great power of the **devil**'s rule.
AP : 0 2 :049(106) [0119] and by these bonds the **devil** has enthralled those who are
AP : 0 2 :050(106) [0119] to destroy the rule of the **devil**, sin, and death; so we
AP : 0 4 :023(110) [0127] weakness and by the **devil**, who drives it to open crimes.
AP : 0 4 :138(126) [0161] own strength to resist the **devil**, who holds enthralled all

Continued ▶

AP : 04 :139(126) [0161] Christ's power is needed for our conflict with the **devil**.
AP : 04 :139(126) [0161] For Christ conquered the **devil** and gave us his promise
AP : 04 :139(126) [0161] of God appeared was to destroy the works of the **devil**."
AP : 04 :189(133) [0175] these works he sanctifies hearts and suppresses the **devil**.
AP : 04 :189(133) [0175] against the rule of the **devil**; in our weakness he displays
AP : 04 :190(133) [0175] which Christ restrained the **devil** and drove him away
AP : 04 :191(133) [0175] God's Word against the **devil**, that the knowledge of God
AP : 04 :192(133) [0175] shows his victory over the **devil**, just as the distribution of
AP : 04 :192(133) [0175] battle of Christ against the **devil**, who is determined that
AP : 04 :250(143) [0191] us alive and enables us to overcome death and the **devil**.
AP : 07 :016(170) [0231] of Christ, the opposite of the kingdom of the **devil**.
AP : 07 :016(170) [0231] are in the power of the **devil** and are members of the
AP : 07 :016(171) [0231] and are members of the **devil**'s kingdom, as Paul teaches
AP : 07 :016(171) [0231] 2:2 when he says that the **devil** "is now at work in the
AP : 07 :016(171) [0231] Christ says (John 8:44), "You are of your father the **devil**.
AP : 07 :016(171) [0231] wicked are ruled by the **devil** and are his captives; they
AP : 07 :017(171) [0231] from the kingdom of the **devil**, it necessarily follows that
AP : 07 :017(171) [0231] to the kingdom of the **devil**, they are not the church.
AP : 07 :019(171) [0233] Christ, for they are members of the kingdom of the **devil**.
AP : 07 :029(173) [0237] kingdom and body of the **devil**, who drives them on and
AP : 07 :050(178) [0245] and are preserved and defended by God against the **devil**.
AP : 12 :055(189) [0267] the kingdom of the **devil**, death, and sin! this was the
AP : 12 :141(204) [0295] demonic doctrines that the **devil** has broadcast in the
AP : 12 :174(210) [0307] from surrendering to the **devil** or offending the Holy
AP : 17 :001(224) [0335] the ungodly to endless torment with the **devil**.
AP : 18 :005(225) [0335] judgment, while the **devil**, who as Paul says (Eph. 2:2) is
AP : 19 :001(226) [0337] of sin is the will of the **devil** and of men turning away
AP : 19 :001(226) [0337] as Christ said about the **devil** (John 8:44), "When he lies,
AP : 20 :008(227) [0341] death terrify them and the **devil** tempts them to despair
AP : 23 :058(247) [0379] (I Tim. 4:1-3); since the **devil** is a murderer (John 8:44),
S1 : PR :005(289) [0457] But how can I stop all the mouths of the **devil**?
S1 : PR :005(289) [0457] I shall let the **devil** — or ultimately the wrath of God —
S1 : PR :006(289) [0457] hand, if one does, the **devil** appears at once to poison and
S2 : 01 :005(292) [0463] and practice against the pope, the **devil**, and the world.
S2 : 01 :005(292) [0463] is lost, and the pope, the **devil**, and all our adversaries
S2 : 02 :012(295) [0465] else than illusions of the **devil**, for purgatory, too, is
S2 : 02 :018(296) [0467] uncertain, harmful will-o'-the-wisps of the **devil**?
S2 : 02 :019(296) [0467] do so simply because the **devil** has possessed the pope to
S2 : 02 :022(296) [0469] and horses that even the **devil** has laughed at such
S2 : 04 :005(299) [0473] better if such a head had not been raised up by the **devil**.
S2 : 04 :014(301) [0475] as we cannot adore the **devil** himself as our lord or God,
S2 : 04 :016(301) [0477] before the pope and the **devil** himself, who does not
S2 : 04 :016(301) [0477] as the angel spoke to the **devil** in Zechariah, "The Lord
S3 : 01 :001(302) [0477] made sinners and became subject to death and the **devil**.
S3 : 03 :017(305) [0483] said Yes (for who but the **devil** himself would want to say
S3 : 03 :018(306) [0483] law or vainly vexed with a sorrowful spirit by the **devil**.
S3 : 03 :042(310) [0491] this and I fear that such a **devil** still dwells in some of
S3 : 08 :005(312) [0495] All this is the old **devil** and the old serpent who made
S3 : 08 :010(313) [0497] apart from such Word and sacrament is of the **devil**.
SC : PR :011(339) [0535] the pope and his officials, and even to the **devil** himself.
SC : PR :020(340) [0537] The **devil** also has a horrible purpose in mind.
SC : PR :023(341) [0537] he has no sin, no flesh, no **devil**, no world, no death, no
SC : PR :023(341) [0539] deeply immersed in them and is held captive by the **devil**.
SC : PR :024(341) [0539] great need and God's gracious help belong to the **devil**.
SC : 02 :004(345) [0545] and from the power of the **devil**, not with silver and gold
SC : 03 :011(347) [0547] and purpose of the **devil**, of the world, and of our flesh
SC : 03 :018(347) [0549] and preserve us that the **devil**, the world, and our flesh
SC : 04 :006(349) [0551] from death and the **devil**, and grants eternal salvation to
LC : PR :010(359) [0569] is so effectual against the **devil**, the world, the flesh, and
LC : PR :010(360) [0571] more potent against the **devil** than to occupy yourself
LC : PR :010(360) [0571] the sign which routs the **devil** and puts him to flight.
LC : PR :011(360) [0571] you obtain from it is to rout the **devil** and evil thoughts.
LC : PR :011(360) [0571] of God which burns the **devil** and gives us immeasurable
LC : PR :012(360) [0571] The **devil** is called the master of a thousand arts.
LC : PR :013(360) [0571] attacks and ambushes of the **devil** with his thousand arts.
LC : PR :014(360) [0571] the constant and furious attacks and assaults of the **devil**.
LC : PR :019(361) [0573] that they have taught the **devil** to death and have become
LC : 01 :012(366) [0583] as to make a pact with the **devil** in order that he may give
LC : 01 :042(370) [0591] grief and want and are opposed and attacked by the **devil**.
LC : 01 :046(370) [0593] deceive; just leave it to the **devil** and the world to deceive
LC : 01 :055(372) [0595] the truth and God's Word and consign it to the **devil**.
LC : 01 :071(374) [0601] very effective against the **devil**, who is ever around us,
LC : 01 :072(374) [0601] To defy the **devil**, I say, we should always keep the holy
LC : 01 :099(378) [0609] plague with which the **devil** bewitches and befuddles the
LC : 01 :100(378) [0609] under the dominion of the **devil**, who neither day nor
LC : 01 :100(379) [0609] Word is not heard, the **devil** breaks in and does his
LC : 01 :102(379) [0609] that in this way the **devil** is cast out and put to flight, this
LC : 01 :120(382) [0615] so thoroughly has the **devil** bewitched us with the false
LC : 01 :121(382) [0615] the pure Word of God to the lying vanities of the **devil**.
LC : 01 :128(382) [0617] But here again the **devil** rules in the world; children
LC : 01 :144(385) [0623] everybody ran in the **devil**'s name into monasteries, on
LC : 01 :163(387) [0627] to arise and lead us to the **devil** — and wring sweat and
LC : 01 :184(390) [0633] Thus by the **devil**'s prompting you acquire many enemies
LC : 01 :208(393) [0639] and all virtues, and fight against wickedness and the **devil**.
LC : 01 :247(398) [0651] Beware of this, I repeat, as of the **devil** himself.
LC : 01 :264(400) [0655] vice of back-biting or slander by which the **devil** rides us.
LC : 02 :027(414) [0685] me from sin, from the **devil**, from death, and from all
LC : 02 :027(414) [0685] and King but was captive under the power of the **devil**.
LC : 02 :028(414) [0685] kinds of good things, the **devil** came and led us into
LC : 02 :031(414) [0685] brought us back from the **devil** to God, from death to
LC : 02 :031(414) [0687] The **devil** and all powers, therefore, must be subject to
LC : 02 :031(414) [0687] us from the wicked world, the **devil**, death, sin, etc.
LC : 02 :052(417) [0691] we were entirely of the **devil**, knowing nothing of God
LC : 03 :002(420) [0697] Besides, the **devil**, along with the world and our flesh,
LC : 03 :014(422) [0701] used to be taught, in the **devil**'s name, in such a way that
LC : 03 :029(424) [0705] This is just what the **devil** wants and works for with all
LC : 03 :030(424) [0707] too weak to cope with the **devil** and all his might and his
LC : 03 :030(424) [0707] to arm themselves in order to stand against the **devil**.
LC : 03 :031(424) [0707] designs by which the **devil** expected to crush us, and the
LC : 03 :031(424) [0707] a far different drama: the **devil** would have destroyed all
LC : 03 :031(424) [0707] both for them and for the **devil**, if we only persevere
LC : 03 :032(424) [0707] indeed be done in spite of the **devil** and all the world."
LC : 03 :044(426) [0709] us called not children of God but children of the **devil**.
LC : 03 :051(426) [0711] us from the power of the **devil** and to bring us to himself
LC : 03 :054(427) [0713] the Holy Spirit, that the **devil**'s kingdom may be
LC : 03 :054(427) [0713] over us, until finally the **devil**'s kingdom shall be utterly
LC : 03 :061(428) [0715] from the power of the **devil** — we must also pray that
LC : 03 :062(428) [0715] It is unbelievable how the **devil** opposes and obstructs
LC : 03 :065(429) [0715] count on having the **devil** with all his angels and the
LC : 03 :067(429) [0717] and not the will of the **devil** or of our enemies, nor of
LC : 03 :068(429) [0717] prevail even though the **devil** and all his host storm and
LC : 03 :069(429) [0717] and beat down all that the **devil**, bishops, tyrants, and
LC : 03 :070(429) [0717] will and purpose of the **devil** and of all our enemies shall
LC : 03 :080(431) [0721] our chief enemy, the **devil**, whose whole purpose and
LC : 03 :101(433) [0727] is of three kinds: of the flesh, the world, and the **devil**.
LC : 03 :104(434) [0727] Then comes the **devil**, who baits and badgers us on all
LC : 03 :104(434) [0727] into our hearts, not by flesh and blood but by the **devil**.
LC : 03 :106(434) [0727] we live in the flesh and have the **devil** prowling about us.
LC : 03 :107(434) [0729] (that is, strong Christians) are tempted by the **devil**.
LC : 03 :109(435) [0729] and heedlessly as if the **devil** were far from us but shall at
LC : 03 :109(435) [0729] kind, and firm in faith, the **devil** is likely in this very hour
LC : 03 :111(435) [0729] make the matter worse and give the **devil** a better opening
LC : 03 :113(435) [0729] to be speaking of the **devil** as the sum of all evil in order
LC : 03 :115(435) [0731] may befall us under the **devil**'s kingdom: poverty, shame,
LC : 03 :115(435) [0731] Since the **devil** is not only a liar but also a murderer, he
LC : 04 :011(437) [0735] Here the **devil** sets to work to blind us with false
LC : 04 :025(439) [0739] from sin, death and the **devil** and to enter into the
LC : 04 :041(441) [0743] victory over death and the **devil**, forgiveness of sin, God's
LC : 04 :047(442) [0743] a question by which the **devil** confuses the world through
LC : 04 :062(444) [0749] lurks a sneaky, seditious **devil** who would like to snatch
LC : 04 :083(446) [0751] us from the jaws of the **devil** and makes God our own,
LC : 05 :023(449) [0757] and temptations of the **devil** and the world that we often
LC : 05 :026(449) [0759] The **devil** is a furious enemy; when he sees that we resist
LC : 05 :044(451) [0763] from experience that the **devil** always sets himself against
LC : 05 :070(454) [0769] and power against death and the **devil** and all evils.
LC : 05 :071(455) [0769] fear of death, and the assaults of the flesh and the **devil**.
LC : 05 :080(456) [0771] and the world, you will surely have the **devil** about you.
LC : 05 :081(456) [0771] Now, what is the **devil**?
LC : 05 :082(456) [0773] in this wicked world, or under the kingdom of the **devil**.
LC : 05 :084(456) [0773] especially because the **devil** so constantly besieges you and
LC : 05 :087(457) [0773] help us to believe, to love, to pray, and to fight the **devil**.
LC : 06 :006(457) [0000] deserve just such a jailer as God's **devil** and hangman.
EP : 01 :002(466) [0779] the difference between God's work and the **devil**'s work.
EP : 09 :004(492) [0827] the power of death, of the **devil**, and of the eternal
EP : 11 :004(494) [0833] source of this is the **devil** and man's wicked and perverse
EP : 11 :013(496) [0835] and thus extinguish the flaming darts of the **devil**.
EP : 11 :016(497) [0837] under the direction of the **devil**, since everything in
SD : 01 :002(509) [0859] (which is a work of the **devil** by which man's nature has
SD : 01 :003(509) [0861] creation in man from the **devil**'s work, the corruption of
SD : 01 :007(510) [0861] (which is the work of the **devil**) entered into the world"
SD : 01 :013(511) [0863] and dominion of the **devil**, so that human nature is
SD : 01 :013(511) [0863] nature is subject to the **devil**'s dominion, abandoned to
SD : 01 :040(515) [0871] handiwork of God; on the contrary, it is the **devil**'s work.
SD : 01 :041(515) [0871] creature; or that, since the **devil** is the author of sin, Satan
SD : 01 :042(515) [0871] in man from the **devil**'s work, we declare that it is by
SD : 01 :061(519) [0879] being corrupted, and the **devil**'s handiwork, the sin which
SD : 02 :007(521) [0883] 8:34), the captive of the **devil** who drives him (Eph. 2:2; II
SD : 02 :029(527) [0893] faith and the Holy Spirit are in the power of the **devil**.
SD : 02 :029(527) [0893] out that Christ helps us and protects us against the **devil**."
SD : 02 :037(528) [0895] we belonged entirely to the **devil** and were completely
SD : 02 :043(529) [0897] are our masters and the **devil** is our god and lord, and
SD : 02 :043(529) [0897] and the property of the **devil** to do and to think what
SD : 02 :044(529) [0897] man performs only the **devil**'s will and what is contrary to
SD : 07 :057(579) [0993] and participating in pagan **devil**-worship and who
SD : 07 :067(582) [0997] dung, by which the **devil** amuses himself and deceives
SD : 08 :021(595) [1023] Luther called this the **devil**'s mask and damned it to the
SD : 08 :025(596) [1023] conquered sin, death, the **devil**, hell, and eternal
SD : 08 :040(598) [1029] this *alloeosis*, for it is the **devil**'s mask since it will finally
SD : 08 :040(599) [1029] is indescribable what the **devil** attempts with this
SD : 09 :002(610) [1051] into hell, conquered the **devil**, destroyed hell's power, and
SD : 09 :002(610) [1051] hell's power, and took from the **devil** all his might.
SD : 09 :003(610) [1053] that neither hell nor the **devil** can take us or any believer
SD : 10 :020(614) [1059] as we cannot adore the **devil** himself as our lord or God,
SD : 11 :006(617) [1065] and wicked will of the **devil** and of men will attempt and
SD : 11 :007(617) [1065] and perverse will of the **devil** and of men, as it is written,
SD : 11 :020(619) [1069] great weakness against the **devil**, the world, and the flesh,
SD : 11 :042(623) [1077] as a tabernacle for the **devil** so that their last state will be
SD : 11 :046(624) [1079] deceit and power of the **devil** and the world it could easily
SD : 11 :076(629) [1089] by which he snatches the elect from the maw of the **devil**.
SD : 11 :079(629) [1089] and the work of the **devil** and of man, who, through the
SD : 11 :079(629) [1089] the instigation of the **devil** and not of God, has made
SD : 11 :080(629) [1089] The **devil** and man himself, and not God, are the cause of
SD : 11 :081(629) [1089] emanates from the **devil** and man through sin, and in no
SD : 11 :091(632) [1093] to reason and the suggestion of the wicked **devil**.

Devils (9)

AL : 17 :003(038) [0051] but ungodly men and **devils** he will condemn to be
AL : 17 :004(038) [0051] an end to the punishments of condemned men and **devils**.
AL : 20 :025(044) [0057] as are the heathen, for **devils** and ungodly men are not
LC : PR :015(360) [0571] mighty enemies as the **devils**, and yet we despise our
LC : 01 :021(367) [0585] help and consolation from creatures, saints, or **devils**.
LC : 01 :125(382) [0617] angels, that it vexes all **devils**, and, besides, that it is the
LC : 05 :012(448) [0755] "Let a hundred thousand **devils**, with all the fanatics, rush
SD : 07 :022(573) [0979] 'Let a hundred thousand **devils** and all the enthusiasts
SD : 08 :083(607) [1045] though death and all the **devils** had been unable to

Devilish (5)

LC : 01 :119(381) [0615] them right for their **devilish** perversity in trampling God's
LC : 01 :188(390) [0635] who desires and does you good is not human but **devilish**.
LC : 01 :315(408) [0671] Just think, is it not a **devilish** presumption on the part of
LC : 03 :047(426) [0711] and warrant for their **devilish** doctrine, we ought
LC : 04 :015(438) [0735] is sheer wickedness and **devilish** blasphemy when our new

Devise (8), Devised (12)

AG : 20 :021(044) [0055] Others **devised** other works for the purpose of earning
AG : 28 :061(091) [0093] apostles and bishops to **devise** new ceremonies which

Continued ▶

AG : 2 8 :074(094) [0093] For many regulations **devised** by men have with the
AL : 2 7 :037(077) [0081] observances and services **devised** by men but that it
AL : 2 8 :061(091) [0093] apostles and bishops to **devise** new ceremonies which
AP : 0 4 :084(119) [0145] Nothing one can **devise** or imagine will refute Paul's
AP : 1 2 :140(204) [0295] commanded but the vain works that men have **devised**.
AP : 1 5 :018(217) [0319] kind of worship of God, **devised** by human authority in
TR : 0 0 :039(327) [0515] of Christ" because he will **devise** doctrines which conflict
TR : 0 0 :046(328) [0517] which are nothing but lies **devised** for the sake of gain.
LC : 0 1 :113(380) [0613] be much nobler than anything we ourselves may **devise**.
LC : 0 1 :114(380) [0613] arrangements we have **devised** without ever asking God's
LC : 0 1 :119(381) [0615] in vain with their self-**devised** works and meanwhile have
LC : 0 1 :298(405) [0665] and better ones are being **devised** daily) under the guise
LC : 0 3 :023(423) [0703] far superior to all others that we might ourselves **devise**.
LC : 0 3 :064(429) [0715] all the arts, tricks, ways, and means that he can **devise**.
LC : 0 4 :006(437) [0733] divine origin, not something **devised** or invented by men.
LC : 0 5 :004(447) [0753] Lord's Supper was not invented or **devised** by any man.
SD : 0 4 :007(552) [0941] that an individual may **devise** according to his own
SD : 0 7 :125(591) [1015] to meet their own self-**devised** standard of preparation,

Devolves (1)
PR : PR :022(012) [0019] the responsibility **devolves** upon the theologians and

Devote (8), Devoted (3), Devotion (18), Devotions (8)
AG : 0 1 :009(056) [0065] among us with greater **devotion** and more earnestness
AL : 0 0 :006(049) [0059] of reverence and **devotion** among the people as the
AL : 2 4 :006(056) [0065] the reverence and **devotion** of public worship, for none
AL : 2 4 :008(057) [0065] and such use of the sacrament nourishes **devotion** to God.
AL : 2 4 :009(057) [0065] is observed with more **devotion** among our adversaries
AL : 2 6 :016(066) [0073] that they were unable to **devote** their attention to a better
AP : 0 4 :010(108) [0123] that form of worship or **devotion** with this view in mind.
AP : 0 4 :212(136) [0179] works, make up new **devotions**, new vows, and new
AP : 0 4 :392(167) [0225] our works and new **devotions**, obscuring the work of
AP : 0 4 :393(167) [0225] by their own works and **devotions**, not by faith for
AP : 0 4 :395(167) [0225] works, and so they multiplied sacrifices and **devotions**.
AP : 0 7 :013(170) [0231] the outward observance of certain **devotions** and rituals.
AP : 0 7 :023(172) [0235] by his leave, institute **devotions** and sacrifices, enact
AP : 0 7 :025(173) [0235] in him and not through **devotions** invented by the pope.
AP : 0 7 :032(174) [0239] human traditions are **devotions** necessary for meriting
AP : 0 7 :032(174) [0239] were really acts of **devotion** rather than outward rules of
AP : 0 7 :034(175) [0239] style of dress is not a **devotion** to God necessary for
AP : 0 7 :035(175) [0241] in promoting rigor of **devotion** and self-abasement."
AP : 0 7 :037(175) [0241] traditions are acts of **devotion** necessary for righteousness
AP : 1 2 :011(184) [0255] How much effort is **devoted** to the endless enumeration
AP : 1 2 :022(185) [0257] to institute new acts of **devotion**, and to make such
AP : 1 2 :022(185) [0257] satisfactions and acts of **devotion** binding upon
AP : 2 4 :054(259) [0403] part of the epistle is **devoted** to the theme that the ancient
AP : 2 7 :027(273) [0429] mercy promised in Christ, and in **devotion** to one's calling
S 2 : 0 2 :008(294) [0465] to communicate himself for the sake of his own **devotion**.
SC : 0 7 :003(352) [0557] or whatever your **devotion** may suggest, you should go to
LC : 0 1 :043(370) [0591] tell me, When men have **devoted** all their care and
LC : 0 1 :086(376) [0605] anyhow, we should **devote** their observance to learning
LC : 0 1 :087(376) [0605] Nothing else than to **devote** it to holy words, holy works,
LC : 0 1 :101(379) [0609] and a new spirit of **devotion**, and it constantly cleanses
LC : 0 1 :103(379) [0611] rest we should diligently **devote** ourselves to God's Word
LC : 0 1 :171(388) [0629] very necessary it is to **devote** serious attention to the
LC : 0 1 :319(408) [0673] effort God requires us to **devote** to learning how to teach
LC : 0 2 :019(412) [0681] ceasing, and, in short, to **devote** all these things to his
LC : 0 3 :026(424) [0705] taught how to prepare for it or how to generate **devotion**.
LC : 0 5 :043(451) [0763] the sacrament, we shall **devote** a little attention to this
EP : 0 6 :004(480) [0807] in their merely human **devotion** they undertake

Devoured (1), Devouring (1)
AP : 0 4 :329(158) [0211] Deut. 4:24, "Your God is a **devouring** fire."
LC : 0 2 :031(414) [0687] dead, swallowed up and **devoured** death, and finally

Devout (27), Devoutly (3)
AG : 2 3 :013(053) [0063] Many **devout** and intelligent people in high station have
AG : 2 4 :010(057) [0065] by learned and **devout** men even before our time.
AG : 2 6 :016(066) [0073] Many **devout** and learned people before our time have
AG : 2 7 :008(072) [0077] rigor displeased many **devout** people in the past, for they
AG : 2 8 :003(081) [0085] by learned and **devout** people in Christendom.
AL : 2 3 :016(054) [0063] man's weakness, and it is **devoutly** to be desired that this
AL : 2 6 :011(065) [0071] the consciences of **devout** people who grieved that they
AL : 2 8 :003(081) [0085] been rebuked in the church by **devout** and learned men.
AP : 0 4 :118(123) [0155] provides a sure and firm consolation for **devout** minds.
AP : 0 4 :167(130) [0169] have better luck than the **devout**, because the wicked
AP : 0 4 :167(130) [0169] the devout, because the wicked persecute the **devout**?
AP : 0 4 :188(133) [0173] Therefore we call upon **devout** minds to consider the
AP : 0 4 :353(161) [0217] The **devout** can understand this teaching better than what
AP : 0 7 :038(176) [0241] How **devout** they are!
AP : 1 1 :002(180) [0249] has encouraged many **devout** minds, and in the beginning
AP : 1 1 :010(182) [0253] has driven many **devout** minds to hopeless despair
AP : 1 2 :083(194) [0275] were not obvious to every **devout** reader of Scripture, and
AP : 1 2 :084(194) [0277] It ought not disturb **devout** minds if our opponents twist
AP : 1 2 :084(194) [0277] position of ours brings **devout** consciences a firm
AP : 1 2 :087(195) [0277] this is clear enough for **devout** consciences, and from this
AP : 1 2 :129(202) [0291] now in order to heal **devout** minds and free them from
AP : 1 2 :178(211) [0307] it is godly and wholesome for the minds of the **devout**.
AP : 1 2 :178(211) [0307] If **devout** men will compare our teaching with the
AP : 1 3 :022(214) [0313] of the sacrament comforts **devout** and troubled minds.
AP : 2 3 :046(246) [0377] commands and gifts, which he wants us to use **devoutly**.
AP : 2 4 :049(258) [0401] our churches the use is more frequent and more **devout**.
S 3 : 0 8 :008(313) [0495] faith (Luke calls him "**devout**" and "God-fearing"), but he
LC : 0 1 :064(373) [0599] upon his name in service of truth and using it **devoutly**.
LC : 0 1 :176(389) [0631] children, no matter how **devout** and holy you may be in
SD : 0 2 :014(523) [0885] very great comfort to all **devout** Christians who perceive

Diabolical (2)
S 2 : 0 4 :003(298) [0471] been and still are purely **diabolical** transactions and deeds
S 2 : 0 4 :014(301) [0475] Finally, it is most **diabolical** for the pope to promote his

Diametrically (5)
AG : 2 6 :029(068) [0075] of the devil, for it is **diametrically** opposed to the Gospel
SD : 0 1 :011(510) [0863] of reason, is by nature **diametrically** opposed to God and
SD : 0 2 :043(529) [0897] will, as directly and **diametrically** contrary to the help and
SD : 0 3 :053(548) [0933] is wrong because it is **diametrically** opposed to Paul's
SD : 0 4 :022(554) [0945] (that is, they are **diametrically** opposed to St. Paul's

Diana (1)
LC : 0 1 :018(367) [0585] women worshiped **Diana** or Lucina, and so forth.

Dichotomy (2)
SD : 0 1 :054(518) [0877] the sense of a perfect **dichotomy** (that is, a division
SD : 0 1 :054(518) [0877] This **dichotomy** was also used by Cyril and Basil.

Didst (5)
AP : 1 2 :107(197) [0283] to the Lord'; then thou **didst** forgive the guilt of my sin."
SD : 0 1 :035(514) [0869] **Didst** thou not pour me out like milk and curdle me like
SD : 0 1 :035(514) [0869] Thou **didst** clothe me with skin and flesh, and knit me
SD : 0 8 :070(605) [1041] with glory and honor and **didst** set him over the works of
SD : 1 1 :074(628) [1087] the next words, "But thou **didst** hear my supplications

Didymus (1)
S 3 : 1 5 :005(317) [0501] Gabriel **Didymus** subscribed

Die (27), Died (24), Dies (3), Dying (5)
AG : 0 3 :002(029) [0045] man, who was truly born, suffered, was crucified, **died**,
AG : 2 8 :045(088) [0089] "If with Christ you **died** to the regulations of the world,
AL : 2 8 :045(088) [0089] Again, "If with Christ you **died** to the elemental spirits of
AP : 0 3 :001(107) [0119] same Christ suffered and **died** to reconcile the Father to
AP : 0 4 :029(111) [0129] a holy life, then 'Christ **died** to no purpose' (Gal. 2:21),
AP : 0 4 :135(125) [0159] care, but supposes that men are born and **die** by chance.
AP : 0 4 :143(126) [0161] to the flesh you will **die**, but if by the Spirit you put to
AP : 0 4 :148(127) [0163] because Christ did not **die** in vain, conquers the terrors of
AP : 0 4 :236(140) [0185] These tumults would **die** down if our opponents did not
AP : 0 7 :035(175) [0239] "If with Christ you **died** to the elemental spirits of
AP : 1 2 :033(186) [0259] Paul says (Gal. 2:19), "I through the law **died** to the law."
AP : 1 2 :046(188) [0263] terrors, like those of the **dying**, which nature could not
AP : 1 2 :056(189) [0267] "The Lord has put away your sin; you shall not **die**."
AP : 2 0 :007(227) [0339] Who would not gladly **die** in the confession of the article
AP : 2 0 :012(228) [0341] man who was sentenced to **die** and then pardoned, "The
AP : 2 1 :026(232) [0349] summoned to console a **dying** doctor of theology, do
AP : 2 1 :026(232) [0349] urge this prayer upon the **dying** man, "Mother of grace,
AP : 2 1 :035(234) [0353] one who calls upon her should **die** without the Eucharist.
AP : 2 4 :071(262) [0409] is the spiritual motivation, **dying** and being made alive.
S 1 : PR :003(289) [0455] articles so that, if I should **die** before a council meets
S 1 : PR :010(290) [0457] how the poor people live or **die**, although Christ died for
S 1 : PR :010(290) [0457] people live or die, although Christ **died** for them too.
S 1 : 0 1 :000(292) [0461] Afterwards he suffered, **died**, was buried, descended to
S 2 : 0 4 :012(300) [0475] to do even if we have to **die** for it in God's name.
S 3 : 0 1 :011(303) [0479] true, Christ would have **died** in vain, for there would be
S 3 : 0 1 :011(303) [0479] he would have had to **die**, or else he would have died only
S 3 : 0 1 :011(303) [0479] die, or else he would have **died** only for the body and not
LC : 0 1 :137(384) [0619] that such wicked people **die** a natural and timely death.
LC : 0 1 :191(391) [0635] me and my followers to **die** of hunger, thirst, and cold, to
LC : 0 1 :242(397) [0649] Your cattle will **die** in the stall.
LC : 0 2 :031(414) [0687] sin; moreover, he suffered, **died**, and was buried that he
LC : 0 2 :062(419) [0695] and we abide in it, having **died** to the world and all evil,
LC : 0 4 :043(442) [0743] skill that people would not **die**, or even though they died
LC : 0 4 :043(442) [0743] die, or even though they **died** would afterward live
EP : 0 8 :008(487) [0819] circumscribed, to suffer, to **die**, to ascend and to descend,
EP : 0 8 :013(488) [0821] man who for us suffered, **died**, was buried, descended into
EP : 0 8 :026(490) [0823] we say that the Son of God **died** for the sins of the world
SD : 0 2 :057(532) [0903] the community of God, **dies** in this condition, and
SD : 0 3 :015(541) [0919] — as he was obligated to suffer and **die** for his person.
SD : 0 3 :015(541) [0919] only in his suffering and **dying**, but also in his
SD : 0 3 :022(543) [0923] they are still sinners and remain sinners until they **die**.
SD : 0 4 :012(553) [0941] grace, so certain that it would **die** a thousand times for it.
SD : 0 4 :032(556) [0947] you live according to the flesh you will **die**" (Rom. 8:13).
SD : 0 7 :033(575) [0983] by it steadfastly and defended it constantly until he **died**.
SD : 0 8 :010(593) [1019] to suffer and **die**, to ascend and descend, to move from
SD : 0 8 :020(595) [1021] it is to suffer and to **die**) that has suffered for the sin of
SD : 0 8 :020(595) [1021] Christian Creed, has truly **died**, although the divine
SD : 0 8 :020(595) [1021] although the divine nature can neither suffer nor **die**.
SD : 0 8 :025(596) [1023] again in death, when he **died** not just like another man
SD : 0 8 :041(599) [1029] surely cannot suffer and **die**, then you must answer and
SD : 0 8 :042(599) [1029] must say that the person (pointing to Christ) suffers, **dies**.
SD : 0 8 :044(599) [1029] If it is not true that God **died** for us, but only a man died,
SD : 0 8 :044(599) [1029] that God died for us, but only a man **died**, we are lost.
SD : 0 8 :044(599) [1031] to his nature God cannot **die**, but since God and man are
SD : 0 8 :044(599) [1031] God's death when that man **dies** who is one thing or one
SD : 0 8 :045(600) [1031] "God suffered," "God **died**," are merely empty words
SD : 0 8 :045(600) [1031] made man, suffered for us, **died**, and redeemed us with
SD : 0 9 :001(610) [1051] Christ, God's Son, who **died**, was buried, and descended
SD : 1 2 :006(633) [1097] in our commitment to this Confession until we **die**.

Diet (9), Diets (2)
PR : PR :002(003) [0007] memory, at the **Diet** of Augsburg in the year 1530,
PR : PR :018(009) [0015] V at the said imperial **diet**, which was afterward collated
AG : PR :001(024) [0039] graciously summoned a **diet** of the empire to convene
AG : PR :015(026) [0041] a public instruction at the **diet** in Spires in 1526, that for
AG : PR :017(026) [0041] instruction at the last **diet** in Spires a year ago, the
AG : PR :018(026) [0041] who were assembled at the **diet** convened in Ratisbon had
AG : PR :021(027) [0043] motives requested in all the **diets** of the empire which
S 1 : PR :012(290) [0459] ten councils and twenty **diets** would not be able to set
TR : 0 0 :082(334) [0529] to the emperor in the **diet** of Augsburg and, by the favor
EP : RN :004(465) [0777] Augsburg during the great **Diet** in the year 1530, together
SD : PR :003(501) [0847] Emperor Charles V at the great **Diet** of Augsburg in 1530.

Dietrich
S 3 : 1 5 :005(317) [0501] I, Master Veit **Dietrich**, minister in Nuremberg, subscribe
TR : 0 0 :082(334) [0529] Master Veit **Dietrich**, of Nuremberg, subscribes
LC : PR :011(360) [0571] such as the one about **Dietrich** of Bern, but as St. Paul

Differ (2), Differed (2), Difference (44), Differences (5), Different (62), Differentiated (3), Differentiating (1), Differently (7)

PR : PR :008(005) [0009] to defend, or to spread a **different** or a new doctrine.
PR : PR :010(006) [0011] explain and decide the **difference** that had arisen with
PR : PR :010(006) [0011] to take toward these **differences** and how by God's grace
PR : PR :011(006) [0011] offensive **differences** might be settled and brought to a
PR : PR :011(006) [0011] they set forth how the **differences** that had occurred were
PR : PR :019(009) [0017] and that a very **different** doctrine by far can be proved
PR : PR :023(012) [0021] we have made no new or **different** confession from the
AG : PR :010(025) [0041] and charitably, our **differences** may be reconciled, and we
AG : 2 6 :030(068) [0075] discipline, their writings reveal something quite **different**.
AG : 2 6 :043(070) [0075] they kept Easter at a time **different** from that in Rome.
AG : 2 6 :043(070) [0075] some regarded this **difference** a divisive of the church,
AG : 2 7 :035(076) [0081] even though some have subsequently **differed** from him.
AG : 2 8 :004(081) [0085] to point out the **difference** between spiritual and
AG : 2 8 :011(082) [0085] with matters altogether **different** from the Gospel.
AG : 2 8 :030(085) [0087] foods, holy days, and the **different** orders of the clergy.
AL : 0 0 :002(047) [0059] Even if there were some **difference** in these, the bishops
AL : 2 4 :040(061) [0069] the number of Masses is **different**, and on account of the
AL : 2 6 :030(068) [0075] But something **different** may be perceived in the writings
AL : 2 6 :043(070) [0075] in the East at a time **different** from that in Rome, and
AL : 2 6 :043(070) [0075] when on account of this **difference** the Romans accused
AL : 2 7 :015(073) [0077] Now everything is **different**, and it is needless to rehearse
AL : 2 7 :035(076) [0081] although others have subsequently **differed** from him.
AL : 2 8 :004(081) [0085] to show the **difference** between the power of the church
AP : 0 4 :012(109) [0123] righteousness, what **difference** is there between
AP : 0 4 :016(109) [0123] reason, there will be no **difference** between philosophical
AP : 0 4 :049(114) [0135] is easy to determine the **difference** between this faith and
AP : 0 4 :194(133) [0175] Therefore there will be **different** rewards for different
AP : 0 4 :194(133) [0175] there will be different rewards for **different** labors.
AP : 0 4 :198(134) [0175] exercises his saints in **different** ways and often puts off
AP : 0 4 :203(135) [0175] But they are put to a **different** use by anyone who cannot
AP : 0 4 :237(140) [0185] But this is completely **different** from those praises of love
AP : 0 4 :306(154) [0207] of righteousness in a **different** way here from the
AP : 0 4 :347(160) [0217] This faith makes the **difference** between those who are
AP : 0 4 :347(160) [0217] Faith makes the **difference** between the worthy and the
AP : 0 7 :014(170) [0231] Then, too, what **difference** will there be between the
AP : 0 7 :022(172) [0235] our Confession that is **different** from what Lyra says
AP : 0 7 :033(174) [0239] But as the **different** length of day and night does not harm
AP : 0 7 :033(174) [0239] is not harmed by **differences** in rites instituted by men,
AP : 0 7 :042(176) [0241] others at another, but this **difference** did no harm to faith.
AP : 0 7 :042(176) [0241] our Passover falls at a **different** time from the Jewish
AP : 0 7 :045(177) [0243] which it appears that a **difference** in human observances
AP : 1 2 :008(183) [0255] For faith makes the **difference** between the contrition of
AP : 1 2 :036(186) [0261] This faith shows the **difference** between the contrition of
AP : 1 2 :112(198) [0285] All of this is totally **different** from the enumeration we
AP : 1 2 :112(198) [0285] **Different** offenses had different canons.
AP : 1 2 :112(198) [0285] Different offenses had **different** canons.
AP : 1 3 :002(211) [0309] think it makes much **difference** if, for purposes of
AP : 1 5 :010(216) [0317] of view there is no **difference** between our traditions and
AP : 1 5 :015(217) [0319] Where is the **difference**?
AP : 1 5 :020(218) [0321] For **different** seasons and various rites serve as reminders
AP : 1 8 :002(225) [0335] good; but what is the **difference** between the Pelagians
AP : 1 8 :009(226) [0337] same time it shows the **difference** between human
AP : 2 4 :045(258) [0399] Daniel describes a vastly **different** desolation, ignorance
AP : 2 4 :045(258) [0401] swamped by the many **different** traditions and ideas and
AP : 2 4 :095(267) [0417] *operato*, they would express themselves far **differently**.
AP : 2 7 :062(280) [0441] But vastly **different** purposes are set forth for
AP : 2 7 :065(280) [0441] if any, must have been **different** from monastic vows.
AP : 2 7 :068(280) [0443] He talks about faith **differently** from the sophists.
AP : 2 8 :002(281) [0443] article we have been arguing about something **different**.
S 2 : 0 4 :009(300) [0473] office (however they may **differ** in gifts) and diligently
S 3 : 0 3 :004(304) [0481] which is to say, "Become **different**, do otherwise, and
S 3 : 0 3 :035(309) [0489] that we must become altogether new and **different** men.
S 3 : 0 3 :036(309) [0489] spend our time weighing, distinguishing, **differentiating**.
TR : 0 0 :010(321) [0505] he says, "makes no **difference** to me" and again, "Those
SC : PR :008(339) [0535] or recite the catechism **differently** from year to year.
SC : PR :009(339) [0535] discuss these topics from **different** angles and in such a
SC : PR :026(341) [0539] has become something **different** from what it was under
LC : PR :016(361) [0573] thing without varying it with anything new or **different**.
LC : PR :016(361) [0573] of nothing better or **different** to learn, though they
LC : 0 1 :033(369) [0589] who think that it makes no great **difference** how they live.
LC : 0 1 :207(393) [0639] man and woman **differently** (as is evident) not for
LC : 0 1 :244(398) [0649] must punish us and teach us morals in a **different** way.
LC : 0 1 :266(401) [0657] There is a great **difference** between judging sin and having
LC : 0 1 :275(402) [0659] It is no **different** from the situation of the physician who,
LC : 0 2 :032(414) [0687] place to explain all these **different** points is not the brief
LC : 0 2 :047(416) [0691] idiomatically, we must express it quite **differently**.
LC : 0 2 :067(419) [0697] that the Creed is a very **different** teaching from the Ten
LC : 0 3 :006(421) [0699] think that it makes no **difference** whether I pray or not,
LC : 0 3 :009(421) [0699] will go and do as I please; what **difference** does it make?"
LC : 0 3 :010(421) [0699] it made no great **difference** if we do not pray, or as
LC : 0 3 :031(424) [0707] have witnessed a far **different** drama: the devil would
LC : 0 3 :107(434) [0729] therefore, is quite a **different** thing from consenting and
LC : 0 4 :017(438) [0735] then: Baptism is a very **different** thing from all other
LC : 0 4 :020(439) [0737] and bones, they look no **different** from Turks and
LC : 0 4 :022(439) [0737] water, the water is no **different** from that which the maid
EP : 0 1 :002(466) [0779] sin is as great as the **difference** between God's work and
EP : 0 1 :019(468) [0783] sin, and that the two cannot be **differentiated** in the mind.
EP : 0 1 :020(468) [0783] to indicate the **difference** between original sin, which
EP : 0 2 :001(469) [0785] may be discussed in four **different** states: (1) before the
EP : 0 6 :007(481) [0807] The **difference**, as far as obedience is concerned, rests
EP : 1 2 :019(499) [0841] 3. That **difference** of faith is sufficient ground for married
SD : PR :005(502) [0847] Confession or to set up a **different** and new confession.
SD : RN :002(503) [0851] prepare nor accept a **different** or a new confession of our
SD : RN :008(505) [0853] as Christians know the **difference** between true and false
SD : 0 1 :001(508) [0859] the Fall allegedly no **difference** whatsoever between man's
SD : 0 1 :030(513) [0867] substance essentially **different** from our nature and
SD : 0 1 :040(515) [0871] This article shows the **difference** irrefutably and clearly,
SD : 0 1 :041(515) [0871] If there were no **difference** whatever between the nature
SD : 0 1 :044(516) [0873] Now, if there were no **difference** between the nature or
SD : 0 1 :047(516) [0873] If there were no **difference** whatever between our
SD : 0 2 :067(534) [0907] is therefore a great **difference** between baptized people
SD : 0 2 :068(534) [0907] is not only a great **difference** between Christians, one
SD : 0 3 :018(542) [0921] senses the two will be **differentiated** from one another.
SD : 0 3 :052(548) [0933] that man is saved in a **different** way or by a different
SD : 0 3 :052(548) [0933] a different way or by a **different** thing from the one by
SD : 0 4 :010(552) [0941] Adam, makes us entirely **different** people in heart, spirit,
SD : 0 5 :022(562) [0959] that there is a vast **difference** between the knowledge of
SD : 0 6 :016(566) [0967] works is due to the **difference** in the individuals who are
SD : 0 7 :029(574) [0981] hold this or that article **differently**, for he did not
SD : 0 7 :038(576) [0985] they also use these **different** formulas, "in the bread,
SD : 0 7 :092(586) [1005] to a strange meaning **different** from the way the letters
SD : 0 7 :098(586) [1005] body of Christ has three **different** modes, or all three
SD : 0 7 :113(589) [1011] are to be given a **different**, new, and strange sense.
SD : 0 8 :011(593) [1019] Christ is not two **different** persons, but one single person,
SD : 0 8 :019(595) [1021] natures in the person of Christ is far **different** from this.
SD : 0 8 :019(595) [1021] person of Christ is far **different**, much higher, and more
SD : 0 8 :048(600) [1031] But it is an entirely **different** matter when, in the third
SD : 0 9 :001(610) [1049] **Different** explanations of the article on Christ's descent
SD : 0 9 :001(610) [1051] descent into hell are **differentiated** as distinct articles, and
SD : 1 0 :005(611) [1053] and are given a **different** color from their true one.
SD : 1 0 :005(611) [1053] that our religion does not **differ** greatly from that of the
SD : 1 0 :031(616) [1063] each other because of a **difference** in ceremonies, when in
SD : 1 1 :004(616) [1063] must carefully note the **difference** between God's eternal
SD : 1 1 :034(622) [1075] although I speak **differently** in my call to them."
SD : 1 1 :035(622) [1075] and intend something **different** in their hearts (Ps. 5:10,
SD : 1 2 :024(634) [1099] 15. That **difference** in faith is sufficient ground for

Difficult (9), Difficulties (2), Difficulty (1)

AP : PR :016(099) [0103] that we must endure **difficulties** and dangers for the glory
AP : 0 4 :350(161) [0217] in which experience testifies how **difficult** a thing faith is.
AP : 1 5 :049(221) [0329] traditions involves many **difficult** and controversial
AP : 1 5 :049(222) [0329] abrogation involves its own **difficulties** and problems.
AP : 2 8 :004(281) [0445] In these very serious and **difficult** controversies the people
LC : 0 1 :055(372) [0595] affairs or in sublime and **difficult** matters of faith and
LC : 0 1 :116(381) [0615] great, laborious, and **difficult** works; we shall see whether
LC : 0 1 :152(386) [0625] How **difficult** do you think it will be for him to pay you
LC : 0 1 :312(407) [0671] orders and the great, **difficult** works which they have
LC : 0 4 :011(438) [0735] does many great and **difficult** works, and we all attach
LC : 0 5 :063(454) [0767] This is **difficult**, for we always have this obstacle and
SD : 0 7 :062(581) [0995] Christ, and hold to it in all **difficulty** and temptation.

Digested (1)

EP : 0 7 :042(486) [0817] flesh with one's teeth and **digested** it like other food.

Digging (1)

S 3 : 0 3 :025(307) [0485] have the discovery and **digging** up of the treasures of the

Dignified (1), Dignity (8)

PR : PR :001(003) [0007] of his station and **dignity**, under whose eyes this
AG : 2 8 :071(093) [0093] of their honor and **dignity** (though it is incumbent on the
AL : 0 0 :006(049) [0059] to the maintenance of **dignity** in public worship and the
AP : 1 2 :124(201) [0289] not add anything to his **dignity** in making use of such
AP : 2 2 :013(238) [0361] are minimizing the real **dignity** of the order, we shall not
AP : 2 4 :099(268) [0419] zealously preserve the **dignity** of the Mass, that we show
TR : 0 0 :018(323) [0509] or Alexandria — he is of the same **dignity** and priesthood.
SC : 0 9 :002(354) [0561] temperate, sensible, **dignified**, hospitable, an apt teacher,
LC : 0 4 :022(439) [0737] the nature and **dignity** of this holy sacrament.

Diligence (20), Diligent (6), Diligently (40)

PR : PR :006(004) [0009] not ceased to apply our **diligence** to the end that the false
PR : PR :013(007) [0013] reflection and careful **diligence**, they brought together in
PR : PR :015(007) [0013] exhorted to consider **diligently** and earnestly the doctrine
PR : PR :018(009) [0015] afterward collated very **diligently** by well-certified persons
PR : PR :023(012) [0021] be faithfully and **diligently** instructed therein, so that the
PR : PR :026(014) [0025] circumstances, through **diligent** visitation of churches and
AG : PR :002(025) [0039] proposed to employ all **diligence** amicably and charitably
AG : PR :016(026) [0041] holy faith but would **diligently** urge it upon the pope to
AG : 2 0 :022(044) [0055] faith in Christ and **diligently** to apply it in order that men
AG : 2 0 :037(046) [0057] love one's neighbor, **diligently** engage in callings which
AG : 0 1 :007(056) [0065] often and with great **diligence** concerning the holy
AG : 2 5 :004(062) [0069] We teach with great **diligence** about this command and
AG : 2 5 :013(063) [0071] preachers on our side **diligently** teach that confession is to
AG : 2 7 :049(079) [0083] good works for others and **diligently** attend to our calling.
AG : 0 0 :005(095) [0095] boasting) that we have **diligently** and with God's help
AL : 0 0 :004(048) [0059] are for the most part **diligently** observed, for it is false and
AL : 2 5 :002(061) [0069] The people are very **diligently** taught concerning faith in
AL : 2 7 :049(079) [0083] meanwhile to be **diligent** in the performance of good
AL : 0 0 :005(095) [0095] that we have guarded **diligently** against the introduction
AP : 0 9 :001(178) [0245] Among us, the Gospel is taught purely and **diligently**.
AP : 1 1 :001(180) [0249] enumerated, one should **diligently** try to recall them and
AP : 1 2 :106(197) [0283] telling him to pay **diligent** attention to his own property
AP : 1 2 :126(201) [0289] in such times to exercise unusual wisdom and **diligence**.
AP : 1 5 :044(221) [0327] it is evident that we **diligently** maintain church discipline,
AP : 1 5 :047(221) [0327] In this we must be **diligent** at all times because God
S 2 : 0 4 :009(300) [0473] may differ in gifts) and **diligently** joined together in unity
TR : 0 0 :014(322) [0507] "Wherefore you must **diligently** observe and practice,
LC : PR :019(361) [0573] the greatest care and **diligence** against the poisonous
LC : PR :020(361) [0573] If they show such **diligence**, then I promise them — and
LC : SP :003(362) [0575] children's sermons and **diligently** drilled in their practice.
LC : 0 1 :043(370) [0591] all their care and **diligence** to scraping together great
LC : 0 1 :056(372) [0595] commandment is and **diligently** shun and avoid every
LC : 0 1 :103(379) [0611] days of rest we should **diligently** devote ourselves to
LC : 0 3 :031(424) [0707] if we only persevere **diligently** and do not become slack.
EP : 0 1 :003(466) [0779] this distinction most **diligently**, because the view that
EP : 0 5 :002(478) [0801] maintained with great **diligence** in the church so that,
EP : 0 6 :003(480) [0805] of the law is to be **diligently** applied not only to
EP : 1 1 :002(494) [0831] and the eternal election of God is to be **diligently** noted.
SD : 0 2 :009(522) [0883] the more zealously and **diligently** they want to
SD : 0 2 :044(529) [0897] and defends them **diligently** and to the best of his ability
SD : 0 2 :055(532) [0903] and when the people **diligently** and earnestly listen to and
SD : 0 2 :070(535) [0909] Christian intentions, and **diligence**, and to fight against
SD : 0 3 :024(543) [0923] we must give especially **diligent** heed that we do not
SD : 0 3 :036(545) [0927] he so earnestly and **diligently** stresses such exclusive
SD : 0 3 :036(546) [0929] should be urged with all **diligence** and seriousness in the

Continued ▶

S D : 0 4 :032(556) [0947] We should often, with all **diligence** and earnestness,
S D : 0 4 :039(558) [0951] avoid with the greatest **diligence** whatever is detrimental
S D : 0 4 :040(558) [0951] works, but are most **diligently** to be admonished and
S D : 0 5 :001(558) [0951] with particular **diligence** lest we confuse the two doctrines
S D : 0 5 :022(562) [0959] Dr. Luther very **diligently** urged this distinction in nearly
S D : 0 5 :024(562) [0961] be urged constantly and **diligently** in the church of God
S D : 0 5 :027(563) [0961] and to maintain with all **diligence** the true and proper
S D : 0 5 :027(563) [0961] law and Gospel, and **diligently** to avoid anything that
S D : 0 6 :004(564) [0963] eyes and continually to urge it upon them with **diligence**.
S D : 0 6 :015(566) [0967] observe with special **diligence** that in speaking of good
S D : 0 7 :002(569) [0971] Some Sacramentarians **diligently** endeavor to employ
S D : 0 7 :030(574) [0981] of God I have most **diligently** traced all these articles
S D : 0 7 :054(579) [0991] are to be regarded **diligently** and earnestly as a special and
S D : 0 7 :068(582) [0997] to explain with great **diligence** who the unworthy guests
S D : 0 8 :035(597) [1027] The following presentation should be noted **diligently**.
S D : 1 1 :021(619) [1069] to God's Word, pray **diligently**, persevere in the grace of
S D : 1 1 :033(621) [1073] of God, follow it, and be **diligent** about it because the
S D : 1 1 :060(626) [1083] we may learn the more **diligently** to recognize and praise
S D : 1 1 :073(628) [1087] love, and should **diligently** seek to "confirm their call and
S D : 1 1 :077(629) [1089] attend on it, hear it with **diligence**, and in no way doubt
S D : 1 1 :083(630) [1091] It is to be considered **diligently** that God punishes sin with

Dim (1)
S D : 0 2 :009(521) [0883] natural intellect still has a **dim** spark of the knowledge

Diminish (3), Diminished (2)
A G : 2 7 :038(077) [0081] What is this but to **diminish** the glory and honor of the
A L : 2 4 :024(058) [0067] the Holy Scriptures and **diminish** the glory of Christ's
A P : 1 2 :125(201) [0289] the future might tend to **diminish** the prestige of the
S D : 0 4 :002(551) [0939] our redeemer, be **diminished** and in order to retain for
S D : 0 8 :049(600) [1031] nature intrinsically **diminished** or augmented thereby.

Diocese (1), Dioceses (1)
P R : P R :027(014) [0025] of Luebeck, administrator of the **diocese** of Verden
S 1 : P R :010(290) [0457] But in the **dioceses** of the papists we see so many vacant

Dionysius (4)
S 3 : 1 5 :005(317) [0501] I, **Dionysius** Melander, subscribe the Confession, the
T R : 0 0 :062(331) [0523] of Bishops Heracles and **Dionysius**, the presbyters always
T R : 0 0 :071(332) [0525] added, many of which **Dionysius** describes; but he is a late
T R : 0 0 :071(332) [0525] But not even this is found in **Dionysius**!

Diphthong (1)
A P : 2 4 :083(264) [0413] Because of the **diphthong**, philologists do not derive it

Dipped (2)
L C : 0 4 :065(444) [0749] consists in being **dipped** into the water, which covers us
L C : 0 4 :065(444) [0749] These two parts, being **dipped** under the water and

Dire (1)
A G : 2 6 :019(067) [0073] of spiritual authority, but **dire** need has compelled them

Direct (11), Directed (22), Directing (2), Direction (6), Directly (3), Directs (11)
P R : P R :010(006) [0011] correct explanation and **direction** might be provided for
P R : P R :020(010) [0017] Christians are to be **directed** in the treatment of the
P R : P R :023(012) [0021] has always been **directed** toward the goal that no other
P R : P R :023(012) [0021] On the contrary, we have **directed** our churches and
A G : 2 7 :020(074) [0079] creation and order also **direct** all to marriage who are not
A G : 2 8 :018(083) [0085] of the two powers, **directing** that both be held in honor as
A G : 2 8 :054(090) [0091] So St. Paul **directed** in I Cor. 11:5 that women should
A G : 2 8 :054(090) [0091] He also **directed** that in the assembly preachers should
A G : 2 8 :065(092) [0093] The apostles **directed** that one should abstain from blood
A P : 0 4 :279(149) [0199] God always, and ask him to **direct** your ways" (4:19).
A P : 2 3 :014(241) [0367] is an express command, **directed** to anyone not suited for
A P : 2 4 :028(254) [0393] declaration, which seems to contradict Moses **directly**?
A P : 2 8 :018(284) [0449] to traditions but is rather **directed** against traditions.
S 2 : 0 2 :001(293) [0463] because it runs into **direct** and violent conflict with this
S 2 : 0 2 :007(294) [0465] abolished because it is a **direct** contradiction to the
S 3 : 0 3 :019(306) [0485] time his attention was **directed** to his own works, and he
S 3 : 0 3 :027(308) [0487] and once again **directed** attention to uncertain human
S 3 : 1 4 :001(315) [0501] monastic vows are in **direct** conflict with the first chief
S 3 : 1 5 :005(317) [0501] from Smalcald **directed** me orally and by a letter which I
L C : 0 1 :050(371) [0593] leads us outward and **directs** the lips and the tongue into
L C : 0 1 :103(379) [0611] three commandments, which are **directed** toward God.
L C : 0 1 :106(379) [0611] humility, and modesty, **directed** (so to speak) toward a
L C : 0 1 :194(391) [0635] And this kindness is **directed**, as I said, especially toward
L C : 0 1 :310(407) [0669] commandments are **directed** especially against envy and
L C : 0 1 :321(408) [0673] of them as a whole ought to be referred and **directed** to it.
L C : 0 2 :054(417) [0693] Toward forgiveness is **directed** everything that is to be
L C : 0 3 :080(431) [0721] especially is this petition **directed** against our chief
L C : 0 3 :087(432) [0723] and, as we have heard, **directing** his attacks against all the
L C : 0 3 :113(435) [0729] of our prayer may be **directed** against our arch-enemy.
L C : 0 3 :117(436) [0731] our bodily welfare and **directs** us to seek and expect help
L C : 0 4 :031(440) [0739] faith, and Christ, who **directs** us and binds us to Baptism.
E P : 0 5 :007(478) [0803] are frightened by the law, **directs** them solely to the merit
E P : 0 5 :008(479) [0803] Thus they are **directed** back to the law, and now they
E P : 0 5 :009(479) [0803] God's wrath which really **directs** people into the law, after
E P : 0 7 :015(483) [0811] this clearly when they **direct** us to take, eat, and drink, all
E P : 1 1 :011(496) [0835] He there **directs** men first to repent, to acknowledge their
E P : 1 1 :016(497) [0837] his reason and under the **direction** of the devil, since
S D : 0 2 :007(521) [0883] and active only in the **direction** of that which is
S D : 0 2 :024(526) [0891] Although he can **direct** the members of his body, can
S D : 0 2 :043(529) [0897] glorifies our free will, as **directly** and diametrically
S D : 0 2 :072(535) [0909] This doctrine **directs** us to the means through which the
S D : 0 3 :067(551) [0937] of our souls depends, we **direct** him for the sake of brevity
S D : 0 4 :022(554) [0945] such propositions are **directly** contrary to the doctrine of
S D : 0 5 :010(560) [0955] This **directs** the sinner to the law, and there he really
S D : 0 7 :066(581) [0997] of desirable brevity we **direct** the Christian reader to our
S D : 0 7 :122(590) [1013] believers are not **directed** to seek the body of Christ in the
S D : 0 8 :029(597) [1025] covenant, to which he has **directed** us through his Word.
S D : 0 8 :050(600) [1031] the testimony of the Scripture points in that **direction**.
S D : 0 8 :063(603) [1037] and terminology in this **direction** in order to cast
S D : 0 9 :001(610) [1051] to which Dr. Luther **directs** us in the sermon that he held
S D : 1 0 :014(613) [1057] will misuse them and misinterpret them in this **direction**.
S D : 1 1 :012(618) [1067] in no other way than to **direct** us thereby to the Word
S D : 1 1 :055(625) [1081] cling solely to his revealed Word, to which he **directs** us.
S D : 1 1 :066(627) [1085] Son, and Holy Spirit, **directs** all men to Christ as to the
S D : 1 1 :093(632) [1093] shall abide by this simple, **direct**, and useful exposition

Dirt (1)
S D : 0 1 :022(512) [0865] off, like a smudge of **dirt** from one's face or paint from

Disability (1)
S D : 0 1 :010(510) [0863] together with a **disability** and ineptitude as far as the

Disabuse (1)
A P : 0 7 :042(176) [0243] the apostles wanted to **disabuse** the people of the foolish

Disadvantage (6), Disadvantages (1)
P R : P R :007(004) [0009] to the very great **disadvantage** of ourselves and of our
P R : P R :009(006) [0011] sustained the further **disadvantage** that, under the name
A G : 2 3 :016(054) [0063] to the church, be of **disadvantage** to the Christian church
A P : 1 5 :051(222) [0329] can be kept without sin or without great **disadvantage**.
A P : 1 5 :052(222) [0329] others, even where this involved some **disadvantage** to us.
S C : P R :017(340) [0537] advantages, and **disadvantages**, as you will find all of this
S C : P R :024(341) [0539] the advantage and **disadvantage**, the benefit and loss, the

Disagree (2), Disagreeing (2), Disagreement (10), Disagreements (2), Disagrees (2)
A G : 0 0 :001(047) [0059] our opponents cannot **disagree** with us in the articles set
A G : 2 6 :044(070) [0075] Irenaeus said, "**Disagreement** in fasting does not destroy
A G : 2 6 :044(070) [0075] in Dist. 12 that such **disagreement** in human ordinances is
A L : 2 6 :044(070) [0075] Irenaeus says, "**Disagreement** about fasting does not
A P : 0 2 :006(101) [0107] To show our **disagreement** with this evil doctrine, we
A P : 0 4 :241(141) [0187] certain minor **disagreements** arose, which would never
A P : 0 4 :291(152) [0203] are therefore obliged to **disagree** with our opponents on
A P : 1 2 :090(195) [0279] important reasons for **disagreeing** with our opponents, we
A P : 2 3 :023(242) [0369] regulation also **disagrees** with the canons of the councils.
A P : 2 3 :060(247) [0379] and natural law; it **disagrees** even with the canons; it is
A P : 2 4 :099(268) [0419] most valid reasons for **disagreeing** with our opponents.
E P : 0 0 :000(463) [0775] Time There Has Been **Disagreement** among Some of the
E P : 0 8 :001(486) [0817] on the Holy Supper a **disagreement** has arisen between
E P : 1 0 :007(494) [0831] the familiar axiom, "**Disagreement** in fasting does not
S D : P R :008(502) [0849] futile hope that these **disagreements** will ultimately lead to
S D : 0 4 :006(552) [0939] order to explain this **disagreement** in a Christian way and
S D : 0 4 :007(552) [0939] is in this article no **disagreement** among us concerning the
S D : 1 0 :031(616) [1063] well-known axiom, "**Disagreement** in fasting should not

Disappears (1)
A P : 2 1 :034(233) [0351] knowledge of Christ **disappears** if we seek out other

Disapproval (2), Disapprove (3), Disapproved (2)
P R : P R :022(012) [0021] for and a cordial **disapproval** of the raging of their
A L : 1 0 :002(034) [0047] They **disapprove** of those who teach otherwise.
A L : 2 4 :040(061) [0069] that it cannot be **disapproved**, especially since the
A P : 0 4 :236(140) [0185] they even intimate their **disapproval** of some open abuse.
A P : 0 7 :030(174) [0237] article, but if we mean "universal rites" they **disapprove** it.
A P : 1 0 :004(179) [0247] Majesty does not **disapprove** this article), but to make
T R : 0 0 :008(321) [0505] The antithesis here shows that lordship is **disapproved**.

Disaster (1)
L C : 0 2 :017(412) [0681] misfortune, warding off all sorts of danger and **disaster**.

Disavowed (1)
S D : 0 7 :001(568) [0971] completely **disavowed** the Augsburg Confession, withdrew

Discard (1), Discarded (1)
S 2 : 0 2 :002(293) [0463] And we can **discard** all human inventions, for Christ
S 2 : 0 2 :012(295) [0465] may consequently be **discarded**, apart entirely from the

Discern (8), Discerned (2), Discerning (2), Discernment (1), Discerns (1)
A G : 1 1 :002(034) [0047] Ps. 19:12, "Who can **discern** his errors?"
A G : 2 5 :008(062) [0069] As the psalmist says, "Who can **discern** his errors?"
A L : 1 1 :002(034) [0047] to the Psalm, "Who can **discern** his errors?" (Ps. 19:12).
A L : 2 5 :007(062) [0069] So the Psalm testifies, "Who can **discern** his errors?"
A L : 0 0 :006(096) [0095] of the doctrine taught among us may be **discerned**.
A P : 0 7 :042(176) [0243] Easter; from them the **discerning** reader can easily judge
A P : 1 1 :008(181) [0251] the statement (Ps. 19:12), "Who can **discern** his errors?"
A P : 1 2 :093(196) [0279] **Discernment** may rightly be demanded of those who have
A P : 2 4 :037(257) [0397] Therefore, as we **discern** the shadow in the Old
A P : 2 7 :020(272) [0425] From that the **discerning** reader will easily be able to
S 3 : 0 7 :001(311) [0493] So it is written, "Who can **discern** his errors?" (Ps. 19:12).
L C : 0 4 :061(444) [0747] blinded that they do not **discern** God's Word and
L C : 0 5 :037(451) [0761] faith of the heart which **discerns** and desires this treasure.
S D : 0 2 :010(522) [0883] understand them because they are spiritually **discerned**."

Discharge (5), Discharging (1)
A L : 2 6 :038(069) [0075] spiritual things and for **discharging** his duty according to
S 3 : 1 0 :002(314) [0497] Communion or **discharge** any office or work in the
S C : 0 1 :020(344) [0543] them to remain and **discharge** their duty to him.
L C : 0 1 :168(388) [0629] earnestly and faithfully **discharge** the duties of their
S D : 0 8 :046(600) [1031] place, as far as the **discharge** of Christ's office is
S D : 1 0 :019(614) [1059] Communion or **discharge** any office or work in the

Disciple (1), Disciples (18)
A G : 2 6 :027(068) [0073] upon the neck of the **disciples** which neither our fathers
A G : 2 8 :042(088) [0089] Peter forbids putting a yoke on the neck of the **disciples**.
A L : 2 6 :027(068) [0073] upon the neck of the **disciples** which neither our fathers
A L : 2 8 :042(088) [0089] putting a yoke on the **disciples** and Paul says that
A P : 1 2 :159(207) [0301] When the **disciples** asked who had sinned in the case of
A P : 2 2 :007(237) [0359] which says that the **disciples** recognized Christ in the
T R : 0 0 :008(320) [0505] was the very question the **disciples** were disputing when
T R : 0 0 :008(321) [0505] child in the midst of the **disciples**, signifying thereby that
T R : 0 0 :009(321) [0505] 20:21 Christ sent his **disciples** out as equals, without
S C : 0 4 :004(348) [0551] "Go therefore and make **disciples** of all nations, baptizing
S C : 0 6 :004(351) [0555] it, and gave it to the **disciples** and said, 'Take, eat; this is
L C : S P :020(364) [0579] Christ said farewell to his **disciples** and sent them forth.

Continued ▶

LC : SP :023(364) [0579] it and gave it to his **disciples**, saying, 'Take and eat, this is
LC : 05 :003(447) [0753] *it, and gave it to his **disciples** and said, 'Take, eat; this is*
LC : 05 :045(452) [0763] are words addressed to **disciples** of Christ; hence whoever
LC : 05 :062(454) [0767] it and I want to be thy **disciple**, no matter how
SD : 07 :042(576) [0987] and apostles, and by their **disciples** and hearers in turn.
SD : 07 :051(578) [0991] He let his **disciples** keep this simple and strict
SD : 07 :064(581) [0995] supper he handed his **disciples** natural bread and natural

Discipline (44), Disciplines (1)
AG : 26 :030(068) [0075] mortification and **discipline**, their writings reveal
AG : 26 :033(069) [0075] as fasting and other **discipline**, so that he does not give
AG : 27 :002(071) [0077] Later, when true **discipline** and doctrine had become
AG : 27 :002(071) [0077] was made to restore **discipline** by means of these vows as
AL : 26 :030(068) [0075] like Jovinian, forbid **discipline** and mortification of the
AL : 26 :033(069) [0075] himself with bodily **discipline**, or bodily exercises and
AL : 26 :034(069) [0075] Such bodily **discipline** ought to be encouraged at all
AL : 26 :038(069) [0075] of sins by that **discipline** but to keep his body in
AL : 27 :002(071) [0077] Afterward, when **discipline** fell into decay, vows were
AL : 27 :002(071) [0077] purpose of restoring **discipline**, as in a carefully planned
AP : 04 :022(110) [0127] For God wants this civil **discipline** to restrain the
AP : 07 :032(174) [0239] than outward rules of **discipline**, completely unrelated to
AP : 07 :033(175) [0239] when they contain a **discipline** that serves to educate and
AP : 12 :120(200) [0287] not see that this was a **discipline**, and a secular one at
AP : 12 :120(200) [0287] were valid not for **discipline** in the church, but for
AP : 12 :121(200) [0287] were instituted for the sake of church **discipline**.
AP : 12 :151(206) [0299] that is, troubles are a **discipline** by which God exercises
AP : 12 :167(208) [0303] matter of ecclesiastical **discipline** established for the sake
AP : 12 :167(208) [0303] did not think that this **discipline** was necessary for the
AP : 12 :175(210) [0307] no longer refers to civil **discipline** but to payment for
AP : 14 :001(214) [0315] instituting ecclesiastical **discipline** in the manner described
AP : 15 :024(218) [0321] human reason interprets fasting and bodily **discipline**.
AP : 15 :039(220) [0325] us of abolishing good ordinances and church **discipline**.
AP : 15 :044(221) [0327] maintain church **discipline**, pious ceremonies, and the
AP : 15 :045(221) [0327] of the body and the **discipline** of the flesh we teach
AP : 15 :045(221) [0327] with which God **disciplines** us effect a genuine and not a
AP : 18 :009(226) [0337] This safeguards outward **discipline**, because all men
AP : 23 :048(246) [0377] we have said before that **discipline** and restraint of the
AP : 23 :049(246) [0377] praised "for the sake of **discipline** and the common weal"
AP : 23 :049(246) [0377] weal" (that is, for the **discipline** of the body and for public
AP : 27 :021(272) [0427] are not impure, are non-obligatory forms of **discipline**.
SC : 06 :010(352) [0557] are a good external **discipline**, but he is truly worthy and
SC : 09 :008(356) [0563] bring them up in the **discipline** and instruction of the
EP : 04 :017(477) [0801] subversive of Christian **discipline** that bald statement that
EP : 04 :018(477) [0801] people to Christian **discipline** and good works, and to
EP : 06 :001(479) [0805] (1) to maintain external **discipline** against unruly and
EP : 06 :008(481) [0807] subversive of Christian **discipline** and true piety the
SD : 04 :008(552) [0941] maintenance of outward **discipline** and which unbelievers
SD : 04 :039(557) [0951] offensive, might weaken **discipline** and decency, and
SD : 06 :001(563) [0963] to maintain external **discipline** and decency against
SD : 06 :009(565) [0965] "If you are left without **discipline** in which all have
SD : 06 :026(568) [0971] contrary to Christian **discipline** and true godliness, the
SD : 10 :001(610) [1053] and decorum or else to preserve Christian **discipline**.
SD : 10 :007(611) [1055] good order, Christian **discipline**, nor evangelical decorum
SD : 10 :009(612) [1055] good order, Christian **discipline**, evangelical decorum,

Disclose (1), Disclosed (1), Discloses (1), Disclosure (1)
AP : 11 :002(180) [0249] of all good men, since it **discloses** a sure and firm
LC : 03 :062(428) [0715] of God's name, are **disclosed** and exposed in all their
EP : 05 :008(478) [0803] 7. Now as to the **disclosure** of sin, as long as men hear
EP : 08 :016(489) [0821] for he did not always **disclose** this majesty, but only when

Disconsolate (2)
EP : 11 :016(497) [0837] life in such a way that **disconsolate** Christians can find no
SD : 05 :012(560) [0957] and lift upright those who are terrified and **disconsolate**."

Discontinue (1), Discontinued (4)
AG : 24 :013(057) [0065] revenues and stipends, were **discontinued** in our churches.
AG : 24 :040(061) [0069] abuse, have been **discontinued**, this manner of holding
AL : 24 :013(057) [0065] private Masses were **discontinued** among us inasmuch as
S2 : 02 :006(293) [0463] the more should it be **discontinued** in order to guard
SD : 10 :014(613) [1057] requiring us to use them or to **discontinue** them.

Discord (8)
PR : PR :004(004) [0007] of false doctrine and **discord** and to bring about
AG : 28 :029(085) [0087] of peace and to prevent **discord** and great disorder in
AL : 00 :003(049) [0059] are trying by the same method to increase the **discord**.
AP : PR :016(099) [0101] We take no pleasure in **discord**, nor are we indifferent to
S1 : PR :012(290) [0459] There is **discord** among princes and political estates.
TR : 00 :058(330) [0521] they are reproached for scandal, schism, and **discord**.
TR : 00 :072(332) [0525] occasion to schism and **discord**, for Paul commands that
SD : 01 :058(519) [0879] but, on the contrary, the **discord** will only be increased

Discouraged (1), Discouraging (1)
SC : 09 :008(356) [0563] lest they become **discouraged**, but bring them up in the
SD : 07 :057(579) [0993] He was **discouraging** them and warning them against

Discourse (1)
SD : 07 :057(579) [0993] of St. Paul's entire **discourse** prove, he had in mind those

Discourteously (1)
LC : 01 :110(380) [0611] and not address them **discourteously**, critically, and

Discover (5), Discovered (3), Discovering (1), Discovers (1), Discovery (1)
AG : 20 :022(044) [0055] Many of them **discovered** that they did not obtain peace
AL : 00 :004(049) [0059] Majesty will undoubtedly **discover** that the forms of
AP : 04 :029(111) [0129] sufficient both for **discovering** how one ought to live, and
AP : 04 :150(127) [0163] God's judgment he will **discover** that this trust in his own
AP : 27 :032(274) [0431] he will undoubtedly **discover** that even with ten thousand
S3 : 03 :025(307) [0485] Here we have the **discovery** and digging up of the
SD : 02 :014(523) [0885] who perceive and **discover** a little spark and a longing for
SD : 02 :068(534) [0907] Christian in his own life **discovers** that at one moment he
SD : 07 :128(591) [1015] may be can easily be **discovered** and identified by name
SD : 09 :001(610) [1051] into hell have been **discovered** among some of our
SD : 11 :025(620) [1071] can and should one **discover**, who the elect are and who

Discredit (1)
PR : PR :004(004) [0007] truth took occasion to **discredit** us and our schools and

Discreetly (1), Discretion (1)
AG : 00 :003(095) [0095] All these things we have **discreetly** passed over for the
AP : 12 :129(202) [0291] to yourself; for men of **discretion** will value this service

Discriminately (1), Discrimination (3)
TR : 00 :009(321) [0505] as equals, without **discrimination**, when he said, "As the
SD : 03 :019(542) [0921] Paul uses the terms **discriminately** when he states, "He
SD : 08 :035(597) [1027] explained with due **discrimination** because the statements
SD : 08 :035(597) [1027] them without due **discrimination**, the doctrine becomes

Discuss (28), Discussed (14), Discusses (6), Discussing (19), Discussion (33), Discussions (14)
PR : PR :007(004) [0009] convention and should **discuss** in a thorough and friendly
PR : PR :013(007) [0013] a Christian fashion they **discussed** with one another the
PR : PR :017(008) [0015] the above-mentioned **discussions** at Naumburg reserved
PR : PR :019(009) [0017] to in the Naumburg **discussions**, is concerned, it is
PR : PR :020(010) [0017] the Holy Supper into a **discussion** of the personal union
PR : PR :020(010) [0017] is concerned, for he cannot comprehend this **discussion**.
AG : PR :010(025) [0041] most gracious lord, to **discuss** with them and their
AG : PR :010(025) [0041] both sides, they may be **discussed** amicably and
AG : 20 :013(043) [0055] from Augustine, who **discusses** this question thoroughly
AG : 27 :001(070) [0075] In **discussing** monastic vows it is necessary to begin by
AG : 28 :061(091) [0093] There are many faulty **discussions** of the transformation
AG : 28 :064(092) [0093] What are such **discussions** but snares of conscience?
AL : 28 :061(091) [0093] There are monstrous **discussions** concerning the mutation
AL : 28 :064(092) [0093] What are **discussions** of this kind but snares of
AL : 00 :001(095) [0095] undue length we have **discussed** only the principle ones.
AP : 02 :013(102) [0109] the scholastics do not often employ in their **discussions**.
AP : 02 :041(105) [0115] In a lengthy **discussion** Augustine refutes the opinion that
AP : 04 :006(108) [0121] By "law" in this **discussion** we mean the commandments
AP : 04 :033(111) [0129] the words that Augustine uses in **discussing** this matter.
AP : 04 :068(116) [0139] and the nature of the faith we have been **discussing**.
AP : 04 :083(119) [0145] But we shall **discuss** this passage later on in considering
AP : 04 :087(119) [0147] basic issue of the whole **discussion**: "We hold that man is
AP : 04 :087(120) [0147] maintains in his lengthy **discussion** on *The Spirit and the*
AP : 04 :087(120) [0147] considered and **discussed** these matters according to the
AP : 04 :088(120) [0149] confirms it with a long **discussion** in Rom. 4 and repeats
AP : 04 :120(124) [0155] about this faith we are **discussing** completely destroys the
AP : 04 :185(132) [0173] This is the case in our **discussion**.
AP : 04 :220(137) [0181] in this text Paul is not **discussing** the mode of
AP : 04 :221(137) [0181] which he systematically **discusses** the mode of
AP : 04 :231(139) [0183] He is obviously **discussing** love of our neighbor.
AP : 04 :279(149) [0199] of faith we have been **discussing**, one which believes that
AP : 04 :303(154) [0205] nor demons can have the faith we are **discussing** here.
AP : 04 :342(160) [0215] it is out of place here to **discuss** what is worthy or
AP : 04 :357(161) [0217] central thought of the **discussion**; they pick out the word
AP : 04 :367(163) [0221] Whenever merit is **discussed**, our opponents immediately
AP : 04 :389(166) [0225] However brief this **discussion** may be, we hope that good
AP : 07 :034(175) [0239] Now, we are not **discussing** whether it is profitable to
AP : 07 :037(175) [0241] we must raise again and **discuss** more fully the issue in
AP : 07 :045(177) [0243] But why **discuss** it?
AP : 11 :006(181) [0251] Now, we are **discussing** what is necessary according to
AP : 11 :010(182) [0253] other major faults, and these we shall presently **discuss**.
AP : 12 :010(184) [0255] that our opponents' **discussions** are very confused and
AP : 12 :013(184) [0257] Here their **discussions** really become confused.
AP : 12 :029(185) [0259] useless and endless **discussions** as to when we are sorry
AP : 12 :055(189) [0267] We shall **discuss** this form of punishment later.
AP : 12 :068(192) [0271] notions we have been **discussing** about the merits of
AP : 12 :077(193) [0275] We **discussed** this issue earlier, in the article on
AP : 12 :093(196) [0279] Since the Fathers **discuss** sometimes one part, sometimes
AP : 12 :098(197) [0281] faith, the two parts of penitence we have **discussed** above.
AP : 12 :112(198) [0285] totally different from the enumeration we are **discussing**.
AP : 12 :116(199) [0287] For this reason we have **discussed** satisfactions in
AP : 12 :137(203) [0293] are not obligatory such as our opponents are **discussing**.
AP : 12 :148(205) [0299] what punishment and revenge is Augustine **discussing**?
AP : 12 :167(208) [0303] before, the patristic **discussions** and conciliar decisions
AP : 12 :178(211) [0307] with the complicated **discussions** of our opponents, they
AP : 13 :023(214) [0313] desecration of Masses, which we shall **discuss** a little later.
AP : 15 :002(215) [0315] Although we have **discussed** traditions at length in Article
AP : 15 :013(216) [0319] What need is there of a long **discussion**?
AP : 15 :052(222) [0329] this whole issue when we **discuss** vows and ecclesiastical
AP : 16 :012(224) [0333] Endless **discussions** about contracts will never satisfy
AP : 18 :010(226) [0337] Augustine **discusses** it too, and more recently William of
AP : 18 :010(226) [0337] more recently William of Paris has **discussed** it very well.
AP : 20 :011(228) [0341] our proofs in our earlier **discussion** of this whole issue.
AP : 21 :016(231) [0347] the common people but **discuss** only the views of the
AP : 23 :006(240) [0365] for some theological **discussion**, but in this one the
AP : 23 :006(240) [0365] is so clear that no **discussion** is necessary, only the
AP : 24 :007(250) [0385] For the present, we forego any **discussion** of their origins.
AP : 24 :010(251) [0387] opponents should be forced to **discuss** the point at issue.
AP : 24 :016(252) [0389] or understood in a **discussion**, and that if he found
AP : 24 :043(257) [0399] Instead, they **discuss** the worship of saints, human
AP : 24 :066(261) [0407] they quote against us, we must also **discuss** the Fathers.
AP : 24 :078(263) [0411] arguments which do not deserve a lengthy **discussion**.
AP : 24 :092(266) [0417] There is no need here of a very lengthy **discussion**.
AP : 24 :092(266) [0417] need ever arises, we shall **discuss** this whole issue more
AP : 27 :010(270) [0423] Since Luther **discussed** this whole issue carefully and fully
AP : 27 :016(271) [0425] As for celibacy, we would rather not **discuss** it.
AP : 27 :035(275) [0431] We have **discussed** this briefly, for on the basis of what
AP : 27 :054(278) [0439] either on philosophical **discussions** or on ceremonial
AP : 27 :055(278) [0439] Here we shall not **discuss** their whole ceremonial worship
AP : 27 :063(280) [0441] We shall not even **discuss** the other evils inherent in
S2 : 02 :014(295) [0467] of) shall we be ready to **discuss** with them whether
S3 : 00 :000(302) [0477] matters which we may **discuss** with learned and sensible
TR : 00 :073(332) [0525] no need, therefore, for **discussion** of the other functions
SC : PR :009(339) [0535] your learning and to **discuss** these topics from different
LC : 01 :053(371) [0595] To **discuss** it briefly, misuse of the divine name occurs
LC : 01 :084(376) [0605] may assemble to hear and **discuss** God's Word and then
LC : 02 :018(412) [0681] But further **discussion** of this subject belongs in the other
LC : 06 :008(458) [0000] which we are **discussing** here there are two other kinds,

Continued ▶

E P : R N :005(465) [0777] which Holy Scripture **discusses** at greater length and
E P : 0 1 :024(469) [0785] be retained in the **discussion** of original sin because they
E P : 0 2 :001(469) [0785] The will of man may be **discussed** in four different states:
E P : 0 2 :016(472) [0791] well to avoid them in a **discussion** of conversion to God.
E P : 0 4 :007(476) [0799] excluded from a **discussion** of the article of man's
E P : 1 1 :022(497) [0837] Confession have been **discussing** and teaching in mutually
S D : 0 1 :030(513) [0867] thesis when we **discussed** the correct doctrine of original
S D : 0 1 :033(514) [0869] must and can consider, **discuss**, and believe these two as
S D : 0 1 :049(517) [0875] We are not **discussing** it here at length but are treating
S D : 0 2 :044(529) [0897] Dr. Luther **discusses** this entire matter in his book *The*
S D : 0 2 :062(533) [0905] But if one is **discussing** the question how God operates in
S D : 0 2 :073(535) [0909] light of the previous **discussion** one can readily recognize,
S D : 0 2 :086(538) [0913] from the preceding **discussion** that this position does not
S D : 0 2 :086(538) [0913] to be avoided in the **discussion** of man's conversion to
S D : 0 3 :029(544) [0925] cannot admit any treatment or **discussion** of works.
S D : 0 3 :042(546) [0931] which the Apology **discusses** in connection with James
S D : 0 3 :054(548) [0933] explain correctly the **discussion** concerning the indwelling
S D : 0 4 :013(553) [0943] among us, we shall **discuss** them no further but shall
S D : 0 4 :014(553) [0943] it is evident that in **discussing** the question whether good
S D : 0 7 :105(588) [1009] word "spiritual" in this **discussion**, we have in mind the
S D : 0 8 :030(597) [1025] This we shall **discuss** in greater detail below.
S D : 0 8 :048(600) [1031] being treated in the **discussion** is this: Do the natures in
S D : 1 1 :002(616) [1063] as it were in passing, but **discuss** and present it in detail in
S D : 1 1 :063(626) [1083] something in the **discussion** on this subject soars too high
S D : 1 1 :064(626) [1083] After a lengthy **discussion** of this article on the basis of
S D : 1 1 :064(626) [1083] and cuts off further **discussion** with the following words:

Disdain (2), Disdained (1), Disdains (1)
L C : 0 1 :027(368) [0587] creatures is not to be **disdained**, nor are we arrogantly to
L C : 0 1 :166(388) [0629] He who despises and **disdains** this is not worthy to hear a
L C : 0 1 :209(393) [0639] we should not despise or **disdain** marriage, as the blind
L C : 0 3 :020(423) [0703] that we may not despise or **disdain** it or pray uncertainly.

Disease (5)
A L : 0 2 :002(029) [0043] And this **disease** or vice of origin is truly sin, which even
A P : 0 2 :006(101) [0107] it and explained it as a **disease** since human nature is born
L C : 0 5 :077(455) [0771] which feels nothing though the **disease** rages and rankles.
S D : 0 1 :005(509) [0861] and dreadful inherited **disease** which has corrupted our
S D : 0 1 :062(519) [0879] original sin a quality or a **disease**, ultimately the worst

Disfavor (2)
L C : 0 1 :153(386) [0625] and blessing than you will with **disfavor** and misfortune.
S D : 0 1 :009(510) [0861] and Eve, are in God's **disfavor** and are children of wrath

Disgrace (16), Disgraced (1), Disgraceful (3), Disgraces (1)
A G : 2 3 :014(054) [0063] cause worse and more **disgraceful** lewdness and vice to
A P : 0 4 :154(128) [0165] What a **disgrace** that an uneducated woman should
A P : 2 3 :001(239) [0363] the Roman Empire be **disgraced** and shamed by the
A P : 2 3 :002(239) [0363] who say that marriage **disgraces** and shames the empire,
A P : 2 3 :002(239) [0363] adorned by the public **disgrace** and the unnatural lusts of
A P : 2 3 :004(239) [0363] your conduct is free of **disgrace** and cruelty, we hope that
A P : 2 8 :026(285) [0451] What **disgrace** there is in celibacy!
T R : 0 0 :043(328) [0517] are shamelessly employed to secure **disgraceful** profits.
L C : P R :006(359) [0569] We Germans have such **disgraceful** people among us and
L C : 0 1 :055(372) [0595] to everyone and who **disgrace** God's name unabashedly
L C : 0 1 :059(372) [0597] cover and gloss over our **disgrace** so that no one may see
L C : 0 1 :059(372) [0597] villainy into righteousness and the **disgrace** into honor.
L C : 0 1 :231(396) [0647] one offense must bear **disgrace** and punishment so as to
L C : 0 1 :255(399) [0653] to live among men in public **disgrace** and contempt.
L C : 0 1 :268(401) [0657] venomous tongue to the **disgrace** and harm of your
L C : 0 1 :270(401) [0657] I might be called a liar and sent away in **disgrace**."
L C : 0 1 :273(401) [0659] some poor man into **disgrace**, from which he could
L C : 0 1 :284(403) [0661] as one who has brought **disgrace** upon himself, and you
L C : 0 1 :288(404) [0663] we should prevent everything that tends to his **disgrace**.
L C : 0 1 :295(404) [0665] this no more a sin or **disgrace** than it is now for a master
L C : 0 3 :044(425) [0709] Just as it is a shame and **disgrace** to an earthly father to

Dish (1)
L C : 0 3 :057(427) [0713] gifts, and the fool asked only for a **dish** of beggar's broth.

Dishonest (3), Dishonestly (2), Dishonesty (4), Dishonor (6), Dishonored (2), Dishonoring (1), Dishonors (1)
A L : 2 8 :036(086) [0089] of Christ's merit is **dishonored** when we suppose that we
A P : 1 2 :123(200) [0289] What good man would not be moved by such **dishonesty**?
A P : 1 2 :123(201) [0289] This is not logic or even sophistry, but sheer **dishonesty**.
A P : 2 1 :042(235) [0355] Therefore it was **dishonest** of our opponents to ignore
S C : P R :018(340) [0537] for many of these are guilty of **dishonesty** and thievery.
S C : 0 1 :014(343) [0541] into our possession by **dishonest** trade or by dealing in
L C : 0 1 :200(392) [0637] it is explicitly forbidden here to **dishonor** his wife.
L C : 0 1 :227(396) [0645] false measures, **dishonest** weights, and bad coins, and
L C : 0 1 :245(398) [0649] things by violence and **dishonesty** must put up with
L C : 0 1 :258(399) [0653] Instead, they speak **dishonestly** with an eye to gaining
L C : 0 3 :021(423) [0703] he angers God, grossly **dishonoring** him and accusing him
L C : 0 3 :041(425) [0709] the worst profanation and **dishonor** of the divine name.
L C : 0 3 :044(425) [0709] reproach, so God is **dishonored** if we who are called by
L C : 0 3 :057(428) [0713] is a great reproach and **dishonor** to God if we, to whom
S D : 0 7 :060(580) [0993] Such a person **dishonors**, abuses, and desecrates him who
S D : 0 7 :088(585) [1003] the Sacramentarians **dishonestly** and maliciously pervert
S D : 1 1 :079(629) [1089] and not of God, has made himself a vessel of **dishonor**.
S D : 1 1 :082(630) [1089] transform the vessels of **dishonor** into vessels of honor
S D : 1 1 :082(630) [1091] have been impure and therefore a vessel of **dishonor**.

Disintegrate (2)
A P : 0 4 :232(140) [0185] lest the church **disintegrate** into various schisms and the
A P : 0 4 :233(140) [0185] will inevitably **disintegrate** if bishops impose heavy

Dislike (2)
A P : 0 4 :073(117) [0141] If they **dislike** the exclusive particle "alone," let them
A P : 0 4 :224(138) [0181] as Paul indicates, they began to **dislike** good teachers.

Dismiss (7), Dismissal (1)
A P : 0 4 :264(146) [0195] Let us therefore **dismiss** Jerome in the interpretation of
A P : 2 3 :023(242) [0369] In those times such a **dismissal** was an act of kindness.
L C : S P :017(363) [0577] his household; he should **dismiss** man-servants and
L C : 0 1 :295(404) [0665] every man had power to **dismiss** his wife publicly by
L C : 0 1 :295(404) [0665] on any flimsy excuse **dismiss** his own wife and estrange
L C : 0 1 :295(404) [0665] it is now for a master to **dismiss** his servants or entice his
L C : 0 1 :305(406) [0667] husband was obliged to **dismiss** her and leave her to the
L C : 0 4 :048(442) [0743] briefly: Let the simple **dismiss** this question from their

Disobedience (16), Disobedient (6), Disobey (1), Disobeys (1)
A P : 0 7 :016(171) [0231] the devil "is now at work in the sons of **disobedience**."
S 1 : P R :012(290) [0459] vice and wickedness, **disobedience** of subjects, domestics,
S 3 : 0 1 :001(302) [0477] Adam, through whose **disobedience** all men were made
S 3 : 0 1 :002(302) [0477] of God's Word, **disobedience** to parents, murder,
S C : 0 1 :022(344) [0543] fear his wrath and not **disobey** these commandments.
S C : 0 5 :020(350) [0553] whether you have been **disobedient**, unfaithful, lazy,
L C : 0 1 :134(383) [0619] the penalty for him who **disobeys** it is that he will perish
L C : 0 1 :137(384) [0619] or broken on the wheel if not because of **disobedience**?
L C : 0 1 :177(389) [0631] we train them, we have unruly and **disobedient** subjects.
L C : 0 1 :305(406) [0667] her, or she became so **disobedient** and hard to live with
L C : 0 2 :028(414) [0685] came and led us into **disobedience**, sin, death, and all
L C : 0 3 :011(421) [0701] that we may not provoke his anger by such **disobedience**.
L C : 0 3 :018(422) [0703] pray, just as he punishes all other kinds of **disobedience**.
E P : 0 3 :003(473) [0793] "For as by one man's **disobedience** many were made
E P : 0 6 :001(479) [0805] against unruly and **disobedient** men, (2) to lead men to a
E P : 1 1 :010(495) [0833] consigned all men to **disobedience**, that he may have
S D : 0 1 :009(510) [0861] of us, because of the **disobedience** of Adam and Eve, are
S D : 0 3 :057(549) [0935] "For as by one man's **disobedience** many will be made
S D : 0 3 :058(550) [0937] thus covered up our **disobedience**, which inheres in our
S D : 0 3 :058(550) [0937] and deeds, so that our **disobedience** is not reckoned to us
S D : 0 4 :032(556) [0947] God is coming upon the sons of **disobedience**" (Col. 3:6).
S D : 0 6 :001(563) [0963] against dissolute and **disobedient** people, (2) and to bring
S D : 1 1 :028(620) [1071] all men under **disobedience** so that he might have mercy
S D : 1 1 :075(628) [1087] his children become **disobedient** and stumble, he arranges

Disorder (3), Disorderly (2)
A G : 2 8 :029(085) [0087] and to prevent discord and great **disorder** in their lands.
A G : 2 8 :055(090) [0091] so that there may be no **disorder** or unbecoming conduct
L C : 0 1 :085(376) [0605] and no one will create **disorder** by unnecessary
L C : 0 1 :217(394) [0643] of the filthy, dissolute, **disorderly** conduct which now is so
S D : 0 2 :046(530) [0899] become dissolute and **disorderly**, lazy and indifferent to

Disowned (1)
A P : 2 7 :067(280) [0443] especially for his own family, he has **disowned** the faith."

Disparage (4), Disparaging (1)
A G : 0 2 :003(029) [0045] his own powers, thus **disparaging** the sufferings and merit
A P : 0 4 :060(115) [0137] when they despise and **disparage** faith and teach men to
A P : 0 4 :193(133) [0175] To **disparage** works like the confession of doctrine,
A P : 0 4 :193(133) [0175] of the flesh would be to **disparage** the outward
A P : 2 3 :048(246) [0377] We do not **disparage** temperances or continence; we have

Dispensation (3), Dispensations (4)
A G : 2 7 :025(074) [0079] with this obligation and have often given **dispensations**,
A G : 2 7 :026(075) [0079] If **dispensations** were granted for the maintenance of
A G : 2 7 :026(075) [0079] much more should **dispensations** be granted for
A L : 2 7 :024(074) [0079] not have granted **dispensations**, for it is not lawful for a
A L : 2 7 :025(074) [0079] we read that they often granted **dispensation** from vows.
S D : 0 5 :022(562) [0959] the letter and is a "**dispensation** of condemnation," but
S D : 0 5 :022(562) [0959] who has faith," "a **dispensation** of righteousness" and "of

Dispense (1), Dispensed (5), Dispensers (1)
A G : 2 7 :024(074) [0079] popes could not have **dispensed** and released men from
A G : 2 8 :033(086) [0087] because the church has **dispensed** from and altered part
A L : 2 8 :033(086) [0087] of the church, for it **dispensed** from one of the Ten
A P : 2 3 :056(247) [0379] Daily the pontiffs **dispense** and change other good laws;
A P : 2 4 :080(264) [0411] ministers of Christ and **dispensers** of the sacraments of
L C : 0 4 :009(437) [0733] thing when the pope **dispensed** indulgences with his
E P : 0 8 :016(489) [0821] of his humiliation he **dispensed** with it and could

Display (4), Displayed (2), Displays (1)
A P : 0 4 :189(133) [0175] rule of the devil; in our weakness he **displays** his strength.
A P : 0 4 :202(134) [0175] to exercise his faith and **display** it to others, inviting them
A P : 0 4 :365(163) [0219] the wrath of God is **displayed**, and hence this belongs to
A P : 0 4 :365(163) [0219] In the proclamation of rewards grace is **displayed**.
A P : 2 7 :008(269) [0421] of the cruelty which the hypocrites among them **display**.
S 1 : P R :012(290) [0459] gluttony, gambling, vain **display**, all manner of vice and
L C : 0 1 :331(410) [0677] them there merely for a **display**, as the Jews did, but we

Displeased (5), Displeases (1), Displeasing (4), Displeasure (9)
A G : 2 6 :017(066) [0073] Augustine was also **displeased** that consciences were
A G : 2 7 :008(072) [0077] Such severity and rigor **displeased** many devout people in
A G : 2 7 :010(072) [0077] monks with even a little understanding were **displeased**.
A L : 2 7 :008(071) [0077] Such rigor **displeased** many good men before our time
A L : 2 7 :010(072) [0077] that it was clearly **displeasing** to those monks in former
A P : 0 2 :038(105) [0115] argue with Augustine if this position **displeases** them!
A P : 1 2 :117(199) [0287] they say that it is done to placate the divine **displeasure**.
A P : 1 2 :118(200) [0287] who are in mortal sin could placate the divine **displeasure**.
A P : 1 2 :144(205) [0297] serve to placate God's **displeasure**, as our opponents
A P : 2 3 :059(247) [0379] are certainly **displeasing** to God, we do not regret our lack
L C : 0 1 :148(385) [0623] but the wrath and **displeasure** of God; there will be no
L C : 0 1 :233(396) [0647] at the risk of God's **displeasure**, not to harm his
L C : 0 1 :305(406) [0667] to make her husband **displeased** with her, or she became
L C : 0 2 :028(414) [0685] under God's wrath and **displeasure**, doomed to eternal
L C : 0 2 :068(420) [0697] for God's wrath and **displeasure** still remain on us
L C : 0 3 :009(421) [0699] and obligation [on pain of God's wrath and **displeasure**].
L C : 0 3 :089(432) [0723] fears God's wrath and **displeasure**, and so it loses the
S D : 0 2 :007(521) [0883] of that which is **displeasing** and contrary to God.
S D : 0 2 :017(524) [0887] for everything which is **displeasing** to God and contrary

Disposal (1), Dispose (2), Disposed (6)
A G : P R :016(026) [0041] Majesty was not **disposed** to render decisions in matters
A P : 0 4 :045(113) [0133] and favorably **disposed** to him because of Christ, this
A P : 0 4 :180(132) [0171] wishes to be favorably **disposed** to us and to justify us,
A P : 0 4 :314(156) [0207] whole issue and bring consolation to well-**disposed** minds.

Continued ▶

S C : P R :012(339) [0535] them that the prince is **disposed** to banish such rude
L C : 0 1 :302(405) [0667] any other means at his **disposal**, until the property is
E P : 0 2 :001(469) [0785] through the Holy Spirit, **dispose** and prepare himself for
E P : 0 2 :011(471) [0789] itself for grace, to **dispose** itself, to apprehend and accept
S D : 0 5 :017(561) [0957] how man ought to be **disposed** in his nature, thoughts,

Disposition (33), Dispositions (1)
P R : P R :008(005) [0009] it was in no way our **disposition** and intention to adopt,
P R : P R :022(012) [0021] that it is in no way our **disposition** and purpose to give
P R : P R :023(012) [0021] As indicated above, our **disposition** and intention has
P R : P R :024(013) [0023] ours it was never our **disposition** or intention — as it is
A P : 0 2 :024(103) [0111] both the defect and the vicious **disposition** that follows.
A P : 0 2 :027(104) [0113] this, the inordinate **disposition** of the parts of the soul.
A P : 0 4 :017(109) [0125] merited for us a certain **disposition** or, as they call it,
A P : 0 4 :017(109) [0125] they understand as a **disposition** inclining us to love God
A P : 0 4 :017(109) [0125] they ascribe to this **disposition**, for they imagine that the
A P : 0 4 :017(109) [0125] of the will before the **disposition** and those after it are of
A P : 0 4 :017(109) [0125] love God, but that this **disposition** stimulates it to do so
A P : 0 4 :017(109) [0125] bid us merit this first **disposition** by our preceding merits.
A P : 0 4 :017(109) [0125] merit an increase of this **disposition** and eternal life by the
A P : 0 4 :018(109) [0125] they talk about this **disposition**, yet without the
A P : 0 4 :019(110) [0125] imagine that after that **disposition** of love a man can earn
A P : 0 4 :019(110) [0125] have him doubt whether the **disposition** is truly present.
A P : 0 4 :020(110) [0125] whether or not the **disposition** is there, because men
A P : 0 4 :066(116) [0139] they talk about the **disposition** of love, they pretend that
A P : 0 4 :081(118) [0143] because he merited for us the **disposition** of love.
A P : 0 4 :081(118) [0143] by which we merit this **disposition**, and then, through this
A P : 0 4 :289(151) [0203] through a certain **disposition** (which is love) infused by
A P : 0 4 :289(151) [0203] with the help of this **disposition** we obey the law of God
A P : 0 4 :312(155) [0207] offers, then the **dispositions** of faith and hope seem to be
A P : 0 4 :316(156) [0209] with the help of a "**disposition**" of love, are a worthy
A P : 0 4 :321(156) [0209] the influence of this **disposition** of love, so that it can be
A P : 0 4 :381(165) [0223] interpret grace as a **disposition** by which we love God, as
A P : 1 3 :018(213) [0313] *operato*,without a good **disposition** in the one using them.
A P : 1 3 :018(213) [0313] without a good **disposition** in our heart, that is, without
A P : 1 3 :023(214) [0313] *operato* without a good **disposition** in the one using
S D : 0 1 :051(517) [0875] means — as it often does — a **disposition** or characteristic.
S D : 0 1 :051(517) [0875] that sin and sinning are man's **disposition** and nature.
S D : 0 2 :007(521) [0883] to its perverse **disposition** and nature the natural free will
S D : 0 2 :017(524) [0887] and corrupted that by **disposition** and nature he is
S D : 0 2 :018(524) [0889] wicked and obstinate **disposition** with which he was

Disproved (1)
A P : P R :009(099) [0101] far from having **disproved** our contentions from the

Disputation (4), Disputations (3), Dispute (12), Disputed (4), Disputes (4), Disputing (1), Disputable (1)
P R : P R :000(001) [0004] Articles about which **Disputation** and Strife Arose after
P R : P R :008(006) [0011] way without any further **disputation** and dissension.
P R : P R :024(013) [0021] of all of the **disputes** which have arisen should come into
P R : P R :024(013) [0023] opinions and dubious, **disputable** imaginations and views
A G : 0 0 :002(048) [0059] The **dispute** and dissension are concerned chiefly with
A G : 0 0 :000(048) [0059] Articles about Matters in **Dispute**, in Which an Account
A G : 2 8 :030(085) [0087] Besides, there is **dispute** as to whether bishops have the
A L : 2 8 :030(085) [0087] Besides, it is **disputed** whether bishops or pastors have the
A P : 2 1 :041(235) [0355] it leads to philosophical **disputes** rather than to piety.
A P : 2 1 :041(235) [0355] and endless **disputations** of the scholastic theologians and
S 1 : P R :013(291) [0459] if we let logs stand and **dispute** about specks, we might
S 1 : 0 1 :000(292) [0461] are not matters of **dispute** or contention, for both parties
S 3 : 0 8 :006(313) [0495] There is no time to **dispute** further about these matters.
T R : 0 0 :008(320) [0505] the disciples were **disputing** when Christ spoke of his
T R : 0 0 :008(321) [0505] when, in a similar **dispute** concerning the kingdom,
T R : 0 0 :021(323) [0509] had for a long time been **disputes** between the bishops of
T R : 0 0 :021(323) [0509] the Roman pontiff, this **dispute** could not have occurred,
T R : 0 0 :081(334) [0527] number of matrimonial **disputes** are so great that they
L C : 0 1 :067(373) [0599] If one party in a **dispute** swears falsely, he will not escape
L C : 0 1 :301(405) [0667] to the property as to put it beyond complaint or **dispute**.
L C : 0 5 :004(447) [0753] occasion to quarrel and **dispute** with those who
E P : 0 9 :001(492) [0827] There has been a **dispute** among some theologians of the
E P : 0 9 :002(492) [0827] should not engage in **disputations** concerning this article,
S D : 0 2 :044(529) [0897] he also takes up several **disputed** points which Erasmus
S D : 0 3 :042(546) [0931] and well the various **disputed** issues which the Apology
S D : 0 4 :030(555) [0947] In the third place, a **disputation** has arisen as to whether
S D : 0 7 :046(577) [0987] sufficient ground for a **disputation** when he heard God's
S D : 1 1 :093(632) [1095] questions and **disputations**, and we reject and condemn
S D : 1 1 :094(632) [1095] articles which have been **disputed** among theologians of

Disqualified (1)
S D : 0 6 :009(565) [0965] I myself should be **disqualified**" (I Cor. 9:27), and again,

Disregard (3), Disregarded (1), Disregards (1)
A G : 2 8 :068(093) [0093] necessary and that **disregard** of them does not injure
S 3 : 0 1 :002(302) [0477] — in short, ignorance or **disregard** of God — and then
L C : 0 1 :016(366) [0585] for him should risk and **disregard** everything else on
L C : 0 1 :177(389) [0631] this commandment is **disregarded**, God terribly punishes
L C : 0 1 :234(397) [0647] A person who willfully **disregards** this commandment

Disrupt (1), Disrupting (1), Disruption (1)
P R : P R :004(003) [0007] situation and amid the **disruption** of well-ordered
A P : 1 4 :002(214) [0315] it how they will answer to God for **disrupting** the church.
S 3 : 1 1 :003(315) [0499] it, and we shall not **disrupt** or hinder God's work, for St.

Disseminate (2)
A L : 0 0 :002(049) [0059] not believe those who **disseminate** astonishing slanders
E P : 0 7 :001(481) [0809] themselves and to **disseminate** their errors under the

Dissension (14), Dissensions (10), Dissent (4), Dissented (2)
P R : P R :008(006) [0011] way without any further disputation and **dissension**.
P R : P R :016(007) [0013] the explanation of the **dissensions** which had arisen was
P R : P R :024(013) [0021] aggravated scandals, **dissensions**, and long-standing
A G : P R :002(025) [0039] might be done about the **dissension** concerning our holy
A G : P R :006(025) [0039] with reference to the said errors, **dissensions**, and abuses.
A G : P R :023(027) [0043] (unless the matters in **dissension** are finally heard,
A G : 0 0 :002(048) [0059] The dispute and **dissension** are concerned chiefly with
A L : 0 0 :002(047) [0059] The whole **dissension** is concerned with a certain few
A L : 0 0 :001(048) [0059] as our churches **dissent** from the church catholic in no
A L : 2 4 :014(057) [0065] them in time, there would now have been less **dissension**.
A L : 2 4 :017(057) [0067] Great **dissensions** have arisen concerning the Mass,
A P : 0 4 :224(138) [0181] Then **dissensions** arose among them and, as Paul
A P : 0 4 :233(140) [0185] **Dissensions** also arise when the people judge their clergy's
A P : 0 4 :241(141) [0187] namely, that if any **dissensions** arise they should be
A P : 0 4 :241(141) [0187] **Dissensions**, it says, grow because of hatred, as we often
A P : 1 2 :090(195) [0279] These **dissensions** in the church certainly give us no
T R : 0 0 :038(327) [0515] and other prophets **dissented** from them, and the apostles
T R : 0 0 :038(327) [0515] them, and the apostles **dissented** from Caiaphas and were
T R : 0 0 :040(327) [0517] the greatest cruelty and puts to death those who **dissent**.
T R : 0 0 :042(328) [0517] To **dissent** from the consensus of so many nations and to
L C : 0 3 :074(430) [0719] For where **dissension**, strife, and war prevail, there our
L C : 0 5 :075(455) [0771] anger, selfishness, **dissension**, party spirit, envy, murder,
E P : 1 1 :001(494) [0831] No public **dissension** has developed among the
E P : 1 1 :001(494) [0831] future date offensive **dissension** concerning it might be
S D : R N :012(506) [0855] published before the **dissensions** arose among the
S D : R N :015(507) [0857] necessary controversy (**dissension** concerning articles of
S D : 0 1 :001(508) [0859] place, there has been **dissension** among a number of
S D : 0 7 :073(582) [0999] misunderstanding and **dissension** among some teachers of
S D : 1 0 :023(615) [1061] To **dissent** from the consensus of so many nations and to
S D : 1 1 :001(616) [1063] and widespread **dissension** among the theologians of the

Dissertation (1)
A P : 0 7 :001(168) [0227] have added a lengthy **dissertation**, that the wicked are not

Dissimilar (3)
A G : 2 6 :045(070) [0075] many examples of **dissimilar** church usages and adds the
A L : 2 6 :045(070) [0075] 9, many examples of **dissimilar** rites are gathered, and
S D : 0 2 :002(520) [0881] and viewed as being in four distinct and **dissimilar** states.

Dissipation (3)
A G : 2 6 :035(069) [0075] be weighed down with **dissipation**," and again, "This kind
A L : 2 6 :035(069) [0075] be weighed down with **dissipation**," and again, "This kind
A P : 1 5 :046(221) [0327] be weighed down with **dissipation**," and Paul says (I Cor.

Dissolute (7), Dissolution (2)
A G : 2 3 :001(051) [0061] immorality and the **dissolute** life of priests who were not
A P : 2 3 :059(247) [0379] of this unjust law, the **dissolution** of existing marriages,
A P : 2 3 :063(248) [0381] 7:2) and forbidding the **dissolution** of existing marriages
L C : 0 1 :217(394) [0643] may be less of the filthy, **dissolute**, disorderly conduct
L C : 0 5 :059(453) [0767] are not so callous and **dissolute** but would like to be
E P : 1 1 :009(495) [0833] lead us into a reckless, **dissolute**, Epicurean life, or drive
S D : 0 2 :046(530) [0899] people have become **dissolute** and disorderly, lazy and
S D : 0 6 :001(563) [0963] and decency against **dissolute** and disobedient people, (2)
S D : 1 1 :089(631) [1093] either despondency or a riotous and **dissolute** life.

Dissolve (4), Dissolved (5)
A G : 2 7 :034(076) [0081] marriage of those who broke them should be **dissolved**.
A G : 2 7 :035(076) [0081] marriage should not be **dissolved**, and St. Augustine is no
A L : 2 3 :013(053) [0063] marriages were also **dissolved**, although this was contrary
A L : 2 7 :034(076) [0081] of persons who violated them ought to be **dissolved**.
A L : 2 7 :035(076) [0081] denies that they should be **dissolved** in *Nuptiarum*,
A P : 2 3 :003(239) [0363] of the councils, they demand that you **dissolve** marriages.
A P : 2 3 :023(242) [0369] not forbid marriage, nor **dissolve** marriages that have
A P : 2 3 :023(242) [0371] of marriages and **dissolve** them once they have been
A P : 2 3 :061(247) [0381] anyone into celibacy or to **dissolve** existing marriages.

Dist (7)
A G : 2 5 :010(063) [0069] the Fathers can be seen in **Dist**. I, *De poenitentia*, where
A G : 2 5 :012(063) [0071] note in *De poenitentia*, **Dist**. 5, also teaches that such
A G : 2 6 :044(070) [0075] and there is a statement in **Dist**. 12 that such disagreement
A L : 2 2 :009(050) [0061] as the canons testify (**Dist**. 3, chap. "Veritate" and the
A L : 2 5 :012(063) [0071] note in *De poenitentia*, **Dist**. 5, in the chapter
A L : 2 6 :044(070) [0075] Pope Gregory indicates in **Dist**. 12 that such diversity
A L : 2 8 :034(086) [0089] The canons concede this throughout the whole of **Dist**. 9.

Distant (8), Distantly (1)
L C : 0 5 :067(454) [0769] greatest good, we act so **distantly** toward it, neglecting it
E P : 0 7 :028(485) [0815] and types of the far-**distant** body and blood of Christ.
S D : 0 7 :002(569) [0973] blood of Christ are as far **distant** from the blessed bread
S D : 0 7 :002(569) [0973] Supper as the highest heaven is **distant** from the earth.
S D : 0 7 :002(569) [0973] and blood of Christ are **distant** from the signs by as great
S D : 0 7 :002(569) [0973] an interval as the earth is **distant** from the highest
S D : 0 7 :115(589) [1011] and types of the far-**distant** body of Christ (for example,
S D : 0 7 :117(589) [1013] and merit of the far-**distant** body of Christ, and that in
S D : 0 7 :119(590) [1013] but that he is as far or as **distant** from it as heaven and

Distinct (20), Distinction (69), Distinctions (12), Distinctly (8)
P R : P R :022(011) [0019] set forth expressly and **distinctly** in this explanation and
A G : 0 1 :006(028) [0043] Spirit, are not necessarily **distinct** persons but that the
A G : 1 5 :004(037) [0049] traditions concerning **distinction** of foods, days, etc., by
A G : 2 6 :000(063) [0071] XXVI. The **Distinction** of Foods
A G : 2 6 :001(063) [0071] and wrote that **distinctions** among foods and similar
A G : 2 6 :006(064) [0071] by prescribed fasts, **distinctions** among foods, vestments,
A G : 2 8 :034(086) [0089] canon law throughout the whole of the ninth **Distinction**.
A L : 0 1 :006(028) [0043] the Holy Spirit are not **distinct** persons since "Word"
A L : 2 6 :000(063) [0071] XXVI. The **Distinction** of Foods
A L : 2 6 :001(063) [0071] in the churches that **distinctions** among foods and similar
A L : 2 6 :006(065) [0071] and righteousness by **distinctions** among foods and
A P : 0 1 :001(100) [0103] are nevertheless three **distinct** and coeternal persons of
A P : 0 4 :019(109) [0125] When they make up a **distinction** between merit of
A P : 0 4 :183(132) [0173] this issue (namely, the **distinction** between the law and the
A P : 0 4 :230(139) [0183] the help of his Holy Spirit to make it clear and **distinct**.
A P : 0 4 :283(150) [0201] habit of the monks, the **distinctions** of foods, and similar
A P : 0 4 :312(155) [0207] If someone wants a **distinction** anyway, we say that the
A P : 0 4 :321(157) [0209] This very **distinction** — that men sometimes acquire the
A P : 0 4 :355(161) [0217] There will be **distinctions** in the glory of the saints.
A P : 1 0 :002(179) [0247] be a sensible writer, says **distinctly** that "the bread is not
A P : 1 2 :009(183) [0255] An academic **distinction** between these two motives is
A P : 1 2 :061(190) [0269] try to make a subtle **distinction** separating absolution

Continued ▶

AP :15 :043(221) [0327] all civil ordinances, the **distinction** between the kingdom
AP :16 :002(222) [0329] whole question of the **distinction** between Christ's
AP :18 :010(226) [0337] This **distinction** is not our invention but the clear teaching
AP :22 :009(237) [0359] Gabriel says that a **distinction** should be made between
AP :22 :013(238) [0361] withhold it to make a **distinction** of orders, this in itself
AP :22 :013(238) [0361] There are other **distinctions** of order between priest and
AP :22 :013(238) [0361] as to why they defend this **distinction** so zealously.
AP :24 :016(252) [0389] that he is very fond of **distinctions** because without them
AP :24 :016(252) [0389] the person making the **distinctions** to cut the members at
AP :24 :017(252) [0389] make a proper **distinction** between sacrament and
AP :24 :020(252) [0389] many proofs for this **distinction** found in the Epistle to
AP :27 :026(273) [0429] does not counsel **distinctions** among clothes or foods, nor
AP :28 :019(284) [0449] it to these trifles, **distinction** of foods and clothing and
S1 :01 :000(291) [0461] and Holy Spirit, three **distinct** persons in one divine
S3 :11 :002(314) [0499] of a woman or abolish **distinctions** of sex altogether, so
TR :00 :033(325) [0513] of Boniface VIII, **Distinction** 22 of the chapter "Omnes,"
TR :00 :063(331) [0523] teaches that the **distinction** between the grades of bishop
TR :00 :064(331) [0523] one thing made a **distinction** between bishops and
TR :00 :065(331) [0523] But since the **distinction** between bishop and pastor is not
LC :01 :105(379) [0611] has given the special **distinction**, above all estates that are
LC :01 :108(380) [0611] must be this sort of inequality and proper **distinctions**.
LC :04 :017(438) [0735] Note the **distinction**, then: Baptism is a very different
LC :05 :058(453) [0767] For this reason we must make a **distinction** among men.
EP :RN :007(465) [0779] In this way the **distinction** between the Holy Scripture of
EP :01 :001(466) [0779] and without any **distinction**, original sin is man's
EP :01 :001(466) [0779] Or if there is a **distinction**, even after the Fall, between
EP :01 :002(466) [0779] confess that there is a **distinction** between man's nature
EP :01 :002(466) [0779] The **distinction** between our nature and original sin is as
EP :01 :003(466) [0779] we must preserve this **distinction** most diligently, because
EP :01 :003(466) [0779] view that admits no **distinction** between our corrupted
EP :01 :007(467) [0781] clearly set forth the **distinction** between the corrupted
EP :01 :019(468) [0783] and without any **distinction** corrupted man's substance,
EP :01 :019(468) [0783] and essence, so that no **distinction** should be made, even
EP :01 :020(468) [0783] to identify without any **distinction** man's nature, person,
EP :01 :024(469) [0785] they clearly show the **distinction** between the essence of a
EP :01 :025(469) [0785] forth very clearly the **distinction** between God's work and
EP :05 :002(478) [0801] and confess that the **distinction** between law and Gospel
EP :06 :005(480) [0807] 4. Concerning the **distinction** between works of the law
EP :11 :002(494) [0831] 1. To start with, the **distinction** between the
EP :12 :029(500) [0843] and Holy Spirit are three **distinct** persons, so each person
EP :12 :029(500) [0843] so each person has its **distinct** divine essence, separate
SD :RN :009(505) [0855] asserts by way of **distinction** that the Word of God is and
SD :RN :015(506) [0857] all times make a sharp **distinction** between needless and
SD :RN :016(507) [0857] be established the most **distinctly** and clearly and may be
SD :RN :019(507) [0857] clearly, and **distinctly** in these theses and antitheses,
SD :01 :002(509) [0859] we must preserve the **distinction** between the nature and
SD :01 :033(514) [0869] one must maintain a **distinction** between (a) our nature as
SD :01 :033(514) [0869] discuss, and believe these two as **distinct** from each other.
SD :01 :034(514) [0869] constrain and compel us to maintain such a **distinction**.
SD :01 :048(517) [0875] there is allegedly no **distinction** whatever between our
SD :01 :048(517) [0875] we must maintain a **distinction** between the nature or
SD :01 :051(517) [0875] to explain carefully and **distinctly** all equivocal terms,
SD :01 :061(519) [0879] only to set forth the **distinction** between God's
SD :02 :002(520) [0881] and viewed as being in four **distinct** and dissimilar states.
SD :03 :042(546) [0931] This correct **distinction** explains usefully and well the
SD :04 :016(554) [0943] is necessary to keep a **distinction** in mind, namely, that
SD :04 :019(554) [0945] must be given to the **distinction** which Paul makes when
SD :05 :001(558) [0951] The **distinction** between law and Gospel is an especially
SD :05 :001(558) [0951] therefore observe this **distinction** with particular diligence
SD :05 :005(559) [0953] apart from the strict **distinction** of law and Gospel, it is
SD :05 :015(561) [0957] side, but in proper order and with the correct **distinction**.
SD :05 :022(562) [0959] diligently urged this **distinction** in nearly all his writings
SD :05 :023(562) [0959] by side in the church of God with the proper **distinction**.
SD :05 :024(562) [0961] world, but with the due **distinction**, so that in the ministry
SD :05 :026(563) [0961] This **distinction** between the law and the Gospel is
SD :05 :027(563) [0961] the true and proper **distinction** between law and Gospel,
SD :05 :027(563) [0961] strictly so called in **distinction** from the law, a
SD :06 :010(565) [0965] necessary to set forth **distinctly** what the Gospel does,
SD :06 :015(566) [0967] to maintain the strict **distinction** between the works of the
SD :06 :016(566) [0967] The **distinction** between works is due to the difference in
SD :07 :037(575) [0985] For as in Christ two **distinct** and untransformed natures
SD :07 :079(584) [1001] to be spoken or sung **distinctly** and clearly before the
SD :07 :123(590) [1015] the making of such a **distinction** among the unworthy
SD :08 :006(592) [1017] Son of God is a separate, **distinct**, and complete divine
SD :08 :007(592) [1017] person there are two **distinct** natures: the divine, which is
SD :08 :011(593) [1019] as to be or constitute a **distinct** person, but that the two
SD :08 :011(593) [1019] spite of the fact that two **distinct** natures, each with its
SD :08 :016(594) [1021] are separated and **distinct** from each other and that in
SD :08 :018(594) [1021] "mixture" in a good sense and with the right **distinction**.
SD :08 :036(598) [1027] place, since in Christ two **distinct** natures are and remain
SD :08 :037(598) [1027] On the contrary, it is **distinctly** explained according to
SD :08 :069(604) [1039] In this way no **distinction** would be made between Christ
SD :09 :001(610) [1051] hell are differentiated as **distinct** articles, and we simply
SD :11 :070(627) [1085] to all men without **distinction** that God wants all men
SD :12 :037(636) [1103] that, as there are three **distinct** persons, Father, Son, and
SD :12 :037(636) [1103] also each person has a **distinct** essence separate from the
SD :12 :037(636) [1103] Trinity, like any three **distinct** and essentially separate

Distinguish (24), Distinguishably (1), Distinguished (9), Distinguishes (9), Distinguishing (2)
PR :PR :024(013) [0021] can be recognized and **distinguished** from adulterated
AG :28 :018(083) [0085] Thus our teachers **distinguish** the two authorities and the
AL :28 :018(083) [0085] this way our teachers **distinguish** the functions of the two
AL :28 :020(084) [0087] authority must be **distinguished** from ecclesiastical
AP :04 :188(133) [0173] And we must **distinguish** between these, as Paul says (II
AP :04 :248(142) [0191] against us when he **distinguishes** between dead and living
AP :04 :321(157) [0209] the work does not **distinguish** between the two kinds of
AP :04 :344(160) [0217] there is nothing to **distinguish** those who are saved from
AP :04 :345(160) [0217] make hope sure and to **distinguish** between those who are
AP :04 :375(164) [0223] overly subtle here in **distinguishing** the righteousness of
AP :07 :014(170) [0231] Yet Paul **distinguishes** the church from the Old
AP :07 :017(171) [0231] kingdom of Christ, is **distinguished** from the kingdom of
AP :13 :006(212) [0311] Hence it is useful to **distinguish** these from the earlier
AP :13 :014(213) [0311] a sacrament, he should **distinguish** it from the preceding
AP :18 :009(226) [0337] we may profitably **distinguish** between civil righteousness
AP :21 :014(230) [0347] Even though they **distinguish** between mediators of
AP :21 :040(235) [0355] Nowhere do they **distinguish** between their teachings and
AP :24 :076(263) [0411] communicant, "Piety **distinguishes** between what is given
AP :27 :062(280) [0441] apparently wanted to **distinguish** them by certain marks
AP :28 :006(282) [0445] power to judge, define, **distinguish**, and establish what is
S2 :04 :014(301) [0475] of the pope is **distinguished** from that of the Holy
S3 :03 :036(309) [0489] spend our time weighing, **distinguishing**, differentiating.
S3 :08 :003(312) [0495] our day who wish to **distinguish** sharply between the
TR :00 :073(332) [0525] Jerome states) that **distinguishes** bishops from the rest of
SC :PR :013(339) [0535] learn to know how to **distinguish** between right and
LC :01 :105(379) [0611] Thus he **distinguishes** father and mother above all other
LC :02 :066(419) [0695] therefore, divide and **distinguish** us Christians from all
LC :03 :033(424) [0707] thing and may clearly **distinguish** between vain babbling
LC :04 :035(441) [0741] as was said, you must **distinguish** Christ's Baptism quite
LC :05 :010(448) [0755] I maintain, which **distinguishes** it from mere bread and
EP :03 :008(474) [0793] renovation of man and **distinguish** it from justification by
SD :RN :005(504) [0851] This symbol **distinguishes** our reformed churches from
SD :RN :016(507) [0857] clearly and may be **distinguished** from all error, and
SD :01 :003(509) [0861] when we carefully **distinguish** his work and creation in
SD :01 :029(513) [0867] corrupted to be **distinguished** from each other in such a
SD :01 :042(515) [0871] reason and in order to **distinguish** God's creature and
SD :01 :044(516) [0873] identical with but must be **distinguished** from each other.
SD :01 :054(518) [0877] self-subsistent essence and can be **distinguished** from it).
SD :03 :042(547) [0931] a true living faith and **distinguish** it from a simulated and
SD :05 :008(559) [0953] sins (Luke 24:46) are **distinguished** from one another, the
SD :07 :021(573) [0979] this sacrament and so **distinguishes** it that it is not mere
SD :08 :019(594) [1021] and ceases to be **distinguishably** either water or honey
SD :10 :008(612) [1055] that we should duly **distinguish** between the two, as it is
SD :11 :052(625) [1079] however, carefully **distinguish** between what God has
SD :11 :079(629) [1089] Paul very carefully **distinguishes** between the work of

Distort (2), Distorted (4), Distortion (3)
AP :02 :001(100) [0105] misinterpret and **distort** a statement that has nothing
AP :04 :286(150) [0201] select the passages on works, and even **distort** these.
AP :04 :288(151) [0203] this way they have also **distorted** the sacraments,
AP :12 :091(195) [0279] our opponents quote in a **distorted** form to obscure faith.
AP :12 :131(202) [0291] is merely a trick and a **distortion** of the Scriptures to suit
AP :12 :135(203) [0293] So it is clearly a wicked **distortion** to apply these passages
AP :12 :149(205) [0299] It is a foolish **distortion** to apply the term "punishments"
AP :24 :014(251) [0389] which they have **distorted**, and to do this we must first set
LC :01 :260(400) [0655] rights to be thwarted or **distorted** but should promote and

Distracted (1)
AP :23 :040(245) [0375] and serving and is not so **distracted** by household chores.

Distress (9), Distressed (2)
PR :PR :009(006) [0011] we found, not without **distress** on our part, that little
AG :23 :003(051) [0061] this step by the great **distress** of their consciences,
AP :12 :151(206) [0299] Isaiah says, "The **distress** in which they cry out is thy
SC :05 :029(351) [0555] heavily burdened or who are **distressed** and sorely tried.
LC :PR :006(359) [0569] both pastors and preachers to suffer **distress** and hunger.
LC :01 :004(365) [0581] you suffer misfortune and **distress**, come and cling to me.
LC :01 :028(368) [0587] but good, especially in **distress** and want, and renounces
LC :02 :023(413) [0683] When we escape **distress** or danger, we should recognize
LC :03 :026(424) [0705] must feel our need, the **distress** that impels and drives us
LC :05 :084(456) [0773] you into misery and **distress** when you least expect it!
SD :07 :071(582) [0997] of Christ, of which the **distressed** father of weak faith

Distribute (7), Distributed (26), Distributes (3), Distribution (5), Distributive (1)
AG :10 :001(034) [0047] of bread and wine and are there **distributed** and received.
AG :22 :006(050) [0061] the sacrament **distributed** the blood of Christ to the
AG :28 :005(081) [0085] sins, and to administer and **distribute** the sacraments.
AL :10 :001(034) [0047] truly present and are **distributed** to those who eat in the
AL :22 :006(050) [0061] the Eucharist and **distribute** the blood of Christ to the
AP :04 :192(133) [0175] the devil, just as the **distribution** of alms by the
AP :04 :308(155) [0207] superior is obviously a kind of **distributive** righteousness.
AP :22 :004(236) [0359] serve the Eucharist and **distribute** the blood of the Lord
AP :24 :086(265) [0413] to be consecrated, the rest was **distributed** to the poor.
AP :27 :046(277) [0435] The **distribution**, control, and possession of property are
S3 :03 :024(307) [0485] The indulgences were **distributed** among the cardinals and
LC :05 :039(451) [0761] daily administered and **distributed** among Christians, may
EP :07 :002(481) [0809] present if they are **distributed** with the bread and the wine
EP :07 :003(482) [0809] and wine are present, **distributed**, and received orally.
EP :07 :006(482) [0809] present and are truly **distributed** and received with the
EP :07 :031(485) [0815] of the absent body and blood of Christ are **distributed**.
EP :12 :024(500) [0843] and by which Christ **distributes** his body and blood.
SD :07 :004(569) [0973] signs of the absent body of Christ, are therein **distributed**.
SD :07 :009(570) [0975] wine and that they are **distributed** and received," and it
SD :07 :014(571) [0977] are truly and essentially present, **distributed**, and received.
SD :07 :016(572) [0977] of the minister who **distributes** the sacrament or of him
SD :07 :016(572) [0977] of Christ are truly **distributed** to the unworthy, too, and
SD :07 :018(572) [0979] with all his benefits, is **distributed** with the bread in
SD :07 :032(574) [0983] though the priests who **distribute** them or those who
SD :07 :054(579) [0991] essential presence and **distribution** of the body and blood
SD :07 :054(579) [0991] himself broke and **distributed**, but also that which we
SD :07 :058(580) [0993] which we break is the **distributed** body of Christ, or the
SD :07 :058(580) [0993] body of Christ **distributed** among those who receive the
SD :07 :075(583) [0999] Christ are truly present, **distributed**, and received by the
SD :07 :075(583) [0999] the bread and cup and **distribute** the blessed bread and
SD :07 :077(583) [0999] it about that we do not **distribute** and receive ordinary
SD :07 :077(583) [0999] blood that are daily **distributed** through our ministry and
SD :07 :082(584) [1001] and blood of Christ are **distributed** to us to eat and to
SD :07 :083(584) [1001] blessed bread is not **distributed**, received, and eaten but is
SD :07 :084(584) [1001] and wine, consecrate it, **distribute** it, receive it, eat and
SD :07 :084(584) [1001] of bread, or of the **distribution** and reception, before our
SD :07 :086(584) [1003] of institution, the **distribution** and reception, or the oral
SD :07 :087(585) [1003] Mass the bread is not **distributed** but is offered up, or
SD :07 :116(589) [1013] and blood of Christ, **distributed** to us, but through the
SD :07 :117(589) [1013] in the Supper there is **distributed** to faith only the virtue,
SD :11 :016(619) [1069] be offered, given, and **distributed** to us through his Word
SD :12 :032(635) [1101] through which Christ **distributes** his body and blood.

Distrust (3), Distrusts (1)
A P : 0 2 :029(104) [0113] of God, unbelief, **distrust**, contempt, and hate of God.
A P : 0 4 :170(130) [0169] The flesh **distrusts** God and trusts in temporal things; in
A P : 0 4 :309(155) [0207] says (Rom. 4:20), "No **distrust** made him waver
A P : 1 2 :167(209) [0305] consumed, that is, that **distrust** of God and similar

Disturb (2), Disturbance (2), Disturbances (2), Disturbed (1), Disturbing (2)
P R : P R :004(003) [0007] and troublesome **disturbances** took place in our beloved
A G : 2 3 :006(052) [0061] torment and frightful **disturbance** of conscience many
A L : 2 4 :016(057) [0067] church, although the **disturbance** was brought about by
A P : 1 2 :084(194) [0277] It ought not **disturb** devout minds if our opponents twist
A P : 1 6 :006(223) [0331] questions were very **disturbing** to Origen, Nazianzus, and
T R : 0 0 :034(325) [0513] and afterwards great **disturbances** to arise in Europe.
L C : 0 1 :037(369) [0591] when God refrains from **disturbing** their security, that he
S D : R N :015(507) [0857] never be allowed to **disturb** the church) and necessary
S D : 0 5 :001(558) [0951] merit of Christ and rob **disturbed** consciences of the

Disunited (1), Disunity (1)
S D : 1 1 :001(616) [1063] as far as we can, **disunity** and schism in this article among
S D : 1 2 :003(633) [1095] Confession, but are so **disunited** that they themselves no

Disuse (5)
A G : 1 1 :001(034) [0047] should be retained and not allowed to fall into **disuse**.
A G : 2 8 :067(092) [0093] of the regulations fall into **disuse** from day to day even
A G : 2 8 :074(094) [0093] passing of time fallen into **disuse** and are not obligatory,
S 3 : 0 8 :001(312) [0493] be allowed to fall into **disuse** in the church, especially for
E P : 1 0 :002(493) [0829] that have fallen into **disuse** and that in themselves are

Diversity (1)
A L : 2 6 :044(070) [0075] in Dist. 12 that such **diversity** does not violate the unity

Divert (1), Diverted (2)
P R : P R :004(004) [0009] their own errors, to **divert** poor, erring consciences from
A P : 0 4 :085(119) [0147] not let themselves be **diverted** from this declaration, that
S D : 0 3 :029(544) [0925] so that we may not be **diverted** (as Satan would very

Divide (3), Divided (17), Divider (2), Dividing (1)
A G : 2 2 :007(050) [0061] himself ordered that the sacrament was not to be **divided**.
A G : 2 8 :015(083) [0085] and again, "Who made me a judge or **divider** over you?"
A L : 2 2 :007(050) [0061] commanded that the sacrament should not be **divided**.
A L : 2 8 :015(083) [0085] and again, "Who made me a judge or **divider** over you?"
A P : 0 4 :005(108) [0121] All Scripture should be **divided** into these two chief
A P : 0 4 :312(155) [0207] these feelings cannot be **divided** in fact the way they are in
S 2 : 0 2 :010(294) [0465] are and remain eternally **divided** and opposed the one to
S 3 : 0 3 :012(305) [0481] repentance the sophists **divided** into three parts —
L C : 0 2 :005(411) [0679] place, the Creed used to be **divided** into twelve articles.
L C : 0 2 :012(412) [0681] be treated more fully and **divided** into as many parts as
L C : 0 2 :031(414) [0687] day, he will completely **divide** and separate us from the
L C : 0 2 :066(419) [0695] of the Creed, therefore, **divide** and distinguish us
E P : 0 5 :002(478) [0801] admonition, the Word of God may be **divided** rightly.
E P : 0 8 :018(489) [0823] and confession do not **divide** the person of Christ, as
E P : 0 8 :018(489) [0823] and thus he actually **divided** the person, as Luther
S D : 0 5 :001(558) [0951] of God may be rightly **divided** and the writings of the
S D : 0 8 :043(599) [1029] But if the works are **divided** and separated, the person
S D : 0 8 :043(599) [1029] neither confounding the natures nor **dividing** the person."
S D : 0 8 :071(605) [1041] majesty, separated or **divided** from the nature and essence
S D : 0 8 :082(607) [1045] the person is already **divided** and I could at once say
S D : 0 8 :083(607) [1045] another and thus had **divided** the person, even though
S D : 0 8 :084(607) [1045] let themselves be separated and **divided** from each other.
S D : 1 2 :027(635) [1101] But they are **divided** into many parties among

Divine (313)
P R : P R :002(003) [0007] was compiled out of the **divine**, prophetic, and apostolic
P R : P R :003(003) [0007] is based solidly on the **divine** Scriptures, and that is also
P R : P R :004(004) [0007] how the adversaries of **divine** truth took occasion to
P R : P R :006(004) [0009] from the right course of **divine** truth which they had once
P R : P R :008(005) [0009] unalterable truth of the **divine** Word, in order thereby to
P R : P R :008(005) [0009] Rather, with **divine** assistance, it was our intention to
P R : P R :008(005) [0011] the truth of the **divine** Word that alone gives salvation, to
P R : P R :010(006) [0011] false doctrine, and clearly to confess the **divine** truth.
P R : P R :011(006) [0011] without violation of **divine** truth, and in this way the
P R : P R :021(011) [0019] and the churches): This **divine** majesty is not ascribed to
P R : P R :021(011) [0019] were being taught that the **divine** and human natures,
P R : P R :021(011) [0019] is equalized with the **divine** nature and is thus negated.
P R : P R :022(011) [0019] the truth of the **divine** Word, and far less do we mean
P R : P R :022(012) [0019] the infallible truth of the **divine** Word and unite with us
P R : P R :024(012) [0021] faith on the basis of the **divine**, prophetic, and apostolic
P R : P R :024(013) [0023] that we have by **divine** precept, on account of the office
P R : P R :024(013) [0023] or to put the light of **divine** truth under a basket or a
P R : P R :024(013) [0023] have an upright love for **divine** truth and for Christian,
P R : P R :025(013) [0023] or formulation, from the **divine** truth that our pious
A G : P R :011(026) [0041] may be done according to **divine** truth we invoke
A G : 0 1 :002(027) [0043] Nicaea, that there is one **divine** essence, which is called
A G : 0 1 :002(027) [0043] three persons in this one **divine** essence, equal in power
A G : 0 1 :003(027) [0043] All three are one **divine** essence, eternal, without division,
A G : 0 3 :002(029) [0045] and that the two natures, **divine** and human, are so
A G : 0 7 :002(032) [0047] be administered in accordance with the **divine** Word.
A G : 2 1 :003(047) [0057] the highest form of **divine** service is sincerely to seek and
A G : 0 0 :001(048) [0059] without any solid basis of **divine** command or Scripture.
A G : 2 3 :013(053) [0063] not only contrary to all **divine**, natural, and civil law, but
A G : 2 3 :021(055) [0063] done contrary not only to **divine** law but also to canon
A G : 2 7 :024(074) [0079] to cancel an obligation which is derived from **divine** law.
A G : 2 8 :017(083) [0085] are not worldly but have **divine** power to destroy
A G : 2 8 :019(083) [0087] it not as bishops by **divine** right, but by human, imperial
A G : 2 8 :021(084) [0087] According to **divine** right, therefore, it is the office of the
A G : 2 8 :028(085) [0087] something contrary to the **divine** Holy Scriptures.
A G : 2 8 :043(088) [0089] are clear passages of **divine** Scripture which forbid the
A G : 2 8 :049(089) [0091] consciences, why does the **divine** Scripture so frequently
A G : 2 8 :063(092) [0093] must not be kept as of **divine** obligation, it must
A G : 2 8 :063(092) [0093] be kept as almost of **divine** obligation, and they prescribe
A G : 0 0 :007(096) [0095] information on the basis of the **divine** Holy Scripture.
A L : 0 1 :001(027) [0043] the unity of the **divine** essence and concerning the three
A L : 0 1 :002(027) [0043] That is to say, there is one **divine** essence, which is called
A L : 0 3 :002(029) [0045] So there are two natures, **divine** and human, inseparably
A L : 2 3 :013(053) [0063] was contrary to all laws, **divine** and human, and contrary
A L : 2 4 :020(058) [0067] of the world nothing of **divine** institution seems ever to
A L : 2 7 :024(074) [0079] an obligation which is plainly derived from **divine** law.
A L : 2 8 :017(083) [0085] are not worldly but have **divine** power to destroy
A L : 2 8 :021(084) [0087] Gospel (or, as they say, by **divine** right) no jurisdiction
A L : 2 8 :022(084) [0087] are therefore bound by **divine** law to be obedient to the
A L : 2 8 :063(092) [0093] Day is not *indeed of* **divine** obligation but is *as it were* of
A L : 2 8 :063(092) [0093] but is *as it were* of **divine** obligation, and they prescribe
A P : 0 1 :001(100) [0103] there is one undivided **divine** essence, and that there are
A P : 0 1 :001(100) [0103] persons of the same **divine** essence, Father, Son, and
A P : 0 4 :130(125) [0157] to the essence of the **divine** law, are impossible without
A P : 0 4 :189(133) [0175] are nevertheless holy and **divine** works, sacrifices, and the
A P : 0 4 :250(143) [0191] it a human power, but a **divine** power that makes us alive
A P : 0 4 :278(149) [0199] that alms merit many **divine** blessings, lighten our
A P : 0 4 :339(159) [0215] believed everything, do not trust in the **divine** promise."
A P : 0 4 :339(159) [0215] works; in the second, trust is a trust in the **divine** promise.
A P : 0 7 :023(172) [0235] men from any laws, **divine**, canonical, or civil, as he
A P : 0 7 :041(176) [0241] If they were of **divine** right, it was unlawful for men to
A P : 0 7 :045(177) [0243] clothing, and similar matters without **divine** command.
A P : 0 7 :046(177) [0243] of Christ's Supper, which is not human but **divine**?
A P : 1 1 :006(181) [0251] are discussing what is necessary according to **divine** law.
A P : 1 1 :006(181) [0251] ought rather show from **divine** law that the enumeration
A P : 1 1 :008(181) [0251] the enumeration of sins is not required by **divine** law.
A P : 1 1 :010(182) [0253] of sins was necessary by **divine** law and yet experienced
A P : 1 2 :011(184) [0255] they imagine that this enumeration is a **divine** command.
A P : 1 2 :012(184) [0255] the pretext that it is by **divine** right, they speak very
A P : 1 2 :012(184) [0255] coldly about absolution, which really is by **divine** right.
A P : 1 2 :014(184) [0257] or similar observances that do not have **divine** command.
A P : 1 2 :023(185) [0257] our opponents command it, is necessary by **divine** right.
A P : 1 2 :088(195) [0277] doubts, he makes the **divine** promise a lie, as John says.
A P : 1 2 :094(196) [0281] the authority of the **divine** promises ought to be sufficient
A P : 1 2 :099(197) [0281] of the keys proclaims to individuals by **divine** authority.
A P : 1 2 :102(197) [0281] that we do not believe that it is necessary by **divine** right.
A P : 1 2 :110(198) [0285] confession is necessary by **divine** right, they will be
A P : 1 2 :116(199) [0285] are not necessary by **divine** law for the forgiveness of
A P : 1 2 :116(199) [0287] were not necessary by **divine** law for the forgiveness of
A P : 1 2 :117(199) [0287] they say that it is done to placate the **divine** displeasure.
A P : 1 2 :118(199) [0287] because it is fitting for **divine** righteousness to punish sin,
A P : 1 2 :118(200) [0287] who are in mortal sin could placate the **divine** displeasure.
A P : 1 2 :147(205) [0297] are not necessary by **divine** law to remit either guilt or
A P : 1 2 :175(210) [0307] necessity commanded by **divine** law, for human authority
A P : 1 2 :175(210) [0307] law, for human authority cannot abrogate **divine** law.
A P : 1 6 :001(222) [0329] God's good creatures and **divine** ordinances in which a
A P : 1 6 :005(223) [0331] us to obey them as **divine** ordinances not only from fear
A P : 2 1 :019(231) [0347] be bestowed on them by **divine** imputation, so that
A P : 2 1 :044(236) [0357] maintain and propagate **divine** things on earth, that is,
A P : 2 2 :001(236) [0357] By **divine** authority and not by human authority, as we
A P : 2 2 :005(236) [0359] decide what he should believe about a **divine** ordinance.
A P : 2 3 :001(239) [0363] and false pretext of **divine** authority for their audacious
A P : 2 3 :003(239) [0363] In opposition to **divine** law, the law of the nations, and
A P : 2 3 :006(240) [0365] because it clashes with **divine** and natural law and
A P : 2 3 :007(240) [0365] love of one sex for the other is truly a **divine** ordinance.
A P : 2 3 :009(240) [0367] because this creation or **divine** ordinance in man is a
A P : 2 3 :012(241) [0367] Natural right is really **divine** right, because it is an
A P : 2 3 :029(243) [0371] Christ calls marriage a **divine** union when he says in
A P : 2 3 :060(247) [0379] It conflicts with **divine** and natural law; it disagrees even
A P : 2 3 :063(248) [0381] They dare to claim **divine** revelation for the law of
A P : 2 7 :033(274) [0431] even by the works of the **divine** law, but must seek the
A P : 2 7 :044(277) [0435] men, and doing so under the pretext of the **divine** name.
S 1 : 0 1 :000(291) [0461] treats the sublime articles of the **divine** majesty, namely:
S 1 : 0 1 :000(291) [0461] distinct persons in one **divine** essence and nature, are one
S 2 : 0 4 :001(298) [0471] of all Christendom by **divine** right or according to God's
S 2 : 0 4 :007(299) [0473] the head of the church by **divine** right or by God's
S 2 : 0 4 :008(299) [0473] of men rather than on a **divine** command, he would very
S 2 : 0 4 :013(300) [0475] to be the head of the Christian church by **divine** right.
S 3 : 0 5 :003(311) [0493] the assistance of the **divine** will, as if the washing takes
S 3 : 1 1 :001(314) [0499] marriage and burden the **divine** estate of priests with
T R : 0 0 :001(320) [0503] the claim that he is by **divine** right above all bishops and
T R : 0 0 :002(320) [0503] Then he adds that by **divine** right he possesses both
T R : 0 0 :005(320) [0503] the Roman bishop is above all bishops by **divine** right.
T R : 0 0 :006(320) [0505] holds that his power is by **divine** right and is even to be
T R : 0 0 :007(320) [0505] Roman bishop is not by **divine** right above all other
T R : 0 0 :010(321) [0505] his superior if Peter had been his superior by **divine** right.
T R : 0 0 :012(322) [0507] had his superiority by **divine** right, it would not have been
T R : 0 0 :014(322) [0507] practice, according to **divine** tradition and apostolic
T R : 0 0 :015(322) [0509] calls this custom a **divine** tradition and an apostolic
T R : 0 0 :020(323) [0509] over the whole church by **divine** right when the church
T R : 0 0 :033(325) [0513] claim that the pope is by **divine** right lord of the
T R : 0 0 :036(326) [0515] that such dominion belongs to the pope by **divine** right.
T R : 0 0 :038(326) [0515] and superiority by **divine** right, obedience would still not
T R : 0 0 :038(326) [0515] the supreme pontifex by **divine** right; nevertheless,
T R : 0 0 :039(327) [0515] the Gospel and will arrogate to himself **divine** authority.
T R : 0 0 :040(327) [0515] pope arrogates to himself a threefold **divine** authority.
T R : 0 0 :040(327) [0517] to have his own doctrine and worship observed as **divine**.
T R : 0 0 :042(328) [0517] But **divine** authority commands us all not to be associated
T R : 0 0 :057(330) [0521] possess the primacy by **divine** right, he should not be
T R : 0 0 :061(330) [0521] this power belongs by **divine** right to all who preside over
T R : 0 0 :065(331) [0523] and pastor is not by **divine** right, it is manifest that
T R : 0 0 :065(331) [0523] by a pastor in his own church is valid by **divine** right.
T R : 0 0 :072(332) [0525] the churches are by **divine** right compelled to ordain
T R : 0 0 :077(333) [0527] By **divine** right temporal magistrates are compelled to
S C : 0 2 :002(345) [0543] of his pure, fatherly, and **divine** goodness and mercy,
L C : 0 1 :040(370) [0591] confidence since the **divine** Majesty comes to us with so
L C : 0 1 :053(371) [0595] it briefly, misuse of the **divine** name occurs most
L C : 0 1 :077(375) [0603] averted the misuse of the **divine** name and taught that its
L C : 0 1 :112(380) [0613] as God's command or as a holy, **divine** word and precept.
L C : 0 1 :120(381) [0615] have a sure text and a **divine** testimony that God has
L C : 0 1 :125(382) [0617] is highly pleasing to the **divine** Majesty and all the angels,
L C : 0 1 :171(388) [0629] is the command of the **divine** Majesty, who will solemnly
L C : 0 1 :174(388) [0629] duty, on pain of losing **divine** grace, to bring up his
L C : 0 1 :180(389) [0631] civil government, that is, **divine** and paternal authority
L C : 0 1 :198(392) [0637] are the true, holy, and **divine** works in which he rejoices

Continued ▶

LC : 01 :207(393) [0639] maintain, and cherish it as a **divine** and blessed estate.
LC : 01 :311(407) [0669] a summary of **divine** teaching on what we are to do to
LC : 03 :041(425) [0709] the worst profanation and dishonor of the **divine** name.
LC : 03 :042(425) [0709] men grossly misuse the **divine** name as a cloak for their
LC : 04 :006(437) [0733] then, that Baptism is of **divine** origin, not something
LC : 04 :014(438) [0735] It is nothing else than a **divine** water, not that the water in
LC : 04 :017(438) [0737] a natural water, but a **divine**, heavenly, holy, and blessed
LC : 04 :018(438) [0737] a sacrament, that is, a holy, **divine** thing and sign.
LC : 04 :021(439) [0737] visibly, and that the **divine** glory and majesty were
LC : 04 :027(440) [0739] it is well described as a **divine**, blessed, fruitful, and
LC : 04 :033(440) [0741] worthy to receive the salutary, **divine** water profitably.
LC : 04 :034(440) [0741] no use, although in itself it is an infinite, **divine** treasure.
LC : 05 :011(448) [0755] or emperor, but of the **divine** Majesty at whose feet every
LC : 05 :012(448) [0755] have less wisdom than the **divine** Majesty has in his little
LC : 06 :014(458) [0000] Thus by **divine** ordinance Christ himself has entrusted
EP : 02 :018(472) [0791] referring to the action of **divine** grace in kindling new
EP : 03 :001(472) [0791] and man since in him the **divine** and human natures are
EP : 03 :003(473) [0793] neither according to the **divine** nature alone nor
EP : 03 :013(474) [0795] our righteousness only according to the **divine** nature, etc.
EP : 03 :016(475) [0795] obedience, but also to his **divine** nature (in so far as it
EP : 03 :018(475) [0795] not God himself but only **divine** gifts dwell in believers.
EP : 05 :003(478) [0801] speaking, the law is a **divine** doctrine which teaches what
EP : 08 :002(487) [0817] person of Christ, do the **divine** and human natures,
EP : 08 :003(487) [0817] asserted that in Christ the **divine** and human natures are
EP : 08 :005(487) [0819] 1. That the **divine** and the human natures are personally
EP : 08 :006(487) [0819] and confess that the **divine** and the human nature are not
EP : 08 :007(487) [0819] 3. The properties of the **divine** nature are omnipotence,
EP : 08 :008(487) [0819] which never become the properties of the **divine** nature.
EP : 08 :009(488) [0819] God and everything **divine** that is said or believed about
EP : 08 :010(488) [0819] not be the case if the **divine** and human natures did not
EP : 08 :011(488) [0821] shared only the name of God with the **divine** nature?
EP : 08 :014(488) [0821] into the unity of his **divine** person and made his own, so
EP : 08 :016(489) [0821] use, revelation, and manifestation of his **divine** majesty.
EP : 08 :021(490) [0823] 2. That the **divine** and human natures are mingled into
EP : 08 :027(490) [0823] infinite essence, like the **divine** nature; that it is
EP : 08 :027(490) [0823] the same manner as the **divine** nature, because this
EP : 08 :028(490) [0825] has become equal to, the **divine** nature in its substance
EP : 08 :029(490) [0825] (something that is not true of the **divine** nature either).
EP : 08 :034(491) [0825] of omnipotence and other properties of the **divine** nature.
EP : 08 :039(491) [0827] Christ according to the **divine** nature, as though in the
EP : 08 :039(491) [0827] on the firm basis of the **divine** Word and our simple
EP : 10 :003(493) [0829] in and for themselves no **divine** worship or even a part of
EP : 10 :009(494) [0831] regarded as in themselves **divine** worship or a part of it.
EP : 11 :008(495) [0833] of the Holy Spirit and **divine** assistance for steadfastness
EP : 12 :021(499) [0841] his flesh received all the **divine** properties in such a way
EP : 12 :021(499) [0841] Christ possess only one **divine** essence, property, will, and
EP : 12 :028(500) [0843] natural God, of one **divine** essence with God the Father
EP : 12 :028(500) [0843] is merely adorned with **divine** majesty and is inferior to
EP : 12 :029(500) [0843] is not only one eternal, **divine** essence, belonging to the
EP : 12 :029(500) [0843] person has its distinct **divine** essence, separate from the
SD : RN :017(507) [0857] certain and solid basis of the holy and **divine** Scriptures.
SD : RN :019(507) [0857] so that the foundation of **divine** truth might be made
SD : 01 :011(510) [0863] lack of good in spiritual, **divine** things, but that at the
SD : 01 :011(510) [0863] against God, especially in **divine** and spiritual matters.
SD : 01 :023(512) [0865] belongs to spiritual and **divine** matters, or that the
SD : 01 :025(512) [0867] good thing in spiritual, **divine** matters, not even the least
SD : 02 :005(521) [0881] is so corrupted that in **divine** things, concerning our
SD : 02 :007(521) [0883] that in spiritual and **divine** things the intellect, heart, and
SD : 02 :010(522) [0885] in spiritual and **divine** things (Eph. 5:8; Acts 26:18).
SD : 02 :015(523) [0885] petitions of the saints for **divine** instruction, illumination,
SD : 02 :015(523) [0887] might rightly comprehend and learn the **divine** doctrine.
SD : 02 :017(523) [0887] of God testifies that in **divine** matters the intellect, heart,
SD : 02 :019(524) [0889] and meditating upon the **divine** Word, or that in outward
SD : 02 :020(525) [0889] In spiritual and **divine** things, however, which concern the
SD : 02 :023(525) [0889] in such a way that by **divine** grace it can be converted to
SD : 02 :025(526) [0891] and alone to the **divine** operation and the Holy Spirit, as
SD : 02 :050(530) [0901] proclamation of his **divine**, eternal law and the wonderful
SD : 02 :059(532) [0905] however, an intellect in **divine** things or a volition that
SD : 02 :061(533) [0905] doing something good and wholesome in **divine** matters.
SD : 02 :061(533) [0905] to do something good in **divine** matters, and he cannot
SD : 02 :061(533) [0905] and he cannot have a mode of acting in **divine** matters.
SD : 02 :066(534) [0907] means be conceded without detriment to the **divine** truth.
SD : 02 :080(536) [0911] without hearing the **divine** Word and without the use of
SD : 02 :089(538) [0915] and the hearing of the **divine** Word, nor did he mean that
SD : 03 :004(540) [0917] not according to the **divine** nature alone or according to
SD : 03 :055(549) [0935] rests neither upon his **divine** nature nor upon his human
SD : 03 :056(549) [0935] had not become man, the **divine** nature alone could not
SD : 03 :056(549) [0935] nature alone, without the **divine** nature, could render
SD : 03 :058(550) [0937] this reason neither the **divine** nor the human nature of
SD : 03 :060(550) [0937] before God only according to his **divine** nature;
SD : 03 :063(550) [0937] of Christ, but also to his **divine** nature in so far as it
SD : 04 :005(552) [0939] that, because of the **divine** order referred to above, new
SD : 04 :010(552) [0941] the Romans, "Faith is a **divine** work in us that transforms
SD : 04 :012(553) [0941] and knowledge of **divine** grace makes us joyous,
SD : 04 :032(556) [0947] true, immutable, and **divine** threats and earnest
SD : 05 :005(559) [0953] promises of the forgiveness of sins but also the **divine** law.
SD : 05 :017(561) [0957] speaking, the law is a **divine** doctrine which reveals the
SD : 07 :001(569) [0971] giving testimony to the **divine** truth by means of our
SD : 07 :004(569) [0973] is, only according to his **divine** nature, but not with his
SD : 07 :006(570) [0973] so only according to his **divine** nature and is not true of
SD : 07 :022(573) [0979] have less wisdom than the **divine** Majesty has in his little
SD : 07 :036(575) [0985] explain that the **divine** essence has not been transformed
SD : 07 :046(577) [0987] not only to reason and to **divine** and natural law but also
SD : 07 :101(587) [1007] one person with God, the **divine**, heavenly mode,
SD : 08 :006(592) [1017] distinct, and complete **divine** person and therefore has
SD : 08 :007(592) [1017] two distinct natures: the **divine**, which is from all
SD : 08 :009(593) [1019] essential properties of the **divine** nature, which
SD : 08 :010(593) [1019] which never will become properties of the **divine** nature.
SD : 08 :011(593) [1019] at the same time both the **divine** and the assumed human
SD : 08 :011(593) [1019] incarnation not only his **divine** nature but also his
SD : 08 :013(594) [1019] man and when the **divine** and human nature were
SD : 08 :014(594) [1019] it, as if both natures, the **divine** and the human, are united
SD : 08 :016(594) [1021] he also held that the **divine** and human natures are
SD : 08 :017(594) [1021] in simple faith that the **divine** and human natures in the
SD : 08 :019(595) [1021] But the union of the **divine** and human natures in the
SD : 08 :019(595) [1021] and union between the **divine** and the human nature in
SD : 08 :020(595) [1021] truly died, although the **divine** nature can neither suffer
SD : 08 :023(595) [1023] and communion of the **divine** and human natures in
SD : 08 :024(595) [1023] He demonstrated his **divine** majesty even in his mother's
SD : 08 :025(596) [1023] and manifested his **divine** majesty according to his good
SD : 08 :025(596) [1023] personally united with the **divine** nature and had
SD : 08 :026(596) [1023] exercise and use of the **divine** majesty according to the
SD : 08 :029(597) [1025] in this manner with the **divine** nature and installed in the
SD : 08 :029(597) [1025] in the exercise of the **divine**, omnipotent majesty and
SD : 08 :030(597) [1025] In him the **divine** and human natures are personally
SD : 08 :031(597) [1025] (that is, the fact that the **divine** and human natures are
SD : 08 :034(597) [1027] "become partakers of the **divine** nature" (II Pet. 1:4),
SD : 08 :034(597) [1027] of participation in the **divine** nature must that be of which
SD : 08 :043(599) [1029] to be two persons, one a **divine** and the other a human
SD : 08 :043(599) [1029] and completely excludes them from the **divine** nature.
SD : 08 :047(600) [1031] nature only, either the **divine** or the human, but according
SD : 08 :049(600) [1031] and properties of the **divine** nature in Christ through the
SD : 08 :049(600) [1031] incarnation, nor was the **divine** nature intrinsically
SD : 08 :051(600) [1031] personally united with the **divine** nature in Christ, the
SD : 08 :055(601) [1033] are not created gifts but **divine** and infinite qualities.
SD : 08 :056(601) [1035] not only according to the **divine** nature but also according
SD : 08 :057(602) [1035] not according to his **divine** nature (according to which he
SD : 08 :059(602) [1035] justification not only the **divine** nature in Christ but also
SD : 08 :061(602) [1035] namely, that such **divine** power, life, might, majesty, and
SD : 08 :061(602) [1035] own essence and all the **divine** properties from eternity to
SD : 08 :061(602) [1035] the Son according to the **divine** nature so that he is of one
SD : 08 :061(602) [1035] For only according to the **divine** nature is Christ equal
SD : 08 :061(603) [1037] Christ the way it is in his **divine** nature, that is, as an
SD : 08 :062(603) [1037] of the properties of the **divine** nature into the human
SD : 08 :062(603) [1037] itself and apart from the **divine** essence, nor in such a way
SD : 08 :064(603) [1039] manifests and exercises his **divine** power, glory, and
SD : 08 :065(604) [1039] of the humiliation the **divine** majesty was concealed and
SD : 08 :066(604) [1039] in Christ only a single **divine** omnipotence, power,
SD : 08 :066(604) [1039] glory, which is the property of the **divine** nature alone.
SD : 08 :067(604) [1039] exalted either as if this **divine** majesty, which is the
SD : 08 :067(604) [1039] is the property of the **divine** nature of the Son of God, is
SD : 08 :067(604) [1039] Man only according to his **divine** nature, or as if this
SD : 08 :067(604) [1039] the human nature has no share in the **divine** majesty.
SD : 08 :071(605) [1041] a kind that thereby the **divine** nature is weakened or
SD : 08 :076(606) [1043] communion that the **divine** and human natures have with
SD : 08 :078(607) [1043] which both natures, the **divine** and the human, belong is
SD : 08 :081(607) [1045] manner, but according to the supernatural, **divine** manner.
SD : 08 :082(607) [1045] he is there as a natural **divine** person and is also naturally
SD : 08 :084(607) [1045] at one single place as a **divine** and human person, and if
SD : 08 :084(607) [1045] mere isolated God and a **divine** person without the
SD : 08 :089(609) [1047] been blended with the **divine** or has been transformed into
SD : 08 :091(609) [1049] has become equal to the **divine** nature in its substance and
SD : 08 :092(609) [1049] provide that through his **divine** omnipotence Christ can
SD : 08 :095(609) [1049] in deed and truth the **divine** power, might, wisdom,
SD : 10 :003(611) [1053] without prejudice to the **divine** truth, even as far as things
SD : 10 :015(613) [1057] increased and be put as **divine** worship not only on a par
SD : 10 :023(615) [1061] But **divine** authority commands us all not be be
SD : 11 :000(616) [1063] XI. Eternal Foreknowledge and **Divine** Election
SD : 11 :002(616) [1063] is set forth out of the **divine** Word and according to the
SD : 11 :003(616) [1063] or reject a teaching of the **divine** Word because some
SD : 11 :006(617) [1065] to the glory of his **divine** name and the salvation of his
SD : 11 :009(617) [1065] this eternal election or **divine** ordering to eternal life only
SD : 11 :026(620) [1071] the secret and hidden abyss of **divine** foreknowledge.
SD : 11 :076(629) [1089] the hearing of his holy, **divine** Word, as with a net by
SD : 11 :096(632) [1095] detract anything from the **divine** truth of the holy
SD : 12 :029(635) [1101] flesh assumed all the **divine** properties in such a way that
SD : 12 :036(635) [1101] God, of one eternal, **divine** essence with God the Father,
SD : 12 :036(635) [1101] but only adorned with **divine** majesty inferior to and
SD : 12 :037(636) [1103] there is not one eternal, **divine** essence of the Father,

Divinely (8), Divinity (2)

AP : 04 :265(146) [0197] and it cannot be driven out unless we are **divinely** taught.
AP : 07 :036(175) [0241] heart to believe (like the **divinely** instituted Word and
AP : 15 :030(219) [0323] to the Gospel, the **divinely** instituted ceremonies of Moses
AP : 21 :011(230) [0345] Evidently some attribute **divinity** to the saints, the power
AP : 21 :023(232) [0349] declares: "It is a **divinely** instituted order that we should
AP : 21 :024(232) [0349] Where is the "**divinely** instituted order that we should
AP : 23 :012(241) [0367] because it is an ordinance **divinely** stamped on nature.
AP : 27 :014(271) [0423] of Moses, which was **divinely** revealed, did not merit the
SD : 07 :085(584) [1001] Christ, or apart from the **divinely** instituted action (that
SD : 08 :041(599) [1029] That is true, but since the **divinity** and humanity are one

Division (9), Divisions (2), Divisive (1)

PR : PR :004(004) [0007] and scandalous **division** in churches and schools so that
AG : 01 :003(027) [0043] essence, eternal, without **division**, without end, of infinite
AG : 22 :012(051) [0061] Because the **division** of the sacrament is contrary to the
AG : 26 :043(070) [0075] this difference a **divisive** of the church, they were
AG : 28 :078(094) [0095] they offer occasion for **division** and schism, which they
AL : 22 :012(050) [0061] Because the **division** of the sacrament does not agree with
AP : 28 :013(283) [0447] We like the old **division** of power into the power of the
EP : 04 :002(475) [0797] The first **division** among some theologians was
EP : 10 :001(492) [0829] There has also been a **division** among theologians of the
SD : PR :008(502) [0849] among us with such **divisions**, while others will not know
SD : RN :019(507) [0857] years a number of **divisions** have occurred among some
SD : 01 :054(518) [0877] dichotomy (that is, a **division** without a middle term), so

Divorce (4), Divorced (1), Divorces (1)

TR : 00 :078(333) [0527] which forbids an innocent person to marry after **divorce**.
LC : 01 :295(404) [0665] by giving her a bill of **divorce** and to take another wife.
LC : 01 :306(406) [0669] Testament married people are forbidden to be **divorced**.
EP : 12 :019(499) [0841] for married people to **divorce** one another, each go his
SD : 11 :075(628) [1087] as it is written, "If a man **divorces** his wife and she goes
SD : 12 :024(634) [1099] for married people to **divorce** each other, to go their

Doctor (4), Doctors (8) (*See also "Dr."*)

AL : 24 :041(061) [0069] are read and the **doctors** expound them on Wednesday

Continued ▶

A P : 0 4 :154(128) [0165] believe God, while a **doctor** of the law does not believe or
A P : 1 3 :018(213) [0313] crowd of scholastic **doctors** who teach that unless there is
A P : 2 1 :026(232) [0349] to console a dying **doctor** of theology, do nothing but
S 1 : P R :008(290) [0457] There was a **doctor** here in Wittenberg, sent from France,
T R : 0 0 :082(334) [0529] List of the **Doctors** and Preachers Who Subscribed the
L C : P R :007(359) [0569] me say that I, too, am a **doctor** and a preacher — yes, and
L C : P R :008(359) [0569] one reading, to become **doctors** above all doctors, to
L C : P R :008(359) [0569] doctors above all **doctors**, to know all there is to be
L C : P R :009(359) [0569] and truly such learned and great **doctors** as they think.
L C : P R :019(361) [0573] not to try to be **doctors** prematurely and to imagine that
S D : 0 1 :054(518) [0877] many other prominent **doctors** of the church, under the

Doctrinal (9)

A P : P R :011(099) [0101] possible to traditional **doctrinal** formulas in order to
A P : 1 2 :128(201) [0291] if you suppose that the **doctrinal** doubts of good men are
S D : P R :005(502) [0847] in this or in subsequent **doctrinal** statements, to depart
S D : R N :009(505) [0853] statements in his **doctrinal** and polemical writings, but in
S D : R N :010(506) [0855] and expositions of **doctrinal** articles, should be rejected.
S D : R N :020(507) [0857] position with the aforementioned **doctrinal** writings.
S D : 0 7 :017(572) [0979] consider what kind of **doctrinal** statement they should
S D : 0 7 :041(576) [0985] than from Dr. Luther's **doctrinal** and polemical writings.
S D : 0 8 :003(592) [1017] refuted this, as his **doctrinal** and polemical writings

Doctrine (313)

P R : P R :000(001) [0004] Confession of the **Doctrine** and Faith of the undersigned
P R : P R :003(003) [0007] fast and loyally to the **doctrine** that is contained in it,
P R : P R :003(003) [0007] recognizing the **doctrine** as the ancient consensus which
P R : P R :004(004) [0007] scatter his seed of false **doctrine** and discord and to bring
P R : P R :004(004) [0007] adulterate the pure **doctrine** of God's Word, sever the
P R : P R :004(004) [0009] of pure evangelical **doctrine**, and to make them more
P R : P R :008(005) [0009] in the future against **doctrine** that is impure, false, and
P R : P R :008(005) [0009] to defend, or to spread a different or a new **doctrine**.
P R : P R :008(005) [0011] of pure evangelical **doctrine** would be constrained to
P R : P R :009(006) [0011] our churches, schools, **doctrine**, faith, and confession.
P R : P R :009(006) [0011] Confession, the contrary **doctrine** about the holy
P R : P R :010(006) [0011] and to reject false **doctrine**, and clearly to confess the
P R : P R :010(006) [0011] they might be preserved from false **doctrine** in the future.
P R : P R :014(007) [0013] in which the Christian **doctrine** set forth in the
P R : P R :014(007) [0013] so that no adulterated **doctrine** might in the future be
P R : P R :015(007) [0013] diligently and earnestly the **doctrine** contained in it.
P R : P R :017(008) [0015] of their erroneous **doctrine** although it never entered our
P R : P R :017(008) [0015] new, false, or erroneous **doctrine** or in the least point to
P R : P R :018(009) [0015] minded to permit any **doctrine** in our lands, churches, and
P R : P R :019(009) [0017] fact that this erroneous **doctrine** is expressly rejected in
P R : P R :019(009) [0017] and that a very different **doctrine** by far can be proved
P R : P R :019(009) [0017] with Evangelical **doctrine** any false and adulterated
P R : P R :022(011) [0019] of false and adulterated **doctrine**, especially in the article
P R : P R :022(012) [0019] rightly instructed in this **doctrine**, they will, through the
P R : P R :023(012) [0021] the goal that no other **doctrine** be treated and taught in
P R : P R :023(012) [0021] understood, and that no **doctrine** be permitted entrance
P R : P R :024(013) [0021] God's Word so that pure **doctrine** can be recognized and
P R : P R :024(013) [0021] from adulterated **doctrine** and so that the way may not be
P R : P R :024(013) [0021] certain formula of pure **doctrine**, to start scandalous
P R : P R :024(013) [0023] is that finally correct **doctrine** will be entirely obscured
A G : 0 0 :000(027) [0043] Articles of Faith and **Doctrine**
A G : 1 0 :002(034) [0047] The contrary **doctrine** is therefore rejected.
A G : 2 0 :022(044) [0055] necessary to preach this **doctrine** about faith in Christ and
A G : 2 3 :022(055) [0063] the teaching that forbids marriage a **doctrine** of the devil.
A G : 2 3 :023(055) [0063] well, for it must be a **doctrine** of the devil to forbid
A G : 2 4 :025(059) [0067] novelty in church **doctrine** that Christ's death should have
A G : 2 6 :029(068) [0075] or marriage are called a **doctrine** of the devil, for it is
A G : 2 7 :002(071) [0077] when true discipline and **doctrine** had become corrupted,
A G : 2 8 :021(084) [0087] forgive sins, judge **doctrine** and condemn doctrine that is
A G : 2 8 :021(084) [0087] doctrine and condemn **doctrine** that is contrary to the
A G : 2 8 :066(092) [0093] chief article of Christian **doctrine**, and this is not
A G : 2 8 :070(093) [0093] he will not preach this **doctrine**, although there is no
A G : 0 0 :005(095) [0095] nothing, either in **doctrine** or in ceremonies, that is
A L : 2 0 :019(043) [0055] to be plagued by the **doctrine** of works when consolation
A L : 2 3 :022(055) [0063] marriage is called a **doctrine** of demons by Paul in I Tim.
A L : 2 5 :006(062) [0069] have shed light on the **doctrine** of repentance and have
A L : 2 6 :004(064) [0071] it has obscured the **doctrine** concerning grace and the
A L : 2 6 :029(068) [0075] prohibition of foods a **doctrine** of demons, for it is in
A L : 2 8 :021(084) [0087] to forgive sins, to reject **doctrine** which is contrary to the
A L : 2 8 :051(089) [0091] necessary to preserve the **doctrine** of Christian liberty in
A L : 2 8 :070(093) [0093] that he will not teach the pure **doctrine** of the Gospel.
A L : 0 0 :005(095) [0095] received among us, in **doctrine** or in ceremonies, that is
A L : 0 0 :006(096) [0095] that a summary of the **doctrine** taught among us may be
A P : P R :017(099) [0103] articles of Christian **doctrine** that the church sorely
A P : 0 1 :002(100) [0103] and defended this **doctrine** and we believe that the Holy
A P : 0 2 :006(101) [0107] with this evil **doctrine**, we made mention of
A P : 0 2 :012(102) [0109] mingled Christian **doctrine** with philosophical views
A P : 0 2 :035(104) [0115] and they add that this **doctrine** was properly condemned
A P : 0 2 :051(107) [0119] We know that our **doctrine** is correct and in agreement
A P : 0 4 :002(107) [0121] controversy the main **doctrine** of Christianity is involved;
A P : 0 4 :003(107) [0121] opponents confuse this **doctrine** miserably, they obscure
A P : 0 4 :004(108) [0121] sources of both kinds of **doctrine**, the opponents' and our
A P : 0 4 :039(112) [0131] in the exposition of our **doctrine** of the righteousness of
A P : 0 4 :186(132) [0173] justifies and by their **doctrine** that because of our love and
A P : 0 4 :193(133) [0175] like the confession of **doctrine**, afflictions, works of
A P : 0 4 :200(134) [0175] At the same time the **doctrine** of penitence is preached to
A P : 0 4 :233(140) [0185] seek after some other kinds of **doctrine** and other clergy.
A P : 0 4 :271(147) [0199] in their treatment of the **doctrine** of penitence, yet we
A P : 0 4 :272(148) [0199] Because the **doctrine** of penitence not only demands new
A P : 0 4 :288(151) [0203] This mode is a **doctrine** of reason.
A P : 0 4 :289(151) [0203] This is obviously a **doctrine** of the law.
A P : 0 4 :300(153) [0205] and trying to destroy the **doctrine** of righteousness by
A P : 0 4 :301(153) [0205] What is this **doctrine** of the law but a doctrine of despair?
A P : 0 4 :301(153) [0205] What is this doctrine of the law but a **doctrine** of despair?
A P : 0 4 :310(155) [0207] comfort comes from this **doctrine** that the highest worship
A P : 0 4 :324(157) [0211] then, do we reject the **doctrine** of the merit of condignity
A P : 0 4 :325(157) [0211] clearly handed down the **doctrine** that we need mercy
A P : 0 4 :377(165) [0223] and what is left of the **doctrine** of justification is nothing
A P : 0 4 :382(165) [0225] If the **doctrine** of faith is omitted, it is vain to say that
A P : 0 4 :387(166) [0225] They teach a **doctrine** of justification derived either from
A P : 0 4 :390(166) [0225] more than enough philosophy with Christian **doctrine**.
A P : 0 4 :397(167) [0227] a very necessary **doctrine** that all Christians should hold
A P : 0 4 :398(167) [0227] does not see that this **doctrine**—that by faith we obtain
A P : 0 4 :398(168) [0227] hear that such a **doctrine** was condemned, how can they
A P : 0 7 :009(169) [0229] We set forth this **doctrine** for a very necessary reason.
A P : 0 7 :021(172) [0233] when they condemn our **doctrine** that the forgiveness of
A P : 0 7 :038(176) [0241] want to keep, apostolic **doctrine** they do not want to
A P : 1 0 :004(179) [0247] that we defend the **doctrine** received in the whole church
A P : 1 2 :003(182) [0253] involving the chief **doctrine** of the Gospel, the true
A P : 1 2 :003(183) [0253] and canonists had overwhelmed the **doctrine** of penitence.
A P : 1 2 :004(183) [0253] Luther's writings the **doctrine** of penitence was very
A P : 1 2 :010(184) [0255] is a great one, the chief **doctrine** of the Gospel, the
A P : 1 2 :016(184) [0257] demonic doctrines the **doctrine** of the righteousness of
A P : 1 2 :016(184) [0257] us to reject the **doctrine** of penitence as taught by the
A P : 1 2 :059(190) [0267] For the **doctrine** of penitence and the doctrine of
A P : 1 2 :059(190) [0267] of penitence and the **doctrine** of justification are very
A P : 1 2 :067(191) [0271] openly condemns this **doctrine** of the forgiveness of sins
A P : 1 2 :078(193) [0275] Our opponents' **doctrine** that men obtain the forgiveness
A P : 1 2 :078(193) [0275] and love, is simply a **doctrine** of the law — and that
A P : 1 2 :089(195) [0279] Such is our opponents' **doctrine** — a doctrine of the law,
A P : 1 2 :089(195) [0279] opponents' doctrine — a **doctrine** of the law, an
A P : 1 2 :089(195) [0279] law, an abrogation of the Gospel, a **doctrine** of despair.
A P : 1 2 :090(195) [0279] On this **doctrine** of penitence, which is quite clear, we are
A P : 1 2 :092(196) [0279] we have listed the **doctrine** of faith among the parts of
A P : 1 2 :116(199) [0287] We must keep the **doctrine** that by faith we obtain the
A P : 1 2 :124(201) [0289] total of all Christian **doctrine**, judges should have been
A P : 1 2 :178(211) [0307] here a summary of our **doctrine** on penitence; we are
A P : 1 4 :002(214) [0315] and condemn the sort of **doctrine** we have confessed, or
A P : 1 5 :003(215) [0315] actually condemn the **doctrine** that we do not merit grace
A P : 1 5 :003(215) [0315] have condemned this **doctrine**, we have an easy and
A P : 1 6 :013(224) [0333] may understand that our **doctrine** does not weaken but
A P : 2 0 :011(228) [0341] record as rejecting our **doctrine** that we obtain the
A P : 2 1 :041(235) [0355] the confusion in the **doctrine** of penitence which ought to
A P : 2 1 :041(235) [0355] upon scholastic **doctrine** because it leads to philosophical
A P : 2 1 :043(235) [0357] been killed and sound **doctrine** crushed, fanatical spirits
A P : 2 1 :044(236) [0357] happened before, nor crush sound **doctrine** in the church.
A P : 2 1 :044(236) [0357] and propagate sound **doctrine** and to defend those who
A P : 2 3 :058(247) [0379] show that this law is a **doctrine** of demons (I Tim. 4:1-3);
A P : 2 3 :063(248) [0381] a law when he calls it a **"doctrine** of demons" (I Tim. 4:1).
A P : 2 4 :045(258) [0401] ideas and could not grasp the sum of Christian **doctrine**.
A P : 2 4 :046(258) [0401] ever understood our opponents' **doctrine** of penitence?
A P : 2 4 :046(258) [0401] Yet this is the principal **doctrine** of the Christian faith.
A P : 2 4 :090(266) [0415] adduce in support of the **doctrine** of satisfaction, which
A P : 2 4 :091(266) [0415] They have crushed the **doctrine** of faith, and under the
A P : 2 4 :096(268) [0417] and utterly destroy the **doctrine** of righteousness by faith.
A P : 2 7 :002(269) [0419] to denounce him for his **doctrine**, which seemed to be
A P : 2 7 :009(269) [0421] The issue is the kind of **doctrine** which the architects of
A P : 2 8 :023(284) [0451] together, still the one **doctrine** of the forgiveness of sins,
S 1 : 0 0 :000(287) [0453] Articles of Christian **doctrine** which were to have been
S 2 : 0 4 :009(300) [0473] together in unity of **doctrine**, faith, sacraments, prayer,
S 3 : 0 8 :001(312) [0495] need to be examined and instructed in Christian **doctrine**.
S 3 : 1 1 :003(315) [0499] for St. Paul says that to do so is a **doctrine** of demons.
T R : 0 0 :006(320) [0505] changes in the sacraments, and concerning **doctrine**.
T R : 0 0 :040(327) [0515] On the other hand, the **doctrine** of the pope conflicts in
T R : 0 0 :040(327) [0515] the right to change the **doctrine** of Christ and the worship
T R : 0 0 :040(327) [0517] wishes to have his own **doctrine** and worship observed as
T R : 0 0 :044(328) [0517] The **doctrine** of repentance has been completely corrupted
T R : 0 0 :082(334) [0529] and cities professing the **doctrine** of the Gospel, we have
L C : S P :005(362) [0575] of all Christian **doctrine** than children and beginners at
L C : S P :019(363) [0579] thus summed up the **doctrine**, life, wisdom, and learning
L C : S P :024(364) [0579] Christian **doctrine**, which we should constantly teach and
L C : 0 1 :055(372) [0595] or in sublime and difficult matters of faith and **doctrine**.
L C : 0 1 :317(408) [0673] before men produce a **doctrine** or social order equal to
L C : 0 2 :001(411) [0679] far we have heard the first part of Christian **doctrine**.
L C : 0 3 :047(426) [0711] warrant for their devilish **doctrine**, we ought constantly to
L C : 0 3 :047(426) [0711] our Gospel and pure **doctrine** and try to suppress it, as
L C : 0 3 :049(426) [0711] sacred and holy in both **doctrine** and life so that he may
L C : 0 4 :049(442) [0745] are not a few whose **doctrine** and life attest that they
L C : 0 5 :039(451) [0761] right interpretation and **doctrine** of the sacrament, there
L C : 0 5 :085(456) [0773] brought up in Christian **doctrine** and a right
E P : R N :002(465) [0777] the fashion in which the **doctrine** of the prophets and
E P : 0 1 :001(466) [0779] *The Pure **Doctrine**, Faith, and Confession according to*
E P : 0 2 :006(470) [0787] *Contrary False **Doctrine***
E P : 0 2 :016(472) [0791] contrary to the **doctrine** of the grace of God, we hold that
E P : 0 2 :016(472) [0791] with the form of sound **doctrine** and that accordingly it is
E P : 0 3 :002(473) [0793] *The Pure **Doctrine** of the Christian Church Against Both*
E P : 0 3 :010(474) [0795] would preserve the pure **doctrine** concerning the
E P : 0 3 :011(474) [0795] *Rejection of the Contrary **Doctrine***
E P : 0 4 :001(475) [0797] in some churches concerning the **doctrine** of good works:
E P : 0 4 :004(476) [0797] *The Pure **Doctrine** of the Christian Church in this*
E P : 0 4 :005(476) [0797] to resolve it, this is our **doctrine**, faith, and confession:
E P : 0 5 :001(478) [0801] *The Pure **Doctrine** of God's Word*
E P : 0 5 :003(478) [0801] the law is a divine **doctrine** which teaches what is right
E P : 0 5 :005(478) [0801] speaking, is the kind of **doctrine** that teaches what a man
E P : 0 5 :006(478) [0803] means the entire **doctrine** of Christ which he proclaimed
E P : 0 5 :010(479) [0805] *Rejected Contrary **Doctrine***
E P : 0 7 :001(481) [0809] at Issue between Our **Doctrine** and the Sacramentarian
E P : 0 7 :001(481) [0809] Doctrine and the Sacramentarian **Doctrine** in This Article
E P : 0 7 :005(482) [0809] *Confession of the Pure **Doctrine** of the Holy Supper*
E P : 0 7 :021(484) [0813] *and Condemned **Doctrine** of the Sacramentarians*
E P : 0 7 :021(484) [0813] and contradictory to the **doctrine** set forth above and to
E P : 0 7 :042(486) [0817] on crediting us with this **doctrine**, against the witness of
E P : 0 8 :018(489) [0823] Our **doctrine**, faith, and confession do not divide the
E P : 0 8 :018(490) [0823] *Contrary False **Doctrine** concerning the Person of Christ*
E P : 0 8 :039(491) [0827] This **doctrine** not only perverts the words of Christ's
E P : 1 0 :002(493) [0829] an agreement with us in **doctrine**, may we with an
E P : 1 0 :002(493) [0829] *The Correct, True **Doctrine** and Confession about this*
E P : 1 0 :007(493) [0831] is mutual agreement in **doctrine** and in all its articles as
E P : 1 0 :007(494) [0831] *False **Doctrine** concerning this Article*
E P : 1 1 :001(494) [0831] *Pure and True **Doctrine** concerning this Article*
E P : 1 1 :011(495) [0835] 10. The **doctrine** of God's eternal election is profitable
E P : 1 1 :013(496) [0835] concern himself with the **doctrine** of the eternal election

Continued ▶

EP : 1 1 :013(496) [0835] which this salutary **doctrine** gives us, namely, that we
EP : 1 1 :015(496) [0835] brief exposition of the **doctrine** of God's eternal election
EP : 1 1 :015(496) [0835] Nor will this **doctrine** ever give anyone occasion either to
EP : 1 1 :015(497) [0837] *False **Doctrine** concerning this Article*
EP : 1 1 :016(497) [0837] if anybody teaches the **doctrine** of the gracious election of
EP : 1 1 :016(497) [0837] find no comfort in this **doctrine** but are driven to doubt
EP : 1 1 :016(497) [0837] he is not teaching the **doctrine** according to the Word and
EP : 1 1 :017(497) [0837] 1. The **doctrine** that God does not want all men to come
EP : 1 1 :018(497) [0837] 2. Furthermore, the **doctrine** that God is not serious
EP : 1 1 :022(497) [0837] only set forth the pure **doctrine** but have also exposed the
EP : 1 2 :006(498) [0839] thus reject the entire **doctrine** of original sin and
EP : 1 2 :031(500) [0843] that this is the **doctrine**, faith and confession of all of us
SD : 0 0 :000(501) [0845] the Summary Formulation of our Christian **Doctrine**
SD : P R :002(501) [0847] reformation as a new **doctrine** and as wholly contrary to
SD : P R :003(501) [0847] then accepted the pure **doctrine** of the holy Gospel and
SD : P R :006(502) [0847] Although the Christian **doctrine** set forth in this
SD : P R :007(502) [0849] to be Christians and gloried in the **doctrine** of Christ.
SD : P R :008(502) [0849] will ultimately lead to the ruin of the pure **doctrine**.
SD : P R :008(502) [0849] will doubt if the pure **doctrine** can coexist among us with
SD : R N :001(503) [0849] which the summarized **doctrine** commonly confessed by
SD : R N :001(503) [0851] churches which confessed the same **doctrine** and religion.
SD : R N :002(503) [0851] faithful to the pure **doctrine** of the Word of God as Dr.
SD : R N :004(504) [0851] times the true Christian **doctrine** as it was correctly and
SD : R N :005(504) [0851] This **doctrine**, drawn from and conformed to the Word
SD : R N :007(505) [0853] In these articles the **doctrine** of the cited Augsburg
SD : R N :008(505) [0853] between true and false **doctrine**, we declare our
SD : R N :008(505) [0853] formulate Christian **doctrine** on the basis of God's Word
SD : R N :009(505) [0853] sum and pattern of the **doctrine** which Dr. Luther of
SD : R N :009(505) [0855] rule and norm of all **doctrine**, and that no human being's
SD : R N :010(506) [0855] pattern of **doctrine** they are to be accepted and used as
SD : R N :010(506) [0855] and common form of **doctrine** which all our Evangelical
SD : R N :011(506) [0855] of our Christian **doctrine** is that they have always and
SD : R N :013(506) [0855] who remained steadfastly in the pure **doctrine**.
SD : R N :014(506) [0855] to preserve the pure **doctrine** and to maintain a
SD : R N :014(506) [0855] the true and wholesome **doctrine** correctly, but also to
SD : R N :015(507) [0857] parts of our Christian **doctrine**, when the contrary error
SD : R N :019(507) [0857] opposing the true **doctrine** to the false doctrine, so that
SD : R N :019(507) [0857] doctrine to the false **doctrine**, so that the foundation of
SD : R N :019(507) [0857] and condemned **doctrine** might be exposed, no matter
SD : R N :020(508) [0859] our adversaries charge, veer from one **doctrine** to another.
SD : 0 1 :004(509) [0861] the true and correct **doctrine** concerning original sin, we
SD : 0 1 :004(509) [0861] short chapters the true **doctrine** and its opposite in theses
SD : 0 1 :015(511) [0865] aforementioned Confessions of our Christian **doctrine**.
SD : 0 1 :016(511) [0865] and preserve this **doctrine** in such a way that we fall
SD : 0 1 :017(511) [0865] as false the opinion and **doctrine** that original sin is only
SD : 0 1 :026(512) [0867] On the other hand, this **doctrine** must also be protected
SD : 0 1 :030(513) [0867] we discussed the correct **doctrine** of original sin, the
SD : 0 1 :043(516) [0873] they also rejected the contrary **doctrine** as patent heresy.
SD : 0 1 :046(516) [0873] Fourthly, concerning the **doctrine** of the resurrection
SD : 0 1 :048(516) [0875] that we must reject this **doctrine** with all its implications
SD : 0 1 :049(517) [0875] simple exposition of the **doctrine** and the contrary
SD : 0 1 :049(517) [0875] and the contrary **doctrine**, the thesis and antithesis, as far
SD : 0 1 :054(518) [0877] of explaining this **doctrine** against heretics, they use them
SD : 0 2 :015(523) [0887] might rightly comprehend and learn the divine **doctrine**.
SD : 0 2 :028(527) [0893] This **doctrine** is founded upon the Word of God and
SD : 0 2 :043(529) [0897] that he will not deviate from his **doctrine** until his death.
SD : 0 2 :043(529) [0897] as sheer error every **doctrine** which glorifies our free will,
SD : 0 2 :046(530) [0899] fashion misused the **doctrine** of the impotence and the
SD : 0 2 :046(530) [0899] free will, as well as the **doctrine** that our conversion and
SD : 0 2 :071(535) [0909] he comes by them), our **doctrine** answers this way: Man's
SD : 0 2 :072(535) [0909] This **doctrine** directs us to the means through which the
SD : 0 2 :073(535) [0909] of the entire **doctrine** of free will it is possible to decide
SD : 0 2 :076(536) [0911] and scholastics, whose **doctrine** was slightly more subtle
SD : 0 2 :086(538) [0913] to the form of sound **doctrine** but rather opposes it and
SD : 0 2 :090(538) [0915] greatly misled by the **doctrine** of the three efficient causes
SD : 0 3 :005(540) [0917] enumeration of those who contradict the pure **doctrine**.
SD : 0 3 :006(540) [0917] of the entire Christian **doctrine**," "without which no poor
SD : 0 3 :007(540) [0917] says specifically of this **doctrine** that a little leaven
SD : 0 3 :007(540) [0919] by side with the true **doctrine**, we clearly segregate,
SD : 0 3 :007(540) [0919] expose, and condemn the false contrary **doctrine**.
SD : 0 3 :042(547) [0931] justifies, it is St. Paul's **doctrine** that faith alone justifies
SD : 0 3 :044(547) [0931] exposition of the **doctrine** of justification by faith, since it
SD : 0 3 :044(547) [0931] The **doctrine** has been set forth in detail in the previously
SD : 0 3 :060(550) [0937] 1. The **doctrine** that Christ is our righteousness before
SD : 0 3 :066(550) [0937] and constantly with the **doctrine** of justification by faith
SD : 0 4 :002(551) [0939] to the form of sound **doctrine** and words which have been
SD : 0 4 :022(554) [0945] directly contrary to the **doctrine** of exclusive terms in the
SD : 0 4 :023(555) [0945] against the pure **doctrine** of salvation by faith alone.
SD : 0 4 :033(556) [0947] without darkening the **doctrine** of faith and justification.
SD : 0 4 :036(557) [0949] words as well as the true **doctrine** itself (II Tim. 1:13).
SD : 0 5 :004(559) [0953] he summarizes his **doctrine** in a few words, "Thus it is
SD : 0 5 :017(561) [0957] the law is a divine **doctrine** which reveals the
SD : 0 5 :018(561) [0957] explains the law and its **doctrine**; nevertheless the true
SD : 0 5 :020(561) [0959] Gospel, however, is that **doctrine** which teaches what a
SD : 0 5 :027(563) [0961] what belongs to one **doctrine** is ascribed to the other, it is
SD : 0 5 :027(563) [0961] would be tangled together and made into one **doctrine**.
SD : 0 6 :002(564) [0963] the law; nor should this **doctrine** in any way be urged on
SD : 0 6 :026(568) [0971] godliness, the erroneous **doctrine** that the law in the
SD : 0 7 :001(569) [0971] Chief Issue between Our **Doctrine** and That of the
SD : 0 7 :009(570) [0975] condemns the contrary **doctrine** (that is, the doctrine of
SD : 0 7 :009(570) [0975] doctrine (that is, the **doctrine** of the Sacramentarians,
SD : 0 7 :028(574) [0981] had departed from this **doctrine** and other Christian
SD : 0 7 :041(576) [0985] the person whose entire **doctrine** in sum and content was
SD : 0 7 :085(584) [1001] this true Christian **doctrine** concerning the Holy Supper
SD : 0 7 :107(588) [1009] to the aforementioned **doctrine**, based as it is on the
SD : 0 7 :112(589) [1011] to, or contrary to the **doctrine** set forth above, based as it
SD : 0 7 :121(590) [1013] 10. Likewise, the **doctrine** that it is not the words and the
SD : 0 7 :123(590) [1013] 12. We also reject the **doctrine** that unbelieving,
SD : 0 7 :124(591) [1015] 13. We also reject the **doctrine** that worthiness does not
SD : 0 7 :128(591) [1015] to, or opposed to the **doctrine** set forth above, well
SD : 0 8 :004(592) [1017] Sacramentarians in the **doctrine** of the Supper of the
SD : 0 8 :031(597) [1025] The **doctrine** of an exchange of properties (that is, of a
SD : 0 8 :035(597) [1027] important that this **doctrine** of the exchange of properties
SD : 0 8 :035(597) [1027] due discrimination, the **doctrine** becomes tangled up and
SD : 0 8 :060(602) [1035] correctly explain this **doctrine** and defend it against all
SD : 0 8 :061(602) [1035] not developed a new **doctrine** of our own, but we accept
SD : 0 8 :063(603) [1037] direction in order to cast suspicion on the pure **doctrine**.
SD : 0 8 :063(603) [1037] a "verbal exchange," the **doctrine** which these people
SD : 0 8 :064(603) [1037] as it explained this **doctrine** on the basis of Scripture,
SD : 0 8 :064(604) [1039] used in explaining this **doctrine**, as we stated above.
SD : 0 8 :071(605) [1041] Creed and to the entire prophetic and apostolic **doctrine**.
SD : 0 8 :088(609) [1047] are inconsistent with the **doctrine** here set forth as
SD : 0 8 :096(609) [1049] contravene the above **doctrine** as being contrary to the
SD : 1 0 :002(611) [1053] an agreement with us in **doctrine**, one may still with a
SD : 1 0 :003(611) [1053] to suppress the pure **doctrine** and gradually to insinuate
SD : 1 0 :005(611) [1053] apostasy from the pure **doctrine** of the Gospel and from
SD : 1 0 :010(612) [1055] to suppress the pure **doctrine** of the holy Gospel, the
SD : 1 0 :010(612) [1055] and actions, the true **doctrine** and all that pertains to it,
SD : 1 0 :012(613) [1057] it to confirm their false **doctrine** that the works of the law
SD : 1 0 :014(613) [1057] and to suppress the pure **doctrine** and Christian liberty,
SD : 1 0 :016(613) [1057] Christian agreement in **doctrine** has not previously been
SD : 1 0 :029(615) [1061] in things indifferent, in **doctrine**, or in whatever else
SD : 1 0 :031(616) [1063] are otherwise agreed in **doctrine** and in all its articles and
SD : 1 1 :012(618) [1067] Scripture presents this **doctrine** in no other way than to
SD : 1 1 :014(619) [1069] as one unit the entire **doctrine** of God's purpose, counsel,
SD : 1 1 :043(623) [1077] and comforting **doctrine**, for it mightily substantiates the
SD : 1 1 :045(624) [1079] This **doctrine** also affords the beautiful and glorious
SD : 1 1 :048(624) [1079] This **doctrine** will also give us the glorious comfort, in
SD : 1 1 :089(631) [1093] as the "book of life," this **doctrine** never occasions either
SD : 1 1 :090(631) [1093] This **doctrine** gives sorrowing and tempted people the
SD : 1 1 :095(632) [1095] any falsification of true **doctrine** or any publicly

Doctrines (61)
PR : P R :006(004) [0009] the false and misleading **doctrines** which have been
PR : P R :022(011) [0019] only false and seductive **doctrines** and their stiff-necked
AG : 0 0 :001(047) [0059] about a summary of the **doctrines** that are preached and
AG : 2 6 :022(067) [0073] worship me, teaching as **doctrines** the precepts of men"
AG : 2 7 :036(076) [0081] worship me, teaching as **doctrines** the precepts of men."
AG : 2 8 :045(088) [0089] are used), according to human precepts and **doctrines**?
AG : 2 8 :049(089) [0091] Why does it call them **doctrines** of the devil?
AL : 2 8 :045(088) [0089] are used), according to human precepts and **doctrines**?
AL : 2 8 :049(089) [0091] Why does it call them **doctrines** of demons?
AL : 0 0 :005(095) [0095] into our churches of any new and ungodly **doctrines**.
AP : 0 2 :049(106) [0119] Blasphemy and wicked **doctrines** fill the world, and by
AP : 0 4 :005(108) [0121] into these two chief **doctrines**, the law and the promises.
AP : 0 4 :007(108) [0121] Of these two **doctrines** our opponents select the law and
AP : 0 4 :396(167) [0225] their spirit, for in some **doctrines** they have condemned a
AP : 0 7 :035(175) [0241] are used), according to human precepts and **doctrines**?
AP : 0 7 :040(176) [0241] In fact, Paul calls such opinions "**doctrines** of demons."
AP : 1 2 :016(184) [0257] and demonic **doctrines** the doctrine of the righteousness
AP : 1 2 :098(197) [0281] the explanation of these **doctrines** and thus far have
AP : 1 2 :141(204) [0295] considers the demonic **doctrines** that the devil has
AP : 1 5 :004(215) [0315] are openly replacing the Gospel with **doctrines** of demons.
AP : 1 5 :004(215) [0315] calls traditions "**doctrines** of demons" (I Tim. 4:1) when
AP : 2 1 :043(235) [0357] a summary of the **doctrines** of the church for the people.
AP : 2 7 :026(273) [0429] of these titles, they are "**doctrines** of demons" (I Tim.
S2 : 0 2 :002(293) [0463] worship me, teaching as **doctrines** the precepts of men'
S3 : 0 1 :011(303) [0479] are thoroughly pagan **doctrines**, and we cannot tolerate
S3 : 1 5 :001(316) [0501] worship me, teaching as **doctrines** the precepts of men"
TR : 0 0 :038(326) [0515] worship, idolatry, and **doctrines** which conflict with the
TR : 0 0 :039(327) [0515] defend godless **doctrines** and godless forms of worship,
TR : 0 0 :039(327) [0515] because he will devise **doctrines** which conflict with the
TR : 0 0 :041(327) [0517] in the impious **doctrines**, blasphemies, and unjust
TR : 0 0 :042(328) [0517] these errors to be **doctrines** of demons and of the
TR : 0 0 :057(330) [0521] forms of worship and **doctrines** which are in conflict with
TR : 0 0 :058(330) [0521] flee from idolatry, impious **doctrines**, and unjust cruelty.
TR : 0 0 :059(330) [0521] the pope and defend his **doctrines** and forms of worship
TR : 0 0 :072(332) [0525] and defend impious **doctrines** and impious forms of
TR : 0 0 :079(333) [0527] pope defend impious **doctrines** and impious forms of
LC : P R :017(361) [0573] sit in judgment upon all **doctrines**, estates, persons, laws,
EP : R N :000(464) [0777] According to Which All **Doctrines** Should Be Judged and
EP : R N :001(464) [0777] according to which all **doctrines** and teachers alike must
EP : R N :006(465) [0779] All **doctrines** should conform to the standards set forth
EP : R N :007(465) [0779] the only touchstone all **doctrines** should and must be
EP : 1 0 :003(493) [0829] worship me, teaching as **doctrines** the precepts of men"
EP : 1 2 :002(498) [0839] in general they profess **doctrines** of a kind that cannot be
SD : P R :001(501) [0847] obscured by human **doctrines** and ordinances under the
SD : R N :000(503) [0849] Indicating How All **Doctrines** Should Be Judged in
SD : R N :006(504) [0853] both to presenting the **doctrines** against the papacy more
SD : 0 1 :016(511) [0865] enumerate the contrary **doctrines** which are rejected and
SD : 0 1 :025(512) [0865] these and similar false **doctrines** because God's Word
SD : 0 2 :073(535) [0909] and condemn such false **doctrines** and errors as these:
SD : 0 5 :001(558) [0951] lest we confuse the two **doctrines** and change the Gospel
SD : 0 5 :015(561) [0957] Thus both **doctrines** are always together, and both of
SD : 0 5 :024(562) [0961] confess that these two **doctrines** must be urged constantly
SD : 0 5 :027(563) [0961] and in order that both **doctrines**, law and Gospel, may
SD : 0 5 :027(563) [0961] them by which the two **doctrines** would be tangled
SD : 0 7 :112(589) [1011] opinions and **doctrines** when are inconsistent with,
SD : 0 8 :062(603) [1037] and similar erroneous **doctrines** have been justly rejected
SD : 1 0 :003(611) [1053] to insinuate their false **doctrines** into our churches again.
SD : 1 0 :008(612) [1055] worship me, teaching for **doctrines** the precepts of men"
SD : 1 0 :014(613) [1057] to confirm false **doctrines**, superstition, and idolatry and
SD : 1 0 :022(615) [1061] in the impious **doctrines**, blasphemies, and unjust
SD : 1 1 :044(623) [1077] opinions and erroneous **doctrines** about the powers of

Document (14), Documents (3)
PR : P R :001(003) [0007] under whose eyes this **document** comes, we, the electors,
PR : P R :011(006) [0011] of God, and produced a **document** in which they set forth
PR : P R :015(007) [0013] of us have had this **document** read article by article to
AP : P R :002(098) [0099] would produce the **document** without hesitation.
AP : P R :004(098) [0099] how could they accept a **document** they had not even seen
AP : 2 1 :040(235) [0355] everywhere else, the Confutation is a deceitful **document**.
EP : 1 1 :001(494) [0831] explanation of it in this **document**, lest as some future
SD : P R :003(501) [0847] In this **document** they gave a clear and unequivocal
SD : R N :009(505) [0853] and generally accepted **documents** as the sum and pattern
SD : R N :012(506) [0855] object to these **documents** but will gladly admit and

Continued ▶

SD : RN :018(507) [0857] that are rejected in the aforementioned **documents**.
SD : RN :020(508) [0859] we now repeat in this **document**, but that it is the same
SD : 0 3 :044(547) [0931] by faith, since it meets the requirements of this **document**.
SD : 0 7 :001(568) [0971] not be included in this **document** in which we intend to
SD : 0 7 :001(569) [0971] of our confession in this **document** and from repeating
SD : 0 7 :111(589) [1011] In this **document** we have intended to set forth primarily
SD : 1 1 :001(616) [1063] of this article in this **document** so that all men may know

Dodge (1), Dodges (1)
AP : 2 4 :096(267) [0417] They often use this **dodge**.
LC : 0 1 :298(405) [0665] We think up artful **dodges** and sly tricks (better and

Doer (2), Doers (6)
AP : 0 4 :122(124) [0157] (Matt. 19:17), "The **doers** of the law will be justified"
AP : 0 4 :252(143) [0191] passage (Rom. 2:13), "the **doers** of the law will be
AP : 0 4 :252(143) [0191] As these words, "the **doers** of the law will be justified,"
AP : 0 4 :252(143) [0191] this sense it is said, "The **doers** of the law will be
LC : 0 1 :094(378) [0607] called holy work unless the **doer** himself is first holy.
LC : 0 1 :094(378) [0607] be performed by which the **doer** himself is made holy;
LC : 0 1 :181(389) [0631] of punishing evil-**doers** to civil magistrates in place of
SD : 1 2 :021(634) [1099] conscience impose the death penalty on evil-**doers**.

Dogkeepers (1)
LC : PR :002(358) [0567] better swineherds or **dogkeepers** than spiritual guides or

Dogmas (1)
AP : 0 4 :383(165) [0225] of history or of **dogmas**, not as the power that grasps the

Dogs (3)
S 2 : 0 2 :022(296) [0469] about the bones of **dogs** and horses that even the devil
LC : PR :003(358) [0567] because, like pigs and **dogs**, they remember no more of
LC : PR :013(360) [0571] but also to be chased out by **dogs** and pelted with dung.

Domestic (11), Domestics (2)
AP : 0 4 :243(141) [0189] for the preservation of **domestic** tranquillity, which
AP : 1 2 :106(197) [0283] is merely giving a bit of **domestic** advice to the head of a
AP : 2 3 :032(244) [0373] by childbirth, and by her other **domestic** duties?
AP : 2 3 :032(244) [0373] and does not praise **domestic** duties apart from faith: "if
AP : 2 3 :043(245) [0375] to good men that **domestic** problems are excluded from
S 1 : PR :012(290) [0459] of subjects, **domestics**, and laborers, extortion in every
LC : 0 1 :142(384) [0621] Likewise he must have **domestics** (man-servants and
LC : 0 1 :225(395) [0643] unfaithful in his or her **domestic** duty and does damage
LC : 0 1 :313(407) [0671] are common, everyday **domestic** duties of one neighbor
LC : 0 3 :073(430) [0719] to the regulation of our **domestic** and our civil or
EP : 1 2 :002(498) [0839] politic and secular administration, or in **domestic** society.
EP : 1 2 :016(499) [0841] *Intolerable Errors which Undermine **Domestic** Society*
SD : 1 2 :009(633) [1097] the churches or in the body politic or in **domestic** society.

Dominated (1), Domination (1), Domineering (2)
AL : 2 8 :076(094) [0095] the bishops to be **domineering** and to coerce the
AP : 2 3 :060(247) [0381] law is not religion but **domination**, for which religion is
S 2 : 0 2 :018(296) [0467] were sought here, too, for Masses **dominated** everything.
TR : 0 0 :011(321) [0507] church, I Peter 5:3, "Not **domineering** over the clergy."

Dominic (1), Dominican (1), Dominicans (2)
AP : 0 4 :211(136) [0179] Anthony, Bernard, **Dominic**, Francis, and other holy
AP : 2 3 :045(245) [0375] thus surpassing the **Dominican** friars, who eat fish.
AP : 2 7 :053(278) [0437] Thus the **Dominicans** made up the rosary of the blessed
S 3 : 0 5 :002(310) [0491] with Thomas and the **Dominicans** who forget the Word

Dominion (13), Dominions (1)
AG : PR :008(025) [0039] our lands, principalities, **dominions**, cities and territories.
AG : 0 3 :004(030) [0045] eternally rule and have **dominion** over all creatures, that
AL : 0 3 :004(030) [0045] forever reign and have **dominion** over all creatures, and
AP : 1 0 :004(180) [0247] knowing that "death no longer has **dominion** over him."
TR : 0 0 :036(326) [0515] pope not only usurped **dominion** contrary to the
TR : 0 0 :036(326) [0515] to believe that such **dominion** belongs to the pope by
LC : 0 1 :018(367) [0585] their trust in power and **dominion** exalted Jupiter as their
LC : 0 1 :100(378) [0609] you are daily under the **dominion** of the devil, who
LC : 0 2 :031(414) [0685] in order to win us and bring us under his **dominion**.
LC : 0 2 :031(414) [0687] heaven and assumed **dominion** at the right hand of the
LC : 0 2 :037(415) [0687] Just as the Son obtains **dominion** by purchasing us
SD : 0 1 :013(511) [0863] misery, the tyranny and **dominion** of the devil, so that
SD : 0 1 :013(511) [0863] is subject to the devil's **dominion**, abandoned to his
SD : 0 1 :019(511) [0865] and is in the kingdom and under the **dominion** of Satan.

Donatists (4)
AG : 0 8 :003(033) [0047] Accordingly the **Donatists** and all others who hold
AL : 0 8 :003(033) [0047] churches condemn the **Donatists** and others like them
AP : 0 7 :029(173) [0237] where we condemn the **Donatists** and the Wycliffites, who
AP : 0 7 :049(178) [0245] should not incite schisms, as the **Donatists** wickedly did.

Donawerda (1)
PR : PR :027(016) [0027] The Council of the City of **Donawerda**

Donkey (1)
SD : 0 6 :024(568) [0969] and recalcitrant **donkey**, is still a part of them and must

Doomed (1)
LC : 0 2 :028(414) [0685] wrath and displeasure, **doomed** to eternal damnation, as

Door (6), Doors (2)
LC : 0 4 :043(442) [0743] free to every man's **door** just such a priceless medicine
LC : 0 5 :035(450) [0761] and placed at everyone's **door**, yes, upon everyone's
EP : 0 5 :011(479) [0805] true comfort, and the **doors** are again opened to the
SD : 0 5 :027(563) [0961] of the law and reopen the **door** to the papacy in the
SD : 0 7 :100(586) [1007] and came through locked **doors**, in the bread and wine in
SD : 1 0 :015(613) [1057] were wrong and sinful, the **door** has been opened to
SD : 1 1 :033(621) [1073] "Strive to enter by the narrow **door**" (Luke 13:23, 24).
SD : 1 1 :066(627) [1085] 14:6), and again, "I am the **door**; if anyone enters by me,

Dost (4)
AP : 1 2 :108(198) [0283] be justified when Thou **dost** justify us and account us
AP : 2 4 :029(255) [0393] and offering thou **dost** not desire; but thou hast given me
AP : 2 4 :029(255) [0393] me thy Word to hear, and **dost** require me to believe it
SD : 0 1 :035(514) [0869] made me together round about, and thou **dost** destroy

Double (5), Doubly (1)
AP : 2 7 :044(277) [0435] Thus they are guilty of a **double** sin — deceiving men, and
AP : 2 7 :053(278) [0437] saints which is guilty of a **double** fault: it arrogates
SC : 0 9 :003(354) [0561] be considered worthy of **double** honor, especially those
LC : 0 1 :056(372) [0597] So from a single lie a **double** one results — indeed,
LC : 0 1 :161(387) [0627] owe it to God to show "**double** honor" to those who
SD : 0 8 :079(607) [1045] certainty and assurance **doubly** sure on this point, he

Doubt (64), Doubted (2), Doubtful (1), Doubting (6), Doubts (13)
PR : PR :003(003) [0007] either controversy or **doubt** in a Christian and unanimous
PR : PR :022(011) [0019] But we have no **doubt** at all that one can find many
PR : PR :022(012) [0021] for it will without **doubt** be required of the persecutors on
PR : PR :024(013) [0023] do not have the slightest **doubt** that all pious people who
AG : 2 3 :002(053) [0063] There is no **doubt** that Pope Pius, as a prudent and
AG : 2 4 :024(058) [0067] Demanded without **doubt** by the necessity of such
AG : 2 8 :070(093) [0093] although there is no **doubt** that it is in accord with the
AL : 0 1 :001(027) [0043] is true and should be believed without any **doubting**.
AP : 0 2 :042(105) [0117] are a neutral thing — **doubt** about God's wrath, his grace,
AP : 0 4 :019(110) [0125] but they would have him **doubt** whether the disposition is
AP : 0 4 :020(110) [0125] consciences waver and **doubt** and then seek to pile up
AP : 0 4 :021(110) [0127] despair because in their **doubt** they can never experience
AP : 0 4 :035(112) [0131] to despise God and to **doubt** his Word with its threats and
AP : 0 4 :119(124) [0155] when they bid them **doubt** whether they have received the
AP : 0 4 :119(124) [0155] believe that they should **doubt** about receiving the
AP : 0 4 :149(127) [0163] If somebody **doubts** that his sins are forgiven, he insults
AP : 0 4 :167(130) [0169] Who does not often **doubt** whether God hears him?
AP : 0 4 :170(130) [0171] because of God's command; and it **doubts** God's mercy.
AP : 0 4 :264(146) [0195] particle expressing **doubt**, and in his commentaries he
AP : 0 4 :301(153) [0205] On these issues consciences are left in **doubt**.
AP : 0 4 :301(153) [0205] the law, they will have to **doubt** whether they have a
AP : 0 4 :301(153) [0205] When will it love God amid these **doubts** and terrors?
AP : 0 4 :319(156) [0209] leaves consciences in **doubt**, so that they can never be
AP : 0 4 :320(156) [0209] Against these **doubts** Paul says (Rom. 5:1), "Since we are
AP : 0 4 :321(157) [0209] of condignity means to **doubt** and to work without faith
AP : 1 0 :003(179) [0247] Who has ever **doubted** that Christ is a vine in this way
AP : 1 2 :062(190) [0269] If the heart **doubts**, it maintains that God's promises are
AP : 1 2 :084(194) [0277] There is no **doubt** that this is Paul's position that we are
AP : 1 2 :088(195) [0277] for Christ's sake, not **doubting** that they are forgiven
AP : 1 2 :088(195) [0277] If anybody **doubts**, he makes the divine promise a lie, as
AP : 1 2 :089(195) [0277] from faith if they always **doubt** whether they have
AP : 1 2 :089(195) [0277] In such **doubt**, how can they call upon God, how can they
AP : 1 2 :089(195) [0279] tossed about in such **doubt**, they never experience what
AP : 1 2 :127(201) [0289] places who have begun to **doubt** because of the
AP : 1 2 :128(201) [0291] many good men to whom such **doubt** is worse than death.
AP : 1 2 :128(201) [0291] that the doctrinal **doubts** of good men are mere petty
AP : 1 2 :128(201) [0291] Such **doubt** cannot help producing the most bitter hatred
AP : 1 2 :129(202) [0291] in order to heal devout minds and free them from **doubt**.
AP : 1 2 :129(202) [0291] if you are kind and heal **doubting** consciences, you can
AP : 1 2 :130(202) [0291] is not because we are in **doubt** about confession that we
AP : 1 2 :130(202) [0291] many places who are in **doubt** about important issues but
AP : 1 5 :017(217) [0319] God, the conscience must **doubt** whether they please
AP : 1 6 :013(224) [0333] them and put them in **doubt** whether the Gospel
AP : 2 2 :001(236) [0357] There can be no **doubt** that the use of both kinds in the
AP : 2 2 :009(237) [0359] This is no **doubt** the main reason for defending the denial
AP : 2 3 :070(249) [0383] Have no **doubt** that as the blood of Abel cried out in
AP : 2 7 :007(269) [0421] Without **doubt**, God will soon avenge these murders.
AP : 2 7 :019(272) [0425] We do not **doubt** that if you had been told about this
AP : 2 8 :004(281) [0445] such minds tortured by **doubt**, they call to arms.
S 1 : PR :006(289) [0457] of the good Gerson, who **doubted** whether one ought to
S 1 : PR :008(290) [0457] been persuaded beyond a **doubt** that among us there is no
S 2 : 0 1 :005(292) [0463] we must be quite certain and have no **doubts** about it.
TR : 0 0 :044(328) [0517] Then they bid us to **doubt** whether forgiveness is
SC : 0 5 :016(349) [0553] himself, by no means **doubting** but firmly believing that
SC : 0 6 :010(352) [0557] believe these words, or **doubts** them, is unworthy and
LC : PR :018(361) [0573] Now, I know beyond a **doubt** that such lazy-bellies and
LC : 0 1 :008(365) [0583] he who has nothing **doubts** and despairs as if he never
LC : 0 1 :277(402) [0661] to his neighbors, he would no **doubt** be told: "You fool!
LC : 0 3 :022(423) [0703] needs, and we shall never **doubt** that our prayer pleases
LC : 0 3 :023(423) [0703] would always be in **doubt**, saying, "I have prayed, but
LC : 0 3 :058(428) [0713] alone expect, without **doubting**, eternal blessings from
LC : 0 3 :119(436) [0731] to it — that is, not to **doubt** that our prayer is surely
LC : 0 3 :121(436) [0731] prayer but remain in **doubt**, saying, "Why should I be so
LC : 0 3 :123(436) [0731] ask in faith, with no **doubting**, for he who doubts is like a
LC : 0 3 :123(436) [0731] no doubting, for he who **doubts** is like a wave of the sea
LC : 0 4 :006(437) [0733] You should not **doubt**, then, that Baptism is of divine
LC : 0 4 :042(442) [0743] them, it may well **doubt** whether they could all be true.
LC : 0 5 :010(448) [0755] and well put that it is **doubtful** if he has said anything
EP : 0 3 :009(474) [0793] still have no reason to **doubt** either the righteousness
EP : 1 1 :016(497) [0837] doctrine but are driven to **doubt** and despair, or in such a
SD : PR :008(502) [0849] be scandalized; some will **doubt** if the pure doctrine can
SD : 0 1 :058(519) [0879] if the clergy are in **doubt** whether or not original sin is a
SD : 0 2 :047(530) [0901] into grave anxiety and **doubt**, and wonder if God has
SD : 0 4 :023(555) [0945] Gospel, give occasion for **doubt**, are dangerous in many
SD : 0 7 :034(575) [0983] understand beyond all **doubt** what the Augsburg
SD : 0 7 :047(578) [0989] Redeemer, without any **doubts** or arguments as to how it
SD : 0 7 :048(578) [0989] supper, there can be no **doubt** that he was speaking of
SD : 0 7 :053(578) [0991] There is therefore no **doubt** that in the other part of the
SD : 1 1 :010(618) [1067] with burdensome **doubts** and say: "Since God has
SD : 1 1 :012(618) [1067] From this it is beyond all **doubt** that the true
SD : 1 1 :036(622) [1075] it with absolute certainty and not **doubt** it in the least.
SD : 1 1 :054(625) [1081] Thus there is no **doubt** that before the world began God
SD : 1 1 :056(625) [1081] Without **doubt** God also knows and has determined for
SD : 1 1 :072(628) [1085] in holy Baptism, and not **doubt** that according to his
SD : 1 1 :073(628) [1087] within themselves, the less they will **doubt** their election.
SD : 1 1 :077(629) [1089] diligence, and in no way **doubt** the drawing of the Father

Dough (2)
SD : 0 1 :038(515) [0871] corrupted by sin, for the **dough** out of which God forms
SD : 0 1 :039(515) [0871] perverted, and sinful **dough** into hell-fire, but out of it he

Down (48)
PR : PR :013(007) [0013] and is necessary for this end and put it **down** in one book.
AG : 2 6 :035(069) [0075] your hearts be weighed **down** with dissipation," and
AG : 2 8 :026(084) [0087] has given me for building up and not for tearing **down**."
AG : 2 8 :042(088) [0089] was given for building up and not for tearing **down**.
AL : 2 6 :035(069) [0075] your hearts be weighed **down** with dissipation," and
AL : 2 8 :026(084) [0087] the authority for building up and not for tearing **down**."
AL : 2 8 :042(088) [0089] was given for building up and not for tearing **down**?
AP : 0 4 :022(110) [0127] and I Tim. 1:9, "The law is laid **down** for the lawless."
AP : 0 4 :236(140) [0185] These tumults would die **down** if our opponents did not
AP : 0 4 :289(151) [0203] of justification, handed **down** by the scholastic
AP : 0 4 :325(157) [0211] have so clearly handed **down** the doctrine that we need
AP : 0 7 :038(176) [0241] are supposed to have been handed **down** by the apostles.
AP : 1 2 :050(189) [0265] and brings to life; he brings **down** to Sheol and raises up."
AP : 1 3 :002(211) [0309] provided what is handed **down** in Scripture is preserved.
AP : 1 5 :046(221) [0327] your hearts be weighed **down** with dissipation," and Paul
AP : 2 1 :018(231) [0347] Ps. 72:11, 15, "May all kings fall **down** before him!
AP : 2 4 :014(251) [0389] to do this we must first set **down** the nature of a sacrifice.
AP : 2 7 :003(269) [0419] number of years written **down** by him in the
AP : 2 8 :016(283) [0449] and they did not set them **down** as though they could not
AP : 2 8 :021(284) [0449] Clearly it does not set **down** the universal commandment
S 2 : 0 3 :002(298) [0471] them or tear them **down** rather than preserve them with
SC : 0 7 :005(353) [0559] Then quickly lie **down** and sleep in peace.
LC : PR :014(360) [0571] walking, standing, lying **down**, or rising, and keep them
LC : 0 1 :037(369) [0591] will not forget his anger **down** to their children's children.
LC : 0 1 :046(370) [0593] despised man, hunted **down** and persecuted, his life
LC : 0 1 :186(390) [0633] murder, nevertheless call **down** curses and imprecations
LC : 0 1 :244(398) [0649] out our chests and purse **down** to the last penny, and then
LC : 0 1 :247(398) [0651] skin and scrape him right **down** to the bone, and you
LC : 0 1 :276(402) [0659] to observe the order laid **down** by the Gospel, Matthew
LC : 0 1 :300(405) [0667] belong much farther **down** in the scale, where the Seventh
LC : 0 3 :011(421) [0701] those who were struck **down** for their sin did not return to
LC : 0 3 :063(428) [0715] us, put us to flight, cut us **down**, and bring us once more
LC : 0 3 :069(429) [0717] now to repulse and beat **down** all that the devil, bishops,
LC : 0 4 :050(443) [0745] him; in short, all this time **down** to the present day no
EP : 0 3 :009(474) [0793] and many shortcomings **down** to their graves, they still
EP : 0 7 :012(483) [0811] only Mary's Son, is so set **down** at the right hand of God,
SD : RN :005(504) [0851] form in which it was set **down** in writing in the year 1530
SD : 0 1 :030(513) [0867] from beginning to end, **down** to the ultimate part
SD : 0 6 :005(564) [0963] that the law is not laid **down** for the just, as St. Paul says
SD : 0 6 :012(566) [0967] brings to life, he brings **down** into Sheol, and raises up."
SD : 0 6 :018(567) [0967] Old Adam clings to them **down** to the grave, the conflict
SD : 0 8 :004(592) [1017] went so far as to load **down** Dr. Luther's teaching, as
SD : 0 8 :044(599) [1029] scale, then his side goes **down** and we go upward like a
SD : 0 8 :084(607) [1045] wherever you put God **down** for me, you must also put
SD : 0 8 :084(607) [1045] for me, you must also put the humanity **down** for me.
SD : 1 1 :004(617) [1065] "I know your sitting **down** and your going out and
SD : 1 1 :012(618) [1067] Word of God is written **down** for us, not for the purpose
SD : 1 1 :034(622) [1075] into my kingdom, but **down** in my heart I am not

Dr. (85) *(See also "Doctor")*
PR : PR :004(003) [0007] and pious person, **Dr.** Martin Luther, and how in this
PR : PR :005(004) [0009] with God's Word, as they were while **Dr.** Luther was
PR : PR :025(014) [0023] Catechism of that highly enlightened man, **Dr.** Luther.
S 1 : 0 0 :000(287) [0453] Written by **Dr.** Martin Luther in the year 1537
S 1 : PR :000(288) [0455] Preface of **Dr.** Martin Luther
S 3 : 1 5 :005(316) [0501] **Dr.** Martin Luther subscribed
S 3 : 1 5 :005(316) [0501] **Dr.** Justus Jonas, rector, subscribed with his own hand
S 3 : 1 5 :005(316) [0501] **Dr.** John Bugenhagen, of Pomerania, subscribed
S 3 : 1 5 :005(316) [0501] **Dr.** Caspar Creutziger subscribed
S 3 : 1 5 :005(317) [0501] I, **Dr.** Urban Rhegius, superintendent of the churches in
S 3 : 1 5 :005(317) [0501] I, **Dr.** John Bugenhagen of Pomerania, again subscribe in
S 3 : 1 5 :005(318) [0501] I, **Dr.** John Lang, preacher of the church in Erfurt, in my
TR : 0 0 :082(334) [0529] I, **Dr.** John Bugenhagen, of Pomerania, subscribe the
TR : 0 0 :082(334) [0529] I also, **Dr.** Urban Rhegius, superintendent of the churches
TR : 0 0 :082(000) [0529] made at Wittenberg with **Dr.** Bucer and others.
TR : 0 0 :082(000) [0529] in the German language by **Dr.** Martin Luther, our most
TR : 0 0 :082(000) [0529] you, most renowned man, **Dr.** John Bugenhagen, most
SC : 0 0 :000(337) [0531] The Small Catechism of **Dr.** Martin Luther for Ordinary
EP : RN :005(465) [0777] of their souls, we subscribe **Dr.** Luther's Small and Large
EP : 0 7 :010(483) [0811] are those which **Dr.** Luther proposed in his *Great*
EP : 0 8 :003(487) [0819] **Dr.** Luther and his followers have contended for the
EP : 0 8 :017(489) [0823] of God's right hand, as **Dr.** Luther says on the basis of
EP : 0 9 :003(492) [0827] teach it in all simplicity, as **Dr.** Luther of blessed memory
EP : 1 2 :031(501) [0843] **Dr.** James Andreae subscribed
EP : 1 2 :031(501) [0843] **Dr.** Nicholas Selnecker subscribed
EP : 1 2 :031(501) [0843] **Dr.** Andrew Musculus subscribed
EP : 1 2 :031(501) [0843] **Dr.** Christopher Koerner subscribed
EP : 1 2 :031(501) [0843] **Dr.** Martin Chemnitz
SD : PR :001(501) [0847] of God and purified by **Dr.** Luther, of blessed and holy
SD : RN :002(503) [0851] of the Word of God as **Dr.** Luther of blessed memory had
SD : RN :005(504) [0851] ministry of that illustrious man of God, **Dr.** Luther.
SD : RN :008(505) [0853] unanimous adherence to **Dr.** Luther's Small and Large
SD : RN :009(505) [0853] of the doctrine which **Dr.** Luther of blessed memory
SD : 0 1 :006(509) [0861] **Dr.** Luther calls this sin "nature-sin" or "person-sin" in
SD : 0 1 :056(518) [0877] being corrected either by **Dr.** Luther or by any other
SD : 0 1 :061(519) [0879] the Word of God, just as **Dr.** Luther in his Latin
SD : 0 2 :023(525) [0889] **Dr.** Luther calls this a "capacity," which he explains as
SD : 0 2 :036(528) [0895] In his Large Catechism **Dr.** Luther writes: "I am also a
SD : 0 2 :040(528) [0895] In **Dr.** Luther's Small Catechism we read: "I believe that
SD : 0 2 :043(529) [0897] include a statement from **Dr.** Luther's *Great Confession*
SD : 0 2 :044(529) [0897] In these words **Dr.** Luther, of sacred and holy memory,
SD : 0 2 :044(529) [0897] **Dr.** Luther discusses this entire matter in his book *The*
SD : 0 3 :006(540) [0917] In the same vein **Dr.** Luther declared: "Where this single
SD : 0 3 :021(542) [0921] righteousness of faith, as **Dr.** Luther used the term in his
SD : 0 3 :028(544) [0925] of the Epistle to the Galatians **Dr.** Luther well states:
SD : 0 3 :041(546) [0931] For **Dr.** Luther's excellent statement remains true: "There
SD : 0 3 :067(551) [0937] for the sake of brevity to **Dr.** Luther's beautiful and
SD : 0 5 :022(562) [0959] **Dr.** Luther very diligently urged this distinction in nearly
SD : 0 6 :009(565) [0965] **Dr.** Luther thoroughly explains this at greater length in
SD : 0 7 :010(571) [0975] **Dr.** Luther clearly presents the same view in the Small
SD : 0 7 :012(571) [0977] in Wittenberg, and **Dr.** Martin Luther and other
SD : 0 7 :017(572) [0979] By common consent **Dr.** Luther drafted the Smalcald
SD : 0 7 :020(572) [0979] **Dr.** Luther explains and confirms this position at greater
SD : 0 7 :029(574) [0981] shall say after my death, 'If **Dr.** Luther were living now,
SD : 0 7 :033(575) [0983] **Dr.** Luther, who understood the true intention of the
SD : 0 7 :034(575) [0983] from the exposition of **Dr.** Luther, as the chief teacher of
SD : 0 7 :038(576) [0985] but a sacramental union, as **Dr.** Luther and our
SD : 0 7 :040(576) [0985] *the Communion* **Dr.** Luther defended with great zeal and
SD : 0 7 :041(576) [0985] Since **Dr.** Luther is rightly to be regarded as the most
SD : 0 7 :041(576) [0985] any other source than from **Dr.** Luther's doctrinal and
SD : 0 7 :087(585) [1003] rule was first formulated and explained by **Dr.** Luther.
SD : 0 7 :091(585) [1005] the basis of God's Word by **Dr.** Luther in his polemical
SD : 0 7 :093(586) [1005] these (the same ones that **Dr.** Luther advanced against the
SD : 0 7 :104(587) [1009] These words of **Dr.** Luther also show clearly in what sense
SD : 0 7 :105(588) [1009] But when **Dr.** Luther or we use the word "spiritual" in this
SD : 0 8 :002(591) [1015] For when **Dr.** Luther maintained with solid arguments
SD : 0 8 :003(592) [1017] **Dr.** Luther contradicted and mightily refuted this, as his
SD : 0 8 :004(592) [1017] went so far as to load down **Dr.** Luther's teaching, as well
SD : 0 8 :017(594) [1021] into one essence but, as **Dr.** Luther writes, into one
SD : 0 8 :021(595) [1021] **Dr.** Luther has explained this thoroughly in his *Great*
SD : 0 8 :026(596) [1025] he laid it aside, and as **Dr.** Luther explains it, he kept it
SD : 0 8 :028(596) [1025] in a mundane way, but as **Dr.** Luther explains, after the
SD : 0 8 :038(598) [1027] suffered for us) and since **Dr.** Luther in his *Great*
SD : 0 8 :038(598) [1027] we shall here quote **Dr.** Luther's own words, so that the
SD : 0 8 :044(599) [1029] Likewise, **Dr.** Luther states in his treatise *Concerning the*
SD : 0 8 :080(607) [1045] of this solid foundation, **Dr.** Luther, of blessed memory,
SD : 0 8 :085(608) [1045] shortly before his death, **Dr.** Luther states: "According to
SD : 0 8 :086(608) [1047] many similar testimonies in **Dr.** Luther's writings,
SD : 0 9 :001(610) [1051] Christian Creed, to which **Dr.** Luther directs us in the
SD : 1 0 :024(615) [1061] In a special opinion **Dr.** Luther exhaustively instructs the
SD : 1 2 :040(636) [1103] **Dr.** James Andreae, subscribed
SD : 1 2 :040(636) [1103] **Dr.** Nicholas Selnecker, subscribed
SD : 1 2 :040(636) [1103] **Dr.** Andrew Musculus, subscribed
SD : 1 2 :040(636) [1103] **Dr.** Christopher Koerner, subscribed
SD : 1 2 :040(636) [1103] **Dr.** Martin Chemnitz

Drach (2)
S 3 : 1 5 :005(317) [0501] Also I, John **Drach**, professor and minister in Marburg,
TR : 0 0 :082(334) [0529] John **Drach**, of Marburg, subscribed

Draft (1), Drafted (6)
S 1 : PR :001(288) [0455] was therefore instructed to **draft** and assemble articles of
S 1 : PR :014(291) [0459] I have **drafted** only a few articles, for, apart from these,
EP : RN :004(465) [0777] thereof and the Articles **drafted** at Smalcald in the year
SD : 0 7 :001(568) [0971] Augsburg Confession was **drafted** and submitted to the
SD : 0 7 :012(571) [0977] and Upper Germany **drafted** the following articles of
SD : 0 7 :017(572) [0979] consent Dr. Luther **drafted** the Smalcald Articles, which
SD : 1 0 :018(614) [1059] Articles, which were **drafted** and adopted in 1537, show

Dragged (1)
LC : 0 1 :059(372) [0597] and his name have to be **dragged** in to turn the villainy

Dragon (2)
S 2 : 0 2 :011(294) [0465] Besides, this **dragon**'s tail — that is, the Mass — has
S 3 : 0 8 :009(313) [0497] in man by the old **dragon**, and it is the source, strength,

Drama (1)
LC : 0 3 :031(424) [0707] witnessed a far different **drama**: the devil would have

Drank (2)
AP : 2 7 :059(279) [0439] (35:6), neither had any possessions nor **drank** any wine.
EP : 0 7 :015(483) [0813] it is written, "And they all **drank** of it" (Mark 14:23).

Draw (22), Drawing (3), Drawn (16), Draws (13)
PR : PR :020(010) [0017] like Luther himself, were **drawn** by adversaries (although
AG : 0 1 :007(056) [0065] that the people may be **drawn** to the Communion and
AG : 2 7 :051(079) [0083] praised above all measure, **draw** many harmful
AL : 0 0 :002(048) [0059] which we have now **drawn** up, for even the canons are
AL : 2 7 :051(079) [0083] The people **draw** many pernicious conclusions from such
AP : 0 4 :082(118) [0145] great high priest,...let us then with confidence **draw** near."
AP : 0 4 :082(118) [0145] By bidding us **draw** near to God with trust not in our
AP : 0 4 :222(137) [0181] No one can **draw** anything more from this text than that
AP : 0 4 :333(158) [0211] without the high priest we cannot **draw** near to the Father
AP : 0 4 :360(162) [0219] Chrysippus-like, they **draw** the following absurd
AP : 2 0 :006(227) [0339] horrible decree has been **drawn** up against us; this would
LC : 0 1 :015(366) [0583] from everything else, and **draw** us to himself, because he
LC : 0 3 :004(420) [0699] necessary to exhort and **draw** people to prayer, as Christ
LC : 0 3 :011(421) [0701] he wishes rather to **draw** us to himself so that we may
LC : 0 3 :022(423) [0703] be encouraged and **drawn** to pray because, in addition to
LC : 0 3 :104(434) [0727] faith, hope, and love, to **draw** us into unbelief, false
LC : 0 4 :015(438) [0735] nothing but the water **drawn** from the well, and then
LC : 0 4 :044(442) [0743] Baptism aright, we must **draw** strength and comfort from
LC : 0 4 :058(444) [0747] and stupid persons **draw** the conclusion that where there
LC : 0 4 :065(444) [0749] which covers us completely, and being **drawn** out again.
LC : 0 5 :064(454) [0769] above, which should most powerfully **draw** and impel us.
EP : 0 2 :013(471) [0789] who imagine that God **draws** men to himself, enlightens
EP : 0 2 :016(472) [0789] such as, "God **draws**, but draws the person who is
EP : 0 2 :016(472) [0789] such as, "God draws, but **draws** the person who is
SD : RN :001(503) [0851] pure Christian religion is **drawn** together out of the Word
SD : RN :004(504) [0851] soundly understood was **drawn** together out of God's
SD : RN :005(504) [0851] This doctrine, **drawn** from and conformed to the Word
SD : RN :010(506) [0855] to which, because it is **drawn** from the Word of God, all
SD : 0 2 :024(525) [0891] reborn, renewed, and **drawn** by the Holy Spirit, he can do
SD : 0 2 :026(526) [0891] come to Christ unless the Father **draws** him (John 6:44).
SD : 0 2 :044(529) [0897] God himself must **draw** man and give him new birth.
SD : 0 2 :050(531) [0901] to eternal salvation, to **draw** them to himself, convert
SD : 0 2 :054(531) [0903] breaks our hearts, and **draws** man, so that through the
SD : 0 2 :060(533) [0905] the Lord God **draws** the person whom he wills to
SD : 0 2 :060(533) [0905] he wills to convert, and **draws** him in such a way that
SD : 0 2 :066(534) [0907] Spirit, the way two horses **draw** a wagon together, such a
SD : 0 2 :080(536) [0911] the holy sacraments, God **draws** man to himself,
SD : 0 2 :086(537) [0913] something," and "God **draws**, but he draws the person
SD : 0 2 :086(537) [0913] and "God draws, but he **draws** the person who wills,"
SD : 0 2 :088(538) [0915] conversion, through the **drawing** of the Holy Spirit, God
SD : 0 3 :035(545) [0927] should and must not be **drawn** or mingled into the article

Continued ▶

S D : 0 3 :036(545) [0929] God they should not be **drawn**, woven, or mingled in.
S D : 0 4 :022(554) [0945] that works are not **drawn** into and mingled with the
S D : 0 4 :037(557) [0949] clear answer: If anyone **draws** good works into the article
S D : 1 0 :018(614) [1059] The following testimonies **drawn** from the Smalcald
S D : 1 1 :010(618) [1065] however, leads many to **draw** and formulate strange,
S D : 1 1 :049(624) [1079] From this Paul **draws** the certain and indubitable
S D : 1 1 :052(625) [1081] in this matter and **draw** our own conclusions and brood,
S D : 1 1 :055(625) [1081] make our own deductions, **draw** conclusions, or brood
S D : 1 1 :076(628) [1087] that no one comes to Christ unless the Father **draw** him.
S D : 1 1 :076(629) [1087] wait for the Father to **draw** him without Word and
S D : 1 1 :076(629) [1087] The Father indeed **draws** by the power of the Holy
S D : 1 1 :077(629) [1089] and in no way doubt the **drawing** of the Father because
S D : 1 1 :077(629) [1089] And this is the **drawing** of the Father.

Dreadful (6), Dreadfully (1)
S 1 : P R :003(289) [0455] But the Roman court is **dreadfully** afraid of a free
S 3 : 0 3 :008(304) [0481] puts it) from the **dreadful** captivity to sin, and this
L C : 0 3 :115(435) [0731] many he hounds to suicide or other **dreadful** catastrophes
E P : 0 7 :034(485) [0815] is unable (a **dreadful** statement!) to cause his body to be
S D : 0 1 :005(509) [0861] the abominable and **dreadful** inherited disease which has
S D : 0 1 :062(519) [0879] how abominable and **dreadful** this quality and accident
S D : 0 2 :021(525) [0889] not see or recognize the **dreadful**, cruel wrath of God

Dream (16), Dreamed (3), Dreaming (1), Dreams (6)
A L : 2 0 :018(043) [0055] and profane men, who **dream** that Christian
A P : 0 4 :018(109) [0125] but should **dream** that they merit the forgiveness of sins
A P : 0 4 :037(112) [0131] men to make up these **dreams** that a man guilty of mortal
A P : 0 4 :222(138) [0181] justification even to be **dreamed** without Christ, the
A P : 0 4 :224(138) [0181] it would be a foolish **dream** to imagine that we are
A P : 0 4 :248(142) [0191] and smug minds who **dream** they have faith but do not.
A P : 0 4 :265(146) [0197] nor understands faith, it **dreams** that the merit of these
A P : 0 7 :020(171) [0233] We are not **dreaming** about some Platonic republic, as
A P : 1 2 :064(191) [0269] Those who **dream** that the heart can find peace without
A P : 1 2 :123(200) [0289] sinfully twist the Word of God to suit their vain **dreams**!
A P : 1 3 :013(212) [0311] to the fanatics who **dream** that the Holy Spirit does not
A P : 1 6 :007(223) [0331] hold it, as in the Jewish **dream** of the messianic kingdom;
A P : 1 8 :010(226) [0337] suppressed by those who **dream** that men can obey the
A P : 2 1 :009(230) [0345] praying, except for the **dream** recorded in the Second
A P : 2 4 :087(265) [0413] have to do with these **dreams** about the efficacy of the act
A P : 2 7 :024(273) [0427] Since they **dream** that they have merits of
A P : 2 7 :038(275) [0433] of life, God pointed in a **dream** to a certain shoemaker in
S 2 : 0 2 :014(295) [0467] St. Augustine never **dreamed** of) shall we be ready to
L C : 0 1 :020(367) [0585] fashion their fancies and **dreams** about God into an idol
L C : 0 4 :063(444) [0749] Baptism merely as an empty sign, as the fanatics **dream**.
E P : 0 2 :008(470) [0787] 1. The mad **dream** of the so-called Stoic philosophers and
E P : 0 4 :018(477) [0801] Such an Epicurean **dream** concerning faith can damn
E P : 0 8 :021(490) [0823] has been changed into the deity, as Eutyches **dreamed**.
S D : 0 4 :015(553) [0943] since many people **dream** up for themselves a dead faith
S D : 0 4 :031(556) [0947] delusion which some **dream** up that it is impossible to
S D : 0 7 :099(586) [1005] mode, as the fanatic spirit **dreams**, for God is not a

Dregs (1)
A P : 2 2 :011(238) [0361] These are the **dregs** of Eck.

Dress (6), Dressed (3)
A G : 1 8 :005(040) [0051] visit a friend, whether to **dress** or undress, whether to
A G : 2 6 :009(065) [0071] fasted in this way, and **dressed** in this way was said to live
A P : 0 7 :034(175) [0239] if the German style of **dress** is not a devotion to God
A P : 0 7 :034(175) [0239] Christ even though they **dress** according to the French
A P : 1 2 :144(205) [0297] Still they **dress** up these works with fancy titles; they call
A P : 1 2 :163(208) [0303] pilgrimage to St. James **dressed** in armor or to perform
S 1 : P R :012(290) [0459] lewdness, extravagance in **dress**, gluttony, gambling, vain
S 2 : 0 2 :015(295) [0467] what they ate, how they **dressed**, and what kind of houses
L C : 0 1 :088(377) [0605] with garlands and **dress** up in our best clothes, but, as has

Drilled (1)
L C : S P :003(362) [0575] children's sermons and diligently **drilled** in their practice.

Drink (60), Drinking (11), Drinks (3)
A G : 1 8 :005(040) [0051] whether or not to eat or **drink** or visit a friend, whether to
A G : 2 2 :001(049) [0059] and order of Christ, "**Drink** of it, all of you" (Matt.
A G : 2 2 :002(049) [0059] commands with clear words that all should **drink** of it.
A G : 2 6 :024(067) [0073] does not mean food and **drink**," and in Col. 2:16 he says,
A G : 2 6 :025(067) [0073] in questions of food and **drink** or with regard to a
A G : 2 8 :044(088) [0089] in questions of food and **drink** or with regard to a festival
A L : 1 8 :005(040) [0051] the field, will to eat and **drink**, will to have a friend, will
A L : 2 2 :001(049) [0059] of the Lord in Matt. 26:27, "**Drink** of it, all of you."
A L : 2 2 :002(049) [0059] with reference to the cup that all should **drink** of it.
A L : 2 4 :012(057) [0065] eats the bread or **drinks** the cup of the Lord in an
A L : 2 6 :024(067) [0073] of God is not food and **drink**," and in Col. 2:16, "Let no
A L : 2 6 :025(067) [0073] in questions of food and **drink** or with regard to a festival
A L : 2 8 :044(088) [0089] in questions of food and **drink** or with regard to a festival
A P : 0 7 :035(175) [0239] in questions of food and **drink** or with regard to a festival
A P : 0 7 :036(175) [0241] does not mean food and **drink** but righteousness and
A P : 0 7 :050(178) [0245] legitimate for them to use the air, light, food, and **drink**.
A P : 1 2 :159(207) [0301] who did not deserve to **drink** the cup must drink it."
A P : 1 2 :159(207) [0301] who did not deserve to drink the cup must **drink** it."
A P : 1 5 :030(219) [0323] in questions of food and **drink** or with regard to a festival
A P : 1 6 :002(222) [0331] make use of medicine or architecture, food or **drink** or air
A P : 2 2 :003(236) [0359] himself, and so eat of the bread and **drink** of the cup."
A P : 2 3 :019(242) [0369] as he wants to nourish our life by using food and **drink**.
A P : 2 4 :021(253) [0391] were the oblation, the **drink** offerings, the thank offering,
A P : 2 4 :035(256) [0397] as you eat this bread and **drink** the cup, you proclaim the
A P : 2 4 :036(257) [0397] burning of the lamb, the **drink** offering, and the offering
A P : 2 4 :036(257) [0397] The **drink** offering symbolizes the sprinkling, that is, the
A P : 2 4 :038(257) [0399] There must be a **drink** offering, namely, the effect of the
A P : 2 8 :007(282) [0445] depends upon food, **drink**, clothing, and similar matters.
A P : 2 8 :007(282) [0445] "The kingdom of God is not food or **drink**."
A P : 2 8 :010(282) [0447] eternal life since food, **drink**, clothing, and the like are
S C : P R :012(339) [0535] them with food and **drink** and should notify them that
S C : P R :022(341) [0537] this," but he said, "Do this, as often as you **drink** it," etc.
S C : 0 6 :002(351) [0555] and wine, given to us Christians to eat and to **drink**.
S C : 0 6 :004(351) [0557] thanks he gave it to them, saying, '**Drink** of it, all of you.
S C : 0 6 :004(351) [0557] Do this, as often as you **drink** it, in remembrance of me.'"
S C : 0 6 :005(352) [0557] What is the benefit of such eating and **drinking**?
S C : 0 6 :007(352) [0557] can bodily eating and **drinking** produce such great
S C : 0 6 :008(352) [0557] Answer: The eating and **drinking** do not in themselves
S C : 0 6 :008(352) [0557] by the bodily eating and **drinking**, are the chief thing in
S C : 0 9 :003(354) [0561] same house, eating and **drinking** what they provide, for
L C : S P :016(363) [0577] them they should not be given anything to eat or **drink**.
L C : S P :023(364) [0579] Do this, as often as you **drink** it, in remembrance of me'"
L C : 0 1 :024(367) [0587] gives us body, life, food, **drink**, nourishment, health,
L C : 0 1 :191(391) [0635] you gave me no food or **drink**, I was a stranger, and you
L C : 0 2 :013(412) [0681] so forth; my food and **drink**, clothing, means of support,
L C : 0 3 :076(431) [0721] God to give us food and **drink**, clothing, house, home,
L C : 0 4 :056(444) [0747] me to go, eat, and **drink**, etc. and that he gives me his
L C : 0 5 :003(447) [0753] Do this, as often as you **drink** it, in remembrance of
L C : 0 5 :008(447) [0755] are commanded by Christ's word to eat and **drink**.
L C : 0 5 :013(448) [0755] '**Drink** of it, all of you, this is the new covenant in my
L C : 0 5 :017(448) [0757] but, "Take, eat and **drink**, this is my body and blood."
L C : 0 5 :022(449) [0757] Christ bids me eat and **drink** in order that the sacrament
L C : 0 5 :034(450) [0761] it and bid you eat and **drink**, that you may take it as your
L C : 0 5 :042(451) [0763] his Christians to eat and **drink** and thereby remember
L C : 0 5 :069(454) [0769] person willfully eats and **drinks** what is forbidden him by
E P : 0 7 :015(483) [0811] direct us to take, eat, and **drink**, all of which took place in
E P : 0 7 :029(485) [0815] as truly as we eat and **drink** bread and wine in the
E P : 0 7 :042(486) [0817] of Christ's body and **drinking** of his blood, which we
S D : 0 7 :010(571) [0975] and wine, given to us Christians to eat and to **drink**."
S D : 0 7 :020(573) [0979] Christ's word commands us Christians to eat and **drink**."
S D : 0 7 :022(573) [0979] **Drink** of it, all of you, this is the new covenant in my
S D : 0 7 :026(573) [0981] but, 'Take, eat and **drink**, this is my body and blood.'
S D : 0 7 :048(578) [0989] and natural wine as well as of oral eating and **drinking**.
S D : 0 7 :053(579) [0991] (namely, what you are **drinking** with your mouth from
S D : 0 7 :054(579) [0991] all who eat this bread and **drink** the cup truly receive and
S D : 0 7 :060(580) [0993] unworthy eating and **drinking** sin grievously against the
S D : 0 7 :060(580) [0993] "Who eats the bread or **drinks** the cup of the Lord in an
S D : 0 7 :063(581) [0995] when all who eat and **drink** the blessed bread and wine in
S D : 0 7 :064(581) [0995] body and blood, and said therewith, "Eat and **drink**."
S D : 0 7 :064(581) [0995] to oral eating and **drinking** — not, however, in a coarse,
S D : 0 7 :074(583) [0999] be it the eating and **drinking** or the faith of the
S D : 0 7 :082(584) [1001] to us to eat and to **drink**, as Paul says, "The cup of
S D : 0 7 :084(584) [1001] it, receive it, eat and **drink** it, and therewith proclaim the
S D : 1 0 :013(613) [1057] in questions of food and **drink**, or with regard to a

Drive (12), Driven (19), Driver (2), Drives (12), Driving (3)
A G : 2 0 :019(043) [0055] poor consciences were **driven** to rely on their own efforts,
A G : 2 0 :020(043) [0055] Some were **driven** by their conscience into monasteries in
A G : 2 0 :032(045) [0057] power of the devil, who **drives** poor human beings into
A G : 2 6 :036(069) [0075] kind of demon cannot be **driven** out by anything but
A G : 2 7 :020(074) [0079] command that urges, **drives**, and compels us to do this,
A L : 2 0 :020(044) [0055] were by their consciences **driven** into the desert, into
A L : 2 1 :001(046) [0057] of David in waging war to **drive** the Turk out of his
A L : 2 6 :036(069) [0075] kind of demon cannot be **driven** out by anything but
A P : 0 4 :020(110) [0125] and the terrors of conscience **drive** out our trust in works.
A P : 0 4 :021(110) [0127] on the other hand, they **drive** to despair because in their
A P : 0 4 :023(110) [0127] weakness and by the devil, who **drives** it to open crimes.
A P : 0 4 :139(126) [0161] deceived and err, nor be **driven** to do anything against
A P : 0 4 :265(146) [0197] of men, and it cannot be **driven** out unless we are divinely
A P : 0 7 :029(173) [0237] body of the devil, who **drives** them on and holds them
A P : 1 1 :010(182) [0253] This teaching has **driven** many devout minds to hopeless
A P : 2 0 :009(228) [0341] and punishments to try to **drive** you away from the
S 2 : 0 2 :004(293) [0463] Why, then, do you **drive** the world into wretchedness and
S 2 : 0 4 :016(301) [0477] but only to damn, murder, and **drive** us to idolatry.
S 3 : 0 3 :002(304) [0479] He **drives** all together into terror and despair.
L C : 0 1 :123(382) [0617] do nothing until they are **driven** with blows; and they
L C : 0 3 :011(421) [0701] he will not cast us out or **drive** us away, even though we
L C : 0 3 :024(423) [0703] our needs, which ought to **drive** and impel us to pray
L C : 0 3 :026(424) [0705] our need, the distress that impels and **drives** us to cry out.
L C : 0 3 :062(428) [0715] when he himself is **driven** out of men's hearts and a
L C : 0 3 :103(434) [0727] us by word and deed and **drives** us to anger and
L C : 0 3 :104(434) [0727] or, on the contrary, to **drive** us into despair, atheism,
L C : 0 3 :111(435) [0729] But prayer can resist him and **drive** him back.
L C : 0 3 :115(435) [0731] many a man's neck and **drives** others to insanity; some he
L C : 0 3 :123(436) [0731] a wave of the sea that is **driven** and tossed by the wind.
L C : 0 5 :044(451) [0763] activity, hounding and **driving** people from it as much as
L C : 0 6 :005(457) [0000] pope and submit to being **driven** and tormented to
L C : 0 6 :017(459) [0000] Thereby the people were **driven** to the point that everyone
L C : 0 6 :023(460) [0000] would need no bailiff to **drive** and beat him but would
L C : 0 6 :025(460) [0000] they have simply **driven** men together in hordes just to
E P : 1 1 :009(495) [0833] Epicurean life, or **drive** men to despair and waken
E P : 1 1 :016(497) [0837] in this doctrine but are **driven** to doubt and despair, or in
S D : 0 1 :013(511) [0863] kinds of blindness, and **drives** them headlong into all
S D : 0 2 :007(521) [0883] captive of the devil who **drives** him (Eph. 2:2; II Tim.
S D : 0 2 :029(527) [0893] He **drives** them into many kinds of manifest sin.
S D : 0 5 :010(559) [0955] law by external works, or **drives** man utterly to despair.
S D : 0 6 :006(564) [0965] free from sins, they would require no law, no **driver**.
S D : 0 6 :006(565) [0965] exhortation, or **driving** by the law they would do what
S D : 0 6 :017(566) [0967] when he is free from this **driver** and is driven by the
S D : 0 6 :017(566) [0967] from this driver and is **driven** by the Spirit of Christ), he
S D : 0 6 :019(567) [0969] as the unconverted are **driven** and coerced into obedience
S D : 1 1 :012(618) [1067] the purpose of thereby **driving** us to despair but in order
S D : 1 1 :074(628) [1087] said in my alarm, I am **driven** far from thy sight" (Ps.
S D : 1 1 :091(631) [1093] no comfort in it but are **driven** to despair, or when

Drop (4)
A P : 1 5 :037(220) [0325] If our people **drop** certain useless traditions, they have
L C : 0 3 :025(423) [0705] prayed whole-heartedly for so much as a **drop** of wine.
E P : 0 3 :002(473) [0793] men are esteemed like a **drop** of water over against the
S D : 0 3 :002(539) [0917] sins of all men are like a **drop** of water compared to the

Drove (2)
A P : 0 4 :190(133) [0175] restrained the devil and **drove** him away from the
L C : 0 1 :102(379) [0609] no other interest or need **drove** us to the Word, yet

Drowned (3), Drowns (1)
S C : 0 4 :012(349) [0551] and evil lusts, should be **drowned** by daily sorrow and

Continued ▶

LC : 0 2 :021(413) [0683] perverse world acts, **drowned** in its blindness, misusing
LC : 0 3 :115(435) [0731] to insanity; some he **drowns**, and many he hounds to
SD : 1 0 :016(613) [1059] his neck and to be **drowned** in the depth of the sea."

Drum (1)
LC : 0 3 :002(420) [0697] upon God incessantly and **drum** into his ears our prayer

Drunk (4), Drunkard (1), Drunkards (1), Drunkenness (2)
SC : 0 9 :002(354) [0561] an apt teacher, no **drunkard**, not violent but gentle, not
LC : 0 1 :096(378) [0607] around in taverns dead **drunk** like swine, but also by that
LC : 0 3 :042(425) [0709] people are adulterers, **drunkards**, gluttons, jealous
LC : 0 3 :102(434) [0727] laziness, gluttony and **drunkenness**, greed and deceit, into
LC : 0 5 :075(455) [0771] spirit, envy, murder, **drunkenness**, carousing, and the
SD : 0 7 :031(574) [0983] I am not **drunk** or irresponsible.
SD : 0 7 :032(574) [0983] Christ are truly eaten and **drunk** in the bread and wine,
SD : 0 7 :105(588) [1009] are received, eaten, and **drunk** spiritually, for although

Dry (2)
LC : 0 1 :238(397) [0647] will hang them not on a green gallows but on a **dry** one.
SD : 0 8 :087(608) [1047] is like a consuming fire on **dry** stubble, will be with them,

Dubious (4)
PR : PR :024(013) [0023] uncertain opinions and **dubious**, disputable imaginations
AP : 2 0 :006(227) [0339] more if we were arguing about **dubious** or trivial matters.
S3 : 0 3 :038(309) [0489] for it consists not of the **dubious**, sinful works which we
SD : RN :019(507) [0857] and that every incorrect, **dubious**, suspicious, and

Duchy (2)
S3 : 1 5 :005(317) [0501] of the churches in the **Duchy** of Lueneburg, subscribe in
TR : 0 0 :082(334) [0529] of the churches in the **Duchy** of Lueneburg, subscribe

Due (43), Dues (1)
PR : PR :001(003) [0007] named below, tender our **due** service, friendship, gracious
PR : PR :016(008) [0013] own volition and with **due** consideration they accepted,
AG : PR :007(025) [0039] Accordingly, after **due** deliberation and counsel, it was
AG : 2 7 :029(075) [0079] of themselves, willingly, and after **due** consideration.
AG : 2 7 :030(075) [0079] be assumed only after **due** consideration and counsel.
AL : 2 0 :014(043) [0055] by grace, were **due** to antecedent merits, for then it would
AP : PR :013(099) [0101] the emperor or the princes, whom I hold in **due** esteem.
AP : 0 4 :024(110) [0127] righteousness of reason its **due** credit; for our corrupt
AP : 0 4 :089(120) [0149] his wages are not reckoned as a gift but are his **due**.
AP : 0 4 :154(128) [0165] him the outward courtesies **due** a guest and a great and
AP : 0 4 :215(137) [0179] not give Christ the honor **due** him, for he has been set
AP : 0 4 :251(143) [0191] say that our propitiation is **due** in part to Christ and in
AP : 0 4 :357(162) [0219] that eternal life is their **due** and that therefore they are
AP : 1 2 :115(199) [0285] as works that are not **due**; we call them canonical
AP : 1 2 :163(208) [0303] and the fruits that are **due**, not to "non-obligatory
AP : 2 7 :028(274) [0429] life if it is maintained by a **due** observance, as by the
AP : 2 7 :034(275) [0431] their own foolish observances the trust that is **due** Christ.
TR : 0 0 :074(332) [0525] and excommunicated them without **due** process of law.
TR : 0 0 :074(332) [0525] power to ban men arbitrarily without **due** process of law!
TR : 0 0 :075(333) [0525] nobody should be condemned without **due** process of law.
SC : 0 8 :007(353) [0559] O Lord, and Thou givest them their food in **due** season.
SC : 0 9 :005(355) [0561] Pay all of them their **dues**, taxes to whom taxes are due,
SC : 0 9 :005(355) [0561] taxes to whom taxes are **due**, revenue to whom revenue is
SC : 0 9 :005(355) [0561] to whom revenue is **due**, respect to whom respect is due,
SC : 0 9 :005(355) [0561] respect to whom respect is **due**, honor to whom honor is
SC : 0 9 :005(355) [0561] is **due**, honor to whom honor is **due**" (Rom. 13:1, 5-7).
SC : 0 9 :012(356) [0563] hand of God, that in **due** time he may exalt you" (I Pet.
LC : PR :020(361) [0573] Then in **due** time they themselves will make the noble
LC : 0 1 :069(374) [0599] children be trained in **due** time to shun falsehood and
LC : 0 1 :070(374) [0601] first gives God the honor **due** him and then the lips do so
LC : 0 1 :141(384) [0621] various kinds of obedience **due** to our superiors, persons
LC : 0 1 :151(386) [0625] gives honor where it is **due**, knows that he pleases God
LC : 0 1 :217(394) [0641] Thus it may in **due** time regain its proper honor, and
EP : 0 4 :010(476) [0799] not coercion but the **due** obedience which genuine
SD : 0 2 :010(522) [0883] ignorance that is in them, **due** to their hardness of heart"
SD : 0 3 :030(544) [0925] comfort and to give **due** honor to the merit of Christ and
SD : 0 3 :035(545) [0927] order to preserve the glory **due** to Christ, the redeemer,
SD : 0 5 :024(562) [0961] of the world, but with the **due** distinction, so that in the
SD : 0 6 :016(566) [0967] between works is **due** to the difference in the individuals
SD : 0 7 :045(577) [0987] them in simple faith and **due** obedience in their strict and
SD : 0 8 :035(597) [1027] treated and explained with **due** discrimination because
SD : 0 8 :035(597) [1027] talks about them without **due** discrimination, the doctrine
SD : 1 1 :046(624) [1079] firmly and certainly — for **due** to the weakness and
SD : 1 1 :087(631) [1091] of God gives God his **due** honor fully and completely.

Duke (23)
PR : PR :027(014) [0025] August, **duke** of Saxony, elector
PR : PR :027(014) [0025] **Duke** Frederick William [of Saxe-Altenburg] and
PR : PR :027(014) [0025] **Duke** John [of Saxe-Weimar] the above two through
PR : PR :027(014) [0025] **Duke** John Casimir [of Saxe-Coburg] and
PR : PR :027(014) [0025] **Duke** John Ernest [of Saxe-Eisenach] the above two
PR : PR :027(014) [0025] Julius, **duke** of Brunswick [-Wolfenbuettel] and
PR : PR :027(014) [0025] Otto, **duke** of Brunswick and Lueneburg [-Harburg]
PR : PR :027(014) [0025] Henry the Younger, **duke** of Brunswick [-Wolfenbuettel]
PR : PR :027(014) [0025] William the Younger, **duke** of Brunswick and Lueneburg
PR : PR :027(014) [0025] Wolf, **duke** of Brunswick [-Grubenhagen] and
PR : PR :027(015) [0025] Ulrich, **duke** of Mecklenburg [-Guestrow]
PR : PR :027(015) [0025] **Duke** John and
PR : PR :027(015) [0025] **Duke** Sigismund August of Mecklenburg [in Ivernack]
PR : PR :027(015) [0025] Louis, **duke** of Wuerttemberg.
AG : 0 0 :007(096) [0095] John, **duke** of Saxony, elector
AG : 0 0 :007(096) [0095] Ernest, **duke** of Lueneburg
AG : 0 0 :007(096) [0095] John Frederick, **duke** of Saxony
AG : 0 0 :007(096) [0095] Francis, **duke** of Lueneburg
AL : 0 0 :017(096) [0095] John, **duke** of Saxony, elector
AL : 0 0 :017(096) [0095] John Frederick, **duke** of Saxony
AL : 0 0 :017(096) [0095] Francis, **duke** of Lueneburg
S3 : 1 5 :005(317) [0501] Conrad Oettinger, preacher of **Duke** Ulric of Pforzheim
TR : 0 0 :082(335) [0529] of Pforzheim, preacher of Ulric, **duke** of Wuerttemberg

Duly (4)
PR : PR :022(012) [0019] theologians and ministers **duly** to remind even those who
AP : 1 4 :001(214) [0315] and the sacraments in the church unless he is **duly** called.
LC : 0 3 :038(425) [0707] the great necessity of **duly** honoring his name and keeping
SD : 1 0 :008(612) [1055] of it, but that we should **duly** distinguish between the

Dung (3)
LC : PR :013(360) [0571] but also to be chased out by dogs and pelted with **dung**.
LC : 0 5 :056(453) [0767] to the bright sun, or as **dung** in contrast to jewels.
SD : 0 7 :067(582) [0997] of Christ as "Satan's **dung**, by which the devil amuses

Duns (1)
AP : 1 2 :068(192) [0271] of great reputation, like **Duns** Scotus, Gabriel Biel, and

Dupes (1)
SD : 0 2 :043(529) [0897] we must remain the **dupes** and captives of sin and the

Duration (1)
EP : 1 1 :004(495) [0833] imposes a limit on its **duration**, so that in spite of its

Duress (1)
AP : 2 7 :057(279) [0439] or because they were under **duress** from their friends.

During (19)
AG : 2 1 :021(027) [0043] which have been held **during** Your Imperial Majesty's
AG : 2 3 :012(053) [0063] decree was almost killed **during** an uprising of the entire
AP : PR :003(098) [0099] **During** the negotiations that followed, it was clear that
AP : PR :006(098) [0101] For **during** the reading some of us had taken notes on the
AP : 1 5 :042(221) [0325] no sermons are preached **during** the whole year, except in
AP : 2 3 :027(243) [0371] which prescribed that **during** the period of their
AP : 2 3 :027(243) [0371] is forbidden only **during** the period of ministration.
S3 : 0 3 :015(305) [0483] those committed **during** the course of a whole year), the
SC : 0 7 :005(353) [0559] Graciously protect me **during** the coming night.
EP : RN :003(465) [0777] — in fact, already **during** their lifetime — false teachers
EP : RN :004(465) [0777] Charles V at Augsburg **during** the great Diet in the year
SD : PR :007(502) [0849] churches, just as **during** the very lifetime of the holy
SD : RN :002(503) [0851] which were kept and used **during** that period when people
SD : 0 7 :029(574) [0981] Hence lest any persons **during** my lifetime or after my
SD : 0 7 :048(578) [0989] command at table and **during** supper, there can be no
SD : 0 7 :064(581) [0995] say, when at table and **during** supper he handed his
SD : 0 8 :026(596) [1025] it, he kept it hidden **during** the state of his humiliation
SD : 0 8 :065(604) [1039] **During** the time of the humiliation the divine majesty was
SD : 0 8 :075(606) [1043] The histories tell us that **during** the time of Emperor

Durlach (1)
PR : PR :027(015) [0025] Margrave Ernest [of Baden-**Durlach**] and

Dust (3)
LC : 0 1 :043(370) [0593] treasures, that these have turned to **dust** and vanished.
SD : 0 1 :035(514) [0869] made me of clay, and wilt thou turn me to **dust** again?
SD : 0 1 :037(514) [0871] we read, "And the **dust** returns to the earth as it was, and

Duty (35), Duties (28), Dutiful (1)
AG : PR :008(025) [0039] Wherefore, in **dutiful** obedience to Your Imperial
AG : 2 6 :038(069) [0075] that one can perform the **duties** required by one's calling.
AG : 2 8 :029(085) [0087] the performance of such **duties**, the princes are obliged,
AL : 1 6 :004(038) [0051] the fear of God and in faith but in forsaking civil **duties**.
AL : 2 0 :002(041) [0053] about all stations and **duties** of life, indicating what
AL : 2 6 :038(069) [0075] and for discharging his **duty** according to his calling.
AL : 2 8 :029(085) [0087] the performance of their **duties**, princes are bound, even
AP : 0 4 :224(138) [0181] them for this and calls them back to the **duties** of love.
AP : 0 4 :226(138) [0183] with God, while love has infinite external **duties** to men.
AP : 0 4 :243(141) [0189] speak so often about this **duty** of love which the
AP : 0 4 :262(145) [0195] defend the poor against injustice, as was the king's **duty**.
AP : 1 3 :002(211) [0309] We believe we have the **duty** not to neglect any of the
AP : 1 6 :007(223) [0331] have them know their **duty** to teach that the spiritual
AP : 2 1 :039(235) [0355] and the preachers do their **duty** in correcting these
AP : 2 3 :032(244) [0373] by childbirth, and by her other domestic **duties**?
AP : 2 3 :032(244) [0373] does not praise domestic **duties** apart from faith: "if she
AP : 2 3 :032(244) [0373] So a woman's **duties** please God because of faith, and a
AP : 2 3 :032(244) [0373] saved if she serves faithfully in these **duties** of her calling.
AP : 2 3 :039(244) [0375] married person does by performing the **duties** of marriage
AP : 2 3 :055(247) [0379] This is the **duty** of public officials, who ought to maintain
AP : 2 4 :081(264) [0411] Greeks it meant "public **duties**," like the taxes collected
AP : 2 4 :081(264) [0411] taken up with public **duties** and immunities: "He will say
AP : 2 4 :081(264) [0411] have found an immunity and have avoided public **duty**."
AP : 2 4 :081(264) [0411] of children does not excuse parents from public **duties**."
AP : 2 4 :083(264) [0413] use of "liturgy" to mean public **duties** or ministrations.
AP : 2 7 :021(272) [0427] teaching and other pious **duties**, not because the works
AP : 2 8 :012(283) [0447] do not perform the **duties** of bishops according to the
S1 : PR :002(289) [0455] free council, as indeed the pope is in **duty** bound to do.
SC : PR :004(338) [0533] and paid no attention at all to the **duties** of your office?
SC : PR :006(338) [0533] that you take the **duties** of your office seriously, that you
SC : PR :025(341) [0539] negligent if you fail to do your **duty** and remain silent.
SC : 0 1 :020(344) [0543] them to remain and discharge their **duty** to him.
SC : 0 5 :022(350) [0553] curse, neglected to do my **duty**, and caused him to suffer
SC : 0 9 :001(354) [0561] [IX] Table of **Duties**
SC : 0 9 :001(354) [0561] *they may be admonished to do their respective **duties***
SC : 0 9 :003(354) [0561] **Duties** Christians Owe Their Teachers and Pastors
SC : 0 9 :005(355) [0561] **Duties** Subjects Owe to Governing Authorities
LC : SP :004(362) [0575] Therefore, it is the **duty** of every head of a household to
LC : SP :017(363) [0577] Every father has the same **duty** to his household; he
LC : 0 1 :122(382) [0615] and never do their **duty** until a rod is laid on their backs,
LC : 0 1 :127(382) [0617] Besides this, it is our **duty** before the world to show
LC : 0 1 :141(384) [0621] superiors, persons whose **duty** it is to command and to
LC : 0 1 :150(386) [0625] their chief glory, it is our **duty** to honor and magnify them
LC : 0 1 :165(387) [0627] Do your **duty**, then, and leave it to God how he will
LC : 0 1 :167(388) [0629] Although the **duty** of superiors is not explicitly stated in
LC : 0 1 :168(388) [0629] faithfully discharge the **duties** of their office, not only to
LC : 0 1 :174(388) [0629] know that it is his chief **duty**, on pain of losing divine
LC : 0 1 :218(394) [0643] and magistrates have the **duty** of so supervising youth
LC : 0 1 :225(395) [0643] in his or her domestic **duty** and does damage or permits
LC : 0 1 :233(396) [0647] know, then, that it is his **duty**, at the risk of God's
LC : 0 1 :274(402) [0659] anyone, yet if they whose **duty** it is fail to do so, they sin

Continued ▶

LC : 0 1 :277(402) [0659] a servant failing to do his **duty**, he takes him to task
LC : 0 1 :313(407) [0671] everyday domestic **duties** of one neighbor toward
LC : 0 2 :019(412) [0681] follows that we are in **duty** bound to love, praise, and
LC : 0 2 :022(413) [0683] themselves in **duty** bound to serve and obey him for all
LC : 0 2 :054(417) [0693] short, the entire Gospel and all the **duties** of Christianity.
LC : 0 3 :005(420) [0699] to know is this: It is our **duty** to pray because God has
LC : 0 3 :006(421) [0699] prayers we teach that there is no **duty** or need to pray.
LC : 0 3 :008(421) [0699] It is our **duty** and obligation to pray if we want to be
LC : 0 3 :008(421) [0699] Christians, just as it is our **duty** and obligation to obey
LC : 0 3 :009(421) [0699] pray or not, but it is my **duty** and obligation (on pain of
LC : 0 3 :039(425) [0709] God our Father, it is our **duty** in every way to behave as
LC : 0 3 :075(430) [0719] should render them the **duties** we owe and do all we can
LC : 0 5 :087(456) [0773] remember that it is his **duty**, by God's injunction and

Dwell (6), Dwelled (1), Dwelling (2), Dwells (38), Dwelt (1)
AP : 0 2 :039(105) [0115] to the law of sin which **dwells** in my members" (Rom.
AP : 0 4 :352(161) [0217] to put on our heavenly **dwelling**, so that by putting it on
AP : 1 0 :003(179) [0247] it not also cause Christ to **dwell** in us bodily through the
AP : 1 2 :094(196) [0281] excellently about faith, **dwelling** especially on the oath in
S 3 : 0 3 :042(310) [0491] and I fear that such a devil still **dwells** in some of them.
LC : PR :015(360) [0571] We must ever live and **dwell** in the midst of such mighty
LC : 0 1 :131(383) [0619] you may have long life in the land where you **dwell**."
LC : 0 5 :076(455) [0771] know that nothing good **dwells** within me, that is, in my
EP : 0 2 :015(471) [0789] out of unwilling people and **dwells** in the willing ones.
EP : 0 3 :002(473) [0791] When he **dwells** in us by faith, over against this indwelling
EP : 0 3 :016(475) [0795] nature (in so far as it **dwells** and works within us), and
EP : 0 3 :018(475) [0795] not God himself but only divine gifts **dwell** in believers.
EP : 0 6 :006(480) [0807] the Spirit of God, who **dwells** in the believers, works
EP : 0 8 :034(491) [0825] Paul's statement, "In him **dwells** the whole fullness of
SD : 0 1 :029(513) [0867] of God, and only the original sin which **dwells** in it is evil.
SD : 0 1 :033(514) [0869] or total man is corrupted, **dwells**) are not identical with
SD : 0 1 :033(514) [0869] with original sin (which **dwells** in man's nature or essence
SD : 0 1 :033(514) [0869] by God and in which sin **dwells** and (b) original sin itself
SD : 0 1 :033(514) [0869] and (b) original sin itself which **dwells** in the nature.
SD : 0 2 :017(524) [0887] know that nothing good **dwells** within me, that is, in my
SD : 0 2 :064(533) [0905] me captive to the law of sin which **dwells** in my members."
SD : 0 3 :002(539) [0917] God, who through faith **dwells** in the elect, impels them to
SD : 0 3 :023(543) [0923] life and because sin still **dwells** in the flesh even in the
SD : 0 3 :054(548) [0935] essential righteousness, **dwells** by faith in the elect who
SD : 0 3 :063(550) [0937] nature in so far as it **dwells** and works within us, and that
SD : 0 3 :065(550) [0937] That not God but only the gifts of God **dwell** in believers.
SD : 0 6 :008(565) [0965] writes, "I know that nothing good **dwells** within me."
SD : 0 7 :005(570) [0973] which the Spirit of Christ **dwells** here upon earth, are
SD : 0 7 :011(571) [0975] to the effect that Christ **dwells** bodily in the Supper
SD : 0 7 :036(575) [0985] phrases as, "The Word **dwelt** in us," or "In Christ the
SD : 0 7 :036(575) [0985] whole fullness of the deity **dwells** bodily," or "God was
SD : 0 7 :063(581) [0995] forgiven, that Christ **dwells** and is efficacious in them;
SD : 0 8 :015(594) [1019] and God the Word who **dwells** in Christ is another.
SD : 0 8 :016(594) [1021] whom the Word of God **dwelled** just as in each of the
SD : 0 8 :016(594) [1021] and God the Word who **dwells** in him another."
SD : 0 8 :030(597) [1025] whole fullness of deity **dwells** bodily (Col. 2:9), and in
SD : 0 8 :034(597) [1027] even we, in whom Christ **dwells** only by grace, have in
SD : 0 8 :034(597) [1027] whole fullness of the deity **dwells** bodily" (Col. 2:9) in
SD : 0 8 :064(603) [1037] the fullness of the deity **dwells** in Christ (Col. 2:9), not as
SD : 0 8 :068(604) [1039] believers and saints), he **dwells**, and since he there has his
SD : 0 8 :068(604) [1039] believers in whom God **dwells**, there likewise the fullness
SD : 0 8 :068(604) [1039] the fullness of deity **dwells** bodily, there likewise are hid
SD : 0 8 :070(604) [1039] he always has with him, **dwells** in believers, he does not
SD : 0 8 :070(605) [1041] likewise, "In him **dwells** the whole fullness of deity
SD : 0 8 :077(606) [1043] because the Godhead which is everywhere **dwells** in them.
SD : 0 8 :079(607) [1045] might be present with us, **dwell** in us, work and be mighty
SD : 1 1 :073(628) [1087] since the Holy Spirit **dwells** in the elect who have come to
SD : 1 1 :073(628) [1087] have come to faith as he **dwells** in his temple, and is not

Each (95)
PR : PR :001(003) [0007] To **each** and every reader, according to the requirements
PR : PR :010(006) [0011] that were expanding with **each** passing day than, on the
PR : PR :015(007) [0013] read article by article to **each** and every theologian,
PR : PR :016(008) [0015] but generally of **each** and every minister and
PR : PR :026(014) [0025] according to our own and **each** community's
AG : PR :006(025) [0039] earnestly requested that **each** of the electors, princes, and
AG : 1 6 :005(038) [0051] of God and that everyone, **each** according to his own
AG : 2 1 :001(046) [0057] are to be an example for us, **each** of us in his own calling.
AG : 2 3 :004(051) [0061] temptation to immorality, **each** man should have his own
AG : 2 7 :019(074) [0079] temptation to immorality, **each** man should have his own
AG : 2 7 :019(074) [0079] have his own wife and **each** woman her own husband."
AL : 2 3 :004(051) [0061] temptation to immorality **each** man should have his own
AP : 0 2 :028(104) [0113] And **each** of these answers includes the other."
AP : 0 4 :194(133) [0175] as Paul says (I Cor. 3:8), "**Each** shall receive his wages
AP : 0 4 :242(141) [0187] When **each** one gave in to his hatred, a major commotion
AP : 0 4 :366(163) [0219] according to I Cor. 3:8, "**Each** shall receive his wages
AP : 1 2 :050(189) [0265] In **each** of these sentences the first part means contrition,
AP : 1 2 :059(190) [0267] personal faith by which **each** individual believes that his
AP : 1 2 :109(198) [0283] of brethren to **each** other, for it commands that the
AP : 2 1 :006(230) [0345] their other virtues, which **each** should imitate in
AP : 2 1 :029(233) [0351] has been said (I Cor. 3:8), "**Each** shall receive his wages
AP : 2 1 :032(233) [0351] hold to the error that **each** saint has a special sphere of
AP : 2 3 :014(241) [0367] temptation to immorality, **each** man should have his own
AP : 2 3 :017(241) [0369] temptation of immorality, **each** man should have his own
AP : 2 3 :017(242) [0369] It is up to **each** man's conscience to decide this matter.
AP : 2 3 :039(244) [0375] **Each** should serve faithfully in what he has been given to
AP : 2 3 :043(245) [0375] too, that Paul commands **each** one to possess his vessel in
AP : 2 3 :063(248) [0381] of Scripture commanding **each** man to have his own wife
AP : 2 4 :007(250) [0385] with the provision that **each** community should be
AP : 2 7 :050(277) [0437] So it is perfection for **each** of us with true faith to obey
AP : 2 7 :051(278) [0437] temptation to immorality, **each** man should have his own
S 2 : 0 2 :026(297) [0469] help to them, assigning to **each** of them a special
S 3 : 0 3 :028(308) [0487] **Each** one, however, held that some of the others were, as
TR : 0 0 :009(321) [0505] He sent out **each** one individually, he said, in the same
TR : 0 0 :014(322) [0507] acquainted with the life of **each** candidate (as we have
SC : 0 1 :012(343) [0541] life in word and deed, **each** one loving and honoring his
SC : 0 9 :015(356) [0563] Let **each** his lesson learn with care
LC : 0 1 :047(371) [0593] Let **each** person be in his station in life according to
LC : 0 1 :053(372) [0595] betroth themselves to **each** other and afterward deny it
LC : 0 1 :073(374) [0601] of commending ourselves **each** day to God — our soul
LC : 0 1 :207(393) [0639] lewdness but to be true to **each** other, be fruitful, beget
LC : 0 1 :219(394) [0643] and harmony, cherishing **each** other whole-heartedly and
LC : 0 1 :220(395) [0643] husbands and wives to love and honor **each** other.
LC : 0 1 :321(408) [0673] be regarded as attached to **each** individual
LC : 0 3 :028(424) [0705] **Each** of us should form the habit from his youth up to
LC : 0 3 :034(425) [0707] that continually beset us, **each** one so great that it should
LC : 0 4 :022(439) [0737] water, must by no means be separated from **each** other.
LC : 0 4 :053(443) [0745] God's Word in and with **each** other; that is, when the
LC : 0 6 :010(458) [0000] second confession, which **each** Christian makes toward
EP : 0 5 :007(478) [0803] Gospel are opposed to **each** other, as when Moses is
EP : 0 7 :027(485) [0815] tokens whereby Christians recognize **each** one another.
EP : 0 8 :002(487) [0817] deed and truth) share with **each** other, and how far does
EP : 0 8 :006(487) [0819] into the other, but that **each** retains its essential
EP : 0 8 :010(488) [0819] did not have a real and true communion with **each** other.
EP : 1 2 :019(499) [0841] to divorce one another, **each** go his own way, and marry
EP : 1 2 :029(500) [0843] three distinct persons, so **each** person has its distinct
EP : 1 2 :029(500) [0843] Some maintain that **each** of the three has the same
SD : RN :016(507) [0857] as correct and true in **each** of the controverted articles of
SD : 0 1 :029(513) [0867] to be distinguished from **each** other in such a way that
SD : 0 1 :033(514) [0869] discuss, and believe these two as distinct from **each** other.
SD : 0 1 :044(516) [0873] identical with but must be distinguished from **each** other.
SD : 0 2 :017(524) [0887] Spirit, and these are opposed to **each** other" (Gal. 5:17).
SD : 0 2 :064(533) [0907] for these are opposed to **each** other, to prevent you from
SD : 0 3 :041(546) [0929] are separated from **each** other in such a way as though on
SD : 0 6 :008(565) [0965] for these are opposed to **each** other, to prevent you from
SD : 0 7 :119(590) [1013] it as heaven and earth are separated from **each** other.
SD : 0 8 :007(592) [1017] be separated, blended with **each** other, or the one changed
SD : 0 8 :007(592) [1017] but in the person of Christ **each** remains in its nature and
SD : 0 8 :008(593) [1017] and unabolished, so that **each** retains its natural
SD : 0 8 :011(593) [1019] that two distinct natures, **each** with its natural essence and
SD : 0 8 :014(594) [1019] human, are united with **each** other like two boards glued
SD : 0 8 :014(594) [1019] allegedly have no communion at all with **each** other.
SD : 0 8 :015(594) [1019] natures have no communion whatsoever with **each** other.
SD : 0 8 :015(594) [1019] the two natures from **each** other and thus make two
SD : 0 8 :016(594) [1021] the Word of God dwelled just as in **each** of the prophets.
SD : 0 8 :016(594) [1021] and distinct from **each** other and that in Christ they have
SD : 0 8 :017(594) [1021] true communion with **each** other, by which the natures
SD : 0 8 :019(594) [1021] have a communion with **each** other, not only after a
SD : 0 8 :019(595) [1021] on the contrary, **each** nature retains its essence and
SD : 0 8 :031(597) [1025] natures are united with **each** other in such a way that they
SD : 0 8 :031(597) [1025] have communion between **each** other without any
SD : 0 8 :032(597) [1025] Since it is true that **each** nature retains its essential
SD : 0 8 :046(600) [1031] of Chalcedon declares, **each** nature according to its own
SD : 0 8 :060(602) [1035] into the other, and since **each** retains its natural and
SD : 0 8 :076(606) [1043] human natures have with **each** other in deed and truth in
SD : 0 8 :084(607) [1045] let themselves be separated and divided from **each** other.
SD : 1 0 :025(615) [1061] a Christian community, **each** individual Christian, and
SD : 1 0 :031(616) [1063] will not condemn **each** other because of a difference in
SD : 1 1 :023(619) [1069] and elected to salvation **each** and every individual among
SD : 1 1 :049(624) [1079] he would conform **each** of his elect to "the image of his
SD : 1 1 :049(624) [1079] of his Son," and that in **each** case the afflictions should
SD : 1 1 :056(625) [1081] and has determined for **each** person the time and hour of
SD : 1 2 :003(633) [1095] who are agreed in **each** and every article of the Augsburg
SD : 1 2 :024(634) [1099] married people to divorce **each** other, to go their separate
SD : 1 2 :037(636) [1103] and Holy Spirit, so also **each** person has a distinct essence

Eager (2), Eagerly (1), Eagerness (1)
S 3 : 0 3 :025(307) [0485] running, for everyone was **eager** to be delivered from the
LC : PR :011(360) [0571] reason alone you should **eagerly** read, recite, ponder, and
LC : 0 1 :072(374) [0601] that he may not be able to injure us as he is **eager** to do.
LC : 0 6 :033(461) [0000] as a hart trembles with **eagerness** for a fresh spring, so I

Ear (1), Ears (14)
AP : 1 3 :005(212) [0309] Word enters through the **ears** to strike the heart, so the
AP : 2 4 :029(255) [0393] dost not desire; but thou hast given me an open **ear**."
LC : 0 1 :100(379) [0609] God's Word in your heart, on your lips, and in your **ears**.
LC : 0 1 :121(382) [0615] were to open our eyes and **ears** and take this to heart so
LC : 0 1 :259(400) [0655] shutting his eyes and **ears** to everything but the evidence
LC : 0 1 :266(401) [0657] of a sin, simply make your **ears** a tomb and bury it until
LC : 0 1 :314(407) [0671] other hand, those other works captivate all eyes and **ears**.
LC : 0 2 :022(413) [0683] we sin daily with eyes and **ears**, hands, body and soul,
LC : 0 3 :002(420) [0697] and drum into his **ears** our prayer that he may give,
EP : 0 2 :004(470) [0787] that men should hear his Word and not stop their **ears**.
EP : 1 1 :008(495) [0833] hear the Word and do not stop their **ears** or despise it.
EP : 1 1 :012(496) [0835] despise it, harden their **ears** and their hearts, and thus bar
SD : 0 1 :038(515) [0871] my body and soul, eyes, **ears**, and all my members, my
SD : 0 2 :026(526) [0891] seeing eyes, and hearing **ears** (Deut. 29:4; Matt. 13:15).
SD : 1 1 :051(624) [1079] likewise, "He who has **ears** to hear, let him hear"; and

Earlier (22), Earliest (2), Early (3)
AG : PR :020(026) [0041] Imperial Majesty, at the **earliest** opportunity and to allow
AP : 0 2 :038(105) [0115] We have said **earlier** that Augustine defines original sin as
AP : 0 4 :073(117) [0141] We said **earlier** that faith is conceived by the Word, and
AP : 0 4 :239(141) [0187] Therefore a little **earlier** (I Pet. 2:4, 5) Peter commands us
AP : 0 4 :278(149) [0199] As we said **earlier** that in penitence we must consider faith
AP : 0 4 :278(149) [0199] death, as we said a little **earlier** about penitence in
AP : 0 4 :348(160) [0217] We have refuted this slander **earlier**.
AP : 0 4 :372(164) [0221] this rule, as we have said **earlier**, all passages on works
AP : 1 2 :048(188) [0265] is faith, abolishing the **earlier** sentence and restoring
AP : 1 2 :059(190) [0267] said enough about this **earlier**, we shall be briefer at this
AP : 1 2 :069(192) [0271] only compiled them from **earlier** ones and transferred
AP : 1 2 :077(193) [0275] We discussed this issue **earlier**, in the article on
AP : 1 2 :102(197) [0281] confession, we have said **earlier** that we do not believe
AP : 1 3 :006(212) [0311] distinguish these from the **earlier** ones which have an
AP : 2 0 :011(228) [0341] find our proofs in our **earlier** discussion of this whole
AP : 2 1 :034(233) [0351] As I have said **earlier**, our whole knowledge of Christ
AP : 2 1 :041(235) [0355] The **earlier** scholastics are usually closer to Scripture than
AP : 2 4 :090(266) [0415] doctrine of satisfaction, which we have refuted **earlier**.
AP : 2 7 :032(274) [0431] We have quoted **earlier** the other things that follow this
AP : 2 7 :035(275) [0431] the basis of what we said **earlier** about justification,
AP : 2 7 :052(278) [0437] On this whole topic we have said enough **earlier**.

Continued ▶

A P : 2 8 :009(282) [0445] **Earlier** they also condemned Article XV, in which we
L C : 0 1 :181(389) [0631] in place of parents; in **early** times, as we read in Moses,
L C : 0 1 :201(392) [0637] Youths were married at the **earliest** age possible.
L C : 0 2 :047(416) [0691] In **early** times the latter phrase was missing, and it is
L C : 0 4 :079(446) [0751] and practice what had **earlier** been begun but abandoned.
S D : 0 7 :001(568) [0971] As **early** as 1530, when the Augsburg Confession was

Earn (15), Earned (13), Earning (6), Earns (2)

A G : 1 5 :003(036) [0049] of propitiating God and **earning** grace are contrary to the
A G : 1 5 :004(037) [0049] by which it is intended to **earn** grace and make
A G : 2 0 :021(044) [0055] works for the purpose of **earning** grace and making
A G : 2 0 :027(045) [0057] we are to rely on them to **earn** grace but that we may do
A G : 2 6 :001(064) [0071] instituted by men serve to **earn** grace and make
A G : 2 6 :002(064) [0071] of which grace would be **earned** if they were observed and
A G : 2 6 :006(064) [0071] taught that grace is to be **earned** by prescribed fasts,
A G : 2 6 :020(067) [0073] is supposed that grace is **earned** through self-chosen
A G : 2 6 :021(067) [0073] that grace cannot be **earned**, God cannot be reconciled,
A G : 2 6 :029(068) [0075] works for the purpose of **earning** forgiveness of sin or
A G : 2 6 :033(069) [0075] to sin, but not as if he **earned** grace by such works.
A G : 2 7 :011(072) [0077] by monastic life one could **earn** forgiveness of sin and
A G : 2 7 :012(072) [0077] monastic life not only **earned** righteousness and
A G : 2 7 :016(073) [0077] God's grace and righteousness before God are **earned**.
A G : 2 7 :044(078) [0081] they were justified and **earned** forgiveness of sins by their
A G : 2 8 :036(086) [0089] when we presume to **earn** grace by such ordinances.
A G : 2 8 :037(087) [0089] grace and everything good might be **earned** from God.
A G : 2 8 :039(087) [0089] of the law, as if in order to **earn** God's grace there had to
A G : 2 8 :043(088) [0089] for the purpose of **earning** God's grace or as if they were
A P : 0 4 :019(110) [0125] of love a man can **earn** the merit of condignity, but they
A P : 0 4 :089(120) [0149] law; for if by these we **earned** justification before God,
A P : 0 4 :146(127) [0163] works, for they say they **earn** grace and eternal life by
A P : 0 4 :155(128) [0165] of propitiation which **earns** the forgiveness of sins that
A P : 0 4 :316(156) [0209] pleases God of itself and **earns** eternal life without
A P : 0 4 :318(156) [0209] teach that good works **earn** grace by the merit of
A P : 0 4 :321(157) [0209] so that it can be sure of **earning** grace by the merit of
A P : 0 4 :332(158) [0211] grace as though they had **earned** it, then they pray like
A P : 0 4 :360(162) [0219] are precious enough to **earn** a reward; therefore works
A P : 1 5 :012(216) [0317] that we must first **earn** our acceptance and justification
A P : 1 8 :006(225) [0335] by the merit of congruity, **earn** the forgiveness of sins and
S 3 : 0 3 :019(306) [0485] for such humiliation would surely **earn** grace before God.
L C : 0 1 :022(367) [0585] but desiring by itself to **earn** or merit everything by works
L C : 0 1 :176(389) [0631] sin and wrath, thus **earning** hell by the way you have
S D : 0 2 :075(536) [0911] spontaneous obedience **earn** the forgiveness of sin and
S D : 1 1 :015(619) [1069] and death Christ has **earned** for us "the righteousness
S D : 1 1 :059(626) [1081] rightfully have deserved, **earned**, and merited because we

Earnest (10), Earnestly (17), Earnestness (8)

P R : P R :012(007) [0013] it with Christian **earnestness** and zeal in view of the office
P R : P R :013(007) [0013] it with particular **earnestness** and Christian zeal, consider
P R : P R :015(007) [0013] consider diligently and **earnestly** the doctrine contained in
A G : P R :001(024) [0039] Majesty indicated an **earnest** desire to deliberate
A G : P R :006(025) [0039] also graciously and **earnestly** requested that each of the
A G : 0 1 :009(056) [0065] devotion and more **earnestness** than among our
A G : 2 6 :004(064) [0071] and yet the Gospel **earnestly** urges them upon us and
A P : 1 4 :002(214) [0315] in some places, despite our **earnest** desire to keep it.
A P : 2 3 :059(247) [0379] Despite our most **earnest** desire to establish harmony, we
S 1 : P R :015(291) [0459] who cry unto Thee and **earnestly** seek Thee according to
S 3 : 0 3 :028(308) [0487] and hard beds and tried **earnestly** and mightily to be
L C : 0 1 :168(388) [0629] above all, they should **earnestly** and faithfully discharge
L C : 0 1 :330(410) [0677] over them with great **earnestness**, who vents his wrath
L C : 0 1 :333(410) [0677] commandments so **earnestly** requires and enjoins under
L C : 0 3 :026(423) [0705] But where there is true prayer there must be **earnestness**.
L C : 0 4 :075(445) [0751] What is repentance but an **earnest** attack on the old man
L C : 0 5 :062(454) [0767] He who **earnestly** desires grace and consolation should
L C : 0 5 :085(456) [0773] them with joy and **earnestness**, practice them from their
E P : 0 5 :009(479) [0803] the Son of God, is an **earnest** and terrifying preaching and
E P : 1 1 :008(495) [0833] He **earnestly** desires that all men should come to him and
S D : 0 1 :061(519) [0879] Genesis 3 likewise writes **earnestly** against a minimizing
S D : 0 2 :055(532) [0903] people diligently and **earnestly** listen to and meditate on
S D : 0 2 :057(532) [0903] the holy sacraments, **earnestly** wills that we hear it, and
S D : 0 2 :066(534) [0907] St. Paul expressly and **earnestly** reminds us, "Working
S D : 0 3 :036(545) [0927] when in this article he so **earnestly** and diligently stresses
S D : 0 4 :031(556) [0947] we must begin by **earnestly** criticizing and rejecting the
S D : 0 4 :032(556) [0947] with all diligence and **earnestness**, repeat and impress
S D : 0 4 :032(556) [0947] and divine threats and **earnest** punishments and
S D : 0 5 :012(560) [0955] where is there a more **earnest** and terrible revelation and
S D : 0 7 :031(574) [0983] or idle talk; I am in dead **earnest**, since by the grace of
S D : 0 7 :040(576) [0985] with great zeal and **earnestness** the formula which Christ
S D : 0 7 :043(576) [0987] our unique teacher, the **earnest** command has been given
S D : 0 7 :047(578) [0989] certain, clear, and **earnest** words and commands of our
S D : 0 7 :054(579) [0991] regarded diligently and **earnestly** as a special and
S D : 1 1 :055(625) [1081] speculations but has **earnestly** warned against it

Earth (126)

A G : 2 8 :004(081) [0085] with all reverence as the two highest gifts of God on **earth**
A G : 2 8 :018(083) [0085] both be held in honor as the highest gifts of God on **earth**
A L : 2 8 :004(081) [0085] in reverence and honor as the chief gifts of God on **earth**.
A P : 0 4 :191(133) [0175] of God might not perish utterly from the **earth**.
A P : 1 2 :176(210) [0307] It is only on **earth**, however, that the keys have the power
A P : 1 2 :176(210) [0307] "Whatever you bind on **earth** shall be bound in heaven,
A P : 1 2 :176(210) [0307] whatever you loose on **earth** shall be loosed in heaven."
A P : 1 2 :178(211) [0309] that these touch neither **earth** nor heaven and they
A P : 2 1 :009(230) [0345] prayed for the church universal while they were on **earth**.
A P : 2 1 :044(236) [0357] divine things on **earth**, that is, the Gospel of Christ, and
A P : 2 3 :008(240) [0365] command to replenish the **earth**, but now that the earth
A P : 2 3 :008(240) [0365] earth, but now that the **earth** has been replenished
A P : 2 3 :008(240) [0367] so this Word makes the **earth** fruitful (Gen. 1:11), "Let
A P : 2 3 :008(240) [0367] (Gen. 1:11), "Let the **earth** put forth vegetation, plants
A P : 2 3 :008(240) [0367] of this ordinance, the **earth** did not begin to bring forth
A P : 2 3 :008(240) [0367] change the nature of the **earth**, so neither vows nor
S 1 : 0 1 :000(291) [0461] nature, are one God, who created heaven and **earth**, etc.
S 2 : 0 1 :005(292) [0461] even if heaven and **earth** and things temporal should be
S 2 : 0 2 :026(297) [0469] and although saints on **earth**, and perhaps also in heaven,
S 2 : 0 2 :027(297) [0469] a Christian and a saint on **earth**, you can pray for me,
S 3 : 0 3 :025(307) [0485] the discovery and digging up of the treasures of the **earth**.
T R : 0 0 :002(320) [0503] bishop of Rome calls himself the vicar of Christ on **earth**.
T R : 0 0 :016(322) [0509] is scattered over all the **earth** and that there are many
T R : 0 0 :024(324) [0511] Christ said, "If two or three of you agree on **earth**," etc.
T R : 0 0 :054(329) [0519] be wise; be warned, O rulers of the **earth**" (Ps. 2:10).
S C : 0 2 :001(344) [0543] *God, the Father almighty, maker of heaven and* ***earth****."*
S C : 0 2 :006(345) [0545] whole Christian church on **earth** and preserves it in union
S C : 0 3 :009(347) [0547] *"Thy will be done, on* ***earth*** *as it is in heaven."*
S C : 0 9 :009(356) [0563] and that you may live long on the **earth**"' (Eph. 6:1-3).
L C : S P :011(363) [0577] in God, the Father almighty, maker of heaven and **earth**:
L C : S P :014(363) [0577] come, thy will be done, on **earth** as it is in heaven.
L C : 0 1 :006(365) [0583] It is the most common idol on **earth**.
L C : 0 1 :016(366) [0585] him should risk and disregard everything else on **earth**.
L C : 0 1 :019(367) [0585] from whom there is truly no god in heaven or on **earth**.
L C : 0 1 :026(368) [0587] kinds of fruits from the **earth** for man's nourishment —
L C : 0 1 :060(372) [0597] is a great mercy that the **earth** still bears and sustains us.
L C : 0 1 :105(379) [0611] all other persons on **earth**, and places them next to
L C : 0 1 :109(380) [0611] and prize them as the most precious treasure on **earth**.
L C : 0 1 :126(382) [0617] he has appointed it to be his representative on **earth**.
L C : 0 1 :133(383) [0619] be well with you and that you may live long on the **earth**."
L C : 0 1 :150(386) [0625] them as the most precious treasure and jewel on **earth**.
L C : 0 1 :156(386) [0625] Somewhere on **earth** there must still be some godly
L C : 0 1 :166(388) [0629] our life or raise from the **earth** a single grain of wheat for
L C : 0 1 :228(396) [0645] is the most common craft and the largest guild on **earth**.
L C : 0 1 :317(408) [0673] that all classes of men on **earth** may accustom themselves
L C : 0 1 :317(408) [0673] a heavenly, angelic man, far above all holiness on **earth**.
L C : 0 1 :324(409) [0675] else in heaven and on **earth** will keep neither this nor any
L C : 0 2 :009(411) [0679] *God, the Father almighty, maker of heaven and* ***earth****."*
L C : 0 2 :011(412) [0681] my God is the Father, who made heaven and **earth**.
L C : 0 2 :011(412) [0681] there is no one else who could create heaven and **earth**."
L C : 0 2 :012(412) [0681] emphasize the words, "maker of heaven and **earth**."
L C : 0 2 :014(412) [0681] night, air, fire, water, the **earth** and all that it brings
L C : 0 2 :019(412) [0681] in heaven and on **earth** besides, is daily given and
L C : 0 2 :051(417) [0691] I believe that there is on **earth** a little holy flock or
L C : 0 2 :059(418) [0693] to increase holiness on **earth** through these two means,
L C : 0 2 :061(419) [0695] a community on **earth**, through which he speaks and does
L C : 0 2 :064(419) [0695] in heaven and on **earth**, he has given us his Son and his
L C : 0 2 :066(419) [0697] distinguish us Christians from all other people on **earth**.
L C : 0 3 :023(423) [0703] prayer to be found on **earth**, for it has the excellent
L C : 0 3 :038(425) [0709] may also be kept holy on **earth** by us and all the world.
L C : 0 3 :040(425) [0709] everything we do on **earth** may be classified as word or
L C : 0 3 :059(428) [0715] *"Thy will be done on* ***earth****, as it is in heaven."*
L C : 0 3 :065(429) [0717] must sacrifice all he has on **earth** — possessions, honor,
L C : 0 3 :070(429) [0717] God could not abide on **earth** nor his name be hallowed.
L C : 0 3 :072(430) [0717] — the needs of our body and our life on **earth**.
L C : 0 3 :076(431) [0719] this petition covers all kinds of relations on **earth**.
L C : 0 3 :080(431) [0721] government or honorable and peaceful relations on **earth**.
L C : 0 3 :115(435) [0731] heartache of which there is so incalculably much on **earth**.
L C : 0 3 :116(435) [0731] is nothing for us to do on **earth** but to pray constantly
L C : 0 4 :016(438) [0735] is a treasure greater and nobler than heaven and **earth**.
L C : 0 4 :039(441) [0743] and grace that heaven and **earth** cannot comprehend it.
L C : 0 4 :046(442) [0743] no other kind of life and no work on **earth** can acquire.
L C : 0 4 :050(443) [0745] present day no man on **earth** could have been a
L C : 0 5 :016(448) [0757] As no saint on **earth**, yes, no angel in heaven can
E P : 0 7 :012(483) [0811] and under his feet everything in heaven and on **earth**.
E P : 0 8 :016(489) [0821] things in heaven and on **earth** and under the earth
E P : 0 8 :016(489) [0821] on earth and under the **earth** beneath his feet and in his
E P : 0 8 :016(489) [0821] in heaven and on **earth** has been given to me," and as St.
E P : 0 8 :029(490) [0825] every place in heaven and **earth** (something that is not
E P : 0 8 :032(491) [0825] is present with us on **earth** in the Word, in the
E P : 0 8 :034(491) [0825] in heaven and on **earth** has been given to me," and St.
E P : 0 8 :035(491) [0825] power in heaven and on **earth**, that is, greater and more
E P : 0 8 :039(491) [0827] power in heaven and on **earth** was restored or again
S D : 0 1 :036(514) [0869] in secret, intricately wrought in the depths of the **earth**.
S D : 0 1 :037(514) [0871] the dust returns to the **earth** as it was, and the spirit
S D : 0 2 :009(521) [0883] most educated people on **earth** read or hear the Gospel of
S D : 0 2 :040(528) [0895] whole Christian church on **earth** and preserves it in union
S D : 0 5 :004(558) [0953] in his public ministry on **earth** and in the New Testament
S D : 0 7 :002(569) [0973] Supper as the highest heaven is distant from the **earth**.
S D : 0 7 :002(569) [0973] as great an interval as the **earth** is distant from the
S D : 0 7 :003(569) [0973] as taking place here on **earth** but only in respect to faith
S D : 0 7 :003(569) [0973] and wine are here on **earth** and not in heaven, so also the
S D : 0 7 :003(569) [0973] now in heaven and not on **earth**, and consequently
S D : 0 7 :005(570) [0973] of Christ dwells here upon **earth**, are united with the body
S D : 0 7 :007(570) [0975] is not in the communion on **earth** but only in heaven).
S D : 0 7 :007(570) [0975] is even now present on **earth** in some invisible and
S D : 0 7 :008(570) [0975] essentially present here on **earth** in the Lord's Supper,
S D : 0 7 :009(571) [0975] and essentially present here on **earth** in the sacrament).
S D : 0 7 :024(573) [0981] As little as a saint on **earth**, or even an angel in heaven,
S D : 0 7 :037(575) [0985] present together here on **earth** in the ordered action of the
S D : 0 7 :043(577) [0987] as he says, "Heaven and **earth** shall pass away, but my
S D : 0 7 :043(577) [0987] authority in heaven and on **earth** has been given to me."
S D : 0 7 :076(583) [0999] and multiply and fill the **earth**,' were spoken only once
S D : 0 7 :088(585) [1003] Christ, in which here on **earth** both the worthy and the
S D : 0 7 :099(586) [1005] when he walked bodily on **earth** and vacated or occupied
S D : 0 7 :119(590) [1013] to Christ's institution on **earth**, but that he is as far or as
S D : 0 7 :119(590) [1013] from it as heaven and **earth** are separated from each
S D : 0 7 :119(590) [1013] can or wills to be with us on **earth** with his human nature.
S D : 0 8 :002(592) [1015] in the Holy Supper on **earth** since such majesty belongs to
S D : 0 8 :026(596) [1023] its exaltation above all creatures in heaven and on **earth**.
S D : 0 8 :027(596) [1025] sea and to the ends of the **earth**, as the prophets foretell
S D : 0 8 :028(596) [1025] which fills heaven and **earth**, in which Christ has been
S D : 0 8 :033(597) [1027] mystery in heaven and on **earth** is the personal union, as
S D : 0 8 :055(601) [1033] in heaven and on **earth**, to have all things given into his
S D : 0 8 :065(604) [1039] saints in heaven and on **earth**, and in yonder life we shall
S D : 0 8 :068(604) [1039] in heaven and on **earth** is given, for the Spirit, who has
S D : 0 8 :070(604) [1039] in heaven and on **earth** has been given to me" (Matt.
S D : 0 8 :070(605) [1041] in heaven and on **earth** has been given to me" (Matt.
S D : 0 8 :071(605) [1041] creature in heaven or on **earth**, is not capable of the
S D : 0 8 :076(606) [1043] being in heaven and on **earth** can say truthfully, "Where
S D : 0 8 :077(606) [1043] would also be with us on **earth** because the Godhead
S D : 0 8 :078(607) [1043] and community on **earth** as mediator, head, king, and
S D : 0 8 :085(608) [1047] in heaven and on **earth** has been given to me' (Matt.

Continued ▶

SD : 08 :092(609) [1049] every place in heaven and **earth**, something which ought
SD : 08 :094(609) [1049] is present with us on **earth** only according to his deity,
SD : 11 :084(630) [1091] throughout all the **earth**") did not perish because God did

Earthly (5)
S2 : 04 :013(300) [0475] far as to claim to be an **earthly** god and even presumed to
SC : 09 :010(356) [0563] to those who are your **earthly** masters, with fear and
LC : 03 :044(425) [0709] and disgrace to an **earthly** father to have a bad, unruly
EP : 02 :003(470) [0787] quicken itself to bodily, **earthly** life, so little can man who
SD : 07 :014(571) [0977] in this sacrament, one heavenly and the other **earthly**.

Ease (5), Easier (3), Easily (43), Easy (22)
AG : 28 :069(093) [0093] The bishops might **easily** retain the obedience of men if
AL : 28 :069(093) [0093] The bishops might **easily** retain the lawful obedience of
AP : 02 :002(100) [0105] This sophistry is **easy** to refute.
AP : 02 :031(104) [0113] The wise reader will **easily** be able to see that when the
AP : 04 :017(109) [0125] as a disposition inclining us to love God more **easily**.
AP : 04 :037(112) [0131] It is **easy** enough for idle men to make up these dreams
AP : 04 :049(114) [0135] It is **easy** to determine the difference between this faith
AP : 04 :051(114) [0135] It will be **easy** to determine what faith is if we pay
AP : 04 :079(117) [0143] It is **easy** to state the minor premise if we know how the
AP : 04 :118(123) [0155] One can **easily** see how necessary it is to understand this
AP : 04 :183(132) [0173] or Gospel) it will be **easy** to refute the opponents'
AP : 04 :219(137) [0179] about love and works, it will be **easy** to answer this.
AP : 04 :236(140) [0185] For themselves they **easily** find forgiveness, but not for
AP : 04 :244(141) [0189] our position more, but the answer is **easy** and clear.
AP : 04 :250(143) [0191] Such a faith is not an **easy** thing, as our opponents
AP : 04 :290(151) [0203] A Christian can **easily** evaluate both modes, since both
AP : 04 :291(152) [0203] reflects on this will **easily** understand that we are justified
AP : 04 :297(153) [0205] reflects on all this will **easily** understand that justification
AP : 04 :303(154) [0205] that pious minds will **easily** understand our teaching and
AP : 04 :303(154) [0205] Sensible people can **easily** see that a faith which believes
AP : 04 :304(154) [0205] The answer to this is **easy**, since even the scholastics
AP : 04 :316(156) [0209] This decision is **easy**.
AP : 04 :343(160) [0217] which intelligent men can **easily** judge when they are
AP : 04 :388(166) [0225] These will be **easy** for good men to evaluate if they
AP : 04 :396(167) [0225] It is **easy** to evaluate their spirit, for in some doctrines
AP : 07 :042(176) [0243] the discerning reader can **easily** judge that the apostles
AP : 11 :006(181) [0251] things so that they might be instructed more **easily**.
AP : 12 :058(190) [0267] It is **easier** to understand the faith proclaimed by the
AP : 12 :083(194) [0275] in order to make our case more **easily** understood.
AP : 12 :098(197) [0281] Good men can **easily** judge the great importance of
AP : 12 :129(202) [0291] they can take care of this **easily** since they hold the keys
AP : 12 :129(202) [0291] As a wise man you can **easily** imagine what will happen if
AP : 13 :003(211) [0309] has been added," we can **easily** determine which are
AP : 15 :003(215) [0315] this doctrine, we have an **easy** and simple case.
AP : 15 :027(219) [0323] interpretations that make them either stricter or **easier**.
AP : 15 :033(220) [0325] in the traditions to **ease** their consciences, yet they do not
AP : 16 :006(223) [0331] though they are very **easy** to answer if we keep certain
AP : 18 :008(226) [0337] Men can **easily** determine this if they consider what their
AP : 20 :006(227) [0339] glory of Christ — we can **easily** ignore the terrors of the
AP : 20 :010(228) [0341] to set his mind at **ease**, for Paul fairly screams, as it were,
AP : 21 :043(235) [0357] the church, and good men can **easily** gauge its outcome.
AP : 23 :044(245) [0375] Such continence is **easy** for the godly and busy.
AP : 23 :059(247) [0379] But our consciences are at **ease**.
AP : 24 :010(251) [0387] is clear, it will be **easy** to evaluate the arguments both
AP : 24 :031(255) [0395] The answer is **easy**.
AP : 24 :041(257) [0399] Now good men can **easily** see the falsity of the charge
AP : 27 :020(272) [0425] the discerning reader will **easily** be able to conclude that
S2 : 04 :008(299) [0473] command, he would very **easily** and quickly be despised
S3 : 03 :021(306) [0485] satisfactions which were **easy** to render, like saying five
SC : PR :007(339) [0533] They are **easily** confused if a teacher employs one form
LC : 01 :013(366) [0583] Thus you can **easily** understand the nature and scope of
LC : 01 :017(366) [0585] the other hand, you can **easily** judge how the world
LC : 01 :018(367) [0585] pleasure, and a life of **ease** venerated Hercules, Mercury,
LC : 01 :065(373) [0599] so understood, you have **easily** solved the question that
LC : 01 :200(392) [0637] commandments are **easily** understood from the preceding
LC : 01 :212(394) [0641] Therefore, to make it **easier** for man to avoid unchastity
LC : 01 :273(401) [0659] honor and good name are **easily** taken away, but not
LC : 01 :273(401) [0659] good name are easily taken away, but not **easily** restored.
LC : 04 :010(437) [0735] this fact everyone can **easily** conclude that it is of much
LC : 05 :015(448) [0757] Hence it is **easy** to answer all kinds of questions which
LC : 05 :051(452) [0765] the sacrament, men can **easily** sense what sort of
LC : 05 :085(456) [0773] training we may more **easily** instill the Ten
LC : 06 :005(457) [0000] we grasp with uncommon **ease** whatever in the Gospel is
EP : 08 :017(489) [0821] he is able and it is **easy** for him to impart to us his true
SD : 01 :022(512) [0865] the spots spoken of can **easily** be washed off, like a
SD : 05 :027(563) [0961] Such a confusion would **easily** darken the merits and
SD : 06 :021(567) [0969] otherwise they can **easily** imagine that their works and life
SD : 07 :024(573) [0979] "Hence it is **easy** to answer all kinds of questions which
SD : 07 :128(591) [1015] views there may be can **easily** be discovered and identified
SD : 08 :035(597) [1027] becomes tangled up and the simple reader is **easily** misled.
SD : 11 :024(620) [1071] we can by the grace of God **easily** orient ourselves in it.
SD : 11 :046(624) [1079] of our flesh it could **easily** slip from our fingers, and
SD : 11 :046(624) [1079] and the world it could **easily** be snatched and taken from

East (6), Eastern (1)
AG : 26 :043(070) [0075] ceremonies, for in the **East** they kept Easter at a time
AL : 26 :043(070) [0075] for Easter was kept in the **East** at a time different from
AL : 26 :043(070) [0075] the Romans accused the **East** of schism, they were
AP : 07 :043(177) [0243] There were some in the **East** who maintained that because
TR : 00 :012(321) [0507] the churches in the **East** and the bishop of Rome should
TR : 00 :012(322) [0507] In fact, all the **Eastern** bishops should forever have sought
TR : 00 :016(322) [0509] are many churches in the **East** today which do not seek

Easter (9)
AG : 26 :043(070) [0075] for in the East they kept **Easter** at a time different from
AG : 28 :057(091) [0091] observance of Sunday, **Easter**, Pentecost, and similar holy
AL : 26 :043(070) [0075] to the Fathers, for **Easter** was kept in the East at a time
AL : 28 :057(091) [0091] observance of Sunday, **Easter**, Pentecost, and similar
AP : 07 :032(174) [0239] as the observance of **Easter**, the use of icons, and the like.
AP : 07 :042(176) [0241] some people celebrated **Easter** at one time and others at
AP : 07 :042(176) [0243] do not correctly compute the time in celebrating **Easter**.
AP : 07 :042(176) [0243] an apostolic decree about **Easter**; from them the
AP : 07 :043(177) [0243] to refer to the time when **Easter** should be celebrated, but

Eat (41), Eaten (3), Eating (34), Eats (6)
AG : 18 :005(040) [0051] fields, whether or not to **eat** or drink or visit a friend,
AG : 28 :032(086) [0087] Acts 15:20, 29, where the **eating** of blood and what is
AG : 28 :065(092) [0093] bondage but forbade such **eating** for a time to avoid
AL : 10 :001(034) [0047] distributed to those who **eat** in the Supper of the Lord.
AL : 18 :005(040) [0051] to labor in the field, will to **eat** and drink, will to have a
AL : 24 :012(057) [0065] when he said, "Whoever **eats** the bread or drinks the cup
AL : 28 :065(092) [0093] bondage but forbade such **eating** for a time to avoid
AP : 12 :164(208) [0303] willing and obedient, you shall **eat** the good of the land."
AP : 13 :004(211) [0309] we are baptized, when we **eat** the Lord's body, when we
AP : 22 :003(236) [0359] examine himself, and so **eat** of the bread and drink of the
AP : 23 :045(245) [0375] thus surpassing the Dominican friars, who **eat** fish.
AP : 24 :029(255) [0393] victims and requires prayer: "Do I **eat** the flesh of bulls?
AP : 24 :035(256) [0397] 11:26), "As often as you **eat** this bread and drink the cup,
S3 : 06 :005(311) [0493] and again, "Let a man so **eat** of the bread" (I Cor. 11:28).
SC : 06 :002(351) [0555] and wine, given to us Christians to **eat** and to drink.
SC : 06 :004(351) [0555] disciples and said, 'Take, **eat**; this is my body which is
SC : 06 :005(352) [0557] What is the benefit of such **eating** and drinking?
SC : 06 :007(352) [0557] How can bodily **eating** and drinking produce such great
SC : 06 :008(352) [0557] Answer: The **eating** and drinking do not in themselves
SC : 06 :008(352) [0557] by the bodily **eating** and drinking, are the chief thing in
SC : 08 :006(353) [0559] [Blessing before **Eating**]
SC : 08 :008(353) [0559] creatures receive enough to **eat** to make them joyful and
SC : 08 :010(353) [0559] [Thanksgiving after **Eating**]
SC : 08 :010(353) [0559] After **eating**, likewise, they should fold their hands
SC : 09 :003(354) [0561] in the same house, **eating** and drinking what they
LC : SP :016(363) [0577] them they should not be given anything to **eat** or drink.
LC : SP :023(364) [0579] disciples, saying, 'Take and **eat**, this is my body, which is
LC : 03 :081(431) [0721] receives a morsel of bread from God and **eats** it in peace.
LC : 04 :056(444) [0747] has commanded me to go, **eat**, and drink, etc. and that he
LC : 05 :003(447) [0753] *disciples and said, 'Take, eat; this is my body, which is*
LC : 05 :008(447) [0755] are commanded by Christ's word to **eat** and drink.
LC : 05 :013(448) [0755] Here we have Christ's word, 'Take, **eat**; this is my body.'
LC : 05 :017(448) [0757] and blood," but, "Take, **eat** and drink, this is my body
LC : 05 :022(449) [0757] Christ bids me **eat** and drink in order that the sacrament
LC : 05 :033(450) [0761] them, those to whom Christ says, "Take and **eat**," etc.
LC : 05 :034(450) [0761] why I give it and bid you **eat** and drink, that you may
LC : 05 :042(451) [0763] his Christians to **eat** and drink and thereby remember
LC : 05 :047(452) [0763] the Jews were obliged to **eat** only once a year, precisely on
LC : 05 :069(454) [0769] a sick person willfully **eats** and drinks what is forbidden
EP : 07 :015(483) [0811] when they direct us to take, **eat**, and drink, all of which
EP : 07 :015(483) [0813] — that is, whoever **eats** this bread eats the body of
EP : 07 :015(483) [0813] — that is, whoever eats this bread **eats** the body of Christ.
EP : 07 :029(485) [0815] of Christ as truly as we **eat** and drink bread and wine in
EP : 07 :042(486) [0817] the Capernaitic **eating** of the body of Christ as though
EP : 07 :042(486) [0817] though supernatural, **eating** of Christ's body and drinking
SD : 07 :006(570) [0975] his true body and blood to **eat** spiritually by faith but not
SD : 07 :007(570) [0975] They interpret "to **eat** Christ's body" as no more than "to
SD : 07 :008(570) [0975] and pious Christians **eat** the bread with their mouths, just
SD : 07 :010(571) [0975] and wine, given to us Christians to **eat** and to drink."
SD : 07 :020(573) [0979] Christ's word commands us Christians to **eat** and drink."
SD : 07 :022(573) [0979] Here we have Christ's word, 'Take **eat**, this is my body.
SD : 07 :026(573) [0981] and blood,' but, 'Take, **eat** and drink, this is my body and
SD : 07 :032(574) [0983] blood of Christ are truly **eaten** and drunk in the bread
SD : 07 :044(577) [0987] proffered bread, "Take, **eat**, this is my body which is given
SD : 07 :048(578) [0989] and natural wine as well as of oral **eating** and drinking.
SD : 07 :054(579) [0991] of Christ, so that all who **eat** this bread and drink the cup
SD : 07 :056(579) [0991] be speaking of a spiritual **eating** but of a sacramental or
SD : 07 :056(579) [0991] of a sacramental or oral **eating** of the body of Christ in
SD : 07 :057(579) [0993] in mind those who were **eating** idol-sacrifices and
SD : 07 :060(580) [0993] who by their unworthy **eating** and drinking sin grievously
SD : 07 :060(580) [0993] St. Paul says, "Who **eats** the bread or drinks the cup of
SD : 07 :061(580) [0995] There is therefore a twofold **eating** of the flesh of Christ.
SD : 07 :061(581) [0995] the sacramental or oral **eating** in the Supper is not only
SD : 07 :062(581) [0995] This spiritual **eating**, however, is precisely faith —
SD : 07 :063(581) [0995] The other **eating** of the body of Christ is oral or
SD : 07 :063(581) [0995] sacramental, when all who **eat** and drink the blessed
SD : 07 :064(581) [0995] true body and blood, and said therewith, "**Eat** and drink."
SD : 07 :064(581) [0995] referring precisely to oral **eating** and drinking — not,
SD : 07 :065(581) [0995] in addition to the oral **eating** he ordains the spiritual
SD : 07 :065(581) [0995] he ordains the spiritual **eating**, when he said, "Do this in
SD : 07 :067(582) [0997] when they call oral **eating** and eating on the part of the
SD : 07 :067(582) [0997] they call oral eating and **eating** on the part of the
SD : 07 :068(582) [0997] by their unworthy oral **eating** of the body of Christ
SD : 07 :074(583) [0999] of the minister, be it the **eating** and drinking or the faith
SD : 07 :082(584) [1001] are distributed to us to **eat** and to drink, as Paul says,
SD : 07 :083(584) [1001] distributed, received, and **eaten** but is locked up, offered
SD : 07 :084(584) [1001] it, distribute it, receive it, **eat** and drink it, and therewith
SD : 07 :086(584) [1003] mean faith, or the oral **eating** alone, but the entire
SD : 07 :086(584) [1003] and reception, or the oral **eating** of the blessed bread and
SD : 07 :088(585) [1003] presence and the oral **eating** of the body of Christ, in
SD : 07 :089(585) [1003] in his words when he says, "Take **eat**, this is my body."
SD : 07 :105(588) [1009] Holy Supper are received, **eaten**, and drunk spiritually,
SD : 07 :105(588) [1009] for although such **eating** occurs with the mouth, the mode
SD : 07 :114(589) [1011] the denial of an oral **eating** of the body and blood of

Eberhard (1)
PR : PR :027(014) [0025] **Eberhard**, bishop of Luebeck, administrator of the diocese

Eccentric (1)
LC : 01 :108(379) [0611] lowly, poor, feeble, and **eccentric** they may be, they are

Ecclesia (2), Ecclesiastical (25)
AG : 28 :041(087) [0089] only about the reservation of **ecclesiastical** penalties.
AL : 14 :000(036) [0049] XIV. **Ecclesiastical** Order
AL : 15 :000(036) [0049] XV. **Ecclesiastical** Rites
AL : 28 :000(081) [0083] XXVIII. **Ecclesiastical** Power
AL : 28 :012(083) [0085] Therefore, **ecclesiastical** and civil power are not to be
AL : 28 :020(084) [0087] must be distinguished from **ecclesiastical** jurisdiction.
AL : 28 :041(087) [0089] only of reserving **ecclesiastical** penalties and not of

Continued ▶

A P : 0 4 :288(151) [0203] the canonists have twisted **ecclesiastical** regulations.
A P : 0 7 :022(172) [0235] or position, whether **ecclesiastical** or secular, because
A P : 1 2 :167(208) [0303] were a matter of **ecclesiastical** discipline established for
A P : 1 4 :000(214) [0315] [Article XIV. **Ecclesiastical** Order]
A P : 1 4 :001(214) [0315] various ranks of the **ecclesiastical** hierarchy, although
A P : 1 4 :001(214) [0315] reasons for instituting **ecclesiastical** discipline in the
A P : 1 4 :005(215) [0315] willingness to keep the **ecclesiastical** and canonical polity,
A P : 1 5 :001(215) [0315] should observe those **ecclesiastical** rites which can be
A P : 1 5 :052(222) [0329] issue when we discuss vows and **ecclesiastical** authority.
A P : 2 8 :000(281) [0443] [Article XXVIII.] **Ecclesiastical** Power
A P : 2 8 :001(281) [0443] the privileges and the **ecclesiastical** estate, and they
S 1 : P R :013(290) [0459] matters of the **ecclesiastical** and secular estates as are
T R : 0 0 :032(325) [0513] would be set up on the pretext of **ecclesiastical** power.
T R : 0 0 :049(329) [0519] and does not allow **ecclesiastical** controversies to be
T R : 0 0 :059(330) [0521] terms what we have to say about **ecclesiastical** power.
T R : 0 0 :077(333) [0527] canon law pertain to **ecclesiastical** courts (as they call
L C : 0 1 :280(403) [0661] public, either before the civil or the **ecclesiastical** court.
L C : 0 2 :047(416) [0691] The word ***ecclesia*** properly means an assembly.
L C : 0 2 :048(416) [0691] not of German but of Greek origin, like the word ***ecclesia***.
S D : 1 0 :000(610) [1053] X. The **Ecclesiastical** Rites That Are Called Adiaphora or

Echo (2)
A P : 0 4 :237(140) [0187] more understanding than the walls that fling back an **echo**
A P : 0 4 :302(154) [0205] the walls of a house, they **echo** the word "love" without

Eck (1)
A P : 2 2 :011(238) [0361] These are the dregs of **Eck**.

Ecumenical (1)
T R : 0 0 :005(320) [0503] universal bishop or, as they put it, the **ecumenical** bishop.

Edict (5), Edicts (1)
A L : 2 3 :012(052) [0063] the Roman pontiff's **edict** on this matter, was almost
A L : 2 3 :013(053) [0063] a harsh manner was the **edict** carried out that not only
A L : 0 0 :006(095) [0095] In keeping with the **edict** of Your Imperial Majesty, we
A P : 0 4 :308(155) [0207] Obedience to the **edict** of a superior is obviously a kind
A P : 1 4 :004(215) [0315] Word of God with their **edicts**, who even butcher anyone
A P : 2 8 :004(281) [0445] questions they set forth an **edict** written in blood,

Edify (1), Edifying (2), Edification (1)
P R : P R :020(010) [0017] is the surest and most **edifying** way as far as the common
E P : 1 0 :004(493) [0829] be most profitable and **edifying** to the community of
S D : R N :015(507) [0857] they destroy rather than **edify**, should never be allowed to
S D : 1 0 :009(612) [1055] evangelical decorum, and the **edification** of the church.

Edition (4)
P R : P R :019(009) [0017] As far as the second **edition** of the Augsburg Confession,
P R : P R :019(009) [0017] of this same second **edition** and in their open writings and
P R : P R :019(009) [0017] or accepted the second **edition** in any other sense than
S D : R N :009(505) [0853] in the Preface to the Latin **edition** of his collected works.

Educate (2), Educated (3), Educating (1), Education (3)
A P : 0 7 :033(175) [0239] a discipline that serves to **educate** and instruct the people
A P : 1 5 :043(221) [0327] affairs, marriage, the **education** and instruction of
S 2 : 0 3 :001(297) [0471] good intentions for the **education** of learned men and
T R : 0 0 :080(334) [0527] the promotion of **education**, the care of the poor, and the
S C : P R :009(339) [0535] preach to intelligent and **educated** people, you are at
S C : P R :019(340) [0537] and parents to rule wisely and **educate** their children.
L C : 0 1 :172(388) [0629] expense in teaching and **educating** our children to serve
L C : 0 2 :012(412) [0681] more advanced and the **educated**, however, all three
S D : 0 2 :009(521) [0883] most gifted and the most **educated** people on earth read

Effect (42), Effected (3), Effecting (1), Effective (5), Effectively (2), Effects (14), Effectual (2), Effectually (1)
A G : P R :001(024) [0039] how with continuing help he might **effectively** be resisted.
A L : 0 8 :002(033) [0047] and the Word are **effectual** by reason of the institution
A L : 0 8 :003(033) [0047] ministry of evil men to be unprofitable and without **effect**.
A L : 1 7 :005(038) [0051] Jewish opinions to the **effect** that before the resurrection
A L : 2 0 :023(044) [0055] the history but also the **effect** of the history, namely, this
A L : 2 3 :002(051) [0061] Platina writes to this **effect**.
A L : 2 7 :027(075) [0079] the obligation or **effect** of a vow while they remain silent
A P : 0 4 :021(110) [0127] can never experience what faith is and how **effective** it is.
A P : 0 4 :078(117) [0143] unrighteous man righteous or **effecting** his regeneration.
A P : 0 4 :116(123) [0155] God" rather than love, which is the **effect** resulting from it
A P : 0 4 :145(127) [0161] which is only one of these **effects** of faith, our opponents
A P : 0 4 :152(127) [0163] sometimes combine cause and **effect** in the same phrase.
A P : 0 4 :179(131) [0171] He writes to the same **effect** in Col. 2:10, "You have come
A P : 0 9 :003(178) [0245] This point by itself can **effectually** confirm good and
A P : 1 2 :037(186) [0261] is love present before faith has **effected** the reconciliation.
A P : 1 3 :005(212) [0309] and the rite have the same **effect**, as Augustine said so
A P : 1 3 :005(212) [0309] Therefore both have the same **effect**.
A P : 1 5 :045(221) [0327] which God disciplines us **effect** a genuine and not a
A P : 2 0 :013(228) [0341] Such argumentation is to make the **effect** the cause.
A P : 2 4 :038(257) [0399] offering, namely, the **effect** of the proclamation, as we are
A P : 2 4 :075(263) [0411] speak of a twofold **effect**, of the comfort for the
S 2 : 0 2 :023(296) [0469] is the claim that relics **effect** indulgences and the
S 3 : 1 5 :001(316) [0501] that human traditions **effect** forgiveness or sins or merit
S C : 0 4 :006(348) [0551] Answer: It **effects** forgiveness of sins, delivers from death
S C : 0 4 :009(349) [0551] How can water produce such great **effects**?
S C : 0 4 :010(349) [0551] water that produces these **effects**, but the Word of God
S C : 0 6 :007(352) [0557] bodily eating and drinking produce such great **effects**?
L C : P R :010(359) [0569] Nothing is so **effectual** against the devil, the world, the
L C : 0 1 :071(374) [0601] useful habit, and very **effective** against the devil, who is
L C : 0 1 :101(379) [0609] these words are not idle or dead, but **effective** and living.
L C : 0 1 :247(398) [0651] They will have an **effect** too heavy for you and all the
L C : 0 2 :037(415) [0687] etc., so the Holy Spirit **effects** our sanctification through
L C : 0 3 :098(433) [0725] Whatever can be **effected** by Baptism and the Lord's
L C : 0 3 :098(433) [0725] signs, this sign also can **effect** to strengthen and gladden
L C : 0 4 :023(439) [0737] that is, what benefits, gifts, and **effects** it brings.
L C : 0 4 :024(439) [0737] most simply, the power, **effect**, benefit, fruit, and purpose
L C : 0 4 :026(440) [0739] water, for ordinary water could not have such an **effect**.
L C : 0 4 :030(440) [0739] In short, whatever God **effects** in us he does through such
L C : 0 4 :065(444) [0749] it, indicate the power and **effect** of Baptism, which is
L C : 0 4 :073(445) [0751] no empty symbol, but the **effect** accompanies it; but
L C : 0 4 :078(446) [0751] only one Baptism, and the **effect** and signification of
L C : 0 5 :033(450) [0761] both of its essence and of its **effect** and benefit.
E P : 0 1 :016(468) [0783] or power to initiate, to **effect**, or to cooperate in
E P : 0 2 :004(470) [0787] Spirit, however, does not **effect** conversion without
E P : 0 2 :019(472) [0791] Holy Spirit's instrument whereby he **effects** conversion.
E P : 0 3 :010(474) [0795] these expressions say in **effect** that we become righteous
E P : 0 7 :008(482) [0811] recitation of the minister **effect** this presence of the body
E P : 0 7 :030(485) [0815] in the Holy Supper is **effected** solely by the external signs
E P : 0 7 :035(485) [0815] of Christ's testament, **effect** and cause this presence of the
E P : 1 2 :023(500) [0841] God seals the adoption of children and **effects** rebirth.
S D : R N :006(504) [0853] more clearly and **effectively** and to forestalling the
S D : 0 1 :010(510) [0863] acts, to begin and to **effect** anything in spiritual matters."
S D : 0 1 :023(512) [0865] or ability to initiate and **effect** something in spiritual
S D : 0 2 :007(521) [0883] begin, accomplish, do, **effect**, or cooperate, but that man
S D : 0 2 :007(521) [0883] himself for it, or help, do, **effect**, or cooperate toward his
S D : 0 2 :024(525) [0891] he can as little begin, **effect**, or cooperate in anything as a
S D : 0 2 :038(528) [0895] sanctifies us therein, and **effects** in us a daily increase in
S D : 0 7 :009(570) [0975] at Augsburg to the **effect** that since the body of Christ
S D : 0 7 :011(571) [0975] Cyril is quoted to the **effect** that Christ dwells bodily in
S D : 0 7 :074(583) [0999] of the communicants, can **effect** the true presence of the
S D : 0 7 :088(585) [1003] faith, or that faith **effects** the presence of Christ's body in
S D : 0 7 :089(585) [1003] that in them it does not **effect** salvation), so whether those
S D : 0 7 :089(585) [1003] This he **effects** not through our faith, but solely through
S D : 0 7 :121(590) [1013] the power allegedly to **effect** a sacrament, the words of
S D : 1 1 :008(617) [1065] a cause which creates, **effects**, helps, and furthers our
S D : 1 1 :017(619) [1069] 3. That he would be **effective** and active in us by his Holy
S D : 1 1 :023(619) [1069] by his grace, gifts, and **effective** working to bring them to
S D : 1 1 :027(620) [1071] Paul testified to the same **effect** when he wrote, "We are
S D : 1 1 :044(624) [1077] Word he would create and **effect** in us everything that
S D : 1 1 :075(628) [1087] it the Holy Spirit wills to **effect** their conversion in them.

Efficacious (19), Efficaciously (4), Efficacy (8)
A G : 0 8 :001(033) [0047] the sacraments are **efficacious** even if the priests who
A P : 0 4 :250(143) [0191] power of God faith is **efficacious** and overcomes death
A P : 0 7 :003(168) [0227] of the church or deny **efficacy** to the sacraments which
A P : 0 7 :003(169) [0227] do not lose their **efficacy** when they are administered by
A P : 0 7 :019(171) [0233] and the sacraments are **efficacious** even when wicked men
A P : 0 7 :028(173) [0237] unworthy men, this does not rob them of their **efficacy**.
A P : 0 7 :047(177) [0243] that the sacraments are **efficacious** even when evil men
A P : 0 9 :001(178) [0245] not useless but is necessary and **efficacious** for salvation.
A P : 1 5 :043(221) [0327] our assurance that it is **efficacious** and is heard, the cross,
A P : 2 4 :087(265) [0413] these dreams about the **efficacy** of the act *ex opere*
A P : 2 8 :018(284) [0449] that the Word is **efficacious** when it is delivered by men
L C : 0 3 :119(436) [0731] But the **efficacy** of prayer consists in our learning also to
S D : 0 2 :022(525) [0889] the gracious and **efficacious** working of the Holy Spirit.
S D : 0 2 :048(530) [0901] Holy Spirit wills to be **efficacious** in us by giving and
S D : 0 2 :052(531) [0901] which he wills to act **efficaciously**, to convert men to
S D : 0 7 :063(581) [0995] Christ dwells and is **efficacious** in them; unbelievers
S D : 0 7 :075(583) [0999] were not only **efficacious** in the first Supper but they still
S D : 0 7 :075(583) [0999] their validity and **efficacious** power in all places where the
S D : 0 7 :076(583) [0999] only once but are ever **efficacious** in nature and make
S D : 0 7 :076(583) [0999] only once, but it is **efficacious** until this day, and until his
S D : 0 7 :078(584) [1001] our speaking or of our **efficacious** word, but because of
S D : 0 7 :089(585) [1003] which always remain **efficacious** in Christendom and
S D : 0 8 :051(601) [1033] and has its power and **efficacy** not only from and
S D : 0 8 :064(603) [1037] power, glory, and **efficacy** in the assumed nature,
S D : 0 8 :064(603) [1039] divine power, glory, and **efficacy**, as the soul does in the
S D : 1 1 :029(621) [1073] he thus calls he will be **efficaciously** active through the
S D : 1 1 :029(621) [1073] Holy Spirit wills to be **efficacious** through the Word, to
S D : 1 1 :039(622) [1075] present with and **efficacious** and active through the Word
S D : 1 1 :040(623) [1077] who wants to work **efficaciously** in them through the
S D : 1 1 :041(623) [1077] Spirit who wills to be **efficaciously** active through the
S D : 1 1 :077(629) [1089] in the Word and to be **efficacious** with his power through

Efficient (4)
E P : 0 2 :019(472) [0791] there are only two **efficient** causes, namely, the Holy
S D : 0 2 :022(525) [0889] by its own natural and **efficient** aptitude, capacity, or
S D : 0 2 :071(535) [0909] is asked concerning the **efficient** cause (that is, who works
S D : 0 2 :090(538) [0915] the doctrine of the three **efficient** causes of unregenerated

Effort (13), Efforts (5)
P R : P R :024(013) [0023] and most necessary **effort** toward concord hidden and
P R : P R :024(013) [0023] necessary, and Christian **effort** and will allow nothing to
P R : P R :026(014) [0025] implementation of this **effort** at concord in our lands,
A G : 2 0 :019(043) [0055] to rely on their own **efforts**, and all sorts of works were
A G : 2 6 :015(066) [0073] so occupied with such **efforts** that they neglected all
A P : 0 4 :330(158) [0211] mercy saves us, our own merits and **efforts** do not save us
A P : 1 2 :011(184) [0255] How much **effort** is devoted to the endless enumeration
A P : 2 1 :043(235) [0357] They make no **effort** to provide a summary of the
S 2 : 0 3 :002(298) [0471] dangerous and needless **effort**, and accordingly the
L C : 0 1 :043(370) [0591] they have wasted their **effort** and toil or, if they have
L C : 0 1 :100(378) [0609] day nor night relaxes his **effort** to steal upon you
L C : 0 1 :166(388) [0629] For the combined **efforts** of the whole world cannot add
L C : 0 1 :172(388) [0629] we must spare no **effort**, time, and expense in teaching
L C : 0 1 :319(408) [0673] order to show how much **effort** God requires us to devote
L C : 0 3 :002(420) [0697] world and our flesh, resists our **efforts** with all his power.
L C : 0 3 :100(433) [0725] about the trouble and **effort** required to retain and
E P : 0 2 :006(470) [0787] his grace our "will and **effort**," our planting, sowing, and
E P : 1 1 :014(496) [0835] we are to put forth every **effort** to live according to the

Effrontery (4)
A P : 2 2 :009(237) [0359] Look at the **effrontery** of the men!
A P : 2 2 :011(238) [0361] Look at the great **effrontery** of the man.
S D : 0 7 :111(589) [1011] of whom have had the **effrontery** to penetrate our
S D : 1 2 :003(632) [1095] have had the **effrontery** to pretend and proclaim to the

Egg (2)
S D : 0 6 :009(565) [0965] of the law as well, to **egg** them on so that they follow the
S D : 1 1 :072(628) [1087] serpent; or if he asks for an **egg**, will give him a scorpion?

Egidius (1)
S 3 : 1 5 :005(318) [0501] And I, **Egidius** Melcher, have subscribed with my hand.

Eighteenth (2)
A G : 2 7 :032(076) [0079] the taking of monastic vows before the **eighteenth** year.
A L : 2 7 :032(076) [0079] and forbids making a vow before the **eighteenth** year.

Eighth (7)
A P : 0 7 :003(168) [0227] That is why we added the **eighth** article, to avoid the
A P : 0 7 :003(169) [0227] The **eighth** article exonerates us enough.
A P : 0 7 :047(177) [0243] They have approved the entire **eighth** article.
S C : 0 1 :015(343) [0541] The **Eighth**
L C : 0 1 :253(399) [0653] The **Eighth** Commandment
S D : 1 1 :033(622) [1073] sin as Paul teaches from the first to the **eighth** chapter.
S D : 1 1 :033(622) [1075] Afterward, when in the **eighth** chapter you are tested

Einbeck (1)
P R : P R :027(016) [0027] The Council of the City of **Einbeck**

Eisenach (3)
P R : P R :027(014) [0025] John Ernest [of Saxe-**Eisenach**] the above two through
A P : 2 7 :001(268) [0419] the Thuringian town of **Eisenach**, there was a Franciscan
S 3 : 1 5 :005(317) [0501] own name and in that of Justus Menius, of **Eisenach**

Eisleben (3)
P R : P R :027(015) [0025] Hoyer Christopher, count of Mansfeld [-**Eisleben**]
P R : P R :027(015) [0025] Peter Ernest the Younger, count of Mansfeld [-**Eisleben**]
S 3 : 1 5 :005(317) [0501] John Agricola, of **Eisleben**, subscribed

Elapse (1)
L C : 0 5 :049(452) [0765] lets a long period of time **elapse** without ever desiring the

Elder (1), Elderly (1), Elders (2)
S C : 0 9 :003(354) [0561] "Let the **elders** who rule well be considered worthy of
S C : 0 9 :012(356) [0563] "You that are younger, be subject to the **elders**.
L C : 0 1 :044(370) [0593] and in the recollections of **elderly** and experienced people.
S D : 1 1 :088(631) [1093] of his call, she was told, 'The **elder** will serve the younger.'

Elect (31), Elected (23), Electing (4), Election (41), Elects (1)
A G : 1 7 :002(038) [0051] joy to believers and the **elect** but to condemn ungodly
A G : 2 8 :028(085) [0087] not obey even regularly **elected** bishops if they err or if
A L : 1 7 :002(038) [0051] To the godly and **elect** he will give eternal life and endless
S 2 : 0 4 :007(299) [0473] a head would then be **elected** by men and it remained in
S 2 : 0 4 :007(299) [0473] to the popes when it deposed three and **elected** a fourth.
T R : 0 0 :005(320) [0505] because he has the right to **elect**, ordain, confirm, and
T R : 0 0 :013(322) [0507] that bishops should be **elected** by their own churches in
T R : 0 0 :014(322) [0507] and a bishop should be **elected** in the presence of the
T R : 0 0 :020(323) [0509] right when the church **elects** him and the custom
T R : 0 0 :067(331) [0523] the right of calling, **electing**, and ordaining ministers.
T R : 0 0 :067(331) [0523] is, therefore, the right of **electing** and ordaining ministers
T R : 0 0 :069(331) [0525] certainly has the right of **electing** and ordaining
T R : 0 0 :070(332) [0525] was a time when the people **elected** pastors and bishops.
T R : 0 0 :070(332) [0525] in to confirm the **election** with the laying on of hands;
T R : 0 0 :072(332) [0525] retains the right of **electing** and ordaining ministers.
E P : 0 1 :006(467) [0781] will not quicken it in the **elect**, will not glorify it or save
E P : 0 3 :007(474) [0793] "Who shall bring any charge against God's **elect**?
E P : 0 4 :013(477) [0799] 8. However, in the **elect** children of God this spontaneity
E P : 0 4 :014(477) [0799] this weakness against his **elect**, as it is written, "There is
E P : 0 4 :019(477) [0801] that the holy ones and the **elect** retain the Holy Spirit
E P : 1 1 :000(494) [0831] XI. God's Eternal Foreknowledge and **Election**
E P : 1 1 :002(494) [0831] and the eternal **election** of God is to be diligently noted.
E P : 1 1 :004(495) [0833] wickedness it must minister to the salvation of his **elect**.
E P : 1 1 :005(495) [0833] or the eternal **election** of God, however, is concerned only
E P : 1 1 :007(495) [0833] saved are inscribed and **elected**, as it is written, "He chose
E P : 1 1 :009(495) [0833] we should not judge this **election** of ours to eternal life on
E P : 1 1 :009(495) [0833] as this: "If God has **elected** me to salvation I cannot be
E P : 1 1 :009(495) [0833] Or, "If I am not **elected** to eternal life, whatever good I do
E P : 1 1 :011(495) [0835] doctrine of God's eternal **election** is profitable and
E P : 1 1 :011(496) [0835] does he speak of the mystery of God's eternal **election**.
E P : 1 1 :012(496) [0835] not lie in God or his **election**, but in their own
E P : 1 1 :013(496) [0835] doctrine of the eternal **election** of God only in so far as it
E P : 1 1 :013(496) [0835] should seek the eternal **election** of the Father, who has
E P : 1 1 :013(496) [0835] know that we have been **elected** to eternal life out of pure
E P : 1 1 :013(496) [0835] us of this gracious **election** not only in mere words, but
E P : 1 1 :015(496) [0835] doctrine of God's eternal **election** gives God his glory
E P : 1 1 :016(497) [0837] doctrine of the gracious **election** of God to eternal life in
E P : 1 1 :020(497) [0837] us a cause of God's **election**, on account of which he has
E P : 1 1 :020(497) [0837] on account of which he has **elected** us to eternal life.
S D : 0 1 :047(516) [0875] and would be and remain in the **elect** in eternal life.
S D : 0 2 :047(530) [0901] wonder if God has really **elected** them and actually
S D : 0 2 :057(532) [0903] himself with God's eternal **election** nor obtain his mercy.
S D : 0 2 :057(532) [0903] Christ, in whom we are **elected**, offers his grace to all men
S D : 0 2 :068(534) [0907] the Spirit continues also in the **elect** and truly reborn.
S D : 0 3 :002(539) [0917] faith dwells in the **elect**, impels them to do what is right,
S D : 0 3 :017(542) [0921] "Who shall bring any charge against God's **elect**?
S D : 0 3 :054(548) [0935] dwells by faith in the **elect** who have been justified
S D : 0 4 :033(556) [0947] to confirm your call and **election**," the Apology states in
S D : 0 6 :006(564) [0963] If believers and the **elect** children of God were perfectly
S D : 0 6 :009(565) [0965] flesh the truly believing, **elect**, and reborn children of God
S D : 0 6 :020(567) [0969] guidance set up a self-**elected** service of God and without
S D : 1 1 :000(616) [1063] XI. Eternal Foreknowledge and Divine **Election**
S D : 1 1 :001(616) [1063] concerning the eternal **election** of the children of God.
S D : 1 1 :004(616) [1063] and the eternal **election** of his children to eternal
S D : 1 1 :005(617) [1065] other hand, the eternal **election** of God or God's
S D : 1 1 :005(617) [1065] of God, who have been **elected** and predestined to eternal
S D : 1 1 :006(617) [1065] and the salvation of his **elect**, and thereby the ungodly are
S D : 1 1 :008(617) [1065] God's eternal **election**, however, not only foresees and
S D : 1 1 :008(617) [1065] the salvation of the **elect**, but by God's gracious will and
S D : 1 1 :009(617) [1065] not to view this eternal **election** or divine ordering to
S D : 1 1 :010(618) [1067] God has foreordained his **elect** to salvation 'before the
S D : 1 1 :013(618) [1067] profitably about eternal **election** or about the
S D : 1 1 :022(619) [1069] life those whom he has **elected**, called, and justified.
S D : 1 1 :023(619) [1069] considered and **elected** to salvation each and every
S D : 1 1 :023(619) [1069] individual among the **elect** who are to be saved through
S D : 1 1 :024(620) [1069] teaching of the eternal **election** of God to adoption and to
S D : 1 1 :024(620) [1069] purpose, foreknowledge, **election**, and ordinance of God
S D : 1 1 :025(620) [1071] salvation: Since only the **elect** "whose names are written
S D : 1 1 :025(620) [1071] one discover, who the **elect** are and who can and should
S D : 1 1 :027(620) [1071] God has foreknown, **elected**, and decreed, he has also
S D : 1 1 :028(620) [1071] to consider our eternal **election** to salvation profitably, we
S D : 1 1 :030(621) [1073] The **elect** are therefore described as follows: "My sheep
S D : 1 1 :031(621) [1073] God gives "witness" to the **elect** "that they are the children
S D : 1 1 :039(622) [1075] that those might be the **elect** who despise God's Word and
S D : 1 1 :040(623) [1077] enlighten, and convert the **elect** through the Word and
S D : 1 1 :043(623) [1077] done any good, God **elected** us to salvation "according to
S D : 1 1 :049(624) [1079] would conform each of his **elect** to "the image of his
S D : 1 1 :065(626) [1083] consider God's eternal **election** in Christ, and not outside
S D : 1 1 :065(627) [1083] testimony we have been **elected** in Christ "before the
S D : 1 1 :065(627) [1083] This **election** is revealed from heaven through the
S D : 1 1 :066(627) [1085] in whom they are to seek the Father's eternal **election**.
S D : 1 1 :067(627) [1085] and thereby our eternal **election** to eternal life when he
S D : 1 1 :070(627) [1085] of God, if he has been **elected** and ordained to eternal
S D : 1 1 :070(627) [1085] of life" and of the eternal **election** of all God's children to
S D : 1 1 :073(628) [1087] Holy Spirit dwells in the **elect** who have come to faith as
S D : 1 1 :073(628) [1087] "confirm their call and **election**" so that the more they
S D : 1 1 :073(628) [1087] within themselves, the less they will doubt their **election**.
S D : 1 1 :073(628) [1087] the Spirit testifies to the **elect** that they are "children of
S D : 1 1 :075(628) [1087] Our **election** to eternal life does not rest on our piety or
S D : 1 1 :076(629) [1089] by which he snatches the **elect** from the maw of the devil.
S D : 1 1 :087(631) [1091] of the eternal and saving **election** of the elect children of
S D : 1 1 :087(631) [1091] and saving election of the **elect** children of God gives God
S D : 1 1 :088(631) [1093] that the cause of our **election** is not only the mercy of
S D : 1 1 :088(631) [1093] us a cause of God's **election** on account of which God has
S D : 1 1 :088(631) [1093] on account of which God has **elected** us unto eternal life.
S D : 1 1 :088(631) [1093] the world was laid") God **elected** us in Christ — "in order
S D : 1 1 :088(631) [1093] that God's purpose of **election** might continue, not
S D : 1 1 :089(631) [1093] to seek their eternal **election** in Christ and in his holy
S D : 1 1 :090(631) [1093] rests in the gracious **election** of God, which he has
S D : 1 1 :091(631) [1093] God's gracious **election** that sorrowing Christians can find

Elector (8), Electors (21)
P R : P R :000(001) [0004] Faith of the undersigned **Electors**, Princes, and Estates
P R : P R :000(001) [0004] of the aforementioned **Electors**, Princes, and Estates for
P R : P R :001(003) [0007] document comes, we, the **electors**, princes, and estates in
P R : P R :007(004) [0009] of a meeting of the **electors** in the year 1558) that we
P R : P R :013(007) [0013] Accordingly we, the **elector** of Saxony, etc., with the
P R : P R :013(007) [0013] believers among the **electors** and princes, convoked a
P R : P R :013(007) [0013] considerable number of **electors**, princes, and estates
P R : P R :018(009) [0015] in the year 1530 by the **electors**, princes, and estates
P R : P R :025(014) [0023] our fellow-members, the **electors** and estates in the Holy
P R : P R :027(014) [0025] Louis, count palatine on the Rhine, **elector**
P R : P R :027(014) [0025] August, duke of Saxony, **elector**
P R : P R :027(014) [0025] John George, margrave of Brandenburg, **elector**
A G : P R :005(025) [0039] as we, the undersigned **elector** and princes and our
A G : P R :005(025) [0039] together with other **electors**, princes, and estates, we have
A G : P R :006(025) [0039] that each of the **electors**, princes, and estates should
A G : P R :009(025) [0039] If the other **electors**, princes, and estates also submit a
A G : P R :012(026) [0041] who represent the **electors**, princes, and estates of the
A G : P R :014(026) [0041] friends (the **electors**, princes, and estates), and every lover
A G : P R :015(026) [0041] gave assurance to the **electors**, princes, and estates of the
A G : P R :018(026) [0041] in Spires a year ago, the **electors**, princes, and estates of
A G : P R :018(026) [0041] with the absent **electors**, princes, and representatives of
A G : P R :021(027) [0043] Christian council as the **electors**, princes, and estates have
A G : 0 0 :007(096) [0095] John, duke of Saxony, **elector**
A L : 0 0 :017(096) [0095] John, duke of Saxony, **elector**
T R : 0 0 :082(000) [0529] Illustrious Prince, the **Elector** of Saxony, and by the other
S D : P R :003(501) [0847] a number of Christian **electors**, princes, and estates who
S D : R N :005(504) [0851] by a number of Christian **electors**, princes, and estates of
S D : R N :007(505) [0853] and most illustrious **electors**, princes, and estates, before
S D : R N :007(505) [0853] Confession, to which the **electors**, princes, and estates

Elegant (1)
L C : 0 1 :025(368) [0587] God by a name more **elegant** and worthy than any found

Element (10), Elemental (2), Elementary (1), Elements (15)
A L : 2 8 :045(088) [0089] Christ you died to the **elemental** spirits of the universe,
A P : 0 2 :004(101) [0105] is the so-called "material **element**" of original sin.
A P : 0 2 :026(103) [0111] correctly expressed both **elements**: lack of ability to trust,
A P : 0 2 :035(105) [0115] remains — or, as they call it, the "material **element**" of sin
A P : 0 2 :035(105) [0115] Concerning this material **element**, he has also said that
A P : 0 2 :051(107) [0119] either the formal **element** of original sin or the so-called
A P : 0 4 :053(114) [0137] that these three **elements** always belong together: the
A P : 0 4 :136(126) [0159] we mean to include both **elements**, namely, the inward
A P : 0 4 :255(144) [0193] They contain two **elements**.
A P : 0 7 :035(175) [0239] Christ you died to the **elemental** spirits of the universe,
A P : 2 2 :008(237) [0359] and were no longer permitted to consecrate the **elements**.
S 3 : 0 5 :001(310) [0491] Word is added to the **element** and it becomes a
L C : 0 4 :001(436) [0733] at least some brief, **elementary** instruction in them
L C : 0 4 :018(438) [0737] Word is added to the **element** or the natural substance, it
L C : 0 5 :010(448) [0755] is joined to the external **element**, it becomes a
L C : 0 5 :010(448) [0755] Word must make the **element** a sacrament; otherwise it
L C : 0 5 :010(448) [0755] a sacrament; otherwise it remains a mere **element**.
L C : 0 5 :014(448) [0755] Word away from the **elements** or view them apart from
E P : 0 7 :040(486) [0817] That the external visible **elements** of bread and wine in
S D : 0 1 :021(512) [0865] of certain accidental **elements** in human nature, in spite
S D : 0 3 :025(543) [0923] essential and necessary **elements** of justification are the
S D : 0 3 :048(548) [0933] of sins and, as a second **element**, renewal or
S D : 0 7 :011(571) [0975] offered with the visible **elements**, the bread and the wine,
S D : 0 7 :023(573) [0979] away or look upon the **elements** without the Word, you
S D : 0 7 :023(573) [0979] words remain with the **elements**, as they should and
S D : 0 7 :076(583) [0999] 'This is my body,' the **elements** set before us in the
S D : 0 7 :082(584) [1001] And thereby the **elements** of bread and wine are hallowed
S D : 0 7 :126(591) [1015] the teaching that the **elements** (the visible forms of the

Elementum (2)
L C : 0 4 :018(438) [0737] *"Accedat verbum ad **elementum** et fit sacramentum."*
L C : 0 5 :010(448) [0755] *"Accedat verbum ad **elementum** et fit sacramentum,"* that

Elevate (1), Elevated (1)
A P : 2 2 :009(237) [0359] the denial of one part: to **elevate** the position of the clergy
S D : 0 8 :012(593) [1019] glorification, it has been **elevated** to the right hand of

Eleven (1), Eleventh (5)
A G : 2 3 :025(055) [0065] He wrote in his **eleventh** letter, "If they are unwilling or
A P : 1 1 :001(180) [0247] They approve the **eleventh** article on retaining absolution
A P : 1 5 :019(217) [0319] In his **eleventh** chapter Daniel says that the invention of
A P : 2 1 :002(229) [0343] Jerome conquered Vigilantius **eleven** hundred years ago."
S D : 1 1 :027(620) [1071] ninth, and even at the **eleventh** hour (Matt. 20:1-16;
S D : 1 1 :033(622) [1075] the ninth, tenth, and **eleventh** chapters will show you how

Eli (3)
A P : 2 2 :010(237) [0359] also mention the case of **Eli**'s sons; after the loss of the
A P : 2 2 :010(237) [0361] when they apply the story of **Eli**'s sons to the sacrament.
A P : 2 2 :010(237) [0361] The story describes **Eli**'s punishment.

Elicited (3), Elicits (2)
A P : 0 2 :012(102) [0109] more than was proper to free will and to "**elicited** acts."
A P : 0 4 :009(108) [0123] in its sorrow over sin **elicits** an act of love to God or does
A P : 0 4 :012(109) [0123] of sins by these **elicited** acts of ours, of what use is Christ?
A P : 0 4 :036(112) [0131] forgiveness of sins by an **elicited** act of love, since it is
A P : 1 2 :075(193) [0273] has attrition or contrition **elicits** an act of love to God, he

Elijah (2)
A P : 2 4 :099(268) [0419] the work the the prophet **Elijah** in condemning the
S 3 : 0 8 :011(313) [0497] and no prophet, whether **Elijah** or Elisha, received the

Eliminate (6), Eliminates (1), Elimination (1)
A P : 0 4 :376(164) [0223] or a Jewish manner they **eliminate** from them the
A P : 1 2 :029(185) [0259] We **eliminate** from contrition those useless and endless
A P : 1 2 :075(193) [0273] of the law, the **elimination** of the Gospel, and the
E P : 0 9 :003(492) [0827] Christian manner, **eliminates** all unnecessary questions,
S D : 0 4 :036(557) [0949] This would **eliminate** much useless wrangling and
S D : 0 7 :085(584) [1001] and to obviate and **eliminate** many kinds of idolatrous
S D : 0 8 :004(592) [1017] ventured to **eliminate** from his Supper the true, essential
S D : 0 8 :038(598) [1027] one nature and wholly **eliminate** the other nature, as if,

Elisha (1)
S 3 : 0 8 :011(313) [0497] whether Elijah or **Elisha**, received the Spirit without the

Eloquence (3)
A P : 2 3 :038(244) [0373] prophecy surpasses **eloquence**, military science surpasses
A P : 2 3 :038(244) [0373] agriculture, and **eloquence** surpasses architecture.
A P : 2 3 :039(244) [0375] But as **eloquence** does not make an orator more righteous

Emanates (1)
S D : 1 1 :081(629) [1089] fits man for damnation **emanates** from the devil and man

Embark (1), Embarked (1)
L C : 0 4 :081(446) [0751] founders" in which we **embarked** when we entered the
S D : 0 4 :015(553) [0943] against conscience or **embark** deliberately on such sins

Embellish (1)
L C : 0 1 :055(372) [0595] all this is an attempt to **embellish** yourself with God's

Embitter (1)
S D : 1 1 :042(623) [1077] grieve and **embitter** the Holy Spirit, become entangled

Emblazoned (1)
L C : 0 3 :075(430) [0719] upright prince were **emblazoned** with a loaf of bread

Embodied (3), Embodies (1), Embodying (1)
P R : P R :023(012) [0021] of God and is **embodied** in the Augsburg Confession and
A P : 0 4 :087(119) [0147] this conclusion, **embodying** the basic issue of the whole
L C : 0 1 :113(380) [0613] God's command, and it **embodies** his highest wisdom,
L C : 0 5 :032(450) [0759] forgiveness of sins," are **embodied** in this sacrament and
S D : R N :011(506) [0855] reason why we have **embodied** the writings above listed —

Embrace (6), Embraced (2), Embraces (4), Embracing (2)
P R : P R :000(001) [0004] Princes, and Estates who **Embrace** the Augsburg
P R : P R :004(004) [0009] papal yoke as well as in **embracing** other errors that
A G : P R :004(025) [0039] side, to have all of us **embrace** and adhere to a single, true
A G : P R :008(025) [0039] communicated, and **embraced** in our lands, principalities,
A P : 0 4 :276(148) [0199] But the faithful **embrace** them and are glad to have signs
A P : 0 7 :013(170) [0231] outward organization **embracing** both the good and the
S 3 : 0 3 :037(309) [0489] he is altogether sinful **embraces** all sins in his confession
T R : 0 0 :052(329) [0519] true teaching must be **embraced** for the glory of God and
L C : 0 1 :014(366) [0583] when our heart **embraces** him and clings to him.
L C : 0 1 :286(403) [0663] in which he means to **embrace** all the commandments
L C : 0 1 :290(404) [0663] commandment, then, **embraces** a great multitude of good
L C : 0 3 :060(428) [0715] These two points **embrace** all that pertains to God's glory
S D : 0 2 :077(536) [0911] for the grace of God, **embrace** and accept it, believe the
S D : 0 3 :043(547) [0931] means and instrument it **embraces** God's grace and the

Embroidered (1)
L C : 0 1 :314(407) [0671] priest stands in a gold-**embroidered** chasuble or a layman

Emerge (1), Emerged (1), Emerging (1)
A P : 0 4 :242(141) [0187] a major commotion **emerged** from an insignificant issue.
L C : 0 1 :050(371) [0593] things that issue and **emerge** from the heart are words.
L C : 0 4 :065(444) [0749] under the water and **emerging** from it, indicate the power

Emergency (1)
T R : 0 0 :067(331) [0523] So in an **emergency** even a layman absolves and becomes

Emich (1)
P R : P R :027(015) [0025] **Emich**, count of Leiningen

Eminence (1), Eminent (3), Eminently (1)
T R : 0 0 :008(321) [0505] a child neither seeks nor takes pre-**eminence** for himself.
S D : 0 2 :045(530) [0899] other writings of this **eminent** and enlightened
S D : 0 7 :041(576) [0985] be regarded as the most **eminent** teacher of the churches
S D : 0 7 :046(577) [0987] law but also to the **eminent** article of faith concerning the
S D : 1 1 :052(625) [1081] This admonition is **eminently** necessary.

Emotions (2)
A P : 0 2 :043(106) [0117] that because of our **emotions** we are neither good nor
S D : 0 2 :070(534) [0909] be new activities and **emotions** in the intellect, will, and

Emperor (43), Emperors (6)
P R : P R :002(003) [0007] predecessors to the then **Emperor** Charles V, of most
P R : P R :008(005) [0009] had been submitted to **Emperor** Charles V in the great
P R : P R :018(008) [0015] which was submitted to **Emperor** Charles V at the great
P R : P R :018(009) [0015] submitted it to **Emperor** Charles V at the said imperial
P R : P R :018(009) [0015] was submitted to the **emperor** and that remained in the
P R : P R :023(012) [0021] in the year 1530 to **Emperor** Charles V, of Christian
P R : P R :025(013) [0023] in the year 1530 to **Emperor** Charles V, of kindest
A G : P R :001(024) [0039] most mighty, invincible **Emperor**, most gracious Lord:
A G : 2 3 :014(053) [0063] most renowned Christian **emperor**, Your Majesty will
A G : 2 8 :002(081) [0085] and depose kings and **emperors** according to their
A G : 2 8 :019(083) [0087] bestowed by Roman **emperors** and kings for the
A L : 2 1 :001(046) [0057] Thus the **emperor** may follow the example of David in
A L : 2 1 :001(047) [0057] out of his country, for like David the **emperor** is a king.
A L : 2 8 :019(083) [0087] granted by kings and **emperors** for the civil
A P : P R :013(099) [0101] not with the **emperor** or the princes, whom I hold in due
A P : 0 2 :002(100) [0105] from the schools, and not from the **emperor**'s council.
A P : 0 4 :236(140) [0185] blood and are asking the **emperor**, this most clement
A P : 0 7 :023(172) [0235] From him the **emperor** and all kings have received their
A P : 1 2 :002(182) [0253] shall we do here, O Charles, most invincible **Emperor**?
A P : 1 2 :003(182) [0253] beg you, most invincible **Emperor** Charles, to hear us out
A P : 2 1 :042(235) [0355] that our most gracious **emperor** take steps to correct the
A P : 2 1 :042(235) [0357] and holy desire of the **emperor**, our opponents are doing
A P : 2 1 :044(235) [0357] Therefore, gracious **Emperor** Charles, for the sake of the
A P : 2 3 :001(239) [0363] but they even urge the **emperor** and the princes not to let
A P : 2 3 :003(239) [0363] your chaste right hand, **Emperor** Charles — you whom
A P : 2 3 :003(239) [0363] most chaste and excellent **Emperor**, they propose laws
A P : 2 7 :018(272) [0425] But look, most clement **Emperor** Charles; look, princes;
S 2 : 0 4 :002(298) [0471] as "most gracious lord," as if he were a king or **emperor**.
S 2 : 0 4 :016(301) [0475] be standing before the **emperor** or the secular authority,
T R : 0 0 :020(323) [0509] the bishops of Rome were confirmed by the **emperors**?
T R : 0 0 :021(323) [0509] over the primacy, **Emperor** Phocas had finally decided
T R : 0 0 :021(323) [0509] nor would a decree of the **emperor** have been necessary.
T R : 0 0 :035(326) [0513] but especially the **emperors** of Germany, with unjust
T R : 0 0 :035(326) [0513] power and deprive the **emperors** of the right to appoint
T R : 0 0 :050(329) [0519] is judged neither by the **emperor**, nor by all the clergy,
T R : 0 0 :082(334) [0529] presented to the **emperor** in the diet of Augsburg and, by
S C : 0 9 :005(355) [0561] whether it be to the **emperor** as supreme, or to governors
L C : 0 1 :209(393) [0641] all, whether those of **emperor**, princes, bishops, or anyone
L C : 0 1 :268(401) [0657] as much authority as the **emperor** and all magistrates.
L C : 0 3 :057(427) [0713] a very rich and mighty **emperor** who bade a poor beggar
L C : 0 3 :077(431) [0721] ask God to endow the **emperor**, kings, and all estates of
L C : 0 5 :011(448) [0755] ordinance of a prince or **emperor**, but of the divine
E P : R N :004(465) [0777] which was delivered to **Emperor** Charles V at Augsburg
S D : P R :003(501) [0847] Word and submitted it to **Emperor** Charles V at the great
S D : P R :005(502) [0847] Confession as it was delivered to **Emperor** Charles in 1530
S D : R N :005(504) [0851] 1530 and submitted to **Emperor** Charles V at Augsburg
S D : 0 7 :001(568) [0971] and submitted to the **emperor**, the Sacramentarians
S D : 0 7 :041(576) [0985] and delivered to **Emperor** Charles V, therefore the true
S D : 0 8 :075(606) [1043] that during the time of **Emperor** Valens there was a

Emphasis (1), Emphasize (4), Emphasized (5), Emphasizing (1), Emphatic (1), Emphatically (2)
A G : 2 6 :020(067) [0073] should and must be **emphasized** in the church, but this
A G : 2 7 :048(078) [0081] faith, which should be **emphasized** above all else in the
A P : 0 4 :266(146) [0197] while Daniel most **emphatically** wants to include faith.
A P : 1 2 :058(190) [0267] two parts in order to **emphasize** the faith that we require
A P : 1 8 :003(225) [0335] we quoted Augustine's **emphatic** refutation of these
A P : 2 1 :038(235) [0355] of saints in order to **emphasize** the honor and the work of
S C : P R :018(340) [0537] of stealing, must be **emphasized** when instructing laborers
L C : 0 1 :232(396) [0647] necessary, therefore, to **emphasize** and explain it to the
L C : 0 1 :325(409) [0675] everywhere, **emphasizing** these two things, fear of God
L C : 0 2 :012(412) [0681] We should **emphasize** the words, "maker of heaven and
L C : 0 4 :022(439) [0737] is the first point to be **emphasized**: the nature and dignity
L C : 0 5 :007(447) [0755] This must always be **emphasized**, for thus we can
L C : 0 6 :016(459) [0000] past we placed all the **emphasis** on our work alone, and
S D : 0 3 :053(548) [0933] works") just as **emphatically** in the article of salvation as

Empire (15)
P R : P R :001(003) [0007] and estates in the Holy **Empire** of the German Nation
P R : P R :002(003) [0007] of all the estates of the **empire**, and published and
P R : P R :018(009) [0015] the custody of the Holy **Empire**, and of which both the
P R : P R :022(011) [0019] inside or outside the Holy **Empire** of the German Nation.
P R : P R :025(014) [0023] in the Holy Roman **Empire**, and also with other Christian
P R : P R :025(014) [0023] ordinances of the Holy **Empire** and of the special treaties
A G : P R :001(024) [0039] summoned a diet of the **empire** to convene here in
A G : P R :015(026) [0041] and estates of the **empire**, especially in a public
A G : P R :018(026) [0041] and estates of the **empire** were, among other things,
A G : P R :021(027) [0043] in all the diets of the **empire** which have been held during
A P : 1 2 :126(201) [0289] take care, indicate a change in the Holy Roman **Empire**.
A P : 2 3 :001(239) [0363] not to let the Roman **Empire** be disgraced and shamed by
A P : 2 3 :002(239) [0363] disgraces and shames the **empire**, as if the church were
T R : 0 0 :082(000) [0529] and estates of the Roman **Empire**, to his Imperial
S D : R N :005(504) [0851] and estates of the Roman **Empire** as the common

Employ (6), Employed (12), Employer (1), Employers (1), Employs (5)
P R : P R :021(010) [0019] and manner of speech **employed** with reference to the
A G : P R :002(025) [0039] end it was proposed to **employ** all diligence amicably and
A G : 0 1 :004(028) [0043] as the Fathers **employed** the term in this connection, not
A L : 0 1 :004(028) [0043] as the ancient Fathers **employed** it in this connection, to
A P : 0 2 :013(102) [0109] the scholastics do not often **employ** in their discussions.
A P : 1 4 :001(214) [0315] With the proviso that we **employ** canonical ordination,
T R : 0 0 :043(328) [0517] they are shamelessly **employed** to secure disgraceful
T R : 0 0 :058(330) [0521] too, is the cruelty which he **employs** against the godly.
T R : 0 0 :074(332) [0525] for themselves alone and have **employed** for gain.
S C : P R :007(339) [0533] confused if a teacher **employs** one form now and another
S C : P R :012(339) [0535] addition, parents and **employers** should refuse to furnish
L C : 0 1 :225(395) [0645] a servant can cheat his **employer** out of thirty or forty
E P : 0 1 :023(469) [0785] should therefore not be **employed** in sermons delivered to
E P : 0 2 :004(470) [0787] without means; he **employs** to this end the preaching and
S D : 0 3 :043(547) [0931] terms which St. Paul **employs**, such as "apart from

Continued ▶

S D : 0 4 :001(551) [0939] One party **employed** such words and formulas as "Good
S D : 0 4 :014(553) [0943] and its Apology often **employ** formulas like these: "Good
S D : 0 6 :012(566) [0965] Then he **employs** the law to instruct the regenerate out of
S D : 0 7 :002(569) [0971] diligently endeavor to **employ** terminology which is as
S D : 0 7 :018(572) [0979] Sacramentarians had **employed** to interpret the
S D : 0 7 :040(576) [0985] the formula which Christ **employed** in the Last Supper.
S D : 0 7 :099(586) [1005] He can still **employ** this mode of presence when he wills
S D : 0 7 :100(586) [1007] He **employed** this mode of presence when he left the
S D : 0 8 :051(601) [1033] nature in Christ is **employed** after its own measure and
S D : 1 0 :012(612) [1057] his Christian liberty he **employed** in other instances

Empty (10), Emptying (1), Emptiness (1)
A P : 0 4 :150(127) [0163] this trust in his own righteousness was wicked and **empty**.
A P : 0 4 :362(162) [0219] not putting forward an **empty** quibble about the term
A P : 1 3 :011(212) [0311] shall not return to me **empty**, but it shall accomplish that
A P : 2 3 :070(249) [0383] Then you will see the **emptiness** of our opponents'
L C : P R :011(360) [0571] Word is not like some **empty** tale, such as the one about
L C : 0 1 :020(367) [0585] into an idol and entrust themselves to an **empty** nothing.
L C : 0 1 :197(392) [0637] their good works and **emptying** the monasteries.
L C : 0 1 :224(395) [0643] the world would soon be **empty**, and there would be a
L C : 0 4 :063(444) [0749] Baptism merely as an **empty** sign, as the fanatics dream.
L C : 0 4 :073(445) [0751] there Baptism is no **empty** symbol, but the effect
S D : 0 8 :044(599) [1031] goes down and we go upward like a light and **empty** pan.
S D : 0 8 :045(600) [1031] "God died," are merely **empty** words which do not

Enable (5), Enabled (1), Enables (6), Enabling (1)
A G : 1 8 :001(039) [0051] of the will which **enables** him to live an outwardly
A G : 1 8 :004(039) [0051] However, this does not **enable** them to act in matters
A L : 1 8 :004(039) [0051] have a free will which **enables** them to make judgments
A L : 1 8 :004(039) [0051] However, this does not **enable** them, without God, to
A L : 2 0 :035(046) [0057] for showing how we are **enabled** to do good works.
A P : 0 4 :250(143) [0191] that makes us alive and **enables** us to overcome death and
A P : 0 4 :351(161) [0217] true knowledge of God, **enabling** us truly to fear him and
S 3 : 0 3 :040(309) [0489] the sins that remain and **enables** man to become truly
S C : 0 3 :013(347) [0547] us aware of his gifts and **enable** us to receive our daily
L C : 0 1 :235(397) [0647] mistress's property, which **enables** you to stuff your craw
E P : 0 1 :022(469) [0785] This **enables** the Manichaeans to conceal their error and
S D : R N :020(507) [0857] This explanation will **enable** the pious reader, as far as is
S D : 0 7 :106(588) [1009] to reason, and will **enable** a Christian heart to rely on and

Enact (2), Enacted (2)
A L : 2 6 :045(070) [0075] of the apostles to **enact** binding laws with respect to holy
A P : 0 4 :288(151) [0203] why the Fathers had **enacted** them, namely, not that we
A P : 0 7 :023(172) [0235] devotions and sacrifices, **enact** whatever laws he pleases,
A P : 1 1 :008(181) [0251] tragic spectacles were **enacted** between the secular and the

Enchiridion (1)
S C : 0 0 :000(337) [0531] **Enchiridion**

Enclosed (4)
L C : 0 4 :016(438) [0735] God has fastened and **enclosed** it and from which he does
L C : 0 4 :019(439) [0737] of a nut) but as that in which God's Word is **enclosed**.
E P : 0 7 :032(485) [0815] the body of Christ is so **enclosed** in heaven that it can in
S D : 0 7 :014(571) [0977] of Christ are locally **enclosed** in the bread, or are in some

Encompassed (1)
A P : 1 2 :149(205) [0299] "The sorrows of death **encompassed** me (II Sam. 22:5).

Encounter (1), Encountered (2)
S 3 : 0 3 :042(310) [0491] I have **encountered** many foolish people like this and I
S C : P R :001(338) [0533] which I recently **encountered** when I was a visitor
L C : 0 1 :273(401) [0659] Therefore, if you **encounter** somebody with a worthless

Encourage (5), Encouraged (9), Encouragement (5), Encourages (6), Encouraging (1)
A L : 2 6 :034(069) [0075] discipline ought to be **encouraged** at all times, and not
A P : 0 4 :045(113) [0133] of conscience it consoles and **encourages** our hearts.
A P : 0 4 :249(143) [0191] of conscience and **encourages** and consoles terrified
A P : 0 4 :293(152) [0203] When the heart is **encouraged** and quickened by faith in
A P : 0 4 :351(161) [0217] we are receiving **encouragement** and comfort in the midst
A P : 1 1 :002(180) [0249] This teaching has **encouraged** many devout minds, and in
A P : 1 1 :009(182) [0251] on faith, which consoles and **encourages** consciences.
A P : 1 2 :056(189) [0267] This voice **encourages** David and by faith it sustains,
A P : 1 2 :057(189) [0267] her penance, the faith that **encouraged** and consoled her.
A P : 1 2 :074(192) [0273] sins, namely, that faith **encourages** our hearts and the
A P : 2 1 :005(230) [0345] after his denial, we are **encouraged** to believe that grace
A P : 2 4 :070(262) [0409] Such a faith **encourages** the contrite mind.
S C : P R :018(340) [0537] order that they may be **encouraged** to be orderly,
S C : 0 1 :020(344) [0543] servants, or cattle, but **encourage** them to remain and
S C : 0 3 :002(346) [0545] Here God would **encourage** us to believe that he is truly
L C : 0 1 :070(374) [0601] constantly urged and **encouraged** to honor God's name
L C : 0 1 :166(387) [0627] This ought to **encourage** us and make our hearts so melt
L C : 0 1 :195(391) [0637] by which he wants to **encourage** and urge us to true,
L C : 0 1 :202(392) [0639] afford no occasion, aid, or **encouragement** to unchastity.
L C : 0 3 :019(423) [0703] all the more urged and **encouraged** to pray because God
L C : 0 3 :022(423) [0703] we should be **encouraged** and drawn to pray because, in
L C : 0 6 :007(457) [0000] preach, exhorting, **encouraging**, and persuading them not
E P : 1 1 :016(497) [0837] and by the **encouragement** of the Scriptures we might
E P : 1 2 :008(498) [0839] of infant Baptism nor **encourage** it, in spite of the
S D : 1 1 :012(618) [1067] steadfastness, by the **encouragement** of the Scriptures we
S D : 1 1 :092(632) [1093] steadfastness and by **encouragement** of the Scriptures we

Encratites (2)
A P : 2 3 :045(245) [0375] among the **Encratites** captured the imagination of the
A P : 2 3 :050(246) [0377] contemptible than the **Encratites**, who seem to have gone

Encumbered (2)
L C : 0 2 :054(418) [0693] yet because we are **encumbered** with our flesh we are
E P : 0 4 :013(477) [0799] but they are still **encumbered** with much weakness, as St.

End (66), Ended (1), Endless (19), Ends (5)
P R : P R :006(004) [0009] apply our diligence to the **end** that the false and
P R : P R :007(004) [0009] this in mind and to this **end** our praiseworthy
P R : P R :013(007) [0013] to and is necessary for this **end** and put it down in one
P R : P R :017(008) [0015] to accomplish the desired **end** of Christian concord, and
P R : P R :018(009) [0015] until our blessed **end** and to appear before the judgment
P R : P R :023(012) [0021] To this **end** the present agreement was proposed,
A G : P R :002(025) [0039] religion, and to this **end** it was proposed to employ all
A G : P R :011(026) [0041] humility and implore him to bestow his grace to this **end**.
A G : 0 1 :003(027) [0043] without division, without **end**, of infinite power, wisdom,
A G : 2 6 :011(065) [0071] Accordingly there was no **end** or limit to the making of
A G : 0 0 :002(095) [0095] Parish ministers also had **endless** quarrels with monks
A L : 1 7 :002(038) [0051] will give eternal life and **endless** joy, but ungodly men and
A L : 1 7 :003(038) [0051] and devils he will condemn to be tormented without **end**.
A L : 1 7 :004(038) [0051] think that there will be an **end** to the punishments of
A L : 2 4 :033(060) [0067] Mass is to be used to this **end**, that the sacrament is
A L : 0 0 :002(095) [0095] There have been **endless** quarrels between parish
A P : P R :015(099) [0101] up all their sophistries, for this would be an **endless** task.
A P : 0 2 :026(103) [0111] which pursues carnal **ends** contrary to the Word of God
A P : 0 4 :030(111) [0129] For even as Christ is 'the **end** of the law,' so likewise he is
A P : 0 4 :087(120) [0147] where he says toward the **end**, "Having therefore
A P : 0 4 :110(123) [0153] Where does this **end** but with the abolition of the promise
A P : 0 4 :372(164) [0221] He is the **end** of the law (Rom. 10:4), and he himself says,
A P : 0 4 :391(166) [0225] not seem so great as to **end** all argument, when there are
A P : 1 2 :005(183) [0253] the *Sentences* are full of **endless** questions which the
A P : 1 2 :011(184) [0255] effort is devoted to the **endless** enumeration of sins, most
A P : 1 2 :016(184) [0257] of satisfactions is **endless**, and we cannot list all the
A P : 1 2 :029(185) [0259] those useless and **endless** discussions as to when we are
A P : 1 2 :137(203) [0293] the sale of Masses, and **endless** observances which make
A P : 1 2 :151(206) [0299] with us, what will be the **end** of those who do not obey
A P : 1 2 :178(211) [0309] the merit of attrition, the **endless** enumeration of
A P : 1 3 :023(214) [0313] From it has come the **endless** desecration of Masses,
A P : 1 6 :012(224) [0333] **Endless** discussions about contracts will never satisfy
A P : 1 7 :001(224) [0335] the ungodly to **endless** torment with the devil.
A P : 2 0 :005(227) [0339] Here we could quote **endless** passages from Scripture and
A P : 2 1 :041(235) [0355] confusions and **endless** disputations of the scholastic
A P : 2 3 :006(240) [0365] morality, for it produces **endless** scandals, sins, and the
A P : 2 3 :054(247) [0379] picture of the times that will precede the **end** of all things.
A P : 2 4 :015(251) [0389] been publishing almost **endless** books about sacrifice, but
A P : 2 4 :064(261) [0405] These errors have sired **endless** others, like the one that
A P : 2 7 :009(270) [0421] openly point to an evil **end**, either because weakness
A P : 2 7 :032(274) [0431] this sentence, but at the **end** Bernard adds: "Let nobody
A P : 2 7 :055(278) [0439] would be more useful than these **endless** babblings.
S 2 : 0 2 :013(295) [0465] what purpose and to what **end** the authors wrote these
S 3 : 0 8 :009(313) [0497] descendants from the beginning to the **end** of the world.
T R : 0 0 :082(000) [0529] not permitted to await the **end** of the assembly, I ask
S C : 0 3 :011(347) [0547] us steadfast in his Word and in faith even to the **end**.
S C : 0 3 :020(348) [0549] he may grant us a blessed **end** and graciously take us from
L C : P R :016(361) [0573] of the world to the **end**, and all prophets and saints have
L C : P R :020(361) [0573] To this **end** may God grant his grace!
L C : S P :020(364) [0579] Matthew and Mark at the **end** of their Gospels where
L C : 0 1 :043(370) [0591] wealth and money, what have they gained in the **end**?
L C : 0 1 :046(371) [0593] which indeed endures for a time but in the **end** is nothing!
L C : 0 1 :067(373) [0599] nothing he does will in the **end** succeed; everything he
L C : 0 1 :076(375) [0603] will come to no good **end**; at best they will remain good
L C : 0 1 :096(378) [0609] of the Word at the **end** of the year as at the beginning.
L C : 0 1 :166(387) [0629] to be willing to run to the **ends** of the world to obtain
L C : 0 1 :186(390) [0633] which, if they came true, would soon put an **end** to him.
L C : 0 1 :326(409) [0675] of a wreath that binds the **end** to the beginning and holds
L C : 0 1 :329(410) [0677] it they depend, so that **end** and beginning are all linked
L C : 0 3 :051(427) [0711] To this **end** he also gave his Holy Spirit to teach us this
L C : 0 3 :064(429) [0715] For this **end** he strives without rest day and night, using
L C : 0 3 :106(434) [0727] even though the tribulation is not removed or **ended**.
L C : 0 4 :028(440) [0739] works and external things contribute nothing to this **end**.
L C : 0 4 :050(443) [0745] church will abide until the **end** of the world, our
L C : 0 4 :050(443) [0745] wickedness, or give his grace and Spirit for such **ends**.
E P : 0 2 :004(470) [0787] means; he employs to this **end** the preaching and the
E P : 1 2 :001(498) [0839] to us, we wish here at the **end** merely to enumerate the
S D : P R :002(501) [0847] and raised no **end** of slanders and insinuations against it.
S D : P R :005(502) [0847] Almighty to abide until our **end** by this repeatedly cited
S D : 0 1 :030(513) [0867] powers from beginning to **end**, down to the ultimate part
S D : 0 2 :006(521) [0883] grace to bring it to an **end**, we submit the following as
S D : 0 2 :014(523) [0885] and to help them to remain in true faith until their **end**.
S D : 0 2 :016(523) [0887] heavenly gifts in us and strengthen us daily until our **end**.
S D : 0 2 :050(530) [0901] To this **end**, in his boundless kindness and mercy, God
S D : 0 4 :030(555) [0947] only he who endures to the **end** will be saved (Matt.
S D : 0 4 :030(555) [0947] we hold our first confidence firm to the **end**" (Heb. 3:14).
S D : 0 4 :034(556) [0949] alone the beginning, the middle, and **end** of everything.
S D : 0 4 :038(557) [0951] right causes and for right **ends** (that is, with the intention
S D : 0 5 :009(559) [0955] terrors of the law may not **end** in despair, the
S D : 0 5 :011(560) [0955] To this **end** Christ has obtained and sent us the Spirit,
S D : 0 5 :024(562) [0961] church of God until the **end** of the world, but with the
S D : 0 5 :024(563) [0961] the Christ who is the **end** of the law (Rom. 10:4), the
S D : 0 7 :029(574) [0981] time, and that there is no **end** to the rage and fury of
S D : 0 7 :044(577) [0987] and obedience until the **end** of the world and which was
S D : 0 7 :077(583) [0999] first Communion until the **end** of the world, make the
S D : 0 8 :027(596) [1025] from sea to sea and to the **ends** of the earth, as the
S D : 1 1 :021(619) [1069] preserve them unto the **end**, if they cling to God's Word,
S D : 1 1 :023(619) [1069] help, further, strengthen, and preserve them to this **end**.
S D : 1 1 :032(621) [1073] will also continue it to the **end** and complete it, if we
S D : 1 1 :032(621) [1073] him but "hold fast until the **end** the substance which has
S D : 1 1 :076(628) [1087] ordinary means or instruments to accomplish this **end**.

Endanger (1), Endangers (1)
A P : 2 3 :006(240) [0365] It obviously **endangers** religion and morality, for it
S C : 0 1 :010(343) [0541] and so we should not **endanger** our neighbor's life, nor

Endeavor (1), Endeavored (1)
E P : 0 7 :001(481) [0809] Nevertheless, they **endeavored** surreptitiously to insinuate
S D : 0 7 :002(569) [0971] diligently **endeavor** to employ terminology which is as

Endow (1), Endowed (4), Endowment (1), Endowments (2), Endows (1)
A G : 2 7 :020(074) [0079] marriage who are not **endowed** with the gift of virginity
A L : 2 0 :029(045) [0057] are so renewed and **endowed** with new affections as to be
T R : 0 0 :081(334) [0527] be established without the **endowments** of the church.
L C : 0 1 :022(367) [0585] how often it has made **endowments**, fasted, celebrated
L C : 0 1 :208(393) [0639] has supplied and **endowed** it with everything in the world

Continued ▶

LC : 03 :077(431) [0721] Again, to ask God to **endow** the emperor, kings, and all
SD : 02 :089(538) [0915] the operation, gift, **endowment**, and work of the Holy
SD : 08 :052(601) [1033] nature in Christ is **endowed** and adorned are created gifts
SD : 08 :073(605) [1041] the Holy Spirit who **endows** them only with created gifts.

Endure (11), Endured (2), Endures (4)
AP : PR :016(099) [0103] therefore, that we must **endure** difficulties and dangers
AP : 04 :167(130) [0169] Who **endures** patiently enough the afflictions that God
AP : 04 :243(141) [0189] which cannot **endure** unless pastors and churches
AP : 12 :124(201) [0289] God will not long **endure** such impudence and malice.
AP : 24 :067(261) [0407] eucharistic sacrifices when the reconciled **endure** them.
AP : 24 :098(268) [0419] this worship of Baal will **endure** together with the papal
SC : 08 :010(354) [0559] for he is good; for his steadfast love **endures** forever.
LC : 01 :046(371) [0593] which indeed **endures** for a time but in the end is
LC : 01 :134(383) [0619] this life can neither be heartily enjoyed nor long **endure**.
LC : 01 :246(398) [0651] We shall **endure** your arrogance and show forgiveness and
LC : 01 :262(400) [0655] Christians, they must **endure** having the world call them
EP : 08 :008(487) [0819] from place to place, to **endure** hunger, thirst, cold, heat,
SD : 01 :062(519) [0879] is that we shall not only **endure** God's eternal wrath and
SD : 04 :030(555) [0947] since only he who **endures** to the end will be saved (Matt.
SD : 11 :006(617) [1065] is to go, how long it is to **endure**, and when and how he
SD : 11 :079(629) [1089] It is written, "God **endured** with much patience the
SD : 11 :080(629) [1089] terms that God "**endured** the vessels of wrath with much

Enemy (11), Enemies (30)
AL : 20 :025(044) [0057] they hate God as an **enemy**, do not call upon him, and
AL : 00 :005(049) [0059] from common rumors or the accusations of our **enemies**.
AP : 15 :039(220) [0325] Our **enemies** falsely accuse us of abolishing good
AP : 21 :026(232) [0349] protect us from the **enemy** and receive us in the hour of
AP : 27 :013(271) [0423] these insults with which our **enemies** attack thy Gospel!
TR : 00 :066(331) [0523] regular bishops become **enemies** of the Gospel and are
SC : PR :019(340) [0537] of the world and are the worst **enemies** of God and man.
LC : PR :015(360) [0571] midst of such mighty **enemies** as the devils, and yet we
LC : 01 :184(390) [0633] you acquire many **enemies** who begrudge you even the
LC : 01 :186(390) [0633] imprecations upon their **enemy**'s head, which, if they
LC : 01 :187(390) [0633] be content to let our **enemies** rave and rage and do their
LC : 01 :187(390) [0633] have given us occasion for anger, namely, our **enemies**.
LC : 01 :194(391) [0635] is directed, as I said, especially toward our **enemies**.
LC : 01 :195(391) [0637] and, in short, love and kindness toward our **enemies**.
LC : 01 :313(407) [0671] patience, love toward **enemies**, chastity, kindness, etc.,
LC : 03 :031(424) [0707] and plots of our **enemies** and checking their murderous
LC : 03 :065(429) [0715] and the world as our **enemies** and must count on their
LC : 03 :067(429) [0717] will of the devil or of our **enemies**, nor of those who
LC : 03 :070(429) [0717] the devil and of all our **enemies** shall and must fail and
LC : 03 :077(431) [0721] the Turks and all our **enemies**; to grant their subjects and
LC : 03 :080(431) [0721] directed against our chief **enemy**, the devil, whose whole
LC : 03 :109(435) [0729] stand, for he is an **enemy** who never stops or becomes
LC : 03 :113(435) [0729] of our prayer may be directed against our arch-**enemy**.
LC : 03 :116(435) [0731] on earth but to pray constantly against this arch-**enemy**.
LC : 05 :026(449) [0759] The devil is a furious **enemy**; when he sees that we resist
LC : 05 :079(455) [0771] you will not acquire **enemies** who harm, wrong, and
EP : 02 :003(470) [0787] but has also become an **enemy** of God, so that he desires
EP : 10 :002(492) [0829] called for, and when the **enemies** of the Gospel have not
EP : 10 :006(493) [0829] we dare not yield to the **enemies** in such indifferent
EP : 10 :006(493) [0831] God sends us and what he lets the **enemies** inflict on us.
EP : 10 :011(494) [0831] understanding with the **enemies** of the holy Gospel (which
SD : 01 :045(516) [0873] his grace but remains the **enemy** of sin throughout
SD : 02 :005(521) [0881] but he is and remains an **enemy** of God until by the
SD : 07 :032(574) [0983] misinterpret them, as the **enemies** of the sacrament do at
SD : 08 :025(596) [1023] one word he struck his **enemies** to the ground, and again
SD : 10 :002(611) [1053] case of confession, when **enemies** of the holy Gospel have
SD : 10 :002(611) [1053] a clear conscience, at the **enemies**' insistent demand,
SD : 10 :010(612) [1055] of confession, as when **enemies** of the Word of God desire
SD : 10 :025(615) [1061] violate love, confirm the **enemies** of God's Word, and
SD : 10 :028(615) [1061] we may yield to **enemies** of the holy Gospel or conform to
SD : 10 :029(615) [1061] deed or action to please **enemies** of the holy Gospel

Enforced (2)
AG : 23 :012(053) [0063] celibacy was at once **enforced** so hastily and indecently
AG : 23 :013(053) [0063] the misgiving that such **enforced** celibacy and such

Engage (11)
AG : 16 :002(037) [0051] evildoers with the sword, **engage** in just wars, serve as
AG : 18 :005(040) [0053] a house, take a wife, **engage** in a trade, or do whatever
AG : 20 :037(046) [0057] one's neighbor, diligently **engage** in callings which are
AG : 23 :001(051) [0061] and who went so far as to **engage** in abominable vices.
AG : 27 :053(079) [0083] keep his possessions and **engage** in business without sin.
AL : 16 :002(037) [0051] just punishments, to **engage** in just wars, to serve as
AL : 16 :003(037) [0051] who forbid Christians to **engage** in these civil functions.
AL : 27 :052(079) [0083] and therefore they **engage** in their married life with a
AL : 27 :053(079) [0083] when they keep their possessions or **engage** in business.
AP : 16 :001(222) [0329] legal punishments, **engage** in just wars, render military
EP : 09 :002(492) [0827] that we should not **engage** in disputations concerning this

Engenders (1)
SD : 02 :089(538) [0915] the Holy Spirit **engenders** no new impulses and begins no

England (1)
AP : 12 :127(201) [0289] In Germany, **England**, Spain, France, Italy, even in Rome

Enhances (1)
AP : 23 :005(239) [0365] their authority, which they think celibacy **enhances**.

Enjoin (1), Enjoined (3), Enjoining (1), Enjoins (4)
AP : 04 :235(140) [0185] Paul often **enjoins** this both here and elsewhere.
AP : 04 :266(146) [0197] Christ when the law is preached and works are **enjoined**.
S2 : 02 :012(295) [0465] has been commanded or **enjoined** upon us with reference
LC : PR :014(360) [0571] Deut. 6:7, 8 solemnly **enjoins** that we should always
LC : 01 :333(410) [0677] so earnestly requires and **enjoins** under threat of his
LC : 02 :019(412) [0681] as he has required and **enjoined** in the Ten
LC : 02 :020(412) [0683] we neither see nor consider what the words **enjoin** on us.
LC : 05 :045(452) [0763] precept and command, **enjoining** all who would be
SD : 04 :016(554) [0943] indicates when it **enjoins** the creature to obey its Creator.

Enjoy (17), Enjoyed (5), Enjoying (1), Enjoyment (1)
LC : 01 :067(373) [0599] will slip through his fingers and will never be **enjoyed**.
LC : 01 :068(374) [0599] of marriage; they never **enjoyed** a happy hour or a
LC : 01 :134(383) [0619] this commandment will **enjoy** good days, happiness, and
LC : 01 :134(383) [0619] this life can neither be heartily **enjoyed** nor long endure.
LC : 01 :242(397) [0649] will be consumed by rust so that you will never **enjoy** it."
LC : 01 :243(398) [0649] that they can never **enjoy** it or pass it on to their children.
LC : 01 :253(399) [0653] happy conscience you can **enjoy** a hundred times more
LC : 02 :021(413) [0683] and greed, pleasure and **enjoyment**, and never once
LC : 02 :038(415) [0689] but put to use and **enjoyed**, God has caused the Word to
LC : 03 :037(425) [0707] children of God and **enjoy** the sacraments, through which
LC : 03 :044(425) [0709] called by his name and **enjoy** his manifold blessings fail to
LC : 03 :072(430) [0719] in order to have and **enjoy** daily bread and, on the
LC : 03 :072(430) [0719] against everything that interferes with **enjoying** it.
LC : 03 :074(430) [0719] retain any of them or **enjoy** them in security or happiness
LC : 03 :075(430) [0719] office of the princes we **enjoy** protection and peace and
LC : 03 :075(430) [0719] those through whom we **enjoy** our possessions in peace
LC : 04 :037(441) [0741] that without it nothing can be received or **enjoyed**.
LC : 05 :034(450) [0761] drink, that you may take it as your own and **enjoy** it."
LC : 05 :035(450) [0761] blessing be offered to him in vain and refuses to **enjoy** it.
LC : 05 :047(452) [0765] for you, which you shall **enjoy** not just on this one
LC : 05 :087(456) [0773] church, they should also **enjoy** this fellowship of the
LC : 06 :005(457) [0000] a Christian ought to do, should **enjoy** none of its benefits.
LC : 06 :006(457) [0000] happen if you wished to **enjoy** the Gospel's benefits but
LC : 06 :006(457) [0000] permission to share and **enjoy** any part of our liberty, but

Enlarge (2), Enlarging (1)
AL : 27 :045(078) [0081] should be inclined to **enlarge** on these claims, how many
AP : 28 :008(282) [0445] dangerous this is and **enlarging** on the sin of those who
LC : 03 :072(430) [0719] You must therefore **enlarge** and extend your thoughts to

Enlighten (3), Enlightened (9), Enlightens (7)
PR : PR :004(003) [0007] Christian death of that **enlightened** and pious person, Dr.
PR : PR :025(014) [0023] Catechism of that highly **enlightened** man, Dr. Luther.
S1 : PR :010(290) [0457] have now been so **enlightened** and supplied with the pure
SC : 02 :006(345) [0545] me through the Gospel, **enlightened** me with his gifts, and
SC : 02 :006(345) [0545] as he calls, gathers, **enlightens**, and sanctifies the whole
LC : 03 :051(427) [0711] his holy Word and to **enlighten** and strengthen us in faith
EP : 02 :013(471) [0789] draws men to himself, **enlightens** them, justifies them, and
SD : 02 :009(522) [0883] until the Holy Spirit **enlightens** and teaches them they
SD : 02 :021(525) [0889] until the Holy Spirit **enlightens**, converts, and regenerates
SD : 02 :040(528) [0895] me through the Gospel, **enlightened** me with his gifts, and
SD : 02 :040(528) [0895] as he calls, gathers, **enlightens**, and sanctifies the whole
SD : 02 :042(529) [0897] us his Holy Spirit, who **enlightens**, sanctifies, and brings
SD : 02 :045(530) [0899] other writings of this eminent and **enlightened** theologian.
SD : 02 :060(533) [0905] reason becomes an **enlightened** one and his resisting will
SD : 02 :063(533) [0905] converted, and thereby **enlightened**, and his will is
SD : 07 :028(574) [0981] Since this highly **enlightened** man foresaw in the Spirit
SD : 11 :017(619) [1069] repentance, and would **enlighten** them in the true faith.
SD : 11 :040(623) [1077] Holy Spirit would call, **enlighten**, and convert the elect
SD : 11 :061(626) [1083] his Word, whereby he **enlightens**, converts, and keeps

Enlisted (1), Enlisting (1), Enlists (1)
AG : PR :004(025) [0039] and church, even as we are all **enlisted** under one Christ.
LC : 01 :141(384) [0621] him; if he is too weak, he **enlists** the help of his friends
LC : 03 :062(428) [0715] all his subjects and even **enlisting** the world and our own

Enlivens (1)
AP : 04 :386(166) [0225] promise of grace, truly **enlivens** the fearful mind, and is

Enmity (8)
AG : 20 :025(044) [0057] of sin, and so they are at **enmity** with God, cannot call
AP : 02 :046(106) [0119] pronounced, "I will put **enmity** between you and the
S2 : 04 :011(300) [0475] Tartars, great as is their **enmity** against Christians, do
LC : 01 :183(390) [0633] harm, and so we have reason to be at **enmity** with them.
LC : 03 :103(434) [0727] but hatred and envy, **enmity**, violence and injustice,
LC : 05 :075(455) [0771] idolatry, sorcery, **enmity**, strife, jealousy, anger,
SD : 01 :011(510) [0863] and is actually **enmity** against God, especially in divine
SD : 02 :022(525) [0889] nature is in recalcitrant **enmity** against God — but out of

Enormous (2)
AP : 21 :034(234) [0353] with abuses that were **enormous** and worse than pagan.
TR : 00 :052(329) [0519] the godly consider the **enormous** errors of the pope's

Enough (85)
AL : 07 :002(032) [0047] unity of the church it is **enough** to agree concerning the
AL : 24 :032(059) [0067] to us; and it is not **enough** to remember the history, for
AP : 02 :003(101) [0105] explanation should be **enough** for any unprejudiced man.
AP : 04 :037(112) [0131] It is easy **enough** for idle men to make up these dreams
AP : 04 :039(112) [0131] We have said **enough** about the righteousness of law or
AP : 04 :051(114) [0135] So it is not **enough** to believe that Christ was born,
AP : 04 :084(119) [0145] could never determine whether we had merited **enough**."
AP : 04 :167(130) [0169] For who loves or fears God **enough**?
AP : 04 :167(130) [0169] Who endures patiently **enough** the afflictions that God
AP : 04 :204(135) [0177] despair because they cannot find works pure **enough**.
AP : 04 :249(142) [0191] have already shown often **enough** what we mean by faith.
AP : 04 :257(144) [0193] of the law were **enough** by itself, why would Christ and
AP : 04 :257(144) [0193] of penitence it is not **enough** to preach the law, the Word
AP : 04 :260(145) [0193] of the law is not **enough** because the law works wrath and
AP : 04 :321(157) [0209] their works are worth **enough** to account them righteous,
AP : 04 :360(162) [0219] works that are precious **enough** to earn a reward;
AP : 04 :376(165) [0223] have a reconciled Father, as we have said often **enough**.
AP : 04 :390(166) [0225] have mingled more than **enough** philosophy with
AP : 07 :003(169) [0227] The eighth article exonerates us **enough**.
AP : 07 :029(173) [0237] have spoken out clearly **enough** in our Confession, where
AP : 07 :029(173) [0237] time being this seemed **enough** to defend the definition of
AP : 07 :030(173) [0237] unity of the church it is **enough** to agree concerning the
AP : 12 :019(185) [0257] 3. To blot out sin, it is **enough** to detest the sin.
AP : 12 :045(188) [0263] For us it is **enough** that he names contrition and faith as
AP : 12 :059(190) [0267] evident that we have said **enough** about this earlier, we
AP : 12 :075(193) [0273] But if the law is **enough** to achieve the forgiveness of sins,
AP : 12 :087(195) [0277] We think this is clear **enough** for devout consciences, and

Continued ▶

AP : 1 2 :095(196) [0281] conscience sees that these works are not good **enough**.
AP : 1 2 :128(201) [0291] You do not pay **enough** attention to the importance of
AP : 1 2 :171(209) [0305] once in a lifetime was **enough** for the sort of public or
AP : 1 2 :174(210) [0305] We have testified often **enough** that penitence ought to
AP : 1 3 :010(212) [0311] Hebrews teaches clearly **enough**, we do not have a
AP : 1 5 :037(220) [0325] they have excuse **enough** now that these are being
AP : 2 0 :005(227) [0339] Fathers, but we have already said **enough** on this subject.
AP : 2 1 :030(233) [0351] not give it for fear that there might not be **enough** for all.
AP : 2 2 :011(238) [0361] we wanted to answer them we would have **enough** to say.
AP : 2 2 :014(238) [0361] which are not cogent **enough** to change Christ's
AP : 2 4 :067(261) [0407] This is **enough** of a general reply to our opponents
AP : 2 7 :009(270) [0421] those who are not old **enough** to make up their own
AP : 2 7 :025(273) [0429] they do not fear him **enough**, they do not believe God
AP : 2 7 :025(273) [0429] do not fear him enough, they do not believe God **enough**.
AP : 2 7 :052(278) [0437] On this whole topic we have said **enough** earlier.
AP : 2 8 :023(285) [0451] for Christ's sake, brings **enough** good to hide all the evils.
S 1 : PR :013(291) [0459] estates, we would find **enough** time to reform the
S 2 : 0 4 :015(301) [0475] articles they will have **enough** to condemn in the council,
S 3 : 0 1 :009(302) [0477] what he ought, but it is **enough** that he does not have an
S 3 : 0 3 :023(307) [0485] one would still not have know whether this was **enough**.
S 3 : 0 3 :036(309) [0489] we might imagine to be good **enough** to pay for our sin.
TR : 0 0 :078(333) [0527] It is **enough** to have pointed out that there are many
SC : 0 8 :008(353) [0559] that all creatures receive **enough** to eat to make them
LC : PR :014(360) [0571] If this were not **enough** to admonish us to read the
LC : PR :014(360) [0571] That alone should be incentive **enough**.
LC : SP :022(364) [0579] It is **enough** for an ordinary person to know this much
LC : SP :026(364) [0579] However, it is not **enough** for them simply to learn and
LC : 0 1 :024(368) [0587] God alone, I have often **enough** repeated, from whom we
LC : 0 1 :166(388) [0629] More than **enough** has now been said to those to whom
LC : 0 1 :178(389) [0631] This is **enough** to serve as a warning; a more extensive
LC : 0 1 :182(389) [0631] This commandment is simple **enough**.
LC : 0 1 :226(395) [0645] and never know **enough** ways to overcharge people and
LC : 0 1 :245(398) [0649] where would we find **enough** gallows and ropes?
LC : 0 1 :249(398) [0651] be alert and resolute **enough** to establish and maintain
LC : 0 1 :250(398) [0651] **Enough** has been said concerning the nature of stealing.
LC : 0 1 :253(399) [0653] this blessing will find wrath and misfortune **enough**.
LC : 0 1 :304(406) [0667] Who is ingenious **enough** to imagine how much he can
LC : 0 1 :332(410) [0677] he will find occasion **enough** to practice the Ten
LC : 0 2 :012(412) [0681] But for young pupils it is **enough** to indicate the most
LC : 0 2 :070(420) [0697] For the present this is **enough** concerning the Creed to lay
LC : 0 2 :070(420) [0697] as we live we shall have **enough** to preach and learn on
LC : 0 3 :014(422) [0701] and men supposed it was **enough** if the act was
LC : 0 3 :015(422) [0701] as these: "I am not holy **enough** or worthy enough; if I
LC : 0 3 :015(422) [0701] holy enough or worthy **enough**; if I were as godly and
LC : 0 3 :027(424) [0705] We all have needs **enough**, but the trouble is that we do
LC : 0 3 :058(428) [0713] not look to God even for **enough** to satisfy the belly, let
LC : 0 3 :100(433) [0725] We have now heard **enough** about the trouble and effort
LC : 0 4 :038(441) [0741] This alone would be **enough**, even though Baptism is an
LC : 0 4 :041(441) [0743] every Christian has **enough** to study and to practice all
LC : 0 4 :041(441) [0743] He always has **enough** to do to believe firmly what
LC : 0 5 :038(451) [0761] **Enough** has been said now for all ordinary instruction on
LC : 0 5 :041(451) [0763] of necessity, and that it is **enough** if they simply believe.
LC : 0 5 :044(451) [0763] and patience it is not **enough** simply to teach and
LC : 0 6 :002(457) [0000] of sin that no one was able to confess purely **enough**.
LC : 0 6 :016(459) [0000] only concerned whether we had confessed purely **enough**.
LC : 0 6 :019(459) [0000] I know this well **enough** anyway; if you are not, I know it
EP : 0 9 :004(492) [0827] It is **enough** to know that Christ went to hell, destroyed
SD : 0 2 :045(530) [0899] man still has **enough** powers to want to accept the Gospel

Enrage (1), Enraged (1)
AL : 2 3 :012(053) [0063] was almost killed by the **enraged** priests in an uprising.
AP : 1 2 :141(204) [0295] opponents, which must **enrage** anyone who considers the

Enrolled (1)
AP : 2 7 :066(280) [0441] forbids that anyone "be **enrolled** as a widow who is under

Ensign (1)
AP : 2 1 :018(231) [0347] of Jesse shall stand as an **ensign** to the peoples; him shall

Enslaved (2)
AP : 0 2 :047(106) [0119] Human nature is **enslaved** and held prisoner by the devil,
SD : 0 2 :044(529) [0897] he writes concerning the **enslaved** will of man against

Ensnare (5), Ensnared (5)
AG : 2 7 :006(071) [0077] of those who were thus **ensnared** and entangled were
AG : 2 7 :015(073) [0077] those who were thus **ensnared** and inveigled into a
AG : 2 8 :042(088) [0089] on Christendom to **ensnare** men's consciences?
AG : 2 8 :049(089) [0091] requirements and thus **ensnare** consciences, why does the
AL : 2 7 :006(071) [0077] Those who were thus **ensnared** were compelled to
AL : 2 8 :042(088) [0089] on the churches and thus **ensnare** consciences when Peter
AP : 1 1 :006(181) [0251] men in such a way as not to **ensnare** their consciences.
AP : 1 1 :007(181) [0251] consciences have been **ensnared** by the part of the
AP : 1 2 :110(198) [0285] lest consciences be **ensnared**; for they will never be at rest
AP : 2 8 :015(283) [0447] These must not **ensnare** consciences as though they were

Ensues (1)
AP : 0 4 :321(157) [0209] to doubt and to work without faith until despair **ensues**.

Entail (1)
LC : 0 1 :266(401) [0657] Knowledge of sin does not **entail** the right to judge it.

Entangled (5)
AG : 2 7 :006(071) [0077] were thus ensnared and **entangled** were pressed and
AL : 2 6 :014(066) [0073] them but rather **entangled** consciences even more.
LC : 0 2 :027(414) [0685] condemned to death and **entangled** in sin and blindness.
LC : 0 3 :106(434) [0729] and even be **entangled** in them, but we pray here that we
SD : 1 1 :042(623) [1077] Holy Spirit, become **entangled** again in the filth of the

Enter (20), Entered (13), Entering (4), Enters (3)
PR : PR :017(008) [0015] although it never **entered** our minds and hearts to want to
PR : PR :025(014) [0023] into which we have **entered** with them, and to
AG : 2 3 :003(051) [0061] some of our priests have **entered** the married state.
AG : 2 3 :026(056) [0065] of the priests and monks **entered** into their estates
AG : 2 7 :005(071) [0077] Many persons also **entered** monastic life ignorantly, for
AG : 2 7 :033(076) [0079] as a majority of them **entered** the cloister in their
AL : 2 7 :005(071) [0077] Many **entered** this kind of life through ignorance, for
AL : 2 7 :015(073) [0077] What happened after such people had **entered** monasteries
AP : 0 2 :051(107) [0119] we have been reluctant to **enter** upon their arguments at
AP : 0 4 :031(111) [0129] and the Spirit, one cannot **enter** the kingdom of God."
AP : 0 4 :122(124) [0157] us the texts, "If you would **enter** life, keep the
AP : 0 4 :123(124) [0157] "If you would **enter** life, keep the commandments."
AP : 0 4 :168(130) [0169] David says (Ps. 143:2), "**Enter** not into judgment with thy
AP : 0 4 :238(140) [0187] It could not have **entered** the mind of any apostle to say
AP : 0 4 :244(142) [0189] None of this ever **entered** into James's mind, though our
AP : 0 4 :270(147) [0197] statement, "If you would **enter** life, keep the
AP : 0 4 :326(157) [0211] Ps. 143:2, "**Enter** not into judgment with thy servant, for
AP : 0 7 :021(172) [0233] sins by their love for God before **entering** a state of grace.
AP : 1 1 :005(181) [0249] says only this: "If any **enter** the church of God and are
AP : 1 2 :078(193) [0275] the passage (Ps. 143:2), "**Enter** not into judgment with thy
AP : 1 3 :005(212) [0309] As the Word **enters** through the ears to strike the heart,
AP : 1 3 :005(212) [0309] the heart, so the rite itself **enters** through the eyes to move
AP : 1 6 :001(222) [0329] render military service, **enter** into legal contracts, own
S 3 : 0 7 :002(312) [0493] As it is written, "**Enter** not into judgment with thy
S 3 : 1 4 :001(316) [0501] life believes that he is **entering** upon a mode of life that is
LC : 0 1 :209(393) [0641] and allow all people to **enter** the estate of marriage, as we
LC : 0 1 :216(394) [0641] their unchaste existence and **enter** the married life.
LC : 0 2 :052(417) [0691] hear God's Word, which is the first step in **entering** it.
LC : 0 4 :025(439) [0739] death and the devil and to **enter** into the kingdom of
LC : 0 4 :067(445) [0749] Now, when we **enter** Christ's kingdom, this corruption
LC : 0 4 :075(445) [0751] attack on the old man and an **entering** upon a new life?
LC : 0 4 :081(446) [0751] we embarked when we **entered** the Christian Church.
EP : 0 8 :016(489) [0821] Thus he **entered** into his glory in such a way that now not
SD : 0 1 :007(510) [0861] is the work of the devil) **entered** into the world" (Rom.
SD : 0 5 :020(561) [0959] through him alone we re-**enter** the good graces of God,
SD : 0 6 :021(567) [0969] (Ps. 119:32), but also, "**Enter** not into judgment with thy
SD : 0 8 :039(598) [1029] suffer these things and **enter** into his glory?' (Luke 24:26).
SD : 1 1 :033(621) [1073] by saying, "Strive to **enter** by the narrow door" (Luke
SD : 1 1 :066(627) [1085] "I am the door; if anyone **enters** by me, he will be saved"
SD : 1 2 :024(634) [1099] separate ways, and to **enter** into a new marriage with

Entertain (1), Entertainment (1)
PR : PR :022(012) [0021] with them, so we **entertain** a corresponding loathing for
LC : 0 1 :096(378) [0609] would to any other **entertainment**, who only from force

Enthralled (2)
AP : 0 2 :049(106) [0119] bonds the devil has **enthralled** those who are wise and
AP : 0 4 :138(126) [0161] the devil, who holds **enthralled** all who have not been

Enthusiasm (3)
S 3 : 0 8 :004(312) [0495] too, is nothing but **enthusiasm**, for the pope boasts that
S 3 : 0 8 :009(313) [0497] In short, **enthusiasm** clings to Adam and his descendants
SD : 0 1 :027(513) [0867] nature, as the Manichaeans imagined in their **enthusiasm**.

Enthusiasts (17)
AP : 1 3 :013(213) [0311] for illumination, as the **enthusiasts** taught formerly and
S 3 : 0 8 :003(312) [0495] be protected from the **enthusiasts** — that is, from the
S 3 : 0 8 :005(312) [0495] the old serpent who made **enthusiasts** of Adam and Eve.
S 3 : 0 8 :006(312) [0495] Even so, the **enthusiasts** of our day condemn the external
EP : 0 2 :013(471) [0789] the error of the **Enthusiasts** who imagine that God draws
SD : 0 2 :004(520) [0881] ancient and modern **enthusiasts** have taught that God
SD : 0 2 :046(530) [0899] Both **enthusiasts** and Epicureans have in an unchristian
SD : 0 2 :080(536) [0911] the church of God, the **enthusiasts** who imagine that
SD : 0 7 :022(573) [0979] devils and all the **enthusiasts** come along and ask, How
SD : 0 7 :022(573) [0979] I know that all the **enthusiasts** and scholars put together
SD : 0 7 :033(575) [0983] Sacramentarians and **enthusiasts**), for that is what they
SD : 0 7 :067(582) [0997] the Sacramentarian **enthusiasts** ridicule the Lord Christ,
SD : 0 7 :097(586) [1005] place, not only, as the **enthusiasts** vainly imagine, the one
SD : 0 7 :099(586) [1005] The passages which the **enthusiasts** adduce concerning
SD : 0 7 :102(587) [1007] Let the **enthusiasts** prove it!
SD : 0 7 :103(587) [1007] what crass fools our **enthusiasts** are, because they concede
SD : 0 7 :103(587) [1009] The **enthusiasts** may indeed think that God is unable to

Entice (4)
SC : 0 1 :020(344) [0543] not abduct, estrange, or **entice** away our neighbor's wife,
LC : 0 1 :295(404) [0665] to dismiss his servants or **entice** his neighbor's from him.
LC : 0 1 :296(405) [0665] it is also forbidden to **entice** anything away from your
LC : 0 1 :306(406) [0669] someone may by trickery **entice** a rich bride away from

Entire (79), Entirely (31), Entirety (1)
PR : PR :022(011) [0019] and far less do we mean **entire** churches inside or outside
PR : PR :024(013) [0023] correct doctrine will be **entirely** obscured and lost and
AG : 2 3 :012(053) [0063] during an uprising of the **entire** body of priests.
AP : 0 4 :121(124) [0155] thereby they destroy the **entire** promise of the free
AP : 0 4 :134(125) [0159] human opinion about the **entire** law, both the moral and
AP : 0 4 :155(128) [0165] therefore, he praises her **entire** act of worship, as the
AP : 0 4 :256(144) [0193] permitted to interpret the **entire** law (Heb. 11:6),
AP : 0 4 :279(149) [0199] Taken in its **entirety**, Tobit's statement shows that faith is
AP : 0 4 :373(164) [0221] outward works but the **entire** righteousness or
AP : 0 7 :047(177) [0243] They have approved the **entire** eighth article.
AP : 2 2 :004(236) [0359] therefore, that the **entire** sacrament was instituted for the
AP : 2 2 :006(237) [0359] who were not permitted to receive the **entire** sacrament.
AP : 2 2 :012(238) [0361] and rage against good men who use the **entire** sacrament?
AP : 2 2 :016(238) [0361] violently persecute anyone that uses the **entire** sacrament.
S 2 : 0 2 :012(295) [0465] be discarded, apart **entirely** from the fact that it is error
S 2 : 0 2 :024(296) [0469] merits of all the saints and the **entire** church.
S 2 : 0 4 :003(298) [0471] to the destruction of the **entire** holy Christian church (in
S 3 : 0 3 :024(307) [0485] for himself alone the right to remit the **entire** satisfaction.
S 3 : 0 3 :039(309) [0489] Accordingly the **entire** building, even when it is most holy
TR : 0 0 :023(324) [0511] is representative of the **entire** company of apostles, as is
TR : 0 0 :024(324) [0511] the representative of the **entire** company of apostles, on
LC : PR :017(361) [0573] Commandments perfectly knows the **entire** Scriptures.
LC : PR :018(361) [0573] Psalm, much less the **entire** Scriptures, yet they pretend to
LC : 0 1 :065(373) [0599] have the substance of the **entire** commandment
LC : 0 1 :075(375) [0601] men may grow up of whom an **entire** land may be proud.
LC : 0 1 :082(376) [0603] It is an **entirely** external matter, like the other ordinances
LC : 0 1 :094(378) [0607] times, persons, and the **entire** outward order of worship

Continued ▶

LC : 0 1 :143(385) [0621] to father and mother, the **entire** household owes them
LC : 0 1 :224(395) [0643] attention to it that the matter is **entirely** out of hand.
LC : 0 1 :242(397) [0649] out of a gulden, your **entire** hoard will be consumed by
LC : 0 1 :325(409) [0675] Thus the **entire** Scriptures have proclaimed and presented
LC : 0 2 :006(411) [0679] shall briefly sum up the **entire** Creed in three articles,
LC : 0 2 :033(415) [0687] Indeed, the **entire** Gospel that we preach depends on the
LC : 0 2 :043(416) [0689] papacy, where faith was **entirely** shoved under the bench
LC : 0 2 :052(417) [0691] this far, we were **entirely** of the devil, knowing nothing of
LC : 0 2 :054(417) [0693] as through all the comforting words of the **entire** Gospel.
LC : 0 2 :054(417) [0693] and, in short, the **entire** Gospel and all the duties of
LC : 0 2 :063(419) [0695] the Creed you have the **entire** essence of God, his will,
LC : 0 3 :073(430) [0719] that belongs to our **entire** life in this world; only for its
LC : 0 3 :113(435) [0729] all evil in order that the **entire** substance of our prayer
LC : 0 4 :030(440) [0739] into the heart, just as the **entire** Gospel is an external,
LC : 0 4 :038(441) [0741] even though Baptism is an **entirely** external thing.
LC : 0 4 :041(442) [0743] of sin, God's grace, the **entire** Christ, and the Holy Spirit
LC : 0 5 :054(453) [0765] be warmed and kindled, and it will not grow **entirely** cold.
LC : 0 5 :080(456) [0771] You will not **entirely** trample him under foot because our
LC : 0 5 :080(456) [0771] our Lord Christ himself could not **entirely** avoid him.
EP : 0 1 :016(468) [0783] essence in man is not **entirely** corrupted, but that man
EP : 0 2 :012(471) [0789] of God perfectly and **entirely** and that this fulfilling
EP : 0 3 :003(473) [0793] On the contrary, the **entire** Christ according to both
EP : 0 5 :006(478) [0803] word "Gospel" means the **entire** doctrine of Christ which
EP : 0 6 :001(480) [0805] to which they should pattern and regulate their **entire** life.
EP : 0 7 :020(484) [0813] and confess that the **entire** worthiness of the guests at this
EP : 1 1 :013(496) [0835] for us or to rob us **entirely** of the glorious comfort which
EP : 1 1 :015(496) [0835] gives God his glory **entirely** and completely, because he
EP : 1 2 :006(498) [0839] They thus reject the **entire** doctrine of original sin and
EP : 1 2 :029(500) [0843] This is an **entirely** new sect, unknown in Christendom
SD : 0 1 :005(509) [0861] inherited disease which has corrupted our **entire** nature.
SD : 0 1 :006(509) [0861] has thoroughly and **entirely** poisoned and corrupted
SD : 0 1 :011(510) [0863] corruption of his **entire** nature in all its powers, especially
SD : 0 1 :023(512) [0865] it has nevertheless not **entirely** lost all the goodness that
SD : 0 1 :031(513) [0869] and condemns man's **entire** corrupted nature unless the
SD : 0 1 :052(517) [0875] birth, your nature, your **entire** essence is sin, that is sinful
SD : 0 1 :053(517) [0877] deeds are sin but that the **entire** nature, person, and
SD : 0 2 :007(521) [0883] but that man is **entirely** and completely dead and
SD : 0 2 :025(526) [0891] natural free will, be it **entirely** or one-half or the least and
SD : 0 2 :037(528) [0895] church we belonged **entirely** to the devil and were
SD : 0 2 :044(529) [0897] Dr. Luther discusses this **entire** matter in his book *The*
SD : 0 2 :073(535) [0909] presentation of the **entire** doctrine of free will it is
SD : 0 2 :085(537) [0913] man resists God **entirely** and is completely the servant of
SD : 0 2 :089(538) [0915] is not only in part, but **entirely**, the operation, gift,
SD : 0 3 :006(540) [0917] is "the chief article of the **entire** Christian doctrine,"
SD : 0 3 :015(541) [0919] on account of this **entire** obedience which, by doing and
SD : 0 3 :037(546) [0929] make or regard them as **entirely** or one-half or even only
SD : 0 3 :039(546) [0929] of sins by sheer grace, **entirely** for the sake of Christ's
SD : 0 3 :045(547) [0933] of our justification before God, either **entirely** or in part.
SD : 0 3 :055(549) [0935] that we must seek our **entire** righteousness apart from our
SD : 0 3 :055(549) [0935] nature but upon the **entire** person of Christ, who as God
SD : 0 3 :057(549) [0935] it is the obedience of the **entire** person, therefore it is a
SD : 0 3 :058(550) [0937] rendered to his Father **entire**, perfect obedience from his
SD : 0 4 :010(552) [0941] the Old Adam, makes us **entirely** different people in
SD : 0 4 :035(557) [0949] or that our works either **entirely** or in part sustain and
SD : 0 5 :004(558) [0953] we understand by it the **entire** teaching of Christ, our
SD : 0 5 :004(559) [0953] Likewise, Paul calls his **entire** teaching "Gospel" (Acts
SD : 0 5 :007(559) [0953] and understood as the **entire** conversion of man, as in
SD : 0 5 :016(561) [0957] but are presenting the **entire** matter nicely and clearly for
SD : 0 5 :027(563) [0961] as referring to the **entire** teaching, a usage that we find
SD : 0 6 :024(568) [0971] the flesh of sin is put off **entirely** and man is completely
SD : 0 7 :041(576) [0985] and as the person whose **entire** doctrine in sum and
SD : 0 7 :046(577) [0989] read, and committed the **entire** matter to God's
SD : 0 7 :057(579) [0993] and context of St. Paul's **entire** discourse prove, he had in
SD : 0 7 :066(581) [0995] Christian teachers and the **entire** holy Christian church
SD : 0 7 :067(582) [0997] Christ, St. Paul, and the **entire** church when they call
SD : 0 7 :083(584) [1001] institution by itself, if the **entire** action of the Lord's
SD : 0 7 :086(584) [1003] oral eating alone, but the **entire** external and visible
SD : 0 8 :026(596) [1023] aside completely and **entirely** the form of a servant
SD : 0 8 :036(598) [1027] separate but to the **entire** person who is simultaneously
SD : 0 8 :038(598) [1027] we are *to ascribe to the* ***entire*** *person what is the property*
SD : 0 8 :038(598) [1027] while they mention the **entire** person, they nevertheless
SD : 0 8 :048(600) [1031] But it is an **entirely** different matter when, in the third
SD : 0 8 :057(602) [1035] accepted rule of the **entire** ancient orthodox church that
SD : 0 8 :064(604) [1039] iron, analogies which the **entire** ancient church used in
SD : 0 8 :071(605) [1041] Creed and to the **entire** prophetic and apostolic doctrine.
SD : 0 8 :073(605) [1041] personal union the **entire** fullness of the Spirit (as the
SD : 0 8 :078(607) [1043] person of Christ, but the **entire** person to which both
SD : 0 9 :002(610) [1051] that after the burial the **entire** person, God and man,
SD : 1 0 :010(612) [1055] of the holy Gospel, the **entire** community of God, yes,
SD : 1 1 :014(619) [1069] take as one unit the **entire** doctrine of God's purpose,
SD : 1 1 :066(627) [1085] Thus the **entire** holy Trinity, God the Father, Son, and
SD : 1 1 :071(627) [1085] his promise, and trust in him completely and **entirely**.
SD : 1 2 :011(634) [1099] they deny and reject the **entire** teaching of original sin and
SD : 1 2 :027(635) [1101] The **entire** sect, however, can be characterized as basically

Entitled (2)
LC : 0 1 :160(387) [0627] are fathers, they are **entitled** to honor, even above all
LC : 0 1 :237(397) [0647] others' possessions and **entitled** to whatever they

Entrance (2)
PR : PR :023(012) [0021] no doctrine be permitted **entrance** which is contrary to
SD : 0 2 :036(528) [0895] still hear it, which is the beginning of my **entrance** into it.

Entreat (1), Entreaties (1), Entreaty (1)
AP : 2 4 :088(265) [0413] to come to offer Thee **entreaties** and supplications and
LC : 0 5 :039(451) [0761] of an admonition and **entreaty** that so great a treasure,
SD : 0 2 :066(534) [0907] with him, then, we **entreat** you not to accept the grace of

Entrust (2), Entrusted (3), Entrusts (1)
SC : PR :006(338) [0533] on the people who are **entrusted** to your care, and that
LC : 0 1 :003(365) [0581] your heart clings and **entrusts** itself is, I say, really your
LC : 0 1 :015(366) [0583] is nothing else than to **entrust** ourselves to him
LC : 0 1 :020(367) [0585] God into an idol and **entrust** themselves to an empty
LC : 0 1 :173(388) [0629] But he has given and **entrusted** children to us with the
LC : 0 6 :014(458) [0000] Christ himself has **entrusted** absolution to his Christian

Entry (1)
SD : 0 4 :034(556) [0949] to faith not only our **entry** into grace but also our present

Enumerate (12), Enumerated (1), Enumerates (1), Enumerating (3), Enumeration (28), Enumerations (1)
AG : 1 1 :001(034) [0047] it is not necessary to **enumerate** all trespasses and sins,
AG : 2 5 :005(062) [0069] without long **enumerations** of sins, with satisfactions, with
AG : 2 5 :009(062) [0069] those which we can **enumerate** we would be helped but
AG : 2 5 :011(063) [0071] does not require a detailed **enumeration** of sins.
AL : 1 1 :001(034) [0047] in confession an **enumeration** of all sins is not necessary,
AL : 2 5 :007(062) [0069] they teach that an **enumeration** of sins is not necessary
AL : 2 5 :007(062) [0069] with a scrupulous **enumeration** of all sins because it is
AL : 2 5 :010(063) [0069] testify that such an **enumeration** is not necessary, for
AP : 0 4 :012(108) [0123] vicious errors that would take a long time to **enumerate**.
AP : 1 1 :001(180) [0249] all sins cannot be **enumerated**, one should diligently try to
AP : 1 1 :001(180) [0249] try to recall them and to **enumerate** those one does recall.
AP : 1 1 :006(181) [0251] With regard to the **enumeration** of sins in confession we
AP : 1 1 :006(181) [0251] the unlearned to **enumerate** certain things so that they
AP : 1 1 :006(181) [0251] divine law that the **enumeration** of sins is necessary to
AP : 1 1 :008(181) [0251] hold therefore that the **enumeration** of sins is not required
AP : 1 1 :010(182) [0253] they believed that an **enumeration** of sins was necessary
AP : 1 2 :011(184) [0255] devoted to the endless **enumeration** of sins, most of them
AP : 1 2 :011(184) [0255] they imagine that this **enumeration** is a divine command.
AP : 1 2 :012(184) [0255] While they demand this **enumeration** under the pretext
AP : 1 2 :023(185) [0257] 7. The **enumeration** of sins in confession, as our
AP : 1 2 :102(197) [0281] As for the **enumeration** of sins in confession, we have said
AP : 1 2 :110(198) [0285] contend that the **enumeration** of sins in confession is
AP : 1 2 :110(198) [0285] the forgiveness of sins without **enumerating** all their sins.
AP : 1 2 :112(198) [0285] of penitence, not about this **enumeration** of secret sins.
AP : 1 2 :112(198) [0285] totally different from the **enumeration** we are discussing.
AP : 1 2 :116(199) [0285] as we do about the **enumeration** of sins, that canonical
AP : 1 2 :178(211) [0309] attrition, the endless **enumeration** of offenses, and
AP : 1 3 :001(211) [0309] But they insist that we **enumerate** seven sacraments.
AP : 1 3 :002(211) [0309] of teaching, the **enumeration** varies, provided what is
AP : 1 3 :002(211) [0309] the Fathers did not always use the same **enumeration**.
AP : 2 4 :016(252) [0389] "sacrifice," as our **enumeration** of the types of sacrifice
AP : 2 4 :020(252) [0389] permitted, we would **enumerate** the many proofs for this
AP : 2 4 :046(258) [0401] Satisfactions and the **enumeration** of sins were a torture
S 1 : PR :012(290) [0459] of peasants — who can **enumerate** everything? — these
S 3 : 0 3 :020(306) [0485] made to rest on his **enumeration** of sins and on his
S 3 : 0 8 :002(312) [0495] However, the **enumeration** of sins should be left free to
TR : 0 0 :045(328) [0517] concerning the **enumeration** of sins which has produced
TR : 0 0 :067(331) [0523] He **enumerates** pastors and teachers among the gifts
TR : 0 0 :078(333) [0527] it would not be profitable to **enumerate** all of them here.
LC : 0 1 :053(371) [0595] though it is impossible to **enumerate** all its misuses.
LC : 0 3 :076(431) [0719] make a long prayer, **enumerating** with many words all the
LC : 0 6 :002(457) [0000] consciences with the **enumeration** of all kinds of sin that
LC : 0 6 :004(457) [0000] released from the torture of **enumerating** all sins in detail.
EP : 1 2 :001(498) [0839] at the end merely to **enumerate** the articles in which they
SD : 0 1 :016(511) [0865] reason we shall briefly **enumerate** the contrary doctrines
SD : 0 3 :005(540) [0917] that is, in the **enumeration** of those who contradict the

Envy (5), Envious (3)
AP : 0 4 :198(134) [0175] fortune of the wicked, like Psalm 37:1, "Be not **envious**."
LC : 0 1 :184(390) [0633] For instance, a neighbor, **envious** that you have received
LC : 0 1 :184(390) [0633] gives vent to his irritation and **envy** by speaking ill of you.
LC : 0 1 :310(407) [0669] directed especially against **envy** and miserable
LC : 0 3 :103(434) [0727] it nothing but hatred and **envy**, enmity, violence and
LC : 0 4 :066(445) [0749] Adam, irascible, spiteful, **envious**, unchaste, greedy, lazy,
LC : 0 4 :067(445) [0749] and the more free from greed, hatred, **envy**, and pride.
LC : 0 5 :075(455) [0771] dissension, party spirit, **envy**, murder, drunkenness,

Epaphroditus (1)
AP : 2 4 :082(264) [0411] In Phil. 2:25 he calls **Epaphroditus** a "minister to my

Ephesus (2)
SD : 0 8 :059(602) [1035] to the Council of **Ephesus** decreed that the flesh of Christ
SD : 0 8 :076(606) [1043] fathers of the Council of **Ephesus** attested when they

Epics (1)
AP : 2 1 :037(234) [0353] fables, which imitate the **epics** and bring only

Epictetus (1)
SD : 0 8 :022(595) [1023] in his *Letter to* ***Epictetus****;* Hilary, *On the Trinity,* Book

Epicurean (5), Epicureans (4)
AP : 0 4 :390(166) [0225] knows that most of them are openly **Epicureans**.
AP : 2 3 :050(246) [0377] These **Epicureans** purposely use religion as a pretext.
EP : 0 4 :018(477) [0801] Such an **Epicurean** dream concerning faith can damn
EP : 1 1 :009(495) [0833] a reckless, dissolute, **Epicurean** life, or drive men to
SD : 0 2 :046(530) [0899] Both enthusiasts and **Epicureans** have in an unchristian
SD : 0 4 :015(553) [0943] and reject a complacent **Epicurean** delusion, since many
SD : 0 4 :031(556) [0947] and rejecting the false **Epicurean** delusion which some
SD : 0 4 :039(558) [0951] a wicked, wild, complacent, and **Epicurean** way of life.
SD : 0 7 :123(590) [1015] alleges that godless **Epicureans** and scoffers at the Word

Epicurus (1)
AP : 0 4 :035(112) [0131] they do these things, as **Epicurus** did not believe that God

Epilepsy (1)
AP : 2 1 :032(233) [0351] Valentine heals **epilepsy**, and George protects knights.

Epilogue (1)
AP : 2 7 :012(271) [0423] they append a horrible **epilogue** in the words: "Therefore

Epiphanius (7)
AP : 0 7 :042(176) [0243] decree is preserved in **Epiphanius**: "Do not calculate, but
AP : 0 7 :042(176) [0243] According to **Epiphanius**, these words are from an
AP : 0 7 :043(177) [0243] his refutation of them **Epiphanius** praises the decree and
AP : 2 3 :045(245) [0375] **Epiphanius** complains that this characteristic among the

Continued ▶

A P : 2 3 :049(246) [0377] the excellent phrase of **Epiphanius**, such observances
A P : 2 4 :008(250) [0385] **Epiphanius** writes that in Asia Minor there were no daily
A P : 2 4 :096(267) [0417] **Epiphanius** testifies that Aerius believed that prayers for

Episcopate (1)
T R : 0 0 :014(322) [0509] in their presence, the **episcopate** might be conferred and

Epistle (22), Epistles (2)
A G : 2 4 :027(059) [0067] For it is written in the **Epistle** to the Hebrews that Christ
A L : 2 3 :025(055) [0065] first book of his letters, **Epistle** XI, are these: "If they are
A L : 2 4 :026(059) [0067] So it is written in the **Epistle** to the Hebrews, "We have
A L : 2 8 :052(089) [0091] as it is written in the **Epistle** to the Galatians, "Do not
A P : 0 4 :087(119) [0147] In the **Epistle** to the Romans, especially, Paul deals with
A P : 0 4 :088(120) [0149] discussion in Rom. 4 and repeats it later in all his **epistles**.
A P : 0 4 :141(126) [0161] John teaches in his first **epistle** (4:19); "We love," he says,
A P : 1 3 :010(212) [0311] As the **Epistle** to the Hebrews teaches clearly enough, we
A P : 2 4 :020(252) [0389] distinction found in the **Epistle** to the Hebrews and
A P : 2 4 :022(253) [0391] death of Christ, as the **Epistle** to the Hebrews teaches
A P : 2 4 :026(254) [0391] The **Epistle** to the Hebrews teaches the same (13:15):
A P : 2 4 :052(259) [0403] They also quote the **Epistle** to the Hebrews (5:1), "Every
A P : 2 4 :053(259) [0403] our position are in the **Epistle** to the Hebrews, our
A P : 2 4 :053(259) [0403] passages from this very **epistle** against us — like this one,
A P : 2 4 :054(259) [0403] a large part of the **epistle** is devoted to the theme that the
A P : 2 4 :058(260) [0405] The whole **Epistle** to the Hebrews supports this
L C : 0 5 :075(455) [0771] good turn to St. Paul's **Epistle** to the Galatians and hear
E P : 0 6 :006(481) [0807] In his **epistles** St. Paul calls it the law of Christ and the
E P : 1 1 :011(496) [0835] order which St. Paul follows in the **Epistle** to the Romans
S D : 0 3 :028(544) [0925] exposition of the **Epistle** to the Galatians Dr. Luther well
S D : 0 3 :067(551) [0937] splendid exposition of St. Paul's **Epistle** to the Galatians.
S D : 0 4 :010(552) [0941] in his Preface to the **Epistle** of St. Paul to the Romans,
S D : 0 6 :009(565) [0965] the Church Postil, on the **Epistle** for the Nineteenth
S D : 1 1 :033(621) [1073] this way: "Follow the order in the **Epistle** to the Romans.

Epitome (1)
E P : 0 0 :000(464) [0775] A Summary **Epitome** of the Articles in Controversy

Epoch (1)
S D : R N :005(504) [0851] as our symbol in this **epoch**, not because this confession

Equal (24), Equality (1), Equalization (4), Equalize (1), Equalized (2), Equally (4), Equals (4)
P R : P R :021(011) [0019] and properties is **equalized** with the divine nature and is
A G : 0 1 :002(027) [0043] in this one divine essence, **equal** in power and alike
A G : 2 7 :011(072) [0077] that monastic vows were **equal** to Baptism, and that by
A L : 2 7 :011(072) [0077] They said that vows were **equal** to Baptism, and they
A P : 0 4 :195(134) [0175] of sins is the same and **equal** to all, as Christ is one, and
A P : 2 4 :093(267) [0417] dead because it applies it **equally** to all the blessed
A P : 2 4 :097(268) [0417] of faith but give **equal** honor to other sacrifices and
A P : 2 7 :009(270) [0421] Are they **equal** to Baptism?
A P : 2 7 :020(272) [0427] says that a monastic profession is **equal** to Baptism.
S 2 : 0 2 :010(294) [0465] he does to be considered **equal** or superior to my
S 2 : 0 4 :009(300) [0473] by having all the bishops **equal** in office (however they
S 2 : 0 4 :013(300) [0475] had to set himself up as **equal** to and above Christ and to
S 3 : 1 4 :001(316) [0501] people boast that a monastic vow is **equal** to Baptism.
T R : 0 0 :008(320) [0505] should be sent forth as **equals** and exercise the ministry
T R : 0 0 :009(321) [0505] sent his disciples out as **equals**, without discrimination,
T R : 0 0 :011(321) [0507] places ministers on an **equality** and teaches that the
T R : 0 0 :023(324) [0511] that the keys were given **equally** to all the apostles and
T R : 0 0 :023(324) [0511] the apostles and that the apostles were sent out as **equals**.
T R : 0 0 :078(333) [0527] are unjust, and **equally** unjust is the tradition which
S C : 0 5 :022(350) [0553] I have quarreled with my **equals**.
L C : 0 1 :108(380) [0611] indeed, we are all **equal** in the sight of God, but among
L C : 0 1 :126(382) [0617] and all other works for our neighbor are not **equal** to this.
L C : 0 1 :317(408) [0673] a doctrine or social order **equal** to that of the Ten
E P : 0 8 :028(490) [0825] level of, and has become **equal** to, the divine nature in its
E P : 1 2 :021(499) [0841] Christ as man is fully **equal** in rank and essential estates
S D : 0 2 :059(532) [0905] And it is **equally** true that prior to his conversion man is
S D : 0 8 :019(594) [1021] sort of blending or **equalization** of the natures, as mead is
S D : 0 8 :028(596) [1025] any blending or **equalization** of the two natures in their
S D : 0 8 :031(597) [1025] any blending or **equalization** of the natures in their
S D : 0 8 :061(602) [1035] he is of one essence with the Father and **equal** with God.
S D : 0 8 :061(602) [1035] divine nature is Christ **equal** with the Father, but
S D : 0 8 :061(603) [1035] that we do not confuse, **equalize**, or abolish the natures in
S D : 0 8 :062(603) [1037] has become intrinsically **equal** with the Godhead, nor in
S D : 0 8 :062(603) [1037] blending, or **equalization** of the natures in Christ or of
S D : 0 8 :068(604) [1039] it could be said with **equal** truth that in all creatures in
S D : 0 8 :071(605) [1041] nature allegedly received **equal** majesty, separated or
S D : 0 8 :091(609) [1049] in Christ has been **equalized** with and has become equal
S D : 0 8 :091(609) [1049] with and has become **equal** to the divine nature in its
S D : 1 1 :057(625) [1081] mind while another in **equal** guilt is again converted.
S D : 1 2 :029(635) [1101] glory he is in every way **equal** in grade and rank of

Equanimity (1)
A P : 2 7 :002(269) [0419] these injuries with **equanimity** for Christ's sake inasmuch

Equip (1), Equipping (1)
A P : 2 4 :081(264) [0411] duties," like the taxes collected for **equipping** a fleet.
L C : P R :014(360) [0571] So he wishes to warn, **equip**, and protect us against them

Equitable (1), Equitably (2), Equity (2)
A G : P R :010(025) [0041] done, such practical and **equitable** ways as may restore
A P : P R :016(099) [0103] and we hope that posterity will judge us more **equitably**.
L C : 0 1 :259(400) [0653] is to administer justice **equitably** in all cases will often
L C : 0 1 :261(400) [0655] set for our jurists: perfect justice and **equity** in every case.
L C : 0 1 :299(405) [0665] without regard for **equity** or for our neighbor's plight.

Equivalent (1)
S D : 0 7 :036(575) [0985] flesh," with such **equivalent** phrases as, "The Word dwelt

Equivocal (1)
S D : 0 1 :051(517) [0875] and distinctly all **equivocal** terms, that is, words and

Era (1)
S D : 1 2 :017(634) [1099] That in the New Testament **era** government service is not

Eradicated (1)
S 3 : 1 3 :001(315) [0499] completely removed or **eradicated**, he will not count or

Erased (1)
A P : 0 4 :350(161) [0217] This handwriting is not **erased** without a great conflict in

Erasmus (2)
S D : 0 2 :044(529) [0897] will of man against **Erasmus** and carefully and in great
S D : 0 2 :044(529) [0897] disputed points which **Erasmus** raised (for example, the

Erecting (1)
L C : 0 1 :021(367) [0585] not consist merely of **erecting** an image and praying to it.

Erfurt (2)
P R : P R :027(016) [0027] The Council of **Erfurt**
S 3 : 1 5 :005(318) [0501] preacher of the church in **Erfurt**, in my own name and in

Erhard (2)
S 3 : 1 5 :005(317) [0501] I, **Erhard** Schnepf, preacher in Stuttgart, subscribe
T R : 0 0 :082(334) [0529] I, **Erhard** Schnepf, subscribe

Ernest (8)
P R : P R :027(014) [0025] Duke John **Ernest** [of Saxe-Eisenach] the above two
P R : P R :027(015) [0025] Margrave **Ernest** [of Baden-Durlach] and
P R : P R :027(015) [0025] George **Ernest**, count and lord of Henneberg
P R : P R :027(015) [0025] Peter **Ernest** the Younger, count of Mansfeld [-Eisleben]
P R : P R :027(015) [0025] Wolf **Ernest**, count of Stolberg
P R : P R :027(015) [0025] **Ernest**, count of Regenstein
A G : 0 0 :007(096) [0095] **Ernest**, duke of Lueneburg
A L : 0 0 :017(096) [0095] **Ernest**, with his own hand

Err (11), Erred (2), Erring (2), Erroneous (27), Erroneously (1), Error (52), Errors (106)
P R : P R :003(003) [0007] many heresies and **errors**, and repeatedly affirmed.
P R : P R :004(004) [0009] as to palliate their own **errors**, to divert poor, erring
P R : P R :004(004) [0009] errors, to divert poor, **erring** consciences from an
P R : P R :004(004) [0009] well as in embracing other **errors** that militate against
P R : P R :009(006) [0011] a way by adherents of **erroneous** opinions which are
P R : P R :009(006) [0011] of Christ and other **erroneous** opinions were now and
P R : P R :017(008) [0015] confirmation of their **erroneous** doctrine although it
P R : P R :017(008) [0015] any new, false, or **erroneous** doctrine or in the least point
P R : P R :019(009) [0017] attempted to hide their **error** concerning the Holy Supper
P R : P R :019(009) [0017] of the fact that this **erroneous** doctrine is expressly
P R : P R :022(011) [0019] thereby those persons who **err** ingenuously and who do
P R : P R :022(012) [0021] to remind even those who **err** ingenuously and ignorantly
P R : P R :024(013) [0021] of so many intrusive **errors**, aggravated scandals,
P R : P R :024(013) [0023] and defend monstrous **errors**, the only possible
A G : P R :006(025) [0039] with reference to the said **errors**, dissensions, and abuses.
A G : 1 1 :002(034) [0047] Ps. 19:12, "Who can discern his **errors**?"
A G : 2 4 :021(058) [0067] same time the abominable **error** was condemned
A G : 2 4 :025(059) [0067] will understand that this **error** is not unjustly condemned.
A G : 2 5 :008(062) [0069] As the psalmist says, "Who can discern his **errors**?"
A G : 2 6 :003(064) [0071] Many harmful **errors** in the church have resulted from
A G : 2 6 :019(067) [0073] about the aforementioned **errors** which have arisen from
A G : 2 7 :060(080) [0083] Gerson censured the **error** of the monks concerning
A G : 2 7 :061(080) [0083] godless opinions and **errors** associated with monastic
A G : 2 8 :028(085) [0087] elected bishops if they **err** or if they teach or command
A G : 2 8 :061(091) [0093] from the false and **erroneous** opinion that in Christendom
A G : 2 8 :062(091) [0093] Such **errors** were introduced into Christendom when the
A L : 1 1 :002(034) [0047] to the Psalm, "Who can discern his **errors**?" (Ps. 19:12).
A L : 2 5 :007(062) [0069] So the Psalm testifies, "Who can discern his **errors**?"
A L : 2 6 :011(065) [0071] This **error** greatly tormented the consciences of devout
A L : 2 6 :019(067) [0073] the churches of these **errors** which had arisen from
A L : 2 7 :055(079) [0083] Others **err** still more, for they judge that all magistracy
A L : 2 7 :060(080) [0083] times Gerson rebuked the **error** of the monks concerning
A L : 2 8 :028(085) [0087] if they should happen to **err** or hold anything contrary to
A L : 2 8 :062(091) [0093] These **errors** crept into the church when the righteousness
A P : P R :004(098) [0099] that we sanction certain manifest abuses and **errors**.
A P : 0 2 :047(106) [0119] with wicked opinions and **errors** and incites it to all kinds
A P : 0 4 :012(108) [0123] there are many vicious **errors** that would take a long time
A P : 0 4 :038(112) [0131] It is an **error**, therefore, for men to trust that by the law
A P : 0 4 :039(112) [0131] will also help refute those **errors** of our opponents that we
A P : 0 4 :135(125) [0159] from us, and this **error** taken away, when God shows us
A P : 0 4 :139(126) [0161] may not be deceived and **err**, nor be driven to do
A P : 0 4 :162(129) [0169] It is an **error** to suppose that he merely merited "initial
A P : 0 4 :253(143) [0191] so simply, contain no **error**, but our opponents twist them
A P : 0 4 :321(157) [0209] teach on this question is full of **errors** and dangers.
A P : 0 4 :376(164) [0223] This **error** obviously destroys the righteousness of faith,
A P : 0 4 :391(166) [0225] are so many manifest **errors** among them, such as the idea
A P : 0 4 :391(167) [0225] falsehood, this teaching has spawned many **errors**.
A P : 0 7 :021(172) [0233] also an open and wicked **error** when our opponents teach
A P : 0 7 :027(173) [0235] that they are pillars of the truth and that they do not **err**.
A P : 0 9 :002(178) [0245] Among the many **errors** of the Anabaptists that we
A P : 1 1 :008(181) [0251] the statement (Ps. 19:12), "Who can discern his **errors**?"
A P : 1 2 :003(183) [0253] corrected many vicious **errors** which through the opinions
A P : 1 2 :007(183) [0255] This is also a vicious **error**.
A P : 1 2 :010(184) [0255] we have listed is full of **error** and hypocrisy; it obscures
A P : 1 2 :069(192) [0271] they quietly approved the **errors** of their superiors,
A P : 1 2 :117(199) [0287] Such **errors** received support from many statements of
A P : 1 5 :011(216) [0317] sake, it is an ungodly **error** to maintain that we merit the
A P : 1 6 :008(223) [0333] is evident from their **erroneous** view that the Gospel is
A P : 2 1 :032(233) [0351] theologians hold to the **error** that each saint has a special
A P : 2 4 :014(251) [0387] many passages of Scripture in defense of their **errors**.
A P : 2 4 :057(260) [0405] It is completely **erroneous** to imagine that the Levitical
A P : 2 4 :062(260) [0405] We therefore reject the **error** of Thomas when he writes,
A P : 2 4 :063(260) [0405] also reject other common **errors**: that the Mass confers
A P : 2 4 :064(261) [0405] These **errors** have sired endless others, like the one that
A P : 2 4 :095(267) [0417] They were men and they could **err** and be deceived.
A P : 2 4 :096(267) [0417] We reject these wicked **errors** which rob Christ's suffering
A P : 2 7 :027(273) [0429] it is a most wicked **error** to believe that evangelical
S 2 : 0 2 :012(295) [0465] apart entirely from the fact that it is **error** and idolatry.
S 3 : 0 1 :003(302) [0477] is therefore nothing but **error** and stupidity, namely,
S 3 : 0 7 :001(311) [0493] So it is written, "Who can discern his **errors**?" (Ps. 19:12).
T R : 0 0 :008(320) [0505] the apostles for this **error** and taught them that no one
T R : 0 0 :037(326) [0515] Since these monstrous **errors** obscure faith and the
T R : 0 0 :040(327) [0517] he defends such horrible **errors** and such impiety with the

Continued ▶

TR : 0 0 :042(328) [0517] The **errors** of the pope's kingdom are manifest, and the
TR : 0 0 :042(328) [0517] declare these **errors** to be doctrines of demons and of the
TR : 0 0 :045(328) [0517] which has produced many **errors** and introduced despair.
TR : 0 0 :048(328) [0519] Such **errors** are not to be taken lightly, for they detract
TR : 0 0 :049(328) [0519] To these **errors**, then, two great sins must be added.
TR : 0 0 :049(328) [0519] the pope defends these **errors** with savage cruelty and
TR : 0 0 :051(329) [0519] tyranny: he defends his **errors** by force and murders, and
TR : 0 0 :052(329) [0519] consider the enormous **errors** of the pope's kingdom and
TR : 0 0 :052(329) [0519] the first place, that these **errors** must be rejected and that
TR : 0 0 :054(329) [0519] and to see to it that **errors** are removed and consciences
TR : 0 0 :056(330) [0521] the rest of the pope's **errors**, so they ought also to rebuke
TR : 0 0 :058(330) [0521] The **errors** of the pope are manifest, and they are not
TR : 0 0 :059(330) [0521] by so strengthening **errors** and other crimes as to impose
LC : 0 4 :057(444) [0747] I — in short, all men — may **err** and deceive, but God's
LC : 0 4 :057(444) [0747] men — may err and deceive, but God's Word cannot **err**.
LC : 0 5 :019(449) [0757] and defense against all **errors** and deceptions that have
EP : RN :000(464) [0777] Be Judged and the **Errors** Which Intruded Should Be
EP : 0 1 :013(467) [0783] reject the Pelagian **error** which asserts that man's nature
EP : 0 1 :017(468) [0783] reject the Manichaean **error** that original sin is an
EP : 0 1 :019(468) [0783] as a Manichaean **error** the teaching that original sin is
EP : 0 1 :022(469) [0785] to conceal their **error** and to mislead many simple people.
EP : 0 2 :007(470) [0787] all the following **errors** as being contrary to the norm of
EP : 0 2 :009(471) [0789] 2. We also reject the **error** of the crass Pelagians who
EP : 0 2 :010(471) [0789] 3. We also reject the **error** of the Semi-Pelagians who
EP : 0 2 :013(471) [0789] we reject and condemn the **error** of the Enthusiasts who
EP : 0 3 :002(473) [0793] *of the Christian Church Against Both These **Errors***
EP : 0 3 :003(473) [0793] opposition to these two **errors** just recounted, we believe,
EP : 0 3 :012(474) [0795] we reject and condemn all the following **errors**:
EP : 0 6 :008(481) [0807] and true piety the **erroneous** teaching that the law is not
EP : 0 7 :001(481) [0809] and to disseminate their **errors** under the name of this
EP : 0 7 :021(484) [0813] all the following **errors**, which are contrary and
EP : 0 8 :018(489) [0823] together in one essence, as Eutyches **erroneously** taught.
EP : 0 8 :019(490) [0823] simple Christian Creed the following **erroneous** articles:
EP : 0 8 :039(491) [0827] unless we refute these **errors** on the firm basis of the
EP : 1 1 :016(497) [0837] Therefore we reject the following **errors**:
EP : 1 1 :021(497) [0837] blasphemous and terrible **errors**, for they rob Christians
EP : 1 1 :022(497) [0837] pure doctrine but have also exposed the contrary **errors**.
EP : 1 2 :001(498) [0839] made no mention of the **errors** held by these factions.
EP : 1 2 :001(498) [0839] result of our silence these **errors** be attributed to us, we
EP : 1 2 :001(498) [0839] the articles in which they **err** and contradict our
EP : 1 2 :001(498) [0839] **Errors** of the Anabaptists
EP : 1 2 :002(498) [0839] some of which teach many **errors**, others teach fewer.
EP : 1 2 :002(498) [0839] ***Errors** which Cannot be Tolerated in the Church*
EP : 1 2 :011(499) [0841] the preaching and the **errors** of the Anabaptists; nor
EP : 1 2 :016(499) [0841] *Intolerable **Errors** which Undermine Domestic Society*
EP : 1 2 :019(499) [0841] **Errors** of the Schwenkfelders
EP : 1 2 :027(500) [0843] **Errors** of the New Arians
EP : 1 2 :028(500) [0843] **Error** of the Anti-Trinitarians
EP : 1 2 :030(500) [0843] together with their **erroneous** implications and
SD : PR :001(501) [0847] memory, and the popish **errors**, abuses, and idolatry were
SD : PR :007(502) [0849] holy apostles frightful **errors** arose among those who
SD : PR :007(502) [0849] knew that these titanic **errors** and the subsequent bitter
SD : PR :009(503) [0849] that the opinions of the **erring** party cannot be tolerated
SD : PR :010(503) [0849] themselves against the **errors** and corruptions that have
SD : RN :000(503) [0849] the Word of God and **Errors** Are to Be Explained and
SD : RN :006(504) [0853] insinuate into the church **errors** that had already been
SD : RN :006(504) [0853] and defended against **errors** and also because it is
SD : RN :007(505) [0853] renouncing the papistic **errors** and idolatries, for having
SD : RN :010(506) [0855] Scriptures, refutations of **errors**, and expositions of
SD : RN :015(507) [0857] when the contrary **error** must be refuted in order to
SD : RN :016(507) [0857] be distinguished from all **error**, and likewise to insure
SD : RN :017(507) [0857] condemn all heresies and **errors** which the primitive,
SD : RN :019(507) [0857] everyone against the **errors** contained here and there in
SD : 0 1 :003(509) [0861] Pelagian and Manichaean **errors**, then (as the Apology
SD : 0 1 :013(511) [0863] of the world with terrible **errors** and heresies, strikes them
SD : 0 1 :016(511) [0865] we fall neither into Pelagian nor into Manichaean **errors**.
SD : 0 1 :020(511) [0865] and condemn the following and related Pelagian **errors**:
SD : 0 1 :026(512) [0867] that reason the following and similar **errors** are rejected:
SD : 0 1 :030(513) [0867] 2. We also condemn the **error** which Augustine attributes
SD : 0 2 :027(526) [0891] to recant his former **erroneous** opinion as he had set it
SD : 0 2 :027(527) [0893] says further on, "I have **erred** when I said that it lies
SD : 0 2 :033(527) [0893] reject the following **errors** concerning free will: "That man
SD : 0 2 :043(529) [0897] and condemn as sheer **error** every doctrine which glorifies
SD : 0 2 :045(530) [0899] Such **erroneous** views are contrary to the Holy Scriptures
SD : 0 2 :073(535) [0909] and condemn such false doctrines and **errors** as these:
SD : 0 2 :075(536) [0909] 2. The **error** of the coarse Pelagians, that by his own
SD : 0 2 :076(536) [0911] 3. The **error** of the papists and scholastics, whose doctrine
SD : 0 2 :081(537) [0911] This **error** St. Augustine condemns in express words in
SD : 0 3 :006(540) [0917] pure, it is impossible to repel any **error** or heretical spirit.
SD : 0 3 :044(547) [0933] that in addition to the **errors** already named we must
SD : 0 3 :044(547) [0933] the following and similar **errors** as contrary to the
SD : 0 3 :052(548) [0933] It is also an **error** when it is taught that man is saved in a
SD : 0 3 :059(550) [0937] the previously mentioned **errors**, the following and all
SD : 0 3 :059(550) [0937] following and all similar **errors** as contrary to the Word
SD : 0 3 :066(550) [0937] These and all similar **errors** we reject unanimously as
SD : 0 4 :036(557) [0949] the aforementioned **error** of the papists, yet, since a
SD : 0 6 :026(568) [0971] and true godliness, the **erroneous** doctrine that the law in
SD : 0 7 :001(569) [0971] against this pernicious **error** which is altogether contrary
SD : 0 7 :026(573) [0981] and defense against all **errors** and deceptions that have so
SD : 0 7 :029(574) [0981] "I see that schisms and **errors** are increasing
SD : 0 7 :029(574) [0981] writings to confirm their **error**, as the Sacramentarians
SD : 0 7 :059(580) [0993] as a basis for their **error** that in the Lord's Supper the
SD : 0 7 :090(585) [1003] a pernicious, impudent **error** when some by a subtle
SD : 0 7 :107(588) [1009] and mouth as false, **erroneous**, and deceiving every error
SD : 0 7 :107(588) [1009] and deceiving every **error** which is inconsistent with or
SD : 0 7 :111(589) [1011] set forth and recite the **errors** preeminently of the
SD : 0 7 :112(589) [1011] and mouth as false, **erroneous**, and deceiving all
SD : 0 7 :119(590) [1013] In support of their **error**, some Sacramentarians have
SD : 0 7 :128(591) [1015] antitheses and rejected **erroneous** views have been
SD : 0 7 :128(591) [1015] opinions or **erroneous** views there may be can easily be
SD : 0 8 :015(594) [1019] This was the **error** and heresy of Nestorius and the
SD : 0 8 :038(598) [1027] hide their pernicious **error** under the words of the formula
SD : 0 8 :038(598) [1027] be forearmed in the best possible way against this **error**.
SD : 0 8 :051(600) [1031] that this opinion is **erroneous** and false, that even their
SD : 0 8 :051(600) [1031] own co-religionists now criticize and reject this **error**.
SD : 0 8 :062(603) [1037] These and similar **erroneous** doctrines have been justly
SD : 0 8 :087(608) [1047] we consider it a pernicious **error** to deprive Christ
SD : 0 8 :088(609) [1047] with mouth and heart all **errors** which are inconsistent
SD : 0 8 :096(609) [1049] reject and condemn these **errors** and all others that
SD : 0 8 :096(610) [1049] and will be well protected against pernicious **errors**.
SD : 1 1 :044(623) [1077] all false opinions and **erroneous** doctrines about the
SD : 1 1 :094(632) [1095] and in which some have **erred** and serious religious
SD : 1 1 :095(632) [1095] of true doctrine or any publicly condemned **errors**.
SD : 1 1 :096(632) [1095] give place to the smallest **error** but will lead the poor
SD : 1 2 :002(632) [1095] Anti-Trinitarians whose **errors** all the churches of the
SD : 1 2 :007(633) [1097] to us the condemned **errors** of the aforementioned
SD : 1 2 :008(633) [1097] no part or share in their **errors**, be they few or many, and
SD : 1 2 :008(633) [1097] and condemn all these **errors** as wrong, heretical, and
SD : 1 2 :008(633) [1097] **Erroneous** Articles of the Anabaptists
SD : 1 2 :009(633) [1097] reject and condemn the **erroneous** and heretical teaching
SD : 1 2 :016(634) [1099] and censure the **errors** of the Anabaptists; neither may
SD : 1 2 :027(635) [1101] holding more and another party holding fewer **errors**.
SD : 1 2 :027(635) [1101] **Erroneous** Articles of the Schwenkfelders
SD : 1 2 :028(635) [1101] We reject and condemn these **errors** of the Schwenkfelders
SD : 1 2 :035(635) [1101] **Erroneous** Articles of the New Arians
SD : 1 2 :036(635) [1101] We reject and condemn the **error** of the New Arians who
SD : 1 2 :036(636) [1101] **Erroneous** Articles of the New Anti-Trinitarians
SD : 1 2 :039(636) [1103] and condemn as false, **erroneous**, heretical, contrary to

Erupt (1)
AP : 1 2 :129(202) [0291] what will happen if this hatred should **erupt** against you.

Esau (1)
SD : 1 1 :088(631) [1093] written, 'Jacob I loved, but **Esau** I hated'" (Rom. 9:11-13;

Escape (11)
AP : 0 4 :103(122) [0151] the sin that none could **escape** and by shedding his blood
AP : 0 4 :364(162) [0219] But to **escape** despair amid afflictions, they should know
S3 : 0 3 :032(308) [0489] any assurance that you will **escape** the wrath to come?"
SC : PR :004(338) [0533] May you **escape** punishment for this!
LC : 0 1 :067(373) [0599] a dispute swears falsely, he will not **escape** punishment.
LC : 0 1 :234(397) [0647] may indeed get by and **escape** the hangman, but he will
LC : 0 1 :234(397) [0647] hangman, but he will not **escape** God's wrath and
LC : 0 1 :307(406) [0669] it is all done "under the hat" so as to **escape** detection.
LC : 0 2 :023(413) [0683] When we **escape** distress or danger, we should recognize
LC : 0 3 :106(434) [0727] For no one can **escape** temptations and allurements as
EP : 1 1 :009(495) [0833] reason, they can hardly **escape** such reflections as this: "If

Especially (112)
PR : PR :020(010) [0017] of our Christian Creed (**especially** those pertaining to the
PR : PR :022(011) [0019] adulterated doctrine, **especially** in the article concerning
AG : PR :015(026) [0041] estates of the empire, **especially** in a public instruction at
AG : 2 0 :011(042) [0055] Paul in many passages, **especially** in Eph. 2:8, 9, "For by
AG : 2 3 :003(051) [0061] of their consciences, **especially** since the Scriptures clearly
AG : 2 3 :016(054) [0063] and the clergy, and **especially** of the pastors and others
AG : 2 3 :021(055) [0063] they are married — and **especially** priests, who above all
AL : 1 3 :001(035) [0049] among men but **especially** to be signs and testimonies of
AL : 1 6 :005(038) [0051] On the contrary, it **especially** requires their preservation
AL : 2 1 :003(047) [0057] Such worship Christ **especially** approves, namely, that in
AL : 2 4 :003(056) [0065] ceremonies are needed **especially** in order that the
AL : 2 4 :040(061) [0069] cannot be disapproved, **especially** since the customary
AL : 2 7 :048(078) [0081] of faith, which ought **especially** to be taught in the
AP : 0 2 :004(101) [0105] in the definition, **especially** now when so many
AP : 0 4 :057(114) [0137] service and worship is **especially** praised throughout the
AP : 0 4 :087(119) [0147] Epistle to the Romans, **especially**, Paul deals with this
AP : 0 4 :262(145) [0195] **Especially** amid the terrors of sin, a human being must
AP : 0 4 :288(151) [0203] the sacraments, **especially** the Mass, through which they
AP : 0 7 :003(169) [0227] and sacraments — **especially** if they have not been
AP : 0 7 :033(175) [0239] and ancient ordinances, **especially** when they contain a
AP : 1 2 :003(182) [0253] good men will see that **especially** on this issue we have
AP : 1 2 :009(183) [0255] eternal punishments — **especially** in those serious, true,
AP : 1 2 :094(196) [0281] about faith, dwelling **especially** on the oath in the
AP : 1 2 :099(197) [0281] we also keep confession, **especially** because of absolution,
AP : 1 2 :161(208) [0303] threat followed so that **especially** through humiliation his
AP : 1 5 :018(217) [0319] but by such rites, and **especially** when they teach that for
AP : 1 5 :034(220) [0325] consciences for good, **especially** from the notion that they
AP : 1 6 :011(224) [0333] praise is dangerous, **especially** because it is so out of
AP : 2 2 :002(236) [0357] ordinance changed, **especially** since he himself calls it his
AP : 2 2 :017(238) [0361] the pontiffs decide, **especially** when Scripture prophesies
AP : 2 3 :004(239) [0365] with us in this case, **especially** when you learn that for
AP : 2 3 :043(245) [0375] marriage moderately, **especially** when they are occupied
AP : 2 3 :053(246) [0379] reasons for changing it, **especially** in these last times.
AP : 2 3 :071(249) [0383] than for anything else, **especially** when the issue is so
AP : 2 4 :052(259) [0403] for the ignorant, **especially** when the pomp of the Old
AP : 2 7 :067(280) [0443] for his relatives, and **especially** for his own family, he has
S1 : PR :014(291) [0459] canons in a council, **especially** when the primary things,
S2 : 0 2 :005(293) [0463] God-fearing people — **especially** if they hear that it is a
S3 : 0 3 :015(305) [0483] could recall all his sins (**especially** those committed during
S3 : 0 6 :004(311) [0493] **Especially** do we condemn and curse in God's name those
S3 : 0 8 :001(312) [0493] disuse in the church, **especially** for the sake of timid
TR : 0 0 :024(324) [0511] he bestows the keys **especially** and immediately on the
TR : 0 0 :024(324) [0511] same reason the church **especially** possesses the right of
TR : 0 0 :035(326) [0513] nations of Europe, but **especially** the emperors of
TR : 0 0 :054(329) [0519] **Especially** does it behoove the chief members of the
TR : 0 0 :056(329) [0521] not of the pontiffs, it is **especially** incumbent on the kings
TR : 0 0 :077(333) [0527] courts (as they call them), **especially** matrimonial cases.
TR : 0 0 :080(334) [0527] establishment of courts, **especially** courts for matrimonial
SC : PR :002(338) [0533] The common people, **especially** those who live in the
SC : PR :006(338) [0533] catechism to the people, **especially** those who are young.
SC : 0 9 :003(354) [0561] worthy of double honor, **especially** those who labor in
LC : PR :013(360) [0571] power, and fruit — **especially** we who would be pastors
LC : PR :019(361) [0573] implore all Christians, **especially** pastors and preachers,
LC : SP :026(364) [0579] also attend preaching, **especially** at the time designated
LC : 0 1 :028(368) [0587] him nothing but good, **especially** in distress and want, and
LC : 0 1 :053(372) [0595] This is **especially** common in marriage matters when two
LC : 0 1 :069(374) [0599] to shun falsehood and **especially** to avoid calling upon

Continued ▶

L C : 0 1 :084(376) [0605] Secondly and most **especially**, we keep holy days so that
L C : 0 1 :089(377) [0605] such matters and deal **especially** with the Ten
L C : 0 1 :095(378) [0607] to hear and learn it, **especially** at the times appointed.
L C : 0 1 :128(382) [0617] **Especially** when an evil hour comes do we rage and
L C : 0 1 :168(388) [0629] subjects, etc., but **especially** to bring them up to the praise
L C : 0 1 :187(390) [0633] a patient, gentle heart, **especially** toward those who have
L C : 0 1 :188(390) [0635] in body and soul, **especially** toward him who wishes or
L C : 0 1 :194(391) [0635] is directed, as I said, **especially** toward our enemies.
L C : 0 1 :211(393) [0641] whom God has **especially** exempted — some who are
L C : 0 1 :219(394) [0643] situation (that is, **especially** in the estate of marriage), but
L C : 0 1 :233(396) [0647] further his interests, **especially** when he takes
L C : 0 1 :289(404) [0663] is what happens now **especially** to the precious Word of
L C : 0 1 :294(404) [0665] **Especially** were these commandments needed because
L C : 0 1 :300(405) [0667] To this class the Jews **especially** claimed to belong, as
L C : 0 1 :310(407) [0669] are directed **especially** against envy and miserable
L C : 0 2 :022(413) [0683] This is **especially** true of those who even fight against the
L C : 0 2 :032(415) [0687] throughout the year, **especially** at the times appointed for
L C : 0 3 :077(431) [0721] all estates of men, and **especially** our princes, counselors,
L C : 0 3 :080(431) [0721] But **especially** is this petition directed against our chief
L C : 0 3 :081(431) [0721] **especially** those of us who have the Word of God and
L C : 0 3 :098(433) [0725] And it has been **especially** instituted for us to use and
L C : 0 3 :104(434) [0727] us on all sides, but **especially** exerts himself where the
L C : 0 4 :038(441) [0741] about this sacrament, **especially** that it is God's ordinance
L C : 0 5 :053(453) [0765] This is the first point, **especially** for the benefit of the cold
L C : 0 5 :055(453) [0765] also is my temptation, **especially** inherited from the old
L C : 0 5 :084(456) [0773] This happens **especially** because the devil so constantly
L C : 0 6 :028(460) [0000] should not be despised, **especially** when we consider our
E P : 0 1 :013(467) [0783] even after the Fall, and **especially** that in spiritual things
E P : 0 2 :014(471) [0789] of the Old Adam, **especially** the rational soul, and that in
E P : 0 4 :008(476) [0799] that all men, but **especially** those who are regenerated and
E P : 0 4 :018(477) [0801] **Especially** in these last times, it is just as necessary to
E P : 0 5 :002(478) [0801] law and Gospel is an **especially** glorious light that is to be
E P : 1 1 :014(496) [0835] **Especially** are we to abide by the revealed Word which
S D : P R :003(502) [0847] the chief articles, **especially** those which were in
S D : 0 1 :011(510) [0863] nature in all its powers, **especially** of the highest and
S D : 0 1 :011(510) [0863] enmity against God, **especially** in divine and spiritual
S D : 0 1 :020(511) [0865] Fall is incorrupt and, **especially**, that in spiritual matters
S D : 0 1 :054(518) [0877] Eusebius, Ambrose, and **especially** Augustine, as well as
S D : 0 2 :044(529) [0897] exposition of Genesis, **especially** of Chapter 26, he
S D : 0 2 :081(537) [0911] of the Old Adam, and **especially** the rational soul, are
S D : 0 3 :024(543) [0923] pure, we must give **especially** diligent heed that we do not
S D : 0 4 :004(551) [0939] "necessary" and "free," **especially** the word "necessary."
S D : 0 5 :001(558) [0951] law and Gospel is an **especially** brilliant light which serves
S D : 0 7 :034(575) [0983] these statements and **especially** from the exposition of
S D : 0 7 :040(576) [0985] *Great Confession* and **especially** in his *Last Confession*
S D : 0 7 :126(591) [1015] truth in all places but **especially** where his community is
S D : 0 8 :068(604) [1039] in whomever he is (**especially** believers and saints), he
S D : 0 8 :068(604) [1039] in whom God is, but **especially** in believers in whom God
S D : 0 8 :086(608) [1047] Dr. Luther's writings, **especially** in the book *That These*
S D : 0 8 :092(609) [1049] wherever he desires and **especially** where he has promised
S D : 1 0 :003(611) [1053] a case of confession, **especially** when the adversaries are
S D : 1 0 :010(612) [1055] Christian, and **especially** the ministers of the Word as the
S D : 1 0 :025(615) [1061] matters of indifference, **especially** in a period of
S D : 1 1 :011(618) [1067] **Especially** when they see their own weakness and the
S D : 1 2 :008(633) [1097] into those places and **especially** at those times where the

Essence (106), Essences (1)
P R : P R :021(011) [0019] nature according to its **essence** and properties is equalized
A G : 0 1 :002(027) [0043] that there is one divine **essence**, which is called and which
A G : 0 1 :002(027) [0043] persons in this one divine **essence**, equal in power and
A G : 0 1 :003(027) [0043] All three are one divine **essence**, eternal, without division,
A L : 0 1 :001(027) [0043] the unity of the divine **essence** and concerning the three
A L : 0 1 :002(027) [0043] say, there is one divine **essence**, which is called and which
A L : 0 1 :003(028) [0043] persons, of the same **essence** and power, who are also
A P : 0 1 :001(100) [0103] is one undivided divine **essence**, and that there are
A P : 0 1 :001(100) [0103] of the same divine **essence**, Father, Son, and Holy Spirit.
A P : 0 4 :130(125) [0157] God, belonging to the **essence** of the divine law, are
A P : 1 6 :010(224) [0333] and blinded them to the **essence** of real perfection.
A P : 1 8 :002(225) [0335] God and perform "the **essence** of the acts" required by his
S 1 : 0 1 :000(291) [0461] persons in one divine **essence** and nature, are one God,
S 2 : 0 4 :014(301) [0475] services (which are the **essence** of the papacy) in
L C : 0 2 :063(419) [0695] Creed you have the entire **essence** of God, his will, and
L C : 0 5 :020(449) [0757] the first part, namely, the **essence** of this sacrament.
L C : 0 5 :033(450) [0761] standpoint both of its **essence** and of its effect and
L C : 0 6 :009(458) [0000] For this is the **essence** of a genuinely Christian life, to
E P : 0 1 :001(466) [0779] nature, substance, and **essence**, or indeed the principal
E P : 0 1 :001(466) [0779] man's substance, nature, **essence**, body, and soul on the
E P : 0 1 :008(467) [0781] Adam's fall man's nature and **essence** are all corrupt."
E P : 0 1 :016(468) [0783] the human nature and **essence** in man is not entirely
E P : 0 1 :019(468) [0783] substance, nature, and **essence**, so that no distinction
E P : 0 1 :020(468) [0783] man's nature, person, or **essence** itself with original sin
E P : 0 1 :021(468) [0783] nature, substance, and **essence** of man in such a way that
E P : 0 1 :022(469) [0785] the term means man's **essence**, as when we say, "God has
E P : 0 1 :022(469) [0785] inheres in the nature or **essence** of a thing, as when we
E P : 0 1 :024(469) [0785] distinction between the **essence** of a particular thing and
E P : 0 2 :014(471) [0789] the substance and **essence** of the Old Adam, especially the
E P : 0 2 :014(471) [0789] he creates out of nothing a new **essence** of the soul.
E P : 0 7 :022(484) [0813] substance and natural **essence** and are thus annihilated, in
E P : 0 8 :006(487) [0819] are not fused into one **essence** and that the one is not
E P : 0 8 :018(489) [0823] together in one **essence**, as Eutyches erroneously taught.
E P : 0 8 :021(490) [0823] are mingled into one **essence** and that the human nature
E P : 0 8 :027(490) [0823] has become an infinite **essence**, like the divine nature;
E P : 0 8 :028(490) [0825] in its substance and **essence**, or in its essential properties.
E P : 1 2 :021(499) [0841] possess only one divine **essence**, property, will, and glory
E P : 1 2 :021(499) [0841] flesh of Christ belongs to the **essence** of the holy Trinity.
E P : 1 2 :028(500) [0843] God, of one divine **essence** with God the Father and the
E P : 1 2 :029(500) [0843] only one eternal, divine **essence**, belonging to the Father,
E P : 1 2 :029(500) [0843] has its distinct divine **essence**, separate from the other
E P : 1 2 :029(500) [0843] the three are unequal in **essence** and properties and that
S D : 0 1 :001(508) [0859] that "man's nature and **essence** are wholly corrupt as a
S D : 0 1 :001(508) [0859] nature, substance, and **essence** of fallen man, at least the
S D : 0 1 :001(508) [0859] and noblest part of his **essence** (namely, his rational soul
S D : 0 1 :001(508) [0859] between man's nature or **essence** and original sin.
S D : 0 1 :002(508) [0859] nature, substance, or **essence** (that is, man's body or
S D : 0 1 :002(509) [0859] between the nature and **essence** of fallen man (that is,
S D : 0 1 :028(513) [0867] it is not itself the proper **essence**, body, or soul of man or
S D : 0 1 :032(513) [0869] so far as our nature and **essence** are the work, the
S D : 0 1 :033(514) [0869] corrupted nature or the **essence** of corrupted man, our
S D : 0 1 :033(514) [0869] sin, by which the nature, **essence**, or total man is
S D : 0 1 :033(514) [0869] (which dwells in man's nature or **essence** and corrupts it).
S D : 0 1 :041(515) [0871] between the nature and **essence** of our body and soul
S D : 0 1 :043(516) [0873] is of one and the same **essence** with us, his brethren,
S D : 0 1 :043(516) [0873] which he assumed is in its **essence** and all its essential
S D : 0 1 :044(516) [0873] between the nature or **essence** of corrupted man and
S D : 0 1 :047(516) [0875] life, instead of this **essence** of our body and soul, we
S D : 0 1 :048(516) [0875] man, its substance, its **essence**, its body or soul, so that
S D : 0 1 :051(517) [0875] the word "nature" means man's **essence**, body and soul.
S D : 0 1 :052(517) [0875] your nature, your entire **essence** is sin, that is sinful and
S D : 0 1 :053(517) [0877] nature, person, and **essence** of man is wholly corrupted
S D : 0 1 :054(518) [0877] (that is, a self-subsisting **essence**) or an accident (that is,
S D : 0 1 :054(518) [0877] another self-subsistent **essence** and can be distinguished
S D : 0 1 :055(518) [0877] or self-subsisting **essence**, in as far as it is a substance, is
S D : 0 1 :055(518) [0877] statement, "Original sin is the nature or **essence** of man."
S D : 0 1 :055(518) [0877] of another self-subsisting **essence**, but is present in
S D : 0 1 :057(518) [0877] either a self-subsisting **essence** or something accidental
S D : 0 2 :081(537) [0911] that the substance and **essence** of the Old Adam, and
S D : 0 2 :081(537) [0911] that the substance or **essence** of man must be laid aside,
S D : 0 3 :022(543) [0923] no unrighteousness in **essence** and life adheres to those
S D : 0 7 :036(575) [0985] explain that the divine **essence** has not been transformed
S D : 0 7 :037(575) [0985] Holy Supper the two **essences**, the natural bread and the
S D : 0 7 :081(584) [1001] of the hearers in the **essence** and benefits of this
S D : 0 7 :101(587) [1007] You must posit this **essence** of Christ since he is one
S D : 0 7 :108(588) [1009] lose their substance and **essence** and are converted into
S D : 0 8 :007(592) [1017] remains in its nature and **essence** through all eternity.
S D : 0 8 :008(593) [1017] that in their nature and **essence** the two natures referred
S D : 0 8 :009(593) [1019] nature and of its natural **essence**), to be intrinsically
S D : 0 8 :011(593) [1019] each with its natural **essence** and properties, are found
S D : 0 8 :017(594) [1021] are not blended into one **essence** but, as Dr. Luther
S D : 0 8 :019(595) [1021] contrary, each nature retains its **essence** and properties.
S D : 0 8 :028(596) [1025] the two natures in their **essence** and essential properties.
S D : 0 8 :031(597) [1025] blending or equalization of the natures in their **essence**).
S D : 0 8 :036(598) [1027] in their natural **essence** and properties, and since both
S D : 0 8 :049(600) [1031] to or detracted from the **essence** and properties of the
S D : 0 8 :061(602) [1035] communicated his own **essence** and all the divine
S D : 0 8 :061(602) [1035] so that he is of one **essence** with the Father and equal
S D : 0 8 :062(603) [1037] apart from the divine **essence**, nor in such a way that the
S D : 0 8 :063(603) [1037] blend the natures in their **essence** and in their essential
S D : 0 8 :068(604) [1039] a spiritual and indivisible **essence** and is therefore
S D : 0 8 :071(605) [1041] that in its substance and **essence** the human nature
S D : 0 8 :071(605) [1041] from the nature and **essence** of the Son of God, as when
S D : 0 8 :071(605) [1041] become an omnipotent **essence** intrinsically or have
S D : 0 8 :072(605) [1041] to the deity he is of one **essence** with the Holy Spirit) in
S D : 0 8 :076(606) [1043] to its nature and **essence** outside of this union, cannot
S D : 0 8 :090(609) [1047] the Deity, as an infinite **essence**, through an essential
S D : 0 8 :091(609) [1049] in its substance and **essence** or in its essential properties.
S D : 1 0 :014(613) [1057] which in their nature and **essence** are and remain of
S D : 1 1 :075(628) [1087] himself because he is changeless in his will and **essence**.
S D : 1 2 :029(635) [1101] in grade and rank of **essence** to the Father and the
S D : 1 2 :029(635) [1101] have but one kind of **essence**, property, will, and glory
S D : 1 2 :029(635) [1101] Christ's flesh belongs to the **essence** of the holy Trinity.
S D : 1 2 :036(635) [1101] of one eternal, divine **essence** with God the Father, but
S D : 1 2 :037(636) [1103] is not one eternal, divine **essence** of the Father, Son, and
S D : 1 2 :037(636) [1103] person has a distinct **essence** separate from the other two.
S D : 1 2 :037(636) [1103] in the Trinity are unequal in their **essence** and properties.

Essential (63), Essentially (19), Essentials (1)
P R : P R :021(011) [0019] majesty intrinsically, **essentially**, formally, habitually, and
A P : 0 4 :274(148) [0199] This is the **essential** proclamation of the Gospel, that we
L C : 0 1 :219(394) [0643] it is above all things **essential** that husband and wife live
L C : 0 3 :061(428) [0715] prayed for what is most **essential** — for the Gospel, for
L C : 0 5 :038(451) [0761] ordinary instruction on the **essentials** of this sacrament.
E P : 0 1 :012(467) [0781] sin but concreated and **essential** properties of human
E P : 0 1 :017(468) [0783] that original sin is an **essential**, self-existing something
E P : 0 1 :020(468) [0783] sin," "person-sin," "**essential** sin," not in order to identify
E P : 0 7 :002(481) [0809] Jesus Christ truly and **essentially** present if they are
E P : 0 7 :004(482) [0809] presence of the true, **essential**, and living body and blood
E P : 0 7 :006(482) [0809] of Christ are truly and **essentially** present and are truly
E P : 0 7 :011(483) [0811] Jesus Christ is true, **essential**, natural, complete God and
E P : 0 7 :033(485) [0815] and blood would be **essentially** present in the Holy
E P : 0 7 :034(485) [0815] to cause his body to be **essentially** present at more than
E P : 0 8 :006(487) [0819] but that each retains its **essential** properties and that they
E P : 0 8 :017(489) [0823] although it is true and **essential**, as the words of Christ's
E P : 0 8 :027(490) [0825] nature, because this **essential** power and property has
E P : 0 8 :028(490) [0825] in its substance and essence, or in its **essential** properties.
E P : 1 2 :021(499) [0841] fully equal in rank and **essential** estates to the Father and
E P : 1 2 :028(500) [0843] That Christ is not a true, **essential**, natural God, of one
E P : 1 2 :029(500) [0843] people who are **essentially** separate from one another.
S D : R N :014(506) [0855] within the church, it is **essential** not only to present the
S D : 0 1 :018(511) [0865] sin but concreated and **essential** attributes of man's
S D : 0 1 :026(512) [0867] sin (as something **essential**) into man's nature, as when
S D : 0 1 :027(512) [0867] or made something **essentially** evil and blended this with
S D : 0 1 :030(513) [0867] some other substance **essentially** different from our
S D : 0 1 :043(516) [0873] in its essence and all its **essential** attributes — sin alone
S D : 0 1 :053(517) [0875] "person-sin," "**essential** sin" to indicate that not only
S D : 0 3 :002(539) [0917] of God, is the **essential** righteousness of God (namely,
S D : 0 3 :002(539) [0917] as the true, natural, **essential** Son of God, who through
S D : 0 3 :025(543) [0923] The only **essential** and necessary elements of justification
S D : 0 3 :054(548) [0933] the indwelling of God's **essential** righteousness in us.
S D : 0 3 :054(548) [0935] who is the eternal and **essential** righteousness, dwells by
S D : 0 7 :002(569) [0973] that the true, **essential** body and blood of Christ are as
S D : 0 7 :003(569) [0973] and partakes truly and **essentially**, but still only
S D : 0 7 :006(570) [0973] Christ is present in his Supper truly, **essentially**, and alive.
S D : 0 7 :008(570) [0975] the body of Christ is **essentially** present here on earth in
S D : 0 7 :009(571) [0975] it is not truly and **essentially** present here on earth in the
S D : 0 7 :011(571) [0975] of Christ are truly and **essentially** present and are truly
S D : 0 7 :014(571) [0977] of Christ are truly and **essentially** present, distributed, and

Continued ▶

SD : 0 7 :014(571) [0977] (that is, an **essential** change of the bread and wine into
SD : 0 7 :049(578) [0989] was speaking of his true, **essential** body, which he gave
SD : 0 7 :049(578) [0989] for us, and of his true, **essential** blood, which was shed
SD : 0 7 :054(579) [0991] to the true and **essential** presence and distribution of the
SD : 0 7 :055(579) [0991] were not truly and **essentially** present and were received
SD : 0 7 :063(581) [0995] and partake of the true, **essential** body and blood of
SD : 0 7 :068(582) [0997] It is **essential** to explain with great diligence who the
SD : 0 7 :088(585) [1003] order to deny the true, **essential** presence and the oral
SD : 0 7 :091(585) [1003] concerning the **essential** and natural properties of the
SD : 0 7 :094(586) [1005] that Jesus Christ is **essential**, natural, true, complete God
SD : 0 7 :113(589) [1011] concerning the true **essential** presence of the body and
SD : 0 7 :119(590) [1013] willing to be truly and **essentially** present with us in the
SD : 0 7 :120(590) [1013] able to achieve the true, **essential** presence of his body and
SD : 0 7 :126(591) [1015] man, who is truly and **essentially** present in the Supper
SD : 0 8 :002(591) [1015] arguments the true, **essential** presence of the body and
SD : 0 8 :004(592) [1017] his Supper the true, **essential** presence of the body and
SD : 0 8 :004(592) [1017] contravenes its natural, **essential** properties, and they
SD : 0 8 :006(592) [1017] from all eternity true, **essential**, and perfect God with the
SD : 0 8 :008(593) [1017] them aside, nor do the **essential** properties of the one
SD : 0 8 :008(593) [1017] nature ever become the **essential** properties of the other.
SD : 0 8 :009(593) [1019] to know everything are **essential** properties of the divine
SD : 0 8 :009(593) [1019] will never become the **essential** properties of the human
SD : 0 8 :012(593) [1019] and retains its natural, **essential** properties but that in
SD : 0 8 :028(596) [1025] the two natures in their essence and **essential** properties.
SD : 0 8 :032(597) [1025] each nature retains its **essential** properties and that these
SD : 0 8 :048(600) [1031] their own natural and **essential** properties (which, as has
SD : 0 8 :050(600) [1031] than its own natural **essential** properties alone, according
SD : 0 8 :051(600) [1033] addition to its natural, **essential**, and abiding properties,
SD : 0 8 :051(601) [1033] to its natural and **essential** properties, or only as far as
SD : 0 8 :060(602) [1035] retains its natural and **essential** properties in such a way
SD : 0 8 :061(603) [1037] it is in his divine nature, that is, as an **essential** property.
SD : 0 8 :062(603) [1037] take place through an **essential** or natural outpouring of
SD : 0 8 :062(603) [1037] aside its natural and **essential** properties and is now either
SD : 0 8 :062(603) [1037] a way that the natural, **essential** properties and acts of
SD : 0 8 :062(603) [1037] in Christ or of their **essential** properties be taught or
SD : 0 8 :063(603) [1037] truth — to describe any **essential**, natural exchange or
SD : 0 8 :063(603) [1037] natures in their essence and in their **essential** properties.
SD : 0 8 :063(603) [1037] blending of the natures and of their **essential** properties.
SD : 0 8 :090(609) [1047] essence, through an **essential** power or property of its
SD : 0 8 :091(609) [1049] in its substance and essence or in its **essential** properties.
SD : 1 2 :026(635) [1099] Christ is not truly and **essentially** God but only possesses
SD : 1 2 :036(635) [1101] that Christ is not a true, **essential**, and natural God, of
SD : 1 2 :037(636) [1103] any three distinct and **essentially** separate human

Esslingen (1)
PR : PR :027(015) [0027] Mayor and Council of the City of **Esslingen**

Establish (20), Established (28), Establishes (1), Establishing (2), Establishment (4)
AG : 1 5 :001(036) [0049] usages that have been **established** by men, it is taught
AG : 1 6 :001(037) [0051] in the world and all **established** rule and laws were
AG : 2 8 :030(085) [0087] in the church or **establish** regulations concerning foods,
AG : 2 8 :034(086) [0087] power to institute or **establish** anything contrary to the
AG : 2 8 :043(088) [0089] which forbid the **establishment** of such regulations for the
AL : 2 8 :013(083) [0085] the forms of government that should be **established**.
AP : 0 4 :030(111) [0129] God, and seeking to **establish** your own, you did not
AP : 0 4 :175(131) [0171] that the law is **established** through faith (Rom. 3:31), this
AP : 0 7 :023(172) [0235] He may **establish** articles of faith, abolish the Scriptures
AP : 1 2 :167(208) [0303] ecclesiastical discipline **established** for the sake of setting
AP : 1 5 :014(217) [0319] prophets forbid the **establishment** of additional
AP : 1 5 :015(217) [0319] If men are allowed to **establish** new rites and if by such
AP : 1 5 :015(217) [0319] as well as the rites **established** by Jeroboam and others
AP : 1 5 :015(217) [0319] If we are permitted to **establish** rites that serve to merit
AP : 1 5 :017(217) [0319] have that religious rites **established** by men without God's
AP : 1 5 :018(217) [0319] of sins, they are simply **establishing** the kingdom of
AP : 1 6 :001(222) [0329] to imperial or other **established** laws, prescribe legal
AP : 1 9 :001(226) [0337] that God alone has **established** all of nature and preserves
AP : 2 1 :018(231) [0347] God our Father, comfort your hearts and **establish** them."
AP : 2 1 :044(236) [0357] honorable ways of **establishing** harmony — ways that will
AP : 2 3 :059(247) [0379] most earnest desire to **establish** harmony, we know that to
AP : 2 4 :012(251) [0387] This position is **established** and proved by the
AP : 2 4 :035(256) [0397] that allegory does not prove or **establish** anything.
AP : 2 4 :089(265) [0413] is no mere peccadillo to **establish** such services in the
AP : 2 8 :006(282) [0445] define, distinguish, and **establish** what is helpful or
S 2 : 0 2 :013(295) [0467] individuals and cannot **establish** an article of faith.
S 2 : 0 2 :015(295) [0467] the Word of God shall **establish** articles of faith and no
S 2 : 0 2 :026(297) [0469] offer sacrifices to them, **establish** churches, altars, and
S 2 : 0 3 :002(298) [0471] life and to the offices and callings **established** by God.
S 2 : 0 4 :010(300) [0475] since it is neither **established** nor commanded by God.
S 3 : 0 6 :003(311) [0493] institution as it was **established** and commanded by
TR : 0 0 :031(325) [0513] sword or the right to **establish**, take possession of, or
TR : 0 0 :078(333) [0527] additional reason why other courts should be **established**.
TR : 0 0 :078(333) [0527] account the magistrates ought to **establish** other courts.
TR : 0 0 :080(334) [0527] of the poor, and the **establishment** of courts, especially
TR : 0 0 :081(334) [0527] but these cannot be **established** without the endowments
LC : 0 1 :017(367) [0585] so wicked that it did not **establish** and maintain some
LC : 0 1 :066(373) [0599] truth and justice are **established**, falsehood is refuted,
LC : 0 1 :207(393) [0639] Significantly he **established** it as the first of all
LC : 0 1 :212(394) [0641] measure, God has **established** marriage, so that everyone
LC : 0 1 :249(398) [0651] and resolute enough to **establish** and maintain order in
LC : 0 2 :050(417) [0691] it has become so **established** in usage that it cannot well
LC : 0 3 :080(431) [0721] and hinders the **establishment** of any kind of government
LC : 0 4 :008(437) [0733] have been instituted, **established**, and confirmed in
LC : 0 5 :001(447) [0753] All these are **established** from the words by which Christ
EP : 0 8 :016(489) [0821] human nature) and was **established** in the full use,
EP : 1 1 :005(495) [0833] salvation is so firmly **established** upon it that the "gates
SD : RN :009(505) [0853] Word and conclusively **established** against the papacy and
SD : RN :016(507) [0857] that the truth may be **established** the most distinctly and
SD : 0 1 :005(509) [0861] the first place, it is an **established** truth that Christians
SD : 0 1 :007(510) [0861] it is also a clearly **established** truth, as Article XIX of the
SD : 0 7 :027(573) [0981] Catechism, which **establishes** the true presence of the
SD : 0 7 :053(579) [0991] covenant, whereby I **establish**, seal, and confirm with you
SD : 0 7 :103(587) [1009] How will they **establish** that kind of speculation?
SD : 0 7 :104(587) [1009] communion which is **established** when in spirit through

Estate (28), Estates (39)
PR : PR :000(001) [0004] Electors, Princes, and **Estates** who Embrace the Augsburg
PR : PR :000(001) [0004] Electors, Princes, and **Estates** for the Instruction and
PR : PR :001(003) [0007] the electors, princes, and **estates** in the Holy Empire of
PR : PR :002(003) [0007] in the presence of all the **estates** of the empire, and
PR : PR :013(007) [0013] of electors, princes, and **estates** adhering to the Augsburg
PR : PR :015(007) [0013] in the case of some other **estates** not of our number, some
PR : PR :018(009) [0015] by the electors, princes, and **estates** referred to above.
PR : PR :025(014) [0023] the electors and **estates** in the Holy Roman Empire, and
AG : PR :005(025) [0039] electors, princes, and **estates**, we have complied with the
AG : PR :006(025) [0039] the electors, princes, and **estates** should commit to writing
AG : PR :009(025) [0039] electors, princes, and **estates** also submit a similar written
AG : PR :012(026) [0041] the electors, princes, and **estates** of the other party do not
AG : PR :014(026) [0041] electors, princes, and **estates**), and every lover of the
AG : PR :015(026) [0041] the electors, princes, and **estates** of the empire, especially
AG : PR :018(026) [0041] the electors, princes, and **estates** of the empire were,
AG : PR :018(026) [0041] and representatives of the **estates**) who were assembled at
AG : PR :021(027) [0043] the electors, princes, and **estates** have with the highest and
AG : 2 0 :002(041) [0053] instructions concerning true Christian **estates** and works.
AG : 2 3 :003(051) [0061] clearly assert that the **estate** of marriage was instituted by
AG : 2 3 :026(056) [0065] monks entered into their **estates** ignorantly when they
AG : 2 7 :016(073) [0077] as far superior to the other **estates** instituted by God.
AG : 2 7 :046(078) [0081] the invented spiritual **estate** of the orders was Christian
AP : 1 6 :003(223) [0331] new laws about the civil **estate**, but commands us to obey
AP : 1 6 :006(223) [0331] not legislate for the civil **estate** but is the forgiveness of
AP : 2 7 :002(269) [0419] threatened the monastic **estate** but had only denounced
AP : 2 7 :018(272) [0425] Emperor Charles; look, princes; look, all you **estates**!
AP : 2 8 :001(281) [0443] and the ecclesiastical **estate**, and they conclude with the
S 1 : PR :012(290) [0459] There is discord among princes and political **estates**.
S 1 : PR :013(290) [0459] ecclesiastical and secular **estates** as are contrary to God,
S 1 : PR :013(291) [0459] spiritual and temporal **estates**, we would find enough time
S 2 : 0 4 :007(299) [0473] of his whole rule and **estate**, together with all his rights
S 3 : 1 1 :001(314) [0499] and burden the divine **estate** of priests with perpetual
TR : 0 0 :082(334) [0529] princes and of the **estates** and cities professing the
TR : 0 0 :082(000) [0529] by the other princes and **estates** of the Roman Empire, to
SC : 0 9 :001(354) [0561] *selected for various **estates** and conditions of men, by*
LC : PR :017(361) [0573] upon all doctrines, **estates**, persons, laws, and everything
LC : 0 1 :093(377) [0607] are the so-called spiritual **estates** who do not know God's
LC : 0 1 :105(379) [0611] distinction, above all **estates** that are beneath it, that he
LC : 0 1 :112(380) [0613] no need to institute monasticism or "spiritual **estates**."
LC : 0 1 :126(382) [0617] For God has exalted this **estate** of parents above all
LC : 0 1 :150(385) [0623] is to be classed with the **estate** of fatherhood, the most
LC : 0 1 :184(390) [0633] God a better house and **estate** or greater wealth and good
LC : 0 1 :197(391) [0637] undermine the "spiritual **estate**" and infringe upon the
LC : 0 1 :206(393) [0639] specifically with the **estate** of marriage and gives occasion
LC : 0 1 :207(393) [0639] maintain, and cherish it as a divine and blessed **estate**.
LC : 0 1 :208(393) [0639] most richly blessed this **estate** above all others and, in
LC : 0 1 :208(393) [0639] world in order that this **estate** might be provided for
LC : 0 1 :209(393) [0639] It is not an **estate** to be placed on a level with the others;
LC : 0 1 :209(393) [0641] as the spiritual and civil **estates** are, these must humble
LC : 0 1 :209(393) [0641] all people to enter the **estate** of marriage, as we shall
LC : 0 1 :210(393) [0641] It is not an exceptional **estate**, but the most universal and
LC : 0 1 :211(393) [0641] is not only an honorable **estate** but also a necessary one,
LC : 0 1 :211(393) [0641] who have been created for it, shall be found in this **estate**.
LC : 0 1 :217(394) [0641] life and know that it is a blessed and God-pleasing **estate**.
LC : 0 1 :219(394) [0643] (that is, especially in the **estate** of marriage), but also to
LC : 0 1 :221(395) [0643] over against all "spiritual **estates**" that are chosen without
LC : 0 1 :301(405) [0667] a large inheritance, real **estate**, etc., they resort to
LC : 0 1 :302(405) [0667] county, or other great **estate**, he practices bribery,
LC : 0 3 :077(431) [0721] emperor, kings, and all **estates** of men, and especially our
LC : 0 4 :020(439) [0737] we speak about the parental **estate** and civil authority.
EP : 1 2 :012(499) [0841] is not a God-pleasing **estate** in the New Testament.
EP : 1 2 :021(499) [0841] in rank and essential **estates** to the Father and to the
SD : PR :003(501) [0847] electors, princes, and **estates** who had then accepted the
SD : RN :005(504) [0851] electors, princes, and **estates** of the Roman Empire as the
SD : RN :007(505) [0853] electors, princes, and **estates**, before the Council in
SD : RN :007(505) [0853] the electors, princes, and **estates** were resolved by God's
SD : 1 2 :017(634) [1099] Testament era government service is not a godly **estate**.

Esteem (11), Esteemed (5)
AG : 2 5 :002(061) [0069] so that they may **esteem** absolution as a great and
AG : 2 6 :004(064) [0071] that faith in Christ is to be **esteemed** far above all works.
AG : 2 8 :004(081) [0085] are to be honored and **esteemed** with all reverence as the
AL : 2 5 :003(061) [0069] Our people are taught to **esteem** absolution highly
AP : PR :013(099) [0101] the emperor or the princes, whom I hold in due **esteem**.
AP : 2 4 :074(263) [0411] gratitude, and a witness of its high **esteem** for God's gifts.
S 2 : 0 2 :028(297) [0471] one will long remember, **esteem**, or honor them out of
S 3 : 0 8 :002(312) [0495] it should be highly **esteemed** and valued, like all other
SC : PR :023(341) [0537] He who does not highly **esteem** the sacrament suggests
SC : 0 1 :008(343) [0541] to anger, but honor, serve, obey, love, and **esteem** them.
SC : 0 9 :003(355) [0561] admonish you, and to **esteem** them very highly in love
LC : 0 1 :109(380) [0611] You are to **esteem** and prize them as the most precious
LC : 0 1 :130(383) [0619] honor to his parents and **esteem** them as those through
LC : 0 1 :322(409) [0673] to be received and **esteemed** as a serious matter to God
EP : 0 3 :002(473) [0793] the sins of all men are **esteemed** like a drop of water over
SD : 1 2 :013(634) [1099] Therefore they do not **esteem** infant Baptism very highly

Estimation (2)
AG : 2 6 :019(067) [0073] which have arisen from a wrong **estimation** of tradition.
AP : 2 1 :028(232) [0351] matter is that in popular **estimation** the blessed Virgin

Estrange (3)
SC : 0 1 :020(344) [0543] we should not abduct, **estrange**, or entice away our
LC : 0 1 :295(404) [0665] dismiss his own wife and **estrange** the other's from him so
LC : 0 1 :306(406) [0669] maid-servant or otherwise **estrange** them with fair words.

Eternal (288)
PR : PR :008(006) [0011] of their souls and their **eternal** welfare to abide by it and
PR : PR :024(013) [0023] against the temporal and **eternal** welfare of our own
PR : PR :024(013) [0023] and the common welfare, both **eternal** and temporal.
AG : 0 1 :002(027) [0043] this one divine essence, equal in power and alike **eternal**:
AG : 0 1 :003(027) [0043] are one divine essence, **eternal**, without division, without

Continued ▶

A G : 0 2 :002(029) [0043] sin and condemns to the **eternal** wrath of God all those
A G : 0 4 :002(030) [0045] and righteousness and **eternal** life are given to us.
A G : 1 6 :004(038) [0051] but an inward and **eternal** mode of existence and
A G : 1 7 :002(038) [0051] up all the dead, to give **eternal** life and everlasting joy to
A G : 1 7 :003(038) [0051] men and the devil to hell and **eternal** punishment.
A G : 1 7 :004(038) [0051] condemned men will not suffer **eternal** pain and torment.
A G : 2 8 :008(082) [0085] imparted no bodily but **eternal** things and gifts, namely,
A G : 2 8 :008(082) [0085] things and gifts, namely, **eternal** righteousness, the Holy
A G : 2 8 :008(082) [0085] eternal righteousness, the Holy Spirit, and **eternal** life.
A G : 2 8 :010(082) [0085] or of bishops bestows **eternal** gifts and is used and
A L : 0 1 :002(027) [0043] called and which is God, **eternal**, incorporeal, indivisible,
A L : 0 2 :002(029) [0043] now damns and brings **eternal** death on those who are
A L : 1 6 :004(038) [0051] The Gospel teaches an **eternal** righteousness of the heart,
A L : 1 7 :002(038) [0051] and elect he will give **eternal** life and endless joy, but
A L : 2 8 :008(082) [0085] given, but rather such **eternal** things as eternal
A L : 2 8 :008(082) [0085] such eternal things as **eternal** righteousness, the Holy
A L : 2 8 :008(082) [0085] as eternal righteousness, the Holy Spirit, and **eternal** life.
A L : 2 8 :010(082) [0085] of the church bestows **eternal** things and is exercised only
A L : 2 8 :011(082) [0085] protects souls from heresies, the devil, and **eternal** death.
A P : 0 2 :005(101) [0107] one is not condemned to **eternal** death because of
A P : 0 4 :005(108) [0121] of sins, justification, and **eternal** life for his sake, or
A P : 0 4 :005(108) [0121] promises forgiveness of sins, justification, and **eternal** life.
A P : 0 4 :017(109) [0125] of this disposition and **eternal** life by the works of the
A P : 0 4 :036(112) [0131] that men who are under **eternal** wrath merit the
A P : 0 4 :036(112) [0131] to be casting us into **eternal** death, human nature cannot
A P : 0 4 :040(112) [0131] are all under sin and subject to **eternal** wrath and death.
A P : 0 4 :062(115) [0139] are under sin and are worthy of **eternal** wrath and death.
A P : 0 4 :079(117) [0143] the terrors of sin and of **eternal** death must be conquered
A P : 0 4 :085(119) [0147] the terrors of sin, against **eternal** death, and against all
A P : 0 4 :095(121) [0149] up, that whoever believes in him may have **eternal** life."
A P : 0 4 :100(121) [0151] it brings forth peace, joy, and **eternal** life in the heart.
A P : 0 4 :128(125) [0157] is overwhelming us with temporal and **eternal** calamities?
A P : 0 4 :131(125) [0159] utterly overlook that **eternal** law, far beyond the senses
A P : 0 4 :132(125) [0159] to bring forth in us **eternal** righteousness and a new and
A P : 0 4 :132(125) [0159] in us eternal righteousness and a new and **eternal** life.
A P : 0 4 :146(127) [0163] for they say they earn grace and **eternal** life by merit.
A P : 0 4 :162(129) [0169] we please God and merit **eternal** life by our keeping of the
A P : 0 4 :196(134) [0175] with Christ, we do not merit **eternal** life by our works.
A P : 0 4 :196(134) [0175] **Eternal** life belongs to the justified, according to the
A P : 0 4 :289(151) [0203] obedience to the law is worthy of grace and **eternal** life.
A P : 0 4 :290(151) [0203] worthy of grace and **eternal** life, although even a weak
A P : 0 4 :297(153) [0205] righteousness, and **eternal** life are assured to us for
A P : 0 4 :297(153) [0205] that God gave us **eternal** life, and this life is in his Son.
A P : 0 4 :301(153) [0205] evils, sufferings in this life and the fear of **eternal** wrath.
A P : 0 4 :310(155) [0207] sees the Son and believes in him should have **eternal** life."
A P : 0 4 :316(156) [0209] God of itself and earns **eternal** life without needing
A P : 0 4 :320(156) [0209] it will count worthy of **eternal** life, if indeed hope ought to
A P : 0 4 :320(156) [0209] that righteousness and **eternal** life are given us freely for
A P : 0 4 :322(157) [0209] church confesses that **eternal** life comes through mercy.
A P : 0 4 :322(157) [0209] *Will,* "God leads us to **eternal** life, not by our merits, but
A P : 0 4 :347(160) [0217] the unworthy because **eternal** life is promised to the
A P : 0 4 :348(160) [0217] works are unnecessary if they do not merit **eternal** life.
A P : 0 4 :348(160) [0217] We say that **eternal** life is promised to the justified, but
A P : 0 4 :352(161) [0217] speak, the beginning of **eternal** life, as Paul says (Rom.
A P : 0 4 :354(161) [0217] justification belongs to faith, so **eternal** life belongs to it.
A P : 0 4 :356(161) [0217] our opponents reply that **eternal** life is called a reward
A P : 0 4 :356(161) [0217] Paul calls **eternal** life a "gift" (Rom. 6:23) because the
A P : 0 4 :356(161) [0217] (John 3:36), "He who believes in the Son has **eternal** life."
A P : 0 4 :357(162) [0219] counted so precious that **eternal** life is their due and that
A P : 0 4 :357(162) [0219] are worthy of grace and **eternal** life without needing
A P : 0 4 :359(162) [0219] are worthy of grace and **eternal** life or whether they
A P : 0 4 :360(162) [0219] attribute to works a worthiness of grace and **eternal** life.
A P : 0 4 :362(162) [0219] We grant that **eternal** life is a reward because it is
A P : 0 4 :362(162) [0219] this gift the promise of **eternal** life has been added,
A P : 0 4 :366(163) [0219] though justification and **eternal** life belong to faith, still
A P : 0 4 :370(163) [0221] works properly merit **eternal** life, since Paul says (Rom.
A P : 0 4 :372(164) [0221] Therefore, when **eternal** life is granted to works, it is
A P : 0 4 :373(164) [0221] faith, and for this reason **eternal** life is granted to
A P : 0 4 :375(164) [0223] but in themselves are not worthy of grace and **eternal** life.
A P : 0 4 :376(164) [0223] they are righteousness that they are worthy of **eternal** life.
A P : 0 4 :378(165) [0223] who teach that we merit **eternal** life by works, omitting
A P : 0 4 :384(166) [0225] what kind of faith obtains **eternal** life, a faith that is firm
A P : 0 7 :015(170) [0231] brings not the shadow of **eternal** things but the eternal
A P : 0 7 :015(170) [0231] of eternal things but the **eternal** blessings themselves, the
A P : 1 2 :007(183) [0255] guilt, but only changes **eternal** punishments into
A P : 1 2 :009(183) [0255] or is running away from **eternal** punishments — especially
A P : 1 2 :013(184) [0257] They imagine that **eternal** punishments are changed into
A P : 1 2 :022(185) [0257] instituted to commute **eternal** to temporal punishments,
A P : 1 2 :029(186) [0259] grant the Holy Spirit and **eternal** life, and to lead us as
A P : 1 2 :108(198) [0283] I am a sinner worthy of **eternal** wrath, and I cannot set
A P : 1 2 :118(199) [0287] sin, he commutes the **eternal** punishment to a temporal
A P : 1 2 :123(200) [0289] compensate for **eternal** punishments; therefore the keys
A P : 1 2 :138(203) [0293] works compensate for **eternal** punishments; it is rash for
A P : 1 2 :138(203) [0293] This remission removes **eternal** death and brings eternal
A P : 1 2 :138(203) [0293] remission removes eternal death and brings **eternal** life.
A P : 1 2 :139(203) [0295] satisfactions can remit **eternal** punishments, or that the
A P : 1 2 :140(204) [0295] only for guilt but also for **eternal** death, according to the
A P : 1 2 :140(204) [0295] our guilt but our penalties redeem us from **eternal** death!
A P : 1 2 :143(204) [0297] pay homage to God and to compensate for **eternal** death.
A P : 1 2 :143(204) [0297] pay homage to God and compensate for **eternal** death.
A P : 1 2 :144(205) [0297] the honor of being a price paid in lieu of **eternal** death.
A P : 1 2 :146(205) [0297] works does not atone for **eternal** death because it is
A P : 1 2 :147(205) [0297] frees the heart from the wrath of God and **eternal** death.
A P : 1 2 :147(205) [0297] The satisfaction for **eternal** death is the death of Christ;
A P : 1 2 :147(205) [0297] to remit either guilt or **eternal** punishment or the
A P : 1 2 :157(207) [0301] we can be freed from **eternal** death only by the payment
A P : 1 2 :157(207) [0301] sin, not as a payment for or a ransom from **eternal** death.
A P : 1 2 :160(208) [0303] but not to pay for **eternal** death; for this God has another
A P : 1 2 :161(208) [0303] the man from obtaining **eternal** life, but the lesson of the
A P : 1 2 :167(209) [0305] not mean a payment for **eternal** punishment, or a
A P : 1 2 :168(209) [0305] the flesh, not to pay for **eternal** punishments but to keep
A P : 1 2 :174(210) [0307] — not to buy off **eternal** punishment but to keep from
A P : 1 2 :174(210) [0307] the penalties of purgatory can remit **eternal** punishments.
A P : 1 6 :002(222) [0331] faith, the beginning of **eternal** righteousness and eternal
A P : 1 6 :002(222) [0331] the beginning of eternal righteousness and **eternal** life.
A P : 1 6 :006(223) [0331] sins and the beginning of **eternal** life in the hearts of
A P : 1 6 :008(223) [0333] that the Gospel brings **eternal** righteousness to hearts,
A P : 1 7 :001(224) [0335] all the dead, granting **eternal** life and eternal joys to the
A P : 1 7 :001(224) [0335] granting eternal life and **eternal** joys to the godly but
A P : 2 4 :034(256) [0397] kill this old flesh and begin a new and **eternal** life in us.
A P : 2 7 :012(270) [0423] according to the Gospel in order to merit **eternal** life.
A P : 2 7 :013(271) [0423] not the statement of the **eternal** Father which Thou who
A P : 2 7 :020(272) [0427] God, which contains a covenant of grace and **eternal** life.
A P : 2 7 :021(272) [0427] themselves are services that justify or merit **eternal** life.
A P : 2 7 :023(272) [0427] through which we merit **eternal** life conflicts with the
A P : 2 7 :023(272) [0427] Christ's sake righteousness and **eternal** life are given to us.
A P : 2 7 :027(274) [0429] of Christ, which is **eternal** life, in these silly observances
A P : 2 7 :028(274) [0429] the monastic life merits **eternal** life if it is maintained by a
A P : 2 7 :029(274) [0431] the Sacred Scriptures the monastic life merits **eternal** life.
A P : 2 7 :030(274) [0431] they say that by a monastic life men merit **eternal** life.
A P : 2 7 :030(274) [0431] the honor of meriting **eternal** life, as he clearly says in
A P : 2 7 :032(274) [0431] In the second place, **eternal** life is given by mercy for
A P : 2 7 :032(274) [0431] no works can you merit **eternal** life, but that this is freely
A P : 2 7 :033(274) [0431] the forgiveness of sins or **eternal** life even by the works of
A P : 2 7 :033(275) [0431] credit for meriting the forgiveness of sins or **eternal** life.
A P : 2 7 :034(275) [0431] the forgiveness of sins or **eternal** life are simply crushing
A P : 2 7 :035(275) [0431] which the forgiveness of sins and **eternal** life are granted.
A P : 2 7 :040(276) [0433] merit a more abundant **eternal** life, and it quotes the
A P : 2 7 :040(276) [0433] because it merits the forgiveness of sins and **eternal** life.
A P : 2 7 :040(276) [0435] the forgiveness of sins or **eternal** life, he is insulting
A P : 2 7 :061(279) [0441] the mercy of God — they would attain **eternal** life.
A P : 2 7 :065(280) [0441] of sins or to secure **eternal** life for us instead of mercy for
A P : 2 7 :069(281) [0443] righteous; that we attain **eternal** life because of them
A P : 2 7 :070(281) [0443] mercy they would attain **eternal** life and not for the sake
A P : 2 8 :006(282) [0445] toward the goal of **eternal** bliss, and that the power to
A P : 2 8 :006(282) [0445] to create laws which are useful for attaining **eternal** life.
A P : 2 8 :009(282) [0445] they also say that traditions are conducive to **eternal** life.
A P : 2 8 :010(282) [0447] that traditions avail for **eternal** righteousness and eternal
A P : 2 8 :010(282) [0447] eternal righteousness and **eternal** life since food, drink,
A P : 2 8 :010(282) [0447] But it is **eternal** things, the Word of God and the Holy
A P : 2 8 :010(282) [0447] and the Holy Spirit, that work **eternal** life in the heart.
A P : 2 8 :010(282) [0447] explain how traditions are conducive to **eternal** life.
A P : 2 8 :021(284) [0449] that they merit forgiveness of sins and **eternal** life.
S 2 : 0 4 :014(301) [0475] murder, and the **eternal** destruction of body and soul are
S C : 0 2 :006(345) [0545] the dead and will grant **eternal** life to me and to all who
S C : 0 4 :006(349) [0551] the devil, and grants **eternal** salvation to all who believe,
S C : 0 4 :010(349) [0551] by his grace and become heirs in hope of **eternal** life.
L C : 0 1 :015(366) [0583] draw us to himself, because he is the one **eternal** good.
L C : 0 1 :016(366) [0585] under penalty of **eternal** wrath, namely, that the heart
L C : 0 1 :024(367) [0587] protection, peace, and all temporal and **eternal** blessings.
L C : 0 1 :025(368) [0587] "good" because he is an **eternal** fountain which overflows
L C : 0 1 :041(370) [0591] For it brings you either **eternal** blessing, happiness, and
L C : 0 1 :041(370) [0591] and salvation, or **eternal** wrath, misery, and woe.
L C : 0 2 :024(413) [0683] us with inexpressible **eternal** treasures through his Son
L C : 0 2 :028(414) [0685] displeasure, doomed to **eternal** damnation, as we had
L C : 0 2 :029(414) [0685] for us until this only and **eternal** Son of God, in his
L C : 0 2 :057(418) [0693] to complete and perfect holiness in a new, **eternal** life.
L C : 0 2 :066(419) [0697] Therefore they remain in **eternal** wrath and damnation,
L C : 0 3 :053(427) [0713] daily growth here and in **eternal** life hereafter to us who
L C : 0 3 :055(427) [0713] blessing, but for an **eternal**, priceless treasure and
L C : 0 3 :056(427) [0713] comprehend — like an **eternal**, inexhaustible fountain
L C : 0 3 :058(428) [0713] expect, without doubting, **eternal** blessings from God.
L C : 0 3 :058(428) [0713] when he promises that which is **eternal** and imperishable?
L C : 0 4 :044(442) [0743] I shall be saved and have **eternal** life, both in soul and
L C : 0 4 :083(446) [0751] until we pass from this present misery to **eternal** glory.
L C : 0 5 :036(450) [0761] Such a gift and **eternal** treasure cannot be seized with the
E P : 0 2 :009(471) [0789] law, and thus merit forgiveness of sins and **eternal** life.
E P : 0 2 :012(471) [0789] righteousness before God whereby we merit **eternal** life.
E P : 0 3 :003(473) [0793] forgiveness of sins and **eternal** life, as it is written, "For as
E P : 0 5 :005(478) [0803] "righteousness that avails before God," and **eternal** life.
E P : 0 8 :022(490) [0823] Christ is not true, natural, and **eternal** God, as Arius held.
E P : 0 8 :039(492) [0827] shall finally have Christ's **eternal** deity denied and we
E P : 0 9 :004(492) [0827] of the devil, and of the **eternal** damnation of the hellish
E P : 1 1 :000(494) [0831] XI. God's **Eternal** Foreknowledge and Election
E P : 1 1 :002(494) [0831] foreknowledge and the **eternal** election of God is to be
E P : 1 1 :005(495) [0833] 4. Predestination or the **eternal** election of God, however,
E P : 1 1 :008(495) [0833] and divine assistance for steadfastness and **eternal** life.
E P : 1 1 :009(495) [0833] this election of ours to **eternal** life on the basis either of
E P : 1 1 :009(495) [0833] Or, "If I am not elected to **eternal** life, whatever good I do
E P : 1 1 :011(495) [0835] 10. The doctrine of God's **eternal** election is profitable
E P : 1 1 :011(496) [0835] does he speak of the mystery of God's **eternal** election.
E P : 1 1 :013(496) [0835] with the doctrine of the **eternal** election of God only in so
E P : 1 1 :013(496) [0835] Christ we should seek the **eternal** election of the Father,
E P : 1 1 :013(496) [0835] who has decreed in his **eternal** counsel that he would save
E P : 1 1 :013(496) [0835] we have been elected to **eternal** life out of pure grace in
E P : 1 1 :015(496) [0835] of the doctrine of God's **eternal** election gives God his
E P : 1 1 :016(497) [0837] election of God to **eternal** life in such a way that
E P : 1 1 :020(497) [0837] on account of which he has elected us to **eternal** life.
E P : 1 2 :029(500) [0843] that there is not only one **eternal**, divine essence,
E P : 1 2 :030(500) [0843] they dearly love their soul's **eternal** welfare and salvation.
S D : P R :007(502) [0849] others even denied that Christ was **eternal** and true God.
S D : R N :008(505) [0853] and laymen who for their **eternal** salvation must as
S D : R N :013(506) [0855] the Word of God as the **eternal** truth, so we introduce and
S D : 0 1 :013(511) [0863] original sin is death, **eternal** damnation, together with
S D : 0 1 :013(511) [0863] spiritual, temporal, and **eternal** misery, the tyranny and
S D : 0 1 :046(516) [0873] shall arise, and that in **eternal** life we shall have and keep
S D : 0 1 :047(516) [0875] Day and that in **eternal** life, instead of this essence of our
S D : 0 1 :047(516) [0875] and would be and remain in the elect in **eternal** life.
S D : 0 1 :062(519) [0879] not only endure God's **eternal** wrath and death but that
S D : 0 2 :009(522) [0883] God and the promise of **eternal** salvation, they cannot by
S D : 0 2 :014(523) [0885] for the grace of God and **eternal** salvation in their hearts.
S D : 0 2 :021(525) [0889] dangers and finally into **eternal** death and damnation.
S D : 0 2 :022(525) [0889] the grace of God, and in **eternal** life, not by its own
S D : 0 2 :049(530) [0901] believes on him should not perish but have **eternal** life."
S D : 0 2 :050(530) [0901] of his divine, **eternal** law and the wonderful counsel
S D : 0 2 :050(530) [0901] only saving Gospel of his **eternal** Son, our only Saviour

Continued ▶

SD : 0 2 :050(531) [0901] Thereby he gathers an **eternal** church for himself out of
SD : 0 2 :050(531) [0901] God's will to call men to **eternal** salvation, to draw them
SD : 0 2 :051(531) [0901] Therefore the **eternal** Father calls out from heaven
SD : 0 2 :057(532) [0903] himself with God's **eternal** election nor obtain his mercy.
SD : 0 2 :075(536) [0911] obedience earn the forgiveness of sin and **eternal** life.
SD : 0 2 :077(536) [0911] forgiveness of sins, and **eternal** life, then the free will by
SD : 0 2 :079(536) [0911] of the law merit righteousness before God and **eternal** life.
SD : 0 3 :009(540) [0919] of God and an heir of **eternal** life) without any merit or
SD : 0 3 :016(541) [0921] of God, adoption, and the inheritance of **eternal** life.
SD : 0 3 :017(542) [0921] from sins and from the **eternal** punishment of these sins
SD : 0 3 :025(543) [0923] with God, adoption, and the inheritance of **eternal** life.
SD : 0 3 :032(545) [0927] and the inheritance of **eternal** life only on account of
SD : 0 3 :033(545) [0927] was pleasing and acceptable to him to **eternal** life, rest?
SD : 0 3 :053(548) [0933] adoption and the inheritance of **eternal** life and salvation.
SD : 0 3 :054(548) [0935] Holy Spirit, who is the **eternal** and essential
SD : 0 3 :056(549) [0935] but had not been true, **eternal** God, the obedience and
SD : 0 3 :056(549) [0935] render satisfaction to the **eternal** and almighty God for
SD : 0 3 :057(549) [0935] race, since it satisfied the **eternal** and immutable
SD : 0 5 :017(561) [0957] with God's wrath and temporal and **eternal** punishment.
SD : 0 5 :023(562) [0959] them into death and **eternal** damnation, but also revived
SD : 0 7 :043(576) [0987] mighty, but himself the **eternal** truth and wisdom and the
SD : 0 7 :045(577) [0987] these words of the **eternal**, truthful, and almighty Son of
SD : 0 7 :062(581) [0995] have a gracious God and **eternal** salvation for the sake of
SD : 0 7 :068(582) [0997] (that is, temporal and **eternal** punishments) and profane
SD : 0 7 :070(582) [0997] be his faith strong or weak, has **eternal** life (John 3:16).
SD : 0 7 :106(588) [1009] of the true and **eternal** God, our Lord and Saviour Jesus
SD : 0 8 :006(592) [1017] simultaneously true **eternal** God, born of the Father from
SD : 0 8 :009(593) [1017] to be almighty, to be **eternal**, to be infinite, to be
SD : 0 8 :025(596) [1023] sin, death, the devil, hell, and **eternal** damnation.
SD : 0 8 :085(608) [1045] human birth, the **eternal** power of God is also given to
SD : 0 8 :085(608) [1047] exchange of qualities has **eternal** power and has created
SD : 1 0 :020(614) [1059] murder, and the **eternal** destruction of body and soul are
SD : 1 1 :000(616) [1063] XI. **Eternal** Foreknowledge and Divine Election
SD : 1 1 :001(616) [1063] concerning the **eternal** election of the children of God.
SD : 1 1 :004(616) [1063] difference between God's **eternal** foreknowledge and the
SD : 1 1 :004(616) [1063] foreknowledge and the **eternal** election of his children to
SD : 1 1 :004(616) [1063] the eternal election of his children to **eternal** salvation.
SD : 1 1 :005(617) [1065] On the other hand, the **eternal** election of God or God's
SD : 1 1 :005(617) [1065] and predestined to **eternal** life "before the foundation of
SD : 1 1 :008(617) [1065] God's **eternal** election, however, not only foresees and
SD : 1 1 :008(617) [1065] many as were ordained to **eternal** life believed" (Acts
SD : 1 1 :009(617) [1065] we are not to view this **eternal** election or divine ordering
SD : 1 1 :009(617) [1065] or divine ordering to **eternal** life only in the secret and
SD : 1 1 :012(618) [1067] of the teaching of God's **eternal** foreknowledge will in no
SD : 1 1 :013(618) [1067] and profitably about **eternal** election or about the
SD : 1 1 :013(618) [1067] of the children of God to **eternal** life, we should accustom
SD : 1 1 :015(619) [1069] righteousness which avails before God" and **eternal** life.
SD : 1 1 :018(619) [1069] into the inheritance of **eternal** life all who in sincere
SD : 1 1 :022(619) [1069] save and glorify in **eternal** life those whom he has elected,
SD : 1 1 :023(619) [1069] In this his **eternal** counsel, purpose, and ordinance God
SD : 1 1 :024(620) [1069] in the teaching of the **eternal** election of God to adoption
SD : 1 1 :024(620) [1069] election of God to adoption and to **eternal** salvation.
SD : 1 1 :024(620) [1069] election, and ordinance of God to **eternal** salvation.
SD : 1 1 :028(620) [1071] we want to consider our **eternal** election to salvation
SD : 1 1 :028(621) [1071] believe on Christ should have **eternal** life" (John 6:40).
SD : 1 1 :030(621) [1073] me; and I give them **eternal** life" (John 10:27, 28), and
SD : 1 1 :035(622) [1075] that God, who is the **eternal** Truth, contradicts himself.
SD : 1 1 :046(624) [1079] my salvation in his **eternal** purpose, which cannot fail or
SD : 1 1 :060(626) [1083] and make ourselves unworthy of **eternal** life (Acts 13:46).
SD : 1 1 :065(626) [1083] consider God's **eternal** election in Christ, and not outside
SD : 1 1 :066(627) [1085] in whom they are to seek the Father's **eternal** election.
SD : 1 1 :067(627) [1085] will and thereby our **eternal** election to eternal life when
SD : 1 1 :067(627) [1085] our eternal election to **eternal** life when he says, "The
SD : 1 1 :067(627) [1085] in him should have **eternal** life" (John 6:40); and again,
SD : 1 1 :070(627) [1085] of God, if he has been elected and ordained to **eternal** life.
SD : 1 1 :070(627) [1085] "book of life" and of the **eternal** election of all God's
SD : 1 1 :070(627) [1085] of all God's children to **eternal** life, and who testifies to
SD : 1 1 :075(628) [1087] Our election to **eternal** life does not rest on our piety or
SD : 1 1 :086(631) [1091] or any other person **eternal** life, or that in his secret
SD : 1 1 :086(631) [1091] God had ordained him to **eternal** damnation so that he
SD : 1 1 :087(631) [1091] and explanation of the **eternal** and saving election of the
SD : 1 1 :088(631) [1093] on account of which God has elected us unto **eternal** life.
SD : 1 1 :089(631) [1093] are taught to seek their **eternal** election in Christ and in
SD : 1 1 :095(632) [1095] to yield anything of the **eternal** and unchangeable truth
SD : 1 2 :029(635) [1101] to the Father and the **eternal** Word, so that the two
SD : 1 2 :036(635) [1101] and natural God, of one **eternal**, divine essence with God
SD : 1 2 :037(636) [1103] that there is not one **eternal**, divine essence of the Father,

Eternally (10)
AG : 0 3 :004(030) [0045] of God, that he may **eternally** rule and have dominion
S 2 : 0 2 :010(294) [0465] we are and remain **eternally** divided and opposed the one
LC : 0 2 :059(418) [0695] our holiness and will **eternally** preserve us in it by means
LC : 0 2 :062(419) [0695] evil, he will finally make us perfectly and **eternally** holy.
LC : 0 3 :052(427) [0711] may all remain together **eternally** in this kingdom which
EP : 0 3 :006(473) [0793] righteous by God the Father, and shall be saved **eternally**.
EP : 1 1 :007(495) [0833] which all who are to be **eternally** saved are inscribed and
SD : 0 2 :014(523) [0885] of God says remains **eternally** true, "Apart from me you
SD : 0 5 :020(561) [0959] and all the punishments of sin, and are saved **eternally**.
SD : 1 1 :022(619) [1069] That, finally, he would **eternally** save and glorify in

Eternity (25)
SC : 0 2 :004(345) [0545] of the Father from **eternity**, and also true man, born of
SC : 0 2 :004(345) [0545] is risen from the dead and lives and reigns to all **eternity**.
LC : 0 1 :040(370) [0591] good things in time and **eternity**, this ought to move and
LC : 0 1 :157(387) [0627] of joy, happiness, and salvation, both here and in **eternity**
LC : 0 3 :053(427) [0711] faith, and secondly, in **eternity**, it comes through the final
EP : 0 8 :007(487) [0819] nature are omnipotence, **eternity**, infinity, and (according
EP : 0 8 :018(489) [0823] is, and remains to all **eternity**, God and man in one
EP : 0 8 :038(491) [0827] what has existed from **eternity**, what is happening
EP : 0 8 :038(491) [0827] everywhere today, nor what will yet take place in **eternity**.
SD : 0 1 :045(516) [0873] grace but remains the enemy of sin throughout **eternity**!
SD : 0 8 :006(592) [1017] has been from all **eternity** true, essential, and perfect God
SD : 0 8 :006(592) [1017] born of the Father from **eternity**, and also a true man,
SD : 0 8 :007(592) [1017] divine, which is from all **eternity**, and the human, which
SD : 0 8 :007(592) [1017] remains in its nature and essence through all **eternity**.
SD : 0 8 :008(593) [1017] and throughout all **eternity** does not lay them aside, nor
SD : 0 8 :009(593) [1019] which throughout **eternity** will never become the essential
SD : 0 8 :026(596) [1023] he retains throughout **eternity**) and has been installed in
SD : 0 8 :057(602) [1035] has everything from all **eternity**) but that the person
SD : 0 8 :061(602) [1035] divine properties from **eternity** to the Son according to
SD : 0 8 :073(605) [1041] he is and remains to all **eternity** his and the Father's own
SD : 0 8 :085(608) [1045] him — in a temporal way, however, and not from **eternity**
SD : 0 8 :085(608) [1045] the deity, existed from **eternity**, but according to our
SD : 0 8 :085(608) [1047] From **eternity** I have this authority from the Father
SD : 1 1 :011(618) [1067] to salvation from **eternity** everything is in vain."
SD : 1 1 :066(627) [1085] Father has decreed from **eternity** that whomever he would

Ethics (3)
AP : 0 2 :043(106) [0117] mingle philosophical and civil **ethics** with the Gospel.
AP : 0 4 :014(109) [0123] aside the Gospel and expounded the **ethics** of Aristotle.
AP : 0 4 :014(109) [0123] wrote so well on natural **ethics** that nothing further needs

Etymology (2)
AP : 2 4 :085(264) [0413] Why such a far-fetched **etymology**, except perhaps to
AP : 2 4 :085(264) [0413] go so far afield for the **etymology** when the term occurs in

Eucharist (8), Eucharistic (5)
AL : 2 2 :006(050) [0061] priests administer the **Eucharist** and distribute the blood
AL : 2 4 :012(057) [0065] unworthily with the **Eucharist** when he said, "Whoever
AP : 2 1 :035(234) [0353] one who calls upon her should die without the **Eucharist**.
AP : 2 2 :004(236) [0359] priests who serve the **Eucharist** and distribute the blood of
AP : 2 4 :019(252) [0389] The other type is the **eucharistic** sacrifice; this does not
AP : 2 4 :021(253) [0391] The **eucharistic** sacrifices were the oblation, the drink
AP : 2 4 :025(253) [0391] The rest are **eucharistic** sacrifices, called "sacrifices of
AP : 2 4 :066(261) [0407] talking about thanksgiving; hence they call it **"eucharist."**
AP : 2 4 :067(261) [0407] have already said that a **eucharistic** sacrifice does not
AP : 2 4 :067(261) [0407] reconciliation but are **eucharistic** sacrifices when the
AP : 2 4 :076(263) [0411] From this term **"eucharist"** arose in the church.
AP : 2 4 :087(265) [0413] offering, as it is called a **eucharist**, because prayers,
S 3 : 1 5 :005(317) [0501] Apology, and the Concord in the matter of the **Eucharist**

Eugubium (1)
TR : 0 0 :018(323) [0509] — whether in Rome or **Eugubium** or Constantinople or

Eunomians (2)
AG : 0 1 :005(028) [0043] Valentinians, Arians, **Eunomians**, Mohammedans, and
AL : 0 1 :005(028) [0043] Valentinians, Arians, **Eunomians**, Mohammedans, and all

Eunuchs (2)
AP : 2 3 :021(242) [0369] have made themselves **eunuchs** for the sake of the
AP : 2 3 :040(245) [0375] who make themselves **eunuchs**, but he adds, "for the sake

Europe (3)
AP : 1 1 :007(181) [0251] whole church throughout **Europe** knows how consciences
TR : 0 0 :034(325) [0513] and afterwards great disturbances to arise in **Europe**.
TR : 0 0 :035(326) [0513] almost all the nations of **Europe**, but especially the

Eusebius (1)
SD : 0 1 :054(518) [0877] not unfamiliar, as did **Eusebius**, Ambrose, and especially

Eutyches (2)
EP : 0 8 :018(489) [0823] together in one essence, as **Eutyches** erroneously taught.
EP : 0 8 :021(490) [0823] has been changed into the deity, as **Eutyches** dreamed.

Evade (2), Evades (1)
AP : 0 4 :109(123) [0153] they have thought up a piece of sophistry to **evade** them.
AP : 0 4 :321(157) [0209] of condignity — was made up to **evade** the Scriptures.
TR : 0 0 :056(330) [0521] rebuke the pope when he **evades** and obstructs true

Evaluate (6), Evaluated (2)
PR : PR :011(006) [0011] articles, examined, **evaluated**, and explained them in the
AP : 0 4 :290(151) [0203] A Christian can easily **evaluate** both modes, since both
AP : 0 4 :388(166) [0225] be easy for good men to **evaluate** if they remember,
AP : 0 4 :396(167) [0225] It is easy to **evaluate** their spirit, for in some doctrines
AP : 1 2 :125(201) [0289] How will the world **evaluate** the Confutation — if it is
AP : 2 4 :010(251) [0387] clear, it will be easy to **evaluate** the arguments both sides
LC : 0 4 :012(438) [0735] Here we must **evaluate** not the person according to the
SD : RN :003(504) [0851] all teachers and teachings are to be judged and **evaluated**.

Evangelical (24)
PR : PR :004(004) [0009] understanding of pure **evangelical** doctrine, and to make
PR : PR :008(005) [0011] the adversaries of pure **evangelical** doctrine would be
PR : PR :019(009) [0017] as concordant with **Evangelical** doctrine any false and
AG : 2 7 :061(080) [0083] means of fulfilling both **evangelical** counsels and
AL : 2 7 :054(079) [0083] They hear that it is an **evangelical** counsel not to take
AL : 2 7 :055(079) [0083] of Christians and in conflict with the **evangelical** counsel.
AP : 0 4 :261(145) [0195] a truly prophetic and **evangelical** voice which Daniel
AP : 0 7 :044(177) [0243] neither to destroy **evangelical** liberty nor to impose a
AP : 1 5 :038(220) [0325] we interpret them in an **evangelical** way, excluding the
AP : 1 6 :004(223) [0331] They called it an **evangelical** state to hold property in
AP : 1 6 :004(223) [0331] and they called it an **evangelical** counsel not to own
AP : 1 6 :007(223) [0331] is forbidden not as an **evangelical** counsel but as a
AP : 2 7 :009(270) [0421] Are they **"evangelical** perfection"?
AP : 2 7 :027(273) [0429] error to believe that **evangelical** perfection is to be found
AP : 2 7 :027(273) [0429] could boast that they have **evangelical** perfection.
AP : 2 7 :035(275) [0431] services," they are not **evangelical** perfection at all.
SD : PR :003(501) [0847] and the teaching of the **Evangelical** Christian churches
SD : PR :007(502) [0849] schisms in the true **Evangelical** churches, just as during
SD : RN :010(506) [0855] doctrine which all our **Evangelical** churches subscribe and
SD : RN :011(506) [0855] them, and that all **Evangelical** churches and schools
SD : 0 1 :056(518) [0877] dependable teacher of our pure **Evangelical** churches.
SD : 1 0 :007(611) [1055] discipline, nor **evangelical** decorum in the church, true
SD : 1 0 :009(612) [1055] Christian discipline, **evangelical** decorum, and the
SD : 1 2 :008(633) [1097] what called itself **evangelical** and was not papistic.

Evangelist (1), Evangelists (3)
TR : 0 0 :062(331) [0523] the time of Mark the **Evangelist** to the time of Bishops

Continued ▶

S C : 0 6 :004(351) [0555] Answer: The holy **evangelists** Matthew, Mark, and Luke,
S D : 0 7 :042(576) [0987] by the holy **evangelists** and apostles, and by their
S D : 0 7 :052(578) [0991] Therefore also all three **evangelists**, Matthew (26:26),

Evasion (1)
A P : 1 5 :030(219) [0323] use their customary **evasion** and say that Paul is talking

Evening (10), Eve (1)
A P : 0 4 :024(110) [0127] says, "Neither the **evening** star nor the morning star is
A P : 2 1 :011(230) [0345] about morning and **evening** knowledge, perhaps because
A P : 2 1 :011(230) [0345] whether they hear us in the morning or in the **evening**.
A P : 2 4 :008(250) [0385] the fourth day, on Sabbath **eve**, and on the Lord's day."
S C : 0 7 :000(352) [0557] [Morning and **Evening** Prayers]
S C : 0 7 :000(352) [0557] *teach his household to say morning and* ***evening*** *prayers*
S C : 0 7 :004(353) [0559] In the **evening**, when you retire, make the sign of the
L C : P R :003(358) [0567] morning, noon, and **evening** they would read, instead, at
L C : 0 1 :073(374) [0601] and saying other prayers for both morning and **evening**.
L C : 0 5 :047(452) [0765] a year, precisely on the **evening** of the fourteenth day of
L C : 0 5 :047(452) [0765] not just on this one **evening** of the year, but frequently,

Eve (6)
S 3 : 0 8 :005(312) [0495] the old serpent who made enthusiasts of Adam and **Eve**.
E P : 0 1 :004(466) [0781] and soul of Adam and **Eve** before the Fall, but also our
S D : 0 1 :009(510) [0861] disobedience of Adam and **Eve**, are in God's disfavor and
S D : 0 1 :027(512) [0867] in the case of Adam and **Eve** man's nature was originally
S D : 0 1 :027(513) [0867] Satan misled Adam and **Eve** through the Fall, and that by
S D : 1 1 :090(631) [1093] readily than Adam and **Eve** did in paradise — yes, would

Event (1), Events (4)
P R : P R :004(003) [0007] what very perilous **events** and troublesome disturbances
A G : 2 0 :025(045) [0057] a knowledge of historical **events** but is a confidence in
A G : 2 0 :026(045) [0057] a knowledge of historical **events** as the devil also
A P : 0 4 :312(155) [0207] hope is properly a future **event**, while faith deals with
A P : 0 7 :040(176) [0241] transmit to posterity the memory of these great **events**.

Eventually (5)
L C : 0 1 :047(371) [0593] and thread (for work, **eventually** to lay them aside) or as
L C : 0 1 :148(385) [0623] in your heart, and **eventually** you will have all kinds of
L C : 0 1 :184(390) [0633] cursing and blows, and **eventually** calamity and murder.
L C : 0 3 :111(435) [0729] will see the temptation cease and **eventually** admit defeat.
L C : 0 5 :053(453) [0765] more callous and cold, and **eventually** spurn it altogether.

Everlasting (9)
A G : 1 7 :002(038) [0051] to give eternal life and **everlasting** joy to believers and the
S C : 0 2 :004(345) [0545] and serve him in **everlasting** righteousness, innocence, and
S C : 0 2 :005(345) [0545] *sins, the resurrection of the body, and the life* ***everlasting***.
L C : S P :013(363) [0577] sins, the resurrection of the body, and the life **everlasting**.
L C : 0 2 :034(415) [0687] *sins, the resurrection of the body, and the life* ***everlasting***.
L C : 0 2 :037(415) [0687] sins, the resurrection of the body, and the life **everlasting**.
L C : 0 2 :041(416) [0689] the resurrection of the body, and the life **everlasting**."
S D : 0 7 :062(581) [0995] righteousness, and **everlasting** life), is presented — and
S D : 0 8 :085(608) [1047] called the almighty and **everlasting** God, who by virtue of

Evidence (15), Evident (54), Evidently (4)
A G : 1 8 :004(039) [0051] In order that it may be **evident** that this teaching is no
A G : 2 2 :010(050) [0061] It is **evident** that such a custom, introduced contrary to
A G : 2 7 :038(077) [0081] It is quite **evident** that the monks have taught and
A G : 0 0 :005(095) [0095] For it is manifest and **evident** (to speak without boasting)
A L : 2 2 :009(050) [0061] But it is **evident** that a custom introduced contrary to the
A L : 2 3 :010(052) [0061] It is also **evident** that in the ancient church priests were
A L : 2 4 :010(057) [0065] However, it is **evident** that for a long time there has been
A L : 2 6 :002(064) [0071] the world thought so is **evident** from the fact that new
A L : 2 7 :038(077) [0081] It is **evident** that the monks have taught that their
A L : 2 8 :031(085) [0087] right to bishops cite as **evidence** the passage, "I have yet
A L : 2 8 :037(086) [0089] It is also **evident** that as a result of this notion traditions
A P : P R :016(099) [0101] our danger; its extent is **evident** from the bitter hatred
A P : 0 2 :023(103) [0111] From this it is **evident** that the ancient definition says just
A P : 0 2 :031(104) [0113] but on so clear an issue there is no need of **evidence**.
A P : 0 2 :032(104) [0113] Modern theologians have **evidently** not paid attention to
A P : 0 4 :039(112) [0131] compel us to cite further **evidence**; this will also help
A P : 0 4 :130(125) [0157] the Holy Spirit; this is **evident** from what we have already
A P : 0 4 :161(129) [0167] it is more clearly **evident** now that this incipient keeping
A P : 0 4 :182(132) [0171] From this it is **evident** that we are justified before God by
A P : 0 4 :195(134) [0175] This is **evident** in terrors of conscience, for we cannot set
A P : 0 4 :198(134) [0175] than the rewards, as is **evident** in Job, in Christ, and in
A P : 0 4 :208(135) [0177] in these places and thus gave **evidence** of their faith.
A P : 0 4 :258(144) [0193] This is **evident** in Isaiah's preaching of penitence: "Cease
A P : 0 4 :298(153) [0205] things are so clear and **evident** that we are astonished to
A P : 0 4 :314(155) [0207] It is **evident** that not with love but with faith we
A P : 0 4 :337(159) [0215] very voice of faith, as is **evident** from the example of
A P : 0 4 :367(163) [0221] degree of the reward is **evidently** commensurate with the
A P : 0 4 :373(164) [0221] is cited as fruit and **evidence** of the righteousness of the
A P : 0 7 :016(170) [0231] It is **evident**, moreover, that the wicked are in the power
A P : 0 7 :036(175) [0241] It is **evident** that human traditions do not quicken the
A P : 0 7 :037(175) [0241] to cite a great deal of **evidence** since it is obvious
A P : 0 9 :003(178) [0245] Secondly, since it is **evident** that God approves the
A P : 1 0 :002(179) [0247] **Evidence** for this is their canon of the Mass, in which the
A P : 1 2 :059(190) [0267] Since it is **evident** that we have said enough about this
A P : 1 2 :113(199) [0285] they had given public **evidence** of their penitence, as far
A P : 1 5 :044(221) [0327] of our churches it is **evident** that we diligently maintain
A P : 1 5 :052(222) [0329] we have shown ample **evidence** of our willingness to
A P : 1 6 :008(223) [0333] these matters has been is **evident** from their erroneous
A P : 2 0 :015(229) [0343] already given ample **evidence** of our conviction that good
A P : 2 1 :011(230) [0345] **Evidently** some attribute divinity to the saints, the power
A P : 2 2 :004(236) [0359] It is **evident**, therefore, that the entire sacrament was
A P : 2 2 :009(237) [0359] this is a human device and its purpose is quite **evident**.
A P : 2 3 :044(245) [0375] But it is all too **evident** that the great crowd of lazy
A P : 2 3 :063(248) [0381] The real author is **evident** in the results, the many
A P : 2 4 :035(256) [0397] with allegories, but it is **evident** that allegory does not
A P : 2 7 :043(276) [0433] It is **evident**, therefore, that they wickedly twist the saying
A P : 2 8 :004(281) [0445] In these **evident** questions they set forth an edict written
T R : 0 0 :016(322) [0509] It is **evident** that the kingdom of Christ is scattered over
T R : 0 0 :058(330) [0521] weighty, compelling, and **evident** reasons for not
T R : 0 0 :061(330) [0521] our adversaries, it is **evident** that this power belongs by
T R : 0 0 :072(332) [0525] From all these facts it is **evident** that the church retains
T R : 0 0 :074(332) [0525] For it is **evident** that the officials (as they are called) have
L C : P R :016(361) [0571] They **evidently** consider themselves much wiser than God
L C : 0 1 :069(374) [0599] It is **evident** that the world today is more wicked than it
L C : 0 1 :207(393) [0639] woman differently (as is **evident**) not for lewdness but to
L C : 0 1 :243(397) [0649] Indeed, we have the **evidence** before our very eyes every
L C : 0 1 :259(400) [0655] to everything but the **evidence** presented, and make his
L C : 0 1 :279(403) [0661] may be confirmed by the **evidence** of two or three
L C : 0 5 :021(449) [0757] This is plainly **evident** from the words just quoted, "This
E P : 0 3 :017(475) [0795] repent and gives no **evidence** of resulting love, but
E P : 0 4 :018(477) [0801] in good works as an **evidence** of their faith and their
S D : 0 1 :044(516) [0873] but not original sin, it is **evident** that even after the Fall
S D : 0 1 :048(516) [0875] From this it is **evident** that we must reject this doctrine
S D : 0 2 :018(524) [0887] From this it is **evident**, as we have pointed out at greater
S D : 0 2 :070(534) [0909] It is, of course, self-**evident** that in true conversion there
S D : 0 2 :086(538) [0913] It is **evident** from the preceding discussion that this
S D : 0 2 :090(539) [0915] previous explanation it is **evident** that conversion to God
S D : 0 4 :014(553) [0943] In the first place, it is **evident** that in discussing the
S D : 0 4 :035(557) [0949] Since it is **evident** from the Word of God that faith is the
S D : 0 7 :067(581) [0997] From these it is **evident** how unjustly and poisonously the
S D : 0 8 :045(600) [1031] From this it is **evident** that it is wrongly put to say or to
S D : 0 8 :061(602) [1035] From this it is **evident** that we do not confuse, equalize,
S D : 1 1 :091(631) [1093] malice, then it is clearly **evident** that this teaching is not

Evil (162), Evildoers (1), Evils (11)
A G : 0 1 :005(028) [0043] gods, one good and one **evil**; also that of the
A G : 0 2 :001(029) [0043] That is, all men are full of **evil** lust and inclinations from
A G : 1 6 :002(037) [0051] existing laws, punish **evildoers** with the sword, engage in
A G : 1 8 :002(039) [0051] heart, or of expelling inborn **evil** lusts from his heart.
A G : 1 8 :004(040) [0051] of this life that they have freedom to choose good or **evil**.
A G : 1 8 :007(040) [0053] man can also undertake **evil**, as when he wills to kneel
A G : 1 9 :000(041) [0053] his support, the will turns away from God to **evil**.
A G : 2 0 :037(046) [0057] are commanded, render obedience, avoid **evil** lusts, etc.
A G : 2 3 :013(053) [0063] occasion for many great and **evil** vices and much scandal.
A G : 2 7 :008(072) [0077] must also have seen what **evils** came from this
A L : 0 1 :005(028) [0043] one good and the other **evil**, and also those of the
A L : 0 8 :001(033) [0047] life many hypocrites and **evil** persons are mingled with
A L : 0 8 :001(033) [0047] they are administered by **evil** men, according to the saying
A L : 0 8 :002(033) [0047] of Christ even if they are administered by **evil** men.
A L : 0 8 :003(033) [0047] denied that the ministry of **evil** men may be used in the
A L : 0 8 :003(033) [0047] thought the ministry of **evil** men to be unprofitable and
A L : 1 8 :004(039) [0051] of this life that they have freedom to choose good or **evil**.
A L : 1 8 :007(040) [0053] On the other hand, by '**evil**' I mean such things as to will
A L : 2 7 :010(072) [0077] To these **evils** was added the fact that vows had such a
A P : 0 2 :002(100) [0105] That is, all men are full of **evil** lusts and inclinations from
A P : 0 2 :005(101) [0107] bear because of his guilt, without any **evil** of their own.
A P : 0 2 :006(101) [0107] our disagreement with this **evil** doctrine, we made
A P : 0 2 :007(101) [0107] that the inclination to **evil** is a quality of the body; in
A P : 0 2 :008(101) [0107] These **evils**, which are most contrary to the law of God,
A P : 0 2 :025(103) [0111] constitution, but the **evil** inclination of man's higher
A P : 0 2 :030(104) [0113] lust at work in our members and bringing forth **evil** fruit.
A P : 0 2 :042(105) [0115] that the inclination to **evil** is a neutral thing, not only will
A P : 0 2 :043(106) [0117] It is no wiser to say that nature is not **evil**.
A P : 0 2 :050(106) [0119] we cannot know his blessings unless we recognize our **evil**.
A P : 0 4 :146(127) [0163] continually brings forth **evil** desires, though the Spirit in
A P : 0 4 :168(130) [0169] the good I want, but the **evil** I do not want is what I do."
A P : 0 4 :169(130) [0169] who do not believe that **evil** desires in the flesh are sins,
A P : 0 4 :200(134) [0175] wicked, whose works are **evil**, and the wrath of God is
A P : 0 4 :258(144) [0193] of penitence: "Cease to do **evil**, learn to do good; seek
A P : 0 4 :258(144) [0193] he says, "Cease to do **evil**," as he denounces ungodly
A P : 0 4 :301(153) [0205] nature so many terrible **evils**, sufferings in this life and the
A P : 0 7 :003(168) [0227] that we separate **evil** men and hypocrites from the
A P : 0 7 :003(168) [0227] to the sacraments which **evil** men or hypocrites
A P : 0 7 :003(169) [0227] this life the hypocrites and **evil** men are mingled with the
A P : 0 7 :003(169) [0227] they are administered by **evil** men; indeed, we may
A P : 0 7 :003(169) [0227] use sacraments that are administered by **evil** men.
A P : 0 7 :012(170) [0231] Hypocrites and **evil** men are indeed associated with the
A P : 0 7 :014(170) [0231] Nevertheless, these **evil** people did not please God.
A P : 0 7 :019(171) [0233] of the kingdom, the weeds are the sons of the **evil** one."
A P : 0 7 :028(173) [0237] the many hypocrites and **evil** men who are mingled with
A P : 0 7 :047(177) [0243] that hypocrites and **evil** men have been mingled with the
A P : 0 7 :047(177) [0243] are efficacious even when **evil** men administer them, for
A P : 1 2 :091(195) [0279] means to lament past **evils** and not to commit again deeds
A P : 1 2 :164(208) [0303] Isa. 1:16-19 teaches: "Cease to do **evil**, learn to do good.
A P : 1 2 :165(208) [0303] to teach that our common **evils** are mitigated by our
A P : 1 8 :005(225) [0335] that men obey their **evil** impulses more often than their
A P : 2 3 :047(246) [0377] The origin of this **evil** is the exaggerated way the monks
A P : 2 7 :009(270) [0421] if they openly point to an **evil** end, either because
A P : 2 7 :063(280) [0441] not even discuss the other **evils** inherent in present-day
A P : 2 8 :023(285) [0451] for Christ's sake, brings enough good to hide all the **evils**.
A P : 2 8 :026(285) [0451] What **evil** there is in the sacrilegious desecration of the
S 2 : 0 2 :001(293) [0463] (even when offered by an **evil** scoundrel) delivers men
S 2 : 0 2 :007(293) [0463] work, even a work of **evil** scoundrels (as the cannon and
S 2 : 0 2 :016(295) [0467] is a consequence of this: **evil** spirits have introduced the
S 3 : 0 1 :002(302) [0477] sin are all the subsequent **evil** deeds which are forbidden
S 3 : 0 1 :005(302) [0477] do good and refrain from **evil** or to refrain from good and
S 3 : 0 1 :005(302) [0477] and refrain from evil or to refrain from good and do **evil**.
S 3 : 0 1 :009(302) [0477] that he does not have an **evil** intention to commit sin, for
S 3 : 0 2 :002(303) [0479] and wicked people who do **evil** whenever they have
S 3 : 0 3 :011(305) [0481] which they consented (for **evil** impulses, lust, and
S 3 : 0 3 :028(308) [0487] chapters fought against **evil** thoughts by fasting, vigils,
S 3 : 0 3 :028(308) [0487] and yet the hereditary **evil** which is born in us did what is
S 3 : 0 3 :029(308) [0487] to repent of when they did not consent to **evil** thoughts?
S 3 : 0 3 :029(308) [0487] should they confess when they refrained from **evil** words?
S 3 : 0 3 :029(308) [0487] when they were innocent of **evil** deeds and could even sell
T R : 0 0 :074(332) [0525] or on account of other **evil** desires, have tormented men
S C : P R :020(340) [0537] plain to them the shocking **evils** they introduce when they
S C : P R :023(341) [0539] in so much that is **evil** and was in need of so much that is
S C : P R :023(341) [0539] is afforded against such **evil** and in which such good is
S C : 0 2 :002(345) [0543] me from all danger, and preserves me from all **evil**.
S C : 0 3 :011(347) [0547] curbs and destroys every **evil** counsel and purpose of the
S C : 0 3 :019(348) [0549] *"But deliver us from* ***evil***.*"*

Continued ▶

S C : 0 3 :020(348) [0549] us from all manner of **evil**, whether it affect body or soul,
S C : 0 4 :012(349) [0551] together with all sins and **evil** lusts, should be drowned by
S C : 0 5 :020(350) [0553] stolen, neglected, or wasted anything, or done other **evil**.
S C : 0 5 :023(350) [0555] my neighbor by speaking **evil** of him, overcharging him,
S C : 0 7 :002(352) [0557] day, too, from all sin and **evil**, that in all my thoughts,
L C : P R :010(359) [0569] world, the flesh, and all **evil** thoughts as to occupy
L C : P R :011(360) [0571] you obtain from it is to rout the devil and **evil** thoughts.
L C : P R :014(360) [0571] a good antidote against their **evil** infection and poison.
L C : S P :014(363) [0577] and lead us not into temptation, but deliver us from **evil**.
L C : 0 1 :024(367) [0587] is he who protects us from **evil**, he who saves and delivers
L C : 0 1 :024(368) [0587] evil, he who saves and delivers us when any **evil** befalls.
L C : 0 1 :024(368) [0587] that is good and by whom we are delivered from all **evil**.
L C : 0 1 :066(373) [0599] not to swear in support of **evil** (that is, to a falsehood) or
L C : 0 1 :066(373) [0599] and separates right from wrong, good from **evil**.
L C : 0 1 :103(379) [0611] in support of lies or any **evil** purpose whatsoever, but use
L C : 0 1 :128(382) [0617] Especially when an **evil** hour comes do we rage and
L C : 0 1 :181(389) [0631] his authority of punishing **evil**-doers to civil magistrates in
L C : 0 1 :183(389) [0633] well knows, the world is **evil** and this life is full of misery.
L C : 0 1 :183(389) [0633] commandments as a boundary between good and **evil**.
L C : 0 1 :186(390) [0633] harm another for any **evil** deed, no matter how much he
L C : 0 1 :188(390) [0635] soul, especially toward him who wishes or does you **evil**.
L C : 0 1 :188(390) [0635] For to do **evil** to somebody who desires and does you
L C : 0 1 :189(390) [0635] a person actually does **evil**, but also when he fails to do
L C : 0 1 :214(394) [0641] do even worse — things too **evil** to mention, as
L C : 0 1 :215(394) [0641] of unchaste thoughts and **evil** desires that they suffer
L C : 0 1 :264(400) [0655] would rather hear **evil** than good about his neighbor.
L C : 0 1 :264(400) [0655] **Evil** though we are, we cannot tolerate having evil spoken
L C : 0 1 :264(400) [0655] we cannot tolerate having **evil** spoken of us; we want the
L C : 0 1 :269(401) [0657] God forbids you to speak **evil** about another even
L C : 0 1 :274(401) [0659] we are absolutely forbidden to speak **evil** of our neighbor.
L C : 0 1 :274(402) [0659] in such a way that **evil** shall not go unpunished.
L C : 0 1 :274(402) [0659] good but only harm and **evil**, yet he does not sin against
L C : 0 1 :275(402) [0659] requires one to report **evil**, to prefer charges, to attest,
L C : 0 1 :275(402) [0659] obligation to reprove **evil** where it is necessary and
L C : 0 1 :278(402) [0661] thing to say, for the **evil** would be corrected and the
L C : 0 1 :285(403) [0661] No one shall speak **evil** of him, whether truly or falsely,
L C : 0 1 :289(404) [0663] as it is not a notorious **evil**, and to defend him against the
L C : 0 2 :017(412) [0681] defends us against every **evil** and misfortune, warding off
L C : 0 2 :017(412) [0681] kind father who cares for us so that no **evil** may befall us.
L C : 0 2 :027(414) [0685] me from sin, from the devil, from death, and from all **evil**.
L C : 0 2 :028(414) [0685] came and led us into disobedience, sin, death, and all **evil**.
L C : 0 2 :036(415) [0687] as the spirit of man, heavenly spirits, and the **evil** spirit.
L C : 0 2 :044(416) [0689] Men and **evil** spirits there were, teaching us to obtain
L C : 0 2 :058(418) [0693] from sin, death, and all **evil**, living in new, immortal and
L C : 0 2 :062(419) [0695] died to the world and all **evil**, he will finally make us
L C : 0 3 :042(425) [0709] also profaned by an openly **evil** life and wicked works,
L C : 0 3 :051(427) [0711] and salvation against sin, death, and an **evil** conscience.
L C : 0 3 :063(428) [0715] itself vile and inclined to **evil**, even when we have accepted
L C : 0 3 :089(432) [0723] is constantly aroused by **evil** desires and devices, so that
L C : 0 3 :102(434) [0727] in short, into all kinds of **evil** lusts which by nature cling
L C : 0 3 :112(435) [0729] *"But deliver us from **evil**.*
L C : 0 3 :113(435) [0729] or keep us from the **Evil** One, or the Wicked One."
L C : 0 3 :113(435) [0729] the devil as the sum of all **evil** in order that the entire
L C : 0 3 :115(435) [0731] petition includes all the **evil** that may befall us under the
L C : 0 3 :118(436) [0731] and delivered from all **evil**, his name must first be
L C : 0 4 :054(443) [0745] deceitfully and with an **evil** purpose, and we baptized him
L C : 0 4 :055(443) [0745] approaches it with an **evil** purpose, and he would not be
L C : 0 4 :069(445) [0749] proverb says very truly, "**Evil** unchecked becomes worse
L C : 0 5 :022(449) [0757] has provided for me against my sins, death, and all **evils**.
L C : 0 5 :070(454) [0769] and power against death and the devil and all **evils**.
E P : R N :007(465) [0779] be understood and judged as good or **evil**, right or wrong.
E P : 0 1 :012(467) [0781] Likewise the teaching that **evil** desires are not sin but
E P : 0 1 :021(468) [0783] such a way that even if no **evil** thought would ever arise in
E P : 0 1 :021(468) [0785] other, actual sins, such as **evil** thoughts, words, and
E P : 0 1 :021(469) [0785] "Out of the heart come **evil** thoughts," etc, and "The
E P : 0 1 :021(469) [0785] "The imagination of man's heart is **evil** from his youth."
E P : 0 2 :003(470) [0787] wills only that which is **evil** and opposed to God, as it is
E P : 0 2 :003(470) [0787] "The imagination of man's heart is **evil** from his youth."
E P : 0 2 :008(471) [0789] acts, and that he commits **evil** deeds and acts like
E P : 1 1 :004(494) [0833] extends alike over good people and **evil** people.
E P : 1 1 :004(494) [0833] But it is not a cause of **evil** or of sin which compels
E P : 1 1 :004(495) [0833] merely controls the **evil** and imposes a limit on its
E P : 1 1 :013(496) [0835] God but are inspired by the **evil** foe in an attempt to
S D : 0 1 :002(508) [0859] and is turned to everything **evil**, and that, because of this
S D : 0 1 :006(509) [0861] a man were to think no **evil**, speak no evil, or do no evil
S D : 0 1 :006(509) [0861] to think no evil, speak no **evil**, or do no evil — which after
S D : 0 1 :006(509) [0861] speak no evil, or do no **evil** — which after the Fall of our
S D : 0 1 :011(510) [0863] uncleanness of the heart and **evil** desires and inclinations.
S D : 0 1 :027(513) [0867] made something essentially **evil** and blended this with
S D : 0 1 :029(513) [0867] of God, and only the original sin which dwells in it is **evil**.
S D : 0 1 :032(513) [0869] because we are sinful and **evil**; not because and in so far
S D : 0 1 :042(515) [0873] words, and deeds are **evil**, is in its origin the handiwork
S D : 0 2 :017(523) [0887] turned and perverted against God and toward all **evil**.
S D : 0 2 :017(524) [0887] of man's heart is **evil** from his youth" (Gen. 8:21).
S D : 0 2 :019(524) [0889] a conception of good or **evil** or freely choose to act or not
S D : 0 2 :032(527) [0893] An **evil** tree cannot bear good fruit, and without faith no
S D : 0 2 :033(527) [0893] to do good and to avoid **evil**," and shortly thereafter,
S D : 0 4 :031(556) [0947] a Christian follows his **evil** lusts without fear and shame,
S D : 0 6 :008(565) [0965] the good I want, but the **evil** I do not want is what I do."
S D : 1 1 :004(616) [1063] foreknowledge — extends to all creatures, good or **evil**.
S D : 1 1 :004(617) [1063] will happen, both good and **evil**, since all things, present
S D : 1 1 :006(617) [1065] and knows in advance the **evil** as well, but not in such a
S D : 1 1 :006(617) [1065] a limit and measure for the **evil** which he does not will —
S D : 1 1 :007(617) [1065] The source and cause of **evil** is not God's foreknowledge
S D : 1 1 :007(617) [1065] neither creates nor works **evil**, nor does he help it along
S D : 1 1 :072(628) [1087] If you then, who are **evil**, know how to give good gifts to
S D : 1 2 :021(634) [1099] conscience impose the death penalty on **evil**-doers.

Evoked (1)
S D : 0 3 :005(540) [0917] were occasioned and **evoked** by the Interim and

Evolved (1)
S 3 : 0 3 :018(306) [0483] and imaginary idea **evolved** by man's own powers

Exact (1), Exacted (1), Exactly (9)
A L : 2 6 :002(064) [0071] men in the churches **exacted** these works as a service
A P : 0 2 :015(102) [0109] the old definition says **exactly** the same thing, "Original
A P : 0 4 :241(141) [0187] It teaches **exactly** the same thing as Paul's statement in
A P : 1 5 :045(221) [0327] of the flesh we teach **exactly** what we said in the
A P : 2 3 :001(239) [0363] This is **exactly** what they say.
L C : 0 1 :047(371) [0593] using all of God's gifts **exactly** as a cobbler uses his
L C : 0 1 :324(409) [0675] This is **exactly** the meaning and right interpretation of the
L C : 0 3 :045(426) [0709] this petition we pray for **exactly** the same thing that God
E P : 0 4 :012(477) [0799] should be understood **exactly** as our Lord and the
S D : 0 7 :017(572) [0979] which agree in the most **exact** way with the words of
S D : 1 1 :055(625) [1081] is also aware and knows **exactly** how many there will be

Exaggerate (2), Exaggerated (1), Exaggerating (1), Exaggeration (2), Exaggerations (1)
A L : 2 7 :017(073) [0077] things without odious **exaggeration** in order that our
A L : 2 7 :022(074) [0079] **Exaggerate** the obligation of a vow as much as one
A L : 2 7 :027(075) [0079] why do our adversaries **exaggerate** the obligation or
A P : 2 2 :005(236) [0359] We are not **exaggerating** here, but we leave it to the
A P : 2 3 :047(246) [0377] origin of this evil is the **exaggerated** way the monks have
A P : 2 7 :047(277) [0437] It is an **exaggeration** to praise it the way the *Extravagant*
S D : 0 4 :036(557) [0949] led to many offensive **exaggerations**, it is safest to follow

Exalt (6), Exaltation (8), Exalted (25), Exalting (1), Exalts (5)
P R : P R :021(010) [0019] right hand of God and is **exalted**, our theologians declare
A G : 2 6 :008(065) [0071] for these traditions were **exalted** far above God's
A G : 2 7 :022(074) [0079] no matter how highly one **exalts** them, it is still
A G : 2 7 :047(078) [0081] Certainly this is **exaltation** of works as a means of
A G : 2 7 :051(079) [0083] from such false **exaltation** of monastic life, for it follows
A L : 2 6 :004(064) [0071] for Christ's sake may be **exalted** far above works and
A L : 2 6 :008(065) [0071] God, for traditions were **exalted** far above the commands
A P : 0 4 :245(142) [0189] he does not omit faith nor **exalt** love in preference to it,
A P : 1 3 :016(213) [0311] so to speak, a more **exalted** position, this would move
S 2 : 0 4 :011(300) [0475] what St. Paul calls **exalting** oneself over and against
S 2 : 0 4 :014(301) [0475] all Christians who do not **exalt** and honor these
T R : 0 0 :036(326) [0515] of Christ, but he even **exalted** himself tyrannically over
T R : 0 0 :039(327) [0515] Christ who opposes and **exalts** himself against every
T R : 0 0 :040(327) [0517] or by anybody, and he **exalts** his authority above the
S C : 0 9 :012(356) [0563] of God, that in due time he may **exalt** you" (I Pet. 5:5, 6).
L C : 0 1 :018(367) [0585] in power and dominion **exalted** Jupiter as their supreme
L C : 0 1 :028(368) [0587] take care to magnify and **exalt** this commandment above
L C : 0 1 :126(382) [0617] For God has **exalted** this estate of parents above all
L C : 0 1 :133(383) [0619] St. Paul also highly **exalts** and praises this
L C : 0 1 :139(384) [0621] since he so highly **exalts** it, so greatly delights in it, so
L C : 0 1 :195(391) [0637] urge us to true, noble, **exalted** deeds, such as gentleness,
L C : 0 1 :333(410) [0677] are to be **exalted** and extolled above all orders,
L C : 0 3 :048(426) [0711] have his glory and praise **exalted** above everything else
L C : 0 3 :049(426) [0711] and life so that he may be praised and **exalted** is us.
L C : 0 4 :007(437) [0733] we regard Baptism as excellent, glorious, and **exalted**.
L C : 0 4 :021(439) [0737] you should honor and **exalt** Baptism on account of the
L C : 0 6 :018(459) [0000] value on our work but **exalt** and magnify God's Word.
E P : 0 8 :009(488) [0819] union and the resultant **exalted** and ineffable sharing
E P : 0 8 :013(488) [0821] into heaven, and was **exalted** to the majesty and
E P : 0 8 :015(488) [0821] is, in deed and in truth) **exalted** to the right hand of the
E P : 0 8 :035(491) [0825] that through the **exaltation** the human nature of Christ
S D : 0 7 :101(587) [1007] according to this **exalted** third mode, where they cannot
S D : 0 8 :012(593) [1019] afterward through the **exaltation** or glorification, it has
S D : 0 8 :013(593) [1019] majesty, to which he was **exalted** according to his
S D : 0 8 :026(596) [1023] from the dead, its **exaltation** above all creatures in heaven
S D : 0 8 :030(597) [1025] union they have such an **exalted**, intimate, and ineffable
S D : 0 8 :034(597) [1027] in Christ, because of this **exalted** mystery, "become
S D : 0 8 :051(600) [1031] it was glorified and **exalted** to the right hand of the
S D : 0 8 :051(601) [1033] through the personal union, glorification, and **exaltation**.
S D : 0 8 :053(601) [1033] union, glorification, or **exaltation** according to his
S D : 0 8 :066(604) [1039] *and through* the assumed **exalted** human nature of
S D : 0 8 :067(604) [1039] nature of Christ has been **exalted** either as if this divine
S D : 0 8 :074(606) [1043] given to him, and he is **exalted** to the right hand of the
S D : 0 9 :003(610) [1051] concern ourselves with **exalted** and acute speculations
S D : 1 2 :029(635) [1101] teach that through the **exaltation** Christ's flesh assumed

Examination (3), Examinations (1), Examine (15), Examined (11)
P R : P R :011(006) [0011] controverted articles, **examined**, evaluated, and explained
A G : 2 5 :001(061) [0069] who have not previously been **examined** and absolved.
A L : 2 4 :006(056) [0065] are admitted unless they are first heard and **examined**.
A L : 2 5 :001(061) [0069] those who have been previously **examined** and absolved.
A P : 0 4 :282(149) [0201] An **examination** of the whole passage shows that it
A P : 1 0 :001(179) [0247] After careful **examination** and consideration of it, we
A P : 1 1 :009(181) [0251] know how profitable it is to **examine** the inexperienced.
A P : 1 2 :110(198) [0285] maintain that some **examination** is useful to instruct men
A P : 1 2 :127(201) [0291] because you refuse to **examine** these questions and
A P : 1 2 :129(202) [0291] that these issues be **examined** and settled now in order to
A P : 1 5 :040(220) [0325] after they have been instructed, **examined**, and absolved.
A P : 1 5 :041(220) [0325] required to instruct and **examine** the youth publicly, a
A P : 2 0 :012(228) [0341] our article, and it is worthwhile to **examine** some of these.
A P : 2 2 :003(236) [0359] on he says, "Let a man **examine** himself, and so eat of the
A P : 2 4 :001(249) [0385] wish for it after they have been **examined** and absolved.
A P : 2 4 :049(258) [0401] this only when they have been instructed and **examined**.
S 3 : 0 3 :018(306) [0483] If we **examine** this in the light, we see that such contrition
S 3 : 0 8 :001(312) [0495] people who need to be **examined** and instructed in
T R : 0 0 :051(329) [0519] and murders, and he forbids a judicial **examinations**.
L C : P R :002(358) [0567] books, or if they have them, to **examine** and read them.
L C : S P :004(362) [0575] head of a household to **examine** his children and servants
L C : 0 1 :028(368) [0587] Search and **examine** your own heart thoroughly and you
L C : 0 1 :275(402) [0659] evil, to prefer charges, to attest, **examine**, and witness.
L C : 0 1 :275(402) [0659] sometimes compelled to **examine** and handle his private
L C : 0 3 :090(432) [0723] others he should **examine** himself in the light of this
L C : 0 5 :050(452) [0765] ever move you to **examine** your inner life and reflect: "See
L C : 0 5 :054(453) [0765] To avoid this, we must **examine** our heart and conscience
L C : 0 5 :083(456) [0773] Just **examine** yourself, look around a little, cling to the
E P : 0 2 :002(470) [0787] them" when he is **examined** concerning spiritual things.
S D : 0 7 :030(574) [0981] the Scriptures, have **examined** them again and again in

Example (85), Examples (24)
A G : 2 1 :001(046) [0057] good works are to be an **example** for us, each of us in his

Continued ▶

AG : 21 :001(046) [0057] fashion imitate the **example** of David in making war on
AG : 26 :010(065) [0071] to his calling — for **example**, that a husband should labor
AG : 26 :045(070) [0075] Book 9, gathers many **examples** of dissimilar church
AG : 28 :029(085) [0087] in various matters (for **example**, in matrimonial cases and
AG : 28 :032(085) [0087] They also cite the **example** in Acts 15:20, 29, where the
AG : 28 :040(087) [0089] bishops were misled by the **example** of the law of Moses.
AG : 28 :041(087) [0089] came into being — for **example**, that it is a mortal sin to
AG : 28 :060(091) [0093] people might have an **example** of Christian liberty and
AL : 21 :001(046) [0057] emperor may follow the **example** of David in waging war
AL : 22 :003(049) [0059] I Cor. 11:20ff. cites an **example** from which it appears
AL : 22 :010(050) [0061] to ancient canons and the **example** of the church.
AL : 24 :040(060) [0069] us is supported by the **example** of the church as seen from
AL : 26 :010(065) [0071] without honor — for **example**, that a father should bring
AL : 26 :045(070) [0075] History, Book 9, many **examples** of dissimilar rites are
AL : 27 :026(075) [0079] monastery, and there is no want of **examples** in our time.
AL : 28 :029(085) [0087] to decide legal cases (for **example**, pertaining to
AL : 28 :032(086) [0087] They also cite the **example** of the apostles who
AL : 28 :040(087) [0089] to have been misled by the **example** of the law of Moses.
AL : 28 :060(091) [0093] that men would have an **example** of Christian liberty and
AP : 04 :058(115) [0137] belong here; for **example**, "If thou, O Lord, shouldst
AP : 04 :154(128) [0165] that this truly powerful **example** moved Christ to chide
AP : 04 :154(128) [0165] and reproves him with the **example** of the woman.
AP : 04 :208(135) [0177] The **examples** of the saints call forth imitation in those
AP : 04 :276(148) [0199] the Lord's Supper, for **example**, are signs that constantly
AP : 04 :337(159) [0215] as is evident from the **example** of Daniel referred to
AP : 07 :011(170) [0229] For **example**, Jerome says, "Therefore the sinner who has
AP : 07 :040(176) [0241] we must consult their writings, not merely their **example**.
AP : 07 :040(176) [0241] so that by these **examples** as well as by instruction they
AP : 07 :043(177) [0243] others to follow the **example** of the chief brethren who
AP : 12 :091(195) [0279] For **example**. "Penitence means to lament past evils and
AP : 12 :107(197) [0283] from time to time; for **example** (Ps. 32:5), "I said, 'I will
AP : 12 :113(199) [0285] the lapsed served as an **example**, as the gloss on the
AP : 12 :117(199) [0287] of the scholastics; for **example**, in defining satisfaction
AP : 12 :120(200) [0287] had been instituted as an **example** and to test those who
AP : 12 :156(207) [0301] God imposes only on them, for the sake of **example**.
AP : 12 :166(208) [0303] Here the **example** of the Ninevites is a case in point.
AP : 12 :167(208) [0303] the sake of setting an **example**; they did not think that
AP : 13 :015(213) [0311] they have God's command, as, for **example**, government.
AP : 15 :020(218) [0321] they provided an **example** of how all things could be done
AP : 15 :024(218) [0321] Then there are the **examples** of the saints; when men
AP : 15 :034(220) [0325] By precept and **example** the apostles compel us to oppose
AP : 15 :036(220) [0325] this was to serve as an **example** to the Pharisees of the
AP : 21 :002(229) [0343] They cite this **example** to prove the invocation of the
AP : 21 :004(229) [0343] thank God for showing **examples** of his mercy, revealing
AP : 21 :010(230) [0345] nor a promise nor an **example** can be shown from
AP : 21 :013(230) [0345] Since they refer to the **example** of the church, we reply
AP : 21 :018(231) [0347] But what precept or **example** can our opponents produce
AP : 21 :021(232) [0349] promise nor a command nor an **example** from Scripture.
AP : 21 :024(232) [0349] Let him produce one **example** or precept from Scripture.
AP : 21 :027(232) [0349] as Christ but to have her **example** considered and
AP : 21 :031(233) [0351] a Word of God nor an **example** from Scripture for this.
AP : 21 :036(234) [0353] have done serve as **examples** to men in their public or
AP : 21 :036(234) [0353] hear of these things and to see some **examples** of mercy.
AP : 21 :036(234) [0353] be useful to recall such **examples** as these which talk
AP : 21 :037(234) [0353] bring only superstitious **examples** of certain prayers,
AP : 22 :007(237) [0359] produce any ancient **examples** to prove their fiction that
AP : 23 :055(247) [0379] the strictest laws and **examples** and to invite men to it.
AP : 24 :072(262) [0409] for the sake of **example**, the way plays celebrate the
AP : 24 :083(264) [0413] Greek authors can find **examples** everywhere of their use
AP : 24 :089(266) [0415] of God and the **example** of Scripture, and to apply to the
AP : 27 :046(277) [0435] Such **examples** have nothing to do with Christian
AP : 27 :049(277) [0437] This sets forth the **example** of obedience in a calling.
AP : 27 :049(277) [0437] and persons; but the **example** of obedience is universal.
AP : 27 :058(279) [0439] quote against us the **example** of the Nazarites from the
AP : 27 :059(279) [0439] Yes, indeed, the **example** of the Rechabites is a beautiful
AP : 27 :060(279) [0441] Besides, **examples** ought to be interpreted according to
AP : 27 :063(280) [0441] Thus the **example** of the Rechabites does not resemble
S3 : 03 :017(306) [0483] Here the **example** of St. Bernard, etc. was cited.
S3 : 03 :028(308) [0487] true, and there are seals, letters, and **examples** to show it.
S3 : 10 :003(314) [0497] as we are taught by the **examples** of the ancient churches
TR : 00 :049(329) [0519] much more impudently by the pontiffs, as **examples** show.
TR : 00 :067(331) [0523] It is like the **example** which Augustine relates of two
SC : PR :018(340) [0537] For **example**, the Seventh Commandment, which treats
SC : PR :018(340) [0537] Always adduce many **examples** from the Scriptures to
SC : 05 :023(350) [0553] I have set a bad **example** by my immodest language and
SC : 05 :024(350) [0555] For **example**, "In particular I confess that I once cursed.
LC : 01 :005(365) [0581] by citing some common **examples** of failure to observe
LC : 01 :018(367) [0585] For **example**, the heathen who put their trust in power
LC : 01 :026(368) [0587] For **example**, he gives to the mother breasts and milk for
LC : 01 :044(370) [0593] **Examples** of this you will find aplenty in all histories and
LC : 01 :051(371) [0595] facts are otherwise — for **example**, where men take oaths
LC : 01 :064(373) [0599] all that is good — for **example**, when we swear properly
LC : 01 :225(395) [0643] Suppose, for **example**, that a man-servant or
LC : 01 :239(397) [0649] The ancient Romans, for **example**, promptly took such
LC : 01 :284(403) [0661] For **example**, we now censure the pope and his teaching,
LC : 01 :301(405) [0667] For **example**, when people wrangle and wrestle over a
LC : 01 :306(406) [0669] Such **examples**, I trust, will not be found among us,
LC : 01 :326(409) [0675] For **example**, in the Second Commandment we are told
LC : 03 :076(431) [0721] For **example**, we might ask God to give us food and
LC : 03 :102(434) [0727] by the association and **example** of other people and by
LC : 03 :107(434) [0729] Youths, for **example**, are tempted chiefly by the flesh;
LC : 05 :015(448) [0757] now trouble men — for **example**, whether even a wicked
EP : 01 :016(468) [0783] spiritual matters — for **example**, the capacity, skill,
EP : 05 :006(478) [0803] apostles also set forth (**examples** of this meaning occur in
SD : 01 :025(512) [0867] least thing (such as, for **example**, producing a good
SD : 02 :015(523) [0887] In Ps. 119, for **example**, David asks God more than ten
SD : 02 :044(529) [0897] Erasmus raised (for **example**, the question of "absolute
SD : 04 :033(556) [0947] Apology offers a fine **example** as to when and how, on
SD : 07 :024(573) [0979] trouble people — for **example**, whether even a wicked
SD : 07 :115(589) [1011] body of Christ (for **example**, just as bread and wine are
SD : 08 :025(596) [1023] of his humiliation — for **example**, at the wedding in Cana
SD : 08 :037(598) [1027] Thus, for **example**, "the Son was descended from David
SD : 08 :039(598) [1027] or vice versa — for **example**, 'Was it not necessary that
SD : 08 :076(606) [1043] be or have — for **example**, that his flesh is truly a
SD : 10 :009(612) [1055] it by his own **example** (Acts 16:3; 21:26; I Cor. 9:10).
SD : 11 :002(616) [1063] and according to the **example** it provides, it neither can
SD : 11 :011(618) [1067] own weakness and the **example** of such as did not
SD : 11 :086(631) [1091] adduces Pharaoh's **example** for the sole purpose of

Exceedingly (2)
AP : 04 :275(148) [0199] external signs of this **exceedingly** great promise, since a
AP : 12 :002(182) [0253] voice of the Gospel, so **exceedingly** salutary and full of

Excellence (1), Excellent (16), Excellently (1)
AP : 04 :033(111) [0129] produces deeds that are **excellent** and praiseworthy in
AP : 04 :224(138) [0181] justified, the Corinthians received many **excellent** gifts.
AP : 04 :244(142) [0189] of their intrinsic **excellence**; that we do not need mercy
AP : 04 :261(145) [0195] For there is the king's **excellent** confession about the God
AP : 12 :094(196) [0281] For Tertullian speaks **excellently** about faith, dwelling
AP : 20 :004(227) [0339] are sure that His Most **Excellent** Imperial Majesty and
AP : 21 :041(235) [0355] We ourselves have heard **excellent** theologians ask for
AP : 23 :003(239) [0363] our most chaste and **excellent** Emperor, they propose
AP : 23 :049(246) [0377] In the **excellent** phrase of Epiphanius, such observances
LC : PR :002(358) [0567] form in the many **excellent** books which are in reality
LC : PR :020(361) [0573] much fruit and God will make **excellent** men of them.
LC : 01 :258(399) [0653] That nation had an **excellent**, orderly government, and
LC : 01 :278(402) [0661] Then you have done a great and **excellent** work.
LC : 02 :024(413) [0683] This is an **excellent** knowledge, but an even greater
LC : 03 :023(423) [0703] on earth, for it has the **excellent** testimony that God loves
LC : 04 :007(437) [0733] we regard Baptism as **excellent**, glorious, and exalted.
LC : 04 :083(446) [0751] we see what a great and **excellent** thing Baptism is, which
SD : 03 :041(546) [0931] For Dr. Luther's **excellent** statement remains true: "There

Except (53), Excepted (5), Excepting (1), Exception (5), Exceptional (1), Exceptions (1)
AG : 01 :002(056) [0065] ceremonies of the Mass, **except** that in certain places
AG : 24 :026(058) [0067] sin, or for any other sin, **except** the one death of Christ.
AG : 24 :040(061) [0069] ceremonies of the Mass **except** that other unnecessary
AG : 28 :009(082) [0085] gifts cannot be obtained **except** through the office of
AL : 16 :006(038) [0051] magistrates and laws **except** when commanded to sin, for
AL : 24 :002(056) [0065] are also retained, **except** that German hymns are
AL : 24 :013(057) [0065] any private Masses were held **except** for the sake of gain.
AL : 24 :041(061) [0069] and all things are done **except** for the solemn
AL : 25 :001(061) [0069] the body of Christ **except** to those who have been
AL : 25 :009(062) [0069] if no sins were forgiven **except** those which are
AL : 27 :020(074) [0079] to marry who are not **excepted** by a singular work of
AL : 28 :009(082) [0085] cannot come about **except** through the ministry of the
AL : 28 :021(084) [0087] Word and sacraments) **except** to forgive sins, to reject
AL : 28 :041(087) [0089] a sin cannot be forgiven **except** by the authority of the
AP : 02 :013(102) [0109] This cannot be adjudged **except** from the Word of God,
AP : 04 :067(116) [0139] deal with God or grasp him **except** through the Word.
AP : 04 :083(119) [0145] We cannot take hold of the name of Christ **except** by faith
AP : 04 :101(121) [0151] the knowledge of Christ **except** to know Christ's
AP : 04 :109(123) [0153] attribute justification to faith **except** on account of love.
AP : 04 :133(125) [0159] Moses cannot be removed **except** by faith, which receives
AP : 04 :217(137) [0179] find peace before God **except** by faith alone, by which it
AP : 04 :330(158) [0211] that is, all trust is vain **except** a trust in mercy; mercy
AP : 04 :372(164) [0221] None can do good works **except** the justified, who are led
AP : 12 :047(188) [0265] peace for the conscience **except** by faith, therefore faith
AP : 12 :073(192) [0273] the forgiveness of sins **except** by the forbearance of God;
AP : 12 :077(193) [0275] of the law or in any other way **except** by faith in Christ.
AP : 15 :042(221) [0325] are preached during the whole year, **except** in Lent.
AP : 16 :001(222) [0329] Our opponents approve Article XVI without **exception**.
AP : 17 :001(224) [0335] Our opponents accept Article XVII without **exception**.
AP : 21 :009(230) [0345] about the dead praying, **except** for the dream recorded in
AP : 24 :056(260) [0405] in the New Testament **except** the one sacrifice of Christ
AP : 24 :085(264) [0413] a far-fetched etymology, **except** perhaps to show off their
AP : 24 :089(266) [0415] cannot be conquered **except** by faith in Christ, as Paul
AP : 27 :032(274) [0431] the forgiveness of sins **except** by God's indulgence;
AP : 27 :038(275) [0433] he did not hear anything, **except** that in the morning he
S2 : 04 :003(298) [0471] transactions and deeds (**except** what pertains to secular
S2 : 04 :010(300) [0475] Christians to be saved **except** by his own power, which
S3 : 03 :034(309) [0489] He says "all men," that is, **excepting** no one who is a man.
S3 : 08 :003(312) [0495] no one his Spirit or grace **except** through or with the
S3 : 08 :010(313) [0497] God will not deal with us **except** through his external
TR : 00 :055(329) [0521] to express an opinion, **except** his followers, whom he has
SC : 09 :004(355) [0561] For there is no authority **except** from God, and those
LC : 01 :027(368) [0587] to take or give anything **except** as God has commanded
LC : 01 :182(389) [0631] It forgives anger **except**, as we have said, to persons who
LC : 01 :210(393) [0641] It is not an **exceptional** estate, but the most universal and
LC : 01 :211(393) [0641] some (although few) **exceptions** whom God has especially
LC : 01 :274(401) [0659] **Exception** is made, however, of civil magistrates,
LC : 01 :274(402) [0659] physically, and yet an **exception** is made of the hangman.
LC : 01 :306(406) [0669] not be found among us, **except** that someone may by
LC : 02 :048(416) [0691] not be called a church **except** for the single reason that
LC : 03 :031(424) [0707] and the Gospel as well, **except** that the prayers of a few
LC : 05 :031(450) [0759] grasp and appropriate it, **except** by steadfastly believing
LC : 05 :034(450) [0761] forgiveness of sins, it cannot be received **except** by faith.
LC : 05 :061(453) [0767] The only **exception** is the person who desires no grace and
EP : 01 :005(466) [0781] be made like his brethren in every respect," sin **excepted**.
EP : 01 :010(467) [0781] No one **except** God alone can separate the corruption of
EP : 11 :013(496) [0835] he would save no one **except** those who acknowledge his
SD : PR :006(502) [0847] unchallenged — **except** for the charges of the papists — it
SD : 01 :043(516) [0873] made like us, his brethren, sin alone **excepted** (Heb. 2:17).
SD : 01 :043(516) [0873] attributes — sin alone **excepted** — identical with ours;
SD : 02 :026(526) [0891] one knows the Father **except** the Son and any one to
SD : 02 :026(526) [0891] can say, Jesus is Lord, **except** by the Holy Spirit" (I Cor.
SD : 07 :005(570) [0973] understand and explain it **except** as something to be
SD : 07 :089(585) [1003] hearers do not believe it (**except** that in them it does not
SD : 07 :126(591) [1015] Of course, no one **except** an Arian heretic can or will
SD : 08 :070(605) [1041] (Heb. 2:7, 8), and "he is **excepted** who put all things

Exchange (13), Exchanged (1)
LC : 01 :224(395) [0643] is transacted and money is **exchanged** for goods or labor.
SD : 07 :004(569) [0973] according to the **exchange** of properties (that is, only
SD : 08 :031(597) [1025] The doctrine of an **exchange** of properties (that is, of a
SD : 08 :032(597) [1025] into another, an **exchange** of properties could not take

Continued ▶

S D : 0 8 :035(597) [1027] that this doctrine of the **exchange** of properties between
S D : 0 8 :062(603) [1037] This **exchange** or communication did not take place
S D : 0 8 :063(603) [1037] the term "real **exchange**" — a communication or exchange
S D : 0 8 :063(603) [1037] — a communication or **exchange** that takes place in deed
S D : 0 8 :063(603) [1037] any essential, natural **exchange** or transfusion which
S D : 0 8 :063(603) [1037] opposition to a "verbal **exchange**," the doctrine which
S D : 0 8 :063(603) [1037] so strongly on this that they will hear no other **exchange**.
S D : 0 8 :063(603) [1037] have spoken of a "real **exchange**" in order to indicate
S D : 0 8 :063(603) [1037] thereby that such an **exchange** has occurred in deed and
S D : 0 8 :085(608) [1047] who by virtue of the **exchange** of qualities has eternal

Exciting (1)
A L : 0 0 :003(049) [0059] By thus **exciting** the minds of good men, they first gave

Exclaim (3)
A P : 0 4 :030(111) [0129] then may I not myself **exclaim**, too—yes, I will exclaim
A P : 0 4 :030(111) [0129] exclaim, too—yes, I will **exclaim** and chide them with a
L C : 0 1 :074(374) [0601] monstrous or fearful and **exclaim**, "Lord God, save us!"

Exclude (17), Excluded (12), Excludes (5), Excluding (1), Exclusion (3), Exclusive (12), Exclusively (10)
P R : P R :018(008) [0015] to commit ourselves **exclusively** and only, in accordance
A G : 2 8 :021(084) [0087] to the Gospel, and **exclude** from the Christian community
A L : 2 8 :021(084) [0087] to the Gospel, and to **exclude** from the fellowship of the
A P : 0 4 :053(114) [0137] the fact that it is free **excludes** our merits and shows that
A P : 0 4 :073(117) [0141] If they dislike the **exclusive** particle "alone," let them
A P : 0 4 :073(117) [0141] them remove the other **exclusive** terms from Paul, too,
A P : 0 4 :073(117) [0141] "it is a gift," etc., for these terms are also **exclusive**.
A P : 0 4 :073(117) [0141] We **exclude** the claim of merit, not the Word or the
A P : 0 4 :074(117) [0143] So they are not **excluded** as though they did not follow,
A P : 0 4 :074(117) [0143] the merit of love or works is **excluded** from justification.
A P : 0 4 :089(120) [0149] Therefore he **excludes** even the merit of works according
A P : 0 4 :221(137) [0181] Thus our opponents **exclude** Christ from justification and
A P : 0 4 :231(139) [0185] the propitiator, to be **excluded**, and hence this view is far
A P : 0 4 :245(142) [0189] Christ, the propitiator, be **excluded** from justification.
A P : 0 4 :257(144) [0193] If our opponents **exclude** the Gospel of Christ from the
A P : 0 4 :281(149) [0201] Yet everywhere they **exclude** Christ and teach that we
A P : 0 4 :290(151) [0203] both modes, since both **exclude** Christ and therefore both
A P : 0 4 :372(164) [0221] know that Christ, the mediator, should not be **excluded**.
A P : 0 4 :394(167) [0225] righteousness to the **exclusion** of the righteousness of
A P : 1 2 :148(205) [0299] Nor do we **exclude** here outward mortification of the
A P : 1 5 :038(220) [0325] in an evangelical way, **excluding** the opinion which holds
A P : 2 3 :043(245) [0375] that domestic problems are **excluded** from their minds.
A P : 2 4 :021(252) [0391] did not have to be **excluded** from the commonwealth.
A P : 2 4 :024(253) [0391] law and prevented the **exclusion** of the sinner from the
S 2 : 0 2 :012(295) [0465] Mass was used almost **exclusively** for the dead although
S 3 : 0 9 :000(314) [0497] excommunication **excludes** those who are manifest and
T R : 0 0 :067(331) [0523] This right is a gift given **exclusively** to the church, and no
T R : 0 0 :067(331) [0523] the gifts belonging **exclusively** to the church, and he adds
L C : 0 1 :293(404) [0663] literally, were given **exclusively** to the Jews; nevertheless,
L C : 0 4 :034(440) [0741] is so potent that it **excludes** and rejects all works that we
L C : 0 4 :035(441) [0741] and they do not **exclude** but rather demand faith, for
L C : 0 5 :059(453) [0767] he should not **exclude** himself from the sacrament," lest
E P : 0 2 :001(469) [0785] question revolves **exclusively** about man's will and ability
E P : 0 3 :010(474) [0795] attention to the "**exclusive** terms," that is, to those
E P : 0 4 :007(476) [0799] should be completely **excluded** from a discussion of the
E P : 0 5 :011(479) [0805] and reproof and not **exclusively** a proclamation of grace.
E P : 0 6 :007(481) [0807] is concerned, rests **exclusively** with man, for the
S D : 0 2 :035(528) [0895] and holy, to the complete **exclusion** of our own powers.
S D : 0 2 :046(530) [0899] and regeneration are **exclusively** the work of God and not
S D : 0 3 :007(540) [0917] Therefore he stresses the **exclusive** terms, that is, the
S D : 0 3 :007(540) [0917] all human works are **excluded**, such as "without the law,"
S D : 0 3 :036(545) [0927] diligently stresses such **exclusive** terms (that is, terms that
S D : 0 3 :036(545) [0927] terms (that is, terms that **exclude** works from the article
S D : 0 3 :036(545) [0927] of works," all of which **exclusive** terms may be
S D : 0 3 :036(545) [0927] terminology does not **exclude** works, however, as though
S D : 0 3 :036(545) [0927] is that good works are **excluded** from the article of
S D : 0 3 :036(545) [0929] understanding of the **exclusive** terms in the article of
S D : 0 3 :037(546) [0929] That thereby there are **excluded** completely from the
S D : 0 3 :038(546) [0929] to serve as the only and **exclusive** means and instrument
S D : 0 3 :038(546) [0929] appropriation we must **exclude** love and every other
S D : 0 3 :043(547) [0931] be justified, and that the **exclusive** terms which St. Paul
S D : 0 3 :043(547) [0931] from works," do not **exclude** works from the article of
S D : 0 3 :053(548) [0933] Paul uses and urges **exclusive** terms (that is, terms that
S D : 0 3 :053(548) [0933] is, terms that wholly **exclude** works and our own merit,
S D : 0 4 :022(554) [0945] to the doctrine of **exclusive** terms in the articles of
S D : 0 4 :022(554) [0945] St. Paul's words which **exclude** our works and merit
S D : 0 8 :043(599) [1029] nature and completely **excludes** them from the divine
S D : 1 1 :024(620) [1069] therein and never be **excluded** or omitted when we speak
S D : 1 1 :052(625) [1081] but we are to adhere **exclusively** to the revealed Word.
S D : 1 1 :089(631) [1093] This does not **exclude** any repentant sinner but invites

Excommunicate (5), Excommunicated (4), Excommunicating (1), Excommunication (7), Excommunications (2)
A L : 2 8 :002(081) [0083] of cases and violent **excommunications** but also have
A L : 0 0 :002(095) [0095] pilgrimages, and misuse of **excommunication**.
A P : 0 7 :003(169) [0227] — especially if they have not been **excommunicated**.
A P : 0 7 :032(174) [0239] some churches have **excommunicated** others because of
A P : 1 1 :004(181) [0249] and the despisers of the sacraments are **excommunicated**.
A P : 1 2 :176(210) [0307] and to denounce and **excommunicate** those who refuse to
A P : 2 2 :016(238) [0361] and who even **excommunicate** and violently persecute
A P : 2 8 :013(283) [0447] the authority to **excommunicate** those who are guilty of
S 3 : 0 9 :000(314) [0497] IX. **Excommunication**
S 3 : 0 9 :000(314) [0497] consider the greater **excommunication**, as the pope calls
S 3 : 0 9 :000(314) [0497] the truly Christian) **excommunication** excludes those who
S 3 : 0 9 :000(314) [0497] with this spiritual penalty or **excommunication**.
T R : 0 0 :031(325) [0513] the sacraments, and **excommunicate** the godless without
T R : 0 0 :035(326) [0513] with unjust **excommunications** and wars, sometimes in
T R : 0 0 :060(330) [0521] jurisdiction, that is, **excommunicate** those who are guilty
T R : 0 0 :074(332) [0525] jurisdiction of **excommunicating** those who are guilty of
T R : 0 0 :074(332) [0525] tormented men and **excommunicated** them without due
E P : 1 2 :026(500) [0843] orderly process of **excommunication** do not take place.
S D : 1 2 :034(635) [1101] orderly process of **excommunication** does not take place

Excuse (8), Excused (3)
A G : 2 7 :033(076) [0079] most monastics have **excuse** and reason for leaving their
A L : 2 7 :033(076) [0079] most monastics have an **excuse** for leaving the monastery
A P : 0 7 :023(172) [0235] whatever laws he pleases, **excuse** and exempt men from
A P : 1 5 :036(220) [0325] traditions, and Christ **excused** them, for this was to serve
A P : 1 5 :037(220) [0325] traditions, they have **excuse** enough now that these are
A P : 2 3 :063(248) [0381] the many murders for which this law provides an **excuse**.
A P : 2 4 :081(264) [0411] of children does not **excuse** parents from public duties."
T R : 0 0 :042(328) [0517] Consequently our consciences are sufficiently **excused**.
L C : 0 1 :295(404) [0665] he might on any flimsy **excuse** dismiss his own wife and
L C : 0 3 :119(436) [0731] that we may never have an **excuse** for failing to pray.
S D : P R :009(503) [0849] the church of God, much less be **excused** and defended.

Execrate (2), Execrated (2)
T R : 0 0 :041(327) [0517] rather to abandon and **execrate** the pope and his
T R : 0 0 :041(328) [0517] should be shunned and **execrated** as accursed, and he
S D : 1 0 :022(615) [1061] rather abandon and **execrate** the pope and his adherents
S D : 1 0 :022(615) [1061] should be shunned and **execrated** as accursed, and he

Execute (3), Executed (1)
S C : 0 9 :004(355) [0561] is the servant of God to **execute** his wrath on the
S D : 0 8 :055(601) [1033] For to give life, to **execute** all judgment, to have all
S D : 0 8 :058(602) [1035] the dead alive and to **execute** judgment has been given to
S D : 1 1 :085(630) [1091] and calloused and God **executed** his judgment on him,

Exempt (1), Exempted (1)
A P : 0 7 :023(172) [0235] he pleases, excuse and **exempt** men from any laws,
L C : 0 1 :211(393) [0641] God has especially **exempted** — some who are unsuited

Exercise (48), Exercised (10), Exercises (16)
A G : 0 1 :002(056) [0065] responses for the instruction and **exercise** of the people.
A G : 2 6 :033(069) [0075] reference to such bodily **exercise** as fasting and other
A G : 2 6 :034(069) [0075] Such bodily **exercise** should not be limited to certain
A G : 2 7 :025(074) [0079] ought to be **exercised** in connection with this obligation
A G : 2 7 :054(079) [0083] to take revenge outside of the **exercise** of their office.
A G : 2 8 :008(082) [0085] of bishops is used and **exercised** only by teaching and
A G : 2 8 :010(082) [0085] gifts and is used and **exercised** only through the office of
A G : 2 8 :076(094) [0095] forbids the bishops to **exercise** lordship as if they had
A L : 1 6 :005(038) [0051] of God and the **exercise** of love in these ordinance.
A L : 2 3 :018(054) [0063] is greater cruelty **exercised** than in opposition to the
A L : 2 6 :033(069) [0075] discipline, or bodily **exercises** and labors, that neither
A L : 2 6 :033(069) [0075] of sins or satisfaction for sins by means of such **exercises**.
A L : 2 8 :008(082) [0085] This power is **exercised** only by teaching or preaching the
A L : 2 8 :010(082) [0085] eternal things and is **exercised** only through the ministry
A P : 0 4 :189(133) [0175] them and in order to **exercise** our faith, to give
A P : 0 4 :198(134) [0175] Yet God **exercises** his saints in different ways and often
A P : 0 4 :202(134) [0175] this work, but to **exercise** his faith and display it to
A P : 0 4 :211(136) [0179] certain kind of life for study or for other useful **exercises**.
A P : 0 4 :211(136) [0179] of Christ, not because of their own spiritual **exercises**.
A P : 0 4 :276(148) [0199] Hence they **exercise** themselves in these signs and
A P : 0 4 :278(149) [0199] Almsgiving is an **exercise** of that faith which accepts
A P : 0 4 :278(149) [0199] death as it becomes ever stronger through such **exercise**.
A P : 0 4 :314(156) [0207] ourselves in the midst of fears and to **exercise** our faith.
A P : 1 2 :126(201) [0289] ought in such times to **exercise** unusual wisdom and
A P : 1 2 :151(206) [0299] purpose, that is, to **exercise** them so that in their
A P : 1 2 :151(206) [0299] are a discipline by which God **exercises** the saints.
A P : 1 2 :161(208) [0303] humiliation his piety might be **exercised** and tested.
A P : 1 2 :161(208) [0303] righteousness, that is, to **exercise** and test the
A P : 1 3 :019(213) [0313] says that circumcision was a sign given to **exercise** faith.
A P : 1 5 :043(221) [0327] through faith, the **exercise** of faith, prayer and our
A P : 1 5 :046(221) [0327] This is the spiritual **exercise** of fear and faith.
A P : 1 5 :046(221) [0327] the cross, a voluntary kind of **exercise** is also necessary.
A P : 1 5 :047(221) [0327] should undertake these **exercises** not as services that
A P : 2 4 :046(258) [0401] were silent about the **exercise** of faith in its struggle with
A P : 2 7 :038(275) [0433] the shoemaker to find out about his **exercises** and gifts.
A P : 2 7 :045(277) [0435] This passage has **exercised** many people because they
A P : 2 7 :055(278) [0439] if they were used as **exercises**, the way lessons are in
A P : 2 7 :058(279) [0439] was intended to **exercise** or show faith before men, not to
A P : 2 7 :058(279) [0439] but to be an outward **exercise** like the other ceremonies
A P : 2 8 :014(283) [0447] according to which he ought to **exercise** his jurisdiction.
A P : 2 8 :014(283) [0447] about when they should **exercise** their jurisdiction,
S 2 : 0 4 :006(299) [0473] use to the church because it **exercises** no Christian office.
S 3 : 0 3 :007(304) [0481] But where the law **exercises** its office alone, without the
T R : 0 0 :008(320) [0505] sent forth as equals and **exercise** the ministry of the
T R : 0 0 :008(320) [0505] "The kings of the Gentiles **exercise** lordship over them.
T R : 0 0 :044(328) [0517] true worship (that is, the **exercise** of faith struggling
T R : 0 0 :051(329) [0519] Thus the pope **exercises** a twofold tyranny: he defends his
T R : 0 0 :060(330) [0521] and, in addition, **exercise** jurisdiction, that is,
T R : 0 0 :074(332) [0525] (as they are called) have **exercised** intolerable
T R : 0 0 :079(333) [0527] pastors and tyrannically **exercise** it alone; and since,
L C : P R :018(361) [0573] but meditations and **exercises** based on the First
L C : P R :019(361) [0573] Let all Christians **exercise** themselves in the Catechism
L C : S P :005(362) [0575] of the Altar and **exercise** all the rights of Christians,
L C : 0 1 :088(377) [0605] ourselves with God's Word and **exercise** ourselves in it.
L C : 0 1 :118(381) [0615] nuns would pay if in the **exercise** of their religion they
L C : 0 1 :182(389) [0631] and they are to be **exercised** upon those who transgress
L C : 0 3 :007(421) [0699] used, may serve as an **exercise** for young children, pupils,
L C : 0 3 :007(421) [0699] called singing or reading **exercise**, it is not really prayer.
L C : 0 5 :037(451) [0761] and children's **exercise** so that one's body may behave
E P : 0 2 :017(472) [0791] conversion, in the daily **exercise** of repentance, the reborn
E P : 0 4 :018(477) [0801] necessary it is that they **exercise** themselves in good
E P : 0 6 :002(480) [0805] that they should **exercise** themselves day and night in the
E P : 0 7 :017(484) [0813] just as much present to **exercise** and manifest his
E P : 0 8 :016(489) [0821] He **exercises** his power everywhere omnipresently, he can
S D : 0 2 :016(523) [0887] and grace, through daily **exercise** in reading his Word and
S D : 0 2 :046(530) [0899] to such Christian **exercises** as prayer, reading, and
S D : 0 2 :072(535) [0909] of God in vain but to **exercise** ourselves in considering
S D : 0 2 :088(538) [0915] is not idle in the daily **exercise** of repentance but
S D : 0 6 :004(564) [0963] law, they should daily **exercise** themselves in the law of
S D : 0 8 :026(596) [1023] installed in the complete **exercise** and use of the divine
S D : 0 8 :029(597) [1025] and installed in the **exercise** of the divine, omnipotent
S D : 0 8 :051(601) [1033] Accordingly, for the **exercise** of Christ's office, the human
S D : 0 8 :064(603) [1037] same he manifests and **exercises** his divine power, glory,
S D : 1 1 :073(628) [1087] of God, but should **exercise** themselves in all Christian

Exert (2), Exertions (1), Exerts (1)
AP : 2 1 :039(235) [0355] that the bishops would **exert** their authority and the
LC : PR :004(359) [0567] and even our utmost **exertions** accomplish but little.
LC : 0 1 :094(378) [0607] in order that God's Word may **exert** its power publicly.
LC : 0 3 :104(434) [0727] on all sides, but especially **exerts** himself where the

Exhausted (1), Exhaustive (1), Exhaustively (1)
LC : 0 1 :080(375) [0603] be refreshed and not be **exhausted** by constant labor.
SD : 0 3 :028(544) [0925] In his beautiful and **exhaustive** exposition of the Epistle
SD : 1 0 :024(615) [1061] opinion Dr. Luther **exhaustively** instructs the church of

Exhibit (1), Exhibited (1), Exhibiting (1), Exhibitions (2)
AL : 0 0 :006(096) [0095] our confession may be **exhibited** in them and that a
AP : 1 2 :116(199) [0285] just as those ancient **exhibitions** of satisfaction in public
AP : 1 2 :120(200) [0287] notice that these public **exhibitions** had been instituted as
SC : PR :009(339) [0535] you are at liberty to **exhibit** your learning and to discuss
SD : RN :013(506) [0855] to the truth and as **exhibiting** the unanimous and correct

Exhort (6), Exhortation (9), Exhorted (1), Exhorting (1), Exhorts (2)
PR : PR :015(007) [0013] had them reminded and **exhorted** to consider diligently
AP : 2 3 :055(247) [0379] of the Gospel should **exhort** the incontinent to marry and
AP : 2 3 :055(247) [0379] to marry and also **exhort** others not to despise the gift of
AP : 2 7 :055(278) [0439] in order to teach and **exhort** the hearers, brief and
TR : 0 0 :054(329) [0519] God expressly **exhorts** kings, "Now therefore, O kings, be
SC : PR :021(340) [0537] too, there is need of **exhortation**, but with this
LC : 0 1 :248(398) [0651] We have now given sufficient warning and **exhortation**.
LC : 0 3 :004(420) [0699] it is very necessary to **exhort** and draw people to prayer,
LC : 0 3 :014(422) [0701] urgently beg and **exhort** everyone to take these words to
LC : 0 5 :044(451) [0763] must also be daily **exhortation**, so on this subject we
LC : 0 5 :067(454) [0769] faithfully summons and **exhorts** us to our highest and
LC : 0 5 :085(456) [0773] Let this serve as an **exhortation**, then, not only for us who
LC : 0 5 :087(457) [0773] Here follows an **exhortation** to confession.
LC : 0 6 :000(457) [0000] A Brief **Exhortation** to Confession [Tappert Only]
LC : 0 6 :007(457) [0000] we must preach, **exhorting**, encouraging, and persuading
EP : 0 4 :018(477) [0801] it is just as necessary to **exhort** people to Christian
SD : 0 4 :033(556) [0947] of the preceding, the **exhortation** to do good works can
SD : 0 6 :006(565) [0965] admonition, **exhortation**, or driving by the law they
SD : 0 6 :006(565) [0965] any admonition, **exhortation**, compulsion, coercion, or

Exile (1)
AP : 2 3 :059(247) [0379] refuse to submit, and the **exile** of poor women and

Exist (19), Existed (3), Existence (12), Existing (10), Exists (19)
AG : 0 1 :004(028) [0043] or a property of another but as that which **exists** of itself.
AG : 1 6 :002(037) [0051] to imperial and other **existing** laws, punish evildoers with
AG : 1 6 :004(038) [0051] and eternal mode of **existence** and righteousness of the
AG : 1 8 :006(040) [0053] None of these is or **exists** without God, but all things are
AG : 2 4 :040(061) [0069] introduced which did not **exist** in the church from ancient
AG : 2 8 :072(093) [0093] burdens which did not **exist** in the church in former times
AL : 1 6 :002(037) [0051] the imperial and other **existing** laws, to award just
AL : 1 8 :006(040) [0053] None of these **exists** without the providence of God;
AL : 2 3 :013(053) [0063] marriages prohibited but **existing** marriages were also
AL : 2 6 :029(068) [0075] righteousness cannot **exist** without such acts of worship.
AP : 0 2 :003(101) [0105] to the flesh we deny the **existence** not only of actual fear
AP : 0 4 :015(109) [0123] that there are books in **existence** which compare certain
AP : 0 4 :048(113) [0135] knowledge and teach that it can **exist** with mortal sin.
AP : 0 4 :064(116) [0139] Therefore this cannot **exist** with mortal sin, but whenever
AP : 0 4 :109(123) [0153] because they imagine that faith can **exist** with mortal sin.
AP : 0 4 :115(123) [0155] idle knowledge, nor can it **exist** with mortal sin; but it is a
AP : 0 4 :142(126) [0161] moreover, has its **existence** in penitence; that is, it is
AP : 0 4 :143(126) [0161] And so it cannot **exist** in those who live according to the
AP : 0 4 :144(127) [0161] obey their lusts, nor does it **exist** together with mortal sin.
AP : 0 4 :349(160) [0217] The faith we speak of has its **existence** in penitence.
AP : 0 7 :009(169) [0229] will abide nevertheless; it **exists** despite the great
AP : 0 7 :020(171) [0233] that this church actually **exists**, made up of true believers
AP : 0 7 :025(173) [0235] There are in **existence** many extravagant and wicked
AP : 1 2 :060(190) [0267] which believes that God **exists**, that punishments hang
AP : 1 3 :021(214) [0313] a faith which believes in a general way that God **exists**.
AP : 1 6 :003(223) [0331] us to obey the **existing** laws, whether they were
AP : 1 9 :001(226) [0337] all of nature and preserves everything that **exists**.
AP : 2 0 :013(228) [0343] as we have said before, faith has its **existence** in penitence.
AP : 2 3 :008(240) [0367] it still does as long as this physical nature of ours **exists**.
AP : 2 3 :008(240) [0367] yearly the fields are clothed as long as this universe **exists**.
AP : 2 3 :059(247) [0379] law, the dissolution of **existing** marriages, the murder of
AP : 2 3 :061(247) [0381] anyone into celibacy or to dissolve **existing** marriages.
AP : 2 3 :063(248) [0381] the dissolution of **existing** marriages (Matt. 19:6).
S2 : 0 4 :005(299) [0473] holy Christian church can **exist** very well without such a
S2 : 0 4 :006(299) [0473] the church must continue to **exist** without the pope.
TR : 0 0 :026(324) [0511] the whole world and **exists** wherever God gives his gifts,
TR : 0 0 :067(331) [0523] For wherever the church **exists**, the right to administer
TR : 0 0 :067(331) [0523] exists, the right to administer the Gospel also **exists**.
SC : 0 2 :002(345) [0543] created me and all that **exists**; that he has given me and
SC : 0 9 :004(355) [0561] from God, and those that **exist** have been instituted by
LC : 0 1 :216(394) [0641] forsake their unchaste **existence** and enter the married
LC : 0 3 :082(431) [0721] our needs and faithfully provides for our daily **existence**.
LC : 0 4 :058(444) [0747] the thing that he misuses has no **existence** or no value?
LC : 0 4 :059(444) [0747] has been wrongly received, it has **existence** and value.
LC : 0 4 :059(444) [0747] not destroy the substance, but confirms its **existence**."
EP : 0 1 :003(466) [0779] against and cannot co-**exist** with the chief articles of our
EP : 0 1 :017(468) [0783] sin is an essential, self-**existing** something which Satan
EP : 0 3 :017(475) [0795] of Christ that can **exist** and remain in a person though he
EP : 0 8 :038(491) [0825] cannot know what has **existed** from eternity, what is
SD : 0 1 :028(513) [0867] is not something which **exists** independently within or
SD : 0 1 :038(515) [0871] created *me* and all that **exists**, that he has given me and
SD : 0 1 :054(518) [0877] term), so that every **existing** thing must either be a
SD : 0 1 :057(518) [0877] person that every **existing** thing is either a substance or an
SD : 0 1 :057(518) [0877] another thing and cannot **exist** or subsist by itself), then
SD : 0 2 :007(521) [0883] powers has remained or **exists** in man by which he could
SD : 0 2 :070(535) [0909] things takes place or **exists**, there is no true conversion.
SD : 0 3 :026(543) [0923] and genuine faith **exists** only in or with true repentance.
SD : 0 7 :100(586) [1007] water, glass, or crystal and **exist** without occupying or
SD : 0 8 :023(595) [1023] person of Christ did not **exist** in deed and truth, all of
SD : 0 8 :032(597) [1027] of natures in the person of Christ did not truly **exist**.
SD : 0 8 :085(608) [1045] has not, like the deity, **existed** from eternity, but
SD : 1 1 :043(623) [1077] before we even **existed**, before we were able to have
SD : 1 1 :050(624) [1079] the church of God shall **exist** and remain against all the

Exonerate (2), Exonerates (1)
AP : 0 2 :002(100) [0105] This will **exonerate** us of the charge of innovation, for it
AP : 0 7 :003(169) [0227] The eighth article **exonerates** us enough.
AP : 2 2 :012(238) [0361] will the reasons he gives **exonerate** those who withhold a

Expanded (2), Expanding (1), Expansion (1)
PR : PR :010(006) [0011] controversies that were **expanding** with each passing day
PR : PR :024(013) [0023] to the increase and **expansion** of God's praise and glory,
AP : 1 5 :023(218) [0321] among the Israelites **expanded** such ceremonies, just as
AP : 1 5 :023(218) [0321] just as they have been **expanded** among us in the

Expect (23), Expectation (2), Expected (5), Expecting (3), Expects (3)
AG : 2 4 :023(058) [0067] of which men **expected** to get everything they needed from
AG : 2 7 :049(079) [0083] need, and confidently **expect** help from him in every
AL : 2 0 :025(045) [0057] do not call upon him, and **expect** no good from him.
AL : 2 0 :037(046) [0057] does not call upon God, **expect** anything of God, or bear
AL : 2 4 :007(056) [0065] in God and ask for and **expect** whatever is good from
AL : 2 7 :049(079) [0083] of God, and assuredly to **expect** from him, help in all
AP : 0 4 :008(108) [0121] hears prayer, and the **expectation** of God's help in death
AP : 0 4 :125(124) [0157] love God, to pray and **expect** help from him, to thank and
AP : 0 4 :312(155) [0207] confused, since it is hope that **expects** what is promised.
AP : 1 5 :003(215) [0315] We **expected** our opponents to defend human traditions
AP : 2 4 :028(254) [0393] Truly and wholeheartedly seek and **expect** help from me."
S1 : PR :001(288) [0455] case, we had reason to **expect** that we might be
S1 : PR :003(289) [0455] meets (which I fully **expect**, for those knaves who shun
S1 : PR :010(290) [0457] no reason to hope or **expect** that a council would improve
S1 : PR :014(291) [0459] It is as if we were to **expect** God to acquiesce in our
S2 : 0 2 :028(297) [0469] and help are no longer **expected**, the saints will cease to
S2 : 0 2 :028(297) [0471] them out of love when there is no **expectation** of return.
S3 : 0 3 :005(304) [0481] from the Lord and to **expect** and accept from him the
LC : PR :004(359) [0567] What, then, can we **expect** if we are sluggish and lazy, as
LC : PR :006(359) [0569] This is what one can **expect** of crazy Germans.
LC : 0 1 :012(366) [0583] They neither **expect** nor seek anything from him.
LC : 0 1 :021(367) [0585] neither cares for God nor **expects** good things from him
LC : 0 1 :024(367) [0587] alone and turn to him, **expecting** from him only good
LC : 0 1 :028(368) [0587] the kind of heart that **expects** from him nothing but
LC : 0 1 :143(385) [0623] that they know is **expected** of them, not from compulsion
LC : 0 1 :226(395) [0645] servants, from whom I **expect** good; but they are the first
LC : 0 1 :235(397) [0647] like a thief, and even **expect** to be revered like noblemen.
LC : 0 2 :001(411) [0679] forth all that we must **expect** and receive from God; in
LC : 0 3 :031(424) [0707] by which the devil **expected** to crush us, and the Gospel
LC : 0 3 :058(428) [0713] satisfy the belly, let alone **expect**, without doubting,
LC : 0 3 :109(435) [0729] us but shall at all times **expect** his blows and parry them.
LC : 0 3 :117(436) [0731] directs us to seek and **expect** help from no one but him.
LC : 0 5 :084(456) [0773] you into misery and distress when you least **expect** it!
LC : 0 6 :024(460) [0000] with repugnance, not **expecting** to receive anything but
SD : RN :007(505) [0853] papists, and for neither **expecting** nor planning to come to
SD : 0 7 :033(575) [0983] will please let me alone and **expect** no fellowship from me.

Expedient (1)
S3 : 0 3 :021(306) [0485] Here the **expedient** was resorted to of imposing small

Expel (2), Expelled (5), Expelling (1), Expels (1)
AG : 1 8 :002(039) [0051] his whole heart, or of **expelling** inborn evil lusts from his
AP : 1 1 :005(181) [0251] If they commune, let them not be permanently **expelled**.
AP : 1 1 :005(181) [0251] If they do not commune, let them be **expelled**."
S3 : 0 3 :040(309) [0489] gift daily cleanses and **expels** the sins that remain and
S3 : 1 0 :002(314) [0497] More than that, they **expel**, persecute, and condemn
LC : 0 2 :056(418) [0693] forgiveness of sin have **expelled** and separated themselves
LC : 0 5 :059(453) [0767] Christian and has to be **expelled** from the congregation,
SD : 0 4 :029(555) [0947] condoned but are to be **expelled** and rejected by our
SD : 1 0 :019(614) [1059] More than that, they **expel**, persecute, and condemn

Expend (1)
AP : 2 1 :001(229) [0343] Nowhere else do they **expend** so much sophistry, but all

Expense (5)
AG : 2 8 :071(093) [0093] peace and unity at the **expense** of their honor and dignity
AL : 2 8 :071(093) [0093] restore concord at the **expense** of their honor (which,
AP : 0 4 :024(110) [0127] it ought not be praised at the **expense** of Christ.
AP : 2 7 :009(270) [0421] be supported at public **expense** without the loss of their
LC : 0 1 :172(388) [0629] no effort, time, and **expense** in teaching and educating

Experience (24), Experienced (9), Experiences (3), Experiencing (1)
PR : PR :013(007) [0013] trustworthy, **experienced**, and learned theologians at
AG : 2 0 :015(043) [0055] yet it is a matter of **experience** that weak and terrified
AG : 2 3 :006(052) [0061] **Experience** has made it all too manifest whether or not it
AG : 2 3 :006(052) [0061] conscience many have **experienced** on their deathbeds on
AL : 2 0 :015(043) [0055] consciences find by **experience** that it offers the greatest
AP : 0 4 :021(110) [0127] doubt they can never **experience** what faith is and how
AP : 0 4 :037(112) [0131] conflict, the conscience **experiences** how vain these
AP : 0 4 :084(119) [0145] **Experienced** consciences can readily understand this.
AP : 0 4 :135(125) [0159] Then we **experience** our failure to believe that God
AP : 0 4 :350(161) [0217] great conflict in which **experience** testifies how difficult a
AP : 0 4 :381(165) [0223] love, which we know by **experience** is weak and unclean.
AP : 1 1 :010(182) [0253] by divine law and yet **experienced** that it was impossible.
AP : 1 2 :009(183) [0255] prophets and certainly **experienced** by those who are truly
AP : 1 2 :089(195) [0279] such doubt, they never **experience** what faith is, and so it
AP : 1 5 :049(221) [0329] we know from actual **experience** that traditions are real
AP : 2 1 :036(234) [0353] a sorcerer; Augustine **experienced** the power of faith in
AP : 2 4 :041(257) [0399] **Experience** shows the sort of tyrants who rule the church.
LC : PR :007(359) [0569] and as learned and **experienced** as any of those who act so
LC : PR :019(361) [0573] they have proved by **experience** that they have taught the
LC : PR :020(361) [0573] them — and their **experience** will bear me out — that they
LC : 0 1 :035(369) [0589] amply shows and as daily **experience** can still teach us.
LC : 0 1 :044(370) [0593] and in the recollections of elderly and **experienced** people.
LC : 0 1 :070(374) [0601] all circumstances and **experiences**, for true honor to
LC : 0 1 :072(374) [0601] myself and learned by **experience** that often sudden, great
LC : 0 1 :138(384) [0621] as we know from **experience**, where there are fine old

Continued ▶

L C : 0 1 :212(394) [0641] as everyone's observation and **experience** testify.
L C : 0 1 :248(398) [0651] this may go his own way until he learns it by **experience**.
L C : 0 3 :083(431) [0721] of time, as indeed we see and **experience** every day.
L C : 0 5 :044(451) [0763] For we know from **experience** that the devil always sets
L C : 0 5 :053(453) [0765] have found in my own **experience**, and as everyone will
L C : 0 5 :075(455) [0771] cannot feel this need or **experience** hunger and thirst for
L C : 0 5 :079(455) [0771] If you have not **experienced** this, then take it from the
L C : 0 6 :001(457) [0000] as we all know from **experience**, there has been no law
S D : 0 2 :054(531) [0903] the wrath of God and **experiences** genuine terror,
S D : 1 1 :073(628) [1087] so that the more they **experience** the power and might of
S D : 1 1 :074(628) [1087] they are no longer **experiencing** any power whatever of
S D : 1 1 :074(628) [1087] regardless of what they **experience** within themselves, they

Expiated (1), Expiation (3), Expiations (1)
A P : 0 4 :082(118) [0145] God put forward as an **expiation**," and Paul adds, "to be
A P : 1 2 :063(191) [0269] God put forward as an **expiation** by his blood, to be
A P : 1 2 :114(199) [0285] heathen had certain **expiations** or sin by which they
A P : 2 4 :023(253) [0391] is a real satisfaction or **expiation** for our sins, as the
S D : 0 5 :020(561) [0959] the curse of the law and **expiated** and paid for all our

Explain (48), Explained (42), Explaining (4), Explains (21), Explanation (36), Explanations (6)
P R : P R :009(006) [0011] our adversaries of this **explanation** and repetition of our
P R : P R :010(006) [0011] and accurately to **explain** and decide the difference that
P R : P R :010(006) [0011] and a correct **explanation** and direction might be
P R : P R :011(006) [0011] evaluated, and **explained** them in the fear of God, and
P R : P R :014(007) [0013] set forth in the **explanation** that had been sent out might
P R : P R :016(007) [0013] had found that the **explanation** of the dissensions which
P R : P R :017(008) [0015] and confession as a final **explanation** of our conviction.
P R : P R :020(010) [0019] by a correct **explanation** of the articles of our Christian
P R : P R :022(011) [0019] and distinctly in this **explanation** and thorough
P R : P R :023(012) [0021] mentioned present **explanation** of the controverted
P R : P R :024(013) [0021] schisms a Christian **explanation** and reconciliation of all
P R : P R :024(013) [0021] Such an **explanation** must be thoroughly grounded in
P R : P R :025(014) [0023] controversies and their **explanations** according to it.
A P : P R :005(098) [0101] objections and **explaining** to His Imperial Majesty why
A P : P R :013(099) [0101] seems too strong, let me **explain** that my quarrel is with
A P : 0 2 :003(101) [0105] This **explanation** should be enough for any unprejudiced
A P : 0 2 :006(101) [0107] we named it and **explained** it as a disease since human
A P : 0 2 :015(102) [0109] questions and do not **explain** what original righteousness
A P : 0 2 :051(107) [0119] themselves and fail to **explain** logically and correctly
A P : 0 4 :185(132) [0173] issues, one or two **explanations**, taken from the sources,
A P : 0 4 :357(162) [0217] "reward" and in their **explanation** do violence not only to
A P : 0 4 :388(166) [0225] of this conflict and have **explained** those issues on which
A P : 0 7 :008(169) [0229] to have been added to **explain** what "church" means,
A P : 1 1 :001(180) [0249] a little later when we **explain** our whole teaching on
A P : 1 1 :002(180) [0249] known that we have so **explained** and extolled the
A P : 1 2 :001(182) [0253] the first part, where we **explain** that those who have fallen
A P : 1 2 :005(183) [0253] which the theologians could never **explain** satisfactorily.
A P : 1 2 :098(197) [0281] concentrated on the **explanation** of these doctrines and
A P : 1 2 :128(202) [0291] healing consciences, refuse to let the issue be **explained**.
A P : 1 2 :158(207) [0301] Scripture **explains** that Job's afflictions were not imposed
A P : 1 2 :163(208) [0303] of grammar when they **explain** "judge" as "to make a
A P : 1 2 :178(211) [0309] and they themselves cannot satisfactorily **explain** them.
A P : 1 6 :013(224) [0333] Our theologians have **explained** this whole matter of
A P : 2 2 :006(236) [0359] do not even try to **explain** to the church why one part of
A P : 2 2 :006(237) [0359] the church a valid **explanation** to instruct those who were
A P : 2 3 :060(247) [0379] We have **explained** why we cannot conscientiously agree
A P : 2 4 :014(251) [0389] Now we shall **explain** the passages of Scripture which
A P : 2 4 :016(252) [0389] them nothing can be **explained** or understood in a
A P : 2 4 :033(256) [0395] In a moment we shall **explain** how even a ceremony is a
A P : 2 4 :066(261) [0407] Now that we have **explained** the Scripture passages that
A P : 2 8 :010(282) [0447] So let our opponents **explain** how traditions are
S C : P R :014(339) [0535] this purpose, take the **explanations** in this booklet, or
S C : P R :014(340) [0535] other brief and fixed **explanations** which you may prefer,
L C : S P :026(364) [0579] so that they may hear it **explained** and may learn the
L C : 0 1 :005(365) [0581] This I must **explain** a little more plainly, so that it may be
L C : 0 1 :029(368) [0589] (**Explanation** of the Appendix to the First
L C : 0 1 :048(371) [0593] We had to **explain** it at length since it is the most
L C : 0 1 :065(373) [0599] have the substance of the entire commandment **explained**.
L C : 0 1 :066(373) [0599] The **explanation** is briefly this: We are not to swear in
L C : 0 1 :178(389) [0631] a more extensive **explanation** will have to await another
L C : 0 1 :182(389) [0631] We hear it **explained** every year in the Gospel, Matthew
L C : 0 1 :182(389) [0631] 5, where Christ himself **explains** and summarizes it: We
L C : 0 1 :232(396) [0647] to emphasize and **explain** it to the common people in
L C : 0 1 :325(409) [0675] He seems to **explain** the whole commandment in one
L C : 0 2 :004(411) [0679] But before we **explain** the advantage and necessity of the
L C : 0 2 :006(411) [0679] of God the Father, **explains** creation; the second, of the
L C : 0 2 :010(411) [0679] Commandments have **explained** that we are to have no
L C : 0 2 :032(414) [0687] But the proper place to **explain** all these different points
L C : 0 2 :049(417) [0691] which someone wished to **explain** what the Christian
L C : 0 2 :065(419) [0695] As we **explained** before, we could never come to
L C : 0 3 :004(420) [0699] Before we **explain** the Lord's Prayer part by part, it is
L C : 0 6 :023(459) [0000] If all this were clearly **explained**, and meanwhile if the
E P : 0 0 :000(463) [0775] Final Restatement and **Explanation** of a Number of
E P : R N :000(464) [0777] Intruded Should Be **Explained** and Decided in a Christian
E P : 0 2 :015(471) [0789] are made without **explanation** that man's will before, in,
E P : 0 4 :005(476) [0797] In order to **explain** this controversy from the ground up
E P : 0 4 :012(477) [0799] the apostles themselves **explain** it, as applying only to the
E P : 0 5 :008(479) [0803] into his own hands and **explains** it spiritually (Matt.
E P : 0 8 :004(487) [0819] To **explain** and to settle this controversy according to our
E P : 0 8 :018(489) [0823] the person, as Luther **explains** it in his treatise *On the*
E P : 0 9 :003(492) [0827] the year 1533, where he **explains** this article in a wholly
E P : 1 1 :001(494) [0831] we have included an **explanation** of it in this document,
E P : 1 1 :022(497) [0837] is a brief and simple **explanation** of the various articles
E P : 1 2 :001(498) [0839] In the preceding **explanation** we have made no mention
S D : P R :010(503) [0849] controverted articles be **explained** on the basis of God's
S D : R N :000(503) [0849] and Errors Are to Be **Explained** and Decided in a
S D : R N :002(503) [0851] of God as Dr. Luther of blessed memory had **explained** it:
S D : R N :007(505) [0853] articles are further **explained** on the basis of God's Word,
S D : R N :010(506) [0855] and used as helpful expositions and **explanations**.
S D : R N :019(507) [0857] wanted to set forth and **explain** our faith and confession
S D : R N :020(507) [0857] This **explanation** will enable the pious reader, as far as is
S D : 0 1 :004(509) [0861] Hence, in order to **explain** this controversy in a Christian
S D : 0 1 :015(511) [0863] in summary form, are **explained** in greater detail in the
S D : 0 1 :051(517) [0875] words, it is necessary to **explain** carefully and distinctly
S D : 0 1 :053(517) [0875] Luther himself **explains** that he uses the terms
S D : 0 1 :054(518) [0877] under the necessity of **explaining** this doctrine against
S D : 0 1 :061(519) [0879] sin if the term is **explained** in harmony with the Word of
S D : 0 1 :062(519) [0879] But at the time he **explained** with special seriousness and
S D : 0 2 :008(521) [0883] confirm the foregoing **explanation** of and summary reply
S D : 0 2 :017(524) [0887] St. Paul **explains** this text: "The mind that is set on the
S D : 0 2 :023(525) [0889] a "capacity," which he **explains** as follows: "When the
S D : 0 2 :081(537) [0911] where he adduces and **explains** St. Paul's words, "Put off
S D : 0 2 :081(537) [0911] be laid aside, he himself **explains** what it means to lay off
S D : 0 2 :082(537) [0913] they are used without **explanation**: that man's will before,
S D : 0 2 :085(537) [0913] way one can and should **explain** and teach the correct
S D : 0 2 :088(538) [0915] It has also been **explained** in sufficient detail above that in
S D : 0 2 :089(538) [0915] way and after the manner set forth and **explained** above.
S D : 0 2 :090(539) [0915] From the previous **explanation** it is evident that
S D : 0 3 :008(540) [0919] Therefore to **explain** this controversy in a Christian way
S D : 0 3 :018(542) [0921] it is necessary to **explain** the term strictly so that the
S D : 0 3 :042(546) [0931] This correct distinction **explains** usefully and well the
S D : 0 3 :044(547) [0933] similar errors as contrary to the preceding **explanation**:
S D : 0 3 :054(548) [0933] We must also **explain** correctly the discussion concerning
S D : 0 3 :066(550) [0937] God as it is set forth, **explained**, and demonstrated from
S D : 0 3 :067(551) [0937] by way of a detailed **explanation** of this high and
S D : 0 4 :006(552) [0939] In order to **explain** this disagreement in a Christian way
S D : 0 4 :013(553) [0943] no further but shall **explain** only the controverted points
S D : 0 4 :021(554) [0945] necessary we must also **explain** why and for what causes
S D : 0 4 :022(555) [0945] merit of Christ, as was **explained** in the preceding
S D : 0 4 :028(555) [0945] who attempted to **explain** the proposition by saying that,
S D : 0 4 :033(556) [0947] In **explaining** II Pet. 1:10, "Be the more zealous to
S D : 0 4 :039(557) [0951] when asserted without **explanation** it is false and
S D : 0 5 :001(558) [0951] and apostles may be **explained** and understood correctly.
S D : 0 5 :010(559) [0955] law into his hands and **explains** it spiritually (Matt.
S D : 0 5 :011(560) [0955] the Paraclete, as Luther **explains** it in his exposition of
S D : 0 5 :013(560) [0957] which cannot be done without the **explanation** of the law.
S D : 0 5 :018(561) [0957] Gospel illustrates and **explains** the law and its doctrine;
S D : 0 5 :022(562) [0959] the law, as previously **explained**, is an office which kills
S D : 0 6 :004(564) [0963] In order to **explain** and definitively to settle this
S D : 0 6 :009(565) [0965] Dr. Luther thoroughly **explains** this at greater length in
S D : 0 7 :001(568) [0971] opinion of some an **explanation** of this article should not
S D : 0 7 :005(570) [0973] did not understand and **explain** it except as something to
S D : 0 7 :013(571) [0977] Master Martin Bucer has **explained** his opinion, and that
S D : 0 7 :020(572) [0979] Dr. Luther **explains** and confirms this position at greater
S D : 0 7 :036(575) [0985] when they reproduce and **explain** the statement, "The
S D : 0 7 :036(575) [0985] Thus the Scriptures **explain** that the divine essence has
S D : 0 7 :045(577) [0987] bound to interpret and **explain** these words of the
S D : 0 7 :050(578) [0989] standpoint of wisdom and intelligence to **explain** them.
S D : 0 7 :050(578) [0991] could creep in, he **explained** things more clearly by
S D : 0 7 :058(580) [0993] Augsburg Confession, **explained** this passage of Paul in
S D : 0 7 :059(580) [0993] and well-founded **explanation** of the noble testimony in
S D : 0 7 :060(580) [0995] understood and **explained** this passage in this way.
S D : 0 7 :068(582) [0997] It is essential to **explain** with great diligence who the
S D : 0 7 :087(585) [1003] rule was first formulated and **explained** by Dr. Luther.
S D : 0 7 :102(587) [1007] But who can **explain** or even conceive how this occurs?
S D : 0 7 :111(589) [1011] our confession and **explanation** concerning the true
S D : 0 8 :005(592) [1017] In order to **explain** this controversy in a Christian way
S D : 0 8 :014(594) [1019] some have incorrectly **explained** it, as if both natures, the
S D : 0 8 :021(595) [1021] Dr. Luther has **explained** this thoroughly in his *Great*
S D : 0 8 :022(595) [1023] this mystery and have **explained** the one through the
S D : 0 8 :026(596) [1025] aside, and as Dr. Luther **explains** it, he kept it hidden
S D : 0 8 :028(596) [1025] way, but as Dr. Luther **explains**, after the manner of the
S D : 0 8 :031(597) [1025] above and as we have **explained** the personal union (that
S D : 0 8 :035(597) [1027] natures be treated and **explained** with due discrimination
S D : 0 8 :037(598) [1027] contrary, it is distinctly **explained** according to which
S D : 0 8 :060(602) [1035] nature, we must correctly **explain** this doctrine and defend
S D : 0 8 :064(603) [1037] orthodox church, as it **explained** this doctrine on the
S D : 0 8 :064(604) [1039] ancient church used in **explaining** this doctrine, as we
S D : 0 9 :001(610) [1049] Different **explanations** of the article on Christ's descent
S D : 1 0 :004(611) [1053] To **explain** this controversy and to settle it definitively by
S D : 1 1 :001(616) [1063] to set forth our **explanation** of this article in this
S D : 1 1 :014(619) [1069] as Paul treats and **explains** this article (Rom. 8:28ff.;
S D : 1 1 :038(622) [1075] a voice from heaven," as the Apology **explains** this article.
S D : 1 1 :064(626) [1083] not try to explore and **explain** everything in this article.
S D : 1 1 :087(631) [1091] This teaching and **explanation** of the eternal and saving
S D : 1 2 :040(636) [1103] that the present **explanation** of all the foregoing
S D : 1 2 :040(636) [1103] articles here **explained**, and none other, is our teaching,

Explicate (1), Explicates (1), Explication (1)
E P : 0 7 :003(482) [0809] In order to **explicate** this controversy, it is necessary to
S D : R N :007(505) [0853] be held) as an **explication** of the Augsburg Confession, to
S D : 0 2 :044(529) [0897] Chapter 26, he repeats and **explicates** the same thought.

Explicit (5), Explicitly (8)
A P : 0 4 :097(121) [0149] He **explicitly** denies justification to the law.
A P : 2 0 :001(226) [0337] This article they **explicitly** reject and condemn.
L C : 0 1 :133(383) [0619] implied, yet in none is it so plainly and **explicitly** stated.
L C : 0 1 :167(388) [0629] duty of superiors is not **explicitly** stated in the Ten
L C : 0 1 :200(392) [0637] Therefore, it is **explicitly** forbidden here to dishonor his
E P : R N :003(465) [0777] (that is, brief and **explicit** confessions) which were
S D : R N :008(505) [0853] a most correct and simple, yet sufficiently **explicit**, form.
S D : 0 7 :002(569) [0973] clearly, honestly, and **explicitly**, they all declare
S D : 0 7 :047(578) [0989] and obedience the **explicit**, certain, clear, and earnest
S D : 0 7 :092(586) [1005] us away from the simple, **explicit**, and clear
S D : 0 7 :110(588) [1011] the laity contrary to the **explicit** command and institution
S D : 0 8 :004(592) [1017] themselves publicly and **explicitly** to the Sacramentarians
S D : 1 2 :001(632) [1095] to which we have not **explicitly** adverted in this statement

Exploitation (1), Exploiters (1)
L C : 0 3 :084(431) [0723] on account of daily **exploitation** and usury in public
L C : 0 3 :084(432) [0723] with, of course; but let **exploiters** and oppressors beware

Explore (4)
S D : 1 1 :026(620) [1071] permit ourselves to try to **explore** the secret and hidden
S D : 1 1 :033(621) [1073] We should not **explore** the abyss of the hidden

Continued ▶

SD : 1 1 :055(625) [1081] has commanded us to **explore** it through our own
SD : 1 1 :064(626) [1083] and should not try to **explore** and explain everything in

Expose (7), Exposed (7)
PR : PR :010(006) [0011] articles in controversy, to **expose** and to reject false
AG : 2 5 :011(063) [0069] not say that you should **expose** yourself in public or
AL : 2 5 :011(063) [0069] not say that you should **expose** yourself in public or
AP : 2 3 :068(249) [0383] the Confutation, lest their fraud and slander be **exposed**.
LC : 0 3 :062(428) [0715] name, are disclosed and **exposed** in all their shame, when
EP : 1 1 :022(497) [0837] pure doctrine but have also **exposed** the contrary errors.
SD : RN :019(507) [0857] doctrine might be **exposed**, no matter where or in what
SD : 0 1 :033(514) [0869] not able to point out and **expose** the nature by itself and
SD : 0 2 :073(535) [0909] can readily recognize, **expose**, reject, and condemn such
SD : 0 3 :007(540) [0919] we clearly segregate, **expose**, and condemn the false
SD : 0 3 :044(547) [0933] named we must criticize, **expose**, and reject the following
SD : 0 7 :015(572) [0977] or carried about and **exposed** in procession, as happens in
SD : 0 7 :087(585) [1003] up, or carried about, or **exposed** for adoration, just as the
SD : 0 7 :087(585) [1003] or to cure leprosy, or is otherwise **exposed** for adoration.

Exposition (31), Expositions (6)
AP : 0 4 :039(112) [0131] Later on, in the **exposition** of our doctrine of the
AP : 1 0 :003(179) [0247] There is a long **exposition** of John 15 in Cyril which
EP : RN :004(465) [0777] consensus and **exposition** of our Christian faith,
EP : RN :008(465) [0779] merely witnesses and **expositions** of the faith, setting forth
EP : 0 1 :001(466) [0779] *to the aforesaid Standard and Comprehensive* ***Exposition***
EP : 1 1 :015(496) [0835] 14. This brief **exposition** of the doctrine of God's eternal
SD : 0 0 :000(501) [0845] Restatement and **Exposition** of a Number of Articles of
SD : RN :010(506) [0855] of errors, and **expositions** of doctrinal articles, should be
SD : RN :010(506) [0855] and used as helpful **expositions** and explanations.
SD : RN :013(506) [0855] us if we derive our **expositions** and decisions in the
SD : 0 1 :024(512) [0865] We shall give our **exposition** concerning the external,
SD : 0 1 :038(514) [0871] In the **exposition** of the First Article of the Creed in the
SD : 0 1 :049(517) [0875] this suffice as a simple **exposition** of the doctrine and the
SD : 0 1 :061(519) [0879] Dr. Luther in his Latin **exposition** of Genesis 3 likewise
SD : 0 1 :062(519) [0879] In his **exposition** of Ps. 90:12 he wrote, "Whether we call
SD : 0 2 :041(529) [0897] And in the **exposition** of the second petition of the Lord's
SD : 0 2 :044(529) [0897] Again, in his splendid **exposition** of Genesis, especially of
SD : 0 2 :083(537) [0913] From the foregoing **exposition** it is clear that when the
SD : 0 3 :028(544) [0925] and exhaustive **exposition** of the Epistle to the Galatians
SD : 0 3 :044(547) [0931] suffice as a summary **exposition** of the doctrine of
SD : 0 3 :067(551) [0937] beautiful and splendid **exposition** of St. Paul's Epistle to
SD : 0 5 :004(558) [0953] term includes both the **exposition** of the law and the
SD : 0 5 :011(560) [0955] Luther explains it in his **exposition** of the Gospel for the
SD : 0 7 :034(575) [0983] and especially from the **exposition** of Dr. Luther, as the
SD : 0 7 :054(579) [0991] confirmation, and **exposition** of the words of Christ
SD : 0 7 :066(581) [0995] and St. Paul's **exposition** of them, all the ancient
SD : 0 7 :121(590) [1013] of the Supper, as shown above in a previous **exposition**.
SD : 0 7 :128(591) [1015] in the foregoing **exposition**; for the sake of desirable
SD : 0 7 :128(591) [1015] from the foregoing **exposition**, for we reject and condemn
SD : 0 8 :086(608) [1047] to these as being clear **expositions** of the majesty of
SD : 1 0 :004(611) [1053] we offer the Christian reader the following **exposition**:
SD : 1 0 :025(615) [1061] From this **exposition** everyone can learn what a Christian
SD : 1 1 :025(620) [1071] for the further **exposition** and the salutary use of the
SD : 1 1 :093(632) [1093] direct, and useful **exposition** which is permanently and
SD : 1 1 :093(632) [1095] are contrary to these true, simple, and useful **expositions**.
SD : 1 1 :095(632) [1095] From our **exposition** friends and foes may clearly
SD : 1 2 :004(633) [1097] and unmistakable **exposition** of all the articles which were

Expound (4), Expounded (8), Expounding (2)
AG : 2 4 :041(061) [0069] were read and **expounded** in Alexandria, and all these
AL : 2 4 :041(061) [0069] are read and the doctors **expound** them on Wednesday
AP : 0 4 :014(109) [0123] aside the Gospel and **expounded** the ethics of Aristotle.
AP : 0 4 :369(163) [0221] take too long we shall **expound** it in another connection.
AP : 0 4 :381(165) [0223] Why not **expound** here God's grace and mercy toward
AP : 1 2 :178(211) [0307] We have **expounded** here a summary of our doctrine on
AP : 2 3 :037(244) [0373] righteousness of faith, as we have **expounded** it above.
SC : PR :017(340) [0535] **Expound** every commandment, petition, and part,
EP : 0 0 :000(464) [0777] Augsburg Confession **Expounded** and Settled in Christian
SD : RN :006(504) [0853] Confession is clearly **expounded** and defended against
SD : RN :020(508) [0859] and afterward **expounded** as occasion demanded and
SD : 0 4 :036(557) [0949] similar formulas in **expounding** Holy Scripture without in
SD : 0 5 :005(559) [0953] with repentance and **expounded** and urged not only the
SD : 0 8 :022(595) [1023] and "union," in **expounding** this mystery and have

Express (17), Expressed (11), Expressing (1), Expression (7), Expressions (12), Expressly (13)
PR : PR :019(009) [0017] erroneous doctrine is **expressly** rejected in the confession
PR : PR :022(011) [0019] have to be set forth **expressly** and distinctly in this
PR : PR :022(011) [0019] are contrary to the **expressed** Word of God and cannot
AG : PR :002(024) [0039] The desire was also **expressed** for deliberation on what
AG : 2 3 :013(053) [0063] in high station have **expressed** similar opinions and the
AP : PR :013(099) [0101] If any **expression** seems too strong, let me explain that
AP : 0 2 :026(103) [0111] we have correctly **expressed** both elements: lack of ability
AP : 0 4 :264(146) [0195] an extraneous particle **expressing** doubt, and in his
AP : 0 4 :266(146) [0197] He uses other words to **express** this same thought, and
AP : 0 4 :399(168) [0227] opinions were being **expressed** about our Confession, a
AP : 0 4 :399(168) [0227] princes regarded this **expression** as unworthy of being
AP : 1 2 :059(190) [0267] Our opponents **expressly** condemn our statement that
AP : 1 2 :122(200) [0289] would be contrary to the **express** commands of the
AP : 1 3 :006(212) [0311] ones which have an **express** command from God and a
AP : 1 6 :007(223) [0331] is not forbidden but **expressly** commanded, and it is a
AP : 1 8 :004(225) [0335] can talk about God and **express** its worship of him in
AP : 2 0 :001(226) [0337] In Article XX they **expressly** state their rejection and
AP : 2 3 :014(241) [0367] This is an **express** command, directed to anyone not
AP : 2 4 :095(267) [0417] *operato*, they would **express** themselves far differently.
AP : 2 7 :027(274) [0429] even Mohammedan **expressions** in the church, finding the
S3 : 0 3 :013(305) [0483] Hence the **expression** in the pulpit when the general
TR : 0 0 :007(320) [0505] In Luke 22:24-27 Christ **expressly** forbids lordship among
TR : 0 0 :010(321) [0505] From this fact he **expressly** argues that his call did not
TR : 0 0 :054(329) [0519] God **expressly** exhorts kings, "Now therefore, O kings, be
TR : 0 0 :055(329) [0521] nobody the right to **express** an opinion, except his
LC : 0 1 :079(375) [0603] hence our common **expression** for "stopping work"
LC : 0 2 :005(411) [0679] nor could they all be clearly **expressed** in so few words.
LC : 0 2 :031(414) [0685] serve to clarify and **express** how and by what means this
LC : 0 2 :035(415) [0687] In it is **expressed** and portrayed the Holy Spirit and his
LC : 0 2 :047(416) [0689] Both **expressions** have the same meaning.
LC : 0 2 :047(416) [0691] idiomatically, we must **express** it quite differently.
LC : 0 2 :049(417) [0691] no German would use or understand such an **expression**.
LC : 0 2 :050(417) [0691] I say in order that the **expression** may be understood; it
LC : 0 3 :027(424) [0705] wishes you to lament and **express** your needs and wants,
LC : 0 3 :068(429) [0717] have been very simply **expressed**, yet we have prayed in
LC : 0 4 :033(440) [0739] beautifully and clearly **expressed** in these same words,
LC : 0 4 :034(440) [0741] So this single **expression**, "He who believes," is so potent
LC : 0 6 :008(458) [0000] These two kinds are **expressed** in the Lord's Prayer when
LC : 0 6 :022(459) [0000] however, to confess and **express** your needs, not for the
EP : 0 2 :016(472) [0789] teachers have used **expressions** such as, "God draws, but
EP : 0 2 :016(472) [0789] Since these **expressions** have been introduced to confirm
EP : 0 2 :016(472) [0791] God, we hold that these **expressions** do not agree with the
EP : 0 3 :010(474) [0795] apostle Paul uses such **expressions** as *"by grace,"*
EP : 0 3 :010(474) [0795] All these **expressions** say in effect that we become
EP : 0 8 :034(491) [0825] That in spite of Christ's **express** assertion, "All authority
EP : 1 2 :008(498) [0839] it, in spite of the **expressed** word of God's promise which
SD : RN :009(505) [0853] Here he **expressly** asserts by way of distinction that the
SD : RN :016(507) [0857] come to a clear and **express** mutual agreement concerning
SD : 0 1 :045(516) [0873] and other similar **expressions** with which we do not want
SD : 0 2 :066(534) [0907] conversion, as St. Paul **expressly** and earnestly reminds
SD : 0 2 :081(537) [0911] Augustine condemns in **express** words in his commentary
SD : 0 4 :037(557) [0951] which, contrary to the **express** Word of God, is being
SD : 0 4 :038(557) [0951] It is God's will and **express** command that believers
SD : 0 7 :036(575) [0985] him," or "God was in Christ," and similar **expressions**.
SD : 0 7 :045(577) [0987] or metaphorical **expressions**, as they appear to our
SD : 0 7 :060(580) [0993] But St. Paul teaches **expressly** that not only godly, pious,
SD : 0 7 :067(582) [0997] These **expressions** are so terrible that a pious Christian
SD : 0 7 :127(591) [1015] questions and **expressions** which are advanced in a
SD : 0 8 :059(602) [1035] of the Son of Man, but **expressly** points to his assumed
SD : 1 1 :052(625) [1079] between what God has **expressly** revealed in his Word and
SD : 1 2 :013(634) [1099] it, contrary to the **express** words of the promise which

Expulsion (2)
EP : 1 2 :026(500) [0843] in which public **expulsion** and the orderly process of
SD : 1 2 :034(635) [1101] in which public **expulsion** or orderly process of

Exquisite (1), Exquisitely (1)
AP : 1 5 :049(221) [0329] as necessary, they bring **exquisite** torture to a conscience
LC : 0 2 :063(419) [0695] his will, and his work **exquisitely** depicted in very short

Extend (6), Extended (2), Extending (1), Extends (9), Extensive (5), Extensively (2), Extent (23)
PR : PR :011(006) [0011] to one another, in **extensive** writings based on God's
AG : 2 7 :028(075) [0079] known to what an **extent** perpetual chastity lies within
AL : 0 0 :005(048) [0059] conscience, they have to some **extent** been corrected.
AL : 2 4 :011(057) [0065] how widely this abuse **extends** in all the churches, by
AL : 2 7 :028(075) [0079] not unknown to what an **extent** perpetual chastity lies in
AL : 2 8 :063(092) [0093] and they prescribe the **extent** to which one is allowed to
AP : PR :016(099) [0101] to our danger; its **extent** is evident from the bitter hatred
AP : 0 4 :007(108) [0121] For to some **extent** human reason naturally understands
AP : 0 4 :023(110) [0127] To some **extent**, reason can produce this righteousness by
AP : 0 4 :181(132) [0171] of the law, to the **extent** that they fulfill the law.
AP : 0 4 :181(132) [0171] And to that **extent** this obedience of the law justifies by
AP : 0 4 :288(151) [0203] understood and, to some **extent**, its requirements can be
AP : 1 2 :076(193) [0273] we could do so to some **extent**, still we must believe that
AP : 1 6 :004(223) [0331] have written **extensively** on this subject because the
AP : 1 8 :004(225) [0335] To some **extent** it can achieve civil righteousness or the
AP : 1 8 :009(226) [0337] righteousness and that, to some **extent**, we can achieve it.
AP : 2 8 :015(283) [0447] we nevertheless added the **extent** to which it is legitimate
AP : 2 8 :021(284) [0449] To the **extent** that they teach wicked things, they should
S1 : PR :012(290) [0459] ascendancy to such an **extent** that ten councils and twenty
SC : PR :020(340) [0537] The **extent** to which parents and governing authorities sin
LC : 0 1 :033(369) [0589] kindness and goodness **extend** to many thousands, lest
LC : 0 1 :178(389) [0631] as a warning; a more **extensive** explanation will have to
LC : 0 1 :192(391) [0635] into a fire, and could **extend** him my hand to pull him
LC : 0 1 :210(393) [0641] Christendom and even **extending** throughout all the
LC : 0 1 :250(399) [0651] narrow limits but must **extend** to all our relations with
LC : 0 1 :262(400) [0655] Next, it **extends** much further when it is applied to
LC : 0 3 :072(430) [0719] therefore enlarge and **extend** your thoughts to include
EP : 0 8 :002(487) [0817] with each other, and how far does this sharing **extend**?
EP : 0 8 :029(490) [0825] of Christ is locally **extended** to every place in heaven and
EP : 1 1 :004(494) [0833] 3. This foreknowledge **extends** alike over good people and
EP : 1 2 :008(498) [0839] of God's promise which **extends** only to those who keep
SD : RN :006(504) [0853] had been submitted, an **extensive** Apology was prepared
SD : RN :009(505) [0853] as appealing to further **extensive** statements in his
SD : 0 2 :003(520) [0881] that he can to some **extent** prepare himself for grace and
SD : 0 2 :026(526) [0891] To some **extent** reason and free will are able to lead an
SD : 0 2 :031(527) [0893] also declare that to a certain **extent** reason has a free will.
SD : 0 2 :077(536) [0911] — though only to a small **extent** and in a weak way —
SD : 0 5 :022(562) [0959] the heathen had to some **extent** a knowledge of God,
SD : 0 7 :066(581) [0997] direct the Christian reader to our more **extensive** writings.
SD : 0 7 :091(585) [1005] have been thoroughly, **extensively**, and definitively
SD : 0 8 :051(601) [1033] as far as their capacity **extends**, but primarily from and
SD : 0 8 :092(609) [1049] of Christ is locally **extended** into every place in heaven
SD : 1 0 :013(613) [1057] yielded to a certain **extent**, Paul criticized them publicly
SD : 1 1 :004(616) [1063] God's foreknowledge — **extends** to all creatures, good or
SD : 1 1 :005(617) [1065] to salvation does not **extend** over both the godly and the
SD : 1 1 :028(620) [1071] of repentance **extends** over all men (Luke 24:47), so also
SD : 1 1 :058(626) [1081] that the punishment **extends** also to their posterity, as
SD : 1 2 :013(634) [1099] of the promise which **extends** only to those who keep the

Extenuate (1)
PR : PR :019(009) [0017] intention to palliate, to **extenuate**, or to confirm as

Exterior (1)
EP : 0 7 :022(484) [0813] of Christ and that only the **exterior** appearance remains.

Exterminate (2), Exterminated (2)
LC : 0 1 :034(369) [0589] the fourth generation, until they are utterly **exterminated**.
LC : 0 3 :054(427) [0713] sin, death, and hell **exterminated**, and that we may live
LC : 0 3 :068(429) [0717] it in their attempt utterly to **exterminate** the Gospel.
LC : 0 3 :069(429) [0717] how to suppress and **exterminate** us so that their will and

External (80), Externally (5)
AG : 0 5 :004(031) [0045] and works without the **external** word of the Gospel.
AL : 0 5 :004(031) [0045] to men without the **external** Word, through their own
AP : 0 4 :008(108) [0121] does not only require **external** works that reason can
AP : 0 4 :018(109) [0125] performs only certain **external** works and meanwhile
AP : 0 4 :226(138) [0183] with God, while love has infinite **external** duties to men.
AP : 0 4 :275(148) [0199] reason is that we need **external** signs of this exceedingly
AP : 0 4 :282(149) [0201] a twofold cleanness, one internal and the other **external**.
AP : 1 2 :142(204) [0295] that God's law deals with **external**, civil righteousness.
AP : 1 2 :142(204) [0295] For though we can do **external** works that God's law
AP : 1 6 :008(223) [0333] the Gospel is something **external**, a new and monastic
AP : 1 8 :004(225) [0335] **Externally**, it can choose to keep the hands from murder,
S 3 : 0 8 :003(312) [0495] which concern the **external**, spoken Word, we must hold
S 3 : 0 8 :003(312) [0495] through or with the **external** Word which comes before.
S 3 : 0 8 :005(312) [0495] He led them from the **external** Word of God to
S 3 : 0 8 :005(312) [0495] and he did this through other **external** words.
S 3 : 0 8 :006(312) [0495] of our day condemn the **external** Word, yet they do not
S 3 : 0 8 :007(313) [0495] to their faith through the **external** Word which preceded.
S 3 : 0 8 :010(313) [0497] with us except through his **external** Word and sacrament.
S 3 : 0 8 :013(313) [0497] But without the **external** Word they were not holy, and
TR : 0 0 :034(325) [0513] was thought to be that **external** government which the
SC : 0 6 :010(352) [0557] preparation are a good **external** discipline, but he is truly
LC : 0 1 :082(376) [0603] It is an entirely **external** matter, like the other ordinances
LC : 0 1 :088(377) [0605] stove and refrain from **external** work, or deck ourselves
LC : 0 1 :092(377) [0607] it, not on account of the **external** work but on account of
LC : 0 1 :202(392) [0639] Not only is the **external** act forbidden, but also every kind
LC : 0 3 :007(421) [0699] Such **external** repetition, when properly used, may serve
LC : 0 4 :007(437) [0733] that Baptism is an **external** thing and that external things
LC : 0 4 :007(437) [0733] an external thing and that **external** things are of no use.
LC : 0 4 :008(437) [0733] But no matter how **external** it may be, here stand God's
LC : 0 4 :019(439) [0737] sacraments and all the **external** things ordained and
LC : 0 4 :019(439) [0737] according to the gross, **external** mask (as we see the shell
LC : 0 4 :028(440) [0739] and that works and **external** things contribute nothing to
LC : 0 4 :029(440) [0739] his Word in this **external** ordinance and offered it to us so
LC : 0 4 :030(440) [0739] on the ground that the object is something **external**.
LC : 0 4 :030(440) [0739] Yes, it must be **external** so that it can be perceived and
LC : 0 4 :030(440) [0739] as the entire Gospel is an **external**, oral proclamation.
LC : 0 4 :030(440) [0739] effects in us he does through such **external** ordinances.
LC : 0 4 :038(441) [0741] even though Baptism is an entirely **external** thing.
LC : 0 4 :064(444) [0749] just this sign and **external** observance for the sacrament
LC : 0 4 :072(445) [0751] So the **external** sign has been appointed not only on
LC : 0 5 :010(448) [0755] Word is joined to the **external** element, it becomes a
LC : 0 5 :037(451) [0761] have their place as an **external** preparation and children's
EP : 0 1 :014(468) [0783] or splashed on **externally** and that underneath man's
EP : 0 1 :015(468) [0783] original sin is only an **external** impediment to man's good
EP : 0 2 :008(471) [0789] compulsion, even in his **external** acts, and that he
EP : 0 6 :001(479) [0805] reasons: (1) to maintain **external** discipline against unruly
EP : 0 7 :020(484) [0813] own virtues or in our internal and **external** preparations.
EP : 0 7 :030(485) [0815] is effected solely by the **external** signs of bread and wine
EP : 0 7 :039(486) [0817] because they are still imperfect in their **external** behavior.
EP : 0 7 :040(486) [0817] 19. That the **external** visible elements of bread and wine
EP : 1 0 :007(493) [0831] it has fewer or more **external** ceremonies not commanded
EP : 1 0 :010(494) [0831] of the Christian liberty which it has in **external** matters.
EP : 1 0 :012(494) [0831] 4. When such **external** ceremonies and indifferent things
SD : 0 1 :012(510) [0863] True, in natural and **external** things which are subject to
SD : 0 1 :021(511) [0865] a simple, insignificant, **external** spot or blemish, merely
SD : 0 1 :022(512) [0865] powers, but only an **external** impediment to them, just as
SD : 0 1 :024(512) [0865] concerning the **external**, temporal, and civil affairs which
SD : 0 1 :033(514) [0869] Just as in the case of **external** leprosy the body which is
SD : 0 1 :060(519) [0879] and all its internal and **external** powers, but that it is
SD : 0 2 :002(520) [0881] his conversion can do in **external** things affecting this
SD : 0 2 :004(520) [0881] (that is, without the **external** preaching and hearing of the
SD : 0 2 :019(524) [0889] or that in outward or **external** secular things he cannot
SD : 0 2 :020(524) [0889] Ps. 91: "In secular and **external** matters affecting the
SD : 0 2 :032(527) [0893] power to perform such **external** works, we declare that in
SD : 0 2 :053(531) [0903] and read this Word **externally** because, as stated above,
SD : 0 2 :053(531) [0903] of a free will in these **external** matters, so that he can go
SD : 0 2 :074(535) [0909] coercion; that even in **external** works man's will has no
SD : 0 2 :074(535) [0909] to achieve a measure of **external** righteousness and
SD : 0 4 :017(554) [0943] so that he does **externally**, for a pretense, something that
SD : 0 5 :010(559) [0955] can fulfill the law by **external** works, or drives man
SD : 0 6 :001(563) [0963] (1) not only to maintain **external** discipline and decency
SD : 0 6 :003(564) [0963] in accord with God's **external** and immutable will.
SD : 0 6 :007(565) [0965] to their nature and to all its internal and **external** powers.
SD : 0 7 :004(569) [0973] Supper was only an **external** sign whereby one can
SD : 0 7 :086(584) [1003] alone, but the entire **external** and visible action of the
SD : 0 7 :115(589) [1011] as bread and wine are **external** food for our body, so the
SD : 0 7 :116(589) [1011] signs, as through an **external** pledge, we are assured that
SD : 0 7 :116(589) [1011] the Supper we receive the **external** sign with our mouth.
SD : 0 7 :116(589) [1013] Christ, distributed to us, but through the **external** signs.
SD : 0 7 :123(590) [1015] of God who are in the **external** community of the church
SD : 1 0 :005(611) [1053] the name and guise of **external** adiaphora and are given a
SD : 1 0 :009(612) [1055] the weak in faith in such **external** matters of indifference
SD : 1 0 :014(613) [1057] longer dealing with the **external** adiaphora which in their
SD : 1 0 :016(613) [1057] or conforming in **external** things, where Christian
SD : 1 1 :034(622) [1075] God intended to say: "**Externally** I do indeed through the

Extinguish (2), Extinguished (5)
AG : 2 6 :006(064) [0071] almost completely **extinguished** by those who have taught
AP : 0 4 :222(138) [0181] that is, faith is **extinguished**, no matter how great it may
AP : 2 1 :030(233) [0351] out with their lamps **extinguished**, they begged the wise
S 3 : 0 3 :018(306) [0483] It did not **extinguish** the lust for sin.
TR : 0 0 :034(325) [0513] of faith and of a spiritual kingdom was **extinguished**.
TR : 0 0 :048(328) [0519] and have utterly **extinguished** the teaching concerning
EP : 1 1 :013(496) [0835] temptations and thus **extinguish** the flaming darts of the

Extol (5), Extolled (4), Extolling (2), Extols (2)
AG : 2 7 :022(074) [0079] No matter how much one **extols** the vow and the
AL : 2 5 :005(062) [0069] were immoderately **extolled**, but nothing was said about
AP : 0 4 :197(134) [0175] Paul **extols** the commandment to honor our parents by
AP : 0 4 :322(157) [0209] he is innocent and by **extolling** himself should perish even
AP : 1 1 :002(180) [0249] have so explained and **extolled** the blessing of absolution
AP : 1 3 :013(212) [0311] It is good to **extol** the ministry of the Word with every
AP : 2 1 :004(229) [0343] greatest gifts, we should **extol** them very highly; we
AP : 2 1 :044(236) [0357] we know you want to **extol** and advance, we implore you
LC : 0 1 :314(407) [0671] a precious work that cannot be sufficiently **extolled**.
LC : 0 1 :333(410) [0677] are to be exalted and **extolled** above all orders,
LC : 0 3 :046(426) [0709] as in our idiom "to praise, **extol**, and honor" in word and
LC : 0 4 :017(438) [0737] no one can sufficiently **extol**, for it contains and conveys
SD : 0 1 :003(509) [0861] Furthermore, we are **extolling** God's honor properly when

Extorted (5), Extortion (1)
AP : 2 7 :009(270) [0421] vows if they have been **extorted** from the unwilling, or
S 1 : PR :012(290) [0459] domestics, and laborers, **extortion** in every trade and on
EP : 0 6 :005(480) [0807] law as long as they are **extorted** from people only under
SD : 0 4 :003(551) [0939] since they are not **extorted** by fear and punishment of the
SD : 0 4 :017(554) [0943] to that which is **extorted** from a person against his will,
SD : 0 6 :016(566) [0967] his good works are **extorted** by the law, just as in the case

Extra (2)
AP : 0 4 :360(162) [0219] suppose that they have **extra** merits which they can give
AP : 0 4 :360(162) [0219] merits than another, therefore some have **extra** merits.

Extraneous (3)
AP : 0 4 :264(146) [0195] Here Jerome adds an **extraneous** particle expressing
EP : 0 1 :018(468) [0783] sin but something **extraneous** and alien within man, and
SD : 0 3 :029(544) [0925] have to do into another **extraneous** matter which does

Extraordinary (3)
AP : 2 3 :007(240) [0365] suspended without an **extraordinary** work of God, it
AP : 2 3 :008(240) [0367] the nature of man without an **extraordinary** act of God.
AP : 2 3 :012(241) [0367] Since only an **extraordinary** act of God can change this

Extravagance (1), Extravagant (3)
AP : 0 7 :025(173) [0235] are in existence many **extravagant** and wicked writings
AP : 2 7 :047(277) [0437] praise it the way the ***Extravagant*** does, saying that
AP : 2 7 :047(277) [0437] to heap such **extravagant** praises upon something that
S 1 : PR :012(290) [0459] Wantonness, lewdness, **extravagance** in dress, gluttony,

Extreme (1), Extremely (3)
AP : 1 3 :006(212) [0309] Confirmation and **extreme** unction are rites received from
LC : 0 1 :258(399) [0653] at present, but among the Jews it was **extremely** common.
SD : 0 2 :020(525) [0889] man is indeed very clever, intelligent, and **extremely** busy.
SD : 0 4 :022(554) [0945] But here we must be **extremely** careful that works are not

Eye (5), Eyes (49)
PR : PR :001(003) [0007] and dignity, under whose **eyes** this document comes, we,
PR : PR :024(013) [0023] away from everyone's **eyes**, or to put the light of divine
AG : 2 7 :048(078) [0081] is obscured when man's **eyes** are dazzled with this curious
AL : 2 7 :048(078) [0081] is obscured when the **eyes** of men are blinded by these
AP : 0 2 :049(106) [0119] those who are wise and righteous in the **eyes** of the world.
AP : 0 4 :033(111) [0129] deeds that are excellent and praiseworthy in human **eyes**.
AP : 0 4 :265(146) [0197] In human **eyes**, works are very impressive.
AP : 0 4 :296(152) [0205] Moses, we must turn our **eyes** to Christ, and believe that
AP : 1 3 :005(212) [0309] the rite itself enters through the **eyes** to move the heart.
AP : 1 3 :005(212) [0309] the rite is received by the **eyes** and is a sort of picture of
AP : 2 2 :008(237) [0359] but they throw sand in the **eyes** of the uninitiated, who
AP : 2 4 :052(259) [0403] priesthood and sacrifices is spread before their **eyes**.
AP : 2 4 :070(262) [0409] the heart to believe through what it presents to the **eyes**.
AP : 2 7 :052(278) [0437] going on before their very **eyes**, our opponents should
S 3 : 0 3 :042(309) [0491] as I saw with my own **eyes** at the time of the uprising)
SC : 0 8 :007(353) [0559] "The **eyes** of all look to Thee, O Lord, and Thou givest
SC : 0 9 :010(356) [0563] Christ; not in the way of **eye**-service, as men-pleasers, but
LC : PR :014(360) [0571] and keep them before our **eyes** and in our hands as a
LC : 0 1 :042(370) [0591] honor, wealth, and every comfort in the **eyes** of the world.
LC : 0 1 :121(382) [0615] if we were to open our **eyes** and ears and take this to
LC : 0 1 :164(387) [0627] Those who keep their **eyes** on God's will and
LC : 0 1 :187(390) [0633] ever before our **eyes** as a mirror in which to see ourselves,
LC : 0 1 :231(396) [0647] should be told that in the **eyes** of God they are the
LC : 0 1 :232(396) [0647] may be continually and urgently kept before their **eyes**.
LC : 0 1 :243(397) [0649] evidence before our very **eyes** every day that no stolen or
LC : 0 1 :248(398) [0651] crowd, but may keep their **eyes** fixed upon God's
LC : 0 1 :258(399) [0653] speak dishonestly with an **eye** to gaining favor, money,
LC : 0 1 :259(400) [0655] be quite blind, shutting his **eyes** and ears to everything
LC : 0 1 :287(403) [0663] No one covers his face, **eyes**, nose, and mouth; we do not
LC : 0 1 :287(403) [0663] Our hands and **eyes**, even the whole body, must help
LC : 0 1 :296(405) [0665] even though in the **eyes** of the world you could do it
LC : 0 1 :307(406) [0669] greed, even though in the **eyes** of the world you might
LC : 0 1 :311(407) [0671] how great or precious it may be in the **eyes** of the world.
LC : 0 1 :313(407) [0671] are not important or impressive in the **eyes** of the world.
LC : 0 1 :314(407) [0671] other hand, those other works captivate all **eyes** and ears.
LC : 0 1 :331(410) [0677] incessantly before our **eyes** and constantly in our
LC : 0 2 :017(412) [0681] we have and see before our **eyes**, but also daily guards
LC : 0 2 :022(413) [0683] For we sin daily with **eyes** and ears, hands, body and
LC : 0 3 :122(436) [0731] That means they have their **eye** not on God's promise but
LC : 0 4 :020(439) [0737] reference to their noses, **eyes**, skin and hair, flesh and
LC : 0 5 :057(453) [0767] If you choose to fix your **eye** on how good and pure you
EP : 0 1 :010(467) [0781] I shall see for myself, and mine **eyes** shall behold him."
EP : 0 5 :008(479) [0803] veil of Moses covers their **eyes**, as a result they fail to
EP : 0 7 :036(485) [0815] but should lift their **eyes** from the bread to heaven and
SD : 0 1 :036(514) [0869] Thy **eyes** behold my uniformed substance; in thy book
SD : 0 1 :038(515) [0871] my body and soul, **eyes**, ears, and all my members, my
SD : 0 2 :020(525) [0889] uses neither mouth nor **eyes** nor senses nor heart,
SD : 0 2 :026(526) [0891] heart, seeing **eyes**, and hearing ears (Deut. 29:4; Matt.
SD : 0 6 :004(564) [0963] before believers' **eyes** and continually to urge it upon them
SD : 0 6 :020(567) [0969] is right in his own **eyes**, but heed all these words which I
SD : 0 7 :022(573) [0979] and look anyone in the **eye** who thinks that he can
SD : 0 7 :084(584) [1001] and reception, before our **eyes** in I Cor. 10:16.
SD : 0 8 :096(609) [1049] to believe, close the **eyes** of reason, take their intellect
SD : 1 1 :004(617) [1063] Again, "Thine **eyes** beheld my unformed substance, in thy

Faber (3)
S 3 : 1 5 :005(317) [0501] Wendal **Faber**, pastor of Seeburg in Mansfeld
S 3 : 1 5 :005(318) [0501] the Rev. Nicholas **Faber**
TR : 0 0 :082(335) [0529] Wendel **Faber**, pastor of Seeburg in Mansfeld

Fables (2)
AP : 21 :037(234) [0353] But the inventors of these **fables**, which imitate the epics
SD : 02 :009(522) [0883] them they consider it all mere foolishness and **fables**.

Fabricate (2), Fabricated (2), Fabrications (1)
PR : PR :008(005) [0011] to desist from their **fabricated** slanders and defamation of
AP : 23 :010(241) [0367] No one could **fabricate** anything more crafty than this
AP : 24 :031(255) [0395] about these shameless **fabrications** of the monks and
AP : 27 :034(275) [0431] they wickedly **fabricate** works of supererogation and sell
S2 : 02 :005(293) [0463] thing which was **fabricated** and invented without God's

Face (22)
PR : PR :022(012) [0021] desire to testify before the **face** of almighty God and the
AP : 04 :021(110) [0127] they look as the Jews did at the veiled **face** of Moses.
AP : 04 :133(125) [0159] the veil that covered the **face** of Moses cannot be removed
AP : 04 :229(139) [0183] they did not see the true **face** of Moses but only his veiled
AP : 04 :229(139) [0183] Moses but only his veiled **face**, just as the Pharisees,
AP : 12 :078(193) [0275] as the Jews looked at Moses' **face** covered by a veil.
AP : 23 :003(239) [0363] the king with the modest **face**, for the saying appears
AP : 23 :003(239) [0363] you, "A man with a modest **face** will reign everywhere."
AP : 23 :006(240) [0365] In the **face** of the clear truth which we have advanced,
S1 : PR :009(290) [0457] Imagine how those will **face** us on the last day, before the
LC : 01 :042(370) [0591] these words, even in the **face** of this apparent
LC : 01 :115(381) [0613] joyfully to boast in the **face** of all who are occupied with
LC : 01 :273(401) [0659] rebuke him straight to his **face** and make him blush for
LC : 01 :287(403) [0663] No one covers his **face**, eyes, nose, and mouth; we do not
LC : 03 :068(429) [0717] may remain steadfast in the **face** of all violence and
EP : 01 :015(468) [0783] spot can be washed from the **face** or color from the wall.
SD : 01 :022(512) [0865] a smudge of dirt from one's **face** or paint from the wall.
SD : 05 :010(560) [0955] veil which "he put over his **face**" remains unremoved, so
SD : 06 :025(568) [0971] just as they will see God **face** to face, so through God's
SD : 06 :025(568) [0971] they will see God face to **face**, so through God's
SD : 08 :065(604) [1039] life we shall behold his glory **face** to face (John 17:24).
SD : 08 :065(604) [1039] life we shall behold his glory face to **face** (John 17:24).

Fact (83), Facts (4)
PR : PR :019(009) [0017] simple folk in spite of the **fact** that this erroneous
AG : 23 :014(053) [0063] take into account that **fact** that, in these last times of
AG : 23 :014(053) [0063] Christian to recognize this **fact** in order that the
AG : 23 :019(054) [0063] great crime, in spite of that **fact** that in the Holy
AG : 26 :017(066) [0073] In **fact**, Augustine was also displeased that consciences
AG : 27 :006(071) [0077] to remain, in spite of the **fact** that even the papal canons
AG : 27 :016(073) [0077] In **fact**, it is called a state of perfection and is regarded as
AG : 27 :044(078) [0081] In **fact**, they have invented a still more indecent and
AG : 28 :033(086) [0087] Besides, they appeal to the **fact** that the Sabbath was
AG : 28 :041(087) [0089] is reserved, in spite of the **fact** that canon law says
AL : 22 :007(050) [0061] In **fact**, Pope Gelasius commanded that the sacrament
AL : 23 :012(052) [0063] In **fact**, they offered such resistance that the archbishop
AL : 26 :002(064) [0071] so is evident from the **fact** that new ceremonies, new
AL : 27 :010(072) [0077] these evils was added the **fact** that vows had such a
AL : 27 :016(073) [0077] In **fact**, they assert that it is a state of perfection, and they
AL : 27 :044(078) [0081] In **fact**, they invented greater absurdities when they
AP : 04 :018(109) [0125] This in spite of the **fact** that the law is never satisfied,
AP : 04 :053(114) [0137] the promise itself, the **fact** that the promise is free, and
AP : 04 :053(114) [0137] is accepted by faith; the **fact** that it is free excludes our
AP : 04 :110(123) [0153] In **fact**, we do not love at all unless our hearts are sure
AP : 04 :141(126) [0161] In **fact**, we add that it is impossible to separate faith from
AP : 04 :297(152) [0205] There are two basic **facts**: First we are not justified by the
AP : 04 :299(153) [0205] and to rely on the sure **fact** that they have a reconciled
AP : 04 :312(155) [0207] cannot be divided in **fact** the way they are in idle
AP : 04 :316(156) [0209] not mention faith or the **fact** that for Christ's sake we
AP : 04 :392(167) [0225] This in spite of the **fact** that prelates and some
AP : 07 :010(170) [0229] only in name and not in **fact**, while the godly are part of
AP : 07 :010(170) [0229] godly are part of the church in **fact** as well as in name.
AP : 07 :012(170) [0231] of Christ and is the church in **fact** as well as in name.
AP : 07 :014(170) [0231] Testament people by the **fact** that the church is a spiritual
AP : 07 :018(171) [0233] The **fact** that the revelation has not yet come does not
AP : 07 :040(176) [0241] In **fact**, Paul calls such opinions "doctrines of demons."
AP : 09 :003(178) [0245] children is shown by the **fact** that God gives the Holy
AP : 11 :005(181) [0249] In **fact**, if everyone rushed in at the same time, the people
AP : 12 :009(183) [0255] motives is possible, but in **fact** they are not so separated
AP : 12 :173(209) [0305] In **fact**, they admit in their schools that it is not a sin to
AP : 13 :023(214) [0313] In **fact**, Augustine says the opposite: that faith in the
AP : 18 :005(225) [0335] men, as we see from the **fact** that even philosophers who
AP : 20 :014(228) [0343] of sins is free; in **fact**, the Pelagians were condemned for
AP : 21 :028(232) [0351] The **fact** of the matter is that in popular estimation the
AP : 21 :033(233) [0351] In **fact**, there is no proof for it either in the Fathers of the
AP : 23 :011(241) [0367] Let us therefore keep this **fact** in mind, taught by
AP : 23 :060(247) [0381] No sane man can argue with these cogent **facts**.
AP : 24 :009(251) [0387] adduce are silenced by the **fact** that the Mass does not
AP : 24 :066(261) [0407] We are aware of the **fact** that the Fathers call the Mass a
AP : 24 :078(263) [0411] does not follow from the **fact** that the Mass is called a
AP : 24 :091(266) [0415] faithful if they ponder the **fact** that the Mass has largely
AP : 27 :007(269) [0421] Another sign is the **fact** that sometimes they are
AP : 27 :041(276) [0435] The **fact** that Christ speaks of leaving wife and children
AP : 27 :067(280) [0441] As a matter of **fact**, the church did not yet know about
S2 : 02 :012(295) [0465] apart entirely from the **fact** that it is error and idolatry.
S3 : 03 :043(310) [0491] holy people, aside from the **fact** that they still possess and
TR : 00 :010(321) [0505] From this **fact** he expressly argues that his call did not
TR : 00 :012(322) [0507] In **fact**, all the Eastern bishops should forever have
TR : 00 :049(329) [0519] In **fact**, he contends that he is above councils and can
TR : 00 :063(331) [0523] The **fact** itself bears witness to this, for the power is the
TR : 00 :072(332) [0525] From all these **facts** it is evident that the church retains
LC : SP :006(362) [0575] wish to be Christians in **fact** as well as in name, both
LC : 01 :025(368) [0587] and pours forth all that is good in name and in **fact**.
LC : 01 :051(371) [0595] or should know that the **facts** are otherwise — for
LC : 02 :052(417) [0691] into it through the **fact** that I have heard and still hear
LC : 03 :012(422) [0701] From the **fact** that prayer is so urgently commanded, we
LC : 04 :010(437) [0735] From this **fact** everyone can easily conclude that it is of
LC : 04 :056(443) [0747] I cannot build on the **fact** that I believe and many people
LC : 05 :052(452) [0765] move and impel you is the **fact** that Christ desires it, and
LC : 05 :077(455) [0771] But the **fact** that we are insensitive to our sin is all the
EP : RN :003(465) [0777] time of the apostles — in **fact**, already during their lifetime
EP : 03 :015(475) [0795] to be made righteous in **fact** before God on account of
EP : 06 :004(480) [0805] In **fact**, it has only begun, and in the spirit of their mind
EP : 08 :025(490) [0823] since really (that is, in **fact**) the deity has nothing in
EP : 08 :031(491) [0825] with the human nature in **fact**, as though it did not
EP : 12 :005(498) [0839] spirituality, which in **fact** is nothing else but a new kind
SD : 01 :005(509) [0861] In **fact**, we must consider this as the chief sin, the root
SD : 01 :027(513) [0867] The **fact** is, that Satan misled Adam and Eve through the
SD : 01 :042(515) [0873] But the **fact** that our nature is corrupted, that our
SD : 03 :004(540) [0917] with God, and the **fact** that we are adopted as God's
SD : 03 :053(548) [0933] one and the same way; in **fact**, that when we are justified
SD : 05 :003(558) [0953] chiefly occasioned by the **fact** that the little word
SD : 05 :012(560) [0955] In **fact**, where is there a more earnest and terrible
SD : 08 :011(593) [1019] person, in spite of the **fact** that two distinct natures, each
SD : 08 :031(597) [1025] personal union (that is, the **fact** that the divine and
SD : 08 :040(599) [1029] a poor Saviour for me, in **fact**, he himself would need a
SD : 11 :004(616) [1063] For the **fact** that God sees and knows everything before it
SD : 11 :028(620) [1071] rigidly and firmly to the **fact** that as the proclamation of
SD : 11 :053(625) [1081] we cannot harmonize — in **fact**, we have no command to
SD : 11 :060(626) [1083] his Spirit, nor his grace; in **fact**, when he does graciously
SD : 11 :088(631) [1093] before we were born (in **fact**, "before the foundation of

Faction (1), Factions (8), Factitious (1)
PR : PR :003(003) [0007] over against both the papacy and all sorts of **factions**.
AP : 04 :232(140) [0185] schisms and the hatreds, **factions**, and heresies that arise
AP : 09 :002(178) [0245] against the wicked and seditious **faction** of these robbers.
AP : 27 :008(269) [0421] opinion of human and "**factitious**" services, as some
EP : 12 :000(498) [0839] XII. Other **Factions** and Sects Which Have Not
EP : 12 :001(498) [0839] made no mention of the errors held by these **factions**.
EP : 12 :002(498) [0839] have split into many **factions**, some of which teach many
SD : 12 :000(632) [1095] XII. Other **Factions** and Sects Which Never Accepted the
SD : 12 :001(632) [1095] As far as the sects and **factions** are concerned which
SD : 12 :007(633) [1097] errors of the aforementioned **factions** and sects.

Factors (2)
AP : 22 :014(238) [0361] of spilling and similar **factors** which are not cogent
SD : 03 :037(546) [0929] only to the smallest degree **factors** in our justification.

Faculty (2), Faculties (3)
SC : 02 :002(345) [0543] my reason and all the **faculties** of my mind, together with
LC : 02 :013(412) [0681] great and small, all the **faculties** of my mind, my reason
SD : 01 :010(510) [0863] and the power, or the **faculty** and the concrete acts, to
SD : 01 :023(512) [0865] poor degree — such as the **faculty**, aptitude, skill, or
SD : 01 :038(515) [0871] great and small, all the **faculties** of my mind, my reason

Fades (1)
AP : 04 :329(158) [0211] grass withers, the flower **fades**, when the breath of the

Fagius (1)
TR : 00 :082(335) [0529] Paul **Fagius**, of Strasbourg

Fail (20), Failed (8), Failing (2), Failings (1), Fails (4), Failure (5), Failures (1)
PR : PR :017(008) [0015] and at Naumburg **failed** to accomplish the desired end of
AG : 20 :033(045) [0057] and blameless lives; they **failed** to accomplish this, and
AP : 02 :012(102) [0109] But thereby they **failed** to see the inner uncleanness of
AP : 02 :051(107) [0119] contradict themselves and **fail** to explain logically and
AP : 04 :120(124) [0155] Whoever **fails** to teach about this faith we are discussing
AP : 04 :121(124) [0155] this faith, our opponents **fail** to see that thereby they
AP : 04 :135(125) [0159] Then we experience our **failure** to believe that God
AP : 04 :177(131) [0171] because of faith our **failure** to keep it is not imputed to
AP : 04 :276(148) [0199] Those who **fail** to do good, do not arouse themselves to
AP : 12 :061(190) [0269] from confession, we **fail** to see what value there is in
AP : 16 :008(223) [0333] Thus they **failed** to see that the Gospel brings eternal
AP : 27 :051(278) [0437] gift of continence, many **fail** in their continence because
S3 : 01 :002(302) [0477] swearing by God's name, **failure** to pray and call upon
S3 : 02 :001(303) [0479] But this purpose **failed** because of the wickedness which
SC : PR :025(341) [0539] other than negligent if you **fail** to do your duty and
LC : PR :012(360) [0571] Time and paper would **fail** me if I were to recount all the
LC : 01 :005(365) [0581] common examples of **failure** to observe this
LC : 01 :097(378) [0609] have God's Word, we still **fail** to remove the abuse of the
LC : 01 :108(379) [0611] of their honor because of their ways or their **failings**.
LC : 01 :140(384) [0621] on other things, and **fails** to perceive and believe how
LC : 01 :176(389) [0631] in this respect and **fail** to bring up your children to
LC : 01 :189(390) [0635] does evil, but also when he **fails** to do good to his
LC : 01 :189(390) [0635] he has the opportunity, **fails** to prevent, protect, and save
LC : 01 :204(392) [0639] Whenever you **fail** to do this (though you could prevent a
LC : 01 :274(402) [0659] yet if they whose duty it is **fail** to do so, they sin as much
LC : 01 :277(402) [0659] the house sees a servant **failing** to do his duty, he takes
LC : 01 :316(408) [0671] They **fail** to see, these miserable, blind people, that no
LC : 03 :021(423) [0703] and promise, which cannot **fail** or deceive me."
LC : 03 :044(425) [0709] his manifold blessings **fail** to teach, speak, and live as
LC : 03 :047(426) [0711] are ungrateful for it and **fail** to live according to it as we
LC : 03 :070(429) [0717] our enemies shall and must **fail** and come to naught, no
LC : 03 :100(433) [0725] is not accomplished without **failures** and stumbling.
LC : 03 :119(436) [0731] that we may never have an excuse for **failing** to pray.
LC : 04 :054(443) [0745] God's Word, even though he **failed** to receive it properly.
EP : 05 :008(479) [0803] their eyes, as a result they **fail** to learn the true nature of
SD : PR :006(502) [0847] either because they **failed** to grasp their true meaning or
SD : 05 :019(561) [0957] the unbelief involved in men's **failure** to believe in Christ.
SD : 05 :020(561) [0959] from God, since man has **failed** to keep the law of God
SD : 07 :125(591) [1015] living faith, but who **fail** to meet their own self-devised
SD : 11 :010(618) [1067] foreknowledge can never **fail** and no one can ever change
SD : 11 :046(624) [1079] purpose, which cannot **fail** or be overthrown, and put it

Faint (2)
LC : 03 :105(434) [0727] not allow us to become **faint** and weary and to fall back
LC : 05 :023(449) [0757] we often grow weary and **faint**, at times even stumble.

Fair (6), Fairer (1), Fairness (4)
AG : 00 :002(048) [0059] the bishops should in all **fairness** act more leniently, even
AG : 23 :026(055) [0065] show great leniency and **fairness** toward those who have
AG : 24 :010(057) [0065] by turning it into a sort of **fair**, by buying and selling it,
AG : 24 :040(061) [0069] Mass ought not in **fairness** be condemned as heretical or
AL : 27 :030(075) [0079] Accordingly it is not **fair** to argue so insistently about the

Continued ▶

A P : 0 4 :353(161) [0217] From these statements the **fair**-minded reader can judge
A P : 0 4 :357(161) [0217] But they are not **fair** judges, for they omit the word "gift."
A P : 0 7 :025(173) [0235] church that way, we would probably have **fairer** judges.
A P : 0 4 :235(140) [0185] of these commands of **fairness**, that in everyday life we
L C : 0 1 :155(386) [0625] therefore, it is only **fair** that we have nothing but
L C : 0 1 :306(406) [0669] maid-servant or otherwise estrange them with **fair** words.

Fairly (1)
A P : 2 0 :010(228) [0341] his mind at ease, for Paul **fairly** screams, as it were, that

Fairy (2)
A P : 2 1 :035(234) [0353] not even compare with the **fairy** tales about the saints
A P : 2 4 :065(261) [0407] in support of the **fairy** tales which they teach so

Faith (1391)
P R : P R :000(001) [0004] of the Doctrine and **Faith** of the undersigned Electors,
P R : P R :003(003) [0007] symbol of their **faith** in the chief articles in controversy
P R : P R :009(006) [0011] were so uncertain of our **faith** and of the confession of
P R : P R :009(006) [0011] our churches, schools, doctrine, **faith**, and confession.
P R : P R :017(008) [0015] of our Christian **faith** and confession as a final
P R : P R :018(009) [0017] we are uncertain of our **faith** and for that reason allegedly
P R : P R :020(010) [0017] basis, but with ingenuous **faith** they are to stay with the
P R : P R :020(010) [0017] assail this our ingenuous **faith** and interpretation of the
P R : P R :020(010) [0017] interpretation and **faith** contradicted the articles of our
P R : P R :023(012) [0021] and confession of the **faith** may be preserved and
P R : P R :024(012) [0021] Christian confession and **faith** on the basis of the divine,
P R : P R :025(014) [0023] in this confession of **faith** and to regulate all religious
A G : 0 0 :000(023) [0037] A Confession of **Faith** Presented in Augsburg by certain
A G : P R :002(025) [0039] concerning our holy **faith** and the Christian religion, and
A G : P R :006(025) [0039] matter pertaining to the **faith** and in conformity with the
A G : P R :008(025) [0039] teaching and of our own **faith**, setting forth how and in
A G : P R :016(026) [0041] pertaining to our holy **faith** but would diligently urge it
A G : 0 0 :000(027) [0043] Articles of **Faith** and Doctrine
A G : 0 2 :001(029) [0043] by nature to have true fear of God and true **faith** in God.
A G : 0 4 :001(030) [0045] for Christ's sake, through **faith**, when we believe that
A G : 0 4 :003(030) [0045] will regard and reckon this **faith** as righteousness, as Paul
A G : 0 5 :001(031) [0045] To obtain such **faith** God instituted the office of the
A G : 0 5 :002(031) [0045] Holy Spirit, who works **faith**, when and where he pleases,
A G : 0 6 :001(031) [0045] among us that such **faith** should produce good fruits and
A G : 0 6 :002(032) [0045] and righteousness through **faith** in Christ, as Christ
A G : 0 6 :003(032) [0047] through works but through **faith** alone, without merit."
A G : 0 7 :004(032) [0047] belongs to your call, one Lord, one **faith**, one baptism."
A G : 1 2 :005(035) [0049] through Christ), and this **faith** will comfort the heart and
A G : 1 2 :010(035) [0049] is not obtained through **faith** but through the
A G : 1 3 :001(035) [0049] the purpose of awakening and strengthening our **faith**.
A G : 1 3 :002(036) [0049] this reason they require **faith**, and they are rightly used
A G : 1 3 :002(036) [0049] when they are received in **faith** and for the purpose of
A G : 1 3 :002(036) [0049] in faith and for the purpose of strengthening **faith**.
A G : 1 5 :003(037) [0049] to the Gospel and the teaching about **faith** in Christ.
A G : 1 6 :004(037) [0051] fear of God and real **faith** in God, for the Gospel does
A G : 2 0 :000(041) [0053] XX. **Faith** and Good Works
A G : 2 0 :005(041) [0053] learned to speak now of **faith**, about which they did not
A G : 2 0 :006(041) [0053] works alone, but they add **faith** in Christ and say that
A G : 2 0 :006(042) [0053] in Christ and say that **faith** and works make us righteous
A G : 2 0 :008(042) [0053] Since the teaching about **faith**, which is the chief article in
A G : 2 0 :009(042) [0053] this happens only through **faith**, that is, when we believe
A G : 2 0 :011(042) [0055] This teaching about **faith** is plainly and clearly treated by
A G : 2 0 :011(042) [0055] have been saved through **faith**; and this is not your own
A G : 2 0 :013(043) [0055] before God through **faith** in Christ and not through
A G : 2 0 :015(043) [0055] works, but only through **faith**, that is, when it is assured
A G : 2 0 :016(043) [0055] "Since we are justified by **faith**, we have peace with God."
A G : 2 0 :022(044) [0055] preach this doctrine about **faith** in Christ and diligently to
A G : 2 0 :022(044) [0055] God is appropriated without merits, through **faith** alone.
A G : 2 0 :023(044) [0055] among us to show that the **faith** here spoken of is not
A G : 2 0 :023(044) [0055] but we mean such true **faith** as believes that we receive
A G : 2 0 :025(044) [0057] the Scriptures speak of **faith** but do not mean by it such
A G : 2 0 :025(044) [0057] Heb. 11:1 teaches about **faith** in such a way as to make it
A G : 2 0 :025(045) [0057] as to make it clear that **faith** is not merely a knowledge of
A G : 2 0 :026(045) [0057] understand the word **"faith"** in the Scriptures to mean
A G : 2 0 :028(045) [0057] It is always **faith** alone that apprehends grace and
A G : 2 0 :029(045) [0057] When through **faith** the Holy Spirit is given, the heart is
A G : 2 0 :034(045) [0057] a man is without true **faith** and the Holy Spirit and
A G : 2 0 :035(046) [0057] this teaching concerning **faith** is not to be accused of
A G : 2 0 :036(046) [0057] For without **faith** and without Christ human nature and
A G : 2 1 :001(046) [0057] rememberance so that our **faith** may be strengthened
A G : 2 1 :001(046) [0057] grace they received and how they were sustained by **faith**.
A G : 0 0 :000(048) [0059] concerning articles of **faith** that is contrary to the Holy
A G : 2 4 :023(058) [0067] Meanwhile **faith** in Christ and true service of God were
A G : 2 4 :028(059) [0067] grace before God through **faith** and not through works.
A G : 2 4 :030(059) [0067] place — but to awaken our **faith** and comfort our
A G : 2 4 :030(059) [0067] the sacrament requires **faith**, and without faith it is used
A G : 2 4 :030(059) [0067] requires faith, and without **faith** it is used in vain.
A G : 2 5 :004(062) [0069] know that through such **faith** we obtain forgiveness of
A G : 2 6 :004(064) [0071] the teaching concerning **faith** are thereby obscured, and
A G : 2 6 :004(064) [0071] precious and know that **faith** in Christ is to be esteemed
A G : 2 6 :005(064) [0071] but that it is only through **faith** in Christ that we obtain
A G : 2 6 :015(066) [0073] important things, such as **faith**, consolation in severe
A G : 2 6 :020(067) [0073] that the teaching about **faith** should and must be
A G : 2 6 :044(070) [0075] does not destroy unity in **faith**," and there is a statement
A G : 2 6 :045(070) [0075] to institute holy days but to teach **faith** and love."
A G : 2 7 :037(077) [0081] in God's sight come from **faith** and trust when we believe
A G : 2 7 :038(077) [0081] of the grace of Christ and deny the righteousness of **faith**?
A G : 2 7 :048(078) [0081] For righteousness of **faith**, which should be emphasized
A G : 2 7 :049(079) [0083] have sincere confidence, **faith**, and trust that for Christ's
A G : 2 8 :009(082) [0085] power of God for salvation to everyone who has **faith**."
A G : 2 8 :037(086) [0089] while teaching concerning **faith** and righteousness of faith
A G : 2 8 :037(086) [0089] faith and righteousness of **faith** has almost been
A G : 2 8 :052(089) [0091] the grace of God through **faith** in Christ without our
A G : 2 8 :062(092) [0093] when the righteousness of **faith** was no longer taught and
A G : 2 8 :064(092) [0093] of the righteousness of **faith** and Christian liberty.
A L : 0 0 :000(027) [0043] Chief Articles of **Faith**
A L : 0 4 :001(030) [0045] for Christ's sake through **faith** when they believe that they
A L : 0 4 :003(030) [0045] This **faith** God imputes for righteousness in his sight
A L : 0 5 :001(031) [0045] that we may obtain this **faith**, the ministry of teaching the
A L : 0 5 :002(031) [0045] the Holy Spirit produces **faith**, where and when it pleases
A L : 0 5 :003(031) [0045] we might receive the promise of the Spirit through **faith**."
A L : 0 6 :001(031) [0045] also teach that this **faith** is bound to bring forth good
A L : 0 6 :001(032) [0045] are apprehended by **faith**, as Christ himself also testifies,
A L : 0 6 :003(032) [0047] works but through **faith** alone, and he shall receive
A L : 0 7 :004(032) [0047] It is as Paul says, "One **faith**, one baptism, one God and
A L : 1 2 :005(034) [0049] of sin, and the other is **faith**, which is born of the Gospel,
A L : 1 2 :010(035) [0049] of sins comes through **faith** but command us to merit
A L : 1 3 :001(035) [0049] to awaken and confirm **faith** in those who use them.
A L : 1 3 :002(035) [0049] should be so used that **faith**, which believes the promises
A L : 1 3 :003(036) [0049] and who do not teach that **faith**, which believes that sins
A L : 1 5 :003(037) [0049] are opposed to the Gospel and the teaching about **faith**.
A L : 1 6 :004(038) [0051] in the fear of God and in **faith** but in forsaking civil
A L : 2 0 :000(041) [0053] XX. **Faith** and Good Works
A L : 2 0 :005(041) [0053] beginning to mention **faith**, about which there used to be
A L : 2 0 :006(041) [0053] works only, but conjoining **faith** with works they say that
A L : 2 0 :006(041) [0053] works they say that we are justified by **faith** and works.
A L : 2 0 :008(042) [0053] as the teaching about **faith** which ought to be the chief
A L : 2 0 :008(042) [0053] the righteousness of **faith** in sermons while only the
A L : 2 0 :008(042) [0053] have instructed our churches concerning **faith** as follows:
A L : 2 0 :009(042) [0053] and grace only by **faith** when we believe that we are
A L : 2 0 :011(042) [0055] This teaching concerning **faith** is everywhere treated in
A L : 2 0 :011(042) [0055] have been saved through **faith**; and this is not because of
A L : 2 0 :013(043) [0055] and the righteousness of **faith** against the merits of
A L : 2 0 :015(043) [0055] by any work but only by **faith** when they are sure that for
A L : 2 0 :016(043) [0055] "Since we are justified by **faith**, we have peace with God."
A L : 2 0 :022(044) [0055] this teaching concerning **faith** in Christ in order that
A L : 2 0 :022(044) [0055] forgiveness of sins are apprehended by **faith** in Christ.
A L : 2 0 :023(044) [0055] that here the term **"faith"** does not signify mere
A L : 2 0 :023(044) [0055] the devil), but it signifies **faith** which believes not only the
A L : 2 0 :026(045) [0057] way concerning the word **"faith"** when he teaches that in
A L : 2 0 :026(045) [0057] the Scriptures the word **"faith"** is to be understood not as
A L : 2 0 :028(045) [0057] It is only by **faith** that forgiveness of sins and grace are
A L : 2 0 :029(045) [0057] and because through **faith** the Holy Spirit is received,
A L : 2 0 :030(045) [0057] Ambrose says, "**Faith** is the mother of the good will and
A L : 2 0 :034(045) [0057] strength alone without **faith** and without the Holy Spirit.
A L : 2 0 :036(046) [0057] For without **faith** human nature cannot possibly do the
A L : 2 0 :037(046) [0057] Without **faith** it does not call upon God, expect anything
A L : 2 0 :038(046) [0057] when there is no **faith** and trust in God, all manner of
A L : 2 1 :001(046) [0057] us so that we imitate their **faith** and good works
A L : 0 0 :001(048) [0059] catholic in no article of **faith** but only omit some few
A L : 2 4 :028(059) [0067] that we are justified before God through **faith** in Christ.
A L : 2 4 :029(059) [0067] comes from the work of the Mass and not from **faith**.
A L : 2 4 :030(059) [0067] Mass was instituted that **faith** on the part of those who
A L : 2 5 :002(061) [0069] taught concerning **faith** in connection with absolution, a
A L : 2 5 :004(062) [0069] are told that God requires **faith** to believe such absolution
A L : 2 5 :004(062) [0069] and are assured that such **faith** truly obtains and receives
A L : 2 5 :005(062) [0069] immoderately extolled, but nothing was said about **faith**.
A L : 2 6 :004(064) [0071] and the righteousness of **faith**, which is the chief part of
A L : 2 6 :004(064) [0071] be well known and that **faith** which believes that sins are
A L : 2 6 :005(064) [0071] works of this sort; it is **faith** which believes that for
A L : 2 6 :007(065) [0071] no mention was made of **faith**; only works of satisfaction
A L : 2 6 :013(066) [0073] the consolation of grace and of the righteousness of **faith**.
A L : 2 6 :015(066) [0073] teachings concerning **faith**, the cross, hope, the
A L : 2 6 :020(067) [0073] and the righteousness of **faith**, and this cannot be
A L : 2 6 :044(070) [0075] does not destroy unity in **faith**," and Pope Gregory
A L : 2 7 :037(077) [0081] but that it comes through **faith** to those who believe that
A L : 2 7 :038(077) [0081] of Christ and obscure and deny the righteousness of **faith**?
A L : 2 7 :048(078) [0081] For righteousness of **faith**, which ought especially to be
A L : 2 7 :049(079) [0083] same time to have great **faith** and to trust that for Christ's
A L : 2 8 :009(082) [0085] to everyone who has **faith**," and Ps. 119:50 states, "Thy
A L : 2 8 :037(086) [0089] the teaching concerning **faith** and the righteousness of
A L : 2 8 :037(086) [0089] and the righteousness of **faith** has been suppressed, for
A L : 2 8 :052(089) [0091] we obtain grace through **faith** in Christ and not through
A L : 2 8 :062(092) [0093] when the righteousness of **faith** was not taught with
A L : 2 8 :064(092) [0093] of the righteousness of **faith** and Christian liberty.
A P : 0 1 :001(100) [0103] This asserts our **faith** and teaching that there is one
A P : 0 2 :001(100) [0105] the fear of God and **faith** is actual guilt, and therefore
A P : 0 2 :002(100) [0105] by nature to have true fear of God or true **faith** in God."
A P : 0 2 :007(101) [0107] but also the absence of the fear of God and of **faith**.
A P : 0 2 :016(102) [0109] commanding fear of God, **faith** and love toward him.
A P : 0 2 :031(104) [0113] when the fear of God and **faith** are lacking, this is not
A P : 0 4 :001(107) [0121] own merits, but freely for Christ's sake, by **faith** in him.
A P : 0 4 :001(107) [0121] the forgiveness of sins by **faith** and by faith in Christ are
A P : 0 4 :001(107) [0121] of sins by faith and by **faith** in Christ are justified.
A P : 0 4 :003(107) [0121] the forgiveness of sins nor **faith** nor grace nor
A P : 0 4 :018(109) [0125] the righteousness of **faith** man can neither have nor
A P : 0 4 :020(110) [0125] the free forgiveness of sins and the righteousness of **faith**.
A P : 0 4 :021(110) [0127] can never experience what **faith** is and how effective it is.
A P : 0 4 :030(111) [0129] righteousness to 'every one who has **faith**' (Rom. 10:4)."
A P : 0 4 :035(112) [0131] 14:23) "whatever does not proceed from **faith** is sin."
A P : 0 4 :036(112) [0131] to love God unless **faith** has first accepted the forgiveness
A P : 0 4 :039(112) [0131] of the righteousness of **faith**, the subject itself will compel
A P : 0 4 :042(113) [0133] who are to be the heirs, **faith** is null and the promise is
A P : 0 4 :043(113) [0133] this promise only by **faith**, the Gospel proclaims the
A P : 0 4 :043(113) [0133] the righteousness of **faith** in Christ, which the law does
A P : 0 4 :044(113) [0133] which we do not accept by works but by **faith** alone.
A P : 0 4 :044(113) [0133] This **faith** brings to God a trust not in our own merits,
A P : 0 4 :045(113) [0133] of Christ, this personal **faith** obtains the forgiveness of
A P : 0 4 :046(113) [0133] the forgiveness of sins, **faith** sets against God's wrath not
A P : 0 4 :046(113) [0133] This **faith** is the true knowledge of Christ, it uses his
A P : 0 4 :047(113) [0133] About this **faith** there is not a syllable in the teaching of
A P : 0 4 :047(113) [0133] which proclaims the righteousness of **faith** in Christ.
A P : 0 4 :047(113) [0133] What Is Justifying **Faith**?
A P : 0 4 :048(113) [0135] opponents imagine that **faith** is only historical knowledge
A P : 0 4 :048(113) [0135] so they say nothing about **faith** by which, as Paul says so
A P : 0 4 :048(114) [0135] The **faith** that justifies, however, is no mere historical
A P : 0 4 :048(114) [0135] we add that to have **faith** means to want and to accept the
A P : 0 4 :049(114) [0135] difference between this **faith** and the righteousness of the
A P : 0 4 :049(114) [0135] **Faith** is that worship which receives God's offered
A P : 0 4 :049(114) [0135] It is by **faith** that God wants to be worshiped, namely,
A P : 0 4 :050(114) [0135] Paul clearly shows that **faith** does not simply mean

Continued ▶

A P : 0 4 :050(114) [0135] is why it depends on **faith**, in order that the promise may
A P : 0 4 :050(114) [0135] For he says that only **faith** can accept the promise.
A P : 0 4 :050(114) [0135] He therefore correlates and connects promise and **faith**.
A P : 0 4 :051(114) [0135] be easy to determine what **faith** is if we pay attention to
A P : 0 4 :053(114) [0135] In speaking of justifying **faith**, therefore, we must
A P : 0 4 :053(114) [0137] promise is accepted by **faith**; the fact that it is free
A P : 0 4 :055(114) [0137] that this requires **faith**, which accepts the promise of
A P : 0 4 :055(114) [0137] at every mention of **faith** we are also thinking of its
A P : 0 4 :056(114) [0137] For **faith** does not justify or save because it is a good
A P : 0 4 :057(114) [0137] the forgiveness of sins by **faith**, just as the saints in the
A P : 0 4 :058(115) [0137] references to mercy and **faith** in the Psalms and the
A P : 0 4 :059(115) [0137] were justified not by the law but by the promise and **faith**.
A P : 0 4 :059(115) [0137] make so little of **faith** when they see it praised everywhere
A P : 0 4 :060(115) [0137] despise and disparage **faith** and teach men to deal with
A P : 0 4 :060(115) [0137] **Faith** in Christ Justifies
A P : 0 4 :061(115) [0137] knowledge, we must tell how **faith** comes into being.
A P : 0 4 :062(115) [0139] of sins and justification, which are received by **faith**.
A P : 0 4 :062(115) [0139] Amid such fears this **faith** brings peace of mind, consoles
A P : 0 4 :064(116) [0139] But we are talking about a **faith** that is not an idle
A P : 0 4 :067(116) [0139] to every one who has **faith**," and (Rom. 10:17), "Faith
A P : 0 4 :067(116) [0139] faith," and (Rom. 10:17), "**Faith** comes from what is
A P : 0 4 :067(116) [0139] From this we can prove that **faith** justifies.
A P : 0 4 :067(116) [0139] Word is received only by **faith**, then it follows that faith
A P : 0 4 :067(116) [0139] received only by faith, then it follows that **faith** justifies.
A P : 0 4 :068(116) [0139] and the nature of the **faith** we have been discussing.
A P : 0 4 :069(116) [0141] Now we shall show that **faith** justifies.
A P : 0 4 :069(116) [0141] then we must defend the proposition, "**Faith** justifies."
A P : 0 4 :070(116) [0141] then we must defend the proposition, "**Faith** justifies."
A P : 0 4 :070(116) [0141] But this can be accepted only by **faith**.
A P : 0 4 :070(116) [0141] anyone who denies that **faith** justifies teaches only the law
A P : 0 4 :071(116) [0141] When we say that **faith** justifies, some may think this
A P : 0 4 :071(116) [0141] the beginning, as though **faith** were the start of
A P : 0 4 :071(116) [0141] Then it would be not **faith**, but the works that follow, by
A P : 0 4 :072(116) [0141] They imagine **faith** is praised so highly because it is this
A P : 0 4 :072(117) [0141] Regarding **faith** we maintain not this, but rather that
A P : 0 4 :072(117) [0141] that because of Christ by **faith** itself we are truly
A P : 0 4 :072(117) [0141] we want to show first that **faith** alone makes a righteous
A P : 0 4 :073(117) [0141] that a man is justified by **faith** apart from works of law,"
A P : 0 4 :073(117) [0141] We said earlier that **faith** is conceived by the Word, and
A P : 0 4 :074(117) [0143] Love and good works must also follow **faith**.
A P : 0 4 :074(117) [0143] We Obtain the Forgiveness of Sins Only by **Faith** in Christ
A P : 0 4 :077(117) [0143] of sins only by **faith** in Christ, not through love, or
A P : 0 4 :077(117) [0143] because of love or works, though love does follow **faith**.
A P : 0 4 :078(117) [0143] we are justified by **faith** alone, justification being
A P : 0 4 :079(118) [0143] By **faith**, when we comfort ourselves by firm trust in the
A P : 0 4 :080(118) [0143] For it is only by **faith** that Christ is accepted as the
A P : 0 4 :080(118) [0143] By **faith** alone, therefore, we obtain the forgiveness of
A P : 0 4 :081(118) [0143] access" to the Father, and he adds, "through **faith**."
A P : 0 4 :081(118) [0145] completely and do away with the whole teaching of **faith**?
A P : 0 4 :081(118) [0145] this happens, he adds that through **faith** we have access.
A P : 0 4 :081(118) [0145] By **faith**, therefore, for Christ's sake we receive the
A P : 0 4 :082(118) [0145] as an expiation," and Paul adds, "to be received by **faith**."
A P : 0 4 :082(118) [0145] benefits us when by **faith** we receive the mercy promised
A P : 0 4 :082(118) [0145] but in Christ, the high priest, this statement requires **faith**.
A P : 0 4 :083(119) [0145] Thus he requires **faith**.
A P : 0 4 :083(119) [0145] We cannot take hold of the name of Christ except by **faith**
A P : 0 4 :084(119) [0145] it can be accepted only by **faith**, since a promise can be
A P : 0 4 :084(119) [0145] by faith, since a promise can be accepted only on **faith**.
A P : 0 4 :084(119) [0145] is why it depends on **faith**, in order that the promise may
A P : 0 4 :084(119) [0145] what was promised to **faith** in Jesus Christ might be given
A P : 0 4 :084(119) [0145] and further that the promise can be accepted by **faith**.
A P : 0 4 :085(119) [0147] for Christ's sake only by **faith**; here they have a certain
A P : 0 4 :086(119) [0147] **Faith** alone justifies because we receive the forgiveness of
A P : 0 4 :086(119) [0147] the forgiveness of sins and the Holy Spirit by **faith** alone.
A P : 0 4 :086(119) [0147] on account of Christ, if they grasp this mercy by **faith**.
A P : 0 4 :086(119) [0147] Scriptures testify that we are accounted righteous by **faith**.
A P : 0 4 :086(119) [0147] testimonies stating that **faith** is the very righteousness by
A P : 0 4 :087(119) [0147] to us for Christ's sake we are justified freely by **faith**.
A P : 0 4 :087(119) [0147] that man is justified by **faith** apart from works of law"
A P : 0 4 :087(120) [0147] precepts of a good life, but through **faith** in Jesus Christ."
A P : 0 4 :088(120) [0149] Paul made the statement "**Faith** justifies" inadvertently,
A P : 0 4 :089(120) [0149] justifies the ungodly, his **faith** is reckoned as
A P : 0 4 :089(120) [0149] Here he clearly says that **faith** itself is accounted for
A P : 0 4 :089(120) [0149] It is **faith**, therefore, that God declares to be
A P : 0 4 :089(120) [0149] justification before God, **faith** would not be accounted
A P : 0 4 :090(120) [0149] Paul says, "We say that **faith** was reckoned to Abraham
A P : 0 4 :091(120) [0149] "Since we are justified by **faith**, we have peace with God,"
A P : 0 4 :092(120) [0149] where he declares that **faith** is the righteousness of the
A P : 0 4 :093(120) [0149] in order to be justified by **faith** in Christ, and not by
A P : 0 4 :093(120) [0149] have been saved through **faith**; and this is not your own
A P : 0 4 :098(121) [0149] But only **faith** takes hold of the name of Christ.
A P : 0 4 :099(121) [0151] Acts 15:9, "He cleansed their hearts by **faith**."
A P : 0 4 :099(121) [0151] Therefore the **faith** of which the apostles speak is not idle
A P : 0 4 :100(121) [0151] Hab. 2:4, "The righteous shall live by his **faith**."
A P : 0 4 :100(121) [0151] men are righteous by the **faith** which believes that God is
A P : 0 4 :100(121) [0151] and he adds that this same **faith** quickens because it
A P : 0 4 :103(122) [0151] It is **faith** therefore that frees men through the blood of
A P : 0 4 :104(122) [0153] works and ascribes it to **faith**, which liberates us through
A P : 0 4 :106(122) [0153] reconciles the justifier by **faith**, not by his own strength
A P : 0 4 :106(122) [0153] Justification is obtained by **faith**."
A P : 0 4 :106(122) [0153] justifier is reconciled by **faith** and that justification is
A P : 0 4 :106(122) [0153] by faith and that justification is obtained by **faith**.
A P : 0 4 :106(122) [0153] says: "By the law we fear God, by **faith** we hope in God.
A P : 0 4 :106(122) [0153] this fear, the soul by **faith** flees to the mercy of God, that
A P : 0 4 :106(122) [0153] but receive consolation by **faith**, and that before we try to
A P : 0 4 :106(122) [0153] we try to keep the law we should receive mercy by **faith**.
A P : 0 4 :107(122) [0153] attribute justification to **faith** and specifically deny it to
A P : 0 4 :109(123) [0153] they say, as referring to "**faith** fashioned by love," that is,
A P : 0 4 :109(123) [0153] attribute justification to **faith** except on account of love.
A P : 0 4 :109(123) [0153] attribute justification to **faith** at all, but only to love,
A P : 0 4 :109(123) [0153] because they imagine that **faith** can exist with mortal sin.
A P : 0 4 :110(123) [0153] If **faith** receives the forgiveness of sins on account of
A P : 0 4 :111(123) [0153] that love should follow **faith**, as Paul also says, "In Christ
A P : 0 4 :111(123) [0155] is of any avail, but **faith** working through love" (Gal.
A P : 0 4 :112(123) [0155] of sins is received by **faith** alone—and we mean faith in
A P : 0 4 :112(123) [0155] faith alone—and we mean **faith** in the true sense of the
A P : 0 4 :112(123) [0155] the word—since the promise can be received only by **faith**
A P : 0 4 :113(123) [0155] But **faith** in the true sense, as the Scriptures use the word,
A P : 0 4 :114(123) [0155] righteous by this **faith** for Christ's sake before we love and
A P : 0 4 :115(123) [0155] This **faith** is no idle knowledge, nor can it exist with
A P : 0 4 :116(123) [0155] And since this **faith** alone receives the forgiveness of sins,
A P : 0 4 :117(123) [0155] was to make clear that by **faith** alone we receive the
A P : 0 4 :117(123) [0155] for Christ's sake, and by **faith** alone are justified, that is,
A P : 0 4 :118(123) [0155] it is to understand this **faith**, for through it alone we
A P : 0 4 :119(124) [0155] heard nothing about this **faith** and who believe that they
A P : 0 4 :120(124) [0155] fails to teach about this **faith** we are discussing completely
A P : 0 4 :121(124) [0155] The scholastics do not say a word about this **faith**.
A P : 0 4 :121(124) [0155] them and rejecting this **faith**, our opponents fail to see
A P : 0 4 :123(124) [0157] Rom. 3:31 Paul says that **faith** does not overthrow but
A P : 0 4 :125(124) [0157] Since **faith** brings the Holy Spirit and produces a new life
A P : 0 4 :125(124) [0157] and regenerated by **faith**, therefore, we begin to fear and
A P : 0 4 :127(125) [0157] the Spirit is received by **faith**, according to Paul's word
A P : 0 4 :127(125) [0157] we might receive the promise of the Spirit through **faith**."
A P : 0 4 :129(125) [0157] love God until we have grasped his mercy by **faith**.
A P : 0 4 :132(125) [0159] keep the law unless by **faith** we have received the Holy
A P : 0 4 :132(125) [0159] Paul says that **faith** does not overthrow but upholds the
A P : 0 4 :133(125) [0159] be removed except by **faith**, which receives the Holy
A P : 0 4 :135(125) [0159] when we are consoled by **faith** through hearing the
A P : 0 4 :138(126) [0161] who holds enthralled all who have not been freed by **faith**.
A P : 0 4 :141(126) [0161] is impossible to separate **faith** from love for God, be it
A P : 0 4 :141(126) [0161] So he indicates that **faith** precedes while love follows.
A P : 0 4 :142(126) [0161] The **faith** of which we are speaking, moreover, has its
A P : 0 4 :142(126) [0161] This **faith** ought to grow and be strengthened in these
A P : 0 4 :144(127) [0161] sin, therefore, such a **faith** does not remain in those who
A P : 0 4 :145(127) [0161] only one of these effects of **faith**, our opponents teach
A P : 0 4 :145(127) [0163] the forgiveness of sins by **faith**, nor that on account of
A P : 0 4 :147(127) [0163] account of love, but on account of Christ by **faith** alone.
A P : 0 4 :148(127) [0163] **Faith** alone, looking to the promise and believing with
A P : 0 4 :150(127) [0163] Therefore it must be **faith** that reconciles and justifies.
A P : 0 4 :152(127) [0163] words when he adds: "Your **faith** has saved you" (v. 50).
A P : 0 4 :153(127) [0163] Therefore he clearly says, "Your **faith** has saved you."
A P : 0 4 :153(127) [0163] But **faith** is that which grasps God's free mercy because
A P : 0 4 :153(128) [0163] anybody denies that this is **faith**, he utterly
A P : 0 4 :153(128) [0163] this is faith, he utterly misunderstands the nature of **faith**.
A P : 0 4 :154(128) [0165] a sign and confession of **faith** that she was looking for the
A P : 0 4 :155(128) [0165] not only alms, but also the righteousness of **faith**.
A P : 0 4 :155(128) [0165] truly worshiped me with **faith** and with the acts and signs
A P : 0 4 :155(128) [0165] me with faith and with the acts and signs of **faith**.
A P : 0 4 :155(128) [0165] he teaches that it is **faith** that properly accepts the
A P : 0 4 :158(129) [0165] that we are justified by **faith**, for it is sure that we receive
A P : 0 4 :158(129) [0165] sure that we receive the forgiveness of sins by **faith** alone.
A P : 0 4 :159(129) [0167] sins and reconciliation by **faith** for Christ's sake, not for
A P : 0 4 :159(129) [0167] necessarily follows that we are justified by **faith** in Christ.
A P : 0 4 :161(129) [0167] not justify, because it is accepted only on account of **faith**.
A P : 0 4 :163(129) [0169] is accounted righteous by **faith** for Christ's sake,
A P : 0 4 :163(129) [0169] This forgiveness is always received by **faith**.
A P : 0 4 :163(129) [0169] it is always received by **faith**; we must always hold that
A P : 0 4 :163(129) [0169] we are accounted righteous by **faith** for the sake of Christ.
A P : 0 4 :166(130) [0169] God for its own sake, but for the sake of **faith** in Christ.
A P : 0 4 :172(130) [0171] works he requires our **faith** that for Christ's sake we
A P : 0 4 :174(131) [0171] law, therefore, we need a **faith** which is sure that for
A P : 0 4 :174(131) [0171] can be grasped only by **faith**, as we have said so often.
A P : 0 4 :175(131) [0171] law is established through **faith** (Rom. 3:31), this should
A P : 0 4 :175(131) [0171] have been regenerated by **faith** receive the Holy Spirit and
A P : 0 4 :177(131) [0171] that being reconciled by **faith** we are accounted righteous
A P : 0 4 :177(131) [0171] pleases God because of **faith**; because of faith our failure
A P : 0 4 :177(131) [0171] of faith; because of **faith** our failure to keep it is not
A P : 0 4 :179(131) [0171] reconciliation through **faith**, though sin still sticks to your
A P : 0 4 :181(132) [0171] imperfect righteousness of the law only because of **faith**.
A P : 0 4 :182(132) [0171] justified before God by **faith** alone, since by faith alone
A P : 0 4 :182(132) [0173] by faith alone, since by **faith** alone we receive the
A P : 0 4 :182(132) [0173] Therefore it is received by **faith** alone, though the keeping
A P : 0 4 :184(132) [0173] we must add that **faith** is necessary, and that they are
A P : 0 4 :184(132) [0173] are commended because of **faith** as its fruit or testimony.
A P : 0 4 :186(132) [0173] But by their denial that **faith** justifies and by their
A P : 0 4 :188(133) [0173] and the reconciliation that comes through **faith** in Christ.
A P : 0 4 :189(133) [0175] in order to exercise our **faith**, to give testimony, and to
A P : 0 4 :189(133) [0175] Because of **faith** they are nevertheless holy and divine
A P : 0 4 :194(133) [0175] we obtain these only by **faith**) but for other physical and
A P : 0 4 :195(134) [0175] are received only by **faith**, not because of any works.
A P : 0 4 :195(134) [0175] "Since we are justified by **faith**, we have peace with God
A P : 0 4 :195(134) [0175] Through him we have obtained access by **faith**."
A P : 0 4 :196(134) [0175] Because **faith** makes us sons of God, moreover, it also
A P : 0 4 :196(134) [0175] It is **faith** that obtains this because it justifies us and has a
A P : 0 4 :201(134) [0175] By **faith** his justification was already accomplished, but
A P : 0 4 :201(134) [0175] be reminded and grow in **faith**, and through his witness
A P : 0 4 :201(134) [0175] his witness testify to his **faith** before others and induce
A P : 0 4 :202(134) [0175] By **faith** Abel offered a more acceptable sacrifice (Heb.
A P : 0 4 :202(134) [0175] he was righteous by **faith**, the sacrifice he made was
A P : 0 4 :202(134) [0175] work, but to exercise his **faith** and display it to others,
A P : 0 4 :203(134) [0175] Good works ought to follow **faith** in this way.
A P : 0 4 :205(135) [0177] But **faith** gives assurance of God's presence when it is sure
A P : 0 4 :206(135) [0177] but did not keep their **faith**, believing that these works
A P : 0 4 :207(135) [0177] those who did away with **faith** in the notion that through
A P : 0 4 :208(135) [0177] in these places and thus gave evidence of their **faith**.
A P : 0 4 :210(136) [0179] might strengthen our **faith** and we might publicly confess
A P : 0 4 :210(136) [0179] might publicly confess our **faith** and announce the
A P : 0 4 :211(136) [0179] believed that through **faith** they were accounted righteous
A P : 0 4 :211(136) [0179] since has copied not the **faith** of the Fathers but only
A P : 0 4 :211(136) [0179] behavior without their **faith** in order by such works to
A P : 0 4 :212(136) [0179] or that freely by **faith** we are accounted righteous for
A P : 0 4 :213(136) [0179] than because of Christ by **faith** — what is this but to rob
A P : 0 4 :214(136) [0179] of the law must follow **faith**; but we still give Christ his
A P : 0 4 :214(136) [0179] accounted righteous before God for Christ's sake by **faith**.
A P : 0 4 :214(136) [0179] the terrors of sin, but **faith** alone can overcome them.
A P : 0 4 :217(137) [0179] before God except by **faith** alone, by which it is sure that

Continued ▶

A P : 0 4 :217(137) [0179] 5:1), "Since we are justified by **faith**, we have peace."
A P : 0 4 :217(137) [0179] therefore it is always received before God by **faith** alone.
A P : 0 4 :218(137) [0179] they quote, "If I have all **faith**, etc., but have not love, I
A P : 0 4 :218(137) [0179] they say, Paul asserts that **faith** alone does not justify.
A P : 0 4 :219(137) [0181] love will not keep his **faith**, be it ever so great, because he
A P : 0 4 :221(137) [0181] other texts that speak of **faith** they always add the
A P : 0 4 :221(137) [0181] be understood in reference to "**faith** formed by love."
A P : 0 4 :221(137) [0181] correction: We need the **faith** that we are accounted
A P : 0 4 :222(138) [0181] "I am nothing"; that is, **faith** is extinguished, no matter
A P : 0 4 :225(138) [0183] that love is preferred to **faith** and hope since Paul says (I
A P : 0 4 :226(138) [0183] **Faith** and hope deal only with God, while love has infinite
A P : 0 4 :227(139) [0183] This virtue is **faith**.
A P : 0 4 :227(139) [0183] As we have often said, **faith** is not merely knowledge but
A P : 0 4 :231(139) [0183] Only **faith** takes hold of Christ, the propitiator.
A P : 0 4 :239(141) [0187] and accuses us, but **faith** in Christ frees us in the midst of
A P : 0 4 :244(141) [0189] is justified by works and not by **faith** alone" (James 2:24).
A P : 0 4 :245(142) [0189] but say nothing about the **faith** by which we take hold of
A P : 0 4 :245(142) [0189] only do they condemn this **faith** in statements and
A P : 0 4 :245(142) [0189] For he does not omit **faith** nor exalt love in preference to
A P : 0 4 :245(142) [0189] Just so Paul includes **faith** and love in presenting a
A P : 0 4 :245(142) [0189] a pure heart and a good conscience and sincere **faith**."
A P : 0 4 :246(142) [0189] here are those that follow **faith** and show that it is not
A P : 0 4 :247(142) [0191] he teaches that we are regenerated and justified by **faith**.
A P : 0 4 :247(142) [0191] For it is only **faith** that takes hold of the promise of
A P : 0 4 :248(142) [0191] between dead and living **faith** and condemns the idle and
A P : 0 4 :248(142) [0191] and smug minds who dream they have **faith** but do not.
A P : 0 4 :249(142) [0191] He says that a **faith** which does not produce good works
A P : 0 4 :249(142) [0191] have already shown often enough what we mean by **faith**.
A P : 0 4 :249(142) [0191] demons have, but about a **faith** that resists the terrors of
A P : 0 4 :250(143) [0191] Such a **faith** is not an easy thing, as our opponents
A P : 0 4 :250(143) [0191] the power of God **faith** is efficacious and overcomes death
A P : 0 4 :250(143) [0191] raised with him through **faith** in the working of God."
A P : 0 4 :250(143) [0191] Since this **faith** is a new life, it necessarily produces new
A P : 0 4 :250(143) [0191] in denying that we are justified by a **faith** without works.
A P : 0 4 :251(143) [0191] he says we are justified by **faith** and works, he certainly
A P : 0 4 :252(143) [0191] by works and not by **faith** alone," for men who have faith
A P : 0 4 :252(143) [0191] alone," for men who have **faith** and good works are
A P : 0 4 :252(143) [0191] the saints are righteous and please God because of **faith**.
A P : 0 4 :252(143) [0191] only the works that **faith** produces, as he shows when he
A P : 0 4 :252(143) [0191] he says of Abraham, "**Faith** was active along with his
A P : 0 4 :252(143) [0191] please him because of **faith** and therefore are a keeping of
A P : 0 4 :255(144) [0193] sins are forgiven without **faith** or that these works are
A P : 0 4 :256(144) [0193] we have been reborn by **faith** in Christ, as Christ says
A P : 0 4 :256(144) [0193] law (Heb. 11:6), "Without **faith** it is impossible to please
A P : 0 4 :257(144) [0193] are forgiven and that by **faith** in Christ we obtain the
A P : 0 4 :258(144) [0193] evil," as he denounces ungodly hearts and requires **faith**.
A P : 0 4 :258(144) [0193] of sins to be received by **faith**, and so he adds a promise.
A P : 0 4 :259(144) [0193] he wants the forgiveness of sins to be received by **faith**.
A P : 0 4 :259(145) [0193] he wishes the forgiveness of sins to be received by **faith**.
A P : 0 4 :261(145) [0195] Thus in Daniel's sermon (4:24) **faith** is required.
A P : 0 4 :261(145) [0195] This presupposes **faith**.
A P : 0 4 :261(145) [0195] him not only to the giving of alms but rather to **faith**.
A P : 0 4 :261(145) [0195] voice which Daniel surely wanted to be received by **faith**.
A P : 0 4 :263(145) [0195] Righteousness is **faith** in the heart.
A P : 0 4 :263(146) [0195] they truly believe and by **faith** conquer sin and death.
A P : 0 4 :264(146) [0197] The text does not say this, but rather requires **faith**.
A P : 0 4 :264(146) [0197] Wherever there is a promise, there **faith** is required.
A P : 0 4 :264(146) [0197] Only **faith** can accept a promise.
A P : 0 4 :265(146) [0197] looks at nor understands **faith**, it dreams that the merit of
A P : 0 4 :266(146) [0197] the teaching of grace and **faith**, while Daniel most
A P : 0 4 :266(146) [0197] while Daniel most emphatically wants to include **faith**.
A P : 0 4 :267(146) [0197] about works but about **faith** as well, as the narrative in
A P : 0 4 :267(146) [0197] he necessarily requires **faith**, which believes that God
A P : 0 4 :269(147) [0197] —and that "without **faith** it is impossible to please
A P : 0 4 :269(147) [0197] God on account of **faith**, since they do not please him
A P : 0 4 :270(147) [0197] When **faith** takes hold of Christ, the mediator, the heart
A P : 0 4 :271(147) [0199] said nothing at all about **faith** in their treatment of the
A P : 0 4 :271(148) [0199] should be received by **faith**, to cheer the terrified
A P : 0 4 :272(148) [0199] the forgiveness of sins, it necessarily requires **faith**.
A P : 0 4 :272(148) [0199] Only **faith** accepts the forgiveness of sins.
A P : 0 4 :272(148) [0199] we should understand that **faith** is required, not merely
A P : 0 4 :272(148) [0199] depending not on the work but on Christ through **faith**.
A P : 0 4 :274(148) [0199] forgiveness of sins by **faith** because of Christ and not
A P : 0 4 :276(148) [0199] *ex opere operato* without **faith**, so almsgiving does not
A P : 0 4 :276(148) [0199] does not justify *ex opere operato* without **faith**.
A P : 0 4 :278(149) [0199] we must consider **faith** and fruits together, so here we say
A P : 0 4 :278(149) [0199] is an exercise of that **faith** which accepts forgiveness of
A P : 0 4 :279(149) [0199] statement shows that **faith** is required before almsgiving:
A P : 0 4 :279(149) [0199] belong to the kind of **faith** we have been discussing, one
A P : 0 4 :282(149) [0201] of the whole passage shows that it requires **faith**.
A P : 0 4 :284(150) [0201] Yet Peter says (Acts 15:9) that hearts are purified by **faith**.
A P : 0 4 :284(150) [0201] many parts, some of which command **faith**, others works.
A P : 0 4 :284(150) [0201] about works and skip the passages about **faith**.
A P : 0 4 :285(150) [0201] that not works but **faith** accepts the promised forgiveness
A P : 0 4 :285(150) [0201] promised forgiveness of sins and righteousness of **faith**.
A P : 0 4 :286(150) [0201] against us in arguing that **faith** does not justify and that
A P : 0 4 :286(150) [0201] scriptural passages on **faith**, select the passages on works,
A P : 0 4 :290(151) [0203] It does not teach that by **faith** in Christ we overcome the
A P : 0 4 :291(152) [0203] access to God through **faith** (Rom. 5:2), and that we
A P : 0 4 :291(152) [0203] It teaches that by **faith** in Christ we receive the
A P : 0 4 :292(152) [0203] promise is received by **faith** alone, as Paul declares in
A P : 0 4 :292(152) [0203] **Faith** alone accepts the forgiveness of sins, justifies, and
A P : 0 4 :293(152) [0203] This **faith** is accounted for righteousness before God
A P : 0 4 :293(152) [0203] and quickened by **faith** in this way, it receives the Holy
A P : 0 4 :293(152) [0203] account of the justifying **faith** that for Christ's sake we
A P : 0 4 :294(152) [0203] we ascribe justification to **faith** rather than to love,
A P : 0 4 :294(152) [0203] love, though love follows **faith** since love is the keeping of
A P : 0 4 :294(152) [0203] law but by the promise, which is received by **faith** only.
A P : 0 4 :295(152) [0203] hold of the promise by **faith**, that for Christ's sake the
A P : 0 4 :297(153) [0205] is to be accepted by **faith**, as John says (1 John 5:10-12):
A P : 0 4 :297(153) [0205] that justification must necessarily be attributed to **faith**.
A P : 0 4 :297(153) [0205] access" to God, adding, "through **faith**" (Rom. 5:2).
A P : 0 4 :297(153) [0205] By **faith** in Christ, therefore, we accept the promise of the
A P : 0 4 :298(153) [0205] justification must necessarily be ascribed to **faith**.
A P : 0 4 :300(153) [0205] trying to destroy the doctrine of righteousness by **faith**.
A P : 0 4 :303(154) [0205] that we are talking about **faith** in Christ and in the
A P : 0 4 :303(154) [0205] the forgiveness of sins, a **faith** that truly and
A P : 0 4 :303(154) [0205] can easily see that a **faith** which believes that God cares
A P : 0 4 :303(154) [0205] nor demons can have the **faith** we are discussing here.
A P : 0 4 :304(154) [0205] thus cannot be ascribed to **faith**, which is in the intellect.
A P : 0 4 :304(154) [0205] God's judgment; just so **faith** is not merely knowledge in
A P : 0 4 :304(154) [0205] Scripture uses the word "**faith**," as this statement of Paul
A P : 0 4 :304(154) [0205] "Since we are justified by **faith**, we have peace with God"
A P : 0 4 :305(154) [0207] Christ's, which is communicated to us through **faith**.
A P : 0 4 :307(154) [0207] is given to us through **faith**, therefore faith is
A P : 0 4 :307(154) [0207] us through faith, therefore **faith** is righteousness in us by
A P : 0 4 :307(154) [0207] as Paul says (Rom. 4:5), "**Faith** is reckoned as
A P : 0 4 :308(155) [0207] of certain carping critics: **faith** is truly righteousness
A P : 0 4 :309(155) [0207] This **faith** gives honor to God, gives him what is properly
A P : 0 4 :309(155) [0207] but he grew strong in his **faith** as he gave glory to God."
A P : 0 4 :312(155) [0207] may quibble that if it is **faith** that wishes for what the
A P : 0 4 :312(155) [0207] then the dispositions of **faith** and hope seem to be
A P : 0 4 :312(155) [0207] In Heb. 11:1 **faith** is defined as "the assurance of things
A P : 0 4 :312(155) [0207] a future event, while **faith** deals with both future and
A P : 0 4 :313(155) [0207] from this the nature of **faith** will be clearly understood, as
A P : 0 4 :313(155) [0207] reconciled, and reborn by **faith**, if indeed we want to
A P : 0 4 :314(155) [0207] not with love but with **faith** we overcome the terrors of
A P : 0 4 :314(156) [0207] Christ we have obtained access to God by **faith**."
A P : 0 4 :314(156) [0207] mediator, rather than by **faith**, but also to cheer ourselves
A P : 0 4 :314(156) [0207] ourselves in the midst of fears and to exercise our **faith**.
A P : 0 4 :315(156) [0207] we can keep the law, our hearts must be reborn by **faith**.
A P : 0 4 :316(156) [0209] First, they do not mention **faith** or the fact that for
A P : 0 4 :316(156) [0209] or the fact that for Christ's sake we please God by **faith**.
A P : 0 4 :318(156) [0209] grace through a good work and not by **faith** in Christ.
A P : 0 4 :319(156) [0209] because of Christ, how will it have peace without **faith**?
A P : 0 4 :320(156) [0209] "Since we are justified by **faith**, we have peace with God";
A P : 0 4 :321(157) [0209] to doubt and to work without **faith** until despair ensues.
A P : 0 4 :324(157) [0209] Looking at his mercy, **faith** comforts and consoles us.
A P : 0 4 :324(157) [0209] to add nothing about this **faith** that takes hold of mercy.
A P : 0 4 :324(157) [0209] that the promise and **faith** are correlative and that only
A P : 0 4 :324(157) [0211] correlative and that only **faith** can take hold of the
A P : 0 4 :324(157) [0211] correlatively requires **faith** and that only faith can take
A P : 0 4 :324(157) [0211] faith and that only **faith** can take hold of this mercy.
A P : 0 4 :324(157) [0211] nothing about justifying **faith** and obscures Christ's glory
A P : 0 4 :337(159) [0215] opponents are deceived with regard to the term "**faith**."
A P : 0 4 :337(159) [0215] their argument that **faith** is worthless would be
A P : 0 4 :337(159) [0215] is the very voice of **faith**, as is evident from the example
A P : 0 4 :338(159) [0215] **Faith** saves because it takes hold of mercy and the promise
A P : 0 4 :341(159) [0215] opponents twist against **faith** statements made in support
A P : 0 4 :341(159) [0215] twist against faith statements made in support of **faith**.
A P : 0 4 :346(160) [0217] mercy is spoken of, **faith** in the promise must be added.
A P : 0 4 :346(160) [0217] This **faith** produces a sure hope, for it rests on the Word
A P : 0 4 :347(160) [0217] This **faith** makes the difference between those who are
A P : 0 4 :347(160) [0217] **Faith** makes the difference between the worthy and the
A P : 0 4 :347(160) [0217] is promised to the justified and it is **faith** that justifies.
A P : 0 4 :348(160) [0217] to the flesh can retain neither **faith** nor righteousness.
A P : 0 4 :349(160) [0217] The **faith** we speak of has its existence in penitence.
A P : 0 4 :350(161) [0217] in which experience testifies how difficult a thing **faith** is.
A P : 0 4 :353(161) [0217] since we teach that this **faith** arises in penitence and
A P : 0 4 :353(161) [0217] if penitence and **faith** amid penitence grow together.
A P : 0 4 :354(161) [0217] as justification belongs to **faith**, so eternal life belongs to
A P : 0 4 :354(161) [0217] "As the outcome of your **faith** you obtain the salvation of
A P : 0 4 :355(161) [0217] spiritual rewards because they please God through **faith**.
A P : 0 4 :357(162) [0219] without needing mercy or the mediator Christ or **faith**.
A P : 0 4 :358(162) [0219] the mediator nor the **faith** that has access to God for
A P : 0 4 :359(162) [0219] God only because of the **faith** that takes hold of Christ,
A P : 0 4 :361(162) [0219] of Christ and the righteousness of **faith** are obscured.
A P : 0 4 :362(162) [0219] accounted righteous by **faith** for Christ's sake and that
A P : 0 4 :362(162) [0219] to God because of **faith**, then we will not argue much
A P : 0 4 :365(163) [0219] Scriptures often include **faith**, since they wish to include
A P : 0 4 :366(163) [0219] and eternal life belong to **faith**, still good works merit
A P : 0 4 :366(163) [0221] of the law that follows **faith** deals with the law, in which a
A P : 0 4 :367(163) [0221] ours, and Christ's merits are communicated to us by **faith**.
A P : 0 4 :368(163) [0221] please God unless we had been accepted because of **faith**.
A P : 0 4 :368(163) [0221] are accepted because of **faith**, this incipient keeping of the
A P : 0 4 :371(164) [0221] works but also the **faith** of the heart, since the Scriptures
A P : 0 4 :372(164) [0221] the mediator Christ and **faith**, according to Heb. 11:6,
A P : 0 4 :372(164) [0221] to Heb. 11:6, "Without **faith** it is impossible to please
A P : 0 4 :373(164) [0221] of the heart and of **faith**, and for this reason eternal life is
A P : 0 4 :374(164) [0223] Such a new birth comes by **faith** amid penitence.
A P : 0 4 :375(164) [0223] please God because of **faith** and the mediator Christ but
A P : 0 4 :376(164) [0223] them the righteousness of **faith** and Christ, the mediator.
A P : 0 4 :376(164) [0223] the righteousness of **faith**, which believes that we have
A P : 0 4 :377(165) [0223] about the righteousness of **faith** dare not be neglected in
A P : 0 4 :378(165) [0223] by works, omitting the **faith** that takes hold of the
A P : 0 4 :379(165) [0223] About this **faith**, which believes that the Father is
A P : 0 4 :381(165) [0223] this is mentioned, **faith** should be added, since we take
A P : 0 4 :381(165) [0223] mercy, reconciliation, and love toward us only by **faith**.
A P : 0 4 :381(165) [0225] please God because of grace; for **faith** takes hold of grace.
A P : 0 4 :382(165) [0225] But why not say something about **faith**?
A P : 0 4 :382(165) [0225] is a propitiation, as Paul says, through **faith** (Rom. 3:25).
A P : 0 4 :382(165) [0225] are consoled by **faith** and believe that our sins are blotted
A P : 0 4 :382(165) [0225] If the doctrine of **faith** is omitted, it is vain to say that
A P : 0 4 :383(165) [0225] The scholastics do not teach the righteousness of **faith**.
A P : 0 4 :383(165) [0225] They interpret **faith** as merely a knowledge of history or
A P : 0 4 :384(166) [0225] save, but that it saves only because of **faith** in the heart.
A P : 0 4 :384(166) [0225] to show what kind of **faith** obtains eternal life, a faith
A P : 0 4 :384(166) [0225] of faith obtains eternal life, a **faith** that is firm and active.
A P : 0 4 :385(166) [0225] No **faith** is firm that does not show itself in confession.
A P : 0 4 :385(166) [0225] please God because of **faith**, as the prayers of the church
A P : 0 4 :386(166) [0225] to him, and reborn by a **faith** that penitently grasps the
A P : 0 4 :386(166) [0225] Through this **faith**, Peter says (I Pet. 1:5), we are
A P : 0 4 :387(166) [0225] need to understand this **faith**, for it brings the fullest
A P : 0 4 :387(166) [0225] that men are justified by **faith** deny that Christ is the
A P : 0 4 :389(166) [0225] for strengthening their **faith** and for teaching and
A P : 0 4 :393(167) [0225] would obscure the righteousness of **faith** in this way.

Continued ▶

A P : 0 4 :393(167) [0225] of the righteousness of **faith** taught that men were
A P : 0 4 :393(167) [0225] own works and devotions, not by **faith** for Christ's sake.
A P : 0 4 :394(167) [0225] of the righteousness of **faith**, and such teachers there will
A P : 0 4 :395(167) [0225] this opinion and taught the righteousness of **faith**.
A P : 0 4 :398(167) [0227] in clear words for saying **faith** is part of penance, by
A P : 0 4 :398(167) [0227] that this doctrine—that by **faith** we obtain the forgiveness
A P : 0 7 :005(169) [0227] mainly an association of **faith** and of the Holy Spirit in
A P : 0 7 :020(171) [0233] Cor. 3:12), that is, the true knowledge of Christ and **faith**.
A P : 0 7 :021(172) [0233] the foundation but that this did not overthrow their **faith**.
A P : 0 7 :021(172) [0233] hand, does overthrow **faith**, as when they condemn our
A P : 0 7 :021(172) [0233] doctrine that the forgiveness of sins is received by **faith**.
A P : 0 7 :021(172) [0233] Similarly, why will **faith** be necessary if sacraments justify
A P : 0 7 :022(172) [0235] as those in lesser stations have apostasized from the **faith**.
A P : 0 7 :022(172) [0235] is true knowledge and the confession of **faith** and truth."
A P : 0 7 :023(172) [0235] may establish articles of **faith**, abolish the Scriptures by
A P : 0 7 :025(173) [0235] of sins through **faith** in him and not through devotions
A P : 0 7 :031(174) [0237] which there can be no **faith** in the heart nor righteousness
A P : 0 7 :031(174) [0237] The righteousness of **faith** is not a righteousness tied to
A P : 0 7 :042(176) [0241] others at another, but this difference did no harm to **faith**.
A P : 0 7 :043(177) [0243] nothing contrary to the **faith** or the rule of the church,
A P : 0 7 :045(177) [0243] human observances does not harm the unity of the **faith**.
A P : 0 7 :045(177) [0243] of the righteousness of **faith** and of the kingdom of God
A P : 1 0 :003(179) [0247] joined to Christ spiritually by true **faith** and sincere love.
A P : 1 1 :002(180) [0249] be sure that by this **faith** we are truly reconciled to God.
A P : 1 1 :002(180) [0249] monks teach nothing about **faith** and free forgiveness.
A P : 1 1 :009(182) [0251] had added one word on **faith**, which consoles and
A P : 1 1 :009(182) [0251] Now, on this **faith** which obtains the forgiveness of sins
A P : 1 2 :001(182) [0253] we say that contrition and **faith** are the parts of
A P : 1 2 :001(182) [0253] and they deny that **faith** is the second part of penitence.
A P : 1 2 :002(182) [0253] of the Gospel, that by **faith** we obtain the forgiveness of
A P : 1 2 :002(182) [0253] If we deny that by **faith** we obtain the forgiveness of sins,
A P : 1 2 :008(183) [0255] must be in reference to **faith** and the Gospel, that Judas
A P : 1 2 :008(183) [0255] For **faith** makes the difference between the contrition of
A P : 1 2 :010(184) [0255] the power of the keys, and the righteousness of **faith**.
A P : 1 2 :012(184) [0257] and they do not mention **faith**, which grasps the
A P : 1 2 :016(184) [0257] of the righteousness of **faith** in Christ and of the blessing
A P : 1 2 :020(185) [0257] of sins because of contrition, not by **faith** in Christ.
A P : 1 2 :025(185) [0259] attitude in the recipient, that is, without **faith** in Christ.
A P : 1 2 :028(185) [0259] given penitence two parts, namely, contrition and **faith**.
A P : 1 2 :034(186) [0261] say nothing about **faith**, but present only the Word that
A P : 1 2 :035(186) [0261] we therefore add **faith** in Christ, that amid these terrors
A P : 1 2 :036(186) [0261] This **faith** strengthens, sustains, and quickens the contrite
A P : 1 2 :036(186) [0261] "Since we are justified by **faith**, we have peace with God."
A P : 1 2 :036(186) [0261] This **faith** obtains the forgiveness of sins.
A P : 1 2 :036(186) [0261] This **faith** justifies before God, as the same passage
A P : 1 2 :036(186) [0261] as the same passage attests, "We are justified by **faith**."
A P : 1 2 :036(186) [0261] This **faith** shows the difference between the contrition of
A P : 1 2 :036(186) [0261] avail because it lacked the **faith** that grasps the
A P : 1 2 :036(186) [0261] avail because it had the **faith** that grasps the forgiveness
A P : 1 2 :037(186) [0261] Nor is love present before **faith** has effected the
A P : 1 2 :037(186) [0261] This **faith** gradually grows and throughout life it struggles
A P : 1 2 :037(187) [0261] But love follows **faith**, as we have said above.
A P : 1 2 :038(187) [0261] as an anxiety joined with **faith**, where faith consoles and
A P : 1 2 :038(187) [0261] joined with faith, where **faith** consoles and sustains the
A P : 1 2 :038(187) [0261] whereas in servile fear **faith** does not sustain the anxious
A P : 1 2 :039(187) [0261] In speaking of **faith**, therefore, we also include absolution
A P : 1 2 :039(187) [0261] include absolution since "**faith** comes from what is
A P : 1 2 :042(187) [0261] Meanwhile this **faith** is nourished in many ways, amid
A P : 1 2 :042(187) [0263] So **faith** is conceived and confirmed through absolution,
A P : 1 2 :045(187) [0263] There are, then, two chief parts here, contrition and **faith**.
A P : 1 2 :045(187) [0263] is not to have the general **faith** that even the demons have
A P : 1 2 :045(188) [0263] sins are denounced; and **faith**, when it is said, "Believe in
A P : 1 2 :045(188) [0263] he names contrition and **faith** as the chief parts of
A P : 1 2 :046(188) [0263] raised with him through **faith** in the working of God"
A P : 1 2 :046(188) [0263] the body of sins, the other is being raised through **faith**.
A P : 1 2 :046(188) [0263] which nature could not bear without the support of **faith**.
A P : 1 2 :047(188) [0263] There are therefore two parts here, contrition and **faith**.
A P : 1 2 :047(188) [0265] the conscience except by **faith**, therefore faith alone
A P : 1 2 :047(188) [0265] except by faith, therefore **faith** alone quickens, according
A P : 1 2 :047(188) [0265] word (Hab. 2:4), "The righteous shall live by his **faith**."
A P : 1 2 :048(188) [0265] This new sentence is **faith**, abolishing the earlier sentence
A P : 1 2 :050(189) [0265] sentences the first part means contrition, the second **faith**.
A P : 1 2 :052(189) [0265] contrition and the **faith** that consoles and justifies.
A P : 1 2 :054(189) [0265] saints were justified by **faith** in this promise, not by their
A P : 1 2 :056(189) [0267] encourages David and by **faith** it sustains, justifies, and
A P : 1 2 :057(189) [0267] added, but contrition and **faith** there must always be in
A P : 1 2 :057(189) [0267] Your **faith** has saved you; go in peace."
A P : 1 2 :057(189) [0267] part of her penance, the **faith** that encouraged and
A P : 1 2 :058(190) [0267] in order to emphasize the **faith** that we require in
A P : 1 2 :058(190) [0267] easier to understand the **faith** proclaimed by the Gospel
A P : 1 2 :059(190) [0267] statement that men obtain the forgiveness of sins by **faith**.
A P : 1 2 :059(190) [0267] but by that personal **faith** by which each individual
A P : 1 2 :060(190) [0267] our opponents talk about **faith** and say that it precedes
A P : 1 2 :060(190) [0267] justifying but the general **faith** which believes that God
A P : 1 2 :060(190) [0267] Beyond such "**faith**" we require everyone to believe that
A P : 1 2 :060(190) [0267] for this personal **faith**, and we set it in opposition to the
A P : 1 2 :060(190) [0269] This **faith** follows on our terrors, overcoming them and
A P : 1 2 :060(190) [0269] To this **faith** we attribute justification and regeneration,
A P : 1 2 :060(190) [0269] We insist that this **faith** is really necessary for the
A P : 1 2 :061(190) [0269] they must maintain that **faith** is part of penitence since
A P : 1 2 :061(190) [0269] of penitence since only **faith** can accept the absolution.
A P : 1 2 :061(190) [0269] That only **faith** can accept the absolution can be proved
A P : 1 2 :061(190) [0269] teaches in Rom. 4:16 that only **faith** accepts a promise.
A P : 1 2 :061(190) [0269] of the forgiveness of sins, it necessarily requires **faith**.
A P : 1 2 :063(191) [0269] accepted by anything but **faith** alone, according to Rom.
A P : 1 2 :063(191) [0269] blood, to be received by **faith**," and Rom. 5:2, "Through
A P : 1 2 :063(191) [0269] him we have obtained access by **faith** to this grace," etc.
A P : 1 2 :064(191) [0269] can find peace without **faith** in Christ do not understand
A P : 1 2 :067(191) [0271] the forgiveness of sins by **faith** for Christ's sake and not
A P : 1 2 :067(191) [0271] good men who hold this **faith** be put to death with all
A P : 1 2 :073(192) [0273] apostle concludes, that a man is justified freely by **faith**."
A P : 1 2 :074(192) [0273] bids us add the personal **faith** that they are forgiven to us
A P : 1 2 :074(192) [0273] of sins, namely, that **faith** encourages our hearts and the
A P : 1 2 :074(193) [0273] the forgiveness of sins by **faith**, or that faith is part of
A P : 1 2 :074(193) [0273] of sins by faith, or that **faith** is part of penitence?
A P : 1 2 :077(193) [0275] of the law or in any other way except by **faith** in Christ.
A P : 1 2 :077(193) [0275] declaring that men are justified by **faith** and not by love.
A P : 1 2 :079(194) [0275] the forgiveness of sins by **faith**, freely for Christ's sake.
A P : 1 2 :080(194) [0275] Only **faith** accepts the promise.
A P : 1 2 :080(194) [0275] for the contrite by **faith** to take hold of the promise of the
A P : 1 2 :081(194) [0275] is why it depends on **faith**, in order that the promise may
A P : 1 2 :081(194) [0275] what was promised to **faith** in Jesus Christ might be given
A P : 1 2 :081(194) [0275] by taking hold through **faith** of the promise of the
A P : 1 2 :082(194) [0275] the forgiveness of sins by **faith** before we keep the law
A P : 1 2 :082(194) [0275] said before, love follows **faith**, for the regenerate receive
A P : 1 2 :084(194) [0277] that we are defending: by **faith** we receive the forgiveness
A P : 1 2 :084(194) [0277] sins for Christ's sake, by **faith** we ought to set against the
A P : 1 2 :085(194) [0277] the forgiveness of sins by **faith** but merit it by our love
A P : 1 2 :086(195) [0277] accept the promise that by **faith** we are reconciled to God
A P : 1 2 :087(195) [0277] said above that men are justified by **faith** and not by love.
A P : 1 2 :088(195) [0277] that such a certainty of **faith** is required in the Gospel;
A P : 1 2 :089(195) [0277] do nothing from **faith** if they always doubt whether they
A P : 1 2 :089(195) [0279] "Whatever does not proceed from **faith** is sin."
A P : 1 2 :089(195) [0279] never experience what **faith** is, and so it is that at last they
A P : 1 2 :091(195) [0279] we set forth contrition and **faith** as the two parts of
A P : 1 2 :091(195) [0279] our opponents quote in a distorted form to obscure **faith**.
A P : 1 2 :091(196) [0279] make no mention of **faith**, and the scholastics add
A P : 1 2 :091(196) [0279] add nothing about **faith** in their interpretation of them.
A P : 1 2 :092(196) [0279] have listed the doctrine of **faith** among the parts of
A P : 1 2 :092(196) [0279] or good works and making no mention of justifying **faith**.
A P : 1 2 :093(196) [0279] only about one but about both parts, contrition and **faith**.
A P : 1 2 :094(196) [0281] speaks excellently about **faith**, dwelling especially on the
A P : 1 2 :094(196) [0281] shows that he requires the **faith** with which we believe him
A P : 1 2 :095(196) [0281] Certainly this **faith** must believe firmly that God freely
A P : 1 2 :095(196) [0281] For if **faith** relies on these works, it immediately becomes
A P : 1 2 :096(196) [0281] we hope for pardon from **faith** just as faith obtains it from
A P : 1 2 :096(196) [0281] pardon from faith just as **faith** obtains it from the written
A P : 1 2 :096(196) [0281] Again, "It is **faith** that covers up our sins."
A P : 1 2 :097(196) [0281] not only about contrition and works, but also about **faith**.
A P : 1 2 :097(197) [0281] the sayings elsewhere about **faith**, they omit them.
A P : 1 2 :098(197) [0281] about contrition and **faith**, the two parts of penitence we
A P : 1 2 :106(197) [0283] neglects the fear of God or **faith** or his concern for God's
A P : 1 2 :114(199) [0285] has a Jewish and heathen **faith**, for even the heathen had
A P : 1 2 :116(199) [0287] keep the doctrine that by **faith** we obtain the forgiveness
A P : 1 2 :116(199) [0287] the righteousness of **faith** be obscured or people think
A P : 1 2 :124(201) [0289] in whose learning and **faith** men could have had greater
A P : 1 2 :125(201) [0289] her as the mistress of the **faith**, she should take care that
A P : 1 2 :131(202) [0291] the body in lusts, and true **faith** is not ungrateful to God
A P : 1 2 :146(205) [0297] **Faith** in Christ overcomes death, just as it overcomes the
A P : 1 2 :147(205) [0297] in the remission of guilt, **faith** frees the heart from the
A P : 1 2 :153(206) [0299] even now, once his **faith** has overcome its terrors, there is
A P : 1 2 :164(208) [0303] of penitence — contrition, **faith**, and good fruits — brings
A P : 1 2 :165(208) [0303] good works done from **faith**, but not, as these men
A P : 1 2 :178(211) [0309] neglected to teach the **faith** that justifies and consoles
A P : 1 3 :005(211) [0309] believe and take hold of **faith**, as Paul says (Rom. 10:17),
A P : 1 3 :005(211) [0309] Paul says (Rom. 10:17), "**Faith** comes from what is
A P : 1 3 :011(212) [0311] to every one who has **faith**" (Rom. 1:16), again, "My word
A P : 1 3 :018(213) [0313] a good disposition in our heart, that is, without **faith**.
A P : 1 3 :019(213) [0313] says that circumcision was a sign given to exercise **faith**.
A P : 1 3 :019(213) [0313] there must be a **faith** which believes these promises and
A P : 1 3 :020(213) [0313] A promise is useless unless **faith** accepts it.
A P : 1 3 :020(213) [0313] therefore, there must be **faith**, so that anyone who uses
A P : 1 3 :020(214) [0313] He should accept this by **faith**, comfort his troubled
A P : 1 3 :021(214) [0313] are talking about personal **faith**, which accepts the
A P : 1 3 :021(214) [0313] being offered, not about a **faith** which believes in a
A P : 1 3 :023(214) [0313] says the opposite: that **faith** in the sacrament, and not the
A P : 1 5 :004(215) [0315] Gospel, the blessing of Christ, and righteousness of **faith**.
A P : 1 5 :005(215) [0317] Gospel teaches that by **faith**, for Christ's sake, we freely
A P : 1 5 :006(215) [0317] men are justified by the **faith** that they have a gracious
A P : 1 5 :006(216) [0317] have been saved through **faith**; and this is not your own
A P : 1 5 :010(216) [0317] the work of Christ and the righteousness of **faith**.
A P : 1 5 :010(216) [0317] that we accept it by **faith**; for only faith can accept a
A P : 1 5 :010(216) [0317] we accept it by faith; for only **faith** can accept a promise.
A P : 1 5 :011(216) [0317] Since it is by **faith** that we accept the forgiveness of sins
A P : 1 5 :011(216) [0317] forgiveness of sins and by **faith** that we have a gracious
A P : 1 5 :016(217) [0319] of the righteousness of **faith**, they believed that by these
A P : 1 5 :017(217) [0319] 14:23), "Whatever does not proceed from **faith** is sin."
A P : 1 5 :018(217) [0319] are freely justified before God by **faith** for Christ's sake.
A P : 1 5 :020(218) [0321] that we are justified by **faith** for Christ's sake, not for the
A P : 1 5 :022(218) [0321] the righteousness of **faith**, it naturally supposes that such
A P : 1 5 :024(218) [0321] copy their outward behavior without copying their **faith**.
A P : 1 5 :025(218) [0321] of the righteousness of **faith** in Christ is obscured and
A P : 1 5 :027(219) [0323] syllable about Christ or **faith** in him or the good works to
A P : 1 5 :032(220) [0325] for justification, they obscure the righteousness of **faith**.
A P : 1 5 :042(221) [0327] about the righteousness of **faith** or about faith in Christ
A P : 1 5 :042(221) [0327] of faith or about **faith** in Christ or about comfort for the
A P : 1 5 :043(221) [0327] penitence, the fear of God, **faith** in Christ, the
A P : 1 5 :043(221) [0327] the righteousness of **faith**, comfort for the conscience
A P : 1 5 :043(221) [0327] the conscience through **faith**, the exercise of faith, prayer
A P : 1 5 :043(221) [0327] faith, the exercise of **faith**, prayer and our assurance that
A P : 1 5 :046(221) [0327] This is the spiritual exercise of fear and **faith**.
A P : 1 5 :050(222) [0329] are necessary over and above the righteousness of **faith**.
A P : 1 6 :002(222) [0331] heart, the fear of God and **faith**, the beginning of eternal
A P : 1 6 :009(224) [0333] of the heart, like a deep fear of God and a strong **faith**.
A P : 1 8 :006(225) [0335] nor trust in God nor the **faith** that God hears, forgives,
A P : 1 8 :006(225) [0335] (Matt. 7:18) and "without **faith** it is impossible to please"
A P : 1 8 :007(225) [0337] for true fear of God, true **faith** in God, true knowledge
A P : 1 8 :008(226) [0337] it is hard to keep this **faith**; for the ungodly it is
A P : 2 0 :003(227) [0339] before God not through **faith** but through their own
A P : 2 0 :008(227) [0341] This **faith** gives support and life to the heart in its hardest
A P : 2 0 :013(228) [0343] and not because of them and which are now kept by **faith**.
A P : 2 0 :013(228) [0343] **Faith** does not remain in those who lose the Holy Spirit
A P : 2 0 :013(228) [0343] as we have said before, **faith** has its existence in
A P : 2 0 :015(229) [0343] conviction that good works must necessarily follow **faith**.
A P : 2 0 :015(229) [0343] the Holy Spirit by **faith**, the keeping of the law necessarily
A P : 2 1 :005(229) [0345] the strengthening of our **faith**: when we see Peter forgiven

Continued ▶

AP : 21 :006(230) [0345] the imitation, first of their **faith** and then of their other
AP : 21 :010(230) [0345] ought to come from **faith**, how do we know that God
AP : 21 :013(230) [0345] uncertain, for prayer without **faith** is not prayer.
AP : 21 :017(231) [0347] Such an invocation, therefore, is not based on **faith**.
AP : 21 :036(234) [0353] means of confirming their **faith** and as an incentive to
AP : 21 :036(234) [0353] experienced the power of **faith** in sickness and constantly
AP : 21 :036(234) [0353] as these which talk about **faith** or fear in the
AP : 21 :037(234) [0355] who know nothing about either **faith** or public affairs.
AP : 23 :030(243) [0371] and by prayer, that is, by **faith** which uses it gratefully as
AP : 23 :031(243) [0373] and holy through **faith** in Christ just as the use of food,
AP : 23 :032(244) [0373] reader note that he adds **faith** and does not praise
AP : 23 :032(244) [0373] duties apart from **faith**: "if she continues," he says, "in
AP : 23 :032(244) [0373] apart from faith: "if she continues," he says, "in **faith**."
AP : 23 :032(244) [0373] above all he requires the **faith** by which a woman accepts
AP : 23 :032(244) [0373] should follow everyone's **faith**, pleasing God because of
AP : 23 :032(244) [0373] follow everyone's faith, pleasing God because of **faith**.
AP : 23 :032(244) [0373] please God because of **faith**, and a believing woman is
AP : 23 :034(244) [0373] that is, to believers in Christ who are righteous by **faith**.
AP : 23 :034(244) [0373] is pure in the godly, through the Word of God and **faith**.
AP : 23 :037(244) [0373] of the righteousness of **faith**, as we have expounded it
AP : 23 :039(244) [0375] of sins and that through **faith** he is accounted righteous
AP : 23 :064(248) [0381] We have said that without **faith** virginity is not pure in
AP : 23 :064(248) [0381] God, and that because of **faith** marriage is pure,
AP : 24 :002(249) [0385] who is ignorant of the **faith** of the church benefits from
AP : 24 :003(250) [0385] by the Word may receive **faith** and fear and so may also
AP : 24 :003(250) [0385] something to learn that will arouse their **faith** and fear.
AP : 24 :012(251) [0387] and by the necessity of **faith** to conquer the terrors of sins
AP : 24 :012(251) [0387] "Since we are justified by **faith**, we have peace" (Rom.
AP : 24 :025(253) [0391] of the Gospel, **faith**, prayer, thanksgiving, confession, the
AP : 24 :026(254) [0393] These are valid, not *ex opere operato* but because of **faith**.
AP : 24 :026(254) [0393] him let us offer," namely, through **faith** in Christ.
AP : 24 :027(254) [0393] it is the righteousness of **faith** in the heart and the fruits
AP : 24 :027(254) [0393] righteousness of faith in the heart and the fruits of **faith**.
AP : 24 :027(254) [0393] worship should be in spirit, in **faith**, and with the heart.
AP : 24 :028(254) [0393] He adds that God had commanded **faith**.
AP : 24 :030(255) [0395] and pure sacrifice; this is **faith**, prayer, thanksgiving,
AP : 24 :032(255) [0395] of the Gospel produces **faith** in those who accept it.
AP : 24 :032(255) [0395] Lord becomes great, like **faith**, prayer, proclamation of
AP : 24 :034(256) [0397] may become offerings acceptable to God through **faith**.
AP : 24 :034(256) [0397] of the Gospel, **faith**, prayer, and things like that, though
AP : 24 :035(256) [0397] of the Gospel, **faith**, prayer, and thanksgiving.
AP : 24 :036(257) [0397] of flour symbolizes **faith**, prayer, and thanksgiving in the
AP : 24 :038(257) [0399] the proclamation of the **faith** which truly believes that by
AP : 24 :043(258) [0399] the law and say nothing about the righteousness of **faith**.
AP : 24 :046(258) [0401] Yet this is the principal doctrine of the Christian **faith**.
AP : 24 :046(258) [0401] never mentioned **faith**, by which we freely receive the
AP : 24 :046(258) [0401] about the exercise of **faith** in its struggle with despair and
AP : 24 :051(259) [0403] of the Gospel, in **faith**, and in its struggles, they should be
AP : 24 :055(259) [0403] had to be justified by **faith** in the promise of the
AP : 24 :057(260) [0405] and the righteousness of **faith**, it corrupts the teaching of
AP : 24 :059(260) [0405] thereby they may receive **faith** and the Holy Spirit and be
AP : 24 :060(260) [0405] the righteousness of **faith** and the idea that the Mass
AP : 24 :060(260) [0405] work or anything else but **faith** in Christ, as we read
AP : 24 :060(260) [0405] "Since we are justified by **faith**, we have peace."
AP : 24 :063(261) [0405] glory of Christ's suffering and the righteousness of **faith**.
AP : 24 :064(261) [0407] though without **faith** the Mass does not even benefit
AP : 24 :068(262) [0409] it does not talk about **faith**, whose true meaning very few
AP : 24 :070(262) [0409] promise is useless unless **faith** accepts it, so the ceremony
AP : 24 :070(262) [0409] is useless without the **faith** which really believes that the
AP : 24 :070(262) [0409] Such a **faith** encourages the contrite mind.
AP : 24 :070(262) [0409] was given to arouse this **faith**, so the sacrament was
AP : 24 :071(262) [0409] of the sacrament, when **faith** gives life to terrified hearts,
AP : 24 :072(262) [0409] the acceptance of them by **faith**, so that they make us
AP : 24 :073(262) [0409] A **faith** that acknowledges mercy makes alive.
AP : 24 :074(262) [0409] Once **faith** has strengthened a conscience to see its
AP : 24 :075(263) [0411] of sins and that it ought to be received by **faith**.
AP : 24 :075(263) [0411] Fathers clearly require **faith** and speak of the
AP : 24 :077(263) [0411] or anyone else without **faith** conflicts with the
AP : 24 :077(263) [0411] else without faith conflicts with the righteousness of **faith**.
AP : 24 :087(265) [0413] provide an advantage *ex opere operato* without **faith**.
AP : 24 :088(265) [0413] service of the mind, fear, **faith**, prayer, thanksgiving, and
AP : 24 :089(266) [0415] to maintain that without **faith**, *ex opere operato*, a
AP : 24 :089(266) [0415] be conquered except by **faith** in Christ, as Paul teaches
AP : 24 :089(266) [0415] (Rom. 5:1), "Being justified by **faith**, we have peace."
AP : 24 :090(266) [0415] The forgiveness of guilt can be accepted only by **faith**.
AP : 24 :090(266) [0415] but a promise and a sacrament requiring **faith**.
AP : 24 :091(266) [0415] forgiveness of guilt and **faith** to vain ideas of
AP : 24 :091(266) [0415] crushed the doctrine of **faith**, and under the pretext of
AP : 24 :092(266) [0415] *opere operato* and without **faith**, it follows that it is
AP : 24 :092(267) [0417] sacrifice nor sacrament nor forgiveness of sins nor **faith**?
AP : 24 :093(267) [0417] who have departed in **faith**, forefathers, fathers,
AP : 24 :096(268) [0417] and utterly destroy the doctrine of righteousness by **faith**.
AP : 24 :097(268) [0417] *opere operato* rather than receiving it freely through **faith**.
AP : 24 :097(268) [0417] the righteousness of **faith** but give equal honor to other
AP : 24 :098(268) [0419] obscure the glory of Christ and the righteousness of **faith**.
AP : 27 :011(270) [0423] forgiveness of sins not by **faith** in Christ, but by monastic
AP : 27 :013(271) [0423] of sins is received freely for Christ's sake, through **faith**.
AP : 27 :013(271) [0423] because of our merits but because of Thee, through **faith**.
AP : 27 :019(272) [0425] attain the forgiveness of sins by **faith** for Christ's sake?
AP : 27 :023(272) [0427] of the righteousness of **faith**, which teaches that for
AP : 27 :023(273) [0427] 14:23): "Whatever does not proceed from **faith** is sin."
AP : 27 :031(274) [0431] but that we receive this freely by **faith**, as has been said.
AP : 27 :032(274) [0431] who accept forgiveness by **faith** and do not set their
AP : 27 :037(275) [0433] in the fear of God, in **faith**, in the love of their neighbor,
AP : 27 :050(277) [0437] for each of us with true **faith** to obey his own calling.
AP : 27 :054(278) [0437] about the righteousness of **faith**, about true penitence,
AP : 27 :055(278) [0439] of teaching, prompting some of them to fear or **faith**.
AP : 27 :058(279) [0439] to exercise or show **faith** before men, not to merit the
AP : 27 :062(280) [0441] them of the teaching of **faith** and immortality — surely a
AP : 27 :064(280) [0441] incur condemnation for having violated their first **faith**."
AP : 27 :067(280) [0441] being supported from public funds and thus lost the **faith**.
AP : 27 :067(280) [0441] This is what he calls "first **faith**" — not a monastic vows,
AP : 27 :067(280) [0441] He uses "**faith**" this way in the same chapter (I Tim. 5:8),
AP : 27 :067(280) [0443] especially for his own family, he has disowned the **faith**."
AP : 27 :068(280) [0443] He talks about **faith** differently from the sophists.
AP : 27 :068(280) [0443] He does not attribute **faith** to people who have a mortal
AP : 27 :068(280) [0443] do not provide for their relatives have rejected the **faith**.
AP : 27 :068(280) [0443] way he says that the wanton women had rejected the **faith**
AP : 27 :070(281) [0443] with services instituted by his Word and done in **faith**.
AP : 28 :007(282) [0445] receive forgiveness of sins freely for Christ's sake by **faith**.
AP : 28 :008(282) [0445] hearts are cleansed by **faith** and then go on to forbid the
AP : 28 :023(284) [0451] of sins, that by **faith** we freely obtain the forgiveness of
S1 : PR :001(288) [0455] assemble articles of our **faith** to serve as a basis for
S1 : PR :002(288) [0455] as the confession of our **faith** if the pope and his
S1 : PR :002(288) [0455] bold as seriously, in good **faith**, and without deception or
S2 : 01 :000(292) [0461] [Article I. Christ and **Faith**]
S2 : 01 :004(292) [0461] clear and certain that such **faith** alone justifies us, as St.
S2 : 01 :004(292) [0461] that a man is justified by **faith** apart from works of law"
S2 : 01 :004(292) [0461] that he justifies him who has **faith** in Jesus" (Rom. 3:26).
S2 : 02 :013(295) [0467] individuals and cannot establish an article of **faith**.
S2 : 02 :015(295) [0467] not do to make articles of **faith** out of the holy Fathers'
S2 : 02 :015(295) [0467] have to become articles of **faith** — as has happened in the
S2 : 02 :015(295) [0467] shall establish articles of **faith** and no one else, not even
S2 : 02 :017(295) [0467] these things as articles of **faith** and had to live according
S2 : 02 :024(296) [0469] by grace, through **faith**, without our work or pennies.
S2 : 02 :029(297) [0471] institution of Christ and may use and receive it in **faith**.
S2 : 04 :009(300) [0473] in unity of doctrine, **faith**, sacraments, prayer, works of
S2 : 04 :012(300) [0475] pope will not permit such **faith** but asserts that one must
S2 : 04 :014(301) [0475] as a mention of Christ, **faith**, and God's commandments.
S3 : 03 :014(305) [0483] There was no mention here of Christ or of **faith**.
S3 : 03 :018(306) [0483] without being able to consider Christ and **faith**.
S3 : 03 :018(306) [0483] man's own powers without **faith** and without knowledge
S3 : 03 :019(306) [0485] Here, again, there was neither **faith** nor Christ.
S3 : 03 :023(306) [0485] placed in it, and neither **faith** nor Christ would have been
S3 : 03 :042(309) [0491] they will persevere in **faith** even if they sin afterwards, and
S3 : 03 :042(310) [0491] not as long as you believe, for **faith** blots out all sins," etc.
S3 : 03 :042(310) [0491] sins after he has received **faith** and the Spirit, he never
S3 : 03 :042(310) [0491] and the Spirit, he never really had the Spirit and **faith**.
S3 : 03 :043(310) [0491] murder, and blasphemy), **faith** and the Spirit have
S3 : 03 :044(310) [0491] the Holy Spirit and **faith** are not present, for St. John
S3 : 08 :007(313) [0495] those who have come to **faith** before they were baptized
S3 : 08 :007(313) [0495] and those who came to **faith** in Baptism came to their
S3 : 08 :007(313) [0495] in Baptism came to their **faith** through the external Word
S3 : 08 :008(313) [0495] acceptable to God in this **faith** (Luke calls him "devout"
S3 : 08 :008(313) [0495] had already come, and his **faith** concerning the coming
S3 : 12 :003(315) [0499] but it consists of the Word of God and true **faith**.
S3 : 13 :001(315) [0499] subject, namely, that by **faith** (as St. Peter says) we get a
S3 : 13 :002(315) [0499] Good works follow such **faith**, renewal, and forgiveness.
S3 : 13 :003(315) [0499] good works do not follow, our **faith** is false and not true.
TR : 00 :006(320) [0505] be regarded as articles of **faith** or commandments of
TR : 00 :028(325) [0511] not on the man but on the **faith** of Peter; and what was
TR : 00 :028(325) [0511] Peter; and what was this **faith** other than "You are the
TR : 00 :029(325) [0513] This **faith** is the foundation of the church.
TR : 00 :031(325) [0513] that we lord it over your **faith**" (II Cor. 1:24), and again,
TR : 00 :034(325) [0513] Knowledge of **faith** and of a spiritual kingdom was
TR : 00 :037(326) [0515] monstrous errors obscure **faith** and the kingdom of
TR : 00 :044(328) [0517] sake and that by this **faith** we obtain the remission of
TR : 00 :044(328) [0517] (that is, the exercise of **faith** struggling against despair).
TR : 00 :048(328) [0519] have utterly extinguished the teaching concerning **faith**.
SC : 02 :006(345) [0545] and preserved me in true **faith**, just as he calls, gathers,
SC : 02 :006(345) [0545] it in union with Jesus Christ in the one true **faith**.
SC : 03 :011(347) [0547] us steadfast in his Word and in **faith** even to the end.
SC : 04 :010(349) [0551] with the water, and our **faith** which relies on the Word of
SC : 05 :026(351) [0555] say: "God be merciful to you and strengthen your **faith**.
SC : 05 :029(351) [0555] and to strengthen the **faith** of those whose consciences are
LC : SP :010(363) [0577] II. The Chief Articles of Our **Faith**
LC : 01 :002(365) [0581] often said, the trust and **faith** of the heart alone make
LC : 01 :003(365) [0581] If your **faith** and trust are right, then your God is the true
LC : 01 :003(365) [0581] For these two belong together, **faith** and God.
LC : 01 :004(365) [0581] is to require true **faith** and confidence of the heart, and
LC : 01 :050(371) [0593] the heart and taught **faith**, so this commandment leads us
LC : 01 :055(372) [0595] or in sublime and difficult matters of **faith** and doctrine.
LC : 01 :069(374) [0599] obedience, no fidelity, no **faith** — only perverse, unbridled
LC : 01 :070(374) [0601] heard above, the heart by **faith** first gives God the honor
LC : 01 :147(385) [0623] sight of God it is really **faith** that makes a person holy;
LC : 01 :147(385) [0623] that makes a person holy; **faith** alone serves him, while
LC : 02 :007(411) [0679] One God and one **faith**, but three persons, and therefore
LC : 02 :043(416) [0689] under the papacy, where **faith** was entirely shoved under
LC : 02 :051(417) [0691] by the Holy Spirit in one **faith**, mind, and understanding.
LC : 02 :053(417) [0693] and become strong in the **faith** and in the fruits of the
LC : 02 :062(419) [0695] increases, and strengthens **faith** through the same Word
LC : 02 :062(419) [0695] We now wait in **faith** for this to be accomplished through
LC : 02 :070(420) [0697] have enough to preach and learn on the subject of **faith**.
LC : 03 :002(420) [0697] and increase in us **faith** and obedience to the Ten
LC : 03 :025(423) [0705] of obedience to God and **faith** in his promise, or out of
LC : 03 :051(427) [0711] and to enlighten and strengthen us in **faith** by his power.
LC : 03 :053(427) [0711] through the Word and **faith**, and secondly, in eternity, it
LC : 03 :054(427) [0713] that it may be received by **faith** and may work and live in
LC : 03 :061(428) [0715] — for the Gospel, for **faith**, and for the Holy Spirit, that
LC : 03 :104(434) [0727] God, to tear us away from **faith**, hope, and love, to draw
LC : 03 :109(435) [0729] patient, kind, and firm in **faith**, the devil is likely in this
LC : 03 :120(436) [0731] affirmation of **faith** on the part of one who does not pray
LC : 03 :120(436) [0731] Where such **faith** is wanting, there can be no true prayer.
LC : 03 :123(436) [0731] prays, let him ask in **faith**, with no doubting, for he who
LC : 04 :028(440) [0739] the new spirits, assert that **faith** alone saves and that
LC : 04 :028(440) [0739] that is in us does it but **faith**, as we shall hear later on.
LC : 04 :029(440) [0739] are unwilling to see that **faith** must have something to
LC : 04 :029(440) [0739] Thus **faith** clings to the water and believes it to be Baptism
LC : 04 :030(440) [0739] so foolish as to separate **faith** from the object to which
LC : 04 :030(440) [0739] from the object to which **faith** is attached and bound on
LC : 04 :030(440) [0739] means he speaks — there **faith** must look and to it faith
LC : 04 :030(440) [0739] speaks — there faith must look and to it **faith** must hold.
LC : 04 :031(440) [0739] rejects God's Word, **faith**, and Christ, who directs us and
LC : 04 :033(440) [0741] will be saved," that is, **faith** alone makes the person
LC : 04 :034(440) [0741] Without **faith** Baptism is of no use, although in itself it is
LC : 04 :034(441) [0741] that whatever is not **faith** contributes nothing toward

Continued ▶

LC : 04 :035(441) [0741] works are of no use for salvation, what becomes of **faith**?"
LC : 04 :035(441) [0741] but rather demand **faith**, for without faith they could not
LC : 04 :035(441) [0741] demand faith, for without **faith** they could not be
LC : 04 :037(441) [0741] which God gives us and **faith** grasps, just as the Lord
LC : 04 :037(441) [0741] and offered to us in the Word and received by **faith**.
LC : 04 :037(441) [0741] they cry out against us as though we preach against **faith**.
LC : 04 :037(441) [0741] Actually, we insist on **faith** alone as so necessary that
LC : 04 :053(443) [0745] the water, Baptism is valid, even though **faith** be lacking.
LC : 04 :053(443) [0745] For my **faith** does not constitute Baptism but receives it.
LC : 04 :053(443) [0745] or used, for it is bound not to our **faith** but to the Word.
LC : 04 :054(443) [0745] baptized him in all good **faith**, we should have to admit
LC : 04 :056(443) [0747] God: "I come here in my **faith**, and in the faith of others,
LC : 04 :056(443) [0747] in my faith, and in the **faith** of others, nevertheless I
LC : 04 :056(444) [0747] on the strength of my own **faith**, but on the strength of
LC : 04 :057(444) [0747] that he may believe, and we pray God to grant him **faith**.
LC : 04 :058(444) [0747] where there is no true **faith**, there also can be no true
LC : 04 :058(444) [0747] I might argue, "If I have no **faith**, then Christ is nothing."
LC : 04 :060(444) [0747] were baptized and he, moreover, did not have true **faith**.
LC : 04 :061(444) [0747] because they see neither **faith** nor obedience, they
LC : 04 :073(445) [0751] Where **faith** is present with its fruits, there Baptism is no
LC : 04 :073(445) [0751] accompanies it; but where **faith** is lacking, it remains a
LC : 04 :084(446) [0753] day he should be found in **faith** and amid its fruits, every
LC : 05 :006(447) [0755] cares so much about our **faith** and conduct that he would
LC : 05 :024(449) [0759] sustenance so that our **faith** may refresh and strengthen
LC : 05 :026(449) [0759] we either renounce our **faith** or yield hand and foot and
LC : 05 :028(449) [0759] can bread and wine forgive sins or strengthen **faith**?"
LC : 05 :034(450) [0761] forgiveness of sins, it cannot be received except by **faith**.
LC : 05 :034(450) [0761] This **faith** he himself demands in the Word when he says,
LC : 05 :037(451) [0761] This is done by the **faith** of the heart which discerns and
LC : 05 :044(451) [0763] matters pertaining to **faith**, love, and patience it is not
LC : 05 :052(452) [0765] be forced by men either to **faith** or to any good work.
LC : 06 :013(458) [0000] sufficiently strong in **faith**, we may at any time and as
EP : RN :003(465) [0777] catholic, Christian **faith** and confessions of the orthodox
EP : RN :004(465) [0777] the schism in matters of **faith** which has occurred in our
EP : RN :004(465) [0777] of our Christian **faith**, particularly against the false
EP : RN :006(465) [0779] as opposed to the unanimous declaration of our **faith**.
EP : RN :008(465) [0779] and expositions of the **faith**, setting forth how at various
EP : 01 :001(466) [0779] *The Pure Doctrine, Faith, and Confession according to*
EP : 01 :003(466) [0779] articles of our Christian **faith**, namely, creation,
EP : 02 :002(470) [0787] It is our teaching, **faith**, and confession that in spiritual
EP : 02 :004(470) [0787] salvation; likewise, that **faith** comes from the hearing of
EP : 03 :000(472) [0791] III. The Righteousness of **Faith** before God
EP : 03 :001(472) [0791] God and saved solely by **faith** in Christ, so that Christ
EP : 03 :002(473) [0791] When he dwells in us by **faith**, over against this indwelling
EP : 03 :005(473) [0793] teach, and confess that **faith** is the only means and
EP : 03 :005(473) [0793] that for Christ's sake such **faith** is reckoned for
EP : 03 :006(473) [0793] and confess that this **faith** is not a mere knowledge of the
EP : 03 :008(474) [0793] of man and distinguish it from justification by **faith**.
EP : 03 :009(474) [0795] reckoned to them through **faith** or the salvation of their
EP : 03 :010(474) [0795] the righteousness of **faith** before God, we must give
EP : 03 :010(474) [0795] become righteous and are saved "alone by **faith**" in Christ
EP : 03 :011(474) [0795] not imagine a kind of **faith** in this connection that could
EP : 03 :011(474) [0795] has been justified by **faith**, a true living faith becomes
EP : 03 :011(474) [0795] by faith, a true living **faith** becomes "active through love"
EP : 03 :011(474) [0795] always follow justifying **faith** and are certainly to be
EP : 03 :011(474) [0795] found with it, since such **faith** is never alone but is always
EP : 03 :015(474) [0795] when the righteousness of **faith** is spoken of in the
EP : 03 :016(475) [0795] 4. That **faith** does not look alone to Christ's obedience,
EP : 03 :017(475) [0795] 5. That **faith** is a kind of trust in the obedience of Christ
EP : 03 :019(475) [0795] 7. That **faith** saves because by faith there is begun in us
EP : 03 :019(475) [0795] faith saves because by **faith** there is begun in us the
EP : 03 :020(475) [0797] 8. That **faith** indeed has the most prominent role in
EP : 03 :022(475) [0797] grace becomes our own by **faith** in the heart and by the
EP : 03 :023(475) [0797] 11. That **faith** does not justify without good works, in
EP : 04 :005(476) [0797] to resolve it, this is our doctrine, **faith**, and confession:
EP : 04 :006(476) [0799] follow genuine **faith** — if it is a living and not a dead
EP : 04 :006(476) [0799] genuine faith — if it is a living and not a dead **faith**.
EP : 04 :007(476) [0799] have been saved through **faith**; and this is not your own
EP : 04 :011(477) [0799] and that he might keep his **faith** even if he deliberately
EP : 04 :015(477) [0799] Spirit, working through **faith**, preserves faith and
EP : 04 :015(477) [0799] working through faith, preserves **faith** and salvation in us.
EP : 04 :018(477) [0801] as an evidence of their **faith** and their gratitude toward
EP : 04 :018(477) [0801] dream concerning **faith** can damn people as much as a
EP : 04 :019(477) [0801] the teaching that **faith** and the indwelling of the Holy
EP : 06 :003(480) [0805] truly converted, regenerated, and justified through **faith**.
EP : 07 :004(482) [0809] Supper but assert that this takes place spiritually by **faith**.
EP : 07 :005(482) [0809] with the thoughts of our **faith** and there, but not in the
EP : 07 :011(483) [0811] article of our Christian **faith**: Jesus Christ is true,
EP : 07 :015(483) [0811] not only spiritually, by **faith**, but also orally — however,
EP : 07 :019(484) [0813] long as he retains a living **faith**, will receive the Holy
EP : 07 :019(484) [0813] who are weak in **faith** but repentant, to comfort them and
EP : 07 :019(484) [0813] to comfort them and to strengthen their weak **faith**.
EP : 07 :020(484) [0813] our own through genuine **faith** and of which we are
EP : 07 :021(484) [0813] above and to our simple **faith** and confession about
EP : 07 :026(485) [0815] we receive the body of Christ only spiritually by **faith**.
EP : 07 :029(485) [0815] assure us that when our **faith** ascends into heaven, it there
EP : 07 :030(485) [0815] and strengthening of our **faith** in the Holy Supper is
EP : 07 :035(485) [0815] 14. That **faith**, and not the omnipotent words of Christ's
EP : 07 :038(486) [0817] not consist only in true **faith** in Christ, but also depends
EP : 07 :039(486) [0817] have a genuine and living **faith** in Christ, can also receive
EP : 07 :042(486) [0817] in no other way than by **faith** and as it is revealed in the
EP : 08 :004(487) [0819] according to our Christian **faith** we teach, believe, and
EP : 08 :017(489) [0823] the basis of our Christian **faith** as we teach this to our
EP : 08 :018(489) [0823] Our doctrine, **faith**, and confession do not divide the
EP : 08 :039(491) [0827] and our simple Christian **faith**, we shall finally have
EP : 09 :002(492) [0827] and reason, but must be apprehended by **faith** alone.
EP : 09 :003(492) [0827] and admonishes all Christians to simplicity of **faith**.
EP : 10 :005(493) [0829] particularly the weak in **faith** are to be spared
EP : 10 :006(493) [0829] a clear-cut confession of **faith** is demanded of us, we dare
EP : 10 :006(493) [0831] as well as preventing offense to the weak in **faith**.
EP : 10 :007(494) [0831] in fasting does not destroy agreement in **faith**."
EP : 12 :007(498) [0839] the use of reason and can confess their **faith** personally.
EP : 12 :019(499) [0841] 3. That difference of **faith** is sufficient ground for married
EP : 12 :019(499) [0841] way, and marry someone else belonging to the same **faith**.
EP : 12 :022(499) [0841] Christ, conversion, repentance, **faith**, and new obedience.
EP : 12 :031(500) [0843] that this is the doctrine, **faith** and confession of all of us
SD : PR :001(501) [0847] articles of our Christian **faith** (which had been hideously
SD : PR :003(501) [0847] witness, setting forth the **faith** and the teaching of the
SD : PR :008(502) [0849] The weak in **faith**, on the other hand, will be scandalized;
SD : RN :002(503) [0851] nor accept a different or a new confession of our **faith**.
SD : RN :004(504) [0851] glorious confessions of the **faith** — succinct, Christian,
SD : RN :016(507) [0857] articles of our Christian **faith**, according to the prophetic
SD : RN :019(507) [0857] set forth and explain our **faith** and confession
SD : 01 :034(514) [0869] articles of our Christian **faith** constrain and compel us to
SD : 01 :041(515) [0871] are contrary to the first article of our Christian **faith**.
SD : 01 :047(516) [0873] article of our Christian **faith**, either that our flesh would
SD : 01 :048(517) [0875] articles of our Christian **faith** show powerfully and
SD : 02 :008(521) [0883] that judgments on articles of **faith** are to be pronounced.
SD : 02 :014(523) [0885] and to help them to remain in true **faith** until their end.
SD : 02 :016(523) [0887] knowledge of God and **faith**, we ought to petition him
SD : 02 :016(523) [0887] he would preserve **faith** and his heavenly gifts in us and
SD : 02 :024(526) [0891] and kindles and creates **faith** and other God-pleasing
SD : 02 :025(526) [0891] ascribe conversion, **faith** in Christ, regeneration, renewal,
SD : 02 :026(526) [0891] He works **faith**, for "It has been granted to you by God
SD : 02 :029(527) [0893] of Christ and without **faith** and the Holy Spirit are in the
SD : 02 :029(527) [0893] we begin our teaching with **faith**, through which the Holy
SD : 02 :031(527) [0893] fear of God, without **faith**, do not trust or believe that
SD : 02 :032(527) [0893] bear good fruit, and without **faith** no one can please God.
SD : 02 :037(528) [0895] and become strong in **faith** and in its fruits, which he
SD : 02 :038(528) [0895] and effects in us a daily increase in **faith** and good works.
SD : 02 :040(528) [0895] and preserved me in true **faith**, just as he calls, gathers,
SD : 02 :040(528) [0895] it in union with Jesus Christ in the one true **faith**."
SD : 02 :042(529) [0897] brings us to Christ in true **faith** and keeps us with him.
SD : 02 :047(530) [0901] feel no strong, ardent **faith** and cordial obedience but
SD : 02 :048(530) [0901] working true repentance, **faith**, and new spiritual power
SD : 02 :050(531) [0901] of their sins and true **faith** in the Son of God, Jesus
SD : 02 :051(531) [0901] "**Faith** comes from what is heard, and what is heard
SD : 02 :054(531) [0903] kindled in him a spark of **faith** which accepts the
SD : 02 :068(534) [0907] ardent in love, strong in **faith** and in hope, and at another
SD : 02 :071(535) [0909] meditation upon it kindles **faith** and other God-pleasing
SD : 03 :000(539) [0917] III. The Righteousness of **Faith** before God
SD : 03 :001(539) [0917] of Christ or of **faith** which God by grace through faith
SD : 03 :001(539) [0917] God by grace through **faith** reckons to poor sinners as
SD : 03 :002(539) [0917] that the righteousness of **faith**, which St. Paul calls the
SD : 03 :002(539) [0917] Son of God, who through **faith** dwells in the elect, impels
SD : 03 :004(540) [0917] that the righteousness of **faith** is forgiveness of sins,
SD : 03 :004(540) [0917] of Christ, which, through **faith** alone, is reckoned by pure
SD : 03 :006(540) [0917] article of justification by **faith** is "the chief article of the
SD : 03 :009(540) [0919] the righteousness of **faith** before God we believe, teach,
SD : 03 :009(540) [0919] of our Christian **faith** and confession described above,
SD : 03 :010(541) [0919] of the Gospel, and **faith** is the only means whereby we can
SD : 03 :011(541) [0919] **Faith** is a gift of God whereby we rightly learn to know
SD : 03 :012(541) [0919] "We are justified by **faith**" (Rom. 3:28), or "faith is
SD : 03 :012(541) [0919] by faith" (Rom. 3:28), or "**faith** is reckoned to us as
SD : 03 :013(541) [0919] For **faith** does not justify because it is so good a work and
SD : 03 :013(541) [0919] be made our own through **faith** if we are to be justified
SD : 03 :014(541) [0919] by grace is reckoned to **faith** or to the believers is the
SD : 03 :016(541) [0921] and accepted by **faith**, so that thus believers have
SD : 03 :017(542) [0921] of Christ which God reckons to **faith** (Phil. 3:9).
SD : 03 :018(542) [0921] follows justification by **faith** will not be confused with
SD : 03 :019(542) [0921] the Holy Spirit works in those who are justified by **faith**.
SD : 03 :020(542) [0921] has brought a person to **faith** and has justified him, a
SD : 03 :020(542) [0921] "He who through **faith** is righteous shall live (Rom. 1:17).
SD : 03 :021(542) [0921] the righteousness of **faith**, as Dr. Luther used the term in
SD : 03 :022(543) [0923] and righteous through **faith** and for the sake of Christ's
SD : 03 :023(543) [0923] mediator, Christ, through **faith** alone, without any work
SD : 03 :023(543) [0923] the righteousness of **faith** before God consists solely in
SD : 03 :024(543) [0923] insert that which precedes **faith** or follows faith into the
SD : 03 :024(543) [0923] precedes faith or follows **faith** into the article of
SD : 03 :025(543) [0923] the merit of Christ, and **faith** which accepts these in the
SD : 03 :026(543) [0923] cannot be genuine saving **faith** in those who live without
SD : 03 :026(543) [0923] precedes and genuine **faith** exists only in or with true
SD : 03 :027(543) [0923] a fruit which certainly and necessarily follows true **faith**.
SD : 03 :027(543) [0923] lost the righteousness of **faith**, as St. John says
SD : 03 :027(543) [0925] says, "We are justified by **faith** apart from works
SD : 03 :027(543) [0925] belong in the article or matter of justification by **faith**.
SD : 03 :029(544) [0925] are justified alone through **faith** in Christ, and not
SD : 03 :030(544) [0925] that the righteousness of **faith** before God consists solely
SD : 03 :030(544) [0925] which we receive only by **faith** in the promise of the
SD : 03 :030(544) [0925] justification before God **faith** trusts neither in contrition
SD : 03 :031(544) [0925] offered to us in the promise of the Gospel, but only **faith**.
SD : 03 :032(544) [0927] believers who through **faith** in Christ have been justified
SD : 03 :032(544) [0927] reckoned righteousness of **faith** and, second, also the
SD : 03 :032(545) [0927] into the article of justification by **faith** before God.
SD : 03 :032(545) [0927] which is reckoned to **faith** can stand before God's
SD : 03 :033(545) [0927] before God through **faith** alone for the sake of the
SD : 03 :034(545) [0927] justifies the ungodly, his **faith** is reckoned as
SD : 03 :036(545) [0927] article of justification by **faith**) as "without works,"
SD : 03 :036(545) [0927] are justified before God and saved "through **faith** alone."
SD : 03 :036(545) [0927] there could well be true **faith** without contrition, or as
SD : 03 :036(545) [0927] and dare not follow true **faith** as certain and unquestioned
SD : 03 :038(546) [0929] 2. That **faith**'s sole office and property is to serve as the
SD : 03 :039(546) [0929] The righteousness of **faith** consists solely in the
SD : 03 :039(546) [0929] applied to us, and made our own solely through **faith**.
SD : 03 :040(546) [0929] the proper order between **faith** and good works is bound
SD : 03 :041(546) [0929] works do not precede **faith**, nor is sanctification prior to
SD : 03 :041(546) [0929] the Holy Spirit kindles **faith** in us in conversion through
SD : 03 :041(546) [0929] **Faith** apprehends the grace of God in Christ whereby the
SD : 03 :041(546) [0929] though on occasion true **faith** could coexist and survive
SD : 03 :041(546) [0931] agreement between **faith** and good works; nevertheless, it
SD : 03 :041(546) [0931] works; nevertheless, it is **faith** alone which apprehends the
SD : 03 :041(546) [0931] And yet **faith** is at no time ever alone."
SD : 03 :042(547) [0931] of the manner in which **faith** justifies, it is St. Paul's
SD : 03 :042(547) [0931] is St. Paul's doctrine that **faith** alone justifies without
SD : 03 :042(547) [0931] of others, a true living **faith** and distinguish it from a
SD : 03 :042(547) [0931] a simulated and dead **faith** (since many lazy and secure

Continued ▶

SD : 0 3 :042(547) [0931] thinking that they have **faith** when they do not have true
SD : 0 3 :042(547) [0931] they do not have true **faith**), the Apology gives the
SD : 0 3 :042(547) [0931] answer: James calls that **faith** dead where all kinds of
SD : 0 3 :042(547) [0931] we are justified by such a **faith** as is without works, which
SD : 0 3 :042(547) [0931] by such a faith as is without works, which is a dead **faith**."
SD : 0 3 :043(547) [0931] But when we ask where **faith** gets the power to justify and
SD : 0 3 :043(547) [0931] and incorrect to answer: **Faith** cannot justify without
SD : 0 3 :043(547) [0931] justify without works; or, **faith** justifies or makes
SD : 0 3 :043(547) [0931] to justify is ascribed to **faith**; or, the presence of good
SD : 0 3 :043(547) [0931] of good works along with **faith** is necessary if men are to
SD : 0 3 :043(547) [0931] **Faith** justifies solely for this reason and on this account,
SD : 0 3 :044(547) [0931] doctrine of justification by **faith**, since it meets the
SD : 0 3 :048(548) [0933] 4. That righteousness by **faith** before God consists of two
SD : 0 3 :049(548) [0933] 5. That **faith** justifies only because righteousness is begun
SD : 0 3 :049(548) [0933] is begun in us by **faith**, or that faith has priority in
SD : 0 3 :049(548) [0933] in us by faith, or that **faith** has priority in justification
SD : 0 3 :051(548) [0933] is made our own through **faith** in the heart, through the
SD : 0 3 :052(548) [0933] justified solely through **faith** without works but that we
SD : 0 3 :053(548) [0933] we are justified through **faith** we simultaneously receive
SD : 0 3 :054(548) [0935] righteousness, dwells by **faith** in the elect who have been
SD : 0 3 :054(549) [0935] is not the righteousness of **faith** of which St. Paul speaks
SD : 0 3 :054(549) [0935] preceding righteousness of **faith**, which is precisely the
SD : 0 3 :057(549) [0935] the Gospel, upon which **faith** depends before God and
SD : 0 3 :057(549) [0935] and which God reckons to **faith**, as it is written, "For as
SD : 0 3 :057(550) [0935] again, "The righteous shall live by his **faith**" (Hab. 2:4).
SD : 0 3 :058(550) [0937] **Faith** thus looks at the person of Christ, how this person
SD : 0 3 :059(550) [0937] of the prophets and apostles, and our Christian **faith**:
SD : 0 3 :062(550) [0937] of the righteousness of **faith**, the words, "to justify" and
SD : 0 3 :063(550) [0937] 4. That **faith** does not look solely to the obedience of
SD : 0 3 :064(550) [0937] 5. That **faith** is such a kind of trust in the obedience of
SD : 0 3 :066(550) [0937] doctrine of justification by **faith** before God as it is set
SD : 0 4 :001(551) [0939] true believers as fruits of **faith** and since faith without
SD : 0 4 :001(551) [0939] as fruits of faith and since **faith** without love is dead,
SD : 0 4 :002(551) [0939] article of our Christian **faith** in which we confess that
SD : 0 4 :002(551) [0939] in which we confess that **faith** alone justifies and saves.
SD : 0 4 :007(552) [0941] to God through **faith** and renewed through the Holy
SD : 0 4 :008(552) [0941] the Lord Christ through **faith**, because the person is
SD : 0 4 :008(552) [0941] do not flow from true **faith**, they are sinful (that is,
SD : 0 4 :008(552) [0941] does not proceed from **faith** is sin" (Rom. 14:23).
SD : 0 4 :009(552) [0941] Hence **faith** alone is the mother and source of the truly
SD : 0 4 :009(552) [0941] reason St. Paul calls them fruits of **faith** or of the Spirit.
SD : 0 4 :010(552) [0941] St. Paul to the Romans, "**Faith** is a divine work in us that
SD : 0 4 :010(552) [0941] Oh, **faith** is a living, busy, active, mighty thing, so that it
SD : 0 4 :011(553) [0941] Likewise, **faith** does not ask if good works are to be
SD : 0 4 :011(553) [0941] but before one can ask, **faith** has already done them and
SD : 0 4 :011(553) [0941] around in search of **faith** and good works without
SD : 0 4 :011(553) [0941] knowing what either **faith** or good works are, and in the
SD : 0 4 :011(553) [0941] and jabbers a great deal about **faith** and good works.
SD : 0 4 :012(553) [0941] **Faith** is a vital, deliberate trust in God's grace, so certain
SD : 0 4 :012(553) [0941] the Holy Spirit works by **faith**, and therefore without any
SD : 0 4 :012(553) [0941] to separate works from **faith** as it is to separate heat and
SD : 0 4 :014(553) [0943] they necessarily follow **faith** and reconciliation"; again,
SD : 0 4 :015(553) [0943] up for themselves a dead **faith** or superstition, without
SD : 0 4 :015(553) [0943] a single heart both a right **faith** and a wicked intention to
SD : 0 4 :015(553) [0943] could have and retain true **faith**, righteousness, and
SD : 0 4 :020(554) [0945] and nonetheless still retain **faith** and God's mercy and his
SD : 0 4 :023(555) [0945] against the pure doctrine of salvation by **faith** alone.
SD : 0 4 :024(555) [0945] Confession, "We are saved without works solely by **faith**."
SD : 0 4 :027(555) [0945] should indeed not put our **faith** in the merit of our
SD : 0 4 :030(555) [0947] are necessary to preserve **faith**, righteousness, and
SD : 0 4 :031(556) [0947] it is impossible to lose **faith** and the gift of righteousness
SD : 0 4 :031(556) [0947] he can nevertheless retain **faith**, the grace of God,
SD : 0 4 :032(556) [0947] who have been justified by **faith** these true, immutable,
SD : 0 4 :033(556) [0947] without darkening the doctrine of **faith** and justification.
SD : 0 4 :033(556) [0949] grace through Christ and which you retain through **faith**!
SD : 0 4 :033(556) [0949] **Faith**, however, does not remain in those who lead a
SD : 0 4 :034(556) [0949] not, however, mean that **faith** accepts righteousness and
SD : 0 4 :034(556) [0949] henceforth preserve **faith**, the righteousness that has been
SD : 0 4 :034(556) [0949] to us, Paul ascribes to **faith** not only our entry into grace
SD : 0 4 :034(556) [0949] words, he attributes to **faith** alone the beginning, the
SD : 0 4 :034(557) [0949] and you stand fast only through **faith**" (Rom 11:20).
SD : 0 4 :034(557) [0949] him, provided you continue in the **faith**" (Col. 1:22).
SD : 0 4 :034(557) [0949] we are guarded through **faith** for a salvation," and again,
SD : 0 4 :034(557) [0949] "As the outcome of your **faith**, you obtain the salvation
SD : 0 4 :035(557) [0949] the Word of God that **faith** is the proper and the only
SD : 0 4 :035(557) [0949] either the righteousness of **faith** that we have received or
SD : 0 4 :035(557) [0949] of faith that we have received or even **faith** itself.
SD : 0 5 :004(559) [0953] under these heads: repentance to God and **faith** in Christ.
SD : 0 5 :008(559) [0953] where repentance and **faith** in Christ (Acts 20:21) or
SD : 0 5 :009(559) [0955] God unless there is added **faith** in Christ, whose merit the
SD : 0 5 :019(561) [0957] teaches and commands **faith** in Christ) is the Word of
SD : 0 5 :019(561) [0957] strictly speaking, teaches about saving **faith** in Christ.
SD : 0 5 :020(561) [0959] of sins through **faith**, are freed from death and all the
SD : 0 5 :022(562) [0959] to everyone who has **faith**," "a dispensation of
SD : 0 5 :024(563) [0961] we might be justified by **faith**" (Gal. 3:24), and hence
SD : 0 6 :021(567) [0969] prescribes good works for **faith** in such a way that, as in a
SD : 0 6 :022(567) [0969] to God through **faith** for Christ's sake (I Pet. 2:5;
SD : 0 6 :023(568) [0969] and condemnation of the law through **faith** in Christ.
SD : 0 7 :003(569) [0973] but only in respect to **faith** (that is, our faith, reminded
SD : 0 7 :003(569) [0973] to faith (that is, our **faith**, reminded and quickened by the
SD : 0 7 :005(570) [0973] according to its power, operation, and benefits, by **faith**).
SD : 0 7 :006(570) [0975] blood to eat spiritually by **faith** but not to receive it orally
SD : 0 7 :008(570) [0975] partake spiritually by **faith** also of the body of Christ
SD : 0 7 :016(572) [0977] they receive it without true repentance and without **faith**.
SD : 0 7 :016(572) [0977] themselves through **faith** in Christ there receive the grace
SD : 0 7 :018(572) [0979] presence of the body of the Lord Christ through **faith**.
SD : 0 7 :029(574) [0981] this treatise to confess my **faith** before God and all the
SD : 0 7 :029(574) [0981] (so help me God!) in this **faith** to depart from this world
SD : 0 7 :032(574) [0983] It does not rest on man's **faith** or unbelief but on the
SD : 0 7 :033(575) [0983] he repeated his **faith** in this article with great fervor and
SD : 0 7 :045(577) [0987] must accept them in simple **faith** and due obedience in
SD : 0 7 :046(577) [0987] to the eminent article of **faith** concerning the promised
SD : 0 7 :050(578) [0989] does in all the articles of **faith** and in the institution of
SD : 0 7 :056(579) [0991] body of Christ through **faith**, as the Sacramentarians
SD : 0 7 :056(579) [0991] bread but that the spirit or **faith** is participation in the
SD : 0 7 :059(580) [0993] when it is laid hold on by **faith**, is a means whereby we
SD : 0 7 :061(580) [0995] than with the spirit and **faith**, in the preaching and
SD : 0 7 :062(581) [0995] however, is precisely **faith** — namely, that we hear, accept
SD : 0 7 :062(581) [0995] that we hear, accept with **faith**, and appropriate to
SD : 0 7 :065(581) [0995] In these words he required **faith**.
SD : 0 7 :066(581) [0997] only spiritually through **faith**, which occurs outside of the
SD : 0 7 :068(582) [0997] their sins, without true **faith**, and without a good
SD : 0 7 :069(582) [0997] Christians, weak in **faith**, who are heartily terrified
SD : 0 7 :069(582) [0997] perceive their weakness in **faith**, deplore it, and heartily
SD : 0 7 :069(582) [0997] a stronger and more cheerful **faith** and a purer obedience.
SD : 0 7 :070(582) [0997] for a man who is weak in **faith**, welcome him, for God
SD : 0 7 :070(582) [0997] on the Son of God, be his **faith** strong or weak, has
SD : 0 7 :071(582) [0997] weakness or certainty of **faith**, be it greater or smaller,
SD : 0 7 :071(582) [0997] distressed father of weak **faith** (Mark 9:24) partook no
SD : 0 7 :071(582) [0997] Paul, and others who had a cheerful and strong **faith**.
SD : 0 7 :072(582) [0997] of Christ, the one through **faith** spiritually, the other
SD : 0 7 :074(583) [0999] eating and drinking or the **faith** of the communicants, can
SD : 0 7 :081(584) [1001] Thereby the **faith** of the hearers in the essence and
SD : 0 7 :086(584) [1003] does not primarily mean **faith**, or the oral eating alone,
SD : 0 7 :088(585) [1003] and internal use of **faith** in order to deny the true,
SD : 0 7 :088(585) [1003] only spiritually through **faith**, or that faith effects the
SD : 0 7 :088(585) [1003] through faith, or that **faith** effects the presence of Christ's
SD : 0 7 :089(585) [1003] It is not our **faith** which makes the sacrament, but solely
SD : 0 7 :089(585) [1003] he effects not through our **faith**, but solely through his
SD : 0 7 :090(585) [1003] rule ascribe to our **faith** the power to achieve the presence
SD : 0 7 :094(586) [1005] first is this article of our **faith**: that Jesus Christ is
SD : 0 7 :101(587) [1007] God is, he must be also, otherwise our **faith** is false.
SD : 0 7 :104(587) [1009] when in spirit through **faith** true believers are
SD : 0 7 :106(588) [1009] Thus our **faith** in this article concerning the true presence
SD : 0 7 :106(588) [1009] confirm and fortify our **faith** in all tensions concerning
SD : 0 7 :114(589) [1011] of only spiritually through **faith** and that in the Supper
SD : 0 7 :116(589) [1011] we are assured that our **faith**, when it turns away from
SD : 0 7 :116(589) [1013] and confirmation of our **faith** in the Supper allegedly take
SD : 0 7 :117(589) [1013] there is distributed to **faith** only the virtue, operation, and
SD : 0 7 :118(590) [1013] only received and partaken of through **faith**, spiritually.
SD : 0 7 :121(590) [1013] omnipotence of Christ but **faith** that achieves the
SD : 0 7 :122(590) [1013] of the Supper and by their **faith** to look to that place in
SD : 0 7 :123(590) [1013] living, and saving **faith**, receive only bread and wine in
SD : 0 7 :124(591) [1015] does not consist in true **faith** alone but also in man's own
SD : 0 7 :125(591) [1015] a true, genuine, living **faith**, but who fail to meet their
SD : 0 8 :017(594) [1021] has always held in simple **faith** that the divine and human
SD : 1 0 :009(612) [1055] and yield to the weak in **faith** in such external matters of
SD : 1 0 :014(613) [1057] article of our Christian **faith**, so that, as the apostle
SD : 1 0 :016(613) [1057] scandalize true believers and weaken them in their **faith**.
SD : 1 0 :025(615) [1061] enemies of God's Word, and scandalize the weak in **faith**.
SD : 1 0 :031(616) [1063] in fasting should not destroy agreement in **faith**."
SD : 1 1 :010(618) [1067] myself with repentance, **faith**, prayer, and godliness.
SD : 1 1 :011(618) [1067] God they have repentance, **faith**, and the good resolve to
SD : 1 1 :012(618) [1067] 10, 12), to strengthen our **faith** and to assure us of our
SD : 1 1 :017(619) [1069] repentance, and would enlighten them in the true **faith**.
SD : 1 1 :018(619) [1069] all who in sincere repentance and true **faith** accept Christ.
SD : 1 1 :028(621) [1071] "comes through **faith** in Christ to all and on all who
SD : 1 1 :040(623) [1077] accept Christ through true **faith**, so he has also ordained
SD : 1 1 :069(627) [1085] Holy Spirit creates true **faith** through the hearing of
SD : 1 1 :069(627) [1085] as the apostle testifies, "**Faith** comes from the hearing of
SD : 1 1 :071(627) [1085] work such repentance and **faith** in us through the Word
SD : 1 1 :073(628) [1087] elect who have come to **faith** as he dwells in his temple,
SD : 1 1 :075(628) [1087] through a right **faith**, he will always show the same old
SD : 1 1 :078(629) [1089] the Word do not come to **faith** and therefore receive the
SD : 1 1 :089(631) [1093] of their sins, and to **faith** in Christ and promises them the
SD : 1 1 :096(632) [1095] raise him up through **faith**, strengthen him in his new
SD : 1 2 :012(634) [1099] and are able to make their own confession of **faith**.
SD : 1 2 :024(634) [1099] 15. That difference in **faith** is sufficient ground for
SD : 1 2 :024(634) [1099] a new marriage with another person of the same **faith**.
SD : 1 2 :030(635) [1101] repentance, and **faith** or works new obedience in them.

Faithful (35)

AL : 0 0 :017(096) [0095] Your Imperial Majesty's **faithful** subjects:
AP : 0 2 :036(105) [0115] is absolved by the sacrament that regenerates the **faithful**.
AP : 0 2 :036(105) [0115] to work those desires against which the **faithful** struggle."
AP : 0 4 :063(115) [0139] is plain and clear, the **faithful** can grasp it, and it has the
AP : 0 4 :119(123) [0155] church from which the **faithful** may receive the sure hope
AP : 0 4 :194(133) [0175] been offered and promised to the works of the **faithful**.
AP : 0 4 :199(134) [0175] praise undoubtedly moves the **faithful** to good works.
AP : 0 4 :276(148) [0199] But the **faithful** embrace them and are glad to have signs
AP : 0 4 :285(150) [0201] greatest consolation to **faithful** consciences and illumines
AP : 0 4 :299(153) [0205] In this teaching, **faithful** consciences see the most
AP : 0 4 :392(167) [0225] the judgment of all the **faithful** are consistently against
AP : 0 4 :392(167) [0225] of Christ has remained with some **faithful** souls.
AP : 0 7 :019(171) [0233] block may not offend the **faithful** and so that we may
AP : 1 2 :178(211) [0309] teach the faith that justifies and consoles **faithful** hearts.
AP : 1 5 :039(220) [0325] it correctly we are more **faithful** to the canons than our
AP : 2 1 :004(229) [0345] just as Christ praises **faithful** businessmen (Matt. 25:21,
AP : 2 1 :044(236) [0357] ways that will not burden **faithful** consciences nor
AP : 2 4 :091(266) [0415] sorrow must seize all the **faithful** if they ponder the fact
AP : 2 4 :091(266) [0415] Therefore we and all **faithful** consciences should be
SC : P R :000(338) [0533] Martin Luther to all **faithful**, godly pastors and
SC : P R :018(340) [0537] to be orderly, **faithful**, obedient, and peaceful.
SC : 0 3 :014(347) [0549] servants, godly and **faithful** rulers, good government;
SC : 0 3 :014(347) [0549] and honor; true friends, **faithful** neighbors, and the like.
SC : 0 5 :023(350) [0553] that I have not been **faithful** in training my children,
LC : 0 1 :112(380) [0613] would have remained **faithful** to this commandment and
LC : 0 3 :052(427) [0711] accepted it may remain **faithful** and grow daily in it and
LC : 0 3 :076(431) [0721] and succeed; to grant us **faithful** neighbors and good
LC : 0 6 :020(459) [0000] to be one, has here the **faithful** advice to go and obtain
SD : R N :002(503) [0851] and unanimously **faithful** to the pure doctrine of the
SD : R N :005(504) [0851] the papacy through the **faithful** ministry of that
SD : R N :007(505) [0853] estates were resolved by God's grace to remain **faithful**.
SD : R N :014(506) [0855] "**Faithful** shepherds," as Luther states, "must both pasture
SD : R N :020(508) [0859] we want to be found **faithful** to the commonly accepted
SD : 0 7 :050(578) [0989] is, of course, no more **faithful** or trustworthy interpreter
SD : 1 1 :032(621) [1073] has called us will be so **faithful** that after "he has begun

Faithfully (20)
PR : PR :023(012) [0021] for the holy ministry be **faithfully** and diligently instructed
AP : PR :009(098) [0101] as we have reported this **faithfully**; far from having
AP : PR :015(099) [0101] we hold to the Gospel of Christ correctly and **faithfully**.
AP : 2 3 :032(244) [0373] is saved if she serves **faithfully** in these duties of her
AP : 2 3 :039(244) [0375] Each should serve **faithfully** in what he has been given to
SC : PR :027(341) [0539] Christ himself will be our reward if we labor **faithfully**.
LC : SP :004(362) [0575] and if they do not know it, to keep them **faithfully** at it.
LC : 0 1 :145(385) [0623] do my daily housework **faithfully**, that is better than the
LC : 0 1 :168(388) [0629] should earnestly and **faithfully** discharge the duties of
LC : 0 1 :175(389) [0631] wives who would **faithfully** bring up their children and
LC : 0 1 :233(396) [0647] he is under obligation **faithfully** to protect his neighbor's
LC : 0 1 :314(407) [0671] tends a little child, or **faithfully** does what she is told, that
LC : 0 3 :082(431) [0721] us in all our needs and **faithfully** provides for our daily
LC : 0 5 :045(452) [0763] be one of them, let him **faithfully** hold to this sacrament,
LC : 0 5 :067(454) [0769] when he tenderly and **faithfully** summons and exhorts us
SD : RN :019(507) [0857] that we might thereby **faithfully** forewarn everyone
SD : RN :020(508) [0859] abide in it loyally and **faithfully** against all the
SD : 0 7 :001(569) [0971] descendants also, and **faithfully** to warn our hearers and
SD : 1 1 :021(619) [1069] grace of God, and use **faithfully** the gifts they have
SD : 1 1 :045(624) [1079] and salvation and so **faithfully** minded about it that "even

Faithfulness (2)
AP : PR :016(099) [0103] that God approves our **faithfulness**, and we hope that
AP : 1 2 :174(210) [0307] and magistrates, **faithfulness** to one's calling, peaceable

Faithless (2)
LC : 0 1 :233(396) [0647] or defraud him by any **faithless** or underhanded business
SD : 0 4 :011(553) [0941] such good works is a **faithless** man, blindly tapping

Fall (77), Fallen (17), Falling (2), Falls (4)
AG : 0 2 :001(029) [0043] among us that since the **fall** of Adam all men who are
AG : 1 1 :001(034) [0047] should be retained and not allowed to **fall** into disuse.
AG : 1 2 :007(035) [0049] persons who have once become godly cannot **fall** again.
AG : 2 3 :025(055) [0065] for them to marry than to **fall** into the fire through their
AG : 2 7 :041(077) [0081] be justified by the law; you have **fallen** away from grace."
AG : 2 7 :042(077) [0081] from Christ and have **fallen** away from God's grace, for
AG : 2 8 :067(092) [0093] many of the regulations **fall** into disuse from day to day
AG : 2 8 :074(094) [0093] with the passing of time **fallen** into disuse and are not
AL : 0 2 :001(029) [0043] also teach that since the **fall** of Adam all men who are
AL : 1 2 :001(034) [0049] that those who have **fallen** after Baptism can receive
AL : 1 2 :009(035) [0049] to absolve those who had **fallen** after Baptism although
AL : 2 3 :025(055) [0065] for them to marry than to **fall** into the fire through their
AL : 2 7 :041(077) [0081] be justified by the law; you have **fallen** away from grace."
AL : 2 7 :042(077) [0081] severed from Christ and **fall** away from grace, for those
AP : 0 2 :002(100) [0105] also taught that since the **fall** of Adam all men who are
AP : 0 4 :030(111) [0129] by the law; you have **fallen** away from grace' (Gal. 5:4);
AP : 0 4 :032(111) [0129] And Rom. 3:23 says, "All **fall** short of the glory of God,"
AP : 0 7 :042(176) [0241] by which our Passover **falls** at a different time from the
AP : 1 2 :001(182) [0253] that those who have **fallen** after Baptism can obtain the
AP : 2 0 :013(228) [0341] their call, that is, lest they **fall** from their call by sinning
AP : 2 1 :018(231) [0347] Ps. 72:11, 15, "May all kings **fall** down before him!
AP : 2 3 :054(246) [0379] vices have preceded the **fall** of many other cities, like
AP : 2 7 :011(270) [0423] be justified by the law; you have **fallen** away from grace."
AP : 2 7 :017(272) [0425] Christ, has cast Christ away, and has **fallen** from Christ.
AP : 2 7 :062(280) [0441] their countrymen, lest they **fall** back into the wickedness
S 2 : 0 2 :010(294) [0465] well aware that if the Mass **falls**, the papacy will fall with
S 2 : 0 2 :010(294) [0465] aware that if the Mass falls, the papacy will **fall** with it.
S 3 : 0 1 :004(302) [0477] 1. That after the **fall** of Adam the natural powers of man
S 3 : 0 2 :004(303) [0479] depths his nature has **fallen** and how corrupt it has
S 3 : 0 3 :043(310) [0491] and strive against it, **fall** into open sin (as David fell into
S 3 : 0 8 :001(312) [0493] by no means be allowed to **fall** into disuse in the church,
LC : PR :006(359) [0569] So they blithely let parishes **fall** into decay, and brazenly
LC : PR :008(359) [0569] They need not fear a **fall**, for they have already fallen all
LC : PR :008(359) [0569] fear a fall, for they have already **fallen** all too horribly.
LC : 0 1 :151(386) [0625] Or he will **fall** victim to the hangman, or perish through
LC : 0 1 :192(391) [0635] in deep water, or **fallen** into a fire, and could extend him
LC : 0 1 :266(401) [0657] pass sentence on him, I **fall** into a greater sin than his.
LC : 0 3 :006(421) [0699] Thus they **fall** into the habit of never praying, alleging
LC : 0 3 :067(429) [0717] poor flesh may not yield or **fall** away through weakness
LC : 0 3 :100(433) [0727] yet such is life that one stands today and **falls** tomorrow.
LC : 0 3 :100(433) [0727] that he will not allow us to **fall** and yield to trials and
LC : 0 3 :105(434) [0727] faint and weary and to **fall** back into sin, shame, and
LC : 0 3 :106(434) [0729] pray here that we may not **fall** into them and be
LC : 0 3 :110(435) [0729] me to pray; let me not **fall** because of temptation."
LC : 0 4 :077(446) [0751] Even though we **fall** from it and sin, nevertheless we
LC : 0 4 :080(446) [0751] which we can no longer use after **falling** again into sin.
LC : 0 4 :082(446) [0751] But it does happen that we slip and **fall** out of the ship.
LC : 0 4 :082(446) [0751] If anybody does **fall** out, he should immediately head for
LC : 0 4 :086(446) [0753] But if anybody **falls** away from his Baptism let him return
EP : 0 1 :001(466) [0779] a distinction, even after the **Fall**, between man's
EP : 0 1 :002(466) [0779] sin, but also as we now have our nature after the **Fall**.
EP : 0 1 :002(466) [0779] Even after the **fall** our nature is and remains a creature of
EP : 0 1 :004(466) [0781] Adam and Eve before the **Fall**, but also our bodies and
EP : 0 1 :004(466) [0781] bodies and souls after the **Fall**, even though they are
EP : 0 1 :008(467) [0781] sings, "Through Adam's **fall** man's nature and essence are
EP : 0 1 :013(467) [0783] uncorrupted even after the **Fall**, and especially that in
EP : 0 1 :019(468) [0783] man's nature itself after the **Fall** and original sin, and that
EP : 0 2 :001(469) [0785] states: (1) before the **Fall**, (2) after the Fall, (3) after
EP : 0 2 :001(469) [0785] the Fall, (2) after the **Fall**, (3) after regeneration, (4) after
EP : 0 2 :001(469) [0785] spiritual matters after the **fall** of our first parents and
EP : 0 4 :019(477) [0801] Spirit even though they **fall** into adultery and other sins
EP : 0 6 :002(480) [0805] parents even before the **Fall** did not live without the law,
EP : 1 0 :002(493) [0829] ceremonies that have **fallen** into disuse and that in
SD : 0 1 :001(508) [0859] corrupt as a result of the **fall** of Adam," so that ever since
SD : 0 1 :001(508) [0859] so that ever since the **Fall** the nature, substance, and
SD : 0 1 :001(508) [0859] substance, and essence of **fallen** man, at least the
SD : 0 1 :001(508) [0859] there is now after the **Fall** allegedly no difference
SD : 0 1 :002(508) [0859] soul), which even after the **Fall** are and remain God's
SD : 0 1 :002(509) [0859] the nature and essence of **fallen** man (that is, between his
SD : 0 1 :002(509) [0859] in us even after the **Fall**) and original sin (which is a work
SD : 0 1 :006(509) [0861] no evil — which after the **Fall** of our first parents is of
SD : 0 1 :006(509) [0861] and because of the **fall** of the first man, our nature or
SD : 0 1 :011(510) [0863] As a result, since the **Fall** man inherits an inborn wicked
SD : 0 1 :016(511) [0865] in such a way that we **fall** neither into Pelagian nor into
SD : 0 1 :020(511) [0865] nature even after the **Fall** is incorrupt and, especially, that
SD : 0 1 :023(512) [0865] and corrupted through the **Fall**, it has nevertheless not
SD : 0 1 :023(512) [0865] it, "Through Adam's **fall** man's nature and being are
SD : 0 1 :026(512) [0867] That now, since the **Fall**, human nature is initially created
SD : 0 1 :027(513) [0867] Adam and Eve through the **Fall**, and that by God's
SD : 0 1 :028(513) [0867] For since the **Fall** human nature is not at first created
SD : 0 1 :032(513) [0869] of God even after the **Fall** but because and in so far as our
SD : 0 1 :034(514) [0869] human nature before the **Fall**, but also that after the Fall
SD : 0 1 :034(514) [0869] Fall, but also that after the **Fall** human nature is God's
SD : 0 1 :038(514) [0871] clearly that even after the **Fall** God is man's creator who
SD : 0 1 :044(516) [0873] evident that even after the **Fall** human nature and original
SD : 0 2 :002(520) [0881] of man's will before the **Fall**, nor what man after the Fall
SD : 0 2 :002(520) [0881] nor what man after the **Fall** and prior to his conversion
SD : 0 2 :002(520) [0881] have remained after the **Fall**, when the Word of God is
SD : 0 2 :005(520) [0881] argued that through the **fall** of our first parents man is so
SD : 0 2 :007(521) [0883] we believe that after the **Fall** and prior to his conversion
SD : 0 2 :019(524) [0889] — not that man since the **Fall** is no longer a rational
SD : 0 2 :022(525) [0889] pure grace, that our poor, **fallen**, and corrupted human
SD : 0 2 :047(530) [0901] despondent hearts may **fall** into grave anxiety and doubt,
SD : 0 2 :053(531) [0903] above, even after the **Fall** man still has something of a free
SD : 0 4 :033(556) [0949] that is, that we do not **fall** from our calling by lapsing
SD : 0 4 :033(556) [0949] heavenly calling, lest you **fall** away and lose the Spirit and
SD : 1 1 :004(617) [1063] And not one of them will **fall** to the ground without your
SD : 1 1 :042(623) [1077] joy," but after that "they **fall** away again" (Luke 8:13).
SD : 1 1 :054(625) [1081] persevere; and who after **falling** away will return and who
SD : 1 1 :074(628) [1087] if perchance they should **fall** into such grave temptation

Fallacious (2), Fallacy (1)
AP : 0 4 :222(137) [0181] It would be a **fallacy** to reason that because it is necessary
AP : 0 4 :246(142) [0189] It is therefore **fallacious** for our opponents to argue from
AP : 0 4 :358(162) [0219] Who cannot see that this is a **fallacious** conclusion?

False (154)
PR : PR :004(003) [0007] to scatter his seed of **false** doctrine and discord and to
PR : PR :005(004) [0009] alive, it happened that **false** teachers insinuated perverted
PR : PR :005(004) [0009] Word of God, so such **false** teachers were also inflicted on
PR : PR :006(004) [0009] to the end that the **false** and misleading doctrines which
PR : PR :008(005) [0009] doctrine that is impure, **false**, and contrary to the Word
PR : PR :010(006) [0011] to expose and to reject **false** doctrine, and clearly to
PR : PR :010(006) [0011] they might be preserved from **false** doctrine in the future.
PR : PR :017(008) [0015] or confirm any new, **false**, or erroneous doctrine or in the
PR : PR :019(009) [0017] Evangelical doctrine any **false** and adulterated teaching
PR : PR :020(010) [0017] and hence must be **false** and incorrect, we should indicate
PR : PR :022(011) [0019] censures, and rejections of **false** and adulterated doctrine,
PR : PR :022(011) [0019] to condemn only **false** and seductive doctrines and their
AG : 0 8 :001(033) [0047] because in this life many **false** Christians, hypocrites, and
AG : 0 1 :007(056) [0065] instruction about other **false** teachings concerning the
AG : 2 7 :039(077) [0081] vows were an improper and **false** service of God.
AG : 2 7 :051(079) [0083] conclusions from such **false** exaltation of monastic life,
AG : 2 7 :062(080) [0083] as all these things are **false**, useless, and invented,
AG : 2 8 :023(084) [0087] for Christ says in Matt. 7:15, "Beware of **false** prophets."
AG : 2 8 :061(091) [0093] which have arisen from the **false** and erroneous opinion
AL : 0 0 :004(048) [0059] observed, for it is **false** and malicious to charge that all
AL : 2 7 :051(079) [0083] conclusions from such **false** commendations of monastic
AL : 2 7 :062(080) [0083] things, since they are **false** and useless, make vows null
AL : 2 8 :023(084) [0087] obedience: "Beware of **false** prophets" (Matt. 7:15), "If an
AL : 2 8 :061(091) [0093] which have arisen from the **false** notion that there must
AP : 0 4 :025(110) [0127] For it is **false** that by our works we merit the forgiveness
AP : 0 4 :026(110) [0127] It is **false**, too, that men are accounted righteous before
AP : 0 4 :027(111) [0127] It is **false**, too, that by its own strength reason can love
AP : 0 4 :028(111) [0129] It is **false**, too, and a reproach to Christ, that men who
AP : 0 4 :255(143) [0193] if our opponents did not read something **false** into them.
AP : 0 4 :275(148) [0199] penitence is hypocritical and **false** if they do not follow.
AP : 0 4 :282(149) [0201] and in place of this **false** cleansing he puts a twofold
AP : 0 7 :048(177) [0245] (Matt. 7:15), "Beware of **false** prophets"; Paul says
AP : 1 2 :016(184) [0257] teachings are clearly **false** and foreign to the Holy
AP : 1 2 :068(192) [0271] by a conspiracy defend the **false** notions we have been
AP : 1 2 :111(198) [0285] this is completely **false**, as well as being impossible.
AP : 1 2 :169(209) [0305] that penitence is **false** if it does not satisfy those whose
AP : 1 3 :020(214) [0313] the testimonies are not **false** but as certain as though
AP : 1 6 :009(224) [0333] It is also **false** to claim that Christian perfection consists
AP : 1 8 :006(225) [0335] Moreover, it is **false** to say that a man does not sin if,
AP : 2 0 :014(228) [0343] This is completely **false**.
AP : 2 1 :022(232) [0349] We are not making **false** charges here.
AP : 2 1 :040(235) [0355] canonists contain many **false** opinions and that the
AP : 2 3 :001(239) [0363] only use the wicked and **false** pretext of divine authority
AP : 2 3 :005(239) [0365] warning (II Pet. 2:1) that **false** prophets would deceive
AP : 2 3 :070(249) [0383] With **false** arguments like these they defend a wicked and
AP : 2 4 :098(268) [0417] A **false** idea about sacrifices clung to the wicked priests in
AP : 2 7 :024(273) [0427] To this they add many other **false** and wicked ideas.
AP : 2 7 :025(273) [0429] Therefore it is **false** for the monks to boast that the
AP : 2 7 :026(273) [0429] It is also **false** that monastic observances are the works of
AP : 2 7 :044(277) [0435] so they quote passages of Scripture under **false** pretenses.
AP : 2 7 :053(278) [0437] as stupid as it is wicked, nourishing a **false** confidence.
AP : 2 7 :056(278) [0439] whole monastic life is full of hypocrisy and **false** opinions.
AP : 2 7 :057(279) [0439] a way of life so full of hypocrisy and **false** opinions.
AP : 2 8 :001(281) [0443] summary: "Everything is **false** that the present article
S 1 : PR :004(289) [0455] our adversaries, but also **false** brethren among those who
S 2 : 0 2 :008(294) [0465] doing because he follows a **false** human opinion and
S 2 : 0 4 :003(298) [0471] on the strength of such **false**, mischievous, blasphemous,
S 3 : 0 1 :002(302) [0477] such as unbelief, **false** belief, idolatry, being without the
S 3 : 0 2 :003(303) [0479] Hypocrites and **false** saints are produced in this way.
S 3 : 0 3 :002(304) [0479] with one blow destroys both open sinners and **false** saints.
S 3 : 0 3 :009(304) [0481] Now we must compare the **false** repentance of the
S 3 : 0 3 :009(304) [0481] The **False** Repentance of the Papists
S 3 : 0 3 :032(308) [0487] in the former group are **false** penitents, and those of you
S 3 : 0 3 :032(308) [0487] penitents, and those of you in the latter are **false** saints.
S 3 : 0 3 :037(309) [0489] our repentance cannot be **false**, uncertain, or partial, for a
S 3 : 1 3 :003(315) [0499] good works do not follow, our faith is **false** and not true.
S 3 : 1 5 :002(316) [0501] sin to break such precepts of men, this, too, is **false**.
TR : 0 0 :004(320) [0503] and hold to be **false**, impious, tyrannical, and injurious to

Continued ▶

TR : 0 0 :033(325) [0513] lord of the kingdoms of the world are **false** and impious.
TR : 0 0 :041(327) [0517] commanded, "Beware of **false** prophets" (Matt. 7:15).
SC : 0 1 :015(343) [0541] *"You shall not bear **false** witness against your neighbor."*
LC : S P :008(362) [0575] 8. You shall not bear **false** witness against your neighbor.
LC : 0 1 :003(365) [0581] other hand, if your trust is **false** and wrong, then you
LC : 0 1 :017(366) [0585] world practices nothing but **false** worship and idolatry.
LC : 0 1 :019(367) [0585] is that their trust is **false** and wrong, for it is not founded
LC : 0 1 :022(367) [0585] There is, moreover, another **false** worship.
LC : 0 1 :035(369) [0589] our day he overthrows all **false** worship so that all who
LC : 0 1 :054(372) [0595] to the conscience, when **false** preachers arise and peddle
LC : 0 1 :067(373) [0599] he may gain by the **false** oath will slip through his fingers
LC : 0 1 :120(382) [0615] bewitched us with the **false** holiness and glamor of our
LC : 0 1 :197(392) [0637] mislead the world with a **false**, hypocritical show of
LC : 0 1 :209(393) [0639] as the blind world and the **false** clergy do, but view it in
LC : 0 1 :227(396) [0645] defective merchandise, **false** measures, dishonest weights,
LC : 0 1 :254(399) [0653] *"You shall not bear **false** witness against your neighbor."*
LC : 0 1 :257(399) [0653] stand ("You shall not bear **false** witness"), this
LC : 0 1 :257(399) [0653] accused and maligned by **false** witnesses and consequently
LC : 0 1 :262(400) [0655] Here, too, everyone bears **false** witness against his
LC : 0 1 :263(400) [0655] **False** witness is clearly a work of the tongue.
LC : 0 1 :263(400) [0655] This applies to **false** preachers with their corrupt teaching
LC : 0 1 :263(400) [0655] and blasphemy, to **false** judges and witnesses with their
LC : 0 1 :271(401) [0657] then, that cannot be adequately proved is **false** witness.
LC : 0 1 :284(403) [0661] can be no question of slander or injustice or **false** witness.
LC : 0 1 :290(404) [0663] the blind world and the **false** saints would recognize
LC : 0 1 :304(406) [0667] this it is clear that all these pretexts and shams are **false**.
LC : 0 2 :066(419) [0697] heathen, Turks, Jews, or **false** Christians and hypocrites,
LC : 0 3 :006(421) [0699] that since we reject **false** and hypocritical prayers we teach
LC : 0 3 :041(425) [0709] name anything that is **false** and deceptive, using his name
LC : 0 3 :047(426) [0709] world is full of sects and **false** teachers, all of whom wear
LC : 0 3 :084(431) [0721] simply on account of **false** coinage, yes, on account of
LC : 0 3 :104(434) [0727] to draw us into unbelief, **false** security, and stubbornness,
LC : 0 4 :011(437) [0735] to work to blind us with **false** appearances and lead us
LC : 0 5 :017(448) [0757] sacrament is not rendered **false** because of an individual's
EP : R N :003(465) [0777] during their lifetime — **false** teachers and heretics invaded
EP : R N :004(465) [0777] particularly against the **false** worship, idolatry, and
EP : 0 1 :010(467) [0781] *Rejection of the Contrary **False** Teaching*
EP : 0 1 :024(469) [0785] familiar and convey no **false** impressions, and they clearly
EP : 0 2 :006(470) [0787] *Contrary **False** Doctrine*
EP : 0 3 :001(473) [0791] Two **false** and mutually contradictory teachings have
EP : 0 4 :015(477) [0801] **False** Antitheses
EP : 0 5 :011(479) [0805] we reject and deem it as **false** and detrimental when men
EP : 0 7 :013(483) [0811] ground is that God's Word is not **false** nor does it lie.
EP : 0 8 :018(490) [0823] *Contrary **False** Doctrine concerning the Person of Christ*
EP : 1 0 :007(494) [0831] ***False** Doctrine concerning this Article*
EP : 1 0 :008(494) [0831] we reject and condemn as **false** and contrary to God's
EP : 1 1 :015(497) [0837] ***False** Doctrine concerning this Article*
EP : 1 2 :030(500) [0843] and condemn as wrong, **false**, heretical, and contrary to
SD : P R :006(502) [0849] even dared to give a **false** interpretation to these articles.
SD : R N :008(505) [0853] between true and **false** doctrine, we declare our
SD : R N :016(507) [0857] what he should reject, flee, and avoid as **false** and wrong.
SD : R N :019(507) [0857] the true doctrine to the **false** doctrine, so that the
SD : 0 1 :017(511) [0865] we condemn and reject as **false** the opinion and doctrine
SD : 0 1 :025(512) [0865] reject these and similar **false** doctrines because God's
SD : 0 2 :073(535) [0909] reject, and condemn such **false** doctrines and errors as
SD : 0 3 :007(540) [0919] expose, and condemn the **false** contrary doctrine.
SD : 0 3 :043(547) [0931] belongs thereto, then it is **false** and incorrect to answer:
SD : 0 3 :044(547) [0931] From these, too, the **false** antitheses become clear,
SD : 0 4 :015(553) [0943] on such sins again, which is impious and **false**.
SD : 0 4 :020(554) [0945] we reject and condemn as **false** the view that good works
SD : 0 4 :025(555) [0945] 1. In the case of the **false** prophets among the Galatians;
SD : 0 4 :029(555) [0947] by our churches as **false** and incorrect and as issues which
SD : 0 4 :031(556) [0947] and rejecting the **false** Epicurean delusion which some
SD : 0 4 :037(557) [0951] themselves, but with the **false** confidence which, contrary
SD : 0 4 :039(557) [0951] without explanation it is **false** and offensive, might
SD : 0 7 :025(573) [0981] sacrament is not rendered **false** because an individual's
SD : 0 7 :066(581) [0997] by unworthy, unbelieving, **false**, and wicked Christians as
SD : 0 7 :096(586) [1005] The third is that the Word of God is not **false** or deceitful.
SD : 0 7 :101(587) [1007] God is, he must be also, otherwise our faith is **false**.
SD : 0 7 :107(588) [1009] with heart and mouth as **false**, erroneous, and deceiving
SD : 0 7 :112(589) [1011] with heart and mouth as **false**, erroneous, and deceiving
SD : 0 8 :051(600) [1031] opinion is erroneous and **false**, that even their own
SD : 1 0 :003(611) [1053] to insinuate their **false** doctrines into our churches again.
SD : 1 0 :011(612) [1055] And again, "But because of **false** brethren secretly
SD : 1 0 :012(612) [1057] But when **false** prophets demanded circumcision and
SD : 1 0 :012(613) [1057] abused it to confirm their **false** doctrine that the works of
SD : 1 0 :013(613) [1057] But he would not yield to **false** apostles who wanted to
SD : 1 0 :014(613) [1057] of indifference to confirm **false** doctrines, superstition,
SD : 1 0 :022(615) [1061] commanded, 'Beware of **false** prophets' (Matt. 7:15).
SD : 1 1 :010(618) [1065] in people's minds either **false** security and impenitence or
SD : 1 1 :012(618) [1067] We must oppose such **false** imagining and thoughts with
SD : 1 1 :044(623) [1077] also completely refutes all **false** opinions and erroneous
SD : 1 1 :050(624) [1079] by the outward prestige of the **false** church (Rom. 9:8ff.).
SD : 1 1 :088(631) [1093] It is therefore **false** and wrong when men teach that the
SD : 1 2 :008(633) [1097] with the open idolatry and **false** beliefs of the papacy,
SD : 1 2 :039(636) [1103] we reject and condemn as **false**, erroneous, heretical,

Falsehood (9), Falsely (12), Falsification (1), Falsified (1), Falsifying (1), Falsity (1)

AG : 2 0 :001(041) [0053] Our teachers have been **falsely** accused of forbidding good
AL : 2 0 :001(041) [0053] Our churches are **falsely** accused of forbidding good
AL : 2 4 :001(056) [0065] Our churches are **falsely** accused of abolishing the Mass.
AL : 2 6 :011(065) [0071] and others like them, **falsely** imagining that the
AP : 0 4 :244(142) [0189] mentioned, our opponents **falsely** add their wicked
AP : 0 4 :391(167) [0225] Despite its obvious **falsehood**, this teaching has spawned
AP : 1 2 :173(210) [0305] Clearly they are **falsifying** the matter when they say that
AP : 1 5 :039(220) [0325] Our enemies **falsely** accuse us of abolishing good
AP : 2 4 :041(257) [0399] men can easily see the **falsity** of the charge that we do
AP : 2 4 :096(267) [0417] ancient heresies and by **falsely** comparing them with our
S 3 : 0 3 :039(309) [0489] is nothing but deceitful **falsehood** and hypocrisy.
LC : 0 1 :051(371) [0595] whatsoever to support **falsehood** or wrong of any kind."
LC : 0 1 :051(371) [0595] appealing to God's name **falsely** or taking his name upon
LC : 0 1 :052(371) [0595] abused than for purposes of **falsehood** and deceit.
LC : 0 1 :064(373) [0599] holy name in support of **falsehood** or wickedness, it
LC : 0 1 :066(373) [0599] of evil (that is, to a **falsehood**) or unnecessarily; but in
LC : 0 1 :066(373) [0599] justice are established, **falsehood** is refuted, people are
LC : 0 1 :067(373) [0599] party in a dispute swears **falsely**, he will not escape
LC : 0 1 :069(374) [0599] in due time to shun **falsehood** and especially to avoid
LC : 0 1 :285(403) [0661] of him, whether truly or **falsely**, unless it is done with
LC : 0 3 :021(423) [0703] grossly dishonoring him and accusing him of **falsehood**.
LC : 0 3 :047(426) [0711] who preach and believe **falsely** and against those who
SD : 0 3 :029(544) [0925] love (as the adversaries **falsely** slander and accuse us) but
SD : 0 7 :119(590) [1013] and maliciously **falsified** the words in Acts 3:21, "Christ
SD : 1 1 :095(632) [1095] or cover up any **falsification** of true doctrine or any

Fame (1)

LC : 0 3 :103(434) [0727] along with fondness for luxury, honor, **fame**, and power.

Familiar (11)

AP : 0 2 :051(107) [0119] to list, in the usual **familiar** phrases, the opinions of the
AP : 0 4 :152(127) [0163] There is a **familiar** figure of speech, called synecdoche, by
AP : 1 3 :023(214) [0313] And Paul's statement is **familiar** (Rom. 10:10), "Man
SC : P R :014(339) [0535] the people have become **familiar** with the text, teach them
LC : S P :006(362) [0575] old, may be well-trained in them and **familiar** with them.
LC : 0 1 :075(375) [0601] may become **familiar** and be constantly practiced.
LC : 0 4 :003(437) [0733] we must above all be **familiar** with the words upon which
LC : 0 5 :002(447) [0753] and go to the sacrament should be **familiar** with them.
EP : 0 1 :024(469) [0785] sin because they are **familiar** and convey no false
EP : 1 0 :007(494) [0831] according to the **familiar** axiom, "Disagreement in fasting
SD : R N :016(507) [0857] likewise to insure that **familiar** terminology may not hide

Familias (1)

LC : 0 1 :142(384) [0621] *patres et matres **familias*** (that is, house-fathers and

Family (15), Families (2)

AL : 1 6 :004(038) [0051] the heart, but it does not destroy the state or the **family**.
AP : 0 4 :232(139) [0185] Similarly, in all **families** and communities harmony
AP : 1 6 :005(223) [0331] destroy the state or the **family** but rather approves them,
AP : 1 6 :013(224) [0333] above the state and the **family**, even though these have
AP : 2 7 :067(280) [0443] especially for his own **family**, he has disowned the faith."
S 1 : P R :014(291) [0459] us in church, state, and **family** that we can never carry
SC : 0 1 :000(342) [0539] *in which the head of the **family** shall teach them to his*
SC : 0 2 :000(344) [0543] *in which the head of the **family** shall teach it to his*
SC : 0 2 :002(345) [0543] house and home, **family** and property; that he provides
SC : 0 3 :000(346) [0545] *in which the head of the **family** shall teach it to his*
SC : 0 4 :000(348) [0551] *in which the head of the **family** shall teach it to his*
SC : 0 6 :000(351) [0555] *in which the head of the **family** shall teach it to his*
SC : 0 7 :000(352) [0557] *How the head of the **family** shall teach his household to*
SC : 0 8 :006(353) [0559] *How the head of the **family** shall teach his household to*
LC : 0 1 :010(366) [0583] wisdom, power, prestige, **family**, and honor, and trusts in
LC : 0 1 :138(384) [0621] where there are fine old **families** who prosper and have
LC : 0 1 :150(385) [0623] is father not of a single **family**, but of as many people as

Famine (3)

LC : 0 1 :060(372) [0597] we deserve: plague, war, **famine**, fire, flood, wayward
LC : 0 1 :151(386) [0625] war, pestilence, or **famine**, or his children will turn out
LC : 0 3 :078(431) [0721] war and bloodshed, **famine**, savage beasts, wicked men,

Fan (1)

AP : 1 2 :123(201) [0289] alienate men's minds and **fan** their hatred, so that the

Fanatic (1), Fanatical (4), Fanatics (6)

AP : 0 9 :003(178) [0245] against the ungodly and **fanatical** opinions of the
AP : 1 3 :013(212) [0311] in opposition to the **fanatics** who dream that the Holy
AP : 1 3 :023(214) [0313] the abuses which this **fanatical** notion, about the
AP : 2 1 :043(235) [0357] sound doctrine crushed, **fanatical** spirits will arise whom
AP : 2 7 :016(271) [0425] By this wicked and **fanatical** notion they bury the blessing
S 3 : 0 3 :042(309) [0491] Some **fanatics** may appear (and perhaps they are already
LC : 0 3 :047(426) [0711] it, as the bishops, tyrants, **fanatics**, and others do.
LC : 0 4 :061(444) [0747] But these **fanatics** are so blinded that they do not discern
LC : 0 4 :063(444) [0749] Baptism merely as an empty sign, as the **fanatics** dream.
LC : 0 5 :012(448) [0755] devils, with all the **fanatics**, rush forward and say, 'How
SD : 0 7 :099(586) [1005] to this mode, as the **fanatic** spirit dreams, for God is not a

Fancier (1), Fancies (1), Fancy (3)

AP : 1 2 :144(205) [0297] dress up these works with **fancy** titles; they call them
AP : 2 7 :059(279) [0441] whose monasteries are **fancier** than kings' palaces and
LC : 0 1 :020(367) [0585] actually fashion their **fancies** and dreams about God into
LC : 0 1 :295(404) [0665] that if anyone took a **fancy** to another's wife, he might on
LC : 0 1 :305(406) [0667] like this: If a man took a **fancy** to another woman, he

Fanning (1)

LC : 0 3 :063(428) [0715] These he stirs up, **fanning** and feeding the flames, in

Fantasies (1)

S 2 : 0 4 :014(301) [0475] other puerilities, **fantasies**, and follies without so much as

Far (137)

PR : P R :008(005) [0009] thereby to warn and, as **far** as we might, to secure our
PR : P R :019(009) [0017] As **far** as the second edition of the Augsburg Confession,
PR : P R :019(009) [0017] a very different doctrine by **far** can be proved therefrom.
PR : P R :019(010) [0017] and others in so **far** as they are in agreement with the
PR : P R :020(010) [0017] and most edifying way as **far** as the common layman is
PR : P R :022(011) [0019] of the divine Word, and **far** less do we mean entire
AG : P R :010(025) [0041] and their associates, in so **far** as this can honorably be
AG : P R :013(026) [0041] omit doing anything, in so **far** as God and conscience
AG : 0 0 :001(047) [0059] of the Roman church (in so **far** as the latter's teaching is
AG : 2 3 :001(051) [0061] continent and who went so **far** as to engage in
AG : 2 6 :004(064) [0071] that faith in Christ is to be esteemed **far** above all works.
AG : 2 6 :008(065) [0071] these traditions were exalted **far** above God's commands.
AG : 2 7 :016(073) [0077] and is regarded as **far** superior to the other estates
AL : 1 8 :008(040) [0053] of God in so **far** as the substance of the acts is concerned.
AL : 0 0 :001(047) [0059] the church of Rome, in so **far** as the ancient church is
AL : 2 3 :002(051) [0061] but that there are now **far** weightier reasons why this
AL : 2 4 :005(056) [0065] the sacrament together, in so **far** as they are fit to do so.
AL : 2 6 :004(064) [0071] sake may be exalted **far** above works and above all other
AL : 2 6 :008(065) [0071] for traditions were exalted **far** above the commands of

Continued ▶

AL : 26 :010(065) [0071] and imperfect works, **far** inferior to those glittering
AL : 27 :013(072) [0077] monastic profession was **far** better than Baptism, and
AL : 27 :016(073) [0077] perfection, and they put it **far** above all other kinds of life
AL : 28 :055(090) [0091] that they keep them; in so **far** as one does not offend
AP : PR :009(099) [0101] reported this faithfully; **far** from having disproved our
AP : 04 :008(108) [0121] also requires other works **far** beyond the reach of reason,
AP : 04 :068(116) [0139] By what we have said so **far** we have sought to show the
AP : 04 :117(123) [0155] What we have shown thus **far**, on the basis of the
AP : 04 :131(125) [0159] overlook that eternal law, **far** beyond the senses and
AP : 04 :135(125) [0159] Only then do we see how **far** we are from keeping the
AP : 04 :138(126) [0161] For human nature is **far** too weak to be able by its own
AP : 04 :175(131) [0171] that we should realize how **far** we are from the perfection
AP : 04 :178(131) [0171] **Far** above our purity—yes, far above the law itself
AP : 04 :178(131) [0171] Far above our purity—yes, **far** above the law itself
AP : 04 :179(131) [0171] "Though you are still **far** away from the perfection of the
AP : 04 :231(139) [0185] and hence this view is **far** removed from his intention.
AP : 04 :270(147) [0199] keeping of the law is impure and **far** from perfect.
AP : 04 :286(150) [0201] So **far** we have reviewed the main passages which our
AP : 04 :296(152) [0205] **Far** away from human reason, far away from Moses, we
AP : 04 :296(152) [0205] away from human reason, **far** away from Moses, we must
AP : 07 :012(170) [0231] with the true church as **far** as outward ceremonies are
AP : 12 :098(197) [0281] of these doctrines and thus **far** have written nothing
AP : 12 :113(199) [0285] public evidence of their penitence, as **far** as was possible.
AP : 12 :142(204) [0295] out everywhere that we are **far** away from the perfection
AP : 16 :013(224) [0333] poverty and humility **far** above the state and the family,
AP : 24 :085(264) [0413] Why such a **far**-fetched etymology, except perhaps to
AP : 24 :085(264) [0413] Why go so **far** afield for the etymology when the term
AP : 24 :095(267) [0417] *operato*, they would express themselves **far** differently.
S1 : PR :001(288) [0455] one hand what and in how **far** we were willing and able to
S2 : 02 :004(293) [0463] sacrament can be had in a **far** better and more blessed
S2 : 04 :003(298) [0473] Christian church (in so **far** as this lies in his power) and
S2 : 04 :013(300) [0475] He went so **far** as to claim to be an earthly god and even
S3 : 02 :002(303) [0479] Accordingly, in so **far** as they are not restrained by
S3 : 03 :016(305) [0483] and to this day they are as **far** from comprehending their
S3 : 06 :004(311) [0493] both forms but even go so **far** as autocratically to
LC : 01 :012(366) [0583] belong those who go so **far** as to make a pact with the
LC : 01 :080(375) [0603] As **far** as outward observance is concerned, the
LC : 01 :103(379) [0611] Thus **far** we have learned the first three commandments,
LC : 01 :110(380) [0613] to them and hold your tongue, even if they go too **far**.
LC : 01 :146(385) [0623] more blessed or holy life, as **far** as your works are
LC : 01 :192(391) [0635] all these crimes, as **far** as you were concerned you have
LC : 01 :226(395) [0645] All these are **far** worse than sneak-thieves, against whom
LC : 01 :229(396) [0645] **Far** from being picklocks and sneak-thieves who loot a
LC : 01 :232(396) [0647] This commandment is very **far**-reaching, as we have
LC : 01 :317(408) [0673] is a heavenly, angelic man, **far** above all holiness on
LC : 01 :332(410) [0677] Commandments, and no one need search **far** for them.
LC : 02 :001(411) [0679] Thus **far** we have heard the first part of Christian
LC : 02 :002(411) [0679] that all human ability is **far** too feeble and weak to keep
LC : 02 :026(413) [0685] This article is very rich and **far**-reaching, but in order to
LC : 02 :052(417) [0691] we had advanced this **far**, we were entirely of the devil,
LC : 03 :023(423) [0703] So this prayer is **far** superior to all others that we might
LC : 03 :030(424) [0707] We are **far** too weak to cope with the devil and all his
LC : 03 :031(424) [0707] would have witnessed a **far** different drama: the devil
LC : 03 :055(427) [0713] It would be **far** too great for any human heart to dare to
LC : 03 :056(427) [0713] claims the honor of giving **far** more abundantly and
LC : 03 :060(428) [0715] Thus **far** we have prayed that God's name may be
LC : 03 :065(429) [0715] fruit, there the blessed holy cross will not be **far** away.
LC : 03 :109(435) [0729] as if the devil were **far** from us but shall at all times
LC : 04 :039(441) [0741] Therefore, it is **far** more glorious than anything else God
LC : 05 :033(450) [0761] So **far** we have treated the sacrament from the standpoint
LC : 05 :041(451) [0763] Thus the majority go so **far** that they have become quite
EP : 01 :023(469) [0785] As **far** as the Latin words *substantia* and *accidens* are
EP : 03 :016(475) [0795] to his divine nature (in so **far** as it dwells and works
EP : 04 :010(476) [0799] genuine believers, in so **far** as they are reborn, render not
EP : 06 :006(481) [0807] regenerated perform in so **far** as they are reborn and do
EP : 06 :007(481) [0807] The difference, as **far** as obedience is concerned, rests
EP : 06 :007(481) [0807] with a willing spirit, in so **far** as he is reborn, does what
EP : 07 :001(481) [0809] we have wished to report as **far** as necessary concerning
EP : 07 :028(485) [0815] images, and types of the **far**-distant body and blood of
EP : 08 :002(487) [0817] with each other, and how **far** does this sharing extend?
EP : 08 :016(489) [0821] Paul states, He ascended "**far** above all the heavens that
EP : 11 :013(496) [0835] election of God only in so **far** as it is revealed in the Word
EP : 12 :021(499) [0841] Father and to the Word as **far** as might, power, majesty,
SD : RN :020(507) [0857] enable the pious reader, as **far** as is necessary, to compare
SD : 01 :010(510) [0863] disability and ineptitude as **far** as the things of God are
SD : 01 :032(513) [0869] evil; not because and in so **far** as our nature and essence
SD : 01 :032(513) [0869] Fall but because and in so **far** as our nature has been
SD : 01 :049(517) [0875] the thesis and antithesis, as **far** as the chief points in this
SD : 01 :055(518) [0877] essence, in as **far** as it is a substance, is either God himself
SD : 02 :007(521) [0883] dead and corrupted as **far** as anything good is concerned.
SD : 02 :063(533) [0905] that which is good, in so **far** as he is reborn or a new
SD : 03 :029(544) [0925] So **far** Luther.
SD : 03 :043(547) [0931] or makes righteous in so **far** as it is associated with love,
SD : 03 :063(550) [0937] to his divine nature in so **far** as it dwells and works within
SD : 04 :038(557) [0951] detrimental to believers as **far** as their salvation is
SD : 06 :010(565) [0965] performs in this matter, as **far** as the good works of
SD : 06 :015(566) [0967] In order as **far** as possible to avoid all
SD : 06 :017(566) [0967] in the law and, in so **far** as he is born anew, he does
SD : 06 :019(567) [0969] As **far** as the Old Adam who still adheres to them is
SD : 07 :002(569) [0973] and blood of Christ are as **far** distant from the blessed
SD : 07 :026(573) [0981] and deceptions that have so **far** arisen or may yet arise."
SD : 07 :027(573) [0981] So **far** the quotation from the Large Catechism, which
SD : 07 :101(587) [1007] one person with God, very **far** beyond creatures, as far as
SD : 07 :101(587) [1007] far beyond creatures, as **far** as God transcends them, and
SD : 07 :103(587) [1009] So **far** Luther.
SD : 07 :115(589) [1011] parables, and types of the **far**-distant body of Christ (for
SD : 07 :117(589) [1013] operation, and merit of the **far**-distant body of Christ,
SD : 07 :119(590) [1013] on earth, but that he is as **far** or as distant from it as
SD : 08 :004(592) [1017] and they went so **far** as to load down Dr. Luther's
SD : 08 :019(595) [1021] natures in the person of Christ is **far** different from this.
SD : 08 :019(595) [1021] in the person of Christ is **far** different, much higher, and
SD : 08 :027(596) [1025] of the apostle (Eph. 4:10), **far** above all heavens that he
SD : 08 :044(600) [1031] So **far** Luther.
SD : 08 :046(600) [1031] In the second place, as **far** as the discharge of Christ's
SD : 08 :050(600) [1031] As **far** as the assumed human nature in the person of
SD : 08 :051(601) [1033] properties, or only as **far** as their capacity extends, but
SD : 10 :003(611) [1053] to the divine truth, even as **far** as things indifferent are
SD : 10 :013(613) [1057] and gave in to the weak as **far** as foods, times, and days
SD : 11 :001(616) [1063] God's grace to prevent, as **far** as we can, disunity and
SD : 11 :006(617) [1065] he does not will — how **far** it is to go, how long it is to
SD : 11 :043(623) [1077] Thus **far** God has revealed the mystery of foreknowledge
SD : 11 :052(625) [1081] which we have spoken thus **far**, there are many points in
SD : 11 :058(625) [1081] limit for us as to how **far** we should go in these and
SD : 11 :062(626) [1083] If we go thus **far** in this article we will remain on the right
SD : 11 :074(628) [1087] in my alarm, I am driven **far** from thy sight" (Ps. 31:22),
SD : 11 :095(632) [1095] Still less by **far** are we minded to whitewash or cover up
SD : 12 :001(632) [1095] As **far** as the sects and factions are concerned which
SD : 12 :006(633) [1097] As **far** as our ministry is concerned, we do not propose to

Fare (2)
SC : 09 :015(356) [0563] And all the household well will **fare**.'
LC : 01 :146(385) [0623] that you will prosper and **fare** well in everything.

Farewell (1)
LC : SP :020(364) [0579] describe how Christ said **farewell** to his disciples and sent

Farmer (1), Farmers (1)
AP : 27 :037(275) [0433] state of perfection than the life of a **farmer** or an artisan.
SC : PR :018(340) [0537] shopkeepers, and even **farmers** and servants, for many of

Farther (2)
LC : 01 :300(405) [0667] masses belong much **farther** down in the scale, where the
LC : 02 :060(418) [0695] *Fleisch* (flesh), we think no **farther** than the butcher shop.

Fashion (24), Fashioned (4), Fashions (1)
PR : PR :005(004) [0009] carried on in a Christian **fashion** and in harmony with
PR : PR :013(007) [0013] In a Christian **fashion** they discussed with one another
PR : PR :026(014) [0025] and composed in timely **fashion** before they become
AG : 21 :001(046) [0057] may in salutary and godly **fashion** imitate the example of
AG : 00 :001(048) [0059] in an unkind and hasty **fashion**, contrary to all Christian
AG : 25 :006(062) [0069] in a more fitting **fashion** than had been done for a long
AP : 04 :109(123) [0153] as referring to "faith **fashioned** by love," that is, they do
AP : 04 :203(135) [0177] he supposes, in human **fashion**, that through these works
S1 : PR :003(289) [0455] council and flees from the light in a shameful **fashion**.
S2 : 02 :002(293) [0463] would speak to them in the following friendly **fashion**:
S3 : 03 :018(306) [0483] his lust or revenge in this **fashion** would sooner have
LC : 01 :020(367) [0585] the heathen actually **fashion** their fancies and dreams
LC : 01 :312(407) [0671] works which they have **fashioned** while they neglect these
EP : 00 :000(464) [0777] and Settled in Christian **Fashion** in Conformity with
EP : RN :002(465) [0777] than as witnesses to the **fashion** in which the doctrine of
EP : 01 :004(466) [0781] is written, "Thy hands **fashioned** and made me, all that I
SD : 01 :004(509) [0861] in a Christian **fashion** and according to the Word of God
SD : 01 :035(514) [0869] Job says: "Thy hands **fashioned** and made me together
SD : 01 :039(515) [0871] out of it he makes and **fashions** our present human
SD : 01 :042(515) [0873] through sin has in this **fashion** corrupted God's
SD : 01 :049(517) [0875] but are treating only the chief points in summary **fashion**.
SD : 01 :056(518) [0877] constantly speaks in this **fashion**: Original sin is not
SD : 01 :062(519) [0879] In this **fashion** Luther used both the term "accident" and
SD : 02 :046(530) [0899] have in an unchristian **fashion** misused the doctrine of the
SD : 03 :015(541) [0919] of the law in so perfect a **fashion** that, reckoning it to us
SD : 04 :020(554) [0945] or to act in a contrary **fashion** and nonetheless still retain
SD : 08 :019(594) [1021] and in a strictly verbal **fashion**, but in deed and in truth.
SD : 08 :051(601) [1033] its own measure and **fashion** along with the other, and
SD : 12 :008(633) [1097] secretly, after the **fashion** of these spirits, into those

Fast (14), Fasted (3)
PR : PR :003(003) [0007] They have held **fast** and loyally to the doctrine that is
AG : 26 :009(065) [0071] way, prayed in this way, **fasted** in this way, and dressed in
AG : 28 :052(089) [0091] Christ has set us free; stand **fast**, therefore, and do not
AP : 04 :269(147) [0197] therefore, we must hold **fast** to these rules: that the law is
AP : 04 :377(165) [0223] therefore obliged to hold **fast** to the Gospel and the
AP : 28 :015(283) [0447] he says (Gal. 5:1), "Stand **fast** in the freedom with which
S1 : PR :001(288) [0455] hand, what we intended to hold **fast** to and persevere in.
LC : 01 :011(366) [0583] had a toothache, he **fasted** to the honor of St. Apollonia;
LC : 01 :022(367) [0585] it has made endowments, **fasted**, celebrated Mass, etc.
LC : 01 :074(374) [0601] used to be trained to **fast** and pray to St. Nicholas and
LC : 03 :061(428) [0715] If we try to hold **fast** these treasures, we must suffer an
LC : 06 :005(457) [0000] and tormented to confess, **fast**, etc., more than ever
LC : 06 :023(460) [0000] him but would run there as **fast** as he could so as not to
EP : 10 :006(493) [0829] Christ has set us free; stand **fast** therefore, and do not
SD : 04 :034(557) [0949] unbelief, and you stand **fast** only through faith" (Rom
SD : 10 :011(612) [1055] Christ has set us free; stand **fast** therefore, and do not
SD : 11 :032(621) [1073] away from him but "hold **fast** until the end the substance

Fastened (2), Fastens (1), Fasting (21), Fasts (16)
AG : 20 :003(041) [0053] pilgrimages, appointed **fasts**, holy days, brotherhoods,
AG : 26 :002(064) [0071] For this reason new **fasts**, new ceremonies, new orders,
AG : 26 :006(064) [0071] be earned by prescribed **fasts**, distinctions among foods,
AG : 26 :033(069) [0075] such bodily exercise as **fasting** and other discipline, so
AG : 26 :036(069) [0075] cannot be driven out by anything but **fasting** and prayer."
AG : 26 :039(069) [0075] Thus **fasting** in itself is not rejected, but what is rejected is
AG : 26 :039(069) [0075] a necessary service of **fasts** on prescribed days and with
AG : 26 :044(070) [0075] said, "Disagreement in **fasting** does not destroy unity in
AG : 28 :037(087) [0089] new holy days and new **fasts** have been prescribed, new
AG : 28 :041(087) [0089] defile the conscience, that **fasting** is a work by which God
AL : 20 :003(041) [0053] holy days, prescribed **fasts**, brotherhoods, pilgrimages,
AL : 26 :002(064) [0071] new holy days, and new **fasts** were daily instituted, and
AL : 26 :008(065) [0071] of certain holy days, rites, **fasts**, and vestments.
AL : 26 :036(069) [0075] cannot be driven out by anything but **fasting** and prayer."
AL : 26 :039(069) [0075] therefore is not **fasting** in itself, but traditions which with
AL : 26 :044(070) [0075] "Disagreement about **fasting** does not destroy unity in
AL : 28 :037(086) [0089] were appointed, more **fasts** prescribed, and new
AL : 28 :041(087) [0089] defile the conscience, that **fasting** which is privative and
AP : 12 :139(203) [0295] that good fruits like true **fasting**, prayer, and charity have
AP : 12 :143(204) [0295] True prayer, charity, and **fasting** have God's command:
AP : 12 :143(204) [0297] Thus certain **fasts** were instituted not to control the flesh

Continued ▶

A P : 1 5 :024(218) [0321] human reason interprets **fasting** and bodily discipline.
A P : 1 5 :024(218) [0321] as Thomas writes, "**Fasting** avails to destroy and prevent
A P : 1 5 :048(221) [0329] Their **fasts** are more luxurious and sumptuous than
A P : 2 1 :037(234) [0353] of certain prayers, **fasts**, and other profitable ceremonies,
A P : 2 3 :018(242) [0369] and to subdue their bodies with labors and **fasting**.
S 1 : P R :013(291) [0459] regulations concerning **fasts**, vestments, tonsures, and
S 2 : 0 2 :026(297) [0469] saints, pray to them, keep **fasts** and festivals for them, say
S 2 : 0 2 :027(297) [0469] to you, invoke you, keep **fasts** and festivals and say
S 3 : 0 3 :021(306) [0485] render, like saying five Our Fathers, **fasting** for a day, etc.
S 3 : 0 3 :028(308) [0487] against evil thoughts by **fasting**, vigils, prayers, Masses,
T R : 0 0 :075(333) [0525] with non-observance of **fasts** or festivals and similar
S C : 0 6 :010(352) [0557] Answer: **Fasting** and bodily preparation are a good
L C : 0 1 :120(381) [0615] they kill themselves with **fasting** and pray on their knees
L C : 0 1 :140(384) [0621] passes over them lightly, **fastens** his attention on other
L C : 0 4 :016(438) [0735] with which God has **fastened** and enclosed it and from
L C : 0 5 :037(450) [0761] **Fasting** and prayer and the like may have their place as
E P : 1 0 :007(494) [0831] axiom, "Disagreement in **fasting** does not destroy
S D : 1 0 :016(613) [1059] have a great millstone **fastened** around his neck and to be
S D : 1 0 :031(616) [1063] axiom, "Disagreement in **fasting** should not destroy

Fastidious (1)
L C : P R :008(359) [0569] These dainty, **fastidious** fellows would like quickly, with

Fat (2)
L C : P R :001(358) [0567] to do but live off the **fat** of the land all their days, as they
L C : 0 1 :162(387) [0627] preacher although in the past they filled ten **fat** paunches.

Fate (2)
A P : 2 7 :006(269) [0421] this way, therefore, the monks are signing their own **fate**.
L C : 0 1 :240(397) [0649] The same **fate** will overtake those who turn the free

Father (229), Fathers (119)
A G : 0 1 :002(027) [0043] God the **Father**, God the Son, God the Holy Spirit.
A G : 0 1 :004(028) [0043] to be understood as the **Fathers** employed the term in this
A G : 0 6 :003(032) [0047] The **Fathers** also teach thus, for Ambrose says, "It is
A G : 2 0 :009(042) [0053] sake, who alone is the mediator who reconciles the **Father**
A G : 2 1 :004(047) [0059] have an advocate with the **Father**, Jesus Christ the
A G : 0 0 :001(047) [0059] in the writings of the **Fathers**), we think that our
A G : 2 2 :004(050) [0061] from history and from writings of the **Fathers**.
A G : 2 3 :010(052) [0061] from the writings of the **Fathers** that it was customary for
A G : 2 4 :035(060) [0067] in I Cor. 11:20ff. and by many statements of the **Fathers**.
A G : 2 5 :010(063) [0069] was also the view of the **Fathers** can be seen in Dist. I, *De*
A G : 2 6 :027(068) [0073] which neither our **fathers** nor we have been able to bear?
A G : 2 6 :042(070) [0075] The ancient **Fathers** maintained such liberty with respect
A G : 2 8 :006(082) [0085] this command, "As the **Father** has sent me, even so I send
A G : 2 8 :048(089) [0091] plant which my heavenly **Father** has not planted will be
A L : 0 1 :003(028) [0043] are also coeternal: the **Father**, the Son, and the Holy
A L : 0 1 :004(028) [0043] is used, as the ancient **Fathers** employed it in this
A L : 0 3 :003(030) [0045] he might reconcile the **Father** to us and be a sacrifice not
A L : 0 3 :004(030) [0045] on the right hand of the **Father**, forever reign and have
A L : 0 6 :003(032) [0047] is also taught by the **Fathers** of the ancient church, for
A L : 0 7 :004(032) [0047] one baptism, one God and **Father** of all," etc. (Eph. 4:5, 6)
A L : 2 0 :009(042) [0053] and propitiation through whom the **Father** is reconciled.
A L : 2 0 :012(043) [0055] whole matter is supported by testimonies of the **Fathers**.
A L : 2 0 :024(044) [0055] knows that he has a **Father** reconciled to him through
A L : 2 1 :004(047) [0059] we have an advocate with the **Father**," etc. (I John 2:1).
A L : 2 4 :040(061) [0069] the Scriptures and the **Fathers**, we are confident that it
A L : 2 6 :010(065) [0071] — for example, that a **father** should bring up his children,
A L : 2 6 :027(068) [0073] which neither our **fathers** nor we have been able to bear?
A L : 2 6 :042(070) [0075] was not unknown to the **Fathers**, for Easter was kept in
A L : 2 8 :006(082) [0085] this command, "As the **Father** has sent me, even so I send
A L : 2 8 :048(089) [0091] plant which my heavenly **Father** has not planted will be
A P : 0 1 :001(100) [0103] of the same divine essence, **Father**, Son, and Holy Spirit.
A P : 0 2 :032(104) [0113] of the Scriptures and the **Fathers** that had been obscured
A P : 0 2 :032(104) [0113] attention to what the **Fathers** meant to say about the
A P : 0 2 :041(105) [0115] This is undoubtedly what the **Fathers** believe.
A P : 0 2 :050(106) [0119] the Holy Scripture and the teachings of the holy **Fathers**.
A P : 0 2 :051(107) [0119] the opinions of the holy **Fathers**, which we also follow.
A P : 0 3 :001(107) [0119] and died to reconcile the **Father** to us; and that he was
A P : 0 4 :029(111) [0129] of ours not only in the Scriptures, but also in the **Fathers**.
A P : 0 4 :054(114) [0137] for mercy, and the holy **Fathers** often say that we are
A P : 0 4 :080(118) [0143] through whom the **Father** is reconciled to us, we cannot
A P : 0 4 :081(118) [0143] obtained access" to the **Father**, and he adds, "through
A P : 0 4 :081(118) [0143] we are reconciled to the **Father** and receive the forgiveness
A P : 0 4 :103(121) [0151] are similar statements here and there in the holy **Fathers**.
A P : 0 4 :141(126) [0161] Christ we come to the **Father**; and having received the
A P : 0 4 :171(130) [0171] not only the Scriptures but also the holy **Fathers**.
A P : 0 4 :211(136) [0179] Francis, and other holy **Fathers** chose a certain kind of
A P : 0 4 :211(136) [0179] not the faith of the **Fathers** but only their behavior
A P : 0 4 :215(137) [0179] propitiator through whom we have access to the **Father**.
A P : 0 4 :238(141) [0187] the propitiator, the **Father** is gracious to us and that the
A P : 0 4 :256(144) [0193] through Christ we have access to the **Father** (Rom. 5:2).
A P : 0 4 :269(147) [0197] obtained access" to the **Father** (Rom. 5:2), not by works
A P : 0 4 :272(148) [0199] trespasses, your heavenly **Father** also will forgive you."
A P : 0 4 :288(151) [0203] not understand why the **Fathers** had enacted them,
A P : 0 4 :292(152) [0203] the promise, in which the **Father** has given the assurance
A P : 0 4 :295(152) [0203] that for Christ's sake the **Father** is reconciled and
A P : 0 4 :299(153) [0205] they have a reconciled **Father** because of Christ, not
A P : 0 4 :310(155) [0207] "This is the will of my **Father**, that everyone who sees the
A P : 0 4 :310(155) [0207] And the **Father** says (Matt. 17:5), "This is my beloved
A P : 0 4 :323(157) [0209] and in the Church **Fathers**, who declare unanimously that
A P : 0 4 :325(157) [0211] regard when the Church **Fathers** have so clearly handed
A P : 0 4 :333(158) [0211] you ask anything of the **Father**, he will give it to you in
A P : 0 4 :333(158) [0211] without the high priest we cannot draw near to the **Father**
A P : 0 4 :367(163) [0221] "Honor your **father** and your mother, that your days may
A P : 0 4 :376(165) [0223] we are led to the **Father** and have a reconciled Father, as
A P : 0 4 :376(165) [0223] and have a reconciled **Father**, as we have said often
A P : 0 4 :379(165) [0223] which believes that the **Father** is propitious to us for
A P : 0 4 :389(166) [0225] Scriptures, with the holy **Fathers** Ambrose, Augustine,
A P : 0 4 :392(167) [0225] The Scriptures, the holy **Fathers**, and the judgment of all
A P : 0 4 :399(168) [0227] Confession, a reverend **father** said that no plan seemed
A P : 0 4 :400(168) [0227] the authority of the holy **Fathers**, and contrary to the
A P : 0 7 :011(170) [0229] The **Fathers** say the same thing in many places.
A P : 0 7 :016(171) [0231] Christ says (John 8:44), "You are of your **father** the devil."
A P : 0 7 :021(172) [0233] The writings of the holy **Fathers** show that even they
A P : 0 7 :023(172) [0235] command; for as the **Father** subjected everything to him,
A P : 1 1 :005(181) [0249] ancient canons and the **Fathers** do not appoint a set time.
A P : 1 2 :016(184) [0257] to the Holy Scriptures as well as the Church **Fathers**:
A P : 1 2 :073(192) [0273] the same thing; nor are testimonies of the **Fathers** lacking.
A P : 1 2 :076(193) [0273] we are reconciled to the **Father**, not because of our
A P : 1 2 :080(194) [0275] that freely for Christ's sake they have a gracious **Father**.
A P : 1 2 :091(195) [0279] in garbled form from the **Fathers** and which our
A P : 1 2 :093(196) [0279] Since the **Fathers** discuss sometimes one part, sometimes
A P : 1 2 :097(196) [0281] are statements in the **Fathers** not only about contrition
A P : 1 2 :097(196) [0281] nor the language of the **Fathers**, they select sayings about
A P : 1 2 :106(197) [0283] commandment given a **father** to the pastor of a church,
A P : 1 2 :113(199) [0285] The holy **Fathers** did not want to accept the lapsed or the
A P : 1 2 :114(199) [0285] The **Fathers** did not believe that by such practices or such
A P : 1 2 :122(200) [0289] statements from the **Fathers** and the canons and conclude
A P : 1 2 :122(200) [0289] the councils, and the **Fathers**; and that even those who
A P : 1 2 :168(209) [0305] Occasionally the **Fathers** take the word "satisfaction"
A P : 1 2 :171(209) [0305] Furthermore, the **Fathers** wrote that once in a lifetime
A P : 1 3 :002(211) [0309] For that matter, the **Fathers** did not always use the same
A P : 1 3 :006(212) [0309] rites received from the **Fathers** which even the church
A P : 1 3 :023(214) [0313] a single word from the **Fathers** that supports the
A P : 1 4 :001(214) [0315] We know that the **Fathers** had good and useful reasons
A P : 1 5 :013(216) [0319] The holy **Fathers** did not institute any traditions for the
A P : 1 5 :014(217) [0319] in the statutes of your **fathers**, nor observe their
A P : 1 5 :019(218) [0319] of these: a god whom his **fathers** did not know he shall
A P : 1 5 :019(218) [0321] a god will be worshiped whom the **fathers** did not know.
A P : 1 5 :020(218) [0321] Although the holy **Fathers** themselves had rites and
A P : 1 5 :021(218) [0321] For these reasons the **Fathers** kept ceremonies, and for
A P : 2 0 :005(227) [0339] from Scripture and the **Fathers**, but we have already said
A P : 2 1 :003(229) [0343] do the rest of the ancient **Fathers** before Gregory mention
A P : 2 1 :003(229) [0343] merits, surely has no support among the ancient **Fathers**.
A P : 2 1 :017(231) [0347] you ask anything of the **Father**, he will give it to you in
A P : 2 1 :018(231) [0347] all may honor the Son, even as they honor the **Father**."
A P : 2 1 :018(231) [0347] himself, and God our **Father**, comfort your hearts and
A P : 2 1 :020(232) [0349] sake and that by his merits we have a gracious **Father**.
A P : 2 1 :033(233) [0351] there is no proof for it either in the **Fathers** of the church.
A P : 2 3 :002(239) [0363] lusts of the holy **fathers** "who look like Curius and live
A P : 2 4 :006(250) [0385] ancient practice, for the **Fathers** of the church before
A P : 2 4 :008(250) [0385] the institutions of the **Fathers** and then quote the
A P : 2 4 :008(250) [0385] and then quote the authority of the **Fathers** against us.
A P : 2 4 :009(250) [0387] the quotations from the **Fathers** and the arguments they
A P : 2 4 :015(252) [0389] the Scriptures or the **Fathers** and use it out of context,
A P : 2 4 :027(254) [0393] will worship the **Father** in spirit and truth, for such the
A P : 2 4 :027(254) [0393] spirit and truth, for such the **Father** seeks to worship him.
A P : 2 4 :028(254) [0393] "I did not speak to your **fathers** or command them
A P : 2 4 :028(254) [0393] God had commanded the **fathers** concerning burnt
A P : 2 4 :032(255) [0395] name of Christ and the **Father**'s mercy promised in
A P : 2 4 :065(261) [0407] have the support of the ancient church and the **Fathers**.
A P : 2 4 :066(261) [0407] they quote against us, we must also discuss the **Fathers**.
A P : 2 4 :066(261) [0407] aware of the fact that the **Fathers** call the Mass a sacrifice;
A P : 2 4 :066(261) [0407] Where do the **Fathers** say anything so monstrous?
A P : 2 4 :067(261) [0407] reply to our opponents regarding what the **Fathers** said.
A P : 2 4 :067(261) [0407] *opere operato* is not to be found anywhere in the **Fathers**.
A P : 2 4 :067(261) [0407] what actually agrees with the **Fathers** and with Scripture.
A P : 2 4 :075(263) [0411] The **Fathers** speak of a twofold effect, of the comfort for
A P : 2 4 :075(263) [0411] of this sort in the **Fathers**, all of which our opponents
A P : 2 4 :075(263) [0411] to others; but the **Fathers** clearly require faith and speak
A P : 2 4 :093(267) [0417] in faith, forefathers, **fathers**, patriarchs, prophets," etc.
A P : 2 4 :094(267) [0417] Our opponents quote the **Fathers** on offerings for the
A P : 2 4 :094(267) [0417] There is also great variety among the **Fathers**.
A P : 2 4 :096(267) [0417] apostles, and holy **Fathers**, namely, that the Mass justifies
A P : 2 7 :013(271) [0423] statement of the eternal **Father** which Thou who are in
A P : 2 7 :013(271) [0423] are in the bosom of the **Father** hast revealed to the world
A P : 2 7 :061(280) [0441] (Ex. 20:12), "Honor your **father** and your mother."
A P : 2 7 :062(280) [0441] than Israelites, their **father** apparently wanted to
S 1 : P R :015(291) [0459] who with Thee and the **Father** liveth and reigneth, blessed
S 1 : 0 1 :000(291) [0461] 1. That **Father**, Son, and Holy Spirit, three distinct
S 1 : 0 1 :000(291) [0461] 2. That the **Father** was begotten by no one, the Son was
S 1 : 0 1 :000(291) [0461] Son was begotten by the **Father**, and the Holy Spirit
S 1 : 0 1 :000(291) [0461] the Holy Spirit proceeded from the **Father** and the Son.
S 1 : 0 1 :000(291) [0461] became man, and neither the **Father** nor the Holy Spirit.
S 2 : 0 2 :013(295) [0465] and some of the **Fathers** who are said to have written
S 2 : 0 2 :015(295) [0467] articles of faith out of the holy **Fathers**' words or works.
S 3 : 0 3 :021(306) [0485] render, like saying five Our **Fathers**, fasting for a day, etc.
S 3 : 1 0 :003(314) [0497] the ancient churches and **Fathers**, we shall and ought
S 3 : 1 5 :005(317) [0501] articles of the reverend **father**, Martin Luther, confess
T R : 0 0 :009(321) [0505] when he said, "As the **Father** has sent me, even so I send
T R : 0 0 :027(324) [0511] Most of the holy **Fathers** (such as Origen, Ambrose,
T R : 0 0 :029(325) [0513] Hilary declares: "The **Father** revealed to Peter that he
T R : 0 0 :031(325) [0513] and also, "As the **Father** has sent me, even so I send
T R : 0 0 :082(000) [0529] most revered **Father** in Christ, that your courtesy may
S C : P R :008(339) [0533] understood by our good **fathers**, who were accustomed to
S C : P R :027(341) [0539] The **Father** of all grace grant it!
S C : 0 1 :007(343) [0541] *"Honor your **father** and your mother."*
S C : 0 1 :021(344) [0543] the iniquity of the **fathers** upon the children to the third
S C : 0 2 :001(344) [0543] *"I believe in God, the **Father** almighty, maker of heaven*
S C : 0 2 :003(345) [0545] *right hand of God, the **Father** almighty, whence he shall*
S C : 0 2 :004(345) [0545] true God, begotten of the **Father** from eternity, and also
S C : 0 3 :001(346) [0545] *"Our **Father** who art in heaven."*
S C : 0 3 :002(346) [0545] that he is truly our **Father** and we are truly his children in
S C : 0 3 :002(346) [0545] even as beloved children approach their dear **father**.
S C : 0 3 :005(346) [0547] Help us to do this, dear **Father** in heaven!
S C : 0 3 :005(346) [0547] From this preserve us, heavenly **Father**!
S C : 0 3 :008(346) [0547] When the heavenly **Father** gives us his Holy Spirit so that
S C : 0 3 :016(347) [0549] petition that our heavenly **Father** may not look upon our
S C : 0 3 :020(348) [0549] as in a summary, that our **Father** in heaven may deliver us
S C : 0 3 :021(348) [0549] to our heavenly **Father** and are heard by him, for he
S C : 0 4 :004(348) [0551] them in the name of the **Father** and of the Son and of the
S C : 0 4 :014(349) [0553] dead by the glory of the **Father**, we too might walk in
S C : 0 5 :020(350) [0553] whether you are a **father** or mother, a son or daughter, a
S C : 0 5 :028(351) [0555] sins in the name of the **Father** and of the Son and of the
S C : 0 7 :001(352) [0557] "In the name of God, the **Father**, the Son, and the Holy

Continued ▶

SC : 07 :002(352) [0557] Thee thanks, heavenly **Father**, through thy dear Son Jesus
SC : 07 :004(353) [0559] "In the name of God, the **Father**, the Son, and the Holy
SC : 07 :005(353) [0559] Thee thanks, heavenly **Father**, through thy dear Son Jesus
SC : 08 :009(353) [0559] "Lord God, heavenly **Father**, bless us, and these thy gifts
SC : 08 :011(354) [0559] thanks, Lord God, our **Father**, for all thy benefits, through
SC : 09 :008(356) [0563] "**Fathers**, do not provoke your children to anger, lest they
SC : 09 :009(356) [0563] 'Honor your **father** and mother' (this is the first
LC : SP :004(362) [0575] 4. You shall honor **father** and mother.
LC : SP :011(363) [0577] I believe in God, the **Father** almighty, maker of heaven
LC : SP :012(363) [0577] right hand of God, the **Father** almighty, whence he shall
LC : SP :013(363) [0577] III. The Prayer, or Our **Father**, Which Christ Taught
LC : SP :014(363) [0577] Our **Father** who art in heaven, hallowed be thy name.
LC : SP :017(363) [0577] Every **father** has the same duty to his household; he
LC : SP :019(363) [0579] terms, for the dear **fathers** or apostles, whoever they
LC : SP :021(364) [0579] them in the name of the **Father** and of the Son and of the
LC : 01 :030(368) [0589] *the iniquity of the **fathers** upon the children to the third*
LC : 01 :104(379) [0611] *"You shall honor your **father** and mother.*
LC : 01 :105(379) [0611] Thus he distinguishes **father** and mother above all other
LC : 01 :108(379) [0611] may be, they are their own **father** and mother, given them
LC : 01 :108(380) [0611] to obey me as your **father** and to acknowledge my
LC : 01 :115(381) [0613] what is pleasing to their **fathers** and mothers, or to those
LC : 01 :116(381) [0615] nobler than obedience to **father** and mother, which God
LC : 01 :125(382) [0617] If we had no **father** and mother, we should wish, on
LC : 01 :125(382) [0617] a block or a stone which we might call **father** and mother.
LC : 01 :135(383) [0619] you are unwilling to obey **father** and mother or to submit
LC : 01 :141(384) [0621] Where a **father** is unable by himself to bring up his child,
LC : 01 :142(384) [0621] they are all called **fathers** because in their responsibility
LC : 01 :142(384) [0621] act in the capacity of **fathers** and ought to have fatherly
LC : 01 :142(384) [0621] *matres familias* (that is, house-**fathers** and house-mothers)
LC : 01 :142(384) [0621] *patres patriae* (that is, **fathers** of the country) to the great
LC : 01 :143(385) [0621] What a child owes to **father** and mother, the entire
LC : 01 :150(385) [0623] In this case a man is **father** not of a single family, but of
LC : 01 :158(387) [0627] we have three kinds of **fathers** presented in this
LC : 01 :158(387) [0627] in this commandment: **fathers** by blood, fathers of a
LC : 01 :158(387) [0627] fathers by blood, **fathers** of a household, and fathers of
LC : 01 :158(387) [0627] blood, fathers of a household, and **fathers** of the nation.
LC : 01 :158(387) [0627] there are also spiritual **fathers** — not like those in the
LC : 01 :158(387) [0627] For the name spiritual **father** belongs only to those who
LC : 01 :159(387) [0627] Paul boasts that he is a **father** in I Cor. 4:15, where he
LC : 01 :159(387) [0627] he says, "I became your **father** in Christ Jesus through the
LC : 01 :160(387) [0627] Since such person are **fathers**, they are entitled to honor,
LC : 01 :164(387) [0627] temporal and spiritual **fathers**, and for the honor they
LC : 01 :167(388) [0629] commandment in which he speaks of **father** and mother.
LC : 01 :173(388) [0629] otherwise God would have no need of **father** and mother.
LC : 01 :185(390) [0633] Here God, like a kind **father**, steps in and intervenes to
LC : 01 :206(393) [0639] "You shall honor **father** and mother"; but here, as I said,
LC : 01 :320(408) [0673] *the iniquity of the **fathers** upon the children to the third*
LC : 01 :323(409) [0675] he shows himself a kind **father** and offers us every grace
LC : 01 :327(409) [0675] We are to honor **father** and mother, masters, and all in
LC : 01 :327(409) [0675] dare not respect or fear **father** or mother wrongly, doing
LC : 01 :327(410) [0675] an angry judge; otherwise, you have a gracious **father**.
LC : 02 :006(411) [0679] first article, of God the **Father**, explains creation; the
LC : 02 :007(411) [0679] "I believe in God the **Father**, who created me; I believe in
LC : 02 :009(411) [0679] *"I believe in God, the **Father** almighty, maker of heaven*
LC : 02 :010(411) [0679] description of God the **Father**, his nature, his will, and his
LC : 02 :011(412) [0681] say, "First, my God is the **Father**, who made heaven and
LC : 02 :013(412) [0681] "I believe in God, the **Father** almighty, maker," etc.?
LC : 02 :017(412) [0681] we confess that God the **Father** not only has given us all
LC : 02 :017(412) [0681] our merit, as a kind **father** who cares for us so that no
LC : 02 :018(412) [0681] two parts of this article, where we say, "**Father** almighty."
LC : 02 :024(413) [0683] For here we see how the **Father** has given himself to us,
LC : 02 :025(413) [0685] *right hand of God, the **Father** almighty, whence he shall*
LC : 02 :028(414) [0685] were created by God the **Father**, and had received from
LC : 02 :030(414) [0685] us free, and restored us to the **Father**'s favor and grace.
LC : 02 :031(414) [0687] and assumed dominion at the right hand of the **Father**.
LC : 02 :036(415) [0687] As the **Father** is called Creator and the Son is called
LC : 02 :043(416) [0689] works and merits and made us acceptable to the **Father**.
LC : 02 :065(419) [0695] come to recognize the **Father**'s favor and grace were it not
LC : 02 :065(419) [0695] for the Lord Christ, who is a mirror of the **Father**'s heart.
LC : 02 :069(420) [0697] Ten Commandments: the **Father** gives us all creation,
LC : 03 :008(421) [0699] obligation to obey our **fathers** and mothers and the civil
LC : 03 :009(421) [0699] for a son to say to his **father**: "What is the use of being
LC : 03 :013(422) [0701] despise obedience to his **father** and mother, but should
LC : 03 :021(423) [0703] "I come to Thee, dear **Father**, and pray not of my own
LC : 03 :032(424) [0707] Christian prays, "Dear **Father**, thy will be done," God
LC : 03 :036(425) [0707] we would say, "Heavenly **Father**, grant that thy name
LC : 03 :039(425) [0709] prayer we call God our **Father**, it is our duty in every way
LC : 03 :044(425) [0709] and disgrace to an earthly **father** to have a bad, unruly
LC : 03 :044(425) [0709] that on his account the **father** suffers scorn and reproach,
LC : 03 :054(427) [0713] is simply to say: "Dear **Father**, we pray Thee, give us thy
LC : 03 :067(429) [0717] "Thy will be done, dear **Father**, and not the will of the
LC : 03 :088(432) [0723] upon God and pray, "Dear **Father**, forgive us our debts."
LC : 03 :096(433) [0725] trespasses, your heavenly **Father** also will forgive you,"
LC : 03 :097(433) [0725] promise and think, "Dear **Father**, I come to Thee praying
LC : 03 :110(435) [0729] from your heart, "Dear **Father**, Thou hast commanded
LC : 03 :114(435) [0729] it all up by saying, "Dear **Father**, help us to get rid of all
LC : 04 :004(437) [0733] *them in the name of the **Father** and of the Son and of the*
LC : 04 :020(439) [0737] the commandment is added, "You shall honor **father** and
LC : 04 :038(441) [0741] "You shall honor your **father** and mother," refers only to
LC : 04 :038(441) [0741] on account of which this flesh is called **father** and mother.
LC : 04 :050(443) [0745] perceived in some of the **fathers**, such as St. Bernard,
LC : 04 :058(444) [0747] I am not obedient, then **father**, mother, and magistrates
EP : 03 :003(473) [0793] man he rendered to his heavenly **Father** into death itself.
EP : 03 :006(473) [0793] and righteous by God the **Father**, and shall be saved
EP : 07 :015(483) [0813] of the leading Church **Fathers**, such as Chrysostom,
EP : 08 :009(488) [0819] The ancient **Fathers** have illustrated this union and
EP : 11 :013(496) [0835] the eternal election of the **Father**, who has decreed in his
EP : 11 :022(497) [0837] the almighty God and **Father** of our Lord Jesus Christ
EP : 12 :021(499) [0841] essential estates to the **Father** and to the Word as far as
EP : 12 :028(500) [0843] essence with God the **Father** and the Holy Spirit, but is
EP : 12 :028(500) [0843] majesty and is inferior to and beside God the **Father**.
EP : 12 :029(500) [0843] essence, belonging to the **Father**, Son, and Holy Spirit,
EP : 12 :029(500) [0843] Spirit, but as God the **Father**, Son, and Holy Spirit are
EP : 12 :029(500) [0843] and that only the **Father** is rightly and truly God.
SD : 01 :007(510) [0861] and birth out of sinful seed from our **father** and mother.
SD : 01 :027(513) [0867] the natural way from a **father** and a mother, now inherit a
SD : 01 :030(513) [0867] the natural way from a **father** and a mother is corrupted
SD : 02 :023(525) [0889] as follows: "When the **Fathers** defend free will, they affirm
SD : 02 :026(526) [0891] come to Christ unless the **Father** draws him (John 6:44).
SD : 02 :026(526) [0891] "No one knows the **Father** except the Son and any one to
SD : 02 :041(529) [0897] "When the heavenly **Father** gives us his Holy Spirit so
SD : 02 :051(531) [0901] Therefore the eternal **Father** calls out from heaven
SD : 03 :011(541) [0919] and holy by God the **Father**, and are saved forever.
SD : 03 :015(541) [0921] in death, Christ rendered for us to his heavenly **Father**.
SD : 03 :022(543) [0923] Christ rendered to his **Father** from his birth until his
SD : 03 :054(548) [0935] true indeed that God the **Father**, Son, and Holy Spirit,
SD : 03 :054(549) [0935] are temples of God the **Father**, Son, and Holy Spirit, who
SD : 03 :056(549) [0935] rendered to his heavenly **Father** even to the most
SD : 03 :058(550) [0937] sin, and in his path to the **Father** rendered to his Father
SD : 03 :058(550) [0937] Father rendered to his **Father** entire, perfect obedience
SD : 05 :004(559) [0953] of God, his heavenly **Father**, as it is written in Mark 1:1,
SD : 07 :058(580) [0993] Therefore our revered **fathers** and forebears, like Luther
SD : 07 :060(580) [0995] The ancient Christian **fathers** and teachers of the church
SD : 07 :071(582) [0997] of which the distressed **father** of weak faith (Mark 9:24)
SD : 07 :099(586) [1005] is not in God or with the **Father** or in heaven according to
SD : 07 :099(586) [1005] world and going to the **Father** speak of this mode of
SD : 08 :006(592) [1017] and perfect God with the **Father** and the Holy Spirit, yet,
SD : 08 :006(592) [1017] eternal God, born of the **Father** from eternity, and also a
SD : 08 :018(594) [1021] on this point from the **Fathers**, if it were necessary, and
SD : 08 :018(594) [1021] The **Fathers** further illustrated the personal union and
SD : 08 :051(600) [1031] and the ancient **Fathers** on the basis of the Scriptures,
SD : 08 :054(601) [1033] and the ancient **Fathers** on the basis of Scriptures, ascribe
SD : 08 :061(602) [1035] same way in which the **Father** communicated his own
SD : 08 :061(602) [1035] he is of one essence with the **Father** and equal with God.
SD : 08 :061(602) [1035] is Christ equal with the **Father**, but according to the
SD : 08 :070(605) [1041] when Jesus knew that "the **Father** had given all things
SD : 08 :072(605) [1041] and confess that God the **Father** gave his Spirit to Christ,
SD : 08 :073(605) [1041] him as well as from the **Father** (and therefore he is and
SD : 08 :073(605) [1041] to all eternity his and the **Father**'s own Spirit, who is
SD : 08 :073(605) [1041] the Spirit (as the ancient **Fathers** say) is communicated to
SD : 08 :074(606) [1043] The **Father** poured out upon him without measure the
SD : 08 :075(606) [1043] taught that the Son, the **Father**'s Word, indeed knows all
SD : 08 :076(606) [1043] as the two hundred **fathers** of the Council of Ephesus
SD : 08 :085(608) [1047] delivered to me by my **Father**' (Matt. 11:27), and 'All
SD : 08 :085(608) [1047] this authority from the **Father** before I became man, but
SD : 10 :017(614) [1059] acknowledge before my **Father** who is in heaven" (Matt.
SD : 11 :004(617) [1063] to the ground without your **Father**'s will" (Matt. 10:29).
SD : 11 :028(621) [1071] "This is the will of the **Father**, that all who believe on
SD : 11 :065(627) [1083] Word when the **Father** says, "This is my beloved Son with
SD : 11 :066(627) [1085] holy Trinity, God the **Father**, Son, and Holy Spirit,
SD : 11 :066(627) [1085] life in whom they are to seek the **Father**'s eternal election.
SD : 11 :066(627) [1085] For the **Father** has decreed from eternity that whomever
SD : 11 :066(627) [1085] "No one comes to the **Father** but by me" (John 14:6), and
SD : 11 :067(627) [1085] is in the bosom of the **Father**" (John 1:18), has proclaimed
SD : 11 :067(627) [1085] 1:18), has proclaimed the **Father**'s will and thereby our
SD : 11 :067(627) [1085] "This is the will of my **Father**, that everyone who sees the
SD : 11 :068(627) [1085] The **Father** wills that all men should hear this
SD : 11 :072(628) [1087] We have his word, "What **father** among you, if his son
SD : 11 :072(628) [1087] more will the heavenly **Father** give the Holy Spirit to
SD : 11 :075(628) [1087] the gracious will of the **Father**, who cannot deny himself
SD : 11 :076(628) [1087] that no one comes to Christ unless the **Father** draw him.
SD : 11 :076(628) [1087] But the **Father** will not do this without means, and he has
SD : 11 :076(629) [1087] not the will of either the **Father** or the Son that any one
SD : 11 :076(629) [1087] and should wait for the **Father** to draw him without Word
SD : 11 :076(629) [1087] The **Father** indeed draws by the power of the Holy Spirit,
SD : 11 :077(629) [1089] doubt the drawing of the **Father** because the Holy Spirit
SD : 11 :077(629) [1089] And this is the drawing of the **Father**.
SD : 12 :006(633) [1097] the almighty God and **Father** of our Lord Jesus Christ has
SD : 12 :029(635) [1101] rank of essence to the **Father** and the eternal Word, so
SD : 12 :036(635) [1101] essence with God the **Father**, but only adorned with divine
SD : 12 :036(635) [1101] with divine majesty inferior to and alongside the **Father**.
SD : 12 :037(636) [1103] divine essence of the **Father**, Son, and Holy Spirit, but
SD : 12 :037(636) [1103] are three distinct persons, **Father**, Son, and Holy Spirit,
SD : 12 :038(636) [1103] 2. That only the **Father** is genuinely and truly God.

Fatherhood (2), Fatherland (2), Fatherless (3), Fatherly (7)

PR : PR :002(003) [0007] appear to our beloved **fatherland**, the German nation, and
PR : PR :004(003) [0007] in our beloved German **fatherland** shortly after the
AP : 04 :258(144) [0193] oppression; defend the **fatherless**, plead for the widow.
AP : 04 :258(144) [0193] these works: "correct oppression, defend the **fatherless**."
AP : 04 :258(144) [0193] oppression, defend the **fatherless**"—they could merit the
SC : 02 :002(345) [0543] he does out of his pure, **fatherly**, and divine goodness and
LC : 01 :105(379) [0611] To **fatherhood** and motherhood God has given the
LC : 01 :142(384) [0621] and ought to have **fatherly** hearts toward their people.
LC : 01 :150(385) [0623] with the estate of **fatherhood**, the most comprehensive of
LC : 01 :158(387) [0627] this title to themselves but performed no **fatherly** office.
LC : 02 :023(413) [0683] and see in them his **fatherly** heart and his boundless love
LC : 02 :064(419) [0695] profound depths of his **fatherly** heart, his sheer,
LC : 03 :083(431) [0721] may recognize in them his **fatherly** goodness toward us.
SD : 11 :075(628) [1087] show the same old **fatherly** heart to all who tremble at his

Fathom (1)

SD : 02 :017(524) [0887] and full of misery that no one can **fathom** it (Jer. 17:9).

Fault (14), Faults (8), Faulty (1)

AG : 28 :061(091) [0093] There are many **faulty** discussions of the transformation
AL : 00 :001(048) [0059] have been adopted by the **fault** of the times although
AL : 25 :005(062) [0069] Accordingly no **fault** is to be found with our churches on
AP : 02 :005(101) [0107] because of one's mother and not by one's own **fault**.
AP : 02 :006(101) [0107] since human nature is born full of corruption and **faults**.
AP : 02 :008(101) [0107] mention the more serious **faults** of human nature,
AP : 02 :011(102) [0109] acknowledge the minor **faults** in human nature and
AP : 02 :011(102) [0109] hate of God, and similar **faults** that we are born with.
AP : 02 :014(102) [0109] sin also involves such **faults** as ignorance of God,
AP : 02 :033(104) [0113] of the grace of Christ unless we acknowledge our **faults**.
AP : 02 :041(105) [0115] that human lust is not a **fault** but is a neutral thing, like

Continued ▶

AP : 04 :233(140) [0185] because of some minor **fault** and then seek after some
AP : 04 :234(140) [0185] best construction on the **faults** of their clergy, when the
AP : 11 :010(182) [0253] there are other major **faults**, and these we shall presently
AP : 27 :053(278) [0437] which is guilty of a double **fault**: it arrogates Christ's
SC : PR :025(341) [0539] the subject, it is your own **fault** if the people treat the
LC : 01 :177(389) [0631] state of things, but we do not see that it is our own **fault**.
LC : 01 :276(402) [0659] you, go and tell him his **fault**, between you and him
LC : 03 :058(428) [0713] The **fault** lies wholly in that shameful unbelief which does
EP : 11 :012(496) [0835] The **fault** does not lie in God or his election, but in their
SD : 04 :037(557) [0951] The **fault**, however, lies not with the good works
SD : 11 :062(626) [1083] "O Israel, it is your own **fault** that you are destroyed, but
SD : 11 :078(629) [1089] It is their own **fault** because they heard the Word of God

Favor (25), Favorably (3), Favors (1)

PR : PR :001(003) [0007] gracious greeting, and **favorably** inclined will, as well as
AG : 06 :001(032) [0045] our trust in them as if thereby to merit **favor** before God.
AG : 27 :037(077) [0081] God receives us into his **favor** for the sake of Christ, his
AL : 04 :002(030) [0045] they are received into **favor** and that their sins are
AL : 05 :003(031) [0045] believe that they are received into **favor** for Christ's sake.
AL : 20 :009(042) [0053] that we are received into **favor** for Christ's sake, who
AL : 27 :037(077) [0081] that they are received by God into **favor** for Christ's sake.
AL : 27 :058(080) [0083] kind of life is one which has God's command in its **favor**.
AL : 28 :067(093) [0093] from day to day even among those who **favor** traditions.
AP : 04 :045(113) [0133] God is reconciled and **favorably** disposed to him because
AP : 04 :180(132) [0171] Christ, God wishes to be **favorably** disposed to us and to
AP : 04 :262(145) [0195] righteousness and your iniquities by **favor** to the poor."
AP : 09 :002(178) [0245] fruit from it, by God's **favor**, that no Anabaptists have
AP : 21 :018(231) [0347] "The richest of the people will sue your **favor**."
AP : 27 :002(269) [0419] we are doing so out of anger or **favor** toward anyone.
S3 : 02 :001(303) [0479] and by the promise and offer of grace and **favor**.
TR : 00 :082(334) [0529] of Augsburg and, by the **favor** of God, all the preachers
LC : 01 :151(386) [0625] know that he shall have no **favor** or blessing from God.
LC : 01 :153(386) [0625] much better with God's **favor**, peace, and blessing than
LC : 01 :155(386) [0625] We spurn **favor** and happiness; therefore, it is only fair
LC : 01 :235(397) [0647] unwilling to do them the **favor** and service of protecting
LC : 01 :247(398) [0651] must live by your **favor**, you skin and scrape him right
LC : 01 :258(399) [0653] with an eye to gaining **favor**, money, prospects, or
LC : 01 :299(405) [0665] law, for as the saying has it, "The law **favors** the vigilant."
LC : 02 :030(414) [0685] us free, and restored us to the Father's **favor** and grace.
LC : 02 :065(419) [0695] to recognize the Father's **favor** and grace were it not for
LC : 03 :010(421) [0699] who are holier and in better **favor** with God than we are.
EP : 05 :007(478) [0803] of God's grace and **favor** acquired through the merits of
EP : 08 :016(489) [0821] in age, wisdom, and **favor** with God and men, for he did

Fear (112), Feared (7), Fearful (5), Fearfully (1), Fearing (6), Fearless (4), Fears (12)

PR : PR :011(006) [0011] and explained them in the **fear** of God, and produced a
PR : PR :018(009) [0015] Christ with joyful and **fearless** hearts and consciences.
AG : 02 :001(029) [0043] by nature to have true **fear** of God and true faith in God.
AG : 16 :004(037) [0051] consists alone of proper **fear** of God and real faith in
AG : 18 :002(039) [0051] acceptable to God, of **fearing** God and believing in God
AG : 18 :004(039) [0051] with their whole heart or **fearing** him), for it is only in
AG : 26 :010(065) [0071] and bring them up in the **fear** of God, that a wife should
AG : 27 :049(078) [0083] perfection: that we **fear** God honestly with our whole
AL : 02 :001(029) [0043] is to say, they are without **fear** of God, are without trust
AL : 16 :004(038) [0051] of the Gospel not in the **fear** of God and in faith but in
AL : 18 :009(040) [0053] inward affections, such as **fear** of God, trust in God,
AL : 20 :015(043) [0055] inexperienced men, God-**fearing** and anxious consciences
AL : 27 :049(078) [0083] perfection: honestly to **fear** God and at the same time to
AP : 02 :001(100) [0105] say that being without the **fear** of God and faith is actual
AP : 02 :002(100) [0105] by nature to have true **fear** of God or true faith in God."
AP : 02 :003(101) [0105] not only of actual **fear** and trust in God but also of the
AP : 02 :003(101) [0105] and cannot produce true **fear** and trust in God.
AP : 02 :003(101) [0105] capacity to produce the **fear** and trust of God, and it
AP : 02 :007(101) [0107] but also the absence of the **fear** of God and of faith.
AP : 02 :008(101) [0107] despising him, lacking **fear** and trust in him, hating his
AP : 02 :014(102) [0109] denied to man's natural powers the **fear** and trust of God.
AP : 02 :014(102) [0109] of God, lack of the **fear** of God and of trust in him,
AP : 02 :016(102) [0109] also the first, commanding **fear** of God, faith and love
AP : 02 :017(102) [0109] a surer knowledge of God, **fear** of God, trust in God, or
AP : 02 :018(103) [0111] the knowledge of God, **fear** of God, and trust in God?
AP : 02 :023(103) [0111] of God, trust in God, **fear** and love of God, or surely the
AP : 02 :023(103) [0111] gifts knowledge of God, **fear** of God, and trust in God.
AP : 02 :023(103) [0111] to natural man not only **fear** and trust of God but also
AP : 02 :024(103) [0111] in its weakness cannot **fear** and love God or believe in
AP : 02 :026(103) [0111] lack of ability to trust, **fear**, or love God; and
AP : 02 :031(104) [0113] able to see that when the **fear** of God and faith are
AP : 02 :033(104) [0113] of itself the heart is lacking in love, **fear**, and trust in God.
AP : 02 :046(106) [0117] For there this **fearful** sentence is pronounced, "I will put
AP : 04 :008(108) [0121] reach of reason, like true **fear** of God, true love of God,
AP : 04 :018(109) [0125] and meanwhile neither **fears** God nor truly believes that
AP : 04 :027(111) [0127] and keep his law, truly **fear** him, truly believe that he
AP : 04 :034(112) [0129] is wrathful at our sin, to **fear** him truly, and to be sure
AP : 04 :045(113) [0133] God's law, love him, truly **fear** him, be sure that he hears
AP : 04 :062(115) [0139] terrifies our consciences with real and serious **fears**.
AP : 04 :062(115) [0139] Amid such **fears** this faith brings peace of mind, consoles
AP : 04 :106(122) [0153] says: "By the law we **fear** God, by faith we hope in God.
AP : 04 :106(122) [0153] But to those who **fear** punishment grace is hidden;
AP : 04 :106(122) [0153] laboring under this **fear**, the soul by faith flees to the
AP : 04 :125(124) [0157] therefore, we begin to **fear** and love God, to pray and
AP : 04 :135(125) [0159] and indifference does not **fear** God or truly believe in his
AP : 04 :135(125) [0159] can think rightly about God, **fear** him, and believe in him.
AP : 04 :141(126) [0161] we call upon him, give thanks to him, **fear** and love him.
AP : 04 :167(130) [0169] For who loves or **fears** God enough?
AP : 04 :239(141) [0187] us in the midst of these **fears** because we know that for
AP : 04 :301(153) [0205] evils, sufferings in this life and the **fear** of eternal wrath.
AP : 04 :314(156) [0207] ourselves in the midst of **fears** and to exercise our faith.
AP : 04 :327(158) [0211] Job 9:28, "I **feared** all my works"; vv. 30-31, "If I wash
AP : 04 :342(160) [0215] servants," since no one **fears**, loves, or trusts God as he
AP : 04 :349(160) [0217] and new impulses, the **fear** and love of God, hatred of
AP : 04 :351(161) [0217] such as knowledge and **fear** of God, love of God, and
AP : 04 :351(161) [0217] God, enabling us truly to **fear** him and to trust that he
AP : 04 :386(166) [0225] grace, truly enlivens the **fearful** mind, and is convinced
AP : 07 :031(174) [0239] are chastity, patience, the **fear** of God, the love of our
AP : 12 :008(183) [0255] that Judas did not love God but **feared** the punishments.
AP : 12 :009(183) [0255] judge whether it **fears** God for his own sake or is running
AP : 12 :029(185) [0259] we love God and when because we **fear** punishment.
AP : 12 :038(187) [0261] Filial **fear** can be clearly defined as an anxiety joined with
AP : 12 :038(187) [0261] heart, whereas in servile **fear** faith does not sustain the
AP : 12 :106(197) [0283] that he neglects the **fear** of God or faith or his concern
AP : 12 :129(202) [0291] here that you ought to **fear** the judgment of God; for the
AP : 12 :149(205) [0299] not to apply them to the **fearful** terrors of conscience of
AP : 15 :043(221) [0327] like these: penitence, the **fear** of God, faith in Christ, the
AP : 15 :046(221) [0327] This is the spiritual exercise of **fear** and faith.
AP : 16 :002(222) [0331] of God in the heart, the **fear** of God and faith, the
AP : 16 :005(223) [0331] ordinances not only from **fear** of punishment but also
AP : 16 :009(224) [0333] of the heart, like a deep **fear** of God and a strong faith.
AP : 18 :006(225) [0335] hearts have neither the **fear** of God nor trust in God nor
AP : 18 :007(225) [0337] spiritual capacity for true **fear** of God, true faith in God,
AP : 21 :030(233) [0351] they could not give it for **fear** that there might not be
AP : 21 :036(234) [0353] which talk about faith or **fear** in the administration of
AP : 23 :006(240) [0365] only the judgment of any honest and God-**fearing** man.
AP : 24 :003(250) [0385] Word may receive faith and **fear** and so may also pray.
AP : 24 :003(250) [0385] something to learn that will arouse their faith and **fear**.
AP : 24 :026(254) [0391] takes hold of God, as it does when it **fears** and trusts him.
AP : 24 :072(262) [0409] He provides food for those who **fear** him."
AP : 24 :088(265) [0413] the service of the mind, **fear**, faith, prayer, thanksgiving,
AP : 27 :025(273) [0429] about God, they do not **fear** him enough, they do not
AP : 27 :027(273) [0429] means to grow in the **fear** of God, in trust in the mercy
AP : 27 :037(275) [0433] that is, growth in the **fear** of God, in faith, in the love of
AP : 27 :055(278) [0439] of teaching, prompting some of them to **fear** or faith.
S1 : PR :011(290) [0457] horrifies me and makes me **fear** that he may cause a
S2 : 02 :005(293) [0463] Christian, sensible, God-**fearing** people — especially if
S3 : 01 :002(302) [0477] being without the **fear** of God, presumption, despair,
S3 : 02 :001(303) [0479] sins by threats and **fear** of punishment and by the
S3 : 03 :042(310) [0491] people like this and I **fear** that such a devil still dwells in
S3 : 08 :008(313) [0495] him "devout" and "God-**fearing**"), but he could not have
SC : PR :022(341) [0537] by telling them: It is to be **feared** that anyone who does
SC : 01 :002(342) [0539] Answer: We should **fear**, love, and trust in God above all
SC : 01 :004(342) [0539] Answer: We should **fear** and love God, and so we should
SC : 01 :006(342) [0541] Answer: We should **fear** and love God, and so we should
SC : 01 :008(343) [0541] Answer: We should **fear** and love God, and so we should
SC : 01 :010(343) [0541] Answer: We should **fear** and love God, and so we should
SC : 01 :012(343) [0541] Answer: We should **fear** and love God, and so we should
SC : 01 :014(343) [0541] Answer: We should **fear** and love God, and so we should
SC : 01 :016(343) [0541] Answer: We should **fear** and love God, and so we should
SC : 01 :018(343) [0541] Answer: We should **fear** and love God, and so we should
SC : 01 :020(344) [0543] Answer: We should **fear** and love God, and so we should
SC : 01 :022(344) [0543] We should therefore **fear** his wrath and not disobey these
SC : 08 :010(354) [0559] pleasure in those who **fear** him, in those who hope in his
SC : 09 :010(356) [0563] your earthly masters, with **fear** and trembling, with
LC : PR :008(359) [0569] They need not **fear** a fall, for they have already fallen all
LC : 01 :007(365) [0583] feels secure, happy, **fearless**, as if he were sitting in the
LC : 01 :011(366) [0583] of St. Apollonia; if he **feared** fire, he sought St. Lawrence
LC : 01 :011(366) [0583] as his patron; if he **feared** the plague, he made a vow to
LC : 01 :034(369) [0589] Therefore he wills to be **feared** and not to be despised.
LC : 01 :061(373) [0597] with punishment but in the reverence and **fear** of God.
LC : 01 :074(374) [0601] anything monstrous or **fearful** and exclaim, "Lord God,
LC : 01 :075(375) [0601] bring up our youth in the **fear** and honor of God so that
LC : 01 :077(375) [0603] in their hearts that they **fear** God more than they do rods
LC : 01 :103(379) [0611] First, we should trust, **fear**, and love him with our whole
LC : 01 :174(388) [0629] bring up his children in the **fear** and knowledge of God,
LC : 01 :218(394) [0643] are grown, will be married honorably in the **fear** of God.
LC : 01 :259(400) [0653] but also a wise, sagacious, brave, and **fearless** man.
LC : 01 :259(400) [0653] a witness should be **fearless**; more than that, he should be
LC : 01 :322(409) [0673] he will watch over them, **fearfully** and terribly punishing
LC : 01 :323(409) [0673] proceed from a heart that **fears** and regards God alone
LC : 01 :323(409) [0673] alone and, because of this **fear**, avoids all that is contrary
LC : 01 :324(409) [0675] means simply, "You shall **fear**, love, and trust me as your
LC : 01 :324(409) [0675] On the one hand, whoever **fears** and loves anything else in
LC : 01 :325(409) [0675] these two things, **fear** of God and trust in God.
LC : 01 :325(409) [0675] pleasure in those who **fear** him, in those who hope in his
LC : 01 :326(409) [0675] we are told to **fear** God and not take his name in vain by
LC : 01 :326(409) [0675] Similarly, this **fear**, love, and trust should impel us not to
LC : 01 :327(409) [0675] you dare not respect or **fear** father or mother wrongly,
LC : 01 :330(410) [0677] like cattle, but in the **fear** and reverence of God.
LC : 02 :021(413) [0683] ourselves, as if we ourselves were to be **feared** and served.
LC : 03 :089(432) [0723] becomes restless; it **fears** God's wrath and displeasure,
LC : 05 :011(448) [0755] and should accept it with all reverence, **fear**, and humility.
LC : 05 :051(452) [0765] from compulsion and **fear** of men's commandments,
LC : 05 :071(455) [0769] are heavy-laden with sin, **fear** of death, and the assaults
LC : 06 :004(457) [0000] without coercion or **fear**, and we are released from the
EP : 04 :012(477) [0799] good works not from a **fear** of punishment, like a slave,
EP : 12 :031(500) [0843] we have advisedly, in true **fear** and invocation of God,
SD : 02 :003(520) [0881] God, to trust God truly, to **fear** and to love him, man
SD : 02 :031(527) [0893] Holy Spirit are without **fear** of God, without faith, do
SD : 02 :068(534) [0907] and at another moment **fearful** and terrified, at one time
SD : 02 :070(535) [0909] learns to know sin, to **fear** the wrath of God, to turn from
SD : 04 :003(551) [0939] they are not extorted by **fear** and punishment of the law
SD : 04 :031(556) [0947] his evil lusts without **fear** and shame, resists the Holy
SD : 06 :016(566) [0967] are commanded, from **fear** of punishment or in hope of
SD : 11 :059(626) [1083] will lead us to live in the **fear** of God and to recognize and
SD : 12 :040(636) [1103] we have advisedly, in the **fear** and invocation of God,

Feast (3), Feasts (1)

AP : 07 :033(174) [0239] the Lord's day, and the other more important **feast** days.
AP : 15 :048(221) [0329] sumptuous than others' **feasts**, and our opponents do not
LC : 05 :048(452) [0765] perverted it and turned it back into a Jewish **feast**).
EP : 07 :020(484) [0813] the guests at this heavenly **feast** is and consists solely and

Febris (1)

AP : 21 :032(233) [0351] that Juno granted riches, **Febris** warded off fever, and

Feeble (6), Feebleness (1)

AL : 20 :034(045) [0057] Such is the **feebleness** of man when he governs himself by
AP : 04 :290(151) [0203] although even a weak and **feeble** keeping of the law is
AP : 18 :005(225) [0335] never stops inciting this **feeble** nature to various offenses.

Continued ▶

L C : 0 1 :108(379) [0611] however lowly, poor, **feeble**, and eccentric they may be,
L C : 0 1 :111(380) [0613] when they are old, sick, **feeble**, or poor; all this you
L C : 0 2 :002(411) [0679] all human ability is far too **feeble** and weak to keep them.
E P : 0 2 :011(471) [0789] (though it be little and **feeble**) to help, to cooperate, to

Feed (5), Feeding (2), Feeds (1)
A P : 0 2 :044(106) [0117] These notions prevailed, **feeding** a trust in human powers
A P : 2 7 :005(269) [0421] richest monasteries just **feed** a lazy crowd that gorges
T R : 0 0 :022(323) [0511] Again, "**Feed** my sheep" (John 21:17), and certain other
T R : 0 0 :030(325) [0513] As to the passages "**Feed** my sheep" (John 21:17) and "Do
L C : 0 1 :128(382) [0617] takes thought how God **feeds**, guards, and protects us and
L C : 0 1 :190(391) [0635] suffer hunger and do not **feed** him, you have let him
L C : 0 3 :063(428) [0715] he stirs up, fanning and **feeding** the flames, in order to
S D : R N :014(506) [0855] "must both pasture or **feed** the lambs and guard against

Feel (40), Feeling (3), Feelings (2), Feels (10), Felt (3)
A G : 2 3 :014(053) [0063] Majesty we therefore **feel** confident that, as a most
A L : 2 6 :013(066) [0073] own lives, because they **felt** that they could not keep the
A P : 0 4 :009(108) [0123] is at rest and he does not **feel** God's wrath or judgment,
A P : 0 4 :036(112) [0131] A heart that really **feels** God's wrath cannot love him
A P : 0 4 :037(112) [0131] they themselves do not **feel** the wrath or judgment of
A P : 0 4 :142(126) [0161] of a conscience that **feels** God's wrath against our sins and
A P : 0 4 :170(130) [0171] battles against such **feelings** in order to suppress and
A P : 0 4 :192(133) [0175] We **feel** the same way about every work done in the most
A P : 0 4 :301(153) [0205] They either do not **feel** this love at all, as our opponents
A P : 0 4 :301(153) [0205] opponents admit, or surely they **feel** that it is very weak.
A P : 0 4 :301(153) [0205] Much more often they **feel** angry at the judgment of God,
A P : 0 4 :312(155) [0207] As long as we **feel** that he is wrathful against us, human
A P : 0 4 :312(155) [0207] we answer that these **feelings** cannot be divided in fact the
A P : 1 2 :029(185) [0259] terror of a conscience that **feels** God's wrath against sin
A P : 1 2 :032(186) [0259] terrors the conscience **feels** God's wrath against sin,
A P : 1 2 :034(186) [0261] real terrors when they **feel** the terrible and indescribable
A P : 1 2 :051(189) [0265] because hearts that do not **feel** God's wrath in their
A P : 1 2 :107(198) [0283] a confession is contrition; **feeling** God's wrath, we confess
A P : 1 2 :151(206) [0299] himself (II Cor. 1:9), "We **felt** that we had received the
A P : 1 2 :158(207) [0301] and wrath, they should not **feel** that God has rejected
A P : 2 8 :018(284) [0449] great and learned men in the church have **felt** about it.
S 3 : 0 3 :043(310) [0491] that they still possess and **feel** original sin and daily
S C : P R :023(341) [0539] of his own accord, he will **feel** constrained to receive it, he
S C : P R :024(341) [0539] that those who do not **feel** and acknowledge their great
S C : 0 5 :024(350) [0555] however, anyone does not **feel** that his conscience is
L C : P R :003(358) [0567] troubles, and they might **feel** a little shame because, like
L C : 0 1 :007(365) [0583] has money and property **feels** secure, happy, fearless, as if
L C : 0 1 :099(378) [0609] sick and tired of it and **feel** that they know it all and need
L C : 0 1 :114(380) [0613] However, men did not **feel** obliged to set forth God's
L C : 0 1 :155(386) [0625] Of course, we keenly **feel** our misfortune, and we grumble
L C : 0 3 :026(424) [0705] We must **feel** our need, the distress that impels and drives
L C : 0 3 :027(424) [0705] enough, but the trouble is that we do not **feel** or see them.
L C : 0 3 :107(434) [0729] To **feel** temptation, therefore, is quite a different thing
L C : 0 3 :107(434) [0729] We must all **feel** it, though not all to the same degree;
L C : 0 3 :108(434) [0729] be harmed by the mere **feeling** of temptation as long as it
L C : 0 3 :108(435) [0729] If we did not **feel** it, it could not be called a temptation.
L C : 0 5 :027(449) [0759] times, when our heart **feels** too sorely pressed, this
L C : 0 5 :041(451) [0763] one should go unless he **feels** a hunger and thirst
L C : 0 5 :055(453) [0765] But suppose you say, "What if I **feel** that I am unfit?"
L C : 0 5 :070(454) [0769] But those who **feel** their weakness, who are anxious to be
L C : 0 5 :072(455) [0769] If you are heavy-laden and **feel** your weakness, go joyfully
L C : 0 5 :074(455) [0771] are unworthy who neither **feel** their infirmities nor admit
L C : 0 5 :075(455) [0771] shall I do if I cannot **feel** this need or experience hunger
L C : 0 5 :075(455) [0771] of mind that they cannot **feel** it, I know no better advice
L C : 0 5 :076(455) [0771] If you cannot **feel** the need, therefore, at least believe the
L C : 0 5 :077(455) [0771] is a leprous flesh which **feels** nothing though the disease
L C : 0 5 :078(455) [0771] In short, the less you **feel** your sins and infirmities, the
L C : 0 5 :081(456) [0773] it, making you unable to **feel** your needs or come to
L C : 0 5 :083(456) [0773] If even then you **feel** nothing, you have all the more need
L C : 0 6 :014(458) [0000] So if there is a heart that **feels** its sin and desires
L C : 0 6 :017(459) [0000] and nobody could **feel** his conscience at peace or have
L C : 0 6 :027(460) [0000] He who **feels** his misery and need will develop such a
S D : 0 2 :046(530) [0899] they are able actually to **feel** and to perceive that God has
S D : 0 2 :047(530) [0901] his within them, since they **feel** no strong, ardent faith and
S D : 0 2 :056(532) [0903] merely on the basis of our **feeling**, how and when we
S D : 0 5 :008(559) [0953] to recognize one's sins, to **feel** heartily sorry for them, and
S D : 0 7 :101(587) [1007] a way that they do not **feel**, touch, measure, or
S D : 1 1 :074(628) [1087] grave temptation that they **feel** that they are no longer

Feet (9)
S 2 : 0 4 :016(301) [0477] we ought not here kiss his **feet** or say, "You are my
L C : 0 2 :031(414) [0687] to him and lie beneath his **feet** until finally, at the last
L C : 0 5 :011(448) [0755] divine Majesty at whose **feet** every knee should bow and
E P : R N :001(464) [0777] "Thy word is a lamp to my **feet** and a light to my path."
E P : 0 7 :012(483) [0811] in his hands and under his **feet** everything in heaven and
E P : 0 8 :016(489) [0821] the earth beneath his **feet** and in his hands, as he himself
S D : 0 1 :062(519) [0879] us from the soles of our **feet** to the crown of our head,
S D : 0 8 :055(601) [1033] have all things under his **feet**, to cleanse from sin, and so
S D : 0 8 :070(605) [1041] thy hands, putting everything in subjection under his **feet**.

Feigned (1)
T R : 0 0 :048(328) [0519] Here they have **feigned** that vows produce righteousness

Fell (9)
A G : 2 0 :033(045) [0057] this, and instead **fell** into many great and open sins.
A G : 2 6 :013(066) [0073] Gerson writes that many **fell** into despair on this account,
A L : 2 6 :013(066) [0073] Gerson writes that many **fell** into despair, and some even
A L : 2 7 :002(071) [0077] Afterward, when discipline **fell** into decay, vows were
A P : 0 4 :108(122) [0153] suppose that these words **fell** from the Holy Spirit
A P : 1 2 :071(192) [0271] saying this, the Holy Spirit **fell** on all who heard the
S 3 : 0 3 :043(310) [0491] into open sin (as David **fell** into adultery, murder, and
S D : 0 2 :022(525) [0889] the wicked spirits who **fell**, he has nevertheless willed, out
S D : 1 1 :011(618) [1067] as did not persevere but **fell** away again, they may think,

Fellow (6), Fellows (5)
P R : P R :013(007) [0013] of some of our **fellow** believers among the electors and
P R : P R :025(014) [0023] and concord with our **fellow**-members, the electors and
A P : 0 4 :354(161) [0217] are children of God and **fellow** heirs with Christ (Rom.
A P : 0 4 :356(161) [0217] makes us sons of God and **fellow** heirs with Christ (Rom.
A P : 0 4 :366(163) [0221] (Col. 1:13), and made **fellow** heirs with Christ (Rom.
L C : P R :008(359) [0569] These dainty, fastidious **fellows** would like quickly, with
L C : P R :016(361) [0573] we not most marvelous **fellows**, therefore, if we imagine,
L C : P R :016(361) [0573] Most marvelous **fellows**, to think we can finish learning in
L C : P R :018(361) [0573] and presumptuous **fellows** do not understand a single
L C : 0 1 :099(378) [0609] way those conceited **fellows** should be chastised who,
L C : 0 1 :180(389) [0631] conduct ourselves individually toward our **fellow** men.

Fellowman (2), Fellowmen (1)
A P : 2 8 :003(281) [0445] they took pleasure in the destruction of their **fellowmen**.
E P : 0 3 :019(475) [0795] which consists in love toward God and our **fellowman**.
S D : 0 3 :023(543) [0923] within them love toward God and their **fellowman**.

Fellowship (14)
A G : P R :004(025) [0039] in unity and in one **fellowship** and church, even as we are
A L : 2 8 :021(084) [0087] to exclude from the **fellowship** of the church ungodly
A P : 0 4 :232(139) [0185] personal perfection but about **fellowship** in the church.
A P : 0 7 :003(168) [0227] from the outward **fellowship** of the church or deny
S 2 : 0 2 :009(294) [0465] his own pleasure apart from the **fellowship** of the church.
S 3 : 0 9 :000(314) [0497] sacrament and other **fellowship** in the church until they
T R : 0 0 :041(328) [0517] unbelievers, for what **fellowship** has light with darkness?"
L C : 0 5 :087(456) [0773] should also enjoy this **fellowship** of the sacrament so that
E P : 1 0 :006(493) [0829] unbelievers, for what **fellowship** has light with darkness?"
S D : 0 7 :033(575) [0983] will please let me alone and expect no **fellowship** from me
S D : 0 7 :057(579) [0993] speaking of a spiritual **fellowship** with Christ, which no
S D : 0 7 :060(580) [0993] and his ilk who have no **fellowship** with Christ, who come
S D : 1 0 :006(611) [1055] and iniquity, or what **fellowship** has light with darkness?
S D : 1 0 :022(615) [1061] unbelievers, for what **fellowship** has light with darkness?'

Female (2)
A G : 2 3 :005(052) [0061] created man as male and **female** according to Gen. 1:27.
S C : 0 9 :010(356) [0563] Laborers and Servants, Male and **Female**

Ferments (1)
S D : 0 3 :007(540) [0917] this doctrine that a little leaven **ferments** the whole lump.

Fervent (1), Fervently (1), Fervor (2)
A P : 0 4 :224(138) [0181] As usual, their zeal was very **fervent** in the beginning.
A P : 2 1 :010(230) [0345] if the saints do pray **fervently** for the church, it does not
L C : P R :009(359) [0569] new and greater light and **fervor**, so that day by day we
S D : 0 7 :033(575) [0983] in this article with great **fervor** and wrote as follows: "I

Festival (7), Festivals (10)
A G : 1 5 :001(036) [0049] them being certain holy days, **festivals**, and the like.
A G : 2 6 :009(065) [0071] life: whoever observed **festivals** in this way, prayed in this
A G : 2 6 :025(068) [0073] of food and drink or with regard to a **festival**," etc.
A G : 2 6 :040(069) [0075] and various canticles, **festivals**, and the like) which serve
A G : 2 8 :044(088) [0089] drink or with regard to a **festival** or a new moon or a
A L : 1 5 :001(036) [0049] Such are certain holy days, **festivals**, and the like.
A L : 2 6 :025(068) [0073] food and drink or with regard to a **festival** or a sabbath."
A L : 2 8 :044(088) [0089] drink or with regard to a **festival** or a new moon or a
A L : 2 8 :057(091) [0091] Sunday, Easter, Pentecost, and similar **festivals** and rites.
A P : 0 7 :035(175) [0239] drink or with regard to a **festival** or a new moon or a
A P : 1 5 :030(219) [0323] drink or with regard to a **festival** or a new moon or a
A P : 2 4 :001(249) [0383] Sunday and on other **festivals**, when the sacrament is
A P : 2 4 :006(250) [0385] one public Mass, and this only on Sundays and **festivals**.
S 2 : 0 2 :026(297) [0469] to them, keep fasts and **festivals** for them, say Masses and
S 2 : 0 2 :027(297) [0469] you, keep fasts and **festivals** and say Masses and offer
T R : 0 0 :075(333) [0525] non-observance of fasts or **festivals** and similar trifles.
S D : 1 0 :013(613) [1057] drink, or with regard to a **festival** or a new moon or a

Fetched (1)
A P : 2 4 :085(264) [0413] Why such a far-**fetched** etymology, except perhaps to

Fetters (3)
A G : 2 7 :004(071) [0077] were imposed, and such **fetters** and burdens were laid on
A L : 2 7 :004(071) [0077] These **fetters** were laid on many, contrary to the canons,
A P : 1 5 :033(220) [0325] standards by which to free themselves from these **fetters**.

Feudal (2)
E P : 1 2 :015(499) [0841] nor pay oath-bound **feudal** homage to his territorial
S D : 1 2 :020(634) [1099] court or pay oath-bound **feudal** homage to his prince or

Fever (1)
A P : 2 1 :032(233) [0351] riches, Febris warded off **fever**, and Castor and Pollux

Few (49), Fewer (4)
P R : P R :016(008) [0015] confession not only of a **few** of our theologians but
A G : 2 3 :005(052) [0061] precept," he indicated that **few** people have the gift of
A G : 2 7 :029(075) [0079] and ability, and there are **few**, whether men or women,
A L : 0 0 :002(047) [0059] is concerned with a certain **few** abuses which have crept
A L : 0 0 :001(048) [0059] faith but only omit some **few** abuses which are new and
A L : 2 6 :034(069) [0075] at all times, and not merely on a **few** prescribed days.
A L : 2 7 :029(075) [0079] How **few** there are who have taken the vow
A L : 2 7 :032(076) [0079] human weakness, adds a **few** years and forbids making a
A L : 2 8 :077(094) [0095] and that they relax some **few** observances which cannot
A P : 0 4 :004(108) [0121] we shall have to say a **few** things by way of preface so
A P : 0 7 :046(177) [0243] whole controversy we shall have a **few** things to say later.
A P : 1 2 :059(190) [0267] We shall therefore add a **few** proofs to show that the
A P : 1 5 :002(215) [0315] of the Confession, we must repeat a **few** things here.
A P : 1 5 :042(221) [0327] A **few** of the better ones are now beginning to talk about
A P : 2 3 :005(239) [0365] know good and well how **few** practice chastity, but they
A P : 2 4 :014(251) [0387] our case, we must add a **few** things because of the way
A P : 2 4 :068(262) [0409] about faith, whose true meaning very **few** understand.
A P : 2 7 :010(270) [0423] shall briefly run through a **few** of our arguments, and in
A P : 2 7 :038(275) [0433] morning he prayed in a **few** words for the whole city and
S 1 : P R :014(291) [0459] I have drafted only a **few** articles, for, apart from these,
L C : 0 1 :009(365) [0583] Very **few** there are who are cheerful, who do not fret and
L C : 0 1 :058(372) [0597] the world that there are **few** who do not use the name of
L C : 0 1 :058(372) [0597] just as there are **few** who trust in God with their whole
L C : 0 1 :211(393) [0641] there are some (although **few**) exceptions whom God has

Continued ▶

L C : 0 1 :224(395) [0643] In a **few** words, this includes taking advantage of our
L C : 0 2 :005(411) [0679] nor could they all be clearly expressed in so **few** words.
L C : 0 2 :007(411) [0679] briefly comprised in these **few** words: "I believe in God
L C : 0 2 :020(412) [0681] to describe in detail how **few** people believe this article.
L C : 0 3 :031(424) [0707] that the prayers of a **few** godly men intervened like an
L C : 0 4 :049(442) [0745] Even today there are not a **few** whose doctrine and life
E P : 0 2 :006(470) [0787] In these **few** words he denies all power to free will and
E P : 0 6 :001(480) [0805] that a controversy has arisen among a **few** theologians.
E P : 0 8 :033(491) [0825] human nature, but only a **few** and only at the place where
E P : 1 0 :007(493) [0831] another because it has **fewer** or more external ceremonies
E P : 1 1 :012(496) [0835] "Many are called, but **few** are chosen," does not mean
E P : 1 2 :002(498) [0839] some of which teach many errors, others teach **fewer**.
S D : 0 2 :002(520) [0881] of the Augsburg Confession for quite a **few** years.
S D : 0 4 :003(551) [0939] In this controversy a very **few** asserted the provocative
S D : 0 4 :003(551) [0939] A **few** theologians also maintained that good works are
S D : 0 4 :036(557) [0949] to this controversy, not a **few** orthodox teachers used
S D : 0 5 :004(559) [0953] his doctrine in a **few** words, "Thus it is written, that the
S D : 0 6 :001(564) [0963] has arisen among a **few** theologians concerning this third
S D : 0 8 :004(592) [1017] But after his death a **few** theologians of the Augsburg
S D : 1 0 :031(616) [1063] Christian liberty one uses **fewer** or more of them, as long
S D : 1 1 :033(621) [1073] will those who are saved be **few**?" by saying, "Strive to
S D : 1 1 :034(622) [1075] why "many are called and **few** are chosen" is not that in
S D : 1 1 :034(622) [1075] heart I am not thinking of all, but only of a certain **few**.
S D : 1 1 :041(623) [1077] "many are called, but **few** are chosen," for few accept the
S D : 1 1 :041(623) [1077] but few are chosen," for **few** accept the Word and obey it;
S D : 1 1 :051(624) [1079] "Many are called, but **few** are chosen" (Matt. 22:14);
S D : 1 2 :004(633) [1097] unanimous opinion with a **few** bare words or our
S D : 1 2 :008(633) [1097] in their errors, be they **few** or many, and that on the
S D : 1 2 :027(635) [1101] holding more and another party holding **fewer** errors.

Fiction (4), Fictions (4), Fictitious (2)
A P : 1 2 :119(200) [0287] whole theory is a recent **fiction**, without authority either
A P : 1 2 :122(200) [0287] opponents prove these **fictions** of theirs in the
A P : 1 2 :137(203) [0293] And yet by these **fictions** they defend monastic orders, the
A P : 2 2 :007(237) [0359] examples to prove their **fiction** that in the beginning of
A P : 2 3 :005(239) [0365] false prophets would deceive people with their **fictions**.
A P : 2 4 :063(261) [0405] the wicked and recent **fictions** of the ignorant monks;
A P : 2 4 :067(261) [0407] Certainly this **fiction** about merit *ex opere operato* is not
S 2 : 0 2 :004(293) [0463] of an unnecessary and **fictitious** matter when the
T R : 0 0 :071(332) [0525] but he is a late and **fictitious** writer, whoever he may be,
S D : 0 7 :102(587) [1007] be where God is and that this mode of being is a **fiction**.

Fidelity (2)
L C : 0 1 :069(374) [0599] no obedience, no **fidelity**, no faith — only perverse,
L C : 0 1 :219(394) [0643] each other whole-heartedly and with perfect **fidelity**.

Field (9), Fields (5)
A G : 1 8 :005(040) [0051] or not to labor in the **fields**, whether or not to eat or
A L : 1 8 :005(040) [0051] is, to will to labor in the **field**, will to eat and drink, will
A P : 0 4 :329(158) [0211] is grass, and all its beauty is like the flower of the **field**.
A P : 0 7 :019(171) [0233] The **field**, he says, is the world, not the church.
A P : 2 1 :002(229) [0343] and say, "On this **field** of battle Jerome conquered
A P : 2 3 :008(240) [0367] beginning, but yearly the **fields** are clothed as long as this
A P : 2 3 :070(249) [0383] is grass, and all its beauty is like the flower of the **field**."
S C : 0 3 :014(347) [0547] house and home, **fields** and flocks, money and property; a
L C : 0 1 :156(386) [0625] not have a penny in the house or a straw in the **field**.
L C : 0 1 :296(405) [0665] as his wife, servants, house, **fields**, meadows, or cattle.
L C : 0 3 :072(430) [0719] bin, but also the broad **fields** and the whole land which
L C : 0 3 :072(430) [0719] bless and preserve it in the **field**, we could never take a
L C : 0 3 :076(431) [0721] the grain and fruits of the **field** to grow and yield richly;
L C : 0 3 :081(431) [0721] not have a straw in the **field**, a penny in the house, or

Fierce (1)
E P : 0 5 :008(479) [0803] heaven" over all sinners and men learn how **fierce** it is.

Fiery (1)
S 3 : 0 3 :030(308) [0487] Here the **fiery** angel St. John, the preacher of true

Fifteen (2)
A G : 2 7 :031(075) [0079] annul vows that are made under the age of **fifteen** years.
A L : 2 7 :031(075) [0079] made before the age of **fifteen** on the ground that before

Fifth (12)
A P : 0 4 :001(107) [0119] In the fourth, **fifth**, and sixth articles, and later in the
A P : 2 3 :026(243) [0371] ***Fifth***, although our opponents do not defend this
S 2 : 0 2 :022(296) [0469] The **fifth** are relics.
S C : 0 1 :009(343) [0541] The **Fifth**
S C : 0 3 :015(347) [0549] The **Fifth** Petition
L C : 0 1 :178(389) [0631] The **Fifth** Commandment
L C : 0 1 :274(402) [0659] We have seen that the **Fifth** Commandment forbids us to
L C : 0 1 :274(402) [0659] and as he warns in the **Fifth** Commandment, he has
L C : 0 3 :084(432) [0723] The **Fifth** Petition
L C : 0 5 :000(447) [0753] [**Fifth** Part:] The Sacrament of the Altar
S D : R N :007(505) [0853] 5. In the **fifth** place, we also commit ourselves to the
S D : 0 5 :011(560) [0955] of the Gospel for the **Fifth** Sunday after Trinity.

Figenbotz (2)
S 3 : 1 5 :005(317) [0501] I, Conrad **Figenbotz**, for the glory of God subscribe that I
T R : 0 0 :082(334) [0529] Conrad **Figenbotz** subscribes to all throughout

Fight (5), Fighting (2), Fought (2)
P R : P R :003(003) [0007] of Christ has believed, **fought** for against many heresies
A P : 1 1 :008(181) [0251] not act as brothers in their **fight** about jurisdiction over
A P : 2 3 :005(240) [0365] All they are actually **fighting** for is their authority; they
A P : 2 4 :010(251) [0387] into side issues, like wrestlers **fighting** for their position.
S 3 : 0 3 :028(308) [0487] monasteries and chapters **fought** against evil thoughts by
L C : 0 1 :208(393) [0639] living, and all virtues, and **fight** against wickedness and
L C : 0 2 :022(413) [0683] true of those who even **fight** against the Word of God.
L C : 0 5 :087(457) [0773] help us to believe, to love, to pray, and to **fight** the devil.
S D : 0 2 :070(535) [0909] and diligence, and to **fight** against the flesh, etc.

Figment (1), Figments (1)
A P : 1 2 :046(188) [0263] understood as a Platonic **figment** but as consolation truly
A P : 2 3 :028(243) [0371] We shall reply to these **figments** one by one.

Figurative (7)
S D : 0 7 :007(570) [0975] the way the letters sound, but as **figurative** speech.
S D : 0 7 :007(570) [0975] sacramentally or in a **figurative** manner, so that nobody
S D : 0 7 :038(576) [0985] we have to do with a **figurative** predication, but with an
S D : 0 7 :038(576) [0985] to be understood as a **figurative**, flowery formula or
S D : 0 7 :045(577) [0987] not as flowery, **figurative**, or metaphorical expressions, as
S D : 0 7 :049(578) [0989] or of his body in a **figurative** sense, or of the virtue of his
S D : 0 7 :113(589) [1011] but through tropes or a **figurative** interpretation are to be

Figure (6), Figures (3)
A P : 0 4 :152(127) [0163] There is a familiar **figure** of speech, called synecdoche, by
A P : 1 0 :002(179) [0247] "the bread is not merely a **figure** but is truly changed into
A P : 2 2 :016(238) [0361] Let them **figure** out how they will account to God for
A P : 2 4 :084(264) [0413] for Paul uses the **figure** of an altar only for illustration.
E P : 0 7 :028(485) [0815] bread and wine are only **figures**, images, and types of the
E P : 0 8 :025(490) [0823] it is only a verbalism and **figure** of speech when we say
S D : 0 7 :007(570) [0975] (that is, a sign or **figure** of the body of Christ which is not
S D : 0 7 :060(580) [0993] signs and symbols and **figures** of the body and blood, but
S D : 0 7 :115(589) [1011] 4. that they are only **figures**, parables, and types of the

Filial (1)
A P : 1 2 :038(187) [0261] **Filial** fear can be clearly defined as an anxiety joined with

Fill (5), Filled (1), Fills (2)
A P : 0 2 :049(106) [0119] and wicked doctrines **fill** the world, and by these bonds
A P : 0 7 :005(169) [0227] is, the whole congregation "of him who **fills** all in all."
S 3 : 0 8 :006(312) [0495] do not remain silent but **fill** the world with their
L C : 0 1 :162(387) [0627] preacher although in the past they **filled** ten fat paunches.
E P : 0 8 :016(489) [0821] "far above all the heavens that he might **fill** all things."
S D : 0 7 :076(583) [0999] fruitful and multiply and **fill** the earth,' were spoken only
S D : 0 8 :027(596) [1025] heavens that he might truly **fill** all things, he is
S D : 0 8 :028(596) [1025] power of God which **fills** heaven and earth, in which

Filth (7), Filthiness (1), Filthy (2)
A P : 2 7 :002(269) [0419] age or on account of the **filth** of the prison, he sent for
A P : 2 7 :034(275) [0431] Christ they worship their own cowls and their own **filth**.
L C : 0 1 :129(383) [0619] he would have perished a hundred times in his own **filth**.
L C : 0 1 :198(392) [0637] holiness is only stench and **filth**, and it merits nothing but
L C : 0 1 :217(394) [0643] there may be less of the **filthy**, dissolute, disorderly
L C : 0 1 :281(403) [0661] and root around in the **filth**, nobody will be reformed.
L C : 0 6 :025(460) [0000] just to show what impure and **filthy** people they were.
L C : 0 6 :026(460) [0000] look to see how full of **filthiness** you are, making of you a
S D : 1 1 :042(623) [1077] entangled again in the **filth** of the world, and decorate
S D : 1 1 :083(630) [1091] themselves again in the **filth** of this world (II Pet. 2:20),

Final (5), Finally (50)
P R : P R :011(006) [0011] **Finally** they took to hand the controverted articles,
P R : P R :013(007) [0013] **Finally**, after invoking almighty God to his praise and
P R : P R :017(008) [0015] faith and confession as a **final** explanation of our
P R : P R :018(008) [0015] informed and possess **final** certainty as to which Christian
P R : P R :024(013) [0023] of which is that **finally** correct doctrine will be entirely
A G : P R :023(027) [0043] matters in dissension are **finally** heard, amicably weighed,
A G : 2 7 :034(076) [0079] **Finally**, although the breaking of monastic vows might be
A L : 2 7 :034(076) [0079] **Finally**, although the violation of vows might be rebuked,
A P : P R :007(098) [0101] They **finally** offered the apology to His Imperial Majesty,
A P : 0 4 :008(108) [0121] **Finally**, it requires obedience to God in death and all
A P : 0 4 :036(112) [0131] **Finally**, it was very foolish of our opponents to write that
A P : 0 4 :045(113) [0133] Spirit, so that we can **finally** obey God's law, love him,
A P : 0 4 :285(150) [0201] **Finally**, we would remind our readers that our opponents
A P : 1 2 :007(183) [0255] what is there that will **finally** bring peace to the
A P : 1 2 :053(189) [0265] by the prophets, and **finally** proclaimed and revealed by
A P : 1 2 :088(195) [0277] **Finally**, when will the conscience find peace if we receive
A P : 1 5 :017(217) [0319] **Finally**, what assurance do we have that religious rites
A P : 1 5 :020(218) [0321] in the churches, and **finally** because they helped instruct
A P : 2 0 :014(228) [0343] **Finally** they say that our opinion was condemned a
A P : 2 3 :036(244) [0373] **Finally**, if they interpret celibacy as a purity that merits
A P : 2 3 :060(247) [0381] and full of danger; **finally**, the whole thing is a fraud.
A P : 2 3 :066(248) [0381] **Finally**, since marriage is pure, it is right to say that those
A P : 2 4 :064(261) [0407] **Finally**, they even transfer it to the dead and free souls
A P : 2 7 :021(272) [0427] **Finally**, they belong to the class of which Paul says
A P : 2 7 :032(274) [0431] he has given this, too; **finally**, that by no works can you
A P : 2 7 :057(279) [0439] **Finally**, the canons themselves release many who took
S 2 : 0 4 :013(300) [0475] the lord of the church, and **finally** of the whole world.
S 2 : 0 4 :014(301) [0475] **Finally**, it is most diabolical for the pope to promote his
S 3 : 0 3 :026(307) [0485] **Finally** the popes forced their way into purgatory, first by
S 3 : 0 4 :000(310) [0491] power of the keys; and **finally**, through the mutual
S 3 : 1 5 :004(316) [0501] **Finally**, there remains the pope's bag of magic tricks
T R : 0 0 :002(320) [0503] **Finally**, he declares that it is necessary for salvation to
T R : 0 0 :020(323) [0509] 11. **Finally**, how can the pope be over the whole church
T R : 0 0 :021(323) [0509] Emperor Phocas had **finally** decided that the primacy
T R : 0 0 :040(327) [0517] **Finally**, he defends such horrible errors and such impiety
T R : 0 0 :069(331) [0523] **Finally**, this is confirmed by the declaration of Peter,
T R : 0 0 :079(333) [0527] it alone; and since, **finally**, they observe unjust laws in
S C : P R :021(340) [0537] **Finally**, now that the people are freed from the tyranny of
S C : 0 3 :018(348) [0549] be so tempted, we may **finally** prevail and gain the
L C : 0 1 :188(390) [0635] anyone may be harmed; **finally**, our heart should harbor
L C : 0 2 :031(414) [0687] and devoured death, and **finally** ascended into heaven and
L C : 0 2 :031(414) [0687] lie beneath his feet until **finally**, at the last day, he will
L C : 0 2 :062(419) [0695] world and all evil, he will **finally** make us perfectly and
L C : 0 3 :053(427) [0711] in eternity, it comes through the **final** revelation.
L C : 0 3 :054(427) [0713] or power over us, until **finally** the devil's kingdom shall
L C : 0 4 :064(444) [0749] **Finally**, we must know what Baptism signifies and why
L C : 0 4 :071(445) [0749] the old man daily decreases until he is **finally** destroyed.
L C : 0 5 :026(449) [0759] does not stop until he has **finally** worn us out so that we
E P : 0 0 :000(463) [0775] Pure, Correct, and **Final** Restatement and Explanation of
E P : 0 8 :016(489) [0821] **Finally**, after his resurrection he laid aside completely the
E P : 0 8 :039(492) [0827] Christian faith, we shall **finally** have Christ's eternal deity
S D : 0 2 :021(525) [0889] a thousand dangers and **finally** into eternal death and
S D : 0 7 :033(575) [0983] This is **final**."
S D : 0 8 :040(598) [1029] devil's mask since it will **finally** construct a kind of Christ
S D : 1 1 :022(619) [1069] 8. That, **finally**, he would eternally save and glorify in

Find (59), Finding (2), Finds (4)

PR : PR :022(011) [0019] doubt at all that one can **find** many pious, innocent
AG : 2 0 :015(043) [0055] and terrified consciences **find** it most comforting and
AG : 2 8 :077(094) [0095] It is not our intention to **find** ways of reducing the
AL : 2 0 :015(043) [0055] and anxious consciences **find** by experience that it offers
AL : 2 5 :009(063) [0069] consciences would never **find** peace, for many sins can
AP : 0 4 :020(110) [0125] doubt and then seek to pile up other works to **find** peace.
AP : 0 4 :204(135) [0177] Secondly, they still do not **find** peace of conscience in
AP : 0 4 :204(135) [0177] despair because they cannot **find** works pure enough.
AP : 0 4 :212(136) [0179] in the hope of **finding** some great work that they can set
AP : 0 4 :217(137) [0179] But the conscience cannot **find** peace before God except
AP : 0 4 :224(138) [0181] must be stilled and the conscience **find** peace before him.
AP : 0 4 :236(140) [0185] For themselves they easily **find** forgiveness, but not for
AP : 0 4 :257(144) [0193] Consciences cannot **find** peace unless they hear the voice
AP : 0 4 :320(156) [0209] What work will it **find** that it will count worthy of eternal
AP : 0 4 :389(166) [0225] hope that good men will **find** it useful for strengthening
AP : 1 2 :064(191) [0269] the wrath of God, but it **finds** peace only when it takes
AP : 1 2 :064(191) [0269] dream that the heart can **find** peace without faith in
AP : 1 2 :088(195) [0277] when will the conscience **find** peace if we receive the
AP : 1 5 :033(220) [0325] yet they do not **find** any sure standards by which to free
AP : 2 0 :010(228) [0341] Anyone who looks will **find** many passages in Scripture to
AP : 2 0 :010(228) [0341] a terrified conscience **find** a work that it thought
AP : 2 0 :011(228) [0341] The reader can **find** our proofs in our earlier discussion
AP : 2 1 :044(236) [0357] of our opponents but to **find** other honorable ways of
AP : 2 4 :015(251) [0389] They **find** the term "sacrifice" in either the Scriptures or
AP : 2 4 :083(264) [0413] the Greek authors can **find** examples everywhere of their
AP : 2 7 :027(274) [0429] in the church, **finding** the perfection of the Gospel and of
AP : 2 7 :038(275) [0433] came to the shoemaker to **find** out about his exercises and
AP : 2 7 :043(277) [0435] of a slender inheritance they **find** the most ample riches.
S 1 : PR :013(291) [0459] estates, we would **find** enough time to reform the
S 3 : 0 2 :004(303) [0479] does not know where to **find** it, and begins to be alienated
SC : PR :017(340) [0537] disadvantages, as you will **find** all of this treated at length
LC : SP :005(362) [0575] — indeed, even now we **find** them daily — yet they come
LC : 0 1 :002(365) [0581] all good and in which we **find** refuge in every time of
LC : 0 1 :028(368) [0587] thoroughly and you will **find** whether or not it clings to
LC : 0 1 :043(370) [0591] You will **find** that they have wasted their effort and toil
LC : 0 1 :044(370) [0593] Examples of this you will **find** aplenty in all histories and
LC : 0 1 :245(398) [0649] Otherwise, where would we **find** enough gallows and
LC : 0 1 :252(399) [0651] good works will here **find** ample opportunity to do things
LC : 0 1 :253(399) [0653] not desire this blessing will **find** wrath and misfortune
LC : 0 1 :258(399) [0653] sit in judgment, we always **find** that, true to the usual
LC : 0 1 :288(404) [0663] and infirmities we **find** in our neighbor, doing our utmost
LC : 0 1 :315(408) [0671] desperate saints to dare to **find** a higher and better way of
LC : 0 1 :318(408) [0673] best, and you will surely **find** so much to do that you will
LC : 0 1 :332(410) [0677] his neighbors, he will **find** occasion enough to practice the
LC : 0 2 :035(415) [0687] it is so precise that we can **find** no substitute for it.
LC : 0 3 :090(432) [0723] He will **find** that he is no better than others, that in the
LC : 0 3 :111(435) [0729] has a serpent's head; if it **finds** an opening into which it
LC : 0 5 :053(453) [0765] and as everyone will **find** in his own case, that if a person
LC : 0 5 :055(453) [0767] pure that God might not **find** the least blemish in us.
LC : 0 5 :075(455) [0771] If you **find** that you are, then for your own good turn to
LC : 0 6 :013(458) [0000] settle it, and yet we do not **find** ourselves sufficiently
EP : 1 1 :016(497) [0837] Christians can **find** no comfort in this doctrine but are
SD : RN :016(507) [0857] truth of God's Word will **find** in the previously mentioned
SD : 0 2 :012(522) [0885] "My Word **finds** no place in you" (John 8:37).
SD : 0 2 :015(523) [0887] We **find** similar prayers in St. Paul's letters (Eph. 1:17,
SD : 0 4 :019(554) [0945] other that in his flesh he **finds** another law which is not
SD : 0 5 :003(558) [0953] on this controversy, we **find** that it was chiefly occasioned
SD : 0 5 :027(563) [0961] teaching, a usage that we **find** occasionally in the Apology
SD : 0 7 :045(577) [0987] words, no matter how appealing our reason may **find** it.
SD : 0 8 :030(597) [1025] the angels marvel at it and **find** their delight and joy in
SD : 0 8 :096(610) [1049] way they will be certain to **find** abiding comfort in all
SD : 1 0 :021(614) [1059] with their own hands, we **find** the following statement:
SD : 1 1 :060(626) [1083] ourselves with them and **find** ourselves in the same
SD : 1 1 :070(627) [1085] sin to come to him and **find** refreshment and be saved.
SD : 1 1 :091(631) [1093] sorrowing Christians can **find** no comfort in it but are

Fine (9)

AP : 0 4 :131(125) [0157] But our opponents are **fine** theologians!
AP : 2 3 :067(248) [0383] **Fine** talk!
SC : PR :003(338) [0533] they have mastered the **fine** art of abusing liberty.
LC : PR :003(358) [0567] Seven Hours, it would be **fine** if every morning, noon,
LC : 0 1 :138(384) [0621] where there are **fine** old families who prosper and have
LC : 0 1 :276(402) [0659] Here you have a **fine**, precious precept for governing the
LC : 0 1 :289(404) [0663] It is a particularly **fine**, noble virtue always to put the
LC : 0 1 :298(405) [0665] We know how to put up a **fine** front to conceal our
SD : 0 4 :033(556) [0947] The Apology offers a **fine** example as to when and how,

Finger (3), Fingers (2)

LC : 0 1 :067(373) [0599] oath will slip through his **fingers** and will never be
LC : 0 5 :012(448) [0755] wisdom than the divine Majesty has in his little **finger**.
SD : 0 7 :022(573) [0979] wisdom than the divine Majesty has in his little **finger**.
SD : 1 1 :046(624) [1079] easily slip from our **fingers**, and through the deceit and
SD : 1 1 :063(626) [1083] must with Paul place our **finger** to our lips and say, "Who

Finish (2), Finished (3)

LC : PR :016(361) [0573] fellows, to think we can **finish** learning in one hour what
LC : PR :016(361) [0573] in one hour what God himself cannot **finish** teaching!
LC : 0 2 :038(415) [0689] The work is **finished** and completed, Christ has acquired
LC : 0 2 :062(419) [0695] when his work has been **finished** and we abide in it,
LC : 0 4 :001(436) [0733] We have now **finished** with the three chief parts of our

Finite (3)

EP : 0 8 :008(487) [0819] be flesh and blood, to be **finite** and circumscribed, to
SD : 0 8 :010(593) [1019] be flesh and blood, to be **finite** and circumscribed, to
SD : 0 8 :052(601) [1033] are created gifts or **finite** qualities, as in the saints, and on

Fire (18)

AG : 2 3 :025(055) [0065] marry than to fall into the **fire** through their lusts, and
AL : 2 3 :025(055) [0065] marry than to fall into the **fire** through their lusts; at least
AP : 0 4 :329(158) [0211] Deut. 4:24, "Your God is a devouring **fire**."
LC : 0 1 :011(366) [0583] St. Apollonia; if he feared **fire**, he sought St. Lawrence as
LC : 0 1 :060(372) [0597] plague, war, famine, **fire**, flood, wayward wives and
LC : 0 1 :192(391) [0635] deep water, or fallen into a **fire**, and could extend him my
LC : 0 2 :014(412) [0681] day and night, air, **fire**, water, the earth and all that it
LC : 0 3 :078(431) [0721] from tempest, hail, **fire**, and flood; from poison,
SD : 0 1 :039(515) [0871] and sinful dough into hell-**fire**, but out of it he makes and
SD : 0 4 :012(553) [0941] from faith as it is to separate heat and light from **fire**."
SD : 0 5 :020(561) [0959] to temporal miseries, and to the punishment of hell-**fire**.
SD : 0 8 :019(594) [1021] body and soul, as well as **fire** and iron, have a
SD : 0 8 :064(603) [1039] soul does in the body and **fire** in glowing iron, analogies
SD : 0 8 :066(604) [1039] is the property of **fire** — but since the fire is united with
SD : 0 8 :066(604) [1039] of fire — but since the **fire** is united with the iron, it
SD : 0 8 :066(604) [1039] of the natural properties of either the **fire** or the iron.
SD : 0 8 :087(608) [1047] sinners is like a consuming **fire** on dry stubble, will be
SD : 1 1 :085(631) [1091] judgment on him, for he was indeed guilty of "hell-**fire**."

Firm (24), Firmer (1), Firmly (19)

PR : PR :000(001) [0004] Appended Declaration, **Firmly** Founded on the Word of
AG : 0 0 :002(048) [0059] although we hope to offer **firm** grounds and reasons why
AP : 0 1 :002(100) [0103] Holy Scriptures testify to it **firmly**, surely, and irrefutably.
AP : 0 4 :048(114) [0135] knowledge, but the **firm** acceptance of God's offer
AP : 0 4 :050(114) [0135] knowledge but is a **firm** acceptance of the promise
AP : 0 4 :079(118) [0143] we comfort ourselves by **firm** trust in the mercy promised
AP : 0 4 :085(119) [0147] they have a certain and **firm** consolation against the
AP : 0 4 :118(123) [0155] alone provides a sure and **firm** consolation for devout
AP : 0 4 :156(128) [0165] and the source of sure and **firm** consolation for pious
AP : 0 4 :165(129) [0169] weakness, and we must **firmly** believe that we are
AP : 0 4 :179(131) [0171] Christ's sake we have a **firm** and sure reconciliation
AP : 0 4 :276(148) [0199] minds to believe more **firmly** that their sins are forgiven.
AP : 0 4 :276(148) [0199] in good works, which thus urge us to believe more **firmly**.
AP : 0 4 :350(160) [0217] to grow and become **firmer** amid good works as well as
AP : 0 4 :384(166) [0225] of faith obtains eternal life, a faith that is **firm** and active.
AP : 0 4 :385(166) [0225] No faith is **firm** that does not show itself in confession.
AP : 1 0 :001(179) [0247] and consideration of it, we **firmly** defend this belief.
AP : 1 1 :002(180) [0249] the absolution and **firmly** believe that the forgiveness of
AP : 1 1 :002(180) [0249] it discloses a sure and **firm** consolation for the
AP : 1 2 :084(194) [0277] devout consciences a **firm** consolation without which no
AP : 1 2 :095(196) [0281] this faith must believe **firmly** that God freely forgives us
AP : 1 3 :004(211) [0309] our hearts should **firmly** believe that God really forgives
AP : 2 3 :013(241) [0367] This is so clear and **firm** as to be irrefutable.
AP : 2 4 :012(251) [0387] This is so **firm** and sure that it can prevail against all the
S 3 : 0 8 :003(312) [0495] Word, we must hold **firmly** to the conviction that God
S 3 : 1 5 :005(317) [0501] and am still preaching and **firmly** believing as above.
TR : 0 0 :044(328) [0517] deprive consciences of a **firm** consolation, and abolish
SC : 0 5 :016(349) [0553] no means doubting but **firmly** believing that our sins are
LC : 0 3 :060(428) [0715] as great need that we keep **firm** hold of these two things
LC : 0 3 :087(432) [0723] possible always to stand **firm** in such a ceaseless conflict.
LC : 0 3 :109(435) [0729] chaste, patient, kind, and **firm** in faith, the devil is likely
LC : 0 4 :040(441) [0743] is lacking is that it should be grasped and held **firmly**.
LC : 0 4 :041(441) [0743] enough to do to believe **firmly** what Baptism promises
LC : 0 5 :063(454) [0767] that it may rest and rely **firmly** upon itself; otherwise it
EP : 0 8 :039(491) [0827] refute these errors on the **firm** basis of the divine Word
EP : 1 1 :005(495) [0833] Our salvation is so **firmly** established upon it that the
SD : 0 4 :002(551) [0939] to retain for believers the **firm** and certain promise of
SD : 0 4 :030(555) [0947] we hold our first confidence **firm** to the end" (Heb. 3:14).
SD : 0 7 :042(576) [0985] above rests on a unique, **firm**, immovable, and
SD : 0 7 :091(585) [1005] *Is My Body" Still Stand Firm*, his *Great* and *Small*
SD : 0 8 :086(608) [1047] *These Words Still Stand Firm* and in his *Great Confession*
SD : 1 1 :028(620) [1071] means cling rigidly and **firmly** to the fact that as the
SD : 1 1 :038(622) [1075] this absolution and **firmly** hold that when we believe the
SD : 1 1 :046(624) [1079] to insure my salvation so **firmly** and certainly — for due

First (262)

PR : PR :011(006) [0011] At **first** the said theologians clearly and correctly
PR : PR :016(008) [0013] and conformable **first** of all to the Word of God and then
PR : PR :019(009) [0017] sense than that of the **first** Augsburg Confession as it was
PR : PR :023(012) [0021] our churches and schools **first** of all to the Holy
AG : PR :005(025) [0039] without boasting that we were among the **first** to arrive.
AG : 2 4 :026(058) [0067] They were taught, **first** of all, that the Scriptures show in
AG : 2 6 :004(064) [0071] In the **first** place, the grace of Christ and the teaching
AG : 2 7 :027(075) [0079] vows must be kept without **first** ascertaining whether a
AG : 2 8 :070(093) [0093] to the ministry unless he **first** swears an oath that he will
AL : 2 0 :036(046) [0057] do the works of the **First** or Second Commandments.
AL : 0 0 :003(049) [0059] minds of good men, they **first** gave occasion to this
AL : 2 3 :004(051) [0061] In the **first** place, this was done because Paul says,
AL : 2 3 :025(055) [0065] His words in the **first** book of his letters, Epistle XI, are
AL : 2 4 :006(056) [0065] are admitted unless they are **first** heard and examined.
AL : 2 6 :004(064) [0071] In the **first** place, it has obscured the doctrine concerning
AL : 2 7 :018(073) [0077] In the **first** place, we teach concerning those who contract
AP : 0 2 :002(100) [0105] not absurd, we ask them **first** to look at the German text
AP : 0 2 :004(101) [0105] **First** we must show why we used these words here.
AP : 0 2 :014(102) [0109] transgressing as they do the **first** table of the Decalogue.
AP : 0 2 :016(102) [0109] Decalogue, but also the **first**, commanding fear of God,
AP : 0 4 :017(109) [0125] They bid us merit this **first** disposition by our preceding
AP : 0 4 :034(112) [0129] they do not see the **first** table, which commands us to love
AP : 0 4 :035(112) [0131] So it does not obey the **first** table.
AP : 0 4 :036(112) [0131] love God unless faith has **first** accepted the forgiveness of
AP : 0 4 :061(115) [0137] **First** of all, lest anyone think that we are speaking of an
AP : 0 4 :069(116) [0141] In the **first** place, we would remind our readers that if we
AP : 0 4 :070(116) [0141] keep the law unless we **first** receive the Holy Spirit.
AP : 0 4 :072(117) [0141] Therefore we want to show **first** that faith alone makes a
AP : 0 4 :076(117) [0143] **First**, forgiveness of sins is the same as justification
AP : 0 4 :100(121) [0151] Here the writer says **first** that men are righteous by the
AP : 0 4 :126(124) [0157] **First**, it is impossible to keep the law without Christ; it is
AP : 0 4 :131(125) [0157] political works; about the **first** table they care nothing, as
AP : 0 4 :141(126) [0161] So John teaches in his **first** epistle (4:19); "We love," he
AP : 0 4 :141(126) [0161] love," he says, "because he **first** loved us," that is, because
AP : 0 4 :145(127) [0163] do not teach that we must **first** receive the forgiveness of
AP : 0 4 :147(127) [0163] To this we must answer, **first** of all, that we do not receive
AP : 0 4 :162(129) [0169] This is so because, **first** of all, Christ does not stop being
AP : 0 4 :204(135) [0177] **First**, it obscures the glory of Christ when men offer these
AP : 0 4 :227(138) [0183] But as even the **first** and greatest law does not justify,
AP : 0 4 :231(139) [0183] to the works of the Second Table rather than the **First**.
AP : 0 4 :245(142) [0189] **First**, we must note that this text is more against our
AP : 0 4 :247(142) [0191] that we should be a kind of **first** fruits of his creatures."

Continued ▶

Continued ▶

SD : 07 :087(585) [1003] abuses that this rule was **first** formulated and explained
SD : 07 :094(586) [1005] "1. The **first** is this article of our faith: that Jesus Christ is
SD : 07 :103(587) [1007] they concede only the **first**, comprehensible mode of
SD : 07 :108(588) [1009] **First**, papistic transubstantiation, when they teach that
SD : 08 :001(591) [1015] It did not at **first** begin among them, however, but
SD : 08 :036(598) [1027] In the **first** place, since in Christ two distinct natures are
SD : 08 :057(602) [1035] 1. In the **first** place, it is a unanimously accepted rule of
SD : 08 :081(607) [1045] of course, according to the **first**, corporeal,
SD : 11 :027(620) [1071] whom he sent out, some at **first**, some at the second, at
SD : 11 :033(621) [1073] Concern yourself **first** with Christ and his Gospel so that
SD : 11 :033(622) [1073] sin as Paul teaches from the **first** to the eighth chapter.
SD : 11 :042(623) [1077] will be worse than the **first** (II Pet. 2:10; Luke 11:24, 25;
SD : 11 :083(630) [1091] will involves both items: **First**, that he would receive into
SD : 12 :029(635) [1101] 1. In the **first** place, that no one has a true knowledge of

Fish (5)
AP : 07 :001(168) [0227] in which there are both good and bad **fish** (Matt. 13:47).
AP : 23 :045(245) [0375] thus surpassing the Dominican friars, who eat **fish**.
LC : 02 :014(412) [0681] it brings forth, birds and **fish**, beasts, grain and all kinds
SD : 11 :072(628) [1087] you, if his son asks for a **fish**, will instead of a fish give
SD : 11 :072(628) [1087] for a fish, will instead of a **fish** give him a serpent; or if he

Fit (12), Fits (2), Fitted (4), Fitting (7), Fittingly (1)
AG : 23 :023(055) [0063] These two statements **fit** together well, for it must be a
AG : 25 :006(062) [0069] repentance in a more **fitting** fashion than had been done
AG : 27 :020(074) [0079] man should be alone; I will make him a helper **fit** for him
AL : 24 :005(056) [0065] the sacrament together, in so far as they are **fit** to do so.
AL : 26 :038(069) [0075] his body in subjection and **fit** for spiritual things and for
AP : 04 :087(120) [0147] ability that the Lord saw **fit** to grant us, we conclude that
AP : 04 :235(140) [0185] perfect or whole when all its parts **fit** together properly."
AP : 04 :236(140) [0185] All this does not **fit** very well with their praises of love; if
AP : 04 :286(150) [0201] maliciously twist the Scriptures to **fit** their own opinions.
AP : 12 :118(199) [0287] and yet, because it is **fitting** for divine righteousness to
AP : 12 :156(207) [0301] where the particular punishment **fits** the particular crime.
AP : 24 :051(259) [0403] ornaments like that are **fitting**, but they are not the
AP : 27 :011(270) [0423] Thus it was **fitting** for us to quote Paul's statement from
S2 : 02 :008(294) [0465] he can do so most **fittingly** and properly in the sacrament
S2 : 04 :008(300) [0473] God would raise up a man **fitted** for such an office.
LC : 01 :117(381) [0615] that he has chosen and **fitted** you to perform a task so
LC : 01 :232(396) [0647] though it might be more **fitting** if the judge, the jailer, or
LC : 03 :075(430) [0719] It would therefore be **fitting** if the coat-of-arms of every
LC : 04 :018(438) [0737] *"Accedat verbum ad elementum et **fit** sacramentum."*
LC : 05 :010(448) [0755] *verbum ad elementum et **fit** sacramentum,"* that is, "When
LC : 05 :058(453) [0767] stay away, for they are not **fit** to receive the forgiveness
EP : 08 :036(491) [0825] not know more than is **fitting** and necessary to perform
SD : 03 :046(548) [0933] make himself worthy and **fit** to have the merit of Christ
SD : 11 :079(629) [1089] the vessels of wrath **fitted** for damnation in order to make
SD : 11 :080(629) [1089] not God, are the cause of their being **fitted** for damnation
SD : 11 :081(629) [1089] which prepares and **fits** man for damnation emanates

Five (5)
S2 : 04 :004(299) [0473] a pope for more that **five** hundred years at the least and
S3 : 03 :021(306) [0485] easy to render, like saying **five** Our Fathers, fasting for a
LC : SP :024(364) [0579] Thus we have, in all, **five** parts covering the whole of
SD : RN :019(507) [0857] within the past twenty-**five** years a number of divisions
SD : 09 :003(610) [1051] With our reason and **five** senses this article cannot be

Fix (5), Fixed (9), Fixes (1)
AP : 07 :050(178) [0245] as this universe and the **fixed** movements of the stars are
AP : 12 :142(204) [0295] to our weakness God has **fixed** a certain limit which man
AP : 12 :143(204) [0297] The same holds when a **fixed** number of prayers or
AP : 15 :028(219) [0323] these precepts and cannot **fix** the mitigation in any
S2 : 04 :008(300) [0473] in Rome or some other **fixed** place, but it could be
SC : PR :007(339) [0533] instructed on the basis of a uniform, **fixed** text and form.
SC : PR :009(339) [0535] the young, adhere to a **fixed** and unchanging form and
SC : PR :014(339) [0535] any other brief and **fixed** explanations which you may
LC : SP :027(364) [0581] into their minds and remain **fixed** in their memories.
LC : 01 :006(365) [0583] and possessions — on which he **fixes** his whole heart.
LC : 01 :012(366) [0583] All these **fix** their heart and trust elsewhere than in the
LC : 01 :040(370) [0591] to move and impel us to **fix** our hearts upon God with
LC : 01 :248(398) [0651] but may keep their eyes **fixed** upon God's
LC : 05 :057(453) [0767] If you choose to **fix** your eye on how good and pure you
SD : 08 :052(601) [1033] to determine and to **fix** the limit of what the human

Flagrant (1)
AG : 23 :001(051) [0061] world concerning the **flagrant** immorality and the

Flames (1)
LC : 03 :063(428) [0715] fanning and feeding the **flames**, in order to hinder us, put

Flaming (4)
AP : 23 :016(241) [0369] and commands it because of these **flaming** passions.
LC : PR :014(360) [0571] "armor" against their "**flaming** darts," and with a good
LC : 03 :104(434) [0727] they are the real "**flaming** darts" which are venomously
EP : 11 :013(496) [0835] and thus extinguish the **flaming** darts of the devil.

Flatter (1), Flatters (1)
AP : 04 :010(108) [0123] this view naturally **flatters** men, it has produced and
AP : 04 :322(157) [0209] "Lest anybody should **flatter** himself that he is innocent

Flaws (1)
AP : 02 :014(102) [0109] These are the chief **flaws** in human nature, transgressing

Flee (13), Fled (1), Fleeing (4), Flees (10)
AG : 27 :057(080) [0083] This, they said, is **fleeing** from the world and seeking a
AL : 27 :057(080) [0083] They called this "**fleeing** from the world" and "seeking a
AP : 02 :008(101) [0107] hating his judgment and **fleeing** it, being angry at him,
AP : 04 :008(108) [0121] all afflictions, yet we try to **flee** these things or turn away
AP : 04 :034(112) [0131] the midst of punishment it **flees** and hates his judgment.
AP : 04 :038(112) [0131] terrified by the law **flees** before God's judgment.
AP : 04 :106(122) [0153] this fear, the soul by faith **flees** to the mercy of God, that
AP : 04 :144(127) [0161] for a heart terrified and **fleeing** from sin, therefore, such a
AP : 04 :176(131) [0171] As long as we **flee** God's judgment and are angry at him,
AP : 04 :204(135) [0177] God, for in their anger they **flee** his judgment and never
AP : 04 :270(147) [0197] the law and therefore **flees** in terror before the judgment
AP : 04 :304(154) [0205] turmoil in the will as it **flees** God's judgment; just so faith
AP : 04 :312(155) [0207] against us, human nature **flees** his wrath and judgment.
AP : 12 :032(186) [0259] sinned; at the same time it **flees** God's horrible wrath, for
AP : 12 :046(188) [0263] consolation truly sustaining a life that **flees** in contrition.
AP : 21 :015(231) [0347] mercy of Christ and they **flee** from Christ and turn to the
S1 : PR :003(289) [0455] of a free council and **flees** from the light in a shameful
S1 : PR :003(289) [0455] who shun the light and **flee** from the day take such
TR : 00 :058(330) [0521] of God that we should **flee** from idolatry, impious
LC : 01 :028(368) [0587] from God, and does it **flee** not to him but from him when
LC : 01 :197(392) [0637] This is why they **fled** to the monasteries, so that they
LC : 03 :010(421) [0699] wicked that it always **flees** from God, thinking that he
LC : 05 :068(454) [0769] from which we should **flee**, but as a pure, wholesome,
EP : 12 :011(499) [0841] for them in any way, but **flee** and avoid them as
SD : RN :014(506) [0855] wolves so that they will **flee** from strange voices and
SD : RN :016(507) [0857] and what he should reject, **flee**, and avoid as false and
SD : 11 :093(632) [1095] will, we shall avoid and **flee** all abstruse and specious
SD : 12 :016(634) [1099] them at all, but one is to **flee** and avoid them as people

Fleece (1), Fleeces (1), Fleecing (1)
LC : 01 :227(396) [0645] a trade and deliberately **fleeces**, skins, and torments him.
LC : 01 :238(397) [0647] let them keep on boldly **fleecing** people as long as they
LC : 01 :241(397) [0649] stand by and let such persons **fleece**, grab, and hoard.

Fleet (1)
AP : 24 :081(264) [0411] duties," like the taxes collected for equipping a **fleet**.

Fleisch (1)
LC : 02 :060(418) [0695] Germans hear the word ***Fleisch*** (flesh), we think no

Flesh (179)
AL : 26 :030(068) [0075] Jovinian, forbid discipline and mortification of the **flesh**.
AP : 02 :003(101) [0105] are born according to the **flesh** we deny the existence not
AP : 02 :029(104) [0113] original sin is ignorance in the mind and lust in the **flesh**.
AP : 02 :036(105) [0115] spiritual regeneration, but it remains in the mortal **flesh**.
AP : 04 :032(111) [0129] mind that is set on the **flesh** is hostile to God; it does not
AP : 04 :032(111) [0129] and those who are in the **flesh** cannot please God."
AP : 04 :033(111) [0129] the mind that is set on the **flesh** is hostile to God, then the
AP : 04 :033(111) [0129] is hostile to God, then the **flesh** sins even when it
AP : 04 :094(120) [0149] nor of the will of the **flesh** nor of the will of man, but of
AP : 04 :135(125) [0159] we recognize how our **flesh** in its smugness and
AP : 04 :143(126) [0161] who live according to the **flesh**, who take pleasure in their
AP : 04 :143(126) [0161] not walk according to the **flesh**, but according to the
AP : 04 :143(126) [0161] are debtors, not to the **flesh**, to live according to the
AP : 04 :143(126) [0161] to live according to the **flesh**—for if you live according to
AP : 04 :143(126) [0161] you live according to the **flesh** you will die, but if by the
AP : 04 :168(130) [0169] with my mind, but with my **flesh** I serve the law of sin."
AP : 04 :169(130) [0169] that evil desires in the **flesh** are sins, about which Paul
AP : 04 :169(130) [0169] "The desires of the **flesh** are against the Spirit, and
AP : 04 :169(130) [0169] Spirit, and the desires of the Spirit are against the **flesh**."
AP : 04 :170(130) [0169] The **flesh** distrusts God and trusts in temporal things; in
AP : 04 :179(131) [0171] through faith, though sin still sticks to your **flesh**."
AP : 04 :189(133) [0175] They take place in a **flesh** that is partly unregenerate and
AP : 04 :193(133) [0175] the mortification of the **flesh** would be to disparage the
AP : 04 :296(152) [0205] In the **flesh** we never satisfy the law.
AP : 04 :319(156) [0209] The **flesh** always lusts against the Spirit (Gal. 5:17).
AP : 04 :329(158) [0211] Zech. 2:13 says, "Be silent, all **flesh**, before the Lord."
AP : 04 :329(158) [0211] Isa. 40:6, 7, "All **flesh** is grass, and all its beauty is like the
AP : 04 :329(158) [0211] blows upon it"; that is, the **flesh** and the righteousness of
AP : 04 :329(158) [0211] the righteousness of the **flesh** cannot stand the judgment
AP : 04 :348(160) [0217] who walk according to the **flesh** can retain neither faith
AP : 07 :014(170) [0231] born according to the **flesh** had promises about physical
AP : 10 :002(179) [0247] is not merely a figure but is truly changed into **flesh**."
AP : 10 :003(179) [0247] with him according to the **flesh**, and we say that this
AP : 10 :003(179) [0247] bodily through the communication of the **flesh** of Christ?"
AP : 12 :046(188) [0263] hands, by putting off the body of the sins of the **flesh**."
AP : 12 :131(202) [0291] where mortifying the **flesh** and good fruits do not follow.
AP : 12 :131(202) [0291] does not produce outwardly the punishing of the **flesh**.
AP : 12 :143(204) [0297] not to control the **flesh** but, as Scotus says, to pay
AP : 12 :152(206) [0299] because of the sin still present and remaining in the **flesh**.
AP : 12 :153(206) [0299] to destroy this sinful **flesh** so that we may rise completely
AP : 12 :168(209) [0305] and restraining the **flesh**, not to pay for eternal
AP : 12 :168(209) [0305] punishments but to keep the **flesh** from alluring us to sin."
AP : 12 :174(210) [0307] and chastisement of the **flesh** instead of adultery and
AP : 15 :024(218) [0321] purpose is to restrain the **flesh**, reason imagines that they
AP : 15 :045(221) [0327] and the discipline of the **flesh** we teach exactly what we
AP : 15 :047(221) [0327] but as restraints on our **flesh**, lest we be overcome by
AP : 15 :047(221) [0327] that we indulge and pamper the desires of our **flesh**.
AP : 15 :048(221) [0329] seasons contributes nothing to the subjection of the **flesh**.
AP : 18 :004(225) [0335] Holy Spirit, Scripture calls the righteousness of the **flesh**.
AP : 22 :010(237) [0361] they believe that Christ's **flesh**, given for the life of the
AP : 23 :070(249) [0383] as Isaiah says (40:6), "All **flesh** is grass, and all its beauty
AP : 24 :029(255) [0393] victims and requires prayer: "Do I eat the **flesh** of bulls?
AP : 24 :034(256) [0397] which should kill this old **flesh** and begin a new and
S3 : 03 :040(309) [0489] life it contends with the sins that remain in the **flesh**.
S3 : 07 :001(311) [0493] (Rom. 7:23) that in his **flesh** he was captive to "the law of
S3 : 08 :002(312) [0495] As long as we are in the **flesh** we shall not be untruthful if
S3 : 13 :001(315) [0499] Although the sin in our **flesh** has not been completely
SC : PR :023(341) [0537] that he has no sin, no **flesh**, no devil, no world, no death,
SC : 03 :011(347) [0547] of the world, and of our **flesh** which would hinder us from
SC : 03 :018(347) [0549] devil, the world, and our **flesh** may not deceive us or
LC : PR :010(359) [0569] the devil, the world, the **flesh**, and all evil thoughts as to
LC : 01 :200(392) [0637] namely, his wife, who is one **flesh** and blood with him.
LC : 01 :212(393) [0641] outside of marriage; for **flesh** and blood remain flesh and
LC : 01 :212(393) [0641] flesh and blood remain **flesh** and blood, and the natural
LC : 02 :054(418) [0693] are encumbered with our **flesh** we are never without sin.
LC : 02 :057(418) [0693] await the time when our **flesh** will be put to death, will be
LC : 02 :060(418) [0695] term "resurrection of the **flesh**," however, is not well
LC : 02 :060(418) [0695] hear the word *Fleisch* (**flesh**), we think no farther than the
LC : 03 :002(420) [0697] with the world and our **flesh**, resists our efforts with all
LC : 03 :062(428) [0715] even enlisting the world and our own **flesh** as his allies.
LC : 03 :063(428) [0715] For our **flesh** is in itself vile and inclined to evil, even

Continued ▶

L C : 0 3 :066(429) [0717] Now, this grieves our **flesh** and the old Adam, for it
L C : 0 3 :067(429) [0717] so that our poor **flesh** may not yield or fall away through
L C : 0 3 :089(432) [0723] For the **flesh** in which we daily live is of such a nature
L C : 0 3 :101(433) [0727] is of three kinds: of the **flesh**, the world, and the devil.
L C : 0 3 :102(434) [0727] We live in the **flesh** and we have the old Adam hanging
L C : 0 3 :104(434) [0727] into our hearts, not by **flesh** and blood but by the devil.
L C : 0 3 :106(434) [0727] as long as we live in the **flesh** and have the devil prowling
L C : 0 3 :107(434) [0729] are tempted chiefly by the **flesh**; older people are tempted
L C : 0 4 :020(439) [0737] noses, eyes, skin and hair, **flesh** and bones, they look no
L C : 0 4 :020(439) [0737] and why I should honor this particular **flesh** and blood.
L C : 0 4 :038(441) [0741] refers only to human **flesh** and blood, yet we look not at
L C : 0 4 :038(441) [0741] yet we look not at the **flesh** and blood but at God's
L C : 0 4 :038(441) [0741] on account of which this **flesh** is called father and
L C : 0 5 :023(449) [0757] born anew, our human **flesh** and blood have not lost their
L C : 0 5 :060(453) [0767] retain many common infirmities in his **flesh** and blood.
L C : 0 5 :071(455) [0769] fear of death, and the assaults of the **flesh** and the devil.
L C : 0 5 :075(455) [0771] bosom and ask whether they are made of **flesh** and blood.
L C : 0 5 :075(455) [0771] what are the fruits of the **flesh**: "The works of the flesh
L C : 0 5 :075(455) [0771] flesh: "The works of the **flesh** are plain: adultery,
L C : 0 5 :076(455) [0771] you, and they know your **flesh** better than you yourself
L C : 0 5 :076(455) [0771] that nothing good dwells within me, that is, in my **flesh**."
L C : 0 5 :076(455) [0771] Paul can speak thus of his **flesh**, let us not pretend to be
L C : 0 5 :077(455) [0771] sign that ours is a leprous **flesh** which feels nothing
L C : 0 5 :080(456) [0771] Besides the **flesh** and the world, you will surely have the
L C : 0 5 :082(456) [0773] believe that we are in the **flesh**, in this wicked world, or
E P : 0 1 :003(466) [0779] sanctification, and the resurrection of our **flesh**.
E P : 0 1 :005(466) [0781] took on himself not alien **flesh**, but our own, and
E P : 0 1 :005(466) [0781] own, and according to our **flesh** has truly become our
E P : 0 1 :005(466) [0781] the children share in **flesh** and blood, he himself likewise
E P : 0 1 :010(467) [0781] by this my skin, and in my **flesh** I shall see God; him I
E P : 0 2 :001(469) [0785] after regeneration, (4) after the resurrection of the **flesh**.
E P : 0 2 :003(470) [0787] mind that is set on the **flesh** is hostile to God; it does not
E P : 0 6 :001(479) [0805] reborn, and although the **flesh** still inheres in them, to
E P : 0 6 :004(480) [0805] constant war against their **flesh** (that is, their corrupt
E P : 0 6 :007(481) [0807] according to the **flesh** — does what is demanded of him
E P : 0 7 :042(486) [0817] though one rent Christ's **flesh** with one's teeth and
E P : 0 8 :008(487) [0819] a corporeal creature, to be **flesh** and blood, to be finite
E P : 1 2 :020(499) [0841] Christ according to the **flesh** is a creature do not have a
E P : 1 2 :021(499) [0841] Christ's glorification his **flesh** received all the divine
E P : 1 2 :021(499) [0841] and glory and that the **flesh** of Christ belongs to the
S D : 0 1 :035(514) [0869] clothe me with skin and **flesh**, and knit me together with
S D : 0 1 :046(516) [0873] the substance of this our **flesh**, but without sin, shall
S D : 0 1 :047(516) [0875] faith, either that our **flesh** would not rise on Judgment
S D : 0 2 :013(523) [0885] the mind that is set on the **flesh** (the natural man's
S D : 0 2 :017(524) [0887] mind that is set on the **flesh** is hostile to God"
S D : 0 2 :017(524) [0887] again, "The desires of the **flesh** are against the Spirit, and
S D : 0 2 :017(524) [0887] within me, that is, in my **flesh**, for I delight in the law of
S D : 0 2 :026(526) [0891] a new and tender heart of **flesh** that we may walk in his
S D : 0 2 :034(528) [0895] the sin remaining in the **flesh** throughout life, as St. Paul
S D : 0 2 :064(533) [0907] my mind, but with my **flesh** the law of sin" (Rom. 7:22,
S D : 0 2 :064(533) [0907] "For the desires of the **flesh** are against the Spirit, and the
S D : 0 2 :064(533) [0907] the Spirit are against the **flesh**; for these are opposed to
S D : 0 2 :068(534) [0907] and warfare of the **flesh** against the Spirit continues also
S D : 0 2 :070(535) [0909] and diligence, and to fight against the **flesh**, etc.
S D : 0 2 :084(537) [0913] say that the desires of the **flesh** are against the Spirit, and
S D : 0 2 :084(537) [0913] that the passions of the **flesh** wage war against the soul,
S D : 0 2 :085(537) [0913] law of God, but with his **flesh** he serves the law of sin
S D : 0 2 :087(538) [0915] bodily resurrection of the **flesh** is to be ascribed to God
S D : 0 3 :023(543) [0923] sin still dwells in the **flesh** even in the case of the
S D : 0 3 :028(544) [0925] wholly pure and perfect on account of our corrupted **flesh**
S D : 0 3 :032(545) [0927] this life on account of the **flesh**, no one can therewith and
S D : 0 4 :008(552) [0941] they are still impure and imperfect in this **flesh** of ours.
S D : 0 4 :019(554) [0945] on the other that in his **flesh** he finds another law which
S D : 0 4 :019(554) [0945] unwilling and recalcitrant **flesh**, Paul says, "I pommel my
S D : 0 4 :019(554) [0945] (that is, killed) their **flesh** with its passions, desires, and
S D : 0 4 :032(556) [0947] you live according to the **flesh** you will die" (Rom. 8:13).
S D : 0 6 :008(565) [0965] "The desires of the **flesh** are against the spirit and the
S D : 0 6 :008(565) [0965] the spirit are against the **flesh**, for these are opposed to
S D : 0 6 :009(565) [0965] of the desires of the **flesh** the truly believing, elect, and
S D : 0 6 :012(566) [0967] and when because of the **flesh** they are lazy, negligent, and
S D : 0 6 :018(567) [0967] the conflict between spirit and **flesh** continues in them.
S D : 0 6 :022(567) [0969] still imperfect and impure because of the sin in our **flesh**.
S D : 0 6 :024(568) [0971] and miseries, until the **flesh** of sin is put off entirely and
S D : 0 7 :011(571) [0975] the Supper through the communication of his **flesh** in us.
S D : 0 7 :036(575) [0985] "The Word became **flesh**," with such equivalent phrases
S D : 0 7 :039(576) [0985] sake of our salvation had **flesh** and blood, so the food
S D : 0 7 :039(576) [0985] and prayer is the true **flesh** and blood of the Lord Jesus
S D : 0 7 :061(580) [0995] There is therefore a twofold eating of the **flesh** of Christ.
S D : 0 8 :006(592) [1017] race, according to the **flesh**, is the Christ, who is God
S D : 0 8 :010(593) [1019] being or a creature, to be **flesh** and blood, to be finite and
S D : 0 8 :011(593) [1019] of God who has assumed **flesh** and has become man, is
S D : 0 8 :033(597) [1027] religion: God was manifested in the **flesh**" (I Tim. 3:16).
S D : 0 8 :037(598) [1027] David according to the **flesh**" (Rom. 1:3), and "Christ was
S D : 0 8 :037(598) [1027] was put to death in the **flesh**" and "suffered for us in the
S D : 0 8 :037(598) [1027] flesh" and "suffered for us in the **flesh**" (I Pet. 3:18; 4:1).
S D : 0 8 :058(602) [1035] the Son of Man and inasmuch as he has **flesh** and blood.
S D : 0 8 :059(602) [1035] says that Christ's **flesh** is a life-giving food, and
S D : 0 8 :059(602) [1035] Ephesus decreed that the **flesh** of Christ has the power to
S D : 0 8 :061(603) [1037] to give life is not in the **flesh** of Christ the way it is in his
S D : 0 8 :073(605) [1041] to Christ according to the **flesh** that is personally united
S D : 0 8 :076(606) [1043] to Christ according to the **flesh** that the flesh, according
S D : 0 8 :076(606) [1043] to the flesh that the **flesh**, according to its nature and
S D : 0 8 :076(606) [1043] — for example, that his **flesh** is truly a life-giving food
S D : 0 8 :076(606) [1043] they stated that Christ's **flesh** is a life-giving flesh, whence
S D : 0 8 :076(606) [1043] flesh is a life-giving **flesh**, whence only this man and no
S D : 0 8 :078(607) [1043] he is our brother and we **flesh** of his flesh and bone of his
S D : 0 8 :078(607) [1043] brother and we flesh of his **flesh** and bone of his bone
S D : 0 8 :079(607) [1045] nature, too, according to which he has **flesh** and blood.
S D : 0 8 :087(608) [1047] by which he is our brother and we are **flesh** of his flesh.
S D : 0 8 :087(608) [1047] by which he is our brother and we are flesh of his **flesh**.
S D : 0 8 :096(610) [1049] rejoice constantly that our **flesh** and blood have in Christ
S D : 1 1 :020(619) [1069] devil, the world, and the **flesh**, guide and lead them in his
S D : 1 1 :028(620) [1071] he has given his **flesh** "for the life of the world"
S D : 1 1 :046(624) [1079] and wickedness of our **flesh** it could easily slip from our
S D : 1 2 :025(635) [1099] Christ did not assume his **flesh** and blood from the virgin
S D : 1 2 :029(635) [1101] that according to the **flesh** or according to his assumed
S D : 1 2 :029(635) [1101] the exaltation Christ's **flesh** assumed all the divine
S D : 1 2 :029(635) [1101] glory and so that Christ's **flesh** belongs to the essence of

Fleshly (2)
A P : 0 4 :266(146) [0197] must be turned from such **fleshly** opinions to the Word of
S D : 0 7 :127(591) [1015] are advanced in a coarse, **fleshly**, Capernaitic way about

Flimsy (1)
L C : 0 1 :295(404) [0665] wife, he might on any **flimsy** excuse dismiss his own wife

Fling (2)
A P : 0 4 :237(140) [0187] more understanding than the walls that **fling** back an
L C : 0 1 :333(410) [0677] Here we can **fling** out the challenge: Let all wise men and

Flock (1), Flocks (3)
A P : 1 2 :106(197) [0283] (Prov. 27:23), "Know well the condition of your **flocks**."
A P : 1 2 :106(197) [0283] and not outward conduct, and "**flocks**" means men.
S C : 0 3 :014(347) [0547] and home, fields and **flocks**, money and property; a pious
L C : 0 2 :051(417) [0691] is on earth a little holy **flock** or community of pure saints

Flood (3), Flooded (1)
A P : 2 3 :054(246) [0379] The destruction in the **flood** and the burning of Sodom
L C : 0 1 :060(372) [0597] Like a great deluge, it has **flooded** all lands.
L C : 0 1 :060(372) [0597] plague, war, famine, fire, **flood**, wayward wives and
L C : 0 3 :078(431) [0721] tempest, hail, fire, and **flood**; from poison, pestilence, and

Floor (1)
A P : 0 7 :001(168) [0227] the church to a threshing **floor** on which chaff and wheat

Flour (3)
A P : 2 4 :036(257) [0397] of the lamb, the drink offering, and the offering of **flour**.
A P : 2 4 :036(257) [0397] The offering of **flour** symbolizes faith, prayer, and
L C : 0 3 :072(430) [0719] not only the oven or the **flour** bin, but also the broad

Flourishes (1)
L C : 0 3 :050(426) [0711] whom his name is hallowed and his kingdom **flourishes**.

Flow (6), Flowed (1), Flowing (1), Flows (2)
L C : P R :012(360) [0571] to recount all the blessings that **flow** from God's Word.
L C : 0 1 :311(407) [0671] true channel through which all good works must **flow**.
L C : 0 6 :033(461) [0000] "As a hart longs for **flowing** streams, so longs my soul for
E P : 0 4 :003(476) [0797] since it does not **flow** from necessity or coercion but from
E P : 0 8 :009(488) [0819] ineffable sharing there **flows** everything human that is
S D : 0 1 :002(509) [0859] inheres in his nature, all actual sins **flow** out of his heart.
S D : 0 4 :003(551) [0939] punishment of the law but **flow** from a spontaneous spirit
S D : 0 4 :008(552) [0941] but since they do not **flow** from true faith, they are sinful
S D : 0 4 :029(555) [0947] as a result of the Interim, **flowed** forth from it, and were
S D : 0 8 :031(597) [1025] of the natures) likewise **flows** from this same foundation,

Flower (3), Flowery (3)
A P : 0 4 :329(158) [0211] is grass, and all its beauty is like the **flower** of the field.
A P : 0 4 :329(158) [0211] The grass withers, the **flower** fades, when the breath of
A P : 2 3 :070(249) [0383] is grass, and all its beauty is like the **flower** of the field."
S D : 0 7 :038(576) [0985] as a figurative, **flowery** formula or quibble about words).
S D : 0 7 :045(577) [0987] and Redeemer, not as **flowery**, figurative, or
S D : 0 7 :050(578) [0989] and union, he uses no **flowery** language but the most

Fly (1), Flight (4)
A P : 2 7 :041(276) [0435] approve of this kind of **flight**, since we know that the
L C : P R :010(360) [0571] the sign which routs the devil and puts him to **flight**.
L C : 0 1 :004(365) [0581] of the heart, and these **fly** straight to the one true God
L C : 0 1 :102(379) [0609] is cast out and put to **flight**, this commandment is
L C : 0 3 :063(428) [0715] to hinder us, put us to **flight**, cut us down, and bring us

Foe (5), Foes (2)
P R : P R :004(003) [0007] government the **foe** of mankind bestirred himself to
A G : P R :001(024) [0039] the Turk, that traditional **foe** of ours and of the Christian
L C : 0 1 :251(399) [0651] we are to help, share, and lend to both friends and **foes**.
L C : 0 1 :285(403) [0661] harm his neighbor, whether friend or **foe**, with his tongue.
L C : 0 3 :062(428) [0715] Therefore, like a furious **foe**, he raves and rages with all
E P : 1 1 :013(496) [0835] but are inspired by the evil **foe** in an attempt to weaken
S D : 1 1 :095(632) [1095] our exposition friends and **foes** may clearly understand

Fold (3)
S C : 0 8 :007(353) [0559] the table, they should reverently **fold** their hands and say:
S C : 0 8 :010(353) [0559] likewise, they should **fold** their hands reverently and say:
L C : 0 1 :236(397) [0647] you have done you will have to pay back thirty-**fold**.

Folk (8)
P R : P R :019(009) [0017] palm them off on simple **folk** in spite of the fact that this
A P : 1 3 :003(211) [0309] though they may instruct or admonish the simple **folk**.
A P : 1 5 :020(218) [0321] and finally because they helped instruct the common **folk**.
A P : 1 5 :020(218) [0321] and various rites serve as reminders for the common **folk**.
L C : 0 2 :048(416) [0691] "church," by which simple **folk** understand not a group of
L C : 0 3 :007(421) [0699] pupils, and simple **folk**; while it may be called singing or
L C : 0 6 :007(458) [0000] confession to instruct and admonish the simple **folk**.
E P : 0 1 :023(469) [0785] unlearned people, but simple **folk** should be spared them.

Follies (1)
S 2 : 0 4 :014(301) [0475] puerilities, fantasies, and **follies** without so much as a

Follow (92), Followed (8), Followers (6), Following (61), Followings (1), Follows (81)
P R : P R :014(007) [0013] in the form that **follows** hereafter, was completed with the
P R : P R :018(008) [0015] to, we have in what **follows** purposed to commit
P R : P R :018(009) [0015] Book of Concord that **follows** hereunder, so that
P R : P R :025(013) [0023] in the Apology that **followed** it, and in the Smalcald
A G : P R :014(026) [0041] assured from what **follows** in the confession which we and
A G : P R :023(027) [0043] position by these or any **following** negotiations (unless
A G : P R :024(027) [0043] it is specifically stated, article by article, in what **follows**.
A G : 1 2 :006(035) [0049] of sin would then **follow**, for these must be the fruits of

Continued ▶

AG : 20 :008(042) [0053] everywhere, our people have been instructed as **follows**:
AG : 24 :023(058) [0067] Thereupon **followed** a debate as to whether one Mass
AG : 24 :034(060) [0067] it is observed among us in the **following** manner:
AG : 27 :034(076) [0079] be censured, it would not **follow** that the marriage of
AG : 27 :039(077) [0081] It **follows** from this that the customary vows were an
AG : 27 :052(079) [0083] of monastic life, for it **follows** that their consciences are
AG : 28 :075(094) [0095] sin, we are bound to **follow** the apostolic rule which
AL : 12 :006(035) [0049] which are the fruits of repentance, are bound to **follow**.
AL : 20 :008(042) [0053] have instructed our churches concerning faith as **follows**:
AL : 21 :001(046) [0057] Thus the emperor may **follow** the example of David in
AL : 22 :009(050) [0061] (Dist. 3, chap. "Veritate" and the **following** chapters).
AL : 27 :033(076) [0079] Whether we **follow** one canon or the other, most
AL : 27 :034(076) [0081] yet it seems not to **follow** of necessity that the marriages
AL : 27 :039(077) [0081] It **follows**, therefore, that the vows thus customarily taken
AL : 28 :050(089) [0091] with the Gospel, it **follows** that it is not lawful for bishops
AL : 28 :075(094) [0095] sin, we are bound to **follow** the apostolic injunction which
AP : PR :003(098) [0099] the negotiations that **followed**, it was clear that our side
AP : 02 :024(103) [0111] that when righteousness is lost, concupiscence **follows**.
AP : 02 :024(103) [0111] both the defect and the vicious disposition that **follows**.
AP : 02 :051(107) [0119] the opinions of the holy Fathers, which we also **follow**.
AP : 04 :009(108) [0123] Here the scholastics have **followed** the philosophers.
AP : 04 :042(113) [0133] keep the law, it would **follow** that we would never obtain
AP : 04 :042(113) [0133] we never keep, it would **follow** that the promise is
AP : 04 :043(113) [0133] free promise, however, it **follows** that we cannot justify
AP : 04 :067(116) [0139] received only by faith, then it **follows** that faith justifies.
AP : 04 :071(116) [0141] faith, but the works that **follow**, by which we would
AP : 04 :074(117) [0143] Love and good works must also **follow** faith.
AP : 04 :074(117) [0143] as though they did not **follow**, but trust in the merit of
AP : 04 :077(117) [0143] because of love or works, though love does **follow** faith.
AP : 04 :080(118) [0143] We prove the minor premise as **follows**.
AP : 04 :111(123) [0153] say, too, that love should **follow** faith, as Paul also says,
AP : 04 :112(123) [0155] of sins on account of the other works that **follow** it.
AP : 04 :114(123) [0155] and keep the law, although love must necessarily **follow**.
AP : 04 :121(124) [0155] In **following** them and rejecting this faith, our opponents
AP : 04 :141(126) [0161] So he indicates that faith precedes while love **follows**.
AP : 04 :151(127) [0163] government, etc.), even though these virtues must **follow**.
AP : 04 :151(127) [0163] of sins on account of love, though it, too, must **follow**.
AP : 04 :155(128) [0165] love, confession, and other good fruits ought to **follow**.
AP : 04 :159(129) [0167] From this it necessarily **follows** that we are justified by
AP : 04 :182(132) [0173] the keeping of the law **follows** with the gift of the Holy
AP : 04 :203(134) [0175] Good works ought to **follow** faith in this way.
AP : 04 :214(136) [0179] keeping of the law must **follow** faith; but we still give
AP : 04 :225(138) [0183] Therefore it **follows** that the greatest and the main virtue
AP : 04 :246(142) [0189] of here are those that **follow** faith and show that it is not
AP : 04 :263(145) [0195] because of the works that **follow** or because of alms, but
AP : 04 :269(147) [0197] It **follows**, therefore, that works are praised for pleasing
AP : 04 :275(148) [0199] a propitiation — for they **follow** reconciliation — but he
AP : 04 :275(148) [0199] that good fruits ought to **follow** of necessity, and so he
AP : 04 :275(148) [0199] penitence is hypocritical and false if they do not **follow**.
AP : 04 :278(149) [0199] by that almsgiving which **follows** justification or
AP : 04 :292(152) [0203] Then love and other good fruits **follow**.
AP : 04 :294(152) [0203] to love, though love **follows** faith since love is the keeping
AP : 04 :360(162) [0219] they draw the **following** absurd conclusion when they
AP : 04 :366(163) [0221] keeping of the law that **follows** faith deals with the law, in
AP : 07 :008(169) [0229] The **following** phrase, "the communion of saints," seems
AP : 07 :017(171) [0231] of the devil, it necessarily **follows** that since the wicked
AP : 07 :023(172) [0235] some such definition of the church as the **following**.
AP : 07 :034(175) [0239] before God, it **follows** that somebody can be righteous
AP : 07 :034(175) [0239] before him, it **follows** that men can be righteous, children
AP : 07 :043(177) [0243] they wanted others to **follow** the example of the chief
AP : 09 :002(178) [0245] Therefore it clearly **follows** that infants should be
AP : 10 :001(179) [0247] Lord's body," it would **follow** that the bread would not be
AP : 12 :007(183) [0255] What **follows** is still more complicated.
AP : 12 :016(184) [0257] The **following** teachings are clearly false and foreign to
AP : 12 :037(187) [0261] But love **follows** faith, as we have said above.
AP : 12 :058(190) [0267] as well as punishments **follow** regeneration and the
AP : 12 :060(190) [0269] This faith **follows** on our terrors, overcoming them and
AP : 12 :066(191) [0271] they are the church and **follow** the consensus of the
AP : 12 :082(194) [0275] as we said before, love **follows** faith, for the regenerate
AP : 12 :116(199) [0287] not because of our works, either preceding or **following**.
AP : 12 :122(200) [0289] prescribed penitence, **following** the statement of Paul,
AP : 12 :131(202) [0291] where mortifying the flesh and good fruits do not **follow**.
AP : 12 :136(203) [0293] Look what **follows**!
AP : 12 :136(203) [0293] Since this necessarily **follows** from our opponents'
AP : 12 :148(205) [0299] of the body which **follows** true sorrow in the mind.
AP : 12 :156(207) [0301] on David it does not **follow** as a universal rule that over
AP : 12 :161(208) [0303] the lesson of the threat **followed** so that especially
AP : 12 :170(209) [0305] Good works ought to **follow** penitence, and penitence
AP : 15 :025(218) [0321] has deceived men, all sorts of troubles **follow**.
AP : 18 :003(225) [0335] How many absurdities **follow** from these Pelagian
AP : 20 :013(228) [0341] about the works that **follow** the forgiveness of sins; he is
AP : 20 :015(229) [0343] conviction that good works must necessarily **follow** faith.
AP : 20 :015(229) [0343] of the law necessarily **follows**, by which love, patience,
AP : 21 :010(230) [0345] the church, it does not **follow** that they should be
AP : 21 :010(230) [0345] of the saints; from this it **follows** that consciences cannot
AP : 21 :027(232) [0349] Christ but to have her example considered and **followed**.
AP : 22 :007(237) [0359] Still it does not **follow** that only one part was given; for
AP : 23 :007(240) [0365] work of God, it **follows** that neither regulations nor vows
AP : 23 :032(244) [0373] particular calling should **follow** everyone's faith, pleasing
AP : 24 :016(252) [0389] making them he would **follow** in his footsteps as those of
AP : 24 :031(255) [0395] to the Mass, it would not **follow** that the Mass justifies *ex*
AP : 24 :035(256) [0397] analogy it does not **follow** at all that there must be a
AP : 24 :056(259) [0403] From this it **follows** that only the sacrifice of Christ
AP : 24 :078(263) [0411] It does not **follow** from the fact that the Mass is called a
AP : 24 :092(266) [0415] and without faith, it **follows** that it is useless to transfer it
AP : 27 :022(272) [0427] ministry of the Word who **follow** these observances
AP : 27 :032(274) [0431] the other things that **follow** this sentence, but at the end
AP : 27 :037(275) [0433] If we **follow** this, the monastic life will be no more a state
AP : 27 :045(277) [0435] you possess and give to the poor; and come, **follow** me."
AP : 27 :048(277) [0437] Perfection consists in that which Christ adds, "**Follow** me
AP : 27 :070(281) [0443] Holy men who **followed** this way of life must have come
AP : 28 :014(283) [0447] Therefore it does not **follow** that since they have a certain
S1 : PR :007(289) [0457] work, has made their **following** smaller and smaller and
S2 : 02 :002(293) [0463] would speak to them in the **following** friendly fashion:
S2 : 02 :008(294) [0465] he is doing because he **follows** a false human opinion and
S2 : 02 :026(297) [0469] do likewise, it does not **follow** that we should invoke
S2 : 04 :003(298) [0471] Hence it **follows** that all the things that the pope has
S3 : 00 :000(302) [0477] The **following** articles treat matters which we may discuss
S3 : 03 :011(305) [0481] From this it **follows** that people did penance only for
S3 : 03 :015(305) [0483] of a whole year), the **following** loophole was resorted to,
S3 : 03 :040(309) [0489] of the Holy Spirit which **follows** the forgiveness of sins.
S3 : 13 :002(315) [0499] Good works **follow** such faith, renewal, and forgiveness.
S3 : 13 :003(315) [0499] if good works do not **follow**, our faith is false and not
TR : 00 :030(325) [0513] it in no wise **follows** that they bestow a special
TR : 00 :039(327) [0515] with those of the pope's kingdom and his **followers**.
TR : 00 :055(329) [0521] an opinion, except his **followers**, whom he has bound by
TR : 00 :062(330) [0523] out that these words are **followed** by, "A bishop must be
TR : 00 :062(330) [0523] by gathering separate **followings** around themselves, rend
SC : PR :010(339) [0535] the Lord's Prayer, etc., **following** the text word for word
LC : 01 :048(371) [0593] fulfillment of all the others will **follow** of its own accord.
LC : 01 :064(373) [0599] or wickedness, it **follows**, conversely that we are
LC : 01 :103(379) [0611] Now **follow** the other seven, which relate to our
LC : 01 :184(390) [0633] Then **follow** cursing and blows, and eventually calamity
LC : 01 :191(391) [0635] permitted me and my **followers** to die of hunger, thirst,
LC : 01 :200(392) [0637] The **following** commandments are easily understood from
LC : 01 :219(394) [0643] chastity always **follows** spontaneously without any
LC : 01 :248(398) [0651] be on their guard and not **follow** the old, wayward
LC : 01 :308(406) [0669] a yard, and at length open injustice and violence **follow**.
LC : 01 :327(409) [0675] So, through the **following** commandments which concern
LC : 02 :001(411) [0679] The Creed properly **follows**, setting forth all that we must
LC : 02 :010(412) [0679] This is taught here and in the **following** articles.
LC : 02 :019(412) [0681] by God, it inevitably **follows** that we are in duty bound to
LC : 02 :037(415) [0687] through the **following**: the communion of saints or
LC : 03 :001(420) [0697] Now **follows** the third part, how we are to pray.
LC : 03 :052(427) [0711] gain recognition and **followers** among other people and
LC : 03 :111(435) [0729] which it can slip, the whole body will irresistibly **follow**.
LC : 04 :031(440) [0739] Hence it **follows** that whoever rejects Baptism rejects
LC : 04 :071(445) [0749] The old man therefore **follows** unchecked the inclinations
LC : 05 :087(457) [0773] Here **follows** an exhortation to confession.
EP : 00 :000(464) [0777] with God's Word in the Recapitulation Here **Following**
EP : 02 :007(470) [0787] and condemn all the **following** errors as being contrary to
EP : 02 :018(472) [0791] cooperates with the Holy Spirit in the works that **follow**.
EP : 03 :011(474) [0795] and the good works that **follow** it do not belong in the
EP : 03 :011(474) [0795] Thus good works always **follow** justifying faith and are
EP : 03 :012(474) [0795] we reject and condemn all the **following** errors:
EP : 04 :006(476) [0799] certainly and indubitably **follow** genuine faith — if it is a
EP : 06 :004(480) [0807] and plagues, to **follow** the Spirit and surrender himself a
EP : 07 :021(484) [0813] and condemn all the **following** errors, which are contrary
EP : 08 :003(487) [0819] Dr. Luther and his **followers** have contended for the
EP : 08 :004(487) [0819] faith we teach, believe, and confess the **following**:
EP : 08 :019(490) [0823] simple Christian Creed the **following** erroneous articles:
EP : 10 :008(494) [0831] and contrary to God's Word the **following** teachings:
EP : 11 :009(495) [0833] As long as men **follow** their reason, they can hardly
EP : 11 :011(495) [0835] the order which St. Paul **follows** in the Epistle to the
EP : 11 :016(497) [0837] Therefore we reject the **following** errors:
SD : RN :007(505) [0853] We **follow** the version as it was initially prepared and
SD : 01 :020(511) [0865] reject and condemn the **following** and related Pelagian
SD : 01 :026(512) [0867] For that reason the **following** and similar errors are
SD : 01 :044(516) [0873] sin, it would have to **follow** that Christ either did not
SD : 01 :047(516) [0873] the other, then it would **follow**, contrary to this article of
SD : 01 :056(518) [0877] schools and churches, **following** the rules of logic, used
SD : 02 :006(521) [0883] an end, we submit the **following** as our teaching, belief,
SD : 02 :008(521) [0883] The **following** reasons from the Word of God support and
SD : 02 :023(525) [0889] which he explains as **follows**: "When the Fathers defend
SD : 02 :028(527) [0893] mentioned, as the **following** testimonies will indicate.
SD : 02 :031(527) [0893] The Apology teaches as **follows** concerning free will: "We
SD : 02 :033(527) [0893] Articles reject the **following** errors concerning free will:
SD : 02 :034(528) [0895] of the Holy Spirit which **follows** upon the forgiveness of
SD : 02 :041(529) [0897] of God come to us?" as **follows**: "When the heavenly
SD : 02 :055(531) [0903] and no conversion would **follow**, if there were not added
SD : 02 :065(534) [0907] From this it **follows** that as soon as the Holy Spirit has
SD : 02 :081(537) [0911] "Put off the old man," as **follows**: "Lest anyone might
SD : 02 :082(537) [0913] 8. We also reject the **following** formulas if they are used
SD : 03 :008(540) [0919] belief, and confession as **follows**: Concerning the
SD : 03 :012(541) [0919] Thus the **following** statements of St. Paul are to be
SD : 03 :018(542) [0921] that the renewal which **follows** justification by faith will
SD : 03 :021(542) [0921] or renewal which **follows** the righteousness of faith, as
SD : 03 :022(543) [0923] that we may or should **follow** in the ways of sin, abide
SD : 03 :024(543) [0923] which precedes faith or **follows** faith into the article of
SD : 03 :027(543) [0923] a fruit which certainly and necessarily **follows** true faith.
SD : 03 :027(544) [0925] justification; rather they **follow** it, since a person must
SD : 03 :028(544) [0925] before God; it rather **follows** justification, because in this
SD : 03 :035(545) [0927] From this it **follows** that although converted persons and
SD : 03 :036(545) [0927] must, and dare not **follow** true faith as certain and
SD : 03 :041(546) [0929] and sanctification the fruits of good works will **follow**.
SD : 03 :041(546) [0931] order in which one thing precedes or **follows** the other.
SD : 03 :042(547) [0931] the Apology gives the **following** answer: James calls that
SD : 03 :042(547) [0931] fruits of the Spirit do not **follow**," and the Latin text of
SD : 03 :044(547) [0933] expose, and reject the **following** and similar errors as
SD : 03 :054(549) [0935] This indwelling **follows** the preceding righteousness of
SD : 03 :059(550) [0937] mentioned errors, the **following** and all similar errors as
SD : 03 :064(550) [0937] (and upon which no love **follows**) but against his
SD : 04 :007(552) [0939] us concerning the **following** points: That it is God's will,
SD : 04 :014(553) [0943] because they necessarily **follow** faith and reconciliation";
SD : 04 :028(555) [0945] case of some of his own **followers** who attempted to
SD : 04 :031(556) [0947] even though a Christian **follows** his evil lusts without fear
SD : 04 :036(557) [0949] it is safest to **follow** the advice of St. Paul to maintain the
SD : 04 :037(557) [0949] salvation, we give the **following** clear answer: If anyone
SD : 04 :038(557) [0951] But it does not **follow** herefrom that one may say without
SD : 05 :016(561) [0957] clearly for the Christian reader, we submit the **following**:
SD : 06 :009(565) [0965] egg them on so that they **follow** the Spirit of God, as it is
SD : 07 :010(571) [0975] Small Catechism in the **following** words: "The Sacrament
SD : 07 :011(571) [0975] quotation from Cyril as **follows**: "Article X has been
SD : 07 :011(571) [0975] of Christ, etc., it would **follow** that the bread is a
SD : 07 :012(571) [0977] Germany drafted the **following** articles of Christian
SD : 07 :017(572) [0977] In the **following** year the leading theologians who were

Continued ▶

SD : 0 7 :020(573) [0979] where he writes as **follows**: "What is the Sacrament of the
SD : 0 7 :029(574) [0981] he appended the **following** protestation to his *Great*
SD : 0 7 :032(574) [0983] **Following** this protestation Luther, of blessed memory,
SD : 0 7 :032(574) [0983] among other articles the **following**: "In the same way I
SD : 0 7 :033(575) [0983] great fervor and wrote as **follows**: "I reckon them all as
SD : 0 7 :059(580) [0993] They write as **follows**: "The bread is participation in the
SD : 0 7 :074(583) [0999] we have reached the **following** fraternal and unanimous
SD : 0 7 :078(583) [1001] happen, but when we **follow** his institution and command
SD : 0 7 :085(584) [1001] of this testament, the **following** useful rule and norm has
SD : 0 7 :093(586) [1005] very beginning in the **following** words): "My grounds, on
SD : 0 7 :093(586) [1005] grounds, on which I rest in this matter, are as **follows**:
SD : 0 8 :004(592) [1017] well as that of those who **follow** it as being in harmony
SD : 0 8 :005(592) [1017] unanimous teaching, belief, and confession are as **follows**:
SD : 0 8 :023(595) [1023] power of God, and everything that **follows** from it.
SD : 0 8 :035(597) [1027] The **following** presentation should be noted diligently.
SD : 0 8 :037(598) [1027] of speaking it does not **follow** that whatever is ascribed to
SD : 0 8 :056(601) [1035] These reasons are the **following**:
SD : 0 8 :073(605) [1041] from the Son), it **follows** that through personal union the
SD : 0 8 :081(607) [1045] there is no God — it must **follow** that according to the
SD : 0 8 :083(607) [1045] For it would **follow** from this that space and place had
SD : 1 0 :004(611) [1053] we offer the Christian reader the **following** exposition:
SD : 1 0 :018(614) [1059] The **following** testimonies drawn from the Smalcald
SD : 1 0 :021(614) [1059] own hands, we find the **following** statement: "No one
SD : 1 1 :003(616) [1063] teaching on this article consists of the **following** points:
SD : 1 1 :012(618) [1067] and thoughts with the **following** clear, certain, and
SD : 1 1 :014(619) [1069] his purpose and counsel God had ordained the **following**:
SD : 1 1 :024(620) [1071] When we **follow** the Scriptures and organize our thinking
SD : 1 1 :025(620) [1071] An answer to the **following** question is necessary for the
SD : 1 1 :030(621) [1073] therefore described as **follows**: "My sheep hear my voice,
SD : 1 1 :030(621) [1073] I know them, and they **follow** me; and I give them eternal
SD : 1 1 :033(621) [1073] this revealed will of God, **follow** it, and be diligent about
SD : 1 1 :033(621) [1073] Luther puts it this way: "**Follow** the order in the Epistle to
SD : 1 1 :052(625) [1081] into these, nor are we to **follow** our own thoughts in this
SD : 1 1 :064(626) [1083] discussion with the **following** words: "O the depth of the
SD : 1 2 :039(636) [1103] attaches to them or **follows** from them, we reject and

Folly (7)
EP : 0 2 :002(470) [0787] Spirit of God, for they are **folly** to him, and he is not able
SD : 0 2 :008(521) [0883] of this perverse world is **folly** with God" and that it is
SD : 0 2 :010(522) [0883] Spirit of God, for they are **folly** to him, and he is not able
SD : 0 2 :010(522) [0883] pleased God through the **folly** of the Gospel that we
SD : 0 2 :012(523) [0885] things) for they are **folly** to him, and he is not able to
SD : 0 2 :024(526) [0891] do, yet he considers it **folly** and cannot believe it.
SD : 0 2 :051(531) [0901] pleased God through the **folly** of what we preach to save

Fond (1), Fondness (1)
AP : 2 4 :016(252) [0389] says that he is very **fond** of distinctions because without
LC : 0 3 :103(434) [0727] and pride, along with **fondness** for luxury, honor, fame,

Fontanus (1)
TR : 0 0 :082(335) [0529] John **Fontanus**, superintendent of Lower Hesse,

Food (53), Foods (23)
AG : 1 5 :004(037) [0049] concerning distinction of **foods**, days, etc., by which it is
AG : 2 6 :000(063) [0071] XXVI. The Distinction of **Foods**
AG : 2 6 :001(063) [0071] that distinctions among **foods** and similar traditions
AG : 2 6 :006(064) [0071] prescribed fasts, distinctions among **foods**, vestments, etc.
AG : 2 6 :024(067) [0073] of God does not mean **food** and drink," and in Col. 2:16
AG : 2 6 :025(067) [0073] on you in questions of **food** and drink or with regard to a
AG : 2 6 :029(068) [0075] prohibitions as forbid **food** or marriage are called a
AG : 2 6 :039(069) [0075] days and with specified **foods**, for this confuses
AG : 2 8 :030(085) [0087] regulations concerning **foods**, holy days, and the different
AG : 2 8 :039(087) [0089] when they attach sin to **foods**, days, and similar things
AG : 2 8 :041(087) [0089] seven hours, that some **foods** defile the conscience, that
AG : 2 8 :044(088) [0089] on you in questions of **food** and drink or with regard to a
AL : 1 5 :004(037) [0049] vows and traditions about **foods** and days, etc., instituted
AL : 2 6 :000(063) [0071] XXVI. The Distinction of **Foods**
AL : 2 6 :001(063) [0071] that distinctions among **foods** and similar human
AL : 2 6 :006(065) [0071] by distinctions among **foods** and similar acts of worship.
AL : 2 6 :024(067) [0073] kingdom of God is not **food** and drink," and in Col. 2:16,
AL : 2 6 :025(067) [0073] on you in questions of **food** and drink or with regard to a
AL : 2 6 :029(068) [0075] calls the prohibition of **foods** a doctrine of demons, for it
AL : 2 6 :039(069) [0075] certain days and certain **foods** as if works of this sort
AL : 2 8 :030(085) [0087] make laws concerning **foods**, holy days, grades or orders
AL : 2 8 :039(087) [0089] when they attach sin to **foods**, days, and similar things
AL : 2 8 :041(087) [0089] to others, that certain **foods** defile the conscience, that
AL : 2 8 :044(088) [0089] on you in questions of **food** and drink or with regard to a
AP : 0 4 :283(150) [0201] monks, the distinctions of **foods**, and similar pompous
AP : 0 4 :370(164) [0221] Matt. 25:35, "I was hungry and you gave me **food**," etc.
AP : 0 4 :373(164) [0221] "You gave me **food**" is cited as fruit and evidence of the
AP : 0 7 :035(175) [0239] on you in questions of **food** and drink or with regard to a
AP : 0 7 :036(175) [0241] of God does not mean **food** and drink but righteousness
AP : 0 7 :039(176) [0241] the observance of days, **food**, and the like a matter of
AP : 0 7 :045(177) [0243] of observances in **food**, days, clothing, and similar
AP : 0 7 :050(178) [0245] legitimate for them to use the air, light, **food**, and drink.
AP : 1 5 :030(219) [0323] on you in questions of **food** and drink or with regard to a
AP : 1 5 :048(221) [0329] prescription of certain **foods** and seasons contributes
AP : 1 6 :002(222) [0331] make use of medicine or architecture, **food** or drink or air
AP : 2 2 :010(237) [0361] life of the world, is their **food** and that they come to life
AP : 2 3 :019(242) [0369] as he wants to nourish our life by using **food** and drink.
AP : 2 3 :030(243) [0371] Paul says marriage, **food**, and similar things are
AP : 2 3 :031(243) [0373] faith in Christ just as the use of **food**, etc. is permissible.
AP : 2 4 :072(262) [0409] He provides **food** for those who fear him."
AP : 2 7 :002(269) [0419] for his doctrine, which seemed to be injuring his **food**.
AP : 2 7 :026(273) [0429] among clothes or **foods**, nor the surrender of property.
AP : 2 7 :026(273) [0429] has been said (I Cor. 8:8), "**Food** does not commend us to
AP : 2 7 :039(276) [0433] and obey the rule in trifles like clothing and **food**.
AP : 2 7 :043(277) [0435] Gospel but for the sake of **food** and leisure; instead of a
AP : 2 7 :069(281) [0443] and the observance of **foods**, lessons, chants, vestments,
AP : 2 8 :007(282) [0445] depends upon **food**, drink, clothing, and similar matters.
AP : 2 8 :007(282) [0445] 14:17), "The kingdom of God is not **food** or drink."
AP : 2 8 :010(282) [0447] and eternal life since **food**, drink, clothing, and the like
AP : 2 8 :019(284) [0449] trifles, distinction of **foods** and clothing and the like.
S2 : 0 4 :014(301) [0475] of churches, vestments, **food**, personnel, and countless
SC : PR :012(339) [0535] to furnish them with **food** and drink and should notify
SC : 0 2 :002(345) [0543] of my mind, together with **food** and clothing, house and
SC : 0 3 :014(347) [0547] our bodily needs, such as **food** and clothing, house and
SC : 0 8 :007(353) [0559] O Lord, and Thou givest them their **food** in due season.
SC : 0 8 :008(353) [0559] Greed and anxiety about **food** prevent such satisfaction.)
SC : 0 8 :010(354) [0559] He gives to the beasts their **food**, and to the young ravens
LC : PR :013(360) [0571] not only to be refused **food** but also to be chased out by
LC : 0 1 :024(367) [0587] he who gives us body, life, **food**, drink, nourishment,
LC : 0 1 :047(371) [0593] avails himself of an inn, **food**, and bed (only for his
LC : 0 1 :150(385) [0623] own parents, God gives us **food**, house and home,
LC : 0 1 :191(391) [0635] and you gave me no **food** or drink, I was a stranger, and
LC : 0 2 :013(412) [0681] and so forth; my **food** and drink, clothing, means of
LC : 0 3 :073(430) [0719] our life requires not only **food** and clothing and other
LC : 0 3 :076(431) [0721] might ask God to give us **food** and drink, clothing,
LC : 0 5 :023(449) [0757] is appropriately called the **food** of the soul since it
LC : 0 5 :024(449) [0759] Supper is given as a daily **food** and sustenance so that
EP : 0 7 :042(486) [0817] flesh with one's teeth and digested it like other **food**.
SD : 0 7 :039(576) [0985] flesh and blood, so the **food** blessed by him through the
SD : 0 7 :048(578) [0989] Christ were spiritual bread or a spiritual **food** for the soul.
SD : 0 7 :115(589) [1011] and wine are external **food** for our body, so the absent
SD : 0 7 :115(589) [1011] of Christ with its merit is spiritual **food** for our souls).
SD : 0 8 :059(602) [1035] flesh is a life-giving **food**, and according to the Council of
SD : 0 8 :076(606) [1043] flesh is truly a life-giving **food** and his blood truly a
SD : 1 0 :013(613) [1057] in to the weak as far as **foods**, times, and days were
SD : 1 0 :013(613) [1057] on you in questions of **food** and drink, or with regard to a

Fool (3), Fools (2)
LC : PR :015(360) [0571] O what mad, senseless **fools** we are!
LC : 0 1 :124(382) [0617] a rule, do very much; one **fool** trains another, and as they
LC : 0 1 :277(402) [0661] to his neighbors, he would no doubt be told: "You **fool**!
LC : 0 3 :057(427) [0713] and princely gifts, and the **fool** asked only for a dish of
SD : 0 7 :103(587) [1007] was to show what crass **fools** our enthusiasts are, because

Foolish (19), Foolishly (1), Foolishness (6)
AP : 0 2 :011(102) [0109] Who cannot see the **foolishness** of our opponents'
AP : 0 4 :036(112) [0131] Finally, it was very **foolish** of our opponents to write that
AP : 0 4 :224(138) [0181] necessary, it would be a **foolish** dream to imagine that we
AP : 0 4 :230(139) [0183] for our part preach the **foolishness** of the Gospel, which
AP : 0 4 :230(139) [0183] But we are not ashamed of the **foolishness** of the Gospel.
AP : 0 4 :258(144) [0193] It would be **foolish** in such a statement to look only at
AP : 0 7 :032(174) [0239] for it is clear that many **foolish** opinions about traditions
AP : 0 7 :032(174) [0239] this issue there are many **foolish** books by the summists
AP : 0 7 :042(177) [0243] the people of the **foolish** notion of having to observe a set
AP : 1 2 :142(204) [0295] the law requires, and it is **foolish** of them to imagine that
AP : 1 2 :149(205) [0299] It is a **foolish** distortion to apply the term "punishments"
AP : 1 6 :013(224) [0333] had been obscured by **foolish** monastic theories which
AP : 2 1 :030(233) [0351] Hilary says of the **foolish** virgins: "Since the foolish
AP : 2 1 :030(233) [0351] virgins: "Since the **foolish** virgins could not go out with
AP : 2 1 :035(234) [0353] Then the **foolish** monks taught the people to call on
AP : 2 3 :004(239) [0365] set against them their own **foolish** and vain opinions.
AP : 2 3 :010(241) [0367] more crafty than this **foolishness**, thought up in order to
AP : 2 7 :034(275) [0431] transferring to their own **foolish** observances the trust
S3 : 0 3 :042(310) [0491] I have encountered many **foolish** people like this and I
LC : 0 1 :038(369) [0591] they become so mad and **foolish** that they justly merit the
LC : 0 1 :277(402) [0659] If he were so **foolish** as to leave the servant at home while
LC : 0 4 :030(440) [0739] Now, these people are so **foolish** as to separate faith from
EP : 0 8 :020(490) [0823] the Son of man another, as Nestorius **foolishly** asserted.
SD : 0 2 :005(521) [0881] but considers it **foolishness**; nor does he of himself
SD : 0 2 :009(522) [0883] them they consider it all mere **foolishness** and fables.
SD : 1 0 :007(611) [1055] Neither are useless and **foolish** spectacles, which serve

Foot (8), Footsteps (2)
AP : 2 1 :035(234) [0353] the whole Psalter every day while standing on one **foot**.
AP : 2 4 :016(252) [0389] them he would follow in his **footsteps** as those of a god.
AP : 2 7 :006(269) [0421] usually "thrown out and trodden under **foot**" (Matt. 5:13)
S3 : 0 3 :035(309) [0489] lost, that from head to **foot** there is no good in us, that
LC : 0 1 :119(381) [0615] commandment under **foot** that they must torture
LC : 0 3 :030(424) [0707] forces arrayed against us, trying to trample us under **foot**.
LC : 0 4 :062(444) [0749] and trample it under **foot** and would, in addition, pervert
LC : 0 5 :026(449) [0759] faith or yield hand and **foot** and become indifferent or
LC : 0 5 :080(456) [0771] trample him under **foot** because our Lord Christ himself
SD : 1 0 :018(614) [1059] who are walking in their **footsteps** intend by the grace of

Forbade (3)
AG : 2 3 :012(053) [0063] at the time not only **forbade** future marriages of priests
AG : 2 8 :065(092) [0093] with such bondage but **forbade** such eating for a time to
AL : 2 8 :065(092) [0093] with such bondage but **forbade** such eating for a time to

Forbear (1), Forbearance (2)
AP : 0 4 :241(141) [0187] be quieted and settled by calmness and **forbearance**.
AP : 1 2 :073(192) [0273] of sins except by the **forbearance** of God; but add further
SC : 0 9 :011(356) [0563] do the same to them, and **forbear** threatening, knowing

Forbid (21), Forbidden (30), Forbidding (8), Forbids (26)
AG : 2 0 :001(041) [0053] have been falsely accused of **forbidding** good works.
AG : 2 0 :035(046) [0057] is not to be accused of **forbidding** good works but is
AG : 2 3 :018(054) [0063] has not only been **forbidden** but has in many places been
AG : 2 3 :022(055) [0063] calls the teaching that **forbids** marriage a doctrine of the
AG : 2 3 :023(055) [0063] a doctrine of the devil to **forbid** marriage and then to be
AG : 2 4 :036(060) [0067] some to Communion and **forbidding** others to approach.
AG : 2 6 :028(068) [0073] Here Peter **forbids** the burdening of consciences with
AG : 2 6 :029(068) [0075] 3 such prohibitions as **forbid** food or marriage are called
AG : 2 6 :030(068) [0075] Jovinian, accused of **forbidding** mortification and
AG : 2 8 :032(086) [0087] the eating of blood and what is strangled was **forbidden**.
AG : 2 8 :042(088) [0089] In Acts 15:10 St. Peter **forbids** putting a yoke on the neck
AG : 2 8 :043(088) [0089] of divine Scripture which **forbid** the establishment of such
AG : 2 8 :046(088) [0089] In Tit. 1:14 St. Paul also **forbids** giving heed to Jewish
AG : 2 8 :049(089) [0091] Scripture so frequently **forbid** the making and keeping of
AG : 2 8 :070(093) [0093] Again, they **forbid** clergymen to marry and admit no one
AG : 2 8 :076(094) [0095] St. Peter **forbids** the bishops to exercise lordship as if
AL : 1 6 :003(037) [0051] the Anabaptists who **forbid** Christians to engage in these
AL : 2 0 :001(041) [0053] churches are falsely accused of **forbidding** good works.

Continued ▶

A L : 2 0 :035(046) [0057] is not to be charged with **forbidding** good works.
A L : 2 3 :002(051) [0061] why priests were **forbidden** to marry but that there are
A L : 2 3 :017(054) [0063] lacking in pastors if marriage continues to be **forbidden**.
A L : 2 6 :017(066) [0073] Augustine also **forbids** the burdening of consciences with
A L : 2 6 :028(068) [0073] Here Peter **forbids** the burdening of consciences with
A L : 2 6 :030(068) [0075] teachers, like Jovinian, **forbid** discipline and mortification
A L : 2 7 :032(076) [0079] adds a few years and **forbids** making a vow before the
A L : 2 8 :023(084) [0087] a command of God that **forbids** obedience: "Beware of
A L : 2 8 :042(088) [0089] consciences when Peter **forbids** putting a yoke on the
A L : 2 8 :076(094) [0095] Peter **forbids** the bishops to be domineering and to coerce
A P : 1 5 :014(217) [0319] throughout the prophets **forbid** the establishment of
A P : 1 5 :031(219) [0323] In Gal. 5:1 Paul **forbids** them to "submit again to
A P : 1 6 :007(223) [0331] The Gospel **forbids** private revenge, and Christ stresses
A P : 1 6 :007(223) [0331] Thus private revenge is **forbidden** not as an evangelical
A P : 1 6 :007(223) [0331] through a judge is not **forbidden** but expressly
A P : 2 3 :023(242) [0369] ancient canons do not **forbid** marriage, nor dissolve
A P : 2 3 :023(242) [0369] They **forbid** the contracting of marriages and dissolve
A P : 2 3 :027(243) [0371] and intercourse is **forbidden** only during the period of
A P : 2 3 :035(244) [0373] not marriage that the law **forbids**, but lust, adultery, and
A P : 2 3 :053(246) [0377] who despise his gift and ordinance and **forbid** marriage.
A P : 2 3 :063(248) [0381] (I Cor. 7:2) and **forbidding** the dissolution of existing
A P : 2 4 :094(267) [0417] We do not **forbid** this, but rather we reject the transfer of
A P : 2 7 :041(276) [0435] the command of God **forbids** deserting wife and children.
A P : 2 7 :066(280) [0441] the other one which **forbids** that anyone "be enrolled as a
A P : 2 8 :008(282) [0445] faith and then go on to **forbid** the imposing of a yoke,
A P : 2 8 :020(284) [0449] When they do so, we are **forbidden** to obey them by the
S 3 : 0 1 :002(302) [0477] evil deeds which are **forbidden** in the Ten
S 3 : 0 2 :002(303) [0479] hate the law because it **forbids** what they desire to do and
S 3 : 1 0 :003(314) [0497] papists have no right to **forbid** or prevent us, not even
S 3 : 1 1 :002(315) [0499] such creatures of God or **forbid** them to live together
S 3 : 1 2 :002(315) [0499] what they command or **forbid** in the name of the church,
T R : 0 0 :007(320) [0505] Christ expressly **forbids** lordship among the apostles
T R : 0 0 :051(329) [0519] and murders, and he **forbids** a judicial examination.
T R : 0 0 :078(333) [0527] is the tradition which **forbids** an innocent person to marry
L C : 0 1 :051(371) [0595] what this commandment **forbids** is appealing to God's
L C : 0 1 :064(373) [0599] Since we are **forbidden** here to use the holy name in
L C : 0 1 :065(373) [0599] why swearing is **forbidden** in the Gospel, and yet Christ,
L C : 0 1 :086(376) [0605] not be so narrow as to **forbid** incidental and unavoidable
L C : 0 1 :181(389) [0631] Therefore what is **forbidden** here applies to private
L C : 0 1 :186(390) [0633] Not only is murder **forbidden**, but also everything that
L C : 0 1 :197(391) [0637] practically the same as **forbidding** their good works and
L C : 0 1 :200(392) [0637] it is explicitly **forbidden** here to dishonor his wife.
L C : 0 1 :202(392) [0639] only is the external act **forbidden**, but also every kind of
L C : 0 1 :213(394) [0641] when they despise and **forbid** marriage, and boast and
L C : 0 1 :223(395) [0643] He has **forbidden** us to rob or pilfer the possessions of
L C : 0 1 :250(399) [0651] On one hand, we are **forbidden** to do our neighbor any
L C : 0 1 :263(400) [0655] It **forbids** all sins of the tongue by which we may injure
L C : 0 1 :263(400) [0655] the tongue against a neighbor, then, is **forbidden** by God.
L C : 0 1 :269(401) [0657] Therefore God **forbids** you to speak evil about another
L C : 0 1 :274(401) [0659] that we are absolutely **forbidden** to speak evil of our
L C : 0 1 :274(402) [0659] the Fifth Commandment **forbids** us to injure anyone
L C : 0 1 :293(404) [0663] vices were sufficiently **forbidden** in commandments
L C : 0 1 :293(404) [0665] that it is sinful and **forbidden** to covet our neighbor's wife
L C : 0 1 :296(405) [0665] higher application) to **forbid** anyone, even with a
L C : 0 1 :296(405) [0665] But here it is also **forbidden** to entice anything away from
L C : 0 1 :306(406) [0669] Testament married people are **forbidden** to be divorced.
L C : 0 3 :033(424) [0707] as Christ himself rejects and **forbids** great wordiness.
L C : 0 4 :086(446) [0753] not recede from us or **forbid** us to return to him even
L C : 0 5 :069(454) [0769] eats and drinks what is **forbidden** him by the physician.
E P : 0 7 :041(486) [0817] which decency **forbids** us to recite and which the
E P : 1 0 :001(492) [0829] neither commanded nor **forbidden** in the Word of God
E P : 1 0 :002(493) [0829] neither commanded nor **forbidden** by God, and thus
E P : 1 0 :003(493) [0829] neither commanded nor **forbidden** in the Word of God,
S D : 1 0 :001(610) [1053] neither commanded nor **forbidden** in the Word of God
S D : 1 0 :002(611) [1053] neither commanded nor **forbidden** by God, and that one
S D : 1 0 :005(611) [1053] and we should avoid as **forbidden** by God, ceremonies
S D : 1 0 :019(614) [1059] what they command or **forbid** in the name of the church,

Force (26), Forced (11), Forces (3), Forcibly (5), Forcing (1)
A G : 2 3 :012(052) [0063] were compelled by **force** to take the vows of celibacy.
A G : 2 7 :029(075) [0079] and sometimes have been compelled and **forced** to do so.
A L : 2 3 :012(052) [0063] priests in Germany compelled by **force** to live in celibacy.
A L : 2 3 :018(054) [0063] of God is in **force**, although the custom of the church is
A L : 2 5 :006(062) [0069] even our adversaries are **forced** to concede to us that our
A P : 1 1 :005(181) [0251] our pastors do not **force** those who are not ready to use
A P : 1 2 :067(191) [0271] teaching be wiped out by **force** and the sword, and that
A P : 1 2 :127(201) [0289] churches should be maintained only by **force** and arms.
A P : 1 4 :002(214) [0315] But the bishops either **force** our priests to forsake and
A P : 2 1 :039(235) [0355] though they intended, by **forcing** our acceptance of the
A P : 2 3 :027(243) [0371] is presented as a proof to **force** perpetual celibacy on
A P : 2 3 :061(247) [0381] need it, but it does not **force** marriage on anyone who
A P : 2 3 :061(247) [0381] freedom; we refuse to **force** anyone into celibacy or to
A P : 2 4 :010(251) [0387] our opponents should be **forced** to discuss the point at
A P : 2 7 :009(270) [0423] of these orders are **forced** to approve and support the
A P : 2 7 :041(276) [0435] government or a tyranny **forces** us to leave or to deny the
A P : 2 7 :056(278) [0439] to these chapters are **forced** to agree with the persecutors
A P : 2 8 :006(282) [0445] to rule and to correct by **force** in order to guide their
S 3 : 0 3 :026(307) [0485] Finally the popes **forced** their way into purgatory, first by
T R : 0 0 :051(329) [0519] he defends his errors by **force** and murders, and he
L C : 0 1 :076(375) [0603] for those who have to be **forced** by means of rods and
L C : 0 1 :090(377) [0605] Wherever this practice is in **force**, a holy day is truly
L C : 0 1 :092(377) [0607] happens the commandment is in **force** and is fulfilled.
L C : 0 1 :094(378) [0607] then, that the power and **force** of this commandment
L C : 0 1 :096(378) [0609] who only from **force** of habit go to hear preaching and
L C : 0 1 :227(396) [0645] everyday business the same fraud prevails in full **force**.
L C : 0 1 :304(406) [0667] taken advantage of and **forced** to sacrifice what he
L C : 0 1 :327(409) [0675] proceeds from the **force** of the First Commandment: We
L C : 0 2 :061(419) [0695] then, is the article which must always remain in **force**.
L C : 0 3 :030(424) [0707] and all his might and his **forces** arrayed against us, trying
L C : 0 5 :026(449) [0759] when he cannot rout us by **force**, he sneaks and skulks
L C : 0 5 :052(452) [0765] But we neither **force** nor compel anyone, nor need anyone
L C : 0 5 :052(452) [0765] should not let yourself be **forced** by men either to faith or
L C : 0 6 :001(457) [0000] oppressive as that which **forced** everyone to make
L C : 0 6 :023(459) [0000] indicated, there would be no need of coercion and **force**.
E P : 1 0 :010(494) [0831] and institutions are **forcibly** imposed upon the
S D : 0 2 :046(530) [0899] God or wait until God **forcibly** converts them against
S D : 0 2 :073(535) [0909] coercion, so that God **forcibly** compels a man to be
S D : 0 4 :004(551) [0939] with which the law **forces** men to do good works.
S D : 0 7 :001(568) [0971] own consciences sought **forcibly** to adduce and pervert
S D : 0 7 :105(588) [1009] ascribe to and **force** upon our churches in spite of our
S D : 1 0 :003(611) [1053] are attempting either by **force** and coercion or by
S D : 1 0 :010(612) [1055] and confirm their idolatry by **force** or chicanery.
S D : 1 0 :015(613) [1057] commandments are **forcibly** imposed on the church as
S D : 1 0 :027(615) [1061] are imposed by **force** on the community of God as
S D : 1 2 :008(633) [1097] simple people, who were **forced** into contact with the

Forchheim (2)
S 3 : 1 5 :005(317) [0501] Master George Helt, of **Forchheim**
T R : 0 0 :082(335) [0529] George Helt, of **Forchheim**

Forearmed (1)
S D : 0 8 :038(598) [1027] church of God may be **forearmed** in the best possible way

Forebears (3)
P R : P R :018(009) [0015] of those sainted **forebears** of ours who themselves
P R : P R :025(013) [0023] truth that our pious **forebears** and we have acknowledged
S D : 0 7 :058(580) [0993] our revered fathers and **forebears**, like Luther and other

Forefathers (1)
A P : 2 4 :093(267) [0417] have departed in faith, **forefathers**, fathers, patriarchs,

Forego (1), Foregoing (8)
A P : 2 4 :007(250) [0385] For the present, we **forego** any discussion of their origins.
E P : 0 3 :001(472) [0791] Because of the **foregoing** a question has arisen, According
S D : 0 1 :030(513) [0867] As stated in a **foregoing** thesis when we discussed the
S D : 0 2 :008(521) [0883] and confirm the **foregoing** explanation of and summary
S D : 0 2 :083(537) [0913] From the **foregoing** exposition it is clear that when the
S D : 0 7 :103(587) [1007] to have denied by the **foregoing** that God may have and
S D : 0 7 :128(591) [1015] and rejected in the **foregoing** exposition; for the sake of
S D : 0 7 :128(591) [1015] by name from the **foregoing** exposition, for we reject and
S D : 1 2 :040(636) [1103] explanation of all the **foregoing** controverted articles here

Foreign (5)
A P : 0 2 :043(106) [0117] philosophy the totally **foreign** idea that because of our
A P : 1 0 :003(179) [0247] this would be completely **foreign** to the sacred Scriptures.
A P : 1 2 :016(184) [0257] are clearly false and **foreign** to the Holy Scriptures as
S 1 : P R :009(290) [0457] lies upon the king and **foreign** peoples as if they were the
S D : 0 1 :030(513) [0867] sin but a strange and **foreign** something within man, so

Foreknowledge (23), Foreknown (4), Foreknows (1)
E P : 1 1 :000(494) [0831] XI. God's Eternal **Foreknowledge** and Election
E P : 1 1 :002(494) [0831] between the **foreknowledge** and the eternal election of
E P : 1 1 :003(494) [0833] 2. God's **foreknowledge** in nothing else than that God
E P : 1 1 :004(494) [0833] 3. This **foreknowledge** extends alike over good people and
E P : 1 1 :004(495) [0833] God's **foreknowledge** merely controls the evil and
S D : 1 1 :000(616) [1063] XI. Eternal **Foreknowledge** and Divine Election
S D : 1 1 :004(616) [1063] God's eternal **foreknowledge** and the eternal election of
S D : 1 1 :004(616) [1063] — what we call God's **foreknowledge** — extends to all
S D : 1 1 :006(617) [1065] God's **foreknowledge** (*praescientia*) sees and knows in
S D : 1 1 :006(617) [1065] acts and works God's **foreknowledge** operates in such a
S D : 1 1 :007(617) [1065] of evil is not God's **foreknowledge** (since God neither
S D : 1 1 :008(617) [1065] not only foresees and **foreknows** the salvation of the
S D : 1 1 :010(618) [1067] and since God's **foreknowledge** can never fail and no
S D : 1 1 :010(618) [1067] if I have been **foreknown** to salvation, it will do me no
S D : 1 1 :010(618) [1067] be saved since God's **foreknowledge** must be carried out.
S D : 1 1 :010(618) [1067] But if I am not **foreknown**, then everything is in vain,
S D : 1 1 :010(618) [1067] etc., since I cannot hinder or alter God's **foreknowledge**."
S D : 1 1 :011(618) [1067] think, "If you are not **foreknown** to salvation from
S D : 1 1 :012(618) [1067] of God's eternal **foreknowledge** will in no way cause or
S D : 1 1 :013(619) [1067] secret, hidden, and inscrutable **foreknowledge** of God.
S D : 1 1 :024(620) [1069] of the purpose, **foreknowledge**, election, and ordinance of
S D : 1 1 :025(620) [1071] teaching of God's **foreknowledge** to salvation: Since only
S D : 1 1 :026(620) [1071] the secret and hidden abyss of divine **foreknowledge**.
S D : 1 1 :027(620) [1071] "Those whom God has **foreknown**, elected, and decreed,
S D : 1 1 :033(621) [1073] abyss of the hidden **foreknowledge** of God, even as Christ
S D : 1 1 :033(622) [1075] will show you how comforting God's **foreknowledge** is."
S D : 1 1 :041(623) [1077] Word is not God's **foreknowledge** but man's own perverse
S D : 1 1 :043(623) [1077] revealed the mystery of **foreknowledge** to us in his Word.

Foremost (4)
A P : 0 4 :059(115) [0137] everywhere as the **foremost** kind of worship, as in Ps.
S D : 0 1 :001(508) [0859] fallen man, at least the **foremost** and noblest part of his
S D : 0 1 :001(508) [0859] its highest degree and **foremost** powers) is original sin
S D : 0 1 :011(510) [0863] of the highest and **foremost** powers of the soul in mind,

Forensic (1)
A P : 0 4 :252(143) [0191] righteous in a **forensic** way, just as in the passage

Foreordained (1)
S D : 1 1 :010(618) [1067] say: "Since God has **foreordained** his elect to salvation

Foresaw (2), Foreseen (1), Foresees (1)
S D : 0 7 :028(574) [0981] highly enlightened man **foresaw** in the Spirit that after his
S D : 1 1 :008(617) [1065] however, not only **foresees** and foreknows the salvation
S D : 1 1 :009(618) [1065] it, than that God has **foreseen** who and how many are to
S D : 1 1 :054(625) [1081] the world began God **foresaw** right well and with utter

Foreshadowed (1)
A P : 2 4 :021(252) [0389] because of what they signified and **foreshadowed**.

Forestalling (1)
S D : R N :006(504) [0853] and effectively and to **forestalling** the possibility that

Foretell (1)
S D : 0 8 :027(596) [1025] earth, as the prophets **foretell** (Ps. 8:6; 93:1; Zech. 9:10)

Forever (27)
AG : 0 7 :001(032) [0047] one holy Christian church will be and remain **forever**.
AL : 0 3 :004(030) [0045] right hand of the Father, **forever** reign and have dominion
AL : 0 7 :001(032) [0047] also teach that one holy church is to continue **forever**.
S 1 : PR :009(290) [0457] the rest, wretchedness and woe will be their lot **forever**.
S 1 : PR :015(291) [0459] Thee and the Father liveth and reigneth, blessed **forever**.
S 2 : 0 2 :006(293) [0463] in order to guard **forever** against such abuses when it is so
TR : 0 0 :012(322) [0507] Eastern bishops should **forever** have sought ordination
SC : PR :005(338) [0533] Woe to you **forever**!
SC : PR :027(341) [0539] him be praise and thanks **forever**, through Christ, our
SC : 0 3 :008(346) [0547] live a godly life, both here in time and hereafter **forever**.
SC : 0 4 :012(349) [0551] cleansed and righteous, to live **forever** in God's presence.
SC : 0 8 :010(354) [0559] for he is good; for his steadfast love endures **forever**.
SC : 0 8 :011(354) [0559] Jesus Christ our Lord, who lives and reigns **forever**.
LC : SP :014(363) [0577] is the kingdom and the power and the glory, **forever**.
LC : 0 1 :164(387) [0627] peace, and afterwards abundance and blessedness **forever**.
LC : 0 3 :054(427) [0713] and that we may live **forever** in perfect righteousness and
LC : 0 4 :025(439) [0739] into the kingdom of Christ and live with him **forever**.
LC : 0 4 :043(442) [0743] or even though they died would afterward live **forever**.
LC : 0 4 :046(442) [0743] shall be saved and live **forever**: the soul through the Word
LC : 0 4 :077(446) [0751] Therefore Baptism remains **forever**.
LC : 0 5 :073(455) [0771] purely and worthily, you must stay away from it **forever**.
EP : 0 1 :010(467) [0781] bear will arise and live **forever**, without original sin and
SD : 0 2 :022(525) [0889] judgment cast away **forever** the wicked spirits who fell, he
SD : 0 2 :049(530) [0901] men should turn themselves to him and be saved **forever**.
SD : 0 3 :011(541) [0919] and holy by God the Father, and are saved **forever**.
SD : 0 3 :015(541) [0919] righteous, and saves us **forever** on account of this entire
SD : 0 6 :025(568) [0971] and with sheer joy, and will rejoice therein **forever**.

Forewarn (2)
SD : RN :019(507) [0857] might thereby faithfully **forewarn** everyone against the
SD : 0 7 :111(589) [1011] and thereby **forewarn** our readers so they can avoid and

Forfeited (1)
LC : 0 5 :059(453) [0767] such a sin that he has **forfeited** the name of Christian and

Forget (7), Forgetful (1), Forgetting (1)
AP : 2 8 :024(285) [0451] good will ceases, and mortals are **forgetful**," said Pindar.
S 3 : 0 3 :037(309) [0489] his confession without omitting or **forgetting** a single one.
S 3 : 0 5 :002(310) [0491] and the Dominicans who **forget** the Word (God's
LC : 0 1 :037(369) [0591] severely that he will not **forget** his anger down to their
LC : 0 1 :128(382) [0617] in the world; children **forget** their parents, as we all forget
LC : 0 1 :128(382) [0617] their parents, as we all **forget** God, and no one takes
LC : 0 1 :128(382) [0617] grumble impatiently and **forget** all the blessings we have
LC : 0 1 :238(397) [0647] God will not **forget** his commandment.
LC : 0 6 :021(459) [0000] for the sake of absolution, let him just **forget** about it.

Forgive (51), Forgives (27), Forgave (2), Forgiving (5), Forgiven (92)
AG : 0 4 :002(030) [0045] for his sake our sin is **forgiven** and righteousness and
AG : 1 2 :005(034) [0049] that sin has been **forgiven** and grace has been obtained
AG : 2 0 :009(042) [0053] believe that our sins are **forgiven** for Christ's sake, who
AG : 2 5 :003(062) [0069] the Word of God, who **forgives** sin, for it is spoken in
AG : 2 8 :005(081) [0085] to preach the Gospel, to **forgive** and retain sins, and to
AG : 2 8 :006(082) [0085] If you **forgive** the sins of any, they are forgiven; if you
AG : 2 8 :006(082) [0085] the sins of any, they are **forgiven**; if you retain the sins of
AG : 2 8 :021(084) [0087] to preach the Gospel, **forgive** sins, judge doctrine and
AG : 2 8 :041(087) [0089] a reserved case sin is not **forgiven** unless forgiveness is
AL : 0 4 :002(030) [0045] and that their sins are **forgiven** on account of Christ, who
AL : 1 2 :005(034) [0049] believes that sins are **forgiven** for Christ's sake, comforts
AL : 1 3 :003(036) [0049] believes that sins are **forgiven**, is required in the use of the
AL : 2 5 :009(062) [0069] But if no sins were **forgiven** except those which are
AL : 2 6 :004(064) [0071] believes that sins are **forgiven** for Christ's sake may be
AL : 2 8 :006(082) [0085] If you **forgive** the sins of any, they are forgiven; if you
AL : 2 8 :006(082) [0085] the sins of any, they are **forgiven**; if you retain the sins of
AL : 2 8 :021(084) [0087] sacraments) except to **forgive** sins, to reject doctrine
AL : 2 8 :041(087) [0089] case a sin cannot be **forgiven** except by the authority of
AP : 0 2 :036(105) [0115] when he says, "Sin is **forgiven** in Baptism, not that it no
AP : 0 2 :036(105) [0115] is in the members is **forgiven** by spiritual regeneration,
AP : 0 2 :036(105) [0115] It is **forgiven** because its guilt is absolved by the
AP : 0 2 :040(105) [0115] of death if it is not **forgiven**, though it is not imputed to
AP : 0 2 :045(106) [0117] the grace of Christ to be **forgiven** and the Holy Spirit to
AP : 0 4 :045(113) [0133] believes that his sins are **forgiven** because of Christ and
AP : 0 4 :057(114) [0137] the Christ, that for his sake God intended to **forgive** sins.
AP : 0 4 :076(117) [0143] Ps. 32:1, "Blessed is he whose transgression is **forgiven**."
AP : 0 4 :082(118) [0145] it is certain that sins are **forgiven** because of Christ, the
AP : 0 4 :103(122) [0151] the Lord Jesus came he **forgave** all men the sin that none
AP : 0 4 :103(122) [0151] whose transgression is **forgiven**, whose sin is covered'
AP : 0 4 :120(124) [0155] promise that sins are **forgiven** freely for Christ's sake)
AP : 0 4 :135(125) [0159] our failure to believe that God **forgives** and hears us.
AP : 0 4 :141(126) [0161] because he gave his Son for us and **forgave** us our sins.
AP : 0 4 :148(127) [0163] full assurance that God **forgives** because Christ did not
AP : 0 4 :149(127) [0163] doubts that his sins are **forgiven**, he insults Christ because
AP : 0 4 :152(127) [0163] which are many, are **forgiven**, because she loved much."
AP : 0 4 :155(128) [0165] which are many, are **forgiven**, because she loved much,"
AP : 0 4 :163(129) [0169] Rom. 4:7), "Blessed is he whose transgression is **forgiven**."
AP : 0 4 :172(130) [0171] of God are kept when what is not kept is **forgiven**."
AP : 0 4 :195(134) [0175] who believe that their sins are **forgiven** for Christ's sake.
AP : 0 4 :203(135) [0175] Christ's sake he is freely **forgiven** and freely has a
AP : 0 4 :205(135) [0177] when it is sure that he freely **forgives** and hears us.
AP : 0 4 :232(139) [0185] unless men cover and **forgive** certain mistakes in their
AP : 0 4 :236(140) [0185] as the poet writes, "I **forgive** myself, says Maenius."
AP : 0 4 :239(141) [0187] because we know that for Christ's sake we are **forgiven**.
AP : 0 4 :242(141) [0187] love covers them up, **forgives**, yields, and does not go to
AP : 0 4 :243(141) [0189] pastors and churches overlook and **forgive** many things.
AP : 0 4 :254(143) [0193] Luke 6:37, **"Forgive**, and you will be forgiven."
AP : 0 4 :254(143) [0193] Luke 6:37, "Forgive, and you will be **forgiven**."
AP : 0 4 :255(144) [0193] do not add that sins are **forgiven** without faith or that
AP : 0 4 :257(144) [0193] for Christ's sake sins are **forgiven** and that by faith in
AP : 0 4 :259(144) [0193] penitence when he says, **"Forgive**," and he adds the
AP : 0 4 :259(144) [0193] he adds the promise, "You will be **forgiven**" (Luke 6:37).
AP : 0 4 :259(144) [0193] not say that when we **forgive**, this merits the forgiveness
AP : 0 4 :260(145) [0193] if we believe that our sins are **forgiven** for Christ's sake.
AP : 0 4 :263(145) [0195] is removed because God **forgives** those who are penitent,
AP : 0 4 :263(145) [0195] from this that God **forgives** because of the works that
AP : 0 4 :263(145) [0195] of his promise he **forgives** those who take hold of that
AP : 0 4 :267(146) [0197] faith, which believes that God freely **forgives** sins.
AP : 0 4 :272(148) [0199] as in Matt. 6:14, "If you **forgive** men their trespasses,
AP : 0 4 :272(148) [0199] trespasses, your heavenly Father also will **forgive** you."
AP : 0 4 :273(148) [0199] I John 2:12, "Your sins are **forgiven** for his sake."
AP : 0 4 :276(148) [0199] minds to believe more firmly that their sins are **forgiven**.
AP : 0 4 :292(152) [0203] that he wishes to **forgive** and to be reconciled for Christ's
AP : 0 4 :295(152) [0203] for Christ's sake the Father is reconciled and **forgiving**.
AP : 0 4 :303(154) [0205] that God cares for us, **forgives** us, and hears us is a
AP : 0 4 :308(155) [0207] for Christ's sake this is **forgiven** us, as Paul says
AP : 0 4 :326(157) [0211] of God, if God does not **forgive** but judges and condemns
AP : 0 4 :331(158) [0211] O Lord, hear; O Lord, **forgive**; O Lord, give heed and
AP : 0 4 :350(161) [0217] that God cares for us, **forgives** us, and hears us for
AP : 0 7 :020(172) [0233] foundation, these are **forgiven** them or even corrected.
AP : 1 2 :006(183) [0255] of the keys accomplish if the sin is **forgiven** already?
AP : 1 2 :007(183) [0255] the power of the keys **forgives** sins before the church but
AP : 1 2 :013(184) [0257] that of these one part is **forgiven** by the power of the keys
AP : 1 2 :022(185) [0257] of the keys does not **forgive** sins before God, but it was
AP : 1 2 :035(186) [0261] that because of Christ their sins are freely **forgiven**.
AP : 1 2 :040(187) [0261] the Word, the keys truly **forgive** sin before him, according
AP : 1 2 :044(187) [0263] Christ means to believe that for his sake sins are **forgiven**.
AP : 1 2 :057(189) [0267] heard the absolution (vv. 48, 50), "Your sins are **forgiven**.
AP : 1 2 :059(190) [0267] which each individual believes that his sins are **forgiven**.
AP : 1 2 :060(190) [0267] require everyone to believe that his sins are **forgiven** him.
AP : 1 2 :065(191) [0271] we believe that our sins are **forgiven** because of Christ.
AP : 1 2 :072(192) [0271] that they are freely **forgiven** because of Christ, not
AP : 1 2 :073(192) [0273] you also believe that through him your sins are **forgiven**.
AP : 1 2 :073(192) [0273] brings in your heart, saying, 'Your sins are **forgiven** you.'
AP : 1 2 :074(192) [0273] general way that sins are **forgiven** by mercy, but he bids
AP : 1 2 :074(192) [0273] add the personal faith that they are **forgiven** to us as well.
AP : 1 2 :075(193) [0273] say that sins are **forgiven** in this way: Because a person
AP : 1 2 :088(195) [0277] "How do we become sure that our sins are **forgiven**?"
AP : 1 2 :088(195) [0277] sure that their sins are **forgiven** freely for Christ's sake,
AP : 1 2 :088(195) [0277] not doubting that they are **forgiven** them personally.
AP : 1 2 :094(196) [0281] him when he swears and are sure that he **forgives** us.
AP : 1 2 :094(196) [0281] is not sure that he is **forgiven**, he denies that God has
AP : 1 2 :095(196) [0281] firmly that God freely **forgives** us because of Christ and
AP : 1 2 :104(197) [0283] have the command to **forgive** sins; they do not have the
AP : 1 2 :105(197) [0283] the voice of the Gospel **forgiving** sins and consoling
AP : 1 2 :107(197) [0283] to the Lord'; then thou didst **forgive** the guilt of my sin."
AP : 1 2 :118(199) [0287] temporal punishment is **forgiven** by the power of the
AP : 1 2 :118(199) [0287] punishments are partly **forgiven** by the power of the keys,
AP : 1 2 :118(200) [0287] of purgatory is **forgiven**; in that case satisfactions would
AP : 1 2 :161(208) [0303] he carry out the threat even when the sin was **forgiven**?
AP : 1 2 :161(208) [0303] is that the sin was **forgiven** so as not to prevent the man
AP : 1 2 :176(210) [0307] have the command to **forgive** the sins of those who are
AP : 1 2 :176(210) [0307] as "to loose" means to **forgive** sins, so "to bind" means
AP : 1 2 :176(210) [0307] to forgive sins, so "to bind" means not to **forgive** sins.
AP : 1 3 :004(211) [0309] believe that God really **forgives** us for Christ's sake.
AP : 1 3 :020(214) [0313] God, by a new miracle, promised his will to **forgive**.
AP : 1 8 :006(225) [0335] the faith that God hears, **forgives**, helps, or saves them.
AP : 1 8 :007(226) [0337] and trust that God considers, hears, and **forgives** us.
AP : 2 0 :010(228) [0341] as it were, that sins are freely **forgiven** for Christ's sake.
AP : 2 1 :005(229) [0345] faith: when we see Peter **forgiven** after his denial, we are
AP : 2 1 :036(234) [0353] Peter was **forgiven** for denying Christ; Cyprian was
AP : 2 1 :036(234) [0353] Christ; Cyprian was **forgiven** for having been a sorcerer;
AP : 2 4 :012(251) [0387] for his sake we are **forgiven**, his merits and righteousness
AP : 2 4 :043(257) [0399] or point out that sins are freely **forgiven** for Christ's sake.
AP : 2 4 :049(258) [0401] to trust and believe that their sins are freely **forgiven**.
AP : 2 4 :076(263) [0411] what is given and what is **forgiven**, and it gives thanks to
AP : 2 4 :076(263) [0411] what is given and what is **forgiven**; it compares the
AP : 2 4 :090(266) [0415] Supper was instituted for the sake of **forgiving** guilt.
AP : 2 7 :017(271) [0425] Moses' place, not by **forgiving** sins on account of our
AP : 2 7 :017(271) [0425] wrath of God for us so that we might be freely **forgiven**.
S 3 : 0 3 :017(306) [0483] on the basis of this good work of his, his sin was **forgiven**.
TR : 0 0 :023(324) [0511] too, it is written, "If you **forgive** the sins," etc. (John
TR : 0 0 :044(328) [0517] who teach that sins are **forgiven** on account of the worth
TR : 0 0 :044(328) [0517] they teach that sins are **forgiven** freely for Christ's sake
SC : 0 2 :006(345) [0545] he daily and abundantly **forgives** all my sins, and the sins
SC : 0 3 :015(347) [0549] *"And **forgive** us our debts, as we also have forgiven our*
SC : 0 3 :015(347) [0549] *us our debts, as we also have **forgiven** our debtors."*
SC : 0 3 :016(347) [0549] on our part will heartily **forgive** and cheerfully do good to
SC : 0 5 :016(350) [0553] that our sins are thereby **forgiven** before God in heaven.
SC : 0 5 :021(350) [0553] and declare that my sins are **forgiven** for God's sake."
SC : 0 5 :028(351) [0555] our Lord Jesus Christ, I **forgive** you your sins in the
SC : 0 7 :005(353) [0559] I beseech Thee to **forgive** all my sin and the wrong which
LC : SP :014(363) [0577] day our daily bread; and **forgive** us our debts, as we also
LC : SP :014(363) [0577] debts, as we also have **forgiven** our debtors; and lead us
LC : 0 1 :182(389) [0631] It **forgives** anger except, as we have said, to persons who
LC : 0 2 :055(418) [0693] God **forgives** us, and we forgive, bear with, and aid one
LC : 0 2 :055(418) [0693] God forgives us, and we **forgive**, bear with, and aid one
LC : 0 3 :085(432) [0723] *"And **forgive** us our debts, as we forgive our debtors."*
LC : 0 3 :085(432) [0723] *"And forgive us our debts, as we **forgive** our debtors."*
LC : 0 3 :088(432) [0723] upon God and pray, "Dear Father, **forgive** us our debts."
LC : 0 3 :088(432) [0723] Not that he does not **forgive** sin even without and before
LC : 0 3 :091(432) [0723] In short, unless God constantly **forgives**, we are lost.
LC : 0 3 :092(432) [0725] deal graciously with us, **forgive** as he has promised, and
LC : 0 3 :092(433) [0725] only come from the knowledge that our sins are **forgiven**.
LC : 0 3 :093(433) [0725] comforting clause is added, "as we **forgive** our debtors."
LC : 0 3 :093(433) [0725] that everything is **forgiven** and pardoned, yet on the
LC : 0 3 :093(433) [0725] yet on the condition that we also **forgive** our neighbor.
LC : 0 3 :094(433) [0725] God everyday and yet he **forgives** it all through grace, we
LC : 0 3 :094(433) [0725] grace, we must always **forgive** our neighbor who does us
LC : 0 3 :095(433) [0725] If you do not **forgive**, do not think that God forgives
LC : 0 3 :095(433) [0725] If you do not forgive, do not think that God **forgives** you.
LC : 0 3 :095(433) [0725] But if you **forgive**, you have the comfort and assurance
LC : 0 3 :095(433) [0725] comfort and assurance that you are **forgiven** in heaven.
LC : 0 3 :096(433) [0725] Not on account of your **forgiving**, for God does it
LC : 0 3 :096(433) [0725] this petition, Luke 6:37, **"Forgive**, and you will be
LC : 0 3 :096(433) [0725] petition, Luke 6:37, "Forgive, and you will be **forgiven**."
LC : 0 3 :096(433) [0725] Matt. 6:14, saying, "If you **forgive** men their trespasses,
LC : 0 3 :096(433) [0725] your heavenly Father also will **forgive** you," etc.

Continued ▶

L C : 0 5 :028(449) [0759] can bread and wine **forgive** sins or strengthen faith?"
L C : 0 6 :008(458) [0000] Prayer when we say, "**Forgive** us our debts, as we forgive
L C : 0 6 :008(458) [0000] "Forgive us our debts, as we **forgive** our debtors," etc.
L C : 0 6 :010(458) [0000] before one another and **forgive** one another before we
L C : 0 6 :012(458) [0000] and to our neighbor are **forgiven** when we forgive our
L C : 0 6 :012(458) [0000] are forgiven when we **forgive** our neighbor and become
L C : 0 6 :016(459) [0000] the absolution was not valid and the sin was not **forgiven**.
E P : 0 3 :004(473) [0793] consists in this, that God **forgives** us our sins purely by
E P : 0 4 :007(476) [0799] whose iniquities are **forgiven**, and whose sins are
S D : 0 1 :014(511) [0863] can be covered up and **forgiven** before God only for the
S D : 0 1 :031(513) [0869] nature unless the sin is **forgiven** for Christ's sake.
S D : 0 2 :031(527) [0893] will hear them, that he **forgives** their sin, or that he will
S D : 0 3 :015(541) [0919] us as righteousness, God **forgives** us our sins, accounts us
S D : 0 3 :023(543) [0923] so that our sins are **forgiven** and covered up and are not
S D : 0 3 :058(550) [0937] our damnation but is **forgiven** and remitted by sheer
S D : 0 5 :002(558) [0953] law of God reproved, has been pardoned and **forgiven**.
S D : 0 5 :021(562) [0959] not to punish sins but to **forgive** them for Christ's sake.
S D : 0 5 :025(563) [0961] believe the Gospel God **forgives** them all their sins
S D : 0 7 :063(581) [0995] that their sins are truly **forgiven**, that Christ dwells and is

Forgiveness (527)
A G : 0 4 :001(030) [0045] that we cannot obtain **forgiveness** of sin and
A G : 0 4 :001(030) [0045] but that we receive **forgiveness** of sin and become
A G : 0 6 :002(032) [0045] For we receive **forgiveness** of sin and righteousness
A G : 0 6 :003(032) [0047] and he shall have **forgiveness** of sins, not through works
A G : 1 2 :001(034) [0049] after Baptism receive **forgiveness** of sin whenever they
A G : 1 2 :010(035) [0049] those who teach that **forgiveness** of sin is not obtained
A G : 2 0 :023(044) [0055] we receive grace and **forgiveness** of sin through Christ.
A G : 2 0 :025(044) [0057] article concerning the **forgiveness** of sin, and so they are
A G : 2 0 :028(045) [0057] faith alone that apprehends grace and **forgiveness** of sin.
A G : 2 4 :030(059) [0067] sacrament grace and **forgiveness** of sin are promised us by
A G : 2 5 :004(062) [0069] that through such faith we obtain **forgiveness** of sins.
A G : 2 6 :029(068) [0075] the purpose of earning **forgiveness** of sin or with the
A G : 2 7 :011(072) [0077] life one could earn **forgiveness** of sin and justification
A G : 2 7 :044(078) [0081] justified and earned **forgiveness** of sins by their vows and
A G : 2 8 :041(087) [0089] is not forgiven unless **forgiveness** is secured from the
A L : 0 6 :001(032) [0045] before God, for **forgiveness** of sins and justification are
A L : 0 6 :003(032) [0047] alone, and he shall receive **forgiveness** of sins by grace."
A L : 1 2 :001(034) [0049] Baptism can receive **forgiveness** of sins whenever they are
A L : 2 0 :009(042) [0053] reconcile God or merit **forgiveness** of sins and grace but
A L : 2 0 :009(042) [0053] but that we obtain **forgiveness** and grace only by faith
A L : 2 0 :022(044) [0055] know that grace and **forgiveness** of sins are apprehended
A L : 2 0 :023(044) [0055] this article of the **forgiveness** of sins — that is, that we
A L : 2 0 :023(044) [0055] righteousness, and **forgiveness** of sins through Christ.
A L : 2 0 :025(044) [0057] this article of the **forgiveness** of sins; hence they hate God
A L : 2 0 :028(045) [0057] It is only by faith that **forgiveness** of sins and grace are
A L : 2 5 :004(062) [0069] faith truly obtains and receives the **forgiveness** of sins.
A L : 2 6 :033(069) [0075] not in order to merit **forgiveness** of sins or satisfaction for
A L : 2 6 :038(069) [0075] his body not to merit **forgiveness** of sins by that discipline
A L : 2 7 :011(072) [0077] that they merited **forgiveness** of sins and justification
A L : 2 7 :044(078) [0081] justified and merited **forgiveness** of sins by their vows and
A P : 0 4 :001(107) [0119] men do not receive the **forgiveness** of sins because of their
A P : 0 4 :001(107) [0121] that men receive the **forgiveness** of sins because of their
A P : 0 4 :001(107) [0121] that men receive the **forgiveness** of sins by faith and by
A P : 0 4 :003(107) [0121] understand neither the **forgiveness** of sins nor faith nor
A P : 0 4 :005(108) [0121] will come and promises **forgiveness** of sins, justification,
A P : 0 4 :005(108) [0121] who came promises **forgiveness** of sins, justification, and
A P : 0 4 :007(108) [0121] law and by it they seek **forgiveness** of sins and
A P : 0 4 :009(108) [0123] teach men to merit the **forgiveness** of sins by doing what
A P : 0 4 :012(109) [0123] If we merit the **forgiveness** of sins by these elicited acts of
A P : 0 4 :015(109) [0123] we could merit the **forgiveness** of sins rather than
A P : 0 4 :016(109) [0123] that we merit **forgiveness** of sins and justification by the
A P : 0 4 :018(109) [0125] they freely receive the **forgiveness** of sins and
A P : 0 4 :018(109) [0125] that they merit the **forgiveness** of sins and are accounted
A P : 0 4 :020(110) [0125] do not know how the **forgiveness** of sins takes place, or
A P : 0 4 :020(110) [0125] the Gospel of the free **forgiveness** of sins and the
A P : 0 4 :025(110) [0127] false that by our works we merit the **forgiveness** of sins.
A P : 0 4 :031(111) [0129] us from our sins or merit for us the **forgiveness** of sins.
A P : 0 4 :036(112) [0131] eternal wrath merit the **forgiveness** of sins by an elicited
A P : 0 4 :036(112) [0131] God unless faith has first accepted the **forgiveness** of sins.
A P : 0 4 :038(112) [0131] not say that by the law men merit the **forgiveness** of sins.
A P : 0 4 :038(112) [0131] law and by their works they merit the **forgiveness** of sins.
A P : 0 4 :040(112) [0131] but the promise of the **forgiveness** of sins and justification
A P : 0 4 :041(113) [0133] merits but offers the **forgiveness** of sins and justification
A P : 0 4 :041(113) [0133] that is, the **forgiveness** of sins is offered freely.
A P : 0 4 :042(113) [0133] If the **forgiveness** of sins depended upon our merits and if
A P : 0 4 :043(113) [0133] the promise of **forgiveness** of sins and justification
A P : 0 4 :045(113) [0133] faith obtains the **forgiveness** of sins and justifies us.
A P : 0 4 :046(113) [0133] By freely accepting the **forgiveness** of sins, faith sets
A P : 0 4 :048(114) [0135] God's offer promising **forgiveness** of sins and
A P : 0 4 :048(114) [0135] the promised offer of **forgiveness** of sins and justification.
A P : 0 4 :051(114) [0135] to the article of the Creed on the **forgiveness** of sins.
A P : 0 4 :051(114) [0135] the purpose of the history, "the **forgiveness** of sins."
A P : 0 4 :051(114) [0135] of our own merits the **forgiveness** of sins is bestowed
A P : 0 4 :057(114) [0137] does not teach the free **forgiveness** of sins, the patriarchs
A P : 0 4 :057(114) [0137] free mercy and the **forgiveness** of sins by faith, just as the
A P : 0 4 :058(115) [0137] He adds, "There is **forgiveness** with thee" (v. 4).
A P : 0 4 :058(115) [0137] thou has promised the **forgiveness** of sins I am sustained
A P : 0 4 :062(115) [0139] that penitence and **forgiveness** of sins should be preached
A P : 0 4 :062(115) [0139] Christ's sake it offers **forgiveness** of sins and justification,
A P : 0 4 :062(115) [0139] promise that for his sake we have the **forgiveness** of sins.
A P : 0 4 :062(115) [0139] us, receives the **forgiveness** of sins, justifies and quickens
A P : 0 4 :070(116) [0141] For the law does not teach the free **forgiveness** of sins.
A P : 0 4 :072(117) [0141] one, that is, that it receives the **forgiveness** of sins.
A P : 0 4 :074(117) [0143] We Obtain the **Forgiveness** of Sins Only by Faith in
A P : 0 4 :075(117) [0143] we suppose, that the **forgiveness** of sins is supremely
A P : 0 4 :076(117) [0143] First, **forgiveness** of sins is the same as justification
A P : 0 4 :077(117) [0143] We obtain the **forgiveness** of sins only by faith in Christ,
A P : 0 4 :079(117) [0143] if we know how the **forgiveness** of sins takes place.
A P : 0 4 :079(117) [0143] as to whether the **forgiveness** of sins and the infusion of
A P : 0 4 :079(117) [0143] In the **forgiveness** of sins, the terrors of sin and of eternal
A P : 0 4 :080(118) [0143] we obtain the **forgiveness** of sins when we comfort our
A P : 0 4 :081(118) [0143] Father and receive the **forgiveness** of sins when we are
A P : 0 4 :081(118) [0145] for Christ's sake we receive the **forgiveness** of sins.
A P : 0 4 :083(118) [0145] believes in him receives **forgiveness** of sins through his
A P : 0 4 :083(118) [0145] We receive the **forgiveness** of sins, he says, through his
A P : 0 4 :084(119) [0145] Fourth, the **forgiveness** of sins is a thing promised for
A P : 0 4 :084(119) [0145] that the promise of the **forgiveness** of sins and
A P : 0 4 :085(119) [0147] that we receive the **forgiveness** of sins for Christ's sake
A P : 0 4 :086(119) [0147] because we receive the **forgiveness** of sins and the Holy
A P : 0 4 :087(120) [0147] works merited the **forgiveness** of sins and justification,
A P : 0 4 :097(121) [0149] that through this man **forgiveness** of sins is proclaimed to
A P : 0 4 :102(121) [0151] of Christ, of the **forgiveness** of sins, and of our gracious
A P : 0 4 :110(123) [0153] If faith receives the **forgiveness** of sins on account of
A P : 0 4 :110(123) [0153] on account of love, the **forgiveness** of sins will always be
A P : 0 4 :110(123) [0153] hearts are sure that the **forgiveness** of sins has been
A P : 0 4 :110(123) [0153] our own love for the **forgiveness** of sins and justification,
A P : 0 4 :110(123) [0153] abolish the Gospel of the free **forgiveness** of sins.
A P : 0 4 :110(123) [0153] they believe that the **forgiveness** of sins is received freely.
A P : 0 4 :112(123) [0155] this that we receive the **forgiveness** of sins by trust in this
A P : 0 4 :112(123) [0155] little as we receive the **forgiveness** of sins on account of
A P : 0 4 :112(123) [0155] For the **forgiveness** of sins is received by faith alone—and
A P : 0 4 :114(123) [0155] because it receives the **forgiveness** of sins and reconciles
A P : 0 4 :116(123) [0155] faith alone receives the **forgiveness** of sins, renders us
A P : 0 4 :117(123) [0155] alone we receive the **forgiveness** of sins for Christ's sake,
A P : 0 4 :119(124) [0155] doubt whether they have received the **forgiveness** of sins.
A P : 0 4 :119(124) [0155] they should doubt about receiving the **forgiveness** of sins?
A P : 0 4 :121(124) [0155] promise of the free **forgiveness** of sins and of the
A P : 0 4 :132(125) [0159] receive the gift of the **forgiveness** of sins and the Holy
A P : 0 4 :135(125) [0159] the Gospel of the **forgiveness** of sins, we receive the Holy
A P : 0 4 :141(126) [0161] having received the **forgiveness** of sins, we become sure
A P : 0 4 :142(126) [0161] our sins and looks for **forgiveness** of sins and deliverance
A P : 0 4 :144(127) [0161] Receiving the **forgiveness** of sins for a heart terrified and
A P : 0 4 :145(127) [0163] must first receive the **forgiveness** of sins by faith, nor that
A P : 0 4 :147(127) [0163] we do not receive the **forgiveness** of sins through love or
A P : 0 4 :150(127) [0163] that he obtains the **forgiveness** of sins because he loves,
A P : 0 4 :151(127) [0163] We do not receive the **forgiveness** of sins by other virtues
A P : 0 4 :151(127) [0163] little do we receive the **forgiveness** of sins on account of
A P : 0 4 :152(127) [0163] of love the woman had merited the **forgiveness** of sins.
A P : 0 4 :154(128) [0163] that she should seek the **forgiveness** of sins from Christ.
A P : 0 4 :154(128) [0163] By looking for the **forgiveness** of sins from him, she truly
A P : 0 4 :154(128) [0165] she was looking for the **forgiveness** of sins from Christ.
A P : 0 4 :154(128) [0165] or seek from him the **forgiveness** of sins and salvation!
A P : 0 4 :155(128) [0165] properly accepts the **forgiveness** of sins, though love,
A P : 0 4 :155(128) [0165] which earns the **forgiveness** of sins that reconciles us to
A P : 0 4 :157(128) [0165] For if the **forgiveness** of sins and reconciliation do not
A P : 0 4 :157(128) [0165] nobody will have the **forgiveness** of sins unless he keeps
A P : 0 4 :158(129) [0165] sure that we receive the **forgiveness** of sins by faith alone.
A P : 0 4 :159(129) [0167] law; but we receive the **forgiveness** of sins and
A P : 0 4 :163(129) [0169] This **forgiveness** is always received by faith.
A P : 0 4 :168(130) [0169] that even the godly must pray for the **forgiveness** of sins.
A P : 0 4 :182(132) [0173] alone we receive the **forgiveness** of sins and reconciliation
A P : 0 4 :186(132) [0173] the free promise of the **forgiveness** of sins for Christ's
A P : 0 4 :186(132) [0173] works we receive the **forgiveness** of sins and
A P : 0 4 :187(133) [0173] If the **forgiveness** of sins were conditional upon our
A P : 0 4 :188(133) [0173] them about the free **forgiveness** of sins and the
A P : 0 4 :194(133) [0175] meritorious—not for the **forgiveness** of sins, grace, or
A P : 0 4 :195(134) [0175] But the **forgiveness** of sins is the same and equal to all, as
A P : 0 4 :195(134) [0175] The **forgiveness** of sins and justification are received only
A P : 0 4 :202(134) [0175] God — not to merit the **forgiveness** of sins and grace
A P : 0 4 :203(135) [0177] works the saints merited grace and the **forgiveness** of sins.
A P : 0 4 :203(135) [0177] he will merit grace and **forgiveness** of sins, appease the
A P : 0 4 :208(135) [0177] to merit grace, righteousness, and the **forgiveness** of sins.
A P : 0 4 :208(135) [0177] to merit grace and **forgiveness** of sins by this deed, but
A P : 0 4 :211(136) [0179] works to merit the **forgiveness** of sins, grace, and
A P : 0 4 :213(136) [0179] that they merit the **forgiveness** of sins and grace and that
A P : 0 4 :214(136) [0179] We do not merit the **forgiveness** of sins, grace, and
A P : 0 4 :222(138) [0181] we receive the promised **forgiveness** of sins — Paul is
A P : 0 4 :236(140) [0185] they easily find **forgiveness**, but not for others, as the
A P : 0 4 :242(141) [0187] that love merits the **forgiveness** of sins in relation to God;
A P : 0 4 :244(142) [0189] works we merit the **forgiveness** of sins; that good works
A P : 0 4 :246(142) [0189] good works we merit grace and the **forgiveness** of sins.
A P : 0 4 :246(142) [0189] and accepted and have obtained the **forgiveness** of sins.
A P : 0 4 :246(142) [0189] we merit grace and **forgiveness** of sins by good works and
A P : 0 4 :253(143) [0193] that works merit the **forgiveness** of sins; that works
A P : 0 4 :257(144) [0193] voice of God, clearly promising the **forgiveness** of sins.
A P : 0 4 :257(144) [0193] that by faith in Christ we obtain the **forgiveness** of sins.
A P : 0 4 :258(144) [0193] could merit the **forgiveness** of sins *ex opere operato*, but
A P : 0 4 :258(144) [0193] time he wants the **forgiveness** of sins to be received by
A P : 0 4 :259(144) [0193] forgive, this merits the **forgiveness** of sins *ex opere*
A P : 0 4 :259(144) [0193] time he wants the **forgiveness** of sins to be received by
A P : 0 4 :259(145) [0193] time he wishes the **forgiveness** of sins to be received by
A P : 0 4 :260(145) [0193] added, that is, that the **forgiveness** of sins is granted to us
A P : 0 4 :260(145) [0195] that by our works we purchase the **forgiveness** of sins.
A P : 0 4 :261(145) [0195] other part Daniel promises the king **forgiveness** of sins.
A P : 0 4 :261(145) [0195] This promise of the **forgiveness** of sins is not the
A P : 0 4 :262(145) [0195] Daniel knew that the **forgiveness** of sins in the Christ was
A P : 0 4 :262(145) [0195] he could not have promised the king **forgiveness** of sins.
A P : 0 4 :264(146) [0195] less authority that the **forgiveness** of sins is uncertain.
A P : 0 4 :264(146) [0195] Gospel promises the **forgiveness** of sins with certainty.
A P : 0 4 :264(146) [0195] were to deny that the **forgiveness** of sins must surely be
A P : 0 4 :264(146) [0195] It signifies that the **forgiveness** of sins is possible, that
A P : 0 4 :264(146) [0195] the human theory that **forgiveness** depends upon works.
A P : 0 4 :265(146) [0197] of these works brings **forgiveness** of sins and justification.
A P : 0 4 :267(147) [0197] say that by these works we merit the **forgiveness** of sins.
A P : 0 4 :268(147) [0197] grant that first come **forgiveness** of sins and justification
A P : 0 4 :269(147) [0197] of them a propitiation that merits the **forgiveness** of sins.
A P : 0 4 :272(148) [0199] but also promises the **forgiveness** of sins, it necessarily
A P : 0 4 :272(148) [0199] Only faith accepts the **forgiveness** of sins.
A P : 0 4 :272(148) [0199] and a promise of the **forgiveness** of sins is added,
A P : 0 4 :273(148) [0199] believes in him receives **forgiveness** of sins through his
A P : 0 4 :273(148) [0199] through his blood, the **forgiveness** of our trespasses."
A P : 0 4 :274(148) [0199] Gospel, that we obtain **forgiveness** of sins by faith
A P : 0 4 :274(148) [0199] such works we merit **forgiveness** of sins or justification.
A P : 0 4 :275(148) [0199] the promise of **forgiveness** of sins with good works.
A P : 0 4 :278(149) [0199] faith which accepts **forgiveness** of sins and overcomes

Continued ▶

Continued ▶

A P : 2 7 :040(276) [0433] because it merits the **forgiveness** of sins and eternal life.
A P : 2 7 :040(276) [0433] by this act to merit the **forgiveness** of sins or eternal life,
A P : 2 7 :054(278) [0437] Gospel about the free **forgiveness** of sins for Christ's
A P : 2 7 :055(278) [0439] of God to merit the **forgiveness** of sins for them and for
A P : 2 7 :058(279) [0439] men, not to merit the **forgiveness** of sins before God or to
A P : 2 7 :058(279) [0439] act of worship to merit **forgiveness** of sins and
A P : 2 7 :058(279) [0439] not meant to merit the **forgiveness** of sins but to be an
A P : 2 7 :061(279) [0441] do not merit the **forgiveness** of sins or justification.
A P : 2 7 :061(279) [0441] that they would merit **forgiveness** of sins by it, or that
A P : 2 7 :062(280) [0441] and that they merit **forgiveness** of sins and justification.
A P : 2 7 :065(280) [0441] idea that they merit **forgiveness** of sin and justification.
A P : 2 7 :065(280) [0441] in order to merit the **forgiveness** of sins or to secure
A P : 2 7 :069(281) [0443] observances merit the **forgiveness** of sins; that because of
A P : 2 7 :070(281) [0443] learning that they had **forgiveness** of sins freely for
A P : 2 8 :007(282) [0445] that we receive **forgiveness** of sins freely for Christ's sake
A P : 2 8 :008(282) [0445] they merited the **forgiveness** of sins or were acts of
A P : 2 8 :009(282) [0445] do not merit the **forgiveness** of sins; here they also say
A P : 2 8 :009(282) [0445] Do they merit **forgiveness** of sins?
A P : 2 8 :011(283) [0447] on the church to merit **forgiveness** of sins or to be acts of
A P : 2 8 :021(284) [0449] that they merit **forgiveness** of sins and eternal life.
A P : 2 8 :023(284) [0451] the one doctrine of the **forgiveness** of sins, that by faith
A P : 2 8 :023(284) [0451] we freely obtain the **forgiveness** of sins for Christ's sake,
S 2 : 0 2 :007(294) [0465] and obtain and merit grace and the **forgiveness** of sins.
S 2 : 0 2 :018(296) [0467] Masses, **forgiveness** of sins, and God's grace were sought
S 2 : 0 2 :018(296) [0467] because we may obtain **forgiveness** and grace in a better
S 2 : 0 2 :023(296) [0469] indulgences and the **forgiveness** of sin and that, like the
S 3 : 0 3 :005(304) [0481] and to expect and accept from him the **forgiveness** of sins.
S 3 : 0 3 :006(304) [0481] "Repentance and the **forgiveness** of sins should be
S 3 : 0 3 :008(304) [0481] offers consolation and **forgiveness** in more ways than
S 3 : 0 3 :012(305) [0481] has merited **forgiveness** and has paid for his sins before
S 3 : 0 3 :032(308) [0487] Both of you need the **forgiveness** of sins, for neither of
S 3 : 0 3 :040(309) [0489] of the Holy Spirit which follows the **forgiveness** of sins.
S 3 : 0 3 :042(309) [0491] the Spirit or the **forgiveness** of sins, or once they have
S 3 : 0 4 :000(310) [0491] word, by which the **forgiveness** of sin (the peculiar
S 3 : 1 3 :002(315) [0499] Good works follow such faith, renewal, and **forgiveness**.
S 3 : 1 5 :001(316) [0501] human traditions effect **forgiveness** or sins or merit
T R : 0 0 :031(325) [0513] Gospel, proclaim the **forgiveness** of sins, administer the
T R : 0 0 :044(328) [0517] they bid us to doubt whether **forgiveness** is obtained.
T R : 0 0 :048(328) [0519] righteousness before God and merit **forgiveness** of sins.
S C : 0 2 :005(345) [0545] *of saints, the **forgiveness** of sins, the resurrection of the*
S C : 0 4 :006(348) [0551] Answer: It effects **forgiveness** of sins, delivers from death
S C : 0 5 :016(349) [0553] receive absolution or **forgiveness** from the confessor as
S C : 0 5 :025(350) [0555] particular, but receive **forgiveness** upon the general
S C : 0 5 :027(351) [0555] you believe that this **forgiveness** is the forgiveness of
S C : 0 5 :027(351) [0555] believe that this forgiveness is the **forgiveness** of God?"
S C : 0 6 :004(351) [0557] which is poured out for many for the **forgiveness** of sins.
S C : 0 6 :006(352) [0557] in the words "for you" and "for the **forgiveness** of sin."
S C : 0 6 :006(352) [0557] By these words the **forgiveness** of sins, life, and salvation
S C : 0 6 :006(352) [0557] for where there is **forgiveness** of sins, there are also life
S C : 0 6 :008(352) [0557] but the words "for you" and "for the **forgiveness** of sins."
S C : 0 6 :008(352) [0557] has what they say and declare: the **forgiveness** of sins.
S C : 0 6 :010(352) [0557] these words: "for you" and "for the **forgiveness** of sins."
L C : S P :013(363) [0577] of saints, the **forgiveness** of sins, the resurrection of the
L C : S P :023(364) [0579] my blood, which is shed for you for the **forgiveness** of sins
L C : 0 1 :246(398) [0651] arrogance and show **forgiveness** and mercy, as the Lord's
L C : 0 2 :034(415) [0687] *of saints, the **forgiveness** of sins, the resurrection of the*
L C : 0 2 :037(415) [0687] Christian church, the **forgiveness** of sins, the resurrection
L C : 0 2 :041(416) [0689] Christian church, the **forgiveness** of sins, the resurrection
L C : 0 2 :054(417) [0693] church we have the **forgiveness** of sins, which is granted
L C : 0 2 :054(417) [0693] Toward **forgiveness** is directed everything that is to be
L C : 0 2 :054(417) [0693] **Forgiveness** is needed constantly, for although God's grace
L C : 0 2 :055(418) [0693] may daily obtain full **forgiveness** of sins through the
L C : 0 2 :055(418) [0693] Christian church, where there is full **forgiveness** of sin.
L C : 0 2 :056(418) [0693] is not) there is no **forgiveness**, and hence no holiness.
L C : 0 2 :056(418) [0693] the Gospel and the **forgiveness** of sin have expelled and
L C : 0 2 :058(418) [0693] Word, daily granting **forgiveness** until we attain to that
L C : 0 2 :058(418) [0693] attain to that life where there will be no more **forgiveness**.
L C : 0 2 :059(418) [0695] means, the Christian church and the **forgiveness** of sins.
L C : 0 2 :062(419) [0695] people, nor has he completed the granting of **forgiveness**.
L C : 0 2 :062(419) [0695] faith through the same Word and the **forgiveness** of sins.
L C : 0 3 :088(432) [0723] there is nothing but **forgiveness**, before we prayed or even
L C : 0 3 :088(432) [0723] here is for us to recognize and accept this **forgiveness**.
L C : 0 3 :090(432) [0723] themselves and be glad that they can attain **forgiveness**.
L C : 0 3 :091(432) [0723] reach the point where he does not need this **forgiveness**.
L C : 0 3 :097(433) [0725] to Thee praying for **forgiveness**, not because I can make
L C : 0 3 :100(433) [0725] we have acquired **forgiveness** and a good conscience, and
L C : 0 4 :041(442) [0743] death and the devil, **forgiveness** of sin, God's grace, the
L C : 0 4 :086(446) [0753] we have once obtained **forgiveness** of sins in Baptism, so
L C : 0 4 :086(446) [0753] of sins in Baptism, so **forgiveness** remains day by day as
L C : 0 5 :003(447) [0753] *which is poured out for you for the **forgiveness** of sins.*
L C : 0 5 :021(449) [0757] given and poured out *for you* for the **forgiveness** of sins."
L C : 0 5 :022(449) [0757] through and in which we obtain the **forgiveness** of sins.
L C : 0 5 :028(449) [0759] are the treasure through which **forgiveness** is obtained.
L C : 0 5 :031(450) [0759] that we cannot have **forgiveness** of sins in the sacrament.
L C : 0 5 :031(450) [0759] was accomplished and **forgiveness** of sins was acquired on
L C : 0 5 :031(450) [0759] do they know of **forgiveness**, and how can they grasp and
L C : 0 5 :032(450) [0759] Christian church, the **forgiveness** of sins," are embodied in
L C : 0 5 :034(450) [0761] he offers and promises **forgiveness** of sins, it cannot be
L C : 0 5 :058(453) [0767] not fit to receive the **forgiveness** of sins since they do not
L C : 0 5 :064(454) [0769] my blood, poured out *for you* for the **forgiveness** of sins."
L C : 0 5 :070(454) [0769] from Christ's lips the **forgiveness** of sins, which contains
L C : 0 6 :008(458) [0000] alone or to our neighbor alone, begging for **forgiveness**.
L C : 0 6 :010(458) [0000] we come into God's presence to beg for **forgiveness**.
L C : 0 6 :029(460) [0000] you show thereby that you can have no **forgiveness** of sin.
E P : 0 3 :009(471) [0789] law, and thus merit **forgiveness** of sins and eternal life.
E P : 0 3 :003(473) [0793] he won for us in the **forgiveness** of sins and eternal life, as
E P : 0 3 :006(473) [0793] by grace, we have **forgiveness** of sins, are regarded as holy
E P : 0 3 :015(475) [0795] sin and to obtain the **forgiveness** of sins, but mean to be
E P : 0 5 :001(478) [0801] which proclaims the **forgiveness** of sins, or is it also a
E P : 0 5 :005(478) [0803] and won for him **forgiveness** of sins, the "righteousness
E P : 0 5 :006(478) [0803] both of repentance and of **forgiveness** of sins.
S D : 0 2 :034(528) [0895] Holy Spirit which follows upon the **forgiveness** of sins.
S D : 0 2 :054(531) [0903] Gospel of the gracious **forgiveness** of sins in Christ there
S D : 0 2 :054(531) [0903] faith which accepts the **forgiveness** of sins for Christ's
S D : 0 2 :075(536) [0911] obedience earn the **forgiveness** of sin and eternal life.
S D : 0 2 :077(536) [0911] offers his grace, the **forgiveness** of sins, and eternal life,
S D : 0 3 :004(540) [0917] of faith is **forgiveness** of sins, reconciliation with God,
S D : 0 3 :011(541) [0919] his obedience we have **forgiveness** of sins by grace, are
S D : 0 3 :016(541) [0921] with God, **forgiveness** of sins, the grace of God,
S D : 0 3 :019(542) [0921] to include both the **forgiveness** of sins solely for Christ's
S D : 0 3 :019(542) [0921] the limited sense of the **forgiveness** of sins and our
S D : 0 3 :025(543) [0923] by which we obtain the **forgiveness** of sins, reconciliation
S D : 0 3 :030(544) [0925] reconciliation or the **forgiveness** of sins, which is
S D : 0 3 :031(544) [0925] merit of Christ, and the **forgiveness** of sins offered to us in
S D : 0 3 :039(546) [0929] consists solely in the **forgiveness** of sins by sheer grace,
S D : 0 3 :043(547) [0931] and who have obtained **forgiveness** of sins through
S D : 0 3 :048(548) [0933] namely, the gracious **forgiveness** of sins and, as a second
S D : 0 3 :054(549) [0935] which is precisely the **forgiveness** of sins and the gracious
S D : 0 3 :062(550) [0937] sins" and "to receive **forgiveness** of sins," but to be made
S D : 0 5 :004(559) [0953] namely, repentance and **forgiveness** of sins (Mark 1:4).
S D : 0 5 :004(559) [0953] that repentance and **forgiveness** of sin should be preached
S D : 0 5 :005(559) [0953] of both repentance and the **forgiveness** of sins.
S D : 0 5 :005(559) [0953] promises of the **forgiveness** of sins but also the divine
S D : 0 5 :008(559) [0953] or repentance and **forgiveness** of sins (Luke 24:46) are
S D : 0 5 :009(559) [0955] does not preach the **forgiveness** of sin to indifferent and
S D : 0 5 :012(560) [0955] and gives nothing but grace and **forgiveness** in Christ.
S D : 0 5 :020(561) [0959] in order to obtain the **forgiveness** of sins from God, since
S D : 0 5 :020(561) [0959] graces of God, obtain **forgiveness** of sins through faith,
S D : 0 5 :027(563) [0961] both of repentance and of **forgiveness** of sins.
S D : 0 5 :027(563) [0961] is the promise of **forgiveness** of sins and justification
S D : 0 7 :049(578) [0989] for us on the tree of the cross for the **forgiveness** of sins.
S D : 0 7 :053(579) [0991] and new covenant, namely, the **forgiveness** of sins."
S D : 0 7 :062(581) [0995] say, the grace of God, **forgiveness** of sins, righteousness,
S D : 0 7 :081(584) [1001] blood of Christ, the **forgiveness** of sins, and all the
S D : 1 1 :027(620) [1071] the preaching of repentance and **forgiveness** of sin.
S D : 1 1 :028(620) [1071] preach "repentance and **forgiveness** of sins in his name

Forgotten (5)

A G : 2 4 :023(058) [0067] faith in Christ and true service of God were **forgotten**.
S 1 : P R :013(291) [0459] crosiers, and similar nonsense would soon be **forgotten**.
S 2 : 0 2 :028(297) [0469] remains will do no harm and will quickly be **forgotten**.
S 3 : 0 3 :019(306) [0483] The sins which had been **forgotten** were pardoned only
L C : 0 1 :326(409) [0675] repeated and never **forgotten**, therefore, you must let

Form (57)

P R : P R :014(007) [0013] Christian Concord, in the **form** that follows hereafter,
P R : P R :018(009) [0015] schools other than in the **form** in which it was once
A G : P R :022(027) [0043] matters, and have done so in legal **form** and procedure.
A G : 1 0 :001(034) [0047] of our Lord under the **form** of bread and wine and are
A G : 2 1 :003(047) [0057] the Scriptures, the highest **form** of divine service is
A P : 0 4 :010(108) [0123] making up this or that **form** of worship or devotion with
A P : 0 4 :281(149) [0201] also quoted in a garbled **form**: "Give alms; and behold,
A P : 0 4 :286(150) [0201] They quote many passages in a garbled **form**.
A P : 0 7 :040(176) [0241] adapted in modified **form** to the Gospel history, like the
A P : 1 2 :055(189) [0267] We shall discuss this **form** of punishment later.
A P : 1 2 :068(192) [0271] statements which the decrees quote in garbled **form**.
A P : 1 2 :091(195) [0279] are quoted in garbled **form** from the Fathers and which
A P : 1 2 :091(195) [0279] our opponents quote in a distorted **form** to obscure faith.
A P : 1 2 :143(204) [0297] God's law but have a set **form** derived from human
A P : 1 5 :019(217) [0319] rites will be the very **form** and constitution of the kingdom
A P : 1 6 :008(223) [0333] external, a new and monastic **form** of government.
A P : 2 1 :025(232) [0349] In some places this **form** of absolution is used: "The
A P : 2 3 :008(240) [0365] The Word of God did not **form** the nature of men to be
A P : 2 4 :068(262) [0407] with a mark that took the **form** of a meal symbolizing the
A P : 2 7 :048(277) [0437] to the text when they quote it in a mutilated **form**.
S 3 : 0 6 :002(311) [0493] hold that it is not to be administered in one **form** only.
S 3 : 0 6 :002(311) [0493] that as much is included under one **form** as under both.
S 3 : 0 6 :003(311) [0493] is included under one **form** as under both, yet
S 3 : 0 6 :003(311) [0493] yet administration in one **form** is not the whole order and
S C : P R :007(339) [0533] he should adopt one **form**, adhere to it, and use it
S C : P R :007(339) [0533] instructed on the basis of a uniform, fixed text and **form**.
S C : P R :007(339) [0533] if a teacher employs one **form** now and another form —
S C : P R :007(339) [0533] form now and another **form** — perhaps with the intention
S C : P R :008(339) [0533] to use the same **form** in teaching the Lord's Prayer, the
S C : P R :008(339) [0535] Choose the **form** that pleases you, therefore, and adhere
S C : P R :009(339) [0535] adhere to a fixed and unchanging **form** and method.
S C : 0 1 :000(342) [0539] *in the plain **form** in which the head of the family shall*
S C : 0 2 :000(344) [0543] The Creed *in the plain **form** in which the head of the*
S C : 0 3 :000(346) [0545] Lord's Prayer *in the plain **form** in which the head of the*
S C : 0 4 :000(348) [0551] *in the plain **form** in which the head of the family shall*
S C : 0 5 :021(350) [0553] Please give me a brief **form** of confession.
S C : 0 5 :029(351) [0555] simply as an ordinary **form** of confession for plain
S C : 0 6 :000(351) [0555] of the Altar *in the plain **form** in which the head of the*
L C : P R :002(358) [0567] them in clear and simple **form** in the many excellent
L C : 0 1 :073(374) [0601] purpose it also helps to **form** the habit of commending
L C : 0 1 :201(392) [0637] was the most common **form** of unchastity among them.
L C : 0 1 :202(392) [0639] applies to every **form** of unchastity, however it is called.
L C : 0 3 :023(423) [0703] or whether I have hit upon the right **form** and mode?"
L C : 0 3 :028(424) [0705] Each of us should **form** the habit from his youth up to
E P : 0 1 :001(466) [0779] (that is, his rational soul in its highest **form** and powers).
E P : 0 2 :016(472) [0791] do not agree with the **form** of sound doctrine and that
E P : 0 8 :016(489) [0821] laid aside completely the **form** of a slave (not the human
E P : 0 8 :033(491) [0825] after he laid aside the **form** of a slave, does not perform
S D : R N :005(504) [0851] Confession (in the **form** in which it was set down in
S D : R N :008(505) [0853] a most correct and simple, yet sufficiently explicit, **form**.
S D : R N :010(506) [0855] certain, and common **form** of doctrine which all our
S D : 0 1 :015(511) [0863] we have given in summary **form**, are explained in greater
S D : 0 2 :086(538) [0913] does not conform to the **form** of sound doctrine but
S D : 0 4 :002(551) [0939] are contrary to the **form** of sound doctrine and words
S D : 0 8 :026(596) [1023] and entirely the **form** of a servant (without, however,
S D : 0 8 :051(600) [1031] power of God, after the **form** of the servant had been laid
S D : 0 8 :065(604) [1039] but now, since the **form** of a slave has been laid aside, it

Formal (4), Formally (1)

P R : P R :021(011) [0019] intrinsically, essentially, **formally**, habitually, and
A P : 0 2 :051(107) [0119] and correctly either the **formal** element of original sin or

Continued ▶

AP : 12 :148(205) [0299] But in a **formal** sense revenge is part of penitence because
AP : 12 :171(209) [0305] for the sort of public or **formal** penitence described by the
AP : 12 :171(209) [0305] other ways besides this **formal** one required in the canons

Formed (4)
AP : 04 :221(137) [0181] be understood in reference to "faith **formed** by love."
SD : 01 :028(513) [0867] seed from which man is **formed** is sinful and corrupted.
SD : 01 :036(514) [0869] them, the days that were **formed** for me, when as yet
SD : 11 :004(617) [1063] them, the days that were **formed** for me, when as yet

Former (26)
PR : PR :020(010) [0017] against the will of the **former**) from a consideration of the
AG : 20 :003(041) [0053] these little was taught in **former** times, when for the most
AG : 20 :005(041) [0053] about which they did not preach at all in **former** times.
AG : 20 :019(043) [0055] In **former** times this comfort was not heard in preaching,
AG : 23 :010(052) [0061] deacons to marry in the Christian church of **former** times.
AG : 25 :005(062) [0069] In **former** times the preachers who taught much about
AG : 26 :001(063) [0071] In **former** times men taught, preached, and wrote that
AG : 27 :016(073) [0077] In **former** times people gathered and adopted monastic
AG : 27 :060(080) [0083] In **former** times Gerson censured the error of the monks
AG : 28 :001(081) [0083] have been written in **former** times about the power of
AG : 28 :072(093) [0093] not exist in the church in **former** times and which were
AL : 20 :007(042) [0053] more tolerable than the **former** one, and it can afford
AL : 23 :026(056) [0065] and as a rule vows used to be so made in **former** times.
AL : 24 :041(061) [0069] In **former** times, even in churches most frequented, Mass
AL : 25 :005(062) [0069] In **former** times satisfactions were immoderately extolled,
AL : 27 :010(072) [0077] to those monks in **former** times who had a little more
AL : 28 :001(081) [0083] In **former** times there has been great controversy about
AP : 18 :009(226) [0337] attributing the **former** to the free will and the latter to the
AP : 28 :024(285) [0451] "The **former** good will ceases, and mortals are forgetful,"
S2 : 03 :001(297) [0471] and monasteries which in **former** times had been founded
S3 : 03 :032(308) [0487] Those of you in the **former** group are false penitents, and
TR : 00 :067(331) [0523] and the latter, after his Baptism, absolved the **former**.
EP : 07 :004(482) [0809] they really retain the **former** crass opinion that in the
SD : 02 :027(526) [0891] him to recant his **former** erroneous opinion as he had set
SD : 08 :051(600) [1031] nature in Christ, the **former** (when it was glorified and
SD : 11 :092(632) [1093] "Whatever was written in **former** days was written for our

Formerly (18)
AG : 24 :035(060) [0067] use, the use which was **formerly** observed in the church
AG : 27 :015(073) [0077] **Formerly** the monasteries had conducted schools of Holy
AL : 20 :004(041) [0053] about such unprofitable works as much as **formerly**.
AL : 27 :015(073) [0077] **Formerly** there had been schools of the Holy Scriptures
AL : 27 :016(073) [0077] **Formerly** people came together in monasteries to learn.
AL : 28 :038(087) [0089] the penitential canons **formerly** increased, and we can
AP : 12 :175(210) [0307] **Formerly** indulgences were the remission of public
AP : 13 :013(213) [0311] as the enthusiasts taught **formerly** and the Anabaptists
AP : 23 :010(241) [0367] the same as saying that **formerly** men were born with a
AP : 24 :079(264) [0411] which shows that **formerly** the Mass was the communion
TR : 00 :077(333) [0527] matrimonial cases had **formerly** belonged to the
LC : 01 :015(366) [0583] as if he said: "What you **formerly** sought from the saints,
LC : 04 :074(445) [0751] the third sacrament, **formerly** called Penance, which is
EP : 12 :010(498) [0839] in those temples where **formerly** papistic Masses were
SD : 04 :002(551) [0939] papists, now as well as **formerly**, to oppose that article of
SD : 05 :002(558) [0953] unbelief, in which they **formerly** had been mired and
SD : 07 :059(580) [0993] this passage, which they **formerly** advanced against the
SD : 12 :015(634) [1099] in which the papistic Mass had **formerly** been read.

Forms (21)
AG : 26 :041(070) [0075] that such outward **forms** of service do not make us
AG : 28 :002(081) [0083] not only introduced new **forms** of worship and burdened
AL : 00 :004(049) [0059] discover that the **forms** of teaching and of ceremonies
AL : 28 :002(081) [0083] only have instituted new **forms** of worship and burdened
AL : 28 :013(083) [0085] civil rulers laws about the **forms** of government that
AP : 04 :288(151) [0203] great peril they add other **forms** of worship to get rid of
AP : 12 :176(210) [0307] penalties or to institute **forms** of worship; they only have
AP : 24 :001(249) [0385] keep traditional liturgical **forms**, such as the order of the
AP : 27 :021(272) [0427] are not impure, are non-obligatory **forms** of discipline.
S3 : 06 :004(311) [0493] who not only omit both **forms** but even go so far as
TR : 00 :038(326) [0515] who defend godless **forms** of worship, idolatry, and
TR : 00 :039(327) [0515] doctrines and godless **forms** of worship, and it is plain
TR : 00 :051(329) [0519] teachings and impious **forms** of worship, and countless
TR : 00 :057(330) [0521] as he defends impious **forms** of worship and doctrines
TR : 00 :059(330) [0521] defend his doctrines and **forms** of worship defile
TR : 00 :072(332) [0525] doctrines and impious **forms** of worship should be
TR : 00 :079(333) [0527] doctrines and impious **forms** of worship and do not
SC : PR :006(338) [0533] this booklet and these **forms** and read them to the people
SD : 01 :038(515) [0871] dough out of which God **forms** and makes man has been
SD : 07 :009(570) [0975] Holy Supper under the **forms** of bread and wine and that
SD : 07 :126(591) [1015] the elements (the visible **forms** of the blessed bread and

Formula (11), Formulas (12)
PR : PR :014(007) [0013] The **Formula** of Christian Concord, in the form that
PR : PR :019(010) [0017] with the norm incorporated in the [**Formula** of] Concord.
PR : PR :020(010) [0017] clearly assert in the **Formula** of Concord itself and in the
PR : PR :020(010) [0017] according to our and the **Formula's** constant intention
PR : PR :024(013) [0021] be bound to any certain **formula** of pure doctrine, to start
AP : PR :011(099) [0101] to traditional doctrinal **formulas** in order to foster the
TR : 00 :082(000) [0529] I have also read the **Formula** of Concord concerning the
EP : 00 :000(463) [0775] **Formula** of Concord, Epitome
SD : RN :001(503) [0849] the church is a summary **formula** and pattern,
SD : 01 :051(517) [0875] that is, words and **formulas** that have two or more
SD : 02 :082(537) [0913] also reject the following **formulas** if they are used without
SD : 02 :086(537) [0913] The **formulas**, "Man's will is not idle in conversion but
SD : 04 :001(551) [0939] such words and **formulas** as "Good works are necessary
SD : 04 :002(551) [0939] propositions and **formulas** are contrary to the form of
SD : 04 :014(553) [0943] Apology often employ **formulas** like these: "Good works
SD : 04 :015(553) [0943] cited propositions and **formulas** when they are used in
SD : 04 :036(557) [0949] used these and similar **formulas** in expounding Holy
SD : 07 :002(569) [0971] close as possible to the **formulas** and speech-patterns of
SD : 07 :035(575) [0983] we at times also use the **formulas** "*under* the bread, *with*
SD : 07 :038(576) [0985] also use these different **formulas**, "in the bread, under the
SD : 07 :038(576) [0985] as a figurative, flowery **formula** or quibble about words).
SD : 07 :040(576) [0985] zeal and earnestness the **formula** which Christ employed
SD : 08 :038(598) [1027] under the words of the **formula** which says we are *to*

Formulate (2), Formulated (4), Formulation (4), Formulations (1)
PR : PR :025(013) [0023] all, either in content or **formulation**, from the divine truth
AP : 16 :003(223) [0331] whether they were **formulated** by heathen or by others,
EP : RN :003(465) [0777] the ancient church **formulated** symbols (that is, brief and
EP : 04 :016(477) [0801] spoken and written **formulations** which teach that good
SD : 00 :000(501) [0845] of God and the Summary **Formulation** of Our Christian
SD : PR :004(502) [0847] and confessions were **formulated** in the Church of God
SD : RN :000(503) [0849] The Summary **Formulation**, Basis, Rule, and Norm,
SD : RN :008(505) [0853] and since they **formulate** Christian doctrine on the basis
SD : 03 :009(540) [0919] with the summary **formulation** of our Christian faith and
SD : 07 :087(585) [1003] that this rule was first **formulated** and explained by Dr.
SD : 11 :010(618) [1065] many to draw and **formulate** strange, dangerous, and

Fornication (4)
AL : 27 :019(074) [0079] of God, "Because of **fornication** let every man have his
AP : 12 :174(210) [0307] of adultery and **fornication**, truthfulness — not to buy off
LC : 01 :214(394) [0641] in open and shameless **fornication** or secretly do even
EP : 02 :008(471) [0789] evil deeds and acts like **fornication**, robbery, murder,

Forsake (6), Forsaken (2), Forsakes (1), Forsaking (4)
AG : 12 :006(035) [0049] of life and the **forsaking** of sin would then follow, for
AG : 16 :004(037) [0051] perfection requires the **forsaking** of house and home, wife
AL : 16 :004(038) [0051] the fear of God and in faith but in **forsaking** civil duties.
AL : 27 :056(080) [0083] be read of men who, **forsaking** marriage and the
AP : 04 :330(158) [0211] (Jonah 2:8), "Those who **forsake** mercy observe lying
AP : 07 :048(177) [0243] We should **forsake** wicked teachers because they no
AP : 12 :090(195) [0279] it is not right for us to **forsake** the cause — not our cause
AP : 14 :002(214) [0315] force our priests to **forsake** and condemn the sort of
AP : 27 :028(274) [0429] to those who have **forsaken** home and brothers (Matt.
AP : 28 :024(285) [0451] Still we will not **forsake** the truth which the church
LC : 01 :028(368) [0587] and want, and renounces and **forsakes** all that is not God?
LC : 01 :216(394) [0641] are even commanded to **forsake** their unchaste existence
EP : 08 :039(491) [0827] he had laid it aside and **forsaken** it even according to his

Forsook (1)
AG : 27 :056(080) [0083] recorded of men who **forsook** wife and child, and also

Forth (126)
PR : PR :011(006) [0011] in which they set **forth** how the differences that had
PR : PR :014(007) [0013] the Christian doctrine set **forth** in the explanation that
PR : PR :022(011) [0019] these have to be set **forth** expressly and distinctly in this
AG : PR :008(025) [0039] of our own faith, setting **forth** how and in what manner,
AG : 00 :001(047) [0059] cannot disagree with us in the articles set **forth** above.
AL : 06 :001(031) [0045] faith is bound to bring **forth** good fruits and that it is
AL : 13 :002(035) [0049] the promises that are set **forth** and offered, is added.
AL : 20 :029(045) [0057] new affections as to be able to bring **forth** good works.
AL : 00 :003(095) [0095] at issue, being briefly set **forth**, may more readily be
AP : 02 :030(104) [0113] lust at work in our members and bringing **forth** evil fruit.
AP : 02 :050(106) [0119] innovations, but have set **forth** the Holy Scripture and
AP : 04 :064(116) [0139] us from death, brings **forth** a new life in our hearts, and is
AP : 04 :064(116) [0139] it appears it brings **forth** good fruits, as we shall point
AP : 04 :080(118) [0143] Since Christ is set **forth** to be the propitiator, through
AP : 04 :080(118) [0143] appease God's wrath by setting **forth** our own works.
AP : 04 :100(121) [0151] quickens because it brings **forth** peace, joy, and eternal
AP : 04 :106(122) [0153] righteousness of law is set **forth** in the statement that he
AP : 04 :132(125) [0159] the Holy Spirit, to bring **forth** in us eternal righteousness
AP : 04 :146(127) [0163] nature continually brings **forth** evil desires, though the
AP : 04 :204(135) [0177] The law always accuses them and brings **forth** wrath.
AP : 04 :208(135) [0177] examples of the saints call **forth** imitation in those who
AP : 04 :215(137) [0179] him, for he has been set **forth** as the propitiator through
AP : 04 :247(142) [0191] his own will he brought us **forth** by the word of truth that
AP : 04 :249(142) [0191] is dead, but it is alive when it brings **forth** good works.
AP : 04 :263(146) [0195] in this way, they bring **forth** fruits worthy of penitence, as
AP : 04 :267(146) [0197] because Daniel clearly sets **forth** a promise, he necessarily
AP : 04 :270(147) [0197] (Ex. 20:6), setting **forth** the most ample promise of the
AP : 04 :293(152) [0203] practice chastity, love toward our neighbor, and so **forth**.
AP : 04 :302(153) [0205] of our opponents come **forth** to describe the love with
AP : 04 :370(164) [0221] have done good will come **forth** to the resurrection of
AP : 07 :009(169) [0229] We set **forth** this doctrine for a very necessary reason.
AP : 12 :035(186) [0261] of Christ ought to be set **forth** to consciences — the
AP : 12 :060(190) [0269] our terrors and brings **forth** peace, joy, and a new life in
AP : 12 :091(195) [0279] We have said why we set **forth** contrition and faith as the
AP : 13 :011(212) [0311] "My word that goes **forth** from my mouth shall not return
AP : 23 :006(240) [0365] the law of celibacy put **forth** by our opponents because it
AP : 23 :008(240) [0367] "Let the earth put **forth** vegetation, plants yielding
AP : 23 :008(240) [0367] did not begin to bring **forth** plants only at the beginning,
AP : 23 :045(245) [0377] from marriage, and this called **forth** the most admiration.
AP : 24 :024(253) [0391] Gospel was promised in order to set **forth** a propitiation.
AP : 24 :070(262) [0409] as Paul calls it (Rom. 4:11), showing **forth** the promise.
AP : 24 :080(264) [0411] who consecrates shows **forth** the body and blood of the
AP : 24 :080(264) [0411] who preaches shows **forth** the gospel to the people, as
AP : 24 :099(268) [0419] We have set **forth** such an important issue with the
AP : 27 :049(277) [0437] This sets **forth** the example of obedience in a calling.
AP : 27 :062(280) [0441] vastly different purposes are set **forth** for monasticism.
AP : 28 :004(281) [0445] evident questions they set **forth** an edict written in blood,
S2 : 02 :011(294) [0465] the Mass — has brought **forth** a brood of vermin and the
TR : 00 :008(320) [0505] apostles should be sent **forth** as equals and exercise the
TR : 00 :032(325) [0513] and that he was led **forth** to be mocked in royal purple
TR : 00 :059(330) [0521] the Apology we have set **forth** in general terms what we
SC : PR :024(341) [0539] need to do is clearly to set **forth** the advantage and
SC : 04 :012(349) [0551] the new man should come **forth** daily and rise up,
LC : SP :020(364) [0579] Christ said farewell to his disciples and sent them **forth**.
LC : 01 :018(367) [0585] women worshiped Diana or Lucina, and so **forth**.
LC : 01 :025(368) [0587] sheer goodness and pours **forth** all that is good in name
LC : 01 :114(380) [0613] did not feel obliged to set **forth** God's commandment in
LC : 01 :157(386) [0625] I have been obliged to set **forth** with such a profusion of
LC : 01 :278(402) [0661] and holy orders step **forth**, with all their works heaped up
LC : 01 :284(403) [0661] which is publicly set **forth** in books and shouted
LC : 01 :310(407) [0669] Therefore he sets it **forth** in plain words: "You shall not
LC : 02 :001(411) [0679] properly follows, setting **forth** all that we must expect and

Continued ▶

LC : 0 2 :013(412) [0681] understanding, and so **forth**; my food and drink,
LC : 0 2 :014(412) [0681] earth and all that it brings **forth**, birds and fish, beasts,
LC : 0 2 :057(418) [0693] and will come **forth** gloriously and arise to complete and
LC : 0 3 :056(427) [0713] which, the more it gushes **forth** and overflows, the more
LC : 0 4 :013(438) [0735] But mad reason rushes **forth** and, because Baptism is not
LC : 0 4 :065(445) [0749] that whatever belongs to the new man may come **forth**.
LC : 0 4 :071(445) [0751] means to plunge into Baptism and daily come **forth** again.
LC : 0 4 :076(446) [0751] old man so that the new may come **forth** and grow strong
EP : RN :006(465) [0779] should conform to the standards set **forth** above.
EP : RN :008(465) [0779] of the faith, setting **forth** how at various times the Holy
EP : 0 1 :007(467) [0781] These points clearly set **forth** the distinction between the
EP : 0 1 :025(469) [0785] This terminology sets **forth** very clearly the distinction
EP : 0 5 :006(478) [0803] which his apostles also set **forth** (examples of this
EP : 0 7 :003(482) [0809] Sacramentarians who set **forth** in clear German words
EP : 0 7 :021(484) [0813] to the doctrine set **forth** above and to our simple faith and
EP : 1 1 :014(496) [0835] we are to put **forth** every effort to live according to the
EP : 1 1 :022(497) [0837] since we have not only set **forth** the pure doctrine but
SD : PR :001(501) [0847] was once more clearly set **forth** on the basis of the Word
SD : PR :003(501) [0847] Christian witness, setting **forth** the faith and the teaching
SD : PR :006(502) [0847] the Christian doctrine set **forth** in this Confession has
SD : RN :006(504) [0853] published in 1531 to set **forth** clearly the true and genuine
SD : RN :007(505) [0853] and reasons are set **forth** at necessary length for
SD : RN :009(505) [0853] blessed memory clearly set **forth** in his writings on the
SD : RN :016(507) [0857] agreement we have set **forth** as a certain and public
SD : RN :019(507) [0857] reasons, we wanted to set **forth** and explain our faith and
SD : 0 1 :004(509) [0861] writings to set **forth** in short chapters the true doctrine
SD : 0 1 :061(519) [0879] The term serves only to set **forth** the distinction between
SD : 0 2 :001(520) [0881] therefore first of all set **forth** the real issue in this
SD : 0 2 :027(526) [0891] opinion as he had set it **forth** in his treatise *Concerning*
SD : 0 2 :048(530) [0901] We shall now set **forth** from the Word of God how man
SD : 0 2 :089(538) [0915] way and after the manner set **forth** and explained above.
SD : 0 2 :090(539) [0915] God, in the manner and degree set **forth** in detail above.
SD : 0 3 :005(540) [0917] which will be set **forth** below in the antitheses, that is, in
SD : 0 3 :041(546) [0931] This has been set **forth** above.
SD : 0 3 :044(547) [0931] The doctrine has been set **forth** in detail in the previously
SD : 0 3 :066(550) [0937] before God as it is set **forth**, explained, and demonstrated
SD : 0 4 :029(555) [0947] of the Interim, flowed **forth** from it, and were made
SD : 0 5 :023(562) [0959] have continually been set **forth** side by side in the church
SD : 0 5 :026(563) [0961] and mightily set **forth** by St. Paul in II Cor. 3:7-9.
SD : 0 6 :010(565) [0965] It is also necessary to set **forth** distinctly what the Gospel
SD : 0 7 :002(569) [0973] when we press them to set **forth** their meaning clearly,
SD : 0 7 :011(571) [0975] And it is not only set **forth** still more clearly in the
SD : 0 7 :017(572) [0979] and true meaning is set **forth** briefly and precisely in
SD : 0 7 :042(576) [0985] Thus the position set **forth** above rests on a unique, firm,
SD : 0 7 :111(589) [1011] we have intended to set **forth** primarily our confession
SD : 0 7 :111(589) [1011] We shall therefore set **forth** and recite the errors
SD : 0 7 :112(589) [1011] to the doctrine set **forth** above, based as it is on the Word
SD : 0 7 :128(591) [1015] to the doctrine set **forth** above, well founded as it is in
SD : 0 8 :047(600) [1031] head, shepherd, and so **forth**, not only according to one
SD : 0 8 :055(601) [1033] cleanse from sin, and so **forth** are not created gifts but
SD : 0 8 :063(603) [1037] To set **forth** correctly the majesty of Christ by way of
SD : 0 8 :064(603) [1037] This fullness shines **forth** with all its majesty, power,
SD : 0 8 :066(604) [1039] But it shines **forth** and manifests itself fully, though
SD : 0 8 :088(609) [1047] with the doctrine here set **forth** as contrary to the
SD : 1 1 :001(616) [1063] we have determined to set **forth** our explanation of this
SD : 1 1 :002(616) [1063] of this article is set **forth** out of the divine Word and
SD : 1 1 :003(616) [1063] we must set **forth** the correct meaning on the basis of
SD : 1 1 :026(620) [1071] will" and has brought it **forth** through Christ so that it
SD : 1 1 :086(631) [1091] purpose of thereby setting **forth** the righteousness of God
SD : 1 1 :087(631) [1091] It sets **forth** that he saves us "according to the purpose"
SD : 1 1 :091(631) [1093] Hence if anyone so sets **forth** this teaching concerning
SD : 1 1 :091(632) [1093] teaching is not being set **forth** according to the Word and
SD : 1 1 :096(632) [1095] for ever through the sole merit of Christ, and so **forth**.
SD : 1 2 :006(633) [1097] We wanted to set **forth** our position so clearly that our

Forthwith (2)
EP : 0 2 :011(471) [0789] his grace, man's will is **forthwith** able by its own natural
SD : 1 0 :014(613) [1057] the adversaries will **forthwith** publicly demand such

Fortified (1), Fortifies (1), Fortify (2)
PR : PR :014(007) [0013] been sent out might be **fortified** with the Word of God
AP : 2 3 :005(240) [0365] and they are trying to **fortify** it with a wicked pretense of
SD : 0 7 :106(588) [1009] they will confirm and **fortify** our faith in all tensions
SD : 1 1 :010(618) [1065] opinions and causes and **fortifies** in people's minds either

Fortress (1), Fortresses (1)
AP : 1 5 :019(218) [0319] shall honor the god of **fortresses** instead of these: a god
LC : 0 1 :185(390) [0633] commandment as a wall, **fortress**, and refuge about our

Fortunate (1), Fortune (3)
AP : 0 2 :042(106) [0117] bad people are more **fortunate** than good people; yielding
AP : 0 4 :198(134) [0175] us against the good **fortune** of the wicked, like Psalm
LC : 0 1 :074(374) [0601] with unexpected good **fortune**, however trivial, he may
LC : 0 1 :184(390) [0633] greater wealth and good **fortune** than he, gives vent to his

Forty (1)
LC : 0 1 :225(395) [0645] his employer out of thirty or **forty** gulden or more a year.

Forward (7)
AP : 0 4 :082(118) [0145] "Whom God put **forward** as an expiation," and
AP : 0 4 :362(162) [0219] We are not putting **forward** an empty quibble about the
AP : 1 2 :006(183) [0255] of our opponents step **forward** and tell us when the
AP : 1 2 :063(191) [0269] "Whom God put **forward** as an expiation by his
LC : 0 1 :116(381) [0615] Let them all come **forward** and boast of their many great,
LC : 0 1 :333(410) [0677] wise men and saints step **forward** and produce, if they
LC : 0 5 :012(448) [0755] with all the fanatics, rush **forward** and say, 'How can

Foster (2)
AP : PR :011(099) [0101] formulas in order to **foster** the attainment of harmony.
AP : 1 5 :051(222) [0329] good reason, and to **foster** harmony those ancient

Fouling (1), Foulness (1)
AP : 0 4 :189(133) [0175] the Holy Spirit motivates, **fouling** it with its impurity.
AP : 1 2 :032(186) [0259] It sees the **foulness** of sin and is genuinely sorry that it

Found (36)
PR : PR :009(006) [0011] In spite of all this we **found**, not without distress on our
PR : PR :014(007) [0013] been received they were **found** to contain all kinds of
PR : PR :016(007) [0013] When they had **found** that the explanation of the
PR : PR :018(009) [0015] Latin copies were afterward **found** to be identical in sense
AG : 2 2 :008(050) [0061] Not a single canon can be **found** which requires the
AG : 2 7 :014(073) [0077] can be denied, for they are **found** in their own books.
AL : 2 5 :005(062) [0069] no fault is to be **found** with our churches on this point,
AL : 0 0 :017(096) [0095] If anything is **found** to be lacking in this confession, we
AP : 0 4 :352(161) [0217] so that by putting it on we may not be **found** naked."
AP : 1 1 :005(181) [0249] church of God and are **found** never to commune, let them
AP : 1 2 :124(201) [0289] judges should have been **found** to deal with such
AP : 2 4 :016(252) [0389] discussion, and that if he **found** someone skilled in
AP : 2 4 :020(252) [0389] proofs for this distinction **found** in the Epistle to the
AP : 2 4 :067(261) [0407] *opere operato* is not to be **found** anywhere in the
AP : 2 4 :081(264) [0411] some unworthy men have **found** an immunity and have
AP : 2 7 :003(269) [0419] Later his friends **found** this same statement about the
AP : 2 7 :027(273) [0429] evangelical perfection is to be **found** in human traditions.
AP : 2 7 :027(273) [0429] Nor is it to be **found** in the observance of other things
AP : 2 7 :036(275) [0433] We remember that this correction is **found** in Gerson.
TR : 0 0 :071(332) [0525] But not even this is **found** in Dionysius!
LC : 0 1 :025(368) [0587] and worthy than any **found** in other languages, a name
LC : 0 1 :043(370) [0593] themselves have never **found** happiness in their wealth,
LC : 0 1 :113(380) [0613] or better teacher to be **found** than God, there can also be
LC : 0 1 :211(393) [0641] who have been created for it, shall be **found** in this estate.
LC : 0 1 :306(406) [0669] I trust, will not be **found** among us, except that someone
LC : 0 3 :023(423) [0703] is no nobler prayer to be **found** on earth, for it has the
LC : 0 4 :084(446) [0753] Every day he should be **found** in faith and amid its fruits,
LC : 0 5 :053(453) [0765] certainly true, as I have **found** in my own experience, and
EP : 0 3 :011(474) [0795] and are certainly to be **found** with it, since such faith is
EP : 1 2 :009(498) [0839] is not truly Christian if sinners are still **found** in it.
SD : RN :019(507) [0857] what books it might be **found** or who may have said it or
SD : RN :020(508) [0859] contrary, we want to be **found** faithful to the commonly
SD : 0 1 :045(516) [0873] people although they are **found** in the writings of the
SD : 0 2 :002(520) [0881] with his free will can be **found** and viewed as being in
SD : 0 8 :011(593) [1019] essence and properties, are **found** unblended in him.
SD : 1 2 :014(634) [1099] congregation in the midst of which sinners are still **found**.

Foundation (25), Foundations (1)
PR : PR :020(010) [0017] only this one basis and **foundation**, namely, the words of
AP : 0 7 :020(171) [0233] what Paul calls the "**foundation**" (I Cor. 3:12), that is, the
AP : 0 7 :020(172) [0233] in it who build on this **foundation** perishing structures of
AP : 0 7 :020(172) [0233] do not overthrow the **foundation**, these are forgiven them
AP : 0 7 :021(172) [0233] stubble on the **foundation** but that this did not overthrow
AP : 0 7 :021(172) [0233] This, too, means to remove Christ as the **foundation**.
AP : 2 0 :008(227) [0339] will have no sure **foundation** when sin and death terrify
S3 : 0 3 :039(309) [0489] an unreal and rotten **foundation** which is called good
TR : 0 0 :029(325) [0513] This faith is the **foundation** of the church.
LC : 0 2 :070(420) [0697] the Creed to lay a **foundation** for the common people
EP : 0 8 :018(489) [0823] testifies, and the sole **foundation** of our comfort, life, and
EP : 1 1 :007(495) [0833] us in him before the **foundation** of the world" (Eph. 1:4).
SD : RN :019(507) [0857] doctrine, so that the **foundation** of divine truth might be
SD : 0 1 :053(517) [0877] corrupted though original sin to its very **foundation**.
SD : 0 8 :031(597) [1025] flows from this same **foundation**, as we have indicated
SD : 0 8 :080(607) [1045] the basis of this solid **foundation**, Dr. Luther, of blessed
SD : 1 1 :005(617) [1065] eternal life "before the **foundation** of the world was laid,"
SD : 1 1 :010(618) [1067] salvation 'before the **foundations** of the world were laid'
SD : 1 1 :012(618) [1067] certain, and unfailing **foundation**: All Scripture, inspired
SD : 1 1 :036(622) [1075] and comforting **foundation**, which daily reminds and
SD : 1 1 :039(622) [1075] and destroy for us the **foundation**, namely, that the Holy
SD : 1 1 :043(623) [1077] of time, "before the **foundation** of the world was laid"
SD : 1 1 :045(624) [1079] it that "even before the **foundation** of the world was laid"
SD : 1 1 :048(624) [1079] his counsel before the **foundation** of the world God has
SD : 1 1 :065(627) [1083] in Christ "before the **foundation** of the world was laid"
SD : 1 1 :088(631) [1093] (in fact, "before the **foundation** of the world was laid")

Founded (10), Founder (1), Founders (1)
PR : PR :000(001) [0004] Declaration, Firmly **Founded** on the Word of God as the
AP : 1 3 :020(213) [0313] The reason for this is clear and well **founded**.
S2 : 0 3 :001(297) [0471] former times had been **founded** with good intentions for
LC : 0 1 :019(367) [0585] and wrong, for it is not **founded** upon the one God, apart
LC : 0 1 :022(367) [0585] Upon it all the religious orders are **founded**.
LC : 0 4 :003(437) [0733] upon which Baptism is **founded** and to which everything
LC : 0 4 :081(446) [0751] ashore after the ship **founders**" in which we embarked
LC : 0 4 :082(446) [0751] The ship does not **founder** since, as we said, it is God's
LC : 0 5 :016(448) [0757] For it is not **founded** on the holiness of men but on the
SD : 0 2 :028(527) [0893] This doctrine is **founded** upon the Word of God and
SD : 0 7 :059(580) [0993] by this simple and well-**founded** explanation of the noble
SD : 0 7 :128(591) [1015] set forth above, well **founded** as it is in God's Word.

Fountain (5), Fountainhead (2)
LC : 0 1 :025(368) [0587] because he is an eternal **fountain** which overflows with
LC : 0 1 :311(407) [0669] They are the true **fountain** from which all good works
LC : 0 1 :329(410) [0677] the chief source and **fountainhead** from which all the
LC : 0 3 :056(427) [0713] an eternal, inexhaustible **fountain** which, the more it
SD : RN :003(503) [0851] as the pure and clear **fountain** of Israel, which is the only
SD : 0 1 :005(509) [0861] as the chief sin, the root and **fountain** of all actual sin.
SD : 0 5 :017(561) [0957] unbelief is a root and **fountainhead** of all culpable sin, the

Four (6), Fourth (27), Fourthly (1)
AG : 2 3 :012(052) [0063] It was only **four** hundred years ago that the priests in
AL : 2 3 :012(052) [0063] (I Tim. 3:2), and not until **four** hundred years ago were
AP : 0 4 :001(107) [0119] In the **fourth**, fifth, and sixth articles, and later in the
AP : 0 4 :084(119) [0145] **Fourth**, the forgiveness of sins is a thing promised for
AP : 0 4 :322(157) [0209] **Fourth**, the whole church confesses that eternal life comes
AP : 2 3 :023(242) [0369] ***Fourth***, the pontifical regulation also disagrees with the
AP : 2 4 :008(250) [0385] apostles to be held on the **fourth** day, on Sabbath eve,
AP : 2 7 :053(278) [0437] **Fourth**, those who live in monasteries are released by such
S2 : 0 2 :021(296) [0467] The **fourth** are fraternities.
S2 : 0 4 :007(299) [0473] to the popes when it deposed three and elected a **fourth**.
S2 : 0 4 :015(301) [0475] In these **four** articles they will have enough to condemn in
S3 : 0 4 :000(310) [0491] Sacrament of the Altar; **fourth**, through the power of the

Continued ▶

TR : 0 0 :014(322) [0507] For Cyprian states in his **fourth** letter to Cornelius:
SC : PR :018(340) [0537] So, too, the **Fourth** Commandment must be stressed when
SC : PR :022(341) [0537] sacrament at least three or **four** times a year despises the
SC : 0 1 :007(343) [0541] The **Fourth**
SC : 0 1 :021(344) [0543] to the third and the **fourth** generation of those who hate
SC : 0 3 :012(347) [0547] The **Fourth** Petition
SC : 0 4 :011(349) [0551] **Fourth**
LC : 0 1 :030(368) [0589] *children to the third and* ***fourth*** *generation of those who*
LC : 0 1 :032(369) [0589] His wrath does not abate until the **fourth** generation.
LC : 0 1 :034(369) [0589] his anger continues to the **fourth** generation, until they
LC : 0 1 :102(379) [0609] The **Fourth** Commandment
LC : 0 1 :137(384) [0621] as we said above, "to the third and **fourth** generation."
LC : 0 1 :206(393) [0639] it above in the **fourth** commandment, "You shall honor
LC : 0 1 :320(408) [0673] *children to the third and* ***fourth*** *generation of them that*
LC : 0 3 :070(430) [0717] The **Fourth** Petition
LC : 0 4 :000(436) [0733] **Fourth** Part: Baptism
EP : 0 2 :001(469) [0785] man may be discussed in **four** different states: (1) before
EP : 0 7 :014(483) [0811] "The **fourth** ground is that God has and knows various
SD : 0 1 :046(516) [0873] **Fourthly**, concerning the doctrine of the resurrection
SD : 0 2 :002(520) [0881] and viewed as being in **four** distinct and dissimilar states.
SD : 0 4 :037(557) [0949] In the **fourth** place, concerning the proposition that good
SD : 0 7 :097(586) [1005] "4. The **fourth** is that God has and knows various ways to

Fourteenth (1)
LC : 0 5 :047(452) [0765] on the evening of the **fourteenth** day of the first full

Fraction (1)
S 2 : 0 4 :015(301) [0475] concede to us even the smallest **fraction** of these articles.

Fragmentary (1)
S 3 : 0 3 :036(309) [0489] is not partial and **fragmentary** like repentance for actual

Frail (1), Frailty (1)
AG : 2 7 :032(076) [0079] still more years to human **frailty**, for it prohibits the
LC : 0 5 :059(453) [0767] even though in other respects they are weak and **frail**.

Frame (1), Framed (1), Framers (1)
AP : 2 0 :002(227) [0337] Here the **framers** of the Confutation have shown their
TR : 0 0 :078(333) [0527] And since they have **framed** certain unjust laws
SD : 0 1 :036(514) [0869] me right well; my **frame** was not hidden from thee when I

France (2)
AP : 1 2 :127(201) [0289] England, Spain, **France**, Italy, even in Rome itself — how
S 1 : PR :008(290) [0457] in Wittenberg, sent from **France**, who reported in our

Francis (5)
AG : 0 0 :007(096) [0095] **Francis**, duke of Lueneburg
AL : 0 0 :017(096) [0095] **Francis**, duke of Lueneburg
AP : 0 4 :211(136) [0179] Bernard, Dominic, **Francis**, and other holy Fathers chose
AP : 2 4 :007(250) [0385] Although St. **Francis** sought to regulate this with the
AP : 2 7 :021(272) [0427] sinning, as did Bernard, **Francis**, and other holy men.

Franciscan (1), Franciscans (1)
AP : 2 7 :001(268) [0419] of Eisenach, there was a **Franciscan** named John Hilten.
S 3 : 0 5 :003(311) [0491] with Scotus and the **Franciscans** who teach that Baptism

Frankenhausen (1)
PR : PR :027(015) [0025] William, count of Schwarzburg [**Frankenhausen**]

Frankfurt (4)
PR : PR :007(004) [0009] agreed to at **Frankfurt**-on-the-Main on the occasion of a
PR : PR :017(008) [0015] and by ourselves at **Frankfurt**-on-the-Main and at
S 3 : 1 5 :005(317) [0501] Master Peter Geltner, preacher in **Frankfurt**, subscribed
TR : 0 0 :082(335) [0529] Peter Geltner, preacher in the church in **Frankfurt**

Frankly (1)
AP : 2 3 :005(239) [0365] write, or act honestly, **frankly**, or openly in this whole

Fraternal (1), Fraternities (1)
S 2 : 0 2 :021(296) [0467] The fourth are **fraternities**.
SD : 0 7 :074(583) [0999] reached the following **fraternal** and unanimous

Fraud (7), Frauds (1), Fraudulent (1)
AP : 1 2 :170(209) [0305] ought to be not a **fraud** but an improvement of the total
AP : 2 3 :060(247) [0381] and full of danger; finally, the whole thing is a **fraud**.
AP : 2 3 :068(249) [0383] the Confutation, lest their **fraud** and slander be exposed.
S 3 : 1 5 :005(316) [0501] and they are not, but are mere mockery and **fraud**.
S 3 : 1 5 :005(316) [0501] Such **frauds**, which are without number, we commend for
LC : 0 1 :227(396) [0645] everyday business the same **fraud** prevails in full force.
LC : 0 1 :296(405) [0665] without accusation or blame for **fraudulent** dealing.
LC : 0 1 :307(406) [0669] not be called stealing or **fraud**, yet it is coveting — that is,
LC : 0 3 :102(434) [0727] and deceit, into acts of **fraud** and deception against our

Frederick (9)
PR : PR :027(014) [0025] Joachim **Frederick**, margrave of Brandenburg,
PR : PR :027(014) [0025] Duke **Frederick** William [of Saxe-Altenburg] and
PR : PR :027(014) [0025] George **Frederick**, margrave of Brandenburg
PR : PR :027(015) [0025] **Frederick**, count of Wuerttemberg and Montbeliard
PR : PR :027(015) [0025] Anarck **Frederick**, baron of Wildenfels
AG : 0 0 :007(096) [0095] John **Frederick**, duke of Saxony
AL : 0 0 :017(096) [0095] John **Frederick**, duke of Saxony
S 3 : 1 5 :005(317) [0501] I, **Frederick** Myconius, pastor of the church in Gotha,
TR : 0 0 :082(335) [0529] **Frederick** Myconius subscribed for himself and for Justus

Free (139), Frees (9)
PR : PR :024(013) [0021] the way may not be left **free** and open to restless,
AG : PR :021(027) [0043] in such a general, **free**, and Christian council as the
AG : 1 8 :004(039) [0051] words of Augustine on **free** will are here quoted from the
AG : 1 8 :004(039) [0051] that all men have a **free** will, for all have a natural, innate
AG : 2 3 :013(053) [0063] himself instituted and left **free** to man) never produced
AG : 2 7 :006(071) [0077] even the papal canons might have set many of them **free**.
AG : 2 7 :036(076) [0081] concerning marriage **frees** and releases many from
AG : 2 8 :052(089) [0091] freedom Christ has set us **free**; stand fast, therefore, and
AL : 1 8 :000(039) [0051] XVIII. **Free** Will
AL : 1 8 :004(039) [0051] that all men have a **free** will which enables them to make
AL : 2 0 :014(043) [0055] it would be a reward for works rather than a **free** gift."
AL : 2 0 :040(046) [0057] good in deed or thought, Nothing **free** from taint of ill."
AL : 2 7 :036(076) [0081] concerning marriage **frees** many from their vows, our
AP : 0 2 :012(102) [0109] more than was proper to **free** will and to "elicited acts."
AP : 0 4 :020(110) [0125] the law, the Gospel of the **free** forgiveness of sins and the
AP : 0 4 :029(111) [0129] capacity, with the help of **free** will, is in itself sufficient
AP : 0 4 :031(111) [0129] says, "If the Son makes you **free**, you will be free indeed."
AP : 0 4 :031(111) [0129] says, "If the Son makes you free, you will be **free** indeed."
AP : 0 4 :031(111) [0129] Therefore reason cannot **free** us from our sins or merit
AP : 0 4 :040(112) [0131] account the law cannot **free** us from sin or justify us, but
AP : 0 4 :043(113) [0133] justification through a **free** promise, however, it follows
AP : 0 4 :053(114) [0137] the fact that the promise is **free**, and the merits of Christ
AP : 0 4 :053(114) [0137] by faith; the fact that it is **free** excludes our merits and
AP : 0 4 :057(114) [0137] the law does not teach the **free** forgiveness of sins, the
AP : 0 4 :057(114) [0137] Therefore they received **free** mercy and the forgiveness of
AP : 0 4 :064(116) [0139] is not an idle thought, but **frees** us from death, brings
AP : 0 4 :070(116) [0141] For the law does not teach the **free** forgiveness of sins.
AP : 0 4 :103(122) [0151] It is faith therefore that **frees** men through the blood of
AP : 0 4 :110(123) [0153] abolish the Gospel of the **free** forgiveness of sins.
AP : 0 4 :115(123) [0155] of the Holy Spirit that **frees** us from death, comforting
AP : 0 4 :121(124) [0155] the entire promise of the **free** forgiveness of sins and of
AP : 0 4 :153(127) [0163] is that which grasps God's **free** mercy because of God's
AP : 0 4 :186(132) [0173] it presents the Gospel, the **free** promise of the forgiveness
AP : 0 4 :186(133) [0173] our opponents simply abolish this **free** promise.
AP : 0 4 :188(133) [0173] we teach them about the **free** forgiveness of sins and the
AP : 0 4 :188(133) [0173] works in such a way as not to remove the **free** promise.
AP : 0 4 :239(141) [0187] Our love does not **free** us from shame when God judges
AP : 0 4 :239(141) [0187] us, but faith in Christ **frees** us in the midst of these fears
AP : 0 4 :277(148) [0199] the same way, "Alms **free** from every sin and from death."
AP : 0 4 :277(148) [0199] Christ, whose prerogative it is to **free** from sin and death.
AP : 0 4 :278(149) [0199] almsgiving does not **free** from sin and death *ex opere*
AP : 0 4 :297(153) [0205] "If the Son makes you **free**, you will be free indeed" (John
AP : 0 4 :297(153) [0205] Son makes you free, you will be **free** indeed" (John 8:36).
AP : 0 4 :322(157) [0209] says in *Grace and Free Will*, "God leads us to eternal life,
AP : 1 1 :002(180) [0249] monks teach nothing about faith and **free** forgiveness.
AP : 1 2 :060(190) [0269] and regeneration, for it **frees** us from our terrors and
AP : 1 2 :129(202) [0291] in order to heal devout minds and **free** them from doubt.
AP : 1 2 :147(205) [0297] remission of guilt, faith **frees** the heart from the wrath of
AP : 1 3 :020(213) [0313] should be certain that the **free** forgiveness of sins,
AP : 1 5 :033(220) [0325] sure standards by which to **free** themselves from these
AP : 1 8 :000(224) [0335] [Article XVIII. **Free** Will]
AP : 1 8 :001(224) [0335] accept Article XVIII on **free** will, but they add several
AP : 1 8 :001(225) [0335] too much be conceded to **free** will, as in Pelagianism, or
AP : 1 8 :007(225) [0337] Although we concede to **free** will the liberty and ability to
AP : 1 8 :009(226) [0337] the former to the **free** will and the latter to the operation
AP : 2 0 :014(228) [0343] the forgiveness of sins is **free**; in fact, the Pelagians were
AP : 2 3 :004(239) [0363] Because your conduct is **free** of disgrace and cruelty, we
AP : 2 3 :022(242) [0369] The matter should be left **free**, and no snares should be
AP : 2 3 :041(245) [0375] The Gospel **frees** us from these Levitical regulations
AP : 2 4 :013(251) [0387] whatever they need in this life, and even **free** the dead.
AP : 2 4 :046(258) [0401] with despair and about the **free** forgiveness of sins for
AP : 2 4 :049(258) [0401] as a seal and witness of the **free** forgiveness of sins and as
AP : 2 4 :064(261) [0407] transfer it to the dead and **free** souls from purgatorial
AP : 2 4 :077(263) [0411] of sins for them or to **free** the souls of the dead.
AP : 2 4 :089(265) [0413] of the ceremony to **free** the souls of the dead, from which
AP : 2 7 :034(275) [0431] the Gospel about the **free** forgiveness of sins and the
AP : 2 7 :054(278) [0437] the Gospel about the **free** forgiveness of sins for Christ's
AP : 2 8 :007(282) [0445] wanted to leave their use **free** when he said (Matt. 15:11),
AP : 2 8 :015(283) [0447] which Christ has set you **free**, and do not submit again to
AP : 2 8 :016(283) [0447] ordinances ought to be left **free**, only that offenses should
AP : 2 8 :016(283) [0449] which they worked hard to **free** the church from the idea
S 1 : PR :002(289) [0455] or treachery to hold a truly **free** council, as indeed the
S 1 : PR :003(289) [0455] is dreadfully afraid of a **free** council and flees from the
S 1 : PR :003(289) [0455] court will ever permit a **free** council, to say nothing of
S 3 : 0 1 :005(302) [0477] 2. Again, that man has a **free** will, either to do good and
S 3 : 0 3 :010(305) [0481] who does as much as he can according to his **free** will.
S 3 : 0 3 :011(305) [0481] works which man with his **free** will might well have
S 3 : 0 3 :018(306) [0483] he would rather have sinned if he had been **free** to do so.
S 3 : 0 8 :002(312) [0495] of sins should be left **free** to everybody to do or not as he
S 3 : 1 1 :003(315) [0499] we desire marriage to be **free**, as God ordained and
SC : 0 9 :010(356) [0563] from the Lord, whether he is a slave or **free**" (Eph. 6:5-8).
LC : PR :003(358) [0567] Now that they are **free** from the useless, bothersome
LC : 0 1 :082(376) [0603] from all of which we are now set **free** through Christ.
LC : 0 1 :154(386) [0625] to be his own master, be **free** from all authority, care
LC : 0 1 :231(396) [0647] rob openly are safe and **free**, unmolested by anyone, even
LC : 0 1 :240(397) [0649] those who turn the **free** public market into a carrion-pit
LC : 0 1 :294(404) [0665] maid-servants were not **free**, as now, to serve for wages
LC : 0 2 :030(414) [0685] of hell, won us, made us **free**, and restored us to the
LC : 0 3 :108(435) [0729] to consent to it is to give it **free** rein and neither resist it
LC : 0 4 :043(442) [0743] Baptism there is brought **free** to every man's door just
LC : 0 4 :067(445) [0749] we become, and the more **free** from greed, hatred, envy,
LC : 0 4 :068(445) [0749] but the old man is given **free** rein and continually grows
LC : 0 5 :046(452) [0763] it'; so he compels no one, but leaves it to our **free** choice."
LC : 0 5 :047(452) [0763] wishes the sacrament to be **free**, not bound to a special
LC : 0 6 :001(457) [0000] We have been set **free** from his coercion and from the
LC : 0 6 :032(460) [0000] to be good Christians, **free** from their sins, and happy in
EP : 0 2 :000(469) [0785] II. **Free** Will
EP : 0 2 :006(470) [0787] he denies all power to **free** will and ascribes everything to
EP : 0 2 :011(471) [0789] is indeed too weak by his **free** will to make a beginning,
EP : 0 2 :016(472) [0791] confirm the role of natural **free** will in conversion
EP : 0 3 :007(473) [0793] in this article "absolve," that is, pronounce **free** from sin.
EP : 0 4 :003(476) [0797] concerning the use of the words "necessary" and "**free**."
EP : 0 4 :011(477) [0799] do good works from a **free** spirit," should not be
EP : 1 0 :006(493) [0829] freedom Christ has set us **free**; stand fast therefore, and
SD : 0 2 :000(519) [0881] II. **Free** Will or Human Powers
SD : 0 2 :001(519) [0881] a controversy concerning **free** will, not only between the
SD : 0 2 :002(520) [0881] Man with his **free** will can be found and viewed as being
SD : 0 2 :002(520) [0881] rules him, nor what man's **free** will is going to be like
SD : 0 2 :007(521) [0883] and nature the natural **free** will is mighty and active only
SD : 0 2 :018(524) [0887] If the natural or carnal **free** will of St. Paul and other
SD : 0 2 :018(524) [0887] we only refer), that the **free** will by its own natural

Continued ▶

SD : 02 :023(525) [0889] "When the Fathers defend **free** will, they affirm a capacity
SD : 02 :023(525) [0889] to God and become truly **free**, a condition for which it
SD : 02 :025(526) [0891] powers of the natural **free** will, be it entirely or one-half
SD : 02 :026(526) [0891] To some extent reason and **free** will are able to lead an
SD : 02 :031(527) [0893] as follows concerning **free** will: "We also declare that to a
SD : 02 :031(527) [0893] also declare that to a certain extent reason has a **free** will.
SD : 02 :031(527) [0893] can be comprehended by reason we have a **free** will."
SD : 02 :032(527) [0893] that in spiritual things our **free** will and reason can do
SD : 02 :033(527) [0893] errors concerning **free** will: "That man has a free will to
SD : 02 :033(527) [0893] free will: "That man has a **free** will to do good and to
SD : 02 :038(528) [0895] mention whatever of our **free** will or of our contribution,
SD : 02 :043(529) [0897] which glorifies our **free** will, as directly and diametrically
SD : 02 :044(529) [0897] holy memory, grants our **free** will no power of its own to
SD : 02 :046(530) [0899] wickedness of our natural **free** will, as well as the doctrine
SD : 02 :053(531) [0903] still has something of a **free** will in these external matters,
SD : 02 :067(534) [0907] — that is, as Christ says, they have again been made **free**.
SD : 02 :073(535) [0909] of the entire doctrine of **free** will it is possible to decide
SD : 02 :075(536) [0911] the Holy Spirit, the **free** will can convert itself to God,
SD : 02 :077(536) [0911] As a result, his **free** will is too weak to make a beginning
SD : 02 :077(536) [0911] and eternal life, then the **free** will by its own natural
SD : 02 :086(538) [0913] view that man's naturally **free** will cooperates in his
SD : 03 :009(540) [0919] and declared utterly **free** from all his sins, and from the
SD : 03 :017(542) [0921] to declare righteous and **free** from sins and from the
SD : 04 :004(551) [0939] words "necessary" and "**free**," especially the word
SD : 04 :014(553) [0943] works are necessary or **free**, both the Augsburg
SD : 04 :017(554) [0943] (Ps. 110:3), who bring **free**-will offerings (Ps. 54:6), not
SD : 04 :018(554) [0943] spirit by those whom the Son of God has set **free**.
SD : 04 :020(554) [0945] view that good works are **free** to believers in the sense
SD : 04 :020(554) [0945] that it lies within their **free** option if they may or want to
SD : 06 :002(564) [0963] temple, and hence are **free**, so that just as the sun
SD : 06 :003(564) [0963] do the will of God from a **free** spirit, nevertheless the
SD : 06 :006(564) [0965] they would be totally **free** from sins, they would require
SD : 06 :017(566) [0967] the law (that is, when he is **free** from this driver and is
SD : 06 :017(566) [0967] anew, he does everything from a **free** and merry spirit.
SD : 10 :005(611) [1053] do we include among truly **free** adiaphora or things
SD : 10 :011(612) [1055] freedom Christ has set us **free**; stand fast therefore, and
SD : 10 :014(613) [1057] and remain of themselves **free** and which accordingly are

Freed (14), Freedom (20), Freeing (1)

AG : 18 :000(039) [0051] XVIII. **Freedom** of the Will
AG : 18 :001(039) [0051] possesses some measure of **freedom** of the will which
AG : 18 :004(040) [0051] of this life that they have **freedom** to choose good or evil.
AG : 28 :052(089) [0091] writes in Gal. 5:1, "For **freedom** Christ has set us free;
AL : 18 :004(039) [0051] of this life that they have **freedom** to choose good or evil.
AL : 27 :006(071) [0077] some could have been **freed** by appealing to the canons.
AP : 04 :133(125) [0159] and where the Spirit of the Lord is, there is **freedom**."
AP : 04 :138(126) [0161] who holds enthralled all who have not been **freed** by faith.
AP : 12 :081(194) [0275] sin, and they cannot be **freed** in any other way than by
AP : 12 :157(207) [0301] teach that we can be **freed** from eternal death only by the
AP : 15 :034(220) [0325] Just so the apostles have **freed** consciences for good,
AP : 18 :004(225) [0335] We are not denying **freedom** to the human will.
AP : 18 :004(225) [0335] The human will has **freedom** to choose among the works
AP : 21 :019(231) [0347] one's friend, the debtor is **freed** by the merit of another as
AP : 21 :041(235) [0355] they saw that he was **freeing** human minds from the
AP : 22 :015(238) [0361] Even if we grant the **freedom** to use one kind or both,
AP : 22 :015(238) [0361] arrogate to itself the **freedom** to call Christ's ordinances
AP : 23 :061(247) [0381] should have this same **freedom**; we refuse to force anyone
AP : 28 :015(283) [0447] "Stand fast in the **freedom** with which Christ has set
SC : PR :021(340) [0537] now that the people are **freed** from the tyranny of the
SC : 02 :004(345) [0545] delivered me and **freed** me from all sins, from death, and
LC : 02 :058(418) [0693] righteousness, completely **freed** from sin, death, and all
LC : 05 :040(451) [0761] been abolished and we are **freed** from his oppression and
LC : 06 :005(457) [0000] take advantage of their **freedom**, acting as if they will
LC : 06 :031(460) [0000] under the command and you must come into **freedom**.
EP : 06 :002(480) [0805] has truly converted are **freed** through Christ from the
EP : 10 :006(493) [0829] Paul writes, "For **freedom** Christ has set us free; stand
SD : 02 :023(525) [0889] affirm a capacity for this **freedom** in such a way that by
SD : 02 :030(527) [0893] any way recognize the **freedom** of the human will in
SD : 02 :074(535) [0909] works man's will has no **freedom** or power whatever to
SD : 05 :020(561) [0959] of sins through faith, are **freed** from death and all the
SD : 06 :004(564) [0963] and justified, have been **freed** and liberated from the
SD : 06 :023(567) [0969] their persons have been **freed** from the curse and
SD : 10 :011(612) [1055] It is written, "For **freedom** Christ has set us free; stand
SD : 10 :011(612) [1055] slipped in to spy out our **freedom** which we have in

Freely (76)

AL : 04 :001(030) [0045] merits, or works but are **freely** justified for Christ's sake
AL : 27 :027(075) [0079] ought to be voluntary and chosen **freely** and deliberately?
AP : 04 :001(107) [0119] of their own merits, but **freely** for Christ's sake, by faith
AP : 04 :015(109) [0123] of sins rather than receiving it **freely** for his merits.
AP : 04 :017(109) [0125] but that this disposition stimulates it to do so more **freely**.
AP : 04 :018(109) [0125] that for his sake they **freely** receive the forgiveness of sins
AP : 04 :024(110) [0127] We **freely** give this righteousness of reason its due credit;
AP : 04 :041(113) [0133] but offers the forgiveness of sins and justification **freely**.
AP : 04 :041(113) [0133] that is, the forgiveness of sins is offered **freely**.
AP : 04 :044(113) [0133] and death, the promise **freely** offers reconciliation for
AP : 04 :046(113) [0133] By **freely** accepting the forgiveness of sins, faith sets
AP : 04 :073(117) [0141] from Paul, too, like "**freely**," "not of works," "it is a gift,"
AP : 04 :087(119) [0147] to us for Christ's sake we are justified **freely** by faith.
AP : 04 :087(120) [0147] that we are saved **freely** by "the gift of God, not
AP : 04 :089(120) [0149] adds that it is accounted **freely** and denies that it could be
AP : 04 :089(120) [0149] it could be accounted **freely** if it were a reward for works.
AP : 04 :110(123) [0153] they believe that the forgiveness of sins is received **freely**.
AP : 04 :120(124) [0155] that sins are forgiven **freely** for Christ's sake) must be
AP : 04 :157(128) [0165] do not come **freely** for Christ's sake, but for the sake of
AP : 04 :195(134) [0175] is one, and it is offered **freely** to all who believe that their
AP : 04 :203(135) [0175] for Christ's sake he is **freely** forgiven and freely has a
AP : 04 :203(135) [0175] sake he is freely forgiven and **freely** has a gracious God.
AP : 04 :205(135) [0177] when it is sure that he **freely** forgives and hears us.
AP : 04 :211(136) [0179] that they received these **freely** because of Christ, the
AP : 04 :212(136) [0179] is the propitiator, or that **freely** by faith we are accounted
AP : 04 :217(137) [0179] that is only promised **freely** because of Christ, and
AP : 04 :267(146) [0197] faith, which believes that God **freely** forgives sins.
AP : 04 :320(156) [0209] and eternal life are given us **freely** for Christ's sake.
AP : 04 :367(163) [0221] Gospel offers justification **freely** because of Christ's
AP : 04 :368(163) [0221] the Gospel offers justification **freely** for Christ's sake.
AP : 11 :002(180) [0249] of sins is granted to us **freely** for Christ's sake and that we
AP : 12 :035(186) [0261] — the Gospel which **freely** promises the forgiveness of sins
AP : 12 :035(186) [0261] that because of Christ their sins are **freely** forgiven.
AP : 12 :072(192) [0271] to believe that they are **freely** forgiven because of Christ,
AP : 12 :073(192) [0273] apostle concludes, that a man is justified **freely** by faith."
AP : 12 :076(193) [0273] and promises the forgiveness of sins **freely** for his sake.
AP : 12 :079(194) [0275] the forgiveness of sins by faith, **freely** for Christ's sake.
AP : 12 :080(194) [0275] sake, and to be sure that **freely** for Christ's sake they have
AP : 12 :088(195) [0277] their sins are forgiven **freely** for Christ's sake, not
AP : 12 :095(196) [0281] believe firmly that God **freely** forgives us because of
AP : 12 :157(207) [0301] the forgiveness of sins **freely** because of Christ, who is the
AP : 15 :005(215) [0317] for Christ's sake, we **freely** receive the forgiveness of sins
AP : 15 :006(215) [0317] God not because of works but **freely** for Christ's sake.
AP : 15 :010(216) [0317] because of our works but **freely** because of Christ,
AP : 15 :018(217) [0319] God, denying that men are **freely** justified before God by
AP : 15 :018(217) [0319] that we are not justified **freely** for his sake but by such
AP : 20 :002(227) [0339] the forgiveness of sins is **freely** given for Christ's sake,
AP : 20 :003(227) [0339] account of our works and not **freely** on account of Christ.
AP : 20 :007(227) [0339] the forgiveness of sins **freely** for Christ's sake and that
AP : 20 :008(227) [0341] in the forgiveness of sins **freely** given for Christ's sake.
AP : 20 :010(228) [0341] as it were, that sins are **freely** forgiven for Christ's sake.
AP : 20 :011(228) [0341] not on account of our works but **freely** for Christ's sake.
AP : 23 :036(244) [0373] are we justified, but **freely** for Christ's sake when we
AP : 24 :043(257) [0399] or point out that sins are **freely** forgiven for Christ's sake.
AP : 24 :046(258) [0401] faith, by which we **freely** receive the forgiveness of sins.
AP : 24 :048(258) [0401] that the forgiveness of sins comes **freely** for Christ's sake.
AP : 24 :049(258) [0401] to trust and believe that their sins are **freely** forgiven.
AP : 24 :097(268) [0417] *opere operato* rather than receiving it **freely** through faith.
AP : 27 :011(270) [0423] of sins is given us **freely** for Christ's sake, as we have said
AP : 27 :013(271) [0423] of sins is received **freely** for Christ's sake, through faith.
AP : 27 :015(271) [0425] the forgiveness of sins **freely** but on account of the works
AP : 27 :017(271) [0425] wrath of God for us so that we might be **freely** forgiven.
AP : 27 :031(274) [0431] but that we receive this **freely** by faith, as has been said.
AP : 27 :032(274) [0431] you merit eternal life, but that this is **freely** given as well."
AP : 27 :070(281) [0443] had forgiveness of sins **freely** for Christ's sake, that for
AP : 28 :007(282) [0445] receive forgiveness of sins **freely** for Christ's sake by
AP : 28 :023(284) [0451] of sins, that by faith we **freely** obtain the forgiveness of
TR : 00 :044(328) [0517] that sins are forgiven **freely** for Christ's sake and that by
LC : 03 :016(422) [0701] The reason is this: I **freely** admit that he is holier in
LC : 03 :096(433) [0725] God does it altogether **freely**, out of pure grace, because
SD : 01 :056(518) [0877] the same terminology **freely** and without incurring
SD : 02 :019(524) [0889] of good or evil or **freely** choose to act or not to act.
SD : 02 :064(533) [0905] will offer themselves **freely** on the day you lead your
SD : 03 :036(545) [0927] "without the law," "**freely**," "not of works," all of which
SD : 04 :017(554) [0943] who offer themselves **freely** (Ps. 110:3), who bring
SD : 11 :087(631) [1093] glorious grace which he **freely** bestowed on us in the

Freeze (1)

LC : 01 :190(391) [0635] you could clothe him, you have let him **freeze** to death.

French (1)

AP : 07 :034(175) [0239] dress according to the **French** rather than the German

Frequency (1), Frequent (5), Frequented (1), Frequently (16)

PR : PR :009(006) [0011] under the name of the **frequently** mentioned Augsburg
AG : 28 :049(089) [0091] the divine Scripture so **frequently** forbid the making and
AL : 24 :041(061) [0069] even in churches most **frequented**, Mass was not held
AP : 02 :051(107) [0119] case our opponents **frequently** do not know what they are
AP : 04 :058(115) [0137] The **frequent** references to mercy and faith in the Psalms
AP : 04 :275(148) [0199] Nevertheless, Christ **frequently** connects the promise of
AP : 04 :282(149) [0201] cleansed before God and justified by **frequent** washings.
AP : 07 :040(176) [0241] **Frequently** the people continued to observe certain Old
AP : 14 :001(214) [0315] matter we have given **frequent** testimony in the assembly
AP : 24 :004(250) [0385] hymns have varied in **frequency**, yet almost everywhere
AP : 24 :049(258) [0401] our churches the use is more **frequent** and more devout.
LC : SP :027(364) [0581] on the Catechism **frequently** is to impress it upon our
LC : 01 :167(388) [0629] Commandments, it is **frequently** dealt with in many other
LC : 01 :301(405) [0667] situation occurs most **frequently** in lawsuits in which
LC : 03 :107(434) [0729] degree; some have more **frequent** and severe temptations
LC : 05 :039(451) [0761] themselves to receive this blessed sacrament **frequently**.
LC : 05 :047(452) [0765] evening of the year, but **frequently**, whenever and
SD : 03 :019(542) [0921] In this latter sense it is **frequently** used in the Apology,
SD : 03 :021(542) [0921] **Frequently** the word "regeneration" means the
SD : 06 :009(565) [0965] of the law, but **frequently** the punishment of the law as
SD : 06 :024(568) [0969] of the law, but **frequently** also with the club of
SD : 08 :018(594) [1021] necessary, and have **frequently** quoted them in our
SD : 11 :060(626) [1083] give us these we **frequently** cast them from us and make

Fresh (1)

LC : 06 :033(461) [0000] with eagerness for a **fresh** spring, so I yearn and tremble

Fret (1), Fretting (1)

AP : 02 :042(106) [0117] from trouble right away; **fretting** because bad people are
LC : 01 :009(365) [0583] are cheerful, who do not **fret** and complain, if they do not

Friars (2)

AP : 23 :045(245) [0375] thus surpassing the Dominican **friars**, who eat fish.
AP : 24 :007(250) [0385] of the mendicant **friars** brought on the multiplication of

Friday (3)

AG : PR :007(025) [0039] present our case in German and Latin today (**Friday**).
AG : 24 :041(061) [0069] on Wednesday and **Friday** the Scriptures were read and
AL : 24 :041(061) [0069] them on Wednesday and **Friday**, and all things are done

Friend (7), Friendly (4), Friends (17), Friendship (5)

PR : PR :001(003) [0007] tender our due service, **friendship**, gracious greeting, and
PR : PR :007(004) [0009] in a thorough and **friendly** way various matters which our
PR : PR :025(014) [0025] to his station, all affection, service, and **friendship**.
AG : PR :012(026) [0041] If, however, our lords, **friends**, and associates who
AG : PR :014(026) [0041] our aforementioned **friends** (the electors, princes, and

Continued ▶

A G : 1 8 :005(040) [0051] to eat or drink or visit a **friend**, whether to dress or
A L : 1 8 :005(040) [0051] and drink, will to have a **friend**, will to clothe oneself,
A P : 0 4 :242(141) [0187] of the mistakes of its **friends**; and that it puts the best
A P : 0 4 :242(141) [0187] says, "Know, but do not hate, the manners of a **friend**."
A P : 2 1 :019(231) [0347] one pays a debt for one's **friend**, the debtor is freed by the
A P : 2 1 :024(232) [0349] at royal courts, where **friends** must be used as
A P : 2 4 :068(262) [0407] the mutual union and **friendship** among Christians
A P : 2 4 :068(262) [0407] banquets are symbols of agreement and **friendship**.
A P : 2 7 :003(269) [0419] Later his **friends** found this same statement about the
A P : 2 7 :009(270) [0421] of life, whom parents or **friends** pushed into the
A P : 2 7 :042(276) [0435] God to leave possessions, **friends**, wife, and children
A P : 2 7 :057(279) [0439] or because they were under duress from their **friends**.
S 2 : 0 2 :002(293) [0463] would speak to them in the following **friendly** fashion:
S C : 0 3 :014(347) [0549] order and honor; true **friends**, faithful neighbors, and the
L C : 0 1 :141(384) [0621] he enlists the help of his **friends** and neighbors; if he
L C : 0 1 :194(391) [0635] To show kindness to our **friends** is but an ordinary
L C : 0 1 :226(395) [0645] my neighbors, my good **friends**, my own servants, from
L C : 0 1 :251(399) [0651] we are to help, share, and lend to both **friends** and foes.
L C : 0 1 :258(399) [0653] an eye to gaining favor, money, prospects, or **friendship**.
L C : 0 1 :259(400) [0655] will often offend good **friends**, relatives, neighbors, and
L C : 0 1 :275(402) [0659] sisters and other good **friends** are under mutual obligation
L C : 0 1 :285(403) [0661] harm his neighbor, whether **friend** or foe, with his tongue.
L C : 0 1 :302(405) [0667] bribery, through **friendly** connections and by any other
L C : 0 1 :322(408) [0673] a wrathful threat and a **friendly** promise, not only to
L C : 0 3 :076(431) [0721] to grant us faithful neighbors and good **friends**, etc.
L C : 0 4 :016(438) [0735] Of course, my **friend**!
L C : 0 4 :059(444) [0747] My **friend**, rather invert the argument and conclude,
S D : 1 1 :095(632) [1095] From our exposition **friends** and foes may clearly

Frighten (1), Frightened (4), Frightens (1), Frightful (3), Frightfully (1)
P R : P R :009(006) [0011] many pious hearts were **frightened** away and deterred
A G : 2 3 :006(052) [0061] terrible torment and **frightful** disturbance of conscience
A G : 2 3 :018(054) [0063] the cause of so much **frightful** and unchristian offense, so
A P : 0 4 :177(131) [0171] the sight of our impurity thoroughly **frightens** us.
A P : 0 4 :303(154) [0205] and wholesome consolation to **frightened** consciences.
A P : 0 4 :382(165) [0225] When **frightened** consciences are consoled by faith and
A P : 2 0 :006(227) [0339] up against us; this would **frighten** us more if we were
L C : 0 3 :025(423) [0705] who howl and growl **frightfully** day and night; not one of
E P : 0 5 :007(478) [0803] consciences that are **frightened** by the law, directs them
S D : P R :007(502) [0849] of the holy apostles **frightful** errors arose among those

Frivolity (3), Frivolous (1), Frivolously (1)
A G : 0 0 :000(049) [0059] in an unchristian and **frivolous** manner but have been
L C : P R :013(360) [0571] Shall we **frivolously** despise this might, blessing, power,
L C : 0 1 :096(378) [0607] who in their greed or **frivolity** neglect to hear God's Word
E P : 1 0 :005(493) [0829] 3. But in this matter all **frivolity** and offenses are to be
S D : 1 0 :009(612) [1055] as it does so without **frivolity** and offense but in an

Front (3)
A P : 2 3 :026(243) [0371] it with pious-sounding phrases to give it a religious **front**.
L C : 0 1 :055(372) [0595] name or to put up a good **front** and justify yourself,
L C : 0 1 :298(405) [0665] know how to put up a fine **front** to conceal our rascality.

Frost (1)
S D : 0 8 :010(593) [1019] to suffer hunger, thirst, **frost**, heat, and similar things are

Frowns (1)
L C : 0 1 :036(369) [0589] not caring whether God **frowns** or smiles, boast defiantly

Fruit (27), Fruitful (7), Fruits (58)
A G : 0 6 :001(031) [0045] should produce good **fruits** and goods works and that we
A G : 1 2 :006(035) [0049] for these must be the **fruits** of repentance, as John says,
A G : 1 2 :006(035) [0049] as John says, "Bear **fruit** that befits repentance" (Matt.
A L : 0 6 :001(031) [0045] bound to bring forth good **fruits** and that it is necessary
A L : 1 2 :006(035) [0049] works, which are the **fruits** of repentance, are bound to
A P : 0 2 :003(101) [0105] not mean only its acts or **fruits**, but the continual
A P : 0 2 :030(104) [0113] lust at work in our members and bringing forth evil **fruit**.
A P : 0 4 :064(116) [0139] it brings forth good **fruits**, as we shall point out later.
A P : 0 4 :155(128) [0165] love, confession, and other good **fruits** ought to follow.
A P : 0 4 :155(128) [0165] does not mean that these **fruits** are the price of
A P : 0 4 :184(132) [0173] are commended because of faith as its **fruit** or testimony.
A P : 0 4 :220(137) [0181] urging to bear good **fruits** lest they lose the Holy Spirit.
A P : 0 4 :221(137) [0181] Paul teaches about the **fruits**, and they omit the many
A P : 0 4 :226(138) [0183] that love is the greatest because it has the most **fruits**.
A P : 0 4 :247(142) [0191] that we should be a kind of first **fruits** of his creatures."
A P : 0 4 :252(143) [0191] heart and then have good **fruits**, which please him
A P : 0 4 :263(146) [0195] this way, they bring forth **fruits** worthy of penitence, as
A P : 0 4 :275(148) [0199] One is that good **fruits** ought to follow of necessity, and
A P : 0 4 :278(149) [0199] must consider faith and **fruits** together, so here we say in
A P : 0 4 :292(152) [0203] Then love and other good **fruits** follow.
A P : 0 4 :365(163) [0219] to include the righteousness of the heart with other **fruits**.
A P : 0 4 :371(164) [0221] but of righteousness in the heart and of its **fruits**.
A P : 0 4 :373(164) [0221] gave me food" is cited as **fruit** and evidence of the
A P : 0 4 :374(164) [0221] lump together the righteousness of the heart and its **fruit**.
A P : 0 4 :374(164) [0221] They often mention the **fruit** to make it clearer to the
A P : 0 4 :375(164) [0223] of the heart from its **fruits**, if only our opponents would
A P : 0 4 :375(164) [0223] would grant that the **fruits** please God because of faith
A P : 0 9 :002(178) [0245] therefore received this **fruit** from it, by God's favor, that
A P : 1 1 :003(180) [0249] about the worth and **fruits** of the sacraments in such a
A P : 1 2 :028(185) [0259] If someone wants to call **fruits** worthy of penitence
A P : 1 2 :045(188) [0263] Christ also includes the **fruits** of penitence or the new life.
A P : 1 2 :058(190) [0267] Worthy **fruits** as well as punishments follow regeneration
A P : 1 2 :122(200) [0289] passages they quote: "Bear **fruit** that befits penitence"
A P : 1 2 :131(202) [0291] must come good **fruits** and good works in every phase of
A P : 1 2 :131(202) [0291] where mortifying the flesh and good **fruits** do not follow.
A P : 1 2 :132(202) [0291] he says (Matt. 3:8), "Bear **fruit** that befits penitence," and
A P : 1 2 :132(202) [0291] about total penitence and total newness of life and **fruits**.
A P : 1 2 :134(203) [0293] life: "Be penitent," "Bear **fruit** that befits penitence,"
A P : 1 2 :135(203) [0293] like "Be penitent" and "Bear **fruit** that befits penitence."
A P : 1 2 :136(203) [0293] "Bear **fruit** that befits penitence" and "Be penitent" will
A P : 1 2 :139(203) [0295] to produce good **fruits**, and that good fruits like true
A P : 1 2 :139(203) [0295] good fruits, and that good **fruits** like true fasting, prayer,
A P : 1 2 :163(208) [0303] of penitence and the **fruits** that are due, not to
A P : 1 2 :164(208) [0303] faith, and good **fruits** — brings about the mitigation of
A P : 1 2 :165(208) [0303] our penitence and its true **fruits**, good works done from
A P : 1 2 :174(210) [0305] often enough that penitence ought to produce good **fruits**.
A P : 1 2 :174(210) [0307] What these **fruit** are, we learn from the commandments —
A P : 1 2 :174(210) [0307] These **fruits** are commanded by God, they should be done
A P : 1 8 :006(225) [0335] bad tree cannot bear good **fruit**" (Matt. 7:18) and
A P : 2 0 :015(229) [0343] chastity, and other **fruits** of the Spirit gradually increase.
A P : 2 3 :007(240) [0365] men were created to be **fruitful** and that one sex should
A P : 2 3 :008(240) [0365] the nature of men to be **fruitful** only at the beginning of
A P : 2 3 :008(240) [0367] Word makes the earth **fruitful** (Gen. 1:11), "Let the earth
A P : 2 4 :021(253) [0391] the thank offering, the first **fruits**, and the tithes.
A P : 2 4 :026(254) [0393] "that is, the **fruit** of lips that acknowledge his name."
A P : 2 4 :027(254) [0393] righteousness of faith in the heart and the **fruits** of faith.
A P : 2 4 :034(256) [0395] are the proclamation of the Gospel and its good **fruits**.
S 1 : P R :006(289) [0457] and malicious tongues and thus destroying the **fruit**.
S 3 : 0 1 :002(302) [0477] The **fruits** of this sin are all the subsequent evil deeds
L C : P R :009(359) [0569] is highly profitable and **fruitful** daily to read it and make
L C : P R :013(360) [0571] might, blessing, power, and **fruit** — especially we who
L C : P R :020(361) [0573] that they will gain much **fruit** and God will make
L C : S P :026(364) [0581] thus the preaching will not be without benefit and **fruit**.
L C : 0 1 :026(368) [0587] grain and all kinds of **fruits** from the earth for man's
L C : 0 1 :075(375) [0601] root, spring up, and bear **fruit**, and men may grow up of
L C : 0 1 :101(379) [0609] use, such is its power that it never departs without **fruit**.
L C : 0 1 :134(383) [0619] This, then, is the **fruit** and the reward, that whoever keeps
L C : 0 1 :207(393) [0639] be true to each other, be **fruitful**, beget children, and
L C : 0 2 :053(417) [0693] become strong in the faith and in the **fruits** of the Spirit.
L C : 0 3 :065(429) [0715] or believed, and bears **fruit**, there the blessed holy cross
L C : 0 3 :076(431) [0721] to cause the grain and **fruits** of the field to grow and yield
L C : 0 4 :024(439) [0737] the power, effect, benefit, **fruit**, and purpose of Baptism is
L C : 0 4 :027(440) [0739] as a divine, blessed, **fruitful**, and gracious water, for
L C : 0 4 :073(445) [0751] faith is present with its **fruits**, there Baptism is no empty
L C : 0 4 :084(446) [0753] in faith and amid its **fruits**, every day he should be
L C : 0 5 :075(455) [0771] and hear what are the **fruits** of the flesh: "The works of
E P : 0 4 :006(476) [0797] 1. That good works, like **fruits** of a good tree, certainly
E P : 0 6 :005(480) [0807] works of the law and **fruits** of the Spirit we believe,
E P : 0 6 :006(480) [0807] 5. **Fruits** of the Spirit, however, are those works which the
S D : 0 2 :032(527) [0893] evil tree cannot bear good **fruit**, and without faith no one
S D : 0 2 :037(528) [0895] become strong in faith and in its **fruits**, which he creates."
S D : 0 2 :068(534) [0907] received only the first **fruits** of the Spirit, and
S D : 0 3 :027(543) [0923] Love is a **fruit** which certainly and necessarily follows
S D : 0 3 :036(545) [0927] certain and unquestioned **fruits**, or as though believers
S D : 0 3 :041(546) [0929] and sanctification the **fruits** of good works will follow.
S D : 0 3 :042(547) [0931] of good works and the **fruits** of the Spirit do not follow,"
S D : 0 4 :001(551) [0939] of true believers as **fruits** of faith and since faith without
S D : 0 4 :008(552) [0941] bad tree cannot bear good **fruit**, and "Whatsoever does
S D : 0 4 :009(552) [0941] reason St. Paul calls them **fruits** of faith or of the Spirit.
S D : 0 4 :015(553) [0943] tree since no good **fruits** appear, yes, even though he were
S D : 0 6 :017(566) [0967] of the law but works and **fruits** of the Spirit, or, as St.
S D : 0 7 :076(583) [0999] Just as the words, 'Be **fruitful** and multiply and fill the

Frustrated (2)
L C : 0 3 :018(422) [0703] allow our prayers to be **frustrated** or lost, for if he did
L C : 0 3 :070(429) [0717] were not broken and **frustrated**, the kingdom of God

Fulda (2)
S 3 : 1 5 :005(317) [0501] Master Adam of **Fulda**, preacher in Hesse
T R : 0 0 :082(335) [0529] own hand both in his name and in that of Adam of **Fulda**

Fulfill (10), Fulfilled (7), Fulfilling (5), Fulfillment (4)
A G : 2 0 :025(045) [0057] confidence in God and in the **fulfillment** of his promises.
A G : 2 7 :061(080) [0083] they are the means of **fulfilling** both evangelical counsels
A P : 0 4 :181(132) [0171] of the law, to the extent that they **fulfill** the law.
A P : 0 4 :289(151) [0203] Therefore love is the **fulfilling** of the law.
L C : 0 1 :048(371) [0593] commandment is kept, **fulfillment** of all the others will
L C : 0 1 :081(376) [0603] commandment could be **fulfilled** by refraining from
L C : 0 1 :092(377) [0607] happens the commandment is in force and is **fulfilled**.
L C : 0 1 :102(379) [0609] this commandment is **fulfilled**, and God is more pleased
L C : 0 1 :312(407) [0671] they were too insignificant or had been **fulfilled** long ago.
L C : 0 1 :317(408) [0673] for they are beyond human power to **fulfill**.
L C : 0 1 :317(408) [0673] Anyone who does **fulfill** them is a heavenly, angelic man,
L C : 0 1 :324(409) [0675] toward God, he has **fulfilled** this commandment and all
L C : 0 2 :068(420) [0697] still remain on us because we cannot **fulfill** his demands.
L C : 0 3 :002(420) [0697] stands in our way and hinders us from **fulfilling** them.
L C : 0 3 :061(428) [0715] hinder and thwart the **fulfillment** of the first two
L C : 0 3 :062(428) [0715] how the devil opposes and obstructs their **fulfillment**.
E P : 0 2 :012(471) [0789] entirely and that this **fulfilling** constitutes our
E P : 0 5 :009(479) [0803] none of which we could **fulfill**, and that we should now
E P : 1 2 :025(500) [0843] can perfectly keep and **fulfill** the law of God in this life.
S D : 0 2 :003(520) [0881] Spirit man is unable to **fulfill** the commandment of God,
S D : 0 3 :030(544) [0925] obedience with which he **fulfilled** the law of God in our
S D : 0 3 :056(549) [0935] his human nature alone **fulfilled** all righteousness but had
S D : 0 5 :010(559) [0955] who believe that they can **fulfill** the law by external
S D : 0 5 :010(560) [0955] and condemns us because we could not **fulfill** or keep it.
S D : 0 7 :046(577) [0989] more ways and means of **fulfilling** the promises
S D : 1 2 :033(635) [1101] God is able to keep and **fulfill** the law of God perfectly in

Full (46), Fullest (1), Fullness (15), Fully (17)
A G : P R :021(026) [0043] above, we offer in **full** obedience, even beyond what is
A G : 0 2 :001(029) [0043] That is, all men are **full** of evil lust and inclinations from
A L : 2 0 :031(045) [0057] Spirit man's powers are **full** of ungodly affections and are
A P : 0 2 :002(100) [0105] That is, all men are **full** of evil lusts and inclinations from
A P : 0 2 :006(101) [0107] since human nature is born **full** of corruption and faults.
A P : 0 4 :102(121) [0151] But the Scripture is **full** of such testimonies.
A P : 0 4 :148(127) [0163] promise and believing with **full** assurance that God
A P : 0 4 :179(131) [0171] in Col. 2:10, "You have come to **fullness** of life in him."
A P : 0 4 :235(140) [0185] the books of the sages are **full** of these commands of
A P : 0 4 :317(156) [0209] Christ "an agent of sin" since he does not justify in **full**.
A P : 0 4 :321(157) [0209] teach on this question is **full** of errors and dangers.
A P : 0 4 :387(166) [0225] faith, for it brings the **fullest** comfort in all afflictions and
A P : 0 7 :005(169) [0227] which is his body, the **fullness**," that is, the whole
A P : 0 7 :029(173) [0237] to twist it, we shall not mind replying more **fully**.
A P : 0 7 :037(175) [0241] again and discuss more **fully** the issue in this controversy,
A P : 1 1 :001(180) [0249] issue we shall speak more **fully** a little later when we

Continued ▶

A P : 1 2 :002(182) [0253] Gospel, so exceedingly salutary and **full** of consolation.
A P : 1 2 :005(183) [0253] on the *Sentences* are **full** of endless questions which the
A P : 1 2 :010(184) [0255] questions we have listed is **full** of error and hypocrisy; it
A P : 2 3 :060(247) [0381] it is superstitious and **full** of danger; finally, the whole
A P : 2 4 :030(255) [0395] But Scripture is **full** of such passages which teach that
A P : 2 4 :092(266) [0417] ever arises, we shall discuss this whole issue more **fully**.
A P : 2 7 :010(270) [0423] whole issue carefully and **fully** in his book called
A P : 2 7 :016(271) [0425] obedience — hypocrisies all, since they are all **full** of
A P : 2 7 :025(273) [0427] All this is **full** of pharisaical vanity.
A P : 2 7 :044(277) [0435] whole monastic system is **full** of counterfeits, so they
A P : 2 7 :056(278) [0439] the whole monastic life is **full** of hypocrisy and false
A P : 2 7 :057(279) [0439] abandon a way of life so **full** of hypocrisy and false
S 1 : P R :003(289) [0455] a council meets (which I **fully** expect, for those knaves
S 1 : P R :013(291) [0459] their hands would be so **full** that their trifling and
S 3 : 0 3 :023(306) [0485] could have been perfect, **full** confidence would have been
S 3 : 0 3 :028(308) [0487] we taught, without sin and **full** of good works, and so we
S 3 : 0 3 :032(308) [0487] All of you are **full** of unbelief, blindness, and ignorance
S 3 : 0 3 :032(308) [0487] present, and from his **fullness** have we all received, grace
S 3 : 0 8 :002(312) [0495] not be untruthful if we say, "I am a poor man, **full** of sin.
T R : 0 0 :022(323) [0511] has been treated **fully** and accurately in the books of our
L C : 0 1 :114(380) [0613] obliged to set forth God's commandment in its **full** glory.
L C : 0 1 :154(386) [0625] think, is the world now so **full** of unfaithfulness, shame,
L C : 0 1 :183(389) [0633] well knows, the world is evil and this life is **full** of misery.
L C : 0 1 :196(391) [0637] minds, we would have our hands **full** of good works to do
L C : 0 1 :215(394) [0641] yet their hearts remain so **full** of unchaste thoughts and
L C : 0 1 :227(396) [0645] everyday business the same fraud prevails in **full** force.
L C : 0 1 :228(396) [0645] it is nothing but a vast, wide stable **full** of great thieves.
L C : 0 1 :313(407) [0671] we shall have our hands **full** to keep these
L C : 0 2 :012(412) [0681] can be treated more **fully** and divided into as many parts
L C : 0 2 :033(415) [0687] and it is so rich and broad that we can never learn it **fully**.
L C : 0 2 :055(418) [0693] that we may daily obtain **full** forgiveness of sins through
L C : 0 2 :055(418) [0693] Christian church, where there is **full** forgiveness of sin.
L C : 0 2 :058(418) [0693] pure and holy people, **full** of goodness and righteousness,
L C : 0 3 :047(426) [0709] we see that the world is **full** of sects and false teachers, all
L C : 0 4 :007(437) [0733] because the world now is **full** of sects who proclaim that
L C : 0 4 :017(438) [0737] extol, for it contains and conveys all the **fullness** of God.
L C : 0 4 :039(441) [0743] ordained; in short, it is so **full** of comfort and grace that
L C : 0 4 :070(445) [0749] When he reaches **full** manhood, the real vices become
L C : 0 5 :036(450) [0761] Since this treasure is **fully** offered in the words, it can be
L C : 0 5 :047(452) [0765] fourteenth day of the first **full** moon, without variation of
L C : 0 6 :026(460) [0000] men should look to see how **full** of filthiness you are,
E P : 0 8 :016(489) [0821] and was established in the **full** use, revelation, and
E P : 0 8 :034(491) [0825] "In him dwells the whole **fullness** of deity bodily" (Col.
E P : 1 2 :021(499) [0841] way that Christ as man is **fully** equal in rank and
S D : 0 1 :003(509) [0861] and to magnify more **fully** Christ's benefits, his precious
S D : 0 2 :017(524) [0887] that is, is so perverted and **full** of misery that no one can
S D : 0 6 :018(567) [0967] however, believers are not **fully** renewed in this life but
S D : 0 7 :001(569) [0971] to make it appear to be in **full** agreement with the
S D : 0 7 :036(575) [0985] or "In Christ the whole **fullness** of the deity dwells
S D : 0 8 :006(592) [1017] yet, when the time had **fully** come, he took the human
S D : 0 8 :030(597) [1025] that in Christ the whole **fullness** of deity dwells bodily
S D : 0 8 :034(597) [1027] that "in Christ the whole **fullness** of the deity dwells
S D : 0 8 :064(603) [1037] that is, because the **fullness** of the deity dwells in Christ
S D : 0 8 :064(603) [1037] This **fullness** shines forth with all its majesty, power,
S D : 0 8 :065(604) [1039] laid aside, it takes place **fully**, mightily, and publicly
S D : 0 8 :066(604) [1039] forth and manifests itself **fully**, though always
S D : 0 8 :068(604) [1039] dwells, there likewise the **fullness** of deity dwells bodily,
S D : 0 8 :070(604) [1039] together with the whole **fullness** of deity which he always
S D : 0 8 :070(605) [1041] "In him dwells the whole **fullness** of deity bodily" (Col.
S D : 0 8 :073(605) [1041] personal union the entire **fullness** of the Spirit (as the
S D : 0 8 :074(605) [1041] This **fullness** demonstrates and manifests itself
S D : 0 8 :081(607) [1045] is and that everything is **full** of Christ through and
S D : 1 1 :087(631) [1091] of God gives God his due honor **fully** and completely.

Fuller (2)
S C : P R :017(340) [0535] the people may have a richer and **fuller** understanding.
L C : S P :005(362) [0575] to know more and have a **fuller** understanding of all

Function (20), Functioning (2), Functions (6)
A G : 2 8 :013(083) [0085] it should not invade the **function** of the other, should not
A G : 2 8 :018(083) [0085] two authorities and the **functions** of the two powers,
A L : 1 6 :003(037) [0051] who forbid Christians to engage in these civil **functions**.
A L : 2 8 :013(083) [0085] it not invade the other's **function**, nor transfer the
A L : 2 8 :018(083) [0085] teachers distinguish the **functions** of the two powers, and
A L : 2 8 :019(084) [0087] This, however, is a **function** other than the ministry of the
A P : 0 7 :048(177) [0245] because they no longer **function** in the place of Christ,
A P : 2 3 :032(243) [0373] is saved by the marital **functions** themselves, by marital
A P : 2 4 :018(252) [0389] baptizes us through a minister **functioning** in his place.
S 2 : 0 2 :026(297) [0469] each of them a special **function**, as the papists teach and
S 3 : 0 2 :004(303) [0479] However, the chief **function** or power of the law is to
S 3 : 0 3 :001(303) [0479] This **function** of the law is retained and taught by the
S 3 : 0 4 :000(310) [0491] of sin (the peculiar **function** of the Gospel) is preached to
S 3 : 0 7 :001(311) [0493] The keys are a **function** and power given to the church by
S 3 : 0 8 :002(312) [0495] valued, like all other **functions** of the Christian church.
T R : 0 0 :073(332) [0525] for discussion of the other **functions** of bishops.
L C : 0 3 :073(430) [0719] and prevented from **functioning** properly, there the
E P : 0 6 :000(479) [0805] VI. The Third **Function** of the Law
E P : 0 6 :001(480) [0805] is concerning the third **function** of the law that a
E P : 1 2 :013(499) [0841] Christian can serve or **function** in any civic office with a
S D : 0 4 :034(556) [0949] and then delegates this **function** to works, as if works
S D : 0 5 :002(558) [0951] they said, is strictly a **function** of the law of God, which
S D : 0 5 :017(561) [0957] to the law, the proper **function** of which is to condemn sin
S D : 0 5 :018(561) [0957] nevertheless the true **function** of the law remains, to
S D : 0 6 :000(563) [0963] VI. The Third **Function** of the Law
S D : 0 6 :001(564) [0963] concerning this third and last **function** of the law.
S D : 0 6 :010(565) [0965] of believers and what **function** the law performs in this
S D : 0 6 :014(566) [0967] But to reprove is the real **function** of the law.

Fundamental (7), Fundamentally (1), Fundamentals (1)
A P : 0 4 :183(132) [0173] of the **fundamentals** in this issue (namely, the distinction
A P : 0 4 :294(152) [0203] From this **fundamental** article it is clear why we ascribe
S 1 : P R :013(290) [0459] were to consider such **fundamental** matters of the
S 2 : 0 2 :001(293) [0463] direct and violent conflict with this **fundamental** article.
S 2 : 0 2 :007(294) [0465] contradiction to the **fundamental** article, which asserts
S 2 : 0 2 :012(295) [0465] too, is contrary to the **fundamental** article that Christ
S 2 : 0 3 :002(298) [0471] conflict with the first, **fundamental** article concerning
S 2 : 0 4 :003(298) [0473] conflict with the first, **fundamental** article which is
S D : 1 2 :005(633) [1097] but that we wanted to help matters **fundamentally**.

Funds (2)
A P : 2 7 :064(280) [0441] supported from public **funds**, "They desire to marry, and
A P : 2 7 :067(280) [0441] being supported from public **funds** and thus lost the faith.

Furious (3), Furiously (2)
A P : 0 4 :298(153) [0205] astonished to see how **furiously** our opponents deny
L C : P R :014(360) [0571] knows the constant and **furious** attacks and assaults of
L C : 0 3 :062(428) [0715] Therefore, like a **furious** foe, he raves and rages with all
L C : 0 3 :068(429) [0717] his host storm and rage **furiously** against it in their
L C : 0 5 :026(449) [0759] The devil is a **furious** enemy; when he sees that we resist

Furnish (3)
P R : P R :017(008) [0015] notice that we would **furnish** further specifications
A G : 2 7 :061(080) [0083] precepts, and that they **furnish** the works of
S C : P R :012(339) [0535] should refuse to **furnish** them with food and drink and

Further (48), Furthermore (36), Furthers (1)
P R : P R :008(006) [0011] way without any **further** disputation and dissension.
P R : P R :009(006) [0011] we sustained the **further** disadvantage that, under the
P R : P R :017(008) [0015] that we would furnish **further** specifications concerning
P R : P R :018(008) [0015] **Furthermore**, lest anybody allow himself to be led astray
P R : P R :020(010) [0017] **Furthermore**, even though a number of theologians, like
P R : P R :022(012) [0019] It is **furthermore** to be hoped that when they are rightly
P R : P R :024(013) [0023] It is **further** apparent to us that many good-hearted
A G : 2 7 :015(073) [0077] **Furthermore**, those who were thus ensnared and inveigled
A G : 0 0 :007(096) [0095] we are ready to present **further** information on the basis
A L : 2 7 :049(078) [0083] **Furthermore**, the commands of God and true service of
A P : P R :011(099) [0101] our contemporaries still **further** from the opponents'
A P : 0 4 :014(109) [0123] on natural ethics that nothing **further** needs to be added.
A P : 0 4 :039(112) [0131] will compel us to cite **further** evidence; this will also help
A P : 0 4 :084(119) [0145] justification is a gift, and **further** that the promise can be
A P : 0 4 :120(124) [0155] **Furthermore**, the Gospel (that is, the promise that sins are
A P : 0 4 :140(126) [0161] We teach, **furthermore**, not only how the law can be
A P : 0 4 :240(141) [0187] **Furthermore**, this statement about love is taken from
A P : 1 2 :118(184) [0257] They add **further** that satisfactions ought to be works of
A P : 1 2 :067(191) [0271] But they go **further** and demand that this teaching be
A P : 1 2 :073(192) [0273] of God; but add **further** that you also believe that through
A P : 1 2 :118(199) [0287] They add **further** that part of this temporal punishment is
A P : 1 2 :140(204) [0295] The death of Christ, **furthermore**, is a satisfaction not
A P : 1 2 :144(204) [0297] pilgrimages, depart even **further** from God's commands;
A P : 1 2 :151(206) [0299] **Furthermore**, the saints are subject to death and to all the
A P : 1 2 :171(209) [0305] **Furthermore**, the Fathers wrote that once in a lifetime
A P : 1 4 :005(215) [0315] **Furthermore**, we want at this point to declare our
A P : 2 0 :015(229) [0343] **Furthermore**, we have already given ample evidence of
A P : 2 1 :018(231) [0347] **Furthermore**, we have the command to call upon Christ,
A P : 2 4 :083(264) [0411] But **further** proofs are unnecessary since anyone who
A P : 2 7 :058(279) [0439] **Furthermore**, just as circumcision or the slaughter of
S 3 : 0 3 :025(307) [0485] The popes went **further** and quickly multiplied the jubilee
S 3 : 0 8 :006(313) [0495] There is no time to dispute **further** about these matters.
T R : 0 0 :045(328) [0517] means of which they have **further** obscured the benefit of
L C : 0 1 :055(372) [0595] Of this there is no need to speak **further**.
L C : 0 1 :227(396) [0645] **Furthermore**, at the market and everyday business the
L C : 0 1 :233(396) [0647] neighbor's property and **further** his interests, especially
L C : 0 1 :251(399) [0651] to promote and **further** our neighbor's interests, and when
L C : 0 1 :262(400) [0655] Next, it extends much **further** when it is applied to
L C : 0 1 :279(402) [0661] Christ teaches **further**: "If he does not listen, take one or
L C : 0 2 :018(412) [0681] But **further** discussion of this subject belongs in the other
L C : 0 2 :024(413) [0683] for us in this life, and, **further**, has showered us with
L C : 0 2 :054(417) [0693] **Further** we believe that in this Christian church we have
L C : 0 3 :022(423) [0703] **Furthermore**, we should be encouraged and drawn to pray
L C : 0 4 :032(440) [0739] Baptism, let us observe **further** who receives these gifts
L C : 0 4 :052(443) [0745] **Further**, we are not primarily concerned whether the
L C : 0 4 :082(446) [0751] Baptism of its value, making it of no **further** use to us.
L C : 0 5 :038(451) [0761] What may be **further** said belongs to another occasion.
L C : 0 5 :049(452) [0765] may just as well take the **further** liberty not to be a
L C : 0 6 :020(459) [0000] **Further**, no one dare oppress you with requirements.
E P : R N :002(465) [0777] in no other way and no **further** than as witnesses to the
E P : 0 1 :005(466) [0781] **Furthermore**, the Son of God assumed into the unity of
E P : 0 1 :015(468) [0783] 5. **Furthermore**, that original sin is only an external
E P : 0 1 :016(468) [0783] 6. **Furthermore**, that the human nature and essence in
E P : 0 4 :008(476) [0799] teach, and confess **further** that all men, but especially
E P : 0 6 :004(480) [0807] This is **further** necessary lest the Old Adam go his own
E P : 1 1 :014(496) [0835] 13. **Furthermore**, we are to put forth every effort to live
E P : 1 1 :018(497) [0837] 2. **Furthermore**, the doctrine that God is not serious about
E P : 1 1 :019(497) [0837] 3. **Furthermore**, that God does not want everybody to be
S D : R N :004(504) [0851] of heretics, we **further** pledge allegiance to the three
S D : R N :007(505) [0853] several articles are **further** explained on the basis of God's
S D : R N :009(505) [0853] regarded as appealing to **further** extensive statements in
S D : 0 1 :003(509) [0861] **Furthermore**, we are extolling God's honor properly when
S D : 0 1 :010(510) [0863] 2. **Furthermore**, that original sin is the complete lack or
S D : 0 1 :060(519) [0879] when someone inquires **further**, What kind of accident is
S D : 0 2 :027(527) [0893] And St. Augustine says **further** on, "I have erred when I
S D : 0 2 :034(527) [0893] Smalcald Articles state **further**: "This repentance
S D : 0 4 :013(553) [0943] we shall discuss them no **further** but shall explain only
S D : 0 4 :023(555) [0945] **Furthermore**, these propositions deprive tempted and
S D : 0 4 :028(555) [0945] 4. **Furthermore**, in the case of some of his own followers
S D : 0 6 :020(567) [0969] Believers, **furthermore**, require the teaching of the law so
S D : 0 6 :021(567) [0969] Believers, **furthermore**, require the teaching of the law in
S D : 0 7 :098(586) [1005] "**Furthermore**, the one body of Christ has three different
S D : 0 7 :110(588) [1011] **Furthermore**, that only one species is administered to the
S D : 0 8 :008(593) [1017] 3. We **furthermore** believe, teach, and confess that in
S D : 0 8 :012(593) [1019] 7. We **furthermore** believe, teach, and confess that the
S D : 0 8 :018(594) [1021] The Fathers **further** illustrated the personal union and
S D : 1 0 :009(612) [1055] We **further** believe, teach, and confess that the
S D : 1 1 :008(617) [1065] effects, helps, and **furthers** our salvation and whatever
S D : 1 1 :009(617) [1065] **Furthermore**, we are not to view this eternal election or
S D : 1 1 :012(618) [1067] **Furthermore**, everything in the Word of God is written

Continued ▶

SD : 11 :023(619) [1069] to salvation and to help, **further**, strengthen, and preserve
SD : 11 :025(620) [1071] is necessary for the **further** exposition and the salutary
SD : 11 :046(624) [1079] **Furthermore**, God wanted to insure my salvation so
SD : 11 :064(626) [1083] silence and cuts off **further** discussion with the following
SD : 11 :095(632) [1095] part to do everything in our power to **further** the same.

Fury (2)
LC : 03 :068(429) [0717] hindrance, in spite of their **fury**, so that they may
SD : 07 :029(574) [0981] and that there is no end to the rage and **fury** of Satan.

Fused (1)
EP : 08 :006(487) [0819] the human nature are not **fused** into one essence and that

Futile (2), Futility (1)
SD : PR :008(502) [0849] us, in the unchristian but **futile** hope that these
SD : 02 :010(522) [0883] God's Spirit, "walk in the **futility** of their minds; they are
SD : 07 :091(585) [1003] imaginary reasons and **futile** counter-arguments of the

Future (21)
PR : PR :008(005) [0009] our posterity in the **future** against doctrine that is
PR : PR :010(006) [0011] they might be preserved from false doctrine in the **future**.
PR : PR :014(007) [0013] doctrine might in the **future** be hidden thereunder and
PR : PR :026(014) [0025] with one another in the **future** in the implementation of
AG : 23 :012(053) [0063] the time not only forbade **future** marriages of priests but
AG : 23 :017(054) [0063] may be a shortage of priests and pastors in the **future**.
AG : 27 :031(076) [0079] determine or arrange the order of one's whole **future** life.
AL : 23 :013(053) [0063] out that not only were **future** marriages prohibited but
AP : 04 :312(155) [0207] of hope is properly a **future** event, while faith deals with
AP : 04 :312(155) [0207] faith deals with both **future** and present things and
AP : 04 :395(167) [0225] a type of what was to happen in the church of the **future**.
AP : 04 :398(167) [0227] When **future** generations hear that such a doctrine was
AP : 12 :125(201) [0289] that now or in the **future** might tend to diminish the
AP : 14 :005(215) [0315] all nations, present and **future**, against the charge that we
AP : 24 :024(253) [0391] were so called only as symbols of a **future** offering.
AP : 24 :054(259) [0403] but only to symbolize the **future** death of Christ alone.
S3 : 15 :005(317) [0501] who are now under him and who may be in the **future**.
TR : 00 :082(334) [0527] be wicked bishops in the **future** who would consume the
EP : 11 :001(494) [0831] document, lest as some **future** date offensive dissension
SD : 04 :038(557) [0951] to reward them gloriously in this and in the **future** life.
SD : 11 :004(617) [1063] all things, present or **future**, are manifest and present to

Gabriel (7)
AP : 04 :210(136) [0179] in those for whom it is offered, as **Gabriel** Biel writes.
AP : 12 :068(192) [0271] like Duns Scotus, **Gabriel** Biel, and the like in addition to
AP : 21 :023(232) [0349] **Gabriel** Biel's interpretation of the canon of the Mass
AP : 21 :023(232) [0349] These are **Gabriel's** own words.
AP : 22 :009(237) [0359] both kinds are not given, **Gabriel** says that a distinction
S3 : 08 :012(313) [0497] the preceding word of **Gabriel**, nor did he leap in his
S3 : 15 :005(317) [0501] **Gabriel** Didymus subscribed

Gain (21), Gained (7), Gaining (5)
AG : 27 :010(072) [0077] Besides, monastic vows **gained** such a reputation, as is
AG : 00 :005(095) [0095] into our churches and **gaining** the upper hand in them.
AL : 24 :010(057) [0065] shamefully profaned and applied to purposes of **gain**.
AL : 24 :013(057) [0065] any private Masses were held except for the sake of **gain**.
AL : 24 :020(058) [0067] to have been so abused for the sake of **gain** as the Mass.
AP : 04 :288(151) [0203] Because this mode of **gaining** justification is reasonable
AP : 12 :124(201) [0289] good men these slanders will not **gain** any adherents.
AP : 15 :004(215) [0315] rites are helpful in **gaining** grace and the forgiveness of
AP : 15 :005(215) [0317] which they seek to **gain** the forgiveness of sins and
AP : 24 :013(251) [0387] can placate God's wrath, **gain** the remission of guilt and
AP : 24 :024(253) [0391] satisfactions since they **gained** the righteousness of the
AP : 28 :024(285) [0451] Originally this **gained** for Luther not only our good will
S1 : PR :012(290) [0459] everything? — these have **gained** the ascendancy to such
S2 : 01 :005(292) [0463] the devil, and all our adversaries will **gain** the victory.
S3 : 03 :044(310) [0491] not permit sin to rule and **gain** the upper hand in such a
TR : 00 :046(328) [0517] which are nothing but lies devised for the sake of **gain**.
TR : 00 :074(332) [0525] for themselves alone and have employed for **gain**.
SC : 01 :018(344) [0541] not seek by craftiness to **gain** possession of our neighbor's
SC : 03 :018(348) [0549] so tempted, we may finally prevail and **gain** the victory.
LC : PR :020(361) [0573] me out — that they will **gain** much fruit and God will
LC : 01 :043(370) [0591] wealth and money, what have they **gained** in the end?
LC : 01 :067(373) [0599] everything he may **gain** by the false oath will slip through
LC : 01 :145(385) [0623] and wages, she would **gain** a treasure such as all who pass
LC : 01 :151(386) [0625] Where he counts on **gaining** a gulden by his
LC : 01 :236(397) [0647] But see what you **gain**.
LC : 01 :238(397) [0649] will neither prosper nor **gain** anything their whole life
LC : 01 :258(399) [0653] with an eye to **gaining** favor, money, prospects, or
LC : 01 :278(402) [0661] "If he listens to you, you have **gained** your brother."
LC : 01 :278(402) [0661] Do you think it is an insignificant thing to **gain** a brother?
LC : 01 :278(402) [0661] can make the boast that they have **gained** one brother!
LC : 01 :301(405) [0667] which someone sets out to **gain** and squeeze something
LC : 01 :301(405) [0667] supports them, and they **gain** such secure title to the
LC : 03 :052(427) [0711] it and in order that it may **gain** recognition and followers

Gaius (1)
AP : 04 :241(141) [0187] Between **Gaius** Caesar and Pompey certain minor

Galatians (7)
AL : 28 :052(089) [0091] in the Epistle to the **Galatians**, "Do not submit again to a
AP : 15 :008(216) [0317] Paul says to the **Galatians** (5:4), "You are severed from
AP : 27 :011(270) [0423] Paul's statement from **Galatians** (Gal. 5:4), "You are
LC : 05 :075(455) [0771] St. Paul's Epistle to the **Galatians** and hear what are the
SD : 03 :028(544) [0925] of the Epistle to the **Galatians** Dr. Luther well states:
SD : 03 :067(551) [0937] splendid exposition of St. Paul's Epistle to the **Galatians**.
SD : 04 :025(555) [0945] 1. In the case of the false prophets among the **Galatians**;

Galilee (1)
SD : 08 :025(596) [1023] the wedding in Cana of **Galilee**, again when he was twelve

Gallows (4)
LC : 01 :224(395) [0643] it, were hanged on the **gallows**, the world would soon be
LC : 01 :224(395) [0643] there would be a shortage of both hangmen and **gallows**.
LC : 01 :238(397) [0647] will hang them not on a green **gallows** but on a dry one.
LC : 01 :245(398) [0649] where would we find enough **gallows** and ropes?

Gambling (1)
S1 : PR :012(290) [0459] in dress, gluttony, **gambling**, vain display, all manner of

Game (1), Games (1)
AP : 24 :081(264) [0411] kind of tax to pay for the **games**, ships, care of the
LC : 01 :245(398) [0649] must put up with another who plays the same **game**.

Gaped (1)
LC : 01 :114(380) [0613] it to heart; they simply **gaped** in astonishment at all the

Garbled (5)
AP : 04 :280(149) [0201] that they are, pick out **garbled** sentences to put something
AP : 04 :281(149) [0201] is also quoted in a **garbled** form: "Give alms; and
AP : 04 :286(150) [0201] They quote many passages in a **garbled** form.
AP : 12 :068(192) [0271] statements which the decrees quote in **garbled** form.
AP : 12 :091(195) [0279] which are quoted in **garbled** form from the Fathers and

Garden (1)
SD : 08 :025(596) [1023] the teachers, again in the **garden** when with one word he

Garlands (1)
LC : 01 :088(377) [0605] or deck ourselves with **garlands** and dress up in our best

Garlic (2)
EP : 01 :015(468) [0783] or loss of the same, just as **garlic** juice, smeared upon a
SD : 01 :022(512) [0865] to them, just as **garlic** juice smeared on a magnet does

Garment (1), Garments (2)
S1 : PR :004(289) [0457] venomous spirits in the **garments** of my labor and thus
LC : 01 :331(410) [0677] on every wall and corner, and even on their **garments**.
LC : 04 :084(446) [0753] his Baptism as the daily **garment** which he is to wear all

Garner (1)
LC : 01 :242(397) [0649] grain will spoil in the **garner** and your beer in the cellar.

Garnishing (1)
LC : 01 :301(405) [0667] so varnishing and **garnishing** them that the law supports

Gates (8)
AP : 04 :085(119) [0147] death, and against all the **gates** of hell (Matt. 16:18).
AP : 04 :260(145) [0193] For it is sure, and no **gates** of hell can overthrow it
AP : 12 :031(186) [0259] days I must depart; I am consigned to the **gates** of Sheol.
AP : 12 :063(191) [0269] very sure, though all the **gates** of hell (Matt. 16:18) cry
AP : 24 :012(251) [0387] and sure that it can prevail against all the **gates** of hell.
EP : 11 :005(495) [0833] upon it that the "**gates** of Hades cannot prevail against" it
SD : 11 :008(617) [1065] it in such a way that "the **gates** of Hades" are not able to
SD : 11 :050(624) [1079] shall exist and remain against all the "**gates** of Hades."

Gather (3), Gathered (18), Gathering (3), Gathers (6)
PR : PR :008(005) [0009] and some of us **gathered** at Naumburg, in Thuringia.
AG : 26 :045(070) [0075] History, Book 9, **gathers** many examples of dissimilar
AG : 27 :016(073) [0077] In former times people **gathered** and adopted monastic
AL : 00 :005(049) [0059] The truth cannot be **gathered** from common rumors or
AL : 26 :014(066) [0073] and theologians **gathered** the traditions together and
AL : 26 :015(066) [0073] so preoccupied with **gathering** traditions that they have
AL : 26 :045(070) [0075] of dissimilar rites are **gathered**, and this statement is
AP : 04 :398(167) [0227] Now in this very **gathering** the authors of the Confutation
AP : 07 :045(177) [0243] similar instances can be **gathered** from the histories in
AP : 24 :086(265) [0413] show that when they **gathered** they brought bread, wine,
S3 : 04 :000(310) [0491] Matt. 18:20, "Where two or three are **gathered**," etc.
TR : 00 :062(330) [0523] lest several persons, by **gathering** separate followings
TR : 00 :068(331) [0523] "Where two or three are **gathered** in my name, there am I
SC : 02 :006(345) [0545] faith, just as he calls, **gathers**, enlightens, and sanctifies
SC : 08 :007(353) [0559] and the whole household **gather** at the table, they should
LC : PR :009(359) [0569] "Where two or three are **gathered** in my name, there am I
LC : 01 :091(377) [0607] consecrated vestments **gathered** together in one heap, they
LC : 01 :243(398) [0649] Though they **gather** a great hoard, they must suffer so
LC : 02 :005(411) [0679] to the Creed were **gathered** together, there would be many
LC : 02 :045(416) [0689] Spirit to create, call, and **gather** the Christian church, and
LC : 02 :053(417) [0693] Through it he **gathers** us, using it to teach and preach the
LC : 02 :062(419) [0695] For he has not yet **gathered** together all his Christian
LC : 03 :025(423) [0705] If we **gathered** all the churches together, with all their
SD : 02 :040(528) [0895] faith, just as he calls, **gathers**, enlightens, and sanctifies
SD : 02 :050(531) [0901] Thereby he **gathers** an eternal church for himself out of
SD : 02 :057(532) [0903] where two or three are **gathered** together in his name and
SD : 02 :058(532) [0903] often would I have **gathered** your children together as a
SD : 02 :058(532) [0903] together as a hen **gathers** her brood under her wings, and
SD : 08 :076(606) [1043] "Where two or three are **gathered** in my name, there am I
SD : 11 :041(623) [1077] often would I have **gathered** you together and you would

Gauge (1)
AP : 21 :043(235) [0357] the church, and good men can easily **gauge** its outcome.

Gelasius (3)
AG : 22 :007(050) [0061] Pope **Gelasius** himself ordered that the sacrament was not
AL : 22 :007(050) [0061] In fact, Pope **Gelasius** commanded that the sacrament
SD : 07 :037(575) [0985] Cyprian, Augustine, Leo, **Gelasius**, Chrysostom, and

Geltner (2)
S3 : 15 :005(317) [0501] Master Peter **Geltner**, preacher in Frankfurt, subscribed
TR : 00 :082(335) [0529] Peter **Geltner**, preacher in the church in Frankfurt

General (32), Generally (6)
PR : PR :007(004) [0009] we should assemble in a **general** convention and should
PR : PR :016(008) [0015] of our theologians but **generally** of each and every
AG : PR :018(026) [0041] proposal concerning a **general** council and acknowledged
AG : PR :019(026) [0041] would not refuse to call a **general** council, and so Your
AG : PR :020(026) [0041] the calling of such a **general** council by the pope, along
AG : PR :021(027) [0043] to participate in such a **general**, free, and Christian
AG : 27 :030(075) [0079] vows inasmuch as it is **generally** conceded that it belongs

Continued ▶

A P : 0 4 :278(149) [0199] as we said a little earlier about penitence in **general**.
A P : 1 2 :045(187) [0263] Gospel is not to have the **general** faith that even the
A P : 1 2 :060(190) [0267] mean justifying but the **general** faith which believes that
A P : 1 2 :074(192) [0273] that we believe in a **general** way that sins are forgiven by
A P : 1 2 :110(198) [0285] many of the most **generally** accepted theologians.
A P : 1 3 :021(214) [0313] a faith which believes in a **general** way that God exists.
A P : 1 6 :013(224) [0333] of magistrates and the value of civil ordinances **generally**.
A P : 2 1 :009(230) [0345] pray for the church in **general**, as they prayed for the
A P : 2 3 :015(241) [0367] to human nature in **general**, applies to priests as well.
A P : 2 4 :067(261) [0407] This is enough of a **general** reply to our opponents
S 3 : 0 3 :013(305) [0483] in the pulpit when the **general** confession was recited to
S 3 : 1 5 :005(317) [0501] the sake of peace and **general** unity among the Christians
T R : 0 0 :059(330) [0521] we have set forth in **general** terms what we have to say
T R : 0 0 :078(333) [0527] too, is the law that in **general** approves all clandestine and
S C : 0 5 :025(351) [0555] forgiveness upon the **general** confession which you make
S C : 0 9 :012(356) [0563] Young Persons in **General**
S C : 0 9 :014(356) [0563] Christians in **General**
L C : 0 1 :105(379) [0611] sisters, and neighbors in **general** he commands nothing
L C : 0 1 :211(393) [0641] by God that in **general** men and women in all conditions,
L C : 0 1 :309(406) [0669] commandments therefore retain their **general** application.
E P : 1 0 :001(492) [0829] in the interest of good order and the **general** welfare.
E P : 1 0 :003(493) [0829] of good order and the **general** welfare, are in and for
E P : 1 2 :002(498) [0839] But in **general** they profess doctrines of a kind that
S D : 0 0 :000(501) [0845] A **General**, Pure, Correct, and Definitive Restatement and
S D : P R :004(504) [0851] allegiance to the three **general** Creeds, the Apostles'; the
S D : P R :009(505) [0853] these publicly and **generally** accepted documents as the
S D : 0 5 :027(563) [0961] however, when it is **generally** understood as referring to
S D : 0 8 :059(602) [1035] not only speaks in **general** terms of the person of the Son
S D : 1 0 :024(615) [1061] to treat ceremonies in **general** and matters of indifference
S D : 1 1 :023(619) [1069] prepared salvation in **general**, but he has also graciously
S D : 1 1 :037(622) [1075] offered not only in **general** but also through the

Generate (1), Generation (10), Generations (5)
P R : P R :024(013) [0023] and views will be transmitted to subsequent **generations**.
A P : 0 2 :036(105) [0115] This view pleased later **generations** so much that they
A P : 0 4 :398(167) [0227] When future **generations** hear that such a doctrine was
T R : 0 0 :051(329) [0519] and countless souls are lost **generation** after generation.
T R : 0 0 :051(329) [0519] and countless souls are lost generation after **generation**.
S C : 0 1 :021(344) [0543] third and the fourth **generation** of those who hate me,
L C : 0 1 :030(369) [0589] *to the third and fourth **generation** of those who hate me,*
L C : 0 1 :032(369) [0589] His wrath does not abate until the fourth **generation**.
L C : 0 1 :034(369) [0589] continues to the fourth **generation**, until they are utterly
L C : 0 1 :039(370) [0591] to a thousand and even many thousands of **generations**.
L C : 0 1 :043(370) [0593] their wealth, nor has it ever lasted to the third **generation**.
L C : 0 1 :137(384) [0621] as we said above, "to the third and fourth **generation**."
L C : 0 1 :138(384) [0621] cut off: and may their name be cut off in one **generation**."
L C : 0 1 :320(408) [0673] *to the third and fourth **generation** of them that hate me;*
L C : 0 1 :320(408) [0673] *I show mercy unto a thousand **generations**."*
L C : 0 3 :026(424) [0705] taught how to prepare for it or how to **generate** devotion.

Generous (1), Generosity (1)
A P : 1 2 :174(210) [0307] the greatest possible **generosity** to the needy, restraint and
A P : 2 4 :076(263) [0411] it gives thanks to the Giver of such a **generous** blessing."

Gentiles (4)
A P : 0 4 :206(135) [0177] The **Gentiles** had sacrifices which they took over from the
A P : 2 4 :034(256) [0395] that the offering of the **Gentiles** may be acceptable,
A P : 2 4 :034(256) [0397] that is, so that the **Gentiles** may become offerings
T R : 0 0 :008(320) [0505] said, "The kings of the **Gentiles** exercise lordship over

Gentium (2)
A L : 2 0 :014(043) [0055] in *De vocatione **gentium*** and elsewhere, for in his *De*
A L : 2 0 :014(043) [0055] for in his *De vocatione **gentium*** he says: "Redemption by

Gentle (4), Gentlemen (1), Gentleness (2), Gentler (1), Gently (1)
A P : 1 4 :004(215) [0315] canons themselves are **gentler** with those who violate
A P : 2 4 :099(268) [0419] of the Mass, we shall not handle the case so **gently**.
S C : 0 9 :002(354) [0561] drunkard, not violent but **gentle**, not quarrelsome, and no
L C : 0 1 :187(390) [0633] anger and have a patient, **gentle** heart, especially toward
L C : 0 1 :195(391) [0637] exalted deeds, such as **gentleness**, patience, and, in short,
L C : 0 1 :229(396) [0645] These men are called **gentlemen** swindlers or big
L C : 0 1 :313(407) [0671] practicing **gentleness**, patience, love toward enemies,
L C : 0 4 :067(445) [0749] longer we live the more **gentle**, patient, and meek we
L C : 0 6 :005(457) [0000] ease whatever in the Gospel is mild and **gentle**.

Genuine (33), Genuinely (8)
P R : P R :018(008) [0015] not know which is the **genuine** Augsburg Confession, and
P R : P R :025(014) [0023] and purpose to live in **genuine** peace and concord with
A G : 1 6 :005(038) [0051] Christian love and **genuine** good works in his station of
A G : 2 0 :038(046) [0057] Such great and **genuine** works cannot be done without
A P : 1 2 :029(185) [0259] say that contrition is the **genuine** terror of a conscience
A P : 1 2 :032(186) [0259] foulness of sin and is **genuinely** sorry that it has sinned;
A P : 1 2 :046(188) [0263] but mortification means **genuine** terrors, like those of the
A P : 1 2 :048(188) [0265] is understood only amid **genuine** sorrows and terrors.
A P : 1 2 :149(205) [0299] satisfactions are more **genuine** punishments than are real
A P : 1 2 :150(206) [0299] thus contrition is a more **genuine** punishment than is
A P : 1 3 :004(211) [0309] The **genuine** sacraments, therefore, are Baptism, the
A P : 1 5 :045(221) [0327] disciplines us effect a **genuine** and not a counterfeit
T R : 0 0 :082(000) [0529] with the belief of the true and **genuine** catholic Church.
L C : 0 6 :009(458) [0000] this is the essence of a **genuinely** Christian life, to
E P : 0 3 :009(474) [0793] that, although the **genuinely** believing and truly
E P : 0 4 :006(476) [0799] and indubitably follow **genuine** faith — if it is a living and
E P : 0 4 :010(476) [0799] the due obedience which **genuine** believers, in so far as
E P : 0 6 :002(480) [0805] although people who **genuinely** believe and whom God
E P : 0 6 :003(480) [0805] also to people who are **genuinely** believing, truly
E P : 0 6 :008(481) [0807] upon Christians and **genuine** believers, but only upon
E P : 0 7 :016(483) [0813] confess that not only the **genuine** believers and those who
E P : 0 7 :019(484) [0813] and confess that no **genuine** believer, no matter how weak
E P : 0 7 :020(484) [0813] make our own through **genuine** faith and of which we are
E P : 0 7 :039(486) [0817] 18. That **genuine** believers, who have a genuine and living
E P : 0 7 :039(486) [0817] believers, who have a **genuine** and living faith in Christ,
E P : 0 8 :018(489) [0823] He denied the **genuine** sharing of the properties of the two
E P : 1 2 :027(500) [0843] or administer true and **genuine** sacraments unless he is
S D : P R :004(502) [0847] this Confession a **genuinely** Christian symbol which all
S D : P R :006(504) [0853] clearly the true and **genuine** meaning of the Augsburg
S D : 0 2 :054(531) [0903] of God and experiences **genuine** terror, contrition, and
S D : 0 3 :022(543) [0923] For **genuine** contrition must precede.
S D : 0 3 :026(543) [0923] Thus there cannot be **genuine** saving faith in those who
S D : 0 3 :026(543) [0923] contrition precedes and **genuine** faith exists only in or
S D : 0 5 :015(561) [0957] law is not sufficient for **genuine** and salutary repentance;
S D : 0 6 :004(564) [0963] Christians, having been **genuinely** converted to God and
S D : 0 7 :125(591) [1015] have and retain a true, **genuine**, living faith, but who fail
S D : 0 8 :002(591) [1015] could not be a true and **genuine** human body if it were
S D : 1 0 :010(612) [1055] order to undermine the **genuine** worship of God and to
S D : 1 1 :013(619) [1067] Christ Jesus, who is the **genuine** and true "book of life" as
S D : 1 2 :035(635) [1101] profitably nor administer **genuine** and true sacraments.
S D : 1 2 :038(636) [1103] 2. That only the Father is **genuinely** and truly God.

Genus (1)
A P : 2 4 :017(252) [0389] The **genus** common to both could be "ceremony" or

George (12)
P R : P R :027(014) [0025] John **George**, margrave of Brandenburg, elector
P R : P R :027(014) [0025] **George** Frederick, margrave of Brandenburg
P R : P R :027(015) [0025] **George** Ernest, count and lord of Henneberg
P R : P R :027(015) [0025] **George**, count and lord of Castell [-Ruedenhausen]
P R : P R :027(015) [0025] **George**, baron of Schoenburg [-Waldenburg]
A G : 0 0 :007(096) [0095] **George**, margrave of Brandenburg
A L : 0 0 :017(096) [0095] **George**, margrave of Brandenburg
A P : 2 1 :032(233) [0351] Valentine heals epilepsy, and **George** protects knights.
S 3 : 1 5 :005(316) [0501] **George** Spalatin, of Altenburg, subscribed
S 3 : 1 5 :005(317) [0501] Master **George** Helt, of Forchheim
T R : 0 0 :082(334) [0529] **George** Spalatin, of Altenburg, subscribed
T R : 0 0 :082(335) [0529] **George** Helt, of Forchheim

Georgental (1)
P R : P R :027(015) [0027] and Council of the City of Muenster-in-St. **Georgental**

Gerard (2)
S 3 : 1 5 :005(317) [0501] **Gerard** Oemcken, superintendent of the church in
T R : 0 0 :082(334) [0529] **Gerard** Oemcken, minister of the church in Minden

German (24), Germans (4), Germany (10)
P R : P R :001(003) [0007] the Holy Empire of the **German** Nation who are named
P R : P R :002(003) [0007] beloved fatherland, the **German** nation, and to light its
P R : P R :002(003) [0007] It was submitted in the **German** and Latin languages by
P R : P R :004(003) [0007] place in our beloved **German** fatherland shortly after the
P R : P R :018(009) [0015] and of which both the **German** and the Latin copies were
P R : P R :022(011) [0019] inside or outside the Holy Empire of the **German** Nation.
A G : P R :006(025) [0039] writing and present, in **German** and Latin, his judgments,
A G : P R :007(025) [0039] present our case in **German** and Latin today (Friday).
A G : P R :009(025) [0041] opinions, in Latin and **German**, we are prepared, in
A G : 2 3 :012(052) [0063] ago that the priests in **Germany** were compelled by force
A G : 2 3 :014(054) [0063] disgraceful lewdness and vice to prevail in **German** lands.
A G : 0 1 :002(056) [0065] that in certain places **German** hymns are sung in addition
A L : 2 3 :012(052) [0063] years ago were priests in **Germany** compelled by force to
A L : 2 3 :014(053) [0063] against the introduction into **Germany** of more vices.
A L : 2 4 :002(056) [0065] also retained, except that **German** hymns are interspersed
A P : 0 2 :002(100) [0105] them first to look at the **German** text of the Confession.
A P : 0 7 :034(175) [0239] Thus if the **German** style of dress is not a devotion to God
A P : 0 7 :034(175) [0239] according to the French rather than the **German** style.
A P : 1 2 :127(201) [0289] In **Germany**, England, Spain, France, Italy, even in Rome
A P : 2 4 :003(250) [0385] it, and we insert **German** hymns to give the common
A P : 2 4 :004(250) [0385] Though **German** hymns have varied in frequency, yet
S 1 : P R :011(290) [0457] of angels to descend on **Germany** and destroy us utterly,
T R : 0 0 :035(326) [0513] the emperors of **Germany**, with unjust excommunications
T R : 0 0 :035(326) [0513] in order to make the **German** bishops subject to their
T R : 0 0 :082(000) [0529] at Smalcald in the **German** language by Dr. Martin
L C : P R :006(359) [0569] This is what one can expect of crazy **Germans**.
L C : P R :006(359) [0569] We **Germans** have such disgraceful people among us and
L C : 0 1 :025(368) [0587] This, I think, is why we **Germans** from ancient times have
L C : 0 1 :230(396) [0645] and daily plunder not only a city or two, but all **Germany**.
L C : 0 2 :048(416) [0691] assembly; it is not of **German** but of Greek origin, like the
L C : 0 2 :049(417) [0691] neither Latin nor **German**, have rendered this
L C : 0 2 :049(417) [0691] of saints," although no **German** would use or understand
L C : 0 2 :060(418) [0695] When we **Germans** hear the word *Fleisch* (flesh), we think
L C : 0 3 :031(424) [0707] devil would have destroyed all **Germany** in its own blood.
L C : 0 3 :036(425) [0707] It is not idiomatic **German**.
E P : 0 7 :003(482) [0809] who set forth in clear **German** words what they believe in
S D : 0 7 :012(571) [0977] of Saxony and Upper **Germany** drafted the following
S D : 0 7 :017(572) [0977] from all parts of **Germany** in Smalcald to consider what

Gerson (12)
A G : 2 6 :013(066) [0073] **Gerson** writes that many fell into despair on this account,
A G : 2 6 :016(066) [0073] **Gerson** and others have complained bitterly about this.
A G : 2 7 :060(080) [0083] In former times **Gerson** censured the error of the monks
A L : 2 6 :013(065) [0073] **Gerson** writes that many fell into despair, and some even
A L : 2 6 :016(066) [0073] Hence **Gerson** and certain other theologians greatly
A L : 2 7 :060(080) [0083] Before our times **Gerson** rebuked the error of the monks
A P : 1 5 :028(219) [0323] How the great **Gerson** suffers as he looks for the degrees
A P : 2 3 :020(242) [0369] **Gerson** testifies that many good men have tried to control
A P : 2 7 :016(271) [0425] **Gerson** indicates how pure this is in most of those who
A P : 2 7 :036(275) [0433] We remember that this correction is found in **Gerson**.
S 1 : P R :006(289) [0457] I often think of the good **Gerson**, who doubted whether
L C : 0 4 :050(443) [0745] such as St. Bernard, **Gerson**, John Hus, and others, and

Gestures (1)
L C : 0 1 :182(389) [0631] or word, by signs or **gestures**, or by aiding and abetting.

Get (18), Gets (2), Getting (1), Got (2), Gotten (1)
A G : 2 4 :023(058) [0067] of which men expected to **get** everything they needed from
A G : 2 8 :042(088) [0089] Where did the bishops **get** the right and power to impose
A L : 2 8 :042(088) [0089] Where did the bishops **get** the right to impose such
A P : 0 4 :288(151) [0203] other forms of worship to **get** rid of the terrors of
A P : 1 2 :146(205) [0297] useless and in this life does not even **get** a taste of death.
A P : 2 0 :012(228) [0341] our opponents have indeed **got** the most out of their logic

Continued ▶

A P : 2 4 :092(266) [0415] But let us **get** back to the issue.
A P : 2 7 :067(280) [0441] not because they were **getting** married (he commands the
S 3 : 0 3 :022(306) [0485] that they would never **get** out of purgatory because,
S 3 : 0 3 :026(307) [0487] In time souls **got** to be so cheap that they were released at
S 3 : 1 3 :001(315) [0499] faith (as St. Peter says) we **get** a new and clean heart and
S 3 : 1 4 :001(316) [0501] to help not only himself but also others to **get** to heaven.
S C : 0 9 :003(354) [0561] proclaim the gospel should **get** their living by the gospel"
L C : P R :009(359) [0569] saints, for God's sake, to **get** it into their heads that they
L C : 0 1 :060(372) [0597] Hence we **get** what we deserve: plague, war, famine, fire,
L C : 0 1 :185(390) [0633] steps in and intervenes to **get** the quarrel settled for the
L C : 0 1 :234(397) [0647] commandment may indeed **get** by and escape the
L C : 0 1 :243(397) [0649] every day that no stolen or ill-**gotten** possession thrives.
L C : 0 1 :299(405) [0665] shrewdest in such affairs **gets** most advantage out of the
L C : 0 1 :317(408) [0673] in order that men may **get** rid of the pernicious abuse
L C : 0 3 :114(435) [0729] "Dear Father, help us to **get** rid of all this misfortune."
L C : 0 4 :043(442) [0743] crowd of rich men no one else could **get** near him.
L C : 0 6 :034(461) [0000] come running after us to **get** it, more than we would like.
S D : 0 3 :043(547) [0931] when we ask where faith **gets** the power to justify and

Giengen (1)
P R : P R :027(016) [0027] Mayor and Council of the City of **Giengen**

Gift (67), Gifted (2), Gifts (80)
A G : 1 8 :003(039) [0051] man does not receive the **gifts** of the Spirit of God."
A G : 2 0 :011(042) [0055] your own doing, it is the **gift** of God — not because of
A G : 2 3 :005(052) [0061] that few people have the **gift** of living in celibacy, and he
A G : 2 3 :006(052) [0061] or vows without a special **gift** or grace of God.
A G : 2 7 :020(074) [0079] are not endowed with the **gift** of virginity by a special act
A G : 2 8 :004(081) [0085] with all reverence as the two highest **gifts** of God on earth
A G : 2 8 :008(082) [0085] but eternal things and **gifts**, namely, eternal
A G : 2 8 :009(082) [0085] These **gifts** cannot be obtained except through the office
A G : 2 8 :010(082) [0085] of bishops bestows eternal **gifts** and is used and exercised
A G : 2 8 :018(083) [0085] both be held in honor as the highest **gifts** of God on earth
A L : 1 8 :002(039) [0051] man does not perceive the **gifts** of the Spirit of God
A L : 2 0 :014(043) [0055] it would be a reward for works rather than a free **gift**."
A L : 2 3 :006(052) [0061] alter his creation without a singular **gift** and work of God.
A L : 2 8 :004(081) [0085] in reverence and honor as the chief **gifts** of God on earth.
A L : 2 8 :018(083) [0085] in honor and acknowledged as **gifts** and blessings of God.
A P : 0 2 :003(101) [0105] in God but also of the possibility and **gift** to produce it.
A P : 0 2 :003(101) [0105] that human nature has the **gift** and capacity to produce
A P : 0 2 :017(102) [0109] constitution, but these **gifts** as well: a surer knowledge of
A P : 0 2 :018(103) [0111] that is, that man received **gifts** like the knowledge of
A P : 0 2 :023(103) [0111] be produced without certain **gifts** and help of grace.
A P : 0 2 :023(103) [0111] clear, we are naming these **gifts** knowledge of God, fear
A P : 0 2 :023(103) [0111] trust of God but also the **gifts** and power to produce
A P : 0 2 :030(104) [0113] man does not receive the **gifts** of the Spirit of God."
A P : 0 4 :063(115) [0139] recipient, as though the **gift** of the Holy Spirit were a
A P : 0 4 :073(117) [0141] (Eph. 2:8, 9), "It is the **gift** of God, not because of works,
A P : 0 4 :073(117) [0141] (Rom. 3:24), "They are justified by his grace as a **gift**."
A P : 0 4 :073(117) [0141] "not of works," "it is a **gift**," etc., for these terms are also
A P : 0 4 :084(119) [0145] of sins and justification is a **gift**, and further that the
A P : 0 4 :087(120) [0147] we are saved freely by "the **gift** of God, not because of
A P : 0 4 :089(120) [0149] his wages are not reckoned as a **gift** but are his due.
A P : 0 4 :093(120) [0149] your own doing, it is the **gift** of God—not because of
A P : 0 4 :103(122) [0151] who is righteous has it as a **gift** because he was justified
A P : 0 4 :132(125) [0159] sake we might receive the **gift** of the forgiveness of sins
A P : 0 4 :139(126) [0161] "He led captivity captive and gave **gifts** to men."
A P : 0 4 :182(132) [0173] keeping of the law follows with the **gift** of the Holy Spirit.
A P : 0 4 :224(138) [0181] justified, the Corinthians received many excellent **gifts**.
A P : 0 4 :356(161) [0217] Paul calls eternal life a "**gift**" (Rom. 6:23) because the
A P : 0 4 :356(161) [0217] as do many later writers, "God crowns his **gifts** in us."
A P : 0 4 :357(161) [0217] But they are not fair judges, for they omit the word "**gift**."
A P : 0 4 :362(162) [0219] justification is strictly a **gift** of God; it is a thing
A P : 0 4 :362(162) [0219] To this **gift** the promise of eternal life has been added,
A P : 0 7 :009(169) [0229] Christ supplies it with the **gifts** he has promised — the
A P : 0 7 :009(170) [0229] of sins, answer to prayer, and the **gift** of the Holy Spirit.
A P : 0 7 :013(170) [0231] of the heart and the **gift** of the Holy Spirit but would
A P : 1 5 :006(216) [0317] not your own doing, it is the **gift** of God" and not of men.
A P : 1 5 :019(218) [0319] with gold and silver, with precious stones and costly **gifts**."
A P : 2 0 :010(228) [0341] justified by his grace as a **gift**" (Rom. 3:24) "in order that
A P : 2 0 :013(228) [0343] call and not to lose its **gifts**, which were given to you
A P : 2 1 :004(229) [0343] men, and giving teachers and other **gifts** to the church.
A P : 2 1 :004(229) [0343] Since these are his greatest **gifts**, we should extol them
A P : 2 1 :004(229) [0343] themselves for using these **gifts**, just as Christ praises
A P : 2 3 :016(241) [0369] those to marry who do not have the **gift** of continence?
A P : 2 3 :019(242) [0369] possible for everyone, it would not require a special **gift**.
A P : 2 3 :019(242) [0369] it does require a special **gift**; therefore, it is not for
A P : 2 3 :021(242) [0369] those who have the **gift** of continence and therefore adds,
A P : 2 3 :022(242) [0369] and about those who do not have the **gift** of continence.
A P : 2 3 :030(243) [0371] that is, by faith which uses it gratefully as a **gift** of God.
A P : 2 3 :038(244) [0373] One **gift** surpasses another.
A P : 2 3 :038(244) [0373] So also virginity is a **gift** that surpasses marriage.
A P : 2 3 :046(246) [0377] of God's commands and **gifts**, which he wants us to use
A P : 2 3 :053(246) [0377] those who despise his **gift** and ordinance and forbid
A P : 2 3 :055(247) [0379] also exhort others not to despise the **gift** of continence.
A P : 2 4 :052(259) [0403] in relation to God, to offer **gifts** and sacrifices for sins."
A P : 2 4 :074(263) [0411] gratitude, and a witness of its high esteem for God's **gifts**.
A P : 2 4 :085(265) [0413] it means the collection or **gifts** of the people rather than
A P : 2 4 :085(265) [0413] of the Passover had to bring some **gift** as a contribution.
A P : 2 7 :027(273) [0429] — but to those who have the **gift**, as has been said above.
A P : 2 7 :038(275) [0433] the shoemaker to find out about his exercises and **gifts**.
A P : 2 7 :051(278) [0437] Since not everyone has the **gift** of continence, many fail in
A P : 2 7 :051(278) [0437] himself because he does not have the **gift** of continence.
A P : 2 8 :002(281) [0443] political ordinances nor the **gifts** and privileges of princes.
S 2 : 0 1 :003(292) [0461] justified by his grace as a **gift**, through the redemption
S 2 : 0 4 :009(300) [0473] they may differ in **gifts**) and diligently joined together in
S 3 : 0 1 :010(303) [0479] the Holy Spirit and his **gifts** are necessary for the
S 3 : 0 3 :040(309) [0489] own powers but with the **gift** of the Holy Spirit which
S 3 : 0 3 :040(309) [0489] This **gift** daily cleanses and expels the sins that remain
S 3 : 1 5 :004(316) [0501] such ceremonies of sponsors who might make **gifts**, etc.
T R : 0 0 :026(324) [0511] wherever God gives his **gifts**, apostles, prophets, pastors,
T R : 0 0 :067(331) [0523] This right is a **gift** given exclusively to the church, and no
T R : 0 0 :067(331) [0523] ascended on high he gave **gifts** to men" (Eph. 4:8, 11, 12).
T R : 0 0 :067(331) [0523] and teachers among the **gifts** belonging exclusively to the
S C : 0 2 :006(345) [0545] enlightened me with his **gifts**, and sanctified and preserved
S C : 0 3 :013(347) [0547] may make us aware of his **gifts** and enable us to receive
S C : 0 4 :005(348) [0551] What **gifts** or benefits does Baptism bestow?
S C : 0 8 :009(353) [0559] bless us, and these thy **gifts** which of thy bountiful
L C : 0 1 :022(367) [0585] to receive anything as a **gift** from God, but desiring by
L C : 0 1 :027(368) [0587] everything as God's **gifts** and thank him for them, as this
L C : 0 1 :047(371) [0593] ahead, using all of God's **gifts** exactly as a cobbler uses
L C : 0 1 :174(388) [0631] of God, and if they are **gifted** to give them opportunity to
L C : 0 1 :211(393) [0641] by a high supernatural **gift** so that they can maintain
L C : 0 2 :021(413) [0683] all the blessings and **gifts** of God solely for its own pride
L C : 0 2 :051(417) [0691] It possesses a variety of **gifts**, yet is united in love without
L C : 0 2 :066(419) [0697] not illuminated and blessed by the **gifts** of the Holy Spirit.
L C : 0 2 :069(420) [0697] to us, with all his **gifts** and his power, to help us keep the
L C : 0 2 :069(420) [0697] creation, Christ all his works, the Holy Spirit all his **gifts**.
L C : 0 3 :057(427) [0713] to give great and princely **gifts**, and the fool asked only
L C : 0 3 :086(432) [0723] are supported by God's **gift** and blessing, nevertheless we
L C : 0 3 :100(433) [0725] to retain and persevere in all the **gifts** for which we pray.
L C : 0 4 :023(439) [0737] that is, what benefits, **gifts**, and effects it brings.
L C : 0 4 :032(440) [0739] further who receives these **gifts** and benefits of Baptism.
L C : 0 4 :041(442) [0743] grace, the entire Christ, and the Holy Spirit with his **gifts**.
L C : 0 4 :050(443) [0745] Baptism through the **gift** of His Holy Spirit, as we have
L C : 0 4 :086(446) [0753] even though we sin, so all his treasures and **gifts** remain.
L C : 0 5 :022(449) [0757] sign — indeed, as the very **gift** he has provided for me
L C : 0 5 :029(449) [0759] blood and that these are yours as your treasure and **gift**.
L C : 0 5 :036(450) [0761] Such a **gift** and eternal treasure cannot be seized with the
L C : 0 5 :070(454) [0769] and Spirit with all his **gifts**, protection, defense, and
L C : 0 6 :023(459) [0000] who hears that a rich **gift**, of money or clothes, is to be
L C : 0 6 :023(460) [0000] run there as fast as he could so as not to miss the **gift**.
E P : 0 2 :002(470) [0787] man does not receive the **gifts** of the Spirit of God, for
E P : 0 3 :006(473) [0793] Christ, but the kind of **gift** of God by which in the Word
E P : 0 3 :018(475) [0795] not God himself but only divine **gifts** dwell in believers.
E P : 0 4 :007(476) [0799] your own doing, it is the **gift** of God — not because of
E P : 1 2 :004(498) [0839] but that he only has more **gifts** of the Holy Spirit than
S D : 0 1 :010(510) [0863] human nature the **gifts** and the power, or the faculty and
S D : 0 2 :003(520) [0881] powers and without the **gift** of the Holy Spirit man is
S D : 0 2 :003(520) [0881] but that without the **gift** of the Holy Spirit he could
S D : 0 2 :009(521) [0883] that when even the most **gifted** and the most educated
S D : 0 2 :010(522) [0883] man does not receive the **gifts** of the Spirit of God, for
S D : 0 2 :012(523) [0885] hold of, or apprehend) the **gifts** of the Spirit of God (that
S D : 0 2 :016(523) [0887] faith and his heavenly **gifts** in us and strengthen us daily
S D : 0 2 :026(526) [0891] "It is the **gift** of God" (Eph. 2:8).
S D : 0 2 :026(526) [0891] In short, every good **gift** comes from God (James 1:17).
S D : 0 2 :026(526) [0891] it, why do you boast as if it were not a **gift**?" (I Cor. 4:7).
S D : 0 2 :034(528) [0895] powers but through the **gift** of the Holy Spirit which
S D : 0 2 :034(528) [0895] This **gift** purifies us and daily sweeps out the remaining
S D : 0 2 :035(528) [0895] ascribe everything to the **gift** of the Holy Spirit, who
S D : 0 2 :040(528) [0895] enlightened me with his **gifts**, and sanctified and preserved
S D : 0 2 :046(530) [0899] wait until God pours his **gifts** into them out of heaven,
S D : 0 2 :047(530) [0901] Holy Spirit to work these **gifts** of his within them, since
S D : 0 2 :056(532) [0903] presence, operations, and **gifts** merely on the basis of our
S D : 0 2 :065(534) [0907] from the new powers and **gifts** which the Holy Spirit has
S D : 0 2 :071(535) [0909] in us, so that they are **gifts** and works of the Holy Spirit
S D : 0 2 :072(535) [0909] and increases these **gifts**, and admonishes us not to
S D : 0 2 :089(538) [0915] but entirely, the operation, **gift**, endowment, and work of
S D : 0 3 :011(541) [0919] Faith is a **gift** of God whereby we rightly learn to know
S D : 0 3 :065(550) [0937] That not God but only the **gifts** of God dwell in believers.
S D : 0 4 :031(556) [0947] to lose faith and the **gift** of righteousness and salvation,
S D : 0 4 :033(556) [0949] and lose the Spirit and his **gifts**, which you have not
S D : 0 8 :052(601) [1033] and contend that the **gifts** with which the human nature in
S D : 0 8 :052(601) [1033] and adorned are created **gifts** or finite qualities, as in the
S D : 0 8 :054(601) [1033] possesses all the created **gifts** which have been given to it.
S D : 0 8 :055(601) [1033] so forth are not created **gifts** but divine and infinite
S D : 0 8 :072(605) [1041] he received the Spirit's **gifts** not by measure, like other
S D : 0 8 :073(605) [1041] the Holy Spirit who endows them only with created **gifts**.
S D : 1 1 :021(619) [1069] of God, and use faithfully the **gifts** they have received.
S D : 1 1 :023(619) [1069] he wills by his grace, **gifts**, and effective working to bring
S D : 1 1 :072(628) [1087] know how to give good **gifts** to your children, how much
S D : 1 2 :026(635) [1099] possesses more and greater **gifts** and glory than other

Girdles (1)
A P : 2 7 :027(274) [0429] receiving another hood or other sandals or other **girdles**."

Girl (2), Girls (4)
A G : 2 7 :008(072) [0077] seen that both boys and **girls** were thrust into monasteries
A L : 2 7 :008(072) [0077] time when they saw that **girls** and boys were thrust into
A L : 2 7 :029(075) [0079] able to judge, boys and **girls** are persuaded, and
S 2 : 0 3 :001(298) [0471] and also well trained **girls** to become mothers,
L C : 0 1 :145(385) [0623] the poor people, a servant **girl** would dance for joy and
L C : 0 1 :314(407) [0671] But when a poor **girl** tends a little child, or faithfully does

Give (183), Gives (70), Gave (48), Givest (1), Giving (24)
P R : P R :008(005) [0011] divine Word that alone **gives** salvation, to commit
P R : P R :022(012) [0021] disposition and purpose to **give** occasion by this Christian
P R : P R :022(012) [0021] they will have to **give** a hard accounting.
A G : P R :015(026) [0041] Majesty graciously **gave** assurance to the electors,
A G : 0 5 :002(031) [0045] as through means, he **gives** the Holy Spirit, who works
A G : 1 7 :002(038) [0051] raise up all the dead, to **give** eternal life and everlasting
A G : 0 0 :000(049) [0059] by our circumstances to **give** an account of them and to
A G : 2 3 :013(053) [0063] any good but rather **gave** occasion for many great and
A G : 2 3 :025(055) [0065] see to it that they do not **give** their brothers and sisters
A G : 2 5 :009(063) [0069] need to compel people to **give** a detailed account of their
A G : 2 6 :019(067) [0073] has compelled them to **give** instruction about the
A G : 2 6 :033(069) [0075] so that he does not **give** occasion to sin, but not as if he
A G : 2 7 :059(080) [0083] matters it was necessary to **give** the people proper
A G : 2 8 :041(087) [0089] (even when it does not **give** offense to others), that it is a
A G : 2 8 :046(088) [0089] St. Paul also forbids **giving** heed to Jewish myths or
A G : 2 8 :055(090) [0091] a way that one does not **give** offense to another and so
A G : 2 8 :068(093) [0093] It is impossible to **give** counsel or help to consciences
A L : 1 7 :002(038) [0051] the godly and elect he will **give** eternal life and endless
A L : 0 0 :003(049) [0059] of good men, they first **gave** occasion to this controversy,
A L : 2 3 :025(055) [0065] lusts; at least they should **give** no offense to their brothers
A L : 2 4 :034(060) [0067] as the Mass is such a **giving** of the sacrament, one

Continued ▶

A L : 2 8 :009(082) [0085] faith," and Ps. 119:50 states, "Thy Word **gives** me life."
A L : 2 8 :041(087) [0089] on holy days, even when it **gives** no offense to others,
A L : 2 8 :046(088) [0089] Tit. 1 Paul also says, "Not **giving** heed to Jewish myths or
A L : 2 8 :077(094) [0095] intention that the bishops **give** up their power to govern,
A P : P R :004(098) [0099] where they could not **give** in to the opponents' point of
A P : P R :010(099) [0101] Therefore I am **giving** my name, so no one can complain
A P : 0 4 :015(109) [0123] Christ had come to **give** some sort of laws by which we
A P : 0 4 :019(110) [0125] For if God necessarily **gives** grace for the merit of
A P : 0 4 :024(110) [0127] We freely **give** this righteousness of reason its due credit;
A P : 0 4 :073(117) [0141] by the Word, and we **give** the highest praise to the
A P : 0 4 :079(118) [0143] thanks be to God, who **gives** us the victory through our
A P : 0 4 :094(120) [0149] believed in his name, he **gave** power to become children
A P : 0 4 :106(122) [0153] the mercy of God, that he may **give** what he commands."
A P : 0 4 :119(123) [0155] Our opponents **give** men bad advice when they bid them
A P : 0 4 :139(126) [0161] "He led captivity captive and **gave** gifts to men."
A P : 0 4 :139(126) [0161] conquered the devil and **gave** us his promise and the Holy
A P : 0 4 :141(126) [0161] us, we call upon him, **give** thanks to him, fear and love
A P : 0 4 :141(126) [0161] us," that is, because he **gave** his Son for us and forgave us
A P : 0 4 :155(128) [0165] passages, like Luke 11:41, "**Give** alms; and behold,
A P : 0 4 :170(130) [0171] and destroy them and to **give** us new spiritual impulses.
A P : 0 4 :189(133) [0175] to exercise our faith, to **give** testimony, and to render
A P : 0 4 :201(134) [0175] circumcision was added to **give** him a sign written in his
A P : 0 4 :204(135) [0177] and propitiation, thus **giving** our works an honor that
A P : 0 4 :205(135) [0177] But faith **gives** assurance of God's presence when it is sure
A P : 0 4 :208(135) [0177] in these places and thus **gave** evidence of their faith.
A P : 0 4 :214(136) [0179] law must follow faith; but we still **give** Christ his honor.
A P : 0 4 :215(137) [0179] believes otherwise does not **give** Christ the honor due
A P : 0 4 :231(139) [0183] Though we could **give** many answers about perfection, we
A P : 0 4 :242(141) [0187] When each one **gave** in to his hatred, a major commotion
A P : 0 4 :261(145) [0195] say that the king should **give** alms, but he includes all of
A P : 0 4 :261(145) [0195] him not only to the **giving** of alms but rather to faith.
A P : 0 4 :281(149) [0201] quoted in a garbled form: "**Give** alms; and behold,
A P : 0 4 :282(149) [0201] the outward cleanness, "**Give** alms from what you have
A P : 0 4 :283(150) [0201] be clean if you are clean inwardly and if you **give** alms.
A P : 0 4 :284(150) [0201] and then the outward **giving** of alms is added (that is, all
A P : 0 4 :297(153) [0205] is the testimony, that God **gave** us eternal life, and this
A P : 0 4 :309(155) [0207] This faith **gives** honor to God, gives him what is properly
A P : 0 4 :309(155) [0207] faith gives honor to God, **gives** him what is properly his;
A P : 0 4 :309(155) [0207] but he grew strong in his faith as he **gave** glory to God."
A P : 0 4 :331(158) [0211] O Lord, forgive; O Lord, **give** heed and act; delay not, for
A P : 0 4 :333(158) [0211] anything of the Father, he will **give** it to you in my name."
A P : 0 4 :336(159) [0215] a refutation, we shall nevertheless **give** a brief answer.
A P : 0 4 :344(160) [0217] To this we must **give** a satisfactory answer.
A P : 0 4 :360(162) [0219] merits which they can **give** to justify others, as when
A P : 0 4 :363(162) [0219] Lord, the righteous judge, will **give** me," etc. (II Tim. 4:8).
A P : 0 4 :370(164) [0221] Matt. 25:35, "I was hungry and you **gave** me food," etc.
A P : 0 4 :373(164) [0221] "You **gave** me food" is cited as fruit and evidence of the
A P : 0 4 :399(168) [0227] better to him than to **give** an answer written in blood to
A P : 0 7 :007(169) [0229] loved the church and **gave** himself up for it, that he might
A P : 0 9 :003(178) [0245] by the fact that God **gives** the Holy Spirit to those who
A P : 1 2 :008(183) [0255] But our opponents **give** the legalistic reply that Judas did
A P : 1 2 :030(186) [0259] Christ **gives** this summary of the Gospel in the last
A P : 1 2 :044(187) [0263] who labor and are heavy-laden, and I will **give** you rest."
A P : 1 2 :077(193) [0275] on justification, where we **gave** our reasons for declaring
A P : 1 2 :090(195) [0279] in the church certainly **give** us no pleasure; therefore if we
A P : 1 2 :106(197) [0283] He is merely **giving** a bit of domestic advice to the head
A P : 1 2 :122(200) [0287] many Scripture passages to **give** the inexperienced the
A P : 1 2 :122(200) [0289] statement of Paul, "He **gave** himself for us to redeem us
A P : 1 2 :146(205) [0297] "Thanks be to God, who **gives** us the victory through our
A P : 1 2 :146(205) [0297] He does not say, "Who **gives** us the victory if we set our
A P : 1 2 :177(210) [0307] authority, which the Lord **gave** for building you up."
A P : 1 5 :020(218) [0321] good order, because they **gave** the people a set time to
A P : 1 5 :041(220) [0325] at all, though even the canons **give** prescriptions about it.
A P : 2 0 :008(227) [0341] This faith **gives** support and life to the heart in its hardest
A P : 2 0 :013(228) [0341] forgiveness of sins; he is **giving** instruction that they
A P : 2 1 :004(229) [0343] Our Confession approves **giving** honor to the saints.
A P : 2 1 :004(229) [0343] his will to save men, and **giving** teachers and other gifts to
A P : 2 1 :017(231) [0347] anything of the Father, he will **give** it to you in my name."
A P : 2 1 :027(232) [0349] in death, does she overcome death, does she **give** life?
A P : 2 1 :030(233) [0351] replied that they could not **give** it for fear that there might
A P : 2 1 :043(235) [0357] They **give** many indications that the state of the church
A P : 2 2 :004(236) [0359] The Council of Toledo **gives** the same testimony, and it
A P : 2 2 :008(237) [0359] our present custom of **giving** the laity only a part of the
A P : 2 2 :012(238) [0361] God, will the reasons he **gives** exonerate those who
A P : 2 3 :026(243) [0371] it with pious-sounding phrases to **give** it a religious front.
A P : 2 3 :040(244) [0375] it justifies but because it **gives** more time for praying,
A P : 2 3 :064(248) [0381] They **give** many quotations to support this.
A P : 2 3 :068(249) [0383] us over and over, and to **give** the impression that our
A P : 2 4 :003(250) [0385] insert German hymns to **give** the common people
A P : 2 4 :019(252) [0389] who have been reconciled **give** thanks or show their
A P : 2 4 :028(254) [0393] But this command I **gave** them, 'Obey my voice, and I
A P : 2 4 :032(255) [0395] Besides, the prophet's own words **give** us his meaning.
A P : 2 4 :032(255) [0395] They call upon God, they **give** thanks to God, they bear
A P : 2 4 :059(260) [0405] when he does work to **give** them new birth and life.
A P : 2 4 :061(260) [0405] passages quoted against us **give** no support to our
A P : 2 4 :071(262) [0409] the sacrament, when faith **gives** life to terrified hearts, is
A P : 2 4 :074(263) [0409] from terror, then it really **gives** thanks for the blessing of
A P : 2 4 :076(263) [0411] what is forgiven, and it **gives** thanks to the Giver of such
A P : 2 4 :076(263) [0411] of our ills, our sin and our death; and it **gives** thanks.
A P : 2 4 :097(268) [0417] righteousness of faith but **give** equal honor to other
A P : 2 7 :002(269) [0419] to recite them here lest we **give** the impression that we are
A P : 2 7 :014(271) [0423] he refuses even more to **give** this credit to human
A P : 2 7 :015(271) [0425] place, so that he does not **give** the forgiveness of sins
A P : 2 7 :030(274) [0431] God does not even **give** his own law the honor of meriting
A P : 2 7 :030(274) [0431] says in Ezek. 20:25, "I **gave** them statutes that were not
A P : 2 7 :036(275) [0433] opponents slyly seek to **give** the impression that they are
A P : 2 7 :045(277) [0435] sell what you possess and **give** to the poor; and come,
A P : 2 8 :005(282) [0445] you will some day have to **give** account of your
A P : 2 8 :021(284) [0449] We **give** the same response to the passage (Matt. 23:3),
A P : 2 8 :025(285) [0451] cruelly persecuting it, will **give** an account for the schism
S 2 : 0 2 :010(294) [0465] to be torn to pieces before he would **give** up the Mass.
S 2 : 0 2 :017(296) [0467] Moreover, the pope **gave** his approval to these things as
S 2 : 0 4 :016(301) [0477] who does not intend to **give** us a hearing but only to
S 3 : 0 3 :019(306) [0483] this: Everybody had to **give** an account of all his sins — an
S 3 : 0 8 :003(312) [0495] the conviction that God **gives** no one his Spirit or grace
S 3 : 1 1 :001(314) [0499] and thereby they **gave** occasion for all sorts of horrible,
T R : 0 0 :022(323) [0511] Again, "I will **give** you the keys" (Matt 16:19).
T R : 0 0 :023(324) [0511] singular number ("I will **give** you the keys" and "whatever
T R : 0 0 :026(324) [0511] and exists wherever God **gives** his gifts, apostles,
T R : 0 0 :031(325) [0513] the first because Christ **gave** the apostles only spiritual
T R : 0 0 :031(325) [0513] He did not **give** them the power of the sword or the right
T R : 0 0 :040(327) [0515] pretext these words, "I will **give** you the keys" (Matt.
T R : 0 0 :067(331) [0523] he ascended on high he **gave** gifts to men" (Eph. 4:8, 11,
T R : 0 0 :071(332) [0525] writers added the words, "I **give** thee the power to
T R : 0 0 :072(332) [0525] of the bishops that **give** occasion to schism and discord,
S C : P R :025(341) [0539] If you do not **give** such admonitions, or if you adopt
S C : 0 1 :004(342) [0539] upon him, pray to him, praise him, and **give** him thanks.
S C : 0 3 :008(346) [0547] When the heavenly Father **gives** us his Holy Spirit so that
S C : 0 3 :012(347) [0547] ***"Give us this day our daily bread."***
S C : 0 5 :021(350) [0553] Please **give** me a brief form of confession.
S C : 0 5 :023(350) [0555] him, overcharging him, **giving** him inferior goods and
S C : 0 6 :004(351) [0555] thanks, he broke it, and **gave** it to the disciples and said,
S C : 0 6 :004(351) [0555] he had given thanks he **gave** it to them, saying, 'Drink of
S C : 0 7 :002(352) [0557] "I **give** Thee thanks, heavenly Father, through thy dear
S C : 0 7 :005(353) [0559] "I **give** Thee thanks, heavenly Father, through thy dear
S C : 0 8 :007(353) [0559] Thee, O Lord, and Thou **givest** them their food in due
S C : 0 8 :010(354) [0559] "O **give** thanks to the Lord, for he is good; for his
S C : 0 8 :010(354) [0559] He **gives** to the beasts their food, and to the young ravens
S C : 0 8 :011(354) [0559] "We **give** Thee thanks, Lord God, our Father, for all thy
S C : 0 9 :003(355) [0561] over your souls, as men who will have to **give** account.
S C : 0 9 :012(356) [0563] 'God opposes the proud, but **gives** grace to the humble.'
L C : P R :011(360) [0571] which burns the devil and **gives** us immeasurable
L C : P R :015(360) [0571] our weapons and armor, too lazy to **give** them a thought!
L C : S P :014(363) [0577] **Give** us this day our daily bread; and forgive us our debts,
L C : S P :023(364) [0579] was betrayed took bread, **gave** thanks, and broke it and
L C : S P :023(364) [0579] thánks, and broke it and **gave** it to his disciples, saying,
L C : S P :026(364) [0581] what they have heard and **give** a good, correct answer
L C : 0 1 :012(366) [0583] devil in order that he may **give** them plenty of money,
L C : 0 1 :024(367) [0587] things; for it is he who **gives** us body, life, food, drink,
L C : 0 1 :026(368) [0587] For example, he **gives** to the mother breasts and milk for
L C : 0 1 :026(368) [0587] milk for her infant, and he **gives** grain and all kinds of
L C : 0 1 :027(368) [0587] should presume to take or **give** anything except as God
L C : 0 1 :063(373) [0599] God at the same time **gives** us to understand that we are
L C : 0 1 :070(374) [0601] the heart by faith first **gives** God the honor due him and
L C : 0 1 :089(377) [0605] every day a holy day and **give** ourselves only to holy
L C : 0 1 :107(379) [0611] and that next to God we **give** them the very highest place.
L C : 0 1 :115(381) [0613] things from sight and **give** first place to this
L C : 0 1 :130(383) [0619] will, without compulsion, **give** all honor to his parents
L C : 0 1 :150(385) [0623] our own parents, God **gives** us food, house and home,
L C : 0 1 :151(386) [0625] to serve, and cheerfully **gives** honor where it is due,
L C : 0 1 :166(387) [0629] in joyful thanks to God for **giving** us such promises.
L C : 0 1 :166(388) [0629] But God can and will **give** you everything abundantly,
L C : 0 1 :170(388) [0629] Everybody acts as if God **gave** us children for our
L C : 0 1 :170(388) [0629] pleasure and amusement, **gave** us servants merely to put
L C : 0 1 :170(388) [0629] like cows or asses, and **gave** us subjects to treat them as
L C : 0 1 :174(388) [0631] and if they are gifted to **give** them opportunity to learn
L C : 0 1 :175(388) [0631] would richly bless us and **give** us grace so that men might
L C : 0 1 :184(390) [0633] and good fortune than he, **gives** vent to his irritation and
L C : 0 1 :191(391) [0635] and thirsty and you **gave** me no food or drink, I was a
L C : 0 1 :206(393) [0639] the estate of marriage and **gives** occasion to speak of it,
L C : 0 1 :226(395) [0645] No one even dares to **give** them a hard look or accuse
L C : 0 1 :247(398) [0651] away whom you ought to **give** aid, he will go away
L C : 0 1 :270(401) [0657] knowledge to yourself and do not **give** it out to others.
L C : 0 1 :295(404) [0665] his wife publicly by **giving** her a bill of divorce and to
L C : 0 1 :307(406) [0669] him against his will, and begrudging what God **gave** him.
L C : 0 1 :308(406) [0669] If you **give** the world an inch, it will take a yard, and at
L C : 0 1 :309(407) [0669] accessory to it, nor **give** occasion for it; we are willingly to
L C : 0 2 :010(411) [0679] These words **give** us a brief description of God the
L C : 0 2 :015(412) [0681] Moreover, he **gives** all physical and temporal blessings —
L C : 0 2 :023(413) [0683] He **gives** us all these things so that we may sense and see
L C : 0 2 :035(415) [0687] as I have said, I cannot **give** a better title than
L C : 0 2 :048(416) [0691] select a special place and **give** the house its name by
L C : 0 2 :067(419) [0697] the Creed tells us what God does for us and **gives** to us.
L C : 0 2 :069(420) [0697] because we see that God **gives** himself completely to us,
L C : 0 2 :069(420) [0697] the Father **gives** us all creation, Christ all his works, the
L C : 0 3 :002(420) [0697] our prayer that he may **give**, preserve, and increase in us
L C : 0 3 :025(423) [0705] anything from him, but only to **give** him something.
L C : 0 3 :051(427) [0711] To this end he also **gave** his Holy Spirit to teach us this
L C : 0 3 :054(427) [0713] Father, we pray Thee, **give** us thy Word, that the Gospel
L C : 0 3 :056(427) [0713] he claims the honor of **giving** far more abundantly and
L C : 0 3 :056(427) [0713] gushes forth and overflows, the more it continues to **give**.
L C : 0 3 :057(427) [0713] desire and was prepared to **give** great and princely gifts,
L C : 0 3 :071(430) [0717] ***"Give us this day our daily bread."***
L C : 0 3 :074(430) [0719] or happiness unless he **gives** us a stable, peaceful
L C : 0 3 :076(431) [0721] we might ask God to **give** us food and drink, clothing,
L C : 0 3 :076(431) [0721] our household well and **give** and preserve to us a good
L C : 0 3 :083(431) [0721] Although he **gives** and provides these blessings
L C : 0 3 :086(432) [0723] who sorely vex us and **give** us occasion for impatience,
L C : 0 3 :088(432) [0723] before our prayer; and he **gave** us the Gospel, in which
L C : 0 3 :106(434) [0727] temptation" when God **gives** us power and strength to
L C : 0 3 :108(435) [0729] But to consent to it is to **give** it free rein and neither resist
L C : 0 3 :111(435) [0729] make the matter worse and **give** the devil a better
L C : 0 4 :037(441) [0741] is a treasure which God **gives** us and faith grasps, just as
L C : 0 4 :050(443) [0745] lies and wickedness, or **give** his grace and Spirit for such
L C : 0 4 :056(444) [0747] drink, etc. and that he **gives** me his body and blood; he
L C : 0 5 :003(447) [0753] *was betrayed took bread, **gave** thanks, broke it, and gave*
L C : 0 5 :003(447) [0753] *gave thanks, broke it, and **gave** it to his disciples and*
L C : 0 5 :003(447) [0753] *the cup, after supper, **gave** thanks, and gave it to them,*
L C : 0 5 :003(447) [0753] *supper, gave thanks, and **gave** it to them, saying, 'This*
L C : 0 5 :017(448) [0757] do, what I institute, what I **give** you and bid you take.
L C : 0 5 :033(450) [0761] words say and what they **give**, for they are not spoken or
L C : 0 5 :034(450) [0761] as if he said, "This is why I **give** it and bid you eat and
L C : 0 5 :079(455) [0771] wrong, and injure you and **give** you occasion for sin and
L C : 0 5 :079(455) [0771] which everywhere **give** this testimony about the world.
L C : 0 5 :083(456) [0773] their prayers, and never **give** up until the stone is removed
E P : 0 2 :006(470) [0787] and watering are in vain unless he "**gives** the growth."

Continued ▶

EP : 0 2 :019(472) [0791] Word, though he cannot **give** it credence and accept it by
EP : 0 3 :010(474) [0795] faith before God, we must **give** special attention to the
EP : 0 3 :010(474) [0795] from our own works and **give** all glory to Christ alone.
EP : 0 3 :017(475) [0795] does not truly repent and **gives** no evidence of resulting
EP : 0 6 :001(479) [0805] still inheres in them, to **give** them on that account a
EP : 0 8 :009(487) [0819] glued together and neither **gives** anything to or takes
EP : 1 1 :013(496) [0835] this salutary doctrine **gives** us, namely, that we know that
EP : 1 1 :015(496) [0835] of God's eternal election **gives** God his glory entirely and
EP : 1 1 :015(496) [0835] Nor will this doctrine ever **give** anyone occasion either to
EP : 1 2 :031(500) [0843] of all of us as we shall **give** account of it on the Last Day
SD : PR :003(501) [0847] In this document they **gave** a clear and unequivocal
SD : PR :006(502) [0849] Confession, even dared to **give** a false interpretation to
SD : 0 1 :024(512) [0865] We shall **give** our exposition concerning the external,
SD : 0 1 :037(514) [0871] was, and the spirit returns to God who **gave** it" (Eccl. 2:7)
SD : 0 1 :060(519) [0879] reason, be it ever so keen, can **give** the right answer.
SD : 0 1 :060(519) [0879] a right understanding and **give** a correct definition of
SD : 0 2 :002(520) [0881] himself for such grace, accept it and **give** his assent to it?
SD : 0 2 :003(520) [0881] himself for grace and **give** his assent to it, though weakly,
SD : 0 2 :013(523) [0885] to believe the Gospel, **give** his assent to it, and accept it as
SD : 0 2 :015(523) [0887] more than ten times to **give** him understanding so that he
SD : 0 2 :018(524) [0889] cannot obey, believe, and **give** assent when the Holy
SD : 0 2 :026(526) [0891] Lord opened her heart to **give** heed to what was said by
SD : 0 2 :026(526) [0891] God "**gives** the repentance" (Acts 5:51; II Tim. 2:25).
SD : 0 2 :026(526) [0891] God **gives** an understanding heart, seeing eyes, and
SD : 0 2 :027(527) [0893] that it is God's work to **give** the ability to achieve
SD : 0 2 :041(529) [0897] the heavenly Father **gives** us his Holy Spirit so that by his
SD : 0 2 :042(529) [0897] Christ, but that God must **give** us his Holy Spirit, who
SD : 0 2 :044(529) [0897] God himself must draw man and **give** him new birth.
SD : 0 2 :048(530) [0901] to be efficacious in us by **giving** and working true
SD : 0 2 :049(530) [0901] so loved the world that he **gave** his only Son, that
SD : 0 2 :055(532) [0903] so that men believe this Word and **give** their assent to it.
SD : 0 2 :055(532) [0903] present with his grace and **gives** what man is unable by
SD : 0 2 :055(532) [0903] what man is unable by his own powers to take or to **give**.
SD : 0 3 :024(543) [0923] to remain pure, we must **give** especially diligent heed that
SD : 0 3 :030(544) [0925] reliable comfort and to **give** due honor to the merit of
SD : 0 3 :042(547) [0931] true faith), the Apology **gives** the following answer:
SD : 0 4 :023(555) [0945] consolation of the Gospel, **give** occasion for doubt, are
SD : 0 4 :037(557) [0949] to salvation, we **give** the following clear answer: If anyone
SD : 0 5 :012(560) [0955] that shows and **gives** nothing but grace and forgiveness in
SD : 0 5 :018(561) [0957] to rebuke sin and to **give** instruction about good works.
SD : 0 5 :027(563) [0961] avoid anything that might **give** occasion for a confusion
SD : 0 6 :011(565) [0965] new life, but it does not **give** the power and ability to
SD : 0 7 :001(569) [0971] nor should refrain from **giving** testimony to the divine
SD : 0 7 :006(570) [0973] the bread and wine Christ **gives** us his true body and
SD : 0 7 :024(573) [0979] priest can administer and **give** the sacrament, and like
SD : 0 7 :024(573) [0979] a rascal receives or **gives** the sacrament, it is the true
SD : 0 7 :026(573) [0981] now doing, instituting, **giving** you, and commanding you
SD : 0 7 :028(574) [0981] to make him suspect by **giving** the impression that he had
SD : 0 7 :046(577) [0989] to his reason, he **gave** God the honor of truthfulness and
SD : 0 7 :048(578) [0989] For since Christ **gave** this command at table and during
SD : 0 7 :049(578) [0989] essential body, which he **gave** into death for us, and of his
SD : 0 7 :053(579) [0991] St. Matthew and St. Mark **give** us, "This (namely, what
SD : 0 7 :054(579) [0991] of Christ which St. Paul **gives** us in I Cor. 10:16 ("The cup
SD : 0 7 :062(581) [0995] he has acquired for us by **giving** his body for us into death
SD : 0 7 :070(582) [0997] are heavy laden, and I will **give** you rest" (Matt. 11:28).
SD : 0 7 :081(584) [1001] of his blood and which he **gives** to us in his testament) is
SD : 0 7 :102(587) [1007] to us, we should not **give** the lie to his words until we
SD : 0 7 :102(587) [1007] They will **give** it up.
SD : 0 8 :053(601) [1033] the Scriptures in this case **give** us clear, certain testimony,
SD : 0 8 :055(601) [1033] For to **give** life, to execute all judgment, to have all
SD : 0 8 :059(602) [1035] that Christ's flesh is a life-**giving** food, and according to
SD : 0 8 :059(602) [1035] decreed that the flesh of Christ has the power to **give** life.
SD : 0 8 :061(603) [1037] Thus also the power to **give** life is not in the flesh of
SD : 0 8 :072(605) [1041] that God the Father **gave** his Spirit to Christ, his beloved
SD : 0 8 :076(606) [1043] his flesh is truly a life-**giving** food and his blood truly a
SD : 0 8 :076(606) [1043] that Christ's flesh is a life-**giving** flesh, whence only this
SD : 1 0 :005(611) [1053] those ceremonies which **give** or (to avoid persecution) are
SD : 1 0 :005(611) [1053] are designed to **give** the impression that our religion does
SD : 1 0 :009(612) [1055] with a good conscience **give** in and yield to the weak in
SD : 1 0 :013(613) [1057] Thus Paul yielded and **gave** in to the weak as far as
SD : 1 0 :030(615) [1061] in such a way as to **give** the impression that the
SD : 1 1 :028(620) [1071] God "loved the world" and **gave** to it his only begotten
SD : 1 1 :028(620) [1071] are heavy-laden, and I will **give** you rest" (Matt. 11:28).
SD : 1 1 :029(621) [1073] of the Spirit — "which **gives** the Spirit" (II Cor. 3:8) and
SD : 1 1 :029(621) [1073] to strengthen us, and to **give** us power and ability, it is
SD : 1 1 :030(621) [1073] and they follow me; and I **give** them eternal life" (John
SD : 1 1 :030(621) [1073] believe on Christ, pray and **give** thanks, are sanctified in
SD : 1 1 :031(621) [1073] Thus the Spirit of God **gives** "witness" to the elect "that
SD : 1 1 :033(621) [1073] it because the Holy Spirit **gives** grace, power, and ability
SD : 1 1 :034(622) [1075] call all of you, to whom I **give** my Word, into my
SD : 1 1 :048(624) [1079] This doctrine will also **give** us the glorious comfort, in
SD : 1 1 :048(624) [1079] grant us patience, **give** us comfort, create hope, and bring
SD : 1 1 :050(624) [1079] This article also **gives** a glorious testimony that the church
SD : 1 1 :057(625) [1081] when we observe that God **gives** his Word at one place
SD : 1 1 :059(626) [1083] deserving, to whom he **gives** and preserves his Word and
SD : 1 1 :060(626) [1083] when he does graciously **give** us these we frequently cast
SD : 1 1 :061(626) [1083] however, to whom God **gives** and preserves his Word,
SD : 1 1 :065(627) [1085] are heavy-laden, and I will **give** you rest" (Matt. 11:28).
SD : 1 1 :072(628) [1085] we should implore God to **give** us his grace, of which he
SD : 1 1 :072(628) [1085] doubt that according to his promise he will **give** it to us.
SD : 1 1 :072(628) [1087] a fish, will instead of a fish **give** him a serpent; or if he
SD : 1 1 :072(628) [1087] serpent; or if he asks for an egg, will **give** him a scorpion?
SD : 1 1 :072(628) [1087] who are evil, know how to **give** good gifts to your
SD : 1 1 :072(628) [1087] will the heavenly Father **give** the Holy Spirit to those who
SD : 1 1 :087(631) [1091] the elect children of God **gives** God his due honor fully
SD : 1 1 :090(631) [1093] This doctrine **gives** sorrowing and tempted people the
SD : 1 1 :096(632) [1095] holy Gospel, that will not **give** place to the smallest error
SD : 1 2 :022(634) [1099] property but is obliged to **give** his property to the
SD : 1 2 :040(636) [1103] of Jesus Christ and for which we shall **give** an account.

Given (209)

AG : 0 4 :002(030) [0045] and righteousness and eternal life are **given** to us.
AG : 1 8 :003(039) [0051] by the Holy Spirit, who is **given** through the Word of
AG : 2 0 :002(041) [0053] well, show that they have **given** good and profitable
AG : 2 0 :023(044) [0055] Instruction is also **given** among us to show that the faith
AG : 2 0 :029(045) [0057] faith the Holy Spirit is **given**, the heart is moved to do
AG : 0 0 :000(048) [0059] in Which an Account Is **Given** of the Abuses Which Have
AG : 2 2 :001(049) [0059] Among us both kinds are **given** to laymen in the
AG : 2 2 :005(050) [0061] mentions that the cup was **given** to laymen in his time.
AG : 2 3 :003(051) [0061] They have **given** as their reason that they have been
AG : 0 1 :007(056) [0065] The people are also **given** instruction about other false
AG : 2 4 :024(058) [0067] instruction was **given** so that our people might know how
AG : 2 6 :011(065) [0071] while traditions were to be **given** the glamorous title of
AG : 2 7 :025(074) [0079] with this obligation and have often **given** dispensations,
AG : 2 7 :057(080) [0083] the commands God has **given** and not by keeping the
AG : 2 8 :002(081) [0083] pretext of the power **given** them by Christ, have not only
AG : 2 8 :026(084) [0087] which the Lord has **given** me for building up and not for
AG : 2 8 :042(088) [0089] that authority was **given** for building up and not for
AG : 2 8 :056(090) [0091] even when no offense is **given** to others, just as no one
AL : 0 5 :002(031) [0045] the Holy Spirit is **given**, and the Holy Spirit produces
AL : 1 6 :002(037) [0051] by magistrates, to marry, to be **given** in marriage.
AL : 0 0 :000(048) [0059] in Which an Account Is **Given** of the Abuses Which Have
AL : 2 2 :001(049) [0059] Supper both kinds are **given** to laymen because this usage
AL : 2 2 :005(050) [0061] places testifies that the blood was **given** to the people.
AL : 2 7 :007(071) [0077] consideration should have been **given** to the weaker sex.
AL : 2 7 :057(080) [0083] the commands he has **given** and not by keeping the
AL : 2 8 :008(082) [0085] bodily things that are thus **given**, but rather such eternal
AL : 2 8 :026(084) [0087] (II Cor. 13:8), and also, "**Given** to me is the authority for
AL : 2 8 :042(088) [0089] says that authority was **given** for building up and not for
AL : 2 8 :056(090) [0091] with her head uncovered, provided no offense is **given**.
AP : 0 2 :035(105) [0115] said that the Holy Spirit, **given** in Baptism, begins to
AP : 0 2 :050(106) [0119] Christ was **given** to us to bear both sin and penalty and to
AP : 0 4 :022(110) [0127] and to preserve it he has **given** laws, learning, teaching,
AP : 0 4 :029(111) [0129] at length that grace is not **given** because of our merits.
AP : 0 4 :040(112) [0131] of sins and justification was **given** because of Christ.
AP : 0 4 :040(112) [0131] He was **given** for us to make satisfaction for the sins of
AP : 0 4 :063(115) [0139] can our opponents say how the Holy Spirit is **given**.
AP : 0 4 :084(119) [0145] in Jesus Christ might be **given** to those who believe."
AP : 0 4 :097(121) [0149] Christ was **given** for us to believe that we are justified
AP : 0 4 :098(121) [0149] other name under heaven **given** among men by which we
AP : 0 4 :132(125) [0159] But Christ was **given** so that for his sake we might receive
AP : 0 4 :132(125) [0159] the law can be kept only when the Holy Spirit is **given**.
AP : 0 4 :264(146) [0195] the forgiveness of sins must surely be **given** by a promise.
AP : 0 4 :283(150) [0201] part: "All things will be clean when you have **given** alms."
AP : 0 4 :285(150) [0201] of Christ, who was surely **given** to us that through him we
AP : 0 4 :291(151) [0203] But the Gospel was not **given** to the world in vain.
AP : 0 4 :292(152) [0203] in which the Father has **given** the assurance that he
AP : 0 4 :296(152) [0205] and believe that he was **given** for us to be justified on his
AP : 0 4 :297(153) [0205] of grace in Christ was not **given** in vain, either, before the
AP : 0 4 :307(154) [0207] righteousness of Christ is **given** to us through faith,
AP : 0 4 :320(156) [0209] and eternal life are **given** us freely for Christ's sake.
AP : 0 4 :377(165) [0223] and the teaching of the promise **given** for Christ's sake.
AP : 0 7 :029(173) [0237] defend the definition of the church which we had **given**.
AP : 0 9 :003(178) [0245] the Holy Spirit would be **given** to none, none would be
AP : 1 2 :028(185) [0259] of the scholastics, we have **given** penitence two parts,
AP : 1 2 :042(187) [0263] clearly state, "This is my body which is **given** for you.
AP : 1 2 :049(188) [0265] me sorely, but he has not **given** me over to death."
AP : 1 2 :053(189) [0265] Scripture; first it was **given** to Adam, later to the
AP : 1 2 :064(191) [0269] mediator, and believes the promises **given** for his sake.
AP : 1 2 :080(194) [0275] clearly the promise was **given** and Christ revealed to us
AP : 1 2 :081(194) [0275] in Jesus Christ might be **given** to those who believe."
AP : 1 2 :106(197) [0283] apply the commandment **given** a father to the pastor of a
AP : 1 2 :113(199) [0285] sinners unless they had **given** public evidence of their
AP : 1 3 :016(213) [0311] the sacraments and thus **given**, so to speak, a more
AP : 1 3 :019(213) [0313] says that circumcision was a sign **given** to exercise faith.
AP : 1 4 :001(214) [0315] On this matter we have **given** frequent testimony in the
AP : 1 5 :026(219) [0323] of record that many have **given** up their administrative
AP : 1 8 :010(226) [0337] and that the Holy Spirit is **given** to them out of regard
AP : 2 0 :002(227) [0339] of sins is freely **given** for Christ's sake, that not our works
AP : 2 0 :005(227) [0339] knows that Christ was **given** to us to be a propitiation for
AP : 2 0 :008(227) [0341] in the forgiveness of sins freely **given** for Christ's sake.
AP : 2 0 :010(228) [0341] forgiveness of sins were **given** on account of our works,
AP : 2 0 :013(228) [0343] lose its gifts, which were **given** to you before your works
AP : 2 0 :014(229) [0343] for maintaining that grace is **given** because of our works.
AP : 2 0 :015(229) [0343] we have already **given** ample evidence of our conviction
AP : 2 2 :006(237) [0359] They should have **given** the church a valid explanation to
AP : 2 2 :007(237) [0359] that only one part was **given**; for by the ordinary usage of
AP : 2 2 :009(237) [0359] why both kinds are not **given**, Gabriel says that a
AP : 2 2 :010(237) [0361] believe that Christ's flesh, **given** for the life of the world,
AP : 2 3 :016(241) [0369] receive this precept, but only those to whom it is **given**."
AP : 2 3 :039(244) [0375] in what he has been **given** to do, believing that for
AP : 2 3 :053(246) [0379] so that we ought to use the remedies God has **given** us.
AP : 2 3 :054(247) [0379] This has **given** us a picture of the times that will precede
AP : 2 4 :029(255) [0393] dost not desire; but thou hast **given** me an open ear."
AP : 2 4 :055(259) [0403] promise of the forgiveness of sins **given** for Christ's sake.
AP : 2 4 :069(262) [0409] is my body, which is **given** for you"; "this is the cup of the
AP : 2 4 :070(262) [0409] As the Word was **given** to arouse this faith, so the
AP : 2 4 :076(263) [0411] between what is **given** and what is forgiven, and it gives
AP : 2 4 :076(263) [0411] is, piety looks at what is **given** and what is forgiven; it
AP : 2 7 :004(269) [0421] how much credence should be **given** to this statement.
AP : 2 7 :011(270) [0423] the forgiveness of sins is **given** us freely for Christ's sake,
AP : 2 7 :023(273) [0427] Christ's sake righteousness and eternal life are **given** to us.
AP : 2 7 :032(274) [0431] place, eternal life is **given** by mercy for Christ's sake to
AP : 2 7 :032(274) [0431] work at all unless he has **given** this, too; finally, that by
AP : 2 7 :032(274) [0431] you merit eternal life, but that this is freely **given** as well."
AP : 2 8 :018(284) [0449] It is a testimony **given** to the apostles so that we may
S 1 : PR :003(289) [0455] which I have previously **given**) to show where I have
S 1 : PR :015(291) [0459] grace which Thou hast **given** us by thy Holy Spirit, who
S 2 : 0 1 :005(292) [0461] in this article can be **given** up or compromised, even if
S 2 : 0 1 :005(292) [0463] other name under heaven **given** among men by which we
S 2 : 0 4 :014(301) [0475] teaching, instructions are **given** concerning the
S 2 : 0 4 :016(301) [0475] summons and were **given** a kindly hearing, but we shall
S 3 : 0 2 :001(303) [0479] maintain that the law was **given** by God first of all to
S 3 : 0 3 :032(308) [0489] brood of vipers, who has **given** you any assurance that
S 3 : 0 6 :001(311) [0493] Christ and that these are **given** and received not only by
S 3 : 0 7 :001(311) [0493] are a function and power **given** to the church by Christ to

Continued ▶

S 3 : 1 1 :002(314) [0499] as the power has been **given** to us or to them to make a
T R : 0 0 :023(324) [0511] you bind") is elsewhere **given** in the plural ("Whatever you
T R : 0 0 :023(324) [0511] show that the keys were **given** equally to all the apostles
T R : 0 0 :026(324) [0511] authority but because of the Word **given** by Christ.
T R : 0 0 :067(331) [0523] This right is a gift **given** exclusively to the church, and no
T R : 0 0 :067(331) [0523] and he adds that they are **given** for the work of ministry
T R : 0 0 :068(331) [0523] testify that the keys were **given** to the church and not
T R : 0 0 :080(334) [0527] that riches have been **given** to bishops as alms for the
T R : 0 0 :080(334) [0527] rule states, "The benefice is **given** because of the office."
S C : 0 2 :002(345) [0543] all that exists; that he has **given** me and still sustains my
S C : 0 6 :002(351) [0555] under the bread and wine, **given** to us Christians to eat
S C : 0 6 :004(351) [0555] bread, and when he had **given** thanks, he broke it, and
S C : 0 6 :004(351) [0555] said, 'Take, eat; this is my body which is **given** for you.
S C : 0 6 :004(351) [0555] supper, and when he had **given** thanks he gave it to them,
S C : 0 6 :006(352) [0557] life, and salvation are **given** to us in the sacrament, for
L C : S P :016(363) [0577] them they should not be **given** anything to eat or drink.
L C : S P :023(364) [0579] 'Take and eat, this is my body, which is **given** for you.
L C : 0 1 :063(373) [0599] it has been revealed and **given** to us precisely for our use
L C : 0 1 :080(375) [0603] the commandment was **given** to the Jews alone.
L C : 0 1 :105(379) [0611] and motherhood God has **given** the special distinction,
L C : 0 1 :108(379) [0611] are their own father and mother, **given** them by God.
L C : 0 1 :125(382) [0617] much more, when he has **given** us living parents, should
L C : 0 1 :130(383) [0619] as those through whom God has **given** him all blessings.
L C : 0 1 :173(388) [0629] But he has **given** and entrusted children to us with the
L C : 0 1 :187(390) [0633] toward those who have **given** us occasion for anger,
L C : 0 1 :219(394) [0643] and cherish the wife or husband whom God has **given**.
L C : 0 1 :248(398) [0651] We have now **given** sufficient warning and exhortation.
L C : 0 1 :293(404) [0663] taken literally, were **given** exclusively to the Jews;
L C : 0 1 :333(411) [0677] other teachings as the greatest treasure God has **given** us.
L C : 0 2 :002(411) [0679] It is **given** in order to help us do what the Ten
L C : 0 2 :013(412) [0681] God; that is, that he has **given** and constantly sustains my
L C : 0 2 :017(412) [0681] the Father not only has **given** us all that we have and see
L C : 0 2 :019(412) [0681] on earth besides, is daily **given** and sustained by God, it
L C : 0 2 :024(413) [0683] we see how the Father has **given** himself to us, with all his
L C : 0 2 :026(413) [0685] is, how he has completely **given** himself to us, withholding
L C : 0 2 :038(415) [0689] in which he has **given** the Holy Spirit to offer and apply
L C : 0 2 :064(419) [0695] and on earth, he has **given** us his Son and his Holy
L C : 0 3 :015(422) [0701] Second Commandment is **given** just as much on my
L C : 0 3 :019(423) [0703] says in Matt. 7:7, 8, "Ask and it will be **given** you," etc.
L C : 0 3 :037(425) [0707] God's name was **given** to us when we became Christians
L C : 0 3 :097(433) [0725] but because Thou hast **given** the promise and hast set thy
L C : 0 4 :006(437) [0733] but revealed and **given** by God himself, so I can also
L C : 0 4 :049(442) [0745] been thus baptized and has **given** them the Holy Spirit.
L C : 0 4 :049(442) [0745] God's grace we have been **given** the power to interpret the
L C : 0 4 :050(443) [0745] he would not have **given** any of them the Holy Spirit nor
L C : 0 4 :068(445) [0749] place but the old man is **given** free rein and continually
L C : 0 4 :076(445) [0751] In Baptism we are **given** the grace, Spirit, and power to
L C : 0 5 :003(447) [0753] *said, 'Take, eat; this is my body, which is **given** for you.*
L C : 0 5 :021(449) [0757] is my body and blood, **given** and poured out *for you* for
L C : 0 5 :024(449) [0759] The Lord's Supper is **given** as a daily food and sustenance
L C : 0 5 :027(449) [0759] of the Lord's Supper is **given** to bring us new strength and
L C : 0 5 :029(449) [0759] than through the words, "**given** and poured out for you."
L C : 0 5 :031(450) [0759] body and blood are not **given** and poured out for us in
L C : 0 5 :034(450) [0761] the Word when he says, "**Given** *for you*" and "poured out
L C : 0 5 :037(451) [0761] But what is **given** in and with the sacrament cannot be
L C : 0 5 :064(454) [0769] words, "This is my body, **given** *for you,*" "This is my
L C : 0 6 :023(460) [0000] money or clothes, is to be **given** out at a certain place; he
L C : 0 6 :024(460) [0000] place, no reason being **given** and no mention of what they
E P : 0 2 :015(471) [0789] and that the Holy Spirit is **given** to such as resist him
E P : 0 6 :001(479) [0805] The law has been **given** to men for three reasons: (1) to
E P : 0 7 :014(483) [0811] modes of being at a **given** place, and not only the single
E P : 0 7 :034(485) [0815] present at more than one place at a single **given** time.
E P : 0 8 :016(489) [0821] and on earth has been **given** to me," and as St. Paul
E P : 0 8 :034(491) [0825] and on earth has been **given** to me," and St. Paul's
E P : 0 8 :035(491) [0825] Christ has indeed been **given** greater power in heaven and
E P : 0 8 :035(491) [0825] of God, and that this has not been **given** to him.
E P : 0 8 :039(491) [0827] "All authority has been **given** to me" (Matt. 28:18), to
S D : 0 1 :015(511) [0863] points, which we have **given** in summary form, are
S D : 0 1 :038(515) [0871] all that exists, that he has **given** me and still sustains my
S D : 0 1 :038(515) [0871] God; that is, that he has **given** and constantly sustains my
S D : 0 2 :010(522) [0885] To you it has been **given** to know the secrets of the
S D : 0 2 :029(527) [0893] which the Holy Spirit is **given**, and by pointing out that
S D : 0 2 :073(535) [0909] Whether the Holy Spirit is **given** to those who resist him?
S D : 0 2 :082(537) [0913] and that the Holy Spirit is **given** to those who resist him.
S D : 0 3 :023(543) [0923] into grace) there is **given** the Holy Spirit, who renews and
S D : 0 4 :019(554) [0945] careful attention must be **given** to the distinction which
S D : 0 5 :012(560) [0957] are not ordained and **given** us to terrify or to condemn
S D : 0 6 :011(565) [0965] Holy Spirit, who is not **given** and received through the
S D : 0 7 :010(571) [0975] under the bread and wine, **given** to us Christians to eat
S D : 0 7 :019(572) [0979] of Jesus Christ which are **given** and received not only by
S D : 0 7 :043(576) [0987] command has been **given** from heaven to all men, "Listen
S D : 0 7 :043(577) [0987] authority in heaven and on earth has been **given** to me."
S D : 0 7 :044(577) [0987] this is my body which is **given** for you," and concerning
S D : 0 7 :050(578) [0991] by adding the words, "**given** for you, shed for you."
S D : 0 7 :098(586) [1005] modes, or all three modes, of being at any **given** place.
S D : 0 7 :113(589) [1011] interpretation are to be **given** a different, new, and
S D : 0 8 :054(601) [1033] possesses all the created gifts which have been **given** to it.
S D : 0 8 :055(601) [1033] earth, to have all things **given** into his hands, to have all
S D : 0 8 :055(601) [1033] properties have been **given** and communicated to the man
S D : 0 8 :058(602) [1035] judgment has been **given** to Christ because he is the Son
S D : 0 8 :060(602) [1035] nature and that it was all **given** and communicated to the
S D : 0 8 :061(602) [1035] and glory were not **given** to Christ's assumed human
S D : 0 8 :068(604) [1039] in heaven and on earth is **given**, for the Spirit, who has
S D : 0 8 :068(604) [1039] for the Spirit, who has all power, has been **given** to them.
S D : 0 8 :070(604) [1039] heaven and on earth has been **given** to me" (Matt. 28:18).
S D : 0 8 :070(605) [1041] and on earth has been **given** to me" (Matt. 28:18);
S D : 0 8 :070(605) [1041] knew that "the Father had **given** all things into his hands"
S D : 0 8 :074(606) [1043] hid in him, all authority is **given** to him, and he is exalted
S D : 0 8 :085(608) [1045] power of God is also **given** to him — in a temporal way,
S D : 0 8 :085(608) [1047] heaven and on earth has been **given** to me' (Matt. 28:18).
S D : 1 0 :005(611) [1053] adiaphora and are **given** a different color from their true
S D : 1 1 :016(619) [1069] Christ are to be offered, **given**, and distributed to us
S D : 1 1 :028(620) [1071] world (John 1:29); he has **given** his flesh "for the life of
S D : 1 1 :057(625) [1081] hardened, blinded, and is **given** over to a perverse mind

Giver (2)
A P : 2 4 :076(263) [0411] and it gives thanks to the **Giver** of such a generous
S D : 0 4 :017(554) [0943] Rom. 6:7) because God loves a cheerful **giver** (II Cor. 9:7)

Glad (6), Gladden (1), Gladly (14)
P R : P R :016(008) [0013] as indicated above, **gladly** and with heartfelt thanks to
A P : 0 4 :276(148) [0199] embrace them and are **glad** to have signs and testimonies
A P : 1 2 :090(195) [0279] with our opponents, we would very **gladly** keep quiet.
A P : 1 5 :038(220) [0325] We **gladly** keep the old traditions set up in the church
A P : 2 0 :007(227) [0339] Who would not **gladly** die in the confession of the article
A P : 2 4 :033(255) [0395] ceremony here, we shall **gladly** concede this, so long as he
S C : 0 1 :006(342) [0541] of the same, but deem it holy and **gladly** hear and learn it.
L C : P R :008(359) [0569] a child and pupil of the Catechism, and I do it **gladly**.
L C : 0 1 :121(382) [0615] I repeat, I should be very **glad** if we were to open our eyes
L C : 0 1 :126(382) [0617] incentive to do cheerfully and **gladly** whatever we can.
L C : 0 1 :143(385) [0623] and reluctantly but **gladly** and cheerfully; and they should
L C : 0 1 :144(385) [0623] privilege of service and be **glad** to acquire masters and
L C : 0 1 :322(409) [0673] who prize them and **gladly** act and live in accordance with
L C : 0 1 :326(409) [0675] Word, but learn it, hear it **gladly**, keep it holy, and honor
L C : 0 1 :330(410) [0677] a spontaneous impulse and desire **gladly** to do God's will.
L C : 0 3 :090(432) [0723] humble themselves and be **glad** that they can attain
L C : 0 3 :098(433) [0725] also can effect to strengthen and **gladden** our conscience.
L C : 0 5 :082(456) [0773] at you, you would be **glad** to come to the sacrament as
L C : 0 6 :007(457) [0000] To others who hear it **gladly**, however, we must preach,
L C : 0 6 :030(460) [0000] a Christian, you should be **glad** to run more than a
S D : P R :012(506) [0855] these documents but will **gladly** admit and accept them as

Glamor (1), Glamorous (2)
A G : 2 6 :011(065) [0071] were to be given the **glamorous** title of alone being holy
A L : 2 6 :009(065) [0071] for themselves the **glamorous** title of comprising the
L C : 0 1 :120(382) [0615] us with the false holiness and **glamor** of our own works.

Glass (1)
S D : 0 7 :100(586) [1007] go through air, water, **glass**, or crystal and exist without

Gleams (1)
L C : 0 1 :314(407) [0671] they are so adorned that everything **gleams** and glitters.

Gleichen (2)
P R : P R :027(015) [0025] Louis, count of **Gleichen** [-Blankenhain]
P R : P R :027(015) [0025] Charles, count of **Gleichen** [-Blankenhain]

Glitters (1), Glittering (1)
A L : 2 6 :010(065) [0071] works, far inferior to those **glittering** observances.
L C : 0 1 :314(407) [0671] they are so adorned that everything gleams and **glitters**.

Glory (95)
P R : P R :013(007) [0013] God to his praise and **glory** and after mature reflection
P R : P R :024(013) [0023] of God's praise and **glory**, to the propagation of that
P R : P R :024(013) [0023] the promotion of God's **glory** and the common welfare,
A G : 2 7 :038(077) [0081] is this but to diminish the **glory** and honor of the grace of
A G : 2 8 :036(086) [0089] and obtain grace, for the **glory** of Christ's merit is
A L : 0 2 :003(029) [0045] sin and who obscure the **glory** of Christ's merit and
A L : 2 4 :024(058) [0067] and diminish the **glory** of Christ's passion, for the passion
A L : 2 7 :038(077) [0081] but to detract from the **glory** of Christ and obscure and
A L : 2 7 :043(077) [0081] own works what properly belongs to the **glory** of Christ.
A L : 2 8 :036(086) [0089] justification, for the **glory** of Christ's merit is dishonored
A P : P R :016(099) [0103] and dangers for the **glory** of Christ and the good of the
A P : 0 4 :003(107) [0121] they obscure the **glory** and the blessings of Christ, and
A P : 0 4 :032(111) [0129] says, "All fall short of the **glory** of God," that is, they lack
A P : 0 4 :103(122) [0151] So let no one **glory** in his works since no one is justified
A P : 0 4 :146(127) [0163] keep the law, though this **glory** properly belongs to
A P : 0 4 :204(135) [0177] First, it obscures the **glory** of Christ when men offer these
A P : 0 4 :230(139) [0183] Because of Christ's **glory** we defend it and we ask Christ
A P : 0 4 :269(147) [0197] they attribute Christ's **glory** to works and make of them a
A P : 0 4 :277(148) [0199] not to take away from the **glory** of Christ, whose
A P : 0 4 :285(150) [0201] and illumines the **glory** of Christ, who was surely given to
A P : 0 4 :299(153) [0205] Christ's **glory** becomes brighter when we teach men to
A P : 0 4 :302(154) [0205] It transfers Christ's **glory** to human works; it leads
A P : 0 4 :309(155) [0207] but he grew strong in his faith as he gave **glory** to God."
A P : 0 4 :317(156) [0209] but a transfer of Christ's **glory** to our works, a destruction
A P : 0 4 :317(156) [0209] to our works, a destruction of his **glory** as mediator?
A P : 0 4 :324(157) [0211] faith and obscures Christ's **glory** and mediatorial work.
A P : 0 4 :326(157) [0211] This absolutely denies any **glory** in man's righteousness,
A P : 0 4 :326(158) [0211] of God's cause and his **glory**, as in Ps. 7:8, "Judge me, O
A P : 0 4 :351(161) [0217] and "beholding the **glory** of the Lord, we are changed into
A P : 0 4 :355(161) [0217] There will be distinctions in the **glory** of the saints.
A P : 0 4 :364(162) [0219] advantage, since they should work for the **glory** of God.
A P : 0 4 :370(164) [0221] to his works"; and v. 10, "**Glory** and honor and peace for
A P : 0 4 :373(164) [0221] That is to say, "**Glory** for him who does good," namely,
A P : 1 2 :139(203) [0295] We believe that God's **glory** and command require
A P : 1 2 :174(210) [0307] should be done to his **glory** and because of his command,
A P : 1 5 :020(218) [0321] They did not obscure the **glory** or work of Christ but
A P : 2 0 :006(227) [0339] and which increases the **glory** of Christ — we can easily
A P : 2 1 :044(235) [0357] for the sake of the **glory** of Christ, which we know you
A P : 2 4 :032(255) [0395] in confession, they do good works for the **glory** of Christ.
A P : 2 4 :063(261) [0405] monks; they destroy the **glory** of Christ's suffering and
A P : 2 4 :096(268) [0417] Christ's suffering of its **glory** and utterly destroy the
A P : 2 4 :098(268) [0419] comes to judge and by the **glory** of his coming destroys
A P : 2 4 :098(268) [0419] command to obscure the **glory** of Christ and the
A P : 2 7 :027(274) [0429] "We are changed from glory to glory, as by the Spirit of
A P : 2 7 :027(274) [0429] are changed from glory to **glory**, as by the Spirit of the
S 3 : 1 5 :005(317) [0501] Conrad Figenbotz, for the **glory** of God subscribe that I
T R : 0 0 :044(328) [0517] Thus they obscure the **glory** of Christ, deprive
T R : 0 0 :048(328) [0519] for they detract from the **glory** of God and bring
T R : 0 0 :052(329) [0519] must be embraced for the **glory** of God and the salvation
T R : 0 0 :054(329) [0519] first care of kings should be to advance the **glory** of God.
T R : 0 0 :059(330) [0521] detract from the **glory** of God, and hinder the welfare of
T R : 0 0 :076(333) [0527] for the reformation of morals and the **glory** of God.
S C : 0 4 :014(349) [0553] from the dead by the **glory** of the Father, we too might
S C : 0 5 :023(350) [0553] my children, servants, and wife to the **glory** of God.
L C : S P :014(363) [0577] is the kingdom and the power and the **glory**, forever.

Continued ▶

LC : 0 1 :114(380) [0613] obliged to set forth God's commandment in its full **glory**.
LC : 0 1 :150(385) [0625] all honor as their chief **glory**, it is our duty to honor and
LC : 0 1 :207(393) [0639] and support and bring them up to the **glory** of God.
LC : 0 2 :023(413) [0683] a desire to use all these blessings to his **glory** and praise.
LC : 0 3 :045(426) [0709] etc., but used rightly to the praise and **glory** of God.
LC : 0 3 :048(426) [0711] hear than to have his **glory** and praise exalted above
LC : 0 3 :049(426) [0711] the world from using his **glory** and name to cloak its lies
LC : 0 3 :060(428) [0715] all that pertains to God's **glory** and to our salvation, in
LC : 0 3 :113(435) [0729] pray for: God's name or **glory**, God's kingdom and will,
LC : 0 4 :020(439) [0737] adorned and clothed with the majesty and **glory** of God.
LC : 0 4 :021(439) [0737] and that the divine **glory** and majesty were manifested
LC : 0 4 :083(446) [0751] until we pass from this present misery to eternal **glory**.
EP : 0 3 :010(474) [0795] from our own works and give all **glory** to Christ alone.
EP : 0 8 :014(488) [0821] "crucified the Lord of **glory**," and in Acts 20:28, We are
EP : 0 8 :016(489) [0821] Thus he entered into his **glory** in such a way that now not
EP : 1 1 :015(496) [0835] election gives God his **glory** entirely and completely,
EP : 1 2 :021(499) [0841] power, majesty, and **glory** are concerned, and that now
EP : 1 2 :021(499) [0841] property, will, and **glory** and that the flesh of Christ
EP : 1 2 :029(500) [0843] wisdom, majesty, and **glory**, just like any three individual
SD : 0 3 :035(545) [0927] in order to preserve the **glory** due to Christ, the
SD : 0 3 :037(546) [0929] works, merit, worthiness, **glory**, and trust in any of our
SD : 0 4 :012(553) [0941] love of God and to his **glory**, who has been so gracious to
SD : 0 4 :034(556) [0949] and our hope of sharing the **glory** of God (Rom. 5:2).
SD : 0 8 :039(598) [1029] suffer these things and enter into his **glory**?' (Luke 24:26).
SD : 0 8 :051(601) [1033] and privileges in majesty, **glory**, power, and might above
SD : 0 8 :051(601) [1033] according to the majesty, **glory**, power, and might which
SD : 0 8 :061(602) [1035] life, might, majesty, and **glory** were not given to Christ's
SD : 0 8 :064(603) [1037] with all its majesty, power, **glory**, and efficacy in the
SD : 0 8 :064(603) [1039] his divine power, **glory**, and efficacy, as the soul does in
SD : 0 8 :065(604) [1039] life we shall behold his **glory** face to face (John 17:24).
SD : 0 8 :066(604) [1039] power, majesty, and **glory**, which is the property of the
SD : 0 8 :070(605) [1041] has crowned him with **glory** and honor and didst set him
SD : 0 8 :095(609) [1049] wisdom, majesty, and **glory**, but has only the bare title
SD : 1 1 :006(617) [1065] it must redound to the **glory** of his divine name and the
SD : 1 1 :079(629) [1089] known the riches of his **glory** in the vessels of mercy,
SD : 1 1 :082(630) [1091] that the Lord himself "has prepared them unto **glory**."
SD : 1 2 :026(635) [1099] more and greater gifts and **glory** than other people.
SD : 1 2 :029(635) [1101] power, in majesty, and in **glory** he is in every way equal in
SD : 1 2 :029(635) [1101] property, will, and **glory** and so that Christ's flesh
SD : 1 2 :037(636) [1103] wisdom, majesty, and **glory**, while others teach that the

Gloried (1)
SD : PR :007(502) [0849] to be Christians and **gloried** in the doctrine of Christ.

Glorification (4)
EP : 1 2 :021(499) [0841] 2. That in Christ's **glorification** his flesh received all the
SD : 0 8 :012(593) [1019] the exaltation or **glorification**, it has been elevated to the
SD : 0 8 :051(601) [1033] through the personal union, **glorification**, and exaltation.
SD : 0 8 :053(601) [1033] the personal union, **glorification**, or exaltation according

Glorified (7), Glorifies (2), Glorify (9)
AG : 2 0 :027(045) [0057] earn grace but that we may do God's will and **glorify** him.
AP : 0 4 :032(111) [0129] of God which acknowledge and **glorify** him.
AP : 0 4 :059(115) [0137] of trouble; I will deliver you, and you shall **glorify** me."
AP : 0 4 :196(134) [0175] "Those whom he justified he also **glorified**" (Rom. 8:30).
AP : 0 4 :362(162) [0219] Rom. 8:30, "Those whom he justified he also **glorified**."
AP : 0 7 :018(171) [0233] is the same, whether now **glorified** or previously afflicted.
AP : 2 4 :029(255) [0393] of trouble; I will deliver you, and you shall **glorify** me."
LC : 0 1 :064(373) [0599] of trouble: I will deliver you and you shall **glorify** me."
LC : 0 1 :206(393) [0639] highly God honors and **glorifies** the married life,
LC : 0 2 :058(418) [0693] and all evil, living in new, immortal and **glorified** bodies.
LC : 0 3 :008(421) [0699] the name of God is **glorified** and used to good purpose.
EP : 0 1 :006(467) [0781] will not quicken it in the elect, will not **glorify** it or save it.
SD : 0 2 :043(529) [0897] every doctrine which **glorifies** our free will, as directly and
SD : 0 8 :051(600) [1031] the former (when it was **glorified** and exalted to the right
SD : 0 8 :085(608) [1047] and John calls it '**glorified**' (John 7:39; 17:10)."
SD : 1 1 :022(619) [1069] would eternally save and **glorify** in eternal life those
SD : 1 1 :059(626) [1083] God and to recognize and **glorify** God's goodness to us
SD : 1 1 :065(627) [1085] Christ says, "He will **glorify** me" (John 16:14) and recall

Glorious (15), Gloriously (3)
PR : PR :023(012) [0021] the Holy Spirit until the **glorious** advent of our only
AP : 1 3 :011(212) [0311] has God's command and **glorious** promises: "The Gospel
S 1 : PR :015(291) [0459] of thine own, and by thy **glorious** advent deliver thy
LC : 0 1 :208(393) [0639] idle curiosity, but it is a **glorious** institution and an object
LC : 0 1 :333(410) [0677] same time he adds such **glorious** promises that he will
LC : 0 2 :057(418) [0693] and will come forth **gloriously** and arise to complete and
LC : 0 4 :007(437) [0733] we regard Baptism as excellent, **glorious**, and exalted.
LC : 0 4 :039(441) [0741] Therefore, it is far more **glorious** than anything else God
EP : 0 1 :006(467) [0781] as his creation, and adorns it **gloriously** as his creation.
EP : 0 5 :002(478) [0801] Gospel is an especially **glorious** light that is to be
EP : 0 9 :001(492) [0827] Christ's suffering or to his **glorious** victory and triumph?
EP : 1 1 :013(496) [0835] to rob us entirely of the **glorious** comfort which this
SD : PR :004(504) [0851] the Athanasian, as the **glorious** confessions of the faith —
SD : 0 4 :038(557) [0951] to reward them **gloriously** in this and in the future life.
SD : 1 1 :045(624) [1079] affords the beautiful and **glorious** comfort that God was
SD : 1 1 :048(624) [1079] will also give us the **glorious** comfort, in times of trial and
SD : 1 1 :050(624) [1079] This article also gives a **glorious** testimony that the church
SD : 1 1 :087(631) [1093] and to the praise of his **glorious** grace which he freely

Gloss (6), Glosses (1)
AP : 0 4 :282(149) [0201] the people," and the **gloss** says that it cleanses from
AP : 0 7 :010(170) [0229] The **gloss** in the *Decrees* says that "the church in the
AP : 1 1 :009(182) [0251] heap of constitutions, **glosses**, summae, and penitential
AP : 1 2 :113(199) [0285] as an example, as the **gloss** on the decree warns, and
AP : 1 2 :121(200) [0287] But the **gloss** on the canons says several times that these
LC : 0 1 :057(372) [0597] will he permit his name to be used to **gloss** over a lie.
LC : 0 1 :059(372) [0597] we like to cover and **gloss** over our disgrace so that no

…ing (4)
… 0 8 :018(594) [1021] analogies of the soul and the body and of **glowing** iron.
… 0 8 :064(603) [1039] in the body and fire in **glowing** iron, analogies which the
… 8 :066(604) [1039] Just as in **glowing** iron there are not two powers of
… :066(604) [1039] through this union the **glowing** iron has the power of

Glued (2)
EP : 0 8 :009(487) [0819] as when two boards are **glued** together and neither gives
SD : 0 8 :014(594) [1019] other like two boards **glued** together, so that in deed and

Gluttons (2), Gluttony (3)
S 1 : PR :012(290) [0459] extravagance in dress, **gluttony**, gambling, vain display,
LC : PR :001(358) [0567] of sheer laziness and **gluttony**, behave in this matter as if
LC : PR :002(358) [0567] Such shameful **gluttons** and servants of their bellies would
LC : 0 3 :042(425) [0709] adulterers, drunkards, **gluttons**, jealous persons, and
LC : 0 3 :102(434) [0727] unchastity, laziness, **gluttony** and drunkenness, greed and

Gnats (1)
S 1 : PR :013(291) [0459] camels and strain out **gnats**, if we let logs stand and

Goal (5)
PR : PR :023(012) [0021] been directed toward the **goal** that no other doctrine be
AP : 1 2 :063(191) [0269] a part of penitence or its **goal** — the "terminus to which,"
AP : 2 8 :006(282) [0445] their subjects toward the **goal** of eternal bliss, and that
AP : 2 8 :006(282) [0445] what is helpful or conducive to the aforementioned **goal**.
LC : 0 1 :261(400) [0655] Here we have a **goal** set for our jurists: perfect justice and

Goats (1)
AP : 2 4 :022(253) [0391] that the blood of bulls and **goats** should take away sins."

God (3083)
PR : PR :000(001) [0004] Founded on the Word of **God** as the Only Norm, of
PR : PR :002(003) [0007] transitory world almighty **God** in his immeasurable love,
PR : PR :004(004) [0007] the pure doctrine of **God**'s Word, sever the bond of
PR : PR :004(004) [0009] embracing other errors that militate against **God**'s Word.
PR : PR :005(004) [0009] in the teaching of **God**'s Word and in agreeable Christian
PR : PR :005(004) [0009] and in harmony with **God**'s Word, as they were while Dr.
PR : PR :005(004) [0009] unadulterated Word of **God**, so such false teachers were
PR : PR :006(004) [0009] Mindful of the office which **God** has committed to us and
PR : PR :008(005) [0009] that is impure, false, and contrary to the Word of **God**.
PR : PR :010(006) [0011] day than, on the basis of **God**'s Word, carefully and
PR : PR :010(006) [0011] differences and how by **God**'s grace they might be
PR : PR :011(006) [0011] writings based on **God**'s Word, how the aforementioned
PR : PR :011(006) [0011] them in the fear of **God**, and produced a document in
PR : PR :012(007) [0013] the office that we bear and that **God** has committed to us.
PR : PR :013(007) [0013] after invoking almighty **God** to his praise and glory and
PR : PR :014(007) [0013] fortified with the Word of **God** against all sorts of
PR : PR :016(008) [0013] first of all to the Word of **God** and then to the Augsburg
PR : PR :016(008) [0013] thanks to almighty **God** testified that of their own volition
PR : PR :018(008) [0015] and unalterable Word of **God**, to that Augsburg
PR : PR :018(009) [0015] By the help of **God**'s grace we, too, intend to persist in
PR : PR :020(010) [0017] to the incarnation of **God**'s Son, his ascension, and his
PR : PR :020(010) [0017] at the right hand of **God**'s almighty power and majesty)
PR : PR :021(010) [0019] seated at the right hand of **God** and is exalted, our
PR : PR :022(011) [0019] to the expressed Word of **God** and cannot coexist with it.
PR : PR :022(012) [0021] before the face of almighty **God** and the whole of
PR : PR :022(012) [0021] solemn and severe throne of **God**'s judgment, and there
PR : PR :023(012) [0021] on the Holy Scriptures of **God** and is embodied in the
PR : PR :023(012) [0021] witnessed publicly before **God** and all mankind that with
PR : PR :024(013) [0021] be thoroughly grounded in **God**'s Word so that pure
PR : PR :024(013) [0023] increase and expansion of **God**'s praise and glory, to the
PR : PR :024(013) [0023] truth and for Christian, **God**-pleasing concord will,
PR : PR :024(013) [0023] and the promotion of **God**'s glory and the common
AG : PR :011(026) [0041] truth we invoke almighty **God** in deepest humility and
AG : PR :013(026) [0041] anything, in so far as **God** and conscience allow, that may
AG : 0 1 :000(027) [0043] I. [**God**]
AG : 0 1 :002(027) [0043] is called and which is truly **God**, and that there are three
AG : 0 1 :002(027) [0043] **God** the Father, God the Son, God the Holy Spirit.
AG : 0 1 :002(027) [0043] God the Father, **God** the Son, God the Holy Spirit.
AG : 0 1 :002(027) [0043] God the Father, God the Son, **God** the Holy Spirit.
AG : 0 2 :001(029) [0043] by nature to have true fear of **God** and true faith in God.
AG : 0 2 :001(029) [0043] by nature to have true fear of God and true faith in **God**.
AG : 0 2 :002(029) [0043] to the eternal wrath of **God** all those who are not born
AG : 0 3 :000(029) [0045] III. [The Son of **God**]
AG : 0 3 :001(029) [0045] also taught among us that **God** the Son became man,
AG : 0 3 :002(029) [0045] there is one Christ, true **God** and true man, who was truly
AG : 0 3 :003(030) [0045] but also for all other sins and to propitiate **God**'s wrath.
AG : 0 3 :004(030) [0045] sits on the right hand of **God**, that he may eternally rule
AG : 0 4 :001(030) [0045] and righteousness before **God** by our own merits, works,
AG : 0 4 :001(030) [0045] become righteous before **God** by grace, for Christ's sake,
AG : 0 4 :003(030) [0045] For **God** will regard and reckon this faith as
AG : 0 5 :001(031) [0045] To obtain such faith **God** instituted the office of the
AG : 0 5 :003(031) [0045] that we have a gracious **God**, not by our own merits but
AG : 0 6 :001(031) [0045] do all such good works as **God** has commanded, but we
AG : 0 6 :001(031) [0045] but we should do them for **God**'s sake and not place our
AG : 0 6 :001(032) [0045] our trust in them as if thereby to merit favor before **God**.
AG : 0 6 :003(032) [0047] says, "It is ordained of **God** that whoever believes in
AG : 0 9 :002(033) [0047] they are committed to **God** and become acceptable to
AG : 1 3 :001(035) [0049] signs and testimonies of **God**'s will toward us for the
AG : 1 5 :003(036) [0049] purpose of propitiating **God** and earning grace are
AG : 1 6 :001(037) [0051] instituted and ordained by **God** for the sake of good
AG : 1 6 :004(037) [0051] alone of proper fear of **God** and real faith in God, for the
AG : 1 6 :004(038) [0051] of God and real faith in **God**, for the Gospel does not
AG : 1 6 :005(038) [0051] be kept as true orders of **God** and that everyone, each
AG : 1 6 :007(038) [0051] without sin, we must obey **God** rather than men (Acts
AG : 1 8 :002(039) [0051] himself acceptable to **God**, of fearing God and believing
AG : 1 8 :002(039) [0051] to God, of fearing **God** and believing in God with his
AG : 1 8 :002(039) [0051] God and believing in **God** with his whole heart, or of
AG : 1 8 :003(039) [0051] given through the Word of **God**, for Paul says in I Cor.
AG : 1 8 :003(039) [0051] man does not receive the gifts of the Spirit of **God**."
AG : 1 8 :004(039) [0051] in matters pertaining to **God** (such as loving God with
AG : 1 8 :004(039) [0051] to God (such as loving **God** with their whole heart or
AG : 1 8 :006(040) [0053] these is or exists without **God**, but all things are from him
AG : 1 9 :000(040) [0053] us that although almighty **God** has created and still
AG : 1 9 :000(041) [0053] all wicked men and despisers of **God** by the perverted will
AG : 1 9 :000(041) [0053] ungodly men; as soon as **God** withdraws his support, the
AG : 1 9 :000(041) [0053] his support, the will turns away from **God** to evil.
AG : 2 0 :006(041) [0053] become righteous before **God** by our works alone, but

Continued ▶

AG : 20 :006(042) [0053] say that faith and works make us righteous before **God**.
AG : 20 :009(042) [0053] cannot reconcile us with **God** or obtain grace for us, for
AG : 20 :010(042) [0055] and seeks his own way to **God**, contrary to the Gospel.
AG : 20 :011(042) [0055] own doing, it is the gift of **God** — not because of works,
AG : 20 :013(043) [0055] and are justified before **God** through faith in Christ and
AG : 20 :015(043) [0055] sake it has a gracious **God**, as Paul says in Rom. 5:1,
AG : 20 :016(043) [0055] "Since we are justified by faith, we have peace with **God**."
AG : 20 :022(044) [0055] may know that the grace of **God** is appropriated without
AG : 20 :024(044) [0055] in Christ he has a gracious **God**, truly knows God, calls
AG : 20 :024(044) [0055] gracious God, truly knows **God**, calls upon him, and is
AG : 20 :024(044) [0057] calls upon him, and is not, like the heathen, without **God**.
AG : 20 :025(044) [0057] so they are at enmity with **God**, cannot call upon him,
AG : 20 :025(045) [0057] but is a confidence in **God** and in the fulfillment of his
AG : 20 :026(045) [0057] to mean confidence in **God**, assurance that God is
AG : 20 :026(045) [0057] in God, assurance that **God** is gracious to us, and not
AG : 20 :027(045) [0057] earn grace but that we may do **God**'s will and glorify him.
AG : 20 :037(046) [0057] do good works, call upon **God**, have patience in suffering,
AG : 21 :002(047) [0057] is one mediator between **God** and men, Christ Jesus"
AG : 21 :002(047) [0057] advocate, and intercessor before **God** (Rom. 8:34).
AG : 00 :001(047) [0059] in grave peril before **God** by misusing his name or Word,
AG : 00 :001(047) [0059] agrees with the pure Word of **God** and Christian truth.
AG : 00 :000(049) [0059] have been compelled by **God**'s command (which is rightly
AG : 22 :010(050) [0061] introduced contrary to **God**'s command and also contrary
AG : 23 :003(051) [0061] was instituted by the Lord **God** to avoid immorality, for
AG : 23 :005(052) [0061] **God** created man as male and female according to Gen.
AG : 23 :006(052) [0061] or change the creation of **God**, the supreme Majesty, by
AG : 23 :006(052) [0061] resolutions or vows without a special gift or grace of **God**.
AG : 23 :008(052) [0061] Since **God**'s Word and command cannot be altered by
AG : 23 :013(053) [0063] of marriage (which **God** himself instituted and left free to
AG : 23 :014(054) [0063] a better or wiser way than **God** himself, who instituted
AG : 23 :018(054) [0063] may marry is based on **God**'s Word and command.
AG : 23 :018(054) [0063] abomination and prevalence, arouse the wrath of **God**.
AG : 23 :019(054) [0063] in the Holy Scriptures **God** commanded that marriage be
AG : 23 :024(055) [0065] or abolish a command of **God**, neither can any vow alter
AG : 23 :024(055) [0065] of God, neither can any vow alter a command of **God**.
AG : 24 :022(058) [0067] of which sin was taken away and **God** was reconciled.
AG : 24 :023(058) [0067] men expected to get everything they needed from **God**.
AG : 24 :023(058) [0067] faith in Christ and true service of **God** were forgotten.
AG : 24 :028(059) [0067] we obtain grace before **God** through faith and not through
AG : 24 :029(059) [0067] all sorts of benefits from **God**, not only for the priest
AG : 25 :003(061) [0069] it, but it is the Word of **God**, who forgives sin, for it is
AG : 25 :003(062) [0069] sin, for it is spoken in **God**'s stead and by God's
AG : 25 :003(062) [0069] for it is spoken in God's stead and by **God**'s command.
AG : 25 :004(062) [0069] We also teach that **God** requires us to believe this
AG : 25 :004(062) [0069] as much as if we heard **God**'s voice from heaven, that we
AG : 25 :011(063) [0071] confess to the Lord **God**, the true judge, in your prayer,
AG : 26 :002(064) [0071] were a necessary service of **God** by means of which grace
AG : 26 :005(064) [0071] we do not become good in **God**'s sight by our works but
AG : 26 :008(065) [0071] obscured the commands of **God**, for these traditions were
AG : 26 :008(065) [0071] these traditions were exalted far above **God**'s commands.
AG : 26 :010(065) [0071] them up in the fear of **God**, that a wife should bear
AG : 26 :011(065) [0071] works, commanded by **God**, were to be regarded as
AG : 26 :012(066) [0073] of the opinion that they were a necessary service of **God**.
AG : 26 :021(067) [0073] grace cannot be earned, **God** cannot be reconciled, and sin
AG : 26 :021(067) [0073] they should not be made into a necessary service of **God**.
AG : 26 :024(067) [0073] "The kingdom of **God** does not mean food and
AG : 26 :027(068) [0073] "Why do you make trial of **God** by putting a yoke upon
AG : 26 :041(070) [0075] make us righteous before **God** and that they are to be
AG : 27 :001(071) [0077] not only to the Word of **God** but also to papal canons.
AG : 27 :011(072) [0077] could earn forgiveness of sin and justification before **God**.
AG : 27 :013(072) [0077] states of life instituted by **God** — whether the office of
AG : 27 :013(073) [0077] calling according to **God**'s Word and command without
AG : 27 :016(073) [0077] such a nature that thereby **God**'s grace and righteousness
AG : 27 :016(073) [0077] God's grace and righteousness before **God** are earned.
AG : 27 :016(073) [0077] as far superior to the other estates instituted by **God**.
AG : 27 :018(073) [0079] marry, for vows cannot nullify **God**'s order and command
AG : 27 :019(073) [0079] **God**'s command in I Cor. 7:2 reads, "Because of the
AG : 27 :020(074) [0079] It is not alone **God**'s command that urges, drives, and
AG : 27 :020(074) [0079] compels us to do this, but **God**'s creation and order also
AG : 27 :020(074) [0079] endowed with the gift of virginity by a special act of **God**.
AG : 27 :020(074) [0079] This appears from **God**'s own words in Gen. 2:18, "It is
AG : 27 :022(074) [0079] them, it is still impossible to abrogate **God**'s command.
AG : 27 :023(074) [0079] and power when they are contrary to **God**'s command!
AG : 27 :036(076) [0081] Although **God**'s command concerning marriage frees and
AG : 27 :036(076) [0081] For all such service of **God** that is chosen and instituted
AG : 27 :036(076) [0081] obtain righteousness and **God**'s grace without the
AG : 27 :036(076) [0081] command and authority of **God** is opposed to God and
AG : 27 :036(076) [0081] of God is opposed to **God** and the holy Gospel and
AG : 27 :036(076) [0081] God and the holy Gospel and contrary to **God**'s command
AG : 27 :037(077) [0081] and godliness in **God**'s sight come from faith and trust
AG : 27 :037(077) [0081] trust when we believe that **God** receives us into his favor
AG : 27 :038(077) [0081] for sin and obtains **God**'s grace and righteousness.
AG : 27 :039(077) [0081] vows were an improper and false service of **God**.
AG : 27 :040(077) [0081] vow, made contrary to **God**'s command, is null and void.
AG : 27 :042(077) [0081] and have fallen away from **God**'s grace, for they rob
AG : 27 :048(078) [0081] with such a service of **God**, invented by men without the
AG : 27 :048(078) [0081] without the command of **God**, and should be taught that
AG : 27 :048(078) [0081] service would make men good and righteous before **God**.
AG : 27 :049(078) [0083] Besides, the commands of **God** and true and proper
AG : 27 :049(078) [0083] true and proper service of **God** are obscured when people
AG : 27 :049(079) [0083] perfection: that we fear **God** honestly with our whole
AG : 27 :049(079) [0083] have a gracious, merciful **God**; that we may and should
AG : 27 :049(079) [0083] and should ask and pray **God** for those things of which
AG : 27 :050(079) [0083] and right service of **God** consist of these things and not of
AG : 27 :057(080) [0083] and seeking a life more pleasing to **God** than the other.
AG : 27 :057(080) [0083] that one is to serve **God** by observing the commands God
AG : 27 :057(080) [0083] observing the commands **God** has given and not by
AG : 27 :058(080) [0083] state of life which has **God**'s command to support it; on
AG : 27 :058(080) [0083] of life which does not have **God**'s command behind it.
AG : 27 :061(080) [0083] men righteous before **God**, that they constitute Christian
AG : 27 :061(080) [0083] which we are not obligated to render to **God**.
AG : 28 :004(081) [0085] taught that because of **God**'s command both authorities
AG : 28 :004(081) [0085] with all reverence as the two highest gifts of **God** on earth
AG : 28 :005(081) [0085] a power and command of **God** to preach the Gospel, to
AG : 28 :008(082) [0085] and preaching the Word of **God** and by administering the
AG : 28 :009(082) [0085] gospel is the power of **God** for salvation to everyone who
AG : 28 :017(083) [0085] and every proud obstacle to the knowledge of **God**."
AG : 28 :018(083) [0085] both be held in honor as the highest gifts of **God** on earth
AG : 28 :021(084) [0087] be done not by human power but by **God**'s Word alone.
AG : 28 :023(084) [0087] to the Gospel, we have **God**'s command not to be
AG : 28 :035(086) [0089] It is patently contrary to **God**'s command and Word to
AG : 28 :037(087) [0089] grace and everything good might be earned from **God**.
AG : 28 :039(087) [0089] also act contrary to **God**'s command when they attach sin
AG : 28 :039(087) [0089] law, as if in order to earn **God**'s grace there had to be a
AG : 28 :039(087) [0089] had to be a service of **God** among Christians like the
AG : 28 :039(087) [0089] Levitical service, and as if **God** had commanded the
AG : 28 :041(087) [0089] fasting is a work by which **God** is reconciled, that in a
AG : 28 :043(088) [0089] for the purpose of earning **God**'s grace or as if they were
AG : 28 :048(089) [0091] He rejects such service of **God** and says, "Every plant
AG : 28 :050(089) [0091] as necessary to propitiate **God** and merit grace are
AG : 28 :050(089) [0091] all proper for the bishops to require such services of **God**.
AG : 28 :052(089) [0091] we obtain the grace of **God** through faith in Christ
AG : 28 :052(089) [0091] we do not merit it by services of **God** instituted by men.
AG : 28 :053(090) [0091] as a means of obtaining **God**'s grace or making
AG : 28 :053(090) [0091] necessary services of **God** and counting it a sin to omit
AG : 28 :061(091) [0093] one must have services of **God** like the Levitical or Jewish
AG : 28 :075(094) [0095] rule which commands us to obey **God** rather than men.
AG : 28 :078(094) [0095] they will answer for it in **God**'s sight, inasmuch as by their
AG : 00 :005(095) [0095] we have diligently and with **God**'s help prevented any new
AL : 01 :000(027) [0043] I. [**God**]
AL : 01 :002(027) [0043] is called and which is **God**, eternal, incorporeal,
AL : 02 :001(029) [0043] they are without fear of **God**, are without trust in God,
AL : 02 :001(029) [0043] of God, are without trust in **God**, and are concupiscent.
AL : 02 :003(029) [0045] man can be justified before **God** by his own strength and
AL : 03 :000(029) [0045] III. [The Son of **God**]
AL : 03 :001(029) [0045] Word — that is, the Son of **God** — took on man's nature
AL : 03 :002(029) [0045] his person, one Christ, true **God** and true man, who was
AL : 04 :001(030) [0045] cannot be justified before **God** by their own strength,
AL : 04 :003(030) [0045] This faith **God** imputes for righteousness in his sight
AL : 05 :002(031) [0045] where and when it pleases **God**, in those who hear the
AL : 05 :003(031) [0045] on account of Christ that **God** justifies those who believe
AL : 06 :001(031) [0045] it is necessary to do the good works commanded by **God**.
AL : 06 :001(031) [0045] We must do so because it is **God**'s will and not because
AL : 06 :001(032) [0045] merit justification before **God**, for forgiveness of sins and
AL : 06 :003(032) [0045] says, "It is ordained of **God** that whoever believes in
AL : 07 :004(032) [0047] faith, one baptism, one **God** and Father of all," etc. (Eph.
AL : 09 :001(033) [0047] salvation, that the grace of **God** is offered through
AL : 09 :002(033) [0047] for being offered to **God** through Baptism they are
AL : 13 :001(035) [0049] testimonies of the will of **God** toward us, intended to
AL : 15 :003(036) [0049] are instituted to propitiate **God**, merit grace, and make
AL : 16 :001(037) [0051] are good works of **God** and that it is right for Christians
AL : 16 :004(038) [0051] Gospel not in the fear of **God** and in faith but in forsaking
AL : 16 :005(038) [0051] as ordinance of **God** and the exercise of love in these
AL : 16 :007(038) [0051] then they ought to obey **God** rather than men (Acts 5:29).
AL : 18 :002(039) [0051] attain the righteousness of **God** — that is, spiritual
AL : 18 :002(039) [0051] the gifts of the Spirit of **God** (I Cor. 2:14); but this
AL : 18 :004(039) [0051] not enable them, without **God**, to begin or (much less) to
AL : 18 :004(039) [0051] things which pertain to **God**, for it is only in acts of this
AL : 18 :006(040) [0053] without the providence of **God**; indeed, it is from and
AL : 18 :008(040) [0053] alone, we are able to love **God** above all things, and can
AL : 18 :008(040) [0053] the commandments of **God** in so far as the substance of
AL : 18 :009(040) [0053] affections, such as fear of **God**, trust in God, patience,
AL : 18 :009(040) [0053] such as fear of God, trust in **God**, patience, etc.]
AL : 19 :000(040) [0053] teach that although **God** creates and preserves nature, the
AL : 19 :000(041) [0053] If not aided by **God**, the will of the wicked turns away
AL : 19 :000(041) [0053] wicked turns away from **God**, as Christ says in John 8:44,
AL : 20 :002(041) [0053] kinds of work are pleasing to **God** in the several callings.
AL : 20 :009(042) [0053] our works cannot reconcile **God** or merit forgiveness of
AL : 20 :010(042) [0055] Christ and seeks a way to **God** without Christ, by human
AL : 20 :014(043) [0055] by the mercy of **God** if justification, which is accomplished
AL : 20 :015(043) [0055] by inexperienced men, **God**-fearing and anxious
AL : 20 :015(043) [0055] are sure that for Christ's sake they have a gracious **God**.
AL : 20 :016(043) [0055] "Since we are justified by faith, we have peace with **God**."
AL : 20 :024(044) [0055] Christ truly knows **God**, knows that God cares for him,
AL : 20 :024(044) [0055] knows God, knows that **God** cares for him, and calls upon
AL : 20 :024(044) [0057] God, knows that God cares for him, and calls upon **God**.
AL : 20 :025(044) [0057] He is not without **God**, as are the heathen, for devils and
AL : 20 :025(044) [0057] of sins; hence they hate **God** as an enemy, do not call
AL : 20 :027(045) [0057] to merit grace by them but because it is the will of **God**.
AL : 20 :031(045) [0057] are too weak to do works which are good in **God**'s sight.
AL : 20 :037(046) [0057] faith it does not call upon **God**, expect anything of God,
AL : 20 :037(046) [0057] God, expect anything of **God**, or bear the cross, but it
AL : 20 :038(046) [0057] is no faith and trust in **God**, all manner of lusts and
AL : 22 :009(050) [0061] to the commands of **God** is not to be approved, as the
AL : 23 :005(052) [0061] suited for celibacy because **God** created man for
AL : 23 :006(052) [0061] alter his creation without a singular gift and work of **God**.
AL : 23 :008(052) [0061] nullify a commandment of **God** and an institution of
AL : 23 :008(052) [0061] nullify a commandment of God and an institution of **God**.
AL : 23 :015(054) [0063] Besides, **God** instituted marriage to be a remedy against
AL : 23 :018(054) [0063] the commandment of **God** is in force, although the
AL : 23 :019(054) [0063] **God** has commanded that marriage be held in honor.
AL : 23 :024(055) [0065] law can nullify a command of **God**, so no vow can do so.
AL : 24 :007(056) [0065] may learn to believe in **God** and ask for and expect
AL : 24 :007(056) [0065] God and ask for and expect whatever is good from **God**.
AL : 24 :008(057) [0065] Such worship pleases **God**, and such use of the sacrament
AL : 24 :008(057) [0065] and such use of the sacrament nourishes devotion to **God**.
AL : 24 :028(059) [0067] that we are justified before **God** through faith in Christ.
AL : 25 :003(062) [0069] because it is the voice of **God** and is pronounced by God's
AL : 25 :003(062) [0069] the voice of God and is pronounced by **God**'s command.
AL : 25 :004(062) [0069] consciences, are told that **God** requires faith to believe
AL : 25 :004(062) [0069] believe such absolution as **God**'s own voice heard from
AL : 25 :011(063) [0071] confess your sins to **God**, the true judge, in your prayer.
AL : 26 :008(065) [0071] obscured the commands of **God**, for traditions were
AL : 26 :008(065) [0071] traditions were exalted far above the commands of **God**.
AL : 26 :010(065) [0071] the commands of **God** pertaining to callings were without
AL : 26 :011(065) [0071] the observances of such men were more pleasing to **God**.

Continued ▶

A L : 2 6 :024(067) [0073] "The kingdom of **God** is not food and drink," and
A L : 2 6 :027(068) [0073] "Why do you make trial of **God** by putting a yoke upon
A L : 2 6 :041(070) [0075] do not justify before **God** and that no sin is committed if
A L : 2 6 :045(070) [0075] but to preach piety toward **God** and good conversation
A L : 2 7 :011(072) [0077] of sins and justification before **God** by this kind of life.
A L : 2 7 :012(072) [0077] only righteousness before **God** but even more, for it was
A L : 2 7 :013(073) [0077] serve their calling in accordance with **God**'s commands.
A L : 2 7 :016(073) [0077] put it far above all other kinds of life instituted by **God**.
A L : 2 7 :018(073) [0079] vows can not nullify the command and institution of **God**.
A L : 2 7 :019(074) [0079] This is the command of **God**, "Because of fornication let
A L : 2 7 :020(074) [0079] it the command only, but **God**'s creation and institution
A L : 2 7 :020(074) [0079] marry who are not excepted by a singular work of **God**.
A L : 2 7 :021(074) [0079] who obey this command and institution of **God** do not sin
A L : 2 7 :022(074) [0079] brought about that a vow abrogates the command of **God**
A L : 2 7 :023(074) [0079] vows valid which are made contrary to **God**'s commands!
A L : 2 7 :036(076) [0081] Although it appears that **God**'s command concerning
A L : 2 7 :036(076) [0081] Every service of **God** that is instituted and chosen by men
A L : 2 7 :036(076) [0081] without the command of **God** is wicked, for Christ says,
A L : 2 7 :037(077) [0081] that they are received by **God** into favor for Christ's sake.
A L : 2 7 :040(077) [0081] vow, taken contrary to the commands of **God**, is invalid.
A L : 2 7 :048(078) [0081] without the command of **God** and to teach that such
A L : 2 7 :049(078) [0083] the commands of **God** and true service of God are
A L : 2 7 :049(078) [0083] of God and true service of **God** are obscured when men
A L : 2 7 :049(078) [0083] perfection: honestly to fear **God** and at the same time to
A L : 2 7 :049(079) [0083] sake we have a gracious **God**, to ask of God, and
A L : 2 7 :049(079) [0083] a gracious God, to ask of **God**, and assuredly to expect
A L : 2 7 :050(079) [0083] and true service of **God** consist of these things and not of
A L : 2 7 :057(080) [0083] They did not perceive that **God** is to be served by
A L : 2 7 :058(080) [0083] kind of life is one which has **God**'s command in its favor.
A L : 2 8 :004(081) [0085] taught that on account of **God**'s command both are to be
A L : 2 8 :004(081) [0085] in reverence and honor as the chief gifts of **God** on earth.
A L : 2 8 :005(081) [0085] is a power or command of **God** to preach the Gospel, to
A L : 2 8 :009(082) [0085] gospel is the power of **God** for salvation to everyone who
A L : 2 8 :018(083) [0085] in honor and acknowledged as gifts and blessings of **God**.
A L : 2 8 :023(084) [0087] have a command of **God** that forbids obedience: "Beware
A L : 2 8 :028(085) [0087] hold anything contrary to the canonical Scriptures of **God**
A L : 2 8 :039(087) [0089] to the command of **God** when they attach sin to foods,
A L : 2 8 :039(087) [0089] to the Levitical, and as if **God** had commissioned the
A L : 2 8 :041(087) [0089] is a work that appeases **God**, that it is a mortal sin to omit
A L : 2 8 :043(088) [0089] the purpose of appeasing **God** or as if they were necessary
A L : 2 8 :075(094) [0095] which commands us to obey **God** rather than men.
A L : 2 8 :078(094) [0095] will answer for it before **God** that by their obstinacy they
A L : 0 0 :017(096) [0095] confession, we are ready, **God** willing, to present ampler
A P : P R :016(099) [0103] We trust that **God** approves our faithfulness, and we hope
A P : P R :018(099) [0103] publicly and thanked **God** for this great blessing, that on
A P : 0 1 :000(100) [0103] [Article I. **God**]
A P : 0 2 :001(100) [0105] being without the fear of **God** and faith is actual guilt,
A P : 0 2 :002(100) [0105] by nature to have true fear of **God** or true faith in God."
A P : 0 2 :002(100) [0105] by nature to have true fear of God or true faith in **God**."
A P : 0 2 :003(101) [0105] of actual fear and trust in **God** but also of the possibility
A P : 0 2 :003(101) [0105] and cannot produce true fear and trust in **God**.
A P : 0 2 :003(101) [0105] the fear and trust of **God**, and it denies that adults actually
A P : 0 2 :007(101) [0107] but also the absence of the fear of **God** and of faith.
A P : 0 2 :008(101) [0107] nature, namely, ignoring **God**, despising him, lacking fear
A P : 0 2 :008(101) [0107] most contrary to the law of **God**, the scholastics do not
A P : 0 2 :008(101) [0107] unimpaired power to love **God** above all things and to
A P : 0 2 :009(102) [0107] To be able to love **God** above all things by one's own
A P : 0 2 :010(102) [0107] that by itself it can love **God** above all things, as the
A P : 0 2 :010(102) [0109] by themselves can love **God** above all things and obey his
A P : 0 2 :011(102) [0109] security, contempt of **God**, hate of God, and similar faults
A P : 0 2 :011(102) [0109] contempt of God, hate of **God**, and similar faults that we
A P : 0 2 :012(102) [0109] men are justified before **God** by philosophical or civic
A P : 0 2 :013(102) [0109] except from the Word of **God**, which the scholastics do
A P : 0 2 :014(102) [0109] denied to man's natural powers the fear and trust of **God**.
A P : 0 2 :014(102) [0109] such faults as ignorance of **God**, contempt of God, lack of
A P : 0 2 :014(102) [0109] of God, contempt of **God**, lack of the fear of God and of
A P : 0 2 :014(102) [0109] of God, lack of the fear of **God** and of trust in him,
A P : 0 2 :016(102) [0109] first, commanding fear of **God**, faith and love toward
A P : 0 2 :017(102) [0109] well: a surer knowledge of **God**, fear of God, trust in God,
A P : 0 2 :017(102) [0109] knowledge of God, fear of **God**, trust in God, or at least
A P : 0 2 :017(102) [0109] God, fear of God, trust in **God**, or at least the inclination
A P : 0 2 :018(102) [0109] was created in the image of **God** and after his likeness
A P : 0 2 :018(103) [0111] in man that would grasp **God** and reflect him, that is, that
A P : 0 2 :018(103) [0111] gifts like the knowledge of **God**, fear of God, and trust in
A P : 0 2 :018(103) [0111] like the knowledge of God, fear of **God**, and trust in God?
A P : 0 2 :018(103) [0111] like the knowledge of God, fear of God, and trust in **God**?
A P : 0 2 :018(103) [0111] So Irenaeus interprets the likeness of **God**.
A P : 0 2 :019(103) [0111] soul is not in the image of **God** in which God is not
A P : 0 2 :019(103) [0111] in the image of God in which **God** is not always present."
A P : 0 2 :020(103) [0111] shows that the image of **God** is the knowledge of God,
A P : 0 2 :020(103) [0111] of God is the knowledge of **God**, righteousness, and truth.
A P : 0 2 :021(103) [0111] is the very likeness of **God** which he put into man.
A P : 0 2 :023(103) [0111] that he has knowledge of **God**, trust in God, fear and love
A P : 0 2 :023(103) [0111] knowledge of God, trust in **God**, fear and love of God, or
A P : 0 2 :023(103) [0111] in God, fear and love of **God**, or surely the power to
A P : 0 2 :023(103) [0111] these gifts knowledge of **God**, fear of God, and trust in
A P : 0 2 :023(103) [0111] gifts knowledge of God, fear of **God**, and trust in God.
A P : 0 2 :023(103) [0111] gifts knowledge of God, fear of God, and trust in **God**.
A P : 0 2 :023(103) [0111] not only fear and trust of **God** but also the gifts and
A P : 0 2 :024(103) [0111] cannot fear and love **God** or believe in him, it seeks and
A P : 0 2 :024(103) [0111] it despises the judgment of **God** in its security, or it hates
A P : 0 2 :025(103) [0111] by the Holy Spirit and a love for **God** above all things.
A P : 0 2 :026(103) [0111] to trust, fear, or love **God**; and concupiscence, which
A P : 0 2 :026(103) [0111] contrary to the Word of **God** (that is, not only the desires
A P : 0 2 :026(103) [0111] and righteousness in which it trusts while it despises **God**).
A P : 0 2 :029(104) [0113] along an ignorance of **God**, unbelief, distrust, contempt,
A P : 0 2 :029(104) [0113] of God, unbelief, distrust, contempt, and hate of **God**.
A P : 0 2 :030(104) [0113] man does not receive the gifts of the Spirit of **God**."
A P : 0 2 :031(104) [0113] see that when the fear of **God** and faith are lacking, this is
A P : 0 2 :033(104) [0113] is mere hypocrisy before **God** unless we acknowledge that
A P : 0 2 :033(104) [0113] of itself the heart is lacking in love, fear, and trust in **God**.
A P : 0 2 :034(104) [0113] all liars," that is, they do not have the right view of **God**.
A P : 0 2 :042(105) [0117] thing — doubt about **God**'s wrath, his grace, and his
A P : 0 2 :043(106) [0117] about the civil courts, not about the judgment of **God**.
A P : 0 2 :046(106) [0117] the commandments of **God** by his own powers, Genesis
A P : 0 4 :008(108) [0121] of reason, like true fear of **God**, true love of God, true
A P : 0 4 :008(108) [0121] fear of God, true love of **God**, true prayer to God, true
A P : 0 4 :008(108) [0121] of God, true prayer to **God**, true conviction that God
A P : 0 4 :008(108) [0121] God, true conviction that **God** hears prayer, and the
A P : 0 4 :008(108) [0121] and the expectation of **God**'s help in death and all
A P : 0 4 :008(108) [0121] it requires obedience to **God** in death and all afflictions,
A P : 0 4 :008(108) [0121] to flee these things or turn away when **God** imposes them.
A P : 0 4 :009(108) [0123] the Holy Spirit reason can love **God** above all things.
A P : 0 4 :009(108) [0123] at rest and he does not feel **God**'s wrath or judgment, he
A P : 0 4 :009(108) [0123] that he wants to love **God** and that he wants to do good
A P : 0 4 :009(108) [0123] to love God and that he wants to do good for **God**'s sake.
A P : 0 4 :009(108) [0123] sin elicits an act of love to **God** or does good for God's
A P : 0 4 :009(108) [0123] elicits an act of love to God or does good for **God**'s sake.
A P : 0 4 :011(108) [0123] order, not of compulsion—**God** grants grace to those who
A P : 0 4 :017(109) [0125] as a disposition inclining us to love **God** more easily.
A P : 0 4 :017(109) [0125] that the will can love **God**, but that this disposition
A P : 0 4 :018(109) [0125] righteous by their own keeping of the law before **God**.
A P : 0 4 :018(109) [0125] meanwhile neither fears **God** nor truly believes that he
A P : 0 4 :018(109) [0125] man can neither have nor understand the love of **God**.
A P : 0 4 :019(110) [0125] For if **God** necessarily gives grace for the merit of
A P : 0 4 :020(110) [0125] or how the judgment of **God** and the terrors of conscience
A P : 0 4 :022(110) [0127] for our part maintain that **God** requires the righteousness
A P : 0 4 :022(110) [0127] Because of **God**'s command, honorable works commanded
A P : 0 4 :022(110) [0127] For **God** wants this civil discipline to restrain the
A P : 0 4 :024(110) [0127] **God** even honors it with material rewards.
A P : 0 4 :026(110) [0127] accounted righteous before **God** because of the
A P : 0 4 :027(111) [0127] strength reason can love **God** above all things and keep
A P : 0 4 :028(111) [0129] the commandments of **God** outside a state of grace do not
A P : 0 4 :030(111) [0129] that comes from **God**, and seeking to establish your own,
A P : 0 4 :030(111) [0129] you did not submit to **God**'s righteousness' (Rom. 10:3).
A P : 0 4 :031(111) [0129] and the Spirit, one cannot enter the kingdom of **God**."
A P : 0 4 :031(111) [0129] does not justify us before **God**, it does not keep the law.
A P : 0 4 :032(111) [0129] fall short of the glory of **God**," that is, they lack the
A P : 0 4 :032(111) [0129] and righteousness of **God** which acknowledge and glorify
A P : 0 4 :032(111) [0129] on the flesh is hostile to **God**; it does not submit to God's
A P : 0 4 :032(111) [0129] God; it does not submit to **God**'s law, indeed it cannot;
A P : 0 4 :032(111) [0129] and those who are in the flesh cannot please **God**."
A P : 0 4 :033(111) [0129] on the flesh is hostile to **God**, then the flesh sins even
A P : 0 4 :033(111) [0129] If it cannot submit to **God**'s law, it is certainly sinning
A P : 0 4 :034(112) [0129] Content with this, they think they satisfy the law of **God**.
A P : 0 4 :034(112) [0129] commands us to love **God**, to be sure that God is wrathful
A P : 0 4 :034(112) [0129] love God, to be sure that **God** is wrathful at our sin, to
A P : 0 4 :034(112) [0129] despises the judgment of **God** in its smugness, or in the
A P : 0 4 :035(112) [0131] inherent in man to despise **God** and to doubt his Word
A P : 0 4 :035(112) [0131] Such people despise **God** when they do these things, as
A P : 0 4 :035(112) [0131] did not believe that **God** cared for him or regarded or
A P : 0 4 :035(112) [0131] This contempt for **God** corrupts works that seem
A P : 0 4 :035(112) [0131] works that seem virtuous, for **God** judges the heart.
A P : 0 4 :036(112) [0131] it is impossible to love **God** unless faith has first accepted
A P : 0 4 :036(112) [0131] A heart that really feels **God**'s wrath cannot love him
A P : 0 4 :036(112) [0131] bring itself to love a wrathful, judging, punishing **God**.
A P : 0 4 :037(112) [0131] of mortal sin can love **God** above all things, since they
A P : 0 4 :037(112) [0131] they themselves do not feel the wrath or judgment of **God**
A P : 0 4 :038(112) [0131] terrified by the law flees before **God**'s judgment.
A P : 0 4 :041(113) [0133] "Now, the righteousness of **God** has been manifested
A P : 0 4 :044(113) [0133] This faith brings to **God** a trust not in our own merits,
A P : 0 4 :045(113) [0133] because of Christ and that **God** is reconciled and
A P : 0 4 :045(113) [0133] so that we can finally obey **God**'s law, love him, truly fear
A P : 0 4 :046(113) [0133] of sins, faith sets against **God**'s wrath not our merits of
A P : 0 4 :048(114) [0135] accounted righteous before **God** do not live in mortal sin.
A P : 0 4 :048(114) [0135] but the firm acceptance of **God**'s offer promising
A P : 0 4 :049(114) [0135] worship which receives **God**'s offered blessing; the
A P : 0 4 :049(114) [0135] the law is that worship which offers **God** our own merits.
A P : 0 4 :049(114) [0135] It is by faith that **God** wants to be worshiped, namely,
A P : 0 4 :057(114) [0137] the Christ, that for his sake **God** intended to forgive sins.
A P : 0 4 :058(115) [0137] Here he comforts himself with his trust in **God**'s mercy.
A P : 0 4 :060(115) [0137] This is how **God** wants to be known and worshiped, that
A P : 0 4 :060(115) [0137] and teach men to deal with **God** only by works and
A P : 0 4 :067(116) [0139] But one cannot deal with **God** or grasp him except
A P : 0 4 :067(116) [0139] Gospel is the power of **God** for salvation to every one
A P : 0 4 :069(116) [0141] merits, that because of him **God** wants to be reconciled to
A P : 0 4 :071(116) [0141] follow, by which we would become acceptable unto **God**.
A P : 0 4 :072(117) [0141] we are truly accounted righteous or acceptable before **God**
A P : 0 4 :073(117) [0141] "It is the gift of **God**, not because of works, lest any man
A P : 0 4 :079(118) [0143] But thanks be to **God**, who gives us the victory through
A P : 0 4 :079(118) [0143] through the law, which shows **God**'s wrath against sin.
A P : 0 4 :080(118) [0143] to us, we cannot appease **God**'s wrath by setting forth our
A P : 0 4 :081(118) [0143] and then, through this love, have access to **God**.
A P : 0 4 :081(118) [0145] set our love or our works against the wrath of **God**.
A P : 0 4 :082(118) [0145] to Rom. 3:25, "Whom **God** put forward as an expiation,"
A P : 0 4 :082(118) [0145] in him and set it against the wrath and judgment of **God**.
A P : 0 4 :082(118) [0145] By bidding us draw near to **God** with trust not in our
A P : 0 4 :084(119) [0145] Paul says (Gal. 3:22), "**God** consigned all things to sin,
A P : 0 4 :086(119) [0147] righteous and children of **God** not on account of their
A P : 0 4 :086(119) [0147] by which we are accounted righteous before **God**.
A P : 0 4 :086(119) [0147] but because it receives **God**'s promise that for Christ's
A P : 0 4 :086(119) [0147] because it believes that "**God** made Christ our wisdom,
A P : 0 4 :087(119) [0147] that when we believe that **God** is reconciled to us for
A P : 0 4 :087(120) [0147] saved freely by "the gift of **God**, not because of works."
A P : 0 4 :087(120) [0147] and David, who had **God**'s command regarding
A P : 0 4 :089(120) [0149] It is faith, therefore, that **God** declares to be
A P : 0 4 :089(120) [0149] earned justification before **God**, faith would not be
A P : 0 4 :091(120) [0149] faith, we have peace with **God**," that is, our consciences
A P : 0 4 :091(120) [0149] tranquil and joyful before **God**, and in Rom. 10:10, "Man
A P : 0 4 :093(120) [0149] own doing, it is the gift of **God**—not because of works,
A P : 0 4 :094(120) [0149] to become children of **God**; who were born, not of blood
A P : 0 4 :094(120) [0149] of the will of the flesh nor of the will of man, but of **God**."
A P : 0 4 :096(121) [0149] Likewise John 3:17, 18, "**God** sent the Son into the world,
A P : 0 4 :097(121) [0149] sake when we believe that **God** is reconciled to us because
A P : 0 4 :100(121) [0151] faith which believes that **God** is propitious; and he adds
A P : 0 4 :101(121) [0151] in Christ, to believe that **God** will certainly accomplish

Continued ▶

AP : 0 4 :103(122) [0151] 'Behold the Lamb of **God**, who takes away the sin
AP : 0 4 :106(122) [0153] says: "By the law we fear **God**, by faith we hope in God.
AP : 0 4 :106(122) [0153] says: "By the law we fear God, by faith we hope in **God**.
AP : 0 4 :106(122) [0153] faith flees to the mercy of **God**, that he may give what he
AP : 0 4 :114(123) [0155] of sins and reconciles us to **God**, we must be accounted
AP : 0 4 :116(123) [0155] renders us acceptable to **God**, and brings the Holy Spirit,
AP : 0 4 :116(123) [0155] makes us acceptable to **God**" rather than love, which is
AP : 0 4 :125(124) [0157] we begin to fear and love **God**, to pray and expect help
AP : 0 4 :128(125) [0157] can the human heart love **God** while it knows that in his
AP : 0 4 :128(125) [0157] always accuses us, it always shows that **God** is wrathful.
AP : 0 4 :129(125) [0157] We cannot love **God** until we have grasped his mercy by
AP : 0 4 :130(125) [0157] of the heart toward **God**, belonging to the essence of the
AP : 0 4 :131(125) [0159] shall love the Lord your **God** with all your heart" (Deut.
AP : 0 4 :134(125) [0159] works satisfy the law of **God** and that sacrifice and ritual
AP : 0 4 :134(125) [0159] sacrifice and ritual justify before **God** *ex opere operato.*
AP : 0 4 :135(125) [0159] error taken away, when **God** shows us our uncleanness
AP : 0 4 :135(125) [0159] indifference does not fear **God** or truly believe in his
AP : 0 4 :135(125) [0159] our failure to believe that **God** forgives and hears us.
AP : 0 4 :135(125) [0159] we can think rightly about **God**, fear him, and believe in
AP : 0 4 :139(126) [0161] for Christ's sake we have a gracious **God** and his promise.
AP : 0 4 :139(126) [0161] and err, nor be driven to do anything against **God**'s will.
AP : 0 4 :139(126) [0161] so that with the help of **God** we, too, might conquer.
AP : 0 4 :139(126) [0161] "The reason the Son of **God** appeared was to destroy the
AP : 0 4 :140(126) [0161] can be kept, but also that **God** is pleased when we keep
AP : 0 4 :141(126) [0161] to separate faith from love for **God**, be it ever so small.
AP : 0 4 :141(126) [0161] that we have a gracious **God** who cares about us, we call
AP : 0 4 :142(126) [0161] of a conscience that feels **God**'s wrath against our sins and
AP : 0 4 :145(127) [0163] account of Christ, the mediator, we have a gracious **God**.
AP : 0 4 :146(127) [0163] to the judgment of **God** they set a trust in their own
AP : 0 4 :148(127) [0163] with full assurance that **God** forgives because Christ did
AP : 0 4 :150(127) [0163] he insults Christ and in **God**'s judgment he will discover
AP : 0 4 :153(127) [0163] faith is that which grasps **God**'s free mercy because of
AP : 0 4 :153(128) [0163] which grasps God's free mercy because of **God**'s Word.
AP : 0 4 :154(128) [0165] woman should believe **God**, while a doctor of the law
AP : 0 4 :155(128) [0165] earns the forgiveness of sins that reconciles us to **God**.
AP : 0 4 :157(128) [0165] And in the judgment of **God** we shall learn that this trust
AP : 0 4 :160(129) [0167] it does not please **God** for its own sake, and it is not
AP : 0 4 :161(129) [0167] accounted righteous before **God** by our own perfection
AP : 0 4 :162(129) [0169] that afterward we please **God** and merit eternal life by our
AP : 0 4 :163(129) [0169] sake we have a gracious **God** in spite of our unworthiness.
AP : 0 4 :164(129) [0169] be sure that it pleases **God**, since we never satisfy the law?
AP : 0 4 :165(129) [0169] is at the right hand of **God**, who indeed intercedes for us"
AP : 0 4 :165(130) [0169] and then imagine that he is righteous before **God**.
AP : 0 4 :166(130) [0169] of the law does not please **God** for its own sake, but for
AP : 0 4 :167(130) [0169] For who loves or fears **God** enough?
AP : 0 4 :167(130) [0169] endures patiently enough the afflictions that **God** sends?
AP : 0 4 :167(130) [0169] history is governed by **God**'s counsels or by chance?
AP : 0 4 :167(130) [0169] Who does not often doubt whether **God** hears him?
AP : 0 4 :168(130) [0169] of myself serve the law of **God** with my mind, but with
AP : 0 4 :168(130) [0169] Even this servant of **God** prays God to avert his
AP : 0 4 :168(130) [0169] Even this servant of God prays **God** to avert his judgment
AP : 0 4 :170(130) [0169] The flesh distrusts **God** and trusts in temporal things; in
AP : 0 4 :170(130) [0171] men for help; it even defies **God**'s will and runs away from
AP : 0 4 :170(130) [0171] ought to bear because of **God**'s command; and it doubts
AP : 0 4 :170(130) [0171] because of God's command; and it doubts **God**'s mercy.
AP : 0 4 :172(130) [0171] the commandments of **God** are kept when what is not
AP : 0 4 :172(131) [0171] for Christ's sake we please **God** and that the works in
AP : 0 4 :172(131) [0171] works in themselves do not have the value to please **God**.
AP : 0 4 :173(131) [0171] does not consist in our own merit, but in **God**'s mercy."
AP : 0 4 :174(131) [0171] is sure that for Christ's sake we have a gracious **God**.
AP : 0 4 :175(131) [0171] Holy Spirit and that their impulses agree with **God**'s law.
AP : 0 4 :176(131) [0171] accounted righteous before **God** on account of our
AP : 0 4 :176(131) [0171] As long as we flee **God**'s judgment and are angry at him,
AP : 0 4 :177(131) [0171] keeping of the law pleases **God** because of faith; because
AP : 0 4 :178(131) [0171] because of our keeping of the law we have a gracious **God**
AP : 0 4 :180(131) [0171] promise, because of Christ, **God** wishes to be favorably
AP : 0 4 :180(132) [0171] of Christ and his promise they have a gracious **God**.
AP : 0 4 :181(132) [0171] But **God** accepts this imperfect righteousness of the law
AP : 0 4 :181(132) [0171] regenerates nor of itself makes us acceptable before **God**.
AP : 0 4 :182(132) [0171] that we are justified before **God** by faith alone, since by
AP : 0 4 :184(132) [0173] works are done without Christ they do not please **God**.
AP : 0 4 :189(133) [0175] should be done because **God** has commanded them and in
AP : 0 4 :190(133) [0175] sacrifices acceptable to **God**, battles by which Christ
AP : 0 4 :191(133) [0175] true sacrifices, battles of **God** to defend the people who
AP : 0 4 :191(133) [0175] defend the people who had **God**'s Word against the devil,
AP : 0 4 :191(133) [0175] that the knowledge of **God** might not perish utterly from
AP : 0 4 :192(133) [0175] is determined that nothing happen to the praise of **God**.
AP : 0 4 :195(134) [0175] ours against the wrath of **God**, as Paul clearly says (Rom.
AP : 0 4 :195(134) [0175] faith, we have peace with **God** through our Lord Jesus
AP : 0 4 :196(134) [0175] faith makes us sons of **God**, moreover, it also makes us
AP : 0 4 :196(134) [0175] which makes us sons of **God** and co-heirs with Christ, we
AP : 0 4 :196(134) [0175] obtains this because it justifies us and has a gracious **God**.
AP : 0 4 :197(134) [0175] parents justifies us before **God**, but rather that when it
AP : 0 4 :198(134) [0175] Yet **God** exercises his saints in different ways and often
AP : 0 4 :198(134) [0175] but to seek the will of **God** rather than the rewards, as is
AP : 0 4 :200(134) [0175] are evil, and the wrath of **God** is revealed, threatening all
AP : 0 4 :202(134) [0175] he made was acceptable to **God** — not to merit the
AP : 0 4 :203(135) [0175] sake he is freely forgiven and freely has a gracious **God**.
AP : 0 4 :203(135) [0175] sins, appease the wrath of **God**, and achieve justification
AP : 0 4 :204(135) [0177] men offer these works to **God** as a price and propitiation,
AP : 0 4 :204(135) [0177] attain the knowledge of **God**, for in their anger they flee
AP : 0 4 :205(135) [0177] But faith gives assurance of **God**'s presence when it is sure
AP : 0 4 :206(135) [0177] were a propitiation and price that reconciled **God** to them
AP : 0 4 :207(135) [0177] them they had a gracious **God**, so to say, *ex opere*
AP : 0 4 :207(135) [0177] the sacrifices that **God** surely commanded as outward
AP : 0 4 :207(135) [0177] that through these works they placated the wrath of **God**.
AP : 0 4 :208(135) [0177] kept thinking up new works beyond **God**'s commandment
AP : 0 4 :209(136) [0177] by this cruel and painful deed to placate the wrath of **God**
AP : 0 4 :211(136) [0179] and had a gracious **God** because of Christ, not because of
AP : 0 4 :212(136) [0179] a propitiation by which **God** is appeased and a price
AP : 0 4 :212(136) [0179] monastic orders beyond **God**'s commandment in the hope
AP : 0 4 :212(136) [0179] that they can set against the wrath and judgment of **God**.
AP : 0 4 :213(136) [0179] accounted righteous before **God** because of them rather
AP : 0 4 :214(136) [0179] accounted righteous before **God** for Christ's sake by faith.
AP : 0 4 :214(136) [0179] pit our works against the wrath and judgment of **God**.
AP : 0 4 :214(136) [0179] mediator, can be pitted against **God**'s wrath and judgment
AP : 0 4 :216(137) [0179] by which we deal with **God**, not with men, and by which
AP : 0 4 :217(137) [0179] cannot find peace before **God** except by faith alone, by
AP : 0 4 :217(137) [0179] by which it is sure that **God** is reconciled to us for Christ's
AP : 0 4 :217(137) [0179] therefore it is always received before **God** by faith alone.
AP : 0 4 :222(138) [0181] the wrath and judgment of **God**; that our love satisfies the
AP : 0 4 :222(138) [0181] our love satisfies the law of **God**; that by our love we have
AP : 0 4 :222(138) [0181] our love we have access to **God** even without Christ, the
AP : 0 4 :222(138) [0181] and believe that for his sake **God** is gracious to us.
AP : 0 4 :223(138) [0181] and can have access to **God** without him as propitiator.
AP : 0 4 :224(138) [0181] that we are justified before **God** by the works of the
AP : 0 4 :224(138) [0181] which we deal with men and not specifically with **God**.
AP : 0 4 :224(138) [0181] our business is with **God**; his wrath must be stilled and
AP : 0 4 :226(138) [0183] and hope deal only with **God**, while love has infinite
AP : 0 4 :226(138) [0183] opponents that the love of **God** and neighbor is the
AP : 0 4 :226(138) [0183] is, "You shall love the Lord your **God**" (Matt. 22:27).
AP : 0 4 :227(139) [0183] merits and, through them, grace and peace from **God**.
AP : 0 4 :228(139) [0183] This obedience toward **God**, this desire to receive the
AP : 0 4 :228(139) [0183] **God** wants us to believe him and to accept blessings from
AP : 0 4 :230(139) [0183] we believe that for Christ's sake **God** is gracious to us.
AP : 0 4 :231(139) [0183] or perfection before **God** to the works of the Second
AP : 0 4 :238(141) [0187] propitiation that reconciles **God** to us; or that love is
AP : 0 4 :239(141) [0187] free us from shame when **God** judges and accuses us, but
AP : 0 4 :242(141) [0187] of sins in relation to **God**; that in place of Christ the
AP : 0 4 :244(142) [0189] and price that reconciles **God** to us; that good works
AP : 0 4 :244(142) [0189] works are accepted before **God** because of their intrinsic
AP : 0 4 :246(142) [0189] works we have access to **God** without Christ, the
AP : 0 4 :250(143) [0191] that through the power of **God** faith is efficacious and
AP : 0 4 :250(143) [0191] also raised with him through faith in the working of **God**."
AP : 0 4 :252(143) [0191] of the saints are righteous and please **God** because of faith
AP : 0 4 :252(143) [0191] will be justified"; that is, **God** pronounces righteous those
AP : 0 4 :253(143) [0193] that works please **God** without Christ, the propitiator;
AP : 0 4 :256(144) [0193] "Without faith it is impossible to please **God**."
AP : 0 4 :257(144) [0193] they hear the voice of **God**, clearly promising the
AP : 0 4 :261(145) [0195] to the king about the one **God** of Israel and converted
AP : 0 4 :261(145) [0195] confession about the **God** of Israel, "There is no other God
AP : 0 4 :261(145) [0195] Israel, "There is no other **God** who can save this way"
AP : 0 4 :262(145) [0195] a very definite Word of **God** to learn to know God's will,
AP : 0 4 :262(145) [0195] of God to learn to know **God**'s will, namely, that he is no
AP : 0 4 :263(145) [0195] or debt is removed because **God** forgives those who are
AP : 0 4 :263(145) [0195] to reason from this that **God** forgives because of the
AP : 0 4 :264(146) [0195] debt can be removed, that the wrath of **God** can be stilled.
AP : 0 4 :266(146) [0197] be turned from such fleshly opinions to the Word of **God**.
AP : 0 4 :266(146) [0197] works may be pleasing to **God**, as Christ says (John 15:5),
AP : 0 4 :267(146) [0197] requires faith, which believes that **God** freely forgives sins.
AP : 0 4 :269(147) [0197] "without faith it is impossible to please **God**" (Heb. 11:6).
AP : 0 4 :269(147) [0197] are praised for pleasing **God** on account of faith, since
AP : 0 4 :270(147) [0197] keep the commandments or please **God** without Christ.
AP : 0 4 :270(147) [0197] as soon as he hears that **God** is reconciled to us for
AP : 0 4 :270(147) [0197] is at peace and begins to love **God** and to keep the law.
AP : 0 4 :270(147) [0197] that now it is pleasing to **God** for the sake of Christ, the
AP : 0 4 :278(149) [0199] Thus **God** is pleased by that almsgiving which follows
AP : 0 4 :279(149) [0199] before almsgiving: "Have **God** in mind all the days of
AP : 0 4 :279(149) [0199] life" (4:5), and later, "Bless **God** always, and ask him to
AP : 0 4 :279(149) [0199] one which believes that **God** is reconciled on account of
AP : 0 4 :279(149) [0199] wants to be justified, sanctified, and governed by **God**.
AP : 0 4 :281(149) [0201] of the law, that for his sake good works please **God**.
AP : 0 4 :282(149) [0201] they are cleansed before **God** and justified by frequent
AP : 0 4 :283(150) [0201] in works commanded by **God**, not in human traditions
AP : 0 4 :285(150) [0201] works cannot be sure that its work will satisfy **God**.
AP : 0 4 :285(150) [0201] we could never be sure that we have a gracious **God**.
AP : 0 4 :288(151) [0203] thinks that it pleases **God** if it does good, but when men
AP : 0 4 :288(151) [0203] many other painful works to appease the wrath of **God**.
AP : 0 4 :288(151) [0203] counteract the terrors of conscience and the wrath of **God**
AP : 0 4 :289(151) [0203] (which is love) infused by **God**, that with the help of this
AP : 0 4 :289(151) [0203] we obey the law of **God** both outwardly and inwardly,
AP : 0 4 :289(151) [0203] Truly the law says, "You shall love the Lord your **God**"
AP : 0 4 :290(151) [0203] teaches that men come to **God** through their own keeping
AP : 0 4 :291(152) [0203] him we have access to **God** through faith (Rom. 5:2), and
AP : 0 4 :291(152) [0203] the mediator and propitiator, against the wrath of **God**.
AP : 0 4 :292(152) [0203] and believes that he has a gracious **God** for Christ's sake.
AP : 0 4 :293(152) [0203] is accounted for righteousness before **God** (Rom. 4:3, 5).
AP : 0 4 :293(152) [0203] we can keep the law, love **God** and his Word, obey God
AP : 0 4 :293(152) [0203] God and his Word, obey **God** in the midst of afflictions,
AP : 0 4 :293(152) [0203] law, these works please **God** on account of the justifying
AP : 0 4 :293(152) [0203] faith that for Christ's sake we have a gracious **God**.
AP : 0 4 :294(152) [0203] We cannot come to **God** without Christ, the mediator;
AP : 0 4 :295(152) [0203] cannot even love an angry **God**; the law always accuses us
AP : 0 4 :295(152) [0203] always accuses us and thus always shows us an angry **God**
AP : 0 4 :297(152) [0205] cannot keep the law of **God** nor love God; and second, we
AP : 0 4 :297(152) [0205] the law of God nor love **God**; and second, we are justified
AP : 0 4 :297(153) [0205] "He who does not believe **God**, has made him a liar,
AP : 0 4 :297(153) [0205] believed in the testimony that **God** has borne to his Son.
AP : 0 4 :297(153) [0205] this is the testimony, that **God** gave us eternal life, and
AP : 0 4 :297(153) [0205] have obtained access" to **God**, adding, "through faith"
AP : 0 4 :297(153) [0205] We are not justified before **God** either by reason or by the
AP : 0 4 :298(153) [0205] we are not justified before **God** by the law but by the
AP : 0 4 :300(153) [0205] Christ against the wrath of **God**, as though we could
AP : 0 4 :300(153) [0205] overcome the wrath of **God** with our love or could love
AP : 0 4 :300(153) [0205] wrath of God with our love or could love an angry **God**.
AP : 0 4 :301(153) [0205] that they have a gracious **God** because they love and keep
AP : 0 4 :301(153) [0205] they will have to doubt whether they have a gracious **God**
AP : 0 4 :301(153) [0205] angry at the judgment of **God**, who visits on human
AP : 0 4 :301(153) [0205] When will it love **God** amid these doubts and terrors?
AP : 0 4 :302(154) [0205] come forth to describe the love with which he loves **God**.
AP : 0 4 :303(154) [0205] a faith which believes that **God** cares for us, forgives us,
AP : 0 4 :303(154) [0205] itself the human mind believes no such thing about **God**.
AP : 0 4 :304(154) [0205] will commands the intellect to assent to the Word of **God**.
AP : 0 4 :304(154) [0205] in the will as it flees **God**'s judgment; just so faith is not
AP : 0 4 :304(154) [0205] are justified by faith, we have peace with **God**" (Rom. 5:1)
AP : 0 4 :306(154) [0207] life in Jesus Christ, whom **God** made our wisdom, our

Continued ▶

A P : 0 4 :306(154) [0207] that in him we might become the righteousness of **God**."
A P : 0 4 :307(154) [0207] we are made acceptable to **God** because of God's
A P : 0 4 :307(154) [0207] to God because of **God**'s imputation and ordinances, as
A P : 0 4 :308(155) [0207] the law can be pleasing to **God** only because this
A P : 0 4 :309(155) [0207] This faith gives honor to **God**, gives him what is properly
A P : 0 4 :309(155) [0207] concerning the promise of **God**, but he grew strong in his
A P : 0 4 :309(155) [0207] but he grew strong in his faith as he gave glory to **God**."
A P : 0 4 :310(155) [0207] receive good things from **God**, while the worship of the
A P : 0 4 :310(155) [0207] of the law is to offer and present our goods to **God**.
A P : 0 4 :310(155) [0207] cannot offer anything to **God** unless we have first been
A P : 0 4 :311(155) [0207] Gospel, and we cannot love **God** unless we have received
A P : 0 4 :314(156) [0207] our love and keeping of the law against the wrath of **God**.
A P : 0 4 :314(156) [0207] Christ we have obtained access to **God** by faith."
A P : 0 4 :314(156) [0207] teaching that we come to **God** by love and merits without
A P : 0 4 :316(156) [0209] or the fact that for Christ's sake we please **God** by faith.
A P : 0 4 :316(156) [0209] righteousness that pleases **God** of itself and earns eternal
A P : 0 4 :317(156) [0209] If we want to please **God** because of our works and not
A P : 0 4 :319(156) [0209] it ought to be pleasing to **God** because of its own work
A P : 0 4 :320(156) [0209] faith, we have peace with **God**"; we ought to be utterly
A P : 0 4 :322(157) [0209] in *Grace and Free Will*, "**God** leads us to eternal life, not
A P : 0 4 :326(157) [0211] the saints and servants of **God**, if God does not forgive
A P : 0 4 :326(157) [0211] and servants of God, if **God** does not forgive but judges
A P : 0 4 :326(158) [0211] against the persecutors of **God**'s Word, not of his
A P : 0 4 :326(158) [0211] He prays for the defense of **God**'s cause and his glory, as
A P : 0 4 :326(158) [0211] can stand the judgment of **God** if he observes our sins, "If
A P : 0 4 :329(158) [0211] Deut. 4:24, "Your **God** is a devouring fire."
A P : 0 4 :329(158) [0211] of the flesh cannot stand the judgment of **God**.
A P : 0 4 :331(158) [0211] for thy own sake, O my **God**, because thy city and thy
A P : 0 4 :331(158) [0211] is, to trust the mercy of **God** and not our merits before
A P : 0 4 :332(158) [0211] if indeed these profane men ever ask **God** for anything!
A P : 0 4 :332(158) [0211] and not on the mercy of **God**, insults Christ, who
A P : 0 4 :333(158) [0211] relies upon the mercy of **God** when we believe that we are
A P : 0 4 :334(158) [0215] words clearly say that **God** saves through mercy and
A P : 0 4 :335(159) [0215] works are worthless to **God**, but that to us they are worth
A P : 0 4 :337(159) [0215] but about trust in **God**'s promise and in his mercy.
A P : 0 4 :339(159) [0215] He does not want us to despair of **God**'s grace and mercy.
A P : 0 4 :342(159) [0215] works are worthless to **God** but worth something to us.
A P : 0 4 :342(159) [0215] of that worthiness whereby **God** obligates himself to
A P : 0 4 :342(160) [0215] since no one fears, loves, or trusts **God** as he ought.
A P : 0 4 :345(160) [0217] The judgment of **God** is another thing altogether.
A P : 0 4 :345(160) [0217] Here mercy has **God**'s clear and certain promise and his
A P : 0 4 :345(160) [0217] to believe that we have a gracious **God** because of Christ.
A P : 0 4 :345(160) [0217] "**God** sent the Son into the world, not to condemn the
A P : 0 4 :346(160) [0217] hope, for it rests on the Word and commandment of **God**.
A P : 0 4 :348(160) [0217] we might begin to do good works and obey **God**'s law.
A P : 0 4 :349(160) [0217] new impulses, the fear and love of **God**, hatred of lust, etc.
A P : 0 4 :350(161) [0217] in the conviction that **God** cares for us, forgives us, and
A P : 0 4 :351(161) [0217] as knowledge and fear of **God**, love of God, and hope.
A P : 0 4 :351(161) [0217] as knowledge and fear of God, love of **God**, and hope.
A P : 0 4 :351(161) [0217] the true knowledge of **God**, enabling us truly to fear him
A P : 0 4 :354(161) [0217] justified are children of **God** and fellow heirs with Christ
A P : 0 4 :355(161) [0217] spiritual rewards because they please **God** through faith.
A P : 0 4 :356(161) [0217] time makes us sons of **God** and fellow heirs with Christ
A P : 0 4 :356(161) [0217] as do many later writers, "**God** crowns his gifts in us."
A P : 0 4 :358(162) [0219] the faith that has access to **God** for Christ's sake, not for
A P : 0 4 :359(162) [0219] life or whether they please **God** only because of the faith
A P : 0 4 :360(162) [0219] therefore works please **God** for their own sake, not for the
A P : 0 4 :362(162) [0219] good works are pleasing to **God** because of faith, then we
A P : 0 4 :362(162) [0219] justification is strictly a gift of **God**; it is a thing promised.
A P : 0 4 :364(162) [0219] advantage, since they should work for the glory of **God**.
A P : 0 4 :364(163) [0219] know that it is the will of **God** to help, rescue, and save
A P : 0 4 :365(163) [0219] punishments the wrath of **God** is displayed, and hence this
A P : 0 4 :366(163) [0221] into the kingdom of **God**'s Son," as Paul says (Col. 1:13),
A P : 0 4 :368(163) [0221] we have been reconciled to **God**, justified, and reborn.
A P : 0 4 :368(163) [0221] the law would not please **God** unless we had been accepted
A P : 0 4 :368(163) [0221] keeping of the law pleases **God** and has its reward, both
A P : 0 4 :372(164) [0221] nor can good works please **God** without the mediator
A P : 0 4 :372(164) [0221] Heb. 11:6, "Without faith it is impossible to please **God**."
A P : 0 4 :375(164) [0223] grant that the fruits please **God** because of faith and the
A P : 0 4 :376(164) [0223] which believes that we have access to **God** not because of
A P : 0 4 :381(165) [0223] that good works please **God** because of grace and that
A P : 0 4 :381(165) [0223] therefore we must place our confidence in **God**'s grace.
A P : 0 4 :381(165) [0223] by which we love **God**, as though the ancients meant to
A P : 0 4 :381(165) [0223] Why not expound here **God**'s grace and mercy toward us?
A P : 0 4 :381(165) [0223] since we take hold of **God**'s mercy, reconciliation, and
A P : 0 4 :381(165) [0223] that good works please **God** because of grace; for faith
A P : 0 4 :382(165) [0225] by Christ's death and that **God** has been reconciled to us
A P : 0 4 :385(166) [0225] other good works please **God** because of faith, as the
A P : 0 4 :386(166) [0225] that we are justified before **God**, reconciled to him, and
A P : 0 4 :386(166) [0225] mind, and is convinced that **God** is reconciled and
A P : 0 4 :391(166) [0225] the idea that we can love **God** above all things by purely
A P : 0 4 :393(167) [0225] men were reconciled to **God** and justified by their own
A P : 0 4 :393(167) [0225] By nature men judge that **God** ought to be appeased by
A P : 0 7 :004(169) [0227] his seat in the temple of **God**" (II Thess. 2:4), that is, that
A P : 0 7 :014(170) [0231] by civil rites but by being **God**'s true people, reborn by
A P : 0 7 :014(170) [0231] were called the people of **God** inasmuch as God had
A P : 0 7 :014(170) [0231] people of God inasmuch as **God** had separated these
A P : 0 7 :014(170) [0231] Nevertheless, these evil people did not please **God**.
A P : 0 7 :015(170) [0231] the righteousness by which we are righteous before **God**.
A P : 0 7 :019(171) [0233] says that the kingdom of **God** is like a net (Matt. 13:47)
A P : 0 7 :021(172) [0233] of sins by their love for **God** before entering a state of
A P : 0 7 :031(174) [0237] in the heart nor righteousness in the heart before **God**.
A P : 0 7 :031(174) [0239] patience, the fear of **God**, the love of our neighbor, and
A P : 0 7 :032(174) [0239] they had come to worship **God** in so many ways, as
A P : 0 7 :032(174) [0239] to the righteousness of the heart or the worship of **God**.
A P : 0 7 :032(174) [0239] of the heart before **God** without these observances.
A P : 0 7 :034(175) [0239] an act of worship necessary for righteousness before **God**.
A P : 0 7 :034(175) [0239] for righteousness before **God**, it follows that somebody
A P : 0 7 :034(175) [0239] be righteous and a child of **God** even if he does not
A P : 0 7 :034(175) [0239] dress is not a devotion to **God** necessary for righteousness
A P : 0 7 :034(175) [0239] be righteous, children of **God**, and the church of Christ
A P : 0 7 :036(175) [0241] are not means by which **God** moves the heart to believe
A P : 0 7 :036(175) [0241] that they are necessary for righteousness before **God**.
A P : 0 7 :036(175) [0241] "The kingdom of **God** does not mean food and
A P : 0 7 :037(175) [0241] acts of devotion necessary for righteousness before **God**.
A P : 0 7 :039(176) [0241] such rites are necessary for righteousness before **God**.
A P : 0 7 :045(177) [0243] and of the kingdom of **God** if they regard as necessary a
A P : 0 7 :050(178) [0245] are truly ordinances of **God** and are preserved by God, so
A P : 0 7 :050(178) [0245] God and are preserved by **God**, so lawful governments are
A P : 0 7 :050(178) [0245] are ordinances of **God** and are preserved and defended by
A P : 0 7 :050(178) [0245] and are preserved and defended by **God** against the devil.
A P : 0 9 :002(178) [0245] this fruit from it, by **God**'s favor, that no Anabaptists
A P : 0 9 :002(178) [0245] people have been armed by **God**'s Word against the
A P : 0 9 :003(178) [0245] since it is evident that **God** approves the Baptism of little
A P : 0 9 :003(178) [0245] That **God** does approve the Baptism of little children is
A P : 0 9 :003(178) [0245] is shown by the fact that **God** gives the Holy Spirit to
A P : 1 1 :002(180) [0249] that it is the command of **God** — yes, the very voice of
A P : 1 1 :002(180) [0249] be sure that by this faith we are truly reconciled to **God**.
A P : 1 1 :005(181) [0249] "If any enter the church of **God** and are found never to
A P : 1 2 :003(182) [0253] true knowledge of Christ, and the true worship of **God**.
A P : 1 2 :006(183) [0255] Good **God**, how great is the darkness!
A P : 1 2 :007(183) [0255] keys forgives sins before the church but not before **God**.
A P : 1 2 :007(183) [0255] does not console us before **God**, what is there that will
A P : 1 2 :008(183) [0255] that Judas did not love **God** but feared the punishments.
A P : 1 2 :009(183) [0255] judge whether it fears **God** for his own sake or is running
A P : 1 2 :017(185) [0257] 1. On the basis of **God**'s covenant, we merit grace by good
A P : 1 2 :021(185) [0257] forgiveness of sins before the church, but not before **God**.
A P : 1 2 :022(185) [0257] not forgive sins before **God**, but it was instituted to
A P : 1 2 :029(185) [0259] are sorry because we love **God** and when because we fear
A P : 1 2 :029(185) [0259] of a conscience that feels **God**'s wrath against sin and is
A P : 1 2 :029(185) [0259] takes place when the Word of **God** denounces sin.
A P : 1 2 :032(186) [0259] terrors the conscience feels **God**'s wrath against sin,
A P : 1 2 :032(186) [0259] at the same time it flees **God**'s horrible wrath, for human
A P : 1 2 :032(186) [0259] cannot bear it unless it is sustained by the Word of **God**.
A P : 1 2 :034(186) [0261] sorrows and terrors men merit grace if they love **God**.
A P : 1 2 :034(186) [0261] Yet how will men love **God** amid such real terrors when
A P : 1 2 :034(186) [0261] they feel the terrible and indescribable wrath of **God**?
A P : 1 2 :036(186) [0261] "Since we are justified by faith, we have peace with **God**."
A P : 1 2 :036(186) [0261] This faith justifies before **God**, as the same passage
A P : 1 2 :040(187) [0261] Because **God** truly quickens through the Word, the keys
A P : 1 2 :046(188) [0263] with him through faith in the working of **God**" (v. 12).
A P : 1 2 :049(188) [0265] in contrition by the Word of **God** which offers us grace.
A P : 1 2 :051(189) [0265] He calls it **God**'s alien work to terrify because God's own
A P : 1 2 :051(189) [0265] work to terrify because **God**'s own proper work is to
A P : 1 2 :051(189) [0265] hearts that do not feel **God**'s wrath in their smugness
A P : 1 2 :053(189) [0265] are the two chief works of **God** in men, to terrify and to
A P : 1 2 :055(189) [0267] Then **God** promised grace and said there would be a seed
A P : 1 2 :060(190) [0267] faith which believes that **God** exists, that punishments
A P : 1 2 :062(190) [0269] to believe absolution but the accusation that **God** is a liar?
A P : 1 2 :062(190) [0269] doubts, it maintains that **God**'s promises are uncertain
A P : 1 2 :062(190) [0269] "He who does not believe **God** has made him a liar
A P : 1 2 :062(191) [0269] believed in the testimony that **God** has borne to his Son."
A P : 1 2 :063(191) [0269] to Rom. 3:25, "Whom **God** put forward as an expiation
A P : 1 2 :064(191) [0269] love against the wrath of **God**, but it finds peace only
A P : 1 2 :072(192) [0271] know, therefore, that **God** commands them to believe that
A P : 1 2 :072(192) [0271] with this command of **God** against despair and against
A P : 1 2 :073(192) [0273] by the forbearance of **God**; but add further that you also
A P : 1 2 :075(193) [0273] elicits an act of love to **God**, he merits the attainment of
A P : 1 2 :075(193) [0273] own works rather than in **God**'s Word and the promise of
A P : 1 2 :078(193) [0275] the wrath and judgment of **God**, according to the passage
A P : 1 2 :084(194) [0277] to set against the wrath of **God** not our works but Christ,
A P : 1 2 :084(194) [0277] which no one can stand before the judgment of **God**.
A P : 1 2 :085(194) [0277] ought to set our love and works against the wrath of **God**.
A P : 1 2 :085(194) [0277] before being reconciled to **God** through Christ, though
A P : 1 2 :086(194) [0277] and to offer our works to **God** before being reconciled to
A P : 1 2 :086(194) [0277] before being reconciled to **God** and becoming the
A P : 1 2 :086(195) [0277] by faith we are reconciled to **God** before we keep the law.
A P : 1 2 :087(195) [0277] works against the wrath of **God** or trust in our love or
A P : 1 2 :088(195) [0277] always accuse us because we never satisfy the law of **God**.
A P : 1 2 :088(195) [0277] unless we know it is **God**'s command and the Gospel itself
A P : 1 2 :089(195) [0277] how can they call upon **God**, how can they be sure that he
A P : 1 2 :089(195) [0279] their whole life is without **God** and without the true
A P : 1 2 :089(195) [0279] life is without God and without the true worship of **God**.
A P : 1 2 :094(196) [0281] "As I live, says the Lord **God**, I have no pleasure in the
A P : 1 2 :094(196) [0281] in the death of the wicked, **God** shows that he requires the
A P : 1 2 :094(196) [0281] is forgiven, he denies that **God** has sworn to the truth; a
A P : 1 2 :094(196) [0281] When **God** says, 'As I live,' he wants to be believed.
A P : 1 2 :094(196) [0281] Oh, blessed are we for whose sake **God** swears an oath!
A P : 1 2 :095(196) [0281] must believe firmly that **God** freely forgives us because of
A P : 1 2 :099(197) [0281] which is the Word of **God** that the power of the keys
A P : 1 2 :106(197) [0283] that he neglects the fear of **God** or faith or his concern for
A P : 1 2 :106(197) [0283] the fear of God or faith or his concern for **God**'s Word.
A P : 1 2 :107(198) [0283] Such confession, made to **God**, is itself contrition.
A P : 1 2 :107(198) [0283] when confession is made to **God**, it must come from the
A P : 1 2 :107(198) [0283] is contrition; feeling **God**'s wrath, we confess that he is
A P : 1 2 :107(198) [0283] and yet we seek mercy because of the promise of **God**.
A P : 1 2 :112(198) [0285] forgiveness of sins before **God** but that satisfactions could
A P : 1 2 :113(199) [0285] are not necessary for the forgiveness of sins before **God**.
A P : 1 2 :114(199) [0285] sin by which they supposed they were reconciled to **God**.
A P : 1 2 :118(199) [0287] in the forgiveness of sin **God** remits the guilt, and yet,
A P : 1 2 :120(200) [0287] not for discipline in the church, but for placating **God**.
A P : 1 2 :123(200) [0289] May **God** destroy these wicked sophists who so sinfully
A P : 1 2 :123(200) [0289] sinfully twist the Word of **God** to suit their vain dreams!
A P : 1 2 :124(201) [0289] **God** will not long endure such impudence and malice.
A P : 1 2 :129(202) [0291] to fear the judgment of **God**; for the members of the
A P : 1 2 :131(202) [0291] faith is not ungrateful to **God** or contemptuous of his
A P : 1 2 :134(203) [0293] refuse, for one may not refuse the commandments of **God**
A P : 1 2 :139(203) [0295] We believe that **God**'s glory and command require
A P : 1 2 :140(204) [0295] — and not even works that **God** has commanded but the
A P : 1 2 :142(204) [0295] to our weakness **God** has fixed a certain limit which man
A P : 1 2 :142(204) [0295] These men imagine that **God**'s law deals with external,
A P : 1 2 :142(204) [0295] that it requires us to love **God** "with all our hearts," etc.
A P : 1 2 :142(204) [0295] can do external works that **God**'s law does not require, it
A P : 1 2 :142(204) [0295] to trust that thereby we make satisfaction to **God**'s law.
A P : 1 2 :143(204) [0295] charity, and fasting have **God**'s command: and where they
A P : 1 2 :143(204) [0297] are not commanded by **God**'s law but have a set form

Continued ▶

A P : 1 2 :143(204) [0297] says, to pay homage to **God** and to compensate for
A P : 1 2 :143(204) [0297] *operato* pay homage to **God** and compensate for eternal
A P : 1 2 :144(204) [0297] depart even further from **God**'s commands; of these there
A P : 1 2 :144(205) [0297] do not serve to placate **God**'s displeasure, as our
A P : 1 2 :145(205) [0297] rank them above the works of **God**'s commandments.
A P : 1 2 :145(205) [0297] they obscure the law of **God** in two ways: first, because
A P : 1 2 :145(205) [0297] and civil works satisfy **God**'s law; and second, because
A P : 1 2 :146(205) [0297] overcomes death, just as it overcomes the wrath of **God**.
A P : 1 2 :146(205) [0297] "Thanks be to **God**, who gives us the victory through our
A P : 1 2 :147(205) [0297] frees the heart from the wrath of **God** and eternal death.
A P : 1 2 :150(206) [0299] object that it is in accord with **God**'s justice to punish sin.
A P : 1 2 :151(206) [0299] with the household of **God**; and if it begins with us, what
A P : 1 2 :151(206) [0299] they may learn to seek **God**'s help and to acknowledge the
A P : 1 2 :151(206) [0299] us rely not on ourselves but on **God** who raises the dead."
A P : 1 2 :151(206) [0299] are a discipline by which **God** exercises the saints.
A P : 1 2 :156(207) [0301] which are the work of **God**, like contrition or terrors of
A P : 1 2 :156(207) [0301] suffer penalties which **God** imposes only on them, for the
A P : 1 2 :156(207) [0301] impose nor remit them; **God** imposes and remits them
A P : 1 2 :158(207) [0301] consciences see only **God**'s punishment and wrath, they
A P : 1 2 :158(207) [0301] they should not feel that **God** has rejected them but they
A P : 1 2 :158(207) [0301] important purposes, that **God** is doing his alien work in
A P : 1 2 :159(207) [0301] sin but "that the works of **God** might be made manifest in
A P : 1 2 :160(207) [0301] past deeds, but works of **God**, intended for our profit,
A P : 1 2 :160(207) [0301] profit, that the power of **God** might be made more
A P : 1 2 :160(207) [0303] Paul says, "The power of **God** is made perfect in
A P : 1 2 :160(207) [0303] It is the will of **God** that our bodies should be sacrifices,
A P : 1 2 :160(208) [0303] for eternal death; for this **God** has another price, the death
A P : 1 2 :161(208) [0303] of David when he says: "If **God** had threatened that
A P : 1 2 :161(208) [0303] Thus **God** imposed physical death on man because of sin,
A P : 1 2 :165(208) [0303] works commanded by **God** should not be transferred to
A P : 1 2 :166(208) [0303] — they were reconciled to **God** and saved their city from
A P : 1 2 :167(209) [0305] that is, that distrust of **God** and similar attitudes are
A P : 1 2 :174(210) [0307] fruits are commanded by **God**, they should be done to his
A P : 1 2 :176(210) [0307] **God**'s command is that the ministers of the Gospel
A P : 1 2 :177(210) [0307] reservation of guilt before **God** in the case of the truly
A P : 1 3 :001(211) [0309] signs and testimonies of **God**'s will toward us, through
A P : 1 3 :003(211) [0309] have the command of **God** and to which the promise of
A P : 1 3 :003(211) [0309] signs instituted without **God**'s command are not sure
A P : 1 3 :004(211) [0309] have the commandment of **God** and the promise of grace,
A P : 1 3 :004(211) [0309] should firmly believe that **God** really forgives us for
A P : 1 3 :005(211) [0309] the Word and the rite **God** simultaneously moves the
A P : 1 3 :006(212) [0311] for salvation since they do not have the command of **God**.
A P : 1 3 :006(212) [0311] an express command from **God** and a clear promise of
A P : 1 3 :011(212) [0311] ministry of the Word has **God**'s command and glorious
A P : 1 3 :011(212) [0311] Gospel is the power of **God** for salvation to every one
A P : 1 3 :012(212) [0311] for we know that **God** approves this ministry and is
A P : 1 3 :014(213) [0311] has the commandment of **God** and also certain promises,
A P : 1 3 :015(213) [0311] a sacrament because it has **God**'s command, then many
A P : 1 3 :015(213) [0311] because they have **God**'s command, as, for example,
A P : 1 3 :016(213) [0311] all the things that have **God**'s command and a promise
A P : 1 3 :016(213) [0311] It has both the command of **God** and many promises.
A P : 1 3 :017(213) [0313] in themselves are signs to which **God** has added promises.
A P : 1 3 :017(213) [0313] things are kept which have **God**'s command and promises.
A P : 1 3 :020(214) [0313] but as certain as though **God**, by a new miracle, promised
A P : 1 3 :021(214) [0313] a faith which believes in a general way that **God** exists.
A P : 1 4 :002(214) [0315] it how they will answer to **God** for disrupting the church.
A P : 1 4 :004(214) [0315] rightly teach the Word of **God** and rightly administer the
A P : 1 4 :004(215) [0315] to destroy the Word of **God** with their edicts, who even
A P : 1 4 :005(215) [0315] our defense, both before **God** and among all nations,
A P : 1 5 :001(215) [0315] instituted to appease **God**, to merit grace, and to make
A P : 1 5 :005(215) [0317] receive the forgiveness of sins and are reconciled to **God**.
A P : 1 5 :005(215) [0317] gain the forgiveness of sins and appease the wrath of **God**.
A P : 1 5 :006(215) [0317] that they have a gracious **God** not because of works but
A P : 1 5 :006(216) [0317] not your own doing, it is the gift of **God**" and not of men.
A P : 1 5 :008(216) [0317] accounted righteous before **God**, then Christ is of no use
A P : 1 5 :009(216) [0317] **God** has appointed Christ as the mediator; he wants to be
A P : 1 5 :009(216) [0317] These men believe that **God** is reconciled and gracious
A P : 1 5 :010(216) [0317] righteousness before **God** and therefore they obscured the
A P : 1 5 :011(216) [0317] that we have a gracious **God** for Christ's sake, it is an
A P : 1 5 :012(216) [0317] words, to the covenant of **God**, promising that he will be
A P : 1 5 :014(216) [0319] that these works please **God** since they do not have
A P : 1 5 :014(217) [0319] please God since they do not have support in **God**'s Word?
A P : 1 5 :014(217) [0319] How will he inform men of **God**'s will without the
A P : 1 5 :014(217) [0319] of God's will without the command and Word of **God**?
A P : 1 5 :014(217) [0319] Does not **God** throughout the prophets forbid the
A P : 1 5 :014(217) [0319] I the Lord am your **God**; walk in my statutes, and be
A P : 1 5 :017(217) [0319] by men without **God**'s command can justify since we can
A P : 1 5 :017(217) [0319] nothing about the will of **God** without the Word of God?
A P : 1 5 :017(217) [0319] nothing about the will of God without the Word of **God**?
A P : 1 5 :017(217) [0319] What if **God** does not approve these acts of worship?
A P : 1 5 :017(217) [0319] Word and testimony of **God**, and Paul says (Rom. 14:23),
A P : 1 5 :017(217) [0319] testimony in the Word of **God**, the conscience must doubt
A P : 1 5 :017(217) [0319] God, the conscience must doubt whether they please **God**.
A P : 1 5 :018(217) [0319] a new kind of worship of **God**, devised by human
A P : 1 5 :018(217) [0319] seeks to be justified before **God**, denying that men are
A P : 1 5 :018(217) [0319] are freely justified before **God** by faith for Christ's sake.
A P : 1 5 :019(218) [0319] "He shall honor the **god** of fortresses instead of these: a
A P : 1 5 :019(218) [0319] instead of these: a **god** whom his fathers did not know he
A P : 1 5 :019(218) [0321] of rites, for he says that a **god** will be worshiped whom
A P : 1 5 :021(218) [0321] What is this but honoring **God** "with gold and silver and
A P : 1 5 :022(218) [0321] supposes that such works justify men and reconcile **God**.
A P : 1 5 :025(218) [0321] the commandments of **God** are obscured; for when men
A P : 1 5 :025(219) [0323] them to the works that **God** commands, like the tasks of
A P : 1 5 :029(219) [0323] rites, let us therefore arm ourselves with the Word of **God**
A P : 1 5 :029(219) [0323] nor justification before **God**, and that they are not
A P : 1 5 :031(219) [0323] do you make a trial of **God** by putting a yoke," etc., Peter
A P : 1 5 :035(220) [0325] claiming any value before **God** for them, just as there is
A P : 1 5 :035(220) [0325] as there is no value before **God** in observing secular
A P : 1 5 :042(221) [0327] But the chief worship of **God** is the preaching of the
A P : 1 5 :043(221) [0327] penitence, the fear of **God**, faith in Christ, the
A P : 1 5 :045(221) [0327] the troubles with which **God** disciplines us effect a genuine
A P : 1 5 :045(221) [0327] this comes, we must obey **God**'s will, as Paul says (Rom.
A P : 1 5 :047(221) [0327] diligent at all times because **God** commands it at all times
A P : 1 6 :001(222) [0329] lawful civil ordinances are **God**'s good creatures and
A P : 1 6 :002(222) [0331] it is the knowledge of **God** in the heart, the fear of God
A P : 1 6 :002(222) [0331] in the heart, the fear of **God** and faith, the beginning of
A P : 1 6 :006(223) [0331] the change of winter and summer as ordinances of **God**.
A P : 1 6 :007(223) [0331] and it is a work of **God** according to Paul (Rom. 13:1ff.).
A P : 1 6 :009(224) [0333] of the heart, like a deep fear of **God** and a strong faith.
A P : 1 6 :012(224) [0333] or of laws, they are legitimate in the sight of **God** as well.
A P : 1 6 :013(224) [0333] even though these have **God**'s command while the
A P : 1 6 :013(224) [0333] the Platonic commune does not have **God**'s command.
A P : 1 8 :002(225) [0335] Holy Spirit men can love **God** and perform "the essence
A P : 1 8 :004(225) [0335] It can talk about **God** and express its worship of him in
A P : 1 8 :006(225) [0335] have neither the fear of **God** nor trust in God nor the faith
A P : 1 8 :006(225) [0335] fear of God nor trust in **God** nor the faith that God hears,
A P : 1 8 :006(225) [0335] in God nor the faith that **God** hears, forgives, helps, or
A P : 1 8 :006(225) [0335] "without faith it is impossible to please" **God** (Heb. 11:6).
A P : 1 8 :007(225) [0337] capacity for true fear of **God**, true faith in God, true
A P : 1 8 :007(225) [0337] fear of God, true faith in **God**, true knowledge and trust
A P : 1 8 :007(226) [0337] knowledge and trust that **God** considers, hears, and
A P : 1 8 :007(226) [0337] his natural powers, "does not perceive the things of **God**."
A P : 1 8 :008(226) [0337] their hearts believe about **God**'s will, whether they really
A P : 1 8 :008(226) [0337] they really believe that **God** regards and hears them.
A P : 1 8 :009(226) [0337] men ought to know that **God** requires this civil
A P : 1 8 :010(226) [0337] men can obey the law of **God** without the Holy Spirit and
A P : 1 9 :001(226) [0337] There we confess that **God** alone has established all of
A P : 1 9 :001(226) [0337] of men turning away from **God**, as Christ said about the
A P : 2 0 :003(227) [0339] men are righteous before **God** not through faith but
A P : 2 0 :005(227) [0339] the other hand, teach that **God** has laid our iniquities on
A P : 2 0 :010(228) [0341] that it thought adequate to placate the wrath of **God**?
A P : 2 1 :004(229) [0343] we should thank **God** for showing examples of his mercy,
A P : 2 1 :010(230) [0345] how do we know that **God** approves such invocation?
A P : 2 1 :012(230) [0345] proved from the Word of **God**, we cannot affirm that the
A P : 2 1 :012(230) [0345] are aware of it or, even if they are, that **God** approves it.
A P : 2 1 :017(231) [0347] there must be a Word of **God** to assure us that God is
A P : 2 1 :017(231) [0347] of God to assure us that **God** is willing to have mercy and
A P : 2 1 :018(231) [0347] Jesus Christ himself, and **God** our Father, comfort your
A P : 2 1 :020(232) [0349] Such trust in **God**'s promise and Christ's merits must be
A P : 2 1 :021(232) [0349] though they have neither **God**'s promise nor a command
A P : 2 1 :029(233) [0351] merits to us, as though **God** were reconciled to us or
A P : 2 1 :031(233) [0351] have neither a Word of **God** nor an example from
A P : 2 1 :031(233) [0351] of Christ because only this has **God**'s promise.
A P : 2 1 :033(233) [0351] if it has no command or proof in the Word of **God**?
A P : 2 1 :036(234) [0353] constantly affirmed that **God** hears the prayers of
A P : 2 1 :044(236) [0357] responsibility before **God** to maintain and propagate
A P : 2 1 :044(236) [0357] **God** demands this when he honors kings with his own
A P : 2 1 :044(236) [0357] of Christ, and as vicars of **God** they should defend the life
A P : 2 2 :012(238) [0361] In the judgment of **God**, will the reasons he gives
A P : 2 2 :016(238) [0361] out how they will account to **God** for their decisions.
A P : 2 3 :004(239) [0365] taken from the Word of **God**, while our opponents set
A P : 2 3 :006(240) [0365] only the judgment of any honest and **God**-fearing man.
A P : 2 3 :007(240) [0365] Since this ordinance of **God** cannot be suspended without
A P : 2 3 :007(240) [0365] an extraordinary work of **God**, it follows that neither
A P : 2 3 :008(240) [0365] The Word of **God** did not form the nature of men to be
A P : 2 3 :008(240) [0367] the nature of man without an extraordinary act of **God**.
A P : 2 3 :009(241) [0367] that ordinance which **God** has built into nature, and
A P : 2 3 :012(241) [0367] an extraordinary act of **God** can change this right, the
A P : 2 3 :012(241) [0367] other is an ordinance of **God**, and therefore it is a right;
A P : 2 3 :018(242) [0369] they order men to pray **God** for continence and to subdue
A P : 2 3 :019(242) [0369] **God** wants the rest to use the universal law of nature
A P : 2 3 :023(242) [0371] (Matt. 19:6), "What **God** has joined together, let no man
A P : 2 3 :028(243) [0371] sanctified by the Word of **God**; that is, it is something
A P : 2 3 :028(243) [0371] which the Word of **God** permits and approves, as the
A P : 2 3 :029(243) [0371] he says in Matt. 19:6, "What **God** has joined together."
A P : 2 3 :030(243) [0371] by the word of **God** and prayer" (I Tim. 4:5): by the Word
A P : 2 3 :030(243) [0371] assures the conscience that **God** approves, and by prayer,
A P : 2 3 :030(243) [0371] that is, by faith which uses it gratefully as a gift of **God**.
A P : 2 3 :032(244) [0373] follow everyone's faith, pleasing **God** because of faith.
A P : 2 3 :032(244) [0373] So a woman's duties please **God** because of faith, and a
A P : 2 3 :033(244) [0373] means that something has **God**'s permission and
A P : 2 3 :033(244) [0373] are pure since they are approved by the Word of **God**.
A P : 2 3 :034(244) [0373] is pure in the godly, through the Word of **God** and faith.
A P : 2 3 :036(244) [0373] when we believe that for his sake **God** is gracious to us.
A P : 2 3 :039(244) [0375] more righteous before **God** than building makes an
A P : 2 3 :039(244) [0375] that through faith he is accounted righteous before **God**.
A P : 2 3 :045(245) [0377] and hardly pleasing to **God**, even though it was not
A P : 2 3 :046(246) [0377] obscures the recognition of **God**'s commands and gifts,
A P : 2 3 :053(246) [0377] So **God** takes revenge against those who despise his gift
A P : 2 3 :053(246) [0379] so that we ought to use the remedies **God** has given us.
A P : 2 3 :054(246) [0379] Sodom and Gomorrah reveal **God**'s wrath at human vice.
A P : 2 3 :059(247) [0379] are certainly displeasing to **God**, we do not regret our lack
A P : 2 3 :063(247) [0381] They say, first, that it was revealed by **God**.
A P : 2 3 :064(248) [0381] is not pure in the sight of **God**, and that because of faith
A P : 2 3 :070(249) [0383] to the judgment of **God**, who will call them to account for
A P : 2 3 :070(249) [0383] **God** will avenge this cruelty.
A P : 2 3 :070(249) [0383] that in the judgment of **God** no perversion of God's Word
A P : 2 3 :070(249) [0383] of God no perversion of **God**'s Word will stand, as Isaiah
A P : 2 3 :071(249) [0383] it is certainly contrary to **God**'s will and Word to break
A P : 2 3 :071(249) [0383] respect for the Word of **God** than for anything else,
A P : 2 4 :013(251) [0387] think they can placate **God**'s wrath, gain the remission of
A P : 2 4 :016(252) [0389] them he would follow in his footsteps as those of a **god**.
A P : 2 4 :018(252) [0389] a ceremony or act in which **God** offers us the content of
A P : 2 4 :018(252) [0389] an act which we offer to **God** but one in which God
A P : 2 4 :018(252) [0389] to God but one in which **God** baptizes us through a
A P : 2 4 :018(252) [0389] Here **God** offers and presents the forgiveness of sins
A P : 2 4 :018(252) [0389] a ceremony or act which we render to **God** to honor him.
A P : 2 4 :019(252) [0389] punishment that reconciles **God** or placates his wrath or
A P : 2 4 :021(252) [0391] of sins in the sight of **God**, but they did on the basis of the
A P : 2 4 :023(253) [0391] was to come to reconcile **God** and make satisfaction for
A P : 2 4 :023(253) [0391] that men might know that **God** does not want our own
A P : 2 4 :023(253) [0391] to placate the wrath of **God** when, amid great calamities,
A P : 2 4 :023(253) [0391] was going to placate **God** for the whole human race.
A P : 2 4 :023(253) [0391] offering to reconcile **God** by his merits instead of ours.
A P : 2 4 :026(254) [0391] holy and acceptable to **God**, which is your spiritual
A P : 2 4 :026(254) [0391] knows and takes hold of **God**, as it does when it fears and

Continued ▶

A P : 2 4 :026(254) [0391] suppose they are offering **God** a work *ex opere operato.*
A P : 2 4 :026(254) [0393] a sacrifice of praise to **God**," with the interpretation, "that
A P : 2 4 :027(254) [0393] **God** is spirit, and those who worship him must worship in
A P : 2 4 :028(254) [0393] I gave them, 'Obey my voice, and I will be your **God**.'"
A P : 2 4 :028(254) [0393] Clearly **God** had commanded the fathers concerning
A P : 2 4 :028(254) [0393] that did not come from **God**, namely, that such worship
A P : 2 4 :028(254) [0393] He adds that **God** had commanded faith.
A P : 2 4 :028(254) [0393] is, "Believe that I am your **God** and that this is the way I
A P : 2 4 :028(254) [0393] Believe that I want to be **God**, the one who justifies and
A P : 2 4 :029(255) [0393] declares that calling upon **God** is really worshiping and
A P : 2 4 :029(255) [0393] The sacrifice acceptable to **God** is a broken spirit; a
A P : 2 4 :029(255) [0393] broken and contrite heart, O **God**, thou wilt not despise."
A P : 2 4 :030(255) [0395] that sacrifices do not reconcile **God** *ex opere operato.*
A P : 2 4 :032(255) [0395] They call upon **God**, they give thanks to God, they bear
A P : 2 4 :032(255) [0395] God, they give thanks to **God**, they bear afflictions in
A P : 2 4 :033(256) [0395] Among the praises of **God** or sacrifices of praise we
A P : 2 4 :034(256) [0395] service of the gospel of **God**, so that the offering of the
A P : 2 4 :034(256) [0397] may become offerings acceptable to **God** through faith.
A P : 2 4 :038(257) [0399] that by the death of Christ **God** has been reconciled.
A P : 2 4 :043(258) [0399] with the claim that these justify men before **God**.
A P : 2 4 :048(258) [0401] By the blessing of **God**, the priests in our churches pay
A P : 2 4 :048(258) [0401] of the good works which **God** commands, and they talk
A P : 2 4 :051(259) [0403] describes as worshiping their **God** with gold and silver.
A P : 2 4 :052(259) [0403] of men in relation to **God**, to offer gifts and sacrifices for
A P : 2 4 :053(259) [0403] of sins in the sight of **God**; as we have already said, they
A P : 2 4 :054(259) [0403] or reconciliation before **God**, but only to symbolize the
A P : 2 4 :057(260) [0405] forgiveness of sins before **God** and that by analogy there
A P : 2 4 :058(260) [0405] that was valid for the sins of others and reconciled **God**.
A P : 2 4 :062(260) [0405] this the church might have a service that reconciles **God**."
A P : 2 4 :068(262) [0409] idea that ignores the chief use of what **God** has instituted.
A P : 2 4 :069(262) [0409] among men, but signs of **God**'s will toward us; so it is
A P : 2 4 :072(262) [0409] we should acknowledge the will and mercy of **God**.
A P : 2 4 :074(263) [0411] itself as praise to **God**, as a demonstration of its gratitude,
A P : 2 4 :074(263) [0411] gratitude, and a witness of its high esteem for **God**'s gifts.
A P : 2 4 :076(263) [0411] compares the greatness of **God**'s blessings with the
A P : 2 4 :080(264) [0411] of the sacraments of **God**," that is, of the Word and
A P : 2 4 :080(264) [0411] ambassadors for Christ, **God** making his appeal through
A P : 2 4 :080(264) [0411] We beseech you on behalf of Christ, be reconciled to **God**
A P : 2 4 :082(264) [0411] but also causes many to thank **God** more abundantly.
A P : 2 4 :089(266) [0413] without the command of **God** and the example of
A P : 2 4 :089(266) [0415] is an abuse of the name of **God** in violation of the Second
A P : 2 4 :089(266) [0415] a sacrifice that reconciles **God** and makes satisfaction for
A P : 2 4 :097(268) [0417] the sacrifices instituted by **God** with this wicked notion in
A P : 2 4 :098(268) [0417] yet the church of **God** was there, condemning wicked
A P : 2 4 :098(268) [0419] services invented against **God**'s command to obscure the
A P : 2 7 :007(269) [0421] Without doubt, **God** will soon avenge these murders.
A P : 2 7 :011(270) [0423] forgiveness of sins before **God** or makes satisfaction for
A P : 2 7 :011(270) [0423] sins before God or makes satisfaction for sins before **God**.
A P : 2 7 :017(271) [0425] against the wrath of **God** for us so that we might be freely
A P : 2 7 :017(271) [0425] against the wrath of **God**; whoever tries to attain to the
A P : 2 7 :020(272) [0427] has neither a command of **God** nor a promise, on the
A P : 2 7 :020(272) [0427] and a promise of **God**, which contains a covenant of grace
A P : 2 7 :023(272) [0427] accounted righteous before **God** and through which we
A P : 2 7 :023(273) [0427] these are services which **God** approves as righteousness
A P : 2 7 :023(273) [0427] when they have no proof for this from the Word of **God**?
A P : 2 7 :025(273) [0427] shall love the Lord your **God** with all your heart" (Deut.
A P : 2 7 :025(273) [0429] not think correctly about **God**, they do not fear him
A P : 2 7 :025(273) [0429] do not fear him enough, they do not believe **God** enough.
A P : 2 7 :026(273) [0429] said (I Cor. 8:8), "Food does not commend us to **God**."
A P : 2 7 :027(273) [0429] Because the kingdom of **God** is righteousness (Rom.
A P : 2 7 :027(273) [0429] to grow in the fear of **God**, in trust in the mercy promised
A P : 2 7 :028(274) [0429] as by the grace of **God** any monk can maintain it.
A P : 2 7 :030(274) [0431] **God** does not even give his own law the honor of meriting
A P : 2 7 :032(274) [0431] and do not set their merits against the judgment of **God**.
A P : 2 7 :032(274) [0431] of sins except by **God**'s indulgence; secondly, that you
A P : 2 7 :037(275) [0433] is, growth in the fear of **God**, in faith, in the love of their
A P : 2 7 :038(275) [0433] that when Anthony asked **God** to show him what progress
A P : 2 7 :038(275) [0433] making in his way of life, **God** pointed in a dream to a
A P : 2 7 :041(276) [0435] without a command of **God**; this Christ does not approve,
A P : 2 7 :041(276) [0435] know that the command of **God** forbids deserting wife
A P : 2 7 :041(276) [0435] happens by a command of **God**, when a government or a
A P : 2 7 :042(276) [0435] this that it is a service to **God** to commit suicide and to
A P : 2 7 :042(276) [0435] and to leave our body without the command of **God**.
A P : 2 7 :042(276) [0435] that it is a service to **God** to leave possessions, friends,
A P : 2 7 :042(276) [0435] friends, wife, and children without the command of **God**.
A P : 2 7 :046(277) [0435] approved by the Word of **God** in the commandment (Ex.
A P : 2 7 :047(277) [0437] of everything for **God** is meritorious and holy and the
A P : 2 7 :052(278) [0437] their traditions, contrary to the clear command of **God**.
A P : 2 7 :052(278) [0437] for setting up traditions contrary to the command of **God**
A P : 2 7 :054(278) [0437] penitence, about works that have the command of **God**.
A P : 2 7 :055(278) [0439] are the worship of **God** to merit the forgiveness of sins for
A P : 2 7 :058(279) [0439] forgiveness of sins before **God** or to justify before God.
A P : 2 7 :058(279) [0439] forgiveness of sins before God or to justify before **God**.
A P : 2 7 :058(279) [0439] up without a Word of **God** as an act of worship to merit
A P : 2 7 :058(279) [0439] which had a Word of **God** and was not meant to merit the
A P : 2 7 :061(279) [0441] Seed, through the mercy of **God** — they would attain
A P : 2 7 :061(280) [0441] for their obedience, which **God** commanded (Ex. 20:12),
A P : 2 7 :069(281) [0443] cinctures — all these are unprofitable services before **God**.
A P : 2 7 :070(281) [0443] of such services, and that **God** is pleased only with
A P : 2 8 :004(281) [0445] unless they act in clear opposition to **God**'s commands.
A P : 2 8 :005(281) [0445] **God** undoubtedly sees and hears them, and it is to him
A P : 2 8 :007(282) [0445] (Rom. 14:17), "The kingdom of **God** is not food or drink."
A P : 2 8 :008(282) [0445] or were acts of worship that pleased **God** as righteousness
A P : 2 8 :008(282) [0445] "Why do you make a trial of **God**?" they say (Acts 15:10).
A P : 2 8 :009(282) [0445] they acts of worship which please **God** as righteousness?
A P : 2 8 :010(282) [0447] things, the Word of **God** and the Holy Spirit, that work
A P : 2 8 :011(283) [0447] acts of worship that please **God** as righteousness or to
A P : 2 8 :014(283) [0447] a definite Word of **God**, which he ought to teach and
A P : 2 8 :021(284) [0449] commands that we must obey **God** rather than men.
A P : 2 8 :021(284) [0449] are the worship of **God**; that they are necessary acts of
A P : 2 8 :025(285) [0451] For we must obey **God** rather than men (Acts 5:29).
S 1 : P R :003(289) [0455] until now and where, by **God**'s grace, I will continue to
S 1 : P R :005(289) [0457] or ultimately the wrath of **God** — answer them as they
S 1 : P R :007(289) [0457] the people on their side, **God** has constantly promoted his
S 1 : P R :009(290) [0457] **God** convert those who are capable of conversion and
S 1 : P R :010(290) [0457] need such a council, for by **God**'s grace our churches have
S 1 : P R :013(290) [0459] estates as are contrary to **God**, their hands would be so
S 1 : P R :013(291) [0459] If we would first carry out **God**'s commands and precepts
S 1 : P R :014(291) [0459] for, apart from these, **God** has laid so many tasks upon us
S 1 : P R :014(291) [0459] which are commanded by **God**, are neither regarded nor
S 1 : P R :014(291) [0459] is as if we were to expect **God** to acquiesce in our
S 1 : P R :014(291) [0459] sins oppress us and keep **God** from being gracious to us,
S 1 : 0 1 :000(291) [0461] and nature, are one **God**, who created heaven and earth,
S 1 : 0 1 :000(292) [0461] seated at the right hand of **God**, will come to judge the
S 2 : 0 1 :001(292) [0461] this, that Jesus Christ, our **God** and Lord, "was put to
S 2 : 0 1 :002(292) [0461] He alone is "the Lamb of **God**, who takes away the sin of
S 2 : 0 1 :002(292) [0461] "**God** has laid upon him the iniquities of us all" (Isa. 53:6)
S 2 : 0 1 :004(292) [0461] and again, "that he [**God**] himself is righteous and
S 2 : 0 2 :001(293) [0463] be done by the Lamb of **God** alone, as has been stated
S 2 : 0 2 :002(293) [0463] They are not commanded by **God**.
S 2 : 0 2 :005(293) [0463] godly, Christian, sensible, **God**-fearing people — especially
S 2 : 0 2 :005(293) [0463] was fabricated and invented without **God**'s Word and will
S 2 : 0 2 :007(294) [0465] themselves and others to **God** and obtain and merit grace
S 2 : 0 2 :007(294) [0465] he does but the Lamb of **God** and the Son of God who
S 2 : 0 2 :007(294) [0465] of God and the Son of **God** who takes away our sin."
S 2 : 0 2 :008(294) [0465] and imagination without the sanction of **God**'s Word.
S 2 : 0 2 :010(294) [0465] So by **God**'s help I would suffer myself to be burned to
S 2 : 0 2 :013(295) [0467] That is the prerogative of **God** alone.
S 2 : 0 2 :015(295) [0467] means that the Word of **God** shall establish articles of
S 2 : 0 2 :018(296) [0467] forgiveness of sins, and **God**'s grace were sought here,
S 2 : 0 2 :018(296) [0467] own parishes, the Word of **God**, their wives and children,
S 2 : 0 2 :023(296) [0469] Mass, etc., their use is a good work and a service of **God**.
S 2 : 0 2 :024(296) [0469] power of the pope but by the preaching of **God**'s Word.
S 2 : 0 2 :026(297) [0469] Such honor belongs to **God** alone.
S 2 : 0 3 :002(298) [0471] life and to the offices and callings established by **God**.
S 2 : 0 3 :002(298) [0471] the prophets call such service of **God** *aven,* that is, vanity.
S 2 : 0 4 :001(298) [0471] right or according to **God**'s Word, for this position
S 2 : 0 4 :003(298) [0471] secular government, where **God** sometimes permits much
S 2 : 0 4 :004(299) [0473] you consider me your **god** and are obedient and subject to
S 2 : 0 4 :007(299) [0473] by divine right or by **God**'s command; suppose that it
S 2 : 0 4 :008(300) [0473] and in whatever church **God** would raise up a man fitted
S 2 : 0 4 :010(300) [0475] since it is neither established nor commanded by **God**.
S 2 : 0 4 :011(300) [0475] what St. Paul calls exalting oneself over and against **God**.
S 2 : 0 4 :012(300) [0475] unwilling to do even if we have to die for it in **God**'s name
S 2 : 0 4 :013(300) [0475] to claim to be an earthly **god** and even presumed to issue
S 2 : 0 4 :014(301) [0475] as a mention of Christ, faith, and **God**'s commandments.
S 2 : 0 4 :014(301) [0475] papacy) in contradiction to **God**, and to damn, slay, and
S 2 : 0 4 :014(301) [0475] devil himself as our lord or **God**, so we cannot suffer his
S 3 : 0 1 :002(302) [0477] being without the fear of **God**, presumption, despair,
S 3 : 0 1 :002(302) [0477] ignorance or disregard of **God** — and then also lying,
S 3 : 0 1 :002(302) [0477] also lying, swearing by **God**'s name, failure to pray and
S 3 : 0 1 :002(302) [0477] to pray and call upon **God**, neglect of God's Word,
S 3 : 0 1 :002(302) [0477] call upon God, neglect of **God**'s Word, disobedience to
S 3 : 0 1 :006(302) [0477] to observe and keep all the commandments of **God**.
S 3 : 0 1 :007(302) [0477] his natural powers to love **God** above all things and his
S 3 : 0 1 :008(302) [0477] if man does what he can, **God** is certain to grant him his
S 3 : 0 2 :001(303) [0479] that the law was given by **God** first of all to restrain sins
S 3 : 0 2 :004(303) [0479] neither has nor cares for **God** or that he worships strange
S 3 : 0 2 :004(303) [0479] it, and begins to be alienated from **God**, to murmur, etc.
S 3 : 0 3 :001(303) [0479] Rom. 1:18, "The wrath of **God** is revealed from heaven
S 3 : 0 3 :001(303) [0479] may be held accountable to **God**, for no human being will
S 3 : 0 3 :002(304) [0479] by means of which **God** with one blow destroys both open
S 3 : 0 3 :005(304) [0481] how they stood before **God** and recognize themselves as
S 3 : 0 3 :008(304) [0481] ways than one, for with **God** there is plenteous redemption
S 3 : 0 3 :010(305) [0481] accordingly, and that **God** will assuredly grant his grace
S 3 : 0 3 :012(305) [0481] merited forgiveness and has paid for his sins before **God**.
S 3 : 0 3 :013(305) [0483] "Prolong my life, Lord **God**, until I make satisfaction for
S 3 : 0 3 :014(305) [0483] works to overcome and blot out their sins before **God**.
S 3 : 0 3 :015(305) [0483] meanwhile the sinner was commended to the grace of **God**
S 3 : 0 3 :016(305) [0483] in order to avail before **God**, this consolation was offered:
S 3 : 0 3 :018(306) [0483] matters which pertain to **God**, seeking consolation in its
S 3 : 0 3 :019(306) [0485] for such humiliation would surely earn grace before **God**.
S 3 : 0 3 :032(308) [0487] unbelief, blindness, and ignorance of **God** and God's will.
S 3 : 0 3 :032(308) [0487] unbelief, blindness, and ignorance of God and **God**'s will.
S 3 : 0 3 :032(308) [0487] No man can be just before **God** without him.
S 3 : 0 3 :033(308) [0489] no, not one; no one understands, no one seeks for **God**.
S 3 : 0 3 :038(309) [0489] of the innocent Lamb of **God** who takes away the sin of
S 3 : 0 3 :045(310) [0491] says, "No one born of **God** commits sin; he cannot sin."
S 3 : 0 4 :000(310) [0491] in more than one way, for **God** is surpassingly rich in his
S 3 : 0 5 :001(310) [0491] else than the Word of **God** in water, commanded by the
S 3 : 0 5 :002(310) [0491] who forget the Word (**God**'s institution) and say that God
S 3 : 0 5 :002(310) [0491] institution) and say that **God** has joined to the water a
S 3 : 0 5 :003(311) [0493] takes place only through **God**'s will and not at all through
S 3 : 0 6 :004(311) [0493] we condemn and curse in **God**'s name those who not only
S 3 : 0 6 :004(311) [0493] against and over Christ, our Lord and **God**, etc.
S 3 : 0 7 :001(311) [0493] which are subtle and secret and which **God** alone perceives
S 3 : 0 7 :002(311) [0493] is not in our power but in **God**'s alone to judge which,
S 3 : 0 8 :003(312) [0495] to the conviction that **God** gives no one his Spirit or grace
S 3 : 0 8 :005(312) [0495] from the external Word of **God** to spiritualizing and to
S 3 : 0 8 :008(313) [0495] he was justified before **God**, and his prayers and alms
S 3 : 0 8 :008(313) [0495] alms were acceptable to **God** in this faith (Luke calls him
S 3 : 0 8 :008(313) [0495] calls him "devout" and "**God**-fearing"), but he could not
S 3 : 0 8 :010(313) [0497] constantly maintain that **God** will not deal with us except
S 3 : 0 8 :011(313) [0497] For even to Moses **God** wished to appear first through
S 3 : 0 8 :013(313) [0497] were moved by the Holy Spirit, yet as holy men of **God**.
S 3 : 1 1 :002(315) [0499] separate such creatures of **God** or forbid them to live
S 3 : 1 1 :003(315) [0499] marriage to be free, as **God** ordained and instituted it, and
S 3 : 1 1 :003(315) [0499] shall not disrupt or hinder **God**'s work, for St. Paul says
S 3 : 1 2 :002(315) [0499] of the church, for, thank **God**, a seven-year-old child
S 3 : 1 2 :003(315) [0499] but it consists of the Word of **God** and true faith.
S 3 : 1 3 :000(315) [0499] How Man Is Justified Before **God**, and His Good Works
S 3 : 1 3 :001(315) [0499] and clean heart and that **God** will and does account us
S 3 : 1 3 :003(315) [0499] are considered apart from **God**'s grace and mercy, but, as
S 3 : 1 3 :003(315) [0499] to say, all is well if we boast that we have a gracious **God**.
S 3 : 1 5 :003(316) [0501] and on which I will stand, **God** willing, until my death.
S 3 : 1 5 :005(316) [0501] for adoration to their **god** and to themselves until they

Continued ▶

S 3 : 1 5 :005(317) [0501] Figenbotz, for the glory of **God** subscribe that I have thus
T R : 0 0 :006(320) [0505] faith or commandments of **God**, binding on the
T R : 0 0 :006(320) [0505] and is even to be preferred to the commandments of **God**.
T R : 0 0 :010(321) [0507] depends on the Word of **God**, that Peter was not superior
T R : 0 0 :025(324) [0511] when he declared Jesus to be the Christ, the Son of **God**.
T R : 0 0 :026(324) [0511] world and exists wherever **God** gives his gifts, apostles,
T R : 0 0 :028(325) [0513] than "You are the Christ, the Son of the living **God**"?
T R : 0 0 :029(325) [0513] that he should say, 'You are the Son of the living **God**.'
T R : 0 0 :038(326) [0515] in Acts, "We must obey **God** rather than men" (Acts
T R : 0 0 :039(327) [0515] against every so-called **god** or object of worship, so that
T R : 0 0 :039(327) [0515] his seat in the temple of **God**, proclaiming himself to be
T R : 0 0 :039(327) [0515] of God, proclaiming himself to be **God**" (II Thess. 2:3, 4).
T R : 0 0 :040(327) [0515] the worship instituted by **God**, and he wishes to have his
T R : 0 0 :040(327) [0517] church or by anybody is to make himself out to be **God**.
T R : 0 0 :048(328) [0519] righteousness before **God** and merit forgiveness of sins.
T R : 0 0 :048(328) [0519] traditions are services of **God** and perfection, and they
T R : 0 0 :048(328) [0519] performed in callings which **God** requires and ordained.
T R : 0 0 :048(328) [0519] detract from the glory of **God** and bring destruction to
T R : 0 0 :052(329) [0519] embraced for the glory of **God** and the salvation of souls.
T R : 0 0 :053(329) [0519] of saints, whose blood **God** will undoubtedly avenge.
T R : 0 0 :054(329) [0519] **God** expressly exhorts kings, "Now therefore, O kings, be
T R : 0 0 :054(329) [0519] first care of kings should be to advance the glory of **God**.
T R : 0 0 :055(329) [0521] and wickedness without any regard for the Word of **God**?
T R : 0 0 :056(330) [0521] judgments and decisions according to the Word of **God**.
T R : 0 0 :058(330) [0521] it is the clear command of **God** that we should flee from
T R : 0 0 :059(330) [0521] detract from the glory of **God**, and hinder the welfare of
T R : 0 0 :076(333) [0527] for the reformation of morals and the glory of **God**.
T R : 0 0 :082(334) [0527] the church know that **God** will require them to pay for
T R : 0 0 :082(334) [0529] and, by the favor of **God**, all the preachers who have been
S C : P R :002(338) [0533] Good **God**, what wretchedness I beheld!
S C : P R :005(338) [0533] Ten Commandments, or a single part of the Word of **God**
S C : P R :006(338) [0533] I therefore beg of you for **God**'s sake, my beloved brethren
S C : P R :018(340) [0537] the Scriptures to show how **God** punished and blessed.
S C : P R :019(340) [0537] waste both the kingdom of **God** and the kingdom of the
S C : P R :019(340) [0537] of the world and are the worst enemies of **God** and man.
S C : P R :020(340) [0537] etc., and tell them that **God** will inflict awful punishments
S C : P R :023(341) [0539] no heaven, no Christ, no **God**, nothing good at all.
S C : P R :024(341) [0539] their great need and **God**'s gracious help belong to the
S C : 0 1 :002(342) [0539] We should fear, love, and trust in **God** above all things.
S C : 0 1 :003(342) [0539] *shall not take the name of the Lord your* **God** *in vain."*
S C : 0 1 :004(342) [0539] We should fear and love **God**, and so we should not use
S C : 0 1 :006(342) [0541] We should fear and love **God**, and so we should not
S C : 0 1 :008(343) [0541] We should fear and love **God**, and so we should not
S C : 0 1 :010(343) [0541] We should fear and love **God**, and so we should not
S C : 0 1 :012(343) [0541] We should fear and love **God**, and so we should lead a
S C : 0 1 :014(343) [0541] We should fear and love **God**, and so we should not rob
S C : 0 1 :016(343) [0541] We should fear and love **God**, and so we should not tell
S C : 0 1 :018(343) [0541] We should fear and love **God**, and so we should not seek
S C : 0 1 :020(344) [0543] We should fear and love **God**, and so we should not
S C : 0 1 :021(344) [0543] What does **God** declare concerning all these
S C : 0 1 :021(344) [0543] He says, "I the Lord your **God** am a jealous God, visiting
S C : 0 1 :021(344) [0543] your God am a jealous **God**, visiting the iniquity of the
S C : 0 1 :022(344) [0543] Answer: **God** threatens to punish all who transgress these
S C : 0 2 :001(344) [0543] *"I believe in* **God**, *the Father almighty, maker of heaven*
S C : 0 2 :002(345) [0543] Answer: I believe that **God** has created me and all that
S C : 0 2 :003(345) [0545] *on the right hand of* **God**, *the Father almighty, whence he*
S C : 0 2 :004(345) [0545] that Jesus Christ, true **God**, begotten of the Father from
S C : 0 3 :002(346) [0545] Answer: Here **God** would encourage us to believe that he
S C : 0 3 :004(346) [0547] Answer: To be sure, **God**'s name is holy in itself, but we
S C : 0 3 :005(346) [0547] Answer: When the Word of **God** is taught clearly and
S C : 0 3 :005(346) [0547] and we, as children of **God**, lead holy lives in accordance
S C : 0 3 :005(346) [0547] than as the Word of **God** teaches, profanes the name of
S C : 0 3 :005(346) [0547] Word of God teaches, profanes the name of **God** among
S C : 0 3 :007(346) [0547] To be sure, the kingdom of **God** comes of itself, without
S C : 0 3 :010(347) [0547] good and gracious will of **God** is done without our
S C : 0 3 :011(347) [0547] Answer: When **God** curbs and destroys every evil counsel
S C : 0 3 :013(347) [0547] Answer: To be sure, **God** provides daily bread, even to the
S C : 0 3 :013(347) [0547] pray in this petition that **God** may make us aware of his
S C : 0 3 :016(347) [0549] we nevertheless pray that **God** may grant us all things by
S C : 0 3 :018(347) [0549] Answer: **God** tempts no one to sin, but we pray in this
S C : 0 3 :018(347) [0549] pray in this petition that **God** may so guard and preserve
S C : 0 4 :002(348) [0551] is water used according to **God**'s command and connected
S C : 0 4 :002(348) [0551] to God's command and connected with **God**'s Word.
S C : 0 4 :003(348) [0551] What is this Word of **God**?
S C : 0 4 :006(349) [0551] all who believe, as the Word and promise of **God** declare.
S C : 0 4 :007(349) [0551] What is this Word and promise of **God**?
S C : 0 4 :010(349) [0551] effects, but the Word of **God** connected with the water,
S C : 0 4 :010(349) [0551] which relies on the Word of **God** connected with the
S C : 0 4 :010(349) [0551] For without the Word of **God** the water is merely water
S C : 0 4 :010(349) [0551] with the Word of **God** it is a Baptism, that is, a gracious
S C : 0 4 :012(349) [0551] cleansed and righteous, to live forever in **God**'s presence.
S C : 0 5 :016(349) [0553] the confessor as from **God** himself, by no means doubting
S C : 0 5 :016(350) [0553] that our sins are thereby forgiven before **God** in heaven.
S C : 0 5 :018(350) [0553] Answer: Before **God** we should acknowledge that we are
S C : 0 5 :021(350) [0553] and declare that my sins are forgiven for **God**'s sake."
S C : 0 5 :022(350) [0553] poor sinner, confess before **God** that I am guilty of all
S C : 0 5 :023(350) [0553] my children, servants, and wife to the glory of **God**.
S C : 0 5 :023(350) [0555] have done contrary to **God**'s commandments and to their
S C : 0 5 :025(351) [0555] which you make to **God** in the presence of the confessor.
S C : 0 5 :026(351) [0555] the confessor shall say: "**God** be merciful to you and
S C : 0 5 :027(351) [0555] believe that this forgiveness is the forgiveness of **God**?"
S C : 0 7 :001(352) [0557] and say, "In the name of **God**, the Father, the Son, and
S C : 0 7 :004(353) [0559] and say, "In the name of **God**, the Father, the Son, and
S C : 0 8 :009(353) [0559] "Lord **God**, heavenly Father, bless us, and these thy gifts
S C : 0 8 :011(354) [0559] give Thee thanks, Lord **God**, our Father, for all thy
S C : 0 9 :003(354) [0561] Do not be deceived; **God** is not mocked" (Gal. 6:6, 7).
S C : 0 9 :004(355) [0561] no authority except from **God**, and those that exist have
S C : 0 9 :004(355) [0561] God, and those that exist have been instituted by **God**.
S C : 0 9 :004(355) [0561] the authorities resists what **God** has appointed, and those
S C : 0 9 :004(355) [0561] vain; he is the servant of **God** to execute his wrath on the
S C : 0 9 :005(355) [0561] that are Caesar's, and to **God** the things that are God's"
S C : 0 9 :005(355) [0561] and to God the things that are **God**'s" (Matt. 22:21).
S C : 0 9 :005(355) [0561] subject, not only to avoid **God**'s wrath but also for the
S C : 0 9 :005(355) [0561] authorities are ministers of **God**, attending to this very
S C : 0 9 :010(356) [0563] of Christ, doing the will of **God** from the heart, rendering
S C : 0 9 :012(356) [0563] toward one another, for '**God** opposes the proud, but
S C : 0 9 :012(356) [0563] under the mighty hand of **God**, that in due time he may
S C : 0 9 :013(356) [0563] alone, has set her hope on **God** and continues in
L C : P R :008(359) [0569] office and the people's souls, yes, even **God** and his Word.
L C : P R :009(359) [0569] presumptuous saints, for **God**'s sake, to get it into their
L C : P R :010(359) [0569] oneself with the Word of **God**, talk about it, and meditate
L C : P R :010(360) [0569] those blessed who "meditate on **God**'s law day and night."
L C : P R :010(360) [0571] to occupy yourself with **God**'s commandments and words
L C : P R :011(360) [0571] For he cannot bear to hear **God**'s Word.
L C : P R :011(360) [0571] **God**'s Word is not like some empty tale, such as the one
L C : P R :011(360) [0571] it is "the power of **God**," indeed, the power of God
L C : P R :011(360) [0571] God," indeed, the power of **God** which burns the devil
L C : P R :012(360) [0571] to recount all the blessings that flow from **God**'s Word.
L C : P R :012(360) [0571] What, then, shall we call **God**'s Word, which routs and
L C : P R :013(360) [0571] Not only do we need **God**'s Word daily as we need our
L C : P R :014(360) [0571] us to read the Catechism daily, there is **God**'s command.
L C : P R :014(360) [0571] Certainly **God** did not require and command this so
L C : P R :016(361) [0573] much wiser than **God** himself, and wiser than all his holy
L C : P R :016(361) [0573] **God** himself is not ashamed to teach it daily, for he knows
L C : P R :016(361) [0573] learning in one hour what **God** himself cannot finish
L C : P R :019(361) [0573] have become wiser than **God** himself and all his saints.
L C : P R :020(361) [0573] will gain much fruit and **God** will make excellent men of
L C : P R :020(361) [0573] To this end may **God** grant his grace!
L C : S P :006(362) [0575] I. The Ten Commandments of **God**
L C : S P :002(362) [0575] 2. You shall not take the name of **God** in vain.
L C : S P :011(363) [0577] I believe in **God**, the Father almighty, maker of heaven
L C : S P :012(363) [0577] sits on the right hand of **God**, the Father almighty,
L C : 0 1 :001(365) [0581] That is, you shall regard me alone as your **God**.
L C : 0 1 :001(365) [0581] What is to have a **god**?
L C : 0 1 :001(365) [0581] What is **God**?
L C : 0 1 :002(365) [0581] Answer: A **god** is that to which we look for all good and
L C : 0 1 :002(365) [0581] To have a **god** is nothing else than to trust and believe
L C : 0 1 :002(365) [0581] and faith of the heart alone make both **God** and an idol.
L C : 0 1 :003(365) [0581] faith and trust are right, then your **God** is the true God.
L C : 0 1 :003(365) [0581] faith and trust are right, then your God is the true **God**.
L C : 0 1 :003(365) [0581] trust is false and wrong, then you have not the true **God**.
L C : 0 1 :003(365) [0581] For these two belong together, faith and **God**.
L C : 0 1 :003(365) [0581] heart clings and entrusts itself is, I say, really your **God**.
L C : 0 1 :004(365) [0581] fly straight to the one true **God** and cling to him alone.
L C : 0 1 :004(365) [0581] you let me alone be your **God**, and never seek another."
L C : 0 1 :005(365) [0581] a person thinks he has **God** and everything he needs when
L C : 0 1 :006(365) [0581] such a man also has a **god** — mammon by name, that is,
L C : 0 1 :008(365) [0583] nothing doubts and despairs as if he never heard of **God**.
L C : 0 1 :010(366) [0583] in them, he also has a **god**, but not the one, true God.
L C : 0 1 :010(366) [0583] in them, he also has a god, but not the one, true **God**.
L C : 0 1 :010(366) [0583] I repeat, to have a **God** properly means to have something
L C : 0 1 :012(366) [0583] fix their heart and trust elsewhere than in the true **God**.
L C : 0 1 :013(366) [0583] and confidence be placed in **God** alone, and in no one else
L C : 0 1 :013(366) [0583] To have **God**, you see, does not mean to lay hands upon
L C : 0 1 :016(366) [0585] true worship which please **God** and which he commands
L C : 0 1 :017(367) [0585] Everyone has set up a **god** of his own, to which he looked
L C : 0 1 :018(367) [0585] and dominion exalted Jupiter as their supreme **god**.
L C : 0 1 :018(367) [0585] Everyone made into a **god** that to which his heart was
L C : 0 1 :018(367) [0585] therefore, to have a **god** means to trust and believe.
L C : 0 1 :019(367) [0585] not founded upon the one **God**, apart from whom there is
L C : 0 1 :019(367) [0585] from whom there is truly no **god** in heaven or on earth.
L C : 0 1 :020(367) [0585] fancies and dreams about **God** into an idol and entrust
L C : 0 1 :021(367) [0585] It neither cares for **God** nor expects good things from him
L C : 0 1 :021(367) [0585] it believe that whatever good it receives comes from **God**.
L C : 0 1 :022(367) [0585] in its own works and presumes to wrest heaven from **God**
L C : 0 1 :022(367) [0585] anything as a gift from **God**, but desiring by itself to earn
L C : 0 1 :022(367) [0585] supererogation, just as if **God** were in our service or debt
L C : 0 1 :023(367) [0585] What is this but making **God** into an idol — indeed, an
L C : 0 1 :023(367) [0585] idol — indeed, an "apple-**god**" — and setting up ourselves
L C : 0 1 :023(367) [0587] indeed, an "apple-god" — and setting up ourselves as **God**
L C : 0 1 :024(367) [0587] We are to trust in **God** alone and turn to him, expecting
L C : 0 1 :024(368) [0587] It is **God** alone, I have often enough repeated, from whom
L C : 0 1 :025(368) [0587] ancient times have called **God** by a name more elegant
L C : 0 1 :026(368) [0587] men, we receive it all from **God** through his command
L C : 0 1 :026(368) [0587] our blessings not from them, but from **God** through them
L C : 0 1 :026(368) [0587] and means through which **God** bestows all blessings.
L C : 0 1 :027(368) [0587] to take or give anything except as **God** has commanded it
L C : 0 1 :027(368) [0587] acknowledge everything as **God**'s gifts and thank him for
L C : 0 1 :027(368) [0587] of receiving good through **God**'s creatures is not to be
L C : 0 1 :027(368) [0587] ways and means than **God** has commanded, for that
L C : 0 1 :027(368) [0587] our blessings from **God** but seeking them from ourselves.
L C : 0 1 :028(368) [0587] and you will find whether or not it clings to **God** alone.
L C : 0 1 :028(368) [0587] and want, and renounces and forsakes all that is not **God**?
L C : 0 1 :028(368) [0587] Then you have the one true **God**.
L C : 0 1 :028(368) [0587] good and help than from **God**, and does it flee not to him
L C : 0 1 :028(368) [0587] Then you have an idol, another **god**.
L C : 0 1 :029(368) [0589] in order to show that **God** will not have this
L C : 0 1 :030(368) [0589] *"For I am the Lord your* **God**, *mighty and jealous, visiting*
L C : 0 1 :032(369) [0589] words, then, how angry **God** is with those who rely on
L C : 0 1 :034(369) [0589] He is a **God** who takes vengeance upon men who turn
L C : 0 1 :036(369) [0589] who, not caring whether **God** frowns or smiles, boast
L C : 0 1 :037(369) [0589] blockheads imagine, when **God** refrains from disturbing
L C : 0 1 :039(370) [0591] mercy to those who cling to **God** alone — sheer goodness
L C : 0 1 :040(370) [0591] us to fix our hearts upon **God** with perfect confidence
L C : 0 1 :041(370) [0591] you ask or desire than **God**'s gracious promise that he will
L C : 0 1 :042(370) [0591] this at all, and does not recognize it as **God**'s Word.
L C : 0 1 :042(370) [0591] sees that those who trust **God** and not mammon suffer
L C : 0 1 :045(370) [0593] was a great king, chosen by **God**, and an upright man; but
L C : 0 1 :045(370) [0593] let his heart depart from **God**, placing his confidence in
L C : 0 1 :046(370) [0593] and prove to be true since **God** cannot lie or deceive; just
L C : 0 1 :047(371) [0593] well and realize that **God** will tolerate no presumption
L C : 0 1 :047(371) [0593] straight ahead, using all of **God**'s gifts exactly as a cobbler
L C : 0 1 :047(371) [0593] station in life according to **God**'s order, allowing none of
L C : 0 1 :048(371) [0593] the heart is right with **God** and this commandment is
L C : 0 1 :049(371) [0593] *"You shall not take the name of* **God** *in vain."*
L C : 0 1 :050(371) [0593] the lips and the tongue into the right relation to **God**.

Continued ▶

L C : 0 1 :050(371) [0593] What it is to have a **God**, so you must learn to grasp
L C : 0 1 :051(371) [0595] misuse or take the name of **God** in vain?" you should
L C : 0 1 :051(371) [0595] briefly: "It is a misuse of **God's** name if we call upon the
L C : 0 1 :051(371) [0595] if we call upon the Lord **God** in any way whatsoever to
L C : 0 1 :051(371) [0595] forbids is appealing to **God's** name falsely or taking his
L C : 0 1 :052(371) [0595] **God's** name cannot be more grievously abused than for
L C : 0 1 :053(371) [0595] and in how many ways **God's** name is abused, though it is
L C : 0 1 :053(372) [0595] himself, swearing by **God's** name or by his own soul.
L C : 0 1 :054(372) [0595] arise and peddle their lying nonsense as the Word of **God**.
L C : 0 1 :055(372) [0595] to embellish yourself with **God's** name or to put up a good
L C : 0 1 :055(372) [0595] everyone and who disgrace **God's** name unabashedly
L C : 0 1 :055(372) [0595] slander the truth and **God's** Word and consign it to the
L C : 0 1 :056(372) [0597] and confirm it by invoking **God's** name and using it as a
L C : 0 1 :057(372) [0597] Therefore **God** has attached to this commandment a
L C : 0 1 :057(372) [0597] As little as **God** will permit the heart that turns away from
L C : 0 1 :058(372) [0597] do not use the name of **God** for lies and all kinds of
L C : 0 1 :058(372) [0597] as there are few who trust in **God** with their whole heart.
L C : 0 1 :059(372) [0597] if anyone is denounced, **God** and his name have to be
L C : 0 1 :061(373) [0597] with punishment but in the reverence and fear of **God**.
L C : 0 1 :062(373) [0597] you understand what it means to take **God's** name in vain
L C : 0 1 :063(373) [0597] you must also know how to use the name of **God** aright.
L C : 0 1 :063(373) [0599] shall not take the name of **God** in vain," God at the same
L C : 0 1 :063(373) [0599] the name of God in vain," **God** at the same time gives us
L C : 0 1 :066(373) [0599] truly good work by which **God** is praised, truth and justice
L C : 0 1 :066(373) [0599] For here **God** himself intervenes and separates right from
L C : 0 1 :069(374) [0599] especially to avoid calling upon **God's** name in its support
L C : 0 1 :069(374) [0601] All this is **God's** wrath and punishment upon such willful
L C : 0 1 :070(374) [0601] and encouraged to honor **God's** name and keep it
L C : 0 1 :070(374) [0601] for true honor to **God's** name consists of looking to it for
L C : 0 1 :070(374) [0601] heart by faith first gives **God** the honor due him and then
L C : 0 1 :071(374) [0601] He hates to hear **God's** name and cannot long remain
L C : 0 1 :072(374) [0601] calamity would befall us if **God** did not preserve us
L C : 0 1 :072(374) [0601] and vanished in the very moment I called upon **God**.
L C : 0 1 :073(374) [0601] ourselves each day to **God** — our soul and body, wife,
L C : 0 1 :074(374) [0601] monstrous or fearful and exclaim, "Lord **God**, save us!"
L C : 0 1 :074(374) [0601] trivial, he may say, "**God** be praised and thanked!" "This
L C : 0 1 :074(374) [0601] and thanked!" "This **God** has bestowed upon me!" etc.
L C : 0 1 :074(375) [0601] pleasing and acceptable to **God** than any monastic life
L C : 0 1 :075(375) [0601] in the fear and honor of **God** so that the First and Second
L C : 0 1 :077(375) [0603] their hearts that they fear **God** more than they do rods
L C : 0 1 :077(375) [0603] We want them to know that **God** is well pleased with the
L C : 0 1 :080(375) [0603] In the Old Testament **God** set apart the seventh day and
L C : 0 1 :083(376) [0603] interpretation of what **God** requires in this
L C : 0 1 :084(376) [0605] to hear and discuss **God's** Word and then praise God with
L C : 0 1 :084(376) [0605] God's Word and then praise **God** with song and prayer.
L C : 0 1 :086(376) [0605] we should devote their observance to learning **God's** Word
L C : 0 1 :087(377) [0605] But **God** wants it to be holy to you.
L C : 0 1 :088(377) [0605] we occupy ourselves with **God's** Word and exercise
L C : 0 1 :089(377) [0605] ourselves daily with **God's** Word and carry it in our hearts
L C : 0 1 :089(377) [0605] our whole life and being according to **God's** Word.
L C : 0 1 :090(377) [0607] neither preach nor practice **God's** Word but teach and live
L C : 0 1 :091(377) [0607] The Word of **God** is the true holy thing above all holy
L C : 0 1 :091(377) [0607] But **God's** Word is the treasure that sanctifies all things.
L C : 0 1 :092(377) [0607] At whatever time **God's** Word is taught, preached, heard,
L C : 0 1 :092(377) [0607] work must be guided by **God's** Word if they are to be
L C : 0 1 :092(377) [0607] by God's Word if they are to be **God**-pleasing or holy.
L C : 0 1 :093(377) [0607] or work done apart from **God's** Word is unholy in the
L C : 0 1 :093(377) [0607] is unholy in the sight of **God**, no matter how splendid and
L C : 0 1 :093(377) [0607] estates who do not know **God's** Word but seek holiness in
L C : 0 1 :094(378) [0607] as we have heard, takes place only through **God's** Word.
L C : 0 1 :094(378) [0607] appointed in order that **God's** Word may exert its power
L C : 0 1 :095(378) [0607] Since so much depends on **God's** Word that no holy day
L C : 0 1 :095(378) [0607] it, we must realize that **God** insists upon a strict
L C : 0 1 :096(378) [0607] or frivolity neglect to hear **God's** Word or lie around in
L C : 0 1 :096(378) [0609] of others who listen to **God's** Word as they would to any
L C : 0 1 :097(378) [0609] no one asked about **God's** Word, and no one taught it
L C : 0 1 :097(378) [0609] Now that we have **God's** Word, we still fail to remove the
L C : 0 1 :098(378) [0609] It is the commandment of **God**, and he will require of you
L C : 0 1 :099(378) [0609] and stealthily take the Word of **God** away from us.
L C : 0 1 :100(379) [0609] you must continually keep **God's** Word in your heart, on
L C : 0 1 :102(379) [0609] is fulfilled, and **God** is more pleased than by any work of
L C : 0 1 :103(379) [0611] three commandments, which are directed toward **God**.
L C : 0 1 :103(379) [0611] but use it for the praise of **God** and the benefit and
L C : 0 1 :103(379) [0611] devote ourselves to **God's** Word so that all our conduct
L C : 0 1 :105(379) [0611] and motherhood **God** has given the special distinction,
L C : 0 1 :107(379) [0611] highly and that next to **God** we give them the very highest
L C : 0 1 :108(379) [0611] to revere their parents as **God's** representatives, and to
L C : 0 1 :108(379) [0611] they are their own father and mother, given them by **God**.
L C : 0 1 :108(379) [0611] they are, but of the will of **God**, who has created and
L C : 0 1 :108(380) [0611] are all equal in the sight of **God**, but among ourselves
L C : 0 1 :108(380) [0611] **God** therefore commands you to be careful to obey me as
L C : 0 1 :111(380) [0613] but with humility and reverence, as in **God's** sight.
L C : 0 1 :112(380) [0613] and no one recognizes it as **God's** command or as a holy,
L C : 0 1 :112(380) [0613] his conscience right toward **God**, saying: "If I am to do
L C : 0 1 :112(380) [0613] to my parents, since **God** himself has commanded it.
L C : 0 1 :113(380) [0613] What **God** commands must be much nobler than anything
L C : 0 1 :113(380) [0613] teacher to be found than **God**, there can also be no better
L C : 0 1 :113(380) [0613] So, if this is **God's** command, and it embodies his highest
L C : 0 1 :114(380) [0613] not feel obliged to set forth **God's** commandment in its
L C : 0 1 :114(380) [0613] we have devised without ever asking **God's** approval.
L C : 0 1 :115(381) [0613] For the love of **God**, therefore, let us at last teach our
L C : 0 1 :115(381) [0613] If they wish to serve **God** with truly good works, they
L C : 0 1 :115(381) [0615] work is well pleasing to my **God** in heaven; this I know
L C : 0 1 :116(381) [0615] father and mother, which **God** has appointed and
L C : 0 1 :116(381) [0615] If **God's** Word and will are placed first and observed,
L C : 0 1 :116(381) [0615] to obedience toward **God** and are not set into opposition
L C : 0 1 :117(381) [0615] rejoice heartily and thank **God** that he has chosen and
L C : 0 1 :117(381) [0615] and holy treasure, the Word and commandment of **God**.
L C : 0 1 :118(381) [0615] they could bring before **God** a single work done in
L C : 0 1 :118(381) [0615] when, standing before **God** and the whole world, they
L C : 0 1 :119(381) [0615] perversity in trampling **God's** commandment under foot
L C : 0 1 :120(381) [0615] a divine testimony that **God** has commanded this;
L C : 0 1 :121(382) [0615] from the pure Word of **God** to the lying vanities of the
L C : 0 1 :122(382) [0615] on their backs, they anger both **God** and their parents.
L C : 0 1 :123(382) [0617] **God** therefore punishes them so that they sink into all
L C : 0 1 :125(382) [0617] the commandments, that **God** would set up a block or a
L C : 0 1 :125(382) [0617] to the sublime worship of **God** described in the previous
L C : 0 1 :126(382) [0617] For **God** has exalted this estate of parents above all
L C : 0 1 :126(382) [0617] This will and pleasure of **God** ought to provide us
L C : 0 1 :128(382) [0617] parents, as we all forget **God**, and no one takes thought
L C : 0 1 :128(382) [0617] no one takes thought how **God** feeds, guards, and protects
L C : 0 1 :129(383) [0617] The perversity of the world **God** knows very well.
L C : 0 1 :130(383) [0619] were right when they said, "**God**, parents, and teachers
L C : 0 1 :130(383) [0619] as those through whom **God** has given him all blessings.
L C : 0 1 :131(383) [0619] this commandment is that **God** has attached to it a lovely
L C : 0 1 :132(383) [0619] you see how important **God** considers this
L C : 0 1 :136(383) [0619] This, in short, is the way **God** will have it: render him
L C : 0 1 :137(384) [0619] by the punishment of **God** they bring upon themselves the
L C : 0 1 :139(384) [0621] well, then, how important **God** considers obedience, since
L C : 0 1 :140(384) [0621] how angry he makes **God** when he neglects this
L C : 0 1 :143(385) [0623] just mentioned, that it is **God's** commandment and is
L C : 0 1 :145(385) [0623] joy and praise and thank **God**; and with her careful work,
L C : 0 1 :147(385) [0623] In the sight of **God** it is really faith that makes a person
L C : 0 1 :148(385) [0623] conscience and a gracious **God** who will reward you a
L C : 0 1 :148(385) [0623] wrath and displeasure of **God**; there will be no peace in
L C : 0 1 :149(385) [0623] take advice remember that **God** is not to be taken lightly.
L C : 0 1 :149(385) [0623] **God** speaks to you and demands obedience.
L C : 0 1 :150(385) [0623] through our own parents, **God** gives us food, house and
L C : 0 1 :151(386) [0625] due, knows that he pleases **God** and receives joy and
L C : 0 1 :151(386) [0625] know that he shall have no favor or blessing from **God**.
L C : 0 1 :152(386) [0625] are so pleasing to **God** and have so rich a reward, we shall
L C : 0 1 :152(386) [0625] But **God's** Word and commandment are despised, as if
L C : 0 1 :153(386) [0625] will live much better with **God's** favor, peace, and blessing
L C : 0 1 :154(386) [0625] So **God** punishes one knave by means of another.
L C : 0 1 :156(386) [0625] some godly people, or else **God** would not grant us so
L C : 0 1 :157(387) [0627] the Word and will of **God** and sincerely accept it.
L C : 0 1 :157(387) [0627] From **God's** Word we could learn how to obtain an
L C : 0 1 :158(387) [0627] to those who govern and guide us by the Word of **God**.
L C : 0 1 :161(387) [0627] of Christians owe it to **God** to show "double honor" to
L C : 0 1 :161(387) [0627] **God** will adequately recompense those who do so and will
L C : 0 1 :163(387) [0627] For this we deserve to have **God** deprive us of his Word
L C : 0 1 :164(387) [0627] who keep their eyes on **God's** will and commandment,
L C : 0 1 :165(387) [0627] duty, then, and leave it to **God** how he will support you
L C : 0 1 :166(387) [0629] hands in joyful thanks to **God** for giving us such
L C : 0 1 :166(388) [0629] But **God** can and will give you everything abundantly,
L C : 0 1 :166(388) [0629] and disdains this is not worthy to hear a word from **God**.
L C : 0 1 :167(388) [0629] passages of Scripture, and **God** intends it to be included
L C : 0 1 :168(388) [0629] **God** does not want to have knaves or tyrants in this office
L C : 0 1 :168(388) [0629] they owe obedience to **God**, and that, above all, they
L C : 0 1 :168(388) [0629] to bring them up to the praise and honor of **God**.
L C : 0 1 :169(388) [0629] and injunction of **God**, who holds you accountable for it.
L C : 0 1 :170(388) [0629] Everybody acts as if **God** gave us children for our pleasure
L C : 0 1 :172(388) [0629] and educating our children to serve **God** and mankind.
L C : 0 1 :173(388) [0629] **God** can provide for them and make them rich without
L C : 0 1 :173(388) [0629] to his will; otherwise **God** would have no need of father
L C : 0 1 :174(388) [0631] the fear and knowledge of **God**, and if they are gifted to
L C : 0 1 :175(388) [0631] If this were done, **God** would richly bless us and give us
L C : 0 1 :177(389) [0631] is disregarded, **God** terribly punishes the world; hence
L C : 0 1 :180(389) [0631] Therefore neither **God** nor the government is included in
L C : 0 1 :181(389) [0631] **God** has delegated his authority of punishing evil-doers to
L C : 0 1 :182(389) [0631] who occupy the place of **God**, that is, parents and rulers.
L C : 0 1 :182(389) [0631] are the prerogatives of **God** and his representatives, and
L C : 0 1 :183(389) [0631] commandment is that, as **God** well knows, the world is
L C : 0 1 :184(390) [0633] you have received from **God** a better house and estate or
L C : 0 1 :185(390) [0633] Here **God**, like a kind father, steps in and intervenes to
L C : 0 1 :187(390) [0633] Therefore **God** wishes to remove the root and source of
L C : 0 1 :191(391) [0635] Therefore **God** rightly calls all persons murderers who do
L C : 0 1 :193(391) [0635] Therefore it is **God's** real intention that we should allow
L C : 0 1 :195(391) [0637] Here again we have **God's** Word by which he wants to
L C : 0 1 :195(391) [0637] that he is our **God**; that is, he wishes to help and protect
L C : 0 1 :198(392) [0637] the works commanded by **God's** Word which are the true,
L C : 0 1 :205(393) [0639] Thus **God** by his commandment wants every husband or
L C : 0 1 :206(393) [0639] note, first, how highly **God** honors and glorifies the
L C : 0 1 :207(393) [0639] and support and bring them up to the glory of **God**.
L C : 0 1 :208(393) [0639] **God** has therefore most richly blessed this estate above all
L C : 0 1 :208(393) [0639] institution and an object of **God's** serious concern.
L C : 0 1 :208(393) [0639] promote knowledge of **God**, godly living, and all virtues,
L C : 0 1 :209(393) [0639] but view it in the light of **God's** Word, by which it is
L C : 0 1 :211(393) [0641] solemnly commanded by **God** that in general men and
L C : 0 1 :211(393) [0641] few) exceptions whom **God** has especially exempted —
L C : 0 1 :212(393) [0641] nature has its way, as **God** implanted it, it is not possible
L C : 0 1 :212(394) [0641] in some measure, **God** has established marriage, so that
L C : 0 1 :212(394) [0641] it — although here, too, **God's** grace is still required to
L C : 0 1 :213(394) [0641] monks, and nuns resist **God's** order and commandment
L C : 0 1 :217(394) [0641] life and know that it is a blessed and **God**-pleasing estate.
L C : 0 1 :218(394) [0643] are grown, will be married honorably in the fear of **God**.
L C : 0 1 :218(394) [0643] Then **God** will add his blessing and grace so that men
L C : 0 1 :219(394) [0643] and cherish the wife or husband whom **God** has given.
L C : 0 1 :221(395) [0643] that are chosen without **God's** Word and commandment.
L C : 0 1 :223(395) [0643] This, too, **God** wants to have protected.
L C : 0 1 :231(396) [0647] be told that in the eyes of **God** they are the greatest
L C : 0 1 :232(396) [0647] and that the wrath of **God** may be continually and
L C : 0 1 :233(396) [0647] it is his duty, at the risk of **God's** displeasure, not to harm
L C : 0 1 :234(397) [0647] but he will not escape **God's** wrath and punishment.
L C : 0 1 :236(397) [0647] of your own — which **God** will let you acquire to your
L C : 0 1 :238(397) [0647] **God** will not forget his commandment.
L C : 0 1 :242(397) [0649] But we shall trust **God**, who takes matters into his own
L C : 0 1 :244(398) [0649] were none of our business, **God** must punish us and teach
L C : 0 1 :245(398) [0649] For **God** is a master of this art; since everyone robs and
L C : 0 1 :246(398) [0649] let him know that this is **God's** commandment and must
L C : 0 1 :247(398) [0651] to bear, for they will reach **God**, who watches over poor,
L C : 0 1 :247(398) [0651] before all the world you may call **God** and me liars.
L C : 0 1 :248(398) [0651] keep their eyes fixed upon **God's** commandment, lest his
L C : 0 1 :249(398) [0651] is only to instruct and reprove by means of **God's** Word.
L C : 0 1 :252(399) [0651] things which are heartily acceptable and pleasing to **God**.
L C : 0 1 :256(399) [0653] Therefore **God** will not have our neighbor deprived of his

Continued ▶

L C : 0 1 :262(400) [0655] Moreover, the Word of **God** must undergo the most
L C : 0 1 :262(400) [0655] truth and the children of **God** and yet consider this no sin
L C : 0 1 :263(400) [0655] the tongue against a neighbor, then, is forbidden by **God**.
L C : 0 1 :268(401) [0657] the judgment and office of **God**, pronouncing the severest
L C : 0 1 :269(401) [0657] Therefore **God** forbids you to speak evil about another
L C : 0 1 :274(402) [0659] yet he does not sin against **God**'s commandment because
L C : 0 1 :274(402) [0659] commandment because **God** of his own accord instituted
L C : 0 1 :289(404) [0663] especially to the precious Word of **God** and its preachers.
L C : 0 1 :290(404) [0663] good works which please **God** most highly and bring
L C : 0 1 :293(404) [0665] **God** therefore added these two commandments to teach
L C : 0 1 :307(406) [0669] be, you must learn that **God** does not wish you to deprive
L C : 0 1 :307(406) [0669] him against his will, and begrudging what **God** gave him.
L C : 0 1 :308(406) [0669] you in possession of it, but **God** will not, for he sees your
L C : 0 1 :310(407) [0669] miserable covetousness, **God**'s purpose being to destroy
L C : 0 1 :310(407) [0669] us and shows just how upright we really are in **God**'s sight
L C : 0 1 :311(407) [0669] what we are to do to make our whole life pleasing to **God**.
L C : 0 1 :311(407) [0671] can be good or pleasing to **God**, no matter how great or
L C : 0 1 :319(408) [0673] to show how much effort **God** requires us to devote to
L C : 0 1 :320(408) [0673] *"I the Lord, your **God**, am a jealous God, visiting the*
L C : 0 1 :320(408) [0673] *your God, am a jealous **God**, visiting the iniquity of the*
L C : 0 1 :322(409) [0673] as a serious matter to **God** because he himself here
L C : 0 1 :323(409) [0673] that fears and regards **God** alone and, because of this
L C : 0 1 :324(409) [0675] "You shall fear, love, and trust me as your one true **God**."
L C : 0 1 :324(409) [0675] such an attitude toward **God**, he has fulfilled this
L C : 0 1 :325(409) [0675] these two things, fear of **God** and trust in God.
L C : 0 1 :325(409) [0675] these two things, fear of God and trust in **God**.
L C : 0 1 :326(409) [0675] we are told to fear **God** and not take his name in vain by
L C : 0 1 :327(409) [0675] to them not on their own account but for **God**'s sake.
L C : 0 1 :327(409) [0675] Rather, ask what **God** wants of you and what he will quite
L C : 0 1 :328(410) [0677] can, purely out of love to **God** and in order to please him,
L C : 0 1 :330(410) [0677] like cattle, but in the fear and reverence of **God**.
L C : 0 1 :330(410) [0677] of the most high **God**, who watches over them with great
L C : 0 1 :330(410) [0677] a spontaneous impulse and desire gladly to do **God**'s will.
L C : 0 1 :333(410) [0677] any work like that which **God** in these commandments so
L C : 0 1 :333(411) [0677] other teachings as the greatest treasure **God** has given us.
L C : 0 2 :001(411) [0679] In it we have seen all that **God** wishes us to do or not to
L C : 0 2 :001(411) [0679] expect and receive from **God**; in brief, it teaches us to
L C : 0 2 :006(411) [0679] The first article, of **God** the Father, explains creation; the
L C : 0 2 :007(411) [0679] few words: "I believe in **God** the Father, who created me;
L C : 0 2 :007(411) [0679] created me; I believe in **God** the Son, who redeemed me; I
L C : 0 2 :007(411) [0679] One **God** and one faith, but three persons, and therefore
L C : 0 2 :009(411) [0679] *"I believe in **God**, the Father almighty, maker of heaven*
L C : 0 2 :010(411) [0679] us a brief description of **God** the Father, his nature, his
L C : 0 2 :010(411) [0679] to have no more than one **God**, it may be asked: "What
L C : 0 2 :010(412) [0679] one God, it may be asked: "What kind of being is **God**?
L C : 0 2 :011(412) [0681] ask a young child, "My boy, what kind of **God** have you?
L C : 0 2 :011(412) [0681] he could say, "First, my **God** is the Father, who made
L C : 0 2 :011(412) [0681] him alone I have no other **God**, for there is no one else
L C : 0 2 :013(412) [0681] these words, "I believe in **God**, the Father almighty,
L C : 0 2 :013(412) [0681] that I am a creature of **God**; that is, that he has given and
L C : 0 2 :017(412) [0681] Moreover, we confess that **God** the Father not only has
L C : 0 2 :019(412) [0681] given and sustained by **God**, it inevitably follows that we
L C : 0 2 :021(413) [0683] the blessings and gifts of **God** solely for its own pride and
L C : 0 2 :021(413) [0683] and never once turning to **God** to thank him or
L C : 0 2 :022(413) [0683] true of those who even fight against the Word of **God**.
L C : 0 2 :023(413) [0683] or danger, we should recognize that this is **God**'s doing.
L C : 0 2 :023(413) [0683] kindled with gratitude to **God** and a desire to use all these
L C : 0 2 :024(413) [0683] we have and receive from **God** and about what we owe
L C : 0 2 :025(413) [0685] *on the right hand of **God**, the Father almighty, whence he*
L C : 0 2 :026(413) [0685] see what we receive from **God** over and above the
L C : 0 2 :027(414) [0685] that Jesus Christ, true Son of **God**, has become my Lord."
L C : 0 2 :028(414) [0685] When we were created by **God** the Father, and had
L C : 0 2 :028(414) [0685] We lay under **God**'s wrath and displeasure, doomed to
L C : 0 2 :029(414) [0685] only and eternal Son of **God**, in his unfathomable
L C : 0 2 :031(414) [0685] us back from the devil to **God**, from death to life, from sin
L C : 0 2 :036(415) [0687] But **God**'s Spirit alone is called Holy Spirit, that is, he
L C : 0 2 :038(415) [0689] put to use and enjoyed, **God** has caused the Word to be
L C : 0 2 :042(416) [0689] and bears every Christian through the Word of **God**.
L C : 0 2 :052(417) [0691] I have heard and still hear **God**'s Word, which is the first
L C : 0 2 :052(417) [0691] of the devil, knowing nothing of **God** and of Christ.
L C : 0 2 :054(417) [0693] constantly, for although **God**'s grace has been won by
L C : 0 2 :054(417) [0693] by the Holy Spirit through **God**'s Word in the unity of the
L C : 0 2 :055(418) [0693] **God** forgives us, and we forgive, bear with, and aid one
L C : 0 2 :063(419) [0695] have the entire essence of **God**, his will, and his work
L C : 0 2 :063(419) [0695] to learn what **God** is and what he thinks and does, yet it
L C : 0 2 :064(419) [0695] In these three articles **God** himself has revealed and
L C : 0 2 :066(419) [0697] worship only the one, true **God**, nevertheless do not know
L C : 0 2 :067(419) [0697] do; the Creed tells us what **God** does for us and gives to
L C : 0 2 :068(420) [0697] make us Christians, for **God**'s wrath and displeasure still
L C : 0 2 :068(420) [0697] pure grace and makes us upright and pleasing to **God**.
L C : 0 2 :069(420) [0697] all the commandments of **God** because we see that God
L C : 0 2 :069(420) [0697] of God because we see that **God** gives himself completely
L C : 0 3 :002(420) [0697] necessary as to call upon **God** incessantly and drum into
L C : 0 3 :005(420) [0699] It is our duty to pray because **God** has commanded it.
L C : 0 3 :005(420) [0699] Commandment, "You shall not take **God**'s name in vain."
L C : 0 3 :006(420) [0699] such as having no other **God**, not killing, not stealing, etc.
L C : 0 3 :006(421) [0699] Who knows whether **God** heeds my prayer or cares to
L C : 0 3 :008(421) [0699] Commandment teaches, is to call upon **God** in every need.
L C : 0 3 :008(421) [0699] This **God** requires of us; he has not left it to our choice.
L C : 0 3 :008(421) [0699] and prayer the name of **God** is glorified and used to good
L C : 0 3 :009(421) [0699] and obligation [on pain of **God**'s wrath and displeasure].
L C : 0 3 :010(421) [0699] who are holier and in better favor with **God** than we are.
L C : 0 3 :010(421) [0699] that it always flees from **God**, thinking that he neither
L C : 0 3 :011(421) [0701] commandment and turn to **God** so that we may not
L C : 0 3 :013(422) [0701] that it befits obedience and the commandment of **God**.
L C : 0 3 :013(422) [0701] regard as demanded by **God** and done in obedience to
L C : 0 3 :013(422) [0701] but it is important because **God** has commanded it."
L C : 0 3 :013(422) [0701] should always approach **God** in obedience to this
L C : 0 3 :014(422) [0701] if the act was performed, whether **God** heard it or not.
L C : 0 3 :016(422) [0701] holy, and pleasing to **God** as those of St. Paul and the
L C : 0 3 :016(422) [0701] **God** does not regard prayer on account of the person, but
L C : 0 3 :017(422) [0703] be based on obedience to **God**, regardless of our person,
L C : 0 3 :018(422) [0703] We must learn that **God** will not have this commandment
L C : 0 3 :019(423) [0703] to pray because **God** has promised that our prayer will
L C : 0 3 :020(423) [0703] For by his Word **God** testifies that our prayer is heartily
L C : 0 3 :021(423) [0703] once again that he angers **God**, grossly dishonoring him
L C : 0 3 :022(423) [0703] and promise, **God** takes the initiative and puts into our
L C : 0 3 :023(423) [0703] for it has the excellent testimony that **God** loves to hear it
L C : 0 3 :025(423) [0705] pray out of obedience to **God** and faith in his promise, or
L C : 0 3 :025(423) [0705] work as a payment to **God**, not willing to receive anything
L C : 0 3 :027(424) [0705] **God** therefore wishes you to lament and express your
L C : 0 3 :028(424) [0705] he should always remind **God** of his commandment and
L C : 0 3 :032(424) [0707] Father, thy will be done," **God** replies from on high, "Yes,
L C : 0 3 :037(425) [0707] **God**'s name was given to us when we became Christians
L C : 0 3 :037(425) [0707] we are called children of **God** and enjoy the sacraments,
L C : 0 3 :037(425) [0707] with himself that all that is **God**'s must serve for our use.
L C : 0 3 :039(425) [0709] Since in this prayer we call **God** our Father, it is our duty
L C : 0 3 :040(425) [0709] Now, the name of **God** is profaned by us either in words
L C : 0 3 :041(425) [0709] preach, teach, and speak in **God**'s name anything that is
L C : 0 3 :042(425) [0709] are called Christians and **God**'s people are adulterers,
L C : 0 3 :042(425) [0709] Here again **God**'s name must be profaned and blasphemed
L C : 0 3 :044(425) [0709] scorn and reproach, so **God** is dishonored if we who are
L C : 0 3 :044(426) [0709] us called not children of **God** but children of the devil.
L C : 0 3 :045(426) [0709] exactly the same thing that **God** demands in the Second
L C : 0 3 :045(426) [0709] etc., but used rightly to the praise and glory of **God**.
L C : 0 3 :045(426) [0709] Whoever uses **God**'s name for any sort of wrong profanes
L C : 0 3 :047(426) [0711] who have the Word of **God** but are ungrateful for it and
L C : 0 3 :048(426) [0711] whole-heartedly, you can be sure that **God** is pleased.
L C : 0 3 :049(426) [0711] in the first petition that **God** would prevent the world
L C : 0 3 :049(426) [0711] but would rather keep **God**'s name sacred and holy in
L C : 0 3 :050(426) [0711] Just as **God**'s name is holy in itself and yet we pray that it
L C : 0 3 :051(426) [0711] What is the kingdom of **God**?
L C : 0 3 :051(426) [0711] in the Creed, namely, that **God** sent his Son, Christ our
L C : 0 3 :052(427) [0711] be realized in us and that **God**'s name may be praised
L C : 0 3 :053(427) [0711] **God**'s kingdom comes to us in two ways: first, it comes
L C : 0 3 :055(427) [0713] treasure and everything that **God** himself possesses.
L C : 0 3 :055(427) [0713] heart to dare to desire if **God** himself had not commanded
L C : 0 3 :056(427) [0713] But because he is **God**, he claims the honor of giving far
L C : 0 3 :057(428) [0713] reproach and dishonor to **God** if we, to whom he offers
L C : 0 3 :058(428) [0713] which does not look to **God** even for enough to satisfy the
L C : 0 3 :058(428) [0713] expect, without doubting, eternal blessings from **God**.
L C : 0 3 :058(428) [0713] and let the kingdom of **God** be the first thing for which
L C : 0 3 :058(428) [0713] "Seek first the kingdom of **God**, and all these things shall
L C : 0 3 :058(428) [0713] For how could **God** allow us to suffer want in temporal
L C : 0 3 :060(428) [0715] far we have prayed that **God**'s name may be hallowed by
L C : 0 3 :060(428) [0715] all that pertains to **God**'s glory and to our salvation, in
L C : 0 3 :060(428) [0715] in which we appropriate **God** with all his treasures.
L C : 0 3 :061(428) [0715] devil — we must also pray that **God**'s will may be done.
L C : 0 3 :062(428) [0715] most specious pretexts of **God**'s name, are disclosed and
L C : 0 3 :063(428) [0715] evil, even when we have accepted and believe **God**'s Word
L C : 0 3 :065(429) [0715] For where **God**'s Word is preached, accepted or believed,
L C : 0 3 :068(429) [0717] interests which concern **God** himself have been very
L C : 0 3 :068(429) [0717] As **God**'s name must be hallowed and his kingdom must
L C : 0 3 :068(429) [0717] all violence and persecution, submitting to the will of **God**
L C : 0 3 :070(429) [0717] frustrated, the kingdom of **God** could not abide on earth
L C : 0 3 :072(430) [0719] For if **God** did not cause grain to grow and did not bless
L C : 0 3 :074(430) [0719] chiefly through them does **God** provide us our daily bread
L C : 0 3 :074(430) [0719] we have received from **God** all good things in abundance,
L C : 0 3 :075(430) [0719] them, that through them **God** may bestow on us still more
L C : 0 3 :076(431) [0721] For example, we might ask **God** to give us food and
L C : 0 3 :077(431) [0721] Again, to ask **God** to endow the emperor, kings, and all
L C : 0 3 :079(431) [0721] all these things come from **God** and that we must pray for
L C : 0 3 :080(431) [0721] away or interfere with all we have received from **God**.
L C : 0 3 :081(431) [0721] receives a morsel of bread from **God** and eats it in peace.
L C : 0 3 :081(431) [0721] power, and our prayer to **God** did not restrain him, surely
L C : 0 3 :081(431) [0721] us who have the Word of **God** and would like to be
L C : 0 3 :082(431) [0721] Thus, you see, **God** wishes to show us how he cares for us
L C : 0 3 :086(432) [0723] Although we have **God**'s Word and believe, although we
L C : 0 3 :086(432) [0723] will and are supported by **God**'s gift and blessing,
L C : 0 3 :088(432) [0723] is great need to call upon **God** and pray, "Dear Father,
L C : 0 3 :089(432) [0723] does not trust and believe **God** and is constantly aroused
L C : 0 3 :089(432) [0723] becomes restless; it fears **God**'s wrath and displeasure,
L C : 0 3 :090(432) [0723] This should serve **God**'s purpose to break our pride and
L C : 0 3 :090(432) [0723] that in the presence of **God** all men must humble
L C : 0 3 :091(432) [0723] In short, unless **God** constantly forgives, we are lost.
L C : 0 3 :092(432) [0723] is really an appeal to **God** not to regard our sins and
L C : 0 3 :092(432) [0725] the heart is not right with **God** and cannot achieve such
L C : 0 3 :093(433) [0725] **God** has promised us assurance that everything is forgiven
L C : 0 3 :094(433) [0725] as we sin greatly against **God** everyday and yet he forgives
L C : 0 3 :095(433) [0725] If you do not forgive, do not think that **God** forgives you.
L C : 0 3 :096(433) [0725] of your forgiving, for **God** does it altogether freely, out of
L C : 0 3 :100(433) [0727] upright and stand before **God** with a good conscience, we
L C : 0 3 :104(433) [0727] Word and the works of **God**, to tear us away from faith,
L C : 0 3 :105(434) [0727] and pray every hour that **God** may not allow us to become
L C : 0 3 :106(434) [0727] not into temptation" when **God** gives us power and
L C : 0 3 :110(435) [0729] Prayer and to appeal to **God** from your heart, "Dear
L C : 0 3 :113(435) [0729] that we pray for: **God**'s name or glory, God's kingdom
L C : 0 3 :113(435) [0729] for: God's name or glory, **God**'s kingdom and will, our
L C : 0 3 :116(435) [0731] For if **God** did not support us, we would not be safe from
L C : 0 3 :117(436) [0731] Thus you see how **God** wants us to pray to him for
L C : 0 3 :119(436) [0731] Thus **God** has briefly set before us all the afflictions that
L C : 0 3 :120(436) [0731] of chance but knows that **God** does not lie since he has
L C : 0 3 :121(436) [0731] with certainty that **God** hears their prayer but remain in
L C : 0 3 :121(436) [0731] should I be so bold as to boast that **God** hears my prayer?
L C : 0 3 :122(436) [0731] they have their eye not on **God**'s promise but on their own
L C : 0 3 :122(436) [0731] so that they despise **God** and accuse him of lying.
L C : 0 3 :123(436) [0731] must not suppose that he will receive anything from **God**."
L C : 0 3 :124(436) [0731] is the importance that **God** attaches to our being certain
L C : 0 4 :006(437) [0733] that these words contain **God**'s commandment and
L C : 0 4 :006(437) [0733] but revealed and given by **God** himself, so I can also boast
L C : 0 4 :006(437) [0733] is no human plaything but is instituted by **God** himself.
L C : 0 4 :008(437) [0733] it may be, here stand **God**'s Word and command which
L C : 0 4 :008(437) [0733] What **God** instituted and commands cannot be useless.
L C : 0 4 :009(437) [0735] and more precious because **God** has commanded it and,
L C : 0 4 :009(437) [0735] "Go baptize," not in your name but "in **God**'s name."

Continued ▶

LC : 04 :010(437) [0735] To be baptized in **God**'s name is to be baptized not by
LC : 04 :010(437) [0735] name is to be baptized not by men but by **God** himself.
LC : 04 :010(437) [0735] by men's hands, it is nevertheless truly **God**'s own act.
LC : 04 :010(437) [0735] what work can man do that is greater than **God**'s work?
LC : 04 :011(437) [0735] and lead us away from **God**'s work to our own.
LC : 04 :012(438) [0735] be as noble and good as if **God** were to pick up a straw.
LC : 04 :014(438) [0735] water comprehended in **God**'s Word and commandment
LC : 04 :014(438) [0735] than other water but that **God**'s Word and commandment
LC : 04 :015(438) [0735] to slander Baptism, ignore **God**'s Word and ordinance,
LC : 04 :016(438) [0735] dare you tamper thus with **God**'s ordinance and tear from
LC : 04 :016(438) [0735] jeweled clasp with which **God** has fastened and enclosed it
LC : 04 :016(438) [0735] the nucleus in the water is **God**'s Word or commandment
LC : 04 :016(438) [0735] or commandment and **God**'s name, and this is a treasure
LC : 04 :017(438) [0735] **God** himself stakes his honor, his power, and his might on
LC : 04 :017(438) [0737] extol, for it contains and conveys all the fullness of **God**.
LC : 04 :019(439) [0737] ordained and instituted by **God** should be regarded not
LC : 04 :019(439) [0737] of a nut) but as that in which **God**'s Word is enclosed.
LC : 04 :020(439) [0737] adorned and clothed with the majesty and glory of **God**.
LC : 04 :021(439) [0737] account of the Word, since **God** himself has honored it by
LC : 04 :022(439) [0737] is present according to **God**'s ordinance, Baptism is a
LC : 04 :026(440) [0739] It shows also (as we said above) that **God**'s name is in it.
LC : 04 :027(440) [0739] And where **God**'s name is, there must also be life and
LC : 04 :029(440) [0739] its incorporation with **God**'s Word and ordinance and the
LC : 04 :029(440) [0739] else is it but believing in **God** as the one who has
LC : 04 :030(440) [0739] In short, whatever **God** effects in us he does through such
LC : 04 :031(440) [0739] that is, the water comprehended in **God**'s ordinance?
LC : 04 :031(440) [0739] rejects Baptism rejects **God**'s Word, faith, and Christ, who
LC : 04 :035(441) [0741] is not our work but **God**'s (for, as was said, you must
LC : 04 :035(441) [0741] **God**'s works, however, are salutary and necessary for
LC : 04 :036(441) [0741] to you if you accept it as **God**'s command and ordinance,
LC : 04 :036(441) [0741] baptized in the name of **God**, you may receive in the water
LC : 04 :037(441) [0741] do but is a treasure which **God** gives us and faith grasps,
LC : 04 :038(441) [0741] especially that it is **God**'s ordinance and is to be held in all
LC : 04 :038(441) [0741] the flesh and blood but at **God**'s commandment in which
LC : 04 :038(441) [0741] to accept and observe Baptism as an ordinance of **God**.
LC : 04 :039(441) [0741] But here we have not only **God**'s commandment and
LC : 04 :039(441) [0741] glorious than anything else **God** has commanded and
LC : 04 :041(442) [0743] devil, forgiveness of sin, **God**'s grace, the entire Christ,
LC : 04 :049(442) [0745] **God** has sanctified many who have been thus baptized
LC : 04 :049(442) [0745] Similarly by **God**'s grace we have been given the power to
LC : 04 :050(442) [0745] Now, if **God** did not accept the Baptism of infants, he
LC : 04 :050(443) [0745] Since **God** has confirmed Baptism through the gift of His
LC : 04 :050(443) [0745] must acknowledge that infant Baptism is pleasing to **God**.
LC : 04 :053(443) [0745] depends upon the Word and commandment of **God**.
LC : 04 :053(443) [0745] is simply water and **God**'s Word in and with each other;
LC : 04 :054(443) [0745] be water together with **God**'s Word, even though he failed
LC : 04 :055(443) [0747] How dare we think that **God**'s Word and ordinance
LC : 04 :056(443) [0747] baptized, must say before **God**: "I come here in my faith,
LC : 04 :056(444) [0747] I may be strong or weak; I leave that in **God**'s hands.
LC : 04 :057(444) [0747] that he may believe, and we pray **God** to grant him faith.
LC : 04 :057(444) [0747] him on that account, but solely on the command of **God**.
LC : 04 :057(444) [0747] Because we know that **God** does not lie.
LC : 04 :057(444) [0747] men — may err and deceive, but **God**'s Word cannot err.
LC : 04 :060(444) [0747] For **God**'s ordinance and Word cannot be changed or
LC : 04 :061(444) [0747] that they do not discern **God**'s Word and commandment.
LC : 04 :062(444) [0749] pervert and nullify all **God**'s work and ordinances.
LC : 04 :064(444) [0749] Baptism signifies and why **God** ordained just this sign and
LC : 04 :082(446) [0751] since, as we said, it is **God**'s ordinance and not a work of
LC : 04 :083(446) [0751] of the devil and makes **God** our own, overcomes and
LC : 05 :004(447) [0753] importance, namely, **God**'s Word and ordinance or
LC : 05 :006(447) [0755] Do you think **God** cares so much about our faith and
LC : 05 :006(447) [0755] temporal things remain as **God** has created and ordered
LC : 05 :007(447) [0755] contrary to the Word of **God**, as human performances.
LC : 05 :009(447) [0755] and wine comprehended in **God**'s Word and connected
LC : 05 :016(448) [0757] founded on the holiness of men but on the Word of **God**.
LC : 05 :032(450) [0761] whole Gospel or Word of **God** apart from the sacrament
LC : 05 :041(451) [0763] despise both the sacrament and the Word of **God**.
LC : 05 :054(453) [0765] act like a person who really desires to be right with **God**.
LC : 05 :055(453) [0767] so perfectly pure that **God** might not find the least blemish
LC : 05 :070(454) [0769] contains and conveys **God**'s grace and Spirit with all his
LC : 05 :071(454) [0769] Thus you have on **God**'s part both the commandment and
LC : 05 :081(456) [0773] who seduces the heart from **God**'s Word and blinds it,
LC : 05 :083(456) [0773] more need to lament both to **God** and to your brother.
LC : 05 :084(456) [0773] you do not see, though **God** grants his grace that you may
LC : 05 :086(456) [0773] Thus the Word of **God** and the Christian church will be
LC : 05 :087(456) [0773] that it is his duty, by **God**'s injunction and command, to
LC : 06 :006(457) [0000] deserve just such a jailer as **God**'s devil and hangman.
LC : 06 :008(458) [0000] practice of confessing to **God** alone or to our neighbor
LC : 06 :010(458) [0000] before we come into **God**'s presence to beg for
LC : 06 :011(458) [0000] they all"; no one does to **God** or his neighbor what he
LC : 06 :012(458) [0000] our debts both to **God** and to our neighbor are forgiven
LC : 06 :014(458) [0000] refuge when it hears in **God**'s Word that through a man
LC : 06 :014(458) [0000] Word that through a man **God** looses and absolves him
LC : 06 :015(459) [0000] second is a work which **God** does, when he absolves me of
LC : 06 :016(459) [0000] were simply a good work with which we could satisfy **God**
LC : 06 :018(459) [0000] value on our work but exalt and magnify **God**'s Word.
LC : 06 :022(459) [0000] a work but to hear what **God** wishes to say to you.
LC : 06 :033(461) [0000] for flowing streams, so longs my soul for thee, O **God**."
LC : 06 :033(461) [0000] so I yearn and tremble for **God**'s Word, absolution, the
LC : 06 :035(461) [0000] in praise and thanks to **God** that we have attained to this
EP : 00 :000(463) [0775] Guidance of the Word of **God** and the Comprehensive
EP : 00 :000(464) [0777] in Conformity with **God**'s Word in the Recapitulation
EP : RN :003(465) [0777] been introduced into the church of **God** contrary to them.
EP : RN :008(465) [0779] in the church of **God** with reference to controverted
EP : 01 :002(466) [0779] only in the beginning when **God** created man pure and
EP : 01 :002(466) [0779] after the fall our nature is and remains a creature of **God**.
EP : 01 :002(466) [0779] as the difference between **God**'s work and the devil's
EP : 01 :004(466) [0781] **God** not only created the body and soul of Adam and Eve
EP : 01 :004(466) [0781] they are corrupted, and **God** still acknowledges them as
EP : 01 :005(466) [0781] Furthermore, the Son of **God** assumed into the unity of
EP : 01 :009(467) [0781] by a rational process, but only from **God**'s Word.
EP : 01 :010(467) [0781] No one except **God** alone can separate the corruption of
EP : 01 :010(467) [0781] and in my flesh I shall see **God**; him I shall see for myself,
EP : 01 :022(469) [0785] essence, as when we say, "**God** has created human nature."
EP : 01 :025(469) [0785] the distinction between **God**'s work and Satan's work.
EP : 01 :025(469) [0785] he can only, with **God**'s permission, corrupt accidentally
EP : 01 :025(469) [0785] corrupt accidentally the substance which **God** has created.
EP : 02 :001(469) [0785] Spirit, dispose and prepare himself for the grace of **God**?
EP : 02 :001(469) [0785] he not accept the grace of **God** offered in the Word and
EP : 02 :001(470) [0787] *concerning this Article on the Basis of God's Word*
EP : 02 :002(470) [0787] the gifts of the Spirit of **God**, for they are folly to him,
EP : 02 :003(470) [0787] not only turned away from **God**, but has also become an
EP : 02 :003(470) [0787] also become an enemy of **God**, so that he desires and wills
EP : 02 :003(470) [0787] is evil and opposed to **God**, as it is written, "The
EP : 02 :003(470) [0787] on the flesh is hostile to **God**; it does not submit to God's
EP : 02 :003(470) [0787] God; it does not submit to **God**'s law, indeed it cannot."
EP : 02 :003(470) [0787] from us; our sufficiency is from **God**" (II Cor. 3:5).
EP : 02 :004(470) [0787] 3. **God** the Holy Spirit, however, does not effect
EP : 02 :004(470) [0787] and the hearing of **God**'s Word, as it is written that the
EP : 02 :004(470) [0787] the Gospel is a "power of **God**" for salvation; likewise,
EP : 02 :004(470) [0787] comes from the hearing of **God**'s Word (Rom. 10:17).
EP : 02 :004(470) [0787] It is **God**'s will that men should hear his Word and not
EP : 02 :006(470) [0787] everything to the grace of **God**, so that no one might
EP : 02 :006(470) [0787] no one might boast in the presence of **God** (I Cor. 9:16).
EP : 02 :007(470) [0787] errors as being contrary to the norm of the Word of **God**:
EP : 02 :009(471) [0789] man can convert himself to **God**, believe the Gospel,
EP : 02 :009(471) [0789] whole-heartedly obey **God**'s law, and thus merit
EP : 02 :011(471) [0789] convert himself to **God**, and whole-heartedly obey God's
EP : 02 :011(471) [0789] and whole-heartedly obey **God**'s law by his own powers,
EP : 02 :012(471) [0789] is able to keep the law of **God** perfectly and entirely and
EP : 02 :012(471) [0789] our righteousness before **God** whereby we merit eternal
EP : 02 :013(471) [0789] who imagine that **God** draws men to himself, enlightens
EP : 02 :013(471) [0789] without the hearing of **God**'s Word and without the use of
EP : 02 :014(471) [0789] in conversion and rebirth **God** wholly destroys the
EP : 02 :015(471) [0789] says, in conversion **God** makes willing people out of
EP : 02 :016(472) [0789] used expressions such as, "**God** draws, but draws the
EP : 02 :016(472) [0791] doctrine of the grace of **God**, we hold that these
EP : 02 :016(472) [0791] well to avoid them in a discussion of conversion to **God**.
EP : 02 :017(472) [0791] of the Holy Spirit, **God** changes stubborn and unwilling
EP : 02 :018(472) [0791] that is, when the Spirit of **God** through the Word that has
EP : 02 :018(472) [0791] and renewed *solely by God's power and activity*, man's
EP : 02 :018(472) [0791] instrument and means of **God** the Holy Spirit, so that man
EP : 02 :019(472) [0791] Spirit and the Word of **God** as the Holy Spirit's
EP : 02 :019(472) [0791] solely by the grace and operation of **God** the Holy Spirit.
EP : 03 :000(472) [0791] III. The Righteousness of Faith before **God**
EP : 03 :001(472) [0791] according to the Word of **God** and the content of the
EP : 03 :001(472) [0791] sinners are justified before **God** and saved solely by faith
EP : 03 :001(472) [0791] He is truly **God** and man since in him the divine and
EP : 03 :002(473) [0793] our righteousness before **God** only according to the
EP : 03 :003(473) [0793] in his obedience which as **God** and man he rendered to his
EP : 03 :004(473) [0793] our righteousness before **God** consists in this, that God
EP : 03 :004(473) [0793] God consists in this, that **God** forgives us our sins purely
EP : 03 :004(473) [0793] we are accepted by **God** into grace and are regarded as
EP : 03 :005(473) [0793] which avails before **God**," and that for Christ's sake such
EP : 03 :006(473) [0793] but the kind of gift of **God** by which in the Word of the
EP : 03 :006(473) [0793] as holy and righteous by **God** the Father, and shall be
EP : 03 :007(474) [0793] likewise, "Who shall bring any charge against **God**'s elect?
EP : 03 :007(474) [0793] It is **God** who justifies" (Rom. 8:33).
EP : 03 :009(474) [0795] the Word of the holy Gospel, they have a gracious **God**.
EP : 03 :010(474) [0795] of faith before **God**, we must give special attention to the
EP : 03 :011(474) [0795] it do not belong in the article of justification before **God**.
EP : 03 :015(475) [0795] righteous in fact before **God** on account of the love and
EP : 03 :018(475) [0795] 6. That not **God** himself but only divine gifts dwell in
EP : 03 :019(475) [0795] which consists in love toward **God** and our fellowman.
EP : 03 :020(475) [0797] our righteousness before **God**, not indeed as if it were the
EP : 03 :020(475) [0797] our righteousness before **God** is incomplete and imperfect
EP : 03 :021(475) [0797] are justified before **God** and saved both by the
EP : 04 :007(476) [0799] as well as from the article of our justification before **God**.
EP : 04 :007(476) [0799] only to the man to whom **God** reckons righteousness
EP : 04 :007(476) [0799] own doing, it is the gift of **God** — not because of works,
EP : 04 :013(477) [0799] in the elect children of **God** this spontaneity is not perfect,
EP : 04 :018(477) [0801] and their gratitude toward **God**, as it is to warn against
EP : 05 :001(478) [0801] *The Pure Doctrine of God's Word*
EP : 05 :002(478) [0801] admonition, the Word of **God** may be divided rightly.
EP : 05 :003(478) [0801] teaches what is right and **God**-pleasing and which
EP : 05 :003(478) [0801] everything that is sinful and contrary to **God**'s will.
EP : 05 :005(478) [0803] "righteousness that avails before **God**," and eternal life.
EP : 05 :007(478) [0803] delightful proclamation of **God**'s grace and favor acquired
EP : 05 :008(479) [0803] Then "**God**'s wrath is revealed from heaven" over all
EP : 05 :009(479) [0803] death of Christ, the Son of **God**, is an earnest and
EP : 05 :009(479) [0803] and advertisement of **God**'s wrath which really directs
EP : 05 :009(479) [0803] time what great things **God** demands of us in the law,
EP : 05 :010(479) [0803] of Christ — proclaims **God**'s wrath and terrifies people, it
EP : 06 :002(480) [0805] believe and whom **God** has truly converted are freed
EP : 06 :002(480) [0805] redeemed by the Son of **God** precisely that they should
EP : 06 :002(480) [0805] the law, for the law of **God** was written into their hearts
EP : 06 :002(480) [0805] their hearts when they were created in the image of **God**.
EP : 06 :004(480) [0807] is necessary for the law of **God** constantly to light their
EP : 06 :004(480) [0807] self-decreed and self-chosen acts of serving **God**.
EP : 06 :005(480) [0807] coercion of punishments and the threat of **God**'s wrath.
EP : 06 :006(480) [0807] works which the Spirit of **God**, who dwells in the
EP : 06 :006(481) [0807] this sense the children of **God** live in the law and walk
EP : 06 :006(481) [0807] God live in the law and walk according to the law of **God**.
EP : 06 :006(481) [0807] Thus **God**'s children are "not under the law, but under
EP : 06 :007(481) [0807] and the same law, namely, the unchangeable will of **God**.
EP : 07 :011(483) [0811] natural, complete **God** and man in one person,
EP : 07 :012(483) [0811] "The second ground is: "**God**'s right hand is everywhere.
EP : 07 :012(483) [0811] set at this right hand of **God** according to his human
EP : 07 :012(483) [0811] down at the right hand of **God**, whence he is able to do
EP : 07 :013(483) [0811] "The third ground is that **God**'s Word is not false nor does
EP : 07 :014(483) [0811] "The fourth ground is that **God** has and knows various
EP : 07 :034(485) [0815] 13. That **God**, even with all his omnipotence, is unable
EP : 07 :041(486) [0817] the righteous judgment of **God** all presumptuous,
EP : 08 :003(487) [0819] names common," so that **God** is called man and a man is
EP : 08 :003(487) [0819] man and a man is called **God**, but that God really (that is,
EP : 08 :003(487) [0819] man is called God, but that **God** really (that is, in deed

Continued ▶

E P : 0 8 :005(487) [0819] Christs, one the Son of **God** and the other the Son of
E P : 0 8 :005(487) [0819] is both the Son of **God** and the Son of man (Luke 1:35;
E P : 0 8 :009(487) [0819] is the highest communion which **God** truly has with man.
E P : 0 8 :009(488) [0819] is said or believed about **God** and everything divine that is
E P : 0 8 :010(488) [0819] teach, and confess that **God** is man and man is God, which
E P : 0 8 :010(488) [0819] God is man and man is **God**, which could not be the case
E P : 0 8 :011(488) [0821] son, truly be called or be **God**, or the Son of the most high
E P : 0 8 :011(488) [0821] or the Son of the most high **God**, if his humanity were not
E P : 0 8 :011(488) [0821] united with the Son of **God** and hence really (that is, in
E P : 0 8 :011(488) [0821] shared only the name of **God** with the divine nature?
E P : 0 8 :012(488) [0821] but the veritable Son of **God**; for this reason she is rightly
E P : 0 8 :012(488) [0821] she is rightly called, and truly is, the mother of **God**.
E P : 0 8 :013(488) [0821] and omnipotent power of **God**, but a man whose human
E P : 0 8 :013(488) [0821] with the Son of **God** that it has become one person with
E P : 0 8 :014(488) [0821] 9. Therefore the Son of **God** has truly suffered for us, but
E P : 0 8 :014(488) [0821] for our reconciliation with **God**, as it is written in I Cor.
E P : 0 8 :014(488) [0821] in Acts 20:28, We are purchased with **God**'s own blood.
E P : 0 8 :015(488) [0821] majesty and power of **God**, because he was assumed into
E P : 0 8 :015(488) [0821] he was assumed into **God** when he was conceived by the
E P : 0 8 :016(489) [0821] wisdom, and favor with **God** and men, for he did not
E P : 0 8 :016(489) [0821] a way that now not only as **God**, but also as man, he
E P : 0 8 :017(489) [0823] *the mode* and property of **God**'s right hand, as Dr. Luther
E P : 0 8 :018(489) [0823] and remains to all eternity, **God** and man in one
E P : 0 8 :019(490) [0823] as contrary to the Word of **God** and our simple Christian
E P : 0 8 :020(490) [0823] 1. That in Christ **God** and man are not one person, but
E P : 0 8 :020(490) [0823] person, but that the Son of **God** is one person and the Son
E P : 0 8 :022(490) [0823] Christ is not true, natural, and eternal **God**, as Arius held.
E P : 0 8 :025(490) [0823] of speech when we say "**God** is man, man is God," since
E P : 0 8 :025(490) [0823] we say "God is man, man is **God**," since really (that is, in
E P : 0 8 :026(490) [0823] we say that the Son of **God** died for the sins of the world
E P : 0 8 :027(490) [0825] has been severed from **God** and communicated to and
E P : 0 8 :031(491) [0825] in the passion the Son of **God** had no communion with
E P : 0 8 :033(491) [0825] 14. That the Son of **God** who assumed the human nature,
E P : 0 8 :035(491) [0825] in the omnipotence of **God**, and that this has not been
E P : 0 8 :035(491) [0825] lies somewhere between **God**'s omnipotence and the
E P : 0 8 :035(491) [0825] a power which is less than **God**'s omnipotence but greater
E P : 0 8 :037(491) [0825] a perfect knowledge of **God** and all his works, though it is
E P : 1 0 :001(492) [0829] forbidden in the Word of **God** but have been introduced
E P : 1 0 :002(493) [0829] nor forbidden by **God**, and thus come to an understanding
E P : 1 0 :003(493) [0829] forbidden in the Word of **God**, but which have been
E P : 1 0 :004(493) [0829] that the community of **God** in every locality and every age
E P : 1 0 :004(493) [0829] be most profitable and edifying to the community of **God**.
E P : 1 0 :006(493) [0831] in consequence what **God** sends us and what he lets the
E P : 1 0 :007(493) [0831] not commanded by **God**, as long as there is mutual
E P : 1 0 :008(494) [0831] as false and contrary to **God**'s Word the following
E P : 1 0 :010(494) [0831] upon the community of **God** as necessary things, in
E P : 1 0 :012(494) [0831] that the community of **God** does not have the liberty to
E P : 1 1 :000(494) [0831] XI. **God**'s Eternal Foreknowledge and Election
E P : 1 1 :002(494) [0831] and the eternal election of **God** is to be diligently noted.
E P : 1 1 :003(494) [0833] 2. **God**'s foreknowledge in nothing else than that God
E P : 1 1 :003(494) [0833] in nothing else than that **God** knows all things before they
E P : 1 1 :003(494) [0833] as it is written, "There is a **God** in heaven who reveals
E P : 1 1 :004(495) [0833] **God**'s foreknowledge merely controls the evil and imposes
E P : 1 1 :005(495) [0833] or the eternal election of **God**, however, is concerned only
E P : 1 1 :005(495) [0833] with the pious children of **God** in whom he is well
E P : 1 1 :006(495) [0833] in the secret counsel of **God**, but it is to be looked for in
E P : 1 1 :007(495) [0833] 6. The Word of **God**, however, leads us to Christ, who is
E P : 1 1 :009(495) [0833] to eternal life on the basis either of reason or **God**'s law.
E P : 1 1 :009(495) [0833] such reflections as this: "If **God** has elected me to salvation
E P : 1 1 :010(495) [0833] which clearly testifies that "**God** has consigned all men to
E P : 1 1 :011(495) [0835] 10. The doctrine of **God**'s eternal election is profitable and
E P : 1 1 :011(495) [0835] with the revealed will of **God** and observes the order
E P : 1 1 :011(496) [0835] in Christ, and to obey **God**, and only then does he speak
E P : 1 1 :011(496) [0835] does he speak of the mystery of **God**'s eternal election.
E P : 1 1 :012(496) [0835] does not mean that **God** does not desire to save everyone.
E P : 1 1 :012(496) [0835] do not hear the Word of **God** at all but willfully despise
E P : 1 1 :012(496) [0835] The fault does not lie in **God** or his election, but in their
E P : 1 1 :013(496) [0835] of the eternal election of **God** only in so far as it is
E P : 1 1 :013(496) [0835] is revealed in the Word of **God**, which shows us Christ as
E P : 1 1 :013(496) [0835] they do not proceed from **God** but are inspired by the evil
E P : 1 1 :013(496) [0835] **God** assures us of this gracious election not only in mere
E P : 1 1 :014(496) [0835] according to the will of **God** and "to confirm our call," as
E P : 1 1 :015(496) [0835] of the doctrine of **God**'s eternal election gives God his
E P : 1 1 :015(496) [0835] God's eternal election gives **God** his glory entirely and
E P : 1 1 :016(497) [0837] of the gracious election of **God** to eternal life in such a
E P : 1 1 :016(497) [0837] to the Word and will of **God**, but in accord with his reason
E P : 1 1 :017(497) [0837] 1. The doctrine that **God** does not want all men to come
E P : 1 1 :018(497) [0837] the doctrine that **God** is not serious about wanting all men
E P : 1 1 :019(497) [0837] 3. Furthermore, that **God** does not want everybody to be
E P : 1 1 :019(497) [0837] regard for their sin, **God** has predestined certain people to
E P : 1 1 :020(497) [0837] it is not only the mercy of **God** and the most holy merit of
E P : 1 1 :020(497) [0837] is also within us a cause of **God**'s election, on account of
E P : 1 1 :021(497) [0837] Hence they should not be tolerated in **God**'s church.
E P : 1 1 :022(497) [0837] guidance of the Word of **God** and the plain Catechism,
E P : 1 1 :022(497) [0837] May the almighty **God** and Father of our Lord Jesus
E P : 1 1 :022(497) [0837] abide in this Christian and **God**-pleasing concord.
E P : 1 2 :004(498) [0839] 2. That Christ is not true **God** but that he only has more
E P : 1 2 :005(498) [0839] our righteousness before **God** does not consist wholly in
E P : 1 2 :006(498) [0839] 4. That in the sight of **God** unbaptized children are not
E P : 1 2 :008(498) [0839] holy and the children of **God** by virtue of their birth from
E P : 1 2 :008(498) [0839] of the expressed word of **God**'s promise which extends
E P : 1 2 :011(499) [0841] way, but flee and avoid them as perverters of **God**'s Word
E P : 1 2 :012(499) [0841] That government is not a **God**-pleasing estate in the New
E P : 1 2 :014(499) [0841] that it has received from **God** for their protection and
E P : 1 2 :022(499) [0841] a means through which **God** the Holy Spirit teaches
E P : 1 2 :023(500) [0841] through which the Lord **God** seals the adoption of
E P : 1 2 :025(500) [0843] again through the Spirit of **God** can perfectly keep and
E P : 1 2 :025(500) [0843] can perfectly keep and fulfill the law of **God** in this life.
E P : 1 2 :028(500) [0843] a true, essential, natural **God**, of one divine essence with
E P : 1 2 :028(500) [0843] of one divine essence with **God** the Father and the Holy
E P : 1 2 :028(500) [0843] majesty and is inferior to and beside **God** the Father.
E P : 1 2 :029(500) [0843] and Holy Spirit, but as **God** the Father, Son, and Holy
E P : 1 2 :029(500) [0843] and that only the Father is rightly and truly **God**.
E P : 1 2 :030(500) [0843] contrary to the Word of **God**, the three Creeds, the
E P : 1 2 :031(500) [0843] but intend by the grace of **God** to abide by it, we have
E P : 1 2 :031(501) [0843] fear and invocation of **God**, subscribed our signatures
S D : 0 0 :000(501) [0845] According to the Word of **God** and the Summary
S D : P R :001(501) [0847] the basis of the Word of **God** and purified by Dr. Luther,
S D : P R :002(501) [0847] contrary to the Word of **God** and Christian institutions,
S D : P R :003(501) [0847] according to the Word of **God**, ordered the preparation of
S D : P R :003(501) [0847] Confession on the basis of **God**'s Word and submitted it
S D : P R :003(502) [0847] Confession, but, thank **God**, it has remained unrefuted
S D : P R :004(502) [0847] accept next to the Word of **God**, just as in ancient times
S D : P R :004(502) [0847] in the Church of **God** when great controversies broke out,
S D : P R :007(502) [0849] others even denied that Christ was eternal and true **God**.
S D : P R :009(503) [0849] tolerated in the church of **God**, much less be excused and
S D : P R :010(503) [0849] explained on the basis of **God**'s Word and of approved
S D : P R :010(503) [0849] agrees with the Word of **God** and the Christian Augsburg
S D : R N :010(503) [0849] with the Word of **God** and Errors Are to Be Explained
S D : P R :001(503) [0851] religion is drawn together out of the Word of **God**.
S D : P R :002(503) [0851] doctrine of the Word of **God** as Dr. Luther of blessed
S D : P R :004(504) [0851] was drawn together out of **God**'s Word in brief articles or
S D : P R :004(504) [0851] based upon the Word of **God** — in which all those heresies
S D : P R :005(504) [0851] special grace our merciful **God** has in these last days
S D : P R :005(504) [0851] ministry of that illustrious man of **God**, Dr. Luther.
S D : P R :005(504) [0851] conformed to the Word of **God**, is summarized in the
S D : P R :005(504) [0851] is taken from the Word of **God** and solidly and well
S D : P R :007(505) [0853] estates were resolved by **God**'s grace to remain faithful.
S D : P R :007(505) [0853] explained on the basis of **God**'s Word, and in addition the
S D : P R :008(505) [0853] doctrine on the basis of **God**'s Word for ordinary laymen
S D : P R :009(505) [0855] his writings on the basis of **God**'s Word and conclusively
S D : P R :009(505) [0855] that the Word of **God** is and should remain the sole rule
S D : P R :010(506) [0855] drawn from the Word of **God**, all other writings are to be
S D : P R :013(506) [0855] position on the Word of **God** as the eternal truth, so we
S D : P R :014(506) [0855] a thorough, lasting, and **God**-pleasing concord within the
S D : P R :016(507) [0857] delights in the truth of **God**'s Word will find in the
S D : P R :016(507) [0857] and apostolic writings of **God**'s Word, and what he should
S D : P R :020(508) [0859] By **God**'s grace we shall continue to abide in it loyally and
S D : 0 1 :002(508) [0859] the Fall are and remain **God**'s handiwork and creation in
S D : 0 1 :002(509) [0859] body and soul, which are **God**'s handiwork and creatures
S D : 0 1 :003(509) [0859] according to the Word of **God** and is purged of all
S D : 0 1 :003(509) [0861] we are extolling **God**'s honor properly when we carefully
S D : 0 1 :004(509) [0861] according to the Word of **God** and to preserve the true
S D : 0 1 :005(509) [0861] the actual transgression of **God**'s commandments but
S D : 0 1 :006(509) [0861] means that in the sight of **God** original sin, like a spiritual
S D : 0 1 :006(509) [0861] of the law of **God**, so that we are "by nature the children
S D : 0 1 :007(510) [0861] Confession teaches, that **God** is not the creator, author, or
S D : 0 1 :007(510) [0861] today, in this corruption, **God** does not create and make
S D : 0 1 :007(510) [0861] with the nature which **God** still creates and makes at the
S D : 0 1 :009(510) [0861] of Adam and Eve, are in **God**'s disfavor and are children
S D : 0 1 :010(510) [0863] paradise or of the image of **God** according to which man
S D : 0 1 :010(510) [0863] and ineptitude as far as the things of **God** are concerned.
S D : 0 1 :011(510) [0863] replaces the lost image of **God** in man with a deep,
S D : 0 1 :011(510) [0863] diametrically opposed to **God** and his highest commands
S D : 0 1 :011(510) [0863] is actually enmity against **God**, especially in divine and
S D : 0 1 :012(510) [0863] them that they amount to nothing in the sight of **God**.
S D : 0 1 :013(511) [0863] of original sin which **God** imposes upon Adam's children
S D : 0 1 :014(511) [0863] up and forgiven before **God** only for the Lord Christ's
S D : 0 1 :019(511) [0865] such a sin in the sight of **God** that apart from Christ every
S D : 0 1 :025(512) [0867] false doctrines because **God**'s Word teaches that man's
S D : 0 1 :025(512) [0867] than that, in the sight of **God** it can by and of itself do
S D : 0 1 :027(513) [0867] the Fall, and that by **God**'s judgment and verdict man lost
S D : 0 1 :029(513) [0867] incorrupt in the sight of **God**, and only the original sin
S D : 0 1 :030(513) [0867] within man, so that **God** by his law does not accuse and
S D : 0 1 :032(513) [0869] human beings created by **God** but because we are sinful
S D : 0 1 :032(513) [0869] and the creature of **God** even after the Fall but because
S D : 0 1 :033(514) [0869] or man himself created by **God** (within which original sin,
S D : 0 1 :033(514) [0869] created and preserved by **God** and in which sin dwells and
S D : 0 1 :034(514) [0869] testifies not only that **God** created human nature before
S D : 0 1 :034(514) [0869] the Fall human nature is **God**'s creature and handiwork
S D : 0 1 :037(514) [0871] was, and the spirit returns to **God** who gave it" (Eccl. 2:7).
S D : 0 1 :038(514) [0871] that even after the Fall **God** is man's creator who creates
S D : 0 1 :038(514) [0871] sin itself, for in that case **God** would be the creator of sin.
S D : 0 1 :038(515) [0871] we confess, "I believe that **God** has created *me* and all that
S D : 0 1 :038(515) [0871] that I am a creature of **God**; that is, that he has given and
S D : 0 1 :038(515) [0871] creature and handiwork of **God** has been miserably
S D : 0 1 :038(515) [0871] the dough out of which **God** forms and makes man has
S D : 0 1 :039(515) [0871] hearts may well ponder **God**'s inexpressible kindness in
S D : 0 1 :040(515) [0871] sin does not come from **God**, nor is God the creator or
S D : 0 1 :040(515) [0871] not come from God, nor is **God** the creator or author of
S D : 0 1 :040(515) [0871] creature or handiwork of **God**; on the contrary, it is the
S D : 0 1 :041(515) [0871] Either that, since **God** is the creator of this our nature, he
S D : 0 1 :042(515) [0871] and in order to distinguish **God**'s creature and handiwork
S D : 0 1 :042(515) [0871] we declare that it is by **God**'s creation that man has a body
S D : 0 1 :042(515) [0871] soul; likewise, that it is **God**'s work that man is able to
S D : 0 1 :042(515) [0871] has in this fashion corrupted **God**'s handiwork in Adam.
S D : 0 1 :043(515) [0873] of Scripture that **God**'s Son assumed our nature, though
S D : 0 1 :044(516) [0873] Since, however, **God**'s Son assumed our nature, but not
S D : 0 1 :045(516) [0873] of Scripture that **God** cleanses man from sin, purifies him,
S D : 0 1 :045(516) [0873] with man himself, since **God** receives man for Christ's
S D : 0 1 :051(517) [0875] Thus in the statement, "**God** creates man's nature," the
S D : 0 1 :055(518) [0877] it is a substance, is either **God** himself or a product and
S D : 0 1 :055(518) [0877] is either God himself or a product and creature of **God**.
S D : 0 1 :058(519) [0879] this reason the churches of **God** will never attain abiding
S D : 0 1 :060(519) [0879] original sin man is in **God**'s sight spiritually lifeless and
S D : 0 1 :061(519) [0879] harmony with the Word of **God**, just as Dr. Luther in his
S D : 0 1 :061(519) [0879] the distinction between **God**'s handiwork, our nature in
S D : 0 1 :061(519) [0879] profoundly and inexpressibly corrupts **God**'s handiwork.
S D : 0 1 :062(519) [0879] we shall not only endure **God**'s eternal wrath and death
S D : 0 2 :002(520) [0881] Fall, when the Word of **God** is preached and the grace of
S D : 0 2 :002(520) [0881] of God is preached and the grace of **God** is offered to him
S D : 0 2 :003(520) [0881] the commandment of **God**, to trust God truly, to fear and
S D : 0 2 :003(520) [0881] of God, to trust **God** truly, to fear and to love him, man
S D : 0 2 :004(520) [0881] have taught that **God** converts man through the Holy
S D : 0 2 :004(520) [0881] hearing of the Word of **God**) and brings them to the
S D : 0 2 :005(521) [0881] understand the Word of **God** when it is preached, but

Continued ▶

S D : 0 2 :005(521) [0881] he of himself approach **God**, but he is and remains an
S D : 0 2 :005(521) [0881] and remains an enemy of **God** until by the power of the
S D : 0 2 :006(521) [0883] according to the Word of **God**, and by God's grace to
S D : 0 2 :006(521) [0883] the Word of God, and by **God**'s grace to bring it to an
S D : 0 2 :007(521) [0883] ready for the grace of **God** or to accept the proffered
S D : 0 2 :007(521) [0883] direction of that which is displeasing and contrary to **God**
S D : 0 2 :008(521) [0883] reasons from the Word of **God** support and confirm the
S D : 0 2 :008(521) [0883] perverse world is folly with **God**" and that it is only from
S D : 0 2 :008(521) [0883] is only from the Word of **God** that judgments on articles
S D : 0 2 :009(521) [0883] knowledge that there is a **God**, as well as of the teaching
S D : 0 2 :009(522) [0883] the Gospel of the Son of **God** and the promise of eternal
S D : 0 2 :010(522) [0883] the gifts of the Spirit of **God**, for they are folly to him,
S D : 0 2 :010(522) [0883] "Since, in the wisdom of **God**, the world did not know
S D : 0 2 :010(522) [0883] the world did not know **God** through its wisdom, it
S D : 0 2 :010(522) [0883] its wisdom, it pleased **God** through the folly of the Gospel
S D : 0 2 :010(522) [0883] are not reborn through **God**'s Spirit, "walk in the futility
S D : 0 2 :010(522) [0883] alienated from the life of **God** because of the ignorance
S D : 0 2 :010(522) [0885] the secrets of the kingdom of **God**" (Matt. 13:13, 11).
S D : 0 2 :010(522) [0885] "No one understands, no one seeks for **God**.
S D : 0 2 :010(522) [0885] neither knows nor regards **God**) and the darkness has not
S D : 0 2 :011(522) [0885] and life, unless the Son of **God** has liberated him from the
S D : 0 2 :012(522) [0885] from us; our sufficiency is from **God**" (II Cor. 3:5).
S D : 0 2 :012(523) [0885] the gifts of the Spirit of **God** (that is, he has no capacity
S D : 0 2 :013(523) [0885] "is hostile to **God**; it does not submit to God's law, indeed
S D : 0 2 :013(523) [0885] God; it does not submit to **God**'s law, indeed it cannot"
S D : 0 2 :014(523) [0885] what the Son of **God** says remains eternally true, "Apart
S D : 0 2 :014(523) [0885] Paul says is also true, "For **God** is at work in you, both to
S D : 0 2 :014(523) [0885] a longing for the grace of **God** and eternal salvation in
S D : 0 2 :014(523) [0885] They know that **God**, who has kindled this beginning of
S D : 0 2 :015(523) [0885] that what they ask of **God** they cannot obtain by their own
S D : 0 2 :015(523) [0887] for example, David asks **God** more than ten times to give
S D : 0 2 :015(523) [0887] meditating on the Word of **God**, but were written in order
S D : 0 2 :015(523) [0887] all things we should thank **God** from our hearts for having
S D : 0 2 :016(523) [0887] And after **God**, through the Holy Spirit in Baptism, has
S D : 0 2 :016(523) [0887] of true knowledge of **God** and faith, we ought to petition
S D : 0 2 :016(523) [0887] Unless **God** himself is our teacher, we cannot study and
S D : 0 2 :017(523) [0887] second place, the Word of **God** testifies that in divine
S D : 0 2 :017(523) [0887] totally turned away from **God**, but is also turned and
S D : 0 2 :017(523) [0887] also turned and perverted against **God** and toward all evil
S D : 0 2 :017(524) [0887] opposed and hostile to **God**, and all too mighty, alive, and
S D : 0 2 :017(524) [0887] which is displeasing to **God** and contrary to his will.
S D : 0 2 :017(524) [0887] on the flesh is hostile to **God**" (Rom. 8:7), and again, "The
S D : 0 2 :017(524) [0887] for I delight in the law of **God** in my inmost self (which
S D : 0 2 :018(524) [0887] wars against the law of **God** even after their regeneration,
S D : 0 2 :018(524) [0887] obstinately opposed and hostile to **God**'s law and will.
S D : 0 2 :018(524) [0889] Spirit offers the grace of **God** and salvation through the
S D : 0 2 :018(524) [0889] born, he defiantly resists **God** and his will unless the Holy
S D : 0 2 :019(524) [0889] or that he is converted to **God** without hearing and
S D : 0 2 :021(525) [0889] dreadful, cruel wrath of **God** over sin and death but
S D : 0 2 :022(525) [0889] And while **God** in his righteous and severe judgment cast
S D : 0 2 :022(525) [0889] conversion, in the grace of **God**, and in eternal life, not by
S D : 0 2 :022(525) [0889] recalcitrant enmity against **God** — but out of pure grace
S D : 0 2 :023(525) [0889] it can be converted to **God** and become truly free, a
S D : 0 2 :024(526) [0891] and hostile to the will of **God** unless the Holy Spirit is
S D : 0 2 :024(526) [0891] and creates faith and other **God**-pleasing virtues and
S D : 0 2 :026(526) [0891] "For **God** is at work in you, both to will and to work"
S D : 0 2 :026(526) [0891] **God** "gives the repentance" (Acts 5:51; II Tim. 2:25).
S D : 0 2 :026(526) [0891] has been granted to you by **God** that you should believe
S D : 0 2 :026(526) [0891] "It is the gift of **God**" (Eph. 2:8).
S D : 0 2 :026(526) [0891] "This is the work of **God**, that you believe in him whom
S D : 0 2 :026(526) [0891] **God** gives an understanding heart, seeing eyes, and
S D : 0 2 :026(526) [0891] **God** removes the hard, stony heart and bestows a new and
S D : 0 2 :026(526) [0891] In short, every good gift comes from **God** (James 1:17).
S D : 0 2 :026(526) [0891] "All our sufficiency is from **God**" (II Cor. 3:6).
S D : 0 2 :027(526) [0891] "The grace of **God** consists merely in this, that God in the
S D : 0 2 :027(527) [0891] merely in this, that **God** in the preaching of the truth
S D : 0 2 :027(527) [0893] and to will, but that it is **God**'s work to give the ability to
S D : 0 2 :028(527) [0893] upon the Word of **God** and accords with the Augsburg
S D : 0 2 :031(527) [0893] Spirit are without fear of **God**, without faith, do not trust
S D : 0 2 :031(527) [0893] do not trust or believe that **God** will hear them, that he
S D : 0 2 :031(527) [0893] them in their troubles; therefore they are without **God**.
S D : 0 2 :032(527) [0893] bear good fruit, and without faith no one can please **God**.
S D : 0 2 :036(528) [0895] I have heard the Word of **God** and still hear it, which is
S D : 0 2 :037(528) [0895] the devil and were completely ignorant of **God** and Christ
S D : 0 2 :039(528) [0895] ascribes this work alone to **God** when he says, "We are his
S D : 0 2 :039(528) [0895] for good works, which **God** prepared beforehand, that we
S D : 0 2 :041(529) [0897] does the kingdom of **God** come to us?" as follows: "When
S D : 0 2 :042(529) [0897] come to Christ, but that **God** must give us his Holy Spirit,
S D : 0 2 :043(529) [0897] masters and the devil is our **god** and lord, and there is no
S D : 0 2 :043(529) [0897] and what is contrary to **God** and his commandments."
S D : 0 2 :044(529) [0897] only the devil's will and what is contrary to the Lord **God**.
S D : 0 2 :044(529) [0897] **God** himself must draw man and give him new birth.
S D : 0 2 :045(530) [0899] to the Holy Scriptures of **God**, the Christian Augsburg
S D : 0 2 :046(530) [0899] are exclusively the work of **God** and not of our own
S D : 0 2 :046(530) [0899] continue wholly to resist **God** or wait until God forcibly
S D : 0 2 :046(530) [0899] to resist God or wait until **God** forcibly converts them
S D : 0 2 :046(530) [0899] but will wait until **God** pours his gifts into them out of
S D : 0 2 :046(530) [0899] to feel and to perceive that **God** has truly converted them.
S D : 0 2 :047(530) [0901] and doubt, and wonder if **God** has really elected them and
S D : 0 2 :048(530) [0901] set forth from the Word of **God** how man is converted to
S D : 0 2 :048(530) [0901] how man is converted to **God**, how and by what means
S D : 0 2 :049(530) [0901] It is not **God**'s will that anyone should be damned but
S D : 0 2 :049(530) [0901] "For **God** so loved the world that he gave his only Son,
S D : 0 2 :050(530) [0901] kindness and mercy, **God** provides for the public
S D : 0 2 :050(531) [0901] of their sins and true faith in the Son of **God**, Jesus Christ
S D : 0 2 :050(531) [0901] And it is **God**'s will to call men to eternal salvation, to
S D : 0 2 :051(531) [0901] since, in the wisdom of **God**, the world did not know God
S D : 0 2 :051(531) [0901] the world did not know **God** through wisdom, it pleased
S D : 0 2 :051(531) [0901] wisdom, it pleased **God** through the folly of what we
S D : 0 2 :052(531) [0901] and the hearing of **God**'s Word are the Holy Spirit's
S D : 0 2 :052(531) [0901] to convert men to **God**, and to work in them both to will
S D : 0 2 :053(531) [0903] who is not yet converted to **God** and regenerated can hear
S D : 0 2 :054(531) [0903] the hearing of his Word) **God** is active, breaks our hearts,
S D : 0 2 :054(531) [0903] his sins and the wrath of **God** and experiences genuine
S D : 0 2 :055(532) [0903] that, when the Word of **God** is preached, pure and
S D : 0 2 :055(532) [0903] unalloyed according to **God**'s command and will, and
S D : 0 2 :055(532) [0903] to and meditate on it, **God** is certainly present with his
S D : 0 2 :057(532) [0903] or read the Word of **God**, but despises the Word and the
S D : 0 2 :057(532) [0903] and the community of **God**, dies in this condition, and
S D : 0 2 :057(532) [0903] comfort himself with **God**'s eternal election nor obtain his
S D : 0 2 :059(532) [0905] with his will resists the Lord **God** until he is converted.
S D : 0 2 :059(532) [0905] the Word and will of **God** until God raises him from the
S D : 0 2 :059(532) [0905] Word and will of God until **God** raises him from the death
S D : 0 2 :060(532) [0905] It is true that **God** does not coerce anyone to piety, for
S D : 0 2 :060(533) [0905] Nevertheless, the Lord **God** draws the person whom he
S D : 0 2 :062(533) [0905] the question how **God** operates in man, it is correct to say
S D : 0 2 :062(533) [0905] to say that the Lord **God** indeed has one mode of acting
S D : 0 2 :063(533) [0905] he delights in the law of **God** according to his inmost self
S D : 0 2 :063(533) [0905] all who are led by the Spirit of **God** are sons of God."
S D : 0 2 :063(533) [0905] all who are led by the Spirit of God are sons of **God**."
S D : 0 2 :064(533) [0905] "For I delight in the law of **God** in my inmost self, but I
S D : 0 2 :064(533) [0907] of myself serve the law of **God** with my mind, but with my
S D : 0 2 :066(534) [0907] we entreat you not to accept the grace of **God** in vain."
S D : 0 2 :066(534) [0907] as much and as long as **God** rules in him through his Holy
S D : 0 2 :066(534) [0907] and leads him, but if **God** should withdraw his gracious
S D : 0 2 :066(534) [0907] could not remain in obedience to **God** for one moment.
S D : 0 2 :067(534) [0907] not only hear the Word of **God** but also are able to assent
S D : 0 2 :070(535) [0909] sin, to fear the wrath of **God**, to turn from sin, to
S D : 0 2 :071(535) [0909] to bring it about that **God** in his immeasurable kindness
S D : 0 2 :071(535) [0909] it kindles faith and other **God**-pleasing virtues in us, so
S D : 0 2 :072(535) [0909] not to receive this grace of **God** in vain but to exercise
S D : 0 2 :073(535) [0909] at all, but merely suffers what **God** accomplishes in him?
S D : 0 2 :073(535) [0909] through coercion, so that **God** forcibly compels a man to
S D : 0 2 :075(536) [0911] will can convert itself to **God**, believe the Gospel, and
S D : 0 2 :075(536) [0911] and obey the law of **God** from the heart, and by this
S D : 0 2 :077(536) [0911] powers to convert itself to **God** and to obey the law of
S D : 0 2 :077(536) [0911] itself to God and to obey the law of **God** from the heart.
S D : 0 2 :077(536) [0911] natural powers can meet **God** and to some degree —
S D : 0 2 :077(536) [0911] itself for the grace of **God**, embrace and accept it, believe
S D : 0 2 :079(536) [0911] can keep the law of **God** perfectly in this life and by such
S D : 0 2 :079(536) [0911] of the law merit righteousness before **God** and eternal life.
S D : 0 2 :080(536) [0911] tolerate in the church of **God**, the enthusiasts who imagine
S D : 0 2 :080(536) [0911] use of the holy sacraments, **God** draws man to himself,
S D : 0 2 :081(537) [0911] and regeneration **God** creates a new heart and a new man
S D : 0 2 :083(537) [0913] and is not prepared by **God** for grace, but wholly resists
S D : 0 2 :085(537) [0913] unregenerated man resists **God** entirely and is completely
S D : 0 2 :085(537) [0913] man delights in the law of **God** according to the inmost
S D : 0 2 :085(537) [0913] mind he serves the law of **God**, but with his flesh he serves
S D : 0 2 :086(537) [0913] also does something," and "**God** draws, but he draws the
S D : 0 2 :086(538) [0913] in his conversion, contrary to the article of **God**'s grace.
S D : 0 2 :086(538) [0913] be avoided in the discussion of man's conversion to **God**.
S D : 0 2 :087(538) [0915] and alone the work of **God**, just as the bodily resurrection
S D : 0 2 :087(538) [0915] flesh is to be ascribed to **God** alone, as was thoroughly
S D : 0 2 :088(538) [0915] drawing of the Holy Spirit, **God** makes willing people out
S D : 0 2 :089(538) [0915] man only suffers that which **God** works in him), he did
S D : 0 2 :090(538) [0915] man's conversion to **God**, particularly as to the manner in
S D : 0 2 :090(538) [0915] these three (the Word of **God** preached and heard, the
S D : 0 2 :090(539) [0915] evident that conversion to **God** is solely of God the Holy
S D : 0 2 :090(539) [0915] to God is solely of **God** the Holy Spirit, who is the true
S D : 0 2 :090(539) [0915] does nothing, but only lets **God** work in him, until he is
S D : 0 2 :090(539) [0915] that which is pleasing to **God**, in the manner and degree
S D : 0 3 :000(539) [0917] III. The Righteousness of Faith before **God**
S D : 0 3 :001(539) [0917] of Christ or of faith which **God** by grace through faith
S D : 0 3 :002(539) [0917] calls the righteousness of **God**, is the essential
S D : 0 3 :002(539) [0917] essential righteousness of **God** (namely, Christ himself as
S D : 0 3 :002(539) [0917] natural, essential Son of **God**, who through faith dwells in
S D : 0 3 :004(540) [0917] to both natures; as **God** and man he has by his perfect
S D : 0 3 :004(540) [0917] of sins, reconciliation with **God**, and the fact that we are
S D : 0 3 :004(540) [0917] that we are adopted as **God**'s children solely on account
S D : 0 3 :008(540) [0919] according to the Word of **God** and to settle it by his
S D : 0 3 :009(540) [0919] of faith before **God** we believe, teach, and confess
S D : 0 3 :009(540) [0919] sinner is justified before **God** (that is, he is absolved and
S D : 0 3 :009(540) [0919] is adopted as a child of **God** and an heir of eternal life)
S D : 0 3 :011(541) [0919] Faith is a gift of **God** whereby we rightly learn to know
S D : 0 3 :011(541) [0919] righteous and holy by **God** the Father, and are saved
S D : 0 3 :013(541) [0919] is so good a work and so **God**-pleasing a virtue, but
S D : 0 3 :015(541) [0919] Christ is not only man, but **God** and man in one undivided
S D : 0 3 :015(541) [0919] it to us as righteousness, **God** forgives us our sins,
S D : 0 3 :016(541) [0921] have reconciliation with **God**, forgiveness of sins, the
S D : 0 3 :016(541) [0921] of sins, the grace of **God**, adoption, and the inheritance of
S D : 0 3 :017(542) [0921] of Christ which **God** reckons to faith (Phil. 3:9).
S D : 0 3 :017(542) [0921] "Who shall bring any charge against **God**'s elect?
S D : 0 3 :017(542) [0921] It is **God** who justifies" (Rom. 8:33), that is, absolves and
S D : 0 3 :019(542) [0921] forgiveness of sins and our adoption as **God**'s children.
S D : 0 3 :019(542) [0921] that is, justification before **God** is regeneration, just as St.
S D : 0 3 :020(542) [0921] of wrath into a child of **God** and thus has translated him
S D : 0 3 :023(543) [0923] merit, are justified before **God** (that is, accepted into
S D : 0 3 :023(543) [0923] creates within them love toward **God** and their fellowman
S D : 0 3 :023(543) [0923] of faith before **God** consists solely in the gracious
S D : 0 3 :025(543) [0923] are the grace of **God**, the merit of Christ, and faith which
S D : 0 3 :025(543) [0923] of sins, reconciliation with **God**, adoption, and the
S D : 0 3 :028(544) [0925] of justification before **God**; it rather follows justification,
S D : 0 3 :029(544) [0925] how a person may be justified before **God** and be saved.
S D : 0 3 :030(544) [0925] of Christ and the grace of **God**, Scripture teaches that the
S D : 0 3 :030(544) [0925] of faith before **God** consists solely in a gracious
S D : 0 3 :030(544) [0925] in justification before **God** faith trusts neither in contrition
S D : 0 3 :030(544) [0925] he fulfilled the law of **God** in our stead and which is
S D : 0 3 :031(544) [0925] and accept the grace of **God**, the merit of Christ, and the
S D : 0 3 :032(545) [0927] into the article of justification by faith before **God**.
S D : 0 3 :032(545) [0927] therewith and thereby stand before the tribunal of **God**.
S D : 0 3 :032(545) [0927] which is reckoned to faith can stand before **God**'s tribunal
S D : 0 3 :032(545) [0927] pleasing and acceptable to **God** and is adopted to sonship
S D : 0 3 :033(545) [0927] was justified before **God** through faith alone for the sake
S D : 0 3 :033(545) [0927] of Abraham before **God**, whereby he had a gracious God
S D : 0 3 :033(545) [0927] whereby he had a gracious **God** and was pleasing and
S D : 0 3 :034(545) [0927] to that person to whom **God** reckons righteousness

Continued ▶

SD : 0 3 :035(545) [0927] of justification before **God**, in order to preserve the glory
SD : 0 3 :036(545) [0927] that we are justified before **God** and saved "through faith
SD : 0 3 :036(545) [0927] of poor sinners before **God** they should not be drawn,
SD : 0 3 :037(546) [0929] of our justification which **God** takes into consideration in
SD : 0 3 :039(546) [0929] our righteousness before **God**, nor are they to be made
SD : 0 3 :041(546) [0929] apprehends the grace of **God** in Christ whereby the person
SD : 0 3 :043(547) [0931] who are reconciled with **God**, and who have obtained
SD : 0 3 :043(547) [0931] to be justified by it before **God**; or, the presence of good
SD : 0 3 :043(547) [0931] instrument it embraces **God**'s grace and the merit of
SD : 0 3 :045(547) [0933] of our justification before **God**, either entirely or in part.
SD : 0 3 :047(548) [0933] real righteousness before **God** is our love or the renewal
SD : 0 3 :048(548) [0933] by faith before **God** consists of two pieces or parts,
SD : 0 3 :049(548) [0933] our righteousness before **God**, in such a way, however,
SD : 0 3 :049(548) [0933] our justification before **God** is incomplete or imperfect
SD : 0 3 :050(548) [0933] are justified before **God** and are righteous both through
SD : 0 3 :052(548) [0933] which he is justified before **God**, as though we are indeed
SD : 0 3 :053(548) [0933] to that man to whom **God** reckons righteousness without
SD : 0 3 :054(548) [0933] the indwelling of **God**'s essential righteousness in us.
SD : 0 3 :054(548) [0935] hand, it is true indeed that **God** the Father, Son, and Holy
SD : 0 3 :054(548) [0935] Christ and reconciled with **God**, since all Christians are
SD : 0 3 :054(549) [0935] Christians are temples of **God** the Father, Son, and Holy
SD : 0 3 :054(549) [0935] hand, this indwelling of **God** is not the righteousness of
SD : 0 3 :054(549) [0935] calls the righteousness of **God**, on account of which we
SD : 0 3 :054(549) [0935] God, on account of which we are declared just before **God**
SD : 0 3 :055(549) [0935] person of Christ, who as **God** and man in his sole, total,
SD : 0 3 :056(549) [0935] had not been true, eternal **God**, the obedience and passion
SD : 0 3 :056(549) [0935] Likewise, if the Son of **God** had not become man, the
SD : 0 3 :056(549) [0935] the eternal and almighty **God** for the sins of all the world.
SD : 0 3 :056(549) [0935] the humanity, could not mediate between **God** and us.
SD : 0 3 :057(549) [0935] and immutable righteousness of **God** revealed in the law.
SD : 0 3 :057(549) [0935] which avails before **God** and is revealed in the Gospel,
SD : 0 3 :057(549) [0935] which faith depends before **God** and which God reckons
SD : 0 3 :057(549) [0935] before God and which **God** reckons to faith, as it is
SD : 0 3 :058(550) [0937] of the person who is **God** and man at the same time.
SD : 0 3 :059(550) [0937] as contrary to the Word of **God**, the teaching of the
SD : 0 3 :060(550) [0937] our righteousness before **God** only according to his divine
SD : 0 3 :063(550) [0937] indwelling our sins are covered up in the sight of **God**.
SD : 0 3 :065(550) [0937] 6. That not **God** but only the gifts of God dwell in
SD : 0 3 :065(550) [0937] That not God but only the gifts of **God** dwell in believers.
SD : 0 3 :066(550) [0937] to the clear Word of **God**, and by God's grace we shall
SD : 0 3 :066(550) [0937] Word of God, and by **God**'s grace we shall remain
SD : 0 3 :066(550) [0937] by faith before **God** as it is set forth, explained, and
SD : 0 3 :066(550) [0937] and demonstrated from **God**'s Word in the Augsburg
SD : 0 3 :067(551) [0937] of justification before **God**, on which the salvation of our
SD : 0 4 :004(551) [0939] all men to be obedient to **God**, but at times it implies the
SD : 0 4 :006(552) [0939] according to the Word of **God**, and by God's grace to
SD : 0 4 :006(552) [0939] the Word of God, and by **God**'s grace to arrive at a
SD : 0 4 :007(552) [0939] following points: That it is **God**'s will, ordinance, and
SD : 0 4 :007(552) [0939] truly good works which **God** himself prescribes and
SD : 0 4 :007(552) [0941] has been reconciled to **God** through faith and renewed
SD : 0 4 :008(552) [0941] pleasing and acceptable to **God**, even though they are still
SD : 0 4 :008(552) [0941] through faith, because the person is acceptable to **God**.
SD : 0 4 :008(552) [0941] of the world, and even **God** will reward them with
SD : 0 4 :008(552) [0941] with sins in the sight of **God**), and God regards them as sin
SD : 0 4 :008(552) [0941] in the sight of God), and **God** regards them as sin and as
SD : 0 4 :008(552) [0941] nature and because the person is not reconciled with **God**.
SD : 0 4 :008(552) [0941] must first be pleasing to **God** — and that alone for Christ's
SD : 0 4 :009(552) [0941] of the truly good and **God**-pleasing works that God will
SD : 0 4 :009(552) [0941] God-pleasing works that **God** will reward both in this and
SD : 0 4 :010(552) [0941] and begets us anew from **God**, kills the Old Adam, makes
SD : 0 4 :012(553) [0941] a vital, deliberate trust in **God**'s grace, so certain that it
SD : 0 4 :012(553) [0941] mettlesome, and merry toward **God** and all creatures.
SD : 0 4 :012(553) [0941] everything for the love of **God** and to his glory, who has
SD : 0 4 :014(553) [0943] of necessity do good works that **God** has commanded."
SD : 0 4 :014(553) [0943] bound to do because of **God**'s ordinance, commandment,
SD : 0 4 :016(554) [0943] as referring to the order of **God**'s immutable will, whose
SD : 0 4 :017(554) [0943] Such works of pretense **God** does not want.
SD : 0 4 :017(554) [0943] Rom. 6:7) because **God** loves a cheerful giver (II Cor.
SD : 0 4 :018(554) [0943] spirit by those whom the Son of **God** has set free.
SD : 0 4 :019(554) [0945] and delights in the law of **God** in his inmost self, and on
SD : 0 4 :020(554) [0945] still retain faith and **God**'s mercy and his grace.
SD : 0 4 :022(555) [0945] solely to the grace of **God** and the merit of Christ, as was
SD : 0 4 :024(555) [0945] solely to the man to whom **God** reckons righteousness
SD : 0 4 :031(556) [0947] retain faith, the grace of **God**, righteousness, and
SD : 0 4 :032(556) [0947] that the unrighteous will not inherit the kingdom of **God**?
SD : 0 4 :032(556) [0947] adulterers will inherit the kingdom of **God**" (I Cor. 6:9).
SD : 0 4 :032(556) [0947] not inherit the kingdom of **God**" (Gal. 5:21; Eph. 5:5).
SD : 0 4 :032(556) [0947] of these the wrath of **God** is coming upon the sons of
SD : 0 4 :034(556) [0949] and our hope of sharing the glory of **God** (Rom. 5:2).
SD : 0 4 :034(557) [0949] "By **God**'s power we are guarded through faith for a
SD : 0 4 :035(557) [0949] evident from the Word of **God** that faith is the proper and
SD : 0 4 :035(557) [0949] but also preserved by **God**, we rightly reject the decree of
SD : 0 4 :037(557) [0949] order to merit the grace of **God** and to be saved thereby,
SD : 0 4 :037(557) [0951] to the express Word of **God**, is being placed upon good
SD : 0 4 :038(557) [0951] is, with the intention that **God** demands of the
SD : 0 4 :038(557) [0951] It is **God**'s will and express command that believers should
SD : 0 4 :038(557) [0951] Spirit works in them, and **God** is willing to be pleased
SD : 0 5 :001(558) [0951] purpose that the Word of **God** may be rightly divided and
SD : 0 5 :002(558) [0951] a function of the law of **God**, which reproves all sins,
SD : 0 5 :002(558) [0953] of the grace and mercy of **God** for Christ's sake, which
SD : 0 5 :002(558) [0953] mired and which the law of **God** reproved, has been
SD : 0 5 :003(558) [0953] in the Holy Scripture of **God** and by ancient and modern
SD : 0 5 :004(559) [0953] of the mercy and grace of **God**, his heavenly Father, as it
SD : 0 5 :004(559) [0953] beginning of the Gospel of Jesus Christ, the Son of **God**."
SD : 0 5 :004(559) [0953] under these heads: repentance to **God** and faith in Christ.
SD : 0 5 :006(559) [0953] of repentance but solely the preaching of **God**'s grace.
SD : 0 5 :009(559) [0955] a salutary conversion to **God** unless there is added faith in
SD : 0 5 :012(560) [0955] our sin and the wrath of **God**, no matter how or when it
SD : 0 5 :012(560) [0955] terrified by the wrath of **God**, as he says in John 16:8,
SD : 0 5 :012(560) [0955] and preaching of **God**'s wrath over sin than the passion
SD : 0 5 :012(560) [0955] proclaims the wrath of **God** and terrifies man, it is not yet
SD : 0 5 :014(560) [0957] law, which reveals sin and **God**'s wrath, but to this office
SD : 0 5 :014(560) [0957] adds the promise of **God**'s grace through the Gospel."
SD : 0 5 :017(561) [0957] and immutable will of **God**, shows how man ought to be
SD : 0 5 :017(561) [0957] pleasing and acceptable to **God**, and threatens the
SD : 0 5 :017(561) [0957] of the law with **God**'s wrath and temporal and eternal
SD : 0 5 :019(561) [0957] unbelief, when a person does not believe the Word of **God**
SD : 0 5 :019(561) [0957] in Christ) is the Word of **God**, the Holy Spirit through the
SD : 0 5 :020(561) [0959] forgiveness of sins from **God**, since man has failed to keep
SD : 0 5 :020(561) [0959] failed to keep the law of **God** and has transgressed it, his
SD : 0 5 :020(561) [0959] subject to the wrath of **God**, to death, to temporal
SD : 0 5 :020(561) [0959] is this, that the Son of **God**, Christ our Lord, himself
SD : 0 5 :020(561) [0959] re-enter the good graces of **God**, obtain forgiveness of sins
SD : 0 5 :021(562) [0959] the mercy and grace of **God** to transgressors of the law
SD : 0 5 :021(562) [0959] and joyful message that **God** wills not to punish sins but
SD : 0 5 :022(562) [0959] the righteousness of **God**," who was "made our
SD : 0 5 :022(562) [0959] to us as righteousness in the strict judgment of **God**.
SD : 0 5 :022(562) [0959] Gospel is "the power of **God** for salvation to everyone
SD : 0 5 :022(562) [0959] between the knowledge of **God** which comes from the the
SD : 0 5 :022(562) [0959] extent a knowledge of **God**, although they neither
SD : 0 5 :023(562) [0959] by side in the church of **God** with the proper distinction.
SD : 0 5 :023(562) [0959] righteous and holy by **God** and through the deceit of the
SD : 0 5 :023(562) [0959] of the serpent transgressed **God**'s laws, became a sinner,
SD : 0 5 :024(562) [0961] diligently in the church of **God** until the end of the world,
SD : 0 5 :025(563) [0961] if they believe the Gospel **God** forgives them all their sins
SD : 0 5 :025(563) [0961] them for his sake as **God**'s children, and out of pure
SD : 0 5 :025(563) [0961] men may abuse the grace of **God** and sin against grace.
SD : 0 5 :027(563) [0961] and reopen the door to the papacy in the church of **God**.
SD : 0 6 :001(563) [0963] The law of **God** serves (1) not only to maintain external
SD : 0 6 :002(564) [0963] liberated by the Son of **God**, have become his Spirit's
SD : 0 6 :002(564) [0963] Holy Spirit spontaneously do what **God** requires of them.
SD : 0 6 :003(564) [0963] inner man do the will of **God** from a free spirit,
SD : 0 6 :003(564) [0963] believers learn to serve **God** not according to their own
SD : 0 6 :003(564) [0963] behavior in accord with **God**'s external and immutable
SD : 0 6 :004(564) [0963] genuinely converted to **God** and justified, have been freed
SD : 0 6 :004(564) [0963] mirror in which the will of **God** and what is pleasing to
SD : 0 6 :005(564) [0963] For the law of **God** is written on their hearts, just as the
SD : 0 6 :005(564) [0963] have been reconciled with **God**, nor may it torture the
SD : 0 6 :005(564) [0963] according to the inner man they delight in the law of **God**
SD : 0 6 :006(564) [0963] and the elect children of **God** were perfectly renewed in
SD : 0 6 :006(565) [0965] do according to the will of **God**, just as the sun, the
SD : 0 6 :006(565) [0965] to the order which **God** instituted for them once and for
SD : 0 6 :006(565) [0965] as the holy angels render **God** a completely spontaneous
SD : 0 6 :009(565) [0965] and reborn children of **God** require in this life not only
SD : 0 6 :009(565) [0965] they follow the Spirit of **God**, as it is written, "It is good
SD : 0 6 :011(565) [0965] indeed tells us that it is **God**'s will and command that we
SD : 0 6 :012(566) [0967] what the acceptable will of **God** is (Rom. 12:2) and in
SD : 0 6 :012(566) [0967] what good works, which **God** has prepared beforehand,
SD : 0 6 :013(566) [0967] is contrary to the law of **God**, and St. Paul says, "All
SD : 0 6 :014(566) [0967] Scripture is inspired by **God** and profitable for teaching,
SD : 0 6 :014(566) [0967] they are rebuked through the Spirit of **God** out of the law
SD : 0 6 :015(566) [0967] in accord with the law of **God** — for otherwise they are
SD : 0 6 :015(566) [0967] the immutable will of **God** according to which man is to
SD : 0 6 :016(566) [0967] about living according to the law and the will of **God**.
SD : 0 6 :017(566) [0967] born anew by the Spirit of **God** and is liberated from the
SD : 0 6 :017(566) [0967] to the immutable will of **God** as it is comprehended in the
SD : 0 6 :018(567) [0967] they delight in the law of **God**; but the law in their
SD : 0 6 :020(567) [0969] up a self-elected service of **God** and without his Word and
SD : 0 6 :021(567) [0969] But the law of **God** prescribes good works for faith in such
SD : 0 6 :022(567) [0969] a perfect and pure obedience if it is to please **God**.
SD : 0 6 :022(567) [0969] of believers are pleasing to **God**, even though in this life
SD : 0 6 :022(567) [0969] sacrifices are acceptable to **God** through faith for Christ's
SD : 0 6 :023(568) [0969] they are acceptable to **God** through Christ because
SD : 0 6 :023(568) [0969] they do what is pleasing to **God** not by coercion of the law
SD : 0 6 :025(568) [0971] But just as they will see **God** face to face, so through
SD : 0 6 :025(568) [0971] face to face, so through **God**'s indwelling Spirit they will
SD : 0 7 :001(569) [0971] With the help of **God** we shall do everything we can to
SD : 0 7 :001(569) [0971] to the holy Word of **God** and to the Augsburg Confession
SD : 0 7 :009(570) [0975] teaches on the basis of **God**'s Word "that the true body
SD : 0 7 :020(572) [0979] length from the Word of **God** in the Large Catechism,
SD : 0 7 :022(573) [0979] from the Word of **God** and declare, 'Let a hundred
SD : 0 7 :024(573) [0981] not based on the holiness of men but on the Word of **God**
SD : 0 7 :027(574) [0981] in the holy Supper from **God**'s Word and confirms that it
SD : 0 7 :029(574) [0981] to confess my faith before **God** and all the world, point by
SD : 0 7 :029(574) [0981] my death and (so help me **God**!) in this faith to depart
SD : 0 7 :030(574) [0981] now, that by the grace of **God** I have most diligently
SD : 0 7 :031(574) [0983] since by the grace of **God** I have learned to know a great
SD : 0 7 :031(574) [0983] and pervert the Word of **God**, what will he not be able to
SD : 0 7 :032(574) [0983] Word and ordinance of **God** — unless they first change
SD : 0 7 :032(574) [0983] — unless they first change **God**'s Word and ordinance
SD : 0 7 :032(575) [0983] and instituted ordinance of **God** but have perverted and
SD : 0 7 :036(575) [0985] deity dwells bodily," or "**God** was with him," or "God was
SD : 0 7 :036(575) [0985] "God was with him," or "**God** was in Christ," and similar
SD : 0 7 :039(576) [0985] through the Word of **God** and for the sake of our
SD : 0 7 :042(576) [0987] in the holy Word of **God** and so understood, taught, and
SD : 0 7 :043(576) [0987] the eternal truth and wisdom and the almighty **God**.
SD : 0 7 :045(577) [0987] and almighty Son of **God**, Jesus Christ, our Lord,
SD : 0 7 :046(577) [0987] disputation when he heard **God**'s words about offering up
SD : 0 7 :046(577) [0989] to his reason, he gave **God** the honor of truthfulness and
SD : 0 7 :046(577) [0989] in his heart that what **God** promised he was also able to
SD : 0 7 :046(577) [0989] words and command of **God** plainly and simply, as the
SD : 0 7 :046(577) [0989] the entire matter to **God**'s omnipotence and wisdom,
SD : 0 7 :046(577) [0989] and wisdom, knowing that **God** had many more ways and
SD : 0 7 :060(580) [0993] and conversion to **God**, and who by their unworthy eating
SD : 0 7 :062(581) [0995] to ourselves the Word of **God**, in which Christ, true God
SD : 0 7 :062(581) [0995] God, in which Christ, true **God** and man, together with
SD : 0 7 :062(581) [0995] (that is to say, the grace of **God**, forgiveness of sins,
SD : 0 7 :062(581) [0995] that we have a gracious **God** and eternal salvation for the
SD : 0 7 :069(582) [0997] wish that they might serve **God** with a stronger and more
SD : 0 7 :070(582) [0997] Likewise, "The power of **God** is made perfect in
SD : 0 7 :070(582) [0997] in faith, welcome him, for **God** has welcomed him" (Rom.
SD : 0 7 :070(582) [0997] believes on the Son of **God**, be his faith strong or weak,
SD : 0 7 :074(583) [0999] to the almighty power of **God** and the Word, institution,
SD : 0 7 :076(583) [0999] mouth of the priest, but by **God**'s power and grace
SD : 0 7 :085(584) [1003] be profitably urged and retained in the church of **God**.
SD : 0 7 :089(585) [1003] institution of our almighty **God** and Saviour, Jesus

Continued ▶

SD : 0 7 :091(585) [1005] refuted on the basis of **God**'s Word by Dr. Luther in his
SD : 0 7 :094(586) [1005] natural, true, complete **God** and man in one person,
SD : 0 7 :095(586) [1005] The second is that the right hand of **God** is everywhere.
SD : 0 7 :096(586) [1005] The third is that the Word of **God** is not false or deceitful.
SD : 0 7 :097(586) [1005] "4. The fourth is that **God** has and knows various ways to
SD : 0 7 :099(586) [1005] proper time by the blessed **God**" (I Tim. 6:15), and, "When
SD : 0 7 :099(586) [1005] He is not in **God** or with the Father or in heaven
SD : 0 7 :099(586) [1005] fanatic spirit dreams, for **God** is not a corporeal space or
SD : 0 7 :101(587) [1007] since he is one person with **God**, the divine, heavenly
SD : 0 7 :101(587) [1007] since he is one person with **God**, very far beyond
SD : 0 7 :101(587) [1007] beyond creatures, as far as **God** transcends them, and you
SD : 0 7 :101(587) [1007] and as near in all creatures as **God** is immanent in them.
SD : 0 7 :101(587) [1007] one indivisible person with **God**, and wherever God is, he
SD : 0 7 :101(587) [1007] with God, and wherever **God** is, he must be also,
SD : 0 7 :102(587) [1007] know indeed that he is in **God** beyond all creatures and is
SD : 0 7 :102(587) [1007] in God beyond all creatures and is one person with **God**.
SD : 0 7 :102(587) [1007] of all the angels in heaven, and is known only to **God**.
SD : 0 7 :102(587) [1007] circumstances be where **God** is and that this mode of
SD : 0 7 :103(587) [1007] by the foregoing that **God** may have and know more
SD : 0 7 :103(587) [1007] to deny in any way that **God**'s power is able to make a
SD : 0 7 :103(587) [1009] who wants to try to prove that **God** is unable to do that?
SD : 0 7 :103(587) [1009] may indeed think that **God** is unable to do it, but who
SD : 0 7 :106(588) [1009] of the true and eternal **God**, our Lord and Saviour Jesus
SD : 0 7 :107(588) [1009] doctrine, based as it is on the Word of **God**:
SD : 0 7 :108(588) [1009] be a sacrament apart from **God**'s command and the
SD : 0 7 :108(588) [1009] it is instituted in the Word of **God**, as was shown above.
SD : 0 7 :110(589) [1011] the basis of the Word of **God** and the testimony of the
SD : 0 7 :112(589) [1011] set forth above, based as it is on the Word of **God**.
SD : 0 7 :123(590) [1015] scoffers at the Word of **God** who are in the external
SD : 0 7 :126(591) [1015] deny Christ himself, true **God** and man, who is truly and
SD : 0 7 :128(591) [1015] set forth above, well founded as it is in **God**'s Word.
SD : 0 8 :002(592) [1017] such majesty belongs to **God** alone and the body of Christ
SD : 0 8 :004(592) [1017] harmony with the Word of **God**, with accusations of
SD : 0 8 :005(592) [1017] according to the Word of **God** and in accordance with our
SD : 0 8 :005(592) [1017] to settle it definitely by **God**'s grace, our unanimous
SD : 0 8 :006(592) [1017] that although the Son of **God** is a separate, distinct, and
SD : 0 8 :006(592) [1017] true, essential, and perfect **God** with the Father and the
SD : 0 8 :006(592) [1017] true eternal **God**, born of the Father from eternity, and
SD : 0 8 :006(592) [1017] flesh, is the Christ, who is **God** over all, blessed for ever"
SD : 0 8 :007(592) [1017] in time into the unity of the person of the Son of **God**.
SD : 0 8 :011(593) [1019] of Christ, or the Son of **God** who has assumed flesh and
SD : 0 8 :015(594) [1019] Christ is one person and **God** the Word who dwells in
SD : 0 8 :016(594) [1021] man in whom the Word of **God** dwelled just as in each of
SD : 0 8 :016(594) [1021] were one individual and **God** the Word who dwells in him
SD : 0 8 :019(595) [1021] union and communion **God** is man and man is God but
SD : 0 8 :019(595) [1021] God is man and man is **God** but without thereby blending
SD : 0 8 :020(595) [1021] the world, but the Son of **God** himself has truly suffered
SD : 0 8 :023(595) [1023] of the almighty power of **God**, and everything that follows
SD : 0 8 :024(595) [1023] truly the Son of the most high **God**, as the angel testifies.
SD : 0 8 :024(595) [1023] she is truly the mother of **God** and yet remained a virgin.
SD : 0 8 :027(596) [1025] present to rule, not only as **God** but also as man, from sea
SD : 0 8 :028(596) [1025] manner of the right hand of **God**, which is not a specific
SD : 0 8 :028(596) [1025] The right hand of **God** is precisely the almighty power of
SD : 0 8 :028(596) [1025] the almighty power of **God** which fills heaven and earth,
SD : 0 8 :033(597) [1027] mystery of our religion: **God** was manifested in the flesh"
SD : 0 8 :034(597) [1027] in such a way that **God** and man are a single person!
SD : 0 8 :036(598) [1027] who is simultaneously **God** and man (whether he is called
SD : 0 8 :036(598) [1027] man (whether he is called **God** or whether he is called
SD : 0 8 :038(598) [1027] so that the church of **God** may be forearmed in the best
SD : 0 8 :042(599) [1029] But this person is truly **God**, and therefore it is correct to
SD : 0 8 :042(599) [1029] and therefore it is correct to say: the Son of **God** suffers.
SD : 0 8 :042(599) [1029] the person who is true **God** suffers in the other part
SD : 0 8 :042(599) [1029] For the Son of **God** truly is crucified for us — that is, this
SD : 0 8 :042(599) [1029] that is, this person who is **God**, for that is what he is —
SD : 0 8 :043(599) [1029] regard our Lord Christ as **God** and man in one person,
SD : 0 8 :044(599) [1029] must know that unless **God** is in the balance and throws
SD : 0 8 :044(599) [1029] way: If it is not true that **God** died for us, but only a man
SD : 0 8 :044(599) [1029] But if **God**'s death and God dead lie in the opposite scale,
SD : 0 8 :044(599) [1029] But if God's death and **God** dead lie in the opposite scale,
SD : 0 8 :044(599) [1031] us, so that it could be said: **God** dead, God's passion,
SD : 0 8 :044(599) [1031] could be said: God dead, **God**'s passion, God's blood,
SD : 0 8 :044(599) [1031] said: God dead, God's passion, **God**'s blood, God's death.
SD : 0 8 :044(599) [1031] said: God dead, God's passion, God's blood, **God**'s death.
SD : 0 8 :044(599) [1031] According to his nature **God** cannot die, but since God
SD : 0 8 :044(599) [1031] God cannot die, but since **God** and man are united in one
SD : 0 8 :044(599) [1031] it is correct to talk about **God**'s death when that man dies
SD : 0 8 :044(599) [1031] that man dies who is one thing or one person with **God**."
SD : 0 8 :045(600) [1031] that the cited locutions, "**God** suffered," "God died," are
SD : 0 8 :045(600) [1031] "God suffered," "**God** died," are merely empty words
SD : 0 8 :045(600) [1031] teaches us that the Son of **God**, who was made man,
SD : 0 8 :049(600) [1031] there is no variation with **God** (James 1:17), nothing was
SD : 0 8 :051(600) [1031] is so clear on the basis of **God**'s Word that this opinion is
SD : 0 8 :051(600) [1031] the majesty and power of **God**, after the form of the
SD : 0 8 :061(602) [1035] he is of one essence with the Father and equal with **God**.
SD : 0 8 :061(602) [1035] according to the assumed human nature he is below **God**.
SD : 0 8 :062(603) [1037] either transformed into the **God**-head or by means of
SD : 0 8 :067(604) [1039] divine nature of the Son of **God**, is to be ascribed in the
SD : 0 8 :068(604) [1039] If that were so, since **God** is a spiritual and indivisible
SD : 0 8 :068(604) [1039] in all creatures in whom **God** is, but especially in believers
SD : 0 8 :068(604) [1039] in believers in whom **God** dwells, there likewise the
SD : 0 8 :070(604) [1039] For while it is true that **God**, together with the whole
SD : 0 8 :071(605) [1041] of the majesty of **God** and all its properties into the
SD : 0 8 :071(605) [1041] and essence of the Son of **God**, as when water, wine, or
SD : 0 8 :071(605) [1041] of the omnipotence of **God** in such a way that it would
SD : 0 8 :072(605) [1041] teach, and confess that **God** the Father gave his Spirit to
SD : 0 8 :073(605) [1041] to the flesh that is personally united with the Son of **God**.
SD : 0 8 :074(606) [1043] to the right hand of the majesty and power of **God**.
SD : 0 8 :078(606) [1043] the majesty and power of **God**, so that, also according to
SD : 0 8 :081(607) [1045] from this man there is no **God** — it must follow that
SD : 0 8 :081(607) [1045] can be everywhere that **God** is and that everything is full
SD : 0 8 :082(607) [1045] For if he was the Son of **God**, he had to be in his mother's
SD : 0 8 :082(607) [1045] and if you can say, 'Here is **God**,' then you must also say,
SD : 0 8 :082(607) [1045] show me one place where **God** is and not the man, then
SD : 0 8 :082(607) [1045] say truthfully, 'Here is **God** who is not man and has never
SD : 0 8 :083(607) [1045] But no **God** like that for me!
SD : 0 8 :084(607) [1045] more than a mere isolated **God** and a divine person
SD : 0 8 :084(607) [1045] wherever you put **God** down for me, you must also put
SD : 0 8 :085(608) [1045] birth, the eternal power of **God** is also given to him — in
SD : 0 8 :085(608) [1047] almighty and everlasting **God**, who by virtue of the
SD : 0 8 :085(608) [1047] because he is one person with the deity and is true **God**.
SD : 0 8 :085(608) [1047] is designated the Son of **God** in power' (Rom. 1:4), and
SD : 0 8 :086(608) [1047] Christ at the right hand of **God** in connection with this
SD : 0 8 :092(609) [1049] the majesty and power of **God**, wherever he desires and
SD : 0 8 :093(609) [1049] with which the Son of **God** had no communion whatever
SD : 0 8 :096(609) [1049] to the pure Word of **God**, the writings of the holy
SD : 0 8 :096(610) [1049] the right hand of the majesty and almighty power of **God**.
SD : 0 9 :001(610) [1051] believe in the Lord Christ, **God**'s Son, who died, was
SD : 0 9 :002(610) [1051] burial the entire person, **God** and man, descended into
SD : 0 9 :003(610) [1051] the right hand of the almighty power and majesty of **God**.
SD : 1 0 :001(610) [1053] forbidden in the Word of **God** but which have been
SD : 1 0 :002(611) [1053] nor forbidden by **God**, and that one may justifiably
SD : 1 0 :004(611) [1053] definitively by the grace of **God**, we offer the Christian
SD : 1 0 :005(611) [1053] avoid as forbidden by **God**, ceremonies which are basically
SD : 1 0 :005(611) [1053] contrary to the Word of **God**, even though they go under
SD : 1 0 :008(612) [1055] themselves no worship of **God** or even a part of it, but
SD : 1 0 :009(612) [1055] that the community of **God** in every place and at every
SD : 1 0 :010(612) [1055] enemies of the Word of **God** desire to suppress the pure
SD : 1 0 :010(612) [1055] the entire community of **God**, yes, every individual
SD : 1 0 :010(612) [1055] of the community of **God**, are obligated to confess
SD : 1 0 :010(612) [1055] and all that pertains to it, according to the Word of **God**.
SD : 1 0 :010(612) [1055] the genuine worship of **God** and to introduce and confirm
SD : 1 0 :015(613) [1057] not only on a par with **God**'s commandments, but even
SD : 1 0 :018(614) [1059] intend by the grace of **God** to abide by this their
SD : 1 0 :019(614) [1059] of the church, for, thank **God**, a seven-year-old child
SD : 1 0 :020(614) [1059] devil himself as our lord or **God**, so we cannot suffer his
SD : 1 0 :021(614) [1061] authority count for more than the Word of **God**."
SD : 1 0 :024(615) [1061] instructs the church of **God** on how we are to treat
SD : 1 0 :025(615) [1061] not provoke the wrath of **God**, violate love, confirm the
SD : 1 0 :025(615) [1061] confirm the enemies of **God**'s Word, and scandalize the
SD : 1 0 :026(615) [1061] as of themselves worship of **God** or a part thereof.
SD : 1 0 :027(615) [1061] imposed by force on the community of **God** as necessary.
SD : 1 0 :030(615) [1061] that the community of **God** does not have the liberty to
SD : 1 1 :001(616) [1063] concerning the eternal election of the children of **God**.
SD : 1 1 :001(616) [1063] Therefore, in order by **God**'s grace to prevent, as far as we
SD : 1 1 :004(616) [1063] the difference between **God**'s eternal foreknowledge and
SD : 1 1 :004(616) [1063] For the fact that **God** sees and knows everything before it
SD : 1 1 :004(616) [1063] it happens — what we call **God**'s foreknowledge —
SD : 1 1 :004(617) [1063] manifest and present to **God**, as it is written, "Are not two
SD : 1 1 :005(617) [1065] the eternal election of **God** or God's predestination to
SD : 1 1 :005(617) [1065] eternal election of God or **God**'s predestination to
SD : 1 1 :005(617) [1065] only over the children of **God**, who have been elected and
SD : 1 1 :006(617) [1065] **God**'s foreknowledge (*praescientia*) sees and knows in
SD : 1 1 :006(617) [1065] a way as though it were **God**'s gracious will that it should
SD : 1 1 :006(617) [1065] in wicked acts and works **God**'s foreknowledge operates
SD : 1 1 :006(617) [1065] operates in such a way that **God** sets a limit and measure
SD : 1 1 :006(617) [1065] For the Lord **God** governs everything in such a way that
SD : 1 1 :007(617) [1065] and cause of evil is not **God**'s foreknowledge (since God
SD : 1 1 :007(617) [1065] God's foreknowledge (since **God** neither creates nor works
SD : 1 1 :007(617) [1065] Likewise, "Thou art not a **God** who delights in
SD : 1 1 :008(617) [1065] **God**'s eternal election, however, not only foresees and
SD : 1 1 :008(617) [1065] of the elect, but by **God**'s gracious will and pleasure in
SD : 1 1 :009(617) [1065] and inscrutable counsel of **God**, as though it comprised
SD : 1 1 :009(618) [1065] with it, than that **God** has foreseen who and how many
SD : 1 1 :010(618) [1067] doubts and say: "Since **God** has foreordained his elect to
SD : 1 1 :010(618) [1067] laid' (Eph. 1:4) and since **God**'s foreknowledge can never
SD : 1 1 :010(618) [1067] and must be saved since **God**'s foreknowledge must be
SD : 1 1 :010(618) [1067] etc., since I cannot hinder or alter **God**'s foreknowledge."
SD : 1 1 :011(618) [1067] though by the grace of **God** they have repentance, faith,
SD : 1 1 :012(618) [1067] All Scripture, inspired by **God**, should minister not to
SD : 1 1 :012(618) [1067] everything in the Word of **God** is written down for us, not
SD : 1 1 :012(618) [1067] right use of the teaching of **God**'s eternal foreknowledge
SD : 1 1 :013(618) [1067] ordering of the children of **God** to eternal life, we should
SD : 1 1 :013(619) [1067] secret, hidden, and inscrutable foreknowledge of **God**.
SD : 1 1 :013(619) [1067] purpose, and ordinance of **God** in Christ Jesus, who is the
SD : 1 1 :014(619) [1069] unit the entire doctrine of **God**'s purpose, counsel, will,
SD : 1 1 :014(619) [1069] in his purpose and counsel **God** had ordained the
SD : 1 1 :015(619) [1069] and reconciled with **God** and that by his innocent
SD : 1 1 :015(619) [1069] righteousness which avails before **God**" and eternal life.
SD : 1 1 :021(619) [1069] the end, if they cling to **God**'s Word, pray diligently,
SD : 1 1 :021(619) [1069] persevere in the grace of **God**, and use faithfully the gifts
SD : 1 1 :023(619) [1069] purpose, and ordinance **God** has not only prepared
SD : 1 1 :024(620) [1069] of the eternal election of **God** to adoption and to eternal
SD : 1 1 :024(620) [1069] election, and ordinance of **God** to eternal salvation.
SD : 1 1 :024(620) [1071] we can by the grace of **God** easily orient ourselves in it.
SD : 1 1 :025(620) [1071] use of the teaching of **God**'s foreknowledge to salvation:
SD : 1 1 :026(620) [1071] Instead we must heed the revealed will of **God**.
SD : 1 1 :027(620) [1071] Paul says, "Those whom **God** has foreknown, elected, and
SD : 1 1 :027(620) [1071] Now, **God** does not call without means but through the
SD : 1 1 :027(620) [1071] in Christ's stead, and **God** is admonishing you through us,
SD : 1 1 :027(620) [1071] you through us, 'Be reconciled to **God**'" (II Cor. 5:20).
SD : 1 1 :028(620) [1071] For **God** "loved the world" and gave to it his only begotten
SD : 1 1 :028(620) [1071] "**God** has included all men under disobedience so that he
SD : 1 1 :029(621) [1073] not regard this call of **God** which takes place through the
SD : 1 1 :029(621) [1073] should know certainly that **God** reveals his will in this
SD : 1 1 :029(621) [1073] (II Cor. 3:8) and a "power of **God**" to save (Rom. 1:16).
SD : 1 1 :029(621) [1073] us power and ability, it is **God**'s will that we should accept
SD : 1 1 :030(621) [1073] are decreed "according to **God**'s purpose" to "the
SD : 1 1 :031(621) [1073] Thus the Spirit of **God** gives "witness" to the elect "that
SD : 1 1 :031(621) [1073] they are the children of **God**," and when they "do not
SD : 1 1 :032(621) [1073] also assures us that **God** who has called us will be so
SD : 1 1 :033(621) [1073] with this revealed will of **God**, follow it, and be diligent
SD : 1 1 :033(621) [1073] hidden foreknowledge of **God**, even as Christ answered
SD : 1 1 :033(622) [1075] will show you how comforting **God**'s foreknowledge is."
SD : 1 1 :034(622) [1075] place through the Word, **God** intended to say: "Externally
SD : 1 1 :035(622) [1075] way it would be taught that **God**, who is the eternal
SD : 1 1 :035(622) [1075] Yet **God** himself punishes men for such wickedness when

Continued ▶

SD : 1 1 :036(622) [1075] to learn and to determine **God's** will toward us and what
SD : 1 1 :038(622) [1075] and teach that it is **God's** command that we "believe this
SD : 1 1 :038(622) [1075] are as truly reconciled with **God** as if we had heard a voice
SD : 1 1 :038(622) [1075] if we could not determine **God's** will toward us from the
SD : 1 1 :039(622) [1075] be the elect who despise **God's** Word and who reject,
SD : 1 1 :040(623) [1077] On the contrary, as **God** has ordained in his counsel that
SD : 1 1 :041(623) [1077] of the Word is not **God's** foreknowledge but man's own
SD : 1 1 :041(623) [1077] of the Holy Spirit which **God** offers to him through the
SD : 1 1 :042(623) [1077] reason for this is not that **God** does not want to impart
SD : 1 1 :043(623) [1077] Thus far **God** has revealed the mystery of foreknowledge
SD : 1 1 :043(623) [1077] to have done any good, **God** elected us to salvation
SD : 1 1 :044(623) [1077] will, for in his counsel **God** has determined and decreed
SD : 1 1 :045(624) [1079] and glorious comfort that **God** was so deeply concerned
SD : 1 1 :046(624) [1079] Furthermore, **God** wanted to insure my salvation so firmly
SD : 1 1 :047(624) [1079] to the purpose of **God**, "who will separate us from the love
SD : 1 1 :047(624) [1079] separate us from the love of **God** in Christ?" (Rom. 8:35).
SD : 1 1 :048(624) [1079] foundation of the world **God** has determined and decreed
SD : 1 1 :049(624) [1079] before the world began **God** ordained in his counsel
SD : 1 1 :049(624) [1079] us from the love of **God** in Christ Jesus" (Rom. 8:28, 29,
SD : 1 1 :050(624) [1079] that the church of **God** shall exist and remain against all
SD : 1 1 :051(624) [1079] "despise the counsel of **God** against themselves" (Luke
SD : 1 1 :052(625) [1079] distinguish between what **God** has expressly revealed in
SD : 1 1 :052(625) [1081] this mystery about which **God** has remained silent and
SD : 1 1 :053(625) [1081] of the question which **God** has revealed to us in his Word.
SD : 1 1 :054(625) [1081] before the world began **God** foresaw right well and with
SD : 1 1 :055(625) [1081] **God** is also aware and knows exactly how many there will
SD : 1 1 :055(625) [1081] But because **God** has reserved this mystery to his own
SD : 1 1 :056(625) [1081] Without doubt **God** also knows and has determined for
SD : 1 1 :056(625) [1081] Word, while we leave the time and hour to **God** (Acts 1:7)
SD : 1 1 :057(625) [1081] when we observe that **God** gives his Word at one place
SD : 1 1 :058(625) [1081] In the case of the one group we are to see **God's** judgment
SD : 1 1 :058(625) [1081] punishment for sin when **God** so severely punishes a land
SD : 1 1 :059(626) [1081] nations and some persons **God** shows his own people
SD : 1 1 :059(626) [1081] we misbehave over against **God's** Word and often sorely
SD : 1 1 :059(626) [1083] us to live in the fear of **God** and to recognize and glorify
SD : 1 1 :059(626) [1083] to recognize and glorify **God's** goodness to us without and
SD : 1 1 :060(626) [1083] is worthy and deserving of **God's** wrath and damnation,
SD : 1 1 :060(626) [1083] wrath and damnation, **God** owes us neither his Word, nor
SD : 1 1 :060(626) [1083] But **God** permits us to behold his righteous and well
SD : 1 1 :060(626) [1083] to recognize and praise **God's** pure and unmerited grace
SD : 1 1 :061(626) [1083] others, however, to whom **God** gives and preserves his
SD : 1 1 :061(626) [1083] converts, and keeps them, **God** commends his pure and
SD : 1 1 :063(626) [1083] and say, "Who are you, a man, to answer back to **God**?"
SD : 1 1 :064(626) [1083] of the revealed Word of **God**, as soon as he comes to the
SD : 1 1 :064(626) [1083] how much of this mystery **God** has reserved for his own
SD : 1 1 :064(626) [1083] depth of the riches and wisdom and knowledge of **God**!
SD : 1 1 :065(626) [1083] accordingly consider **God's** eternal election in Christ, and
SD : 1 1 :066(627) [1085] the entire holy Trinity, **God** the Father, Son, and Holy
SD : 1 1 :067(627) [1085] he says, "The kingdom of **God** is at hand; repent and
SD : 1 1 :067(627) [1085] (John 6:40); and again, "**God** so loved the world," etc.
SD : 1 1 :069(627) [1085] through the hearing of **God's** Word, as the apostle
SD : 1 1 :069(627) [1085] comes from the hearing of **God's** Word" (Rom. 10:17)
SD : 1 1 :070(627) [1085] the secret counsel of **God**, if he has been elected and
SD : 1 1 :070(627) [1085] the eternal election of all **God's** children to eternal life,
SD : 1 1 :070(627) [1085] without distinction that **God** wants all men who are laden
SD : 1 1 :072(628) [1085] in it, we should implore **God** to give us his grace, of which
SD : 1 1 :073(628) [1087] the commandments of **God**, believers likewise should not
SD : 1 1 :073(628) [1087] the urgings of the Spirit of **God**, but should exercise
SD : 1 1 :073(628) [1087] to the elect that they are "children of **God**" (Rom. 8:16).
SD : 1 1 :074(628) [1087] of the indwelling Spirit of **God** and say with David, "I had
SD : 1 1 :078(629) [1089] damnation is not that **God** did not want them to be saved
SD : 1 1 :078(629) [1089] they heard the Word of **God** not to learn but only to
SD : 1 1 :079(629) [1089] between the work of **God**, who alone prepares vessels of
SD : 1 1 :079(629) [1089] of the devil and not of **God**, has made himself a vessel of
SD : 1 1 :079(629) [1089] It is written, "**God** endured with much patience the vessels
SD : 1 1 :080(629) [1089] unmistakable terms that **God** "endured the vessels of
SD : 1 1 :080(629) [1089] He does not say that **God** made them vessels of wrath.
SD : 1 1 :080(629) [1089] and man himself, and not **God**, are the cause of their
SD : 1 1 :081(629) [1089] the devil and man through sin, and in no way from **God**.
SD : 1 1 :081(629) [1089] Since **God** does not want any man to be damned, how
SD : 1 1 :081(629) [1089] **God** is not the cause of sin, nor is he the cause of the
SD : 1 1 :081(629) [1089] And as **God** does not will sin and has no pleasure in sin,
SD : 1 1 :081(629) [1089] "As I live, says the Lord **God**, I have no pleasure in the
SD : 1 1 :082(630) [1089] with clear words that **God's** power and operation can
SD : 1 1 :082(630) [1091] this of the damned, whom **God** has not prepared but who
SD : 1 1 :083(630) [1091] considered diligently that **God** punishes sin with sin, that
SD : 1 1 :083(630) [1091] and deliberate sins **God** punishes with obduracy and
SD : 1 1 :083(630) [1091] as if it had never been **God's** gracious will that such people
SD : 1 1 :083(630) [1091] **God's** revealed will involves both items: First, that he
SD : 1 1 :084(630) [1091] did not perish because **God** did not want to grant him
SD : 1 1 :084(630) [1091] salvation or because it was **God's** good pleasure that he
SD : 1 1 :084(630) [1091] For **God** "is not wishing that any should perish," nor has
SD : 1 1 :085(630) [1091] But that **God** hardened Pharaoh's heart so that Pharaoh
SD : 1 1 :085(630) [1091] But after **God** arranged to have his Word proclaimed and
SD : 1 1 :085(630) [1091] and warnings, **God** withdrew his hand from him, and so
SD : 1 1 :085(630) [1091] and calloused and **God** executed his judgment on him, for
SD : 1 1 :086(631) [1091] forth the righteousness of **God** which God manifests
SD : 1 1 :086(631) [1091] of God which **God** manifests toward the impenitent and
SD : 1 1 :086(631) [1091] he want us to infer that **God** had not wanted to grant
SD : 1 1 :086(631) [1091] that in his secret counsel **God** had ordained him to eternal
SD : 1 1 :087(631) [1091] of the elect children of **God** gives God his due honor fully
SD : 1 1 :087(631) [1091] elect children of God gives **God** his due honor fully and
SD : 1 1 :088(631) [1093] is not only the mercy of **God** and the most holy merit of
SD : 1 1 :088(631) [1093] is also within us a cause of **God's** election on account of
SD : 1 1 :088(631) [1093] on account of which **God** has elected us unto eternal life.
SD : 1 1 :088(631) [1093] of the world was laid") **God** elected us in Christ — "in
SD : 1 1 :088(631) [1093] in Christ — "in order that **God's** purpose of election might
SD : 1 1 :090(631) [1093] in the gracious election of **God**, which he has revealed to
SD : 1 1 :091(631) [1093] this teaching concerning **God's** gracious election that
SD : 1 1 :091(632) [1093] to the Word and will of **God** but according to reason and
SD : 1 1 :093(632) [1093] and well grounded in **God's** revealed will, we shall avoid
SD : 1 1 :095(632) [1095] and unchangeable truth of **God** for the sake of temporal
SD : 1 1 :096(632) [1095] as will not violate **God's** honor, that will not detract
SD : 1 2 :006(633) [1097] And we desire by **God's** grace to remain steadfastly in our
SD : 1 2 :006(633) [1097] in which the almighty **God** and Father of our Lord Jesus
SD : 1 2 :010(633) [1097] our righteousness before **God** does not depend alone on
SD : 1 2 :010(634) [1097] and in our own piety, in which we walk before **God**.
SD : 1 2 :011(634) [1099] are not sinners before **God** but righteous and innocent,
SD : 1 2 :013(634) [1099] are holy and children of **God** even without and prior to
SD : 1 2 :016(634) [1099] and avoid them as people who pervert the Word of **God**.
SD : 1 2 :026(635) [1099] is not truly and essentially **God** but only possesses more
SD : 1 2 :030(635) [1101] is not a means whereby **God** the Holy Spirit teaches men
SD : 1 2 :031(635) [1101] a means whereby the Lord **God** seals the adoption of sons
SD : 1 2 :033(635) [1101] again through the Spirit of **God** is able to keep and fulfill
SD : 1 2 :033(635) [1101] able to keep and fulfill the law of **God** perfectly in this life
SD : 1 2 :036(635) [1101] true, essential, and natural **God**, of one eternal, divine
SD : 1 2 :036(635) [1101] divine essence with **God** the Father, but only adorned
SD : 1 2 :038(636) [1103] 2. That only the Father is genuinely and truly **God**.
SD : 1 2 :039(636) [1103] contrary to the Word of **God**, to the three Creeds, to the
SD : 1 2 :040(636) [1103] in the presence of **God** and of all Christendom among
SD : 1 2 :040(636) [1103] and confession in which by **God's** grace we shall appear
SD : 1 2 :040(636) [1103] but we intend through **God's** grace to abide by it.
SD : 1 2 :040(636) [1103] the fear and invocation of **God**, subscribed our signatures

Godfrey (1)

PR : PR :027(015) [0025] **Godfrey**, count of Oettingen

Godhead (8)

LC : 0 2 :006(411) [0679] the three persons of the **Godhead**, to whom all that we
LC : 0 2 :026(413) [0685] second person of the **Godhead**, and we see what we
EP : 0 3 :002(473) [0791] Christ is our righteousness only according to his **Godhead**
EP : 0 3 :002(473) [0793] against this indwelling **Godhead**, the sins of all men are
SD : 0 8 :062(603) [1037] equal with the **Godhead**, nor in such a way that the
SD : 0 8 :071(605) [1041] be denied and completely transformed into the **Godhead**.
SD : 0 8 :073(605) [1041] Christ according to the **Godhead** is the second person in
SD : 0 8 :077(606) [1043] us on earth because the **Godhead** which is everywhere

Godless (18), Godlessly (1)

AG : 1 7 :005(039) [0051] possess a worldly kingdom and annihilate all the **godless**.
AG : 2 7 :061(080) [0083] Thus there are many **godless** opinions and errors
AG : 0 0 :005(095) [0095] prevented any new and **godless** teaching from creeping
AP : 2 1 :043(235) [0357] the church with their **godless** teachings and overthrow the
S3 : 0 3 :041(309) [0491] the Gospel, and yet it is called a heresy by **godless** saints.
TR : 0 0 :031(325) [0513] and excommunicate the **godless** without physical
TR : 0 0 :038(326) [0515] pontiffs who defend **godless** forms of worship, idolatry,
TR : 0 0 :038(327) [0515] divine right; nevertheless, **godless** high priests were not to
TR : 0 0 :039(327) [0515] their adherents defend **godless** doctrines and godless
TR : 0 0 :039(327) [0515] godless doctrines and **godless** forms of worship, and it is
EP : 0 7 :002(481) [0809] or unworthy, godly or **godless**, believers or unbelievers,
EP : 1 1 :015(496) [0835] either to despair or to lead a reckless and **godless** life.
SD : 0 3 :017(542) [0921] to those who acquit the **godless** for a bribe, and deprive
SD : 0 7 :033(575) [0983] natural body, which the **godless** or Judas receive orally as
SD : 0 7 :056(579) [0991] Christ in which both the godly and the **godless** participate
SD : 0 7 :060(580) [0993] also the unworthy and **godless** hypocrites, like Judas and
SD : 0 7 :089(585) [1003] true Gospel even when **godless** hearers do not believe it
SD : 0 7 :123(590) [1015] which alleges that **godless** Epicureans and scoffers at the
SD : 0 8 :016(594) [1021] Antioch in Syria, taught **godlessly** that the Lord Christ

Godliness (10), Godly (69)

AG : 0 8 :001(033) [0047] sinners remain among the **godly**, the sacraments are
AG : 1 2 :007(035) [0049] persons who have once become **godly** cannot fall again.
AG : 1 7 :005(039) [0051] of the dead, saints and **godly** men will possess a worldly
AG : 2 1 :001(046) [0057] may in salutary and **godly** fashion imitate the example of
AG : 0 0 :002(048) [0059] confession is seen to be **godly** and Christian, the bishops
AG : 2 6 :016(066) [0073] strife in the church that **godly** people were thereby
AG : 2 7 :012(072) [0077] righteousness and **godliness**, but also that by means of
AG : 2 7 :037(077) [0081] that righteousness and **godliness** in God's sight come from
AL : 1 7 :002(038) [0051] To the **godly** and elect he will give eternal life and endless
AL : 1 7 :005(038) [0051] of the dead the **godly** will take possession of the kingdom
AP : PR :019(099) [0103] and to restore them to a **godly** and abiding harmony.
AP : 0 4 :168(130) [0169] let every one who is **godly** offer prayer to thee" (Ps. 32:6).
AP : 0 4 :168(130) [0169] he show that even the **godly** must pray for the forgiveness
AP : 0 4 :303(154) [0205] and that it will bring **godly** and wholesome consolation to
AP : 0 4 :399(168) [0227] they have hitherto shown toward many **godly** men.
AP : 0 7 :010(170) [0229] sense includes both the **godly** and the wicked," and that
AP : 0 7 :010(170) [0229] and not in fact, while the **godly** are part of the church in
AP : 0 9 :003(178) [0245] confirm good and **godly** minds against the ungodly and
AP : 1 2 :003(182) [0253] have taught what is true, **godly**, salutary, and necessary
AP : 1 2 :011(184) [0255] And to torture **godly** minds still more, they imagine that
AP : 1 2 :058(189) [0267] From all these passages **godly** readers can see that we put
AP : 1 2 :090(195) [0279] teaching is more **godly** and salutary for consciences.
AP : 1 2 :130(202) [0291] We know that it is true, **godly**, and beneficial to godly
AP : 1 2 :130(202) [0291] that it is true, godly, and beneficial to **godly** consciences.
AP : 1 2 :151(206) [0299] In the **godly** they have another and better purpose, that
AP : 1 2 :178(211) [0307] we are certain that it is **godly** and wholesome for the
AP : 1 4 :003(214) [0315] we know that our confession is true, **godly**, and catholic.
AP : 1 7 :001(224) [0335] and eternal joys to the **godly** but condemning the ungodly
AP : 2 1 :041(235) [0355] and was teaching things profitable for **godliness**.
AP : 2 2 :001(236) [0357] in the Lord's Supper is **godly** and in accord with the
AP : 2 3 :005(240) [0365] are trying to fortify it with a wicked pretense of **godliness**.
AP : 2 3 :034(244) [0373] so marriage is pure in the **godly**, through the Word of
AP : 2 3 :044(245) [0375] Such continence is easy for the **godly** and busy.
AP : 2 3 :047(246) [0377] We could mention cases of **godly** consciences being very
AP : 2 4 :051(259) [0401] of the churches is **godly**, practical, and clear teaching, the
AP : 2 4 :051(259) [0401] and clear teaching, the **godly** use of the sacraments,
AP : 2 4 :076(263) [0411] of Cyprian about the **godly** communicant, "Piety
S2 : 0 2 :005(293) [0463] rabble, but also for all **godly**, Christian, sensible,
S3 : 0 3 :003(304) [0481] Here no one is **godly**," etc.
S3 : 0 6 :001(311) [0493] and received not only by **godly** but also by wicked
TR : 0 0 :052(329) [0519] Therefore, let the **godly** consider the enormous errors of
TR : 0 0 :058(330) [0521] too, is the cruelty which he employs against the **godly**.
TR : 0 0 :058(330) [0521] Therefore all the **godly** have weighty, compelling, and
TR : 0 0 :058(330) [0521] are a comfort to the **godly** when, as often happens, they
TR : 0 0 :059(330) [0521] guilty of the blood of the **godly** whom the pope
TR : 0 0 :076(333) [0527] restore this jurisdiction to **godly** pastors and see to it that
TR : 0 0 :079(333) [0527] and do not ordain **godly** teachers but rather support the
SC : PR :000(338) [0533] Martin Luther to all faithful, **godly** pastors and preachers.

Continued ▶

SC : 03 :008(346) [0547] his holy Word and live a **godly** life, both here in time and
SC : 03 :014(347) [0549] trustworthy servants, **godly** and faithful rulers, good
SC : 09 :005(355) [0561] a quiet and peaceable life, **godly** and respectful in every
LC : 01 :114(380) [0613] see, we should have had **godly** children, properly taught,
LC : 01 :137(384) [0621] The **godly** and the obedient, however, are blessed.
LC : 01 :149(385) [0623] will not be inclined to **godliness**, we deliver to the
LC : 01 :156(386) [0625] there must still be some **godly** people, or else God would
LC : 01 :175(389) [0631] bring up their children and servants to be **godly**.
LC : 01 :208(393) [0639] knowledge of God, **godly** living, and all virtues, and fight
LC : 01 :216(394) [0641] that the monastic life is **godly**, yet it is not in their power
LC : 01 :262(400) [0655] Wherever there are **godly** preachers and Christians, they
LC : 03 :015(422) [0701] enough; if I were as **godly** and holy as St. Peter or St.
LC : 03 :031(424) [0707] that the prayers of a few **godly** men intervened like an
LC : 03 :039(425) [0709] both our teaching and our life are **godly** and Christian.
LC : 03 :044(425) [0709] teach, speak, and live as **godly** and heavenly children with
EP : 07 :002(481) [0809] they worthy or unworthy, **godly** or godless, believers or
SD : 02 :014(523) [0885] this beginning of true **godliness** in their heart, wills to
SD : 02 :041(529) [0897] grace we may believe his holy Word and live a **godly** life."
SD : 06 :003(564) [0963] and norm for achieving a **godly** life and behavior in
SD : 06 :026(568) [0971] discipline and true **godliness**, the erroneous doctrine that
SD : 07 :019(572) [0979] and received not only by **godly** but also by wicked
SD : 07 :056(579) [0991] Christ in which both the **godly** and the godless
SD : 07 :060(580) [0993] expressly that not only **godly**, pious, and believing
SD : 07 :066(581) [0997] and wicked Christians as well as by the **godly** and pious.
SD : 08 :064(603) [1037] (Col. 2:9), not as in other **godly** human beings or in the
SD : 11 :005(617) [1065] not extend over both the **godly** and the ungodly, but only
SD : 11 :010(618) [1067] myself with repentance, faith, prayer, and **godliness**.
SD : 11 :011(618) [1067] faith, and the good resolve to lead a **godly** life.
SD : 11 :012(618) [1067] to urge us to **godliness** (Eph. 1:15ff.; John 15:16, 17
SD : 11 :073(628) [1087] Christian virtues, in all **godliness**, modesty, temperance,
SD : 12 :017(634) [1099] Testament era government service is not a **godly** estate.

Gods (9)

AG : 01 :005(028) [0043] assert that there are two **gods**, one good and one evil; also
AP : 21 :044(236) [0357] own name and calls them **gods** (Ps. 82:6), "I say, 'You are
AP : 21 :044(236) [0357] and calls them gods (Ps. 82:6), "I say, 'You are **gods**.'"
S3 : 02 :004(303) [0479] that he worships strange **gods** — something that he would
SC : 01 :001(342) [0539] *"You shall have no other **gods**."*
LC : SP :001(362) [0575] 1. You shall have no other **gods** before me.
LC : 01 :000(365) [0581] *"You shall have no other **gods**."*
LC : 01 :324(409) [0675] "You shall have no other **gods**," means simply, "You shall
LC : 01 :325(409) [0675] Lord takes pleasure in those who have no other **gods**."

Go (80), Goes (15), Going (10), Gone (5), Went (8)

PR : PR :022(011) [0019] These people **go** their way in the simplicity of their
AG : 23 :001(051) [0061] remain continent and who **went** so far as to engage in
AG : 26 :023(067) [0073] Christ says, "Not what **goes** into the mouth defiles a
AG : 28 :056(090) [0091] offense to others she **goes** out with uncovered head.
AL : 26 :023(067) [0073] Christ says, "Not what **goes** into the mouth defiles a
AL : 28 :007(082) [0085] Mark 16:15 he also said, "**Go** and preach the gospel to the
AL : 28 :056(090) [0091] say that a woman sins by **going** out in public with her
AP : PR :010(099) [0101] with others, but as it was **going** through the press I added
AP : 02 :005(101) [0107] They **go** on to say that one is not condemned to eternal
AP : 04 :072(117) [0141] or, as the common saying **goes**, "the beginning is half of
AP : 04 :164(129) [0169] Therefore we must always **go** back to the promise.
AP : 04 :242(141) [0187] forgives, yields, and does not **go** to the limit of the law.
AP : 12 :031(186) [0259] "For my iniquities have **gone** over my head; they weigh
AP : 12 :057(189) [0267] Your faith has saved you; **go** in peace."
AP : 12 :067(191) [0271] But they **go** further and demand that this teaching be
AP : 12 :144(205) [0297] one making a trip in armor and another **going** barefoot.
AP : 13 :011(212) [0311] again, "My word that **goes** forth from my mouth shall
AP : 16 :004(223) [0331] counsel not to own property and not to **go** to court.
AP : 20 :009(227) [0341] not yield to the wicked, but **go** on still more boldly,"
AP : 20 :011(228) [0341] They have **gone** on record as rejecting our doctrine that
AP : 21 :030(233) [0351] foolish virgins could not **go** out with their lamps
AP : 23 :050(246) [0377] who seem to have **gone** astray through some sort of
AP : 23 :059(247) [0379] We would have to **go** along with our opponents in the
AP : 24 :023(253) [0391] that a human victim was **going** to placate God for the
AP : 24 :075(263) [0411] says about the comfort: "**Go** to him and be absolved, for
AP : 24 :085(264) [0413] Why **go** so far afield for the etymology when the term
AP : 24 :093(267) [0417] itself but the prayers and everything that **goes** on there.
AP : 27 :038(275) [0433] The next day Anthony **went** into the city and came to the
AP : 27 :045(277) [0435] "If you would be perfect, **go**, sell what you possess and
AP : 27 :052(278) [0437] dangers and scandals **going** on before their very eyes, our
AP : 28 :004(281) [0445] want instruction in order to have a sure way to **go**.
AP : 28 :007(282) [0445] said (Matt. 15:11), "What **goes** into the mouth does not
AP : 28 :008(282) [0445] cleansed by faith and then **go** on to forbid the imposing
S2 : 04 :013(300) [0475] He **went** so far as to claim to be an earthly god and even
S3 : 01 :009(302) [0477] 6. Again, when a man **goes** to the sacrament there is no
S3 : 03 :016(305) [0483] substitute for contrition when people **went** to confession.
S3 : 03 :025(307) [0485] The popes **went** further and quickly multiplied the jubilee
S3 : 03 :033(308) [0489] All have turned aside, together they have **gone** wrong."
S3 : 06 :004(311) [0493] omit both forms but even **go** so far as autocratically to
TR : 00 :031(325) [0513] For Christ said, "**Go** therefore and teach them to observe
SC : 04 :004(348) [0551] our Lord Christ said, "**Go** therefore and make disciples of
SC : 05 :028(351) [0555] **Go** in peace."
SC : 07 :003(352) [0557] may suggest, you should **go** to your work joyfully.
LC : SP :016(363) [0577] in the morning, when they **go** to their meals, and they go
LC : SP :016(363) [0577] go to their meals, and they **go** to bed at night; until they
LC : SP :021(364) [0579] "**Go** and teach all nations, and baptize them in the name
LC : 01 :012(366) [0583] this class belong those who **go** so far as to make a pact
LC : 01 :028(368) [0587] it flee not to him but from him when things **go** wrong?
LC : 01 :057(372) [0597] turns away from him to **go** unpunished, so little will he
LC : 01 :096(378) [0609] only from force of habit **go** to hear preaching and depart
LC : 01 :110(380) [0613] to them and hold your tongue, even if they **go** too far.
LC : 01 :120(381) [0615] melt with joy when it can **go** to work and do what is
LC : 01 :123(382) [0617] That is the way things **go** in the world now, as everyone
LC : 01 :180(389) [0631] we leave our own house and **go** out among our neighbors
LC : 01 :235(397) [0647] But you **go** your own way, take your wages like a thief,
LC : 01 :247(398) [0651] ought to give aid, he will **go** away wretched and dejected,
LC : 01 :248(398) [0651] heed or believe this may **go** his own way until he learns it
LC : 01 :274(402) [0659] in such a way that evil shall not **go** unpunished.
LC : 01 :276(402) [0659] brother sins against you, **go** and tell him his fault,
LC : 01 :276(402) [0659] he saw the wrongdoing, to **go** and reprove the man
LC : 01 :277(402) [0659] servant at home while he **went** out on the streets to
LC : 01 :314(407) [0671] Otherwise, why should monks and nuns **go** into cloisters?
LC : 01 :332(410) [0677] looks, and even wherever he **goes** or wherever he stands.
LC : 03 :009(421) [0699] I will **go** and do as I please; what difference does it
LC : 03 :066(429) [0717] whatever befalls us, and let **go** whatever is taken from us.
LC : 03 :102(434) [0727] around our necks; he **goes** to work and lures us daily into
LC : 03 :109(435) [0729] Then we shall not **go** about securely and heedlessly as if
LC : 04 :004(437) [0733] *"**Go** into all the world, and teach all nations, baptizing*
LC : 04 :009(437) [0735] So the words read, "**Go**, baptize," not in your name but
LC : 04 :038(441) [0741] more than these words, "**Go** and baptize," we would still
LC : 04 :056(444) [0747] Just so, I **go** to the Sacrament of the Altar not on the
LC : 04 :056(444) [0747] he has commanded me to **go**, eat, and drink, etc. and that
LC : 04 :059(444) [0747] The saying **goes**, *"Abusus non tollit, sed confirmat*
LC : 05 :002(447) [0753] wishes to be a Christian and **go** to the sacrament should
LC : 05 :022(449) [0757] In other words, we **go** to the sacrament because we
LC : 05 :040(451) [0763] two, three, or more years **go** by without receiving the
LC : 05 :041(451) [0763] taught that no one should **go** unless he feels a hunger and
LC : 05 :041(451) [0763] Thus the majority **go** so far that they have become quite
LC : 05 :056(453) [0767] this, such people refuse to **go** to the sacrament and wait
LC : 05 :057(453) [0767] nothing will prick your conscience, you will never **go**.
LC : 05 :062(454) [0767] should compel himself to **go** and allow no one to deter
LC : 05 :072(455) [0769] and feel your weakness, **go** joyfully to the sacrament and
LC : 05 :078(455) [0771] more reason you have to **go** to the sacrament and seek a
LC : 05 :082(456) [0773] The only reason we **go** about so securely and heedlessly is
LC : 06 :005(457) [0000] will never need or desire to **go** to confession any more.
LC : 06 :020(459) [0000] here the faithful advice to **go** and obtain this precious
LC : 06 :021(459) [0000] is this: If anybody does not **go** to confession willingly and
LC : 06 :021(459) [0000] Yes, and if anybody **goes** about relying on the purity of
LC : 06 :024(460) [0000] How else would the beggar **go** but with repugnance, not
LC : 06 :025(460) [0000] Who could thus **go** to confession willingly?
LC : 06 :026(460) [0000] poor and miserable, then **go** and make use of the healing
LC : 06 :027(460) [0000] and do not come of their own accord, we let **go** their way.
LC : 06 :032(460) [0000] when I urge you to **go** to confession, I am simply urging
EP : 06 :004(480) [0807] necessary lest the Old Adam **go** his own self-willed way.
EP : 09 :001(492) [0827] to our simple Christian Creed, did Christ **go** to hell?
EP : 09 :004(492) [0827] to know that Christ **went** to hell, destroyed hell for all
EP : 12 :019(499) [0841] divorce one another, each **go** his own way, and marry
SD : 02 :002(520) [0881] nor what man's free will is **going** to be like after he will
SD : 02 :010(522) [0885] aside, together they have **gone** wrong; no one does good,
SD : 02 :053(531) [0903] matters, so that he can **go** to church, listen to the sermon,
SD : 02 :089(538) [0915] anything about what is **going** on or perceive or will
SD : 07 :057(579) [0993] and who likewise were **going** to the table of the Lord and
SD : 07 :068(582) [0997] are, namely, those who **go** to this sacrament without true
SD : 07 :099(586) [1005] leaving the world and **going** to the Father speak of this
SD : 07 :100(586) [1007] likewise light and heat **go** through air, water, glass, or
SD : 08 :004(592) [1017] properties, and they **went** so far as to load down Dr.
SD : 08 :044(599) [1029] scale, then his side **goes** down and we go upward like a
SD : 08 :044(599) [1029] his side goes down and we **go** upward like a light and
SD : 08 :044(599) [1031] Of course, he can also **go** up again or jump out of his
SD : 08 :086(608) [1047] of brevity we here merely **go** on record as having appealed
SD : 10 :005(611) [1053] of God, even though they **go** under the name and guise of
SD : 11 :004(617) [1065] sitting down and your **going** out and coming in, and your
SD : 11 :006(617) [1065] not will — how far it is to **go**, how long it is to endure,
SD : 11 :058(625) [1081] us as to how far we should **go** in these and similar
SD : 11 :062(626) [1083] If we **go** thus far in this article we will remain on the right
SD : 11 :063(626) [1083] subject soars too high and **goes** beyond these limits, we
SD : 11 :075(628) [1087] divorces his wife and she **goes** from him and becomes
SD : 12 :024(634) [1099] to divorce each other, to **go** their separate ways, and to

Goettingen (1)

PR : PR :027(016) [0027] The Council of the City of **Goettingen**

Gold (11), Golden (5)

AP : 15 :019(218) [0319] know he shall honor with **gold** and silver, with precious
AP : 15 :021(218) [0321] but honoring God "with **gold** and silver and precious
AP : 24 :034(256) [0395] Levi and refine them like **gold** and silver, till they present
AP : 24 :051(259) [0401] Candles, **golden** vessels, and ornaments like that are
AP : 24 :051(259) [0403] describes as worshiping their God with **gold** and silver.
AP : 24 :064(261) [0407] of merit, like the money-changers with **gold** or silver.
AP : 27 :005(269) [0421] degenerated as from a **golden** age to an iron age, or as the
AP : 27 :046(277) [0435] for throwing a great weight of **gold** into the sea.
SC : 02 :004(345) [0545] devil, not with silver and **gold** but with his holy and
LC : 01 :144(385) [0623] consciences and know how to do truly **golden** works.
LC : 01 :264(400) [0655] of us; we want the **golden** compliments of the whole
LC : 01 :314(407) [0671] when a priest stands in a **gold**-embroidered chasuble or a
LC : 02 :031(414) [0687] owed, not with silver and **gold** but with his own precious
LC : 04 :020(439) [0737] I say, is the **golden** chain about his neck, yes, the crown
LC : 04 :059(444) [0747] **Gold** remains no less gold if a harlot wears it in sin and
LC : 04 :059(444) [0747] Gold remains no less **gold** if a harlot wears it in sin and

Gomorrah (2)

AP : 23 :054(246) [0379] burning of Sodom and **Gomorrah** reveal God's wrath at
S1 : PR :011(290) [0457] utterly, like Sodom and **Gomorrah**, because we mock him

Good (623)

PR : PR :008(005) [0011] of us and that other **good**-hearted people would have
PR : PR :013(007) [0013] they brought together in **good** order, by the singular
PR : PR :024(013) [0023] apparent to us that many **good**-hearted Christian
AG : PR :019(026) [0041] were progressing toward a **good**, Christian
AG : 01 :005(028) [0043] there are two gods, one **good** and one evil; also that of
AG : 06 :001(031) [0045] such faith should produce **good** fruits and good works
AG : 06 :001(031) [0045] produce good fruits and **good** works and that we must
AG : 06 :001(031) [0045] that we must do all such **good** works as God has
AG : 15 :001(036) [0049] contribute to peace and **good** order in the church, among
AG : 16 :001(037) [0051] by God for the sake of **good** order, and that Christians
AG : 16 :005(038) [0051] Christian love and genuine **good** works in his station of
AG : 18 :004(040) [0051] of this life that they have freedom to choose **good** or evil.
AG : 18 :005(040) [0051] By **good** I mean what they are capable of by nature:
AG : 18 :005(040) [0053] a trade, or do whatever else may be **good** and profitable.
AG : 20 :000(041) [0053] XX. Faith and **Good** Works
AG : 20 :001(041) [0053] have been falsely accused of forbidding **good** works.
AG : 20 :002(041) [0053] show that they have given **good** and profitable accounts
AG : 20 :025(044) [0057] upon him, and have no hope of receiving **good** from him.

Continued ▶

AG : 2 0 :027(045) [0057] also taught among us that **good** works should and must
AG : 2 0 :029(045) [0057] Spirit is given, the heart is moved to do **good** works.
AG : 2 0 :035(046) [0057] be accused of forbidding **good** works but is rather to be
AG : 2 0 :035(046) [0057] praised for teaching that **good** works are to be done and
AG : 2 0 :036(046) [0057] are much too weak to do **good** works, call upon God,
AG : 2 1 :001(046) [0057] Moreover, their **good** works are to be an example for us,
AG : 2 3 :006(052) [0061] What **good** has resulted?
AG : 2 3 :013(053) [0063] man) never produced any **good** but rather gave occasion
AG : 2 6 :005(064) [0071] that we do not become **good** in God's sight by our works
AG : 2 6 :010(065) [0071] hand, other necessary **good** works were considered
AG : 2 7 :020(074) [0079] in Gen. 2:18, "It is not **good** that the man should be
AG : 2 7 :044(078) [0081] namely, that they could apply their **good** works to others.
AG : 2 7 :048(078) [0081] a service would make men **good** and righteous before
AG : 2 7 :049(079) [0083] and that meanwhile we do **good** works for others and
AG : 2 7 :058(080) [0083] That is a **good** and perfect state of life which has God's
AG : 2 8 :037(087) [0089] grace and everything **good** might be earned from God.
AG : 2 8 :053(090) [0091] in the churches is done in **good** order, but not as a means
AG : 0 0 :003(095) [0095] over for the common **good** in order that the chief points
AL : 0 1 :005(028) [0043] two principles, one **good** and the other evil, and also
AL : 0 6 :001(031) [0045] is bound to bring forth **good** fruits and that it is necessary
AL : 0 6 :001(031) [0045] it is necessary to do the **good** works commanded by God.
AL : 1 2 :006(035) [0049] Then **good** works, which are the fruits of repentance, are
AL : 1 5 :001(036) [0049] which contribute to peace and **good** order in the church.
AL : 1 6 :001(037) [0051] civil ordinances are **good** works of God and that it is
AL : 1 8 :004(039) [0051] of this life that they have freedom to choose **good** or evil.
AL : 1 8 :005(040) [0051] By '**good**' I mean the acts which spring from the good in
AL : 1 8 :005(040) [0051] which spring from the **good** in nature, that is, to will to
AL : 1 8 :005(040) [0053] arts, or will to do whatever **good** pertains to this life.
AL : 2 0 :000(041) [0053] XX. Faith and **Good** Works
AL : 2 0 :001(041) [0053] churches are falsely accused of forbidding **good** works.
AL : 2 0 :002(041) [0053] that they have taught to **good** purpose about all stations
AL : 2 0 :025(045) [0057] do not call upon him, and expect no **good** from him.
AL : 2 0 :027(045) [0057] that it is necessary to do **good** works, not that we should
AL : 2 0 :029(045) [0057] new affections as to be able to bring forth **good** works.
AL : 2 0 :030(045) [0057] "Faith is the mother of the **good** will and the right deed."
AL : 2 0 :031(045) [0057] are too weak to do works which are **good** in God's sight.
AL : 2 0 :035(046) [0057] is not to be charged with forbidding **good** works.
AL : 2 0 :035(046) [0057] for showing how we are enabled to do **good** works.
AL : 2 0 :040(046) [0057] man hath naught, Nothing **good** in deed or thought,
AL : 2 1 :001(046) [0057] we imitate their faith and **good** works according to our
AL : 0 0 :005(048) [0059] not be approved with a **good** conscience, they have to
AL : 0 0 :003(049) [0059] thus exciting the minds of **good** men, they first gave
AL : 2 4 :007(056) [0065] God and ask for and expect whatever is **good** from God.
AL : 2 4 :010(057) [0065] grievous complaint by all **good** men that Masses were
AL : 2 6 :040(069) [0075] are profitable for maintaining **good** order in the church.
AL : 2 6 :045(070) [0075] piety toward God and **good** conversation among men."
AL : 2 7 :008(071) [0077] rigor displeased many **good** men before our time when
AL : 2 7 :020(074) [0079] in Gen. 2:18, "It is not **good** that the man should be
AL : 2 7 :049(079) [0083] in the performance of **good** works for others and to
AL : 2 7 :058(080) [0083] A **good** and perfect kind of life is one which has God's
AL : 2 8 :053(090) [0091] church may be done in **good** order, but not that by means
AL : 2 8 :069(093) [0093] traditions which cannot be kept with a **good** conscience.
AL : 2 8 :071(093) [0093] honor (which, however, **good** pastors ought to do), but
AP : PR :016(099) [0103] for the glory of Christ and the **good** of the church.
AP : PR :018(099) [0103] Many **good** men have testified publicly and thanked God
AP : 0 2 :002(100) [0105] But to show all **good** men that our teaching on this point
AP : 0 2 :042(106) [0117] are more fortunate than **good** people; yielding to anger,
AP : 0 2 :043(106) [0117] emotions we are neither **good** nor bad, neither to be
AP : 0 4 :009(108) [0123] to love God and that he wants to do **good** for God's sake.
AP : 0 4 :009(108) [0123] elicits an act of love to God or does **good** for God's sake.
AP : 0 4 :024(110) [0127] nature has no greater **good** than this, as Aristotle
AP : 0 4 :056(114) [0137] or save because it is a **good** work in itself, but only
AP : 0 4 :064(116) [0139] it appears it brings forth **good** fruits, as we shall point
AP : 0 4 :074(117) [0143] Love and **good** works must also follow faith.
AP : 0 4 :087(120) [0147] by the precepts of a **good** life, but through faith in Jesus
AP : 0 4 :106(122) [0153] a justified man is there a **good** work by the performance
AP : 0 4 :136(126) [0159] inward spiritual impulses and the outward **good** works.
AP : 0 4 :136(126) [0159] that we do not require **good** works, whereas we not only
AP : 0 4 :140(126) [0161] So it is clear that we require **good** works.
AP : 0 4 :155(128) [0165] love, confession, and other **good** fruits ought to follow.
AP : 0 4 :168(130) [0169] "I do not do the **good** I want, but the evil I do not
AP : 0 4 :172(130) [0171] Therefore even in **good** works he requires our faith that
AP : 0 4 :189(133) [0175] **Good** works should be done because God has commanded
AP : 0 4 :189(133) [0175] For these reasons **good** works must necessarily be done.
AP : 0 4 :194(133) [0175] We teach that **good** works are meritorious—not for the
AP : 0 4 :198(134) [0175] console us against the **good** fortune of the wicked, like
AP : 0 4 :199(134) [0175] praise undoubtedly moves the faithful to **good** works.
AP : 0 4 :200(134) [0175] Therefore we praise **good** works and require them, and
AP : 0 4 :203(134) [0175] **Good** works ought to follow faith in this way.
AP : 0 4 :214(136) [0179] and teach, therefore, that **good** works must necessarily be
AP : 0 4 :220(137) [0181] needed urging to bear **good** fruits lest they lose the Holy
AP : 0 4 :224(138) [0181] as Paul indicates, they began to dislike **good** teachers.
AP : 0 4 :236(140) [0185] priests and other **good** men if they even intimate their
AP : 0 4 :244(142) [0189] wicked opinions that by **good** works we merit the
AP : 0 4 :244(142) [0189] forgiveness of sins; that **good** works are a propitiation
AP : 0 4 :244(142) [0189] reconciles God to us; that **good** works conquer the terrors
AP : 0 4 :244(142) [0189] of sin and death; that **good** works are accepted before
AP : 0 4 :245(142) [0189] from a pure heart and a **good** conscience and sincere
AP : 0 4 :246(142) [0189] did not hold that by our **good** works we merit grace and
AP : 0 4 :246(142) [0189] and forgiveness of sins by **good** works and that by our
AP : 0 4 :249(142) [0191] which does not produce **good** works is dead, but it is alive
AP : 0 4 :249(142) [0191] is dead, but it is alive when it brings forth **good** works.
AP : 0 4 :252(143) [0191] men who have faith and **good** works are certainly
AP : 0 4 :252(143) [0191] As we have said, the **good** works of the saints are
AP : 0 4 :252(143) [0191] their heart and then have **good** fruits, which please him
AP : 0 4 :258(144) [0193] to do evil, learn to do **good**; seek justice, correct
AP : 0 4 :262(145) [0195] righteous, then to do **good** and to defend the poor
AP : 0 4 :266(146) [0197] that we may be able to do **good** and that our works may
AP : 0 4 :268(147) [0197] by our prayers and **good** works, indeed by our complete
AP : 0 4 :269(147) [0197] Whenever **good** works are praised and the law preached,
AP : 0 4 :275(148) [0199] the promise of forgiveness of sins with **good** works.
AP : 0 4 :275(148) [0199] He does not mean that **good** works are a propitiation —
AP : 0 4 :275(148) [0199] One is that **good** fruits ought to follow of necessity, and
AP : 0 4 :276(148) [0199] is written and pictured in **good** works, which thus urge us
AP : 0 4 :276(148) [0199] Those who fail to do **good**, do not arouse themselves to
AP : 0 4 :281(149) [0201] of the law, that for his sake **good** works please God.
AP : 0 4 :288(151) [0203] that men merit grace by **good** works — first by the merit
AP : 0 4 :288(151) [0203] it pleases God if it does **good**, but when men are in great
AP : 0 4 :292(152) [0203] Then love and other **good** fruits follow.
AP : 0 4 :300(153) [0205] Let all **good** men beware, therefore, of yielding to their
AP : 0 4 :308(155) [0207] Our **good** works or obedience to the law can be pleasing
AP : 0 4 :310(155) [0207] of the Gospel is to receive **good** things from God, while
AP : 0 4 :316(156) [0209] They imagine that **good** works, done with the help of a
AP : 0 4 :318(156) [0209] our opponents teach that **good** works earn grace by the
AP : 0 4 :318(156) [0209] must seek grace through a **good** work and not by faith in
AP : 0 4 :319(156) [0209] stilled; for the law always accuses us, even in **good** works.
AP : 0 4 :323(157) [0209] that even if we have **good** works we need mercy in them.
AP : 0 4 :325(157) [0211] the doctrine that we need mercy even in our **good** works.
AP : 0 4 :332(158) [0211] they have love and **good** works, and ask for grace as
AP : 0 4 :334(159) [0215] as a payment which he owes to us for our **good** works.
AP : 0 4 :348(160) [0217] will raise the cry that **good** works are unnecessary if they
AP : 0 4 :348(160) [0217] Of course, **good** works are necessary.
AP : 0 4 :348(160) [0217] we might begin to do **good** works and obey God's law.
AP : 0 4 :350(160) [0217] and become firmer amid **good** works as well as
AP : 0 4 :353(161) [0217] we very definitely require **good** works, since we teach that
AP : 0 4 :356(161) [0217] merited by the merit of condignity through **good** works.
AP : 0 4 :359(162) [0219] about the issue whether **good** works of themselves are
AP : 0 4 :362(162) [0219] for Christ's sake and that **good** works are pleasing to God
AP : 0 4 :365(163) [0219] When they talk about **good** works, the Scriptures often
AP : 0 4 :366(163) [0219] life belong to faith, still **good** works merit other rewards,
AP : 0 4 :370(163) [0221] Our opponents urge that **good** works properly merit
AP : 0 4 :370(164) [0221] and honor and peace for every one who does **good**."
AP : 0 4 :370(164) [0221] "Those who have done **good** will come forth to the
AP : 0 4 :372(164) [0221] None can do **good** works except the justified, who are led
AP : 0 4 :372(164) [0221] Spirit of Christ; nor can **good** works please God without
AP : 0 4 :373(164) [0221] "Glory for him who does **good**," namely, for the righteous
AP : 0 4 :381(165) [0223] in the schools that **good** works please God because of
AP : 0 4 :381(165) [0223] in grace and that **good** works please God because of
AP : 0 4 :382(165) [0225] they also boast that our **good** works are valid by virtue of
AP : 0 4 :385(166) [0225] Thus other **good** works please God because of faith, as
AP : 0 4 :388(166) [0225] These will be easy for **good** men to evaluate if they
AP : 0 4 :389(166) [0225] may be, we hope that **good** men will find it useful for
AP : 0 7 :001(168) [0227] in which there are both **good** and bad fish (Matt. 13:47).
AP : 0 7 :013(170) [0231] embracing both the **good** and the wicked, then men would
AP : 0 7 :019(171) [0233] in Matt. 13:38 that "the **good** seed means the sons of the
AP : 0 7 :021(172) [0233] *opere operato*, without a **good** attitude in the one using
AP : 0 7 :032(174) [0239] For **good** and valid reasons, these vary according to the
AP : 0 9 :003(178) [0245] can effectually confirm **good** and godly minds against the
AP : 1 1 :002(180) [0249] the highest praise of all **good** men, since it discloses a sure
AP : 1 1 :006(181) [0251] It is, of course, a **good** practice to accustom the unlearned
AP : 1 1 :009(181) [0251] **Good** pastors know how profitable it is to examine the
AP : 1 2 :003(182) [0253] All **good** men will see that especially on this issue we have
AP : 1 2 :004(183) [0253] All **good** men of all classes, even the theologians, admit
AP : 1 2 :006(183) [0255] **Good** God, how great is the darkness!
AP : 1 2 :010(184) [0255] Here we appeal to the judgment of all **good** and wise men.
AP : 1 2 :016(184) [0257] All **good** men will understand, therefore, that good and
AP : 1 2 :016(184) [0257] therefore, that **good** and proper reasons prompted us to
AP : 1 2 :017(185) [0257] we merit grace by **good** works done apart from grace.
AP : 1 2 :029(186) [0259] eternal life, and to lead us as regenerated men to do **good**.
AP : 1 2 :067(191) [0271] and the sword, and that **good** men who hold this faith be
AP : 1 2 :090(195) [0279] we are happy to have all **good** men judge and decide
AP : 1 2 :092(196) [0279] requiring contrition or **good** works and making no
AP : 1 2 :095(196) [0281] conscience sees that these works are not **good** enough.
AP : 1 2 :098(197) [0281] **Good** men can easily judge the great importance of
AP : 1 2 :122(200) [0289] a people of his own who are zealous for **good** deeds."
AP : 1 2 :123(200) [0289] What **good** man would not be moved by such dishonesty?
AP : 1 2 :124(201) [0289] We hope that among **good** men these slanders will not
AP : 1 2 :128(201) [0291] There are many **good** men to whom such doubt is worse
AP : 1 2 :128(201) [0291] the doctrinal doubts of **good** men are mere petty anxiety.
AP : 1 2 :131(202) [0291] regeneration) must come **good** fruits and good works in
AP : 1 2 :131(202) [0291] must come good fruits and **good** works in every phase of
AP : 1 2 :131(202) [0291] where mortifying the flesh and **good** fruits do not follow.
AP : 1 2 :139(203) [0295] penitence to produce **good** fruits, and that good fruits like
AP : 1 2 :139(203) [0295] good fruits, and that **good** fruits like true fasting, prayer,
AP : 1 2 :164(208) [0303] — contrition, faith, and **good** fruits — brings about the
AP : 1 2 :164(208) [0303] Isa. 1:16-19 teaches: "Cease to do evil, learn to do **good**.
AP : 1 2 :164(208) [0303] willing and obedient, you shall eat the **good** of the land."
AP : 1 2 :165(208) [0303] and its true fruits, **good** works done from faith, but not,
AP : 1 2 :170(209) [0305] **Good** works ought to follow penitence, and penitence
AP : 1 2 :174(210) [0305] often enough that penitence ought to produce **good** fruits.
AP : 1 3 :013(212) [0311] It is **good** to extol the ministry of the Word with every
AP : 1 3 :018(213) [0313] *opere operato*, without a **good** disposition in the one
AP : 1 3 :018(213) [0313] by a ceremony without a **good** disposition in our heart,
AP : 1 3 :020(214) [0313] For that matter, what **good** would such miracles or
AP : 1 3 :023(214) [0313] *opere operato* without a **good** disposition in the one using
AP : 1 4 :001(214) [0315] know that the Fathers had **good** and useful reasons for
AP : 1 5 :001(215) [0315] conducive to tranquillity and **good** order in the church.
AP : 1 5 :013(216) [0319] them for the sake of **good** order and tranquility in the
AP : 1 5 :020(218) [0321] they were profitable for **good** order, because they gave
AP : 1 5 :022(218) [0321] This **good** order is very becoming in the church and is
AP : 1 5 :027(219) [0323] or faith in him or the **good** works to be performed in
AP : 1 5 :034(220) [0325] knot, he solved it for **good** by cutting it with his sword.
AP : 1 5 :034(220) [0325] have freed consciences for **good**, especially from the
AP : 1 5 :039(220) [0325] accuse us of abolishing **good** ordinances and church
AP : 1 5 :041(220) [0325] youth publicly, a custom that produces very **good** results.
AP : 1 5 :042(221) [0327] beginning to talk about **good** works, but they say nothing
AP : 1 5 :044(221) [0327] pious ceremonies, and the **good** customs of the church.
AP : 1 5 :051(222) [0329] accustomed rites without **good** reason, and to foster
AP : 1 6 :001(222) [0329] civil ordinances are God's **good** creatures and divine
AP : 1 6 :012(224) [0333] will never satisfy **good** consciences unless they keep the
AP : 1 6 :013(224) [0333] so clearly that many **good** men involved in politics and in
AP : 1 8 :002(225) [0335] Well and **good**; but what is the difference between the
AP : 1 8 :006(225) [0335] "a bad tree cannot bear **good** fruit" (Matt. 7:18) and
AP : 2 0 :000(226) [0337] [Article XX. **Good** Works]
AP : 2 0 :001(226) [0337] men do not merit the forgiveness of sins by **good** works.
AP : 2 0 :012(228) [0341] "Confirm your call by **good** works"; therefore works

Continued ▶

A P : 2 0 :013(228) [0341] Do **good** works to persevere in your call and not to lose
A P : 2 0 :015(229) [0343] of our conviction that **good** works must necessarily follow
A P : 2 1 :039(235) [0355] **Good** men everywhere have been hoping that the bishops
A P : 2 1 :042(235) [0355] If they really had the **good** of the church at heart at this
A P : 2 1 :043(235) [0357] nor the church, and **good** men can easily gauge its
A P : 2 1 :043(235) [0357] After the **good** clergy have been killed and sound doctrine
A P : 2 2 :006(237) [0359] This is what **good** religious men ought to do.
A P : 2 2 :012(238) [0361] and rage against **good** men who use the entire sacrament?
A P : 2 3 :002(239) [0363] the impudence of these **good**-for-nothings who say that
A P : 2 3 :005(239) [0365] They know **good** and well how few practice chastity, but
A P : 2 3 :020(242) [0369] Gerson testifies that many **good** men have tried to
A P : 2 3 :025(243) [0371] tyranny, and with **good** reason: Daniel says that it is
A P : 2 3 :043(245) [0375] At the same time **good** men will know how to use
A P : 2 3 :043(245) [0375] is often so burdensome to **good** men that domestic
A P : 2 3 :043(245) [0375] **Good** men know, too, that Paul commands each one to
A P : 2 3 :051(246) [0377] this alone should keep **good** men from approving a
A P : 2 3 :052(246) [0377] **Good** men have been complaining about this burden for a
A P : 2 3 :053(246) [0377] other laws if the common **good** demanded it, why was
A P : 2 3 :053(246) [0379] There are so many **good** reasons for changing it,
A P : 2 3 :056(247) [0379] dispense and change other **good** laws; on this one law of
A P : 2 4 :007(250) [0385] been that for a long time **good** men have wanted some
A P : 2 4 :025(253) [0391] of the saints, yes, all the **good** works of the saints.
A P : 2 4 :032(255) [0395] in confession, they do **good** works for the glory of Christ.
A P : 2 4 :034(256) [0395] are the proclamation of the Gospel and its **good** fruits.
A P : 2 4 :041(257) [0399] Now **good** men can easily see the falsity of the charge
A P : 2 4 :042(257) [0399] to someone else to merit for him grace and every **good**.
A P : 2 4 :048(258) [0401] to it the teaching of the **good** works which God
A P : 2 4 :061(260) [0405] **Good** men in every country can see this.
A P : 2 4 :064(261) [0407] success, to merchants for **good** business, to hunters for
A P : 2 4 :064(261) [0407] business, to hunters for **good** hunting, and things like
A P : 2 4 :099(268) [0419] about the Mass to let all **good** men understand that we
A P : 2 4 :099(268) [0419] We want all **good** men to be warned not to help our
A P : 2 7 :007(269) [0421] sometimes they are responsible for murdering **good** men.
A P : 2 7 :008(269) [0421] monasteries there are some **good** men who have a
A P : 2 7 :009(270) [0423] to the saints, and the conspiracies against **good** men?
A P : 2 7 :022(272) [0427] there are still some **good** men serving the ministry of the
A P : 2 7 :029(274) [0431] case; that is the way these **good**-for-nothings quote the
A P : 2 7 :030(274) [0431] statutes that were not **good** and ordinances by which they
A P : 2 7 :032(274) [0431] that you cannot have any **good** work at all unless he has
A P : 2 7 :056(278) [0439] reasons that release **good** men from this way of life.
A P : 2 8 :005(281) [0445] and hear the pitiful complaints of many **good** men.
A P : 2 8 :023(285) [0451] for Christ's sake, brings enough **good** to hide all the evils.
A P : 2 8 :024(285) [0451] for Luther not only our **good** will but that of many who
A P : 2 8 :024(285) [0451] "The former **good** will ceases, and mortals are forgetful,"
S 1 : P R :002(288) [0455] so bold as seriously, in **good** faith, and without deception
S 1 : P R :006(289) [0457] I often think of the **good** Gerson, who doubted whether
S 1 : P R :006(289) [0457] doubted whether one ought to make **good** writings public.
S 2 : 0 2 :021(296) [0467] and open sale) all Masses, **good** works, etc. for the
S 2 : 0 2 :022(296) [0469] Even if there were some **good** in them, relics should long
S 2 : 0 2 :023(296) [0469] Mass, etc., their use is a **good** work and a service of God.
S 2 : 0 3 :001(297) [0471] had been founded with **good** intentions for the education
S 2 : 0 4 :003(298) [0471] sometimes permits much **good** to come to a people
S 2 : 0 4 :008(299) [0473] head would depend on the **good** pleasure of men rather
S 3 : 0 1 :004(302) [0477] right understanding and a **good** will, as the philosophers
S 3 : 0 1 :005(302) [0477] a free will, either to do **good** and refrain from evil or to
S 3 : 0 1 :005(302) [0477] and refrain from evil or to refrain from **good** and do evil.
S 3 : 0 1 :009(302) [0477] there is no need of a **good** intention to do what he ought,
S 3 : 0 1 :010(303) [0479] gifts are necessary for the performance of a **good** work.
S 3 : 0 3 :017(305) [0483] and, on the basis of this **good** work of his, his sin was
S 3 : 0 3 :028(308) [0487] without sin and full of **good** works, and so we shared our
S 3 : 0 3 :028(308) [0487] and so we shared our **good** works with others and sold
S 3 : 0 3 :032(308) [0487] None of you is **good**.
S 3 : 0 3 :035(309) [0489] head to foot there is no **good** in us, that we must become
S 3 : 0 3 :036(309) [0489] we might imagine to be **good** enough to pay for our sin.
S 3 : 0 3 :039(309) [0489] that is built on our **good** works, for all of this is
S 3 : 0 3 :039(309) [0489] which is called **good** works or the law, although no good
S 3 : 0 3 :039(309) [0489] or the law, although no **good** work but only wicked
S 3 : 1 3 :000(315) [0499] How Man Is Justified Before God, and His **Good** Works
S 3 : 1 3 :002(315) [0499] **Good** works follow such faith, renewal, and forgiveness.
S 3 : 1 3 :003(315) [0499] this we must add that if **good** works do not follow, our
T R : 0 0 :076(333) [0527] And since we have **good** reason for not obeying, it is
T R : 0 0 :080(334) [0527] they cannot possess these alms with a **good** conscience.
S C : P R :002(338) [0533] **Good** God, what wretchedness I beheld!
S C : P R :008(339) [0533] well understood by our **good** fathers, who were
S C : P R :023(341) [0539] no heaven, no Christ, no God, nothing **good** at all.
S C : P R :023(341) [0539] in need of so much that is **good**, he would not neglect the
S C : P R :023(341) [0539] against such evil and in which such **good** is bestowed.
S C : 0 3 :010(347) [0547] Answer: To be sure, the **good** and gracious will of God is
S C : 0 3 :011(347) [0547] This is his **good** and gracious will.
S C : 0 3 :014(347) [0547] a pious spouse and **good** children, trustworthy servants,
S C : 0 3 :014(347) [0549] godly and faithful rulers, **good** government; seasonable
S C : 0 3 :016(347) [0549] forgive and cheerfully do **good** to those who may sin
S C : 0 6 :010(352) [0557] bodily preparation are a **good** external discipline, but he
S C : 0 8 :008(353) [0559] enough to eat to make them joyful and of **good** cheer.
S C : 0 8 :010(354) [0559] to the Lord, for he is **good**; for his steadfast love endures
S C : 0 9 :003(354) [0561] taught the word share all **good** things with him who
S C : 0 9 :010(356) [0563] rendering service with a **good** will as to the Lord and not
S C : 0 9 :010(356) [0563] knowing that whatever **good** anyone does, he will receive
L C : P R :014(360) [0571] and command this so solemnly without **good** reason.
L C : P R :014(360) [0571] us against them with **good** "armor" against their "flaming
L C : P R :014(360) [0571] darts," and with a **good** antidote against their evil
L C : S P :026(364) [0581] have heard and give a **good**, correct answer when they are
L C : 0 1 :002(365) [0581] to which we look for all **good** and in which we find refuge
L C : 0 1 :004(365) [0581] "Whatever **good** thing you lack, look to me for it and seek
L C : 0 1 :015(366) [0583] draw us to himself, because he is the one eternal **good**.
L C : 0 1 :015(366) [0585] to help you and to lavish all **good** upon you richly."
L C : 0 1 :021(367) [0585] cares for God nor expects **good** things from him
L C : 0 1 :021(367) [0585] it believe that whatever **good** it receives comes from God.
L C : 0 1 :024(367) [0587] expecting from him only **good** things; for it is he who
L C : 0 1 :024(368) [0587] whom we receive all that is **good** and by whom we are
L C : 0 1 :025(368) [0587] derived from the word "**good**" because he is an eternal
L C : 0 1 :025(368) [0587] and pours forth all that is **good** in name and in fact.
L C : 0 1 :026(368) [0587] Although much that is **good** comes to us from men, we
L C : 0 1 :026(368) [0587] — have received the command to do us all kinds of **good**.
L C : 0 1 :027(368) [0587] this way of receiving **good** through God's creatures is not
L C : 0 1 :028(368) [0587] from him nothing but **good**, especially in distress and
L C : 0 1 :028(368) [0587] it hopes to receive more **good** and help than from God,
L C : 0 1 :040(370) [0591] Certainly, if we desire all **good** things in time and
L C : 0 1 :047(371) [0593] allowing none of these **good** things to be his lord or idol.
L C : 0 1 :055(372) [0595] God's name or to put up a **good** front and justify
L C : 0 1 :064(373) [0599] of truth and all that is **good** — for example, when we
L C : 0 1 :066(373) [0599] but in support of the **good** and for the advantage of our
L C : 0 1 :066(373) [0599] This is a truly **good** work by which God is praised, truth
L C : 0 1 :066(373) [0599] and separates right from wrong, **good** from evil.
L C : 0 1 :069(374) [0599] are allowed to do as they please, no **good** will come of it.
L C : 0 1 :074(374) [0601] meets with unexpected **good** fortune, however trivial, he
L C : 0 1 :075(375) [0601] Then some **good** may take root, spring up, and bear
L C : 0 1 :076(375) [0603] and blows will come to no **good** end; at best they will
L C : 0 1 :076(375) [0603] at best they will remain **good** only as long as the rod is on
L C : 0 1 :112(380) [0613] place, notice what a great, **good**, and holy work is here
L C : 0 1 :112(380) [0613] God, saying: "If I am to do **good** and holy works, I know
L C : 0 1 :113(380) [0613] we wish to perform truly **good** works, and by
L C : 0 1 :115(381) [0613] to serve God with truly **good** works, they must do what is
L C : 0 1 :127(382) [0617] kindness and for all the **good** things we have received
L C : 0 1 :134(383) [0619] commandment will enjoy **good** days, happiness, and
L C : 0 1 :134(383) [0619] child, livelihood, peace, **good** government, etc., without
L C : 0 1 :148(385) [0623] have everything that is **good** — shelter and protection in
L C : 0 1 :162(387) [0627] cannot now support one **good** preacher although in the
L C : 0 1 :183(389) [0633] commandments as a boundary between **good** and evil.
L C : 0 1 :184(390) [0633] or greater wealth and **good** fortune than he, gives vent to
L C : 0 1 :184(390) [0633] you even the least **good**, whether physical or spiritual.
L C : 0 1 :188(390) [0635] who desires and does you **good** is not human but
L C : 0 1 :189(390) [0635] also when he fails to do **good** to his neighbor, or, though
L C : 0 1 :190(391) [0635] It will do you no **good** to plead that you did not
L C : 0 1 :196(391) [0637] minds, we would have our hands full of **good** works to do
L C : 0 1 :197(391) [0637] same as forbidding their **good** works and emptying the
L C : 0 1 :197(392) [0637] to suffer wrong from anyone or do anyone any **good**.
L C : 0 1 :221(395) [0643] you have another precious **good** work — indeed, many
L C : 0 1 :226(395) [0645] are my neighbors, my **good** friends, my own servants,
L C : 0 1 :226(395) [0645] from whom I expect **good**; but they are the first to
L C : 0 1 :229(396) [0645] lords and honorable, **good** citizens, and yet with a great
L C : 0 1 :252(399) [0651] who seeks and desires **good** works will here find ample
L C : 0 1 :255(399) [0653] us, namely, our honor and **good** name, for it is
L C : 0 1 :259(400) [0655] all cases will often offend **good** friends, relatives,
L C : 0 1 :264(400) [0655] would rather hear evil than **good** about his neighbor.
L C : 0 1 :270(401) [0657] deprived of his honor and **good** name unless these have
L C : 0 1 :273(401) [0659] For honor and **good** name are easily taken away, but not
L C : 0 1 :274(402) [0659] does not do his neighbor **good** but only harm and evil,
L C : 0 1 :275(402) [0659] and sisters and other **good** friends are under mutual
L C : 0 1 :285(403) [0663] his tongue to speak only **good** of everyone, to cover his
L C : 0 1 :290(404) [0663] a great multitude of **good** works which please God most
L C : 0 1 :291(404) [0663] a man that can do greater **good** or greater harm, in
L C : 0 1 :311(407) [0669] fountain from which all **good** works must spring, the true
L C : 0 1 :311(407) [0671] true channel through which all **good** works must flow.
L C : 0 1 :311(407) [0671] deed, no conduct can be **good** or pleasing to God, no
L C : 0 1 :322(409) [0673] bless, and bestow all **good** things on those who prize them
L C : 0 1 :328(410) [0677] contrary, you should do **good** to all men, help them and
L C : 0 1 :333(410) [0677] that he will shower us with all **good** things and blessings.
L C : 0 2 :015(412) [0681] and temporal blessings — **good** government, peace,
L C : 0 2 :028(414) [0685] from him all kinds of **good** things, the devil came and led
L C : 0 2 :030(414) [0685] of life and righteousness and every **good** and blessing.
L C : 0 3 :008(421) [0699] the name of God is glorified and used to **good** purpose.
L C : 0 3 :025(423) [0705] at best, of doing a **good** work as a payment to God, not
L C : 0 3 :032(424) [0707] For whenever a **good** Christian prays, "Dear Father, thy
L C : 0 3 :038(425) [0709] we have, and praying, as **good** children, that his name,
L C : 0 3 :039(425) [0709] in every way to behave as **good** children so that he may
L C : 0 3 :061(428) [0715] In a **good** government there is need not only for good
L C : 0 3 :061(428) [0715] there is need not only for **good** builders and rulers, but
L C : 0 3 :074(430) [0719] received from God all **good** things in abundance, we
L C : 0 3 :075(430) [0719] may bestow on us still more blessings and **good** things.
L C : 0 3 :076(431) [0721] give and preserve to us a **good** wife, children, and
L C : 0 3 :076(431) [0721] to grant us faithful neighbors and **good** friends, etc.
L C : 0 3 :079(431) [0721] It is **good** to impress upon the common people that all
L C : 0 3 :100(433) [0725] forgiveness and a **good** conscience, and have been wholly
L C : 0 3 :100(433) [0727] stand before God with a **good** conscience, we must pray
L C : 0 3 :113(435) [0729] will, our daily bread, a **good** and cheerful conscience, etc.
L C : 0 4 :012(438) [0735] would not be as noble and **good** as if God were to pick up
L C : 0 4 :036(441) [0741] Baptism in such a manner that it does you any **good**.
L C : 0 4 :054(443) [0745] and we baptized him in all **good** faith, we should have to
L C : 0 4 :066(445) [0749] with all vices and by nature has nothing **good** in him.
L C : 0 5 :052(452) [0765] be forced by men either to faith or to any **good** work.
L C : 0 5 :057(453) [0767] to fix your eye on how **good** and pure you are, to work
L C : 0 5 :058(453) [0767] since they do not desire it and do not want to be **good**.
L C : 0 5 :059(453) [0767] but would like to be **good**, should not absent themselves,
L C : 0 5 :067(454) [0769] our highest and greatest **good**, we act so distantly toward
L C : 0 5 :069(454) [0769] people nothing can be **good** or wholesome, just as when a
L C : 0 5 :075(455) [0771] are, then for your own **good** turn to St. Paul's Epistle to
L C : 0 5 :076(455) [0771] "For I know that nothing **good** dwells within me, that is,
L C : 0 5 :079(455) [0771] as if you want to become **good** and cling to the Gospel,
L C : 0 6 :016(459) [0000] confession were simply a **good** work with which we could
L C : 0 6 :018(459) [0000] dare not come and say how **good** or how wicked you are.
L C : 0 6 :032(460) [0000] who really want to be **good** Christians, free from their
E P : R N :007(465) [0779] be understood and judged as **good** or evil, right or wrong.
E P : 0 1 :013(467) [0783] things its natural powers remained wholly **good** and pure.
E P : 0 1 :014(468) [0783] unimpaired its powers for **good** even in spiritual things.
E P : 0 1 :015(468) [0783] impediment to man's **good** spiritual powers and not the
E P : 0 1 :016(468) [0783] man still has something **good** about him even in spiritual
E P : 0 1 :022(469) [0785] times the word means the **good** or bad quality which
E P : 0 3 :011(474) [0795] justification and the **good** works that follow it do not
E P : 0 3 :011(474) [0795] Thus **good** works always follow justifying faith and are
E P : 0 3 :023(475) [0797] does not justify without **good** works, in such a way that
E P : 0 3 :023(475) [0797] works, in such a way that **good** works are necessary for
E P : 0 4 :000(475) [0797] IV. **Good** Works
E P : 0 4 :000(475) [0797] Chief Issue in the Controversy Concerning **Good** Works
E P : 0 4 :001(475) [0797] in some churches concerning the doctrine of **good** works:
E P : 0 4 :002(475) [0797] one party asserted that **good** works are necessary to

Continued ▶

E P : 0 4 :002(475) [0797] to be saved without **good** works; and that no one has ever
E P : 0 4 :002(475) [0797] and that no one has ever been saved without **good** works.
E P : 0 4 :002(475) [0797] other party asserted that **good** works are detrimental to
E P : 0 4 :004(476) [0797] be admonished to do **good** works solely on the basis of
E P : 0 4 :006(476) [0797] 1. That **good** works, like fruits of a good tree, certainly
E P : 0 4 :006(476) [0797] works, like fruits of a **good** tree, certainly and indubitably
E P : 0 4 :007(476) [0799] teach, and confess that **good** works should be completely
E P : 0 4 :008(476) [0799] by the Holy Spirit, are obligated to do **good** works.
E P : 0 4 :011(477) [0799] "The regenerated do **good** works from a free spirit,"
E P : 0 4 :011(477) [0799] to do or not to do **good** and that he might keep his faith
E P : 0 4 :012(477) [0799] spirit which does **good** works not from a fear of
E P : 0 4 :015(477) [0799] The **good** works are testimonies of the Holy Spirit's
E P : 0 4 :016(477) [0801] which teach that **good** works are necessary to salvation;
E P : 0 4 :016(477) [0801] ever been saved without **good** works; likewise, that it is
E P : 0 4 :016(477) [0801] that it is impossible to be saved without **good** works.
E P : 0 4 :017(477) [0801] that bald statement that **good** works are detrimental to
E P : 0 4 :018(477) [0801] Christian discipline and **good** works, and to remind them
E P : 0 4 :018(477) [0801] exercise themselves in **good** works as an evidence of their
E P : 0 4 :018(477) [0801] to warn against mingling **good** works in the article of
E P : 1 0 :001(492) [0829] church in the interest of **good** order and the general
E P : 1 0 :003(493) [0829] solely for the sake of **good** order and the general welfare,
E P : 1 1 :004(494) [0833] extends alike over **good** people and evil people.
E P : 1 1 :009(495) [0833] to eternal life, whatever **good** I do is of no avail;
E P : 1 2 :013(499) [0841] in any civic office with a **good** and clear conscience.
E P : 1 2 :015(499) [0841] swear an oath with a **good** conscience nor pay
E P : 1 2 :017(499) [0841] a Christian cannot with a **good** conscience hold or
E P : 1 2 :018(499) [0841] a Christian cannot with a **good** conscience be an
S D : P R :010(506) [0855] does not mean that other **good**, useful, and pure books,
S D : 0 1 :002(508) [0859] he is dead to that which is **good** and is turned to
S D : 0 1 :011(510) [0863] is not only a total lack of **good** in spiritual, divine things,
S D : 0 1 :020(511) [0865] in spiritual matters it is **good**, pure, and in its natural
S D : 0 1 :022(512) [0865] absence of man's spiritual **good** powers, but only an
S D : 0 1 :023(512) [0865] birth something that is **good** — even though in only a
S D : 0 1 :025(512) [0867] can of and by itself do no **good** thing in spiritual, divine
S D : 0 1 :025(512) [0867] thing (such as, for example, producing a **good** thought).
S D : 0 1 :027(512) [0867] originally created pure, **good**, and holy, sin did not
S D : 0 1 :060(519) [0879] that nothing pure nor **good** has remained in itself and all
S D : 0 1 :060(519) [0879] and with all his powers dead indeed to that which is **good**.
S D : 0 2 :007(521) [0883] dead and corrupted as far as anything **good** is concerned.
S D : 0 2 :010(522) [0885] gone wrong; no one does **good**, not even one" (Rom.
S D : 0 2 :012(522) [0885] ability to think anything **good** or right in spiritual
S D : 0 2 :014(523) [0885] to will and to work for his **good** pleasure" (Phil. 2:13).
S D : 0 2 :017(524) [0887] incapable, and dead to **good**, but also that by original sin
S D : 0 2 :017(524) [0887] "I know that nothing **good** dwells within me, that is, in
S D : 0 2 :019(524) [0889] have a conception of **good** or evil or freely choose to act
S D : 0 2 :026(526) [0891] us in Christ Jesus for **good** works (Eph. 2:10); and makes
S D : 0 2 :026(526) [0891] In short, every **good** gift comes from God (James 1:17).
S D : 0 2 :032(527) [0893] An evil tree cannot bear **good** fruit, and without faith no
S D : 0 2 :032(527) [0893] either to initiate something **good** or by itself to cooperate.
S D : 0 2 :033(527) [0893] man has a free will to do **good** and to avoid evil," and
S D : 0 2 :033(527) [0893] Holy Spirit and his grace are necessary for **good** works."
S D : 0 2 :038(528) [0895] and effects in us a daily increase in faith and **good** works.
S D : 0 2 :039(528) [0895] where they desire to do the **good** and delight in it
S D : 0 2 :039(528) [0895] in it (indeed, actually do **good** deeds and grow in
S D : 0 2 :039(528) [0895] created in Christ Jesus for **good** works, which God
S D : 0 2 :048(530) [0901] power and ability for **good** in our hearts, and how we are
S D : 0 2 :059(532) [0905] or a volition that wills what is **good** and wholesome).
S D : 0 2 :061(533) [0905] mode of doing something **good** and wholesome in divine
S D : 0 2 :061(533) [0905] no power to do something **good** in divine matters, and he
S D : 0 2 :062(533) [0905] by which he does anything **good** in spiritual matters.
S D : 0 2 :063(533) [0905] then he wills that which is **good**, in so far as he is reborn
S D : 0 2 :063(533) [0905] And immediately he does **good**, as much and as long as
S D : 0 2 :064(533) [0905] does that which is **good**, as David says, "Your people will
S D : 0 2 :066(534) [0907] the converted man does **good**, as much and as long as
S D : 0 2 :070(535) [0909] of grace in Christ, to have **good** spiritual thoughts,
S D : 0 2 :076(536) [0911] out toward that which is **good** and toward his own
S D : 0 2 :076(536) [0911] comes to the aid of the **good** work which man began by
S D : 0 2 :077(536) [0911] dead toward that which is **good**, but only grievously
S D : 0 2 :083(537) [0913] no change at all for the **good** in the intellect, will, and
S D : 0 2 :090(539) [0915] Holy Spirit in subsequent **good** works by doing that
S D : 0 3 :013(541) [0919] not justify because it is so **good** a work and so
S D : 0 3 :027(543) [0925] For **good** works do not precede justification; rather they
S D : 0 3 :027(544) [0925] must first be righteous before he can do **good** works.
S D : 0 3 :029(544) [0925] grant that we must teach about love and **good** works too.
S D : 0 3 :029(544) [0925] when we deal with **good** works apart from this matter of
S D : 0 3 :029(544) [0925] a person should also do **good** works and love, but how a
S D : 0 3 :032(545) [0927] righteousness of the new obedience or of **good** works.
S D : 0 3 :032(545) [0927] after he has done many **good** works and leads the best
S D : 0 3 :033(545) [0927] from idolatry and had no **good** works, but also afterward
S D : 0 3 :033(545) [0927] with many resplendent **good** works (Rom. 4:3; Gen. 15:6;
S D : 0 3 :035(545) [0927] love, virtues, and **good** works, these should and must not
S D : 0 3 :036(545) [0927] contrition, or as though **good** works should, must, and
S D : 0 3 :036(545) [0927] or as though believers must or dare do nothing **good**.
S D : 0 3 :036(545) [0927] The point is that **good** works are excluded from the
S D : 0 3 :039(546) [0929] virtues, nor other **good** works are our righteousness
S D : 0 3 :040(546) [0929] order between faith and **good** works is bound to be
S D : 0 3 :041(546) [0929] For **good** works do not precede faith, nor is sanctification
S D : 0 3 :041(546) [0929] and sanctification the fruits of **good** works will follow.
S D : 0 3 :041(546) [0931] between faith and **good** works; nevertheless, it is faith
S D : 0 3 :042(547) [0931] dead where all kinds of **good** works and the fruits of the
S D : 0 3 :043(547) [0931] James is speaking of the **good** works of those who are
S D : 0 3 :043(547) [0931] faith; or, the presence of **good** works along with faith is
S D : 0 3 :043(547) [0931] God; or, the presence of **good** works is necessary in the
S D : 0 3 :045(547) [0933] 1. That our love or our **good** works are a meritorious
S D : 0 3 :046(548) [0933] 2. That by **good** works man must make himself worthy
S D : 0 3 :062(550) [0937] them by the Holy Spirit and the consequent **good** works.
S D : 0 4 :000(551) [0939] IV. **Good** Works
S D : 0 4 :001(551) [0939] A controversy concerning **good** works has likewise arisen
S D : 0 4 :001(551) [0939] words and formulas as "**Good** works are necessary to
S D : 0 4 :001(551) [0939] to be saved without **good** works," and "No one has been
S D : 0 4 :001(551) [0939] has been saved without **good** works," since good works
S D : 0 4 :001(551) [0939] good works," since **good** works are required of true
S D : 0 4 :002(551) [0939] on the contrary that **good** works are indeed necessary —
S D : 0 4 :003(551) [0939] or principle "that **good** works are detrimental to
S D : 0 4 :003(551) [0939] also maintained that **good** works are not necessary but
S D : 0 4 :003(551) [0939] took the contrary view that **good** works are necessary.
S D : 0 4 :004(551) [0939] with which the law forces men to do **good** works.
S D : 0 4 :007(552) [0939] that believers walk in **good** works; that only those are
S D : 0 4 :007(552) [0939] that only those are truly **good** works which God himself
S D : 0 4 :007(552) [0941] traditions; that truly **good** works are not done by a
S D : 0 4 :007(552) [0941] says, "has been created in Christ Jesus for **good** works."
S D : 0 4 :008(552) [0941] us as to how and why the **good** works of believers are
S D : 0 4 :008(552) [0941] A bad tree cannot bear **good** fruit, and "Whatsoever does
S D : 0 4 :009(552) [0941] and source of the truly **good** and God-pleasing works
S D : 0 4 :010(553) [0941] impossible for it not to be constantly doing what is **good**.
S D : 0 4 :011(553) [0941] faith does not ask if **good** works are to be done, but
S D : 0 4 :011(553) [0941] does not perform such **good** works is a faithless man,
S D : 0 4 :011(553) [0941] in search of faith and **good** works without knowing what
S D : 0 4 :011(553) [0941] what either faith or **good** works are, and in the meantime
S D : 0 4 :011(553) [0941] and jabbers a great deal about faith and **good** works.
S D : 0 4 :012(553) [0941] willing and desirous to do **good** to everyone, to serve
S D : 0 4 :014(553) [0943] the question whether **good** works are necessary or free,
S D : 0 4 :014(553) [0943] formulas like these: "**Good** works are necessary"; again,
S D : 0 4 :014(553) [0943] "It is necessary to do **good** works because they necessarily
S D : 0 4 :014(553) [0943] and must of necessity do **good** works that God has
S D : 0 4 :015(553) [0943] repentance and without **good** works, as if there could
S D : 0 4 :015(553) [0943] unfruitful tree since no **good** fruits appear, yes, even
S D : 0 4 :018(554) [0943] say and teach that truly **good** works are to be done
S D : 0 4 :018(554) [0943] the proposition that **good** works are spontaneous.
S D : 0 4 :020(554) [0945] as false the view that **good** works are free to believers in
S D : 0 4 :021(554) [0945] when we teach that **good** works are necessary we must
S D : 0 4 :022(554) [0945] the propositions that **good** works are necessary for the
S D : 0 4 :022(554) [0945] to be saved without **good** works, since such propositions
S D : 0 4 :023(555) [0945] confidence in one's own **good** works, and are adopted by
S D : 0 4 :028(555) [0947] that, although we require **good** works as necessary to
S D : 0 4 :030(555) [0947] has arisen as to whether **good** works preserve salvation or
S D : 0 4 :033(556) [0947] the exhortation to do **good** works can be instilled without
S D : 0 4 :033(556) [0947] teaches why we should do **good** works, namely, that we
S D : 0 4 :033(556) [0949] He says: 'Do **good** works so that you remain in your
S D : 0 4 :035(557) [0949] opinion, namely, that our **good** works preserve salvation,
S D : 0 4 :037(557) [0949] the proposition that **good** works are supposed to be
S D : 0 4 :037(557) [0949] answer: If anyone draws **good** works into the article of
S D : 0 4 :037(557) [0949] assurance of salvation on **good** works in order to merit
S D : 0 4 :037(557) [0951] times in Phil. 3:7ff. that **good** works not only are useless
S D : 0 4 :037(557) [0951] however, lies not with the **good** works themselves, but
S D : 0 4 :037(557) [0951] express Word of God, is being placed upon **good** works.
S D : 0 4 :038(557) [0951] any qualifications that **good** works are detrimental to
S D : 0 4 :038(557) [0951] For when **good** works are done on account of right
S D : 0 4 :038(557) [0951] that believers should do **good** works which the Holy
S D : 0 4 :040(558) [0951] not to be deterred from **good** works, but are most
S D : 0 4 :040(558) [0951] to apply themselves to **good** works, we cannot and should
S D : 0 5 :018(561) [0957] to rebuke sin and to give instruction about **good** works.
S D : 0 5 :020(561) [0959] him alone we re-enter the **good** graces of God, obtain
S D : 0 5 :021(562) [0959] is called, the Gospel, a **good** and joyful message that God
S D : 0 6 :002(564) [0963] obedience (that is, in what **good** works they should walk)
S D : 0 6 :008(565) [0965] writes, "I know that nothing **good** dwells within me."
S D : 0 6 :008(565) [0965] again, "I do not do the **good** I want, but the evil I do not
S D : 0 6 :009(565) [0965] God, as it is written, "It is **good** for me that I was afflicted
S D : 0 6 :010(565) [0965] this matter, as far as the **good** works of believers are
S D : 0 6 :012(566) [0967] (Rom. 12:2) and in what **good** works, which God has
S D : 0 6 :015(566) [0967] that in speaking of **good** works that are in accord with
S D : 0 6 :015(566) [0967] for otherwise they are not **good** works — the word "law"
S D : 0 6 :016(566) [0967] strict sense, because his **good** works are extorted by the
S D : 0 6 :021(567) [0969] in connection with their **good** works, because otherwise
S D : 0 6 :021(567) [0969] the law of God prescribes **good** works for faith in such a
S D : 0 6 :021(567) [0969] them that in this life our **good** works are imperfect and
S D : 0 6 :021(567) [0969] been born anew to do **good** works, he holds up before
S D : 0 6 :022(567) [0969] teach us how and why the **good** works of believers are
S D : 0 6 :023(568) [0969] Though their **good** works are still imperfect and impure,
S D : 0 7 :068(582) [0997] true faith, and without a **good** intention to improve their
S D : 0 8 :018(594) [1021] the term "mixture" in a **good** sense and with the right
S D : 0 8 :025(596) [1023] majesty according to his **good** pleasure, when and how he
S D : 1 0 :001(610) [1053] into the church with **good** intentions for the sake of good
S D : 1 0 :001(610) [1053] intentions for the sake of **good** order and decorum or else
S D : 1 0 :007(611) [1055] which serve neither **good** order, Christian discipline, nor
S D : 1 0 :009(612) [1055] and salutary for **good** order, Christian discipline,
S D : 1 0 :009(612) [1055] us how we can with a **good** conscience give in and yield to
S D : 1 1 :004(616) [1063] foreknowledge — extends to all creatures, **good** or evil.
S D : 1 1 :004(617) [1063] or will happen, both **good** and evil, since all things,
S D : 1 1 :011(618) [1067] repentance, faith, and the **good** resolve to lead a godly
S D : 1 1 :021(619) [1069] and increase in them the **good** work which he has begun,
S D : 1 1 :032(621) [1073] after "he has begun the **good** work in us" he will also
S D : 1 1 :042(623) [1077] to those in whom he has "begun the **good** work."
S D : 1 1 :043(623) [1077] able to have done any **good**, God elected us to salvation
S D : 1 1 :049(624) [1079] must "work together for **good**" since they are "called
S D : 1 1 :072(628) [1087] are evil, know how to give **good** gifts to your children,
S D : 1 1 :082(630) [1089] of the house, ready for any **good** work" (II Tim. 2:21).
S D : 1 1 :084(630) [1091] or because it was God's **good** pleasure that he should be
S D : 1 1 :087(631) [1093] without our merit and **good** works, as it is written, "He
S D : 1 1 :088(631) [1093] before we had done any **good**, but even before we were
S D : 1 2 :020(634) [1099] a Christian cannot with a **good** conscience swear an oath
S D : 1 2 :022(634) [1099] no Christian can with a **good** conscience hold or possess
S D : 1 2 :023(634) [1099] no Christian can with a **good** conscience be an innkeeper,

Goodness (18)

A G : 0 1 :003(028) [0043] power, wisdom, and **goodness**, one creator and preserver
A L : 0 1 :002(027) [0043] power, wisdom, and **goodness**, the maker and preserver
S 3 : 0 1 :009(302) [0477] sin, for such is the **goodness** of man's nature and such is
S C : 0 2 :002(345) [0543] fatherly, and divine **goodness** and mercy, without any
S C : 0 8 :009(353) [0559] which of thy bountiful **goodness** Thou hast bestowed on
L C : 0 1 :025(368) [0587] overflows with sheer **goodness** and pours forth all that is
L C : 0 1 :033(369) [0589] hand, his kindness and **goodness** extend to many
L C : 0 1 :039(370) [0591] to God alone — sheer **goodness** and blessing, not only for
L C : 0 1 :114(380) [0613] have had an object lesson in **goodness** and happiness.
L C : 0 2 :017(412) [0681] out of pure love and **goodness**, without our merit, as a
L C : 0 2 :029(414) [0685] in his unfathomable **goodness**, had mercy on our misery

Continued 5

L C : 0 2 :058(418) [0693] and holy people, full of **goodness** and righteousness,
L C : 0 3 :083(431) [0721] may recognize in them his fatherly **goodness** toward us.
L C : 0 3 :090(432) [0723] if anybody boasts of his **goodness** and despises others he
S D : 0 1 :021(512) [0865] has and retains its **goodness** and powers also in spiritual
S D : 0 1 :023(512) [0865] not entirely lost all the **goodness** that belongs to spiritual
S D : 0 1 :030(513) [0867] and affecting the **goodness**, truth, holiness, and
S D : 1 1 :059(626) [1083] and glorify God's **goodness** to us without and contrary to

Goods (10)
A G : 2 8 :011(082) [0085] it protects body and **goods** from the power of others.
A L : 2 8 :011(082) [0085] not souls but bodies and **goods** from manifest harm, and
A P : 0 4 :310(155) [0207] of the law is to offer and present our **goods** to God.
A P : 2 4 :083(264) [0413] which means public **goods**; thus the verb means to care
A P : 2 4 :083(264) [0413] the verb means to care for or to administer public **goods**.
S C : 0 5 :023(350) [0555] him, giving him inferior **goods** and short measure."
L C : 0 1 :224(395) [0643] is transacted and money is exchanged for **goods** or labor.
L C : 0 1 :240(397) [0649] and privilege to sell his **goods** as dearly as he pleases
L C : 0 2 :026(413) [0685] and above the temporal **goods** mentioned above — that
S D : 0 2 :036(528) [0895] and partaker in it of all the **goods** which it possesses.

Gordian (1)
A P : 1 5 :034(220) [0325] could not untie the **Gordian** knot, he solved it for good by

Gorges (1)
A P : 2 7 :005(269) [0421] feed a lazy crowd that **gorges** itself on the public alms of

Goslar (1)
P R : P R :027(015) [0027] The Council of the City of **Goslar**

Gospel (500)
P R : P R :002(003) [0007] light of his holy **Gospel** and of the Word that alone brings
P R : P R :004(004) [0007] and perceptibly impede the course of the holy **Gospel**.
A G : 0 5 :001(031) [0045] ministry, that is, provided the **Gospel** and the sacraments.
A G : 0 5 :002(031) [0045] when and where he pleases, in those who hear the **Gospel**.
A G : 0 5 :003(031) [0045] And the **Gospel** teaches that we have a gracious God, not
A G : 0 5 :004(031) [0045] and works without the external word of the **Gospel**.
A G : 0 7 :001(032) [0047] believers among who the **Gospel** is preached in its purity
A G : 0 7 :001(032) [0047] holy sacraments are administered according to the **Gospel**
A G : 0 7 :002(032) [0047] Christian church that the **Gospel** be preached in
A G : 1 2 :005(034) [0049] same time to believe the **Gospel** and absolution (namely,
A G : 1 5 :003(036) [0049] grace are contrary to the **Gospel** and the teaching about
A G : 1 5 :004(037) [0049] satisfaction for sin, are useless and contrary to the **Gospel**
A G : 1 6 :004(038) [0051] real faith in God, for the **Gospel** does not teach an
A G : 1 6 :005(038) [0051] The **Gospel** does not overthrow civil authority, the state,
A G : 2 0 :010(042) [0055] and seeks his own way to God, contrary to the **Gospel**.
A G : 2 6 :004(064) [0071] obscured, and yet the **Gospel** earnestly urges them upon
A G : 2 6 :020(067) [0073] The **Gospel** demands that the teaching about faith should
A G : 2 6 :029(068) [0075] opposed to the **Gospel** to institute or practice such works
A G : 2 7 :012(072) [0077] counsels included in the **Gospel** were kept, and so
A G : 2 7 :036(076) [0081] to God and the holy **Gospel** and contrary to God's
A G : 2 8 :005(081) [0085] that according to the **Gospel** the power of keys or the
A G : 2 8 :005(081) [0085] of God to preach the **Gospel**, to forgive and retain sins,
A G : 2 8 :009(082) [0085] for St. Paul says, "The **gospel** is the power of God for
A G : 2 8 :011(082) [0085] with matters altogether different from the **Gospel**.
A G : 2 8 :012(083) [0085] commission to preach the **Gospel** and administer the
A G : 2 8 :019(084) [0087] has nothing at all to do with the office of the **Gospel**.
A G : 2 8 :021(084) [0087] the bishop to preach the **Gospel**, forgive sins, judge
A G : 2 8 :021(084) [0087] that is contrary to the **Gospel**, and exclude from the
A G : 2 8 :023(084) [0087] anything contrary to the **Gospel**, we have God's command
A G : 2 8 :024(084) [0087] should preach to you a **gospel** contrary to that which we
A G : 2 8 :034(086) [0089] anything contrary to the **Gospel**, as has been indicated
A G : 2 8 :050(089) [0091] grace are contrary to the **Gospel**, it is not at all proper for
A G : 2 8 :052(089) [0091] For the chief article of the **Gospel** must be maintained,
A G : 2 8 :059(091) [0091] after the revelation of the **Gospel** all ceremonies of the old
A G : 2 8 :070(093) [0093] there is no doubt that it is in accord with the holy **Gospel**.
A L : 0 5 :001(031) [0045] ministry of teaching the **Gospel** and administering the
A L : 0 5 :002(031) [0045] and when it pleases God, in those who hear the **Gospel**.
A L : 0 7 :001(032) [0047] of saints in which the **Gospel** is taught purely and the
A L : 0 7 :002(032) [0047] the teaching of the **Gospel** and the administration of the
A L : 1 2 :005(034) [0049] which is born of the **Gospel**, or of absolution, believes
A L : 1 5 :003(037) [0049] sins are opposed to the **Gospel** and the teaching about
A L : 1 5 :004(037) [0049] for sins, are useless and contrary to the **Gospel**.
A L : 1 6 :004(038) [0051] the perfection of the **Gospel** not in the fear of God and in
A L : 1 6 :004(038) [0051] The **Gospel** teaches an eternal righteousness of the heart,
A L : 2 0 :019(043) [0055] works when consolation from the **Gospel** was not heard.
A L : 2 6 :004(064) [0071] is the chief part of the **Gospel** and ought above all else to
A L : 2 6 :020(067) [0073] For the **Gospel** compels us to insist in the church on the
A L : 2 6 :029(068) [0075] it is in conflict with the **Gospel** to institute or practice
A L : 2 7 :012(072) [0077] only of the precepts but also of the counsels of the **Gospel**
A L : 2 8 :005(081) [0085] that according to the **Gospel** the power of keys or the
A L : 2 8 :005(081) [0085] of God to preach the **Gospel**, to remit and retain sins, and
A L : 2 8 :007(082) [0085] said, "Go and preach the **gospel** to the whole creation."
A L : 2 8 :008(082) [0085] teaching or preaching the **Gospel** and by administering the
A L : 2 8 :009(082) [0085] for Paul says, "The **gospel** is the power of God for
A L : 2 8 :011(082) [0085] is concerned with other things than the **Gospel**.
A L : 2 8 :011(082) [0085] penalties, while the **Gospel** protects souls from heresies,
A L : 2 8 :012(083) [0085] commission to preach the **Gospel** and administer the
A L : 2 8 :019(083) [0087] a commission of the **Gospel**, but by human right granted
A L : 2 8 :019(084) [0087] is a function other than the ministry of the **Gospel**.
A L : 2 8 :021(084) [0087] Hence according to the **Gospel** (or, as they say, by divine
A L : 2 8 :021(084) [0087] which is contrary to the **Gospel**, and to exclude from the
A L : 2 8 :023(084) [0087] anything contrary to the **Gospel**, churches have a
A L : 2 8 :024(084) [0087] should preach any other **Gospel**, let him be accursed"
A L : 2 8 :034(086) [0089] have power to institute anything contrary to the **Gospel**.
A L : 2 8 :050(089) [0091] are in conflict with the **Gospel**, it follows that it is not
A L : 2 8 :052(089) [0091] the chief article of the **Gospel**, namely, that we obtain
A L : 2 8 :059(091) [0091] after the revelation of the **Gospel** all ceremonies of the
A L : 2 8 :066(092) [0093] one must consider what the perpetual aim of the **Gospel** is
A L : 2 8 :070(093) [0093] that he will not teach the pure doctrine of the **Gospel**.
A L : 2 8 :077(094) [0095] thing, that they allow the **Gospel** to be taught purely and
A P : P R :015(099) [0101] that we hold to the **Gospel** of Christ correctly and
A P : 0 2 :043(106) [0117] mingle philosophical and civil ethics with the **Gospel**.
A P : 0 4 :014(109) [0123] sermons, laid aside the **Gospel** and expounded the ethics
A P : 0 4 :020(110) [0125] teaching of the law, the **Gospel** of the free forgiveness of
A P : 0 4 :043(113) [0133] The **Gospel** is, strictly speaking, the promise of
A P : 0 4 :043(113) [0133] promise only by faith, the **Gospel** proclaims the
A P : 0 4 :047(113) [0133] the righteousness of the **Gospel**, which proclaims the
A P : 0 4 :062(115) [0139] The **Gospel** declares that all men are under sin and are
A P : 0 4 :067(116) [0139] says (Rom. 1:16), "The **Gospel** is the power of God for
A P : 0 4 :070(116) [0141] only the law and does away with Christ and the **Gospel**.
A P : 0 4 :101(121) [0151] promises which by the **Gospel** he has spread throughout
A P : 0 4 :110(123) [0153] completely abolish the **Gospel** of the free forgiveness of
A P : 0 4 :120(124) [0155] Furthermore, the **Gospel** (that is, the promise that sins are
A P : 0 4 :120(124) [0155] faith we are discussing completely destroys the **Gospel**.
A P : 0 4 :135(125) [0159] faith through hearing the **Gospel** of the forgiveness of
A P : 0 4 :163(129) [0169] of the righteousness of the **Gospel** is through the promise.
A P : 0 4 :183(132) [0173] law and the promises or **Gospel**) it will be easy to refute
A P : 0 4 :186(132) [0173] in others it presents the **Gospel**, the free promise of the
A P : 0 4 :189(133) [0175] And in order to keep the **Gospel** among men, he visibly
A P : 0 4 :223(138) [0181] let them abolish the **Gospel**, if Christ is unnecessary and
A P : 0 4 :230(139) [0183] the foolishness of the **Gospel**, which reveals another
A P : 0 4 :230(139) [0183] But we are not ashamed of the foolishness of the **Gospel**.
A P : 0 4 :238(141) [0187] law rather than of the **Gospel** which promises us
A P : 0 4 :247(142) [0191] just said that regeneration takes place through the **Gospel**.
A P : 0 4 :247(142) [0191] been regenerated by the **Gospel**, he teaches that we are
A P : 0 4 :256(144) [0193] We must keep the **Gospel** promise that through Christ we
A P : 0 4 :257(144) [0193] by itself, why would Christ and the **Gospel** be necessary?
A P : 0 4 :257(144) [0193] it is necessary to add the **Gospel** promise, that for Christ's
A P : 0 4 :257(144) [0193] opponents exclude the **Gospel** of Christ from the
A P : 0 4 :260(145) [0193] The preaching of the **Gospel** must be added, that is, that
A P : 0 4 :260(145) [0193] need would there be of Christ, what need of the **Gospel**?
A P : 0 4 :260(145) [0195] reject Christ, destroy the **Gospel**, and maliciously twist the
A P : 0 4 :264(146) [0195] Let us remember that the **Gospel** promises the forgiveness
A P : 0 4 :264(146) [0195] be an abolition of the **Gospel** if we were to deny that the
A P : 0 4 :266(146) [0197] We see that the **Gospel** and the promise of Christ are
A P : 0 4 :269(147) [0197] intended to abolish the **Gospel** of Christ, the propitiator.
A P : 0 4 :271(148) [0199] is so mad as to deny that absolution is the spoken **Gospel**.
A P : 0 4 :274(148) [0199] proclamation of the **Gospel**, that we obtain forgiveness of
A P : 0 4 :274(148) [0199] this proclamation of the **Gospel** by twisting those passages
A P : 0 4 :281(149) [0201] and over we say that the **Gospel** of Christ must be added
A P : 0 4 :286(150) [0203] the law in such a way as to hide the **Gospel** of Christ.
A P : 0 4 :287(150) [0203] or from the teaching of the law rather than the **Gospel**.
A P : 0 4 :287(150) [0203] one based upon the **Gospel** or the promise of Christ.
A P : 0 4 :291(151) [0203] But the **Gospel** was not given to the world in vain.
A P : 0 4 :291(152) [0203] The **Gospel** shows another way.
A P : 0 4 :293(152) [0203] in conformity with the **Gospel**, and any sound mind can
A P : 0 4 :298(153) [0205] unless he wants utterly to abolish Christ and the **Gospel**?
A P : 0 4 :308(155) [0207] truly righteousness because it is obedience to the **Gospel**.
A P : 0 4 :308(155) [0207] this obedience to the **Gospel** takes hold of Christ, the
A P : 0 4 :310(155) [0207] and worship of the **Gospel** is to receive good things from
A P : 0 4 :310(155) [0207] highest worship in the **Gospel** is the desire to receive
A P : 0 4 :311(155) [0207] the law; they do not talk about obedience to the **Gospel**.
A P : 0 4 :311(155) [0207] been reborn through the **Gospel**, and we cannot love God
A P : 0 4 :313(155) [0207] teach the righteousness of the **Gospel** and not of the law.
A P : 0 4 :345(160) [0217] Properly speaking, the **Gospel** is the command to believe
A P : 0 4 :366(163) [0221] The righteousness of the **Gospel**, which deals with the
A P : 0 4 :367(163) [0221] justification, though the **Gospel** offers justification freely
A P : 0 4 :368(163) [0221] must remember that the **Gospel** offers justification freely
A P : 0 4 :377(165) [0223] obliged to hold fast to the **Gospel** and the teaching of the
A P : 0 4 :387(166) [0225] and propitiator, deny the promise of grace and the **Gospel**
A P : 0 4 :388(166) [0225] by the law but by the **Gospel**, the promise of grace offered
A P : 0 4 :390(166) [0225] more important than the **Gospel** of Christ, and everybody
A P : 0 4 :400(168) [0227] those who teach the **Gospel** of Christ, not among those
A P : 0 4 :400(168) [0227] opinions against the **Gospel**, as the Lord says, "My sheep
A P : 0 4 :400(168) [0227] opinions contrary to the **Gospel**, contrary to the authority
A P : 0 7 :005(169) [0227] the pure teaching of the **Gospel** and the administration of
A P : 0 7 :005(169) [0227] of the sacraments in harmony with the **Gospel** of Christ.
A P : 0 7 :008(169) [0229] association of the same **Gospel** or teaching and of the
A P : 0 7 :010(170) [0229] world who agree on the **Gospel** and have the same Christ,
A P : 0 7 :015(170) [0231] But the **Gospel** brings not the shadow of eternal things
A P : 0 7 :016(170) [0231] According to the **Gospel**, therefore, only those are the true
A P : 0 7 :020(171) [0233] marks, the pure teaching of the **Gospel** and the sacraments
A P : 0 7 :020(171) [0233] for it retains the pure **Gospel** and what Paul calls the
A P : 0 7 :027(173) [0235] care anything for the **Gospel** or think it worth reading?
A P : 0 7 :028(173) [0237] who truly believe the **Gospel** of Christ and who have the
A P : 0 7 :030(173) [0237] the teaching of the **Gospel** and the administration of the
A P : 0 7 :040(176) [0241] in modified form to the **Gospel** history, like the Passover
A P : 0 7 :048(177) [0245] is preaching to you a **gospel** contrary to that which you
A P : 0 9 :001(178) [0245] Among us, the **Gospel** is taught purely and diligently.
A P : 1 1 :002(180) [0249] yes, the very voice of the **Gospel** — that we should believe
A P : 1 1 :004(181) [0249] this according to both the **Gospel** and the ancient canons.
A P : 1 2 :002(182) [0253] is the very voice of the **Gospel**, that by faith we obtain the
A P : 1 2 :002(182) [0253] This voice of the **Gospel** these writers of the Confutation
A P : 1 2 :002(182) [0253] condemn the voice of the **Gospel**, so exceedingly salutary
A P : 1 2 :003(182) [0253] the chief doctrine of the **Gospel**, the true knowledge of
A P : 1 2 :003(182) [0253] shed much light on the **Gospel** and have corrected many
A P : 1 2 :008(183) [0255] reference to faith and the **Gospel**, that Judas did not
A P : 1 2 :008(183) [0255] himself with the **Gospel** and the promise of Christ.
A P : 1 2 :010(184) [0255] the chief doctrine of the **Gospel**, the forgiveness of sins.
A P : 1 2 :029(185) [0259] the proclamation of the **Gospel** is to denounce sin, to offer
A P : 1 2 :030(186) [0259] gives this summary of the **Gospel** in the last chapter of
A P : 1 2 :034(186) [0261] alone, this is the teaching of the law, not of the **Gospel**.
A P : 1 2 :035(186) [0261] amid these terrors the **Gospel** of Christ ought to be set
A P : 1 2 :035(186) [0261] to consciences — the **Gospel** which freely promises the
A P : 1 2 :039(187) [0261] and offers the **Gospel** through absolution, which is the
A P : 1 2 :039(187) [0261] through absolution, which is the true voice of the **Gospel**.
A P : 1 2 :039(187) [0261] Hearing the **Gospel** and hearing absolution strengthens
A P : 1 2 :042(187) [0261] the proclamation of the **Gospel** and the use of the
A P : 1 2 :042(187) [0263] the hearing of the **Gospel**, so that it may not succumb in
A P : 1 2 :045(187) [0263] Mark 1:15 Christ says, "Repent, and believe in the **Gospel**
A P : 1 2 :045(187) [0263] For to believe in the **Gospel** is not to have the general faith
A P : 1 2 :045(188) [0263] of sins has been granted us; this is revealed in the **Gospel**.
A P : 1 2 :045(188) [0263] and faith, when it is said, "Believe in the **Gospel**."
A P : 1 2 :053(189) [0265] The other part is the **Gospel**, that is, the promise of grace
A P : 1 2 :058(190) [0267] faith proclaimed by the **Gospel** when it is contrasted with
A P : 1 2 :075(193) [0273] the elimination of the **Gospel**, and the abolition of the

Continued ▶

AP : 12 :075(193) [0273] the forgiveness of sins, what need is there of the **Gospel**?
AP : 12 :076(193) [0273] away from the law to the **Gospel**, away from trust in their
AP : 12 :076(193) [0273] and in Christ; for the **Gospel** shows us Christ and
AP : 12 :077(193) [0275] Christ and abrogate the **Gospel** if we believe that we
AP : 12 :085(194) [0277] of the law and not of the **Gospel**, to imagine that a man is
AP : 12 :088(195) [0277] God's command and the **Gospel** itself that they should be
AP : 12 :088(195) [0277] of faith is required in the **Gospel**; our opponents leave
AP : 12 :089(195) [0279] law, an abrogation of the **Gospel**, a doctrine of despair.
AP : 12 :105(197) [0283] which is the voice of the **Gospel** forgiving sins and
AP : 12 :122(200) [0289] express commands of the **Gospel**, the councils, and the
AP : 12 :141(204) [0295] knowledge of law and **Gospel**, penitence and quickening,
AP : 12 :151(206) [0299] will be the end of those who do not obey the **gospel**?"
AP : 12 :172(209) [0305] satisfactions contrary to the clear teaching of the **Gospel**.
AP : 12 :172(209) [0305] have already shown, the **Gospel** does not command that
AP : 12 :173(209) [0305] works, why cite the clear teaching of the **Gospel**?
AP : 12 :173(209) [0305] If the **Gospel** commanded us to buy off punishment by
AP : 12 :173(210) [0305] the clear teaching of the **Gospel** compels us to assume
AP : 12 :174(210) [0307] the confession of the **Gospel**, the teaching of the Gospel,
AP : 12 :174(210) [0307] the teaching of the **Gospel**, obedience to parents and
AP : 12 :176(210) [0307] that the ministers of the **Gospel** absolve those who are
AP : 13 :009(212) [0311] are called to preach the **Gospel** and administer the
AP : 13 :011(212) [0311] glorious promises: "The **Gospel** is the power of God for
AP : 15 :001(215) [0315] to make satisfaction for sin are contrary to the **Gospel**.
AP : 15 :004(215) [0315] are openly replacing the **Gospel** with doctrines of demons.
AP : 15 :004(215) [0315] This obscures the **Gospel**, the blessing of Christ, and
AP : 15 :005(215) [0317] The **Gospel** teaches that by faith, for Christ's sake, we
AP : 15 :006(215) [0317] the teaching of the **Gospel**, for Paul clearly teaches
AP : 15 :025(218) [0321] The **Gospel** of the righteousness of faith in Christ is
AP : 15 :030(219) [0323] If, according to the **Gospel**, the divinely instituted
AP : 15 :042(221) [0327] the chief worship of God is the preaching of the **Gospel**.
AP : 15 :042(221) [0327] and walk out on them after the reading of the **Gospel**.
AP : 15 :042(221) [0327] they even attack this most salutary part of the **Gospel**.
AP : 15 :051(222) [0329] the true teaching of the **Gospel** because of an abuse of
AP : 16 :003(222) [0331] The **Gospel** does not introduce any new laws about the
AP : 16 :004(223) [0331] seriously obscure the **Gospel** and the spiritual kingdom;
AP : 16 :005(223) [0331] For the **Gospel** does not destroy the state or the family
AP : 16 :006(223) [0331] on the grounds that their **Gospel** would destroy the
AP : 16 :006(223) [0331] The **Gospel** does not legislate for the civil estate but is the
AP : 16 :007(223) [0331] The **Gospel** forbids private revenge, and Christ stresses
AP : 16 :008(223) [0333] erroneous view that the **Gospel** is something external, a
AP : 16 :008(223) [0333] they failed to see that the **Gospel** brings eternal
AP : 16 :010(224) [0333] the theory that the **Gospel** requires us to hold property in
AP : 16 :013(224) [0333] in doubt whether the **Gospel** permitted such public and
AP : 18 :008(226) [0337] terrified hearts hear the **Gospel** and receive consolation.
AP : 21 :035(234) [0353] teach or confess the **Gospel**, must be strong of soul
AP : 21 :036(234) [0353] great danger, taught the **Gospel**, battled against heretics.
AP : 21 :044(236) [0357] on earth, that is, the **Gospel** of Christ, and as vicars of
AP : 23 :040(245) [0375] that is, to make room for hearing or teaching the **Gospel**.
AP : 23 :041(245) [0375] The **Gospel** frees us from these Levitical regulations about
AP : 23 :055(247) [0379] preachers of the **Gospel** should exhort the incontinent to
AP : 23 :061(247) [0381] The **Gospel** permits marriage for those who need it, but it
AP : 23 :064(248) [0381] apply here because the **Gospel** requires purity of the heart
AP : 24 :024(253) [0391] after the revelation of the **Gospel** they had to stop;
AP : 24 :024(253) [0391] propitiations, since the **Gospel** was promised in order to
AP : 24 :025(253) [0391] the proclamation of the **Gospel**, faith, prayer,
AP : 24 :030(255) [0395] and proclamation of the **Gospel**, suffering because of the
AP : 24 :030(255) [0395] of the Gospel, suffering because of the **Gospel**, etc.
AP : 24 :032(255) [0395] the proclamation of the **Gospel**, which makes known the
AP : 24 :032(255) [0395] The proclamation of the **Gospel** produces faith in those
AP : 24 :032(255) [0395] faith, prayer, proclamation of the **Gospel**, confession, etc.
AP : 24 :034(256) [0395] are the proclamation of the **Gospel** and its good fruits.
AP : 24 :034(256) [0395] priestly service of the **gospel** of God, so that the offering
AP : 24 :034(256) [0397] the proclamation of the **Gospel**, which should kill this old
AP : 24 :034(256) [0397] the proclamation of the **Gospel**, faith, prayer, and things
AP : 24 :035(256) [0397] the proclamation of the **Gospel**, faith, prayer, and
AP : 24 :036(257) [0397] not only the ceremony but the proclamation of the **Gospel**
AP : 24 :036(257) [0397] the proclamation of the **Gospel**, as Peter says (I Pet. 1:2);
AP : 24 :038(257) [0399] and made alive when the **Gospel** sprinkles us with the
AP : 24 :040(257) [0399] and not preaching the **Gospel**, being put to death and
AP : 24 :041(257) [0399] regard for religion and the preaching of the **Gospel**.
AP : 24 :043(257) [0399] they do not preach the **Gospel** or console consciences or
AP : 24 :045(258) [0401] a vastly different desolation, ignorance of the **Gospel**.
AP : 24 :048(258) [0401] the Word, they teach the **Gospel** of the blessing of Christ,
AP : 24 :049(258) [0401] the proclamation of the **Gospel** and the proper use of the
AP : 24 :051(259) [0403] the proclamation of the **Gospel**, in faith, and in its
AP : 24 :059(260) [0405] but it offers to others the **Gospel** and the sacraments so
AP : 24 :080(264) [0411] preaches shows forth the **gospel** to the people, as Paul
AP : 24 :089(266) [0415] it is an insult to the **Gospel** to maintain that without faith,
AP : 24 :091(266) [0415] is a contamination of the **Gospel**, a corruption of the use
AP : 24 :098(268) [0419] who truly believe the **Gospel** should reject those wicked
AP : 27 :011(270) [0423] is an open insult to the **Gospel**, which teaches that the
AP : 27 :012(270) [0423] closely according to the **Gospel** in order to merit eternal
AP : 27 :013(271) [0423] these insults with which our enemies attack thy **Gospel**!
AP : 27 :013(271) [0423] not the true voice of the **Gospel**, if it is not the statement
AP : 27 :013(271) [0423] truly the teaching of the **Gospel** that we receive the
AP : 27 :017(271) [0425] monks "pattern their lives more closely after the **Gospel**"!
AP : 27 :023(272) [0427] life conflicts with the **Gospel** of the righteousness of faith,
AP : 27 :026(273) [0429] observances are the works of the counsels of the **Gospel**.
AP : 27 :026(273) [0429] For the **Gospel** does not counsel distinctions among
AP : 27 :027(274) [0429] the perfection of the **Gospel** and of the kingdom of
AP : 27 :034(275) [0431] are simply crushing the **Gospel** about the free forgiveness
AP : 27 :039(276) [0433] try to pattern their lives more closely with the **Gospel**.
AP : 27 :039(276) [0433] more closely after the **Gospel** because they do not have
AP : 27 :041(276) [0435] or a tyranny forces us to leave or to deny the **Gospel**.
AP : 27 :041(276) [0435] adds the phrase "for the **Gospel**" (Mark 10:29) to show
AP : 27 :041(276) [0435] who bear injury because of the confession of the **Gospel**.
AP : 27 :042(276) [0435] We should leave our body, too, for the **Gospel**.
AP : 27 :043(277) [0435] not for the sake of the **Gospel** but for the sake of food
AP : 27 :046(277) [0435] The poverty of the **Gospel** (Matt. 5:3) does not consist in
AP : 27 :054(278) [0437] hear nor preach the **Gospel** about the free forgiveness of
AP : 28 :003(281) [0445] in the observance of their traditions than of the **Gospel**.
AP : 28 :008(282) [0445] traditions apart from the **Gospel** as though they merited
AP : 28 :011(283) [0447] The **Gospel** clearly testifies that traditions should not be
AP : 28 :012(283) [0447] we have said what power the **Gospel** grants to bishops.
AP : 28 :012(283) [0447] bishops according to the **Gospel**, though they may well be
AP : 28 :012(283) [0447] But we are talking about a bishop according to the **Gospel**
AP : 28 :020(284) [0449] requires obedience to the **Gospel**; it does not create an
AP : 28 :020(284) [0449] not create an authority for bishops apart from the **Gospel**.
AP : 28 :020(284) [0449] traditions contrary to the **Gospel**, nor interpret their
AP : 28 :020(284) [0449] their traditions in a manner contrary to the **Gospel**.
AP : 28 :020(284) [0449] "If anyone preaches another **Gospel**, let him be accursed."
S3 : 03 :004(304) [0481] adds the consoling promise of grace in the **Gospel**.
S3 : 03 :004(304) [0481] and believe in the **Gospel**," which is to say, "Become
S3 : 03 :007(304) [0481] the addition of the **Gospel**, there is only death and hell,
S3 : 03 :008(304) [0481] Moreover, the **Gospel** offers consolation and forgiveness
S3 : 03 :039(309) [0489] preaches in the **Gospel**, and which we also preach.
S3 : 03 :041(309) [0491] heaven, revealed in the **Gospel**, and yet it is called a heresy
S3 : 04 :000(310) [0491] IV. The **Gospel**
S3 : 04 :000(310) [0491] We shall now return to the **Gospel**, which offers council
S3 : 04 :000(310) [0491] peculiar function of the **Gospel**) is preached to the whole
S3 : 08 :001(312) [0493] by Christ in the **Gospel**, is a consolation and help against
S3 : 10 :001(314) [0497] about the church and the **Gospel**, they might be permitted
S3 : 15 :005(316) [0501] if he would allow the **Gospel**, we, too, may concede to him
S3 : 15 :005(318) [0501] the names of my other co-workers in the **Gospel**, namely:
TR : 00 :007(320) [0505] let us show from the **Gospel** that the Roman bishop is not
TR : 00 :008(320) [0505] equals and exercise the ministry of the **Gospel** in common
TR : 00 :010(321) [0505] he at once preached the **Gospel** without consulting Peter.
TR : 00 :031(325) [0513] command to preach the **Gospel**, proclaim the forgiveness
TR : 00 :032(325) [0513] despised (that is, after the **Gospel** was suppressed) when
TR : 00 :034(325) [0513] The ministry of the **Gospel** was neglected.
TR : 00 :038(326) [0515] idolatry, and doctrines which conflict with the **Gospel**.
TR : 00 :038(326) [0515] should preach to you a **gospel** contrary to that which we
TR : 00 :039(327) [0515] which conflict with the **Gospel** and will arrogate to
TR : 00 :040(327) [0515] in many ways with the **Gospel**, and the pope arrogates to
TR : 00 :048(328) [0519] darkness has the teaching about vows covered the **Gospel**!
TR : 00 :057(330) [0521] and doctrines which are in conflict with the **Gospel**.
TR : 00 :060(330) [0521] The **Gospel** requires of those who preside over the
TR : 00 :060(330) [0521] that they preach the **Gospel**, remit sins, administer the
TR : 00 :066(331) [0523] become enemies of the **Gospel** and are unwilling to
TR : 00 :067(331) [0523] exists, the right to administer the **Gospel** also exists.
TR : 00 :082(334) [0529] the doctrine of the **Gospel**, we have reread the articles of
SC : PR :003(338) [0533] beasts, and now that the **Gospel** has been restored they
SC : PR :022(341) [0537] is no Christian who does not hear and believe the **Gospel**.
SC : 02 :006(345) [0545] has called me through the **Gospel**, enlightened me with his
SC : 09 :003(354) [0561] those who proclaim the **gospel** should get their living by
SC : 09 :003(354) [0561] gospel should get their living by the **gospel**" (I Cor. 9:14).
LC : PR :003(358) [0567] and gratitude to the **Gospel**, through which they have
LC : PR :003(358) [0567] remember no more of the **Gospel** than this rotten,
LC : PR :004(359) [0567] common people take the **Gospel** altogether too lightly,
LC : 01 :065(373) [0599] is forbidden in the **Gospel**, and yet Christ, St. Paul, and
LC : 01 :081(375) [0603] day, as we read in the **Gospel** — as if the commandment
LC : 01 :097(378) [0609] Mass or the reading of the **Gospel**; no one asked about
LC : 01 :159(387) [0627] became your father in Christ Jesus through the **Gospel**."
LC : 01 :182(389) [0631] every year in the **Gospel**, Matthew 5, where Christ himself
LC : 01 :276(402) [0659] order laid down by the **Gospel**, Matthew 19, where Christ
LC : 01 :286(403) [0663] Christ indicates in the **Gospel**, and in which he means to
LC : 01 :305(406) [0669] for we read even in the **Gospel** that King Herod took his
LC : 02 :033(415) [0687] Indeed, the entire **Gospel** that we preach depends on the
LC : 02 :038(415) [0689] through the preaching of the **Gospel** by the Holy Spirit.
LC : 02 :054(417) [0693] as through all the comforting words of the entire **Gospel**.
LC : 02 :054(417) [0693] and, in short, the entire **Gospel** and all the duties of
LC : 02 :056(418) [0693] church (that is, where the **Gospel** is not) there is no
LC : 02 :056(418) [0693] rather than through the **Gospel** and the forgiveness of sin
LC : 03 :031(424) [0707] to crush us, and the **Gospel** as well, except that the
LC : 03 :047(426) [0711] attack and persecute our **Gospel** and pure doctrine and
LC : 03 :054(427) [0713] us thy Word, that the **Gospel** may be sincerely preached
LC : 03 :061(428) [0715] most essential — for the **Gospel**, for faith, and for the
LC : 03 :068(429) [0717] it in their attempt utterly to exterminate the **Gospel**.
LC : 03 :069(429) [0717] bishops, tyrants, and heretics can do against our **Gospel**.
LC : 03 :088(432) [0723] and he gave us the **Gospel**, in which there is nothing but
LC : 03 :089(432) [0723] and so it loses the comfort and confidence of the **Gospel**.
LC : 03 :096(433) [0725] grace, because he has promised it, as the **Gospel** teaches.
LC : 04 :030(440) [0739] heart, just as the entire **Gospel** is an external, oral
LC : 05 :031(450) [0759] by steadfastly believing the Scriptures and the **Gospel**?
LC : 05 :032(450) [0759] Now, the whole **Gospel** and the article of the Creed, "I
LC : 05 :032(450) [0761] the very words which we hear everywhere in the **Gospel**.
LC : 05 :032(450) [0761] dare say that the whole **Gospel** or Word of God apart
LC : 05 :040(451) [0761] of people who hear the **Gospel**, now that the pope's
LC : 05 :079(455) [0771] good and cling to the **Gospel**, and see whether you will
LC : 06 :005(457) [0000] uncommon ease whatever in the **Gospel** is mild and gentle
LC : 06 :005(457) [0000] in the presence of the **Gospel** or to have any part of it.
LC : 06 :005(457) [0000] who will not believe the **Gospel**, live according to it, and
LC : 06 :006(457) [0000] you wished to enjoy the **Gospel**'s benefits but did nothing
LC : 06 :006(457) [0000] who will not obey the **Gospel** deserve just such a jailer as
LC : 06 :007(458) [0000] precious and comforting treasure which the **Gospel** offers.
LC : 06 :029(460) [0000] And this is a sure sign that you also despise the **Gospel**.
LC : 06 :030(460) [0000] to do with him, nor may he have any share in the **Gospel**.
EP : RN :001(464) [0777] should preach to you a **gospel** contrary to that which we
EP : 02 :004(470) [0787] as it is written that the **Gospel** is a "power of God" for
EP : 02 :009(471) [0789] to God, believe the **Gospel**, whole-heartedly obey God's
EP : 02 :011(471) [0789] to apprehend and accept it, and to believe the **Gospel**.
EP : 03 :006(473) [0793] which in the Word of the **Gospel** we recognize Christ
EP : 03 :009(474) [0795] and the Word of the holy **Gospel**, they have a gracious
EP : 04 :004(476) [0797] to do good works solely on the basis of the **Gospel**.
EP : 05 :000(477) [0801] V. Law and **Gospel**
EP : 05 :001(477) [0801] preaching of the Holy **Gospel** strictly speaking only a
EP : 05 :001(478) [0801] condemned not in the law but wholly through the **Gospel**?
EP : 05 :002(478) [0801] between law and **Gospel** is an especially glorious light that
EP : 05 :005(478) [0801] 4. But the **Gospel**, strictly speaking, is the kind of doctrine
EP : 05 :006(478) [0803] 5. The word "**Gospel**" is not used in a single sense in Holy
EP : 05 :006(478) [0803] that when the word "**Gospel**" means the entire doctrine of
EP : 05 :006(478) [0803] to say or write that the **Gospel** is a proclamation both of
EP : 05 :007(478) [0803] 6. But when the law and **Gospel** are opposed to each
EP : 05 :007(478) [0803] as a preacher of the **Gospel**, then we believe, teach, and
EP : 05 :007(478) [0803] and confess that the **Gospel** is not a proclamation of
EP : 05 :010(479) [0803] the preaching of the **Gospel** but the preaching of Moses

Continued ▶

E P : 0 5 :010(479) [0803] And this is the preaching of the **Gospel**, strictly speaking.
E P : 0 5 :011(479) [0805] when men teach that the **Gospel**, strictly speaking, is a
E P : 0 5 :011(479) [0805] Thereby the **Gospel** is again changed into a teaching of
E P : 1 0 :002(492) [0829] when the enemies of the **Gospel** have not come to an
E P : 1 0 :006(493) [0829] that the truth of the **Gospel** might be preserved for you"
E P : 1 0 :006(493) [0829] do with the truth of the **Gospel**, Christian liberty, and the
E P : 1 0 :011(494) [0831] the enemies of the holy **Gospel** (which serve to impair the
E P : 1 1 :010(495) [0833] Christ from the Holy **Gospel** alone, which clearly testifies
E P : 1 1 :013(496) [0835] proclamation of the Holy **Gospel**, Christ opens and
E P : 1 1 :017(497) [0837] all men to come to repentance and to believe the **Gospel**.
E P : 1 1 :021(497) [0837] they have in the holy **Gospel** and in the use of the holy
E P : 1 2 :011(499) [0841] who preach the **Gospel** according to the Augsburg
S D : P R :003(501) [0847] pure doctrine of the holy **Gospel** and had allowed their
S D : 0 2 :009(521) [0883] on earth read or hear the **Gospel** of the Son of God and
S D : 0 2 :010(522) [0883] through the folly of the **Gospel** that we preach to save
S D : 0 2 :013(523) [0885] able truly to believe the **Gospel**, give his assent to it, and
S D : 0 2 :018(524) [0889] offers the grace of God and salvation through the **Gospel**.
S D : 0 2 :024(526) [0891] of his body, can hear the **Gospel** and meditate on it to a
S D : 0 2 :027(527) [0891] will; but to assent to this **Gospel** when it is preached is our
S D : 0 2 :030(527) [0893] man by his own powers turn to the **Gospel** or to Christ?
S D : 0 2 :040(528) [0895] has called me through the **Gospel**, enlightened me with his
S D : 0 2 :044(529) [0897] not once think to turn to the holy **Gospel** and to accept it.
S D : 0 2 :045(530) [0899] to want to accept the **Gospel** and to comfort himself with
S D : 0 2 :050(530) [0901] the holy and only saving **Gospel** of his eternal Son, our
S D : 0 2 :054(531) [0903] meditation upon the holy **Gospel** of the gracious
S D : 0 2 :054(531) [0903] sake and comforts itself with the promise of the **Gospel**.
S D : 0 2 :071(535) [0909] us and has his holy **Gospel** preached to us, through which
S D : 0 2 :075(536) [0911] itself to God, believe the **Gospel**, and obey the law of God
S D : 0 2 :077(536) [0911] and has called us by the **Gospel** and offers his grace, the
S D : 0 2 :077(536) [0911] and accept it, believe the **Gospel**, and by its own powers
S D : 0 3 :010(541) [0919] us in the promise of the **Gospel**, and faith is the only
S D : 0 3 :011(541) [0919] in the Word of the **Gospel** and to trust in him, that solely
S D : 0 3 :013(541) [0919] the merit of Christ in the promise of the holy **Gospel**.
S D : 0 3 :016(541) [0921] Holy Spirit through the **Gospel** and in the sacraments,
S D : 0 3 :025(543) [0923] in the promise of the **Gospel**, whereby the righteousness
S D : 0 3 :030(544) [0925] we receive only by faith in the promise of the **Gospel**.
S D : 0 3 :031(544) [0925] offered to us in the promise of the **Gospel**, but only faith.
S D : 0 3 :038(546) [0929] grace and the merit of Christ in the promise of the **Gospel**
S D : 0 3 :039(546) [0929] us in the promise of the **Gospel** and received, accepted,
S D : 0 3 :041(546) [0929] in us in conversion through the hearing of the **Gospel**.
S D : 0 3 :043(547) [0931] grace and the merit of Christ in the promise of the **Gospel**
S D : 0 3 :057(549) [0935] God and is revealed in the **Gospel**, upon which faith
S D : 0 4 :023(555) [0945] of the consolation of the **Gospel**, give occasion for doubt,
S D : 0 5 :000(558) [0951] V. Law and **Gospel**
S D : 0 5 :001(558) [0951] between law and **Gospel** is an especially brilliant light
S D : 0 5 :001(558) [0951] confuse the two doctrines and change the **Gospel** into law.
S D : 0 5 :001(558) [0951] have in the holy **Gospel** when it is preached purely and
S D : 0 5 :002(558) [0951] strictly speaking, the **Gospel** is not only a proclamation of
S D : 0 5 :002(558) [0951] strictly speaking, the **Gospel** is not a proclamation of
S D : 0 5 :002(558) [0953] unbelief, whereas the **Gospel** in its strict sense is a
S D : 0 5 :003(558) [0953] fact that the little word "**Gospel**" does not always have
S D : 0 5 :004(559) [0953] "The beginning of the **Gospel** of Jesus Christ, the Son of
S D : 0 5 :004(559) [0953] his apostles to preach the **Gospel** in all the world (Mark
S D : 0 5 :004(559) [0953] calls his entire teaching "**Gospel**" (Acts 20:24) and
S D : 0 5 :005(559) [0953] And when the word "**Gospel**" is used in its broad sense
S D : 0 5 :005(559) [0953] distinction of law and **Gospel**, it is correct to define the
S D : 0 5 :006(559) [0953] however, the word "**Gospel**" is also used in another (that
S D : 0 5 :006(559) [0953] said, "Repent and believe in the **Gospel**" (Mark 1:15).
S D : 0 5 :009(559) [0955] proclamation of the holy **Gospel** offers to all penitent
S D : 0 5 :009(559) [0955] For the **Gospel** does not preach the forgiveness of sin to
S D : 0 5 :009(559) [0955] the proclamation of the **Gospel** must be added so that it
S D : 0 5 :011(560) [0955] it in his exposition of the **Gospel** for the Fifth Sunday
S D : 0 5 :012(560) [0955] On the other hand, the **Gospel** is a proclamation that
S D : 0 5 :012(560) [0955] and the preachers of the **Gospel**, just as Christ himself
S D : 0 5 :012(560) [0955] man, it is not yet the **Gospel** nor Christ's own
S D : 0 5 :012(560) [0957] For the **Gospel** and Christ are not ordained and given us
S D : 0 5 :014(560) [0957] adds the promise of God's grace through the **Gospel**."
S D : 0 5 :015(561) [0957] salutary repentance; the **Gospel** must also be added to it."
S D : 0 5 :015(561) [0957] and sorrow not from the law but solely from the **Gospel**.
S D : 0 5 :018(561) [0957] But it is also true that the **Gospel** illustrates and explains
S D : 0 5 :019(561) [0957] Since the **Gospel** (which alone, strictly speaking, teaches
S D : 0 5 :019(561) [0957] Nevertheless, this **Gospel** alone, strictly speaking, teaches
S D : 0 5 :020(561) [0959] The **Gospel**, however, is that doctrine which teaches what
S D : 0 5 :020(561) [0959] The content of the **Gospel** is this, that the Son of God,
S D : 0 5 :021(562) [0959] is, and is called, the **Gospel**, a good and joyful message
S D : 0 5 :022(562) [0959] condemnation," but the **Gospel** is "the power of God for
S D : 0 5 :022(562) [0959] which comes from the the **Gospel** and that which is taught
S D : 0 5 :025(563) [0961] the proclamation of the **Gospel** of our Lord Christ will
S D : 0 5 :025(563) [0961] that if they believe the **Gospel** God forgives them all their
S D : 0 5 :026(563) [0961] between the law and the **Gospel** is thoroughly and
S D : 0 5 :027(563) [0961] both doctrines, law and **Gospel**, may not be mingled
S D : 0 5 :027(563) [0961] between law and **Gospel**, and diligently to avoid anything
S D : 0 5 :027(563) [0961] once more make the **Gospel** a teaching of law, as
S D : 0 5 :027(563) [0961] which they have in the **Gospel** against the terrors of the
S D : 0 5 :027(563) [0961] wrong to make of the **Gospel**, strictly so called in
S D : 0 5 :027(563) [0961] in the Apology too, the **Gospel** is a proclamation both of
S D : 0 5 :027(563) [0961] strictly speaking, the **Gospel** is the promise of forgiveness
S D : 0 6 :010(565) [0965] forth distinctly what the **Gospel** does, creates, and works
S D : 0 6 :011(566) [0965] the preaching of the **Gospel** (Gal. 3:2, 14), who renews the
S D : 0 6 :014(566) [0967] and comforts them with the preaching of the holy **Gospel**.
S D : 0 6 :022(567) [0969] But the **Gospel** teaches us that our spiritual sacrifices are
S D : 0 6 :024(568) [0971] punishments, just as he will no longer require the **Gospel**.
S D : 0 7 :018(572) [0979] as with the Word of the **Gospel**, and that the sacramental
S D : 0 7 :059(580) [0993] just as the Word of the **Gospel**, when it is laid hold on by
S D : 0 7 :061(580) [0995] and contemplation of the **Gospel** as well as in the Lord's
S D : 0 7 :089(585) [1003] Just as the **Gospel** is and remains the true Gospel even
S D : 0 7 :089(585) [1003] is and remains the true **Gospel** even when godless hearers
S D : 1 0 :002(611) [1053] when enemies of the holy **Gospel** have not come to an
S D : 1 0 :005(611) [1055] the pure doctrine of the **Gospel** and from true religion has
S D : 1 0 :010(612) [1055] pure doctrine of the holy **Gospel**, the entire community of
S D : 1 0 :011(612) [1057] that the truth of the **gospel** might be preserved for you"
S D : 1 0 :012(613) [1057] so that the truth of the **Gospel** might be preserved.
S D : 1 0 :013(613) [1057] straightforward about the truth of the **Gospel** (Gal. 2:14).
S D : 1 0 :014(613) [1057] testifies, the truth of the **Gospel** might be preserved (Gal.
S D : 1 0 :019(614) [1059] about the church and the **Gospel**, they might be permitted
S D : 1 0 :028(615) [1061] to enemies of the holy **Gospel** or conform to their
S D : 1 0 :029(615) [1061] enemies of the holy **Gospel** contrary and in opposition to
S D : 1 1 :028(620) [1071] men (Luke 24:47), so also does the promise of the **Gospel**.
S D : 1 1 :028(621) [1073] have this promise of the **Gospel** proclaimed to them (Luke
S D : 1 1 :030(621) [1073] "the inheritance" hear the **Gospel**, believe on Christ, pray
S D : 1 1 :033(621) [1073] first with Christ and his **Gospel** so that you learn to know
S D : 1 1 :037(622) [1075] has the promises of the **Gospel** offered not only in general
S D : 1 1 :067(627) [1085] repent and believe in the **Gospel**" (Mark 1:15); and again
S D : 1 1 :089(631) [1093] in Christ and in his holy **Gospel** as the "book of life," this
S D : 1 1 :096(632) [1095] divine truth of the holy **Gospel**, that will not give place to
S D : 1 2 :008(633) [1097] pure Word of the holy **Gospel** was allowed neither room
S D : 1 2 :008(633) [1097] and confessors of the **Gospel** were being persecuted, where
S D : 1 2 :016(634) [1099] church who preach the **Gospel** according to the Augsburg

Gospels (1)
L C : S P :020(364) [0579] Mark at the end of their **Gospels** where they describe how

Gossip (3), Gossiped (1), Gossips (2)
L C : 0 1 :267(401) [0657] Learning a bit of **gossip** about someone else, they spread
L C : 0 1 :273(401) [0659] a worthless tongue who **gossips** and slanders someone,
L C : 0 1 :276(402) [0659] to spread slander and **gossip** about your neighbor but
L C : 0 1 :279(403) [0661] with personally and not **gossiped** about behind his back.
L C : 0 1 :281(403) [0661] But if you **gossip** about someone in every corner and root
L C : 0 1 :282(403) [0661] It would serve such **gossips** right to have their sport

Gotha (1)
S 3 : 1 5 :005(317) [0501] pastor of the church in **Gotha**, Thuringia, subscribe in my

Govern (14), Governed (5), Governing (8)
A G : 2 6 :010(065) [0071] and magistrates should **govern** land and people, etc.
A L : 2 6 :010(065) [0071] bear children, that a prince should **govern** his country.
A L : 2 8 :077(094) [0095] give up their power to **govern**, but we ask for this one
A P : 0 4 :139(126) [0161] that the Holy Spirit may **govern** and defend us, so that
A P : 0 4 :167(130) [0169] whether history is **governed** by God's counsels or by
A P : 0 4 :191(133) [0175] in waging war and in **governing** the state are holy works,
A P : 0 4 :279(149) [0199] wants to be justified, sanctified, and **governed** by God.
S 2 : 0 4 :009(300) [0473] church cannot be better **governed** and maintained than by
S 2 : 0 4 :009(300) [0473] priests of Alexandria **governed** the churches together and
S 2 : 0 4 :014(301) [0475] pope or Antichrist, to **govern** us as our head or lord, for
S 3 : 1 0 :003(314) [0497] that it was originally **governed** without bishops by priests
T R : 0 0 :030(325) [0513] to preach the Word or **govern** the church with the Word.
S C : P R :019(340) [0537] also take pains to urge **governing** authorities and parents
S C : P R :020(340) [0537] to which parents and **governing** authorities sin in this
S C : 0 9 :004(355) [0561] **Governing** Authorities
S C : 0 9 :004(355) [0561] "Let every person be subject to the **governing** authorities.
S C : 0 9 :005(355) [0561] Duties Subjects Owe to **Governing** Authorities
S C : 0 9 :005(355) [0561] "Let every person be subject to the **governing** authorities.
L C : 0 1 :141(384) [0621] persons whose duty it is to command and to **govern**.
L C : 0 1 :142(384) [0621] derive from them their power and authority to **govern**.
L C : 0 1 :158(387) [0627] only to those who **govern** and guide us by the Word of
L C : 0 1 :168(388) [0629] power and authority to **govern**) merely to receive
L C : 0 1 :173(388) [0629] that we train and **govern** them according to his will;
L C : 0 1 :276(402) [0659] precious precept for **governing** the tongue which ought to
L C : 0 3 :061(428) [0715] Holy Spirit, that he may **govern** us who have been
L C : 0 3 :077(431) [0721] and prosperity to **govern** well and to be victorious over
S D : 1 0 :020(614) [1059] pope or Antichrist, to **govern** us as our head or lord, for

Government (54), Governments (5)
P R : P R :004(003) [0007] of well-ordered **government** the foe of mankind bestirred
A G : P R :018(026) [0041] of the imperial **government** (together with the absent
A G : 1 6 :000(037) [0051] XVI. Civil **Government**
A G : 1 6 :001(037) [0051] among us that all **government** in the world and all
A G : 2 7 :055(079) [0083] for Christians, even in the **government**, to avenge wrong.
A G : 2 8 :010(082) [0085] not interfere at all with **government** or temporal
A G : 2 8 :013(083) [0085] obedience to **government**, should not make or prescribe
A L : 2 8 :010(082) [0085] it interferes with civil **government** as little as the art of
A L : 2 8 :010(082) [0085] as the art of singing interferes with civil **government**.
A L : 2 8 :011(082) [0085] For civil **government** is concerned with other things than
A L : 2 8 :013(083) [0085] about the forms of **government** that should be
A P : 0 4 :022(110) [0127] laws, learning, teaching, **governments**, and penalties.
A P : 0 4 :151(127) [0163] or obedience to the **government**, etc.), even though these
A P : 0 7 :005(169) [0227] rites like other civic **governments**, however, but it is
A P : 0 7 :010(170) [0229] it to mean an outward **government** of certain nations.
A P : 0 7 :050(178) [0245] by God, so lawful **governments** are ordinances of God
A P : 1 3 :015(213) [0311] they have God's command, as, for example, **government**.
A P : 1 4 :002(214) [0315] abolition of canonical **government** in some places, despite
A P : 1 5 :026(219) [0323] positions in the **government** and their marriages because
A P : 1 6 :001(222) [0329] take an oath when the **government** requires it, or contract
A P : 1 6 :006(223) [0331] It not only approves **governments** but subjects us to
A P : 1 6 :007(223) [0331] should usurp the **government** from those who hold it,
A P : 1 6 :007(223) [0331] spiritual kingdom does not change the civil **government**.
A P : 1 6 :008(223) [0333] external, a new and monastic form of **government**.
A P : 1 6 :008(223) [0333] to hearts, while it approves the civil **government**.
A P : 2 7 :041(276) [0435] of God, when a **government** or a tyranny forces us to
S 1 : P R :008(290) [0457] there is no church, no **government**, and no state of
S 2 : 0 3 :001(298) [0471] necessary for secular **government** in cities and states, and
S 2 : 0 4 :001(298) [0471] a human institution (that is, a secular **government**).
S 2 : 0 4 :003(298) [0471] pertains to secular **government**, where God sometimes
S 2 : 0 4 :014(301) [0475] of his papal **government**, as I have demonstrated in many
T R : 0 0 :034(325) [0513] to be that external **government** which the pope had set
T R : 0 0 :038(326) [0515] such pontiffs and such **government** ought to be regarded
S C : 0 3 :014(347) [0549] faithful rulers, good **government**; seasonable weather,
L C : 0 1 :069(374) [0599] There is no **government**, no obedience, no fidelity, no
L C : 0 1 :134(383) [0619] peace, good **government**, etc., without which this life can
L C : 0 1 :150(385) [0623] obedience to the civil **government**, which, as we have
L C : 0 1 :180(389) [0631] spiritual and the civil **government**, that is, divine and
L C : 0 1 :180(389) [0631] neither God nor the **government** is included in this
L C : 0 1 :181(389) [0631] here applies to private individuals, not to **governments**.
L C : 0 1 :239(397) [0649] Of course, if our **government** were well regulated, such
L C : 0 1 :258(399) [0653] an excellent, orderly **government**, and even now, where
L C : 0 1 :258(399) [0653] where there is such a **government**, instances of this sin

Continued ▶

LC : 0 1 :294(404) [0665] under the Jewish **government** man-servants and
LC : 0 2 :015(412) [0681] temporal blessings — good **government**, peace, security.
LC : 0-3 :061(428) [0715] In a good **government** there is need not only for good
LC : 0 3 :074(430) [0719] authorities and the **government**, for chiefly through them
LC : 0 3 :074(430) [0719] unless he gives us a stable, peaceful **government**.
LC : 0 3 :080(431) [0721] of any kind of **government** or honorable and peaceful
EP : 1 2 :012(499) [0841] 1. That **government** is not a God-pleasing estate in the
EP : 1 2 :014(499) [0841] use an office of the **government** against wicked people,
EP : 1 2 :014(499) [0841] may not call upon the **government** to use the power that
EP : 1 2 :016(499) [0841] New Testament the **government** cannot with a clear
SD : 1 0 :020(614) [1059] body and soul are characteristic of his papal **government**."
SD : 1 2 :017(634) [1099] New Testament era **government** service is not a godly
SD : 1 2 :018(634) [1099] hold an office in the **government** with an inviolate
SD : 1 2 :019(634) [1099] use an office of the **government** against wicked persons as
SD : 1 2 :019(634) [1099] nor may a subject call upon the **government** for help.
SD : 1 2 :021(634) [1099] 12. That the **government** cannot with an inviolate

Governors (1)
SC : 0 9 :005(355) [0561] as supreme, or to **governors** as sent by him to punish

Governs (5)
AG : 2 0 :034(045) [0057] and the Holy Spirit and **governs** himself by his own
AL : 2 0 :034(045) [0057] of man when he **governs** himself by human strength alone
AP : 0 7 :005(169) [0227] renews, consecrates, and **governs** by his Spirit, as Paul
AP : 0 7 :008(169) [0229] spirit, who renews, consecrates, and **governs** their hearts.
SD : 1 1 :006(617) [1065] For the Lord God **governs** everything in such a way that

Grab (1)
LC : 0 1 :241(397) [0649] stand by and let such persons fleece, **grab**, and hoard.

Grace (428)
PR : PR :002(003) [0007] in his immeasurable love, **grace**, and mercy toward
PR : PR :010(006) [0011] and how by God's **grace** they might be preserved from
PR : PR :013(007) [0013] order, by the singular **grace** of the Holy Spirit, everything
PR : PR :018(009) [0015] By the help of God's **grace** we, too, intend to persist in
PR : PR :024(013) [0021] consciences through the **grace** of the Holy Spirit, the
PR : PR :025(014) [0023] we are minded by the **grace** of the Holy Spirit to abide
AG : PR :011(026) [0041] humility and implore him to bestow his **grace** to this end.
AG : 0 3 :005(030) [0045] on them life and every **grace** and blessing, and that he
AG : 0 4 :001(030) [0045] righteous before God by **grace**, for Christ's sake, through
AG : 0 9 :001(033) [0047] Baptism is necessary and that **grace** is offered through it.
AG : 1 2 :005(035) [0049] sin has been forgiven and **grace** has been obtained
AG : 1 5 :003(036) [0049] God and earning **grace** are contrary to the Gospel and the
AG : 1 5 :004(037) [0049] it is intended to earn **grace** and make satisfaction for sin,
AG : 1 8 :002(039) [0051] But without the **grace**, help, and activity of the Holy
AG : 2 0 :009(042) [0053] us with God or obtain **grace** for us, for this happens only
AG : 2 0 :010(042) [0055] or that he can merit **grace**, despises Christ and seeks his
AG : 2 0 :011(042) [0055] in Eph. 2:8, 9, "For by **grace** you have been saved through
AG : 2 0 :013(043) [0055] namely, that we obtain **grace** and are justified before God
AG : 2 0 :020(044) [0055] that there they might merit **grace** through monastic life.
AG : 2 0 :021(044) [0055] the purpose of earning **grace** and making satisfaction for
AG : 2 0 :022(044) [0055] men may know that the **grace** of God is appropriated
AG : 2 0 :023(044) [0055] as believes that we receive **grace** and forgiveness of sin
AG : 2 0 :027(045) [0057] to rely on them to earn **grace** but that we may do God's
AG : 2 0 :028(045) [0057] faith alone that apprehends **grace** and forgiveness of sin.
AG : 2 1 :001(046) [0057] when we see what **grace** they received and how they were
AG : 2 3 :006(052) [0061] or vows without a special gift or **grace** of God.
AG : 2 4 :028(059) [0067] taught that we obtain **grace** before God through faith and
AG : 2 4 :029(059) [0067] by those who think that **grace** is obtained through the
AG : 2 4 :029(059) [0067] to remove sin and obtain **grace** and all sorts of benefits
AG : 2 4 :030(059) [0067] through the sacrament **grace** and forgiveness of sin are
AG : 2 6 :001(064) [0071] by men serve to earn **grace** and make satisfaction for sin.
AG : 2 6 :002(064) [0071] of God by means of which **grace** would be earned if they
AG : 2 6 :004(064) [0071] In the first place, the **grace** of Christ and the teaching
AG : 2 6 :005(064) [0071] faith in Christ that we obtain **grace** for Christ's sake.
AG : 2 6 :006(064) [0071] who have taught that **grace** is to be earned by prescribed
AG : 2 6 :013(066) [0073] heard anything of the consolation of the **grace** of Christ.
AG : 2 6 :020(067) [0073] if it is supposed that **grace** is earned through self-chosen
AG : 2 6 :021(067) [0073] It is therefore taught that **grace** cannot be earned, God
AG : 2 6 :027(068) [0073] be saved through the **grace** of the Lord Jesus, just as they
AG : 2 6 :033(069) [0075] to sin, but not as if he earned **grace** by such works.
AG : 2 6 :038(069) [0075] of mortification to merit **grace** but to keep the body in
AG : 2 7 :016(073) [0077] nature that thereby God's **grace** and righteousness before
AG : 2 7 :036(076) [0081] righteousness and God's **grace** without the command and
AG : 2 7 :038(077) [0081] for sin and obtains God's **grace** and righteousness.
AG : 2 7 :038(077) [0081] glory and honor of the **grace** of Christ and deny the
AG : 2 7 :041(077) [0081] be justified by the law; you have fallen away from **grace**."
AG : 2 7 :042(077) [0081] fallen away from God's **grace**, for they rob Christ, who
AG : 2 8 :035(086) [0089] for sins and obtain **grace**, for the glory of Christ's merit is
AG : 2 8 :036(086) [0089] when we presume to earn **grace** by such ordinances.
AG : 2 8 :037(087) [0089] order that by such works **grace** and everything good
AG : 2 8 :039(087) [0089] if in order to earn God's **grace** there had to be a service of
AG : 2 8 :043(088) [0089] purpose of earning God's **grace** or as if they were
AG : 2 8 :050(089) [0091] propitiate God and merit **grace** are contrary to the
AG : 2 8 :052(089) [0091] that we obtain the **grace** of God through faith in Christ
AG : 2 8 :053(090) [0091] means of obtaining God's **grace** or making satisfaction
AL : 0 6 :003(032) [0047] alone, and he shall receive forgiveness of sins by **grace**."
AL : 0 9 :001(033) [0047] for salvation, that the **grace** of God is offered through
AL : 0 9 :002(033) [0047] to God through Baptism they are received into his **grace**.
AL : 1 2 :010(035) [0049] but command us to merit **grace** through satisfactions of
AL : 1 5 :003(036) [0049] to propitiate God, merit **grace**, and make satisfaction for
AL : 1 5 :004(037) [0049] etc., instituted to merit **grace** and make satisfaction for
AL : 2 0 :009(042) [0053] forgiveness of sins and **grace** but that we obtain
AL : 2 0 :009(042) [0053] we obtain forgiveness and **grace** only by faith when we
AL : 2 0 :010(042) [0055] trusts that he merits **grace** by works despises the merit
AL : 2 0 :010(042) [0055] despises the merit and **grace** of Christ and seeks a way to
AL : 2 0 :011(042) [0055] as in Eph. 2:8, "For by **grace** you have been saved
AL : 2 0 :013(043) [0055] Augustine defends **grace** and the righteousness of faith
AL : 2 0 :014(043) [0055] which is accomplished by **grace**, were due to antecedent
AL : 2 0 :020(044) [0055] hope that there they might merit **grace** by monastic life.
AL : 2 0 :021(044) [0055] of another kind to merit **grace** and make satisfaction for
AL : 2 0 :022(044) [0055] but know that **grace** and forgiveness of sins are
AL : 2 0 :023(044) [0055] — that is, that we have **grace**, righteousness, and
AL : 2 0 :027(045) [0057] we should trust to merit **grace** by them but because it is
AL : 2 0 :028(045) [0057] forgiveness of sins and **grace** are apprehended, and
AL : 2 6 :001(064) [0071] are profitable to merit **grace** and make satisfactions for
AL : 2 6 :002(064) [0071] service necessary to merit **grace** and sorely terrified the
AL : 2 6 :004(064) [0071] the doctrine concerning **grace** and the righteousness of
AL : 2 6 :005(064) [0071] believes that for Christ's sake we are received into **grace**.
AL : 2 6 :006(064) [0071] it is necessary to merit **grace** and righteousness by
AL : 2 6 :013(066) [0073] heard the consolation of **grace** and of the righteousness
AL : 2 6 :020(067) [0073] the teaching concerning **grace** and the righteousness of
AL : 2 6 :020(067) [0073] suppose that they merit **grace** by observances of their own
AL : 2 6 :021(067) [0073] that we cannot merit **grace** or make satisfaction for sins
AL : 2 6 :027(068) [0073] be saved through the **grace** of the Lord Jesus, just as they
AL : 2 6 :029(068) [0075] the purpose of meriting **grace** through them or with the
AL : 2 7 :016(073) [0077] of life was instituted to merit **grace** and righteousness.
AL : 2 7 :036(076) [0081] to merit justification and **grace** without the command of
AL : 2 7 :038(077) [0081] satisfaction for sins and merit **grace** and justification.
AL : 2 7 :041(077) [0081] be justified by the law; you have fallen away from **grace**."
AL : 2 7 :042(077) [0081] Christ and fall away from **grace**, for those who ascribe
AL : 2 8 :037(087) [0089] thought that they would merit **grace** by these works.
AL : 2 8 :052(089) [0091] namely, that we obtain **grace** through faith in Christ and
AP : 0 2 :008(101) [0107] at him, despairing of his **grace**, trusting in temporal
AP : 0 2 :010(102) [0107] What need is there for the **grace** of Christ if we can
AP : 0 2 :023(103) [0111] be produced without certain gifts and help of **grace**.
AP : 0 2 :033(104) [0113] the magnitude of the **grace** of Christ unless we
AP : 0 2 :042(105) [0117] about God's wrath, his **grace**, and his Word; anger at his
AP : 0 2 :044(106) [0117] and obscuring the knowledge of the **grace** of Christ.
AP : 0 2 :045(106) [0117] neutral, but they need the **grace** of Christ to be forgiven
AP : 0 4 :003(107) [0121] of sins nor faith nor **grace** nor righteousness, our
AP : 0 4 :011(108) [0123] of compulsion—God grants **grace** to those who do this.
AP : 0 4 :017(109) [0125] or, as they call it, "initial **grace**," which they understand
AP : 0 4 :019(110) [0125] if God necessarily gives **grace** for the merit of congruity,
AP : 0 4 :021(110) [0127] trust in works and a contempt for the **grace** of Christ.
AP : 0 4 :028(111) [0129] of God outside a state of **grace** do not sin.
AP : 0 4 :029(111) [0129] maintains at length that **grace** is not given because of our
AP : 0 4 :029(111) [0129] In *Nature and Grace* he says: "If natural capacity, with
AP : 0 4 :030(111) [0129] have fallen away from **grace**' (Gal. 5:4); for 'being
AP : 0 4 :041(113) [0133] "If it is by works, it is no longer on the basis of **grace**."
AP : 0 4 :073(117) [0141] (Rom. 3:24), "They are justified by his **grace** as a gift."
AP : 0 4 :079(117) [0143] of sins and the infusion of **grace** are the same thing, yet
AP : 0 4 :084(119) [0145] the promise may rest on **grace** and be guaranteed," as
AP : 0 4 :093(120) [0149] Eph. 2:8, "For by **grace** you have been saved through
AP : 0 4 :103(122) [0151] but where sin increased, **grace** abounded all the more'
AP : 0 4 :106(122) [0153] who fear punishment **grace** is hidden; laboring under this
AP : 0 4 :116(123) [0155] Spirit, it should be called "**grace** that makes us acceptable
AP : 0 4 :146(127) [0163] for they say they earn **grace** and eternal life by merit.
AP : 0 4 :149(127) [0163] though Paul says that **grace** abounded more than sin
AP : 0 4 :162(129) [0169] he merely merited "initial **grace**" and that afterward we
AP : 0 4 :194(133) [0175] the forgiveness of sins, **grace**, or justification (for we
AP : 0 4 :202(134) [0175] forgiveness of sins and **grace** through this work, but to
AP : 0 4 :203(135) [0177] works the saints merited **grace** and the forgiveness of
AP : 0 4 :203(135) [0177] works he will merit **grace** and forgiveness of sins, appease
AP : 0 4 :208(135) [0177] who hope that by similar actions they can obtain **grace**.
AP : 0 4 :208(135) [0177] in order thereby to merit **grace**, righteousness, and the
AP : 0 4 :208(135) [0177] the high places to merit **grace** and forgiveness of sins by
AP : 0 4 :211(136) [0179] to merit the forgiveness of sins, **grace**, and righteousness.
AP : 0 4 :213(136) [0179] forgiveness of sins and **grace** and that we are accounted
AP : 0 4 :214(136) [0179] the forgiveness of sins, **grace**, and righteousness through
AP : 0 4 :216(137) [0179] by which we take hold of **grace** and peace of conscience.
AP : 0 4 :227(139) [0183] merits and, through them, **grace** and peace from God.
AP : 0 4 :236(140) [0185] Moreover, it comes in poor **grace** for our opponents to
AP : 0 4 :246(142) [0189] our good works we merit **grace** and the forgiveness of
AP : 0 4 :246(142) [0189] James teaches we merit **grace** and forgiveness of sins by
AP : 0 4 :266(146) [0197] of the teaching of **grace** and faith, while Daniel most
AP : 0 4 :285(150) [0201] him we might have **grace**, righteousness, and peace.
AP : 0 4 :286(150) [0201] by our works we merit **grace** and the forgiveness of sins.
AP : 0 4 :288(151) [0203] them, is that men merit **grace** by good works — first by
AP : 0 4 :288(151) [0203] they seek righteousness, **grace**, and salvation *ex opere*
AP : 0 4 :289(151) [0203] obedience to the law is worthy of **grace** and eternal life.
AP : 0 4 :290(151) [0203] a righteousness worthy of **grace** and eternal life, although
AP : 0 4 :297(153) [0205] in vain; the promise of **grace** in Christ was not given in
AP : 0 4 :303(154) [0205] truly and wholeheartedly accepts the promise of **grace**.
AP : 0 4 :310(155) [0207] to receive forgiveness of sins, **grace**, and righteousness.
AP : 0 4 :318(156) [0209] that good works earn **grace** by the merit of condignity, as
AP : 0 4 :318(156) [0209] often does, we must seek **grace** through a good work and
AP : 0 4 :321(157) [0209] can be sure of earning **grace** by the merit of condignity?
AP : 0 4 :322(157) [0209] Augustine says in *Grace and Free Will*, "God leads us to
AP : 0 4 :332(158) [0211] good works, and ask for **grace** as though they had earned
AP : 0 4 :338(159) [0215] mercy and the promise of **grace**, even though our works
AP : 0 4 :339(159) [0215] He does not want us to despair of God's **grace** and mercy.
AP : 0 4 :340(159) [0215] Ambrose has clearly said, "**Grace** is to be recognized, but
AP : 0 4 :341(159) [0215] We should trust the promise of **grace**, not our own nature.
AP : 0 4 :342(159) [0215] himself to bestow his **grace** upon us, though it is out of
AP : 0 4 :357(162) [0219] they are worthy of **grace** and eternal life without needing
AP : 0 4 :359(162) [0219] themselves are worthy of **grace** and eternal life or whether
AP : 0 4 :360(162) [0219] attribute to works a worthiness of **grace** and eternal life.
AP : 0 4 :365(163) [0219] In the proclamation of rewards **grace** is displayed.
AP : 0 4 :365(163) [0219] so they sometimes offer **grace** with other rewards, as in
AP : 0 4 :366(163) [0221] deals with the promise of **grace**, receives justification and
AP : 0 4 :375(164) [0223] but in themselves are not worthy of **grace** and eternal life.
AP : 0 4 :376(164) [0223] reason that works merit **grace** by the merit of congruity
AP : 0 4 :381(165) [0223] please God because of **grace** and that therefore we must
AP : 0 4 :381(165) [0223] therefore we must place our confidence in God's **grace**.
AP : 0 4 :381(165) [0223] Here they interpret **grace** as a disposition by which we
AP : 0 4 :381(165) [0223] Why not expound here God's **grace** and mercy toward us?
AP : 0 4 :381(165) [0223] must put our confidence in **grace** and that good works
AP : 0 4 :381(165) [0223] please God because of **grace**; for faith takes hold of
AP : 0 4 :381(165) [0225] please God because of grace; for faith takes hold of **grace**.
AP : 0 4 :383(165) [0225] grasps the promise of **grace** and righteousness, quickening
AP : 0 4 :386(166) [0225] grasps the promise of **grace**, truly enlivens the fearful
AP : 0 4 :387(166) [0225] propitiator, deny the promise of **grace** and the Gospel.
AP : 0 4 :388(166) [0225] but by the Gospel, the promise of **grace** offered in Christ.
AP : 0 4 :392(167) [0225] seek forgiveness of sins, **grace**, and righteousness through
AP : 0 7 :021(172) [0233] sins by their love for God before entering a state of **grace**.

Continued ▶

GRACE 238 GRACE

A P : 1 2 :008(183) [0255] They teach that by contrition we merit **grace**.
A P : 1 2 :008(183) [0255] and men like them attain **grace** even though they were
A P : 1 2 :012(184) [0255] that the sacrament grants **grace** *ex opere operato*,
A P : 1 2 :017(185) [0257] God's covenant, we merit **grace** by good works done
A P : 1 2 :017(185) [0257] we merit grace by good works done apart from **grace**.
A P : 1 2 :018(185) [0257] 2. We merit **grace** through attrition.
A P : 1 2 :025(185) [0259] of penitence obtains **grace** *ex opere operato*, without the
A P : 1 2 :034(186) [0261] sorrows and terrors men merit **grace** if they love God.
A P : 1 2 :049(188) [0265] in contrition by the Word of God which offers us **grace**.
A P : 1 2 :053(189) [0265] Gospel, that is, the promise of **grace** granted in Christ.
A P : 1 2 :055(189) [0267] Then God promised **grace** and said there would be a seed
A P : 1 2 :063(191) [0269] him we have obtained access by faith to this **grace**," etc.
A P : 1 2 :081(194) [0275] the promise may rest on **grace** and be guaranteed"; and in
A P : 1 2 :103(197) [0281] in the area of blessing or **grace**, not of judgment or law.
A P : 1 2 :146(205) [0297] In addition, they obscure penitence and **grace**.
A P : 1 3 :003(211) [0309] to which the promise of **grace** has been added," we can
A P : 1 3 :003(211) [0309] since men do not have the authority to promise **grace**.
A P : 1 3 :003(211) [0309] are not sure signs of **grace**, even though they may instruct
A P : 1 3 :004(211) [0309] God and the promise of **grace**, which is the heart of the
A P : 1 3 :006(212) [0311] express command from God and a clear promise of **grace**.
A P : 1 3 :014(213) [0311] Testament," testimonies of **grace** and the forgiveness of
A P : 1 3 :018(213) [0313] the sacraments confer **grace** *ex opere operato*, without a
A P : 1 5 :001(215) [0315] to appease God, to merit **grace**, and to make satisfaction
A P : 1 5 :003(215) [0315] that we do not merit **grace** or the forgiveness of sins by
A P : 1 5 :004(215) [0315] are helpful in gaining **grace** and the forgiveness of sins.
A P : 1 5 :006(216) [0317] teaches (Eph. 2:8), "By **grace** you have been saved
A P : 1 5 :012(216) [0317] already justified do merit **grace** by observing these
A P : 1 5 :015(217) [0319] if by such rites they merit **grace**, we shall have to approve
A P : 1 5 :015(217) [0319] rites that serve to merit **grace** or righteousness, why did
A P : 1 5 :018(217) [0319] rites merit justification, **grace**, and the forgiveness of sins,
A P : 1 5 :021(218) [0321] to merit the forgiveness of sins, **grace** and justification.
A P : 1 8 :002(225) [0335] Holy Spirit men can merit **grace** and justification by
A P : 1 8 :006(225) [0335] sin if, outside the state of **grace**, he does the works
A P : 2 0 :010(228) [0341] "We are justified by his **grace** as a gift" (Rom. 3:24) "in
A P : 2 0 :014(229) [0343] for maintaining that **grace** is given because of our works.
A P : 2 1 :005(230) [0345] to believe that **grace** does indeed abound more than sin
A P : 2 1 :026(232) [0349] dying man, "Mother of **grace**, protect us from the enemy
A P : 2 3 :045(245) [0377] thought they would merit **grace** by performing these
A P : 2 4 :009(251) [0387] the Mass does not confer **grace** *ex opere operato*, nor
A P : 2 4 :011(251) [0387] Supper does not grant **grace** *ex opere operato* and does
A P : 2 4 :042(257) [0399] to someone else to merit for him **grace** and every good.
A P : 2 4 :063(260) [0405] that the Mass confers **grace** *ex opere operato* on one who
A P : 2 4 :066(261) [0407] that the Mass confers **grace** *ex opere operato* or that it
A P : 2 4 :069(262) [0409] to define the New Testament sacraments as signs of **grace**.
A P : 2 4 :069(262) [0409] New Testament, the Word is the added promise of **grace**.
A P : 2 4 :078(263) [0411] a sacrifice that it grants **grace** *ex opere operato* or that it
A P : 2 7 :011(270) [0423] be justified by the law; you have fallen away from **grace**."
A P : 2 7 :020(272) [0427] God, which contains a covenant of **grace** and eternal life.
A P : 2 7 :028(274) [0429] due observance, as by the grace of God any monk can
S 1 : P R :003(289) [0455] now and where, by God's **grace**, I will continue to stand.
S 1 : P R :010(290) [0457] a council, for by God's **grace** our churches have now been
S 1 : P R :015(291) [0459] Thee according to the **grace** which Thou hast given us by
S 2 : 0 1 :003(292) [0461] "they are justified by his **grace** as a gift, through the
S 2 : 0 2 :007(294) [0465] God and obtain and merit **grace** and the forgiveness of
S 2 : 0 2 :018(296) [0467] of sins, and God's **grace** were sought here, too, for
S 2 : 0 2 :018(296) [0467] obtain forgiveness and **grace** in a better way and may
S 2 : 0 2 :024(296) [0469] of Christ are obtained by **grace**, through faith, without
S 3 : 0 1 :008(302) [0477] does what he can, God is certain to grant him his **grace**.
S 3 : 0 2 :001(303) [0479] and by the promise and offer of **grace** and favor.
S 3 : 0 3 :004(304) [0481] adds the consoling promise of **grace** in the Gospel.
S 3 : 0 3 :005(304) [0481] to be prepared to receive **grace** from the Lord and to
S 3 : 0 3 :010(305) [0481] will assuredly grant his **grace** to the man who does as
S 3 : 0 3 :015(305) [0483] the sinner was commended to the **grace** of God.
S 3 : 0 3 :019(306) [0485] for such humiliation would surely earn **grace** before God.
S 3 : 0 3 :032(308) [0487] from his fullness have we all received, **grace** upon grace.
S 3 : 0 3 :032(308) [0487] from his fullness have we all received, grace upon **grace**.
S 3 : 0 4 :000(310) [0491] is surpassingly rich in his **grace**: First, through the spoken
S 3 : 0 8 :003(312) [0495] gives no one his Spirit or **grace** except through or with
S 3 : 1 3 :002(315) [0499] and holy through the pure **grace** and mercy which have
S 3 : 1 3 :003(315) [0499] apart from God's **grace** and mercy, but, as it is written,
S C : P R :000(338) [0533] **Grace**, mercy, and peace in Jesus Christ, our Lord, from
S C : P R :023(341) [0539] suggests that he needs no **grace**, no life, no paradise, no
S C : P R :026(341) [0539] It is now a ministry of **grace** and salvation.
S C : P R :027(341) [0539] The Father of all **grace** grant it!
S C : 0 1 :022(344) [0543] other hand, he promises **grace** and every blessing to all
S C : 0 3 :008(346) [0547] Holy Spirit so that by his **grace** we may believe his holy
S C : 0 3 :016(347) [0549] pray that God may grant us all things by his **grace**.
S C : 0 4 :010(349) [0551] might be justified by his **grace** and become heirs in hope
S C : 0 5 :022(350) [0553] For all this I am sorry and pray for **grace**.
S C : 0 8 :006(353) [0559] **[Grace at Table]**
S C : 0 9 :006(355) [0561] you are joint heirs of the **grace** of life, in order that your
S C : 0 9 :012(356) [0563] 'God opposes the proud, but gives **grace** to the humble.'
L C : P R :020(361) [0573] To this end may God grant his **grace**!
L C : 0 1 :073(374) [0601] us the custom of saying **grace** and returning thanks at
L C : 0 1 :174(388) [0629] on pain of losing divine **grace**, to bring up his children in
L C : 0 1 :175(388) [0631] richly bless us and give us **grace** so that men might be
L C : 0 1 :212(394) [0641] although here, too, God's **grace** is still required to keep
L C : 0 1 :218(394) [0643] will add his blessing and **grace** so that men may have joy
L C : 0 1 :323(409) [0675] a kind father and offers us every **grace** and blessing.
L C : 0 2 :030(414) [0685] us free, and restored us to the Father's favor and **grace**.
L C : 0 2 :044(416) [0689] teaching us to obtain **grace** and be saved by our works.
L C : 0 2 :054(417) [0693] for although God's **grace** has been won by Christ, and
L C : 0 2 :065(419) [0695] the Father's favor and **grace** were it not for the Lord
L C : 0 2 :068(420) [0697] But the Creed brings pure **grace** and makes us upright
L C : 0 3 :011(421) [0701] our misery and plight, and pray for **grace** and help.
L C : 0 3 :011(421) [0701] and assuage his wrath and seek **grace** by their prayers.]
L C : 0 3 :052(427) [0711] come into the kingdom of **grace** and become partakers of
L C : 0 3 :094(433) [0725] he forgives it all through **grace**, we must always forgive
L C : 0 3 :096(433) [0725] freely, out of pure **grace**, because he has promised it, as
L C : 0 4 :039(441) [0743] is so full of comfort and **grace** that heaven and earth
L C : 0 4 :041(442) [0743] forgiveness of sin, God's **grace**, the entire Christ, and the
L C : 0 4 :049(442) [0745] Similarly by God's **grace** we have been given the power to
L C : 0 4 :050(443) [0745] wickedness, or give his **grace** and Spirit for such ends.
L C : 0 4 :076(445) [0751] Baptism we are given the **grace**, Spirit, and power to
L C : 0 5 :061(453) [0767] the person who desires no **grace** and absolution and has
L C : 0 5 :062(454) [0767] He who earnestly desires **grace** and consolation should
L C : 0 5 :070(454) [0769] and conveys God's **grace** and Spirit with all his gifts,
L C : 0 5 :084(456) [0773] though God grants his **grace** that you may become more
L C : 0 6 :009(458) [0000] we ought and a plea for **grace** and a happy conscience?
L C : 0 6 :009(458) [0000] to acknowledge that we are sinners and to pray for **grace**.
E P : 0 2 :001(469) [0785] Spirit, dispose and prepare himself for the **grace** of God?
E P : 0 2 :001(469) [0785] or can he not accept the **grace** of God offered in the Word
E P : 0 2 :004(470) [0787] solely through the **grace** and power of the Holy Spirit, for
E P : 0 2 :006(470) [0787] Without his **grace** our "will and effort," our planting,
E P : 0 2 :006(470) [0787] ascribes everything to the **grace** of God, so that no one
E P : 0 2 :009(471) [0789] own powers, without the **grace** of the Holy Spirit, man
E P : 0 2 :010(471) [0789] not complete it without the **grace** of the Holy Spirit.
E P : 0 2 :011(471) [0789] and in it has offered his **grace**, man's will is forthwith able
E P : 0 2 :011(471) [0789] to prepare itself for **grace**, to dispose itself, to apprehend
E P : 0 2 :016(472) [0791] to the doctrine of the **grace** of God, we hold that these
E P : 0 2 :018(472) [0791] to the action of divine **grace** in kindling new movements
E P : 0 2 :018(472) [0791] man not only lays hold on **grace** but also cooperates with
E P : 0 2 :019(472) [0791] powers but solely by the **grace** and operation of God the
E P : 0 3 :004(473) [0793] us our sins purely by his **grace**, without any preceding,
E P : 0 3 :004(473) [0793] are accepted by God into **grace** and are regarded as
E P : 0 3 :006(473) [0793] of his obedience, by **grace**, we have forgiveness of sins,
E P : 0 3 :010(474) [0795] such expressions as "*by grace*," "without merit," "without
E P : 0 3 :022(475) [0797] 10. That the promise of **grace** becomes our own by faith
E P : 0 4 :007(476) [0799] And again, "For by **grace** you have been saved through
E P : 0 4 :010(476) [0799] they are "no longer under the law but under **grace**."
E P : 0 5 :001(477) [0801] only a preaching of **grace** which proclaims the forgiveness
E P : 0 5 :007(478) [0803] proclamation of God's **grace** and favor acquired through
E P : 0 5 :010(479) [0803] office — namely, to preach **grace**, to comfort, to make
E P : 0 5 :011(479) [0805] and reproof and not exclusively a proclamation of **grace**.
E P : 0 6 :006(481) [0807] "not under the law, but under **grace**" (Rom. 7:23; 8:1, 14).
E P : 1 1 :013(496) [0835] to eternal life out of pure **grace** in Christ without any
E P : 1 1 :015(496) [0835] because he out of pure **grace** alone, without any merit of
E P : 1 1 :022(497) [0837] Jesus Christ grant us the **grace** of his Holy Spirit that we
E P : 1 2 :031(500) [0843] to it but intend by the **grace** of God to abide by it, we
S D : P R :001(501) [0847] By the special **grace** and mercy of the Almighty, the
S D : P R :005(502) [0847] we are determined by the **grace** of the Almighty to abide
S D : P R :005(504) [0851] 3. By a special **grace** our merciful God has in these last
S D : P R :007(505) [0853] estates were resolved by God's **grace** to remain faithful.
S D : P R :020(508) [0859] By God's **grace** we shall continue to abide in it loyally and
S D : 0 1 :045(516) [0873] for Christ's sake into his **grace** but remains the enemy of
S D : 0 2 :002(520) [0881] God is preached and the **grace** of God is offered to him.
S D : 0 2 :002(520) [0881] prepare himself for such **grace**, accept it and give his
S D : 0 2 :003(520) [0881] extent prepare himself for **grace** and give his assent to it,
S D : 0 2 :005(521) [0881] and heard, purely out of **grace** and without any
S D : 0 2 :006(521) [0883] of God, and by God's **grace** to bring it to an end, we
S D : 0 2 :007(521) [0883] make himself ready for the **grace** of God or to accept the
S D : 0 2 :007(521) [0883] or to accept the proffered **grace**, nor that he has any
S D : 0 2 :007(521) [0883] he has any capacity for **grace** by and for himself or can
S D : 0 2 :014(523) [0885] and a longing for the **grace** of God and eternal salvation
S D : 0 2 :016(523) [0887] by the same Spirit and **grace**, through daily exercise in
S D : 0 2 :018(524) [0889] the Holy Spirit offers the **grace** of God and salvation
S D : 0 2 :022(525) [0889] out of particular and pure **grace**, that our poor, fallen,
S D : 0 2 :022(525) [0889] in conversion, in the **grace** of God, and in eternal life, not
S D : 0 2 :022(525) [0889] God — but out of pure **grace** through the gracious and
S D : 0 2 :023(525) [0889] such a way that by divine **grace** it can be converted to
S D : 0 2 :027(526) [0891] *Predestination*, "The **grace** of God consists merely in this,
S D : 0 2 :033(527) [0893] the Holy Spirit and his **grace** are necessary for good
S D : 0 2 :041(529) [0897] Holy Spirit so that by his **grace** we may believe his holy
S D : 0 2 :043(529) [0897] contrary to the help and **grace** of our Lord Jesus Christ.
S D : 0 2 :055(532) [0903] should question this **grace** and operation of the Holy
S D : 0 2 :055(532) [0903] certainly present with his **grace** and gives what man is
S D : 0 2 :057(532) [0903] we are elected, offers his **grace** to all men in the Word and
S D : 0 2 :066(534) [0907] we entreat you not to accept the **grace** of God in vain."
S D : 0 2 :070(535) [0909] and accept the promise of **grace** in Christ, to have good
S D : 0 2 :072(535) [0909] us not to receive this **grace** of God in vain but to exercise
S D : 0 2 :077(536) [0911] the Gospel and offers his **grace**, the forgiveness of sins,
S D : 0 2 :077(536) [0911] and prepare itself for the **grace** of God, embrace and
S D : 0 2 :078(536) [0911] to prepare oneself for **grace** does not come from man's
S D : 0 2 :083(537) [0913] not prepared by God for **grace**, but wholly resists the
S D : 0 2 :083(537) [0913] of the Holy Spirit is able to accept the offered **grace**.
S D : 0 2 :086(538) [0913] in his conversion, contrary to the article of God's **grace**.
S D : 0 3 :001(539) [0917] or of faith which God by **grace** through faith reckons to
S D : 0 3 :004(540) [0917] alone, is reckoned by pure **grace** to all true believers as
S D : 0 3 :006(540) [0917] or rightly understand the riches of the **grace** of Christ."
S D : 0 3 :007(540) [0917] as "without the law," "without works," "by **grace** alone."
S D : 0 3 :008(540) [0919] God and to settle it by his **grace**, we affirm our teaching,
S D : 0 3 :009(541) [0919] works, by sheer **grace**, solely through the merit of the
S D : 0 3 :011(541) [0919] forgiveness of sins by **grace**, are accounted righteous and
S D : 0 3 :014(541) [0919] righteousness which by **grace** is reckoned to faith or to
S D : 0 3 :016(541) [0921] forgiveness of sins, the **grace** of God, adoption, and the
S D : 0 3 :023(543) [0923] And to those who by sheer **grace**, for the sake of the only
S D : 0 3 :023(543) [0923] God (that is, accepted into **grace**) there is given the Holy
S D : 0 3 :025(543) [0923] of justification are the **grace** of God, the merit of Christ,
S D : 0 3 :030(544) [0925] merit of Christ and the **grace** of God, Scripture teaches
S D : 0 3 :030(544) [0925] bestowed upon us by pure **grace** because of the unique
S D : 0 3 :031(544) [0925] receive and accept the **grace** of God, the merit of Christ,
S D : 0 3 :038(546) [0929] and appropriate the **grace** and the merit of Christ in the
S D : 0 3 :039(546) [0929] of sins by sheer **grace**, entirely for the sake of Christ's
S D : 0 3 :041(546) [0929] Faith apprehends the **grace** of God in Christ whereby the
S D : 0 3 :043(547) [0931] it embraces God's **grace** and the merit of Christ in the
S D : 0 3 :051(548) [0933] that the promise of **grace** is made our own through faith
S D : 0 3 :053(548) [0933] own merit, such as "by **grace**" and "without works") just
S D : 0 3 :058(550) [0937] and remitted by sheer **grace** for Christ's sake alone.
S D : 0 3 :066(550) [0937] of God, and by God's **grace** we shall remain steadfastly
S D : 0 4 :006(552) [0939] of God, and by God's **grace** to arrive at a complete
S D : 0 4 :012(553) [0941] deliberate trust in God's **grace**, so certain that it would
S D : 0 4 :012(553) [0941] and knowledge of divine **grace** makes us joyous,
S D : 0 4 :020(554) [0945] still retain faith and God's mercy and his **grace**.
S D : 0 4 :022(555) [0945] everything solely to the **grace** of God and the merit of
S D : 0 4 :031(556) [0947] retain faith, the **grace** of God, righteousness, and
S D : 0 4 :033(556) [0949] have come to you by **grace** through Christ and which you

Continued ▶

SD : 04 :034(556) [0949] not only our entry into **grace** but also our present state of
SD : 04 :034(556) [0949] also our present state of **grace** and our hope of sharing
SD : 04 :037(557) [0949] in order to merit the **grace** of God and to be saved
SD : 05 :002(558) [0951] only a proclamation of **grace** but also at the same time a
SD : 05 :002(558) [0953] is a proclamation of the **grace** and mercy of God for
SD : 05 :004(559) [0953] of the mercy and **grace** of God, his heavenly Father, as it
SD : 05 :006(559) [0953] of repentance but solely the preaching of God's **grace**.
SD : 05 :011(560) [0955] own work (that is, to comfort and to preach about **grace**).
SD : 05 :012(560) [0955] and gives nothing but **grace** and forgiveness in Christ.
SD : 05 :014(560) [0957] adds the promise of God's **grace** through the Gospel."
SD : 05 :021(562) [0959] offers the mercy and **grace** of God to transgressors of the
SD : 05 :025(563) [0961] children, and out of pure **grace**, without any merit of
SD : 05 :025(563) [0961] that men may abuse the **grace** of God and sin against
SD : 05 :025(563) [0961] men may abuse the grace of God and sin against **grace**.
SD : 06 :017(567) [0967] are no longer under law but under **grace** (Rom. 6:14; 8:2).
SD : 06 :023(567) [0969] under the law but under **grace** because their persons have
SD : 07 :016(572) [0977] in Christ there receive the **grace** and merits of Christ, are
SD : 07 :030(574) [0981] then as now, that by the **grace** of God I have most
SD : 07 :031(574) [0983] dead earnest, since by the **grace** of God I have learned to
SD : 07 :050(578) [0989] and signs of **grace** or sacraments, such as circumcision,
SD : 07 :062(581) [0995] for us (that is to say, the **grace** of God, forgiveness of
SD : 07 :076(583) [0999] but by God's power and **grace** through the words that he
SD : 08 :005(592) [1017] it definitely by God's **grace**, our unanimous teaching,
SD : 08 :034(597) [1027] Christ dwells only by **grace**, have in Christ, because of
SD : 10 :004(611) [1053] settle it definitively by the **grace** of God, we offer the
SD : 10 :018(614) [1059] footsteps intend by the **grace** of God to abide by this their
SD : 11 :001(616) [1063] in order by God's **grace** to prevent, as far as we can,
SD : 11 :011(618) [1067] too, even though by the **grace** of God they have
SD : 11 :021(619) [1069] diligently, persevere in the **grace** of God, and use
SD : 11 :023(619) [1069] recounted he wills by his **grace**, gifts, and effective
SD : 11 :024(620) [1071] this light, we can by the **grace** of God easily orient
SD : 11 :032(621) [1073] he has promised his **grace** (I Cor. 1:8; Phil. 1:6ff.; II Pet.
SD : 11 :033(621) [1073] the Holy Spirit gives **grace**, power, and ability through
SD : 11 :033(621) [1073] Gospel so that you learn to know your sins and his **grace**.
SD : 11 :042(623) [1077] not want to impart the **grace** of perseverance to those in
SD : 11 :043(623) [1077] and merit, purely by **grace** and solely for Christ's sake.
SD : 11 :043(623) [1077] to his purpose" by **grace** in Christ (Rom. 9:11; II Tim.
SD : 11 :060(626) [1083] nor his Spirit, nor his **grace**; in fact, when he does
SD : 11 :060(626) [1083] God's pure and unmerited **grace** toward the "vessels of
SD : 11 :061(626) [1083] God commends his pure and unmerited **grace** and mercy.
SD : 11 :062(626) [1083] is help for you is pure **grace** on my part" (Hos. 13:9).
SD : 11 :072(628) [1085] God to give us his **grace**, of which he has assured us in
SD : 11 :083(630) [1091] that he would receive into **grace** all who repent and
SD : 11 :087(631) [1093] the praise of his glorious **grace** which he freely bestowed
SD : 12 :006(633) [1097] And we desire by God's **grace** to remain steadfastly in our
SD : 12 :040(636) [1103] in which by God's **grace** we shall appear with intrepid
SD : 12 :040(636) [1103] but we intend through God's **grace** to abide by it.

Graces (1)
SD : 05 :020(561) [0959] we re-enter the good **graces** of God, obtain forgiveness of

Gracious (83), Graciously (16)
PR : PR :001(003) [0007] due service, friendship, **gracious** greeting, and favorably
PR : PR :008(005) [0009] and declare to our most **gracious** lord, His Roman
AG : PR :001(024) [0039] most mighty, invincible Emperor, most **gracious** Lord:
AG : PR :001(024) [0039] Your Imperial Majesty **graciously** summoned a diet of the
AG : PR :006(025) [0039] Imperial Majesty also **graciously** and earnestly requested
AG : PR :010(025) [0041] Majesty, our most **gracious** lord, to discuss with them and
AG : PR :014(026) [0041] these questions will be **graciously** and sufficiently assured
AG : PR :015(026) [0041] Your Imperial Majesty **graciously** gave assurance to the
AG : PR :020(026) [0041] Your Imperial Majesty **graciously** offered to promote and
AG : 05 :003(031) [0045] teaches that we have a **gracious** God, not by our own
AG : 20 :015(043) [0055] for Christ's sake it has a **gracious** God, as Paul says in
AG : 20 :024(044) [0055] that in Christ he has a **gracious** God, truly knows God,
AG : 20 :026(045) [0057] assurance that God is **gracious** to us, and not merely such
AG : 23 :014(053) [0063] Your Majesty will **graciously** take into account that fact
AG : 27 :049(079) [0083] Christ's sake we have a **gracious**, merciful God; that we
AG : 28 :074(093) [0093] bishops ought to be so **gracious** as to temper these
AL : 20 :015(043) [0055] are sure that for Christ's sake they have a **gracious** God.
AL : 00 :001(049) [0059] Imperial Majesty will **graciously** hear both what has been
AL : 27 :049(079) [0083] Christ's sake we have a **gracious** God, to ask of God, and
AP : 04 :102(121) [0151] of sins, and of our **gracious** acceptance for Christ's sake.
AP : 04 :139(126) [0161] Christ's sake we have a **gracious** God and his promise.
AP : 04 :141(126) [0161] sure that we have a **gracious** God who cares about us, we
AP : 04 :145(127) [0163] account of Christ, the mediator, we have a **gracious** God.
AP : 04 :163(129) [0169] for his sake we have a **gracious** God in spite of our
AP : 04 :174(131) [0171] is sure that for Christ's sake we have a **gracious** God.
AP : 04 :178(131) [0171] of our keeping of the law we have a **gracious** God.
AP : 04 :180(132) [0171] of Christ and his promise they have a **gracious** God.
AP : 04 :196(134) [0175] obtains this because it justifies us and has a **gracious** God.
AP : 04 :203(135) [0175] sake he is freely forgiven and freely has a **gracious** God.
AP : 04 :207(135) [0177] of them they had a **gracious** God, so to say, *ex opere*
AP : 04 :211(136) [0179] righteous and had a **gracious** God because of Christ, not
AP : 04 :222(138) [0181] and believe that for his sake God is **gracious** to us.
AP : 04 :230(139) [0183] we believe that for Christ's sake God is **gracious** to us.
AP : 04 :238(141) [0187] propitiator, the Father is **gracious** to us and that the
AP : 04 :285(150) [0201] we could never be sure that we have a **gracious** God.
AP : 04 :292(152) [0203] and believes that he has a **gracious** God for Christ's sake.
AP : 04 :293(152) [0203] faith that for Christ's sake we have a **gracious** God.
AP : 04 :301(153) [0205] believe that they have a **gracious** God because they love
AP : 04 :301(153) [0205] will have to doubt whether they have a **gracious** God.
AP : 04 :345(160) [0217] to believe that we have a **gracious** God because of Christ.
AP : 12 :031(186) [0259] And in Ps. 6:2, 3, "Be **gracious** to me, O Lord, for I am
AP : 12 :080(194) [0275] that freely for Christ's sake they have a **gracious** Father.
AP : 15 :006(215) [0317] faith that they have a **gracious** God not because of works
AP : 15 :009(216) [0317] mediator; he wants to be **gracious** to us through him, not
AP : 15 :009(216) [0317] God is reconciled and **gracious** because of the traditions
AP : 15 :011(216) [0317] by faith that we have a **gracious** God for Christ's sake, it
AP : 15 :012(216) [0317] promising that he will be **gracious** to us for Christ's sake,
AP : 21 :020(232) [0349] sake and that by his merits we have a **gracious** Father.
AP : 21 :042(235) [0355] would ask that our most **gracious** emperor take steps to
AP : 21 :044(235) [0357] Therefore, **gracious** Emperor Charles, for the sake of the
AP : 23 :036(244) [0373] when we believe that for his sake God is **gracious** to us.
AP : 24 :072(262) [0409] to be remembered; the Lord is **gracious** and merciful.
S1 : PR :014(291) [0459] keep God from being **gracious** to us, for we do not repent
S2 : 04 :002(298) [0471] address him as "most **gracious** lord," as if he were a king
S2 : 04 :016(301) [0475] where we responded to a **gracious** summons and were
S2 : 04 :016(301) [0477] feet or say, "You are my **gracious** lord," but we ought
S3 : 13 :003(315) [0499] to say, all is well if we boast that we have a **gracious** God.
SC : PR :024(341) [0539] great need and God's **gracious** help belong to the devil.
SC : 03 :010(347) [0547] To be sure, the good and **gracious** will of God is done
SC : 03 :011(347) [0547] This is his good and **gracious** will.
SC : 03 :020(348) [0549] us a blessed end and **graciously** take us from this world
SC : 04 :010(349) [0551] it is a Baptism, that is, a **gracious** water of life and a
SC : 07 :005(353) [0559] Christ, that Thou hast this day **graciously** protected me.
SC : 07 :005(353) [0559] **Graciously** protect me during the coming night.
LC : 01 :032(369) [0589] again, how kind and **gracious** he is to those who trust and
LC : 01 :040(370) [0591] comes to us with so **gracious** an offer, so cordial an
LC : 01 :041(370) [0591] ask or desire than God's **gracious** promise that he will be
LC : 01 :148(385) [0623] joyful conscience and a **gracious** God who will reward
LC : 01 :252(399) [0653] Moreover, he **graciously** lavishes upon them a wonderful
LC : 01 :327(410) [0675] an angry judge; otherwise, you have a **gracious** father.
LC : 03 :092(432) [0725] deserve, but to deal **graciously** with us, forgive as he has
LC : 04 :027(440) [0739] blessed, fruitful, and **gracious** water, for through the
LC : 05 :035(450) [0761] nothing, for he lets this **gracious** blessing be offered to him
LC : 05 :064(454) [0769] Here stand the **gracious** and lovely words, "This is my
LC : 05 :066(454) [0769] us, to which he most **graciously** invites us in other places,
EP : 03 :009(474) [0795] the Word of the holy Gospel, they have a **gracious** God.
EP : 11 :013(496) [0835] God assures us of this **gracious** election not only in mere
EP : 11 :016(497) [0837] the doctrine of the **gracious** election of God to eternal life
SD : 01 :003(509) [0861] precious merits, and the Holy Spirit's **gracious** activity.
SD : 02 :022(525) [0889] pure grace through the **gracious** and efficacious working
SD : 02 :054(531) [0903] the holy Gospel of the **gracious** forgiveness of sins in
SD : 02 :066(534) [0907] God should withdraw his **gracious** hand man could not
SD : 03 :023(543) [0923] God consists solely in the **gracious** reckoning of Christ's
SD : 03 :030(544) [0925] God consists solely in a **gracious** reconciliation or the
SD : 03 :033(545) [0927] God, whereby he had a **gracious** God and was pleasing
SD : 03 :048(548) [0933] or parts, namely, the **gracious** forgiveness of sins and, as a
SD : 03 :054(549) [0935] of sins and the **gracious** acceptance of poor sinners on
SD : 04 :012(553) [0941] of God and to his glory, who has been so **gracious** to him.
SD : 05 :005(559) [0953] and urged not only the **gracious** promises of the
SD : 07 :062(581) [0995] assurance that we have a **gracious** God and eternal
SD : 11 :006(617) [1065] as though it were God's **gracious** will that it should
SD : 11 :008(617) [1065] the elect, but by God's **gracious** will and pleasure in
SD : 11 :018(619) [1069] he would justify and **graciously** accept into the adoption
SD : 11 :023(619) [1069] general, but he has also **graciously** considered and elected
SD : 11 :060(626) [1083] in fact, when he does **graciously** give us these we
SD : 11 :075(628) [1087] merit of Christ and the **gracious** will of the Father, who
SD : 11 :083(630) [1091] it had never been God's **gracious** will that such people
SD : 11 :090(631) [1093] salvation rests in the **gracious** election of God, which he
SD : 11 :091(631) [1093] concerning God's **gracious** election that sorrowing

Grade (1), Grades (2)
AL : 28 :030(085) [0087] foods, holy days, **grades** or orders of ministers, etc.
TR : 00 :063(331) [0523] distinction between the **grades** of bishop and presbyter
SD : 12 :029(635) [1101] he is in every way equal in **grade** and rank of essence to

Gradually (5)
AL : 27 :003(071) [0077] other observances were **gradually** added in addition to
AP : 12 :037(186) [0261] This faith **gradually** grows and throughout life it struggles
AP : 20 :015(229) [0343] chastity, and other fruits of the Spirit **gradually** increase.
TR : 00 :020(323) [0509] him and the custom **gradually** prevailed that the bishops
SD : 10 :003(611) [1053] the pure doctrine and **gradually** to insinuate their false

Grain (7)
SC : 09 :003(354) [0561] when it is treading out the **grain**,' and 'The laborer
LC : 01 :026(368) [0587] her infant, and he gives **grain** and all kinds of fruits from
LC : 01 :166(388) [0629] life or raise from the earth a single **grain** of wheat for us.
LC : 01 :242(397) [0649] blessing over them: "Your **grain** will spoil in the garner
LC : 02 :014(412) [0681] birds and fish, beasts, **grain** and all kinds of produce.
LC : 03 :072(430) [0719] For if God did not cause **grain** to grow and did not bless
LC : 03 :076(431) [0721] sound body; to cause the **grain** and fruits of the field to

Grammar (3)
AP : 04 :072(117) [0141] Thus one can say that **grammar** produces the teachers of
AP : 12 :106(197) [0283] is a neat one, worthy of these men who despise **grammar**.
AP : 12 :163(208) [0303] for their neglect of **grammar** when they explain "judge" as

Grand (1), Grandmother (1)
LC : 06 :015(459) [0000] This is the surpassingly **grand** and noble thing that makes
SD : 08 :041(599) [1029] Dame Reason, the **grandmother** of the *alloeosis*, would

Grant (46), Granted (29), Granting (4), Grants (10)
AG : 27 :026(075) [0079] If dispensations were **granted** for the maintenance of
AG : 27 :026(075) [0079] should dispensations be **granted** for necessities of men's
AL : 20 :008(042) [0053] (for everybody must **grant** that there has been profound
AL : 27 :024(074) [0079] pontiffs would not have **granted** dispensations, for it is
AL : 27 :025(074) [0079] we read that they often **granted** dispensation from vows.
AL : 28 :019(083) [0087] but by human right **granted** by kings and emperors for
AP : 04 :011(108) [0123] not of compulsion—God **grants** grace to those who do
AP : 04 :075(117) [0143] Even our opponents will **grant**, we suppose, that the
AP : 04 :087(120) [0147] that the Lord saw fit to **grant** us, we conclude that a man
AP : 04 :110(123) [0153] sure that the forgiveness of sins has been **granted** to us.
AP : 04 :147(127) [0163] may ask: Since we also **grant** that love is the work of the
AP : 04 :222(137) [0181] This we **grant**.
AP : 04 :238(141) [0187] to us and that the merits of Christ are **granted** to us.
AP : 04 :260(145) [0193] the forgiveness of sins is **granted** to us if we believe that
AP : 04 :268(147) [0197] then they will have to **grant** that first come forgiveness of
AP : 04 :278(149) [0199] We also **grant** that alms merit many divine blessings,
AP : 04 :354(161) [0217] Our opponents **grant** that the justified are children of God
AP : 04 :362(162) [0219] If our opponents will **grant** that we are accounted
AP : 04 :362(162) [0219] We **grant** that eternal life is a reward because it is
AP : 04 :372(164) [0221] when eternal life is **granted** to works, it is granted to the
AP : 04 :372(164) [0221] life is granted to works, it is **granted** to the justified.
AP : 04 :373(164) [0221] and for this reason eternal life is **granted** to righteousness.
AP : 04 :375(164) [0223] only our opponents would **grant** that the fruits please

Continued ▶

A P : 0 4 :384(166) [0225] that our opponents will **grant** that the mere act of
A P : 0 7 :028(173) [0237] Nevertheless, we **grant** that the many hypocrites and evil
A P : 1 1 :002(180) [0249] the forgiveness of sins is **granted** to us freely for Christ's
A P : 1 2 :012(184) [0255] that the sacrament **grants** grace *ex opere operato,*
A P : 1 2 :029(186) [0259] for Christ's sake, to **grant** the Holy Spirit and eternal life,
A P : 1 2 :036(186) [0261] grasps the forgiveness of sins **granted** for Christ's sake.
A P : 1 2 :036(186) [0261] grasps the forgiveness of sins **granted** for Christ's sake.
A P : 1 2 :045(188) [0263] of sins has been **granted** us; this is revealed in the Gospel.
A P : 1 2 :053(189) [0265] Gospel, that is, the promise of grace **granted** in Christ.
A P : 1 2 :063(191) [0269] our opponents will **grant** that the forgiveness of sins is
A P : 1 2 :066(191) [0271] nor to the church do we **grant** the authority to issue
A P : 1 2 :074(192) [0273] our hearts and the Holy Spirit **grants** them peace.
A P : 1 2 :079(193) [0275] of the forgiveness of sins **granted** for Christ's sake, and he
A P : 1 2 :080(194) [0275] of the forgiveness of sins **granted** for Christ's sake, and to
A P : 1 2 :148(205) [0299] We **grant** that revenge or punishment is necessary for
A P : 1 2 :177(210) [0307] their judgment when they **grant** that in the hour of death
A P : 1 7 :001(224) [0335] and raise all the dead, **granting** eternal life and eternal
A P : 2 1 :008(230) [0345] Besides, we **grant** that the angels pray for us.
A P : 2 1 :009(230) [0345] We also **grant** that the saints in heaven pray for the
A P : 2 1 :027(232) [0349] **Granted** that blessed Mary prays for the church, does she
A P : 2 1 :032(233) [0351] Thus Anne **grants** riches, Sebastian wards off pestilence,
A P : 2 1 :032(233) [0351] thought that Juno **granted** riches, Febris warded off
A P : 2 2 :006(237) [0359] to deny one part, and they refuse to **grant** both kinds.
A P : 2 2 :015(238) [0361] Even if we **grant** the freedom to use one kind or both,
A P : 2 4 :011(251) [0387] Lord's Supper does not **grant** grace *ex opere operato* and
A P : 2 4 :078(263) [0411] is called a sacrifice that it **grants** grace *ex opere operato*
A P : 2 7 :035(275) [0431] which the forgiveness of sins and eternal life are **granted**.
A P : 2 8 :012(283) [0447] we have said what power the Gospel **grants** to bishops.
S 2 : 0 2 :024(296) [0469] indulgences, which are **granted** to the living and the dead
S 3 : 0 1 :008(302) [0477] does what he can, God is certain to **grant** him his grace.
S 3 : 0 3 :010(305) [0481] that God will assuredly **grant** his grace to the man who
S 3 : 0 3 :024(307) [0485] bishops so that one could **grant** them for a hundred
T R : 0 0 :009(321) [0505] Wherefore he **granted** to none a prerogative or lordship
T R : 0 0 :055(329) [0521] contrary to his will and **grants** nobody the right to
S C : P R :027(341) [0539] The Father of all grace **grant** it!
S C : 0 2 :006(345) [0545] and all the dead and will **grant** eternal life to me and to
S C : 0 3 :016(347) [0549] pray that God may **grant** us all things by his grace.
S C : 0 3 :020(348) [0549] of death comes, he may **grant** us a blessed end and
S C : 0 4 :006(349) [0551] death and the devil, and **grants** eternal salvation to all
L C : P R :020(361) [0573] To this end may God **grant** his grace!
L C : 0 1 :156(386) [0625] people, or else God would not **grant** us so many blessings!
L C : 0 1 :216(394) [0641] Even **granting** that the monastic life is godly, yet it is not
L C : 0 2 :054(417) [0693] of sins, which is **granted** through the holy sacraments and
L C : 0 2 :058(418) [0693] through the Word, daily **granting** forgiveness until we
L C : 0 2 :062(419) [0695] people, nor has he completed the **granting** of forgiveness.
L C : 0 3 :020(423) [0703] assuredly be heard and **granted**, so that we may not
L C : 0 3 :036(425) [0707] say, "Heavenly Father, **grant** that thy name alone may be
L C : 0 3 :067(429) [0717] from coming; and **grant** that whatever we must suffer on
L C : 0 3 :076(431) [0721] prosper and succeed; to **grant** us faithful neighbors and
L C : 0 3 :077(431) [0721] and all our enemies; to **grant** their subjects and the people
L C : 0 3 :092(432) [0725] he has promised, and thus **grant** us a happy and cheerful
L C : 0 3 :119(436) [0731] doubt that our prayer is surely heard and will be **granted**.
L C : 0 3 :120(436) [0731] does not lie since he has promised to **grant** his requests.
L C : 0 4 :057(444) [0747] that he may believe, and we pray God to **grant** him faith.
L C : 0 5 :049(452) [0765] you see that we are not **granted** liberty to despise the
L C : 0 5 :084(456) [0773] do not see, though God **grants** his grace that you may
E P : 1 1 :022(497) [0837] of our Lord Jesus Christ **grant** us the grace of his Holy
S D : 0 1 :035(514) [0869] Thou has **granted** me life and steadfast love; and thy care
S D : 0 2 :026(526) [0891] faith, for "It has been **granted** to you by God that you
S D : 0 2 :032(527) [0893] Therefore, though we **grant** that it lies within our power
S D : 0 2 :044(529) [0897] sacred and holy memory, **grants** our free will no power of
S D : 0 3 :029(544) [0925] "We certainly **grant** that we must teach about love and
S D : 0 7 :014(572) [0977] use of the sacrament, they **grant** that through
S D : 1 1 :048(624) [1079] us in all our necessities, **grant** us patience, give us
S D : 1 1 :084(630) [1091] God did not want to **grant** him salvation or because it
S D : 1 1 :086(631) [1091] God had not wanted to **grant** Pharaoh or any other

Grasp (21), Grasped (7), Grasps (7)
A G : 2 7 :017(073) [0077] order that one may better **grasp** and understand what our
A P : 0 2 :018(103) [0111] in man that would **grasp** God and reflect him, that is,
A P : 0 4 :063(115) [0139] and clear, the faithful can **grasp** it, and it has the
A P : 0 4 :067(116) [0139] cannot deal with God or **grasp** him except through the
A P : 0 4 :086(119) [0147] on account of Christ, if they **grasp** this mercy by faith.
A P : 0 4 :129(125) [0157] love God until we have **grasped** his mercy by faith.
A P : 0 4 :153(127) [0163] But faith is that which **grasps** God's free mercy because
A P : 0 4 :174(131) [0171] For mercy can be **grasped** only by faith, as we have said
A P : 0 4 :227(139) [0183] a desire to accept and **grasp** what is offered in the
A P : 0 4 :293(152) [0203] with the Gospel, and any sound mind can **grasp** them.
A P : 0 4 :383(165) [0225] not as the power that **grasps** the promise of grace and
A P : 0 4 :386(166) [0225] by a faith that penitently **grasps** the promise of grace,
A P : 1 2 :005(183) [0253] The people could **grasp** neither the sum of the matter nor
A P : 1 2 :012(184) [0257] not mention faith, which **grasps** the absolution and
A P : 1 2 :036(186) [0261] it lacked the faith that **grasps** the forgiveness of sins
A P : 1 2 :036(186) [0261] it had the faith that **grasps** the forgiveness of sins granted
A P : 1 8 :004(225) [0335] the works and things which reason by itself can **grasp**.
A P : 1 8 :004(225) [0335] things that the senses can **grasp**, it also retains a choice in
A P : 2 4 :045(258) [0401] and ideas and could not **grasp** the sum of Christian
L C : 0 1 :042(370) [0591] Accordingly, we must **grasp** these words, even in the face
L C : 0 1 :050(371) [0595] God, so you must learn to **grasp** simply the meaning of
L C : 0 2 :042(416) [0689] kindles hearts so that they **grasp** and accept it, cling to it,
L C : 0 4 :029(440) [0739] it to us so that we may **grasp** the treasure it contains?
L C : 0 4 :030(440) [0739] it can be perceived and **grasped** by the senses and thus
L C : 0 4 :035(441) [0741] demand faith, for without faith they could not be **grasped**.
L C : 0 4 :037(441) [0741] God gives us and faith **grasps**, just as the Lord Christ
L C : 0 4 :040(441) [0743] is lacking is that it should be **grasped** and held firmly.
L C : 0 4 :045(442) [0743] the Word is spoken so that the soul may **grasp** it.
L C : 0 5 :031(450) [0759] and how can they **grasp** and appropriate it, except by
L C : 0 5 :036(450) [0761] in the words, it can be **grasped** and appropriated only by
L C : 0 5 :037(451) [0761] the sacrament cannot be **grasped** and appropriated by the
L C : 0 6 :005(457) [0000] benefits us, and we **grasp** with uncommon ease whatever
S D : P R :006(502) [0847] because they failed to **grasp** their true meaning or because
S D : 0 2 :012(523) [0885] actually has it, does not **grasp**, take hold of, or
S D : 0 3 :038(546) [0929] which we receive, **grasp**, accept, apply to ourselves, and

Grass (3)
A P : 0 4 :329(158) [0211] Isa. 40:6, 7, "All flesh is **grass**, and all its beauty is like the
A P : 0 4 :329(158) [0211] The **grass** withers, the flower fades, when the breath of
A P : 2 3 :070(249) [0383] says (40:6), "All flesh is **grass**, and all its beauty is like the

Gratefully (1), Gratified (1), Gratify (1)
P R : P R :012(006) [0013] of us, we not only were **gratified** by it but we also
A P : 2 3 :030(243) [0371] that is, by faith which uses it **gratefully** as a gift of God.
L C : 0 1 :307(406) [0669] him suffer loss while you **gratify** your greed, even though

Gratis (3)
A P : 0 4 :339(159) [0215] does not denounce the promise that offers mercy **gratis**.
A P : 0 4 :366(163) [0221] promise of grace, receives justification and new life **gratis**.
A P : 0 4 :366(163) [0221] reward is offered and owed, not **gratis** but for our works.

Gratitude (8)
A P : 2 4 :019(252) [0389] thanks or show their **gratitude** for the forgiveness of sins
A P : 2 4 :074(263) [0411] a demonstration of its **gratitude**, and a witness of its high
S C : P R :027(341) [0539] with little reward or **gratitude** from the world.
L C : P R :003(358) [0567] might show honor and **gratitude** to the Gospel, through
L C : 0 1 :127(382) [0617] the world to show **gratitude** for the kindness and for all
L C : 0 2 :023(413) [0683] and kindled with **gratitude** to God and a desire to use all
L C : 0 6 :022(459) [0000] treasure to be accepted with all praise and **gratitude**.
E P : 0 4 :018(477) [0801] of their faith and their **gratitude** toward God, as it is to

Grave (10), Graves (2), Gravest (1)
A G : 0 0 :001(047) [0059] souls and consciences in **grave** peril before God by
A G : 2 3 :002(053) [0063] man, made this statement because of **grave** misgivings.
A G : 0 0 :002(095) [0095] the past there have been **grave** complaints about
A L : 0 0 :002(095) [0095] There have been **grave** complaints about indulgences,
A P : 1 2 :090(195) [0279] if we did not have **grave** and important reasons for
S 2 : 0 2 :028(297) [0469] to be molested in their **graves** and in heaven, for no one
L C : 0 1 :009(366) [0583] clings and cleaves to our nature all the way to the **grave**.
L C : 0 6 :001(457) [0000] to make confession on pain of the **gravest** mortal sin.
E P : 0 3 :009(474) [0793] down to their **graves**, they still have no reason to doubt
S D : 0 2 :047(530) [0901] hearts may fall into **grave** anxiety and doubt, and wonder
S D : 0 6 :018(567) [0967] to them down to the **grave**, the conflict between spirit and
S D : 0 7 :100(586) [1007] when he left the closed **grave** and came through locked
S D : 1 1 :074(628) [1087] they should fall into such **grave** temptation that they feel

Gray (1)
A G : 2 7 :050(079) [0083] not of mendicancy or wearing a black or **gray** cowl, etc.

Great (218), Greater (61), Greatest (45), Greatly (13), Greatness (3)
P R : P R :007(004) [0009] interpreting to the very **great** disadvantage of ourselves
P R : P R :008(005) [0009] Emperor Charles V in the **great** imperial assembly at
P R : P R :018(008) [0015] Emperor Charles V at the **great** imperial assembly in
P R : P R :022(012) [0021] of the persecutors on the **great** day of the Lord before the
A G : 2 0 :015(043) [0055] this teaching is held in **great** contempt among untried
A G : 2 0 :033(045) [0057] this, and instead fell into many **great** and open sins.
A G : 2 0 :038(046) [0057] Such **great** and genuine works cannot be done without
A G : 2 3 :003(051) [0061] to take this step by the **great** distress of their consciences,
A G : 2 3 :013(053) [0063] gave occasion for many **great** and evil vices and much
A G : 2 3 :016(054) [0063] weakness and to prevent and avoid **greater** offense.
A G : 2 3 :018(054) [0063] punished, as if it were a **great** crime, in spite of that fact
A G : 2 3 :026(055) [0065] all the canons show **great** leniency and fairness toward
A G : 0 1 :009(056) [0065] observed among us with **greater** devotion and more
A G : 0 1 :007(056) [0065] instructed often and with **great** diligence concerning the
A G : 2 5 :002(061) [0069] they may esteem absolution as a **great** and precious thing.
A G : 2 5 :004(062) [0069] We teach with **great** diligence about this command and
A G : 2 6 :002(064) [0071] they were observed and a **great** sin committed if they were
A G : 2 6 :004(064) [0071] of Christ as something **great** and precious and know that
A G : 2 8 :029(085) [0087] and to prevent discord and **great** disorder in their lands.
A G : 2 8 :033(086) [0087] of the church is indeed **great** because the church has
A L : 0 1 :001(027) [0043] Our churches teach with **great** unanimity that the decree
A L : 2 0 :015(043) [0055] that it offers the **greatest** consolation because the
A L : 2 0 :022(044) [0055] Hence there was very **great** need to treat of and to restore
A L : 2 3 :018(054) [0063] thing that nowhere is **greater** cruelty exercised than in
A L : 2 3 :020(055) [0063] heathen, have adorned marriage with the **greatest** praise.
A L : 2 4 :001(056) [0065] among us and is celebrated with the **greatest** reverence.
A L : 2 4 :007(056) [0065] of the sacrament and the **great** consolation it offers to
A L : 2 4 :017(057) [0067] **Great** dissensions have arisen concerning the Mass,
A L : 2 4 :040(061) [0069] and on account of the **great** and manifest abuses it would
A L : 2 5 :004(062) [0069] are reminded of the **great** consolation it brings to terrified
A L : 2 5 :006(062) [0069] doctrine of repentance and have treated it with **great** care.
A L : 2 5 :013(063) [0071] us on account of the **great** benefit of absolution and
A L : 2 6 :005(064) [0071] Paul therefore lays the **greatest** weight on this article and
A L : 2 6 :011(065) [0071] This error **greatly** tormented the consciences of devout
A L : 2 6 :012(065) [0071] place, traditions brought **great** dangers to consciences, for
A L : 2 6 :016(066) [0073] certain other theologians **greatly** lamented that they were
A L : 2 6 :019(067) [0073] There was **great** need to warn the churches of these errors
A L : 2 7 :032(076) [0079] Another canon, making a **greater** concession to human
A L : 2 7 :044(078) [0081] In fact, they invented **greater** absurdities when they
A L : 2 7 :049(079) [0083] at the same time to have **great** faith and to trust that for
A L : 2 8 :001(081) [0083] times there has been **great** controversy about the power
A L : 2 8 :002(081) [0083] From this confusion **great** wars and tumults have
A L : 2 8 :033(086) [0087] **Great**, they say, is the power of the church, for it
A P : P R :018(099) [0103] and thanked God for this **great** blessing, that on many
A P : 0 2 :019(103) [0111] And after saying a **great** deal about it, Ambrose says,
A P : 0 2 :049(106) [0119] history itself shows the **great** power of the devil's rule.
A P : 0 2 :051(107) [0119] reluctant to enter upon their arguments at **great** length.
A P : 0 4 :024(110) [0127] corrupt nature has no **greater** good than this, as Aristotle
A P : 0 4 :060(115) [0137] This is the **greatest** consolation in all afflictions, and our
A P : 0 4 :065(116) [0139] From such a **great** crowd of writers, let them produce one
A P : 0 4 :082(118) [0145] "Since then we have a **great** high priest,...let us then with
A P : 0 4 :135(125) [0159] shows us our uncleanness and the **greatness** of our sin.
A P : 0 4 :149(127) [0163] he thinks that his sin is **greater** and stronger than the
A P : 0 4 :154(128) [0163] Nothing **greater** could she ascribe to him.
A P : 0 4 :154(128) [0165] outward courtesies due a guest and a **great** and holy man.
A P : 0 4 :197(134) [0175] it takes place in the justified it merits other **great** rewards.
A P : 0 4 :212(136) [0179] the hope of finding some **great** work that they can set
A P : 0 4 :218(137) [0179] Here they celebrate a **great** victory.

Continued ▶

A P : 0 4 :219(137) [0181] his faith, be it ever so **great**, because he will not keep the
A P : 0 4 :222(138) [0181] is extinguished, no matter how **great** it may have been.
A P : 0 4 :225(138) [0183] Paul says (I Cor. 13:13), "The **greatest** of these is love."
A P : 0 4 :225(138) [0183] it follows that the **greatest** and the main virtue should
A P : 0 4 :226(138) [0183] indicates that love is the **greatest** because it has the most
A P : 0 4 :226(138) [0183] God and neighbor is the **greatest** virtue because the great
A P : 0 4 :226(138) [0183] greatest virtue because the **great** commandment is, "You
A P : 0 4 :226(138) [0183] The **greatest** virtue, they say, justifies.
A P : 0 4 :227(138) [0183] But as even the first and **greatest** law does not justify,
A P : 0 4 :227(138) [0183] not justify, neither does the **greatest** virtue of the law.
A P : 0 4 :229(139) [0183] Thus the **great** and learned scholastics proclaimed the
A P : 0 4 :241(141) [0187] as we often see the **greatest** tragedies come from the most
A P : 0 4 :275(148) [0199] signs of this exceedingly **great** promise, since a terrified
A P : 0 4 :276(148) [0199] glad to have signs and testimonies of this **great** promise.
A P : 0 4 :285(150) [0201] This offers the **greatest** consolation to faithful consciences
A P : 0 4 :288(151) [0203] but when men are in **great** peril they add other forms of
A P : 0 4 :300(153) [0205] Such **great** blessings our opponents take from the church
A P : 0 4 :303(154) [0205] does not come without a **great** battle in the human heart.
A P : 0 4 :310(155) [0207] and reborn. The **greatest** possible comfort comes from
A P : 0 4 :331(158) [0211] our righteousness, but on the ground of thy **great** mercy.
A P : 0 4 :345(160) [0217] This can be a **great** problem to the human mind.
A P : 0 4 :350(161) [0217] is not erased without a **great** conflict in which experience
A P : 0 4 :356(161) [0217] it is written, "Your reward is **great** in heaven."
A P : 0 4 :391(166) [0225] ought not seem so **great** as to end all argument, when
A P : 0 7 :009(169) [0229] it exists despite the **great** multitude of the wicked, and
A P : 0 7 :037(175) [0241] is not necessary to cite a **great** deal of evidence since it is
A P : 0 7 :040(176) [0241] transmit to posterity the memory of these **great** events.
A P : 1 1 :007(181) [0251] What **great** tortures for the most pious minds!
A P : 1 1 :009(182) [0253] The **greater** part deals with sins against human traditions,
A P : 1 2 :006(183) [0255] Good God, how **great** is the darkness!
A P : 1 2 :009(183) [0255] in those serious, true, and **great** terrors described in the
A P : 1 2 :010(184) [0255] Yet the issue at hand is a **great** one, the chief doctrine of
A P : 1 2 :068(192) [0271] side some theologians of **great** reputation, like Duns
A P : 1 2 :068(192) [0271] be right; for there is a **great** crowd of worthless
A P : 1 2 :069(192) [0271] be kept in mind that no **great** authority attaches to the
A P : 1 2 :098(197) [0281] men can easily judge the **great** importance of preserving
A P : 1 2 :124(201) [0289] men could have had **greater** confidence than in that of the
A P : 1 2 :126(201) [0289] predicted there would be the **greatest** danger for religion.
A P : 1 2 :144(205) [0297] of these there is a **great** variety, with one making a trip in
A P : 1 2 :150(206) [0299] that contrition can be so **great** as to make satisfaction
A P : 1 2 :174(210) [0307] murder and hatred, the **greatest** possible generosity to the
A P : 1 2 :178(211) [0309] have made up a **great** deal about the merit of attrition,
A P : 1 3 :018(213) [0313] notion is taught with **great** authority throughout the
A P : 1 5 :028(219) [0323] How the **great** Gerson suffers as he looks for the degrees
A P : 1 5 :031(219) [0323] that to put this burden on the church is a **great** sin.
A P : 1 5 :051(222) [0329] can be kept without sin or without **great** disadvantage.
A P : 1 5 :052(222) [0329] We believed that the **greatest** possible public harmony,
A P : 1 8 :003(225) [0335] notions which the schools teach with **great** authority!
A P : 1 8 :005(225) [0335] But so **great** is the power of concupiscence that men obey
A P : 2 1 :004(229) [0343] Since these are his **greatest** gifts, we should extol them
A P : 2 1 :023(232) [0349] books and sermons there are even **greater** absurdities.
A P : 2 1 :033(233) [0351] could be taught with **great** moderation, the precedent still
A P : 2 1 :035(234) [0353] strong of soul because they have to undergo **great** danger.
A P : 2 1 :036(234) [0353] The **great** things that the saints have done serve as
A P : 2 1 :036(234) [0353] helped kings in time of **great** danger, taught the Gospel,
A P : 2 2 :004(236) [0359] not be hard to collect a **great** multitude of testimonies.
A P : 2 2 :011(238) [0361] Look at the **great** effrontery of the man.
A P : 2 3 :002(239) [0363] history can one read of **greater** brazenness than that of
A P : 2 3 :032(243) [0373] of celibacy, what **greater** honor could he bestow than to
A P : 2 3 :035(244) [0373] There may be **greater** purity of heart in a married man
A P : 2 3 :044(245) [0375] is all too evident that the **great** crowd of lazy priests in
A P : 2 3 :071(249) [0383] own sake, but they have **greater** respect for the Word of
A P : 2 4 :014(251) [0387] The Confutation has a **great** deal to say about sacrifice,
A P : 2 4 :023(253) [0391] wrath of God when, amid **great** calamities, it seemed to
A P : 2 4 :031(255) [0395] to its setting my name is **great** among the nations, and in
A P : 2 4 :032(255) [0395] They say, first, that the name of the Lord will be **great**.
A P : 2 4 :032(255) [0395] the name of the Lord becomes **great** among the nations.
A P : 2 4 :032(255) [0395] of the Lord becomes **great**, like faith, prayer,
A P : 2 4 :033(256) [0395] by which the name of the Lord really becomes **great**.
A P : 2 4 :050(259) [0401] appearances, our church attendance is **greater** than theirs.
A P : 2 4 :076(263) [0411] it compares the **greatness** of God's blessings with the
A P : 2 4 :076(263) [0411] God's blessings with the **greatness** of our ills, our sin and
A P : 2 4 :094(267) [0417] There is also **great** variety among the Fathers.
A P : 2 4 :099(268) [0419] This is a **great** cause and a great issue, not inferior to the
A P : 2 4 :099(268) [0419] This is a great cause and a **great** issue, not inferior to the
A P : 2 4 :099(268) [0419] important issue with the **greatest** moderation, and now
A P : 2 7 :016(271) [0425] no class of men has **greater** license than the monks.
A P : 2 7 :046(277) [0435] Aristippus for throwing a **great** weight of gold into the
A P : 2 8 :003(281) [0445] They demand **greater** strictness in the observance of their
A P : 2 8 :018(284) [0449] This is the way many **great** and learned men in the church
S 1 : P R :013(291) [0459] and tomfoolery with albs, **great** tonsures, broad
S 1 : 0 1 :000(292) [0461] it is not necessary to treat them at **greater** length.
S 2 : 0 2 :001(293) [0463] must be regarded as the **greatest** and most horrible
S 2 : 0 2 :019(296) [0467] practices in order that **great** multitudes of people may
S 2 : 0 4 :011(300) [0475] Turks nor the Tartars, **great** as is their enmity against
S 3 : 0 3 :003(304) [0481] are and no matter how **great**, wise, mighty, and holy you
S 3 : 0 3 :019(306) [0483] his sins — an impossibility and the source of **great** torture.
S 3 : 0 7 :002(312) [0493] alone to judge which, how **great**, and how many our sins
S 3 : 0 9 :000(314) [0497] We consider the **greater** excommunication, as the pope
S 3 : 1 3 :003(315) [0499] we cannot boast of the **great** merit in our works if they
T R : 0 0 :008(320) [0505] with you; rather let the **greatest** among you become as
T R : 0 0 :015(322) [0509] bishop of Rome in the **greater** part of the world, whether
T R : 0 0 :016(323) [0509] and the churches in the **greater** part of the world never
T R : 0 0 :018(323) [0509] that you want, the world is **greater** than the city.
T R : 0 0 :034(325) [0513] church, and afterwards **great** disturbances to arise in
T R : 0 0 :037(326) [0515] that they have been **great** plagues in the church.
T R : 0 0 :040(327) [0517] such impiety with the **greatest** cruelty and puts to death
T R : 0 0 :049(328) [0519] To these errors, then, two **great** sins must be added.
T R : 0 0 :053(329) [0519] should also know how **great** a crime it is to support
T R : 0 0 :081(334) [0527] disputes are so **great** that they require special courts, but
T R : 0 0 :082(000) [0529] But although in so **great** a number of most learned men
S C : P R :018(340) [0537] Lay the **greatest** weight on those commandments or other
S C : P R :024(341) [0539] and acknowledge their **great** need and God's gracious help
S C : P R :027(341) [0539] It subjects us to **greater** burdens and labors, dangers and
S C : 0 3 :018(348) [0549] despair, and other **great** and shameful sins, but that,
S C : 0 4 :009(349) [0551] How can water produce such **great** effects?
S C : 0 5 :024(350) [0555] burdened by such or by **greater** sins, he should not
S C : 0 6 :007(352) [0557] bodily eating and drinking produce such **great** effects?
L C : P R :001(358) [0567] Some because of their **great** and lofty learning, others
L C : P R :009(359) [0569] and truly such learned and **great** doctors as they think.
L C : P R :009(359) [0569] bestows ever new and **greater** light and fervor, so that day
L C : P R :009(359) [0569] day we relish and appreciate the Catechism more **greatly**.
L C : P R :019(361) [0573] themselves with the **greatest** care and diligence against the
L C : 0 1 :010(366) [0583] too, if anyone boasts of **great** learning, wisdom, power,
L C : 0 1 :022(367) [0585] This is the **greatest** idolatry that has been practiced up to
L C : 0 1 :033(369) [0589] who think that it makes no **great** difference how they live.
L C : 0 1 :043(370) [0591] to scraping together **great** wealth and money, what have
L C : 0 1 :043(370) [0591] or, if they have amassed **great** treasures, that these have
L C : 0 1 :045(370) [0593] Saul was a **great** king, chosen by God, and an upright
L C : 0 1 :047(371) [0593] object; he makes no **greater** demand of us than a hearty
L C : 0 1 :054(372) [0595] The **greatest** abuse, however, occurs in spiritual matters,
L C : 0 1 :056(372) [0595] of the holy name as the **greatest** sin that can be committed
L C : 0 1 :056(372) [0595] itself a gross sin, but it is **greatly** aggravated when we
L C : 0 1 :060(372) [0597] Like a **great** deluge, it has flooded all lands.
L C : 0 1 :060(372) [0597] It is a **great** mercy that the earth still bears and sustains
L C : 0 1 :072(374) [0601] that often sudden, **great** calamity was averted and
L C : 0 1 :103(379) [0611] Among these the first and **greatest** is:
L C : 0 1 :106(379) [0611] For it is a much **greater** thing to honor than to love.
L C : 0 1 :107(379) [0611] to honor, we must truly regard as high and **great**.
L C : 0 1 :112(380) [0613] place, notice what a **great**, good, and holy work is here
L C : 0 1 :113(380) [0613] And because there is no **greater** or better teacher to be
L C : 0 1 :115(381) [0613] has, in the first place, the **great** comfort of being able
L C : 0 1 :116(381) [0615] and boast of their many **great**, laborious, and difficult
L C : 0 1 :116(381) [0615] a single work that is **greater** and nobler than obedience to
L C : 0 1 :117(381) [0615] sure that you regard it as **great** and precious, not on
L C : 0 1 :118(381) [0615] O how **great** a price all the Carthusian monks and nuns
L C : 0 1 :125(382) [0617] besides, that it is the **greatest** work that we can do, next to
L C : 0 1 :132(383) [0619] intended for our **greatest** welfare, to lead us to a quiet,
L C : 0 1 :139(384) [0621] he so highly exalts it, so **greatly** delights in it, so richly
L C : 0 1 :142(385) [0621] of the country) to the **great** shame of us would-be
L C : 0 1 :145(385) [0623] such as all who pass for the **greatest** saints do not have.
L C : 0 1 :184(390) [0633] house and estate or **greater** wealth and good fortune than
L C : 0 1 :197(391) [0637] It would too **greatly** undermine the "spiritual estate" and
L C : 0 1 :200(392) [0637] possession of his can we inflict a **greater** injury upon him.
L C : 0 1 :214(394) [0641] who under the guise of **great** sanctity avoid marriage and
L C : 0 1 :221(395) [0643] work — indeed, many and **great** works — which you can
L C : 0 1 :228(396) [0645] it is nothing but a vast, wide stable full of **great** thieves.
L C : 0 1 :229(396) [0645] chairs and are called **great** lords and honorable, good
L C : 0 1 :229(396) [0645] citizens, and yet with a **great** show of legality they rob and
L C : 0 1 :230(396) [0645] an attack against the **great**, powerful arch-thieves who
L C : 0 1 :231(396) [0647] eyes of God they are the **greatest** thieves, and that he will
L C : 0 1 :243(398) [0649] Though they gather a **great** hoard, they must suffer so
L C : 0 1 :266(401) [0657] There is a **great** difference between judging sin and having
L C : 0 1 :266(401) [0657] pass sentence on him, I fall into a **greater** sin than his.
L C : 0 1 :278(402) [0661] Then you have done a **great** and excellent work.
L C : 0 1 :287(403) [0663] we invest with the **greater** honor; and our unpresentable
L C : 0 1 :287(403) [0663] our unpresentable parts are treated with **greater** modesty."
L C : 0 1 :290(404) [0663] then, embraces a **great** multitude of good works which
L C : 0 1 :291(404) [0663] or in a man that can do **greater** good or greater harm, in
L C : 0 1 :291(404) [0663] can do greater good or **greater** harm, in spiritual or in
L C : 0 1 :300(405) [0667] to belong, as many **great** nobles, lords, and princes do
L C : 0 1 :302(405) [0667] city, county, or other **great** estate, he practices bribery,
L C : 0 1 :311(407) [0671] to God, no matter how **great** or precious it may be in the
L C : 0 1 :312(407) [0671] Let us see, now, how our **great** saints can boast of their
L C : 0 1 :312(407) [0671] spiritual orders and the **great**, difficult works which they
L C : 0 1 :314(407) [0671] Aided by **great** pomp, splendor, and magnificent
L C : 0 1 :330(410) [0677] watches over them with **great** earnestness, who vents his
L C : 0 1 :333(410) [0677] under threat of his **greatest** wrath and punishment, while
L C : 0 1 :333(411) [0677] all other teachings as the **greatest** treasure God has given
L C : 0 2 :013(412) [0681] and life, my members **great** and small, all the faculties of
L C : 0 2 :024(413) [0683] is an excellent knowledge, but an even **greater** treasure.
L C : 0 2 :060(418) [0695] However, this is not of **great** importance, as long as the
L C : 0 3 :010(421) [0699] as though it made no **great** difference if we do not pray,
L C : 0 3 :027(424) [0705] heart to stronger and **greater** desires and spread your
L C : 0 3 :031(424) [0707] has accomplished such **great** results in the past, parrying
L C : 0 3 :033(424) [0707] all to value prayer as a **great** and precious thing and may
L C : 0 3 :033(424) [0707] as Christ himself rejects and forbids **great** wordiness.
L C : 0 3 :034(425) [0707] beset us, each one so **great** that it should impel us to keep
L C : 0 3 :038(425) [0707] that we are under the **great** necessity of duly honoring his
L C : 0 3 :038(425) [0707] regarding it as the **greatest** treasure and most sacred thing
L C : 0 3 :047(426) [0709] See, then, what a **great** need there is for this kind of
L C : 0 3 :055(427) [0713] It would be far too **great** for any human heart to dare to
L C : 0 3 :056(427) [0713] that we ask many and **great** things of him; and on the
L C : 0 3 :057(427) [0713] and was prepared to give **great** and princely gifts, and the
L C : 0 3 :057(427) [0713] Just so, it is a **great** reproach and dishonor to God if we,
L C : 0 3 :060(428) [0715] But there is just as **great** need that we keep firm hold of
L C : 0 3 :074(430) [0719] Indeed, the **greatest** need of all is to pray for our civil
L C : 0 3 :088(432) [0723] Here again there is **great** need to call upon God and pray,
L C : 0 3 :094(433) [0725] Inasmuch as we sin **greatly** against God everyday and yet
L C : 0 3 :105(434) [0727] These are the **great**, grievous perils and temptations which
L C : 0 4 :007(437) [0733] It is of the **greatest** importance that we regard Baptism as
L C : 0 4 :009(437) [0733] used to consider it a **great** thing when the pope dispensed
L C : 0 4 :009(437) [0735] regard Baptism as much **greater** and more precious
L C : 0 4 :010(437) [0735] that it is of much **greater** value than the work of any man
L C : 0 4 :010(437) [0735] what work can man do that is **greater** than God's work?
L C : 0 4 :011(438) [0735] a Carthusian does many **great** and difficult works, and we
L C : 0 4 :011(438) [0735] works, and we all attach **greater** importance to our own
L C : 0 4 :016(438) [0735] and this is a treasure **greater** and nobler than heaven and
L C : 0 4 :032(440) [0739] place, having learned the **great** benefit and power of
L C : 0 4 :046(442) [0743] No **greater** jewel, therefore, can adorn our body and soul
L C : 0 4 :083(446) [0751] Thus we see what a **great** and excellent thing Baptism is,
L C : 0 5 :004(447) [0753] first learn what is of **greatest** importance, namely, God's
L C : 0 5 :022(449) [0757] because we receive there a **great** treasure, through and in
L C : 0 5 :028(449) [0759] themselves with their **great** learning and wisdom,
L C : 0 5 :030(449) [0759] Yet, however **great** the treasure may be in itself, it must
L C : 0 5 :039(451) [0761] of the sacrament, there is **great** need also of an

Continued ▶

LC : 0 5 :039(451) [0761] and entreaty that so **great** a treasure, which is daily
LC : 0 5 :056(453) [0767] unworthiness with this **great** and precious blessing, and it
LC : 0 5 :067(454) [0769] us to our highest and **greatest** good, we act so distantly
LC : 0 6 :002(457) [0000] Moreover, it so **greatly** burdened and tortured
LC : 0 6 :008(458) [0000] which have an even **greater** right to be called the
LC : 0 6 :022(459) [0000] and cherishing it as a **great** and wonderful treasure to be
LC : 0 6 :024(460) [0000] from this, but only a **greater** hostility to the command.
LC : 0 6 :028(460) [0000] be despised, especially when we consider our **great** need.
EP : RN :004(465) [0777] V at Augsburg during the **great** Diet in the year 1530,
EP : RN :005(465) [0777] Scripture discusses at **greater** length and which a
EP : 0 1 :002(466) [0779] and original sin is as **great** as the difference between
EP : 0 5 :002(478) [0801] is to be maintained with **great** diligence in the church so
EP : 0 5 :009(479) [0803] for the first time what **great** things God demands of us in
EP : 0 7 :010(483) [0811] those which Dr. Luther proposed in his ***Great** Confession.*
EP : 0 8 :035(491) [0825] has indeed been given **greater** power in heaven and on
EP : 0 8 :035(491) [0825] and on earth, that is, **greater** and more than all angels and
EP : 0 8 :035(491) [0825] God's omnipotence but **greater** than the power of other
EP : 1 1 :013(496) [0835] comfort ourselves in our **greatest** temptations and thus
SD : PR :003(501) [0847] Emperor Charles V at the **great** Diet of Augsburg in
SD : PR :004(502) [0847] the Church of God when **great** controversies broke out,
SD : PR :007(505) [0853] which we prepared in the **great** assembly of theologians
SD : 0 1 :012(510) [0863] and ability, although **greatly** weakened since the inherited
SD : 0 1 :014(511) [0863] inherited damage is so **great** and terrible that in baptized
SD : 0 1 :015(511) [0863] form, are explained in **greater** detail in the
SD : 0 1 :023(512) [0865] man's nature has been **greatly** weakened and corrupted
SD : 0 1 :038(515) [0871] and life, my members **great** and small, all the faculties of
SD : 0 1 :062(519) [0879] special seriousness and **great** zeal and impressed on
SD : 0 2 :014(523) [0885] passage is of very **great** comfort to all devout Christians
SD : 0 2 :014(523) [0885] to support them in their **great** weakness and to help them
SD : 0 2 :018(524) [0887] we have pointed out at **greater** length in the article on
SD : 0 2 :043(529) [0897] from Dr. Luther's ***Great** Confession Concerning the Holy*
SD : 0 2 :044(529) [0897] and carefully and in **great** detail presents and
SD : 0 2 :056(532) [0903] happens under cover of **great** weakness, we should be
SD : 0 2 :065(534) [0907] Holy Spirit, even though we still do so in **great** weakness.
SD : 0 2 :067(534) [0907] There is therefore a **great** difference between baptized
SD : 0 2 :067(534) [0907] to it and accept it, even though it be in **great** weakness.
SD : 0 2 :068(534) [0907] Again, there is not only a **great** difference between
SD : 0 2 :090(538) [0915] universities have been **greatly** misled by the doctrine of
SD : 0 4 :011(553) [0941] he chatters and jabbers a **great** deal about faith and good
SD : 0 4 :039(558) [0951] ought to avoid with the **greatest** diligence whatever is
SD : 0 5 :001(558) [0951] themselves in their **greatest** temptations against the
SD : 0 5 :002(558) [0951] of repentance, which rebukes the **greatest** sin, unbelief.
SD : 0 5 :010(560) [0955] heaven over all sinners and shows how **great** this wrath is.
SD : 0 6 :009(565) [0965] explains this at **greater** length in the summer portion of
SD : 0 7 :002(569) [0973] from the signs by as **great** an interval as the earth is
SD : 0 7 :020(572) [0979] confirms this position at **greater** length from the Word of
SD : 0 7 :029(574) [0981] protestation to his ***Great** Confession:* "I see that schisms
SD : 0 7 :031(574) [0983] of God I have learned to know a **great** deal about Satan.
SD : 0 7 :033(575) [0983] faith in this article with **great** fervor and wrote as follows:
SD : 0 7 :040(576) [0985] In both his ***Great** Confession* and especially in his *Last*
SD : 0 7 :040(576) [0985] Dr. Luther defended with **great** zeal and earnestness the
SD : 0 7 :044(577) [0987] selected his words with **great** deliberation and care in
SD : 0 7 :044(577) [0987] was to be observed with **great** reverence and obedience
SD : 0 7 :068(582) [0997] essential to explain with **great** diligence who the unworthy
SD : 0 7 :069(582) [0997] because of their many and **great** sins, who consider
SD : 0 7 :069(582) [0997] of Christ because of their **great** impurity, and who
SD : 0 7 :071(582) [0997] or certainty of faith, be it **greater** or smaller, but solely in
SD : 0 7 :091(585) [1005] *Still Stand Firm,* his ***Great*** and *Small Confessions*
SD : 0 8 :021(595) [1021] this thoroughly in his ***Great** Confession concerning the*
SD : 0 8 :030(597) [1025] This we shall discuss in **greater** detail below.
SD : 0 8 :033(597) [1027] of the holy Trinity, the **greatest** mystery in heaven and on
SD : 0 8 :033(597) [1027] union, as Paul says, "**Great** indeed is the mystery of our
SD : 0 8 :038(598) [1027] since Dr. Luther in his ***Great** Confession concerning the*
SD : 0 8 :051(600) [1033] properties, special, high, **great**, supernatural,
SD : 0 8 :075(606) [1043] Against this sect Gregory the **Great** also wrote.
SD : 0 8 :081(607) [1045] In the ***Great** Confession concerning the Holy Supper* he
SD : 0 8 :086(608) [1047] *Stand Firm* and in his ***Great** Confession concerning the*
SD : 1 0 :005(611) [1053] religion does not differ **greatly** from that of the papists,
SD : 1 0 :016(613) [1059] better for him to have a **great** millstone fastened around
SD : 1 1 :020(619) [1069] protect them in their **great** weakness against the devil, the
SD : 1 1 :053(625) [1081] we take much **greater** delight in concerning ourselves with
SD : 1 1 :064(626) [1083] The **great** apostle Paul shows us that we cannot and
SD : 1 1 :075(628) [1087] Would not that land be **greatly** polluted?
SD : 1 1 :078(629) [1089] and therefore receive the **greater** damnation is not that
SD : 1 2 :010(634) [1097] this piety rests for the **greater** part on their own peculiar
SD : 1 2 :026(635) [1099] only possesses more and **greater** gifts and glory than

Greed (8), Greedy (2)
AP : 2 7 :004(269) [0421] hypocrisy, ambition, and **greed** there is in the
AP : 2 7 :046(277) [0435] but in the absence of **greed** and of trust in riches.
SC : 0 8 :008(353) [0559] **Greed** and anxiety about food prevent such satisfaction.)
LC : 0 1 :096(378) [0607] like those who in their **greed** or frivolity neglect to hear
LC : 0 1 :307(406) [0669] while you gratify your **greed**, even though in the eyes of
LC : 0 2 :021(413) [0683] for its own pride and **greed**, pleasure and enjoyment, and
LC : 0 3 :102(434) [0727] and drunkenness, **greed** and deceit, into acts of fraud and
LC : 0 4 :066(445) [0749] envious, unchaste, **greedy**, lazy, proud, yes, and
LC : 0 4 :067(445) [0749] and the more free from **greed**, hatred, envy, and pride.
LC : 0 4 :070(445) [0749] a man was proud and **greedy**, this year he is much more

Greek (12)
AP : 1 0 :002(179) [0247] of Christ, but that the **Greek** Church has taken and still
AP : 2 2 :004(236) [0359] In the **Greek** churches this practice still remains, and once
AP : 2 4 :006(250) [0385] Even today, **Greek** parishes have no private Masses but
AP : 2 4 :083(264) [0413] anyone who reads the **Greek** authors can find examples
AP : 2 4 :088(265) [0413] The **Greek** canon also says much about an offering; but it
AP : 2 4 :093(267) [0417] The **Greek** canon does not apply the offering as a
TR : 0 0 :015(322) [0509] of the world, whether in **Greek** or Latin churches, it is
LC : SP :001(362) [0575] times it has been called in **Greek**, a "catechism" — that is,
LC : 0 2 :048(416) [0691] is not of German but of **Greek** origin, like the word
LC : 0 3 :113(435) [0729] In the **Greek** this petition reads, "Deliver or keep us from
SD : 0 2 :012(523) [0885] not receive (or, as the **Greek** word actually has it, does not
SD : 0 7 :011(571) [0975] the Roman but also the **Greek** Church has taught the

Greeks (5)
AP : 2 4 :023(253) [0391] The **Greeks** called them either "refuse" or "offscouring."
AP : 2 4 :079(263) [0411] The **Greeks** call the Mass "liturgy," and this, they say,
AP : 2 4 :081(264) [0411] To the **Greeks** it meant "public duties," like the taxes
AP : 2 4 :093(267) [0417] it seems that the **Greeks** offer it only as a thanksgiving
S2 : 0 4 :004(299) [0473] that the churches of the **Greeks** and of many other

Green (1)
LC : 0 1 :238(397) [0647] will hang them not on a **green** gallows but on a dry one.

Greeting (1), Greetings (1)
PR : PR :001(003) [0007] friendship, gracious **greeting**, and favorably inclined will,
AP : PR :000(098) [0099] **Greetings** from Philip Melanchthon to the reader.

Gregory (11)
AL : 2 4 :035(060) [0067] for before the time of **Gregory** the ancients do not mention
AL : 2 6 :044(070) [0075] unity in faith," and Pope **Gregory** indicates in Dist. 12
AP : 1 2 :161(208) [0303] This is how **Gregory** interprets the punishment of David
AP : 1 2 :169(209) [0305] Thus **Gregory** says about restitution that penitence is false
AP : 2 1 :003(229) [0343] of the ancient Fathers before **Gregory** mention invocation
AP : 2 4 :006(250) [0385] of the church before **Gregory** make no mention of private
AP : 2 4 :094(267) [0417] support at most from **Gregory** and the more recent
TR : 0 0 :019(323) [0509] patriarch of Alexandria, **Gregory** objected to having
EP : 0 7 :015(483) [0813] Cyprian, Leo I, **Gregory**, Ambrose, Augustine.
SD : 0 8 :022(595) [1023] Book IX; Basil and **Gregory** of Nyssa, in Theodoret; John
SD : 0 8 :075(606) [1043] Against this sect **Gregory** the Great also wrote.

Grief (6)
AP : 1 2 :149(206) [0299] unspeakable power of the **grief** that comes over even the
S1 : PR :010(290) [0457] everywhere that our hearts would break with **grief**.
LC : 0 1 :042(370) [0591] and not mammon suffer **grief** and want and are opposed
LC : 0 1 :137(384) [0619] the misfortune and **grief** that we behold, for it seldom
LC : 0 1 :149(385) [0623] then take shame, misery, and **grief** for your reward.
LC : 0 3 :065(429) [0715] inflicting every possible misfortune and **grief** upon us.

Grieve (5), Grieved (1), Grieves (1)
AL : 2 6 :011(065) [0071] of devout people who **grieved** that they were bound to an
S3 : 0 3 :018(306) [0483] involved was obliged to **grieve**, but he would rather have
LC : 0 3 :066(429) [0717] Now, this **grieves** our flesh and the old Adam, for it
SD : 0 2 :069(534) [0907] in themselves and thus **grieve** the Holy Spirit within them
SD : 0 2 :083(537) [0913] do not receive the Holy Spirit but **grieve** and lose him.
SD : 1 1 :042(623) [1077] the holy commandment, **grieve** and embitter the Holy
SD : 1 1 :059(626) [1083] God's Word and often sorely **grieve** the Holy Spirit.

Grievous (4), Grievously (3)
AG : 2 6 :012(065) [0071] have turned out to be a **grievous** burden to consciences,
AL : 2 4 :010(057) [0065] has been open and very **grievous** complaint by all good
LC : 0 1 :052(371) [0595] name cannot be more **grievously** abused than for
LC : 0 3 :105(434) [0727] These are the great, **grievous** perils and temptations which
SD : 0 2 :072(535) [0909] in considering what a **grievous** sin it is to hinder and
SD : 0 2 :077(536) [0911] which is good, but only **grievously** wounded and
SD : 0 7 :060(580) [0993] eating and drinking sin **grievously** against the body and

Grim (2)
LC : 0 1 :135(383) [0619] you will not obey him, then obey the **grim** reaper, Death!
LC : 0 1 :149(385) [0623] godliness, we deliver to the hangman and the **grim** reaper.

Groan (1), Groanings (1)
AP : 1 2 :031(186) [0259] spent and crushed; I **groan** because of the tumult of my
SD : 1 1 :031(621) [1073] for them "with inexpressible **groanings**" (Rom. 8:16-26).

Grocery (1)
LC : 0 1 :224(395) [0643] at the market, in a **grocery** shop, butcher stall, wine- and

Gropes (1)
S3 : 0 3 :018(306) [0483] we see how blind reason **gropes** about in matters which

Groschen (1)
LC : 0 1 :316(408) [0671] I haven't a single **groschen** to pay, but I promise to pay

Gross (4), Grosser (1), Grossly (4)
AP : 0 2 :049(106) [0119] In others, even **grosser** vices appear.
S3 : 0 7 :001(311) [0493] loose sins, not only the **gross** and manifest sins but also
LC : 0 1 :056(372) [0595] and deceive is in itself a **gross** sin, but it is greatly
LC : 0 1 :081(375) [0603] this commandment too narrowly and **grossly** misused it.
LC : 0 1 :096(378) [0607] not only by those who **grossly** misuse and desecrate the
LC : 0 3 :021(423) [0703] that he angers God, **grossly** dishonoring him and accusing
LC : 0 3 :042(425) [0709] Likewise, when men **grossly** misuse the divine name as a
LC : 0 4 :019(439) [0737] not according to the **gross**, external mask (as we see the
SD : 0 7 :105(588) [1009] conception of a **gross**, carnal presence which the

Ground (16), Grounded (4), Grounds (7)
PR : PR :024(013) [0021] must be thoroughly **grounded** in God's Word so that pure
AG : 0 0 :001(047) [0059] Since this teaching is **grounded** clearly on the Holy
AG : 0 0 :002(048) [0059] we hope to offer firm **grounds** and reasons why we have
AL : 2 7 :031(075) [0079] the age of fifteen on the **ground** that before that age a
AP : 0 4 :331(158) [0211] before thee on the **ground** of our righteousness, but on
AP : 0 4 :331(158) [0211] our righteousness, but on the **ground** of thy great mercy.
AP : 0 4 :337(159) [0215] before thee on the **ground** of our righteousness," etc.
AP : 0 4 :338(159) [0215] On these **grounds** we are not bothered by the argument,
AP : 1 5 :003(215) [0315] opponents to defend human traditions on other **grounds**.
AP : 1 6 :006(223) [0331] the Christians on the **grounds** that their Gospel would
TR : 0 0 :005(320) [0503] In order that the **ground** of this our assertion may be
LC : 0 4 :030(440) [0739] and bound on the **ground** that the object is something
EP : 0 4 :005(476) [0797] controversy from the **ground** up and to resolve it, this is
EP : 0 7 :010(483) [0811] 5. The **grounds** on which we stand in this controversy
EP : 0 7 :011(483) [0811] "The first **ground** is this article of our Christian faith:
EP : 0 7 :012(483) [0811] "The second **ground** is: "God's right hand is everywhere.
EP : 0 7 :013(483) [0811] "The third **ground** is that God's Word is not false nor
EP : 0 7 :014(483) [0811] "The fourth **ground** is that God has and knows various
EP : 1 2 :019(499) [0841] of faith is sufficient **ground** for married people to divorce
SD : PR :005(504) [0851] the Word of God and solidly and well **grounded** therein.

Continued ▶

SD : PR :007(505) [0853] and in addition the **grounds** and reasons are set forth at
SD : 0 7 :046(577) [0987] certainly had sufficient **ground** for a disputation when he
SD : 0 7 :093(586) [1005] following words): "My **grounds**, on which I rest in this
SD : 0 8 :025(596) [1023] struck his enemies to the **ground**, and again in death,
SD : 1 1 :004(617) [1063] of them will fall to the **ground** without your Father's will"
SD : 1 1 :093(632) [1093] permanently and well **grounded** in God's revealed will, we
SD : 1 2 :024(634) [1099] in faith is sufficient **ground** for married people to divorce

Group (5)
AP : 1 6 :013(224) [0333] so that those outside our **group** may understand that our
S3 : 0 3 :032(308) [0487] of you in the former **group** are false penitents, and those
LC : 0 2 :048(416) [0691] folk understand not a **group** of people but a consecrated
LC : 0 2 :048(416) [0691] the single reason that the **group** of people assembles
SD : 1 1 :058(625) [1081] In the case of the one **group** we are to see God's

Groves (1)
AP : 2 4 :097(268) [0417] worship of Baal; in Judah they even sacrificed in **groves**.

Grow (24), Growing (5), Grown (2), Grows (4), Growth (3), Grew (3)
AG : 2 3 :014(053) [0063] prophesy, the world is **growing** worse and men are
AG : 2 4 :023(058) [0067] Out of this **grew** countless multiplication of Masses, by
AL : 2 3 :014(053) [0063] as the world is **growing** old and man's nature is becoming
AP : 0 4 :142(126) [0161] This faith ought to **grow** and be strengthened in these
AP : 0 4 :201(134) [0175] he might be reminded and **grow** in faith, and through his
AP : 0 4 :241(141) [0187] Dissensions, it says, **grow** because of hatred, as we often
AP : 0 4 :309(155) [0207] promise of God, but he **grew** strong in his faith as he gave
AP : 0 4 :350(160) [0217] It ought to **grow** and become firmer amid good works as
AP : 0 4 :353(161) [0217] in penitence and ought to **grow** continually in penitence.
AP : 0 4 :353(161) [0217] if penitence and faith amid penitence **grow** together.
AP : 1 2 :037(186) [0261] This faith gradually **grows** and throughout life it struggles
AP : 2 3 :053(246) [0379] Nature is **growing** older and progressively weaker, so that
AP : 2 7 :027(273) [0429] perfection means to **grow** in the fear of God, in trust in
AP : 2 7 :037(275) [0433] seek perfection, that is, **growth** in the fear of God, in
TR : 0 0 :012(322) [0507] of the Roman bishop **grew** out of a decision of a council
LC : 0 1 :075(375) [0601] bear fruit, and men may **grow** up of whom an entire land
LC : 0 1 :134(383) [0619] life means not merely to **grow** old but to have everything
LC : 0 1 :218(394) [0643] and, when they are **grown**, will be married honorably in
LC : 0 1 :243(397) [0649] scratch day and night and yet **grow** not a penny richer!
LC : 0 2 :053(417) [0693] causing it daily to **grow** and become strong in the faith
LC : 0 2 :057(418) [0693] has begun and is **growing** daily, we await the time when
LC : 0 2 :070(420) [0697] and thus advance and **grow** richer in understanding.
LC : 0 3 :052(427) [0711] may remain faithful and **grow** daily in it and in order that
LC : 0 3 :053(427) [0713] it may come by daily **growth** here and in eternal life
LC : 0 3 :072(430) [0719] God did not cause grain to **grow** and did not bless and
LC : 0 3 :076(431) [0721] and fruits of the field to **grow** and yield richly; to help us
LC : 0 4 :068(445) [0749] free rein and continually **grows** stronger, Baptism is not
LC : 0 4 :069(445) [0749] are outside of Christ can only **grow** worse day by day.
LC : 0 4 :070(445) [0749] Vice thus **grows** and increases in him from his youth up.
LC : 0 4 :070(445) [0749] vice, becomes vicious and unchaste as he **grows**.
LC : 0 4 :076(446) [0751] old man so that the new may come forth and **grow** strong.
LC : 0 4 :084(446) [0753] be suppressing the old man and **growing** up in the new.
LC : 0 5 :023(449) [0757] the world that we often **grow** weary and faint, at times
LC : 0 5 :024(449) [0759] not weaken in the struggle but **grow** continually stronger.
LC : 0 5 :054(453) [0765] be warmed and kindled, and it will not **grow** entirely cold.
LC : 0 5 :067(454) [0769] it so long that we **grow** quite cold and callous and lose all
LC : 0 5 :085(456) [0773] not only for us who are **grown** and advanced in years,
EP : 0 2 :006(470) [0787] and watering are in vain unless he "gives the **growth**."
SD : 0 2 :037(528) [0895] sanctification so that we **grow** daily and become strong in
SD : 0 2 :039(528) [0895] do good deeds and **grow** in sanctification), nevertheless,
SD : 0 7 :076(583) [0999] nature and make things **grow** and multiply, so this word

Growl (1), Growling (1)
LC : 0 3 :025(423) [0705] priests, who howl and **growl** frightfully day and night;
LC : 0 3 :033(424) [0707] useless howling and **growling**, as Christ himself rejects

Grubenhagen (1)
PR : PR :027(014) [0025] Wolf, duke of Brunswick [-**Grubenhagen**] and Lueneburg.

Grudge (1)
LC : 0 1 :160(387) [0627] out of the country and **grudge** them as much as a piece of

Grumble (2), Grumbled (1)
SC : 0 5 :022(350) [0553] I have **grumbled** and sworn at my mistress, etc.
LC : 0 1 :128(382) [0617] comes do we rage and **grumble** impatiently and forget all
LC : 0 1 :155(386) [0625] our misfortune, and we **grumble** and complain of

Guaranteed (5)
AP : 0 4 :050(114) [0135] on faith, in order that the promise may be **guaranteed**."
AP : 0 4 :084(119) [0145] rest on grace and be **guaranteed**," as though he were to
AP : 1 2 :081(194) [0275] rest on grace and be **guaranteed**"; and in Gal. 3:22, "The
AP : 2 0 :010(228) [0341] order that the promise may be **guaranteed**" (Rom. 4:16).
AP : 2 0 :010(228) [0341] conditional on our works, it would not be **guaranteed**.

Guard (13), Guarded (4), Guardian (3), Guardians (4), Guarding (1), Guards (2)
PR : PR :022(011) [0019] may know that he must **guard** himself against them.
PR : PR :027(014) [0025] [of Saxe-Weimar] the above two through their **guardian**.
PR : PR :027(014) [0025] Saxe-Eisenach] the above two through their **guardians**.
PR : PR :027(015) [0025] [in Ivernack] the above two through their **guardians**.
PR : PR :027(015) [0025] [-Hachberg] the above two through their **guardians**.
AL : 0 0 :005(095) [0095] is manifest that we have **guarded** diligently against the
AP : 0 4 :386(166) [0225] says (I Pet. 1:5), we are "**guarded** for a salvation ready to
AP : 2 3 :055(247) [0379] it was appropriate to **guard** marriage with the strictest
AP : 2 7 :002(269) [0419] prison, he sent for the **guardian** to tell him of his illness.
AP : 2 7 :002(269) [0419] a pharisaical hatred, the **guardian** began to denounce him
S2 : 0 2 :006(293) [0463] discontinued in order to **guard** forever against such
SC : 0 3 :018(347) [0549] petition that God may so **guard** and preserve us that the
LC : PR :019(361) [0573] put it into practice, **guarding** themselves with the greatest
LC : 0 1 :128(382) [0617] thought how God feeds, **guards**, and protects us and how
LC : 0 1 :200(392) [0637] They all teach us to **guard** against harming our neighbor
LC : 0 1 :205(393) [0639] every husband or wife **guarded** and protected from any
LC : 0 1 :226(395) [0645] against whom we can **guard** with lock and bolt, or if we
LC : 0 1 :226(395) [0645] But against the others no one can **guard**.
LC : 0 1 :248(398) [0651] that they may be on their **guard** and not follow the old,
LC : 0 1 :260(400) [0655] promote and resolutely **guard** them, whether he be judge
LC : 0 1 :284(403) [0661] so that everyone may know how to **guard** against it.
LC : 0 2 :017(412) [0681] our eyes, but also daily **guards** and defends us against
LC : 0 3 :061(428) [0715] but also for defenders, protectors, and vigilant **guardians**.
EP : 1 2 :030(500) [0843] degree and low, must **guard** against these if they dearly
SD : PR :010(503) [0849] truth may know how to **guard** and protect themselves
SD : PR :014(506) [0855] or feed the lambs and **guard** against wolves so that they
SD : 0 4 :034(557) [0949] "By God's power we are **guarded** through faith for a

Guenther (1)
PR : PR :027(015) [0025] John **Guenther**, count of Schwarzburg [-Sondershausen]

Guest (2), Guests (8)
AP : 0 4 :154(128) [0165] outward courtesies due a **guest** and a great and holy man.
EP : 0 7 :017(484) [0813] judgment on unrepentant **guests** as he is to work life and
EP : 0 7 :017(484) [0813] consolation in the hearts of believing and worthy **guests**.
EP : 0 7 :018(484) [0813] one kind of unworthy **guest**, namely, those who do not
EP : 0 7 :020(484) [0813] entire worthiness of the **guests** at this heavenly feast is and
EP : 0 7 :038(486) [0817] That the worthiness of the **guests** at this heavenly meal
SD : 0 7 :068(582) [0997] who the unworthy **guests** at this Supper are, namely,
SD : 0 7 :123(590) [1015] are only two kinds of **guests** at this heavenly meal, the
SD : 0 7 :125(591) [1015] this sacrament for judgment, just as unworthy **guests**.
SD : 1 1 :027(620) [1071] And the **guests** whom the king invites to his son's

Guestrow (1)
PR : PR :027(015) [0025] Ulrich, duke of Mecklenburg [-**Guestrow**]

Guidance (4)
PR : PR :022(012) [0019] they will, through the **guidance** of the Holy Spirit, turn to
EP : 0 0 :000(463) [0775] Reconciled under the **Guidance** of the Word of God and
EP : 1 1 :022(497) [0837] From it, under the **guidance** of the Word of God and the
SD : 0 6 :020(567) [0969] of the Holy Spirit's **guidance** set up a self-elected service

Guide (6), Guided (1), Guides (3)
AG : 2 8 :031(085) [0087] Spirit of truth comes, he will **guide** you into all the truth."
AG : 2 8 :047(088) [0091] "Let them alone; they are blind **guides**" (Matt. 15:14).
AL : 2 8 :031(086) [0087] Spirit of truth comes, he will **guide** you into all the truth."
AP : 1 2 :126(201) [0289] on a watchtower to **guide** religious affairs, ought in such
AP : 2 8 :006(282) [0445] by force in order to **guide** their subjects toward the goal
LC : PR :002(358) [0567] or dogkeepers than spiritual **guides** or pastors.
LC : 0 1 :092(377) [0607] life and work must be **guided** by God's Word if they are
LC : 0 1 :158(387) [0627] to those who govern and **guide** us by the Word of God.
SD : 0 2 :066(534) [0907] through his Holy Spirit, **guides** and leads him, but if God
SD : 1 1 :020(619) [1069] the world, and the flesh, **guide** and lead them in his ways,

Guild (1)
LC : 0 1 :228(396) [0645] is the most common craft and the largest **guild** on earth.

Guilt (48), Guiltless (2), Guilty (22)
AG : 2 4 :012(057) [0065] sacrament unworthily is **guilty** of the body and blood of
AG : 2 8 :041(087) [0089] of the reservation of **guilt** but speaks only about the
AL : 0 3 :003(030) [0045] not only for original **guilt** but also for all actual sins of
AL : 2 4 :012(057) [0065] unworthy manner will be **guilty** of profaning the body
AL : 2 4 :019(058) [0067] Lord will not hold him **guiltless** who takes his name in
AL : 2 4 :025(058) [0067] not only for original **guilt** but also for others sins.
AL : 2 8 :041(087) [0089] ecclesiastical penalties and not of reserving **guilt**.
AP : 0 2 :001(100) [0105] of God and faith is actual **guilt**, and therefore they deny
AP : 0 2 :001(100) [0105] guilt, and therefore they deny that it is original **guilt**.
AP : 0 2 :005(101) [0107] bear because of his **guilt**, without any evil of their own.
AP : 0 2 :031(104) [0113] this is not merely actual **guilt** but an abiding deficiency in
AP : 0 2 :035(105) [0115] that Baptism removes the **guilt** of original sin, even
AP : 0 2 :036(105) [0115] It is forgiven because its **guilt** is absolved by the
AP : 0 4 :037(112) [0131] these dreams that a man **guilty** of mortal sin can love God
AP : 0 4 :084(119) [0145] merit, for he says that all are **guilty** and consigned to sin.
AP : 0 4 :103(121) [0151] is, by the law sin is recognized but its **guilt** is not relieved.
AP : 0 4 :210(136) [0179] removes the burden of **guilt** and punishment in those for
AP : 0 4 :267(147) [0197] unless the heart first receives remission of **guilt**.
AP : 0 4 :305(154) [0205] way to mean "to absolve a **guilty** man and pronounce him
AP : 1 2 :007(183) [0255] the keys does not remove **guilt**, but only changes eternal
AP : 1 2 :024(185) [0257] of purgatory, or they profit as a payment to blot out **guilt**.
AP : 1 2 :027(185) [0259] punishment but also the **guilt** ought to be reserved in the
AP : 1 2 :107(198) [0283] to the Lord'; then thou didst forgive the **guilt** of my sin."
AP : 1 2 :118(199) [0287] to the remission of **guilt**, though they imagine that they
AP : 1 2 :118(199) [0287] of sin God remits the **guilt**, and yet, because it is fitting
AP : 1 2 :137(203) [0293] which make satisfaction for punishment, if not for **guilt**.
AP : 1 2 :140(204) [0295] a satisfaction not only for **guilt** but also for eternal death,
AP : 1 2 :140(204) [0295] satisfaction redeems our **guilt** but our penalties redeem us
AP : 1 2 :147(205) [0297] carry on idle speculations about the remission of **guilt**.
AP : 1 2 :147(205) [0297] how, in the remission of **guilt**, faith frees the heart from
AP : 1 2 :147(205) [0297] divine law to remit either **guilt** or eternal punishment or
AP : 1 2 :167(208) [0305] for the remission either of the **guilt** or of the punishment.
AP : 1 2 :177(210) [0307] not the reservation of **guilt** before God in the case of the
AP : 1 5 :024(218) [0321] writes, "Fasting avails to destroy and prevent **guilt**."
AP : 2 4 :009(251) [0387] of venial or mortal sins, of **guilt**, or of punishment.
AP : 2 4 :013(251) [0387] gain the remission of **guilt** and punishment, secure
AP : 2 4 :019(252) [0389] a work of satisfaction for **guilt** and punishment that
AP : 2 4 :063(261) [0405] the remission of sins, **guilt**, and punishment for those to
AP : 2 4 :066(261) [0407] the remission of sins, of **guilt**, and of punishment for
AP : 2 4 :090(266) [0415] Supper was instituted for the sake of forgiving **guilt**.
AP : 2 4 :090(266) [0415] forgiveness of sins, which necessarily implies real **guilt**.
AP : 2 4 :090(266) [0415] not make satisfaction for **guilt**; otherwise, the Mass would
AP : 2 4 :090(266) [0415] The forgiveness of **guilt** can be accepted only by faith.
AP : 2 4 :091(266) [0415] of the remission of **guilt** and faith to vain ideas of
AP : 2 4 :091(266) [0415] said (I Cor. 11:27), are "**guilty** of the body and blood of
AP : 2 4 :091(266) [0415] debased the forgiveness of **guilt** and the body and blood
AP : 2 4 :092(266) [0415] for either punishment or **guilt**, *ex opere operato* and
AP : 2 4 :096(267) [0417] merits the forgiveness of **guilt** and punishment even for
AP : 2 4 :098(268) [0417] to merit the forgiveness of **guilt** and punishment for the
AP : 2 7 :044(277) [0435] Thus they are **guilty** of a double sin — deceiving men, and
AP : 2 7 :053(278) [0437] worship of saints which is **guilty** of a double fault: it
AP : 2 8 :013(283) [0447] those who are **guilty** of public offenses or to absolve them
S3 : 0 3 :025(307) [0485] of all penalty and **guilt**, and the people came running, for
S3 : 0 3 :028(308) [0487] did not think they were **guilty** of actual sins — that is, of

Continued ▶

TR : 0 0 :059(330) [0521] make themselves **guilty** of the blood of the godly whom
TR : 0 0 :060(330) [0521] those who are **guilty** of notorious crimes and absolve
TR : 0 0 :074(332) [0525] those who are **guilty** of manifest crimes belongs to all
SC : PR :018(340) [0537] for many of these are **guilty** of dishonesty and thievery.
SC : PR :019(340) [0537] do so, and that they are **guilty** of damnable sin if they do
SC : 0 5 :018(350) [0553] acknowledge that we are **guilty** of all manner of sins,
SC : 0 5 :022(350) [0553] sinner, confess before God that I am **guilty** of all sins.
LC : 0 1 :057(372) [0597] Lord will not hold him **guiltless** who takes his name in
LC : 0 1 :204(393) [0639] of yours, you are just as **guilty** as the culprit himself.
LC : 0 1 :268(401) [0657] his neighbor of such **guilt** assumes as much authority as
LC : 0 1 :269(401) [0657] even though, to your certain knowledge, he is **guilty**.
LC : 0 1 :280(403) [0661] whom you can convict the **guilty** one and on whose
LC : 0 6 :010(458) [0000] We are to confess our **guilt** before one another and
LC : 0 6 :011(458) [0000] besides our universal **guilt** there is also a particular one,
EP : 0 5 :005(478) [0803] satisfied and paid for all **guilt** and without man's merit
SD : 0 7 :060(580) [0993] and blood, but becomes **guilty** of profaning the body and
SD : 1 1 :057(625) [1081] mind while another in equal **guilt** is again converted.
SD : 1 1 :085(631) [1091] judgment on him, for he was indeed **guilty** of "hell-fire."

Guise (3)
LC : 0 1 :214(394) [0641] as those who under the **guise** of great sanctity avoid
LC : 0 1 :298(405) [0665] ones are being devised daily) under the **guise** of justice.
SD : 1 0 :005(611) [1053] go under the name and **guise** of external adiaphora and

Gulden (4)
LC : 0 1 :151(386) [0625] he counts on gaining a **gulden** by his unfaithfulness, he
LC : 0 1 :225(395) [0645] his employer out of thirty or forty **gulden** or more a year.
LC : 0 1 :242(397) [0649] anyone out of a **gulden**, your entire hoard will be
LC : 0 1 :316(408) [0671] single groschen to pay, but I promise to pay ten **gulden**."

Gushes (1)
LC : 0 3 :056(427) [0713] which, the more it **gushes** forth and overflows, the more

Gymnasium (1)
AP : 2 4 :081(264) [0411] ships, care of the **gymnasium**, and similar public

Habit (11), Habitually (1)
PR : PR :021(011) [0019] essentially, formally, **habitually**, and subjectively (to use
AP : 0 2 :027(104) [0113] it is not a pure privation, but also a corrupt **habit**."
AP : 0 4 :283(150) [0201] sprinkling with water, the **habit** of the monks, the
AP : 1 0 :003(179) [0247] not only according to the **habit** which we understand as
LC : SP :016(363) [0577] should be taught the **habit** of reciting them daily when
LC : 0 1 :071(374) [0601] is a blessed and useful **habit**, and very effective against
LC : 0 1 :073(374) [0601] it also helps to form the **habit** of commending ourselves
LC : 0 1 :081(375) [0603] themselves were in the **habit** of doing on that day, as we
LC : 0 1 :096(378) [0609] who only from force of **habit** go to hear preaching and
LC : 0 1 :332(410) [0677] is to make them his daily **habit** in all circumstances, in all
LC : 0 3 :006(421) [0699] Thus they fall into the **habit** of never praying, alleging
LC : 0 3 :028(424) [0705] of us should form the **habit** from his youth up to pray

Hachberg (1)
PR : PR :027(015) [0025] James of Baden [-**Hachberg**] the above two through their

Hades (3)
EP : 1 1 :005(495) [0833] upon it that the "gates of **Hades** cannot prevail against" it
SD : 1 1 :008(617) [1065] a way that "the gates of **Hades**" are not able to do
SD : 1 1 :050(624) [1079] God shall exist and remain against all the "gates of **Hades**

Hail (2)
LC : 0 3 :078(431) [0721] livelihood, from tempest, **hail**, fire, and flood; from
LC : 0 3 :080(431) [0721] why he sends tempest and **hail** to destroy crops and

Hair (1), Hairs (1)
LC : 0 4 :020(439) [0737] their noses, eyes, skin and **hair**, flesh and bones, they look
SD : 0 7 :067(582) [0997] part of the unworthy "two **hairs** of a horse's tail and an

Half (6), Halfway (1), Half-way (2), Half-dead (1)
AP : 0 4 :072(117) [0141] saying goes, "the beginning is **half** of everything."
S3 : 0 3 :016(305) [0483] attrite (which I might call **half**-way or partially
LC : 0 1 :303(406) [0667] him until he acquires a **half** or more of it; and yet this
LC : 0 2 :058(418) [0693] Now we are only **halfway** pure and holy.
LC : 0 5 :056(453) [0767] passes into another and one **half** year into yet another.
SD : 0 2 :007(521) [0883] either altogether or **half**-way or in the tiniest or smallest
SD : 0 2 :025(526) [0891] will, be it entirely or one-**half** or the least and tiniest part,
SD : 0 2 :077(536) [0911] is good, but only grievously wounded and **half-dead**.
SD : 0 3 :037(546) [0929] them as entirely or one-**half** or even only to the smallest
SD : 0 8 :078(607) [1043] Not part or only one-**half** of the person of Christ, but the

Hall (2)
PR : PR :027(015) [0027] Mayor and Council of the City of Schwaebisch-**Hall**
TR : 0 0 :082(000) [0529] John Brentz, Minister of **Hall** (Triglotta text only)

Hallow (1), Hallowed (11), Hallowing (1)
SC : 0 3 :003(346) [0547] ***"Hallowed** be thy name."*
SC : 0 3 :011(347) [0547] would hinder us from **hallowing** his name and prevent the
LC : SP :014(363) [0577] Our Father who art in heaven, **hallowed** be thy name.
LC : 0 1 :064(373) [0599] Thus his name is **hallowed**, as we pray in the Lord's
LC : 0 1 :097(378) [0609] had been properly **hallowed** if one heard a Mass or the
LC : 0 3 :035(425) [0707] ***"Hallowed** be thy name."*
LC : 0 3 :046(426) [0709] namely, that "to **hallow**" means the same as in our idiom
LC : 0 3 :050(426) [0711] whom his name is **hallowed** and his kingdom flourishes.
LC : 0 3 :060(428) [0715] God's name may be **hallowed** by us and that his kingdom
LC : 0 3 :068(429) [0717] As God's name must be **hallowed** and his kingdom must
LC : 0 3 :070(429) [0717] God could not abide on earth nor his name be **hallowed**.
LC : 0 3 :118(436) [0731] his name must first be **hallowed** in us, his kingdom come
SD : 0 7 :082(584) [1001] of bread and wine are **hallowed** or blessed in this holy

Hamburg (2)
PR : PR :027(016) [0027] The Council of the City of **Hamburg**
TR : 0 0 :082(335) [0529] superintendent in **Hamburg**, subscribed with his own hand

Hamelin (1)
PR : PR :027(016) [0027] Mayor and Council of the City of **Hamelin**

Hammer (2)
S3 : 0 3 :002(304) [0479] This is the **hammer** of which Jeremiah speaks, "Is not my
S3 : 0 3 :002(304) [0479] "Is not my word like a **hammer** which breaks the rock in

Hanau (1)
PR : PR :027(015) [0025] Philip, count of **Hanau** [-Lichtenburg]

Hand (132), Hands (43)
PR : PR :011(006) [0011] Finally they took to **hand** the controverted articles,
PR : PR :016(008) [0013] publicly attested this with their hearts, lips, and **hands**.
PR : PR :020(010) [0017] his session at the right **hand** of God's almighty power and
PR : PR :021(010) [0019] it is seated at the right **hand** of God and is exalted, our
AG : 0 3 :004(030) [0045] and sits on the right **hand** of God, that he may eternally
AG : 1 2 :009(035) [0049] Condemned on the other **hand** are the Novatians who
AG : 1 8 :007(040) [0053] On the other **hand**, by his own choice man can also
AG : 2 6 :010(065) [0071] On the other **hand**, other necessary good works were
AG : 2 7 :058(080) [0083] to support it; on the other **hand**, that is a dangerous state
AG : 2 8 :023(084) [0087] On the other **hand**, if they teach, introduce, or institute
AG : 0 0 :005(095) [0095] into our churches and gaining the upper **hand** in them.
AL : 0 3 :004(030) [0045] heaven to sit on the right **hand** of the Father, forever
AL : 1 8 :007(040) [0053] On the other **hand**, by 'evil' I mean such things as to will
AL : 1 8 :009(040) [0053] works (for it can keep the **hands** from theft and murder),
AL : 0 0 :017(096) [0095] Ernest, with his own **hand**
AP : 0 4 :021(110) [0127] consciences, on the other **hand**, they drive to despair
AP : 0 4 :081(118) [0145] Paul, on the other **hand**, teaches that we have access (that
AP : 0 4 :165(129) [0169] Christ, "who is at the right **hand** of God, who indeed
AP : 0 4 :234(140) [0185] On the other **hand**, perfection (that is, the integrity of the
AP : 0 4 :314(156) [0207] it is well to have it at **hand** and keep it in mind, not only
AP : 0 4 :327(158) [0211] snow, and cleanse my **hands** with lye, yet thou wilt plunge
AP : 0 7 :021(172) [0233] maintain, on the other **hand**, does overthrow faith, as
AP : 1 2 :010(184) [0255] Yet the issue at **hand** is a great one, the chief doctrine of
AP : 1 2 :036(186) [0261] and Saul on the one **hand** and that of Peter and David on
AP : 1 2 :046(188) [0263] made without **hands**, by putting off the body of the sins
AP : 1 2 :061(190) [0269] If, on the other **hand**, they do not separate the reception
AP : 1 3 :012(212) [0311] either to calling the laying on of **hands** a sacrament.
AP : 1 5 :005(215) [0317] opponents, on the other **hand**, set up these traditions as
AP : 1 5 :043(221) [0327] our churches, on the other **hand**, all sermons deal with
AP : 1 5 :049(221) [0329] On the other **hand**, their abrogation involves its own
AP : 1 8 :004(225) [0335] it can choose to keep the **hands** from murder, adultery, or
AP : 2 0 :005(227) [0339] opponents, on the other **hand**, teach that God has laid
AP : 2 3 :003(239) [0363] with your chaste right **hand**, Emperor Charles — you
AP : 2 4 :044(258) [0399] opponents wring their **hands** over "the desolation of the
S1 : PR :001(288) [0455] to indicate, on the one **hand** what and in how far we were
S1 : PR :001(288) [0455] papists and, on the other **hand**, what we intended to hold
S1 : PR :006(289) [0457] On the other **hand**, if one does, the devil appears at once
S1 : PR :013(291) [0459] are contrary to God, their **hands** would be so full that
S1 : 0 1 :000(292) [0461] he is seated at the right **hand** of God, will come to judge
S3 : 0 3 :030(308) [0487] On the one **hand** there are some who think, "We have
S3 : 0 3 :031(308) [0487] and on the other **hand** there are others who suppose, "We
S3 : 0 3 :044(310) [0491] to rule and gain the upper **hand** in such a way that sin is
S3 : 1 5 :005(316) [0501] Dr. Justus Jonas, rector, subscribed with his own **hand**
S3 : 1 5 :005(318) [0501] the Rev. Andrew Menser (I Subscribe with my **hand**)
S3 : 1 5 :005(318) [0501] And I, Egidius Melcher, have subscribed with my **hand**.
TR : 0 0 :014(322) [0509] might be conferred and **hands** imposed on him."
TR : 0 0 :040(327) [0515] On the one **hand**, it is manifest that the pope rules in the
TR : 0 0 :040(327) [0515] On the other **hand**, the doctrine of the pope conflicts in
TR : 0 0 :059(330) [0521] On the other **hand**, those who agree with the pope and
TR : 0 0 :070(332) [0525] with the laying on of **hands**; nor was ordination anything
TR : 0 0 :082(334) [0529] Agricola, minister in Chur, subscribed with his own **hand**
TR : 0 0 :082(335) [0529] Philip Melanchthon subscribes with his own **hand**
TR : 0 0 :082(335) [0529] subscribes with his own **hand** both in his name and in
TR : 0 0 :082(335) [0529] John Schlagenhaufen subscribes with his own **hand**
TR : 0 0 :082(335) [0529] in Hamburg, subscribed with his own **hand**
SC : PR :023(341) [0539] On the other **hand**, he suggests that he needs no grace, no
SC : 0 1 :022(344) [0543] On the other **hand**, he promises grace and every blessing
SC : 0 2 :003(345) [0545] *and is seated on the right **hand** of God, the Father*
SC : 0 6 :010(352) [0557] On the other **hand**, he who does not believe these words,
SC : 0 7 :002(352) [0557] Into thy **hands** I commend my body and soul and all that
SC : 0 7 :005(353) [0559] Into thy **hands** I commend my body and soul and all that
SC : 0 8 :007(353) [0559] the table, they should reverently fold their **hands** and say:
SC : 0 8 :007(353) [0559] Thou openest thy **hand**; Thou satisfiest the desire of every
SC : 0 8 :010(353) [0559] likewise, they should fold their **hands** reverently and say:
SC : 0 9 :012(356) [0563] under the mighty **hand** of God, that in due time he may
LC : PR :014(360) [0571] our eyes and in our **hands** as a constant token and sign.
LC : SP :012(363) [0577] and sits on the right **hand** of God, the Father almighty,
LC : 0 1 :003(365) [0581] On the other **hand**, if your trust is false and wrong, then
LC : 0 1 :008(365) [0583] On the other **hand**, he who has nothing doubts and
LC : 0 1 :013(366) [0583] see, does not mean to lay **hands** upon him, or put him
LC : 0 1 :017(366) [0585] On the other **hand**, you can easily judge how the world
LC : 0 1 :026(368) [0587] Creatures are only the **hands**, channels, and means
LC : 0 1 :033(369) [0589] On the other **hand**, his kindness and goodness extend to
LC : 0 1 :046(370) [0593] David, on the other **hand**, was a poor, despised man,
LC : 0 1 :070(374) [0601] On the other **hand**, children should be constantly urged
LC : 0 1 :101(379) [0609] On the other **hand**, when we seriously ponder the Word,
LC : 0 1 :122(382) [0615] On the other **hand**, when they are obstinate and never do
LC : 0 1 :134(383) [0619] On the other **hand**, the penalty for him who disobeys it is
LC : 0 1 :136(383) [0619] blessing; on the other **hand**, if you provoke him to anger,
LC : 0 1 :138(384) [0621] On the other **hand**, it is written of the wicked in Ps.
LC : 0 1 :151(386) [0625] On the other **hand**, if he will not do so in love, but
LC : 0 1 :166(387) [0627] honor that we lift our **hands** in joyful thanks to God for
LC : 0 1 :182(389) [0631] We must not kill, either by **hand**, heart, or word, by signs
LC : 0 1 :188(390) [0633] This means, first, by **hand** or by deed; next, we should
LC : 0 1 :192(391) [0635] and could extend him my **hand** to pull him out and save
LC : 0 1 :196(391) [0637] minds, we would have our **hands** full of good works to
LC : 0 1 :224(395) [0643] attention to it that the matter is entirely out of **hand**.
LC : 0 1 :242(397) [0649] we shall trust God, who takes matters into his own **hands**.
LC : 0 1 :247(398) [0651] man who must live from **hand** to mouth, you act as if
LC : 0 1 :250(399) [0651] commandments: On one **hand**, we are forbidden to do
LC : 0 1 :251(399) [0651] On the other **hand**, we are commanded to promote and
LC : 0 1 :274(402) [0659] the law into their own **hands** without such a commission.
LC : 0 1 :287(403) [0663] Our **hands** and eyes, even the whole body, must help
LC : 0 1 :288(404) [0663] On the other **hand**, we should prevent everything that

Continued ▶

LC : 0 1 :303(405) [0667] out of another's **hand** so that the victim is helpless to
LC : 0 1 :313(407) [0671] me that we shall have our **hands** full to keep these
LC : 0 1 :314(407) [0671] On the other **hand**, those other works captivate all eyes
LC : 0 1 :324(409) [0675] On the one **hand**, whoever fears and loves anything else in
LC : 0 2 :022(413) [0683] daily with eyes and ears, **hands**, body and soul, money
LC : 0 2 :025(413) [0685] *and is seated on the right* ***hand*** *of God, the Father*
LC : 0 2 :031(414) [0687] and assumed dominion at the right **hand** of the Father.
LC : 0 3 :078(431) [0721] On the other **hand**, to protect us from all kinds of harm
LC : 0 3 :083(431) [0721] received them from his **hand** and may recognize in them
LC : 0 3 :083(431) [0721] When he withdraws his **hand**, nothing can prosper or last
LC : 0 4 :010(437) [0735] it is performed by men's **hands**, it is nevertheless truly
LC : 0 4 :036(441) [0741] This the **hand** cannot do, nor the body, but the heart
LC : 0 4 :056(444) [0747] I may be strong or weak; I leave that in God's **hands**.
LC : 0 4 :071(445) [0749] On the other **hand**, when we become Christians, the old
LC : 0 5 :026(449) [0759] our faith or yield **hand** and foot and become indifferent
LC : 0 5 :036(450) [0761] a gift and eternal treasure cannot be seized with the **hand**.
LC : 0 5 :075(455) [0771] that they put their **hands** to their bosom and ask whether
LC : 0 6 :035(461) [0000] however, let us lift up our **hands** in praise and thanks to
EP : 0 1 :001(466) [0779] body, and soul on the one **hand**, and original sin on the
EP : 0 1 :001(466) [0779] original sin on the other **hand**, so that man's nature is one
EP : 0 1 :004(466) [0781] as it is written, "Thy **hands** fashioned and made me, all
EP : 0 1 :008(467) [0781] 3. On the other **hand**, we believe, teach, and confess that
EP : 0 2 :017(472) [0791] On the other **hand**, it is correct to say that in conversion,
EP : 0 5 :008(479) [0803] the law into his own **hands** and explains it spiritually
EP : 0 7 :012(483) [0811] "The second ground is: "God's right **hand** is everywhere.
EP : 0 7 :012(483) [0811] and truly set at this right **hand** of God according to his
EP : 0 7 :012(483) [0811] presently and has in his **hands** and under his feet
EP : 0 7 :012(483) [0811] is so set down at the right **hand** of God, whence he is able
EP : 0 8 :015(488) [0821] truth) exalted to the right **hand** of the omnipotent majesty
EP : 0 8 :016(489) [0821] beneath his feet and in his **hands**, as he himself testifies,
EP : 0 8 :017(489) [0823] property of God's right **hand**, as Dr. Luther says on the
EP : 1 1 :013(496) [0835] of our own, and that no one can pluck us out of his **hand**.
EP : 1 2 :031(501) [0843] of God, subscribed our signatures with our own **hands**.
SD : PR :008(502) [0849] weak in faith, on the other **hand**, will be scandalized;
SD : 0 1 :026(512) [0867] 1. On the other **hand**, this doctrine must also be protected
SD : 0 1 :035(514) [0869] Job says: "Thy **hands** fashioned and made me together
SD : 0 1 :047(516) [0873] body and soul on the one **hand** and original sin on the
SD : 0 2 :004(520) [0881] On the other **hand**, both ancient and modern enthusiasts
SD : 0 2 :047(530) [0901] On the other **hand**, despondent hearts may fall into grave
SD : 0 2 :055(531) [0903] On the one **hand**, it is true that both the preacher's
SD : 0 2 :055(532) [0903] On the other **hand**, neither the preacher nor the hearer
SD : 0 2 :066(534) [0907] withdraw his gracious **hand** man could not remain in
SD : 0 2 :080(536) [0911] 6. On the other **hand**, we must condemn with all
SD : 0 3 :022(543) [0923] Nor, on the other **hand**, does this mean that we may or
SD : 0 3 :054(548) [0935] On the one **hand**, it is true indeed that God the Father,
SD : 0 3 :054(549) [0935] But, on the other **hand**, this indwelling of God is not the
SD : 0 4 :019(554) [0945] when he says on the one **hand** (Rom. 7:22, 23) that he is
SD : 0 5 :010(559) [0955] takes the law into his **hands** and explains it spiritually
SD : 0 5 :012(560) [0955] On the other **hand**, the Gospel is a proclamation that
SD : 0 7 :009(570) [0975] Confession, on the other **hand**, teaches on the basis of
SD : 0 7 :060(580) [0995] and in deed laid violent **hands** upon the body of Christ
SD : 0 7 :069(582) [0997] on the other **hand**, are those timid, perturbed Christians,
SD : 0 7 :095(586) [1005] The second is that the right **hand** of God is everywhere.
SD : 0 7 :106(588) [1009] On the other **hand** they will overthrow and refute all the
SD : 0 8 :010(593) [1019] 5. On the other **hand**, to be a corporeal being or a
SD : 0 8 :012(593) [1019] been elevated to the right **hand** of majesty, power, and
SD : 0 8 :023(595) [1023] human nature at the right **hand** of the almighty power of
SD : 0 8 :028(596) [1025] the manner of the right **hand** of God, which is not a
SD : 0 8 :028(596) [1025] The right **hand** of God is precisely the almighty power of
SD : 0 8 :039(598) [1029] performs a sleight-of-**hand** trick and substitutes the
SD : 0 8 :051(600) [1031] and exalted to the right **hand** and majesty and power of
SD : 0 8 :055(601) [1033] all things given into his **hands**, to have all things under
SD : 0 8 :070(605) [1041] given all things into his **hands**" (John 13:3); likewise, "In
SD : 0 8 :070(605) [1041] him over the works of thy **hands**, putting everything in
SD : 0 8 :074(606) [1043] he is exalted to the right **hand** of the majesty and power
SD : 0 8 :078(606) [1043] his humanity at the right **hand** of the majesty and power
SD : 0 8 :086(608) [1047] of Christ at the right **hand** of God in connection with this
SD : 0 8 :092(609) [1049] he has placed at the right **hand** of the majesty and power
SD : 0 8 :096(610) [1049] to sit so high at the right **hand** of the majesty and
SD : 0 9 :003(610) [1051] made to sit at the right **hand** of the almighty power and
SD : 1 0 :016(613) [1057] idolatry, and on the other **hand**, it will sadden and
SD : 1 0 :021(614) [1059] with their own **hands**, we find the following statement:
SD : 1 1 :005(617) [1065] On the other **hand**, the eternal election of God or God's
SD : 1 1 :008(617) [1065] my sheep out of my **hand**" (John 10:28), and again, "As
SD : 1 1 :046(624) [1079] and taken from our **hands** — that he ordained my
SD : 1 1 :046(624) [1079] into the almighty **hand** of our Saviour, Jesus Christ, out
SD : 1 1 :067(627) [1085] kingdom of God is at **hand**; repent and believe in the
SD : 1 1 :085(630) [1091] God withdrew his **hand** from him, and so his heart
SD : 1 1 :090(631) [1093] that their salvation does not rest in their own **hands**.
SD : 1 1 :090(631) [1093] us in Christ, out of whose **hand** "no one can pluck" us
SD : 1 2 :040(636) [1103] of God, subscribed our signatures with our own **hands**.

Handed (5), Handedly (1)
AP : 0 4 :289(151) [0203] mode of justification, **handed** down by the scholastic
AP : 0 4 :325(157) [0211] Fathers have so clearly **handed** down the doctrine that we
AP : 0 7 :038(176) [0241] are supposed to have been **handed** down by the apostles.
AP : 1 3 :002(211) [0309] varies, provided what is **handed** down in Scripture is
LC : 0 1 :226(395) [0645] who act high-**handedly** and never know enough ways to
SD : 0 7 :064(581) [0995] and during supper he **handed** his disciples natural bread

Handful (1)
LC : 0 4 :015(438) [0735] then babble, "How can a **handful** of water help the soul?"

Handiwork (14)
EP : 0 1 :004(466) [0781] them as his **handiwork**, as it is written, "Thy hands
SD : 0 1 :002(508) [0859] Fall are and remain God's **handiwork** and creation in us.
SD : 0 1 :002(509) [0859] soul, which are God's **handiwork** and creatures in us even
SD : 0 1 :034(514) [0869] is God's creature and **handiwork** (Deut. 32:6; Isa. 45:11;
SD : 0 1 :038(515) [0871] that this creature and **handiwork** of God has been
SD : 0 1 :040(515) [0871] sin the creature or **handiwork** of God; on the contrary, it
SD : 0 1 :041(515) [0871] would also become his **handiwork** and creature; or that,
SD : 0 1 :041(515) [0871] have to be Satan's **handiwork** or creature if our corrupted
SD : 0 1 :042(515) [0871] God's creature and **handiwork** in man from the devil's
SD : 0 1 :042(515) [0873] evil, is in its origin the **handiwork** of Satan, who through
SD : 0 1 :042(515) [0873] has in this fashion corrupted God's **handiwork** in Adam.
SD : 0 1 :061(519) [0879] between God's **handiwork**, our nature in spite of its
SD : 0 1 :061(519) [0879] and the devil's **handiwork**, the sin which inheres in and
SD : 0 1 :061(519) [0879] profoundly and inexpressibly corrupts God's **handiwork**.

Handle (6)
AG : 2 8 :045(088) [0089] to regulations, 'Do not **handle**, Do not taste, Do not
AL : 2 8 :045(088) [0089] to regulations, 'Do not **handle**, Do not taste, Do not
AP : 0 7 :035(175) [0241] to regulations, 'Do not **handle**, Do not taste, Do not
AP : 2 4 :099(268) [0419] of the Mass, we shall not **handle** the case so gently.
LC : 0 1 :275(402) [0659] compelled to examine and **handle** his private parts.
LC : 0 5 :005(447) [0755] and inviolate even if we use and **handle** it unworthily.

Handwriting (2)
AP : 0 4 :350(161) [0217] This **handwriting** is not erased without a great conflict in
TR : 0 0 :082(000) [0529] testify in this my own **handwriting** that I thus hold,

Hang (2), Hanged (2), Hanging (1), Hangman (9), Hangmen (1), Hangs (1)
AP : 1 2 :060(190) [0267] God exists, that punishments **hang** over the wicked, etc.
LC : 0 1 :055(372) [0595] (these belong in the **hangman**'s school, not ours), but also
LC : 0 1 :135(383) [0619] to them, then obey the **hangman**; and if you will not obey
LC : 0 1 :136(383) [0619] he will send upon you both death and the **hangman**.
LC : 0 1 :137(384) [0619] who must daily be **hanged**, beheaded, or broken on the
LC : 0 1 :149(385) [0623] godliness, we deliver to the **hangman** and the grim reaper.
LC : 0 1 :151(386) [0625] he will fall victim to the **hangman**, or perish through war,
LC : 0 1 :224(395) [0643] to admit it, were **hanged** on the gallows, the world would
LC : 0 1 :224(395) [0643] there would be a shortage of both **hangmen** and gallows.
LC : 0 1 :232(396) [0647] if the judge, the jailer, or the **hangman** did the preaching.
LC : 0 1 :234(397) [0647] get by and escape the **hangman**, but he will not escape
LC : 0 1 :238(397) [0647] He will **hang** them not on a green gallows but on a dry
LC : 0 1 :274(402) [0659] physically, and yet an exception is made of the **hangman**.
LC : 0 3 :102(434) [0727] we have the old Adam **hanging** around our necks; he goes
LC : 0 5 :071(454) [0769] by your own need, which **hangs** around your neck and
LC : 0 6 :006(457) [0000] deserve just such a jailer as God's devil and **hangman**.

Hanover (3)
PR : PR :027(014) [0025] Younger, duke of Brunswick and Lueneburg [-**Hanover**].
PR : PR :027(016) [0027] Mayor and Council of the City of **Hanover**.
S3 : 1 5 :005(317) [0501] in the name of my brethren and of the church of **Hanover**

Happen (20), Happened (8), Happening (1), Happens (32)
PR : PR :005(004) [0009] were still alive, it **happened** that false teachers insinuated
AG : 2 0 :009(042) [0053] grace for us, for this **happens** only through faith, that is,
AG : 2 0 :034(045) [0057] This is what **happens** when a man is without true faith
AL : 2 7 :015(073) [0077] What **happened** after such people had entered
AL : 2 8 :028(085) [0087] be obeyed if they should **happen** to err or hold anything
AP : 0 2 :044(106) [0117] As often **happens**, these ideas did not remain purely
AP : 0 4 :062(115) [0139] This **happens** if they believe Christ's promise that for his
AP : 0 4 :079(118) [0143] consciences; this **happens** through the law, which shows
AP : 0 4 :081(118) [0145] And to show how this **happens**, he adds that through
AP : 0 4 :126(124) [0157] This cannot **happen** until, being justified and
AP : 0 4 :192(133) [0175] is determined that nothing **happen** to the praise of God.
AP : 0 4 :224(138) [0181] neither what justification is nor how it **happens**.
AP : 0 4 :224(138) [0181] None of this **happens** through the works of the Second
AP : 0 4 :395(167) [0225] The same thing **happened** among the people of Israel.
AP : 0 4 :395(167) [0225] is a type of what was to **happen** in the church of the
AP : 0 7 :032(174) [0239] they debated how it **happened** that they had come to
AP : 1 2 :011(184) [0255] All this **happens** in the first step.
AP : 1 2 :011(184) [0255] What **happens** when we come to confession?
AP : 1 2 :065(191) [0271] And this **happens** when we believe that our sins are
AP : 1 2 :129(202) [0291] easily imagine what will **happen** if this hatred should
AP : 1 2 :164(208) [0303] condemnation really **happens** in contrition and in a
AP : 2 1 :044(236) [0357] innocent men, as has **happened** before, nor crush sound
AP : 2 3 :071(249) [0383] Whatever **happens**, our princes can have a clear
AP : 2 4 :059(260) [0405] This does not **happen** by the transfer of one man's work
AP : 2 7 :002(269) [0419] of them have already **happened**, and others seem to be
AP : 2 7 :041(276) [0435] One **happens** without a call, without a command of God;
AP : 2 7 :041(276) [0435] of leaving is that which **happens** by a command of God,
S1 : PR :004(289) [0457] Imagine what will **happen** after I am dead!
S2 : 0 2 :010(294) [0465] would permit this to **happen**, they would put us all to
S2 : 0 2 :015(295) [0467] articles of faith — as has **happened** in the case of relics.
TR : 0 0 :058(330) [0521] the godly when, as often **happens**, they are reproached
LC : 0 1 :092(377) [0607] Where that **happens** the commandment is in force and is
LC : 0 1 :137(384) [0619] we behold, for it seldom **happens** that such wicked people
LC : 0 1 :225(395) [0643] or permits damage to **happen** when it could have been
LC : 0 1 :225(395) [0645] am not speaking of what **happens** inadvertently and
LC : 0 1 :289(404) [0663] This is what **happens** now especially to the precious Word
LC : 0 1 :303(405) [0667] The same thing **happens** in ordinary business affairs,
LC : 0 1 :304(406) [0667] Yet no one wishes this to **happen** to himself.
LC : 0 4 :082(446) [0751] But it does **happen** that we slip and fall out of the ship.
LC : 0 5 :084(456) [0773] This **happens** especially because the devil so constantly
LC : 0 6 :006(457) [0000] What would **happen** if you wished to enjoy the Gospel's
EP : 0 2 :008(471) [0789] taught that whatever **happens** must so happen and could
EP : 0 2 :008(471) [0789] happens must so **happen** and could not happen
EP : 0 2 :008(471) [0789] so happen and could not **happen** otherwise, that man
EP : 0 8 :038(491) [0827] from eternity, what is **happening** everywhere today, nor
EP : 0 9 :001(492) [0827] Did it **happen** before or after his death?
EP : 1 1 :003(494) [0833] all things before they **happen**, as it is written, "There is a
SD : 0 2 :056(532) [0903] often is hidden, and **happens** under cover of great
SD : 0 2 :074(535) [0909] that everything must **happen** as it does; that man acts
SD : 0 5 :012(560) [0955] matter how or when it **happens**, is the proclamation of
SD : 0 5 :027(563) [0961] a teaching of law, as **happened** in the papacy, and thus
SD : 0 7 :015(572) [0977] and exposed in procession, as **happens** in the papacy.
SD : 0 7 :072(582) [0997] the other orally, which **happens** in the case of both the
SD : 0 7 :078(583) [1001] of Christ,' nothing would **happen**, but when we follow his
SD : 0 7 :082(584) [1001] which we bless," which **happens** precisely through the
SD : 0 7 :102(587) [1007] But how this **happens**, we do not know; it transcends
SD : 0 8 :041(599) [1029] personal union, all that **happens** to the humanity, and
SD : 1 1 :004(616) [1063] everything before it **happens** — what we call God's
SD : 1 1 :004(617) [1063] is or shall be, all that **happens** or will happen, both good
SD : 1 1 :004(617) [1063] all that happens or will **happen**, both good and evil, since
SD : 1 1 :006(617) [1065] though it were God's gracious will that it should **happen**.

Happy (11), Happiness (11)
A P : 1 2 :090(195) [0279] is quite clear, we are **happy** to have all good men judge
S 1 : P R :010(290) [0457] I should be very **happy** to see a true council assemble in
L C : 0 1 :007(365) [0583] and property feels secure, **happy**, fearless, as if he were
L C : 0 1 :018(367) [0585] who strove for riches, **happiness**, pleasure, and a life of
L C : 0 1 :041(370) [0591] either eternal blessing, **happiness**, and salvation, or
L C : 0 1 :043(370) [0593] have never found **happiness** in their wealth, nor has it
L C : 0 1 :068(374) [0599] they never enjoyed a **happy** hour or a healthful day
L C : 0 1 :114(380) [0613] have had an object lesson in goodness and **happiness**.
L C : 0 1 :121(382) [0615] would have more **happiness**, love, kindness, and harmony
L C : 0 1 :125(382) [0617] parents, should we be **happy** to show them honor and
L C : 0 1 :134(383) [0619] will enjoy good days, **happiness**, and prosperity.
L C : 0 1 :134(383) [0619] it is that he will perish sooner and never be **happy** in life.
L C : 0 1 :151(386) [0625] God and receives joy and **happiness** for his reward.
L C : 0 1 :155(386) [0625] We spurn favor and **happiness**; therefore, it is only fair
L C : 0 1 :157(387) [0627] an abundance of joy, **happiness**, and salvation, both here
L C : 0 1 :218(394) [0643] men may have joy and **happiness** in their married life.
L C : 0 1 :253(399) [0653] Thus with a **happy** conscience you can enjoy a hundred
L C : 0 3 :074(430) [0719] them in security or **happiness** unless he gives us a stable,
L C : 0 3 :092(432) [0725] and thus grant us a **happy** and cheerful conscience to
L C : 0 6 :009(458) [0000] we ought and a plea for grace and a **happy** conscience?
L C : 0 6 :019(459) [0000] so that you may attain a **happy** heart and conscience.
L C : 0 6 :032(460) [0000] free from their sins, and **happy** in their conscience,

Harangue (1)
A P : 2 4 :002(249) [0385] In a long **harangue** about the use of Latin in the Mass,

Harass (1), Harassed (2)
A L : 2 6 :032(068) [0075] To be **harassed** by various afflictions and to be crucified
T R : 0 0 :035(326) [0513] transfer kingdoms, and **harass** the kings of almost all the
T R : 0 0 :075(333) [0525] connection they often **harassed** innocent and honest men.

Harbor (1)
L C : 0 1 :188(390) [0635] finally, our heart should **harbor** no hostility or malice

Harburg (1)
P R : P R :027(014) [0025] Otto, duke of Brunswick and Lueneburg [-**Harburg**]

Hard (12), Harden (5), Hardened (4), Hardest (1), Hardly (5), Hardness (1)
P R : P R :022(012) [0021] they will have to give a **hard** accounting.
A G : 2 3 :017(054) [0063] If this **hard** prohibition of marriage is to continue longer,
A L : 2 4 :013(057) [0065] among us inasmuch as **hardly** any private Masses were
A P : 0 4 :165(130) [0169] It is **hard** to understand how a man can do away with
A P : 1 8 :001(224) [0335] several proofs which are **hardly** applicable in this matter.
A P : 1 8 :008(226) [0337] Even for the saints it is **hard** to keep this faith; for the
A P : 2 0 :008(227) [0341] and life to the heart in its **hardest** struggle against
A P : 2 2 :004(236) [0359] and it would not be **hard** to collect a great multitude of
A P : 2 3 :045(245) [0377] profane and unclean and **hardly** pleasing to God, even
A P : 2 8 :016(283) [0449] in which they worked **hard** to free the church from the
S 3 : 0 3 :028(308) [0487] coarse clothing, and **hard** beds and tried earnestly and
S 3 : 0 8 :008(313) [0495] him captive with the **hardened**, unbelieving Jews, but he
S C : P R :016(340) [0535] that they will **hardly** remember anything at all.
L C : 0 1 :080(375) [0603] They were to abstain from **hard** work and to rest, so that
L C : 0 1 :226(395) [0645] even dares to give them a **hard** look or accuse them of
L C : 0 1 :305(406) [0667] so disobedient and **hard** to live with that her husband was
E P : 1 1 :009(495) [0833] their reason, they can **hardly** escape such reflections as
E P : 1 1 :012(496) [0835] but willfully despise it, **harden** their ears and their hearts,
S D : 0 2 :010(522) [0883] is in them, due to their **hardness** of heart" (Eph. 4:17, 18).
S D : 0 2 :019(524) [0889] of unregenerated man to a **hard** stone which resists rather
S D : 0 2 :026(526) [0891] God removes the **hard**, stony heart and bestows a new
S D : 1 1 :039(622) [1075] Acts 13:40f., 46), or who **harden** their hearts when they
S D : 1 1 :040(623) [1077] his counsel that he would **harden**, reject, and condemn all
S D : 1 1 :057(625) [1081] or that one becomes **hardened**, blinded, and is given over
S D : 1 1 :059(626) [1083] his Word and whom he does not **harden** and reject.
S D : 1 1 :083(630) [1091] and that he would **harden**, blind, and for ever damn them
S D : 1 1 :085(630) [1091] But that God **hardened** Pharaoh's heart so that Pharaoh
S D : 1 1 :085(630) [1091] and so his heart became **hardened** and calloused and God

Harlot (2)
L C : 0 4 :059(444) [0747] remains no less gold if a **harlot** wears it in sin and shame.
S D : 1 1 :075(628) [1087] You have played the **harlot** with many lovers; yet return

Harm (35), Harmed (4), Harmful (10), Harming (2), Harms (1)
A G : 2 6 :003(064) [0071] Many **harmful** errors in the church have resulted from
A G : 2 7 :051(079) [0083] all measure, draw many **harmful** conclusions from such
A L : 2 6 :003(064) [0071] traditions much **harm** has resulted in the church.
A L : 2 8 :011(082) [0085] and goods from manifest **harm**, and constrains men with
A L : 2 8 :068(093) [0093] be necessary and that no **harm** is done to consciences even
A P : 0 4 :103(121) [0151] law would seem to be **harmful** since it has made all men
A P : 0 4 :290(151) [0203] The second contains much that is **harmful**.
A P : 0 7 :033(174) [0239] of day and night does not **harm** the unity of the church,
A P : 0 7 :033(174) [0239] unity of the church is not **harmed** by differences in rites
A P : 0 7 :042(176) [0241] others at another, but this difference did no **harm** to faith.
A P : 0 7 :045(177) [0243] human observances does not **harm** the unity of the faith.
A P : 2 3 :052(246) [0377] It is no secret how **harmful** this law has been to public
S 2 : 0 2 :018(296) [0467] unnecessary, uncertain, **harmful** will-o'-the-wisps of the
S 2 : 0 2 :019(296) [0467] abortive, uncertain, and even **harmful** thing.
S 2 : 0 2 :028(297) [0469] that remains will do no **harm** and will quickly be
S 3 : 0 3 :042(310) [0491] if they sin afterwards, and such sin will not **harm** them.
T R : 0 0 :051(329) [0519] The latter does more **harm** than all the punishments, for
S C : 0 1 :010(343) [0541] life, nor cause him any **harm**, but help and befriend him
S C : 0 5 :020(350) [0553] whether you have **harmed** anyone by word or deed; and
S C : 0 7 :002(352) [0557] protected me through the night from all **harm** and danger.
L C : 0 1 :176(389) [0631] Think what deadly **harm** you do when you are negligent
L C : 0 1 :183(390) [0633] many people who do us **harm**, and so we have reason to
L C : 0 1 :185(390) [0633] so that no one may do him bodily **harm** or injury.
L C : 0 1 :186(390) [0633] is that no one should **harm** another for any evil deed, no
L C : 0 1 :188(390) [0633] is this: In the first place, we should not **harm** anyone.
L C : 0 1 :188(390) [0633] to advocate or advise **harming** anyone; again, we should
L C : 0 1 :188(390) [0635] whereby anyone may be **harmed**; finally, our heart should
L C : 0 1 :189(391) [0635] and save him from suffering bodily **harm** or injury.
L C : 0 1 :193(391) [0635] allow no man to suffer **harm**, but show to everyone all
L C : 0 1 :200(392) [0637] us to guard against **harming** our neighbor in any way.
L C : 0 1 :233(396) [0647] God's displeasure, not to **harm** his neighbor, take
L C : 0 1 :259(400) [0655] and powerful who are in a position to help or **harm** him.
L C : 0 1 :268(401) [0657] tongue to the disgrace and **harm** of your neighbor.
L C : 0 1 :274(402) [0659] neighbor good but only **harm** and evil, yet he does not
L C : 0 1 :285(403) [0661] No one shall **harm** his neighbor, whether friend or foe,
L C : 0 1 :291(404) [0663] do greater good or greater **harm**, in spiritual or in
L C : 0 1 :309(407) [0669] commanded not to desire **harm** to our neighbor, nor
L C : 0 1 :328(410) [0675] to do your neighbor no **harm**, injury, or violence, nor in
L C : 0 2 :055(418) [0693] sees to it that it does not **harm** us because we are in the
L C : 0 3 :029(424) [0705] aware what damage and **harm** he suffers when prayer is in
L C : 0 3 :078(431) [0721] us from all kinds of **harm** to our body and our
L C : 0 3 :094(433) [0725] our neighbor who does us **harm**, violence, and injustice,
L C : 0 3 :108(434) [0729] But we cannot be **harmed** by the mere feeling of
L C : 0 3 :118(436) [0731] shame and from everything else that **harms** or injures us.
L C : 0 5 :068(454) [0769] the sacrament as a **harmful** thing from which we should
L C : 0 5 :069(454) [0769] unchristian lives receive it to their **harm** and damnation.
L C : 0 5 :079(455) [0771] not acquire enemies who **harm**, wrong, and injure you
L C : 0 6 :017(459) [0000] and bitter, to the manifest **harm** and destruction of souls.
E P : 0 7 :004(482) [0809] the most **harmful** kind, who in part talk our language
S D : 0 4 :037(557) [0951] an impediment to such a person but are actually **harmful**.
S D : 0 9 :003(610) [1053] can take us or any believer in Christ captive or **harm** us.
S D : 1 1 :010(618) [1067] salvation, it will do me no **harm** if I live in all kinds of sin

Harmony (24), Harmonies (1), Harmonize (1)
P R : P R :005(004) [0009] Christian fashion and in **harmony** with God's Word, as
A P : P R :011(099) [0101] formulas in order to foster the attainment of **harmony**.
A P : P R :012(099) [0101] they are after neither truth no **harmony**, but our blood.
A P : P R :019(099) [0103] and to restore them to a godly and abiding **harmony**.
A P : 0 4 :232(139) [0185] and communities **harmony** should be nurtured by mutual
A P : 0 4 :232(140) [0185] the church to preserve **harmony**, to bear, if need be, with
A P : 0 4 :233(140) [0185] For **harmony** will inevitably disintegrate if bishops
A P : 0 7 :005(169) [0227] of the sacraments in **harmony** with the Gospel of Christ.
A P : 0 7 :043(177) [0243] but for the sake of **harmony** they wanted others to follow
A P : 1 5 :051(222) [0329] reason, and to foster **harmony** those ancient customs
A P : 1 5 :052(222) [0329] greatest possible public **harmony**, without offense to
A P : 1 6 :011(224) [0333] because it is so out of **harmony** with the Scriptures.
A P : 2 1 :044(236) [0357] ways of establishing **harmony** — ways that will not burden
A P : 2 3 :059(247) [0379] desire to establish **harmony**, we know that to satisfy our
A P : 2 7 :005(269) [0421] degenerates into bad **harmonies** which, Plato says, cause
L C : 0 1 :121(382) [0615] love, kindness, and **harmony** in their houses, and children
L C : 0 1 :219(394) [0643] together in love and **harmony**, cherishing each other
S D : 0 1 :061(519) [0879] the term is explained in **harmony** with the Word of God,
S D : 0 3 :006(540) [0917] pure, in beautiful **harmony**, and without any schisms.
S D : 0 7 :066(581) [0995] Hence, in **harmony** with these words of Christ's
S D : 0 8 :004(592) [1017] who follow it as being in **harmony** with the Word of
S D : 1 1 :053(625) [1081] which we cannot **harmonize** — in fact, we have no
S D : 1 1 :095(632) [1095] of temporal peace, tranquility, and outward **harmony**.
S D : 1 1 :095(632) [1095] would such peace and **harmony** last, because it would be
S D : 1 1 :095(632) [1095] and deep love for true **harmony** and are cordially inclined
S D : 1 1 :096(632) [1095] We desire such **harmony** as will not violate God's honor,

Harried (1)
L C : 0 3 :105(434) [0727] attacked, hunted, and **harried** on all sides, we are

Harry (1)
L C : 0 1 :160(387) [0627] of honoring them is to **harry** them out of the country and

Harsh (3), Harshest (1), Harshly (1)
A L : 0 0 :001(047) [0059] teachers are to be regarded as heretics judge too **harshly**.
A L : 2 3 :013(053) [0063] In such a **harsh** manner was the edict carried out that not
A P : 0 4 :242(141) [0187] relations it is not peevish, **harsh**, or implacable; that it
S C : 0 9 :006(355) [0561] your wives, and do not be **harsh** with them" (Col. 3:19).
L C : 0 1 :268(401) [0657] and sentence, for the **harshest** verdict a judge can

Hart (3)
L C : 0 6 :032(461) [0000] bread just like a hunted **hart**, burning with heat and
L C : 0 6 :033(461) [0000] as Ps. 42:2 says, "As a **hart** longs for flowing streams, so
L C : 0 6 :033(461) [0000] That is, as a **hart** trembles with eagerness for a fresh

Hasten (1), Hastily (1), Hasty (1)
A G : 0 0 :001(048) [0059] act in an unkind and **hasty** fashion, contrary to all
A G : 2 3 :012(053) [0063] was at once enforced so **hastily** and indecently that the
S C : P R :023(341) [0539] sacrament, for he will **hasten** to it of his own accord, he

Hat (1), Hats (1)
S 1 : P R :013(291) [0459] bishops' and cardinals' **hats** and crosiers, and similar
L C : 0 1 :307(406) [0669] it is all done "under the **hat**" so as to escape detection.

Hate (10), Hated (1), Hateful (1), Hates (4), Hating (1), Hatred (19), Hatreds (1)
A G : 0 0 :004(095) [0095] said or introduced out of **hatred** or for the purpose of
A L : 2 0 :025(044) [0057] of sins; hence they **hate** God as an enemy, do not call
A L : 0 0 :002(049) [0059] people in order to inflame the **hatred** of men against us.
A L : 2 6 :018(067) [0073] matter rashly or out of **hatred** for the bishops, as some
A L : 2 7 :045(078) [0081] If out of **hatred** anybody should be inclined to enlarge on
A P : P R :016(099) [0103] is evident from the bitter **hatred** inflaming our
A P : 0 2 :008(101) [0107] fear and trust in him, **hating** his judgment and fleeing it,
A P : 0 2 :011(102) [0109] contempt of God, **hate** of God, and similar faults that we
A P : 0 2 :024(103) [0111] of God in its security, or it **hates** him in its terror.
A P : 0 2 :029(104) [0113] of God, unbelief, distrust, contempt, and **hate** of God.
A P : 0 4 :034(112) [0131] the midst of punishment it flees and **hates** his judgment.
A P : 0 4 :232(140) [0185] various schisms and the **hatreds**, factions, and heresies
A P : 0 4 :240(141) [0187] shows what it means: "**Hatred** stirs up strife, but love
A P : 0 4 :241(141) [0187] it says, grow because of **hatred**, as we often see the
A P : 0 4 :242(141) [0187] each one gave in to his **hatred**, a major commotion
A P : 0 4 :242(141) [0187] arisen in the church simply from the **hatred** of the clergy.
A P : 0 4 :242(141) [0187] says, "Know, but do not **hate**, the manners of a friend."
A P : 0 4 :349(160) [0217] impulses, the fear and love of God, **hatred** of lust, etc.
A P : 1 2 :123(201) [0289] men's minds and fan their **hatred**, so that the uninitiated
A P : 1 2 :128(201) [0291] producing the most bitter **hatred** against those who,
A P : 1 2 :129(202) [0291] what will happen if this **hatred** should erupt against you.
A P : 1 2 :137(203) [0293] We **hate** to waste any more words in refuting these silly
A P : 1 2 :174(210) [0307] instead of murder and **hatred**, the greatest possible
A P : 2 3 :044(245) [0375] boy who is used to being lazy **hates** those who are busy."

Continued ▶

A P : 2 7 :002(269) [0419] with a pharisaical **hatred**, the guardian began to
A P : 2 7 :009(270) [0421] of religion, but actually for the sake of appetite or **hatred**?
S 3 : 0 2 :002(303) [0479] Some, who **hate** the law because it forbids what they
S C : 0 1 :021(344) [0543] generation of those who **hate** me, but showing steadfast
L C : 0 1 :030(369) [0589] *generation of those who **hate** me, and showing mercy to*
L C : 0 1 :038(369) [0591] means when he says, "who **hate** me," that is, those who
L C : 0 1 :071(374) [0601] He **hates** to hear God's name and cannot long remain
L C : 0 1 :188(390) [0635] or malice toward anyone in a spirit of anger and **hatred**.
L C : 0 1 :320(408) [0673] *generation of them that **hate** me; but to those who love*
L C : 0 3 :103(434) [0727] there is in it nothing but **hatred** and envy, enmity,
L C : 0 4 :067(445) [0749] and the more free from greed, **hatred**, envy, and pride.
L C : 0 6 :003(457) [0000] even though nothing was more **hateful** to them.
S D : 1 1 :088(631) [1093] I loved, but Esau I **hated**'" (Rom. 9:11-13; Gen. 25:23;

Haven (1)
L C : 0 1 :316(408) [0671] if I boasted, "Of course, I **haven**'t a single groschen to

Head (49), Heads (7)
A G : 2 8 :054(090) [0091] that women should cover their **heads** in the assembly.
A G : 2 8 :056(090) [0091] offense to others she goes out with uncovered **head**.
A L : 2 8 :054(090) [0091] women should cover their **heads** in the assembly and that
A L : 2 8 :056(090) [0091] out in public with her **head** uncovered, provided no
A P : 0 4 :098(121) [0149] builders, but which has become the **head** of the corner.
A P : 0 4 :400(168) [0227] words or in the words of its **head**, our Lord Jesus Christ?
A P : 0 7 :005(169) [0227] he has made him the **head** over all things for the church,
A P : 1 2 :031(186) [0259] have gone over my **head**; they weigh like a burden too
A P : 1 2 :106(197) [0283] of domestic advice to the **head** of a household, telling him
A P : 2 4 :021(252) [0389] can be classified under one or another of these **heads**.
S 2 : 0 4 :001(298) [0471] The pope is not the **head** of all Christendom by divine
S 2 : 0 4 :005(299) [0473] very well without such a **head**, and it would have
S 2 : 0 4 :005(299) [0473] much better if such a **head** had not been raised up by the
S 2 : 0 4 :007(299) [0473] the claim that he is the **head** of the church by divine right
S 2 : 0 4 :007(299) [0473] were necessary to have a **head**, to whom all others should
S 2 : 0 4 :007(299) [0473] and suppose that such a **head** would then be elected by
S 2 : 0 4 :007(299) [0473] in their power and choice to change or depose this **head**.
S 2 : 0 4 :008(299) [0473] as subjection to such a **head** would depend on the good
S 2 : 0 4 :009(300) [0473] all of us live under one **head**, Christ, and by having all the
S 2 : 0 4 :009(300) [0475] Christendom, until the pope raised his **head** over them all.
S 2 : 0 4 :013(300) [0475] of his wishing to be the **head** of the Christian church by
S 2 : 0 4 :013(300) [0475] to proclaim himself the **head**, and then the lord of the
S 2 : 0 4 :014(301) [0475] to govern us as our **head** or lord, for deception, murder,
S 3 : 0 3 :026(307) [0487] be so cheap that they were released at six pence a **head**.
S 3 : 0 3 :035(309) [0489] all utterly lost, that from **head** to foot there is no good in
T R : 0 0 :014(322) [0507] the people for whom a **head** is to be ordained, and a
S C : 0 1 :000(342) [0539] *plain form in which the **head** of the family shall teach*
S C : 0 2 :000(344) [0543] *plain form in which the **head** of the family shall teach it to*
S C : 0 3 :000(346) [0545] *plain form in which the **head** of the family shall teach it to*
S C : 0 4 :000(348) [0551] *plain form in which the **head** of the family shall teach it to*
S C : 0 6 :000(351) [0555] *plain form in which the **head** of the family shall teach it to*
S C : 0 7 :000(352) [0557] *How the **head** of the family shall teach his household to*
S C : 0 8 :006(353) [0559] *How the **head** of the family shall teach his household to*
L C : P R :009(359) [0569] sake, to get it into their **heads** that they are not really and
L C : S P :004(362) [0575] it is the duty of every **head** of a household to examine his
L C : 0 1 :031(369) [0589] one which stands at the **head** of the list because it is of the
L C : 0 1 :031(369) [0589] the utmost importance for a man to have the right **head**.
L C : 0 1 :031(369) [0589] For where the **head** is right, the whole life must be right,
L C : 0 1 :186(390) [0633] upon their enemy's **head**, which, if they came true, would
L C : 0 1 :230(396) [0645] what would become of the **head** and chief protector of all
L C : 0 2 :051(417) [0691] or community of pure saints under one **head**, Christ.
L C : 0 3 :111(435) [0729] For he has a serpent's **head**; if it finds an opening into
L C : 0 4 :020(439) [0737] yes, the crown on his **head**, which shows me how and why
L C : 0 4 :082(446) [0751] he should immediately **head** for the ship and cling to it
L C : 0 5 :087(456) [0773] Therefore let every **head** of a household remember that it
S D : 0 1 :008(510) [0861] The Apology summarizes the matter under these **heads**:
S D : 0 1 :062(519) [0879] feet to the crown of our **head**, inasmuch as this befell a
S D : 0 5 :004(559) [0953] it under these **heads**: repentance to God and faith in
S D : 0 5 :023(562) [0959] would bruise the serpent's **head**; likewise, of the seed of
S D : 0 7 :044(577) [0987] of Christians with Christ their **head** and with one another.
S D : 0 8 :047(600) [1031] king, high priest, **head**, shepherd, and so forth, not only
S D : 0 8 :062(603) [1037] transformed into the God-**head** or by means of these
S D : 0 8 :078(607) [1043] on earth as mediator, **head**, king, and high priest.
S D : 0 8 :087(608) [1047] and indwelling of their **head**, king, and high priest, who
S D : 0 8 :096(609) [1049] all heretics break their **heads**, we admonish all Christians
S D : 1 0 :020(614) [1059] to govern us as our **head** or lord, for deception, murder,

Headings (1)
L C : 0 5 :001(447) [0753] Baptism under three **headings**, so we must deal with the

Headlong (2)
A P : 0 4 :020(110) [0125] and so they run **headlong** into despair, unless they hear,
S D : 0 1 :013(511) [0863] blindness, and drives them **headlong** into all sorts of vice.

Heal (4), Healed (4), Healing (4), Heals (2)
A P : 0 4 :263(146) [0195] 4:27), "Behold, there will be a **healing** of your offenses."
A P : 1 2 :031(186) [0259] I am languishing; O Lord, **heal** me, for my bones are
A P : 1 2 :128(202) [0291] though they ought to be **healing** consciences, refuse to let
A P : 1 2 :129(202) [0291] settled now in order to **heal** devout minds and free them
A P : 1 2 :129(202) [0291] But if you are kind and **heal** doubting consciences, you
A P : 2 1 :032(233) [0351] off pestilence, Valentine **heals** epilepsy, and George
A P : 2 1 :042(235) [0355] is most anxious for the **healing** and improving of the
S 2 : 0 1 :005(292) [0463] "And with his stripes we are **healed**" (Isa. 53:5).
T R : 0 0 :054(329) [0519] to it that errors are removed and consciences are **healed**.
L C : 0 5 :068(454) [0769] For where the soul is **healed**, the body has benefited also.
L C : 0 6 :026(460) [0000] miserable, then go and make use of the **healing** medicine.
S D : 0 1 :014(511) [0863] and renovation can **heal** man's nature, which original sin
S D : 0 2 :037(528) [0895] through which he **heals** us and which he uses to proclaim
S D : 0 5 :023(562) [0959] for our iniquities and with whose stripes we are **healed**."

Health (4), Healthful (1)
A P : 0 2 :041(105) [0115] is a neutral thing, like the color of the skin or ill **health**.
S C : 0 3 :014(347) [0549] weather, peace and **health**, order and honor; true friends,
L C : 0 1 :024(367) [0587] drink, nourishment, **health**, protection, peace, and all
L C : 0 1 :068(374) [0599] a happy hour or a **healthful** day thereafter, and thus they
L C : 0 1 :134(383) [0619] pertains to long life — **health**, wife and child, livelihood,

Heap (3), Heaped (2)
A P : 0 7 :001(168) [0227] chaff and wheat are **heaped** together (Matt. 3:12) and
A P : 1 1 :009(182) [0251] is not a syllable in this **heap** of constitutions, glosses,
A P : 2 7 :047(277) [0437] It is highly dangerous to **heap** such extravagant praises
L C : 0 1 :091(377) [0607] gathered together in one **heap**, they could not help us in
L C : 0 1 :278(402) [0661] with all their works **heaped** up together, and see if they

Hear (120), Heard (74), Hearing (33), Hears (40)
A G : P R :002(025) [0039] and charitably to **hear**, understand, and weigh the
A G : P R :023(027) [0043] in dissension are finally **heard**, amicably weighed,
A G : 0 5 :002(031) [0045] when and where he pleases, in those who **hear** the Gospel.
A G : 2 0 :019(043) [0055] this comfort was not **heard** in preaching, but poor
A G : 2 1 :002(047) [0057] He alone has promised to **hear** our prayers.
A G : 2 5 :004(062) [0069] as much as if we **heard** God's voice from heaven, that we
A G : 2 6 :013(066) [0073] because they had not **heard** anything of the consolation
A G : 2 7 :051(079) [0083] the common people, **hearing** the state of celibacy praised
A G : 2 7 :053(079) [0083] When the common man **hears** that only mendicants are
A G : 2 7 :054(079) [0083] When the people **hear** that it is only a counsel not to take
A G : 2 8 :022(084) [0087] of Christ in Luke 10:16, "He who **hears** you hears me."
A G : 2 8 :022(084) [0087] of Christ in Luke 10:16, "He who hears you **hears** me."
A G : 0 0 :002(095) [0095] with monks about the **hearing** of confessions, about
A L : 0 5 :002(031) [0045] and when it pleases God, in those who **hear** the Gospel.
A L : 2 0 :019(043) [0055] works when consolation from the Gospel was not **heard**.
A L : 2 1 :003(047) [0057] to be prayed to, and he has promised to **hear** our prayers.
A L : 0 0 :001(049) [0059] Majesty will graciously **hear** both what has been changed
A L : 2 4 :006(056) [0065] are admitted unless they are first **heard** and examined.
A L : 2 5 :004(062) [0069] as God's own voice **heard** from heaven, and are assured
A L : 2 6 :013(066) [0073] meanwhile, they had never **heard** the consolation of grace
A L : 2 7 :049(078) [0083] are obscured when men **hear** that only monks are in a
A L : 2 7 :052(079) [0083] They **hear** celibacy praised above measure, and therefore
A L : 2 7 :053(079) [0083] They **hear** that only mendicants are perfect, and therefore
A L : 2 7 :054(079) [0083] They **hear** that it is an evangelical counsel not to take
A L : 2 8 :022(084) [0087] according to the text, "He who **hears** you hears me."
A L : 2 8 :022(084) [0087] according to the text, "He who hears you **hears** me."
A L : 2 8 :054(090) [0091] in the church should be **heard** one after another.
A P : P R :002(098) [0099] Confutation; for we had **heard** that it condemned many
A P : 0 4 :002(107) [0121] Majesty kindly to **hear** us out on this important issue.
A P : 0 4 :008(108) [0121] true conviction that God **hears** prayer, and the
A P : 0 4 :014(109) [0123] We have **heard** of some who, in their sermons, laid aside
A P : 0 4 :020(110) [0125] into despair, unless they **hear**, beyond the teaching of the
A P : 0 4 :027(111) [0127] him, truly believe that he **hears** prayer, willingly obey him
A P : 0 4 :034(112) [0129] our sin, to fear him truly, and to be sure that he **hears** us.
A P : 0 4 :035(112) [0131] believe that God cared for him or regarded or **heard** him.
A P : 0 4 :045(113) [0133] fear him, be sure that he **hears** us, and obey him in all
A P : 0 4 :067(116) [0139] and (Rom. 10:17), "Faith comes from what is **heard**."
A P : 0 4 :119(124) [0155] sustain those who have **heard** nothing about this faith and
A P : 0 4 :135(125) [0159] our failure to believe that God forgives and **hears** us.
A P : 0 4 :135(125) [0159] by faith through **hearing** the Gospel of the forgiveness of
A P : 0 4 :167(130) [0169] Who does not often doubt whether God **hears** him?
A P : 0 4 :204(135) [0177] flee his judgment and never believe that he **hears** them.
A P : 0 4 :205(135) [0177] when it is sure that he freely forgives and **hears** us.
A P : 0 4 :209(135) [0177] The people **heard** that Abraham had offered up his son.
A P : 0 4 :257(144) [0193] find peace unless they **hear** the voice of God, clearly
A P : 0 4 :270(147) [0197] the law as soon as he **hears** that God is reconciled to us
A P : 0 4 :303(154) [0205] for us, forgives us, and **hears** us is a supernatural thing,
A P : 0 4 :331(158) [0211] O Lord, **hear**; O Lord, forgive; O Lord, give heed and
A P : 0 4 :333(158) [0211] we believe that we are **heard** because of Christ the high
A P : 0 4 :350(161) [0217] cares for us, forgives us, and **hears** us for Christ's sake.
A P : 0 4 :351(161) [0217] to fear him and to trust that he cares for us and **hears** us.
A P : 0 4 :358(162) [0219] We **hear** the term "reward": therefore we need neither
A P : 0 4 :360(162) [0219] conclusion when they **hear** this one word "reward": "It is
A P : 0 4 :360(162) [0219] out, dear reader, you have not yet **heard** the whole sorites.
A P : 0 4 :364(163) [0219] The strong **hear** the mention of punishments and rewards
A P : 0 4 :398(168) [0227] When future generations **hear** that such a doctrine was
A P : 0 4 :399(168) [0227] We have **heard** in this assembly that when opinions were
A P : 0 4 :400(168) [0227] as the Lord says, "My sheep **hear** my voice" (John 10:27).
A P : 0 7 :028(173) [0237] testifies (Luke 10:16), "He who **hears** you hears me."
A P : 0 7 :028(173) [0237] testifies (Luke 10:16), "He who hears you **hears** me."
A P : 0 7 :047(177) [0243] to the word (Luke 10:16), "He who **hears** you hears me."
A P : 0 7 :047(177) [0243] to the word (Luke 10:16), "He who hears you **hears** me."
A P : 1 1 :002(180) [0249] They have **heard** that it is the command of God — yes,
A P : 1 1 :005(181) [0249] the people could not be **heard** and instructed properly.
A P : 1 2 :003(182) [0253] Emperor Charles, to **hear** us out patiently and to consider
A P : 1 2 :039(187) [0261] "faith comes from what is **heard**," as Paul says
A P : 1 2 :039(187) [0261] **Hearing** the Gospel and hearing absolution strengthens
A P : 1 2 :039(187) [0261] Hearing the Gospel and **hearing** absolution strengthens
A P : 1 2 :040(187) [0261] statement (Luke 10:16), "He who **hears** you, hears me."
A P : 1 2 :040(187) [0261] statement (Luke 10:16), "He who hears you, **hears** me."
A P : 1 2 :042(187) [0263] absolution, through the **hearing** of the Gospel, so that it
A P : 1 2 :056(189) [0267] Then he **hears** the absolution (II Sam. 12:14), "The Lord
A P : 1 2 :057(189) [0267] Later she **heard** the absolution (vv. 48, 50), "Your sins are
A P : 1 2 :071(192) [0271] this, the Holy Spirit fell on all who **heard** the word."
A P : 1 2 :089(195) [0277] call upon God, how can they be sure that he **hears** them?
A P : 1 2 :103(197) [0281] objects that a judge must **hear** a case before pronouncing
A P : 1 2 :106(197) [0283] "know" here means to **hear** confessions, "condition"
A P : 1 2 :123(201) [0289] that when the uninitiated **hear** this they will conclude that
A P : 1 2 :130(202) [0291] issues but do not **hear** teachers capable of setting their
A P : 1 3 :005(212) [0309] says (Rom. 10:17), "Faith comes from what is **heard**."
A P : 1 5 :043(221) [0327] it is efficacious and is **heard**, the cross, respect for rulers
A P : 1 8 :006(225) [0335] nor the faith that God **hears**, forgives, helps, or saves
A P : 1 8 :007(226) [0337] and trust that God considers, **hears**, and forgives us.
A P : 1 8 :008(226) [0337] they really believe that God regards and **hears** them.
A P : 1 8 :008(226) [0337] being when terrified hearts **hear** the Gospel and receive
A P : 2 1 :010(230) [0345] Scripture, that the saints **hear** the individual's prayers?
A P : 2 1 :011(230) [0345] are not sure whether they **hear** us in the morning or in the
A P : 2 1 :017(231) [0347] be sure that we shall be **heard** if we invoke the saints.
A P : 2 1 :020(232) [0349] certain that we are **heard** for Christ's sake and that by his
A P : 2 1 :036(234) [0353] It is truly worthwhile to **hear** of these things and to see
A P : 2 1 :036(234) [0353] affirmed that God **hears** the prayers of believers.
A P : 2 1 :041(235) [0355] We ourselves have **heard** excellent theologians ask for
A P : 2 2 :008(237) [0359] who when they **hear** the phrase "lay communion"
A P : 2 3 :040(245) [0375] that is, to make room for **hearing** or teaching the Gospel.

Continued ▶

AP : 24 :002(249) [0385] the church benefits from **hearing** a Mass that he does not
AP : 24 :002(249) [0385] they imagine that mere **hearing** is a beneficial act of
AP : 24 :005(250) [0385] that men benefit from **hearing** lessons they do not
AP : 24 :023(253) [0391] perhaps because they had **heard** that a human victim was
AP : 24 :029(255) [0393] offered me thy Word to **hear**, and dost require me to
AP : 24 :075(263) [0411] **Hear** his own words (John 6:35), 'I am the bread of life;
AP : 27 :010(270) [0423] It is worthwhile to **hear** how they twist our arguments and
AP : 27 :027(274) [0429] It is terrible to read and **hear** such pharisaical and even
AP : 27 :038(275) [0433] with the man he did not **hear** anything, except that in the
AP : 27 :054(278) [0437] Meanwhile they neither **hear** nor preach the Gospel
AP : 28 :005(281) [0445] tears of the sufferers and **hear** the pitiful complaints of
AP : 28 :005(282) [0445] God undoubtedly sees and **hears** them, and it is to him
AP : 28 :018(284) [0449] the statement, "He who **hears** you hears me"
AP : 28 :018(284) [0449] "He who hears you **hears** me" (Luke 10:16), is not
AP : 28 :019(284) [0449] "He who **hears** you **hears** me" cannot be applied to
AP : 28 :019(284) [0449] "He who **hears** you **hears** me" cannot be applied to
AP : 28 :019(284) [0449] a way that he might be **heard**, because he says, "hears
AP : 28 :019(284) [0449] way that he might be heard, because he says, "**hears** me."
AP : 28 :019(284) [0449] his voice, His Word to be **heard**, not human traditions.
AP : 28 :021(284) [0449] that they teach wicked things, they should not be **heard**.
S1 : PR :010(290) [0457] Those people cannot **hear** Christ speak to them as the
S2 : 02 :005(293) [0463] people — especially if they **hear** that it is a dangerous
S2 : 04 :016(301) [0475] and were given a kindly **hearing**, but we shall stand
S2 : 04 :016(301) [0477] not intend to give us a **hearing** but only to damn,
S3 : 03 :003(304) [0481] Here man must **hear** such a judgment as this: "You are
S3 : 03 :008(304) [0481] the Word, the sacraments, and the like, as we shall **hear**.
S3 : 03 :027(307) [0487] these people, as we have **heard** above, are uncertain and
S3 : 08 :007(313) [0495] of reason must first have **heard**, "He who believes and is
S3 : 08 :008(313) [0495] had long since **heard** from the Jews about the coming
S3 : 08 :008(313) [0495] if the Word and his **hearing** of it had not preceded.
S3 : 12 :002(315) [0499] believers and sheep who **hear** the voice of their Shepherd.
SC : PR :022(341) [0537] is no Christian who does not **hear** and believe the Gospel.
SC : 01 :006(342) [0541] of the same, but deem it holy and gladly **hear** and learn it.
SC : 03 :021(348) [0549] heavenly Father and are **heard** by him, for he himself
SC : 03 :021(348) [0549] commanded us to pray like this and promised to **hear** us.
SC : 05 :021(350) [0553] "Dear Pastor, please **hear** my confession and declare that
LC : PR :011(360) [0571] For he cannot bear to **hear** God's Word.
LC : PR :016(361) [0573] after reading or **hearing** it once, that we know it all and
LC : SP :026(364) [0579] so that they may **hear** it explained and may learn the
LC : SP :026(364) [0581] to repeat what they have **heard** and give a good, correct
LC : 01 :008(365) [0583] nothing doubts and despairs as if he never **heard** of God.
LC : 01 :031(369) [0589] (as we shall **hear** later), yet they are attached precisely to
LC : 01 :038(369) [0591] They refuse to **hear** what is preached or spoken to them.
LC : 01 :070(374) [0601] Thus, as we have **heard** above, the heart by faith first
LC : 01 :071(374) [0601] He hates to **hear** God's name and cannot long remain
LC : 01 :074(374) [0601] when they see or **hear** anything monstrous or fearful and
LC : 01 :081(376) [0603] intention, but, as we shall **hear**, it meant that we should
LC : 01 :084(376) [0605] that they may assemble to **hear** and discuss God's Word
LC : 01 :092(377) [0607] Word is taught, preached, **heard**, read, or pondered, there
LC : 01 :094(378) [0607] holy; this, as we have **heard**, takes place only through
LC : 01 :095(378) [0607] his Word and refuse to **hear** and learn it, especially at the
LC : 01 :096(378) [0607] or frivolity neglect to **hear** God's Word or lie around in
LC : 01 :096(378) [0609] from force of habit go to **hear** preaching and depart again
LC : 01 :097(378) [0609] properly hallowed if one **heard** a Mass or the reading of
LC : 01 :098(378) [0609] not only about **hearing** the Word but also about learning
LC : 01 :098(378) [0609] of how you have **heard** and learned and honored his
LC : 01 :099(378) [0609] be chastised who, after **hearing** a sermon or two, become
LC : 01 :100(379) [0609] idle and the Word is not **heard**, the devil breaks in and
LC : 01 :101(379) [0609] ponder the Word, **hear** it, and put it to use, such is its
LC : 01 :166(388) [0629] and disdains this is not worthy to **hear** a word from God.
LC : 01 :182(389) [0631] We **hear** it explained every year in the Gospel, Matthew
LC : 01 :209(393) [0641] all people to enter the estate of marriage, as we shall **hear**.
LC : 01 :264(400) [0655] everyone would rather **hear** evil than good about his
LC : 01 :264(400) [0655] Yet we cannot bear to **hear** the best spoken of others.
LC : 01 :266(401) [0657] I may see and **hear** that my neighbor sins, but to make
LC : 01 :272(401) [0659] or at any rate be reproved in secret, as we shall **hear**.
LC : 01 :289(404) [0663] upon all we may **hear** about our neighbor, as long as it is
LC : 01 :314(407) [0671] and candles until nothing else can be seen or **heard**.
LC : 01 :316(408) [0671] and the Lord's Prayer must help us, as we shall **hear**.
LC : 01 :321(408) [0673] Commandment, as we **heard** above, this appendix was
LC : 01 :326(409) [0675] his Word, but learn it, **hear** it gladly, keep it holy, and
LC : 02 :001(411) [0679] Thus far we have **heard** the first part of Christian
LC : 02 :020(412) [0683] We all pass over it, **hear** it, and recite it, but we neither
LC : 02 :024(413) [0683] through his Son and the Holy Spirit, as we shall **hear**.
LC : 02 :052(417) [0691] the fact that I have **heard** and still hear God's Word,
LC : 02 :052(417) [0691] that I have heard and still **hear** God's Word, which is the
LC : 02 :060(418) [0695] When we Germans **hear** the word *Fleisch* (flesh), we think
LC : 03 :001(420) [0697] We have **heard** what we are to do and believe.
LC : 03 :006(421) [0699] knows whether God heeds my prayer or cares to **hear** it?
LC : 03 :014(422) [0701] if the act was performed, whether God **heard** it or not.
LC : 03 :020(423) [0703] him and will assuredly be **heard** and granted, so that we
LC : 03 :022(423) [0703] that our prayer pleases him and will assuredly be **heard**.
LC : 03 :023(423) [0703] it has the excellent testimony that God loves to **hear** it.
LC : 03 :044(426) [0709] the result that he must **hear** us called not children of God
LC : 03 :048(426) [0711] nothing he would rather **hear** than to have his glory and
LC : 03 :087(432) [0723] side and, as we have **heard**, directing his attacks against
LC : 03 :100(433) [0725] We have now **heard** enough about the trouble and effort
LC : 03 :102(434) [0727] example of other people and by things we **hear** and see.
LC : 03 :119(436) [0731] doubt that our prayer is surely **heard** and will be granted.
LC : 03 :121(436) [0731] with certainty that God **hears** their prayer but remain in
LC : 03 :121(436) [0731] I be so bold as to boast that God **hears** my prayer?
LC : 04 :028(440) [0739] that is in us does it but faith, as we shall **hear** later on.
LC : 05 :032(450) [0761] the very words which we **hear** everywhere in the Gospel.
LC : 05 :033(450) [0761] wood but to those who **hear** them, those to whom Christ
LC : 05 :040(451) [0761] A lot of people who **hear** the Gospel, now that the
LC : 05 :064(454) [0769] the commandment, as we **heard** above, which should
LC : 05 :075(455) [0771] to the Galatians and **hear** what are the fruits of the flesh:
LC : 06 :007(457) [0000] To others who **hear** it gladly, however, we must preach,
LC : 06 :014(458) [0000] here a sure refuge when it **hears** in God's Word that
LC : 06 :022(459) [0000] performing a work but to **hear** what God wishes to say to
LC : 06 :023(459) [0000] miserable beggar who **hears** that a rich gift, of money or
LC : 06 :030(460) [0000] if anyone refuses to **hear** and heed the warning of our
EP : 02 :004(470) [0787] the preaching and the **hearing** of God's Word, as it is
EP : 02 :004(470) [0787] faith comes from the **hearing** of God's Word
EP : 02 :004(470) [0787] God's will that men should **hear** his Word and not stop
EP : 02 :013(471) [0789] means, without the **hearing** of God's Word and without
EP : 02 :018(472) [0791] the Word that has been **heard** or through the use of the
EP : 02 :019(472) [0791] Man should **hear** this Word, though he cannot give it
EP : 05 :008(478) [0803] of sin, as long as men **hear** only the law and hear nothing
EP : 05 :008(478) [0803] men hear only the law and **hear** nothing about Christ, the
EP : 11 :008(495) [0833] and it is his will that they **hear** the Word and do not stop
EP : 11 :012(496) [0835] is that men either do not **hear** the Word of God at all but
EP : 11 :012(496) [0835] in them; or, if they do **hear** the Word, they cast it to the
EP : 12 :010(498) [0839] 8. That no one should **hear** sermons or attend services in
EP : 12 :022(499) [0841] the Word preached and **heard** — is not a means through
SD : 02 :004(520) [0881] external preaching and **hearing** of the Word of God) and
SD : 02 :005(521) [0881] which is preached and **heard**, purely out of grace and
SD : 02 :009(521) [0883] people on earth read or **hear** the Gospel of the Son of
SD : 02 :010(522) [0885] they do not see, and **hearing** they do not hear, nor do
SD : 02 :010(522) [0885] and hearing they do not **hear**, nor do they understand.
SD : 02 :015(523) [0887] and lazy in reading, **hearing**, and meditating on the Word
SD : 02 :019(524) [0889] to God without **hearing** and meditating upon the divine
SD : 02 :024(526) [0891] members of his body, can **hear** the Gospel and meditate
SD : 02 :026(526) [0891] Likewise, "Lydia **heard** us; the Lord opened her heart to
SD : 02 :026(526) [0891] heart, seeing eyes, and **hearing** ears (Deut. 29:4;
SD : 02 :031(527) [0893] or believe that God will **hear** them, that he forgives their
SD : 02 :036(528) [0895] through this, that I have **heard** the Word of God and still
SD : 02 :036(528) [0895] the Word of God and still **hear** it, which is the beginning
SD : 02 :046(530) [0899] they will refuse to heed, **hear**, or read the Word and the
SD : 02 :050(531) [0901] his holy Word (when one **hears** it preached or reads it)
SD : 02 :051(531) [0901] comes from what is **heard**, and what is heard comes by
SD : 02 :051(531) [0901] what is heard, and what is **heard** comes by the preaching
SD : 02 :052(531) [0901] who would be saved must **hear** this preaching, for the
SD : 02 :052(531) [0901] the preaching and the **hearing** of God's Word are the
SD : 02 :053(531) [0903] God and regenerated can **hear** and read this Word
SD : 02 :054(531) [0903] the preaching and the **hearing** of his Word) God is active,
SD : 02 :055(532) [0903] the Word preached and **heard** illuminates and converts
SD : 02 :056(532) [0903] that the Word which is **heard** and preached is an office
SD : 02 :057(532) [0903] If a person will not **hear** preaching or read the Word of
SD : 02 :057(532) [0903] earnestly wills that we **hear** it, and has promised that,
SD : 02 :058(532) [0903] Holy Spirit and will not **hear**, no injustice is done him if
SD : 02 :067(534) [0907] As a result, they not only **hear** the Word of God but also
SD : 02 :080(536) [0911] without means, without **hearing** the divine Word and
SD : 02 :089(538) [0915] the preaching and the **hearing** of the divine Word, nor did
SD : 02 :090(538) [0915] of God preached and **heard**, the Holy Spirit, and man's
SD : 02 :090(539) [0915] the preaching and the **hearing** of his holy Word as his
SD : 03 :041(546) [0929] in us in conversion through the **hearing** of the Gospel.
SD : 07 :013(571) [0977] "We have **heard** how Master Martin Bucer has explained
SD : 07 :046(577) [0987] for a disputation when he **heard** God's words about
SD : 07 :062(581) [0995] faith — namely, that we **hear**, accept with faith, and
SD : 08 :063(603) [1037] so strongly on this that they will **hear** no other exchange.
SD : 10 :015(613) [1057] the church to preserve, as we have just **heard**.
SD : 10 :019(614) [1059] believers and sheep who **hear** the voice of their
SD : 11 :017(619) [1069] Word when it is preached, **heard**, and meditated on,
SD : 11 :030(621) [1073] as follows: "My sheep **hear** my voice, and I know them,
SD : 11 :030(621) [1073] to "the inheritance" **hear** the Gospel, believe on Christ,
SD : 11 :038(622) [1075] with God as if we had **heard** a voice from heaven," as the
SD : 11 :039(622) [1075] Word when it is proclaimed, **heard**, and meditated upon.
SD : 11 :039(623) [1075] their hearts when they **hear** it (Heb. 4:2, 7), resist the
SD : 11 :051(624) [1079] "He who has ears to **hear**, let him hear"; and "Take heed
SD : 11 :051(625) [1079] has ears to hear, let him **hear**"; and "Take heed how ye
SD : 11 :051(625) [1079] ears to hear, let him hear"; and "Take heed how ye **hear**."
SD : 11 :068(627) [1085] wills that all men should **hear** this proclamation and
SD : 11 :069(627) [1085] true faith through the **hearing** of God's Word, as the
SD : 11 :069(627) [1085] "Faith comes from the **hearing** of God's Word"
SD : 11 :074(628) [1087] words, "But thou didst **hear** my supplications when I cried
SD : 11 :076(629) [1087] any one should refuse to **hear** or should despise the
SD : 11 :076(629) [1089] he does this through the **hearing** of his holy, divine
SD : 11 :077(629) [1089] must therefore attend on it, **hear** it with diligence, and in
SD : 11 :078(629) [1089] The reason why all who **hear** the Word do not come to
SD : 11 :078(629) [1089] own fault because they **heard** the Word of God not to
SD : 12 :015(634) [1099] 6. That one may not **hear** or attend on a sermon in those
SD : 12 :030(635) [1101] Word proclaimed and **heard**, is not a means whereby God

Hearer (3), Hearers (7)

AP : 24 :002(249) [0385] quibble about how a **hearer** who is ignorant of the faith
AP : 27 :055(278) [0439] to teach and exhort the **hearers**, brief and pointed lessons
EP : 07 :042(486) [0817] in order to make our teaching obnoxious to their **hearers**.
SD : PR :004(502) [0847] orthodox teachers and **hearers** pledged themselves to
SD : 02 :055(531) [0903] and watering and the **hearer**'s running and willing would
SD : 02 :055(532) [0903] the preacher nor the **hearer** should question this grace and
SD : 07 :001(569) [0971] faithfully to warn our **hearers** and other pious Christians
SD : 07 :042(576) [0987] and apostles, and by their disciples and **hearers** in turn.
SD : 07 :081(584) [1001] Thereby the faith of the **hearers** in the essence and
SD : 07 :089(585) [1003] Gospel even when godless **hearers** do not believe it

Hearsay (1)

LC : 01 :269(401) [0657] if you are not sure but have it only from **hearsay**.

Heart (239), Hearts (114)

PR : PR :009(006) [0011] allegation many pious **hearts** were frightened away and
PR : PR :010(006) [0011] for simple and pious **hearts**, so that they might know
PR : PR :016(008) [0013] publicly attested this with their **hearts**, lips, and hands.
PR : PR :017(008) [0015] entered our minds and **hearts** to want to introduce,
PR : PR :018(009) [0015] Christ with joyful and fearless **hearts** and consciences.
PR : PR :022(011) [0019] in the simplicity of their **hearts**, do not understand the
PR : PR :024(013) [0021] assured of this in our **hearts** and Christian consciences
PR : PR :027(014) [0025] have with one mind and **heart** subscribed our names
AG : 12 :005(035) [0049] this faith will comfort the **heart** and again set it at rest.
AG : 16 :004(038) [0051] eternal mode of existence and righteousness of the **heart**.
AG : 18 :004(039) [0051] God with their whole **heart** or fearing him), for it is only
AG : 18 :002(039) [0051] in God with his whole **heart**, or of expelling inborn evil
AG : 18 :002(039) [0051] heart, or of expelling inborn evil lusts from his **heart**.
AG : 20 :029(045) [0057] Holy Spirit is given, the **heart** is moved to do good
AG : 20 :031(045) [0057] when it is without the Holy Spirit, the **heart** is too weak.
AG : 25 :008(062) [0069] Jeremiah also says, "The **heart** is desperately corrupt; who

Continued ▶

A G : 2 6 :035(069) [0075] to yourselves lest your **hearts** be weighed down with
A G : 2 7 :049(079) [0083] honestly with our whole **hearts**, and yet have sincere
A L : 0 3 :004(030) [0045] the Holy Spirit into their **hearts** to rule, comfort, and
A L : 1 6 :004(038) [0051] righteousness of the **heart**, but it does not destroy the
A L : 1 8 :003(039) [0051] is wrought in the **heart** when the Holy Spirit is received
A L : 2 0 :026(045) [0057] as confidence which consoles and lifts up terrified **hearts**.
A L : 2 0 :029(045) [0057] Holy Spirit is received, **hearts** are so renewed and
A L : 2 0 :038(046) [0057] all manner of lusts and human devices rule in the **heart**.
A L : 2 5 :008(062) [0069] Jeremiah also says, "The **heart** of man is corrupt and
A L : 2 6 :035(069) [0075] to yourselves lest your **hearts** be weighed down with
A P : 0 2 :033(104) [0113] that of itself the **heart** is lacking in love, fear, and trust in
A P : 0 4 :034(112) [0129] Holy Spirit, the human **heart** either despises the
A P : 0 4 :035(112) [0131] do them with a wicked **heart**, and (Rom. 14:23) "whatever
A P : 0 4 :035(112) [0131] works that seem virtuous, for God judges the **heart**.
A P : 0 4 :036(112) [0131] A **heart** that really feels God's wrath cannot love him
A P : 0 4 :045(113) [0133] of conscience it consoles and encourages our **hearts**.
A P : 0 4 :046(113) [0133] it regenerates our **hearts**, it precedes our keeping of the
A P : 0 4 :062(115) [0139] For these, our **hearts** must again receive consolation.
A P : 0 4 :064(116) [0139] forth a new life in our **hearts**, and is a work of the Holy
A P : 0 4 :079(118) [0143] must be conquered in our **hearts**, as Paul says in
A P : 0 4 :080(118) [0143] when we comfort our **hearts** with trust in the mercy
A P : 0 4 :092(120) [0149] "Man believes with his **heart** and so is justified," where he
A P : 0 4 :092(120) [0149] he declares that faith is the righteousness of the **heart**.
A P : 0 4 :099(121) [0151] Acts 15:9, "He cleansed their **hearts** by faith."
A P : 0 4 :100(121) [0151] it brings forth peace, joy, and eternal life in the **heart**.
A P : 0 4 :106(122) [0153] Here he teaches that our **hearts** are terrified by the law
A P : 0 4 :110(123) [0153] not love at all unless our **hearts** are sure that the
A P : 0 4 :123(124) [0157] prophet (Jer. 31:33), "I will put my law upon their **hearts**."
A P : 0 4 :124(124) [0157] the law that deals with the thoughts of the **heart**.
A P : 0 4 :125(124) [0157] produces a new life in our **hearts**, it must also produce
A P : 0 4 :125(124) [0157] it must also produce spiritual impulses in our **hearts**.
A P : 0 4 :125(124) [0157] he says (Jer. 31:33), "I will put my law upon their **hearts**."
A P : 0 4 :125(124) [0157] our neighbor because our **hearts** have spiritual and holy
A P : 0 4 :128(125) [0157] too, how can the human **heart** love God while it knows
A P : 0 4 :130(125) [0157] still the impulses of the **heart** toward God, belonging to
A P : 0 4 :131(125) [0159] love the Lord your God with all your **heart**" (Deut. 6:5).
A P : 0 4 :144(127) [0161] forgiveness of sins for a **heart** terrified and fleeing from
A P : 0 4 :170(130) [0171] The Holy Spirit in our **hearts** battles against such feelings
A P : 0 4 :189(133) [0175] these works he sanctifies **hearts** and suppresses the devil.
A P : 0 4 :203(135) [0175] believe and be sure in his **heart** that for Christ's sake he is
A P : 0 4 :219(137) [0181] (Jer. 31:33), "I will put my law within their **hearts**."
A P : 0 4 :245(142) [0189] that issues from a pure **heart** and a good conscience and
A P : 0 4 :246(142) [0189] show that it is not dead but living and active in the **heart**.
A P : 0 4 :249(143) [0191] conscience and encourages and consoles terrified **hearts**.
A P : 0 4 :252(143) [0191] believe him from their **heart** and then have good fruits,
A P : 0 4 :253(143) [0193] works regenerate our **hearts**; that works are a
A P : 0 4 :258(144) [0193] evil," as he denounces ungodly **hearts** and requires faith.
A P : 0 4 :261(145) [0195] is, redeem your sins by changing your **heart** and works.
A P : 0 4 :263(145) [0195] Righteousness is faith in the **heart**.
A P : 0 4 :267(147) [0197] of punishment unless the **heart** first receives remission of
A P : 0 4 :270(147) [0197] Christ, the mediator, the **heart** is at peace and begins to
A P : 0 4 :284(150) [0201] Yet Peter says (Acts 15:9) that **hearts** are purified by faith.
A P : 0 4 :284(150) [0201] of the Scripture; for if **hearts** are clean and then the
A P : 0 4 :288(151) [0203] to the uncleanness of the **heart**, reason thinks that it
A P : 0 4 :292(152) [0203] of penitence, he takes **heart** and believes that he has a
A P : 0 4 :293(152) [0203] When the **heart** is encouraged and quickened by faith in
A P : 0 4 :303(154) [0205] does not come without a great battle in the human **heart**.
A P : 0 4 :315(156) [0207] we can keep the law, our **hearts** must be reborn by faith.
A P : 0 4 :326(157) [0211] does not forgive but judges and condemns their **hearts**.
A P : 0 4 :327(158) [0211] can say, 'I have made my **heart** clean, I am pure from my
A P : 0 4 :365(163) [0219] to include the righteousness of the **heart** with other fruits.
A P : 0 4 :371(164) [0221] but also the faith of the **heart**, since the Scriptures do not
A P : 0 4 :371(164) [0221] but of righteousness in the **heart** and of its fruits.
A P : 0 4 :373(164) [0221] of the righteousness of the **heart** and of faith, and for this
A P : 0 4 :374(164) [0221] lump together the righteousness of the **heart** and its fruit.
A P : 0 4 :375(164) [0223] the righteousness of the **heart** from its fruits, if only our
A P : 0 4 :383(165) [0225] quickening the **heart** amid the terrors of sin and death.
A P : 0 4 :383(166) [0225] "Man believes with his **heart** and so is justified, and he
A P : 0 4 :384(166) [0225] save, but that it saves only because of faith in the **heart**.
A P : 0 7 :005(169) [0227] association of faith and of the Holy Spirit in men's **hearts**.
A P : 0 7 :008(169) [0229] spirit, who renews, consecrates, and governs their **hearts**.
A P : 0 7 :013(170) [0231] is the righteousness of the **heart** and the gift of the Holy
A P : 0 7 :031(174) [0237] can be no faith in the **heart** nor righteousness in the heart
A P : 0 7 :031(174) [0237] in the heart nor righteousness in the **heart** before God.
A P : 0 7 :031(174) [0237] this righteousness of the **heart** is something that quickens
A P : 0 7 :031(174) [0237] of the heart is something that quickens the **heart**.
A P : 0 7 :032(174) [0239] to the righteousness of the **heart** or the worship of God.
A P : 0 7 :032(174) [0239] be no righteousness of the **heart** before God without these
A P : 0 7 :036(175) [0241] The righteousness of the **heart** is a spiritual thing that
A P : 0 7 :036(175) [0241] of the heart is a spiritual thing that quickens men's **hearts**.
A P : 0 7 :036(175) [0241] do not quicken the **heart**, are not works of the Holy
A P : 0 7 :036(175) [0241] by which God moves the **heart** to believe (like the divinely
A P : 0 7 :036(175) [0241] that do not pertain to the **heart** and "perish as they are
A P : 1 2 :031(186) [0259] and crushed; I groan because of the tumult of my **heart**."
A P : 1 2 :038(187) [0261] and sustains the anxious **heart**, whereas in servile fear
A P : 1 2 :038(187) [0261] in servile fear faith does not sustain the anxious **heart**.
A P : 1 2 :044(187) [0263] Holy Spirit quickens our **hearts** through the Word of
A P : 1 2 :048(188) [0265] nor read the sentence of the law written in their **hearts**.
A P : 1 2 :048(188) [0265] earlier sentence and restoring peace and life to the **heart**.
A P : 1 2 :049(189) [0265] This sustains and quickens the **heart**.
A P : 1 2 :051(189) [0265] and quickening because **hearts** that do not feel God's
A P : 1 2 :060(190) [0269] and brings forth peace, joy, and a new life in the **heart**.
A P : 1 2 :062(190) [0269] If the **heart** doubts, it maintains that God's promises are
A P : 1 2 :064(191) [0269] Those who dream that the **heart** can find peace without
A P : 1 2 :073(192) [0273] Holy Spirit brings in your **heart**, saying, 'Your sins are
A P : 1 2 :074(192) [0273] that faith encourages our **hearts** and the Holy Spirit
A P : 1 2 :107(198) [0283] it must come from the **heart** and not just from the voice,
A P : 1 2 :142(204) [0295] to love God "with all our **hearts**," etc. (Deut. 6:5) and
A P : 1 2 :147(205) [0297] of guilt, faith frees the **heart** from the wrath of God and
A P : 1 2 :149(205) [0299] genuine punishments than are real terrors in the **heart**.
A P : 1 2 :151(206) [0299] help and to acknowledge the unbelief in their **hearts**.
A P : 1 2 :170(209) [0305] Chrysostom says, "In the **heart** contrition, in the mouth
A P : 1 2 :178(211) [0309] teach the faith that justifies and consoles faithful **hearts**.
A P : 1 3 :001(211) [0309] us, through which he moves men's **hearts** to believe.
A P : 1 3 :004(211) [0309] of grace, which is the **heart** of the New Testament.
A P : 1 3 :004(211) [0309] we are absolved, our **hearts** should firmly believe that
A P : 1 3 :005(211) [0309] simultaneously moves the **heart** to believe and take hold
A P : 1 3 :005(212) [0309] the ears to strike the **heart**, so the rite itself enters through
A P : 1 3 :005(212) [0309] the rite itself enters through the eyes to move the **heart**.
A P : 1 3 :018(213) [0313] a good disposition in our **heart**, that is, without faith.
A P : 1 3 :023(214) [0313] "Man believes with his **heart** and so is justified."
A P : 1 5 :046(221) [0327] to yourselves lest your **hearts** be weighed down with
A P : 1 6 :002(222) [0331] knowledge of God in the **heart**, the fear of God and faith,
A P : 1 6 :006(223) [0331] and the beginning of eternal life in the **hearts** of believers.
A P : 1 6 :008(223) [0333] eternal righteousness to **hearts**, while it approves the civil
A P : 1 6 :009(224) [0333] but attitudes of the **heart**, like a deep fear of God and a
A P : 1 8 :006(225) [0335] the Holy Spirit human **hearts** have neither the fear of God
A P : 1 8 :007(226) [0337] table, which the human **heart** cannot perform without the
A P : 1 8 :008(226) [0337] they consider what their **hearts** believe about God's will,
A P : 1 8 :008(226) [0337] into being when terrified **hearts** hear the Gospel and
A P : 2 0 :008(227) [0341] support and life to the **heart** in its hardest struggle
A P : 2 1 :018(231) [0347] God our Father, comfort your **hearts** and establish them."
A P : 2 1 :042(235) [0355] the good of the church at **heart** at this point, they would
A P : 2 2 :010(237) [0361] and strengthen terrified **hearts** when they believe that
A P : 2 3 :035(244) [0373] as the purity of the **heart** and the mortification of lust; it
A P : 2 3 :035(244) [0373] may be greater purity of **heart** in a married man like
A P : 2 3 :064(248) [0381] requires purity of the **heart** and not ceremonies of the
A P : 2 3 :064(248) [0381] It is possible that the **heart** of married men like Abraham
A P : 2 3 :064(248) [0381] be taken to mean purity of the **heart** and total penitence.
A P : 2 4 :012(251) [0387] death and to comfort our **hearts** with the knowledge of
A P : 2 4 :027(254) [0393] righteousness of faith in the **heart** and the fruits of faith.
A P : 2 4 :027(254) [0393] worship should be in spirit, in faith, and with the **heart**.
A P : 2 4 :029(255) [0393] a broken and contrite **heart**, O God, thou wilt not
A P : 2 4 :033(256) [0395] the worship of the **heart**, by which the name of the Lord
A P : 2 4 :034(256) [0397] requires sacrifices of the **heart**, not the ceremonial
A P : 2 4 :036(257) [0397] symbolizes faith, prayer, and thanksgiving in the **heart**.
A P : 2 4 :039(257) [0399] the daily sacrifice of the **heart**, for in the New Testament
A P : 2 4 :059(260) [0405] ministry of the Spirit, the Holy Spirit works in the **heart**.
A P : 2 4 :070(262) [0409] was instituted to move the **heart** to believe through what
A P : 2 4 :071(262) [0409] faith gives life to terrified **hearts**, is the worship of the
A P : 2 7 :025(273) [0427] your God with all your **heart**" (Deut. 6:5), and again,
A P : 2 7 :027(273) [0429] and life in the **heart**, therefore perfection means to
A P : 2 7 :069(281) [0443] sake of showing pious **hearts** why they should reject the
A P : 2 7 :069(281) [0443] And let every pious **heart** know and be sure that such
A P : 2 8 :003(281) [0443] listen to the complaints of churches and pious **hearts**!
A P : 2 8 :008(282) [0445] the apostles say that **hearts** are cleansed by faith and then
A P : 2 8 :010(282) [0445] Do they make **hearts** alive?
A P : 2 8 :010(282) [0447] and the Holy Spirit, that work eternal life in the **heart**.
S 1 : P R :010(290) [0457] everywhere that our **hearts** would break with grief.
S 3 : 0 3 :002(304) [0479] (true sorrow of the **heart**, suffering, and pain of death).
S 3 : 0 8 :004(312) [0495] are in the shrine of his **heart**," and he claims that
S 3 : 1 3 :001(315) [0499] we get a new and clean **heart** and that God will and does
S C : P R :013(339) [0535] whether he is a believer or, at **heart**, a scoundrel or knave.
S C : 0 6 :010(352) [0557] for the words "for you" require truly believing **hearts**.
S C : 0 9 :010(356) [0563] with singleness of **heart**, as to Christ; not in the way of
S C : 0 9 :010(356) [0563] the will of God from the **heart**, rendering service with a
L C : 0 1 :002(365) [0581] else than to trust and believe him with our whole **heart**.
L C : 0 1 :002(365) [0581] the trust and faith of the **heart** alone make both God and
L C : 0 1 :003(365) [0581] That to which your **heart** clings and entrusts itself is, I
L C : 0 1 :004(365) [0581] and confidence of the **heart**, and these fly straight to the
L C : 0 1 :004(365) [0581] Only let your **heart** cling to no one else."
L C : 0 1 :006(365) [0583] and possessions — on which he fixes his whole **heart**.
L C : 0 1 :010(366) [0583] to have something in which the **heart** trusts completely.
L C : 0 1 :012(366) [0583] All these fix their **heart** and trust elsewhere than in the
L C : 0 1 :013(366) [0583] requires that man's whole **heart** and confidence be placed
L C : 0 1 :014(366) [0583] of him when our **heart** embraces him and clings to
L C : 0 1 :015(366) [0583] cling to him with all our **heart** is nothing else than to
L C : 0 1 :016(366) [0585] wrath, namely, that the **heart** should know no other
L C : 0 1 :018(367) [0585] made into a god that to which his **heart** was inclined.
L C : 0 1 :021(367) [0585] It is primarily in the **heart**, which pursues other things
L C : 0 1 :028(368) [0587] and examine your own **heart** thoroughly and you will find
L C : 0 1 :028(368) [0587] Do you have the kind of **heart** that expects from him
L C : 0 1 :028(368) [0587] the contrary, does your **heart** cling to something else,
L C : 0 1 :029(368) [0589] so that they may take them to **heart** and remember them.
L C : 0 1 :032(369) [0589] who trust and believe him alone with their whole **heart**.
L C : 0 1 :040(370) [0591] and impel us to fix our **hearts** upon God with perfect
L C : 0 1 :045(370) [0593] his throne and he let his **heart** depart from God, placing
L C : 0 1 :048(371) [0593] as I said before, where the **heart** is right with God and
L C : 0 1 :050(371) [0593] inwardly instructed the **heart** and taught faith, so this
L C : 0 1 :050(371) [0593] things that issue and emerge from the **heart** are words.
L C : 0 1 :051(371) [0595] upon our lips when our **heart** knows or should know that
L C : 0 1 :056(372) [0595] Let us take to **heart** how important this commandment is
L C : 0 1 :057(372) [0597] as God will permit the **heart** that turns away from him to
L C : 0 1 :058(372) [0597] as there are few who trust in God with their whole **heart**.
L C : 0 1 :070(374) [0601] we have heard above, the **heart** by faith first gives God
L C : 0 1 :071(374) [0601] remain when it is uttered and invoked from the **heart**.
L C : 0 1 :077(375) [0603] takes such root in their **hearts** that they fear God more
L C : 0 1 :089(377) [0605] God's Word and carry it in our **hearts** and on our lips.
L C : 0 1 :099(378) [0609] and befuddles the **hearts** of many so that he may take us
L C : 0 1 :100(378) [0609] and to kindle in your **heart** unbelief and wicked thoughts
L C : 0 1 :100(379) [0609] keep God's Word in your **heart**, on your lips, and in your
L C : 0 1 :100(379) [0609] For where the **heart** stands idle and the Word is not
L C : 0 1 :101(379) [0609] and it constantly cleanses the **heart** and its meditations.
L C : 0 1 :103(379) [0611] love him with our whole **heart** all the days of our lives.
L C : 0 1 :107(379) [0611] by our actions, both of **heart** and of body, that we respect
L C : 0 1 :114(380) [0613] could not lay it to **heart**; they simply gaped in
L C : 0 1 :118(381) [0615] could say with a joyful **heart** in his presence, "Now I know
L C : 0 1 :120(381) [0615] Should not the **heart** leap and melt with joy when it can
L C : 0 1 :121(382) [0615] and ears and take this to **heart** so that we may not again
L C : 0 1 :121(382) [0615] and children would win their parents' **hearts** completely.
L C : 0 1 :142(384) [0621] and ought to have fatherly **hearts** toward their people.
L C : 0 1 :148(385) [0623] will be no peace in your **heart**, and eventually you will
L C : 0 1 :152(386) [0625] our blessings and we shall have all that our **hearts** desire.
L C : 0 1 :157(386) [0625] someone may take it to **heart**, so that we may be delivered
L C : 0 1 :166(387) [0627] us and make our **hearts** so melt for joy and love toward
L C : 0 1 :166(388) [0629] everything abundantly, according to your **heart**'s desire.

Continued ▶

LC : 0 1 :182(389) [0631] not kill, either by hand, **heart**, or word, by signs or
LC : 0 1 :184(390) [0633] we see such people, our **hearts** in turn rage and we are
LC : 0 1 :187(390) [0633] and have a patient, gentle **heart**, especially toward those
LC : 0 1 :188(390) [0635] be harmed; finally, our **heart** should harbor no hostility
LC : 0 1 :202(392) [0639] Your **heart**, your lips, and your whole body are to be
LC : 0 1 :212(394) [0641] too, God's grace is still required to keep the **heart** pure.
LC : 0 1 :215(394) [0641] from the act, yet their **hearts** remain so full of unchaste
LC : 0 1 :247(398) [0651] over poor, sorrowful **hearts**, and he will not leave them
LC : 0 1 :308(406) [0669] for he sees your wicked **heart** and the deceitfulness of the
LC : 0 1 :310(407) [0669] Above all, he wants our **hearts** to be pure, even though as
LC : 0 1 :323(409) [0673] actions proceed from a **heart** that fears and regards God
LC : 0 1 :324(409) [0675] Wherever a man's **heart** has such an attitude toward
LC : 0 1 :330(410) [0677] this and take it to **heart**, there will arise a spontaneous
LC : 0 2 :021(413) [0683] believed it with our whole **heart**, we would also act
LC : 0 2 :023(413) [0683] see in them his fatherly **heart** and his boundless love
LC : 0 2 :023(413) [0683] Thus our **hearts** will be warmed and kindled with
LC : 0 2 :038(415) [0689] us and bestowed on our **hearts** through the preaching of
LC : 0 2 :042(416) [0689] he illumines and kindles **hearts** so that they grasp and
LC : 0 2 :043(416) [0689] does not awaken understanding in the **heart**, all is lost.
LC : 0 2 :064(419) [0695] depths of his fatherly **heart**, his sheer, unutterable love.
LC : 0 2 :065(419) [0695] for the Lord Christ, who is a mirror of the Father's **heart**.
LC : 0 2 :067(419) [0697] moreover, are inscribed in the **hearts** of all men.
LC : 0 3 :010(421) [0699] Indeed, the human **heart** is by nature so desperately
LC : 0 3 :014(422) [0701] to take these words to **heart** and in no case to despise
LC : 0 3 :020(423) [0703] awaken and kindle in our **hearts** a desire and love to
LC : 0 3 :027(424) [0705] that you may kindle your **heart** to stronger and greater
LC : 0 3 :055(427) [0713] too great for any human **heart** to dare to desire if God
LC : 0 3 :062(428) [0715] is driven out of men's **hearts** and a breach is made in his
LC : 0 3 :092(432) [0725] Where the **heart** is not right with God and cannot achieve
LC : 0 3 :092(433) [0725] a confident and joyful **heart** can only come from the
LC : 0 3 :102(434) [0727] this often wounds and inflames even an innocent **heart**.
LC : 0 3 :104(434) [0727] venomously shot into our **hearts**, not by flesh and blood
LC : 0 3 :109(435) [0729] send such a shaft into my **heart** that I can scarcely stand,
LC : 0 3 :110(435) [0729] appeal to God from your **heart**, "Dear Father, Thou hast
LC : 0 4 :030(440) [0739] and thus brought into the **heart**, just as the entire Gospel
LC : 0 4 :036(441) [0741] cannot do, nor the body, but the **heart** must believe it.
LC : 0 5 :027(449) [0759] For such times, when our **heart** feels too sorely pressed,
LC : 0 5 :036(450) [0761] it can be grasped and appropriated only by the **heart**.
LC : 0 5 :037(451) [0761] is done by the faith of the **heart** which discerns and
LC : 0 5 :054(453) [0765] we must examine our **heart** and conscience and act like a
LC : 0 5 :054(453) [0765] do this, the more will our **heart** be warmed and kindled,
LC : 0 5 :081(456) [0773] A liar who seduces the **heart** from God's Word and blinds
LC : 0 5 :083(456) [0773] never give up until the stone is removed from your **heart**.
LC : 0 6 :014(458) [0000] So if there is a **heart** that feels its sin and desires
LC : 0 6 :019(459) [0000] so that you may attain a happy **heart** and conscience.
EP : 0 1 :021(468) [0783] would ever arise in the **heart** of corrupted man, no idle
EP : 0 1 :021(468) [0785] it is written, "Out of the **heart** come evil thoughts," etc,
EP : 0 1 :021(469) [0785] "The imagination of man's **heart** is evil from his youth."
EP : 0 2 :003(470) [0787] "The imagination of man's **heart** is evil from his youth."
EP : 0 2 :004(470) [0787] with this Word and opens **hearts** so that, like Lydia in
EP : 0 3 :022(475) [0797] our own by faith in the **heart** and by the confession of the
EP : 0 6 :002(480) [0805] God was written into their **hearts** when they were created
EP : 0 7 :003(482) [0809] what they believe in their **hearts**, namely, that in the Holy
EP : 0 7 :017(484) [0813] and consolation in the **hearts** of believing and worthy
EP : 1 1 :009(495) [0833] to despair and waken dangerous thoughts in their **hearts**.
EP : 1 1 :012(496) [0835] their ears and their **hearts**, and thus bar the ordinary way
EP : 1 1 :022(497) [0837] that we may all be of one **heart** in him and constantly
SD : PR :004(502) [0847] themselves to these symbols with **heart** and mouth.
SD : PR :002(503) [0851] way we have from our **hearts** and with our mouths
SD : 0 1 :002(509) [0859] inheres in his nature, all actual sins flow out of his **heart**.
SD : 0 1 :011(510) [0863] and foremost powers of the soul in mind, **heart**, and will.
SD : 0 1 :011(510) [0863] uncleanness of the **heart** and evil desires and inclinations.
SD : 0 1 :011(510) [0863] us inherits from Adam a **heart**, sensation, and mind-set
SD : 0 1 :039(515) [0871] At this point all Christian **hearts** may well ponder God's
SD : 0 2 :007(521) [0883] divine things the intellect, **heart**, and will of unregenerated
SD : 0 2 :010(522) [0883] is in them, due to their hardness of **heart**" (Eph. 4:17, 18).
SD : 0 2 :012(522) [0885] denies to the intellect, **heart**, and will of the natural man
SD : 0 2 :014(523) [0885] for the grace of God and eternal salvation in their **hearts**.
SD : 0 2 :014(523) [0885] of true godliness in their **heart**, wills to continue to
SD : 0 2 :015(523) [0887] thank God from our **hearts** for having liberated us from
SD : 0 2 :017(523) [0887] matters the intellect, **heart**, and will of a natural,
SD : 0 2 :017(524) [0887] imagination of man's **heart** is evil from his youth"
SD : 0 2 :017(524) [0887] "The **heart** of man is deceitful and desperately wicked,"
SD : 0 2 :019(524) [0889] Scriptures compare the **heart** of unregenerated man to a
SD : 0 2 :020(525) [0889] nor eyes nor senses nor **heart**, inasmuch as man does not
SD : 0 2 :026(526) [0891] to receive inwardly a new **heart**, mind, and spirit, is solely
SD : 0 2 :026(526) [0891] opens the intellect and the **heart** to understand the
SD : 0 2 :026(526) [0891] us; the Lord opened her **heart** to give heed to what was
SD : 0 2 :026(526) [0891] gives an understanding **heart**, seeing eyes, and hearing
SD : 0 2 :026(526) [0891] removes the hard, stony **heart** and bestows a new and
SD : 0 2 :026(526) [0891] bestows a new and tender **heart** of flesh that we may walk
SD : 0 2 :031(527) [0893] And shortly thereafter: "**Hearts** which are without the
SD : 0 2 :044(529) [0897] Without this our **heart** of itself does not once think to
SD : 0 2 :047(530) [0901] other hand, despondent **hearts** may fall into grave anxiety
SD : 0 2 :048(530) [0901] ability for good in our **hearts**, and how we are to relate
SD : 0 2 :050(531) [0901] race and works in the **hearts** of men true repentance and
SD : 0 2 :054(531) [0903] God is active, breaks our **hearts**, and draws man, so that
SD : 0 2 :054(531) [0903] and sorrow in his **heart**, and through the preaching of and
SD : 0 2 :054(531) [0903] Spirit, who works all of this, is introduced into the **heart**.
SD : 0 2 :055(532) [0903] illuminates and converts **hearts** so that men believe this
SD : 0 2 :056(532) [0903] of our feeling, how and when we perceive it in our **hearts**.
SD : 0 2 :056(532) [0903] is potent and active in our **hearts** (II Cor. 2:14ff.).
SD : 0 2 :060(533) [0905] This the Scriptures call the creation of a new **heart**.
SD : 0 2 :070(535) [0909] in the intellect, will, and **heart**, so that the heart learns to
SD : 0 2 :070(535) [0909] will, and heart, so that the **heart** learns to know sin, to
SD : 0 2 :075(536) [0911] the law of God from the **heart**, and by this spontaneous
SD : 0 2 :077(536) [0911] itself to God and to obey the law of God from the **heart**.
SD : 0 2 :081(537) [0911] God creates a new **heart** and a new man in such a way
SD : 0 2 :083(537) [0913] in the intellect, will, and **heart**, when man in no way
SD : 0 2 :083(537) [0913] in the intellect, will, and **heart** of man whereby man
SD : 0 2 :089(538) [0915] through the Word in the intellect, will, and **heart** of man.
SD : 0 3 :051(548) [0933] own through faith in the **heart**, through the confession
SD : 0 4 :003(551) [0939] but flow from a spontaneous spirit and a joyful **heart**.
SD : 0 4 :010(552) [0941] different people in **heart**, spirit, mind, and all our powers,
SD : 0 4 :015(553) [0943] be in a single **heart** both a right faith and a wicked
SD : 0 4 :017(554) [0943] with obedience from the **heart** (II Cor. 9:7, Rom. 6:7)
SD : 0 5 :009(559) [0955] to indifferent and secure **hearts**, but to the "oppressed" or
SD : 0 5 :024(562) [0961] its threats will terrify the **hearts** of the unrepentant and
SD : 0 6 :005(564) [0963] of God is written on their **hearts**, just as the first man
SD : 0 6 :011(566) [0965] of the Gospel (Gal. 3:2, 14), who renews the **heart**.
SD : 0 6 :023(568) [0969] spontaneously from the **heart** by the renewal of the Holy
SD : 0 7 :044(577) [0987] comfort for all sorrowing **hearts**, and a true bond and
SD : 0 7 :046(577) [0989] most certainly in his **heart** that what God promised he
SD : 0 7 :050(578) [0989] his words and **heart** and intention and is best qualified
SD : 0 7 :106(588) [1009] will enable a Christian **heart** to rely on and trust in them
SD : 0 7 :107(588) [1009] reject and condemn with **heart** and mouth as false,
SD : 0 7 :112(589) [1011] reject and condemn with **heart** and mouth as false,
SD : 0 8 :088(609) [1047] condemn with mouth and **heart** all errors which are
SD : 0 9 :003(610) [1053] Then we shall retain the **heart** of this article and derive
SD : 1 1 :011(618) [1067] may well come to pious **hearts**, too, even though by the
SD : 1 1 :017(619) [1069] on, would convert **hearts** to true repentance, and would
SD : 1 1 :034(622) [1075] kingdom, but down in my **heart** I am not thinking of all,
SD : 1 1 :035(622) [1075] something different in their **hearts** (Ps. 5:10, 11; 12:3, 4).
SD : 1 1 :039(622) [1075] or who harden their **hearts** when they hear it
SD : 1 1 :042(623) [1077] world, and decorate their **hearts** as a tabernacle for the
SD : 1 1 :070(627) [1085] adversary is accustomed to tempt and vex pious **hearts**.
SD : 1 1 :075(628) [1087] the same old fatherly **heart** to all who tremble at his
SD : 1 1 :083(630) [1091] Pet. 2:20), prepare their **hearts** for Satan (Luke 11:24,
SD : 1 1 :085(630) [1091] God hardened Pharaoh's **heart** so that Pharaoh continued
SD : 1 1 :085(630) [1091] hand from him, and so his **heart** became hardened and
SD : 1 2 :040(636) [1103] shall appear with intrepid **hearts** before the judgment seat

Heartache (1)
LC : 0 3 :115(435) [0731] all the tragic misery and **heartache** of which there is so

Hearted (2), Heartedly (9), Heartfelt (1), Heartily (8), Hearty (2)
PR : PR :008(005) [0011] us and that other good-**hearted** people would have been
PR : PR :016(008) [0013] above, gladly and with **heartfelt** thanks to almighty God
PR : PR :024(013) [0023] to us that many good-**hearted** Christian persons, of high
SC : 0 3 :016(347) [0549] we on our part will **heartily** forgive and cheerfully do
LC : 0 1 :047(371) [0593] demand of us than a **hearty** trust in him for all blessings.
LC : 0 1 :107(379) [0611] whom we are whole-**heartedly** to honor, we must truly
LC : 0 1 :117(381) [0615] You should rejoice **heartily** and thank God that he has
LC : 0 1 :134(383) [0619] this life can neither be **heartily** enjoyed nor long endure.
LC : 0 1 :187(390) [0633] to his will and with **hearty** confidence and prayer commit
LC : 0 1 :219(394) [0643] each other whole-**heartedly** and with perfect fidelity.
LC : 0 1 :252(399) [0651] to do things which are **heartily** acceptable and pleasing to
LC : 0 3 :020(423) [0703] that our prayer is **heartily** pleasing to him and will
LC : 0 3 :025(423) [0705] never prayed whole-**heartedly** for so much as a drop of
LC : 0 3 :048(426) [0711] pray the petition whole-**heartedly**, you can be sure that
LC : 0 3 :121(436) [0731] they dare not whole-**heartedly** add "yes" and conclude
LC : 0 4 :033(440) [0741] be received unless we believe them whole-**heartedly**.
EP : 0 2 :009(471) [0789] the Gospel, whole-**heartedly** obey God's law, and thus
EP : 0 2 :011(471) [0789] to God, and whole-**heartedly** obey God's law by his own
SD : PR :004(502) [0847] we again whole-**heartedly** subscribe this Christian and
SD : 0 5 :008(559) [0953] one's sins, to feel **heartily** sorry for them, and to desist
SD : 0 7 :069(582) [0997] weak in faith, who are **heartily** terrified because of their
SD : 0 7 :069(582) [0997] in faith, deplore it, and **heartily** wish that they might

Heat (5)
LC : 0 6 :032(461) [0000] hunted hart, burning with **heat** and thirst, as Ps. 42:2
EP : 0 8 :008(487) [0819] hunger, thirst, cold, **heat**, and the like, which never
SD : 0 4 :012(553) [0941] from faith as it is to separate **heat** and light from fire."
SD : 0 7 :100(586) [1007] space; likewise light and **heat** go through air, water, glass,
SD : 0 8 :010(593) [1019] suffer hunger, thirst, frost, **heat**, and similar things are

Heathen (20)
AG : 2 0 :024(044) [0057] calls upon him, and is not, like the **heathen**, without God.
AL : 2 0 :025(044) [0057] without God, as are the **heathen**, for devils and ungodly
AL : 2 3 :020(055) [0063] states, even among the **heathen**, have adorned marriage
AP : 0 4 :288(151) [0203] The **heathen** and the Israelites sacrificed human victims
AP : 0 7 :014(170) [0231] separated from the **heathen** not by civil rites but by being
AP : 1 2 :114(199) [0285] this has a Jewish and **heathen** faith, for even the heathen
AP : 1 2 :114(199) [0285] faith, for even the **heathen** had certain expiations or sin
AP : 1 5 :015(217) [0319] religious rites of all the **heathen**, as well as the rites
AP : 1 5 :015(217) [0319] why did not the **heathen** and Israelites have the same
AP : 1 5 :016(217) [0319] Yet the rites of the **heathen** and the Israelites were
AP : 1 6 :003(223) [0331] they were formulated by **heathen** or by others, and in this
AP : 2 4 :023(253) [0391] at the customs which the **heathen** adopted from their
LC : 0 1 :018(367) [0585] For example, the **heathen** who put their trust in power
LC : 0 1 :018(367) [0585] in the mind of all the **heathen**, therefore, to have a god
LC : 0 1 :020(367) [0585] Accordingly the **heathen** actually fashion their fancies and
LC : 0 1 :035(369) [0589] he has destroyed both **heathen** and Jews; just so in our
LC : 0 1 :194(391) [0635] is but an ordinary **heathen** virtue, as Christ says in
LC : 0 2 :066(419) [0697] church, whether **heathen**, Turks, Jews, or false Christians
LC : 0 4 :020(439) [0737] bones, they look no different from Turks and **heathen**.
SD : 0 5 :022(562) [0959] the natural law even the **heathen** had to some extent a

Heaven (135)
AG : 0 3 :004(030) [0045] third day, ascended into **heaven**, and sits on the right
AG : 2 5 :004(062) [0069] heard God's voice from **heaven**, that we should joyfully
AG : 2 8 :016(083) [0085] commonwealth is in **heaven**," and in II Cor. 10:4, 5, "The
AG : 2 8 :024(084) [0087] if we, or an angel from **heaven**, should preach to you a
AL : 0 3 :004(030) [0045] he ascended into **heaven** to sit on the right hand of the
AL : 2 5 :004(062) [0069] own voice heard from **heaven**, and are assured that such
AL : 2 8 :016(083) [0085] commonwealth is in **heaven**," and in II Cor. 10:4, 5, "The
AL : 2 8 :024(084) [0087] "If an angel from **heaven** should preach any other
AP : 0 4 :098(121) [0149] is no other name under **heaven** given among men by
AP : 0 4 :198(134) [0175] righteousness' sake, for theirs is the kingdom of **heaven**."
AP : 0 4 :254(143) [0193] the poor in spirit, for theirs is the kingdom of **heaven**."
AP : 0 4 :356(161) [0217] it is written, "Your reward is great in **heaven**."
AP : 1 2 :040(187) [0261] less than we would believe a voice coming from **heaven**.
AP : 1 2 :129(202) [0291] so, of course, can open **heaven** for themselves whenever
AP : 1 2 :176(210) [0307] earth shall be bound in **heaven**, and whatever you loose
AP : 1 2 :176(210) [0307] whatever you loose on earth shall be loosed in **heaven**."
AP : 1 2 :178(211) [0309] touch neither earth nor **heaven** and they themselves

Continued ▶

AP : 2 1 :009(230) [0345] grant that the saints in **heaven** pray for the church in
AP : 2 3 :021(242) [0369] sake of the kingdom of **heaven**" (Matt. 19:12), let him
AP : 2 3 :040(245) [0375] sake of the kingdom of **heaven**" (Matt. 19:12), that is, to
AP : 2 8 :018(284) [0449] that we should not look for another word from **heaven**.
S 1 : 0 1 :000(291) [0461] nature, are one God, who created **heaven** and earth, etc.
S 1 : 0 1 :000(292) [0461] dead, and ascended to **heaven**; and he is seated at the
S 2 : 0 1 :005(292) [0461] or compromised, even if **heaven** and earth and things
S 2 : 0 1 :005(292) [0463] is no other name under **heaven** given among men by
S 2 : 0 2 :026(297) [0469] Although angels in **heaven** pray for us (as Christ himself
S 2 : 0 2 :026(297) [0469] and perhaps also in **heaven**, do likewise, it does not follow
S 2 : 0 2 :028(297) [0469] in their graves and in **heaven**, for no one will long
S 2 : 0 4 :013(300) [0475] even presumed to issue orders to the angels in **heaven**.
S 3 : 0 3 :001(303) [0479] of God is revealed from **heaven** against all ungodliness
S 3 : 0 3 :028(308) [0487] that they were more than we ourselves needed for **heaven**.
S 3 : 0 3 :041(309) [0491] It is a teaching from **heaven**, revealed in the Gospel, and
S 3 : 1 4 :001(316) [0501] to help not only himself but also others to get to **heaven**.
TR : 0 0 :038(326) [0515] "If an angel from **heaven** should preach to you a gospel
SC : PR :023(341) [0539] no life, no paradise, no **heaven**, no Christ, no God,
SC : 0 2 :001(344) [0543] *God, the Father almighty, maker of* ***heaven*** *and earth."*
SC : 0 2 :003(345) [0545] *dead, he ascended into* ***heaven****, and is seated on the right*
SC : 0 3 :001(346) [0545] *"Our Father who art in* ***heaven****."*
SC : 0 3 :005(346) [0547] Help us to do this, dear Father in **heaven**!
SC : 0 3 :009(347) [0547] *"Thy will be done, on earth as it is in* ***heaven****."*
SC : 0 3 :020(348) [0549] that our Father in **heaven** may deliver us from all manner
SC : 0 3 :020(348) [0549] take us from this world of sorrow to himself in **heaven**.
SC : 0 5 :016(350) [0553] that our sins are thereby forgiven before God in **heaven**.
SC : 0 9 :011(356) [0563] Master and yours is in **heaven**, and that there is no
LC : SP :011(363) [0577] in God, the Father almighty, maker of **heaven** and earth:
LC : SP :012(363) [0577] dead, he ascended into **heaven**, and sits on the right hand
LC : SP :014(363) [0577] Our Father who art in **heaven**, hallowed be thy name.
LC : SP :014(363) [0577] come, thy will be done, on earth as it is in **heaven**.
LC : 0 1 :019(367) [0585] from whom there is truly no god in **heaven** or on earth.
LC : 0 1 :022(367) [0585] its own works and presumes to wrest **heaven** from God.
LC : 0 1 :115(381) [0615] pleasing to my God in **heaven**; this I know for certain."
LC : 0 1 :247(398) [0651] he can complain to no one else, he will cry to **heaven**.
LC : 0 1 :324(409) [0675] loves anything else in **heaven** and on earth will keep
LC : 0 2 :009(411) [0679] *God, the Father almighty, maker of* ***heaven*** *and earth."*
LC : 0 2 :011(412) [0681] my God is the Father, who made **heaven** and earth.
LC : 0 2 :011(412) [0681] there is no one else who could create **heaven** and earth."
LC : 0 2 :012(412) [0681] emphasize the words, "maker of **heaven** and earth."
LC : 0 2 :019(412) [0681] and everything in **heaven** and on earth besides, is daily
LC : 0 2 :025(413) [0683] *dead, he ascended into* ***heaven****, and is seated on the right*
LC : 0 2 :029(414) [0685] and wretchedness and came from **heaven** to help us.
LC : 0 2 :031(414) [0687] and finally ascended into **heaven** and assumed dominion
LC : 0 2 :064(419) [0695] upon us everything in **heaven** and on earth, he has given
LC : 0 3 :038(425) [0709] which is already holy in **heaven**, may also be kept holy on
LC : 0 3 :059(428) [0715] *"Thy will be done on earth, as it is in* ***heaven****."*
LC : 0 3 :095(433) [0725] comfort and assurance that you are forgiven in **heaven**.
LC : 0 4 :016(438) [0735] is a treasure greater and nobler than **heaven** and earth.
LC : 0 4 :021(439) [0737] and deeds and has confirmed it by wonders from **heaven**.
LC : 0 4 :039(441) [0743] comfort and grace that **heaven** and earth cannot
LC : 0 5 :016(448) [0757] on earth, yes, no angel in **heaven** can transform bread and
LC : 0 5 :066(454) [0769] he brought from **heaven** for us, to which he most
EP : RN :001(464) [0777] "Even if an angel from **heaven** should preach to you a
EP : 0 5 :008(479) [0803] wrath is revealed from **heaven**" over all sinners and men
EP : 0 7 :005(482) [0809] confined to the highest **heaven** above, whither we should
EP : 0 7 :012(483) [0811] and under his feet everything in **heaven** and on earth.
EP : 0 7 :029(485) [0815] our faith ascends into **heaven**, it there partakes of the
EP : 0 7 :032(485) [0815] Christ is so enclosed in **heaven** that it can in no way be
EP : 0 7 :036(485) [0815] eyes from the bread to **heaven** and there seek the body of
EP : 0 8 :013(488) [0821] the dead, ascended into **heaven**, and was exalted to the
EP : 0 8 :016(489) [0821] and has all things in **heaven** and on earth and under the
EP : 0 8 :016(489) [0821] "All authority in **heaven** and on earth has been given to
EP : 0 8 :029(490) [0825] to every place in **heaven** and earth (something that is not
EP : 0 8 :034(491) [0825] "All authority in **heaven** and on earth has been given to
EP : 0 8 :035(491) [0825] given greater power in **heaven** and on earth, that is,
EP : 0 8 :039(491) [0827] his ascension all power in **heaven** and on earth was
EP : 1 1 :003(494) [0833] "There is a God in **heaven** who reveals mysteries, and he
EP : 1 2 :003(498) [0839] virgin Mary, but brought them with him from **heaven**.
EP : 1 2 :020(499) [0841] understanding of Christ as the reigning king of **heaven**.
SD : 0 2 :046(530) [0899] his gifts into them out of **heaven**, without means, and
SD : 0 2 :051(531) [0901] Father calls out from **heaven** concerning his beloved Son
SD : 0 5 :007(559) [0953] so, there will be joy in **heaven** over one sinner who
SD : 0 5 :010(560) [0955] he reveals his wrath from **heaven** over all sinners and
SD : 0 6 :006(565) [0965] moon, and all the stars of **heaven** regularly run their
SD : 0 7 :002(569) [0973] Supper as the highest **heaven** is distant from the earth.
SD : 0 7 :003(569) [0973] Christ which is there in **heaven**, yes, of Christ himself and
SD : 0 7 :003(569) [0973] here on earth and not in **heaven**, so also the body of
SD : 0 7 :003(569) [0973] body of Christ is now in **heaven** and not on earth, and
SD : 0 7 :005(570) [0973] are united with the body of Christ, which is in **heaven**.
SD : 0 7 :006(570) [0973] blood, which is now in **heaven** and nowhere else, and that
SD : 0 7 :007(570) [0975] is not in the communion on earth but only in **heaven**).
SD : 0 7 :008(570) [0975] by faith also of the body of Christ which is up in **heaven**.
SD : 0 7 :009(571) [0975] Christ has ascended into **heaven** it is not truly and
SD : 0 7 :024(573) [0981] or even an angel in **heaven**, can change bread and wine
SD : 0 7 :043(576) [0987] has been given from **heaven** to all men, "Listen to him."
SD : 0 7 :043(577) [0987] promises, as he says, "**Heaven** and earth shall pass away,
SD : 0 7 :043(577) [0987] again, "All authority in **heaven** and on earth has been
SD : 0 7 :099(586) [1005] or with the Father or in **heaven** according to this mode,
SD : 0 7 :102(587) [1007] of all the angels in **heaven**, and is known only to God.
SD : 0 7 :119(590) [1013] of his bodily ascension to **heaven** Christ is so confined
SD : 0 7 :119(590) [1013] by a certain space in **heaven** that he is neither able nor
SD : 0 7 :119(590) [1013] or as distant from it as **heaven** and earth are separated
SD : 0 7 :119(590) [1013] must take possession of **heaven**," to read "Christ must be
SD : 0 7 :119(590) [1013] must be received by **heaven**" — that is, Christ must be so
SD : 0 7 :119(590) [1013] comprehended by or in **heaven** that he in no way can or
SD : 0 7 :122(590) [1013] to look to that place in **heaven** where Christ is present
SD : 0 8 :002(591) [1015] at the same time in **heaven** and in the Holy Supper on
SD : 0 8 :026(596) [1023] its exaltation above all creatures in **heaven** and on earth.
SD : 0 8 :027(596) [1025] since he ascended into **heaven**, not just like some other
SD : 0 8 :028(596) [1025] is not a specific place in **heaven**, as the Sacramentarians
SD : 0 8 :028(596) [1025] power of God which fills **heaven** and earth, in which
SD : 0 8 :033(597) [1027] the greatest mystery in **heaven** and on earth is the
SD : 0 8 :055(601) [1033] to have all authority in **heaven** and on earth, to have all
SD : 0 8 :065(604) [1039] before all the saints in **heaven** and on earth, and in
SD : 0 8 :068(604) [1039] to them all authority in **heaven** and on earth is given, for
SD : 0 8 :070(604) [1039] say, "All authority in **heaven** and on earth has been given
SD : 0 8 :070(605) [1041] nature, "All authority in **heaven** and on earth has been
SD : 0 8 :071(605) [1041] every other creature in **heaven** or on earth, is not capable
SD : 0 8 :076(606) [1043] no other human being in **heaven** and on earth can say
SD : 0 8 :077(606) [1043] Paul, and all the saints in **heaven** would also be with us
SD : 0 8 :085(608) [1047] and 'All authority in **heaven** and on earth has been given
SD : 0 8 :092(609) [1049] into every place in **heaven** and earth, something which
SD : 1 0 :017(614) [1059] before my Father who is in **heaven**" (Matt. 10:32).
SD : 1 1 :038(622) [1075] had heard a voice from **heaven**," as the Apology explains
SD : 1 1 :065(627) [1083] election is revealed from **heaven** through the proclaimed
SD : 1 2 :025(635) [1099] from the virgin Mary but brought it along from **heaven**.
SD : 1 2 :029(635) [1101] the reigning king of **heaven**, who believes that according

Heavenly (37), Heavens (7)

AG : 2 8 :048(089) [0091] "Every plant which my **heavenly** Father has not planted
AL : 2 8 :048(089) [0091] "Every plant which my **heavenly** Father has not planted
AP : 0 4 :272(148) [0199] their trespasses, your **heavenly** Father also will forgive
AP : 0 4 :352(161) [0217] "We long to put on our **heavenly** dwelling, so that by
SC : 0 3 :005(346) [0547] From this preserve us, **heavenly** Father!
SC : 0 3 :008(346) [0547] Answer: When the **heavenly** Father gives us his Holy
SC : 0 3 :016(347) [0549] in this petition that our **heavenly** Father may not look
SC : 0 3 :021(348) [0549] are acceptable to our **heavenly** Father and are heard by
SC : 0 7 :002(352) [0557] "I give Thee thanks, **heavenly** Father, through thy dear
SC : 0 7 :005(353) [0559] "I give Thee thanks, **heavenly** Father, through thy dear
SC : 0 8 :009(353) [0559] "Lord God, **heavenly** Father, bless us, and these thy gifts
LC : 0 1 :317(408) [0673] does fulfill them is a **heavenly**, angelic man, far above all
LC : 0 2 :014(412) [0681] moon, and stars in the **heavens**, day and night, air, fire,
LC : 0 2 :036(415) [0687] as the spirit of man, **heavenly** spirits, and the evil spirit.
LC : 0 3 :036(425) [0707] tongue we would say, "**Heavenly** Father, grant that thy
LC : 0 3 :044(425) [0709] and live as godly and **heavenly** children with the result
LC : 0 3 :096(433) [0725] their trespasses, your **heavenly** Father also will forgive
LC : 0 4 :017(438) [0737] water, but a divine, **heavenly**, holy, and blessed water —
LC : 0 4 :017(438) [0737] of the Word, which is a **heavenly**, holy Word which no
LC : 0 4 :021(439) [0737] it was a jest that the **heavens** opened when Christ allowed
EP : 0 3 :003(473) [0793] man he rendered to his **heavenly** Father into death itself.
EP : 0 7 :015(483) [0811] union in a supernatural and **heavenly** manner.
EP : 0 7 :020(484) [0813] of the guests at this **heavenly** feast is and consists solely
EP : 0 7 :038(486) [0817] of the guests at this **heavenly** meal does not consist only
EP : 0 8 :016(489) [0821] "far above all the **heavens** that he might fill all things."
SD : 0 2 :011(522) [0885] to obtain spiritual and **heavenly** righteousness and life,
SD : 0 2 :016(523) [0887] preserve faith and his **heavenly** gifts in us and strengthen
SD : 0 2 :041(529) [0897] as follows: "When the **heavenly** Father gives us his Holy
SD : 0 3 :015(541) [0921] in death, Christ rendered for us to his **heavenly** Father.
SD : 0 3 :056(549) [0935] which he rendered to his **heavenly** Father even to the
SD : 0 4 :033(556) [0949] that you remain in your **heavenly** calling, lest you fall
SD : 0 5 :004(559) [0953] and grace of God, his **heavenly** Father, as it is written in
SD : 0 7 :002(569) [0973] interval as the earth is distant from the highest **heavens**."
SD : 0 7 :003(569) [0973] up and ascends above all **heavens** and receives and
SD : 0 7 :014(571) [0977] in this sacrament, one **heavenly** and the other earthly.
SD : 0 7 :091(585) [1005] writings, *Against the* ***Heavenly*** *Prophets, That These*
SD : 0 7 :101(587) [1007] with God, the divine, **heavenly** mode, according to which
SD : 0 7 :105(588) [1009] spiritual, supernatural, **heavenly** mode according to which
SD : 0 7 :116(589) [1011] and rises above all **heavens**, partakes up there of the body
SD : 0 7 :123(590) [1015] kinds of guests at this **heavenly** meal, the worthy and the
SD : 0 7 :127(591) [1015] the supernatural and **heavenly** mysteries of this Supper.
SD : 0 8 :027(596) [1025] far above all **heavens** that he might truly fill all
SD : 0 8 :051(600) [1033] unsearchable, ineffable, **heavenly** prerogatives and
SD : 1 1 :072(628) [1087] how much more will the **heavenly** Father give the Holy

Heavily (2), Heavy (13)

AP : 0 4 :233(140) [0185] if bishops impose **heavy** burdens on the people or have no
AP : 1 2 :031(186) [0259] over my head; they weigh like a burden too **heavy** for me.
AP : 1 2 :044(187) [0263] me, all who labor and are **heavy**-laden, and I will give you
AP : 1 2 :044(187) [0263] Labor and being **heavy**-laden mean contrition, anxiety,
AP : 1 2 :175(210) [0307] of public penitence so as not to burden men too **heavily**.
S 3 : 0 3 :025(307) [0485] eager to be delivered from the **heavy**, unbearable burden.
SC : 0 5 :029(351) [0555] whose consciences are **heavily** burdened or who are
LC : 0 1 :247(398) [0651] will have an effect too **heavy** for you and all the world to
LC : 0 5 :066(454) [0769] me, all who labor and are **heavy**-laden, and I will refresh
LC : 0 5 :071(455) [0769] those who labor and are **heavy**-laden with sin, fear of
LC : 0 5 :072(455) [0769] If you are **heavy**-laden and feel your weakness, go joyfully
SD : 0 7 :070(582) [0997] me, all who labor and are **heavy** laden, and I will give you
SD : 1 1 :028(620) [1071] unto me, all who are **heavy**-laden, and I will give you
SD : 1 1 :065(627) [1085] "Come to me, all who are **heavy**-laden, and I will give you
SD : 1 1 :089(631) [1093] all poor, burdened, and **heavy**-laden sinners to

Hebrew (3)

AP : 2 4 :085(264) [0413] is derived from *mizbeach*, the **Hebrew** term for altar.
AP : 2 4 :085(264) [0413] except perhaps to show off their knowledge of **Hebrew**?
LC : 0 1 :079(375) [0603] is so called from the **Hebrew** word "Sabbath," which

Hebrews (9)

AG : 2 4 :027(059) [0067] in the Epistle to the **Hebrews** that Christ offered himself
AL : 2 4 :026(059) [0067] in the Epistle to the **Hebrews**, "We have been sanctified
AP : 1 3 :010(212) [0311] As the Epistle to the **Hebrews** teaches clearly enough, we
AP : 2 4 :020(252) [0389] found in the Epistle to the **Hebrews** and elsewhere.
AP : 2 4 :022(253) [0391] as the Epistle to the **Hebrews** teaches (10:4), "It is
AP : 2 4 :026(254) [0391] The Epistle to the **Hebrews** teaches the same (13:15):
AP : 2 4 :052(259) [0403] quote the Epistle to the **Hebrews** (5:1), "Every high priest
AP : 2 4 :053(259) [0403] are in the Epistle to the **Hebrews**, our opponents twist
AP : 2 4 :058(260) [0405] The whole Epistle to the **Hebrews** supports this

Heed (18), Heeded (2), Heedlessly (3), Heeds (2)

AG : 2 6 :035(069) [0075] this in Luke 21:34, "Take **heed** to yourselves lest your
AG : 2 8 :046(088) [0089] Paul also forbids giving **heed** to Jewish myths or to
AL : 2 6 :035(069) [0075] Christ commands, "Take **heed** to yourselves lest your
AL : 2 8 :046(088) [0089] Paul also says, "Not giving **heed** to Jewish myths or to
AP : 0 4 :331(158) [0211] forgive; O Lord, give **heed** and act; delay not, for thy own
AP : 1 5 :046(221) [0327] says (Luke 21:34), "Take **heed** to yourselves lest your
LC : 0 1 :044(370) [0593] Just ponder and **heed** them.

Continued ▶

L C : 0 1 :140(384) [0621] in the past was neither **heeded** nor taught under the
L C : 0 1 :170(388) [0629] The trouble is that no one perceives or **heeds** this.
L C : 0 1 :248(398) [0651] He who will not **heed** or believe this may go his own way
L C : 0 1 :317(408) [0673] themselves to look only to these precepts and **heed** them.
L C : 0 3 :006(421) [0699] Who knows whether God **heeds** my prayer or cares to
L C : 0 3 :109(435) [0729] go about securely and **heedlessly** as if the devil were far
L C : 0 5 :039(451) [0761] among Christians, may not be **heedlessly** passed by .
L C : 0 5 :082(456) [0773] about so securely and **heedlessly** is that we neither
L C : 0 6 :030(460) [0000] refuses to hear and **heed** the warning of our preaching, we
E P : 0 2 :004(470) [0787] Lydia in Acts 16:14, they **heed** it and thus are converted
S D : 0 2 :026(526) [0891] the Scriptures and to **heed** the Word, as we read in Luke
S D : 0 2 :026(526) [0891] opened her heart to give **heed** to what was said by Paul"
S D : 0 2 :046(530) [0899] matters, they will refuse to **heed**, hear, or read the Word
S D : 0 3 :024(543) [0923] give especially diligent **heed** that we do not mingle or
S D : 0 6 :020(567) [0969] right in his own eyes, but **heed** all these words which I
S D : 1 0 :006(611) [1055] words of Paul must be **heeded**: "Do not be mismated with
S D : 1 1 :026(620) [1071] Instead we must **heed** the revealed will of God.
S D : 1 1 :051(625) [1079] ears to hear, let him hear"; and "Take **heed** how ye hear."

Heilbronn (1)
P R : P R :027(016) [0027] Mayor and Council of the City of **Heilbronn**

Heir (1), Heirs (8)
A P : 0 4 :042(113) [0133] the law who are to be the **heirs**, faith is null and the
A P : 0 4 :196(134) [0175] of God, moreover, it also makes us co-**heirs** with Christ.
A P : 0 4 :196(134) [0175] us sons of God and co-**heirs** with Christ, we do not merit
A P : 0 4 :354(161) [0217] children of God and fellow **heirs** with Christ (Rom. 8:17).
A P : 0 4 :356(161) [0217] us sons of God and fellow **heirs** with Christ (Rom. 8:17),
A P : 0 4 :366(163) [0221] 1:13), and made fellow **heirs** with Christ (Rom. 8:17).
S C : 0 4 :010(349) [0551] by his grace and become **heirs** in hope of eternal life.
S C : 0 9 :006(355) [0561] sex, since you are joint **heirs** of the grace of life, in order
S D : 0 3 :009(540) [0919] as a child of God and an **heir** of eternal life) without any

Hell (33)
A G : 0 3 :004(030) [0045] Christ also descended into **hell**, truly rose from the dead
A G : 1 7 :003(038) [0051] men and the devil to **hell** and eternal punishment.
A L : 0 3 :004(030) [0045] He also descended into **hell**, and on the third day truly
A P : 0 4 :085(119) [0147] death, and against all the gates of **hell** (Matt. 16:18).
A P : 0 4 :260(145) [0193] it is sure, and no gates of **hell** can overthrow it
A P : 1 2 :063(191) [0269] though all the gates of **hell** (Matt. 16:18) cry out against
A P : 2 4 :012(251) [0387] and sure that it can prevail against all the gates of **hell**.
S 1 : 0 1 :000(292) [0461] was buried, descended to **hell**, rose from the dead, and
S 3 : 0 3 :007(304) [0481] there is only death and **hell**, and man must despair like
S C : P R :023(341) [0539] has no sin, no flesh, no devil, no world, no death, no **hell**.
S C : 0 2 :003(345) [0545] *buried: he descended into* ***hell****, the third day he rose from*
L C : S P :012(363) [0577] buried: he descended into **hell**, the third day he rose from
L C : 0 1 :176(389) [0631] and wrath, thus earning **hell** by the way you have reared
L C : 0 2 :025(413) [0683] *buried: he descended into* ***hell****, the third day he rose from*
L C : 0 2 :030(414) [0685] creatures, from the jaws of **hell**, won us, made us free, and
L C : 0 3 :054(427) [0713] and sin, death, and **hell** exterminated, and that we may
E P : 0 8 :013(488) [0821] was buried, descended into **hell**, rose from the dead,
E P : 0 9 :000(492) [0827] IX. Christ's Descent into **Hell**
E P : 0 9 :001(492) [0827] to our simple Christian Creed, did Christ go to **hell**?
E P : 0 9 :004(492) [0827] know that Christ went to **hell**, destroyed hell for all
E P : 0 9 :004(492) [0827] went to hell, destroyed **hell** for all believers, and has
S D : 0 1 :039(515) [0871] and sinful dough into **hell**-fire, but out of it he makes and
S D : 0 5 :020(561) [0959] to temporal miseries, and to the punishment of **hell**-fire.
S D : 0 8 :021(595) [1023] this the devil's mask and damned it to the depths of **hell**.
S D : 0 8 :025(596) [1023] sin, death, the devil, **hell**, and eternal damnation.
S D : 0 9 :000(610) [1049] IX. Christ's Descent into **Hell**
S D : 0 9 :001(610) [1051] on Christ's descent into **hell** have been discovered among
S D : 0 9 :001(610) [1051] Son, who died, was buried, and descended into **hell**."
S D : 0 9 :001(610) [1051] burial and the descent into **hell** are differentiated as
S D : 0 9 :002(610) [1051] and man, descended into **hell**, conquered the devil,
S D : 0 9 :002(610) [1051] the devil, destroyed **hell**'s power, and took from the devil
S D : 0 9 :003(610) [1053] it the comfort that neither **hell** nor the devil can take us
S D : 1 1 :085(631) [1091] judgment on him, for he was indeed guilty of "**hell**-fire."

Hellish (2)
L C : 0 6 :003(457) [0000] made sheer anguish and a **hellish** torture since people had
E P : 0 9 :004(492) [0827] devil, and of the eternal damnation of the **hellish** jaws.

Help (113), Helped (8), Helping (1), Helps (6)
P R : P R :014(007) [0013] was completed with the **help** of such memoranda.
P R : P R :018(009) [0015] By the **help** of God's grace we, too, intend to persist in
P R : P R :023(012) [0021] our posterity through the **help** and assistance of the Holy
A G : P R :001(024) [0039] and how with continuing **help** he might effectively be
A G : 1 8 :002(039) [0051] But without the grace, **help**, and activity of the Holy
A G : 2 0 :035(046) [0057] be done and for offering **help** as to how they may be
A G : 2 0 :038(046) [0057] be done without the **help** of Christ, as he himself says in
A G : 2 1 :002(047) [0057] that we are to invoke saints or seek **help** from them.
A G : 2 5 :009(062) [0069] which we can enumerate we would be **helped** but little.
A G : 2 7 :049(079) [0083] and confidently expect **help** from him in every affliction
A G : 2 8 :068(093) [0093] to give counsel or **help** to consciences unless this
A G : 2 8 :078(094) [0095] and schism, which they should in truth **help** to prevent.
A G : 0 0 :005(095) [0095] diligently and with God's **help** prevented any new and
A L : 2 0 :037(046) [0057] or bear the cross, but it seeks and trusts in man's **help**.
A L : 2 1 :002(047) [0057] to the saints or seek their **help**, for the only mediator,
A L : 2 7 :049(079) [0083] to expect from him, **help** in all things which are to be
A P : 0 2 :023(103) [0111] be produced without certain gifts and **help** of grace.
A P : 0 2 :048(106) [0119] without Christ's **help**, so we cannot buy our way out of
A P : 0 4 :008(108) [0121] the expectation of God's **help** in death and all afflictions.
A P : 0 4 :029(111) [0129] natural capacity, with the **help** of free will, is in itself
A P : 0 4 :039(112) [0131] evidence; this will also **help** refute those errors of our
A P : 0 4 :125(124) [0157] God, to pray and expect **help** from him, to thank and
A P : 0 4 :139(126) [0161] Spirit, so that with the **help** of God we, too, might
A P : 0 4 :170(130) [0169] it looks to men for **help**; it even defies God's will and runs
A P : 0 4 :230(139) [0183] and we ask Christ for the **help** of his Holy Spirit to make
A P : 0 4 :289(151) [0203] by God, that with the **help** of this disposition we obey the
A P : 0 4 :299(153) [0205] but because Christ still **helps** us to keep the law.
A P : 0 4 :315(156) [0207] also clear that without the **help** of Christ we cannot keep
A P : 0 4 :316(156) [0209] good works, done with the **help** of a "disposition" of love,
A P : 0 4 :364(163) [0219] that it is the will of God to **help**, rescue, and save them.
A P : 1 2 :031(186) [0259] I cry for **help** until morning; like a lion he breaks all my
A P : 1 2 :128(201) [0291] Such doubt cannot **help** producing the most bitter hatred
A P : 1 2 :151(206) [0299] may learn to seek God's **help** and to acknowledge the
A P : 1 5 :020(218) [0321] and finally because they **helped** instruct the common
A P : 1 6 :013(224) [0333] testified how they were **helped** after the theories of the
A P : 1 8 :006(225) [0335] the faith that God hears, forgives, **helps**, or saves them.
A P : 2 1 :010(230) [0345] does not teach us to invoke the saints or to ask their **help**.
A P : 2 1 :023(232) [0349] should take refuge in the **help** of the saints, so that we
A P : 2 1 :024(232) [0349] should take refuge in the **help** of the saints," as this man
A P : 2 1 :030(233) [0351] Now one can be **helped** by the works or merits of others,
A P : 2 1 :036(234) [0353] troubles and dangers, **helped** kings in time of great
A P : 2 1 :043(235) [0357] This way of doing things **helps** neither their position nor
A P : 2 4 :028(254) [0393] me when I show mercy and **help** you, for I do not need
A P : 2 4 :028(254) [0393] Truly and wholeheartedly seek and expect **help** from me."
A P : 2 4 :029(255) [0393] thy promises of willingness to show mercy and to **help**."
A P : 2 4 :099(268) [0419] men to be warned not to **help** our opponents in defending
S 1 : P R :015(291) [0459] But **help** us, poor and wretched souls who cry unto Thee
S 2 : 0 2 :010(294) [0465] So by God's **help** I would suffer myself to be burned to
S 2 : 0 2 :012(295) [0465] Christ alone, and not the work of man, can **help** souls.
S 2 : 0 2 :026(297) [0469] and attribute all sorts of **help** to them, assigning to each
S 2 : 0 2 :028(297) [0469] and physical benefit and **help** are no longer expected, the
S 2 : 0 4 :007(299) [0473] he could, Christendom would not be **helped** in any way.
S 3 : 0 2 :004(303) [0479] anxiously desires **help** but does not know where to find
S 3 : 0 3 :027(307) [0487] Even this did not **help**, however, for although the pope
S 3 : 0 4 :000(310) [0491] which offers council and **help** against sin in more than
S 3 : 0 8 :001(312) [0493] is a consolation and **help** against sin and a bad
S 3 : 1 4 :001(316) [0501] by means of his work to **help** not only himself but also
S C : P R :006(338) [0533] to your care, and that you **help** me to teach the catechism
S C : P R :024(341) [0539] great need and God's gracious **help** belong to the devil.
S C : 0 1 :010(343) [0541] cause him any harm, but **help** and befriend him in every
S C : 0 1 :014(343) [0541] in shoddy wares, but **help** him to improve and protect his
S C : 0 1 :018(344) [0541] but be of service and **help** to him so that he may keep
S C : 0 3 :005(346) [0547] **Help** us to do this, dear Father in heaven!
L C : P R :011(360) [0571] and gives us immeasurable strength, comfort, and **help**.
L C : P R :017(361) [0573] he can counsel, **help**, comfort, judge, and make decisions
L C : 0 1 :004(365) [0581] one who will satisfy you and **help** you out of every need.
L C : 0 1 :012(366) [0583] them plenty of money, **help** them in love affairs, protect
L C : 0 1 :015(366) [0585] as the one who wishes to **help** you and to lavish all good
L C : 0 1 :017(367) [0585] own, to which he looked for blessings, **help**, and comfort.
L C : 0 1 :021(367) [0585] other things and seeks **help** and consolation from
L C : 0 1 :021(367) [0585] to trust that he wants to **help**, nor does it believe that
L C : 0 1 :022(367) [0585] conscience which seeks **help**, comfort, and salvation in its
L C : 0 1 :028(368) [0587] to receive more good and **help** than from God, and does
L C : 0 1 :041(370) [0591] blessing and will protect and **help** you in every need?
L C : 0 1 :069(374) [0601] men whom no teaching or punishment can **help**.
L C : 0 1 :073(374) [0601] For this purpose it also **helps** to form the habit of
L C : 0 1 :074(374) [0601] "**Help**, dear Lord Christ!" etc.
L C : 0 1 :091(377) [0607] one heap, they could not **help** us in the slightest degree,
L C : 0 1 :111(380) [0613] serving them, **helping** them, and caring for them when
L C : 0 1 :141(384) [0621] is too weak, he enlists the **help** of his friends and
L C : 0 1 :173(388) [0629] make them rich without our **help**, as indeed he does daily.
L C : 0 1 :195(391) [0637] God; that is, he wishes to **help** and protect us, so that he
L C : 0 1 :205(393) [0639] chastely himself and to **help** his neighbor do the same.
L C : 0 1 :251(399) [0651] he suffers want we are to **help**, share, and lend to both
L C : 0 1 :252(399) [0653] richly rewarded for all the **help** and kindness we show to
L C : 0 1 :259(400) [0655] and powerful who are in a position to **help** or harm him.
L C : 0 1 :260(400) [0655] is that everyone should **help** his neighbor maintain his
L C : 0 1 :280(403) [0661] If this does not **help**, then bring the matter before the
L C : 0 1 :287(403) [0663] eyes, even the whole body, must **help** cover and veil them.
L C : 0 1 :288(404) [0663] our utmost to serve and **help** him to promote his honor.
L C : 0 1 :316(408) [0671] and the Lord's Prayer must **help** us, as we shall hear.
L C : 0 1 :316(408) [0671] we must seek and pray for **help** and receive it continually.
L C : 0 1 :328(410) [0677] do good to all men, **help** them and promote their
L C : 0 2 :002(411) [0679] It is given in order to **help** us do what the Ten
L C : 0 2 :014(412) [0681] he makes all creation **help** provide the comforts and
L C : 0 2 :029(414) [0685] There was no counsel, no **help**, no comfort for us until
L C : 0 2 :029(414) [0685] and wretchedness and came from heaven to **help** us.
L C : 0 2 :069(420) [0697] his gifts and his power, to **help** us keep the Ten
L C : 0 3 :011(421) [0701] our misery and plight, and pray for grace and **help**.
L C : 0 3 :076(431) [0721] grow and yield richly; to **help** us manage our household
L C : 0 3 :106(434) [0729] We cannot **help** but suffer tribulations, and even be
L C : 0 3 :108(435) [0729] free rein and neither resist it nor pray for **help** against it.
L C : 0 3 :110(435) [0729] At such times your only **help** or comfort is to take refuge
L C : 0 3 :111(435) [0729] if you attempt to **help** yourself by your own thoughts and
L C : 0 3 :114(435) [0729] by saying, "Dear Father, **help** us to get rid of all this
L C : 0 3 :117(436) [0731] directs us to seek and expect **help** from no one but him.
L C : 0 4 :015(438) [0735] then babble, "How can a handful of water **help** the soul?"
L C : 0 5 :070(454) [0769] to be rid of it and desire **help**, should regard and use the
L C : 0 5 :087(457) [0773] For they must all **help** us to believe, to love, to pray, and
L C : 0 6 :019(459) [0000] and allow yourself to be **helped** so that you may attain a
E P : 0 2 :011(471) [0789] it be little and feeble) to **help**, to cooperate, to prepare
E P : 1 1 :008(495) [0833] all men should come to him and let themselves be **helped**.
S D : 0 2 :007(521) [0883] prepare himself for it, or **help**, do, effect, or cooperate
S D : 0 2 :014(523) [0885] great weakness and to **help** them to remain in true faith
S D : 0 2 :029(527) [0893] pointing out that Christ **helps** us and protects us against
S D : 0 2 :031(527) [0893] their sin, or that he will **help** them in their troubles;
S D : 0 2 :043(529) [0897] contrary to the **help** and grace of our Lord Jesus Christ.
S D : 0 2 :071(535) [0909] contribute anything or **help** in any way (I Cor. 2:4-12);
S D : 0 2 :077(536) [0911] and in a weak way — **help** and cooperate and prepare
S D : 0 7 :001(569) [0971] With the **help** of God we shall do everything we can to
S D : 0 7 :029(574) [0981] it until my death and (so **help** me God!) in this faith to
S D : 1 1 :007(617) [1065] works evil, nor does he **help** it along and promote it), but
S D : 1 1 :008(617) [1065] which creates, effects, **helps**, and furthers our salvation
S D : 1 1 :023(619) [1069] them to salvation and to **help**, further, strengthen, and
S D : 1 1 :062(626) [1083] destroyed, but that there is **help** for you is pure grace on
S D : 1 1 :074(628) [1087] my supplications when I cried to thee for **help**" (Ps. 31:23)
S D : 1 2 :005(633) [1097] but that we wanted to **help** matters fundamentally.
S D : 1 2 :019(634) [1099] nor may a subject call upon the government for **help**.

Helper (1), Helpers (1)
A G : 2 7 :020(074) [0079] man should be alone; I will make him a **helper** fit for him
S 2 : 0 2 :026(297) [0469] ways, regard them as **helpers** in time of need, and

Helpful (3)
AP : 1 5 :004(215) [0315] that religious rites are **helpful** in gaining grace and the
AP : 2 8 :006(282) [0445] and establish what is **helpful** or conducive to the
SD : PR :010(506) [0855] be accepted and used as **helpful** expositions and

Helpless (1)
LC : 0 1 :303(405) [0667] another's hand so that the victim is **helpless** to prevent it.

Helt (2)
S3 : 1 5 :005(317) [0501] Master George **Helt**, of Forchheim
TR : 0 0 :082(335) [0529] George **Helt**, of Forchheim

Hen (1)
SD : 0 2 :058(532) [0903] your children together as a **hen** gathers her brood under

Hence (85), Henceforth (7)
PR : PR :020(010) [0017] and veracious, and **hence** he is able to accomplish what
PR : PR :020(010) [0017] power and majesty) and **hence** must be false and
AG : 2 8 :013(083) [0085] **Hence** it should not invade the function of the other,
AL : 2 0 :022(044) [0055] **Hence** there was very great need to treat of and to restore
AL : 2 0 :025(044) [0057] of the forgiveness of sins; **hence** they hate God as an
AL : 2 0 :035(046) [0057] **Hence** it may readily be seen that this teaching is not to be
AL : 2 6 :016(066) [0073] **Hence** Gerson and certain other theologians greatly
AL : 2 6 :021(067) [0073] **Hence** observances of this kind are not to be thought of
AL : 2 8 :021(084) [0087] **Hence** according to the Gospel (or, as they say, by divine
AP : 0 2 :004(101) [0105] **Hence** it belongs in the definition, especially now when so
AP : 0 4 :222(137) [0181] **Hence** this passage from Paul is not against us; only our
AP : 0 4 :231(139) [0185] to be excluded, and **hence** this view is far removed from
AP : 0 4 :276(148) [0199] **Hence** they exercise themselves in these signs and
AP : 0 4 :365(163) [0219] of God is displayed, and **hence** this belongs to the
AP : 1 3 :003(211) [0309] **Hence** signs instituted without God's command are not
AP : 1 3 :006(212) [0311] **Hence** it is useful to distinguish these from the earlier ones
AP : 2 1 :017(231) [0347] is no such promise, and **hence** consciences cannot be sure
AP : 2 3 :016(241) [0369] **Hence** Paul speaks of marriage as a remedy and
AP : 2 3 :068(249) [0383] are well aware of this; **hence** they refuse to show us a
AP : 2 4 :066(261) [0407] talking about thanksgiving; **hence** they call it "eucharist."
AP : 2 4 :097(268) [0417] **Hence** they increased the services and sacrifices.
AP : 2 7 :020(272) [0425] **Hence** it is also an intolerable blasphemy when Thomas
AP : 2 7 :021(272) [0427] **Hence** the saints can use them without sinning, as did
AP : 2 7 :026(273) [0429] **Hence** they are neither justifying services nor perfection.
AP : 2 7 :058(279) [0439] **Hence** it is not right to compare monasticism, thought up
AP : 2 7 :069(281) [0443] **Hence** the vows themselves and the observance of foods,
S2 : 0 4 :003(298) [0471] **Hence** it follows that all the things that the pope has
S3 : 0 3 :013(305) [0483] **Hence** the expression in the pulpit when the general
SC : PR :008(339) [0535] that pleases you, therefore, and adhere to it **henceforth**.
LC : SP :001(362) [0575] **Hence** from ancient times it has been called in Greek, a
LC : 0 1 :060(372) [0597] **Hence** we get what we deserve: plague, war, famine, fire,
LC : 0 1 :079(375) [0603] is, to cease from labor; **hence** our common expression for
LC : 0 1 :120(381) [0615] **Hence** you have a sure text and a divine testimony that
LC : 0 1 :177(389) [0631] punishes the world; **hence** there is no longer any civil
LC : 0 1 :303(406) [0667] **Hence** the sayings, "First come, first served," and "Every
LC : 0 2 :007(411) [0679] **Hence** the Creed may be briefly comprised in these few
LC : 0 2 :019(412) [0681] **Hence**, since everything we possess, and everything in
LC : 0 2 :056(418) [0693] is not) there is no forgiveness, and **hence** no holiness.
LC : 0 4 :027(440) [0739] **Hence** it is well described as a divine, blessed, fruitful, and
LC : 0 4 :031(440) [0739] **Hence** it follows that whoever rejects Baptism rejects
LC : 0 5 :015(448) [0757] **Hence** it is easy to answer all kinds of questions which
LC : 0 5 :031(450) [0759] in the Lord's Supper and **hence** that we cannot have
LC : 0 5 :045(452) [0763] to disciples of Christ; **hence** whoever would be one of
EP : 0 5 :011(479) [0805] 1. **Hence** we reject and deem it as false and detrimental
EP : 0 8 :011(488) [0821] with the Son of God and **hence** really (that is, in deed and
EP : 0 8 :039(491) [0827] **Hence**, unless we refute these errors on the firm basis of
EP : 1 1 :021(497) [0837] **Hence** they should not be tolerated in God's church.
SD : 0 1 :002(509) [0859] **Hence**, they say, we must preserve the distinction between
SD : 0 1 :004(509) [0861] **Hence**, in order to explain this controversy in a Christian
SD : 0 1 :028(513) [0867] **Hence** original sin is not something which exists
SD : 0 1 :043(516) [0873] **Hence** all the ancient orthodox teachers held that
SD : 0 1 :045(516) [0873] **Hence** it is unchristian and abominable to say that
SD : 0 2 :007(521) [0883] **Hence** according to its perverse disposition and nature the
SD : 0 2 :061(533) [0905] is dead in sin (Eph. 2:5); **hence** there can be in him no
SD : 0 2 :085(537) [0913] **Hence** the unregenerated man resists God entirely and is
SD : 0 3 :032(545) [0927] **Hence** even after his renewal, after he has done many
SD : 0 3 :055(549) [0935] **Hence**, since in our churches the theologians of the
SD : 0 4 :002(551) [0939] **Hence**, they held, these propositions should not be
SD : 0 4 :009(552) [0941] **Hence** faith alone is the mother and source of the truly
SD : 0 4 :029(555) [0947] **Hence** and for these reasons it is right for our churches to
SD : 0 4 :034(556) [0949] as if works should **henceforth** preserve faith, the
SD : 0 4 :039(557) [0951] **Hence** our churches condemn and reject this proposition,
SD : 0 5 :024(563) [0961] by faith" (Gal. 3:24), and **hence** points and leads not away
SD : 0 6 :002(564) [0963] his Spirit's temple, and **hence** are free, so that just as the
SD : 0 6 :003(564) [0963] by the Holy Spirit and **hence** according to the inner man
SD : 0 6 :009(565) [0965] **Hence**, because of the desires of the flesh the truly
SD : 0 6 :026(568) [0971] **Hence** we reject and condemn, as pernicious and contrary
SD : 0 7 :001(569) [0971] **Hence** we neither could nor should refrain from giving
SD : 0 7 :024(573) [0979] "**Hence** it is easy to answer all kinds of questions which
SD : 0 7 :029(574) [0981] **Hence** let no one rashly reject ... during my lifetime or after my
SD : 0 7 :029(574) [0981] **Hence** if any one shall say after my death, 'If Dr. Luther
SD : 0 7 :048(578) [0989] **Hence** there can be no metaphor (that is, a change in
SD : 0 7 :066(581) [0995] **Hence**, in harmony with these words of Christ's institution
SD : 0 8 :006(592) [1017] way that Christ Jesus is **henceforth** in *one* person
SD : 0 8 :007(592) [1017] teach, and confess that **henceforth** in this single undivided
SD : 0 8 :007(592) [1017] person of Christ will **henceforth** never be separated,
SD : 0 8 :011(593) [1019] neither nature in Christ **henceforth** subsists for itself so as
SD : 0 8 :016(594) [1021] **Hence** he also held that the divine and human natures are
SD : 0 8 :026(596) [1023] **Hence** also the human nature has, after the resurrection
SD : 0 8 :062(603) [1037] acts of both natures are **henceforth** of the same kind or
SD : 0 8 :067(604) [1039] **Hence** we do not understand the testimonies of the
SD : 0 8 :087(608) [1047] **Hence** we consider it a pernicious error to deprive Christ
SD : 0 9 :001(610) [1051] **Hence** we let matters rest on the simple statement of our
SD : 1 0 :016(613) [1057] **Hence** yielding or conforming in external things, where
SD : 1 1 :013(618) [1067] **Hence** if we wish to think or speak correctly and
SD : 1 1 :028(620) [1071] **Hence** if we want to consider our eternal election to
SD : 1 1 :039(622) [1075] **Hence**, as was mentioned before, there is no basis for the
SD : 1 1 :075(628) [1087] **Hence** when his children become disobedient and
SD : 1 1 :079(629) [1089] **Hence** Paul very carefully distinguishes between the work
SD : 1 1 :084(630) [1091] **Hence** Pharaoh (of whom we read, "For this purpose have
SD : 1 1 :091(631) [1093] **Hence** if anyone so sets forth this teaching concerning
SD : 1 2 :011(634) [1099] and innocent, and **hence** in their innocence they will be

Henneberg (1)
PR : PR :027(015) [0025] Ernest, count and lord of **Henneberg** [-Schleusingen]

Henry (3)
PR : PR :027(014) [0025] **Henry** the Younger, duke of Brunswick [-Wolfenbuettel]
PR : PR :027(015) [0025] **Henry**, count and lord of Castell [-Remlingen]
PR : PR :027(015) [0025] **Henry**, baron of Limpurg [-Schmiedelfeld], Semperfrei

Heracles (1)
TR : 0 0 :062(331) [0523] to the time of Bishops **Heracles** and Dionysius, the

Hercules (2)
AP : 2 4 :072(262) [0409] way plays celebrate the memory of **Hercules** or Ulysses.
LC : 0 1 :018(367) [0585] a life of ease venerated **Hercules**, Mercury, Venus, or

Hereafter (4)
PR : PR :014(007) [0013] in the form that follows **hereafter**, was completed with the
AP : 0 4 :368(163) [0221] pleases God and has its reward, both here and **hereafter**.
SC : 0 3 :008(346) [0547] live a godly life, both here in time and **hereafter** forever.
LC : 0 3 :053(427) [0713] here and in eternal life **hereafter** to us who have attained

Hereby (5)
PR : PR :001(003) [0007] humble, and willing service, and **hereby** declare:
PR : PR :019(009) [0017] We have therefore desired **hereby** to attest and affirm
LC : 0 6 :021(459) [0000] **Hereby** we abolish the pope's tyranny, commandments,
EP : RN :003(465) [0777] to these, and we **hereby** reject all heresies and teachings
SD : 0 2 :044(529) [0897] We **hereby** appeal to these writings and refer others to

Hereditary (3)
AG : 0 2 :002(029) [0043] inborn sickness and **hereditary** sin is truly sin and
S3 : 0 1 :003(302) [0477] This **hereditary** sin is so deep a corruption of nature that
S3 : 0 3 :028(308) [0487] to be holy, and yet the **hereditary** evil which is born in us

Herefrom (1)
SD : 0 4 :038(557) [0951] But it does not follow **herefrom** that one may say without

Herein (2)
SD : 0 8 :061(602) [1035] orthodox church made **herein** on the basis of sound
SD : 0 9 :001(610) [1051] **Herein** the burial and the descent into hell are

Hereon (1)
PR : PR :027(014) [0025] hereto and ordered our privy seals impressed **hereon**.

Heresy (14), Heresies (16)
PR : PR :003(003) [0007] fought for against many **heresies** and errors, and
AG : 0 1 :005(028) [0043] Therefore all the **heresies** which are contrary to this
AG : 0 1 :005(028) [0043] Among these are the **heresy** of the Manichaeans, who
AL : 0 1 :005(028) [0043] churches condemn all **heresies** which have sprung up
AL : 2 8 :011(082) [0085] protects souls from **heresies**, the devil, and eternal death.
AP : 0 4 :232(140) [0185] hatreds, factions, and **heresies** that arise from such
AP : 0 4 :242(141) [0187] Many **heresies** have arisen in the church simply from the
AP : 2 3 :067(248) [0383] is horrible: the marriage of priests is the Jovinian **heresy**.
AP : 2 3 :067(248) [0383] This is a new charge, that marriage is a **heresy**!
AP : 2 3 :067(248) [0383] of priests is the Jovinian **heresy** or that the church
AP : 2 3 :068(249) [0383] was to raise the cry of **heresy** against us over and over,
AP : 2 4 :096(267) [0417] They cite ancient **heresies** and by falsely comparing them
AP : 2 4 :096(267) [0417] for wickedly defending a **heresy** that clearly conflicts with
S2 : 0 4 :007(299) [0473] the attacks of sects and **heresies**; and suppose that such a
S3 : 0 3 :041(309) [0491] the Gospel, and yet it is called a **heresy** by godless saints.
S3 : 0 6 :004(311) [0493] slander the use of both as **heresy** and thus set themselves
S3 : 0 8 :009(313) [0497] and power of all **heresy**, including that of the papacy and
LC : 0 2 :050(417) [0691] uprooted, and it would be next to **heresy** to alter a word.
EP : RN :003(465) [0777] and we hereby reject all **heresies** and teachings which
EP : 0 8 :039(491) [0827] but it opens a way for the accursed Arian **heresy**.
SD : PR :004(504) [0851] God — in which all those **heresies** which at that time had
SD : PR :005(504) [0851] the papacy and from other condemned sects and **heresies**.
SD : PR :017(507) [0857] reject and condemn all **heresies** and errors which the
SD : PR :018(507) [0857] all the sects and **heresies** that are rejected in the
SD : 0 1 :013(511) [0863] with terrible errors and **heresies**, strikes them with other
SD : 0 1 :043(516) [0873] they also rejected the contrary doctrine as patent **heresy**.
SD : 0 8 :004(592) [1017] with accusations of almost all the monstrous old **heresies**.
SD : 0 8 :015(594) [1019] This was the error and **heresy** of Nestorius and the
SD : 0 8 :017(594) [1021] to this condemned **heresy** the Christian church has always
SD : 0 8 :060(602) [1035] explain this doctrine and defend it against all **heresies**.

Heretic (2), Heretics (13)
AL : 0 0 :001(047) [0059] teachers are to be regarded as **heretics** judge too harshly.
AP : 1 2 :123(201) [0289] that such terrible **heretics**, who reject penitence, should be
AP : 2 1 :036(234) [0353] great danger, taught the Gospel, battled against **heretics**.
AP : 2 3 :045(245) [0375] Many **heretics** have misunderstood the law of Moses;
S3 : 1 0 :003(314) [0497] who are ordained by **heretics** shall also be regarded as
TR : 0 0 :072(332) [0525] when the bishops are **heretics** or refuse to administer
LC : 0 1 :262(400) [0655] the world call them **heretics**, apostates, even seditious and
LC : 0 3 :069(429) [0717] bishops, tyrants, and **heretics** can do against our Gospel.
LC : 0 4 :002(437) [0733] and defended against **heretics** and sectarians we shall
EP : RN :003(465) [0777] lifetime — false teachers and **heretics** invaded the church.
SD : PR :004(504) [0851] the aberrations of **heretics**, we further pledge allegiance to
SD : 0 1 :054(518) [0877] this doctrine against **heretics**, they use them in the sense
SD : 0 7 :126(591) [1015] no one except an Arian **heretic** can or will deny Christ
SD : 0 8 :016(594) [1021] "A contemporary of the **heretic** Manes by the name of
SD : 0 8 :096(609) [1049] a mystery over which all **heretics** break their heads, we

Heretical (8)
AG : 0 0 :001(048) [0059] as if our teaching were **heretical**, act in an unkind and
AG : 2 4 :040(061) [0069] not in fairness be condemned as **heretical** or unchristian.
TR : 0 0 :038(326) [0515] clearly teach that a **heretical** pope is not to be obeyed.
EP : 1 2 :030(500) [0843] as wrong, false, **heretical**, and contrary to the Word of

Continued ▶

SD : 0 3 :006(540) [0917] pure, it is impossible to repel any error or **heretical** spirit.
SD : 1 2 :008(633) [1097] these errors as wrong, **heretical**, and contrary to our
SD : 1 2 :009(633) [1097] the erroneous and **heretical** teaching of the Anabaptists
SD : 1 2 :039(636) [1103] as false, erroneous, **heretical**, contrary to the Word of

Hereto (1), Heretofore (1)
PR : PR :027(014) [0025] subscribed our names **hereto** and ordered our privy seals
S 3 : 1 3 :001(315) [0499] can change what I have **heretofore** constantly taught on

Hereunder (1)
PR : PR :018(009) [0015] of Concord that follows **hereunder**, so that everyone may

Herewith (6)
AG : PR :023(027) [0043] summons) as we **herewith** publicly witness and assert.
EP : 0 7 :042(486) [0817] 21. Accordingly, we **herewith** condemn without any
SD : PR :004(502) [0847] **Herewith** we again whole-heartedly subscribe this
SD : 0 2 :043(529) [0897] "I **herewith** reject and condemn as sheer error every
SD : 0 7 :091(586) [1005] desire to have them considered as appealed to **herewith**.
SD : 0 8 :003(592) [1017] Supper, to which we **herewith** publicly profess our

Heritage (1)
LC : SP :006(362) [0575] parts which have been **heritage** of Christendom from

Hermit (1), Hermits (1)
AP : 1 6 :009(224) [0333] David, and Daniel were no less perfect than any **hermit**.
AP : 2 7 :038(275) [0433] In the histories of the **hermits** there are stories of

Herod (1)
LC : 0 1 :305(406) [0669] in the Gospel that King **Herod** took his brother's wife

Hesitate (1), Hesitation (1)
AP : PR :002(098) [0099] would produce the document without **hesitation**.
AP : 1 2 :070(192) [0271] Let us not **hesitate**, therefore, to oppose this statement of

Hesse (4)
AG : 0 0 :007(096) [0095] Philip, landgrave of **Hesse**
AL : 0 0 :017(096) [0095] Philip, landgrave of **Hesse**, subscribes
S 3 : 1 5 :005(317) [0501] Master Adam of Fulda, preacher in **Hesse**
TR : 0 0 :082(335) [0529] Fontanus, superintendent of Lower **Hesse**, subscribed

Hid (3), Hidden (16), Hide (5), Hiding (1)
PR : PR :014(007) [0013] might in the future be **hidden** thereunder and that a pure
PR : PR :019(009) [0017] some have attempted to **hide** their error concerning the
PR : PR :024(013) [0023] effort toward concord **hidden** and concealed in darkness,
AP : PR :017(099) [0103] here how they lay **hidden** under all sorts of dangerous
AP : 0 4 :106(122) [0153] fear punishment grace is **hidden**; laboring under this fear,
AP : 0 4 :286(150) [0203] the law in such a way as to **hide** the Gospel of Christ.
AP : 0 7 :018(171) [0233] whether it be revealed or **hidden** under the cross, just as
AP : 0 7 :019(171) [0233] us that the church is **hidden** under a crowd of wicked men
AP : 2 8 :023(285) [0451] for Christ's sake, brings enough good to **hide** all the evils.
S 3 : 0 3 :015(305) [0483] to, namely, that when a **hidden** sin was afterwards
LC : 0 1 :106(379) [0611] (so to speak) toward a majesty **hidden** within them.
LC : 0 2 :038(415) [0689] But if the work remained **hidden** and no one knew of it,
EP : 0 8 :037(491) [0825] it is written that in him are **hid** "all the treasures of
SD : PR :016(507) [0857] terminology may not **hide** and conceal something, we
SD : 0 1 :036(514) [0869] well; my frame was not **hidden** from thee when I was
SD : 0 2 :056(532) [0903] Spirit's activity often is **hidden**, and happens under cover
SD : 0 8 :026(596) [1025] explains it, he kept it **hidden** during the state of his
SD : 0 8 :038(598) [1027] as open Sacramentarians **hide** their pernicious error
SD : 0 8 :068(604) [1039] bodily, there likewise are **hid** all treasures of wisdom and
SD : 0 8 :074(606) [1043] treasures of wisdom are **hid** in him, all authority is given
SD : 1 1 :013(618) [1067] the absolute, secret, **hidden**, and inscrutable
SD : 1 1 :026(620) [1071] to explore the secret and **hidden** abyss of divine
SD : 1 1 :033(621) [1073] explore the abyss of the **hidden** foreknowledge of God,
SD : 1 1 :064(626) [1083] has reserved for his own **hidden** wisdom, Paul
SD : 1 2 :005(633) [1097] we were not proposing or **hiding** anything with intent to

Hideously (1)
SD : PR :001(501) [0847] faith (which had been **hideously** obscured by human

Hierarchy (2)
AP : 1 2 :129(202) [0291] for the members of the **hierarchy** suppose that they can
AP : 1 4 :001(214) [0315] of the ecclesiastical **hierarchy**, although they were created

High (48), Higher (6), Highest (28), Highly (29), Height (2)
PR : PR :024(013) [0023] Christian persons, of **high** station and low, are sighing
PR : PR :025(014) [0023] Small Catechism of that **highly** enlightened man, Dr.
AG : PR :021(027) [0043] and estates have with the **highest** and best motives
AG : 2 0 :004(041) [0053] these useless works so **highly** as they once did, and they
AG : 2 1 :003(047) [0057] to the Scriptures, the **highest** form of divine service is
AG : 2 3 :001(051) [0061] Among all people, both of **high** and of low degree, there
AG : 2 3 :013(053) [0063] and intelligent people in **high** station have expressed
AG : 2 3 :020(055) [0063] Marriage has also been **highly** praised in the imperial
AG : 2 7 :013(072) [0077] monastic vows were praised more **highly** than Baptism.
AG : 2 7 :022(074) [0079] no matter how **highly** one exalts them, it is still
AG : 2 8 :004(081) [0085] with all reverence as the two **highest** gifts of God on earth
AG : 2 8 :018(083) [0085] both be held in honor as the **highest** gifts of God on earth
AL : 2 5 :003(061) [0069] to esteem absolution **highly** because it is the voice of God
AP : 0 2 :025(103) [0111] evil inclination of man's **higher** capacities to carnal
AP : 0 4 :057(114) [0137] they knew that our works could not pay so **high** a price.
AP : 0 4 :072(116) [0141] faith is praised so **highly** because it is this kind of
AP : 0 4 :073(117) [0141] Word, and we give the **highest** praise to the ministry of
AP : 0 4 :082(118) [0145] then we have a great **high** priest,...let us then with
AP : 0 4 :082(118) [0145] merits but in Christ, the **high** priest, this statement
AP : 0 4 :154(128) [0163] This is the **highest** way of worshiping Christ.
AP : 0 4 :165(130) [0169] because of Christ's promise, he insults this **high** priest.
AP : 0 4 :208(135) [0177] Israel had seen the prophets sacrifice on the **high** places.
AP : 0 4 :208(135) [0177] did not sacrifice on the **high** places to merit grace and
AP : 0 4 :229(139) [0183] We cannot deny that love is the **highest** work of the law.
AP : 0 4 :229(139) [0183] proclaimed the **highest** work of the law, and to it they
AP : 0 4 :310(155) [0207] this doctrine that the **highest** worship in the Gospel is the
AP : 0 4 :318(156) [0209] It is **highly** absurd when our opponents teach that good
AP : 0 4 :332(158) [0211] insults Christ, who intercedes for us as our **high** priest.
AP : 0 4 :333(158) [0211] because of Christ the **high** priest, as he himself says
AP : 0 4 :333(158) [0211] says, because without the **high** priest we cannot draw
AP : 0 7 :016(171) [0231] people), for they held **high** positions and they sacrificed
AP : 1 1 :002(180) [0249] brought Luther the **highest** praise of all good men, since
AP : 1 1 :009(182) [0253] against human traditions, which is the **height** of vanity.
AP : 1 2 :129(202) [0291] for men of discretion will value this service **highly**.
AP : 1 6 :009(224) [0333] were wealthy and held **high** positions, Abraham, David,
AP : 2 1 :004(229) [0343] we should extol them very **highly**; we should also praise
AP : 2 1 :024(232) [0349] as our intercessor and **high** priest, why seek others?
AP : 2 1 :027(232) [0349] she is worthy of the **highest** honors, she does not want to
AP : 2 1 :035(234) [0353] which are being taught in public on the **highest** authority.
AP : 2 2 :010(237) [0359] sons; after the loss of the **high** priesthood, they were
AP : 2 4 :052(259) [0403] the Hebrews (5:1), "Every **high** priest chosen from among
AP : 2 4 :052(259) [0403] Testament has priests and **high** priests, it must also have
AP : 2 4 :053(259) [0403] which says that "every **high** priest is appointed to offer
AP : 2 4 :053(259) [0403] itself adds immediately that Christ is the **high** priest.
AP : 2 4 :074(263) [0411] gratitude, and a witness of its **high** esteem for God's gifts.
AP : 2 7 :025(273) [0427] It is the **height** of wickedness to believe that they satisfy
AP : 2 7 :047(277) [0437] It is **highly** dangerous to heap such extravagant praises
S 3 : 0 8 :002(312) [0495] the contrary, it should be **highly** esteemed and valued,
TR : 0 0 :038(326) [0515] The Levitical **high** priest was the supreme pontifex by
TR : 0 0 :038(327) [0515] nevertheless, godless **high** priests were not to be obeyed.
TR : 0 0 :062(331) [0523] number, set him in a **higher** place, and called him bishop.
TR : 0 0 :067(331) [0523] "When he ascended on **high** he gave gifts to men"
SC : PR :023(341) [0537] He who does not **highly** esteem the sacrament suggests
SC : 0 9 :003(355) [0561] and to esteem them very **highly** in love because of their
SC : 0 9 :005(355) [0561] kings and all who are in **high** positions, that we may lead
LC : PR :007(359) [0569] experienced as any of those who act so **high** and mighty.
LC : PR :009(359) [0569] in this life), yet it is **highly** profitable and fruitful daily to
LC : 0 1 :036(369) [0589] who thought themselves to be so **high** and mighty.
LC : 0 1 :061(373) [0597] this as well as the other commandments in **high** regard.
LC : 0 1 :105(379) [0611] he commands nothing **higher** than that we love them.
LC : 0 1 :107(379) [0611] we respect them very **highly** and that next to God we give
LC : 0 1 :107(379) [0611] and that next to God we give them the very **highest** place.
LC : 0 1 :107(379) [0611] to honor, we must truly regard as **high** and great.
LC : 0 1 :113(380) [0613] and it embodies his **highest** wisdom, then I shall never
LC : 0 1 :125(382) [0617] For we know that it is **highly** pleasing to the divine
LC : 0 1 :133(383) [0619] St. Paul also **highly** exalts and praises this
LC : 0 1 :139(384) [0621] obedience, since he so **highly** exalts it, so greatly delights
LC : 0 1 :206(393) [0639] carefully note, first, how **highly** God honors and glorifies
LC : 0 1 :208(393) [0639] For it is of the **highest** importance to him that persons be
LC : 0 1 :211(393) [0641] whom he has released by a **high** supernatural gift so that
LC : 0 1 :226(395) [0645] and day-laborers who act **high**-handedly and never know
LC : 0 1 :240(397) [0649] New burdens and **high** prices are imposed.
LC : 0 1 :290(404) [0663] which please God most **highly** and bring abundant
LC : 0 1 :296(405) [0665] also have a broader and **higher** application) to forbid
LC : 0 1 :315(408) [0671] saints to dare to find a **higher** and better way of life than
LC : 0 1 :330(410) [0677] of the most **high** God, who watches over them with great
LC : 0 1 :333(410) [0677] obvious once again how **highly** these Ten
LC : 0 2 :002(411) [0679] above, they are set on so **high** a plane that all human
LC : 0 3 :012(422) [0701] means despise our prayers, but rather prize them **highly**.
LC : 0 3 :013(422) [0701] and I can revere it **highly**, not because of my worthiness,
LC : 0 3 :032(424) [0707] God replies from on **high**, "Yes, dear child, it shall indeed
LC : 0 5 :061(453) [0767] must learn that it is the **highest** wisdom to realize that
LC : 0 5 :067(454) [0769] and exhorts us to our **highest** and greatest good, we act so
EP : 0 1 :001(466) [0779] (that is, his rational soul in its **highest** form and powers).
EP : 0 7 :005(482) [0809] it is confined to the **highest** heaven above, whither we
EP : 0 8 :009(487) [0819] the contrary, here is the **highest** communion which God
EP : 0 8 :011(488) [0821] or the Son of the most **high** God, if his humanity were not
EP : 0 8 :014(488) [0821] he could suffer and be our **high** priest for our
EP : 0 8 :015(488) [0821] was personally united with the Son of the Most **High**.
EP : 0 8 :018(489) [0823] holy Trinity this is the **highest** mystery, as the apostles
EP : 1 2 :008(498) [0839] Anabaptists neither think **highly** of infant Baptism nor
EP : 1 2 :030(500) [0843] All pious Christians, of **high** degree and low, must guard
SD : PR :019(507) [0857] anyone be misled by the **high** regard in which these
SD : 0 1 :001(508) [0859] his rational soul in its **highest** degree and foremost
SD : 0 1 :011(510) [0863] powers, especially of the **highest** and foremost powers of
SD : 0 1 :011(510) [0863] mind-set which, in its **highest** powers and the light of
SD : 0 1 :011(510) [0863] opposed to God and his **highest** commands and is
SD : 0 1 :059(519) [0879] settle this offensive and **highly** detrimental controversy
SD : 0 3 :067(551) [0937] explanation of this **high** and important article of
SD : 0 7 :002(569) [0973] wine in the Supper as the **highest** heaven is distant from
SD : 0 7 :002(569) [0973] interval as the earth is distant from the **highest** heavens."
SD : 0 7 :028(574) [0981] Since this **highly** enlightened man foresaw in the Spirit
SD : 0 8 :019(595) [1021] is far different, much **higher**, and more ineffable, since on
SD : 0 8 :024(595) [1023] truly the Son of the most **high** God, as the angel testifies.
SD : 0 8 :035(597) [1027] It is **highly** important that this doctrine of the exchange
SD : 0 8 :047(600) [1031] mediator, redeemer, king, **high** priest, head, shepherd,
SD : 0 8 :051(600) [1033] properties, special, **high**, great, supernatural,
SD : 0 8 :078(607) [1043] on earth as mediator, head, king, and **high** priest.
SD : 0 8 :087(608) [1047] robs Christians of their **highest** comfort, afforded them in
SD : 0 8 :087(608) [1047] of their head, king, and **high** priest, who has promised
SD : 0 8 :096(610) [1049] Christ been made to sit so **high** at the right hand of the
SD : 1 1 :063(626) [1083] on this subject soars too **high** and goes beyond these
SD : 1 2 :013(634) [1099] infant Baptism very **highly** and do not advocate it,

Highpriest (2)
AG : 2 1 :002(047) [0057] only saviour, the only **highpriest**, advocate, and
AL : 2 1 :002(047) [0057] mediator, propitiation, **highpriest**, and intercessor whom

Hilary (5)
AP : 2 1 :030(233) [0351] **Hilary** says of the foolish virgins: "Since the foolish
TR : 0 0 :027(324) [0511] Ambrose, Cyprian, **Hilary**, and Bede) interpret the
TR : 0 0 :029(325) [0513] **Hilary** declares: "The Father revealed to Peter that he
LC : 0 5 :059(453) [0767] As St. **Hilary** has said, "Unless a man has committed such
SD : 0 8 :022(595) [1023] in his *Letter to Epictetus; Hilary*, *On the Trinity*, Book

Hildesheim (1)
PR : PR :027(016) [0027] The whole administration of the City of **Hildesheim**

Hilten (2)
AP : 2 7 :001(268) [0419] of Eisenach, there was a Franciscan named John **Hilten**.
AP : 2 7 :002(269) [0419] Then with a sigh **Hilten** omitted all mention of his illness

Hinder (9), Hindered (4), Hinders (3), Hindrance (4), Hindrances (1)
A G : P R :020(026) [0041] and to allow no **hindrance** to be put in the way.
A G : 2 6 :016(066) [0073] people were thereby **hindered** from coming to a right
A L : 2 6 :016(066) [0073] that they were so **hindered** by these bickerings about
A P : 0 4 :189(133) [0175] partly unregenerate and **hinders** what the Holy Spirit
S 3 : 1 1 :003(315) [0499] we shall not disrupt or **hinder** God's work, for St. Paul
T R : 0 0 :059(330) [0521] the glory of God, and **hinder** the welfare of the church by
S C : 0 3 :011(347) [0547] of our flesh which would **hinder** us from hallowing his
S C : 0 9 :006(355) [0561] order that your prayers may not be **hindered**" (I Pet. 3:7).
L C : 0 1 :212(393) [0641] their way without let or **hindrance**, as everyone's
L C : 0 3 :002(420) [0697] stands in our way and **hinders** us from fulfilling them.
L C : 0 3 :015(422) [0701] We allow ourselves to be **hindered** and deterred by such
L C : 0 3 :061(428) [0715] from all who venture to **hinder** and thwart the fulfillment
L C : 0 3 :063(428) [0715] the flames, in order to **hinder** us, put us to flight, cut us
L C : 0 3 :068(429) [0717] done among us without **hindrance**, in spite of their fury,
L C : 0 3 :080(431) [0721] but he also prevents and **hinders** the establishment of any
L C : 0 5 :023(449) [0757] There are so many **hindrances** and temptations of the
L C : 0 5 :049(452) [0765] a person, with nothing to **hinder** him, lets a long period
L C : 0 5 :063(454) [0767] have this obstacle and **hindrance** to contend with, that we
S D : 0 2 :072(535) [0909] what a grievous sin it is to **hinder** and resist such
S D : 1 1 :010(618) [1067] one can ever change or **hinder** it (Isa. 14:27; Rom. 9:19,
S D : 1 1 :010(618) [1067] etc., since I cannot **hinder** or alter God's foreknowledge."

Hirelings (1)
A P : 1 5 :040(220) [0325] unwilling celebrants and **hirelings** perform Mass, and they

History (26), Historical (6), Histories (4)
A G : 2 0 :023(044) [0055] who also believe the **history** of Christ's suffering and his
A G : 2 0 :025(045) [0057] merely a knowledge of **historical** events but is a
A G : 2 0 :026(045) [0057] such a knowledge of **historical** events as the devil also
A G : 2 2 :004(050) [0061] be demonstrated from **history** and from writings of the
A G : 2 3 :010(052) [0061] be demonstrated from **history** and from the writings of
A G : 2 3 :018(054) [0063] Besides, **history** demonstrates both that priests were
A G : 2 4 :041(061) [0069] to the Tripartite **History**, Book 9, on Wednesday and
A G : 2 6 :045(070) [0075] Moreover, the Tripartite **History**, Book 9, gathers many
A L : 2 0 :023(044) [0055] mere knowledge of the **history** (such as is in the ungodly
A L : 2 0 :023(044) [0055] believes not only the **history** but also the effect of the
A L : 2 0 :023(044) [0055] but also the effect of the **history**, namely, this article of
A L : 2 4 :032(059) [0067] enough to remember the **history**, for the Jews and the
A L : 2 4 :041(061) [0069] day; as the Tripartite **History** testifies in Book 9, "Again,
A L : 2 6 :045(070) [0075] In the Tripartite **History**, Book 9, many examples of
A P : 0 2 :049(106) [0119] World **history** itself shows the great power of the devil's
A P : 0 4 :017(109) [0125] a knowledge of the **history** about Christ and claim that he
A P : 0 4 :048(113) [0135] that faith is only **historical** knowledge and teach that it
A P : 0 4 :048(114) [0135] however, is no mere **historical** knowledge, but the firm
A P : 0 4 :050(114) [0135] does not simply mean **historical** knowledge but is a firm
A P : 0 4 :051(114) [0135] the purpose of the **history**, "the forgiveness of sins."
A P : 0 4 :061(115) [0137] are speaking of an idle **historical** knowledge, we must tell
A P : 0 4 :167(130) [0169] often wonder whether **history** is governed by God's
A P : 0 4 :337(159) [0215] meant the knowledge of **history** that the wicked and
A P : 0 4 :337(159) [0215] about a knowledge of **history**, however, but about trust in
A P : 0 4 :383(165) [0225] as merely a knowledge of **history** or of dogmas, not as the
A P : 0 4 :395(167) [0225] The **history** of the people of Israel is a type of what was to
A P : 0 7 :040(176) [0241] form to the Gospel **history**, like the Passover and
A P : 0 7 :045(177) [0243] be gathered from the **histories** in which it appears that a
A P : 2 3 :002(239) [0363] Where in any **history** can one read of greater brazenness
A P : 2 7 :004(269) [0419] **History** will show how much credence should be given to
A P : 2 7 :038(275) [0433] In the **histories** of the hermits there are stories of
T R : 0 0 :011(321) [0507] Testimony from **History**
L C : 0 1 :035(369) [0589] in all the records of **history**, as Scripture amply shows and
L C : 0 1 :044(370) [0593] will find aplenty in all **histories** and in the recollections of
S D : 0 8 :075(606) [1043] The **histories** tell us that during the time of Emperor
S D : 1 1 :059(626) [1081] Thus in the **history** of some nations and some persons

Hit (1)
L C : 0 3 :023(423) [0703] him, or whether I have **hit** upon the right form and

Hitherto (7)
P R : P R :018(008) [0015] of our lands have **hitherto** at all times adhered and
A G : 2 4 :013(057) [0065] Masses, which had **hitherto** been held under compulsion
A G : 2 7 :001(071) [0075] what opinions have **hitherto** been held concerning them,
A L : 2 2 :012(051) [0061] processions which were **hitherto** held are also omitted
A P : 0 4 :399(168) [0227] knows, they have **hitherto** shown toward many godly
S 3 : 1 5 :005(317) [0501] confess that I have **hitherto** thus believed and taught, and
S D : 0 1 :062(519) [0879] head, inasmuch as this befell a **hitherto** perfect nature."

Hoard (3)
L C : 0 1 :241(397) [0649] stand by and let such persons fleece, grab, and **hoard**.
L C : 0 1 :242(397) [0649] of a gulden, your entire **hoard** will be consumed by rust
L C : 0 1 :243(398) [0649] they gather a great **hoard**, they must suffer so many

Hof (1)
S 3 : 1 5 :005(317) [0501] I, Stephen Agricola, minister in **Hof**, subscribe

Hold (127), Holding (7), Holdings (1), Holds (13), Held (55)
P R : P R :003(003) [0007] They have **held** fast and loyally to the doctrine that is
P R : P R :004(004) [0007] and in this way **hold** back and perceptibly impede the
A G : P R :021(027) [0043] empire which have been **held** during Your Imperial
A G : 0 1 :001(027) [0043] We unanimously **hold** and teach, in accordance with the
A G : 0 1 :006(028) [0043] old and new, who **hold** that there is only one person and
A G : 0 2 :003(029) [0045] original sin is sin, for they **hold** that natural man is made
A G : 0 8 :003(033) [0047] and all others who **hold** contrary views are condemned.
A G : 2 0 :015(043) [0055] Although this teaching is **held** in great contempt among
A G : 2 3 :019(054) [0063] God commanded that marriage be **held** in honor.
A G : 2 4 :013(057) [0065] which had hitherto been **held** under compulsion for the
A G : 2 4 :023(058) [0067] as to whether one Mass **held** for many people merited as
A G : 2 4 :023(058) [0067] merited as much as a special Mass **held** for an individual.
A G : 2 4 :034(060) [0067] are present, Mass is **held** and those who desire it are
A G : 2 4 :040(061) [0069] Masses which were **held** in addition to the parochial
A G : 2 4 :040(061) [0069] this manner of **holding** Mass ought not in fairness be
A G : 2 4 :041(061) [0069] people, Mass was not **held** on every day that the people
A G : 2 4 :041(061) [0069] Alexandria, and all these services were **held** without Mass.
A G : 2 7 :001(071) [0075] have hitherto been **held** concerning them, what kind of
A G : 2 7 :031(075) [0079] They **hold** that before this age one does not possess
A G : 2 8 :018(083) [0085] directing that both be **held** in honor as the highest gifts of
A L : 1 6 :002(037) [0051] it is right for Christians to **hold** civil office, to sit as
A L : 1 6 :002(037) [0051] make legal contracts, to **hold** property, to swear oaths
A L : 2 2 :008(050) [0061] only a custom of quite recent times that **holds** otherwise.
A L : 2 2 :012(051) [0061] which were hitherto **held** are also omitted among us.
A L : 2 3 :019(054) [0063] God has commanded that marriage be **held** in honor.
A L : 2 4 :013(057) [0065] any private Masses were **held** except for the sake of gain.
A L : 2 4 :019(058) [0067] written, "The Lord will not **hold** him guiltless who takes
A L : 2 4 :041(061) [0069] frequented, Mass was not **held** every day; as the
A L : 2 8 :004(081) [0085] command both are to be **held** in reverence and honor as
A L : 2 8 :005(081) [0085] Our teachers **hold** that according to the Gospel the power
A L : 2 8 :018(083) [0085] command that both be **held** in honor and acknowledged
A L : 2 8 :028(085) [0087] should happen to err or **hold** anything contrary to the
A L : 2 8 :058(091) [0091] Those who **hold** that the observance of the Lord's Day in
A L : 2 8 :068(093) [0093] canons are kept without **holding** them to be necessary and
A P : P R :013(099) [0101] the emperor or the princes, whom I **hold** in due esteem.
A P : P R :015(099) [0101] to all nations that we **hold** to the Gospel of Christ
A P : 0 2 :047(106) [0119] nature is enslaved and **held** prisoner by the devil, who
A P : 0 4 :069(116) [0141] readers that if we must **hold** to the proposition, "Christ is
A P : 0 4 :073(117) [0141] says (Rom. 3:28), "We **hold** that a man is justified by faith
A P : 0 4 :083(119) [0145] We cannot take **hold** of the name of Christ except by
A P : 0 4 :087(119) [0147] the whole discussion: "We **hold** that man is justified by
A P : 0 4 :098(121) [0149] But only faith takes **hold** of the name of Christ.
A P : 0 4 :136(126) [0159] Therefore we also **hold** that the keeping of the law should
A P : 0 4 :138(126) [0161] to resist the devil, who **holds** enthralled all who have not
A P : 0 4 :154(128) [0163] way, and in this way to worship and take **hold** of him.
A P : 0 4 :163(129) [0169] by faith; we must always **hold** that we are accounted
A P : 0 4 :216(137) [0179] men, and by which we take **hold** of grace and peace of
A P : 0 4 :222(138) [0181] only when we take **hold** of Christ, the propitiator, and
A P : 0 4 :227(138) [0183] virtue justifies which takes **hold** of Christ, communicating
A P : 0 4 :231(139) [0183] Only faith takes **hold** of Christ, the propitiator.
A P : 0 4 :245(142) [0189] the faith by which we take **hold** of Christ, the propitiator.
A P : 0 4 :246(142) [0189] James did not **hold** that by our good works we merit
A P : 0 4 :247(142) [0191] it is only faith that takes **hold** of the promise of Christ
A P : 0 4 :247(142) [0191] Thus James does not **hold** that we are regenerated by our
A P : 0 4 :263(145) [0195] promise he forgives those who take **hold** of that promise.
A P : 0 4 :263(145) [0195] They do not take **hold** of it unless they truly believe and
A P : 0 4 :266(146) [0197] We must first take **hold** of the promise so that we may be
A P : 0 4 :269(147) [0197] therefore, we must **hold** fast to these rules: that the law is
A P : 0 4 :270(147) [0197] When faith takes **hold** of Christ, the mediator, the heart
A P : 0 4 :295(152) [0203] we must first take **hold** of the promise by faith, that for
A P : 0 4 :308(155) [0207] to the Gospel takes **hold** of Christ, the propitiator, and is
A P : 0 4 :313(155) [0207] reasons that compel us to **hold** that we are justified,
A P : 0 4 :324(157) [0209] to add nothing about this faith that takes **hold** of mercy.
A P : 0 4 :324(157) [0211] that only faith can take **hold** of the promise, so we say
A P : 0 4 :324(157) [0211] faith and that only faith can take **hold** of this mercy.
A P : 0 4 :331(158) [0211] Daniel teaches us to take **hold** of mercy when we pray,
A P : 0 4 :338(159) [0215] saves because it takes **hold** of mercy and the promise of
A P : 0 4 :344(160) [0217] Let us therefore **hold** to the church's confession that we
A P : 0 4 :345(160) [0217] who are not, we must **hold** that we are saved through
A P : 0 4 :359(162) [0219] of the faith that takes **hold** of Christ, the mediator.
A P : 0 4 :377(165) [0223] We are therefore obliged to **hold** fast to the Gospel and
A P : 0 4 :378(165) [0223] omitting the faith that takes **hold** of the mediator Christ.
A P : 0 4 :381(165) [0223] be added, since we take **hold** of God's mercy,
A P : 0 4 :381(165) [0225] please God because of grace; for faith takes **hold** of grace.
A P : 0 4 :397(167) [0227] that all Christians should **hold** and believe, namely, "We
A P : 0 7 :004(169) [0227] that is, that he will rule and **hold** office in the church.
A P : 0 7 :016(171) [0231] people), for they **held** high positions and they sacrificed
A P : 0 7 :017(171) [0233] are mingled with the church and **hold** office in the church.
A P : 0 7 :028(173) [0237] outward marks, and therefore **hold** office in the church.
A P : 0 7 :029(173) [0237] of the devil, who drives them on and **holds** them captive.
A P : 0 7 :042(176) [0241] of Nicaea, certain nations **held** tenaciously to the custom
A P : 0 7 :050(178) [0245] to priests the right to **hold** property or other possessions.
A P : 0 7 :050(178) [0245] The right to **hold** property is a civil ordinance.
A P : 1 1 :008(181) [0251] We **hold** therefore that the enumeration of sins is not
A P : 1 2 :064(191) [0269] peace only when it takes **hold** of Christ, the mediator, and
A P : 1 2 :067(191) [0271] and that good men who **hold** this faith be put to death
A P : 1 2 :080(194) [0275] contrite by faith to take **hold** of the promise of the
A P : 1 2 :081(194) [0275] other way than by taking **hold** through faith of the
A P : 1 2 :087(195) [0277] We must take **hold** of the promise of the forgiveness of
A P : 1 2 :106(197) [0283] with the increase of his **holdings** that he neglects the fear
A P : 1 2 :129(202) [0291] of this easily since they **hold** the keys and so, of course,
A P : 1 2 :143(204) [0297] The same **holds** when a fixed number of prayers or
A P : 1 2 :148(205) [0299] that penitence is so called because it **holds** punishment.
A P : 1 2 :169(209) [0305] as long as he unjustly **holds** on to another man's
A P : 1 3 :005(211) [0309] heart to believe and take **hold** of faith, as Paul says
A P : 1 5 :038(220) [0325] way, excluding the opinion which **holds** that they justify.
A P : 1 6 :001(222) [0329] might legitimately **hold** public office, render verdicts
A P : 1 6 :004(223) [0331] it an evangelical state to **hold** property in common, and
A P : 1 6 :007(223) [0331] from those who **hold** it, as in the Jewish dream of the
A P : 1 6 :009(224) [0333] Christian perfections consists in not **holding** property.
A P : 1 6 :009(224) [0333] they were wealthy and **held** high positions, Abraham,
A P : 1 6 :010(224) [0333] that the Gospel requires us to **hold** property in common!
A P : 1 6 :011(224) [0333] does not command **holding** property in common, but by
A P : 2 0 :003(227) [0339] been theologians who **held** that after the forgiveness of
A P : 2 1 :003(229) [0343] our opponents now **hold** about the application of merits,
A P : 2 1 :032(233) [0351] Even the theologians **hold** to the error that each saint has
A P : 2 4 :008(250) [0385] by the apostles to be **held** on the fourth day, on Sabbath
A P : 2 4 :013(251) [0387] Yet this notion has taken **hold** among the people and has
A P : 2 4 :026(254) [0391] the spirit knows and takes **hold** of God, as it does when it
A P : 2 4 :050(259) [0401] and clear sermons **hold** an audience, but neither the
S 1 : P R :001(288) [0455] and it is not yet known where it will or can be **held**.
S 1 : P R :001(288) [0455] hand, what we intended to **hold** fast to and persevere in.
S 1 : P R :002(289) [0455] deception or treachery to **hold** a truly free council, as
S 2 : 0 1 :004(292) [0461] in Romans 3, "For we **hold** that a man is justified by faith
S 2 : 0 2 :001(293) [0463] papal idolatries, for it is **held** that this sacrifice or work
S 3 : 0 3 :001(303) [0479] "The whole world may be **held** accountable to God, for
S 3 : 0 3 :028(308) [0487] Each one, however, **held** that some of the others were, as
S 3 : 0 3 :042(309) [0491] time of the uprising) who **hold** that once they have
S 3 : 0 5 :004(311) [0493] As for infant Baptism, we **hold** that children should be
S 3 : 0 6 :001(311) [0493] We **hold** that the bread and the wine in the Supper are
S 3 : 0 6 :002(311) [0493] We also **hold** that it is not to be administered in one form

Continued ▶

S 3 : 0 8 :003(312) [0495] spoken Word, we must **hold** firmly to the conviction that
S 3 : 0 8 :008(313) [0495] coming Messiah did not **hold** him captive with the
S 3 : 1 5 :005(316) [0501] concerning the pope I **hold** that, if he would allow the
T R : 0 0 :004(320) [0503] we acknowledge and **hold** to be false, impious,
T R : 0 0 :006(320) [0505] of men, because he **holds** that his power is by divine right
T R : 0 0 :017(323) [0509] synods were called and **held** in which the bishop of Rome
T R : 0 0 :030(325) [0513] This commission Peter **holds** in common with the rest of
T R : 0 0 :055(329) [0521] Even if the pope should **hold** synods, how can the church
T R : 0 0 :082(000) [0529] handwriting that I thus **hold**, confess, and constantly will
S C : P R :023(341) [0539] deeply immersed in them and is **held** captive by the devil.
L C : 0 1 :014(366) [0583] We lay **hold** of him when our heart embraces him
L C : 0 1 :057(372) [0597] "for the Lord will not **hold** him guiltless who takes his
L C : 0 1 :061(373) [0597] required and trained to **hold** this as well as the other
L C : 0 1 :110(380) [0613] but submit to them and **hold** your tongue, even if they go
L C : 0 1 :169(388) [0629] and injunction of God, who **holds** you accountable for it.
L C : 0 1 :230(396) [0645] treasures of the whole world and **holds** them to this day?
L C : 0 1 :270(401) [0657] before the proper authorities, then **hold** your tongue.
L C : 0 1 :276(402) [0659] reprove the man personally, otherwise to **hold** his tongue.
L C : 0 1 :303(406) [0667] adversity or debt cannot **hold** on to his property, nor yet
L C : 0 1 :326(409) [0675] the end to the beginning and **holds** everything together.
L C : 0 2 :013(412) [0681] Answer: I **hold** and believe that I am a creature of God;
L C : 0 3 :021(423) [0703] This you can **hold** up to him and say, "I come to Thee,
L C : 0 3 :060(428) [0715] need that we keep firm **hold** of these two things and never
L C : 0 3 :061(428) [0715] If we try to **hold** fast these treasures, we must suffer an
L C : 0 4 :030(440) [0739] speaks — there faith must look and to it faith must **hold**.
L C : 0 4 :038(441) [0741] that it is God's ordinance and is to be **held** in all honor.
L C : 0 4 :040(441) [0743] is lacking is that it should be grasped and **held** firmly.
L C : 0 5 :045(452) [0763] of them, let him faithfully **hold** to this sacrament, not
E P : 0 2 :016(472) [0791] of the grace of God, we **hold** that these expressions do
E P : 0 2 :018(472) [0791] the holy sacraments takes **hold** of man's will and works
E P : 0 2 :018(472) [0791] so that man not only lays **hold** on grace but also
E P : 0 3 :002(473) [0791] One party has **held** that Christ is our righteousness only
E P : 0 3 :002(473) [0793] Others, however, **held** that Christ is our righteousness
E P : 0 4 :003(476) [0797] The other party **held** with reference to the word
E P : 0 7 :042(486) [0817] of Christ's testament, we **hold** and believe in a true,
E P : 0 8 :022(490) [0823] Christ is not true, natural, and eternal God, as Arius **held**.
E P : 1 2 :001(498) [0839] made no mention of the errors **held** by these factions.
E P : 1 2 :017(499) [0841] with a good conscience **hold** or possess private property
S D : P R :007(505) [0853] it would ultimately be **held**) as an explication of the
S D : P R :019(507) [0857] by the high regard in which these theologians were **held**.
S D : 0 1 :013(511) [0863] abandoned to his power, and **held** captive in his servitude.
S D : 0 1 :038(515) [0871] the Large Catechism, "I **hold** and believe that I am a
S D : 0 1 :043(516) [0873] ancient orthodox teachers **held** that according to his
S D : 0 1 :055(518) [0877] people have always **held** that whatever does not subsist by
S D : 0 2 :003(520) [0881] The one party **held** and taught that, although by his own
S D : 0 2 :012(523) [0885] has it, does not grasp, take **hold** of, or apprehend) the
S D : 0 2 :074(535) [0909] and Manichaeans in **holding** that everything must happen
S D : 0 3 :003(539) [0917] the other side some have **held** and taught that Christ is
S D : 0 3 :004(539) [0917] the Augsburg Confession **held** unanimously that Christ is
S D : 0 3 :013(541) [0919] virtue, but because it lays **hold** on and accepts the merit
S D : 0 3 :022(543) [0923] and regenerated, but we **hold** that Christ with his perfect
S D : 0 4 :002(551) [0939] They **held** that therefore the preceding propositions and
S D : 0 4 :002(551) [0939] Hence, they **held**, these propositions should not be
S D : 0 4 :030(555) [0947] share in Christ only if we **hold** our first confidence firm to
S D : 0 6 :002(564) [0963] This one party taught and **held** that the regenerated do
S D : 0 6 :004(564) [0963] It is necessary to **hold** this constantly before believers'
S D : 0 6 :021(567) [0969] to do good works, he **holds** up before them precisely the
S D : 0 7 :004(569) [0973] When this did not **hold** water, they confessed that the
S D : 0 7 :006(570) [0973] and boasted that they **hold** no other opinion than that the
S D : 0 7 :016(572) [0977] "Secondly, they **hold** that it is the institution of this
S D : 0 7 :016(572) [0977] Therefore they **hold** that, where Christ's institution and
S D : 0 7 :029(574) [0981] now, he would teach and **hold** this or that article
S D : 0 7 :059(580) [0993] the Gospel, when it is laid **hold** on by faith, is a means
S D : 0 7 :062(581) [0995] sake of Jesus Christ, and **hold** to it in all difficulty and
S D : 0 8 :016(594) [1021] Hence he also **held** that the divine and human natures are
S D : 0 8 :017(594) [1021] church has always **held** in simple faith that the divine and
S D : 0 8 :064(603) [1037] We therefore **hold** and teach with the ancient orthodox
S D : 0 9 :001(610) [1051] us in the sermon that he **held** in the castle at Torgau in
S D : 1 0 :002(610) [1053] The one party **held** that even in a period of persecution
S D : 1 0 :028(615) [1061] the opinion of those who **hold** that in a period of
S D : 1 0 :029(615) [1061] 4. Likewise we **hold** it to be a culpable sin when in a
S D : 1 1 :009(618) [1065] damned, or that he merely **held** a sort of military muster:
S D : 1 1 :010(618) [1067] even though I were to **hold** to the Word, repent, believe,
S D : 1 1 :032(621) [1073] turn away from him but "**hold** fast until the end the
S D : 1 1 :038(622) [1075] this absolution and firmly **hold** that when we believe the
S D : 1 1 :043(623) [1077] If we stay with this and **hold** ourselves thereto, it is indeed
S D : 1 1 :045(624) [1079] of the world was laid" he **held** counsel and ordained
S D : 1 2 :018(634) [1099] 9. That no Christian can **hold** an office in the government
S D : 1 2 :022(634) [1099] with a good conscience **hold** or possess private property
S D : 1 2 :027(635) [1101] They **hold** other similar articles.
S D : 1 2 :027(635) [1101] with one party **holding** more and another party holding
S D : 1 2 :027(635) [1101] holding more and another party **holding** fewer errors.

Hole (1)
S D : 0 7 :018(572) [0979] every subterfuge and loop-**hole** which the

Holiday (2), Holidays (1)
L C : 0 1 :079(375) [0603] Our word "holy day" or "**holiday**" is so called from the
L C : 0 1 :079(375) [0603] work" literally means "observing a holy day or **holiday**."
L C : 0 1 :086(376) [0605] Since we observe **holidays** anyhow, we should devote

Holier (4), Holiest (1), Holiness (26)
A P : 1 5 :026(219) [0323] they regarded these observances as better and **holier**.
A P : 2 3 :043(245) [0375] each one to possess his vessel in **holiness** (I Thess. 4:4).
A P : 2 3 :065(248) [0381] Paul calls possessing one's vessel in **holiness** (I Thess. 4:4).
S 3 : 1 2 :003(315) [0499] Its **holiness** does not consist of surplices, tonsures, albs,
L C : 0 1 :074(375) [0601] to God than any monastic life and Carthusian **holiness**.
L C : 0 1 :093(377) [0607] know God's Word but seek **holiness** in their own works.
L C : 0 1 :120(381) [0615] this is better than the **holiness** of all the Carthusians, even
L C : 0 1 :120(382) [0615] us with the false **holiness** and glamor of our own works.
L C : 0 1 :145(385) [0623] that is better than the **holiness** and austere life of all the
L C : 0 1 :197(391) [0637] estate" and infringe upon the **holiness** of the Carthusians.
L C : 0 1 :197(392) [0637] hypocritical show of **holiness**, while they have thrown this
L C : 0 1 :198(392) [0637] to them all human **holiness** is only stench and filth, and it
L C : 0 1 :317(408) [0673] a heavenly, angelic man, far above all **holiness** on earth.
L C : 0 1 :318(408) [0673] attention to any other works or other kind of **holiness**.
L C : 0 2 :054(417) [0693] been won by Christ, and **holiness** has been wrought by
L C : 0 2 :056(418) [0693] is not) there is no forgiveness, and hence no **holiness**.
L C : 0 2 :056(418) [0693] all who seek to merit **holiness** through their works rather
L C : 0 2 :057(418) [0693] Meanwhile, since **holiness** has begun and is growing
L C : 0 2 :057(418) [0693] to complete and perfect **holiness** in a new, eternal life.
L C : 0 2 :059(418) [0693] and daily to increase **holiness** on earth through these two
L C : 0 2 :059(418) [0695] will instantly perfect our **holiness** and will eternally
L C : 0 3 :010(421) [0699] for those who are **holier** and in better favor with God
L C : 0 3 :015(422) [0701] He can boast of no better or **holier** commandment than I.
L C : 0 3 :016(422) [0701] to God as those of St. Paul and the **holiest** of saints.
L C : 0 3 :016(422) [0701] I freely admit that he is **holier** in respect to his person,
L C : 0 4 :046(442) [0743] it we obtain perfect **holiness** and salvation, which no
L C : 0 5 :016(448) [0757] it is not founded on the **holiness** of men but on the Word
S D : 0 1 :010(510) [0863] created in truth, **holiness**, and righteousness, together
S D : 0 1 :030(513) [0867] the goodness, truth, **holiness**, and righteousness imparted
S D : 0 6 :020(567) [0969] back on their own **holiness** and piety and under the
S D : 0 7 :024(573) [0981] is not based on the **holiness** of men but on the Word of

Holy (801)
P R : P R :001(003) [0007] princes, and estates in the **Holy** Empire of the German
P R : P R :002(003) [0007] unadulterated light of his **holy** Gospel and of the Word
P R : P R :004(004) [0007] and perceptibly impede the course of the **holy** Gospel.
P R : P R :005(004) [0009] just as, while the **holy** apostles were still alive, it happened
P R : P R :009(006) [0011] doctrine about the **holy** sacrament of the body and the
P R : P R :013(007) [0013] the singular grace of the **Holy** Spirit, everything that
P R : P R :018(009) [0015] in the custody of the **Holy** Empire, and of which both the
P R : P R :019(009) [0017] their error concerning the **Holy** Supper as well as other
P R : P R :020(010) [0017] a consideration of the **Holy** Supper into a discussion of
P R : P R :022(011) [0019] inside or outside the **Holy** Empire of the German Nation.
P R : P R :022(012) [0019] in blasphemies against the **Holy** Supper as it is celebrated
P R : P R :022(012) [0019] the guidance of the **Holy** Spirit, turn to the infallible truth
P R : P R :023(012) [0021] which is based on the **Holy** Scriptures of God and is
P R : P R :023(012) [0021] schools first of all to the **Holy** Scriptures and the Creeds,
P R : P R :023(012) [0021] in the church and for the **holy** ministry be faithfully and
P R : P R :023(012) [0021] help and assistance of the **Holy** Spirit until the glorious
P R : P R :024(013) [0021] through the grace of the **Holy** Spirit, the most acute and
P R : P R :025(014) [0023] minded by the grace of the **Holy** Spirit to abide and
P R : P R :025(014) [0023] electors and estates in the **Holy** Roman Empire, and also
P R : P R :025(014) [0023] of the ordinances of the **Holy** Empire and of the special
A G : P R :002(025) [0039] dissension concerning our **holy** faith and the Christian
A G : P R :008(025) [0039] manner, on the basis of the **Holy** Scriptures, these things
A G : P R :016(026) [0041] matters pertaining to our **holy** faith but would diligently
A G : 0 1 :002(027) [0043] God the Father, God the Son, God the **Holy** Spirit.
A G : 0 1 :006(028) [0043] two, the Word and the **Holy** Spirit, are not necessarily
A G : 0 1 :006(028) [0043] word or voice and that the **Holy** Spirit is a movement
A G : 0 2 :002(029) [0043] are not born again through Baptism and the **Holy** Spirit.
A G : 0 3 :004(030) [0045] that through the **Holy** Spirit he may sanctify, purify,
A G : 0 5 :002(031) [0045] means, he gives the **Holy** Spirit, who works faith, when
A G : 0 5 :004(031) [0045] others who teach that the **Holy** Spirit comes to us through
A G : 0 7 :001(032) [0047] taught among us that one **holy** Christian church will be
A G : 0 7 :001(032) [0047] in its purity and the **holy** sacraments are administered
A G : 1 0 :000(034) [0047] X. The **Holy** Supper of Our Lord
A G : 1 5 :001(036) [0049] among them being certain **holy** days, festivals, and the
A G : 1 8 :002(039) [0051] help, and activity of the **Holy** Spirit man is not capable of
A G : 1 8 :003(039) [0051] is accomplished by the **Holy** Spirit, who is given through
A G : 2 0 :003(041) [0053] appointed fasts, **holy** days, brotherhoods, etc.
A G : 2 0 :029(045) [0057] When through faith the **Holy** Spirit is given, the heart is
A G : 2 0 :031(045) [0057] when it is without the **Holy** Spirit, the heart is too weak.
A G : 2 0 :034(045) [0057] without true faith and the **Holy** Spirit and governs himself
A G : 0 0 :001(047) [0059] is grounded clearly on the **Holy** Scriptures and is not
A G : 0 0 :000(048) [0059] that is contrary to the **Holy** Scriptures or what is common
A G : 2 3 :019(054) [0063] of that fact that in the **Holy** Scriptures God commanded
A G : 0 1 :007(056) [0065] diligence concerning the **holy** sacrament, why it was
A G : 2 4 :030(059) [0067] In the third place, the **holy** sacrament was not instituted
A G : 2 4 :034(060) [0067] On **holy** days, and at other times when communicants are
A G : 2 6 :011(065) [0071] glamorous title of alone being **holy** and perfect works.
A G : 2 6 :031(068) [0075] taught concerning the **holy** cross that Christians are
A G : 2 6 :045(070) [0075] of the apostles to institute **holy** days but to teach faith
A G : 2 7 :015(073) [0077] had conducted schools of **Holy** Scripture and other
A G : 2 7 :036(076) [0081] opposed to God and the **holy** Gospel and contrary to
A G : 2 8 :006(082) [0085] Receive the **Holy** Spirit.
A G : 2 8 :008(082) [0085] eternal righteousness, the **Holy** Spirit, and eternal life.
A G : 2 8 :009(082) [0085] and of administering the **holy** sacraments, for St. Paul
A G : 2 8 :028(085) [0087] something contrary to the divine **Holy** Scriptures.
A G : 2 8 :030(085) [0087] concerning foods, **holy** days, and the different orders of
A G : 2 8 :037(086) [0089] Almost every day new **holy** days and new fasts have been
A G : 2 8 :041(087) [0089] sin to do manual work on **holy** days (even when it does
A G : 2 8 :049(089) [0091] Is it possible that the **Holy** Spirit warned against them for
A G : 2 8 :057(091) [0091] Easter, Pentecost, and similar **holy** days and usages.
A G : 2 8 :059(091) [0091] much mistaken, for the **Holy** Scriptures have abrogated
A G : 2 8 :070(093) [0093] is no doubt that it is in accord with the **holy** Gospel.
A G : 0 0 :005(095) [0095] that is contrary to **Holy** Scripture or the universal
A G : 0 0 :007(096) [0095] information on the basis of the divine **Holy** Scripture.
A L : 0 1 :003(028) [0043] also coeternal: the Father, the Son, and the **Holy** Spirit.
A L : 0 1 :006(028) [0043] that the Word and the **Holy** Spirit are not distinct persons
A L : 0 2 :002(029) [0043] are not born again through Baptism and the **Holy** Spirit.
A L : 0 3 :004(030) [0045] in him by sending the **Holy** Spirit into their hearts to rule,
A L : 0 5 :002(031) [0045] through instruments, the **Holy** Spirit is given, and the
A L : 0 5 :002(031) [0045] Spirit is given, and the **Holy** Spirit produces faith, where
A L : 0 5 :004(031) [0045] others who think that the **Holy** Spirit comes to men
A L : 0 7 :001(032) [0047] also teach that one **holy** church is to continue forever.
A L : 1 2 :007(035) [0049] been justified can lose the **Holy** Spirit, and also those who
A L : 1 5 :001(036) [0049] Such are certain **holy** days, festivals, and the like.
A L : 1 8 :002(039) [0051] the power, without the **Holy** Spirit, to attain the
A L : 1 8 :003(039) [0051] in the heart when the **Holy** Spirit is received through the
A L : 1 8 :008(040) [0053] who teach that without the **Holy** Spirit, by the power of
A L : 2 0 :003(041) [0053] works, such as particular **holy** days, prescribed fasts,
A L : 2 0 :029(045) [0057] because through faith the **Holy** Spirit is received, hearts
A L : 2 0 :031(045) [0057] For without the **Holy** Spirit man's powers are full of
A L : 2 0 :034(045) [0057] strength alone without faith and without the **Holy** Spirit.

Continued ▶

A L : 2 4 :024(058) [0067] that they depart from the **Holy** Scriptures and diminish
A L : 2 4 :034(060) [0067] among us on every **holy** day, and on other days, if any
A L : 2 4 :038(060) [0069] let the deacons receive **Holy** Communion from the bishop
A L : 2 6 :002(064) [0071] new orders, new **holy** days, and new fasts were daily
A L : 2 6 :008(065) [0071] the observance of certain **holy** days, rites, fasts, and
A L : 2 6 :040(069) [0075] of lessons in the Mass, **holy** days, etc.) which are
A L : 2 6 :045(070) [0075] laws with respect to **holy** days but to preach piety toward
A L : 2 7 :015(073) [0077] had been schools of the **Holy** Scriptures and other
A L : 2 7 :057(080) [0083] "fleeing from the world" and "seeking a **holy** kind of life."
A L : 2 8 :006(082) [0085] Receive the **Holy** Spirit.
A L : 2 8 :008(082) [0085] as eternal righteousness, the **Holy** Spirit, and eternal life.
A L : 2 8 :030(085) [0087] laws concerning foods, **holy** days, grades or orders of
A L : 2 8 :037(086) [0089] from time to time more **holy** days were appointed, more
A L : 2 8 :041(087) [0089] sin to do manual work on **holy** days, even when it gives
A L : 2 8 :049(089) [0091] Was it in vain that the **Holy** Spirit warned against these?
A L : 2 8 :063(092) [0093] the extent to which one is allowed to work on **holy** days.
A P : P R :009(099) [0101] in opposition to the clear Scripture of the **Holy** Spirit.
A P : 0 1 :001(100) [0103] of the same divine essence, Father, Son, and **Holy** Spirit.
A P : 0 1 :002(100) [0103] and we believe that the **Holy** Scriptures testify to it firmly,
A P : 0 2 :010(102) [0109] What need is there for the **Holy** Spirit if human powers
A P : 0 2 :025(103) [0111] not been quenched by the **Holy** Spirit and a love for God
A P : 0 2 :035(105) [0115] he has also said that the **Holy** Spirit, given in Baptism,
A P : 0 2 :045(106) [0117] Christ to be forgiven and the **Holy** Spirit to be mortified.
A P : 0 2 :050(106) [0119] but have set forth the **Holy** Scripture and the teachings of
A P : 0 2 :050(106) [0119] the Holy Scripture and the teachings of the **holy** Fathers.
A P : 0 2 :051(107) [0119] the opinions of the **holy** Fathers, which we also follow.
A P : 0 4 :009(108) [0123] maintain that without the **Holy** Spirit reason can love God
A P : 0 4 :029(111) [0129] and also for leading a **holy** life, then 'Christ died to no
A P : 0 4 :031(111) [0129] be born again through the **Holy** Spirit, then the
A P : 0 4 :034(112) [0129] But without the **Holy** Spirit, the human heart either
A P : 0 4 :035(112) [0131] things without the **Holy** Spirit; for they do them with a
A P : 0 4 :045(113) [0133] us and brings us the **Holy** Spirit, so that we can finally
A P : 0 4 :054(114) [0137] pleas for mercy, and the **holy** Fathers often say that we
A P : 0 4 :063(115) [0139] can our opponents say how the **Holy** Spirit is given.
A P : 0 4 :063(115) [0139] the sacraments bestow the **Holy** Spirit *ex opere operato*
A P : 0 4 :063(115) [0139] as though the gift of the **Holy** Spirit were a minor matter.
A P : 0 4 :064(116) [0139] a new life in our hearts, and is a work of the **Holy** Spirit.
A P : 0 4 :070(116) [0141] cannot keep the law unless we first receive the **Holy** Spirit
A P : 0 4 :086(119) [0147] the forgiveness of sins and the **Holy** Spirit by faith alone.
A P : 0 4 :099(121) [0151] but a thing that receives the **Holy** Spirit and justifies us.
A P : 0 4 :103(121) [0151] are similar statements here and there in the **holy** Fathers.
A P : 0 4 :108(122) [0153] that these words fell from the **Holy** Spirit unawares?
A P : 0 4 :115(123) [0155] sin; but it is a work of the **Holy** Spirit that frees us from
A P : 0 4 :116(123) [0155] to God, and brings the **Holy** Spirit, it should be called
A P : 0 4 :125(124) [0157] Since faith brings the **Holy** Spirit and produces a new life
A P : 0 4 :125(124) [0157] because our hearts have spiritual and **holy** impulses.
A P : 0 4 :126(124) [0157] being justified and regenerated, we receive the **Holy** Spirit
A P : 0 4 :126(124) [0157] it is impossible to keep the law without the **Holy** Spirit.
A P : 0 4 :130(125) [0157] without Christ and the **Holy** Spirit, still the impulses of
A P : 0 4 :130(125) [0157] are impossible without the **Holy** Spirit; this is evident
A P : 0 4 :132(125) [0159] forgiveness of sins and the **Holy** Spirit, to bring forth in
A P : 0 4 :132(125) [0159] the law unless by faith we have received the **Holy** Spirit.
A P : 0 4 :132(125) [0159] the law can be kept only when the **Holy** Spirit is given.
A P : 0 4 :133(125) [0159] removed except by faith, which receives the **Holy** Spirit.
A P : 0 4 :135(125) [0159] of sins, we receive the **Holy** Spirit, so that we can think
A P : 0 4 :135(126) [0159] Christ and without the **Holy** Spirit we cannot keep the
A P : 0 4 :139(126) [0161] therefore we pray that the **Holy** Spirit may govern and
A P : 0 4 :139(126) [0161] us his promise and the **Holy** Spirit, so that with the help
A P : 0 4 :147(127) [0163] love is the work of the **Holy** Spirit and since it is
A P : 0 4 :154(128) [0165] outward courtesies due a guest and a great and **holy** man.
A P : 0 4 :170(130) [0171] The **Holy** Spirit in our hearts battles against such feelings
A P : 0 4 :171(130) [0171] not only the Scriptures but also the **holy** Fathers.
A P : 0 4 :175(131) [0171] by faith receive the **Holy** Spirit and that their impulses
A P : 0 4 :182(132) [0173] keeping of the law follows with the gift of the **Holy** Spirit.
A P : 0 4 :189(133) [0175] and hinders what the **Holy** Spirit motivates, fouling it
A P : 0 4 :189(133) [0175] faith they are nevertheless **holy** and divine works,
A P : 0 4 :190(133) [0175] teachers of the church are **holy** works, true sacrifices
A P : 0 4 :191(133) [0175] in governing the state are **holy** works, true sacrifices,
A P : 0 4 :192(133) [0175] by the Corinthians was a **holy** work (I Cor. 16:1), a
A P : 0 4 :211(136) [0179] Francis, and other **holy** Fathers chose a certain kind of
A P : 0 4 :219(137) [0181] it ever so great, because he will not keep the **Holy** Spirit.
A P : 0 4 :220(137) [0181] urging to bear good fruits lest they lose the **Holy** Spirit.
A P : 0 4 :230(139) [0183] Christ for the help of his **Holy** Spirit to make it clear and
A P : 0 4 :293(152) [0203] quickened by faith in this way, it receives the **Holy** Spirit.
A P : 0 4 :349(160) [0217] are reborn and receive the **Holy** Spirit, that this new life
A P : 0 4 :389(166) [0225] Scriptures, with the **holy** Fathers Ambrose, Augustine,
A P : 0 4 :392(167) [0225] The Scriptures, the **holy** Fathers, and the judgment of all
A P : 0 4 :400(168) [0227] to the authority of the **holy** Fathers, and contrary to the
A P : 0 7 :005(169) [0227] association of faith and of the **Holy** Spirit in men's hearts.
A P : 0 7 :007(169) [0229] saying that it should be purified in order to be **holy**.
A P : 0 7 :007(169) [0229] such thing, that it might be **holy** and without blemish."
A P : 0 7 :007(169) [0229] us to believe that there is a **holy**, catholic church.
A P : 0 7 :007(169) [0229] Certainly the wicked are not a **holy** church!
A P : 0 7 :008(169) [0229] teaching and of the same **Holy** spirit, who renews,
A P : 0 7 :009(170) [0229] of sins, answer to prayer, and the gift of the **Holy** Spirit.
A P : 0 7 :010(170) [0229] the same Christ, the same **Holy** Spirit, and the same
A P : 0 7 :013(170) [0231] heart and the gift of the **Holy** Spirit but would think of it
A P : 0 7 :014(170) [0231] but by being God's true people, reborn by the **Holy** Spirit.
A P : 0 7 :015(170) [0231] blessings themselves, the **Holy** Spirit and the
A P : 0 7 :021(172) [0233] The writings of the **holy** Fathers show that even they
A P : 0 7 :022(172) [0233] it will always have the **Holy** Spirit, so it also has the
A P : 0 7 :022(172) [0235] properly speaking, is that which has the **Holy** Spirit.
A P : 0 7 :028(173) [0237] believe the Gospel of Christ and who have the **Holy** Spirit
A P : 0 7 :031(174) [0239] are they wrought by the **Holy** Spirit, as are chastity,
A P : 0 7 :036(175) [0241] heart, are not works of the **Holy** Spirit (like love of
A P : 0 7 :036(175) [0241] but righteousness and peace and joy in the **Holy** Spirit."
A P : 0 9 :003(178) [0245] fact that God gives the **Holy** Spirit to those who were
A P : 0 9 :003(178) [0245] Baptism were useless, the **Holy** Spirit would be given to
A P : 1 0 :000(179) [0247] [Article X. The **Holy** Supper]
A P : 1 2 :016(184) [0257] false and foreign to the **Holy** Scriptures as well as the
A P : 1 2 :029(186) [0259] Christ's sake, to grant the **Holy** Spirit and eternal life, and
A P : 1 2 :044(187) [0263] When we believe, the **Holy** Spirit quickens our hearts
A P : 1 2 :071(192) [0271] The testimony of the **Holy** Spirit was added to this
A P : 1 2 :071(192) [0271] was still saying this, the **Holy** Spirit fell on all who heard
A P : 1 2 :073(192) [0273] This is the witness that the **Holy** Spirit brings in your
A P : 1 2 :074(192) [0273] our hearts and the **Holy** Spirit grants them peace.
A P : 1 2 :082(194) [0275] the regenerate receive the **Holy** Spirit and therefore begin
A P : 1 2 :113(199) [0285] The **holy** Fathers did not want to accept the lapsed or the
A P : 1 2 :126(201) [0289] take care, indicate a change in the **Holy** Roman Empire.
A P : 1 2 :132(202) [0291] 12:1), "Present your bodies as a living sacrifice, **holy**," etc.
A P : 1 2 :139(203) [0295] But nowhere in **Holy** Scripture are we told that only
A P : 1 2 :174(210) [0307] surrendering to the devil or offending the **Holy** Spirit.
A P : 1 3 :013(212) [0311] who dream that the **Holy** Spirit does not come through
A P : 1 5 :013(216) [0319] The **holy** Fathers did not institute any traditions for the
A P : 1 5 :020(218) [0321] Although the **holy** Fathers themselves had rites and
A P : 1 8 :002(225) [0335] believe that without the **Holy** Spirit men can love God
A P : 1 8 :002(225) [0335] and that without the **Holy** Spirit men can merit grace and
A P : 1 8 :004(225) [0335] on its own without the **Holy** Spirit, Scripture calls the
A P : 1 8 :006(225) [0335] Without the **Holy** Spirit human hearts have neither the
A P : 1 8 :007(226) [0337] the human heart cannot perform without the **Holy** Spirit.
A P : 1 8 :009(226) [0337] to the operation of the **Holy** Spirit in the regenerate.
A P : 1 8 :009(226) [0337] and the teaching of the **Holy** Spirit; and it points out the
A P : 1 8 :009(226) [0337] Holy Spirit; and it points out the need for the **Holy** Spirit.
A P : 1 8 :010(226) [0337] law of God without the **Holy** Spirit and that the Holy
A P : 1 8 :010(226) [0337] Holy Spirit and that the **Holy** Spirit is given to them out
A P : 2 0 :013(228) [0343] in those who lose the **Holy** Spirit and reject penitence; as
A P : 2 0 :015(229) [0343] when we have received the **Holy** Spirit by faith, the
A P : 2 1 :042(235) [0357] this most honorable and **holy** desire of the emperor, our
A P : 2 3 :002(239) [0363] the unnatural lusts of the **holy** fathers "who look like
A P : 2 3 :031(243) [0373] marriage is permissible and **holy** through faith in Christ
A P : 2 4 :026(254) [0391] teaches in I Pet. 2:5, "A **holy** priesthood, to offer spiritual
A P : 2 4 :026(254) [0391] refers to the operation of the **Holy** Spirit within us.
A P : 2 4 :026(254) [0391] bodies as a living sacrifice, **holy** and acceptable to God,
A P : 2 4 :034(256) [0395] sanctified by the **Holy** Spirit," that is, so that the Gentiles
A P : 2 4 :039(257) [0399] of things, for the **Holy** Spirit who puts us to death and
A P : 2 4 :059(260) [0405] may receive faith and the **Holy** Spirit and be put to death
A P : 2 4 :059(260) [0405] ministry of the Spirit, the **Holy** Spirit works in the heart.
A P : 2 4 :070(262) [0409] For the **Holy** Spirit works through the Word and the
A P : 2 4 :084(264) [0413] to argue that since the **Holy** Scriptures mention an altar,
A P : 2 4 :096(267) [0417] prophets, apostles, and **holy** Fathers, namely, that the
A P : 2 7 :013(271) [0423] is a witness, the **Holy** Spirit is a witness, thy whole church
A P : 2 7 :021(272) [0427] sinning, as did Bernard, Francis, and other **holy** men.
A P : 2 7 :047(277) [0437] God is meritorious and **holy** and the way of perfection.
A P : 2 7 :051(278) [0437] the commandment of the **Holy** Spirit (I Cor. 7:2),
A P : 2 7 :070(281) [0443] **Holy** men who followed this way of life must have come
A P : 2 8 :010(282) [0447] the Word of God and the **Holy** Spirit, that work eternal
S 1 : P R :015(291) [0459] Thou hast given us by thy **Holy** Spirit, who with Thee and
S 1 : 0 1 :000(291) [0461] 1. That Father, Son, and **Holy** Spirit, three distinct
S 1 : 0 1 :000(291) [0461] by the Father, and the **Holy** Spirit proceeded from the
S 1 : 0 1 :000(291) [0461] became man, and neither the Father nor the **Holy** Spirit.
S 1 : 0 1 :000(291) [0461] he was conceived by the **Holy** Spirit, without the
S 1 : 0 1 :000(292) [0461] of man, and was born of the pure, **holy**, and virgin Mary.
S 2 : 0 2 :015(295) [0467] articles of faith out of the **holy** Fathers' words or works.
S 2 : 0 2 :029(297) [0471] that we may retain the **holy** sacrament in its purity and
S 2 : 0 4 :003(298) [0471] destruction of the entire **holy** Christian church (in so far
S 2 : 0 4 :004(299) [0473] Yet it is manifest that the **holy** church was without a pope
S 2 : 0 4 :005(299) [0473] The **holy** Christian church can exist very well without
S 2 : 0 4 :014(301) [0475] from that of the **Holy** Scriptures, or is compared with
S 3 : 0 1 :010(303) [0479] the Scriptures that the **Holy** Spirit and his gifts are
S 3 : 0 3 :001(303) [0479] says in John 16:8, "The **Holy** Spirit will convince the
S 3 : 0 3 :003(304) [0481] great, wise, mighty, and **holy** you may think yourselves.
S 3 : 0 3 :024(307) [0485] Here the **holy** see in Rome came to the aid of the poor
S 3 : 0 3 :028(308) [0487] and mightily to be **holy**, and yet the hereditary evil which
S 3 : 0 3 :039(309) [0489] even when it is most **holy** and beautiful, is nothing but
S 3 : 0 3 :040(309) [0489] but with the gift of the **Holy** Spirit which follows the
S 3 : 0 3 :040(309) [0489] remain and enables man to become truly pure and **holy**.
S 3 : 0 3 :043(310) [0491] and to teach that when **holy** people, aside from the fact
S 3 : 0 3 :044(310) [0491] This is so because the **Holy** Spirit does not permit sin to
S 3 : 0 3 :044(310) [0491] sin is committed, but the **Holy** Spirit represses and
S 3 : 0 3 :044(310) [0491] does what it wishes, the **Holy** Spirit and faith are not
S 3 : 0 4 :000(310) [0491] third, through the **holy** Sacrament of the Altar; fourth,
S 3 : 0 8 :013(313) [0497] but were moved by the **Holy** Spirit, yet as holy men of
S 3 : 0 8 :013(313) [0497] were moved by the Holy Spirit, yet as **holy** men of God.
S 3 : 0 8 :013(313) [0497] Word they were not **holy**, and the Holy Spirit would not
S 3 : 0 8 :013(313) [0497] were not holy, and the **Holy** Spirit would not have moved
S 3 : 0 8 :013(313) [0497] They were **holy**, St. Peter says, because the Holy Spirit
S 3 : 0 8 :013(313) [0497] St. Peter says, because the **Holy** Spirit spoke through
S 3 : 1 2 :002(315) [0499] the church is, namely, **holy** believers and sheep who hear
S 3 : 1 2 :003(315) [0499] So children pray, "I believe in one **holy** Christian church."
S 3 : 1 2 :003(315) [0499] over and above the **Holy** Scriptures, but it consists of the
S 3 : 1 3 :001(315) [0499] altogether righteous and **holy** for the sake of Christ, our
S 3 : 1 3 :002(315) [0499] and shall be righteous and **holy** through the pure grace
S 3 : 1 5 :004(316) [0501] a ridicule and mockery of **holy** Baptism which should not
T R : 0 0 :027(324) [0511] Most of the **holy** Fathers (such as Origen, Ambrose,
T R : 0 0 :082(000) [0529] that all these agree with **Holy** Scripture, and with the
S C : P R :003(338) [0533] baptized, and receive the **holy** sacrament, they do not
S C : 0 1 :005(342) [0541] *"Remember the Sabbath day, to keep it* ***holy***.*"*
S C : 0 1 :006(342) [0541] of the same, but deem it **holy** and gladly hear and learn
S C : 0 2 :003(345) [0545] *who was conceived by the* ***Holy*** *Spirit, born of the virgin*
S C : 0 2 :004(345) [0545] and gold but with his **holy** and precious blood and with
S C : 0 2 :005(345) [0545] *"I believe in the* ***Holy*** *Spirit, the holy Christian church,*
S C : 0 2 :005(345) [0545] *in the Holy Spirit, the* ***holy*** *Christian church, the*
S C : 0 2 :006(345) [0545] But the **Holy** Spirit has called me through the Gospel,
S C : 0 3 :004(346) [0547] To be sure, God's name is **holy** in itself, but we pray in
S C : 0 3 :004(346) [0547] we pray in this petition that it may also be **holy** for us.
S C : 0 3 :005(346) [0547] as children of God, lead **holy** lives in accordance with it.
S C : 0 3 :008(346) [0547] Father gives us his **Holy** Spirit so that by his grace we
S C : 0 3 :008(346) [0547] grace we may believe his **holy** Word and live a godly life,
S C : 0 4 :000(348) [0551] [IV] The Sacrament of **Holy** Baptism
S C : 0 4 :004(348) [0551] of the Father and of the Son and of the **Holy** Spirit."
S C : 0 4 :010(349) [0551] of regeneration in the **Holy** Spirit, as St. Paul wrote to
S C : 0 4 :010(349) [0551] and renewal in the **Holy** Spirit, which he poured out upon
S C : 0 5 :028(351) [0555] name of the Father and of the Son and of the **Holy** Spirit.
S C : 0 6 :004(351) [0555] Answer: The **holy** evangelists Matthew, Mark, and Luke,
S C : 0 7 :001(352) [0557] name of God, the Father, the Son, and the **Holy** Spirit.
S C : 0 7 :002(352) [0557] Let thy **holy** angel have charge of me, that the wicked one

Continued ▶

S C : 0 7 :004(353) [0559] name of God, the Father, the Son, and the **Holy** Spirit.
S C : 0 7 :005(353) [0559] Let thy **holy** angels have charge of me, that the wicked
L C : P R :009(359) [0569] and meditation the **Holy** Spirit is present and bestows
L C : P R :010(360) [0571] This, indeed, is the true **holy** water, the sign which routs
L C : P R :016(361) [0573] and wiser than all his **holy** angels, prophets, apostles, and
L C : P R :018(361) [0573] a brief compend and summary of all the **Holy** Scriptures.
L C : S P :003(362) [0575] 3. You shall keep the Sabbath day **holy**.
L C : S P :012(363) [0577] who was conceived by the **Holy** Spirit, born of the virgin
L C : S P :013(363) [0577] I believe in the **Holy** Spirit, the holy Christian church, the
L C : S P :013(363) [0577] in the Holy Spirit, the **holy** Christian church, the
L C : S P :020(364) [0579] Baptism and the **holy** Body and Blood of Christ,
L C : S P :021(364) [0579] and of the Son and of the **Holy** Spirit" (Matt. 28:19).
L C : 0 1 :056(372) [0595] avoid every misuse of the **holy** name as the greatest sin
L C : 0 1 :064(373) [0599] forbidden here to use the **holy** name in support of
L C : 0 1 :072(374) [0601] we should always keep the **holy** name on our lips so that
L C : 0 1 :078(375) [0603] *"You shall sanctify the* ***holy*** *day."*
L C : 0 1 :079(375) [0603] Our word "**holy** day" or "holiday" is so called from the
L C : 0 1 :079(375) [0603] work" literally means "observing a **holy** day or holiday."
L C : 0 1 :080(375) [0603] he commanded it to be kept **holy** above all other days.
L C : 0 1 :081(376) [0603] meant that we should sanctify the **holy** day or day of rest.
L C : 0 1 :083(376) [0603] we point out that we keep **holy** days not for the sake of
L C : 0 1 :084(376) [0605] most especially, we keep **holy** days so that people may
L C : 0 1 :087(376) [0605] "You shall sanctify the **holy** day" means, answer: "It
L C : 0 1 :087(376) [0605] the holy day" means, answer: "It means to keep it **holy**."
L C : 0 1 :087(376) [0605] What is meant by "keeping it **holy**"?
L C : 0 1 :087(376) [0605] else than to devote it to **holy** words, holy works, holy life.
L C : 0 1 :087(376) [0605] else than to devote it to holy words, **holy** works, holy life.
L C : 0 1 :087(376) [0605] else than to devote it to holy words, holy works, **holy** life.
L C : 0 1 :087(377) [0605] the day needs no sanctification, for it was created **holy**.
L C : 0 1 :087(377) [0605] But God wants it to be **holy** to you.
L C : 0 1 :087(377) [0605] So it becomes **holy** or unholy on your account, according
L C : 0 1 :087(377) [0605] as you spend the day in doing **holy** or unholy things.
L C : 0 1 :089(377) [0605] should make every day a **holy** day and give ourselves only
L C : 0 1 :089(377) [0605] and give ourselves only to **holy** activities — that is, occupy
L C : 0 1 :090(377) [0605] Wherever this practice is in force, a **holy** day is truly kept.
L C : 0 1 :090(377) [0607] Where it is not, it cannot be called a Christian **holy** day.
L C : 0 1 :090(377) [0607] without sanctifying the **holy** day because they neither
L C : 0 1 :091(377) [0607] Word of God is the true **holy** thing above all holy things.
L C : 0 1 :091(377) [0607] Word of God is the true holy thing above all **holy** things.
L C : 0 1 :091(377) [0607] of all the saints or all the **holy** and consecrated vestments
L C : 0 1 :092(377) [0607] by God's Word if they are to be God-pleasing or **holy**.
L C : 0 1 :093(377) [0607] be altogether covered with **holy** relics, as are the so-called
L C : 0 1 :094(378) [0607] so that this day should have its own particular **holy** work.
L C : 0 1 :094(378) [0607] are not properly called **holy** work unless the doer himself
L C : 0 1 :094(378) [0607] called holy work unless the doer himself is first **holy**.
L C : 0 1 :094(378) [0607] the doer himself is made **holy**; this, as we have heard,
L C : 0 1 :095(378) [0607] on God's Word that no **holy** day is sanctified without it,
L C : 0 1 :096(378) [0607] misuse and desecrate the **holy** day, like those who in their
L C : 0 1 :097(378) [0609] remove the abuse of the **holy** day, for we permit ourselves
L C : 0 1 :103(379) [0611] we should not misuse his **holy** name in support of lies or
L C : 0 1 :103(379) [0611] Thirdly, on **holy** days or days of rest we should diligently
L C : 0 1 :112(380) [0613] what a great, good, and **holy** work is here assigned to
L C : 0 1 :112(380) [0613] as God's command or as a **holy**, divine word and precept.
L C : 0 1 :112(380) [0613] lived according to these words must also be **holy** men.
L C : 0 1 :112(380) [0613] "If I am to do good and **holy** works, I know of none
L C : 0 1 :117(381) [0615] place within that jewel and **holy** treasure, the Word and
L C : 0 1 :128(383) [0617] and considers this, unless he is led to it by the **Holy** Spirit.
L C : 0 1 :146(385) [0623] you lead a more blessed or **holy** life, as far as your works
L C : 0 1 :147(385) [0623] faith that makes a person **holy**; faith alone serves him,
L C : 0 1 :176(389) [0631] no matter how devout and **holy** you may be in other
L C : 0 1 :198(392) [0637] Word which are the true, **holy**, and divine works in which
L C : 0 1 :230(396) [0645] of all thieves, the **Holy** See at Rome, and all its retinue,
L C : 0 1 :278(402) [0661] Let all monks and **holy** orders step forth, with all their
L C : 0 1 :326(409) [0675] but learn it, hear it gladly, keep it **holy**, and honor it.
L C : 0 2 :006(411) [0679] redemption; the third, of the **Holy** Spirit, sanctification.
L C : 0 2 :007(411) [0679] me; I believe in the **Holy** Spirit, who sanctifies me."
L C : 0 2 :024(413) [0683] through his Son and the **Holy** Spirit, as we shall hear.
L C : 0 2 :025(413) [0683] *who was conceived by the* ***Holy*** *Spirit, born of the virgin*
L C : 0 2 :031(414) [0687] born without sin, of the **Holy** Spirit and the Virgin, that
L C : 0 2 :034(415) [0687] *"I believe in the* ***Holy*** *Spirit, the holy Christian Church,*
L C : 0 2 :034(415) [0687] *in the Holy Spirit, the* ***holy*** *Christian Church, the*
L C : 0 2 :035(415) [0687] and portrayed the **Holy** Spirit and his office, which is that
L C : 0 2 :035(415) [0687] Holy Spirit and his office, which is that he makes us **holy**.
L C : 0 2 :035(415) [0687] concentrate on the term "**Holy** Spirit," because it is so
L C : 0 2 :036(415) [0687] God's Spirit alone is called **Holy** Spirit, that is, he who
L C : 0 2 :036(415) [0687] on account of his work the **Holy** Spirit must be called
L C : 0 2 :036(415) [0687] Spirit must be called Sanctifier, the One who makes **holy**.
L C : 0 2 :037(415) [0687] resurrection, etc., so the **Holy** Spirit effects our
L C : 0 2 :037(415) [0687] he first leads us into his **holy** community, placing us upon
L C : 0 2 :038(415) [0689] through the preaching of the Gospel by the **Holy** Spirit.
L C : 0 2 :038(415) [0689] in which he has given the **Holy** Spirit to offer and apply to
L C : 0 2 :040(416) [0689] words, "I believe in the **Holy** Spirit"? you can answer, "I
L C : 0 2 :040(416) [0689] answer, "I believe that the **Holy** Spirit makes me holy, as
L C : 0 2 :040(416) [0689] that the Holy Spirit makes me **holy**, as his name implies."
L C : 0 2 :042(416) [0689] The **Holy** Spirit reveals and preaches that Word, and by it
L C : 0 2 :043(416) [0689] Christ as the Lord, or the **Holy** Spirit as the Sanctifier.
L C : 0 2 :044(416) [0689] There was no **Holy** Spirit present to reveal this truth and
L C : 0 2 :045(416) [0689] not preached, there is no **Holy** Spirit to create, call, and
L C : 0 2 :047(416) [0689] The Creed calls the **holy** Christian church a *communio*
L C : 0 2 :048(417) [0691] or best and most clearly of all, "a **holy** Christian people."
L C : 0 2 :049(417) [0691] only of saints, or, still more clearly, "a **holy** community."
L C : 0 2 :051(417) [0691] there is on earth a little **holy** flock or community of pure
L C : 0 2 :051(417) [0691] It is called together by the **Holy** Spirit in one faith, mind,
L C : 0 2 :052(417) [0691] I was brought to it by the **Holy** Spirit and incorporated
L C : 0 2 :053(417) [0691] Until the last day the **Holy** Spirit remains with the holy
L C : 0 2 :053(417) [0691] Spirit remains with the **holy** community or Christian
L C : 0 2 :054(417) [0693] is granted through the **holy** sacraments and absolution as
L C : 0 2 :054(417) [0693] has been wrought by the **Holy** Spirit through God's Word
L C : 0 2 :055(418) [0693] Although we have sin, the **Holy** Spirit sees to it that it
L C : 0 2 :058(418) [0693] Now we are only halfway pure and **holy**.
L C : 0 2 :058(418) [0693] The **Holy** Spirit must continue to work in us through the
L C : 0 2 :058(418) [0693] only perfectly pure and **holy** people, full of goodness and
L C : 0 2 :059(418) [0693] the office and work of the **Holy** Spirit, to begin and daily
L C : 0 2 :061(419) [0695] is accomplished, but the **Holy** Spirit carries on his work
L C : 0 2 :062(419) [0695] evil, he will finally make us perfectly and eternally **holy**.
L C : 0 2 :064(419) [0695] given us his Son and his **Holy** Spirit, through whom he
L C : 0 2 :065(419) [0695] of Christ, had it not been revealed by the **Holy** Spirit.
L C : 0 2 :066(419) [0697] not illuminated and blessed by the gifts of the **Holy** Spirit.
L C : 0 2 :067(420) [0697] the Creed; it must be taught by the **Holy** Spirit alone.
L C : 0 2 :069(420) [0697] creation, Christ all his works, the **Holy** Spirit all his gifts.
L C : 0 3 :005(420) [0699] are required to praise the **holy** name and pray or call
L C : 0 3 :015(422) [0701] as these: "I am not **holy** enough or worthy enough; if I
L C : 0 3 :015(422) [0701] if I were as godly and **holy** as St. Peter or St. Paul, then I
L C : 0 3 :016(422) [0701] I offer is just as precious, **holy**, and pleasing to God as
L C : 0 3 :036(425) [0707] Father, grant that thy name alone may be **holy**."
L C : 0 3 :037(425) [0707] But what is it to pray that his name may become **holy**?
L C : 0 3 :037(425) [0707] Is it not already **holy**?
L C : 0 3 :037(425) [0707] Answer: Yes, in itself it is **holy**, but not our use of it.
L C : 0 3 :038(425) [0707] his name and keeping it **holy** and sacred, regarding it as
L C : 0 3 :038(425) [0709] his name, which is already **holy** in heaven, may also be
L C : 0 3 :038(425) [0709] heaven, may also be kept **holy** on earth by us and all the
L C : 0 3 :039(425) [0709] How does it become **holy** among us?
L C : 0 3 :045(426) [0709] and desecrates this **holy** name, as in the past a church was
L C : 0 3 :045(426) [0709] rendering unholy by misuse that which is **holy** in itself.
L C : 0 3 :047(426) [0711] all of whom wear the **holy** name as a cloak and warrant
L C : 0 3 :049(426) [0711] God's name sacred and **holy** in both doctrine and life so
L C : 0 3 :050(426) [0711] Just as God's name is **holy** in itself and yet we pray that it
L C : 0 3 :050(426) [0711] yet we pray that it may be **holy** among us, so also his
L C : 0 3 :051(427) [0711] this end he also gave his **Holy** Spirit to teach us this
L C : 0 3 :051(427) [0711] teach us this through his **holy** Word and to enlighten and
L C : 0 3 :052(427) [0711] may be praised through his **holy** Word and our Christian
L C : 0 3 :052(427) [0711] So we pray that, led by the **Holy** Spirit, many may come
L C : 0 3 :054(427) [0713] Word and the power of the **Holy** Spirit, that the devil's
L C : 0 3 :061(428) [0715] for faith, and for the **Holy** Spirit, that he may govern us
L C : 0 3 :065(429) [0715] fruit, there the blessed **holy** cross will not be far away.
L C : 0 3 :067(429) [0717] persecute and suppress thy **holy** Word or prevent thy
L C : 0 4 :004(437) [0733] *of the Father and of the Son and of the* ***Holy*** *Spirit."*
L C : 0 4 :017(438) [0737] but a divine, heavenly, **holy**, and blessed water — praise it
L C : 0 4 :017(438) [0737] Word, which is a heavenly, **holy** Word which no one can
L C : 0 4 :018(438) [0737] a sacrament, that is, a **holy**, divine thing and sign.
L C : 0 4 :021(439) [0737] to be baptized, that the **Holy** Spirit descended visibly, and
L C : 0 4 :022(439) [0737] the nature and dignity of this **holy** sacrament.
L C : 0 4 :041(442) [0743] grace, the entire Christ, and the **Holy** Spirit with his gifts.
L C : 0 4 :049(442) [0745] been thus baptized and has given them the **Holy** Spirit.
L C : 0 4 :049(442) [0745] doctrine and life attest that they have the **Holy** Spirit.
L C : 0 4 :049(442) [0745] know Christ, which is impossible without the **Holy** Spirit.
L C : 0 4 :050(443) [0745] given any of them the **Holy** Spirit nor any part of him; in
L C : 0 4 :050(443) [0745] through the gift of His **Holy** Spirit, as we have perceived
L C : 0 4 :050(443) [0745] and others, and since the **holy** Christian church will abide
L C : 0 4 :051(443) [0745] this article, "I believe one **Holy** Christian church, the
L C : 0 5 :001(447) [0753] As we treated **Holy** Baptism under three headings, so we
L C : 0 5 :032(450) [0759] Creed, "I believe in the **holy** Christian church, the
L C : 0 5 :061(453) [0767] we are worthy and **holy**, nor do we come to confession
L C : 0 5 :076(455) [0771] of his flesh, let us not pretend to be better or more **holy**.
E P : R N :002(465) [0777] names, should not be put on a par with **Holy** Scripture.
E P : R N :005(465) [0777] contain everything which **Holy** Scripture discusses at
E P : R N :007(465) [0779] distinction between the **Holy** Scripture of the Old and
E P : R N :007(465) [0779] writings is maintained, and **Holy** Scripture remains the
E P : R N :008(465) [0779] writings are not judges like **Holy** Scripture, but merely
E P : R N :008(465) [0779] how at various times the **Holy** Scriptures were understood
E P : 0 1 :002(466) [0779] God created man pure and **holy** and without sin, but also
E P : 0 2 :001(469) [0785] he is reborn through the **Holy** Spirit, dispose and prepare
E P : 0 2 :001(469) [0785] of God offered in the Word and the **holy** sacraments?
E P : 0 2 :004(470) [0787] 3. God the **Holy** Spirit, however, does not effect
E P : 0 2 :004(470) [0787] The **Holy** Spirit is present with this Word and opens
E P : 0 2 :004(470) [0787] grace and power of the **Holy** Spirit, for man's conversion
E P : 0 2 :009(471) [0789] without the grace of the **Holy** Spirit, man can convert
E P : 0 2 :010(471) [0789] could not complete it without the grace of the **Holy** Spirit
E P : 0 2 :011(471) [0789] own powers, yet after the **Holy** Spirit has made the
E P : 0 2 :013(471) [0789] God's Word and without the use of the **holy** sacraments.
E P : 0 2 :015(471) [0789] after conversion resists the **Holy** Spirit, and that the Holy
E P : 0 2 :015(471) [0789] Holy Spirit, and that the **Holy** Spirit is given to such as
E P : 0 2 :017(472) [0791] the attraction of the **Holy** Spirit, God changes stubborn
E P : 0 2 :017(472) [0791] in all the works which the **Holy** Spirit performs through
E P : 0 2 :018(472) [0791] or through the use of the **holy** sacraments takes hold of
E P : 0 2 :018(472) [0791] But after the **Holy** Spirit has performed and accomplished
E P : 0 2 :018(472) [0791] and means of God the **Holy** Spirit, so that man not only
E P : 0 2 :018(472) [0791] also cooperates with the **Holy** Spirit in the works that
E P : 0 2 :019(472) [0791] causes, namely, the **Holy** Spirit and the Word of God as
E P : 0 2 :019(472) [0791] the Word of God as the **Holy** Spirit's instrument whereby
E P : 0 2 :019(472) [0791] solely by the grace and operation of God the **Holy** Spirit.
E P : 0 3 :006(473) [0793] of sins, are regarded as **holy** and righteous by God the
E P : 0 3 :009(474) [0795] and the Word of the **holy** Gospel, they have a gracious
E P : 0 3 :010(474) [0795] is, to those words of the **holy** apostle Paul which separate
E P : 0 3 :010(474) [0795] Thus the **holy** apostle Paul uses such expressions as *"by*
E P : 0 3 :015(475) [0795] love and virtue that the **Holy** Spirit has infused and the
E P : 0 4 :008(476) [0799] and renewed by the **Holy** Spirit, are obligated to do good
E P : 0 4 :015(477) [0799] our works but only the **Holy** Spirit, working through
E P : 0 4 :015(477) [0799] are testimonies of the **Holy** Spirit's presence and
E P : 0 4 :019(477) [0801] and the indwelling of the **Holy** Spirit are not lost through
E P : 0 4 :019(477) [0801] malicious sin, but that the **holy** ones and the elect retain
E P : 0 4 :019(477) [0801] and the elect retain the **Holy** Spirit even though they fall
E P : 0 5 :001(477) [0801] Is the preaching of the **Holy** Gospel strictly speaking only
E P : 0 5 :006(478) [0803] used in a single sense in **Holy** Scripture, and this was the
E P : 0 5 :011(479) [0805] merit of Christ and the **Holy** Scriptures are obscured,
E P : 0 7 :000(481) [0807] VII. The **Holy** Supper of Christ
E P : 0 7 :002(481) [0809] The question is, In the **Holy** Communion are the true
E P : 0 7 :003(482) [0809] hearts, namely, that in the **Holy** Supper only bread and
E P : 0 7 :004(482) [0809] and blood of Christ in the **Holy** Supper but assert that
E P : 0 7 :004(482) [0809] crass opinion that in the **Holy** Supper nothing but bread
E P : 0 7 :005(482) [0809] the bread and wine of the **Holy** Supper, seek the body and
E P : 0 7 :005(482) [0809] *the Pure Doctrine of the* ***Holy*** *Supper Against the*
E P : 0 7 :006(482) [0809] and confess that in the **Holy** Supper the body and blood
E P : 0 7 :008(482) [0811] and blood of Christ in the **Holy** Supper, but it is to be
E P : 0 7 :009(483) [0811] in the celebration of the **Holy** Supper the words of
E P : 0 7 :018(484) [0813] The unworthy use of the **holy** sacrament increases,

Continued ▶

EP : 07 :019(484) [0813] faith, will receive the **Holy** Supper to his condemnation,
EP : 07 :020(484) [0813] and alone in the most **holy** obedience and complete merit
EP : 07 :022(484) [0813] the bread and wine in the **Holy** Supper lose their
EP : 07 :026(485) [0815] 5. That in the **holy** sacrament the body of Christ is not
EP : 07 :027(485) [0815] That bread and wine in the **Holy** Supper are no more than
EP : 07 :030(485) [0815] of our faith in the **Holy** Supper is effected solely by the
EP : 07 :031(485) [0815] 10. That in the **Holy** Supper only the power, operation,
EP : 07 :032(485) [0815] still less in all places, where his **Holy** Supper is observed.
EP : 07 :033(485) [0815] essentially present in the **Holy** Supper, nor could he have
EP : 07 :035(485) [0815] of the body and blood of Christ in the **Holy** Supper.
EP : 07 :036(485) [0815] the bread and wine of the **Holy** Supper, but should lift
EP : 07 :037(485) [0815] 16. That in the **Holy** Supper unbelieving and impenitent
EP : 07 :040(486) [0817] of bread and wine in the **holy** sacrament should be
EP : 08 :001(486) [0817] the controversy on the **Holy** Supper a disagreement has
EP : 08 :015(488) [0821] he was conceived by the **Holy** Spirit in his mother's womb
EP : 08 :017(489) [0823] which are present in the **Holy** Supper, *not according to*
EP : 08 :018(489) [0823] Next to the **holy** Trinity this is the highest mystery, as the
EP : 10 :007(493) [0831] as in the right use of the **holy** sacraments, according to
EP : 10 :011(494) [0831] with the enemies of the **holy** Gospel (which serve to
EP : 11 :008(495) [0833] and operation of the **Holy** Spirit and divine assistance for
EP : 11 :010(495) [0833] about Christ from the **Holy** Gospel alone, which clearly
EP : 11 :012(496) [0835] the ordinary way for the **Holy** Spirit, so that he cannot
EP : 11 :013(496) [0835] the proclamation of the **Holy** Gospel, Christ opens and
EP : 11 :013(496) [0835] and has sealed it with his **holy** sacraments, of which we
EP : 11 :020(497) [0837] mercy of God and the most **holy** merit of Christ, but that
EP : 11 :021(497) [0837] that they have in the **holy** Gospel and in the use of the
EP : 11 :021(497) [0837] in the holy Gospel and in the use of the **holy** sacraments.
EP : 11 :022(497) [0837] grant us the grace of his **Holy** Spirit that we may all be of
EP : 12 :004(498) [0839] only has more gifts of the **Holy** Spirit than any other holy
EP : 12 :004(498) [0839] more gifts of the Holy Spirit than any other **holy** person.
EP : 12 :008(498) [0839] of Christian parents are **holy** and the children of God by
EP : 12 :021(499) [0841] flesh of Christ belongs to the essence of the **holy** Trinity.
EP : 12 :022(499) [0841] through which God the **Holy** Spirit teaches people and
EP : 12 :024(500) [0843] That bread and wine in the **Holy** Supper are not means
EP : 12 :028(500) [0843] God the Father and the **Holy** Spirit, but is merely adorned
EP : 12 :029(500) [0843] to the Father, Son, and **Holy** Spirit, but as God the
EP : 12 :029(500) [0843] God the Father, Son, and **Holy** Spirit are three distinct
SD : PR :001(501) [0847] Dr. Luther, of blessed and **holy** memory, and the popish
SD : PR :003(501) [0847] the pure doctrine of the **holy** Gospel and had allowed
SD : PR :007(502) [0849] the very lifetime of the **holy** apostles frightful errors arose
SD : PR :007(502) [0849] The **holy** apostles were compelled vigorously to denounce
SD : PR :006(505) [0853] clear and irrefutable testimonies from the **Holy** Scriptures
SD : PR :010(506) [0855] as interpretations of the **Holy** Scriptures, refutations of
SD : PR :017(507) [0857] certain and solid basis of the **holy** and divine Scriptures.
SD : 01 :003(509) [0861] his precious merits, and the **Holy** Spirit's gracious activity
SD : 01 :014(511) [0863] Likewise, only the **Holy** Spirit's regeneration and
SD : 01 :027(512) [0867] created pure, good, and **holy**, sin did not invade their
SD : 01 :028(513) [0867] at first created pure and **holy** and is corrupted only
SD : 01 :029(513) [0867] nature is allegedly pure, **holy**, righteous, and incorrupt in
SD : 01 :033(514) [0869] According to the **Holy** Scriptures we must and can
SD : 01 :045(516) [0873] in the name of the **holy** Trinity, is sanctified and saved,
SD : 01 :050(517) [0875] of sound words, as the **Holy** Scriptures and the
SD : 01 :060(519) [0879] **Holy** Scripture alone can lead to a right understanding
SD : 02 :002(520) [0881] spiritual things after the **Holy** Spirit has regenerated him
SD : 02 :003(520) [0881] and without the gift of the **Holy** Spirit man is unable to
SD : 02 :003(520) [0881] without the gift of the **Holy** Spirit he could accomplish
SD : 02 :004(520) [0881] converts man through the **Holy** Spirit without any means
SD : 02 :005(521) [0881] until by the power of the **Holy** Spirit, through the Word
SD : 02 :009(522) [0883] or believe, and until the **Holy** Spirit enlightens and
SD : 02 :015(523) [0887] and illuminated us through Baptism and the **Holy** Spirit.
SD : 02 :016(523) [0887] after God, through the **Holy** Spirit in Baptism, has kindled
SD : 02 :017(524) [0887] my inmost self (which the **Holy** Spirit has regenerated),
SD : 02 :018(524) [0889] and give assent when the **Holy** Spirit offers the grace of
SD : 02 :018(524) [0889] God and his will unless the **Holy** Spirit illuminates and
SD : 02 :019(524) [0889] For this reason the **Holy** Scriptures compare the heart of
SD : 02 :021(525) [0889] and preach" until the **Holy** Spirit enlightens, converts,
SD : 02 :022(525) [0889] the gracious and efficacious working of the **Holy** Spirit.
SD : 02 :024(525) [0891] and drawn by the **Holy** Spirit, he can do nothing in
SD : 02 :024(526) [0891] the will of God unless the **Holy** Spirit is active in him and
SD : 02 :025(526) [0891] In the third place, **Holy** Scriptures ascribe conversion,
SD : 02 :025(526) [0891] divine operation and the **Holy** Spirit, as the Apology
SD : 02 :026(526) [0891] mind, and spirit, is solely the work of the **Holy** Spirit.
SD : 02 :026(526) [0891] The **Holy** Spirit is a Spirit "of regeneration and renewal"
SD : 02 :026(526) [0891] Jesus is Lord, except by the **Holy** Spirit" (I Cor. 12:3).
SD : 02 :029(527) [0893] and without faith and the **Holy** Spirit are in the power of
SD : 02 :029(527) [0893] faith, through which the **Holy** Spirit is given, and by
SD : 02 :031(527) [0893] which are without the **Holy** Spirit are without fear of
SD : 02 :033(527) [0893] for the position that the **Holy** Spirit and his grace are
SD : 02 :034(528) [0895] but through the gift of the **Holy** Spirit which follows upon
SD : 02 :034(528) [0895] sin and operates to make man truly pure and **holy**."
SD : 02 :035(528) [0895] to the gift of the **Holy** Spirit, who purifies and daily
SD : 02 :035(528) [0895] man more pious and **holy**, to the complete exclusion of
SD : 02 :036(528) [0895] The **Holy** Spirit has brought me thereto and has
SD : 02 :037(528) [0895] Until the Last Day, the **Holy** Spirit remains with the holy
SD : 02 :037(528) [0895] Spirit remains with the **holy** community of Christendom,
SD : 02 :038(528) [0895] ascribes everything to the **Holy** Spirit, namely, that
SD : 02 :039(528) [0895] will and power, but the **Holy** Spirit, as St. Paul says,
SD : 02 :040(528) [0895] But the **Holy** Spirit has called me through the Gospel,
SD : 02 :041(529) [0897] Father gives us his **Holy** Spirit so that by his grace we
SD : 02 :041(529) [0897] grace we may believe his **holy** Word and live a godly life."
SD : 02 :042(529) [0897] that God must give us his **Holy** Spirit, who enlightens,
SD : 02 :043(529) [0897] *Confession Concerning the Holy Supper* in which he
SD : 02 :044(529) [0897] Dr. Luther, of sacred and **holy** memory, grants our free
SD : 02 :044(529) [0897] not once think to turn to the **holy** Gospel and to accept it.
SD : 02 :045(530) [0899] views are contrary to the **Holy** Scriptures of God, the
SD : 02 :046(530) [0899] altogether the work of the **Holy** Spirit and they can do
SD : 02 :047(530) [0901] purposes through his **Holy** Spirit to work these gifts of his
SD : 02 :048(530) [0901] the oral Word and the **holy** sacraments) the Holy Spirit
SD : 02 :048(530) [0901] the holy sacraments) the **Holy** Spirit wills to be efficacious
SD : 02 :050(530) [0901] redemption, namely, the **holy** and only saving Gospel of
SD : 02 :050(531) [0901] way — namely, through his **holy** Word (when one hears it
SD : 02 :052(531) [0901] of God's Word are the **Holy** Spirit's instrument in, with,
SD : 02 :054(531) [0903] and meditation upon the **holy** Gospel of the gracious
SD : 02 :054(531) [0903] And in this way the **Holy** Spirit, who works all of this, is
SD : 02 :055(531) [0903] and operation of the **Holy** Spirit, who through the Word
SD : 02 :055(532) [0903] grace and operation of the **Holy** Spirit, but should be
SD : 02 :056(532) [0903] pass judgment on the **Holy** Spirit's presence, operations,
SD : 02 :056(532) [0903] the contrary, because the **Holy** Spirit's activity often is
SD : 02 :056(532) [0903] an office and work of the **Holy** Spirit, whereby he
SD : 02 :057(532) [0903] men in the Word and the **holy** sacraments, earnestly wills
SD : 02 :057(532) [0903] themselves with his **holy** Word, he is in the midst of
SD : 02 :058(532) [0903] the instruments of the **Holy** Spirit and will not hear, no
SD : 02 :058(532) [0903] is done him if the **Holy** Spirit does not illuminate him but
SD : 02 :060(533) [0905] who always resist the **Holy** Spirit and oppose and
SD : 02 :063(533) [0905] much and as long as the **Holy** Spirit motivates him, as St.
SD : 02 :064(533) [0905] This impulse of the **Holy** Spirit is no coercion or
SD : 02 :065(534) [0907] that as soon as the **Holy** Spirit has initiated his work of
SD : 02 :065(534) [0907] through the Word and the **holy** sacraments, it is certain
SD : 02 :065(534) [0907] by the power of the **Holy** Spirit, even though we still do
SD : 02 :065(534) [0907] powers and gifts which the **Holy** Spirit has begun in us in
SD : 02 :066(534) [0907] rules in him through his **Holy** Spirit, guides and leads
SD : 02 :066(534) [0907] cooperates alongside the **Holy** Spirit, the way two horses
SD : 02 :069(534) [0907] and thus grieve the **Holy** Spirit within them and lose him,
SD : 02 :071(535) [0909] anticipates us and has his **holy** Gospel preached to us,
SD : 02 :071(535) [0909] to us, through which the **Holy** Spirit wills to work such
SD : 02 :071(535) [0909] so that they are gifts and works of the **Holy** Spirit alone.
SD : 02 :072(535) [0909] means through which the **Holy** Spirit wills to begin and
SD : 02 :072(535) [0909] is to hinder and resist such operations of the **Holy** Spirit.
SD : 02 :073(535) [0909] his conversion resists the **Holy** Spirit, and if he does
SD : 02 :073(535) [0909] Whether the **Holy** Spirit is given to those who resist him?
SD : 02 :075(536) [0911] powers, without the **Holy** Spirit, the free will can convert
SD : 02 :076(536) [0911] weak to complete it, the **Holy** Spirit comes to the aid of
SD : 02 :077(536) [0911] Nevertheless, after the **Holy** Spirit has made the beginning
SD : 02 :077(536) [0911] powers cooperate with the **Holy** Spirit in the continuation
SD : 02 :078(536) [0911] but solely through the operation of the **Holy** Spirit.
SD : 02 :080(536) [0911] and without the use of the **holy** sacraments, God draws
SD : 02 :082(537) [0913] after conversion resists the **Holy** Spirit, and that the Holy
SD : 02 :082(537) [0913] Holy Spirit, and that the **Holy** Spirit is given to those who
SD : 02 :083(537) [0913] it is clear that when the **Holy** Spirit's activity produces no
SD : 02 :083(537) [0913] of change through the **Holy** Spirit's activity in the
SD : 02 :083(537) [0913] such working of the **Holy** Spirit is able to accept the
SD : 02 :083(537) [0913] perseveringly resist the **Holy** Spirit's activities and
SD : 02 :083(537) [0913] Word, do not receive the **Holy** Spirit but grieve and lose
SD : 02 :087(538) [0915] above from clear passages of **Holy** Scripture.
SD : 02 :088(538) [0915] the drawing of the **Holy** Spirit, God makes willing people
SD : 02 :088(538) [0915] in all the works that the **Holy** Spirit does through us.
SD : 02 :089(538) [0915] that in conversion the **Holy** Spirit engenders no new
SD : 02 :089(538) [0915] and work of the **Holy** Spirit alone, who accomplishes and
SD : 02 :090(538) [0915] preached and heard, the **Holy** Spirit, and man's will)
SD : 02 :090(539) [0915] God is solely of God the **Holy** Spirit, who is the true
SD : 02 :090(539) [0915] and the hearing of his **holy** Word as his ordinary means
SD : 02 :090(539) [0915] dead, in whom the **Holy** Spirit works conversion and
SD : 02 :090(539) [0915] he cooperates with the **Holy** Spirit in subsequent good
SD : 03 :010(541) [0919] The **Holy** Spirit offers these treasures to us in the promise
SD : 03 :011(541) [0919] accounted righteous and **holy** by God the Father, and are
SD : 03 :013(541) [0919] the merit of Christ in the promise of the **holy** Gospel.
SD : 03 :015(541) [0919] us our sins, accounts us **holy** and righteous, and saves us
SD : 03 :016(541) [0921] is offered to us by the **Holy** Spirit through the Gospel and
SD : 03 :017(542) [0921] meaning of the word in the **Holy** Scriptures of the Old
SD : 03 :019(542) [0921] renewal which the **Holy** Spirit works in those who are
SD : 03 :019(542) [0921] regeneration and renewing in the **Holy** Spirit" (Titus 3:5).
SD : 03 :020(542) [0921] For when the **Holy** Spirit has brought a person to faith
SD : 03 :022(543) [0923] we teach that through the **Holy** Spirit's work we are
SD : 03 :022(543) [0923] they are regarded as **holy** and righteous through faith and
SD : 03 :023(543) [0923] grace) there is given the **Holy** Spirit, who renews and
SD : 03 :028(544) [0925] and a work of the **Holy** Spirit, it does not belong to the
SD : 03 :033(545) [0927] also afterward when the **Holy** Spirit had renewed and
SD : 03 :041(546) [0929] First the **Holy** Spirit kindles faith in us in conversion
SD : 03 :041(546) [0929] the person is justified, the **Holy** Spirit next renews and
SD : 03 :047(548) [0933] or the renewal which the **Holy** Spirit works and is within
SD : 03 :054(548) [0935] God the Father, Son, and **Holy** Spirit, who is the eternal
SD : 03 :054(549) [0935] God the Father, Son, and **Holy** Spirit, who impels them
SD : 03 :056(549) [0935] had been conceived by the **Holy** Spirit without sin and
SD : 03 :058(550) [0937] perfect obedience from his **holy** birth to his death in the
SD : 03 :062(550) [0937] poured into them by the **Holy** Spirit and the consequent
SD : 04 :007(552) [0941] and renewed through the **Holy** Spirit, or, as St. Paul says,
SD : 04 :010(552) [0941] and all our powers, and brings the **Holy** Spirit with it.
SD : 04 :012(553) [0941] This the **Holy** Spirit works by faith, and therefore without
SD : 04 :014(553) [0943] Likewise, **Holy** Scripture itself uses words like "necessity,"
SD : 04 :031(556) [0947] fear and shame, resists the **Holy** Spirit, and deliberately
SD : 04 :033(556) [0949] lead a wicked life, lose the **Holy** Spirit, and reject
SD : 04 :034(557) [0949] "He will present you **holy** and blameless and
SD : 04 :036(557) [0949] formulas in expounding **Holy** Scripture without in any
SD : 04 :038(557) [0951] do good works which the **Holy** Spirit works in them, and
SD : 05 :001(558) [0951] and the writings of the **holy** prophets and apostles may be
SD : 05 :001(558) [0951] otherwise have in the **holy** Gospel when it is preached
SD : 05 :003(558) [0953] a twofold way, both in the **Holy** Scripture of God and by
SD : 05 :007(559) [0953] is not used in a single sense in **Holy** Scripture.
SD : 05 :007(559) [0953] In some passages of **Holy** Writ the word is used and
SD : 05 :009(559) [0955] proclamation of the **holy** Gospel offers to all penitent
SD : 05 :012(560) [0955] he says in John 16:8, 'The **Holy** Spirit will convince the
SD : 05 :013(560) [0957] again: "Christ says, 'The **Holy** Spirit will convince the
SD : 05 :019(561) [0957] is the Word of God, the **Holy** Spirit through the office of
SD : 05 :023(562) [0959] The descendants of the **holy** patriarchs, like the
SD : 05 :023(562) [0959] was created righteous and **holy** by God and through the
SD : 06 :001(563) [0963] born anew through the **Holy** Spirit, who have been
SD : 06 :002(564) [0963] and impulse of the **Holy** Spirit spontaneously do what
SD : 06 :003(564) [0963] indeed motivated by the **Holy** Spirit and hence according
SD : 06 :003(564) [0963] spirit, nevertheless the **Holy** Spirit uses the written law on
SD : 06 :006(565) [0965] or necessity, and as the **holy** angels render God a
SD : 06 :007(565) [0965] and although the **Holy** Spirit has begun the mortification
SD : 06 :011(565) [0965] It is the **Holy** Spirit, who is not given and received
SD : 06 :012(566) [0967] and recalcitrant, the **Holy** Spirit reproves them through
SD : 06 :012(566) [0967] In this way the **Holy** Spirit simultaneously performs both
SD : 06 :012(566) [0967] as it is written, "When the **Holy** Spirit shall come, he will
SD : 06 :014(566) [0967] and comforts them with the preaching of the **holy** Gospel.

Continued ▶

SD : 0 6 :020(567) [0969] under the pretext of the **Holy** Spirit's guidance set up a
SD : 0 6 :021(567) [0969] that their works and life are perfectly pure and **holy**.
SD : 0 6 :023(568) [0969] from the heart by the renewal of the **Holy** Spirit.
SD : 0 7 :000(568) [0971] The **Holy** Supper
SD : 0 7 :001(569) [0971] altogether contrary to the **holy** Word of God and to the
SD : 0 7 :002(569) [0973] and confess that in the **Holy** Supper the body of Christ is
SD : 0 7 :009(570) [0975] are really present in the **Holy** Supper under the forms of
SD : 0 7 :011(571) [0975] truly present, but only the **Holy** Spirit, then when Paul
SD : 0 7 :011(571) [0975] the bodily presence of Christ in the **Holy** Communion."
SD : 0 7 :013(571) [0977] the cities, concerning the **holy** sacrament of the body and
SD : 0 7 :016(572) [0977] says, for they misuse the **holy** sacrament since they
SD : 0 7 :027(574) [0981] and blood of Christ in the **holy** Supper from God's Word
SD : 0 7 :037(575) [0985] united, so in the **Holy** Supper the two essences, the
SD : 0 7 :042(576) [0987] institution recorded in the **holy** Word of God and so
SD : 0 7 :042(576) [0987] and transmitted by the **holy** evangelists and apostles, and
SD : 0 7 :050(578) [0989] kinds of sacrifice in the Old Testament, and **holy** Baptism.
SD : 0 7 :066(581) [0995] teachers and the entire **holy** Christian church teach
SD : 0 7 :082(584) [1001] hallowed or blessed in this **holy** use, so that therewith the
SD : 0 7 :085(584) [1001] doctrine concerning the **Holy** Supper and to obviate and
SD : 0 7 :088(585) [1003] of Christ's body in the **Holy** Supper and that therefore the
SD : 0 7 :091(585) [1005] *concerning the **Holy** Supper*, and other writings of his.
SD : 0 7 :105(588) [1009] Christ is present in the **Holy** Supper, not only to work
SD : 0 7 :105(588) [1009] and blood of Christ in the **Holy** Supper are received,
SD : 0 7 :106(588) [1009] and blood of Christ in the **Holy** Supper is built upon the
SD : 0 7 :108(588) [1009] bread and wine in the **Holy** Supper completely lose their
SD : 0 7 :121(590) [1013] the body of Christ in the **Holy** Supper, whence some omit
SD : 0 7 :123(590) [1015] and wine in the use of the **Holy** Supper and not the body
SD : 0 8 :002(592) [1015] time in heaven and in the **Holy** Supper on earth since
SD : 0 8 :003(592) [1017] writings concerning the **Holy** Supper, to which we
SD : 0 8 :006(592) [1017] with the Father and the **Holy** Spirit, yet, when the time
SD : 0 8 :021(595) [1021] *Confession concerning the **Holy** Supper* against the
SD : 0 8 :028(596) [1025] maintain without proof from the **Holy** Scriptures.
SD : 0 8 :029(596) [1025] his body and blood in the **Holy** Supper according to the
SD : 0 8 :033(597) [1027] Next to the article of the **holy** Trinity, the greatest
SD : 0 8 :038(598) [1027] *Confession concerning the **Holy** Supper* has written about
SD : 0 8 :051(600) [1031] The **Holy** Scriptures, and the ancient Fathers on the basis
SD : 0 8 :061(602) [1035] of sound passages of the **Holy** Scriptures, namely, that
SD : 0 8 :069(604) [1039] human nature and other **holy** people, and thus Christ
SD : 0 8 :072(605) [1041] is of one essence with the **Holy** Spirit) in such a manner
SD : 0 8 :073(605) [1041] can do things through the **Holy** Spirit who endows them
SD : 0 8 :073(605) [1041] the second person in the **holy** Trinity and the Holy Spirit
SD : 0 8 :073(605) [1041] the holy Trinity and the **Holy** Spirit proceeds from him as
SD : 0 8 :079(607) [1045] point, he instituted his **Holy** Supper that he might be
SD : 0 8 :081(607) [1045] *Confession concerning the **Holy** Supper* he writes about
SD : 0 8 :086(608) [1047] and in his *Great Confession concerning the **Holy** Supper.*
SD : 0 8 :086(608) [1047] as of his covenant in the **Holy** Supper in connection with
SD : 0 8 :092(609) [1049] his presence in his Word, as in the **Holy** Communion.
SD : 0 8 :094(609) [1049] and in the right use of the **holy** sacraments Christ is
SD : 0 8 :096(609) [1049] of God, the writings of the **holy** prophets and apostles,
SD : 0 8 :096(609) [1049] Since the **Holy** Scriptures call Christ a mystery over which
SD : 0 8 :096(609) [1049] their reason, but with the **holy** apostles simply to believe,
SD : 1 0 :002(611) [1053] when enemies of the **holy** Gospel have not come to an
SD : 1 0 :010(612) [1055] the pure doctrine of the **holy** Gospel, the entire
SD : 1 0 :015(613) [1057] well, an article which the **Holy** Spirit through the mouth
SD : 1 0 :015(613) [1057] through the mouth of the **holy** apostle so seriously
SD : 1 0 :019(614) [1059] the church is, namely, **holy** believers and sheep who hear
SD : 1 0 :028(615) [1061] may yield to enemies of the **holy** Gospel or conform to
SD : 1 0 :029(615) [1061] to please enemies of the **holy** Gospel contrary and in
SD : 1 0 :031(616) [1063] the right use of the **holy** sacraments, according to the
SD : 1 1 :002(616) [1063] detrimental, because the **Holy** Scriptures mention this
SD : 1 1 :017(619) [1069] and active in us by his **Holy** Spirit through the Word
SD : 1 1 :029(621) [1073] And because the **Holy** Spirit wills to be efficacious
SD : 1 1 :032(621) [1073] In the same vein **Holy** Scripture also assures us that God
SD : 1 1 :033(621) [1073] about it because the **Holy** Spirit gives grace, power, and
SD : 1 1 :039(622) [1075] namely, that the **Holy** Spirit wills to be certainly present
SD : 1 1 :039(623) [1075] it (Heb. 4:2, 7), resist the **Holy** Spirit (Acts 7:51), remain
SD : 1 1 :040(623) [1077] in his counsel that the **Holy** Spirit would call, enlighten,
SD : 1 1 :040(623) [1077] and persistently resist the **Holy** Spirit who wants to work
SD : 1 1 :041(623) [1077] and instrument of the **Holy** Spirit which God offers to
SD : 1 1 :041(623) [1077] the call and resists the **Holy** Spirit who wills to be
SD : 1 1 :042(623) [1077] turn away from the **holy** commandment, grieve and
SD : 1 1 :042(623) [1077] grieve and embitter the **Holy** Spirit, become entangled
SD : 1 1 :044(624) [1077] that by the power of his **Holy** Spirit through the Word he
SD : 1 1 :059(626) [1083] God's Word and often sorely grieve the **Holy** Spirit.
SD : 1 1 :065(627) [1085] And of the **Holy** Spirit Christ says, "He will glorify me"
SD : 1 1 :066(627) [1085] Thus the entire **holy** Trinity, God the Father, Son, and
SD : 1 1 :066(627) [1085] God the Father, Son, and **Holy** Spirit, directs all men to
SD : 1 1 :069(627) [1085] may come to Christ, the **Holy** Spirit creates true faith
SD : 1 1 :071(627) [1085] by our own powers, the **Holy** Spirit wills to work such
SD : 1 1 :072(628) [1085] which he has assured us in **holy** Baptism, and not doubt
SD : 1 1 :072(628) [1087] heavenly Father give the **Holy** Spirit to those who ask
SD : 1 1 :073(628) [1087] Next, since the **Holy** Spirit dwells in the elect who have
SD : 1 1 :075(628) [1087] Word, and through it the **Holy** Spirit wills to effect their
SD : 1 1 :076(629) [1087] draws by the power of the **Holy** Spirit, but according to
SD : 1 1 :076(629) [1089] through the hearing of his **holy**, divine Word, as with a
SD : 1 1 :077(629) [1089] of the Father because the **Holy** Spirit wills to be present
SD : 1 1 :078(629) [1089] it, and they resisted the **Holy** Spirit who wanted to work
SD : 1 1 :083(630) [1091] turn away from the **holy** commandment and involve
SD : 1 1 :083(630) [1091] and outrage the **Holy** Spirit (Heb. 10:29), and that he
SD : 1 1 :086(631) [1091] The **holy** apostle adduces Pharaoh's example for the sole
SD : 1 1 :088(631) [1093] mercy of God and the most **holy** merit of Christ, but that
SD : 1 1 :089(631) [1093] in Christ and in his **holy** Gospel as the "book of life," this
SD : 1 1 :089(631) [1093] and promises them the **Holy** Spirit to cleanse and renew
SD : 1 1 :092(632) [1093] and hope is contrary to the **Holy** Spirit's will and intent.
SD : 1 1 :096(632) [1095] the divine truth of the **holy** Gospel, that will not give
SD : 1 2 :008(633) [1097] the pure Word of the **holy** Gospel was allowed neither
SD : 1 2 :013(634) [1099] and believing parents, are **holy** and children of God even
SD : 1 2 :029(635) [1101] Christ's flesh belongs to the essence of the **holy** Trinity.
SD : 1 2 :030(635) [1101] a means whereby God the **Holy** Spirit teaches men the
SD : 1 2 :032(635) [1101] the bread and wine in the **Holy** Supper are not means
SD : 1 2 :037(636) [1103] of the Father, Son, and **Holy** Spirit, but that, as there are
SD : 1 2 :037(636) [1103] persons, Father, Son, and **Holy** Spirit, so also each person

Homage (5)
AP : 1 2 :143(204) [0297] as Scotus says, to pay **homage** to God and to compensate
AP : 1 2 :143(204) [0297] *ex opere operato* pay **homage** to God and compensate for
LC : 0 1 :168(388) [0629] power and authority to govern) merely to receive **homage**.
EP : 1 2 :015(499) [0841] pay oath-bound feudal **homage** to his territorial sovereign
SD : 1 2 :020(634) [1099] pay oath-bound feudal **homage** to his prince or liege

Home (14), Homes (1)
AG : 1 6 :004(037) [0051] forsaking of house and **home**, wife and child, and the
AP : 2 7 :028(274) [0429] those who have forsaken **home** and brothers
SC : 0 1 :018(344) [0541] neighbor's inheritance or **home**, nor to obtain them under
SC : 0 2 :002(345) [0543] and clothing, house and **home**, family and property; that
SC : 0 3 :014(347) [0547] and clothing, house and **home**, fields and flocks, money
LC : 0 1 :114(380) [0613] would have remained at **home** in obedience and service to
LC : 0 1 :150(385) [0625] gives us food, house and **home**, protection and security.
LC : 0 1 :175(389) [0631] citizens, virtuous and **home**-loving wives who would
LC : 0 1 :244(398) [0649] and ravage house and **home** and outrage and kill wife and
LC : 0 1 :277(402) [0659] as to leave the servant at **home** while he went out on the
LC : 0 1 :332(410) [0677] Thus, both for himself at **home**, and abroad among his
LC : 0 2 :013(412) [0681] of support, wife and child, servants, house and **home**, etc.
LC : 0 3 :065(429) [0717] honor, house and **home**, wife and children, body and life.
LC : 0 3 :076(431) [0721] drink, clothing, house, **home**, and a sound body; to cause
SD : PR :008(505) [0853] the schools, and the **homes** of those churches which

Honest (13), Honestly (6), Honesty (1)
AG : 2 3 :006(052) [0061] What **honest** and chaste manner of life, what Christian,
AG : 2 3 :018(054) [0063] vice that even some **honest** men among the cathedral
AG : 2 7 :049(079) [0083] that we fear God **honestly** with our whole hearts, and yet
AL : 2 0 :033(045) [0057] they tried to live **honest** lives, were not able to do so but
AL : 2 7 :049(078) [0083] is Christian perfection: **honestly** to fear God and at the
AP : 0 2 :001(100) [0105] are lacking not only in judgment but also in **honesty**.
AP : 0 4 :154(128) [0165] the Pharisee, this wise and **honest** but unbelieving man.
AP : 0 4 :284(150) [0201] An **honest** reader would not pick out the commands
AP : 1 1 :003(180) [0249] opponents, if they are but **honest**, will undoubtedly
AP : 2 3 :005(239) [0365] not speak, write, or act **honestly**, frankly, or openly in
AP : 2 3 :006(240) [0365] only the judgment of any **honest** and God-fearing man.
S2 : 0 2 :008(294) [0465] This is not **honest**, for if he really desires to commune, he
S3 : 1 1 :002(315) [0499] God or forbid them to live together **honestly** in marriage.
TR : 0 0 :075(333) [0525] connection they often harassed innocent and **honest** men.
SC : 0 9 :005(355) [0561] be obedient, to be ready for any **honest** work" (Tit. 3:1).
LC : PR :002(358) [0567] are not so upright and **honest** as to buy these books, or if
LC : 0 1 :225(395) [0643] common people so that we may see how **honest** we are.
LC : 0 1 :300(405) [0667] wish to be commended as **honest** and virtuous because
LC : 0 1 :303(406) [0667] as illegally acquired, but rather as **honestly** purchased.
SD : 0 7 :002(569) [0973] their meaning clearly, **honestly**, and explicitly, they all

Honey (2)
SD : 0 8 :019(594) [1021] as mead is made out of **honey** and water and ceases to be
SD : 0 8 :019(595) [1021] either water or **honey** but is a blended beverage.

Honor (141), Honorable (14), Honorably (4), Honored (7), Honoring (6), Honors (5)
AG : PR :010(025) [0041] in so far as this can **honorably** be done, such practical and
AG : 1 8 :001(039) [0051] to live an outwardly **honorable** life and to make choices
AG : 2 0 :033(045) [0057] who undertook to lead **honorable** and blameless lives;
AG : 2 3 :006(052) [0061] Christian, upright, and **honorable** sort of conduct has
AG : 2 3 :019(054) [0063] God commanded that marriage be held in **honor**.
AG : 2 7 :038(077) [0081] to diminish the glory and **honor** of the grace of Christ and
AG : 2 7 :043(077) [0081] who alone justifies, of his **honor** and bestow this honor
AG : 2 7 :043(077) [0081] his honor and bestow this **honor** upon their vows and
AG : 2 8 :004(081) [0085] and powers are to be **honored** and esteemed with all
AG : 2 8 :018(083) [0085] that both be held in **honor** as the highest gifts of God on
AG : 2 8 :071(093) [0093] at the expense of their **honor** and dignity (though it is
AL : 2 0 :003(041) [0053] pilgrimages, services in **honor** of saints, rosaries,
AL : 2 3 :019(055) [0063] God has commanded that marriage be held in **honor**.
AL : 2 6 :010(065) [0071] to callings were without **honor** — for example, that a
AL : 2 8 :004(081) [0085] be held in reverence and **honor** as the chief gifts of God
AL : 2 8 :018(083) [0085] that both be held in **honor** and acknowledged as gifts and
AL : 2 8 :071(093) [0093] at the expense of their **honor** (which, however, good
AP : 0 4 :002(107) [0121] and magnifies the **honor** of Christ and brings to pious
AP : 0 4 :022(110) [0127] of God's command, **honorable** works commanded in the
AP : 0 4 :024(110) [0127] God even **honors** it with material rewards.
AP : 0 4 :156(128) [0165] an important issue, the **honor** of Christ and the source of
AP : 0 4 :157(128) [0165] we rob Christ of his **honor** as mediator and propitiator.
AP : 0 4 :197(134) [0175] the commandment to **honor** our parents by referring to
AP : 0 4 :204(135) [0177] thus giving our works an **honor** that belongs only to
AP : 0 4 :213(136) [0179] but to rob Christ of his **honor** as mediator and
AP : 0 4 :214(136) [0179] law must follow faith; but we still give Christ his **honor**.
AP : 0 4 :215(137) [0179] does not give Christ the **honor** due him, for he has been
AP : 0 4 :309(155) [0207] This faith gives **honor** to God, gives him what is properly
AP : 0 4 :367(163) [0221] "**Honor** your father and your mother, that your days may
AP : 0 4 :370(164) [0221] and v. 10, "Glory and **honor** and peace for every one who
AP : 1 2 :043(187) [0263] and clear, it adds to the **honor** of the power of the keys
AP : 1 2 :078(193) [0275] Nor should the **honor** of Christ be transferred to our
AP : 1 2 :144(205) [0297] they ascribe to them the **honor** of being a price paid in
AP : 1 5 :009(216) [0317] Thus they rob Christ of his **honor** as the mediator.
AP : 1 5 :018(217) [0319] They take **honor** away from Christ when they teach that
AP : 1 5 :019(218) [0319] says (11:38): "He shall **honor** the god of fortresses instead
AP : 1 5 :019(218) [0319] did not know he shall **honor** with gold and silver, with
AP : 1 5 :021(218) [0321] What is this but **honoring** God "with gold and silver and
AP : 2 0 :004(227) [0339] of attributing the **honor** of Christ to our works is
AP : 2 1 :001(229) [0343] that the saints should be **honored** and that the living
AP : 2 1 :002(229) [0343] about invoking, but only about **honoring**, the saints.
AP : 2 1 :004(229) [0343] Our Confession approves giving **honor** to the saints.
AP : 2 1 :004(229) [0343] This **honor** is threefold.
AP : 2 1 :005(229) [0345] The second **honor** is the strengthening of our faith: when
AP : 2 1 :006(230) [0345] The third **honor** is the imitation, first of their faith and
AP : 2 1 :007(230) [0345] do not require these real **honors**; they only argue about
AP : 2 1 :011(230) [0345] not thought this up to **honor** the saints but to defend
AP : 2 1 :014(230) [0345] it transfers to the saints **honor** belonging to Christ alone.
AP : 2 1 :018(231) [0347] Christ says, "That all may **honor** the Son, even as they
AP : 2 1 :018(231) [0347] all may honor the Son, even as they **honor** the Father."
AP : 2 1 :027(232) [0349] is worthy of the highest **honors**, she does not want to be

Continued ▶

A P : 2 1 :031(233) [0351] transfer to the saints the **honor** that belongs to Christ.
A P : 2 1 :038(235) [0355] in order to emphasize the **honor** and the work of Christ.
A P : 2 1 :042(235) [0357] of supporting this most **honorable** and holy desire of the
A P : 2 1 :044(236) [0357] but to find other **honorable** ways of establishing harmony
A P : 2 1 :044(236) [0357] demands this when he **honors** kings with his own name
A P : 2 3 :032(243) [0373] of celibacy, what greater **honor** could he bestow than to
A P : 2 4 :018(252) [0389] a ceremony or act which we render to God to **honor** him.
A P : 2 4 :029(255) [0393] calling upon God is really worshiping and **honoring** him.
A P : 2 4 :097(268) [0417] only the sacrifice of Christ is **honored** as a propitiation.
A P : 2 4 :097(268) [0417] of faith but give equal **honor** to other sacrifices and
A P : 2 7 :011(270) [0423] take away from Christ's **honor** and crucify him again.
A P : 2 7 :030(274) [0431] even give his own law the **honor** of meriting eternal life,
A P : 2 7 :061(280) [0441] commanded (Ex. 20:12), "**Honor** your father and your
S 2 : 0 2 :026(297) [0469] Such **honor** belongs to God alone.
S 2 : 0 2 :027(297) [0469] offer sacrifices in your **honor**, or trust in you for my
S 2 : 0 2 :027(297) [0469] other ways in which I can **honor**, love, and thank you in
S 2 : 0 2 :028(297) [0469] If such idolatrous **honor** is withdrawn from angels and
S 2 : 0 2 :028(297) [0469] and dead saints, the **honor** that remains will do no harm
S 2 : 0 2 :028(297) [0471] remember, esteem, or **honor** them out of love when there
S 2 : 0 4 :014(301) [0475] who do not exalt and **honor** these abominations of his
S 3 : 0 0 :000(302) [0477] of conscience but only about money, **honor**, and power.
S C : 0 1 :007(343) [0541] ***"Honor** your father and your mother."*
S C : 0 1 :008(343) [0541] them to anger, but **honor**, serve, obey, love, and esteem
S C : 0 1 :012(343) [0541] each one loving and **honoring** his wife or her husband.
S C : 0 3 :014(347) [0549] and health, order and **honor**; true friends, faithful
S C : 0 9 :003(354) [0561] worthy of double **honor**, especially those who labor in
S C : 0 9 :005(355) [0561] to whom respect is due, **honor** to whom honor is due"
S C : 0 9 :005(355) [0561] is due, honor to whom **honor** is due" (Rom. 13:1, 5-7).
S C : 0 9 :006(355) [0561] your wives, bestowing **honor** on the woman as the weaker
S C : 0 9 :009(356) [0563] '**Honor** your father and mother' (this is the first
L C : P R :003(358) [0567] this way they might show **honor** and gratitude to the
L C : S P :004(362) [0575] 4. You shall **honor** father and mother.
L C : 0 1 :010(366) [0583] prestige, family, and **honor**, and trusts in them, he also
L C : 0 1 :011(366) [0583] he fasted to the **honor** of St. Apollonia; if he feared fire,
L C : 0 1 :016(366) [0585] here you have the true **honor** and the true worship which
L C : 0 1 :042(370) [0591] money, prestige, nor **honor**, and can scarcely even keep
L C : 0 1 :042(370) [0591] have power, prestige, **honor**, wealth, and every comfort in
L C : 0 1 :053(372) [0595] money, property, and **honor**, whether publicly in court or
L C : 0 1 :059(372) [0597] villainy into righteousness and the disgrace into **honor**.
L C : 0 1 :070(374) [0601] urged and encouraged to **honor** God's name and keep it
L C : 0 1 :070(374) [0601] and experiences, for true **honor** to God's name consists of
L C : 0 1 :070(374) [0601] faith first gives God the **honor** due him and then the lips
L C : 0 1 :075(375) [0601] our youth in the fear and **honor** of God so that the First
L C : 0 1 :098(378) [0609] how you have heard and learned and **honored** his Word.
L C : 0 1 :104(379) [0611] *"You shall **honor** your father and mother.*
L C : 0 1 :105(379) [0611] us not simply to love our parents but also to **honor** them.
L C : 0 1 :106(379) [0611] For it is a much greater thing to **honor** than to love.
L C : 0 1 :106(379) [0611] **Honor** includes not only love but also deference, humility,
L C : 0 1 :107(379) [0611] we are whole-heartedly to **honor**, we must truly regard as
L C : 0 1 :108(379) [0611] to be deprived of their **honor** because of their ways or
L C : 0 1 :109(380) [0611] this commandment requires concerning **honor** to parents.
L C : 0 1 :111(380) [0613] You are also to **honor** them by your actions (that is, with
L C : 0 1 :112(380) [0613] better than to show all **honor** and obedience to my
L C : 0 1 :123(382) [0617] no sense of modesty or **honor**; they do nothing until they
L C : 0 1 :125(382) [0617] should we be happy to show them **honor** and obedience.
L C : 0 1 :130(383) [0619] compulsion, give all **honor** to his parents and esteem them
L C : 0 1 :142(385) [0621] way, or at least do not treat and **honor** them as such.
L C : 0 1 :143(385) [0623] mistresses, but also to **honor** them as their own parents
L C : 0 1 :150(385) [0625] name and title with all **honor** as their chief glory, it is our
L C : 0 1 :150(386) [0625] glory, it is our duty to **honor** and magnify them as the
L C : 0 1 :151(386) [0625] and cheerfully gives **honor** where it is due, knows that he
L C : 0 1 :160(387) [0627] fathers, they are entitled to **honor**, even above all others.
L C : 0 1 :160(387) [0627] for the world's way of **honoring** them is to harry them
L C : 0 1 :161(387) [0627] to God to show "double **honor**" to those who watch over
L C : 0 1 :164(387) [0627] and spiritual fathers, and for the **honor** they render them.
L C : 0 1 :166(387) [0627] those to whom we owe **honor** that we lift our hands in
L C : 0 1 :168(388) [0629] does he assign them this **honor** (that is, power and
L C : 0 1 :168(388) [0629] to bring them up to the praise and **honor** of God.
L C : 0 1 :203(392) [0639] to aid and assist him so that he may retain his **honor**.
L C : 0 1 :206(393) [0639] first, how highly God **honors** and glorifies the married
L C : 0 1 :206(393) [0639] "You shall **honor** father and mother"; but here, as I said,
L C : 0 1 :207(393) [0639] he also wishes us to **honor**, maintain, and cherish it as a
L C : 0 1 :211(393) [0641] that it is not only an **honorable** estate but also a necessary
L C : 0 1 :217(394) [0643] due time regain its proper **honor**, and there may be less
L C : 0 1 :218(394) [0643] are grown, will be married **honorably** in the fear of God.
L C : 0 1 :220(394) [0643] husbands and wives to love and **honor** each other.
L C : 0 1 :229(396) [0645] called great lords and **honorable**, good citizens, and yet
L C : 0 1 :231(396) [0647] unmolested by anyone, even claiming **honor** from men.
L C : 0 1 :231(396) [0647] so as to make the others look respectable and **honorable**.
L C : 0 1 :255(399) [0653] to us, namely, our **honor** and good name, for it is
L C : 0 1 :256(399) [0653] of his reputation, **honor**, and character any more than of
L C : 0 1 :257(399) [0653] consequently punished in his body, property, or **honor**.
L C : 0 1 :261(400) [0655] account of anyone's money, property, **honor**, or power.
L C : 0 1 :270(401) [0657] should be deprived of his **honor** and good name unless
L C : 0 1 :273(401) [0659] For **honor** and good name are easily taken away, but not
L C : 0 1 :278(402) [0661] would be corrected and the neighbor's **honor** maintained.
L C : 0 1 :285(403) [0663] them, and to cloak and veil them with his own **honor**.
L C : 0 1 :287(403) [0663] which we think less **honorable** we invest with the greater
L C : 0 1 :287(403) [0663] we invest with the greater **honor**; and our unpresentable
L C : 0 1 :287(403) [0663] do not need to, for they are our most **honorable** members.
L C : 0 1 :288(404) [0663] our utmost to serve and help him to promote his **honor**.
L C : 0 1 :296(405) [0665] world you could do it **honorably**, without accusation or
L C : 0 1 :300(405) [0667] about questions of **honor** and right when it comes to
L C : 0 1 :305(406) [0669] and yet posed as an **honorable**, upright man, as St. Mark
L C : 0 1 :307(406) [0669] of the world you might **honorably** retain the property.
L C : 0 1 :326(409) [0675] but learn it, hear it gladly, keep it holy, and **honor** it.
L C : 0 1 :327(409) [0675] We are to **honor** father and mother, masters, and all in
L C : 0 1 :328(410) [0675] his wife, his property, his **honor** or rights, as these things
L C : 0 2 :021(413) [0683] we had life, riches, power, **honor**, and such things of
L C : 0 3 :038(425) [0707] great necessity of duly **honoring** his name and keeping it
L C : 0 3 :039(425) [0707] he may receive from us not shame but **honor** and praise.
L C : 0 3 :046(426) [0709] our idiom "to praise, extol, and **honor**" in word and deed.
L C : 0 3 :056(427) [0713] he is God, he claims the **honor** of giving far more
L C : 0 3 :062(428) [0715] lies and abominations, **honored** under the most specious
L C : 0 3 :065(429) [0717] on earth — possessions, **honor**, house and home, wife and
L C : 0 3 :075(430) [0719] Rulers are worthy of all **honor**, and we should render
L C : 0 3 :080(431) [0721] kind of government or **honorable** and peaceful relations
L C : 0 3 :103(434) [0727] along with fondness for luxury, **honor**, fame, and power.
L C : 0 4 :017(438) [0735] God himself stakes his **honor**, his power, and his might on
L C : 0 4 :020(439) [0737] the commandment is added, "You shall **honor** father and
L C : 0 4 :020(439) [0737] me how and why I should **honor** this particular flesh and
L C : 0 4 :021(439) [0737] much more, you should **honor** and exalt Baptism on
L C : 0 4 :021(439) [0737] since God himself has **honored** it by words and deeds and
L C : 0 4 :038(441) [0741] that it is God's ordinance and is to be held in all **honor**.
L C : 0 4 :038(441) [0741] "You shall **honor** your father and mother," refers only to
L C : 0 5 :043(451) [0763] who cherish and **honor** the sacrament will of their own
S D : 0 1 :003(509) [0861] we are extolling God's **honor** properly when we carefully
S D : 0 2 :074(535) [0909] righteousness and **honorable** behavior and to avoid
S D : 0 3 :030(544) [0925] comfort and to give due **honor** to the merit of Christ and
S D : 0 5 :022(562) [0959] neither understood nor **honored** him rightly (Rom. 1:21).
S D : 0 7 :046(577) [0989] reason, he gave God the **honor** of truthfulness and
S D : 0 8 :070(605) [1041] him with glory and **honor** and didst set him over the
S D : 1 1 :079(629) [1089] alone prepares vessels of **honor**, and the work of the devil
S D : 1 1 :082(630) [1089] dishonor into vessels of **honor** when he writes, "If any one
S D : 1 1 :087(631) [1091] of God gives God his due **honor** fully and completely.
S D : 1 1 :096(632) [1095] as will not violate God's **honor**, that will not detract

Hood (3)

A P : 0 4 :361(162) [0219] as when a monk's **hood** is placed on a dead man.
A P : 2 4 :068(261) [0407] just as a certain type of **hood** is the mark of a particular
A P : 2 7 :027(274) [0429] receiving another **hood** or other sandals or other girdles."

Hoop (1)

L C : 0 1 :326(409) [0675] like the clasp or the **hoop** of a wreath that binds the end

Hope (55), Hoped (5), Hopeless (1), Hopes (2), Hoping (1)

P R : P R :008(005) [0011] in the confidence and **hope** that thereby the adversaries
P R : P R :018(009) [0015] We also **hope** that from now on our adversaries will spare
P R : P R :022(012) [0019] It is furthermore to be **hoped** that when they are rightly
A G : 0 7 :004(032) [0047] you were called to the one **hope** that belongs to your call,
A G : 2 0 :020(044) [0055] into monasteries in the **hope** that there they might merit
A G : 2 0 :025(044) [0057] upon him, and have no **hope** of receiving good from him.
A G : 0 0 :002(048) [0059] to traditions, although we **hope** to offer firm grounds and
A G : 2 4 :025(059) [0067] Accordingly it is to be **hoped** that everyone will
A L : 2 0 :020(044) [0055] into monasteries, in the **hope** that there they might merit
A L : 2 6 :015(066) [0073] faith, the cross, **hope**, the importance of civil affairs, and
A P : P R :016(099) [0103] our faithfulness, and we **hope** that posterity will judge us
A P : 0 4 :058(115) [0137] for his word, my soul **hopes** in the Lord," that is, because
A P : 0 4 :106(122) [0153] says: "By the law we fear God, by faith we **hope** in God.
A P : 0 4 :119(123) [0155] which the faithful may receive the sure **hope** of salvation.
A P : 0 4 :208(135) [0177] imitation in those who **hope** that by similar actions they
A P : 0 4 :212(136) [0179] commandment in the **hope** of finding some great work
A P : 0 4 :225(138) [0183] is preferred to faith and **hope** since Paul says
A P : 0 4 :226(138) [0183] Faith and **hope** deal only with God, while love has
A P : 0 4 :286(150) [0203] We **hope** we have shown all this to the satisfaction of
A P : 0 4 :303(154) [0205] We **hope** that pious minds will easily understand our
A P : 0 4 :312(155) [0207] dispositions of faith and **hope** seem to be confused, since
A P : 0 4 :312(155) [0207] to be confused, since it is **hope** that expects what is
A P : 0 4 :312(155) [0207] faith is defined as "the assurance of things **hoped** for."
A P : 0 4 :312(155) [0207] we say that the object of **hope** is properly a future event,
A P : 0 4 :313(155) [0207] We **hope** that from this the nature of faith will be clearly
A P : 0 4 :320(156) [0209] of eternal life, if indeed **hope** ought to be sustained by
A P : 0 4 :320(156) [0209] he says (Rom. 4:18), "In **hope** he believed against hope."
A P : 0 4 :320(156) [0209] he says (Rom. 4:18), "In hope he believed against **hope**."
A P : 0 4 :344(160) [0217] point someone may say, "**Hope** will be uncertain if we are
A P : 0 4 :345(160) [0217] Precisely in order to make **hope** sure and to distinguish
A P : 0 4 :346(160) [0217] This faith produces a sure **hope**, for it rests on the Word
A P : 0 4 :346(160) [0217] If our **hope** were to rest on works, then it would really be
A P : 0 4 :351(161) [0217] as knowledge and fear of God, love of God, and **hope**.
A P : 0 4 :389(166) [0225] discussion may be, we **hope** that good men will find it
A P : 1 1 :010(182) [0253] many devout minds to **hopeless** despair because they
A P : 1 2 :096(196) [0281] in such a way that we **hope** for pardon from faith just as
A P : 1 2 :124(201) [0289] We **hope** that among good men these slanders will not
A P : 2 1 :039(235) [0355] everywhere have been **hoping** that the bishops would
A P : 2 3 :004(239) [0365] disgrace and cruelty, we **hope** that you will deal kindly
S 1 : P R :003(289) [0455] of that party have lost **hope** that the Roman court will
S 1 : P R :010(290) [0457] and we have no reason to **hope** or expect that a council
S 2 : 0 4 :015(301) [0475] and we must rely on the **hope** that Christ, our Lord, has
S 3 : 0 3 :014(305) [0483] Rather, men **hoped** by their own works to overcome and
S 3 : 0 3 :036(309) [0489] sure: We cannot pin our **hope** on anything that we are,
S C : 0 4 :010(349) [0551] by his grace and become heirs in **hope** of eternal life.
S C : 0 8 :010(354) [0559] who fear him, in those who **hope** in his steadfast love."
S C : 0 9 :013(356) [0563] left all alone, has set her **hope** on God and continues in
L C : 0 1 :015(366) [0583] the saints, or what you **hoped** to receive from mammon
L C : 0 1 :028(368) [0587] else, from which it **hopes** to receive more good and help
L C : 0 1 :157(386) [0625] profusion of words in the **hope** that someone may take it
L C : 0 1 :325(409) [0675] fear him, in those who **hope** in his mercy" (Ps. 147:11).
L C : 0 3 :104(434) [0727] tear us away from faith, **hope**, and love, to draw us into
L C : 0 4 :057(444) [0747] with the purpose and **hope** that he may believe, and we
E P : 0 3 :011(474) [0795] never alone but is always accompanied by love and **hope**.
E P : 1 1 :016(497) [0837] the encouragement of the Scriptures we might have **hope**.
S D : P R :008(502) [0849] the unchristian but futile **hope** that these disagreements
S D : 0 2 :068(534) [0907] strong in faith and in **hope**, and at another time cold and
S D : 0 4 :034(556) [0949] state of grace and our **hope** of sharing the glory of God
S D : 0 6 :016(566) [0967] fear of punishment or in **hope** of reward, he is still under
S D : 1 1 :012(618) [1067] of the Scriptures we might have **hope**" (Rom. 15:4).
S D : 1 1 :030(621) [1073] sanctified in love, have **hope**, patience, and comfort in
S D : 1 1 :048(624) [1079] give us comfort, create **hope**, and bring everything to such
S D : 1 1 :092(632) [1093] of the Scriptures we might have **hope**" (Rom. 15:4).
S D : 1 1 :092(632) [1093] removes this comfort and **hope** is contrary to the Holy

Hordes (1)

L C : 0 6 :025(460) [0000] driven men together in **hordes** just to show what impure

Horoscopes (1)

A P : 2 1 :034(234) [0353] sorcerers imagine that **horoscopes** carved at a particular

Horrendous (1)

S D : 0 7 :008(570) [0975] anathematize and condemn as a **horrendous** blasphemy.

Horrible (18), Horribly (2), Horrifies (1)
A P : 0 4 :304(154) [0205] intellect but are also a **horrible** turmoil in the will as it
A P : 1 2 :032(186) [0259] same time it flees God's **horrible** wrath, for human nature
A P : 1 2 :094(196) [0281] to the truth; a more **horrible** blasphemy than this cannot
A P : 1 2 :140(204) [0295] How **horrible** it is, then, to say that Christ's satisfaction
A P : 2 0 :006(227) [0339] We see that a **horrible** decree has been drawn up against
A P : 2 3 :067(248) [0383] Their third argument is **horrible**: the marriage of priests is
A P : 2 4 :047(258) [0401] In addition, they **horribly** profaned the Mass and
A P : 2 4 :089(266) [0415] It is **horrible** to attribute as much to the work of a priest
A P : 2 7 :012(271) [0423] To this they append a **horrible** epilogue in the words:
A P : 2 8 :004(281) [0445] threatening men with **horrible** punishments unless they
S 1 : P R :011(290) [0457] This **horrifies** me and makes me fear that he may cause a
S 2 : 0 2 :001(293) [0463] as the greatest and most **horrible** abomination because it
S 3 : 1 1 :001(314) [0499] occasion for all sorts of **horrible**, abominable, and
T R : 0 0 :006(320) [0505] What is even more **horrible** is that he adds that it is
T R : 0 0 :034(325) [0513] This notion has caused **horrible** darkness to descend over
T R : 0 0 :040(327) [0517] Finally, he defends such **horrible** errors and such impiety
T R : 0 0 :047(328) [0517] many abuses and what **horrible** idolatry it has produced!
T R : 0 0 :055(329) [0521] whom he has bound by **horrible** oaths and curses to
S C : P R :020(340) [0537] The devil also has a **horrible** purpose in mind.
L C : P R :008(359) [0569] fear a fall, for they have already fallen all too **horribly**.
S D : 1 1 :085(630) [1091] his preceding sin and his **horrible** tyranny with which he

Horse (2), Horses (2)
S 2 : 0 2 :022(296) [0469] the bones of dogs and **horses** that even the devil has
S C : 0 8 :010(354) [0559] not in the strength of the **horse**, nor his pleasure in the
S D : 0 2 :066(534) [0907] Holy Spirit, the way two **horses** draw a wagon together,
S D : 0 7 :067(582) [0997] unworthy "two hairs of a **horse**'s tail and an invention of

Hospitable (1)
S C : 0 9 :002(354) [0561] sensible, dignified, **hospitable**, an apt teacher, no

Host (3), Hosts (1)
A P : 2 1 :008(230) [0345] angel prays, "O Lord of **hosts**, how long wilt thou have no
A P : 2 4 :093(267) [0417] service" does not mean the **host** itself but the prayers and
L C : 0 3 :068(429) [0717] the devil and all his **host** storm and rage furiously against
S D : 0 2 :064(533) [0905] will offer themselves freely on the day you lead your **host**."

Hostile (9), Hostility (2)
A P : 0 4 :032(111) [0129] that is set on the flesh is **hostile** to God; it does not
A P : 0 4 :033(111) [0129] that is set on the flesh is **hostile** to God, then the flesh
A P : 1 5 :051(222) [0329] and become more **hostile** to the true teaching of the
L C : 0 1 :188(390) [0635] heart should harbor no **hostility** or malice toward anyone
L C : 0 6 :024(460) [0000] from this, but only a greater **hostility** to the command.
E P : 0 2 :003(470) [0787] that is set on the flesh is **hostile** to God; it does not
S D : 0 2 :013(523) [0885] man's understanding) "is **hostile** to God; it does not
S D : 0 2 :017(524) [0887] wicked, opposed and **hostile** to God, and all too mighty,
S D : 0 2 :017(524) [0887] that is set on the flesh is **hostile** to God" (Rom. 8:7), and
S D : 0 2 :018(524) [0887] obstinately opposed and **hostile** to God's law and will.
S D : 0 2 :024(526) [0891] he is resistant and **hostile** to the will of God unless the

Hounding (1)
L C : 0 5 :044(451) [0763] other Christian activity, **hounding** and driving people

Hounds (1)
L C : 0 3 :115(435) [0731] he drowns, and many he **hounds** to suicide or other

Hour (22), Hours (4)
A G : 2 8 :041(087) [0089] sin to omit the seven **hours**, that some foods defile the
A L : 2 8 :041(087) [0089] sin to omit the canonical **hours**, that in a reserved case a
A P : 0 4 :119(124) [0155] For in the **hour** of death, what will sustain those who
A P : 1 2 :177(210) [0307] when they grant that in the **hour** of death the reservation
A P : 2 1 :026(232) [0349] us from the enemy and receive us in the **hour** of death."
S C : 0 3 :020(348) [0549] and that at last, when the **hour** of death comes, he may
L C : P R :003(358) [0567] babbling of the Seven **Hours**, it would be fine if every
L C : P R :016(361) [0573] can finish learning in one **hour** what God himself cannot
L C : 0 1 :068(374) [0599] never enjoyed a happy **hour** or a healthful day thereafter,
L C : 0 1 :089(377) [0605] we must set apart several **hours** a week for the young, and
L C : 0 1 :128(382) [0617] Especially when an evil **hour** comes do we rage and
L C : 0 1 :166(388) [0629] world cannot add an **hour** to our life or raise from the
L C : 0 1 :244(398) [0649] of soldiers upon us; in one **hour** they clean out our chests
L C : 0 3 :081(431) [0721] a penny in the house, or even our life for one **hour** —
L C : 0 3 :098(433) [0725] to use and practice every **hour**, keeping it with us at all
L C : 0 3 :105(434) [0727] to cry out and pray every **hour** that God may not allow
L C : 0 3 :109(435) [0729] devil is likely in this very **hour** to send such a shaft into
L C : 0 3 :116(435) [0731] us, we would not be safe from him for a single **hour**.
L C : 0 4 :055(443) [0745] take it again the selfsame **hour**, as if he had not really
L C : 0 5 :081(456) [0773] A murderer who begrudges you every **hour** of your life.
L C : 0 5 :084(456) [0773] and body, so that you cannot be safe from him one **hour**.
S D : 0 7 :044(577) [0987] our sin, in this sad, last **hour** of his life, this truthful and
S D : 1 1 :027(620) [1071] and even at the eleventh **hour** (Matt. 20:1-16; 22:2-14).
S D : 1 1 :056(625) [1081] each person the time and **hour** of his call and conversion.
S D : 1 1 :056(625) [1081] Word, while we leave the time and **hour** to God (Acts 1:7)
S D : 1 1 :090(631) [1093] — yes, would be losing it every moment and **hour**.

House (29), Household (25), Housekeepers (1), Houses (3), Housework (1)
A G : 1 6 :004(037) [0051] requires the forsaking of **house** and home, wife and child,
A G : 1 8 :005(040) [0051] whether to build a **house**, take a wife, engage in a trade,
A L : 1 8 :005(040) [0051] oneself, will to build a **house**, will to marry, will to keep
A P : 0 4 :302(154) [0205] about; like the walls of a **house**, they echo the word
A P : 1 2 :106(197) [0283] advice to the head of a **household**, telling him to pay
A P : 1 2 :151(206) [0299] to begin with the **household** of God; and if it begins with
A P : 1 5 :025(219) [0323] administration of the **household**, married life, and the
A P : 2 3 :040(245) [0375] and serving and is not so distracted by **household** chores.
A P : 2 7 :040(276) [0433] (Matt. 19:29), "Every one who has left **houses**," etc.
S 2 : 0 2 :015(295) [0467] and what kind of **houses** they lived in would have to
S 2 : 0 3 :001(298) [0471] well trained girls to become mothers, **housekeepers**, etc.
S 3 : 0 3 :025(307) [0485] until every church and **house** was reached by jubilee
S C : 0 1 :000(342) [0539] *the head of the family shall teach them to his* ***household***
S C : 0 1 :017(343) [0541] *"You shall not covet your neighbor's* ***house****."*
S C : 0 2 :000(344) [0543] *the head of the family shall teach it to his* ***household***
S C : 0 2 :002(345) [0543] with food and clothing, **house** and home, family and
S C : 0 3 :000(346) [0545] *the head of the family shall teach it to his* ***household***
S C : 0 3 :014(347) [0547] as food and clothing, **house** and home, fields and flocks,
S C : 0 4 :000(348) [0551] *the head of the family shall teach it to his* ***household***
S C : 0 6 :000(351) [0555] *the head of the family shall teach it to his* ***household***
S C : 0 7 :000(352) [0557] *family shall teach his* ***household*** *to say morning and*
S C : 0 8 :006(353) [0559] *family shall teach his* ***household*** *to offer blessing and*
S C : 0 8 :007(353) [0559] children and the whole **household** gather at the table, they
S C : 0 9 :002(354) [0561] must manage his own **household** well, keeping his
S C : 0 9 :003(354) [0561] "Remain in the same **house**, eating and drinking what
S C : 0 9 :015(356) [0563] And all the **household** well will fare.'
L C : S P :004(362) [0575] duty of every head of a **household** to examine his children
L C : S P :009(363) [0577] 9. You shall not covet your neighbor's **house**.
L C : S P :017(363) [0577] the same duty to his **household**; he should dismiss
L C : 0 1 :121(382) [0615] and harmony in their **houses**, and children would win
L C : 0 1 :142(384) [0621] and maid-servants) under him to manage his **household**.
L C : 0 1 :142(384) [0621] and mistresses of the **household** *patres et matres familias*
L C : 0 1 :142(384) [0621] *et matres familias* (that is, **house**-fathers and
L C : 0 1 :142(384) [0621] *matres familias* (that is, house-fathers and **house**-mothers)
L C : 0 1 :143(385) [0621] and mother, the entire **household** owes them likewise.
L C : 0 1 :145(385) [0623] "If I do my daily **housework** faithfully, that is better than
L C : 0 1 :150(385) [0623] God gives us food, **house** and home, protection and
L C : 0 1 :154(386) [0625] Indeed, in your own **household** you must suffer ten times
L C : 0 1 :156(386) [0625] not have a penny in the **house** or a straw in the field.
L C : 0 1 :158(387) [0627] by blood, fathers of a **household**, and fathers of the
L C : 0 1 :180(389) [0631] we leave our own **house** and go out among our neighbors
L C : 0 1 :184(390) [0633] from God a better **house** and estate or greater wealth and
L C : 0 1 :236(397) [0647] yourself and have a **house** of your own — which God will
L C : 0 1 :244(398) [0649] they burn and ravage **house** and home and outrage and
L C : 0 1 :277(402) [0659] can learn from the daily management of the **household**.
L C : 0 1 :277(402) [0659] When the master of the **house** sees a servant failing to do
L C : 0 1 :292(404) [0663] *"You shall not covet your neighbor's* ***house****."*
L C : 0 1 :296(405) [0665] such as his wife, servants, **house**, fields, meadows, or
L C : 0 2 :013(412) [0681] of support, wife and child, servants, **house** and home, etc.
L C : 0 2 :048(416) [0691] a group of people but a consecrated **house** or building.
L C : 0 2 :048(416) [0691] But the **house** should not be called a church except for
L C : 0 2 :048(416) [0691] special place and give the **house** its name by virtue of the
L C : 0 3 :065(429) [0717] — possessions, honor, **house** and home, wife and
L C : 0 3 :076(431) [0721] food and drink, clothing, **house**, home, and a sound
L C : 0 3 :076(431) [0721] to help us manage our **household** well and give and
L C : 0 3 :081(431) [0721] the field, a penny in the **house**, or even our life for one
L C : 0 5 :087(456) [0773] let every head of a **household** remember that it is his
S D : 0 2 :051(531) [0901] you will be saved, you and your **household**" (Acts 11:14).
S D : 1 1 :082(630) [1089] useful to the master of the **house**, ready for any good

How (360)
P R : P R :004(003) [0007] Dr. Martin Luther, and **how** in this anguished situation
P R : P R :004(004) [0007] Everybody also knows **how** the adversaries of divine truth
P R : P R :010(006) [0011] these differences and **how** by God's grace they might be
P R : P R :011(006) [0011] based on God's Word, **how** the aforementioned offensive
P R : P R :011(006) [0011] in which they set forth **how** the differences that had
A G : P R :001(024) [0039] the Christian religion, and **how** with continuing help he
A G : P R :008(025) [0039] own faith, setting forth **how** and in what manner, on the
A G : 2 0 :035(046) [0057] done and for offering help as to **how** they may be done.
A G : 2 1 :001(046) [0057] grace they received and **how** they were sustained by faith.
A G : 2 3 :016(054) [0063] **How** would the marriage of priests and the clergy, and
A G : 0 1 :007(056) [0065] why it was instituted, and **how** it is to be used (namely, as
A G : 2 4 :024(058) [0067] our people might know **how** the sacrament is to be used
A G : 2 4 :036(060) [0067] For Chrysostom reports **how** the priest stood every day,
A G : 2 5 :004(062) [0069] and power of keys and **how** comforting and necessary it
A G : 2 6 :014(066) [0073] summists and canonists **how** consciences have been
A G : 2 7 :001(071) [0077] in the monasteries, and **how** many of the daily
A G : 2 7 :022(074) [0079] No matter **how** much one extols the vow and the
A G : 2 7 :022(074) [0079] the obligation, no matter **how** highly one exalts them, it
A G : 2 7 :023(074) [0079] **How** much less must be their obligation, lawfulness, and
A G : 2 7 :026(075) [0079] of temporal interests, **how** much more should
A G : 2 7 :045(078) [0081] them into their teeth, **how** many items could be assembled
A G : 2 8 :078(094) [0095] petition, let them consider **how** they will answer for it in
A L : 2 0 :035(046) [0057] commended for showing **how** we are enabled to do good
A L : 2 4 :011(057) [0065] It is also well known **how** widely this abuse extends in all
A L : 2 4 :011(057) [0065] revenues or stipends, and **how** many celebrate Masses
A L : 2 7 :001(071) [0077] of monasteries was and **how** many things were done in
A L : 2 7 :023(074) [0079] **How** much less are those vows valid which are made
A L : 2 7 :029(075) [0079] **How** few there are who have taken the vow spontaneously
A L : 2 7 :045(078) [0081] to enlarge on these claims, **how** many things could be
A L : 2 8 :078(094) [0095] do this, they must see to it **how** they will answer for it
A P : P R :004(098) [0099] In a religious issue, **how** could they accept a document
A P : P R :017(099) [0103] We need not describe here **how** they lay hidden under all
A P : 0 4 :019(110) [0125] **How** is one to know whether one has the merit of
A P : 0 4 :020(110) [0125] men who do not know **how** the forgiveness of sins takes
A P : 0 4 :020(110) [0125] of sins takes place, or **how** the judgment of God and the
A P : 0 4 :021(110) [0127] can never experience what faith is and **how** effective it is.
A P : 0 4 :029(111) [0129] both for discovering **how** one ought to live, and also for
A P : 0 4 :037(112) [0131] the conscience experiences **how** vain these philosophical
A P : 0 4 :060(115) [0137] This is **how** God wants to be known and worshiped, that
A P : 0 4 :061(115) [0137] knowledge, we must tell **how** faith comes into being.
A P : 0 4 :063(115) [0139] can our opponents say **how** the Holy Spirit is given.
A P : 0 4 :065(116) [0139] on the *Sentences* that tells **how** regeneration takes place.
A P : 0 4 :069(116) [0141] For **how** will Christ be the mediator if we do not use him
A P : 0 4 :079(117) [0143] minor premise if we know **how** the forgiveness of sins
A P : 0 4 :079(118) [0143] **How**?
A P : 0 4 :081(118) [0145] And to show **how** this happens, he adds that through
A P : 0 4 :083(118) [0145] **How** could he say it any more plainly?
A P : 0 4 :118(123) [0155] One can easily see **how** necessary it is to understand this
A P : 0 4 :128(125) [0157] Then, too, **how** can the human heart love God while it
A P : 0 4 :135(125) [0159] Only then do we see **how** far we are from keeping the
A P : 0 4 :135(125) [0159] Then we recognize **how** our flesh in its smugness and
A P : 0 4 :136(126) [0159] we not only require them but show **how** they can be done.
A P : 0 4 :140(126) [0161] furthermore, not only **how** the law can be kept, but also
A P : 0 4 :164(129) [0169] they have kept the law, **how** can our conscience be sure
A P : 0 4 :165(130) [0169] It is hard to understand **how** a man can do away with
A P : 0 4 :175(131) [0171] that we should realize **how** far we are from the perfection
A P : 0 4 :207(135) [0177] Here we see **how** vehemently the prophets rebuke the
A P : 0 4 :222(138) [0181] is extinguished, no matter **how** great it may have been.
A P : 0 4 :224(138) [0181] neither what justification is nor **how** it happens.

Continued ▶

A P : 0 4 :226(138) [0183] **How** will they conclude from this that love justifies?
A P : 0 4 :230(139) [0183] We know **how** repulsive this teaching is to the judgment
A P : 0 4 :245(142) [0189] **How** much better is James's teaching!
A P : 0 4 :267(146) [0197] This, then, is **how** we reply to the words of Daniel: Since
A P : 0 4 :277(148) [0199] is hyperbole; but that is **how** it ought to be understood so
A P : 0 4 :298(153) [0205] we are astonished to see **how** furiously our opponents
A P : 0 4 :300(153) [0205] teaching does not mention **how** we must set Christ
A P : 0 4 :302(154) [0205] **How** confused and unclear their teaching is!
A P : 0 4 :304(154) [0205] This is **how** Scripture uses the word "faith," as this
A P : 0 4 :319(156) [0209] and not because of Christ, **how** will it have peace without
A P : 0 4 :321(156) [0209] Third, **how** will the conscience know when a work has
A P : 0 4 :336(159) [0215] Look **how** this childish sophistry delights our opponents!
A P : 0 4 :350(161) [0217] **How** often our aroused conscience tempts us to despair
A P : 0 4 :350(161) [0217] in which experience testifies **how** difficult a thing faith is.
A P : 0 4 :398(168) [0227] doctrine was condemned, **how** can they ascribe any
A P : 0 7 :027(173) [0235] **How** many of them care anything for the Gospel or think
A P : 0 7 :029(173) [0237] Nor do we see **how** it could be defined otherwise, since
A P : 0 7 :032(174) [0239] Later they debated **how** it happened that they had come
A P : 0 7 :038(176) [0241] **How** devout they are!
A P : 1 1 :007(181) [0251] throughout Europe knows **how** consciences have been
A P : 1 1 :009(181) [0251] Good pastors know **how** profitable it is to examine the
A P : 1 2 :006(183) [0255] Good God, **how** great is the darkness!
A P : 1 2 :011(184) [0255] **How** much effort is devoted to the endless enumeration of
A P : 1 2 :024(185) [0257] This is **how** uninformed people understand it.
A P : 1 2 :031(186) [0259] But thou, O Lord — **how** long?"
A P : 1 2 :034(186) [0261] Yet **how** will men love God amid such real terrors when
A P : 1 2 :049(188) [0265] while the second describes **how** we are revived in
A P : 1 2 :052(189) [0265] We cannot see **how** the nature of penitence could be
A P : 1 2 :062(190) [0269] We do not see **how** anyone can be said to receive
A P : 1 2 :064(191) [0269] what the forgiveness of sins is nor **how** it comes to us.
A P : 1 2 :074(192) [0273] And he teaches us **how** to be sure of the forgiveness of
A P : 1 2 :088(195) [0277] with penitence, "**How** do we become sure that our sins are
A P : 1 2 :089(195) [0277] In such doubt, **how** can they call upon God, how can they
A P : 1 2 :089(195) [0277] can they call upon God, **how** can they be sure that he
A P : 1 2 :122(200) [0287] Look **how** our opponents prove these fictions of theirs in
A P : 1 2 :125(201) [0289] **How** will the world evaluate the Confutation — if it is ever
A P : 1 2 :127(201) [0289] even in Rome itself — **how** many do you think there are
A P : 1 2 :127(201) [0291] **How** much silent indignation is there because you refuse
A P : 1 2 :140(204) [0295] **How** horrible it is, then, to say that Christ's satisfaction
A P : 1 2 :147(205) [0297] They do not see **how**, in the remission of guilt, faith frees
A P : 1 2 :161(208) [0303] This is **how** Gregory interprets the punishment of David
A P : 1 3 :018(213) [0313] much more necessary to know **how** to use the sacraments.
A P : 1 4 :002(214) [0315] Let them see to it **how** they will answer to God for
A P : 1 5 :014(216) [0319] of sins or righteousness, **how** will he know that these
A P : 1 5 :014(217) [0319] **How** will he inform men of God's will without the
A P : 1 5 :017(217) [0319] **How**, then, can our opponents maintain that they justify?
A P : 1 5 :020(218) [0321] provided an example of **how** all things could be done
A P : 1 5 :024(218) [0321] This is **how** human reason interprets fasting and bodily
A P : 1 5 :028(219) [0323] **How** the great Gerson suffers as he looks for the degrees
A P : 1 5 :030(219) [0323] of Moses do not justify, **how** much less do the traditions
A P : 1 6 :008(223) [0331] **How** poor the judgment of many writers in these matters
A P : 1 6 :010(224) [0333] **How** they have praised the theory that the Gospel requires
A P : 1 6 :013(224) [0333] in business have testified **how** they were helped after the
A P : 1 8 :003(225) [0335] **How** many absurdities follow from these Pelagian notions
A P : 2 1 :008(230) [0345] prays, "O Lord of hosts, **how** long wilt thou have no
A P : 2 1 :010(230) [0345] ought to come from faith, **how** do we know that God
A P : 2 1 :010(230) [0345] **How** do we know, without proof from Scripture, that the
A P : 2 2 :015(238) [0361] to use one kind or both, **how** can they make the
A P : 2 2 :016(238) [0361] Let them figure out **how** they will account to God for
A P : 2 3 :005(239) [0365] They know good and well **how** few practice chastity, but
A P : 2 3 :043(245) [0375] time good men will know **how** to use marriage
A P : 2 3 :052(246) [0377] It is no secret **how** harmful this law has been to public
A P : 2 3 :052(246) [0377] been to public morals and **how** productive of vices and
A P : 2 4 :002(249) [0385] opponents quibble about **how** a hearer who is ignorant of
A P : 2 4 :028(254) [0393] **How** are we to think the Jews accepted this declaration,
A P : 2 4 :032(255) [0395] This is **how** the name of the Lord becomes great among
A P : 2 4 :033(256) [0395] a moment we shall explain **how** even a ceremony is a
A P : 2 4 :073(262) [0409] are the ones worthy of it, and **how** they ought to use it.
A P : 2 4 :080(264) [0411] says (I Cor. 4:1), "This is **how** one should regard us, as
A P : 2 7 :004(269) [0419] History will show **how** much credence should be given to
A P : 2 7 :004(269) [0421] Everyone knows **how** much hypocrisy, ambition, and
A P : 2 7 :004(269) [0421] is in the monasteries; **how** ignorant and cruel these
A P : 2 7 :004(269) [0421] illiterate men are; and **how** vain they are in their sermons
A P : 2 7 :010(270) [0423] It is worthwhile to hear **how** they twist our arguments and
A P : 2 7 :011(270) [0423] But listen **how** the architects of the Confutation slip away
A P : 2 7 :013(271) [0423] O Christ, **how** long wilt Thou bear these insults with
A P : 2 7 :014(271) [0425] the forgiveness of sins, **how** much less do these silly
A P : 2 7 :016(271) [0425] Gerson indicates **how** pure this is in most of those who
A P : 2 7 :016(271) [0425] And **how** many of them strive to be continent?
A P : 2 7 :018(272) [0425] **How** impudent our opponents are!
A P : 2 7 :023(273) [0427] **How** can they maintain that these are services which God
A P : 2 8 :008(282) [0445] of a yoke, showing **how** dangerous this is and enlarging
A P : 2 8 :010(282) [0447] let our opponents explain **how** traditions are conducive to
S 1 : P R :001(288) [0455] the one hand what and in **how** far we were willing and
S 1 : P R :005(289) [0457] But **how** can I stop all the mouths of the devil?
S 1 : P R :009(290) [0457] Imagine **how** those will face us on the last day, before the
S 1 : P R :010(290) [0457] nor the canons care **how** the poor people live or die,
S 2 : 0 2 :006(293) [0463] **How** much the more should it be discontinued in order to
S 2 : 0 2 :015(295) [0467] Otherwise what they ate, **how** they dressed, and what kind
S 3 : 0 2 :004(303) [0479] his nature has fallen and **how** corrupt it has become.
S 3 : 0 3 :003(304) [0481] who you are and no matter **how** great, wise, mighty, and
S 3 : 0 3 :005(304) [0481] that they might know **how** they stood before God and
S 3 : 0 3 :016(305) [0483] since nobody knew **how** much contrition he had to
S 3 : 0 3 :018(306) [0483] Here we see **how** blind reason gropes about in matters
S 3 : 0 3 :021(306) [0485] for nobody could know **how** much he was to do for one
S 3 : 0 7 :002(312) [0493] alone to judge which, **how** great, and how many our sins
S 3 : 0 7 :002(312) [0493] to judge which, how great, and **how** many our sins are.
S 3 : 1 3 :000(315) [0499] XIII. **How** Man Is Justified Before God, and His Good
S 3 : 1 3 :001(315) [0499] I do not know **how** I can change what I have heretofore
S 3 : 1 5 :003(316) [0501] I do not know **how** I can change or concede anything in
T R : 0 0 :020(323) [0509] 11. Finally, **how** can the pope be over the whole church
T R : 0 0 :047(328) [0517] the invocation of saints — **how** many abuses and what
T R : 0 0 :048(328) [0519] **How** many profligate acts have sprung from the tradition
T R : 0 0 :053(329) [0519] they should also know **how** great a crime it is to support
T R : 0 0 :055(329) [0521] pope should hold synods, **how** can the church be purified
S C : P R :004(338) [0533] **How** will you bishops answer for it before Christ that you
S C : P R :013(339) [0535] the people learn to know **how** to distinguish between
S C : P R :018(340) [0537] the Scriptures to show **how** God punished and blessed.
S C : P R :025(341) [0539] **How** can they be other than negligent if you fail to do
S C : 0 3 :005(346) [0547] **How** is this done?
S C : 0 3 :008(346) [0547] **How** is this done?
S C : 0 3 :011(347) [0547] **How** is this done?
S C : 0 4 :009(349) [0551] **How** can water produce such great effects?
S C : 0 5 :015(349) [0553] ***How** Plain People Are to Be Taught to Confess*
S C : 0 6 :007(352) [0557] **How** can bodily eating and drinking produce such great
S C : 0 7 :000(352) [0557] ***How** the head of the family shall teach his household to*
S C : 0 8 :006(353) [0559] ***How** the head of the family shall teach his household to*
L C : S P :020(364) [0579] where they describe **how** Christ said farewell to his
L C : 0 1 :001(365) [0581] What does this mean, and **how** is it to be understood?
L C : 0 1 :010(366) [0583] Notice, again, **how** presumptuous, secure, and proud
L C : 0 1 :010(366) [0583] of such possessions, and **how** despondent when they lack
L C : 0 1 :017(366) [0585] hand, you can easily judge **how** the world practices
L C : 0 1 :022(367) [0585] It keeps account **how** often it has made endowments,
L C : 0 1 :032(369) [0589] from these words, then, **how** angry God is with those who
L C : 0 1 :032(369) [0589] but himself, and again, **how** kind and gracious he is to
L C : 0 1 :033(369) [0589] who think that it makes no great difference **how** they live.
L C : 0 1 :050(371) [0593] As I have taught above **how** to answer the question,
L C : 0 1 :051(371) [0595] If you are asked, "**How** do you understand the Second
L C : 0 1 :053(371) [0595] readily infer when and in **how** many ways God's name is
L C : 0 1 :056(372) [0595] Let us take to heart **how** important this commandment is
L C : 0 1 :063(373) [0597] you must also know **how** to use the name of God aright.
L C : 0 1 :088(377) [0605] **How** does this sanctifying take place?
L C : 0 1 :093(377) [0607] sight of God, no matter **how** splendid and brilliant it may
L C : 0 1 :098(378) [0609] of you an accounting of **how** you have heard and learned
L C : 0 1 :118(381) [0615] O **how** great a price all the Carthusian monks and nuns
L C : 0 1 :125(382) [0617] **How** much more, when he has given us living parents,
L C : 0 1 :128(382) [0617] and no one takes thought **how** God feeds, guards, and
L C : 0 1 :128(382) [0617] and protects us and **how** many blessings of body and soul
L C : 0 1 :132(383) [0619] Here you see **how** important God considers this
L C : 0 1 :139(384) [0621] Learn well, then, **how** important God considers
L C : 0 1 :140(384) [0621] for no one will believe **how** necessary is this
L C : 0 1 :140(384) [0621] to perceive and believe **how** angry he makes God when he
L C : 0 1 :140(384) [0621] this commandment, and **how** precious and acceptable a
L C : 0 1 :144(385) [0623] consciences and know **how** to do truly golden works.
L C : 0 1 :146(385) [0623] **How** can you lead a more blessed or holy life, as far as
L C : 0 1 :152(386) [0625] **How** difficult do you think it will be for him to pay you
L C : 0 1 :157(387) [0627] God's Word we could learn **how** to obtain an abundance
L C : 0 1 :165(387) [0627] then, and leave it to God **how** he will support you and
L C : 0 1 :167(388) [0629] the nature of their office, **how** they should treat those
L C : 0 1 :170(388) [0629] were no concern of ours what they learn or **how** they live.
L C : 0 1 :171(388) [0629] nor is it recognized **how** very necessary it is to devote
L C : 0 1 :176(389) [0631] own children, no matter **how** devout and holy you may
L C : 0 1 :180(389) [0631] our neighbors to learn **how** we should conduct ourselves
L C : 0 1 :186(390) [0633] for any evil deed, no matter **how** much he deserves it.
L C : 0 1 :192(391) [0635] **How** would I appear before all the world in any other
L C : 0 1 :197(392) [0637] Everybody would see **how** the monks mock and mislead
L C : 0 1 :206(393) [0639] let us carefully note, first, **how** highly God honors and
L C : 0 1 :213(394) [0641] From this you see **how** the papal rabble, priests, monks,
L C : 0 1 :225(395) [0643] common people so that we may see **how** honest we are.
L C : 0 1 :243(397) [0649] **How** many people scrape and scratch day and night and
L C : 0 1 :246(398) [0651] But beware **how** you deal with the poor, of whom there
L C : 0 1 :284(403) [0661] so that everyone may know **how** to guard against it.
L C : 0 1 :298(405) [0665] We know **how** to put up a fine front to conceal our
L C : 0 1 :304(406) [0667] enough to imagine **how** much he can acquire by such
L C : 0 1 :310(407) [0669] accuses us and shows just **how** upright we really are in
L C : 0 1 :311(407) [0671] pleasing to God, no matter **how** great or precious it may
L C : 0 1 :312(407) [0671] Let us see, now, **how** our great saints can boast of their
L C : 0 1 :319(408) [0673] in order to show **how** much effort God requires us to
L C : 0 1 :319(408) [0673] us to devote to learning **how** to teach and practice the Ten
L C : 0 1 :322(409) [0673] he himself here declares **how** important the
L C : 0 1 :322(409) [0673] are to him and **how** strictly he will watch over them,
L C : 0 1 :322(409) [0673] and again, **how** richly he will reward, bless, and bestow
L C : 0 1 :329(410) [0677] Thus you see **how** the First Commandment is the chief
L C : 0 1 :333(410) [0677] it is obvious once again **how** highly these Ten
L C : 0 2 :002(411) [0679] we may know where and **how** to obtain strength for this
L C : 0 2 :010(412) [0679] **How** can we praise or portray or describe him in such a
L C : 0 2 :020(412) [0681] were to describe in detail **how** few people believe this
L C : 0 2 :024(413) [0683] For here we see **how** the Father has given himself to us,
L C : 0 2 :026(413) [0685] mentioned above — that is, **how** he has completely given
L C : 0 2 :026(413) [0685] of the article; from it we shall learn **how** we are redeemed.
L C : 0 2 :031(414) [0685] to clarify and express **how** and by what means this
L C : 0 2 :031(414) [0685] accomplished — that is, **how** much it cost Christ and what
L C : 0 2 :037(415) [0687] **How** does this sanctifying take place?
L C : 0 2 :041(416) [0689] **How** does he do this?
L C : 0 3 :001(420) [0697] Now follows the third part, **how** we are to pray.
L C : 0 3 :003(420) [0697] we may know what and **how** to pray, our Lord Christ
L C : 0 3 :022(423) [0703] Thus we see **how** sincerely he is concerned over our
L C : 0 3 :026(424) [0705] not need to be taught **how** to prepare for it or how to
L C : 0 3 :026(424) [0705] taught how to prepare for it or **how** to generate devotion.
L C : 0 3 :039(425) [0709] **How** does it become holy among us?
L C : 0 3 :058(428) [0713] For **how** could God allow us to suffer want in temporal
L C : 0 3 :062(428) [0715] It is unbelievable **how** the devil opposes and obstructs
L C : 0 3 :069(429) [0717] let them plot and plan **how** to suppress and exterminate
L C : 0 3 :070(429) [0717] come to naught, no matter **how** proud, secure, and
L C : 0 3 :076(431) [0719] Let us outline very briefly **how** comprehensively this
L C : 0 3 :082(431) [0721] God wishes to show us **how** he cares for us in all our
L C : 0 3 :084(431) [0721] **How** much trouble there now is in the world simply on
L C : 0 3 :117(436) [0731] Thus you see **how** God wants us to pray to him for
L C : 0 4 :002(436) [0733] **How** it is to be maintained and defended against heretics
L C : 0 4 :008(437) [0733] But no matter **how** external it may be, here stand God's
L C : 0 4 :012(438) [0735] all the monks, no matter **how** precious and dazzling they
L C : 0 4 :014(438) [0735] Now you can understand **how** to answer properly the
L C : 0 4 :015(438) [0735] well, and then babble, "**How** can a handful of water help
L C : 0 4 :016(438) [0735] But **how** dare you tamper thus with God's ordinance and
L C : 0 4 :020(439) [0737] his head, which shows me **how** and why I should honor
L C : 0 4 :023(439) [0737] know what Baptism is and **how** it is to be regarded, we

Continued ▶

L C : 0 4 :026(439) [0739] Here you see again **how** precious and important a thing
L C : 0 4 :043(442) [0743] Just think **how** the world would snow and rain money
L C : 0 4 :055(443) [0747] **How** dare we think that God's Word and ordinance
L C : 0 5 :006(447) [0755] and ordered them, regardless of **how** we treat them.
L C : 0 5 :012(448) [0755] rush forward and say, '**How** can bread and wine be
L C : 0 5 :028(449) [0759] bellowing and blustering, "**How** can bread and wine
L C : 0 5 :031(450) [0759] **How** should we know that this has been accomplished
L C : 0 5 :031(450) [0759] know of forgiveness, and **how** can they grasp and
L C : 0 5 :057(453) [0767] choose to fix your eye on **how** good and pure you are, to
L C : 0 5 :062(454) [0767] be thy disciple, no matter **how** insignificant my
L C : 0 5 :082(456) [0773] If you could see **how** many daggers, spears, and arrows
L C : 0 5 :084(456) [0773] **How** quickly can he bring you into misery and distress
L C : 0 6 :003(457) [0000] what confession is and **how** useful and comforting it is.
L C : 0 6 :004(457) [0000] the advantage of knowing **how** to use confession
L C : 0 6 :018(459) [0000] dare not come and say **how** good or how wicked you are.
L C : 0 6 :018(459) [0000] dare not come and say how good or **how** wicked you are.
L C : 0 6 :024(460) [0000] **How** else would the beggar go but with repugnance, not
L C : 0 6 :024(460) [0000] just letting everyone see **how** poor and miserable his is?
L C : 0 6 :026(460) [0000] men should look to see **how** full of filthiness you are,
E P : R N :008(465) [0779] of the faith, setting forth **how** at various times the Holy
E P : R N :008(465) [0779] controverted articles, and **how** contrary teachings were
E P : 0 4 :018(477) [0801] works, and to remind them **how** necessary it is that they
E P : 0 5 :008(479) [0803] heaven" over all sinners and men learn **how** fierce it is.
E P : 0 7 :019(484) [0813] believer, no matter **how** weak he may be, as long as he
E P : 0 8 :002(487) [0817] share with each other, and **how** far does this sharing
E P : 0 8 :011(488) [0821] For **how** could the man, Mary's son, truly be called or be
E P : 0 8 :036(491) [0825] certain limitations as to **how** much he is supposed to
E P : 0 9 :001(492) [0827] raised were: When and **how**, according to our simple
E P : 0 9 :004(492) [0827] **How** this took place is something that we should postpone
S D : P R :010(503) [0849] about the truth may know **how** to guard and protect
S D : R N :010(503) [0849] and Norm, Indicating **How** All Doctrines Should Be
S D : 0 1 :062(519) [0879] impressed on everyone **how** abominable and dreadful this
S D : 0 2 :030(527) [0893] This being the case, **how** can man by his own powers turn
S D : 0 2 :041(529) [0897] answers the question, "**How** does the kingdom of God
S D : 0 2 :044(529) [0897] necessity"), indicates **how** he intended his statements to be
S D : 0 2 :048(530) [0901] from the Word of God **how** man is converted to God, how
S D : 0 2 :048(530) [0901] man is converted to God, **how** and by what means
S D : 0 2 :048(530) [0901] good in our hearts, and **how** we are to relate ourselves to
S D : 0 2 :056(532) [0903] on the basis of our feeling, **how** and when we perceive it
S D : 0 2 :058(532) [0903] be lost, as it is written, "**How** often would I have gathered
S D : 0 2 :062(533) [0905] is discussing the question **how** God operates in man, it is
S D : 0 2 :071(535) [0909] acquires these things, and **how** he comes by them), our
S D : 0 2 :072(535) [0909] all this, reminds us also **how** he preserves, strengthens,
S D : 0 3 :007(540) [0917] zeal in order to indicate **how** very important it is that this
S D : 0 3 :029(544) [0925] good works and love, but **how** a person may be justified
S D : 0 3 :042(547) [0931] the question is asked, **how** a Christian can identify, either
S D : 0 3 :058(550) [0937] at the person of Christ, **how** this person was placed under
S D : 0 4 :008(552) [0941] among us as to **how** and why the good works of believers
S D : 0 4 :030(556) [0947] declare well and in detail **how** righteousness and salvation
S D : 0 4 :033(556) [0947] example as to when and **how**, on the basis of the
S D : 0 5 :010(560) [0955] heaven over all sinners and shows **how** great this wrath is.
S D : 0 5 :010(560) [0955] see the law spiritually, or **how** much it requires of us, or
S D : 0 5 :010(560) [0955] much it requires of us, or **how** severely it curses and
S D : 0 5 :012(560) [0955] wrath of God, no matter **how** or when it happens, is the
S D : 0 5 :017(561) [0957] will of God, shows **how** man ought to be disposed in his
S D : 0 5 :023(562) [0959] themselves not only **how** man in the beginning was
S D : 0 6 :022(567) [0969] It does not teach us **how** and why the good works of
S D : 0 7 :013(571) [0977] "We have heard **how** Master Martin Bucer has explained
S D : 0 7 :022(573) [0979] come along and ask, **How** can bread and wine be the body
S D : 0 7 :043(576) [0987] knows very well what and **how** he must speak, and he is
S D : 0 7 :045(577) [0987] these words, no matter **how** appealing our reason may
S D : 0 7 :047(578) [0989] doubts or arguments as to **how** it is to be reconciled with
S D : 0 7 :047(578) [0989] is to be reconciled with our reason or **how** it is possible.
S D : 0 7 :067(581) [0997] From these it is evident **how** unjustly and poisonously the
S D : 0 7 :101(587) [1007] or comprehend him, **how** much more marvelously will he
S D : 0 7 :102(587) [1007] But who can explain or even conceive **how** this occurs?
S D : 0 7 :102(587) [1007] But **how** this happens, we do not know; it transcends
S D : 0 7 :102(587) [1007] his words until we know **how** to prove certainly that the
S D : 0 7 :103(587) [1009] **How** will they establish that kind of speculation?
S D : 0 7 :106(588) [1009] no matter **how** appealing and attractive they may appear
S D : 0 7 :113(589) [1011] views, no matter **how** manifold and various they may be.
S D : 0 8 :025(596) [1023] to his good pleasure, when and **how** he wanted to.
S D : 0 9 :003(610) [1051] exalted and acute speculations about **how** this occurred.
S D : 0 9 :003(610) [1051] than the preceding one, **how** Christ has been made to sit
S D : 1 0 :009(612) [1055] Paul instructs us **how** we can with a good conscience give
S D : 1 0 :024(615) [1061] the church of God on **how** we are to treat ceremonies in
S D : 1 1 :006(617) [1065] which he does not will — **how** far it is to go, how long it is
S D : 1 1 :006(617) [1065] will — how far it is to go, **how** long it is to endure, and
S D : 1 1 :006(617) [1065] to endure, and when and **how** he will interfere with it and
S D : 1 1 :009(618) [1065] God has foreseen who and **how** many are to be saved,
S D : 1 1 :009(618) [1065] are to be saved, who and **how** many are to be damned, or
S D : 1 1 :025(620) [1071] book of life" will be saved, **how** can and should one
S D : 1 1 :031(621) [1073] when they "do not know **how** to pray as we ought," he
S D : 1 1 :033(622) [1075] chapters will show you **how** comforting God's
S D : 1 1 :041(623) [1077] the Word, as Christ says, "**How** often would I have
S D : 1 1 :045(624) [1079] "according to his purpose" **how** he would bring me
S D : 1 1 :051(625) [1079] ears to hear, let him hear"; and "Take heed **how** ye hear."
S D : 1 1 :055(625) [1081] aware and knows exactly **how** many there will be on
S D : 1 1 :058(625) [1081] a definite limit for us as to **how** far we should go in these
S D : 1 1 :064(626) [1083] the point where he shows **how** much of this mystery God
S D : 1 1 :064(626) [1083] **How** unsearchable are his judgements and how inscrutable
S D : 1 1 :064(626) [1083] are his judgements and **how** inscrutable his ways!
S D : 1 1 :072(628) [1087] then, who are evil, know **how** to give good gifts to your
S D : 1 1 :072(628) [1087] gifts to your children, **how** much more will the heavenly
S D : 1 1 :081(629) [1089] any man to be damned, **how** could he prepare man for

Howl (1), Howling (1)
L C : 0 3 :025(423) [0705] of monks and priests, who **howl** and growl frightfully day
L C : 0 3 :033(424) [0707] the utterly useless **howling** and growling, as Christ

Hoya (1)
P R : P R :027(015) [0025] Otto, count of **Hoya** [-Nienburg] and Burghausen

Hoyer (2)
P R : P R :027(015) [0025] John **Hoyer**, count of Mansfeld [-Artern]
P R : P R :027(015) [0025] **Hoyer** Christopher, count of Mansfeld [-Eisleben]

Huge (1)
A P : 1 5 :027(219) [0323] There are **huge** tomes, even whole libraries, that do not

Hugo (1)
A P : 0 2 :029(104) [0113] **Hugo** teaches the same thing when he says that original sin

Human (429)
P R : P R :021(010) [0019] to the majesty of the **human** nature in the person of
P R : P R :021(011) [0019] is not ascribed to the **human** nature of Christ outside the
P R : P R :021(011) [0019] that the divine and **human** natures, together with their
P R : P R :021(011) [0019] mixed together and the **human** nature according to its
A G : 0 3 :002(029) [0045] two natures, divine and **human**, are so inseparably united
A G : 2 0 :032(045) [0057] the devil, who drives poor **human** beings into many sins.
A G : 2 0 :034(045) [0057] and governs himself by his own **human** strength alone.
A G : 2 0 :036(046) [0057] faith and without Christ **human** nature and human
A G : 2 0 :036(046) [0057] Christ human nature and **human** strength are much too
A G : 2 3 :006(052) [0061] whether or not it lies in **human** power and ability to
A G : 2 3 :006(052) [0061] Majesty, by means of **human** resolutions or vows without
A G : 2 3 :008(052) [0061] cannot be altered by any **human** vows or laws, our priests
A G : 2 3 :015(054) [0063] marriage to aid **human** infirmity and prevent unchastity.
A G : 2 3 :016(054) [0063] and rigor for the sake of **human** weakness and to prevent
A G : 2 3 :024(055) [0065] However, just as no **human** law can alter or abolish a
A G : 2 5 :008(062) [0069] Our wretched **human** nature is so deeply submerged in
A G : 2 6 :005(064) [0071] of Moses and against **human** tradition so that we should
A G : 2 6 :021(067) [0073] be atoned for by observing the said **human** traditions.
A G : 2 6 :044(070) [0075] such disagreement in **human** ordinances is not in conflict
A G : 2 7 :028(075) [0079] chastity lies within **human** power and ability, and there
A G : 2 7 :032(076) [0079] still more years to **human** frailty, for it prohibits the
A G : 2 8 :019(083) [0087] by divine right, but by **human**, imperial right, bestowed
A G : 2 8 :021(084) [0087] this is to be done not by **human** power but by God's
A G : 2 8 :029(085) [0087] and in tithes), they have these by virtue of **human** right.
A G : 2 8 :037(086) [0089] because of this notion **human** ordinances have multiplied
A G : 2 8 :039(087) [0089] those who institute **human** ordinances also act contrary to
A G : 2 8 :045(088) [0089] are used), according to **human** precepts and doctrines?
A G : 2 8 :047(088) [0089] those who urge **human** ordinances on people, "Let them
A G : 2 8 :049(089) [0091] forbid the making and keeping of **human** regulations?
A G : 2 8 :064(092) [0093] to lighten and mitigate **human** regulations, yet there can
A G : 2 8 :075(094) [0095] to mitigate or abrogate **human** regulations which are not
A L : 0 3 :002(029) [0045] two natures, divine and **human**, inseparably conjoined in
A L : 0 7 :003(032) [0047] It is not necessary that **human** traditions or rites and
A L : 1 5 :003(036) [0049] are also admonished that **human** traditions which are
A L : 2 0 :010(042) [0055] God without Christ, by **human** strength, although Christ
A L : 2 0 :014(043) [0055] and the preeminence of **human** works would not be
A L : 2 0 :034(045) [0057] he governs himself by **human** strength alone without faith
A L : 2 0 :036(046) [0057] For without faith **human** nature cannot possibly do the
A L : 2 0 :038(046) [0057] all manner of lusts and **human** devices rule in the heart.
A L : 2 3 :013(053) [0063] to all laws, divine and **human**, and contrary even to the
A L : 2 3 :015(054) [0063] marriage to be a remedy against **human** infirmity.
A L : 2 3 :024(055) [0065] Just as no **human** law can nullify a command of God, so
A L : 2 5 :012(063) [0071] admits that such confession is of **human** right.
A L : 2 6 :001(064) [0071] among foods and similar **human** traditions are works
A L : 2 6 :005(064) [0071] puts aside the law and **human** traditions in order to show
A L : 2 6 :021(067) [0073] for sins by the observance of **human** traditions.
A L : 2 6 :042(070) [0075] Such liberty in **human** terms was not unknown to the
A L : 2 7 :032(076) [0079] a greater concession to **human** weakness, adds a few
A L : 2 8 :019(083) [0087] of the Gospel, but by **human** right granted by kings and
A L : 2 8 :021(084) [0087] doing all this without **human** power, simply by the Word.
A L : 2 8 :029(085) [0087] matrimony, tithes, etc.), bishops have this by **human** right.
A L : 2 8 :045(088) [0089] are used), according to **human** precepts and doctrines?
A L : 2 8 :074(094) [0093] inasmuch as many **human** traditions have been changed
A P : 0 2 :003(101) [0105] definition denies that **human** nature has the gift and
A P : 0 2 :005(101) [0107] vice or corruption in **human** nature, but only the
A P : 0 2 :006(101) [0107] it as a disease since **human** nature is born full of
A P : 0 2 :008(101) [0107] more serious faults of **human** nature, namely, ignoring
A P : 0 2 :008(101) [0107] They even attribute to **human** nature unimpaired power
A P : 0 2 :010(102) [0107] If **human** nature has such powers that by itself it can love
A P : 0 2 :010(102) [0109] for the Holy Spirit if **human** powers by themselves can
A P : 0 2 :011(102) [0109] the minor faults in **human** nature and ignore the major
A P : 0 2 :012(102) [0109] they failed to see the inner uncleanness of **human** nature.
A P : 0 2 :014(102) [0109] are the chief flaws in **human** nature, transgressing as they
A P : 0 2 :031(104) [0113] but an abiding deficiency in an unrenewed **human** nature.
A P : 0 2 :041(105) [0115] refutes the opinion that **human** lust is not a fault but is a
A P : 0 2 :044(106) [0117] feeding a trust in **human** powers and obscuring the
A P : 0 2 :045(106) [0117] of original sin and of **human** weakness, he taught that the
A P : 0 2 :046(106) [0117] There **human** nature is subjected not only to death and
A P : 0 2 :047(106) [0119] **Human** nature is enslaved and held prisoner by the devil,
A P : 0 3 :001(107) [0119] the Word assumed the **human** nature into the unity of his
A P : 0 4 :007(108) [0121] For to some extent **human** reason naturally understands
A P : 0 4 :033(111) [0129] deeds that are excellent and praiseworthy in **human** eyes.
A P : 0 4 :034(112) [0129] the Holy Spirit, the **human** heart either despises the
A P : 0 4 :036(112) [0131] us into eternal death, **human** nature cannot bring itself to
A P : 0 4 :128(125) [0157] Then, too, how can the **human** heart love God while it
A P : 0 4 :134(125) [0159] By the "veil" Paul means **human** opinion about the entire
A P : 0 4 :138(126) [0161] For **human** nature is far too weak to be able by its own
A P : 0 4 :203(135) [0177] saints, he supposes, in **human** fashion, that through these
A P : 0 4 :229(139) [0183] **Human** wisdom looks at the law and seeks righteousness
A P : 0 4 :229(139) [0183] Deceived by **human** wisdom, they did not see the true
A P : 0 4 :230(139) [0183] about love is more plausible; for this is **human** wisdom.
A P : 0 4 :242(141) [0187] He means that in **human** relations it is not peevish,
A P : 0 4 :250(143) [0191] imagine; nor is it a **human** power, but a divine power that
A P : 0 4 :262(145) [0195] amid the terrors of sin, a **human** being must have a very
A P : 0 4 :264(146) [0195] adding to them the **human** theory that forgiveness
A P : 0 4 :265(146) [0197] In **human** eyes, works are very impressive.
A P : 0 4 :265(146) [0197] **Human** reason naturally admires them; because it sees
A P : 0 4 :283(150) [0201] by God, not in **human** traditions like the ablutions in
A P : 0 4 :286(150) [0201] Everywhere they add **human** opinions to what the words
A P : 0 4 :287(150) [0203] is derived either from **human** reason or from the teaching
A P : 0 4 :288(151) [0203] the Israelites sacrificed **human** victims and undertook

Continued ▶

AP : 04 :296(152) [0205] Far away from **human** reason, far away from Moses, we
AP : 04 :297(152) [0205] by the law because **human** nature cannot keep the law of
AP : 04 :301(153) [0205] of God, who visits on **human** nature so many terrible
AP : 04 :302(154) [0205] Christ's glory to **human** works; it leads consciences into
AP : 04 :303(154) [0205] does not come without a great battle in the **human** heart.
AP : 04 :303(154) [0205] thing, for of itself the **human** mind believes no such thing
AP : 04 :312(155) [0207] he is wrathful against us, **human** nature flees his wrath
AP : 04 :345(160) [0217] This can be a great problem to the **human** mind.
AP : 04 :345(160) [0217] In courts of **human** judgment a right or debt is certain,
AP : 04 :393(167) [0225] Scriptures predicted that **human** traditions and the
AP : 04 :400(168) [0227] us since they defend **human** opinions contrary to the
AP : 07 :010(170) [0229] whether they have the same **human** traditions or not.
AP : 07 :027(173) [0237] only what agrees with **human** reason and regard the rest
AP : 07 :030(174) [0237] It is not necessary that **human** traditions or rites and
AP : 07 :031(174) [0237] we say, a similarity of **human** rites, whether universal or
AP : 07 :031(174) [0237] To this quickening **human** traditions, whether universal
AP : 07 :032(174) [0237] Some have thought that **human** traditions are devotions
AP : 07 :034(175) [0239] the observance of **human** traditions is an act of worship
AP : 07 :034(175) [0239] unity of the church that **human** traditions be alike
AP : 07 :034(175) [0239] If **human** traditions are not acts of worship necessary for
AP : 07 :035(175) [0241] are used), according to **human** precepts and doctrines?
AP : 07 :036(175) [0241] It is evident that **human** traditions do not quicken the
AP : 07 :037(175) [0241] the question whether **human** traditions are acts of
AP : 07 :045(177) [0243] that a difference in **human** observances does not harm the
AP : 07 :046(177) [0243] They require uniform **human** ceremonies for the unity of
AP : 07 :046(177) [0243] of Christ's Supper, which is not **human** but divine?
AP : 11 :008(181) [0251] judge that it, like other **human** traditions, is not an act of
AP : 11 :009(182) [0253] deals with sins against **human** traditions, which is the
AP : 12 :011(184) [0255] of sins, most of them against **human** traditions!
AP : 12 :032(186) [0259] God's horrible wrath, for **human** nature cannot bear it
AP : 12 :142(204) [0295] and condemns every aspect of lust in **human** nature.
AP : 12 :143(204) [0297] a set form derived from **human** tradition, such works
AP : 12 :143(204) [0297] such works belong to the **human** traditions of which
AP : 12 :145(205) [0297] second, because they add **human** traditions, whose works
AP : 12 :147(205) [0297] works but works of **human** tradition, which Christ calls
AP : 12 :162(208) [0303] is, the performance of **human** traditions which they say
AP : 12 :165(208) [0303] to the satisfaction and performance of **human** traditions.
AP : 12 :175(210) [0307] Now, if **human** authority can remit satisfactions and
AP : 12 :175(210) [0307] by divine law, for **human** authority cannot abrogate
AP : 13 :014(213) [0311] in the very beginning, at the creation of the **human** race.
AP : 14 :001(214) [0315] although they were created by **human** authority.
AP : 15 :000(215) [0315] [Article XV.] **Human** Traditions in the Church
AP : 15 :001(215) [0315] part, where we say that **human** traditions instituted to
AP : 15 :003(215) [0315] our opponents to defend **human** traditions on other
AP : 15 :003(215) [0315] of sins by the observance of **human** traditions.
AP : 15 :007(216) [0317] merit the forgiveness of sins by these **human** observances.
AP : 15 :018(217) [0319] the notion that these **human** rites merit justification,
AP : 15 :018(217) [0319] of God, devised by **human** authority in opposition to
AP : 15 :018(217) [0319] of Antichrist if it maintains that **human** rites justify.
AP : 15 :019(217) [0319] that the invention of **human** rites will be the very form
AP : 15 :020(218) [0321] for Christ's sake, not for the sake of these **human** rites.
AP : 15 :020(218) [0321] They observed these **human** rites because they were
AP : 15 :021(218) [0321] innumerable similar observances in the **human** traditions.
AP : 15 :022(218) [0321] But because **human** reason does not understand the
AP : 15 :024(218) [0321] This is how **human** reason interprets fasting and bodily
AP : 15 :029(219) [0323] and righteousness in **human** rites, let us therefore arm
AP : 15 :030(219) [0323] perfectly clear that he is talking about **human** traditions.
AP : 15 :042(221) [0327] preach, they talk about **human** traditions, the worship of
AP : 15 :050(222) [0329] us for teaching that **human** traditions do not merit the
AP : 18 :004(225) [0335] We are not denying freedom to the **human** will.
AP : 18 :004(225) [0335] The **human** will has freedom to choose among the works
AP : 18 :004(225) [0335] Since **human** nature still has reason and judgment about
AP : 18 :006(225) [0335] Without the Holy Spirit **human** hearts have neither the
AP : 18 :007(226) [0337] the first table, which the **human** heart cannot perform
AP : 18 :009(226) [0337] the difference between **human** righteousness and spiritual
AP : 21 :041(235) [0355] saw that he was freeing **human** minds from the
AP : 22 :001(236) [0357] authority and not by **human** authority, as we suppose our
AP : 22 :009(237) [0359] as possible, this is a **human** device and its purpose is quite
AP : 23 :008(240) [0367] Just as **human** regulations cannot change the nature of
AP : 23 :008(240) [0367] so neither vows nor **human** regulations can change the
AP : 23 :009(241) [0367] has built into nature, and **human** regulations cannot
AP : 23 :015(241) [0367] should marry — as though priests were not **human** beings.
AP : 23 :015(241) [0367] that whatever applies to **human** nature in general, applies
AP : 23 :016(241) [0369] Because **human** authority, regulations, and vows cannot
AP : 23 :054(246) [0379] Sodom and Gomorrah reveal God's wrath at **human** vice.
AP : 23 :056(247) [0379] though it is obviously a matter of simple **human** right.
AP : 24 :023(253) [0391] they offered up **human** sacrifices, perhaps because they
AP : 24 :023(253) [0391] they had heard that a **human** victim was going to placate
AP : 24 :023(253) [0391] was going to placate God for the whole **human** race.
AP : 24 :026(254) [0391] of cattle but also with **human** works offered *ex opere*
AP : 24 :043(257) [0399] the worship of saints, **human** satisfactions, and human
AP : 24 :043(257) [0399] human satisfactions, and **human** traditions with the claim
AP : 27 :008(269) [0421] a moderate opinion of **human** and "factitious" services, as
AP : 27 :014(271) [0423] more to give this credit to **human** traditions, as he clearly
AP : 27 :020(272) [0427] It is madness to put a **human** tradition, which has neither
AP : 27 :026(273) [0429] These are **human** traditions, about all of which it has been
AP : 27 :027(273) [0429] evangelical perfection is to be found in **human** traditions.
AP : 27 :033(275) [0431] observances, mere **human** traditions, deserve the credit
AP : 27 :035(275) [0431] penance, and **human** traditions, it is quite clear that
AP : 27 :039(276) [0433] ascribing perfection to **human** traditions if they say that
AP : 27 :047(277) [0437] is therefore merely a **human** tradition, it is a useless
AP : 28 :007(282) [0445] keep the teaching that **human** traditions are useless acts
AP : 28 :016(283) [0449] from the idea that **human** rites are necessary acts of
AP : 28 :019(284) [0449] his voice, His Word to be heard, not **human** traditions.
AP : 28 :021(284) [0449] are wicked things: that **human** traditions are the worship
S2 : 02 :002(293) [0463] "1. After all, they are a purely **human** invention.
S2 : 02 :002(293) [0463] And we can discard all **human** inventions, for Christ
S2 : 02 :007(293) [0463] be nothing else than a **human** work, even a work of evil
S2 : 02 :008(294) [0465] because he follows a false **human** opinion and
S2 : 02 :013(295) [0467] Now, this is nothing but a **human** opinion of certain
S2 : 02 :014(295) [0467] papists make use of such **human** opinions to make men
S2 : 02 :021(296) [0469] Not only is this mere **human** trumpery, utterly
S2 : 03 :002(298) [0471] Besides, like other **human** inventions, all this is without
S2 : 04 :001(298) [0471] voluntarily or through a **human** institution (that is, a
S2 : 04 :005(299) [0473] often) the papacy is a **human** invention, and it is not
S2 : 04 :014(301) [0475] monastic life, and **human** works and services (which are
S3 : 03 :001(303) [0479] to God, for no **human** being will be justified in his sight."
S3 : 03 :027(308) [0487] once again directed attention to uncertain **human** works.
S3 : 15 :000(316) [0501] XV. **Human** Traditions
S3 : 15 :001(316) [0501] of the papists that **human** traditions effect forgiveness or
S3 : 15 :005(316) [0501] which he possesses by **human** right, making this
TR : 00 :012(322) [0507] of a council and is of **human** right, for if the bishop of
TR : 00 :048(328) [0519] merit from Christ to **human** traditions and have utterly
TR : 00 :063(331) [0523] bishop and presbyter (or pastor) is by **human** authority.
TR : 00 :067(331) [0523] to the church, and no **human** authority can take it away
TR : 00 :077(333) [0527] too, the bishops have by **human** right only, and they have
SC : PR :005(338) [0533] on the observance of **human** laws, yet you do not take the
SC : 09 :005(355) [0561] the Lord's sake to every **human** institution, whether it be
LC : 01 :180(389) [0631] yet their right to take **human** life is not abrogated.
LC : 01 :188(390) [0635] who desires and does you good is not **human** but devilish.
LC : 01 :198(392) [0637] In contrast to them all **human** holiness is only stench and
LC : 01 :264(400) [0655] It is a common vice of **human** nature that everyone would
LC : 01 :317(408) [0673] for they are beyond **human** power to fulfill.
LC : 02 :002(411) [0679] so high a plane that all **human** ability is far too feeble and
LC : 02 :067(420) [0697] No **human** wisdom can comprehend the Creed; it must be
LC : 03 :010(421) [0699] Indeed, the **human** heart is by nature so desperately
LC : 03 :055(427) [0713] be far too great for any **human** heart to dare to desire if
LC : 04 :006(437) [0733] boast that Baptism is no **human** plaything but is instituted
LC : 04 :038(441) [0741] mother," refers only to **human** flesh and blood, yet we
LC : 05 :007(447) [0755] contrary to the Word of God, as **human** performances.
LC : 05 :023(449) [0757] are first born anew, our **human** flesh and blood have not
EP : 01 :003(466) [0779] between our corrupted **human** nature and original sin
EP : 01 :005(466) [0781] of his person this same **human** nature, though without
EP : 01 :008(467) [0781] not a slight corruption of **human** nature, but that it is so
EP : 01 :012(467) [0781] essential properties of **human** nature, or the teaching that
EP : 01 :016(468) [0783] 6. Furthermore, that the **human** nature and essence in
EP : 01 :017(468) [0783] into and mingled with **human** nature, as when poison and
EP : 01 :020(468) [0783] sin, which inheres in **human** nature, and the other
EP : 01 :022(469) [0785] as when we say, "God has created **human** nature."
EP : 03 :001(472) [0791] in him the divine and **human** natures are personally
EP : 03 :002(473) [0793] before God only according to the **human** nature.
EP : 03 :003(473) [0793] nature alone nor according to the **human** nature alone.
EP : 03 :014(474) [0795] righteousness only according to the **human** nature, etc.
EP : 06 :004(480) [0807] way lest in their merely **human** devotion they undertake
EP : 07 :012(483) [0811] of God according to his **human** nature, rules presently
EP : 07 :012(483) [0811] No other **human** being, no angel, but only Mary's Son, is
EP : 07 :033(485) [0815] properties of his assumed **human** nature could neither
EP : 07 :042(486) [0817] we cannot comprehend with our **human** sense or reason.
EP : 08 :002(487) [0817] Christ, do the divine and **human** natures, together with
EP : 08 :003(487) [0817] in Christ the divine and **human** natures are personally
EP : 08 :005(487) [0819] That the divine and the **human** natures are personally
EP : 08 :006(487) [0819] that the divine and the **human** nature are not fused into
EP : 08 :007(487) [0819] etc., which never become properties of the **human** nature.
EP : 08 :008(487) [0819] 4. The attributes of the **human** nature are to be a
EP : 08 :009(488) [0819] there flows everything **human** that is said or believed
EP : 08 :010(488) [0819] the case if the divine and **human** natures did not have a
EP : 08 :013(488) [0821] of God, but a man whose **human** nature has such a
EP : 08 :014(488) [0821] to the property of the **human** nature which he assumed
EP : 08 :015(488) [0821] of man according to his **human** nature is really (that is, in
EP : 08 :015(488) [0821] mother's womb and his **human** nature was personally
EP : 08 :016(489) [0821] form of a slave (not the **human** nature) and was
EP : 08 :017(489) [0823] *mode or property of the **human** nature* but *according to*
EP : 08 :018(489) [0823] we deny or abolish the **human** nature in the person of
EP : 08 :021(490) [0823] 2. That the divine and **human** natures are mingled into
EP : 08 :021(490) [0823] one essence and that the **human** nature has been changed
EP : 08 :023(490) [0823] Christ did not have a true **human** nature with a body and
EP : 08 :027(490) [0823] 8. That Christ's **human** nature has become an infinite
EP : 08 :027(490) [0825] and communicated to and infused into the **human** nature.
EP : 08 :028(490) [0825] 9. That the **human** nature has been raised to the level of,
EP : 08 :029(490) [0825] 10. That the **human** nature of Christ is locally extended to
EP : 08 :030(490) [0825] of the property of the **human** nature it is impossible for
EP : 08 :031(491) [0825] no communion with the **human** nature in fact, as though
EP : 08 :032(491) [0825] not at all concern his **human** nature; and that after Christ
EP : 08 :032(491) [0825] anything to do with us according to his **human** nature.
EP : 08 :033(491) [0825] of God who assumed the **human** nature, after he laid
EP : 08 :033(491) [0825] in, through, and with his **human** nature, but only a few
EP : 08 :033(491) [0825] at the place where the **human** nature is locally present.
EP : 08 :034(491) [0825] Christ, according to the **human** nature, is wholly
EP : 08 :035(491) [0825] 16. That according to his **human** nature Christ has indeed
EP : 08 :035(491) [0825] the exaltation the **human** nature of Christ received a
EP : 08 :036(491) [0825] 17. That according to his **human** spirit Christ has certain
EP : 08 :038(491) [0825] 19. That according to his **human** spirit Christ cannot
EP : 10 :009(494) [0831] 1. That **human** precepts and institutions in the church are
SD : PR :001(501) [0847] hideously obscured by **human** doctrines and ordinances
SD : PR :009(505) [0855] all doctrine, and that no **human** being's writings dare be
SD : 01 :003(509) [0861] from the devil's work, the corruption of **human** nature.
SD : 01 :006(509) [0861] of course impossible for **human** nature in this life —
SD : 01 :006(509) [0861] and entirely poisoned and corrupted **human** nature.
SD : 01 :010(510) [0863] sin denies to unrenewed **human** nature the gifts and the
SD : 01 :011(510) [0863] 3. That original sin in **human** nature is not only a total
SD : 01 :013(511) [0863] of the devil, so that **human** nature is subject to the devil's
SD : 01 :020(511) [0865] That **human** nature even after the Fall is incorrupt and,
SD : 01 :021(512) [0865] accidental elements in **human** nature, in spite of which
SD : 01 :021(512) [0865] which and beneath which **human** nature has and retains
SD : 01 :023(512) [0865] corrupted,"but that **human** nature has of and from man's
SD : 01 :024(512) [0865] which are subject to **human** reason in the next article.
SD : 01 :026(512) [0867] That now, since the Fall, **human** nature is initially created
SD : 01 :027(513) [0867] perverted and corrupted **human** nature (as was indicated
SD : 01 :028(513) [0867] For since the Fall **human** nature is not at first created
SD : 01 :029(513) [0867] are original sin and the **human** nature that has been
SD : 01 :030(513) [0867] whole nature of every **human** being born in the natural
SD : 01 :030(513) [0867] This does not mean that **human** nature has been totally
SD : 01 :032(513) [0869] not because we are **human** beings created by God but
SD : 01 :034(514) [0869] only that God created **human** nature before the Fall, but
SD : 01 :034(514) [0869] also that after the Fall **human** nature is God's creature
SD : 01 :039(515) [0871] and fashions our present **human** nature, which is so

Continued ▶

SD : 01 :043(516) [0873] according to his assumed **human** nature Christ is of one
SD : 01 :043(516) [0873] his brethren, because the **human** nature which he assumed
SD : 01 :044(516) [0873] that even after the Fall **human** nature and original sin are
SD : 01 :060(519) [0879] no sophist, indeed, no **human** reason, be it ever so keen,
SD : 01 :060(519) [0879] and such a corruption of **human** nature that nothing pure
SD : 01 :062(519) [0879] did not simply sully **human** nature but corrupted it so
SD : 02 :000(519) [0881] II. Free Will or **Human** Powers
SD : 02 :019(524) [0889] than yields in any way to **human** touch, or to an unhewn
SD : 02 :022(525) [0889] fallen, and corrupted **human** nature should again become
SD : 02 :022(525) [0889] or capability — our **human** nature is in recalcitrant enmity
SD : 02 :025(526) [0891] in no way to the **human** powers of the natural free will,
SD : 02 :029(527) [0893] the article states that "**human** reason and power without
SD : 02 :030(527) [0893] the freedom of the **human** will in spiritual matters.
SD : 02 :045(530) [0899] with it, and that thus the **human** will cooperates in
SD : 02 :050(531) [0901] for himself out of the **human** race and works in the hearts
SD : 03 :003(539) [0917] is our righteousness only according to his **human** nature.
SD : 03 :004(540) [0917] alone or according to the **human** nature alone but
SD : 03 :007(540) [0917] is, the terms by which all **human** works are excluded, such
SD : 03 :055(549) [0935] our own and all other **human** merits, works, virtues, and
SD : 03 :055(549) [0935] nature nor upon his **human** nature but upon the entire
SD : 03 :056(549) [0935] been born and had in his **human** nature alone fulfilled all
SD : 03 :056(549) [0935] and passion of the **human** nature could not be reckoned
SD : 03 :056(549) [0935] nor the passion of the **human** nature alone, without the
SD : 03 :057(549) [0935] and reconciliation of the **human** race, since it satisfied the
SD : 03 :058(550) [0937] neither the divine nor the **human** nature of Christ by
SD : 03 :061(550) [0937] is our righteousness only according to his **human** nature.
SD : 04 :007(552) [0941] or that are based on **human** traditions; that truly good
SD : 07 :036(575) [0985] transformed into the **human** nature but that both
SD : 07 :045(577) [0987] permit any objection or **human** contradiction, spun out
SD : 07 :045(577) [0987] spun out of **human** reason, to turn us away from these
SD : 07 :076(583) [0999] No **human** being, but only Christ himself who was
SD : 07 :091(585) [1003] natural properties of the **human** body, concerning the
SD : 07 :092(586) [1005] not permit any clever **human** opinions, no matter what
SD : 07 :119(590) [1013] can or wills to be with us on earth with his **human** nature.
SD : 07 :120(590) [1013] properties of his assumed **human** nature neither permit
SD : 08 :002(591) [1015] not be a true and genuine **human** body if it were present
SD : 08 :004(592) [1017] is to be attributed to the **human** nature in the person of
SD : 08 :006(592) [1017] fully come, he took the **human** nature into the unity of
SD : 08 :007(592) [1017] from all eternity, and the **human**, which was assumed in
SD : 08 :009(593) [1019] become the essential properties of the **human** nature.
SD : 08 :010(593) [1019] are properties of the **human** nature, which never will
SD : 08 :011(593) [1019] divine and the assumed **human** nature, so that after the
SD : 08 :011(593) [1019] but also his assumed **human** nature belong to the total
SD : 08 :012(593) [1019] confess that the assumed **human** nature in Christ not only
SD : 08 :013(594) [1019] and when the divine and **human** nature were personally
SD : 08 :014(594) [1019] the divine and the **human**, are united with each other like
SD : 08 :016(594) [1021] held that the divine and **human** natures are separated and
SD : 08 :017(594) [1021] faith that the divine and **human** natures in the person of
SD : 08 :019(595) [1021] union of the divine and **human** natures in the person of
SD : 08 :019(595) [1021] the divine and the **human** nature in the person of Christ
SD : 08 :020(595) [1021] it is not only the bare **human** nature (whose property it is
SD : 08 :020(595) [1021] according to the assumed **human** nature) and, in the
SD : 08 :023(595) [1023] of the divine and **human** natures in Christ, according to
SD : 08 :023(595) [1023] of Christ according to his **human** nature at the right hand
SD : 08 :024(595) [1023] a mere, ordinary **human** being, but a human being who is
SD : 08 :024(595) [1023] human being, but a **human** being who is truly the Son of
SD : 08 :025(596) [1023] The **human** nature could not have accomplished this if it
SD : 08 :026(596) [1023] Hence also the **human** nature has, after the resurrection
SD : 08 :026(596) [1023] however, laying aside the **human** nature, which he retains
SD : 08 :026(596) [1023] divine majesty according to the assumed **human** nature.
SD : 08 :029(597) [1025] No other **human** being can do this, since no human being
SD : 08 :029(597) [1025] can do this, since no **human** being is united in this
SD : 08 :030(597) [1025] In him the divine and **human** natures are personally
SD : 08 :031(597) [1025] fact that the divine and **human** natures are united with
SD : 08 :038(598) [1027] if, for instance, only the **human** nature had suffered for
SD : 08 :039(598) [1027] trick and substitutes the **human** nature for Christ.
SD : 08 :040(598) [1029] if I believe that only the **human** nature suffered for me,
SD : 08 :043(599) [1029] a divine and the other a **human** person, since Zwingli
SD : 08 :043(599) [1029] the passion only to the **human** nature and completely
SD : 08 :047(600) [1031] either the divine or the **human**, but according to both
SD : 08 :050(600) [1031] As far as the assumed **human** nature in the person of
SD : 08 :050(600) [1031] union with the deity the **human** nature has nothing else
SD : 08 :050(600) [1031] or can be ascribed to the **human** nature in Christ which
SD : 08 :051(600) [1031] mightily that, because the **human** nature in Christ is
SD : 08 :051(601) [1033] of Christ's office, the **human** nature in Christ is employed
SD : 08 :051(601) [1033] and might which the **human** nature has received through
SD : 08 :052(601) [1033] the gifts with which the **human** nature in Christ is
SD : 08 :052(601) [1033] fix the limit of what the **human** nature in Christ could or
SD : 08 :053(601) [1033] according to his assumed **human** nature and of what his
SD : 08 :053(601) [1033] and of what his assumed **human** nature is capable over
SD : 08 :053(601) [1033] it and not argue that the **human** nature in Christ is not
SD : 08 :054(601) [1033] and true that Christ's **human** nature in and by itself
SD : 08 :054(601) [1033] ascribe to the assumed **human** nature in Christ.
SD : 08 :056(601) [1035] nature but also according to the assumed **human** nature.
SD : 08 :057(602) [1035] this in time according to the assumed **human** nature.
SD : 08 :059(602) [1035] points to his assumed **human** nature when it states, "The
SD : 08 :060(602) [1035] all this according to his **human** nature and that it was all
SD : 08 :060(602) [1035] communicated to the assumed **human** nature in Christ.
SD : 08 :061(602) [1035] given to Christ's assumed **human** nature in the same way
SD : 08 :061(602) [1035] according to the assumed **human** nature he is below God.
SD : 08 :062(603) [1037] divine nature into the **human** nature in such a way that
SD : 08 :062(603) [1037] in such a way that the **human** nature in Christ has
SD : 08 :064(603) [1037] of Scripture, that the **human** nature in Christ has received
SD : 08 :064(603) [1037] not as in other godly **human** beings or in the angels, but
SD : 08 :066(604) [1039] *and through* the assumed exalted **human** nature of Christ.
SD : 08 :067(604) [1039] the majesty to which the **human** nature of Christ has been
SD : 08 :067(604) [1039] this majesty is in Christ's **human** nature only in such a
SD : 08 :067(604) [1039] in deed and in truth the **human** nature has no share in the
SD : 08 :069(604) [1039] Christ according to his **human** nature and other holy
SD : 08 :069(604) [1039] of his majesty, which as a **human** being and according to
SD : 08 :069(604) [1039] and according to his **human** nature he has received above
SD : 08 :070(605) [1041] also according to the **human** nature, "All authority in
SD : 08 :071(605) [1041] all its properties into the **human** nature of Christ of such
SD : 08 :071(605) [1041] and essence the **human** nature allegedly received equal
SD : 08 :071(605) [1041] For the **human** nature, like every other creature in heaven
SD : 08 :071(605) [1041] Thereby Christ's **human** nature would be denied and
SD : 08 :072(605) [1041] according to the assumed **human** nature (whence he is
SD : 08 :072(605) [1041] according to his assumed **human** nature (according to the
SD : 08 :074(606) [1041] with all power in, with, and through the **human** nature.
SD : 08 :075(606) [1043] according to his assumed **human** nature many things are
SD : 08 :076(606) [1043] that the divine and **human** natures have with each other
SD : 08 :076(606) [1043] this man and no other **human** being in heaven and on
SD : 08 :077(606) [1043] presence only to Christ, and to no other **human** being.
SD : 08 :078(606) [1043] with this same assumed **human** nature of his, Christ can
SD : 08 :078(607) [1043] both natures, the divine and the **human**, belong is present.
SD : 08 :078(607) [1043] to and with his assumed **human** nature, according to
SD : 08 :080(607) [1045] the majesty of Christ according to the **human** nature.
SD : 08 :084(607) [1045] place as a divine and **human** person, and if at all other
SD : 08 :085(608) [1045] to the second, temporal, **human** birth, the eternal power
SD : 08 :085(608) [1047] me, Jesus of Nazareth, Mary's son, born a **human** being.
SD : 08 :087(608) [1047] in his assumed **human** nature, and who can therefore
SD : 08 :089(609) [1047] of the personal union the **human** nature has allegedly
SD : 08 :090(609) [1047] 2. Likewise, that the **human** nature in Christ is
SD : 08 :091(609) [1049] 3. Likewise, that the **human** nature in Christ has been
SD : 08 :092(609) [1049] or destroying his true **human** nature, Christ's
SD : 08 :093(609) [1049] Likewise, that the mere **human** nature of Christ alone,
SD : 08 :094(609) [1049] not involve his assumed **human** nature in any way
SD : 08 :095(609) [1049] that the assumed **human** nature in Christ does not share
SD : 10 :015(613) [1057] article is weakened and **human** commandments are
SD : 11 :015(619) [1069] That through Christ the **human** race has truly been
SD : 12 :029(635) [1101] according to his assumed **human** nature Christ is a
SD : 12 :037(636) [1103] and essentially separate **human** persons, have the same

Humanity (27)

EP : 08 :003(487) [0819] in common with the **humanity** and that the humanity
EP : 08 :003(487) [0819] humanity and that the **humanity** really has nothing in
EP : 08 :011(488) [0821] most high God, if his **humanity** were not personally and
EP : 08 :025(490) [0823] in common with the **humanity**, nor the humanity with the
EP : 08 :025(490) [0823] with the humanity, nor the **humanity** with the deity.
EP : 08 :031(490) [0825] 12. That only the mere **humanity** suffered for us and
SD : 03 :056(549) [0935] deity alone, without the **humanity**, could not mediate
SD : 08 :011(593) [1019] and that without his **humanity** no less than without his
SD : 08 :013(593) [1019] exalted according to his **humanity**, only after his
SD : 08 :028(596) [1025] according to his **humanity** in deed and in truth without
SD : 08 :039(598) [1027] after all belongs to the **humanity**, or vice versa — for
SD : 08 :041(599) [1029] since the divinity and **humanity** are one person in Christ,
SD : 08 :041(599) [1029] union, all that happens to the **humanity**, and vice versa.
SD : 08 :042(599) [1029] God suffers in the other part (namely, in the **humanity**).
SD : 08 :042(599) [1029] this person, I say, is crucified according to the **humanity**.
SD : 08 :062(603) [1037] in such a way that the **humanity** of Christ has them of
SD : 08 :077(606) [1043] this presence of Christ in no way involves his **humanity**.
SD : 08 :078(606) [1043] according to his **humanity** at the right hand of the
SD : 08 :081(607) [1045] also according to the **humanity** — not, of course,
SD : 08 :084(607) [1045] isolated God and a divine person without the **humanity**.
SD : 08 :084(607) [1045] for me, you must also put the **humanity** down for me.
SD : 08 :084(608) [1045] and never separates the assumed **humanity** from himself."
SD : 08 :085(608) [1045] For the **humanity** of Christ has not, like the deity, existed
SD : 08 :085(608) [1047] that the deity and the **humanity** were united in one person
SD : 08 :085(608) [1047] time according to the **humanity** and concealed it until my
SD : 08 :087(608) [1047] deprive Christ according to his **humanity** of this majesty.
SD : 08 :092(609) [1049] 4. Likewise, that the **humanity** of Christ is locally

Humble (11), Humbled (1)

PR : PR :001(003) [0007] as our most respectful, **humble**, and willing service, and
AL : 27 :050(079) [0083] things and not of celibacy, mendicancy, or **humble** attire.
AP : 04 :192(133) [0175] work done in the most **humble** occupation and in private
S3 : 02 :004(303) [0479] he is terror-stricken and **humbled**, becomes despondent
TR : 00 :082(000) [0529] And in my **humble** opinion I judge that all these agree
SC : 09 :012(356) [0563] 'God opposes the proud, but gives grace to the **humble**.'
SC : 09 :012(356) [0563] **Humble** yourselves therefore under the mighty hand of
LC : 01 :209(393) [0641] estates are, these must **humble** themselves and allow all
LC : 02 :022(413) [0683] this article would **humble** and terrify us all if we believed
LC : 03 :011(421) [0701] himself so that we may **humble** ourselves before him,
LC : 03 :090(432) [0723] God's purpose to break our pride and keep us **humble**.
LC : 03 :090(432) [0723] of God all men must **humble** themselves and be glad that

Humbug (2)

S3 : 10 :001(314) [0497] done without pretense, **humbug**, and unchristian
SD : 10 :019(614) [1059] done without pretense, **humbug**, and un-Christian

Humiliated (1), Humiliation (8), Humility (11)

AG : PR :011(026) [0041] almighty God in deepest **humility** and implore him to
AG : 27 :048(078) [0081] spirituality and sham of poverty, **humility**, and chastity.
AL : 27 :048(078) [0081] and this pretense of poverty, **humility**, and chastity.
AP : 12 :161(208) [0303] of his sin he would be **humiliated** by his son, why did he
AP : 12 :161(208) [0303] especially through **humiliation** his piety might be
AP : 12 :170(209) [0305] in the mouth confession, in the deed complete **humility**."
AP : 16 :013(224) [0333] hypocritical poverty and **humility** far above the state and
S3 : 03 :019(306) [0485] for his sins, for such **humiliation** would surely earn grace
TR : 00 :018(323) [0509] power of riches or the **humility** of poverty that makes a
SC : 09 :012(356) [0563] all of you, with **humility** toward one another, for 'God
LC : 01 :106(379) [0611] love but also deference, **humility**, and modesty, directed
LC : 01 :111(380) [0613] only cheerfully, but with **humility** and reverence, as in
LC : 05 :011(448) [0755] and should accept it with all reverence, fear, and **humility**.
EP : 08 :016(489) [0821] But in the state of his **humiliation** he dispensed with it
EP : 08 :039(491) [0827] though in the state of **humiliation** he had laid it aside and
SD : 07 :047(578) [0989] we are to believe in all **humility** and obedience the
SD : 08 :025(596) [1023] also in the state of his **humiliation** — for example, at the
SD : 08 :026(596) [1025] during the state of his **humiliation** and did not use it at
SD : 08 :051(600) [1033] aside and after the **humiliation**) received, in addition to
SD : 08 :065(604) [1039] During the time of the **humiliation** the divine majesty was

Hundred (16), Hundredfold (2)

AG : 23 :012(052) [0063] It was only four **hundred** years ago that the priests in
AL : 23 :012(052) [0063] and not until four **hundred** years ago were priests in
AP : 21 :002(229) [0343] Jerome conquered Vigilantius eleven **hundred** years ago."

Continued ▶

A P : 2 7 :043(277) [0435] they will receive a **hundredfold** in this life applies here.
S 2 : 0 4 :004(299) [0473] pope for more that five **hundred** years at the least and
S 3 : 0 3 :023(307) [0485] in this way for a **hundred** years, one would still not have
S 3 : 0 3 :024(307) [0485] for seven years in a single case, then for a **hundred**, etc.
S 3 : 0 3 :024(307) [0485] could grant them for a **hundred** years, another for a
S 3 : 0 3 :024(307) [0485] years, another for a **hundred** days, but the pope reserved
L C : P R :012(360) [0571] indeed, be master of more than a **hundred** thousand arts.
L C : 0 1 :129(383) [0619] he would have perished a **hundred** times in his own filth.
L C : 0 1 :148(385) [0623] and a gracious God who will reward you a **hundredfold**.
L C : 0 1 :253(399) [0653] you can enjoy a **hundred** times more than you could
L C : 0 4 :078(446) [0751] immersed in water a **hundred** times, it would nevertheless
L C : 0 5 :012(448) [0755] and declare: "Let a **hundred** thousand devils, with all the
L C : 0 6 :030(460) [0000] glad to run more than a **hundred** miles for confession,
S D : 0 7 :022(573) [0979] God and declare, 'Let a **hundred** thousand devils and all
S D : 0 8 :076(606) [1043] beverage, as the two **hundred** fathers of the Council of

Hungary (1)
A G : P R :018(026) [0041] (His Royal Majesty of **Hungary** and Bohemia, etc.) and

Hunger (11), Hungry (6)
A P : 0 4 :254(143) [0193] Isa. 58:7, 9, "Share your bread with the **hungry**.
A P : 0 4 :259(145) [0193] your bread with the **hungry**," he requires the new life.
A P : 0 4 :370(164) [0221] life"; Matt. 25:35, "I was **hungry** and you gave me food,"
A P : 2 4 :075(263) [0411] comes to me shall not **hunger**, and he who believes in me
L C : P R :006(359) [0569] both pastors and preachers to suffer distress and **hunger**.
L C : P R :020(361) [0573] Only then, **hungry** and thirsty, will they truly relish what
L C : 0 1 :111(380) [0613] them to suffer want or **hunger**, but will place them above
L C : 0 1 :190(391) [0635] If you see anyone suffer **hunger** and do not feed him, you
L C : 0 1 :191(391) [0635] He will say: "I was **hungry** and thirsty and you gave me
L C : 0 1 :191(391) [0635] my followers to die of **hunger**, thirst, and cold, to be torn
L C : 0 5 :041(451) [0763] go unless he feels a **hunger** and thirst impelling him to it.
L C : 0 5 :075(455) [0771] this need or experience **hunger** and thirst for the
L C : 0 5 :084(456) [0773] more sensitive to it and more **hungry** for the sacrament.
L C : 0 6 :032(461) [0000] their conscience, already have the true **hunger** and thirst.
E P : 0 8 :008(487) [0819] place to place, to endure **hunger**, thirst, cold, heat, and
S D : 0 8 :010(593) [1019] to another, to suffer **hunger**, thirst, frost, heat, and
S D : 1 1 :030(621) [1073] them, they nevertheless **hunger** and thirst after

Hunted (3), Hunters (1), Hunting (1)
A P : 2 4 :064(261) [0407] for good business, to **hunters** for good hunting, and
A P : 2 4 :064(261) [0407] to hunters for good **hunting**, and things like that.
L C : 0 1 :046(370) [0593] a poor, despised man, **hunted** down and persecuted, his
L C : 0 3 :105(434) [0727] which we are attacked, **hunted**, and harried on all sides,
L C : 0 6 :032(461) [0000] at the bread just like a **hunted** hart, burning with heat and

Hurries (1)
L C : 0 1 :303(406) [0667] sell it without loss — he **hurries** and worries him until he

Hurt (2)
L C : 0 1 :144(385) [0623] indulgences, to their own **hurt** and with a bad conscience.
L C : 0 1 :246(398) [0651] will not want, and you will **hurt** yourself more than

Hus (1)
L C : 0 4 :050(443) [0745] St. Bernard, Gerson, John **Hus**, and others, and since the

Husband (10), Husbands (6)
A G : 2 6 :010(065) [0071] — for example, that a **husband** should labor to support
A G : 2 7 :019(074) [0079] have his own wife and each woman her own **husband**."
A P : 2 3 :031(243) [0371] says, "The unbelieving **husband** is consecrated through
A P : 2 3 :066(248) [0381] requires impure celibates to become pure **husbands**.
S C : 0 1 :012(343) [0541] each one loving and honoring his wife or her **husband**.
S C : 0 9 :006(355) [0561] **Husbands**
S C : 0 9 :006(355) [0561] "You **husbands**, live considerately with your wives,
S C : 0 9 :006(355) [0561] "**Husbands**, love your wives, and do not be harsh with
S C : 0 9 :007(355) [0563] be submissive to your **husbands**, as Sarah obeyed
L C : 0 1 :205(393) [0639] wants every **husband** or wife guarded and protected from
L C : 0 1 :219(394) [0643] and cherish the wife or **husband** whom God has given.
L C : 0 1 :219(394) [0643] all things essential that **husband** and wife live together in
L C : 0 1 :220(394) [0643] so urgently admonishes **husbands** and wives to love and
L C : 0 1 :255(399) [0653] own body, our wife or **husband**, and our temporal
L C : 0 1 :305(406) [0667] of ways, to make her **husband** displeased with her, or she
L C : 0 1 :305(406) [0667] to live with that her **husband** was obliged to dismiss her

Hymn (3), Hymns (5)
A G : 0 1 :002(056) [0065] in certain places German **hymns** are sung in addition to
A L : 2 4 :002(056) [0065] except that German **hymns** are interspersed here and
A P : 2 4 :003(250) [0385] it, and we insert German **hymns** to give the common
A P : 2 4 :004(250) [0385] Though German **hymns** have varied in frequency, yet
S C : 0 7 :003(352) [0557] After singing a **hymn** (possibly a hymn on the Ten
S C : 0 7 :003(352) [0557] a hymn (possibly a **hymn** on the Ten Commandments) or
L C : S P :025(364) [0579] some Psalms and some **hymns**, based on these subjects, to
S D : 0 1 :023(512) [0865] is not the way the **hymn** which we sing in our churches

Hyperbole (1)
A P : 0 4 :277(148) [0199] shall not say that this is **hyperbole**; but that is how it

Hypocrisy (14), Hypocrisies (1), Hypocrites (24), Hypocritical (7)
A G : 0 8 :001(033) [0047] many false Christians, **hypocrites**, and even open sinners
A L : 0 8 :001(033) [0047] since in this life many **hypocrites** and evil persons are
A P : 0 2 :033(104) [0113] of man is mere **hypocrisy** before God unless we
A P : 0 4 :020(110) [0125] Smug **hypocrites** always believe that they have the merit
A P : 0 4 :021(110) [0127] In smug **hypocrites**, who think that they are keeping the
A P : 0 4 :134(125) [0159] the ceremonial; that is, **hypocrites** think that outward and
A P : 0 4 :137(126) [0161] The results show that **hypocrites** who try to keep the law
A P : 0 4 :275(148) [0199] warns that penitence is **hypocritical** and false if they do
A P : 0 4 :321(157) [0209] Rather, smug **hypocrites** simply believe that their works
A P : 0 4 :371(164) [0221] do not speak of **hypocrisy** but of righteousness in the
A P : 0 4 :374(164) [0223] that a new life and new birth are required, not **hypocrisy**.
A P : 0 7 :003(168) [0227] separate evil men and **hypocrites** from the outward
A P : 0 7 :003(168) [0227] the sacraments which evil men or **hypocrites** administer.
A P : 0 7 :003(169) [0227] that in this life the **hypocrites** and evil men are mingled
A P : 0 7 :012(170) [0231] **Hypocrites** and evil men are indeed associated with the
A P : 0 7 :028(173) [0237] we grant that the many **hypocrites** and evil men who are
A P : 0 7 :047(177) [0243] There we confess that **hypocrites** and evil men have been
A P : 1 2 :010(184) [0255] is full of error and **hypocrisy**; it obscures the blessing of
A P : 1 2 :065(191) [0271] **Hypocrites** therefore must be put to shame, for they trust
A P : 1 2 :108(198) [0283] to be blameless when **hypocrites** judge Thee to be
A P : 1 2 :132(202) [0293] talking about those **hypocritical** satisfactions which the
A P : 1 6 :010(224) [0333] men with this outward **hypocrisy** and blinded them to the
A P : 1 6 :013(224) [0333] theories which put a **hypocritical** poverty and humility far
A P : 2 3 :032(243) [0373] In contrast to the **hypocrisy** of celibacy, what greater
A P : 2 3 :046(246) [0377] that through such **hypocrisy** they are pure and righteous.
A P : 2 7 :004(269) [0421] knows how much **hypocrisy**, ambition, and greed there is
A P : 2 7 :008(269) [0421] of the cruelty which the **hypocrites** among them display.
A P : 2 7 :016(271) [0425] and obedience — **hypocrisies** all, since they are all full of
A P : 2 7 :056(278) [0439] whole monastic life is full of **hypocrisy** and false opinions.
A P : 2 7 :057(279) [0439] a way of life so full of **hypocrisy** and false opinions.
A P : 2 7 :069(281) [0443] they should reject the **hypocrisy** and the sham worship of
S 3 : 0 3 :003(303) [0479] **Hypocrites** and false saints are produced in this way.
S 3 : 0 3 :018(306) [0483] cases like this, such repentance surely was pure **hypocrisy**.
S 3 : 0 3 :027(307) [0487] as we have heard above, are uncertain and **hypocritical**.
S 3 : 0 3 :032(308) [0489] And you **hypocrites** who think you do not need to
S 3 : 0 3 :039(309) [0489] is nothing but deceitful falsehood and **hypocrisy**.
L C : 0 1 :102(379) [0609] pleased than by any work of **hypocrisy**, however brilliant.
L C : 0 1 :197(392) [0637] the world with a false, **hypocritical** show of holiness,
L C : 0 1 :197(392) [0637] and bragged of their **hypocritical** calling and works as
L C : 0 2 :066(419) [0697] or false Christians and **hypocrites**, even though they
L C : 0 3 :006(421) [0699] we reject false and **hypocritical** prayers we teach that
E P : 0 5 :008(479) [0803] either conceited **hypocrites**, like the Pharisees, or they
S D : 0 2 :024(526) [0891] it, as Pharisees and **hypocrites** do, yet he considers it folly
S D : 0 7 :008(570) [0975] blessed bread even by **hypocrites** or counterfeit
S D : 0 7 :060(580) [0993] unworthy and godless **hypocrites**, like Judas and his ilk
S D : 0 7 :088(585) [1003] and unbelieving **hypocrites** do not receive the body of

Hypognosticon (2)
A G : 1 8 :004(039) [0051] here quoted from the third book of his ***Hypognosticon:***
A L : 1 8 :004(039) [0051] In Book III of his ***Hypognosticon*** Augustine said these

Icons (1)
A P : 0 7 :032(174) [0239] as the observance of Easter, the use of **icons**, and the like.

Idea (24), Ideal (1), Ideas (15)
A P : 0 2 :043(106) [0117] the totally foreign **idea** that because of our emotions we
A P : 0 2 :043(106) [0117] Yet these **ideas** appear in the scholastics, who improperly
A P : 0 2 :044(106) [0117] As often happens, these **ideas** did not remain purely
A P : 0 4 :014(109) [0123] If the opponents' **ideas** are correct, this was perfectly
A P : 0 4 :204(135) [0177] We condemn this wicked **idea** about works.
A P : 0 4 :206(135) [0177] This wicked **idea** about works has always clung to the
A P : 0 4 :209(136) [0179] offer up his son with the **idea** that this work was a price
A P : 0 4 :213(136) [0179] maintain these wicked and unscriptural **ideas** about works
A P : 0 4 :391(166) [0225] among them, such as the **idea** that we can love God above
A P : 0 7 :043(177) [0243] were called Audians, from the originator of this **idea**.
A P : 1 2 :068(192) [0271] about the merits of attrition and works and similar **ideas**.
A P : 1 2 :122(200) [0287] the impression that this **idea** has authority in Scripture,
A P : 1 5 :027(219) [0323] are obsessed with the **idea** that such observances are
A P : 1 5 :034(220) [0325] accept traditions with the **idea** that they merit
A P : 1 5 :037(220) [0325] For such an **idea** of traditions is wicked.
A P : 1 6 :004(223) [0331] had broadcast many dangerous **ideas** through the church.
A P : 1 6 :004(223) [0331] These **ideas** seriously obscure the Gospel and the spiritual
A P : 2 1 :031(233) [0351] cannot accept either their **ideas** about venerating the
A P : 2 4 :005(250) [0385] Out with such pharisaic **ideas**!
A P : 2 4 :015(252) [0389] attaching their own **ideas** to it as if it meant whatever they
A P : 2 4 :028(254) [0393] is condemning is an **idea** of sacrifices that did not come
A P : 2 4 :029(255) [0393] 15 also condemns the **idea** of sacrifices *ex opere operato.*
A P : 2 4 :033(256) [0395] propound the pharisaic **idea** of ceremonies *ex opere*
A P : 2 4 :039(257) [0399] With the rejection of the **idea** that ceremonies work *ex*
A P : 2 4 :045(258) [0401] different traditions and **ideas** and could not grasp the sum
A P : 2 4 :060(260) [0405] of faith and the **idea** that the Mass justifies *ex opere*
A P : 2 4 :061(260) [0405] to our opponents' wicked **idea** that the Mass justifies *ex*
A P : 2 4 :068(262) [0407] But this is a secular **idea** that ignores the chief use of
A P : 2 4 :075(263) [0411] twist in support of their **idea** that sacraments work *ex*
A P : 2 4 :091(266) [0415] of guilt and faith to vain **ideas** of satisfactions.
A P : 2 4 :094(267) [0417] support the opponents' **idea** of the transfer *ex opere*
A P : 2 4 :098(268) [0417] A false **idea** about sacrifices clung to the wicked priests in
A P : 2 7 :011(270) [0423] This **idea** is an open insult to the Gospel, which teaches
A P : 2 7 :022(272) [0427] Word who follow these observances without wicked **ideas**.
A P : 2 7 :024(273) [0427] To this they add many other false and wicked **ideas**.
A P : 2 7 :065(280) [0441] of worship and with the **idea** that they merit forgiveness
A P : 2 7 :069(281) [0443] and be sure that such **ideas** as this are plain, damnable
A P : 2 8 :016(283) [0449] free the church from the **idea** that human rites are
S 3 : 0 3 :018(306) [0483] an artificial and imaginary **idea** evolved by man's own
L C : 0 1 :310(407) [0669] though as long as we live here we cannot reach that **ideal**.

Identical (6)
P R : P R :018(009) [0015] Latin copies were afterward found to be **identical** in sense.
S D : 0 1 :033(514) [0869] dwells) are not **identical** with original sin (which dwells in
S D : 0 1 :041(515) [0871] nature were unqualifiedly **identical** with sin itself.
S D : 0 1 :043(516) [0873] — sin alone excepted — **identical** with ours; they also
S D : 0 1 :044(516) [0873] and original sin are not **identical** with but must be
S D : 0 8 :062(603) [1037] natures are henceforth of the same kind or even **identical**.

Identify (3), Identified (5)
A G : 1 3 :001(035) [0049] which people might be **identified** outwardly as Christians,
E P : 0 1 :020(468) [0783] sin," not in order to **identify** without any distinction
E P : 0 7 :001(481) [0807] among the theologians **identified** with the Augsburg
S D : 0 1 :038(514) [0871] man cannot be **identified** unqualifiedly with sin itself, for
S D : 0 1 :045(516) [0873] Sin thus cannot be **identified** with man himself, since God
S D : 0 3 :042(547) [0931] how a Christian can **identify**, either in his own case or in
S D : 0 7 :004(569) [0973] sign whereby one can **identify** Christians, and that
S D : 0 7 :128(591) [1015] easily be discovered and **identified** by name from the

Idiom (1), Idiomatic (1), Idiomatically (3)
L C : 0 2 :047(416) [0691] If it is to be rendered **idiomatically**, we must express it
L C : 0 2 :049(417) [0691] To speak **idiomatically**, we ought to say "a community of
L C : 0 2 :060(418) [0695] **Idiomatically** we would say "resurrection of the body."
L C : 0 3 :036(425) [0707] It is not **idiomatic** German.
L C : 0 3 :046(426) [0709] means the same as in our **idiom** "to praise, extol, and

Idle (23), Idleness (2), Idly (1)
A L : 2 6 :033(069) [0075] that neither plenty nor **idleness** may tempt him to sin, but
A P : 0 4 :020(110) [0125] business is the invention of **idle** men who do not know
A P : 0 4 :037(112) [0131] It is easy enough for **idle** men to make up these dreams
A P : 0 4 :061(115) [0137] that we are speaking of an **idle** historical knowledge, we
A P : 0 4 :064(116) [0139] about a faith that is not an **idle** thought, but frees us from
A P : 0 4 :079(117) [0143] Our **idle** opponents quibble as to whether the forgiveness
A P : 0 4 :099(121) [0151] the apostles speak is not **idle** knowledge, but a thing that
A P : 0 4 :115(123) [0155] This faith is no **idle** knowledge, nor can it exist with
A P : 0 4 :248(142) [0191] faith and condemns the **idle** and smug minds who dream
A P : 0 4 :249(142) [0191] We are not talking about **idle** knowledge, such as even
A P : 0 4 :312(155) [0207] in fact the way they are in **idle** scholastic speculations.
A P : 1 2 :147(205) [0297] Our opponents carry on **idle** speculations about the
A P : 1 5 :047(221) [0327] become complacent and **idle** with the result that we
L C : 0 1 :090(377) [0607] spend a day in rest and **idleness**, too, and so can the
L C : 0 1 :100(379) [0609] For where the heart stands **idle** and the Word is not
L C : 0 1 :101(379) [0609] For these words are not **idle** or dead, but effective and
L C : 0 1 :208(393) [0639] life is no matter for jest or **idle** curiosity, but it is a
E P : 0 1 :021(468) [0783] heart of corrupted man, no **idle** word were spoken, or no
E P : 0 2 :016(472) [0789] or, "Man's will is not **idle** in conversion, but does
E P : 0 2 :017(472) [0791] reborn will of man is not **idle** but cooperates in all the
S D : 0 2 :086(537) [0913] "Man's will is not **idle** in conversion but also does
S D : 0 2 :088(538) [0915] man's reborn will is not **idle** in the daily exercise of
S D : 0 7 :031(574) [0983] this out to be a joke or **idle** talk; I am in dead earnest,
S D : 1 1 :073(628) [1087] in his temple, and is not **idle** in them but urges them to
S D : 1 1 :073(628) [1087] likewise should not be **idle**, still less oppose the urgings of
S D : 1 2 :006(633) [1097] do not propose to look on **idly** or stand by silently while

Idol (9), Idolaters (4), Idolatries (3), Idolatrous (2), Idolatry (26), Idols (1)
A G : 1 8 :007(040) [0053] he wills to kneel before an **idol**, commit murder, etc."
A L : 1 8 :007(040) [0053] as to will to worship an **idol**, will to commit murder," etc.
A P : 0 1 :002(100) [0103] the church of Christ but are **idolaters** and blasphemers.
A P : 1 5 :014(217) [0319] their ordinances, nor defile yourselves with their **idols**.
S 2 : 0 2 :001(293) [0463] precious of the papal **idolatries**, for it is held that this
S 2 : 0 2 :011(294) [0465] a brood of vermin and the poison of manifold **idolatries**.
S 2 : 0 2 :012(295) [0465] apart entirely from the fact that it is error and **idolatry**.
S 2 : 0 2 :019(296) [0467] own merits and (what is worst of all) become **idolaters**.
S 2 : 0 2 :026(297) [0469] This is **idolatry**.
S 2 : 0 2 :028(297) [0469] If such **idolatrous** honor is withdrawn from angels and
S 2 : 0 4 :016(301) [0477] but only to damn, murder, and drive us to **idolatry**.
S 3 : 0 1 :002(302) [0477] as unbelief, false belief, **idolatry**, being without the fear of
S 3 : 0 3 :020(306) [0485] torture, rascality, and **idolatry** which such confession has
T R : 0 0 :038(326) [0515] forms of worship, **idolatry**, and doctrines which conflict
T R : 0 0 :043(328) [0517] The **idolatry** in the profanation of Masses is manifest, for
T R : 0 0 :047(328) [0519] many abuses and what horrible **idolatry** it has produced!
T R : 0 0 :054(329) [0519] power for the support of **idolatry** and countless other
T R : 0 0 :058(330) [0521] that we should flee from **idolatry**, impious doctrines, and
T R : 0 0 :059(330) [0521] defile themselves with **idolatry** and blasphemous
L C : 0 1 :002(365) [0581] and faith of the heart alone make both God and an **idol**.
L C : 0 1 :006(365) [0583] It is the most common **idol** on earth.
L C : 0 1 :017(367) [0585] world practices nothing but false worship and **idolatry**.
L C : 0 1 :020(367) [0585] dreams about God into an **idol** and entrust themselves to
L C : 0 1 :021(367) [0585] So it is with all **idolatry**.
L C : 0 1 :021(367) [0585] **Idolatry** does not consist merely of erecting an image and
L C : 0 1 :022(367) [0585] This is the greatest **idolatry** that has been practiced up to
L C : 0 1 :023(367) [0585] but making God into an **idol** — indeed, an "apple-god" —
L C : 0 1 :028(368) [0587] Then you have an **idol**, another god.
L C : 0 1 :035(369) [0589] rooted out all **idolatry**, and on that account he has
L C : 0 1 :047(371) [0593] allowing none of these good things to be his lord or **idol**.
L C : 0 5 :075(455) [0771] impurity, licentiousness, **idolatry**, sorcery, enmity, strife,
E P : R N :004(465) [0777] the false worship, **idolatry**, and superstition of the papacy
E P : 1 0 :006(493) [0831] sanctioning of public **idolatry**, as well as preventing
S D : P R :001(501) [0847] the popish errors, abuses, and **idolatry** were condemned.
S D : P R :007(505) [0853] the papistic errors and **idolatries**, for having no
S D : 0 3 :033(545) [0927] was first converted from **idolatry** and had no good
S D : 0 4 :032(556) [0947] neither the immoral, nor **idolaters**, nor adulterers will
S D : 0 7 :057(579) [0993] those who were eating **idol**-sacrifices and participating in
S D : 0 7 :085(584) [1001] many kinds of **idolatrous** misuse and perversion of this
S D : 1 0 :010(612) [1055] and confirm their **idolatry** by force or chicanery.
S D : 1 0 :014(613) [1057] superstition, and **idolatry** and to suppress the pure
S D : 1 0 :015(613) [1057] door has been opened to **idolatry**, and ultimately the
S D : 1 0 :016(613) [1057] will support the **idolaters** in their idolatry, and on the
S D : 1 0 :016(613) [1057] the idolaters in their **idolatry**, and on the other hand, it
S D : 1 2 :008(633) [1097] contact with the open **idolatry** and false beliefs of the

Ignoble (1)
S D : 1 1 :082(630) [1089] himself from what is **ignoble**, then he will be a vessel for

Ignominious (2)
S D : 0 3 :022(543) [0923] his birth until his **ignominious** death on the cross for us,
S D : 0 3 :056(549) [0935] even to the most **ignominious** death of the cross, is

Ignorance (14), Ignorant (12), Ignorantly (3)
P R : P R :022(012) [0021] err ingenuously and **ignorantly** of the danger to their
A G : 2 3 :026(056) [0065] into their estates **ignorantly** when they were young.
A G : 2 7 :005(071) [0077] entered monastic life **ignorantly**, for although they were
A L : 2 4 :014(057) [0065] The bishops were not **ignorant** of these abuses.
A L : 2 7 :005(071) [0077] kind of life through **ignorance**, for although they were
A P : 0 2 :014(102) [0109] involves such faults as **ignorance** of God, contempt of
A P : 0 2 :029(104) [0113] says that original sin is **ignorance** in the mind and lust in
A P : 0 2 :029(104) [0113] birth we bring along an **ignorance** of God, unbelief,
A P : 0 2 :029(104) [0113] He includes these things in the term "**ignorance**."
A P : 0 4 :030(111) [0129] (Gal. 5:4); for 'being **ignorant** of the righteousness that
A P : 1 5 :016(217) [0319] because, in their **ignorance** of the righteousness of faith,
A P : 2 1 :040(235) [0355] opinions and that the **ignorance** and negligence of the
A P : 2 3 :049(246) [0377] as lessons for the **ignorant** and not as services that justify.
A P : 2 3 :050(246) [0377] as a pretext to put something over on the **ignorant**.
A P : 2 3 :068(249) [0383] best way to arouse the **ignorant** was to raise the cry of
A P : 2 4 :002(249) [0385] how a hearer who is **ignorant** of the faith of the church
A P : 2 4 :045(258) [0399] a vastly different desolation, **ignorance** of the Gospel.
A P : 2 4 :052(259) [0403] argument for the **ignorant**, especially when the pomp of
A P : 2 4 :063(261) [0405] recent fictions of the **ignorant** monks; they destroy the
A P : 2 7 :004(269) [0421] in the monasteries; how **ignorant** and cruel these illiterate
S 3 : 0 1 :002(302) [0477] blindness — in short, **ignorance** or disregard of God —
S 3 : 0 1 :011(303) [0479] misunderstanding and **ignorance** concerning sin and
S 3 : 0 3 :032(308) [0487] unbelief, blindness, and **ignorance** of God and God's will.
L C : S P :005(362) [0575] old people who were so **ignorant** that they knew nothing
S D : 0 2 :009(521) [0883] nevertheless, it is so **ignorant**, blind, and perverse
S D : 0 2 :010(522) [0883] of God because of the **ignorance** that is in them, due to
S D : 0 2 :015(523) [0887] and passages about our **ignorance** and impotence were
S D : 0 2 :015(523) [0887] us from the darkness of **ignorance** and the bondage of sin
S D : 0 2 :037(528) [0895] devil and were completely **ignorant** of God and Christ.

Ignore (10), Ignored (3), Ignores (1), Ignoring (1)
A G : 2 8 :078(094) [0095] unwilling to do this and **ignore** our petition, let them
A L : 2 7 :009(072) [0077] authority of the canons was utterly **ignored** and despised.
A P : 0 2 :008(101) [0107] human nature, namely, **ignoring** God, despising him,
A P : 0 2 :011(102) [0109] minor faults in human nature and **ignore** the major ones.
A P : 0 4 :340(159) [0215] is to be recognized, but nature is not to be **ignored**."
A P : 2 0 :006(227) [0339] of Christ — we can easily **ignore** the terrors of the world
A P : 2 1 :039(235) [0355] opponents completely **ignore** even the obvious offenses,
A P : 2 1 :042(235) [0355] of our opponents to **ignore** abuses when they required us
A P : 2 4 :068(262) [0409] this is a secular idea that **ignores** the chief use of what
T R : 0 0 :037(326) [0515] of Christ, they are under no circumstances to be **ignored**.
L C : 0 1 :114(380) [0613] They were able to **ignore** it and skip lightly over it, and so
L C : 0 1 :244(398) [0649] But because we **ignore** this and act as if it were none of
L C : 0 4 :015(438) [0735] order to slander Baptism, **ignore** God's Word and
L C : 0 6 :027(460) [0000] But those who **ignore** it and do not come of their own
L C : 0 6 :034(461) [0000] and other people who **ignore** such a treasure and bar

Ilk (1)
S D : 0 7 :060(580) [0993] like Judas and his **ilk** who have no fellowship with

Ill (6), Illness (2), Ills (3)
A L : 2 0 :040(046) [0057] good in deed or thought, Nothing free from taint of **ill**."
A P : 0 2 :041(105) [0115] is a neutral thing, like the color of the skin or **ill** health.
A P : 0 2 :046(106) [0117] death and other physical **ills**, but also to the rule of the
A P : 0 2 :047(106) [0119] death, other physical **ills**, and the tyranny of the devil
A P : 2 4 :076(263) [0411] with the greatness of our **ills**, our sin and our death; and
A P : 2 7 :002(269) [0419] But at last, when he became **ill** either on account of age
A P : 2 7 :002(269) [0419] prison, he sent for the guardian to tell him of his **illness**.
A P : 2 7 :002(269) [0419] omitted all mention of his **illness** and said that he was
S C : 0 5 :020(350) [0553] unfaithful, lazy, **ill**-tempered, or quarrelsome; whether
L C : 0 1 :184(390) [0633] gives vent to his irritation and envy by speaking **ill** of you.
L C : 0 1 :243(397) [0649] every day that no stolen or **ill**-gotten possession thrives.

Illegal (3), Illegally (1)
A P : 2 1 :043(235) [0357] They defend obvious abuses with new and **illegal** cruelty.
A P : 2 2 :002(236) [0357] If it is **illegal** to annul a man's testament, it is much more
A P : 2 2 :002(236) [0357] man's testament, it is much more **illegal** to annul Christ's.
L C : 0 1 :303(406) [0667] not be considered as **illegally** acquired, but rather as

Illegitimate (1)
S D : 0 6 :009(565) [0965] then you are **illegitimate** children and not sons"

Illiterate (1)
A P : 2 7 :004(269) [0421] ignorant and cruel these **illiterate** men are; and how vain

Illuminate (2), Illuminated (5), Illuminates (4), Illumination (6), Illumine (1), Illumined (2), Illumines (4)
A P : 0 4 :002(107) [0121] properly understood, it **illumines** and magnifies the honor
A P : 0 4 :285(150) [0201] faithful consciences and **illumines** the glory of Christ, who
A P : 1 2 :043(187) [0263] and the sacraments, it **illumines** the blessing of Christ,
A P : 1 2 :053(189) [0265] to the patriarchs, then **illumined** by the prophets, and
A P : 1 2 :074(192) [0273] These words of Bernard marvelously **illumine** our case.
A P : 1 3 :013(213) [0311] but only waiting for **illumination**, as the enthusiasts
A P : 1 6 :002(222) [0329] have profitably **illumined** this whole question of the
L C : 0 1 :326(409) [0675] Commandment is to **illuminate** and impart its splendor to
L C : 0 2 :042(416) [0689] that Word, and by it he **illumines** and kindles hearts so
L C : 0 2 :066(419) [0697] besides, they are not **illuminated** and blessed by the gifts
S D : 0 2 :015(523) [0885] for divine instruction, **illumination**, and sanctification.
S D : 0 2 :015(523) [0887] having reborne and **illuminated** us through Baptism and
S D : 0 2 :018(524) [0889] his will unless the Holy Spirit **illuminates** and rules him.
S D : 0 2 :024(525) [0891] But before man is **illuminated**, converted, reborn,
S D : 0 2 :055(532) [0903] preached and heard **illuminates** and converts hearts so
S D : 0 2 :058(532) [0903] Holy Spirit does not **illuminate** him but lets him remain
S D : 0 2 :059(532) [0905] from the death of sin, **illuminates** him, and renews him.
S D : 0 2 :080(536) [0911] draws man to himself, **illuminates**, justifies, and saves
S D : 0 8 :066(604) [1039] are not two powers of **illumination** and combustion — the
S D : 0 8 :066(604) [1039] — the power of **illumination** and combustion is the
S D : 0 8 :066(604) [1039] manifests its power of **illumination** and combustion in
S D : 0 8 :066(604) [1039] iron has the power of **illumination** and combustion
S D : 1 1 :029(621) [1073] so that they may be **illuminated**, converted, and saved.
S D : 1 1 :034(622) [1075] Word are not to be **illuminated** or converted, but are to

Illusion (1), Illusions (1)
S 2 : 0 2 :012(295) [0465] as nothing else than **illusions** of the devil, for purgatory,
S D : 1 0 :005(611) [1053] intended to create the **illusion** (or are demanded or agreed

Illustrate (2), Illustrated (2), Illustrates (1), Illustration (2), Illustrations (1), Illustrious (6)
A P : 2 4 :084(264) [0413] for Paul uses the figure of an altar only for **illustration**.
S 1 : P R :008(290) [0457] Let me **illustrate** this.
T R : 0 0 :082(334) [0529] command of the most **illustrious** princes and of the
T R : 0 0 :082(000) [0529] Augsburg by the Most **Illustrious** Prince, the Elector of
L C : 0 3 :012(422) [0701] Take an **illustration** from the other commandments.
E P : 0 8 :009(488) [0819] ancient Fathers have **illustrated** this union and sharing of
S D : P R :005(504) [0851] faithful ministry of that **illustrious** man of God, Dr.
S D : P R :007(505) [0853] in the name of the **illustrious** and most illustrious
S D : P R :007(505) [0853] the illustrious and most **illustrious** electors, princes, and
S D : P R :011(506) [0855] that the chief and most **illustrious** theologians of that
S D : 0 5 :018(561) [0957] true that the Gospel **illustrates** and explains the law and
S D : 0 7 :100(586) [1007] To use some imperfect **illustrations**, my vision penetrates
S D : 0 8 :018(594) [1021] The Fathers further **illustrated** the personal union and
S D : 0 8 :078(606) [1043] that the cited passages **illustrate** the majesty of the man

Image (9), Images (2)

A P : 0 2 :018(102) [0109] man was created in the **image** of God and after his
A P : 0 2 :019(103) [0111] "That soul is not in the **image** of God in which God is not
A P : 0 2 :020(103) [0111] Paul shows that the **image** of God is the knowledge
A P : 0 2 :022(103) [0111] with which Augustine's interpretation of the **image** agrees.
A P : 2 1 :034(234) [0353] From invocation the next step was to **images**.
L C : 0 1 :021(367) [0585] not consist merely of erecting an **image** and praying to it.
E P : 0 6 :002(480) [0805] their hearts when they were created in the **image** of God.
E P : 0 7 :028(485) [0815] wine are only figures, **images**, and types of the far-distant
S D : 0 1 :010(510) [0863] of paradise or of the **image** of God according to which
S D : 0 1 :011(510) [0863] time it replaces the lost **image** of God in man with a
S D : 1 1 :049(624) [1079] each of his elect to "the **image** of his Son," and that in

Imaginable (1), Imaginary (2), Imagination (7), Imaginations (3), Imagine (60), Imagined (5), Imagines (4), Imagining (3)

P R : P R :024(013) [0023] dubious, disputable **imaginations** and views will be
A G : 2 0 :010(042) [0055] Whoever **imagines** that he can accomplish this by works,
A L : 2 6 :011(065) [0071] others like them, falsely **imagining** that the observances
A P : 0 4 :009(108) [0123] or judgment, he can **imagine** that he wants to love God
A P : 0 4 :017(109) [0125] this disposition, for they **imagine** that the acts of the will
A P : 0 4 :017(109) [0125] They **imagine** that the will can love God, but that this
A P : 0 4 :019(110) [0125] They **imagine** that after that disposition of love a man can
A P : 0 4 :048(113) [0135] Our opponents **imagine** that faith is only historical
A P : 0 4 :063(115) [0139] They **imagine** that the sacraments bestow the Holy Spirit
A P : 0 4 :072(116) [0141] They **imagine** faith is praised so highly because it is this
A P : 0 4 :081(118) [0143] completely buried, they **imagine** that we have access
A P : 0 4 :084(119) [0145] one can devise or **imagine** will refute Paul's argument.
A P : 0 4 :109(123) [0153] to love, because they **imagine** that faith can exist with
A P : 0 4 :165(130) [0169] and mediator, and then **imagine** that he is righteous
A P : 0 4 :224(138) [0181] be a foolish dream to **imagine** that we are justified before
A P : 0 4 :250(143) [0191] thing, as our opponents **imagine**; nor is it a human
A P : 0 4 :290(151) [0203] precedes our love, but it **imagines** that we produce an act
A P : 0 4 :290(151) [0203] Then it **imagines** that this very keeping of the law without
A P : 0 4 :316(156) [0209] They **imagine** that good works, done with the help of a
A P : 1 2 :007(183) [0255] Some of them **imagine** that the power of the keys does
A P : 1 2 :009(184) [0255] they are not so separated as these clever sophists **imagine**.
A P : 1 2 :011(184) [0255] minds still more, they **imagine** that this enumeration is a
A P : 1 2 :013(184) [0257] They **imagine** that eternal punishments are changed into
A P : 1 2 :085(194) [0277] not of the Gospel, to **imagine** that a man is justified by
A P : 1 2 :086(194) [0277] But our opponents **imagine** that we are members of
A P : 1 2 :094(196) [0281] a more horrible blasphemy than this cannot be **imagined**.
A P : 1 2 :118(199) [0287] of guilt, though they **imagine** that they do contribute to
A P : 1 2 :120(200) [0287] they superstitiously **imagined** that satisfactions were valid
A P : 1 2 :129(202) [0291] wise man you can easily **imagine** what will happen if this
A P : 1 2 :132(202) [0293] which the scholastics **imagine** avail as a payment for the
A P : 1 2 :142(204) [0295] Here are men who **imagine** that we can keep the law in
A P : 1 2 :142(204) [0295] These men **imagine** that God's law deals with external,
A P : 1 2 :142(204) [0295] it is foolish of them to **imagine** that we can do even more.
A P : 1 2 :148(205) [0299] or price, as our opponents **imagine** satisfactions to be.
A P : 1 2 :165(208) [0303] but not, as these men **imagine**, by works done in mortal
A P : 1 3 :001(211) [0309] among men, as some **imagine**, but are rather signs and
A P : 1 5 :024(218) [0321] the flesh, reason **imagines** that they are to be rites which
A P : 2 1 :034(234) [0353] power, just as sorcerers **imagine** that horoscopes carved
A P : 2 2 :008(237) [0359] immediately **imagine** that it means our present custom of
A P : 2 3 :005(240) [0365] is their authority; they **imagine** that this is in danger and
A P : 2 3 :045(245) [0375] the Encratites captured the **imagination** of the unwary.
A P : 2 4 :002(249) [0385] Apparently they **imagine** that mere hearing is a beneficial
A P : 2 4 :040(257) [0399] Our opponents **imagine** that it symbolizes the ceremony
A P : 2 4 :057(260) [0405] completely erroneous to **imagine** that the Levitical
A P : 2 4 :068(261) [0407] Some clever people **imagine** that the Lord's Supper was
A P : 2 4 :085(264) [0413] They also **imagine** that "Mass' is derived from *mizbeach*,
A P : 2 7 :024(273) [0427] They **imagine** that they observe both precepts and
A P : 2 7 :045(277) [0435] people because they **imagined** that perfection consists in
A P : 2 7 :055(278) [0439] But now they **imagine** that these ceremonies are the
A P : 2 7 :062(280) [0441] They **imagine** that the works of monasticism are acts of
S 1 : P R :004(289) [0457] **Imagine** what will happen after I am dead!
S 1 : P R :009(290) [0457] **Imagine** how those will face us on the last day, before the
S 2 : 0 2 :008(294) [0465] human opinion and **imagination** without the sanction of
S 3 : 0 2 :003(303) [0479] and presumptuous, **imagining** that they can and do keep
S 3 : 0 3 :018(306) [0483] is an artificial and **imaginary** idea evolved by man's own
S 3 : 0 3 :036(309) [0489] is left that we might **imagine** to be good enough to pay
S 3 : 0 8 :005(312) [0495] and to their own **imaginations**, and he did this through
L C : P R :009(359) [0569] I implore them not to **imagine** that they have learned
L C : P R :016(361) [0573] fellows, therefore, if we **imagine**, after reading or hearing
L C : P R :019(361) [0573] prematurely and to **imagine** that they know everything.
L C : P R :019(361) [0573] Vain **imaginations**, like new cloth, suffer shrinkage!
L C : 0 1 :037(369) [0589] because such blockheads **imagine**, when God refrains from
L C : 0 1 :169(388) [0629] Therefore do not **imagine** that the parental office is a
L C : 0 1 :227(396) [0645] Who can even describe or **imagine** it all?
L C : 0 1 :250(399) [0651] or wrong in any way **imaginable**, whether by damaging,
L C : 0 1 :304(406) [0667] is ingenious enough to **imagine** how much he can acquire
L C : 0 3 :057(427) [0713] **Imagine** a very rich and mighty emperor who bade a poor
L C : 0 4 :006(437) [0733] spun out of any man's **imagination** but revealed and given
E P : 0 1 :021(469) [0785] etc, and "The **imagination** of man's heart is evil from his
E P : 0 2 :003(470) [0787] as it is written, "The **imagination** of man's heart is evil
E P : 0 2 :013(471) [0789] of the Enthusiasts who **imagine** that God draws men to
E P : 0 3 :011(474) [0795] we should not **imagine** a kind of faith in this connection
E P : 0 8 :023(490) [0823] nature with a body and a soul, as Marcion **imagined**.
E P : 0 8 :035(491) [0825] other creatures) and they **imagine** that through the
S D : 0 1 :027(513) [0867] nature, as the Manichaeans **imagined** in their enthusiasm.
S D : 0 2 :007(521) [0883] believe, accept, **imagine**, will, begin, accomplish, do,
S D : 0 2 :017(524) [0887] "The **imagination** of man's heart is evil from his youth"
S D : 0 2 :080(536) [0911] God, the enthusiasts who **imagine** that without means,
S D : 0 2 :081(536) [0911] 7. Likewise those who **imagine** that in conversion and
S D : 0 6 :021(567) [0969] otherwise they can easily **imagine** that their works and life
S D : 0 7 :007(570) [0975] so that nobody will **imagine** that the reality is joined to
S D : 0 7 :032(575) [0983] and changed it according to their own **imagination**."
S D : 0 7 :091(585) [1003] All the **imaginary** reasons and futile counter-arguments
S D : 0 7 :097(586) [1005] as the enthusiasts vainly **imagine**, the one which the
S D : 1 1 :012(618) [1067] must oppose such false **imagining** and thoughts with the

Imitate (7), Imitated (2), Imitates (1), Imitation (2)

A G : 2 1 :001(046) [0057] and godly fashion **imitate** the example of David in
A L : 2 1 :001(046) [0057] to us so that we **imitate** their faith and good works
A P : 0 4 :203(135) [0177] Then he **imitates** them in the delusion that by similar
A P : 0 4 :206(135) [0177] They **imitated** their works but did not keep their faith,
A P : 0 4 :207(135) [0177] of the Old Testament **imitated** these sacrifices with the
A P : 0 4 :208(135) [0177] of the saints call forth **imitation** in those who hope that
A P : 1 5 :024(218) [0321] when men strive to **imitate** them, they copy their outward
A P : 2 1 :006(230) [0345] The third honor is the **imitation**, first of their faith and
A P : 2 1 :006(230) [0345] which each should **imitate** in accordance with his calling.
A P : 2 1 :036(234) [0353] faith and as an incentive to **imitate** them in public affairs.
A P : 2 1 :037(234) [0353] of these fables, which **imitate** the epics and bring only
A P : 2 7 :049(277) [0437] of Abraham to sacrifice his son, are not for us to **imitate**.

Immanent (1)

S D : 0 7 :101(587) [1007] and as near in all creatures as God is **immanent** in them.

Immeasurable (3)

P R : P R :002(003) [0007] almighty God in his **immeasurable** love, grace, and mercy
L C : P R :011(360) [0571] the devil and gives us **immeasurable** strength, comfort,
S D : 0 2 :071(535) [0909] about that God in his **immeasurable** kindness and mercy

Immediate (1), Immediately (20)

A P : 0 4 :184(132) [0173] the law we answer **immediately** that the law cannot be
A P : 0 4 :266(146) [0197] and our opponents **immediately** twist his words to mean
A P : 0 4 :367(163) [0221] our opponents **immediately** apply it not to the other
A P : 0 4 :390(166) [0225] We ought not assume **immediately** that the church of
A P : 1 2 :095(196) [0281] on these works, it **immediately** becomes unsure because
A P : 1 2 :113(199) [0285] people to communion **immediately** was improper.
A P : 2 2 :008(237) [0359] "lay communion" **immediately** imagine that it means our
A P : 2 2 :017(238) [0361] that the church **immediately** approves or accepts
A P : 2 4 :053(259) [0403] Scripture itself adds **immediately** that Christ is the high
A P : 2 7 :062(280) [0441] too, the custom had an **immediate** purpose: since they
S 3 : 0 3 :004(304) [0481] the New Testament **immediately** adds the consoling
T R : 0 0 :024(324) [0511] keys especially and **immediately** on the church, and for
L C : 0 3 :096(433) [0725] Christ repeats it **immediately** after the Lord's Prayer in
L C : 0 4 :082(446) [0751] fall out, he should **immediately** head for the ship and
E P : R N :003(465) [0777] 2. **Immediately** after the time of the apostles — in fact,
S D : 0 1 :039(515) [0871] in that he does not **immediately** cast this corrupted,
S D : 0 2 :063(533) [0905] And **immediately** he does good, as much and as long as
S D : 0 5 :014(560) [0957] but to this office it **immediately** adds the promise of
S D : 0 6 :005(564) [0963] just as the first man **immediately** after his creation
S D : 0 8 :026(596) [1023] He had this majesty **immediately** at his conception even in
S D : 1 1 :064(626) [1083] hidden wisdom, Paul **immediately** commands silence and

Immense (1)

E P : 0 3 :002(473) [0793] like a drop of water over against the **immense** ocean.

Immersed (2)

S C : P R :023(341) [0539] although he is deeply **immersed** in them and is held
L C : 0 4 :078(446) [0751] Even if we were **immersed** in water a hundred times, it

Immoderate (2), Immoderately (1)

A L : 2 5 :005(062) [0069] satisfactions were **immoderately** extolled, but nothing
A P : 0 2 :028(104) [0113] sin is, it is correct to answer that it is **immoderate** lust.
A P : 2 7 :036(275) [0433] were offended by the **immoderate** praises of the monastic

Immodest (2)

S C : 0 5 :022(350) [0553] I have also been **immodest** in word and deed.
S C : 0 5 :023(350) [0553] set a bad example by my **immodest** language and actions.

Immoral (2), Immorality (11)

A G : 2 3 :001(051) [0061] concerning the flagrant **immorality** and the dissolute life
A G : 2 3 :003(051) [0061] the Lord God to avoid **immorality**, for Paul says,
A G : 2 3 :004(051) [0061] of the temptation to **immorality**, each man should have
A G : 2 3 :018(054) [0063] such terrible, shocking **immorality** and abominable vice
A G : 2 7 :019(074) [0079] of the temptation to **immorality**, each man should have
A L : 2 3 :004(051) [0061] of the temptation to **immorality** each man should have
A P : 2 3 :014(241) [0367] of the temptation to **immorality**, each man should have
A P : 2 3 :017(241) [0369] of the temptation of **immorality**, each man should have
A P : 2 3 :063(248) [0381] of the temptation to **immorality** (I Cor. 7:2) and
A P : 2 3 :070(249) [0383] like these they defend a wicked and **immoral** law.
A P : 2 7 :051(278) [0437] of the temptation to **immorality**, each man should have
L C : 0 5 :075(455) [0771] are plain: adultery, **immorality**, impurity, licentiousness,
S D : 0 4 :032(556) [0947] be deceived; neither the **immoral**, nor idolaters, nor

Immortal (1), Immortality (1)

A P : 2 7 :062(280) [0441] teaching of faith and **immortality** — surely a lawful
L C : 0 2 :058(418) [0693] and all evil, living in new, **immortal** and glorified bodies.

Immovable (1)

S D : 0 7 :042(576) [0985] on a unique, firm, **immovable**, and indubitable rock of

Immunity (3), Immunities (1)

A P : 2 4 :081(264) [0411] with public duties and **immunities**: "He will say that some
A P : 2 4 :081(264) [0411] men have found an **immunity** and have avoided public
A P : 2 4 :081(264) [0411] Pertinax on the law of **immunity** shows: "Even though
A P : 2 8 :001(281) [0443] article states about the **immunity** of churches and

Immutable (8)

S D : 0 3 :057(549) [0935] the eternal and **immutable** righteousness of God revealed
S D : 0 4 :004(551) [0939] word may refer to the **immutable** order which obligates
S D : 0 4 :016(554) [0943] to the order of God's **immutable** will, whose debtors we
S D : 0 4 :032(556) [0947] by faith these true, **immutable**, and divine threats and
S D : 0 5 :017(561) [0957] the righteousness and **immutable** will of God, shows how
S D : 0 6 :003(564) [0963] in accord with God's external and **immutable** will.
S D : 0 6 :015(566) [0967] meaning, namely, the **immutable** will of God according to
S D : 0 6 :017(566) [0967] lives according to the **immutable** will of God as it is

Impair (2), Impairment (1)

A L : 2 8 :074(093) [0093] for such change does not **impair** the unity of the church
E P : 1 0 :011(494) [0831] Gospel (which serve to **impair** the truth) in such
S D : 0 1 :060(519) [0879] sin is an inexpressible **impairment** and such a corruption

Impalpable (1), Impalpably (1)

S D : 0 7 :007(570) [0975] on earth in some invisible and **impalpable** manner.
S D : 0 7 :008(570) [0975] although invisibly and **impalpably**, and is orally received

Impart (4), Imparted (3), Imparts (1)
AG : 2 8 :008(082) [0085] In this way are **imparted** no bodily but eternal things and
AL : 1 2 :002(034) [0049] that the church ought to **impart** absolution to those who
LC : 0 1 :326(409) [0675] is to illuminate and **impart** its splendor to all the others.
LC : 0 2 :062(419) [0695] through the Word, and **imparts**, increases, and
LC : 0 5 :022(449) [0757] the words are there through which this is **imparted**!
EP : 0 8 :017(489) [0821] and it is easy for him to **impart** to us his true body and
SD : 0 1 :030(513) [0867] and righteousness **imparted** at creation to our nature in
SD : 1 1 :042(623) [1077] God does not want to **impart** the grace of perseverance to

Impartial (1)
SD : PR :012(506) [0855] therefore regarded as **impartial**, none of the parties in the

Impatient (1), Impatiently (1), Impatience (2)
LC : 0 1 :128(382) [0617] we rage and grumble **impatiently** and forget all the
LC : 0 3 :086(432) [0723] give us occasion for **impatience**, wrath, vengeance, etc.
LC : 0 3 :103(434) [0727] by word and deed and drives us to anger and **impatience**.
LC : 0 5 :026(449) [0759] yield hand and foot and become indifferent or **impatient**.

Impede (1), Impedes (2), Impediment (3)
PR : PR :004(004) [0007] back and perceptibly **impede** the course of the holy
EP : 0 1 :015(468) [0783] sin is only an external **impediment** to man's good
EP : 0 1 :015(468) [0783] smeared upon a magnet, **impedes** but does not remove
SD : 0 1 :022(512) [0865] but only an external **impediment** to them, just as garlic
SD : 0 1 :022(512) [0865] natural power but only **impedes** it; or that the spots
SD : 0 4 :037(557) [0951] only are useless and an **impediment** to such a person but

Impel (8), Impelled (2), Impelling (2), Impels (5)
AG : 2 3 :003(051) [0061] that they have been **impelled** and moved to take this step
AL : 2 0 :032(045) [0057] power of the devil, who **impels** men to various sins,
LC : 0 1 :040(370) [0591] this ought to move and **impel** us to fix our hearts upon
LC : 0 1 :125(382) [0617] and strongest reason **impelling** us to keep this
LC : 0 1 :129(383) [0617] he reminds and **impels** everyone to consider what his
LC : 0 1 :326(409) [0675] love, and trust should **impel** us not to despise his Word,
LC : 0 3 :024(423) [0703] which ought to drive and **impel** us to pray without
LC : 0 3 :026(424) [0705] our need, the distress that **impels** and drives us to cry
LC : 0 3 :034(425) [0707] one so great that it should **impel** us to keep praying for it
LC : 0 5 :041(451) [0763] go unless he feels a hunger and thirst **impelling** him to it.
LC : 0 5 :043(451) [0763] of their own accord urge and **impel** themselves to come.
LC : 0 5 :052(452) [0765] What should move and **impel** you is the fact that Christ
LC : 0 5 :064(454) [0769] above, which should most powerfully draw and **impel** us.
LC : 0 5 :071(454) [0769] part, you ought to be **impelled** by your own need, which
LC : 0 6 :023(459) [0000] own conscience would **impel** him and make him so
SD : 0 3 :002(539) [0917] faith dwells in the elect, **impels** them to do what is right,
SD : 0 3 :054(549) [0935] Son, and Holy Spirit, who **impels** them to do rightly.

Impenitence (5), Impenitent (9)
PR : PR :005(004) [0009] our own and the ungrateful world's **impenitence** and sin.
AP : 0 4 :200(134) [0175] wrath of God is revealed, threatening all the **impenitent**.
S3 : 0 9 :000(314) [0497] who are manifest and **impenitent** sinners from the
EP : 0 6 :003(480) [0805] to unbelievers and the **impenitent** but also to people who
EP : 0 6 :007(481) [0807] for the penitent and **impenitent**, for regenerated and
EP : 0 6 :008(481) [0807] upon unbelievers, non-Christians, and the **impenitent**.
EP : 0 7 :037(485) [0815] Supper unbelieving and **impenitent** Christians do not
EP : 1 1 :016(497) [0837] in such a way that the **impenitent** are strengthened in
SD : 1 1 :010(618) [1065] false security and **impenitence** or anxiety and despair.
SD : 1 1 :012(618) [1067] not to security and **impenitence** but "to reproof,
SD : 1 1 :012(618) [1067] in no way cause or support either **impenitence** or despair.
SD : 1 1 :083(630) [1091] subsequent impurity, **impenitence**, and deliberate sins
SD : 1 1 :086(631) [1091] manifests toward the **impenitent** and despisers of his
SD : 1 1 :091(631) [1093] to despair, or when **impenitent** sinners are strengthened in

Imperfect (19)
AG : 2 6 :011(065) [0071] regarded as secular and **imperfect**, while traditions were
AL : 2 6 :010(065) [0071] regarded as secular and **imperfect** works, far inferior to
AL : 2 6 :011(065) [0071] they were bound to an **imperfect** kind of life — in
AP : 0 4 :181(132) [0171] But God accepts this **imperfect** righteousness of the law
AP : 1 2 :167(209) [0305] or a satisfaction, but the cleansing of **imperfect** souls.
S3 : 1 3 :002(315) [0499] Whatever is still sinful or **imperfect** in these works will
EP : 0 3 :020(475) [0797] God is incomplete and **imperfect** without such love and
EP : 0 7 :039(486) [0817] because they are still **imperfect** in their external behavior.
SD : 0 3 :023(543) [0923] renewal remains **imperfect** in this life and because sin still
SD : 0 3 :032(545) [0927] or renewal in us is **imperfect** and impure in this life on
SD : 0 3 :035(545) [0927] our new obedience is **imperfect** and impure, in order to
SD : 0 3 :049(548) [0933] God is incomplete or **imperfect** without such love and
SD : 0 4 :008(552) [0941] they are still impure and **imperfect** in this flesh of ours.
SD : 0 6 :021(567) [0969] life our good works are **imperfect** and impure, so that we
SD : 0 6 :021(567) [0969] that his works are still **imperfect** and impure (Rom. 7:18,
SD : 0 6 :022(567) [0969] in this life they are still **imperfect** and impure because of
SD : 0 6 :023(568) [0969] good works are still **imperfect** and impure, they are
SD : 0 6 :024(568) [0971] They belong to this **imperfect** life.
SD : 0 7 :100(586) [1007] To use some **imperfect** illustrations, my vision penetrates

Imperial (56)
PR : PR :008(005) [0009] Charles V in the great **imperial** assembly at Augsburg in
PR : PR :008(005) [0009] lord, His Roman **Imperial** Majesty, and to everyone else
PR : PR :018(008) [0015] Charles V at the great **imperial** assembly in Augsburg in
PR : PR :018(009) [0015] Charles V at the said **imperial** diet, which was afterward
AG : 0 0 :000(023) [0037] Princes and Cities to His **Imperial** Majesty Charles V
AG : PR :001(024) [0039] A short time ago Your **Imperial** Majesty graciously
AG : PR :006(025) [0039] in conformity with the **imperial** summons, Your Imperial
AG : PR :006(025) [0039] summons, Your **Imperial** Majesty also graciously and
AG : PR :008(025) [0039] obedience to Your **Imperial** Majesty, we offer and present
AG : PR :010(025) [0041] in obedience to Your **Imperial** Majesty, our most gracious
AG : PR :011(026) [0041] is in accord with Your **Imperial** Majesty's aforementioned
AG : PR :012(026) [0041] intended by Your **Imperial** Majesty's summons, if no
AG : PR :014(026) [0041] Of this Your **Imperial** Majesty, our aforementioned
AG : PR :015(026) [0041] In the past Your **Imperial** Majesty graciously gave
AG : PR :016(026) [0041] there stated Your **Imperial** Majesty was not disposed to
AG : PR :018(026) [0041] and notified by Your **Imperial** Majesty's viceroy (His
AG : PR :018(026) [0041] etc.) and by Your **Imperial** Majesty's orator and
AG : PR :018(026) [0041] that Your **Imperial** Majesty's viceroy, administrators, and
AG : PR :018(026) [0041] and councilors of the **imperial** government (together with
AG : PR :019(026) [0041] relations between Your **Imperial** Majesty and the pope
AG : PR :019(026) [0041] understanding, Your **Imperial** Majesty was sure that the
AG : PR :020(026) [0041] council, and so Your **Imperial** Majesty graciously offered
AG : PR :020(026) [0041] pope, along with Your **Imperial** Majesty, at the earliest
AG : PR :021(027) [0043] have been held during Your **Imperial** Majesty's reign.
AG : PR :023(027) [0043] accordance with Your **Imperial** Majesty's summons) as we
AG : 1 6 :002(037) [0051] sentence according to **imperial** and other existing laws,
AG : 2 1 :001(046) [0057] So His **Imperial** Majesty may in salutary and godly
AG : 0 0 :000(049) [0059] cases in order that Your **Imperial** Majesty may perceive
AG : 2 3 :014(053) [0063] In loyalty to Your **Imperial** Majesty we therefore feel
AG : 2 3 :020(055) [0063] highly praised in the **imperial** laws and in all states in
AG : 2 8 :019(083) [0087] right, but by human, **imperial** right, bestowed by Roman
AG : 0 0 :007(096) [0095] Your **Imperial** Majesty's most obedient servants:
AL : 1 6 :002(037) [0051] to decide matters by the **imperial** and other existing laws,
AL : 0 0 :001(049) [0059] we pray that Your **Imperial** Majesty will graciously hear
AL : 0 0 :002(049) [0059] Your **Imperial** Majesty should not believe those who
AL : 0 0 :004(049) [0059] Your **Imperial** Majesty will undoubtedly discover that the
AL : 2 8 :002(081) [0085] of this world and take away the **imperial** power.
AL : 0 0 :006(095) [0095] with the edict of Your **Imperial** Majesty, we have desired
AL : 0 0 :017(096) [0095] Your **Imperial** Majesty's faithful subjects:
AP : PR :001(098) [0099] His **Imperial** Majesty had this read before the assembly of
AP : PR :004(098) [0099] When we could not, His **Imperial** Majesty again ordered
AP : PR :005(098) [0101] and explaining to His **Imperial** Majesty why we could not
AP : PR :007(098) [0101] the apology to His **Imperial** Majesty, to show him that
AP : PR :007(098) [0101] the Confutation, but his **Imperial** Majesty did not receive
AP : 0 2 :001(100) [0105] at the very outset His **Imperial** Majesty will see that the
AP : 0 2 :035(104) [0115] His **Imperial** Majesty will recognize an obvious slander
AP : 0 2 :051(106) [0119] believe, will satisfy His **Imperial** Majesty about the
AP : 0 4 :002(107) [0121] We therefore ask His **Imperial** Majesty kindly to hear us
AP : 1 0 :004(179) [0247] on this subject (his **Imperial** Majesty does not disapprove
AP : 1 2 :122(200) [0287] that they dared to thrust upon his **Imperial** Majesty.
AP : 1 6 :001(222) [0329] verdicts according to **imperial** or other established laws,
AP : 2 0 :004(227) [0339] that His Most Excellent **Imperial** Majesty and many of
S2 : 0 4 :014(301) [0475] has been taken from the **imperial**, pagan law and is a
TR : 0 0 :035(326) [0513] Clementines, "When the **imperial** throne is vacant, the
TR : 0 0 :082(000) [0529] estates of the Roman Empire, to his **Imperial** Majesty.
LC : 0 3 :057(427) [0713] made a mockery of his **imperial** majesty's command and

Imperil (1)
SD : 1 0 :028(615) [1061] to their practices, since this serves to **imperil** the truth.

Imperishable (1)
LC : 0 3 :058(428) [0713] when he promises that which is eternal and **imperishable**?

Impiety (4), Impious (16), Impiously (1)
PR : PR :020(010) [0017] and condemn them as **impiety**, as if our ingenuous
AL : 0 1 :006(028) [0043] person and craftily and **impiously** argue that the Word
AL : 2 0 :032(045) [0057] men to various sins, **impious** opinions, and manifest
AL : 2 7 :061(080) [0083] So there are many **impious** opinions which are associated
TR : 0 0 :004(320) [0503] and hold to be false, **impious**, tyrannical, and injurious to
TR : 0 0 :033(325) [0513] lord of the kingdoms of the world are false and **impious**.
TR : 0 0 :036(326) [0515] attach salvation to these **impious** and nefarious opinions
TR : 0 0 :040(327) [0517] horrible errors and such **impiety** with the greatest cruelty
TR : 0 0 :041(327) [0517] participants in the **impious** doctrines, blasphemies, and
TR : 0 0 :042(328) [0517] with and not to support **impiety** and unjust cruelty.
TR : 0 0 :051(329) [0519] are not able to remove **impious** teachings and impious
TR : 0 0 :051(329) [0519] impious teachings and **impious** forms of worship, and
TR : 0 0 :057(330) [0521] inasmuch as he defends **impious** forms of worship and
TR : 0 0 :058(330) [0521] flee from idolatry, **impious** doctrines, and unjust cruelty.
TR : 0 0 :072(332) [0525] who teach and defend **impious** doctrines and impious
TR : 0 0 :072(332) [0525] impious doctrines and **impious** forms of worship should
TR : 0 0 :079(333) [0527] of the pope defend **impious** doctrines and impious forms
TR : 0 0 :079(333) [0527] impious doctrines and **impious** forms of worship and do
SD : 0 4 :015(553) [0943] on such sins again, which is **impious** and false.
SD : 1 0 :022(615) [1061] participants in the **impious** doctrines, blasphemies, and
SD : 1 0 :023(615) [1061] with and not to support **impiety** and unjust cruelty."

Implacable (1)
AP : 0 4 :242(141) [0187] not peevish, harsh, or **implacable**; that it covers up some

Implanted (4)
AP : 0 2 :018(102) [0111] and righteousness was **implanted** in man that would grasp
S3 : 0 8 :009(313) [0497] It is a poison **implanted** and inoculated in man by the old
LC : 0 1 :212(393) [0641] has its way, as God **implanted** it, it is not possible to
LC : 0 4 :029(440) [0739] God as the one who has **implanted** his Word in this

Implementation (1)
PR : PR :026(014) [0025] in the future in the **implementation** of this effort at

Implore (5)
AG : PR :011(026) [0041] in deepest humility and **implore** him to bestow his grace
AP : 2 1 :044(236) [0357] extol and advance, we **implore** you not to agree to the
LC : PR :009(359) [0569] I **implore** them not to imagine that they have learned
LC : PR :019(361) [0573] Therefore, I once again **implore** all Christians, especially
SD : 1 1 :072(628) [1085] in it, we should **implore** God to give us his grace, of which

Imply (1), Implying (1), Implied (1), Implies (4), Implications (3)
AP : 2 4 :090(266) [0415] forgiveness of sins, which necessarily **implies** real guilt.
S2 : 0 2 :029(297) [0471] condemn the Mass, its **implications**, and its consequences
LC : 0 1 :133(383) [0619] also have a promise **implied**, yet in none is it so plainly
LC : 0 2 :040(416) [0689] that the Holy Spirit makes me holy, as his name **implies**."
LC : 0 5 :047(452) [0763] "as often as you do it," **imply** that we should do it often.
EP : 1 2 :030(500) [0843] with their erroneous **implications** and conclusions, we
SD : 0 1 :048(516) [0875] doctrine with all its **implications** and conclusions, as when
SD : 0 4 :004(551) [0939] to God, but at times it **implies** the coercion with which
SD : 0 4 :016(554) [0943] not to be understood as **implying** compulsion but only as
SD : 0 7 :088(585) [1003] This **implies** that for the unworthy it is no sacrament, and

Import (2), Importance (11), Important (46), Imported (1)
AG : 2 3 :002(053) [0063] there were now more **important**, better, and weightier
AG : 2 5 :013(063) [0071] is its chief and most **important** part), for the consolation
AG : 2 6 :015(066) [0073] teachings about more **important** things, such as faith,
AL : 2 0 :002(041) [0053] and others of like **import** bear witness that they have

Continued ▶

AL : 26 :015(066) [0073] the cross, hope, the **importance** of civil affairs, and the
AP : 02 :032(104) [0113] and brought to light **important** teachings of the
AP : 04 :002(107) [0121] Majesty kindly to hear us out on this **important** issue.
AP : 04 :072(117) [0141] For beginnings are very **important**; or, as the common
AP : 04 :156(128) [0165] are debating about an **important** issue, the honor of
AP : 04 :175(131) [0171] Even more **important**, it must be added that we should
AP : 04 :260(145) [0195] We must always keep this **important** teaching in view.
AP : 04 :390(166) [0225] is obviously more **important** than the Gospel of Christ,
AP : 07 :033(174) [0239] the Lord's day, and the other more **important** feast days.
AP : 12 :003(182) [0253] carefully this most **important** issue, involving the chief
AP : 12 :090(195) [0279] did not have grave and **important** reasons for disagreeing
AP : 12 :098(197) [0281] easily judge the great **importance** of preserving the true
AP : 12 :124(201) [0289] over to these sophists such an **important** assignment.
AP : 12 :124(201) [0289] to deal with such **important**, numerous, and varied
AP : 12 :125(201) [0289] to see to it that on such **important** issues they did not
AP : 12 :127(201) [0291] that have arisen on the most **important** questions?
AP : 12 :128(201) [0291] attention to the **importance** of religion if you suppose
AP : 12 :130(202) [0291] who are in doubt about **important** issues but do not hear
AP : 12 :158(207) [0301] that troubles have other and more **important** purposes.
AP : 12 :158(207) [0301] at these other and more **important** purposes, that God is
AP : 12 :165(208) [0303] A statement that is **important** and wholesome with regard
AP : 16 :013(224) [0333] The **importance** of this had been obscured by foolish
AP : 24 :087(265) [0413] to raise such quibbles about such an **important** issue.
AP : 24 :099(268) [0419] have set forth such an **important** issue with the greatest
LC : 01 :031(369) [0589] it is of the utmost **importance** for a man to have the right
LC : 01 :048(371) [0593] had to explain it at length since it is the most **important**.
LC : 01 :056(372) [0595] us take to heart how **important** this commandment is and
LC : 01 :116(381) [0615] to be considered more **important** than the will and word
LC : 01 :132(383) [0619] Here you see how **important** God considers this
LC : 01 :139(384) [0621] Learn well, then, how **important** God considers
LC : 01 :188(390) [0633] the common people, the **import** of the commandment
LC : 01 :208(393) [0639] For it is of the highest **importance** to him that persons be
LC : 01 :209(393) [0641] **Important** as the spiritual and civil estates are, these must
LC : 01 :313(407) [0671] But such works are not **important** or impressive in the
LC : 01 :322(409) [0673] here declares how **important** the commandments are to
LC : 02 :060(418) [0695] this is not of great **importance**, as long as the words are
LC : 03 :013(422) [0701] to nothing; but it is **important** because God has
LC : 03 :017(422) [0703] is the first and most **important** point, that all our prayers
LC : 03 :124(436) [0731] Behold, such is the **importance** that God attaches to our
LC : 04 :007(437) [0733] It is of the greatest **importance** that we regard Baptism as
LC : 04 :011(438) [0735] we all attach greater **importance** to our own achievements
LC : 04 :026(439) [0739] again how precious and **important** a thing Baptism should
LC : 05 :004(447) [0753] what is of greatest **importance**, namely, God's Word and
EP : 01 :022(469) [0785] It is **important** to observe that the word "nature" has
SD : PR :006(502) [0847] from it in several **important** and significant articles, either
SD : PR :009(503) [0849] deal with weighty and **important** matters, and they are of
SD : PR :008(505) [0853] 6. Since these **important** matters also concern ordinary
SD : 03 :007(540) [0917] to indicate how very **important** it is that this article, side
SD : 03 :055(549) [0935] on the Lord Christ, it is **important** to consider carefully in
SD : 03 :067(551) [0937] of this high and **important** article of justification before
SD : 04 :029(555) [0947] when it was particularly **important** to have a clear and
SD : 04 :030(555) [0947] course, is a serious and **important** question since only he
SD : 04 :030(555) [0947] For this reason it is **important** to declare well and in
SD : 07 :006(570) [0973] As a result many **important** people were deceived by the
SD : 08 :035(597) [1027] It is highly **important** that this doctrine of the exchange
SD : 12 :006(633) [1097] Augsburg Confession is **imported** into our churches and

Impose (19), Imposed (11), Imposes (5), Imposing (3), Imposition (1)
AG : 27 :003(071) [0077] other requirements were **imposed**, and such fetters and
AG : 28 :042(088) [0089] the right and power to **impose** such requirements on
AL : 28 :042(088) [0089] bishops get the right to **impose** such traditions on the
AP : 04 :008(108) [0121] flee these things or turn away when God **imposes** them.
AP : 04 :233(140) [0185] disintegrate if bishops **impose** heavy burdens on the
AP : 07 :039(176) [0241] They did not want to **impose** such a burden on
AP : 07 :042(176) [0243] apostles did not want to **impose** an ordinance on the
AP : 07 :044(177) [0243] evangelical liberty nor to **impose** a necessity upon
AP : 11 :008(181) [0251] We do not want to **impose** on our people's consciences
AP : 12 :022(185) [0257] punishments, to **impose** certain satisfactions upon
AP : 12 :138(203) [0295] you bind" refer to **imposing** penalties but to retaining the
AP : 12 :156(207) [0301] penalties which God **imposes** only on them, for the sake
AP : 12 :156(207) [0301] the keys can neither **impose** nor remit them; God imposes
AP : 12 :156(207) [0301] nor remit them; God **imposes** and remits them apart from
AP : 12 :156(207) [0301] the particular penalty **imposed** on David it does not
AP : 12 :158(207) [0301] afflictions were not **imposed** on him because of his past
AP : 12 :161(208) [0303] Thus God **imposed** physical death on man because of sin,
AP : 12 :173(209) [0305] in their satisfactions they **impose** non-obligatory works.
AP : 12 :176(210) [0307] do not have the power to **impose** penalties or to institute
AP : 16 :003(223) [0331] mad of Carlstadt to try to **impose** on us the judicial laws
AP : 23 :041(245) [0375] not make it necessary to **impose** perpetual celibacy on
AP : 23 :042(245) [0375] circumcision and tried to **impose** the law of Moses on
AP : 28 :003(281) [0445] Then they **impose** intolerable burdens on them, as though
AP : 28 :008(282) [0445] then go on to forbid the **imposing** of a yoke, showing how
AP : 28 :011(283) [0447] traditions should not be **imposed** on the church to merit
S3 : 03 :021(306) [0485] was resorted to of **imposing** small satisfactions which
TR : 00 :014(322) [0509] might be conferred and hands **imposed** on him."
TR : 00 :059(330) [0521] and other crimes as to **impose** them on all posterity.
LC : 01 :240(397) [0649] New burdens and high prices are **imposed**.
LC : 06 :001(457) [0000] intolerable burden he **imposed** upon the Christian
EP : 10 :010(494) [0831] institutions are forcibly **imposed** upon the community of
EP : 11 :004(495) [0833] controls the evil and **imposes** a limit on its duration, so
SD : 01 :013(511) [0863] original sin which God **imposes** upon Adam's children
SD : 06 :005(564) [0963] that the law cannot **impose** its curse upon those who
SD : 10 :010(612) [1055] should we tolerate the **imposition** of such ceremonies on
SD : 10 :013(613) [1057] apostles who wanted to **impose** such things on
SD : 10 :015(613) [1057] are forcibly **imposed** on the church as necessary and as
SD : 10 :027(615) [1061] commandments are **imposed** by force on the community
SD : 12 :021(634) [1099] an inviolate conscience **impose** the death penalty on

Impossible (47), Impossibility (2)
AG : 11 :002(034) [0047] enumerate all trespasses and sins, for this is **impossible**.
AG : 25 :007(062) [0069] compelled to recount sins in detail, for this is **impossible**.
AG : 27 :022(074) [0079] exalts them, it is still **impossible** to abrogate God's
AG : 28 :068(093) [0093] It is **impossible** to give counsel or help to consciences
AG : 28 :075(094) [0095] If, however, this is **impossible** and they cannot be
AL : 25 :007(062) [0069] of all sins because it is **impossible** to recount all of them.
AL : 26 :012(065) [0071] consciences, for it was **impossible** to keep all traditions,
AL : 28 :075(094) [0095] However, if it is **impossible** to obtain a relaxation of
AP : 02 :042(105) [0115] unanimity may be **impossible**, no one has dared to say
AP : 04 :036(112) [0131] act of love, since it is **impossible** to love God unless faith
AP : 04 :106(122) [0153] nor by the letter of that same law, for this is **impossible**.
AP : 04 :126(124) [0157] First, it is **impossible** to keep the law without Christ; it is
AP : 04 :126(124) [0157] without Christ; it is **impossible** to keep the law without
AP : 04 :130(125) [0157] of the divine law, are **impossible** without the Holy Spirit;
AP : 04 :141(126) [0161] fact, we add that it is **impossible** to separate faith from
AP : 04 :256(144) [0193] "Without faith it is **impossible** to please God."
AP : 04 :269(147) [0197] that "without faith it is **impossible** to please God"
AP : 04 :372(164) [0221] Heb. 11:6, "Without faith it is **impossible** to please God."
AP : 11 :008(181) [0251] commands the **impossible**, namely, that we make
AP : 11 :010(182) [0253] by divine law and yet experienced that it was **impossible**.
AP : 12 :111(198) [0285] this is completely false, as well as being **impossible**.
AP : 18 :006(225) [0335] and "without faith it is **impossible** to please" God
AP : 18 :008(226) [0337] is hard to keep this faith; for the ungodly it is **impossible**.
AP : 24 :012(251) [0387] and proved by the **impossibility** of our obtaining the
AP : 24 :022(253) [0391] teaches (10:4), "It is **impossible** that the blood of bulls and
S2 : 04 :007(299) [0473] accept this (which is **impossible**), he would have to suffer
S3 : 03 :010(304) [0481] It was **impossible** for them to teach correctly about
S3 : 03 :019(306) [0483] of all his sins — an **impossibility** and the source of great
S3 : 03 :023(307) [0485] But such confidence was **impossible**.
TR : 00 :016(322) [0509] 7. Such superiority is **impossible**, for it is not possible for
TR : 00 :016(322) [0509] as such superiority is **impossible** and the churches in the
LC : PR :009(359) [0569] perfect (though that is **impossible** in this life), yet it is
LC : 01 :053(371) [0595] is abused, though it is **impossible** to enumerate all its
LC : 03 :105(434) [0727] Otherwise it is **impossible** to overcome even the least
LC : 04 :049(442) [0745] know Christ, which is **impossible** without the Holy
LC : 06 :017(459) [0000] so purely (which was **impossible**), and nobody could feel
EP : 04 :002(475) [0797] to salvation; that it is **impossible** to be saved without
EP : 04 :016(477) [0801] likewise, that it is **impossible** to be saved without good
EP : 08 :030(490) [0825] the human nature it is **impossible** for Christ to be present
SD : 01 :006(509) [0861] parents is of course **impossible** for human nature in this
SD : 03 :006(540) [0917] not remain pure, it is **impossible** to repel any error or
SD : 04 :001(551) [0939] to salvation," and "It is **impossible** to be saved without
SD : 04 :010(553) [0941] thing, so that it is **impossible** for it not to be constantly
SD : 04 :012(553) [0941] It is therefore as **impossible** to separate works from faith
SD : 04 :015(553) [0943] to continue and abide in sin, which is **impossible**.
SD : 04 :022(554) [0945] salvation, or that it is **impossible** to be saved without
SD : 04 :031(556) [0947] dream up that it is **impossible** to lose faith and the gift of
SD : 07 :046(577) [0989] although this seemed **impossible** to his reason, he gave
SD : 08 :020(595) [1021] is unthinkable and **impossible**, it is not only the bare

Impotence (2), Impotent (3)
LC : 05 :030(449) [0759] never be an unfruitful, vain thing, **impotent** and useless.
SD : 02 :015(523) [0887] our ignorance and **impotence** were not written so that we
SD : 02 :017(524) [0887] man is not only weak, **impotent**, incapable, and dead to
SD : 02 :046(530) [0899] the doctrine of the **impotence** and the wickedness of our
SD : 07 :089(585) [1003] abrogated nor rendered **impotent** by either the worthiness

Imprecations (1)
LC : 01 :186(390) [0633] call down curses and **imprecations** upon their enemy's

Impress (8), Impressed (10), Impression (12), Impressions (2), Impressive (2)
PR : PR :027(014) [0025] hereto and ordered our privy seals **impressed** hereon.
AP : 04 :019(110) [0125] in order to avoid the **impression** that they are outright
AP : 04 :048(114) [0135] To avoid the **impression** that it is merely knowledge, we
AP : 04 :265(146) [0197] In human eyes, works are very **impressive**.
AP : 07 :003(168) [0227] article, to avoid the **impression** that we separate evil men
AP : 11 :007(181) [0251] These terrors made no **impression** on wild and profane
AP : 12 :122(200) [0287] the inexperienced the **impression** that this idea has
AP : 16 :010(224) [0333] The monks **impressed** men with this outward hypocrisy
AP : 22 :013(238) [0361] But to avoid the **impression** that we are minimizing the
AP : 23 :068(249) [0383] over, and to give the **impression** that our cause had been
AP : 27 :002(269) [0419] here lest we give the **impression** that we are doing so out
AP : 27 :036(275) [0433] slyly seek to give the **impression** that they are modifying
LC : SP :027(364) [0581] frequently is to **impress** it upon our youth, not in a lofty
LC : 01 :029(368) [0589] stressed and **impressed** upon young people so that they
LC : 01 :037(369) [0591] that everyone shall be **impressed** and see that this is no
LC : 01 :061(373) [0597] and continually **impress** it upon them, so that they may
LC : 01 :140(384) [0621] it may be thoroughly **impressed** upon the young people,
LC : 01 :145(385) [0623] If this truth could be **impressed** upon the poor people, a
LC : 01 :161(387) [0627] Yet there is need to **impress** upon the common people
LC : 01 :188(390) [0633] Briefly, then, to **impress** it unmistakably upon the
LC : 01 :196(391) [0637] could be thoroughly **impressed** on people's minds, we
LC : 01 :213(394) [0641] common people with lying words and wrong **impressions**.
LC : 01 :248(398) [0651] But it needs to be **impressed** upon the young people so
LC : 01 :313(407) [0671] are not important or **impressive** in the eyes of the world.
LC : 02 :023(413) [0683] daily to study this article and **impress** it upon our minds.
LC : 03 :027(424) [0705] serve to remind us and **impress** upon us not to become
LC : 03 :079(431) [0721] It is good to **impress** upon the common people that all
EP : 01 :024(469) [0785] and convey no false **impressions**, and they clearly show
SD : 01 :062(519) [0879] and great zeal and **impressed** on everyone how
SD : 02 :089(538) [0915] or wax when a seal is **impressed** into it, for these do not
SD : 04 :032(556) [0947] earnestness, repeat and **impress** upon Christians who
SD : 07 :028(574) [0981] suspect by giving the **impression** that he had departed
SD : 10 :005(611) [1053] are designed to give the **impression** that our religion does
SD : 10 :030(615) [1061] a way as to give the **impression** that the community of

Improper (4), Improperly (4)
AG : 27 :039(077) [0081] vows were an **improper** and false service of God.
AG : 28 :001(081) [0083] and some have **improperly** confused the power of bishops
AL : 28 :001(081) [0083] and some have **improperly** confused the power of the
AP : 02 :043(106) [0117] in the scholastics, who **improperly** mingle philosophical
AP : 04 :280(149) [0201] the common rule it is **improper** in an argument to judge
AP : 12 :113(199) [0285] people to communion immediately was **improper**.
AP : 12 :120(200) [0287] and the secular **improperly**, so also in the case of
LC : 03 :009(421) [0699] It would be **improper** for a son to say to his father:

Improve (5), Improved (1), Improvement (6), Improvements (1), Improving (2)
AG : PR :019(026) [0041] and the pope were **improving** and were progressing

Continued ▶

A G : 2 3 :006(052) [0061] power and ability to **improve** or change the creation of
A P : 1 2 :028(185) [0259] (Matt. 3:8) and an **improvement** of the whole life and
A P : 1 2 :170(209) [0305] to be not a fraud but an **improvement** of the total life.
A P : 2 1 :042(235) [0355] most anxious for the healing and **improving** of the church
S 1 : P R :010(290) [0457] or expect that a council would **improve** our conditions.
S C : P R :007(339) [0533] with the intention of making **improvements** — later on.
S C : 0 1 :014(343) [0541] wares, but help him to **improve** and protect his income
L C : 0 1 :113(380) [0613] his highest wisdom, then I shall never **improve** upon it."
L C : 0 1 :155(386) [0625] punishment and that we are not one bit **improved** by it.
L C : 0 1 :283(403) [0661] for your neighbor's **improvement** or from the love of
L C : 0 1 :285(403) [0661] it is done with proper authority or for his **improvement**.
S D : 0 3 :022(543) [0923] without repentance, conversion, and **improvement**.
S D : 0 7 :068(582) [0997] a good intention to **improve** their life and who by their
S D : 1 1 :012(618) [1067] "to reproof, correction, and **improvement**" (II Tim. 3:16).

Impudence (3), Impudent (4), Impudently (3)
A P : 1 2 :124(201) [0289] God will not long endure such **impudence** and malice.
A P : 2 0 :002(227) [0339] of the Confutation who so **impudently** blaspheme Christ.
A P : 2 3 :002(239) [0363] reader consider the **impudence** of these good-for-nothings
A P : 2 3 :063(248) [0381] Just look at these **impudent** rascals!
A P : 2 7 :018(272) [0425] How **impudent** our opponents are!
A P : 2 7 :024(273) [0427] But look at the **impudence** of our opponents!
A P : 2 7 :029(274) [0431] of all, they make the **impudent** claim that according to
T R : 0 0 :049(329) [0519] the canons sometimes **impudently** declare — yet this was
T R : 0 0 :049(329) [0519] was done much more **impudently** by the pontiffs, as
S D : 0 7 :090(585) [1003] therefore a pernicious, **impudent** error when some by a

Impulse (6), Impulses (15)
A P : 0 2 :035(105) [0115] begins to mortify lust and to create new **impulses** in man.
A P : 0 4 :125(124) [0157] it must also produce spiritual **impulses** in our hearts.
A P : 0 4 :125(124) [0157] What these **impulses** are, the prophet shows when he says
A P : 0 4 :125(124) [0157] because our hearts have spiritual and holy **impulses**.
A P : 0 4 :130(125) [0157] the Holy Spirit, still the **impulses** of the heart toward
A P : 0 4 :136(126) [0159] the inward spiritual **impulses** and the outward good
A P : 0 4 :170(130) [0171] and destroy them and to give us new spiritual **impulses**.
A P : 0 4 :175(131) [0171] Holy Spirit and that their **impulses** agree with God's law.
A P : 0 4 :250(143) [0191] life, it necessarily produces new **impulses** and new works.
A P : 0 4 :349(160) [0217] new works and new **impulses**, the fear and love of God,
A P : 0 4 :351(161) [0217] terrors, other spiritual **impulses** increase, such as
A P : 0 4 :379(165) [0223] at least wrought by the **impulse** of the love they talk
A P : 1 8 :005(225) [0335] that men obey their evil **impulses** more often than their
S 3 : 0 3 :011(305) [0481] they consented (for evil **impulses**, lust, and inclinations
S 3 : 0 8 :013(313) [0497] did not prophesy by the **impulse** of man but were moved
L C : 0 1 :330(410) [0677] will arise a spontaneous **impulse** and desire gladly to do
S D : 0 2 :064(533) [0905] This **impulse** of the Holy Spirit is no coercion or
S D : 0 2 :083(537) [0913] Spirit's activities and **impulses**, which take place through
S D : 0 2 :089(538) [0915] Spirit engenders no new **impulses** and begins no spiritual
S D : 0 6 :002(564) [0963] without any outside **impulse**, they, too, through the
S D : 0 6 :002(564) [0963] the inspiration and **impulse** of the Holy Spirit

Impure (19), Impurity (6)
P R : P R :008(005) [0009] against doctrine that is **impure**, false, and contrary to the
A L : 2 3 :018(054) [0063] known, and although **impure** celibacy causes many
A P : 0 4 :160(129) [0167] is indeed righteousness; but in us it is weak and **impure**.
A P : 0 4 :177(131) [0171] the sight of our **impurity** thoroughly frightens us.
A P : 0 4 :189(133) [0175] the Holy Spirit motivates, fouling it with its **impurity**.
A P : 0 4 :270(147) [0199] keeping of the law is **impure** and far from perfect.
A P : 2 3 :022(242) [0369] **Impure** continence does not please Christ.
A P : 2 3 :026(243) [0371] as though marriage were **impure** and sinful or as though
A P : 2 3 :034(244) [0373] As virginity is **impure** in the ungodly, therefore, so
A P : 2 3 :041(245) [0375] frees us from these Levitical regulations about **impurity**.
A P : 2 3 :066(248) [0381] of the Lord," requires **impure** celibates to become pure
A P : 2 7 :021(272) [0427] provided they are not **impure**, are non-obligatory forms
L C : 0 5 :075(455) [0771] adultery, immorality, **impurity**, licentiousness, idolatry,
L C : 0 6 :025(460) [0000] hordes just to show what **impure** and filthy people they
S D : 0 3 :032(545) [0927] in us is imperfect and **impure** in this life on account of the
S D : 0 3 :035(545) [0927] is imperfect and **impure**, in order to supply tempted
S D : 0 4 :008(552) [0941] even though they are still **impure** and imperfect in this
S D : 0 4 :008(552) [0941] them as sin and as **impure** because of our corrupted
S D : 0 6 :021(567) [0969] works are imperfect and **impure**, so that we must say with
S D : 0 6 :021(567) [0969] his works are still imperfect and **impure** (Rom. 7:18, 19).
S D : 0 6 :022(567) [0969] are still imperfect and **impure** because of the sin in our
S D : 0 6 :023(568) [0969] are still imperfect and **impure**, they are acceptable to God
S D : 0 7 :069(582) [0997] because of their great **impurity**, and who perceive their
S D : 1 1 :082(630) [1089] beforehand have been **impure** and therefore a vessel of
S D : 1 1 :083(630) [1091] of their subsequent **impurity**, impenitence, and deliberate

Imputation (5), Imputed (5), Imputes (2)
A L : 0 4 :003(030) [0045] This faith God **imputes** for righteousness in his sight
A P : 0 2 :036(105) [0115] Baptism, not that it no longer is, but it is not **imputed**."
A P : 0 2 :036(105) [0115] sin is — that is, remains — even though it is not **imputed**.
A P : 0 2 :040(105) [0115] though it is not **imputed** to those who are in Christ.
A P : 0 4 :163(129) [0169] Thus also the **imputation** of the righteousness of the
A P : 0 4 :168(130) [0169] is the man to whom the Lord **imputes** no iniquity."
A P : 0 4 :168(130) [0169] always sin that could be **imputed** to us; about this he says
A P : 0 4 :177(131) [0171] failure to keep it is not **imputed** to us, although the sight
A P : 0 4 :306(154) [0207] our righteousness is the **imputation** of someone else's
A P : 0 4 :307(154) [0207] faith, therefore faith is righteousness in us by **imputation**.
A P : 0 4 :307(154) [0207] God because of God's **imputation** and ordinances, as
A P : 2 1 :019(231) [0347] on them by divine **imputation**, so that through them we

Inability (1)
A P : 0 2 :014(102) [0109] the fear of God and of trust in him, **inability** to love him.

Inadvertently (2)
A P : 0 4 :088(120) [0149] "Faith justifies" **inadvertently**, he reinforces and confirms
L C : 0 1 :225(395) [0645] of what happens **inadvertently** and unintentionally — a

Inane (1)
A P : 1 2 :062(190) [0269] it maintains that God's promises are uncertain and **inane**.

Inborn (5)
A G : 0 2 :002(029) [0043] Moreover, this **inborn** sickness and hereditary sin is truly
A G : 1 8 :002(039) [0051] heart, or of expelling **inborn** evil lusts from his heart.
S D : 0 1 :002(509) [0859] this corruption and this **inborn** sin which inheres in his
S D : 0 1 :011(510) [0863] the Fall man inherits an **inborn** wicked stamp, an interior
S D : 0 1 :030(513) [0867] who sins because of his **inborn** original sin but a strange

Incalculably (1)
L C : 0 3 :115(435) [0731] heartache of which there is so **incalculably** much on earth.

Incandescent (1)
E P : 0 8 :009(488) [0819] by the analogy of **incandescent** iron and the union of

Incapable (4)
E P : 0 8 :034(491) [0825] human nature, is wholly **incapable** of omnipotence and
S D : 0 2 :017(524) [0887] only weak, impotent, **incapable**, and dead to good, but
S D : 0 8 :002(592) [1017] to God alone and the body of Christ is **incapable** of it.
S D : 0 8 :052(601) [1033] or should be capable or **incapable** without being

Incarnate (1), Incarnation (4)
P R : P R :020(010) [0017] those pertaining to the **incarnation** of God's Son, his
S D : 0 7 :039(576) [0985] Christ, our Saviour, was **incarnate** through the Word of
S D : 0 8 :011(593) [1019] confess that after the **incarnation** neither nature in Christ
S D : 0 8 :011(593) [1019] so that after the **incarnation** not only his divine nature
S D : 0 8 :049(600) [1031] in Christ through the **incarnation**, nor was the divine

Incense (4)
A P : 2 4 :031(255) [0395] and in every place **incense** is offered to my name, and a
A P : 2 4 :032(255) [0395] Therefore "**incense**" and "a pure offering" do not refer to
L C : P R :010(360) [0569] will never offer up any **incense** or other savor more
L C : 0 1 :314(407) [0671] There is burning of **incense**, singing and ringing of bells,

Incentive (5)
A P : 0 4 :364(162) [0219] It is not an **incentive** to work for their own advantage,
A P : 2 1 :036(234) [0353] their faith and as an **incentive** to imitate them in public
L C : P R :014(360) [0571] That alone should be **incentive** enough.
L C : 0 1 :126(382) [0617] us sufficient reason and **incentive** to do cheerfully and
L C : 0 1 :131(383) [0619] all this, another strong **incentive** for us to keep this

Incessant (3), Incessantly (6)
L C : P R :013(360) [0571] daily against the daily, **incessant** attacks and ambushes of
L C : 0 1 :215(394) [0641] desires that they suffer **incessant** ragings of secret
L C : 0 1 :331(410) [0677] we are to keep them **incessantly** before our eyes and
L C : 0 3 :002(420) [0697] as to call upon God **incessantly** and drum into his ears
L C : 0 3 :109(435) [0729] must be armed and prepared for **incessant** attacks.
L C : 0 3 :115(435) [0731] but also a murderer, he **incessantly** seeks our life and
L C : 0 4 :065(445) [0749] For we must keep at it **incessantly**, always purging out
L C : 0 6 :009(458) [0000] should and must take place **incessantly** as long as we live.
S D : 0 2 :016(523) [0887] ought to petition him **incessantly** that by the same Spirit

Inch (1)
L C : 0 1 :308(406) [0669] If you give the world an **inch**, it will take a yard, and at

Inchoate (5)
S D : 0 3 :023(543) [0923] But because of the **inchoate** renewal remains imperfect in
S D : 0 3 :032(544) [0927] and, second, also the **inchoate** righteousness of the new
S D : 0 3 :032(545) [0927] For because this **inchoate** righteousness or renewal in us
S D : 0 3 :050(548) [0933] and through their own **inchoate** new obedience, or in part
S D : 0 3 :050(548) [0933] righteousness and in part by the **inchoate** new obedience.

Incidental (1), Incidentally (1)
A P : 2 3 :062(247) [0381] arguments, we have **incidentally** recited and refuted the
L C : 0 1 :086(376) [0605] so narrow as to forbid **incidental** and unavoidable work.

Incipient (9)
A P : 0 4 :161(129) [0167] evident now that this **incipient** keeping of the law does
A P : 0 4 :166(130) [0169] The **incipient** keeping of the law does not please God for
A P : 0 4 :174(131) [0171] In the **incipient** keeping of the law, therefore, we need a
A P : 0 4 :177(131) [0171] The **incipient** keeping of the law pleases God because of
A P : 0 4 :214(136) [0179] be done since our **incipient** keeping of the law must follow
A P : 0 4 :270(147) [0199] even though its **incipient** keeping of the law is impure and
A P : 0 4 :368(163) [0221] because of faith, this **incipient** keeping of the law pleases
E P : 0 3 :021(475) [0797] to them and by the **incipient** new obedience, or in part by
E P : 0 3 :021(475) [0797] righteousness and in part by our **incipient** new obedience.

Incite (1), Incited (2), Incites (3), Inciting (1)
A P : 0 2 :047(106) [0119] opinions and errors and **incites** it to all kinds of sins.
A P : 0 7 :049(178) [0245] or people, we should not **incite** schisms, as the Donatists
A P : 0 7 :050(178) [0245] seditious those who have **incited** schisms because they
A P : 1 8 :005(225) [0335] the ungodly, never stops **inciting** this feeble nature to
L C : 0 3 :102(434) [0727] us and to which we are **incited** by the association and
L C : 0 5 :052(452) [0765] He invites and **incites** you; if you despise this, you must
S D : 0 2 :029(527) [0893] is much too weak for Satan, who **incites** men to sin."

Inclination (6), Inclinations (6), Inclined (9), Inclining (1)
P R : P R :001(003) [0007] greeting, and favorably **inclined** will, as well as our most
A G : 0 2 :001(029) [0043] are full of evil lust and **inclinations** from their mothers'
A G : 2 7 :045(078) [0081] If one were **inclined** to count up all these claims for the
A G : 2 8 :060(091) [0091] and it was the more **inclined** and pleased to do this in
A L : 2 7 :045(078) [0081] anybody should be **inclined** to enlarge on these claims,
A P : 0 2 :002(100) [0105] full of evil lusts and **inclinations** from their mothers'
A P : 0 2 :003(101) [0105] its acts or fruits, but the continual **inclination** of nature.
A P : 0 2 :007(101) [0107] They argue that the **inclination** to evil is a quality of the
A P : 0 2 :017(102) [0109] in God, or at least the **inclination** and power to do these
A P : 0 2 :025(103) [0111] but the evil **inclination** of man's higher capacities to
A P : 0 2 :042(105) [0115] claim that the **inclination** to evil is a neutral thing, not
A P : 0 4 :017(109) [0125] as a disposition **inclining** us to love God more easily.
A P : 2 0 :005(227) [0339] We are not **inclined** to mention here the type of works
S 3 : 0 3 :011(305) [0481] evil impulses, lust, and **inclinations** they did not consider
L C : 0 1 :018(367) [0585] made into a god that to which his heart was **inclined**.
L C : 0 1 :149(385) [0623] and who will not be **inclined** to godliness, we deliver to
L C : 0 1 :212(393) [0641] blood, and the natural **inclinations** and stimulations have
L C : 0 1 :214(394) [0641] has so little love and **inclination** for chastity as those who
L C : 0 3 :063(428) [0715] flesh is in itself vile and **inclined** to evil, even when we
L C : 0 4 :071(445) [0749] follows unchecked the **inclinations** of his nature if he is
S D : 0 1 :011(510) [0863] uncleanness of the heart and evil desires and **inclinations**.
S D : 1 1 :095(632) [1095] and are cordially **inclined** and determined on our part to

Include (15), Included (17), Includes (16), Including (3)
A G : 2 7 :012(072) [0077] and the counsels **included** in the Gospel were kept, and so
A P : 0 2 :001(100) [0105] what original sin **includes**, they viciously misinterpret and
A P : 0 2 :024(103) [0111] Thus Augustine **includes** both the defect and the vicious
A P : 0 2 :028(104) [0113] And each of these answers **includes** the other."
A P : 0 2 :029(104) [0113] He **includes** these things in the term "ignorance."
A P : 0 2 :036(105) [0115] generations so much that they **included** it in the decretals.
A P : 0 4 :136(126) [0159] But we mean to **include** both elements, namely, the
A P : 0 4 :155(128) [0165] often do when they **include** many things in one phrase.
A P : 0 4 :155(128) [0165] He **includes** the whole act of worship; but meanwhile he
A P : 0 4 :245(142) [0189] Just so Paul **includes** faith and love in presenting a
A P : 0 4 :261(145) [0195] should give alms, but he **includes** all of penitence when he
A P : 0 4 :266(146) [0197] while Daniel most emphatically wants to **include** faith.
A P : 0 4 :365(163) [0219] the Scriptures often **include** faith, since they wish to
A P : 0 4 :365(163) [0219] faith, since they wish to **include** the righteousness of the
A P : 0 7 :010(170) [0229] in the larger sense **includes** both the godly and the
A P : 1 1 :007(181) [0251] added to it later, **including** the circumstances of the sins.
A P : 1 2 :039(187) [0261] faith, therefore, we also **include** absolution since "faith
A P : 1 2 :045(188) [0263] says that Christ also **includes** the fruits of penitence or the
A P : 1 2 :063(191) [0269] sins should properly be **included** as one of the parts of
A P : 1 5 :030(219) [0323] This **includes** both the law of Moses and the traditions of
A P : 2 4 :033(255) [0395] It somebody wants to **include** the ceremony here, we
A P : 2 4 :033(256) [0395] or sacrifices of praise we **include** the proclamation of the
A P : 2 8 :006(282) [0445] article of the Confessions we **included** various subjects.
S 3 : 0 5 :004(311) [0493] for they, too, are **included** in the promise of redemption
S 3 : 0 6 :002(311) [0493] that as much is **included** under one form as under both.
S 3 : 0 6 :003(311) [0493] were true that as much is **included** under one form as
S 3 : 0 8 :009(313) [0497] and power of all heresy, **including** that of the papacy and
L C : 0 1 :106(379) [0611] Honor **includes** not only love but also deference,
L C : 0 1 :167(388) [0629] and God intends it to be **included** in this commandment
L C : 0 1 :180(389) [0631] nor the government is **included** in this commandment, yet
L C : 0 1 :224(395) [0643] In a few words, this **includes** taking advantage of our
L C : 0 3 :072(430) [0719] extend your thoughts to **include** not only the oven or the
L C : 0 3 :073(430) [0719] it briefly, this petition **includes** everything that belongs to
L C : 0 3 :076(431) [0721] enumerating with many words all the things it **includes**.
L C : 0 3 :115(435) [0731] this petition **includes** all the evil that may befall us under
L C : 0 5 :065(454) [0769] Ponder, then, and **include** yourself personally in the
L C : 0 6 :010(458) [0000] toward his neighbor, is **included** in the Lord's prayer.
L C : 0 6 :014(458) [0000] kind of confession is not **included** in the commandment
E P : 1 1 :001(494) [0831] treated, we have **included** an explanation of it in this
S D : P R :012(506) [0855] We have **included** these confessions also because all were
S D : 0 1 :052(517) [0875] in a wider sense to **include** the concrete person or subject
S D : 0 2 :043(529) [0897] We shall also **include** a statement from Dr. Luther's
S D : 0 3 :019(542) [0921] used, in the first place, to **include** both the forgiveness of
S D : 0 5 :002(558) [0951] which reproves all sins, **including** unbelief, whereas the
S D : 0 5 :004(558) [0953] Here the term **includes** both the exposition of the law and
S D : 0 5 :006(559) [0953] Here it does not **include** the proclamation of repentance
S D : 0 7 :001(568) [0971] article should not be **included** in this document in which
S D : 1 0 :005(611) [1053] Nor do we **include** among truly free adiaphora or things
S D : 1 1 :024(619) [1069] the Scriptures all this is **included** in the teaching of the
S D : 1 1 :024(620) [1069] should be understood as **included** therein and never be
S D : 1 1 :028(620) [1071] "God has **included** all men under disobedience so that he

Income (1)
S C : 0 1 :014(343) [0541] help him to improve and protect his **income** and property.

Incompetent (3)
S C : P R :002(338) [0533] many pastors are quite **incompetent** and unfitted for
L C : S P :002(362) [0575] of his craft is rejected and considered **incompetent**.
S D : 0 2 :012(522) [0885] "They are all **incompetent**" (Rom. 3:12).

Incomplete (3)
E P : 0 3 :020(475) [0797] before God is **incomplete** and imperfect without such love
E P : 0 6 :004(480) [0805] regeneration and renewal is **incomplete** in this world.
S D : 0 3 :049(548) [0933] before God is **incomplete** or imperfect without such love

Incomprehensible (2)
S D : 0 7 :064(581) [0995] manner, but in a supernatural, **incomprehensible** manner.
S D : 0 7 :100(586) [1005] is, secondly, the **incomprehensible**, spiritual mode of

Inconsiderable (2)
A G : 2 7 :035(076) [0081] St. Augustine is no **inconsiderable** authority in the
A L : 2 7 :035(076) [0081] his authority is not **inconsiderable**, although others have

Inconsistent (4)
S D : 0 7 :107(588) [1009] every error which is **inconsistent** with or opposed and
S D : 0 7 :112(589) [1011] doctrines which are **inconsistent** with, opposed to, or
S D : 0 7 :128(591) [1015] everything that is **inconsistent** with, contrary to, or
S D : 0 8 :088(609) [1047] all errors which are **inconsistent** with the doctrine here set

Incontinent (1)
A P : 2 3 :055(247) [0379] should exhort the **incontinent** to marry and also exhort

Incorporated (7), Incorporates (1), Incorporation (2)
P R : P R :018(009) [0015] we have ordered the **incorporation** of the Augsburg
P R : P R :019(010) [0017] with the norm **incorporated** in the [Formula of]
L C : 0 2 :052(417) [0691] by the Holy Spirit and **incorporated** into it through the
L C : 0 3 :037(425) [0707] through which he so **incorporates** us with himself that all
L C : 0 4 :029(440) [0739] but through its **incorporation** with God's Word and
S D : P R :008(505) [0853] he prepared them and **incorporated** them in his published
S D : 0 2 :036(528) [0895] me thereto and has **incorporated** me therein through this,
S D : 0 7 :016(572) [0977] merits of Christ, are **incorporated** into Christ, and are
S D : 0 7 :059(580) [0993] with Christ and are **incorporated** into the body of Christ,
S D : 0 7 :104(587) [1009] true believers are **incorporated** into Christ and become

Incorporeal (1)
A L : 0 1 :002(027) [0043] which is God, eternal, **incorporeal**, indivisible, of infinite

Incorrect (5), Incorrectly (1)
P R : P R :020(010) [0017] hence must be false and **incorrect**, we should indicate and
L C : 0 4 :082(446) [0751] Therefore the statement is **incorrect**.
S D : P R :019(507) [0857] article and that every **incorrect**, dubious, suspicious, and
S D : 0 3 :043(547) [0931] then it is false and **incorrect** to answer: Faith cannot
S D : 0 4 :029(555) [0947] churches as false and **incorrect** and as issues which in
S D : 0 8 :014(594) [1019] as some have **incorrectly** explained it, as if both natures,

Incorrupt (2)
S D : 0 1 :020(511) [0865] even after the Fall is **incorrupt** and, especially, that in
S D : 0 1 :029(513) [0867] holy, righteous, and **incorrupt** in the sight of God, and

Increase (16), Increased (7), Increases (8), Increasing (1), Increasingly (1)
P R : P R :006(004) [0009] insinuating themselves **increasingly** into them might be
P R : P R :024(013) [0023] and profitable to the **increase** and expansion of God's
A L : 0 0 :003(049) [0059] are trying by the same method to **increase** the discord.
A L : 2 4 :006(056) [0065] This likewise **increases** the reverence and devotion of
A L : 2 4 :021(058) [0067] opinion which infinitely **increased** private Masses,
A L : 2 8 :038(087) [0089] canons formerly **increased**, and we can still see some
A P : 0 4 :010(108) [0123] it has produced and **increased** many types of worship in
A P : 0 4 :011(108) [0123] To support and **increase** trust in such works, the
A P : 0 4 :017(109) [0125] they bid us merit an **increase** of this disposition and
A P : 0 4 :103(122) [0151] says, 'Law came in, to **increase** the trespass; but where sin
A P : 0 4 :103(122) [0151] trespass; but where sin **increased**, grace abounded all the
A P : 0 4 :136(126) [0159] the law should begin in us and **increase** more and more.
A P : 0 4 :351(161) [0217] other spiritual impulses **increase**, such as knowledge and
A P : 1 2 :106(197) [0283] so preoccupied with the **increase** of his holdings that he
A P : 2 0 :006(227) [0339] must defend and which **increases** the glory of Christ — we
A P : 2 0 :015(229) [0343] chastity, and other fruits of the Spirit gradually **increase**.
A P : 2 4 :097(268) [0417] Hence they **increased** the services and sacrifices.
S 3 : 0 2 :005(303) [0479] and Rom. 5:20, "Law came in to **increase** the trespass."
L C : 0 2 :053(417) [0693] By it he creates and **increases** sanctification, causing it
L C : 0 2 :059(418) [0693] to begin and daily to **increase** holiness on earth through
L C : 0 2 :062(419) [0695] the Word, and imparts, **increases**, and strengthens faith
L C : 0 3 :002(420) [0697] may give, preserve, and **increase** in us faith and obedience
L C : 0 4 :070(445) [0749] Vice thus grows and **increases** in him from his youth up.
E P : 0 7 :018(484) [0813] of the holy sacrament **increases**, magnifies, and
E P : 0 8 :016(489) [0821] could therefore truly **increase** in age, wisdom, and favor
S D : 0 1 :058(519) [0879] the discord will only be **increased** and deepened if the
S D : 0 2 :037(528) [0895] whereby he initiates and **increases** sanctification so that
S D : 0 2 :038(528) [0895] and effects in us a daily **increase** in faith and good works.
S D : 0 2 :072(535) [0909] strengthens, and **increases** these gifts, and admonishes us
S D : 0 7 :029(574) [0981] schisms and errors are **increasing** proportionately with
S D : 1 0 :009(612) [1055] change, to reduce, or to **increase** ceremonies according to
S D : 1 0 :015(613) [1057] of men will be **increased** and be put as divine worship not
S D : 1 1 :021(619) [1069] also strengthen and **increase** in them the good work which

Incumbent (3), Incumbents (1)
A G : 2 1 :001(046) [0057] the Turk, for both are **incumbents** of a royal office which
A G : 2 8 :071(093) [0093] dignity (though it is **incumbent** on the bishops to do this,
T R : 0 0 :056(329) [0521] pontiffs, it is especially **incumbent** on the kings to restrain
S D : 0 1 :016(511) [0865] It is **incumbent** upon us to maintain and preserve this

Incur (2), Incurring (1)
A P : 2 7 :064(280) [0441] to marry, and so they **incur** condemnation for having
S C : 0 9 :004(355) [0561] has appointed, and those who resist will **incur** judgment.
S D : 0 1 :056(518) [0877] freely and without **incurring** suspicion, and for that

Indecent (1), Indecently (2)
A G : 2 3 :012(053) [0063] enforced so hastily and **indecently** that the pope at the
A G : 2 7 :044(078) [0081] invented a still more **indecent** and absurd claim, namely,
S C : 0 5 :024(350) [0555] On one occasion I also spoke **indecently**.

Indeed (103)
A G : 2 8 :033(086) [0087] power of the church is **indeed** great because the church
A L : 1 8 :006(040) [0053] the providence of God; **indeed**, it is from and through him
A L : 2 8 :063(092) [0093] of the Lord's Day is not ***indeed*** of divine obligation but is
A P : 0 4 :031(111) [0129] says, "If the Son makes you free, you will be free **indeed**."
A P : 0 4 :032(111) [0129] not submit to God's law, **indeed** it cannot; and those who
A P : 0 4 :109(123) [0153] **Indeed**, they do not attribute justification to faith at all,
A P : 0 4 :160(129) [0167] to the law is perfect, it is **indeed** righteousness; but in us
A P : 0 4 :165(129) [0169] right hand of God, who **indeed** intercedes for us"
A P : 0 4 :268(147) [0197] prayers and good works, **indeed** by our complete
A P : 0 4 :297(153) [0205] Son makes you free, you will be free **indeed**" (John 8:36).
A P : 0 4 :313(155) [0207] and reborn by faith, if **indeed** we want to teach the
A P : 0 4 :320(156) [0209] worthy of eternal life, if **indeed** hope ought to be
A P : 0 4 :332(158) [0211] do when they pray, if **indeed** these profane men ever ask
A P : 0 4 :337(159) [0215] **Indeed**, this confession that our works are worthless is the
A P : 0 4 :382(165) [0225] of Christ's suffering, then **indeed** Christ's suffering
A P : 0 7 :003(169) [0227] administered by evil men; **indeed**, we may legitimately use
A P : 0 7 :012(170) [0231] and evil men are **indeed** associated with the true church
A P : 0 7 :035(175) [0241] These have **indeed** an appearance of wisdom in
A P : 1 5 :022(218) [0321] "have an appearance of wisdom," and **indeed** they have.
A P : 2 0 :003(227) [0339] There have **indeed** been theologians who held that after
A P : 2 0 :012(228) [0341] that our opponents have **indeed** got the most out of their
A P : 2 1 :005(230) [0345] to believe that grace does **indeed** abound more than sin
A P : 2 4 :091(266) [0415] **Indeed**, the bitterest kind of sorrow must seize all the
A P : 2 7 :026(273) [0429] **Indeed**, when they are proposed under the cover of these
A P : 2 7 :028(274) [0429] **Indeed**, Christ has promised this in abundance to those
A P : 2 7 :040(276) [0433] **Indeed**, such leaving is accursed; for if someone leaves his
A P : 2 7 :052(278) [0437] It is **indeed** strange that with such dangers and scandals
A P : 2 7 :059(279) [0439] Yes, **indeed**, the example of the Rechabites is a beautiful
S 1 : P R :002(289) [0455] a truly free council, as **indeed** the pope is in duty bound
S 2 : 0 2 :004(293) [0463] more blessed manner — **indeed**, the only blessed manner
T R : 0 0 :035(326) [0513] **Indeed**, it is even written in the Clementines, "When the
L C : P R :006(359) [0569] **Indeed**, even among the nobility there are some louts and
L C : P R :010(360) [0571] This, **indeed**, is the true holy water, the sign which routs
L C : P R :011(360) [0571] it is "the power of God," **indeed**, the power of God which
L C : P R :012(360) [0571] It must, **indeed**, be master of more than a hundred
L C : S P :005(362) [0575] nothing of these things — **indeed**, even now we find them
L C : 0 1 :023(367) [0585] God into an idol — **indeed**, an "apple-god" — and setting
L C : 0 1 :046(371) [0593] their appearance, which **indeed** endures for a time but in
L C : 0 1 :056(372) [0597] a single lie a double one results — **indeed**, manifold lies.
L C : 0 1 :089(377) [0605] **Indeed**, we Christians should make every day a holy day
L C : 0 1 :091(377) [0607] **Indeed**, it is the only one we Christians acknowledge and
L C : 0 1 :108(380) [0611] In other respects, **indeed**, we are all equal in the sight of
L C : 0 1 :126(382) [0617] parents above all others; **indeed**, he has appointed it to be
L C : 0 1 :154(386) [0625] **Indeed**, in your own household you must suffer ten times

Continued ▶

L C : 0 1 :173(388) [0629] make them rich without our help, as **indeed** he does daily.
L C : 0 1 :216(394) [0641] by this commandment; **indeed**, all poor, captive
L C : 0 1 :221(395) [0643] precious good work — **indeed**, many and great works —
L C : 0 1 :230(396) [0645] **Indeed**, what would become of the head and chief
L C : 0 1 :234(397) [0647] this commandment may **indeed** get by and escape the
L C : 0 1 :243(397) [0649] **Indeed**, we have the evidence before our very eyes every
L C : 0 2 :033(415) [0687] **Indeed**, the entire Gospel that we preach depends on the
L C : 0 3 :010(421) [0699] **Indeed**, the human heart is by nature so desperately
L C : 0 3 :032(424) [0707] "Yes, dear child, it shall **indeed** be done in spite of the
L C : 0 3 :074(430) [0719] **Indeed**, the greatest need of all is to pray for our civil
L C : 0 3 :083(431) [0721] for any length of time, as **indeed** we see and experience
L C : 0 3 :104(434) [0727] These are snares and nets; **indeed**, they are the real
L C : 0 4 :022(439) [0737] cooks with and could **indeed** be called a bathkeeper's
L C : 0 4 :030(440) [0739] matter where he speaks — **indeed**, no matter for what
L C : 0 4 :056(443) [0747] confess, "The Baptism **indeed** was right, but unfortunately
L C : 0 4 :081(446) [0751] **Indeed**, St. Jerome is responsible for this view, for he
L C : 0 5 :014(448) [0755] It is true, **indeed**, that if you take the Word away from
L C : 0 5 :022(449) [0757] a sure pledge and sign — **indeed**, as the very gift he has
L C : 0 5 :043(451) [0763] **Indeed**, true Christians who cherish and honor the
L C : 0 5 :047(452) [0763] **Indeed**, the very words, "as often as you do it," imply that
L C : 0 5 :051(452) [0765] **Indeed**, since we show such an aversion toward the
L C : 0 6 :009(458) [0000] **Indeed**, the whole Lord's Prayer is nothing else than such
E P : 0 1 :001(466) [0779] and essence, or **indeed** the principal and best part of his
E P : 0 2 :003(470) [0787] God; it does not submit to God's law, **indeed** it cannot."
E P : 0 2 :011(471) [0789] his conversion man is **indeed** too weak by his free will to
E P : 0 3 :020(475) [0797] 8. That faith **indeed** has the most prominent role in
E P : 0 3 :020(475) [0797] before God, not **indeed** as if it were the primary cause of
E P : 0 6 :004(480) [0805] 3. For although they are **indeed** reborn and have been
E P : 0 8 :035(491) [0825] human nature Christ has **indeed** been given greater power
S D : 0 1 :060(519) [0879] no papist, no sophist, **indeed**, no human reason, be it ever
S D : 0 1 :060(519) [0879] and with all his powers dead **indeed** to that which is good.
S D : 0 2 :013(523) [0885] not submit to God's law, **indeed** it cannot" (Rom. 8:7).
S D : 0 2 :020(525) [0889] needs of the body, man is **indeed** very clever, intelligent,
S D : 0 2 :039(528) [0895] good and delight in it (**indeed**, actually do good deeds and
S D : 0 2 :062(533) [0905] to say that the Lord God **indeed** has one mode of acting
S D : 0 3 :020(542) [0921] him, a regeneration has **indeed** taken place because he
S D : 0 3 :032(544) [0927] It is **indeed** correct to say that believers who through faith
S D : 0 3 :052(548) [0933] God, as though we are **indeed** justified solely through
S D : 0 3 :054(548) [0935] On the one hand, it is true **indeed** that God the Father,
S D : 0 4 :002(551) [0939] that good works are **indeed** necessary — not for salvation,
S D : 0 4 :008(552) [0941] require to perform, are **indeed** praiseworthy in the sight
S D : 0 4 :027(555) [0945] We should **indeed** not put our faith in the merit of our
S D : 0 6 :003(564) [0963] true believers are **indeed** motivated by the Holy Spirit and
S D : 0 6 :011(565) [0965] The law **indeed** tells us that it is God's will and command
S D : 0 7 :023(573) [0979] It is true **indeed** that if you take the Word away or look
S D : 0 7 :032(574) [0983] They, **indeed** have only bread and wine, for they do not
S D : 0 7 :076(583) [0999] multiply, so this word was **indeed** spoken only once, but
S D : 0 7 :101(587) [1007] to which all creatures are **indeed** much more penetrable
S D : 0 7 :102(587) [1007] We know **indeed** that he is in God beyond all creatures
S D : 0 7 :103(587) [1009] The enthusiasts may **indeed** think that God is unable to
S D : 0 8 :033(597) [1027] as Paul says, "Great **indeed** is the mystery of our religion:
S D : 0 8 :075(606) [1043] Son, the Father's Word, **indeed** knows all things, but that
S D : 1 1 :027(620) [1071] but through the Word, as **indeed** he has commanded the
S D : 1 1 :034(622) [1075] to say: "Externally I do **indeed** through the Word call all
S D : 1 1 :043(623) [1077] ourselves thereto, it is **indeed** a useful, salutary, and
S D : 1 1 :058(625) [1081] It is **indeed** a well deserved punishment for sin when God
S D : 1 1 :076(628) [1087] It is **indeed** correct and true what Scripture states, that no
S D : 1 1 :076(629) [1087] The Father **indeed** draws by the power of the Holy
S D : 1 1 :085(631) [1091] judgment on him, for he was **indeed** guilty of "hell-fire."

Independently (1)
S D : 0 1 :028(513) [0867] which exists **independently** within or apart from man's

Indescribable (3)
A P : 1 2 :034(186) [0261] they feel the terrible and **indescribable** wrath of God?
L C : 0 6 :025(460) [0000] rich alms and this **indescribable** treasure; they have
S D : 0 8 :040(599) [1029] In short it is **indescribable** what the devil attempts with

Indicate (22), Indicated (18), Indicates (14), Indicating (3), Indication (1), Indications (1)
P R : P R :016(008) [0013] had been presented, as **indicated** above, gladly and with
P R : P R :020(010) [0017] and incorrect, we should **indicate** and demonstrate by a
P R : P R :023(012) [0021] As **indicated** above, our disposition and intention has
A G : P R :001(024) [0039] summons Your Majesty **indicated** an earnest desire to
A G : 0 8 :001(033) [0047] for as Christ himself **indicated**, "The Pharisees sit on
A G : 1 6 :003(037) [0051] teach that none of the things **indicated** above is Christian.
A G : 2 0 :025(044) [0057] as has just been **indicated**, the Scriptures speak of faith
A G : 0 0 :000(049) [0059] account of them and to **indicate** our reasons for
A G : 2 3 :005(052) [0061] receive this precept," he **indicated** that few people have
A G : 2 4 :037(060) [0067] The ancient canons also **indicate** that one man officiated
A G : 2 6 :038(069) [0075] it, and by this he **indicated** that it is not the purpose of
A G : 2 7 :060(080) [0083] perfection and **indicated** that it was an innovation of his
A G : 2 8 :034(086) [0089] the Gospel, as has been **indicated** above and as is taught
A G : 0 0 :001(095) [0095] undue length we have **indicated** only the principal ones.
A L : 2 0 :002(041) [0053] and duties of life, **indicating** what manners of life and
A L : 2 6 :044(070) [0075] and Pope Gregory **indicates** in Dist. 12 that such diversity
A P : 0 4 :141(126) [0161] So he **indicates** that faith precedes while love follows.
A P : 0 4 :224(138) [0181] them and, as Paul **indicates**, they began to dislike good
A P : 0 4 :226(138) [0183] to our neighbor, and he **indicates** that love is the greatest
A P : 0 4 :259(145) [0193] of penitence, as the text **indicates**; but at the same time he
A P : 1 2 :126(201) [0289] unless you take care, **indicate** a change in the Holy
A P : 2 1 :043(235) [0357] They give many **indications** that the state of the church
A P : 2 2 :008(237) [0359] use lay communion, this **indicated** that they had been
A P : 2 2 :010(237) [0361] They say this **indicates** the use of one kind, and they add,
A P : 2 4 :029(255) [0393] this is a right sacrifice, **indicating** that other sacrifices are
A P : 2 7 :016(271) [0425] Gerson **indicates** how pure this is in most of those who
S 1 : 0 0 :000(287) [0453] and which were to **indicate** what we could or could not
S 1 : P R :001(288) [0455] deliberations and to **indicate**, on the one hand what and
L C : 0 1 :286(403) [0663] be the one which Christ **indicates** in the Gospel, and in
L C : 0 2 :012(412) [0681] pupils it is enough to **indicate** the most necessary points,
L C : 0 3 :027(424) [0705] and others is quite amply **indicated** in the Lord's Prayer.
L C : 0 4 :065(444) [0749] and emerging from it, **indicate** the power and effect of
L C : 0 6 :023(459) [0000] confession were clearly **indicated**, there would be no need
E P : 0 1 :020(468) [0783] by such terminology to **indicate** the difference between
S D : R N :000(503) [0849] Basis, Rule, and Norm, **Indicating** How All Doctrines
S D : 0 1 :006(509) [0861] "person-sin" in order to **indicate** that even though a man
S D : 0 1 :027(513) [0867] human nature (as was **indicated** above) that all men,
S D : 0 1 :038(514) [0871] These passages **indicate** clearly that even after the Fall
S D : 0 1 :053(517) [0875] "essential sin" to **indicate** that not only thoughts, words,
S D : 0 2 :015(523) [0885] By these petitions they **indicate** that what they ask of God
S D : 0 2 :028(527) [0893] mentioned, as the following testimonies will **indicate**.
S D : 0 2 :030(527) [0893] These statements **indicate** clearly that the Augsburg
S D : 0 2 :042(529) [0897] These testimonies **indicate** clearly that we cannot by our
S D : 0 2 :044(529) [0897] of "absolute necessity"), **indicates** how he intended his
S D : 0 3 :007(540) [0917] with such zeal in order to **indicate** how very important it
S D : 0 3 :027(543) [0923] does not love, this **indicates** certainly that he is not
S D : 0 3 :027(543) [0925] works (Rom. 3:28), he **indicates** thereby that neither the
S D : 0 4 :014(553) [0943] "should," and "must" to **indicate** what we are bound to do
S D : 0 4 :016(554) [0943] as his commandment **indicates** when it enjoins the
S D : 0 4 :038(557) [0951] they are an **indication** of salvation in believers
S D : 0 5 :027(563) [0961] But the Apology also **indicates** that, strictly speaking, the
S D : 0 6 :012(566) [0967] of it and to show and **indicate** to them in the Ten
S D : 0 6 :021(567) [0969] a mirror, it shows and **indicates** to them that in this life
S D : 0 6 :026(568) [0971] manner and measure **indicated** above is not to be urged
S D : 0 7 :035(575) [0983] and to **indicate** the sacramental union between the
S D : 0 7 :038(576) [0985] Thereby they wished to **indicate** that, even though they
S D : 0 8 :031(597) [1025] foundation, as we have **indicated** above and as we have
S D : 0 8 :048(600) [1031] (which, as has been **indicated** above, they have and
S D : 0 8 :063(603) [1037] exchange" in order to **indicate** thereby that such an

Indifference (15), Indifferent (22)
A L : 2 6 :017(066) [0073] they are to be as things **indifferent**, for these are his
A P : P R :016(099) [0101] in discord, nor are we **indifferent** to our danger; its extent
A P : 0 4 :135(125) [0159] in its smugness and **indifference** does not fear God or
A P : 2 2 :015(238) [0361] to call Christ's ordinances matters of **indifference**.
A P : 2 7 :058(279) [0439] but should be regarded simply as a matter of **indifference**.
L C : 0 4 :006(437) [0733] not to regard it as an **indifferent** matter, then, like putting
L C : 0 5 :026(449) [0759] yield hand and foot and become **indifferent** or impatient.
L C : 0 5 :044(451) [0763] in preaching, lest people become **indifferent** and bored.
L C : 0 5 :053(453) [0765] benefit of the cold and **indifferent**, that they may come to
E P : 1 0 :000(492) [0829] X. Church Usages, Called Adiaphora or **Indifferent** Things
E P : 1 0 :002(493) [0829] that in themselves are **indifferent** things and are neither
E P : 1 0 :002(493) [0829] with them in such ceremonies and **indifferent** things?
E P : 1 0 :006(493) [0829] to the enemies in such **indifferent** things, as the apostle
E P : 1 0 :006(493) [0829] no longer a question of **indifferent** things, but a matter
E P : 1 0 :011(494) [0831] the truth) in such **indifferent** things and ceremonies.
E P : 1 0 :012(494) [0831] ceremonies and **indifferent** things are abolished in a way
S D : 0 2 :046(530) [0899] disorderly, lazy and **indifferent** to such Christian
S D : 0 5 :009(559) [0955] forgiveness of sin to **indifferent** and secure hearts, but to
S D : 1 0 :000(610) [1053] Rites That Are Called Adiaphora or Things **Indifferent**
S D : 1 0 :002(611) [1053] themselves matters of **indifference** and that are neither
S D : 1 0 :002(611) [1053] to them in such adiaphora or matters of **indifference**.
S D : 1 0 :003(611) [1053] even as far as things **indifferent** are concerned, in a period
S D : 1 0 :005(611) [1053] consider as matters of **indifference**, and we should avoid
S D : 1 0 :005(611) [1053] adiaphora or things **indifferent** those ceremonies which
S D : 1 0 :005(611) [1053] such rites matters of **indifference** when these ceremonies
S D : 1 0 :007(611) [1055] in the church, true adiaphora or things **indifferent**.
S D : 1 0 :008(612) [1055] adiaphora or things **indifferent**, as defined above, are in
S D : 1 0 :009(612) [1055] external matters of **indifference** (Rom. 14) and
S D : 1 0 :010(612) [1055] even in matters of **indifference**, nor should we tolerate the
S D : 1 0 :012(612) [1057] time was a matter of **indifference** and which in his
S D : 1 0 :013(613) [1057] even in matters that were in themselves **indifferent**.
S D : 1 0 :014(613) [1057] such matters of **indifference** to confirm false doctrines,
S D : 1 0 :018(614) [1059] such matters of **indifference**, and we who are walking in
S D : 1 0 :024(615) [1061] in general and matters of **indifference** in particular.
S D : 1 0 :025(615) [1061] in matters of **indifference**, especially in a period of
S D : 1 0 :029(615) [1061] whether in things **indifferent**, in doctrine, or in whatever
S D : 1 0 :030(615) [1061] whereby matters of **indifference** are abolished in such a

Indignation (2)
A P : 0 2 :042(105) [0117] anger at his judgments; **indignation** because he does not
A P : 1 2 :127(201) [0291] How much silent **indignation** is there because you refuse

Indiscriminately (1)
A P : 2 8 :003(281) [0445] kinds of people to the priesthood quite **indiscriminately**.

Indispensable (3)
A P : 0 4 :398(167) [0227] most true and certain and **indispensable** for all Christians?
L C : 0 1 :255(399) [0653] more treasure which is **indispensable** to us, namely, our
L C : 0 1 :287(403) [0663] to be weaker are **indispensable**, and those parts of the

Individual (20), Individually (4), Individuals (11)
P R : P R :024(013) [0021] to restless, contentious **individuals**, who do not want to
A G : 2 4 :023(058) [0067] merited as much as a special Mass held for an **individual**.
A G : 2 8 :008(082) [0085] (to many persons or to **individuals**, depending on one's
A L : 2 4 :023(058) [0067] a special Mass said for **individuals**, and this produced
A L : 2 8 :008(082) [0085] either to many or to **individuals**, depending on one's
A P : 1 2 :059(190) [0267] faith by which each **individual** believes that his sins are
A P : 1 2 :099(197) [0281] of the keys proclaims to **individuals** by divine authority.
A P : 2 1 :010(230) [0345] Scripture, that the saints hear the **individual**'s prayers?
A P : 2 1 :013(230) [0345] church is not the same as the invocation of **individuals**.
A P : 2 4 :085(265) [0413] **Individuals** coming to the celebration of the Passover had
S 2 : 0 2 :013(295) [0467] opinion of certain **individuals** and cannot establish an
T R : 0 0 :009(321) [0505] He sent out each one **individually**, he said, in the same
T R : 0 0 :024(324) [0511] of one particular **individual** but to the whole church, as is
T R : 0 0 :026(324) [0511] valid because of any **individual**'s authority but because of
T R : 0 0 :068(331) [0523] not merely to certain **individuals**: "Where two or three are
L C : 0 1 :180(389) [0631] conduct ourselves **individually** toward our fellow men.
L C : 0 1 :181(389) [0631] here applies to private **individuals**, not to governments.
L C : 0 1 :279(403) [0661] So the **individual** is to be dealt with personally and not
L C : 0 1 :321(408) [0673] as attached to each **individual** commandment, penetrating
L C : 0 5 :017(448) [0757] false because of an **individual**'s unworthiness or unbelief.
E P : 0 8 :005(487) [0819] of man, but a single **individual** is both the Son of God
E P : 1 2 :005(498) [0839] is built on one's own **individual** self-chosen spirituality,
E P : 1 2 :029(500) [0843] just like any three **individual** people who are essentially
S D : 0 2 :068(534) [0907] the Spirit, but even the **individual** Christian in his own
S D : 0 4 :007(552) [0941] and not those that an **individual** may devise according to

Continued ▶

SD : 0 6 :016(566) [0967] to the difference in the **individuals** who are concerned
SD : 0 7 :017(572) [0979] the theologians collectively and **individually** subscribed.
SD : 0 7 :025(573) [0981] rendered false because an **individual's** person or unbelief.
SD : 0 8 :016(594) [1021] as if Christ were one **individual** and God the Word who
SD : 1 0 :010(612) [1055] of God, yes, every **individual** Christian, and especially the
SD : 1 0 :025(615) [1061] community, each **individual** Christian, and particularly
SD : 1 1 :023(619) [1069] each and every **individual** among the elect who are to be
SD : 1 1 :037(622) [1075] and by which he confirms it to every believer **individually**.
SD : 1 1 :038(622) [1075] in Article XI, we retain **individual** absolution and teach
SD : 1 1 :045(624) [1079] concerned about every **individual** Christian's conversion,

Indivisible (5), Indivisibly (1)
AL : 0 1 :002(027) [0043] eternal, incorporeal, **indivisible**, of infinite power,
EP : 0 8 :018(489) [0823] to all eternity, God and man in one **indivisible** person.
SD : 0 7 :037(575) [0985] natures are **indivisibly** united, so in the Holy Supper the
SD : 0 7 :101(587) [1007] For he is one **indivisible** person with God, and wherever
SD : 0 8 :068(604) [1039] God is a spiritual and **indivisible** essence and is therefore
SD : 0 8 :082(607) [1045] is, it is the single, **indivisible** person, and if you can say,

Indolence (2)
LC : 0 1 :099(378) [0609] called *acidia* — that is, **indolence** or satiety — a malignant
LC : 0 3 :067(429) [0717] not yield or fall away through weakness or **indolence**."

Indomitably (1)
SD : 0 7 :062(581) [0995] — and that we rest **indomitably**, with certain trust and

Indubitable (4), Indubitably (1)
EP : 0 4 :006(476) [0799] tree, certainly and **indubitably** follow genuine faith — if it
SD : 0 7 :042(576) [0985] firm, immovable, and **indubitable** rock of truth in the
SD : 0 7 :048(578) [0989] manifest, certain, and **indubitable**, can and should be
SD : 0 7 :050(578) [0989] appropriate, simple, **indubitable**, and clear words, just as
SD : 1 1 :049(624) [1079] draws the certain and **indubitable** conclusion that neither

Induce (2), Induced (2)
AG : 0 1 :006(028) [0043] that the Holy Spirit is a movement **induced** in creatures.
AP : 0 4 :201(134) [0175] to his faith before others and **induce** them to believe.
LC : 0 5 :043(451) [0763] to be Christians, may be **induced** to see the reason and
LC : 0 6 :023(459) [0000] which ought to move and **induce** us to confession were

Indulge (2), Indulgence (5), Indulgences (22), Indulgent (1)
AG : 2 5 :005(062) [0069] with satisfactions, with **indulgences**, with pilgrimages and
AG : 0 0 :002(095) [0095] complaints about **indulgences**, pilgrimages, and misuse of
AL : 0 0 :002(095) [0095] complaints about **indulgences**, pilgrimages, and misuse of
AL : 0 0 :002(095) [0095] have been troubled in many ways by **indulgence** sellers.
AP : 1 2 :015(184) [0257] They sell **indulgences**, which they interpret as the
AP : 1 2 :015(184) [0257] the dead not only by **indulgences** but also by the sacrifice
AP : 1 2 :026(185) [0259] of the keys, through **indulgences**, souls are delivered from
AP : 1 2 :131(202) [0291] soul do not permit the **indulgence** of the body in lusts,
AP : 1 2 :135(203) [0293] such satisfactions that **indulgences** remit, as the chapter
AP : 1 2 :135(203) [0293] But **indulgences** do not release us from commandments
AP : 1 2 :175(210) [0307] Formerly **indulgences** were the remission of public
AP : 1 2 :175(210) [0307] Still the name **indulgences** remains.
AP : 1 2 :175(210) [0307] for penalties; so also "**indulgence**" has been misinterpreted
AP : 1 5 :047(221) [0327] with the result that we **indulge** and pamper the desires of
AP : 2 1 :023(232) [0349] In **indulgences** they claim to apply the merits of the
AP : 2 7 :032(274) [0431] of sins except by God's **indulgence**; secondly, that you
S 2 : 0 2 :023(296) [0469] claim that relics effect **indulgences** and the forgiveness of
S 2 : 0 2 :024(296) [0469] belongs to the precious **indulgences**, which are granted to
S 3 : 0 3 :024(307) [0485] to the aid of the poor church and invented **indulgences**.
S 3 : 0 3 :024(307) [0485] The **indulgences** were distributed among the cardinals and
S 3 : 0 3 :025(307) [0485] church and house was reached by jubilee **indulgences**.
S 3 : 0 3 :026(307) [0487] afterwards by offering **indulgences** for the dead through
S 3 : 0 3 :027(307) [0487] on and trust in such **indulgences**, he again introduced
S 3 : 0 3 :027(307) [0487] to benefit from the **indulgence** or jubilee year must be
S 3 : 0 3 :027(308) [0487] with his power and **indulgences**, and once again directed
TR : 0 0 :046(328) [0517] Out of these arose **indulgences**, which are nothing but lies
SC : 0 9 :013(356) [0563] whereas she who is self-**indulgent** is dead even while she
LC : 0 1 :144(385) [0623] pilgrimages, and after **indulgences**, to their own hurt and
LC : 0 1 :214(394) [0641] marriage and either **indulge** in open and shameless
LC : 0 4 :009(437) [0733] the pope dispensed **indulgences** with his letters and bulls

Indwelling (12)
EP : 0 3 :002(473) [0793] faith, over against this **indwelling** Godhead, the sins of all
EP : 0 3 :016(475) [0795] us), and that by such **indwelling** our sins are covered up.
EP : 0 4 :015(477) [0799] testimonies of the Holy Spirit's presence and **indwelling**.
EP : 0 4 :019(477) [0801] that faith and the **indwelling** of the Holy Spirit are not
SD : 0 3 :054(548) [0933] concerning the **indwelling** of God's essential righteousness
SD : 0 3 :054(549) [0935] on the other hand, this **indwelling** of God is not the
SD : 0 3 :054(549) [0935] This **indwelling** follows the preceding righteousness of
SD : 0 3 :063(550) [0937] us, and that by such **indwelling** our sins are covered up in
SD : 0 6 :006(564) [0965] in this life through the **indwelling** Spirit in such a way
SD : 0 6 :025(568) [0971] face, so through God's **indwelling** Spirit they will do his
SD : 0 8 :087(608) [1047] of the presence and **indwelling** of their head, king, and
SD : 1 1 :074(628) [1087] power whatever of the **indwelling** Spirit of God and say

Ineffable (5)
EP : 0 8 :009(488) [0819] resultant exalted and **ineffable** sharing there flows
EP : 0 8 :013(488) [0821] has such a profound and **ineffable** union and communion
SD : 0 8 :019(595) [1021] much higher, and more **ineffable**, since on account of this
SD : 0 8 :030(597) [1025] exalted, intimate, and **ineffable** communion that even the
SD : 0 8 :051(600) [1033] unsearchable, **ineffable**, heavenly prerogatives and

Inept (1), Ineptitude (1)
LC : 0 3 :029(424) [0705] and coldly that they become daily more **inept** at praying.
SD : 0 1 :010(510) [0863] with a disability and **ineptitude** as far as the things of God

Inequality (1)
LC : 0 1 :108(380) [0611] must be this sort of **inequality** and proper distinctions.

Inevitably (7)
AP : 0 4 :233(140) [0185] For harmony will **inevitably** disintegrate if bishops
LC : 0 1 :045(370) [0593] crown and power, he **inevitably** perished with all that he
LC : 0 1 :046(370) [0593] life nowhere secure, yet **inevitably** he remained safe from
LC : 0 1 :216(394) [0641] if they remain they will **inevitably** sin more and more
LC : 0 1 :258(399) [0653] a poor man is **inevitably** oppressed, loses his case, and
LC : 0 2 :019(412) [0681] sustained by God, it **inevitably** follows that we are in duty
LC : 0 6 :017(459) [0000] the point that everyone **inevitably** despaired of confessing

Inexhaustible (1)
LC : 0 3 :056(427) [0713] — like an eternal, **inexhaustible** fountain which, the more

Inexorable (1)
AP : 2 3 :056(247) [0379] they are adamant and **inexorable**, though it is obviously a

Inexperienced (9)
AL : 2 0 :015(043) [0055] is despised by **inexperienced** men, God-fearing and
AL : 2 0 :018(043) [0055] Accordingly **inexperienced** and profane men, who dream
AP : 0 4 :280(149) [0201] sentences to put something over on the **inexperienced**.
AP : 0 4 :374(164) [0223] make it clearer to the **inexperienced** and to show that a
AP : 0 7 :033(175) [0239] to educate and instruct the people and the **inexperienced**.
AP : 1 1 :009(182) [0251] know how profitable it is to examine the **inexperienced**.
AP : 1 2 :114(199) [0285] tend to beguile the **inexperienced** into thinking that by
AP : 1 2 :122(200) [0287] passages to give the **inexperienced** the impression that
SC : PR :007(339) [0533] Young and **inexperienced** people must be instructed on

Inexpressible (8), Inexpressibly (1)
LC : 0 2 :024(413) [0683] has showered us with **inexpressible** eternal treasures
LC : 0 3 :057(428) [0713] and pledges so many **inexpressible** blessings, despise them
LC : 0 4 :026(439) [0739] being, for in it we obtain such an **inexpressible** treasure.
SD : 0 1 :002(508) [0859] deep, and **inexpressible** corruption thereof, in the sense
SD : 0 1 :011(510) [0863] inscrutable, and **inexpressible** corruption of his entire
SD : 0 1 :039(515) [0871] may well ponder God's **inexpressible** kindness in that he
SD : 0 1 :060(519) [0879] that original sin is an **inexpressible** impairment and such
SD : 0 1 :061(519) [0879] most profoundly and **inexpressibly** corrupts God's
SD : 1 1 :031(621) [1073] for them "with **inexpressible** groanings" (Rom. 8:16-26).

Infallible (2)
PR : PR :018(008) [0015] with the pure, **infallible**, and unalterable Word of God, to
PR : PR :022(012) [0019] Holy Spirit, turn to the **infallible** truth of the divine Word

Infant (9), Infants (5)
AG : 0 9 :003(033) [0047] who teach that **infant** Baptism is not right are rejected.
AP : 0 9 :002(178) [0245] is offered to all — men, women, children, and **infants**.
AP : 0 9 :002(178) [0245] it clearly follows that **infants** should be baptized because
S 3 : 0 5 :004(311) [0493] As for **infant** Baptism, we hold that children should be
LC : 0 1 :026(368) [0587] breasts and milk for her **infant**, and he gives grain and all
LC : 0 4 :046(442) [0743] [**Infant** Baptism]
LC : 0 4 :047(442) [0743] world through his sects, the question of **infant** Baptism.
LC : 0 4 :049(442) [0743] That the Baptism of **infants** is pleasing to Christ is
LC : 0 4 :050(443) [0745] not accept the Baptism of **infants**, he would not have
LC : 0 4 :050(443) [0745] must acknowledge that **infant** Baptism is pleasing to
LC : 0 4 :055(443) [0745] As we said, even if **infants** did not believe — which,
LC : 0 4 :057(444) [0747] We do the same in **infant** Baptism.
EP : 1 2 :008(498) [0839] neither think highly of **infant** Baptism nor encourage it, in
SD : 1 2 :013(634) [1099] they do not esteem **infant** Baptism very highly and do not

Infection (2)
LC : PR :014(360) [0571] a good antidote against their evil **infection** and poison.
LC : PR :019(361) [0573] against the poisonous **infection** of such security or vanity.

Infer (3)
AP : 0 4 :253(143) [0193] which our opponents shamelessly **infer** from his words.
LC : 0 1 :053(371) [0595] this everyone can readily **infer** when and in how many
SD : 1 1 :086(631) [1091] no way does he want us to **infer** that God had not wanted

Inferior (6)
AL : 2 6 :010(065) [0071] and imperfect works, far **inferior** to those glittering
AP : 2 4 :099(268) [0419] and a great issue, not **inferior** to the work the the prophet
TR : 0 0 :018(323) [0509] of poverty that makes a bishop superior or **inferior**."
SC : 0 5 :023(350) [0555] him, giving him **inferior** goods and short measure.
EP : 1 2 :028(500) [0843] divine majesty and is **inferior** to and beside God the
SD : 1 2 :036(635) [1101] with divine majesty **inferior** to and alongside the Father.

Infinite (13), Infinitely (2), Infinity (1)
AG : 0 1 :003(027) [0043] division, without end, of **infinite** power, wisdom, and
AL : 0 1 :002(027) [0043] indivisible, of **infinite** power, wisdom, and goodness, the
AL : 2 4 :021(058) [0067] added an opinion which **infinitely** increased private
AL : 2 4 :023(058) [0067] and this produced that **infinite** proliferation of Masses to
AP : 0 4 :226(138) [0183] with God, while love has **infinite** external duties to men.
AP : 0 7 :009(169) [0229] We see the **infinite** dangers that threaten the church with
AP : 0 7 :009(169) [0229] There is an **infinite** number of ungodly within the church
AP : 2 4 :013(251) [0387] the people and has **infinitely** multiplied the Masses.
AP : 2 4 :089(265) [0413] souls of the dead, from which they make **infinite** profits.
LC : 0 4 :034(440) [0741] no use, although in itself it is an **infinite**, divine treasure.
EP : 0 8 :007(487) [0819] omnipotence, eternity, **infinity**, and (according to its
EP : 0 8 :027(490) [0823] nature has become an **infinite** essence, like the divine
SD : 0 7 :047(578) [0989] these words is himself **infinite** Wisdom and Truth and can
SD : 0 8 :009(593) [1017] to be eternal, to be **infinite**, to be everywhere at the same
SD : 0 8 :055(601) [1033] are not created gifts but divine and **infinite** qualities.
SD : 0 8 :090(609) [1047] way as the Deity, as an **infinite** essence, through an

Infirm (1), Infirmities (5), Infirmity (2)
AG : 2 3 :014(053) [0063] worse and men are becoming weaker and more **infirm**.
AG : 2 3 :015(054) [0063] marriage to aid human **infirmity** and prevent unchastity.
AL : 2 3 :015(054) [0063] marriage to be a remedy against human **infirmity**.
LC : 0 1 :285(403) [0663] his neighbor's sins and **infirmities**, to overlook them, and
LC : 0 1 :288(404) [0663] whatever blemishes and **infirmities** we find in our
LC : 0 5 :060(453) [0767] retain many common **infirmities** in his flesh and blood.
LC : 0 5 :074(455) [0771] who neither feel their **infirmities** nor admit to being
LC : 0 5 :078(455) [0771] you feel your sins and **infirmities**, the more reason you

Inflame (1), Inflamed (3), Inflames (2), Inflaming (1)
AL : 0 0 :002(049) [0059] the people in order to **inflame** the hatred of men against
AP : PR :016(099) [0103] evident from the bitter hatred **inflaming** our opponents.
AP : 2 3 :013(241) [0367] which lust did not remove from nature but only **inflamed**.
AP : 2 3 :016(241) [0369] desire and the lust that **inflames** it come together;

Continued ▶

A P : 2 3 :064(248) [0381] was purer and less **inflamed** with lust than that of many
A P : 2 7 :002(269) [0419] **Inflamed** with a pharisaical hatred, the guardian began to
L C : 0 3 :102(434) [0727] this often wounds and **inflames** even an innocent heart.

Inflict (5), Inflicted (2), Inflicting (1)

P R : P R :005(004) [0009] false teachers were also **inflicted** on our churches because
A P : 1 2 :152(206) [0299] So troubles are **inflicted** on account of present sin
S C : P R :020(340) [0537] tell them that God will **inflict** awful punishments on them
L C : 0 1 :151(386) [0625] strangers and tyrants will **inflict** injury, injustice, and
L C : 0 1 :200(392) [0637] possession of his can we **inflict** a greater injury upon him.
L C : 0 3 :065(429) [0715] and must count on their **inflicting** every possible
E P : 1 0 :006(493) [0831] God sends us and what he lets the enemies **inflict** on us.
E P : 1 2 :016(499) [0841] with a clear conscience **inflict** capital punishment upon

Influence (1), Influential (1)

A P : 0 4 :321(156) [0209] performed under the **influence** of this disposition of love,
S D : 0 1 :013(511) [0863] He misleads many **influential** and wise men of the world

Inform (2), Informed (3)

P R : P R :018(008) [0015] clearly and thoroughly **informed** and possess final
A G : P R :018(026) [0041] among other things, **informed** and notified by Your
A P : 1 5 :014(217) [0319] How will he **inform** men of God's will without the
A P : 2 8 :006(282) [0445] by which our opponents **inform** us that bishops have the
L C : 0 1 :083(376) [0603] of intelligent and well **informed** Christians, for these have

Information (4)

P R : P R :012(006) [0013] When **information** about this Christian undertaking
A G : 0 0 :007(096) [0095] to present further **information** on the basis of the divine
A L : 0 0 :017(096) [0095] to present ampler **information** according to the
S D : 0 7 :052(578) [0991] who received the same **information** after Christ's

Infringe (1)

L C : 0 1 :197(391) [0637] the "spiritual estate" and **infringe** upon the holiness of the

Infused (4), Infuses (1), Infusion (1)

A P : 0 4 :079(117) [0143] of sins and the **infusion** of grace are the same thing, yet
A P : 0 4 :289(151) [0203] (which is love) **infused** by God, that with the help of this
E P : 0 1 :017(468) [0783] something which Satan **infused** into and mingled with
E P : 0 3 :015(475) [0795] that the Holy Spirit has **infused** and the works resulting
E P : 0 8 :027(490) [0825] and communicated to and **infused** into the human nature.
S D : 0 1 :026(512) [0867] and that afterward Satan **infuses** and blends original sin

Ingenious (1), Ingenuous (4), Ingenuously (2)

P R : P R :020(010) [0017] other basis, but with **ingenuous** faith they are to stay with
P R : P R :020(010) [0017] assail this our **ingenuous** faith and interpretation of the
P R : P R :020(010) [0017] as impiety, as if our **ingenuous** interpretation and faith
P R : P R :020(010) [0019] Creed that our **ingenuous** understanding of the words of
P R : P R :022(011) [0019] those persons who err **ingenuously** and who do not
P R : P R :022(012) [0021] even those who err **ingenuously** and ignorantly of the
L C : 0 1 :304(406) [0667] Who is **ingenious** enough to imagine how much he can

Inhabitants (1)

L C : 0 1 :150(385) [0623] many people as he has **inhabitants**, citizens, or subjects.

Inhere (1), Inherent (2), Inheres (11)

A P : 0 4 :035(112) [0131] It is **inherent** in man to despise God and to doubt his
A P : 2 7 :063(280) [0441] discuss the other evils **inherent** in present-day
E P : 0 1 :001(466) [0779] and original sin, which **inheres** in the corrupted nature
E P : 0 1 :020(468) [0783] original sin, which **inheres** in human nature, and the
E P : 0 1 :021(468) [0783] which man commits; it **inheres** in the nature, substance,
E P : 0 1 :022(469) [0785] or bad quality which **inheres** in the nature or essence of a
E P : 0 1 :022(469) [0785] man but something which **inheres** in the nature or
E P : 0 6 :001(479) [0805] although the flesh still **inheres** in them, to give them on
E P : 0 6 :004(480) [0805] of this Old Adam, who **inheres** in people's intellect, will,
S D : 0 1 :002(509) [0859] this inborn sin which **inheres** in his nature, all actual sins
S D : 0 1 :052(517) [0875] soul in which sin is and **inheres**) because through sin man
S D : 0 1 :061(519) [0879] handiwork, the sin which **inheres** in and most profoundly
S D : 0 3 :022(543) [0923] sins which throughout this life still **inhere** in our nature.
S D : 0 3 :058(550) [0937] our disobedience, which **inheres** in our nature, in its

Inherit (4), Inheritance (10), Inherited (6), Inherits (2)

A P : 2 7 :043(277) [0435] instead of a slender **inheritance** they find the most ample
S C : 0 1 :018(344) [0541] of our neighbor's **inheritance** or home, nor to obtain them
L C : 0 1 :301(405) [0667] wrestle over a large **inheritance**, real estate, etc., they
L C : 0 5 :055(453) [0765] temptation, especially **inherited** from the old order under
S D : 0 1 :005(509) [0861] and dreadful **inherited** disease which has corrupted our
S D : 0 1 :008(510) [0861] and understand the true nature of this **inherited** damage.
S D : 0 1 :009(510) [0861] 1. That this **inherited** damage is the reason why all of us,
S D : 0 1 :011(510) [0863] since the Fall man **inherits** an inborn wicked stamp, an
S D : 0 1 :011(510) [0863] By nature every one of us **inherits** from Adam a heart,
S D : 0 1 :012(510) [0863] weakened since the **inherited** malady has so poisoned and
S D : 0 1 :014(511) [0863] 5. This **inherited** damage is so great and terrible that in
S D : 0 1 :027(513) [0867] and a mother, now **inherit** a nature with the same lack
S D : 0 1 :042(515) [0873] This corruption has come upon us by **inheritance**.
S D : 0 3 :016(541) [0921] of God, adoption, and the **inheritance** of eternal life.
S D : 0 3 :025(543) [0923] with God, adoption, and the **inheritance** of eternal life.
S D : 0 3 :032(545) [0927] to sonship and the **inheritance** of eternal life only on
S D : 0 3 :053(548) [0933] adoption and the **inheritance** of eternal life and salvation.
S D : 0 4 :032(556) [0947] that the unrighteous will not **inherit** the kingdom of God?
S D : 0 4 :032(556) [0947] nor adulterers will **inherit** the kingdom of God"
S D : 0 4 :032(556) [0947] do such things shall not **inherit** the kingdom of God"
S D : 1 1 :018(619) [1069] children and into the **inheritance** of eternal life all who in
S D : 1 1 :030(621) [1073] God's purpose" to "the **inheritance**" hear the Gospel,

Inhuman (1)

S D : 1 1 :085(630) [1091] many, various, and most **inhuman** devices contrary to the

Iniquities (9), Iniquity (8)

A L : 2 7 :040(077) [0081] As the canon says, no vow ought to bind men to **iniquity**.
A P : 0 4 :058(115) [0137] O Lord, shouldst mark **iniquities**, Lord, who shall stand?"
A P : 0 4 :168(130) [0169] is the man to whom the Lord imputes no **iniquity**."
A P : 0 4 :261(145) [0195] he says, "Redeem your **iniquities** by showing mercy to the
A P : 0 4 :262(145) [0195] righteousness and your **iniquities** by favor to the poor."
A P : 0 4 :326(158) [0211] O Lord, shouldst mark **iniquities**, Lord, who could
A P : 1 2 :031(186) [0259] in Ps. 38:4, 8, "For my **iniquities** have gone over my
A P : 1 2 :122(200) [0289] us to redeem us from all **iniquity** and to purify himself a
A P : 2 0 :005(227) [0339] "The Lord has laid on him the **iniquity** of us all."
A P : 2 0 :005(227) [0339] that God has laid our **iniquities** on our works and not on
S 2 : 0 1 :002(292) [0461] has laid upon him the **iniquities** of us all" (Isa. 53:6).
S C : 0 1 :021(344) [0543] jealous God, visiting the **iniquity** of the fathers upon the
L C : 0 1 :030(368) [0589] *and jealous, visiting the* ***iniquity*** *of the fathers upon the*
L C : 0 1 :320(408) [0673] *jealous God, visiting the* ***iniquity*** *of the fathers upon the*
E P : 0 4 :007(476) [0799] are those whose **iniquities** are forgiven, and whose sins
S D : 0 5 :023(562) [0959] and bruised for our **iniquities** and with whose stripes we
S D : 1 0 :006(611) [1055] have righteousness and **iniquity**, or what fellowship has

Initial (2), Initially (2), Initiate (3), Initiated (1), Initiates (1), Initiative (2)

A P : 0 4 :017(109) [0125] or, as they call it, "**initial** grace," which they understand
A P : 0 4 :162(129) [0169] that he merely merited "**initial** grace" and that afterward
L C : 0 2 :070(420) [0697] they may on their own **initiative** learn more, relating these
L C : 0 3 :022(423) [0703] promise, God takes the **initiative** and puts into our
E P : 0 1 :016(468) [0783] capability, or power to **initiate**, to effect, or to cooperate
S D : P R :007(505) [0853] the version as it was **initially** prepared and published for
S D : 0 1 :023(512) [0865] skill, or ability to **initiate** and effect something in
S D : 0 1 :026(512) [0867] Fall, human nature is **initially** created perfect and pure,
S D : 0 2 :032(527) [0893] will any ability either to **initiate** something good or by
S D : 0 2 :037(528) [0895] his Word, whereby he **initiates** and increases
S D : 0 2 :065(534) [0907] as the Holy Spirit has **initiated** his work of regeneration

Injunction (4), Injunctions (1)

A L : 2 8 :075(094) [0095] to follow the apostolic **injunction** which commands us to
L C : 0 1 :169(388) [0629] commandment and **injunction** of God, who holds you
L C : 0 1 :293(404) [0665] when they obeyed the **injunctions** and prohibitions
L C : 0 4 :039(441) [0741] God's commandment and **injunction**, but also his promise
L C : 0 5 :087(456) [0773] it is his duty, by God's **injunction** and command, to teach

Injure (5), Injured (1), Injures (1), Injuries (2), Injuring (3), Injurious (1), Injury (13)

A G : 2 8 :068(093) [0093] and that disregard of them does not **injure** consciences.
A G : 0 0 :004(095) [0095] or for the purpose of **injuring** anybody, but we have
A L : 0 0 :004(095) [0095] been said or related for the purpose of **injuring** anybody.
A P : 2 2 :016(238) [0361] which has suffered this **injury** because it could not obtain
A P : 2 7 :002(269) [0419] for his doctrine, which seemed to be **injuring** his food.
A P : 2 7 :002(269) [0419] he was bearing these **injuries** with equanimity for Christ's
A P : 2 7 :041(276) [0435] rather to bear the **injury**, to let property, wife, and
A P : 2 7 :041(276) [0435] not about those who do **injury** to wife and children but
A P : 2 7 :041(276) [0435] but about those who bear **injury** because of the confession
T R : 0 0 :004(320) [0503] be false, impious, tyrannical, and **injurious** to the church.
S C : 0 5 :023(350) [0553] I have **injured** my neighbor by speaking evil of him, over
L C : 0 1 :072(374) [0601] that he may not be able to **injure** us as he is eager to do.
L C : 0 1 :151(386) [0625] and tyrants will inflict **injury**, injustice, and violence upon
L C : 0 1 :185(390) [0633] so that no one may do him bodily harm or **injury**.
L C : 0 1 :187(390) [0633] that no one willingly suffers **injury** from another.
L C : 0 1 :189(391) [0635] and save him from suffering bodily harm or **injury**.
L C : 0 1 :200(392) [0637] possession of his can we inflict a greater **injury** upon him.
L C : 0 1 :250(399) [0651] to do our neighbor any **injury** or wrong in any way
L C : 0 1 :263(400) [0655] tongue by which we may **injure** or offend our neighbor.
L C : 0 1 :274(402) [0659] forbids us to **injure** anyone physically, and yet an
L C : 0 1 :304(406) [0667] forced to sacrifice what he cannot spare without **injury**.
L C : 0 1 :310(407) [0669] all the roots and causes of our **injuries** to our neighbors.
L C : 0 1 :328(410) [0675] your neighbor no harm, **injury**, or violence, nor in any
L C : 0 3 :115(435) [0731] his anger by causing accidents and **injury** to our bodies.
L C : 0 3 :118(436) [0731] shame and from everything else that harms or **injures** us.
L C : 0 5 :079(455) [0771] who harm, wrong, and **injure** you and give you occasion

Injustice (10)

A P : 0 4 :262(145) [0195] defend the poor against **injustice**, as was the king's duty.
L C : 0 1 :151(386) [0625] will inflict injury, **injustice**, and violence upon him.
L C : 0 1 :155(386) [0625] violence, and **injustice**; but we are unwilling to see that we
L C : 0 1 :253(399) [0653] than you could scrape together by perfidy and **injustice**.
L C : 0 1 :284(403) [0661] can be no question of slander or **injustice** or false witness.
L C : 0 1 :308(406) [0669] a yard, and at length open **injustice** and violence follow.
L C : 0 3 :094(433) [0725] us harm, violence, and **injustice**, bears malice toward us,
L C : 0 3 :103(434) [0727] enmity, violence and **injustice**, perfidy, vengeance,
S D : 0 2 :058(532) [0903] and will not hear, no **injustice** is done him if the Holy
S D : 1 1 :061(626) [1083] No **injustice** is done to those who are punished and

Ink (1)

A P : 0 4 :399(168) [0227] answer written in blood to our Confession written in **ink**.

Inmost (7)

S D : 0 2 :017(524) [0887] in the law of God in my **inmost** self (which the Holy
S D : 0 2 :063(533) [0905] the law of God according to his **inmost** self (Rom. 7:22).
S D : 0 2 :064(533) [0905] in the law of God in my **inmost** self, but I see in my
S D : 0 2 :085(537) [0913] of God according to the **inmost** self, though he also sees
S D : 0 4 :019(554) [0945] in the law of God in his **inmost** self, and on the other that
S D : 0 6 :018(567) [0967] According to the **inmost** self they delight in the law of
S D : 0 6 :023(568) [0969] according to their **inmost** self they do what is pleasing to

Inn (1), Innkeeper (2)

L C : 0 1 :047(371) [0593] avails himself of an **inn**, food, and bed (only for his
E P : 1 2 :018(499) [0841] good conscience be an **innkeeper**, a merchant, or a cutler.
S D : 1 2 :023(634) [1099] good conscience be an **innkeeper**, a merchant, or a cutler.

Innate (2)

A G : 1 8 :004(039) [0051] for all have a natural, **innate** understanding and reason.
E P : 0 1 :021(468) [0785] through original sin, **innate** in us through our sinful seed

Inner (4)

A P : 0 2 :012(102) [0109] they failed to see the **inner** uncleanness of human nature.
L C : 0 5 :050(452) [0765] move you to examine your **inner** life and reflect: "See
S D : 0 6 :003(564) [0963] hence according to the **inner** man do the will of God from
S D : 0 6 :005(564) [0963] for according to the **inner** man they delight in the law of

Innocence (4), Innocent (22)

P R : P R :022(011) [0019] can find many pious, **innocent** people even in those
A G : 2 3 :021(055) [0063] one begin to persecute **innocent** people simply because

Continued ▶

A P : 0 2 :037(105) [0115] words in order by this device to crush an **innocent** man.
A P : 0 4 :322(157) [0209] flatter himself that he is **innocent** and by extolling himself
A P : 0 4 :329(158) [0211] Num. 14:18, "And the **innocent** will not be innocent."
A P : 0 4 :329(158) [0211] Num. 14:18, "And the innocent will not be **innocent**."
A P : 1 4 :002(214) [0315] of cruelty, they kill the unfortunate and **innocent** men.
A P : 2 1 :044(236) [0357] nor persecute **innocent** men, as has happened before, nor
A P : 2 1 :044(236) [0357] God they should defend the life and safety of the **innocent**
A P : 2 3 :003(239) [0363] marriage, you sentence **innocent** men to cruel
A P : 2 3 :070(249) [0383] the blood of the many **innocent** victims of their rage will
S 3 : 0 3 :029(308) [0487] render when they were **innocent** of evil deeds and could
S 3 : 0 3 :038(309) [0489] and blood of the **innocent** Lamb of God who takes away
T R : 0 0 :075(333) [0525] connection they often harassed **innocent** and honest men.
T R : 0 0 :078(333) [0527] which forbids an **innocent** person to marry after divorce.
S C : 0 2 :004(345) [0545] blood and with his **innocent** sufferings and death, in
S C : 0 2 :004(345) [0545] righteousness, **innocence**, and blessedness, even as he is
L C : 0 1 :257(399) [0653] of justice, where a poor, **innocent** man is accused and
L C : 0 3 :102(434) [0727] this often wounds and inflames even an **innocent** heart.
E P : 1 2 :006(498) [0839] but are righteous and **innocent**, and that as long as they
E P : 1 2 :006(498) [0839] will be saved in this **innocence** without Baptism (which
S D : 0 3 :017(542) [0921] a bribe, and deprive the **innocent** of his right" (Isa. 5:22).
S D : 1 1 :015(619) [1069] with God and that by his **innocent** obedience, suffering,
S D : 1 2 :008(633) [1097] accepted in their **innocence** what called itself evangelical
S D : 1 2 :011(634) [1099] God but righteous and **innocent**, and hence in their
S D : 1 2 :011(634) [1099] and hence in their **innocence** they will be saved without

Innovation (3), Innovations (1)
A G : 2 7 :060(080) [0083] that it was an **innovation** of his time to speak of monastic
A P : 0 2 :002(100) [0105] us of the charge of **innovation**, for it says: "It is also
A P : 0 2 :050(106) [0119] not introduced any **innovations**, but have set forth the
L C : 0 1 :085(376) [0605] no one will create disorder by unnecessary **innovation**.

Innumerable (1)
A P : 1 5 :021(218) [0321] ornaments, and **innumerable** similar observances in the

Inoculated (1)
S 3 : 0 8 :009(313) [0497] a poison implanted and **inoculated** in man by the old

Inordinate (1)
A P : 0 2 :027(104) [0113] and besides this, the **inordinate** disposition of the parts of

Inquires (2)
A L : 2 8 :020(084) [0087] When one **inquires** about the jurisdiction of bishops,
S D : 0 1 :060(519) [0879] however, when someone **inquires** further, What kind of

Insanity (1)
L C : 0 3 :115(435) [0731] neck and drives others to **insanity**; some he drowns, and

Inscribed (2)
L C : 0 2 :067(419) [0697] moreover, are **inscribed** in the hearts of all men.
E P : 1 1 :007(495) [0833] be eternally saved are **inscribed** and elected, as it is

Inscrutable (6)
P R : P R :021(011) [0019] of the personal union, which is an **inscrutable** mystery.
A L : 2 5 :008(062) [0069] also says, "The heart of man is corrupt and **inscrutable**."
S D : 0 1 :011(510) [0863] bottomless, **inscrutable**, and inexpressible corruption of
S D : 1 1 :009(617) [1065] only in the secret and **inscrutable** counsel of God, as
S D : 1 1 :013(618) [1067] secret, hidden, and **inscrutable** foreknowledge of God.
S D : 1 1 :064(626) [1083] are his judgements and how **inscrutable** his ways!

Insensitive (1)
L C : 0 5 :077(455) [0771] But the fact that we are **insensitive** to our sin is all the

Inseparable (2), Inseparably (2)
A G : 0 3 :002(029) [0045] and human, are so **inseparably** united in one person that
A L : 0 3 :002(029) [0045] divine and human, **inseparably** conjoined in the unity of
E P : 0 7 :011(483) [0811] God and man in one person, **inseparable** and undivided.
S D : 0 7 :094(586) [1005] God and man in one person, undivided and **inseparable**.

Insert (2)
A P : 2 4 :003(250) [0385] and understand it, and we **insert** German hymns to give
S D : 0 3 :024(543) [0923] that we do not mingle or **insert** that which precedes faith

Inside (1)
P R : P R :022(011) [0019] we mean entire churches **inside** or outside the Holy

Insidious (1)
L C : P R :005(359) [0567] Besides, a shameful and **insidious** plague of security and

Insight (1)
S D : 0 5 :010(560) [0955] to know his sin, an **insight** that Moses could never have

Insignificant (6)
A P : 0 4 :242(141) [0187] a major commotion emerged from an **insignificant** issue.
L C : 0 1 :278(402) [0661] Do you think it is an **insignificant** thing to gain a
L C : 0 1 :312(407) [0671] as if they were too **insignificant** or had been fulfilled long
L C : 0 5 :062(454) [0767] thy disciple, no matter how **insignificant** my worthiness."
E P : 0 1 :014(467) [0783] original sin is a slight, **insignificant** spot or blemish that
S D : 0 1 :021(511) [0865] sin is only a simple, **insignificant**, external spot or

Insinuate (3), Insinuated (2), Insinuating (1), Insinuations (1)
P R : P R :005(004) [0009] that false teachers **insinuated** perverted teachings into the
P R : P R :006(004) [0009] and which are **insinuating** themselves increasingly into
E P : 0 7 :001(481) [0809] surreptitiously to **insinuate** themselves and to disseminate
S D : P R :002(501) [0847] and raised no end of slanders and **insinuations** against it.
S D : P R :006(504) [0853] undertake to **insinuate** into the church errors that had
S D : 1 0 :003(611) [1053] and gradually to **insinuate** their false doctrines into our
S D : 1 2 :008(633) [1097] For the most part they **insinuated** themselves secretly,

Insist (17), Insisted (3), Insistent (1), Insistently (3), Insists (3)
A G : 2 6 :004(064) [0071] upon us and strongly **insists** that we regard the merit of
A G : 2 7 :027(075) [0079] then, do our opponents **insist** so strongly that vows must
A G : 2 7 :030(075) [0079] to argue so rashly and **insistently** about the obligation of
A G : 2 8 :033(086) [0087] to and urged so **insistently** as the change of the Sabbath,
A G : 2 8 :069(093) [0093] of men if they did not **insist** on the observance of
A L : 0 0 :001(047) [0059] Since this is so, those who **insist** that our teachers are to
A L : 2 6 :020(067) [0073] the Gospel compels us to **insist** in the church on the
A L : 2 7 :030(075) [0079] is not fair to argue so **insistently** about the obligation
A L : 2 8 :069(093) [0093] of men if they did not **insist** on the observance of
A P : P R :004(098) [0099] opponents stubbornly **insisted** that we sanction certain
A P : 0 4 :236(140) [0185] if our opponents did not **insist** so bitterly on certain
A P : 1 2 :060(190) [0269] We **insist** that this faith is really necessary for the
A P : 1 3 :001(211) [0309] But they **insist** that we enumerate seven sacraments.
A P : 1 5 :032(220) [0323] But the apostles **insisted** that Christian liberty remain in
A P : 1 5 :050(222) [0329] champion; everywhere he **insists** that these observances
A P : 2 7 :066(280) [0441] If our opponents **insist** upon misapplying this passage to
S C : P R :005(338) [0533] in the Lord's Supper and **insist** on the observance of
S C : P R :013(339) [0535] we should nevertheless **insist** that the people learn to know
S C : P R :023(341) [0539] to receive it, he will **insist** that you administer it to him.
L C : 0 1 :095(378) [0607] we must realize that God **insists** upon a strict observance
L C : 0 1 :298(405) [0665] dare to boast of it, and **insist** that it should be called not
L C : 0 1 :321(408) [0673] it before the young and **insist** that they learn and
L C : 0 4 :037(441) [0741] Actually, we **insist** on faith alone as so necessary that
E P : 0 7 :042(486) [0817] deliberately **insist** on crediting us with this doctrine,
S D : 0 4 :029(555) [0947] churches to continue to **insist** that the aforementioned
S D : 0 8 :063(603) [1037] They have **insisted** so strongly on this that they will hear
S D : 1 0 :002(611) [1053] at the enemies' **insistent** demand, restore once more

Insolence (2), Insolent (2)
L C : 0 1 :225(395) [0645] even become defiant and **insolent** and dare anyone to call
L C : 0 1 :235(397) [0647] Many of you are even **insolent** toward masters and
L C : 0 1 :237(397) [0647] whom we are obliged to suffer such intolerable **insolence**.
L C : 0 1 :239(397) [0649] well regulated, such **insolence** might soon be checked.

Inspiration (1), Inspired (3)
E P : 1 1 :013(496) [0835] from God but are **inspired** by the evil foe in an attempt to
S D : 0 6 :002(564) [0963] they, too, through the **inspiration** and impulse of the
S D : 0 6 :014(566) [0967] says, "All Scripture is **inspired** by God and profitable for
S D : 1 1 :012(618) [1067] All Scripture, **inspired** by God, should minister not to

Installed (3)
S D : 0 8 :026(596) [1023] eternity) and has been **installed** in the complete exercise
S D : 0 8 :028(596) [1025] which Christ has been **installed** according to his humanity
S D : 0 8 :029(597) [1025] the divine nature and **installed** in the exercise of the

Instance (4), Instances (5)
A G : 2 7 :056(080) [0083] Many **instances** are also recorded of men who forsook
A P : 0 7 :045(177) [0243] Many similar **instances** can be gathered from the histories
A P : 1 2 :155(207) [0301] From these **instances** they construct the universal rule
L C : 0 1 :184(390) [0633] For **instance**, a neighbor, envious that you have received
L C : 0 1 :258(399) [0653] is such a government, **instances** of this sin still occur.
S D : 0 7 :083(584) [1001] it is not observed (if, for **instance**, the blessed bread is not
S D : 0 7 :108(588) [1009] sacrament (when, for **instance**, the bread is locked up in
S D : 0 8 :038(598) [1027] other nature, as if, for **instance**, only the human nature
S D : 1 0 :012(612) [1057] liberty he employed in other **instances** (Acts 16:3).

Instantly (1)
L C : 0 2 :059(418) [0695] from this life, he will **instantly** perfect our holiness and

Instead (27)
A G : 2 0 :033(045) [0057] to accomplish this, and **instead** fell into many great and
A L : 2 0 :003(041) [0053] **Instead**, they urged childish and needless works, such as
A P : 0 4 :047(113) [0133] righteousness of the law **instead** of the righteousness of
A P : 0 4 :081(118) [0143] **Instead**, as though Christ were completely buried, they
A P : 0 4 :224(138) [0181] own opinions into them **instead** of deriving the meaning
A P : 1 2 :174(210) [0307] peaceable conduct **instead** of murder and hatred, the
A P : 1 2 :174(210) [0307] chastisement of the flesh **instead** of adultery and
A P : 1 5 :007(216) [0317] to set up another justifier and mediator **instead** of Christ?
A P : 1 5 :019(218) [0319] the god of fortresses **instead** of these: a god whom his
A P : 1 6 :007(223) [0331] the messianic kingdom; **instead**, he would have them
A P : 2 1 :042(235) [0357] **Instead** of supporting this most honorable and holy desire
A P : 2 3 :045(245) [0377] these works and services **instead** of using wine or meat or
A P : 2 4 :023(253) [0391] offering to reconcile God by his merits **instead** of ours.
A P : 2 4 :043(257) [0399] **Instead**, they discuss the worship of saints, human
A P : 2 7 :034(275) [0431] **Instead** of Christ they worship their own cowls and their
A P : 2 7 :043(277) [0435] sake of food and leisure; **instead** of a slender inheritance
A P : 2 7 :065(280) [0441] secure eternal life for us **instead** of mercy for Christ's
A P : 2 8 :004(281) [0445] **Instead** of alleviating such minds tortured by doubt, they
L C : P R :003(358) [0567] evening they would read, **instead**, at least a page or two
L C : 0 1 :144(385) [0623] neglected and despised; **instead**, everybody ran in the
L C : 0 1 :258(399) [0653] **Instead**, they speak dishonestly with an eye to gaining
L C : 0 3 :075(430) [0719] with a loaf of bread **instead** of a lion or a wreath of rue,
L C : 0 6 :003(457) [0000] **Instead**, it was made sheer anguish and a hellish torture
S D : 0 1 :047(516) [0875] and that in eternal life, **instead** of this essence of our body
S D : 1 1 :026(620) [1071] **Instead** we must heed the revealed will of God.
S D : 1 1 :072(628) [1087] son asks for a fish, will **instead** of a fish give him a
S D : 1 2 :037(636) [1103] and terminology, and **instead** teach that there is not one

Instigation (1)
S D : 1 1 :079(629) [1089] man, who, through the **instigation** of the devil and not of

Instill (1), Instilled (1)
L C : 0 5 :085(456) [0773] we may more easily **instill** the Ten Commandments, the
S D : 0 4 :033(556) [0947] do good works can be **instilled** without darkening the

Institute (24), Instituted (106), Instituting (4)
A G : 0 5 :001(031) [0045] obtain such faith God **instituted** the office of the
A G : 0 7 :003(032) [0047] church that ceremonies, **instituted** by men, should be
A G : 1 3 :001(035) [0049] the sacraments were **instituted** not only to be signs by
A G : 1 5 :003(036) [0049] and traditions **instituted** by men for the purpose of
A G : 1 6 :001(037) [0051] rule and laws were **instituted** and ordained by God for the
A G : 2 3 :003(051) [0061] estate of marriage was **instituted** by the Lord God to
A G : 2 3 :013(053) [0063] (which God himself **instituted** and left free to man) never
A G : 2 3 :015(054) [0063] than God himself, who **instituted** marriage to aid human
A G : 0 1 :007(056) [0065] sacrament, why it was **instituted**, and how it is to be used
A G : 2 4 :021(058) [0067] original sin, and had **instituted** the Mass as a sacrifice for
A G : 2 4 :030(059) [0067] holy sacrament was not **instituted** to make provision for a

Continued ▶

AG : 2 5 :012(063) [0071] by the Scriptures, but was **instituted** by the church.
AG : 2 6 :001(063) [0071] which had been **instituted** by men serve to earn grace and
AG : 2 6 :029(068) [0075] to the Gospel to **institute** or practice such works for the
AG : 2 6 :045(070) [0075] of the apostles to **institute** holy days but to teach faith
AG : 2 7 :013(072) [0077] by all other states of life **instituted** by God — whether the
AG : 2 7 :016(073) [0077] as far superior to the other estates **instituted** by God.
AG : 2 7 :036(076) [0081] God that is chosen and **instituted** by men to obtain
AG : 2 8 :023(084) [0087] they teach, introduce, or **institute** anything contrary to
AG : 2 8 :034(086) [0087] do not have power to **institute** or establish anything
AG : 2 8 :037(087) [0089] of saints have been **instituted** in order that by such works
AG : 2 8 :039(087) [0089] Again, those who **institute** human ordinances also act
AG : 2 8 :039(087) [0089] apostles and bishops to **institute** it, as some have written.
AG : 2 8 :050(089) [0091] as have been **instituted** as necessary to propitiate God and
AG : 2 8 :052(089) [0091] we do not merit it by services of God **instituted** by men.
AL : 0 5 :001(031) [0045] Gospel and administering the sacraments was **instituted**.
AL : 0 7 :003(032) [0047] or rites and ceremonies, **instituted** by men, should be
AL : 1 3 :001(035) [0049] the sacraments were **instituted** not merely to be marks of
AL : 1 5 :003(036) [0049] traditions which are **instituted** to propitiate God, merit
AL : 1 5 :004(037) [0049] foods and days, etc., **instituted** to merit grace and make
AL : 2 3 :015(054) [0063] Besides, God **instituted** marriage to be a remedy against
AL : 2 4 :021(058) [0067] for original sin and had **instituted** the Mass in which an
AL : 2 4 :030(059) [0067] Therefore the Mass was **instituted** that faith on the part
AL : 2 6 :002(064) [0071] new fasts were daily **instituted**, and the learned men in the
AL : 2 6 :029(068) [0075] with the Gospel to **institute** or practice such works for the
AL : 2 7 :016(073) [0077] this kind of life was **instituted** to merit grace and
AL : 2 7 :016(073) [0077] put it far above all other kinds of life **instituted** by God.
AL : 2 7 :036(076) [0081] service of God that is **instituted** and chosen by men to
AL : 2 8 :002(081) [0083] the keys, not only have **instituted** new forms of worship
AL : 2 8 :034(086) [0087] do not have power to **institute** anything contrary to the
AL : 2 8 :037(086) [0089] and new orders **instituted** because the authors of these
AL : 2 8 :039(087) [0089] had commissioned the apostles and bishops to **institute** it.
AL : 2 8 :050(089) [0091] which have been **instituted** as necessary or instituted with
AL : 2 8 :050(089) [0091] as necessary or **instituted** with the intention of meriting
AL : 2 8 :050(089) [0091] not lawful for bishops to **institute** such services or require
AL : 2 8 :052(089) [0091] certain observances or acts of worship **instituted** by men.
AL : 2 8 :058(091) [0091] of the Sabbath was **instituted** by the church's authority as
AP : 0 4 :210(136) [0179] the Lord's Supper was **instituted** in the church so that as
AP : 0 7 :023(172) [0235] Scriptures by his leave, **institute** devotions and sacrifices,
AP : 0 7 :030(174) [0237] or rites and ceremonies, **instituted** by men, should be
AP : 0 7 :033(174) [0239] by differences in rites **instituted** by men, although we like
AP : 0 7 :036(175) [0241] believe (like the divinely **instituted** Word and
AP : 1 2 :022(185) [0257] before God, but it was **instituted** to commute eternal to
AP : 1 2 :022(185) [0257] upon consciences, to **institute** new acts of devotion, and
AP : 1 2 :120(200) [0287] exhibitions had been **instituted** as an example and to test
AP : 1 2 :121(200) [0287] these observances were **instituted** for the sake of church
AP : 1 2 :143(204) [0297] Thus certain fasts were **instituted** not to control the flesh
AP : 1 2 :176(210) [0307] impose penalties or to **institute** forms of worship; they
AP : 1 3 :002(211) [0309] rites and ceremonies **instituted** in Scripture, whatever
AP : 1 3 :003(211) [0309] By this definition, rites **instituted** by men are not
AP : 1 3 :003(211) [0309] Hence signs **instituted** without God's command are not
AP : 1 3 :014(213) [0311] Matrimony was first **instituted** not in the New Testament
AP : 1 4 :001(214) [0315] and useful reasons for **instituting** ecclesiastical discipline
AP : 1 5 :001(215) [0315] that human traditions **instituted** to appease God, to merit
AP : 1 5 :013(216) [0319] The holy Fathers did not **institute** any traditions for the
AP : 1 5 :013(216) [0319] They **instituted** them for the sake of good order and
AP : 1 5 :014(216) [0319] If somebody wants to **institute** certain works to merit the
AP : 1 5 :018(217) [0319] not necessary that rites **instituted** by men be everywhere
AP : 1 5 :030(219) [0323] the Gospel, the divinely **instituted** ceremonies of Moses
AP : 1 5 :031(219) [0323] have the power to **institute** rites as though they justified
AP : 2 1 :023(232) [0349] declares: "It is a divinely **instituted** order that we should
AP : 2 1 :024(232) [0349] Where is the "divinely **instituted** order that we should
AP : 2 2 :001(236) [0357] For Christ **instituted** both kinds, and he did not do so
AP : 2 2 :002(236) [0357] If Christ **instituted** it for all of the church, why is one kind
AP : 2 2 :003(236) [0359] the words of him who **instituted** the sacrament; previously
AP : 2 2 :004(236) [0359] the entire sacrament was **instituted** for the whole church.
AP : 2 2 :010(237) [0361] The sacrament was **instituted** to console and strengthen
AP : 2 3 :019(242) [0369] of nature which he has **instituted**, for he does not want us
AP : 2 4 :034(256) [0397] though it was for these that the ceremony was **instituted**.
AP : 2 4 :035(256) [0397] the ceremony was **instituted** because of them and ought
AP : 2 4 :041(257) [0399] world, and they have **instituted** new worship in the
AP : 2 4 :054(259) [0403] sacrifices were not **instituted** to merit the forgiveness of
AP : 2 4 :068(261) [0407] that the Lord's Supper was **instituted** for two reasons.
AP : 2 4 :068(262) [0409] idea that ignores the chief use of what God has **instituted**.
AP : 2 4 :070(262) [0409] so the sacrament was **instituted** to move the heart to
AP : 2 4 :071(262) [0409] For such use Christ **instituted** it, as he commanded
AP : 2 4 :089(266) [0415] Supper which was **instituted** for commemoration and
AP : 2 4 :090(266) [0415] the Lord's Supper was **instituted** for the sake of forgiving
AP : 2 4 :092(266) [0417] and it is not safe to **institute** services in the church
AP : 2 4 :097(268) [0417] perform the sacrifices **instituted** by God with this wicked
AP : 2 7 :070(281) [0443] only with services **instituted** by his Word and done in
AP : 2 8 :011(283) [0447] bishops have the power to **institute** such acts of worship.
AP : 2 8 :014(283) [0447] bishops may **institute** new acts of worship, for worship
S 2 : 0 2 :012(295) [0465] dead although Christ **instituted** the sacrament for the
S 3 : 0 3 :026(307) [0487] into purgatory, first by **instituting** Masses and vigils for
S 3 : 0 8 :001(312) [0493] of the keys, which was **instituted** by Christ in the Gospel,
S 3 : 1 1 :003(315) [0499] as God ordained and **instituted** it, and we shall not
TR : 0 0 :016(323) [0509] with it, it is quite apparent that it was not **instituted**.
TR : 0 0 :040(327) [0515] Christ and the worship **instituted** by God, and he wishes
SC : 0 6 :002(351) [0555] Answer: **Instituted** by Christ himself, it is the true body
SC : 0 9 :004(355) [0561] God, and those that exist have been **instituted** by God.
LC : S P :020(364) [0579] say about the sacraments which Christ himself **instituted**.
LC : 0 1 :094(378) [0607] of worship are therefore **instituted** and appointed in order
LC : 0 1 :112(380) [0613] have been no need to **institute** monasticism or "spiritual
LC : 0 1 :274(402) [0659] God of his own accord **instituted** that office, and as he
LC : 0 3 :098(433) [0725] it has been especially **instituted** for us to use and practice
LC : 0 4 :001(436) [0733] us to speak of our two sacraments, **instituted** by Christ.
LC : 0 4 :006(437) [0733] is no human plaything but is **instituted** by God himself.
LC : 0 4 :008(437) [0733] which have been **instituted**, established, and confirmed in
LC : 0 4 :008(437) [0733] What God **instituted** and commands cannot be useless.
LC : 0 4 :019(439) [0737] things ordained and **instituted** by God should be regarded
LC : 0 4 :023(439) [0737] for what purpose it was **instituted**, that is, what benefits,
LC : 0 5 :001(447) [0753] established from the words by which Christ **instituted** it.
LC : 0 5 :004(447) [0755] It was **instituted** by Christ without man's counsel or
LC : 0 5 :017(448) [0757] what I now do, what I **institute**, what I give you and bid
LC : 0 5 :020(449) [0757] sacrament was really **instituted**, for it is most necessary
LC : 0 5 :042(451) [0763] or compelled, lest we **institute** a new slaughter of souls.
LC : 0 5 :042(451) [0763] Christ did not **institute** it to be treated merely as a
LC : 0 5 :047(452) [0765] Christ means to say: "I **institute** a Passover or Supper for
LC : 0 5 :065(454) [0769] as well have kept quiet and not **instituted** a sacrament.
EP : 0 7 :019(484) [0813] for Christ **instituted** this Supper particularly for
SD : 0 6 :006(565) [0965] to the order which God **instituted** for them once and for
SD : 0 7 :010(571) [0975] Sacrament of the Altar, **instituted** by Christ himself, is
SD : 0 7 :016(572) [0977] For it was **instituted** to testify that those who truly repent
SD : 0 7 :025(573) [0981] by which it has been **instituted** and has become a
SD : 0 7 :026(573) [0981] what I am now doing, **instituting**, giving you, and
SD : 0 7 :032(575) [0983] also have the Word and **instituted** ordinance of God but
SD : 0 7 :044(577) [0987] care in ordaining and **instituting** this most venerable
SD : 0 7 :070(582) [0997] sacrament was **instituted** and ordained primarily for
SD : 0 7 :073(583) [0999] that there is no sacrament apart from the **instituted** use.
SD : 0 7 :085(584) [1001] apart from the use **instituted** by Christ, or apart from the
SD : 0 7 :085(584) [1001] apart from the divinely **instituted** action (that is, if one
SD : 0 7 :108(588) [1009] use for which it is **instituted** in the Word of God, as was
SD : 0 8 :079(607) [1045] sure on this point, he **instituted** his Holy Supper that he

Institution (52), Institutions (5)

PR : P R :020(010) [0017] namely, the words of **institution** of Christ's testament.
PR : P R :022(012) [0019] according to Christ's **institution** and as we concordantly
AG : 2 2 :011(050) [0061] according to Christ's **institution** or to compel them to act
AG : 2 2 :012(051) [0061] is contrary to the **institution** of Christ, the customary
AG : 2 8 :058(091) [0091] Sabbath as a necessary **institution** are very much
AL : 0 8 :002(033) [0047] by reason of the **institution** and commandment of Christ
AL : 2 2 :012(051) [0061] does not agree with the **institution** of Christ, the
AL : 2 3 :008(052) [0061] a commandment of God and an **institution** of God.
AL : 2 4 :020(058) [0067] world nothing of divine **institution** seems ever to have
AL : 2 7 :018(073) [0079] can not nullify the command and **institution** of God.
AL : 2 7 :020(074) [0079] but God's creation and **institution** also compel those to
AL : 2 7 :021(074) [0079] obey this command and **institution** of God do not sin.
AP : 2 2 :001(236) [0357] and in accord with the **institution** of Christ and the words
AP : 2 4 :008(250) [0385] them, they change the **institutions** of the Fathers and then
S 2 : 0 2 :004(293) [0463] blessed manner — according to the **institution** of Christ.
S 2 : 0 2 :008(294) [0465] sacrament administered according to Christ's **institution**.
S 2 : 0 2 :029(297) [0471] according to the **institution** of Christ and may use and
S 2 : 0 4 :001(298) [0471] or through a human **institution** (that is, a secular
S 3 : 0 5 :001(310) [0491] commanded by the **institution** of Christ; or as Paul says,
S 3 : 0 5 :002(310) [0491] forget the Word (God's **institution**) and say that God has
S 3 : 0 6 :003(311) [0493] the whole order and **institution** as it was established and
SC : 0 9 :005(355) [0561] sake to every human **institution**, whether it be to the
LC : 0 1 :207(393) [0639] it as the first of all **institutions**, and he created man and
LC : 0 1 :208(393) [0639] but it is a glorious **institution** and an object of God's
EP : 0 7 :009(483) [0811] the words of Christ's **institution** should under no
EP : 1 0 :009(494) [0831] human precepts and **institutions** in the church are to be
EP : 1 0 :010(494) [0831] precepts, and **institutions** are forcibly imposed upon the
SD : P R :002(501) [0847] of God and Christian **institutions**, attacked it violently
SD : 0 7 :016(572) [0977] they hold that it is the **institution** of this sacrament,
SD : 0 7 :016(572) [0977] that, where Christ's **institution** and command are
SD : 0 7 :042(576) [0987] of truth in the words of **institution** recorded in the holy
SD : 0 7 :048(578) [0989] All circumstances of the **institution** of this Supper testify
SD : 0 7 :050(578) [0989] In the **institution** of his last will and testament and of his
SD : 0 7 :050(578) [0989] of faith and in the **institution** of other covenant-signs and
SD : 0 7 :064(581) [0995] what Christ's words of **institution** say, when at table and
SD : 0 7 :066(581) [0995] these words of Christ's **institution** and St. Paul's
SD : 0 7 :074(583) [0999] of God and the Word, **institution**, and ordinance of our
SD : 0 7 :075(583) [0999] he spoke in the first **institution** were not only efficacious
SD : 0 7 :075(583) [0999] according to Christ's **institution** and where his words are
SD : 0 7 :075(583) [0999] wherever we observe his **institution** and speak his words
SD : 0 7 :075(583) [0999] by the virtue of the first **institution**, which he wants to be
SD : 0 7 :077(583) [0999] his command and **institution** can and does bring it about
SD : 0 7 :078(583) [1001] but when we follow his **institution** and command in the
SD : 0 7 :079(584) [1001] the words of **institution** are to be spoken or sung
SD : 0 7 :082(584) [1001] the repetition and recitation of the words of **institution**.
SD : 0 7 :083(584) [1001] of Christ's words of **institution** by itself, if the entire
SD : 0 7 :085(584) [1001] from the words of **institution**: Nothing has the character
SD : 0 7 :085(584) [1001] not observe Christ's **institution** as he ordained it, it is no
SD : 0 7 :086(584) [1003] or words of **institution**, the distribution and reception, or
SD : 0 7 :089(585) [1003] solely the Word and **institution** of our almighty God and
SD : 0 7 :110(588) [1011] to the explicit command and **institution** of Christ, etc.
SD : 0 7 :113(589) [1011] that the words of **institution** are not to be simply
SD : 0 7 :119(590) [1013] according to Christ's **institution** on earth, but that he is as
SD : 0 7 :121(590) [1013] omit the words of **institution** in the administration of the
SD : 0 7 :121(590) [1013] the words of **institution** cannot and should not in any
SD : 0 7 :122(590) [1013] the words of Christ's **institution** believers are not directed
SD : 0 8 :002(591) [1015] basis of the words of **institution**, the Zwinglians countered

Instruct (13), Instructed (22), Instructing (3), Instruction (33), Instructions (4), Instructs (3)

PR : P R :000(001) [0004] and Estates for the **Instruction** and Admonition of their
PR : P R :022(012) [0019] when they are rightly **instructed** in this doctrine, they
PR : P R :023(012) [0021] faithfully and diligently **instructed** therein, so that the
PR : P R :024(013) [0023] needed consolation and **instruction** of poor, misguided
AG : P R :015(026) [0041] especially in a public **instruction** at the diet in Spires in
AG : P R :017(026) [0041] by means of a written **instruction** at the last diet in Spires
AG : 1 5 :002(036) [0049] these observances with **instruction** so that consciences
AG : 2 0 :002(041) [0053] accounts and **instructions** concerning true Christian
AG : 2 0 :008(042) [0053] everywhere, our people have been **instructed** as follows:
AG : 2 0 :023(044) [0055] **Instruction** is also given among us to show that the faith
AG : 0 0 :001(047) [0059] for proper Christian **instruction**, the consolation of
AG : 0 1 :007(056) [0065] the people are **instructed** often and with great diligence
AG : 0 1 :007(056) [0065] people are also given **instruction** about other false
AG : 0 1 :002(056) [0065] Latin responses for the **instruction** and exercise of the
AG : 2 4 :024(058) [0067] of such circumstances, **instruction** was given so that our
AG : 2 5 :002(061) [0069] the people are carefully **instructed** concerning the
AG : 2 6 :019(067) [0073] compelled them to give **instruction** about the
AG : 2 6 :041(070) [0075] however, the people are **instructed** that such outward
AG : 2 7 :059(080) [0083] it was necessary to give the people proper **instruction**.
AL : 2 0 :008(042) [0053] our teachers have **instructed** our churches concerning
AL : 2 4 :002(056) [0065] These are added for the **instruction** of the people, for
AL : 2 8 :004(081) [0085] for the sake of **instructing** consciences, to show the

Continued ▶

A P : 0 2 :034(104) [0113] "After I was **instructed**, I smote upon my thigh"
A P : 0 4 :261(145) [0195] One part **instructs** about the new life and its works.
A P : 0 4 :322(157) [0209] perish even more, he is **instructed** and taught that he sins
A P : 0 7 :033(175) [0239] serves to educate and **instruct** the people and the
A P : 0 7 :040(176) [0241] examples as well as by **instruction** they might transmit to
A P : 1 1 :003(180) [0249] Our clergy **instruct** the people about the worth and fruits
A P : 1 1 :005(181) [0249] the people could not be heard and **instructed** properly.
A P : 1 1 :006(181) [0251] things so that they might be **instructed** more easily.
A P : 1 2 :110(198) [0285] examination is useful to **instruct** men better, still it must
A P : 1 2 :127(201) [0289] Men are demanding **instruction** in religion.
A P : 1 3 :003(211) [0309] even though they may **instruct** or admonish the simple
A P : 1 5 :020(218) [0321] and finally because they helped **instruct** the common folk.
A P : 1 5 :040(220) [0325] after they have been **instructed**, examined, and absolved.
A P : 1 5 :041(220) [0325] churches are required to **instruct** and examine the youth
A P : 1 5 :043(221) [0327] the education and **instruction** of children, chastity, and
A P : 2 0 :013(228) [0341] of sins; he is giving **instruction** that they should be done
A P : 2 2 :006(237) [0359] a valid explanation to **instruct** those who were not
A P : 2 4 :016(252) [0389] for they despise these **instructions** and mutilate the
A P : 2 4 :049(258) [0401] this only when they have been **instructed** and examined.
A P : 2 4 :049(258) [0401] They are **instructed** about the proper use of the
A P : 2 7 :005(269) [0421] schools of Christian **instruction**, they have degenerated as
A P : 2 8 :004(281) [0445] desperately want **instruction** in order to have a sure way
S 1 : P R :001(288) [0455] I was therefore **instructed** to draft and assemble articles
S 2 : 0 4 :014(301) [0475] with such teaching, **instructions** are given concerning the
S 3 : 0 3 :012(305) [0483] the sophists thus **instructed** the people to place their
S 3 : 0 8 :001(312) [0495] need to be examined and **instructed** in Christian doctrine.
S C : P R :007(339) [0533] people must be **instructed** on the basis of a uniform, fixed
S C : P R :011(339) [0535] refuse to receive your **instructions**, tell them that they
S C : P R :018(340) [0537] be emphasized when **instructing** laborers and
S C : P R :018(340) [0537] must be stressed when **instructing** children and the
S C : 0 9 :008(356) [0563] up in the discipline and **instruction** of the Lord"
L C : S P :001(362) [0575] undertaken for the **instruction** of children and uneducated
L C : S P :001(362) [0575] in Greek, a "catechism" — that is, **instruction** for children.
L C : S P :003(362) [0575] should be thoroughly **instructed** in the various parts of
L C : S P :015(363) [0577] are the most necessary parts of Christian **instruction**.
L C : 0 1 :050(371) [0593] has inwardly **instructed** the heart and taught faith, so this
L C : 0 1 :099(378) [0609] feel that they know it all and need no more **instruction**.
L C : 0 1 :175(389) [0631] also have soundly **instructed** citizens, virtuous and
L C : 0 1 :249(398) [0651] responsibility is only to **instruct** and reprove by means of
L C : 0 1 :319(408) [0673] the first part, both for **instruction** and for admonition.
L C : 0 4 :001(436) [0733] some brief, elementary **instruction** in them because
L C : 0 5 :013(448) [0755] and see who dares to **instruct** Christ and alter what he
L C : 0 5 :038(451) [0761] now for all ordinary **instruction** on the essentials of this
L C : 0 5 :044(451) [0763] simply to teach and **instruct**, but there must also be daily
L C : 0 6 :007(458) [0000] about confession to **instruct** and admonish the simple
E P : 1 1 :016(497) [0837] was written for our **instruction** that by steadfastness and
S D : 0 1 :059(519) [0879] that every one be rightly **instructed** in these issues.
S D : 0 2 :015(523) [0885] of the saints for divine **instruction**, illumination, and
S D : 0 5 :018(561) [0957] to rebuke sin and to give **instruction** about good works.
S D : 0 6 :003(564) [0963] written law on them to **instruct** them, and thereby even
S D : 0 6 :006(565) [0965] without any **instruction**, admonition, exhortation, or
S D : 0 6 :012(566) [0967] he employs the law to **instruct** the regenerate out of it and
S D : 0 6 :024(568) [0969] not only with the **instruction**, admonition, urging, and
S D : 1 0 :009(612) [1055] Paul **instructs** us how we can with a good conscience give
S D : 1 0 :024(615) [1061] Dr. Luther exhaustively **instructs** the church of God on
S D : 1 1 :092(632) [1093] was written for our **instruction**, that by steadfastness and

Instrument (10), Instruments (4)
A L : 0 5 :002(031) [0045] as through **instruments**, the Holy Spirit is given, and the
L C : 0 1 :132(383) [0619] to himself, but also an **instrument** intended for our
E P : 0 2 :018(472) [0791] new will becomes an **instrument** and means of God the
E P : 0 2 :019(472) [0791] as the Holy Spirit's **instrument** whereby he effects
E P : 0 3 :005(473) [0793] is the only means and **instrument** whereby we accept
S D : 0 2 :004(520) [0881] any means or created **instruments** (that is, without the
S D : 0 2 :052(531) [0901] are the Holy Spirit's **instrument** in, with, and through
S D : 0 2 :058(532) [0903] a person despises the **instruments** of the Holy Spirit and
S D : 0 2 :090(539) [0915] of his holy Word as his ordinary means and **instrument**.
S D : 0 3 :031(544) [0925] virtue the means and **instrument** with and through which
S D : 0 3 :038(546) [0929] exclusive means and **instrument** with and through which
S D : 0 3 :043(547) [0931] that as a means and **instrument** it embraces God's grace
S D : 1 1 :041(623) [1077] perverts the means and **instrument** of the Holy Spirit
S D : 1 1 :076(628) [1087] the ordinary means or **instruments** to accomplish this

Insufficient (1)
A P : 0 4 :342(160) [0215] servants" means "**insufficient** servants," since no one

Insult (5), Insulting (1), Insults (5)
A P : 0 4 :149(127) [0163] his sins are forgiven, he **insults** Christ because he thinks
A P : 0 4 :150(127) [0163] sins because he loves, he **insults** Christ and in God's
A P : 0 4 :165(130) [0169] because of Christ's promise, he **insults** this high priest.
A P : 0 4 :332(158) [0211] not on the mercy of God, **insults** Christ, who intercedes
A P : 1 2 :002(182) [0253] of sins, what is this but to **insult** the blood and death of
A P : 1 2 :077(193) [0275] Truly, we **insult** Christ and abrogate the Gospel if we
A P : 2 4 :089(266) [0415] For one thing, it is an **insult** to the Gospel to maintain
A P : 2 7 :011(270) [0423] This idea is an open **insult** to the Gospel, which teaches
A P : 2 7 :013(271) [0423] wilt Thou bear these **insults** with which our enemies
A P : 2 7 :030(274) [0431] In addition, they **insult** Christ when they say that by a
A P : 2 7 :040(276) [0435] forgiveness of sins or eternal life, he is **insulting** Christ.

Insure (3)
S D : P R :016(507) [0857] Nevertheless, to **insure** that the truth may be established
S D : P R :016(507) [0857] all error, and likewise to **insure** that familiar terminology
S D : 1 1 :046(624) [1079] God wanted to **insure** my salvation so firmly and

Integrally (1), Integrated (1)
A P : 0 4 :051(114) [0135] The rest must be **integrated** with this article, namely, that
S D : 0 7 :084(584) [1001] death), must be kept **integrally** and inviolately, just as St.

Integrity (6)
A P : 0 4 :234(140) [0185] perfection (that is, the **integrity** of the church) is preserved
A P : 0 4 :326(158) [0211] and according to the **integrity** that is in me."
A P : 1 2 :125(201) [0289] men of learning and **integrity** do the investigating on
L C : 0 1 :258(400) [0653] of the world that men of **integrity** seldom preside in
L C : 0 1 :259(400) [0653] all, to be a man of **integrity**, and not only upright but also
L C : 0 4 :060(444) [0747] valid and retains its **integrity**, even if only one person

Intellect (21)
A P : 0 4 :304(154) [0205] thus cannot be ascribed to faith, which is in the **intellect**.
A P : 0 4 :304(154) [0205] the will commands the **intellect** to assent to the Word of
A P : 0 4 :304(154) [0205] merely thoughts in the **intellect** but are also a horrible
A P : 0 4 :304(154) [0205] merely knowledge in the **intellect** but also trust in the
E P : 0 6 :004(480) [0805] who inheres in people's **intellect**, will, and all their
E P : 0 7 :042(486) [0817] Here we take our **intellect** captive in obedience to Christ,
S D : 0 2 :002(520) [0881] the unregenerated man's **intellect** and will can do in his
S D : 0 2 :007(521) [0883] and divine things the **intellect**, heart, and will of
S D : 0 2 :009(521) [0883] man's reason or natural **intellect** still has a dim spark of
S D : 0 2 :012(522) [0885] Scripture denies to the **intellect**, heart, and will of the
S D : 0 2 :017(523) [0887] in divine matters the **intellect**, heart, and will of a
S D : 0 2 :026(526) [0891] He opens the **intellect** and the heart to understand the
S D : 0 2 :059(532) [0905] rational creature with an **intellect** and will (not, however,
S D : 0 2 :059(532) [0905] will (not, however, an **intellect** in divine things or a
S D : 0 2 :070(534) [0909] and emotions in the **intellect**, will, and heart, so that the
S D : 0 2 :083(537) [0913] at all for the good in the **intellect**, will, and heart, when
S D : 0 2 :083(537) [0913] Spirit's activity in the **intellect**, will, and heart of man
S D : 0 2 :089(538) [0915] through the Word in the **intellect**, will, and heart of man.
S D : 0 2 :090(539) [0915] The unconverted man's **intellect** and will are only that
S D : 0 2 :090(539) [0915] since they are the **intellect** and will of a man who is
S D : 0 8 :096(609) [1049] eyes of reason, take their **intellect** captive to obey Christ,

Intelligence (2), Intelligent (12)
A G : 2 3 :002(053) [0063] Many devout and **intelligent** people in high station have
A G : 2 3 :013(053) [0063] Pius, as a prudent and **intelligent** man, made this
A P : 0 4 :012(108) [0123] But let the **intelligent** reader just consider this.
A P : 0 4 :343(160) [0217] of our opponents which **intelligent** men can easily judge
A P : 1 3 :017(213) [0313] No **intelligent** person will quibble about the number of
A P : 2 3 :002(239) [0363] First, let the **intelligent** reader consider the impudence of
S C : P R :009(339) [0535] When you preach to **intelligent** and educated people, you
L C : 0 1 :083(376) [0603] days not for the sake of **intelligent** and well informed
S D : P R :010(503) [0849] with Christian **intelligence** can see which opinion in the
S D : 0 1 :055(518) [0877] basis all scholars and **intelligent** people have always held
S D : 0 1 :057(518) [0877] by any really **intelligent** person that every existing thing is
S D : 0 2 :020(525) [0889] man is indeed very clever, **intelligent**, and extremely busy.
S D : 0 7 :034(575) [0983] Confession, every **intelligent** person who loves truth and
S D : 0 7 :050(578) [0989] standpoint of wisdom and **intelligence** to explain them.

Intend (12), Intended (23), Intending (1), Intends (2), Intent (4), Intention (40), Intentions (4)
P R : P R :008(005) [0009] way our disposition and **intention** to adopt, to defend, or
P R : P R :008(005) [0009] assistance, it was our **intention** to remain and abide
P R : P R :009(006) [0011] the contrary, this well-**intended** action of ours was again
P R : P R :017(008) [0015] and well-**intended** agreements reached by our
P R : P R :018(009) [0015] of God's grace we, too, **intend** to persist in this confession
P R : P R :019(009) [0017] was our purpose and **intention** to palliate, to extenuate,
P R : P R :020(010) [0017] the Formula's constant **intention** Christians are to be
P R : P R :022(011) [0019] is not our purpose and **intention** to mean thereby those
P R : P R :022(011) [0019] we do not by any means **intend** to tolerate in our lands,
P R : P R :023(012) [0021] our disposition and **intention** has always been directed
P R : P R :024(013) [0023] never our disposition or **intention** — as it is not now — to
A G : P R :012(026) [0041] with the procedure **intended** by Your Imperial Majesty's
A G : 1 5 :004(037) [0049] days, etc., by which it is **intended** to earn grace and make
A G : 2 6 :045(070) [0075] "It was not the **intention** of the apostles to institute holy
A G : 2 8 :077(094) [0095] It is not our **intention** to find ways of reducing the
A L : 1 3 :001(035) [0049] will of God toward us, **intended** to awaken and confirm
A L : 0 0 :001(049) [0059] although contrary to the **intent** of the canons, we pray
A L : 2 3 :021(055) [0063] to death, contrary to the **intent** of the canons, for no
A L : 2 6 :045(070) [0075] is made: "It was not the **intention** of the apostles to enact
A L : 2 8 :050(089) [0091] or instituted with the **intention** of meriting justification
A L : 2 8 :077(094) [0095] It is not our **intention** that the bishops give up their
A P : 0 2 :006(101) [0107] with the best of **intentions** we named it and explained it
A P : 0 2 :017(102) [0109] righteousness was **intended** to involve not only a balanced
A P : 0 2 :024(103) [0111] This is precisely the **intention** of Augustine's definition
A P : 0 4 :057(114) [0137] the Christ, that for his sake God **intended** to forgive sins.
A P : 0 4 :231(139) [0185] and hence this view is far removed from his **intention**.
A P : 0 4 :269(147) [0197] the law is certainly not **intended** to abolish the Gospel of
A P : 0 4 :321(157) [0209] we have said above, the **intention** of the one performing
A P : 0 7 :040(176) [0241] the apostles' wish and **intention**, therefore, we must
A P : 0 7 :043(177) [0243] for the apostles did not **intend** it to refer to the time when
A P : 1 2 :160(207) [0301] but works of God, **intended** for our profit, that the power
A P : 1 2 :173(209) [0305] All of this is **intended** to put something over on the
A P : 2 1 :039(235) [0355] offenses, as though they **intended**, by forcing our
A P : 2 7 :058(279) [0439] of the Nazarites was **intended** to exercise or show faith
S 1 : P R :001(288) [0455] the other hand, what we **intended** to hold fast to and
S 2 : 0 3 :001(297) [0471] founded with good **intentions** for the education of learned
S 2 : 0 4 :016(301) [0477] himself, who does not **intend** to give us a hearing but only
S 3 : 0 1 :009(302) [0477] is no need of a good **intention** to do what he ought, but it
S 3 : 0 1 :009(302) [0477] he does not have an evil **intention** to commit sin, for such
S 3 : 0 3 :014(305) [0483] With this **intention** we, too, became priests and monks,
S C : P R :007(339) [0533] — perhaps with the **intention** of making improvements —
S C : 0 5 :029(351) [0555] This is **intended** simply as an ordinary form of confession
L C : 0 1 :037(369) [0591] He **intends** that everyone shall be impressed and see that
L C : 0 1 :081(376) [0603] This was not its **intention**, but, as we shall hear, it meant
L C : 0 1 :132(383) [0619] but also an instrument **intended** for our greatest welfare,
L C : 0 1 :167(388) [0629] of Scripture, and God **intends** it to be included in this
L C : 0 1 :193(391) [0635] it is God's real **intention** that we should allow no man to
L C : 0 1 :321(408) [0673] this appendix was **intended** to apply to all the
L C : 0 3 :018(422) [0703] or lost, for if he did not **intend** to answer you, he would
L C : 0 4 :034(440) [0741] we may do with the **intention** of meriting salvation
L C : 0 5 :002(447) [0753] For we do not **intend** to admit to the sacrament and
L C : 0 5 :061(453) [0767] and absolution and has no **intention** to amend his life.
E P : 0 3 :011(474) [0795] co-persist with a wicked **intention** to sin and to act
E P : 1 2 :031(500) [0843] contrary to it but **intend** by the grace of God to abide by
S D : P R :005(502) [0847] And we do not **intend**, either in this or in subsequent
S D : P R :010(506) [0855] Our **intention** was only to have a single, universally
S D : 0 2 :044(529) [0897] indicates how he **intended** his statements to be
S D : 0 2 :070(535) [0909] thoughts, Christian **intentions**, and diligence, and to fight
S D : 0 3 :026(543) [0923] and have a wicked **intention** to remain and abide in sin,
S D : 0 3 :036(545) [0927] And this is St. Paul's **intention** when in this article he so

Continued ▶

SD : 0 3 :041(546) [0931] by side with a wicked **intention**, but this merely shows the
SD : 0 4 :015(553) [0943] right faith and a wicked **intention** to continue and abide
SD : 0 4 :036(557) [0949] without in any way **intending** to confirm the
SD : 0 4 :038(557) [0951] ends (that is, with the **intention** that God demands of the
SD : 0 6 :005(564) [0963] contrary, it is St. Paul's **intention** that the law cannot
SD : 0 7 :001(568) [0971] document in which we **intend** to deal only with those
SD : 0 7 :001(569) [0971] from repeating the true **intention** and the right
SD : 0 7 :018(572) [0979] sacramental union is **intended** to mean nothing more than
SD : 0 7 :033(575) [0983] who understood the true **intention** of the Augsburg
SD : 0 7 :034(575) [0983] real meaning and **intention** in this article have always
SD : 0 7 :041(576) [0985] the true meaning and **intention** of the Augsburg
SD : 0 7 :050(578) [0989] his words and heart and **intention** and is best qualified
SD : 0 7 :068(582) [0997] and without a good **intention** to improve their life and
SD : 0 7 :111(589) [1011] this document we have **intended** to set forth primarily our
SD : 1 0 :001(610) [1053] the church with good **intentions** for the sake of good
SD : 1 0 :005(611) [1053] these ceremonies are **intended** to create the illusion (or
SD : 1 0 :005(611) [1053] or agreed to with that **intention**) that these two opposing
SD : 1 0 :018(614) [1059] walking in their footsteps **intend** by the grace of God to
SD : 1 1 :034(622) [1075] through the Word, God **intended** to say: "Externally I do
SD : 1 1 :035(622) [1075] one thing and think and **intend** something different in
SD : 1 1 :092(632) [1093] and hope is contrary to the Holy Spirit's will and **intent**.
SD : 1 1 :095(632) [1095] that we have no **intention** (since we have no authority to
SD : 1 1 :095(632) [1095] to the truth and actually **intended** for its suppression.
SD : 1 2 :002(632) [1095] had not for that reason **intended** to make special and
SD : 1 2 :005(633) [1097] or hiding anything with **intent** to deceive and that our
SD : 1 2 :040(636) [1103] to this confession, but we **intend** through God's grace to

Intercedes (3), Intercession (4), Intercessions (2)
AP : 0 4 :165(129) [0169] hand of God, who indeed **intercedes** for us" (Rom. 8:34).
AP : 0 4 :332(158) [0211] God, insults Christ, who **intercedes** for us as our high
AP : 2 1 :014(230) [0347] between mediators of **intercession** and mediators of
AP : 2 1 :015(231) [0347] from Scripture for calling them mediators of **intercession**.
AP : 2 1 :031(233) [0351] put our trust in the **intercession** of Christ because only
SC : 0 9 :005(355) [0561] prayers, **intercessions**, and thanksgivings be made for all
SC : 0 9 :014(356) [0563] prayers, **intercessions**, and thanksgivings be made for all
LC : 0 3 :084(432) [0723] they lose the common **intercession** of the church, and let
SD : 1 1 :031(621) [1073] pray as we ought," he **intercedes** for them "with

Intercessor (4), Intercessors (3)
AG : 2 1 :002(047) [0057] advocate, and **intercessor** before God (Rom. 8:34).
AL : 2 1 :002(047) [0057] highpriest, and **intercessor** whom the Scriptures set before
AP : 2 1 :014(230) [0345] and make the saints propitiators as well as **intercessors**.
AP : 2 1 :016(231) [0347] the saints not only **intercessors** but propitiators, that is,
AP : 2 1 :024(232) [0349] royal courts, where friends must be used as **intercessors**.
AP : 2 1 :024(232) [0349] has appointed a certain **intercessor**, he does not want
AP : 2 1 :024(232) [0349] been appointed as our **intercessor** and high priest, why

Intercourse (5)
AP : 2 3 :027(243) [0371] is permitted and **intercourse** is forbidden only during the
AP : 2 3 :027(243) [0371] ministry, and marital **intercourse** did not keep them from
AP : 2 3 :032(243) [0373] themselves, by marital **intercourse**, by childbirth, and by
AP : 2 3 :041(245) [0375] **Intercourse** contrary to these laws was uncleanness; now
AP : 2 3 :065(248) [0381] moderation in marital **intercourse** and of what Paul calls

Interest (5), Interests (6)
AG : 2 7 :026(075) [0079] maintenance of temporal **interests**, how much more
TR : 0 0 :054(329) [0519] to have regard for the **interests** of the church and to see to
SC : PR :005(338) [0533] do not take the slightest **interest** in teaching the people
LC : 0 1 :102(379) [0609] Even if no other **interest** or need drove us to the Word,
LC : 0 1 :233(396) [0647] property and further his **interests**, especially when he
LC : 0 1 :251(399) [0651] further our neighbor's **interests**, and when he suffers want
LC : 0 1 :328(410) [0677] them and promote their **interests**, however and whenever
LC : 0 3 :068(429) [0717] in these three petitions **interests** which concern God
EP : 1 0 :001(492) [0829] into the church in the **interest** of good order and the
SD : 0 4 :018(554) [0943] It was chiefly in this **interest** that many defended the
SD : 0 7 :066(581) [0997] long to list here, in the **interest** of desirable brevity we

Interfere (5), Interfered (3), Interferes (3), Interfering (1)
PR : PR :015(007) [0013] special circumstances **interfered**, as they did in the case of
AG : 2 8 :010(082) [0085] of preaching, it does not **interfere** at all with government
AL : 2 8 :010(082) [0085] ministry of the Word, it **interferes** with civil government
AL : 2 8 :010(082) [0085] as the art of singing **interferes** with civil government.
AL : 2 8 :013(083) [0085] lawful obedience, nor **interfere** with judgments concerning
LC : 0 1 :250(399) [0651] withholding, or **interfering** with his possessions and
LC : 0 1 :266(401) [0657] If I **interfere** and pass sentence on him, I fall into a
LC : 0 3 :072(430) [0719] against everything that **interferes** with enjoying it.
LC : 0 3 :073(430) [0719] these two relations are **interfered** with and prevented from
LC : 0 3 :073(430) [0719] of life are also **interfered** with, and life itself cannot be
LC : 0 3 :080(431) [0721] it is to take away or **interfere** with all we have received
SD : 1 1 :006(617) [1065] and when and how he will **interfere** with it and punish it.

Interim (3)
SD : PR :019(507) [0857] on account of the **Interim** and for other reasons, we
SD : 0 3 :005(540) [0917] and evoked by the **Interim** and otherwise, which will be
SD : 0 4 :029(555) [0947] again as a result of the **Interim**, flowed forth from it, and

Interior (1)
SD : 0 1 :011(510) [0863] wicked stamp, an **interior** uncleanness of the heart and

Intermediate (1)
EP : 0 8 :035(491) [0825] they invent an **intermediate** power (that is, a power that

Internal (5)
AP : 0 4 :282(149) [0201] a twofold cleanness, one **internal** and the other external.
EP : 0 7 :020(484) [0813] own virtues or in our **internal** and external preparations.
SD : 0 1 :060(519) [0879] in itself and all its **internal** and external powers, but that
SD : 0 6 :007(565) [0965] to their nature and to all its **internal** and external powers.
SD : 0 7 :088(585) [1003] only to the spiritual and **internal** use of faith in order to

Interpret (27), Interpretation (29), Interpretations (2), Interpreted (12), Interpreter (1), Interpreters (1), Interpreting (2), Interprets (11)
PR : PR :003(003) [0007] in a Christian and unanimous **interpretation** thereof.
PR : PR :007(004) [0009] adversaries had been **interpreting** to the very great
PR : PR :009(006) [0011] again understood and **interpreted** in such a way by
PR : PR :016(008) [0013] the correct Christian **interpretation** of the Augsburg
PR : PR :020(010) [0017] ingenuous faith and **interpretation** of the words of the
PR : PR :020(010) [0017] as if our ingenuous **interpretation** and faith contradicted
AG : PR :003(025) [0039] not have been rightly **interpreted** or treated by either
AG : 2 0 :012(042) [0055] That no new **interpretation** is here introduced can be
AG : 2 2 :003(049) [0059] these words and **interpret** them as if they apply only to
AL : 2 0 :012(043) [0055] have invented a new **interpretation** of Paul, this whole
AL : 2 8 :054(090) [0091] the assembly and that **interpreters** in the church should be
AP : 0 2 :018(103) [0111] So Irenaeus **interprets** the likeness of God.
AP : 0 2 :022(103) [0111] with which Augustine's **interpretation** of the image agrees.
AP : 0 4 :087(120) [0147] This our opponents **interpret** as referring to Levitical
AP : 0 4 :109(123) [0153] They should be **interpreted**, so they say, as referring to
AP : 0 4 :152(127) [0163] But he **interprets** his own words when he adds: "Your
AP : 0 4 :185(132) [0173] rule I have just stated **interprets** all the passages they
AP : 0 4 :224(138) [0181] text if we remove the **interpretation** that our opponents
AP : 0 4 :235(140) [0185] Ambrose **interprets** the text this way: "Just as a building
AP : 0 4 :256(144) [0193] must be permitted to **interpret** the entire law (Heb. 11:6),
AP : 0 4 :259(144) [0193] We must **interpret** all similar passages in the same way.
AP : 0 4 :264(146) [0195] dismiss Jerome in the **interpretation** of this text, though
AP : 0 4 :269(147) [0197] those Pharisees, who **interpret** the law in such a way that
AP : 0 4 :280(149) [0201] own context, they often yield their own **interpretation**.
AP : 0 4 :342(159) [0215] a childish quibble to **interpret** "unworthy servants" as
AP : 0 4 :372(164) [0221] said earlier, all passages on works can be **interpreted**.
AP : 0 4 :376(164) [0223] position, that by **interpreting** such passages of the
AP : 0 4 :381(165) [0223] Here they **interpret** grace as a disposition by which we
AP : 0 4 :383(165) [0225] They **interpret** faith as merely a knowledge of history or
AP : 0 7 :039(176) [0241] We should **interpret** those rites just as the apostles
AP : 0 7 :043(177) [0243] He **interprets** it the same way that we do; for the apostles
AP : 1 2 :015(184) [0257] indulgences, which they **interpret** as the remission of
AP : 1 2 :066(191) [0271] the prophets should be **interpreted** as the consensus of the
AP : 1 2 :091(196) [0279] add nothing about faith in their **interpretation** of them.
AP : 1 2 :106(197) [0283] According to their **interpretation**, "know" here means to
AP : 1 2 :106(197) [0283] The **interpretation** surely is a neat one, worthy of these
AP : 1 2 :106(197) [0283] church, he should surely **interpret** "condition" as meaning
AP : 1 2 :136(203) [0293] these passages will have to be **interpreted** in a new way.
AP : 1 2 :157(207) [0301] have troubles, Scripture **interprets** them as the
AP : 1 2 :161(208) [0303] This is how Gregory **interprets** the punishment of David
AP : 1 3 :007(212) [0311] Our opponents do not **interpret** the priesthood in
AP : 1 3 :011(212) [0311] If ordination is **interpreted** in relation to the ministry of
AP : 1 3 :012(212) [0311] If ordination is **interpreted** this way, we shall not object
AP : 1 5 :024(218) [0321] is how human reason **interprets** fasting and bodily
AP : 1 5 :027(219) [0323] together with **interpretations** that make them either
AP : 1 5 :028(219) [0323] comes from this strict **interpretation** of the traditions.
AP : 1 5 :038(220) [0325] tranquillity, and we **interpret** them in an evangelical way,
AP : 2 1 :023(232) [0349] Gabriel Biel's **interpretation** of the canon of the Mass
AP : 2 3 :016(241) [0369] He **interprets** himself a little later when he says (v. 9), "It
AP : 2 3 :036(244) [0373] Finally, if they **interpret** celibacy as a purity that merits
AP : 2 4 :023(253) [0391] Isaiah **interprets** the law to mean that the death of Christ
AP : 2 4 :023(253) [0391] Paul **interprets** the same word as "sin" in Rom. 8:3, "As a
AP : 2 4 :026(254) [0393] to God," with the **interpretation**, "that is, the fruit of lips
AP : 2 4 :058(260) [0405] whole Epistle to the Hebrews supports this **interpretation**.
AP : 2 7 :010(270) [0423] *Vows*, we want to be **interpreted** here as reiterating that
AP : 2 7 :060(279) [0441] examples ought to be **interpreted** according to the rule,
AP : 2 8 :017(283) [0449] This is the simple way to **interpret** traditions.
AP : 2 8 :020(284) [0449] to the Gospel, nor **interpret** their traditions in a manner
S3 : 0 8 :003(312) [0495] who therefore judge, **interpret**, and twist the Scriptures or
TR : 0 0 :023(324) [0511] we shall respond briefly by way of **interpretation**.
TR : 0 0 :027(324) [0511] Hilary, and Bede) **interpret** the statement "on this rock" in
SC : 0 1 :016(343) [0541] speak well of him, and **interpret** charitably all that he
LC : 0 1 :081(375) [0603] however, the Jews **interpreted** this commandment too
LC : 0 1 :083(376) [0603] people a Christian **interpretation** of what God requires in
LC : 0 1 :274(402) [0659] parents, for we must **interpret** this commandment in such
LC : 0 1 :293(404) [0663] The Jews did not **interpret** them as referring to unchastity
LC : 0 1 :296(404) [0665] Therefore, I say, they **interpreted** these commandments
LC : 0 1 :324(409) [0675] meaning and right **interpretation** of the first and chief
LC : 0 2 :049(417) [0691] but a comment or **interpretation** by which someone
LC : 0 4 :049(442) [0745] been given the power to **interpret** the Scriptures and to
LC : 0 4 :082(446) [0751] This **interpretation** deprives Baptism of its value, making
LC : 0 5 :039(451) [0761] we have the right **interpretation** and doctrine of the
SD : PR :006(502) [0849] even dared to give a false **interpretation** to these articles.
SD : PR :010(506) [0855] pure books, such as **interpretations** of the Holy
SD : 0 4 :027(555) [0945] who advanced this **interpretation**: We should indeed not
SD : 0 7 :007(570) [0975] They **interpret** "to eat Christ's body" as no more than "to
SD : 0 7 :007(570) [0975] They **interpret** the word "is" sacramentally or in a
SD : 0 7 :018(572) [0979] had employed to **interpret** the aforementioned articles of
SD : 0 7 :045(577) [0987] are therefore bound to **interpret** and explain these words
SD : 0 7 :046(577) [0987] or if it was to receive a tolerable and loose **interpretation**.
SD : 0 7 :050(578) [0989] faithful or trustworthy **interpreter** of the words of Jesus
SD : 0 7 :052(578) [0991] proffered bread without any **interpretation** and change.
SD : 0 7 :088(585) [1003] and necessary rule and **interpret** it as referring only to the
SD : 0 7 :113(589) [1011] tropes or a figurative **interpretation** are to be given a
SD : 1 1 :092(632) [1093] it is certain that any **interpretation** of the Scriptures which

Interspersed (1)
AL : 2 4 :002(056) [0065] German hymns are **interspersed** here and there among the

Interval (1)
SD : 0 7 :002(569) [0973] the signs by as great an **interval** as the earth is distant

Intervened (1), Intervenes (3)
S3 : 0 3 :030(308) [0487] St. John, the preacher of true repentance, **intervenes**.
LC : 0 1 :066(373) [0599] For here God himself **intervenes** and separates right from
LC : 0 1 :185(390) [0633] father, steps in and **intervenes** to get the quarrel settled
LC : 0 3 :031(424) [0707] of a few godly men **intervened** like an iron wall on our

Intimate (2)
AP : 0 4 :236(140) [0185] good men if they even **intimate** their disapproval of some
SD : 0 8 :030(597) [1025] have such an exalted, **intimate**, and ineffable communion

Intolerable (12)
AL : 0 0 :004(049) [0059] among us are not so **intolerable** as those ungodly and
AP : 1 2 :172(209) [0305] Confutation say it is **intolerable** to abolish satisfactions

Continued ▶

A P : 2 0 :004(227) [0339] the honor of Christ to our works is **intolerable**.
A P : 2 1 :014(230) [0345] This is completely **intolerable**, for it transfers to the saints
A P : 2 7 :020(272) [0425] Hence it is also an **intolerable** blasphemy when Thomas
A P : 2 8 :003(281) [0445] Then they impose **intolerable** burdens on them, as though
T R : 0 0 :074(332) [0525] called) have exercised **intolerable** arbitrariness and, either
L C : 0 1 :237(397) [0647] whom we are obliged to suffer such **intolerable** insolence.
L C : 0 1 :255(399) [0653] good name, for it is **intolerable** to live among men in
L C : 0 6 :001(457) [0000] coercion and from the **intolerable** burden he imposed
E P : 1 2 :011(499) [0841] ***Intolerable** Articles in the Body Politic*
E P : 1 2 :016(499) [0841] ***Intolerable** Errors which Undermine Domestic Society*

Intrepid (1)
S D : 1 2 :040(636) [1103] we shall appear with **intrepid** hearts before the judgment

Intricate (1), Intricately (1)
A P : 1 2 :010(184) [0255] opponents' discussions are very confused and **intricate**.
S D : 0 1 :036(514) [0869] being made in secret, **intricately** wrought in the depths of

Intrinsic (2), Intrinsically (8)
P R : P R :021(011) [0019] to have this majesty **intrinsically**, essentially, formally,
A P : 0 4 :244(142) [0189] God because of their **intrinsic** excellence; that we do not
E P : 1 1 :004(495) [0833] so that in spite of its **intrinsic** wickedness it must minister
S D : 0 7 :061(580) [0995] It is **intrinsically** useful, salutary, and necessary to
S D : 0 8 :009(593) [1019] natural essence), to be **intrinsically** present, and to know
S D : 0 8 :049(600) [1031] was the divine nature **intrinsically** diminished or
S D : 0 8 :062(603) [1037] properties has become **intrinsically** equal with the
S D : 0 8 :071(605) [1041] an omnipotent essence **intrinsically** or have omnipotent
S D : 0 8 :071(605) [1041] intrinsically or have omnipotent properties **intrinsically**.
S D : 0 8 :076(606) [1043] of this union, cannot **intrinsically** be or have — for

Introduce (10), Introduced (33), Introducing (1), Introduction (3)
P R : P R :006(004) [0009] which have been **introduced** into our lands and territories
P R : P R :009(006) [0011] were now and again **introduced** into our churches and
P R : P R :017(008) [0015] and hearts to want to **introduce**, palliate, or confirm any
P R : P R :024(013) [0023] at will and to **introduce** and defend monstrous errors, the
A G : 2 0 :012(042) [0055] interpretation is here **introduced** can be demonstrated
A G : 0 0 :000(049) [0059] of them having been **introduced** with violence), we are
A G : 2 2 :008(050) [0061] only one kind was **introduced**, although Cardinal
A G : 2 2 :010(050) [0061] that such a custom, **introduced** contrary to God's
A G : 2 4 :040(060) [0069] no novelty has been **introduced** which did not exist in the
A G : 2 8 :002(081) [0083] Christ, have not only **introduced** new forms of worship
A G : 2 8 :023(084) [0087] hand, if they teach, **introduce**, or institute anything
A G : 2 8 :030(085) [0087] have the power to **introduce** ceremonies in the church or
A G : 2 8 :062(091) [0093] Such errors were **introduced** into Christendom when the
A G : 2 8 :072(093) [0093] times and which were **introduced** contrary to the custom
A G : 2 8 :073(093) [0093] was some reason for **introducing** them, but they are not
A G : 0 0 :004(095) [0095] has been said or **introduced** out of hatred or for the
A G : 0 0 :005(095) [0095] very clear that we have **introduced** nothing, either in
A L : 2 2 :009(050) [0061] evident that a custom **introduced** contrary to the
A L : 2 3 :014(053) [0063] against the **introduction** into Germany of more vices.
A L : 2 4 :023(058) [0067] Thus was **introduced** a debate on whether one Mass said
A L : 2 8 :030(085) [0087] have the right to **introduce** ceremonies in the church and
A L : 2 8 :072(093) [0093] which are new and were **introduced** contrary to the
A L : 2 8 :073(093) [0093] when they were **introduced**, but they are not adapted to
A L : 0 0 :005(095) [0095] diligently against the **introduction** into our churches of
A P : 0 2 :050(106) [0119] They have not **introduced** any innovations, but have set
A P : 1 6 :003(223) [0331] The Gospel does not **introduce** any new laws about the
A P : 2 3 :049(246) [0377] as certain rites were **introduced** as lessons for the
A P : 2 4 :047(258) [0401] profaned the Mass and **introduced** much wicked worship
A P : 2 4 :097(268) [0417] In Israel they **introduced** the worship of Baal; in Judah
S 2 : 0 2 :016(295) [0467] of this: evil spirits have **introduced** the knavery of
S 3 : 0 3 :027(307) [0487] indulgences, he again **introduced** uncertainty when he
T R : 0 0 :045(328) [0517] which has produced many errors and **introduced** despair.
S C : P R :020(340) [0537] the shocking evils they **introduce** when they refuse their
S C : 0 3 :000(346) [0545] **[Introduction]**
E P : R N :003(465) [0777] which have been **introduced** into the church of God
E P : 0 2 :016(472) [0789] expressions have been **introduced** to confirm the role of
E P : 1 0 :001(492) [0829] of God but have been **introduced** into the church in the
E P : 1 0 :003(493) [0829] but which have been **introduced** solely for the sake of
E P : 1 1 :001(494) [0831] concerning it might be **introduced** into the church.
S D : P R :013(506) [0855] the eternal truth, so we **introduce** and cite these writings
S D : 0 2 :054(531) [0903] Spirit, who works all of this, is **introduced** into the heart.
S D : 0 2 :086(538) [0913] person who wills," were **introduced** to support the view
S D : 0 3 :032(545) [0927] with one another or **introduced** simultaneously into the
S D : 0 4 :039(557) [0951] and decency, and might **introduce** and confirm a wicked,
S D : 0 8 :019(594) [1021] Yet there is not **introduced** thereby any sort of blending
S D : 1 0 :001(610) [1053] but which have been **introduced** into the church with
S D : 1 0 :010(612) [1055] worship of God and to **introduce** and confirm their

Intruded (1), Intrusive (1)
P R : P R :024(013) [0021] the presence of so many **intrusive** errors, aggravated
E P : R N :000(464) [0777] and the Errors Which **Intruded** Should Be Explained and

Invade (3), Invaded (3)
A G : 2 8 :013(083) [0085] Hence it should not **invade** the function of the other,
A L : 2 8 :013(083) [0085] Let it not **invade** the other's function, nor transfer the
E P : R N :003(465) [0777] lifetime — false teachers and heretics **invaded** the church.
E P : 0 3 :001(473) [0791] contradictory teachings have **invaded** some churches.
S D : P R :010(503) [0849] the errors and corruptions that have **invaded** our midst.
S D : 0 1 :027(512) [0867] and holy, sin did not **invade** their nature in such a way

Invalid (6)
A L : 2 7 :040(077) [0081] vow, taken contrary to the commands of God, is **invalid**.
A P : 2 7 :066(280) [0441] Thus vows made before that age must be **invalid**.
L C : 0 4 :052(443) [0745] for in the latter case Baptism does not become **invalid**.
L C : 0 4 :053(443) [0745] Baptism does not become **invalid** even if it is wrongly
L C : 0 4 :055(443) [0747] should be wrong and **invalid** because we use it wrongly?
L C : 0 4 :061(444) [0749] conclude that these ordinances are in themselves **invalid**.

Inveigled (1)
A G : 2 7 :015(073) [0077] were thus ensnared and **inveigled** into a monastery

Invent (2), Invented (34), Invention (8), Inventions (4), Inventors (1), Invents (1)
A G : 2 6 :002(064) [0071] orders, and the like were **invented** daily, and were
A G : 2 6 :032(068) [0075] this is true and real rather than **invented** mortification.
A G : 2 7 :002(071) [0077] monastic vows were **invented**, and the attempt was made
A G : 2 7 :013(073) [0077] God's Word and command without **invented** spirituality.
A G : 2 7 :037(077) [0081] precepts and services **invented** by men but that
A G : 2 7 :038(077) [0081] and preached that their **invented** spiritual life makes
A G : 2 7 :044(078) [0081] In fact, they have **invented** a still more indecent and
A G : 2 7 :046(078) [0081] the people that the **invented** spiritual estate of the orders
A G : 2 7 :048(078) [0081] such a service of God, **invented** by men without the
A G : 2 7 :057(080) [0083] given and not by keeping the commands **invented** by men.
A G : 2 7 :062(080) [0083] are false, useless, and **invented**, monastic vows are null
A L : 2 0 :012(042) [0055] object that we have **invented** a new interpretation of
A L : 2 0 :021(044) [0055] Others **invented** works of another kind to merit grace and
A L : 2 6 :032(068) [0075] Christ is true and real, rather than **invented**, mortification.
A L : 2 7 :038(077) [0081] have taught that their **invented** observances make
A L : 2 7 :044(078) [0081] In fact, they **invented** greater absurdities when they
A L : 2 7 :046(078) [0081] men that their **invented** observances were a state of
A L : 2 7 :048(078) [0081] people a certain service **invented** by men without the
A L : 2 7 :057(080) [0083] given and not by keeping the commands **invented** by men.
A P : 0 4 :020(110) [0125] whole business is the **invention** of idle men who do not
A P : 0 4 :285(150) [0201] and constantly **invents** other works and services until it
A P : 0 4 :344(160) [0217] reason the scholastics **invented** the term "merit of
A P : 0 7 :025(173) [0235] in him and not through devotions **invented** by the pope.
A P : 1 2 :015(184) [0257] profitable way of buying off satisfactions was **invented**.
A P : 1 2 :131(202) [0291] scholastics because these are obviously later **inventions**.
A P : 1 5 :019(217) [0319] Daniel says that the **invention** of human rites will be the
A P : 1 5 :019(218) [0319] Here he is describing the **invention** of rites, for he says
A P : 1 8 :010(226) [0337] distinction is not our **invention** but the clear teaching of
A P : 2 1 :037(234) [0353] But the **inventors** of these fables, which imitate the epics
A P : 2 1 :037(234) [0355] the miracles they have **invented** about rosaries and
A P : 2 4 :098(268) [0419] those wicked services **invented** against God's command to
A P : 2 7 :029(274) [0431] monasticism is a recent **invention**, they still cite the
S 2 : 0 2 :002(293) [0463] "1. After all, they are a purely human **invention**.
S 2 : 0 2 :002(293) [0463] can discard all human **inventions**, for Christ says, 'In vain
S 2 : 0 2 :005(293) [0463] was fabricated and **invented** without God's Word and
S 2 : 0 2 :022(296) [0469] much nonsense has been **invented** about the bones of
S 2 : 0 3 :002(298) [0471] blasphemous services, **invented** by men, which claim to be
S 2 : 0 3 :002(298) [0471] like other human **inventions**, all this is without
S 2 : 0 4 :005(299) [0473] the papacy is a human **invention**, and it is not
S 3 : 0 3 :018(306) [0483] according to its own **inventions**, without being able to
S 3 : 0 3 :024(307) [0485] to the aid of the poor church and **invented** indulgences.
S 3 : 0 3 :025(307) [0485] profitable, the pope **invented** the jubilee year and attached
S 3 : 1 2 :003(315) [0499] theirs which they have **invented** over and above the Holy
T R : 0 0 :045(328) [0517] concerning sin and have **invented** a tradition concerning
T R : 0 0 :045(328) [0517] They have also **invented** satisfactions, by means of which
S C : 0 5 :024(350) [0555] should he search for and **invent** other sins, for this would
L C : 0 4 :006(437) [0733] divine origin, not something devised or **invented** by men.
L C : 0 5 :004(447) [0753] Lord's Supper was not **invented** or devised by any man.
E P : 0 8 :035(491) [0825] Therefore they **invent** an intermediate power (that is, a
S D : 0 7 :067(582) [0997] of a horse's tail and an **invention** of which even Satan

Invert (1), Inverted (1)
L C : 0 4 :059(444) [0747] My friend, rather **invert** the argument and conclude,
L C : 0 6 :031(460) [0000] the compulsion must be **inverted**; we must come under

Invest (1), Investigate (3), Investigating (1), Investigation (2)
P R : P R :008(005) [0011] the more seriously to **investigate** the truth of the divine
A P : 0 4 :306(154) [0207] or judicial **investigation** of a man's own righteousness,
A P : 1 2 :104(197) [0283] they do not have the command to **investigate** secret sins.
A P : 1 2 :105(197) [0283] consoling consciences, does not need an **investigation**.
A P : 1 2 :125(201) [0289] and integrity do the **investigating** on religious questions.
L C : 0 1 :287(403) [0663] think less honorable we **invest** with the greater honor; and
E P : 1 1 :006(495) [0833] 5. We are not to **investigate** this predestination in the

Invincible (3)
A G : P R :001(024) [0039] serene, most mighty, **invincible** Emperor, most gracious
A P : 1 2 :002(182) [0253] shall we do here, O Charles, most **invincible** Emperor?
A P : 1 2 :003(182) [0253] therefore beg you, most **invincible** Emperor Charles, to

Inviolate (5), Inviolately (1)
L C : 0 5 :005(447) [0755] remain unimpaired and **inviolate** even if we use and
E P : 1 0 :002(493) [0829] may we with an **inviolate** conscience yield to their
S D : 0 7 :084(584) [1001] be kept integrally and **inviolately**, just as St. Paul sets the
S D : 1 2 :018(634) [1099] an office in the government with an **inviolate** conscience.
S D : 1 2 :019(634) [1099] Christian may with an **inviolate** conscience use an office
S D : 1 2 :021(634) [1099] cannot with an **inviolate** conscience impose the death

Invisible (3), Invisibly (1)
A G : 0 1 :003(028) [0043] creator and preserver of all things visible and **invisible**.
A L : 0 1 :002(027) [0043] maker and preserver of all things, visible and **invisible**.
S D : 0 7 :007(570) [0975] present on earth in some **invisible** and impalpable
S D : 0 7 :008(570) [0975] Lord's Supper, although **invisibly** and impalpably, and is

Invite (2), Invited (1), Invites (5), Invitation (4), Inviting (3)
A G : 2 4 :036(060) [0067] priest stood every day, **inviting** some to Communion and
A L : 2 4 :036(060) [0067] stands daily at the altar, **inviting** some to Communion
A P : 0 4 :202(134) [0175] his faith and display it to others, **inviting** them to believe.
A P : 1 1 :003(180) [0249] in such a way as to **invite** them to use the sacraments
A P : 1 2 :094(196) [0281] what Tertullian says: "He **invites** us to salvation with an
A P : 2 3 :055(247) [0379] the strictest laws and examples and to **invite** men to it.
S 3 : 1 5 :004(316) [0501] of altar stones, the **invitation** to such ceremonies of
L C : 0 1 :040(370) [0591] an offer, so cordial an **invitation**, and so rich a promise.
L C : 0 5 :052(452) [0765] He **invites** and incites you; if you despise this, you must
L C : 0 5 :066(454) [0769] which he most graciously **invites** us in other places, as
L C : 0 5 :071(455) [0769] reason for this command and **invitation** and promise.
L C : 0 6 :024(460) [0000] Suppose, now, that the **invitation** were changed into a
S D : 1 1 :027(620) [1071] guests whom the king **invites** to his son's wedding he calls
S D : 1 1 :051(624) [1079] of those men who were **invited** shall taste my banquet"
S D : 1 1 :089(631) [1093] any repentant sinner but **invites** and calls all poor,

Invoke (8), Invoked (4), Invoking (3), Invocation (28)
P R : P R :013(007) [0013] Finally, after **invoking** almighty God to his praise and
A G : P R :011(026) [0041] to divine truth we **invoke** almighty God in deepest

Continued ▶

A G : 2 1 :002(047) [0057] Scriptures that we are to **invoke** saints or seek help from
A P : 2 1 :000(229) [0343] [Article XXI. The **Invocation** of the Saints]
A P : 2 1 :001(229) [0343] because we do not require the **invocation** of the saints.
A P : 2 1 :001(229) [0343] on this account the **invocation** of the departed saints were
A P : 2 1 :002(229) [0343] cite this example to prove the **invocation** of the dead.
A P : 2 1 :002(229) [0343] is not a syllable about **invoking**, but only about
A P : 2 1 :003(229) [0343] the ancient Fathers before Gregory mention **invocation**.
A P : 2 1 :003(229) [0343] The theory of **invocation**, together with the theories our
A P : 2 1 :007(230) [0345] they only argue about **invocation**, which, even if it were
A P : 2 1 :010(230) [0345] church, it does not follow that they should be **invoked**.
A P : 2 1 :010(230) [0345] does not teach us to **invoke** the saints or to ask their
A P : 2 1 :010(230) [0345] from Scripture for the **invocation** of the saints; from this
A P : 2 1 :010(230) [0345] that consciences cannot be sure about such **invocation**.
A P : 2 1 :010(230) [0345] how do we know that God approves such **invocation**?
A P : 2 1 :012(230) [0345] argument that since **invocation** cannot be proved from
A P : 2 1 :013(230) [0345] prayers mention the saints, but they do not **invoke** them.
A P : 2 1 :013(230) [0345] Besides, this novel **invocation** in the church is not the
A P : 2 1 :013(230) [0345] church is not the same as the **invocation** of individuals.
A P : 2 1 :014(230) [0345] our opponents require **invocation** in the veneration of the
A P : 2 1 :017(231) [0347] be sure that we shall be heard if we **invoke** the saints.
A P : 2 1 :017(231) [0347] Such an **invocation**, therefore, is not based on faith.
A P : 2 1 :018(231) [0347] produce from Scripture for the **invocation** of the saints?
A P : 2 1 :021(232) [0349] tell us, first of all, to **invoke** the saints, though they have
A P : 2 1 :028(233) [0351] Men have **invoked** her, trusted in her mercy, and sought
A P : 2 1 :031(233) [0351] put our trust in the **invocation** of the saints, though they
A P : 2 1 :033(233) [0351] supposing that the **invocation** of the saints could be
A P : 2 1 :034(234) [0353] Afterwards came **invocation**, with abuses that were
A P : 2 1 :034(234) [0353] From **invocation** the next step was to images.
A P : 2 1 :038(234) [0355] we do not require the **invocation** of saints and condemn
S 2 : 0 2 :025(297) [0469] The **Invocation** of Saints
S 2 : 0 2 :025(297) [0469] The **invocation** of saints is also one of the abuses of the
S 2 : 0 2 :025(297) [0469] Even if the **invocation** of saints were a precious practice
S 2 : 0 2 :026(297) [0469] not follow that we should **invoke** angels and saints, pray
S 2 : 0 2 :027(297) [0469] this account pray to you, **invoke** you, keep fasts and
T R : 0 0 :047(328) [0517] Then there is the **invocation** of saints — how many abuses
L C : 0 1 :011(366) [0583] saint and worshiped and **invoked** him in time of need.
L C : 0 1 :056(372) [0597] and confirm it by **invoking** God's name and using it as a
L C : 0 1 :071(374) [0601] remain when it is uttered and **invoked** from the heart.
L C : 0 3 :008(421) [0699] By **invocation** and prayer the name of God is glorified
E P : 1 2 :031(500) [0843] in true fear and **invocation** of God, subscribed our
S D : 1 2 :040(636) [1103] in the fear and **invocation** of God, subscribed our

Involve (6), Involved (13), Involves (6), Involving (5)
A G : 2 7 :027(075) [0079] For a vow must **involve** what is possible and voluntary
A L : 2 7 :031(076) [0079] judgment to make a decision **involving** the rest of his life.
A P : P R :002(098) [0099] and consciences are **involved**, we assumed that the
A P : 0 2 :014(102) [0109] that original sin also **involves** such faults as ignorance of
A P : 0 2 :017(102) [0109] was intended to **involve** not only a balanced physical
A P : 0 4 :002(107) [0121] of Christianity is **involved**; when it is properly
A P : 0 4 :264(146) [0195] though the promise is **involved** even in the word
A P : 0 7 :034(175) [0239] Another issue is **involved**.
A P : 1 2 :003(182) [0253] most important issue, **involving** the chief doctrine of the
A P : 1 5 :049(221) [0329] This subject of traditions **involves** many difficult and
A P : 1 5 :049(221) [0329] hand, their abrogation **involves** its own difficulties and
A P : 1 5 :052(222) [0329] others, even where this **involved** some disadvantage to us.
A P : 1 6 :013(224) [0333] that many good men **involved** in politics and in business
S 3 : 0 3 :018(306) [0483] The person **involved** was obliged to grieve, but he would
S 3 : 1 1 :001(314) [0499] and countless sins, in which they are still **involved**.
T R : 0 0 :075(333) [0525] punished persons **involved** in adultery, but in this
S C : P R :023(341) [0539] he believed that he was **involved** in so much that is evil
L C : 0 1 :053(371) [0595] business and in matters **involving** money, property, and
L C : 0 1 :313(407) [0671] chastity, kindness, etc., and all that these virtues **involve**.
E P : 0 4 :010(476) [0799] are to be understood as **involving** not coercion but the
S D : P R :007(502) [0849] controversies would **involve** serious offense for both the
S D : 0 1 :030(513) [0867] to the ultimate part **involving** and affecting the goodness,
S D : 0 1 :060(519) [0879] It **involves** another question, however, when someone
S D : 0 5 :019(561) [0957] rebukes the unbelief **involved** in men's failure to believe in
S D : 0 8 :077(606) [1043] this presence of Christ in no way **involves** his humanity.
S D : 0 8 :094(609) [1049] this presence does not **involve** his assumed human nature
S D : 1 1 :001(616) [1063] at other places and has **involved** our people also.
S D : 1 1 :009(617) [1065] that nothing more is **involved** in it, or that nothing more
S D : 1 1 :083(630) [1091] God's revealed will **involves** both items: First, that he
S D : 1 1 :083(630) [1091] holy commandment and **involve** themselves again in the

Inward (4), Inwardly (7)
A G : 1 6 :004(038) [0051] and temporal but an **inward** and eternal mode of
A L : 1 8 :009(040) [0053] yet it cannot produce the **inward** affections, such as fear
A P : 0 4 :136(126) [0159] elements, namely, the **inward** spiritual impulses and the
A P : 0 4 :282(149) [0201] that they be cleansed **inwardly** and then adds concerning
A P : 0 4 :283(150) [0201] be clean if you are clean **inwardly** and if you give alms.
A P : 0 4 :284(150) [0201] men are completely clean, outwardly as well as **inwardly**.
A P : 0 4 :289(151) [0203] God both outwardly and **inwardly**, and that such
A P : 1 2 :131(202) [0291] there is no penitence **inwardly** which does not produce
L C : 0 1 :050(371) [0593] Commandment has **inwardly** instructed the heart and
E P : 0 1 :008(467) [0781] in man's body or soul, in his **inward** or outward powers.
S D : 0 2 :026(526) [0891] be born anew, to receive **inwardly** a new heart, mind, and

Irascible (1)
L C : 0 4 :066(445) [0749] born in us from Adam, **irascible**, spiteful, envious,

Irenaeus (6)
A G : 2 6 :044(070) [0075] **Irenaeus** said, "Disagreement in fasting does not destroy
A L : 2 6 :044(070) [0075] **Irenaeus** says, "Disagreement about fasting does not
A P : 0 2 :018(103) [0111] So **Irenaeus** interprets the likeness of God.
A P : 0 4 :103(121) [0151] In a letter to a certain **Irenaeus**, Ambrose says: "But the
S D : 0 7 :014(571) [0977] with the words of **Irenaeus**, that there are two things in
S D : 0 8 :022(595) [1023] one through the other (**Irenaeus**, Book IV, chap. 3;

Irenic (1)
P R : P R :010(006) [0011] When a number of pious, **irenic**, and learned theologians

Iron (11)
A P : 2 7 :005(269) [0421] as from a golden age to an **iron** age, or as the Platonic
L C : 0 3 :031(424) [0707] a few godly men intervened like an **iron** wall on our side?
E P : 0 8 :009(488) [0819] analogy of incandescent **iron** and the union of body and
S D : 0 8 :018(594) [1021] analogies of the soul and the body and of glowing **iron**.
S D : 0 8 :019(594) [1021] soul, as well as fire and **iron**, have a communion with
S D : 0 8 :064(603) [1039] body and fire in glowing **iron**, analogies which the entire
S D : 0 8 :066(604) [1039] Just as in glowing **iron** there are not two powers of
S D : 0 8 :066(604) [1039] the fire is united with the **iron**, it demonstrates and
S D : 0 8 :066(604) [1039] in and through the **iron** in such a way that on that
S D : 0 8 :066(604) [1039] this union the glowing **iron** has the power of illumination
S D : 0 8 :066(604) [1039] of the natural properties of either the fire or the **iron**.

Irrational (2)
S C : P R :003(338) [0533] as if they were pigs and **irrational** beasts, and now that
S D : 0 2 :062(533) [0905] of action to work in **irrational** creatures or in a stone or

Irrefutable (5), Irrefutably (3)
A P : 0 1 :002(100) [0103] Holy Scriptures testify to it firmly, surely, and **irrefutably**.
A P : 0 4 :105(122) [0153] "subtle," and others "**irrefutable**" — read them and reread
A P : 2 3 :013(241) [0367] This is so clear and firm as to be **irrefutable**.
S D : P R :006(505) [0853] with clear and **irrefutable** testimonies from the Holy
S D : 0 1 :040(515) [0871] shows the difference **irrefutably** and clearly, because
S D : 0 1 :055(518) [0877] the unquestioned and **irrefutable** axioms in theology that
S D : 0 1 :057(518) [0877] Since it is **irrefutably** true, attested and demonstrated by
S D : 0 8 :056(601) [1033] are three strong and **irrefutable** arguments which show

Irrelevant (2)
A P : 0 4 :131(125) [0157] as though it were **irrelevant**, or at best they require only
A P : 1 2 :103(197) [0281] sentence, that is **irrelevant** because the ministry of

Irreligiously (1)
A P : 0 2 :004(101) [0105] now when so many philosophize about it **irreligiously**.

Irreproachable (1)
S D : 0 4 :034(557) [0949] and blameless and **irreproachable** before him, provided

Irresistibly (1)
L C : 0 3 :111(435) [0729] which it can slip, the whole body will **irresistibly** follow.

Irresponsible (1)
S D : 0 7 :031(574) [0983] I am not drunk or **irresponsible**.

Irreverence (1)
A P : 0 4 :154(128) [0165] He charges him with **irreverence** and reproves him with

Irritation (1)
L C : 0 1 :184(390) [0633] he, gives vent to his **irritation** and envy by speaking ill of

Isaac (3)
S D : 0 7 :046(577) [0987] the promised seed, Christ, who was to be born of **Isaac**.
S D : 0 7 :046(577) [0989] of the blessed seed of **Isaac**, although this seemed
S D : 0 7 :046(577) [0989] concerning the seed of **Isaac** than he could comprehend

Isaiah (11)
A P : 0 4 :258(144) [0193] This is evident in **Isaiah**'s preaching of penitence: "Cease
A P : 0 4 :259(144) [0193] Similarly, when **Isaiah** says (Isa. 58:7) "Share your bread
A P : 1 2 :065(191) [0271] quotes the words from **Isaiah** (28:16), "He who believes in
A P : 1 2 :151(206) [0299] **Isaiah** says, "The distress in which they cry out is thy
A P : 1 2 :158(207) [0301] to do his proper work, as **Isaiah** teaches in a long sermon
A P : 2 0 :005(227) [0339] **Isaiah** says (53:6), "The Lord has laid on him the iniquity
A P : 2 1 :018(231) [0347] **Isaiah** says (11:10), "In that day the root of Jesse shall
A P : 2 3 :064(248) [0381] **Isaiah**'s words, "Purify yourselves, you who bear the
A P : 2 3 :070(249) [0383] God's Word will stand, as **Isaiah** says (40:6), "All flesh is
A P : 2 4 :023(253) [0391] **Isaiah** interprets the law to mean that the death of Christ
A P : 2 4 :023(253) [0391] **Isaiah** and Paul mean that Christ became a sacrificial

Isna (1)
P R : P R :027(016) [0027] Mayor and Council of the City of **Isna**

Isolated (1)
S D : 0 8 :084(607) [1045] more than a mere **isolated** God and a divine person

Israel (12), Israelites (6)
A P : 0 4 :208(135) [0177] The people of **Israel** had seen the prophets sacrifice on the
A P : 0 4 :261(145) [0195] about the one God of **Israel** and converted him not only
A P : 0 4 :261(145) [0195] about the God of **Israel**, "There is no other God who can
A P : 0 4 :262(145) [0195] was promised not only to the **Israelites** but to all nations.
A P : 0 4 :288(151) [0203] The heathen and the **Israelites** sacrificed human victims
A P : 0 4 :395(167) [0225] The same thing happened among the people of **Israel**.
A P : 0 4 :395(167) [0225] history of the people of **Israel** is a type of what was to
A P : 1 5 :015(217) [0319] did not the heathen and **Israelites** have the same privilege?
A P : 1 5 :016(217) [0319] of the heathen and the **Israelites** were condemned
A P : 1 5 :023(218) [0321] people among the **Israelites** expanded such ceremonies,
A P : 2 4 :097(268) [0417] In **Israel** they introduced the worship of Baal; in Judah
A P : 2 4 :098(268) [0417] priests in Judah, and in **Israel** the worship of Baal
A P : 2 7 :062(280) [0441] were nomads rather than **Israelites**, their father apparently
S D : P R :003(503) [0851] pure and clear fountain of **Israel**, which is the only true
S D : 0 5 :023(562) [0959] restore the kingdom of **Israel** and be a light to the
S D : 1 1 :007(617) [1065] of men, as it is written, "**Israel**, thou hast plunged thyself
S D : 1 1 :062(626) [1083] path, as it is written, "O **Israel**, it is your own fault that
S D : 1 1 :085(630) [1091] oppressed the children of **Israel** by many, various, and

Issue (68), Issues (16)
P R : P R :022(011) [0019] do not understand the **issues**, and take no pleasure in
A G : P R :010(025) [0041] Thus the matters at **issue** between us may be
A G : 0 0 :003(095) [0095] that the chief points at **issue** may better be perceived.
A L : 0 0 :003(095) [0095] so that the chief points at **issue**, being briefly set forth,
A P : P R :004(098) [0099] In a religious **issue**, how could they accept a document
A P : 0 2 :007(101) [0107] By such questions they miss the main **issue**.
A P : 0 2 :031(104) [0113] but on so clear an **issue** there is no need of evidence.
A P : 0 4 :002(107) [0121] Majesty kindly to hear us out on this important **issue**.
A P : 0 4 :087(119) [0147] embodying the basic **issue** of the whole discussion: "We
A P : 0 4 :156(128) [0165] about an important **issue**, the honor of Christ and the
A P : 0 4 :183(132) [0173] the fundamentals in this **issue** (namely, the distinction

Continued ▶

A P : 0 4 :185(132) [0173] and dangerous **issues** produce many and varied solutions.
A P : 0 4 :185(132) [0173] But in just and sure **issues**, one or two explanations, taken
A P : 0 4 :242(141) [0187] a major commotion emerged from an insignificant **issue**.
A P : 0 4 :245(142) [0189] of our charge is love that **issues** from a pure heart and a
A P : 0 4 :301(153) [0205] On these **issues** consciences are left in doubt.
A P : 0 4 :314(156) [0207] us much about the whole **issue** and bring consolation to
A P : 0 4 :359(162) [0219] We do contend about the **issue** whether good works of
A P : 0 4 :388(166) [0225] and have explained those **issues** on which our opponents
A P : 0 7 :029(173) [0237] On this **issue** we have spoken out clearly enough in our
A P : 0 7 :032(174) [0239] On this **issue** there are many foolish books by the
A P : 0 7 :034(175) [0239] Another **issue** is involved.
A P : 0 7 :037(175) [0241] and discuss more fully the **issue** in this controversy,
A P : 1 1 :001(180) [0249] On this whole **issue** we shall speak more fully a little later
A P : 1 2 :003(182) [0253] this most important **issue**, involving the chief doctrine of
A P : 1 2 :003(182) [0253] see that especially on this **issue** we have taught what is
A P : 1 2 :010(184) [0255] Yet the **issue** at hand is a great one, the chief doctrine of
A P : 1 2 :059(190) [0267] For this is the chief **issue** on which we clash with our
A P : 1 2 :066(191) [0271] we grant the authority to **issue** decrees contrary to this
A P : 1 2 :077(193) [0275] We discussed this **issue** earlier, in the article on
A P : 1 2 :125(201) [0289] it that on such important **issues** they did not write
A P : 1 2 :128(202) [0291] healing consciences, refuse to let the **issue** be explained.
A P : 1 2 :129(202) [0291] demand that these **issues** be examined and settled now in
A P : 1 2 :130(202) [0291] doubt about important **issues** but do not hear teachers
A P : 1 4 :003(214) [0315] In this **issue** our consciences are clear and we dare not
A P : 1 5 :052(222) [0329] to say about this whole **issue** when we discuss vows and
A P : 2 0 :002(226) [0337] What can we say about an **issue** that is so clear?
A P : 2 0 :009(227) [0341] This **issue** is so weighty that we shrink from no danger on
A P : 2 0 :011(228) [0341] our proofs in our earlier discussion of this whole **issue**.
A P : 2 0 :011(228) [0341] have treated this **issue** has compelled us to register a
A P : 2 3 :071(249) [0383] break up marriages and to **issue** savage and cruel
A P : 2 3 :071(249) [0383] for anything else, especially when the **issue** is so clear.
A P : 2 4 :010(251) [0387] We want to remind our readers of the real **issue**.
A P : 2 4 :010(251) [0387] deal only with the point at **issue** and not wander off into
A P : 2 4 :010(251) [0387] not wander off into side **issues**, like wrestlers fighting for
A P : 2 4 :010(251) [0387] opponents should be forced to discuss the point at **issue**.
A P : 2 4 :010(251) [0387] Once the real **issue** of the controversy is clear, it will be
A P : 2 4 :023(253) [0391] Let this stand in this **issue**, then, that the death of Christ
A P : 2 4 :087(265) [0413] to raise such quibbles about such an important **issue**.
A P : 2 4 :092(266) [0415] But let us get back to the **issue**.
A P : 2 4 :092(266) [0417] ever arises, we shall discuss this whole **issue** more fully.
A P : 2 4 :099(268) [0419] a great cause and a great **issue**, not inferior to the work
A P : 2 4 :099(268) [0419] forth such an important **issue** with the greatest
A P : 2 7 :009(269) [0421] The **issue** is the kind of doctrine which the architects of
A P : 2 7 :010(270) [0423] discussed this whole **issue** carefully and fully in his book
A P : 2 8 :006(282) [0445] That is the **issue** in controversy.
S 2 : 0 2 :010(294) [0465] the Mass will be the decisive **issue** in the council.
S 2 : 0 4 :013(300) [0475] god and even presumed to **issue** orders to the angels in
L C : 0 1 :050(371) [0593] The first things that **issue** and emerge from the heart are
E P : 0 1 :000(466) [0779] The Question at **Issue**
E P : 0 2 :000(469) [0785] The Question at **Issue** in This Controversy
E P : 0 3 :000(472) [0791] The Question at **Issue**
E P : 0 4 :000(475) [0797] The Chief **Issue** in the Controversy Concerning Good
E P : 0 4 :004(476) [0797] At first this was merely a semantic **issue**.
E P : 0 5 :000(477) [0801] The Chief Question at **Issue** in This Controversy
E P : 0 6 :000(479) [0805] The Chief Question at **Issue** in This Controversy
E P : 0 7 :001(481) [0809] The Chief Question at **Issue** between Our Doctrine and
E P : 0 8 :001(487) [0817] The Chief Question at **Issue** in This Controversy
E P : 0 9 :000(492) [0827] The Chief Question at **Issue** in the Controversy about
E P : 1 0 :001(492) [0829] The Chief Question at **Issue** in this Controversy
S D : P R :010(503) [0849] in the controverted **issues** agrees with the Word of God
S D : P R :016(507) [0857] and abiding answer in the controverted **issues**, to wit:
S D : 0 1 :059(519) [0879] that every one be rightly instructed in these **issues**.
S D : 0 1 :062(519) [0879] "accident" and the term "quality" when treating this **issue**.
S D : 0 2 :001(520) [0881] first of all set forth the real **issue** in this controversy.
S D : 0 2 :002(520) [0881] The chief **issue** is solely and alone what the unregenerated
S D : 0 2 :002(520) [0881] This is the **issue** which has been argued by some of the
S D : 0 2 :008(521) [0883] to the questions and **issues** stated at the beginning of this
S D : 0 3 :029(544) [0925] much like) from the main **issue** with which we here have
S D : 0 3 :042(546) [0931] well the various disputed **issues** which the Apology
S D : 0 4 :005(551) [0939] of time, however, the **issue** ceased to be only a semantic
S D : 0 4 :029(555) [0947] false and incorrect and as **issues** which in times of
S D : 0 7 :001(569) [0971] The Chief **Issue** between Our Doctrine and That of the
S D : 1 1 :048(624) [1079] bring everything to such an **issue** that we shall be saved.

Italian (1), Italy (1)
A P : 1 2 :127(201) [0289] England, Spain, France, **Italy**, even in Rome itself — how
T R : 0 0 :035(326) [0513] in order to occupy **Italian** cities and sometimes in order to

Items (2)
A G : 2 7 :045(078) [0081] their teeth, how many **items** could be assembled which
S D : 1 1 :083(630) [1091] will involves both **items**: First, that he would receive into

Ivernack (1)
P R : P R :027(015) [0025] of Mecklenburg [in **Ivernack**] the above two through

Jabbers (1)
S D : 0 4 :011(553) [0941] meantime he chatters and **jabbers** a great deal about faith

Jacob (3)
A P : 2 3 :035(244) [0373] man like Abraham or **Jacob** than in many others who are
A P : 2 3 :064(248) [0381] men like Abraham and **Jacob**, who were polygamists, was
S D : 1 1 :088(631) [1093] As it is written, '**Jacob** I loved, but Esau I hated'"

Jailer (2), Jailers (1)
L C : 0 1 :232(396) [0647] fitting if the judge, the **jailer**, or the hangman did the
L C : 0 2 :030(414) [0685] Those tyrants and **jailers** now have been routed, and their
L C : 0 6 :006(457) [0000] Gospel deserve just such a **jailer** as God's devil and

James (23)
P R : P R :027(015) [0025] Margrave **James** of Baden [-Hachberg] the above two
A P : 0 4 :244(141) [0189] From **James** they quote the text, "You see that a man is
A P : 0 4 :244(141) [0189] The words of **James** will cause no trouble if our
A P : 0 4 :244(142) [0189] of this ever entered into **James**'s mind, though our
A P : 0 4 :244(142) [0189] uphold it under the pretext that this is what **James** meant.
A P : 0 4 :245(142) [0189] How much better is **James**'s teaching!
A P : 0 4 :246(142) [0189] **James** did not hold that by our good works we merit
A P : 0 4 :246(142) [0189] argue from this text that **James** teaches we merit grace
A P : 0 4 :247(142) [0191] Third, **James** has just said that regeneration takes place
A P : 0 4 :247(142) [0191] Thus **James** does not hold that we are regenerated by our
A P : 0 4 :248(142) [0191] From this it is clear that **James** is not against us when he
A P : 0 4 :250(143) [0191] Accordingly, **James** is correct in denying that we are
A P : 0 4 :252(143) [0191] maintain the same about **James**'s words, "A man is
A P : 0 4 :252(143) [0191] **James** preaches only the works that faith produces, as he
A P : 0 4 :253(143) [0193] **James** says none of this, which our opponents shamelessly
A P : 1 2 :149(206) [0299] seek out the church of St. **James** or the basilica of St.
A P : 1 2 :163(208) [0303] make a pilgrimage to St. **James** dressed in armor or to
L C : 0 3 :123(436) [0731] receive nothing, as St. **James** says, "If anyone prays, let
E P : 1 2 :031(501) [0843] Dr. **James** Andreae subscribed
S D : 0 3 :042(547) [0931] the following answer: **James** calls that faith dead where
S D : 0 3 :042(547) [0931] of the Apology states, "**James** teaches correctly when he
S D : 0 3 :043(547) [0931] as the Apology declares, **James** is speaking of the good
S D : 1 2 :040(636) [1103] Dr. **James** Andreae, subscribed

Januarius (1)
A L : 2 6 :017(066) [0073] prudently admonishes **Januarius** that he should know that

Jaundiced (1)
S D : P R :003(502) [0847] The adversaries took a **jaundiced** view of this Confession,

Jaws (3)
L C : 0 2 :030(414) [0685] lost creatures, from the **jaws** of hell, won us, made us
L C : 0 4 :083(446) [0751] which snatches us from the **jaws** of the devil and makes
E P : 0 9 :004(492) [0827] devil, and of the eternal damnation of the hellish **jaws**.

Jealous (4), Jealously (1), Jealousy (1)
A G : 2 8 :067(093) [0093] among those who observe such ordinance most **jealously**.
S C : 0 1 :021(344) [0543] the Lord your God am a **jealous** God, visiting the iniquity
L C : 0 1 :030(368) [0589] *your God, mighty and* ***jealous****, visiting the iniquity of the*
L C : 0 1 :320(408) [0673] *Lord, your God, am a* ***jealous*** *God, visiting the iniquity*
L C : 0 3 :042(425) [0709] drunkards, gluttons, **jealous** persons, and slanderers.
L C : 0 5 :075(455) [0771] sorcery, enmity, strife, **jealousy**, anger, selfishness,

Jeremiah (7)
A G : 2 5 :008(062) [0069] **Jeremiah** also says, "The heart is desperately corrupt; who
A L : 2 5 :008(062) [0069] **Jeremiah** also says, "The heart of man is corrupt and
A P : 1 2 :159(207) [0301] In **Jeremiah** (49:12) it is said, "Those who did not deserve
A P : 2 4 :028(254) [0393] and sacrifices, but what **Jeremiah** is condemning is an idea
A P : 2 7 :059(279) [0439] the Rechabites who, as **Jeremiah** writes (35:6), neither had
S 3 : 0 3 :002(304) [0479] is the hammer of which **Jeremiah** speaks, "Is not my word
T R : 0 0 :038(327) [0515] So **Jeremiah** and other prophets dissented from them, and

Jeroboam (1)
A P : 1 5 :015(217) [0319] the rites established by **Jeroboam** and others over and

Jerome (20)
A G : 2 2 :006(050) [0061] St. **Jerome** also states that the priests who administered
A L : 2 2 :006(050) [0061] The same is testified by **Jerome**, who said, "The priests
A P : 0 4 :173(131) [0171] Against the Pelagians, **Jerome** writes, "We are righteous,
A P : 0 4 :264(146) [0195] Here **Jerome** adds an extraneous particle expressing
A P : 0 4 :264(146) [0195] Let us therefore dismiss **Jerome** in the interpretation of
A P : 0 7 :011(170) [0229] For example, **Jerome** says, "Therefore the sinner who has
A P : 2 1 :002(229) [0343] They also refer to **Jerome**'s controversy with Vigilantius
A P : 2 1 :002(229) [0343] "On this field of battle **Jerome** conquered Vigilantius
A P : 2 1 :002(229) [0343] the controversy between **Jerome** and Vigilantius there is
A P : 2 2 :004(236) [0359] in the Latin church, as Cyprian and **Jerome** attest.
A P : 2 2 :004(236) [0359] on Zephaniah, **Jerome** says, "The priests who serve the
S 2 : 0 4 :009(300) [0473] So St. **Jerome** writes that the priests of Alexandria
S 3 : 0 3 :028(308) [0487] we slept (as St. Augustine, St. **Jerome**, and others confess)
S 3 : 1 0 :003(314) [0497] St. **Jerome**, too, wrote concerning the church in
T R : 0 0 :018(323) [0509] 9. **Jerome** says, "If it is authority that you want, the world
T R : 0 0 :062(330) [0521] Accordingly **Jerome** teaches clearly that in the apostolic
T R : 0 0 :062(330) [0523] And **Jerome** observes: "One man was chosen over the rest
T R : 0 0 :063(331) [0523] **Jerome** therefore teaches that the distinction between the
T R : 0 0 :073(332) [0525] which is the one thing (as **Jerome** states) that distinguishes
L C : 0 4 :081(446) [0751] Indeed, St. **Jerome** is responsible for this view, for he

Jerusalem (1)
A P : 2 1 :008(230) [0345] hosts, how long wilt thou have no mercy on **Jerusalem**?"

Jesse (1)
A P : 2 1 :018(231) [0347] "In that day the root of **Jesse** shall stand as an ensign to

Jest (3)
L C : 0 1 :208(393) [0639] Married life is no matter for **jest** or idle curiosity, but it is
L C : 0 3 :018(422) [0703] commandment treated as a **jest** but will be angry and
L C : 0 4 :021(439) [0737] Do you think it was a **jest** that the heavens opened when

Jesus (113)
P R : P R :018(009) [0015] seat of our Lord **Jesus** Christ with joyful and fearless
P R : P R :023(012) [0021] advent of our only Redeemer and Saviour **Jesus** Christ.
A G : 1 7 :001(038) [0051] among us that our Lord **Jesus** Christ will return on the
A G : 2 1 :002(047) [0057] God and men, Christ **Jesus**" (I Tim. 2:5), who is the only
A G : 2 1 :003(047) [0059] and call upon this same **Jesus** Christ in every time of
A G : 2 1 :004(047) [0059] advocate with the Father, **Jesus** Christ the righteous"
A G : 2 6 :027(068) [0073] through the grace of the Lord **Jesus**, just as they will."
A L : 2 4 :026(059) [0067] offering of the body of **Jesus** Christ once for all," and
A L : 2 6 :027(068) [0073] through the grace of the Lord **Jesus**, just as they will."
A P : 0 4 :079(118) [0143] who gives us the victory through our Lord **Jesus** Christ."
A P : 0 4 :084(119) [0145] was promised to faith in **Jesus** Christ might be given to
A P : 0 4 :087(120) [0147] precepts of a good life, but through faith in **Jesus** Christ."
A P : 0 4 :093(120) [0149] have believed in Christ **Jesus**, in order to be justified by
A P : 0 4 :103(122) [0151] but when the Lord **Jesus** came he forgave all men the sin
A P : 0 4 :103(122) [0151] grace abounded all the more' (Rom. 5:20) through **Jesus**.
A P : 0 4 :111(123) [0155] Paul also says, "In Christ **Jesus** neither circumcision nor
A P : 0 4 :143(126) [0161] those who are in Christ **Jesus**, who do not walk according
A P : 0 4 :195(134) [0175] we have peace with God through our Lord **Jesus** Christ.

Continued ▶

A P : 0 4 :306(154) [0207] the source of your life in **Jesus** Christ, whom God made
A P : 0 4 :308(155) [0207] now no condemnation for those who are in Christ **Jesus**."
A P : 0 4 :400(168) [0227] words or in the words of its head, our Lord **Jesus** Christ?
A P : 1 2 :081(194) [0275] was promised to faith in **Jesus** Christ might be given to
A P : 1 2 :146(205) [0297] who gives us the victory through our Lord **Jesus** Christ."
A P : 2 1 :018(231) [0347] prays, "May our Lord **Jesus** Christ himself, and God our
A P : 2 1 :025(232) [0349] "The passion of our Lord **Jesus** Christ and the merits of
A P : 2 4 :022(253) [0391] the offering of the body of **Jesus** Christ once for all."
A P : 2 4 :036(257) [0397] Spirit for obedience to **Jesus** Christ and for sprinkling
S 1 : P R :015(291) [0459] Dear Lord **Jesus** Christ, assemble a council of thine own,
S 2 : 0 0 :000(292) [0461] to the office and work of **Jesus** Christ, or to our
S 2 : 0 1 :001(292) [0461] chief article is this, that **Jesus** Christ, our God and Lord,
S 2 : 0 1 :003(292) [0461] which is in Christ **Jesus**, by his blood" (Rom. 3:23-25).
S 2 : 0 1 :004(292) [0461] that he justifies him who has faith in **Jesus**" (Rom. 3:26).
S 2 : 0 2 :010(294) [0465] considered equal or superior to my Saviour, **Jesus** Christ.
S 2 : 0 3 :002(298) [0471] article concerning redemption in **Jesus** Christ.
S 2 : 0 4 :001(298) [0471] this position belongs only to one, namely, to **Jesus** Christ.
S 2 : 0 4 :003(298) [0473] which is concerned with redemption in **Jesus** Christ.
T R : 0 0 :025(324) [0511] made when he declared **Jesus** to be the Christ, the Son of
T R : 0 0 :082(000) [0529] and constantly will teach, through **Jesus** Christ, our Lord.
S C : P R :000(338) [0533] Grace, mercy, and peace in **Jesus** Christ, our Lord, from
S C : 0 2 :003(345) [0545] *"And in* ***Jesus*** *Christ, his only son, our Lord: who was*
S C : 0 2 :004(345) [0545] Answer: I believe that **Jesus** Christ, true God, begotten of
S C : 0 2 :006(345) [0545] I cannot believe in **Jesus** Christ, my Lord, or come to
S C : 0 2 :006(345) [0545] preserves it in union with **Jesus** Christ in the one true
S C : 0 4 :010(349) [0551] upon us richly through **Jesus** Christ our Saviour, so that
S C : 0 5 :028(351) [0555] the command of our Lord **Jesus** Christ, I forgive you your
S C : 0 6 :002(351) [0555] and blood of our Lord **Jesus** Christ, under the bread and
S C : 0 6 :004(351) [0555] write thus: "Our Lord **Jesus** Christ, on the night when he
S C : 0 7 :002(352) [0557] through thy dear Son **Jesus** Christ, that Thou hast
S C : 0 7 :005(353) [0559] through thy dear Son **Jesus** Christ, that Thou hast this
S C : 0 8 :009(353) [0559] Thou hast bestowed on us, through **Jesus** Christ our Lord
S C : 0 8 :011(354) [0559] all thy benefits, through **Jesus** Christ our Lord, who lives
L C : S P :012(363) [0577] And in **Jesus** Christ, his only Son, our Lord: who was
L C : S P :023(364) [0579] "Our Lord **Jesus** Christ on the night when he was betrayed
L C : 0 1 :159(387) [0627] became your father in Christ **Jesus** through the Gospel."
L C : 0 2 :025(413) [0683] *"And in* ***Jesus*** *Christ, his only Son, our Lord: who was*
L C : 0 2 :026(414) [0685] concentrate on these words, "in **Jesus** Christ, our Lord."
L C : 0 2 :027(414) [0685] Article, concerning **Jesus** Christ?" answer briefly, "I
L C : 0 2 :027(414) [0685] briefly, "I believe that **Jesus** Christ, true Son of God, has
L C : 0 2 :030(414) [0685] place has been taken by **Jesus** Christ, the Lord of life and
L C : 0 5 :003(447) [0753] *"Our Lord* ***Jesus*** *Christ on the night when he was betrayed*
E P : 0 4 :014(477) [0799] for those who are in Christ **Jesus**" (Rom. 8:1).
E P : 0 7 :002(481) [0809] and blood of our Lord **Jesus** Christ truly and essentially
E P : 0 7 :008(482) [0811] and alone to the almighty power of our Lord **Jesus** Christ.
E P : 0 7 :011(483) [0811] of our Christian faith: **Jesus** Christ is true, essential,
E P : 1 1 :010(495) [0833] and believe on the Lord **Jesus** Christ (I Tim. 2:6; I John
E P : 1 1 :022(497) [0837] and Father of our Lord **Jesus** Christ grant us the grace of
E P : 1 2 :031(500) [0843] righteous judge, our Lord **Jesus** Christ, and that we shall
S D : 0 2 :026(526) [0891] 51:12); creates us in Christ **Jesus** for good works
S D : 0 2 :026(526) [0891] "No one can say, **Jesus** is Lord, except by the Holy Spirit"
S D : 0 2 :039(528) [0895] created in Christ **Jesus** for good works, which God
S D : 0 2 :040(528) [0895] I cannot believe in **Jesus** Christ, my Lord, or come to
S D : 0 2 :040(528) [0895] preserves it in union with **Jesus** Christ in the one true
S D : 0 2 :043(529) [0897] contrary to the help and grace of our Lord **Jesus** Christ.
S D : 0 2 :050(530) [0901] Son, our only Saviour and Redeemer, **Jesus** Christ.
S D : 0 2 :050(531) [0901] of their sins and true faith in the Son of God, **Jesus** Christ
S D : 0 3 :057(550) [0935] and "the blood of **Jesus**, his Son, cleanses us from
S D : 0 4 :007(552) [0941] says, "has been created in Christ **Jesus** for good works."
S D : 0 5 :004(559) [0953] beginning of the Gospel of **Jesus** Christ, the Son of God."
S D : 0 5 :022(562) [0959] solely on the Lord **Jesus** Christ, "who was put to death for
S D : 0 7 :010(571) [0975] and blood of our Lord **Jesus** Christ, under the bread and
S D : 0 7 :019(572) [0979] true body and blood of **Jesus** Christ which are given and
S D : 0 7 :029(574) [0981] appear before the judgment seat of our Lord **Jesus** Christ.
S D : 0 7 :039(576) [0985] but we believe that just as **Jesus** Christ, our Saviour, was
S D : 0 7 :039(576) [0985] is the true flesh and blood of the Lord **Jesus** Christ."
S D : 0 7 :043(576) [0987] is our Lord and Saviour **Jesus** Christ concerning whom,
S D : 0 7 :044(577) [0987] Creator and Redeemer **Jesus** Christ, selected his words
S D : 0 7 :045(577) [0987] and almighty Son of God, **Jesus** Christ, our Lord,
S D : 0 7 :048(578) [0989] of our Lord and Saviour **Jesus** Christ, which in
S D : 0 7 :050(578) [0989] of the words of **Jesus** Christ than the Lord Christ himself,
S D : 0 7 :060(580) [0993] of profaning the body and blood of the Lord **Jesus** Christ.
S D : 0 7 :062(581) [0995] salvation for the sake of **Jesus** Christ, and hold to it in all
S D : 0 7 :074(583) [0999] Word, institution, and ordinance of our Lord **Jesus** Christ
S D : 0 7 :075(583) [0999] and almighty words of **Jesus** Christ which he spoke in the
S D : 0 7 :089(585) [1003] God and Saviour, **Jesus** Christ, which always remain
S D : 0 7 :090(585) [1003] the omnipotence of our Lord and Saviour, **Jesus** Christ.
S D : 0 7 :094(586) [1005] article of our faith: that **Jesus** Christ is essential, natural,
S D : 0 7 :106(588) [1009] true and eternal God, our Lord and Saviour **Jesus** Christ.
S D : 0 8 :002(591) [1015] of the body and blood of **Jesus** Christ in the Lord's
S D : 0 8 :006(592) [1017] in such a way that Christ **Jesus** is henceforth in *one* person
S D : 0 8 :029(597) [1025] both natures in Christ, the way **Jesus**, the son of Mary, is.
S D : 0 8 :059(602) [1035] it states, "The blood of **Jesus** his Son cleanses us from all
S D : 0 8 :070(605) [1041] likewise, when **Jesus** knew that "the Father had
S D : 0 8 :085(608) [1047] according to our calendar **Jesus** the son of Mary is 1543
S D : 0 8 :085(608) [1047] To me, **Jesus** of Nazareth, Mary's son, born a human
S D : 1 0 :011(612) [1055] which we have in Christ **Jesus**, that they might bring us
S D : 1 1 :005(617) [1065] in love to be his sons through **Jesus** Christ" (Eph. 1:4, 5).
S D : 1 1 :008(617) [1065] will and pleasure in Christ **Jesus** it is also a cause which
S D : 1 1 :013(619) [1067] of God in Christ **Jesus**, who is the genuine and true "book
S D : 1 1 :046(624) [1079] hand of our Saviour, **Jesus** Christ, out of which no one
S D : 1 1 :049(624) [1079] the love of God in Christ **Jesus**" (Rom. 8:28, 29, 35, 38,
S D : 1 1 :087(631) [1093] love to be his son through **Jesus** Christ, according to the
S D : 1 2 :006(633) [1097] and Father of our Lord **Jesus** Christ has appointed us
S D : 1 2 :040(636) [1103] the judgment seat of **Jesus** Christ and for which we shall

Jew (1), Jewish (14), Jews (24)
A G : 1 7 :005(038) [0051] Rejected, too, are certain **Jewish** opinions which are even
A G : 2 8 :046(088) [0089] forbids giving heed to **Jewish** myths or to commands of
A G : 2 8 :061(091) [0093] God like the Levitical or **Jewish** services and that Christ
A L : 1 7 :005(038) [0051] who are now spreading **Jewish** opinions to the effect that
A L : 2 4 :032(059) [0067] the history, for the **Jews** and the ungodly can also
A L : 2 8 :046(088) [0089] says, "Not giving heed to **Jewish** myths or to commands
A P : 0 4 :021(110) [0127] at which they look as the **Jews** did at the veiled face of
A P : 0 4 :376(164) [0223] a philosophical or a **Jewish** manner they eliminate from
A P : 0 7 :019(171) [0233] about the whole **Jewish** nation and says that the true
A P : 0 7 :042(176) [0241] Passover falls at a different time from the **Jewish** Passover
A P : 0 7 :042(176) [0241] held tenaciously to the custom of using the **Jewish** time.
A P : 0 7 :043(177) [0243] be celebrated with the **Jews**; they were called Audians,
A P : 1 2 :053(189) [0265] by Christ among the **Jews**, and spread by the apostles
A P : 1 2 :078(193) [0275] misunderstood, as the **Jews** looked at Moses' face covered
A P : 1 2 :114(199) [0285] believes this has a **Jewish** and heathen faith, for even the
A P : 1 6 :007(223) [0331] who hold it, as in the **Jewish** dream of the messianic
A P : 2 4 :010(251) [0387] Aeschines reminded the **Jews** that both parties in a
A P : 2 4 :028(254) [0393] How are we to think the **Jews** accepted this declaration,
S 3 : 0 8 :008(313) [0495] long since heard from the **Jews** about the coming Messiah
S 3 : 0 8 :008(313) [0495] the hardened, unbelieving **Jews**, but he knew that he now
S 3 : 0 8 :008(313) [0497] Messiah and not deny or persecute him as the **Jews** did.
L C : 0 1 :035(369) [0589] both heathen and **Jews**; just so in our day he overthrows
L C : 0 1 :080(375) [0603] the commandment was given to the **Jews** alone.
L C : 0 1 :081(375) [0603] In time, however, the **Jews** interpreted this commandment
L C : 0 1 :085(376) [0605] time, as it was among the **Jews**, when it had to be
L C : 0 1 :201(392) [0637] because among the **Jewish** people marriage was
L C : 0 1 :258(399) [0653] at present, but among the **Jews** it was extremely common.
L C : 0 1 :293(404) [0663] given exclusively to the **Jews**; nevertheless, in part they
L C : 0 1 :293(404) [0663] The **Jews** did not interpret them as referring to unchastity
L C : 0 1 :294(404) [0665] needed because under the **Jewish** government
L C : 0 1 :300(405) [0667] To this class the **Jews** especially claimed to belong, as
L C : 0 1 :331(410) [0677] merely for a display, as the **Jews** did, but we are to keep
L C : 0 2 :066(419) [0697] whether heathen, Turks, **Jews**, or false Christians and
L C : 0 4 :054(443) [0745] Even though a **Jew** should today come deceitfully and
L C : 0 5 :047(452) [0763] the Passover, which the **Jews** were obliged to eat only
L C : 0 5 :048(452) [0765] perverted it and turned it back into a **Jewish** feast).
S D : 0 2 :060(533) [0905] describes the obstinate **Jews** (Acts 7:51), will not be
S D : 0 7 :060(580) [0993] as certainly as did the **Jews** when they actually and in deed
S D : 1 1 :058(626) [1081] extends also to their posterity, as with the **Jews**.

Jewel (3), Jeweled (1), Jewels (1)
L C : 0 1 :117(381) [0615] it has its place within that **jewel** and holy treasure, the
L C : 0 1 :150(386) [0625] them as the most precious treasure and **jewel** on earth.
L C : 0 4 :016(438) [0735] tear from it the precious **jeweled** clasp with which God
L C : 0 4 :046(442) [0743] No greater **jewel**, therefore, can adorn our body and soul
L C : 0 5 :056(453) [0767] to the bright sun, or as dung in contrast to **jewels**.

Joachim (1)
P R : P R :027(014) [0025] **Joachim** Frederick, margrave of Brandenburg,

Job (3)
A P : 0 4 :198(134) [0175] rewards, as is evident in **Job**, in Christ, and in other
A P : 1 2 :158(207) [0301] Scripture explains that **Job**'s afflictions were not imposed
S D : 0 1 :035(514) [0869] **Job** says: "Thy hands fashioned and made me together

John (63)
P R : P R :019(009) [0017] Philip Melanchthon or of [**John**] Brenz, Urban Rhegius,
P R : P R :019(009) [0017] Brenz, Urban Rhegius, [**John** Bugenhagen] of
P R : P R :027(014) [0025] **John** George, margrave of Brandenburg, elector
P R : P R :027(014) [0025] **John**, bishop of Meissen
P R : P R :027(014) [0025] Duke **John** [of Saxe-Weimar] the above two through
P R : P R :027(014) [0025] Duke **John** Casimir [of Saxe-Coburg] and
P R : P R :027(014) [0025] Duke **John** Ernest [of Saxe-Eisenach] the above two
P R : P R :027(015) [0025] Duke **John** and
P R : P R :027(015) [0025] **John** Guenther, count of Schwarzburg [-Sondershausen].
P R : P R :027(015) [0025] **John** Hoyer, count of Mansfeld [-Artern].
P R : P R :027(015) [0025] **John**, count of Oldenburg and Delmenhorst.
A G : 1 2 :006(035) [0049] fruits of repentance, as **John** says, "Bear fruit that befits
A G : 0 0 :007(096) [0095] **John**, duke of Saxony, elector
A G : 0 0 :007(096) [0095] **John** Frederick, duke of Saxony
A L : 0 0 :017(096) [0095] **John**, duke of Saxony, elector
A L : 0 0 :017(096) [0095] **John** Frederick, duke of Saxony
A P : 0 4 :103(122) [0151] sin of the whole world, as **John** testified when he said
A P : 0 4 :141(126) [0161] So **John** teaches in his first epistle (4:19); "We love," he
A P : 0 4 :263(146) [0195] worthy of penitence, as **John** the Baptist says (Matt. 3:8).
A P : 0 4 :297(153) [0205] to be accepted by faith, as **John** says (1 John 5:10-12): "He
A P : 0 4 :356(161) [0217] with Christ (Rom. 8:17), as **John** says (John 3:36), "He
A P : 0 7 :001(168) [0227] from the church since **John** compared the church to a
A P : 0 7 :019(171) [0233] Thus **John** speaks (Matt. 3:12) about the whole Jewish
A P : 1 2 :088(195) [0277] doubts, he makes the divine promise a lie, as **John** says.
A P : 1 2 :132(202) [0291] This, we say, is what **John** means when he says
A P : 1 2 :159(207) [0301] prophets were killed, and **John** the Baptist, and other
A P : 2 7 :001(268) [0419] of Eisenach, there was a Franciscan named **John** Hilten
S 3 : 0 3 :005(304) [0481] **John**, who preceded Christ, is called a preacher of
S 3 : 0 3 :005(304) [0481] That is, **John** was to accuse them all and convince them
S 3 : 0 3 :030(308) [0487] Here the fiery angel St. **John**, the preacher of true
S 3 : 0 3 :032(308) [0487] But **John** says: "Repent, both of you.
S 3 : 0 3 :039(309) [0489] is the repentance which **John** preaches, which Christ
S 3 : 0 3 :045(310) [0491] are not present, for St. **John** says, "No one born of God
S 3 : 0 3 :045(310) [0491] also true, as the same St. **John** writes, "If we say we have
S 3 : 0 8 :012(313) [0497] **John** the Baptist was not conceived without the preceding
S 3 : 1 5 :005(316) [0501] Dr. **John** Bugenhagen, of Pomerania, subscribed
S 3 : 1 5 :005(317) [0501] **John** Agricola, of Eisleben, subscribed
S 3 : 1 5 :005(317) [0501] Also I, **John** Drach, professor and minister in Marburg,
S 3 : 1 5 :005(317) [0501] I, **John** Schlagenhaufen, pastor of the church in Koethen,
S 3 : 1 5 :005(317) [0501] I, Dr. **John** Bugenhagen of Pomerania, again subscribe in
S 3 : 1 5 :005(317) [0501] in the name of Master **John** Brenz, who on his departure
S 3 : 1 5 :005(317) [0501] I, **John** Aepinus, subscribe
S 3 : 1 5 :005(317) [0501] Likewise I, **John** Amsterdam, of Bremen
S 3 : 1 5 :005(318) [0501] I, Dr. **John** Lang, preacher of the church in Erfurt, in my
S 3 : 1 5 :005(318) [0501] the Rev. **John** Thall
S 3 : 1 5 :005(318) [0501] the Rev. **John** Kilian
T R : 0 0 :023(324) [0511] In **John**, too, it is written, "If you forgive the sins," etc.
T R : 0 0 :062(330) [0523] Again, Peter and **John** call themselves presbyters.
T R : 0 0 :082(334) [0529] I, Dr. **John** Bugenhagen, of Pomerania, subscribe the
T R : 0 0 :082(334) [0529] **John** Drach, of Marburg, subscribed
T R : 0 0 :082(335) [0529] in the name of Master **John** Brenz, as he commanded me
T R : 0 0 :082(335) [0529] **John** Schlagenhaufen subscribes with his own hand
T R : 0 0 :082(335) [0529] **John** Aepinus, superintendent in Hamburg, subscribed

Continued ▶

TR : 0 0 :082(335) [0529] **John** Amsterdam, of Bremen, did the same
TR : 0 0 :082(335) [0529] **John** Fontanus, superintendent of Lower Hesse,
TR : 0 0 :082(000) [0529] most renowned man, Dr. **John** Bugenhagen, most revered
TR : 0 0 :082(000) [0529] **John** Brentz, Minister of Hall (Triglotta text only)]
LC : 0 4 :050(443) [0745] as St. Bernard, Gerson, **John** Hus, and others, and since
SD : 0 3 :027(543) [0923] the righteousness of faith, as St. **John** says (I John 3:14).
SD : 0 5 :005(559) [0953] For **John**, Christ, and the apostles began in their
SD : 0 8 :022(595) [1023] of Nyssa, in Theodoret; **John** Damascene, Book III, chap.
SD : 0 8 :059(602) [1035] **John** is saying in this passage that in the work or matter
SD : 0 8 :085(608) [1047] in power' (Rom. 1:4), and **John** calls it 'glorified'

Join (1), Joined (10), Joining (2), Joint (2), Jointly (1)
AP : 1 0 :003(179) [0247] do not deny that we are **joined** to Christ spiritually by
AP : 1 2 :038(187) [0261] defined as an anxiety **joined** with faith, where faith
AP : 1 2 :052(189) [0265] makes a practice of **joining** these two, terror and
AP : 2 2 :003(236) [0359] who would use the Lord's Supper should use it **jointly**.
AP : 2 2 :010(238) [0361] food and that they come to life by being **joined** to Christ.
AP : 2 3 :023(242) [0371] "What God has **joined** together, let no man put
AP : 2 3 :029(243) [0371] he says in Matt. 19:6, "What God has **joined** together."
AP : 2 4 :016(252) [0389] to cut the members at the **joint**, lest like an unskilled cook
AP : 2 4 :018(252) [0389] content of the promise **joined** to the ceremony; thus
S2 : 0 4 :009(300) [0473] in gifts) and diligently **joined** together in unity of
S3 : 0 5 :002(310) [0491] and say that God has **joined** to the water a spiritual
SC : 0 9 :006(355) [0561] weaker sex, since you are **joint** heirs of the grace of life, in
LC : 0 4 :029(440) [0739] Word and ordinance and the **joining** of his name to it.
LC : 0 5 :010(448) [0755] is, "When the Word is **joined** to the external element, it
SD : 0 7 :007(570) [0975] that the reality is **joined** to the symbols in such a way that
SD : 1 1 :074(628) [1087] they should nevertheless **join** David in the next words,

Joke (2), Joking (1)
LC : 0 1 :246(398) [0651] God's commandment and must not be treated as a **joke**.
LC : 0 1 :247(398) [0651] Such a man's sighs and cries will be no **joking** matter.
SD : 0 7 :031(574) [0983] one make this out to be a **joke** or idle talk; I am in dead

Jonas (1)
S3 : 1 5 :005(316) [0501] Dr. Justus **Jonas**, rector, subscribed with his own hand

Jovinian (7)
AG : 2 6 :030(068) [0075] our teachers are, like **Jovinian**, accused of forbidding
AL : 2 6 :030(068) [0075] that our teachers, like **Jovinian**, forbid discipline and
AP : 2 3 :037(244) [0373] marriage on the same level with virginity, as **Jovinian** did.
AP : 2 3 :067(248) [0383] is horrible: the marriage of priests is the **Jovinian** heresy.
AP : 2 3 :067(248) [0383] In **Jovinian**'s time the world still did not know the law of
AP : 2 3 :067(248) [0383] marriage of priests is the **Jovinian** heresy or that the
AP : 2 3 :069(249) [0383] our position in the **Jovinian** controversy on the relative

Joy (20), Joyful (12), Joyfully (6), Joyous (1), Joys (1)
PR : PR :018(009) [0015] Lord Jesus Christ with **joyful** and fearless hearts and
AG : 1 7 :002(038) [0051] eternal life and everlasting **joy** to believers and the elect
AG : 2 5 :004(062) [0069] heaven, that we should **joyfully** comfort ourselves with
AL : 1 7 :002(038) [0051] give eternal life and endless **joy**, but ungodly men and
AP : 0 4 :091(120) [0149] are tranquil and **joyful** before God, and in Rom. 10:10,
AP : 0 4 :100(121) [0151] it brings forth peace, **joy**, and eternal life in the heart.
AP : 0 7 :036(175) [0241] but righteousness and peace and **joy** in the Holy Spirit."
AP : 1 2 :060(190) [0269] and brings forth peace, **joy**, and a new life in the heart.
AP : 1 7 :001(224) [0335] eternal life and eternal **joys** to the godly but condemning
SC : 0 7 :003(352) [0557] may suggest, you should go to your work **joyfully**.
SC : 0 8 :008(353) [0559] enough to eat to make them **joyful** and of good cheer.
SC : 0 9 :003(355) [0561] Let them do this **joyfully**, and not sadly, for that would
LC : 0 1 :115(381) [0613] comfort of being able **joyfully** to boast in the face of all
LC : 0 1 :118(381) [0615] and could say with a **joyful** heart in his presence, "Now I
LC : 0 1 :120(381) [0615] heart leap and melt with **joy** when it can go to work and
LC : 0 1 :122(382) [0617] of this treasure and **joy** of conscience and lay up for
LC : 0 1 :144(385) [0623] in order to have such **joyful** consciences and know how to
LC : 0 1 :145(385) [0623] girl would dance for **joy** and praise and thank God; and
LC : 0 1 :148(385) [0623] Lord and, what is more, a **joyful** conscience and a
LC : 0 1 :151(386) [0625] pleases God and receives **joy** and happiness for his
LC : 0 1 :157(387) [0627] to obtain an abundance of **joy**, happiness, and salvation,
LC : 0 1 :166(387) [0627] make our hearts so melt for **joy** and love toward those to
LC : 0 1 :166(387) [0627] that we lift our hands in **joyful** thanks to God for giving
LC : 0 1 :218(394) [0643] so that men may have **joy** and happiness in their married
LC : 0 1 :221(395) [0643] works — which you can **joyfully** set over against all
LC : 0 3 :092(433) [0725] But such a confident and **joyful** heart can only come from
LC : 0 5 :051(452) [0765] commandments, without **joy** and love and even without
LC : 0 5 :072(455) [0769] feel your weakness, go **joyfully** to the sacrament and
LC : 0 5 :085(456) [0773] they will receive them with **joy** and earnestness, practice
LC : 0 6 :024(460) [0000] Not much **joy** or comfort would come from this, but only
LC : 0 6 :027(460) [0000] a desire for confession that he will run toward it with **joy**.
EP : 0 5 :007(478) [0803] a comforting and **joyful** message which does not reprove
SD : 0 2 :068(534) [0907] that at one moment he is **joyful** in the Spirit and at
SD : 0 4 :003(551) [0939] but flow from a spontaneous spirit and a **joyful** heart.
SD : 0 4 :012(553) [0941] of divine grace makes us **joyous**, mettlesome, and merry
SD : 0 5 :007(559) [0953] "Even so, there will be **joy** in heaven over one sinner who
SD : 0 5 :021(562) [0959] the Gospel, a good and **joyful** message that God wills not
SD : 0 6 :025(568) [0971] completely, and with sheer **joy**, and will rejoice therein
SD : 0 8 :030(597) [1025] and find their delight and **joy** in looking into it, as St.
SD : 1 1 :042(623) [1077] "receive the Word with **joy**," but after that "they fall away

Jubilee (5)
S3 : 0 3 :025(307) [0485] the pope invented the **jubilee** year and attached it to
S3 : 0 3 :025(307) [0485] went further and quickly multiplied the **jubilee** years.
S3 : 0 3 :025(307) [0485] church and house was reached by **jubilee** indulgences.
S3 : 0 3 :026(307) [0487] indulgences for the dead through bulls and **jubilee** years.
S3 : 0 3 :027(307) [0487] from the indulgence or **jubilee** year must be contrite,

Judah (2)
AP : 2 4 :097(268) [0417] the worship of Baal; in **Judah** they even sacrificed in
AP : 2 4 :098(268) [0417] to the wicked priests in **Judah**, and in Israel the worship

Judaism (3), Judaizing (1)
AP : 0 7 :042(176) [0241] had been converted from **Judaism**, and so, after the
AP : 0 7 :043(177) [0243] had been converted from **Judaism** but kept their customs.
AP : 1 3 :018(213) [0313] It is sheer **Judaism** to believe that we are justified by a
AP : 1 5 :004(215) [0315] opponents are openly **Judaizing**; they are openly replacing

Judas (10)
AP : 1 2 :008(183) [0255] Why did not Saul, **Judas**, and men like them attain grace
AP : 1 2 :008(183) [0255] faith and the Gospel, that **Judas** did not believe nor
AP : 1 2 :008(183) [0255] between the contrition of **Judas** and that of Peter.
AP : 1 2 :008(183) [0255] the legalistic reply that **Judas** did not love God but feared
AP : 1 2 :036(186) [0261] between the contrition of **Judas** and Saul on the one hand
AP : 1 2 :036(186) [0261] The contrition of **Judas** and Saul did not avail because it
S3 : 0 3 :007(304) [0481] death and hell, and man must despair like Saul and **Judas**.
EP : 0 5 :008(479) [0803] like the Pharisees, or they despair, as **Judas** did, etc.
SD : 0 7 :033(575) [0983] which the godless or **Judas** receive orally as well as St.
SD : 0 7 :060(580) [0993] godless hypocrites, like **Judas** and his ilk who have no

Judge (70), Judged (19), Judging (3)
AG : 0 3 :006(030) [0045] will return openly to **judge** the living and the dead, as
AG : 2 5 :011(063) [0071] to the Lord God, the true **judge**, in your prayer, telling
AG : 2 8 :015(083) [0085] and again, "Who made me a **judge** or divider over you?"
AG : 2 8 :021(084) [0087] the Gospel, forgive sins, **judge** doctrine and condemn
AL : 0 3 :006(030) [0045] will openly come again to **judge** the living and the dead,
AL : 0 0 :001(047) [0059] teachers are to be regarded as heretics **judge** too harshly.
AL : 0 0 :006(049) [0059] However, it can readily be **judged** that nothing
AL : 2 5 :011(063) [0071] confess your sins to God, the true **judge**, in your prayer.
AL : 2 6 :012(065) [0071] traditions, and yet men **judged** these observances to be
AL : 2 7 :005(071) [0077] in years, they were unable to **judge** their own strength.
AL : 2 7 :025(074) [0079] pontiffs have prudently **judged** that leniency should be
AL : 2 7 :029(075) [0079] Before they are able to **judge**, boys and girls are
AL : 2 7 :055(079) [0083] err still more, for they **judge** that all magistracy and all
AL : 2 8 :015(083) [0085] and again, "Who made me a **judge** or divider over you?"
AL : 2 8 :056(090) [0091] for salvation or by **judging** that those who omit them
AP : PR :009(098) [0101] what our opponents have **judged**, as we have reported
AP : PR :016(099) [0103] and we hope that posterity will **judge** us more equitably.
AP : PR :019(099) [0103] to Christ, who will one day **judge** these controversies.
AP : 0 4 :036(112) [0131] bring itself to love a wrathful, **judging**, punishing God.
AP : 0 4 :233(140) [0185] also arise when the people **judge** their clergy's behavior
AP : 0 4 :268(147) [0197] to the words, "If we **judged** ourselves, we would not be
AP : 0 4 :268(147) [0197] we would not be **judged** by the Lord" (I Cor. 11:31); "If
AP : 0 4 :280(149) [0201] in an argument to **judge** or reply to a single passage
AP : 0 4 :322(157) [0209] praiseworthy, if it is to be **judged** without mercy."
AP : 0 4 :326(158) [0211] his glory, as in Ps. 7:8, "**Judge** me, O Lord, according to
AP : 0 4 :343(160) [0217] intelligent men can easily **judge** when they are brought to
AP : 0 4 :353(161) [0217] fair-minded reader can **judge** that we very definitely
AP : 0 4 :363(162) [0219] the Lord, the righteous **judge**, will give me," etc. (II Tim.
AP : 0 4 :375(164) [0223] No sane man can **judge** otherwise.
AP : 0 4 :393(167) [0225] By nature men **judge** that God ought to be appeased by
AP : 0 4 :399(168) [0227] One can also **judge** their spirit from the unheard of
AP : 0 7 :042(176) [0243] reader can easily **judge** that the apostles wanted to
AP : 1 1 :008(181) [0251] *Omnis utriusque*, for we **judge** that it, like other human
AP : 1 2 :009(183) [0255] can a terrified conscience **judge** whether it fears God for
AP : 1 2 :067(192) [0271] From this we can **judge** what sort of church it is that is
AP : 1 2 :090(195) [0279] to have all good men **judge** and decide whether our
AP : 1 2 :098(197) [0281] Good men can easily **judge** the great importance of
AP : 1 2 :103(197) [0281] someone objects that a **judge** must hear a case before
AP : 1 2 :108(198) [0283] when hypocrites **judge** Thee to be unrighteous in
AP : 1 2 :163(208) [0303] us (I Cor. 11:31), "If we **judged** ourselves truly, we should
AP : 1 2 :163(208) [0303] truly, we should not be **judged**" by the Lord; but the word
AP : 1 2 :163(208) [0303] the Lord; but the word "**judge**" refers to the whole
AP : 1 2 :163(208) [0303] when they explain "**judge**" as "to make a pilgrimage to St.
AP : 1 2 :163(208) [0303] "**Judge**" means all of penitence; it means to "condemn
AP : 1 6 :007(223) [0331] Public redress through a **judge** is not forbidden but
AP : 2 1 :028(233) [0351] not a propitiator but only a terrible **judge** and avenger.
AP : 2 4 :098(268) [0419] until Christ comes to **judge** and by the glory of his
AP : 2 8 :006(282) [0445] rule requires the power to **judge**, define, distinguish, and
AP : 2 8 :011(283) [0447] consciences so that their omission is **judged** to be a sin.
S1 : PR :009(290) [0457] Christ, the lord and **judge** of us all, knows very well that
S1 : 0 1 :000(292) [0461] hand of God, will come to **judge** the living and the dead,
S3 : 0 7 :002(311) [0493] but in God's alone to **judge** which, how great, and how
S3 : 0 8 :003(312) [0495] Word and who therefore **judge**, interpret, and twist the
TR : 0 0 :040(327) [0517] pope is unwilling to be **judged** by the church or by
TR : 0 0 :040(327) [0517] Such unwillingness to be **judged** by the church or by
TR : 0 0 :050(329) [0519] states, "No one shall **judge** the supreme see, for the judge
TR : 0 0 :050(329) [0519] the supreme see, for the **judge** is judged neither by the
TR : 0 0 :050(329) [0519] see, for the judge is **judged** neither by the emperor, nor by
TR : 0 0 :082(000) [0529] in my humble opinion I **judge** that all these agree with
SC : 0 2 :003(345) [0545] *whence he shall come to* ***judge*** *the living and the dead.*"
LC : PR :017(361) [0573] counsel, help, comfort, **judge**, and make decisions in both
LC : SP :012(363) [0577] whence he shall come to **judge** the living and the dead.
LC : 0 1 :017(366) [0585] other hand, you can easily **judge** how the world practices
LC : 0 1 :232(396) [0647] be more fitting if the **judge**, the jailer, or the hangman did
LC : 0 1 :259(400) [0653] A **judge** ought, above all, to be a man of integrity, and
LC : 0 1 :260(400) [0655] them, whether he be **judge** or witness, let the
LC : 0 1 :265(400) [0655] nobody has the right to **judge** and reprove his neighbor
LC : 0 1 :265(401) [0657] unless he has been authorized to **judge** and reprove.
LC : 0 1 :266(401) [0657] great difference between **judging** sin and having
LC : 0 1 :266(401) [0657] Knowledge of sin does not entail the right to **judge** it.
LC : 0 1 :266(401) [0657] until you are appointed a **judge** and authorized to
LC : 0 1 :267(401) [0657] are not content just to know but rush ahead and **judge**.
LC : 0 1 :268(401) [0657] for the harshest verdict a **judge** can pronounce is to
LC : 0 1 :270(401) [0657] reply: "Why don't you bring it before the regular **judge**?"
LC : 0 1 :274(402) [0659] own person the right to **judge** and condemn anyone, yet
LC : 0 1 :280(403) [0661] on whose testimony the **judge** can base his decision and
LC : 0 1 :284(403) [0661] sin is so public that the **judge** and the whole world are
LC : 0 1 :308(406) [0669] The **judge** and the public may have to leave you in
LC : 0 1 :327(410) [0675] that, you have an angry **judge**; otherwise, you have a
LC : 0 2 :025(413) [0685] *whence he shall come to* ***judge*** *the living and the dead.*"
LC : 0 2 :065(419) [0695] from him we see nothing but an angry and terrible **Judge**.
EP : RN :000(464) [0777] All Doctrines Should Be **Judged** and the Errors Which
EP : RN :001(464) [0777] must be appraised and **judged**, as it is written in
EP : RN :007(465) [0779] remains the only **judge**, rule, and norm according to
EP : RN :007(465) [0779] must be understood and **judged** as good or evil, right or
EP : 0 7 :017(484) [0813] accept him even contrary to their will as a strict **judge**.
EP : 0 8 :036(491) [0825] is fitting and necessary to perform his office as **judge**.
EP : 1 1 :009(495) [0833] Therefore we should not **judge** this election of ours to
EP : 1 2 :031(500) [0843] Day before the righteous **judge**, our Lord Jesus Christ,

Continued ▶

SD : RN :000(503) [0849] All Doctrines Should Be **Judged** in Conformity with the
SD : PR :003(504) [0851] all teachers and teachings are to be **judged** and evaluated.
SD : PR :010(506) [0855] are to be approved and accepted, **judged** and regulated.

Judges (13)
AG : 1 6 :002(037) [0051] or serve as princes and **judges**, render decisions and pass
AL : 1 6 :002(037) [0051] hold civil office, to sit as **judges**, to decide matters by the
AP : 0 4 :035(112) [0131] works that seem virtuous, for God **judges** the heart.
AP : 0 4 :212(136) [0179] The world **judges** this way about all works, that they are a
AP : 0 4 :239(141) [0187] us from shame when God **judges** and accuses us, but faith
AP : 0 4 :326(157) [0211] God does not forgive but **judges** and condemns their
AP : 0 4 :357(161) [0217] But they are not fair **judges**, for they omit the word "gift."
AP : 0 7 :025(173) [0235] church that way, we would probably have fairer **judges**.
AP : 1 2 :124(201) [0289] of all Christian doctrine, **judges** should have been found
AP : 2 7 :028(274) [0429] the unworthy verdict our **judges** have rendered in the
LC : 0 1 :258(399) [0653] The reason is this: Where **judges**, mayors, princes, or
LC : 0 1 :263(400) [0655] and blasphemy, to false **judges** and witnesses with their
EP : RN :008(465) [0779] other writings are not **judges** like Holy Scripture, but

Judgement (1), Judgements (1), Judgment (116), Judgments (13)
PR : PR :013(007) [0013] reserve their considered **judgment** concerning every part
PR : PR :014(007) [0013] When the requested **judgments** had been received they
PR : PR :018(009) [0015] to appear before the **judgment** seat of our Lord Jesus
PR : PR :022(012) [0021] solemn and severe throne of God's **judgment**, and there
AG : PR :002(025) [0039] and weigh the **judgments**, opinions, and beliefs of the
AG : PR :006(025) [0039] German and Latin, his **judgments**, opinions, and beliefs
AG : PR :009(025) [0041] statement of their **judgments** and opinions, in Latin and
AG : 1 7 :000(038) [0051] XVII. [The Return of Christ to **Judgment**]
AG : 1 7 :001(038) [0051] on the last day for **judgment** and will raise up all the
AG : 2 6 :025(067) [0073] says, "Let no one pass **judgment** on you in questions of
AG : 2 8 :044(088) [0089] "Let no one pass **judgment** on you in questions of
AL : 1 7 :000(038) [0051] XVII. [The Return of Christ for **Judgment**]
AL : 1 7 :001(038) [0051] Christ will appear for **judgment** and will raise up all the
AL : 1 8 :004(039) [0051] enables them to make **judgments** according to reason.
AL : 2 0 :018(043) [0055] righteousness, have bad **judgment** concerning this
AL : 2 6 :025(067) [0073] "Let no one pass **judgment** on you in questions of
AL : 2 7 :031(076) [0079] seem to have sufficient **judgment** to make a decision
AL : 2 8 :013(083) [0085] nor interfere with **judgments** concerning any civil
AL : 2 8 :044(088) [0089] says, "Let no one pass **judgment** on you in questions of
AP : 0 2 :001(100) [0105] are lacking not only in **judgment** but also in honesty.
AP : 0 2 :008(101) [0107] trust in him, hating his **judgment** and fleeing it, being
AP : 0 2 :024(103) [0111] either it despises the **judgment** of God in its security, or it
AP : 0 2 :042(105) [0117] his Word; anger at his **judgments**; indignation because he
AP : 0 2 :043(106) [0117] about the civil courts, not about the **judgment** of God.
AP : 0 4 :007(108) [0121] since it has the same **judgment** naturally written in the
AP : 0 4 :009(108) [0123] not feel God's wrath or **judgment**, he can imagine that he
AP : 0 4 :020(110) [0125] takes place, or how the **judgment** of God and the terrors
AP : 0 4 :034(112) [0129] heart either despises the **judgment** of God in its
AP : 0 4 :034(112) [0131] the midst of punishment it flees and hates his **judgment**.
AP : 0 4 :037(112) [0131] themselves do not feel the wrath or **judgment** of God.
AP : 0 4 :038(112) [0131] terrified by the law flees before God's **judgment**.
AP : 0 4 :082(118) [0145] in him and set it against the wrath and **judgment** of God.
AP : 0 4 :146(127) [0163] In opposition to the **judgment** of God they set a trust in
AP : 0 4 :150(127) [0163] Christ and in God's **judgment** he will discover that this
AP : 0 4 :157(128) [0165] And in the **judgment** of God we shall learn that this trust
AP : 0 4 :168(130) [0169] 143:2), "Enter not into **judgment** with thy servant; for no
AP : 0 4 :168(130) [0169] Even this servant of God prays God to avert his **judgment**.
AP : 0 4 :176(131) [0171] As long as we flee God's **judgment** and are angry at him,
AP : 0 4 :204(135) [0177] their anger they flee his **judgment** and never believe that
AP : 0 4 :212(136) [0179] that they can set against the wrath and **judgment** of God.
AP : 0 4 :214(136) [0179] pit our works against the wrath and **judgment** of God.
AP : 0 4 :214(136) [0179] mediator, can be pitted against God's wrath and **judgment**
AP : 0 4 :222(138) [0181] against the wrath and **judgment** of God; that our love
AP : 0 4 :230(139) [0183] this teaching is to the **judgment** of reason and law and
AP : 0 4 :270(147) [0197] in terror before the **judgment** and punishment of the law,
AP : 0 4 :301(153) [0205] they feel angry at the **judgment** of God, who visits on
AP : 0 4 :304(154) [0205] the will as it flees God's **judgment**; just so faith is not
AP : 0 4 :312(155) [0207] against us, human nature flees his wrath and **judgment**.
AP : 0 4 :326(157) [0211] 143:2, "Enter not into **judgment** with thy servant, for no
AP : 0 4 :326(158) [0211] no one can stand the **judgment** of God if he observes our
AP : 0 4 :329(158) [0211] of the flesh cannot stand the **judgment** of God.
AP : 0 4 :345(160) [0217] In courts of human **judgment** a right or debt is certain,
AP : 0 4 :345(160) [0217] The **judgment** of God is another thing altogether.
AP : 0 4 :392(167) [0225] holy Fathers, and the **judgment** of all the faithful are
AP : 0 4 :400(168) [0227] The **judgments** of our opponents will not bother us since
AP : 0 7 :035(175) [0239] "Let no one pass **judgment** on you in questions of
AP : 1 1 :005(181) [0251] an unworthy manner receive **judgment** upon themselves.
AP : 1 2 :010(184) [0255] Here we appeal to the **judgment** of all good and wise
AP : 1 2 :069(192) [0271] In this they showed no **judgment**, but like petty public
AP : 1 2 :078(193) [0275] against the wrath and **judgment** of God, according to the
AP : 1 2 :078(193) [0275] 143:2), "Enter not into **judgment** with thy servant; for no
AP : 1 2 :084(194) [0277] which no one can stand before the **judgment** of God.
AP : 1 2 :103(197) [0281] in the area of blessing or grace, not of **judgment** or law.
AP : 1 2 :108(198) [0283] justified in thy sentence and blameless in thy **judgment**."
AP : 1 2 :108(198) [0283] our merits against Thy **judgment**, but we shall be justified
AP : 1 2 :125(201) [0289] will posterity think about these slanderous **judgments**?
AP : 1 2 :129(202) [0291] you ought to fear the **judgment** of God; for the members
AP : 1 2 :129(202) [0291] We are talking about the **judgments** of men and the silent
AP : 1 2 :151(206) [0299] the time has come for **judgment** to begin with the
AP : 1 2 :177(210) [0307] are right in their **judgment** when they grant that in the
AP : 1 5 :030(219) [0323] says: "Let no one pass **judgment** on you in questions of
AP : 1 6 :008(223) [0331] How poor the **judgment** of many writers in these matters
AP : 1 7 :000(224) [0335] [Article XVII. Christ's Return to **Judgment**]
AP : 1 8 :004(225) [0335] still has reason and **judgment** about the things that the
AP : 1 8 :005(225) [0335] often than their sound **judgment**, while the devil, who as
AP : 2 1 :016(231) [0347] As to the rest even the uninitiated can pass **judgment**.
AP : 2 2 :012(238) [0361] In the **judgment** of God, will the reasons he gives
AP : 2 3 :006(240) [0365] is necessary, only the **judgment** of any honest and
AP : 2 3 :023(242) [0369] of the synods but the private **judgment** of the popes.
AP : 2 3 :070(249) [0383] position contrary to the **judgment** of God, who will call
AP : 2 3 :070(249) [0383] understand that in the **judgment** of God no perversion of
AP : 2 4 :003(250) [0385] point, but we leave it up to the **judgment** of the reader.
AP : 2 7 :032(274) [0431] and do not set their merits against the **judgment** of God.
AP : 2 7 :057(279) [0439] vows without proper **judgment** because they were
AP : 2 8 :027(285) [0451] Now we leave it to the **judgment** of all pious people
S 1 : PR :009(290) [0457] the last day, before the **judgment** seat of Christ, who in
S 2 : 0 4 :014(301) [0475] transactions and **judgments**, as the papal decretals show.
S 3 : 0 3 :003(304) [0481] man must hear such a **judgment** as this: "You are all of no
S 3 : 0 7 :002(312) [0493] written, "Enter not into **judgment** with thy servant, for no
TR : 0 0 :014(322) [0509] the brethren and by the **judgment** of the bishops
TR : 0 0 :049(328) [0519] is that the pope wrests **judgment** from the church and
TR : 0 0 :056(329) [0521] of the power of making **judgments** and decisions
TR : 0 0 :056(330) [0521] understanding and true **judgment** on the part of the
SC : 0 9 :004(355) [0561] has appointed, and those who resist will incur **judgment**.
LC : PR :017(361) [0573] He is qualified to sit in **judgment** upon all doctrines,
LC : 0 1 :181(389) [0631] their own children to **judgment** and sentence them to
LC : 0 1 :191(391) [0635] upon them in the day of **judgment**, as Christ himself
LC : 0 1 :258(399) [0653] others in authority sit in **judgment**, we always find that,
LC : 0 1 :268(401) [0657] else than usurping the **judgment** and office of God,
LC : 0 5 :074(455) [0771] Christ pronounces the **judgment**, "If you are pure and
LC : 0 5 :078(455) [0771] the Scriptures, which pronounce this **judgment** upon you.
EP : 0 7 :002(482) [0809] for life and salvation, the unbelievers for **judgment**?
EP : 0 7 :016(484) [0813] and salvation but to their **judgment** and condemnation.
EP : 0 7 :017(484) [0813] and manifest his **judgment** on unrepentant guests as he is
EP : 0 7 :041(486) [0817] to the righteous **judgment** of God all presumptuous,
SD : 0 1 :027(513) [0867] Fall, and that by God's **judgment** and verdict man lost
SD : 0 1 :047(516) [0875] flesh would not rise on **Judgment** Day and that in eternal
SD : 0 2 :008(521) [0883] the Word of God that **judgments** on articles of faith are to
SD : 0 2 :022(525) [0889] his righteous and severe **judgment** cast away forever the
SD : 0 2 :056(532) [0903] not and cannot pass **judgment** on the Holy Spirit's
SD : 0 5 :022(562) [0959] to us as righteousness in the strict **judgment** of God.
SD : 0 6 :012(566) [0967] belongs) of sin and of righteousness and of **judgment**."
SD : 0 6 :021(567) [0969] but also, "Enter not into **judgment** with thy servant; for
SD : 0 7 :016(572) [0977] But they receive it for **judgment**, as St. Paul says, for they
SD : 0 7 :029(574) [0981] to appear before the **judgment** seat of our Lord Jesus
SD : 0 7 :031(574) [0983] for me before the Last **Judgment** at the coming of the
SD : 0 7 :057(579) [0993] blood of Christ to their own **judgment** and condemnation.
SD : 0 7 :063(581) [0995] it orally, too, but to their **judgment** and damnation.
SD : 0 7 :068(582) [0997] burden themselves with **judgment** (that is, temporal and
SD : 0 7 :105(588) [1009] in believers but also to wreak **judgment** on unbelievers.
SD : 0 7 :123(590) [1015] not the body and the blood of Christ for their **judgment**.
SD : 0 7 :125(591) [1015] this sacrament for **judgment**, just as unworthy guests.
SD : 0 8 :055(601) [1033] give life, to execute all **judgment**, to have all authority in
SD : 0 8 :058(602) [1035] alive and to execute **judgment** has been given to Christ
SD : 1 0 :013(613) [1057] let no one pass **judgment** on you in questions of food and
SD : 1 1 :026(620) [1071] We should not pass **judgment** on the basis of our reason,
SD : 1 1 :058(625) [1081] the case of the one group we are to see God's **judgment**.
SD : 1 1 :060(626) [1083] and well deserved **judgement** over certain lands, nations,
SD : 1 1 :064(626) [1083] unsearchable are his **judgements** and how inscrutable his
SD : 1 1 :085(630) [1091] and God executed his **judgment** on him, for he was indeed
SD : 1 2 :040(636) [1103] hearts before the **judgment** seat of Jesus Christ and for

Judicial (5)
AP : 0 4 :305(154) [0205] "justify" is used in a **judicial** way to mean "to absolve a
AP : 0 4 :306(154) [0207] the philosophical or **judicial** investigation of a man's own
AP : 1 6 :003(223) [0331] to try to impose on us the **judicial** laws of Moses.
TR : 0 0 :051(329) [0519] and murders, and he forbids a **judicial** examination.
TR : 0 0 :051(329) [0519] for when proper **judicial** process has been taken away, the

Juice (2)
EP : 0 1 :015(468) [0783] of the same, just as garlic **juice**, smeared upon a magnet,
SD : 0 1 :022(512) [0865] to them, just as garlic **juice** smeared on a magnet does

Julian (3)
AP : 0 2 :036(105) [0115] Against **Julian**, Augustine says: "That law which is in the
AP : 1 6 :006(223) [0331] **Julian** the Apostate, Celsus, and many others opposed the
SD : 0 2 :023(525) [0889] written in a similar vein in his second book *Against **Julian***

Julius (1)
PR : PR :027(014) [0025] **Julius**, duke of Brunswick [-Wolfenbuettel] and

Jump (1)
SD : 0 8 :044(599) [1031] Of course, he can also go up again or **jump** out of his pan.

Juno (1)
AP : 2 1 :032(233) [0351] The Romans thought that **Juno** granted riches, Febris

Jupiter (1)
LC : 0 1 :018(367) [0585] power and dominion exalted **Jupiter** as their supreme god

Jurisdiction (26)
AG : 2 8 :029(085) [0087] other power and **jurisdiction** bishops may have in various
AL : 2 8 :020(084) [0087] one inquires about the **jurisdiction** of bishops, therefore,
AL : 2 8 :020(084) [0087] must be distinguished from ecclesiastical **jurisdiction**.
AL : 2 8 :021(084) [0087] by divine right) no **jurisdiction** belongs to the bishops as
AL : 2 8 :029(085) [0087] any other power or **jurisdiction** to decide legal cases (for
AP : 1 1 :008(181) [0251] brothers in their fight about **jurisdiction** over confessions!
AP : 2 8 :013(283) [0447] into the power of the order and the power of **jurisdiction**.
AP : 2 8 :013(283) [0447] also has the power of **jurisdiction**, namely, the authority
AP : 2 8 :014(283) [0447] according to which he ought to exercise his **jurisdiction**.
AP : 2 8 :014(283) [0447] they have a certain **jurisdiction** bishops may institute new
AP : 2 8 :014(283) [0447] worship, for worship does not belong to their **jurisdiction**.
AP : 2 8 :014(283) [0447] should exercise their **jurisdiction**, namely, when anyone
TR : 0 0 :040(327) [0517] in this life but also the **jurisdiction** over souls after this
TR : 0 0 :059(330) [0521] The Power and **Jurisdiction** of Bishops
TR : 0 0 :060(330) [0521] in addition, exercise **jurisdiction**, that is, excommunicate
TR : 0 0 :073(332) [0525] Something, however, must be said about **jurisdiction**.
TR : 0 0 :074(332) [0525] that the common **jurisdiction** of excommunicating those
TR : 0 0 :076(333) [0525] reserved this **jurisdiction** for themselves and have
TR : 0 0 :076(333) [0525] need, on account of this **jurisdiction**, to obey the bishops.
TR : 0 0 :076(333) [0527] is right to restore this **jurisdiction** to godly pastors and
TR : 0 0 :077(333) [0527] There remains **jurisdiction** in those cases which according
TR : 0 0 :077(333) [0527] to obey the bishops on account of this **jurisdiction** either.
TR : 0 0 :079(333) [0527] they have wrested **jurisdiction** from the pastors and
TR : 0 0 :082(334) [0529] and the power and **jurisdiction** of the bishops which was
TR : 0 0 :082(000) [0529] the Papacy and the Power and **Jurisdiction** of Bishops.
LC : 0 1 :262(400) [0655] it is applied to spiritual **jurisdiction** or administration.

Jurists (5)

A P : 2 3 :009(240) [0367] man is a natural right, the **jurists** have said wisely and
A P : 2 3 :011(241) [0367] and wisely put by the **jurists**: The union of man and
S 3 : 0 3 :041(309) [0491] pope, the theologians, the **jurists**, and all men understand
L C : 0 1 :261(400) [0655] we have a goal set for our **jurists**: perfect justice and
L C : 0 1 :299(405) [0665] In this we are abetted by **jurists** and lawyers who twist

Just (201)

P R : P R :005(004) [0009] Nevertheless, **just** as, while the holy apostles were still
P R : P R :013(007) [0013] controversy and also the **just** cited written agreement
P R : P R :022(012) [0021] For **just** as Christian charity causes us to have special
P R : P R :024(013) [0023] Therefore, **just** as from the very beginning of this
A G : 0 7 :004(032) [0047] one body and one Spirit, **just** as you were called to the
A G : 1 6 :002(037) [0051] with the sword, engage in **just** wars, serve as soldiers, buy
A G : 2 0 :025(044) [0057] Therefore, as has **just** been indicated, the Scriptures speak
A G : 0 0 :001(047) [0059] This is **just** about a summary of the doctrines that are
A G : 2 3 :024(055) [0065] However, **just** as no human law can alter or abolish a
A G : 2 6 :027(068) [0073] through the grace of the Lord Jesus, **just** as they will."
A G : 2 8 :056(090) [0091] offense is given to others, **just** as no one would say that a
A L : 1 6 :002(037) [0051] existing laws, to award **just** punishments, to engage in
A L : 1 6 :002(037) [0051] punishments, to engage in **just** wars, to serve as soldiers,
A L : 2 3 :018(054) [0063] deserve the punishments of **just** magistrates, yet it is a
A L : 2 3 :024(055) [0065] **Just** as no human law can nullify a command of God, so
A L : 2 6 :027(068) [0073] through the grace of the Lord Jesus, **just** as they will."
A P : 0 2 :023(103) [0111] the ancient definition says **just** what we do when we deny
A P : 0 2 :048(106) [0119] **Just** as the devil cannot be conquered without Christ's
A P : 0 4 :012(108) [0123] But let the intelligent reader **just** consider this.
A P : 0 4 :057(114) [0137] of sins by faith, **just** as the saints in the New Testament.
A P : 0 4 :112(123) [0155] or on account of this love, **just** as little as we receive the
A P : 0 4 :151(127) [0163] **Just** as little do we receive the forgiveness of sins on
A P : 0 4 :185(132) [0173] But in **just** and sure issues, one or two explanations, taken
A P : 0 4 :185(132) [0173] The rule I have **just** stated interprets all the passages they
A P : 0 4 :192(133) [0175] his victory over the devil, **just** as the distribution of alms
A P : 0 4 :229(139) [0183] but only his veiled face, **just** as the Pharisees,
A P : 0 4 :235(140) [0185] the text this way: "**Just** as a building is said to be perfect
A P : 0 4 :245(142) [0189] **Just** so Paul includes faith and love in presenting a
A P : 0 4 :247(142) [0191] Third, James has **just** said that regeneration takes place
A P : 0 4 :250(143) [0191] **Just** so Paul says that through the power of God faith is
A P : 0 4 :251(143) [0191] but only the nature of the **just** who have already been
A P : 0 4 :252(143) [0191] in a forensic way, **just** as in the passage (Rom. 2:13), "the
A P : 0 4 :276(148) [0199] **Just** as the Lord's Supper does not justify *ex opere*
A P : 0 4 :282(149) [0201] **Just** so some pope — I am not sure which — said that
A P : 0 4 :304(154) [0205] as it flees God's judgment; **just** so faith is not merely
A P : 0 4 :317(156) [0209] continually and not **just** at the beginning of justification.
A P : 0 4 :354(161) [0217] **Just** as justification belongs to faith, so eternal life
A P : 0 4 :365(163) [0219] **Just** so they sometimes offer grace with other rewards, as
A P : 0 7 :018(171) [0233] or hidden under the cross, **just** as Christ is the same,
A P : 0 7 :022(172) [0233] **Just** as the church has the promise that it will always have
A P : 0 7 :039(176) [0241] should interpret those rites **just** as the apostles themselves
A P : 0 7 :050(178) [0245] to use civil ordinances **just** as it is legitimate for them to
A P : 0 9 :002(178) [0245] **Just** as there salvation is offered to all, so Baptism is
A P : 1 2 :096(196) [0281] hope for pardon from faith **just** as faith obtains it from
A P : 1 2 :107(198) [0283] from the heart and not **just** from the voice, as in a play.
A P : 1 2 :116(199) [0285] for the forgiveness of sins, **just** as those ancient
A P : 1 2 :120(200) [0287] And **just** as elsewhere they often confused the spiritual
A P : 1 2 :135(203) [0293] Thirdly, it is **just** such satisfactions that indulgences
A P : 1 2 :146(205) [0297] Christ overcomes death, **just** as it overcomes the wrath of
A P : 1 2 :150(206) [0299] me, O Lord, but in **just** measure; not in thy anger, lest
A P : 1 2 :176(210) [0307] **Just** as "to loose" means to forgive sins, so "to bind"
A P : 1 5 :023(218) [0321] such ceremonies, **just** as they have been expanded among
A P : 1 5 :034(220) [0325] **Just** so the apostles have freed consciences for good,
A P : 1 5 :035(220) [0325] before God for them, **just** as there is no value before God
A P : 1 6 :001(222) [0329] punishments, engage in **just** wars, render military service,
A P : 1 6 :002(222) [0331] nation in which we live, **just** as it lets us make use of
A P : 1 6 :006(223) [0331] but subjects us to them, **just** as we are necessarily
A P : 2 1 :004(229) [0343] for using these gifts, **just** as Christ praises faithful
A P : 2 1 :022(232) [0349] on account of them **just** as we are by Christ's merits.
A P : 2 1 :034(234) [0353] sort of magical power, **just** as sorcerers imagine that
A P : 2 3 :008(240) [0367] **Just** so this Word makes the earth fruitful (Gen. 1:11),
A P : 2 3 :008(240) [0367] **Just** as human regulations cannot change the nature of the
A P : 2 3 :019(242) [0369] using the remedy he offers, **just** as he wants to nourish
A P : 2 3 :031(243) [0373] through faith in Christ **just** as the use of food, etc. is
A P : 2 3 :049(246) [0377] and for public morality), **just** as certain rites were
A P : 2 3 :057(247) [0379] They cruelly kill men **just** because they are married.
A P : 2 3 :060(247) [0381] domination, for which religion is **just** a wicked pretext.
A P : 2 3 :063(247) [0381] **Just** look at these impudent rascals!
A P : 2 4 :052(259) [0403] or sacrifice for sins, **just** as the Old Testament did.
A P : 2 4 :064(261) [0405] are transferred to many **just** as when they are transferred
A P : 2 4 :067(261) [0407] comes from the reconciled, **just** as afflictions do not merit
A P : 2 4 :068(261) [0407] and witness of profession, **just** as a certain type of hood is
A P : 2 4 :080(264) [0411] of the Lord to the people, **just** as a minister who preaches
A P : 2 7 :005(269) [0421] of the richest monasteries **just** feed a lazy crowd that
A P : 2 7 :049(277) [0437] Callings are personal, **just** as matters of business
A P : 2 7 :058(279) [0439] Furthermore, **just** as circumcision or the slaughter of
S 1 : P R :013(291) [0459] about specks, we might **just** as well be satisfied with such
S 2 : 0 4 :007(299) [0473] This is **just** the way in which the Council of Constance
S 2 : 0 4 :014(301) [0475] Accordingly, **just** as we cannot adore the devil himself as
S 3 : 0 2 :003(303) [0479] their own powers, as was **just** said above concerning the
S 3 : 0 3 :029(308) [0487] and Pharisees in Christ's time were **just** such saints.
S 3 : 0 3 :032(308) [0487] No man can be **just** before God without him.
T R : 0 0 :008(321) [0505] primacy among ministers, **just** as a child neither seeks nor
T R : 0 0 :071(332) [0525] writer, whoever he may be, **just** as the writings of
S C : P R :022(341) [0537] and is no Christian, **just** as he is no Christian who does
S C : 0 2 :006(345) [0545] preserved me in true faith, **just** as he calls, gathers,
L C : S P :002(362) [0575] admitted to a sacrament, **just** as a craftsman who does
L C : 0 1 :022(367) [0585] works of supererogation, **just** as if God were in our
L C : 0 1 :035(369) [0589] both heathen and Jews; **just** so in our day he overthrows
L C : 0 1 :036(369) [0589] all they have trusted in, **just** as all others have perished
L C : 0 1 :037(369) [0589] **Just** because such blockheads imagine, when God refrains
L C : 0 1 :044(370) [0593] **Just** ponder and heed them.
L C : 0 1 :046(370) [0593] God cannot lie or deceive; **just** leave it to the devil and
L C : 0 1 :058(372) [0597] all kinds of wickedness, **just** as there are few who trust in
L C : 0 1 :128(382) [0617] **Just** so we act toward our parents, and there is no child
L C : 0 1 :143(385) [0623] should do it for the reason **just** mentioned, that it is
L C : 0 1 :192(391) [0635] It is **just** as if I saw someone wearily struggling in deep
L C : 0 1 :197(392) [0637] life would be considered **just** as acceptable, and even
L C : 0 1 :204(393) [0639] concern of yours, you are **just** as guilty as the culprit
L C : 0 1 :224(395) [0643] As I have **just** said, a person steals not only when he robs
L C : 0 1 :238(397) [0647] **Just** let them keep on boldly fleecing people as long as
L C : 0 1 :245(398) [0649] steal, depend on it that **just** as much will be stolen from
L C : 0 1 :267(401) [0657] who are not content **just** to know but rush ahead and
L C : 0 1 :275(402) [0659] **Just** so, magistrates, parents, even brothers and sisters
L C : 0 1 :310(407) [0669] accuses us and shows **just** how upright we really are in
L C : 0 1 :315(408) [0671] **Just** think, is it not a devilish presumption on the part of
L C : 0 1 :318(408) [0673] **Just** concentrate upon them and test yourself thoroughly,
L C : 0 2 :037(415) [0687] Answer: **Just** as the Son obtains dominion by purchasing
L C : 0 3 :008(421) [0699] we want to be Christians, **just** as it is our duty and
L C : 0 3 :009(421) [0699] **Just** so, it is not left to my choice here whether to pray or
L C : 0 3 :015(422) [0701] Commandment is given **just** as much on my account as on
L C : 0 3 :016(422) [0701] say: "The prayer I offer is **just** as precious, holy, and
L C : 0 3 :018(422) [0703] us if we do not pray, **just** as he punishes all other kinds of
L C : 0 3 :029(424) [0705] This is **just** what the devil wants and works for with all
L C : 0 3 :044(425) [0709] **Just** as it is a shame and disgrace to an earthly father to
L C : 0 3 :050(426) [0711] **Just** as God's name is holy in itself and yet we pray that it
L C : 0 3 :057(427) [0713] **Just** so, it is a great reproach and dishonor to God if we,
L C : 0 3 :060(428) [0715] But there is **just** as great need that we keep firm hold of
L C : 0 3 :067(429) [0717] Therefore, there is **just** as much need in this case as in
L C : 0 4 :030(440) [0739] brought into the heart, **just** as the entire Gospel is an
L C : 0 4 :036(441) [0741] **Just** by allowing the water to be poured over you, you do
L C : 0 4 :037(441) [0741] gives us and faith grasps, **just** as the Lord Christ upon the
L C : 0 4 :038(441) [0741] **Just** so, if we had nothing more than these words, "Go
L C : 0 4 :043(442) [0743] **Just** think how the world would snow and rain money
L C : 0 4 :043(442) [0743] free to every man's door **just** such a priceless medicine
L C : 0 4 :056(444) [0747] **Just** so, I go to the Sacrament of the Altar not on the
L C : 0 4 :064(444) [0749] and why God ordained **just** this sign and external
L C : 0 5 :005(447) [0755] Therefore, **just** as the Ten Commandments, the Lord's
L C : 0 5 :016(448) [0757] Christ's body and blood) **just** as truly as when one uses it
L C : 0 5 :021(449) [0757] evident from the words **just** quoted, "This is my body and
L C : 0 5 :032(450) [0761] sacrament are of no value **just** as little as they dare say
L C : 0 5 :035(450) [0761] confidently believe that it is **just** as the words tell you.
L C : 0 5 :047(452) [0765] which you shall enjoy not **just** on this one evening of the
L C : 0 5 :049(452) [0765] want such liberty, you may **just** as well take the further
L C : 0 5 :049(452) [0765] or pray, for the one is **just** as much Christ's
L C : 0 5 :065(454) [0769] me; otherwise Christ might **just** as well have kept quiet
L C : 0 5 :069(454) [0769] be good or wholesome, **just** as when a sick person
L C : 0 5 :079(455) [0771] **Just** begin to act as if you want to become good and cling
L C : 0 5 :083(456) [0773] **Just** examine yourself, look around a little, cling to the
L C : 0 6 :006(457) [0000] obey the Gospel deserve **just** such a jailer as God's devil
L C : 0 6 :016(459) [0000] second part; it was **just** as if our confession were simply a
L C : 0 6 :021(459) [0000] for the sake of absolution, let him **just** forget about it.
L C : 0 6 :021(459) [0000] purity of his confession, let him **just** stay away from it.
L C : 0 6 :024(460) [0000] to receive anything but **just** letting everyone see how poor
L C : 0 6 :025(460) [0000] men together in hordes **just** to show what impure and
L C : 0 6 :031(460) [0000] ourselves to be compelled, **just** as we are compelled to
L C : 0 6 :032(461) [0000] They snatch at the bread **just** like a hunted hart, burning
E P : 0 1 :015(468) [0783] or loss of the same, **just** as garlic juice, smeared upon a
E P : 0 3 :003(473) [0793] to these two errors **just** recounted, we believe, teach, and
E P : 0 4 :018(477) [0801] in these last times, it is **just** as necessary to exhort people
E P : 0 6 :007(481) [0807] the unregenerated man — **just** like the regenerated
E P : 0 7 :017(484) [0813] He is **just** as much present to exercise and manifest his
E P : 1 2 :029(500) [0843] majesty, and glory, **just** like any three individual people
S D : P R :004(502) [0847] next to the Word of God, **just** as in ancient times
S D : P R :007(502) [0849] true Evangelical churches, **just** as during the very lifetime
S D : P R :005(504) [0851] We appeal to it **just** as in the ancient church it was
S D : P R :013(506) [0855] from these writings, for **just** as we base our position on
S D : 0 1 :022(512) [0865] impediment to them, **just** as garlic juice smeared on a
S D : 0 1 :028(513) [0867] man's corrupted nature, **just** as it is not itself the proper
S D : 0 1 :033(514) [0869] **Just** as in the case of external leprosy the body which is
S D : 0 1 :061(519) [0879] with the Word of God, **just** as Dr. Luther in his Latin
S D : 0 2 :011(522) [0885] **Just** as little as a person who is physically dead can by his
S D : 0 2 :039(528) [0895] and doing (Phil. 2:13), **just** as the apostle ascribes this
S D : 0 2 :040(528) [0895] preserved me in true faith, **just** as he calls, gathers,
S D : 0 2 :087(538) [0915] alone the work of God, **just** as the bodily resurrection of
S D : 0 3 :019(542) [0921] God is regeneration, **just** as St. Paul uses the terms
S D : 0 3 :053(548) [0933] and "without works") **just** as emphatically in the article of
S D : 0 3 :054(549) [0935] on account of which we are declared **just** before God.
S D : 0 5 :012(560) [0955] preachers of the Gospel, **just** as Christ himself did, confirm
S D : 0 6 :002(564) [0963] and hence are free, so that **just** as the sun spontaneously
S D : 0 6 :005(564) [0963] is not laid down for the **just**, as St. Paul says (I Tim. 1:9),
S D : 0 6 :005(564) [0963] is written on their hearts, **just** as the first man
S D : 0 6 :006(565) [0965] to the will of God, **just** as the sun, the moon, and all the
S D : 0 6 :016(566) [0967] are extorted by the law, **just** as in the case of
S D : 0 6 :019(567) [0969] his will and by coercion, **just** as the unconverted are
S D : 0 6 :024(568) [0971] threats and punishments, **just** as he will no longer require
S D : 0 6 :025(568) [0971] But **just** as they will see God face to face, so through
S D : 0 7 :003(569) [0973] For **just** as the bread and wine are here on earth and not
S D : 0 7 :008(570) [0975] bread with their mouths, **just** so certainly do they partake
S D : 0 7 :024(573) [0981] Christ's body and blood) **just** as much as when one does
S D : 0 7 :039(576) [0985] but we believe that **just** as Jesus Christ, our Saviour, was
S D : 0 7 :045(577) [0987] obedience in their strict and clear sense, **just** as they read.
S D : 0 7 :050(578) [0989] and clear words, **just** as he does in all the articles of faith
S D : 0 7 :059(580) [0993] are united with Christ, **just** as the Word of the Gospel,
S D : 0 7 :067(582) [0997] would be ashamed," **just** as they describe the majesty of
S D : 0 7 :076(583) [0999] **Just** as the words, 'Be fruitful and multiply and fill the
S D : 0 7 :084(584) [1001] integrally and inviolately, **just** as St. Paul sets the whole
S D : 0 7 :087(585) [1003] or exposed for adoration, **just** as the baptismal water is
S D : 0 7 :089(585) [1003] **Just** as the Gospel is and remains the true Gospel even
S D : 0 7 :115(589) [1011] of Christ (for example, **just** as bread and wine are
S D : 0 7 :125(591) [1015] this sacrament for judgment, **just** as unworthy guests.
S D : 0 8 :016(594) [1021] the Word of God dwelled **just** as in each of the prophets.
S D : 0 8 :016(594) [1021] have no communion at all, **just** as if Christ were one
S D : 0 8 :025(596) [1023] in death, when he died not **just** like another man but in
S D : 0 8 :027(596) [1025] ascended into heaven, not **just** like some other saint but,
S D : 0 8 :066(604) [1039] **Just** as in glowing iron there are not two powers of
S D : 0 9 :001(610) [1051] some of our theologians **just** as among the ancient
S D : 1 0 :015(613) [1057] the church to preserve, as we have **just** heard.

Continued ▶

Continued ▶

S D : 0 3 :039(546) [0929] with the article of **justification** as pertinent or necessary to
S D : 0 3 :040(546) [0929] as well as between **justification** and renewal or
S D : 0 3 :041(546) [0929] precede faith, nor is sanctification prior to **justification**.
S D : 0 3 :041(546) [0929] however, as though **justification** and sanctification are
S D : 0 3 :043(547) [0931] in the article of **justification**, or for our justification, as a
S D : 0 3 :043(547) [0931] or for our **justification**, as a cause without which a person
S D : 0 3 :043(547) [0931] do not exclude works from the article of **justification**.
S D : 0 3 :044(547) [0931] of the doctrine of **justification** by faith, since it meets the
S D : 0 3 :045(547) [0933] basis or cause of our **justification** before God, either
S D : 0 3 :049(548) [0933] faith has priority in **justification** but that renewal and
S D : 0 3 :049(548) [0933] cause but that our **justification** before God is incomplete
S D : 0 3 :053(548) [0933] of salvation as he does in the article of **justification**.
S D : 0 3 :055(549) [0935] in this matter of **justification**: Our righteousness rests
S D : 0 3 :066(550) [0937] with the doctrine of **justification** by faith before God as it
S D : 0 3 :067(551) [0937] important article of **justification** before God, on which
S D : 0 4 :022(554) [0945] and mingled with the article of **justification** and salvation.
S D : 0 4 :022(554) [0945] terms in the articles of **justification** and salvation (that is,
S D : 0 4 :022(554) [0945] from the article of **justification** and salvation and ascribe
S D : 0 4 :029(555) [0947] of the article of **justification**, were raised again as a result
S D : 0 4 :033(556) [0947] without darkening the doctrine of faith and **justification**.
S D : 0 4 :037(557) [0949] into the article of **justification** and rests his righteousness
S D : 0 5 :022(562) [0959] and raised for our **justification**," who "was made sin
S D : 0 5 :027(563) [0961] forgiveness of sins and **justification** through Christ,
S D : 0 8 :059(602) [1035] work or matter of our **justification** not only the divine
S D : 1 1 :014(619) [1069] our redemption, call, **justification**, and salvation, as Paul

Justified (187)
A G : 2 0 :013(043) [0055] we obtain grace and are **justified** before God through
A G : 2 0 :016(043) [0055] Rom. 5:1, "Since we are **justified** by faith, we have peace
A G : 2 7 :041(077) [0081] you who would be **justified** by the law; you have fallen
A G : 2 7 :042(077) [0081] way, those who would be **justified** by vows are severed
A G : 2 7 :044(078) [0081] preached that they were **justified** and earned forgiveness
A L : 0 2 :003(029) [0045] that man can be **justified** before God by his own strength
A L : 0 4 :001(030) [0045] that men cannot be **justified** before God by their own
A L : 0 4 :001(030) [0045] or works but are freely **justified** for Christ's sake through
A L : 1 2 :007(035) [0049] who have once been **justified** can lose the Holy Spirit, and
A L : 2 0 :006(041) [0053] They teach that we are **justified** not by works only, but
A L : 2 0 :006(041) [0053] works they say that we are **justified** by faith and works.
A L : 2 0 :016(043) [0055] Rom. 5:1, "Since we are **justified** by faith, we have peace
A L : 2 4 :028(059) [0067] also teach that we are **justified** before God through faith
A L : 2 7 :041(077) [0081] you who would be **justified** by the law; you have fallen
A L : 2 7 :042(077) [0081] those who would be **justified** by vows are severed from
A L : 2 7 :044(078) [0081] taught that they were **justified** and merited forgiveness of
A L : 2 8 :036(086) [0089] we suppose that we are **justified** by such observances.
A P : 0 2 :012(102) [0109] taught that men are **justified** before God by philosophical
A P : 0 4 :001(107) [0121] of sins by faith and by faith in Christ are **justified**.
A P : 0 4 :012(109) [0123] If we can be **justified** by reason and its works, what need
A P : 0 4 :030(111) [0129] you who would be **justified** by the law; you have fallen
A P : 0 4 :048(113) [0135] says so often, men are **justified**, because those who are
A P : 0 4 :059(115) [0137] the patriarchs, too, were **justified** not by the law but by
A P : 0 4 :072(117) [0141] And "to be **justified**" means to make unrighteous men
A P : 0 4 :073(117) [0141] "We hold that a man is **justified** by faith apart from
A P : 0 4 :073(117) [0141] (Rom. 3:24), "They are **justified** by his grace as a gift."
A P : 0 4 :078(117) [0143] Therefore we are **justified** by faith alone, justification
A P : 0 4 :087(119) [0147] to us for Christ's sake we are **justified** freely by faith.
A P : 0 4 :087(119) [0147] "We hold that man is **justified** by faith apart from works
A P : 0 4 :087(120) [0147] If any works **justified**, therefore, surely these works,
A P : 0 4 :087(120) [0147] that a man is not **justified** by the precepts of a good life,
A P : 0 4 :091(120) [0149] he says, "Since we are **justified** by faith, we have peace
A P : 0 4 :092(120) [0149] with his heart and so is **justified**," where he declares that
A P : 0 4 :093(120) [0149] Jesus, in order to be **justified** by faith in Christ, and not
A P : 0 4 :097(121) [0149] every one that believes is **justified** from everything from
A P : 0 4 :097(121) [0149] which you could not be **justified** by the law of Moses."
A P : 0 4 :097(121) [0149] for us to believe that we are **justified** because of him.
A P : 0 4 :103(121) [0151] works of the law none is **justified**, that is, by the law sin is
A P : 0 4 :103(122) [0151] glory in his works since no one is **justified** by his deeds.
A P : 0 4 :103(122) [0151] has it as a gift because he was **justified** after being washed.
A P : 0 4 :106(122) [0153] Only in a **justified** man is there a good work by the
A P : 0 4 :117(123) [0155] and by faith alone are **justified**, that is, out of unrighteous
A P : 0 4 :122(124) [0157] doers of the law will be **justified**" (Rom. 2:13), and many
A P : 0 4 :125(124) [0157] After we have been **justified** and regenerated by faith,
A P : 0 4 :126(124) [0157] happen until, being **justified** and regenerated, we receive
A P : 0 4 :158(129) [0165] it is clear that we are **justified** by faith, for it is sure that
A P : 0 4 :159(129) [0167] mistaken when they think that we are **justified** by the law.
A P : 0 4 :159(129) [0167] We are not **justified** by the law; but we receive the
A P : 0 4 :159(129) [0167] necessarily follows that we are **justified** by faith in Christ.
A P : 0 4 :163(129) [0169] of anything against me, but I am not thereby **justified**."
A P : 0 4 :182(132) [0171] it is evident that we are **justified** before God by faith
A P : 0 4 :195(134) [0175] 5:1), "Since we are **justified** by faith, we have peace with
A P : 0 4 :196(134) [0175] life belongs to the **justified**, according to the saying,
A P : 0 4 :196(134) [0175] saying, "Those whom he **justified** he also glorified" (Rom.
A P : 0 4 :197(134) [0175] when it takes place in the **justified** it merits other great
A P : 0 4 :201(134) [0175] circumcision in order to be **justified** (Rom. 4:9-22).
A P : 0 4 :217(137) [0179] 5:1), "Since we are **justified** by faith, we have peace."
A P : 0 4 :218(137) [0179] quote to prove that we are **justified** by love and works.
A P : 0 4 :220(137) [0181] people who, upon being **justified**, needed urging to bear
A P : 0 4 :222(138) [0181] love justifies, for we are **justified** only when we take hold
A P : 0 4 :224(138) [0181] Upon being **justified**, the Corinthians received many
A P : 0 4 :224(138) [0181] to imagine that we are **justified** before God by the works
A P : 0 4 :244(141) [0189] "You see that a man is **justified** by works and not by faith
A P : 0 4 :245(142) [0189] They teach that a man is **justified** by love and works but
A P : 0 4 :246(142) [0189] about the works of the **justified**, who have already been
A P : 0 4 :247(142) [0191] he teaches that we are regenerated and **justified** by faith.
A P : 0 4 :250(143) [0191] in denying that we are **justified** by a faith without works.
A P : 0 4 :251(143) [0191] When he says we are **justified** by faith and works, he
A P : 0 4 :251(143) [0191] of the just who have already been **justified** and reborn.
A P : 0 4 :252(143) [0191] "To be **justified**" here does not mean that a wicked man is
A P : 0 4 :252(143) [0191] (Rom. 2:13), "the doers of the law will be **justified**."
A P : 0 4 :252(143) [0191] doers of the law will be **justified**," contain nothing
A P : 0 4 :252(143) [0191] words, "A man is **justified** by works and not by faith
A P : 0 4 :252(143) [0191] doers of the law will be **justified**"; that is, God
A P : 0 4 :257(144) [0193] It is clear that we are not **justified** by the law.
A P : 0 4 :279(149) [0199] and which wants to be **justified**, sanctified, and governed
A P : 0 4 :282(149) [0201] cleansed before God and **justified** by frequent washings.
A P : 0 4 :291(152) [0203] understand that we are **justified** neither by reason nor by
A P : 0 4 :292(152) [0203] we teach that a man is **justified** when, with his conscience
A P : 0 4 :294(152) [0203] Paul teaches that we are **justified** not by the law but by
A P : 0 4 :296(152) [0205] that he was given for us to be **justified** on his account.
A P : 0 4 :297(152) [0205] facts: First we are not **justified** by the law because human
A P : 0 4 :297(152) [0205] God; and second, we are **justified** by the promise, in
A P : 0 4 :297(153) [0205] We are not **justified** before God either by reason or by the
A P : 0 4 :298(153) [0205] Since we are not **justified** before God by the law but by
A P : 0 4 :304(154) [0205] shows, "Since we are **justified** by faith, we have peace with
A P : 0 4 :313(155) [0207] us to hold that we are **justified**, reconciled, and reborn by
A P : 0 4 :313(155) [0207] who teach that we are **justified** by love teach the
A P : 0 4 :317(156) [0209] (Gal. 2:17) that if a man **justified** in Christ must then seek
A P : 0 4 :320(156) [0209] 5:1), "Since we are **justified** by faith, we have peace with
A P : 0 4 :347(160) [0217] life is promised to the **justified** and it is faith that
A P : 0 4 :348(160) [0217] life is promised to the **justified**, but those who walk
A P : 0 4 :348(160) [0217] We are **justified** for this very purpose, that, being
A P : 0 4 :354(161) [0217] opponents grant that the **justified** are children of God and
A P : 0 4 :362(162) [0219] Rom. 8:30, "Those whom he **justified** he also glorified."
A P : 0 4 :363(162) [0219] The crown is owed to the **justified** because of the
A P : 0 4 :366(163) [0221] Those who merit this are **justified** before they keep the
A P : 0 4 :368(163) [0221] we have been reconciled to God, **justified**, and reborn.
A P : 0 4 :372(164) [0221] life is granted to works, it is granted to the **justified**.
A P : 0 4 :372(164) [0221] good works except the **justified**, who are led by the Spirit
A P : 0 4 :383(166) [0225] with his heart and so is **justified**, and he confesses with
A P : 0 4 :386(166) [0225] we conclude that we are **justified** before God, reconciled
A P : 0 4 :387(166) [0225] who deny that men are **justified** by faith deny that Christ
A P : 0 4 :388(166) [0225] and that we are not **justified** by the law but by the
A P : 0 4 :393(167) [0225] reconciled to God and **justified** by their own works and
A P : 0 7 :039(176) [0241] us to believe that we are **justified** by such rites or that
A P : 1 2 :036(186) [0261] 5:1), "Since we are **justified** by faith, we have peace with
A P : 1 2 :036(186) [0261] as the same passage attests, "We are **justified** by faith."
A P : 1 2 :054(189) [0265] For all the saints were **justified** by faith in this promise,
A P : 1 2 :073(192) [0273] apostle concludes, that a man is **justified** freely by faith."
A P : 1 2 :077(193) [0275] declaring that men are **justified** by faith and not by love.
A P : 1 2 :079(193) [0275] contends that we are not **justified** by the law; to the law
A P : 1 2 :079(194) [0275] be useless if we were **justified** by the law before the
A P : 1 2 :085(194) [0277] to imagine that a man is **justified** by the law before being
A P : 1 2 :086(194) [0277] They want to be **justified** by the law and to offer our
A P : 1 2 :087(195) [0277] said above that men are **justified** by faith and not by
A P : 1 2 :108(198) [0283] sinned, so that thou art **justified** in thy sentence and
A P : 1 2 :108(198) [0283] I declare Thee to be **justified** in condemning and
A P : 1 2 :108(198) [0283] but we shall be **justified** when Thou dost justify us and
A P : 1 3 :009(212) [0311] Men are not **justified**, therefore, because of any other
A P : 1 3 :018(213) [0313] to believe that we are **justified** by a ceremony without a
A P : 1 3 :019(213) [0313] that Abraham was **justified** by circumcision, but says that
A P : 1 3 :023(214) [0313] 10:10), "Man believes with his heart and so is **justified**."
A P : 1 5 :006(215) [0317] at length that men are **justified** by the faith that they have
A P : 1 5 :008(216) [0317] from Christ, you who would be **justified** by the law."
A P : 1 5 :012(216) [0317] those who are already **justified** do merit grace by
A P : 1 5 :018(217) [0319] by which it seeks to be **justified** before God, denying that
A P : 1 5 :018(217) [0319] that men are freely **justified** before God by faith for
A P : 1 5 :018(217) [0319] teach that we are not **justified** freely for his sake but by
A P : 1 5 :020(218) [0321] but taught that we are **justified** by faith for Christ's sake,
A P : 1 5 :031(219) [0323] rites as though they **justified** or were necessary for
A P : 2 0 :010(228) [0341] He says, "We are **justified** by his grace as a gift" (Rom.
A P : 2 3 :036(244) [0361] nor by marriage are we **justified**, but freely for Christ's
A P : 2 4 :012(251) [0387] "Since we are **justified** by faith, we have peace" (Rom.
A P : 2 4 :055(259) [0403] New, the saints had to be **justified** by faith in the promise
A P : 2 4 :060(260) [0405] 5:1), "Since we are **justified** by faith, we have peace."
A P : 2 4 :089(266) [0415] (Rom. 5:1), "Being **justified** by faith, we have peace."
A P : 2 7 :011(270) [0423] you who would be **justified** by the law; you have fallen
A P : 2 7 :061(279) [0441] an act of worship that **justified**, or that because of it —
S 2 : 0 1 :003(292) [0461] sinned," and "they are **justified** by his grace as a gift,
S 2 : 0 1 :004(292) [0461] we hold that a man is **justified** by faith apart from works
S 3 : 0 3 :001(303) [0479] to God, for no human being will be **justified** in his sight."
S 3 : 0 8 :008(313) [0495] through whom he was **justified** before God, and his
S 3 : 0 8 :008(313) [0495] have believed and been **justified** if the Word and his
S 3 : 1 3 :000(315) [0499] XIII. How Man Is **Justified** Before God, and His Good
S C : 0 4 :010(349) [0551] so that we might be **justified** by his grace and become
E P : 0 3 :001(472) [0791] that we poor sinners are **justified** before God and saved
E P : 0 3 :011(474) [0795] after a person has been **justified** by faith, a true living
E P : 0 3 :015(475) [0795] "to justify" and "to be **justified**" do not mean to absolve
E P : 0 3 :021(475) [0797] 9. That believers are **justified** before God and saved both
E P : 0 3 :023(475) [0797] that unless they are present a person cannot be **justified**.
E P : 0 6 :003(480) [0805] truly converted, regenerated, and **justified** through faith.
S D : 0 3 :004(540) [0917] redeemed us from our sins, **justified** and saved us.
S D : 0 3 :009(540) [0919] that a poor sinner is **justified** before God (that is, he is
S D : 0 3 :012(541) [0919] as synonymous: "We are **justified** by faith" (Rom. 3:28),
S D : 0 3 :012(541) [0919] when he says that we are **justified** by the obedience of
S D : 0 3 :013(541) [0919] our own through faith if we are to be **justified** thereby.
S D : 0 3 :019(542) [0921] the Holy Spirit works in those who are **justified** by faith.
S D : 0 3 :020(542) [0921] a person to faith and has **justified** him, a regeneration has
S D : 0 3 :022(543) [0923] work we are reborn and **justified**, we do not mean that
S D : 0 3 :022(543) [0923] to those who have been **justified** and regenerated, but we
S D : 0 3 :023(543) [0923] any work or merit, are **justified** before God (that is,
S D : 0 3 :027(543) [0923] certainly that he is not **justified** but is still in death, or
S D : 0 3 :027(543) [0925] St. Paul says, "We are **justified** by faith apart from works
S D : 0 3 :029(544) [0925] how a person may be **justified** before God and be saved.
S D : 0 3 :029(544) [0925] with St. Paul that we are **justified** alone through faith in
S D : 0 3 :032(544) [0927] in Christ have been **justified** possess in this life, first, the
S D : 0 3 :033(545) [0927] says that Abraham was **justified** before God through faith
S D : 0 3 :036(545) [0927] the assertion that we are **justified** before God and saved
S D : 0 3 :041(546) [0929] the grace of God in Christ whereby the person is **justified**.
S D : 0 3 :041(546) [0929] After the person is **justified**, the Holy Spirit next renews
S D : 0 3 :042(547) [0931] he denies that we are **justified** by such a faith as is
S D : 0 3 :043(547) [0931] of those who are already **justified** through Christ, who are
S D : 0 3 :043(547) [0931] if men are to be **justified** by it before God; or, the
S D : 0 3 :043(547) [0931] a person cannot be **justified**, and that the exclusive terms
S D : 0 3 :050(548) [0933] that the believers are **justified** before God and are
S D : 0 3 :052(548) [0933] the one by which he is **justified** before God, as though we
S D : 0 3 :052(548) [0933] as though we are indeed **justified** solely through faith
S D : 0 3 :053(548) [0933] fact, that when we are **justified** through faith we

Continued ▶

SD : 0 3 :054(548) [0935] the elect who have been **justified** through Christ and
SD : 0 3 :062(550) [0937] "to justify" and "to be **justified**" do not mean "to absolve
SD : 0 4 :032(556) [0947] who have been **justified** by faith these true, immutable,
SD : 0 5 :024(563) [0961] came, that we might be **justified** by faith" (Gal. 3:24), and
SD : 0 6 :004(564) [0963] converted to God and **justified**, have been freed and
SD : 1 1 :019(619) [1069] in love all who are thus **justified**, as St. Paul says
SD : 1 1 :022(619) [1069] life those whom he has elected, called, and **justified**.
SD : 1 1 :043(623) [1077] the article that we are **justified** and saved without our

Justifier (5)
AP : 0 4 :106(122) [0153] He reconciles the **justifier** by faith, not by his own
AP : 0 4 :106(122) [0153] he clearly says that the **justifier** is reconciled by faith and
AP : 0 4 :389(166) [0225] confesses that Christ is the propitiator and the **justifier**.
AP : 0 4 :392(167) [0225] him not the propitiator and **justifier**, but only a legislator.
AP : 1 5 :007(216) [0317] but to set up another **justifier** and mediator instead of

Justifies (66)
AG : 2 7 :043(077) [0081] rob Christ, who alone **justifies**, of his honor and bestow
AL : 0 5 :003(031) [0045] of Christ that God **justifies** those who believe that they
AL : 2 7 :048(078) [0081] of God and to teach that such service **justifies** men.
AP : 0 4 :045(113) [0133] faith obtains the forgiveness of sins and **justifies** us.
AP : 0 4 :048(114) [0135] The faith that **justifies**, however, is no mere historical
AP : 0 4 :060(115) [0137] Faith in Christ **Justifies**
AP : 0 4 :061(115) [0139] we shall show that it **justifies** and what this means, and
AP : 0 4 :062(115) [0139] receives the forgiveness of sins, **justifies** and quickens us.
AP : 0 4 :067(116) [0139] From this we can prove that faith **justifies**.
AP : 0 4 :067(116) [0139] received only by faith, then it follows that faith **justifies**.
AP : 0 4 :069(116) [0141] Now we shall show that faith **justifies**.
AP : 0 4 :069(116) [0141] then we must defend the proposition, "Faith **justifies**."
AP : 0 4 :070(116) [0141] then we must defend the proposition, "Faith **justifies**."
AP : 0 4 :070(116) [0141] who denies that faith **justifies** teaches only the law and
AP : 0 4 :071(116) [0141] When we say that faith **justifies**, some may think this
AP : 0 4 :086(119) [0147] Faith alone **justifies** because we receive the forgiveness of
AP : 0 4 :088(120) [0149] the statement "Faith **justifies**" inadvertently, he reinforces
AP : 0 4 :089(120) [0149] but trusts in him who **justifies** the ungodly, his faith is
AP : 0 4 :099(121) [0151] but a thing that receives the Holy Spirit and **justifies** us.
AP : 0 4 :145(127) [0163] effects of faith, our opponents teach that love **justifies**.
AP : 0 4 :147(127) [0163] is the keeping of the law, why do we deny that it **justifies**?
AP : 0 4 :150(127) [0163] Therefore it must be faith that reconciles and **justifies**.
AP : 0 4 :181(132) [0171] this obedience of the law **justifies** by the righteousness of
AP : 0 4 :186(132) [0173] by their denial that faith **justifies** and by their doctrine
AP : 0 4 :196(134) [0175] obtains this because it **justifies** us and has a gracious
AP : 0 4 :197(134) [0175] obedience to parents **justifies** us before God, but rather
AP : 0 4 :210(136) [0179] the Mass is a work that **justifies** *ex opere operato* and
AP : 0 4 :222(137) [0181] therefore not stealing **justifies**; for justification is not the
AP : 0 4 :222(138) [0181] he is not saying that love **justifies** but that "I am
AP : 0 4 :222(138) [0181] not believe that love **justifies**, for we are justified only
AP : 0 4 :226(138) [0183] How will they conclude from this that love **justifies**?
AP : 0 4 :226(138) [0183] The greatest virtue, they say, **justifies**.
AP : 0 4 :227(138) [0183] But that virtue **justifies** which takes hold of Christ,
AP : 0 4 :231(139) [0183] this they argue that love **justifies** since it makes men
AP : 0 4 :235(140) [0185] "perfection" that love **justifies**, when Paul is speaking of
AP : 0 4 :242(141) [0187] it is our propitiation; or that it regenerates and **justifies**.
AP : 0 4 :292(152) [0203] accepts the forgiveness of sins, **justifies**, and regenerates.
AP : 0 4 :347(160) [0217] is promised to the justified and it is faith that **justifies**.
AP : 1 2 :036(186) [0261] This faith **justifies** before God, as the same passage
AP : 1 2 :052(189) [0265] contrition and the faith that consoles and **justifies**.
AP : 1 2 :056(189) [0265] David and by faith it sustains, **justifies**, and quickens him.
AP : 1 2 :178(211) [0309] to teach the faith that **justifies** and consoles faithful
AP : 1 3 :023(214) [0313] faith in the sacrament, and not the sacrament, **justifies**.
AP : 2 3 :040(244) [0375] virginity because it **justifies** but because it gives more time
AP : 2 4 :028(254) [0393] to be God, the one who **justifies** and saves, because of my
AP : 2 4 :031(255) [0395] not follow that the Mass **justifies** *ex opere operato* or
AP : 2 4 :035(256) [0397] must be a ceremony that **justifies** *ex opere operato* or
AP : 2 4 :060(260) [0405] the idea that the Mass **justifies** *ex opere operato* or that it
AP : 2 4 :061(260) [0405] wicked idea that the Mass **justifies** *ex opere operato*.
AP : 2 4 :096(267) [0417] namely, that the Mass **justifies** *ex opere operato* and that
S2 : 0 1 :004(292) [0461] that such faith alone **justifies** us, as St. Paul says in
S2 : 0 1 :004(292) [0461] is righteous and that he **justifies** him who has faith in
EP : 0 2 :013(471) [0789] himself, enlightens them, **justifies** them, and saves them
EP : 0 3 :007(473) [0793] "He who **justifies** the wicked and he who condemns the
EP : 0 3 :007(474) [0793] It is God who **justifies**" (Rom. 8:33).
SD : 0 2 :080(536) [0911] man to himself, illuminates, **justifies**, and saves him.
SD : 0 3 :017(542) [0921] "He who **justifies** the wicked and he who condemns the
SD : 0 3 :017(542) [0921] It is God who **justifies**" (Rom. 8:33), that is, absolves and
SD : 0 3 :034(545) [0927] work, but trusts him who **justifies** the ungodly, his faith is
SD : 0 3 :042(547) [0931] manner in which faith **justifies**, it is St. Paul's doctrine
SD : 0 3 :042(547) [0931] doctrine that faith alone **justifies** without works when, as
SD : 0 3 :043(547) [0931] without works; or, faith **justifies** or makes righteous in so
SD : 0 3 :043(547) [0931] Faith **justifies** solely for this reason and on this account,
SD : 0 3 :049(548) [0933] 5. That faith **justifies** only because righteousness is begun
SD : 0 4 :002(551) [0939] in which we confess that faith alone **justifies** and saves.
SD : 0 5 :025(563) [0961] without any merit of their own, **justifies** and saves them.

Justify (67)
AG : 2 7 :061(080) [0083] monastic vows: that they **justify** and render men
AL : 1 3 :003(036) [0049] teach that the sacraments **justify** by the outward act and
AL : 2 6 :041(070) [0075] such observances do not **justify** before God and that no
AL : 2 7 :061(080) [0083] with vows: that they **justify**, that they constitute Christian
AP : 0 3 :001(107) [0119] he was raised to rule, **justify**, and sanctify the believers,
AP : 0 4 :031(111) [0129] of reason does not **justify** us before God, it does not keep
AP : 0 4 :038(112) [0131] It does not **justify**, because a conscience terrified by the
AP : 0 4 :040(112) [0131] free us from sin or **justify** us, but the promise of the
AP : 0 4 :043(113) [0133] however, it follows that we cannot **justify** ourselves.
AP : 0 4 :056(114) [0137] For faith does not **justify** or save because it is a good
AP : 0 4 :087(120) [0147] these works, having a command, would have to **justify**.
AP : 0 4 :097(121) [0149] The law, he says, does not **justify**.
AP : 0 4 :101(121) [0151] Isa. 53:11, "By his knowledge he shall **justify** many."
AP : 0 4 :134(125) [0159] that sacrifice and ritual **justify** before God *ex opere*
AP : 0 4 :157(129) [0165] because the law does not **justify** so long as it can accuse
AP : 0 4 :161(129) [0167] of the law does not **justify**, because it is accepted only on
AP : 0 4 :178(131) [0171] justification elsewhere, our love and works do not **justify**.
AP : 0 4 :180(132) [0171] disposed to us and to **justify** us, not because of the law or
AP : 0 4 :181(132) [0171] love and works do not **justify**; still they are virtues, in
AP : 0 4 :181(132) [0171] Therefore it does not **justify**; that is, it neither reconciles
AP : 0 4 :218(137) [0179] they say, Paul asserts that faith alone does not **justify**.
AP : 0 4 :225(138) [0183] that the greatest and the main virtue should **justify**.
AP : 0 4 :227(138) [0183] and greatest law does not **justify**, neither does the greatest
AP : 0 4 :276(148) [0199] Lord's Supper does not **justify** *ex opere operato* without
AP : 0 4 :276(148) [0199] so almsgiving does not **justify** *ex opere operato* without
AP : 0 4 :286(150) [0201] that faith does not **justify** and that by our works we merit
AP : 0 4 :305(154) [0205] In this passage "**justify**" is used in a judicial way to mean
AP : 0 4 :317(156) [0209] Christ "an agent of sin" since he does not **justify** in full.
AP : 0 4 :360(162) [0219] which they can give to **justify** others, as when monks sell
AP : 0 4 :376(164) [0223] that is, that they **justify**, and because they are
AP : 0 7 :021(172) [0233] necessary if sacraments **justify** *ex opere operato*, without
AP : 1 2 :053(189) [0265] in men, to terrify and to **justify** and quicken the terrified.
AP : 1 2 :108(198) [0283] justified when Thou dost **justify** us and account us
AP : 1 5 :017(217) [0319] God's command can **justify** since we can affirm nothing
AP : 1 5 :017(217) [0319] How, then, can our opponents maintain that they **justify**?
AP : 1 5 :018(217) [0319] of Antichrist if it maintains that human rites **justify**.
AP : 1 5 :022(218) [0321] supposes that such works **justify** men and reconcile God.
AP : 1 5 :024(218) [0321] they are to be rites which **justify**, as Thomas writes,
AP : 1 5 :030(219) [0323] of Moses do not **justify**, how much less do the traditions
AP : 1 5 :030(219) [0323] justify, how much less do the traditions of men **justify**?
AP : 1 5 :034(220) [0325] that traditions do not **justify**; that they are not necessary
AP : 1 5 :038(220) [0325] way, excluding the opinion which holds that they **justify**.
AP : 1 5 :047(221) [0327] not as services that **justify** but as restraints on our flesh,
AP : 1 5 :050(222) [0329] these observances neither **justify** nor are necessary over
AP : 2 3 :049(246) [0377] as lessons for the ignorant and not as services that **justify**.
AP : 2 4 :033(256) [0395] but it does not **justify** *ex opere operato* or merit the
AP : 2 4 :043(258) [0399] with the claim that these **justify** men before God.
AP : 2 7 :021(272) [0427] themselves are services that **justify** or merit eternal life.
AP : 2 7 :024(273) [0427] they teach that these observances are services that **justify**.
AP : 2 7 :058(279) [0439] forgiveness of sins before God or to **justify** before God.
S1 : PR :014(291) [0459] repent and we even try to **justify** all our abominations.
S2 : 0 2 :008(294) [0465] Somebody may seek to **justify** himself by saying that he
S3 : 0 3 :002(304) [0479] He allows no one to **justify** himself.
LC : 0 1 :055(372) [0595] put up a good front and **justify** yourself, whether in
LC : 0 1 :056(372) [0595] when we attempt to **justify** and confirm it by invoking
EP : 0 3 :007(473) [0793] of Scripture the word "**justify**" means in this article
EP : 0 3 :015(475) [0795] apostles, the words "to **justify**" and "to be justified" do
EP : 0 3 :023(475) [0797] 11. That faith does not **justify** without good works, in
SD : 0 3 :013(541) [0919] For faith does not **justify** because it is so good a work and
SD : 0 3 :017(541) [0921] Accordingly the word "**justify**" here means to declare
SD : 0 3 :043(547) [0931] faith gets the power to **justify** and save, and what belongs
SD : 0 3 :043(547) [0931] to answer: Faith cannot **justify** without works; or, faith
SD : 0 3 :043(547) [0931] which love the power to **justify** is ascribed to faith; or, the
SD : 0 3 :062(550) [0937] of faith, the words, "to **justify**" and "to be justified" do
SD : 1 1 :018(619) [1069] 4. That he would **justify** and graciously accept into the
SD : 1 1 :040(623) [1077] Word and that he would **justify** and save all who accept
SD : 1 1 :096(632) [1095] new obedience, and thus **justify** and save him for ever

Justifying (8)
AP : 0 4 :047(113) [0133] What Is **Justifying** Faith?
AP : 0 4 :053(114) [0135] In speaking of **justifying** faith, therefore, we must
AP : 0 4 :293(152) [0203] God on account of the **justifying** faith that for Christ's
AP : 0 4 :324(157) [0211] teaches nothing about **justifying** faith and obscures
AP : 1 2 :060(190) [0267] they do not mean **justifying** but the general faith which
AP : 1 2 :092(196) [0279] or good works and making no mention of **justifying** faith.
AP : 2 7 :026(273) [0429] Hence they are neither **justifying** services nor perfection.
EP : 0 3 :011(474) [0795] works always follow **justifying** faith and are certainly to

Justly (6)
AP : 1 2 :107(198) [0283] we confess that he is **justly** wrathful and cannot be
LC : 0 1 :038(369) [0591] mad and foolish that they **justly** merit the wrath they
SD : 0 5 :015(561) [0957] Therefore we **justly** condemn the Antinomians or
SD : 0 7 :059(580) [0993] We are **justly** astonished that some are so rash that they
SD : 0 7 :121(590) [1013] For while we **justly** criticize and condemn the papistic
SD : 0 8 :062(603) [1037] doctrines have been **justly** rejected and condemned in the

Justin (2)
SD : 0 7 :037(575) [0985] ancient teachers, like **Justin**, Cyprian, Augustine, Leo,
SD : 0 7 :039(576) [0985] As **Justin** says, "We receive this not as ordinary bread or

Justinian (1)
TR : 0 0 :077(333) [0527] *Codex* and *Novellae* of **Justinian** that decisions in

Justus (3)
S3 : 1 5 :005(316) [0501] Dr. **Justus** Jonas, rector, subscribed with his own hand
S3 : 1 5 :005(317) [0501] my own name and in that of **Justus** Menius, of Eisenach
TR : 0 0 :082(335) [0529] Myconius subscribed for himself and for **Justus** Menius

Kaufbeuren (1)
PR : PR :027(016) [0027] Mayor and Council of the City of **Kaufbeuren**

Keen (1), Keenly (1)
LC : 0 1 :155(386) [0625] Of course, we **keenly** feel our misfortune, and we grumble
SD : 0 1 :060(519) [0879] reason, be it ever so **keen**, can give the right answer.

Keep (168), Keeper (1), Keeping (55), Keeps (14), Kept (55)
PR : PR :024(013) [0023] — as it is not now — to **keep** this salutary and most
AG : PR :007(025) [0039] last Wednesday that, in **keeping** with Your Majesty's
AG : 1 6 :005(038) [0051] requires that all these be **kept** as true orders of God and
AG : 2 1 :001(046) [0057] us that saints should be **kept** in rememberance so that our
AG : 2 3 :025(055) [0065] who were unable to **keep** their vows of chastity should
AG : 2 3 :025(055) [0065] are unwilling or unable to **keep** their chastity, it is better
AG : 2 6 :012(065) [0071] for it was not possible to **keep** all the traditions, and yet
AG : 2 6 :038(069) [0075] to merit grace but to **keep** the body in such a condition
AG : 2 6 :043(070) [0075] for in the East they **kept** Easter at a time different from
AG : 2 7 :012(072) [0077] in the Gospel were **kept**, and so monastic vows were
AG : 2 7 :027(075) [0079] that vows must be **kept** without first ascertaining whether
AG : 2 7 :053(079) [0083] uncertain whether he can **keep** his possessions and engage
AG : 2 7 :057(080) [0083] has given and not by **keeping** the commands invented by
AG : 2 8 :049(089) [0091] forbid the making and **keeping** of human regulations?
AG : 2 8 :055(090) [0091] the Christian assembly to **keep** such ordinances for the

Continued ▶

A G : 2 8 :060(091) [0093] and might know that the **keeping** neither of the Sabbath
A G : 2 8 :063(092) [0093] Sunday must not be **kept** as of divine obligation, it must
A G : 2 8 :063(092) [0093] it must nevertheless be **kept** as almost of divine
A G : 2 8 :069(093) [0093] of regulations which cannot be **kept** without sin.
A G : 0 0 :006(095) [0095] In **keeping** with the summons, we have desired to present
A L : 1 8 :005(040) [0051] will to marry, will to **keep** cattle, will to learn various
A L : 1 8 :008(040) [0053] all things, and can also **keep** the commandments of God
A L : 1 8 :009(040) [0053] outward works (for it can **keep** the hands from theft and
A L : 2 3 :025(055) [0065] that women who did not **keep** the chastity which they had
A L : 2 4 :036(060) [0067] inviting some to Communion and **keeping** others away.
A L : 2 6 :012(065) [0071] for it was impossible to **keep** all traditions, and yet men
A L : 2 6 :013(066) [0073] felt that they could not **keep** the traditions and,
A L : 2 6 :038(069) [0075] by that discipline but to **keep** his body in subjection and
A L : 2 6 :040(069) [0075] traditions are nevertheless **kept** among us (such as the
A L : 2 6 :043(070) [0075] Fathers, for Easter was **kept** in the East at a time
A L : 2 7 :053(079) [0083] conscience when they **keep** their possessions or engage in
A L : 2 7 :057(080) [0083] he has given and not by **keeping** the commands invented
A L : 2 8 :055(090) [0091] tranquility and that they **keep** them; in so far as one does
A L : 2 8 :060(091) [0093] would know that the **keeping** neither of the Sabbath nor
A L : 2 8 :068(093) [0093] recognizes that canons are **kept** without holding them to
A L : 2 8 :069(093) [0093] traditions which cannot be **kept** with a good conscience.
A L : 2 8 :075(094) [0095] which cannot be **kept** without sin, we are bound to follow
A L : 2 8 :077(094) [0095] some few observances which cannot be **kept** without sin.
A L : 0 0 :006(095) [0095] In **keeping** with the edict of Your Imperial Majesty, we
A P : 0 4 :018(109) [0125] righteous by their own **keeping** of the law before God.
A P : 0 4 :021(110) [0127] who think that they are **keeping** the law, they arouse
A P : 0 4 :027(111) [0127] God above all things and **keep** his law, truly fear him,
A P : 0 4 :028(111) [0129] to Christ, that men who **keep** the commandments of God
A P : 0 4 :031(111) [0129] does not justify us before God, it does not **keep** the law.
A P : 0 4 :040(112) [0131] Therefore men cannot **keep** the law by their own
A P : 0 4 :042(113) [0133] For since we do not **keep** the law, it would follow that we
A P : 0 4 :042(113) [0133] the law, which we never **keep**, it would follow that the
A P : 0 4 :046(113) [0133] regenerates our hearts, it precedes our **keeping** of the law.
A P : 0 4 :070(116) [0141] Again, we cannot **keep** the law unless we first receive the
A P : 0 4 :106(122) [0153] statement that he who **keeps** the law will live in it, so that
A P : 0 4 :106(122) [0153] his weakness one may attain to it, **keep** it, and live in it.
A P : 0 4 :106(122) [0153] and that before we try to **keep** the law we should receive
A P : 0 4 :114(123) [0155] sake before we love and **keep** the law, although love must
A P : 0 4 :121(124) [0157] Love and the **Keeping** of the Law
A P : 0 4 :122(124) [0157] "If you would enter life, **keep** the commandments"
A P : 0 4 :122(124) [0157] what we believe about love and the **keeping** of the law.
A P : 0 4 :123(124) [0157] "If you would enter life, **keep** the commandments."
A P : 0 4 :124(124) [0157] that we should begin to **keep** the law ever more and
A P : 0 4 :126(124) [0157] First, it is impossible to **keep** the law without Christ; it is
A P : 0 4 :126(124) [0157] Christ; it is impossible to **keep** the law without the Holy
A P : 0 4 :132(125) [0159] we cannot correctly **keep** the law unless by faith we have
A P : 0 4 :132(125) [0159] because the law can be **kept** only when the Holy Spirit is
A P : 0 4 :135(125) [0159] Only then do we see how far we are from **keeping** the law.
A P : 0 4 :135(126) [0159] and without the Holy Spirit we cannot **keep** the law.
A P : 0 4 :136(126) [0159] we also hold that the **keeping** of the law should begin in
A P : 0 4 :137(126) [0161] that hypocrites who try to **keep** the law by their own
A P : 0 4 :140(126) [0161] only how the law can be **kept**, but also that God is
A P : 0 4 :140(126) [0161] God is pleased when we **keep** it—not because we live up
A P : 0 4 :146(127) [0163] They claim to **keep** the law, though this glory properly
A P : 0 4 :147(127) [0163] because it is the **keeping** of the law, why do we deny that
A P : 0 4 :157(128) [0165] of sins unless he **keeps** the whole law, because the law
A P : 0 4 :159(129) [0165] they say that love is the **keeping** of the law, and obedience
A P : 0 4 :159(129) [0167] sake, not for the sake of love or the **keeping** of the law.
A P : 0 4 :160(129) [0167] When this **keeping** of the law and obedience to the law is
A P : 0 4 :161(129) [0167] now that this incipient **keeping** of the law does not
A P : 0 4 :161(129) [0167] our own perfection and **keeping** of the law, but only
A P : 0 4 :162(129) [0169] God and merit eternal life by our **keeping** of the law.
A P : 0 4 :164(129) [0169] because they have **kept** the law, how can our conscience
A P : 0 4 :165(130) [0169] because of his own **keeping** of the law rather than because
A P : 0 4 :166(130) [0169] The incipient **keeping** of the law does not please God for
A P : 0 4 :172(130) [0171] of God are **kept** when what is not kept is forgiven."
A P : 0 4 :172(130) [0171] of God are kept when what is not **kept** is forgiven."
A P : 0 4 :174(131) [0171] In the incipient **keeping** of the law, therefore, we need a
A P : 0 4 :176(131) [0171] God on account of our **keeping** of the law; for our
A P : 0 4 :177(131) [0171] The incipient **keeping** of the law pleases God because of
A P : 0 4 :177(131) [0171] of faith our failure to **keep** it is not imputed to us,
A P : 0 4 :178(131) [0171] and not because of our **keeping** of the law we have a
A P : 0 4 :180(132) [0171] or our works: this promise we must always **keep** in view.
A P : 0 4 :181(132) [0171] still they are virtues, in **keeping** with the righteousness of
A P : 0 4 :182(132) [0173] faith alone, though the **keeping** of the law follows with
A P : 0 4 :184(132) [0173] that the law cannot be **kept** without Christ, and that if
A P : 0 4 :189(133) [0175] And in order to **keep** the Gospel among men, he visibly
A P : 0 4 :206(135) [0177] their works but did not **keep** their faith, believing that
A P : 0 4 :208(135) [0177] conscience at rest, they **kept** thinking up new works
A P : 0 4 :214(136) [0179] done since our incipient **keeping** of the law must follow
A P : 0 4 :219(137) [0181] be renewed and begin to **keep** the law, according to the
A P : 0 4 :219(137) [0181] casts away love will not **keep** his faith, be it ever so great,
A P : 0 4 :219(137) [0181] it ever so great, because he will not **keep** the Holy Spirit.
A P : 0 4 :245(142) [0189] in preference to it, but **keeps** it, lest Christ, the
A P : 0 4 :252(143) [0191] because of faith and therefore are a **keeping** of the law.
A P : 0 4 :256(144) [0193] law there are two things we must always **keep** in mind.
A P : 0 4 :256(144) [0193] First, we cannot **keep** the law unless we have been reborn
A P : 0 4 :256(144) [0193] We must **keep** the Gospel promise that through Christ we
A P : 0 4 :260(145) [0195] We must always **keep** this important teaching in view.
A P : 0 4 :269(147) [0197] rules: that the law is not **kept** without Christ—as he
A P : 0 4 :270(147) [0197] "If you would enter life, **keep** the commandments"
A P : 0 4 :270(147) [0197] realize that no one can **keep** the commandments or please
A P : 0 4 :270(147) [0197] of those who love me and **keep** my commandments"
A P : 0 4 :270(147) [0197] But without Christ this law is not **kept**.
A P : 0 4 :270(147) [0197] But a man **keeps** the law as soon as he hears that God is
A P : 0 4 :270(147) [0197] is at peace and begins to love God and to **keep** the law.
A P : 0 4 :270(147) [0199] even though its incipient **keeping** of the law is impure and
A P : 0 4 :290(151) [0203] God through their own **keeping** of the law and not
A P : 0 4 :290(151) [0203] imagines that this very **keeping** of the law with[out] Christ,
A P : 0 4 :290(151) [0203] even a weak and feeble **keeping** of the law is rare, even
A P : 0 4 :293(152) [0203] his renewal we can **keep** the law, love God and his Word,
A P : 0 4 :294(152) [0203] love follows faith since love is the **keeping** of the law.
A P : 0 4 :295(152) [0203] Later we begin to **keep** the law.
A P : 0 4 :297(152) [0205] human nature cannot **keep** the law of God nor love God;
A P : 0 4 :299(153) [0205] but because Christ still helps us to **keep** the law.
A P : 0 4 :301(153) [0205] God because they love and **keep** the law, they will have to
A P : 0 4 :314(156) [0207] cannot set our love and **keeping** of the law against the
A P : 0 4 :314(156) [0207] well to have it at hand and **keep** it in mind, not only to
A P : 0 4 :315(156) [0207] help of Christ we cannot **keep** the law, as he himself says
A P : 0 4 :315(156) [0207] So before we can **keep** the law, our hearts must be reborn
A P : 0 4 :366(163) [0221] The **keeping** of the law that follows faith deals with the
A P : 0 4 :366(163) [0221] who merit this are justified before they **keep** the law.
A P : 0 4 :368(163) [0221] Although **keeping** the law thus merits a reward, since a
A P : 0 4 :368(163) [0221] We neither do nor can **keep** the law before we have been
A P : 0 4 :368(163) [0221] This **keeping** of the law would not please God unless we
A P : 0 4 :368(163) [0221] of faith, this incipient **keeping** of the law pleases God and
A P : 0 4 :388(166) [0225] that the law cannot be **kept** without Christ, and that we
A P : 0 7 :038(176) [0241] rites they want to **keep**, apostolic doctrine they do not
A P : 0 7 :038(176) [0241] want to keep, apostolic doctrine they do not want to **keep**
A P : 0 7 :043(177) [0243] had been converted from Judaism but **kept** their customs.
A P : 1 2 :037(186) [0261] For the law is not **kept** without Christ, according to the
A P : 1 2 :069(192) [0271] of quotations, it must be **kept** in mind that no great
A P : 1 2 :076(193) [0273] Nor can we **keep** the law before we have been reconciled
A P : 1 2 :080(194) [0275] because we cannot **keep** the law, and therefore we must
A P : 1 2 :080(194) [0275] must be reconciled by the promise before we **keep** the law.
A P : 1 2 :082(194) [0275] of sins by faith before we **keep** the law although, as we
A P : 1 2 :082(194) [0275] the Holy Spirit and therefore begin to **keep** the law.
A P : 1 2 :086(194) [0277] contends that we cannot **keep** the law without Christ.
A P : 1 2 :086(195) [0277] by faith we are reconciled to God before we **keep** the law.
A P : 1 2 :087(195) [0277] promise of the forgiveness of sins before we **keep** the law.
A P : 1 2 :088(195) [0277] the forgiveness of sins because we love or **keep** the law?
A P : 1 2 :090(195) [0279] with our opponents, we would very gladly **keep** quiet.
A P : 1 2 :099(197) [0281] For we also **keep** confession, especially because of
A P : 1 2 :116(199) [0287] We must **keep** the doctrine that by faith we obtain the
A P : 1 2 :125(201) [0289] to you, Campegius, in **keeping** with your wisdom, to see
A P : 1 2 :142(204) [0295] who imagine that we can **keep** the law in such a way as to
A P : 1 2 :168(209) [0305] punishments but to **keep** the flesh from alluring us to
A P : 1 2 :169(209) [0305] Anyone who **keeps** on stealing is not really sorry that he
A P : 1 2 :174(210) [0307] eternal punishment but to **keep** from surrendering to the
A P : 1 3 :017(213) [0313] so long as those things are **kept** which have God's
A P : 1 4 :002(214) [0315] This **keeps** our priests from acknowledging such bishops.
A P : 1 4 :002(214) [0315] in some places, despite our earnest desire to **keep** it.
A P : 1 4 :005(215) [0315] declare our willingness to **keep** the ecclesiastical and
A P : 1 5 :021(218) [0321] these reasons the Fathers **kept** ceremonies, and for the
A P : 1 5 :021(218) [0321] the same reasons we also believe in **keeping** traditions.
A P : 1 5 :027(219) [0323] because they cannot **keep** the requirements in every
A P : 1 5 :038(220) [0325] We gladly **keep** the old traditions set up in the church
A P : 1 5 :051(222) [0329] ancient customs should be **kept** which can be kept
A P : 1 5 :051(222) [0329] be kept which can be **kept** without sin or without great
A P : 1 6 :006(223) [0331] are very easy to answer if we **keep** certain things in mind.
A P : 1 6 :012(224) [0333] consciences unless they **keep** the rule in mind, that a
A P : 1 8 :004(225) [0335] it can choose to **keep** the hands from murder, adultery, or
A P : 1 8 :008(226) [0337] for the saints it is hard to **keep** this faith; for the ungodly
A P : 2 0 :013(228) [0343] and not because of them and which are now **kept** by faith.
A P : 2 0 :015(229) [0343] Holy Spirit by faith, the **keeping** of the law necessarily
A P : 2 2 :010(237) [0361] say that the laity has been **kept** from the one kind as a
A P : 2 2 :010(238) [0361] that the laity has been **kept** from the one kind as a
A P : 2 2 :013(238) [0361] orders, this in itself should **keep** us from agreeing with
A P : 2 3 :011(241) [0367] Let us therefore **keep** this fact in mind, taught by
A P : 2 3 :027(243) [0371] and marital intercourse did not **keep** them from praying.
A P : 2 3 :044(245) [0375] voluptuously, cannot even **keep** this Levitical continence.
A P : 2 3 :051(246) [0377] morals; this alone should **keep** good men from approving
A P : 2 4 :001(249) [0383] not abolish the Mass but religiously **keep** and defend it.
A P : 2 4 :001(249) [0385] We **keep** traditional liturgical forms, such as the order of
A P : 2 4 :003(250) [0385] out that our churches **keep** the Latin lessons and prayers.
A P : 2 4 :003(250) [0385] Therefore we **keep** Latin for the sake of those who study
A P : 2 4 :042(257) [0399] the Mass our opponents **keep** only the ceremony, which
A P : 2 4 :049(258) [0401] Thus, since we **keep** both the proclamation of the Gospel
A P : 2 4 :085(265) [0413] Originally the Christians **kept** this practice.
A P : 2 4 :086(265) [0413] With this practice they also **kept** the term "Mass" as the
A P : 2 7 :009(269) [0421] defending, not the question whether vows should be **kept**.
A P : 2 7 :009(269) [0421] legitimate vows should be **kept**, but we are arguing about
A P : 2 8 :007(282) [0445] In the church we must **keep** this teaching, that we receive
A P : 2 8 :007(282) [0445] We must also **keep** the teaching that human traditions are
S 1 : P R :005(289) [0457] to what I write and who **keep** themselves busy by
S 1 : P R :007(289) [0457] and try by their lies to **keep** the people on their side, God
S 1 : P R :014(291) [0459] our sins oppress us and **keep** God from being gracious to
S 2 : 0 2 :026(297) [0469] and saints, pray to them, **keep** fasts and festivals for
S 2 : 0 2 :027(297) [0469] pray to you, invoke you, **keep** fasts and festivals and say
S 2 : 0 4 :014(301) [0475] In **keeping** with such teaching, instructions are given
S 3 : 0 1 :006(302) [0477] powers to observe and **keep** all the commandments of
S 3 : 0 2 :003(303) [0479] that they can and do **keep** the law by their own powers,
S 3 : 0 3 :039(309) [0489] and although no one **keeps** the law (as Christ says in John
S C : 0 1 :005(342) [0541] *"Remember the Sabbath day, to keep it holy."*
S C : 0 1 :018(344) [0541] service and help to him so that he may **keep** what is his.
S C : 0 1 :021(344) [0543] of those who love me and **keep** my commandments."
S C : 0 1 :022(344) [0543] promises grace and every blessing to all who **keep** them.
S C : 0 3 :011(347) [0547] he strengthens us and **keeps** us steadfast in his Word and
S C : 0 7 :002(352) [0557] I beseech Thee to **keep** me this day, too, from all sin and
S C : 0 9 :002(354) [0561] his own household well, **keeping** his children submissive
S C : 0 9 :003(355) [0561] to them; for they are **keeping** watch over your souls, as
L C : P R :014(360) [0571] lying down, or rising, and **keep** them before our eyes and
L C : P R :016(361) [0573] to teach, and he always **keeps** on teaching this one thing
L C : S P :004(362) [0575] and if they do not know it, to **keep** them faithfully at it.
L C : S P :003(362) [0575] 3. You shall **keep** the Sabbath day holy.
L C : 0 1 :022(367) [0585] It **keeps** account how often it has made endowments,
L C : 0 1 :030(369) [0589] *of those who love me and keep my commandments."*
L C : 0 1 :042(370) [0591] and can scarcely even **keep** alive; meanwhile, those who
L C : 0 1 :048(371) [0593] and this commandment is **kept**, fulfillment of all the
L C : 0 1 :070(374) [0601] to honor God's name and **keep** it constantly upon their
L C : 0 1 :072(374) [0601] I say, we should always **keep** the holy name on our lips so
L C : 0 1 :080(375) [0603] he commanded it to **be kept** holy above all other days.
L C : 0 1 :083(376) [0603] we point out that we **keep** holy days not for the sake of
L C : 0 1 :083(376) [0603] We **keep** them, first, for the sake of bodily need.
L C : 0 1 :084(376) [0605] and most especially, we **keep** holy days so that people
L C : 0 1 :087(376) [0605] the holy day" means, answer: "It means to **keep** it holy."

Continued ▶

LC : 0 1 :087(376) [0605] What is meant by "**keeping** it holy"?
LC : 0 1 :090(377) [0605] Wherever this practice is in force, a holy day is truly **kept**.
LC : 0 1 :100(379) [0609] you must continually **keep** God's Word in your heart, on
LC : 0 1 :125(382) [0617] strongest reason impelling us to **keep** this commandment.
LC : 0 1 :131(383) [0619] strong incentive for us to **keep** this commandment is that
LC : 0 1 :134(383) [0619] the reward, that whoever **keeps** this commandment will
LC : 0 1 :164(387) [0627] Those who **keep** their eyes on God's will and
LC : 0 1 :187(390) [0633] He wants us to **keep** this commandment ever before our
LC : 0 1 :212(394) [0641] too, God's grace is still required to **keep** the heart pure.
LC : 0 1 :230(396) [0645] Yes, we might well **keep** quiet here about various petty
LC : 0 1 :232(396) [0647] may be continually and urgently **kept** before their eyes.
LC : 0 1 :238(397) [0647] Just let them **keep** on boldly fleecing people as long as
LC : 0 1 :248(398) [0651] wayward crowd, but may **keep** their eyes fixed upon
LC : 0 1 :270(401) [0657] **Keep** your knowledge to yourself and do not give it out to
LC : 0 1 :293(404) [0663] They thought they were **keeping** the commandments when
LC : 0 1 :313(407) [0671] have our hands full to **keep** these commandments,
LC : 0 1 :316(408) [0671] can achieve so much as to **keep** one of the Ten
LC : 0 1 :316(408) [0671] one of the Ten Commandments as it ought to be **kept**.
LC : 0 1 :320(408) [0673] *to those who love me and* **keep** *my commandments, I*
LC : 0 1 :321(408) [0673] I said that we should **keep** it before the young and insist
LC : 0 1 :321(408) [0673] and compelled to **keep** these Ten Commandments.
LC : 0 1 :324(409) [0675] heaven and on earth will **keep** neither this nor any other.
LC : 0 1 :326(409) [0675] but learn it, hear it gladly, **keep** it holy, and honor it.
LC : 0 1 :330(410) [0677] the contrary, abundantly rewards those who **keep** them.
LC : 0 1 :331(410) [0677] Jews did, but we are to **keep** them incessantly before our
LC : 0 2 :002(411) [0679] all human ability is far too feeble and weak to **keep** them.
LC : 0 2 :003(411) [0679] could by our own strength **keep** the Ten Commandments
LC : 0 2 :003(411) [0679] as they ought to be **kept**, we would need neither the Creed
LC : 0 2 :031(414) [0685] from sin to righteousness, and now **keeps** us safe there.
LC : 0 2 :069(420) [0697] and his power, to help us **keep** the Ten Commandments:
LC : 0 3 :002(420) [0697] situation that no one can **keep** the Ten Commandments
LC : 0 3 :010(421) [0699] (This should be **kept** in mind above all things so that you
LC : 0 3 :034(425) [0707] that it should impel us to **keep** praying for it all our lives.
LC : 0 3 :038(425) [0707] honoring his name and **keeping** it holy and sacred,
LC : 0 3 :038(425) [0709] in heaven, may also be **kept** holy on earth by us and all
LC : 0 3 :049(426) [0711] but would rather **keep** God's name sacred and holy in
LC : 0 3 :060(428) [0715] just as great need that we **keep** firm hold of these two
LC : 0 3 :075(430) [0719] and quietness, since otherwise we could not **keep** a penny.
LC : 0 3 :090(432) [0723] God's purpose to break our pride and **keep** us humble.
LC : 0 3 :098(433) [0725] and practice every hour, **keeping** it with us at all times.
LC : 0 3 :113(435) [0729] petition reads, "Deliver or **keep** us from the Evil One, or
LC : 0 4 :035(441) [0741] Baptism quite clearly from a bath-**keeper**'s baptism).
LC : 0 4 :065(445) [0749] For we must **keep** at it incessantly, always purging out
LC : 0 5 :005(447) [0755] and value even if we never **keep**, pray, or believe them, so
LC : 0 5 :041(451) [0763] Some let themselves be **kept** and deterred from it because
LC : 0 5 :065(454) [0769] might just as well have **kept** quiet and not instituted a
LC : 0 6 :018(459) [0000] therefore take care to **keep** the two parts clearly separate.
LC : 0 6 :025(460) [0000] preachers have in the past **kept** silence about this
EP : 0 2 :012(471) [0789] conversion man is able to **keep** the law of God perfectly
EP : 0 4 :011(477) [0799] do good and that he might **keep** his faith even if he
EP : 0 5 :005(478) [0801] what a man who has not **kept** the law and is condemned
EP : 0 7 :033(485) [0815] Supper, nor could he have **kept** such a promise, since the
EP : 1 2 :008(498) [0839] extends only to those who **keep** his covenant and do not
EP : 1 2 :025(500) [0843] Spirit of God can perfectly **keep** and fulfill the law of God
SD : PR :002(503) [0851] and which were **kept** and used during that period when
SD : 0 1 :046(516) [0873] life we shall have and **keep** precisely this soul, although
SD : 0 1 :050(517) [0875] procedure is to use and **keep** the pattern of sound words,
SD : 0 2 :042(529) [0897] brings us to Christ in true faith and **keeps** us with him.
SD : 0 2 :079(536) [0911] after his conversion can **keep** the law of God perfectly in
SD : 0 3 :015(541) [0919] law in our stead and his **keeping** of the law in so perfect a
SD : 0 4 :016(554) [0943] however, it is necessary to **keep** a distinction in mind,
SD : 0 5 :010(560) [0955] and condemns us because we could not fulfill or **keep** it.
SD : 0 5 :020(561) [0959] since man has failed to **keep** the law of God and has
SD : 0 7 :051(578) [0991] He let his disciples **keep** this simple and strict
SD : 0 7 :084(584) [1001] the Lord's death), must be **kept** integrally and inviolately,
SD : 0 8 :026(596) [1025] Dr. Luther explains it, he **kept** it hidden during the state
SD : 0 8 :071(605) [1041] something that belongs to it without **keeping** it for itself.
SD : 1 1 :045(624) [1079] how he would bring me thereto and **keep** me therein.
SD : 1 1 :052(625) [1081] has not revealed but has **kept** reserved solely to his own
SD : 1 1 :061(626) [1083] enlightens, converts, and **keeps** them, God commends his
SD : 1 2 :013(634) [1099] extends only to those who **keep** the covenant and do not
SD : 1 2 :033(635) [1101] Spirit of God is able to **keep** and fulfill the law of God

Kempten (1)
PR : PR :027(016) [0027] Mayor and Council of the City of **Kempten**

Keys (51)
AG : 2 5 :004(062) [0069] command and power of **keys** and how comforting and
AG : 2 8 :005(081) [0085] the Gospel the power of **keys** or the power of bishops is a
AG : 2 8 :008(082) [0085] This power of **keys** or of bishops is used and exercised
AL : 2 5 :004(062) [0069] The power of **keys** is praised, and people are reminded of
AL : 2 8 :002(081) [0083] on the power of the **keys**, not only have instituted new
AL : 2 8 :005(081) [0085] the Gospel the power of **keys** or the power of bishops is a
AP : 1 1 :002(180) [0249] and the power of the **keys** that many troubled consciences
AP : 1 2 :006(183) [0255] what does the power of the **keys** accomplish if the sin is
AP : 1 2 :006(183) [0255] still more and wickedly minimize the power of the **keys**.
AP : 1 2 :007(183) [0255] that the power of the **keys** does not remove guilt, but only
AP : 1 2 :007(183) [0255] the salutary power of the **keys** would be a ministry not of
AP : 1 2 :007(183) [0255] that the power of the **keys** forgives sins before the church
AP : 1 2 :007(183) [0255] For if the power of the **keys** does not console us before
AP : 1 2 :010(184) [0255] of Christ, the power of the **keys**, and the righteousness of
AP : 1 2 :013(184) [0257] by the power of the **keys** and another part is redeemed by
AP : 1 2 :021(185) [0257] 5. The power of the **keys** has validity for the forgiveness
AP : 1 2 :022(185) [0257] 6. The power of the **keys** does not forgive sins before
AP : 1 2 :026(185) [0259] 10. By the power of the **keys**, through indulgences, souls
AP : 1 2 :039(187) [0261] The power of the **keys** administers and offers the Gospel
AP : 1 2 :040(187) [0261] through the Word, the **keys** truly forgive sin before him,
AP : 1 2 :043(187) [0263] honor of the power of the **keys** and the sacraments, it
AP : 1 2 :099(197) [0281] God that the power of the **keys** proclaims to individuals
AP : 1 2 :101(197) [0281] neither the forgiveness of sins nor the power of the **keys**.
AP : 1 2 :118(199) [0287] by the power of the **keys**, and the rest must be bought off
AP : 1 2 :118(199) [0287] by the power of the **keys**, unless they say that part of the
AP : 1 2 :123(200) [0289] punishments; therefore the **keys** have the command to
AP : 1 2 :129(202) [0291] easily since they hold the **keys** and so, of course, can open
AP : 1 2 :138(203) [0293] is no command for the **keys** to commute certain
AP : 1 2 :139(203) [0295] or that the power of the **keys** carries with it the command
AP : 1 2 :154(206) [0301] say that the power of the **keys** remits part of the
AP : 1 2 :154(206) [0301] They also say that the **keys** remit both the satisfactions
AP : 1 2 :154(206) [0301] Clearly the power of the **keys** does not remove these
AP : 1 2 :156(207) [0301] do with the power of the **keys** because the keys can
AP : 1 2 :156(207) [0301] of the keys because the **keys** can neither impose nor remit
AP : 1 2 :156(207) [0301] remits them apart from the administration of the **keys**.
AP : 1 2 :176(210) [0307] earth, however, that the **keys** have the power to bind and
AP : 1 2 :176(210) [0307] As we have said above, the **keys** do not have the power to
S3 : 0 4 :000(310) [0491] through the power of the **keys**; and finally, through the
S3 : 0 7 :000(311) [0493] VII. The **Keys**
S3 : 0 7 :001(311) [0493] The **keys** are a function and power given to the church by
S3 : 0 8 :001(312) [0493] or the power of the office of the **keys**, which was instituted by Christ
S3 : 0 8 :002(312) [0495] from the office of the **keys**, it should not be neglected; on
TR : 0 0 :022(323) [0511] Again, "I will give you the **keys**" (Matt 16:19).
TR : 0 0 :023(324) [0511] ("I will give you the **keys**" and "whatever you bind") is
TR : 0 0 :023(324) [0511] These words show that the **keys** were given equally to all
TR : 0 0 :024(324) [0511] to acknowledge that the **keys** do not belong to the person
TR : 0 0 :024(324) [0511] for after speaking of the **keys** in Matt. 18:19, Christ said,
TR : 0 0 :024(324) [0511] Therefore, he bestows the **keys** especially and immediately
TR : 0 0 :036(326) [0515] that he can transfer the **keys** of a worldly kingdom by the
TR : 0 0 :040(327) [0515] these words, "I will give you the **keys**" (Matt. 16:19).
TR : 0 0 :068(331) [0523] which testify that the **keys** were given to the church and

Kilian (1)
S3 : 1 5 :005(318) [0501] the Rev. John **Kilian**

Kill (11), Killed (7), Killing (3), Kills (4)
AG : 2 3 :012(052) [0063] papal decree was almost **killed** during an uprising of the
AL : 2 3 :012(052) [0063] this matter, was almost **killed** by the enraged priests in an
AP : 1 2 :050(189) [0265] I Sam. 2:6, "The Lord **kills** and brings to life; he brings
AP : 1 2 :152(206) [0299] because in the saints they **kill** and wipe out lust so that
AP : 1 2 :152(206) [0299] of sin"; that is, it is being **killed** because of the sin still
AP : 1 2 :159(207) [0301] Thus the prophets were **killed**, and John the Baptist, and
AP : 1 4 :002(214) [0315] unheard of cruelty, they **kill** the unfortunate and innocent
AP : 2 1 :043(235) [0357] good clergy have been **killed** and sound doctrine crushed,
AP : 2 3 :057(247) [0379] They cruelly **kill** men just because they are married.
AP : 2 3 :070(249) [0383] breaking up marriages and torturing and **killing** priests.
AP : 2 4 :034(256) [0397] the Gospel, which should **kill** this old flesh and begin a
SC : 0 1 :009(343) [0541] *"You shall not* **kill**.*"*
LC : SP :005(362) [0575] 5. You shall not **kill**.
LC : 0 1 :120(381) [0615] even though they **kill** themselves with fasting and pray on
LC : 0 1 :179(389) [0631] *"You shall not* **kill**.*"*
LC : 0 1 :182(389) [0631] it: We must not **kill**, either by hand, heart, or word, by
LC : 0 1 :188(390) [0633] commandment against **killing** is this: In the first place, we
LC : 0 1 :190(391) [0635] you know ways and means to do so, you have **killed** him.
LC : 0 1 :244(398) [0649] house and home and outrage and **kill** wife and children.
LC : 0 3 :006(420) [0699] as having no other God, not **killing**, not stealing, etc.
LC : 0 5 :068(454) [0769] were a poison which would **kill** us if we ate of it?
SD : 0 4 :010(552) [0941] begets us anew from God, **kills** the Old Adam, makes us
SD : 0 4 :019(554) [0945] have crucified (that is, **killed**) their flesh with its passions,
SD : 0 5 :022(562) [0959] is an office which **kills** through the letter and is a
SD : 0 6 :012(566) [0967] performs both offices, "he **kills** and brings to life, he

Kind (100), Kindest (1), Kindly (3), Kindness (14)
PR : PR :021(010) [0019] Turning to the **kind** and manner of speech employed with
PR : PR :025(013) [0023] Emperor Charles V, of **kindest** memory, in the Apology
AG : 2 2 :008(050) [0061] be found which requires the reception of only one **kind**.
AG : 2 2 :008(050) [0061] of receiving only one **kind** was introduced, although
AG : 2 6 :036(069) [0075] and again, "This **kind** of demon cannot be driven out by
AG : 2 7 :001(071) [0075] concerning them, what **kind** of life as lived in the
AG : 2 8 :063(092) [0093] and they prescribe the **kind** and amount of work that may
AG : 2 8 :070(093) [0093] the sacrament in one **kind** and prohibit administration in
AL : 1 5 :002(036) [0049] as if observances of this **kind** were necessary for
AL : 2 0 :021(044) [0055] works of another **kind** to merit grace and make
AL : 2 6 :011(065) [0071] bound to an imperfect **kind** of life — in marriage, in the
AL : 2 6 :016(066) [0073] to devote their attention to a better **kind** of teaching.
AL : 2 6 :021(067) [0073] Hence observances of this **kind** are not to be thought of
AL : 2 6 :036(069) [0075] and again, "This **kind** of demon cannot be driven out by
AL : 2 7 :005(071) [0077] Many entered this **kind** of life through ignorance, for
AL : 2 7 :011(072) [0077] of sins and justification before God by this **kind** of life.
AL : 2 7 :016(073) [0077] Now they pretend that this **kind** of life was instituted to
AL : 2 7 :057(080) [0083] "fleeing from the world" and "seeking a holy **kind** of life."
AL : 2 7 :058(080) [0083] A good and perfect **kind** of life is one which has God's
AL : 2 8 :064(092) [0093] What are discussions of this **kind** but snares of conscience
AP : 0 4 :002(107) [0121] ask His Imperial Majesty **kindly** to hear us out on this
AP : 0 4 :059(115) [0137] as the foremost **kind** of worship, as in Ps. 50:15: "Call
AP : 0 4 :072(116) [0141] is praised so highly because it is this **kind** of beginning.
AP : 0 4 :211(136) [0179] Fathers chose a certain **kind** of life for study or for other
AP : 0 4 :247(142) [0191] truth that we should be a **kind** of first fruits of his
AP : 0 4 :279(149) [0199] properly belong to the **kind** of faith we have been
AP : 0 4 :308(155) [0207] a superior is obviously a **kind** of distributive
AP : 0 4 :384(166) [0225] in order to show what **kind** of faith obtains eternal life, a
AP : 1 0 :003(179) [0247] do deny that we have no **kind** of connection with him
AP : 1 2 :129(202) [0291] But if you are **kind** and heal doubting consciences, you
AP : 1 3 :013(212) [0311] Word with every possible **kind** of praise in opposition to
AP : 1 5 :018(217) [0319] of Antichrist is a new **kind** of worship of God, devised by
AP : 1 5 :035(220) [0325] if soldiers wear one **kind** of uniform and scholars
AP : 1 5 :046(221) [0327] by the cross, a voluntary **kind** of exercise is also
AP : 2 2 :002(236) [0357] of the church, why is one **kind** taken away from part of
AP : 2 2 :008(237) [0359] But this was not the use of only one **kind**.
AP : 2 2 :010(237) [0361] indicates the use of one **kind**, and they add, "Thus our
AP : 2 2 :010(237) [0361] the one part offered by the priest, that is, with one **kind**."
AP : 2 2 :010(237) [0361] laity has been kept from the one **kind** as a punishment?
AP : 2 2 :010(238) [0361] laity has been kept from the one **kind** as a punishment.
AP : 2 2 :015(238) [0361] the freedom to use one **kind** or both, how can they make
AP : 2 2 :015(238) [0361] can they make the withholding of one **kind** mandatory?
AP : 2 3 :004(239) [0365] we hope that you will deal **kindly** with us in this case,
AP : 2 3 :023(242) [0369] In those times such a dismissal was an act of **kindness**.
AP : 2 4 :081(264) [0411] says that "liturgy" is a **kind** of tax to pay for the games,
AP : 2 4 :091(266) [0415] Indeed, the bitterest **kind** of sorrow must seize all the

Continued ▶

AP : 27 :009(269) [0421] The issue is the **kind** of doctrine which the architects of
AP : 27 :041(276) [0435] does not approve of this **kind** of flight, since we know
AP : 27 :041(276) [0435] The other **kind** of leaving is that which happens by a
AP : 27 :041(276) [0435] This **kind** of leaving Christ approves.
AP : 28 :019(284) [0449] and contains the deepest **kind** of comfort and teaching,
S2 : 02 :015(295) [0467] they dressed, and what **kind** of houses they lived in would
S2 : 02 :027(297) [0469] one particular necessity only, but in every **kind** of need.
S2 : 04 :016(301) [0475] and were given a **kindly** hearing, but we shall stand
LC : 01 :028(368) [0587] Do you have the **kind** of heart that expects from him
LC : 01 :032(369) [0589] himself, and again, how **kind** and gracious he is to those
LC : 01 :033(369) [0589] On the other hand, his **kindness** and goodness extend to
LC : 01 :051(371) [0595] whatsoever to support falsehood or wrong of any **kind**."
LC : 01 :060(372) [0597] and children and servants, and troubles of every **kind**.
LC : 01 :076(375) [0603] they can be trained with **kind** and pleasant methods, for
LC : 01 :077(375) [0603] This **kind** of training takes such root in their hearts that
LC : 01 :081(376) [0603] be fulfilled by refraining from manual labor of any **kind**.
LC : 01 :121(382) [0615] more happiness, love, **kindness**, and harmony in their
LC : 01 :127(382) [0617] show gratitude for the **kindness** and for all the good
LC : 01 :137(384) [0619] to be brought up in **kindness**; consequently, by the
LC : 01 :185(390) [0633] Here God, like a **kind** father, steps in and intervenes to
LC : 01 :193(391) [0635] suffer harm, but show to everyone all **kindness** and love.
LC : 01 :194(391) [0635] And this **kindness** is directed, as I said, especially toward
LC : 01 :194(391) [0635] To show **kindness** to our friends is but an ordinary
LC : 01 :195(391) [0637] and, in short, love and **kindness** toward our enemies.
LC : 01 :202(392) [0639] forbidden, but also every **kind** of cause, motive, and
LC : 01 :242(397) [0649] he will pronounce this **kind** of blessing over them: "Your
LC : 01 :252(399) [0653] for all the help and **kindness** we show to our neighbor, as
LC : 01 :252(399) [0653] Prov. 19:17, "He who is **kind** to the poor lends to the
LC : 01 :268(401) [0657] pronouncing the severest **kind** of verdict and sentence, for
LC : 01 :313(407) [0671] enemies, chastity, **kindness**, etc., and all that these virtues
LC : 01 :318(408) [0673] attention to any other works or other **kind** of holiness.
LC : 01 :323(409) [0675] he shows himself a **kind** father and offers us every grace
LC : 02 :010(412) [0679] one God, it may be asked: "What **kind** of being is God?
LC : 02 :011(412) [0681] ask a young child, "My boy, what **kind** of God have you?
LC : 02 :017(412) [0681] without our merit, as a **kind** father who cares for us so
LC : 03 :007(421) [0699] It is quite true that the **kind** of babbling and bellowing
LC : 03 :047(426) [0709] then, what a great need there is for this **kind** of prayer!
LC : 03 :080(431) [0721] the establishment of any **kind** of government or
LC : 03 :109(435) [0729] I am chaste, patient, **kind**, and firm in faith, the devil is
LC : 04 :046(442) [0743] salvation, which no other **kind** of life and no work on
LC : 06 :009(458) [0000] This **kind** of confession should and must take place
LC : 06 :014(458) [0000] This **kind** of confession is not included in the
EP : 01 :011(467) [0781] wrongdoing, without any **kind** of corruption of our own
EP : 03 :006(473) [0793] about Christ, but the **kind** of gift of God by which in the
EP : 03 :011(474) [0795] we should not imagine a **kind** of faith in this connection
EP : 03 :017(475) [0795] 5. That faith is a **kind** of trust in the obedience of Christ
EP : 05 :005(478) [0801] strictly speaking, is the **kind** of doctrine that teaches what
EP : 06 :004(480) [0805] their corrupt nature and **kind**), which clings to them until
EP : 07 :004(482) [0809] the most harmful **kind**, who in part talk our language
EP : 07 :018(484) [0813] that there is only one **kind** of unworthy guest, namely,
EP : 07 :024(484) [0815] administration of only one **kind** of the sacrament to the
EP : 08 :009(487) [0819] or connection of such a **kind** that neither nature has
EP : 12 :002(498) [0839] they profess doctrines of a **kind** that cannot be tolerated
EP : 12 :005(498) [0839] which in fact is nothing else but a new **kind** of monkery.
SD : 01 :039(515) [0871] God's inexpressible **kindness** in that he does not
SD : 01 :060(519) [0879] inquires further, What **kind** of accident is original sin?
SD : 02 :050(530) [0901] end, in his boundless **kindness** and mercy, God provides
SD : 02 :071(535) [0909] God in his immeasurable **kindness** and mercy anticipates
SD : 02 :083(537) [0913] For conversion is that **kind** of change through the Holy
SD : 03 :032(545) [0927] works and leads the best **kind** of life, a person is pleasing
SD : 03 :039(546) [0929] nor under any **kind** of pretense, title, or name are they to
SD : 03 :064(550) [0937] 5. That faith is such a **kind** of trust in the obedience of
SD : 07 :017(572) [0977] Smalcald to consider what **kind** of doctrinal statement
SD : 07 :103(587) [1009] How will they establish that **kind** of speculation?
SD : 08 :034(597) [1027] nature" (II Pet. 1:4), what **kind** of participation in the
SD : 08 :035(597) [1027] are not all of the same **kind** and mode, and if one talks
SD : 08 :040(598) [1029] it will finally construct a **kind** of Christ after whom I
SD : 08 :062(603) [1037] natures are henceforth of the same **kind** or even identical.
SD : 08 :071(605) [1041] nature of Christ of such a **kind** that thereby the divine
SD : 12 :010(634) [1097] and self-chosen spirituality as on a **kind** of new monkery.
SD : 12 :027(635) [1101] as basically nothing else than a new **kind** of monkery.
SD : 12 :029(635) [1101] of Christ have but one **kind** of essence, property, will, and

Kindle (3), Kindled (5), Kindles (4), Kindling (1)
LC : 01 :100(378) [0609] you unawares and to **kindle** in your heart unbelief and
LC : 02 :023(413) [0683] will be warmed and **kindled** with gratitude to God and a
LC : 02 :042(416) [0689] by it he illumines and **kindles** hearts so that they grasp
LC : 03 :020(423) [0703] ought to awaken and **kindle** in our hearts a desire and
LC : 03 :027(424) [0705] but in order that you may **kindle** your heart to stronger
LC : 05 :054(453) [0765] our heart be warmed and **kindled**, and it will not grow
EP : 02 :018(472) [0791] action of divine grace in **kindling** new movements within
SD : 02 :014(523) [0885] know that God, who has **kindled** this beginning of true
SD : 02 :016(523) [0887] Spirit in Baptism, has **kindled** and wrought a beginning
SD : 02 :024(526) [0891] is active in him and **kindles** and creates faith and other
SD : 02 :054(531) [0903] of sins in Christ there is **kindled** in him a spark of faith
SD : 02 :071(535) [0909] our meditation upon it **kindles** faith and other
SD : 03 :041(546) [0929] First the Holy Spirit **kindles** faith in us in conversion

Kinds (61)
PR : PR :014(007) [0013] were found to contain all **kinds** of Christian, necessary,
PR : PR :026(014) [0025] in order that all **kinds** of scandal might be obviated.
AG : 22 :000(049) [0059] XXII. Both **Kinds** in the Sacrament
AG : 22 :001(049) [0059] Among us both **kinds** are given to laymen in the
AG : 22 :003(050) [0061] of the congregation in Corinth received both **kinds**.
AG : 28 :070(093) [0093] in one kind and prohibit administration in both **kinds**.
AL : 20 :002(041) [0053] manners of life and what **kinds** of work are pleasing to
AL : 22 :000(049) [0059] XXII. Both **Kinds**
AL : 22 :001(049) [0059] of the Lord's Supper both **kinds** are given to laymen
AL : 22 :003(050) [0061] it appears that a whole congregation used both **kinds**.
AL : 22 :011(050) [0061] preferred to use both **kinds** in the sacrament, they should
AL : 27 :016(073) [0077] put it far above all other **kinds** of life instituted by God.
AP : 02 :047(106) [0119] opinions and errors and incites it to all **kinds** of sins.
AP : 04 :004(108) [0121] that the sources of both **kinds** of doctrine, the opponents'
AP : 04 :233(140) [0185] seek after some other **kinds** of doctrine and other clergy.
AP : 04 :321(157) [0209] work does not distinguish between the two **kinds** of merit.
AP : 16 :007(223) [0331] Now the various **kinds** of public redress are court
AP : 22 :000(236) [0357] [Article XXII.] The Lord's Supper Under Both **Kinds**
AP : 22 :001(236) [0357] doubt that the use of both **kinds** in the Lord's Supper is
AP : 22 :001(236) [0357] For Christ instituted both **kinds**, and he did not do so
AP : 22 :003(236) [0357] the text clearly shows that this was the use of both **kinds**.
AP : 22 :006(237) [0359] to deny one part, and they refuse to grant both **kinds**.
AP : 22 :009(237) [0359] the reasons why both **kinds** are not given, Gabriel says
AP : 22 :016(238) [0361] of withholding both **kinds** in the sacrament and who even
AP : 24 :099(268) [0419] make us compile all **kinds** of abuses of the Mass, we shall
AP : 27 :041(276) [0435] There are two **kinds** of leaving.
AP : 28 :003(281) [0445] They admit all **kinds** of people to the priesthood quite
TR : 00 :075(332) [0525] And in what **kinds** of cases they have abused this power!
LC : 01 :026(368) [0587] — have received the command to do us all **kinds** of good.
LC : 01 :026(368) [0587] and he gives grain and all **kinds** of fruits from the earth
LC : 01 :058(372) [0597] of God for lies and all **kinds** of wickedness, just as there
LC : 01 :123(382) [0617] so that they sink into all **kinds** of trouble and misery.
LC : 01 :141(384) [0621] be said about the various **kinds** of obedience due to our
LC : 01 :148(385) [0623] you will have all **kinds** of trouble and misfortune.
LC : 01 :158(387) [0627] Thus we have three **kinds** of fathers presented in this
LC : 01 :202(392) [0639] mess and cesspool of all **kinds** of vice and lewdness
LC : 01 :234(397) [0647] beggar and will suffer all **kinds** of troubles and
LC : 01 :326(409) [0675] deceiving, and other **kinds** of corruption and wickedness,
LC : 02 :014(412) [0681] birds and fish, beasts, grain and all **kinds** of produce.
LC : 02 :028(414) [0685] had received from him all **kinds** of good things, the devil
LC : 02 :036(415) [0687] Many other **kinds** of spirits are mentioned in the
LC : 03 :018(422) [0703] pray, just as he punishes all other **kinds** of disobedience.
LC : 03 :072(430) [0719] provide for us our daily bread and all **kinds** of sustenance.
LC : 03 :076(431) [0721] this petition covers all **kinds** of relations on earth.
LC : 03 :078(431) [0721] to protect us from all **kinds** of harm to our body and our
LC : 03 :101(433) [0727] *Bekoerunge*) is of three **kinds**: of the flesh, the world, and
LC : 03 :102(434) [0727] — in short, into all **kinds** of evil lusts which by nature
LC : 05 :015(448) [0757] it is easy to answer all **kinds** of questions which now
LC : 05 :026(449) [0759] everywhere, trying all **kinds** of tricks, and does not stop
LC : 06 :002(457) [0000] the enumeration of all **kinds** of sin that no one was able
LC : 06 :008(458) [0000] here there are two other **kinds**, which have an even
LC : 06 :008(458) [0000] These two **kinds** are expressed in the Lord's Prayer when
EP : 07 :003(482) [0809] first of all, that there are two **kinds** of Sacramentarians.
SD : 01 :013(511) [0863] strikes them with other **kinds** of blindness, and drives
SD : 02 :029(527) [0893] He drives them into many **kinds** of manifest sin.
SD : 03 :042(547) [0931] that faith dead where all **kinds** of good works and the
SD : 07 :024(573) [0979] it is easy to answer all **kinds** of questions which now
SD : 07 :050(578) [0989] as circumcision, the many **kinds** of sacrifice in the Old
SD : 07 :085(584) [1001] and eliminate many **kinds** of idolatrous misuse and
SD : 07 :123(590) [1015] There are only two **kinds** of guests at this heavenly meal,
SD : 11 :010(618) [1067] me no harm if I live in all **kinds** of sin and vice without

King (28)
AG : 27 :026(075) [0079] as in the case of the **king** of Aragon and many others.
AL : 21 :001(047) [0057] out of his country, for like David the emperor is a **king**.
AL : 27 :026(075) [0079] known is the case of the **king** of Aragon, who was recalled
AP : 04 :261(145) [0195] only mean to say that the **king** should give alms, but he
AP : 04 :261(145) [0195] many things to the **king** about the one God of Israel and
AP : 04 :261(145) [0195] For there is the **king**'s excellent confession about the God
AP : 04 :261(145) [0195] other part Daniel promises the **king** forgiveness of sins.
AP : 04 :262(145) [0195] he could not have promised the **king** forgiveness of sins.
AP : 04 :262(145) [0195] defend the poor against injustice, as was the **king**'s duty.
AP : 21 :024(232) [0349] But if a **king** has appointed a certain intercessor, he does
AP : 23 :003(239) [0363] ancient prophecies call the **king** with the modest face, for
AP : 28 :014(283) [0447] a definite law, nor that of a **king** to act above the law.
S1 : PR :008(290) [0457] in our presence that his **king** had been persuaded beyond
S1 : PR :009(290) [0457] such big lies upon the **king** and foreign peoples as if they
S2 : 04 :002(298) [0471] as "most gracious lord," as if he were a **king** or emperor.
LC : 01 :045(370) [0593] Saul was a great **king**, chosen by God, and an upright
LC : 01 :046(370) [0593] inevitably he remained safe from Saul and became **king**.
LC : 01 :252(399) [0653] show to our neighbor, as **King** Solomon teaches in Prov.
LC : 01 :305(406) [0669] even in the Gospel that **King** Herod took his brother's
LC : 02 :027(414) [0685] this I had no Lord and **King** but was captive under the
LC : 03 :051(426) [0711] to himself and rule us as a **king** of righteousness, life, and
EP : 11 :003(494) [0833] he has made known to **King** Nebuchadnezzar what will be
EP : 12 :020(499) [0841] understanding of Christ as the reigning **king** of heaven.
SD : 08 :047(600) [1031] our mediator, redeemer, **king**, high priest, head,
SD : 08 :078(607) [1043] on earth as mediator, head, **king**, and high priest.
SD : 08 :087(608) [1047] indwelling of their head, **king**, and high priest, who has
SD : 11 :027(620) [1071] And the guests whom the **king** invites to his son's
SD : 12 :029(635) [1101] of Christ, the reigning **king** of heaven, who believes that

Kings (23)
AG : 00 :000(023) [0037] of thy testimonies before **kings**, and shall not be put to
AG : 28 :002(081) [0083] to set up and depose **kings** and emperors according to
AG : 28 :013(083) [0085] not set up and depose **kings**, should not annul temporal
AG : 28 :019(083) [0087] by Roman emperors and **kings** for the temporal
AL : 28 :019(083) [0087] human right granted by **kings** and emperors for the civil
AP : 07 :023(172) [0235] him the emperor and all **kings** have received their power
AP : 21 :018(231) [0347] Ps. 72:11, 15, "May all **kings** fall down before him!
AP : 21 :036(234) [0353] and dangers, helped **kings** in time of great danger, taught
AP : 21 :044(236) [0357] this when he honors **kings** with his own name and calls
AP : 24 :041(257) [0399] They wage war like the **kings** of the world, and they have
AP : 27 :059(279) [0441] are fancier than **kings**' palaces and who live most
TR : 00 :008(320) [0505] Accordingly he said, "The **kings** of the Gentiles exercise
TR : 00 :035(326) [0513] kingdoms, and harass the **kings** of almost all the nations
TR : 00 :036(326) [0515] but he even exalted himself tyrannically over all **kings**.
TR : 00 :039(327) [0515] the church and not of the **kings** of nations, and he calls
TR : 00 :050(329) [0519] nor by all the clergy, nor by **kings**, nor by the people."
TR : 00 :054(329) [0519] of the church, the **kings** and the princes, to have regard
TR : 00 :054(329) [0519] God expressly exhorts **kings**, "Now therefore, O kings, be
TR : 00 :054(329) [0519] kings, "Now therefore, O **kings**, be wise; be warned, O
TR : 00 :054(329) [0519] For the first care of **kings** should be to advance the glory
TR : 00 :056(329) [0521] incumbent on the **kings** to restrain the license of the
SC : 09 :005(355) [0561] be made for all men, for **kings** and all who are in high
LC : 03 :077(431) [0721] to endow the emperor, **kings**, and all estates of men, and

Kingdom (110), Kingdoms (8)
A G : 1 7 :005(039) [0051] will possess a worldly **kingdom** and annihilate all the
A G : 2 6 :024(067) [0073] in Rom. 14:17, "The **kingdom** of God does not mean food
A L : 1 7 :005(039) [0051] take possession of the **kingdom** of the world, the ungodly
A L : 2 6 :024(067) [0073] in Rom. 14:17, "The **kingdom** of God is not food and
A L : 2 8 :002(081) [0083] undertaken to transfer **kingdoms** of this world and take
A L : 2 8 :013(083) [0085] nor transfer the **kingdoms** of the world, nor abrogate the
A L : 2 8 :014(083) [0085] Christ says, "My **kingdom** is not of this world," and
A P : 0 4 :031(111) [0129] and the Spirit, one cannot enter the **kingdom** of God."
A P : 0 4 :198(134) [0175] righteousness' sake, for theirs is the **kingdom** of heaven."
A P : 0 4 :254(143) [0193] the poor in spirit, for theirs is the **kingdom** of heaven."
A P : 0 4 :366(163) [0221] "transferred into the **kingdom** of God's Son," as Paul says
A P : 0 7 :013(170) [0231] not understand that the **kingdom** of Christ is the
A P : 0 7 :016(170) [0231] Besides the church is the **kingdom** of Christ, the opposite
A P : 0 7 :016(170) [0231] of Christ, the opposite of the **kingdom** of the devil.
A P : 0 7 :016(171) [0231] members of the devil's **kingdom**, as Paul teaches in Eph.
A P : 0 7 :016(171) [0231] which is truly the **kingdom** of Christ, is, precisely
A P : 0 7 :017(171) [0231] which is truly the **kingdom** of Christ, is distinguished
A P : 0 7 :017(171) [0231] distinguished from the **kingdom** of the devil, it necessarily
A P : 0 7 :017(171) [0231] wicked belong to the **kingdom** of the devil, they are not
A P : 0 7 :017(171) [0233] because the **kingdom** of Christ has not yet been revealed,
A P : 0 7 :018(171) [0233] come does not make the wicked the **kingdom** of Christ.
A P : 0 7 :018(171) [0233] Spirit is always the same **kingdom** of Christ, whether it be
A P : 0 7 :019(171) [0233] means the sons of the **kingdom**, the weeds are the sons of
A P : 0 7 :019(171) [0233] when he says that the **kingdom** of God is like a net
A P : 0 7 :019(171) [0233] they are not the true **kingdom** of Christ and members of
A P : 0 7 :019(171) [0233] Christ, for they are members of the **kingdom** of the devil.
A P : 0 7 :022(172) [0235] they are not, properly speaking, the **kingdom** of Christ.
A P : 0 7 :023(172) [0235] whole world, of all the **kingdoms** of the world, and of all
A P : 0 7 :024(172) [0235] definition of the papal **kingdom** rather than of the church
A P : 0 7 :026(173) [0235] define the church as anything but such a papal **kingdom**.
A P : 0 7 :029(173) [0237] wicked belong to the **kingdom** and body of the devil, who
A P : 0 7 :036(175) [0241] in Rom. 14:17, "The **kingdom** of God does not mean food
A P : 0 7 :045(177) [0243] of faith and of the **kingdom** of God if they regard as
A P : 1 2 :055(189) [0267] that would destroy the **kingdom** of the devil, death, and
A P : 1 2 :176(210) [0307] It is of a spiritual **kingdom** that Christ is speaking.
A P : 1 5 :018(217) [0319] they are simply establishing the **kingdom** of Antichrist.
A P : 1 5 :018(217) [0319] The **kingdom** of Antichrist is a new kind of worship of
A P : 1 5 :018(217) [0319] Thus the **kingdom** of Mohammed has rites and works by
A P : 1 5 :018(217) [0319] will also be a part of the **kingdom** of Antichrist if it
A P : 1 5 :019(217) [0319] very form and constitution of the **kingdom** of Antichrist.
A P : 1 5 :043(221) [0327] distinction between the **kingdom** of Christ (or the
A P : 1 5 :043(221) [0327] Christ (or the spiritual **kingdom**) and political affairs,
A P : 1 6 :002(222) [0329] between Christ's **kingdom** and a political kingdom.
A P : 1 6 :002(222) [0331] between Christ's kingdom and a political **kingdom**.
A P : 1 6 :002(222) [0331] Christ's **kingdom** is spiritual; it is the knowledge of God
A P : 1 6 :004(223) [0331] Gospel and the spiritual **kingdom**; they are also
A P : 1 6 :007(223) [0331] dream of the messianic **kingdom**; instead, he would have
A P : 1 6 :007(223) [0331] teach that the spiritual **kingdom** does not change the civil
A P : 2 3 :021(242) [0369] for the sake of the **kingdom** of heaven" (Matt. 19:12), let
A P : 2 3 :025(243) [0371] of Antichrist's **kingdom** to despise women (11:37).
A P : 2 3 :040(245) [0375] "for the sake of the **kingdom** of heaven" (Matt. 19:12),
A P : 2 4 :041(257) [0399] religion they usurp the **kingdom** of the world, and they
A P : 2 4 :091(266) [0415] It is the **kingdom** of tyrants who transferred the blessed
A P : 2 4 :098(268) [0419] glory of his coming destroys the **kingdom** of Antichrist.
A P : 2 7 :027(273) [0429] Because the **kingdom** of God is righteousness
A P : 2 7 :027(274) [0429] of the Gospel and of the **kingdom** of Christ, which is
A P : 2 7 :046(277) [0435] Thus David was poor in a very rich **kingdom**.
A P : 2 8 :007(282) [0445] says (Rom. 14:17), "The **kingdom** of God is not food or
T R : 0 0 :002(320) [0503] that is, the authority to bestow and transfer **kingdoms**.
T R : 0 0 :008(321) [0505] dispute concerning the **kingdom**, Christ put a child in the
T R : 0 0 :016(322) [0509] It is evident that the **kingdom** of Christ is scattered over
T R : 0 0 :031(325) [0513] take possession of, or transfer the **kingdoms** of the world.
T R : 0 0 :031(325) [0513] or possess a worldly **kingdom**, for he said, "My kingship
T R : 0 0 :032(325) [0513] come after his spiritual **kingdom** was despised (that is,
T R : 0 0 :032(325) [0513] when another worldly **kingdom** would be set up on the
T R : 0 0 :033(325) [0513] divine right lord of the **kingdoms** of the world are false
T R : 0 0 :034(325) [0513] of faith and of a spiritual **kingdom** was extinguished.
T R : 0 0 :035(326) [0513] popes began to seize **kingdoms** for themselves, transfer
T R : 0 0 :035(326) [0513] for themselves, transfer **kingdoms**, and harass the kings
T R : 0 0 :036(326) [0515] the keys of a worldly **kingdom** by the authority of Christ
T R : 0 0 :037(326) [0515] obscure faith and the **kingdom** of Christ, they are under
T R : 0 0 :039(327) [0515] with those of the pope's **kingdom** and his followers.
T R : 0 0 :040(327) [0515] that he has set up this **kingdom** for himself on the pretext
T R : 0 0 :041(327) [0517] pope and his adherents as the **kingdom** of the Antichrist.
T R : 0 0 :042(328) [0517] The errors of the pope's **kingdom** are manifest, and the
T R : 0 0 :052(329) [0519] enormous errors of the pope's **kingdom** and his tyranny.
S C : P R :019(340) [0537] and lay waste both the **kingdom** of God and the kingdom
S C : P R :019(340) [0537] of God and the **kingdom** of the world and are the worst
S C : 0 2 :004(345) [0545] his, live under him in his **kingdom**, and serve him in
S C : 0 3 :006(346) [0547] *"Thy **kingdom** come."*
S C : 0 3 :007(346) [0547] Answer: To be sure, the **kingdom** of God comes of itself,
S C : 0 3 :011(347) [0547] the coming of his **kingdom**, and when he strengthens us
L C : S P :014(363) [0577] Thy **kingdom** come, thy will be done, on earth as it is in
L C : S P :014(363) [0577] For thine is the **kingdom** and the power and the glory,
L C : 0 3 :049(426) [0711] *"Thy **kingdom** come."*
L C : 0 3 :049(426) [0711] Here we ask that his **kingdom** may come.
L C : 0 3 :050(426) [0711] among us, so also his **kingdom** comes of itself without
L C : 0 3 :050(426) [0711] whom his name is hallowed and his **kingdom** flourishes.
L C : 0 3 :051(426) [0711] What is the **kingdom** of God?
L C : 0 3 :052(427) [0711] many may come into the **kingdom** of grace and become
L C : 0 3 :052(427) [0711] eternally in this **kingdom** which has now made its
L C : 0 3 :053(427) [0711] God's **kingdom** comes to us in two ways: first, it comes
L C : 0 3 :054(427) [0713] So we pray that thy **kingdom** may prevail among us
L C : 0 3 :054(427) [0713] Spirit, that the devil's **kingdom** may be overthrown and
L C : 0 3 :054(427) [0713] until finally the devil's **kingdom** shall be utterly destroyed
L C : 0 3 :058(428) [0713] unbelief and let the **kingdom** of God be the first thing for
L C : 0 3 :058(428) [0713] teaches, "Seek first the **kingdom** of God, and all these
L C : 0 3 :060(428) [0715] by us and that his **kingdom** may prevail among us.
L C : 0 3 :062(428) [0715] out of men's hearts and a breach is made in his **kingdom**.
L C : 0 3 :067(429) [0717] Word or prevent thy **kingdom** from coming; and grant
L C : 0 3 :068(429) [0717] be hallowed and his **kingdom** must come even without
L C : 0 3 :070(429) [0717] and frustrated, the **kingdom** of God could not abide on
L C : 0 3 :113(435) [0729] name or glory, God's **kingdom** and will, our daily bread,
L C : 0 3 :115(435) [0731] us under the devil's **kingdom**: poverty, shame, death,
L C : 0 3 :118(436) [0731] be hallowed in us, his **kingdom** come among us, and his
L C : 0 4 :025(439) [0739] and to enter into the **kingdom** of Christ and live with him
L C : 0 4 :067(445) [0749] when we enter Christ's **kingdom**, this corruption must
L C : 0 5 :082(456) [0773] in this wicked world, or under the **kingdom** of the devil.
S D : 0 1 :019(511) [0865] damnation and is in the **kingdom** and under the dominion
S D : 0 2 :010(522) [0885] know the secrets of the **kingdom** of God" (Matt. 13:13,
S D : 0 2 :041(529) [0897] question, "How does the **kingdom** of God come to us?" as
S D : 0 4 :032(556) [0947] that the unrighteous will not inherit the **kingdom** of God?
S D : 0 4 :032(556) [0947] adulterers will inherit the **kingdom** of God" (I Cor. 6:9).
S D : 0 4 :032(556) [0947] shall not inherit the **kingdom** of God" (Gal. 5:21;
S D : 0 5 :023(562) [0959] who should restore the **kingdom** of Israel and be a light to
S D : 1 0 :022(615) [1061] the pope and his adherents as the **kingdom** of Antichrist.
S D : 1 1 :034(622) [1075] give my Word, into my **kingdom**, but down in my heart I
S D : 1 1 :067(627) [1085] life when he says, "The **kingdom** of God is at hand;

Kingship (2)
A G : 2 8 :014(083) [0085] Christ himself said, "My **kingship** is not of this world,"
T R : 0 0 :031(325) [0513] for he said, "My **kingship** is not of this world"

Kirche (2)
L C : 0 2 :048(416) [0691] accustomed to the term ***Kirche***, "church," by which simple
L C : 0 2 :048(416) [0691] Thus the word "church" (***Kirche***) really means nothing else

Kirchner (1)
S 3 : 1 5 :005(318) [0501] the Rev. Master Sigismund **Kirchner**

Kiss (1)
S 2 : 0 4 :016(301) [0477] we ought not here **kiss** his feet or say, "You are my

Kiswetter (1)
S 3 : 1 5 :005(318) [0501] the Rev. Wolfgang **Kiswetter**

Knave (4), Knavery (2), Knaves (4)
S 1 : P R :003(289) [0455] I fully expect, for those **knaves** who shun the light and
S 2 : 0 2 :016(295) [0467] have introduced the **knavery** of appearing as spirits of the
S 2 : 0 2 :022(296) [0469] horses that even the devil has laughed at such **knavery**.
S C : P R :013(339) [0535] whether he is a believer or, at heart, a scoundrel or **knave**.
L C : 0 1 :154(386) [0625] So God punishes one **knave** by means of another.
L C : 0 1 :155(386) [0625] see that we ourselves are **knaves** who have roundly
L C : 0 1 :168(388) [0629] does not want to have **knaves** or tyrants in this office and
L C : 0 1 :232(396) [0647] Christians but chiefly to **knaves** and scoundrels, though it
L C : 0 1 :270(401) [0657] Besides, you act like a **knave**, for no man should be
L C : 0 5 :016(448) [0757] is: Even though a **knave** should receive or administer it, it

Knee (1), Kneel (1), Kneeling (2), Knees (2)
A G : 1 8 :007(040) [0053] evil, as when he wills to **kneel** before an idol, commit
S C : 0 7 :002(352) [0557] Then, **kneeling** or standing, say the Apostles' Creed and
S C : 0 7 :005(353) [0559] Then, **kneeling** or standing, say the Apostles' Creed and
L C : 0 1 :120(381) [0615] with fasting and pray on their **knees** without ceasing"?
L C : 0 1 :314(407) [0671] a layman remains on his **knees** a whole day in church,
L C : 0 5 :011(448) [0755] Majesty at whose feet every **knee** should bow and confess

Knights (2)
A P : 2 1 :032(233) [0351] Valentine heals epilepsy, and George protects **knights**.
A P : 2 1 :032(233) [0351] off fever, and Castor and Pollux protected **knights**.

Knit (1)
S D : 0 1 :035(514) [0869] me with skin and flesh, and **knit** me together with bones

Knot (1)
A P : 1 5 :034(220) [0325] not untie the Gordian **knot**, he solved it for good by

Know (240), Knowest (1), Knowing (11), Knowingly (1), Known (33), Knows (56), Knew (18)
P R : P R :004(004) [0007] Everybody also **knows** how the adversaries of divine truth
P R : P R :009(006) [0011] we nor our theologians **knew** which version was the true
P R : P R :010(006) [0011] hearts, so that they might **know** what attitude to take
P R : P R :018(008) [0015] that we ourselves do not **know** which is the genuine
P R : P R :022(011) [0019] order that everybody may **know** that he must guard
A G : 2 0 :015(043) [0055] is, when it is assured and **knows** that for Christ's sake it
A G : 2 0 :022(044) [0055] it in order that men may **know** that the grace of God is
A G : 2 0 :024(044) [0055] Whoever **knows** that in Christ he has a gracious God,
A G : 2 0 :024(044) [0055] has a gracious God, truly **knows** God, calls upon him,
A G : 2 2 :008(050) [0061] Nobody **knows** when or through whom this custom of
A G : 2 3 :005(052) [0061] of living in celibacy, and he certainly **knew** man's nature.
A G : 2 3 :006(052) [0061] It is well **known** what terrible torment and frightful
A G : 0 1 :003(056) [0065] to teach the people what they need to **know** about Christ.
A G : 2 4 :010(057) [0065] in many ways, as is well **known**, by turning it into a sort
A G : 2 4 :024(058) [0067] so that our people might **know** how the sacrament is to
A G : 2 4 :029(059) [0067] of this work, for it is well **known** that the Mass is used to
A G : 2 5 :004(062) [0069] and that we should **know** that through such faith we
A G : 2 5 :008(062) [0069] it is unable to perceive or **know** them all, and if we were
A G : 2 6 :004(064) [0071] great and precious and **know** that faith in Christ is to be
A G : 2 7 :010(072) [0077] a reputation, as is well **known**, that many monks with
A G : 2 7 :028(075) [0079] Yet it is commonly **known** to what an extent perpetual
A G : 2 8 :060(091) [0091] so that the people might **know** when they ought to
A G : 2 8 :060(091) [0093] liberty and might **know** that the keeping neither of the
A L : 2 0 :022(044) [0055] of consolation but **know** that grace and forgiveness of
A L : 2 0 :024(044) [0055] Whoever **knows** that he has a Father reconciled to him
A L : 2 0 :024(044) [0055] him through Christ truly **knows** God, knows that God
A L : 2 0 :024(044) [0055] Christ truly knows God, **knows** that God cares for him,
A L : 0 0 :001(047) [0059] far as the ancient church is **known** to us from its writers.
A L : 2 2 :004(050) [0061] It is not **known** when or by whom it was changed,
A L : 2 3 :018(054) [0063] of the church is well **known**, and although impure
A L : 2 4 :011(057) [0065] It is also well **known** how widely this abuse extends in all
A L : 2 6 :004(064) [0071] of Christ may be well **known** and that faith which
A L : 2 6 :017(066) [0073] Januarius that he should **know** that they are to be as
A L : 2 7 :015(073) [0077] and it is needless to rehearse what is well **known**.
A L : 2 7 :026(075) [0079] Well **known** is the case of the king of Aragon, who was
A L : 2 8 :021(084) [0087] whose wickedness is **known**, doing all this without human
A L : 2 8 :060(091) [0091] so that the people may **know** when they ought to
A L : 2 8 :060(091) [0093] liberty and would **know** that the keeping neither of the

Continued ▶

A P : 0 2 :025(103) [0111] They do not **know** what they are talking about when they
A P : 0 2 :033(104) [0113] is a necessity, nor can we **know** the magnitude of the
A P : 0 2 :035(105) [0115] Our opponents **know** what Luther meant by this
A P : 0 2 :037(105) [0115] Our opponents **know** that this is what Luther believes and
A P : 0 2 :039(105) [0115] 7:7), "I should not have **known** lust if the law had not
A P : 0 2 :050(106) [0119] and death; so we cannot **know** his blessings unless we
A P : 0 2 :051(107) [0119] We **know** that our doctrine is correct and in agreement
A P : 0 2 :051(107) [0119] frequently do not **know** what they are talking about.
A P : 0 4 :019(110) [0125] They do not **know** what they are talking about.
A P : 0 4 :019(110) [0125] How is one to **know** whether one has the merit of
A P : 0 4 :020(110) [0125] of idle men who do not **know** how the forgiveness of sins
A P : 0 4 :057(114) [0137] of sins, the patriarchs **knew** the promise of the Christ,
A P : 0 4 :057(114) [0137] price for our sins, they **knew** that our works could not
A P : 0 4 :060(115) [0137] is how God wants to be **known** and worshiped, that we
A P : 0 4 :079(117) [0143] the minor premise if we **know** how the forgiveness of sins
A P : 0 4 :097(121) [0149] Acts 13:38, 39, "Let it be **known** to you therefore,
A P : 0 4 :101(121) [0151] of Christ except to **know** Christ's blessings, the promises
A P : 0 4 :101(121) [0151] And to **know** these blessings is rightly and truly to believe
A P : 0 4 :128(125) [0157] heart love God while it **knows** that in his terrible wrath he
A P : 0 4 :139(126) [0161] We **know** that for Christ's sake we have a gracious God
A P : 0 4 :230(139) [0183] We **know** how repulsive this teaching is to the judgment
A P : 0 4 :239(141) [0187] of these fears because we **know** that for Christ's sake we
A P : 0 4 :242(141) [0187] common proverb says, "**Know**, but do not hate, the
A P : 0 4 :262(145) [0195] Daniel **knew** that the forgiveness of sins in the Christ was
A P : 0 4 :262(145) [0195] Word of God to learn to **know** God's will, namely, that
A P : 0 4 :270(147) [0197] It **knows** that now it is pleasing to God for the sake of
A P : 0 4 :302(154) [0205] They do not **know** what they are talking about; like the
A P : 0 4 :306(154) [0207] made him to be sin who **knew** no sin, so that in him we
A P : 0 4 :321(156) [0207] how will the conscience **know** when a work has been
A P : 0 4 :323(157) [0209] But the point is well **known** and has many clear
A P : 0 4 :363(162) [0219] This promise the saints must **know**.
A P : 0 4 :364(163) [0219] afflictions, they should **know** that it is the will of God to
A P : 0 4 :372(164) [0221] are mentioned, we must **know** that Christ, the mediator,
A P : 0 4 :381(165) [0223] in our love, which we **know** by experience is weak and
A P : 0 4 :381(165) [0223] they teach that we cannot **know** whether it is present.
A P : 0 4 :385(166) [0225] It is well **known** that every prayer closes with this phrase:
A P : 0 4 :389(166) [0225] We **know** that what we have said agrees with the
A P : 0 4 :390(166) [0225] of Christ, and everybody **knows** that most of them are
A P : 0 4 :399(168) [0227] which, as everyone **knows**, they have hitherto shown
A P : 0 4 :400(168) [0227] the church, therefore, we **know** that the church of Christ
A P : 0 4 :400(168) [0227] of him who is the truth and who **knows** his body best."
A P : 0 7 :009(170) [0229] that we may not despair but may **know** all this.
A P : 0 7 :019(171) [0233] and so that we may **know** that the Word and the
A P : 0 7 :040(176) [0241] justification but to let the people **know** when to assemble.
A P : 1 0 :002(179) [0247] We **know** that not only the Roman Church affirms the
A P : 1 0 :003(179) [0247] perhaps that we do not **know** the power of the mystical
A P : 1 0 :004(180) [0247] of the living Christ, **knowing** that "death no longer has
A P : 1 1 :002(180) [0249] It is well **known** that we have so explained and extolled
A P : 1 1 :007(181) [0251] throughout Europe **knows** how consciences have been
A P : 1 1 :009(181) [0251] Good pastors **know** how profitable it is to examine the
A P : 1 2 :048(188) [0265] the sentence by which we **know** that we have been
A P : 1 2 :072(192) [0271] Let pious consciences **know**, therefore, that God
A P : 1 2 :073(192) [0273] Let them **know** that this is what the saints in the church
A P : 1 2 :084(194) [0277] We **know** that what we have said is what Paul really and
A P : 1 2 :084(194) [0277] and truly means; we **know** that this position of ours
A P : 1 2 :088(195) [0277] quieted unless we **know** it is God's command and the
A P : 1 2 :106(197) [0283] Solomon (Prov. 27:23), "**Know** well the condition of your
A P : 1 2 :106(197) [0283] to their interpretation, "**know**" here means to hear
A P : 1 2 :112(198) [0285] be prescribed without **knowing** the character of the
A P : 1 2 :130(202) [0291] We **know** that it is true, godly, and beneficial to godly
A P : 1 3 :012(212) [0311] wholeheartedly, for we **know** that God approves this
A P : 1 3 :018(213) [0313] much more necessary to **know** how to use the
A P : 1 4 :001(214) [0315] We **know** that the Fathers had good and useful reasons
A P : 1 4 :003(214) [0315] this teaching, for we **know** that our confession is true,
A P : 1 4 :004(214) [0315] We **know** that the church is present among those who
A P : 1 5 :014(216) [0319] how will he **know** that these works please God since they
A P : 1 5 :019(218) [0319] whom his fathers did not **know** he shall honor with gold
A P : 1 5 :019(218) [0321] a god will be worshiped whom the fathers did not **know**.
A P : 1 5 :029(219) [0323] Let us **know** that they merit neither the forgiveness of
A P : 1 5 :030(219) [0323] Our opponents do not **know** what they are talking about.
A P : 1 5 :049(221) [0329] questions, and we **know** from actual experience that
A P : 1 6 :007(223) [0331] he would have them **know** their duty to teach that the
A P : 1 8 :009(226) [0337] because all men ought to **know** that God requires this
A P : 2 0 :005(227) [0339] proofs to anyone who **knows** that Christ was given to us
A P : 2 0 :008(227) [0341] to despair unless they **know** that they must believe in the
A P : 2 0 :010(228) [0341] works, when would we **know** that we had attained it,
A P : 2 1 :010(230) [0345] from faith, how do we **know** that God approves such
A P : 2 1 :010(230) [0345] How do we **know**, without proof from Scripture, that the
A P : 2 1 :031(233) [0351] We **know** that we must put our trust in the intercession
A P : 2 1 :031(233) [0351] We **know** that the merits of Christ are our only
A P : 2 1 :037(234) [0355] are clowns who **know** nothing about either faith or public
A P : 2 1 :044(236) [0357] glory of Christ, which we **know** you want to extol and
A P : 2 2 :008(237) [0359] Our opponents **know** this very well, but they throw sand
A P : 2 3 :005(239) [0365] They **know** good and well how few practice chastity, but
A P : 2 3 :043(245) [0375] same time good men will **know** how to use marriage
A P : 2 3 :043(245) [0375] Good men **know**, too, that Paul commands each one to
A P : 2 3 :043(245) [0375] They **know** that sometimes they must withdraw to have
A P : 2 3 :044(245) [0375] We all **know** the verse, "The boy who is used to being lazy
A P : 2 3 :050(246) [0377] religious reasons, for they **know** that chastity is not the
A P : 2 3 :059(247) [0379] We **know** we are laying ourselves open to the charge of
A P : 2 3 :059(247) [0379] to establish harmony, we **know** that to satisfy our
A P : 2 3 :065(248) [0381] Besides, the saints will **know** the value of moderation in
A P : 2 3 :067(248) [0383] the world still did not **know** the law of perpetual
A P : 2 4 :023(253) [0391] sins, so that men might **know** that God does not want our
A P : 2 4 :026(254) [0391] in which the spirit **knows** and takes hold of God, as it
A P : 2 4 :028(254) [0393] is the way I want you to **know** me when I show mercy and
A P : 2 4 :032(255) [0395] the Gospel, which makes **known** the name of Christ and
A P : 2 4 :094(267) [0417] We **know** that the ancients spoke of prayer for the dead.
A P : 2 7 :001(268) [0419] Those who **knew** him testify that he was a mild old man,
A P : 2 7 :004(269) [0421] Everyone **knows** how much hypocrisy, ambition, and
A P : 2 7 :029(274) [0431] Though everyone **knows** that monasticism is a recent
A P : 2 7 :041(276) [0435] kind of flight, since we **know** that the command of God
A P : 2 7 :067(280) [0441] of fact, the church did not yet **know** about these vows.
A P : 2 7 :069(281) [0443] And let every pious heart **know** and be sure that such
A P : 2 8 :017(283) [0449] We should **know** that they are not necessary acts of
S 1 : P R :001(288) [0455] Mantua, and it is not yet **known** where it will or can be
S 1 : P R :004(289) [0455] and listen, although they **know** very well that I teach
S 1 : P R :009(290) [0457] lord and judge of us all, **knows** very well that they lie and
S 2 : 0 2 :008(294) [0465] and he does not **know** what he is doing because he
S 3 : 0 2 :004(303) [0479] desires help but does not **know** where to find it, and
S 3 : 0 3 :005(304) [0481] in order that they might **know** how they stood before God
S 3 : 0 3 :010(304) [0481] repentance because they did not **know** what sin really is.
S 3 : 0 3 :016(305) [0483] Moreover, since nobody **knew** how much contrition he
S 3 : 0 3 :019(306) [0483] he could never **know** when he had made a sufficiently
S 3 : 0 3 :021(306) [0485] for nobody could **know** how much he was to do for one
S 3 : 0 3 :023(307) [0485] one would still not have **know** whether this was enough.
S 3 : 0 3 :027(307) [0487] Moreover, nobody **knew** which soul was in purgatory,
S 3 : 0 3 :027(307) [0487] in purgatory, and nobody **knew** which of those in
S 3 : 0 3 :032(308) [0487] of sins, for neither of you **knows** what sin really is, to say
S 3 : 0 3 :043(310) [0491] is therefore necessary to **know** and to teach that when
S 3 : 0 8 :003(312) [0495] and the spirit without **knowing** what they say or teach.
S 3 : 0 8 :008(313) [0495] unbelieving Jews, but he **knew** that he now had to be
S 3 : 1 2 :002(315) [0499] a seven-year-old child **knows** what the church is, namely,
S 3 : 1 3 :001(315) [0499] I do not **know** how I can change what I have heretofore
S 3 : 1 5 :003(316) [0501] I do not **know** how I can change or concede anything in
T R : 0 0 :052(329) [0519] They should **know**, in the first place, that these errors
T R : 0 0 :053(329) [0519] place, they should also **know** how great a crime it is to
T R : 0 0 :062(331) [0523] their number one who is **known** to be active and name
T R : 0 0 :082(334) [0527] who defraud the church **know** that God will require them
S C : P R :003(338) [0533] sacrament, they do not **know** the Lord's Prayer, the
S C : P R :013(339) [0535] that the people learn to **know** how to distinguish between
S C : P R :013(339) [0535] in a city is bound to **know** and observe the laws under
S C : 0 5 :029(351) [0555] A confessor will **know** additional passages of the
S C : 0 9 :010(356) [0563] Lord and not to men, **knowing** that whatever good
S C : 0 9 :011(356) [0563] and forbear threatening, **knowing** that he who is both
L C : P R :008(359) [0569] above all doctors, to **know** all there is to be known.
L C : P R :008(359) [0569] above all doctors, to know all there is to be **known**.
L C : P R :009(359) [0569] even though they think they **know** them ever so well.
L C : P R :014(360) [0571] He **knows** our danger and need.
L C : P R :014(360) [0571] He **knows** the constant and furious attacks and assaults
L C : P R :016(361) [0573] to teach it daily, for he **knows** of nothing better to teach,
L C : P R :016(361) [0573] All the saints **know** of nothing better or different to
L C : P R :016(361) [0573] or hearing it once, that we **know** it all and need not read
L C : P R :017(361) [0573] is certain: anyone who **knows** the Ten Commandments
L C : P R :017(361) [0573] Commandments perfectly **knows** the entire Scriptures.
L C : P R :018(361) [0573] Now, I **know** beyond a doubt that such lazy-bellies and
L C : P R :018(361) [0573] yet they pretend to **know** and despise the Catechism,
L C : P R :019(361) [0573] prematurely and to imagine that they **know** everything.
L C : P R :020(361) [0573] Catechism, the less they **know** of it and the more they
L C : S P :002(362) [0575] a craftsman who does not **know** the rules and practices of
L C : S P :004(362) [0575] of it, and if they do not **know** it, to keep them faithfully
L C : S P :005(362) [0575] were so ignorant that they **knew** nothing of these things —
L C : S P :005(362) [0575] to the sacrament ought to **know** more and have a fuller
L C : S P :017(363) [0577] if they do not **know** these things and are unwilling to
L C : S P :020(364) [0579] we ought also to **know** what to say about the sacraments
L C : S P :022(364) [0579] for an ordinary person to **know** this much about Baptism
L C : 0 1 :016(366) [0585] that the heart should **know** no other consolation or
L C : 0 1 :036(369) [0589] Before they **know** it they will be wrecked, along with all
L C : 0 1 :051(371) [0595] our lips when our heart **knows** or should know that the
L C : 0 1 :051(371) [0595] heart knows or should **know** that the facts are otherwise
L C : 0 1 :055(372) [0595] crass ones who are well **known** to everyone and who
L C : 0 1 :059(372) [0597] over our disgrace so that no one may see it or **know** it.
L C : 0 1 :063(373) [0597] addition, you must also **know** how to use the name of
L C : 0 1 :077(375) [0603] We want them to **know** that God is well pleased with the
L C : 0 1 :093(377) [0607] estates who do not **know** God's Word but seek holiness in
L C : 0 1 :099(378) [0609] of it and feel that they **know** it all and need no more
L C : 0 1 :100(378) [0609] Even though you **know** the Word perfectly and have
L C : 0 1 :112(380) [0613] good and holy works, I **know** of none better than to show
L C : 0 1 :115(381) [0613] Every child who **knows** and does this has, in the first
L C : 0 1 :115(381) [0615] pleasing to my God in heaven; this I **know** for certain."
L C : 0 1 :118(381) [0615] in his presence, "Now I **know** that this work is well
L C : 0 1 :125(382) [0617] For we **know** that it is highly pleasing to the divine
L C : 0 1 :129(383) [0617] The perversity of the world God **knows** very well.
L C : 0 1 :138(384) [0621] Again, as we **know** from experience, where there are fine
L C : 0 1 :140(384) [0621] words, and everyone thinks he already **knows** them well.
L C : 0 1 :143(385) [0623] do everything that they **know** is expected of them, not
L C : 0 1 :144(385) [0623] joyful consciences and **know** how to do truly golden
L C : 0 1 :151(386) [0625] honor where it is due, **knows** that he pleases God and
L C : 0 1 :151(386) [0625] resists authority, let him **know** that he shall have no favor
L C : 0 1 :174(388) [0629] Therefore let everybody **know** that it is his chief duty, on
L C : 0 1 :183(389) [0631] is that, as God well **knows**, the world is evil and this life
L C : 0 1 :190(391) [0635] save him although you **know** ways and means to do so,
L C : 0 1 :198(392) [0637] **Know**, however, that it is the works commanded by God's
L C : 0 1 :217(394) [0641] a love for married life and **know** that it is a blessed and
L C : 0 1 :226(395) [0645] high-handedly and never **know** enough ways to
L C : 0 1 :233(396) [0647] Let every one **know**, then, that it is his duty, at the risk of
L C : 0 1 :246(398) [0649] to learn a lesson, let him **know** that this is God's
L C : 0 1 :267(401) [0657] are not content just to **know** but rush ahead and judge.
L C : 0 1 :284(403) [0661] so that everyone may **know** how to guard against it.
L C : 0 1 :298(405) [0665] We **know** how to put up a fine front to conceal our
L C : 0 1 :305(406) [0667] They **knew** tricks like this: If a man took a fancy to
L C : 0 2 :001(411) [0679] from God; in brief, it teaches us to **know** him perfectly.
L C : 0 2 :002(411) [0679] the other so that we may **know** where and how to obtain
L C : 0 2 :010(412) [0679] or describe him in such a way as to make him **known**?"
L C : 0 2 :011(412) [0681] What do you **know** about him?" he could say, "First, my
L C : 0 2 :026(413) [0685] Here we learn to **know** the second person of the
L C : 0 2 :038(415) [0689] you nor I could ever **know** anything of Christ, or believe
L C : 0 2 :038(415) [0689] hidden and no one **knew** of it, it would have been all in
L C : 0 2 :052(417) [0691] entirely of the devil, **knowing** nothing of God and of
L C : 0 2 :065(419) [0695] But neither could we **know** anything of Christ, had it not
L C : 0 2 :066(419) [0697] God, nevertheless do not **know** what his attitude is
L C : 0 3 :003(420) [0697] That we may **know** what and how to pray, our Lord
L C : 0 3 :005(420) [0699] The first thing to **know** is this: It is our duty to pray
L C : 0 3 :006(421) [0699] Who **knows** whether God heeds my prayer or cares to
L C : 0 3 :023(423) [0703] "I have prayed, but who **knows** whether it pleased him, or
L C : 0 3 :028(424) [0705] and promise, **knowing** that he will not have them

Continued ▶

L C : 0 3 :030(424) [0705] This we must **know**, that all our safety and protection
L C : 0 3 :120(436) [0731] as a matter of chance but **knows** that God does not lie
L C : 0 4 :002(436) [0733] ourselves to that which is necessary for us to **know**.
L C : 0 4 :016(438) [0735] Who does not **know** that water is water, if such a
L C : 0 4 :023(439) [0737] place, since we now **know** what Baptism is and how it is
L C : 0 4 :025(439) [0737] To be saved, we **know**, is nothing else than to be delivered
L C : 0 4 :028(440) [0739] Our **know**-it-alls, the new spirits, assert that faith alone
L C : 0 4 :038(441) [0741] three things that must be **known** about this sacrament,
L C : 0 4 :049(442) [0745] the Scriptures and to **know** Christ, which is impossible
L C : 0 4 :056(444) [0747] This I **know**, however, that he has commanded me to go,
L C : 0 4 :057(444) [0747] Because we **know** that God does not lie.
L C : 0 4 :064(444) [0749] Finally, we must **know** what Baptism signifies and why
L C : 0 5 :002(447) [0753] it to those who do not **know** what they seek or why they
L C : 0 5 :012(448) [0755] Still I **know** that all the spirits and scholars put together
L C : 0 5 :020(449) [0757] is most necessary that we **know** what we should seek and
L C : 0 5 :028(449) [0759] Yet they **know** that we do not claim this of bread and
L C : 0 5 :030(450) [0759] the Word, otherwise we could never **know** of it or seek it.
L C : 0 5 :031(450) [0759] How should we **know** that this has been accomplished
L C : 0 5 :031(450) [0759] Whence do they **know** of forgiveness, and how can they
L C : 0 5 :044(451) [0763] For we **know** from experience that the devil always sets
L C : 0 5 :075(455) [0771] that they cannot feel it, I **know** no better advice than to
L C : 0 5 :076(455) [0771] not lie to you, and they **know** your flesh better than you
L C : 0 5 :076(455) [0771] in Rom. 7:18, "For I **know** that nothing good dwells
L C : 0 5 :079(455) [0771] If you do not **know**, ask your neighbors about it.
L C : 0 5 :087(456) [0773] have taught to his children the things they ought to **know**.
L C : 0 6 :004(457) [0000] have the advantage of **knowing** how to use confession
L C : 0 6 :005(457) [0000] Everyone **knows** this now.
L C : 0 6 :019(459) [0000] If you are a Christian, I **know** this well enough anyway; if
L C : 0 6 :019(459) [0000] well enough anyway; if you are not, I **know** it still better.
L C : 0 6 :027(460) [0000] However, they ought to **know** that we do not regard them
E P : R N :005(465) [0777] and which a Christian must **know** for his salvation.
E P : 0 5 :009(479) [0803] for them, so they now **know** for the first time what great
E P : 0 6 :006(481) [0807] spontaneously as if they **knew** of no command, threat, or
E P : 0 7 :014(483) [0811] is that God has and **knows** various modes of being at a
E P : 0 8 :016(489) [0821] God, but also as man, he **knows** all things, can do all
E P : 0 8 :016(489) [0821] he can do everything, and he **knows** everything.
E P : 0 8 :036(491) [0825] much he is supposed to **know**, and that he does not know
E P : 0 8 :036(491) [0825] and that he does not **know** more than is fitting and
E P : 0 8 :038(491) [0825] spirit Christ cannot **know** what has existed from eternity,
E P : 0 9 :004(492) [0827] It is enough to **know** that Christ went to hell, destroyed
E P : 1 1 :003(494) [0833] else than that God **knows** all things before they happen,
E P : 1 1 :003(494) [0833] and he has made **known** to King Nebuchadnezzar what
E P : 1 1 :013(496) [0835] gives us, namely, that we **know** that we have been elected
S D : P R :007(502) [0849] writings, though they **knew** that these titanic errors and
S D : P R :008(502) [0849] while others will not **know** which of the contending
S D : P R :010(503) [0849] about the truth may **know** how to guard and protect
S D : P R :002(503) [0851] to those public and well-**known** symbols or common
S D : P R :008(505) [0853] must as Christians **know** the difference between true and
S D : 0 1 :008(510) [0861] Thirdly, reason does not **know** and understand the true
S D : 0 1 :036(514) [0869] Thou **knowest** me right well; my frame was not hidden
S D : 0 2 :008(521) [0883] philosophy, but we also **know** that "the wisdom of this
S D : 0 2 :010(522) [0883] of God, the world did not **know** God through its wisdom,
S D : 0 2 :010(522) [0885] you it has been given to **know** the secrets of the kingdom
S D : 0 2 :010(522) [0885] blind world which neither **knows** nor regards God) and
S D : 0 2 :014(523) [0885] They **know** that God, who has kindled this beginning of
S D : 0 2 :017(524) [0887] "We **know** that the law is spiritual; but I am carnal, sold
S D : 0 2 :017(524) [0887] St. Paul says, "I **know** that nothing good dwells within
S D : 0 2 :021(525) [0889] carnal security — even **knowingly** and willingly — and
S D : 0 2 :026(526) [0891] "No one **knows** the Father except the Son and any one to
S D : 0 2 :051(531) [0901] of God, the world did not **know** God through wisdom, it
S D : 0 2 :054(531) [0903] of the law man learns to **know** his sins and the wrath of
S D : 0 2 :070(535) [0909] so that the heart learns to **know** sin, to fear the wrath of
S D : 0 2 :089(538) [0915] into it, for these do not **know** anything about what is
S D : 0 3 :011(541) [0919] we rightly learn to **know** Christ as our redeemer in the
S D : 0 4 :011(553) [0941] and good works without **knowing** what either faith or
S D : 0 4 :032(556) [0947] "Do you not **know** that the unrighteous will not inherit
S D : 0 5 :010(560) [0955] there he really learns to **know** his sin, an insight that
S D : 0 5 :012(560) [0955] those who as yet neither **know** their sins nor are terrified
S D : 0 5 :022(562) [0959] "was made sin though he **knew** no sin, so that in him we
S D : 0 6 :008(565) [0965] this the apostle writes, "I **know** that nothing good dwells
S D : 0 7 :011(571) [0975] And we **know** that not only the Roman but also the
S D : 0 7 :022(573) [0979] I **know** that all the enthusiasts and scholars put together
S D : 0 7 :031(574) [0983] I **know** what I am saying, and I well realize what this will
S D : 0 7 :031(574) [0983] of God I have learned to **know** a great deal about Satan.
S D : 0 7 :043(576) [0987] He **knows** very well what and how he must speak, and he
S D : 0 7 :046(577) [0989] and wisdom, **knowing** that God had many more ways and
S D : 0 7 :097(586) [1005] is that God has and **knows** various ways to be present at a
S D : 0 7 :102(587) [1007] We **know** indeed that he is in God beyond all creatures
S D : 0 7 :102(587) [1007] this happens, we do not **know**; it transcends nature and
S D : 0 7 :102(587) [1007] of all the angels in heaven, and is **known** only to God.
S D : 0 7 :102(587) [1007] lie to his words until we **know** how to prove certainly
S D : 0 7 :103(587) [1007] that God may have and **know** more modes whereby
S D : 0 8 :009(593) [1019] present, and to **know** everything are essential properties
S D : 0 8 :043(599) [1029] to the other nature, all of which scholars **know** right well.
S D : 0 8 :044(599) [1029] "We Christians must **know** that unless God is in the
S D : 0 8 :053(601) [1033] to realize that no one can **know** better and more
S D : 0 8 :053(601) [1033] us as much as we need to **know** in this life, and wherever
S D : 0 8 :070(605) [1041] likewise, when Jesus **knew** that "the Father had given all
S D : 0 8 :073(605) [1041] as a man he therefore **knows** and can do only certain
S D : 0 8 :073(605) [1041] way in which other saints **know** and can do things
S D : 0 8 :074(606) [1043] The result is not that he **knows** only certain things and
S D : 0 8 :074(606) [1043] things and does not **know** certain other things, or that he
S D : 0 8 :074(606) [1043] other things, but that he **knows** and can do everything.
S D : 0 8 :075(606) [1043] Father's Word, indeed **knows** all things, but that
S D : 1 0 :019(614) [1059] a seven-year-old child **knows** what the church is, namely,
S D : 1 0 :031(616) [1063] according to the well-**known** axiom, "Disagreement in
S D : 1 1 :001(616) [1063] so that all men may **know** what we teach, believe, and
S D : 1 1 :004(616) [1063] fact that God sees and **knows** everything before it
S D : 1 1 :004(616) [1063] He sees and **knows** in advance all that is or shall be, all
S D : 1 1 :004(617) [1065] And again, "I **know** your sitting down and your going
S D : 1 1 :006(617) [1065] (*praescientia*) sees and **knows** in advance the evil as well,
S D : 1 1 :006(617) [1065] To be sure, he sees and **knows** beforehand whatever the
S D : 1 1 :025(620) [1071] how can and should one **know**, and wherefrom and
S D : 1 1 :026(620) [1071] has revealed and "made **known** to us the mystery of his
S D : 1 1 :029(621) [1073] as a deception, but should **know** certainly that God
S D : 1 1 :030(621) [1073] hear my voice, and I **know** them, and they follow me; and
S D : 1 1 :031(621) [1073] and when they "do not **know** how to pray as we ought,"
S D : 1 1 :033(621) [1073] Gospel so that you learn to **know** your sins and his grace.
S D : 1 1 :054(625) [1081] and that he still **knows**, who of those who are called will
S D : 1 1 :055(625) [1081] God is also aware and **knows** exactly how many there
S D : 1 1 :056(625) [1081] Without doubt God also **knows** and has determined for
S D : 1 1 :064(626) [1083] For who has **known** the mind of the Lord?" — that is,
S D : 1 1 :072(628) [1087] If you then, who are evil, **know** how to give good gifts to
S D : 1 1 :079(629) [1089] in order to make **known** the riches of his glory in the
S D : 1 1 :090(631) [1093] abiding comfort of **knowing** that their salvation does not
S D : 1 2 :003(633) [1095] they themselves no longer **know** what the Augsburg

Knowledge (96)
P R : P R :004(003) [0007] is a matter of common **knowledge**, patent and
A G : 2 0 :025(044) [0057] do not mean by it such **knowledge** as the devil and
A G : 2 0 :025(045) [0057] faith is not merely a **knowledge** of historical events but is
A G : 2 0 :026(045) [0057] and not merely such a **knowledge** of historical events as
A G : 2 6 :016(066) [0073] hindered from coming to a right **knowledge** of Christ.
A G : 2 8 :017(083) [0085] and every proud obstacle to the **knowledge** of God."
A L : 1 2 :004(034) [0049] the conscience with a **knowledge** of sin, and the other is
A L : 2 0 :023(044) [0055] does not signify mere **knowledge** of the history (such as is
A L : 2 0 :026(045) [0057] be understood not as **knowledge**, such as is in the
A P : 0 2 :017(102) [0109] gifts as well: a surer **knowledge** of God, fear of God, trust
A P : 0 2 :018(103) [0111] received gifts like the **knowledge** of God, fear of God, and
A P : 0 2 :020(103) [0111] image of God is the **knowledge** of God, righteousness,
A P : 0 2 :023(103) [0111] also denies that he has **knowledge** of God, trust in God,
A P : 0 2 :023(103) [0111] are naming these gifts **knowledge** of God, fear of God,
A P : 0 2 :044(106) [0117] and obscuring the **knowledge** of the grace of Christ.
A P : 0 4 :017(109) [0125] opponents require a **knowledge** of the history about
A P : 0 4 :046(113) [0133] This faith is the true **knowledge** of Christ, it uses his
A P : 0 4 :048(113) [0135] faith is only historical **knowledge** and teach that it can
A P : 0 4 :048(114) [0135] is no mere historical **knowledge**, but the firm acceptance
A P : 0 4 :048(114) [0135] that it is merely **knowledge**, we add that to have faith
A P : 0 4 :050(114) [0135] simply mean historical **knowledge** but is a firm
A P : 0 4 :061(115) [0137] of an idle historical **knowledge**, we must tell how faith
A P : 0 4 :099(121) [0151] speak is not idle **knowledge**, but a thing that receives the
A P : 0 4 :101(121) [0151] Isa. 53:11, "By his **knowledge** he shall justify many."
A P : 0 4 :101(121) [0151] But what is the **knowledge** of Christ except to know
A P : 0 4 :115(123) [0155] This faith is no idle **knowledge**, nor can it exist with
A P : 0 4 :191(133) [0175] the devil, that the **knowledge** of God might not perish
A P : 0 4 :204(135) [0177] people never attain the **knowledge** of God, for in their
A P : 0 4 :227(139) [0183] faith is not merely **knowledge** but rather a desire to
A P : 0 4 :249(142) [0191] not talking about idle **knowledge**, such as even the
A P : 0 4 :304(154) [0205] so faith is not merely **knowledge** in the intellect but also
A P : 0 4 :337(159) [0215] If it meant the **knowledge** of history that the wicked and
A P : 0 4 :337(159) [0215] are not talking about a **knowledge** of history, however,
A P : 0 4 :351(161) [0217] increase, such as **knowledge** and fear of God, love of
A P : 0 4 :351(161) [0217] II Cor. 3:18), "in **knowledge**," and "beholding the
A P : 0 4 :351(161) [0217] is, we acquire the true **knowledge** of God, enabling us
A P : 0 4 :383(165) [0225] faith as merely a **knowledge** of history or of dogmas, not
A P : 0 4 :392(167) [0225] Therefore the **knowledge** of Christ has remained with
A P : 0 4 :398(168) [0227] can they ascribe any **knowledge** of Christ to those who
A P : 0 7 :020(171) [0233] that is, the true **knowledge** of Christ and faith.
A P : 0 7 :022(172) [0235] in whom there is true **knowledge** and the confession of
A P : 1 2 :003(182) [0253] of the Gospel, the true **knowledge** of Christ, and the true
A P : 1 2 :141(204) [0295] church to suppress the **knowledge** of law and Gospel,
A P : 1 6 :002(222) [0331] is spiritual; it is the **knowledge** of God in the heart, the
A P : 1 8 :007(225) [0337] true faith in God, true **knowledge** and trust that God
A P : 2 1 :011(230) [0345] morning and evening **knowledge**, perhaps because they
A P : 2 1 :034(233) [0351] said earlier, our whole **knowledge** of Christ disappears if
A P : 2 3 :046(246) [0377] It surpasses the **knowledge** of Christ by making men
A P : 2 4 :012(251) [0387] our hearts with the **knowledge** of Christ; for his sake we
A P : 2 4 :085(264) [0413] except perhaps to show off their **knowledge** of Hebrew?
S 2 : 0 2 :025(297) [0469] first, chief article and undermines **knowledge** of Christ.
S 3 : 0 2 :004(303) [0479] not have believed before without a **knowledge** of the law.
S 3 : 0 3 :018(306) [0483] powers without faith and without **knowledge** of Christ.
T R : 0 0 :034(325) [0513] **Knowledge** of faith and of a spiritual kingdom was
S C : P R :002(338) [0533] the country, have no **knowledge** whatever of Christian
S C : 0 5 :018(350) [0553] sins of which we have **knowledge** and which trouble us.
S C : 0 5 :025(350) [0555] If you have **knowledge** of no sin at all (which is quite
L C : P R :009(359) [0569] Even if their **knowledge** of Catechism were perfect
L C : S P :002(362) [0575] the minimum of **knowledge** required of a Christian.
L C : S P :025(364) [0579] subjects, to supplement and confirm their **knowledge**.
L C : 0 1 :096(378) [0609] again with as little **knowledge** of the Word at the end of
L C : 0 1 :174(388) [0629] children in the fear and **knowledge** of God, and if they
L C : 0 1 :187(390) [0633] of us, and it is common **knowledge** that no one willingly
L C : 0 1 :208(393) [0639] the world, promote **knowledge** of God, godly living, and
L C : 0 1 :266(401) [0657] between judging sin and having **knowledge** of sin.
L C : 0 1 :266(401) [0657] **Knowledge** of sin does not entail the right to judge it.
L C : 0 1 :269(401) [0657] even though, to your certain **knowledge**, he is guilty.
L C : 0 1 :270(401) [0657] Keep your **knowledge** to yourself and do not give it out to
L C : 0 2 :024(413) [0683] This is an excellent **knowledge**, but an even greater
L C : 0 2 :069(420) [0697] Through this **knowledge** we come to love and delight in
L C : 0 3 :092(433) [0725] only come from the **knowledge** that our sins are forgiven.
L C : 0 6 :035(461) [0000] we have attained to this blessed **knowledge** of confession.
E P : 0 3 :006(473) [0793] this faith is not a mere **knowledge** of the stories about
E P : 0 6 :001(479) [0805] (2) to lead men to a **knowledge** of their sin, (3) after they
E P : 0 8 :037(491) [0825] as yet have a perfect **knowledge** of God and all his works,
E P : 0 8 :037(491) [0825] "all the treasures of wisdom and **knowledge**" (Col. 2:3).
E P : 1 2 :022(499) [0841] in them the saving **knowledge** of Christ, conversion,
S D : 0 2 :009(521) [0883] has a dim spark of the **knowledge** that there is a God, as
S D : 0 2 :016(523) [0887] a beginning of true **knowledge** of God and faith, we
S D : 0 2 :050(531) [0901] true repentance and **knowledge** of their sins and true faith
S D : 0 4 :012(553) [0941] such confidence and **knowledge** of divine grace makes us
S D : 0 5 :009(559) [0953] This **knowledge** comes from the law, but it is not
S D : 0 5 :017(561) [0957] sin and to lead to a **knowledge** of sin" (Rom. 3:20; 7:7).
S D : 0 5 :022(562) [0959] difference between the **knowledge** of God which comes
S D : 0 5 :022(562) [0959] had to some extent a **knowledge** of God, although they
S D : 0 5 :024(562) [0961] and bring them to a **knowledge** of their sin and to
S D : 0 6 :001(563) [0963] to bring people to a **knowledge** of their sin through the
S D : 0 8 :068(604) [1039] of wisdom and **knowledge**, and to them all authority in

Continued ▶

SD : 0 8 :072(605) [1041] counsel and might and **knowledge**" (Isa. 11:2; 61:1) does
SD : 0 8 :074(606) [1043] really and truly has received all **knowledge** and all power.
SD : 1 1 :052(625) [1081] kept reserved solely to his own wisdom and **knowledge**.
SD : 1 1 :064(626) [1083] depth of the riches and wisdom and **knowledge** of God!
SD : 1 1 :083(630) [1091] should come to the **knowledge** of the truth and be saved.
SD : 1 1 :089(631) [1093] to repentance, to a **knowledge** of their sins, and to faith in
SD : 1 2 :029(635) [1101] that no one has a true **knowledge** of Christ, the reigning
SD : 1 2 :030(635) [1101] teaches men the saving **knowledge** of Christ, conversion,

Koerner (2)
EP : 1 2 :031(501) [0843] Dr. Christopher **Koerner** subscribed
SD : 1 2 :040(636) [1103] Dr. Christopher **Koerner**, subscribed

Koethen (1)
S 3 : 1 5 :005(317) [0501] pastor of the church in **Koethen**, subscribe

Kyria (1)
LC : 0 2 :048(416) [0691] In that language the word is ***kyria***, and in Latin *curia*.

Labor (23), Laborer (2), Laborers (5), Laboring (1), Laborious (1), Labors (6)
AG : 1 8 :005(040) [0051] nature: whether or not to **labor** in the fields, whether or
AG : 2 6 :010(065) [0071] that a husband should **labor** to support his wife and
AL : 1 8 :005(040) [0051] nature, that is, to will to **labor** in the field, will to eat and
AL : 2 6 :033(069) [0075] or bodily exercises and **labors**, that neither plenty nor
AP : 0 4 :106(122) [0153] grace is hidden; **laboring** under this fear, the soul by faith
AP : 0 4 :190(133) [0175] The dangers, **labors**, and sermons of the apostle Paul,
AP : 0 4 :191(133) [0175] David's **labors** in waging war and in governing the state
AP : 0 4 :194(133) [0175] "Each shall receive his wages according to his **labor**."
AP : 0 4 :194(133) [0175] there will be different rewards for different **labors**.
AP : 0 4 :366(163) [0221] "Each shall receive his wages according to his **labor**."
AP : 1 2 :006(183) [0255] Here they **labor** still more and wickedly minimize the
AP : 1 2 :044(187) [0263] "Come to me, all who **labor** and are heavy-laden, and I
AP : 1 2 :044(187) [0263] **Labor** and being heavy-laden mean contrition, anxiety,
AP : 2 1 :018(231) [0347] "Come to me, all who **labor**," which is certainly addressed
AP : 2 1 :029(233) [0351] his wages according to his **labor**"; that is, they cannot
AP : 2 3 :018(242) [0369] and to subdue their bodies with **labors** and fasting.
S 1 : P R :004(289) [0457] in the garments of my **labor** and thus mislead the poor
S 1 : P R :012(290) [0459] subjects, domestics, and **laborers**, extortion in every trade
SC : P R :007(339) [0533] In this way all the time and **labor** will be lost.
SC : P R :018(340) [0537] when instructing **laborers** and shopkeepers, and even
SC : P R :027(341) [0539] us to greater burdens and **labors**, dangers and
SC : P R :027(341) [0539] Christ himself will be our reward if we **labor** faithfully.
SC : 0 9 :003(354) [0561] they provide, for the **laborer** deserves his wages"
SC : 0 9 :003(354) [0561] especially those who **labor** in preaching and teaching; for
SC : 0 9 :003(354) [0561] out the grain,' and 'The **laborer** deserves his wages'"
SC : 0 9 :003(354) [0561] to respect those who **labor** among you and who are over
SC : 0 9 :010(356) [0563] **Laborers** and Servants, Male and Female
LC : 0 1 :079(375) [0603] rest, that is, to cease from **labor**; hence our common
LC : 0 1 :080(375) [0603] be refreshed and not be exhausted by constant **labor**.
LC : 0 1 :081(376) [0603] be fulfilled by refraining from manual **labor** of any kind.
LC : 0 1 :116(381) [0615] of their many great, **laborious**, and difficult works; we
LC : 0 1 :224(395) [0643] is transacted and money is exchanged for goods or **labor**.
LC : 0 1 :226(395) [0645] workmen, and day-**laborers** who act high-handedly and
LC : 0 1 :237(397) [0647] be with artisans and day-**laborers**, from whom we are
LC : 0 3 :084(431) [0723] business, trading, and **labor** on the part of those who
LC : 0 5 :066(454) [0769] "Come to me, all who **labor** and are heavy-laden, and I
LC : 0 5 :071(455) [0769] sick," that is, those who **labor** and are heavy-laden with
SD : 0 7 :070(582) [0997] "Come unto me, all who **labor** and are heavy laden, and I

Labyrinthine (1), Labyrinths (2)
AP : 1 1 :007(181) [0251] What **labyrinths**!
AP : 1 2 :028(185) [0259] consciences from these **labyrinths** of the scholastics, we
AP : 2 1 :041(235) [0355] human minds from the **labyrinthine** confusions and

Lack (19), Lacked (1), Lacking (14), Lacks (1)
AG : 0 0 :007(096) [0095] should consider that it is **lacking** in some respect, we are
AL : 2 3 :017(054) [0063] churches will soon be **lacking** in pastors if marriage
AL : 0 0 :017(096) [0095] anything is found to be **lacking** in this confession, we are
AP : 0 2 :001(100) [0105] of the Confutation are **lacking** not only in judgment but
AP : 0 2 :008(101) [0107] God, despising him, **lacking** fear and trust in him, hating
AP : 0 2 :014(102) [0109] of God, contempt of God, **lack** of the fear of God and of
AP : 0 2 :015(102) [0109] thing, "Original sin is the **lack** of original righteousness."
AP : 0 2 :023(103) [0111] Thus when the ancient definition says that sin is **lack** of
AP : 0 2 :026(103) [0111] expressed both elements: **lack** of ability to trust, fear, or
AP : 0 2 :028(104) [0113] to answer that it is the **lack** of proper righteousness.
AP : 0 2 :031(104) [0113] of God and faith are **lacking**, this is not merely actual
AP : 0 2 :033(104) [0113] that of itself the heart is **lacking** in love, fear, and trust in
AP : 0 2 :051(107) [0119] controversy, we shall not **lack** men to reply in defense of
AP : 0 4 :032(111) [0129] glory of God," that is, they **lack** the wisdom and
AP : 1 2 :036(186) [0261] did not avail because it **lacked** the faith that grasps the
AP : 1 2 :073(192) [0273] same thing; nor are testimonies of the Fathers **lacking**.
AP : 2 3 :059(247) [0379] God, we do not regret our **lack** of an alliance with such
S 3 : 0 3 :021(306) [0485] penance that was still **lacking** man was referred to
SC : P R :006(338) [0533] Let those who **lack** the qualifications to do better at least
LC : 0 1 :004(365) [0581] "Whatever good thing you **lack**, look to me for it and seek
LC : 0 1 :010(366) [0583] despondent when they **lack** them or are deprived of them.
LC : 0 1 :253(399) [0653] for your needs and will let you **lack** or want for nothing.
LC : 0 2 :044(416) [0689] What was **lacking** here?
LC : 0 3 :057(428) [0713] blessings, despise them or **lack** confidence that we shall
LC : 0 4 :040(441) [0743] is not the treasure that is **lacking**; rather, what is lacking
LC : 0 4 :040(441) [0743] lacking; rather, what is **lacking** is that it should be
LC : 0 4 :053(443) [0745] the water, Baptism is valid, even though faith be **lacking**.
LC : 0 4 :073(445) [0751] it; but where faith is **lacking**, it remains a mere unfruitful
LC : 0 5 :079(455) [0771] do not think that there will be any **lack** of sins and needs.
SD : 0 1 :002(508) [0859] in the sense that man **lacks** the righteousness in which he
SD : 0 1 :010(510) [0863] original sin is the complete **lack** or absence of the original
SD : 0 1 :011(510) [0863] nature is not only a total **lack** of good in spiritual, divine
SD : 0 1 :019(511) [0865] that the above-mentioned **lack** and damage allegedly are
SD : 0 1 :027(513) [0867] This deprivation and **lack**, this corruption and wounding
SD : 0 1 :027(513) [0867] now inherit a nature with the same **lack** and corruption.

Laden (10)
AP : 1 2 :044(187) [0263] who labor and are heavy-**laden**, and I will give you rest."
AP : 1 2 :044(187) [0263] Labor and being heavy-**laden** mean contrition, anxiety,
LC : 0 5 :066(454) [0769] who labor and are heavy-**laden**, and I will refresh you."
LC : 0 5 :071(455) [0769] who labor and are heavy-**laden** with sin, fear of death,
LC : 0 5 :072(455) [0769] If you are heavy-**laden** and feel your weakness, go joyfully
SD : 0 7 :070(582) [0997] who labor and are heavy **laden**, and I will give you rest"
SD : 1 1 :028(620) [1071] me, all who are heavy-**laden**, and I will give you rest"
SD : 1 1 :065(627) [1085] to me, all who are heavy-**laden**, and I will give you rest"
SD : 1 1 :070(627) [1085] wants all men who are **laden** and burdened with sin to
SD : 1 1 :089(631) [1093] burdened, and heavy-**laden** sinners to repentance, to a

Laity (8)
AP : 2 2 :008(237) [0359] custom of giving the **laity** only a part of the sacrament.
AP : 2 2 :009(237) [0359] a distinction should be made between **laity** and clergy.
AP : 2 2 :010(237) [0361] and they add, "Thus our **laity** should be satisfied with the
AP : 2 2 :010(237) [0361] also want to say that the **laity** has been kept from the one
AP : 2 2 :010(238) [0361] opponents argue that the **laity** has been kept from the one
EP : R N :005(465) [0777] matters also concern the **laity** and the salvation of their
EP : 0 7 :024(484) [0815] of the sacrament to the **laity** and the withholding of the
SD : 0 7 :110(588) [1011] is administered to the **laity** contrary to the explicit

Lamb (8), Lambs (1)
AP : 0 4 :103(122) [0151] (John 1:29), 'Behold the **Lamb** of God, who takes away
AP : 2 4 :036(257) [0397] the burning of the **lamb**, the drink offering, and the
AP : 2 4 :036(257) [0397] The burning of the **lamb** symbolizes the death of Christ.
AP : 2 4 :036(257) [0397] with the blood of the **lamb**, by the proclamation of the
S 2 : 0 1 :002(292) [0461] He alone is "the **Lamb** of God, who takes away the sin of
S 2 : 0 2 :001(293) [0463] and must be done by the **Lamb** of God alone, as has been
S 2 : 0 2 :007(294) [0465] and what he does but the **Lamb** of God and the Son of
S 3 : 0 3 :038(309) [0489] and blood of the innocent **Lamb** of God who takes away
SD : P R :014(506) [0855] both pasture or feed the **lambs** and guard against wolves

Lament (6), Lamented (2)
AL : 2 6 :016(066) [0073] theologians greatly **lamented** that they were so hindered
AP : 1 2 :091(195) [0279] "Penitence means to **lament** past evils and not to commit
AP : 1 2 :091(196) [0279] not to commit again deeds that ought to be **lamented**."
LC : 0 3 :011(421) [0701] ourselves before him, **lament** our misery and plight, and
LC : 0 3 :027(424) [0705] therefore wishes you to **lament** and express your needs
LC : 0 5 :083(456) [0773] have all the more need to **lament** both to God and to
LC : 0 6 :015(458) [0000] my work and act, when I **lament** my sin and desire
LC : 0 6 :019(459) [0000] what you must do is to **lament** your need and allow

Lamp (2), Lamps (1)
AP : 2 1 :030(233) [0351] not go out with their **lamps** extinguished, they begged the
AP : 2 1 :030(233) [0351] of others, for everyone must buy oil for his own **lamp**."
EP : R N :001(464) [0777] 119:105, "Thy word is a **lamp** to my feet and a light to my

Land (10), Lands (17)
PR : P R :000(001) [0004] and Admonition of their **Lands**, Churches, Schools, and
PR : P R :006(004) [0009] been introduced into our **lands** and territories and which
PR : P R :015(007) [0013] and schoolmaster in our **lands** and territories and have
PR : P R :016(008) [0015] minister and schoolmaster in our **lands** and territories.
PR : P R :018(008) [0015] and schools of our **lands** have hitherto at all times
PR : P R :018(009) [0015] permit any doctrine in our **lands**, churches, and schools
PR : P R :022(011) [0019] intend to tolerate in our **lands**, churches, and schools
PR : P R :023(012) [0021] treated and taught in our **lands**, territories, schools, and
PR : P R :026(014) [0025] effort at concord in our **lands**, according to our own and
AG : P R :008(025) [0039] and embraced in our **lands**, principalities, dominions,
AG : 2 3 :014(054) [0063] disgraceful lewdness and vice to prevail in German **lands**.
AG : 2 6 :010(065) [0071] and magistrates should govern **land** and people, etc.
AG : 2 8 :019(084) [0087] and kings for the temporal administration of their **lands**.
AG : 2 8 :029(085) [0087] and to prevent discord and great disorder in their **lands**.
AL : 2 8 :019(084) [0087] and emperors for the civil administration of their **lands**.
AP : 0 4 :367(163) [0221] days may be long in the **land**" (Ex. 20:12); here, too, the
AP : 1 2 :164(208) [0303] willing and obedient, you shall eat the good of the **land**."
S 3 : 0 3 :025(307) [0485] their legates out into all **lands** until every church and
SC : P R :012(339) [0535] is disposed to banish such rude people from his **land**.
LC : P R :001(358) [0567] but live off the fat of the **land** all their days, as they used
LC : 0 1 :060(372) [0597] Like a great deluge, it has flooded all **lands**.
LC : 0 1 :075(375) [0601] men may grow up of whom an entire **land** may be proud.
LC : 0 1 :131(383) [0619] you may have long life in the **land** where you dwell."
LC : 0 3 :072(430) [0719] broad fields and the whole **land** which produce and
SD : 1 1 :058(626) [1081] God so severely punishes a **land** or a people for contempt
SD : 1 1 :060(626) [1083] judgement over certain **lands**, nations, and people so
SD : 1 1 :075(628) [1087] Would not that **land** be greatly polluted?

Landau (1)
PR : P R :027(015) [0027] Mayor and Council of the City of **Landau**

Landgrave (2)
AG : 0 0 :007(096) [0095] Philip, **landgrave** of Hesse
AL : 0 0 :017(096) [0095] Philip, **landgrave** of Hesse, subscribes

Lang (1)
S 3 : 1 5 :005(318) [0501] I, Dr. John **Lang**, preacher of the church in Erfurt, in my

Language (13), Languages (2)
PR : P R :002(003) [0007] the German and Latin **languages** by our pious and
AL : 2 4 :004(056) [0065] that in church a **language** should be used which is
AP : 0 4 :262(145) [0195] In his own **language** Daniel's words speak even more
AP : 0 4 :357(162) [0217] to Scripture but also to the very usage of the **language**.
AP : 1 2 :097(196) [0281] of penitence nor the **language** of the Fathers, they select
AP : 2 2 :007(237) [0359] by the ordinary usage of **language**, naming one part also
AP : 2 4 :004(250) [0385] almost everywhere the people sang in their own **language**.
TR : 0 0 :082(000) [0529] Smalcald in the German **language** by Dr. Martin Luther,
SC : 0 5 :023(350) [0553] set a bad example by my immodest **language** and actions.
LC : 0 1 :025(368) [0587] any found in other **languages**, a name derived from the
LC : 0 1 :077(375) [0603] we preach to children, we must also speak their **language**.
LC : 0 2 :048(416) [0691] In that **language** the word is *kyria*, and in Latin *curia*.
LC : 0 3 :046(426) [0709] as we understand the **language**, namely, that "to hallow"
EP : 0 7 :004(482) [0809] who in part talk our **language** very plausibly and claim to
SD : 0 7 :050(578) [0989] he uses no flowery **language** but the most appropriate,

Languish (1), Languishing (1)
AP : 1 2 :031(186) [0259] me, O Lord, for I am **languishing**; O Lord, heal me, for
LC : 0 1 :192(391) [0635] your neighbor to **languish** and perish in his misfortune.

Lantern (1)
LC : 0 5 :056(453) [0767] it appears like a dark **lantern** in contrast to the bright

Lapsed (3), Lapsing (1)
AP : 1 2 :112(198) [0285] Because the **lapsed** or notorious sinners were not accepted
AP : 1 2 :113(199) [0285] not want to accept the **lapsed** or the notorious sinners
AP : 1 2 :113(199) [0285] Chastising the **lapsed** served as an example, as the gloss
SD : 0 4 :033(556) [0949] we do not fall from our calling by **lapsing** again into sin.

Large (15), Largely (1), Larger (2), Largest (1)
PR : PR :025(014) [0023] Smalcald Articles and the **Large** and Small Catechism of
AG : 2 4 :041(061) [0069] In times past, even in **large** churches where there were
AP : 0 7 :010(170) [0229] that "the church in the **larger** sense includes both the
AP : 1 2 :069(192) [0271] anyone be moved by this **large** number of quotations, it
AP : 2 4 :054(259) [0403] Therefore a **large** part of the epistle is devoted to the
AP : 2 4 :091(266) [0415] fact that the Mass has **largely** been transferred to the dead
S1 : PR :007(289) [0457] and smaller and ours ever **larger**, and has caused, and
SC : PR :017(340) [0535] brief catechism, take up a **large** catechism so that the
LC : 0 1 :228(396) [0645] is the most common craft and the **largest** guild on earth.
LC : 0 1 :301(405) [0667] wrangle and wrestle over a **large** inheritance, real estate,
LC : 0 3 :077(431) [0721] subjects and the people at **large** to live together in
EP : RN :005(465) [0777] Dr. Luther's Small and **Large** Catechisms as both of them
SD : PR :008(505) [0853] to Dr. Luther's Small and **Large** Catechisms, as he
SD : PR :011(506) [0855] Articles, and Luther's **Large** and Small Catechisms — in
SD : 0 1 :038(515) [0871] Similarly we confess in the **Large** Catechism, "I hold and
SD : 0 2 :036(528) [0895] In his **Large** Catechism Dr. Luther writes: "I am also a
SD : 0 2 :045(530) [0899] the Smalcald Articles, the **Large** and Small Catechisms of
SD : 0 7 :020(572) [0979] the Word of God in the **Large** Catechism, where he writes
SD : 0 7 :027(573) [0981] the quotation from the **Large** Catechism, which establishes

Lash (1)
AP : 0 2 :035(104) [0113] Here our opponents **lash** out at Luther because he wrote

Last (44), Lasted (1), Lasting (1)
PR : PR :002(003) [0007] In these **last** times of this transitory world almighty God
AG : PR :007(025) [0039] and counsel, it was decided **last** Wednesday that, in
AG : PR :017(026) [0041] a written instruction at the **last** diet in Spires a year ago,
AG : 1 7 :001(038) [0051] Christ will return on the **last** day for judgment and will
AG : 2 3 :014(053) [0063] that fact that, in these **last** times of which the Scriptures
AP : 0 4 :021(110) [0127] And at **last** they despair utterly.
AP : 0 4 :062(115) [0139] In the **last** chapter of Luke (24:47) Christ commands that
AP : 1 2 :030(186) [0259] of the Gospel in the **last** chapter of Luke (24:47), "That
AP : 1 2 :089(195) [0279] faith is, and so it is that at **last** they rush into despair.
AP : 1 2 :126(201) [0289] that these are the **last** times, in which Christ predicted
AP : 2 3 :053(246) [0379] reasons for changing it, especially in these **last** times.
AP : 2 4 :015(251) [0389] For the **last** ten years our opponents have been publishing
AP : 2 7 :002(269) [0419] But at **last**, when he became ill either on account of age
S1 : PR :001(288) [0455] a council to meet in Mantua **last** year, in Whitsuntide.
S1 : PR :009(290) [0457] those will face us on the **last** day, before the judgment
SC : 0 2 :006(345) [0545] of all believers, and on the **last** day he will raise me and
SC : 0 3 :020(348) [0549] or reputation, and that at **last**, when the hour of death
LC : 0 1 :043(370) [0593] their wealth, nor has it ever **lasted** to the third generation.
LC : 0 1 :115(381) [0613] of God, therefore, let us at **last** teach our young people to
LC : 0 1 :244(398) [0649] and purse down to the **last** penny, and then by way of
LC : 0 1 :300(405) [0665] This **last** commandment, then, is addressed not to those
LC : 0 2 :031(414) [0687] his feet until finally, at the **last** day, he will completely
LC : 0 2 :053(417) [0691] Until the **last** day the Holy Spirit remains with the holy
LC : 0 2 :059(418) [0695] us in it by means of the **last** two parts of this article.
LC : 0 2 :061(419) [0695] Spirit carries on his work unceasingly until the **last** day.
LC : 0 3 :083(431) [0721] nothing can prosper or **last** for any length of time, as
LC : 0 3 :111(435) [0729] The **Last** Petition
LC : 0 3 :118(436) [0731] But this petition he has put **last**, for if we are to be
EP : 0 4 :018(477) [0801] Especially in these **last** times, it is just as necessary to
EP : 1 2 :031(500) [0843] give account of it on the **Last** Day before the righteous
SD : PR :005(504) [0851] merciful God has in these **last** days brought to light the
SD : PR :014(506) [0855] to maintain a thorough, **lasting**, and God-pleasing
SD : 0 2 :037(528) [0895] Until the **Last** Day, the Holy Spirit remains with the holy
SD : 0 6 :001(564) [0963] concerning this third and **last** function of the law.
SD : 0 7 :031(574) [0983] will mean for me before the **Last** Judgment at the coming
SD : 0 7 :033(575) [0983] before his death, in his **last** confession, he repeated his
SD : 0 7 :040(576) [0985] and especially in his ***Last** Confession Concerning the*
SD : 0 7 :040(576) [0985] the formula which Christ employed in the **Last** Supper.
SD : 0 7 :044(577) [0987] After the **Last** Supper, as he was about to begin his bitter
SD : 0 7 :044(577) [0987] for our sin, in this sad, **last** hour of his life, this truthful
SD : 0 7 :050(578) [0989] In the institution of his **last** will and testament and of his
SD : 0 7 :054(579) [0991] which Christ blessed in the **Last** Supper and not only the
SD : 0 7 :099(586) [1005] and as he will on the **Last** Day, as St. Paul says, "This will
SD : 0 8 :085(608) [1045] In his tract *Concerning the **Last** Words of David*, which
SD : 1 1 :042(623) [1077] for the devil so that their **last** state will be worse than the
SD : 1 1 :095(632) [1095] such peace and harmony **last**, because it would be

Late (2)
AL : 2 4 :016(057) [0067] Now when it is too **late** they are beginning to complain
TR : 0 0 :071(332) [0525] describes; but he is a **late** and fictitious writer, whoever he

Latin (22), Latins (1)
PR : PR :002(003) [0007] in the German and **Latin** languages by our pious and
PR : PR :018(009) [0015] both the German and the **Latin** copies were afterward
AG : PR :006(025) [0039] present, in German and **Latin**, his judgments, opinions,
AG : PR :007(025) [0039] present our case in German and **Latin** today (Friday).
AG : PR :009(025) [0041] and opinions, in **Latin** and German, we are prepared, in
AG : 0 1 :002(056) [0065] are sung in addition to the **Latin** responses for the
AL : 2 4 :002(056) [0065] interspersed here and there among the parts sung in **Latin**.
AP : 0 2 :003(101) [0105] In this sense the **Latin** definition denies that human nature
AP : 2 2 :004(236) [0359] once it prevailed in the **Latin** church, as Cyprian and
AP : 2 4 :002(249) [0385] harangue about the use of **Latin** in the Mass, our clever
AP : 2 4 :003(250) [0385] out that our churches keep the **Latin** lessons and prayers.
AP : 2 4 :003(250) [0385] Therefore we keep **Latin** for the sake of those who study
AP : 2 4 :023(253) [0391] The **Latins** offered a sacrificial victim to placate the wrath
TR : 0 0 :014(322) [0507] in the West and in the **Latin** churches, as Cyprian and
TR : 0 0 :015(322) [0509] world, whether in Greek or **Latin** churches, it is quite
LC : 0 2 :048(416) [0691] In that language the word is *kyria*, and in **Latin** *curia*.
LC : 0 2 :049(417) [0691] who understand neither **Latin** nor German, have rendered
EP : 0 1 :023(469) [0785] As far as the **Latin** words *substantia* and *accidens* are
SD : PR :009(505) [0853] them in the Preface to the **Latin** edition of his collected
SD : 0 1 :010(510) [0863] As the **Latin** words put it, "The description of original sin
SD : 0 1 :054(517) [0877] Concerning the use of the **Latin** terms *substantia* and
SD : 0 1 :061(519) [0879] just as Dr. Luther in his **Latin** exposition of Genesis 3
SD : 0 3 :042(547) [0931] do not follow," and the **Latin** text of the Apology states,

Latter (20)
AG : 0 0 :001(047) [0059] church (in so far as the **latter**'s teaching is reflected in the
AP : 0 7 :037(175) [0241] assembled much of it in the **latter** part of our Confession.
AP : 1 2 :045(187) [0263] denounces our sins, in the **latter** part he consoles us and
AP : 1 8 :009(226) [0337] to the free will and the **latter** to the operation of the Holy
S1 : PR :002(288) [0455] The **latter** accepted them, unanimously adopted them as
S3 : 0 3 :032(308) [0487] penitents, and those of you in the **latter** are false saints.
TR : 0 0 :051(329) [0519] The **latter** does more harm than all the punishments, for
TR : 0 0 :067(331) [0523] (a catechumen), and the **latter**, after his Baptism, absolved
LC : 0 1 :231(396) [0647] But the **latter** should be told that in the eyes of God they
LC : 0 1 :305(406) [0669] brother's wife while the **latter** was still living, and yet
LC : 0 2 :047(416) [0691] In early times the **latter** phrase was missing, and it is
LC : 0 2 :067(419) [0697] The **latter** teach us what we ought to do; the Creed tells
LC : 0 3 :023(423) [0703] For in the **latter** our conscience would always be in
LC : 0 4 :052(443) [0745] believes or not, for in the **latter** case Baptism does not
EP : 0 7 :001(481) [0807] themselves from the **latter** at the very outset when the
EP : 1 1 :003(494) [0833] what will be in the **latter** days" (Daniel 2:28).
SD : 0 1 :051(517) [0875] It is in this **latter** sense that Luther writes that sin and
SD : 0 3 :019(542) [0921] In this **latter** sense it is frequently used in the Apology,
SD : 0 4 :004(551) [0939] At first this **latter** controversy arose about the words
SD : 0 5 :011(560) [0955] and for this reason the **latter** is called the Paraclete, as

Laughed (2), Laughing (1)
S2 : 0 2 :022(296) [0469] horses that even the devil has **laughed** at such knavery.
S3 : 0 3 :018(306) [0483] would sooner have **laughed** than wept, unless perchance
LC : 0 1 :037(369) [0591] and see that this is no **laughing** matter with him.

Launch (1)
LC : 0 1 :230(396) [0645] petty thieves in order to **launch** an attack against the

Lavish (1), Lavishes (1)
LC : 0 1 :015(366) [0585] wishes to help you and to **lavish** all good upon you
LC : 0 1 :252(399) [0653] Moreover, he graciously **lavishes** upon them a wonderful

Law (700)
AG : 2 3 :013(053) [0063] divine, natural, and civil **law**, but was also utterly
AG : 2 3 :021(055) [0063] contrary not only to divine **law** but also to canon law.
AG : 2 3 :021(055) [0063] contrary not only to divine law but also to canon **law**.
AG : 2 3 :024(055) [0065] However, just as no human **law** can alter or abolish a
AG : 2 6 :005(064) [0071] mightily against the **law** of Moses and against human
AG : 2 7 :024(074) [0079] to cancel an obligation which is derived from divine **law**.
AG : 2 7 :041(077) [0081] would be justified by the **law**; you have fallen away from
AG : 2 8 :027(085) [0087] Canon **law** requires the same in Part II, Question 7, in the
AG : 2 8 :034(086) [0089] and as is taught by canon **law** throughout the whole of
AG : 2 8 :039(087) [0089] with the bondage of the **law**, as if in order to earn God's
AG : 2 8 :040(087) [0089] bishops were misled by the example of the **law** of Moses.
AG : 2 8 :041(087) [0089] spite of the fact that canon **law** says nothing of the
AG : 2 8 :051(089) [0091] that bondage to the **law** is not necessary for justification,
AG : 2 8 :059(091) [0091] the Gospel all ceremonies of the old **law** may be omitted.
AG : 2 8 :061(091) [0093] the transformation of the **law**, of the ceremonies of the
AG : 2 8 :074(094) [0095] disuse and are not obligatory, as papal **law** itself testifies.
AL : 2 3 :008(052) [0061] ought to marry, for no **law** of man and no vow can nullify
AL : 2 3 :024(055) [0065] Just as no human **law** can nullify a command of God, so
AL : 2 6 :005(064) [0071] article and puts aside the **law** and human traditions in
AL : 2 6 :022(067) [0073] the purifications of the **law**, and he says, "In vain do they
AL : 2 7 :024(074) [0079] an obligation which is plainly derived from divine **law**.
AL : 2 7 :041(077) [0081] would be justified by the **law**; you have fallen away from
AL : 2 8 :022(084) [0087] therefore bound by divine **law** to be obedient to the
AL : 2 8 :039(087) [0089] with the bondage of the **law**, as if in order to merit
AL : 2 8 :040(087) [0089] to have been misled by the example of the **law** of Moses.
AL : 2 8 :051(089) [0091] that bondage to the **law** is not necessary for justification,
AL : 2 8 :059(091) [0091] Gospel all ceremonies of the Mosaic **law** can be omitted.
AL : 2 8 :061(091) [0093] the mutation of the **law**, concerning ceremonies of the
AL : 2 8 :061(091) [0093] ceremonies of the new **law**, concerning the change of the
AP : 0 2 :008(101) [0107] are most contrary to the **law** of God, the scholastics do
AP : 0 2 :036(105) [0115] Augustine says: "That **law** which is in the members is
AP : 0 2 :039(105) [0115] not have known lust if the **law** had not said, 'You shall
AP : 0 2 :039(105) [0115] in my members another **law** at war with the law of my
AP : 0 2 :039(105) [0115] law at war with the **law** of my mind and making me
AP : 0 2 :039(105) [0115] making me captive to the **law** of sin which dwells in my
AP : 0 4 :005(108) [0121] into these two chief doctrines, the **law** and the promises.
AP : 0 4 :005(108) [0121] In some places it presents the **law**.
AP : 0 4 :006(108) [0121] By "**law**" in this discussion we mean the commandments
AP : 0 4 :007(108) [0121] our opponents select the **law** and by it they seek
AP : 0 4 :007(108) [0121] naturally understands the **law** since it has the same
AP : 0 4 :017(109) [0125] of this disposition and eternal life by the works of the **law**.
AP : 0 4 :018(109) [0125] righteous by their own keeping of the **law** before God.
AP : 0 4 :018(109) [0125] in spite of the fact that the **law** is never satisfied, that
AP : 0 4 :020(110) [0125] beyond the teaching of the **law**, the Gospel of the free
AP : 0 4 :021(110) [0127] of reason or of **law**, at which they look as the Jews did at
AP : 0 4 :021(110) [0127] that they are keeping the **law**, they arouse presumption, a
AP : 0 4 :022(110) [0127] to Gal. 3:24, "The **law** is a custodian," and I Tim. 1:9,
AP : 0 4 :022(110) [0127] and I Tim. 1:9, "The **law** is laid down for the lawless."
AP : 0 4 :027(111) [0127] all things and keep his **law**, truly fear him, truly believe
AP : 0 4 :030(111) [0129] would be justified by the **law**; you have fallen away from
AP : 0 4 :030(111) [0129] as Christ is 'the end of the **law**,' so likewise he is the
AP : 0 4 :031(111) [0129] does not justify us before God, it does not keep the **law**.
AP : 0 4 :032(111) [0129] does not submit to God's **law**, indeed it cannot; and those
AP : 0 4 :033(111) [0129] it cannot submit to God's **law**, it is certainly sinning even
AP : 0 4 :034(112) [0129] Content with this, they think they satisfy the **law** of God.
AP : 0 4 :038(112) [0131] Paul says (Rom. 4:15), "The **law** brings wrath."
AP : 0 4 :038(112) [0131] He does not say that by the **law** men merit the forgiveness
AP : 0 4 :038(112) [0131] For the **law** always accuses and terrifies consciences.
AP : 0 4 :038(112) [0131] conscience terrified by the **law** flees before God's
AP : 0 4 :038(112) [0131] men to trust that by the **law** and by their works they
AP : 0 4 :039(112) [0131] about the righteousness of **law** or of reason which our

Continued ▸

AP : 04 :040(112) [0131] men cannot keep the **law** by their own strength, and they
AP : 04 :040(112) [0131] On this account the **law** cannot free us from sin or justify
AP : 04 :041(113) [0133] manifested apart from **law**" (Rom. 3:21), that is, the
AP : 04 :042(113) [0133] and if reconciliation were by the **law**, it would be useless.
AP : 04 :042(113) [0133] since we do not keep the **law**, it would follow that we
AP : 04 :042(113) [0133] it is the adherents of the **law** who are to be the heirs, faith
AP : 04 :042(113) [0133] upon our merits and the **law**, which we never keep, it
AP : 04 :043(113) [0133] of faith in Christ, which the **law** does not teach.
AP : 04 :043(113) [0133] And this is not the righteousness of the **law**.
AP : 04 :044(113) [0133] For the **law** requires our own works and our own
AP : 04 :045(113) [0133] we can finally obey God's **law**, love him, truly fear him,
AP : 04 :046(113) [0133] regenerates our hearts, it precedes our keeping of the **law**.
AP : 04 :047(113) [0133] the righteousness of the **law** instead of the righteousness
AP : 04 :049(114) [0135] between this faith and the righteousness of the **law**.
AP : 04 :049(114) [0135] the righteousness of the **law** is that worship which offers
AP : 04 :057(114) [0137] Even though the **law** does not teach the free forgiveness
AP : 04 :059(115) [0137] were justified not by the **law** but by the promise and
AP : 04 :070(116) [0141] over and above the **law**," then we must defend the
AP : 04 :070(116) [0141] For the **law** does not teach the free forgiveness of sins.
AP : 04 :070(116) [0141] Again, we cannot keep the **law** unless we first receive the
AP : 04 :070(116) [0141] justifies teaches only the **law** and does away with Christ
AP : 04 :073(117) [0141] faith apart from works of **law**," and again (Eph. 2:8, 9),
AP : 04 :079(118) [0143] "The sting of death is sin, and the power of sin is **law**.
AP : 04 :079(118) [0143] this happens through the **law**, which shows God's wrath
AP : 04 :087(119) [0147] justified by faith apart from works of **law**" (Rom. 3:28).
AP : 04 :087(120) [0147] is talking about the whole **law**, not only about
AP : 04 :087(120) [0147] is talking about the whole **law**, as Augustine correctly
AP : 04 :089(120) [0149] according to the moral **law**; for if by these we earned
AP : 04 :093(120) [0149] justified by faith in Christ, and not by works of the **law**."
AP : 04 :097(121) [0149] which you could not be justified by the **law** of Moses."
AP : 04 :097(121) [0149] The **law**, he says, does not justify.
AP : 04 :097(121) [0149] He explicitly denies justification to the **law**.
AP : 04 :102(121) [0151] some places it teaches the **law**; in others it teaches the
AP : 04 :103(121) [0151] to him through the **law**; for by the commandment of the
AP : 04 :103(121) [0151] the commandment of the **law** all are accused and by the
AP : 04 :103(121) [0151] and by the works of the **law** none is justified, that is, by
AP : 04 :103(121) [0151] is justified, that is, by the **law** sin is recognized but its
AP : 04 :103(121) [0151] The **law** would seem to be harmful since it has made all
AP : 04 :103(122) [0151] This is what Paul says, '**Law** came in, to increase the
AP : 04 :106(122) [0153] says: "The righteousness of **law** is set forth in the
AP : 04 :106(122) [0153] that he who keeps the **law** will live in it, so that by
AP : 04 :106(122) [0153] nor by the letter of that same **law**, for this is impossible.
AP : 04 :106(122) [0153] Augustine says: "By the **law** we fear God, by faith we
AP : 04 :106(122) [0153] hearts are terrified by the **law** but receive consolation by
AP : 04 :106(122) [0153] before we try to keep the **law** we should receive mercy by
AP : 04 :110(123) [0153] with the abolition of the promise and a return to the **law**?
AP : 04 :114(123) [0155] we love and keep the **law**, although love must necessarily
AP : 04 :121(124) [0157] Love and the Keeping of the **Law**
AP : 04 :122(124) [0157] "The doers of the **law** will be justified" (Rom. 2:13),
AP : 04 :122(124) [0157] and many similar passages regarding the **law** and works.
AP : 04 :122(124) [0157] what we believe about love and the keeping of the **law**.
AP : 04 :123(124) [0157] prophet (Jer. 31:33), "I will put my **law** upon their hearts."
AP : 04 :123(124) [0157] says that faith does not overthrow but upholds the **law**.
AP : 04 :124(124) [0157] we should begin to keep the **law** ever more and more.
AP : 04 :124(124) [0157] but of Decalogue, the **law** that deals with the thoughts of
AP : 04 :125(124) [0157] he says (Jer. 31:33), "I will put my **law** upon their hearts."
AP : 04 :126(124) [0157] it is impossible to keep the **law** without Christ; it is
AP : 04 :126(124) [0157] it is impossible to keep the **law** without the Holy Spirit.
AP : 04 :128(125) [0157] The **law** always accuses us, it always shows that God is
AP : 04 :130(125) [0157] the outward works of the **law**, without Christ and the
AP : 04 :130(125) [0157] to the essence of the divine **law**, are impossible without
AP : 04 :131(125) [0159] overlook that eternal **law**, far beyond the senses and
AP : 04 :132(125) [0159] cannot correctly keep the **law** unless by faith we have
AP : 04 :132(125) [0159] overthrow but upholds the **law** (Rom. 3:31) because the
AP : 04 :132(125) [0159] (Rom. 3:31) because the **law** can be kept only when the
AP : 04 :134(125) [0159] opinion about the entire **law**, both the moral and the
AP : 04 :134(125) [0159] and civil works satisfy the **law** of God and that sacrifice
AP : 04 :135(125) [0159] Only then do we see how far we are from keeping the **law**.
AP : 04 :135(126) [0159] and without the Holy Spirit we cannot keep the **law**.
AP : 04 :136(126) [0159] that the keeping of the **law** should begin in us and
AP : 04 :137(126) [0161] who try to keep the **law** by their own strength cannot
AP : 04 :140(126) [0161] not only how the **law** can be kept, but also that God is
AP : 04 :145(127) [0163] From this it is clear that they teach only the **law**.
AP : 04 :146(127) [0163] They claim to keep the **law**, though this glory properly
AP : 04 :146(127) [0163] life we cannot satisfy the **law**, because our unspiritual
AP : 04 :147(127) [0163] it is the keeping of the **law**, why do we deny that it
AP : 04 :151(127) [0163] sins by other virtues of the **law** or on account of them
AP : 04 :154(128) [0165] God, while a doctor of the **law** does not believe or accept
AP : 04 :157(128) [0165] unless he keeps the whole **law**, because the law does not
AP : 04 :157(128) [0165] the whole law, because the **law** does not justify so long as
AP : 04 :159(129) [0165] love is the keeping of the **law**, and obedience to the law
AP : 04 :159(129) [0165] law, and obedience to the **law** certainly is righteousness.
AP : 04 :159(129) [0167] mistaken when they think that we are justified by the **law**.
AP : 04 :159(129) [0167] We are not justified by the **law**; but we receive the
AP : 04 :159(129) [0167] sake, not for the sake of love or the keeping of the **law**.
AP : 04 :160(129) [0167] When this keeping of the **law** and obedience to the law is
AP : 04 :160(129) [0167] law and obedience to the **law** is perfect, it is indeed
AP : 04 :161(129) [0167] incipient keeping of the **law** does not justify, because it is
AP : 04 :161(129) [0167] and keeping of the **law**, but only because of Christ.
AP : 04 :162(129) [0169] God and merit eternal life by our keeping of the **law**.
AP : 04 :164(129) [0169] because they have kept the **law**, how can our conscience
AP : 04 :164(129) [0169] be sure that it pleases God, since we never satisfy the **law**?
AP : 04 :165(130) [0169] of his own keeping of the **law** rather than because of
AP : 04 :166(130) [0169] and the church proclaim that the **law** cannot be satisfied.
AP : 04 :166(130) [0169] incipient keeping of the **law** does not please God for its
AP : 04 :167(130) [0169] Without this, the **law** always accuses us.
AP : 04 :168(130) [0169] "I of myself serve the **law** of God with my mind,
AP : 04 :168(130) [0169] with my mind, but with my flesh I serve the **law** of sin."
AP : 04 :168(130) [0169] Here he openly says that he serves the **law** of sin.
AP : 04 :174(131) [0171] incipient keeping of the **law**, therefore, we need a faith
AP : 04 :175(131) [0171] says, therefore, that the **law** is established through faith
AP : 04 :175(131) [0171] Holy Spirit and that their impulses agree with God's **law**.
AP : 04 :175(131) [0171] realize how far we are from the perfection of the **law**.
AP : 04 :176(131) [0171] of our keeping of the **law**; for our conscience to be at
AP : 04 :177(131) [0171] because of Christ, not because of the **law** or our works.
AP : 04 :177(131) [0171] incipient keeping of the **law** pleases God because of faith;
AP : 04 :178(131) [0171] purity—yes, far above the **law** itself—should be placed the
AP : 04 :178(131) [0171] of our keeping of the **law** we have a gracious God.
AP : 04 :179(131) [0171] us from the curse of the **law**, being made a curse for us."
AP : 04 :179(131) [0171] That is, the **law** condemns all men, but by undergoing the
AP : 04 :179(131) [0171] took away the right of the **law** to accuse and condemn
AP : 04 :179(131) [0171] accounted righteous, the **law** cannot accuse or condemn
AP : 04 :179(131) [0171] them, even though they have not really satisfied the **law**.
AP : 04 :179(131) [0171] from the perfection of the **law**, still the remnants of your
AP : 04 :180(132) [0171] us, not because of the **law** or our works: this promise we
AP : 04 :181(132) [0171] the righteousness of the **law**, to the extent that they fulfill
AP : 04 :181(132) [0171] of the law, to the extent that they fulfill the **law**.
AP : 04 :181(132) [0171] this obedience of the **law** justifies by the righteousness of
AP : 04 :181(132) [0171] of the law justifies by the righteousness of the **law**.
AP : 04 :181(132) [0171] imperfect righteousness of the **law** only because of faith.
AP : 04 :182(132) [0173] promised because of Christ, not because of the **law**.
AP : 04 :182(132) [0173] though the keeping of the **law** follows with the gift of the
AP : 04 :183(132) [0173] the distinction between the **law** and the promises or
AP : 04 :183(132) [0173] they quote passages about **law** and works but omit
AP : 04 :184(132) [0173] their statements about the **law** we answer immediately
AP : 04 :184(132) [0173] immediately that the **law** cannot be kept without Christ,
AP : 04 :185(132) [0173] interprets all the passages they quote on **law** and works.
AP : 04 :186(132) [0173] the Scripture presents the **law**, while in others it presents
AP : 04 :188(133) [0173] Later we add the teaching of the **law**.
AP : 04 :188(133) [0173] Scriptures ascribe to the **law** and what they ascribe to the
AP : 04 :204(135) [0177] The **law** always accuses them and brings forth wrath.
AP : 04 :214(136) [0179] incipient keeping of the **law** must follow faith; but we still
AP : 04 :219(137) [0181] and begin to keep the **law**, according to the statement
AP : 04 :219(137) [0181] (Jer. 31:33), "I will put my **law** within their hearts."
AP : 04 :221(137) [0181] justification and teach only the righteousness of the **law**.
AP : 04 :222(138) [0181] that our love satisfies the **law** of God; that by our love we
AP : 04 :227(138) [0183] even the first and greatest **law** does not justify, neither
AP : 04 :227(138) [0183] not justify, neither does the greatest virtue of the **law**.
AP : 04 :229(139) [0183] they teach and require the righteousness of the **law**.
AP : 04 :229(139) [0183] We cannot deny that love is the highest work of the **law**.
AP : 04 :229(139) [0183] wisdom looks at the **law** and seeks righteousness in it.
AP : 04 :229(139) [0183] the highest work of the **law**, and to it they attributed
AP : 04 :230(139) [0183] judgment of reason and **law** and that the teaching of the
AP : 04 :230(139) [0183] that the teaching of the **law** about love is more plausible;
AP : 04 :238(141) [0187] be a righteousness of the **law** rather than of the Gospel
AP : 04 :242(141) [0187] forgives, yields, and does not go to the limit of the **law**.
AP : 04 :252(143) [0191] (Rom. 2:13), "the doers of the **law** will be justified."
AP : 04 :252(143) [0191] words, "the doers of the **law** will be justified," contain
AP : 04 :252(143) [0191] is said, "The doers of the **law** will be justified"; that is,
AP : 04 :252(143) [0191] because of faith and therefore are a keeping of the **law**.
AP : 04 :255(144) [0193] is the proclamation of the **law** or of penitence, which
AP : 04 :256(144) [0193] In the preaching of the **law** there are two things we must
AP : 04 :256(144) [0193] First, we cannot keep the **law** unless we have been reborn
AP : 04 :256(144) [0193] to interpret the entire **law** (Heb. 11:6), "Without faith it is
AP : 04 :257(144) [0193] It is clear that we are not justified by the **law**.
AP : 04 :257(144) [0193] if the preaching of the **law** were enough by itself, why
AP : 04 :257(144) [0193] not enough to preach the **law**, the Word that convicts of
AP : 04 :257(144) [0193] For the **law** works wrath; it only accuses; it only terrifies
AP : 04 :260(145) [0193] the preaching of the **law** is not enough because the law
AP : 04 :260(145) [0193] is not enough because the **law** works wrath and
AP : 04 :261(145) [0195] is not the preaching of the **law**, but a truly prophetic and
AP : 04 :266(146) [0197] promise of Christ when the **law** is preached and works are
AP : 04 :269(147) [0197] works are praised and the **law** preached, therefore, we
AP : 04 :269(147) [0197] fast to these rules: that the **law** is not kept without
AP : 04 :269(147) [0197] The teaching of the **law** is certainly not intended to
AP : 04 :269(147) [0197] who interpret the **law** in such a way that they attribute
AP : 04 :270(147) [0197] setting forth the most ample promise of the **law**.
AP : 04 :270(147) [0197] But without Christ this **law** is not kept.
AP : 04 :270(147) [0197] which does not satisfy the **law** and therefore flees in
AP : 04 :270(147) [0197] and punishment of the **law**, "for the law brings wrath"
AP : 04 :270(147) [0197] of the law, "for the **law** brings wrath" (Rom. 4:15).
AP : 04 :270(147) [0197] But a man keeps the **law** as soon as he hears that God is
AP : 04 :270(147) [0197] us for Christ's sake even though we cannot satisfy the **law**.
AP : 04 :270(147) [0197] is at peace and begins to love God and to keep the **law**.
AP : 04 :270(147) [0199] its incipient keeping of the **law** is impure and far from
AP : 04 :274(148) [0199] those passages which teach about the **law** or works.
AP : 04 :277(149) [0199] that without Christ the teaching of the **law** has no value.
AP : 04 :280(149) [0201] single passage without taking the whole **law** into account.
AP : 04 :281(149) [0201] to the preaching of the **law**, that for his sake good works
AP : 04 :281(149) [0201] teach that we merit justification by the works of the **law**.
AP : 04 :285(150) [0201] The **law** always accuses.
AP : 04 :286(150) [0203] They teach the **law** in such a way as to hide the Gospel of
AP : 04 :287(150) [0203] or from the teaching of the **law** rather than the Gospel.
AP : 04 :287(150) [0203] the other based upon the **law**, neither one based upon the
AP : 04 :289(151) [0203] disposition we obey the **law** of God both outwardly and
AP : 04 :289(151) [0203] that such obedience to the **law** is worthy of grace and
AP : 04 :289(151) [0203] This is obviously a doctrine of the **law**.
AP : 04 :289(151) [0203] Truly the **law** says, "You shall love the Lord your God"
AP : 04 :289(151) [0203] Therefore love is the fulfilling of the **law**.
AP : 04 :290(151) [0203] their own keeping of the **law** and not through Christ, the
AP : 04 :290(151) [0203] this very keeping of the **law** with[out] Christ, the
AP : 04 :290(151) [0203] and feeble keeping of the **law** is rare, even among saints.
AP : 04 :291(152) [0203] that we are justified neither by reason nor by the **law**.
AP : 04 :292(152) [0203] righteousness is not by the **law** but by the promise, in
AP : 04 :293(152) [0203] renewal we can keep the **law**, love God and his Word,
AP : 04 :293(152) [0203] from the perfection of the **law**, these works please God on
AP : 04 :294(152) [0203] love follows faith since love is the keeping of the **law**.
AP : 04 :294(152) [0203] we are justified not by the **law** but by the promise, which
AP : 04 :295(152) [0203] love an angry God; the **law** always accuses us and thus
AP : 04 :295(152) [0205] Later we begin to keep the **law**.
AP : 04 :296(152) [0205] In the flesh we never satisfy the **law**.
AP : 04 :296(152) [0205] righteous because of the **law** but because of Christ, whose
AP : 04 :297(152) [0205] we are not justified by the **law** because human nature
AP : 04 :297(152) [0205] nature cannot keep the **law** of God nor love God; and
AP : 04 :297(153) [0205] in vain, either, before the **law** and outside the law from
AP : 04 :297(153) [0205] the law and outside the **law** from the very beginning of

Continued ▶

A P : 0 4 :297(153) [0205] not justified before God either by reason or by the **law**.
A P : 0 4 :298(153) [0205] before God by the **law** but by the promise, justification
A P : 0 4 :299(153) [0205] but because Christ still helps us to keep the **law**.
A P : 0 4 :301(153) [0205] they love and keep the **law**, they will have to doubt
A P : 0 4 :301(153) [0205] What is this doctrine of the **law** but a doctrine of despair?
A P : 0 4 :308(155) [0207] works or obedience to the **law** can be pleasing to God
A P : 0 4 :308(155) [0207] We do not satisfy the **law**, but for Christ's sake this is
A P : 0 4 :310(155) [0207] while the worship of the **law** is to offer and present our
A P : 0 4 :311(155) [0207] about obedience to the **law**; they do not talk about
A P : 0 4 :311(155) [0207] Yet we cannot obey the **law** unless we have been reborn
A P : 0 4 :313(155) [0207] teach the righteousness of the Gospel and not of the **law**.
A P : 0 4 :313(155) [0207] the righteousness of the **law**, they do not teach us to use
A P : 0 4 :314(156) [0207] our love and keeping of the **law** against the wrath of God.
A P : 0 4 :315(156) [0207] Christ we cannot keep the **law**, as he himself says
A P : 0 4 :315(156) [0207] So before we can keep the **law**, our hearts must be reborn
A P : 0 4 :319(156) [0209] can never be stilled; for the **law** always accuses us, even in
A P : 0 4 :348(160) [0217] we might begin to do good works and obey God's **law**.
A P : 0 4 :366(163) [0221] The keeping of the **law** that follows faith deals with the
A P : 0 4 :366(163) [0221] faith deals with the **law**, in which a reward is offered and
A P : 0 4 :366(163) [0221] who merit this are justified before they keep the **law**.
A P : 0 4 :367(163) [0221] (Ex. 20:12); here, too, the **law** offers a reward for a certain
A P : 0 4 :368(163) [0221] Although keeping the **law** thus merits a reward, since a
A P : 0 4 :368(163) [0221] properly belongs to the **law**, still we must remember that
A P : 0 4 :368(163) [0221] do nor can keep the **law** before we have been reconciled
A P : 0 4 :368(163) [0221] This keeping of the **law** would not please God unless we
A P : 0 4 :368(163) [0221] incipient keeping of the **law** pleases God and has its
A P : 0 4 :369(163) [0221] based on the nature of the **law**, but since it would take too
A P : 0 4 :372(164) [0221] Whenever **law** and works are mentioned, we must know
A P : 0 4 :372(164) [0221] He is the end of the **law** (Rom. 10:4), and he himself says,
A P : 0 4 :377(165) [0223] justification is nothing more than the teaching of the **law**.
A P : 0 4 :387(166) [0225] justification derived either from reason or from the **law**.
A P : 0 4 :388(166) [0225] works is quoted, that the **law** cannot be kept without
A P : 0 4 :388(166) [0225] we are not justified by the **law** but by the Gospel, the
A P : 0 4 :394(167) [0225] is the righteousness of the **law**, understood as civic
A P : 0 7 :031(174) [0237] as the righteousness of the **law** was tied to the Mosaic
A P : 1 1 :006(181) [0251] are discussing what is necessary according to divine **law**.
A P : 1 1 :006(181) [0251] rather show from divine **law** that the enumeration of sins
A P : 1 1 :008(181) [0251] the enumeration of sins is not required by divine **law**.
A P : 1 1 :008(181) [0251] by Panormitanus and other learned in the canon **law**.
A P : 1 1 :010(182) [0253] was necessary by divine **law** and yet experienced that it
A P : 1 2 :033(186) [0259] Paul says (Gal. 2:19), "I through the **law** died to the law."
A P : 1 2 :033(186) [0259] Paul says (Gal. 2:19), "I through the law died to the **law**."
A P : 1 2 :034(186) [0259] For the **law** only accuses and terrifies the conscience.
A P : 1 2 :034(186) [0261] alone, this is the teaching of the **law**, not of the Gospel.
A P : 1 2 :034(186) [0261] when amid such terrors they show men only the **law**?
A P : 1 2 :037(186) [0261] For the **law** is not kept without Christ, according to the
A P : 1 2 :048(188) [0265] nor read the sentence of the **law** written in their hearts.
A P : 1 2 :053(189) [0265] One part is the **law**, which reveals, denounces, and
A P : 1 2 :075(193) [0273] but the teaching of the **law**, the elimination of the
A P : 1 2 :075(193) [0273] They require only the **law** and our works because the law
A P : 1 2 :075(193) [0273] the law and our works because the **law** demands love.
A P : 1 2 :075(193) [0273] But if the **law** is enough to achieve the forgiveness of sins,
A P : 1 2 :076(193) [0273] consciences away from the **law** to the Gospel, away from
A P : 1 2 :076(193) [0273] Nor can we keep the **law** before we have been reconciled
A P : 1 2 :077(193) [0275] of sins because of the **law** or in any other way except by
A P : 1 2 :078(193) [0275] is simply a doctrine of the **law** — and that misunderstood,
A P : 1 2 :079(193) [0275] we are not justified by the **law**; to the law he opposes the
A P : 1 2 :079(193) [0275] justified by the law; to the **law** he opposes the promise of
A P : 1 2 :079(194) [0275] Paul calls us away from the **law** to this promise.
A P : 1 2 :079(194) [0275] if we were justified by the **law** before the promise or if we
A P : 1 2 :080(194) [0275] we cannot keep the **law**, and therefore we must be
A P : 1 2 :080(194) [0275] must be reconciled by the promise before we keep the **law**.
A P : 1 2 :082(194) [0275] by faith before we keep the **law** although, as we said
A P : 1 2 :082(194) [0275] the Holy Spirit and therefore begin to keep the **law**.
A P : 1 2 :085(194) [0277] This is a teaching of the **law** and not of the Gospel, to
A P : 1 2 :085(194) [0277] a man is justified by the **law** before being reconciled to
A P : 1 2 :086(194) [0277] want to be justified by the **law** and to offer our works to
A P : 1 2 :086(194) [0277] contends that we cannot keep the **law** without Christ.
A P : 1 2 :086(195) [0277] by faith we are reconciled to God before we keep the **law**.
A P : 1 2 :087(195) [0277] promise of the forgiveness of sins before we keep the **law**.
A P : 1 2 :088(195) [0277] the forgiveness of sins because we love or keep the **law**?
A P : 1 2 :088(195) [0277] For the **law** will always accuse us because we never satisfy
A P : 1 2 :088(195) [0277] always accuse us because we never satisfy the **law** of God.
A P : 1 2 :088(195) [0277] As Paul says (Rom. 4:15), "The **law** brings wrath."
A P : 1 2 :089(195) [0279] — a doctrine of the **law**, an abrogation of the Gospel, a
A P : 1 2 :103(197) [0281] in the area of blessing or grace, not of judgment or **law**.
A P : 1 2 :116(199) [0285] are not necessary by divine **law** for the forgiveness of
A P : 1 2 :116(199) [0287] not necessary by divine **law** for the forgiveness of sins.
A P : 1 2 :141(204) [0295] suppress the knowledge of **law** and Gospel, penitence and
A P : 1 2 :142(204) [0295] Regarding the **law** they say that in condescension to our
A P : 1 2 :142(204) [0295] that we can keep the **law** in such a way as to do even
A P : 1 2 :142(204) [0295] we are far away from the perfection that the **law** requires.
A P : 1 2 :142(204) [0295] men imagine that God's **law** deals with external, civil
A P : 1 2 :142(204) [0295] no one does as much as the **law** requires, and it is foolish
A P : 1 2 :142(204) [0295] external works that God's **law** does not require, it is vain
A P : 1 2 :142(204) [0295] to trust that thereby we make satisfaction to God's **law**.
A P : 1 2 :143(204) [0297] not commanded by God's **law** but have a set form derived
A P : 1 2 :145(205) [0297] this way they obscure the **law** of God in two ways: first,
A P : 1 2 :145(205) [0297] civil works satisfy God's **law**; and second, because they
A P : 1 2 :145(205) [0297] whose works they rank above the works of the **law**.
A P : 1 2 :147(205) [0297] are not necessary by divine **law** to remit either guilt or
A P : 1 2 :153(206) [0299] sting of death is sin, and the power of sin is the **law**."
A P : 1 2 :175(210) [0307] commanded by divine **law**, for human authority cannot
A P : 1 2 :175(210) [0307] law, for human authority cannot abrogate divine **law**.
A P : 1 5 :008(216) [0317] from Christ, you who would be justified by the **law**."
A P : 1 5 :008(216) [0317] if by the observance of the **law** you think you deserve to
A P : 1 5 :008(216) [0317] believes he is righteous by his own observance of the **law**?
A P : 1 5 :010(216) [0317] With the removal of the **law** and of the traditions, he
A P : 1 5 :015(217) [0319] by Jeroboam and others over and above the **law**.
A P : 1 5 :030(219) [0323] This includes both the **law** of Moses and the traditions of
A P : 1 5 :030(219) [0323] and say that Paul is talking only about the **law** of Moses.
A P : 1 5 :032(220) [0323] lest the observances of the **law** or traditions be regarded
A P : 1 8 :007(225) [0337] the outward works of the **law**, we do not ascribe to it the
A P : 1 8 :010(226) [0337] that men can obey the **law** of God without the Holy
A P : 2 0 :015(229) [0343] We do not overthrow the **law**, Paul says (Rom. 3:31), but
A P : 2 0 :015(229) [0343] by faith, the keeping of the **law** necessarily follows, by
A P : 2 2 :011(238) [0361] reason; but whatever the theologians say, let that be **law**!
A P : 2 2 :017(238) [0361] of Ezekiel (7:26), "The **law** perishes from the priest."
A P : 2 3 :001(239) [0363] defense of the pontifical **law**, but they even urge the
A P : 2 3 :003(239) [0363] In opposition to divine **law**, the law of the nations, and
A P : 2 3 :003(239) [0363] to divine law, the **law** of the nations, and the canons of
A P : 2 3 :006(240) [0365] We cannot approve the **law** of celibacy put forth by our
A P : 2 3 :006(240) [0365] with divine and natural **law** and conflicts with the very
A P : 2 3 :010(241) [0367] thought up in order to circumvent the natural **law**.
A P : 2 3 :019(242) [0369] rest to use the universal **law** of nature which he has
A P : 2 3 :027(243) [0371] ceremonies of the Mosaic **law** which prescribed that
A P : 2 3 :035(244) [0373] it is not marriage that the **law** forbids, but lust, adultery,
A P : 2 3 :042(245) [0375] If anybody supports the **law** of celibacy in order to
A P : 2 3 :042(245) [0375] and tried to impose the **law** of Moses on Christians.
A P : 2 3 :045(245) [0375] have misunderstood the **law** of Moses; therefore they
A P : 2 3 :051(246) [0377] many reasons for rejecting the **law** of perpetual celibacy.
A P : 2 3 :051(246) [0377] But even if the **law** were not unjust, it is dangerous to
A P : 2 3 :052(246) [0377] no secret how harmful this **law** has been to public morals
A P : 2 3 :053(246) [0379] demanded it, why was not the same done to this **law**?
A P : 2 3 :056(247) [0379] good laws; on this one **law** of celibacy they are adamant
A P : 2 3 :057(247) [0379] Now they are making the **law** even more unbearable in
A P : 2 3 :058(247) [0379] murders show that this **law** is a doctrine of demons
A P : 2 3 :058(247) [0379] (John 8:44), he uses these murders to defend his **law**.
A P : 2 3 :059(247) [0379] the defense of this unjust **law**, the dissolution of existing
A P : 2 3 :060(247) [0379] their defense of the pontifical **law** of perpetual celibacy.
A P : 2 3 :060(247) [0379] with divine and natural **law**; it disagrees even with the
A P : 2 3 :060(247) [0381] The real purpose of the **law** is not religion but
A P : 2 3 :062(247) [0381] review their weighty arguments in defense of the **law**.
A P : 2 3 :063(248) [0381] divine revelation for the **law** of perpetual celibacy, though
A P : 2 3 :063(248) [0381] the real author of such a **law** when he calls it a "doctrine
A P : 2 3 :063(248) [0381] the many murders for which this **law** provides an excuse.
A P : 2 3 :064(248) [0381] purity of the heart and not ceremonies of the **law**.
A P : 2 3 :066(248) [0381] Thus the same **law**, "Purify yourselves, you who bear the
A P : 2 3 :067(248) [0383] the world still did not know the **law** of perpetual celibacy.
A P : 2 3 :070(249) [0383] like these they defend a wicked and immoral **law**.
A P : 2 4 :021(252) [0391] basis of the justice of the **law**; thus those for whom they
A P : 2 4 :023(253) [0391] Isaiah interprets the **law** to mean that the death of Christ
A P : 2 4 :023(253) [0391] as the ceremonies of the **law** were not; therefore he says
A P : 2 4 :024(253) [0391] of the ceremonial **law** and prevented the exclusion of the
A P : 2 4 :043(258) [0399] The better ones teach the **law** and say nothing about the
A P : 2 4 :081(264) [0411] It is an old word, ordinarily used in public **law**.
A P : 2 4 :081(264) [0411] rescript of Pertinax on the **law** of immunity shows: "Even
A P : 2 7 :011(270) [0423] would be justified by the **law**; you have fallen away from
A P : 2 7 :012(270) [0423] They apply the passage in Paul only to the **law** of Moses.
A P : 2 7 :014(271) [0423] Paul denies that by the **law** of Moses men merit the
A P : 2 7 :014(271) [0423] If the **law** of Moses, which was divinely revealed, did not
A P : 2 7 :015(271) [0425] that Paul abolished the **law** of Moses and that Christ took
A P : 2 7 :016(271) [0425] those who observe this **law** of Christ, the monks come
A P : 2 7 :017(272) [0425] the works of the Mosaic **law** or of the Decalogue or the
A P : 2 7 :030(274) [0431] does not even give his own **law** the honor of meriting
A P : 2 7 :033(274) [0431] by the works of the divine **law**, but must seek the mercy
A P : 2 7 :051(277) [0437] marriage of priests that the **law** of nature in men cannot
A P : 2 8 :014(283) [0447] to act without a definite **law**, nor that of a king to act
A P : 2 8 :014(283) [0447] a definite law, nor that of a king to act above the **law**.
S 2 : 0 1 :004(292) [0461] apprehended by any work, **law**, or merit, it is clear and
S 2 : 0 1 :004(292) [0461] faith apart from works of **law**" (Rom. 3:28), and again,
S 2 : 0 4 :014(301) [0475] from the imperial, pagan **law** and is a teaching concerning
S 3 : 0 2 :000(303) [0479] II. The **Law**
S 3 : 0 2 :001(303) [0479] Here we maintain that the **law** was given by God first of
S 3 : 0 2 :002(303) [0479] Some, who hate the **law** because it forbids what they
S 3 : 0 2 :002(303) [0479] they act against the **law** even more than before.
S 3 : 0 2 :003(303) [0479] they can and do keep the **law** by their own powers, as was
S 3 : 0 2 :004(303) [0479] function or power of the **law** is to make original sin
S 3 : 0 2 :004(303) [0479] So the **law** must tell him that he neither has nor cares for
S 3 : 0 2 :004(303) [0479] not have believed before without a knowledge of the **law**.
S 3 : 0 2 :005(303) [0479] meant by Rom. 4:15, "The **law** brings wrath," and
S 3 : 0 2 :005(303) [0479] wrath," and Rom. 5:20, "**Law** came in to increase the
S 3 : 0 3 :001(303) [0479] This function of the **law** is retained and taught by the New
S 3 : 0 3 :004(304) [0481] To this office of the **law** the New Testament immediately
S 3 : 0 3 :007(304) [0481] But where the **law** exercises its office alone, without the
S 3 : 0 3 :008(304) [0481] As St. Paul says, the **law** slays through sin.
S 3 : 0 3 :018(306) [0483] was really smitten by the **law** or vainly vexed with a
S 3 : 0 3 :039(309) [0489] called good works or the **law**, although no good work but
S 3 : 0 3 :039(309) [0489] although no one keeps the **law** (as Christ says in John
S 3 : 0 3 :040(309) [0489] 7:23, he wars with the **law** in his members, and he does
S 3 : 0 7 :001(311) [0493] 7:23) that in his flesh he was captive to "the **law** of sin."
S 3 : 0 8 :002(312) [0495] I see in my members another **law**," etc. (Rom. 7:23).
S 3 : 0 8 :012(312) [0495] his churches is spirit and **law**, even when it is above and
T R : 0 0 :074(332) [0525] and excommunicated them without due process of **law**.
T R : 0 0 :074(332) [0525] power to ban men arbitrarily without due process of **law**!
T R : 0 0 :075(333) [0525] nobody should be condemned without due process of **law**.
T R : 0 0 :077(333) [0527] which according to canon **law** pertain to ecclesiastical
T R : 0 0 :078(333) [0527] Unjust, too, is the **law** that in general approves all
T R : 0 0 :078(333) [0527] The **law** concerning the celibacy of priests is likewise
S C : P R :021(340) [0537] receive the sacrament, no **law** is to be made concerning it,
S C : P R :022(341) [0537] accord and without any **law**, the people will desire the
S C : P R :023(341) [0539] to compel him by any **law** to receive the sacrament, for he
S C : P R :024(341) [0539] you are not to make a **law** of this, as the pope has done.
L C : P R :010(360) [0569] blessed who "meditate on God's **law** day and night."
L C : 0 1 :274(402) [0659] much as those who take the **law** into their own hands
L C : 0 1 :299(405) [0665] who twist and stretch the **law** to suit their purpose,
L C : 0 1 :299(405) [0665] most advantage out of the **law**, for as the saying has it,
L C : 0 1 :299(405) [0665] law, for as the saying has it, "The **law** favors the vigilant."
L C : 0 1 :301(405) [0667] garnishing them that the **law** supports them, and they
L C : 0 1 :305(406) [0667] prevalent in the time of the **law**, for we read even in the
L C : 0 6 :001(457) [0000] there has been no **law** quite so oppressive as that which
E P : 0 2 :003(470) [0787] God; it does not submit to God's **law**, indeed it cannot."
E P : 0 2 :009(471) [0789] obey God's **law**, and thus merit forgiveness of sins and
E P : 0 2 :011(471) [0789] obey God's **law** by his own powers, yet after the Holy
E P : 0 2 :012(471) [0789] man is able to keep the **law** of God perfectly and entirely
E P : 0 3 :010(474) [0795] merit," "without the **law**," "without works," "not by

Continued ▶

E P : 0 4 :004(476) [0797] party contended that the **law** should not be preached at
E P : 0 4 :010(476) [0799] or compulsion of the **law** but from a spontaneous spirit
E P : 0 4 :010(476) [0799] they are "no longer under the **law** but under grace."
E P : 0 5 :000(477) [0801] V. **Law** and Gospel
E P : 0 5 :001(478) [0801] is condemned not in the **law** but wholly through the
E P : 0 5 :002(478) [0801] the distinction between **law** and Gospel is an especially
E P : 0 5 :003(478) [0801] that, strictly speaking, the **law** is a divine doctrine which
E P : 0 5 :004(478) [0801] sin is and belongs to the proclamation of the **law**.
E P : 0 5 :005(478) [0801] man who has not kept the **law** and is condemned by it
E P : 0 5 :007(478) [0803] 6. But when the **law** and Gospel are opposed to each
E P : 0 5 :007(478) [0803] of as a teacher of the **law** in contrast to Christ as a
E P : 0 5 :007(478) [0803] that are frightened by the **law**, directs them solely to the
E P : 0 5 :008(478) [0803] long as men hear only the **law** and hear nothing about
E P : 0 5 :008(479) [0803] true nature of sin from the **law**, and thus they become
E P : 0 5 :008(479) [0803] Therefore Christ takes the **law** into his own hands and
E P : 0 5 :008(479) [0803] are directed back to the **law**, and now they learn from it
E P : 0 5 :009(479) [0803] directs people into the **law**, after the veil of Moses has
E P : 0 5 :009(479) [0803] God demands of us in the **law**, none of which we could
E P : 0 5 :010(479) [0803] of Moses and the **law**, and therefore it is an "alien work"
E P : 0 5 :011(479) [0805] into a teaching of the **law**, the merit of Christ and the
E P : 0 6 :000(479) [0805] VI. The Third Function of the **Law**
E P : 0 6 :001(479) [0805] The **law** has been given to men for three reasons: (1) to
E P : 0 6 :001(480) [0805] the third function of the **law** that a controversy has arisen
E P : 0 6 :001(480) [0805] is whether or not the **law** is to be urged upon reborn
E P : 0 6 :002(480) [0805] curse and coercion of the **law**, they are not on that
E P : 0 6 :002(480) [0805] that account without the **law**; on the contrary, they have
E P : 0 6 :002(480) [0805] exercise themselves day and night in the **law** (Ps. 119:1).
E P : 0 6 :002(480) [0805] did not live without the **law**, for the law of God was
E P : 0 6 :002(480) [0805] without the law, for the **law** of God was written into their
E P : 0 6 :003(480) [0805] that the preaching of the **law** is to be diligently applied
E P : 0 6 :004(480) [0807] it is necessary for the **law** of God constantly to light their
E P : 0 6 :004(480) [0807] and threats of the **law**, but also by its punishments and
E P : 0 6 :005(480) [0807] between works of the **law** and fruits of the Spirit we
E P : 0 6 :005(480) [0807] done according to the **law** are, and are called, works of
E P : 0 6 :005(480) [0807] are called, works of the **law** as long as they are extorted
E P : 0 6 :006(481) [0807] children of God live in the **law** and walk according to the
E P : 0 6 :006(481) [0807] God live in the law and walk according to the **law** of God.
E P : 0 6 :006(481) [0807] epistles St. Paul calls it the **law** of Christ and the law of
E P : 0 6 :006(481) [0807] St. Paul calls it the law of Christ and the **law** of the mind.
E P : 0 6 :006(481) [0807] children are "not under the **law**, but under grace"
E P : 0 6 :007(481) [0807] unregenerated people the **law** is and remains one and the
E P : 0 6 :007(481) [0807] remains one and the same **law**, namely, the unchangeable
E P : 0 6 :007(481) [0807] is demanded of him by the **law** under coercion and
E P : 0 6 :007(481) [0807] does what no threat of the **law** could ever have wrung
E P : 0 6 :008(481) [0807] teaching that the **law** is not to be urged, in the manner
E P : 1 1 :009(495) [0833] to eternal life on the basis either of reason or God's **law**.
E P : 1 2 :025(500) [0843] can perfectly keep and fulfill the **law** of God in this life.
S D : P R :007(502) [0849] saved by the works of the **law** (Acts 15:1-5, 10, 24); some
S D : 0 1 :006(509) [0861] and condemnation of the **law** of God, so that we are "by
S D : 0 1 :030(513) [0867] man, so that God by his **law** does not accuse and
S D : 0 1 :031(513) [0869] of this corruption the **law** accuses and condemns man's
S D : 0 1 :032(513) [0869] The **law**, however, accuses and condemns our nature, not
S D : 0 2 :009(521) [0883] as of the teaching of the **law** (Rom. 1:19-21, 28, 32),
S D : 0 2 :013(523) [0885] does not submit to God's **law**, indeed it cannot"
S D : 0 2 :017(524) [0887] "We know that the **law** is spiritual; but I am carnal, sold
S D : 0 2 :017(524) [0887] my flesh, for I delight in the **law** of God in my inmost self
S D : 0 2 :017(524) [0887] in my members another **law** at war with the law of my
S D : 0 2 :017(524) [0887] law at war with the **law** of my mind and making me
S D : 0 2 :017(524) [0887] making me captive to the **law** of sin" (Rom. 7:18, 22, 23).
S D : 0 2 :018(524) [0887] persons wars against the **law** of God even after their
S D : 0 2 :018(524) [0887] obstinately opposed and hostile to God's **law** and will.
S D : 0 2 :034(528) [0895] that he wars with the **law** in his members and that
S D : 0 2 :050(530) [0901] of his divine, eternal **law** and the wonderful counsel
S D : 0 2 :054(531) [0903] the preaching of the **law** man learns to know his sins and
S D : 0 2 :063(533) [0905] man, and he delights in the **law** of God according to his
S D : 0 2 :064(533) [0905] "For I delight in the **law** of God in my inmost self, but I
S D : 0 2 :064(533) [0905] in my members another **law** at war with the law of my
S D : 0 2 :064(533) [0905] law at war with the **law** of my mind and making me
S D : 0 2 :064(533) [0905] making me captive to the **law** of sin which dwells in my
S D : 0 2 :064(533) [0907] then, I of myself serve the **law** of God with my mind, but
S D : 0 2 :064(533) [0907] mind, but with my flesh the **law** of sin" (Rom. 7:22, 23,
S D : 0 2 :075(536) [0911] the Gospel, and obey the **law** of God from the heart, and
S D : 0 2 :077(536) [0911] itself to God and to obey the **law** of God from the heart.
S D : 0 2 :079(536) [0911] conversion can keep the **law** of God perfectly in this life
S D : 0 2 :079(536) [0911] perfect obedience of the **law** merit righteousness before
S D : 0 2 :084(537) [0913] against the soul, and the **law** in our members is at war
S D : 0 2 :084(537) [0913] law in our members is at war with the **law** of our mind.
S D : 0 2 :085(537) [0913] man delights in the **law** of God according to the inmost
S D : 0 2 :085(537) [0913] sees in his members the **law** of sin at war with the law of
S D : 0 2 :085(537) [0913] members the law of sin at war with the **law** of his mind.
S D : 0 2 :085(537) [0913] For that reason with the **law** of his mind he serves the law
S D : 0 2 :085(537) [0913] of his mind he serves the **law** of God, but with his flesh he
S D : 0 2 :085(537) [0913] with his flesh he serves the **law** of sin (Rom. 7:22, 23, 25).
S D : 0 3 :007(540) [0917] such as "without the **law**," "without works," "by grace
S D : 0 3 :014(541) [0919] Christ when he satisfied the **law** for us and paid for our
S D : 0 3 :015(541) [0919] he was as little under the **law** — since he is the Lord of the
S D : 0 3 :015(541) [0919] since he is the Lord of the **law** — as he was obligated to
S D : 0 3 :015(541) [0919] subjection to the **law** in our stead and his keeping of the
S D : 0 3 :015(541) [0919] and his keeping of the **law** in so perfect a fashion that,
S D : 0 3 :029(544) [0925] through the works of the **law** or through love — not in
S D : 0 3 :029(544) [0925] off every reference to the **law** and the works of the law in
S D : 0 3 :029(544) [0925] to the law and the works of the **law** in this conjunction."
S D : 0 3 :030(544) [0925] with which he fulfilled the **law** of God in our stead and
S D : 0 3 :036(545) [0927] works," "without the **law**," "freely," "not of works," all of
S D : 0 3 :057(549) [0935] and immutable righteousness of God revealed in the **law**.
S D : 0 3 :058(550) [0937] was placed under the **law** for us, bore our sin, and in his
S D : 0 4 :003(551) [0939] and punishment of the **law** but flow from a spontaneous
S D : 0 4 :004(551) [0939] coercion with which the **law** forces men to do good
S D : 0 4 :019(554) [0945] willing and delights in the **law** of God in his inmost self,
S D : 0 4 :019(554) [0945] his flesh he finds another **law** which is not only unwilling
S D : 0 4 :019(554) [0945] but actually wars against the **law** of his mind.
S D : 0 5 :000(558) [0951] V. **Law** and Gospel
S D : 0 5 :001(558) [0951] The distinction between **law** and Gospel is an especially
S D : 0 5 :001(558) [0951] the two doctrines and change the Gospel into **law**.
S D : 0 5 :001(558) [0951] their greatest temptations against the terrors of the **law**.
S D : 0 5 :002(558) [0951] is strictly a function of the **law** of God, which reproves all
S D : 0 5 :002(558) [0953] been mired and which the **law** of God reproved, has been
S D : 0 5 :004(558) [0953] both the exposition of the **law** and the proclamation of
S D : 0 5 :005(559) [0953] the strict distinction of **law** and Gospel, it is correct to
S D : 0 5 :005(559) [0953] promises of the forgiveness of sins but also the divine **law**.
S D : 0 5 :009(559) [0955] knowledge comes from the **law**, but it is not sufficient for
S D : 0 5 :009(559) [0955] who have been terrified by the proclamation of the **law**.
S D : 0 5 :009(559) [0955] or the terrors of the **law** may not end in despair, the
S D : 0 5 :010(559) [0955] The mere preaching of the **law** without Christ either
S D : 0 5 :010(559) [0955] that they can fulfill the **law** by external works, or drives
S D : 0 5 :010(559) [0955] Therefore Christ takes the **law** into his hands and
S D : 0 5 :010(560) [0955] directs the sinner to the **law**, and there he really learns to
S D : 0 5 :010(560) [0955] so that they do not see the **law** spiritually, or how much it
S D : 0 5 :011(560) [0955] through the office of the **law**, must also convince the
S D : 0 5 :012(560) [0955] how or when it happens, is the proclamation of the **law**.
S D : 0 5 :012(560) [0955] the proclamation of the **law** and begin with the law in the
S D : 0 5 :012(560) [0955] the law and begin with the **law** in the case of those who as
S D : 0 5 :012(560) [0957] but it is Moses and the **law** pronounced upon the
S D : 0 5 :013(560) [0957] which cannot be done without the explanation of the **law**."
S D : 0 5 :014(560) [0957] performs the office of the **law**, which reveals sin and
S D : 0 5 :015(561) [0957] "The preaching of the **law** is not sufficient for genuine and
S D : 0 5 :015(561) [0957] cast the preaching of the **law** out of the churches and
S D : 0 5 :015(561) [0957] and sorrow not from the **law** but solely from the Gospel.
S D : 0 5 :017(561) [0957] that, strictly speaking, the **law** is a divine doctrine which
S D : 0 5 :017(561) [0957] the transgressors of the **law** with God's wrath and
S D : 0 5 :017(561) [0957] sin is and belongs to the **law**, the proper function of which
S D : 0 5 :017(561) [0957] of all culpable sin, the **law** reproves unbelief also.
S D : 0 5 :018(561) [0957] illustrates and explains the **law** and its doctrine;
S D : 0 5 :018(561) [0957] the true function of the **law** remains, to rebuke sin and to
S D : 0 5 :019(561) [0957] is the way in which the **law** rebukes unbelief, when a
S D : 0 5 :019(561) [0957] through the office of the **law** rebukes the unbelief
S D : 0 5 :020(561) [0959] man has failed to keep the **law** of God and has
S D : 0 5 :020(561) [0959] and deeds war against the **law**, and he is therefore subject
S D : 0 5 :020(561) [0959] and bore the curse of the **law** and expiated and paid for
S D : 0 5 :021(562) [0959] God to transgressors of the **law** strictly speaking is, and is
S D : 0 5 :022(562) [0959] Thus the **law**, as previously explained, is an office which
S D : 0 5 :022(562) [0959] by and learned from the **law**, since from the natural law
S D : 0 5 :022(562) [0959] since from the natural **law** even the heathen had to some
S D : 0 5 :024(562) [0961] the proclamation of the **law** and its threats will terrify the
S D : 0 5 :024(563) [0961] Rather, since "the **law** was our custodian until Christ
S D : 0 5 :024(563) [0961] Christ who is the end of the **law** (Rom. 10:4), the
S D : 0 5 :026(563) [0961] distinction between the **law** and the Gospel is thoroughly
S D : 0 5 :027(563) [0961] order that both doctrines, **law** and Gospel, may not be
S D : 0 5 :027(563) [0961] proper distinction between **law** and Gospel, and diligently
S D : 0 5 :027(563) [0961] the Gospel a teaching of **law**, as happened in the papacy,
S D : 0 5 :027(563) [0961] against the terrors of the **law** and reopen the door to the
S D : 0 5 :027(563) [0961] in distinction from the **law**, a proclamation of repentance
S D : 0 5 :027(563) [0961] Christ, whereas the **law** is a message that rebukes and
S D : 0 6 :000(563) [0963] VI. The Third Function of the **Law**
S D : 0 6 :001(563) [0963] The **law** of God serves (1) not only to maintain external
S D : 0 6 :001(563) [0963] of their sin through the **law**, (3) but those who have been
S D : 0 6 :001(564) [0963] away, learn from the **law** to live and walk in the law.
S D : 0 6 :001(564) [0963] away, learn from the law to live and walk in the **law**.
S D : 0 6 :001(564) [0963] concerning this third and last function of the **law**.
S D : 0 6 :002(564) [0963] should walk) from the **law**; nor should this doctrine in
S D : 0 6 :002(564) [0963] urged on the basis of the **law**, since they have been
S D : 0 6 :003(564) [0963] Holy Spirit uses the written **law** on them to instruct
S D : 0 6 :003(564) [0963] according to his written **law** and Word, which is a certain
S D : 0 6 :004(564) [0963] from the curse of the **law**, they should daily exercise
S D : 0 6 :004(564) [0963] exercise themselves in the **law** of the Lord, as it is
S D : 0 6 :004(564) [0963] man whose delight is in the **law** of the Lord, and on his
S D : 0 6 :004(564) [0963] of the Lord, and on his **law** he meditates day and night"
S D : 0 6 :004(564) [0963] For the **law** is a mirror in which the will of God and what
S D : 0 6 :005(564) [0963] It is true that the **law** is not laid down for the just, as St.
S D : 0 6 :005(564) [0963] as though the righteous should live without the **law**.
S D : 0 6 :005(564) [0963] For the **law** of God is written on their hearts, just as the
S D : 0 6 :005(564) [0963] his creation received a **law** according to which he should
S D : 0 6 :005(564) [0963] Paul's intention that the **law** cannot impose its curse upon
S D : 0 6 :005(564) [0963] to the inner man they delight in the **law** of God.
S D : 0 6 :006(564) [0965] free from sins, they would require no **law**, no driver.
S D : 0 6 :006(565) [0965] or driving by the **law** they would do what they are
S D : 0 6 :008(565) [0965] in my members another **law** at war with the law of my
S D : 0 6 :008(565) [0965] law at war with the **law** of my mind and making me
S D : 0 6 :008(565) [0965] of my mind and making me captive to the **law** of sin."
S D : 0 6 :009(565) [0965] and threatening of the **law**, but frequently the
S D : 0 6 :009(565) [0965] the punishment of the **law** as well, to egg them on so that
S D : 0 6 :010(565) [0965] and what function the **law** performs in this matter, as far
S D : 0 6 :011(565) [0965] The **law** indeed tells us that it is God's will and command
S D : 0 6 :011(565) [0965] and received through the **law** but through the preaching
S D : 0 6 :012(566) [0965] Then he employs the **law** to instruct the regenerate out of
S D : 0 6 :012(566) [0967] the Holy Spirit reproves them through the **law**.
S D : 0 6 :013(566) [0967] that is contrary to the **law** of God, and St. Paul says, "All
S D : 0 6 :014(566) [0967] But to reprove is the real function of the **law**.
S D : 0 6 :014(566) [0967] are rebuked through the Spirit of God out of the **law**.
S D : 0 6 :015(566) [0967] between the works of the **law** and those of the Spirit, we
S D : 0 6 :015(566) [0967] that are in accord with the **law** of God — for otherwise
S D : 0 6 :015(566) [0967] good works — the word "**law**" here has but one meaning,
S D : 0 6 :016(566) [0967] about living according to the **law** and the will of God.
S D : 0 6 :016(566) [0967] lives according to the **law**, and does its works merely
S D : 0 6 :016(566) [0967] punishment or in hope of reward, he is still under the **law**.
S D : 0 6 :016(566) [0967] such a man "works of the **law**" in the strict sense, because
S D : 0 6 :016(566) [0967] works are extorted by the **law**, just as in the case of
S D : 0 6 :017(566) [0967] and is liberated from the **law** (that is, when he is free from
S D : 0 6 :017(566) [0967] it is comprehended in the **law** and, in so far as he is born
S D : 0 6 :017(566) [0967] speaking, not works of the **law** but works and fruits of
S D : 0 6 :017(567) [0967] as St. Paul calls them, the **law** of the mind and the law of
S D : 0 6 :017(567) [0967] Paul calls them, the law of the mind and the **law** of Christ
S D : 0 6 :017(567) [0967] people are no longer under **law** but under grace
S D : 0 6 :018(567) [0967] self they delight in the **law** of God; but the law in their
S D : 0 6 :018(567) [0967] in the law of God; but the **law** in their members is at war
S D : 0 6 :018(567) [0967] in their members is at war against the **law** of their mind.

Continued ▶

SD : 06 :018(567) [0969] they are never without the **law**, they are not under but in
SD : 06 :018(567) [0969] are not under but in the **law**, they live and walk in the law
SD : 06 :018(567) [0969] they live and walk in the **law** of the Lord, and yet do
SD : 06 :018(567) [0969] Lord, and yet do nothing by the compulsion of the **law**.
SD : 06 :019(567) [0969] coerced not only with the **law** but also with miseries, for
SD : 06 :019(567) [0969] by the threats of the **law** (I Cor. 9:27; Rom. 7:18, 19).
SD : 06 :020(567) [0969] require the teaching of the **law** so that they will not be
SD : 06 :021(567) [0969] require the teaching of the **law** in connection with their
SD : 06 :021(567) [0969] But the **law** of God prescribes good works for faith in
SD : 06 :021(567) [0969] he himself learns from the **law** that his works are still
SD : 06 :022(567) [0969] The **law** demands a perfect and pure obedience if it is to
SD : 06 :023(567) [0969] are not under the **law** but under grace because their
SD : 06 :023(567) [0969] and condemnation of the **law** through faith in Christ.
SD : 06 :023(568) [0969] God not by coercion of the **law** but willingly and
SD : 06 :024(568) [0969] and threatening of the **law**, but frequently also with the
SD : 06 :024(568) [0971] either the preaching of the **law** or its threats and
SD : 06 :026(568) [0971] doctrine that the **law** in the manner and measure
SD : 07 :046(577) [0987] and to divine and natural **law** but also to the eminent
SD : 10 :012(613) [1057] that the works of the **law** are necessary for righteousness
SD : 11 :026(620) [1071] or on the basis of the **law**, or on the basis of some
SD : 12 :033(635) [1101] able to keep and fulfill the **law** of God perfectly in this

Laws (57)
AG : 16 :001(037) [0051] all established rule and **laws** were instituted and ordained
AG : 16 :002(037) [0051] and other existing **laws**, punish evildoers with the sword,
AG : 16 :006(038) [0051] obey its commands and **laws** in all that can be done
AG : 23 :008(052) [0061] by any human vows or **laws**, our priests and other clergy
AG : 23 :020(055) [0063] praised in the imperial **laws** and in all states in which
AG : 23 :020(055) [0063] and in all states in which there have been **laws** and justice.
AG : 28 :013(083) [0085] not annul temporal **laws** or undermine obedience to
AG : 28 :013(083) [0085] to the temporal power **laws** concerning worldly matters.
AG : 28 :035(086) [0089] and Word to make **laws** out of opinions or to require
AL : 16 :002(037) [0051] and other existing **laws**, to award just punishments, to
AL : 16 :006(038) [0051] obey their magistrates and **laws** except when commanded
AL : 23 :013(053) [0063] this was contrary to all **laws**, divine and human, and
AL : 23 :020(055) [0063] The **laws** of all well-ordered states, even among the
AL : 26 :045(070) [0075] apostles to enact binding **laws** with respect to holy days
AL : 28 :013(083) [0085] world, nor abrogate the **laws** of civil rulers, nor abolish
AL : 28 :013(083) [0085] prescribe to civil rulers **laws** about the forms of
AL : 28 :030(085) [0087] in the church and make **laws** concerning foods, holy
AP : 04 :006(108) [0121] nothing about the ceremonial and civil **laws** of Moses.
AP : 04 :015(109) [0123] come to give some sort of **laws** by which we could merit
AP : 04 :022(110) [0127] to preserve it he has given **laws**, learning, teaching,
AP : 04 :236(140) [0185] They are writing **laws** in blood and are asking the
AP : 04 :236(140) [0185] clement prince, that these **laws** should be promulgated.
AP : 07 :023(172) [0235] sacrifices, enact whatever **laws** he pleases, excuse and
AP : 07 :023(172) [0235] and exempt men from any **laws**, divine, canonical, or
AP : 16 :001(222) [0329] or other established **laws**, prescribe legal punishments,
AP : 16 :003(223) [0331] not introduce any new **laws** about the civil estate, but
AP : 16 :003(223) [0331] us to obey the existing **laws**, whether they were
AP : 16 :003(223) [0331] to try to impose on us the judicial **laws** of Moses.
AP : 16 :006(223) [0331] subjected to the **laws** of the seasons and to the change of
AP : 16 :012(224) [0333] may legitimately make use of civil ordinances and **laws**.
AP : 16 :012(224) [0333] of magistrates or of **laws**, they are legitimate in the sight
AP : 23 :003(239) [0363] Emperor, they propose **laws** which no barbarous
AP : 23 :041(245) [0375] In addition, the Levitical **laws** about uncleanness do not
AP : 23 :041(245) [0375] contrary to these **laws** was uncleanness; now it is not, for
AP : 23 :053(246) [0377] to change other **laws** if the common good demanded it,
AP : 23 :055(247) [0379] marriage with the strictest **laws** and examples and to
AP : 23 :056(247) [0379] and change other good **laws**; on this one law of celibacy
AP : 23 :064(248) [0381] ceremonies and purity **laws** of the Old Testament do not
AP : 27 :015(271) [0425] of the works of other **laws** that have now been thought
AP : 27 :051(278) [0437] law of nature in men cannot be repealed by vows or **laws**.
AP : 27 :051(278) [0437] Nor can any vows or any **laws** abolish the commandment
AP : 27 :065(280) [0441] condemns all worship, all **laws**, all works, if they are
AP : 28 :006(282) [0445] the authority to create **laws** which are useful for attaining
S3 : 08 :004(312) [0495] the pope boasts that "all **laws** are in the shrine of his
S3 : 10 :003(314) [0497] according to their own **laws**, for their laws state that
S3 : 10 :003(314) [0497] their own laws, for their **laws** state that those who are
TR : 00 :006(320) [0505] the authority to make **laws** concerning worship,
TR : 00 :006(320) [0505] his decrees, and his **laws** to be regarded as articles of faith
TR : 00 :078(333) [0527] have framed certain unjust **laws** concerning marriage and
TR : 00 :078(333) [0527] of conscience in their **laws**, but it would not be profitable
TR : 00 :078(333) [0527] are many unjust papal **laws** on matrimonial questions and
TR : 00 :079(333) [0527] they observe unjust **laws** in matrimonial cases; there are
SC : PR :005(338) [0533] the observance of human **laws**, yet you do not take the
SC : PR :013(339) [0535] to know and observe the **laws** under whose protection he
SC : PR :025(341) [0539] or if you adopt odious **laws** on the subject, it is your own
LC : PR :017(361) [0573] doctrines, estates, persons, **laws**, and everything else in
SD : 05 :023(562) [0959] transgressed God's **laws**, became a sinner, corrupted

Lawful (17), Lawfully (1), Lawfulness (1), Lawless (1), Lawlessness (1), Lawsuits (1), Lawyers (1)
AG : 27 :023(074) [0079] be their obligation, **lawfulness**, and power when they are
AL : 16 :001(037) [0051] Our churches teach that **lawful** civil ordinances are good
AL : 23 :003(051) [0061] and taught that it was **lawful** for them to contract
AL : 23 :009(052) [0061] our priests teach that it is **lawful** for them to have wives.
AL : 27 :004(071) [0077] to the canons, before they had attained a **lawful** age.
AL : 27 :018(073) [0077] matrimony that it is **lawful** for all who are not suited for
AL : 27 :024(074) [0079] dispensations, for it is not **lawful** for a man to annul an
AL : 28 :013(083) [0085] of civil rulers, nor abolish **lawful** obedience, nor interfere
AL : 28 :050(089) [0091] it follows that it is not **lawful** for bishops to institute such
AL : 28 :053(090) [0091] teachers reply that it is **lawful** for bishops or pastors to
AL : 28 :069(093) [0093] might easily retain the **lawful** obedience of men if they did
AP : 04 :022(110) [0127] and I Tim. 1:9, "The law is laid down for the **lawless**."
AP : 07 :050(178) [0245] are preserved by God, so **lawful** governments are
AP : 16 :001(222) [0329] marriage — in short, that **lawful** civil ordinances are
AP : 23 :033(244) [0373] These passages teach that marriage is a **lawful** thing.
AP : 23 :034(244) [0373] Paul says about **lawful** things (Tit. 1:15), "To the pure all
AP : 27 :051(278) [0437] such a vow is not **lawful** for anybody whose weakness
AP : 27 :062(280) [0441] of faith and immortality — surely a **lawful** purpose.
TR : 00 :012(322) [0507] it would not have been **lawful** for the council to withdraw
LC : 01 :249(398) [0651] To restrain open **lawlessness** is the responsibility of
LC : 01 :299(405) [0665] abetted by jurists and **lawyers** who twist and stretch the
LC : 01 :301(405) [0667] most frequently in **lawsuits** in which someone sets out to
LC : 01 :302(405) [0667] seal of the prince attesting that it was acquired **lawfully**.

Lawrence (1)
LC : 01 :011(366) [0583] fire, he sought St. **Lawrence** as his patron; if he feared the

Lay (19), Laying (5), Lays (4), Laid (30)
AG : 27 :004(071) [0077] fetters and burdens were **laid** on many before they had
AL : 26 :005(064) [0071] Paul therefore **lays** the greatest weight on this article and
AL : 27 :004(071) [0077] These fetters were **laid** on many, contrary to the canons,
AP : PR :017(099) [0103] not describe here how they **lay** hidden under all sorts of
AP : 04 :014(109) [0123] who, in their sermons, **laid** aside the Gospel and
AP : 04 :022(110) [0127] and I Tim. 1:9, "The law is **laid** down for the lawless."
AP : 04 :058(115) [0137] his sins, but he does not **lay** claim to any merit of his
AP : 04 :363(162) [0219] words apply, "There is **laid** up for me the crown of
AP : 13 :012(212) [0311] object either to calling the **laying** on of hands a
AP : 20 :005(227) [0339] says (53:6), "The Lord has **laid** on him the iniquity of us
AP : 20 :005(227) [0339] hand, teach that God has **laid** our iniquities on our works
AP : 22 :008(237) [0359] They also refer to "**lay** communion."
AP : 22 :008(237) [0359] were commanded to use **lay** communion, this indicated
AP : 22 :008(237) [0359] when they hear the phrase "**lay** communion" immediately
AP : 23 :059(247) [0379] We know we are **laying** ourselves open to the charge of
AP : 24 :049(258) [0401] daily sacrifice, we could **lay** more claim to observing it
S1 : PR :014(291) [0459] apart from these, God has **laid** so many tasks upon us in
S2 : 01 :002(292) [0461] "God has **laid** upon him the iniquities of us all"
TR : 00 :070(332) [0525] the election with the **laying** on of hands; nor was
SC : PR :018(340) [0537] **Lay** the greatest weight on those commandments or other
SC : PR :019(340) [0537] neglect they undermine and **lay** waste both the kingdom
LC : 01 :013(366) [0583] you see, does not mean to **lay** hands upon him, or put him
LC : 01 :014(366) [0583] We **lay** hold of him when our heart embraces him
LC : 01 :047(371) [0593] (for work, eventually to **lay** them aside) or as a traveler
LC : 01 :114(380) [0613] and so children could not **lay** it to heart; they simply
LC : 01 :122(382) [0615] do their duty until a rod is **laid** on their backs, they anger
LC : 01 :122(382) [0617] and joy of conscience and **lay** up for themselves nothing
LC : 01 :244(398) [0649] He **lays** on us one affliction after another, or he quarters
LC : 01 :276(402) [0659] be to observe the order **laid** down by the Gospel, Matthew
LC : 02 :028(414) [0685] We **lay** under God's wrath and displeasure, doomed to
LC : 02 :070(420) [0697] concerning the Creed to **lay** a foundation for the common
LC : 06 :013(458) [0000] and as often as we wish **lay** our complaint before a
EP : 02 :018(472) [0791] so that man not only **lays** hold on grace but also
EP : 08 :016(489) [0821] after his resurrection he **laid** aside completely the form of
EP : 08 :033(491) [0825] the human nature, after he **laid** aside the form of a slave,
EP : 08 :039(491) [0827] of humiliation he had **laid** it aside and forsaken it even
SD : 02 :081(537) [0911] or essence of man must be **laid** aside, he himself explains
SD : 02 :081(537) [0911] explains what it means to **lay** off the old man and put on
SD : 02 :081(537) [0913] man by adding, 'Therefore **lay** aside lies and speak the
SD : 02 :081(537) [0913] Behold, this is **laying** off the old man and putting on the
SD : 03 :013(541) [0919] a virtue, but because it **lays** hold on and accepts the merit
SD : 06 :005(564) [0963] is true that the law is not **laid** down for the just, as St.
SD : 07 :015(572) [0977] use, as when the bread is **laid** aside or reserved in the
SD : 07 :059(580) [0993] of the Gospel, when it is **laid** hold on by faith, is a means
SD : 07 :060(580) [0995] they actually and in deed **laid** violent hands upon the
SD : 08 :008(593) [1017] all eternity does not **lay** them aside, nor do the essential
SD : 08 :026(596) [1023] This is precisely that he has **laid** aside completely and
SD : 08 :026(596) [1023] (without, however, **laying** aside the human nature, which
SD : 08 :026(596) [1025] as the apostle testifies, he **laid** it aside, and as Dr. Luther
SD : 08 :051(600) [1033] of the servant had been **laid** aside and after the
SD : 08 :062(603) [1037] in Christ has completely **laid** aside its natural and
SD : 08 :065(604) [1039] form of a slave has been **laid** aside, it takes place fully,
SD : 11 :005(617) [1065] of the world was **laid**," as St. Paul says, "Even as he chose
SD : 11 :010(618) [1067] of the world were **laid**' (Eph. 1:4) and since God's
SD : 11 :043(623) [1077] of the world was **laid**" (Eph. 1:4), before we even existed,
SD : 11 :045(624) [1079] of the world was **laid**" he held counsel and ordained
SD : 11 :065(627) [1083] of the world was **laid**" (Eph. 1:4), as it is written, "He has
SD : 11 :088(631) [1093] of the world was **laid**") God elected us in Christ — "in

Layman (4), Laymen (5)
PR : PR :020(010) [0017] as far as the common **layman** is concerned, for he cannot
AG : 22 :001(049) [0059] us both kinds are given to **laymen** in the sacrament.
AG : 22 :005(050) [0061] mentions that the cup was given to **laymen** in his time.
AL : 22 :001(049) [0059] both kinds are given to **laymen** because this usage has the
TR : 00 :067(331) [0523] in an emergency even a **layman** absolves and becomes the
LC : 01 :314(407) [0671] chasuble or a **layman** remains on his knees a whole day in
EP : RN :005(465) [0777] They are "the **layman**'s Bible" and contain everything
SD : PR :008(505) [0853] ordinary people and **laymen** who for their eternal
SD : PR :008(505) [0853] God's Word for ordinary **laymen** in a most correct and

Lazy (14), Laziness (3)
AP : 23 :044(245) [0375] that the great crowd of **lazy** priests in the confraternities,
AP : 23 :044(245) [0375] boy who is used to being **lazy** hates those who are busy."
AP : 27 :005(269) [0421] monasteries just feed a **lazy** crowd that gorges itself on
SC : 05 :020(350) [0553] disobedient, unfaithful, **lazy**, ill-tempered, or
LC : PR :001(358) [0567] others because of sheer **laziness** and gluttony, behave in
LC : PR :004(359) [0567] if we are sluggish and **lazy**, as we used to be under the
LC : PR :009(359) [0569] Therefore, I beg these **lazy**-bellies and presumptuous
LC : PR :015(360) [0571] our weapons and armor, too **lazy** to give them a thought!
LC : PR :018(361) [0573] beyond a doubt that such **lazy**-bellies and presumptuous
LC : 01 :225(395) [0645] suppose that through **laziness**, carelessness, or malice a
LC : 03 :102(434) [0727] us daily into unchastity, **laziness**, gluttony and
LC : 04 :066(445) [0749] envious, unchaste, greedy, **lazy**, proud, yes, and
LC : 05 :040(451) [0761] men are becoming listless and **lazy** about its observance.
SD : 02 :015(523) [0887] might become remiss and **lazy** in reading, hearing, and
SD : 02 :046(530) [0899] dissolute and disorderly, **lazy** and indifferent to such
SD : 03 :042(547) [0931] and dead faith (since many **lazy** and secure Christians
SD : 06 :012(566) [0967] of the flesh they are **lazy**, negligent, and recalcitrant, the

Lead (29), Leader (1), Leaders (5), Leadership (1), Leading (5), Leads (12), Led (15)
PR : PR :018(008) [0015] allow himself to be **led** astray by the unwarranted
AG : 20 :033(045) [0057] who undertook to **lead** honorable and blameless lives;
AL : 28 :047(089) [0091] "Let them alone; they are blind and **leaders** of the blind."
AP : PR :011(099) [0101] here, even though I could **lead** our contemporaries still
AP : 04 :029(111) [0129] to live, and also for **leading** a holy life, then 'Christ died

Continued ▶

A P : 0 4 :139(126) [0161] teaches (Ps. 68:18), "He **led** captivity captive and gave
A P : 0 4 :302(154) [0205] glory to human works; it **leads** consciences into either
A P : 0 4 :322(157) [0209] *and Free Will,* "God **leads** us to eternal life, not by our
A P : 0 4 :372(164) [0221] the justified, who are **led** by the Spirit of Christ; nor can
A P : 0 4 :376(165) [0223] priestly mediation we are **led** to the Father and have a
A P : 1 2 :029(186) [0259] and eternal life, and to **lead** us as regenerated men to do
A P : 2 1 :041(235) [0355] doctrine because it **leads** to philosophical disputes rather
A P : 2 8 :020(284) [0449] quote the statement (Heb. 13:17), "Obey your **leaders**."
S 3 : 0 8 :005(312) [0495] He **led** them from the external Word of God to
T R : 0 0 :008(320) [0505] Who was to be the **leader** and, as it were, the vicar of
T R : 0 0 :032(325) [0513] with thorns and that he was **led** forth to be mocked in
S C : 0 1 :012(343) [0541] God, and so we should **lead** a chaste and pure life in word
S C : 0 3 :005(346) [0547] we, as children of God, **lead** holy lives in accordance with
S C : 0 3 :017(347) [0549] *"And **lead** us not into temptation."*
S C : 0 9 :003(355) [0561] "Obey your **leaders** and submit to them; for they are
S C : 0 9 :005(355) [0561] positions, that we may **lead** a quiet and peaceable life,
L C : S P :014(363) [0577] forgiven our debtors; and **lead** us not into temptation,
L C : S P :025(364) [0579] Thus our youth will be **led** into the Scriptures so they
L C : 0 1 :050(371) [0593] so this commandment **leads** us outward and directs the
L C : 0 1 :121(382) [0615] that we may not again be **led** astray from the pure Word
L C : 0 1 :128(383) [0617] considers this, unless he is **led** to it by the Holy Spirit.
L C : 0 1 :132(383) [0619] our greatest welfare, to **lead** us to a quiet, pleasant, and
L C : 0 1 :146(385) [0623] How can you **lead** a more blessed or holy life, as far as
L C : 0 1 :163(387) [0627] of lies to arise and **lead** us to the devil — and wring sweat
L C : 0 1 :172(388) [0629] both civil and spiritual **leadership**, we must spare no
L C : 0 1 :186(390) [0633] forbidden, but also everything that may **lead** to murder.
L C : 0 1 :217(394) [0641] our young people may be **led** to acquire a love for
L C : 0 2 :028(414) [0685] things, the devil came and **led** us into disobedience, sin,
L C : 0 2 :037(415) [0687] In other words, he first **leads** us into his holy community,
L C : 0 3 :052(427) [0711] So we pray that, **led** by the Holy Spirit, many may come
L C : 0 3 :099(433) [0725] *"And **lead** us not into temptation."*
L C : 0 3 :106(434) [0727] This, then, is "**leading** us not into temptation" when God
L C : 0 4 :011(437) [0735] with false appearances and **lead** us away from God's work
L C : 0 4 :029(440) [0739] but these **leaders** of the blind are unwilling to see that
L C : 0 5 :069(454) [0769] despise the sacrament and **lead** unchristian lives receive it
E P : R N :004(465) [0777] the year 1537, which the **leading** theologians approved by
E P : 0 6 :001(479) [0805] disobedient men, (2) to **lead** men to a knowledge of their
E P : 0 7 :015(483) [0813] teaching of the **leading** Church Fathers, such as
E P : 1 1 :007(495) [0833] Word of God, however, **leads** us to Christ, who is "the
E P : 1 1 :009(495) [0833] This would either **lead** us into a reckless, dissolute,
E P : 1 1 :015(496) [0835] either to despair or to **lead** a reckless and godless life.
S D : P R :008(502) [0849] will ultimately **lead** to the ruin of the pure doctrine.
S D : 0 1 :003(509) [0861] Apology declares) we are **led** to understand better and to
S D : 0 1 :060(519) [0879] Holy Scripture alone can **lead** to a right understanding
S D : 0 2 :026(526) [0891] and free will are able to **lead** an outwardly virtuous life.
S D : 0 2 :063(533) [0905] Paul says, "For all who are **led** by the Spirit of God are
S D : 0 2 :064(533) [0905] will offer themselves freely on the day you **lead** your host."
S D : 0 2 :066(534) [0907] Holy Spirit, guides and **leads** him, but if God should
S D : 0 3 :012(541) [0919] man's act of righteousness **leads** to acquittal and life for
S D : 0 3 :032(545) [0927] many good works and **leads** the best kind of life, a person
S D : 0 4 :033(556) [0949] not remain in those who **lead** a wicked life, lose the Holy
S D : 0 4 :036(557) [0949] arose on this point which **led** to many offensive
S D : 0 5 :009(559) [0955] becomes a "contrition that **leads** to salvation"
S D : 0 5 :017(561) [0957] is to condemn sin and to **lead** to a knowledge of sin"
S D : 0 5 :024(563) [0961] and hence points and **leads** not away from but toward the
S D : 0 7 :017(572) [0977] In the following year the **leading** theologians who were
S D : 0 7 :092(586) [1005] prestige they may have, to **lead** us away from the simple,
S D : 1 0 :010(612) [1055] of the Word as the **leaders** of the community of God, are
S D : 1 1 :010(618) [1065] Such a view, however, **leads** many to draw and formulate
S D : 1 1 :011(618) [1067] faith, and the good resolve to **lead** a godly life.
S D : 1 1 :020(619) [1069] and the flesh, guide and **lead** them in his ways, raise them
S D : 1 1 :059(626) [1083] This will **lead** us to live in the fear of God and to
S D : 1 1 :096(632) [1095] the smallest error but will **lead** the poor sinner to true and

Leap (2)
S 3 : 0 8 :013(313) [0497] of Gabriel, nor did he **leap** in his mother's womb until
L C : 0 1 :120(381) [0615] Should not the heart **leap** and melt with joy when it can

Learn (82), Learned (39), Learners (1), Learning (21), Learns (6)
P R : P R :010(006) [0011] of pious, irenic, and **learned** theologians noted these
P R : P R :013(007) [0013] experienced, and **learned** theologians at Torgau in the
A G : 2 0 :005(041) [0053] did, and they have also **learned** to speak now of faith,
A G : 2 4 :010(057) [0065] were often condemned by **learned** and devout men even
A G : 2 6 :005(064) [0071] so that we should **learn** that we do not become good in
A G : 2 6 :016(066) [0073] Many devout and **learned** people before our time have
A G : 2 7 :015(073) [0077] and inveigled into a monastery **learned** little about Christ.
A G : 2 7 :015(073) [0077] and other branches of **learning** which are profitable to the
A G : 2 7 :016(073) [0077] life for the purpose of **learning** the Scriptures, but now it
A G : 2 7 :023(074) [0079] **Learned** men say that a vow made contrary to papal
A G : 2 8 :003(081) [0085] been condemned by **learned** and devout people in
A L : 1 8 :005(040) [0053] will to keep cattle, will to **learn** various useful arts, or will
A L : 2 4 :007(056) [0065] that they may **learn** to believe in God and ask for and
A L : 2 6 :002(064) [0071] daily instituted, and the **learned** men in the churches
A L : 2 7 :015(073) [0077] and other branches of **learning** which were profitable to
A L : 2 7 :016(073) [0077] Formerly people came together in monasteries to **learn**.
A L : 2 8 :003(081) [0085] been rebuked in the church by devout and **learned** men.
A P : 0 4 :022(110) [0127] it he has given laws, **learning**, teaching, governments, and
A P : 0 4 :157(128) [0165] judgment of God we shall **learn** that this trust was vain
A P : 0 4 :198(134) [0175] Thus they **learn** not to trust in their own righteousness,
A P : 0 4 :229(139) [0183] Thus the great and **learned** scholastics proclaimed the
A P : 0 4 :258(144) [0193] "Cease to do evil, **learn** to do good; seek justice, correct
A P : 0 4 :262(145) [0195] definite Word of God to **learn** to know God's will,
A P : 0 4 :350(161) [0217] No one **learns** this without many severe struggles.
A P : 1 1 :008(181) [0251] by Panormitanus and other **learned** in the canon law.
A P : 1 2 :041(187) [0261] penitence, as even the more **learned** of the scholastics say.
A P : 1 2 :124(201) [0289] varied subjects in whose **learning** and faith men could
A P : 1 2 :125(201) [0289] take care that men of **learning** and integrity do the
A P : 1 2 :151(206) [0299] temptations they may **learn** to seek God's help and to
A P : 1 2 :164(208) [0303] Isa. 1:16-19 teaches: "Cease to do evil, **learn** to do good.
A P : 1 2 :174(210) [0307] What these fruit are, we **learn** from the commandments —
A P : 1 5 :040(220) [0325] the Psalms, it is not to **learn** or pray but for the sake of
A P : 1 5 :040(220) [0325] the Psalms in order to **learn**; the people sing, too, in
A P : 1 5 :040(220) [0325] the people sing, too, in order to **learn** or to worship.
A P : 2 0 :012(228) [0341] courses, for they have **learned** the trick of deducing from
A P : 2 1 :041(235) [0355] before, there were many **learned** and outstanding men
A P : 2 3 :004(239) [0365] case, especially when you **learn** that for our position we
A P : 2 4 :003(250) [0385] is that men may **learn** the Scriptures and that those who
A P : 2 4 :003(250) [0385] people something to **learn** that will arouse their faith and
A P : 2 4 :043(258) [0399] who want to look more **learned** take up philosophical
A P : 2 7 :070(281) [0443] in such observances, **learning** that they had forgiveness of
A P : 2 8 :018(284) [0449] the way many great and **learned** men in the church have
S 2 : 0 3 :001(297) [0471] for the education of **learned** men and decent women
S 3 : 0 0 :000(302) [0477] we may discuss with **learned** and sensible men, or even
S 3 : 0 6 :002(311) [0493] resort to the specious **learning** of the sophists and the
T R : 0 0 :082(000) [0529] great a number of most **learned** men who have now
S C : P R :009(339) [0535] at liberty to exhibit your **learning** and to discuss these
S C : P R :013(339) [0535] insist that the people **learn** to know how to distinguish
S C : P R :016(340) [0535] When the **learners** have a proper understanding of the
S C : 0 1 :006(342) [0541] of the same, but deem it holy and gladly hear and **learn** it.
S C : 0 9 :015(356) [0563] Let each his lesson **learn** with care
L C : P R :001(358) [0567] of their great and lofty **learning**, others because of sheer
L C : P R :006(359) [0569] have everything in books and can **learn** it all by ourselves.
L C : P R :007(359) [0569] a preacher — yes, and as **learned** and experienced as any
L C : P R :008(359) [0569] children and begin **learning** their ABC's, which they
L C : P R :009(359) [0569] not really and truly such **learned** and great doctors as
L C : P R :009(359) [0569] imagine that they have **learned** these parts of the
L C : P R :016(361) [0573] better or different to **learn**, though they cannot learn it to
L C : P R :016(361) [0573] to learn, though they cannot **learn** it to perfection.
L C : P R :016(361) [0573] to think we can finish **learning** in one hour what God
L C : P R :016(361) [0573] saints have been busy **learning** it and have always
L C : P R :019(361) [0573] to read and teach, to **learn** and meditate and ponder.
L C : P R :020(361) [0573] the less they know of it and the more they have to **learn**.
L C : S P :004(362) [0575] ascertain what they have **learned** of it, and if they do not
L C : S P :006(362) [0575] be satisfied if they **learned** the three parts which have been
L C : S P :015(363) [0577] We should **learn** to repeat them word for word.
L C : S P :017(363) [0577] do not know these things and are unwilling to **learn** them.
L C : S P :018(363) [0577] unruly that he refuses to **learn** these three parts in which
L C : S P :019(363) [0579] life, wisdom, and **learning** which constitute the
L C : S P :024(364) [0579] not assume that they will **learn** and retain this teaching
L C : S P :025(364) [0579] parts have been well **learned**, you may assign them also
L C : S P :026(364) [0579] for them simply to **learn** and repeat these parts verbatim.
L C : S P :026(364) [0579] hear it explained and may **learn** the meaning of every
L C : S P :027(364) [0581] youth, not in a lofty and **learned** manner but briefly and
L C : 0 1 :010(366) [0583] anyone boasts of great **learning**, wisdom, power, prestige,
L C : 0 1 :032(369) [0589] **Learn** from these words, then, how angry God is with
L C : 0 1 :042(370) [0591] contradiction, and **learn** that they neither lie nor deceive
L C : 0 1 :047(371) [0593] Let us therefore **learn** the first commandment well and
L C : 0 1 :050(371) [0593] have a God, so you must **learn** to grasp simply the
L C : 0 1 :072(374) [0601] I have tried it myself and **learned** by experience that often
L C : 0 1 :086(376) [0605] should devote their observance to **learning** God's Word.
L C : 0 1 :095(378) [0607] and refuse to hear and **learn** it, especially at the times
L C : 0 1 :098(378) [0609] hearing the Word but also about **learning** and retaining it.
L C : 0 1 :098(378) [0609] how you have heard and **learned** and honored his Word.
L C : 0 1 :103(379) [0611] Thus far we have **learned** the first three commandments,
L C : 0 1 :109(380) [0611] First, then, **learn** what this commandment requires
L C : 0 1 :139(384) [0621] **Learn** well, then, how important God considers
L C : 0 1 :157(387) [0627] God's Word we could **learn** how to obtain an abundance
L C : 0 1 :170(388) [0629] were no concern of ours what they **learn** or how they live.
L C : 0 1 :174(388) [0631] give them opportunity to **learn** and study so that they
L C : 0 1 :180(389) [0631] among our neighbors to **learn** how we should conduct
L C : 0 1 :187(390) [0633] Thus we may **learn** to calm our anger and have a patient,
L C : 0 1 :246(398) [0649] Whoever is willing to **learn** a lesson, let him know that
L C : 0 1 :248(398) [0651] this may go his own way until he **learns** it by experience.
L C : 0 1 :267(401) [0657] **Learning** a bit of gossip about someone else, they spread
L C : 0 1 :277(402) [0659] This lesson you can **learn** from the daily management of
L C : 0 1 :307(406) [0669] things may be, you must **learn** that God does not wish
L C : 0 1 :319(408) [0673] requires us to devote to **learning** how to teach and
L C : 0 1 :321(408) [0673] young and insist that they **learn** and remember it so that
L C : 0 1 :326(409) [0675] to despise his Word, but **learn** it, hear it gladly, keep it
L C : 0 2 :002(411) [0679] it is as necessary to **learn** this part as it is the other so
L C : 0 2 :004(411) [0679] for very simple persons to **learn** to understand the Creed
L C : 0 2 :016(412) [0681] Thus we **learn** from this article that none of us has his life
L C : 0 2 :024(413) [0683] ordinary people need to **learn** at first, both about what we
L C : 0 2 :026(413) [0685] Here we **learn** to know the second person of the
L C : 0 2 :026(413) [0685] of the article; from it we shall **learn** how we are redeemed.
L C : 0 2 :033(415) [0687] and it is so rich and broad that we can never **learn** it fully.
L C : 0 2 :040(416) [0689] **Learn** this article, then, as clearly as possible.
L C : 0 2 :063(419) [0695] sought painstakingly to **learn** what God is and what he
L C : 0 2 :070(420) [0697] may on their own initiative **learn** more, relating these
L C : 0 2 :070(420) [0697] Catechism all that they **learn** in the Scriptures, and thus
L C : 0 2 :070(420) [0697] have enough to preach and **learn** on the subject of faith.
L C : 0 3 :018(422) [0703] We must **learn** that God will not have this commandment
L C : 0 3 :033(424) [0707] in order that men may **learn** above all to value prayer as a
L C : 0 3 :051(426) [0711] Answer: Simply what we **learned** in the Creed, namely,
L C : 0 3 :119(436) [0731] of prayer consists in our **learning** also to say "Amen" to it
L C : 0 4 :002(437) [0733] heretics and sectarians we shall leave to the **learned**.
L C : 0 4 :023(439) [0737] be regarded, we must also **learn** for what purpose it was
L C : 0 4 :032(440) [0739] the third place, having **learned** the great benefit and
L C : 0 4 :048(442) [0743] this question from their minds and refer it to the **learned**.
L C : 0 5 :004(447) [0753] of Baptism, we shall first **learn** what is of greatest
L C : 0 5 :028(449) [0759] with their great **learning** and wisdom, bellowing and
L C : 0 5 :061(453) [0767] with such misgivings must **learn** that it is the highest
L C : 0 6 :005(457) [0000] Unfortunately, men have **learned** in only too well; they do
E P : 0 1 :024(469) [0785] In schools and **learned** circles these words can profitably
E P : 0 5 :008(479) [0803] as a result they fail to **learn** the true nature of sin from
E P : 0 5 :008(479) [0803] heaven" over all sinners and men **learn** how fierce it is.
E P : 0 5 :008(479) [0803] to the law, and now they **learn** from it for the first time
E P : 1 1 :010(495) [0833] 9. We must **learn** about Christ from the Holy Gospel
S D : 0 1 :008(510) [0861] something that has to be **learned** and believed from the
S D : 0 2 :015(523) [0887] might rightly comprehend and **learn** the divine doctrine.
S D : 0 2 :016(523) [0887] we cannot study and **learn** anything pleasing to him and
S D : 0 2 :054(531) [0903] preaching of the law man **learns** to know his sins and the
S D : 0 2 :070(535) [0909] heart, so that the heart **learns** to know sin, to fear the
S D : 0 3 :011(541) [0919] God whereby we rightly **learn** to know Christ as our
S D : 0 5 :010(560) [0955] law, and there he really **learns** to know his sin, an insight
S D : 0 5 :022(562) [0959] which is taught by and **learned** from the law, since from

Continued ▶

SD : 0 6 :001(564) [0963] has been taken away, **learn** from the law to live and walk
SD : 0 6 :002(564) [0963] the regenerated do not **learn** the new obedience (that is, in
SD : 0 6 :003(564) [0963] even true believers **learn** to serve God not according to
SD : 0 6 :009(565) [0965] was afflicted that I might **learn** thy statutes" (Ps. 119:71).
SD : 0 6 :021(567) [0969] and he himself **learns** from the law that his works
SD : 0 7 :031(574) [0983] the grace of God I have **learned** to know a great deal
SD : 0 7 :054(579) [0991] From these words we **learn** clearly that not only the cup
SD : 1 0 :025(615) [1061] exposition everyone can **learn** what a Christian
SD : 1 1 :033(621) [1073] his Gospel so that you **learn** to know your sins and his
SD : 1 1 :036(622) [1075] and admonishes us to **learn** and to determine God's will
SD : 1 1 :060(626) [1083] condemnation, we may **learn** the more diligently to
SD : 1 1 :078(629) [1089] the Word of God not to **learn** but only to despise,

Least (36)
PR : PR :017(008) [0015] doctrine or in the **least** point to depart from the Augsburg
AL : 2 3 :025(055) [0065] fire through their lusts; at **least** they should give no
AP : 0 2 :017(102) [0109] of God, trust in God, or at **least** the inclination and
AP : 0 2 :027(103) [0113] the more recent ones — at **least** the more sensible among
AP : 0 4 :241(141) [0187] on civil war if either had yielded the **least** bit to the other.
AP : 0 4 :379(165) [0223] done by the reason or at **least** wrought by the impulse of
AP : 1 2 :106(197) [0283] That at **least** would be more consistent.
AP : 1 5 :040(220) [0325] were an act of worship or at **least** worth some reward.
S 2 : 0 4 :004(299) [0473] five hundred years at the **least** and that the churches of
S 3 : 0 3 :016(305) [0483] repentant), he should at **least** be attrite (which I might
TR : 0 0 :082(000) [0529] that I am of all the **least**, yet, as I am not permitted to
SC : PR :006(338) [0533] to do better at **least** take this booklet and these forms and
SC : PR :022(341) [0537] receive the sacrament at **least** three or four times a year
LC : PR :003(358) [0567] would read, instead, at **least** a page or two from the
LC : PR :009(359) [0569] Catechism perfectly, or at **least** sufficiently, even though
LC : SP :004(362) [0575] children and servants at **least** once a week and ascertain
LC : 0 1 :085(376) [0605] common people can do, at **least** one day in the week must
LC : 0 1 :089(377) [0605] week for the young, and at **least** a day for the whole
LC : 0 1 :142(385) [0621] in the same way, or at **least** do not treat and honor them
LC : 0 1 :184(390) [0633] begrudge you even the **least** good, whether physical or
LC : 0 1 :301(405) [0667] arguments have the **least** semblance of right, so
LC : 0 2 :063(419) [0695] he thinks and does, yet it has never succeeded in the **least**.
LC : 0 3 :025(423) [0705] night; not one of them thinks of asking for the **least** thing.
LC : 0 3 :074(430) [0719] there our daily bread is taken away, or at **least** reduced.
LC : 0 3 :103(434) [0727] No one is willing to be the **least**, but everyone wants to sit
LC : 0 3 :105(434) [0727] it is impossible to overcome even the **least** temptation.
LC : 0 4 :001(436) [0733] Christian ought to have at **least** some brief, elementary
LC : 0 5 :050(452) [0765] I would surely have at **least** a little longing to do what my
LC : 0 5 :055(453) [0767] pure that God might not find the **least** blemish in us.
LC : 0 5 :076(455) [0771] feel the need, therefore, at **least** believe the Scriptures.
LC : 0 5 :078(455) [0771] so utterly dead in sin, at **least** believe the Scriptures,
LC : 0 5 :084(456) [0773] you into misery and distress when you **least** expect it!
SD : 0 1 :001(508) [0859] essence of fallen man, at **least** the foremost and noblest
SD : 0 1 :025(512) [0867] matters, not even the **least** thing (such as, for example,
SD : 0 2 :025(526) [0891] entirely or one-half or the **least** and tiniest part, but
SD : 1 1 :036(622) [1075] it with absolute certainty and not doubt it in the **least**.

Leave (24), Leaves (4), Leaving (9), Left (24)
PR : PR :024(013) [0021] so that the way may not be **left** free and open to restless,
AG : 2 3 :013(053) [0063] God himself instituted and **left** free to man) never
AG : 2 7 :033(076) [0079] excuse and reason for **leaving** their monasteries inasmuch
AL : 2 7 :033(076) [0079] have an excuse for **leaving** the monastery because a
AP : 0 4 :282(149) [0201] alms from what you have **left** over, and thus all things
AP : 0 4 :301(153) [0205] On these issues consciences are **left** in doubt.
AP : 0 4 :319(156) [0209] the opponents' teaching **leaves** consciences in doubt, so
AP : 0 4 :341(159) [0215] We **leave** these thorny questions to the schools.
AP : 0 4 :377(165) [0223] be understood, and what is **left** of the doctrine of
AP : 0 7 :023(172) [0235] the Scriptures by his **leave**, institute devotions and
AP : 1 2 :088(195) [0277] Gospel; our opponents **leave** consciences wavering and
AP : 1 2 :106(197) [0283] to his own property and **leave** other people's alone, but
AP : 2 2 :005(236) [0359] exaggerating here, but we **leave** it to the prudent reader to
AP : 2 3 :022(242) [0369] The matter should be **left** free, and no snares should be
AP : 2 4 :003(250) [0385] belabor this point, but we **leave** it up to the judgment of
AP : 2 4 :056(260) [0405] is no other such sacrifice **left** in the New Testament
AP : 2 7 :003(269) [0419] in the commentaries he **left** on certain passages in Daniel.
AP : 2 7 :025(273) [0427] a way that there are merits **left** over, when these
AP : 2 7 :039(276) [0433] they really believe that they have merits **left** over.
AP : 2 7 :040(276) [0433] (Matt. 19:29), "Every one who has **left** houses," etc.
AP : 2 7 :040(276) [0433] not mean to say that **leaving** parents or wife or brothers
AP : 2 7 :040(276) [0433] Indeed, such **leaving** is accursed; for if someone leaves his
AP : 2 7 :040(276) [0433] accursed; for if someone **leaves** his parents or or his wife
AP : 2 7 :041(276) [0435] There are two kinds of **leaving**.
AP : 2 7 :041(276) [0435] that Christ speaks of **leaving** wife and children makes it
AP : 2 7 :041(276) [0435] The other kind of **leaving** is that which happens by a
AP : 2 7 :041(276) [0435] or a tyranny forces us to **leave** or to deny the Gospel.
AP : 2 7 :041(276) [0435] This kind of **leaving** Christ approves.
AP : 2 7 :042(276) [0435] We should **leave** our body, too, for the Gospel.
AP : 2 7 :042(276) [0435] to commit suicide and to **leave** our body without the
AP : 2 7 :042(276) [0435] it is a service to God to **leave** possessions, friends, wife,
AP : 2 8 :007(282) [0445] Christ wanted to **leave** their use free when he said
AP : 2 8 :016(283) [0447] ordinances ought to be **left** free, only that offenses should
AP : 2 8 :027(285) [0451] Now we **leave** it to the judgment of all pious people
S 2 : 0 2 :013(295) [0467] He **leaves** it undecided whether or not there is a purgatory
S 3 : 0 3 :036(309) [0489] repentance, for nothing is **left** that we might imagine to
S 3 : 0 8 :002(312) [0495] of sins should be **left** free to everybody to do or not as he
TR : 0 0 :062(330) [0521] from Titus, "This is why I **left** you in Crete, that you
SC : 0 9 :013(356) [0563] who is a real widow, and is **left** all alone, has set her hope
LC : 0 1 :046(370) [0593] cannot lie or deceive; just **leave** it to the devil and the
LC : 0 1 :057(372) [0597] no one shall a violation be condoned or **left** unpunished.
LC : 0 1 :165(387) [0627] Do your duty, then, and **leave** it to God how he will
LC : 0 1 :180(389) [0631] In this commandment we **leave** our own house and go
LC : 0 1 :247(398) [0651] sorrowful hearts, and he will not **leave** them unavenged.
LC : 0 1 :277(402) [0659] If we were so foolish as to **leave** the servant at home while
LC : 0 1 :305(406) [0667] was obliged to dismiss her and **leave** her to the other man.
LC : 0 1 :308(406) [0669] the public may have to **leave** you in possession of it, but
LC : 0 1 :309(407) [0669] for it; we are willingly to **leave** him what is his, and
LC : 0 3 :008(421) [0699] This God requires of us; he has not **left** it to our choice.
LC : 0 3 :009(421) [0699] Just so, it is not **left** to my choice here whether to pray or
LC : 0 4 :002(437) [0733] heretics and sectarians we shall **leave** to the learned.
LC : 0 4 :056(444) [0747] I may be strong or weak; I **leave** that in God's hands.
LC : 0 5 :046(452) [0763] it'; so he compels no one, but **leaves** it to our free choice."
LC : 0 6 :014(458) [0000] like the other two but is **left** to everyone to use whenever
LC : 0 6 :020(459) [0000] no such comfort, we shall **leave** you to another's power.
EP : 0 4 :011(477) [0799] as though it were **left** to the regenerated person's option
SD : 0 6 :009(565) [0965] and again, "If you are **left** without discipline in which all
SD : 0 7 :099(586) [1005] concerning Christ's **leaving** the world and going to the
SD : 0 7 :100(586) [1007] mode of presence when he **left** the closed grave and came
SD : 0 8 :070(605) [1041] in subjection to him, he **left** nothing outside his control"
SD : 1 1 :056(625) [1081] with the Word, while we **leave** the time and hour to God

Leaven (1)
SD : 0 3 :007(540) [0917] this doctrine that a little **leaven** ferments the whole lump.

Lechery (2)
AG : 2 3 :003(051) [0061] adultery, and other **lechery**, some of our priests have
SD : 0 2 :074(536) [0909] doing such wicked acts as **lechery**, robbery, and murder.

Lecturing (1)
S 1 : PR :004(289) [0455] I am still writing, preaching, and **lecturing** every day.

Legal (9), Legalistic (3), Legality (2), Legally (2)
AG : PR :022(027) [0043] matters, and have done so in **legal** form and procedure.
AL : 1 6 :002(037) [0051] serve as soldiers, to make **legal** contracts, to hold
AL : 2 6 :022(067) [0073] which was seen to be **legalistic** and to have a relationship
AL : 2 8 :029(085) [0087] or jurisdiction to decide **legal** cases (for example,
AP : 0 4 :265(146) [0197] This **legalistic** opinion clings by nature to the minds of
AP : 1 2 :008(183) [0255] our opponents give the **legalistic** reply that Judas did not
AP : 1 2 :048(188) [0265] the bond which stood against us with its **legal** demands.
AP : 1 6 :001(222) [0329] established laws, prescribe **legal** punishments, engage in
AP : 1 6 :001(222) [0329] military service, enter into **legal** contracts, own property,
AP : 1 6 :006(223) [0331] by its prohibition of **legal** redress and by other teachings
S 1 : PR :012(290) [0459] in like a deluge and have taken on the color of **legality**.
S 2 : 0 2 :021(296) [0467] themselves to transfer (by **legal** and open sale) all Masses,
SC : 0 1 :018(344) [0541] them under pretext of **legal** right, but be of service and
LC : 0 1 :229(396) [0645] and yet with a great show of **legality** they rob and steal.
LC : 0 1 :295(404) [0665] the other's from him so that he might **legally** take her.
LC : 0 1 :302(405) [0667] away from the owner and **legally** awarded to him with

Legates (1)
S 3 : 0 3 :025(307) [0485] So they sent their **legates** out into all lands until every

Legends (1)
AP : 2 1 :037(234) [0355] ceremonies, or the **legends**, as they call them, and the

Legions (1)
AP : 1 2 :070(192) [0271] prophets, to the many **legions** of commentators on the

Legislate (1), Legislator (1)
AP : 0 4 :392(167) [0225] him not the propitiator and justifier, but only a **legislator**.
AP : 1 6 :006(223) [0331] The Gospel does not **legislate** for the civil estate but is the

Legitimacy (2), Legitimate (11), Legitimately (3)
AP : 0 7 :003(169) [0227] men; indeed, we may **legitimately** use sacraments that are
AP : 0 7 :050(178) [0245] It is **legitimate** for Christians to use civil ordinances just
AP : 0 7 :050(178) [0245] ordinances just as it is **legitimate** for them to use the air,
AP : 1 6 :001(222) [0329] that a Christian might **legitimately** hold public office,
AP : 1 6 :002(222) [0331] make outward use of the **legitimate** political ordinances
AP : 1 6 :012(224) [0333] that a Christian may **legitimately** make use of civil
AP : 1 6 :012(224) [0333] or of laws, they are **legitimate** in the sight of God as well.
AP : 2 2 :016(238) [0361] writers who defend the **legitimacy** of withholding both
AP : 2 3 :047(246) [0377] very troubled about the **legitimacy** of being married.
AP : 2 7 :009(269) [0421] We maintain that **legitimate** vows should be kept, but we
AP : 2 7 :009(270) [0421] Are vows made with these notions in mind **legitimate**?
AP : 2 7 :009(270) [0421] Are vows **legitimate** that have been taken with the pretext
AP : 2 7 :009(270) [0421] Are vows **legitimate** if they openly point to an evil end,
AP : 2 7 :011(270) [0423] it certainly is not a **legitimate** vow if the one making it
AP : 2 8 :015(283) [0447] the extent to which it is **legitimate** for them to create
TR : 0 0 :035(326) [0513] throne is vacant, the pope is the **legitimate** successor."

Legs (1)
SC : 0 8 :010(354) [0559] nor his pleasure in the **legs** of a man; but the Lord takes

Leiningen (1)
PR : PR :027(015) [0025] Emich, count of **Leiningen**

Leisure (3)
AP : 2 7 :021(272) [0427] advantage, to have more **leisure** for teaching and other
AP : 2 7 :043(277) [0435] for the sake of food and **leisure**; instead of a slender
LC : 0 1 :089(377) [0605] have this much time and **leisure**, we must set apart

Leita (1)
AP : 2 4 :083(264) [0413] means prayers, but from ***leita***, which means public goods;

Lend (2), Lends (1)
AP : 2 1 :030(233) [0351] extinguished, they begged the wise ones to **lend** them oil.
LC : 0 1 :251(399) [0651] we are to help, share, and **lend** to both friends and foes.
LC : 0 1 :252(399) [0653] who is kind to the poor **lends** to the Lord, and he will

Length (25), Lengthy (7)
AG : 0 0 :001(095) [0095] prolixity and undue **length** we have indicated only the
AL : 0 0 :001(095) [0095] to avoid undue **length** we have discussed only the
AP : 0 2 :004(101) [0105] Later on we shall show at **length** that our definition
AP : 0 2 :041(105) [0115] In a **lengthy** discussion Augustine refutes the opinion that
AP : 0 2 :051(107) [0119] reluctant to enter upon their arguments at great **length**.
AP : 0 4 :029(111) [0129] Augustine maintains at **length** that grace is not given
AP : 0 4 :087(120) [0147] maintains in his **lengthy** discussion on *The Spirit and the*
AP : 0 7 :001(168) [0227] And they have added a **lengthy** dissertation, that the
AP : 0 7 :003(168) [0227] to defend ourselves at any **length** against this slander.
AP : 0 7 :033(174) [0239] But as the different **length** of day and night does not harm
AP : 1 2 :083(194) [0275] we want to avoid being **lengthy** in order to make our case
AP : 1 5 :002(215) [0315] discussed traditions at **length** in Article XXVI of the
AP : 1 5 :006(215) [0317] have previously shown at **length** that men are justified by

Continued ▶

AP : 2 4 :078(263) [0411] arguments which do not deserve a **lengthy** discussion.
AP : 2 4 :092(266) [0417] There is no need here of a very **lengthy** discussion.
AP : 2 7 :011(270) [0423] freely for Christ's sake, as we have said at **length** above.
AP : 2 7 :020(272) [0425] we have above shown at **length** the wickedness of the
S 1 : 0 1 :000(292) [0461] it is not necessary to treat them at greater **length**.
SC : PR :017(340) [0537] find all of this treated at **length** in the many books written
LC : 0 1 :048(371) [0593] We had to explain it at **length** since it is the most
LC : 0 1 :308(406) [0669] it will take a yard, and at **length** open injustice and
LC : 0 2 :032(415) [0687] appointed for dealing at **length** with such articles as the
LC : 0 3 :073(430) [0719] life itself cannot be maintained for any **length** of time.
LC : 0 3 :083(431) [0721] prosper or last for any **length** of time, as indeed we see
EP : RN :005(465) [0777] discusses at greater **length** and which a Christian must
SD : PR :007(505) [0853] are set forth at necessary **length** for renouncing the
SD : 0 1 :049(517) [0875] not discussing it here at **length** but are treating only the
SD : 0 2 :018(524) [0887] pointed out at greater **length** in the article on original sin
SD : 0 6 :009(565) [0965] explains this at greater **length** in the summer portion of
SD : 0 7 :020(572) [0979] this position at greater **length** from the Word of God in
SD : 0 7 :110(588) [1011] have been refuted at **length** in the common Confession of
SD : 1 1 :064(626) [1083] After a **lengthy** discussion of this article on the basis of

Leniency (3), Lenient (1), Leniently (1)
AG : 0 0 :002(048) [0059] in all fairness act more **leniently**, even if there were some
AG : 2 3 :026(055) [0065] the canons show great **leniency** and fairness toward those
AL : 0 0 :002(047) [0059] should have been so **lenient** as to bear with us on account
AL : 2 7 :025(074) [0079] prudently judged that **leniency** should be observed in
AP : 0 4 :243(141) [0189] this duty of love which the philosophers call "**leniency**."

Lent (1)
AP : 1 5 :042(221) [0325] are preached during the whole year, except in **Lent**.

Leo (5)
AP : 0 2 :035(104) [0115] add that this doctrine was properly condemned by **Leo** X.
AP : 0 4 :397(167) [0227] The bull of **Leo** X has condemned a very necessary
AP : 1 2 :067(191) [0271] **Leo** quite openly condemns this doctrine of the
EP : 0 7 :015(483) [0813] as Chrysostom, Cyprian, **Leo** I, Gregory, Ambrose,
SD : 0 7 :037(575) [0985] Cyprian, Augustine, **Leo**, Gelasius, Chrysostom, and

Leprosy (5), Leprous (2)
LC : 0 5 :077(455) [0771] it is a sign that ours is a **leprous** flesh which feels nothing
SD : 0 1 :006(509) [0861] sin, like a spiritual **leprosy**, has thoroughly and entirely
SD : 0 1 :033(514) [0869] a spiritual poison and **leprosy**, has so poisoned and
SD : 0 1 :033(514) [0869] as in the case of external **leprosy** the body which is
SD : 0 1 :033(514) [0869] the body which is **leprous** and the leprosy on or in the
SD : 0 1 :033(514) [0869] which is leprous and the **leprosy** on or in the body are
SD : 0 7 :087(585) [1003] bells, or to cure **leprosy**, or is otherwise exposed for

Leptines (1)
AP : 2 4 :081(264) [0411] As Demosthenes' oration ***Leptines*** shows, it is completely

Less (39), Lesser (2)
PR : PR :022(011) [0019] the divine Word, and far **less** do we mean entire churches
AG : 2 7 :023(074) [0079] How much **less** must be their obligation, lawfulness, and
AL : 1 8 :004(039) [0051] God, to begin or (much **less**) to accomplish anything in
AL : 2 4 :014(057) [0065] them in time, there would now have been **less** dissension.
AL : 2 7 :023(074) [0079] How much **less** are those vows valid which are made
AP : 0 4 :105(122) [0153] them, they contribute **less** to an understanding of Paul
AP : 0 4 :139(126) [0161] Nothing **less** than Christ's power is needed for our
AP : 0 4 :228(139) [0183] the offered promise, is no **less** an act of worship than is
AP : 0 4 :264(146) [0195] he maintains with even **less** authority that the forgiveness
AP : 0 7 :022(172) [0235] pontiffs as well as those in **lesser** stations have apostasized
AP : 1 2 :040(187) [0261] of the one absolving no **less** than we would believe a voice
AP : 1 5 :030(219) [0323] do not justify, how much **less** do the traditions of men
AP : 1 6 :009(224) [0333] David, and Daniel were no **less** perfect than any hermit.
AP : 2 3 :064(248) [0381] polygamists, was purer and **less** inflamed with lust than
AP : 2 7 :004(269) [0421] there are other signs, no **less** sure than oracles, which
AP : 2 7 :014(271) [0425] of sins, how much **less** do these silly observances merit
AP : 2 7 :033(275) [0431] promised in Christ, much **less** do monastic observances,
S 2 : 0 4 :004(299) [0473] This is nothing **less** than to say, "Although you believe in
S 3 : 0 9 :000(314) [0497] However, the **lesser** (that is, the truly Christian)
LC : PR :018(361) [0573] a single Psalm, much **less** the entire Scriptures, yet they
LC : PR :020(361) [0573] with the Catechism, the **less** they know of it and the more
LC : 0 1 :217(394) [0643] honor, and there may be **less** of the filthy, dissolute,
LC : 0 1 :287(403) [0663] of the body which we think **less** honorable we invest with
LC : 0 4 :059(444) [0747] Gold remains no **less** gold if a harlot wears it in sin and
LC : 0 5 :012(448) [0755] scholars put together have **less** wisdom than the divine
LC : 0 5 :078(455) [0771] In short, the **less** you feel your sins and infirmities, the
EP : 0 7 :032(485) [0815] time in may places, still **less** in all places, where his Holy
EP : 0 8 :030(490) [0825] more than one place, still **less** to be present with his body
EP : 0 8 :035(491) [0825] received a power which is **less** than God's omnipotence
SD : PR :009(503) [0849] the church of God, much **less** be excused and defended.
SD : 0 2 :009(522) [0883] with their reason, the **less** they understand or believe, and
SD : 0 2 :013(523) [0885] Much **less** will he be able truly to believe the Gospel, give
SD : 0 4 :037(557) [0951] himself, who declares no **less** than three times in Phil.
SD : 0 7 :022(573) [0979] scholars put together have **less** wisdom than the divine
SD : 0 7 :071(582) [0997] (Mark 9:24) partook no **less** than Abraham, Paul, and
SD : 0 8 :011(593) [1019] without his humanity no **less** than without his deity the
SD : 1 1 :002(616) [1063] and unnecessary, still **less** offensive and detrimental,
SD : 1 1 :055(625) [1081] it in the Word, still **less** has commanded us to explore it
SD : 1 1 :073(628) [1087] should not be idle, still **less** oppose the urgings of the
SD : 1 1 :073(628) [1087] within themselves, the **less** they will doubt their election.
SD : 1 1 :095(632) [1095] Still **less** by far are we minded to whitewash or cover up

Lesson (5), Lessons (10)
AL : 2 6 :040(069) [0075] us (such as the order of **lessons** in the Mass, holy days,
AP : 0 7 :040(176) [0241] they also observed other rites and a sequence of **lessons**.
AP : 1 2 :161(208) [0303] eternal life, but the **lesson** of the threat followed so that
AP : 2 3 :049(246) [0377] rites were introduced as **lessons** for the ignorant and not
AP : 2 4 :001(249) [0385] such as the order of the **lessons**, prayers, vestments, etc.
AP : 2 4 :003(250) [0385] out that our churches keep the Latin **lessons** and prayers.
AP : 2 4 :005(250) [0385] men benefit from hearing **lessons** they do not understand,
AP : 2 7 :055(278) [0439] ceremonial worship — **lessons**, chants, and the like —
AP : 2 7 :055(278) [0439] as exercises, the way **lessons** are in school, with the
AP : 2 7 :055(278) [0439] brief and pointed **lessons** would be more useful than these
AP : 2 7 :069(281) [0443] the observance of foods, **lessons**, chants, vestments,
SC : 0 9 :015(356) [0563] Let each his **lesson** learn with care
LC : 0 1 :114(380) [0613] have had an object **lesson** in goodness and happiness.
LC : 0 1 :246(398) [0649] is willing to learn a **lesson**, let him know that this is God's
LC : 0 1 :277(402) [0659] This **lesson** you can learn from the daily management of

Lest (56)
PR : PR :018(008) [0015] Furthermore, **lest** anybody allow himself to be led astray
PR : PR :022(012) [0021] to warn them against it, **lest** one blind person let himself
AG : 2 0 :011(042) [0055] — not because of works, **lest** any man should boast," etc.
AG : 2 6 :035(069) [0075] "Take heed to yourselves **lest** your hearts be weighed
AL : 2 0 :012(042) [0055] **Lest** anyone should captiously object that we have
AL : 2 2 :003(049) [0059] **Lest** anybody should captiously object that this refers
AL : 2 6 :035(069) [0075] "Take heed to yourselves **lest** your hearts be weighed
AP : 0 4 :008(108) [0121] death and all afflictions, **lest** we try to flee these things or
AP : 0 4 :061(115) [0137] First of all, **lest** anyone think that we are speaking of an
AP : 0 4 :073(117) [0141] God, not because of works, **lest** any man should boast,"
AP : 0 4 :088(120) [0149] And **lest** we suppose that Paul made the statement "Faith
AP : 0 4 :093(120) [0149] God—not because of works, **lest** any man should boast."
AP : 0 4 :220(137) [0181] urging to bear good fruits **lest** they lose the Holy Spirit.
AP : 0 4 :232(140) [0185] cover up minor mistakes, **lest** the church disintegrate into
AP : 0 4 :245(142) [0189] to it, but keeps it, **lest** Christ, the propitiator, be excluded
AP : 0 4 :322(157) [0209] on the Lord's Prayer: "**Lest** anybody should flatter himself
AP : 0 7 :010(170) [0229] says "the church catholic" **lest** we take it to mean an
AP : 1 2 :069(192) [0271] **Lest** anyone be moved by this large number of quotations,
AP : 1 2 :110(198) [0285] still it must be controlled, **lest** consciences be ensnared;
AP : 1 2 :116(199) [0287] satisfactions in particular, **lest** by their adoption the
AP : 1 2 :150(206) [0299] measure; not in thy anger, **lest** thou bring me to nothing."
AP : 1 5 :032(220) [0323] remain in the church, **lest** the observances of the law or
AP : 1 5 :046(221) [0327] "Take heed to yourselves **lest** your hearts be weighed
AP : 1 5 :047(221) [0327] as restraints on our flesh, **lest** we be overcome by satiety
AP : 1 5 :051(222) [0329] be used moderately, **lest** the weak be offended and
AP : 1 6 :007(223) [0331] Christ stresses this so often **lest** the apostles think that
AP : 1 8 :001(225) [0335] They also add a caution, **lest** too much be conceded to
AP : 2 0 :013(228) [0341] confirm their call, that is, **lest** they fall from their call by
AP : 2 3 :068(249) [0383] a copy of the Confutation, **lest** their fraud and slander be
AP : 2 4 :016(252) [0389] the members at the joint, **lest** like an unskilled cook he
AP : 2 4 :099(268) [0419] desecration of the Mass **lest** they burden themselves with
AP : 2 7 :002(269) [0419] want to recite them here **lest** we give the impression that
AP : 2 7 :062(280) [0441] from their countrymen, **lest** they fall back into the
TR : 0 0 :062(330) [0523] the rest to prevent schism, **lest** several persons, by
SC : 0 9 :008(356) [0563] your children to anger, **lest** they become discouraged, but
LC : 0 1 :033(369) [0589] extend to many thousands, **lest** men live in security and
LC : 0 1 :248(398) [0651] God's commandment, **lest** his wrath and punishment
LC : 0 1 :323(409) [0673] that is contrary to his will, **lest** he be moved to wrath;
LC : 0 3 :084(432) [0723] and oppressors beware **lest** they lose the common
LC : 0 3 :084(432) [0723] and let them take care **lest** this petition of the Lord's
LC : 0 5 :042(451) [0763] be coerced or compelled, **lest** we institute a new slaughter
LC : 0 5 :044(451) [0763] be persistent in preaching, **lest** people become indifferent
LC : 0 5 :059(453) [0767] from the sacrament," **lest** he deprive himself of life.
EP : 0 4 :007(476) [0799] — not because of works, **lest** any man should boast"
EP : 0 6 :004(480) [0807] to light their way **lest** in their merely human devotion
EP : 0 6 :004(480) [0807] This is further necessary **lest** the Old Adam go his own
EP : 1 1 :001(494) [0831] of it in this document, **lest** as some future date offensive
EP : 1 2 :001(498) [0839] But **lest** as a result of our silence these errors be attributed
SD : PR :019(507) [0857] of certain theologians, **lest** anyone be misled by the high
SD : 0 2 :081(537) [0911] the old man," as follows: "**Lest** anyone might think that
SD : 0 4 :002(551) [0939] be tolerated in the church, **lest** the merit of Christ, our
SD : 0 4 :033(556) [0949] in your heavenly calling, **lest** you fall away and lose the
SD : 0 5 :001(558) [0951] with particular diligence **lest** we confuse the two doctrines
SD : 0 6 :009(565) [0965] my body and subdue it, **lest** after preaching to others I
SD : 0 7 :029(574) [0981] Hence **lest** any persons during my lifetime or after my
SD : 1 1 :050(624) [1079] us what the true church is, **lest** we be offended by the

Letter (14), Letters (13)
AG : 2 3 :025(055) [0065] He wrote in his eleventh **letter**, "If they are unwilling or
AG : 2 8 :028(085) [0087] writes in his reply to the **letters** of Petilian that one should
AG : 2 8 :067(092) [0093] observed according to the **letter**, and many of the
AL : 2 3 :025(055) [0065] in the first book of his **letters**, Epistle XI, are these: "If
AL : 2 8 :028(085) [0087] also says in reply to the **letters** of Petilian that not even
AL : 2 8 :067(092) [0093] observed according to the **letter**, and many of them
AP : 0 4 :087(120) [0147] on *The Spirit and the **Letter***, where he says toward the
AP : 0 4 :103(121) [0151] In a **letter** to a certain Irenaeus, Ambrose says: "But the
AP : 0 4 :106(122) [0153] In *The Spirit and the **Letter*** he says: "The righteousness of
AP : 0 4 :106(122) [0153] own strength nor by the **letter** of that same law, for this is
AP : 1 1 :009(182) [0251] of constitutions, glosses, summae, and penitential **letters**.
AP : 1 5 :030(219) [0323] some proofs for this, and Paul's **letters** abound in them.
S 1 : PR :005(289) [0457] twisting and corrupting my every word and **letter**?
S 3 : 0 3 :028(308) [0487] true, and there are seals, **letters**, and examples to show it.
S 3 : 0 8 :003(312) [0495] sharply between the **letter** and the spirit without knowing
S 3 : 1 5 :005(317) [0501] me orally and by a **letter** which I have shown to these
TR : 0 0 :014(322) [0507] states in his fourth **letter** to Cornelius: "Wherefore you
TR : 0 0 :039(327) [0515] the Antichrist in his **letter** to the Thessalonians Paul calls
TR : 0 0 :062(330) [0521] that in the apostolic **letters** all who preside over the
LC : 0 1 :302(405) [0667] awarded to him with **letters** patent and the seal of the
LC : 0 4 :009(437) [0733] indulgences with his **letters** and bulls and consecrated
LC : 0 4 :009(437) [0733] solely by virtue of his **letters** and seals, then we ought to
SD : 0 2 :015(523) [0887] prayers in St. Paul's **letters** (Eph. 1:17, 18; Col. 1:9, 11;
SD : 0 5 :022(562) [0959] which kills through the **letter** and is a "dispensation of
SD : 0 7 :007(570) [0975] not strictly, the way the **letters** sound, but as figurative
SD : 0 7 :092(586) [1005] from the way the **letters** read, but, as stated above, we
SD : 0 8 :022(595) [1023] 3; Anthanasius in his ***Letter** to Epictetus;* Hilary, *On the*

Letting (2)
LC : 0 1 :307(406) [0669] of anything that is his, **letting** him suffer loss while you
LC : 0 6 :024(460) [0000] receive anything but just **letting** everyone see how poor

Leutkirch (1)
PR : PR :027(016) [0027] Mayor and Council of the City of **Leutkirch**

Level (9)
AP : 2 1 :023(232) [0349] salvation, they are being put on the same **level** as Christ.
AP : 2 1 :027(232) [0349] want to be put on the same **level** as Christ but to have her

Continued ▶

A P : 2 3 :037(244) [0373] put marriage on the same **level** with virginity, as Jovinian
A P : 2 3 :038(244) [0373] We do not put marriage on the same **level** with virginity.
A P : 2 3 :069(249) [0383] and virginity on the same **level**, but neither virginity nor
A P : 2 7 :020(272) [0427] a promise, on the same **level** with an ordinance of Christ
A P : 2 7 :038(275) [0433] of others which put various ways of life on the same **level**.
L C : 0 1 :209(393) [0639] an estate to be placed on a **level** with the others; it
E P : 0 8 :028(490) [0825] has been raised to the **level** of, and has become equal to,

Levi (2)
A P : 2 4 :034(256) [0395] he will purify the sons of **Levi** and refine them like gold
A P : 2 4 :034(256) [0395] The offerings of the sons of **Levi** (that is, of those who

Levitical (26)
A G : 2 8 :039(087) [0089] Christians like the **Levitical** service, and as if God had
A G : 2 8 :061(091) [0093] services of God like the **Levitical** or Jewish services and
A L : 2 8 :039(087) [0089] Christians similar to the **Levitical**, and as if God had
A L : 2 8 :061(091) [0093] in the church like the **Levitical** service and that Christ
A P : 0 4 :087(120) [0147] interpret as referring to **Levitical** ceremonies, but Paul is
A P : 1 3 :007(212) [0311] a priesthood like the **Levitical** to offer sacrifices and merit
A P : 1 3 :010(212) [0311] enough, we do not have a priesthood like the **Levitical**.
A P : 2 3 :041(245) [0375] for the analogy with the **Levitical** priests, we have already
A P : 2 3 :041(245) [0375] In addition, the **Levitical** laws about uncleanness do not
A P : 2 3 :041(245) [0375] frees us from these **Levitical** regulations about impurity.
A P : 2 3 :042(245) [0375] consciences with these **Levitical** observances, we must
A P : 2 3 :044(245) [0375] voluptuously, cannot even keep this **Levitical** continence.
A P : 2 4 :021(252) [0389] All the **Levitical** sacrifices can be classified under one or
A P : 2 4 :024(253) [0391] The **Levitical** propitiatory sacrifices were so called only as
A P : 2 4 :026(254) [0391] contrast is not only with **Levitical** worship, where cattle
A P : 2 4 :027(254) [0393] Thus it abrogates **Levitical** worship.
A P : 2 4 :030(255) [0395] With the abrogation of **Levitical** worship, the New
A P : 2 4 :034(256) [0397] sacrifices for sin offered by a **Levitical** priesthood.
A P : 2 4 :035(256) [0397] From the **Levitical** analogy it does not follow at all that
A P : 2 4 :052(259) [0403] are nothing but a misinterpretation of the **Levitical** order.
A P : 2 4 :053(259) [0403] words talk about the **Levitical** priesthood and say that it
A P : 2 4 :053(259) [0403] The **Levitical** sacrifices for sin did not merit the
A P : 2 4 :057(260) [0405] to imagine that the **Levitical** sacrifices merited the
A P : 2 4 :059(260) [0405] has no sacrifices like the **Levitical** which could be
T R : 0 0 :026(324) [0511] and persons, as the **Levitical** priesthood is, but is spread
T R : 0 0 :038(326) [0515] The **Levitical** high priest was the supreme pontifex by

Lewdness (5)
A G : 2 3 :014(054) [0063] and more disgraceful **lewdness** and vice to prevail in
S 1 : P R :012(290) [0459] Wantonness, **lewdness**, extravagance in dress, gluttony,
L C : 0 1 :201(392) [0637] public prostitution and **lewdness** tolerated as they are
L C : 0 1 :202(392) [0639] of all kinds of vice and **lewdness** among us, this
L C : 0 1 :207(393) [0639] (as is evident) not for **lewdness** but to be true to each

Liar (8), Liars (4)
A P : 0 2 :034(104) [0113] consternation, men are all **liars**," that is, they do not have
A P : 0 4 :297(153) [0205] God, has made him a **liar**, because he has not believed in
A P : 1 2 :062(190) [0269] believe absolution but the accusation that God is a **liar**?
A P : 1 2 :062(191) [0269] God has made him a **liar** because he has not believed in
A P : 2 7 :025(273) [0429] (Ps. 116:11), "All men are **liars**"; that is, they do not think
L C : 0 1 :055(372) [0595] Also to be counted among **liars** are blasphemers, not only
L C : 0 1 :247(398) [0651] before all the world you may call God and me **liars**.
L C : 0 1 :270(401) [0657] I might be called a **liar** and sent away in disgrace."
L C : 0 1 :270(401) [0657] you cannot prove, even if it is true, you appear as a **liar**.
L C : 0 3 :115(435) [0731] the devil is not only a **liar** but also a murderer, he
L C : 0 5 :081(456) [0773] than what the Scriptures call him, a **liar** and a murderer.
L C : 0 5 :081(456) [0773] A **liar** who seduces the heart from God's Word and blinds

Liberal (1), Liberally (1)
A P : 2 7 :024(273) [0427] of supererogation, these **liberal** men then sell them to
L C : 0 3 :056(427) [0713] more abundantly and **liberally** than anyone can

Liberated (7), Liberates (1), Liberation (2)
A P : 0 4 :104(122) [0153] it to faith, which **liberates** us through the blood of Christ.
A P : 1 2 :175(210) [0307] been misinterpreted as a **liberation** of souls from
A P : 2 4 :074(262) [0409] a conscience to see its **liberation** from terror, then it really
E P : 0 4 :012(477) [0799] as applying only to the **liberated** spirit which does good
S D : 0 2 :011(522) [0885] the Son of God has **liberated** him from the death of sin
S D : 0 2 :015(523) [0887] our hearts for having **liberated** us from the darkness of
S D : 0 2 :067(534) [0907] again, and now have a **liberated** will — that is, as Christ
S D : 0 6 :002(564) [0963] since they have been **liberated** by the Son of God, have
S D : 0 6 :004(564) [0963] have been freed and **liberated** from the curse of the law,
S D : 0 6 :017(566) [0967] the Spirit of God and is **liberated** from the law (that is,

Liberty (33)
A G : 2 6 :042(070) [0075] Fathers maintained such **liberty** with respect to outward
A G : 2 8 :051(089) [0091] the teaching of Christian **liberty** in Christendom, namely,
A G : 2 8 :060(091) [0093] an example of Christian **liberty** and might know that the
A G : 2 8 :064(092) [0093] of the righteousness of faith and Christian **liberty**.
A L : 1 8 :001(039) [0051] that man's will has some **liberty** for the attainment of
A L : 2 6 :042(070) [0075] Such **liberty** in human terms was not unknown to the
A L : 2 8 :051(089) [0091] the doctrine of Christian **liberty** in the churches, namely,
A L : 2 8 :060(091) [0093] an example of Christian **liberty** and would know that the
A L : 2 8 :064(092) [0093] of the righteousness of faith and Christian **liberty**.
A P : 0 7 :044(177) [0243] to destroy evangelical **liberty** nor to impose a necessity
A P : 1 5 :032(220) [0323] insisted that Christian **liberty** remain in the church, lest
A P : 1 5 :051(222) [0329] Nevertheless, **liberty** in these matters should be used
A P : 1 5 :051(222) [0329] teaching of the Gospel because of an abuse of **liberty**.
A P : 1 8 :001(225) [0335] as in Pelagianism, or all **liberty** be denied it, as in
A P : 1 8 :004(225) [0335] things, as well as the **liberty** and ability to achieve civil
A P : 1 8 :007(225) [0337] concede to free will the **liberty** and ability to do the
S C : P R :003(338) [0533] they have mastered the fine art of abusing **liberty**.
S C : P R :009(339) [0535] people, you are at **liberty** to exhibit your learning and to
L C : P R :003(359) [0567] than this rotten, pernicious, shameful, carnal **liberty**.
L C : 0 5 :041(451) [0763] that it is a matter of **liberty**, not of necessity, and that it is
L C : 0 5 :049(452) [0765] that we are not granted **liberty** to despise the sacrament.
L C : 0 5 :049(452) [0765] If you want such **liberty**, you may just as well take the
L C : 0 5 :049(452) [0765] as well take the further **liberty** not to be a Christian; then
L C : 0 6 :006(457) [0000] and enjoy any part of our **liberty**, but we shall let the
E P : 1 0 :006(493) [0831] of the Gospel, Christian **liberty**, and the sanctioning of
E P : 1 0 :010(494) [0831] violation of the Christian **liberty** which it has in external
E P : 1 0 :012(494) [0831] of God does not have the **liberty** to avail itself of one or
S D : 1 0 :012(612) [1057] which in his Christian **liberty** he employed in other
S D : 1 0 :014(613) [1057] doctrine and Christian **liberty**, or they will misuse them
S D : 1 0 :015(613) [1057] the article of Christian **liberty** as well, an article which the
S D : 1 0 :030(615) [1061] of God does not have the **liberty** to use one or more
S D : 1 0 :030(616) [1061] as may in Christian **liberty** be most beneficial to the
S D : 1 0 :031(616) [1063] when in Christian **liberty** one uses fewer or more of them,

Libidos (1)
A P : 2 3 :003(239) [0363] ask you to defend these **libidos** of theirs with your chaste

Libraries (1)
A P : 1 5 :027(219) [0323] huge tomes, even whole **libraries**, that do not contain a

License (2)
A P : 2 7 :016(271) [0425] no class of men has greater **license** than the monks.
T R : 0 0 :056(329) [0521] the kings to restrain the **license** of the pontiffs and see to

Licentiate (1)
S 3 : 1 5 :005(318) [0501] the Rev. **Licentiate** Louis Platz, of Melsungen

Licentiousness (1)
L C : 0 5 :075(455) [0771] impurity, **licentiousness**, idolatry, sorcery, enmity, strife,

Lichtenburg (1)
P R : P R :027(015) [0025] Philip, count of Hanau -[**Lichtenburg**]

Lie (24), Lied (2), Lies (37), Lying (10)
A G : 1 9 :000(041) [0053] John 8:44, "When the devil **lies**, he speaks according to
A G : 2 3 :006(052) [0061] manifest whether or not it **lies** in human power and
A G : 2 7 :028(075) [0079] extent perpetual chastity **lies** within human power and
A L : 1 9 :000(041) [0053] John 8:44, "When the devil **lies**, he speaks according to
A L : 2 7 :028(075) [0079] to what an extent perpetual chastity **lies** in man's power.
A P : 0 4 :133(125) [0159] Moses is read a veil **lies** over their minds; but when a man
A P : 0 4 :330(158) [0211] forsake mercy observe **lying** vanities"; that is, all trust is
A P : 1 2 :016(184) [0257] of faith in Christ and of the blessing of Christ **lies** buried.
A P : 1 2 :088(195) [0277] doubts, he makes the divine promise a **lie**, as John says.
A P : 1 9 :001(226) [0337] (John 8:44), "When he **lies**, he speaks according to his
A P : 2 3 :067(248) [0383] So it is a shameless **lie** to say that the marriage of priests
A P : 2 4 :095(267) [0417] to support the obvious **lies** which our opponents teach
S 1 : P R :007(289) [0457] shamefully and try by their **lies** to keep the people on
S 1 : P R :007(289) [0457] and still causes, them and their **lies** to be put to shame.
S 1 : P R :009(290) [0457] have urged such big **lies** upon the king and foreign
S 1 : P R :009(290) [0457] of us all, knows very well that they **lie** and have lied.
S 1 : P R :009(290) [0457] of us all, knows very well that they lie and have **lied**.
S 2 : 0 2 :016(295) [0467] and, with unspeakable **lies** and cunning, of demanding
S 2 : 0 2 :022(296) [0469] so many manifest **lies** and so much nonsense has been
S 2 : 0 4 :003(298) [0473] church (in so far as this **lies** in his power) and come into
S 2 : 0 4 :014(301) [0475] the pope to promote his **lies** about Masses, purgatory,
S 3 : 0 1 :002(302) [0477] of God — and then also **lying**, swearing by God's name,
T R : 0 0 :046(328) [0517] which are nothing but **lies** devised for the sake of gain.
S C : 0 1 :004(342) [0539] swear, practice magic, **lie**, or deceive, but in every time of
S C : 0 1 :016(343) [0541] and so we should not tell **lies** about our neighbor, nor
S C : 0 7 :005(353) [0559] Then quickly **lie** down and sleep in peace.
L C : P R :014(360) [0571] sitting, walking, standing, **lying** down, or rising, and keep
L C : 0 1 :042(370) [0591] and learn that they neither **lie** nor deceive but will yet
L C : 0 1 :046(370) [0593] be true since God cannot **lie** or deceive; just leave it to the
L C : 0 1 :051(371) [0595] men take oaths in court and one side **lies** against the other
L C : 0 1 :054(372) [0595] arise and peddle their **lying** nonsense as the Word of
L C : 0 1 :056(372) [0595] For to **lie** and deceive is in itself a gross sin, but it is
L C : 0 1 :056(372) [0597] So from a single **lie** a double one results — indeed,
L C : 0 1 :056(372) [0597] a single lie a double one results — indeed, manifold **lies**.
L C : 0 1 :057(372) [0597] will he permit his name to be used to gloss over a **lie**.
L C : 0 1 :058(372) [0597] use the name of God for **lies** and all kinds of wickedness,
L C : 0 1 :062(373) [0597] briefly, it is either simply to **lie** and assert under his name
L C : 0 1 :071(374) [0601] who is ever around us, **lying** in wait to lure us into sin and
L C : 0 1 :096(378) [0607] to hear God's Word or **lie** around in taverns dead drunk
L C : 0 1 :103(379) [0611] holy name in support of **lies** or any evil purpose
L C : 0 1 :121(382) [0615] the pure Word of God to the **lying** vanities of the devil.
L C : 0 1 :163(387) [0627] again allow preachers of **lies** to arise and lead us to the
L C : 0 1 :165(387) [0627] it, and has never yet **lied**, he will not lie to you either.
L C : 0 1 :165(387) [0627] it, and has never yet lied, he will not **lie** to you either.
L C : 0 1 :213(394) [0641] the common people with **lying** words and wrong
L C : 0 1 :263(400) [0655] in court and their **lying** and malicious talk outside of
L C : 0 1 :326(409) [0675] name in vain by cursing, **lying**, deceiving, and other kinds
L C : 0 2 :031(414) [0687] must be subject to him and **lie** beneath his feet until
L C : 0 3 :041(425) [0709] using his name to cloak **lies** and make them acceptable;
L C : 0 3 :049(426) [0711] glory and name to cloak its **lies** and wickedness, but
L C : 0 3 :058(428) [0713] The fault **lies** wholly in that shameful unbelief which does
L C : 0 3 :062(428) [0715] beyond measure when his **lies** and abominations, honored
L C : 0 3 :080(431) [0721] may deceive men with his **lies** and bring them under his
L C : 0 3 :120(436) [0731] knows that God does not **lie** since he has promised to
L C : 0 3 :122(436) [0731] so that they despise God and accuse him of **lying**.
L C : 0 4 :050(443) [0745] with himself, support **lies** and wickedness, or give his
L C : 0 4 :056(444) [0747] me his body and blood; he will not **lie** or deceive me.
L C : 0 4 :057(444) [0747] Because we know that God does not **lie**.
L C : 0 5 :014(448) [0757] from the lips of Christ, so it is; he cannot **lie** or deceive."
L C : 0 5 :076(455) [0771] They will not **lie** to you, and they know your flesh better
L C : 0 5 :084(456) [0773] besieges you and **lies** in wait to trap and destroy you,
E P : 0 7 :013(483) [0811] ground is that God's Word is not false nor does it **lie**.
E P : 0 8 :035(491) [0825] (that is, a power that **lies** somewhere between God's
E P : 1 1 :012(496) [0835] The fault does not **lie** in God or his election, but in their
S D : 0 2 :027(527) [0893] is our own work and **lies** within our own power."
S D : 0 2 :027(527) [0893] erred when I said that it **lies** within our power to believe
S D : 0 2 :032(527) [0893] though we grant that it **lies** within our power to perform
S D : 0 2 :081(537) [0913] by adding, 'Therefore lay aside **lies** and speak the truth.'
S D : 0 4 :020(554) [0945] believers in the sense that it **lies** within their free option if
S D : 0 4 :037(557) [0951] The fault, however, **lies** not with the good works
S D : 0 7 :023(573) [0979] lips speak and declare, since he cannot **lie** or deceive.
S D : 0 7 :102(587) [1007] us, we should not give the **lie** to his words until we know
S D : 0 8 :044(599) [1029] God's death and God dead **lie** in the opposite scale, then

Liege (3)
LC : 01 :022(367) [0585] were in our service or debt and we were his **liege** lords.
EP : 12 :015(499) [0841] feudal homage to his territorial sovereign or **liege**-lord.
SD : 12 :020(634) [1099] pay oath-bound feudal homage to his prince or **liege** lord.

Lieu (1)
AP : 12 :144(205) [0297] the honor of being a price paid in **lieu** of eternal death.

Life (483) (*See also "live" etc., below.*)
AG : 03 :005(030) [0045] he may bestow on them **life** and every grace and blessing,
AG : 04 :002(030) [0045] and righteousness and eternal **life** are given to us.
AG : 08 :001(033) [0047] saints, yet because in this **life** many false Christians,
AG : 12 :006(035) [0049] Amendment of **life** and the forsaking of sin would then
AG : 16 :005(038) [0051] love and genuine good works in his station of **life**.
AG : 17 :002(038) [0051] all the dead, to give eternal **life** and everlasting joy to
AG : 18 :001(039) [0051] an outwardly honorable **life** and to make choices among
AG : 18 :004(040) [0051] in the outward acts of this **life** that they have freedom to
AG : 20 :008(042) [0053] article in the Christian **life**, has been neglected so long (as
AG : 20 :020(044) [0055] that there they might merit grace through monastic **life**.
AG : 23 :001(051) [0061] and the dissolute **life** of priests who were not able to
AG : 23 :006(052) [0061] and chaste manner of **life**, what Christian, upright, and
AG : 26 :009(065) [0071] was regarded as Christian **life**: whoever observed festivals
AG : 26 :009(065) [0071] in this way was said to live a spiritual and Christian **life**.
AG : 27 :001(071) [0075] them, what kind of **life** as lived in the monasteries, and
AG : 27 :002(071) [0077] In the days of St. Augustine monastic **life** was voluntary.
AG : 27 :005(071) [0077] also entered monastic **life** ignorantly, for although they
AG : 27 :011(072) [0077] and that by monastic **life** one could earn forgiveness of sin
AG : 27 :012(072) [0077] they added that monastic **life** not only earned
AG : 27 :012(072) [0077] also that by means of this **life** both the precepts and the
AG : 27 :013(072) [0077] be obtained by monastic **life** than by all other states of
AG : 27 :013(072) [0077] than by all other states of **life** instituted by God —
AG : 27 :016(073) [0077] and adopted monastic **life** for the purpose of learning the
AG : 27 :016(073) [0077] it is claimed that monastic **life** is of such a nature that
AG : 27 :031(076) [0079] determine or arrange the order of one's whole future **life**.
AG : 27 :038(077) [0081] their invented spiritual **life** makes satisfaction for sin and
AG : 27 :043(077) [0081] and bestow this honor upon their vows and monastic **life**.
AG : 27 :044(078) [0081] by their vows and their monastic **life** and observances.
AG : 27 :049(079) [0083] calling and station in **life**; and that meanwhile we do good
AG : 27 :051(079) [0083] exaltation of monastic **life**, for it follows that their
AG : 27 :057(080) [0083] the world and seeking a **life** more pleasing to God than
AG : 27 :058(080) [0083] a good and perfect state of **life** which has God's command
AG : 27 :058(080) [0083] that is a dangerous state of **life** which does not have
AG : 27 :060(080) [0083] his time to speak of monastic **life** as a state of perfection.
AG : 28 :008(082) [0085] eternal righteousness, the Holy Spirit, and eternal **life**.
AL : 08 :001(033) [0047] However, since in this **life** many hypocrites and evil
AL : 12 :008(035) [0049] may attain such perfection in this **life** that they cannot sin.
AL : 17 :002(038) [0051] elect he will give eternal **life** and endless joy, but ungodly
AL : 18 :004(039) [0051] for it is only in acts of this **life** that they have freedom to
AL : 18 :005(040) [0053] arts, or will to do whatever good pertains to this **life**.
AL : 20 :002(041) [0053] all stations and duties of **life**, indicating what manners of
AL : 20 :002(041) [0053] what manners of **life** and what kinds of work are pleasing
AL : 20 :010(042) [0055] "I am the way, and the truth, and the **life**" (John 14:6).
AL : 20 :020(044) [0055] hope that there they might merit grace by monastic **life**.
AL : 26 :009(065) [0071] title of comprising the spiritual **life** and the perfect life.
AL : 26 :009(065) [0071] title of comprising the spiritual life and the perfect **life**.
AL : 26 :011(065) [0071] to an imperfect kind of **life** — in marriage, in the
AL : 27 :005(071) [0077] Many entered this kind of **life** through ignorance, for
AL : 27 :011(072) [0077] of sins and justification before God by this kind of **life**.
AL : 27 :012(072) [0077] they added that monastic **life** merited not only
AL : 27 :013(072) [0077] Baptism, and that monastic **life** was more meritorious
AL : 27 :013(072) [0077] more meritorious than the **life** of magistrates, pastors, and
AL : 27 :016(073) [0077] pretend that this kind of **life** was instituted to merit grace
AL : 27 :016(073) [0077] put it far above all other kinds of **life** instituted by God.
AL : 27 :031(076) [0079] judgment to make a decision involving the rest of his **life**.
AL : 27 :051(079) [0083] from such false commendations of monastic **life**.
AL : 27 :052(079) [0083] engage in their married **life** with a troubled conscience.
AL : 27 :054(079) [0083] vengeance in their private **life** since they are told that this
AL : 27 :057(080) [0083] "fleeing from the world" and "seeking a holy kind of **life**."
AL : 27 :058(080) [0083] A good and perfect kind of **life** is one which has God's
AL : 27 :060(080) [0083] in his day to say that monastic **life** is a state of perfection.
AL : 28 :008(082) [0085] as eternal righteousness, the Holy Spirit, and eternal **life**.
AL : 28 :009(082) [0085] faith," and Ps. 119:50 states, "Thy Word gives me **life**."
AP : 04 :005(108) [0121] justification, and eternal **life** for his sake, or when, in the
AP : 04 :005(108) [0121] promises forgiveness of sins, justification, and eternal **life**.
AP : 04 :017(109) [0125] of this disposition and eternal **life** by the works of the law.
AP : 04 :029(111) [0129] and also for leading a holy **life**, then 'Christ died to no
AP : 04 :062(115) [0139] For this consolation is a new and spiritual **life**.
AP : 04 :064(116) [0139] death, brings forth a new **life** in our hearts, and is a work
AP : 04 :087(120) [0147] by the precepts of a good **life**, but through faith in Jesus
AP : 04 :095(121) [0149] up, that whoever believes in him may have eternal **life**."
AP : 04 :100(121) [0151] it brings forth peace, joy, and eternal **life** in the heart.
AP : 04 :122(124) [0157] texts, "If you would enter **life**, keep the commandments"
AP : 04 :123(124) [0157] "If you would enter **life**, keep the
AP : 04 :125(124) [0157] Spirit and produces a new **life** in our hearts, it must also
AP : 04 :132(125) [0159] in us eternal righteousness and a new and eternal **life**.
AP : 04 :146(127) [0163] for they say they earn grace and eternal **life** by merit.
AP : 04 :146(127) [0163] In this **life** we cannot satisfy the law, because our
AP : 04 :162(129) [0169] God and merit eternal **life** by our keeping of the law.
AP : 04 :179(131) [0171] in Col. 2:10, "You have come to fullness of **life** in him."
AP : 04 :192(133) [0175] done in the most humble occupation and in private **life**.
AP : 04 :194(133) [0175] spiritual rewards in this **life** and in that which is to come,
AP : 04 :196(134) [0175] with Christ, we do not merit eternal **life** by our works.
AP : 04 :196(134) [0175] Eternal **life** belongs to the justified, according to the
AP : 04 :211(136) [0179] chose a certain kind of **life** for study or for other useful
AP : 04 :235(140) [0185] fairness, that in everyday **life** we should put up with many
AP : 04 :245(142) [0189] summary of the Christian **life** (I Tim. 1:5), "The aim of
AP : 04 :250(143) [0191] Since this faith is a new **life**, it necessarily produces new
AP : 04 :258(144) [0193] he commands these works as necessary to the new **life**.
AP : 04 :259(144) [0193] but he requires a new **life**, which is certainly necessary.
AP : 04 :259(145) [0193] your bread with the hungry," he requires the new **life**.
AP : 04 :261(145) [0195] One part instructs about the new **life** and its works.
AP : 04 :270(147) [0197] "If you would enter **life**, keep the commandments"
AP : 04 :274(148) [0199] are required, since a new **life** is certainly required; but
AP : 04 :278(149) [0199] almsgiving that it is the whole newness of **life** which saves.
AP : 04 :279(149) [0199] mind all the days of your **life**" (4:5), and later, "Bless God
AP : 04 :289(151) [0203] obedience to the law is worthy of grace and eternal **life**.
AP : 04 :290(151) [0203] worthy of grace and eternal **life**, although even a weak
AP : 04 :297(153) [0205] righteousness, and eternal **life** are assured to us for
AP : 04 :297(153) [0205] that God gave us eternal **life**, and this life is in his Son.
AP : 04 :297(153) [0205] that God gave us eternal life, and this **life** is in his Son.
AP : 04 :297(153) [0205] He who has the Son, has **life**; he who has not the Son,
AP : 04 :297(153) [0205] the Son, has life; he who has not the Son, has not **life**."
AP : 04 :301(153) [0205] evils, sufferings in this **life** and the fear of eternal wrath.
AP : 04 :306(154) [0207] "He is the source of your **life** in Jesus Christ, whom God
AP : 04 :310(155) [0207] sees the Son and believes in him should have eternal **life**."
AP : 04 :316(156) [0209] of itself and earns eternal **life** without needing Christ, the
AP : 04 :320(156) [0209] will count worthy of eternal **life**, if indeed hope ought to
AP : 04 :320(156) [0209] righteousness and eternal **life** are given us freely for
AP : 04 :322(157) [0209] church confesses that eternal **life** comes through mercy.
AP : 04 :322(157) [0209] "God leads us to eternal **life**, not by our merits, but
AP : 04 :322(157) [0209] he says, "Woe to the **life** of men, however praiseworthy, if
AP : 04 :347(160) [0217] unworthy because eternal **life** is promised to the justified
AP : 04 :348(160) [0217] works are unnecessary if they do not merit eternal **life**.
AP : 04 :348(160) [0217] We say that eternal **life** is promised to the justified, but
AP : 04 :349(160) [0217] Holy Spirit, that this new **life** might have new works and
AP : 04 :352(161) [0217] the beginning of eternal **life**, as Paul says (Rom. 8:10), "If
AP : 04 :354(161) [0217] justification belongs to faith, so eternal **life** belongs to it.
AP : 04 :356(161) [0217] reply that eternal **life** is called a reward and that therefore
AP : 04 :356(161) [0217] Paul calls eternal **life** a "gift" (Rom. 6:23) because the
AP : 04 :356(161) [0217] (John 3:36), "He who believes in the Son has eternal **life**."
AP : 04 :357(162) [0219] so precious that eternal **life** is their due and that therefore
AP : 04 :357(162) [0219] worthy of grace and eternal **life** without needing mercy or
AP : 04 :359(162) [0219] worthy of grace and eternal **life** or whether they please
AP : 04 :360(162) [0219] attribute to works a worthiness of grace and eternal **life**.
AP : 04 :362(162) [0219] We grant that eternal **life** is a reward because it is
AP : 04 :362(162) [0219] gift the promise of eternal **life** has been added, according
AP : 04 :366(163) [0219] justification and eternal **life** belong to faith, still good
AP : 04 :366(163) [0221] promise of grace, receives justification and new **life** gratis.
AP : 04 :370(164) [0221] properly merit eternal **life**, since Paul says (Rom. 2:6),
AP : 04 :370(164) [0221] forth to the resurrection of **life**"; Matt. 25:35, "I was
AP : 04 :372(164) [0221] Therefore, when eternal **life** is granted to works, it is
AP : 04 :373(164) [0221] and for this reason eternal **life** is granted to
AP : 04 :374(164) [0223] and to show that a new **life** and new birth are required,
AP : 04 :375(164) [0223] but in themselves are not worthy of grace and eternal **life**.
AP : 04 :376(164) [0223] they are righteousness that they are worthy of eternal **life**.
AP : 04 :378(165) [0223] teach that we merit eternal **life** by works, omitting the
AP : 04 :384(166) [0225] of faith obtains eternal **life**, a faith that is firm and active.
AP : 07 :003(169) [0227] We concede that in this **life** the hypocrites and evil men
AP : 07 :017(171) [0231] In this **life**, nevertheless, because the kingdom of Christ
AP : 07 :028(173) [0237] mingled with them in this **life** share an association in the
AP : 10 :003(179) [0247] are truly branches, deriving **life** from him for ourselves?
AP : 12 :007(183) [0255] would be a ministry not of **life** and of the Spirit, but only
AP : 12 :028(185) [0259] improvement of the whole **life** and character a third part,
AP : 12 :029(186) [0259] the Holy Spirit and eternal **life**, and to lead us as
AP : 12 :037(187) [0261] grows and throughout **life** it struggles with sin to conquer
AP : 12 :045(188) [0263] Christ also includes the fruits of penitence or the new **life**.
AP : 12 :046(188) [0263] consolation truly sustaining a **life** that flees in contrition.
AP : 12 :048(188) [0265] earlier sentence and restoring peace and **life** to the heart.
AP : 12 :050(189) [0265] Lord kills and brings to **life**; he brings down to Sheol and
AP : 12 :060(190) [0269] and brings forth peace, joy, and a new **life** in the heart.
AP : 12 :089(195) [0279] So their whole **life** is without God and without the true
AP : 12 :131(202) [0291] come good fruits and good works in every phase of **life**.
AP : 12 :132(202) [0291] about total penitence and total newness of **life** and fruits.
AP : 12 :134(203) [0293] referring to this **life**: "Be penitent," "Bear fruit that befits
AP : 12 :136(203) [0293] will mean "Suffer the penalties of purgatory after this **life**.
AP : 12 :137(203) [0293] the whole newness of **life**, and not about observances and
AP : 12 :138(203) [0293] remission removes eternal death and brings eternal **life**.
AP : 12 :146(205) [0297] it is useless and in this **life** does not even get a taste of
AP : 12 :148(205) [0299] itself takes place by constantly mortifying the old **life**.
AP : 12 :161(208) [0303] man from obtaining eternal **life**, but the lesson of the
AP : 12 :164(208) [0303] really happens in contrition and in a changed **life**.
AP : 12 :170(209) [0305] to be not a fraud but an improvement of the total **life**.
AP : 13 :014(213) [0311] but these apply to physical **life** and not strictly to the New
AP : 15 :025(219) [0323] of the household, married **life**, and the rearing of
AP : 16 :002(222) [0331] the beginning of eternal righteousness and eternal **life**.
AP : 16 :006(223) [0331] and the beginning of eternal **life** in the hearts of believers.
AP : 17 :001(224) [0335] the dead, granting eternal **life** and eternal joys to the
AP : 20 :008(227) [0341] faith gives support and **life** to the heart in its hardest
AP : 21 :027(232) [0349] in death, does she overcome death, does she give **life**?
AP : 21 :036(234) [0353] in their public or private **life**, as a means of confirming
AP : 21 :044(236) [0357] God they should defend the **life** and safety of the
AP : 22 :010(237) [0361] Christ's flesh, given for the **life** of the world, is their food
AP : 22 :010(237) [0361] food and that they come to **life** by being joined to Christ.
AP : 23 :019(242) [0369] as he wants to nourish our **life** by using food and drink.
AP : 24 :013(251) [0387] whatever they need in this **life**, and even free the dead.
AP : 24 :034(256) [0397] kill this old flesh and begin a new and eternal **life** in us.
AP : 24 :059(260) [0405] when he does work to give them new birth and **life**.
AP : 24 :071(262) [0409] when faith gives **life** to terrified hearts, is the worship of
AP : 24 :075(263) [0411] 'I am the bread of **life**; he who comes to me shall
AP : 24 :095(267) [0417] If they came back to **life** now and saw their sayings being
AP : 27 :009(270) [0421] minds about their way of **life**, whom parents or friends
AP : 27 :012(270) [0423] according to the Gospel in order to merit eternal **life**.
AP : 27 :014(271) [0425] of sins, opposed as they are to the customs of public **life**?
AP : 27 :020(272) [0427] God, which contains a covenant of grace and eternal **life**.
AP : 27 :021(272) [0427] themselves are services that justify or merit eternal **life**.
AP : 27 :023(272) [0427] which we merit eternal **life** conflicts with the Gospel of
AP : 27 :023(272) [0427] Christ's sake righteousness and eternal **life** are given to us.
AP : 27 :024(273) [0427] services than other ways of **life**, that is, that they merit
AP : 27 :025(273) [0429] observance of a monastic **life** satisfies the
AP : 27 :027(273) [0429] (Rom. 14:17) and **life** in the heart, therefore perfection
AP : 27 :027(274) [0429] of Christ, which is eternal **life**, in these silly observances
AP : 27 :028(274) [0429] that the monastic **life** merits eternal life if it is maintained
AP : 27 :028(274) [0429] monastic life merits eternal **life** if it is maintained by a
AP : 27 :029(274) [0431] the Sacred Scriptures the monastic **life** merits eternal life.
AP : 27 :029(274) [0431] the Sacred Scriptures the monastic life merits eternal **life**.
AP : 27 :029(274) [0431] Where do the Sacred Scriptures talk about monastic **life**?

Continued ▶

AP : 2 7 :030(274) [0431] they say that by a monastic **life** men merit eternal life.
AP : 2 7 :030(274) [0431] they say that by a monastic life men merit eternal **life**.
AP : 2 7 :030(274) [0431] honor of meriting eternal **life**, as he clearly says in Ezek.
AP : 2 7 :030(274) [0431] good and ordinances by which they could not have **life**."
AP : 2 7 :031(274) [0431] it is sure that the monastic **life** does not merit the
AP : 2 7 :032(274) [0431] the second place, eternal **life** is given by mercy for
AP : 2 7 :032(274) [0431] can you merit eternal **life**, but that this is freely given as
AP : 2 7 :033(274) [0431] of sins or eternal **life** even by the works of the divine law,
AP : 2 7 :033(275) [0431] credit for meriting the forgiveness of sins or eternal **life**.
AP : 2 7 :034(275) [0431] teach that the monastic **life** merits the forgiveness of sins
AP : 2 7 :034(275) [0431] of sins or eternal **life** are simply crushing the Gospel
AP : 2 7 :035(275) [0431] which the forgiveness of sins and eternal **life** are granted.
AP : 2 7 :036(275) [0433] deny that the monastic **life** is perfection, but they say that
AP : 2 7 :036(275) [0433] praises of the monastic **life**; but since they did not dare to
AP : 2 7 :037(275) [0433] follow this, the monastic **life** will be no more a state of
AP : 2 7 :037(275) [0433] state of perfection than the **life** of a farmer or an artisan.
AP : 2 7 :038(275) [0433] of others which put various ways of **life** on the same level.
AP : 2 7 :038(275) [0433] was making in his way of **life**, God pointed in a dream to
AP : 2 7 :040(276) [0433] a more abundant eternal **life**, and it quotes the passage
AP : 2 7 :040(276) [0433] of Scripture has nothing to do with the monastic **life**.
AP : 2 7 :040(276) [0433] because it merits the forgiveness of sins and eternal **life**.
AP : 2 7 :040(276) [0435] forgiveness of sins or eternal **life**, he is insulting Christ.
AP : 2 7 :041(276) [0435] wife, and children, even **life** itself, be taken from us.
AP : 2 7 :043(276) [0435] in applying it to monastic **life**, unless perhaps the
AP : 2 7 :043(277) [0435] they will receive a hundredfold in this **life** applies here.
AP : 2 7 :056(278) [0439] Thus the whole monastic **life** is full of hypocrisy and false
AP : 2 7 :056(278) [0439] reasons that release good men from this way of **life**.
AP : 2 7 :057(279) [0439] to abandon a way of **life** so full of hypocrisy and false
AP : 2 7 :061(279) [0441] not observe their way of **life** out of the belief that they
AP : 2 7 :061(279) [0441] the mercy of God — they would attain eternal **life**.
AP : 2 7 :065(280) [0441] of sins or to secure eternal **life** for us instead of mercy for
AP : 2 7 :069(281) [0443] that we attain eternal **life** because of them rather than
AP : 2 7 :070(281) [0443] who followed this way of **life** must have come to reject
AP : 2 7 :070(281) [0443] they would attain eternal **life** and not for the sake of such
AP : 2 8 :006(282) [0445] to create laws which are useful for attaining eternal **life**.
AP : 2 8 :009(282) [0445] they also say that traditions are conducive to eternal **life**.
AP : 2 8 :010(282) [0447] righteousness and eternal **life** since food, drink, clothing,
AP : 2 8 :010(282) [0447] and the Holy Spirit, that work eternal **life** in the heart.
AP : 2 8 :010(282) [0447] explain how traditions are conducive to eternal **life**.
AP : 2 8 :021(284) [0449] that they merit forgiveness of sins and eternal **life**.
S 1 : PR :010(290) [0457] of the various callings of **life**, and with true works, that
S 2 : 0 2 :001(293) [0463] their sins, both here in this **life** and yonder in purgatory,
S 2 : 0 3 :002(298) [0471] to the ordinary Christian **life** and to the offices and
S 2 : 0 4 :014(301) [0475] purgatory, monastic **life**, and human works and services
S 3 : 0 3 :013(305) [0483] the people: "Prolong my **life**, Lord God, until I make
S 3 : 0 3 :013(305) [0483] until I make satisfaction for my sins and amend my **life**."
S 3 : 0 3 :040(309) [0489] until death, for all through **life** it contends with the sins
S 3 : 1 4 :001(316) [0501] takes the vows of monastic **life** believes that he is entering
S 3 : 1 4 :001(316) [0501] is entering upon a mode of **life** that is better than that of
TR : 0 0 :014(322) [0507] acquainted with the **life** of each candidate (as we have
TR : 0 0 :040(327) [0517] to loose and bind in this **life** but also the jurisdiction over
TR : 0 0 :040(327) [0517] this life but also the jurisdiction over souls after this **life**.
SC : PR :023(341) [0539] that he needs no grace, no **life**, no paradise, no heaven, no
SC : 0 1 :010(343) [0541] endanger our neighbor's **life**, nor cause him any harm,
SC : 0 1 :010(343) [0541] harm, but help and befriend him in every necessity of **life**.
SC : 0 1 :012(343) [0541] lead a chaste and pure **life** in word and deed, each one
SC : 0 2 :002(345) [0543] with all the necessities of **life**, protects me from all
SC : 0 2 :005(345) [0545] *sins, the resurrection of the body, and the* ***life*** *everlasting.*
SC : 0 2 :006(345) [0545] dead and will grant eternal **life** to me and to all who
SC : 0 3 :008(346) [0547] holy Word and live a godly **life**, both here in time and
SC : 0 4 :010(349) [0551] that is, a gracious water of **life** and a washing of
SC : 0 4 :010(349) [0551] by his grace and become heirs in hope of eternal **life**.
SC : 0 4 :014(349) [0553] glory of the Father, we too might walk in newness of **life**."
SC : 0 5 :023(350) [0555] to God's commandments and to their action in **life**, etc.
SC : 0 6 :006(352) [0557] the forgiveness of sins, **life**, and salvation are given to us
SC : 0 6 :006(352) [0557] is forgiveness of sins, there are also **life** and salvation.
SC : 0 9 :005(355) [0561] lead a quiet and peaceable **life**, godly and respectful in
SC : 0 9 :006(355) [0561] joint heirs of the grace of **life**, in order that your prayers
LC : PR :009(359) [0569] that is impossible in this **life**), yet it is highly profitable
LC : SP :013(363) [0577] sins, the resurrection of the body, and the **life** everlasting.
LC : SP :019(363) [0579] summed up the doctrine, **life**, wisdom, and learning which
LC : 0 1 :018(367) [0585] happiness, pleasure, and a **life** of ease venerated
LC : 0 1 :024(367) [0587] it is he who gives us body, **life**, food, drink, nourishment,
LC : 0 1 :031(369) [0589] head is right, the whole **life** must be right, and vice versa.
LC : 0 1 :046(370) [0593] down and persecuted, his **life** nowhere secure, yet
LC : 0 1 :047(371) [0593] person be in his station in **life** according to God's order,
LC : 0 1 :074(375) [0601] to God than any monastic **life** and Carthusian holiness.
LC : 0 1 :077(375) [0603] consists not only of words but also of practice and **life**.
LC : 0 1 :087(376) [0605] else than to devote it to holy words, holy works, holy **life**.
LC : 0 1 :089(377) [0605] we may regulate our whole **life** and being according to
LC : 0 1 :092(377) [0607] repeat that all our **life** and work must be guided by God's
LC : 0 1 :103(379) [0611] so that all our conduct and **life** may be regulated by it.
LC : 0 1 :128(382) [0617] all the blessings we have received throughout our **life**.
LC : 0 1 :129(383) [0617] has received his body and **life** from them and that he has
LC : 0 1 :131(383) [0619] "That you may have long **life** in the land where you
LC : 0 1 :132(383) [0619] welfare, to lead us to a quiet, pleasant, and blessed **life**.
LC : 0 1 :134(383) [0619] it is that he will perish sooner and never be happy in **life**.
LC : 0 1 :134(383) [0619] Scriptures, to have long **life** means not merely to grow old
LC : 0 1 :134(383) [0619] that pertains to long **life** — health, wife and child,
LC : 0 1 :134(383) [0619] etc., without which this **life** can neither be heartily
LC : 0 1 :145(385) [0623] better than the holiness and austere **life** of all the monks"?
LC : 0 1 :146(385) [0623] a more blessed or holy **life**, as far as your works are
LC : 0 1 :164(387) [0627] for a year or two, but long **life**, sustenance, and peace,
LC : 0 1 :166(388) [0629] cannot add an hour to our **life** or raise from the earth a
LC : 0 1 :180(389) [0631] yet their right to take human **life** is not abrogated.
LC : 0 1 :183(389) [0633] well knows, the world is evil and this **life** is full of misery.
LC : 0 1 :190(391) [0635] of the service by which his **life** might have been saved.
LC : 0 1 :191(391) [0635] and aid to men in need and in peril of body and **life**.
LC : 0 1 :197(392) [0637] the ordinary Christian **life** would be considered just as
LC : 0 1 :197(392) [0637] works as "the most perfect **life**," so that they might live a
LC : 0 1 :197(392) [0637] they might live a nice, soft **life** without the cross and
LC : 0 1 :206(393) [0639] and glorifies the married **life**, sanctioning and protecting
LC : 0 1 :208(393) [0639] Married **life** is no matter for jest or idle curiosity, but it is
LC : 0 1 :211(393) [0641] are unsuited for married **life** and others whom he has
LC : 0 1 :215(394) [0641] of secret passion, which can be avoided in married **life**.
LC : 0 1 :216(394) [0641] their unchaste existence and enter the married **life**.
LC : 0 1 :216(394) [0641] granting that the monastic **life** is godly, yet it is not in
LC : 0 1 :217(394) [0641] acquire a love for married **life** and know that it is a
LC : 0 1 :217(394) [0643] shameful vices resulting from contempt of married **life**.
LC : 0 1 :218(394) [0643] men may have joy and happiness in their married **life**.
LC : 0 1 :238(397) [0649] neither prosper nor gain anything their whole **life** long.
LC : 0 1 :311(407) [0669] what we are to do to make our whole **life** pleasing to God.
LC : 0 1 :315(408) [0671] a higher and better way of **life** than the Ten
LC : 0 1 :315(408) [0671] said, that this is a simple **life** for the ordinary man,
LC : 0 2 :013(412) [0681] my body, soul, and **life**, my members great and small, all
LC : 0 2 :014(412) [0681] comforts and necessities of **life** — sun, moon, and stars in
LC : 0 2 :016(412) [0681] that none of us has his **life** of himself, or anything else
LC : 0 2 :021(413) [0683] brag and boast as if we had **life**, riches, power, honor, and
LC : 0 2 :024(413) [0683] provided for us in this **life**, and, further, has showered us
LC : 0 2 :030(414) [0685] Jesus Christ, the Lord of **life** and righteousness and every
LC : 0 2 :030(414) [0685] his righteousness, wisdom, power, **life**, and blessedness.
LC : 0 2 :031(414) [0685] to God, from death to **life**, from sin to righteousness, and
LC : 0 2 :034(415) [0687] *sins, the resurrection of the body, and the* ***life*** *everlasting.*
LC : 0 2 :037(415) [0687] sins, the resurrection of the body, and the **life** everlasting.
LC : 0 2 :041(416) [0689] the resurrection of the body, and the **life** everlasting."
LC : 0 2 :057(418) [0693] to complete and perfect holiness in a new, eternal **life**.
LC : 0 2 :058(418) [0693] until we attain to that **life** where there will be no more
LC : 0 2 :058(418) [0693] In that **life** are only perfectly pure and holy people, full of
LC : 0 2 :059(418) [0695] when we pass from this **life**, he will instantly perfect our
LC : 0 3 :001(420) [0697] The best and most blessed **life** consists of these things.
LC : 0 3 :039(425) [0709] both our teaching and our **life** are godly and Christian.
LC : 0 3 :042(425) [0709] profaned by an openly evil **life** and wicked works, when
LC : 0 3 :049(426) [0711] holy in both doctrine and **life** so that he may be praised
LC : 0 3 :051(426) [0711] as a king of righteousness, **life**, and salvation against sin,
LC : 0 3 :053(427) [0713] growth here and in eternal **life** hereafter to us who have
LC : 0 3 :065(429) [0717] honor, house and home, wife and children, body and **life**.
LC : 0 3 :072(430) [0717] — the needs of our body and our **life** on earth.
LC : 0 3 :073(430) [0719] that belongs to our entire **life** in this world; only for its
LC : 0 3 :073(430) [0719] Now, our **life** requires not only food and clothing and
LC : 0 3 :073(430) [0719] there the necessities of **life** are also interfered with, and
LC : 0 3 :073(430) [0719] also interfered with, and **life** itself cannot be maintained
LC : 0 3 :074(430) [0719] us our daily bread and all the comforts of this **life**.
LC : 0 3 :081(431) [0721] a penny in the house, or even our **life** for one hour —
LC : 0 3 :086(432) [0723] This petition has to do with our poor, miserable **life**.
LC : 0 3 :091(432) [0723] that he will ever in this **life** reach the point where he does
LC : 0 3 :100(433) [0725] wholly absolved, yet such is **life** that one stands today and
LC : 0 3 :105(434) [0727] as we remain in this vile **life** in which we are attacked,
LC : 0 3 :115(435) [0731] he incessantly seeks our **life** and vents his anger by
LC : 0 4 :027(440) [0739] where God's name is, there must also be **life** and salvation.
LC : 0 4 :029(440) [0739] is sheer salvation and **life**, not through the water, as we
LC : 0 4 :041(441) [0743] Christian has enough to study and to practice all his **life**.
LC : 0 4 :044(442) [0743] be saved and have eternal **life**, both in soul and body."
LC : 0 4 :046(442) [0743] which no other kind of **life** and no work on earth can
LC : 0 4 :049(442) [0745] whose doctrine and **life** attest that they have the Holy
LC : 0 4 :065(445) [0749] of which actions must continue in us our whole **life** long.
LC : 0 4 :065(445) [0749] Thus a Christian **life** is nothing else than a daily Baptism,
LC : 0 4 :068(445) [0749] Where this amendment of **life** does not take place but the
LC : 0 4 :075(445) [0751] attack on the old man and an entering upon a new **life**?
LC : 0 4 :075(445) [0751] only announces this new **life** but also produces, begins,
LC : 0 5 :025(449) [0759] For the new **life** should be one that continually develops
LC : 0 5 :050(452) [0765] you to examine your inner **life** and reflect: "See what sort
LC : 0 5 :059(453) [0767] from the sacrament," lest he deprive himself of **life**.
LC : 0 5 :061(453) [0767] and absolution and has no intention to amend his **life**.
LC : 0 5 :081(456) [0773] A murderer who begrudges you every hour of your **life**.
LC : 0 6 :009(458) [0000] of a genuinely Christian **life**, to acknowledge that we are
EP : 0 2 :003(470) [0787] itself to bodily, earthly **life**, so little can man who through
EP : 0 2 :003(470) [0787] raise himself to spiritual **life**, as it is written, "When we
EP : 0 2 :009(471) [0789] law, and thus merit forgiveness of sins and eternal **life**.
EP : 0 2 :012(471) [0789] righteousness before God whereby we merit eternal **life**.
EP : 0 3 :003(473) [0793] of sins and eternal **life**, as it is written, "For as by one
EP : 0 5 :005(478) [0803] "righteousness that avails before God," and eternal **life**.
EP : 0 6 :001(480) [0805] to which they should pattern and regulate their entire **life**.
EP : 0 7 :002(482) [0809] the believers for **life** and salvation, the unbelievers for
EP : 0 7 :016(484) [0813] they receive them not to **life** and salvation but to their
EP : 0 7 :017(484) [0813] guests as he is to work **life** and consolation in the hearts
EP : 0 8 :018(489) [0823] the sole foundation of our comfort, **life**, and salvation.
EP : 0 9 :004(492) [0827] cannot comprehend in this **life** but which we simply
EP : 1 1 :007(495) [0833] Christ, who is "the book of **life**" in which all who are to
EP : 1 1 :008(495) [0833] and divine assistance for steadfastness and eternal **life**.
EP : 1 1 :009(495) [0833] election of ours to eternal **life** on the basis either of reason
EP : 1 1 :009(495) [0833] dissolute, Epicurean **life**, or drive men to despair and
EP : 1 1 :009(495) [0833] I am not elected to eternal **life**, whatever good I do is of
EP : 1 1 :013(496) [0835] Word of God, which shows us Christ as the "book of **life**."
EP : 1 1 :013(496) [0835] been elected to eternal **life** out of pure grace in Christ
EP : 1 1 :015(496) [0835] either to despair or to lead a reckless and godless **life**.
EP : 1 1 :016(497) [0837] election of God to eternal **life** in such a way that
EP : 1 1 :020(497) [0837] on account of which he has elected us to eternal **life**.
EP : 1 2 :025(500) [0843] can perfectly keep and fulfill the law of God in this **life**.
SD : 0 1 :006(509) [0861] for human nature in this **life** — nevertheless man's nature
SD : 0 1 :014(511) [0863] is only begun in this **life**, not to be completed until the life
SD : 0 1 :014(511) [0863] in this life, not to be completed until the **life** yonder.
SD : 0 1 :035(514) [0869] Thou has granted me **life** and steadfast love; and thy care
SD : 0 1 :038(515) [0871] my body, soul, and **life**, my members great and small, all
SD : 0 1 :046(516) [0873] arise, and that in eternal **life** we shall have and keep
SD : 0 1 :047(516) [0875] Day and that in eternal **life**, instead of this essence of our
SD : 0 1 :047(516) [0875] and would be and remain in the elect in eternal **life**.
SD : 0 2 :002(520) [0881] affecting this temporal **life**, nor what man can do in
SD : 0 2 :010(522) [0883] alienated from the **life** of God because of the ignorance
SD : 0 2 :011(522) [0885] himself to regain temporal **life**, so little can a man who is
SD : 0 2 :011(522) [0885] heavenly righteousness and **life**, unless the Son of God
SD : 0 2 :022(525) [0889] of God, and in eternal **life**, not by its own natural and
SD : 0 2 :026(526) [0891] and free will are able to lead an outwardly virtuous **life**.
SD : 0 2 :034(528) [0895] in the flesh throughout **life**, as St. Paul says in Rom.
SD : 0 2 :039(528) [0895] while still in this **life**, reach the point where they desire to
SD : 0 2 :041(529) [0897] grace we may believe his holy Word and live a godly **life**."
SD : 0 2 :043(529) [0897] ourselves for righteousness and **life** or seek after it.

Continued ▶

SD : 0 2 :049(530) [0901] believes on him should not perish but have eternal **life**."
SD : 0 2 :068(534) [0907] But since in this **life** we have received only the first fruits
SD : 0 2 :068(534) [0907] Christian in his own **life** discovers that at one moment he
SD : 0 2 :075(536) [0911] obedience earn the forgiveness of sin and eternal **life**.
SD : 0 2 :077(536) [0911] of sins, and eternal **life**, then the free will by its own
SD : 0 2 :079(536) [0911] of God perfectly in this **life** and by such perfect obedience
SD : 0 2 :079(536) [0911] of the law merit righteousness before God and eternal **life**.
SD : 0 3 :009(540) [0919] God and an heir of eternal **life**) without any merit or
SD : 0 3 :012(541) [0919] leads to acquittal and **life** for all men" (Rom. 5:18).
SD : 0 3 :015(541) [0919] by doing and suffering, in **life** and in death, Christ
SD : 0 3 :016(541) [0921] of God, adoption, and the inheritance of eternal **life**.
SD : 0 3 :020(542) [0921] him from death into **life**, as it is written, "When we were
SD : 0 3 :022(543) [0923] in essence and **life** adheres to those who have been
SD : 0 3 :022(543) [0923] sins which throughout this **life** still inhere in our nature.
SD : 0 3 :023(543) [0923] remains imperfect in this **life** and because sin still dwells
SD : 0 3 :025(543) [0923] with God, adoption, and the inheritance of eternal **life**.
SD : 0 3 :028(544) [0925] because in this **life** sanctification is never wholly pure and
SD : 0 3 :032(544) [0927] justified possess in this **life**, first, the reckoned
SD : 0 3 :032(545) [0927] and impure in this **life** on account of the flesh, no one can
SD : 0 3 :032(545) [0927] and leads the best kind of **life**, a person is pleasing and
SD : 0 3 :032(545) [0927] the inheritance of eternal **life** only on account of Christ's
SD : 0 3 :033(545) [0927] was pleasing and acceptable to him to eternal **life**, rest?
SD : 0 3 :053(548) [0933] adoption and the inheritance of eternal **life** and salvation.
SD : 0 4 :033(556) [0949] those who lead a wicked **life**, lose the Holy Spirit, and
SD : 0 4 :038(557) [0951] to reward them gloriously in this and in the future **life**.
SD : 0 4 :039(558) [0951] a wicked, wild, complacent, and Epicurean way of **life**.
SD : 0 6 :003(564) [0963] norm for achieving a godly **life** and behavior in accord
SD : 0 6 :006(564) [0965] perfectly renewed in this **life** through the indwelling Spirit
SD : 0 6 :007(565) [0965] But in this **life** Christians are not renewed perfectly and
SD : 0 6 :009(565) [0965] of God require in this **life** not only the daily teaching and
SD : 0 6 :011(565) [0965] we should walk in the new **life**, but it does not give the
SD : 0 6 :012(566) [0967] "he kills and brings to **life**, he brings down into Sheol, and
SD : 0 6 :015(566) [0967] according to which man is to conduct himself in this **life**.
SD : 0 6 :018(567) [0967] not fully renewed in this **life** but the Old Adam clings to
SD : 0 6 :021(567) [0969] that their works and **life** are perfectly pure and holy.
SD : 0 6 :021(567) [0969] to them that in this **life** our good works are imperfect and
SD : 0 6 :022(567) [0969] God, even though in this **life** they are still imperfect and
SD : 0 6 :024(568) [0971] They belong to this imperfect **life**.
SD : 0 7 :044(577) [0987] in this sad, last hour of his **life**, this truthful and almighty
SD : 0 7 :062(581) [0995] and everlasting **life**), is presented — and that we rest
SD : 0 7 :068(582) [0997] intention to improve their **life** and who by their unworthy
SD : 0 7 :070(582) [0997] be his faith strong or weak, has eternal **life** (John 3:16).
SD : 0 7 :099(586) [1005] and, "When Christ who is our **life** appears" (Col. 3:4).
SD : 0 7 :105(588) [1009] only to work comfort and **life** in believers but also to
SD : 0 8 :053(601) [1033] as we need to know in this **life**, and wherever the
SD : 0 8 :055(601) [1033] For to give **life**, to execute all judgment, to have all
SD : 0 8 :059(602) [1035] says that Christ's flesh is a **life**-giving food, and according
SD : 0 8 :059(602) [1035] decreed that the flesh of Christ has the power to give **life**.
SD : 0 8 :061(602) [1035] that such divine power, **life**, might, majesty, and glory
SD : 0 8 :061(603) [1037] Thus also the power to give **life** is not in the flesh of
SD : 0 8 :065(604) [1039] on earth, and in yonder **life** we shall behold his glory face
SD : 0 8 :076(606) [1043] that his flesh is truly a **life**-giving food and his blood truly
SD : 0 8 :076(606) [1043] that Christ's flesh is a **life**-giving flesh, whence only this
SD : 1 1 :005(617) [1065] and predestined to eternal **life** "before the foundation of
SD : 1 1 :008(617) [1065] as were ordained to eternal **life** believed" (Acts 13:48).
SD : 1 1 :009(617) [1065] divine ordering to eternal **life** only in the secret and
SD : 1 1 :011(618) [1067] faith, and the good resolve to lead a godly **life**.
SD : 1 1 :013(618) [1067] children of God to eternal **life**, we should accustom
SD : 1 1 :013(619) [1067] genuine and true "book of **life**" as it is revealed to us
SD : 1 1 :015(619) [1069] righteousness which avails before God" and eternal **life**.
SD : 1 1 :018(619) [1069] the inheritance of eternal **life** all who in sincere
SD : 1 1 :022(619) [1069] save and glorify in eternal **life** those whom he has elected,
SD : 1 1 :025(620) [1071] are written in the book of **life**" will be saved, how can and
SD : 1 1 :028(620) [1071] has given his flesh "for the **life** of the world" (John 6:51);
SD : 1 1 :028(621) [1071] believe on Christ should have eternal **life**" (John 6:40).
SD : 1 1 :030(621) [1073] me; and I give them eternal **life**" (John 10:27, 28), and
SD : 1 1 :049(624) [1079] anguish, neither death nor **life**, etc. can separate us from
SD : 1 1 :060(626) [1083] and make ourselves unworthy of eternal **life** (Acts 13:46).
SD : 1 1 :066(627) [1085] to Christ as to the book of **life** in whom they are to seek
SD : 1 1 :067(627) [1085] eternal election to eternal **life** when he says, "The kingdom
SD : 1 1 :067(627) [1085] in him should have eternal **life**" (John 6:40); and again,
SD : 1 1 :070(627) [1085] of God, if he has been elected and ordained to eternal **life**.
SD : 1 1 :070(627) [1085] Christ, who is the "book of **life**" and of the eternal
SD : 1 1 :070(627) [1085] God's children to eternal **life**, and who testifies to all men
SD : 1 1 :075(628) [1087] Our election to eternal **life** does not rest on our piety or
SD : 1 1 :086(631) [1091] or any other person eternal **life**, or that in his secret
SD : 1 1 :088(631) [1093] on account of which God has elected us unto eternal **life**.
SD : 1 1 :089(631) [1093] Gospel as the "book of **life**," this doctrine never occasions
SD : 1 1 :089(631) [1093] either despondency or a riotous and dissolute **life**.
SD : 1 2 :033(635) [1101] to keep and fulfill the law of God perfectly in this **life**.

Lifeless (3), Lifetime (4)
AP : 1 2 :171(209) [0305] wrote that once in a **lifetime** was enough for the sort of
EP : RN :003(465) [0777] already during their **lifetime** — false teachers and heretics
SD : PR :007(502) [0849] just as during the very **lifetime** of the holy apostles
SD : 0 1 :060(519) [0879] in God's sight spiritually **lifeless** and with all his powers
SD : 0 2 :010(522) [0885] sick, but that he is truly **lifeless** and "dead" (Eph. 2:1, 5;
SD : 0 2 :020(525) [0889] a log or a stone, like a **lifeless** statue which uses neither
SD : 0 7 :029(574) [0981] any persons during my **lifetime** or after my death appeal

Lift (4), Lifted (2), Lifts (2)
AL : 2 0 :026(045) [0057] as confidence which consoles and **lifts** up terrified hearts.
AP : 0 4 :095(121) [0149] John 3:14, 15, "As Moses **lifted** up the serpent in the
AP : 0 4 :095(121) [0149] must the Son of man be **lifted** up, that whoever believes in
LC : 0 1 :166(387) [0627] we owe honor that we **lift** our hands in joyful thanks to
LC : 0 6 :035(461) [0000] ourselves, however, let us **lift** up our hands in praise and
EP : 0 7 :036(485) [0815] Holy Supper, but should **lift** their eyes from the bread to
SD : 0 5 :012(560) [0957] us, but to comfort and **lift** upright those who are terrified
SD : 0 7 :003(569) [0973] as by the preached Word, **lifts** itself up and ascends above

Light (42), Lighten (2), Lightened (1), Lightly (6)
PR : PR :002(003) [0007] and unadulterated **light** of his holy Gospel and of the
PR : PR :002(003) [0007] German nation, and to **light** its way out of papistic
PR : PR :024(013) [0023] eyes, or to put the **light** of divine truth under a basket or
AG : 2 8 :064(092) [0093] they undertake to **lighten** and mitigate human
AG : 0 0 :001(095) [0095] The others can readily be weighed in the **light** of these.
AL : 2 5 :006(062) [0069] our teachers have shed **light** on the doctrine of repentance
AL : 2 7 :048(078) [0081] It is no **light** offense in the church to recommend to the
AP : 0 2 :032(104) [0113] cleansed and brought to **light** important teachings of the
AP : 0 4 :268(147) [0197] that chasten us are **lightened** by our prayers and good
AP : 0 4 :278(149) [0199] many divine blessings, **lighten** our punishments, and
AP : 0 4 :343(160) [0217] men can easily judge when they are brought to **light**.
AP : 0 7 :029(173) [0237] All this is clearer than the **light** of noonday; if our
AP : 0 7 :050(178) [0245] legitimate for them to use the air, **light**, food, and drink.
AP : 1 2 :003(182) [0253] have shed much **light** on the Gospel and have corrected
S1 : PR :003(289) [0455] council and flees from the **light** in a shameful fashion.
S1 : PR :003(289) [0455] knaves who shun the **light** and flee from the day take such
S3 : 0 3 :018(306) [0483] If we examine this in the **light**, we see that such contrition
TR : 0 0 :041(328) [0517] unbelievers, for what fellowship has **light** with darkness?"
TR : 0 0 :048(328) [0519] errors are not to be taken **lightly**, for they detract from
SC : 0 5 :020(350) [0553] on your condition in the **light** of the Ten
LC : PR :004(359) [0567] the Gospel altogether too **lightly**, and even our utmost
LC : PR :009(359) [0569] ever new and greater **light** and fervor, so that day by day
LC : 0 1 :028(368) [0587] commandment above all things and not make **light** of it.
LC : 0 1 :029(368) [0589] this commandment taken **lightly** but will strictly watch
LC : 0 1 :114(380) [0613] able to ignore it and skip **lightly** over it, and so children
LC : 0 1 :130(383) [0619] views the matter in this **light** will, without compulsion,
LC : 0 1 :140(384) [0621] So he passes over them **lightly**, fastens his attention on
LC : 0 1 :149(385) [0623] take advice remember that God is not to be taken **lightly**.
LC : 0 1 :192(391) [0635] all the world in any other **light** than as a murderer and a
LC : 0 1 :209(393) [0639] do, but view it in the **light** of God's Word, by which it is
LC : 0 1 :283(403) [0661] not sneak about in secret, shunning the **light** of day.
LC : 0 3 :090(432) [0723] he should examine himself in the **light** of this petition.
LC : 0 4 :080(446) [0751] Baptism only in the **light** of a work performed once for
EP : RN :001(464) [0777] "Thy word is a lamp to my feet and a **light** to my path."
EP : 0 5 :002(478) [0801] is an especially glorious **light** that is to be maintained with
EP : 0 6 :004(480) [0807] law of God constantly to **light** their way lest in their
EP : 1 0 :006(493) [0829] for what fellowship has **light** with darkness?"
SD : PR :005(504) [0851] these last days brought to **light** the truth of his Word
SD : 0 1 :011(510) [0863] its highest powers and the **light** of reason, is by nature
SD : 0 2 :010(522) [0885] "The **light** shines in the darkness (that is, in the dark,
SD : 0 2 :073(535) [0909] In the **light** of the previous discussion one can readily
SD : 0 4 :012(553) [0941] from faith as it is to separate heat and **light** from fire."
SD : 0 5 :001(558) [0951] is an especially brilliant **light** which serves the purpose
SD : 0 5 :023(562) [0959] of Israel and be a **light** to the nations, "who was wounded
SD : 0 7 :030(574) [0983] again and again in the **light** thereof, and have wanted to
SD : 0 7 :100(586) [1007] my vision penetrates air, **light**, or water and does not
SD : 0 7 :100(586) [1007] nor vacates space; likewise **light** and heat go through air,
SD : 0 8 :044(599) [1029] goes down and we go upward like a **light** and empty pan.
SD : 1 0 :006(611) [1055] and iniquity, or what fellowship has **light** with darkness?
SD : 1 0 :022(615) [1061] unbelievers, for what fellowship has **light** with darkness?'
SD : 1 1 :024(620) [1071] about this article in this **light**, we can by the grace of God

Lighting (1)
LC : 0 1 :314(407) [0671] and ringing of bells, **lighting** of tapers and candles until

Likely (2), Likeness (4)
AP : 0 2 :018(102) [0109] in the image of God and after his **likeness** (Gen. 1:27).
AP : 0 2 :018(103) [0111] So Irenaeus interprets the **likeness** of God.
AP : 0 2 :021(103) [0111] righteousness is the very **likeness** of God which he put
AP : 0 4 :351(161) [0217] we are changed into his **likeness**"; that is, we acquire the
AP : 2 7 :022(272) [0427] It is **likely** that here and there in the monasteries there are
LC : 0 3 :109(435) [0729] firm in faith, the devil is **likely** in this very hour to send

Limbs (1)
SC : 0 2 :002(345) [0543] my body and soul, all my **limbs** and senses, my reason

Limit (7), Limitations (4), Limited (3), Limits (5)
AG : 2 6 :011(065) [0071] there was no end or **limit** to the making of such
AG : 2 6 :034(069) [0075] exercise should not be **limited** to certain specified days
AP : 0 4 :242(141) [0187] forgives, yields, and does not go to the **limit** of the law.
AP : 1 2 :142(204) [0295] God has fixed a certain **limit** which man is bound to
AP : 1 5 :028(219) [0323] for the degrees and **limitations** of these precepts and
AP : 2 1 :041(235) [0355] theologians ask for **limitations** upon scholastic doctrine
AP : 2 4 :007(250) [0385] long time good men have wanted some **limits** set to them.
AP : 2 4 :020(252) [0389] If the **limits** of this book permitted, we would enumerate
S1 : PR :003(289) [0455] a little and allow **limitations** to be placed on his tyranny.
LC : 0 1 :250(399) [0651] to be confined to narrow **limits** but must extend to all our
EP : 0 8 :036(491) [0825] Christ has certain **limitations** as to how much he is
EP : 1 1 :004(495) [0833] the evil and imposes a **limit** on its duration, so that in
SD : 0 1 :023(512) [0865] though in only a small, **limited**, and poor degree — such
SD : 0 3 :019(542) [0921] word is also used in the **limited** sense of the forgiveness of
SD : 0 7 :103(587) [1009] Who has seen the **limits** of his power?
SD : 0 8 :052(601) [1033] determine and to fix the **limit** of what the human nature
SD : 1 1 :006(617) [1065] a way that God sets a **limit** and measure for the evil which
SD : 1 1 :058(625) [1081] Paul sets a definite **limit** for us as to how far we should go
SD : 1 1 :063(626) [1083] and goes beyond these **limits**, we must with Paul place

Limpurg (1)
PR : PR :027(015) [0025] Henry, baron of **Limpurg** [-Schmiedelfeld], Semperfrei

Lindau (1)
PR : PR :027(016) [0027] Mayor and Council of the City of **Lindau**

Line (1)
SD : 1 0 :031(616) [1063] 6. In **line** with the above, churches will not condemn each

Linked (1), Linking (1)
AP : 0 4 :232(139) [0185] and unbroken chain **linking** the many members of the
LC : 0 1 :329(410) [0677] that end and beginning are all **linked** and bound together.

Lion (3)
AP : 1 2 :031(186) [0259] help until morning; like a **lion** he breaks all my bones."
S2 : 0 4 :004(298) [0473] in which he roars like a **lion** (as the angel in Rev. 10:3
LC : 0 3 :075(430) [0719] a loaf of bread instead of a **lion** or a wreath of rue, or if a

Lips (17)
PR : PR :016(008) [0013] publicly attested this with their hearts, **lips**, and hands.
AP : 0 4 :383(166) [0225] justified, and he confesses with his **lips** and so is saved."
AP : 2 4 :026(254) [0393] "that is, the fruit of **lips** that acknowledge his name."
LC : 0 1 :050(371) [0593] us outward and directs the **lips** and the tongue into the
LC : 0 1 :051(371) [0595] taking his name upon our **lips** when our heart knows or
LC : 0 1 :070(374) [0601] it constantly upon their **lips** in all circumstances and
LC : 0 1 :070(374) [0601] the honor due him and then the **lips** do so by confession.
LC : 0 1 :072(374) [0601] keep the holy name on our **lips** so that he may not be able
LC : 0 1 :089(377) [0605] God's Word and carry it in our hearts and on our **lips**.
LC : 0 1 :100(379) [0609] God's Word in your heart, on your **lips**, and in your ears.
LC : 0 1 :202(392) [0639] Your heart, your **lips**, and your whole body are to be
LC : 0 5 :014(448) [0757] For as we have it from the **lips** of Christ, so it is; he
LC : 0 5 :063(454) [0767] than upon the words that proceed from Christ's **lips**.
LC : 0 5 :070(454) [0769] you receive from Christ's **lips** the forgiveness of sins,
EP : 0 3 :022(475) [0797] and by the confession of the **lips**, along with other virtues.
SD : 0 7 :023(573) [0979] For it must be as Christ's **lips** speak and declare, since he
SD : 1 1 :063(626) [1083] place our finger to our **lips** and say, "Who are you, a

List (9), Listed (7), Listing (1), Lists (2)
AP : 0 2 :027(104) [0113] of the defects that I have **listed**, as well as of
AP : 0 2 :051(107) [0119] it worthwhile rather to **list**, in the usual familiar phrases,
AP : 1 1 :009(182) [0251] They only recite **lists** of sins.
AP : 1 2 :010(184) [0255] on the questions we have **listed** is full of error and
AP : 1 2 :016(184) [0257] satisfactions is endless, and we cannot **list** all the abuses.
AP : 1 2 :092(196) [0279] Therefore we have **listed** the doctrine of faith among the
AP : 1 2 :141(204) [0295] We are very sorry to have to **list** these silly opinions of
AP : 1 3 :016(213) [0311] Ultimately, if we should **list** as sacraments all the things
AP : 1 3 :017(213) [0313] Alms could be **listed** here, as well as afflictions, which in
AP : 1 5 :027(219) [0323] Who could even **list** them all?
AP : 2 1 :016(231) [0347] the present we shall not **list** the abuses among the
AP : 2 1 :037(234) [0355] There is no point in **listing** here the miracles they have
AP : 2 4 :036(257) [0397] Num. 28:4ff. **lists** three parts of this daily sacrifice, the
TR : 0 0 :082(334) [0529] **List** of the Doctors and Preachers Who Subscribed the
LC : 0 1 :031(369) [0589] stands at the head of the **list** because it is of the utmost
SD : PR :011(506) [0855] the writings above **listed** — the Augsburg confession, the
SD : 0 3 :036(545) [0929] the article of justification **listed** above) consists solely
SD : 0 7 :032(574) [0983] of blessed memory, **listed** among other articles the
SD : 0 7 :066(581) [0997] testimonies are too long to **list** here, in the interest of

Listen (16), Listened (1), Listeners (1), Listening (1), Listens (1)
AP : 0 4 :033(111) [0129] but only attentive **listening**—to use the words that
AP : 0 4 :310(155) [0207] beloved Son, with whom I am well pleased; **listen** to him."
AP : 1 0 :003(179) [0247] **Listen** to Paul say, 'We are all one body in Christ' Rom.
AP : 2 3 :052(246) [0377] but none of the popes **listened** to these complaints.
AP : 2 7 :011(270) [0423] But **listen** how the architects of the Confutation slip away
AP : 2 7 :028(274) [0429] Now **listen** to the unworthy verdict our judges have
AP : 2 7 :055(278) [0439] purpose of teaching the **listeners** and, in the process of
AP : 2 8 :003(281) [0443] our opponents would only **listen** to the complaints of
S 1 : PR :004(289) [0455] They let me look on and **listen**, although they know very
LC : 0 1 :096(378) [0609] multitude of others who **listen** to God's Word as they
LC : 0 1 :097(378) [0609] to and admonished but we **listen** without serious concern.
LC : 0 1 :278(402) [0661] the same passage, "If he **listens** to you, you have gained
LC : 0 1 :279(402) [0661] further: "If he does not **listen**, take one or two others
SD : 0 2 :051(531) [0901] and the remission of sins, "**Listen** to him" (Matt. 17:5).
SD : 0 2 :053(531) [0903] that he can go to church, **listen** to the sermon, or not
SD : 0 2 :053(531) [0903] can go to church, listen to the sermon, or not **listen** to it.
SD : 0 2 :055(532) [0903] diligently and earnestly **listen** to and meditate on it, God
SD : 0 7 :043(576) [0987] has been given from heaven to all men, "**Listen** to him."
SD : 1 1 :065(627) [1083] with whom I am well pleased; **listen** to him" (Luke 3:22).
SD : 1 1 :070(627) [1085] the contrary, they should **listen** to Christ, who is the

Listless (1)
LC : 0 5 :040(451) [0761] that men are becoming **listless** and lazy about its

Lite (1)
AP : 2 4 :083(264) [0413] do not derive it from ***lite***, which means prayers, but from

Litera (1)
AG : 2 0 :013(043) [0055] His whole book, *De spiritu et* ***litera***, proves this.

Literal (2), Literally (3)
LC : 0 1 :079(375) [0603] for "stopping work" **literally** means "observing a holy day
LC : 0 1 :082(376) [0603] according to its **literal**, outward sense, this
LC : 0 1 :293(404) [0663] commandments, taken **literally**, were given exclusively to
EP : 0 7 :007(482) [0811] no other way than in their **literal** sense, and not as though
SD : 0 7 :046(577) [0987] was to be understood **literally** or if it was to receive a

Little (76)
PR : PR :009(006) [0011] distress on our part, that **little** account was taken by our
AG : 2 0 :003(041) [0053] About these **little** was taught in former times, when for
AG : 2 0 :007(042) [0053] This teaching may offer a **little** more comfort than the
AG : 2 5 :009(063) [0069] which we can enumerate we would be helped but **little**.
AG : 2 7 :010(072) [0077] many monks with even a **little** understanding were
AG : 2 7 :015(073) [0077] and inveigled into a monastery learned **little** about Christ.
AL : 2 0 :003(041) [0053] Concerning such things preachers used to teach **little**.
AL : 2 0 :014(043) [0055] of Christ would become of **little** value and the
AL : 2 7 :010(072) [0077] in former times who had a **little** more understanding.
AL : 2 8 :010(082) [0085] with civil government as **little** as the art of singing
AP : 0 4 :059(115) [0137] our opponents make so **little** of faith when they see it
AP : 0 4 :106(122) [0153] A **little** later Augustine says: "By the law we fear God, by
AP : 0 4 :106(122) [0153] A **little** later we shall quote several other statements.
AP : 0 4 :112(123) [0155] of this love, just as **little** as we receive the forgiveness of
AP : 0 4 :140(126) [0161] because we are in Christ, as we shall show a **little** later.
AP : 0 4 :151(127) [0163] Just as **little** do we receive the forgiveness of sins on
AP : 0 4 :168(130) [0169] to us; about this he says a **little** later, "Therefore let every
AP : 0 4 :239(141) [0187] Therefore a **little** earlier (I Pet. 2:4, 5) Peter commands us
AP : 0 4 :278(149) [0199] and death, as we said a **little** earlier about penitence in
AP : 0 9 :002(178) [0245] the promise of salvation also applies to **little** children.
AP : 0 9 :003(178) [0245] approves the Baptism of **little** children, the Anabaptists
AP : 0 9 :003(178) [0245] when they condemn the Baptism of **little** children.
AP : 0 9 :003(178) [0245] approve the Baptism of **little** children is shown by the
AP : 1 0 :003(179) [0247] A **little** later he says, "Therefore we must consider that
AP : 1 1 :001(180) [0249] we shall speak more fully a **little** later when we explain
AP : 1 3 :023(214) [0313] desecration of Masses, which we shall discuss a **little** later.
AP : 2 1 :040(235) [0355] in their party with a **little** sense would admit that the
AP : 2 3 :016(241) [0369] He interprets himself a **little** later when he says (v. 9), "It
AP : 2 4 :022(253) [0391] A **little** later it says about the will of Christ (v. 10), "By
AP : 2 4 :088(265) [0413] So it says a **little** later: "We offer Thee this reasonable and
AP : 2 7 :021(272) [0427] Paul says (I Tim. 4:8), "Bodily training is of **little** value."
S 1 : PR :003(289) [0455] might be, and are not a **little** troubled on this account, for
S 1 : PR :003(289) [0455] to be reformed a **little** and allow limitations to be placed
S 3 : 1 1 :002(314) [0499] As **little** as the power has been given to us or to them to
S 3 : 1 1 :002(314) [0499] of sex altogether, so **little** have they had the power to
SC : PR :027(341) [0539] and temptations, with **little** reward or gratitude from the
LC : PR :003(358) [0567] and they might feel a **little** shame because, like pigs and
LC : PR :004(359) [0567] and even our utmost exertions accomplish but **little**.
LC : 0 1 :005(365) [0581] This I must explain a **little** more plainly, so that it may be
LC : 0 1 :023(367) [0587] reasoning, however, is a **little** too subtle to be understood
LC : 0 1 :057(372) [0597] As **little** as God will permit the heart that turns away from
LC : 0 1 :057(372) [0597] him to go unpunished, so **little** will he permit his name to
LC : 0 1 :096(378) [0609] and depart again with as **little** knowledge of the Word at
LC : 0 1 :118(381) [0615] blush with shame before a **little** child that has lived
LC : 0 1 :214(394) [0641] For no one has so **little** love and inclination for chastity
LC : 0 1 :224(395) [0643] vice, but people pay so **little** attention to it that the
LC : 0 1 :225(395) [0643] Let us make it a **little** clearer for the common people so
LC : 0 1 :231(396) [0647] Meanwhile the **little** sneak-thieves who have committed
LC : 0 1 :258(399) [0653] to concern us only a **little** at present, but among the Jews
LC : 0 1 :314(407) [0671] when a poor girl tends a **little** child, or faithfully does
LC : 0 2 :031(414) [0685] of this article, that the **little** word "Lord" simply means
LC : 0 2 :051(417) [0691] that there is on earth a **little** holy flock or community of
LC : 0 5 :012(448) [0755] wisdom than the divine Majesty has in his **little** finger.
LC : 0 5 :032(450) [0761] are of no value just as **little** as they dare say that the
LC : 0 5 :043(451) [0763] sacrament, we shall devote a **little** attention to this point.
LC : 0 5 :050(452) [0765] surely have at least a **little** longing to do what my Lord
LC : 0 5 :083(456) [0773] yourself, look around a **little**, cling to the Scriptures.
LC : 0 6 :018(459) [0000] We should set **little** value on our work but exalt and
EP : 0 2 :003(470) [0787] As **little** as a corpse can quicken itself to bodily, earthly
EP : 0 2 :003(470) [0787] to bodily, earthly life, so **little** can man who through sin
EP : 0 2 :011(471) [0789] something (though it be **little** and feeble) to help, to
SD : PR :009(503) [0849] a mere semantic problem of **little** or no consequence.
SD : 0 2 :011(522) [0885] Just as **little** as a person who is physically dead can by his
SD : 0 2 :011(522) [0885] to regain temporal life, so **little** can a man who is
SD : 0 2 :014(523) [0885] perceive and discover a **little** spark and a longing for the
SD : 0 2 :024(525) [0891] or regeneration he can as **little** begin, effect, or cooperate
SD : 0 3 :007(540) [0917] of this doctrine that a **little** leaven ferments the whole
SD : 0 3 :015(541) [0919] person, he was as **little** under the law — since he is the
SD : 0 5 :003(558) [0953] by the fact that the **little** word "Gospel" does not always
SD : 0 5 :007(559) [0953] Again, the **little** word "repentance" is not used in a single
SD : 0 7 :022(573) [0979] wisdom than the divine Majesty has in his **little** finger.
SD : 0 7 :024(573) [0981] As **little** as a saint on earth, or even an angel in heaven,
SD : 0 7 :024(573) [0981] and blood of Christ, so **little** can anyone alter or change
SD : 1 0 :005(611) [1055] or will allegedly result **little** by little from these
SD : 1 0 :005(611) [1055] will allegedly result little by **little** from these ceremonies.
SD : 1 0 :016(613) [1059] causes one of these **little** ones who believe in me to sin, it

Liturgical (1), Liturgy (7)
AG : 2 6 :040(069) [0075] traditions (such as the **liturgy** of the Mass and various
AP : 1 5 :039(220) [0325] our churches the public **liturgy** is more decent than in
AP : 2 4 :001(249) [0385] We keep traditional **liturgical** forms, such as the order of
AP : 2 4 :079(264) [0411] Greeks call the Mass "**liturgy**," and this, they say, means
AP : 2 4 :079(264) [0411] But let us talk about the term "**liturgy**."
AP : 2 4 :081(264) [0411] Thus the term "**liturgy**" squares well with the ministry.
AP : 2 4 :081(264) [0411] Demosthenes says that "**liturgy**" is a kind of tax to pay
AP : 2 4 :083(264) [0413] of their use of "**liturgy**" to mean public duties or

Live (106), Lived (7), Lives (22), Liveth (1), Living (60) (*See also "life," above.*)
PR : PR :025(014) [0023] resolved and purpose to **live** in genuine peace and
AG : PR :004(025) [0039] a single, true religion and **live** together in unity and in one
AG : 0 3 :006(030) [0045] openly to judge the **living** and the dead, as stated in the
AG : 1 8 :001(039) [0051] will which enables him to **live** an outwardly honorable life
AG : 2 0 :033(045) [0057] honorable and blameless **lives**; they failed to accomplish
AG : 2 3 :005(052) [0061] people have the gift of **living** in celibacy, and he certainly
AG : 2 4 :022(058) [0067] into a sacrifice for the **living** and the dead, a sacrifice by
AG : 2 4 :029(059) [0067] for the whole world and for others, both **living** and dead.
AG : 2 4 :034(060) [0067] sins of others, whether **living** or dead, but should be a
AG : 2 6 :009(065) [0071] in this way was said to **live** a spiritual and Christian life.
AG : 2 7 :001(071) [0075] them, what kind of life as **lived** in the monasteries, and
AG : 2 8 :045(088) [0089] of the world, why do you **live** as if you still belonged to
AL : 0 3 :006(030) [0045] come again to judge the **living** and the dead, etc.,
AL : 2 0 :033(045) [0057] who, although they tried to **live** honest lives, were not
AL : 2 0 :033(045) [0057] they tried to live honest **lives**, were not able to do so but
AL : 2 3 :012(052) [0063] priests in Germany compelled by force to **live** in celibacy.
AL : 2 4 :022(058) [0067] takes away the sins of the **living** and the dead.
AL : 2 4 :029(059) [0067] takes away the sins of the **living** and the dead by a
AL : 2 6 :013(066) [0073] some even took their own **lives**, because they felt that they
AL : 2 8 :045(088) [0089] the universe, why do you **live** as if you still belonged to
AP : 0 4 :029(111) [0129] how one ought to **live**, and also for leading a holy life,
AP : 0 4 :048(114) [0135] accounted righteous before God do not **live** in mortal sin.
AP : 0 4 :100(121) [0151] Hab. 2:4, "The righteous shall **live** by his faith."
AP : 0 4 :106(122) [0153] he who keeps the law will **live** in it, so that by recognizing
AP : 0 4 :106(122) [0153] his weakness one may attain to it, keep it, and **live** in it.
AP : 0 4 :106(122) [0153] a good work by the performance of which he can **live**.
AP : 0 4 :140(126) [0161] we keep it—not because we **live** up to it but because we
AP : 0 4 :143(126) [0161] cannot exist in those who **live** according to the flesh, who
AP : 0 4 :143(126) [0161] debtors, not to the flesh, to **live** according to the
AP : 0 4 :143(126) [0161] to the flesh—for if you **live** according to the flesh you will
AP : 0 4 :143(127) [0161] you put to death the deeds of the body, you will **live**."
AP : 0 4 :167(130) [0169] Who **lives** up to the requirements of his calling?
AP : 0 4 :168(130) [0169] thy servant; for no man **living** is righteous before thee."
AP : 0 4 :236(140) [0185] of love; if our opponents **lived** up to them, they would
AP : 0 4 :236(140) [0185] and most of which are not **lived** up to even by those who
AP : 0 4 :246(142) [0189] show that it is not dead but **living** and active in the heart.
AP : 0 4 :248(142) [0191] between dead and **living** faith and condemns the idle and
AP : 0 4 :326(157) [0211] thy servant, for no man **living** is righteous before thee."
AP : 0 7 :006(169) [0229] criticize our description, which speaks of **living** members.

Continued ▶

A P : 0 7 :012(170) [0231] define that which is the **living** body of Christ and is the
A P : 0 7 :013(170) [0231] makes us members, and **living** members, of the church.
A P : 0 7 :035(175) [0239] the universe, why do you **live** as if you still belonged to
A P : 1 0 :004(180) [0247] about the presence of the **living** Christ, knowing that
A P : 1 2 :015(184) [0257] not only from the **living** but even more from the dead.
A P : 1 2 :047(188) [0265] word (Hab. 2:4), "The righteous shall **live** by his faith."
A P : 1 2 :055(189) [0265] These two parts also appear in the **lives** of the saints.
A P : 1 2 :078(193) [0275] thy servant; for no man **living** is righteous before thee."
A P : 1 2 :094(196) [0281] prophet (Ez. 33:11), "As I **live**, says the Lord God, I have
A P : 1 2 :094(196) [0281] wicked, but that the wicked turn from his way and **live**."
A P : 1 2 :094(196) [0281] When God says, 'As I **live**,' he wants to be believed.
A P : 1 2 :132(202) [0291] 12:1), "Present your bodies as a **living** sacrifice, holy," etc.
A P : 1 6 :002(222) [0331] of the nation in which we **live**, just as it lets us make use
A P : 2 1 :001(229) [0343] be honored and that the **living** saints should pray for
A P : 2 3 :002(239) [0363] fathers "who look like Curius and **live** like Bacchantes."
A P : 2 3 :044(245) [0375] where they can **live** voluptuously, cannot even keep this
A P : 2 4 :011(251) [0387] merit for others, whether **living** or dead, forgiveness of
A P : 2 4 :026(254) [0391] "Present your bodies as a **living** sacrifice, holy and
A P : 2 4 :064(261) [0407] without faith the Mass does not even benefit **living** people.
A P : 2 4 :089(266) [0415] for commemoration and preaching among the **living**.
A P : 2 4 :096(267) [0417] Mass there was an offering for the **living** and the dead.
A P : 2 7 :012(270) [0423] for Christ's sake and try to **live** more closely according to
A P : 2 7 :017(271) [0425] the monks "pattern their **lives** more closely after the
A P : 2 7 :039(276) [0433] monks try to pattern their **lives** more closely with the
A P : 2 7 :039(276) [0433] that monks pattern their **lives** more closely after the
A P : 2 7 :053(278) [0437] Fourth, those who **live** in monasteries are released by
A P : 2 7 :059(279) [0441] than kings' palaces and who **live** most sumptuously.
S 1 : P R :003(289) [0455] the council), those who **live** after me may have my
S 1 : P R :005(289) [0457] I should reply to everything while I am still **living**.
S 1 : P R :008(290) [0457] of matrimony, but that all **live** promiscuously like cattle
S 1 : P R :010(290) [0457] care how the poor people **live** or die, although Christ died
S 1 : P R :015(291) [0459] with Thee and the Father **liveth** and reigneth, blessed
S 1 : 0 1 :000(292) [0461] will come to judge the **living** and the dead, etc., as the
S 2 : 0 2 :012(295) [0465] Christ instituted the sacrament for the **living** alone.
S 2 : 0 2 :015(295) [0467] what kind of houses they **lived** in would have to become
S 2 : 0 2 :017(296) [0467] as articles of faith and had to **live** according to them.
S 2 : 0 2 :021(296) [0469] good works, etc. for the benefit of the **living** and the dead.
S 2 : 0 2 :024(296) [0469] which are granted to the **living** and the dead (for money)
S 2 : 0 4 :009(300) [0473] than by having all of us **live** under one head, Christ, and
S 3 : 0 7 :002(312) [0493] thy servant, for no man **living** is righteous before thee"
S 3 : 1 1 :002(315) [0499] of God or forbid them to **live** honestly in
T R : 0 0 :028(325) [0513] than "You are the Christ, the Son of the **living** God"?
T R : 0 0 :029(325) [0513] that he should say, 'You are the Son of the **living** God.'
T R : 0 0 :071(332) [0525] thee the power to sacrifice for the **living** and the dead."
S C : P R :002(338) [0533] especially those who **live** in the country, have no
S C : P R :003(338) [0533] Ten Commandments, they **live** as if they were pigs and
S C : P R :013(339) [0535] of those among whom they **live** and make their living.
S C : P R :013(339) [0535] of those among whom they live and make their **living**.
S C : P R :013(339) [0535] under whose protection he **lives**, no matter whether he is
S C : 0 2 :003(345) [0545] *whence he shall come to judge the* ***living*** *and the dead."*
S C : 0 2 :004(345) [0545] in order that I may be his, **live** under him in his kingdom,
S C : 0 2 :004(345) [0545] is risen from the dead and **lives** and reigns to all eternity.
S C : 0 3 :005(346) [0547] as children of God, lead holy **lives** in accordance with it.
S C : 0 3 :005(346) [0547] But whoever teaches and **lives** otherwise than as the Word
S C : 0 3 :008(346) [0547] believe his holy Word and **live** a godly life, both here in
S C : 0 4 :012(349) [0551] cleansed and righteous, to **live** forever in God's presence.
S C : 0 8 :007(353) [0559] thy hand; Thou satisfiest the desire of every **living** thing."
S C : 0 8 :008(353) [0559] the desire of every **living** thing" means that all creatures
S C : 0 9 :003(354) [0561] gospel should get their **living** by the gospel" (I Cor. 9:14).
S C : 0 8 :011(354) [0559] Jesus Christ our Lord, who **lives** and reigns forever.
S C : 0 9 :006(355) [0561] "You husbands, **live** considerately with your wives,
S C : 0 9 :009(356) [0563] with you and that you may **live** long on the earth'"
S C : 0 9 :013(356) [0563] self-indulgent is dead even while she **lives**" (I Tim. 5:5, 6).
L C : P R :001(358) [0567] and had nothing to do but **live** off the fat of the land all
L C : P R :015(360) [0571] We must ever **live** and dwell in the midst of such mighty
L C : S P :012(363) [0577] whence he shall come to judge the **living** and the dead.
L C : 0 1 :033(369) [0589] many thousands, lest men **live** in security and commit
L C : 0 1 :033(369) [0589] who think that it makes no great difference how they **live**.
L C : 0 1 :090(377) [0607] nor practice God's Word but teach and **live** contrary to it.
L C : 0 1 :101(379) [0609] these words are not idle or dead, but effective and **living**.
L C : 0 1 :103(379) [0611] love him with our whole heart all the days of our **lives**.
L C : 0 1 :112(380) [0613] to all that they who **lived** according to these words must
L C : 0 1 :118(381) [0615] the merits of their whole **lives** they are not worthy to
L C : 0 1 :118(381) [0615] a little child that has **lived** according to this
L C : 0 1 :124(382) [0617] another, and as they have **lived**, so live their children
L C : 0 1 :124(382) [0617] and as they have lived, so **live** their children after them.
L C : 0 1 :125(382) [0617] when he has given us **living** parents, should we be happy
L C : 0 1 :133(383) [0619] be well with you and that you may **live** long on the earth."
L C : 0 1 :137(384) [0621] They **live** long in peace and quietness.
L C : 0 1 :153(386) [0625] You will **live** much better with God's favor, peace, and
L C : 0 1 :170(388) [0629] were no concern of ours what they learn or how they **live**.
L C : 0 1 :183(390) [0633] We must **live** among many people who do us harm, and
L C : 0 1 :197(392) [0637] life," so that they might **live** a nice, soft life without the
L C : 0 1 :205(393) [0639] is required both to **live** chastely himself and to help his
L C : 0 1 :208(393) [0639] knowledge of God, godly **living**, and all virtues, and fight
L C : 0 1 :219(394) [0643] everyone not only to **live** chastely in thought, word, and
L C : 0 1 :219(394) [0643] that husband and wife **live** together in love and harmony,
L C : 0 1 :247(398) [0651] meet a poor man who must **live** from hand to mouth, you
L C : 0 1 :247(398) [0651] you act as if everyone must **live** by your favor, you skin
L C : 0 1 :255(399) [0651] for it is intolerable to **live** among men in public disgrace
L C : 0 1 :305(406) [0667] so disobedient and hard to **live** with that her husband was
L C : 0 1 :305(406) [0669] while the latter was still **living**, and yet posed as an
L C : 0 1 :310(407) [0669] even though as long as we **live** here we cannot reach that
L C : 0 1 :322(409) [0673] them and gladly act and **live** in accordance with them.
L C : 0 2 :025(413) [0685] *whence he shall come to judge the* ***living*** *and the dead."*
L C : 0 2 :055(418) [0693] to comfort and revive our consciences as long as we **live**.
L C : 0 2 :058(418) [0693] sin, death, and all evil, **living** in new, immortal and
L C : 0 2 :070(420) [0697] For as long as we **live** we shall have enough to preach and
L C : 0 3 :034(425) [0707] that it should impel us to keep praying for it all our **lives**.
L C : 0 3 :044(425) [0709] fail to teach, speak, and **live** as godly and heavenly
L C : 0 3 :047(426) [0711] ungrateful for it and fail to **live** according to it as we
L C : 0 3 :052(427) [0711] be praised through his holy Word and our Christian **lives**.
L C : 0 3 :054(427) [0713] it may be received by faith and may work and **live** in us.
L C : 0 3 :054(427) [0713] and that we may **live** forever in perfect righteousness and
L C : 0 3 :073(430) [0719] people among whom we **live** and move — in short,
L C : 0 3 :077(431) [0721] and the people at large to **live** together in obedience,
L C : 0 3 :086(432) [0723] and transgress because we **live** in the world among people
L C : 0 3 :089(432) [0723] the flesh in which we daily **live** is of such a nature that it
L C : 0 3 :102(433) [0727] We **live** in the flesh and we have the old Adam hanging
L C : 0 3 :106(434) [0727] allurements as long as we **live** in the flesh and have the
L C : 0 4 :025(439) [0739] into the kingdom of Christ and **live** with him forever.
L C : 0 4 :043(442) [0743] or even though they died would afterward **live** forever.
L C : 0 4 :043(442) [0743] which swallows up death and saves the **lives** of all men.
L C : 0 4 :046(442) [0743] soul shall be saved and **live** forever: the soul through the
L C : 0 4 :067(445) [0749] so that the longer we **live** the more gentle, patient, and
L C : 0 4 :075(445) [0751] If you **live** in repentance, therefore, you are walking in
L C : 0 4 :086(446) [0753] day by day as long as we **live**, that is, as long as we carry
L C : 0 5 :069(454) [0769] and lead unchristian **lives** receive it to their harm and
L C : 0 6 :005(457) [0000] will not believe the Gospel, **live** according to it, and do
L C : 0 6 :009(458) [0000] should and must take place incessantly as long as we **live**.
E P : 0 1 :010(467) [0781] we now bear will arise and **live** forever, without original
E P : 0 3 :011(474) [0795] justified by faith, a true **living** faith becomes "active
E P : 0 4 :006(476) [0799] genuine faith — if it is a **living** and not a dead faith.
E P : 0 6 :002(480) [0805] before the Fall did not **live** without the law, for the law of
E P : 0 6 :006(481) [0807] sense the children of God **live** in the law and walk
E P : 0 7 :004(482) [0809] of the true, essential, and **living** body and blood of Christ
E P : 0 7 :019(484) [0813] be, as long as he retains a **living** faith, will receive the
E P : 0 7 :023(484) [0815] of the Mass for the sins of the **living** and the dead.
E P : 0 7 :039(486) [0817] who have a genuine and **living** faith in Christ, can also
E P : 1 1 :014(496) [0835] to put forth every effort to **live** according to the will of
S D : 0 1 :042(515) [0871] anything, for "in him we **live** and move and are"
S D : 0 2 :041(529) [0897] grace we may believe his holy Word and **live** a godly life."
S D : 0 2 :049(530) [0901] "As I **live**, I have no pleasure in the death of the wicked,
S D : 0 2 :049(530) [0901] that the wicked turn from his way and **live**" (Ezek. 33:11).
S D : 0 3 :020(542) [0921] "He who through faith is righteous shall **live** (Rom. 1:17).
S D : 0 3 :026(543) [0923] saving faith in those who **live** without contrition and
S D : 0 3 :042(547) [0931] the case of others, a true **living** faith and distinguish it
S D : 0 3 :057(550) [0935] again, "The righteous shall **live** by his faith" (Hab. 2:4).
S D : 0 4 :010(552) [0941] Oh, faith is a **living**, busy, active, mighty thing, so that it
S D : 0 4 :032(556) [0947] "If you **live** according to the flesh you will die"
S D : 0 6 :001(564) [0963] away, learn from the law to **live** and walk in the law.
S D : 0 6 :005(564) [0963] as though the righteous should **live** without the law.
S D : 0 6 :016(566) [0967] who are concerned about **living** according to the law and
S D : 0 6 :016(566) [0967] as a person is not reborn, **lives** according to the law, and
S D : 0 6 :017(566) [0967] by the Spirit of Christ), he **lives** according to the
S D : 0 6 :018(567) [0969] under but in the law, they **live** and walk in the law of the
S D : 0 6 :021(567) [0969] thy servant; for no man **living** is righteous before thee"
S D : 0 7 :029(574) [0981] death, 'If Dr. Luther were **living** now, he would teach and
S D : 0 7 :109(588) [1011] of the sacrifice of the Mass for the **living** and for the dead.
S D : 0 7 :123(590) [1013] not have a right, truthful, **living**, and saving faith, receive
S D : 0 7 :125(591) [1015] retain a true, genuine, **living** faith, but who fail to meet
S D : 1 1 :010(618) [1067] it will do me no harm if I **live** in all kinds of sin and vice
S D : 1 1 :059(626) [1083] This will lead us to **live** in the fear of God and to
S D : 1 1 :081(629) [1089] is written in Ezekiel, "As I **live**, says the Lord God, I have
S D : 1 1 :081(630) [1089] wicked turn from his way and **live**" (Ezek. 18:23; 33:11).
S D : 1 1 :084(630) [1091] this purpose have I let you **live** to show you my power, so
S D : 1 1 :084(630) [1091] wicked, but that the wicked turn from his way and **live**."

Livelihood (2)
L C : 0 1 :134(383) [0619] health, wife and child, **livelihood**, peace, good
L C : 0 3 :078(431) [0721] to our body and our **livelihood**, from tempest, hail, fire,

Lo (1)
L C : 0 1 :120(381) [0615] is commanded, saying, "**Lo**, this is better than the holiness

Load (1)
S D : 0 8 :004(592) [1017] and they went so far as to **load** down Dr. Luther's

Loaf (4)
A P : 1 0 :003(179) [0247] body, for we all partake of the same **loaf** (I Cor. 10:17).
L C : 0 3 :072(430) [0719] we could never take a **loaf** of bread from the oven to set
L C : 0 3 :075(430) [0719] were emblazoned with a **loaf** of bread instead of a lion or
L C : 0 3 :075(430) [0719] or a wreath of rue, or if a **loaf** of bread were stamped on

Loathe (1), Loathing (1)
P R : P R :022(012) [0021] a corresponding **loathing** for and a cordial disapproval of
L C : 0 1 :258(399) [0653] course of the world, men are **loathe** to offend anyone.

Local (2), Locality (1), Locally (4)
E P : 0 7 :014(483) [0811] single mode which the philosophers call ***local*** or spatial."
E P : 0 8 :029(490) [0825] human nature of Christ is **locally** extended to every place
E P : 0 8 :033(491) [0825] at the place where the human nature is **locally** present.
E P : 1 0 :004(493) [0829] of God in every **locality** and every age has authority to
S D : 0 7 :014(571) [0977] and blood of Christ are **locally** enclosed in the bread, or
S D : 0 7 :097(586) [1005] the one which the philosophers call **local** or spatial.
S D : 0 8 :092(609) [1049] the humanity of Christ is **locally** extended into every

Lock (1), Locked (4)
L C : 0 1 :226(395) [0645] whom we can guard with **lock** and bolt, or if we catch
S D : 0 7 :083(584) [1001] received, and eaten but is **locked** up, offered up, or
S D : 0 7 :087(585) [1003] but is offered up, or **locked** up, or carried about, or
S D : 0 7 :100(586) [1007] grave and came through **locked** doors, in the bread and
S D : 0 7 :108(588) [1009] for instance, the bread is **locked** up in the tabernacle or is

Locutions (1)
S D : 0 8 :045(600) [1031] or to write that the cited **locutions**, "God suffered," "God

Loewenstein (1)
P R : P R :027(015) [0025] Louis, count of **Loewenstein**

Lofty (2)
L C : P R :001(358) [0567] because of their great and **lofty** learning, others because
L C : S P :027(364) [0581] upon our youth, not in a **lofty** and learned manner but

Log (2), Logs (1)
S 1 : P R :013(291) [0459] strain out gnats, if we let **logs** stand and dispute about

Continued ▶

SD : 02 :020(525) [0889] like Lot's wife, yes, like a **log** or a stone, like a lifeless
SD : 02 :022(525) [0889] destiny for which only man, no stone or **log**, was created.

Logic (5), Logically (1)

AP : 02 :051(107) [0119] and fail to explain **logically** and correctly either the
AP : 04 :357(162) [0219] Such **logic** is completely new.
AP : 12 :123(201) [0289] Who ever taught these asses such **logic**?
AP : 12 :123(201) [0289] This is not **logic** or even sophistry, but sheer dishonesty.
AP : 20 :012(228) [0341] got the most out of their **logic** courses, for they have
SD : 01 :056(518) [0877] following the rules of **logic**, used the same terminology

Lombard (4)

AP : 02 :021(103) [0111] Peter **Lombard** is not afraid to say that original
AP : 12 :119(200) [0287] Not even Peter **Lombard** speaks this way about
AP : 12 :122(200) [0287] though it was unknown in the time of Peter **Lombard**.
AP : 12 :139(203) [0295] Peter **Lombard**'s statement about remitting part of the

Long (107), Longer (36), Longs (2)

PR : PR :024(013) [0021] scandals, dissensions, and **long**-standing schisms a
PR : PR :024(013) [0023] or postpone its printing and publication any **longer**.
AG : 20 :004(041) [0053] Our opponents no **longer** praise these useless works so
AG : 20 :008(042) [0053] life, has been neglected so **long** (as all must admit) while
AG : 22 :004(050) [0061] in the church for a **long** time, as can be demonstrated from
AG : 23 :012(053) [0063] also broke up the marriages which were of **long** standing.
AG : 23 :017(054) [0063] of marriage is to continue **longer**, there may be a shortage
AG : 25 :005(062) [0069] consciences without **long** enumerations of sins, with
AG : 25 :006(062) [0069] a more fitting fashion than had been done for a **long** time.
AG : 28 :003(081) [0085] Such outrage has **long** since been condemned by learned
AG : 28 :062(092) [0093] of faith was no **longer** taught and preached with clarity
AG : 28 :064(092) [0093] or mitigation as **long** as the opinion remains and prevails
AG : 28 :064(092) [0093] opinion will remain as **long** as there is no understanding
AL : 20 :008(042) [0053] in the church, has so **long** been neglected (for everybody
AL : 22 :004(050) [0061] This usage continued in the church for a **long** time.
AL : 24 :010(057) [0065] it is evident that for a **long** time there has been open and
AL : 24 :016(057) [0067] become so manifest that they could no **longer** be borne.
AL : 24 :018(058) [0067] is being punished for such **long** continued profanations of
AL : 28 :003(081) [0085] These wrongs have **long** since been rebuked in the church
AL : 28 :064(092) [0093] can never be achieved as **long** as the opinion remains that
AP : 02 :036(105) [0115] Baptism, not that it no **longer** is, but it is not imputed."
AP : 04 :009(108) [0123] As **long** as a man's mind is at rest and he does not feel
AP : 04 :012(108) [0123] vicious errors that would take a **long** time to enumerate.
AP : 04 :019(110) [0125] merit of congruity, it is no **longer** merit of congruity but
AP : 04 :041(113) [0133] "If it is by works, it is no **longer** on the basis of grace."
AP : 04 :088(120) [0149] and confirms it with a **long** discussion in Rom. 4 and
AP : 04 :157(129) [0165] the law does not justify so **long** as it can accuse us.
AP : 04 :166(130) [0169] Again, what need is there for a **long** argument?
AP : 04 :176(131) [0171] As **long** as we flee God's judgment and are angry at him,
AP : 04 :262(145) [0195] to know God's will, namely, that he is no **longer** angry.
AP : 04 :293(152) [0203] Even though they are a **long** way from the perfection of
AP : 04 :312(155) [0207] As **long** as we feel that he is wrathful against us, human
AP : 04 :352(161) [0217] again (II Cor. 5:2, 3), "We **long** to put on our heavenly
AP : 04 :367(163) [0221] that your days may be **long** in the land" (Ex. 20:12); here,
AP : 04 :369(163) [0221] but since it would take too **long** we shall expound it in
AP : 07 :048(177) [0245] teachers because they no **longer** function in the place of
AP : 10 :003(179) [0247] There is a **long** exposition of John 15 in Cyril which
AP : 10 :004(180) [0247] knowing that "death no **longer** has dominion over him."
AP : 12 :031(186) [0259] But thou, O Lord — how **long**?"
AP : 12 :113(199) [0285] These practices have **long** since become antiquated, nor
AP : 12 :124(201) [0289] God will not **long** endure such impudence and malice.
AP : 12 :153(206) [0299] its terrors, there is no **longer** that sting and sense of wrath
AP : 12 :153(206) [0299] is a real punishment as **long** as it is present; without this
AP : 12 :158(207) [0301] as Isaiah teaches in a **long** sermon in his twenty-eighth
AP : 12 :169(209) [0305] a thief and a robber as **long** as he unjustly holds on to
AP : 12 :169(209) [0305] as it is written (Eph. 4:28), "Let the thief no **longer** steal."
AP : 12 :175(210) [0307] The term "satisfaction" no **longer** refers to civil discipline
AP : 13 :017(213) [0313] or the terminology, so **long** as those things are kept which
AP : 15 :013(216) [0319] What need is there of a **long** discussion?
AP : 21 :008(230) [0345] "O Lord of hosts, how **long** wilt thou have no mercy on
AP : 21 :041(235) [0355] **Long** before, there were many learned and outstanding
AP : 22 :008(237) [0359] unfrocked and were no **longer** permitted to consecrate the
AP : 23 :008(240) [0367] but it still does as **long** as this physical nature of ours
AP : 23 :008(240) [0367] yearly the fields are clothed as **long** as this universe exists.
AP : 23 :010(241) [0367] was commanded but that it is no **longer** commanded.
AP : 23 :052(246) [0377] about this burden for a **long** time, either for themselves
AP : 23 :061(247) [0381] to remain continent, as **long** as he is really continent.
AP : 24 :002(249) [0385] In a **long** harangue about the use of Latin in the Mass,
AP : 24 :007(250) [0385] have they been that for a **long** time good men have
AP : 24 :033(255) [0395] gladly concede this, so **long** as he does not mean that by
AP : 27 :013(271) [0423] O Christ, how **long** wilt Thou bear these insults with
S2 : 02 :022(296) [0469] in them, relics should **long** since have been condemned.
S2 : 02 :028(297) [0469] benefit and help are no **longer** expected, the saints will
S2 : 02 :028(297) [0471] in heaven, for no one will **long** remember, esteem, or
S3 : 03 :042(310) [0491] you will, it matters not as **long** as you believe, for faith
S3 : 06 :005(311) [0493] of bread without any **longer** being real bread, for that
S3 : 08 :002(312) [0495] As **long** as we are in the flesh we shall not be untruthful if
S3 : 08 :008(313) [0495] (Acts 10:1ff.) had **long** since heard from the Jews about
TR : 00 :021(323) [0509] when there had for a **long** time been disputes between the
TR : 00 :055(329) [0521] the church be purified as **long** as the pope does not
TR : 00 :077(333) [0527] they have not had it for **long**, for it appears from the
SC : 09 :009(356) [0563] you and that you may live **long** on the earth'"
LC : PR :008(359) [0569] ABC's, which they think they have outgrown **long** ago.
LC : PR :020(361) [0573] noble confession that the **longer** they work with the
LC : 01 :067(373) [0599] Though it may take a **long** time, nothing he does will in
LC : 01 :071(374) [0601] God's name and cannot **long** remain when it is uttered
LC : 01 :076(375) [0601] to bring up children, so **long** as they can be trained with
LC : 01 :076(375) [0603] will remain good only as **long** as the rod is on their
LC : 01 :083(376) [0603] and trades the whole week **long** — should retire for a day
LC : 01 :131(383) [0619] "That you may have **long** life in the land where you
LC : 01 :133(383) [0619] be well with you and that you may live **long** on the earth."
LC : 01 :134(383) [0619] in the Scriptures, to have **long** life means not merely to
LC : 01 :134(383) [0619] everything that pertains to **long** life — health, wife and
LC : 01 :134(383) [0619] this life can neither be heartily enjoyed nor **long** endure.
LC : 01 :137(384) [0621] They live **long** in peace and quietness.
LC : 01 :164(387) [0627] for a year or two, but **long** life, sustenance, and peace,
LC : 01 :177(389) [0631] world; hence there is no **longer** any civil order, peace, or
LC : 01 :234(397) [0647] and arrogant course for a **long** time, still he will remain a
LC : 01 :238(397) [0647] them keep on boldly fleecing people as **long** as they can.
LC : 01 :238(397) [0649] neither prosper nor gain anything their whole life **long**.
LC : 01 :242(397) [0649] and scraped for a **long** time, he will pronounce this kind
LC : 01 :289(404) [0663] about our neighbor, as **long** as it is not a notorious evil,
LC : 01 :310(407) [0669] be pure, even though as **long** as we live here we cannot
LC : 01 :312(407) [0671] they were too insignificant or had been fulfilled **long** ago.
LC : 01 :317(408) [0673] It will be a **long** time before men produce a doctrine or
LC : 02 :032(415) [0687] sermons, but rather the **longer** sermons throughout the
LC : 02 :055(418) [0693] to comfort and revive our consciences as **long** as we live.
LC : 02 :060(418) [0695] of great importance, as **long** as the words are rightly
LC : 02 :070(420) [0697] For as **long** as we live we shall have enough to preach and
LC : 03 :076(431) [0719] Out of it one might make a **long** prayer, enumerating with
LC : 03 :105(434) [0727] As **long** as we remain in this vile life in which we are
LC : 03 :106(434) [0727] and allurements as **long** as we live in the flesh and have
LC : 03 :108(435) [0729] feeling of temptation as **long** as it is contrary to our will
LC : 04 :065(445) [0749] of which actions must continue in us our whole life **long**.
LC : 04 :067(445) [0749] daily decrease so that the **longer** we live the more gentle,
LC : 04 :080(446) [0751] the opinion, which has **long** prevailed among us, that our
LC : 04 :080(446) [0751] past which we can no **longer** use after falling again into
LC : 04 :086(446) [0753] remains day by day as **long** as we live, that is, as long as
LC : 04 :086(446) [0753] long as we live, that is, as **long** as we carry the old Adam
LC : 05 :042(451) [0763] from the sacrament over a **long** period of time are not to
LC : 05 :049(452) [0765] to hinder him, lets a **long** period of time elapse without
LC : 05 :067(454) [0769] toward it, neglecting it so **long** that we grow quite cold
LC : 06 :009(458) [0000] should and must take place incessantly as **long** as we live.
LC : 06 :033(461) [0000] Ps. 42:2 says, "As a hart **longs** for flowing streams, so
LC : 06 :033(461) [0000] for flowing streams, so **longs** my soul for thee, O God."
EP : 04 :010(476) [0799] because they are "no **longer** under the law but under
EP : 05 :008(478) [0803] to the disclosure of sin, as **long** as men hear only the law
EP : 05 :010(479) [0803] 8. Nevertheless, as **long** as all this — namely, the passion
EP : 06 :005(480) [0807] called, works of the law as **long** as they are extorted from
EP : 07 :019(484) [0813] how weak he may be, as **long** as he retains a living faith,
EP : 08 :032(491) [0825] suffering and death he no **longer** has anything to do with
EP : 10 :006(493) [0829] In such a case it is no **longer** a question of indifferent
EP : 10 :007(493) [0831] commanded by God, as **long** as there is mutual
EP : 11 :009(495) [0833] As **long** as men follow their reason, they can hardly
EP : 12 :006(498) [0839] and innocent, and that as **long** as they have not achieved
SD : 02 :019(524) [0889] man since the Fall is no **longer** a rational creature, or
SD : 02 :063(533) [0905] does good, as much and as **long** as the Holy Spirit
SD : 02 :066(534) [0907] does good, as much and as **long** as God rules in him
SD : 03 :029(544) [0925] Therefore, while and as **long** as we have to do with this
SD : 05 :012(560) [0955] But as **long** as all this proclaims the wrath of God and
SD : 06 :016(566) [0967] For as **long** as a person is not reborn, lives according to
SD : 06 :017(567) [0967] Paul, such people are no **longer** under law but under
SD : 06 :024(568) [0971] There he will no **longer** require either the preaching of the
SD : 06 :024(568) [0971] punishments, just as he will no **longer** require the Gospel.
SD : 07 :001(568) [0971] Augsburg Confession no **longer** secretly but in part
SD : 07 :066(581) [0997] these testimonies are too **long** to list here, in the interest
SD : 07 :108(588) [1009] substance and is no **longer** bread, the body of Christ is
SD : 08 :051(601) [1033] the adversaries cannot and dare not any **longer** deny.
SD : 10 :009(612) [1055] to its circumstances, as **long** as it does so without frivolity
SD : 10 :014(613) [1057] For here we are no **longer** dealing with the external
SD : 10 :031(616) [1063] fewer or more of them, as **long** as they are otherwise
SD : 11 :006(617) [1065] — how far it is to go, how **long** it is to endure, and when
SD : 11 :074(628) [1087] they feel that they are no **longer** experiencing any power
SD : 11 :080(629) [1089] his will, he would not have needed any **long**-suffering.
SD : 12 :003(633) [1095] that they themselves no **longer** know what the Augsburg

Longing (3)

PR : PR :024(013) [0023] of Christian concord and have a particular **longing** for it.
LC : 05 :050(452) [0765] have at least a little **longing** to do what my Lord has
SD : 02 :014(523) [0885] a little spark and a **longing** for the grace of God and

Look (57), Looked (4), Looking (7), Looks (9)

PR : PR :011(006) [0011] that the adversaries were **looking** for could be abolished
AL : 26 :018(066) [0073] therefore, must not be **looked** upon as having taken up
AP : 02 :002(100) [0105] we ask them first to **look** at the German text of the
AP : 04 :021(110) [0127] or of law, at which they **look** as the Jews did at the veiled
AP : 04 :131(125) [0157] They **look** at the second table and political works; about
AP : 04 :142(126) [0161] wrath against our sins and **looks** for forgiveness of sins
AP : 04 :148(127) [0163] Faith alone, **looking** to the promise and believing with
AP : 04 :154(128) [0163] By **looking** for the forgiveness of sins from him, she truly
AP : 04 :154(128) [0165] of faith that she was **looking** for the forgiveness of sins
AP : 04 :170(130) [0169] things; in trouble it **looks** to men for help; it even defies
AP : 04 :229(139) [0183] Human wisdom **looks** at the law and seeks righteousness
AP : 04 :258(144) [0193] in such a statement to **look** only at these works: "correct
AP : 04 :264(146) [0195] omit the promises and **look** only at the commandments,
AP : 04 :265(146) [0197] only works and neither **looks** at nor understands faith, it
AP : 04 :324(157) [0209] **Looking** at his mercy, faith comforts and consoles us.
AP : 04 :336(159) [0215] **Look** how this childish sophistry delights our opponents!
AP : 04 :360(162) [0219] **Look** out, dear reader, you have not yet heard the whole
AP : 12 :078(193) [0275] as the Jews **looked** at Moses' face covered by a veil.
AP : 12 :079(194) [0275] He asks us to **look** at this promise, which would certainly
AP : 12 :122(200) [0287] **Look** how our opponents prove these fictions of theirs in
AP : 12 :136(203) [0293] **Look** what follows!
AP : 12 :158(207) [0301] They should **look** at these other and more important
AP : 15 :028(219) [0323] great Gerson suffers as he **looks** for the degrees and
AP : 15 :033(220) [0325] Many **look** for loopholes in the traditions to ease their
AP : 15 :039(220) [0325] than in theirs, and if you **look** at it correctly we are more
AP : 20 :010(228) [0341] Anyone who **looks** will find many passages in Scripture to
AP : 21 :034(233) [0353] Let us **look** at this as it really is.
AP : 22 :009(237) [0359] **Look** at the effrontery of the men!
AP : 22 :011(238) [0361] **Look** at the great effrontery of the man.
AP : 23 :002(239) [0363] of the holy fathers "who **look** like Curius and live like
AP : 23 :008(240) [0365] **Look** at their clever argument!
AP : 23 :063(247) [0381] Just **look** at these impudent rascals!
AP : 24 :023(253) [0391] word more readily if we **look** at the customs which the
AP : 24 :037(257) [0397] so in the New we should **look** for what it represents and
AP : 24 :039(257) [0399] New Testament we should **look** for the substance of
AP : 24 :043(258) [0399] preachers who want to **look** more learned take up

Continued ▶

A P : 2 4 :058(260) [0405] Christ if we were to **look** for some other satisfaction that
A P : 2 4 :076(263) [0411] That is, piety **looks** at what is given and what is forgiven;
A P : 2 7 :018(272) [0425] But **look**, most clement Emperor Charles; look, princes;
A P : 2 7 :018(272) [0425] clement Emperor Charles; **look**, princes; look, all you
A P : 2 7 :018(272) [0425] Emperor Charles; look, princes; **look**, all you estates!
A P : 2 7 :024(273) [0427] But **look** at the impudence of our opponents!
A P : 2 8 :018(284) [0449] and that we should not **look** for another word from
S 1 : P R :004(289) [0455] They let me **look** on and listen, although they know very
S C : 0 3 :016(347) [0549] heavenly Father may not **look** upon our sins, and on
S C : 0 8 :007(353) [0559] "The eyes of all **look** to Thee, O Lord, and Thou givest
L C : P R :016(361) [0571] **Look** at these bored, presumptuous saints who will not or
L C : 0 1 :002(365) [0581] A god is that to which we **look** for all good and in which
L C : 0 1 :004(365) [0581] good thing you lack, **look** to me for it and seek it from
L C : 0 1 :015(366) [0585] turn to me for all this; **look** upon me as the one who
L C : 0 1 :017(367) [0585] of his own, to which he **looked** for blessings, help, and
L C : 0 1 :070(374) [0601] God's name consists of **looking** to it for all consolation
L C : 0 1 :226(395) [0645] dares to give them a hard **look** or accuse them of theft.
L C : 0 1 :228(396) [0645] If we **look** at mankind in all its conditions, it is nothing
L C : 0 1 :231(396) [0647] so as to make the others **look** respectable and honorable.
L C : 0 1 :297(405) [0665] all he can and lets others **look** out for themselves.
L C : 0 1 :303(406) [0667] and "Every man must **look** out for himself while others
L C : 0 1 :317(408) [0673] accustom themselves to **look** only to these precepts and
L C : 0 1 :332(410) [0677] written everywhere he **looks**, and even wherever he goes
L C : 0 3 :058(428) [0713] unbelief which does not **look** to God even for enough to
L C : 0 4 :020(439) [0737] hair, flesh and bones, they **look** no different from Turks
L C : 0 4 :030(440) [0739] speaks — there faith must **look** and to it faith must hold.
L C : 0 4 :038(441) [0741] flesh and blood, yet we **look** not at the flesh and blood
L C : 0 5 :079(455) [0771] Again, **look** about you and see whether you are also in
L C : 0 5 :083(456) [0773] Just examine yourself, **look** around a little, cling to the
L C : 0 6 :024(460) [0000] and no mention of what they were to **look** for or receive.
L C : 0 6 :026(460) [0000] not say that men should **look** to see how full of filthiness
E P : 0 3 :016(475) [0795] 4. That faith does not **look** alone to Christ's obedience,
E P : 1 1 :006(495) [0833] of God, but it is to be **looked** for in his Word, where he
S D : 0 3 :058(550) [0937] Faith thus **looks** at the person of Christ, how this person
S D : 0 3 :063(550) [0937] 4. That faith does not **look** solely to the obedience of
S D : 0 7 :022(573) [0979] abide by these words and **look** anyone in the eye who
S D : 0 7 :023(573) [0979] take the Word away or **look** upon the elements without
S D : 0 7 :122(590) [1013] wine of the Supper, but to **look** away from the bread of
S D : 0 7 :122(590) [1013] and by their faith to **look** to that place in heaven where
S D : 0 8 :030(597) [1025] their delight and joy in **looking** into it, as St. Peter
S D : 1 2 :006(633) [1097] we do not propose to **look** on idly or stand by silently

Loop (1), Loophole (1), Loopholes (1)
A P : 1 5 :033(220) [0325] Many look for **loopholes** in the traditions to ease their
S 3 : 0 3 :015(305) [0483] year), the following **loophole** was resorted to, namely,
S D : 0 7 :018(572) [0979] up every subterfuge and **loop**-hole which the

Loose (7), Loosed (1), Looses (1)
A P : 1 2 :138(203) [0293] when he says (Matt. 18:18), "Whatever you **loose**," etc.
A P : 1 2 :176(210) [0307] the power to bind and **loose**, according to the statement
A P : 1 2 :176(210) [0307] heaven, and whatever you **loose** on earth shall be loosed
A P : 1 2 :176(210) [0307] whatever you loose on earth shall be **loosed** in heaven."
A P : 1 2 :176(210) [0307] Just as "to **loose**" means to forgive sins, so "to bind"
S 3 : 0 7 :001(311) [0493] by Christ to bind and **loose** sins, not only the gross and
T R : 0 0 :040(327) [0517] not only the power to **loose** and bind in this life but also
L C : 0 6 :014(458) [0000] that through a man God **looses** and absolves him from
S D : 0 7 :046(577) [0987] or if it was to receive a tolerable and **loose** interpretation.

Loot (1)
L C : 0 1 :229(396) [0645] and sneak-thieves who **loot** a cash box, they sit in office

Lord (339)
P R : P R :018(009) [0015] the judgment seat of our **Lord** Jesus Christ with joyful
P R : P R :020(010) [0017] in the treatment of the **Lord**'s Supper to this and only this
P R : P R :022(011) [0019] the article concerning the **Lord**'s Supper, these have to be
P R : P R :022(012) [0021] on the great day of the **Lord** before the solemn and severe
A G : 0 3 :006(030) [0045] The same **Lord** Christ will return openly to judge the
A G : 0 7 :004(032) [0047] belongs to your call, one **Lord**, one faith, one baptism."
A G : 1 0 :000(034) [0047] X. The Holy Supper of Our **Lord**
A G : 1 0 :001(034) [0047] in the Supper of our **Lord** under the form of bread and
A G : 1 7 :001(038) [0051] taught among us that our **Lord** Jesus Christ will return on
A G : 2 2 :011(050) [0061] to act contrary to the arrangement of our **Lord** Christ.
A G : 2 3 :003(051) [0061] was instituted by the **Lord** God to avoid immorality, for
A G : 2 4 :021(058) [0067] it was taught that our **Lord** Christ has by his death made
A G : 2 5 :011(063) [0069] obey the prophet who says, 'Show your way to the **Lord**.'
A G : 2 5 :011(063) [0071] Therefore confess to the **Lord** God, the true judge, in your
A G : 2 6 :027(068) [0073] through the grace of the **Lord** Jesus, just as they will."
A G : 2 8 :026(084) [0087] "the authority which the **Lord** has given me for building
A L : 1 0 :000(034) [0047] X. **Lord**'s Supper
A L : 1 0 :001(034) [0047] are distributed to those who eat in the Supper of the **Lord**
A L : 2 2 :001(049) [0059] In the sacrament of the **Lord**'s Supper both kinds are
A L : 2 2 :001(049) [0059] has the command of the **Lord** in Matt. 26:27, "Drink of it,
A L : 2 4 :012(057) [0065] or drinks the cup of the **Lord** in an unworthy manner will
A L : 2 4 :012(057) [0065] be guilty of profaning the body and blood of the **Lord**."
A L : 2 4 :019(058) [0067] it is written, "The **Lord** will not hold him guiltless who
A L : 2 4 :037(060) [0067] received the body of the **Lord** from him, for the words of
A L : 2 5 :011(063) [0069] obey the prophet who says, 'Show your way to the **Lord**.'
A L : 2 6 :027(068) [0073] through the grace of the **Lord** Jesus, just as they will."
A L : 2 8 :033(086) [0087] from the Sabbath to the **Lord**'s Day — contrary to the
A L : 2 8 :058(091) [0091] that the observance of the **Lord**'s Day in place of the
A L : 2 8 :060(091) [0091] the church designated the **Lord**'s Day for this purpose,
A L : 2 8 :063(092) [0093] that the observance of the **Lord**'s Day is not *indeed* of
A P : 0 4 :058(115) [0137] for example, "If thou, O **Lord**, shouldst mark iniquities,
A P : 0 4 :058(115) [0137] shouldst mark iniquities, **Lord**, who shall stand?"
A P : 0 4 :058(115) [0137] word, my soul hopes in the **Lord**," that is, because thou
A P : 0 4 :079(118) [0143] who gives us the victory through our **Lord** Jesus Christ."
A P : 0 4 :087(120) [0147] to the ability that the **Lord** saw fit to grant us, we
A P : 0 4 :103(122) [0151] men sinners, but when the **Lord** Jesus came he forgave all
A P : 0 4 :131(125) [0159] "You shall love the **Lord** your God with all your heart"
A P : 0 4 :133(125) [0159] but when a man turns to the **Lord** the veil is removed.
A P : 0 4 :133(125) [0159] Now, the **Lord** is the Spirit, and where the Spirit of the
A P : 0 4 :133(125) [0159] and where the Spirit of the **Lord** is, there is freedom."
A P : 0 4 :168(130) [0169] is the man to whom the **Lord** imputes no iniquity."
A P : 0 4 :195(134) [0175] we have peace with God through our **Lord** Jesus Christ.
A P : 0 4 :210(136) [0179] Thus the **Lord**'s Supper was instituted in the church so
A P : 0 4 :210(136) [0179] "As often as you do this, you proclaim the **Lord**'s death."
A P : 0 4 :226(138) [0183] is, "You shall love the **Lord** your God" (Matt. 22:27).
A P : 0 4 :254(143) [0193] Then you shall call, and the **Lord** will answer."
A P : 0 4 :258(144) [0193] reason together, says the **Lord**: though your sins are like
A P : 0 4 :268(147) [0197] would not be judged by the **Lord**" (I Cor. 11:31); "If you
A P : 0 4 :276(148) [0199] Baptism and the **Lord**'s Supper, for example, are signs
A P : 0 4 :276(148) [0199] Just as the **Lord**'s Supper does not justify *ex opere*
A P : 0 4 :289(151) [0203] Truly the law says, "You shall love the **Lord** your God"
A P : 0 4 :322(157) [0209] in his commentary on the **Lord**'s Prayer: "Lest anybody
A P : 0 4 :326(158) [0211] as in Ps. 7:8, "Judge me, O **Lord**, according to my
A P : 0 4 :326(158) [0211] our sins, "If thou, O **Lord**, shouldst mark iniquities, Lord,
A P : 0 4 :326(158) [0211] O Lord, shouldst mark iniquities, **Lord**, who could stand?"
A P : 0 4 :328(158) [0211] And in the **Lord**'s Prayer the saints pray for the
A P : 0 4 :329(158) [0211] Zech. 2:13 says, "Be silent, all flesh, before the **Lord**."
A P : 0 4 :329(158) [0211] when the breath of the **Lord** blows upon it"; that is, the
A P : 0 4 :331(158) [0211] O **Lord**, hear; O Lord, forgive; O Lord, give heed and act;
A P : 0 4 :331(158) [0211] O Lord, hear; O **Lord**, forgive; O Lord, give heed and act;
A P : 0 4 :331(158) [0211] hear; O Lord, forgive; O **Lord**, give heed and act; delay
A P : 0 4 :351(161) [0217] the glory of the **Lord**, we are changed into his likeness";
A P : 0 4 :363(162) [0219] righteousness, which the **Lord**, the righteous judge, will
A P : 0 4 :385(166) [0225] prayer closes with this phrase: "through Christ our **Lord**."
A P : 0 4 :400(168) [0227] against the Gospel, as the **Lord** says, "My sheep hear my
A P : 0 4 :400(168) [0227] words or in the words of its head, our **Lord** Jesus Christ?
A P : 0 7 :033(174) [0239] the order of the Mass, the **Lord**'s day, and the other more
A P : 0 7 :046(177) [0243] of Christ in the use of the **Lord**'s Supper, which certainly
A P : 1 0 :001(179) [0247] our belief that in the **Lord**'s Supper the body and blood
A P : 1 0 :001(179) [0247] is "a participation in the **Lord**'s body," it would follow
A P : 1 0 :001(179) [0247] but only in his spirit if the **Lord**'s body were not truly
A P : 1 0 :004(179) [0247] whole church — that in the **Lord**'s Supper the body and
A P : 1 1 :003(180) [0249] absolution and the **Lord**'s Supper, many times a year.
A P : 1 2 :031(186) [0259] 3, "Be gracious to me, O **Lord**, for I am languishing; O
A P : 1 2 :031(186) [0259] for I am languishing; O **Lord**, heal me, for my bones are
A P : 1 2 :031(186) [0259] But thou, O **Lord** — how long?"
A P : 1 2 :042(187) [0263] of sins, as the words in the **Lord**'s Supper clearly state,
A P : 1 2 :048(188) [0265] David (II Sam. 12:13), "I have sinned against the **Lord**."
A P : 1 2 :049(188) [0265] Ps. 118:18, "The **Lord** has chastened me sorely, but he has
A P : 1 2 :050(189) [0265] I Sam. 2:6, "The **Lord** kills and brings to life; he brings
A P : 1 2 :051(189) [0265] Isa. 28:21, "The **Lord** will be wroth, to do his deed —
A P : 1 2 :056(189) [0267] he says (II Sam. 12:13), "I have sinned against the **Lord**."
A P : 1 2 :056(189) [0267] (II Sam. 12:14), "The **Lord** has put away your sin; you
A P : 1 2 :094(196) [0281] "As I live, says the **Lord** God, I have no pleasure in
A P : 1 2 :094(196) [0281] we if we do not believe the **Lord** even when he swears an
A P : 1 2 :107(197) [0283] my transgressions to the **Lord**'; then thou didst forgive the
A P : 1 2 :146(205) [0297] who gives us the victory through our **Lord** Jesus Christ."
A P : 1 2 :150(206) [0299] when he prays (Ps. 6:1), "O **Lord**, rebuke me not in thy
A P : 1 2 :150(206) [0299] Jer. 10:24, "Correct me, O **Lord**, but in just measure; not
A P : 1 2 :163(208) [0303] not be judged" by the **Lord**; but the word "judge" refers to
A P : 1 2 :177(210) [0307] "Our authority, which the **Lord** gave for building you up."
A P : 1 3 :004(211) [0309] are Baptism, the **Lord**'s Supper, and absolution (which is
A P : 1 3 :004(211) [0309] baptized, when we eat the **Lord**'s body, when we are
A P : 1 3 :020(213) [0313] that anyone who uses the **Lord**'s Supper uses it this way.
A P : 1 5 :014(217) [0319] I the **Lord** am your God; walk in my statutes, and be
A P : 1 5 :040(220) [0325] Every **Lord**'s Day many in our circles use the Lord's
A P : 1 5 :040(220) [0325] many in our circles use the **Lord**'s Supper, but only after
A P : 2 0 :005(227) [0339] Isaiah says (53:6), "The **Lord** has laid on him the iniquity
A P : 2 1 :008(230) [0345] where the angel prays, "O **Lord** of hosts, how long wilt
A P : 2 1 :018(231) [0347] Paul prays, "May our **Lord** Jesus Christ himself, and
A P : 2 1 :025(232) [0349] used: "The passion of our **Lord** Jesus Christ and the
A P : 2 2 :000(236) [0357] [Article XXII.] The **Lord**'s Supper Under Both Kinds
A P : 2 2 :001(236) [0357] use of both kinds in the **Lord**'s Supper is godly and in
A P : 2 2 :003(236) [0357] he had received from the **Lord** what he was delivering, but
A P : 2 2 :003(236) [0359] those who would use the **Lord**'s Supper should use it
A P : 2 2 :004(236) [0359] and distribute the blood of the **Lord** to the people."
A P : 2 3 :040(245) [0375] unmarried man is anxious about the affairs of the **Lord**."
A P : 2 3 :045(245) [0375] from wine, even in the **Lord**'s Supper; they abstained from
A P : 2 3 :064(248) [0381] "Purify yourselves, you who bear the vessels of the **Lord**."
A P : 2 3 :064(248) [0381] who bear the vessels of the **Lord**," must be taken to mean
A P : 2 3 :066(248) [0381] who bear the vessels of the **Lord**," requires impure
A P : 2 4 :008(250) [0385] on the fourth day, on Sabbath eve, and on the **Lord**'s day
A P : 2 4 :011(251) [0387] our position that the **Lord**'s Supper does not grant grace
A P : 2 4 :029(255) [0393] "Offer right sacrifices, and put your trust in the **Lord**."
A P : 2 4 :029(255) [0393] of thanksgiving and call on the name of the **Lord**."
A P : 2 4 :032(255) [0395] They say, first, that the name of the **Lord** will be great.
A P : 2 4 :032(255) [0395] is how the name of the **Lord** becomes great among the
A P : 2 4 :032(255) [0395] which the name of the **Lord** becomes great, like faith,
A P : 2 4 :033(256) [0395] way, the reception of the **Lord**'s Supper itself can be praise
A P : 2 4 :033(256) [0395] not only about the **Lord**'s Supper, and he does not
A P : 2 4 :033(256) [0395] heart, by which the name of the **Lord** really becomes great
A P : 2 4 :034(256) [0395] and silver, till they present right offerings to the **Lord**."
A P : 2 4 :035(256) [0397] bread and drink the cup, you proclaim the **Lord**'s death."
A P : 2 4 :062(260) [0405] writes, "The body of the **Lord**, once offered on the cross
A P : 2 4 :068(261) [0407] people imagine that the **Lord**'s Supper was instituted for
A P : 2 4 :072(262) [0409] to be remembered; the **Lord** is gracious and merciful.
A P : 2 4 :080(264) [0411] the body and blood of the **Lord** to the people, just as a
A P : 2 4 :087(265) [0413] not about prayers, but really about the **Lord**'s Supper.
A P : 2 4 :088(265) [0413] the body and blood of the **Lord** in particular, but about
A P : 2 4 :089(266) [0415] to apply to the dead the **Lord**'s Supper which was
A P : 2 4 :090(266) [0415] Surely the **Lord**'s Supper was instituted for the sake of
A P : 2 4 :091(266) [0415] Cor. 11:27), are "guilty of the body and blood of the **Lord**
A P : 2 4 :091(266) [0415] the body and blood of the **Lord** for their own sacrilegious
A P : 2 4 :093(267) [0417] the body and blood of the **Lord**, but about the other parts
A P : 2 4 :094(267) [0417] we reject the transfer of the **Lord**'s Supper to the dead *ex*
A P : 2 7 :003(269) [0419] one will come," he said, "in the year of our **Lord** 1516.
A P : 2 7 :025(273) [0427] saints, "You shall love the **Lord** your God with all your
A P : 2 7 :027(274) [0429] changed from glory to glory, as by the Spirit of the **Lord**."
A P : 2 7 :032(274) [0431] stand up against the **Lord** who comes at him with twenty
S 1 : P R :009(290) [0457] Christ, the **lord** and judge of us all, knows very well that
S 1 : P R :015(291) [0459] Dear **Lord** Jesus Christ, assemble a council of thine own,
S 2 : 0 1 :001(292) [0461] Jesus Christ, our God and **Lord**, "was put to death for our
S 2 : 0 4 :015(301) [0475] the hope that Christ, our **Lord**, has attacked his
S 2 : 0 4 :016(301) [0477] devil in Zechariah, "The **Lord** rebuke you, O Satan"

Continued ▶

S 3 : 0 3 :005(304) [0481] to receive grace from the **Lord** and to expect and accept
S 3 : 0 3 :013(305) [0483] people: "Prolong my life, **Lord** God, until I make
S 3 : 0 6 :004(311) [0493] against and over Christ, our **Lord** and God, etc.
S 3 : 1 3 :003(315) [0499] "Let him who boasts, boast of the **Lord**" (I Cor. 1:31).
T R : 0 0 :082(000) [0529] and constantly will teach, through Jesus Christ, our **Lord**.
S C : P R :000(338) [0533] peace in Jesus Christ, our **Lord**, from Martin Luther to all
S C : P R :003(338) [0533] they do not know the **Lord's** Prayer, the Creed, or the Ten
S C : P R :005(338) [0533] withhold the cup in the **Lord's** Supper and insist on the
S C : P R :005(338) [0533] in teaching the people the **Lord's** Prayer, the Creed, the
S C : P R :007(339) [0533] the Creed, the **Lord's** Prayer, the sacraments, etc.
S C : P R :008(339) [0535] same form in teaching the **Lord's** Prayer, the Creed, and
S C : P R :010(339) [0535] the Creed, the **Lord's** Prayer, etc., following the text word
S C : P R :027(341) [0539] be praise and thanks forever, through Christ, our **Lord**.
S C : 0 1 :003(342) [0539] *shall not take the name of the **Lord** your God in vain."*
S C : 0 1 :021(344) [0543] Answer: He says, "I the **Lord** your God am a jealous God,
S C : 0 2 :003(345) [0545] *Christ, his only son, our **Lord**: who was conceived by the*
S C : 0 2 :004(345) [0545] of the virgin Mary, is my **Lord**, who has redeemed me, a
S C : 0 2 :006(345) [0545] I cannot believe in Jesus Christ, my **Lord**, or come to him.
S C : 0 3 :000(346) [0545] [III] The **Lord's** Prayer *in the plain form in which the*
S C : 0 4 :004(348) [0551] in Matthew 28:19, our **Lord** Christ said, "Go therefore
S C : 0 4 :008(349) [0551] in Mark 16:16, our **Lord** Christ said, "He who believes
S C : 0 5 :018(350) [0553] of which we are not aware, as we do in the **Lord's** Prayer.
S C : 0 5 :028(351) [0555] to the command of our **Lord** Jesus Christ, I forgive you
S C : 0 6 :002(351) [0555] body and blood of our **Lord** Jesus Christ, under the bread
S C : 0 6 :004(351) [0555] St. Paul, write thus: "Our **Lord** Jesus Christ, on the night
S C : 0 7 :002(352) [0557] or standing, say the Apostles' Creed and the **Lord's** Prayer
S C : 0 7 :005(353) [0559] or standing, say the Apostles' Creed and the **Lord's** Prayer
S C : 0 8 :007(353) [0559] eyes of all look to Thee, O **Lord**, and Thou givest them
S C : 0 8 :009(353) [0559] Then the **Lord's** Prayer should be said, and afterwards
S C : 0 8 :009(353) [0559] "**Lord** God, heavenly Father, bless us, and these thy gifts
S C : 0 8 :009(353) [0559] Thou hast bestowed on us, through Jesus Christ our **Lord**
S C : 0 8 :010(354) [0559] "O give thanks to the **Lord**, for he is good; for his
S C : 0 8 :010(354) [0559] the legs of a man; but the **Lord** takes pleasure in those
S C : 0 8 :011(354) [0559] Then the **Lord's** Prayer should be said, and afterwards
S C : 0 8 :011(354) [0559] "We give Thee thanks, **Lord** God, our Father, for all thy
S C : 0 8 :011(354) [0559] through Jesus Christ our **Lord**, who lives and reigns
S C : 0 9 :003(354) [0561] "The **Lord** commanded that those who proclaim the
S C : 0 9 :003(354) [0561] who are over you in the **Lord** and admonish you, and to
S C : 0 9 :005(355) [0561] "Be subject for the **Lord's** sake to every human institution
S C : 0 9 :008(356) [0563] and instruction of the **Lord**" (Eph. 6:4; Col. 3:21).
S C : 0 9 :009(356) [0563] "Children, obey your parents in the **Lord**, for this is right.
S C : 0 9 :010(356) [0563] with a good will as to the **Lord** and not to men, knowing
S C : 0 9 :010(356) [0563] the same again from the **Lord**, whether he is a slave or
L C : P R :003(358) [0567] Bible and would pray the **Lord's** Prayer for themselves
L C : P R :007(359) [0569] recite word for word the **Lord's** Prayer, the Ten
L C : S P :012(363) [0577] Christ, his only Son, our **Lord**: who was conceived by the
L C : S P :023(364) [0579] "Our **Lord** Jesus Christ on the night when he was betrayed
L C : 0 1 :030(368) [0589] *"For I am the **Lord** your God, mighty and jealous, visiting*
L C : 0 1 :051(371) [0595] name if we call upon the **Lord** God in any way whatsoever
L C : 0 1 :057(372) [0597] a solemn threat: "for the **Lord** will not hold him guiltless
L C : 0 1 :064(373) [0599] his name is hallowed, as we pray in the **Lord's** Prayer.
L C : 0 1 :074(374) [0601] monstrous or fearful and exclaim, "**Lord** God, save us!"
L C : 0 1 :074(374) [0601] "Help, dear **Lord** Christ!" etc.
L C : 0 1 :089(377) [0605] Ten Commandments, the Creed, and the **Lord's** Prayer.
L C : 0 1 :148(385) [0623] and protection in the **Lord** and, what is more, a joyful
L C : 0 1 :246(398) [0651] show forgiveness and mercy, as the **Lord's** Prayer teaches.
L C : 0 1 :252(399) [0653] to the poor lends to the **Lord**, and he will repay him for
L C : 0 1 :253(399) [0653] Here you have a rich **Lord**.
L C : 0 1 :316(408) [0671] Both the Creed and the **Lord's** Prayer must help us, as we
L C : 0 1 :320(408) [0673] *"I the **Lord**, your God, am a jealous God, visiting the*
L C : 0 1 :325(409) [0675] as when he says, "The **Lord** takes pleasure in those who
L C : 0 1 :325(409) [0675] verse, as if to say, "The **Lord** takes pleasure in those who
L C : 0 2 :003(411) [0679] we would need neither the Creed nor the **Lord's** Prayer.
L C : 0 2 :021(413) [0683] to thank him or acknowledge him as **Lord** and Creator.
L C : 0 2 :025(413) [0683] *Christ, his only Son, our **Lord**: who was conceived by the*
L C : 0 2 :026(414) [0685] concentrate on these words, "in Jesus Christ, our **Lord**."
L C : 0 2 :027(414) [0685] that Jesus Christ, true Son of God, has become my **Lord**."
L C : 0 2 :027(414) [0685] What is it to "become a **Lord**"?
L C : 0 2 :027(414) [0685] Before this I had no **Lord** and King but was captive under
L C : 0 2 :030(414) [0685] taken by Jesus Christ, the **Lord** of life and righteousness
L C : 0 2 :031(414) [0685] that the little word "**Lord**" simply means the same as
L C : 0 2 :031(414) [0685] that he might become **Lord** over sin; moreover, he
L C : 0 2 :031(414) [0687] All this in order to become my **Lord**.
L C : 0 2 :038(415) [0689] him and take him as our **Lord**, unless these were first
L C : 0 2 :039(415) [0689] than to bring us to the **Lord** Christ to receive this
L C : 0 2 :043(416) [0689] recognized Christ as the **Lord**, or the Holy Spirit as the
L C : 0 2 :043(416) [0689] believed that Christ is our **Lord** in the sense that he won
L C : 0 2 :045(416) [0689] church, and outside it no one can come to the **Lord** Christ
L C : 0 2 :065(419) [0695] grace were it not for the **Lord** Christ, who is a mirror of
L C : 0 2 :066(419) [0697] for they do not have the **Lord** Christ, and, besides, they
L C : 0 3 :000(420) [0697] Third Part: The **Lord's** Prayer
L C : 0 3 :003(420) [0697] what and how to pray, our **Lord** Christ himself has taught
L C : 0 3 :004(420) [0699] Before we explain the **Lord's** Prayer part by part, it is very
L C : 0 3 :027(424) [0705] and others is quite amply indicated in the **Lord's** Prayer.
L C : 0 3 :034(425) [0707] Now we shall treat the **Lord's** Prayer very briefly and
L C : 0 3 :051(426) [0711] sent his Son, Christ our **Lord**, into the world to redeem
L C : 0 3 :084(432) [0723] lest this petition of the **Lord's** Prayer be turned against
L C : 0 3 :096(433) [0725] it immediately after the **Lord's** Prayer in Matt. 6:14,
L C : 0 3 :098(433) [0725] by Baptism and the **Lord's** Supper, which are appointed
L C : 0 3 :110(435) [0729] is to take refuge in the **Lord's** Prayer and to appeal to God
L C : 0 4 :003(437) [0733] subject, namely, where the **Lord** Christ says in Matt.
L C : 0 4 :006(437) [0733] the Creed, and the **Lord's** Prayer are not spun out of any
L C : 0 4 :037(441) [0741] faith grasps, just as the **Lord** Christ upon the cross is not
L C : 0 4 :054(443) [0745] partake unworthily of the **Lord's** Supper receive the true
L C : 0 5 :003(447) [0753] *"Our **Lord** Jesus Christ on the night when he was betrayed*
L C : 0 5 :004(447) [0753] For the **Lord's** Supper was not invented or devised by any
L C : 0 5 :005(447) [0755] Ten Commandments, the **Lord's** Prayer, and the Creed
L C : 0 5 :008(447) [0755] body and blood of the **Lord** Christ in and under the bread
L C : 0 5 :024(449) [0759] The **Lord's** Supper is given as a daily food and sustenance
L C : 0 5 :027(449) [0759] this comfort of the **Lord's** Supper is given to bring us new
L C : 0 5 :031(450) [0759] poured out for us in the **Lord's** Supper and hence that we
L C : 0 5 :045(452) [0763] coerced by men, but to obey and please the **Lord** Christ.
L C : 0 5 :050(452) [0765] longing to do what my **Lord** has commanded me to do."
L C : 0 5 :071(454) [0769] the commandment and the promise of the **Lord** Christ.
L C : 0 5 :080(456) [0771] under foot because our **Lord** Christ himself could not
L C : 0 5 :085(456) [0773] the Creed, and the **Lord's** Prayer into the young so that
L C : 0 6 :008(458) [0000] kinds are expressed in the **Lord's** Prayer when we say,
L C : 0 6 :009(458) [0000] Indeed, the whole **Lord's** Prayer is nothing else than such
L C : 0 6 :010(458) [0000] toward his neighbor, is included in the **Lord's** prayer.
L C : 0 6 :012(458) [0000] Thus we have in the **Lord's** Prayer a twofold absolution:
E P : 0 3 :007(474) [0793] an abomination to the **Lord**" (Prov. 17:15); likewise,
E P : 0 4 :012(477) [0799] understood exactly as our **Lord** and the apostles
E P : 0 4 :014(477) [0799] for Christ's sake the **Lord** does not reckon this weakness
E P : 0 7 :002(481) [0809] body and blood of our **Lord** Jesus Christ truly and
E P : 0 7 :008(482) [0811] and alone to the almighty power of our **Lord** Jesus Christ.
E P : 0 8 :014(488) [0821] They have "crucified the **Lord** of glory," and in Acts
E P : 1 1 :010(495) [0833] repent and believe on the **Lord** Jesus Christ (I Tim. 2:6;
E P : 1 1 :022(497) [0837] God and Father of our **Lord** Jesus Christ grant us the
E P : 1 2 :023(500) [0841] means through which the **Lord** God seals the adoption of
E P : 1 2 :031(500) [0843] the righteous judge, our **Lord** Jesus Christ, and that we
S D : 0 1 :014(511) [0863] and forgiven before God only for the **Lord** Christ's sake.
S D : 0 2 :026(526) [0891] "Lydia heard us; the **Lord** opened her heart to give heed
S D : 0 2 :026(526) [0891] "No one can say, Jesus is **Lord**, except by the Holy Spirit"
S D : 0 2 :040(528) [0895] I cannot believe in Jesus Christ, my **Lord**, or come to him.
S D : 0 2 :041(529) [0897] the second petition of the **Lord's** Prayer Luther answers
S D : 0 2 :043(529) [0897] contrary to the help and grace of our **Lord** Jesus Christ.
S D : 0 2 :044(529) [0897] only the devil's will and what is contrary to the **Lord** God.
S D : 0 2 :059(532) [0905] with his will resists the **Lord** God until he is converted.
S D : 0 2 :060(533) [0905] Nevertheless, the **Lord** God draws the person whom he
S D : 0 2 :062(533) [0905] it is correct to say that the **Lord** God indeed has one mode
S D : 0 3 :009(541) [0919] resurrection of Christ, our **Lord**, whose obedience is
S D : 0 3 :015(541) [0919] the law — since he is the **Lord** of the law — as he was
S D : 0 3 :017(542) [0921] are both alike an abomination to the **Lord**" (Prov. 17:15).
S D : 0 3 :055(549) [0935] solely and alone on the **Lord** Christ, it is important to
S D : 0 4 :008(552) [0941] is so for the sake of the **Lord** Christ through faith, because
S D : 0 5 :004(558) [0953] teaching of Christ, our **Lord**, which in his public ministry
S D : 0 5 :010(560) [0955] "When a man turns to the **Lord**, the veil is removed"
S D : 0 5 :020(561) [0959] Son of God, Christ our **Lord**, himself assumed and bore
S D : 0 5 :022(562) [0959] confidence solely on the **Lord** Jesus Christ, "who was put
S D : 0 5 :025(563) [0961] of the Gospel of our **Lord** Christ will once more comfort
S D : 0 6 :001(563) [0963] have been converted to the **Lord** and from whom the veil
S D : 0 6 :004(564) [0963] in the law of the **Lord**, as it is written, "Blessed is the man
S D : 0 6 :004(564) [0963] delight is in the law of the **Lord**, and on his law he
S D : 0 6 :018(567) [0969] and walk in the law of the **Lord**, and yet do nothing by
S D : 0 7 :004(569) [0973] they alleged that the **Lord's** Supper was only an external
S D : 0 7 :004(569) [0973] they confessed that the **Lord** Christ is truly present in the
S D : 0 7 :006(570) [0973] opinion than that the **Lord** Christ is present in his Supper
S D : 0 7 :008(570) [0975] here on earth in the **Lord's** Supper, although invisibly and
S D : 0 7 :010(571) [0975] body and blood of our **Lord** Jesus Christ, under the bread
S D : 0 7 :011(571) [0975] we confess that in the **Lord's** Supper the body and blood
S D : 0 7 :018(572) [0979] presence of the body of the **Lord** Christ through faith.
S D : 0 7 :029(574) [0981] appear before the judgment seat of our **Lord** Jesus Christ.
S D : 0 7 :031(574) [0983] the Last Judgment at the coming of the **Lord** Christ.
S D : 0 7 :033(575) [0983] will not believe that the **Lord's** bread in the Supper is his
S D : 0 7 :035(575) [0983] St. Paul (the bread in the **Lord's** Supper "is true body of
S D : 0 7 :039(576) [0985] is the true flesh and blood of the **Lord** Jesus Christ."
S D : 0 7 :043(576) [0987] It is our **Lord** and Saviour Jesus Christ concerning whom,
S D : 0 7 :044(577) [0987] this truthful and almighty **Lord**, our Creator and
S D : 0 7 :045(577) [0987] of God, Jesus Christ, our **Lord**, Creator, and Redeemer,
S D : 0 7 :047(578) [0989] The **Lord** who has spoken these words is himself infinite
S D : 0 7 :048(578) [0989] that these words of our **Lord** and Saviour Jesus Christ,
S D : 0 7 :050(578) [0989] of Jesus Christ than the **Lord** Christ himself, who best
S D : 0 7 :057(579) [0993] going to the table of the **Lord** and partaking of the body
S D : 0 7 :059(580) [0993] for their error that in the **Lord's** Supper the body of
S D : 0 7 :060(580) [0993] Christ, who come to the **Lord's** table without true
S D : 0 7 :060(580) [0993] or drinks the cup of the **Lord** in an unworthy manner"
S D : 0 7 :060(580) [0993] of profaning the body and blood of the **Lord** Jesus Christ.
S D : 0 7 :061(580) [0995] of the Gospel as well as in the **Lord's** Supper.
S D : 0 7 :063(581) [0995] bread and wine in the **Lord's** Supper receive and partake
S D : 0 7 :067(582) [0997] enthusiasts ridicule the **Lord** Christ, St. Paul, and the
S D : 0 7 :074(583) [0999] Word, institution, and ordinance of our **Lord** Jesus Christ
S D : 0 7 :078(583) [1001] and command in the **Lord's** Supper and say, 'This is my
S D : 0 7 :083(584) [1001] if the entire action of the **Lord's** Supper as Christ ordained
S D : 0 7 :084(584) [1001] therewith proclaim the **Lord's** death), must be kept
S D : 0 7 :090(585) [1003] to the omnipotence of our **Lord** and Saviour, Jesus
S D : 0 7 :100(587) [1007] the bread and wine in the **Lord's** Supper, and, as people
S D : 0 7 :106(588) [1009] true and eternal God, our **Lord** and Saviour Jesus Christ.
S D : 0 8 :002(591) [1015] of Jesus Christ in the **Lord's** Supper on the basis of the
S D : 0 8 :004(592) [1017] of the Supper of the **Lord**, did operate with and use the
S D : 0 8 :016(594) [1021] taught godlessly that the **Lord** Christ was a mere man in
S D : 0 8 :043(599) [1029] Therefore we regard our **Lord** Christ as God and man in
S D : 0 8 :053(601) [1033] more thoroughly than the **Lord** Christ himself what Christ
S D : 0 8 :072(605) [1041] not rest upon Christ the **Lord** according to his assumed
S D : 0 9 :001(610) [1051] year 1533, "I believe in the **Lord** Christ, God's Son, who
S D : 1 0 :006(611) [1055] be separate from them, says the **Lord**" (II Cor. 6:14, 17).
S D : 1 1 :006(617) [1065] For the **Lord** God governs everything in such a way that
S D : 1 1 :028(621) [1071] "The **Lord** is not wishing that any should perish, but that
S D : 1 1 :028(621) [1071] "He is simultaneously one **Lord** of all, rich toward all who
S D : 1 1 :033(621) [1073] answered the question, "**Lord**, will those who are saved be
S D : 1 1 :064(626) [1083] has known the mind of the **Lord**?" — that is, outside and
S D : 1 1 :075(628) [1087] lovers; yet return again to me, says the **Lord**" (Jer. 3:1).
S D : 1 1 :081(629) [1089] Ezekiel, "As I live, says the **Lord** God, I have no pleasure
S D : 1 1 :082(630) [1091] says specifically that the **Lord** himself "has prepared them
S D : 1 2 :006(633) [1097] God and Father of our **Lord** Jesus Christ has appointed
S D : 1 2 :031(635) [1101] not a means whereby the **Lord** God seals the adoption of

Lord (22), Lords (8)

P R : P R :008(005) [0009] to our most gracious **lord**, His Roman Imperial Majesty,
P R : P R :027(015) [0025] George Ernest, count and **lord** of Henneberg
P R : P R :027(015) [0025] George, count and **lord** of Castell [-Ruedenhausen]
P R : P R :027(015) [0025] Henry, count and **lord** of Castell [-Remlingen]
A G : P R :001(024) [0039] most mighty, invincible Emperor, most gracious **Lord**:
A G : P R :010(025) [0041] Majesty, our most gracious **lord**, to discuss with them and
A G : P R :012(026) [0041] If, however, our **lords**, friends, and associates who
A G : 2 7 :013(073) [0077] preacher, of ruler, prince, **lord**, or the like, all of whom
A P : 0 7 :023(172) [0235] the pope must be **lord** of the whole world, of all the

Continued ▶

S 2 : 0 4 :002(298) [0471] him as “most gracious **lord**,” as if he were a king or
S 2 : 0 4 :013(300) [0475] the head, and then the **lord** of the church, and finally of
S 2 : 0 4 :014(301) [0475] the devil himself as our **lord** or God, so we cannot suffer
S 2 : 0 4 :014(301) [0475] govern us as our head or **lord**, for deception, murder, and
S 2 : 0 4 :016(301) [0477] say, “You are my gracious **lord**,” but we ought rather
S 3 : 1 0 :002(314) [0497] They are temporal **lords** and princes who are unwilling to
T R : 0 0 :031(325) [0513] also said, “Not that we **lord** it over your faith”
T R : 0 0 :033(325) [0513] the pope is by divine right **lord** of the kingdoms of the
S C : 0 9 :007(355) [0563] husbands, as Sarah obeyed Abraham, calling him **lord**.
L C : 0 1 :022(367) [0585] were in our service or debt and we were his liege **lords**.
L C : 0 1 :047(371) [0593] allowing none of these good things to be his **lord** or idol.
L C : 0 1 :229(396) [0645] chairs and are called great **lords** and honorable, good
L C : 0 1 :230(396) [0645] who consort with **lords** and princes and daily plunder not
L C : 0 1 :237(397) [0647] They act as if they were **lords** over others' possessions and
L C : 0 1 :300(405) [0667] belong, as many great nobles, **lords**, and princes do now.
E P : 1 2 :015(499) [0841] feudal homage to his territorial sovereign or liege-**lord**.
S D : 0 2 :043(529) [0897] the devil is our god and **lord**, and there is no power or
S D : 1 0 :019(614) [1059] They are temporal **lords** and princes who are unwilling to
S D : 1 0 :020(614) [1059] the devil himself as our **lord** or God, so we cannot suffer
S D : 1 0 :020(614) [1059] govern us as our head or **lord**, for deception, murder, and
S D : 1 2 :020(634) [1099] pay oath-bound feudal homage to his prince or liege **lord**.

Lordship (10)
A G : 2 8 :076(094) [0095] the bishops to exercise **lordship** as if they had power to
T R : 0 0 :007(320) [0505] Christ expressly forbids **lordship** among the apostles.
T R : 0 0 :008(320) [0505] that no one should have **lordship** or superiority among
T R : 0 0 :008(320) [0505] “The kings of the Gentiles exercise **lordship** over them.
T R : 0 0 :008(321) [0505] The antithesis here shows that **lordship** is disapproved.
T R : 0 0 :009(321) [0505] he granted to none a prerogative or **lordship** over the rest.
T R : 0 0 :011(321) [0507] ministers should assume **lordship** or authority over the
T R : 0 0 :015(322) [0509] attribute superiority and **lordship** to the bishop of Rome.
S D : 1 0 :020(614) [1059] article on the primacy or **lordship** of the pope, the
S D : 1 0 :021(614) [1061] “No one should assume **lordship** or authority over the

Lose (22), Loses (2), Losing (2), Loss (10), Lost (29)
P R : P R :024(013) [0023] be entirely obscured and **lost** and nothing beyond
A L : 1 2 :007(035) [0049] once been justified can **lose** the Holy Spirit, and also
A P : 0 2 :024(103) [0111] that when righteousness is **lost**, concupiscence follows.
A P : 0 4 :220(137) [0181] urging to bear good fruits lest they **lose** the Holy Spirit.
A P : 0 7 :003(169) [0227] The sacraments do not **lose** their efficacy when they are
A P : 2 0 :004(227) [0339] These theologians have **lost** all sense of shame if they dare
A P : 2 0 :013(228) [0343] in your call and not to **lose** its gifts, which were given to
A P : 2 0 :013(228) [0343] not remain in those who **lose** the Holy Spirit and reject
A P : 2 2 :010(237) [0359] case of Eli's sons; after the **loss** of the high priesthood,
A P : 2 4 :020(252) [0389] others, we must never **lose** sight of these two types of
A P : 2 7 :009(270) [0421] public expense without the **loss** of their private
A P : 2 7 :067(280) [0441] being supported from public funds and thus **lost** the faith.
S 1 : P R :003(289) [0455] of that party have **lost** hope that the Roman court will
S 1 : P R :003(289) [0455] to see all Christendom **lost** and all souls damned rather
S 1 : P R :015(291) [0459] The pope and his adherents are **lost**.
S 2 : 0 1 :005(292) [0463] Otherwise all is **lost**, and the pope, the devil, and all our
S 3 : 0 3 :005(304) [0481] stood before God and recognize themselves as **lost** men.
S 3 : 0 3 :035(309) [0489] that we are all utterly **lost**, that from head to foot there is
S 3 : 0 6 :005(311) [0493] and wine surrender or **lose** their natural substance and
T R : 0 0 :051(329) [0519] and countless souls are **lost** generation after generation.
S C : P R :007(339) [0533] In this way all the time and labor will be **lost**.
S C : P R :024(341) [0539] the benefit and **loss**, the blessing and danger connected
S C : 0 2 :004(345) [0545] who has redeemed me, a **lost** and condemned creature,
S C : 0 5 :022(350) [0553] neglected to do my duty, and caused him to suffer **loss**.
L C : 0 1 :012(366) [0583] protect their cattle, recover **lost** possessions, etc., as
L C : 0 1 :151(386) [0625] a gulden by his unfaithfulness, he will **lose** ten elsewhere.
L C : 0 1 :174(388) [0629] his chief duty, on pain of **losing** divine grace, to bring up
L C : 0 1 :224(395) [0643] neighbor in any sort of dealing that results in **loss** to him.
L C : 0 1 :226(395) [0645] One would ten times rather **lose** the money from one's
L C : 0 1 :235(397) [0647] them the favor and service of protecting them from **loss**.
L C : 0 1 :258(399) [0653] is inevitably oppressed, **loses** his case, and suffers
L C : 0 1 :303(406) [0667] nor yet sell it without **loss** — he hurries and worries him
L C : 0 1 :307(406) [0669] is his, letting him suffer **loss** while you gratify your greed,
L C : 0 2 :030(414) [0685] He has snatched us, poor **lost** creatures, from the jaws of
L C : 0 2 :038(415) [0689] no one knew of it, it would have been all in vain, all **lost**.
L C : 0 2 :043(416) [0689] does not awaken understanding in the heart, all is **lost**.
L C : 0 3 :018(422) [0703] prayers to be frustrated or **lost**, for if he did not intend to
L C : 0 3 :084(432) [0723] beware lest they **lose** the common intercession of the
L C : 0 3 :089(432) [0723] and displeasure, and so it **loses** the comfort and
L C : 0 3 :091(432) [0723] In short, unless God constantly forgives, we are **lost**.
L C : 0 5 :023(449) [0757] our human flesh and blood have not **lost** their old skin.
L C : 0 5 :067(454) [0769] quite cold and callous and **lose** all desire and love for it.
L C : 0 6 :007(457) [0000] persuading them not to **lose** this precious and comforting
E P : 0 1 :015(468) [0783] complete deprivation or **loss** of the same, just as garlic
E P : 0 4 :019(477) [0801] of the Holy Spirit are not **lost** through malicious sin, but
E P : 0 7 :022(484) [0813] wine in the Holy Supper **lose** their substance and natural
E P : 0 8 :039(492) [0827] deity denied and we shall **lose** Christ altogether along
S D : 0 1 :011(510) [0863] same time it replaces the **lost** image of God in man with a
S D : 0 1 :023(512) [0865] nevertheless not entirely **lost** all the goodness that belongs
S D : 0 1 :027(513) [0867] judgment and verdict man **lost** the concreated
S D : 0 1 :027(513) [0867] Satan brought about, this **loss** has so perverted and
S D : 0 2 :058(532) [0903] of his unbelief and be **lost**, as it is written, “How often
S D : 0 2 :069(534) [0907] Spirit within them and **lose** him, they dare not be
S D : 0 2 :083(537) [0913] do not receive the Holy Spirit but grieve and **lose** him.
S D : 0 3 :027(543) [0923] death, or that he has again **lost** the righteousness of faith,
S D : 0 4 :030(556) [0947] are preserved in us so that we do not **lose** them again.
S D : 0 4 :031(556) [0947] up that it is impossible to **lose** faith and the gift of
S D : 0 4 :033(556) [0949] lest you fall away and **lose** the Spirit and his gifts, which
S D : 0 4 :033(556) [0949] who lead a wicked life, **lose** the Holy Spirit, and reject
S D : 0 7 :108(588) [1009] Holy Supper completely **lose** their substance and essence
S D : 0 7 :108(588) [1009] which they allege has **lost** its natural substance and is no
S D : 0 8 :044(599) [1029] that God died for us, but only a man died, we are **lost**.
S D : 1 1 :084(630) [1091] God's good pleasure that he should be damned and **lost**.
S D : 1 1 :090(631) [1093] were the case, they would **lose** it more readily than Adam
S D : 1 1 :090(631) [1093] paradise — yes, would be **losing** it every moment and

Lot (3)
S 1 : P R :009(290) [0457] the rest, wretchedness and woe will be their **lot** forever.
L C : 0 5 :040(451) [0761] A **lot** of people who hear the Gospel, now that the
S D : 0 2 :020(525) [0889] is like a pillar of salt, like **Lot**'s wife, yes, like a log or a

Loud (1), Loudly (1)
A G : 2 3 :001(051) [0061] degree, there has been **loud** complaint throughout the
A P : 2 7 :065(280) [0441] For Paul **loudly** condemns all worship, all laws, all

Louis (6)
P R : P R :027(014) [0025] **Louis**, count palatine on the Rhine, elector
P R : P R :027(014) [0025] Philip **Louis**, palsgrave [of Pfalz-Neuburg]
P R : P R :027(015) [0025] **Louis**, duke of Wuerttemberg
P R : P R :027(015) [0025] **Louis**, count of Gleichen [-Blankenhain]
P R : P R :027(015) [0025] **Louis**, count of Loewenstein
S 3 : 1 5 :005(318) [0501] the Rev. Licentiate **Louis** Platz, of Melsungen

Loutish (1), Louts (1)
L C : P R :006(359) [0569] the nobility there are some **louts** and skinflints who
L C : 0 1 :152(386) [0625] are despised, as if they came from some **loutish** peddler.

Love (345)
P R : P R :002(003) [0007] God in his immeasurable **love**, grace, and mercy toward
P R : P R :024(013) [0023] who have an upright **love** for divine truth and for
A G : 1 6 :005(038) [0051] calling, manifest Christian **love** and genuine good works
A G : 2 0 :037(046) [0057] have patience in suffering, **love** one's neighbor, diligently
A G : 0 0 :001(048) [0059] to all Christian unity and **love**, and do so without any
A G : 2 6 :045(070) [0075] to institute holy days but to teach faith and **love**.”
A G : 2 8 :055(090) [0091] ordinances for the sake of **love** and peace, to be obedient
A L : 1 6 :005(038) [0051] of God and the exercise of **love** in these ordinance.
A L : 1 8 :008(040) [0053] alone, we are able to **love** God above all things, and can
A L : 2 8 :055(090) [0091] ordinances for the sake of **love** and tranquility and that
A P : 0 2 :008(101) [0107] unimpaired power to **love** God above all things and to
A P : 0 2 :009(102) [0107] To be able to **love** God above all things by one's own
A P : 0 2 :010(102) [0107] powers that by itself it can **love** God above all things, as
A P : 0 2 :010(102) [0109] powers by themselves can **love** God above all things and
A P : 0 2 :014(102) [0109] the fear of God and of trust in him, inability to **love** him.
A P : 0 2 :016(102) [0109] commanding fear of God, faith and **love** toward him.
A P : 0 2 :023(103) [0111] God, trust in God, fear and **love** of God, or surely the
A P : 0 2 :024(103) [0111] weakness cannot fear and **love** God or believe in him, it
A P : 0 2 :025(103) [0111] by the Holy Spirit and a **love** for God above all things.
A P : 0 2 :026(103) [0111] of ability to trust, fear, or **love** God; and concupiscence,
A P : 0 2 :033(104) [0113] of itself the heart is lacking in **love**, fear, and trust in God.
A P : 0 4 :008(108) [0121] like true fear of God, true **love** of God, true prayer to
A P : 0 4 :009(108) [0123] the Holy Spirit reason can **love** God above all things.
A P : 0 4 :009(108) [0123] imagine that he wants to **love** God and that he wants to
A P : 0 4 :009(108) [0123] over sin elicits an act of **love** to God or does good for
A P : 0 4 :017(109) [0125] as a disposition inclining us to **love** God more easily.
A P : 0 4 :017(109) [0125] imagine that the will can **love** God, but that this
A P : 0 4 :018(109) [0125] man can neither have nor understand the **love** of God.
A P : 0 4 :019(110) [0125] after that disposition of **love** a man can earn the merit of
A P : 0 4 :027(111) [0127] own strength reason can **love** God above all things and
A P : 0 4 :034(112) [0129] which commands us to **love** God, to be sure that God is
A P : 0 4 :036(112) [0131] of sins by an elicited act of **love**, since it is impossible to
A P : 0 4 :036(112) [0131] since it is impossible to **love** God unless faith has first
A P : 0 4 :036(112) [0131] feels God's wrath cannot **love** him unless it sees that he is
A P : 0 4 :036(112) [0131] cannot bring itself to **love** a wrathful, judging, punishing
A P : 0 4 :037(112) [0131] guilty of mortal sin can **love** God above all things, since
A P : 0 4 :045(113) [0133] finally obey God's law, **love** him, truly fear him, be sure
A P : 0 4 :046(113) [0133] wrath not our merits of **love**, but Christ the mediator and
A P : 0 4 :066(116) [0139] about the disposition of **love**, they pretend that one
A P : 0 4 :074(117) [0143] **Love** and good works must also follow faith.
A P : 0 4 :074(117) [0143] but trust in the merit of **love** or works is excluded from
A P : 0 4 :077(117) [0143] in Christ, not through **love**, or because of love or works,
A P : 0 4 :077(117) [0143] love, or because of **love** or works, though love does follow
A P : 0 4 :077(117) [0143] because of love or works, though **love** does follow faith.
A P : 0 4 :081(118) [0143] because he merited for us the disposition of **love**.
A P : 0 4 :081(118) [0143] and then, through this **love**, have access to God.
A P : 0 4 :081(118) [0145] We cannot set our **love** or our works against the wrath of
A P : 0 4 :083(118) [0145] merits, our contrition, attrition, **love**, worship, or works.
A P : 0 4 :109(123) [0153] to “faith fashioned by **love**,” that is, they do not attribute
A P : 0 4 :109(123) [0153] attribute justification to faith except on account of **love**.
A P : 0 4 :109(123) [0153] to faith at all, but only to **love**, because they imagine that
A P : 0 4 :110(123) [0153] of sins on account of **love**, the forgiveness of sins will
A P : 0 4 :110(123) [0153] be unsure, for we never **love** as much as we should.
A P : 0 4 :110(123) [0153] In fact, we do not **love** at all unless our hearts are sure
A P : 0 4 :110(123) [0153] us to trust in our own **love** for the forgiveness of sins and
A P : 0 4 :110(123) [0153] nor understand this **love** unless they believe that the
A P : 0 4 :111(123) [0153] We say, too, that **love** should follow faith, as Paul also
A P : 0 4 :111(123) [0155] of any avail, but faith working through **love**” (Gal. 5:6).
A P : 0 4 :112(123) [0155] of sins by trust in this **love** or on account of this love, just
A P : 0 4 :112(123) [0155] love or on account of this **love**, just as little as we receive
A P : 0 4 :114(123) [0155] Christ's sake before we **love** and keep the law, although
A P : 0 4 :114(123) [0155] and keep the law, although **love** must necessarily follow.
A P : 0 4 :116(123) [0155] to God” rather than **love**, which is the effect resulting from
A P : 0 4 :121(124) [0157] **Love** and the Keeping of the Law
A P : 0 4 :122(124) [0157] say what we believe about **love** and the keeping of the
A P : 0 4 :123(124) [0157] And again, “If I have not **love**, I am nothing” (I Cor.
A P : 0 4 :125(124) [0157] we begin to fear and **love** God, to pray and expect help
A P : 0 4 :125(124) [0157] Then we also begin to **love** our neighbor because our
A P : 0 4 :128(125) [0157] how can the human heart **love** God while it knows that in
A P : 0 4 :129(125) [0157] We cannot **love** God until we have grasped his mercy by
A P : 0 4 :131(125) [0159] of all creatures: “You shall **love** the Lord your God with
A P : 0 4 :141(126) [0161] to separate faith from **love** for God, be it ever so small.
A P : 0 4 :141(126) [0161] we call upon him, give thanks to him, fear and **love** him.
A P : 0 4 :141(126) [0161] his first epistle (4:19); “We **love**,” he says, “because he
A P : 0 4 :141(126) [0161] So he indicates that faith precedes while **love** follows.
A P : 0 4 :145(127) [0161] Selecting **love**, which is only one of these effects of faith,
A P : 0 4 :145(127) [0161] effects of faith, our opponents teach that **love** justifies.
A P : 0 4 :145(127) [0163] this is on account of our **love**, though they do not and
A P : 0 4 :145(127) [0163] do not and cannot say what the nature of this **love** is.
A P : 0 4 :147(127) [0163] Since we also grant that **love** is the work of the Holy
A P : 0 4 :147(127) [0163] of sins through **love** or on account of love, but on
A P : 0 4 :147(127) [0163] love or on account of **love**, but on account of Christ by
A P : 0 4 :151(127) [0163] of sins on account of **love**, though it, too, must follow.

Continued ▶

A P : 0 4 :152(127) [0163] say that by her works of **love** the woman had merited the
A P : 0 4 :154(128) [0163] And the account here shows what he calls "**love**."
A P : 0 4 :154(128) [0163] Christ used the word "**love**" not toward the woman but
A P : 0 4 :155(128) [0165] of sins, though **love**, confession, and other good fruits
A P : 0 4 :157(128) [0165] but for the sake of our **love**, nobody will have the
A P : 0 4 :159(129) [0165] right when they say that **love** is the keeping of the law,
A P : 0 4 :159(129) [0167] sake, not for the sake of **love** or the keeping of the law.
A P : 0 4 :178(131) [0171] justification elsewhere, our **love** and works do not justify.
A P : 0 4 :181(132) [0171] elsewhere than in our **love** and works, love and works do
A P : 0 4 :181(132) [0171] in our love and works, **love** and works do not justify; still
A P : 0 4 :186(132) [0173] that because of our **love** and works we receive the
A P : 0 4 :218(137) [0179] quote to prove that we are justified by **love** and works.
A P : 0 4 :218(137) [0179] "If I have all faith, etc., but have not **love**, I am nothing."
A P : 0 4 :219(137) [0179] what we believe about **love** and works, it will be easy to
A P : 0 4 :219(137) [0179] In this text Paul requires **love**.
A P : 0 4 :219(137) [0181] Whoever casts away **love** will not keep his faith, be it ever
A P : 0 4 :221(137) [0181] be understood in reference to "faith formed by **love**."
A P : 0 4 :222(137) [0181] anything more from this text than that **love** is necessary.
A P : 0 4 :222(138) [0181] For he is not saying that **love** justifies but that "I am
A P : 0 4 :222(138) [0181] He is not saying that **love** conquers the terrors of sin and
A P : 0 4 :222(138) [0181] death; that we can set our **love** against the wrath and
A P : 0 4 :222(138) [0181] of God; that our **love** satisfies the law of God; that by our
A P : 0 4 :222(138) [0181] law of God; that by our **love** we have access to God even
A P : 0 4 :222(138) [0181] propitiator; that by our **love** we receive the promised
A P : 0 4 :222(138) [0181] He does not believe that **love** justifies, for we are justified
A P : 0 4 :223(138) [0181] is unnecessary and by our **love** we can conquer death and
A P : 0 4 :224(138) [0181] them for this and calls them back to the duties of **love**.
A P : 0 4 :225(138) [0183] They object that **love** is preferred to faith and hope since
A P : 0 4 :225(138) [0183] Paul says (I Cor. 13:13), "The greatest of these is **love**."
A P : 0 4 :226(138) [0183] speaks specifically about **love** to our neighbor, and he
A P : 0 4 :226(138) [0183] and he indicates that **love** is the greatest because it has the
A P : 0 4 :226(138) [0183] deal only with God, while **love** has infinite external duties
A P : 0 4 :226(138) [0183] to our opponents that the **love** of God and neighbor is the
A P : 0 4 :226(138) [0183] is, "You shall **love** the Lord your God" (Matt. 22:27).
A P : 0 4 :226(138) [0183] How will they conclude from this that **love** justifies?
A P : 0 4 :228(139) [0183] offered promise, is no less an act of worship than is **love**.
A P : 0 4 :229(139) [0183] attribute justification to **love** because everywhere they
A P : 0 4 :229(139) [0183] We cannot deny that **love** is the highest work of the law.
A P : 0 4 :230(139) [0183] teaching of the law about **love** is more plausible; for this
A P : 0 4 :231(139) [0183] cited against us Col. 3:14, "**love**, which is the bond of
A P : 0 4 :231(139) [0183] From this they argue that **love** justifies since it makes men
A P : 0 4 :231(139) [0183] He is obviously discussing **love** of our neighbor.
A P : 0 4 :231(139) [0183] If it is **love** that makes men perfect, Christ, the
A P : 0 4 :232(139) [0185] He says that **love** is a bond and unbroken chain linking
A P : 0 4 :232(140) [0185] commands that there be **love** in the church to preserve
A P : 0 4 :235(140) [0185] the word "perfection" that **love** justifies, when Paul is
A P : 0 4 :236(140) [0185] to talk so much about **love** when they never show it.
A P : 0 4 :236(140) [0185] well with their praises of **love**; if our opponents lived up
A P : 0 4 :237(140) [0185] from those praises of **love** which they recite from Paul;
A P : 0 4 :238(140) [0187] statement (I Pet. 4:8), "**Love** covers a multitude of sins."
A P : 0 4 :238(140) [0187] too, is talking here about **love** to the neighbor, for he
A P : 0 4 :238(140) [0187] this statement with the commandment of mutual **love**.
A P : 0 4 :238(140) [0187] any apostle to say that our **love** conquers sin and death;
A P : 0 4 :238(140) [0187] of Christ, the mediator, **love** is the propitiation that
A P : 0 4 :238(141) [0187] God to us; or that **love** is righteousness without Christ,
A P : 0 4 :238(141) [0187] even if there were such a **love**, it would be a righteousness
A P : 0 4 :239(141) [0187] Our **love** does not free us from shame when God judges
A P : 0 4 :240(141) [0187] this statement about **love** is taken from Proverbs (10:12),
A P : 0 4 :240(141) [0187] means: "Hatred stirs up strife, but **love** covers all offenses.
A P : 0 4 :242(141) [0187] people's when it says, "**Love** covers all offenses," namely,
A P : 0 4 :242(141) [0187] these offenses occur, **love** covers them up, forgives,
A P : 0 4 :242(141) [0187] Peter does not mean that **love** merits the forgiveness of
A P : 0 4 :243(141) [0189] so often about this duty of **love** which the philosophers
A P : 0 4 :245(142) [0189] that a man is justified by **love** and works but say nothing
A P : 0 4 :245(142) [0189] not omit faith nor exalt **love** in preference to it, but keeps
A P : 0 4 :245(142) [0189] so Paul includes faith and **love** in presenting a summary
A P : 0 4 :245(142) [0189] "The aim of our charge is **love** that issues from a pure
A P : 0 4 :270(147) [0197] states, "Showing steadfast **love** to thousands of those who
A P : 0 4 :270(147) [0197] to thousands of those who **love** me and keep my
A P : 0 4 :270(147) [0197] is at peace and begins to **love** God and to keep the law.
A P : 0 4 :284(150) [0201] (that is, all the works of **love**), then men are completely
A P : 0 4 :289(151) [0203] disposition (which is **love**) infused by God, that with the
A P : 0 4 :289(151) [0203] Truly the law says, "You shall **love** the Lord your God"
A P : 0 4 :289(151) [0203] (Deut. 6:5) and "You shall **love** your neighbor"
A P : 0 4 :289(151) [0203] Therefore **love** is the fulfilling of the law.
A P : 0 4 :290(151) [0203] of sins precedes our **love**, but it imagines that we produce
A P : 0 4 :290(151) [0203] that we produce an act of **love** whereby we merit the
A P : 0 4 :292(152) [0203] Then **love** and other good fruits follow.
A P : 0 4 :293(152) [0203] we can keep the law, **love** God and his Word, obey God
A P : 0 4 :293(152) [0203] and practice chastity, **love** toward our neighbor, and so
A P : 0 4 :294(152) [0203] to faith rather than to **love**, though love follows faith
A P : 0 4 :294(152) [0203] than to love, though **love** follows faith since love is the
A P : 0 4 :294(152) [0203] love follows faith since **love** is the keeping of the law.
A P : 0 4 :294(152) [0203] of sin because of our **love** but because of Christ.
A P : 0 4 :295(152) [0203] We cannot even **love** an angry God; the law always
A P : 0 4 :297(152) [0205] keep the law of God nor **love** God; and second, we are
A P : 0 4 :300(153) [0205] the wrath of God with our **love** or could love an angry
A P : 0 4 :300(153) [0205] wrath of God with our love or could **love** an angry God.
A P : 0 4 :301(153) [0205] gracious God because they **love** and keep the law, they
A P : 0 4 :301(153) [0205] They either do not feel this **love** at all, as our opponents
A P : 0 4 :301(153) [0205] When will it **love** God amid these doubts and terrors?
A P : 0 4 :302(153) [0205] come forth to describe the **love** with which he loves God.
A P : 0 4 :302(154) [0205] they echo the word "**love**" without understanding it.
A P : 0 4 :311(155) [0207] Gospel, and we cannot **love** God unless we have received
A P : 0 4 :313(155) [0207] that we are justified by **love** teach the righteousness of the
A P : 0 4 :314(155) [0207] It is evident that not with **love** but with faith we
A P : 0 4 :314(156) [0207] since we cannot set our **love** and keeping of the law
A P : 0 4 :314(156) [0207] that we come to God by **love** and merits without Christ,
A P : 0 4 :316(156) [0209] help of a "disposition" of **love**, are a worthy righteousness
A P : 0 4 :321(156) [0209] of this disposition of **love**, so that it can be sure of
A P : 0 4 :332(158) [0211] worthy because they have **love** and good works, and ask
A P : 0 4 :349(160) [0217] new impulses, the fear and **love** of God, hatred of lust,
A P : 0 4 :351(161) [0217] as knowledge and fear of God, **love** of God, and hope.
A P : 0 4 :376(164) [0223] merit of congruity or, if **love** is added, by the merit of
A P : 0 4 :379(165) [0223] least wrought by the impulse of the **love** they talk about.
A P : 0 4 :381(165) [0223] a disposition by which we **love** God, as though the
A P : 0 4 :381(165) [0223] put confidence in our **love**, which we know by experience
A P : 0 4 :381(165) [0223] they advise us to trust our **love** when they teach that we
A P : 0 4 :381(165) [0223] mercy, reconciliation, and **love** toward us only by faith.
A P : 0 4 :388(166) [0225] whenever a passage on **love** or works is quoted, that the
A P : 0 4 :391(166) [0225] as the idea that we can **love** God above all things by
A P : 0 7 :021(172) [0233] of sins by their **love** for God before entering a state of
A P : 0 7 :031(174) [0239] the fear of God, the **love** of our neighbor, and the works
A P : 0 7 :031(174) [0239] of God, the love of our neighbor, and the works of **love**.
A P : 0 7 :036(175) [0241] of the Holy Spirit (like **love** of neighbor, chastity, etc.),
A P : 1 0 :003(179) [0247] joined to Christ spiritually by true faith and sincere **love**.
A P : 1 0 :003(179) [0247] which we understand as **love**, but also by a natural
A P : 1 2 :008(183) [0255] reply that Judas did not **love** God but feared the
A P : 1 2 :029(185) [0259] we are sorry because we **love** God and when because we
A P : 1 2 :034(186) [0261] sorrows and terrors men merit grace if they **love** God.
A P : 1 2 :034(186) [0261] Yet how will men **love** God amid such real terrors when
A P : 1 2 :037(186) [0261] Nor is **love** present before faith has effected the
A P : 1 2 :037(187) [0261] But **love** follows faith, as we have said above.
A P : 1 2 :064(191) [0269] pit our works or our **love** against the wrath of God, but it
A P : 1 2 :075(193) [0273] contrition elicits an act of **love** to God, he merits the
A P : 1 2 :075(193) [0273] the law and our works because the law demands **love**.
A P : 1 2 :075(193) [0273] the forgiveness of sins because of our contrition or **love**.
A P : 1 2 :076(193) [0273] of our contrition or **love**, for there is no other mediator
A P : 1 2 :077(193) [0275] declaring that men are justified by faith and not by **love**.
A P : 1 2 :078(193) [0275] by their contrition and **love**, and should trust their
A P : 1 2 :078(193) [0275] trust their contrition and **love**, is simply a doctrine of the
A P : 1 2 :078(193) [0275] Even supposing that **love** and works are present, neither
A P : 1 2 :078(193) [0275] works are present, neither **love** nor works can be a
A P : 1 2 :082(194) [0275] as we said before, **love** follows faith, for the regenerate
A P : 1 2 :085(194) [0277] by faith but merit it by our **love** and works, and that we
A P : 1 2 :085(194) [0277] that we ought to set our **love** and works against the wrath
A P : 1 2 :087(195) [0277] said above that men are justified by faith and not by **love**.
A P : 1 2 :087(195) [0277] For we must not set our **love** or works against the wrath
A P : 1 2 :087(195) [0277] of God or trust in our **love** or works, but only in Christ,
A P : 1 2 :088(195) [0277] the forgiveness of sins because we **love** or keep the law?
A P : 1 2 :142(204) [0295] see that it requires us to **love** God "with all our hearts,"
A P : 1 5 :043(221) [0327] of children, chastity, and all the works of **love**.
A P : 1 6 :003(223) [0331] or by others, and in this obedience to practice **love**.
A P : 1 8 :002(225) [0335] the Holy Spirit men can **love** God and perform "the
A P : 2 0 :015(229) [0343] follows, by which **love**, patience, chastity, and other fruits
A P : 2 3 :007(240) [0365] about so-called "natural **love**," the desire which was
A P : 2 3 :007(240) [0365] This **love** of one sex for the other is truly a divine
A P : 2 3 :013(241) [0367] which is called "natural **love**," which lust did not remove
A P : 2 4 :068(262) [0409] only about the practice of **love**, which even profane and
A P : 2 7 :025(273) [0427] all the saints, "You shall **love** the Lord your God with all
A P : 2 7 :037(275) [0433] of God, in faith, in the **love** of their neighbor, and similar
S 2 : 0 2 :027(297) [0469] ways in which I can honor, **love**, and thank you in
S 2 : 0 2 :028(297) [0471] or honor them out of **love** when there is no expectation
S 2 : 0 4 :009(300) [0473] of doctrine, faith, sacraments, prayer, works of **love**, etc.
S 3 : 0 1 :007(302) [0477] by his natural powers to **love** God above all things and
S 3 : 1 0 :001(314) [0497] permitted (for the sake of **love** and unity, but not of
T R : 0 0 :030(325) [0513] (John 21:17) and "Do you **love** me more than these?"
S C : 0 1 :002(342) [0539] Answer: We should fear, **love**, and trust in God above all
S C : 0 1 :004(342) [0539] We should fear and **love** God, and so we should not use
S C : 0 1 :006(342) [0541] We should fear and **love** God, and so we should not
S C : 0 1 :008(343) [0541] We should fear and **love** God, and so we should not
S C : 0 1 :008(343) [0541] to anger, but honor, serve, obey, **love**, and esteem them.
S C : 0 1 :010(343) [0541] We should fear and **love** God, and so we should not
S C : 0 1 :012(343) [0541] We should fear and **love** God, and so we should lead a
S C : 0 1 :014(343) [0541] We should fear and **love** God, and so we should not rob
S C : 0 1 :016(343) [0541] We should fear and **love** God, and so we should not tell
S C : 0 1 :018(343) [0541] We should fear and **love** God, and so we should not seek
S C : 0 1 :020(344) [0543] We should fear and **love** God, and so we should not
S C : 0 1 :021(344) [0543] me, but showing steadfast **love** to thousands of those who
S C : 0 1 :021(344) [0543] to thousands of those who **love** me and keep my
S C : 0 1 :022(344) [0543] We should therefore **love** him, trust in him, and cheerfully
S C : 0 8 :010(354) [0559] for he is good; for his steadfast **love** endures forever.
S C : 0 8 :010(354) [0559] who fear him, in those who hope in his steadfast **love**."
S C : 0 9 :003(355) [0561] esteem them very highly in **love** because of their work.
S C : 0 9 :006(355) [0561] "Husbands, **love** your wives, and do not be harsh with
S C : 0 9 :014(356) [0563] this sentence: 'You shall **love** your neighbor as yourself'"
L C : 0 1 :012(366) [0583] of money, help them in **love** affairs, protect their cattle,
L C : 0 1 :030(369) [0589] *thousands of those who* ***love*** *me and keep my*
L C : 0 1 :103(379) [0611] we should trust, fear, and **love** him with our whole heart
L C : 0 1 :105(379) [0611] us not simply to **love** our parents but also to honor them.
L C : 0 1 :105(379) [0611] he commands nothing higher than that we **love** them.
L C : 0 1 :106(379) [0611] For it is a much greater thing to honor than to **love**.
L C : 0 1 :106(379) [0611] Honor includes not only **love** but also deference,
L C : 0 1 :115(381) [0613] For the **love** of God, therefore, let us at last teach our
L C : 0 1 :121(382) [0615] have more happiness, **love**, kindness, and harmony in
L C : 0 1 :136(383) [0619] render him obedience and **love** and service, and he will
L C : 0 1 :151(386) [0625] if he will not do so in **love**, but despises or rebelliously
L C : 0 1 :166(387) [0627] hearts so melt for joy and **love** toward those to whom we
L C : 0 1 :190(391) [0635] you have withheld your **love** from him and robbed him of
L C : 0 1 :193(391) [0635] suffer harm, but show to everyone all kindness and **love**.
L C : 0 1 :195(391) [0637] patience, and, in short, **love** and kindness toward our
L C : 0 1 :214(394) [0641] For no one has so little **love** and inclination for chastity
L C : 0 1 :217(394) [0641] may be led to acquire a **love** for married life and know
L C : 0 1 :219(394) [0643] of marriage), but also to **love** and cherish the wife or
L C : 0 1 :219(394) [0643] and wife live together in **love** and harmony, cherishing
L C : 0 1 :220(394) [0643] husbands and wives to **love** and honor each other.
L C : 0 1 :283(403) [0661] improvement or from the **love** of truth, you would not
L C : 0 1 :313(407) [0671] gentleness, patience, **love** toward enemies, chastity,
L C : 0 1 :320(408) [0673] *hate me; but to those who* ***love*** *me and keep my*
L C : 0 1 :324(409) [0675] simply, "You shall fear, **love**, and trust me as your one
L C : 0 1 :326(409) [0675] which spring from that **love** and trust which the First
L C : 0 1 :326(409) [0675] Similarly, this fear, **love**, and trust should impel us not to
L C : 0 1 :328(410) [0677] you can, purely out of **love** to God and in order to please
L C : 0 2 :017(412) [0681] All this he does out of pure **love** and goodness, without
L C : 0 2 :019(412) [0681] we are in duty bound to **love**, praise, and thank him
L C : 0 2 :023(413) [0683] them his fatherly heart and his boundless **love** toward us.

Continued ▶

L C : 0 2 :051(417) [0691] of gifts, yet is united in **love** without sect or schism.
L C : 0 2 :064(419) [0695] depths of his fatherly heart, his sheer, unutterable **love**.
L C : 0 2 :066(419) [0697] They cannot be confident of his **love** and blessing.
L C : 0 2 :069(420) [0697] knowledge we come to **love** and delight in all the
L C : 0 3 :020(423) [0703] awaken and kindle in our hearts a desire and **love** to pray.
L C : 0 3 :104(434) [0727] from faith, hope, and **love**, to draw us into unbelief, false
L C : 0 5 :044(451) [0763] matters pertaining to faith, **love**, and patience it is not
L C : 0 5 :051(452) [0765] without joy and **love** and even without regard for Christ's
L C : 0 5 :067(454) [0769] quite cold and callous and lose all desire and **love** for it.
L C : 0 5 :087(457) [0773] all help us to believe, to **love**, to pray, and to fight the
L C : 0 6 :034(461) [0000] and such a desire and **love** for it would be aroused that
E P : 0 3 :011(474) [0795] true living faith becomes "active through **love**" (Gal. 5:6).
E P : 0 3 :011(474) [0795] never alone but is always accompanied by **love** and hope.
E P : 0 3 :015(475) [0795] God on account of the **love** and virtue that the Holy
E P : 0 3 :017(475) [0795] no evidence of resulting **love**, but continues to sin against
E P : 0 3 :019(475) [0795] renewal which consists in **love** toward God and our
E P : 0 3 :020(475) [0797] but that also renewal and **love** belong to our
E P : 0 3 :020(475) [0797] incomplete and imperfect without such **love** and renewal.
E P : 0 4 :012(477) [0799] like a slave, but out of a **love** of righteousness, like a child
E P : 1 2 :030(500) [0843] against these if they dearly **love** their soul's eternal
S D : 0 1 :035(514) [0869] me life and steadfast **love**; and thy care has preserved my
S D : 0 2 :003(520) [0881] God truly, to fear and to **love** him, man nevertheless still
S D : 0 2 :068(534) [0907] at one time ardent in **love**, strong in faith and in hope,
S D : 0 3 :023(543) [0923] and creates within them **love** toward God and their
S D : 0 3 :027(543) [0923] **Love** is a fruit which certainly and necessarily follows true
S D : 0 3 :027(543) [0923] For if a person does not **love**, this indicates certainly that
S D : 0 3 :029(544) [0925] grant that we must teach about **love** and good works too.
S D : 0 3 :029(544) [0925] also do good works and **love**, but how a person may be
S D : 0 3 :029(544) [0925] of the law or through **love** — not in such a way as if we
S D : 0 3 :029(544) [0925] utterly rejected works and **love** (as the adversaries falsely
S D : 0 3 :030(544) [0925] neither in contrition nor in **love** nor in other virtues, but
S D : 0 3 :031(544) [0925] Neither is contrition nor **love** nor any other virtue the
S D : 0 3 :035(545) [0927] of renewal, sanctification, **love**, virtues, and good works,
S D : 0 3 :038(546) [0929] we must exclude **love** and every other virtue or work.
S D : 0 3 :043(547) [0931] far as it is associated with **love**, on account of which love
S D : 0 3 :043(547) [0931] love, on account of which **love** the power to justify is
S D : 0 3 :045(547) [0933] 1. That our **love** or our good works are a meritorious
S D : 0 3 :047(548) [0933] before God is our **love** or the renewal which the Holy
S D : 0 3 :049(548) [0933] but that renewal and **love** likewise belong to our
S D : 0 3 :049(548) [0933] incomplete or imperfect without such **love** and renewal.
S D : 0 3 :062(550) [0937] on account of the **love** and virtues which are poured into
S D : 0 3 :064(550) [0937] (and upon which no **love** follows) but against his
S D : 0 4 :001(551) [0939] and since faith without **love** is dead, although such love is
S D : 0 4 :001(551) [0939] is dead, although such **love** is not a cause of salvation.
S D : 0 4 :012(553) [0941] suffer everything for the **love** of God and to his glory,
S D : 1 0 :019(614) [1059] permitted (for the sake of **love** and unity, but not of
S D : 1 0 :025(615) [1061] the wrath of God, violate **love**, confirm the enemies of
S D : 1 1 :005(617) [1065] in him, he destined us in **love** to be his sons through Jesus
S D : 1 1 :019(619) [1069] he also would sanctify in **love** all who are thus justified,
S D : 1 1 :030(621) [1073] thanks, are sanctified in **love**, have hope, patience, and
S D : 1 1 :047(624) [1079] will separate us from the **love** of God in Christ?" (Rom.
S D : 1 1 :049(624) [1079] can separate us from the **love** of God in Christ Jesus"
S D : 1 1 :073(628) [1087] patience, and brotherly **love**, and should diligently seek to
S D : 1 1 :087(631) [1093] written, "He destined us in **love** to be his son through
S D : 1 1 :095(632) [1095] sincere delight in and deep **love** for true harmony and are
S D : 1 2 :039(636) [1103] these as dearly as they **love** their soul's welfare and

Loved (10), Loves (10), Lovely (2), Lover (2), Lovers (1), Loving (3)
A G : P R :014(026) [0041] and estates), and every **lover** of the Christian religion who
A G : 1 8 :004(039) [0051] to God (such as **loving** God with their whole heart or
A P : 0 2 :024(103) [0111] in him, it seeks and **loves** carnal things; either it despises
A P : 0 4 :129(125) [0157] Only then does he become an object that can be **loved**.
A P : 0 4 :141(126) [0161] he says, "because he first **loved us**," that is, because he
A P : 0 4 :150(127) [0163] of sins because he **loves**, he insults Christ and in God's
A P : 0 4 :152(127) [0163] which are many, are forgiven, because she **loved** much."
A P : 0 4 :155(128) [0165] are forgiven, because she **loved** much," that is, because
A P : 0 4 :167(130) [0169] For who **loves** or fears God enough?
A P : 0 4 :167(130) [0169] Who **loves** his neighbor as himself?
A P : 0 4 :302(153) [0205] come forth to describe the love with which he **loves** God.
A P : 0 4 :342(160) [0215] since no one fears, **loves**, or trusts God as he ought.
A P : 0 7 :007(169) [0229] He says, "Christ **loved** the church and gave himself up for
S C : 0 1 :012(343) [0541] word and deed, each one **loving** and honoring his wife or
S C : 0 9 :002(354) [0561] but gentle, not quarrelsome, and no **lover** of money.
L C : 0 1 :131(383) [0619] God has attached to it a **lovely** promise, "That you may
L C : 0 1 :175(389) [0631] virtuous and home-**loving** wives who would faithfully
L C : 0 1 :324(409) [0675] hand, whoever fears and **loves** anything else in heaven
L C : 0 3 :023(423) [0703] it has the excellent testimony that God **loves** to hear it.
L C : 0 5 :064(454) [0769] stand the gracious and **lovely** words, "This is my body,
S D : 0 2 :049(530) [0901] "For God so **loved** the world that he gave his only Son,
S D : 0 4 :017(554) [0943] Rom. 6:7) because God **loves** a cheerful giver
S D : 0 7 :034(575) [0983] intelligent person who **loves** truth and peace can
S D : 1 1 :028(620) [1071] For God "**loved** the world" and gave to it his only
S D : 1 1 :065(627) [1083] as it is written, "He has **loved** us in the Beloved"
S D : 1 1 :067(627) [1085] and again, "God so **loved** the world," etc. (John 3:16).
S D : 1 1 :075(628) [1087] the harlot with many **lovers**; yet return again to me, says
S D : 1 1 :088(631) [1093] As it is written, 'Jacob I **loved**, but Esau I hated'"

Low (4), Lower (2), Lowly (1)
P R : P R :024(013) [0023] of high station and **low**, are sighing anxiously for this
A G : 2 3 :001(051) [0061] both of high and of **low** degree, there has been loud
A P : 0 2 :023(103) [0111] the obedience of man's **lower** powers, but also denies that
T R : 0 0 :082(335) [0529] Fontanus, superintendent of **Lower** Hesse, subscribed
L C : 0 1 :108(379) [0611] remember that, however **lowly**, poor, feeble, and eccentric
L C : 0 5 :084(456) [0773] you have sunk twice as **low** as any other poor sinner and
E P : 1 2 :030(500) [0843] of high degree and **low**, must guard against these if they

Loyally (3), Loyalty (1)
P R : P R :003(003) [0007] They have held fast and **loyally** to the doctrine that is
P R : P R :008(005) [0009] to remain and abide **loyally** by the truth once recognized
A G : 2 3 :014(053) [0063] In **loyalty** to Your Imperial Majesty we therefore feel
S D : P R :020(508) [0859] continue to abide in it **loyally** and faithfully against all

Lucian (1)
A P : 2 1 :037(234) [0355] many things that resemble the "true stories" of **Lucian**.

Lucid (1)
S D : 1 2 :004(633) [1097] but to present a clear, **lucid**, and unmistakable exposition

Lucina (1)
L C : 0 1 :018(367) [0585] pregnant women worshiped Diana or **Lucina**, and so

Luck (3)
A P : 0 4 :167(130) [0169] the wicked have better **luck** than the devout, because the
L C : 0 1 :033(369) [0589] and commit themselves to **luck**, like brutes who think
L C : 0 3 :014(422) [0701] that is to stake prayer on **luck** and to mumble aimlessly.

Luebeck (2)
P R : P R :027(014) [0025] Eberhard, bishop of **Luebeck**, administrator of the diocese
P R : P R :027(015) [0025] Mayor and Council of the City of **Luebeck**

Lueneburg (11)
P R : P R :027(014) [0025] duke of Brunswick [-Wolfenbuettel] and **Lueneburg**
P R : P R :027(014) [0025] Otto, duke of Brunswick and **Lueneburg** [-Harburg]
P R : P R :027(014) [0025] duke of Brunswick [-Wolfenbuettel] and **Lueneburg**
P R : P R :027(014) [0025] Younger, duke of Brunswick and **Lueneburg** [-Hanover]
P R : P R :027(014) [0025] Wolf, duke of Brunswick [-Grubenhagen] and **Lueneburg**
P R : P R :027(016) [0027] Mayor and Council of the City of **Lueneburg**
A G : 0 0 :007(096) [0095] Ernest, duke of **Lueneburg**
A G : 0 0 :007(096) [0095] Francis, duke of **Lueneburg**
A L : 0 0 :017(096) [0095] Francis, duke of **Lueneburg**
S 3 : 1 5 :005(317) [0501] in the Duchy of **Lueneburg**, subscribe in my own name
T R : 0 0 :082(334) [0529] of the churches in the Duchy of **Lueneburg**, subscribe

Luke (3)
S 3 : 0 8 :008(313) [0495] to God in this faith (**Luke** calls him "devout" and
S C : 0 6 :004(351) [0555] Matthew, Mark, and **Luke**, and also St. Paul, write thus:
S D : 0 7 :053(579) [0991] sacrament the words of **Luke** and Paul, "This cup is the

Lump (3), Lumps (1)
A P : 0 4 :374(164) [0221] In this way the Scriptures **lump** together the
S 3 : 0 3 :036(309) [0489] and what is not sin, but **lumps** everything together and
S D : 0 2 :024(526) [0891] in anything as a stone, a block, or a **lump** of clay could.
S D : 0 3 :007(540) [0917] this doctrine that a little leaven ferments the whole **lump**.

Lure (2), Lures (1), Luring (1)
L C : 0 1 :071(374) [0601] around us, lying in wait to **lure** us into sin and shame,
L C : 0 1 :306(406) [0669] among us for a person to **lure** away another's
L C : 0 1 :307(406) [0669] your neighbor's property, **luring** it away from him against
L C : 0 3 :102(434) [0727] he goes to work and **lures** us daily into unchastity,

Lurks (1)
L C : 0 4 :062(444) [0749] Here **lurks** a sneaky, seditious devil who would like to

Lust (27), Lusts (16)
A G : 0 2 :001(029) [0043] is, all men are full of evil **lust** and inclinations from their
A G : 1 8 :002(039) [0051] heart, or of expelling inborn evil **lusts** from his heart.
A G : 2 0 :037(046) [0057] are commanded, render obedience, avoid evil **lusts**, etc.
A G : 2 3 :025(055) [0065] into the fire through their **lusts**, and they should see to it
A L : 2 0 :038(046) [0057] in God, all manner of **lusts** and human devices rule in the
A L : 2 3 :025(055) [0065] into the fire through their **lusts**; at least they should give
A P : 0 2 :002(100) [0105] is, all men are full of evil **lusts** and inclinations from their
A P : 0 2 :028(104) [0113] sin is, it is correct to answer that it is immoderate **lust**.
A P : 0 2 :029(104) [0113] original sin is ignorance in the mind and **lust** in the flesh.
A P : 0 2 :030(104) [0113] (Rom. 7:5) he mentions **lust** at work in our members and
A P : 0 2 :035(105) [0115] Baptism, begins to mortify **lust** and to create new
A P : 0 2 :039(105) [0115] "I should not have known **lust** if the law had not said,
A P : 0 2 :039(105) [0115] known lust if the law had not said, 'You shall not **lust**.'"
A P : 0 2 :040(105) [0115] For they clearly call **lust** sin, by nature worthy of death if
A P : 0 2 :041(105) [0115] the opinion that human **lust** is not a fault but is a neutral
A P : 0 4 :045(113) [0133] It mortifies our **lust**.
A P : 0 4 :143(126) [0161] the flesh, who take pleasure in their **lusts** and obey them.
A P : 0 4 :144(127) [0161] in those who obey their **lusts**, nor does it exist together
A P : 0 4 :167(130) [0169] Who is not tempted by **lust**?
A P : 0 4 :319(156) [0209] The flesh always **lusts** against the Spirit (Gal. 5:17).
A P : 0 4 :349(160) [0217] impulses, the fear and love of God, hatred of **lust**, etc.
A P : 1 2 :046(188) [0263] because in these troubles our natural **lust** is purged away.
A P : 1 2 :131(202) [0291] indulgence of the body in **lusts**, and true faith is not
A P : 1 2 :142(204) [0295] and condemns every aspect of **lust** in human nature.
A P : 1 2 :152(206) [0299] they kill and wipe out **lust** so that the Spirit may renew
A P : 2 3 :002(239) [0363] disgrace and the unnatural **lusts** of the holy fathers "who
A P : 2 3 :007(240) [0365] not talking about sinful **lust** but about so-called "natural
A P : 2 3 :013(241) [0367] not talking about sinful **lust** but about the desire which is
A P : 2 3 :013(241) [0367] "natural love," which **lust** did not remove from nature but
A P : 2 3 :016(241) [0369] natural desire and the **lust** that inflames it come together;
A P : 2 3 :016(241) [0369] abolish either nature or **lust**, they cannot abolish the
A P : 2 3 :035(244) [0373] proper contrast is between **lust** and purity understood as
A P : 2 3 :035(244) [0373] and the mortification of **lust**; it is not marriage that the
A P : 2 3 :035(244) [0373] that the law forbids, but **lust**, adultery, and promiscuity.
A P : 2 3 :052(246) [0377] morals and how productive of vices and shameful **lusts**.
A P : 2 3 :063(248) [0381] the many unnatural **lusts** and the many murders for which
A P : 2 3 :064(248) [0381] and less inflamed with **lust** than that of many celibates
S 3 : 0 3 :011(305) [0481] (for evil impulses, **lust**, and inclinations they did not
S 3 : 0 3 :018(306) [0483] sinner who reflected on his **lust** or revenge in this fashion
S 3 : 0 3 :018(306) [0483] It did not extinguish the **lust** for sin.
S C : 0 4 :012(349) [0551] with all sins and evil **lusts**, should be drowned by daily
L C : 0 3 :102(434) [0727] short, into all kinds of evil **lusts** which by nature cling to
S D : 0 4 :031(556) [0947] a Christian follows his evil **lusts** without fear and shame,

Luther (109)
P R : P R :000(001) [0004] blessed Death of Martin **Luther**, Prepared for Publication
P R : P R :004(003) [0007] pious person, Dr. Martin **Luther**, and how in this
P R : P R :005(004) [0009] with God's Word, as they were while Dr. **Luther** was alive.
P R : P R :020(010) [0017] of theologians, like **Luther** himself, were drawn by
P R : P R :025(014) [0023] Catechism of that highly enlightened man, Dr. **Luther**.
A P : 0 2 :035(104) [0113] our opponents lash out at **Luther** because he wrote that
A P : 0 2 :035(105) [0115] opponents know what **Luther** meant by this statement
A P : 0 2 :037(105) [0115] know that this is what **Luther** believes and teaches; and

Continued ▶

AP : 02 :038(105) [0115] and not a sin, while **Luther** contends that it is a sin.
AP : 02 :045(106) [0117] So when **Luther** wanted to show the magnitude of original
AP : 11 :002(180) [0249] in the beginning brought **Luther** the highest praise of all
AP : 12 :004(183) [0253] admit that before **Luther**'s writings the doctrine of
AP : 21 :041(235) [0355] **Luther** was not the first to complain about public abuses.
AP : 21 :041(235) [0355] Those who sided with **Luther** from the outset did so
AP : 27 :010(270) [0423] Since **Luther** discussed this whole issue carefully and fully
AP : 28 :024(285) [0451] Originally this gained for **Luther** not only our good will
S1 : 00 :000(287) [0453] Written by Dr. Martin **Luther** in the year 1537
S1 : PR :000(288) [0455] Preface of Dr. Martin **Luther**
S3 : 15 :005(316) [0501] Dr. Martin **Luther** subscribed
S3 : 15 :005(317) [0501] reverend father, Martin **Luther**, confess that I have
TR : 00 :082(000) [0529] language by Dr. Martin **Luther**, our most revered
SC : 00 :000(337) [0531] Catechism of Dr. Martin **Luther** for Ordinary Pastors and
SC : PR :000(338) [0533] our Lord, from Martin **Luther** to all faithful, godly
LC : PR :000(358) [0567] Martin **Luther**'s Preface
EP : RN :005(465) [0777] souls, we subscribe Dr. **Luther**'s Small and Large
EP : 01 :020(468) [0783] **Luther** calls original sin "nature-sin," "person-sin,"
EP : 02 :018(472) [0791] 9. Likewise **Luther**'s statement that man's will in
EP : 07 :010(483) [0811] are those which Dr. **Luther** proposed in his *Great*
EP : 08 :003(487) [0819] Dr. **Luther** and his followers have contended for the
EP : 08 :017(489) [0823] God's right hand, as Dr. **Luther** says on the basis of our
EP : 08 :018(489) [0823] divided the person, as **Luther** explains it in his treatise *On*
EP : 09 :003(492) [0827] it in all simplicity, as Dr. **Luther** of blessed memory
EP : 12 :030(500) [0843] the Smalcald Articles, and the Catechisms of **Luther**.
SD : PR :001(501) [0847] God and purified by Dr. **Luther**, of blessed and holy
SD : PR :002(503) [0851] the Word of God as Dr. **Luther** of blessed memory had
SD : PR :005(504) [0851] ministry of that illustrious man of God, Dr. **Luther**.
SD : PR :008(505) [0853] adherence to Dr. **Luther**'s Small and Large Catechisms,
SD : PR :009(505) [0853] of the doctrine which Dr. **Luther** of blessed memory
SD : PR :011(506) [0855] Smalcald Articles, and **Luther**'s Large and Small
SD : PR :014(506) [0855] "Faithful shepherds," as **Luther** states, "must both pasture
SD : 01 :006(509) [0861] Dr. **Luther** calls this sin "nature-sin" or "person-sin" in
SD : 01 :033(514) [0869] Although, in **Luther**'s words, original sin, like a spiritual
SD : 01 :051(517) [0875] is in this latter sense that **Luther** writes that sin and
SD : 01 :052(517) [0875] Thus **Luther** can say, "Your birth, your nature, your
SD : 01 :053(517) [0875] **Luther** himself explains that he uses the terms
SD : 01 :056(518) [0877] corrected either by Dr. **Luther** or by any other dependable
SD : 01 :061(519) [0879] Word of God, just as Dr. **Luther** in his Latin exposition
SD : 01 :062(519) [0879] In this fashion **Luther** used both the term "accident" and
SD : 02 :020(524) [0889] It is as **Luther** says in his comments on Ps. 91: "In secular
SD : 02 :023(525) [0889] Dr. **Luther** calls this a "capacity," which he explains as
SD : 02 :036(528) [0895] his Large Catechism Dr. **Luther** writes: "I am also a part
SD : 02 :040(528) [0895] In Dr. **Luther**'s Small Catechism we read: "I believe that
SD : 02 :041(529) [0897] of the Lord's Prayer **Luther** answers the question, "How
SD : 02 :043(529) [0897] a statement from Dr. **Luther**'s *Great Confession*
SD : 02 :044(529) [0897] In these words Dr. **Luther**, of sacred and holy memory,
SD : 02 :044(529) [0897] Dr. **Luther** discusses this entire matter in his book *The*
SD : 02 :045(530) [0899] and Small Catechisms of **Luther**, and other writings of
SD : 02 :089(538) [0915] Again, when **Luther** says that man behaves in a purely
SD : 03 :006(540) [0917] In the same vein Dr. **Luther** declared: "Where this single
SD : 03 :021(542) [0921] of faith, as Dr. **Luther** used the term in his book *On the*
SD : 03 :028(544) [0925] of the Epistle to the Galatians Dr. **Luther** well states:
SD : 03 :029(544) [0925] So far **Luther**.
SD : 03 :041(546) [0931] For Dr. **Luther**'s excellent statement remains true: "There
SD : 03 :067(551) [0937] the sake of brevity to Dr. **Luther**'s beautiful and splendid
SD : 04 :010(552) [0941] For, as **Luther** writes in his Preface to the Epistle of St.
SD : 04 :024(555) [0945] **Luther** also has rejected and condemned these
SD : 05 :011(560) [0955] is called the Paraclete, as **Luther** explains it in his
SD : 05 :017(561) [0957] For, as **Luther** says against the nomoclasts, "Everything
SD : 05 :022(562) [0959] Dr. **Luther** very diligently urged this distinction in nearly
SD : 06 :009(565) [0965] Dr. **Luther** thoroughly explains this at greater length in
SD : 07 :010(571) [0975] Dr. **Luther** clearly presents the same view in the Small
SD : 07 :012(571) [0977] and Dr. Martin **Luther** and other theologians of both
SD : 07 :017(572) [0979] By common consent Dr. **Luther** drafted the Smalcald
SD : 07 :020(572) [0979] Dr. **Luther** explains and confirms this position at greater
SD : 07 :029(574) [0981] after my death, 'If Dr. **Luther** were living now, he would
SD : 07 :032(574) [0983] this protestation **Luther**, of blessed memory, listed among
SD : 07 :033(575) [0983] Dr. **Luther**, who understood the true intention of the
SD : 07 :034(575) [0983] the exposition of Dr. **Luther**, as the chief teacher of the
SD : 07 :038(576) [0985] union, as Dr. **Luther** and our theologians call it in the
SD : 07 :040(576) [0985] *the Communion* Dr. **Luther** defended with great zeal and
SD : 07 :041(576) [0985] Since Dr. **Luther** is rightly to be regarded as the most
SD : 07 :041(576) [0985] source than from Dr. **Luther**'s doctrinal and polemical
SD : 07 :058(580) [0993] and forebears, like **Luther** and other pure teachers of the
SD : 07 :077(583) [0999] And **Luther** states: "This his command and institution can
SD : 07 :087(585) [1003] rule was first formulated and explained by Dr. **Luther**.
SD : 07 :091(585) [1005] of God's Word by Dr. **Luther** in his polemical writings,
SD : 07 :093(586) [1005] (the same ones that Dr. **Luther** advanced against the
SD : 07 :103(587) [1009] So far **Luther**.
SD : 07 :104(587) [1009] These words of Dr. **Luther** also show clearly in what sense
SD : 07 :105(588) [1009] But when Dr. **Luther** or we use the word "spiritual" in this
SD : 08 :002(591) [1015] For when Dr. **Luther** maintained with solid arguments the
SD : 08 :003(592) [1017] Dr. **Luther** contradicted and mightily refuted this, as his
SD : 08 :004(592) [1017] far as to load down Dr. **Luther**'s teaching, as well as that
SD : 08 :017(594) [1021] one essence but, as Dr. **Luther** writes, into one person.
SD : 08 :021(595) [1021] Dr. **Luther** has explained this thoroughly in his *Great*
SD : 08 :021(595) [1023] **Luther** called this the devil's mask and damned it to the
SD : 08 :026(596) [1025] laid it aside, and as Dr. **Luther** explains it, he kept it
SD : 08 :028(596) [1025] mundane way, but as Dr. **Luther** explains, after the
SD : 08 :038(598) [1027] for us) and since Dr. **Luther** in his *Great Confession*
SD : 08 :038(598) [1027] we shall here quote Dr. **Luther**'s own words, so that the
SD : 08 :044(599) [1029] Likewise, Dr. **Luther** states in his treatise *Concerning the*
SD : 08 :044(600) [1031] So far **Luther**.
SD : 08 :080(607) [1045] this solid foundation, Dr. **Luther**, of blessed memory, has
SD : 08 :085(608) [1045] before his death, Dr. **Luther** states: "According to the
SD : 08 :086(608) [1047] similar testimonies in Dr. **Luther**'s writings, especially in
SD : 09 :001(610) [1051] Creed, to which Dr. **Luther** directs us in the sermon that
SD : 10 :024(615) [1061] In a special opinion Dr. **Luther** exhaustively instructs the
SD : 11 :033(621) [1073] **Luther** puts it this way: "Follow the order in the Epistle
SD : 12 :039(636) [1103] Apology, to the Smalcald Articles, to **Luther**'s Catechisms

Luxuries (1), Luxurious (1), Luxury (1)
AP : 15 :048(221) [0329] Their fasts are more **luxurious** and sumptuous than
TR : 00 :082(334) [0527] alms of the churches for **luxuries** and would neglect the
LC : 03 :103(434) [0727] along with fondness for **luxury**, honor, fame, and power.

Lydia (2)
EP : 02 :004(470) [0787] opens hearts so that, like **Lydia** in Acts 16:14, they heed
SD : 02 :026(526) [0891] Likewise, "**Lydia** heard us; the Lord opened her heart to

Lye (1)
AP : 04 :327(158) [0211] and cleanse my hands with **lye**, yet thou wilt plunge me

Lyra (2)
AP : 07 :022(172) [0235] So **Lyra** testifies when he says: "The church is not made
AP : 07 :022(172) [0235] our Confession that is different from what **Lyra** says here?

Mad (6), Madness (1)
AP : 04 :271(148) [0199] of our opponents is so **mad** as to deny that absolution is
AP : 16 :003(223) [0331] It was **mad** of Carlstadt to try to impose on us the
AP : 27 :020(272) [0427] It is **madness** to put a human tradition, which has neither
LC : PR :015(360) [0571] O what **mad**, senseless fools we are!
LC : 01 :038(369) [0591] descends, they become so **mad** and foolish that they justly
LC : 04 :013(438) [0735] But **mad** reason rushes forth and, because Baptism is not
EP : 02 :008(470) [0787] 1. The **mad** dream of the so-called Stoic philosophers and

Maenius (1)
AP : 04 :236(140) [0185] as the poet writes, "I forgive myself, says **Maenius**."

Magdeburg (3)
PR : PR :027(014) [0025] administrator of the archdiocese of **Magdeburg**
S3 : 15 :005(316) [0501] Nicholas Amsdorf, of **Magdeburg**, subscribed
TR : 00 :082(334) [0529] Nicholas Amsdorf, of **Magdeburg**, subscribed

Magic (2), Magical (1), Magicians (1)
AP : 21 :034(234) [0353] contained some sort of **magical** power, just as sorcerers
S3 : 15 :004(316) [0501] remains the pope's bag of **magic** tricks which contains
SC : 01 :004(342) [0539] to curse, swear, practice **magic**, lie, or deceive, but in
LC : 01 :012(366) [0583] lost possessions, etc., as **magicians** and sorcerers do.

Magistracy (2), Magistrate (3), Magistrates (20)
AG : 26 :010(065) [0071] that a prince and **magistrates** should govern land and
AL : 16 :002(037) [0051] when required by **magistrates**, to marry, to be given in
AL : 16 :006(038) [0051] bound to obey their **magistrates** and laws except when
AL : 23 :018(054) [0063] punishments of just **magistrates**, yet it is a marvelous
AL : 26 :011(065) [0071] — in marriage, in the **magistracy**, or in other civil
AL : 27 :013(072) [0077] than the life of **magistrates**, pastors, and the like who,
AL : 27 :055(079) [0083] for they judge that all **magistracy** and all civil offices are
AL : 00 :017(096) [0095] Senate and **magistrate** of Nuremberg
AP : 12 :174(210) [0307] to parents and **magistrates**, faithfulness to one's calling,
AP : 16 :012(224) [0333] have the approval of **magistrates** or of laws, they are
AP : 16 :013(224) [0333] the authority of **magistrates** and the value of civil
AP : 20 :012(228) [0341] then pardoned, "The **magistrate** commands that from
TR : 00 :077(333) [0527] cases had formerly belonged to the **magistrate**.
TR : 00 :077(333) [0527] divine right temporal **magistrates** are compelled to make
TR : 00 :078(333) [0527] on this account the **magistrates** ought to establish other
LC : 01 :181(389) [0631] evil-doers to civil **magistrates** in place of parents; in early
LC : 01 :218(394) [0643] Therefore parents and **magistrates** have the duty of so
LC : 01 :249(398) [0651] is the responsibility of princes and **magistrates**.
LC : 01 :268(401) [0657] as much authority as the emperor and all **magistrates**.
LC : 01 :274(401) [0659] made, however, of civil **magistrates**, preachers, and
LC : 01 :275(402) [0659] Just so, **magistrates**, parents, even brothers and sisters
LC : 03 :028(424) [0705] him, such as preachers, **magistrates**, neighbors, servants;
LC : 03 :077(431) [0721] princes, counselors, **magistrates**, and officials, with
LC : 04 :058(444) [0747] then father, mother, and **magistrates** are nothing."
LC : 04 :061(444) [0747] or in the pot, and **magistrates** only as ordinary people.

Magnet (4)
EP : 01 :015(468) [0783] juice, smeared upon a **magnet**, impedes but does not
EP : 01 :015(468) [0783] natural powers of the **magnet**; likewise the view that this
SD : 01 :022(512) [0865] garlic juice smeared on a **magnet** does not destroy the
SD : 01 :022(512) [0865] does not destroy the **magnet**'s natural power but only

Magnificent (4)
AP : 04 :105(122) [0153] T00 with all their **magnificent** titles — for some are called
AP : 23 :018(242) [0369] they not apply these **magnificent** commandments to
LC : 01 :314(407) [0671] pomp, splendor, and **magnificent** buildings, they are so
LC : 06 :018(459) [0000] wanted to perform a **magnificent** work to present to him,

Magnify (4), Magnifying (1), Magnifies (2)
AP : 04 :002(107) [0121] it illumines and **magnifies** the honor of Christ and brings
LC : 01 :028(368) [0587] then, take care to **magnify** and exalt this commandment
LC : 01 :150(386) [0625] our duty to honor and **magnify** them as the most precious
LC : 06 :018(459) [0000] value on our work but exalt and **magnify** God's Word.
LC : 06 :022(459) [0000] should concentrate on, **magnifying** and cherishing it as a
EP : 07 :018(484) [0813] sacrament increases, **magnifies**, and aggravates this
SD : 01 :003(509) [0861] understand better and to **magnify** more fully Christ's

Magnitude (2)
AP : 02 :033(104) [0113] nor can we know the **magnitude** of the grace of Christ
AP : 02 :045(106) [0117] wanted to show the **magnitude** of original sin and of

Maid (10), Maidservant (2)
SC : 01 :019(344) [0543] *his manservant, or his* ***maidservant****, or his ox, or his ass,*
SC : 05 :022(350) [0553] as a manservant or **maidservant**, etc., I am unfaithful to
LC : SP :010(363) [0577] his wife, man-servant, **maid**-servant, cattle, or anything
LC : SP :017(363) [0577] dismiss man-servants and **maid**-servants if they do not
LC : 01 :083(376) [0603] — man-servants and **maid**-servants who have attended to
LC : 01 :142(384) [0621] (man-servants and **maid**-servants) under him to manage
LC : 01 :143(385) [0623] man-servants and **maid**-servants should take care not
LC : 01 :225(395) [0643] that a man-servant or **maid**-servant is unfaithful in his or
LC : 01 :292(404) [0663] *his wife, man-servant,* ***maid****-servant, cattle, or anything*
LC : 01 :294(404) [0665] man-servants and **maid**-servants were not free, as now, to
LC : 01 :306(406) [0669] another's man-servant or **maid**-servant or otherwise
LC : 04 :022(439) [0737] from that which the **maid** cooks with and could indeed be

Main (11), Mainly (1)

AP : PR :006(098) [0101] us had taken notes on the **main** points of its
AP : PR :015(099) [0101] I have assembled the **main** arguments, to testify to all
AP : 02 :007(101) [0107] By such questions they miss the **main** issue.
AP : 04 :002(107) [0121] In this controversy the **main** doctrine of Christianity is
AP : 04 :225(138) [0183] that the greatest and the **main** virtue should justify.
AP : 04 :286(150) [0201] far we have reviewed the **main** passages which our
AP : 07 :005(169) [0227] however, but it is **mainly** an association of faith and of
AP : 22 :009(237) [0359] This is no doubt the **main** reason for defending the denial
AP : 24 :053(259) [0403] Though the **main** proofs for our position are in the
SD : 03 :029(544) [0925] At this point the **main** question with which we have to do
SD : 03 :029(544) [0925] very much like) from the **main** issue with which we here
SD : 08 :035(598) [1027] it can be comprehended under three **main** points.

Maintain (68), Maintained (21), Maintaining (3), Maintains (5), Maintenance (5)

AG : 23 :023(055) [0063] then to be so bold as to **maintain** such a teaching with the
AG : 26 :042(070) [0075] The ancient Fathers **maintained** such liberty with respect
AG : 26 :043(070) [0075] it was not necessary to **maintain** uniformity in such
AG : 27 :008(072) [0077] thrust into monasteries to provide for their **maintenance**.
AG : 27 :026(075) [0079] were granted for the **maintenance** of temporal interests,
AG : 28 :033(086) [0087] for thereby they wish to **maintain** that the power of the
AG : 28 :052(089) [0091] of the Gospel must be **maintained**, namely, that we obtain
AL : 00 :006(049) [0059] so much to the **maintenance** of dignity in public worship
AL : 23 :023(055) [0063] of marriage is **maintained** by means of such penalties.
AL : 26 :040(069) [0075] are profitable for **maintaining** good order in the church.
AL : 27 :008(072) [0077] monasteries for their **maintenance** and saw what
AL : 28 :029(085) [0087] to their subjects for the sake of **maintaining** public peace.
AP : 01 :002(100) [0103] We steadfastly **maintain** that those who believe otherwise
AP : 02 :038(105) [0115] But they **maintain** that concupiscence is a penalty and
AP : 04 :009(108) [0123] is, civil works—and **maintain** that without the Holy Spirit
AP : 04 :022(110) [0127] We for our part **maintain** that God requires the
AP : 04 :029(111) [0129] Pelagians, Augustine **maintains** at length that grace is not
AP : 04 :070(116) [0141] Therefore we must **maintain** that the promise of Christ is
AP : 04 :072(117) [0141] Regarding faith we **maintain** not this, but rather that
AP : 04 :087(120) [0147] as Augustine correctly **maintains** in his lengthy discussion
AP : 04 :213(136) [0179] Our opponents **maintain** these wicked and unscriptural
AP : 04 :252(143) [0191] to our position, so we **maintain** the same about James's
AP : 04 :264(146) [0195] in his commentaries he **maintains** with even less authority
AP : 04 :274(148) [0199] opponents maliciously **maintain** that by such works we
AP : 04 :379(165) [0223] Everywhere they **maintain** that we are acceptable and
AP : 07 :021(172) [0233] of what our opponents **maintain**, on the other hand, does
AP : 07 :028(173) [0237] Scriptures, therefore, we **maintain** that the church in the
AP : 07 :034(175) [0239] observe traditions that have been **maintained** elsewhere.
AP : 07 :043(177) [0243] some in the East who **maintained** that because of this
AP : 12 :061(190) [0269] then they must **maintain** that faith is part of penitence
AP : 12 :062(190) [0269] If the heart doubts, it **maintains** that God's promises are
AP : 12 :110(198) [0285] of confession and **maintain** that some examination is
AP : 12 :111(198) [0285] our opponents have **maintained** that complete confession
AP : 12 :127(201) [0289] churches should be **maintained** only by force and arms.
AP : 14 :001(214) [0315] to our deep desire to **maintain** the church polity and
AP : 15 :011(216) [0317] it is an ungodly error to **maintain** that we merit the
AP : 15 :017(217) [0319] How, then, can our opponents **maintain** that they justify?
AP : 15 :017(217) [0319] They cannot **maintain** this without the Word and
AP : 15 :018(217) [0319] of Antichrist if it **maintains** that human rites justify.
AP : 15 :021(218) [0321] when our opponents **maintain** that traditions have
AP : 15 :044(221) [0327] that we diligently **maintain** church discipline, pious
AP : 20 :014(229) [0343] were condemned for **maintaining** that grace is given
AP : 21 :029(233) [0351] We **maintain** that we dare not trust in the transfer of the
AP : 21 :043(235) [0357] of the church, which we are very anxious to **maintain**.
AP : 21 :044(236) [0357] before God to **maintain** and propagate sound doctrine
AP : 21 :044(236) [0357] They should take care to **maintain** and propagate divine
AP : 22 :006(237) [0359] These men **maintain** that it is right to deny one part, and
AP : 22 :013(238) [0361] otherwise we might want to **maintain** their practice.
AP : 23 :005(239) [0365] religion as a pretext to **maintain** their authority, which
AP : 23 :015(241) [0367] We **maintain** that whatever applies to human nature in
AP : 23 :055(247) [0379] of public officials, who ought to **maintain** public order.
AP : 24 :089(266) [0415] insult to the Gospel to **maintain** that without faith, *ex*
AP : 27 :009(269) [0421] We **maintain** that legitimate vows should be kept, but we
AP : 27 :023(273) [0427] How can they **maintain** that these are services which God
AP : 27 :028(274) [0429] merits eternal life if it is **maintained** by a due observance,
AP : 27 :028(274) [0429] as by the grace of God any monk can **maintain** it.
AP : 27 :042(276) [0435] So it is silly to **maintain** that it is a service to God to leave
AP : 27 :057(279) [0439] Not even the canons **maintain** that such vows are really
AP : 28 :009(282) [0445] XV, in which we **maintained** that traditions do not merit
S2 : 04 :009(300) [0473] be better governed and **maintained** than by having all of
S3 : 02 :001(303) [0479] Here we **maintain** that the law was given by God first of
S3 : 08 :010(313) [0497] and must constantly **maintain** that God will not deal with
LC : 01 :017(367) [0585] it did not establish and **maintain** some sort of worship.
LC : 01 :207(393) [0639] also wishes us to honor, **maintain**, and cherish it as a
LC : 01 :211(393) [0641] gift so that they can **maintain** chastity outside of
LC : 01 :213(394) [0641] and vow that they will **maintain** perpetual chastity while
LC : 01 :216(394) [0641] is not in their power to **maintain** chastity, and if they
LC : 01 :249(398) [0651] enough to establish and **maintain** order in all areas of
LC : 01 :256(399) [0651] would have every man **maintain** his self-respect before his
LC : 01 :260(400) [0655] everyone should help his neighbor **maintain** his rights.
LC : 01 :278(402) [0661] would be corrected and the neighbor's honor **maintained**.
LC : 03 :073(430) [0719] and life itself cannot be **maintained** for any length of
LC : 04 :002(437) [0733] How it is to be **maintained** and defended against heretics
LC : 05 :010(448) [0755] It is the Word, I **maintain**, which distinguishes it from
EP : RN :007(465) [0779] all other writings is **maintained**, and Holy Scripture
EP : 05 :002(478) [0801] light that is to be **maintained** with great diligence in the
EP : 06 :001(479) [0805] for three reasons: (1) to **maintain** external discipline
EP : 11 :016(497) [0837] we believe and **maintain** that if anybody teaches the
EP : 12 :029(500) [0843] Some **maintain** that each of the three has the same
EP : 12 :029(500) [0843] Others **maintain** that the three are unequal in essence and
SD : PR :014(506) [0855] pure doctrine and to **maintain** a thorough, lasting, and
SD : 01 :002(508) [0859] They **maintained** that original sin is something in man's
SD : 01 :016(511) [0865] incumbent upon us to **maintain** and preserve this doctrine
SD : 01 :033(514) [0869] speak strictly, one must **maintain** a distinction between
SD : 01 :034(514) [0869] constrain and compel us to **maintain** such a distinction.
SD : 01 :048(517) [0875] mightily why we must **maintain** a distinction between the
SD : 01 :054(517) [0877] and *accidens*, we **maintain** that the assemblies of the
SD : 02 :077(536) [0911] of the synergists, who **maintain** that in spiritual things
SD : 03 :004(540) [0917] Therefore they **maintained** that the righteousness of faith
SD : 03 :040(546) [0929] works is bound to be **maintained** and preserved, as well
SD : 04 :003(551) [0939] A few theologians also **maintained** that good works are
SD : 04 :008(552) [0941] which belong to the **maintenance** of outward discipline
SD : 04 :036(557) [0949] advice of St. Paul to **maintain** the pattern of sound words
SD : 05 :002(558) [0951] other party, however, **maintained** and contended that,
SD : 05 :027(563) [0961] necessary to urge and to **maintain** with all diligence the
SD : 06 :001(563) [0963] serves (1) not only to **maintain** external discipline and
SD : 06 :015(566) [0967] to teach and to **maintain** the strict distinction between the
SD : 07 :014(571) [0977] Therefore they **maintain** and teach that with the bread
SD : 07 :015(572) [0977] For they do not **maintain** that the body of Christ is
SD : 07 :085(584) [1001] To **maintain** this true Christian doctrine concerning the
SD : 08 :002(591) [1015] For when Dr. Luther **maintained** with solid arguments
SD : 08 :028(596) [1025] as the Sacramentarians **maintain** without proof from the

Majesty (113)

PR : PR :008(005) [0009] His Roman Imperial **Majesty**, and to everyone else that it
PR : PR :020(010) [0017] almighty power and **majesty**) and hence must be false and
PR : PR :021(010) [0019] with reference to the **majesty** of the human nature in the
PR : PR :021(011) [0019] churches): This divine **majesty** is not ascribed to the
PR : PR :021(011) [0019] it is alleged to have this **majesty** intrinsically, essentially,
AG : 00 :000(023) [0037] Princes and Cities to His Imperial **Majesty** Charles V
AG : PR :001(024) [0039] time ago Your Imperial **Majesty** graciously summoned a
AG : PR :001(024) [0039] In the summons Your **Majesty** indicated an earnest desire
AG : PR :006(025) [0039] Your Imperial **Majesty** also graciously and earnestly
AG : PR :007(025) [0039] in keeping with Your **Majesty**'s wish, we should present
AG : PR :008(025) [0039] to Your Imperial **Majesty**, we offer and present a
AG : PR :010(025) [0041] to Your Imperial **Majesty**, our most gracious lord, to
AG : PR :011(026) [0041] with Your Imperial **Majesty**'s aforementioned summons.
AG : PR :012(026) [0041] by Your Imperial **Majesty**'s summons, if no amicable and
AG : PR :014(026) [0041] Of this Your Imperial **Majesty**, our aforementioned
AG : PR :015(026) [0041] the past Your Imperial **Majesty** graciously gave assurance
AG : PR :016(026) [0041] stated Your Imperial **Majesty** was not disposed to render
AG : PR :018(026) [0041] by Your Imperial **Majesty**'s viceroy (His Royal Majesty
AG : PR :018(026) [0041] viceroy (His Royal **Majesty** of Hungary and Bohemia,
AG : PR :018(026) [0041] and by Your Imperial **Majesty**'s orator and appointed
AG : PR :018(026) [0041] that Your Imperial **Majesty**'s viceroy, administrators, and
AG : PR :019(026) [0041] between Your Imperial **Majesty** and the pope were
AG : PR :019(026) [0041] Your Imperial **Majesty** was sure that the pope would not
AG : PR :020(026) [0041] and so Your Imperial **Majesty** graciously offered to
AG : PR :020(026) [0041] with Your Imperial **Majesty**, at the earliest opportunity
AG : PR :021(027) [0043] have been held during Your Imperial **Majesty**'s reign.
AG : PR :023(027) [0043] with Your Imperial **Majesty**'s summons) as we herewith
AG : 21 :001(046) [0057] So His Imperial **Majesty** may in salutary and godly
AG : 00 :000(049) [0059] order that Your Imperial **Majesty** may perceive that we
AG : 23 :006(052) [0061] of God, the supreme **Majesty**, by means of human
AG : 23 :014(053) [0063] loyalty to Your Imperial **Majesty** we therefore feel
AG : 23 :014(053) [0063] Christian emperor, Your **Majesty** will graciously take into
AG : 00 :007(096) [0095] Your Imperial **Majesty**'s most obedient servants:
AL : 00 :001(049) [0059] pray that Your Imperial **Majesty** will graciously hear both
AL : 00 :002(049) [0059] Your Imperial **Majesty** should not believe those who
AL : 00 :004(049) [0059] Your Imperial **Majesty** will undoubtedly discover that the
AL : 00 :006(095) [0095] edict of Your Imperial **Majesty**, we have desired to
AL : 00 :017(096) [0095] Your Imperial **Majesty**'s faithful subjects:
AP : PR :001(098) [0099] His Imperial **Majesty** had this read before the assembly
AP : PR :004(098) [0099] could not, His Imperial **Majesty** again ordered our
AP : PR :005(098) [0101] to His Imperial **Majesty** why we could not accept the
AP : PR :007(098) [0101] apology to His Imperial **Majesty**, to show him that very
AP : PR :007(098) [0101] Confutation, but his Imperial **Majesty** did not receive it.
AP : 02 :001(100) [0105] very outset His Imperial **Majesty** will see that the authors
AP : 02 :035(104) [0115] His Imperial **Majesty** will recognize an obvious slander
AP : 02 :051(106) [0119] will satisfy His Imperial **Majesty** about the childish and
AP : 04 :002(107) [0121] ask His Imperial **Majesty** kindly to hear us out on this
AP : 10 :004(179) [0247] this subject (his Imperial **Majesty** does not disapprove
AP : 12 :122(200) [0287] that they dared to thrust upon his Imperial **Majesty**.
AP : 20 :004(227) [0339] Most Excellent Imperial **Majesty** and many of the princes
S1 : 01 :000(291) [0461] treats the sublime articles of the divine **majesty**, namely:
TR : 00 :082(000) [0529] estates of the Roman Empire, to his Imperial **Majesty**.
LC : 01 :040(370) [0591] since the divine **Majesty** comes to us with so gracious an
LC : 01 :106(379) [0611] (so to speak) toward a **majesty** hidden within them.
LC : 01 :116(381) [0615] and commanded next to obedience to his own **majesty**.
LC : 01 :125(382) [0617] pleasing to the divine **Majesty** and all the angels, that it
LC : 01 :171(388) [0629] command of the divine **Majesty**, who will solemnly call us
LC : 03 :057(427) [0713] mockery of his imperial **majesty**'s command and was
LC : 04 :020(439) [0737] adorned and clothed with the **majesty** and glory of God.
LC : 04 :021(439) [0737] that the divine glory and **majesty** were manifested
LC : 05 :011(448) [0755] but of the divine **Majesty** at whose feet every knee should
LC : 05 :012(448) [0755] wisdom than the divine **Majesty** has in his little finger.
EP : 08 :003(487) [0819] in common with the deity, its **majesty**, and its properties.
EP : 08 :013(488) [0821] and was exalted to the **majesty** and omnipotent power of
EP : 08 :015(488) [0821] hand of the omnipotent **majesty** and power of God,
EP : 08 :016(489) [0821] to the personal union he always possessed this **majesty**.
EP : 08 :016(489) [0821] not always disclose this **majesty**, but only when it pleased
EP : 08 :016(489) [0821] use, revelation, and manifestation of his divine **majesty**.
EP : 12 :021(499) [0841] as far as might, power, **majesty**, and glory are concerned,
EP : 12 :028(500) [0843] adorned with divine **majesty** and is inferior to and beside
EP : 12 :029(500) [0843] same power, wisdom, **majesty**, and glory, just like any
SD : 07 :022(573) [0979] wisdom than the divine **Majesty** has in his little finger.
SD : 07 :067(582) [0997] just as they describe the **majesty** of Christ as "Satan's
SD : 08 :002(592) [1017] on earth since such **majesty** belongs to God alone and the
SD : 08 :012(593) [1019] to the right hand of **majesty**, power, and might over every
SD : 08 :013(593) [1019] did not receive this **majesty**, to which he was exalted
SD : 08 :023(595) [1023] that is said about the **majesty** of Christ according to his
SD : 08 :024(595) [1023] demonstrated his divine **majesty** even in his mother's
SD : 08 :025(596) [1023] manifested his divine **majesty** according to his good
SD : 08 :026(596) [1023] and use of the divine **majesty** according to the assumed
SD : 08 :026(596) [1023] He had this **majesty** immediately at his conception even
SD : 08 :029(597) [1025] the divine, omnipotent **majesty** and power through and in
SD : 08 :051(600) [1031] to the right hand of the **majesty** and power of God, after
SD : 08 :051(601) [1033] and privileges in **majesty**, glory, power, and might above
SD : 08 :051(601) [1033] and according to the **majesty**, glory, power, and might
SD : 08 :054(601) [1033] do not measure up to the **majesty** which the Scriptures,
SD : 08 :061(602) [1035] divine power, life, might, **majesty**, and glory were not

Continued ▶

SD : 0 8 :063(603) [1037] To set forth correctly the **majesty** of Christ by way of
SD : 0 8 :064(603) [1037] Christ has received this **majesty** according to the manner
SD : 0 8 :064(603) [1037] shines forth with all its **majesty**, power, glory, and
SD : 0 8 :065(604) [1039] humiliation the divine **majesty** was concealed and
SD : 0 8 :066(604) [1039] omnipotence, power, **majesty**, and glory, which is the
SD : 0 8 :067(604) [1039] which speak of the **majesty** to which the human nature of
SD : 0 8 :067(604) [1039] either as if this divine **majesty**, which is the property of
SD : 0 8 :067(604) [1039] nature, or as if this **majesty** is in Christ's human nature
SD : 0 8 :067(604) [1039] the human nature has no share in the divine **majesty**.
SD : 0 8 :068(604) [1039] since he there has his **majesty** with and about him at all
SD : 0 8 :069(604) [1039] would be robbed of his **majesty**, which as a human being
SD : 0 8 :071(605) [1041] an outpouring of the **majesty** of God and all its properties
SD : 0 8 :071(605) [1041] allegedly received equal **majesty**, separated or divided
SD : 0 8 :074(606) [1043] to the right hand of the **majesty** and power of God.
SD : 0 8 :078(606) [1043] passages illustrate the **majesty** of the man Christ, which
SD : 0 8 :078(606) [1043] at the right hand of the **majesty** and power of God, so
SD : 0 8 :080(607) [1045] has written about the **majesty** of Christ according to the
SD : 0 8 :086(608) [1047] clear expositions of the **majesty** of Christ at the right
SD : 0 8 :087(608) [1047] deprive Christ according to his humanity of this **majesty**.
SD : 0 8 :092(609) [1049] at the right hand of the **majesty** and power of God,
SD : 0 8 :095(609) [1049] power, might, wisdom, **majesty**, and glory, but has only
SD : 0 8 :096(610) [1049] at the right hand of the **majesty** and almighty power of
SD : 0 9 :003(610) [1051] right hand of the almighty power and **majesty** of God.
SD : 1 2 :029(635) [1101] in might, in power, in **majesty**, and in glory he is in every
SD : 1 2 :036(635) [1101] only adorned with divine **majesty** inferior to and
SD : 1 2 :037(636) [1103] same power, wisdom, **majesty**, and glory, while others

Major (3)
AP : 0 2 :011(102) [0109] minor faults in human nature and ignore the **major** ones.
AP : 0 4 :242(141) [0187] gave in to his hatred, a **major** commotion emerged from
AP : 1 1 :010(182) [0253] penitence there are other **major** faults, and these we shall

Majority (6)
AG : 2 7 :033(076) [0079] inasmuch as a **majority** of them entered the cloister in
AL : 2 7 :033(076) [0079] monastery because a **majority** of them took vows before
AP : 0 4 :395(167) [0225] The **majority** of the people believed that they merited the
LC : 0 5 :041(451) [0763] Thus the **majority** go so far that they have become quite
SD : 1 1 :034(622) [1075] For it is my will that the **majority** of those whom I call
SD : 1 1 :041(623) [1077] Word and obey it; the **majority** despise the Word and

Make (219), Maker (6), Makes (76), Making (43), Made (169)
PR : PR :004(004) [0009] doctrine, and to **make** them more compliant in submitting
PR : PR :018(009) [0017] for that reason allegedly **make** a new confession almost
PR : PR :023(012) [0021] articles we have **made** no new or different confession from
AG : PR :022(027) [0043] We have at various times **made** our protestations and
AG : 0 2 :003(029) [0045] hold that natural man is **made** righteous by his own
AG : 1 2 :010(035) [0049] through faith but through the satisfactions **made** by man.
AG : 1 5 :004(037) [0049] to earn grace and **make** satisfaction for sin, are useless
AG : 1 7 :005(039) [0051] which are even now **making** an appearance and which
AG : 1 8 :001(039) [0051] honorable life and to **make** choices among the things that
AG : 1 8 :002(039) [0051] man is not capable of **making** himself acceptable to God,
AG : 2 0 :006(042) [0053] say that faith and works **make** us righteous before God.
AG : 2 0 :021(044) [0055] purpose of earning grace and **making** satisfaction for sins.
AG : 2 0 :025(044) [0057] faith in such a way as to **make** it clear that faith is not
AG : 2 1 :001(046) [0057] the example of David in **making** war on the Turk, for
AG : 2 3 :006(052) [0061] Experience has **made** it all too manifest whether or not it
AG : 2 3 :013(053) [0063] the popes had themselves **made** and to the decisions of
AG : 2 3 :002(053) [0063] and intelligent man, **made** this statement because of grave
AG : 2 3 :026(055) [0065] toward those who have **made** vows in their youth — and
AG : 0 1 :002(056) [0065] changes have been **made** in the public ceremonies of the
AG : 2 4 :021(058) [0067] Christ has by his death **made** satisfaction only for
AG : 2 4 :027(059) [0067] once and by this offering **made** satisfaction for all sin.
AG : 2 4 :025(059) [0067] Christ's death should have **made** satisfaction only for
AG : 2 4 :030(059) [0067] was not instituted to **make** provision for a sacrifice for sin
AG : 2 4 :040(061) [0069] change has been **made** in the public ceremonies of the
AG : 2 6 :001(064) [0071] by men serve to earn grace and **make** satisfaction for sin.
AG : 2 6 :011(065) [0071] was no end or limit to the **making** of such traditions.
AG : 2 6 :021(067) [0073] they should not be **made** into a necessary service of God.
AG : 2 6 :027(068) [0073] Peter says, "Why do you **make** trial of God by putting a
AG : 2 6 :039(069) [0075] but what is rejected is **making** a necessary service of fasts
AG : 2 6 :041(070) [0075] forms of service do not **make** us righteous before God
AG : 2 7 :002(071) [0077] and the attempt was **made** to restore discipline by means
AG : 2 7 :020(074) [0079] man should be alone; I will **make** him a helper fit for him
AG : 2 7 :023(074) [0079] men say that a vow **made** contrary to papal canons is not
AG : 2 7 :031(075) [0079] annul vows that are **made** under the age of fifteen years.
AG : 2 7 :038(077) [0081] invented spiritual life **makes** satisfaction for sin and
AG : 2 7 :040(077) [0081] for an ungodly vow, **made** contrary to God's command,
AG : 2 7 :048(078) [0081] that such a service would **make** men good and righteous
AG : 2 8 :013(083) [0085] government, should not **make** or prescribe to the
AG : 2 8 :015(083) [0085] world," and again, "Who **made** me a judge or divider over
AG : 2 8 :035(086) [0089] command and Word to **make** laws out of opinions or to
AG : 2 8 :035(086) [0089] be observed in order to **make** satisfaction for sins and
AG : 2 8 :049(089) [0091] so frequently forbid the **making** and keeping of human
AG : 2 8 :053(090) [0091] bishops or pastors may **make** regulations so that
AG : 2 8 :053(090) [0091] obtaining God's grace or **making** satisfaction for sins, nor
AG : 0 0 :005(095) [0095] in order that it may be **made** very clear that we have
AL : 0 1 :002(027) [0043] and goodness, the **maker** and preserver of all things,
AL : 0 4 :002(030) [0045] of Christ, who by his death **made** satisfaction for our sins.
AL : 1 5 :003(036) [0049] God, merit grace, and **make** satisfaction for sins are
AL : 1 5 :004(037) [0049] to merit grace and **make** satisfaction for sins, are useless
AL : 1 6 :002(037) [0051] to serve as soldiers, to **make** legal contracts, to hold
AL : 1 8 :004(039) [0051] will which enables them to **make** judgments according to
AL : 2 0 :021(044) [0055] kind to merit grace and **make** satisfaction for sins.
AL : 2 3 :013(053) [0063] to the canons, both those **made** by the popes and those
AL : 2 3 :013(053) [0063] by the popes and those **made** by the most celebrated
AL : 2 3 :026(056) [0065] toward those who have **made** vows before attaining a
AL : 2 3 :026(056) [0065] and as a rule vows used to be so **made** in former times.
AL : 2 4 :021(058) [0067] Christ had by his passion **made** satisfaction for original
AL : 2 4 :021(058) [0067] an oblation should be **made** for daily sins, mortal and
AL : 2 4 :023(058) [0067] proliferation of Masses to which reference has been **made**
AL : 2 6 :001(064) [0071] profitable to merit grace and **make** satisfactions for sins.
AL : 2 6 :007(065) [0071] no mention was **made** of faith; only works of satisfaction
AL : 2 6 :021(067) [0073] we cannot merit grace or **make** satisfaction for sins by the
AL : 2 6 :027(068) [0073] Peter says, "Why do you **make** trial of God by putting a
AL : 2 6 :045(070) [0075] and this statement is **made**: "It was not the intention of
AL : 2 7 :013(072) [0077] Thus they **made** men believe that the monastic profession
AL : 2 7 :013(073) [0077] like who, without man-**made** observances, serve their
AL : 2 7 :023(074) [0079] vows valid which are **made** contrary to God's commands!
AL : 2 7 :030(075) [0079] to the nature of a vow to **make** a promise which is not
AL : 2 7 :031(075) [0079] Many canons annul vows **made** before the age of fifteen
AL : 2 7 :031(076) [0079] sufficient judgment to **make** a decision involving the rest
AL : 2 7 :032(076) [0079] Another canon, **making** a greater concession to human
AL : 2 7 :032(076) [0079] a few years and forbids **making** a vow before the
AL : 2 7 :038(077) [0081] invented observances **make** satisfaction for sins and merit
AL : 2 7 :062(080) [0083] since they are false and useless, **make** vows null and void.
AL : 2 8 :015(083) [0085] world," and again, "Who **made** me a judge or divider over
AL : 2 8 :030(085) [0087] in the church and **make** laws concerning foods, holy
AL : 2 8 :033(086) [0087] No case is **made** more of than this change of the
AL : 2 8 :035(086) [0089] for the purpose of **making** satisfaction for sins or meriting
AL : 2 8 :043(088) [0089] which prohibit the **making** of traditions for the purpose
AL : 2 8 :049(089) [0091] does Scripture so often prohibit the **making** of traditions?
AL : 2 8 :053(090) [0091] for bishops or pastors to **make** regulations so that things
AL : 2 8 :053(090) [0091] that by means of these we **make** satisfaction for sins, nor
AP : PR :011(099) [0101] I have always **made** it a point to stick as closely as
AP : 0 2 :006(101) [0107] with this evil doctrine, we **made** mention of
AP : 0 2 :023(103) [0111] To **make** ourselves clear, we are naming these gifts
AP : 0 2 :039(105) [0115] the law of my mind and **making** me captive to the law of
AP : 0 4 :010(108) [0123] has always been **making** up this or that form of worship
AP : 0 4 :019(109) [0125] When they **make** up a distinction between merit of
AP : 0 4 :031(111) [0129] says, "If the Son **makes** you free, you will be free
AP : 0 4 :037(112) [0131] enough for idle men to **make** up these dreams that a man
AP : 0 4 :040(112) [0131] He was given for us to **make** satisfaction for the sins of
AP : 0 4 :052(114) [0135] for our sins if our merits **make** satisfaction for them?
AP : 0 4 :059(115) [0137] that our opponents **make** so little of faith when they see it
AP : 0 4 :072(117) [0141] though it is his own art that **makes** everyone an artist.
AP : 0 4 :072(117) [0141] "to be justified" means to **make** unrighteous men
AP : 0 4 :072(117) [0141] first that faith alone **makes** a righteous man out of an
AP : 0 4 :078(117) [0143] being understood as **making** an unrighteous man
AP : 0 4 :081(118) [0143] they would not have us **make** use of him now as our
AP : 0 4 :086(119) [0147] it believes that "God **made** Christ our wisdom, our
AP : 0 4 :088(120) [0149] lest we suppose that Paul **made** the statement "Faith
AP : 0 4 :103(121) [0151] to be harmful since it has **made** all men sinners, but when
AP : 0 4 :116(123) [0155] be called "grace that **makes** us acceptable to God" rather
AP : 0 4 :117(123) [0155] the Scriptures, was to **make** clear that by faith alone we
AP : 0 4 :117(123) [0155] out of unrighteous we are **made** righteous and regenerated
AP : 0 4 :179(131) [0171] us from the curse of the law, being **made** a curse for us."
AP : 0 4 :181(132) [0171] regenerates nor of itself **makes** us acceptable before God.
AP : 0 4 :196(134) [0175] Because faith **makes** us sons of God, moreover, it also
AP : 0 4 :196(134) [0175] of God, moreover, it also **makes** us co-heirs with Christ.
AP : 0 4 :196(134) [0175] our justification, which **makes** us sons of God and
AP : 0 4 :202(134) [0175] by faith, the sacrifice he **made** was acceptable to God —
AP : 0 4 :212(136) [0179] choose other works, **make** up new devotions, new vows,
AP : 0 4 :230(139) [0183] the help of his Holy Spirit to **make** it clear and distinct.
AP : 0 4 :231(139) [0183] they argue that love justifies since it **makes** men perfect.
AP : 0 4 :231(139) [0183] If it is love that **makes** men perfect, Christ, the
AP : 0 4 :235(140) [0185] And so it does not **make** sense when our opponents argue
AP : 0 4 :250(143) [0191] but a divine power that **makes** us alive and enables us to
AP : 0 4 :252(143) [0191] mean that a wicked man is **made** righteous but that he is
AP : 0 4 :260(145) [0195] Scriptures to suit the man-**made** theory that by our works
AP : 0 4 :269(147) [0197] glory to works and **make** of them a propitiation that
AP : 0 4 :291(152) [0203] It compels us to **make** use of Christ in justification.
AP : 0 4 :297(153) [0205] does not believe God, has **made** him a liar, because he
AP : 0 4 :297(153) [0205] Christ says, "If the Son **makes** you free, you will be free
AP : 0 4 :299(153) [0205] when we teach men to **make** use of him as mediator and
AP : 0 4 :306(154) [0207] Jesus Christ, whom God **made** our wisdom, our
AP : 0 4 :306(154) [0207] "For our sake he **made** him to be sin who knew no
AP : 0 4 :307(154) [0207] That is, by it we are **made** acceptable to God because of
AP : 0 4 :309(155) [0207] (Rom. 4:20), "No distrust **made** him waver concerning the
AP : 0 4 :317(156) [0209] elsewhere, he thereby **makes** Christ "an agent of sin" since
AP : 0 4 :321(157) [0209] merit of condignity — was **made** up to evade the
AP : 0 4 :327(158) [0211] "Who can say, 'I have **made** my heart clean, I am pure
AP : 0 4 :335(159) [0215] this point our opponents **make** a marvelous play on
AP : 0 4 :341(159) [0215] twist against faith statements **made** in support of faith.
AP : 0 4 :345(160) [0217] Precisely in order to **make** hope sure and to distinguish
AP : 0 4 :347(160) [0217] This faith **makes** the difference between those who are
AP : 0 4 :347(160) [0217] Faith **makes** the difference between the worthy and the
AP : 0 4 :356(161) [0217] sake at the same time **makes** us sons of God and fellow
AP : 0 4 :366(163) [0221] Paul says (Col. 1:13), and **made** fellow heirs with Christ
AP : 0 4 :374(164) [0221] often mention the fruit to **make** it clearer to the
AP : 0 4 :392(167) [0225] the work of Christ and **making** of him not the propitiator
AP : 0 7 :005(169) [0227] To **make** it recognizable, this association has outward
AP : 0 7 :005(169) [0227] "And he has **made** him the head over all things
AP : 0 7 :010(170) [0229] It is, rather, **made** up of men scattered throughout the
AP : 0 7 :013(170) [0231] what it is that chiefly **makes** us members, and living
AP : 0 7 :018(171) [0233] has not yet come does not **make** the wicked the kingdom
AP : 0 7 :020(171) [0233] church actually exists, **made** up of true believers and
AP : 0 7 :022(172) [0235] says: "The church is not **made** up of men by reason of
AP : 0 7 :022(172) [0235] Therefore the church is **made** up of those persons in
AP : 0 7 :039(176) [0241] on consciences, nor to **make** the observance of days,
AP : 0 7 :042(176) [0243] them; even if they have **made** a mistake, do not let this
AP : 1 0 :004(179) [0247] this article), but to **make** clear to all our readers that we
AP : 1 1 :001(180) [0249] that confession should be **made** annually, and that even
AP : 1 1 :007(181) [0251] These terrors **made** no impression on wild and profane
AP : 1 1 :008(181) [0251] namely, that we **make** confession of all our sins.
AP : 1 2 :008(183) [0255] For faith **makes** the difference between the contrition of
AP : 1 2 :022(185) [0257] acts of devotion, and to **make** such satisfactions and acts
AP : 1 2 :043(187) [0263] Christ, and it teaches us to **make** use of Christ as our
AP : 1 2 :044(187) [0263] must show that Scripture **makes** them the chief parts in
AP : 1 2 :046(188) [0263] with a circumcision **made** without hands, by putting off
AP : 1 2 :051(189) [0265] But he terrifies, he says, to **make** room for consolation
AP : 1 2 :052(189) [0265] In this way Scripture **makes** a practice of joining these
AP : 1 2 :061(190) [0269] If they try to **make** a subtle distinction separating
AP : 1 2 :062(191) [0269] does not believe God has **made** him a liar because he has
AP : 1 2 :067(192) [0271] what sort of church it is that is **made** up of such men.
AP : 1 2 :083(194) [0275] being lengthy in order to **make** our case more easily
AP : 1 2 :088(195) [0277] If anybody doubts, he **makes** the divine promise a lie, as

Continued ▶

A P : 1 2 :091(196) [0279] These statements **make** no mention of faith, and the
A P : 1 2 :092(196) [0279] parts of penitence in order to **make** it more conspicuous.
A P : 1 2 :092(196) [0279] or good works and **making** no mention of justifying
A P : 1 2 :096(196) [0281] Ambrose **makes** this very clear statement about
A P : 1 2 :106(197) [0283] our opponents **make** passages of Scripture mean
A P : 1 2 :107(198) [0283] Such confession, **made** to God, is itself contrition.
A P : 1 2 :107(198) [0283] For when confession is **made** to God, it must come from
A P : 1 2 :109(198) [0283] specific confession to be **made** to priests but of the
A P : 1 2 :112(198) [0285] certain satisfactions, they **made** confession to the priests
A P : 1 2 :124(201) [0289] anything to his dignity in **making** use of such defenders
A P : 1 2 :137(203) [0293] observances which **make** satisfaction for punishment, if
A P : 1 2 :142(204) [0295] of supererogation, he can **make** satisfaction for the sins
A P : 1 2 :142(204) [0295] to trust that thereby we **make** satisfaction to God's law.
A P : 1 2 :144(205) [0297] a great variety, with one **making** a trip in armor and
A P : 1 2 :150(206) [0299] can be so great as to **make** satisfaction unnecessary; thus
A P : 1 2 :151(206) [0299] of death; but that was to **make** us rely not on ourselves
A P : 1 2 :154(206) [0301] penalties on account of which the satisfactions are **made**.
A P : 1 2 :154(207) [0301] do they add that we must **make** satisfaction in purgatory?
A P : 1 2 :159(207) [0301] works of God might be **made** manifest in him"
A P : 1 2 :160(207) [0301] power of God might be **made** more manifest in our
A P : 1 2 :160(207) [0303] "The power of God is **made** perfect in weakness"
A P : 1 2 :163(208) [0303] explain "judge" as "to **make** a pilgrimage to St. James
A P : 1 2 :178(211) [0309] that our opponents have **made** up a great deal about the
A P : 1 3 :002(211) [0309] We do not think it **makes** much difference if, for
A P : 1 3 :009(212) [0311] priests are not called to **make** sacrifices that merit
A P : 1 5 :001(215) [0315] to merit grace, and to **make** satisfaction for sin are
A P : 1 5 :027(219) [0323] with interpretations that **make** them either stricter or
A P : 1 5 :030(219) [0323] He **makes** it perfectly clear that he is talking about human
A P : 1 5 :031(219) [0323] Acts 15:10, "Why do you **make** a trial of God by putting
A P : 1 6 :002(222) [0331] At the same time it lets us **make** outward use of the
A P : 1 6 :002(222) [0331] we live, just as it lets us **make** use of medicine or
A P : 1 6 :009(224) [0333] What **makes** for Christian perfection is not contempt of
A P : 1 6 :012(224) [0333] Christian may legitimately **make** use of civil ordinances
A P : 2 0 :013(228) [0341] Such argumentation is to **make** the effect the cause.
A P : 2 1 :014(230) [0345] of the saints to others and **make** the saints propitiators as
A P : 2 1 :014(230) [0347] It **makes** them mediators and propitiators.
A P : 2 1 :014(231) [0347] they obviously **make** the saints mediators of redemption.
A P : 2 1 :015(231) [0347] Thus they actually **make** them mediators of redemption.
A P : 2 1 :016(231) [0347] prove that they actually **make** the saints not only
A P : 2 1 :018(231) [0347] May prayer be **made** for him continually!"
A P : 2 1 :019(231) [0347] must be authorized to **make** satisfaction for others and to
A P : 2 1 :022(232) [0349] We are not **making** false charges here.
A P : 2 1 :023(232) [0349] What is this if not to **make** the saints propitiators?
A P : 2 1 :038(234) [0355] monstrous and ungodly tales because they **make** money.
A P : 2 1 :043(235) [0357] They **make** no effort to provide a summary of the
A P : 2 2 :009(237) [0359] a distinction should be **made** between laity and clergy.
A P : 2 2 :013(238) [0361] If they withhold it to **make** a distinction of orders, this in
A P : 2 2 :015(238) [0361] or both, how can they **make** the withholding of one kind
A P : 2 3 :008(240) [0367] Just so this Word **makes** the earth fruitful (Gen. 1:11),
A P : 2 3 :021(242) [0369] those "who have **made** themselves eunuchs for the sake of
A P : 2 3 :037(244) [0373] But no such outcry will **make** us surrender the truth of
A P : 2 3 :039(244) [0375] as eloquence does not **make** an orator more righteous
A P : 2 3 :039(244) [0375] before God than building **makes** an architect, so the
A P : 2 3 :040(245) [0375] commend those who **make** themselves eunuchs, but he
A P : 2 3 :040(245) [0375] (Matt. 19:12), that is, to **make** room for hearing or
A P : 2 3 :041(245) [0375] that this does not **make** it necessary to impose perpetual
A P : 2 3 :046(246) [0377] knowledge of Christ by **making** men believe that through
A P : 2 3 :057(247) [0379] Now they are **making** the law even more unbearable in
A P : 2 4 :006(250) [0385] church before Gregory **make** no mention of private
A P : 2 4 :016(252) [0389] someone skilled in **making** them he would follow in his
A P : 2 4 :016(252) [0389] He tells the person **making** the distinctions to cut the
A P : 2 4 :016(252) [0389] our enumeration of the types of sacrifice will **make** clear.
A P : 2 4 :017(252) [0389] The theologians **make** a proper distinction between
A P : 2 4 :023(253) [0391] he says (53:10), "When he **makes** himself an offering for
A P : 2 4 :023(253) [0391] to reconcile God and **make** satisfaction for our sins, so
A P : 2 4 :032(255) [0395] of the Gospel, which **makes** known the name of Christ
A P : 2 4 :038(257) [0399] put to death, and **made** alive when the Gospel sprinkles
A P : 2 4 :039(257) [0399] the Holy Spirit who puts us to death and **makes** us alive.
A P : 2 4 :040(257) [0399] the Gospel, being put to death and **made** alive.
A P : 2 4 :042(257) [0399] which they put on in public as a money-**making** venture.
A P : 2 4 :042(257) [0399] Then they **make** the claim that this work can be
A P : 2 4 :055(259) [0403] teaches, "When he **makes** himself an offering for
A P : 2 4 :059(260) [0405] and the Holy Spirit and be put to death and **made** alive.
A P : 2 4 :066(261) [0407] They **make** clear that they are talking about
A P : 2 4 :067(261) [0407] But to **make** the whole matter as clear as possible, we
A P : 2 4 :071(262) [0409] is the spiritual motivation, dying and being **made** alive.
A P : 2 4 :072(262) [0409] acceptance of them by faith, so that they **make** us alive.
A P : 2 4 :073(262) [0409] A faith that acknowledges mercy **makes** alive.
A P : 2 4 :073(262) [0409] use of the sacrament is to **make** clear that terrified
A P : 2 4 :080(264) [0411] for Christ, God **making** his appeal through us.
A P : 2 4 :088(265) [0413] This is what it says: "And **make** us worthy to come to
A P : 2 4 :088(265) [0413] It prays that we might be **made** worthy to offer prayers
A P : 2 4 :089(265) [0413] souls of the dead, from which they **make** infinite profits.
A P : 2 4 :089(266) [0415] that reconciles God and **makes** satisfaction for sins.
A P : 2 4 :090(266) [0415] Nevertheless, it does not **make** satisfaction for guilt;
A P : 2 4 :096(267) [0417] wicked to whom it is applied, if they **make** no objection.
A P : 2 4 :099(268) [0419] But if our opponents **make** us compile all kinds of abuses
A P : 2 7 :004(269) [0421] sermons and in thinking up new ways of **making** money.
A P : 2 7 :009(270) [0421] Are vows **made** with these notions in mind legitimate?
A P : 2 7 :009(270) [0421] who are not old enough to **make** up their own minds
A P : 2 7 :011(270) [0423] legitimate vow if the one **making** it supposes that by it he
A P : 2 7 :011(270) [0423] of sins before God or **makes** satisfaction for sins before
A P : 2 7 :029(274) [0431] which, first of all, they **make** the impudent claim that
A P : 2 7 :038(275) [0433] what progress he was **making** in his way of life, God
A P : 2 7 :041(276) [0435] leaving wife and children **makes** it even clearer that he
A P : 2 7 :053(278) [0437] Thus the Dominicans **made** up the rosary of the blessed
A P : 2 7 :057(279) [0439] that monastic vows, as **made** until now, are not vows,
A P : 2 7 :066(280) [0441] Thus vows **made** before that age must be invalid.
A P : 2 8 :008(282) [0445] "Why do you **make** a trial of God?" they say (Acts 15:10).
A P : 2 8 :010(282) [0445] Do they **make** hearts alive?
A P : 2 8 :026(285) [0451] the time being we have **made** this reply to the
S 1 : P R :006(289) [0457] doubted whether one ought to **make** good writings public.
S 1 : P R :007(289) [0457] promoted his work, has **made** their following smaller and
S 1 : P R :011(290) [0457] This horrifies me and **makes** me fear that he may cause a
S 2 : 0 2 :010(294) [0465] possible for the papists to **make** concessions to us in all
S 2 : 0 2 :014(295) [0467] But our papists **make** use of such human opinions to
S 2 : 0 2 :014(295) [0467] such human opinions to **make** men believe their
S 2 : 0 2 :015(295) [0467] It will not do to **make** articles of faith out of the holy
S 2 : 0 2 :018(296) [0467] not been commanded to **make** pilgrimages, nor are they
S 3 : 0 1 :001(302) [0477] disobedience all men were **made** sinners and became
S 3 : 0 2 :002(303) [0479] what they are unwilling to do, are **made** worse thereby.
S 3 : 0 2 :004(303) [0479] or power of the law is to **make** original sin manifest and
S 3 : 0 3 :012(305) [0481] repents, confesses, and **makes** satisfaction has merited
S 3 : 0 3 :013(305) [0483] my life, Lord God, until I **make** satisfaction for my sins
S 3 : 0 3 :019(306) [0483] never know when he had **made** a sufficiently complete or
S 3 : 0 3 :019(306) [0485] and the better he would **make** satisfaction for his sins, for
S 3 : 0 3 :020(306) [0485] for his consolation was **made** to rest on his enumeration
S 3 : 0 3 :027(307) [0487] year must be contrite, **make** confession, and pay money."
S 3 : 0 5 :004(311) [0493] redemption which Christ **made**, and the church should
S 3 : 0 8 :005(312) [0495] and the old serpent who **made** enthusiasts of Adam and
S 3 : 1 1 :002(314) [0499] given to us or to them to **make** a woman out of a man or
S 3 : 1 5 :003(316) [0501] If anybody wishes to **make** some concessions, let him do
S 3 : 1 5 :004(316) [0501] such ceremonies of sponsors who might **make** gifts, etc.
S 3 : 1 5 :005(316) [0501] by human right, **making** this concession for the sake of
T R : 0 0 :006(320) [0505] himself the authority to **make** laws concerning worship,
T R : 0 0 :010(321) [0505] be something," he says, "**makes** no difference to me" and
T R : 0 0 :018(323) [0509] humility of poverty that **makes** a bishop superior or
T R : 0 0 :025(324) [0511] confession which Peter **made** when he declared Jesus to
T R : 0 0 :035(326) [0513] and sometimes in order to **make** the German bishops
T R : 0 0 :040(327) [0517] church or by anybody is to **make** himself out to be God.
T R : 0 0 :056(329) [0521] deprived of the power of **making** judgments and decisions
T R : 0 0 :059(330) [0521] blasphemous opinions, **make** themselves guilty of the
T R : 0 0 :064(331) [0523] Afterwards one thing **made** a distinction between bishops
T R : 0 0 :077(333) [0527] are compelled to **make** these decisions if the bishops are
T R : 0 0 :082(000) [0529] the Sacrament, **made** at Wittenberg with Dr. Bucer and
S C : P R :007(339) [0533] with the intention of **making** improvements — later on.
S C : P R :013(339) [0535] of those among whom they live and **make** their living.
S C : P R :020(340) [0537] **Make** very plain to them the shocking evils they introduce
S C : P R :021(340) [0537] no law is to be **made** concerning it, and no time or place
S C : P R :024(341) [0539] you are not to **make** a law of this, as the pope has done.
S C : 0 2 :001(344) [0543] *God, the Father almighty,* ***maker*** *of heaven and earth."*
S C : 0 3 :013(347) [0547] petition that God may **make** us aware of his gifts and
S C : 0 4 :004(348) [0551] said, "Go therefore and **make** disciples of all nations,
S C : 0 5 :022(350) [0553] I have **made** my master angry, caused him to curse,
S C : 0 5 :025(351) [0555] confession which you **make** to God in the presence of the
S C : 0 7 :001(352) [0557] morning, when you rise, **make** the sign of the cross and
S C : 0 7 :004(353) [0559] evening, when you retire, **make** the sign of the cross and
S C : 0 8 :008(353) [0559] receive enough to eat to **make** them joyful and of good
S C : 0 9 :005(355) [0561] and thanksgivings be **made** for all men, for kings and all
S C : 0 9 :014(356) [0563] and thanksgivings be **made** for all men" (I Tim. 2:1).
L C : P R :002(358) [0567] of their bellies would **make** better swineherds or
L C : P R :009(359) [0569] daily to read it and **make** it the subject of meditation and
L C : P R :017(361) [0573] help, comfort, judge, and **make** decisions in both
L C : P R :020(361) [0573] much fruit and God will **make** excellent men of them.
L C : P R :020(361) [0573] time they themselves will **make** the noble confession that
L C : S P :011(363) [0577] in God, the Father almighty, **maker** of heaven and earth:
L C : S P :025(364) [0579] will be led into the Scriptures so they **make** progress daily
L C : 0 1 :002(365) [0581] and faith of the heart alone **make** both God and an idol.
L C : 0 1 :011(366) [0583] he feared the plague, he **made** a vow to St. Sebastian or
L C : 0 1 :012(366) [0583] those who go so far as to **make** a pact with the devil in
L C : 0 1 :018(367) [0585] Everyone **made** into a god that to which his heart was
L C : 0 1 :022(367) [0585] account how often it has **made** endowments, fasted,
L C : 0 1 :023(367) [0585] What is this but **making** God into an idol — indeed, an
L C : 0 1 :028(368) [0587] commandment above all things and not **make** light of it.
L C : 0 1 :033(369) [0589] brutes who think that it **makes** no great difference how
L C : 0 1 :047(371) [0593] in any other object; he **makes** no greater demand of us
L C : 0 1 :089(377) [0605] we Christians should **make** every day a holy day and give
L C : 0 1 :092(377) [0607] but on account of the Word which **makes** us all saints.
L C : 0 1 :094(378) [0607] which the doer himself is **made** holy; this, as we have
L C : 0 1 :117(381) [0615] trivial and contemptible, **make** sure that you regard it as
L C : 0 1 :140(384) [0621] and believe how angry he **makes** God when he neglects
L C : 0 1 :147(385) [0623] God it is really faith that **makes** a person holy; faith alone
L C : 0 1 :161(387) [0627] and to treat them well and **make** provision for them.
L C : 0 1 :166(387) [0627] to encourage us and **make** our hearts so melt for joy and
L C : 0 1 :173(388) [0629] can provide for them and **make** them rich without our
L C : 0 1 :212(394) [0641] Therefore, to **make** it easier for man to avoid unchastity
L C : 0 1 :219(394) [0643] one of the chief ways to **make** chastity attractive and
L C : 0 1 :225(395) [0643] Let us **make** it a little clearer for the common people so
L C : 0 1 :231(396) [0647] and punishment so as to **make** the others look respectable
L C : 0 1 :259(400) [0655] evidence presented, and **make** his decision accordingly.
L C : 0 1 :266(401) [0657] my neighbor sins, but to **make** him the talk of the town is
L C : 0 1 :266(401) [0657] aware of a sin, simply **make** your ears a tomb and bury it
L C : 0 1 :270(401) [0657] do not trust yourself to **make** your charges before the
L C : 0 1 :273(401) [0659] him straight to his face and **make** him blush for shame.
L C : 0 1 :274(401) [0659] Exception is **made**, however, of civil magistrates,
L C : 0 1 :274(402) [0659] physically, and yet an exception is **made** of the hangman.
L C : 0 1 :278(402) [0661] and see if they can **make** the boast that they have gained
L C : 0 1 :305(406) [0667] of a number of ways, to **make** her husband displeased
L C : 0 1 :311(407) [0669] on what we are to do to **make** our whole life pleasing to
L C : 0 1 :332(410) [0677] Everyone is to **make** them his daily habit in all
L C : 0 2 :006(411) [0679] But to **make** it most clear and simple for teaching to
L C : 0 2 :009(411) [0679] *God, the Father almighty,* ***maker*** *of heaven and earth."*
L C : 0 2 :010(412) [0679] or describe him in such a way as to **make** him known?"
L C : 0 2 :011(412) [0681] my God is the Father, who **made** heaven and earth.
L C : 0 2 :012(412) [0681] emphasize the words, "**maker** of heaven and earth."
L C : 0 2 :013(412) [0681] "I believe in God, the Father almighty, **maker**," etc.?
L C : 0 2 :014(412) [0681] Besides, he **makes** all creation help provide the comforts
L C : 0 2 :030(414) [0685] the jaws of hell, won us, **made** us free, and restored us to
L C : 0 2 :031(414) [0687] was buried that he might **make** satisfaction for me and
L C : 0 2 :035(415) [0687] Holy Spirit and his office, which is that he **makes** us holy.
L C : 0 2 :036(415) [0687] Spirit must be called Sanctifier, the One who **makes** holy.
L C : 0 2 :040(416) [0689] that the Holy Spirit **makes** me holy, as his name implies."
L C : 0 2 :043(416) [0689] our works and merits and **made** us acceptable to the
L C : 0 2 :062(419) [0695] and all evil, he will finally **make** us perfectly and eternally
L C : 0 2 :068(420) [0697] do not by themselves **make** us Christians, for God's wrath
L C : 0 2 :068(420) [0697] brings pure grace and **makes** us upright and pleasing to

Continued ▶

LC : 03 :006(421) [0699] Let no one think that it **makes** no difference whether I
LC : 03 :009(421) [0699] will go and do as I please; what difference does it **make**?"
LC : 03 :010(421) [0699] praying, as though it **made** no great difference if we do
LC : 03 :011(421) [0701] By this commandment he **makes** it clear that he will not
LC : 03 :041(425) [0709] his name to cloak lies and **make** them acceptable; this is
LC : 03 :052(427) [0711] kingdom which has now **made** its appearance among us.
LC : 03 :057(427) [0713] and a scoundrel who had **made** a mockery of his imperial
LC : 03 :062(428) [0715] out of men's hearts and a breach is **made** in his kingdom.
LC : 03 :076(431) [0719] Out of it one might **make** a long prayer, enumerating with
LC : 03 :097(433) [0725] not because I can **make** satisfaction or merit anything by
LC : 03 :097(433) [0725] hast set thy seal to it, **making** it as certain as an
LC : 03 :104(434) [0727] His purpose is to **make** us scorn and despise both the
LC : 03 :111(435) [0729] counsels, you will only **make** the matter worse and give
LC : 04 :011(437) [0735] It **makes** a much more splendid appearance when a
LC : 04 :033(440) [0741] that is, faith alone **makes** the person worthy to receive the
LC : 04 :082(446) [0751] Baptism of its value, **making** it of no further use to us.
LC : 04 :083(446) [0751] the jaws of the devil and **makes** God our own, overcomes
LC : 04 :085(446) [0753] we must practice the work that **makes** us Christians.
LC : 05 :010(448) [0755] The Word must **make** the element a sacrament; otherwise
LC : 05 :058(453) [0767] For this reason we must **make** a distinction among men.
LC : 05 :060(453) [0767] No one will **make** such progress that he does not retain
LC : 05 :075(455) [0771] bosom and ask whether they are **made** of flesh and blood.
LC : 05 :081(456) [0773] Word and blinds it, **making** you unable to feel your needs
LC : 06 :001(457) [0000] which forced everyone to **make** confession on pain of the
LC : 06 :003(457) [0000] Instead, it was **made** sheer anguish and a hellish torture
LC : 06 :003(457) [0000] since people had to **make** confession even though nothing
LC : 06 :004(457) [0000] now been removed and **made** voluntary so that we may
LC : 06 :010(458) [0000] which each Christian **makes** toward his neighbor, is
LC : 06 :015(459) [0000] and noble thing that **makes** confession so wonderful and
LC : 06 :016(459) [0000] the confession was not **made** perfectly and in complete
LC : 06 :017(459) [0000] confession was not only **made** useless to us but it also
LC : 06 :023(459) [0000] would impel him and **make** him so anxious that he would
LC : 06 :026(460) [0000] full of filthiness you are, **making** of you a mirror for
LC : 06 :026(460) [0000] miserable, then go and **make** use of the healing medicine.
EP : 01 :004(466) [0781] hands fashioned and **made** me, all that I am round
EP : 01 :005(466) [0781] Therefore he had to be **made** like his brethren in every
EP : 01 :019(468) [0783] no distinction should be **made**, even in the mind, between
EP : 02 :003(470) [0787] our trespasses, he **made** us alive together with Christ."
EP : 02 :010(471) [0789] of his own powers could **make** a beginning of his
EP : 02 :011(471) [0789] weak by his free will to **make** a beginning, convert
EP : 02 :011(471) [0789] after the Holy Spirit has **made** the beginning through the
EP : 02 :015(471) [0789] when these statements are **made** without explanation that
EP : 02 :015(471) [0789] says, in conversion God **makes** willing people out of
EP : 03 :003(473) [0793] disobedience many were **made** sinners, so by *one man's*
EP : 03 :003(473) [0793] *obedience* many will be **made** righteous" (Rom. 5:19).
EP : 03 :008(474) [0793] (rebirth) and *vivificatio* (**making** alive) are used in place
EP : 03 :015(475) [0795] of sins, but mean to be **made** righteous in fact before God
EP : 05 :010(479) [0803] — namely, to preach grace, to comfort, to **make** alive.
EP : 07 :020(484) [0813] merit of Christ, which we **make** our own through genuine
EP : 07 :042(486) [0817] many protests, in order to **make** our teaching obnoxious
EP : 08 :003(487) [0819] that the "personal union **makes** merely the names
EP : 08 :014(488) [0821] of his divine person and **made** his own, so that he could
EP : 10 :006(493) [0831] we have no concessions to **make**, but we should witness
EP : 10 :011(494) [0831] is required, one may **make** concessions to or come to an
EP : 11 :003(494) [0833] mysteries, and he has **made** known to King
EP : 12 :001(498) [0839] explanation we have **made** no mention of the errors held
SD : PR :015(506) [0857] that we shall at all times **make** a sharp distinction between
SD : PR :019(507) [0857] of divine truth might be **made** apparent in every article
SD : 01 :007(510) [0861] this corruption, God does not create and **make** sin in us.
SD : 01 :007(510) [0861] God still creates and **makes** at the present time, original
SD : 01 :027(512) [0867] way that Satan created or **made** something essentially
SD : 01 :035(514) [0869] hands fashioned and **made** me together round about, and
SD : 01 :035(514) [0869] Remember that thou hast **made** me of clay, and wilt thou
SD : 01 :036(514) [0869] David says: "I will praise thee, for I am wonderfully **made**
SD : 01 :036(514) [0869] thee when I was being **made** in secret, intricately wrought
SD : 01 :038(515) [0871] of which God forms and **makes** man has been corrupted
SD : 01 :039(515) [0871] hell-fire, but out of it he **makes** and fashions our present
SD : 01 :041(515) [0871] nature, he has created and **made** original sin, which thus
SD : 01 :043(515) [0873] in every respect he was **made** like us, his brethren, sin
SD : 02 :007(521) [0883] man by which he could **make** himself ready for the grace
SD : 02 :011(522) [0885] liberated him from the death of sin and **made** him alive.
SD : 02 :017(524) [0887] the law of my mind and **making** me captive to the law of
SD : 02 :026(526) [0891] works (Eph. 2:10); and **makes** us new creatures
SD : 02 :034(528) [0895] sin and operates to **make** man truly pure and holy."
SD : 02 :035(528) [0895] who purifies and daily **makes** man more pious and holy,
SD : 02 :038(528) [0895] words the Catechism **makes** no mention whatever of our
SD : 02 :042(529) [0897] These testimonies **make** no mention whatever of our will
SD : 02 :064(533) [0905] the law of my mind and **making** me captive to the law of
SD : 02 :067(534) [0907] — that is, as Christ says, they have again been **made** free.
SD : 02 :077(536) [0911] his free will is too weak to **make** a beginning and by its
SD : 02 :077(536) [0911] after the Holy Spirit has **made** the beginning and has
SD : 02 :088(538) [0915] of the Holy Spirit, God **makes** willing people out of
SD : 03 :010(541) [0919] accept, apply them to ourselves, and **make** them our own.
SD : 03 :013(541) [0919] be applied to us and to be **made** our own through faith if
SD : 03 :019(542) [0921] where the statement is **made**, "Justification is
SD : 03 :020(542) [0921] that is, being **made** alive, has sometimes been used in the
SD : 03 :020(542) [0921] our trespasses, he **made** us alive together with Christ"
SD : 03 :037(546) [0929] matter, or rely on them, or **make** or regard them as
SD : 03 :039(546) [0929] God, nor are they to be **made** and posited to be a part or
SD : 03 :039(546) [0929] applied to us, and **made** our own solely through faith.
SD : 03 :042(547) [0931] it applies to us and **makes** our own the merits of Christ.
SD : 03 :043(547) [0931] or, faith justifies or **makes** righteous in so far as it is
SD : 03 :046(548) [0933] by good works man must **make** himself worthy and fit to
SD : 03 :051(548) [0933] the promise of grace is **made** our own through faith in the
SD : 03 :051(548) [0933] the confession which we **make** with our mouth, and
SD : 03 :057(549) [0935] disobedience many will be **made** sinners, so by one man's
SD : 03 :057(550) [0935] obedience many will be **made** righteous" (Rom. 5:19), and
SD : 03 :062(550) [0937] of sins," but to be **made** really and truly righteous on
SD : 04 :010(552) [0941] God, kills the Old Adam, **makes** us entirely different
SD : 04 :012(553) [0941] of divine grace **makes** us joyous, mettlesome, and merry
SD : 04 :019(554) [0945] distinction which Paul **makes** when he says on the one
SD : 04 :029(555) [0947] forth from it, and were **made** matters of controversy.
SD : 05 :022(562) [0959] justification," who "was **made** sin though he knew no sin,
SD : 05 :022(562) [0959] of God," who was "**made** our righteousness," and whose
SD : 05 :027(563) [0961] would be tangled together and **made** into one doctrine.
SD : 05 :027(563) [0961] of Christ, once more **make** the Gospel a teaching of law,
SD : 05 :027(563) [0961] dangerous and wrong to **make** of the Gospel, strictly so
SD : 06 :008(565) [0965] the law of my mind and **making** me captive to the law of
SD : 07 :001(569) [0971] Confession so as to **make** it appear to be in full
SD : 07 :016(572) [0977] performed by Christ, that **makes** it valid in Christendom,
SD : 07 :021(573) [0979] Word, I say, is what **makes** this sacrament and so
SD : 07 :028(574) [0981] death some would try to **make** him suspect by giving the
SD : 07 :031(574) [0983] Let no one **make** this out to be a joke or idle talk; I am in
SD : 07 :070(582) [0997] "The power of God is **made** perfect in weakness."
SD : 07 :076(583) [0999] was crucified for us, can **make** of the bread and wine set
SD : 07 :076(583) [0999] efficacious in nature and **make** things grow and multiply,
SD : 07 :077(583) [0999] until the end of the world, **make** the bread the body and
SD : 07 :083(584) [1001] offered up, or carried about), does not **make** a sacrament.
SD : 07 :089(585) [1003] It is not our faith which **makes** the sacrament, but solely
SD : 07 :099(586) [1005] Paul says, "This will be **made** manifest at the proper time
SD : 07 :103(587) [1007] God's power is able to **make** a body be simultaneously in
SD : 07 :123(590) [1015] Therefore we reject the **making** of such a distinction
SD : 08 :015(594) [1019] from each other and thus **make** two Christs, so that
SD : 08 :019(594) [1021] of the natures, as mead is **made** out of honey and water
SD : 08 :035(597) [1027] the statements that we **make** about the person of Christ,
SD : 08 :045(600) [1031] the Son of God, who was **made** man, suffered for us,
SD : 08 :050(600) [1031] which it is in every respect **made** like his brethren, and
SD : 08 :058(602) [1035] that the power to **make** the dead alive and to execute
SD : 08 :061(602) [1035] ancient orthodox church **made** herein on the basis of
SD : 08 :064(603) [1039] no distinction would be **made** between Christ according
SD : 08 :079(607) [1045] To **make** certainty and assurance doubly sure on this
SD : 08 :096(610) [1049] blood have in Christ been **made** to sit so high at the right
SD : 09 :003(610) [1051] one, how Christ has been **made** to sit at the right hand of
SD : 11 :026(620) [1071] For he has revealed and "**made** known to us the mystery
SD : 11 :039(623) [1077] in Christ (Mark 16:16), **make** only an outward pretense
SD : 11 :055(625) [1081] of our speculations, to **make** our own deductions, draw
SD : 11 :060(626) [1083] cast them from us and **make** ourselves unworthy of
SD : 11 :079(629) [1089] devil and not of God, has **made** himself a vessel of
SD : 11 :079(629) [1089] for damnation in order to **make** known the riches of his
SD : 11 :080(629) [1089] He does not say that God **made** them vessels of wrath.
SD : 12 :002(632) [1095] that reason intended to **make** special and detailed
SD : 12 :012(634) [1099] of reason and are able to **make** their own confession of

Malady (1)
SD : 01 :012(510) [0863] since the inherited **malady** has so poisoned and tainted

Male (2)
AG : 23 :005(052) [0061] God created man as **male** and female according to Gen.
SC : 09 :010(356) [0563] Laborers and Servants, **Male** and Female

Malice (6), Malicious (5), Maliciously (6)
AG : 26 :018(067) [0073] these matters out of **malice** or contempt of spiritual
AL : 00 :004(048) [0059] for it is false and **malicious** to charge that all ceremonies
AL : 00 :004(049) [0059] as those ungodly and **malicious** men represent.
AP : 04 :260(145) [0195] the Gospel, and **maliciously** twist the Scriptures to suit
AP : 04 :274(148) [0199] here our opponents **maliciously** maintain that by such
AP : 04 :286(150) [0201] Our opponents **maliciously** twist the Scriptures to fit their
AP : 12 :124(201) [0289] God will not long endure such impudence and **malice**.
S1 : PR :006(289) [0457] venomous and **malicious** tongues and thus destroying the
LC : 01 :188(390) [0635] harbor no hostility or **malice** toward anyone in a spirit of
LC : 01 :225(395) [0645] laziness, carelessness, or **malice** a servant wastes and
LC : 01 :263(400) [0655] court and their lying and **malicious** talk outside of court.
LC : 03 :094(433) [0725] harm, violence, and injustice, bears **malice** toward us, etc.
EP : 04 :019(477) [0801] are not lost through **malicious** sin, but that the holy ones
SD : 07 :088(585) [1003] dishonestly and **maliciously** pervert this useful and
SD : 07 :119(590) [1013] have deliberately and **maliciously** falsified the words in
SD : 08 :063(603) [1037] own conscience, have **maliciously** and wickedly twisted
SD : 11 :091(631) [1093] are strengthened in their **malice**, then it is clearly evident

Malignant (1)
LC : 01 :099(378) [0609] or satiety — a **malignant**, pernicious plague with which

Maligned (1)
LC : 01 :257(399) [0653] man is accused and **maligned** by false witnesses and

Mammon (6)
LC : 01 :006(365) [0581] a man also has a god — **mammon** by name, that is, money
LC : 01 :009(365) [0583] do not fret and complain, if they do not have **mammon**.
LC : 01 :015(366) [0585] hoped to receive from **mammon** or anything else, turn to
LC : 01 :036(369) [0589] boast defiantly of their **mammon** and believe that they
LC : 01 :042(370) [0591] who trust God and not **mammon** suffer grief and want
LC : 01 :042(370) [0591] those who serve **mammon** have power, prestige, honor,

Man (643) *(See also "men" and "mankind," below.)*
PR : PR :025(014) [0023] Catechism of that highly enlightened **man**, Dr. Luther.
AG : 02 :003(029) [0045] for they hold that natural **man** is made righteous by his
AG : 03 :001(029) [0045] that God the Son became **man**, born of the virgin Mary,
AG : 03 :002(029) [0045] Christ, true God and true **man**, who was truly born,
AG : 12 :010(035) [0049] through faith but through the satisfactions made by **man**.
AG : 18 :001(039) [0051] also taught among us that **man** possesses some measure of
AG : 18 :002(039) [0051] activity of the Holy Spirit **man** is not capable of making
AG : 18 :003(039) [0051] in I Cor. 2:14, "Natural **man** does not receive the gifts of
AG : 18 :007(040) [0053] hand, by his own choice **man** can also undertake evil, as
AG : 20 :011(042) [0055] — not because of works, lest any **man** should boast," etc.
AG : 20 :034(045) [0057] is what happens when a **man** is without true faith and the
AG : 23 :004(051) [0061] to immorality, each **man** should have his own wife"
AG : 23 :005(052) [0061] of living in celibacy, and he certainly knew **man**'s nature.
AG : 23 :005(052) [0061] God created **man** as male and female according to Gen.
AG : 23 :013(053) [0063] instituted and left free to **man**) never produced any good
AG : 23 :002(053) [0063] a prudent and intelligent **man**, made this statement
AG : 24 :037(060) [0067] also indicate that one **man** officiated and communicated
AG : 25 :003(061) [0069] the voice or word of the **man** who speaks it, but it is the
AG : 26 :023(067) [0073] Christ says, "Not what goes into the mouth defiles a **man**
AG : 27 :019(074) [0079] to immorality, each **man** should have his own wife"
AG : 27 :020(074) [0079] "It is not good that the **man** should be alone; I will make
AG : 27 :024(074) [0079] such obligation, for no **man** has the right to cancel an

Continued ▶

A G : 2 7 :048(078) [0081] church, is obscured when **man**'s eyes are dazzled with this
A G : 2 7 :053(079) [0083] When the common **man** hears that only mendicants are
A L : 0 2 :003(029) [0045] by contending that **man** can be justified before God by
A L : 0 3 :001(029) [0045] the Son of God — took on **man**'s nature in the womb of
A L : 0 3 :002(029) [0045] Christ, true God and true **man**, who was born of the
A L : 1 8 :001(039) [0051] Our churches teach that **man**'s will has some liberty for
A L : 1 8 :002(039) [0051] — because natural **man** does not perceive the gifts of the
A L : 2 0 :031(045) [0057] without the Holy Spirit **man**'s powers are full of ungodly
A L : 2 0 :034(045) [0057] Such is the feebleness of **man** when he governs himself by
A L : 2 0 :037(046) [0057] or bear the cross, but it seeks and trusts in **man**'s help.
A L : 2 0 :040(046) [0057] "Where Thou art not, **man** hath naught, Nothing good in
A L : 2 3 :004(051) [0061] to immorality each **man** should have his own wife"
A L : 2 3 :005(052) [0061] because God created **man** for procreation (Gen. 1:28).
A L : 2 3 :006(052) [0061] Moreover, it is not in **man**'s power to alter his creation
A L : 2 3 :008(052) [0061] to marry, for no law of **man** and no vow can nullify a
A L : 2 3 :011(052) [0063] Paul said that a married **man** should be chosen to be
A L : 2 3 :014(053) [0063] world is growing old and **man**'s nature is becoming
A L : 2 3 :016(054) [0063] and then on account of **man**'s weakness, and it is devoutly
A L : 2 5 :008(062) [0069] also says, "The heart of **man** is corrupt and inscrutable."
A L : 2 6 :023(067) [0073] Christ says, "Not what goes into the mouth defiles a **man**
A L : 2 7 :013(073) [0077] and the like who, without **man**-made observances, serve
A L : 2 7 :019(074) [0079] "Because of fornication let every **man** have his own wife."
A L : 2 7 :020(074) [0079] Gen. 2:18, "It is not good that the **man** should be alone."
A L : 2 7 :024(074) [0079] for it is not lawful for a **man** to annul an obligation which
A L : 2 7 :028(075) [0079] to what an extent perpetual chastity lies in **man**'s power.
A P : 0 2 :003(101) [0105] explanation should be enough for any unprejudiced **man**.
A P : 0 2 :014(102) [0109] and denied to **man**'s natural powers the fear and trust of
A P : 0 2 :018(102) [0109] shows when it says that **man** was created in the image of
A P : 0 2 :018(103) [0111] was implanted in **man** that would grasp God and reflect
A P : 0 2 :018(103) [0111] reflect him, that is, that **man** received gifts like the
A P : 0 2 :021(103) [0111] is the very likeness of God which he put into **man**.
A P : 0 2 :023(103) [0111] denies the obedience of **man**'s lower powers, but also
A P : 0 2 :023(103) [0111] when we deny to natural **man** not only fear and trust of
A P : 0 2 :025(103) [0111] but the evil inclination of **man**'s higher capacities to
A P : 0 2 :025(103) [0111] attribute to **man** a concupiscence that has not been
A P : 0 2 :030(104) [0113] Cor. 2:14, "The unspiritual **man** does not receive the gifts
A P : 0 2 :033(104) [0113] All the righteousness of **man** is mere hypocrisy before
A P : 0 2 :035(105) [0115] begins to mortify lust and to create new impulses in **man**.
A P : 0 2 :037(105) [0115] words in order by this device to crush an innocent **man**.
A P : 0 2 :045(106) [0117] remnants of original sin in **man** are not in their nature
A P : 0 2 :046(106) [0117] when they teach that **man** can obey the commandments
A P : 0 4 :009(108) [0123] As long as a **man**'s mind is at rest and he does not feel
A P : 0 4 :018(109) [0125] the righteousness of faith **man** can neither have nor
A P : 0 4 :019(110) [0125] that disposition of love a **man** can earn the merit of
A P : 0 4 :030(111) [0129] he is the Saviour of **man**'s corrupted nature, for
A P : 0 4 :035(112) [0131] It is inherent in **man** to despise God and to doubt his
A P : 0 4 :037(112) [0131] up these dreams that a **man** guilty of mortal sin can love
A P : 0 4 :045(113) [0133] Therefore, when a **man** believes that his sins are forgiven
A P : 0 4 :072(117) [0141] alone makes a righteous **man** out of an unrighteous one,
A P : 0 4 :073(117) [0141] "We hold that a **man** is justified by faith apart from
A P : 0 4 :073(117) [0141] because of works, lest any **man** should boast," and again
A P : 0 4 :078(117) [0143] as making an unrighteous **man** righteous or effecting his
A P : 0 4 :087(119) [0147] discussion: "We hold that **man** is justified by faith apart
A P : 0 4 :087(120) [0147] us, we conclude that a **man** is not justified by the precepts
A P : 0 4 :092(120) [0149] God, and in Rom. 10:10, "**Man** believes with his heart
A P : 0 4 :093(120) [0149] God—not because of works, lest any **man** should boast."
A P : 0 4 :094(120) [0149] of the will of the flesh nor of the will of **man**, but of God."
A P : 0 4 :095(121) [0149] so must the Son of **man** be lifted up, that whoever
A P : 0 4 :097(121) [0149] brethren, that through this **man** forgiveness of sins is
A P : 0 4 :106(122) [0153] Only in a justified **man** is there a good work by the
A P : 0 4 :133(125) [0159] their minds; but when a **man** turns to the Lord the veil is
A P : 0 4 :154(128) [0165] outward courtesies due a guest and a great and holy **man**.
A P : 0 4 :154(128) [0165] the Pharisee, this wise and honest but unbelieving **man**.
A P : 0 4 :165(130) [0169] hard to understand how a **man** can do away with Christ,
A P : 0 4 :168(130) [0169] with thy servant; for no **man** living is righteous before
A P : 0 4 :168(130) [0169] (Ps. 32:2), "Blessed is the **man** to whom the Lord imputes
A P : 0 4 :244(141) [0189] the text, "You see that a **man** is justified by works and
A P : 0 4 :245(142) [0189] They teach that a **man** is justified by love and works but
A P : 0 4 :252(143) [0191] not mean that a wicked **man** is made righteous but that
A P : 0 4 :252(143) [0191] about James's words, "A **man** is justified by works and
A P : 0 4 :260(145) [0195] the Scriptures to suit the **man**-made theory that by our
A P : 0 4 :270(147) [0197] But a **man** keeps the law as soon as he hears that God is
A P : 0 4 :292(152) [0203] stated, we teach that a **man** is justified when, with his
A P : 0 4 :305(154) [0205] mean "to absolve a guilty **man** and pronounce him
A P : 0 4 :306(154) [0207] judicial investigation of a **man**'s own righteousness, which
A P : 0 4 :317(156) [0209] says (Gal. 2:17) that if a **man** justified in Christ must then
A P : 0 4 :326(157) [0211] with thy servant, for no **man** living is righteous before
A P : 0 4 :326(157) [0211] denies any glory in **man**'s righteousness, even to all the
A P : 0 4 :361(162) [0219] as when a monk's hood is placed on a dead **man**.
A P : 0 4 :370(164) [0221] "He will render to every **man** according to his works"; and
A P : 0 4 :373(164) [0221] "He will render to every **man** according to his works," we
A P : 0 4 :373(164) [0221] for him who does good," namely, for the righteous **man**.
A P : 0 4 :375(164) [0223] No sane **man** can judge otherwise.
A P : 0 4 :383(166) [0225] Paul says (Rom. 10:10), "**Man** believes with his heart and
A P : 1 2 :073(192) [0273] apostle concludes, that a **man** is justified freely by faith."
A P : 1 2 :078(193) [0275] with thy servant; for no **man** living is righteous before
A P : 1 2 :085(194) [0277] Gospel, to imagine that a **man** is justified by the law
A P : 1 2 :123(200) [0289] What good **man** would not be moved by such dishonesty?
A P : 1 2 :129(202) [0291] As a wise **man** you can easily imagine what will happen if
A P : 1 2 :142(204) [0295] fixed a certain limit which **man** is bound to observe,
A P : 1 2 :159(207) [0301] in the case of the blind **man**, Christ replied that the reason
A P : 1 2 :161(208) [0303] so as not to prevent the **man** from obtaining eternal life,
A P : 1 2 :161(208) [0303] physical death on **man** because of sin, and even after the
A P : 1 2 :162(208) [0303] the calamities common to **man** — that is, the performance
A P : 1 2 :169(209) [0305] as long as he unjustly holds on to another **man**'s property
A P : 1 3 :023(214) [0313] is familiar (Rom. 10:10), "**Man** believes with his heart and
A P : 1 5 :012(216) [0317] "No one adds even to a **man**'s covenant."
A P : 1 8 :006(225) [0335] it is false to say that a **man** does not sin if, outside the
A P : 1 8 :007(226) [0337] (I Cor. 2:14), "The natural **man**," that is, the man who
A P : 1 8 :007(226) [0337] natural man," that is, the **man** who uses only his natural
A P : 2 0 :012(228) [0341] we could say to a **man** who was sentenced to die and then
A P : 2 1 :024(232) [0349] take refuge in the help of the saints," as this **man** says?
A P : 2 1 :026(232) [0349] prayer upon the dying **man**, "Mother of grace, protect us
A P : 2 2 :002(236) [0357] If it is illegal to annul a **man**'s testament, it is much more
A P : 2 2 :003(236) [0359] Later on he says, "Let a **man** examine himself, and so eat
A P : 2 2 :011(238) [0361] Look at the great effrontery of the **man**.
A P : 2 3 :003(239) [0363] appears about you, "A **man** with a modest face will reign
A P : 2 3 :006(240) [0365] only the judgment of any honest and God-fearing **man**.
A P : 2 3 :008(240) [0367] can change the nature of **man** without an extraordinary
A P : 2 3 :009(240) [0367] or divine ordinance in **man** is a natural right, the jurists
A P : 2 3 :009(240) [0367] correctly that the union of **man** and woman is by natural
A P : 2 3 :011(241) [0367] the jurists: The union of **man** and woman is by natural
A P : 2 3 :014(241) [0367] to immorality, each **man** should have his own wife."
A P : 2 3 :016(241) [0369] Ever since **man** sinned, natural desire and the lust that
A P : 2 3 :017(242) [0369] of immorality, each **man** should have his own wife,"
A P : 2 3 :017(242) [0369] It is up to each **man**'s conscience to decide this matter.
A P : 2 3 :023(242) [0371] "What God has joined together, let no **man** put asunder."
A P : 2 3 :035(244) [0373] of heart in a married **man** like Abraham or Jacob than in
A P : 2 3 :040(245) [0375] Cor. 7:32), "The unmarried **man** is anxious about the
A P : 2 3 :060(247) [0381] No sane **man** can argue with these cogent facts.
A P : 2 3 :063(248) [0381] commanding each **man** to have his own wife because of
A P : 2 4 :059(260) [0405] by the transfer of one **man**'s work to another *ex opere*
A P : 2 7 :001(269) [0419] that he was a mild old **man**, serious but not morose.
A P : 2 7 :038(275) [0433] his conversation with the **man** he did not hear anything,
A P : 2 7 :050(277) [0437] perfection for this young **man** to believe and obey this
A P : 2 7 :051(278) [0437] to immorality, each **man** should have his own wife."
A P : 2 8 :007(282) [0445] "What goes into the mouth does not defile a **man**."
S 1 : 0 1 :000(291) [0461] That only the Son became **man**, and neither the Father
S 1 : 0 1 :000(291) [0461] 4. That the Son became **man** in this manner: he was
S 1 : 0 1 :000(291) [0461] without the cooperation of **man**, and was born of the
S 2 : 0 1 :004(292) [0461] 3, "For we hold that a **man** is justified by faith apart from
S 2 : 0 2 :012(295) [0465] Christ alone, and not the work of **man**, can help souls.
S 2 : 0 4 :008(300) [0473] God would raise up a **man** fitted for such an office.
S 3 : 0 1 :001(302) [0477] sin had its origin in one **man**, Adam, through whose
S 3 : 0 1 :004(302) [0477] the natural powers of **man** have remained whole and
S 3 : 0 1 :004(302) [0477] and uncorrupted, and that **man** by nature possesses a
S 3 : 0 1 :005(302) [0477] 2. Again, that **man** has a free will, either to do good and
S 3 : 0 1 :006(302) [0477] 3. Again, that **man** is able by his natural powers to
S 3 : 0 1 :007(302) [0477] 4. Again, that **man** is able by his natural powers to love
S 3 : 0 1 :008(302) [0477] 5. Again, if **man** does what he can, God is certain to
S 3 : 0 1 :009(302) [0477] 6. Again, when a **man** goes to the sacrament there is no
S 3 : 0 1 :009(302) [0477] such is the goodness of **man**'s nature and such is the
S 3 : 0 1 :011(303) [0479] be no defect or sin in **man** for which he would have had
S 3 : 0 2 :001(303) [0479] because of the wickedness which sin has worked in **man**.
S 3 : 0 2 :004(303) [0479] sin manifest and show **man** to what utter depths his
S 3 : 0 3 :003(304) [0481] Here **man** must hear such a judgment as this: "You are
S 3 : 0 3 :007(304) [0481] only death and hell, and **man** must despair like Saul and
S 3 : 0 3 :010(305) [0481] that the natural powers of **man** have remained whole and
S 3 : 0 3 :010(305) [0481] grant his grace to the **man** who does as much as he can
S 3 : 0 3 :011(305) [0481] and wicked works which **man** with his free will might
S 3 : 0 3 :012(305) [0481] added consolation that a **man** who properly repents,
S 3 : 0 3 :018(306) [0483] imaginary idea evolved by **man**'s own powers without
S 3 : 0 3 :019(306) [0483] pardoned only when a **man** remembered them and
S 3 : 0 3 :020(306) [0485] A **man** did not become aware of the power of absolution,
S 3 : 0 3 :021(306) [0485] that was still lacking **man** was referred to purgatory.
S 3 : 0 3 :023(306) [0485] confidence was placed in **man**'s own works of
S 3 : 0 3 :032(308) [0487] No **man** can be just before God without him.
S 3 : 0 3 :034(309) [0489] He says "all men," that is, excepting no one who is a **man**.
S 3 : 0 3 :040(309) [0489] that remain and enables **man** to become truly pure and
S 3 : 0 6 :005(311) [0493] and again, "Let a **man** so eat of the bread" (I Cor. 11:28).
S 3 : 0 7 :002(312) [0493] with thy servant, for no **man** living is righteous before
S 3 : 0 8 :002(312) [0495] not be untruthful if we say, "I am a poor **man**, full of sin.
S 3 : 0 8 :009(313) [0497] and inoculated in **man** by the old dragon, and it is the
S 3 : 0 8 :013(313) [0497] by the impulse of **man** but were moved by the Holy
S 3 : 1 1 :002(314) [0499] make a woman out of a **man** or a man out of a woman or
S 3 : 1 1 :002(314) [0499] woman out of a man or a **man** out of a woman or abolish
S 3 : 1 3 :000(315) [0499] XIII. How **Man** Is Justified Before God, and His Good
S 3 : 1 3 :002(315) [0499] The whole **man**, in respect both of his person and of his
T R : 0 0 :025(324) [0511] built on the authority of a **man** but on the ministry of the
T R : 0 0 :028(325) [0511] built his church not on the **man** but on the faith of Peter;
T R : 0 0 :039(327) [0515] nations, and he calls that **man** "an adversary of Christ"
T R : 0 0 :062(330) [0523] Jerome observes: "One **man** was chosen over the rest to
T R : 0 0 :082(000) [0529] I ask you, most renowned **man**, Dr. John Bugenhagen,
S C : P R :019(340) [0537] of the world and are the worst enemies of God and **man**.
S C : 0 2 :004(345) [0545] eternity, and also true **man**, born of the virgin Mary, is
S C : 0 4 :012(349) [0551] to death, and that the new **man** should come forth daily
S C : 0 8 :010(354) [0559] pleasure in the legs of a **man**; but the Lord takes pleasure
L C : S P :010(363) [0577] shall not covet his wife, **man**-servant, maid-servant,
L C : S P :017(363) [0577] he should dismiss **man**-servants and maid-servants if they
L C : 0 1 :006(365) [0581] Surely such a **man** also has a god — mammon by name,
L C : 0 1 :013(366) [0583] It requires that **man**'s whole heart and confidence be
L C : 0 1 :026(368) [0587] of fruits from the earth for **man**'s nourishment — things
L C : 0 1 :031(369) [0589] the utmost importance for a **man** to have the right head.
L C : 0 1 :041(370) [0591] be careful not to regard this as if it were spoken by **man**.
L C : 0 1 :045(370) [0593] by God, and an upright **man**; but once he was secure on
L C : 0 1 :046(370) [0593] was a poor, despised **man**, hunted down and persecuted,
L C : 0 1 :059(372) [0597] Nor **man** is so arrogant as to boast before the whole
L C : 0 1 :080(375) [0603] and to rest, so that both **man** and beast might be
L C : 0 1 :083(376) [0603] the common people — **man**-servants and maid-servants
L C : 0 1 :142(384) [0621] he must have domestics (**man**-servants and
L C : 0 1 :143(385) [0621] Therefore **man**-servants and maid-servants should take
L C : 0 1 :150(385) [0623] In this case a **man** is father not of a single family, but of
L C : 0 1 :152(386) [0625] Let us see, though, whether you are the **man** to defy him.
L C : 0 1 :160(387) [0627] be "the refuse of the world, and every **man**'s offscouring."
L C : 0 1 :193(391) [0635] that we should allow no **man** to suffer harm, but show to
L C : 0 1 :207(393) [0639] and he created **man** and woman differently (as is evident)
L C : 0 1 :212(394) [0641] to make it easier for **man** to avoid unchastity in some
L C : 0 1 :224(395) [0643] not only when he robs a **man**'s strongbox or his pocket,
L C : 0 1 :225(395) [0643] for example, that a **man**-servant or maid-servant is
L C : 0 1 :247(398) [0651] If, when you meet a poor **man** who must live from hand
L C : 0 1 :247(398) [0651] Such a **man**'s sighs and cries will be no joking matter.
L C : 0 1 :256(399) [0653] he would have every **man** maintain his self-respect before
L C : 0 1 :257(399) [0653] where a poor, innocent **man** is accused and maligned by
L C : 0 1 :258(399) [0653] Consequently, a poor **man** is inevitably oppressed, loses
L C : 0 1 :259(400) [0653] ought, above all, to be a **man** of integrity, and not only
L C : 0 1 :259(400) [0653] but also a wise, sagacious, brave, and fearless **man**.

Continued ▶

LC : 0 1 :259(400) [0653] be fearless; more than that, he should be an upright **man**.
LC : 0 1 :270(401) [0657] act like a knave, for no **man** should be deprived of his
LC : 0 1 :273(401) [0659] would bring some poor **man** into disgrace, from which he
LC : 0 1 :276(402) [0659] to go and reprove the **man** personally, otherwise to hold
LC : 0 1 :291(404) [0663] There is nothing about a **man** or in a man that can do
LC : 0 1 :291(404) [0663] about a man or in a **man** that can do greater good or
LC : 0 1 :292(404) [0663] *shall not covet his wife, **man**-servant, maid-servant,*
LC : 0 1 :294(404) [0665] the Jewish government **man**-servants and maid-servants
LC : 0 1 :295(404) [0665] Moreover, every **man** had power to dismiss his wife
LC : 0 1 :303(406) [0667] profit — let us say, when a **man** because of adversity or
LC : 0 1 :303(406) [0667] first served," and "Every **man** must look out for himself
LC : 0 1 :305(406) [0667] knew tricks like this: If a **man** took a fancy to another
LC : 0 1 :305(406) [0667] was obliged to dismiss her and leave her to the other **man**.
LC : 0 1 :305(406) [0669] posed as an honorable, upright **man**, as St. Mark testifies.
LC : 0 1 :306(406) [0669] to lure away another's **man**-servant or maid-servant or
LC : 0 1 :315(408) [0671] life for the ordinary **man**, whereas theirs is for the saints
LC : 0 1 :316(408) [0671] blind people, that no **man** can achieve so much as to keep
LC : 0 1 :317(408) [0673] and still clings to every **man**, and that all classes of men
LC : 0 1 :317(408) [0673] is a heavenly, angelic **man**, far above all holiness on
LC : 0 1 :324(409) [0675] Wherever a **man**'s heart has such an attitude toward
LC : 0 1 :328(410) [0677] and occasion to do so and no **man** may reprove you.
LC : 0 2 :031(414) [0687] That is to say, he became **man**, conceived and born
LC : 0 2 :036(415) [0687] such as the spirit of **man**, heavenly spirits, and the evil
LC : 0 3 :115(435) [0731] He breaks many a **man**'s neck and drives others to
LC : 0 4 :006(437) [0733] are not spun out of any **man**'s imagination but revealed
LC : 0 4 :010(437) [0735] of much greater value than the work of any **man** or saint.
LC : 0 4 :010(437) [0735] For what work can **man** do that is greater than God's
LC : 0 4 :020(439) [0737] mother," I see another **man**, adorned and clothed with the
LC : 0 4 :043(442) [0743] is brought free to every **man**'s door just such a priceless
LC : 0 4 :050(443) [0745] to the present day no **man** on earth could have been a
LC : 0 4 :060(444) [0747] and Word cannot be changed or altered by **man**.
LC : 0 4 :065(445) [0749] resurrection of the new **man**, both of which actions must
LC : 0 4 :065(445) [0749] that whatever belongs to the new **man** may come forth.
LC : 0 4 :066(445) [0749] What is the old **man**?
LC : 0 4 :068(445) [0749] not take place but the old **man** is given free rein and
LC : 0 4 :070(445) [0749] If a year ago a **man** was proud and greedy, this year he is
LC : 0 4 :071(445) [0749] The old **man** therefore follows unchecked the inclinations
LC : 0 4 :071(445) [0749] become Christians, the old **man** daily decreases until he is
LC : 0 4 :075(445) [0751] earnest attack on the old **man** and an entering upon a new
LC : 0 4 :076(446) [0751] power to suppress the old **man** so that the new may come
LC : 0 4 :077(446) [0751] access to it so that we may again subdue the old **man**.
LC : 0 4 :083(446) [0751] daily strengthens the new **man**, always remains until we
LC : 0 4 :084(446) [0753] be suppressing the old **man** and growing up in the new.
LC : 0 5 :004(447) [0753] Lord's Supper was not invented or devised by any **man**.
LC : 0 5 :004(447) [0755] by Christ without **man**'s counsel or deliberation.
LC : 0 5 :023(449) [0757] the soul since it nourishes and strengthens the new **man**.
LC : 0 5 :026(449) [0759] him and attack the old **man**, and when he cannot rout us
LC : 0 5 :059(453) [0767] Hilary has said, "Unless a **man** has committed such a sin
LC : 0 6 :011(458) [0000] the proverb says, "If one **man** is upright, so are they all";
LC : 0 6 :014(458) [0000] God's Word that through a **man** God looses and absolves
LC : 0 6 :015(459) [0000] of my sins through a word placed in the mouth of a **man**.
LC : 0 6 :023(459) [0000] A **man**'s own conscience would impel him and make him
LC : 0 6 :031(460) [0000] We compel no **man**, but allow ourselves to be compelled,
EP : 0 1 :001(466) [0779] distinction, original sin is **man**'s corrupted nature,
EP : 0 1 :001(466) [0779] after the Fall, between **man**'s substance, nature, essence,
EP : 0 1 :001(466) [0779] on the other hand, so that **man**'s nature is one thing and
EP : 0 1 :002(466) [0779] is a distinction between **man**'s nature and original sin, not
EP : 0 1 :002(466) [0779] when God created **man** pure and holy and without sin,
EP : 0 1 :008(467) [0781] has survived in **man**'s body or soul, in his inward or
EP : 0 1 :008(467) [0781] "Through Adam's fall **man**'s nature and essence are all
EP : 0 1 :012(467) [0783] sin on account of which **man** outside of Christ is a child
EP : 0 1 :013(467) [0783] error which asserts that **man**'s nature is uncorrupted even
EP : 0 1 :014(468) [0783] and that underneath **man**'s nature has retained
EP : 0 1 :015(468) [0783] an external impediment to **man**'s good spiritual powers
EP : 0 1 :016(468) [0783] nature and essence in **man** is not entirely corrupted, but
EP : 0 1 :016(468) [0783] corrupted, but that **man** still has something good about
EP : 0 1 :018(468) [0783] that it is not the natural **man** himself who commits sin
EP : 0 1 :018(468) [0783] and alien within **man**, and that therefore not the nature
EP : 0 1 :018(468) [0783] not the nature of **man** but only the original sin which is in
EP : 0 1 :019(468) [0783] any distinction corrupted **man**'s substance, nature, and
EP : 0 1 :019(468) [0783] even in the mind, between **man**'s nature itself after the
EP : 0 1 :020(468) [0783] without any distinction **man**'s nature, person, or essence
EP : 0 1 :021(468) [0783] sin is not a sin which **man** commits; it inheres in the
EP : 0 1 :021(468) [0783] substance, and essence of **man** in such a way that even if
EP : 0 1 :021(468) [0783] in the heart of corrupted **man**, no idle word were spoken,
EP : 0 1 :021(468) [0785] took place, nevertheless **man**'s nature is corrupted
EP : 0 1 :021(469) [0785] and "The imagination of **man**'s heart is evil from his
EP : 0 1 :022(469) [0785] Sometimes the term means **man**'s essence, as when we
EP : 0 1 :022(469) [0785] the nature or quality of a **man** to sin," or, "Man's nature
EP : 0 1 :022(469) [0785] or quality of a man to sin," or, "**Man**'s nature is sin."
EP : 0 1 :022(469) [0785] not mean the substance of **man** but something which
EP : 0 1 :023(469) [0785] and, besides, they are unknown to the common **man**.
EP : 0 2 :001(469) [0785] The will of **man** may be discussed in four different states:
EP : 0 2 :001(469) [0785] revolves exclusively about **man**'s will and ability in the
EP : 0 2 :001(469) [0785] is, What powers does **man** possess in spiritual matters
EP : 0 2 :001(469) [0785] Can **man** by his own powers, before he is reborn through
EP : 0 2 :002(470) [0787] that in spiritual matters **man**'s understanding and reason
EP : 0 2 :002(470) [0787] Cor. 2:14, "The unspiritual **man** does not receive the gifts
EP : 0 2 :003(470) [0787] teach, and confess that **man**'s unregenerated will is not
EP : 0 2 :003(470) [0787] "The imagination of **man**'s heart is evil from his youth."
EP : 0 2 :003(470) [0787] earthly life, so little can **man** who through sin is
EP : 0 2 :004(470) [0787] of the Holy Spirit, for **man**'s conversion is the Spirit's
EP : 0 2 :008(471) [0789] not happen otherwise, that **man** always acts only under
EP : 0 2 :009(471) [0789] grace of the Holy Spirit, **man** can convert himself to
EP : 0 2 :010(471) [0789] who teach that **man** by virtue of his own powers could
EP : 0 2 :011(471) [0789] while before his conversion **man** is indeed too weak by
EP : 0 2 :011(471) [0789] in it has offered his grace, **man**'s will is forthwith able by
EP : 0 2 :012(471) [0789] that after his conversion **man** is able to keep the law of
EP : 0 2 :015(471) [0789] without explanation that **man**'s will before, in, and after
EP : 0 2 :016(472) [0789] who is willing," or, "**Man**'s will is not idle in conversion,
EP : 0 2 :017(472) [0791] the reborn will of **man** is not idle but cooperates in all the
EP : 0 2 :018(472) [0791] Luther's statement that **man**'s will in conversion behaves
EP : 0 2 :018(472) [0791] sacraments takes hold of **man**'s will and works the new
EP : 0 2 :018(472) [0791] this and the will of **man** has been changed and renewed
EP : 0 2 :018(472) [0791] *God's power and activity,* **man**'s new will becomes an
EP : 0 2 :018(472) [0791] the Holy Spirit, so that **man** not only lays hold on grace
EP : 0 2 :019(472) [0791] Prior to **man**'s conversion there are only two efficient
EP : 0 2 :019(472) [0791] **Man** should hear this Word, though he cannot give it
EP : 0 3 :001(472) [0791] He is truly God and **man** since in him the divine and
EP : 0 3 :003(473) [0793] which as God and **man** he rendered to his heavenly
EP : 0 3 :003(473) [0793] is written, "For as by one **man**'s disobedience many were
EP : 0 3 :003(473) [0793] made sinners, so by *one **man**'s obedience* many will be
EP : 0 3 :008(474) [0793] refer to the renovation of **man** and distinguish it from
EP : 0 4 :007(476) [0799] discussion of the article of **man**'s salvation as well as from
EP : 0 4 :007(476) [0799] pertains only to the **man** to whom God reckons
EP : 0 4 :007(476) [0799] because of works, lest any **man** should boast"
EP : 0 5 :005(478) [0801] that teaches what a **man** who has not kept the law and is
EP : 0 5 :005(478) [0803] for all guilt and without **man**'s merit has obtained and
EP : 0 6 :007(481) [0807] rests exclusively with **man**, for the unregenerated man —
EP : 0 6 :007(481) [0807] man, for the unregenerated **man** — just like the
EP : 0 7 :008(482) [0811] teach, and confess that no **man**'s work nor the recitation
EP : 0 7 :011(483) [0811] complete God and **man** in one person, inseparable and
EP : 0 8 :003(487) [0819] so that God is called **man** and a man is called God, but
EP : 0 8 :003(487) [0819] God is called man and a **man** is called God, but that God
EP : 0 8 :005(487) [0819] and the other the Son of **man**, but a single individual is
EP : 0 8 :005(487) [0819] Son of God and the Son of **man** (Luke 1:35; Rom. 9:5).
EP : 0 8 :009(487) [0819] is the highest communion which God truly has with **man**.
EP : 0 8 :009(488) [0819] divine that is said or believed about Christ the **man**.
EP : 0 8 :009(488) [0819] iron and the union of body and soul in **man**.
EP : 0 8 :010(488) [0819] and confess that God is **man** and man is God, which
EP : 0 8 :010(488) [0819] that God is man and **man** is God, which could not be the
EP : 0 8 :011(488) [0821] For how could the **man**, Mary's son, truly be called or be
EP : 0 8 :012(488) [0821] a plain, ordinary, mere **man** but the veritable Son of
EP : 0 8 :013(488) [0821] a plain, ordinary, mere **man** who for us suffered, died,
EP : 0 8 :013(488) [0821] power of God, but a **man** whose human nature has such a
EP : 0 8 :015(488) [0821] confess that the Son of **man** according to his human
EP : 0 8 :016(489) [0821] only as God, but also as **man**, he knows all things, can do
EP : 0 8 :018(489) [0823] to all eternity, God and **man** in one indivisible person.
EP : 0 8 :020(490) [0823] 1. That in Christ God and **man** are not one person, but
EP : 0 8 :020(490) [0823] one person and the Son of **man** another, as Nestorius
EP : 0 8 :025(490) [0823] when we say "God is **man**, man is God," since really (that
EP : 0 8 :025(490) [0823] when we say "God is man, **man** is God," since really (that
EP : 0 8 :026(490) [0823] of the world or that the Son of **man** has become almighty.
EP : 1 1 :004(495) [0833] of this is the devil and **man**'s wicked and perverse will.
EP : 1 1 :004(495) [0833] Neither is it the cause of **man**'s perdition; for this man
EP : 1 1 :004(495) [0833] of man's perdition; for this **man** himself is responsible.
EP : 1 2 :021(499) [0841] such a way that Christ as **man** is fully equal in rank and
SD : PR :005(504) [0851] ministry of that illustrious **man** of God, Dr. Luther.
SD : 0 1 :001(508) [0859] One side contended that "**man**'s nature and essence are
SD : 0 1 :001(508) [0859] and essence of fallen **man**, at least the foremost and
SD : 0 1 :001(508) [0859] whatsoever between **man**'s nature or essence and original
SD : 0 1 :002(508) [0859] strictly speaking, is not **man**'s nature, substance, or
SD : 0 1 :002(508) [0859] or essence (that is, **man**'s body or soul), which even after
SD : 0 1 :002(508) [0859] sin is something in **man**'s nature, in his body, soul, and
SD : 0 1 :002(508) [0859] thereof, in the sense that **man** lacks the righteousness in
SD : 0 1 :002(509) [0859] and essence of fallen **man** (that is, between his body and
SD : 0 1 :002(509) [0859] work of the devil by which **man**'s nature has become
SD : 0 1 :003(509) [0861] his work and creation in **man** from the devil's work, the
SD : 0 1 :006(509) [0861] that even though a **man** were to think no evil, speak no
SD : 0 1 :006(509) [0861] in this life — nevertheless **man**'s nature and person would
SD : 0 1 :006(509) [0861] of the fall of the first **man**, our nature or person is under
SD : 0 1 :007(510) [0861] Satan's scheme, "by one **man** sin (which is the work of the
SD : 0 1 :010(510) [0863] of God according to which **man** was originally created in
SD : 0 1 :011(510) [0863] the lost image of God in **man** with a deep, wicked,
SD : 0 1 :011(510) [0863] As a result, since the Fall **man** inherits an inborn wicked
SD : 0 1 :012(510) [0863] which are subject to reason **man** still possesses a measure
SD : 0 1 :014(511) [0863] and renovation can heal **man**'s nature, which original sin
SD : 0 1 :018(511) [0865] but concreated and essential attributes of **man**'s nature.
SD : 0 1 :022(512) [0865] deprivation or absence of **man**'s spiritual good powers,
SD : 0 1 :023(512) [0865] who teach that, though **man**'s nature has been greatly
SD : 0 1 :023(512) [0865] it, "Through Adam's fall **man**'s nature and being are
SD : 0 1 :023(512) [0865] nature has of and from **man**'s natural birth something
SD : 0 1 :025(512) [0867] God's Word teaches that **man**'s corrupted nature can of
SD : 0 1 :026(512) [0867] something essential) into **man**'s nature, as when poison is
SD : 0 1 :027(512) [0867] the case of Adam and Eve **man**'s nature was originally
SD : 0 1 :027(513) [0867] judgment and verdict **man** lost the concreated
SD : 0 1 :028(513) [0867] the seed from which **man** is formed is sinful and
SD : 0 1 :028(513) [0867] within or apart from **man**'s corrupted nature, just as it is
SD : 0 1 :028(513) [0867] the proper essence, body, or soul of **man** or man himself.
SD : 0 1 :028(513) [0867] the proper essence, body, or soul of man or **man** himself.
SD : 0 1 :029(513) [0867] other in such a way that **man**'s nature is allegedly pure,
SD : 0 1 :030(513) [0867] it is not the corrupted **man** himself who sins because of
SD : 0 1 :030(513) [0867] foreign something within **man**, so that God by his law
SD : 0 1 :030(513) [0867] not accuse and condemn **man**'s nature, corrupted by sin,
SD : 0 1 :031(513) [0869] accuses and condemns **man**'s entire corrupted nature
SD : 0 1 :033(514) [0869] poisoned and corrupted **man**'s whole nature that within
SD : 0 1 :033(514) [0869] the essence of corrupted **man**, our body and soul or man
SD : 0 1 :033(514) [0869] man, our body and soul or **man** himself created by God
SD : 0 1 :033(514) [0869] nature, essence, or total **man** is corrupted, dwells) are not
SD : 0 1 :033(514) [0869] sin (which dwells in **man**'s nature or essence and corrupts
SD : 0 1 :038(514) [0871] even after the Fall God is **man**'s creator who creates body
SD : 0 1 :038(514) [0871] Therefore the corrupted **man** cannot be identified
SD : 0 1 :038(515) [0871] God forms and makes **man** has been corrupted and
SD : 0 1 :042(515) [0871] creature and handiwork in **man** from the devil's work, we
SD : 0 1 :042(515) [0871] is by God's creation that **man** has a body and soul;
SD : 0 1 :042(515) [0871] that it is God's work that **man** is able to think, to speak,
SD : 0 1 :044(516) [0873] or essence of corrupted **man** and original sin, it would
SD : 0 1 :045(516) [0873] that God cleanses **man** from sin, purifies him, and
SD : 0 1 :045(516) [0873] cannot be identified with **man** himself, since God receives
SD : 0 1 :045(516) [0873] himself, since God receives **man** for Christ's sake into his
SD : 0 1 :048(516) [0875] very nature of corrupted **man**, its substance, its essence,
SD : 0 1 :048(517) [0875] the nature or substance of **man**, which is corrupted by
SD : 0 1 :048(517) [0875] sin, and the sin by and through which **man** is corrupted.
SD : 0 1 :051(517) [0875] statement, "God creates **man**'s nature," the word "nature"
SD : 0 1 :051(517) [0875] the word "nature" means **man**'s essence, body and soul.
SD : 0 1 :051(517) [0875] that sin and sinning are **man**'s disposition and nature.

Continued ▶

SD : 0 1 :052(517) [0875] person or subject (that is, **man** himself with the body and
SD : 0 1 :052(517) [0875] because through sin **man** is corrupted, poisoned, and
SD : 0 1 :053(517) [0877] person, and essence of **man** is wholly corrupted though
SD : 0 1 :054(517) [0877] since they are not the common **man**'s vocabulary.
SD : 0 1 :055(518) [0877] statement, "Original sin is the nature or essence of **man**."
SD : 0 1 :056(518) [0877] Original sin is not **man**'s nature itself, but an accidental
SD : 0 1 :060(519) [0879] that through original sin **man** is in God's sight spiritually
SD : 0 2 :002(520) [0881] **Man** with his free will can be found and viewed as being
SD : 0 2 :002(520) [0881] not concerning the state of **man**'s will before the Fall, nor
SD : 0 2 :002(520) [0881] before the Fall, nor what **man** after the Fall and prior to
SD : 0 2 :002(520) [0881] temporal life, nor what **man** can do in spiritual things
SD : 0 2 :002(520) [0881] and rules him, nor what **man**'s free will is going to be like
SD : 0 2 :002(520) [0881] what the unregenerated **man**'s intellect and will can do in
SD : 0 2 :002(520) [0881] Can **man** prepare himself for such grace, accept it and
SD : 0 2 :003(520) [0881] the gift of the Holy Spirit **man** is unable to fulfill the
SD : 0 2 :003(520) [0881] to fear and to love him, **man** nevertheless still has so
SD : 0 2 :004(520) [0881] taught that God converts **man** through the Holy Spirit
SD : 0 2 :005(521) [0881] fall of our first parents **man** is so corrupted that in divine
SD : 0 2 :007(521) [0883] and will of unregenerated **man** cannot by any native or
SD : 0 2 :007(521) [0883] or cooperate, but that **man** is entirely and completely
SD : 0 2 :007(521) [0883] has remained or exists in **man** by which he could make
SD : 0 2 :009(521) [0883] the first place, although **man**'s reason or natural intellect
SD : 0 2 :010(522) [0883] Cor. 2:14, "The unspiritual **man** does not receive the gifts
SD : 0 2 :010(522) [0885] Scripture calls the natural **man** simply "darkness" in
SD : 0 2 :010(522) [0885] Scripture teaches that the **man** who is "in sin" is not only
SD : 0 2 :011(522) [0885] life, so little can a **man** who is spiritually dead, in sin,
SD : 0 2 :012(522) [0885] and will of the natural **man** every capacity, aptitude,
SD : 0 2 :012(522) [0885] "The unspiritual **man** does not receive (or, as the Greek
SD : 0 2 :013(523) [0885] on the flesh (the natural **man**'s understanding) "is hostile
SD : 0 2 :017(523) [0887] a natural, unregenerated **man** is not only totally turned
SD : 0 2 :017(523) [0887] Again, that **man** is not only weak, impotent, incapable,
SD : 0 2 :017(524) [0887] "The imagination of **man**'s heart is evil from his youth"
SD : 0 2 :017(524) [0887] "The heart of **man** is deceitful and desperately wicked,"
SD : 0 2 :018(524) [0887] regeneration, the will of **man** prior to his conversion will
SD : 0 2 :018(524) [0889] powers can do nothing for **man**'s conversion,
SD : 0 2 :019(524) [0889] heart of unregenerated **man** to a hard stone which resists
SD : 0 2 :019(524) [0889] animal — not that **man** since the Fall is no longer a
SD : 0 2 :020(524) [0889] and needs of the body, **man** is indeed very clever,
SD : 0 2 :020(525) [0889] the salvation of his soul, **man** is like a pillar of salt, like
SD : 0 2 :021(525) [0889] nor heart, inasmuch as **man** does not see or recognize the
SD : 0 2 :021(525) [0889] converts, and regenerates **man**, a destiny for which only
SD : 0 2 :022(525) [0889] a destiny for which only **man**, no stone or log, was
SD : 0 2 :024(525) [0891] But before **man** is illuminated, converted, reborn,
SD : 0 2 :030(527) [0893] the contrary, it declares that **man** is the captive of Satan.
SD : 0 2 :030(527) [0893] being the case, how can **man** by his own powers turn to
SD : 0 2 :032(527) [0893] does not ascribe to **man**'s will any ability either to initiate
SD : 0 2 :033(527) [0893] concerning free will: "That **man** has a free will to do good
SD : 0 2 :034(528) [0895] sin and operates to make **man** truly pure and holy."
SD : 0 2 :035(528) [0895] purifies and daily makes **man** more pious and holy, to the
SD : 0 2 :044(529) [0897] that blind and captive **man** performs only the devil's will
SD : 0 2 :044(529) [0897] cooperation on the part of our will in **man**'s conversion.
SD : 0 2 :044(529) [0897] God himself must draw **man** and give him new birth.
SD : 0 2 :044(529) [0897] the enslaved will of **man** against Erasmus and carefully
SD : 0 2 :045(530) [0899] that unregenerated **man** still has enough powers to want
SD : 0 2 :048(530) [0901] the Word of God how **man** is converted to God, how and
SD : 0 2 :053(531) [0903] above, even after the Fall **man** still has something of a
SD : 0 2 :054(531) [0903] our hearts, and draws **man**, so that through the preaching
SD : 0 2 :054(531) [0903] the preaching of the law **man** learns to know his sins and
SD : 0 2 :055(532) [0903] his grace and gives what **man** is unable by his own
SD : 0 2 :059(532) [0905] case it is correct to say that **man** is not a stone or a block.
SD : 0 2 :059(532) [0905] is being done to it, as a **man** does who with his will resists
SD : 0 2 :059(532) [0905] prior to his conversion **man** is still a rational creature with
SD : 0 2 :060(533) [0905] him in such a way that **man**'s darkened reason becomes
SD : 0 2 :061(533) [0905] that before his conversion **man** has a mode of acting in
SD : 0 2 :061(533) [0905] Prior to his conversion **man** is dead in sin (Eph. 2:5);
SD : 0 2 :062(533) [0905] how God operates in **man**, it is correct to say that the
SD : 0 2 :062(533) [0905] has one mode of acting in **man** as a rational creature and
SD : 0 2 :062(533) [0905] one cannot ascribe to **man** prior to his conversion any
SD : 0 2 :063(533) [0905] But after a **man** is converted, and thereby enlightened,
SD : 0 2 :063(533) [0905] as he is reborn or a new **man**, and he delights in the law
SD : 0 2 :064(533) [0905] because the converted **man** spontaneously does that which
SD : 0 2 :066(534) [0907] than that the converted **man** does good, as much and as
SD : 0 2 :066(534) [0907] his gracious hand **man** could not remain in obedience to
SD : 0 2 :066(534) [0907] as though the converted **man** cooperates alongside the
SD : 0 2 :071(535) [0909] things in us, from where **man** acquires these things, and
SD : 0 2 :071(535) [0909] doctrine answers this way: **Man**'s natural powers cannot
SD : 0 2 :073(535) [0909] Confession: Whether **man** before, in, or after his
SD : 0 2 :073(535) [0909] Whether **man** in his conversion behaves and is like a
SD : 0 2 :073(535) [0909] God forcibly compels a **man** to be converted against his
SD : 0 2 :074(535) [0909] happen as it does; that **man** acts only under coercion;
SD : 0 2 :074(535) [0909] even in external works **man**'s will has no freedom or
SD : 0 2 :074(536) [0909] vices; or that the will of **man** is coerced into doing such
SD : 0 2 :076(536) [0911] that by his natural powers **man** can start out toward that
SD : 0 2 :076(536) [0911] and that thereupon, since **man** is too weak to complete it,
SD : 0 2 :076(536) [0911] of the good work which **man** began by his natural
SD : 0 2 :077(536) [0911] that in spiritual things **man** is not wholly dead toward
SD : 0 2 :078(536) [0911] grace does not come from **man**'s own natural powers but
SD : 0 2 :079(536) [0911] and the monks that **man** after his conversion can keep the
SD : 0 2 :080(536) [0911] sacraments, God draws **man** to himself, illuminates,
SD : 0 2 :081(537) [0911] a new heart and a new **man** in such a way that the
SD : 0 2 :081(537) [0911] words, "Put off the old **man**," as follows: "Lest anyone
SD : 0 2 :081(537) [0911] substance or essence of **man** must be laid aside, he
SD : 0 2 :081(537) [0911] it means to lay off the old **man** and put on the new man
SD : 0 2 :081(537) [0911] man and put on the new **man** by adding, 'Therefore lay
SD : 0 2 :081(537) [0913] this is laying off the old **man** and putting on the new
SD : 0 2 :081(537) [0913] is laying off the old man and putting on the new **man**."
SD : 0 2 :082(537) [0913] without explanation: that **man**'s will before, in, and after
SD : 0 2 :083(537) [0913] will, and heart, when **man** in no way believes the promise
SD : 0 2 :083(537) [0913] will, and heart of **man** whereby man through such
SD : 0 2 :083(537) [0913] and heart of man whereby **man** through such working of
SD : 0 2 :085(537) [0913] Hence the unregenerated **man** resists God entirely and is
SD : 0 2 :085(537) [0913] But the regenerated **man** delights in the law of God
SD : 0 2 :086(537) [0913] The formulas, "**Man**'s will is not idle in conversion but
SD : 0 2 :086(538) [0913] to support the view that **man**'s naturally free will
SD : 0 2 :086(538) [0913] be avoided in the discussion of **man**'s conversion to God.
SD : 0 2 :088(538) [0915] that after such conversion **man**'s reborn will is not idle in
SD : 0 2 :089(538) [0915] when Luther says that **man** behaves in a purely passive
SD : 0 2 :089(538) [0915] conversion (that is, that **man** does not do anything toward
SD : 0 2 :089(538) [0915] toward it and that **man** only suffers that which God
SD : 0 2 :089(538) [0915] is his understanding that **man** of himself or by his natural
SD : 0 2 :089(538) [0915] his conversion, and that **man**'s conversion is not only in
SD : 0 2 :089(538) [0915] through the Word in the intellect, will, and heart of **man**.
SD : 0 2 :089(538) [0915] **Man** is, as it were, the subject which suffers.
SD : 0 2 :089(538) [0915] That is, **man** does or works nothing; he only suffers —
SD : 0 2 :090(538) [0915] causes of unregenerated **man**'s conversion to God,
SD : 0 2 :090(538) [0915] and heard, the Holy Spirit, and **man**'s will) concur.
SD : 0 2 :090(539) [0915] The unconverted **man**'s intellect and will are only that
SD : 0 2 :090(539) [0915] the intellect and will of a **man** who is spiritually dead, in
SD : 0 3 :004(540) [0917] both natures; as God and **man** he has by his perfect
SD : 0 3 :012(541) [0919] mediator, or that "one **man**'s act of righteousness leads to
SD : 0 3 :015(541) [0919] Since Christ is not only **man**, but God and man in one
SD : 0 3 :015(541) [0919] only man, but God and **man** in one undivided person, he
SD : 0 3 :046(548) [0933] 2. That by good works **man** must make himself worthy
SD : 0 3 :052(548) [0933] when it is taught that **man** is saved in a different way or
SD : 0 3 :053(548) [0933] salvation belongs to that **man** to whom God reckons
SD : 0 3 :055(549) [0935] of Christ, who as God and **man** in his sole, total, and
SD : 0 3 :056(549) [0935] of God had not become **man**, the divine nature alone
SD : 0 3 :057(549) [0935] is written, "For as by one **man**'s disobedience many will
SD : 0 3 :057(550) [0935] be made sinners, so by one **man**'s obedience many will be
SD : 0 3 :058(550) [0937] of the person who is God and **man** at the same time.
SD : 0 4 :011(553) [0941] good works is a faithless **man**, blindly tapping around in
SD : 0 4 :012(553) [0941] without any coercion a **man** is willing and desirous to do
SD : 0 4 :024(555) [0945] of salvation solely to the **man** to whom God reckons
SD : 0 5 :007(559) [0953] as the entire conversion of **man**, as in Luke 13:5, "Unless
SD : 0 5 :010(559) [0955] law by external works, or drives **man** utterly to despair.
SD : 0 5 :010(560) [0955] "When a **man** turns to the Lord, the veil is removed"
SD : 0 5 :012(560) [0955] wrath of God and terrifies **man**, it is not yet the Gospel
SD : 0 5 :017(561) [0957] will of God, shows how **man** ought to be disposed in his
SD : 0 5 :020(561) [0959] which teaches what a **man** should believe in order to
SD : 0 5 :020(561) [0959] of sins from God, since **man** has failed to keep the law of
SD : 0 5 :023(562) [0959] themselves not only how **man** in the beginning was
SD : 0 6 :003(564) [0963] according to the inner **man** do the will of God from a free
SD : 0 6 :004(564) [0963] is written, "Blessed is the **man** whose delight is in the law
SD : 0 6 :005(564) [0963] hearts, just as the first **man** immediately after his creation
SD : 0 6 :005(564) [0963] for according to the inner **man** they delight in the law of
SD : 0 6 :015(566) [0967] of God according to which **man** is to conduct himself in
SD : 0 6 :016(566) [0967] calls the works of such a **man** "works of the law" in the
SD : 0 6 :020(567) [0969] "You shall not do every **man** whatever is right in his own
SD : 0 6 :021(567) [0969] with thy servant; for no **man** living is righteous before
SD : 0 6 :024(568) [0971] sin is put off entirely and **man** is completely renewed in
SD : 0 7 :028(574) [0981] this highly enlightened **man** foresaw in the Spirit that
SD : 0 7 :032(574) [0983] It does not rest on **man**'s faith or unbelief but on the
SD : 0 7 :043(576) [0987] He is not a mere **man** or an angel; he is not only truthful,
SD : 0 7 :062(581) [0995] Christ, true God and **man**, together with all the benefits
SD : 0 7 :070(582) [0997] Likewise, "As for a **man** who is weak in faith, welcome
SD : 0 7 :074(583) [0999] among ourselves: No **man**'s word or work, be it the merit
SD : 0 7 :094(586) [1005] true, complete God and **man** in one person, undivided
SD : 0 7 :124(591) [1015] in true faith alone but also in **man**'s own preparation.
SD : 0 7 :126(591) [1015] himself, true God and **man**, who is truly and essentially
SD : 0 8 :006(592) [1017] eternity, and also a true **man**, born of the most blessed
SD : 0 8 :011(593) [1019] has assumed flesh and has become **man**, is not complete.
SD : 0 8 :013(594) [1019] womb and became **man** and when the divine and human
SD : 0 8 :016(594) [1021] Lord Christ was a mere **man** in whom the Word of God
SD : 0 8 :019(595) [1021] and communion God is **man** and man is God but without
SD : 0 8 :019(595) [1021] God is man and **man** is God but without thereby blending
SD : 0 8 :025(596) [1023] died not just like another **man** but in such a way that by
SD : 0 8 :027(596) [1025] only as God but also as **man**, from sea to sea and to the
SD : 0 8 :034(597) [1027] in such a way that God and **man** are a single person!
SD : 0 8 :036(598) [1027] simultaneously God and **man** (whether he is called God
SD : 0 8 :036(598) [1027] (whether he is called God or whether he is called **man**).
SD : 0 8 :043(599) [1029] Lord Christ as God and **man** in one person, neither
SD : 0 8 :044(599) [1029] that God died for us, but only a **man** died, we are lost.
SD : 0 8 :044(599) [1031] unless he had become a **man** like us, so that it could be
SD : 0 8 :044(599) [1031] die, but since God and **man** are united in one person, it is
SD : 0 8 :044(599) [1031] God's death when that **man** dies who is one thing or one
SD : 0 8 :045(600) [1031] of God, who was made **man**, suffered for us, died, and
SD : 0 8 :055(601) [1033] and communicated to the **man** Christ (John 5:21, 27;
SD : 0 8 :058(602) [1035] because he is the Son of **Man** and inasmuch as he has
SD : 0 8 :059(602) [1035] the person of the Son of **Man**, but expressly points to his
SD : 0 8 :067(604) [1039] the person of the Son of **Man** only according to his divine
SD : 0 8 :070(604) [1039] no other creature, whether **man** or angel, can or should
SD : 0 8 :073(605) [1041] such a manner that as **man** he therefore knows and can
SD : 0 8 :074(606) [1043] and power, so that as a **man**, through the personal union,
SD : 0 8 :076(606) [1043] flesh, whence only this **man** and no other human being in
SD : 0 8 :078(606) [1043] the majesty of the **man** Christ, which Christ received
SD : 0 8 :081(607) [1045] of Christ: "Since he is a **man** like this — and apart from
SD : 0 8 :081(607) [1045] this — and apart from this **man** there is no God — it must
SD : 0 8 :082(607) [1045] mother's womb naturally and personally and become **man**
SD : 0 8 :082(607) [1045] he is, then he must be **man** there, too, since he is not two
SD : 0 8 :082(607) [1045] then you must also say, 'Christ the **man** is present too.'
SD : 0 8 :082(607) [1045] where God is and not the **man**, then the person is already
SD : 0 8 :082(607) [1045] 'Here is God who is not **man** and has never become
SD : 0 8 :082(607) [1045] is God who is not man and has never become **man**.'
SD : 0 8 :085(608) [1047] united in one person this **man**, Mary's son, is and is called
SD : 0 8 :085(608) [1047] Father before I became **man**, but when I became man I
SD : 0 8 :085(608) [1047] man, but when I became **man** I received it in time
SD : 0 8 :087(608) [1047] them, but that he, he, the **man** who has spoken with
SD : 0 9 :002(610) [1051] entire person, God and **man**, descended into hell,
SD : 1 1 :041(623) [1077] God's foreknowledge but **man**'s own perverse will, which
SD : 1 1 :063(626) [1083] and say, "Who are you, a **man**, to answer back to God?"
SD : 1 1 :075(628) [1087] him, as it is written, "If a **man** divorces his wife and she
SD : 1 1 :075(628) [1087] him and becomes another **man**'s wife, may he receive her
SD : 1 1 :079(629) [1089] work of the devil and of **man**, who, through the
SD : 1 1 :080(629) [1089] The devil and **man** himself, and not God, are the cause of
SD : 1 1 :081(629) [1089] which prepares and fits **man** for damnation emanates
SD : 1 1 :081(629) [1089] from the devil and **man** through sin, and in no way from

Continued ▶

SD : 1 1 :081(629) [1089] God does not want any **man** to be damned, how could he
SD : 1 1 :081(629) [1089] to be damned, how could he prepare **man** for damnation?
SD : 1 1 :081(629) [1089] The only cause of **man**'s damnation is sin, for the "wages

Men (533)
PR : PR :023(012) [0021] particularly that the young **men** who are being trained for
AG : 0 2 :001(029) [0043] since the fall of Adam all **men** who are born according to
AG : 0 2 :001(029) [0043] That is, all **men** are full of evil lust and inclinations from
AG : 0 7 :003(032) [0047] ceremonies, instituted by **men**, should be observed
AG : 0 8 :001(033) [0047] them are wicked **men**, for as Christ himself indicated,
AG : 1 5 :001(036) [0049] have been established by **men**, it is taught among us that
AG : 1 5 :003(036) [0049] traditions instituted by **men** for the purpose of
AG : 1 6 :007(038) [0051] sin, we must obey God rather than **men** (Acts 5:29).
AG : 1 7 :003(038) [0051] but to condemn ungodly **men** and the devil to hell and
AG : 1 7 :004(038) [0051] the devil and condemned **men** will not suffer eternal pain
AG : 1 7 :005(039) [0051] the dead, saints and godly **men** will possess a worldly
AG : 1 8 :004(039) [0051] "We concede that all **men** have a free will, for all have a
AG : 1 9 :000(040) [0053] sin is caused in all wicked **men** and despisers of God by
AG : 1 9 :000(041) [0053] devil and of all ungodly **men**; as soon as God withdraws
AG : 2 0 :022(044) [0055] to apply it in order that **men** may know that the grace of
AG : 2 0 :025(044) [0057] it such knowledge as the devil and ungodly **men** possess.
AG : 2 1 :002(047) [0057] mediator between God and **Men**, Christ Jesus"
AG : 2 3 :005(051) [0061] in Matt. 19:11, "Not all **men** can receive this precept," he
AG : 2 3 :014(053) [0063] is growing worse and **men** are becoming weaker and more
AG : 2 3 :018(054) [0063] vice that even some honest **men** among the cathedral
AG : 2 4 :010(057) [0065] by learned and devout **men** even before our time.
AG : 2 4 :023(058) [0067] the performance of which **men** expected to get everything
AG : 2 6 :001(063) [0071] In former times **men** taught, preached, and wrote that
AG : 2 6 :001(064) [0071] had been instituted by **men** serve to earn grace and make
AG : 2 6 :022(067) [0073] teaching as doctrines the precepts of **men**" (Matt. 15:9).
AG : 2 7 :007(071) [0077] convents than in those of **men**, though it would have been
AG : 2 7 :023(074) [0079] Learned **men** say that a vow made contrary to papal
AG : 2 7 :024(074) [0079] dispensed and released **men** from such obligation, for no
AG : 2 7 :026(075) [0079] dispensations be granted for necessities of **men**'s souls!
AG : 2 7 :029(075) [0079] and there are few, whether **men** or women, who have
AG : 2 7 :036(076) [0081] chosen and instituted by **men** to obtain righteousness and
AG : 2 7 :036(077) [0081] worship me, teaching as doctrines the precepts of **men**."
AG : 2 7 :037(077) [0081] and services invented by **men** but that righteousness and
AG : 2 7 :048(078) [0081] of God, invented by **men** without the command of God,
AG : 2 7 :048(078) [0081] such a service would make **men** good and righteous
AG : 2 7 :056(080) [0083] are also recorded of **men** who forsook wife and child, and
AG : 2 7 :057(080) [0083] given and not by keeping the commands invented by **men**.
AG : 2 7 :061(080) [0083] they justify and render **men** righteous before God, that
AG : 2 8 :042(088) [0089] on Christendom to ensnare **men**'s consciences?
AG : 2 8 :046(088) [0089] myths or to commands of **men** who reject the truth.
AG : 2 8 :052(089) [0091] we do not merit it by services of God instituted by **men**.
AG : 2 8 :053(090) [0091] sins, nor in order to bind **men**'s consciences by
AG : 2 8 :069(093) [0093] retain the obedience of **men** if they did not insist on the
AG : 2 8 :074(094) [0093] regulations devised by **men** have with the passing of time
AG : 2 8 :075(094) [0095] rule which commands us to obey God rather than **men**.
AL : 0 2 :001(029) [0043] since the fall of Adam all **men** who are propagated
AL : 0 3 :003(030) [0045] only for original guilt but also for all actual sins of **men**.
AL : 0 4 :001(030) [0045] churches also teach that **men** cannot be justified before
AL : 0 5 :004(031) [0045] the Holy Spirit comes to **men** without the external Word,
AL : 0 7 :003(032) [0047] ceremonies, instituted by **men**, should be alike
AL : 0 8 :001(033) [0047] are administered by evil **men**, according to the saying of
AL : 0 8 :002(033) [0047] of Christ even if they are administered by evil **men**.
AL : 0 8 :003(033) [0047] that the ministry of evil **men** may be used in the church
AL : 0 8 :003(033) [0047] the ministry of evil **men** to be unprofitable and without
AL : 1 3 :001(035) [0049] marks of profession among **men** but especially to be signs
AL : 1 5 :002(036) [0049] Nevertheless, **men** are admonished not to burden
AL : 1 6 :007(038) [0051] then they ought to obey God rather than **men** (Acts 5:29).
AL : 1 7 :003(038) [0051] endless joy, but ungodly **men** and devils he will condemn
AL : 1 7 :004(038) [0051] an end to the punishments of condemned **men** and devils.
AL : 1 8 :004(039) [0051] "We concede that all **men** have a free will which enables
AL : 1 9 :000(041) [0053] will of the wicked, that is, of the devil and ungodly **men**.
AL : 2 0 :015(043) [0055] despised by inexperienced **men**, God-fearing and anxious
AL : 2 0 :015(043) [0055] because the consciences of **men** cannot be pacified by any
AL : 2 0 :018(043) [0055] and profane **men**, who dream that Christian
AL : 2 0 :023(044) [0055] **Men** are also admonished that here the term "faith" does
AL : 2 0 :025(044) [0057] for devils and ungodly **men** are not able to believe this
AL : 2 0 :032(045) [0057] of the devil, who impels **men** to various sins, impious
AL : 0 0 :002(049) [0059] people in order to inflame the hatred of **men** against us.
AL : 0 0 :003(049) [0059] exciting the minds of good **men**, they first gave occasion
AL : 0 0 :004(049) [0059] as those ungodly and malicious **men** represent.
AL : 2 3 :005(051) [0061] place, Christ said, "Not all **men** can receive this precept"
AL : 2 3 :005(051) [0061] which he declared that all **men** are not suited for celibacy
AL : 2 3 :010(052) [0061] that in the ancient church priests were married **men**.
AL : 2 3 :021(055) [0063] But now **men**, and even priests, are cruelly put to death,
AL : 2 4 :010(057) [0065] complaint by all good **men** that Masses were being
AL : 2 4 :011(057) [0065] by what manner of **men** Masses are celebrated only for
AL : 2 4 :018(058) [0067] many centuries by the very **men** who were able to correct
AL : 2 6 :002(064) [0071] instituted, and the learned **men** in the churches exacted
AL : 2 6 :011(065) [0071] the observances of such **men** were more pleasing to God.
AL : 2 6 :012(065) [0071] keep all traditions, and yet **men** judged these observances
AL : 2 6 :020(067) [0073] cannot be understood if **men** suppose that they merit
AL : 2 6 :022(067) [0073] "In vain do they worship me with the precepts of **men**."
AL : 2 6 :041(069) [0075] At the same time **men** are warned that such observances
AL : 2 6 :045(070) [0075] piety toward God and good conversation among **men**."
AL : 2 7 :007(071) [0077] more than in those of **men**, although more consideration
AL : 2 7 :008(071) [0077] displeased many good **men** before our time when they saw
AL : 2 7 :013(072) [0077] Thus they made **men** believe that the monastic profession
AL : 2 7 :036(076) [0081] instituted and chosen by **men** to merit justification and
AL : 2 7 :036(077) [0081] "In vain do they worship me with the precepts of **men**."
AL : 2 7 :037(077) [0081] and services devised by **men** but that it comes through
AL : 2 7 :040(077) [0081] As the canon says, no vow ought to bind **men** to iniquity.
AL : 2 7 :046(078) [0081] all this, they persuaded **men** that their invented
AL : 2 7 :048(078) [0081] certain service invented by **men** without the command of
AL : 2 7 :048(078) [0081] of God and to teach that such service justifies **men**.
AL : 2 7 :048(078) [0081] obscured when the eyes of **men** are blinded by these
AL : 2 7 :049(078) [0083] of God are obscured when **men** hear that only monks are
AL : 2 7 :056(080) [0083] Cases can be read of **men** who, forsaking marriage and
AL : 2 7 :057(080) [0083] given and not by keeping the commands invented by **men**.
AL : 2 7 :059(080) [0083] Concerning such things it was necessary to admonish **men**
AL : 2 8 :003(081) [0085] been rebuked in the church by devout and learned **men**.
AL : 2 8 :011(082) [0085] harm, and constrains **men** with the sword and physical
AL : 2 8 :032(086) [0087] apostles who commanded **men** to abstain from blood and
AL : 2 8 :046(088) [0089] myths or to commands of **men** who reject the truth."
AL : 2 8 :052(089) [0091] certain observances or acts of worship instituted by **men**.
AL : 2 8 :060(091) [0091] the additional reason that **men** would have an example of
AL : 2 8 :068(093) [0093] even if the usage of **men** changes in such matters.
AL : 2 8 :069(093) [0093] the lawful obedience of **men** if they did not insist on the
AL : 2 8 :075(094) [0095] which commands us to obey God rather than **men**.
AP : PR :018(099) [0103] Many good **men** have testified publicly and thanked God
AP : 0 2 :002(100) [0105] But to show all good **men** that our teaching on this point
AP : 0 2 :002(100) [0105] since the fall of Adam all **men** who are born according to
AP : 0 2 :002(100) [0105] That is, all **men** are full of evil lusts and inclinations from
AP : 0 2 :012(102) [0109] They taught that **men** are justified before God by
AP : 0 2 :034(104) [0113] said in my consternation, **men** are all liars," that is, they
AP : 0 2 :043(106) [0117] Pious **men** have confessed to these things, as the Psalms
AP : 0 2 :051(107) [0119] we shall not lack **men** to reply in defense of the truth, for
AP : 0 4 :001(107) [0119] us for teaching that **men** do not receive the forgiveness of
AP : 0 4 :001(107) [0121] us both for denying that **men** receive the forgiveness of
AP : 0 4 :001(107) [0121] and for affirming that **men** receive the forgiveness of sins
AP : 0 4 :009(108) [0123] way the scholastics teach **men** to merit the forgiveness of
AP : 0 4 :010(108) [0123] this view naturally flatters **men**, it has produced and
AP : 0 4 :013(109) [0123] us for teaching that **men** ought to seek some
AP : 0 4 :018(109) [0125] Thus they bury Christ; **men** should not use him as
AP : 0 4 :020(110) [0125] is the invention of idle **men** who do not know how the
AP : 0 4 :020(110) [0125] is there, because **men** naturally trust their own
AP : 0 4 :026(110) [0127] It is false, too, that **men** are accounted righteous before
AP : 0 4 :028(111) [0129] a reproach to Christ, that **men** who keep the
AP : 0 4 :035(112) [0131] Therefore **men** really sin even when they do virtuous
AP : 0 4 :036(112) [0131] opponents to write that **men** who are under eternal wrath
AP : 0 4 :037(112) [0131] It is easy enough for idle **men** to make up these dreams
AP : 0 4 :038(112) [0131] not say that by the law **men** merit the forgiveness of sins.
AP : 0 4 :038(112) [0131] is an error, therefore, for **men** to trust that by the law and
AP : 0 4 :040(112) [0131] Therefore **men** cannot keep the law by their own
AP : 0 4 :048(113) [0135] as Paul says so often, **men** are justified, because those
AP : 0 4 :060(115) [0137] disparage faith and teach **men** to deal with God only by
AP : 0 4 :062(115) [0139] Gospel declares that all **men** are under sin and are worthy
AP : 0 4 :072(117) [0141] means to make unrighteous **men** righteous or to
AP : 0 4 :085(119) [0147] So pious **men** should not let themselves be diverted from
AP : 0 4 :098(121) [0149] under heaven given among **men** by which we must be
AP : 0 4 :100(121) [0151] the writer says first that **men** are righteous by the faith
AP : 0 4 :103(121) [0151] since it has made all **men** sinners, but when the Lord
AP : 0 4 :103(122) [0151] Jesus came he forgave all **men** the sin that none could
AP : 0 4 :103(122) [0151] faith therefore that frees **men** through the blood of
AP : 0 4 :110(123) [0153] For **men** can neither render nor understand this love
AP : 0 4 :117(123) [0155] unrighteous we are made righteous and regenerated **men**.
AP : 0 4 :119(123) [0155] Our opponents give **men** bad advice when they bid them
AP : 0 4 :135(125) [0159] care, but supposes that **men** are born and die by chance.
AP : 0 4 :139(126) [0161] "He led captivity captive and gave gifts to **men**."
AP : 0 4 :170(130) [0169] in trouble it looks to **men** for help; it even defies God's
AP : 0 4 :179(131) [0171] is, the law condemns all **men**, but by undergoing the
AP : 0 4 :189(133) [0175] to keep the Gospel among **men**, he visibly pits the witness
AP : 0 4 :193(133) [0175] the outward administration of Christ's rule among **men**.
AP : 0 4 :204(135) [0177] the glory of Christ when **men** offer these works to God as
AP : 0 4 :212(136) [0179] pacify the conscience, **men** constantly choose other
AP : 0 4 :216(137) [0179] we deal with God, not with **men**, and by which we take
AP : 0 4 :224(138) [0181] which we deal with **men** and not specifically with God.
AP : 0 4 :226(138) [0183] with God, while love has infinite external duties to **men**.
AP : 0 4 :231(139) [0183] they argue that love justifies since it makes **men** perfect.
AP : 0 4 :231(139) [0183] If it is love that makes **men** perfect, Christ, the
AP : 0 4 :232(139) [0185] preserve tranquility unless **men** cover and forgive certain
AP : 0 4 :236(140) [0185] priests and other good **men** if they even intimate their
AP : 0 4 :252(143) [0191] not by faith alone," for **men** who have faith and good
AP : 0 4 :256(144) [0193] Secondly, though **men** can at most do certain outward
AP : 0 4 :265(146) [0197] by nature to the minds of **men**, and it cannot be driven
AP : 0 4 :272(148) [0199] Matt. 6:14, "If you forgive **men** their trespasses, your
AP : 0 4 :280(149) [0201] But our opponents, clever **men** that they are, pick out
AP : 0 4 :284(150) [0201] all the works of love), then **men** are completely clean,
AP : 0 4 :288(151) [0203] according to them, is that **men** merit grace by good works
AP : 0 4 :288(151) [0203] if it does good, but when **men** are in great peril they add
AP : 0 4 :288(151) [0203] Later on **men** thought up monastic orders, which
AP : 0 4 :290(151) [0203] any warrant it teaches that **men** come to God through
AP : 0 4 :299(153) [0205] brighter when we teach **men** to make use of him as
AP : 0 4 :300(153) [0205] Let all good **men** beware, therefore, of yielding to their
AP : 0 4 :321(157) [0209] very distinction — that **men** sometimes acquire the merit
AP : 0 4 :322(157) [0209] he says, "Woe to the life of **men**, however praiseworthy, if
AP : 0 4 :332(158) [0211] if indeed these profane **men** ever ask God for anything!
AP : 0 4 :332(158) [0211] in Luke 18:11 who says, "I am not like other **men**."
AP : 0 4 :343(160) [0217] which intelligent **men** can easily judge when they are
AP : 0 4 :368(163) [0221] Since **men** are accepted because of faith, this incipient
AP : 0 4 :387(166) [0225] Those who deny that **men** are justified by faith deny that
AP : 0 4 :388(166) [0225] These will be easy for good **men** to evaluate if they
AP : 0 4 :389(166) [0225] may be, we hope that good **men** will find it useful for
AP : 0 4 :393(167) [0225] of faith taught that **men** were reconciled to God and
AP : 0 4 :393(167) [0225] By nature **men** judge that God ought to be appeased by
AP : 0 4 :399(168) [0227] they have hitherto shown toward many godly **men**.
AP : 0 7 :003(168) [0227] that we separate evil **men** and hypocrites from the
AP : 0 7 :003(168) [0227] the sacraments which evil **men** or hypocrites administer.
AP : 0 7 :003(169) [0227] life the hypocrites and evil **men** are mingled with the
AP : 0 7 :003(169) [0227] are administered by evil **men**; indeed, we may legitimately
AP : 0 7 :003(169) [0227] use sacraments that are administered by evil **men**.
AP : 0 7 :005(169) [0227] association of faith and of the Holy Spirit in **men**'s hearts.
AP : 0 7 :010(170) [0229] It is, rather, made up of **men** scattered throughout the
AP : 0 7 :012(170) [0231] Hypocrites and evil **men** are indeed associated with the
AP : 0 7 :013(170) [0231] good and the wicked, then **men** would not understand
AP : 0 7 :019(171) [0233] under a crowd of wicked **men** so that this stumbling block
AP : 0 7 :019(171) [0233] are efficacious even when wicked **men** administer them.
AP : 0 7 :019(171) [0233] that though these wicked **men** participate in the outward
AP : 0 7 :020(171) [0233] believers and righteous **men** scattered throughout the
AP : 0 7 :021(172) [0233] our opponents teach that **men** merit the forgiveness of
AP : 0 7 :022(172) [0233] church is not made up of **men** by reason of their power or
AP : 0 7 :023(172) [0235] excuse and exempt **men** from any laws, divine, canonical,

Continued ▶

AP : 0 7 :028(173) [0237] many hypocrites and evil **men** who are mingled with them
AP : 0 7 :028(173) [0237] administered by unworthy **men**, this does not rob them of
AP : 0 7 :029(173) [0237] who believed that **men** sinned if they received the
AP : 0 7 :029(173) [0237] the sacraments from unworthy **men** in the church.
AP : 0 7 :030(174) [0237] ceremonies, instituted by **men**, should be alike
AP : 0 7 :033(174) [0239] in rites instituted by **men**, although we like it when
AP : 0 7 :034(175) [0239] before him, it follows that **men** can be righteous, children
AP : 0 7 :036(175) [0241] of the heart is a spiritual thing that quickens **men**'s hearts.
AP : 0 7 :041(176) [0241] right, it was unlawful for **men** to assume the right to
AP : 0 7 :046(177) [0243] But see what religious **men** our opponents are!
AP : 0 7 :047(177) [0243] that hypocrites and evil **men** have been mingled with the
AP : 0 7 :047(177) [0243] efficacious even when evil **men** administer them, for
AP : 0 9 :002(178) [0245] Baptism is offered to all — **men**, women, children, and
AP : 1 1 :002(180) [0249] highest praise of all good **men**, since it discloses a sure
AP : 1 1 :006(181) [0251] in confession we teach **men** in such a way as not to
AP : 1 1 :007(181) [0251] terrors made no impression on wild and profane **men**.
AP : 1 2 :003(182) [0253] All good **men** will see that especially on this issue we have
AP : 1 2 :004(183) [0253] All good **men** of all classes, even the theologians, admit
AP : 1 2 :008(183) [0255] did not Saul, Judas, and **men** like them attain grace even
AP : 1 2 :010(184) [0255] Here we appeal to the judgment of all good and wise **men**.
AP : 1 2 :016(184) [0257] All good **men** will understand, therefore, that good and
AP : 1 2 :029(186) [0259] eternal life, and to lead us as regenerated **men** to do good.
AP : 1 2 :032(186) [0259] against sin, unknown to **men** who walk in carnal security.
AP : 1 2 :034(186) [0261] these sorrows and terrors **men** merit grace if they love
AP : 1 2 :034(186) [0261] Yet how will **men** love God amid such real terrors when
AP : 1 2 :034(186) [0261] when amid such terrors they show **men** only the law?
AP : 1 2 :048(188) [0265] Wicked and smug **men** do not say this seriously, for they
AP : 1 2 :053(189) [0265] two chief works of God in **men**, to terrify and to justify
AP : 1 2 :059(190) [0267] our statement that **men** obtain the forgiveness of sins by
AP : 1 2 :067(191) [0271] the sword, and that good **men** who hold this faith be put
AP : 1 2 :067(192) [0271] what sort of church it is that is made up of such **men**.
AP : 1 2 :076(193) [0273] We, on the contrary, call **men**'s consciences away from
AP : 1 2 :077(193) [0275] reasons for declaring that **men** are justified by faith and
AP : 1 2 :078(193) [0275] opponents' doctrine that **men** obtain the forgiveness of
AP : 1 2 :081(194) [0275] That is, all **men** are under sin, and they cannot be freed in
AP : 1 2 :087(195) [0277] why we said above that **men** are justified by faith and not
AP : 1 2 :090(195) [0279] are happy to have all good **men** judge and decide whether
AP : 1 2 :098(197) [0281] Good **men** can easily judge the great importance of
AP : 1 2 :106(197) [0283] and not outward conduct, and "flocks" means **men**.
AP : 1 2 :106(197) [0283] is a neat one, worthy of these **men** who despise grammar.
AP : 1 2 :110(198) [0285] is useful to instruct **men** better, still it must be controlled,
AP : 1 2 :114(199) [0285] practices or such works **men** merit the forgiveness of sins.
AP : 1 2 :123(201) [0289] tricks they try to alienate **men**'s minds and fan their
AP : 1 2 :124(201) [0289] We hope that among good **men** these slanders will not
AP : 1 2 :124(201) [0289] whose learning and faith **men** could have had greater
AP : 1 2 :125(201) [0289] she should take care that **men** of learning and integrity do
AP : 1 2 :127(201) [0289] **Men** are demanding instruction in religion.
AP : 1 2 :128(201) [0291] There are many good **men** to whom such doubt is worse
AP : 1 2 :128(201) [0291] the doctrinal doubts of good **men** are mere petty anxiety.
AP : 1 2 :129(202) [0291] about the judgments of **men** and the silent desires of all
AP : 1 2 :129(202) [0291] all nations to yourself; for **men** of discretion will value
AP : 1 2 :132(202) [0293] even when they come from **men** in mortal sin.
AP : 1 2 :140(204) [0295] commanded but the vain works that **men** have devised.
AP : 1 2 :142(204) [0295] Here are **men** who imagine that we can keep the law in
AP : 1 2 :142(204) [0295] These **men** imagine that God's law deals with external,
AP : 1 2 :143(204) [0297] "In vain do they worship me with the precepts of **men**."
AP : 1 2 :165(208) [0303] faith, but not, as these **men** imagine, by works done in
AP : 1 2 :175(210) [0307] of public penitence so as not to burden **men** too heavily.
AP : 1 2 :178(211) [0307] If devout **men** will compare our teaching with the
AP : 1 3 :001(211) [0309] marks of profession among **men**, as some imagine, but
AP : 1 3 :001(211) [0309] us, through which he moves **men**'s hearts to believe.
AP : 1 3 :003(211) [0309] rites instituted by **men** are not sacraments in the strict
AP : 1 3 :003(211) [0309] in the strict sense since **men** do not have the authority to
AP : 1 3 :009(212) [0311] **Men** are not justified, therefore, because of any other
AP : 1 3 :016(213) [0313] a more exalted position, this would move **men** to pray.
AP : 1 4 :002(214) [0315] of cruelty, they kill the unfortunate and innocent **men**.
AP : 1 4 :005(215) [0315] Thus **men** may read that, despite our protest against the
AP : 1 5 :005(215) [0317] "In vain do they worship me with the precepts of **men**."
AP : 1 5 :006(215) [0317] shown at length that **men** are justified by the faith that
AP : 1 5 :006(216) [0317] not your own doing, it is the gift of God" and not of **men**.
AP : 1 5 :007(216) [0317] They say that **men** merit the forgiveness of sins by these
AP : 1 5 :009(216) [0317] These **men** believe that God is reconciled and gracious
AP : 1 5 :014(217) [0319] How will he inform **men** of God's will without the
AP : 1 5 :015(217) [0319] If **men** are allowed to establish new rites and if by such
AP : 1 5 :017(217) [0319] rites established by **men** without God's command can
AP : 1 5 :018(217) [0319] before God, denying that **men** are freely justified before
AP : 1 5 :018(217) [0319] necessary that rites instituted by **men** be everywhere alike.
AP : 1 5 :022(218) [0321] supposes that such works justify **men** and reconcile God.
AP : 1 5 :024(218) [0321] So **men** are deceived by the appearance of wisdom and
AP : 1 5 :024(218) [0321] of the saints; when **men** strive to imitate them, they copy
AP : 1 5 :025(218) [0321] righteousness has deceived **men**, all sorts of troubles
AP : 1 5 :025(218) [0321] are obscured; for when **men** regard these works as perfect
AP : 1 5 :030(219) [0323] Moses and the traditions of **men**, so that our opponents
AP : 1 5 :030(219) [0323] justify, how much less do the traditions of **men** justify?
AP : 1 5 :032(220) [0325] If **men** believe that these observances merit justification
AP : 1 6 :010(224) [0333] The monks impressed **men** with this outward hypocrisy
AP : 1 6 :013(224) [0333] so clearly that many good **men** involved in politics and in
AP : 1 8 :002(225) [0335] without the Holy Spirit **men** can love God and perform
AP : 1 8 :002(225) [0335] without the Holy Spirit **men** can merit grace and
AP : 1 8 :005(225) [0335] of concupiscence that **men** obey their evil impulses more
AP : 1 8 :005(225) [0335] is rare among **men**, as we see from the fact that even
AP : 1 8 :008(226) [0337] **Men** can easily determine this if they consider what their
AP : 1 8 :009(226) [0337] discipline, because all **men** ought to know that God
AP : 1 8 :010(226) [0337] by those who dream that **men** can obey the law of God
AP : 1 9 :001(226) [0337] the will of the devil and of **men** turning away from God,
AP : 2 0 :001(226) [0337] of our statement that **men** do not merit the forgiveness of
AP : 2 0 :003(227) [0339] the forgiveness of sins **men** are righteous before God not
AP : 2 1 :004(229) [0343] revealing his will to save **men**, and giving teachers and
AP : 2 1 :015(231) [0347] **Men** suppose that Christ is more severe and the saints
AP : 2 1 :028(233) [0351] **Men** have invoked her, trusted in her mercy, and sought
AP : 2 1 :034(234) [0353] **Men** venerated these and thought they contained some
AP : 2 1 :036(234) [0353] done serve as examples to **men** in their public or private
AP : 2 1 :039(235) [0355] Good **men** everywhere have been hoping that the bishops
AP : 2 1 :041(235) [0355] learned and outstanding **men** who deplored the abuses of
AP : 2 1 :043(235) [0357] nor the church, and good **men** can easily gauge its
AP : 2 1 :044(236) [0357] nor persecute innocent **men**, as has happened before, nor
AP : 2 2 :006(237) [0359] This is what good religious **men** ought to do.
AP : 2 2 :006(237) [0359] These **men** maintain that it is right to deny one part, and
AP : 2 2 :009(237) [0359] Look at the effrontery of the **men**!
AP : 2 2 :012(238) [0361] and rage against good **men** who use the entire sacrament?
AP : 2 3 :002(239) [0363] Most of the things these **men** do with utter abandon
AP : 2 3 :003(239) [0363] you sentence innocent **men** to cruel punishments,
AP : 2 3 :007(240) [0365] Gen. 1:28 teaches that **men** were created to be fruitful and
AP : 2 3 :008(240) [0365] did not form the nature of **men** to be fruitful only at the
AP : 2 3 :010(241) [0367] as saying that formerly **men** were born with a sex and
AP : 2 3 :016(241) [0369] (Matt. 19:11), "Not all **men** can receive this precept, but
AP : 2 3 :018(242) [0369] Here they order **men** to pray God for continence and to
AP : 2 3 :019(242) [0369] He wants **men** to be chaste by using the remedy he offers,
AP : 2 3 :020(242) [0369] testifies that many good **men** have tried to control their
AP : 2 3 :043(245) [0375] At the same time good **men** will know how to use
AP : 2 3 :043(245) [0375] so burdensome to good **men** that domestic problems are
AP : 2 3 :043(245) [0375] Good **men** know, too, that Paul commands each one to
AP : 2 3 :046(246) [0377] of Christ by making **men** believe that through such
AP : 2 3 :051(246) [0377] alone should keep good **men** from approving a burden
AP : 2 3 :052(246) [0377] Good **men** have been complaining about this burden for
AP : 2 3 :055(247) [0379] the strictest laws and examples and to invite **men** to it.
AP : 2 3 :057(247) [0379] They cruelly kill **men** just because they are married.
AP : 2 3 :064(248) [0381] that the heart of married **men** like Abraham and Jacob,
AP : 2 4 :003(250) [0385] ceremonies is that **men** may learn the Scriptures and that
AP : 2 4 :005(250) [0385] written or suggested that **men** benefit from hearing
AP : 2 4 :007(250) [0385] that for a long time good **men** have wanted some limits
AP : 2 4 :023(253) [0391] for our sins, so that **men** might know that God does not
AP : 2 4 :026(254) [0391] with any worship where **men** suppose they are offering
AP : 2 4 :041(257) [0399] Now good **men** can easily see the falsity of the charge
AP : 2 4 :043(258) [0399] with the claim that these justify **men** before God.
AP : 2 4 :052(259) [0403] priest chosen from among **men** is appointed to act on
AP : 2 4 :052(259) [0403] to act on behalf of **men** in relation to God, to offer gifts
AP : 2 4 :061(260) [0405] Good **men** in every country can see this.
AP : 2 4 :068(262) [0409] even profane and secular **men** understand; it does not talk
AP : 2 4 :069(262) [0409] are not only signs among **men**, but signs of God's will
AP : 2 4 :081(264) [0411] say that some unworthy **men** have found an immunity
AP : 2 4 :095(267) [0417] They were **men** and they could err and be deceived.
AP : 2 4 :097(268) [0417] Carnal **men** cannot stand it when only the sacrifice of
AP : 2 4 :099(268) [0419] the Mass to let all good **men** understand that we most
AP : 2 4 :099(268) [0419] We want all good **men** to be warned not to help our
AP : 2 4 :099(268) [0419] Mass lest they burden themselves with other **men**'s sin.
AP : 2 7 :004(269) [0421] and cruel these illiterate **men** are; and how vain they are
AP : 2 7 :007(269) [0421] sometimes they are responsible for murdering good **men**.
AP : 2 7 :008(269) [0421] there are some good **men** who have a moderate opinion
AP : 2 7 :009(270) [0423] to the saints, and the conspiracies against good **men**?
AP : 2 7 :014(271) [0423] that by the law of Moses **men** merit the forgiveness of
AP : 2 7 :016(271) [0425] though no class of **men** has greater license than the
AP : 2 7 :019(272) [0425] But what is surer than that **men** attain the forgiveness of
AP : 2 7 :021(272) [0427] sinning, as did Bernard, Francis, and other holy **men**.
AP : 2 7 :022(272) [0427] there are still some good **men** serving the ministry of the
AP : 2 7 :023(273) [0427] "In vain do they worship me with the precepts of **men**."
AP : 2 7 :024(273) [0427] supererogation, these liberal **men** then sell them to others.
AP : 2 7 :025(273) [0429] says (Ps. 116:11), "All **men** are liars"; that is, they do not
AP : 2 7 :030(274) [0431] they say that by a monastic life **men** merit eternal life.
AP : 2 7 :036(275) [0433] It seems that wise **men** were offended by the immoderate
AP : 2 7 :037(275) [0433] All **men**, whatever their calling, ought to seek perfection,
AP : 2 7 :044(277) [0435] of a double sin — deceiving **men**, and doing so under the
AP : 2 7 :051(278) [0437] that the law of nature in **men** cannot be repealed by vows
AP : 2 7 :056(278) [0439] reasons that release good **men** from this way of life.
AP : 2 7 :058(279) [0439] But those **men** did not undertake their vows with the
AP : 2 7 :058(279) [0439] or show faith before **men**, not to merit the forgiveness of
AP : 2 7 :069(281) [0443] "In vain do they worship me with the precepts of **men**."
AP : 2 7 :070(281) [0443] Holy **men** who followed this way of life must have come
AP : 2 8 :004(281) [0445] in blood, threatening **men** with horrible punishments
AP : 2 8 :005(281) [0445] and hear the pitiful complaints of many good **men**.
AP : 2 8 :018(284) [0449] many great and learned **men** in the church have felt
AP : 2 8 :018(284) [0449] when it is delivered by **men** and that we should not look
AP : 2 8 :021(284) [0449] commands that we must obey God rather than **men**.
AP : 2 8 :025(285) [0451] For we must obey God rather than **men** (Acts 5:29).
S 2 : 0 1 :005(292) [0463] under heaven given among **men** by which we must be
S 2 : 0 2 :001(293) [0463] an evil scoundrel) delivers **men** from their sins, both here
S 2 : 0 2 :002(293) [0463] teaching as doctrines the precepts of **men**' (Matt. 15:9).
S 2 : 0 2 :007(294) [0463] for by means of the Mass **men** try to reconcile themselves
S 2 : 0 2 :014(295) [0467] human opinions to make **men** believe their shameful,
S 2 : 0 3 :001(297) [0471] the education of learned **men** and decent women should
S 2 : 0 3 :002(298) [0471] services, invented by **men**, which claim to be superior to
S 2 : 0 4 :007(299) [0473] would then be elected by **men** and it remained in their
S 2 : 0 4 :008(299) [0473] on the good pleasure of **men** rather than on a divine
S 3 : 0 0 :000(302) [0477] with learned and sensible **men**, or even among ourselves.
S 3 : 0 1 :001(302) [0477] whose disobedience all **men** were made sinners and
S 3 : 0 3 :001(303) [0479] and wickedness of **men**." and in Rom. 3:19, 20, "The
S 3 : 0 3 :005(304) [0481] stood before God and recognize themselves as lost **men**.
S 3 : 0 3 :014(305) [0483] Rather, **men** hoped by their own works to overcome and
S 3 : 0 3 :034(309) [0489] 17:30, "Now he commands all **men** everywhere to repent."
S 3 : 0 3 :034(309) [0489] He says "all **men**," that is, excepting no one who is a
S 3 : 0 3 :035(309) [0489] that we must become altogether new and different **men**.
S 3 : 0 3 :041(309) [0491] theologians, the jurists, and all **men** understand nothing.
S 3 : 0 8 :013(313) [0497] were moved by the Holy Spirit, yet as holy **men** of God.
S 3 : 1 5 :001(316) [0501] doctrines the precepts of **men**" (Matt. 15:9), and it is
S 3 : 1 5 :001(316) [0501] written in Titus 1:14, "They are **men** who reject the truth."
S 3 : 1 5 :002(316) [0501] sin to break such precepts of **men**, this, too, is false.
TR : 0 0 :006(320) [0505] on the consciences of **men**, because he holds that his
TR : 0 0 :038(326) [0515] Acts, "We must obey God rather than **men**" (Acts 5:29).
TR : 0 0 :067(331) [0523] ascended on high he gave gifts to **men**" (Eph. 4:8, 11, 12).
TR : 0 0 :074(332) [0525] desires, have tormented **men** and excommunicated them
TR : 0 0 :074(332) [0525] to have the power to ban **men** arbitrarily without due
TR : 0 0 :075(333) [0525] connection they often harassed innocent and honest **men**.
TR : 0 0 :082(000) [0529] a number of most learned **men** who have now assembled
SC : 0 9 :001(354) [0561] *estates and conditions of* **men**, *by which they may be*
SC : 0 9 :003(355) [0561] watch over your souls, as **men** who will have to give
SC : 0 9 :005(355) [0561] be made for all **men**, for kings and all who are in high

Continued ▶

S C : 0 9 :010(356) [0563] the way of eye-service, as **men**-pleasers, but as servants of
S C : 0 9 :010(356) [0563] as to the Lord and not to **men**, knowing that whatever
S C : 0 9 :014(356) [0563] and thanksgivings be made for all **men**" (I Tim. 2:1).
L C : P R :020(361) [0573] much fruit and God will make excellent **men** of them.
L C : 0 1 :026(368) [0587] is good comes to us from **men**, we receive it all from God
L C : 0 1 :033(369) [0589] to many thousands, lest **men** live in security and commit
L C : 0 1 :034(369) [0589] who takes vengeance upon **men** who turn away from
L C : 0 1 :043(370) [0591] it out, and tell me, When **men** have devoted all their care
L C : 0 1 :051(371) [0595] — for example, where **men** take oaths in court and one
L C : 0 1 :069(374) [0601] — only perverse, unbridled **men** whom no teaching or
L C : 0 1 :075(375) [0601] up, and bear fruit, and **men** may grow up of whom an
L C : 0 1 :112(380) [0613] lived according to these words must also be holy **men**.
L C : 0 1 :114(380) [0613] However, **men** did not feel obliged to set forth God's
L C : 0 1 :130(383) [0619] The wise **men** of old were right when they said, "God,
L C : 0 1 :172(388) [0629] want qualified and capable **men** for both civil and
L C : 0 1 :175(388) [0631] and give us grace so that **men** might be trained who
L C : 0 1 :180(389) [0631] conduct ourselves individually toward our fellow **men**.
L C : 0 1 :191(391) [0635] offer counsel and aid to **men** in need and in peril of body
L C : 0 1 :211(393) [0641] by God that in general **men** and women in all conditions,
L C : 0 1 :218(394) [0643] blessing and grace so that **men** may have joy and
L C : 0 1 :229(396) [0645] These **men** are called gentlemen swindlers or big
L C : 0 1 :231(396) [0647] unmolested by anyone, even claiming honor from **men**.
L C : 0 1 :249(398) [0651] may not themselves be charged with other **men**'s sins.
L C : 0 1 :255(399) [0653] intolerable to live among **men** in public disgrace and
L C : 0 1 :258(399) [0653] usual course of the world, **men** are loathe to offend
L C : 0 1 :258(400) [0653] of the world that **men** of integrity seldom preside in
L C : 0 1 :286(403) [0663] "Whatever you wish that **men** would do to you, do so to
L C : 0 1 :317(408) [0673] and repeat in order that **men** may get rid of the
L C : 0 1 :317(408) [0673] man, and that all classes of **men** on earth may accustom
L C : 0 1 :317(408) [0673] will be a long time before **men** produce a doctrine or
L C : 0 1 :328(410) [0677] you should do good to all **men**, help them and promote
L C : 0 1 :330(410) [0677] These are not trifles of **men** but the commandments of
L C : 0 1 :330(410) [0677] Where **men** consider this and take it to heart, there will
L C : 0 1 :331(410) [0677] Old Testament commands **men** to write the Ten
L C : 0 1 :333(410) [0677] the challenge: Let all wise **men** and saints step forward
L C : 0 2 :044(416) [0689] **Men** and evil spirits there were, teaching us to obtain
L C : 0 2 :063(419) [0695] all the wisdom, understanding, and reason of **men**.
L C : 0 2 :067(419) [0697] moreover, are inscribed in the hearts of all **men**.
L C : 0 3 :014(422) [0701] any attention to it, and **men** supposed it was enough if
L C : 0 3 :031(424) [0707] the prayers of a few godly **men** intervened like an iron
L C : 0 3 :033(424) [0707] admonition in order that **men** may learn above all to
L C : 0 3 :041(425) [0709] then, it is profaned when **men** preach, teach, and speak in
L C : 0 3 :042(425) [0709] Likewise, when **men** grossly misuse the divine name as a
L C : 0 3 :062(428) [0715] he himself is driven out of **men**'s hearts and a breach is
L C : 0 3 :077(431) [0721] kings, and all estates of **men**, and especially our princes,
L C : 0 3 :078(431) [0721] and bloodshed, famine, savage beasts, wicked **men**, etc.
L C : 0 3 :080(431) [0721] so that he may deceive **men** with his lies and bring them
L C : 0 3 :083(431) [0721] even for wicked **men** and rogues, yet he wishes us to pray
L C : 0 3 :090(432) [0723] in the presence of God all **men** must humble themselves
L C : 0 3 :096(433) [0725] saying, "If you forgive **men** their trespasses, your heavenly
L C : 0 4 :006(437) [0733] divine origin, not something devised or invented by **men**.
L C : 0 4 :010(437) [0735] name is to be baptized not by **men** but by God himself.
L C : 0 4 :010(437) [0735] it is performed by **men**'s hands, it is nevertheless truly
L C : 0 4 :043(442) [0743] the pressing crowd of rich **men** no one else could get near
L C : 0 4 :043(442) [0743] which swallows up death and saves the lives of all **men**.
L C : 0 4 :057(444) [0747] and I — in short, all **men** — may err and deceive, but
L C : 0 5 :015(448) [0757] which now trouble **men** — for example, whether even a
L C : 0 5 :016(448) [0757] founded on the holiness of **men** but on the Word of God.
L C : 0 5 :040(451) [0761] For we see that **men** are becoming listless and lazy about
L C : 0 5 :045(452) [0763] compulsion, coerced by **men**, but to obey and please the
L C : 0 5 :051(452) [0765] toward the sacrament, **men** can easily sense what sort of
L C : 0 5 :051(452) [0765] compulsion and fear of **men**'s commandments, without
L C : 0 5 :052(452) [0765] let yourself be forced by **men** either to faith or to any
L C : 0 5 :058(453) [0767] For this reason we must make a distinction among **men**.
L C : 0 5 :061(453) [0767] come as poor, miserable **men**, precisely because we are
L C : 0 6 :005(457) [0000] Unfortunately, **men** have learned in only too well; they do
L C : 0 6 :025(460) [0000] they have simply driven **men** together in hordes just to
L C : 0 6 :026(460) [0000] contrary, do not say that **men** should look to see how full
E P : 0 2 :004(470) [0787] It is God's will that **men** should hear his Word and not
E P : 0 2 :013(471) [0789] imagine that God draws **men** to himself, enlightens them,
E P : 0 3 :002(473) [0793] Godhead, the sins of all **men** are esteemed like a drop of
E P : 0 4 :008(476) [0799] confess further that all **men**, but especially those who are
E P : 0 5 :008(478) [0803] of sin, as long as **men** hear only the law and hear nothing
E P : 0 5 :008(479) [0803] heaven" over all sinners and **men** learn how fierce it is.
E P : 0 5 :011(479) [0805] and detrimental when **men** teach that the Gospel, strictly
E P : 0 6 :001(479) [0805] The law has been given to **men** for three reasons: (1) to
E P : 0 6 :001(479) [0805] unruly and disobedient **men**, (2) to lead men to a
E P : 0 6 :001(479) [0805] men, (2) to lead **men** to a knowledge of their sin, (3) after
E P : 0 8 :016(489) [0821] and favor with God and **men**, for he did not always
E P : 1 0 :003(493) [0829] teaching as doctrines the precepts of **men**" (Matt. 15:9).
E P : 1 1 :008(495) [0833] He earnestly desires that all **men** should come to him and
E P : 1 1 :009(495) [0833] Epicurean life, or drive **men** to despair and waken
E P : 1 1 :009(495) [0833] As long as **men** follow their reason, they can hardly
E P : 1 1 :010(495) [0833] "God has consigned all **men** to disobedience, that he may
E P : 1 1 :011(496) [0835] He there directs **men** first to repent, to acknowledge their
E P : 1 1 :012(496) [0835] of condemnation is that **men** either do not hear the Word
E P : 1 1 :017(497) [0837] God does not want all **men** to come to repentance and to
E P : 1 1 :018(497) [0837] serious about wanting all **men** to come to him when he
S D : 0 1 :013(511) [0863] many influential and wise **men** of the world with terrible
S D : 0 1 :027(513) [0867] indicated above) that all **men**, conceived and born in the
S D : 0 2 :029(527) [0893] is much too weak for Satan, who incites **men** to sin."
S D : 0 2 :045(530) [0899] Therefore **men** teach wrongly when they pretend that
S D : 0 2 :049(530) [0901] be damned but that all **men** should turn themselves to him
S D : 0 2 :050(531) [0901] and works in the hearts of **men** true repentance and
S D : 0 2 :050(531) [0901] And it is God's will to call **men** to eternal salvation, to
S D : 0 2 :052(531) [0901] efficaciously, to convert **men** to God, and to work in them
S D : 0 2 :055(532) [0903] converts hearts so that **men** believe this Word and give
S D : 0 2 :057(532) [0903] offers his grace to all **men** in the Word and the holy
S D : 0 3 :002(539) [0917] the sins of all **men** are like a drop of water compared to
S D : 0 3 :012(541) [0919] leads to acquittal and life for all **men**" (Rom. 5:18).
S D : 0 3 :043(547) [0931] with faith is necessary if **men** are to be justified by it
S D : 0 4 :004(551) [0939] obligates and binds all **men** to be obedient to God, but at
S D : 0 4 :004(551) [0939] with which the law forces **men** to do good works.
S D : 0 5 :019(561) [0957] the unbelief involved in **men**'s failure to believe in Christ.
S D : 0 5 :025(563) [0961] this does not mean that **men** may abuse the grace of God
S D : 0 7 :024(573) [0981] based on the holiness of **men** but on the Word of God.
S D : 0 7 :043(576) [0987] has been given from heaven to all **men**, "Listen to him."
S D : 0 7 :067(582) [0997] by which the devil amuses himself and deceives **men**."
S D : 0 8 :087(608) [1047] with us as with **men** and his brethren, he wills to be with
S D : 1 0 :008(612) [1055] teaching for doctrines the precepts of **men**" (Matt. 15:9).
S D : 1 0 :015(613) [1057] the commandments of **men** will be increased and be put
S D : 1 0 :017(614) [1059] acknowledges me before **men**, I also will acknowledge
S D : 1 0 :026(615) [1061] the commandments of **men** are to be considered as of
S D : 1 1 :001(616) [1063] this document so that all **men** may know what we teach,
S D : 1 1 :006(617) [1065] wicked will of the devil and of **men** will attempt and do.
S D : 1 1 :007(617) [1065] will of the devil and of **men**, as it is written, "Israel, thou
S D : 1 1 :028(620) [1071] extends over all **men** (Luke 24:47), so also does the
S D : 1 1 :028(620) [1071] "God has included all **men** under disobedience so that he
S D : 1 1 :035(622) [1075] Yet God himself punishes **men** for such wickedness when
S D : 1 1 :051(624) [1079] "I tell you, none of those **men** who were invited shall taste
S D : 1 1 :066(627) [1085] and Holy Spirit, directs all **men** to Christ as to the book
S D : 1 1 :068(627) [1085] The Father wills that all **men** should hear this
S D : 1 1 :070(627) [1085] and who testifies to all **men** without distinction that God
S D : 1 1 :070(627) [1085] that God wants all **men** who are laden and burdened with
S D : 1 1 :088(631) [1093] false and wrong when **men** teach that the cause of our
S D : 1 2 :030(635) [1101] the Holy Spirit teaches **men** the saving knowledge of

Manage (4), Managed (2), Management (1)
P R : P R :005(004) [0009] might have been well **managed** and carried on in a
A P : 2 1 :001(229) [0343] sophistry, but all they **manage** to prove is that the saints
S C : 0 9 :002(354) [0561] He must **manage** his own household well, keeping his
L C : 0 1 :142(384) [0621] and maid-servants) under him to **manage** his household.
L C : 0 1 :277(402) [0659] can learn from the daily **management** of the household.
L C : 0 1 :305(406) [0667] to another woman, he **managed**, either personally or
L C : 0 3 :076(431) [0721] yield richly; to help us **manage** our household well and

Mandatory (1)
A P : 2 2 :015(238) [0361] can they make the withholding of one kind **mandatory**?

Manes (1)
S D : 0 8 :016(594) [1021] of the heretic **Manes** by the name of Paul, a native of

Manhood (1)
L C : 0 4 :070(445) [0749] When he reaches full **manhood**, the real vices become

Manichaean (5), Manichaeans (9), Manichaeism (1)
A G : 0 1 :005(028) [0043] are the heresy of the **Manichaeans**, who assert that there
A L : 0 1 :005(028) [0043] such as that of the **Manichaeans**, who posited two
A P : 1 8 :001(225) [0335] Pelagianism, or all liberty be denied it, as in **Manichaeism**
E P : 0 1 :017(468) [0783] 7. We also reject the **Manichaean** error that original sin is
E P : 0 1 :019(468) [0783] and condemn as a **Manichaean** error the teaching that
E P : 0 1 :022(469) [0785] This enables the **Manichaeans** to conceal their error and
E P : 0 2 :008(471) [0787] philosophers and of **Manichaeans** who taught that
S D : 0 1 :003(509) [0861] of all Pelagian and **Manichaean** errors, then (as the
S D : 0 1 :016(511) [0865] we fall neither into Pelagian nor into **Manichaean** errors.
S D : 0 1 :026(512) [0867] also be protected against any **Manichaean** aberrations.
S D : 0 1 :027(513) [0867] their nature, as the **Manichaeans** imagined in their
S D : 0 1 :030(513) [0867] attributes to the **Manichaeans**, that it is not the corrupted
S D : 0 1 :045(516) [0873] are found in the writings of the modern **Manichaeans**.
S D : 0 1 :055(518) [0877] writings against the **Manichaeans**, Augustine, in accord
S D : 0 2 :074(535) [0909] of the Stoics and **Manichaeans** in holding that everything

Manifest (42), Manifestation (1), Manifested (4), Manifestly (4), Manifests (5)
A G : 1 6 :005(038) [0051] to his own calling, **manifest** Christian love and genuine
A G : 0 0 :000(048) [0059] From the above it is **manifest** that nothing is taught in
A G : 2 3 :006(052) [0061] has made it all too **manifest** whether or not it lies in
A G : 0 1 :009(056) [0065] Without boasting, it is **manifest** that the Mass is observed
A G : 2 4 :029(059) [0067] **Manifestly** contrary to this teaching is the misuse of the
A G : 2 8 :021(084) [0087] the ungodly whose wicked conduct is **manifest**.
A G : 0 0 :005(095) [0095] For it is **manifest** and evident (to speak without boasting)
A L : 2 0 :032(045) [0057] to various sins, impious opinions, and **manifest** crimes.
A L : 2 0 :033(045) [0057] able to do so but were defiled by many **manifest** crimes.
A L : 2 2 :002(049) [0059] Christ has here **manifestly** commanded with reference to
A L : 2 4 :016(057) [0067] which had become so **manifest** that they could no longer
A L : 2 4 :040(061) [0069] account of the great and **manifest** abuses it would
A L : 2 8 :011(082) [0085] bodies and goods from **manifest** harm, and constrains
A L : 0 0 :005(095) [0095] For it is **manifest** that we have guarded diligently against
A P : P R :004(098) [0099] that we sanction certain **manifest** abuses and errors.
A P : 0 4 :041(113) [0133] of God has been **manifested** apart from law" (Rom. 3:21),
A P : 0 4 :391(166) [0225] when there are so many **manifest** errors among them,
A P : 0 4 :396(167) [0225] condemned a truth so **manifest** and clear that their
A P : 1 2 :159(207) [0301] works of God might be made **manifest** in him" (John 9:3).
A P : 1 2 :160(207) [0301] of God might be made more **manifest** in our weakness.
S 1 : P R :006(289) [0457] However, what such persons accomplish is **manifest**.
S 2 : 0 2 :022(296) [0469] this connection so many **manifest** lies and so much
S 2 : 0 4 :004(299) [0473] Yet it is **manifest** that the holy church was without a pope
S 2 : 0 4 :005(299) [0473] **Manifestly** (to repeat what has already been said often)
S 3 : 0 2 :004(303) [0479] is to make original sin **manifest** and show man to what
S 3 : 0 3 :003(304) [0481] Whether you are **manifest** sinners or saints, you must all
S 3 : 0 7 :001(311) [0493] not only the gross and **manifest** sins but also those which
S 3 : 0 9 :000(314) [0497] excludes those who are **manifest** and impenitent sinners
T R : 0 0 :031(325) [0513] Moreover, it is **manifest** that Christ was not sent to wield
T R : 0 0 :039(327) [0515] But it is **manifest** that the Roman pontiffs and their
T R : 0 0 :040(327) [0515] On the one hand, it is **manifest** that the pope rules in the
T R : 0 0 :042(328) [0517] the pope's kingdom are **manifest**, and the Scriptures
T R : 0 0 :043(328) [0517] profanation of Masses is **manifest**, for in addition to
T R : 0 0 :058(330) [0521] errors of the pope are **manifest**, and they are not trifling.
T R : 0 0 :058(330) [0521] **Manifest**, too, is the cruelty which he employs against the
T R : 0 0 :065(331) [0523] not by divine right, it is **manifest** that ordination
T R : 0 0 :074(332) [0525] those who are guilty of **manifest** crimes belongs to all
L C : 0 1 :284(403) [0661] For when an affair is **manifest** to everybody there can be
L C : 0 4 :021(439) [0737] the divine glory and majesty were **manifested** everywhere?
L C : 0 6 :017(459) [0000] and bitter, to the **manifest** harm and destruction of souls.
E P : 0 7 :017(484) [0813] present to exercise and **manifest** his judgment on
E P : 0 8 :016(489) [0821] use, revelation, and **manifestation** of his divine majesty.
S D : 0 1 :033(514) [0869] sin by itself as two **manifestly** separate things,

Continued ▶

SD : 0 2 :029(527) [0893] He drives them into many kinds of **manifest** sin.
SD : 0 2 :074(535) [0909] behavior and to avoid **manifest** sins and vices; or that the
SD : 0 7 :048(578) [0989] are simple, clear, **manifest**, certain, and indubitable, can
SD : 0 7 :054(579) [0991] as a special and **manifest** testimony to the true and
SD : 0 7 :099(586) [1005] says, "This will be made **manifest** at the proper time by
SD : 0 8 :025(596) [1023] all his miracles and **manifested** his divine majesty
SD : 0 8 :033(597) [1027] our religion: God was **manifested** in the flesh"
SD : 0 8 :064(603) [1037] *through* the same he **manifests** and exercises his divine
SD : 0 8 :066(604) [1039] But it shines forth and **manifests** itself fully, though
SD : 0 8 :066(604) [1039] it demonstrates and **manifests** its power of illumination
SD : 0 8 :074(606) [1041] demonstrates and **manifests** itself spontaneously and with
SD : 1 1 :004(617) [1063] present or future, are **manifest** and present to God, as it is
SD : 1 1 :086(631) [1091] of God which God **manifests** toward the impenitent and

Manifold (5)
AP : 0 4 :275(148) [0199] since a terrified conscience needs **manifold** consolations.
S 2 : 0 2 :011(294) [0465] a brood of vermin and the poison of **manifold** idolatries.
LC : 0 1 :056(372) [0597] a single lie a double one results — indeed, **manifold** lies.
LC : 0 3 :044(425) [0709] his name and enjoy his **manifold** blessings fail to teach,
SD : 0 7 :113(589) [1011] views, no matter how **manifold** and various they may be.

Manipulated (1)
AP : 2 1 :034(234) [0353] Virgin which was **manipulated** like a puppet so that it

Mankind (6)
PR : PR :002(003) [0007] and mercy toward **mankind** has permitted the pure,
PR : PR :004(003) [0007] government the foe of **mankind** bestirred himself to
PR : PR :023(012) [0021] before God and all **mankind** that with the repeatedly
LC : 0 1 :172(388) [0629] and educating our children to serve God and **mankind**.
LC : 0 1 :228(396) [0645] If we look at **mankind** in all its conditions, it is nothing
LC : 0 3 :002(420) [0697] **Mankind** is in such a situation that no one can keep the

Manner (59)
PR : PR :021(010) [0019] Turning to the kind and **manner** of speech employed with
AG : PR :008(025) [0039] forth how and in what **manner**, on the basis of the Holy
AG : 0 0 :000(049) [0059] unchristian and frivolous **manner** but have been
AG : 2 3 :006(052) [0061] What honest and chaste **manner** of life, what Christian,
AG : 2 4 :034(060) [0067] it is observed among us in the following **manner**:
AG : 2 4 :040(061) [0069] been discontinued, this **manner** of holding Mass ought
AL : 2 0 :038(046) [0057] and trust in God, all **manner** of lusts and human devices
AL : 2 3 :013(053) [0063] In such a harsh **manner** was the edict carried out that not
AL : 2 4 :011(057) [0065] all the churches, by what **manner** of men Masses are
AL : 2 4 :012(057) [0065] the Lord in an unworthy **manner** will be guilty of
AP : 0 4 :065(116) [0139] conversion of the wicked or the **manner** of regeneration?
AP : 0 4 :068(116) [0139] have sought to show the **manner** of regeneration and the
AP : 0 4 :251(143) [0191] Nor does he describe the **manner** of justification, but only
AP : 0 4 :376(164) [0223] or a Jewish **manner** they eliminate from them the
AP : 1 1 :005(181) [0251] receive in an unworthy **manner** receive judgment upon
AP : 1 4 :001(214) [0315] discipline in the **manner** described by the ancient canons.
AP : 2 8 :020(284) [0449] their traditions in a **manner** contrary to the Gospel.
S 1 : PR :012(290) [0459] vain display, all **manner** of vice and wickedness,
S 1 : 0 1 :000(291) [0461] Son became man in this **manner**: he was conceived by the
S 2 : 0 2 :004(293) [0463] better and more blessed **manner** — indeed, the only
S 2 : 0 2 :004(293) [0463] indeed, the only blessed **manner** — according to the
TR : 0 0 :049(329) [0519] controversies to be decided in the proper **manner**.
SC : PR :006(338) [0533] read them to the people word for word in this **manner**:
SC : 0 3 :020(348) [0549] may deliver us from all **manner** of evil, whether it affect
SC : 0 5 :018(350) [0553] that we are guilty of all **manner** of sins, even those of
LC : SP :027(364) [0581] in a lofty and learned **manner** but briefly and very
LC : SP :028(365) [0581] in the plainest possible **manner** say about them as much
LC : 0 4 :021(439) [0737] In the same **manner**, and even much more, you should
LC : 0 4 :036(441) [0741] Baptism in such a **manner** that it does you any good.
EP : 0 6 :008(481) [0807] is not to be urged, in the **manner** and measure above
EP : 0 7 :005(482) [0809] Christ is present in any **manner** or way, since in their
EP : 0 7 :015(483) [0811] not in a Capernaitic **manner**, but because of the
EP : 0 7 :015(483) [0811] union in a supernatural and heavenly **manner**.
EP : 0 8 :027(490) [0823] omnipresent in the same **manner** as the divine nature,
EP : 0 9 :003(492) [0827] in a wholly Christian **manner**, eliminates all unnecessary
SD : PR :009(505) [0853] and Christian terms and **manner** in which he himself
SD : 0 2 :089(538) [0915] in the way and after the **manner** set forth and explained
SD : 0 2 :090(538) [0915] particularly as to the **manner** in which these three (the
SD : 0 2 :090(539) [0915] pleasing to God, in the **manner** and degree set forth in
SD : 0 3 :042(547) [0931] If we speak of the **manner** in which faith justifies, it is St.
SD : 0 6 :026(568) [0971] that the law in the **manner** and measure indicated above
SD : 0 7 :007(570) [0975] or in a figurative **manner**, so that nobody will imagine
SD : 0 7 :007(570) [0975] on earth in some invisible and impalpable **manner**.
SD : 0 7 :024(573) [0981] so in the most worthy **manner**, for the sacrament is not
SD : 0 7 :060(580) [0993] the Lord in an unworthy **manner**" (I Cor. 11:27) sins not
SD : 0 7 :064(581) [0995] carnal, Capernaitic **manner**, but in a supernatural,
SD : 0 7 :064(581) [0995] manner, but in a supernatural, incomprehensible **manner**.
SD : 0 7 :103(587) [1007] places, even in a corporeal and comprehensible **manner**.
SD : 0 8 :006(592) [1017] his person, not in such a **manner** that there are now two
SD : 0 8 :019(594) [1021] other, not only after a **manner** of speaking and in a
SD : 0 8 :028(596) [1025] Luther explains, after the **manner** of the right hand of
SD : 0 8 :029(597) [1025] being is united in this **manner** with the divine nature and
SD : 0 8 :064(603) [1037] majesty according to the **manner** of the personal union,
SD : 0 8 :073(605) [1041] Holy Spirit) in such a **manner** that as a man he therefore
SD : 0 8 :081(607) [1045] to the third supernatural **manner**, he is and can be
SD : 0 8 :081(607) [1045] comprehensible **manner**, but according to the
SD : 0 8 :081(607) [1045] manner, but according to the supernatural, divine **manner**
SD : 1 1 :023(619) [1069] also ordained that in the **manner** just recounted he wills
SD : 1 1 :049(624) [1079] in a most comforting **manner** when he points out that

Manners (2)
AL : 2 0 :002(041) [0053] of life, indicating what **manners** of life and what kinds of
AP : 0 4 :242(141) [0187] says, "Know, but do not hate, the **manners** of a friend."

Manservant (2)
SC : 0 1 :019(344) [0543] *neighbor's wife, or his* **manservant**, *or his maidservant, or*
SC : 0 5 :022(350) [0553] presence that, as a **manservant** or maidservant, etc., I am

Mansfeld (9)
PR : PR :027(015) [0025] John Hoyer, count of **Mansfeld** [-Artern]
PR : PR :027(015) [0025] Bruno, count of **Mansfeld** [-Bronstedt]
PR : PR :027(015) [0025] Hoyer Christopher, count of **Mansfeld** [-Eisleben]
PR : PR :027(015) [0025] Peter Ernest the Younger, count of **Mansfeld** [-Eisleben]
PR : PR :027(015) [0025] Christopher, count of **Mansfeld**
S 3 : 1 5 :005(317) [0501] Michael Caelius, preacher in **Mansfeld**, subscribed
S 3 : 1 5 :005(317) [0501] Wendal Faber, pastor of Seeburg in **Mansfeld**
TR : 0 0 :082(335) [0529] Michael Caelius, preacher in **Mansfeld**
TR : 0 0 :082(335) [0529] Wendel Faber, pastor of Seeburg in **Mansfeld**

Mantua (4)
S 1 : 0 0 :000(287) [0453] party at the council in **Mantua**, or wherever else the
S 1 : PR :001(288) [0455] a council to meet in **Mantua** last year, in Whitsuntide.
S 1 : PR :001(288) [0455] the council from **Mantua**, and it is not yet known where it
SD : PR :007(505) [0853] before the Council in **Mantua** (or wherever it would

Manual (3)
AG : 2 8 :041(087) [0089] it is a mortal sin to do **manual** work on holy days (even
AL : 2 8 :041(087) [0089] it is a mortal sin to do **manual** work on holy days, even
LC : 0 1 :081(376) [0603] be fulfilled by refraining from **manual** labor of any kind.

Manuals (1)
LC : PR :002(358) [0567] in reality what the old **manuals** claimed in their titles to

Manufacture (1)
PR : PR :025(013) [0023] we are not minded to **manufacture** anything new by this

Marburg (2)
S 3 : 1 5 :005(317) [0501] John Drach, professor and minister in **Marburg**, subscribe
TR : 0 0 :082(334) [0529] John Drach, of **Marburg**, subscribed

Marcion (1)
EP : 0 8 :023(490) [0823] nature with a body and a soul, as **Marcion** imagined.

Marginal (2)
AG : 2 5 :012(063) [0071] The **marginal** note in *De poenitentia*, Dist. 5, also teaches
AL : 2 5 :012(063) [0071] The **marginal** note in *De poenitentia*, Dist. 5, in the

Margrave (7)
PR : PR :027(014) [0025] John George, **margrave** of Brandenburg, elector
PR : PR :027(014) [0025] Joachim Frederick, **margrave** of Brandenburg,
PR : PR :027(014) [0025] George Frederick, **margrave** of Brandenburg
PR : PR :027(015) [0025] **Margrave** Ernest [of Baden-Durlach] and
PR : PR :027(015) [0025] **Margrave** James of Baden [-Hachberg] the above two
AG : 0 0 :007(096) [0095] George, **margrave** of Brandenburg
AL : 0 0 :017(096) [0095] George, **margrave** of Brandenburg

Marital (5)
AP : 2 3 :027(243) [0371] public ministry, and **marital** intercourse did not keep
AP : 2 3 :032(243) [0373] woman is saved by the **marital** functions themselves, by
AP : 2 3 :032(243) [0373] functions themselves, by **marital** intercourse, by
AP : 2 3 :065(248) [0381] value of moderation in **marital** intercourse and of what
LC : 0 1 :219(394) [0643] For **marital** chastity it is above all things essential that

Mark (14), Marks (13)
AL : 1 3 :001(035) [0049] not merely to be **marks** of profession among men but
AP : 0 4 :058(115) [0137] thou, O Lord, shouldst **mark** iniquities, Lord, who shall
AP : 0 4 :326(158) [0211] thou, O Lord, shouldst **mark** iniquities, Lord, who could
AP : 0 7 :003(169) [0227] of the church's **marks** — that is, Word, confession, and
AP : 0 7 :005(169) [0227] association has outward **marks**, the pure teaching of the
AP : 0 7 :007(169) [0229] also added the outward **marks**, the Word and the
AP : 0 7 :019(171) [0233] in the outward **marks**, still they are not the true kingdom
AP : 0 7 :020(171) [0233] And we add its **marks**, the pure teaching of the Gospel
AP : 0 7 :028(173) [0237] in the outward **marks**, are members of the church
AP : 0 7 :028(173) [0237] in the outward **marks**, and therefore hold office in the
AP : 1 3 :001(211) [0309] sacraments are no more **marks** of profession among men,
AP : 2 4 :068(261) [0407] it was supposed to be a **mark** and witness of profession,
AP : 2 4 :068(261) [0407] certain type of hood is the **mark** of a particular monastic
AP : 2 4 :068(262) [0407] to be very pleased with a **mark** that took the form of a
AP : 2 7 :062(280) [0441] them by certain **marks** from their countrymen, lest they
AP : 2 7 :062(280) [0441] By these **marks** he wanted to remind them of the teaching
TR : 0 0 :038(327) [0515] [The **Marks** of the Antichrist]
TR : 0 0 :039(327) [0515] and it is plain that the **marks** of the Antichrist coincide
TR : 0 0 :062(331) [0523] from the time of **Mark** the Evangelist to the time of
SC : 0 6 :004(351) [0555] holy evangelists Matthew, **Mark**, and Luke, and also St.
LC : SP :020(364) [0579] the texts of Matthew and **Mark** at the end of their
LC : 0 1 :024(367) [0587] people so that they may **mark** well and remember the
LC : 0 1 :305(406) [0669] posed as an honorable, upright man, as St. **Mark** testifies.
LC : 0 5 :019(448) [0757] **Mark** this and remember it well.
SD : 0 5 :006(559) [0953] in the first chapter of St. **Mark**, where Christ said,
SD : 0 7 :026(573) [0981] **Mark** this and remember it well, for on these words rest
SD : 0 7 :053(579) [0991] of St. Matthew and St. **Mark** give us, "This (namely,

Market (6)
S 3 : 0 3 :025(307) [0485] yield money and the bull **market** became profitable, the
LC : 0 1 :053(372) [0595] in court or in the **market** or elsewhere, when a person
LC : 0 1 :224(395) [0643] of his neighbor at the **market**, in a grocery shop, butcher
LC : 0 1 :227(396) [0645] Furthermore, at the **market** and everyday business the
LC : 0 1 :240(397) [0649] who turn the free public **market** into a carrion-pit and a
LC : 0 1 :240(397) [0649] Everyone misuses the **market** in his own willful,

Marriage (102), Marriages (15), Married (34), Marry (28), Marrying (1)
AG : 1 6 :002(037) [0051] take required oaths, possess property, be **married**, etc.
AG : 1 6 :005(038) [0051] authority, the state, and **marriage** but requires that all
AG : 2 3 :000(051) [0061] XXIII. The **Marriage** of Priests
AG : 2 3 :003(051) [0061] some of our priests have entered the **married** state.
AG : 2 3 :003(051) [0061] assert that the estate of **marriage** was instituted by the
AG : 2 3 :004(051) [0061] and again, "It is better to **marry** than to be aflame with
AG : 2 3 :010(052) [0061] priests and deacons to **marry** in the Christian church of
AG : 2 3 :011(052) [0063] "A bishop must be above reproach, **married** only once."
AG : 2 3 :012(053) [0063] not only forbade future **marriages** of priests but also
AG : 2 3 :012(053) [0063] but also broke up the **marriages** which were of long
AG : 2 3 :002(053) [0063] and such prohibition of **marriage** (which God himself
AG : 2 3 :002(053) [0063] for prohibiting the **marriage** of clergymen, there were
AG : 2 3 :013(053) [0063] and weightier reasons for permitting them to be **married**.

Continued ▶

AG : 2 3 :014(053) [0063] that the prohibition of **marriage** may not cause worse and
AG : 2 3 :015(054) [0063] himself, who instituted **marriage** to aid human infirmity
AG : 2 3 :016(054) [0063] How would the **marriage** of priests and the clergy, and
AG : 2 3 :017(054) [0063] this hard prohibition of **marriage** is to continue longer,
AG : 2 3 :018(054) [0063] and clergymen may **marry** is based on God's Word and
AG : 2 3 :018(054) [0063] both that priests were **married** and that the vow of
AG : 2 3 :018(054) [0063] that Christian **marriage** has not only been forbidden but
AG : 2 3 :019(054) [0063] God commanded that **marriage** be held in honor.
AG : 2 3 :020(054) [0063] **Marriage** has also been highly praised in the imperial laws
AG : 2 3 :021(055) [0063] simply because they are **married** — and especially priests,
AG : 2 3 :022(055) [0063] the teaching that forbids **marriage** a doctrine of the devil.
AG : 2 3 :023(055) [0063] of the devil to forbid **marriage** and then to be so bold as
AG : 2 3 :025(055) [0065] were unable to keep their vows of chastity should **marry**.
AG : 2 3 :025(055) [0065] it is better for them to **marry** than to fall into the fire
AG : 2 6 :029(068) [0075] as forbid food or **marriage** are called a doctrine of the
AG : 2 7 :018(073) [0077] to those who desire to **marry** that all those who are not
AG : 2 7 :018(073) [0079] right, and authority to **marry**, for vows cannot nullify
AG : 2 7 :020(074) [0079] order also direct all to **marriage** who are not endowed
AG : 2 7 :034(076) [0081] not follow that the **marriage** of those who broke them
AG : 2 7 :035(076) [0081] Chapter I, that such a **marriage** should not be dissolved,
AG : 2 7 :036(076) [0081] command concerning **marriage** frees and releases many
AG : 2 7 :052(079) [0083] their consciences are troubled because they are **married**.
AG : 2 8 :070(093) [0093] they forbid clergymen to **marry** and admit no one to the
AL : 1 6 :002(037) [0051] by magistrates, to **marry**, to be given in marriage.
AL : 1 6 :002(037) [0051] by magistrates, to marry, to be given in **marriage**.
AL : 1 8 :005(040) [0051] to build a house, will to **marry**, will to keep cattle, will to
AL : 2 3 :000(051) [0061] XXIII. The **Marriage** of Priests
AL : 2 3 :002(051) [0061] priests were forbidden to **marry** but that there are now
AL : 2 3 :004(051) [0061] and again, "It is better to **marry** than to be aflame with
AL : 2 3 :007(052) [0061] for celibacy ought to **marry**, for no law of man and no
AL : 2 3 :010(052) [0061] that in the ancient church priests were **married** men.
AL : 2 3 :011(052) [0063] Paul said that a **married** man should be chosen to be
AL : 2 3 :013(053) [0063] not only were future **marriages** prohibited but existing
AL : 2 3 :013(053) [0063] prohibited but existing **marriages** were also dissolved,
AL : 2 3 :015(054) [0063] Besides, God instituted **marriage** to be a remedy against
AL : 2 3 :016(054) [0063] that this be done in the case of sacerdotal **marriage**.
AL : 2 3 :017(054) [0063] be lacking in pastors if **marriage** continues to be
AL : 2 3 :018(054) [0063] exercised than in opposition to the **marriage** of priests.
AL : 2 3 :019(054) [0063] God has commanded that **marriage** be held in honor.
AL : 2 3 :020(055) [0063] heathen, have adorned **marriage** with the greatest praise.
AL : 2 3 :021(055) [0063] intent of the canons, for no other cause than **marriage**.
AL : 2 3 :022(055) [0063] To prohibit **marriage** is called a doctrine of demons by
AL : 2 3 :023(055) [0063] that the prohibition of **marriage** is maintained by means
AL : 2 3 :025(055) [0065] keep the chastity which they had promised should **marry**.
AL : 2 3 :025(055) [0065] it is better for them to **marry** than to fall into the fire
AL : 2 6 :011(065) [0071] kind of life — in **marriage**, in the magistracy, or in other
AL : 2 7 :018(073) [0079] not suited for celibacy to **marry**, for vows can not nullify
AL : 2 7 :020(074) [0079] also compel those to **marry** who are not excepted by a
AL : 2 7 :034(076) [0081] of necessity that the **marriages** of persons who violated
AL : 2 7 :036(076) [0081] command concerning **marriage** frees many from their
AL : 2 7 :052(079) [0083] they engage in their **married** life with a troubled
AL : 2 7 :056(080) [0083] of men who, forsaking **marriage** and the administration
AP : 1 5 :025(219) [0323] of the household, **married** life, and the rearing of
AP : 1 5 :026(219) [0323] government and their **marriages** because they regarded
AP : 1 5 :043(221) [0327] and political affairs, **marriage**, the education and
AP : 1 6 :001(222) [0329] requires it, or contract **marriage** — in short, that lawful
AP : 2 3 :000(239) [0363] [Article XXIII. The **Marriage** of Priests]
AP : 2 3 :001(239) [0363] be disgraced and shamed by the **marriage** of priests.
AP : 2 3 :002(239) [0363] who say that **marriage** disgraces and shames the empire,
AP : 2 3 :003(239) [0363] of the councils, they demand that you dissolve **marriages**.
AP : 2 3 :003(239) [0363] merely because of their **marriage**, you sentence innocent
AP : 2 3 :007(240) [0365] nor vows can abolish the right to contract **marriage**.
AP : 2 3 :008(240) [0365] earth has been replenished **marriage** is not commanded.
AP : 2 3 :009(240) [0367] the right to contract **marriage** must always remain.
AP : 2 3 :010(241) [0367] to say that originally **marriage** was commanded but that
AP : 2 3 :012(241) [0367] right, the right to contract **marriage** necessarily remains.
AP : 2 3 :013(241) [0367] remedy even more, and **marriage** is necessary for a
AP : 2 3 :015(241) [0367] that priests should **marry** — as though priests were not
AP : 2 3 :016(241) [0369] commanding those to **marry** who do not have the gift of
AP : 2 3 :016(241) [0369] says (v. 9), "It is better to **marry** than to be aflame with
AP : 2 3 :016(241) [0369] together; therefore **marriage** is more necessary now than
AP : 2 3 :016(241) [0369] Hence Paul speaks of **marriage** as a remedy and
AP : 2 3 :016(241) [0369] statement, "It is better to **marry** than to be aflame with
AP : 2 3 :016(241) [0369] Thus anyone who is aflame retains the right to **marry**.
AP : 2 3 :023(242) [0369] canons do not forbid **marriage**, nor dissolve marriages
AP : 2 3 :023(242) [0369] marriage, nor dissolve **marriages** that have been
AP : 2 3 :023(242) [0369] from the public ministry who **married** while in office.
AP : 2 3 :023(242) [0371] the contracting of **marriages** and dissolve them once they
AP : 2 3 :024(243) [0371] for they do allow **marriage** under certain circumstances;
AP : 2 3 :026(243) [0371] it is pure, as though **marriage** were impure and sinful or
AP : 2 3 :026(243) [0371] though celibacy merited justification more than **marriage**.
AP : 2 3 :027(243) [0371] in this very analogy **marriage** is permitted and intercourse
AP : 2 3 :028(243) [0371] admit that for believers **marriage** is pure because it has
AP : 2 3 :029(243) [0371] Christ calls **marriage** a divine union when he says in
AP : 2 3 :030(243) [0371] Paul says **marriage**, food, and similar things are
AP : 2 3 :031(243) [0371] wife"; that is, the use of **marriage** is permissible and holy
AP : 2 3 :033(244) [0373] These passages teach that **marriage** is a lawful thing.
AP : 2 3 :033(244) [0373] and approval, then **marriages** are pure since they are
AP : 2 3 :034(244) [0373] ungodly, therefore, so **marriage** is pure in the godly,
AP : 2 3 :035(244) [0373] of lust; it is not **marriage** that the law forbids, but lust,
AP : 2 3 :035(244) [0373] purity of heart in a **married** man like Abraham or Jacob
AP : 2 3 :036(244) [0373] justification more than **marriage** does, we shall really
AP : 2 3 :036(244) [0373] by virginity nor by **marriage** are we justified, but freely
AP : 2 3 :037(244) [0373] may cry out that we put **marriage** on the same level with
AP : 2 3 :038(244) [0373] We do not put **marriage** on the same level with virginity.
AP : 2 3 :038(244) [0373] So also virginity is a gift that surpasses **marriage**.
AP : 2 3 :039(244) [0375] any more than the **married** person does by performing the
AP : 2 3 :039(244) [0375] married person does by performing the duties of **marriage**
AP : 2 3 :043(245) [0375] will know how to use **marriage** moderately, especially
AP : 2 3 :045(245) [0375] contemptuously about **marriage** and admiringly about
AP : 2 3 :045(245) [0377] also abstained from **marriage**, and this called forth the
AP : 2 3 :045(245) [0377] of using wine or meat or **marriage**, which seemed profane
AP : 2 3 :047(246) [0377] very troubled about the legitimacy of being **married**.
AP : 2 3 :053(246) [0377] who despise his gift and ordinance and forbid **marriage**.
AP : 2 3 :055(247) [0379] appropriate to guard **marriage** with the strictest laws and
AP : 2 3 :055(247) [0379] exhort the incontinent to **marry** and also exhort others
AP : 2 3 :057(247) [0379] They cruelly kill men just because they are **married**.
AP : 2 3 :059(247) [0379] dissolution of existing **marriages**, the murder of priests
AP : 2 3 :061(247) [0381] The Gospel permits **marriage** for those who need it, but it
AP : 2 3 :061(247) [0381] it, but it does not force **marriage** on anyone who wants to
AP : 2 3 :061(247) [0381] anyone into celibacy or to dissolve existing **marriages**.
AP : 2 3 :063(248) [0381] the dissolution of existing **marriages** (Matt. 19:6).
AP : 2 3 :064(248) [0381] that because of faith **marriage** is pure, according to the
AP : 2 3 :064(248) [0381] possible that the heart of **married** men like Abraham and
AP : 2 3 :066(248) [0381] Finally, since **marriage** is pure, it is right to say that those
AP : 2 3 :066(248) [0381] continent in celibacy should **marry** in order to be pure.
AP : 2 3 :067(248) [0383] is horrible: the **marriage** of priests is the Jovinian heresy.
AP : 2 3 :067(248) [0383] This is a new charge, that **marriage** is a heresy!
AP : 2 3 :067(248) [0383] lie to say that the **marriage** of priests is the Jovinian
AP : 2 3 :067(248) [0383] or that the church condemned **marriage** at that time.
AP : 2 3 :069(249) [0383] on the relative value of **marriage** and celibacy.
AP : 2 3 :069(249) [0383] We do not put **marriage** and virginity on the same level,
AP : 2 3 :069(249) [0383] but neither virginity nor **marriage** merits justification.
AP : 2 3 :070(249) [0383] for breaking up **marriages** and torturing and killing
AP : 2 3 :071(249) [0383] had done wrong in **marrying**, it is certainly contrary to
AP : 2 3 :071(249) [0383] and Word to break up **marriages** and to issue savage and
AP : 2 7 :051(277) [0437] in connection with the **marriage** of priests that the law of
AP : 2 7 :059(279) [0441] the Rechabites were **married**; though our monks abound
AP : 2 7 :064(280) [0441] funds, "They desire to **marry**, and so they incur
AP : 2 7 :067(280) [0441] they were getting **married** (he commands the younger
AP : 2 7 :067(280) [0441] the younger ones to **marry**, v. 14), but because they
S 3 : 1 1 :000(314) [0499] XI. The **Marriage** of Priests
S 3 : 1 1 :001(314) [0499] nor right to prohibit **marriage** and burden the divine
S 3 : 1 1 :002(315) [0499] God or forbid them to live together honestly in **marriage**.
S 3 : 1 1 :003(315) [0499] the contrary, we desire **marriage** to be free, as God
TR : 0 0 :062(330) [0523] by, "A bishop must be **married** only once" (Titus 1:5-7).
TR : 0 0 :078(333) [0527] unjust laws concerning **marriage** and apply them in their
TR : 0 0 :078(333) [0527] which forbids an innocent person to **marry** after divorce.
SC : 0 9 :002(354) [0561] must be above reproach, **married** only once, temperate,
LC : 0 1 :053(372) [0595] is especially common in **marriage** matters when two
LC : 0 1 :068(374) [0599] broke their promise of **marriage**; they never enjoyed a
LC : 0 1 :201(392) [0637] among the Jewish people **marriage** was obligatory.
LC : 0 1 :201(392) [0637] Youths were **married** at the earliest age possible.
LC : 0 1 :206(393) [0639] with the estate of **marriage** and gives occasion to speak of
LC : 0 1 :206(393) [0639] honors and glorifies the **married** life, sanctioning and
LC : 0 1 :208(393) [0639] **Married** life is no matter for jest or idle curiosity, but it is
LC : 0 1 :209(393) [0639] not despise or disdain **marriage**, as the blind world and
LC : 0 1 :209(393) [0641] all people to enter the estate of **marriage**, as we shall hear.
LC : 0 1 :211(393) [0641] who are unsuited for **married** life and others whom he
LC : 0 1 :211(393) [0641] so that they can maintain chastity outside of **marriage**.
LC : 0 1 :212(393) [0641] chaste outside of **marriage**; for flesh and blood remain
LC : 0 1 :212(394) [0641] God has established **marriage**, so that everyone may have
LC : 0 1 :213(394) [0641] they despise and forbid **marriage**, and boast and vow that
LC : 0 1 :214(394) [0641] of great sanctity avoid **marriage** and either indulge in
LC : 0 1 :215(394) [0641] of secret passion, which can be avoided in **married** life.
LC : 0 1 :216(394) [0641] of chastity apart from **marriage** are condemned and
LC : 0 1 :216(394) [0641] their unchaste existence and enter the **married** life.
LC : 0 1 :217(394) [0641] led to acquire a love for **married** life and know that it is a
LC : 0 1 :217(394) [0643] shameful vices resulting from contempt of **married** life.
LC : 0 1 :218(394) [0643] they are grown, will be **married** honorably in the fear of
LC : 0 1 :218(394) [0643] men may have joy and happiness in their **married** life.
LC : 0 1 :219(394) [0643] in the estate of **marriage**), but also to love and cherish the
LC : 0 1 :306(406) [0669] in the New Testament **married** people are forbidden to be
EP : 1 2 :019(499) [0841] is sufficient ground for **married** people to divorce one
EP : 1 2 :019(499) [0841] each go his own way, and **marry** someone else belonging
SD : 1 2 :024(634) [1099] is sufficient ground for **married** people to divorce each
SD : 1 2 :024(634) [1099] and to enter into a new **marriage** with another person of

Marshaling (1)

LC : 0 3 :062(428) [0715] his power and might, **marshaling** all his subjects and even

Martin (15)

PR : PR :000(001) [0004] the blessed Death of **Martin** Luther, Prepared for
PR : PR :004(003) [0007] and pious person, Dr. **Martin** Luther, and how in this
S 1 : 0 0 :000(287) [0453] Written by Dr. **Martin** Luther in the year 1537
S 1 : PR :000(288) [0455] Preface of Dr. **Martin** Luther
S 3 : 1 5 :005(316) [0501] Dr. **Martin** Luther subscribed
S 3 : 1 5 :005(317) [0501] of the reverend father, **Martin** Luther, confess that I have
TR : 0 0 :082(334) [0529] **Martin** Bucer
TR : 0 0 :082(000) [0529] German language by Dr. **Martin** Luther, our most revered
SC : 0 0 :000(337) [0531] Small Catechism of Dr. **Martin** Luther for Ordinary
SC : PR :000(338) [0533] Christ, our Lord, from **Martin** Luther to all faithful,
LC : PR :000(358) [0567] **Martin** Luther's Preface
EP : 1 2 :031(501) [0843] Dr. **Martin** Chemnitz
SD : 0 7 :012(571) [0977] in Wittenberg, and Dr. **Martin** Luther and other
SD : 0 7 :013(571) [0977] have heard how Master **Martin** Bucer has explained his
SD : 1 2 :040(636) [1103] Dr. **Martin** Chemnitz

Marvel (1), Marvelous (7), Marvelously (2)

AL : 2 0 :005(041) [0053] faith, about which there used to be **marvelous** silence.
AL : 2 3 :018(054) [0063] magistrates, yet it is a **marvelous** thing that nowhere is
AP : 0 4 :335(159) [0215] our opponents make a **marvelous** play on Christ's words.
AP : 1 2 :074(192) [0273] These words of Bernard **marvelously** illumine our case.
AP : 1 2 :106(197) [0283] By a **marvelous** transformation, our opponents make
AP : 2 1 :035(234) [0353] But all these **marvelous** tales about statues and pictures
LC : PR :016(361) [0573] Are we not most **marvelous** fellows, therefore, if we
LC : PR :016(361) [0573] Most **marvelous** fellows, to think we can finish learning
SD : 0 7 :101(587) [1007] him, how much more **marvelously** will he be present in
SD : 0 8 :030(597) [1025] that even the angels **marvel** at it and find their delight and

Mary (23)

AG : 0 3 :001(029) [0045] man, born of the virgin **Mary**, and that the two natures,
AL : 0 3 :001(029) [0045] on man's nature in the womb of the blessed virgin **Mary**.
AL : 0 3 :002(030) [0045] was born of the virgin **Mary**, truly suffered, was crucified,
AP : 2 1 :025(232) [0349] of the most blessed virgin **Mary** and of all the saints be to
AP : 2 1 :027(232) [0349] Granted that blessed **Mary** prays for the church, does she

Continued ▶

A P : 2 1 :027(232) [0349] What does Christ do if blessed **Mary** does all this?
S 1 : 0 1 :000(292) [0461] of man, and was born of the pure, holy, and virgin **Mary**.
S 3 : 0 8 :013(313) [0497] nor did he leap in his mother's womb until **Mary** spoke.
S C : 0 2 :003(345) [0545] *Spirit, born of the virgin **Mary**, suffered under Pontius*
S C : 0 2 :004(345) [0545] man, born of the virgin **Mary**, is my Lord, who has
L C : S P :012(363) [0577] Spirit, born of the virgin **Mary**, suffered under Pontius
L C : 0 2 :025(413) [0683] *Spirit, born of the virgin **Mary**, suffered under Pontius*
E P : 0 7 :012(483) [0811] being, no angel, but only **Mary**'s Son, is so set down at
E P : 0 8 :011(488) [0821] For how could the man, **Mary**'s son, truly be called or be
E P : 0 8 :012(488) [0821] teach, and confess that **Mary** conceived and bore not only
E P : 1 2 :003(498) [0839] and blood from the virgin **Mary**, but brought them with
S D : 0 8 :006(592) [1017] of the most blessed virgin **Mary**, as it is written, "Of their
S D : 0 8 :024(595) [1023] of the natures, **Mary**, the most blessed virgin, did not
S D : 0 8 :029(597) [1025] both natures in Christ, the way Jesus, the son of **Mary**, is.
S D : 0 8 :085(608) [1047] calendar Jesus the son of **Mary** is 1543 years old this
S D : 0 8 :085(608) [1047] in one person this man, **Mary**'s son, is and is called the
S D : 0 8 :085(608) [1047] To me, Jesus of Nazareth, **Mary**'s son, born a human
S D : 1 2 :025(635) [1099] and blood from the virgin **Mary** but brought it along from

Mask (3)
L C : 0 4 :019(439) [0737] to the gross, external **mask** (as we see the shell of a nut)
S D : 0 8 :021(595) [1023] called this the devil's **mask** and damned it to the depths
S D : 0 8 :040(598) [1029] for it is the devil's **mask** since it will finally construct a

Mass (134), Masses (39)
A G : 0 1 :000(056) [0065] XXIV. The **Mass**
A G : 0 1 :001(056) [0065] We are unjustly accused of having abolished the **Mass**.
A G : 0 1 :009(056) [0065] it is manifest that the **Mass** is observed among us with
A G : 0 1 :007(056) [0065] the people may be drawn to the Communion and **Mass**.
A G : 0 1 :002(056) [0065] public ceremonies of the **Mass**, except that in certain
A G : 2 4 :010(057) [0065] our time, however, the **Mass** came to be misused in many
A G : 2 4 :013(057) [0065] such mercenary **Masses** and private Masses, which had
A G : 2 4 :013(057) [0065] Masses and private **Masses**, which had hitherto been held
A G : 2 4 :021(058) [0067] sin, and had instituted the **Mass** as a sacrifice for other
A G : 2 4 :022(058) [0067] This transformed the **Mass** into a sacrifice for the living
A G : 2 4 :023(058) [0067] debate as to whether one **Mass** held for many people
A G : 2 4 :023(058) [0067] merited as much as a special **Mass** held for an individual.
A G : 2 4 :023(058) [0067] multiplication of **Masses**, by the performance of which
A G : 2 4 :029(059) [0067] is the misuse of the **Mass** by those who think that grace is
A G : 2 4 :029(059) [0067] it is well known that the **Mass** is used to remove sin and
A G : 2 4 :034(060) [0067] Inasmuch, then, as the **Mass** is not a sacrifice to remove
A G : 2 4 :034(060) [0067] are present, **Mass** is held and those who desire it are
A G : 2 4 :035(060) [0067] Thus the **Mass** is preserved among us in its proper use,
A G : 2 4 :040(061) [0069] public ceremonies of the **Mass** except that other
A G : 2 4 :040(061) [0069] that other unnecessary **Masses** which were held in
A G : 2 4 :040(061) [0069] addition to the parochial **Mass**, probably through abuse,
A G : 2 4 :040(061) [0069] this manner of holding **Mass** ought not in fairness be
A G : 2 4 :041(061) [0069] there were many people, **Mass** was not held on every day
A G : 2 4 :041(061) [0069] Alexandria, and all these services were held without **Mass**
A G : 2 6 :040(069) [0075] (such as the liturgy of the **Mass** and various canticles,
A L : 2 4 :000(056) [0065] XXIV. The **Mass**
A L : 2 4 :001(056) [0065] Our churches are falsely accused of abolishing the **Mass**.
A L : 2 4 :001(056) [0065] Actually, the **Mass** is retained among us and is celebrated
A L : 2 4 :009(057) [0065] does not appear that the **Mass** is observed with more
A L : 2 4 :010(057) [0065] by all good men that **Masses** were being shamefully
A L : 2 4 :011(057) [0065] by what manner of men **Masses** are celebrated only for
A L : 2 4 :011(057) [0065] and how many celebrate **Masses** contrary to the canons.
A L : 2 4 :013(057) [0065] this sin, private **Masses** were discontinued among us
A L : 2 4 :013(057) [0065] as hardly any private **Masses** were held except for the
A L : 2 4 :017(057) [0067] have arisen concerning the **Mass**, concerning the
A L : 2 4 :018(058) [0067] profanations of the **Mass** as have been tolerated in the
A L : 2 4 :020(058) [0067] to have been so abused for the sake of gain as the **Mass**.
A L : 2 4 :021(058) [0067] increased private **Masses**, namely, that Christ had by his
A L : 2 4 :021(058) [0067] sin and had instituted the **Mass** in which an oblation
A L : 2 4 :022(058) [0067] common opinion that the **Mass** is a work by which its
A L : 2 4 :023(058) [0067] a debate on whether one **Mass** said for many people is
A L : 2 4 :023(058) [0067] worth as much as a special **Mass** said for individuals, and
A L : 2 4 :023(058) [0067] infinite proliferation of **Masses** to which reference has
A L : 2 4 :029(059) [0067] Now, if the **Mass** takes away the sins of the living and the
A L : 2 4 :029(059) [0067] comes from the work of the **Mass** and not from faith.
A L : 2 4 :030(059) [0067] Therefore the **Mass** was instituted that faith on the part
A L : 2 4 :033(060) [0067] Consequently the **Mass** is to be used to this end, that the
A L : 2 4 :034(060) [0067] Inasmuch as the **Mass** is such a giving of the sacrament,
A L : 2 4 :034(060) [0067] sacrament, one common **Mass** is observed among us on
A L : 2 4 :035(060) [0067] do not mention private **Masses** but speak often of the
A L : 2 4 :035(060) [0067] private Masses but speak often of the common **Mass**.
A L : 2 4 :037(060) [0067] person or other celebrated **Mass** and the rest of the
A L : 2 4 :040(060) [0069] Since, therefore, the **Mass** among us is supported by the
A L : 2 4 :040(061) [0069] Only the number of **Masses** is different, and on account
A L : 2 4 :041(061) [0069] churches most frequented, **Mass** was not held every day;
A L : 2 6 :040(069) [0075] the order of lessons in the **Mass**, holy days, etc.) which
A P : 0 4 :010(108) [0123] and the abuses of the **Mass**; someone has always been
A P : 0 4 :210(136) [0179] opponents claim that the **Mass** is a work that justifies *ex*
A P : 0 4 :288(151) [0203] sacraments, especially the **Mass**, through which they seek
A P : 0 7 :033(174) [0239] observe the order of the **Mass**, the Lord's day, and the
A P : 1 0 :002(179) [0247] this is their canon of the **Mass**, in which the priest clearly
A P : 1 2 :015(184) [0257] only by indulgences but also by the sacrifice of the **Mass**.
A P : 1 2 :137(203) [0293] orders, the sale of **Masses**, and endless observances which
A P : 1 3 :023(214) [0313] endless desecration of **Masses**, which we shall discuss a
A P : 1 5 :040(220) [0325] and hirelings perform **Mass**, and they often do so only for
A P : 2 1 :023(232) [0349] of the canon of the **Mass** confidently declares: "It is a
A P : 2 1 :041(235) [0355] deplored the abuses of the **Mass**, the trust in monastic
A P : 2 4 :000(249) [0383] [Article XXIV.] The **Mass**
A P : 2 4 :001(249) [0383] we do not abolish the **Mass** but religiously keep and
A P : 2 4 :001(249) [0383] In our churches **Mass** is celebrated every Sunday and on
A P : 2 4 :002(249) [0385] the use of Latin in the **Mass**, our clever opponents quibble
A P : 2 4 :002(249) [0385] benefits from hearing a **Mass** that he does not
A P : 2 4 :006(250) [0385] catholic in our having only the public or common **Mass**.
A P : 2 4 :006(250) [0385] parishes have no private **Masses** but only one public
A P : 2 4 :006(250) [0385] Masses but only one public **Mass**, and this only on
A P : 2 4 :006(250) [0385] The monasteries have public, though daily, **Mass**.
A P : 2 4 :006(250) [0385] before Gregory make no mention of private **Masses**.
A P : 2 4 :007(250) [0385] multiplication of private **Masses**; so superstitious and so
A P : 2 4 :007(250) [0385] a single common daily **Mass**, reasons of piety or of profit
A P : 2 4 :008(250) [0385] Minor there were no daily **Masses** but Communion was
A P : 2 4 :009(250) [0387] many statements to prove that the **Mass** is a sacrifice.
A P : 2 4 :009(251) [0387] by the fact that the **Mass** does not confer grace *ex opere*
A P : 2 4 :009(251) [0387] Confutation and in all their other books about the **Mass**.
A P : 2 4 :013(251) [0387] notion about the working of the **Mass** *ex opere operato*.
A P : 2 4 :013(251) [0387] the people and has infinitely multiplied the **Masses**.
A P : 2 4 :013(251) [0387] With the work of these **Masses** they think they can placate
A P : 2 4 :031(255) [0395] and apply it to the **Mass**, and for this they quote patristic
A P : 2 4 :031(255) [0395] were a reference to the **Mass**, it would not follow that the
A P : 2 4 :031(255) [0395] would not follow that the **Mass** justifies *ex opere operato*
A P : 2 4 :035(256) [0397] the Old Testament, so the **Mass** ought to be the daily
A P : 2 4 :035(256) [0397] perfectly willing for the **Mass** to be understood as a daily
A P : 2 4 :035(256) [0397] this means the whole **Mass**, the ceremony and also the
A P : 2 4 :042(257) [0399] For in the **Mass** our opponents keep only the ceremony,
A P : 2 4 :047(258) [0401] horribly profaned the **Mass** and introduced much wicked
A P : 2 4 :052(259) [0403] The services of the **Mass** and the rest of the papal order
A P : 2 4 :060(260) [0405] faith and the idea that the **Mass** justifies *ex opere*
A P : 2 4 :061(260) [0405] wicked idea that the **Mass** justifies *ex opere operato*.
A P : 2 4 :063(260) [0405] common errors: that the **Mass** confers grace *ex opere*
A P : 2 4 :064(261) [0405] others, like the one that **Masses** are valid when they are
A P : 2 4 :064(261) [0407] They sell the **Mass** as a price for success, to merchants for
A P : 2 4 :064(261) [0407] though without faith the **Mass** does not even benefit living
A P : 2 4 :066(261) [0407] that the Fathers call the **Mass** a sacrifice; but they do not
A P : 2 4 :066(261) [0407] they do not mean that the **Mass** confers grace *ex opere*
A P : 2 4 :077(263) [0411] The Term **"Mass"**
A P : 2 4 :078(263) [0411] From the names for the **Mass** they take arguments which
A P : 2 4 :078(263) [0411] from the fact that the **Mass** is called a sacrifice that it
A P : 2 4 :079(264) [0411] The Greeks call the **Mass** "liturgy," and this, they say,
A P : 2 4 :079(264) [0411] shows that formerly the **Mass** was the communion of
A P : 2 4 :084(264) [0413] mention an altar, the **Mass** must be a sacrifice; for Paul
A P : 2 4 :085(264) [0413] They also imagine that **"Mass"** is derived from *mizbeach*,
A P : 2 4 :086(265) [0413] they also kept the term **"Mass"** as the name for the
A P : 2 4 :086(265) [0413] of such contributions the **Mass** was called *agape* in some
A P : 2 4 :087(265) [0413] For even though the **Mass** is called an offering, what does
A P : 2 4 :088(265) [0413] [**Mass** for the Dead]
A P : 2 4 :090(266) [0415] for guilt; otherwise, the **Mass** would be on a par with the
A P : 2 4 :090(266) [0415] Therefore the **Mass** is not a satisfaction but a promise
A P : 2 4 :091(266) [0415] ponder the fact that the **Mass** has largely been transferred
A P : 2 4 :092(266) [0415] Since the **Mass** is not a satisfaction for either punishment
A P : 2 4 :093(267) [0417] the other parts of the **Mass**, namely, prayers and
A P : 2 4 :096(267) [0417] he denied that in the **Mass** there was an offering for the
A P : 2 4 :096(267) [0417] Fathers, namely, that the **Mass** justifies *ex opere operato*
A P : 2 4 :098(268) [0417] namely, the abuse of the **Mass**, which they apply in order
A P : 2 4 :099(268) [0419] briefly said this about the **Mass** to let all good men
A P : 2 4 :099(268) [0419] preserve the dignity of the **Mass**, that we show its proper
A P : 2 4 :099(268) [0419] their desecration of the **Mass** lest they burden themselves
A P : 2 4 :099(268) [0419] all kinds of abuses of the **Mass**, we shall not handle the
A P : 2 7 :009(270) [0423] support the abuses of the **Mass**, the wicked services to the
A P : 2 7 :053(278) [0437] as the desecration of the **Mass** by its application to the
A P : 2 8 :026(285) [0451] is in the sacrilegious desecration of the **Mass** for profit!
S 2 : 0 2 :000(293) [0463] Article II. [The **Mass**]
S 2 : 0 2 :001(293) [0463] The **Mass** in the papacy must be regarded as the greatest
S 2 : 0 2 :001(293) [0463] sacrifice or work of the **Mass** (even when offered by an
S 2 : 0 2 :002(293) [0463] "Why do you cling so tenaciously to your **Masses**?
S 2 : 0 2 :003(293) [0463] "2. The **Mass** is unnecessary, and so it can be omitted
S 2 : 0 2 :005(293) [0463] be told openly that the **Mass**, as trumpery, can be omitted
S 2 : 0 2 :005(293) [0463] that one can be saved in a better way without the **Mass**.
S 2 : 0 2 :005(293) [0463] Will the **Mass** not then collapse of itself — not only for
S 2 : 0 2 :006(293) [0463] the buying and selling of **Masses**, it would be prudent to
S 2 : 0 2 :006(293) [0463] prudent to do without the **Mass** for no other reason than
S 2 : 0 2 :006(293) [0463] more useful, and more certain without the **Mass**.
S 2 : 0 2 :007(293) [0463] "5. The **Mass** is and can be nothing else than a human
S 2 : 0 2 :007(294) [0463] for by means of the **Mass** men try to reconcile themselves
S 2 : 0 2 :007(294) [0465] it is not the celebrant of a **Mass** and what he does but the
S 2 : 0 2 :010(294) [0465] This article concerning the **Mass** will be the decisive issue
S 2 : 0 2 :010(294) [0465] to be torn to pieces before he would give up the **Mass**.
S 2 : 0 2 :010(294) [0465] allow a celebrant of the **Mass** and what he does to be
S 2 : 0 2 :010(294) [0465] are well aware that if the **Mass** falls, the papacy will fall
S 2 : 0 2 :011(294) [0465] dragon's tail — that is, the **Mass** — has brought forth a
S 2 : 0 2 :012(294) [0465] occupied with requiem **Masses**, with vigils, with the
S 2 : 0 2 :012(295) [0465] with soul-baths that the **Mass** was used almost exclusively
S 2 : 0 2 :014(295) [0467] accursed traffic in **Masses** which are offered for souls in
S 2 : 0 2 :014(295) [0467] traffic in purgatorial **Masses** (which St. Augustine never
S 2 : 0 2 :016(295) [0467] cunning, of demanding **Masses**, vigils, pilgrimages, and
S 2 : 0 2 :017(296) [0467] things as well as to the **Mass** and all the other
S 2 : 0 2 :018(296) [0467] **Masses**, forgiveness of sins, and God's grace were sought
S 2 : 0 2 :018(296) [0467] were sought here, too, for **Masses** dominated everything.
S 2 : 0 2 :021(296) [0467] legal and open sale) all **Masses**, good works, etc. for the
S 2 : 0 2 :023(296) [0469] of sin and that, like the **Mass**, etc., their use is a good
S 2 : 0 2 :026(297) [0469] festivals for them, say **Masses** and offer sacrifices to
S 2 : 0 2 :027(297) [0469] and festivals and say **Masses** and offer sacrifices in your
S 2 : 0 2 :029(297) [0471] but must condemn the **Mass**, its implications, and its
S 2 : 0 4 :014(301) [0475] to promote his lies about **Masses**, purgatory, monastic
S 3 : 0 3 :026(307) [0487] first by instituting **Masses** and vigils for the dead and
S 3 : 0 3 :028(308) [0487] by fasting, vigils, prayers, **Masses**, coarse clothing, and
T R : 0 0 :043(328) [0517] in the profanation of **Masses** is manifest, for in addition
L C : 0 1 :022(367) [0585] it has made endowments, fasted, celebrated **Mass**, etc.
L C : 0 1 :097(378) [0609] hallowed if one heard a **Mass** or the reading of the
L C : 0 1 :300(405) [0667] For the common **masses** belong much farther down in the
E P : 0 7 :023(484) [0815] papistic sacrifice of the **Mass** for the sins of the living and
E P : 1 2 :010(498) [0839] where formerly papistic **Masses** were read and celebrated.
S D : 0 7 :087(585) [1003] as when in the papistic **Mass** the bread is not distributed
S D : 0 7 :109(588) [1011] of the sacrifice of the **Mass** for the living and for the
S D : 1 2 :015(634) [1099] in which the papistic **Mass** had formerly been read.

Master (30), Mastered (2), Masters (11)
P R : P R :019(009) [0017] profitable writings of **Master** Philip Melanchthon or of
S 3 : 1 5 :005(317) [0501] I, **Master** Veit Dietrich, minister in Nuremberg, subscribe
S 3 : 1 5 :005(317) [0501] **Master** George Helt, of Forchheim
S 3 : 1 5 :005(317) [0501] **Master** Adam of Fulda, preacher in Hesse
S 3 : 1 5 :005(317) [0501] **Master** Anthony Corvinus
S 3 : 1 5 :005(317) [0501] subscribe in the name of **Master** John Brenz, who on his

Continued ▶

S 3 : 1 5 :005(317) [0501] **Master** Peter Geltner, preacher in Frankfurt, subscribed
S 3 : 1 5 :005(318) [0501] the Rev. **Master** Sigismund Kirchner
TR : 0 0 :082(334) [0529] **Master** Veit Dietrich, of Nuremberg, subscribes
TR : 0 0 :082(335) [0529] subscribe in the name of **Master** John Brenz, as he
S C : P R :003(338) [0533] been restored they have **mastered** the fine art of abusing
S C : 0 5 :020(350) [0553] a son or daughter, a **master** or servant; whether you have
S C : 0 5 :022(350) [0553] I am unfaithful to my **master**, for here and there I have
S C : 0 5 :022(350) [0553] I have made my **master** angry, caused him to curse,
S C : 0 5 :023(350) [0553] A **master** or mistress may say: "In particular I confess in
S C : 0 5 :023(350) [0555] **Masters** and mistresses should add whatever else they
S C : 0 9 :010(356) [0563] who are your earthly **masters**, with fear and trembling,
S C : 0 9 :011(356) [0563] **Masters** and Mistresses
S C : 0 9 :011(356) [0563] "**Masters**, do the same to them, and forbear threatening,
S C : 0 9 :011(356) [0563] that he who is both their **Master** and yours is in heaven,
L C : P R :005(359) [0567] which they can absorb and **master** at one reading.
L C : P R :008(359) [0569] daily, yet I cannot **master** it as I wish, but must remain a
L C : P R :012(360) [0571] The devil is called the **master** of a thousand arts.
L C : P R :012(360) [0571] routs and destroys this **master** of a thousand arts with all
L C : P R :012(360) [0571] It must, indeed, be **master** of more than a hundred
L C : 0 1 :100(378) [0609] and have already **mastered** everything, still you are daily
L C : 0 1 :142(384) [0621] Thus all who are called **masters** stand in the place of
L C : 0 1 :142(384) [0621] other peoples called the **masters** and mistresses of the
L C : 0 1 :143(385) [0623] not only to obey their **masters** and mistresses, but also to
L C : 0 1 :144(385) [0623] and be glad to acquire **masters** and mistresses in order to
L C : 0 1 :154(386) [0625] wishes to be his own **master**, be free from all authority,
L C : 0 1 :154(386) [0625] defraud or despise your **master**, another person comes
L C : 0 1 :225(395) [0645] to the vexation and annoyance of his **master** or mistress.
L C : 0 1 :235(397) [0647] to take care of your **master**'s or mistress's property, which
L C : 0 1 :235(397) [0647] are even insolent toward **masters** and mistresses and
L C : 0 1 :245(398) [0649] For God is a **master** of this art; since everyone robs and
L C : 0 1 :277(402) [0659] When the **master** of the house sees a servant failing to do
L C : 0 1 :294(404) [0665] they had they were their **master**'s property, the same as
L C : 0 1 :295(404) [0665] than it is now for a **master** to dismiss his servants or
L C : 0 1 :327(409) [0675] father and mother, **masters**, and all in authority, being
S D : 0 2 :043(529) [0897] death and sin are our **masters** and the devil is our god and
S D : 0 7 :013(571) [0977] "We have heard how **Master** Martin Bucer has explained
S D : 1 1 :082(630) [1089] and useful to the **master** of the house, ready for any good

Match (1)
L C : 0 3 :031(424) [0707] prayer alone we shall be a **match** both for them and for

Material (5)
A P : 0 2 :004(101) [0105] is the so-called "**material** element" of original sin.
A P : 0 2 :035(105) [0115] remains — or, as they call it, the "**material** element" of sin.
A P : 0 2 :035(105) [0115] Concerning this **material** element, he has also said that
A P : 0 4 :024(110) [0127] God even honors it with **material** rewards.
L C : 0 1 :168(388) [0629] only to provide for the **material** support of their children,

Matres (1)
L C : 0 1 :142(384) [0621] the household *patres et* ***matres*** *familias* (that is,

Matrimonial (7), Matrimony (6)
A G : 2 8 :029(085) [0087] (for example, in **matrimonial** cases and in tithes), they
A L : 2 3 :003(051) [0061] taught that it was lawful for them to contract **matrimony**.
A L : 2 7 :018(073) [0077] those who contract **matrimony** that it is lawful for all who
A L : 2 8 :029(085) [0087] example, pertaining to **matrimony**, tithes, etc.), bishops
A P : 1 3 :014(213) [0311] **Matrimony** was first instituted not in the New Testament
A P : 1 3 :015(213) [0311] If **matrimony** should be called a sacrament because it has
S 1 : P R :008(290) [0457] and no state of **matrimony**, but that all live
TR : 0 0 :077(333) [0527] courts (as they call them), especially **matrimonial** cases.
TR : 0 0 :077(333) [0527] that decisions in **matrimonial** cases had formerly belonged
TR : 0 0 :078(333) [0527] unjust papal laws on **matrimonial** questions and that on
TR : 0 0 :079(333) [0527] observe unjust laws in **matrimonial** cases; there are
TR : 0 0 :080(334) [0527] of courts, especially courts for **matrimonial** cases.
TR : 0 0 :081(334) [0527] variety and number of **matrimonial** disputes are so great

Matthew (3)
S C : 0 6 :004(351) [0555] The holy evangelists **Matthew**, Mark, and Luke, and also
L C : S P :020(364) [0579] according to the texts of **Matthew** and Mark at the end of
S D : 0 7 :053(579) [0991] what the words of St. **Matthew** and St. Mark give us,

Mature (1)
P R : P R :013(007) [0013] and glory and after **mature** reflection and careful

Maw (1), Maws (1)
S 3 : 0 3 :025(307) [0485] money they swallowed, the wider became their **maws**.
S D : 1 1 :076(629) [1089] by which he snatches the elect from the **maw** of the devil.

Maybe (1)
A P : 1 2 :109(198) [0283] **Maybe** someone will quote James 5:16, "Confess your sins

Mayence (2)
A G : 2 3 :012(052) [0063] that an archbishop of **Mayence** who had published the
A L : 2 3 :012(052) [0063] that the archbishop of **Mayence**, when about to publish

Mayor (25), Mayors (1)
P R : P R :027(015) [0025] **Mayor** and Council of the City of Luebeck
P R : P R :027(015) [0027] **Mayor** and Council of the City of Landau
P R : P R :027(015) [0027] **Mayor** and Council of the City of Muenster-in-St.
P R : P R :027(015) [0027] **Mayor** and Council of the City of Ulm
P R : P R :027(015) [0027] **Mayor** and Council of the City of Esslingen
P R : P R :027(015) [0027] **Mayor** and Council of the City of Noerdlingen
P R : P R :027(015) [0027] **Mayor** and Council of Rothenburg-on-the-Tauber
P R : P R :027(015) [0027] **Mayor** and Council of the City of Schwaebisch-Hall
P R : P R :027(016) [0027] **Mayor** and Council of the City of Heilbronn
P R : P R :027(016) [0027] **Mayor** and Council of the City of Memmingen
P R : P R :027(016) [0027] **Mayor** and Council of the City of Lindau
P R : P R :027(016) [0027] **Mayor** and Council of the City of Schweinfurt
P R : P R :027(016) [0027] **Mayor** and Council of the City of Wimpfen
P R : P R :027(016) [0027] **Mayor** and Council of the City of Giengen
P R : P R :027(016) [0027] **Mayor** and Council of Bopfingen
P R : P R :027(016) [0027] **Mayor** and Council of the City of Aalen
P R : P R :027(016) [0027] **Mayor** and Council of the City of Kaufbeuren
P R : P R :027(016) [0027] **Mayor** and Council of the City of Isna
P R : P R :027(016) [0027] **Mayor** and Council of the City of Kempten
P R : P R :027(016) [0027] **Mayor** and Council of the City of Lueneburg
P R : P R :027(016) [0027] **Mayor** and Council of the City of Leutkirch
P R : P R :027(016) [0027] **Mayor** and Council of the City of Hamelin
P R : P R :027(016) [0027] **Mayor** and Council of the City of Hanover
A G : 0 0 :007(096) [0095] **Mayor** and council of Nuremburg
A G : 0 0 :007(096) [0095] **Mayor** and council or Reutlingen
L C : 0 1 :258(399) [0653] is this: Where judges, **mayors**, princes, or others in

Mead (1)
S D : 0 8 :019(594) [1021] of the natures, as **mead** is made out of honey and water

Meadows (1)
L C : 0 1 :296(405) [0665] as his wife, servants, house, fields, **meadows**, or cattle.

Meal (3), Meals (2)
A P : 2 4 :068(262) [0407] that took the form of a **meal** symbolizing the mutual
L C : S P :016(363) [0577] when they go to their **meals**, and they go to bed at night;
L C : 0 1 :073(374) [0601] and returning thanks at **meals** and saying other prayers
E P : 0 7 :038(486) [0817] the guests at this heavenly **meal** does not consist only in
S D : 0 7 :123(590) [1015] of guests at this heavenly **meal**, the worthy and the

Mean (107), Means (176), Meant (16)
P R : P R :022(011) [0019] why condemnations cannot by any **means** be avoided.
P R : P R :022(011) [0019] purpose and intention to **mean** thereby those persons who
P R : P R :022(011) [0019] Word, and far less do we **mean** entire churches inside or
P R : P R :022(011) [0019] On the contrary, we **mean** specifically to condemn only
P R : P R :022(011) [0019] These we do not by any **means** intend to tolerate in our
P R : P R :026(014) [0025] the supervision of printers, and other salutary **means**.
A G : P R :017(026) [0041] Again, by **means** of a written instruction at the last diet in
A G : 0 5 :002(031) [0045] these, as through **means**, he gives the Holy Spirit, who
A G : 1 8 :005(040) [0051] By good I **mean** what they are capable of by nature:
A G : 2 0 :022(044) [0055] discovered that they did not obtain peace by such **means**.
A G : 2 0 :023(044) [0055] from the dead, but we **mean** such true faith as believes
A G : 2 0 :025(044) [0057] speak of faith but do not **mean** by it such knowledge as
A G : 2 0 :026(045) [0057] in the Scriptures to **mean** confidence in God, assurance
A G : 2 3 :006(052) [0061] the supreme Majesty, by **means** of human resolutions or
A G : 2 4 :022(058) [0067] the dead, a sacrifice by **means** of which sin was taken
A G : 2 6 :002(064) [0071] service of God by **means** of which grace would be earned
A G : 2 6 :024(067) [0073] kingdom of God does not **mean** food and drink," and in
A G : 2 7 :002(071) [0077] to restore discipline by **means** of these vows as if in a
A G : 2 7 :012(072) [0077] but also that by **means** of this life both the precepts and
A G : 2 7 :047(078) [0081] exaltation of works as a **means** of attaining justification.
A G : 2 7 :061(080) [0083] that they are the **means** of fulfilling both evangelical
A G : 2 8 :053(090) [0091] good order, but not as a **means** of obtaining God's grace
A L : 1 8 :005(040) [0051] By 'good' I **mean** the acts which spring from the good in
A L : 1 8 :007(040) [0053] the other hand, by 'evil' I **mean** such things as to will to
A L : 2 3 :023(055) [0063] of marriage is maintained by **means** of such penalties.
A L : 2 6 :033(069) [0075] of sins or satisfaction for sins by **means** of such exercises.
A L : 2 8 :053(090) [0091] order, but not that by **means** of these we make
A P : 0 2 :003(101) [0105] we do not **mean** only its acts or fruits, but the continual
A P : 0 2 :024(103) [0111] It **means** that when righteousness is lost, concupiscence
A P : 0 2 :029(104) [0113] He **means** that at birth we bring along an ignorance of
A P : 0 2 :032(104) [0113] to what the Fathers **meant** to say about the deficiency.
A P : 0 2 :035(105) [0115] know what Luther **meant** by this statement that original
A P : 0 4 :006(108) [0121] in this discussion we **mean** the commandments of the
A P : 0 4 :048(114) [0135] we add that to have faith **means** to want and to accept the
A P : 0 4 :050(114) [0135] that faith does not simply **mean** historical knowledge but
A P : 0 4 :061(115) [0139] it justifies and what this **means**, and we shall answer our
A P : 0 4 :069(116) [0141] But to believe **means** to trust in Christ's merits, that
A P : 0 4 :072(117) [0141] And "to be justified" **means** to make unrighteous men
A P : 0 4 :098(121) [0151] For "name" here **means** that which is cited as the cause of
A P : 0 4 :112(123) [0155] by faith alone—and we **mean** faith in the true sense of the
A P : 0 4 :134(125) [0159] By the "veil" Paul **means** human opinion about the entire
A P : 0 4 :136(126) [0159] But we **mean** to include both elements, namely, the
A P : 0 4 :154(128) [0163] Truly to believe **means** to think of Christ in this way, and
A P : 0 4 :155(128) [0165] He does not **mean** that these fruits are the price of
A P : 0 4 :161(129) [0167] that justification does not **mean** merely the beginning of
A P : 0 4 :175(131) [0171] should not be taken to **mean** only that those who have
A P : 0 4 :197(134) [0175] He does not **mean** to say that obedience to parents
A P : 0 4 :240(141) [0187] clearly shows what it **means**: "Hatred stirs up strife, but
A P : 0 4 :242(141) [0187] Peter does not **mean** that love merits the forgiveness of
A P : 0 4 :242(141) [0187] He **means** that in human relations it is not peevish,
A P : 0 4 :244(142) [0189] uphold it under the pretext that this is what James **meant**.
A P : 0 4 :249(142) [0191] have already shown often enough what we **mean** by faith.
A P : 0 4 :251(143) [0191] he certainly does not **mean** that we are regenerated by
A P : 0 4 :252(143) [0191] be justified" here does not **mean** that a wicked man is
A P : 0 4 :261(145) [0195] Daniel did not only **mean** to say that the king should give
A P : 0 4 :266(146) [0197] twist his words to **mean** the very opposite of the teaching
A P : 0 4 :275(148) [0199] He does not **mean** that good works are a propitiation —
A P : 0 4 :283(150) [0201] He **means** that outward cleanness is to be sought in
A P : 0 4 :285(150) [0201] This is what Paul really and truly **means**.
A P : 0 4 :305(154) [0205] used in a judicial way to **mean** "to absolve a guilty man
A P : 0 4 :321(157) [0209] the merit of condignity **means** to doubt and to work
A P : 0 4 :337(159) [0215] If it **meant** the knowledge of history that the wicked and
A P : 0 4 :342(160) [0215] "Unworthy servants" **means** "insufficient servants," since
A P : 0 4 :371(164) [0221] must be taken to **mean** not only outward works but also
A P : 0 4 :381(165) [0223] as though the ancients **meant** to say that we should put
A P : 0 7 :008(169) [0229] to explain what "church" **means**, namely, the assembly of
A P : 0 7 :010(170) [0229] catholic" lest we take it to **mean** an outward government
A P : 0 7 :019(171) [0233] that "the good seed **means** the sons of the kingdom,
A P : 0 7 :021(172) [0233] This, too, **means** to remove Christ as the foundation.
A P : 0 7 :030(174) [0237] If we **mean** "particular rites" they approve our article, but
A P : 0 7 :030(174) [0237] our article, but if we **mean** "universal rites" they
A P : 0 7 :031(174) [0237] We do not quite understand what our opponents **mean**.
A P : 0 7 :036(175) [0241] What he **means** is this.
A P : 0 7 :036(175) [0241] etc.), and are not **means** by which God moves the heart to
A P : 0 7 :036(175) [0241] kingdom of God does not **mean** food and drink but
A P : 1 2 :044(187) [0263] and being heavy-laden **mean** contrition, anxiety, and the
A P : 1 2 :044(187) [0263] To come to Christ **means** to believe that for his sake sins
A P : 1 2 :046(188) [0263] but mortification **means** genuine terrors, like those of the
A P : 1 2 :050(189) [0265] sentences the first part **means** contrition, the second

Continued ▶

A P : 1 2 :060(190) [0267] penitence, they do not **mean** justifying but the general
A P : 1 2 :081(194) [0275] This is what Paul **means** when he says in Rom. 4:16,
A P : 1 2 :084(194) [0277] what Paul really and truly **means**; we know that this
A P : 1 2 :091(195) [0279] For example. "Penitence **means** to lament past evils and
A P : 1 2 :106(197) [0283] passages of Scripture **mean** whatever they want them to
A P : 1 2 :106(197) [0283] of Scripture mean whatever they want them to **mean**.
A P : 1 2 :106(197) [0283] "know" here **means** to hear confessions, "condition"
A P : 1 2 :106(197) [0283] confessions, "condition" **means** the secrets of conscience
A P : 1 2 :106(197) [0283] and not outward conduct, and "flocks" **means** men.
A P : 1 2 :132(202) [0291] we say, is what John **means** when he says (Matt. 3:8),
A P : 1 2 :136(203) [0293] and "Be penitent" will **mean** "Suffer the penalties of
A P : 1 2 :140(204) [0295] death," should be taken to **mean** not Christ but our
A P : 1 2 :154(207) [0301] but if this is what they **mean**, why do they add that we
A P : 1 2 :163(208) [0303] "Judge" **means** all of penitence; it means to "condemn
A P : 1 2 :163(208) [0303] means all of penitence; it **means** to "condemn sins."
A P : 1 2 :166(208) [0303] By their penitence — we **mean** the whole process of
A P : 1 2 :167(209) [0305] connection they did not **mean** a payment for eternal
A P : 1 2 :168(209) [0305] says, "True satisfaction **means** cutting off the causes of
A P : 1 2 :176(210) [0307] Just as "to loose" **means** to forgive sins, so "to bind"
A P : 1 2 :176(210) [0307] to forgive sins, so "to bind" **means** not to forgive sins.
A P : 1 5 :037(220) [0325] are being required as a **means** of meriting justification.
A P : 2 0 :003(227) [0339] nevertheless, they did not **mean** to say that we receive the
A P : 2 1 :036(234) [0353] public or private life, as a **means** of confirming their faith
A P : 2 2 :008(237) [0359] imagine that it **means** our present custom of giving the
A P : 2 3 :007(240) [0365] the desire which was **meant** to be in uncorrupted nature.
A P : 2 3 :018(242) [0369] are only clowning; they do not **mean** this seriously.
A P : 2 3 :033(244) [0373] If purity **means** that something has God's permission and
A P : 2 3 :064(248) [0381] Lord," must be taken to **mean** purity of the heart and
A P : 2 4 :015(252) [0389] own ideas to it as if it **meant** whatever they want it to
A P : 2 4 :015(252) [0389] ideas to it as if it meant whatever they want it to **mean**.
A P : 2 4 :023(253) [0391] interprets the law to **mean** that the death of Christ is a
A P : 2 4 :023(253) [0391] word he uses here (*'asam*) **means** a victim sacrificed for
A P : 2 4 :023(253) [0391] the Old Testament this **meant** that a victim was to come
A P : 2 4 :023(253) [0391] Isaiah and Paul **mean** that Christ became a sacrificial
A P : 2 4 :033(255) [0395] so long as he does not **mean** that by itself, or *ex opere*
A P : 2 4 :035(256) [0397] sacrifice, provided this **means** the whole Mass, the
A P : 2 4 :066(261) [0407] sacrifice; but they do not **mean** that the Mass confers
A P : 2 4 :072(262) [0409] This **means** that in the ceremony we should acknowledge
A P : 2 4 :079(264) [0411] the Mass "liturgy," and this, they say, **means** "sacrifice."
A P : 2 4 :080(264) [0411] It does not really **mean** a sacrifice but a public service.
A P : 2 4 :081(264) [0411] To the Greeks it **meant** "public duties," like the taxes
A P : 2 4 :082(264) [0411] to my need," which surely does not **mean** a sacrificer.
A P : 2 4 :083(264) [0413] of their use of "liturgy" to **mean** public duties or
A P : 2 4 :083(264) [0413] derive it from *lite,* which **means** prayers, but from *leita,*
A P : 2 4 :083(264) [0413] but from *leita,* which **means** public goods; thus the verb
A P : 2 4 :083(264) [0413] goods; thus the verb **means** to care for or to administer
A P : 2 4 :085(265) [0413] in Deut. 16:10, where it **means** the collection or gifts of
A P : 2 4 :088(265) [0413] service" (Rom. 12:1) Paul **meant** the service of the mind,
A P : 2 4 :093(267) [0417] service" does not **mean** the host itself but the prayers and
A P : 2 7 :027(273) [0429] therefore perfection **means** to grow in the fear of God, in
A P : 2 7 :040(276) [0433] Christ does not **mean** to say that leaving parents or wife
A P : 2 7 :058(279) [0439] Word of God and was not **meant** to merit the forgiveness
A P : 2 8 :015(283) [0447] acts of worship but a **means** of preserving order in the
S 2 : 0 2 :007(294) [0463] subject declare), for by **means** of the Mass men try to
S 2 : 0 2 :015(295) [0467] This **means** that the Word of God shall establish articles
S 3 : 0 2 :005(303) [0479] This is what is **meant** by Rom. 4:15, "The law brings
S 3 : 0 3 :002(304) [0479] is the thunderbolt by **means** of which God with one blow
S 3 : 0 8 :001(312) [0493] absolution should by no **means** be allowed to fall into
S 3 : 1 4 :001(316) [0501] Christian and proposes by **means** of his work to help not
T R : 0 0 :005(320) [0503] define what the papists **mean** when they say that the
T R : 0 0 :005(320) [0503] They **mean** that the pope is the universal bishop or, as
T R : 0 0 :045(328) [0517] invented satisfactions, by **means** of which they have
T R : 0 0 :080(334) [0527] which needs these **means** for the support of ministers, the
S C : P R :014(339) [0535] become familiar with the text, teach them what it **means**.
S C : 0 1 :002(342) [0539] What does this **mean**?
S C : 0 1 :004(342) [0539] What does this **mean**?
S C : 0 1 :006(342) [0541] What does this **mean**?
S C : 0 1 :008(343) [0541] What does this **mean**?
S C : 0 1 :010(343) [0541] What does this **mean**?
S C : 0 1 :012(343) [0541] What does this **mean**?
S C : 0 1 :014(343) [0541] What does this **mean**?
S C : 0 1 :016(343) [0541] What does this **mean**?
S C : 0 1 :018(343) [0541] What does this **mean**?
S C : 0 1 :020(344) [0543] What does this **mean**?
S C : 0 1 :022(344) [0543] What does this **mean**?
S C : 0 2 :002(344) [0543] What does this **mean**?
S C : 0 2 :004(345) [0545] What does this **mean**?
S C : 0 2 :006(345) [0545] What does this **mean**?
S C : 0 3 :002(346) [0545] What does this **mean**?
S C : 0 3 :004(346) [0547] What does this **mean**?
S C : 0 3 :007(346) [0547] What does this **mean**?
S C : 0 3 :010(347) [0547] What does this **mean**?
S C : 0 3 :013(347) [0547] What does this **mean**?
S C : 0 3 :014(347) [0547] What is **meant** by daily bread?
S C : 0 3 :016(347) [0549] What does this **mean**?
S C : 0 3 :018(347) [0549] What does this **mean**?
S C : 0 3 :020(348) [0549] What does this **mean**?
S C : 0 3 :021(348) [0549] What does this **mean**?
S C : 0 3 :021(348) [0549] Answer: It **means** that I should be assured that such
S C : 0 3 :021(348) [0549] "Amen, amen" **means** "Yes, yes, it shall be so."
S C : 0 5 :016(349) [0553] from God himself, by no **means** doubting but firmly
S C : 0 5 :022(350) [0553] I **mean** to do better."
S C : 0 8 :008(353) [0559] of every living thing" **means** that all creatures receive
L C : 0 1 :001(365) [0581] What does this **mean**, and how is it to be understood?
L C : 0 1 :010(366) [0583] to have a God properly **means** to have something in
L C : 0 1 :013(366) [0583] God, you see, does not **mean** to lay hands upon him, or
L C : 0 1 :018(367) [0585] therefore, to have a god **means** to trust and believe.
L C : 0 1 :026(368) [0587] the hands, channels, and **means** through which God
L C : 0 1 :027(368) [0587] to seek other ways and **means** than God has commanded,
L C : 0 1 :038(369) [0591] are also the people he **means** when he says, "who hate
L C : 0 1 :051(371) [0595] What does it **mean** to misuse or take the name of God in
L C : 0 1 :057(372) [0597] This **means** that in no one shall a violation be condoned
L C : 0 1 :062(373) [0597] you understand what it **means** to take God's name in
L C : 0 1 :064(373) [0599] All this is what we **mean** by calling upon his name in
L C : 0 1 :069(374) [0599] as I have before, that by **means** of warning and threat,
L C : 0 1 :076(375) [0603] who have to be forced by **means** of rods and blows will
L C : 0 1 :079(375) [0603] which properly **means** to rest, that is, to cease from
L C : 0 1 :079(375) [0603] "stopping work" literally **means** "observing a holy day or
L C : 0 1 :081(376) [0603] but, as we shall hear, it **meant** that we should sanctify the
L C : 0 1 :087(376) [0605] sanctify the holy day" **means**, answer: "It means to keep it
L C : 0 1 :087(376) [0605] the holy day" means, answer: "It **means** to keep it holy."
L C : 0 1 :087(376) [0605] What is **meant** by "keeping it holy"?
L C : 0 1 :129(383) [0617] By **means** of commandments, therefore, he reminds and
L C : 0 1 :134(383) [0619] to have long life **means** not merely to grow old but to
L C : 0 1 :154(386) [0625] So God punishes one knave by **means** of another.
L C : 0 1 :188(390) [0633] This **means**, first, by hand or by deed; next, we should
L C : 0 1 :188(390) [0635] use nor sanction any **means** or methods whereby anyone
L C : 0 1 :190(391) [0635] you know ways and **means** to do so, you have killed him.
L C : 0 1 :202(392) [0639] but also every kind of cause, motive, and **means**.
L C : 0 1 :224(395) [0643] else than to acquire another's property by unjust **means**.
L C : 0 1 :245(398) [0649] the other, he punishes one thief by **means** of another.
L C : 0 1 :249(398) [0651] is only to instruct and reprove by **means** of God's Word.
L C : 0 1 :286(403) [0663] Gospel, and in which he **means** to embrace all the
L C : 0 1 :302(405) [0667] and by any other **means** at his disposal, until the property
L C : 0 1 :324(409) [0675] have no other gods," **means** simply, "You shall fear, love,
L C : 0 2 :013(412) [0681] What is **meant** by these words, "I believe in God, the
L C : 0 2 :013(412) [0681] food and drink, clothing, **means** of support, wife and
L C : 0 2 :027(414) [0685] It **means** that he has redeemed me from sin, from the
L C : 0 2 :031(414) [0685] little word "Lord" simply **means** the same as Redeemer,
L C : 0 2 :031(414) [0685] express how and by what **means** this redemption was
L C : 0 2 :040(416) [0689] are asked, What do you **mean** by the words, "I believe in
L C : 0 2 :041(416) [0689] By what **means**?
L C : 0 2 :047(416) [0691] The word *ecclesia* properly **means** an assembly.
L C : 0 2 :048(416) [0691] "church" *(Kirche)* really **means** nothing else than a
L C : 0 2 :059(418) [0695] earth through these two **means**, the Christian church and
L C : 0 2 :059(418) [0695] preserve us in it by **means** of the last two parts of this
L C : 0 3 :012(422) [0701] that we should by no **means** despise our prayers, but
L C : 0 3 :033(424) [0707] We by no **means** reject prayer, but we do denounce the
L C : 0 3 :046(426) [0709] namely, that "to hallow" **means** the same as in our idiom
L C : 0 3 :064(429) [0715] all the arts, tricks, ways, and **means** that he can devise.
L C : 0 3 :066(429) [0717] and the old Adam, for it **means** that we must remain
L C : 0 3 :122(436) [0731] That **means** they have their eye not on God's promise but
L C : 0 4 :018(438) [0737] This **means** that when the Word is added to the element
L C : 0 4 :022(439) [0737] the water, must by no **means** be separated from each
L C : 0 4 :030(440) [0739] what purpose or by what **means** he speaks — there faith
L C : 0 4 :071(445) [0751] This is what it **means** to plunge into Baptism and daily
L C : 0 5 :039(451) [0761] What I **mean** is that those who claim to be Christians
L C : 0 5 :047(452) [0765] Christ **means** to say: "I institute a Passover or Supper for
E P : 0 1 :022(469) [0785] Sometimes the term **means** man's essence, as when we
E P : 0 1 :022(469) [0785] At other times the word **means** the good or bad quality
E P : 0 1 :022(469) [0785] word "nature" does not **mean** the substance of man but
E P : 0 2 :004(470) [0787] effect conversion without **means**; he employs to this end
E P : 0 2 :013(471) [0789] and saves them without **means**, without the hearing of
E P : 0 2 :018(472) [0791] an instrument and **means** of God the Holy Spirit, so that
E P : 0 3 :005(473) [0793] that faith is the only **means** and instrument whereby we
E P : 0 3 :007(473) [0793] the word "justify" **means** in this article "absolve," that is,
E P : 0 3 :008(474) [0793] and then they **mean** the same thing, even though
E P : 0 3 :015(475) [0795] "to be justified" do not **mean** to absolve or to be absolved
E P : 0 3 :015(475) [0795] forgiveness of sins, but **mean** to be made righteous in fact
E P : 0 5 :006(478) [0803] when the word "Gospel" **means** the entire doctrine of
E P : 0 7 :005(482) [0809] them the word "spiritual" **means** no more than the
E P : 0 8 :039(491) [0827] to me" (Matt. 28:18), to **mean** that in the resurrection and
E P : 1 1 :012(496) [0835] few are chosen," does not **mean** that God does not desire
E P : 1 2 :022(499) [0841] and heard — is not a **means** through which God the Holy
E P : 1 2 :023(500) [0841] water of Baptism is not a **means** through which the Lord
E P : 1 2 :024(500) [0843] the Holy Supper are not **means** through and by which
S D : P R :010(506) [0855] This, of course, does not **mean** that other good, useful,
S D : 0 1 :006(509) [0861] This **means** that in the sight of God original sin, like a
S D : 0 1 :030(513) [0867] This does not **mean** that human nature has been totally
S D : 0 1 :051(517) [0875] the word "nature" **means** man's essence, body and soul.
S D : 0 1 :051(517) [0875] the term "nature" **means** — as it often does — a
S D : 0 2 :004(520) [0881] Holy Spirit without any **means** or created instruments
S D : 0 2 :046(530) [0899] out of heaven, without **means**, and they are able actually
S D : 0 2 :048(530) [0901] God, how and by what **means** (namely, the oral Word
S D : 0 2 :048(530) [0901] how we are to relate ourselves to and use these **means**.
S D : 0 2 :050(531) [0901] them through this **means** and in no other way — namely,
S D : 0 2 :054(531) [0903] Through this **means** (namely, the preaching and the
S D : 0 2 :066(534) [0907] such a view could by no **means** be conceded without
S D : 0 2 :072(535) [0909] doctrine directs us to the **means** through which the Holy
S D : 0 2 :080(536) [0911] who imagine that without **means**, without hearing the
S D : 0 2 :081(537) [0911] himself explains what it **means** to lay off the old man and
S D : 0 2 :089(538) [0915] works in him), he did not **mean** that conversion takes
S D : 0 2 :089(538) [0915] divine Word, nor did he **mean** that in conversion the
S D : 0 2 :090(539) [0915] of his holy Word as his ordinary **means** and instrument.
S D : 0 3 :010(541) [0919] and faith is the only **means** whereby we can apprehend,
S D : 0 3 :017(541) [0921] the word "justify" here **means** to declare righteous and
S D : 0 3 :021(542) [0921] the word "regeneration" **means** the sanctification or
S D : 0 3 :022(543) [0923] and justified, we do not **mean** that after regeneration no
S D : 0 3 :022(543) [0923] the other hand, does this **mean** that we may or should
S D : 0 3 :031(544) [0925] nor any other virtue the **means** and instrument with and
S D : 0 3 :038(546) [0929] as the only and exclusive **means** and instrument with and
S D : 0 3 :043(547) [0931] on this account, that as a **means** and instrument it
S D : 0 3 :062(550) [0937] "to be justified" do not **mean** "to absolve from sins" and
S D : 0 4 :034(556) [0949] It does not, however, **mean** that faith accepts
S D : 0 4 :035(557) [0949] the proper and the only **means** whereby righteousness and
S D : 0 5 :008(559) [0953] the phrase "to repent" **means** nothing more than truly to
S D : 0 5 :025(563) [0961] But this does not **mean** that men may abuse the grace of
S D : 0 7 :001(569) [0971] to the divine truth by **means** of our confession in this
S D : 0 7 :018(572) [0979] union is intended to **mean** nothing more than the
S D : 0 7 :031(574) [0983] well realize what this will **mean** for me before the Last
S D : 0 7 :046(577) [0989] had many more ways and **means** of fulfilling the promises
S D : 0 7 :056(579) [0991] body of Christ, and that **means** that all who receive the
S D : 0 7 :059(580) [0993] is the church), or it is the **means** whereby believers are
S D : 0 7 :059(580) [0993] laid hold on by faith, is a **means** whereby we are
S D : 0 7 :086(584) [1003] does not primarily **mean** faith, or the oral eating alone,
S D : 0 7 :104(587) [1009] this word "spiritual" **means** precisely that spiritual

Continued ▶

SD : 0 8 :044(599) [1029] I **mean** that this way: If it is not true that God died for
SD : 0 8 :062(603) [1037] into the God-head or by **means** of these communicated
SD : 0 8 :077(606) [1043] these testimonies to **mean** that only the deity of Christ is
SD : 0 8 :085(608) [1047] This is what he **means** when he says, 'All things have been
SD : 1 1 :014(619) [1069] This **means** that we must always take as one unit the
SD : 1 1 :027(620) [1071] God does not call without **means** but through the Word,
SD : 1 1 :028(620) [1071] profitably, we must by all **means** cling rigidly and firmly
SD : 1 1 :041(623) [1077] rejects or perverts the **means** and instrument of the Holy
SD : 1 1 :076(628) [1087] will not do this without **means**, and he has ordained
SD : 1 1 :076(628) [1087] as the ordinary **means** or instruments to accomplish this
SD : 1 2 :003(633) [1097] Augsburg Confession really is and what it really **means**.
SD : 1 2 :030(635) [1101] and heard, is not a **means** whereby God the Holy Spirit
SD : 1 2 :031(635) [1101] water of Baptism is not a **means** whereby the Lord God
SD : 1 2 :032(635) [1101] the Holy Supper are not **means** through which Christ

Meaning (45), Meanings (2)
AP : 0 4 :224(138) [0181] instead of deriving the **meaning** from the texts
AP : 0 4 :231(139) [0183] about perfection, we shall simply present Paul's **meaning**.
AP : 0 4 :283(150) [0201] Our opponents twist his **meaning** by sophistically
AP : 0 4 :342(159) [0215] "unworthy servants" as **meaning** that works are worthless
AP : 0 7 :045(177) [0243] misunderstand the **meaning** of the righteousness of faith
AP : 1 2 :106(197) [0283] surely interpret "condition" as **meaning** outward conduct.
AP : 2 4 :023(253) [0391] We can understand the **meaning** of the word more readily
AP : 2 4 :032(255) [0395] Besides, the prophet's own words give us his **meaning**.
AP : 2 4 :039(257) [0399] we can see that their real **meaning** is spiritual worship and
AP : 2 4 :068(262) [0409] about faith, whose true **meaning** very few understand.
AP : 2 4 :092(267) [0417] who understand the **meaning** of neither sacrifice nor
S3 : 0 3 :016(305) [0483] are as far from comprehending their **meaning** as I am.
LC : SP :026(364) [0579] it explained and may learn the **meaning** of every part.
LC : 0 1 :004(365) [0581] The **meaning** is: "See to it that you let me alone be your
LC : 0 1 :024(367) [0587] well and remember the **meaning** of this commandment:
LC : 0 1 :050(371) [0595] to grasp simply the **meaning** of this and all the other
LC : 0 1 :052(371) [0595] as the plain and simple **meaning** of this commandment.
LC : 0 1 :086(376) [0605] This, then, is the plain **meaning** of this commandment:
LC : 0 1 :257(399) [0653] In its first and simplest **meaning**, as the words stand
LC : 0 1 :261(400) [0655] and its plainest **meaning**, applying to all that takes place
LC : 0 1 :324(409) [0675] This is exactly the **meaning** and right interpretation of the
LC : 0 2 :024(413) [0683] Such, very briefly, is the **meaning** of this article.
LC : 0 2 :047(416) [0691] Both expressions have the same **meaning**.
EP : 0 1 :022(469) [0785] to observe that the word "nature" has several **meanings**.
EP : 0 5 :006(478) [0803] forth (examples of this **meaning** occur in Mark 1:15 and
EP : 0 7 :025(485) [0815] are dark sayings whose **meaning** must first be sought in
SD : PR :004(502) [0847] abide by the plain, clear, and pure **meaning** of its words.
SD : PR :006(502) [0847] failed to grasp their true **meaning** or because they did not
SD : PR :010(503) [0849] and so that well-**meaning** Christians who are really
SD : PR :006(504) [0853] the true and genuine **meaning** of the Augsburg
SD : PR :020(508) [0859] accepted Christian **meaning** of the Augsburg Confession
SD : 0 1 :051(517) [0875] have two or more accepted **meanings** in common use.
SD : 0 3 :017(542) [0921] is the usual usage and **meaning** of the word in the Holy
SD : 0 4 :018(554) [0943] With this **meaning** and in this sense it is right to say and
SD : 0 5 :003(558) [0953] have one and the same **meaning** but is used in a twofold
SD : 0 6 :015(566) [0967] "law" here has but one **meaning**, namely, the immutable
SD : 0 7 :002(569) [0973] them to set forth their **meaning** clearly, honestly, and
SD : 0 7 :017(572) [0979] the correct and true **meaning** is set forth briefly and
SD : 0 7 :034(575) [0983] Confession's real **meaning** and intention in this article
SD : 0 7 :041(576) [0985] V, therefore the true **meaning** and intention of the
SD : 0 7 :048(578) [0989] in their usual, strict, and commonly accepted **meaning**.
SD : 0 7 :048(578) [0989] (that is, a change in **meaning**) in the word "bread," as
SD : 0 7 :049(578) [0989] (that is, a change in **meaning**) in the word "body."
SD : 0 7 :053(579) [0991] have no other **meaning** than what the words of St.
SD : 0 7 :092(586) [1005] testament to a strange **meaning** different from the way the
SD : 1 1 :003(616) [1063] must set forth the correct **meaning** on the basis of
SD : 1 2 :006(633) [1097] natural, and proper **meaning** of the Augsburg

Meantime (1), Meanwhile (27)
AG : 0 1 :002(056) [0065] **Meanwhile** no conspicuous changes have been made in
AG : 2 4 :023(058) [0067] **Meanwhile** faith in Christ and true service of God were
AG : 2 7 :049(079) [0083] station in life; and that **meanwhile** we do good works for
AL : 2 6 :010(065) [0071] **Meanwhile** the commands of God pertaining to callings
AL : 2 6 :013(066) [0073] keep the traditions and, **meanwhile**, they had never heard
AL : 2 7 :049(079) [0083] with our callings; **meanwhile** to be diligent in the
AP : 0 4 :018(109) [0125] external works and **meanwhile** neither fears God nor truly
AP : 0 4 :034(112) [0129] **Meanwhile** they do not see the first table, which
AP : 0 4 :155(128) [0165] act of worship; but **meanwhile** he teaches that it is faith
AP : 0 7 :019(171) [0233] **Meanwhile** he teaches that though these wicked men
AP : 1 2 :042(187) [0261] **Meanwhile** this faith is nourished in many ways, amid
AP : 2 3 :055(247) [0379] **Meanwhile**, preachers of the Gospel should exhort the
AP : 2 4 :098(268) [0419] **Meanwhile** all those who truly believe the Gospel should
AP : 2 7 :054(278) [0437] **Meanwhile** they neither hear nor preach the Gospel about
AP : 2 8 :003(281) [0443] **Meanwhile** they neglect the state of the churches, and they
S3 : 0 3 :015(305) [0483] of, confessed, etc., but **meanwhile** the sinner was
TR : 0 0 :080(334) [0527] **Meanwhile** they defraud the church, which needs these
LC : 0 1 :042(370) [0591] even keep alive; **meanwhile**, those who serve mammon
LC : 0 1 :119(381) [0615] self-devised works and **meanwhile** have only scorn and
LC : 0 1 :231(396) [0647] **Meanwhile** the little sneak-thieves who have committed
LC : 0 1 :246(398) [0651] The upright, **meanwhile**, will not want, and you will hurt
LC : 0 2 :057(418) [0693] **Meanwhile**, since holiness has begun and is growing
LC : 0 3 :093(433) [0725] **Meanwhile**, a necessary but comforting clause is added,
LC : 0 4 :045(442) [0743] but the water, and **meanwhile** the Word is spoken so that
LC : 0 5 :026(449) [0759] **Meanwhile** it must suffer much opposition.
LC : 0 5 :071(454) [0769] **Meanwhile**, on your part, you ought to be impelled by
LC : 0 6 :023(459) [0000] clearly explained, and **meanwhile** if the needs which
SD : 0 4 :011(553) [0941] works are, and in the **meantime** he chatters and jabbers a

Measure (21), Measures (2)
AG : 1 8 :001(039) [0051] that man possesses some **measure** of freedom of the will
AG : 2 7 :051(079) [0083] praised above all **measure**, draw many harmful
AL : 1 8 :009(040) [0053] nature is able in some **measure** to perform the outward
AL : 2 7 :052(079) [0083] celibacy praised above **measure**, and therefore they
AL : 2 8 :040(087) [0089] pontiffs seem in some **measure** to have been misled by the
AP : 1 2 :150(206) [0299] me, O Lord, but in just **measure**; not in thy anger, lest
SC : 0 5 :023(350) [0555] him, giving him inferior goods and short **measure**."
LC : 0 1 :212(394) [0641] unchastity in some **measure**, God has established
LC : 0 1 :227(396) [0645] merchandise, false **measures**, dishonest weights, and bad
LC : 0 2 :063(419) [0695] But here you have everything in richest **measure**.
LC : 0 3 :062(428) [0715] It pains him beyond **measure** when his lies and
EP : 0 6 :008(481) [0807] in the manner and **measure** above described, upon
SD : 0 1 :012(510) [0863] man still possesses a **measure** of reason, power, and
SD : 0 2 :074(535) [0909] whatever to achieve a **measure** of external righteousness
SD : 0 6 :026(568) [0971] law in the manner and **measure** indicated above is not to
SD : 0 7 :101(587) [1007] they do not feel, touch, **measure**, or comprehend him, how
SD : 0 7 :101(587) [1007] mode, where they cannot **measure** or comprehend him
SD : 0 7 :101(587) [1007] present to himself, **measures** and comprehends them.
SD : 0 8 :051(601) [1033] employed after its own **measure** and fashion along with
SD : 0 8 :054(601) [1033] But these do not **measure** up to the majesty which the
SD : 0 8 :072(605) [1041] the Spirit's gifts not by **measure**, like other saints.
SD : 0 8 :074(606) [1043] out upon him without **measure** the Spirit of wisdom and
SD : 1 1 :006(617) [1065] God sets a limit and **measure** for the evil which he does

Meat (2)
AP : 2 3 :045(245) [0375] they abstained from the **meat** of all animals, thus
AP : 2 3 :045(245) [0377] instead of using wine or **meat** or marriage, which seemed

Mecklenburg (2)
PR : PR :027(015) [0025] Ulrich, duke of **Mecklenburg** [-Guestrow]
PR : PR :027(015) [0025] Sigismund August of **Mecklenburg** [in Ivernack] the

Mediate (1), Mediation (2), Mediatorial (1), Mediators (9)
AP : 0 4 :324(157) [0211] faith and obscures Christ's glory and **mediatorial** work.
AP : 0 4 :376(165) [0223] through his priestly **mediation** we are led to the Father
AP : 2 1 :014(230) [0347] It makes them **mediators** and propitiators.
AP : 2 1 :014(230) [0347] distinguish between **mediators** of intercession and
AP : 2 1 :014(230) [0347] of intercession and **mediators** of redemption, they
AP : 2 1 :014(231) [0347] they obviously make the saints **mediators** of redemption.
AP : 2 1 :015(231) [0347] from Scripture for calling them **mediators** of intercession.
AP : 2 1 :015(231) [0347] Thus they actually make them **mediators** of redemption.
AP : 2 1 :016(231) [0347] but propitiators, that is, **mediators** of redemption.
AP : 2 1 :034(233) [0351] if we seek out other **mediators** besides Christ and put our
AP : 2 3 :040(245) [0375] commends virginity for the sake of **mediation** and study.
AP : 2 4 :058(260) [0405] be setting up other **mediators** besides Christ if we were to
SD : 0 3 :056(549) [0935] the humanity, could not **mediate** between God and us.

Mediator (64)
AG : 2 0 :009(042) [0053] sake, who alone is the **mediator** who reconciles the
AG : 2 1 :002(047) [0057] "For there is one **mediator** between God and men, Christ
AL : 2 0 :009(042) [0053] been ordained to be the **mediator** and propitiation
AL : 2 1 :002(047) [0057] their help, for the only **mediator**, propitiation, highpriest,
AP : 0 4 :018(109) [0125] should not use him as **mediator** and believe that for his
AP : 0 4 :040(112) [0131] has been appointed as the **mediator** and the propitiator.
AP : 0 4 :046(113) [0133] merits of love, but Christ the **mediator** and propitiator.
AP : 0 4 :069(116) [0141] "Christ is the **mediator**," then we must defend the
AP : 0 4 :069(116) [0141] how will Christ be the **mediator** if we do not use him as
AP : 0 4 :069(116) [0141] if we do not use him as **mediator** in our justification and
AP : 0 4 :080(118) [0143] it is only by faith that Christ is accepted as the **mediator**.
AP : 0 4 :081(118) [0143] that Christ is the **mediator** and propitiator because he
AP : 0 4 :081(118) [0143] would not have us make use of him now as our **mediator**.
AP : 0 4 :145(127) [0163] account of Christ, the **mediator**, we have a gracious God.
AP : 0 4 :157(128) [0165] we rob Christ of his honor as **mediator** and propitiator.
AP : 0 4 :162(129) [0169] Christ does not stop being the **mediator** after our renewal.
AP : 0 4 :163(129) [0169] Christ remains the **mediator**.
AP : 0 4 :165(130) [0169] the propitiator and **mediator**, and then imagine that he is
AP : 0 4 :213(136) [0179] to rob Christ of his honor as **mediator** and propitiator?
AP : 0 4 :214(136) [0179] because of our works without Christ, the **mediator**.
AP : 0 4 :214(136) [0179] Only Christ, the **mediator**, can be pitted against God's
AP : 0 4 :238(140) [0187] in place of Christ, the **mediator**, love is the propitiation
AP : 0 4 :238(141) [0187] or that love is righteousness without Christ, the **mediator**.
AP : 0 4 :242(141) [0187] in place of Christ the **mediator** it is our propitiation; or
AP : 0 4 :269(147) [0197] (Rom. 5:2), not by works without Christ, the **mediator**.
AP : 0 4 :270(147) [0197] hold of Christ, the **mediator**, the heart is at peace and
AP : 0 4 :270(147) [0199] the sake of Christ, the **mediator**, even though its incipient
AP : 0 4 :291(152) [0203] we should set him, the **mediator** and propitiator, against
AP : 0 4 :294(152) [0203] God without Christ, the **mediator**; nor do we receive
AP : 0 4 :299(153) [0205] men to make use of him as **mediator** and propitiator.
AP : 0 4 :313(155) [0207] not teach us to use Christ as the **mediator** in justification.
AP : 0 4 :314(156) [0207] without Christ, the **mediator**, rather than by faith, but
AP : 0 4 :316(156) [0209] earns eternal life without needing Christ, the **mediator**.
AP : 0 4 :317(156) [0209] to our works, a destruction of his glory as **mediator**?
AP : 0 4 :317(156) [0209] For he is the **mediator** continually and not just at the
AP : 0 4 :357(162) [0219] without needing mercy or the **mediator** Christ or faith.
AP : 0 4 :358(162) [0219] need neither Christ the **mediator** nor the faith that has
AP : 0 4 :359(162) [0219] of the faith that takes hold of Christ, the **mediator**.
AP : 0 4 :360(162) [0219] their own sake, not for the sake of Christ, the **mediator**.
AP : 0 4 :372(164) [0221] know that Christ, the **mediator**, should not be excluded.
AP : 0 4 :372(164) [0221] please God without the **mediator** Christ and faith,
AP : 0 4 :375(164) [0223] because of faith and the **mediator** Christ but in
AP : 0 4 :376(164) [0223] them the righteousness of faith and Christ, the **mediator**.
AP : 0 4 :378(165) [0223] omitting the faith that takes hold of the **mediator** Christ.
AP : 0 4 :387(166) [0225] deny that Christ is the **mediator** and propitiator, deny the
AP : 1 2 :043(187) [0263] us to make use of Christ as our **mediator** and propitiator.
AP : 1 2 :064(191) [0269] hold of Christ, the **mediator**, and believes the promises
AP : 1 2 :076(193) [0273] for there is no other **mediator** or propitiator but Christ.
AP : 1 2 :076(193) [0275] works but because of Christ, the **mediator** and propitiator
AP : 1 2 :084(194) [0277] the wrath of God not our works but Christ, the **mediator**.
AP : 1 2 :087(195) [0277] in our love or works, but only in Christ, the **mediator**.
AP : 1 5 :005(215) [0317] traditions as another **mediator** through which they seek to
AP : 1 5 :007(216) [0317] to set up another justifier and **mediator** instead of Christ?
AP : 1 5 :009(216) [0317] appointed Christ as the **mediator**; he wants to be gracious
AP : 1 5 :009(216) [0317] Thus they rob Christ of his honor as the **mediator**.
AP : 2 4 :057(260) [0405] it replaces Christ as our **mediator** and propitiator with
S3 : 1 3 :001(315) [0499] righteous and holy for the sake of Christ, our **mediator**.
SD : 0 3 :012(541) [0919] of Christ, our only **mediator**, or that "one man's act of
SD : 0 3 :023(543) [0923] for the sake of the only **mediator**, Christ, through faith
SD : 0 3 :028(544) [0925] a blessing of Christ, the **mediator**, and a work of the Holy
SD : 0 3 :030(544) [0925] merit of Christ, the **mediator**, and which we receive only
SD : 0 3 :033(545) [0927] alone for the sake of the **Mediator** without the addition of
SD : 0 8 :047(600) [1031] Thus Christ is our **mediator**, redeemer, king, high priest,
SD : 0 8 :078(607) [1043] community on earth as **mediator**, head, king, and high

Medicine (6)
A L : 2 4 :033(060) [0067] "Because I always sin, I ought always take the **medicine**."
A P : 0 2 :007(101) [0107] the serpent's breath, and whether **medicine** can cure it.
A P : 1 6 :002(222) [0331] as it lets us make use of **medicine** or architecture, food or
L C : 0 4 :043(442) [0743] just such a priceless **medicine** which swallows up death
L C : 0 5 :068(454) [0769] wholesome, soothing **medicine** which aids and quickens
L C : 0 6 :026(460) [0000] miserable, then go and make use of the healing **medicine**.

Meditate (7), Meditated (2), Meditates (1), Meditating (2), Meditation (5), Meditations (2)
L C : P R :009(359) [0569] and make it the subject of **meditation** and conversation.
L C : P R :009(359) [0569] conversation, and **meditation** the Holy Spirit is present
L C : P R :010(360) [0569] with the Word of God, talk about it, and **meditate** on it.
L C : P R :010(360) [0569] calls those blessed who "**meditate** on God's law day and
L C : P R :010(360) [0571] and words and to speak, sing, and **meditate** on them.
L C : P R :014(360) [0571] that we should always **meditate** upon his precepts
L C : P R :018(361) [0573] the whole Psalter but **meditations** and exercises based on
L C : P R :019(361) [0573] to read and teach, to learn and **meditate** and ponder.
L C : 0 1 :101(379) [0609] and it constantly cleanses the heart and its **meditations**.
S D : 0 2 :015(523) [0887] reading, hearing, and **meditating** on the Word of God,
S D : 0 2 :019(524) [0889] without hearing and **meditating** upon the divine Word, or
S D : 0 2 :024(526) [0891] can hear the Gospel and **meditate** on it to a certain
S D : 0 2 :046(530) [0899] exercises as prayer, reading, and Christian **meditation**.
S D : 0 2 :054(531) [0903] the preaching of and **meditation** upon the holy Gospel of
S D : 0 2 :055(532) [0903] earnestly listen to and **meditate** on it, God is certainly
S D : 0 2 :071(535) [0909] of his Word and our **meditation** upon it kindles faith and
S D : 0 6 :004(564) [0963] Lord, and on his law he **meditates** day and night"
S D : 1 1 :017(619) [1069] is preached, heard, and **meditated** on, would convert
S D : 1 1 :039(622) [1075] Word when it is proclaimed, heard, and **meditated** upon.

Meek (1)
L C : 0 4 :067(445) [0749] more gentle, patient, and **meek** we become, and the more

Meet (5), Meeting (1), Meets (3)
P R : P R :007(004) [0009] on the occasion of a **meeting** of the electors in the year
S 1 : P R :001(288) [0455] Paul III called a council to **meet** in Mantua last year, in
S 1 : P R :003(289) [0455] die before a council **meets** (which I fully expect, for those
S 2 : 0 2 :009(294) [0465] of the church, to **meet** his own private need and thus trifle
L C : 0 1 :074(374) [0601] Thus, too, if anyone **meets** with unexpected good
L C : 0 1 :247(398) [0651] If, when you **meet** a poor man who must live from hand
S D : 0 2 :077(536) [0911] own natural powers can **meet** God and to some degree —
S D : 0 3 :044(547) [0931] by faith, since it **meets** the requirements of this
S D : 0 7 :125(591) [1015] faith, but who fail to **meet** their own self-devised standard

Meissen (1)
P R : P R :027(014) [0025] John, bishop of **Meissen**

Melanchthon (4)
P R : P R :019(009) [0017] of Master Philip **Melanchthon** or of [John] Brenz, Urban
A P : P R :000(098) [0099] Greetings from Philip **Melanchthon** to the reader.
S 3 : 1 5 :005(316) [0501] I, Philip **Melanchthon**, regard the above articles as right
T R : 0 0 :082(335) [0529] Philip **Melanchthon** subscribes with his own hand

Melander (2)
S 3 : 1 5 :005(317) [0501] I, Dionysius **Melander**, subscribe the Confession, the
T R : 0 0 :082(335) [0529] David **Melander**, subscribed

Melcher (1)
S 3 : 1 5 :005(318) [0501] And I, Egidius **Melcher**, have subscribed with my hand

Melchior (1)
S 3 : 1 5 :005(318) [0501] the Rev. **Melchior** Weitmann

Melsungen (1)
S 3 : 1 5 :005(318) [0501] the Rev. Licentiate Louis Platz, of **Melsungen**

Melt (2), Melts (1)
A P : 1 2 :049(188) [0265] Ps. 119:28, "My soul **melts** away for sorrow; strengthen
L C : 0 1 :120(381) [0615] not the heart leap and **melt** with joy when it can go to
L C : 0 1 :166(387) [0627] us and make our hearts so **melt** for joy and love toward

Member (3), Members (45)
P R : P R :025(014) [0023] concord with our fellow-**members**, the electors and
A P : 0 2 :030(104) [0113] lust at work in our **members** and bringing forth evil fruit.
A P : 0 2 :036(105) [0115] law which is in the **members** is forgiven by spiritual
A P : 0 2 :039(105) [0115] And again, "I see in my **members** another law at war with
A P : 0 2 :039(105) [0115] the law of sin which dwells in my **members**" (Rom. 7:23).
A P : 0 4 :232(139) [0185] chain linking the many **members** of the church with one
A P : 0 7 :003(169) [0227] with the church and are **members** of the church according
A P : 0 7 :005(169) [0227] in whom Christ is not active are not **members** of Christ.
A P : 0 7 :005(169) [0227] admit, that the wicked are dead **members** of the church.
A P : 0 7 :006(169) [0229] criticize our description, which speaks of living **members**.
A P : 0 7 :013(170) [0231] is that chiefly makes us **members**, and living members, of
A P : 0 7 :013(170) [0231] makes us members, and living **members**, of the church.
A P : 0 7 :016(171) [0231] of the devil and are **members** of the devil's kingdom, as
A P : 0 7 :019(171) [0233] kingdom of Christ and **members** of Christ, for they are
A P : 0 7 :019(171) [0233] of Christ, for they are **members** of the kingdom of the
A P : 0 7 :028(173) [0237] the outward marks, are **members** of the church according
A P : 1 2 :086(194) [0277] imagine that we are **members** of Moses rather than of
A P : 1 2 :122(200) [0289] (Matt. 3:8); "Yield your **members** to righteousness"
A P : 1 2 :129(202) [0291] of God; for the **members** of the hierarchy suppose that
A P : 1 2 :132(202) [0291] "Yield your **members** to righteousness," and
A P : 1 2 :134(203) [0293] befits penitence," "Yield your **members** to righteousness."
A P : 2 4 :016(252) [0389] distinctions to cut the **members** at the joint, lest like an
A P : 2 4 :016(252) [0389] unskilled cook he sever the **member** at the wrong place.
A P : 2 4 :016(252) [0389] and mutilate the various **members** of the concept
A P : 2 7 :009(270) [0421] or because the **members** of these orders are forced to
S 1 : P R :013(290) [0459] If **members** of a council were to consider such
S 3 : 0 3 :040(309) [0489] wars with the law in his **members**, and he does this not
S 3 : 0 8 :002(312) [0495] I see in my **members** another law," etc. (Rom. 7:23).
T R : 0 0 :054(329) [0519] it behoove the chief **members** of the church, the kings and
L C : 0 1 :287(403) [0663] do not need to, for they are our most honorable **members**.
L C : 0 1 :287(403) [0663] But the weakest **members**, of which we are ashamed, we
L C : 0 1 :291(404) [0663] this smallest and weakest of his **members**, the tongue.
L C : 0 2 :013(412) [0681] body, soul, and life, my **members** great and small, all the
L C : 0 2 :052(417) [0691] I also am a part and **member**, a participant and
S D : 0 1 :038(515) [0871] eyes, ears, and all my **members**, my reason and all my
S D : 0 1 :038(515) [0871] body, soul, and life, my **members** great and small, all the
S D : 0 2 :017(524) [0887] but I see in my **members** another law at war with the law
S D : 0 2 :024(526) [0891] he can direct the **members** of his body, can hear the
S D : 0 2 :034(528) [0895] wars with the law in his **members** and that he does so not
S D : 0 2 :036(528) [0895] "I am also a part and **member** of this Christian church, a
S D : 0 2 :037(528) [0895] For before we became **members** of the Christian church
S D : 0 2 :064(533) [0905] self, but I see in my **members** another law at war with the
S D : 0 2 :064(533) [0907] me captive to the law of sin which dwells in my **members**."
S D : 0 2 :084(537) [0913] soul, and the law in our **members** is at war with the law
S D : 0 2 :085(537) [0913] he also sees in his **members** the law of sin at war with the
S D : 0 6 :008(565) [0965] Likewise, "I see in my **members** another law at war with
S D : 0 6 :018(567) [0967] God; but the law in their **members** is at war against the
S D : 0 7 :104(587) [1009] Christ and become true, spiritual **members** of his body.

Memmingen (1)
P R : P R :027(016) [0027] Mayor and Council of the City of **Memmingen**

Memoranda (2), Memorandum (1)
P R : P R :007(004) [0009] (on the basis of a **memorandum** agreed to at
P R : P R :014(007) [0013] necessary, and useful **memoranda** on the way in which
P R : P R :014(007) [0013] was completed with the help of such **memoranda**.

Memorial (2)
A P : 2 4 :038(257) [0397] the ceremony is a **memorial** of the death of Christ,
S D : 0 7 :044(577) [0987] was to be an abiding **memorial** of his bitter passion and

Memory (15), Memories (1)
P R : P R :002(003) [0007] V, of most praiseworthy **memory**, at the Diet of
P R : P R :023(012) [0021] year 1530 to Emperor Charles V, of Christian **memory**.
P R : P R :025(013) [0023] Charles V, of kindest **memory**, in the Apology that
A L : 2 5 :011(063) [0071] your tongue but with the **memory** of your conscience."
A P : 0 7 :040(176) [0241] transmit to posterity the **memory** of these great events.
A P : 2 4 :072(262) [0409] way plays celebrate the **memory** of Hercules or Ulysses.
S C : P R :010(339) [0535] these things after you and retain them in their **memory**.
L C : S P :027(364) [0581] into their minds and remain fixed in their **memories**.
L C : 0 1 :331(410) [0677] and constantly in our **memory**, and practice them in all
E P : 0 9 :003(492) [0827] as Dr. Luther of blessed **memory** taught in his sermon
S D : P R :001(501) [0847] of blessed and holy **memory**, and the popish errors,
S D : P R :002(503) [0851] of God as Dr. Luther of blessed **memory** had explained it:
S D : P R :009(505) [0853] Dr. Luther of blessed **memory** clearly set forth in his
S D : 0 2 :044(529) [0897] of sacred and holy **memory**, grants our free will no power
S D : 0 7 :032(574) [0983] Luther, of blessed **memory**, listed among other articles
S D : 0 8 :080(607) [1045] Dr. Luther, of blessed **memory**, has written about the

Mend (2)
S 3 : 0 9 :000(314) [0497] in the church until they **mend** their ways and avoid sin.
L C : 0 1 :038(369) [0591] senses and cause them to **mend** their ways before

Mendacious (1)
P R : P R :010(006) [0011] way to counteract the **mendacious** calumnies and the

Mendicancy (2), Mendicant (1), Mendicants (2)
A G : 2 7 :050(079) [0083] things and not of **mendicancy** or wearing a black or gray
A G : 2 7 :053(079) [0083] man hears that only **mendicants** are perfect, he is
A L : 2 7 :050(079) [0083] things and not of celibacy, **mendicancy**, or humble attire.
A L : 2 7 :053(079) [0083] They hear that only **mendicants** are perfect, and therefore
A P : 2 4 :007(250) [0385] the prevalence of the **mendicant** friars brought on the

Menius (2)
S 3 : 1 5 :005(317) [0501] my own name and in that of Justus **Menius**, of Eisenach
T R : 0 0 :082(335) [0529] Myconius subscribed for himself and for Justus **Menius**

Menser (1)
S 3 : 1 5 :005(318) [0501] the Rev. Andrew **Menser** (I Subscribe with my hand)

Mention (42), Mentioned (39), Mentions (8)
P R : P R :008(005) [0009] took up the repeatedly **mentioned** Augsburg Confession,
P R : P R :009(006) [0011] name of the frequently **mentioned** Augsburg Confession,
P R : P R :017(008) [0015] The above-**mentioned** and well-intended agreements
P R : P R :017(008) [0015] present at the above-**mentioned** discussions at Naumburg
P R : P R :023(012) [0021] with the repeatedly **mentioned** present explanation of the
A G : P R :021(026) [0043] should be such as we **mentioned** above, we offer in full
A G : 1 6 :004(037) [0051] renunciation of such activities as are **mentioned** above.
A G : 2 2 :005(050) [0061] several places Cyprian **mentions** that the cup was given to
A G : 2 2 :008(050) [0061] Cardinal Cusanus **mentions** when the use was approved.
A G : 2 5 :005(062) [0069] about confession never **mentioned** a word concerning
A G : 2 7 :017(073) [0077] All this is **mentioned**, without misrepresentation, in order
A G : 0 0 :001(094) [0095] we could have **mentioned** many more abuses and wrongs,
A G : 0 0 :005(095) [0095] necessary to adduce and **mention** in order that it may be
A L : 2 0 :005(041) [0053] are even beginning to **mention** faith, about which there
A L : 2 2 :004(050) [0061] Cardinal Cusanus **mentions** when the change was
A L : 2 4 :035(060) [0067] the ancients do not **mention** private Masses but speak
A L : 2 6 :007(065) [0071] of repentance no **mention** was made of faith; only works
A L : 0 0 :001(094) [0095] more abuses could be **mentioned**, to avoid undue length
A P : 0 2 :006(101) [0107] evil doctrine, we made **mention** of concupiscence; with
A P : 0 2 :007(101) [0107] We have **mentioned** not only concupiscence but also the
A P : 0 2 :008(101) [0107] original sin, they do not **mention** the more serious faults
A P : 0 2 :008(101) [0107] to the law of God, the scholastics do not even **mention**.
A P : 0 2 :014(102) [0109] of original sin we also **mentioned** concupiscence and
A P : 0 2 :030(104) [0113] For Paul sometimes **mentions** the deficiency, as in
A P : 0 2 :030(104) [0113] Elsewhere (Rom. 7:5) he **mentions** lust at work in our
A P : 0 4 :055(114) [0137] And so at every **mention** of mercy we must remember
A P : 0 4 :055(114) [0137] Similarly, at every **mention** of faith we are also thinking
A P : 0 4 :087(120) [0147] Paul also **mentions** Abraham and David, who had God's
A P : 0 4 :244(142) [0189] Wherever works are **mentioned**, our opponents falsely
A P : 0 4 :267(146) [0197] Although he **mentions** works in connection with
A P : 0 4 :300(153) [0205] teaching does not **mention** how we must set Christ
A P : 0 4 :316(156) [0209] First, they do not **mention** faith or the fact that for
A P : 0 4 :357(162) [0217] Because a "reward" is **mentioned**, they argue that our
A P : 0 4 :364(163) [0219] The strong hear the **mention** of punishments and rewards

Continued ▶

AP : 04 :372(164) [0221] law and works are **mentioned**, we must know that Christ,
AP : 04 :374(164) [0221] They often **mention** the fruit to make it clearer to the
AP : 04 :381(165) [0223] Whenever this is **mentioned**, faith should be added, since
AP : 12 :012(184) [0257] and they do not **mention** faith, which grasps the
AP : 12 :091(196) [0279] statements make no **mention** of faith, and the scholastics
AP : 12 :092(196) [0279] or good works and making no **mention** of justifying faith.
AP : 12 :107(197) [0283] The Psalms **mention** confession from time to time; for
AP : 12 :112(198) [0285] The church writers do **mention** confession, but they are
AP : 20 :005(227) [0339] We are not inclined to **mention** here the type of works
AP : 21 :003(229) [0343] the ancient Fathers before Gregory **mention** invocation.
AP : 21 :013(230) [0345] The ancient prayers **mention** the saints, but they do not
AP : 21 :034(233) [0353] the saints were first **mentioned**, as in the ancient prayers,
AP : 22 :007(237) [0359] They quote passages that **mention** bread, like Luke 24:35,
AP : 22 :010(237) [0359] confutation they also **mention** the case of Eli's sons; after
AP : 23 :002(239) [0363] abandon cannot even be **mentioned** without blushing.
AP : 23 :047(246) [0377] We could **mention** cases of godly consciences being very
AP : 24 :003(250) [0385] We **mention** this only in passing in order to point out
AP : 24 :006(250) [0385] before Gregory make no **mention** of private Masses.
AP : 24 :046(258) [0401] Our opponents never **mentioned** faith, by which we freely
AP : 24 :079(264) [0411] Why do they not **mention** the old term "communion,"
AP : 24 :084(264) [0413] the Holy Scriptures **mention** an altar, the Mass must be a
AP : 27 :002(269) [0419] a sigh Hilten omitted all **mention** of his illness and said
S2 : 02 :013(295) [0467] a purgatory and merely **mentions** that his mother asked
S2 : 04 :014(301) [0475] without so much as a **mention** of Christ, faith, and God's
S3 : 03 :014(305) [0483] There was no **mention** here of Christ or of faith.
TR : 00 :082(000) [0529] if it be necessary, to all that I have above **mentioned**.
SC : 05 :024(350) [0555] he should simply **mention** one or two sins of which he is
SC : 05 :025(350) [0555] unlikely), you should **mention** none in particular, but
LC : SP :028(365) [0581] shall take up the above-**mentioned** parts one by one and
LC : 01 :143(385) [0623] do it for the reason just **mentioned**, that it is God's
LC : 01 :201(392) [0637] Adultery is particularly **mentioned** because among the
LC : 01 :214(394) [0641] — things too evil to **mention**, as unfortunately has been
LC : 02 :016(412) [0681] else that has been **mentioned** here or can be mentioned,
LC : 02 :016(412) [0681] here or can be **mentioned**, nor can he by himself preserve
LC : 02 :026(413) [0685] the temporal goods **mentioned** above — that is, how he
LC : 02 :036(415) [0687] kinds of spirits are **mentioned** in the Scriptures, such as
LC : 06 :024(460) [0000] being given and no **mention** of what they were to look for
EP : 07 :003(482) [0809] it is necessary to **mention**, first of all, that there are two
EP : 12 :001(498) [0839] we have made no **mention** of the errors held by these
SD : PR :016(507) [0857] find in the previously **mentioned** writings what he should
SD : 01 :019(511) [0865] 3. Or that the above-**mentioned** lack and damage
SD : 01 :050(517) [0875] and the above-**mentioned** books use them in treating this
SD : 02 :028(527) [0893] other writings before **mentioned**, as the following
SD : 02 :038(528) [0895] the Catechism makes no **mention** whatever of our free
SD : 02 :039(528) [0895] nevertheless, as **mentioned** above, we do this not of our
SD : 02 :042(529) [0897] testimonies make no **mention** whatever of our will and
SD : 02 :059(532) [0905] his conversion, as was **mentioned** above, and in this
SD : 03 :044(547) [0931] set forth in detail in the previously **mentioned** writings.
SD : 03 :057(549) [0935] Since, as was **mentioned** above, it is the obedience of the
SD : 03 :059(550) [0937] to the previously **mentioned** errors, the following and all
SD : 07 :038(576) [0985] call it in the above-**mentioned** articles of agreement of
SD : 08 :038(598) [1027] *nature* (for while they **mention** the entire person, they
SD : 11 :002(616) [1063] the Holy Scriptures **mention** this article not only once,
SD : 11 :039(622) [1075] Hence, as was **mentioned** before, there is no basis for the
SD : 12 :002(632) [1095] special and detailed **mention** of them, although it now

Mercenary (4)
AG : 24 :013(057) [0065] such **mercenary** Masses and private Masses, which had
AP : 21 :041(235) [0355] observances, the **mercenary** worship of the saints, the
AP : 24 :007(250) [0385] so superstitious and so **mercenary** have they been that for
AP : 24 :049(258) [0401] in their churches **mercenary** priests use the sacrament.

Merchandise (1)
LC : 01 :227(396) [0645] another with defective **merchandise**, false measures,

Merchant (2), Merchants (1)
AP : 24 :064(261) [0407] a price for success, to **merchants** for good business, to
EP : 12 :018(499) [0841] good conscience be an innkeeper, a **merchant**, or a cutler.
SD : 12 :023(634) [1099] good conscience be an innkeeper, a **merchant**, or a cutler.

Mercury (1)
LC : 01 :018(367) [0585] ease venerated Hercules, **Mercury**, Venus, or others, while

Mercy (123), Merciful (5)
PR : PR :002(003) [0007] love, grace, and **mercy** toward mankind has permitted the
AG : 27 :049(079) [0083] sake we have a gracious, **merciful** God; that we may and
AL : 20 :014(043) [0055] not be superseded by the **mercy** of God if justification,
AP : 04 :044(113) [0133] own merits, but only in the promise of **mercy** in Christ.
AP : 04 :053(114) [0137] blessing is offered only by **mercy**; the merits of Christ are
AP : 04 :054(114) [0137] contains many pleas for **mercy**, and the holy Fathers
AP : 04 :054(114) [0137] the holy Fathers often say that we are saved by **mercy**.
AP : 04 :055(114) [0137] so at every mention of **mercy** we must remember that this
AP : 04 :055(114) [0137] this requires faith, which accepts the promise of **mercy**.
AP : 04 :055(114) [0137] we are also thinking of its object, the promised **mercy**.
AP : 04 :056(114) [0137] in itself, but only because it accepts the promised **mercy**.
AP : 04 :057(114) [0137] they received free **mercy** and the forgiveness of sins by
AP : 04 :058(115) [0137] The frequent references to **mercy** and faith in the Psalms
AP : 04 :058(115) [0137] Here he comforts himself with his trust in God's **mercy**.
AP : 04 :060(115) [0137] them because of his **mercy** rather than because of our own
AP : 04 :079(118) [0143] by firm trust in the **mercy** promised because of Christ.
AP : 04 :080(118) [0143] hearts with trust in the **mercy** promised for Christ's sake.
AP : 04 :081(118) [0143] comforted by trust in the **mercy** promised for Christ's
AP : 04 :082(118) [0145] by faith we receive the **mercy** promised in him and set it
AP : 04 :086(119) [0147] of their own purity but by **mercy** on account of Christ, if
AP : 04 :086(119) [0147] on account of Christ, if they grasp this **mercy** by faith.
AP : 04 :106(122) [0153] soul by faith flees to the **mercy** of God, that he may give
AP : 04 :106(122) [0153] we try to keep the law we should receive **mercy** by faith.
AP : 04 :129(125) [0157] love God until we have grasped his **mercy** by faith.
AP : 04 :149(127) [0163] sin (Rom. 5:20), that **mercy** is more powerful than sin.
AP : 04 :153(127) [0163] which grasps God's free **mercy** because of God's Word.
AP : 04 :170(130) [0171] because of God's command; and it doubts God's **mercy**.
AP : 04 :173(131) [0171] does not consist in our own merit, but in God's **mercy**."
AP : 04 :174(131) [0171] For **mercy** can be grasped only by faith, as we have said
AP : 04 :244(142) [0189] that we do not need **mercy** and Christ, the propitiator.
AP : 04 :254(143) [0193] Dan. 4:27, "Redeem your sins by showing **mercy**."
AP : 04 :255(143) [0193] (v. 7), "Blessed are the **merciful**, for they shall obtain
AP : 04 :255(143) [0193] "Blessed are the merciful, for they shall obtain **mercy**."
AP : 04 :261(145) [0195] iniquities by showing **mercy** to the oppressed," that is,
AP : 04 :279(149) [0199] on account of his **mercy** and which wants to be justified,
AP : 04 :322(157) [0209] church confesses that eternal life comes through **mercy**.
AP : 04 :322(157) [0209] life, not by our merits, but according to his **mercy**."
AP : 04 :322(157) [0209] praiseworthy, if it is to be judged without **mercy**."
AP : 04 :323(157) [0209] that even if we have good works we need **mercy** in them.
AP : 04 :324(157) [0209] Looking at his **mercy**, faith comforts and consoles us.
AP : 04 :324(157) [0209] to add nothing about this faith that takes hold of **mercy**.
AP : 04 :324(157) [0211] here that the promised **mercy** correlatively requires faith
AP : 04 :324(157) [0211] faith and that only faith can take hold of this **mercy**.
AP : 04 :325(157) [0211] the doctrine that we need **mercy** even in our good works.
AP : 04 :330(158) [0211] "Those who forsake **mercy** observe lying vanities";
AP : 04 :330(158) [0211] is vain except a trust in **mercy**; mercy saves us, our own
AP : 04 :330(158) [0211] except a trust in mercy; **mercy** saves us, our own merits
AP : 04 :331(158) [0211] our righteousness, but on the ground of thy great **mercy**.
AP : 04 :331(158) [0211] teaches us to take hold of **mercy** when we pray, that is, to
AP : 04 :331(158) [0211] pray, that is, to trust the **mercy** of God and not our
AP : 04 :332(158) [0211] and not on the **mercy** of God, insults Christ, who
AP : 04 :333(158) [0211] prayer relies upon the **mercy** of God when we believe that
AP : 04 :334(158) [0215] that God saves through **mercy** and because of his
AP : 04 :337(159) [0215] but about trust in God's promise and in his **mercy**.
AP : 04 :338(159) [0215] because it takes hold of **mercy** and the promise of grace,
AP : 04 :338(159) [0215] the whole church we teach that we are saved by **mercy**.
AP : 04 :339(159) [0215] He does not want us to despair of God's grace and **mercy**.
AP : 04 :339(159) [0215] does not denounce the promise that offers **mercy** gratis.
AP : 04 :344(160) [0217] the church's confession that we are saved through **mercy**.
AP : 04 :344(160) [0217] if we are saved through **mercy** and if, prior to salvation,
AP : 04 :345(160) [0217] are not, we must hold that we are saved through **mercy**.
AP : 04 :345(160) [0217] a right or debt is certain, while **mercy** is uncertain.
AP : 04 :345(160) [0217] Here **mercy** has God's clear and certain promise and his
AP : 04 :346(160) [0217] So whenever **mercy** is spoken of, faith in the promise
AP : 04 :357(162) [0219] life without needing **mercy** or the mediator Christ or
AP : 04 :381(165) [0223] Why not expound here God's grace and **mercy** toward us?
AP : 04 :381(165) [0223] we take hold of God's **mercy**, reconciliation, and love
AP : 12 :074(192) [0273] that sins are forgiven by **mercy**, but he bids us add the
AP : 12 :107(198) [0283] works, and yet we seek **mercy** because of the promise of
AP : 12 :108(198) [0283] justify us and account us righteous through Thy **mercy**."
AP : 21 :004(229) [0343] showing examples of his **mercy**, revealing his will to save
AP : 21 :008(230) [0345] hosts, how long wilt thou have no **mercy** on Jerusalem?"
AP : 21 :015(231) [0347] to the saints the trust we should have in Christ's **mercy**.
AP : 21 :015(231) [0347] so they trust more in the **mercy** of the saints than in the
AP : 21 :015(231) [0347] of the saints than in the **mercy** of Christ and they flee
AP : 21 :017(231) [0347] God is willing to have **mercy** and to answer those who
AP : 21 :020(232) [0349] of merits are therefore the sources of trust in **mercy**.
AP : 21 :021(232) [0349] have us trust more in the **mercy** of the saints than in the
AP : 21 :021(232) [0349] of the saints than in the **mercy** of Christ, though Christ
AP : 21 :028(233) [0351] her, trusted in her **mercy**, and sought through her to
AP : 21 :036(234) [0353] hear of these things and to see some examples of **mercy**.
AP : 24 :028(254) [0393] to know me when I show **mercy** and help you, for I do
AP : 24 :029(255) [0393] thy promises of willingness to show **mercy** and to help."
AP : 24 :032(255) [0395] of Christ and the Father's **mercy** promised in Christ.
AP : 24 :072(262) [0409] to be remembered; the Lord is gracious and **merciful**.
AP : 24 :072(262) [0409] we should acknowledge the will and **mercy** of God.
AP : 24 :073(262) [0409] A faith that acknowledges **mercy** makes alive.
AP : 27 :027(273) [0429] of God, in trust in the **mercy** promised in Christ, and in
AP : 27 :032(274) [0431] eternal life is given by **mercy** for Christ's sake to those
AP : 27 :033(275) [0431] law, but must seek the **mercy** promised in Christ, much
AP : 27 :034(275) [0431] of sins and the promised **mercy** available in Christ and
AP : 27 :034(275) [0431] Although they need **mercy** themselves, they wickedly
AP : 27 :061(279) [0441] Seed, through the **mercy** of God — they would attain
AP : 27 :065(280) [0441] eternal life for us instead of **mercy** for Christ's sake.
AP : 27 :069(281) [0443] of them rather than because of Christ through **mercy**.
AP : 27 :070(281) [0443] that for Christ's sake by **mercy** they would attain eternal
S3 : 13 :002(315) [0499] the pure grace and **mercy** which have been poured out
S3 : 13 :003(315) [0499] from God's grace and **mercy**, but, as it is written, "Let him
SC : PR :000(338) [0533] Grace, **mercy**, and peace in Jesus Christ, our Lord, from
SC : 02 :002(345) [0543] and divine goodness and **mercy**, without any merit or
SC : 05 :026(351) [0555] shall say: "God be **merciful** to you and strengthen your
LC : 01 :030(369) [0589] *hate me, and showing* **mercy** *to many thousands of those*
LC : 01 :039(370) [0591] the promise that assures **mercy** to those who cling to God
LC : 01 :060(372) [0597] It is a great **mercy** that the earth still bears and sustains
LC : 01 :155(386) [0625] that we have nothing but unhappiness without **mercy**.
LC : 01 :246(398) [0651] and show forgiveness and **mercy**, as the Lord's Prayer
LC : 01 :320(408) [0673] *commandments, I show* **mercy** *unto a thousand*
LC : 01 :325(409) [0675] fear him, in those who hope in his **mercy**" (Ps. 147:11).
LC : 02 :029(414) [0685] goodness, had **mercy** on our misery and wretchedness and
LC : 04 :086(446) [0753] As Christ, the **mercy**-seat, does not recede from us or
EP : 11 :010(495) [0833] that he may have **mercy** upon all" (Rom. 11:32), and that
EP : 11 :020(497) [0837] that it is not only the **mercy** of God and the most holy
SD : PR :001(501) [0847] By the special grace and **mercy** of the Almighty, the
SD : PR :005(504) [0851] 3. By a special grace our **merciful** God has in these last
SD : 02 :050(530) [0901] boundless kindness and **mercy**, God provides for the
SD : 02 :057(532) [0903] himself with God's eternal election nor obtain his **mercy**.
SD : 02 :071(535) [0909] kindness and **mercy** anticipates us and has his holy
SD : 04 :020(554) [0945] still retain faith and God's **mercy** and his grace.
SD : 05 :002(558) [0953] of the grace and **mercy** of God for Christ's sake, which
SD : 05 :004(559) [0953] the proclamation of the **mercy** and grace of God, his
SD : 05 :021(562) [0959] and which offers the **mercy** and grace of God to
SD : 11 :028(620) [1071] so that he might have **mercy** on all" (Rom. 11:32).
SD : 11 :060(626) [1083] pure and unmerited grace toward the "vessels of **mercy**."
SD : 11 :061(626) [1083] God commends his pure and unmerited grace and **mercy**.
SD : 11 :079(629) [1089] his glory in the vessels of **mercy**, which he has prepared
SD : 11 :082(630) [1091] Concerning "the vessels of **mercy**" he says specifically that
SD : 11 :087(631) [1093] of his will through sheer **mercy** in Christ without our
SD : 11 :088(631) [1093] election is not only the **mercy** of God and the most holy

Mere (41), Merely (60)
AG : 20 :025(045) [0057] it clear that faith is not **merely** a knowledge of historical
AG : 20 :026(045) [0057] gracious to us, and not **merely** such a knowledge of

Continued ▶

AL : 13 :001(035) [0049] were instituted not **merely** to be marks of profession
AL : 20 :023(044) [0055] "faith" does not signify **mere** knowledge of the history
AL : 26 :034(069) [0075] at all times, and not **merely** on a few prescribed days.
AP : 02 :016(102) [0109] contains not **merely** the second table of the Decalogue,
AP : 02 :025(103) [0111] Concupiscence is not **merely** a corruption of the physical
AP : 02 :031(104) [0113] are lacking, this is not **merely** actual guilt but an abiding
AP : 02 :033(104) [0113] righteousness of man is **mere** hypocrisy before God unless
AP : 04 :048(114) [0135] justifies, however, is no **mere** historical knowledge, but
AP : 04 :048(114) [0135] the impression that it is **merely** knowledge, we add that to
AP : 04 :161(129) [0167] does not mean **merely** the beginning of our renewal, but
AP : 04 :162(129) [0169] error to suppose that he **merely** merited "initial grace" and
AP : 04 :227(139) [0183] often said, faith is not **merely** knowledge but rather a
AP : 04 :272(148) [0199] that faith is required, not **merely** works, as in Matt. 6:14,
AP : 04 :304(154) [0205] of sin and death are not **merely** thoughts in the intellect
AP : 04 :304(154) [0205] just so faith is not **merely** knowledge in the intellect but
AP : 04 :373(164) [0221] we must understand not **merely** outward works but the
AP : 04 :383(165) [0225] They interpret faith as **merely** a knowledge of history or
AP : 04 :384(166) [0225] will grant that the **mere** act of confessing does not save,
AP : 07 :005(169) [0227] The church is not **merely** an association of outward ties
AP : 07 :040(176) [0241] we must consult their writings, not **merely** their example.
AP : 10 :002(179) [0247] that "the bread is not **merely** a figure but is truly changed
AP : 12 :074(192) [0273] He does not **merely** require that we believe in a general
AP : 12 :106(197) [0283] He is **merely** giving a bit of domestic advice to the head
AP : 12 :128(201) [0291] the doctrinal doubts of good men are **mere** petty anxiety.
AP : 12 :131(202) [0291] Therefore this is **merely** a trick and a distortion of the
AP : 12 :143(204) [0297] satisfaction to the **mere** performance of these acts, for
AP : 13 :001(211) [0309] the sacraments are no **mere** marks of profession among
AP : 23 :003(239) [0363] And **merely** because of their marriage, you sentence
AP : 24 :002(249) [0385] they imagine that **mere** hearing is a beneficial act of
AP : 24 :005(250) [0385] simply *ex opere operato,* by the **mere** doing or observing.
AP : 24 :053(259) [0403] already said, they were **merely** a picture of the sacrifice of
AP : 24 :089(265) [0413] It is no **mere** peccadillo to establish such services in the
AP : 27 :033(275) [0431] do monastic observances, **mere** human traditions, deserve
AP : 27 :047(277) [0437] of property is therefore **merely** a human tradition, it is a
AP : 27 :053(278) [0437] blessed Virgin, which is **mere** babbling, as stupid as it is
S2 : 02 :013(295) [0467] there is a purgatory and **merely** mentions that his mother
S2 : 02 :021(296) [0469] Not only is this **mere** human trumpery, utterly
S3 : 09 :000(314) [0497] as the pope calls it, to be **merely** a civil penalty which
S3 : 15 :005(316) [0501] and they are not, but are **mere** mockery and fraud.
TR : 00 :068(331) [0523] to the church and not **merely** to certain individuals:
SC : 04 :002(348) [0551] Answer: Baptism is not **merely** water, but it is water used
SC : 04 :010(349) [0551] Word of God the water is **merely** water and no Baptism.
LC : 01 :021(367) [0585] Idolatry does not consist **merely** of erecting an image and
LC : 01 :061(373) [0597] may be brought up not **merely** with punishment but in
LC : 01 :134(383) [0619] have long life means not **merely** to grow old but to have
LC : 01 :168(388) [0629] power and authority to govern) **merely** to receive homage.
LC : 01 :170(388) [0629] gave us servants **merely** to put them to work like cows or
LC : 01 :197(392) [0637] as if they were not commandments but **mere** counsels.
LC : 01 :331(410) [0677] we are to have them there **merely** for a display, as the
LC : 03 :108(434) [0729] cannot be harmed by the **mere** feeling of temptation as
LC : 04 :063(444) [0749] Word, regarding Baptism **merely** as an empty sign, as the
LC : 04 :073(445) [0751] where faith is lacking, it remains a **mere** unfruitful sign.
LC : 05 :009(447) [0755] of Baptism that it is not **mere** water, so we say here that
LC : 05 :009(447) [0755] bread and wine, but not **mere** bread or wine such as is
LC : 05 :010(448) [0755] which distinguishes it from **mere** bread and wine and
LC : 05 :010(448) [0755] a sacrament; otherwise it remains a **mere** element.
LC : 05 :042(451) [0763] institute it to be treated **merely** as a spectacle, but
LC : 05 :051(452) [0765] attended the sacrament **merely** from compulsion and fear
EP : RN :008(465) [0779] like Holy Scripture, but **merely** witnesses and expositions
EP : 03 :006(473) [0793] that this faith is not a **mere** knowledge of the stories
EP : 04 :004(476) [0797] At first this was **merely** a semantic issue.
EP : 06 :004(480) [0807] their way lest in their **merely** human devotion they
EP : 08 :003(487) [0819] "personal union makes **merely** the names common," so
EP : 08 :012(488) [0821] not only a plain, ordinary, **mere** man but the veritable
EP : 08 :013(488) [0821] was not a plain, ordinary, **mere** man who for us suffered,
EP : 08 :031(490) [0825] 12. That only the **mere** humanity suffered for us and
EP : 11 :004(495) [0833] God's foreknowledge **merely** controls the evil and
EP : 11 :013(496) [0835] election not only in **mere** words, but also with his oath,
EP : 11 :019(497) [0837] to be saved, but that **merely** by an arbitrary counsel,
EP : 12 :001(498) [0839] we wish here at the end **merely** to enumerate the articles
EP : 12 :028(500) [0843] the Holy Spirit, but is **merely** adorned with divine majesty
SD : PR :009(503) [0849] not, as some may think, **mere** misunderstandings or
SD : PR :009(503) [0849] so that the strife reflects a **mere** semantic problem of little
SD : PR :001(503) [0851] It based these not on **mere** private writings, but on such
SD : 01 :021(512) [0865] external spot or blemish, **merely** splashed on, or a
SD : 02 :009(522) [0883] them they consider it all **mere** foolishness and fables.
SD : 02 :027(527) [0891] grace of God consists **merely** in this, that God in the
SD : 02 :056(532) [0903] operations, and gifts **merely** on the basis of our feeling,
SD : 02 :073(535) [0909] does nothing at all, but **merely** suffers what God
SD : 03 :041(546) [0931] wicked intention, but this **merely** shows the order in
SD : 05 :010(559) [0955] The **mere** preaching of the law without Christ either
SD : 06 :016(566) [0967] law, and does its works **merely** because they are
SD : 07 :004(569) [0973] that nothing more than **mere** bread and wine, which are
SD : 07 :021(573) [0979] it that it is not **mere** bread and wine but is and is called
SD : 07 :043(576) [0987] He is not a **mere** man or an angel; he is not only truthful,
SD : 07 :091(586) [1005] sake of desirable brevity, **merely** refer the Christian
SD : 07 :108(588) [1009] of Christ, so that only the **mere** species of bread and
SD : 08 :016(594) [1021] the Lord Christ was a **mere** man in whom the Word of
SD : 08 :024(595) [1023] virgin, did not conceive a **mere**, ordinary human being,
SD : 08 :045(600) [1031] "God died," are **merely** empty words which do not
SD : 08 :056(601) [1033] communication is not **merely** a matter of words but is to
SD : 08 :063(603) [1037] We have used this term **merely** in opposition to a "verbal
SD : 08 :063(603) [1037] all only a mode of speech, **mere** words, titles, and names.
SD : 08 :067(604) [1039] only in such a way that it **merely** shares the bare titles and
SD : 08 :084(607) [1045] be nothing more than a **mere** isolated God and a divine
SD : 08 :086(608) [1047] sake of brevity we here **merely** go on record as having
SD : 08 :093(609) [1049] 5. Likewise, that the **mere** human nature of Christ alone,
SD : 11 :009(618) [1065] to be damned, or that he **merely** held a sort of military
SD : 12 :005(633) [1097] our agreement was not a **mere** pretense but that we

Merit (272), Merits (132)

AG : 02 :003(029) [0045] thus disparaging the sufferings and **merit** of Christ.
AG : 04 :001(030) [0045] before God by our own **merits**, works, or satisfactions,
AG : 05 :003(031) [0045] God, not by our own **merits** but by the merit of Christ,
AG : 05 :003(031) [0045] our own merits but by the **merit** of Christ, when we
AG : 06 :001(032) [0045] our trust in them as if thereby to **merit** favor before God.
AG : 06 :003(032) [0047] through works but through faith alone, without **merit**."
AG : 20 :010(042) [0055] by works, or that he can **merit** grace, despises Christ and
AG : 20 :020(044) [0055] that there they might **merit** grace through monastic life.
AG : 20 :022(044) [0055] God is appropriated without **merits**, through faith alone.
AG : 26 :004(064) [0071] insists that we regard the **merit** of Christ as something
AG : 26 :038(069) [0075] of mortification to **merit** grace but to keep the body in
AG : 27 :013(072) [0077] also claimed that more **merit** could be obtained by
AG : 28 :036(086) [0089] for the glory of Christ's **merit** is blasphemed when we
AG : 28 :050(089) [0091] to propitiate God and **merit** grace are contrary to the
AG : 28 :052(089) [0091] in Christ without our **merits**; we do not merit it by
AG : 28 :052(089) [0091] our merits; we do not **merit** it by services of God
AL : 02 :003(029) [0045] the glory of Christ's **merit** and benefits by contending
AL : 04 :001(030) [0045] by their own strength, **merits**, or works but are freely
AL : 05 :003(031) [0045] on account of our own **merits** but on account of Christ
AL : 06 :001(032) [0045] we rely on such works to **merit** justification before God,
AL : 12 :010(035) [0049] faith but command us to **merit** grace through
AL : 15 :003(036) [0049] to propitiate God, **merit** grace, and make satisfaction for
AL : 15 :004(037) [0049] days, etc., instituted to **merit** grace and make satisfaction
AL : 20 :009(042) [0053] cannot reconcile God or **merit** forgiveness of sins and
AL : 20 :010(042) [0055] whoever trusts that he **merits** grace by works despises the
AL : 20 :010(042) [0055] by works despises the **merit** and grace of Christ and seeks
AL : 20 :013(043) [0055] and the righteousness of faith against the **merits** of works.
AL : 20 :014(043) [0055] were due to antecedent **merits**, for then it would be a
AL : 20 :020(044) [0055] hope that there they might **merit** grace by monastic life.
AL : 20 :021(044) [0055] works of another kind to **merit** grace and make
AL : 20 :027(045) [0057] that we should trust to **merit** grace by them but because it
AL : 26 :001(064) [0071] which are profitable to **merit** grace and make
AL : 26 :002(064) [0071] as a service necessary to **merit** grace and sorely terrified
AL : 26 :004(064) [0071] in it, so that the **merit** of Christ may be well known and
AL : 26 :006(064) [0071] that it is necessary to **merit** grace and righteousness by
AL : 26 :020(067) [0073] if men suppose that they **merit** grace by observances of
AL : 26 :021(067) [0073] taught that we cannot **merit** grace or make satisfaction
AL : 26 :033(069) [0075] to sin, but not in order to **merit** forgiveness of sins or
AL : 26 :038(069) [0075] pommeled his body not to **merit** forgiveness of sins by
AL : 27 :016(073) [0077] of life was instituted to **merit** grace and righteousness.
AL : 27 :036(076) [0081] and chosen by men to **merit** justification and grace
AL : 27 :038(077) [0081] satisfaction for sins and **merit** grace and justification.
AL : 28 :036(086) [0089] for the glory of Christ's **merit** is dishonored when we
AL : 28 :037(087) [0089] thought that they would **merit** grace by these works.
AL : 28 :039(087) [0089] the law, as if in order to **merit** justification there had to
AP : 04 :001(107) [0119] sins because of their own **merits**, but freely for Christ's
AP : 04 :001(107) [0121] of sins because of their **merits**, and for affirming that men
AP : 04 :009(108) [0123] scholastics teach men to **merit** the forgiveness of sins by
AP : 04 :012(109) [0123] If we **merit** the forgiveness of sins by these elicited acts of
AP : 04 :015(109) [0123] of laws by which we could **merit** the forgiveness of sins
AP : 04 :015(109) [0123] of sins rather than receiving it freely for his **merits**.
AP : 04 :016(109) [0123] of the opponents that we **merit** forgiveness of sins and
AP : 04 :017(109) [0125] They bid us **merit** this first disposition by our preceding
AP : 04 :017(109) [0125] bid us merit this first disposition by our preceding **merits**.
AP : 04 :017(109) [0125] Then they bid us **merit** an increase of this disposition and
AP : 04 :018(109) [0125] should dream that they **merit** the forgiveness of sins and
AP : 04 :019(109) [0125] up a distinction between **merit** of congruity and merit of
AP : 04 :019(109) [0125] merit of congruity and **merit** of condignity, they are only
AP : 04 :019(110) [0125] gives grace for the **merit** of congruity, it is no longer
AP : 04 :019(110) [0125] congruity, it is no longer **merit** of congruity but merit of
AP : 04 :019(110) [0125] it is no longer merit of congruity but **merit** of condignity.
AP : 04 :019(110) [0125] love a man can earn the **merit** of condignity, but they
AP : 04 :019(110) [0125] know whether one has the **merit** of congruity or the merit
AP : 04 :019(110) [0125] one has the merit of congruity or the **merit** of condignity?
AP : 04 :020(110) [0125] believe that they have the **merit** of condignity, whether or
AP : 04 :020(110) [0125] that they have the **merit** of condignity, and so they run
AP : 04 :025(110) [0127] false that by our works we **merit** the forgiveness of sins.
AP : 04 :029(111) [0129] at length that grace is not given because of our **merits**.
AP : 04 :031(111) [0129] free us from our sins or **merit** for us the forgiveness of
AP : 04 :036(112) [0131] are under eternal wrath **merit** the forgiveness of sins by an
AP : 04 :038(112) [0131] not say that by the law men **merit** the forgiveness of sins.
AP : 04 :038(112) [0131] law and by their works they **merit** the forgiveness of sins.
AP : 04 :041(113) [0133] not conditional upon our **merits** but offers the forgiveness
AP : 04 :041(113) [0133] Reconciliation does not depend upon our **merits**.
AP : 04 :042(113) [0133] sins depended upon our **merits** and if reconciliation were
AP : 04 :042(113) [0133] conditional upon our **merits** and the law, which we never
AP : 04 :044(113) [0133] a trust not in our own **merits**, but only in the promise of
AP : 04 :046(113) [0133] God's wrath not our **merits** of love, but Christ the
AP : 04 :049(114) [0135] the law is that worship which offers God our own **merits**.
AP : 04 :051(114) [0135] not because of our own **merits** the forgiveness of sins is
AP : 04 :052(114) [0135] offered for our sins if our **merits** make satisfaction for
AP : 04 :053(114) [0137] promise is free, and the **merits** of Christ as the price and
AP : 04 :053(114) [0137] it is free excludes our **merits** and shows that the blessing
AP : 04 :053(114) [0137] only by mercy; the **merits** of Christ are the price because
AP : 04 :058(115) [0137] his sins, but he does not lay claim to any **merit** of his own.
AP : 04 :060(115) [0137] of his mercy rather than because of our own **merits**.
AP : 04 :060(115) [0137] teach men to deal with God only by works and **merits**.
AP : 04 :066(116) [0139] of love, they pretend that one **merits** it by works.
AP : 04 :069(116) [0141] means to trust in Christ's **merits**, that because of him God
AP : 04 :073(117) [0141] We exclude the claim of **merit**, not the Word or the
AP : 04 :074(117) [0143] follow, but trust in the **merit** of love or works is excluded
AP : 04 :081(118) [0143] own works, by which we **merit** this disposition, and then,
AP : 04 :082(118) [0145] God with trust not in our **merits** but in Christ, the high
AP : 04 :083(118) [0145] not for the sake of our **merits**, our contrition, attrition,
AP : 04 :084(119) [0145] "If it depended on our **merits**, the promise would be
AP : 04 :084(119) [0145] Here he denies us any **merit**, for he says that all are guilty
AP : 04 :089(120) [0149] he excludes even the **merit** of works according to the
AP : 04 :146(127) [0163] for they say they earn grace and eternal life by **merit**.
AP : 04 :162(129) [0169] we please God and **merit** eternal life by our keeping of the
AP : 04 :173(131) [0171] does not consist in our own **merit**, but in God's mercy."
AP : 04 :193(133) [0175] Let us add a word here about reward and **merit**.
AP : 04 :196(134) [0175] Because our works do not **merit** our justification, which
AP : 04 :196(134) [0175] with Christ, we do not **merit** eternal life by our works.
AP : 04 :197(134) [0175] it takes place in the justified it **merits** other great rewards.
AP : 04 :202(134) [0175] to God — not to **merit** the forgiveness of sins and grace

Continued ▶

AP : 04 :203(135) [0177] by similar works he will **merit** grace and forgiveness of
AP : 04 :208(135) [0177] action in order thereby to **merit** grace, righteousness, and
AP : 04 :208(135) [0177] on the high places to **merit** grace and forgiveness of sins
AP : 04 :211(136) [0179] in order by such works to **merit** the forgiveness of sins,
AP : 04 :213(136) [0179] and to claim that they **merit** the forgiveness of sins and
AP : 04 :214(136) [0179] We do not **merit** the forgiveness of sins, grace, and
AP : 04 :227(139) [0183] to us Christ's **merits** and, through them, grace and peace
AP : 04 :238(141) [0187] to us and that the **merits** of Christ are granted to us.
AP : 04 :242(141) [0187] does not mean that love **merits** the forgiveness of sins in
AP : 04 :244(142) [0189] read into them their opinion about the **merit** of works.
AP : 04 :244(142) [0189] that by good works we **merit** the forgiveness of sins; that
AP : 04 :246(142) [0189] by our good works we **merit** grace and the forgiveness of
AP : 04 :246(142) [0189] that James teaches we **merit** grace and forgiveness of sins
AP : 04 :253(143) [0193] conclusions: that works **merit** the forgiveness of sins; that
AP : 04 :258(144) [0193] fatherless"—they could **merit** the forgiveness of sins *ex*
AP : 04 :259(144) [0193] when we forgive, this **merits** the forgiveness of sins *ex*
AP : 04 :265(146) [0197] faith, it dreams that the **merit** of these works brings
AP : 04 :267(147) [0197] say that by these works we **merit** the forgiveness of sins.
AP : 04 :269(147) [0197] of them a propitiation that **merits** the forgiveness of sins.
AP : 04 :274(148) [0199] that by such works we **merit** forgiveness of sins or
AP : 04 :278(149) [0199] We also grant that alms **merit** many divine blessings,
AP : 04 :278(149) [0199] our punishments, and **merit** a defense for us in the perils
AP : 04 :281(149) [0201] Christ and teach that we **merit** justification by the works
AP : 04 :285(150) [0201] they teach that works **merit** the forgiveness of sins,
AP : 04 :286(150) [0201] and that by our works we **merit** grace and the forgiveness
AP : 04 :288(151) [0203] to them, is that men **merit** grace by good works — first by
AP : 04 :288(151) [0203] good works — first by the **merit** of congruity, then by the
AP : 04 :288(151) [0203] by the merit of congruity, then by the **merit** of condignity.
AP : 04 :290(151) [0203] an act of love whereby we **merit** the forgiveness of sins.
AP : 04 :296(152) [0205] because of Christ, whose **merits** are conferred on us if we
AP : 04 :314(156) [0207] come to God by love and **merits** without Christ, the
AP : 04 :316(156) [0209] reject our opponents' teaching on the **merit** of condignity.
AP : 04 :318(156) [0209] works earn grace by the **merit** of condignity, as though
AP : 04 :320(156) [0209] life, if indeed hope ought to be sustained by **merits**?
AP : 04 :321(157) [0209] can be sure of earning grace by the **merit** of condignity?
AP : 04 :321(157) [0209] men sometimes acquire the **merit** of congruity and
AP : 04 :321(157) [0209] and sometimes the **merit** of condignity — was made up to
AP : 04 :321(157) [0209] work does not distinguish between the two kinds of **merit**.
AP : 04 :321(157) [0209] To acquire the **merit** of condignity means to doubt and to
AP : 04 :322(157) [0209] to eternal life, not by our **merits**, but according to his
AP : 04 :324(157) [0209] wrongly when they praise **merits** in such a way as to add
AP : 04 :324(157) [0211] reject the doctrine of the **merit** of condignity since it
AP : 04 :330(158) [0211] mercy saves us, our own **merits** and efforts do not save
AP : 04 :331(158) [0211] to trust the mercy of God and not our **merits** before him.
AP : 04 :344(160) [0217] the scholastics invented the term "**merit** of condignity."
AP : 04 :348(160) [0217] works are unnecessary if they do not **merit** eternal life.
AP : 04 :355(161) [0217] Afterwards works **merit** other bodily and spiritual
AP : 04 :356(161) [0217] it is merited by the **merit** of condignity through good
AP : 04 :360(162) [0219] that they have extra **merits** which they can give to justify
AP : 04 :360(162) [0219] as when monks sell the **merits** of their orders to others.
AP : 04 :360(162) [0219] Since one has more **merits** than another, therefore some
AP : 04 :360(162) [0219] merits than another, therefore some have extra **merits**.
AP : 04 :360(162) [0219] Those who **merit** them can transfer these merits to
AP : 04 :360(162) [0219] who merit them can transfer these **merits** to others."
AP : 04 :362(162) [0219] — not because of our **merits** but because of the promise.
AP : 04 :366(163) [0219] to faith, still good works **merit** other rewards, both bodily
AP : 04 :366(163) [0221] Those who **merit** this are justified before they keep the
AP : 04 :367(163) [0221] Whenever **merit** is discussed, our opponents immediately
AP : 04 :367(163) [0221] freely because of Christ's **merits**, not ours, and Christ's
AP : 04 :367(163) [0221] not ours, and Christ's **merits** are communicated to us by
AP : 04 :367(163) [0221] Works and afflictions **merit** not justification but other
AP : 04 :368(163) [0221] keeping the law thus **merits** a reward, since a reward
AP : 04 :370(163) [0221] that good works properly **merit** eternal life, since Paul
AP : 04 :376(164) [0223] they reason that works **merit** grace by the merit of
AP : 04 :376(164) [0223] works merit grace by the **merit** of congruity or, if love is
AP : 04 :376(164) [0223] or, if love is added, by the **merit** of condignity; that is,
AP : 04 :378(165) [0223] those who teach that we **merit** eternal life by works,
AP : 07 :021(172) [0233] opponents teach that men **merit** the forgiveness of sins by
AP : 12 :008(183) [0255] They teach that by contrition we **merit** grace.
AP : 12 :017(185) [0257] of God's covenant, we **merit** grace by good works done
AP : 12 :018(185) [0257] 2. We **merit** grace through attrition.
AP : 12 :034(186) [0261] sorrows and terrors men **merit** grace if they love God.
AP : 12 :055(189) [0267] this punishment does not **merit** the forgiveness of sin.
AP : 12 :056(189) [0267] added here, but it does not **merit** the forgiveness of sins.
AP : 12 :065(191) [0271] him and not because of any **merits** or works of our own.
AP : 12 :068(192) [0271] been discussing about the **merits** of attrition and works
AP : 12 :075(193) [0273] an act of love to God, he **merits** the attainment of the
AP : 12 :085(194) [0277] of sins by faith but **merit** it by our love and works, and
AP : 12 :108(198) [0283] set my righteousness or my **merits** against Thy wrath.
AP : 12 :108(198) [0283] Yes, we cannot set our **merits** against Thy judgment, but
AP : 12 :114(199) [0285] practices or such works men **merit** the forgiveness of sins.
AP : 12 :114(199) [0285] that by these works they **merit** the forgiveness of sins.
AP : 12 :148(205) [0299] penitence, but not as a **merit** or price, as our opponents
AP : 12 :157(207) [0301] we should not mingle the **merit** of satisfactions with this.
AP : 12 :178(211) [0309] up a great deal about the **merit** of attrition, the endless
AP : 13 :007(212) [0311] to offer sacrifices and **merit** the forgiveness of sins for the
AP : 13 :009(212) [0311] to make sacrifices that **merit** forgiveness of sins for the
AP : 15 :001(215) [0315] to appease God, to **merit** grace, and to make satisfaction
AP : 15 :003(215) [0315] doctrine that we do not **merit** grace or the forgiveness of
AP : 15 :007(216) [0317] They say that men **merit** the forgiveness of sins by these
AP : 15 :011(216) [0317] error to maintain that we **merit** the forgiveness of sins by
AP : 15 :012(216) [0317] that though we do not **merit** the forgiveness of sins, those
AP : 15 :012(216) [0317] are already justified do **merit** grace by observing these
AP : 15 :012(216) [0317] for his sake but must first **merit** this by other
AP : 15 :014(216) [0319] institute certain works to **merit** the forgiveness of sins or
AP : 15 :015(217) [0319] and if by such rites they **merit** grace, we shall have to
AP : 15 :015(217) [0319] rites that serve to **merit** grace or righteousness, why did
AP : 15 :018(217) [0319] that these human rites **merit** justification, grace, and the
AP : 15 :021(218) [0321] purpose, namely, to **merit** the forgiveness of sins, grace
AP : 15 :029(219) [0323] Let us know that they **merit** neither the forgiveness of
AP : 15 :032(220) [0325] that these observances **merit** justification or are necessary
AP : 15 :034(220) [0325] especially from the notion that they **merit** justification.
AP : 15 :034(220) [0325] traditions with the idea that they **merit** justification.
AP : 15 :050(222) [0329] human traditions do not **merit** the forgiveness of sins, and
AP : 18 :002(225) [0335] the Holy Spirit men can **merit** grace and justification by
AP : 18 :006(225) [0335] that such works, by the **merit** of congruity, earn the
AP : 18 :010(226) [0337] to them out of regard for the **merit** of this obedience.
AP : 20 :001(226) [0337] that men do not **merit** the forgiveness of sins by good
AP : 20 :007(227) [0339] and that our works do not **merit** the forgiveness of sins?
AP : 20 :012(228) [0341] works"; therefore works **merit** the forgiveness of sins!
AP : 21 :003(229) [0343] about the application of **merits**, surely has no support
AP : 21 :014(230) [0345] they even apply the **merits** of the saints to others and
AP : 21 :019(231) [0347] a propitiator is this: His **merits** must be authorized to
AP : 21 :019(231) [0347] accounted righteous as though the **merits** were our own.
AP : 21 :019(231) [0347] the debtor is freed by the **merit** of another as though it
AP : 21 :019(231) [0347] Thus the **merits** of Christ are bestowed on us so that when
AP : 21 :019(231) [0347] by our trust in Christ's **merits** as though we had merits of
AP : 21 :019(231) [0347] in Christ's merits as though we had **merits** of our own.
AP : 21 :020(231) [0349] and the bestowal of **merits** are therefore the sources of
AP : 21 :020(232) [0349] promise and Christ's **merits** must be the basis for prayer.
AP : 21 :020(232) [0349] sake and that by his **merits** we have a gracious Father.
AP : 21 :022(232) [0349] They tell us, secondly, to trust in the **merits** of the saints.
AP : 21 :022(232) [0349] on account of them just as we are by Christ's **merits**.
AP : 21 :023(232) [0349] indulgences they claim to apply the **merits** of the saints.
AP : 21 :023(232) [0349] so that we may be saved by their **merits** and vows."
AP : 21 :025(232) [0349] Lord Jesus Christ and the **merits** of the most blessed
AP : 21 :025(232) [0349] not only by Christ's **merits** but also by the merits of other
AP : 21 :025(232) [0349] by Christ's merits but also by the **merits** of other saints.
AP : 21 :029(233) [0351] the transfer of the saints' **merits** to us, as though God
AP : 21 :029(233) [0351] of sins only by Christ's **merits** when we believe in him.
AP : 21 :029(233) [0351] they cannot bestow their **merits** on one another, like the
AP : 21 :029(233) [0351] like the monks who peddle the **merits** of their orders.
AP : 21 :030(233) [0351] be helped by the works or **merits** of others, for everyone
AP : 21 :031(233) [0351] They apply the **merits** of the saints in the same way as the
AP : 21 :031(233) [0351] in the same way as the **merits** of Christ and thus transfer
AP : 21 :031(233) [0351] We know that the **merits** of Christ are our only
AP : 21 :031(233) [0351] righteous by the **merits** of the blessed Virgin or of the
AP : 23 :036(244) [0373] celibacy as a purity that **merits** justification more than
AP : 23 :039(244) [0375] so the virgin does not **merit** justification by virginity any
AP : 23 :040(245) [0375] not say that virginity **merits** salvation or the forgiveness
AP : 23 :045(245) [0377] They thought they would **merit** grace by performing these
AP : 23 :069(249) [0383] but neither virginity nor marriage **merits** justification.
AP : 24 :009(251) [0387] *ex opere operato*, nor **merit** for others the forgiveness of
AP : 24 :011(251) [0387] *operato* and does not **merit** for others, whether living or
AP : 24 :012(251) [0387] sake we are forgiven, his **merits** and righteousness are
AP : 24 :019(252) [0389] or placates his wrath or **merits** the forgiveness of sins for
AP : 24 :019(252) [0389] sacrifice; this does not **merit** the forgiveness of sins or
AP : 24 :021(252) [0391] They did not **merit** the forgiveness of sins in the sight of
AP : 24 :023(253) [0391] righteousness but the **merits** of another (namely, of
AP : 24 :023(253) [0391] offering to reconcile God by his **merits** instead of ours.
AP : 24 :025(253) [0391] can they be transferred to **merit** the forgiveness of sins or
AP : 24 :031(255) [0395] *opere operato* or that it **merits** the forgiveness of sin when
AP : 24 :033(256) [0395] *ex opere operato* or **merit** the forgiveness of sins when it
AP : 24 :035(256) [0397] *ex opere operato* or that **merits** the forgiveness of sins
AP : 24 :042(257) [0399] to someone else to **merit** for him grace and every good.
AP : 24 :053(259) [0403] sacrifices for sin did not **merit** the forgiveness of sins in
AP : 24 :054(259) [0403] were not instituted to **merit** the forgiveness of sins or
AP : 24 :056(259) [0403] therefore, did not **merit** reconciliation — unless by
AP : 24 :057(260) [0405] completely negates the **merit** of Christ's suffering and the
AP : 24 :060(260) [0405] *opere operato* or that it **merits** the forgiveness of sins for
AP : 24 :063(261) [0405] who uses it, or that it **merits** the remission of sins, guilt,
AP : 24 :064(261) [0405] scholastics have scales of **merit**, like the money-changers
AP : 24 :066(261) [0407] *opere operato* or that it **merits** the remission of sins, of
AP : 24 :067(261) [0407] sacrifice does not **merit** reconciliation but comes from the
AP : 24 :067(261) [0407] just as afflictions do not **merit** reconciliation but are
AP : 24 :067(261) [0407] this fiction about **merit** *ex opere operato* is not to be
AP : 24 :077(263) [0411] others *ex opere operato* to **merit** the forgiveness of sins
AP : 24 :078(263) [0411] *opere operato* or that it **merits** the forgiveness of sins for
AP : 24 :087(265) [0413] supposed applicability to **merit** the forgiveness of sins for
AP : 24 :096(267) [0417] *opere operato* and that it **merits** the forgiveness of guilt
AP : 24 :098(268) [0417] apply in order by it to **merit** the forgiveness of guilt and
AP : 27 :009(269) [0421] Do those services **merit** the forgiveness of sins and
AP : 27 :009(270) [0421] Do they have **merits** of supererogation?
AP : 27 :009(270) [0421] Do these **merits** save others when they are transferred to
AP : 27 :011(270) [0423] it supposes that by it he **merits** the forgiveness of sins
AP : 27 :012(270) [0423] according to the Gospel in order to **merit** eternal life.
AP : 27 :013(271) [0423] of sins not because of our **merits** but because of Thee,
AP : 27 :014(271) [0423] by the law of Moses men **merit** the forgiveness of sins, he
AP : 27 :014(271) [0425] divinely revealed, did not **merit** the forgiveness of sins,
AP : 27 :014(271) [0425] do these silly observances **merit** the forgiveness of sins,
AP : 27 :017(271) [0425] works but by setting his **merits** and his propitiation
AP : 27 :017(271) [0425] Whoever sets his own **merits**, in addition to Christ's
AP : 27 :017(272) [0425] of sins because of his own **merits** by doing the works of
AP : 27 :020(272) [0425] conclude that we do not **merit** the forgiveness of sins by
AP : 27 :021(272) [0427] themselves are services that justify or **merit** eternal life.
AP : 27 :023(272) [0427] and through which we **merit** eternal life conflicts with the
AP : 27 :024(273) [0427] of life, that is, that they **merit** forgiveness of sins and
AP : 27 :024(273) [0427] dream that they have **merits** of supererogation, these
AP : 27 :025(273) [0427] such a way that there are **merits** left over, when these
AP : 27 :028(274) [0429] that the monastic life **merits** eternal life if it is maintained
AP : 27 :029(274) [0431] the Sacred Scriptures the monastic life **merits** eternal life.
AP : 27 :030(274) [0431] they say that by a monastic life men **merit** eternal life.
AP : 27 :031(274) [0431] the monastic life does not **merit** the forgiveness of sins
AP : 27 :032(274) [0431] faith and do not set their **merits** against the judgment of
AP : 27 :032(274) [0431] that by no works can you **merit** eternal life, but that this
AP : 27 :033(274) [0431] Since we do not **merit** the forgiveness of sins or eternal
AP : 27 :034(275) [0431] that the monastic life **merits** the forgiveness of sins or
AP : 27 :039(276) [0433] They sell **merits** and transfer them to others under the
AP : 27 :039(276) [0433] they really believe that they have **merits** left over.
AP : 27 :040(276) [0433] says that monks **merit** a more abundant eternal life, and
AP : 27 :040(276) [0433] we should do because it **merits** the forgiveness of sins and
AP : 27 :040(276) [0433] wife in order by this act to **merit** the forgiveness of sins or
AP : 27 :055(278) [0439] are the worship of God to **merit** the forgiveness of sins
AP : 27 :058(279) [0439] faith before men, not to **merit** the forgiveness of sins
AP : 27 :058(279) [0439] as an act of worship to **merit** forgiveness of sins and
AP : 27 :058(279) [0439] God and was not meant to **merit** the forgiveness of sins

Continued ▶

A P : 2 7 :061(279) [0441] our observances do not **merit** the forgiveness of sins or
A P : 2 7 :061(279) [0441] the belief that they would **merit** forgiveness of sins by it,
A P : 2 7 :062(280) [0441] of worship and that they **merit** forgiveness of sins and
A P : 2 7 :065(280) [0441] with the idea that they **merit** forgiveness of sin and
A P : 2 7 :065(280) [0441] are observed in order to **merit** the forgiveness of sins or to
A P : 2 7 :069(281) [0443] that these observances **merit** the forgiveness of sins; that
A P : 2 8 :009(282) [0445] that traditions do not **merit** the forgiveness of sins; here
A P : 2 8 :009(282) [0445] Do they **merit** forgiveness of sins?
A P : 2 8 :011(283) [0447] imposed on the church to **merit** forgiveness of sins or to
A P : 2 8 :021(284) [0449] acts of worship; that they **merit** forgiveness of sins and
S 2 : 0 1 :004(292) [0461] by any work, law, or **merit**, it is clear and certain that
S 2 : 0 2 :007(294) [0465] to God and obtain and **merit** grace and the forgiveness of
S 2 : 0 2 :019(296) [0467] from Christ to their own **merits** and (what is worst of all)
S 2 : 0 2 :024(296) [0469] which the pope sells the **merits** of Christ together with the
S 2 : 0 2 :024(296) [0469] with the superabundant **merits** of all the saints and the
S 2 : 0 2 :024(296) [0469] to the first article, for the **merits** of Christ are obtained by
S 2 : 0 2 :024(296) [0469] us without our money or **merit**, not by the power of the
S 3 : 1 3 :003(315) [0499] cannot boast of the great **merit** in our works if they are
S 3 : 1 5 :001(316) [0501] forgiveness or sins or **merit** salvation is unchristian and to
T R : 0 0 :048(328) [0519] righteousness before God and **merit** forgiveness of sins.
T R : 0 0 :048(328) [0519] they have transferred **merit** from Christ to human
S C : 0 2 :002(345) [0543] and mercy, without any **merit** or worthiness on my part.
S C : 0 3 :016(347) [0549] prayers, for we neither **merit** nor deserve those things for
L C : 0 1 :022(367) [0585] by itself to earn or **merit** everything by works of
L C : 0 1 :038(369) [0591] and foolish that they justly **merit** the wrath they receive.
L C : 0 1 :118(381) [0615] and confess that with the **merits** of their whole lives they
L C : 0 1 :156(386) [0625] If it depended on our **merits**, we would not have a penny
L C : 0 1 :198(392) [0637] stench and filth, and it **merits** nothing but wrath and
L C : 0 2 :017(412) [0681] goodness, without our **merit**, as a kind father who cares
L C : 0 2 :043(416) [0689] without our works and **merits** and made us acceptable to
L C : 0 2 :056(418) [0693] Therefore, all who seek to **merit** holiness through their
L C : 0 3 :097(433) [0725] I can make satisfaction or **merit** anything by my works,
L C : 0 4 :011(438) [0735] greater importance to our own achievements and **merits**.
E P : 0 2 :009(471) [0789] obey God's law, and thus **merit** forgiveness of sins and
E P : 0 2 :012(471) [0789] righteousness before God whereby we **merit** eternal life.
E P : 0 3 :004(473) [0793] or subsequent work, **merit**, or worthiness, and reckons to
E P : 0 3 :010(474) [0795] Paul which separate the **merit** of Christ completely from
E P : 0 3 :010(474) [0795] as *"by grace,"* "without **merit**," "without the law,"
E P : 0 4 :018(477) [0801] and Pharisaic confidence in one's own works and **merit**.
E P : 0 5 :005(478) [0803] guilt and without man's **merit** has obtained and won for
E P : 0 5 :007(478) [0803] directs them solely to the **merit** of Christ, and raises them
E P : 0 5 :007(478) [0803] grace and favor acquired through the **merits** of Christ.
E P : 0 5 :011(479) [0805] a teaching of the law, the **merit** of Christ and the Holy
E P : 0 7 :005(482) [0809] spirit, or the power of Christ's absent body, or his **merit**.
E P : 0 7 :020(484) [0813] obedience and complete **merit** of Christ, which we make
E P : 0 7 :031(485) [0815] the power, operation, and **merit** of the absent body and
E P : 1 1 :013(496) [0835] in Christ without any **merit** of our own, and that no one
E P : 1 1 :015(496) [0835] grace alone, without any **merit** of ours, saves us
E P : 1 1 :020(497) [0837] of God and the most holy **merit** of Christ, but that there
E P : 1 2 :005(498) [0839] wholly in the unique **merit** of Christ, but in renewal and
S D : 0 1 :003(509) [0861] benefits, his precious **merits**, and the Holy Spirit's
S D : 0 1 :006(509) [0861] we are redeemed from this state through Christ's **merit**.
S D : 0 2 :079(536) [0911] obedience of the law **merit** righteousness before God and
S D : 0 3 :009(540) [0919] eternal life) without any **merit** or worthiness on our part,
S D : 0 3 :009(541) [0919] grace, solely through the **merit** of the total obedience, the
S D : 0 3 :013(541) [0919] hold on and accepts the **merit** of Christ in the promise of
S D : 0 3 :013(541) [0919] This **merit** has to be applied to us and to be made our
S D : 0 3 :023(543) [0923] without any work or **merit**, are justified before God (that
S D : 0 3 :025(543) [0923] are the grace of God, the **merit** of Christ, and faith which
S D : 0 3 :030(544) [0925] to give due honor to the **merit** of Christ and the grace of
S D : 0 3 :030(544) [0925] because of the unique **merit** of Christ, the mediator, and
S D : 0 3 :031(544) [0925] the grace of God, the **merit** of Christ, and the forgiveness
S D : 0 3 :037(546) [0929] all our own works, **merit**, worthiness, glory, and trust in
S D : 0 3 :038(546) [0929] the grace and the **merit** of Christ in the promise of the
S D : 0 3 :039(546) [0929] for the sake of Christ's **merit**, which treasures are offered
S D : 0 3 :042(547) [0931] it applies to us and makes our own the **merits** of Christ.
S D : 0 3 :043(547) [0931] God's grace and the **merit** of Christ in the promise of the
S D : 0 3 :046(548) [0933] worthy and fit to have the **merit** of Christ applied to him.
S D : 0 3 :053(548) [0933] works and our own **merit**, such as "by grace" and
S D : 0 3 :054(549) [0935] sinners on account of the obedience and **merit** of Christ.
S D : 0 3 :055(549) [0935] own and all other human **merits**, works, virtues, and
S D : 0 4 :002(551) [0939] in the church, lest the **merit** of Christ, our redeemer, be
S D : 0 4 :022(554) [0945] exclude our works and **merit** completely from the article
S D : 0 4 :022(555) [0945] the grace of God and the **merit** of Christ, as was
S D : 0 4 :027(555) [0945] not put our faith in the **merit** of our works, but we must
S D : 0 4 :037(557) [0949] on good works in order to **merit** the grace of God and to
S D : 0 5 :001(558) [0951] This would darken the **merit** of Christ and rob disturbed
S D : 0 5 :009(559) [0955] faith in Christ, whose **merit** the comforting proclamation
S D : 0 5 :025(563) [0961] of pure grace, without any **merit** of their own, justifies
S D : 0 5 :027(563) [0961] would easily darken the **merits** and benefits of Christ,
S D : 0 7 :016(572) [0977] receive the grace and **merits** of Christ, are incorporated
S D : 0 7 :071(582) [0997] smaller, but solely in the **merits** of Christ, of which the
S D : 0 7 :074(583) [0999] word or work, be it the **merit** or the speaking of the
S D : 0 7 :115(589) [1011] body of Christ with its **merit** is spiritual food for our
S D : 0 7 :117(589) [1013] the virtue, operation, and **merit** of the far-distant body of
S D : 0 8 :059(602) [1035] does not refer only to the **merit** that was once achieved on
S D : 1 1 :016(619) [1069] 2. That this **merit** and these benefits of Christ are to be
S D : 1 1 :043(623) [1077] without our works and **merit**, purely by grace and solely
S D : 1 1 :075(628) [1087] or virtue but solely on the **merit** of Christ and the
S D : 1 1 :087(631) [1093] in Christ without our **merit** and good works, as it is
S D : 1 1 :088(631) [1093] of God and the most holy **merit** of Christ, but that there
S D : 1 1 :096(632) [1095] for ever through the sole **merit** of Christ, and so forth.
S D : 1 2 :010(633) [1097] on the sole obedience and **merit** of Christ but in renewal

Merited (22), Meriting (10), Meritorious (5)
A G : 2 4 :023(058) [0067] held for many people **merited** as much as a special Mass
A L : 2 6 :029(068) [0075] works for the purpose of **meriting** grace through them or
A L : 2 7 :011(072) [0077] they taught that they **merited** forgiveness of sins and
A L : 2 7 :012(072) [0077] added that monastic life **merited** not only righteousness
A L : 2 7 :013(072) [0077] monastic life was more **meritorious** than the life of
A L : 2 7 :044(078) [0081] they were justified and **merited** forgiveness of sins by
A L : 2 8 :035(086) [0089] satisfaction for sins or **meriting** justification, for the glory
A L : 2 8 :050(089) [0091] with the intention of **meriting** justification are in conflict
A P : 0 4 :017(109) [0125] Christ and claim that he **merited** for us a certain
A P : 0 4 :081(118) [0143] propitiator because he **merited** for us the disposition of
A P : 0 4 :084(119) [0145] could never determine whether we had **merited** enough."
A P : 0 4 :087(120) [0147] If moral works **merited** the forgiveness of sins and
A P : 0 4 :152(127) [0163] of love the woman had **merited** the forgiveness of sins.
A P : 0 4 :162(129) [0169] suppose that he merely **merited** "initial grace" and that
A P : 0 4 :194(133) [0175] that good works are **meritorious**—not for the forgiveness
A P : 0 4 :203(135) [0177] these works the saints **merited** grace and the forgiveness
A P : 0 4 :356(161) [0217] and that therefore it is **merited** by the merit of condignity
A P : 0 4 :395(167) [0225] people believed that they **merited** the forgiveness of sins
A P : 0 7 :032(174) [0239] are devotions necessary for **meriting** justification.
A P : 1 5 :010(216) [0317] were thought of as works **meriting** righteousness before
A P : 1 5 :013(216) [0319] for the purpose of **meriting** the forgiveness of sins or
A P : 1 5 :016(217) [0319] that by these they **merited** the forgiveness of sins and
A P : 1 5 :037(220) [0325] are being required as a means of **meriting** justification.
A P : 2 3 :026(243) [0371] or as though celibacy **merited** justification more than
A P : 2 4 :056(259) [0403] by analogy, since they **merited** civil reconciliation — but
A P : 2 4 :057(260) [0405] the Levitical sacrifices **merited** the forgiveness of sins
A P : 2 4 :097(268) [0417] similar notion that they **merited** the forgiveness of sins by
A P : 2 7 :030(274) [0431] own law the honor of **meriting** eternal life, as he clearly
A P : 2 7 :033(275) [0431] deserve the credit for **meriting** the forgiveness of sins or
A P : 2 7 :047(277) [0437] everything for God is **meritorious** and holy and the way
A P : 2 8 :008(282) [0445] Gospel as though they **merited** the forgiveness of sins or
S 3 : 0 3 :012(305) [0481] makes satisfaction has **merited** forgiveness and has paid
L C : 0 3 :010(421) [0699] we are sinners and have **merited** nothing but wrath.
L C : 0 4 :034(440) [0741] do with the intention of **meriting** salvation through them.
S D : 0 3 :037(546) [0929] either the cause or the **meritorious** basis of our
S D : 0 3 :045(547) [0933] our good works are a **meritorious** basis or cause of our
S D : 1 1 :059(626) [1081] deserved, earned, and **merited** because we misbehave over

Merry (2)
S D : 0 4 :012(553) [0941] joyous, mettlesome, and **merry** toward God and all
S D : 0 6 :017(566) [0967] anew, he does everything from a free and **merry** spirit.

Mess (1)
L C : 0 1 :202(392) [0639] as there is a shameful **mess** and cesspool of all kinds of

Message (5)
E P : 0 5 :007(478) [0803] a comforting and joyful **message** which does not reprove
S D : 0 2 :051(531) [0901] will declare to you a **message** by which you will be saved,
S D : 0 5 :021(562) [0959] a good and joyful **message** that God wills not to punish
S D : 0 5 :027(563) [0961] whereas the law is a **message** that rebukes and condemns
S D : 0 8 :027(596) [1025] and confirmed the **message** by the signs that attended it

Messengers (1)
S D : 1 1 :027(620) [1071] he calls through the **messengers** whom he sent out, some

Messiah (9), Messianic (1)
A P : 0 4 :005(108) [0121] when it promises that the **Messiah** will come and promises
A P : 0 4 :154(128) [0163] from him, she truly acknowledged him as the **Messiah**.
A P : 0 4 :154(128) [0165] him as the **Messiah**, though he did show him the outward
A P : 0 4 :154(128) [0165] not believe or accept the **Messiah** or seek from him the
A P : 1 6 :007(223) [0331] Jewish dream of the **messianic** kingdom; instead, he
S 3 : 0 8 :008(313) [0495] Jews about the coming **Messiah** through whom he was
S 3 : 0 8 :008(313) [0495] to reveal to him that the **Messiah**, in whose coming he had
S 3 : 0 8 :008(313) [0495] concerning the coming **Messiah** did not hold him captive
S 3 : 0 8 :008(313) [0497] saved by the present **Messiah** and not deny or persecute
S D : 0 8 :072(605) [1041] (whence he is called **Messiah**, or the Anointed) in such a

Met (1)
A P : 0 4 :288(151) [0203] and, to some extent, its requirements can be **met**.

Metaphor (1), Metaphorical (1)
S D : 0 7 :045(577) [0987] flowery, figurative, or **metaphorical** expressions, as they
S D : 0 7 :048(578) [0989] Hence there can be no **metaphor** (that is, a change in

Method (2), Methods (4)
A L : 0 0 :003(049) [0059] are trying by the same **method** to increase the discord.
S C : P R :009(339) [0535] adhere to a fixed and unchanging form and **method**.
L C : 0 1 :075(375) [0601] With childish and playful **methods** like these we may
L C : 0 1 :076(375) [0603] with kind and pleasant **methods**, for those who have to be
L C : 0 1 :188(390) [0635] sanction any means or **methods** whereby anyone may be
S D : 1 0 :003(611) [1053] or by surreptitious **methods** to suppress the pure doctrine

Metonymy (1)
S D : 0 7 :049(578) [0989] likewise precluded a **metonymy** (that is, a change in

Mettlesome (1)
S D : 0 4 :012(553) [0941] grace makes us joyous, **mettlesome**, and merry toward

Michael (2)
S 3 : 1 5 :005(317) [0501] **Michael** Caelius, preacher in Mansfeld, subscribed
T R : 0 0 :082(335) [0529] **Michael** Caelius, preacher in Mansfeld

Middle (2)
S D : 0 1 :054(518) [0877] is, a division without a **middle** term), so that every
S D : 0 4 :034(556) [0949] alone the beginning, the **middle**, and end of everything.

Midst (18)
A P : 0 4 :034(112) [0129] in its smugness, or in the **midst** of punishment it flees and
A P : 0 4 :232(139) [0185] men cover and forgive certain mistakes in their **midst**.
A P : 0 4 :239(141) [0187] in Christ frees us in the **midst** of these fears because we
A P : 0 4 :293(152) [0203] Word, obey God in the **midst** of afflictions, and practice
A P : 0 4 :314(156) [0207] to cheer ourselves in the **midst** of fears and to exercise
A P : 0 4 :351(161) [0217] and comfort in the **midst** of our terrors, other spiritual
A P : 1 2 :123(201) [0289] who reject penitence, should be removed from their **midst**.
A P : 1 2 :158(207) [0301] When in the **midst** of troubles terrified consciences see
A P : 2 1 :035(234) [0353] In the **midst** of her tortures, Barbara asks for a reward —
T R : 0 0 :008(321) [0505] Christ put a child in the **midst** of the disciples, signifying
T R : 0 0 :068(331) [0523] my name, there am I in the **midst** of them" (Matt. 18:20).
L C : P R :009(359) [0569] gathered in my name, there am I in the **midst** of them."
L C : P R :015(360) [0571] ever live and dwell in the **midst** of such mighty enemies as
L C : 0 1 :007(365) [0583] fearless, as if he were sitting in the **midst** of paradise.

Continued ▶

SD : PR :010(503) [0849] the errors and corruptions that have invaded our **midst**.
SD : 0 2 :057(532) [0903] with his holy Word, he is in the **midst** of them.
SD : 0 8 :076(606) [1043] name, there am I in the **midst** of them," likewise, "I am
SD : 1 2 :014(634) [1099] or congregation in the **midst** of which sinners are still

Might (175)

PR : PR :004(004) [0007] and schools so that he **might** thereby adulterate the pure
PR : PR :005(004) [0009] our churches and schools **might** have been preserved in
PR : PR :005(004) [0009] concord and that they **might** have been well managed and
PR : PR :006(004) [0009] increasingly into them **might** be checked and that our
PR : PR :006(004) [0009] and that our subjects **might** be preserved from straying
PR : PR :008(005) [0009] to warn and, as far as we **might**, to secure our posterity in
PR : PR :008(005) [0009] This we did that we **might** testify and declare to our most
PR : PR :010(006) [0011] mouths of the adversaries **might** be stopped by solid
PR : PR :010(006) [0011] explanation and direction **might** be provided for simple
PR : PR :010(006) [0011] pious hearts, so that they **might** know what attitude to
PR : PR :010(006) [0011] how by God's grace they **might** be preserved from false
PR : PR :011(006) [0011] offensive differences **might** be settled and brought to a
PR : PR :014(007) [0013] that had been sent out **might** be fortified with the Word
PR : PR :014(007) [0013] no adulterated doctrine **might** in the future be hidden
PR : PR :014(007) [0013] declaration of the truth **might** be transmitted to our
PR : PR :017(008) [0015] one or if at any time it **might** become necessary to do so.
PR : PR :019(009) [0017] adulterated teaching that **might** be concealed therein,
PR : PR :026(014) [0025] in order that all kinds of scandal **might** be obviated.
AG : PR :001(024) [0039] how with continuing help he **might** effectively be resisted.
AG : PR :002(025) [0039] for deliberation on what **might** be done about the
AG : 1 3 :001(035) [0049] be signs by which people **might** be identified outwardly as
AG : 2 0 :020(044) [0055] the hope that there they **might** merit grace through
AG : 2 2 :003(049) [0059] In order that no one **might** question these words and
AG : 2 4 :024(058) [0067] given so that our people **might** know how the sacrament
AG : 2 7 :006(071) [0077] even the papal canons **might** have set many of them free.
AG : 2 7 :034(076) [0079] of monastic vows **might** be censured, it would not follow
AG : 2 8 :037(087) [0089] grace and everything good **might** be earned from God.
AG : 2 8 :060(091) [0091] day so that the people **might** know when they ought to
AG : 2 8 :060(091) [0091] in order that the people **might** have an example of
AG : 2 8 :060(091) [0093] of Christian liberty and **might** know that the keeping
AG : 2 8 :069(093) [0093] The bishops **might** easily retain the obedience of men if
AL : 0 3 :003(030) [0045] dead, and buried, that he **might** reconcile the Father to us
AL : 0 5 :003(031) [0045] Gal. 3:14, "That we **might** receive the promise of the
AL : 2 0 :020(044) [0055] the hope that there they **might** merit grace by monastic
AL : 2 7 :034(076) [0079] the violation of vows **might** be rebuked, yet it seems not
AL : 2 8 :069(093) [0093] The bishops **might** easily retain the lawful obedience of
AP : 0 4 :004(108) [0121] the opponents' and our own, **might** be recognized.
AP : 0 4 :084(119) [0145] to faith in Jesus Christ **might** be given to those who
AP : 0 4 :096(121) [0149] world, but that the world **might** be saved through him.
AP : 0 4 :127(125) [0157] (Gal. 3:14), "That we **might** receive the promise of the
AP : 0 4 :132(125) [0159] so that for his sake we **might** receive the gift of the
AP : 0 4 :139(126) [0161] so that with the help of God we, too, **might** conquer.
AP : 0 4 :191(133) [0175] the knowledge of God **might** not perish utterly from the
AP : 0 4 :201(134) [0175] in his body by which he **might** be reminded and grow in
AP : 0 4 :210(136) [0179] Christ, the remembrance **might** strengthen our faith and
AP : 0 4 :210(136) [0179] our faith and we **might** publicly confess our faith and
AP : 0 4 :285(150) [0201] us that through him we **might** have grace, righteousness,
AP : 0 4 :306(154) [0207] no sin, so that in him we **might** become the righteousness
AP : 0 4 :345(160) [0217] world, but that the world **might** be saved through him.
AP : 0 4 :348(160) [0217] that, being righteous, we **might** begin to do good works
AP : 0 4 :349(160) [0217] Spirit, that this new life **might** have new works and new
AP : 0 4 :369(163) [0221] We **might** say more on the term "reward," based on the
AP : 0 7 :007(169) [0229] himself up for it, that he **might** sanctify it, having cleansed
AP : 0 7 :007(169) [0229] the word, that the church **might** be presented before him
AP : 0 7 :007(169) [0229] or any such thing, that it **might** be holy and without
AP : 0 7 :040(176) [0241] well as by instruction they **might** transmit to posterity the
AP : 0 9 :002(178) [0245] the promise of salvation **might** be applied to them
AP : 1 1 :006(181) [0251] certain things so that they **might** be instructed more
AP : 1 2 :081(194) [0275] to faith in Jesus Christ **might** be given to those who
AP : 1 2 :112(198) [0285] so that these satisfactions **might** be suited to their
AP : 1 2 :125(201) [0289] that now or in the future **might** tend to diminish the
AP : 1 2 :127(201) [0291] that we be conquered and destroyed by armed **might**?
AP : 1 2 :159(207) [0301] "that the works of God **might** be made manifest in him"
AP : 1 2 :160(207) [0301] that the power of God **might** be made more manifest in
AP : 1 2 :161(208) [0303] humiliation his piety **might** be exercised and tested.
AP : 1 3 :015(213) [0311] other states or offices **might** also be called sacraments
AP : 1 5 :012(216) [0317] Someone **might** say in this connection that though we do
AP : 1 6 :001(222) [0329] confessed that a Christian **might** legitimately hold public
AP : 2 1 :030(233) [0351] not give it for fear that there **might** not be enough for all.
AP : 2 2 :013(238) [0361] even though otherwise we **might** want to maintain their
AP : 2 4 :023(253) [0391] for our sins, so that men **might** know that God does not
AP : 2 4 :062(260) [0405] so that in this the church **might** have a service that
AP : 2 4 :088(265) [0413] It prays that we **might** be made worthy to offer prayers
AP : 2 7 :017(271) [0425] wrath of God for us so that we **might** be freely forgiven.
AP : 2 8 :019(284) [0449] in such a way that he **might** be heard, because he says,
S 1 : PR :001(288) [0455] reason to expect that we **might** be summoned to appear
S 1 : PR :003(289) [0455] offended, as well they **might** be, and are not a little
S 1 : PR :006(289) [0457] does not, many souls that **might** have been saved are
S 1 : PR :010(290) [0457] many things and many people **might** derive benefit from it
S 1 : PR :013(291) [0459] dispute about specks, we **might** just as well be satisfied
S 2 : 0 4 :007(299) [0473] the unity of Christendom **might** better be preserved
S 3 : 0 3 :005(304) [0481] sinners in order that they **might** know how they stood
S 3 : 0 3 :011(305) [0481] which man with his free will **might** well have avoided.
S 3 : 0 3 :014(305) [0483] priests and monks, that we **might** set ourselves against sin.
S 3 : 0 3 :016(305) [0483] at least be attrite (which I **might** call half-way or partially
S 3 : 0 3 :017(305) [0483] be sorry for his sin (which **might** have been committed,
S 3 : 0 3 :036(309) [0489] for nothing is left that we **might** imagine to be good
S 3 : 1 0 :001(314) [0497] and the Gospel, they **might** be permitted (for the sake of
S 3 : 1 5 :004(316) [0501] such ceremonies of sponsors who **might** make gifts, etc.
TR : 0 0 :014(322) [0509] presence, the episcopate **might** be conferred and hands
TR : 0 0 :062(330) [0523] you in Crete, that you **might** appoint presbyters in every
TR : 0 0 :062(331) [0523] way in which an army **might** select a commander for
SC : 0 4 :010(349) [0551] our Saviour, so that we **might** be justified by his grace
SC : 0 4 :014(349) [0553] glory of the Father, we too **might** walk in newness of life."
LC : PR :003(358) [0567] In this way they **might** show honor and gratitude to the
LC : PR :003(358) [0567] and troubles, and they **might** feel a little shame because,
LC : PR :012(360) [0571] master of a thousand arts with all his wiles and **might**?
LC : PR :013(360) [0571] we frivolously despise this **might**, blessing, power, and
LC : 0 1 :080(375) [0603] that both man and beast **might** be refreshed and not be
LC : 0 1 :125(382) [0617] a block or a stone which we **might** call father and mother.
LC : 0 1 :175(388) [0631] give us grace so that men **might** be trained who would be
LC : 0 1 :190(391) [0635] of the service by which his life **might** have been saved.
LC : 0 1 :197(392) [0637] perfect life," so that they **might** live a nice, soft life
LC : 0 1 :197(392) [0637] monasteries, so that they **might** not have to suffer wrong
LC : 0 1 :208(393) [0639] in order that this estate **might** be provided for richly and
LC : 0 1 :230(396) [0645] Yes, we **might** well keep quiet here about various petty
LC : 0 1 :232(396) [0647] and scoundrels, though it **might** be more fitting if the
LC : 0 1 :239(397) [0649] well regulated, such insolence **might** soon be checked.
LC : 0 1 :270(401) [0657] prove it publicly; I **might** be called a liar and sent away in
LC : 0 1 :295(404) [0665] to another's wife, he **might** on any flimsy excuse dismiss
LC : 0 1 :295(404) [0665] the other's from him so that he **might** legally take her.
LC : 0 1 :307(406) [0669] the eyes of the world you **might** honorably retain the
LC : 0 2 :031(414) [0687] and the Virgin, that he **might** become Lord over sin;
LC : 0 2 :031(414) [0687] and was buried that he **might** make satisfaction for me
LC : 0 2 :038(415) [0689] In order that this treasure **might** not be buried but put to
LC : 0 3 :023(423) [0703] far superior to all others that we **might** ourselves devise.
LC : 0 3 :029(424) [0705] and works for with all his **might**, for he is well aware
LC : 0 3 :030(424) [0707] with the devil and all his **might** and his forces arrayed
LC : 0 3 :057(427) [0713] to ask for whatever he **might** desire and was prepared to
LC : 0 3 :062(428) [0715] with all his power and **might**, marshaling all his subjects
LC : 0 3 :076(431) [0719] Out of it one **might** make a long prayer, enumerating with
LC : 0 3 :076(431) [0721] For example, we **might** ask God to give us food and
LC : 0 4 :012(438) [0735] and dazzling they **might** appear, they would not be as
LC : 0 4 :017(438) [0735] himself stakes his honor, his power, and his **might** on it.
LC : 0 4 :020(439) [0737] Someone **might** come and say, "Why should I think more
LC : 0 4 :058(444) [0747] Likewise I **might** argue, "If I have no faith, then Christ is
LC : 0 5 :055(453) [0767] perfectly pure that God **might** not find the least blemish
LC : 0 5 :065(454) [0769] and me; otherwise Christ **might** just as well have kept
EP : 0 2 :006(470) [0787] of God, so that no one **might** boast in the presence of
EP : 0 4 :011(477) [0799] to do good and that he **might** keep his faith even if he
EP : 0 8 :016(489) [0821] "far above all the heavens that he **might** fill all things."
EP : 1 0 :006(493) [0829] the truth of the Gospel **might** be preserved for you"
EP : 1 1 :001(494) [0831] dissension concerning it **might** be introduced into the
EP : 1 1 :016(497) [0837] the encouragement of the Scriptures we **might** have hope.
EP : 1 2 :021(499) [0841] and to the Word as far as **might**, power, majesty, and
SD : PR :006(504) [0853] Confession someone **might** surreptitiously undertake to
SD : PR :019(507) [0857] of divine truth **might** be made apparent in every article
SD : PR :019(507) [0857] and condemned doctrine **might** be exposed, no matter
SD : PR :019(507) [0857] where or in what books it **might** be found or who may
SD : PR :019(507) [0857] We did this so that we **might** thereby faithfully forewarn
SD : 0 1 :039(515) [0871] his beloved Son he **might** cleanse it from sin, sanctify it,
SD : 0 2 :015(523) [0887] understanding so that he **might** rightly comprehend and
SD : 0 2 :015(523) [0887] not written so that we **might** become remiss and lazy in
SD : 0 2 :081(537) [0911] as follows: "Lest anyone **might** think that the substance
SD : 0 2 :089(538) [0915] it by his power and **might** through the Word in the
SD : 0 3 :037(546) [0929] of our works, so that we **might** or should not view our
SD : 0 4 :039(557) [0951] it is false and offensive, **might** weaken discipline and
SD : 0 4 :039(557) [0951] and decency, and **might** introduce and confirm a wicked,
SD : 0 5 :022(562) [0959] no sin, so that in him we **might** become the righteousness
SD : 0 5 :024(563) [0961] until Christ came, that we **might** be justified by faith"
SD : 0 5 :027(563) [0961] to avoid anything that **might** give occasion for a
SD : 0 6 :009(565) [0965] that I was afflicted that I **might** learn thy statutes"
SD : 0 7 :069(582) [0997] heartily wish that they **might** serve God with a stronger
SD : 0 8 :012(593) [1019] of majesty, power, and **might** over every name that is
SD : 0 8 :027(596) [1025] above all heavens that he **might** truly fill all things, he is
SD : 0 8 :051(601) [1033] majesty, glory, power, and **might** above every name that
SD : 0 8 :051(601) [1033] majesty, glory, power, and **might** which the human nature
SD : 0 8 :061(602) [1035] such divine power, life, **might**, majesty, and glory were
SD : 0 8 :072(605) [1041] of counsel and **might** and knowledge" (Isa. 11:2; 61:1)
SD : 0 8 :079(607) [1045] his Holy Supper that he **might** be present with us, dwell in
SD : 0 8 :095(609) [1049] truth the divine power, **might**, wisdom, majesty, and
SD : 0 9 :002(610) [1051] hell's power, and took from the devil all his **might**.
SD : 1 0 :011(612) [1057] in Christ Jesus, that they **might** bring us into bondage: to
SD : 1 0 :011(612) [1057] the truth of the gospel **might** be preserved for you"
SD : 1 0 :012(613) [1057] so that the truth of the Gospel **might** be preserved.
SD : 1 0 :014(613) [1057] the truth of the Gospel **might** be preserved (Gal. 2:5).
SD : 1 0 :019(614) [1059] and the Gospel, they **might** be permitted (for the sake of
SD : 1 1 :012(618) [1067] of the Scriptures we **might** have hope" (Rom. 15:4).
SD : 1 1 :028(620) [1071] disobedience so that he **might** have mercy on all"
SD : 1 1 :039(622) [1075] assumption that those **might** be the elect who despise
SD : 1 1 :073(628) [1087] experience the power and **might** of the Spirit within
SD : 1 1 :086(631) [1091] damnation so that he could not and **might** not be saved.
SD : 1 1 :088(631) [1093] God's purpose of election **might** continue, not because of
SD : 1 1 :092(632) [1093] of the Scriptures we **might** have hope" (Rom. 15:4).
SD : 1 2 :029(635) [1101] in such a way that in **might**, in power, in majesty, and in

Mightier (1), Mightily (9), Mighty (16)

AG : PR :001(024) [0039] Most serene, most **mighty**, invincible Emperor, most
AG : 2 6 :005(064) [0071] St. Paul contended **mightily** against the law of Moses and
S 3 : 0 3 :001(304) [0481] matter how great, wise, **mighty**, and holy you may think
S 3 : 0 3 :028(308) [0487] and tried earnestly and **mightily** to be holy, and yet the
SC : 0 9 :012(356) [0563] therefore under the **mighty** hand of God, that in due time
LC : PR :007(359) [0569] experienced as any of those who act so high and **mighty**.
LC : PR :015(360) [0571] in the midst of such **mighty** enemies as the devils, and yet
LC : 0 1 :030(368) [0589] *I am the Lord your God, **mighty** and jealous, visiting the*
LC : 0 1 :036(369) [0589] who thought themselves to be so high and **mighty**.
LC : 0 1 :039(370) [0591] these threats are, much **mightier** is the comfort in the
LC : 0 3 :057(427) [0713] Imagine a very rich and **mighty** emperor who bade a poor
SD : 0 1 :043(515) [0873] redemption we have the **mighty** testimony of Scripture
SD : 0 1 :048(517) [0875] show powerfully and **mightily** why we must maintain a
SD : 0 2 :007(521) [0883] the natural free will is **mighty** and active only in the
SD : 0 2 :017(524) [0887] hostile to God, and all too **mighty**, alive, and active for
SD : 0 3 :002(539) [0917] are like a drop of water compared to the **mighty** ocean.
SD : 0 4 :010(552) [0941] is a living, busy, active, **mighty** thing, so that it is
SD : 0 5 :026(563) [0961] Gospel is thoroughly and **mightily** set forth by St. Paul in
SD : 0 7 :043(576) [0987] only truthful, wise, and **mighty**, but himself the eternal
SD : 0 7 :043(577) [0987] speak, and he is able **mightily** to accomplish and achieve
SD : 0 8 :003(592) [1017] Luther contradicted and **mightily** refuted this, as his
SD : 0 8 :051(600) [1033] of the Scriptures, testify **mightily** that, because the human
SD : 0 8 :065(604) [1039] it takes place fully, **mightily**, and publicly before all the

Continued ▶

SD : 0 8 :079(607) [1045] dwell in us, work and be **mighty** in us according to that
SD : 1 1 :043(623) [1077] doctrine, for it **mightily** substantiates the article that we
SD : 1 1 :051(624) [1079] This article also contains **mighty** admonitions and

Mild (2), Mildly (2)
AP : 2 1 :015(231) [0347] To put it **mildly**, even this obscures the work of Christ
AP : 2 2 :009(237) [0359] To put it as **mildly** as possible, this is a human device and
AP : 2 7 :001(268) [0419] him testify that he was a **mild** old man, serious but not
LC : 0 6 :005(457) [0000] ease whatever in the Gospel is **mild** and gentle.

Miles (1)
LC : 0 6 :030(460) [0000] run more than a hundred **miles** for confession, not under

Military (4)
AP : 1 6 :001(222) [0329] in just wars, render **military** service, enter into legal
AP : 1 6 :007(223) [0331] are court decisions, punishments, wars, **military** service.
AP : 2 3 :038(244) [0373] surpasses eloquence, **military** science surpasses
SD : 1 1 :009(618) [1065] he merely held a sort of **military** muster: This one shall be

Militate (1), Militates (1)
PR : PR :004(004) [0009] embracing other errors that **militate** against God's Word.
EP : 0 1 :003(466) [0779] nature and original sin **militates** against and cannot

Milk (2)
LC : 0 1 :026(368) [0587] to the mother breasts and **milk** for her infant, and he
SD : 0 1 :035(514) [0869] thou not pour me out like **milk** and curdle me like

Millstone (1)
SD : 1 0 :016(613) [1059] for him to have a great **millstone** fastened around his neck

Mind (69), Minded (6), Mindful (3), Minds (39)
PR : PR :006(004) [0009] **Mindful** of the office which God has committed to us and
PR : PR :007(004) [0009] With this in **mind** and to this end our praiseworthy
PR : PR :017(008) [0015] it never entered our **minds** and hearts to want to
PR : PR :018(009) [0015] may see that we were not **minded** to permit any doctrine
PR : PR :024(013) [0023] We are accordingly **mindful** of the obligation that we
PR : PR :025(013) [0023] again that we are not **minded** to manufacture anything
PR : PR :025(014) [0023] On the contrary, we are **minded** by the grace of the Holy
PR : PR :027(014) [0025] whereof we have with one **mind** and heart subscribed our
AL : 0 0 :003(049) [0059] By thus exciting the **minds** of good men, they first gave
AP : 0 2 :029(104) [0113] original sin is ignorance in the **mind** and lust in the flesh.
AP : 0 2 :039(105) [0115] at war with the law of my **mind** and making me captive to
AP : 0 4 :007(108) [0121] it has the same judgment naturally written in the **mind**.
AP : 0 4 :009(108) [0123] As long as a man's **mind** is at rest and he does not feel
AP : 0 4 :010(108) [0123] that form of worship or devotion with this view in **mind**.
AP : 0 4 :032(111) [0129] And Rom. 8:7, 8, "The **mind** that is set on the flesh is
AP : 0 4 :033(111) [0129] If the **mind** that is set on the flesh is hostile to God, then
AP : 0 4 :062(115) [0139] this faith brings peace of **mind**, consoles us, receives the
AP : 0 4 :115(123) [0155] us from death, comforting and quickening terrified **minds**.
AP : 0 4 :118(123) [0155] provides a sure and firm consolation for devout **minds**.
AP : 0 4 :133(125) [0159] read a veil lies over their **minds**; but when a man turns to
AP : 0 4 :156(128) [0165] consolation for pious **minds**—whether we should put our
AP : 0 4 :168(130) [0169] the law of God with my **mind**, but with my flesh I serve
AP : 0 4 :188(133) [0173] we call upon devout **minds** to consider the promises, and
AP : 0 4 :238(140) [0187] not have entered the **mind** of any apostle to say that our
AP : 0 4 :244(142) [0189] ever entered into James's **mind**, though our opponents
AP : 0 4 :248(142) [0191] the idle and smug **minds** who dream they have faith but
AP : 0 4 :256(144) [0193] law there are two things we must always keep in **mind**.
AP : 0 4 :265(146) [0197] clings by nature to the **minds** of men, and it cannot be
AP : 0 4 :266(146) [0197] The **mind** must be turned from such fleshly opinions to
AP : 0 4 :276(148) [0199] and confirm terrified **minds** to believe more firmly that
AP : 0 4 :279(149) [0199] almsgiving: "Have God in **mind** all the days of your life"
AP : 0 4 :293(152) [0203] with the Gospel, and any sound **mind** can grasp them.
AP : 0 4 :303(154) [0205] We hope that pious **minds** will easily understand our
AP : 0 4 :303(154) [0205] for of itself the human **mind** believes no such thing about
AP : 0 4 :314(156) [0207] whole issue and bring consolation to well-disposed **minds**.
AP : 0 4 :314(156) [0207] it at hand and keep it in **mind**, not only to refute the
AP : 0 4 :345(160) [0217] This can be a great problem to the human **mind**.
AP : 0 4 :353(161) [0217] these statements the fair-**minded** reader can judge that we
AP : 0 4 :386(166) [0225] truly enlivens the fearful **mind**, and is convinced that God
AP : 0 4 :396(167) [0225] Therefore let not pious **minds** be troubled by the crowd
AP : 0 4 :400(168) [0227] Fathers, and contrary to the testimony of pious **minds**.
AP : 0 7 :029(173) [0237] to twist it, we shall not **mind** replying more fully.
AP : 0 7 :042(176) [0243] say that no one should **mind** if his brethren do not
AP : 0 9 :003(178) [0245] confirm good and godly **minds** against the ungodly and
AP : 1 1 :002(180) [0249] encouraged many devout **minds**, and in the beginning
AP : 1 1 :007(181) [0251] What great tortures for the most pious **minds**!
AP : 1 1 :010(182) [0253] has driven many devout **minds** to hopeless despair
AP : 1 2 :011(184) [0255] And to torture godly **minds** still more, they imagine that
AP : 1 2 :069(192) [0271] it must be kept in **mind** that no great authority attaches to
AP : 1 2 :084(194) [0277] ought not disturb devout **minds** if our opponents twist
AP : 1 2 :123(201) [0289] they try to alienate men's **minds** and fan their hatred, so
AP : 1 2 :129(202) [0291] in order to heal devout **minds** and free them from doubt.
AP : 1 2 :148(205) [0299] of the body which follows true sorrow in the **mind**.
AP : 1 2 :178(211) [0307] it is godly and wholesome for the **minds** of the devout.
AP : 1 3 :022(214) [0313] of the sacrament comforts devout and troubled **minds**.
AP : 1 5 :027(219) [0323] When **minds** are obsessed with the idea that such
AP : 1 6 :006(223) [0331] are very easy to answer if we keep certain things in **mind**.
AP : 1 6 :011(224) [0333] was obviously out of his **mind** in claiming that priests
AP : 1 6 :012(224) [0333] they keep the rule in **mind**, that a Christian may
AP : 2 0 :010(228) [0341] in Scripture to set his **mind** at ease, for Paul fairly
AP : 2 1 :011(230) [0345] power to perceive the unspoken thought of our **minds**.
AP : 2 1 :041(235) [0355] he was freeing human **minds** from the labyrinthine
AP : 2 3 :011(241) [0367] therefore keep this fact in **mind**, taught by Scripture and
AP : 2 3 :043(245) [0375] that domestic problems are excluded from their **minds**.
AP : 2 4 :070(262) [0409] Such a faith encourages the contrite **mind**.
AP : 2 4 :088(265) [0413] meant the service of the **mind**, fear, faith, prayer,
AP : 2 4 :097(268) [0417] instituted by God with this wicked notion in **mind**.
AP : 2 7 :009(270) [0421] Are vows made with these notions in **mind** legitimate?
AP : 2 7 :009(270) [0421] to make up their own **minds** about their way of life, whom
AP : 2 8 :004(281) [0445] of alleviating such **minds** tortured by doubt, they call to
SC : PR :020(340) [0537] The devil also has a horrible purpose in **mind**.
SC : 0 2 :002(345) [0543] and all the faculties of my **mind**, together with food and
LC : SP :027(364) [0581] deeply into their **minds** and remain fixed in their
LC : 0 1 :018(367) [0585] Even in the **mind** of all the heathen, therefore, to have a
LC : 0 1 :077(375) [0603] it may sink into their **minds**, for when we preach to
LC : 0 1 :196(391) [0637] impressed on people's **minds**, we would have our hands
LC : 0 2 :013(412) [0681] all the faculties of my **mind**, my reason and
LC : 0 2 :023(413) [0683] daily to study this article and impress it upon our **minds**.
LC : 0 2 :051(417) [0691] by the Holy Spirit in one faith, **mind**, and understanding.
LC : 0 3 :010(421) [0699] This should be kept in **mind** above all things so that you
LC : 0 4 :048(442) [0743] this question from their **minds** and refer it to the learned.
LC : 0 5 :075(455) [0771] persons in such a state of **mind** that they cannot feel it, I
EP : 0 1 :019(468) [0783] be made, even in the **mind**, between man's nature itself
EP : 0 1 :019(468) [0783] sin, and that the two cannot be differentiated in the **mind**.
EP : 0 2 :003(470) [0787] Likewise, "The **mind** that is set on the flesh is hostile to
EP : 0 6 :004(480) [0805] in the spirit of their **mind**, such regeneration and renewal
EP : 0 6 :004(480) [0805] and in the spirit of their **mind** the believers are in a
EP : 0 6 :006(481) [0807] St. Paul calls it the law of Christ and the law of the **mind**.
SD : 0 1 :011(510) [0863] and foremost powers of the soul in **mind**, heart, and will.
SD : 0 1 :011(510) [0863] a heart, sensation, and **mind**-set which, in its highest
SD : 0 1 :038(515) [0871] all the faculties of my **mind**, my reason and
SD : 0 2 :010(522) [0883] in the futility of their **minds**; they are darkened in their
SD : 0 2 :013(523) [0885] For the **mind** that is set on the flesh (the natural man's
SD : 0 2 :017(524) [0887] explains this text: "The **mind** that is set on the flesh is
SD : 0 2 :017(524) [0887] at war with the law of my **mind** and making me captive to
SD : 0 2 :026(526) [0891] inwardly a new heart, **mind**, and spirit, is solely the work
SD : 0 2 :026(526) [0891] "Then he opened their **minds** to understand the
SD : 0 2 :064(533) [0905] at war with the law of my **mind** and making me captive to
SD : 0 2 :064(533) [0907] the law of God with my **mind**, but with my flesh the law
SD : 0 2 :084(537) [0913] law in our members is at war with the law of our **mind**.
SD : 0 2 :085(537) [0913] members the law of sin at war with the law of his **mind**.
SD : 0 2 :085(537) [0913] reason with the law of his **mind** he serves the law of God,
SD : 0 4 :010(552) [0941] people in heart, spirit, **mind**, and all our powers, and
SD : 0 4 :016(554) [0943] to keep a distinction in **mind**, namely, that when the word
SD : 0 4 :019(554) [0945] but actually wars against the law of his **mind**.
SD : 0 6 :007(565) [0965] in the spirit of their **minds**, nevertheless the Old Adam
SD : 0 6 :008(565) [0965] at war with the law of my **mind** and making me captive to
SD : 0 6 :017(567) [0967] Paul calls them, the law of the **mind** and the law of Christ.
SD : 0 6 :018(567) [0967] in their members is at war against the law of their **mind**.
SD : 0 7 :057(579) [0993] discourse prove, he had in **mind** those who were eating
SD : 0 7 :105(588) [1009] discussion, we have in **mind** the spiritual, supernatural,
SD : 1 0 :017(614) [1059] We are to be particularly **mindful** that Christ says, "So
SD : 1 1 :010(618) [1065] and fortifies in people's **minds** either false security and
SD : 1 1 :045(624) [1079] and so faithfully **minded** about it that "even before the
SD : 1 1 :057(625) [1081] given over to a perverse **mind** while another in equal guilt
SD : 1 1 :064(626) [1083] For who has known the **mind** of the Lord?" — that is,
SD : 1 1 :095(632) [1095] Still less by far are we **minded** to whitewash or cover up

Minden (2)
S3 : 1 5 :005(317) [0501] Gerard Oemcken, superintendent of the church in **Minden**
TR : 0 0 :082(334) [0529] Gerard Oemcken, minister of the church in **Minden**

Mine (6)
SC : 0 7 :002(352) [0557] hands I commend my body and soul and all that is **mine**.
SC : 0 7 :005(353) [0559] hands I commend my body and soul and all that is **mine**.
LC : 0 3 :016(422) [0703] which all the saints base their prayer, I, too, base **mine**.
LC : 0 5 :022(449) [0757] the sacrament may be **mine** and may be a source of
LC : 0 5 :062(454) [0767] of any worthiness of **mine**, but on account of thy Word,
EP : 0 1 :010(467) [0781] I shall see for myself, and **mine** eyes shall behold him."

Mingle (5), Mingled (15), Mingling (1)
AG : 2 8 :012(083) [0085] temporal, are not to be **mingled** or confused, for the
AL : 0 8 :001(033) [0047] and evil persons are **mingled** with believers, it is allowable
AP : 0 2 :012(102) [0109] The scholastics **mingled** Christian doctrine with
AP : 0 2 :043(106) [0117] who improperly **mingle** philosophical and civil ethics with
AP : 0 4 :390(166) [0225] the theologians have **mingled** more than enough
AP : 0 7 :003(169) [0227] and evil men are **mingled** with the church and are
AP : 0 7 :017(171) [0233] been revealed, they are **mingled** with the church and hold
AP : 0 7 :028(173) [0237] and evil men who are **mingled** with them in this life share
AP : 0 7 :047(177) [0243] and evil men have been **mingled** with the church and that
AP : 1 2 :157(207) [0301] Therefore we should not **mingle** the merit of satisfactions
S3 : 0 9 :000(314) [0497] Preachers should not **mingle** civil punishments with this
EP : 0 1 :017(468) [0783] Satan infused into and **mingled** with human nature, as
EP : 0 4 :018(477) [0801] as it is to warn against **mingling** good works in the article
EP : 0 8 :018(489) [0823] Nor do we **mingle** the natures and their properties
EP : 0 8 :021(490) [0823] and human natures are **mingled** into one essence and that
SD : 0 3 :024(543) [0923] heed that we do not **mingle** or insert that which precedes
SD : 0 3 :035(545) [0927] must not be drawn or **mingled** into the article of
SD : 0 3 :036(545) [0929] God they should not be drawn, woven, or **mingled** in.
SD : 0 3 :039(546) [0929] or name are they to be **mingled** with the article of
SD : 0 4 :022(554) [0945] are not drawn into and **mingled** with the article of
SD : 0 5 :027(563) [0961] and Gospel, may not be **mingled** together and confused so

Minimize (5), Minimizing (2)
AP : 0 2 :007(101) [0107] of original sin and therefore **minimize** original sin.
AP : 0 2 :043(106) [0117] it is not right to twist it in order to **minimize** original sin.
AP : 0 2 :046(106) [0117] Although the scholastics **minimize** both sin and its
AP : 1 2 :006(183) [0255] still more and wickedly **minimize** the power of the keys.
AP : 2 2 :013(238) [0361] impression that we are **minimizing** the real dignity of the
SD : 0 1 :061(519) [0879] does not in any way **minimize** original sin if the term is
SD : 0 1 :061(519) [0879] writes earnestly against a **minimizing** of original sin.

Minimum (1)
LC : SP :002(362) [0575] contents represent the **minimum** of knowledge required

Minister (27), Ministers (33)
PR : PR :015(007) [0013] and every theologian, **minister**, and schoolmaster in our
PR : PR :016(008) [0015] of each and every **minister** and schoolmaster in our lands
PR : PR :018(009) [0017] our churches and their **ministers** the onerous burden of
PR : PR :022(012) [0019] the theologians and **ministers** duly to remind even those
AG : 2 3 :016(054) [0063] and others who are to **minister** to the church, be of
AG : 2 8 :022(084) [0087] On this account parish **ministers** and churches are bound
AG : 2 8 :055(090) [0091] the bishops and parish **ministers** in such matters, and to
AG : 0 0 :002(095) [0095] Parish **ministers** also had endless quarrels with monks
AL : 2 8 :030(085) [0087] foods, holy days, grades or orders of **ministers**, etc.

Continued ▶

A L : 0 0 :002(095) [0095] quarrels between parish **ministers** and monks about
A P : 0 7 :028(173) [0237] we may not be offended by the unworthiness of **ministers**.
A P : 0 7 :047(177) [0243] administer them, for **ministers** act in Christ's stead and do
A P : 1 2 :104(197) [0283] The **ministers** of the church therefore have the command
A P : 1 2 :176(210) [0307] command is that the **ministers** of the Gospel absolve
A P : 1 3 :012(212) [0311] command to appoint **ministers**; to this we must subscribe
A P : 1 5 :041(220) [0325] circles the pastors and **ministers** of the churches are
A P : 2 4 :018(252) [0389] baptizes us through a **minister** functioning in his place.
A P : 2 4 :080(264) [0411] with our position that a **minister** who consecrates shows
A P : 2 4 :080(264) [0411] to the people, just as a **minister** who preaches shows forth
A P : 2 4 :080(264) [0411] one should regard us, as **ministers** of Christ and
A P : 2 4 :082(264) [0411] he calls Epaphroditus a "**minister** to my need," which
S 2 : 0 3 :001(297) [0471] preachers, and other **ministers** in the church, others who
S 3 : 0 9 :000(314) [0497] which does not concern us **ministers** of the church.
S 3 : 1 0 :002(314) [0497] must not be deprived of **ministers** on their account.
S 3 : 1 5 :005(317) [0501] I, Stephen Agricola, **minister** in Hof, subscribe
S 3 : 1 5 :005(317) [0501] Drach, professor and **minister** in Marburg, subscribe
S 3 : 1 5 :005(317) [0501] I, Andrew Osiander, **minister** in Nuremberg, subscribe
S 3 : 1 5 :005(317) [0501] I, Master Veit Dietrich, **minister** in Nuremberg, subscribe
S 3 : 1 5 :005(317) [0501] I, Brixius Northanus, **minister** of the church of Christ
T R : 0 0 :008(321) [0505] be no primacy among **ministers**, just as a child neither
T R : 0 0 :011(321) [0507] I Cor. 3:4-8 Paul places **ministers** on an equality and
T R : 0 0 :011(321) [0507] and teaches that the church is above the **ministers**.
T R : 0 0 :011(321) [0507] or authority over the church or the other **ministers**.
T R : 0 0 :011(321) [0507] Peter nor the other **ministers** should assume lordship or
T R : 0 0 :025(324) [0511] addresses Peter as a **minister** and says, "On this rock,"
T R : 0 0 :064(331) [0523] should ordain the **ministers** in a number of churches.
T R : 0 0 :067(331) [0523] the right of calling, electing, and ordaining **ministers**.
T R : 0 0 :067(331) [0523] electing and ordaining **ministers** must of necessity also
T R : 0 0 :067(331) [0523] absolves and becomes the **minister** and pastor of another.
T R : 0 0 :069(331) [0525] certainly has the right of electing and ordaining **ministers**.
T R : 0 0 :072(332) [0525] retains the right of electing and ordaining **ministers**.
T R : 0 0 :072(332) [0525] compelled to ordain pastors and **ministers** for themselves.
T R : 0 0 :080(334) [0527] means for the support of **ministers**, the promotion of
T R : 0 0 :082(334) [0529] Stephen Agricola, **minister** in Chur, subscribed with his
T R : 0 0 :082(334) [0529] Gerard Oemcken, **minister** of the church in Minden
T R : 0 0 :082(335) [0529] Brixius Northanus, **minister** in Soest
T R : 0 0 :082(335) [0529] Boniface Wolfart, **minister** of the Word in the church in
T R : 0 0 :082(000) [0529] John Brentz, **Minister** of Hall (Triglotta text only)]
S C : 0 9 :005(355) [0561] for the authorities are **ministers** of God, attending to this
E P : 0 7 :008(482) [0811] nor the recitation of the **minister** effect this presence of
E P : 1 1 :004(495) [0833] wickedness it must **minister** to the salvation of his elect.
E P : 1 2 :027(500) [0843] 8. That a **minister** of the church cannot teach profitably
S D : 0 7 :016(572) [0977] or unworthiness of the **minister** who distributes the
S D : 0 7 :074(583) [0999] or the speaking of the **minister**, be it the eating and
S D : 0 7 :089(585) [1003] or unworthiness of the **minister** or the unbelief of him
S D : 1 0 :010(612) [1055] and especially the **ministers** of the Word as the leaders of
S D : 1 0 :019(614) [1059] must not be deprived of **ministers** on their account."
S D : 1 1 :012(618) [1067] inspired by God, should **minister** not to security and
S D : 1 2 :016(634) [1099] to do with those **ministers** of the church who preach the
S D : 1 2 :035(635) [1101] 7. That a **minister** of the church who is himself not truly

Ministration (3), Ministrations (1)
A P : 2 3 :027(243) [0371] the period of their **ministration** the priests of the Old
A P : 2 3 :027(243) [0371] is forbidden only during the period of **ministration**.
A P : 2 3 :027(243) [0371] Besides, prayer is one thing and **ministration** another.
A P : 2 4 :083(264) [0413] use of "liturgy" to mean public duties or **ministrations**.

Ministry (53)
P R : P R :023(012) [0021] church and for the holy **ministry** be faithfully and
A G : 0 5 :000(031) [0045] V. [The Office of the **Ministry**]
A G : 0 5 :001(031) [0045] the office of the **ministry**, that is, provided the Gospel and
A G : 2 8 :070(093) [0093] and admit no one to the **ministry** unless he first swears an
A L : 0 5 :000(031) [0045] V. [The **Ministry** of the Church]
A L : 0 5 :001(031) [0045] may obtain this faith, the **ministry** of teaching the Gospel
A L : 0 8 :003(033) [0047] who have denied that the **ministry** of evil men may be
A L : 0 8 :003(033) [0047] who have thought the **ministry** of evil men to be
A L : 2 8 :009(082) [0085] except through the **ministry** of the Word and sacraments,
A L : 2 8 :010(082) [0085] only through the **ministry** of the Word, it interferes with
A L : 2 8 :019(084) [0087] is a function other than the **ministry** of the Gospel.
A L : 2 8 :021(084) [0087] has been committed the **ministry** of the Word and
A L : 2 8 :070(093) [0093] will admit no one to the **ministry** unless he swears that he
A P : 0 4 :073(117) [0141] we give the highest praise to the **ministry** of the Word.
A P : 1 2 :007(183) [0255] of the keys would be a **ministry** not of life and of the
A P : 1 2 :103(197) [0281] is irrelevant because the **ministry** of absolution is in the
A P : 1 3 :007(212) [0311] in reference to the **ministry** of the Word or the
A P : 1 3 :011(212) [0311] in relation to the **ministry** of the Word, we have no
A P : 1 3 :011(212) [0311] The **ministry** of the Word has God's command and
A P : 1 3 :012(212) [0311] know that God approves this **ministry** and is present in it.
A P : 1 3 :013(212) [0311] It is good to extol the **ministry** of the Word with every
A P : 2 3 :023(242) [0369] those from the public **ministry** who married while in
A P : 2 3 :027(243) [0371] carrying on their public **ministry**, and marital intercourse
A P : 2 4 :048(258) [0401] pay attention to the **ministry** of the Word, they teach the
A P : 2 4 :059(260) [0405] the New Testament is a **ministry** of the Spirit, as Paul
A P : 2 4 :059(260) [0405] The **ministry** of the Spirit contradicts any such transfer *ex*
A P : 2 4 :059(260) [0405] Through the **ministry** of the Spirit, the Holy Spirit works
A P : 2 4 :059(260) [0405] Therefore this **ministry** benefits people when he does
A P : 2 4 :081(264) [0411] Thus the term "liturgy" squares well with the **ministry**.
A P : 2 7 :022(272) [0427] good men serving the **ministry** of the Word who follow
A P : 2 8 :013(283) [0447] of the order, namely, the **ministry** of Word and
T R : 0 0 :008(320) [0505] equals and exercise the **ministry** of the Gospel in
T R : 0 0 :010(321) [0507] that the authority of the **ministry** depends on the Word
T R : 0 0 :025(324) [0511] of a man but on the **ministry** of the confession which
T R : 0 0 :025(324) [0511] minister and says, "On this rock," that is, on this **ministry**.
T R : 0 0 :026(324) [0511] Besides, the **ministry** of the New Testament is not bound
T R : 0 0 :026(324) [0511] Nor is this **ministry** valid because of any individual's
T R : 0 0 :034(325) [0513] The **ministry** of the Gospel was neglected.
T R : 0 0 :040(327) [0515] of the church and the **ministry**, offering as pretext these
T R : 0 0 :067(331) [0523] given for the work of **ministry** and for building up the
T R : 0 0 :082(334) [0527] the churches for luxuries and would neglect the **ministry**.
S C : P R :026(341) [0539] It is now a **ministry** of grace and salvation.
L C : 0 1 :086(376) [0605] therefore, should be the **ministry** of the Word for the sake
E P : 0 5 :006(478) [0803] in his teaching **ministry** and which his apostles also set
E P : 1 2 :022(499) [0841] 3. That the **ministry** of the church — the Word preached
S D : P R :005(504) [0851] through the faithful **ministry** of that illustrious man of
S D : 0 2 :038(528) [0895] namely, that through the **ministry** he brings us into the
S D : 0 5 :004(558) [0953] Lord, which in his public **ministry** on earth and in the
S D : 0 5 :024(562) [0961] so that in the **ministry** of the New Testament the
S D : 0 7 :077(583) [0999] are daily distributed through our **ministry** and office."
S D : 1 1 :029(621) [1073] which we are called is a **ministry** of the Spirit — "which
S D : 1 2 :006(633) [1097] As far as our **ministry** is concerned, we do not propose to
S D : 1 2 :030(635) [1101] 2. That the **ministry** of the church, the Word proclaimed

Minor (9)
A P : 0 2 :011(102) [0109] They acknowledge the **minor** faults in human nature and
A P : 0 4 :063(115) [0139] as though the gift of the Holy Spirit were a **minor** matter.
A P : 0 4 :079(117) [0143] It is easy to state the **minor** premise if we know how the
A P : 0 4 :080(118) [0143] We prove the **minor** premise as follows.
A P : 0 4 :232(140) [0185] the brethren, to cover up **minor** mistakes, lest the church
A P : 0 4 :233(140) [0185] them because of some **minor** fault and then seek after
A P : 0 4 :241(141) [0187] and Pompey certain **minor** disagreements arose, which
A P : 0 4 :378(165) [0223] It is then no **minor** matter about which we are arguing
A P : 2 4 :008(250) [0385] writes that in Asia **Minor** there were no daily Masses but

Miracle (1), Miracles (3)
A P : 1 3 :020(214) [0313] as though God, by a new **miracle**, promised his will to
A P : 1 3 :020(214) [0313] what good would such **miracles** or promises do an
A P : 2 1 :037(234) [0355] point in listing here the **miracles** they have invented
S D : 0 8 :025(596) [1023] Christ performed all his **miracles** and manifested his

Mired (1)
S D : 0 5 :002(558) [0953] they formerly had been **mired** and which the law of God

Mirror (5), Mirrors (1)
A P : 2 1 :037(234) [0355] they call them, and the **mirrors** and the rosaries, all of
L C : 0 1 :187(390) [0633] ever before our eyes as a **mirror** in which to see ourselves,
L C : 0 2 :065(419) [0695] for the Lord Christ, who is a **mirror** of the Father's heart.
L C : 0 6 :026(460) [0000] you are, making of you a **mirror** for contemplating
S D : 0 6 :004(564) [0963] For the law is a **mirror** in which the will of God and what
S D : 0 6 :021(567) [0969] such a way that, as in a **mirror**, it shows and indicates to

Misapply (3), Misapplying (1)
A P : 2 4 :096(267) [0417] Our opponents also **misapply** against us the
A P : 2 7 :066(280) [0441] opponents insist upon **misapplying** this passage to vows,
A P : 2 7 :066(280) [0441] to vows, they must also **misapply** the other one which
A P : 2 8 :019(284) [0449] and teaching, and they **misapply** it to these trifles,

Misbehave (1)
S D : 1 1 :059(626) [1081] and merited because we **misbehave** over against God's

Mischievous (1)
S 2 : 0 4 :003(298) [0471] strength of such false, **mischievous**, blasphemous, usurped

Misconstrued (1), Misconstruing (1)
L C : 0 1 :289(404) [0663] in their neighbor, **misconstruing** and twisting things in the
S D : 1 1 :083(630) [1091] This must not be **misconstrued** as if it had never been

Misdeeds (1)
A P : 1 2 :158(207) [0301] were not imposed on him because of his past **misdeeds**.

Misery (19), Miserable (9), Miserably (5), Miseries (3)
A P : 0 4 :003(107) [0121] confuse this doctrine **miserably**, they obscure the glory
A P : 1 2 :094(196) [0281] Oh, most **miserable** are we if we do not believe the Lord
S 3 : 0 3 :022(306) [0485] Here, too, there was nothing but anguish and **misery**.
L C : 0 1 :041(370) [0591] and salvation, or eternal wrath, **misery**, and woe.
L C : 0 1 :060(372) [0597] Where else could so much **misery** come from?
L C : 0 1 :068(374) [0599] and thus they **miserably** perished, body, soul, and
L C : 0 1 :120(382) [0615] is the plight and the **miserable** blindness of the world that
L C : 0 1 :123(382) [0617] so that they sink into all kinds of trouble and **misery**.
L C : 0 1 :149(385) [0623] then take shame, **misery**, and grief for your reward.
L C : 0 1 :154(386) [0625] now so full of unfaithfulness, shame, **misery**, and murder?
L C : 0 1 :157(386) [0627] from the blindness and **misery** in which we are so deeply
L C : 0 1 :183(389) [0633] well knows, the world is evil and this life is full of **misery**.
L C : 0 1 :310(407) [0669] against envy and **miserable** covetousness, God's purpose
L C : 0 1 :316(408) [0671] They fail to see, these **miserable**, blind people, that no
L C : 0 2 :029(414) [0685] had mercy on our **misery** and wretchedness and came
L C : 0 3 :011(421) [0701] before him, lament our **misery** and plight, and pray for
L C : 0 3 :086(432) [0723] This petition has to do with our poor, **miserable** life.
L C : 0 3 :115(435) [0731] in short, all the tragic **misery** and heartache of which
L C : 0 4 :083(446) [0751] until we pass from this present **misery** to eternal glory.
L C : 0 5 :061(453) [0767] we come as poor, **miserable** men, precisely because we are
L C : 0 5 :084(456) [0773] much in need of the sacrament to combat your **misery**.
L C : 0 5 :084(456) [0773] This **misery**, unfortunately, you do not see, though God
L C : 0 5 :084(456) [0773] can he bring you into **misery** and distress when you least
L C : 0 6 :023(459) [0000] and act like a poor **miserable** beggar who hears that a rich
L C : 0 6 :024(460) [0000] just letting everyone see how poor and **miserable** he is?
L C : 0 6 :026(460) [0000] If you are poor and **miserable**, then go and make use of
L C : 0 6 :027(460) [0000] He who feels his **misery** and need will develop such a
S D : 0 1 :013(511) [0863] temporal, and eternal **misery**, the tyranny and dominion
S D : 0 1 :038(515) [0871] of God has been **miserably** corrupted by sin, for the
S D : 0 1 :039(515) [0871] nature, which is so **miserably** corrupted by sin, in order
S D : 0 2 :017(524) [0887] by original sin he is so **miserably** perverted, poisoned, and
S D : 0 2 :017(524) [0887] so perverted and full of **misery** that no one can fathom it
S D : 0 2 :047(530) [0901] obedience but only weakness and anxiety and **misery**.
S D : 0 5 :020(561) [0959] to death, to temporal **miseries**, and to the punishment of
S D : 0 6 :019(567) [0969] the law but also with **miseries**, for he does everything
S D : 0 6 :024(568) [0969] club of punishments and **miseries**, until the flesh of sin is

Misfortune (13), Misfortunes (2)
L C : 0 1 :004(365) [0581] whenever you suffer **misfortunes** and distress, come and
L C : 0 1 :122(382) [0617] and lay up for themselves nothing but **misfortune**.
L C : 0 1 :137(384) [0619] upon themselves the **misfortune** and grief that we behold,
L C : 0 1 :148(385) [0623] you will have all kinds of trouble and **misfortune**.
L C : 0 1 :153(386) [0625] and blessing than you will with disfavor and **misfortune**.
L C : 0 1 :155(386) [0625] we keenly feel our **misfortune**, and we grumble and
L C : 0 1 :192(391) [0635] your neighbor to languish and perish in his **misfortune**.

Continued ▶

LC : 0 1 :234(397) [0647] and will suffer all kinds of troubles and **misfortunes**.
LC : 0 1 :243(398) [0649] so many troubles and **misfortunes** that they can never
LC : 0 1 :253(399) [0653] this blessing will find wrath and **misfortune** enough.
LC : 0 1 :258(400) [0653] It is the universal **misfortune** of the world that men of
LC : 0 2 :017(412) [0681] against every evil and **misfortune**, warding off all sorts of
LC : 0 3 :065(429) [0715] inflicting every possible **misfortune** and grief upon us.
LC : 0 3 :114(435) [0729] "Dear Father, help us to get rid of all this **misfortune**."
SD : 1 1 :007(617) [1065] plunged thyself into **misfortune**, but in me alone is thy

Misgiving (1), Misgivings (2)
AG : 2 3 :013(053) [0063] opinions and the **misgiving** that such enforced celibacy
AG : 2 3 :002(053) [0063] man, made this statement because of grave **misgivings**.
LC : 0 5 :061(453) [0767] People with such **misgivings** must learn that it is the

Misguided (1)
PR : PR :024(013) [0023] and instruction of poor, **misguided** consciences.

Misinterpret (6), Misinterpretation (4), Misinterpreted (2)
AP : 0 2 :001(100) [0105] they viciously **misinterpret** and distort a statement that
AP : 0 4 :283(149) [0201] Our opponents **misinterpret** the universal particle "all."
AP : 1 2 :175(210) [0307] has been **misinterpreted** as a liberation of souls from
AP : 2 4 :023(253) [0391] adopted from their **misinterpretation** of the patriarchal
AP : 2 4 :031(255) [0395] Our opponents **misinterpret** this passage and apply it to
AP : 2 4 :052(259) [0403] are nothing but a **misinterpretation** of the Levitical order.
AP : 2 4 :088(265) [0413] It is a **misinterpretation** to translate this as "reasonable
LC : 0 1 :262(400) [0655] it is contradicted, perverted, misused, and **misinterpreted**.
EP : 0 8 :039(491) [0827] 20. They **misinterpret** and blasphemously pervert the
SD : 0 2 :044(529) [0897] against all misunderstandings and **misinterpretation**.
SD : 0 7 :032(574) [0983] and ordinance and **misinterpret** them, as the enemies of
SD : 1 0 :014(613) [1057] will misuse them and **misinterpret** them in this direction.

Mislead (4), Misleading (1), Misleads (1), Misled (8)
PR : PR :006(004) [0009] end that the false and **misleading** doctrines which have
PR : PR :022(012) [0021] it, lest one blind person let himself be **misled** by another.
AG : 2 8 :040(087) [0089] that some bishops were **misled** by the example of the law
AL : 2 8 :040(087) [0089] measure to have been **misled** by the example of the law of
S 1 : PR :004(289) [0457] of my labor and thus **mislead** the poor people in my
SC : 0 3 :018(347) [0549] may not deceive us or **mislead** us into unbelief, despair,
LC : 0 1 :197(392) [0637] the monks mock and **mislead** the world with a false,
EP : 0 1 :022(469) [0785] to conceal their error and to **mislead** many simple people.
EP : 0 8 :001(486) [0817] the Calvinists (who have **misled** some other theologians
SD : PR :019(507) [0857] lest anyone be **misled** by the high regard in which these
SD : 0 1 :013(511) [0863] He **misleads** many influential and wise men of the world
SD : 0 1 :027(513) [0867] The fact is, that Satan **misled** Adam and Eve through the
SD : 0 2 :090(538) [0915] have been greatly **misled** by the doctrine of the three
SD : 0 8 :035(597) [1027] becomes tangled up and the simple reader is easily **misled**.

Mismated (4)
TR : 0 0 :041(328) [0517] Cor. 6:14, "Do not be **mismated** with unbelievers, for
EP : 1 0 :006(493) [0829] "Do not be **mismated** with unbelievers, for what
SD : 1 0 :006(611) [1055] must be heeded: "Do not be **mismated** with unbelievers.
SD : 1 0 :022(615) [1061] II Cor. 6:14, 'Do not be **mismated** with unbelievers, for

Misquote (1)
AP : 2 3 :068(249) [0383] So they often **misquote** these tribunals of the church.

Misrepresentation (2)
AG : 2 7 :017(073) [0077] mentioned, without **misrepresentation**, in order that one
AP : 0 7 :002(168) [0227] be said so carefully that it can avoid **misrepresentation**.

Miss (2), Missing (1)
AP : 0 2 :007(101) [0107] By such questions they **miss** the main issue.
LC : 0 2 :047(416) [0691] the latter phrase was **missing**, and it is unintelligible in
LC : 0 6 :023(460) [0000] run there as fast as he could so as not to **miss** the gift.

Mistake (3), Mistaken (5), Mistakes (3)
AG : 2 8 :058(091) [0091] are very much **mistaken**, for the Holy Scriptures have
AL : 2 8 :058(091) [0091] the church's authority as a necessary thing are **mistaken**.
AP : 0 4 :159(129) [0167] But they are **mistaken** when they think that we are
AP : 0 4 :232(139) [0185] men cover and forgive certain **mistakes** in their midst.
AP : 0 4 :232(140) [0185] to cover up minor **mistakes**, lest the church disintegrate
AP : 0 4 :242(141) [0187] it covers up some of the **mistakes** of its friends; and that
AP : 0 7 :042(176) [0243] even if they have made a **mistake**, do not let this bother
AP : 0 7 :042(177) [0243] even if there has been a **mistake** in the calculations.
AP : 0 7 :044(177) [0243] even if there has been a **mistake** in the calculations.
AP : 1 2 :127(201) [0289] You are **mistaken** if you suppose that churches should be
AP : 1 2 :149(205) [0299] Our opponents are badly **mistaken** if they think that

Mistress (5), Mistresses (6)
AP : 1 2 :125(201) [0289] to recognize her as the **mistress** of the faith, she should
SC : 0 5 :022(350) [0553] I have grumbled and sworn at my **mistress**, etc.
SC : 0 5 :023(350) [0553] A master or **mistress** may say: "In particular I confess in
SC : 0 5 :023(350) [0555] Masters and **mistresses** should add whatever else they
SC : 0 9 :011(356) [0563] Masters and **Mistresses**
LC : 0 1 :142(384) [0621] called the masters and **mistresses** of the household *patres*
LC : 0 1 :143(385) [0623] obey their masters and **mistresses**, but also to honor them
LC : 0 1 :144(385) [0623] to acquire masters and **mistresses** in order to have such
LC : 0 1 :225(395) [0645] to the vexation and annoyance of his master or **mistress**.
LC : 0 1 :235(397) [0647] care of your master's or **mistress**'s property, which
LC : 0 1 :235(397) [0647] toward masters and **mistresses** and unwilling to do them

Misunderstand (3), Misunderstanding (9), Misunderstandings (3), Misunderstands (1), Misunderstood (2)
PR : PR :014(007) [0013] all sorts of perilous **misunderstanding**, so that no
PR : PR :021(010) [0019] words (so that all **misunderstanding** and scandal on this
AL : 2 6 :019(067) [0073] which had arisen from **misunderstanding** of traditions.
AL : 2 8 :074(093) [0093] that some were adopted out of **misunderstanding**.
AP : 0 2 :007(101) [0107] the scholastics **misunderstand** the patristic definition of
AP : 0 4 :153(128) [0163] this is faith, he utterly **misunderstands** the nature of faith.
AP : 0 7 :043(177) [0243] and he criticizes the Audians for **misunderstanding** it.
AP : 0 7 :045(177) [0243] completely **misunderstand** the meaning of the
AP : 1 2 :078(193) [0275] of the law — and that **misunderstood**, as the Jews looked
AP : 2 3 :045(245) [0375] Many heretics have **misunderstood** the law of Moses;
S 3 : 0 1 :011(303) [0479] have resulted from **misunderstanding** and ignorance
SD : PR :009(503) [0849] may think, mere **misunderstandings** or contentions about
SD : 0 2 :044(529) [0897] ability against all **misunderstandings** and
SD : 0 6 :015(566) [0967] to avoid all **misunderstandings**, to teach and to maintain
SD : 0 7 :050(578) [0991] And so that no **misunderstanding** could creep in, he
SD : 0 7 :073(582) [0999] has also arisen a **misunderstanding** and dissension among
SD : 1 1 :003(616) [1063] people misuse and **misunderstand** it; on the contrary,
SD : 1 1 :003(616) [1063] such misuse and **misunderstanding**, we must set forth the

Misuse (22), Misused (6), Misuses (3), Misusing (2)
AG : 0 0 :001(047) [0059] peril before God by **misusing** his name or Word, nor
AG : 2 4 :010(057) [0065] the Mass came to be **misused** in many ways, as is well
AG : 2 4 :029(059) [0067] to this teaching is the **misuse** of the Mass by those who
AG : 0 0 :002(095) [0095] about indulgences, pilgrimages, and **misuse** of the ban.
AL : 0 0 :002(095) [0095] pilgrimages, and **misuse** of excommunication.
LC : 0 1 :051(371) [0595] What does it mean to **misuse** or take the name of God in
LC : 0 1 :051(371) [0595] answer briefly: "It is a **misuse** of God's name if we call
LC : 0 1 :053(371) [0595] though it is impossible to enumerate all its **misuses**.
LC : 0 1 :053(371) [0595] To discuss it briefly, **misuse** of the divine name occurs
LC : 0 1 :056(372) [0595] shun and avoid every **misuse** of the holy name as the
LC : 0 1 :077(375) [0603] Thus we have averted the **misuse** of the divine name and
LC : 0 1 :077(375) [0603] richly reward it, even as he will terribly punish its **misuse**.
LC : 0 1 :081(375) [0603] this commandment too narrowly and grossly **misused** it.
LC : 0 1 :096(378) [0607] by those who grossly **misuse** and desecrate the holy day,
LC : 0 1 :103(379) [0611] Secondly, we should not **misuse** his holy name in support
LC : 0 1 :240(397) [0649] Everyone **misuses** the market in his own willful,
LC : 0 1 :262(400) [0655] it is contradicted, perverted, **misused**, and misinterpreted.
LC : 0 2 :021(413) [0683] in its blindness, **misusing** all the blessings and gifts of God
LC : 0 3 :042(425) [0709] when men grossly **misuse** the divine name as a cloak for
LC : 0 3 :045(426) [0709] thus rendering unholy by **misuse** that which is holy in
LC : 0 4 :058(444) [0747] should, the thing that he **misuses** has no existence or no
LC : 0 4 :059(444) [0747] *substantiam*," that is, "**Misuse** does not destroy the
LC : 0 5 :016(448) [0757] can change or alter the sacrament, even if it is **misused**.
SD : 0 2 :046(530) [0899] an unchristian fashion **misused** the doctrine of the
SD : 0 7 :016(572) [0977] as St. Paul says, for they **misuse** the holy sacrament since
SD : 0 7 :024(573) [0981] alter or change the sacrament, even though it is **misused**.
SD : 0 7 :029(574) [0981] my death appeal to me or **misuse** my writings to confirm
SD : 0 7 :032(574) [0983] them do not believe or otherwise **misuse** the sacrament.
SD : 0 7 :057(579) [0993] which no one could **misuse** and against which no one
SD : 0 7 :085(584) [1001] many kinds of idolatrous **misuse** and perversion of this
SD : 1 0 :014(613) [1057] liberty, or they will **misuse** them and misinterpret them in
SD : 1 1 :003(616) [1063] because some people **misuse** and misunderstand it; on the
SD : 1 1 :003(616) [1063] in order to avert such **misuse** and misunderstanding, we

Mitigate (4), Mitigated (1), Mitigation (5), Mitigations (2)
AG : 2 6 :014(066) [0073] traditions and sought **mitigations** to relieve consciences,
AG : 2 8 :064(092) [0093] undertake to lighten and **mitigate** human regulations, yet
AG : 2 8 :064(092) [0093] be no moderation or **mitigation** as long as the opinion
AG : 2 8 :068(093) [0093] consciences unless this **mitigation** is practiced, that one
AG : 2 8 :075(094) [0095] cannot be persuaded to **mitigate** or abrogate human
AL : 2 6 :014(066) [0073] together and sought **mitigations** to relieve consciences;
AL : 2 8 :064(092) [0093] Although they try to **mitigate** the traditions, moderation
AL : 2 8 :068(093) [0093] consciences unless this **mitigation** is practiced, that one
AL : 2 8 :074(093) [0093] of the bishops to **mitigate** these regulations now, for such
AP : 1 2 :164(208) [0303] — brings about the **mitigation** of public and private
AP : 1 2 :165(208) [0303] our common evils are **mitigated** by our penitence and its
AP : 1 5 :028(219) [0323] and cannot fix the **mitigation** in any definite degree!

Mixed (3), Mixture (1)
PR : PR :021(011) [0019] respective properties, are **mixed** together and the human
AP : 0 4 :282(149) [0201] said that sprinkling water **mixed** with salt "sanctifies and
EP : 0 1 :017(468) [0783] with human nature, as when poison and wine are **mixed**.
SD : 0 8 :018(594) [1021] often used the term "**mixture**" in a good sense and with

Mizbeach (1)
AP : 2 4 :085(264) [0413] "Mass" is derived from ***mizbeach***, the Hebrew term for

Mock (3), Mocked (2), Mockery (3)
S 1 : PR :011(290) [0457] Gomorrah, because we **mock** him so shamefully with the
S 3 : 1 5 :004(316) [0501] is a ridicule and **mockery** of holy Baptism which should
S 3 : 1 5 :005(316) [0501] and they are not, but are mere **mockery** and fraud.
TR : 0 0 :032(325) [0513] he was led forth to be **mocked** in royal purple signified
SC : 0 9 :003(354) [0561] Do not be deceived; God is not **mocked**" (Gal. 6:6, 7).
LC : 0 1 :197(392) [0637] would see how the monks **mock** and mislead the world
LC : 0 3 :031(424) [0707] Now they may confidently ridicule and **mock**.
LC : 0 3 :057(427) [0713] who had made a **mockery** of his imperial majesty's

Mode (36), Modes (6)
AG : 1 6 :004(038) [0051] but an inward and eternal **mode** of existence and
AP : 0 4 :220(137) [0181] this text Paul is not discussing the **mode** of justification.
AP : 0 4 :221(137) [0181] he systematically discusses the **mode** of justification.
AP : 0 4 :287(150) [0203] They teach two **modes** of justification, one based upon
AP : 0 4 :288(151) [0203] The first **mode** of justification, according to them, is that
AP : 0 4 :288(151) [0203] This **mode** is a doctrine of reason.
AP : 0 4 :288(151) [0203] Because this **mode** of gaining justification is reasonable
AP : 0 4 :289(151) [0203] The other **mode** of justification, handed down by the
AP : 0 4 :290(151) [0203] can easily evaluate both **modes**, since both exclude Christ
S 3 : 1 4 :001(316) [0501] that he is entering upon a **mode** of life that is better than
LC : 0 3 :023(423) [0703] or whether I have hit upon the right form and **mode**?"
EP : 0 7 :014(483) [0811] has and knows various **modes** of being at a given place,
EP : 0 7 :014(483) [0811] and not only the single **mode** which the philosophers call
EP : 0 8 :017(489) [0823] *not according to the **mode** or property of the human*
EP : 0 8 :017(489) [0823] but *according to the **mode*** and property of God's right
SD : 0 2 :061(533) [0905] his conversion man has a **mode** of acting in the sense of a
SD : 0 2 :061(533) [0905] of acting in the sense of a **mode** of doing something good
SD : 0 2 :061(533) [0905] and he cannot have a **mode** of acting in divine matters.
SD : 0 2 :062(533) [0905] Lord God indeed has one **mode** of acting in man as a
SD : 0 2 :062(533) [0905] creature and another **mode** of action to work in
SD : 0 2 :062(533) [0905] to his conversion any **mode** of acting by which he does
SD : 0 7 :098(586) [1005] Christ has three different **modes**, or all three modes, of
SD : 0 7 :098(586) [1005] modes, or all three **modes**, of being at any given place.
SD : 0 7 :099(586) [1005] corporeal **mode** of presence, as when he walked bodily on
SD : 0 7 :099(586) [1005] He can still employ this **mode** of presence when he wills

Continued ▶

SD : 0 7 :099(586) [1005] heaven according to this **mode**, as the fanatic spirit
SD : 0 7 :099(586) [1005] and going to the Father speak of this **mode** of presence.
SD : 0 7 :100(586) [1005] spiritual **mode** of presence according to which he neither
SD : 0 7 :100(586) [1007] He employed this **mode** of presence when he left the
SD : 0 7 :101(587) [1007] God, the divine, heavenly **mode**, according to which all
SD : 0 7 :101(587) [1007] to him than they are according to the second **mode**.
SD : 0 7 :101(587) [1007] according to the second **mode** he can be present in and
SD : 0 7 :101(587) [1007] to this exalted third **mode**, where they cannot measure or
SD : 0 7 :102(587) [1007] be where God is and that this **mode** of being is a fiction.
SD : 0 7 :103(587) [1007] may have and know more **modes** whereby Christ's body
SD : 0 7 :103(587) [1007] the first, comprehensible **mode** of presence to the body of
SD : 0 7 :103(587) [1007] to prove that even this **mode** is contrary to our view.
SD : 0 7 :105(588) [1009] supernatural, heavenly **mode** according to which Christ is
SD : 0 7 :105(588) [1009] such eating occurs with the mouth, the **mode** is spiritual.
SD : 0 8 :035(597) [1027] all of the same kind and **mode**, and if one talks about
SD : 0 8 :037(598) [1027] But in this **mode** of speaking it does not follow that
SD : 0 8 :063(603) [1037] that it is all only a **mode** of speech, mere words, titles, and

Moderate (1), Moderately (3), Moderation (5)
AG : 2 8 :064(092) [0093] yet there can be no **moderation** or mitigation as long as
AL : 2 8 :064(092) [0093] mitigate the traditions, **moderation** can never be achieved
AP : PR :013(099) [0101] Now, I have written as **moderately** as I could.
AP : 1 5 :051(222) [0329] matters should be used **moderately**, lest the weak be
AP : 2 1 :033(233) [0351] be taught with great **moderation**, the precedent still would
AP : 2 3 :043(245) [0375] how to use marriage **moderately**, especially when they are
AP : 2 3 :065(248) [0381] will know the value of **moderation** in marital intercourse
AP : 2 4 :099(268) [0419] issue with the greatest **moderation**, and now we have
AP : 2 7 :008(269) [0421] good men who have a **moderate** opinion of human and

Modern (7)
AP : 0 2 :032(104) [0113] by the sophistic arguments of **modern** theologians.
AP : 0 2 :032(104) [0113] **Modern** theologians have evidently not paid attention to
EP : RN :002(464) [0777] writings of ancient and **modern** teachers, whatever their
EP : 0 2 :016(472) [0789] Some ancient and **modern** teachers have used expressions
SD : 0 1 :045(516) [0873] are found in the writings of the **modern** Manichaeans.
SD : 0 2 :004(520) [0881] hand, both ancient and **modern** enthusiasts have taught
SD : 0 5 :003(558) [0953] Scripture of God and by ancient and **modern** theologians.

Modest (2), Modesty (4)
AP : 2 3 :003(239) [0363] call the king with the **modest** face, for the saying appears
AP : 2 3 :003(239) [0363] you, "A man with a **modest** face will reign everywhere."
LC : 0 1 :106(379) [0611] deference, humility, and **modesty**, directed (so to speak)
LC : 0 1 :123(382) [0617] they have no sense of **modesty** or honor; they do nothing
LC : 0 1 :287(403) [0663] our unpresentable parts are treated with greater **modesty**."
SD : 1 1 :073(628) [1087] virtues, in all godliness, **modesty**, temperance, patience,

Modified (1), Modifying (2)
AP : 0 7 :040(176) [0241] the apostles adapted in **modified** form to the Gospel
AP : 2 7 :036(275) [0433] that they are **modifying** the common notion about
AP : 2 7 :039(276) [0433] our opponents are now **modifying** their praises about

Mohammed (1), Mohammedan (1), Mohammedanism (1), Mohammedans (4)
AG : 0 1 :005(028) [0043] Arians, Eunomians, **Mohammedans**, and others like
AL : 0 1 :005(028) [0043] Arians, Eunomians, **Mohammedans**, and all others like
AP : 0 4 :229(139) [0183] just as the Pharisees, philosophers, and **Mohammedans**.
AP : 1 5 :018(217) [0319] Thus the kingdom of **Mohammed** has rites and works by
AP : 2 7 :027(273) [0429] monks among the **Mohammedans** could boast that they
AP : 2 7 :027(274) [0429] pharisaical and even **Mohammedan** expressions in the
S3 : 0 8 :009(313) [0497] including that of the papacy and **Mohammedanism**.

Molest (1), Molestation (1), Molested (1)
PR : PR :022(012) [0021] agreement for any **molestation** and persecution of poor,
S2 : 0 2 :028(297) [0469] saints will cease to be **molested** in their graves and in
LC : 0 1 :328(410) [0675] violence, nor in any way **molest** him, either in his person,

Moment (13), Momentous (2)
AG : 2 7 :009(072) [0077] that in such a **momentous** matter the canons were not
AL : 2 7 :009(072) [0077] that in such a **momentous** matter the authority of the
AP : 2 3 :002(239) [0363] We shall review their arguments in a **moment**.
AP : 2 4 :033(256) [0395] In a **moment** we shall explain how even a ceremony is a
LC : 0 1 :072(374) [0601] and vanished in the very **moment** I called upon God.
LC : 0 5 :082(456) [0773] and arrows are at every **moment** aimed at you, you would
EP : 1 0 :006(493) [0829] submission even for a **moment**, that the truth of the
SD : 0 1 :028(513) [0867] sin, but in the first **moment** of our conception the seed
SD : 0 2 :066(534) [0907] could not remain in obedience to God for one **moment**.
SD : 0 2 :068(534) [0907] discovers that at one **moment** he is joyful in the Spirit and
SD : 0 2 :068(534) [0907] Spirit and at another **moment** fearful and terrified, at one
SD : 0 8 :085(608) [1047] But from the **moment** that the deity and the humanity
SD : 1 0 :011(612) [1057] submission even for a **moment**, that the truth of the
SD : 1 0 :012(613) [1057] not yield, not even for a **moment**, so that the truth of the
SD : 1 1 :090(631) [1093] — yes, would be losing it every **moment** and hour.

Monarchy (1)
AP : 0 7 :023(172) [0235] is the supreme outward **monarchy** of the whole world in

Monastery (7), Monasteries (27)
AG : 2 0 :020(044) [0055] their conscience into **monasteries** in the hope that there
AG : 2 7 :001(071) [0077] of life as lived in the **monasteries**, and how many of the
AG : 2 7 :008(072) [0077] girls were thrust into **monasteries** to provide for their
AG : 2 7 :015(073) [0077] and inveigled into a **monastery** learned little about
AG : 2 7 :015(073) [0077] Formerly the **monasteries** had conducted schools of Holy
AG : 2 7 :015(073) [0077] so that pastors and bishops were taken from **monasteries**.
AG : 2 7 :033(076) [0079] for leaving their **monasteries** inasmuch as a majority of
AG : 2 7 :056(080) [0083] and also their civil office, to take shelter in a **monastery**.
AL : 2 0 :020(044) [0055] into the desert, into **monasteries**, in the hope that there
AL : 2 7 :001(071) [0077] what the condition of **monasteries** was and how many
AL : 2 7 :001(071) [0077] were done in these **monasteries** every day that were
AL : 2 7 :008(072) [0077] boys were thrust into **monasteries** for their maintenance
AL : 2 7 :015(073) [0077] What happened after such people had entered **monasteries**
AL : 2 7 :016(073) [0077] Formerly people came together in **monasteries** to learn.
AL : 2 7 :026(075) [0079] was recalled from a **monastery**, and there is no want of
AL : 2 7 :033(076) [0079] excuse for leaving the **monastery** because a majority of
AL : 2 7 :056(080) [0083] administration of the state, withdrew into a **monastery**.
AP : 1 5 :023(218) [0321] as they have been expanded among us in the **monasteries**.
AP : 2 1 :034(234) [0353] In one **monastery** we saw a statue of the blessed Virgin
AP : 2 4 :006(250) [0385] The **monasteries** have public, though daily, Mass.
AP : 2 7 :004(269) [0421] greed there is in the **monasteries**; how ignorant and cruel
AP : 2 7 :005(269) [0421] Some of the richest **monasteries** just feed a lazy crowd
AP : 2 7 :008(269) [0421] here and there in the **monasteries** there are some good
AP : 2 7 :009(270) [0421] friends pushed into the **monastery** to be supported at
AP : 2 7 :022(272) [0427] here and there in the **monasteries** there are still some good
AP : 2 7 :053(278) [0437] those who live in **monasteries** are released by such wicked
AP : 2 7 :059(279) [0441] to our monks, whose **monasteries** are fancier than kings'
S2 : 0 2 :021(296) [0467] Here **monasteries**, chapters, and vicars have obligated
S2 : 0 3 :000(297) [0471] Article III. [Chapters and **Monasteries**]
S2 : 0 3 :001(297) [0471] The chapters and **monasteries** which in former times had
S3 : 0 3 :028(308) [0487] monks and priests in **monasteries** and chapters fought
LC : 0 1 :144(385) [0623] the devil's name into **monasteries**, on pilgrimages, and
LC : 0 1 :197(392) [0637] their good works and emptying the **monasteries**.
LC : 0 1 :197(392) [0637] is why they fled to the **monasteries**, so that they might

Monastic (83), Monasticism (11), Monastics (2)
AG : 1 5 :004(037) [0049] Accordingly **monastic** vows and other traditions
AG : 2 0 :003(041) [0053] the cult of saints, **monasticism**, pilgrimages, appointed
AG : 2 0 :020(044) [0055] that there they might merit grace through **monastic** life.
AG : 2 7 :000(070) [0075] XXVII. **Monastic** Vows
AG : 2 7 :001(070) [0075] In discussing **monastic** vows it is necessary to begin by
AG : 2 7 :002(071) [0077] In the days of St. Augustine **monastic** life was voluntary.
AG : 2 7 :002(071) [0077] had become corrupted, **monastic** vows were invented, and
AG : 2 7 :003(071) [0077] In addition to **monastic** vows many other requirements
AG : 2 7 :005(071) [0077] persons also entered **monastic** life ignorantly, for
AG : 2 7 :010(072) [0077] Besides, **monastic** vows gained such a reputation, as is
AG : 2 7 :011(072) [0077] It was claimed that **monastic** vows were equal to
AG : 2 7 :011(072) [0077] to Baptism, and that by **monastic** life one could earn
AG : 2 7 :012(072) [0077] more, they added that **monastic** life not only earned
AG : 2 7 :013(072) [0077] were kept, and so **monastic** vows were praised more
AG : 2 7 :013(072) [0077] could be obtained by **monastic** life than by all other states
AG : 2 7 :016(073) [0077] gathered and adopted **monastic** life for the purpose of
AG : 2 7 :016(073) [0077] now it is claimed that **monastic** life is of such a nature
AG : 2 7 :029(075) [0079] women, who have taken **monastic** vows of themselves,
AG : 2 7 :029(075) [0079] were persuaded to take **monastic** vows, and sometimes
AG : 2 7 :032(076) [0079] prohibits the taking of **monastic** vows before the
AG : 2 7 :033(076) [0079] of this provision most **monastics** have excuse and reason
AG : 2 7 :034(076) [0079] the breaking of **monastic** vows might be censured, it
AG : 2 7 :036(076) [0081] and releases many from **monastic** vows, our teachers
AG : 2 7 :036(076) [0081] still more reasons why **monastic** vows are null and void.
AG : 2 7 :043(077) [0081] and bestow this honor upon their vows and **monastic** life.
AG : 2 7 :044(078) [0081] by their vows and their **monastic** life and observances.
AG : 2 7 :051(079) [0083] such false exaltation of **monastic** life, for it follows that
AG : 2 7 :060(080) [0083] of his time to speak of **monastic** life as a state of
AG : 2 7 :061(080) [0083] errors associated with **monastic** vows: that they justify
AG : 2 7 :062(080) [0083] useless, and invented, **monastic** vows are null and void.
AL : 2 0 :003(041) [0053] in honor of saints, rosaries, **monasticism**, and the like.
AL : 2 0 :020(044) [0055] hope that there they might merit grace by **monastic** life.
AL : 2 7 :000(070) [0075] XXVII. **Monastic** Vows
AL : 2 7 :001(070) [0075] among us concerning **monastic** vows will be better
AL : 2 7 :012(072) [0077] more, they added that **monastic** life merited not only
AL : 2 7 :013(072) [0077] men believe that the **monastic** profession was far better
AL : 2 7 :013(072) [0077] than Baptism, and that **monastic** life was more
AL : 2 7 :033(076) [0079] or the other, most **monastics** have an excuse for leaving
AL : 2 7 :051(079) [0083] from such false commendations of **monastic** life.
AL : 2 7 :060(080) [0083] in his day to say that **monastic** life is a state of perfection.
AP : 0 4 :010(108) [0123] in the church, like **monastic** vows and the abuses of the
AP : 0 4 :212(136) [0179] new vows, and new **monastic** orders beyond God's
AP : 0 4 :288(151) [0203] on men thought up **monastic** orders, which competed in
AP : 1 2 :137(203) [0293] fictions they defend **monastic** orders, the sale of Masses,
AP : 1 6 :008(223) [0333] external, a new and **monastic** form of government.
AP : 1 6 :013(224) [0333] obscured by foolish **monastic** theories which put a
AP : 2 1 :026(232) [0349] of us have seen a certain **monastic** theologian, summoned
AP : 2 1 :041(235) [0355] of the Mass, the trust in **monastic** observances, the
AP : 2 4 :068(261) [0407] of hood is the mark of a particular **monastic** profession.
AP : 2 7 :000(268) [0419] [Article XXVII.] **Monastic** Vows
AP : 2 7 :002(269) [0419] that threatened the **monastic** estate but had only
AP : 2 7 :003(269) [0419] about the decline of the **monastic** regime and this same
AP : 2 7 :004(269) [0421] oracles, which threaten a change in the **monastic** regime.
AP : 2 7 :010(270) [0423] fully in his book called ***Monastic Vows***, we want to be
AP : 2 7 :011(270) [0423] faith in Christ, but by **monastic** works, take away from
AP : 2 7 :012(271) [0423] has here been charged against **monasticism** is wicked."
AP : 2 7 :018(272) [0425] has been charged against **monasticism** here is wicked."
AP : 2 7 :020(272) [0425] we do not merit the forgiveness of sins by **monastic** works.
AP : 2 7 :020(272) [0427] Thomas says that a **monastic** profession is equal to
AP : 2 7 :025(273) [0429] that the observance of a **monastic** life satisfies the
AP : 2 7 :026(273) [0429] It is also false that **monastic** observances are the works of
AP : 2 7 :028(274) [0429] Scriptures that the **monastic** life merits eternal life if it is
AP : 2 7 :029(274) [0431] the Sacred Scriptures the **monastic** life merits eternal life.
AP : 2 7 :029(274) [0431] Where do the Sacred Scriptures talk about **monastic** life?
AP : 2 7 :029(274) [0431] everyone knows that **monasticism** is a recent invention,
AP : 2 7 :030(274) [0431] when they say that by a **monastic** life men merit eternal
AP : 2 7 :031(274) [0431] place, it is sure that the **monastic** life does not merit the
AP : 2 7 :033(275) [0431] in Christ, much less do **monastic** observances, mere
AP : 2 7 :034(275) [0431] who teach that the **monastic** life merits the forgiveness of
AP : 2 7 :035(275) [0431] it is quite clear that **monastic** vows are not a price for
AP : 2 7 :036(275) [0433] They deny that the **monastic** life is perfection, but they
AP : 2 7 :036(275) [0433] praises of the **monastic** life; but since they did not dare to
AP : 2 7 :037(275) [0433] If we follow this, the **monastic** life will be no more a state
AP : 2 7 :040(276) [0433] of Scripture has nothing to do with the **monastic** life.
AP : 2 7 :043(276) [0435] Christ in applying it to **monastic** life, unless perhaps the
AP : 2 7 :044(277) [0435] But as the whole **monastic** system is full of counterfeits,
AP : 2 7 :051(277) [0437] Third, in **monastic** vows chastity is promised.
AP : 2 7 :056(278) [0439] Thus the whole **monastic** life is full of hypocrisy and false
AP : 2 7 :057(279) [0439] for the stand that **monastic** vows, as made until now, are
AP : 2 7 :058(279) [0439] not right to compare **monasticism**, thought up without a
AP : 2 7 :062(280) [0441] vastly different purposes are set forth for **monasticism**.
AP : 2 7 :062(280) [0441] that the works of **monasticism** are acts of worship and
AP : 2 7 :063(280) [0441] of the Rechabites does not resemble **monasticism**.
AP : 2 7 :063(280) [0441] the other evils inherent in present-day **monasticism**.

Continued ▶

A P : 2 7 :065(280) [0441] does not support **monastic** vows, taken for wicked acts of
A P : 2 7 :065(280) [0441] if any, must have been different from **monastic** vows.
A P : 2 7 :067(280) [0441] calls "first faith" — not a **monastic** vows, but Christianity.
S 2 : 0 4 :014(301) [0475] Masses, purgatory, **monastic** life, and human works and
S 3 : 1 4 :000(315) [0501] XIV. **Monastic** Vows
S 3 : 1 4 :001(315) [0501] Since **monastic** vows are in direct conflict with the first
S 3 : 1 4 :001(316) [0501] takes the vows of **monastic** life believes that he is entering
S 3 : 1 4 :001(316) [0501] people boast that a **monastic** vow is equal to Baptism.
L C : 0 1 :074(375) [0601] to God than any **monastic** life and Carthusian holiness.
L C : 0 1 :112(380) [0613] no need to institute **monasticism** or "spiritual estates."
L C : 0 1 :216(394) [0641] deceived by their **monastic** vows are even commanded to
L C : 0 1 :216(394) [0641] Even granting that the **monastic** life is godly, yet it is not

Monetary (1)
A G : 2 4 :010(057) [0065] it in almost all churches for a **monetary** consideration.

Money (32)
A P : 1 5 :040(220) [0325] perform Mass, and they often do so only for the **money**.
A P : 2 1 :038(234) [0355] monstrous and ungodly tales because they make **money**.
A P : 2 4 :042(257) [0399] which they put on in public as a **money**-making venture.
A P : 2 4 :064(261) [0405] scales of merit, like the **money**-changers with gold or
A P : 2 7 :004(269) [0421] sermons and in thinking up new ways of making **money**.
S 2 : 0 2 :024(296) [0469] living and the dead (for **money**) and by which the pope
S 2 : 0 2 :024(296) [0469] offered to us without our **money** or merit, not by the
S 3 : 0 0 :000(302) [0477] of conscience but only about **money**, honor, and power.
S 3 : 0 3 :025(307) [0485] When this began to yield **money** and the bull market
S 3 : 0 3 :025(307) [0485] The more **money** they swallowed, the wider became their
S 3 : 0 3 :027(307) [0487] year must be contrite, make confession, and pay **money**."
S 3 : 0 3 :027(307) [0487] So the pope took the **money**, consoled the people with his
S C : 0 1 :014(343) [0541] rob our neighbor of his **money** or property, nor bring
S C : 0 3 :014(347) [0547] home, fields and flocks, **money** and property; a pious
S C : 0 9 :002(354) [0561] but gentle, not quarrelsome, and no lover of **money**.
L C : 0 1 :005(365) [0581] he needs when he has **money** and property; in them he
L C : 0 1 :006(365) [0581] by name, that is, **money** and possessions — on which he
L C : 0 1 :007(365) [0583] He who has **money** and property feels secure, happy,
L C : 0 1 :012(366) [0583] may give them plenty of **money**, help them in love affairs,
L C : 0 1 :042(370) [0591] They have neither **money**, prestige, nor honor, and can
L C : 0 1 :043(370) [0591] great wealth and **money**, what have they gained in the
L C : 0 1 :053(371) [0595] and in matters involving **money**, property, and honor,
L C : 0 1 :164(387) [0627] have bread, clothing, and **money** for a year or two, but
L C : 0 1 :172(388) [0629] not think only of amassing **money** and property for them.
L C : 0 1 :224(395) [0643] is transacted and **money** is exchanged for goods or labor.
L C : 0 1 :226(395) [0645] would ten times rather lose the **money** from one's purse.
L C : 0 1 :256(399) [0653] any more than of his **money** and possessions; he would
L C : 0 1 :258(399) [0653] an eye to gaining favor, **money**, prospects, or friendship.
L C : 0 1 :261(400) [0655] on account of anyone's **money**, property, honor, or
L C : 0 2 :022(413) [0683] hands, body and soul, **money** and property, and with all
L C : 0 4 :043(442) [0743] how the world would snow and rain **money** upon him!
L C : 0 6 :023(459) [0000] hears that a rich gift, of **money** or clothes, is to be given

Monk (2), Monkery (3), Monks (64)
A G : 2 3 :026(056) [0065] most of the priests and **monks** entered into their estates
A G : 2 7 :010(072) [0077] well known, that many **monks** with even a little
A G : 2 7 :038(077) [0081] is quite evident that the **monks** have taught and preached
A G : 2 7 :044(078) [0081] One cannot deny that the **monks** have taught and
A G : 2 7 :045(078) [0081] be assembled which the **monks** themselves are now
A G : 2 7 :049(078) [0083] when people are told that **monks** alone are in a state of
A G : 2 7 :060(080) [0083] censured the error of the **monks** concerning perfection
A G : 0 0 :002(095) [0095] had endless quarrels with **monks** about the hearing of
A L : 2 6 :011(065) [0071] — and admired the **monks** and others like them, falsely
A L : 2 7 :010(072) [0077] displeasing to those **monks** in former times who had a
A L : 2 7 :038(077) [0081] It is evident that the **monks** have taught that their
A L : 2 7 :044(078) [0081] cannot be denied that the **monks** taught that they were
A L : 2 7 :045(078) [0081] be collected of which even the **monks** are now ashamed!
A L : 2 7 :049(078) [0083] when men hear that only **monks** are in a state of
A L : 2 7 :060(080) [0083] rebuked the error of the **monks** concerning perfection and
A L : 2 7 :061(080) [0083] perfection, that the **monks** observe both the counsels and
A L : 2 7 :061(080) [0083] the precepts, and that **monks** do works of
A L : 0 0 :002(095) [0095] parish ministers and **monks** about parochial rights,
A P : P R :001(098) [0099] of theologians and **monks** prepared a Confutation of it.
A P : P R :013(099) [0101] with the theologians and **monks** who wrote the
A P : P R :017(099) [0103] in the writings of the **monks**, canonists, and scholastic
A P : 0 4 :283(150) [0201] water, the habit of the **monks**, the distinctions of foods,
A P : 0 4 :360(162) [0219] to justify others, as when **monks** sell the merits of their
A P : 0 4 :361(162) [0219] of this transfer, as when a **monk**'s hood is placed on a
A P : 0 4 :390(166) [0225] or bishops or some theologians or **monks** advance.
A P : 0 4 :392(167) [0225] some theologians and **monks** in the church have taught
A P : 1 1 :002(180) [0249] since the scholastics and **monks** teach nothing about faith
A P : 1 6 :004(223) [0331] this subject because the **monks** had broadcast many
A P : 1 6 :010(224) [0333] The **monks** impressed men with this outward hypocrisy
A P : 1 6 :013(224) [0333] after the theories of the **monks** had troubled them and
A P : 2 1 :029(233) [0351] on one another, like the **monks** who peddle the merits of
A P : 2 1 :035(234) [0353] Then the foolish **monks** taught the people to call on
A P : 2 1 :038(234) [0355] Bishops, theologians, and **monks** applaud these
A P : 2 3 :047(246) [0377] is the exaggerated way the **monks** have praised celibacy.
A P : 2 4 :013(251) [0387] The **monks** and scholastics have brought this pharisaic
A P : 2 4 :031(255) [0395] shameless fabrications of the **monks** and scholastics.
A P : 2 4 :063(261) [0405] fictions of the ignorant **monks**; they destroy the glory of
A P : 2 7 :006(269) [0421] this way, therefore, the **monks** are signing their own fate.
A P : 2 7 :012(270) [0423] And they add that the **monks** observe everything for
A P : 2 7 :016(271) [0425] this law of Christ, the **monks** come closer in their
A P : 2 7 :016(271) [0425] no class of men has greater license than the **monks**.
A P : 2 7 :017(271) [0425] this sham, to be sure, the **monks** "pattern their lives more
A P : 2 7 :025(273) [0429] it is false for the **monks** to boast that the observance of a
A P : 2 7 :027(273) [0429] If it were, even the **monks** among the Mohammedans
A P : 2 7 :028(274) [0429] as by the grace of God any **monk** can maintain it.
A P : 2 7 :039(276) [0433] itself they say that **monks** try to pattern their lives more
A P : 2 7 :039(276) [0433] traditions if they say that **monks** pattern their lives more
A P : 2 7 :040(276) [0433] Confutation says that **monks** merit a more abundant
A P : 2 7 :043(277) [0435] Many become **monks** not for the sake of the Gospel but
A P : 2 7 :057(279) [0439] by the tricks of the **monks** or because they were under
A P : 2 7 :058(279) [0439] as we have said, we condemn in the vows of the **monks**.
A P : 2 7 :059(279) [0441] beautiful parallel to our **monks**, whose monasteries are
A P : 2 7 :059(279) [0441] were married; though our **monks** abound in every
A P : 2 7 :069(281) [0443] the sham worship of the **monks**, which Christ cancels with
S 3 : 0 3 :014(305) [0483] too, became priests and **monks**, that we might set
S 3 : 0 3 :028(308) [0487] myself who wished to be **monks** and priests in
L C : 0 1 :118(381) [0615] a price all the Carthusian **monks** and nuns would pay if in
L C : 0 1 :145(385) [0623] better than the holiness and austere life of all the **monks**"?
L C : 0 1 :197(391) [0637] But this would be no preaching for **monks**.
L C : 0 1 :197(392) [0637] would see how the **monks** mock and mislead the world
L C : 0 1 :213(394) [0641] the papal rabble, priests, **monks**, and nuns resist God's
L C : 0 1 :278(402) [0661] Let all **monks** and holy orders step forth, with all their
L C : 0 1 :314(407) [0671] Otherwise, why should **monks** and nuns go into cloisters?
L C : 0 3 :025(423) [0705] rejected the prayers of **monks** and priests, who howl and
L C : 0 4 :012(438) [0735] all the works of all the **monks**, no matter how precious
E P : 1 2 :005(498) [0839] which in fact is nothing else but a new kind of **monkery**.
S D : 0 2 :079(536) [0911] of the papists and the **monks** that man after his
S D : 1 2 :010(634) [1097] and self-chosen spirituality as on a kind of new **monkery**.
S D : 1 2 :027(635) [1101] as basically nothing else than a new kind of **monkery**.

Monstrance (1), Monstrous (7)
P R : P R :024(013) [0023] introduce and defend **monstrous** errors, the only possible
A L : 2 8 :061(091) [0093] There are **monstrous** discussions concerning the mutation
A P : 2 1 :038(234) [0355] monks applaud these **monstrous** and ungodly tales
A P : 2 4 :066(261) [0407] Where do the Fathers say anything so **monstrous**?
T R : 0 0 :037(326) [0515] Since these **monstrous** errors obscure faith and the
L C : 0 1 :074(374) [0601] see or hear anything **monstrous** or fearful and exclaim,
L C : 0 3 :045(426) [0709] in it, or when a **monstrance** or a relic was profaned, thus
S D : 0 8 :004(592) [1017] with accusations of almost all the **monstrous** old heresies.

Montbeliard (1)
P R : P R :027(015) [0025] Frederick, count of Wuerttemberg and **Montbeliard**

Month (1), Monthly (1)
P R : P R :018(009) [0017] make a new confession almost every year or every **month**.
S 2 : 0 2 :012(294) [0465] vigils, with the weekly, **monthly**, and yearly celebrations

Moon (8)
A G : 2 8 :044(088) [0089] or with regard to a festival or a new **moon** or a sabbath.
A L : 2 8 :044(088) [0089] or with regard to a festival or a new **moon** or a sabbath."
A P : 0 7 :035(175) [0239] or with regard to a festival or a new **moon** or a sabbath.
A P : 1 5 :030(219) [0323] or with regard to a festival or a new **moon** or a sabbath.
L C : 0 2 :014(412) [0681] necessities of life — sun, **moon**, and stars in the heavens,
L C : 0 5 :047(452) [0765] day of the first full **moon**, without variation of a single
S D : 0 6 :006(565) [0965] God, just as the sun, the **moon**, and all the stars of heaven
S D : 1 0 :013(613) [1057] to a festival or a new **moon** or a sabbath" (Col. 2:16).

Moral (3), Morality (2), Morals (6)
A P : 0 4 :087(120) [0147] If **moral** works merited the forgiveness of sins and
A P : 0 4 :089(120) [0149] of works according to the **moral** law; for if by these we
A P : 0 4 :134(125) [0159] the entire law, both the **moral** and the ceremonial; that is,
A P : 2 3 :006(240) [0365] endangers religion and **morality**, for it produces endless
A P : 2 3 :006(240) [0365] scandals, sins, and the corruption of public **morals**.
A P : 2 3 :049(246) [0377] the body and for public **morality**), just as certain rites
A P : 2 3 :051(246) [0377] to public and private **morals**; this alone should keep good
A P : 2 3 :052(246) [0377] law has been to public **morals** and how productive of
A P : 2 3 :052(246) [0377] its satires Rome still reads and recognizes its own **morals**.
T R : 0 0 :076(333) [0527] for the reformation of **morals** and the glory of God.
L C : 0 1 :244(398) [0649] must punish us and teach us **morals** in a different way.

Morning (12)
A P : 0 4 :024(110) [0127] the evening star nor the **morning** star is more beautiful
A P : 1 2 :031(186) [0259] I cry for help until **morning**; like a lion he breaks all my
A P : 2 1 :011(230) [0345] They argue about **morning** and evening knowledge,
A P : 2 1 :011(230) [0345] whether they hear us in the **morning** or in the evening.
A P : 2 7 :038(275) [0433] except that in the **morning** he prayed in a few words for
S C : 0 7 :000(352) [0557] [**Morning** and Evening Prayers]
S C : 0 7 :000(352) [0557] *teach his household to say **morning** and evening prayers*
S C : 0 7 :001(352) [0557] In the **morning**, when you rise, make the sign of the cross
L C : P R :003(358) [0567] it would be fine if every **morning**, noon, and evening they
L C : P R :007(359) [0569] Every **morning**, and whenever else I have time, I read and
L C : S P :016(363) [0577] when they rise in the **morning**, when they go to their
L C : 0 1 :073(374) [0601] and saying other prayers for both **morning** and evening.

Morose (1)
A P : 2 7 :001(269) [0419] that he was a mild old man, serious but not **morose**.

Morsel (2)
L C : 0 3 :057(428) [0713] them and scarcely venture to ask for a **morsel** of bread.
L C : 0 3 :081(431) [0721] that anyone receives a **morsel** of bread from God and eats

Mortal (26), Mortality (1), Mortals (1)
A G : 2 8 :041(087) [0089] for example, that it is a **mortal** sin to do manual work on
A G : 2 8 :041(087) [0089] to others), that it is a **mortal** sin to omit the seven hours,
A L : 2 4 :021(058) [0067] oblation should be made for daily sins, **mortal** and venial.
A L : 2 8 :041(087) [0089] as this, that it is a **mortal** sin to do manual work on holy
A L : 2 8 :041(087) [0089] appeases God, that it is a **mortal** sin to omit the
A P : 0 2 :005(101) [0107] only the subjection to **mortality** that Adam's descendants
A P : 0 2 :036(105) [0115] spiritual regeneration, but it remains in the **mortal** flesh.
A P : 0 4 :037(112) [0131] that a man guilty of **mortal** sin can love God above all
A P : 0 4 :048(113) [0135] knowledge and teach that it can exist with **mortal** sin.
A P : 0 4 :048(114) [0135] accounted righteous before God do not live in **mortal** sin.
A P : 0 4 :064(116) [0139] this cannot exist with **mortal** sin, but whenever it appears
A P : 0 4 :109(123) [0153] because they imagine that faith can exist with **mortal** sin.
A P : 0 4 :115(123) [0155] nor can it exist with **mortal** sin; but it is a work of the
A P : 0 4 :144(127) [0161] obey their lusts, nor does it exist together with **mortal** sin.
A P : 1 2 :118(200) [0287] who have relapsed into **mortal** sin, as though those who
A P : 1 2 :118(200) [0287] though those who are in **mortal** sin could placate the
A P : 1 2 :132(202) [0293] even when they come from men in **mortal** sin.
A P : 1 2 :140(204) [0295] to abolish death, even when they are done in **mortal** sin.
A P : 1 2 :143(204) [0297] for they teach that they avail even for those in **mortal** sin.
A P : 1 2 :162(208) [0303] so that even those in **mortal** sin can buy off their
A P : 1 2 :165(208) [0303] not, as these men imagine, by works done in **mortal** sin.
A P : 2 4 :009(251) [0387] forgiveness of venial or **mortal** sins, of guilt, or of
A P : 2 7 :068(280) [0443] to people who have a **mortal** sin; therefore he says that

Continued ▶

AP : 28 :024(285) [0451] good will ceases, and **mortals** are forgetful," said Pindar.
S3 : 03 :022(306) [0485] years of penance were required for a single **mortal** sin.
S3 : 15 :002(316) [0501] papists say that it is a **mortal** sin to break such precepts
LC : 01 :099(378) [0609] to be classed among the **mortal** sins and was called
LC : 06 :001(457) [0000] to make confession on pain of the gravest **mortal** sin.

Mortify (1), Mortifying (6), Mortification (15), Mortified (1), Mortifies (1)
AG : 26 :030(068) [0075] accused of forbidding **mortification** and discipline, their
AG : 26 :032(068) [0075] this is true and real rather than invented **mortification**.
AG : 26 :038(069) [0075] is not the purpose of **mortification** to merit grace but to
AL : 26 :030(068) [0075] Jovinian, forbid discipline and **mortification** of the flesh.
AL : 26 :032(068) [0075] Christ is true and real, rather than invented, **mortification**.
AP : 02 :035(105) [0115] in Baptism, begins to **mortify** lust and to create new
AP : 02 :045(106) [0117] Christ to be forgiven and the Holy Spirit to be **mortified**.
AP : 04 :045(113) [0133] It **mortifies** our lust.
AP : 04 :193(133) [0175] of charity, and the **mortification** of the flesh would be to
AP : 12 :046(188) [0263] always names these two parts, **mortifying** and quickening.
AP : 12 :046(188) [0263] **Mortifying**, quickening, putting off the body of sins, being
AP : 12 :046(188) [0263] changes; but **mortification** means genuine terrors, like
AP : 12 :058(190) [0267] when it is contrasted with contrition and **mortification**.
AP : 12 :131(202) [0291] or contrition where **mortifying** the flesh and good fruits
AP : 12 :148(205) [0299] itself takes place by constantly **mortifying** the old life.
AP : 12 :148(205) [0299] exclude here outward **mortification** of the body which
AP : 12 :157(207) [0301] interprets them as the **mortification** of present sin, not as
AP : 12 :168(209) [0305] the public rite and use it to denote the real **mortification**.
AP : 12 :168(209) [0305] causes of sin, that is, **mortifying** and restraining the flesh,
AP : 15 :045(221) [0327] With regard to the **mortifying** of the body and the
AP : 15 :045(221) [0327] us effect a genuine and not a counterfeit **mortification**.
AP : 15 :046(221) [0327] Besides this **mortification** brought on by the cross, a
AP : 23 :035(244) [0373] of the heart and the **mortification** of lust; it is not
SD : 06 :007(565) [0965] Spirit has begun the **mortification** of the Old Adam and

Mosaic (4)
AL : 28 :059(091) [0091] Gospel all ceremonies of the **Mosaic** law can be omitted.
AP : 07 :031(174) [0237] of the law was tied to the **Mosaic** ceremonies, because this
AP : 23 :027(243) [0371] to the ceremonies of the **Mosaic** law which prescribed
AP : 27 :017(272) [0425] doing the works of the **Mosaic** law or of the Decalogue or

Moses (42)
AG : 08 :001(033) [0047] indicated, "The Pharisees sit on **Moses'** seat" (Matt. 23:2).
AG : 26 :005(064) [0071] mightily against the law of **Moses** and against human
AG : 26 :028(068) [0073] outward ceremonies, whether of **Moses** or of another.
AG : 28 :040(087) [0089] bishops were misled by the example of the law of **Moses**.
AL : 08 :001(033) [0047] and Pharisees sit on **Moses'** seat," etc. (Matt. 23:2).
AL : 26 :028(068) [0073] with numerous rites, whether of **Moses** or of others.
AL : 28 :040(087) [0089] to have been misled by the example of the law of **Moses**.
AP : 04 :006(108) [0121] nothing about the ceremonial and civil laws of **Moses**.
AP : 04 :021(110) [0127] they look as the Jews did at the veiled face of **Moses**.
AP : 04 :095(121) [0149] John 3:14, 15, "As **Moses** lifted up the serpent in the
AP : 04 :097(121) [0149] which you could not be justified by the law of **Moses**."
AP : 04 :133(125) [0159] that covered the face of **Moses** cannot be removed except
AP : 04 :133(125) [0159] to this day whenever **Moses** is read a veil lies over their
AP : 04 :229(139) [0183] not see the true face of **Moses** but only his veiled face,
AP : 04 :296(152) [0205] reason, far away from **Moses**, we must turn our eyes to
AP : 12 :078(193) [0275] as the Jews looked at **Moses'** face covered by a veil.
AP : 12 :086(194) [0277] that we are members of **Moses** rather than of Christ.
AP : 15 :010(216) [0317] between our traditions and the ceremonies of **Moses**.
AP : 15 :010(216) [0317] the ceremonies of **Moses** as well as traditions because they
AP : 15 :030(219) [0323] includes both the law of **Moses** and the traditions of men,
AP : 15 :030(219) [0323] and say that Paul is talking only about the law of **Moses**.
AP : 15 :030(219) [0323] instituted ceremonies of **Moses** do not justify, how much
AP : 16 :003(223) [0331] to try to impose on us the judicial laws of **Moses**.
AP : 23 :042(245) [0375] and tried to impose the law of **Moses** on Christians.
AP : 23 :045(245) [0375] misunderstood the law of **Moses**; therefore they have
AP : 24 :028(254) [0393] declaration, which seems to contradict **Moses** directly?
AP : 27 :012(270) [0423] They apply the passage in Paul only to the law of **Moses**.
AP : 27 :014(271) [0423] denies that by the law of **Moses** men merit the forgiveness
AP : 27 :014(271) [0423] If the law of **Moses**, which was divinely revealed, did not
AP : 27 :015(271) [0425] Paul abolished the law of **Moses** and that Christ took its
AP : 27 :017(271) [0425] Christ takes **Moses'** place, not by forgiving sins on
S3 : 08 :011(313) [0497] For even to **Moses** God wished to appear first through the
LC : 01 :181(389) [0631] early times, as we read in **Moses**, parents had to bring
EP : 05 :007(478) [0803] to each other, as when **Moses** is spoken of as a teacher of
EP : 05 :008(478) [0803] about Christ, the veil of **Moses** covers their eyes, as a
EP : 05 :008(479) [0803] acknowledgment which **Moses** could never have wrung
EP : 05 :009(479) [0803] the law, after the veil of **Moses** has been removed for
EP : 05 :010(479) [0803] but the preaching of **Moses** and the law, and therefore it
SD : 05 :010(560) [0955] his sin, an insight that **Moses** could never have wrung out
SD : 05 :010(560) [0955] testifies that although "**Moses** is read," the veil which "he
SD : 05 :012(560) [0955] proclamation, but it is **Moses** and the law pronounced
SD : 06 :001(563) [0963] from whom the veil of **Moses** has been taken away, learn

Mother (47), Motherhood (1), Mothers (7)
AG : 02 :001(029) [0043] inclinations from their **mothers'** wombs and are unable by
AL : 20 :030(045) [0057] says, "Faith is the **mother** of the good will and the right
AL : 26 :010(065) [0071] up his children, that a **mother** should bear children, that a
AP : 02 :002(100) [0105] inclinations from their **mothers'** wombs and are unable by
AP : 02 :005(101) [0107] because of one's **mother** and not by one's own fault.
AP : 04 :367(163) [0221] your father and your **mother**, that your days may be long
AP : 21 :026(232) [0349] upon the dying man, "**Mother** of grace, protect us from
AP : 23 :032(244) [0373] about the whole class of **mothers**, and above all he
AP : 27 :061(280) [0441] (Ex. 20:12), "Honor your father and your **mother**."
S2 : 02 :013(295) [0467] merely mentions that his **mother** asked that she be
S2 : 03 :001(298) [0471] well trained girls to become **mothers**, housekeepers, etc.
S3 : 08 :013(313) [0497] nor did he leap in his **mother's** womb until Mary spoke.
SC : 01 :007(343) [0541] *"Honor your father and your **mother**."*
SC : 05 :020(350) [0553] you are a father or **mother**, a son or daughter, a master
SC : 09 :009(356) [0563] 'Honor your father and **mother**' (this is the first
LC : SP :004(362) [0575] 4. You shall honor father and **mother**.
LC : 01 :026(368) [0587] example, he gives to the **mother** breasts and milk for her
LC : 01 :104(379) [0611] *"You shall honor your father and **mother**.*
LC : 01 :105(379) [0611] To fatherhood and **motherhood** God has given the
LC : 01 :105(379) [0611] distinguishes father and **mother** above all other persons
LC : 01 :108(379) [0611] are their own father and **mother**, given them by God.
LC : 01 :115(381) [0613] to their fathers and **mothers**, or to those who have
LC : 01 :116(381) [0615] obedience to father and **mother**, which God has
LC : 01 :125(382) [0617] If we had no father and **mother**, we should wish, on
LC : 01 :125(382) [0617] a block or a stone which we might call father and **mother**.
LC : 01 :135(383) [0619] to obey father and **mother** or to submit to them, then
LC : 01 :142(384) [0621] *matres familias* (that is, house-fathers and house-**mothers**)
LC : 01 :143(385) [0621] child owes to father and **mother**, the entire household
LC : 01 :167(388) [0629] commandment in which he speaks of father and **mother**.
LC : 01 :173(388) [0629] otherwise God would have no need of father and **mother**.
LC : 01 :206(393) [0639] shall honor father and **mother**"; but here, as I said, he has
LC : 01 :327(409) [0675] are to honor father and **mother**, masters, and all in
LC : 01 :327(409) [0675] respect or fear father or **mother** wrongly, doing or
LC : 02 :042(416) [0689] It is the **mother** that begets and bears every Christian
LC : 02 :048(416) [0691] In our **mother** tongue therefore it ought to be called "a
LC : 03 :008(421) [0699] to obey our fathers and **mothers** and the civil authorities.
LC : 03 :013(422) [0701] to his father and **mother**, but should always reflect: "This
LC : 03 :036(425) [0707] In our **mother** tongue we would say, "Heavenly Father,
LC : 04 :020(439) [0737] **mother**," I see another man, adorned and clothed with the
LC : 04 :038(441) [0741] honor your father and **mother**," refers only to human
LC : 04 :038(441) [0741] on account of which this flesh is called father and **mother**.
LC : 04 :058(444) [0747] obedient, then father, **mother**, and magistrates are
EP : 08 :012(488) [0821] she is rightly called, and truly is, the **mother** of God.
EP : 08 :015(488) [0821] by the Holy Spirit in his **mother's** womb and his human
SD : 01 :007(510) [0861] and birth out of sinful seed from our father and **mother**.
SD : 01 :027(513) [0867] way from a father and a **mother**, now inherit a nature
SD : 01 :030(513) [0867] way from a father and a **mother** is corrupted and
SD : 04 :009(552) [0941] Hence faith alone is the **mother** and source of the truly
SD : 07 :100(587) [1007] as people believe, when he was born of his **mother**, etc.
SD : 08 :013(593) [1019] he was conceived in his **mother's** womb and became man
SD : 08 :024(595) [1023] majesty even in his **mother's** womb in that he was born of
SD : 08 :024(595) [1023] Therefore she is truly the **mother** of God and yet
SD : 08 :026(596) [1023] conception even in his **mother's** womb, but, as the apostle
SD : 08 :082(607) [1045] as his conception in his **mother's** womb proves
SD : 08 :082(607) [1045] God, he had to be in his **mother's** womb naturally and

Motive (1), Motives (2), Motivated (1), Motivates (2), Motivation (1)
AG : PR :021(027) [0043] with the highest and best **motives** requested in all the
AP : 04 :189(133) [0175] what the Holy Spirit **motivates**, fouling it with its
AP : 12 :009(183) [0255] between these two **motives** is possible, but in fact they are
AP : 24 :071(262) [0409] is the spiritual **motivation**, dying and being made alive.
LC : 01 :202(392) [0639] but also every kind of cause, **motive**, and means.
SD : 02 :063(533) [0905] long as the Holy Spirit **motivates** him, as St. Paul says,
SD : 06 :003(564) [0963] believers are indeed **motivated** by the Holy Spirit and

Mouth (23), Mouths (5)
PR : PR :010(006) [0011] In this way the **mouths** of the adversaries might be
AG : 26 :023(067) [0073] Christ says, "Not what goes into the **mouth** defiles a man."
AL : 26 :023(067) [0073] Christ says, "Not what goes into the **mouth** defiles a man."
AP : 12 :170(209) [0305] heart contrition, in the **mouth** confession, in the deed
AP : 13 :011(212) [0311] that goes forth from my **mouth** shall not return to me
AP : 28 :007(282) [0445] "What goes into the **mouth** does not defile a man."
S1 : PR :005(289) [0457] But how can I stop all the **mouths** of the devil?
LC : 01 :247(398) [0651] must live from hand to **mouth**, you act as if everyone
LC : 01 :287(403) [0663] his face, eyes, nose, and **mouth**; we do not need to, for
LC : 03 :022(423) [0703] and puts into our **mouths** the very words we are to use.
LC : 06 :015(459) [0000] of my sins through a word placed in the **mouth** of a man.
EP : 07 :004(482) [0809] bread and wine are present and received with the **mouth**.
EP : 07 :026(485) [0815] bread, but that with the **mouth** we receive only bread and
SD : PR :004(502) [0847] themselves to these symbols with heart and **mouth**.
SD : PR :002(503) [0851] our hearts and with our **mouths** declared in mutual
SD : 02 :020(525) [0889] statue which uses neither **mouth** nor eyes nor senses nor
SD : 03 :051(548) [0933] which we make with our **mouth**, and through other
SD : 07 :006(570) [0975] by faith but not to receive it orally with the **mouth**.
SD : 07 :008(570) [0975] eat the bread with their **mouths**, just so certainly do they
SD : 07 :053(579) [0991] are drinking with your **mouth** from the cup) is my blood
SD : 07 :076(583) [0999] words are spoken by the **mouth** of the priest, but by
SD : 07 :105(588) [1009] such eating occurs with the **mouth**, the mode is spiritual.
SD : 07 :107(588) [1009] condemn with heart and **mouth** as false, erroneous, and
SD : 07 :112(589) [1011] condemn with heart and **mouth** as false, erroneous, and
SD : 07 :114(589) [1011] that in the Supper our **mouth** receives only bread and
SD : 07 :116(589) [1011] the Supper we receive the external sign with our **mouth**.
SD : 08 :088(609) [1047] reject and condemn with **mouth** and heart all errors which
SD : 10 :015(613) [1057] Holy Spirit through the **mouth** of the holy apostle so

Move (11), Moved (10), Movement (2), Movements (2), Moves (5)
AG : 01 :006(028) [0043] that the Holy Spirit is a **movement** induced in creatures.
AG : 20 :029(045) [0057] Spirit is given, the heart is **moved** to do good works.
AG : 23 :003(051) [0061] have been impelled and **moved** to take this step by the
AL : 01 :006(028) [0043] and "Spirit" signifies a **movement** which is produced in
AP : 02 :044(106) [0117] purely academic, but **moved** out among the people.
AP : 04 :154(128) [0165] truly powerful example **moved** Christ to chide the
AP : 04 :199(134) [0175] Such praise undoubtedly **moves** the faithful to good
AP : 07 :036(175) [0241] not means by which God **moves** the heart to believe (like
AP : 07 :050(178) [0245] universe and the fixed **movements** of the stars are truly
AP : 12 :069(192) [0271] Lest anyone be **moved** by this large number of
AP : 12 :123(200) [0289] What good man would not be **moved** by such dishonesty?
AP : 13 :001(211) [0309] us, through which he **moves** men's hearts to believe.
AP : 13 :005(211) [0309] rite God simultaneously **moves** the heart to believe and
AP : 13 :005(212) [0309] the rite itself enters through the eyes to **move** the heart.
AP : 13 :016(213) [0313] a more exalted position, this would **move** men to pray.
AP : 24 :070(262) [0409] was instituted to **move** the heart to believe through what
S3 : 08 :013(313) [0497] impulse of man but were **moved** by the Holy Spirit, yet as
S3 : 08 :013(313) [0497] Spirit would not have **moved** them to speak while they
LC : 01 :040(370) [0591] and eternity, this ought to **move** and impel us to fix our
LC : 01 :149(385) [0623] Whoever will not be **moved** by this, and who will not be
LC : 01 :323(409) [0673] to his will, lest he be **moved** to wrath; and, conversely,
LC : 03 :073(430) [0719] among whom we live and **move** — in short, everything
LC : 05 :050(452) [0765] should ever **move** you to examine your inner life and
LC : 05 :052(452) [0765] What should **move** and impel you is the fact that Christ
LC : 06 :023(459) [0000] the needs which ought to **move** and induce us to
EP : 02 :018(472) [0791] grace in kindling new **movements** within the will, that is,
EP : 08 :008(487) [0819] ascend and to descend, to **move** from place to place, to

Continued ▶

SD : 0 1 :042(515) [0871] for "in him we live and move and are" (Acts 17:28).
SD : 0 2 :059(532) [0905] not resist the person who moves it, neither does it
SD : 0 8 :010(593) [1019] to ascend and descend, to move from one place to

Mud (1)
LC : 0 1 :267(401) [0657] it like pigs that roll in the **mud** and root around in it with

Muehlhausen (1)
PR : PR :027(016) [0027] The Council of **Muehlhausen**

Muenster (1)
PR : PR :027(015) [0027] and Council of the City of **Muenster**-in-St. Georgental

Muenzer (1)
S 3 : 0 8 :003(312) [0495] **Muenzer** did this, and many still do it in our day who

Multiply (5), Multiplication (2), Multiplied (5)
AG : 2 4 :023(058) [0067] of this grew countless **multiplication** of Masses, by the
AG : 2 8 :037(086) [0089] human ordinances have **multiplied** beyond calculation
AG : 2 8 :042(088) [0089] Why, then, do they **multiply** sins with such requirements?
AL : 2 8 :037(086) [0089] notion traditions have **multiplied** in the church almost
AL : 2 8 :042(088) [0089] Why do they **multiply** sin with such traditions?
AP : 0 4 :395(167) [0225] works, and so they **multiplied** sacrifices and devotions.
AP : 2 4 :007(250) [0385] friars brought on the **multiplication** of private Masses; so
AP : 2 4 :013(251) [0387] the people and has infinitely **multiplied** the Masses.
AP : 2 7 :055(278) [0439] That is why they **multiply** these ceremonies.
S 3 : 0 3 :025(307) [0485] went further and quickly **multiplied** the jubilee years.
SD : 0 7 :076(583) [0999] words, 'Be fruitful and **multiply** and fill the earth,' were
SD : 0 7 :076(583) [0999] make things grow and **multiply**, so this word was indeed

Multitude (6), Multitudes (1)
AP : 0 4 :238(140) [0187] statement (I Pet. 4:8), "Love covers a **multitude** of sins."
AP : 0 7 :009(169) [0229] exists despite the great **multitude** of the wicked, and
AP : 2 2 :004(236) [0359] not be hard to collect a great **multitude** of testimonies.
S 1 : PR :014(291) [0459] is the use of adopting a **multitude** of decrees and canons
S 2 : 0 2 :019(296) [0467] in order that great **multitudes** of people may turn aside
LC : 0 1 :096(378) [0607] swine, but also by that **multitude** of others who listen to
LC : 0 1 :290(404) [0663] then, embraces a great **multitude** of good works which

Mumble (1)
LC : 0 3 :014(422) [0701] that is to stake prayer on luck and to **mumble** aimlessly.

Mummeries (1)
S 1 : PR :014(291) [0459] to acquiesce in our **mummeries** while we trample his

Mundane (2)
EP : 0 8 :017(489) [0823] This presence is not **mundane** or Capernaitic although it
SD : 0 8 :028(596) [1025] does not take place in a **mundane** way, but as Dr. Luther

Murder (23), Murdered (1), Murderer (7), Murderers (2), Murdering (1), Murderous (2), Murders (5)
AG : 1 8 :007(040) [0053] he wills to kneel before an idol, commit **murder**, etc."
AG : 2 3 :023(055) [0063] that the devil is a **murderer** from the beginning (John
AL : 1 8 :007(040) [0053] as to will to worship an idol, will to commit **murder**," etc.
AL : 1 8 :009(040) [0053] the hands from theft and **murder**), yet it cannot produce
AP : 1 2 :174(210) [0307] conduct instead of **murder** and hatred, the greatest
AP : 1 8 :004(225) [0335] choose to keep the hands from **murder**, adultery, or theft.
AP : 2 3 :058(247) [0379] Such **murders** show that this law is a doctrine of demons
AP : 2 3 :058(247) [0379] since the devil is a **murderer** (John 8:44), he uses these
AP : 2 3 :058(247) [0379] (John 8:44), he uses these **murders** to defend his law.
AP : 2 3 :059(247) [0379] of existing marriages, the **murder** of priests who refuse to
AP : 2 3 :059(247) [0379] our lack of an alliance with such **murderous** opponents.
AP : 2 3 :063(248) [0381] lusts and the many **murders** for which this law provides
AP : 2 7 :007(269) [0421] sometimes they are responsible for **murdering** good men.
AP : 2 7 :007(269) [0421] Without doubt, God will soon avenge these **murders**.
S 2 : 0 4 :014(301) [0475] or lord, for deception, **murder**, and the eternal destruction
S 2 : 0 4 :016(301) [0477] but only to damn, **murder**, and drive us to idolatry.
S 3 : 0 1 :002(302) [0477] disobedience to parents, **murder**, unchastity, theft, deceit,
S 3 : 0 3 :043(310) [0491] David fell into adultery, **murder**, and blasphemy), faith
TR : 0 0 :051(329) [0519] his errors by force and **murders**, and he forbids a judicial
TR : 0 0 :053(329) [0519] unjust cruelty in the **murder** of saints, whose blood God
TR : 0 0 :054(329) [0519] and countless other crimes and for the **murder** of saints.
LC : 0 1 :154(386) [0625] now so full of unfaithfulness, shame, misery, and **murder**?
LC : 0 1 :184(390) [0633] cursing and blows, and eventually calamity and **murder**.
LC : 0 1 :186(390) [0633] Not only is **murder** forbidden, but also everything that
LC : 0 1 :186(390) [0633] forbidden, but also everything that may lead to **murder**.
LC : 0 1 :186(390) [0633] may not actually commit **murder**, nevertheless call down
LC : 0 1 :191(391) [0635] rightly calls all persons **murderers** who do not offer
LC : 0 1 :192(391) [0635] to reproach such persons as **murderers** and bloodhounds?
LC : 0 1 :192(391) [0635] in any other light than as a **murderer** and a scoundrel?
LC : 0 1 :268(401) [0657] is to declare somebody a thief, a **murderer**, a traitor, etc.
LC : 0 3 :031(424) [0707] and checking their **murderous** and seditious designs by
LC : 0 3 :045(426) [0709] to be desecrated when a **murder** or any other crime had
LC : 0 3 :080(431) [0721] so much contention, **murder**, sedition, and war, why he
LC : 0 3 :115(435) [0731] only a liar but also a **murderer**, he incessantly seeks our
LC : 0 5 :075(455) [0771] party spirit, envy, **murder**, drunkenness, carousing, and
LC : 0 5 :081(456) [0773] than what the Scriptures call him, a liar and a **murderer**.
LC : 0 5 :081(456) [0773] A **murderer** who begrudges you every hour of your life.
EP : 0 2 :008(471) [0789] fornication, robbery, **murder**, theft, and similar sins
SD : 0 2 :074(536) [0909] doing such wicked acts as lechery, robbery, and **murder**.
SD : 0 7 :060(580) [0995] violent hands upon the body of Christ and **murdered** him.
SD : 1 0 :020(614) [1059] or lord, for deception, **murder**, and the eternal destruction

Murmur (1)
S 3 : 0 2 :004(303) [0479] it, and begins to be alienated from God, to **murmur**, etc.

Musculus (2)
EP : 1 2 :031(501) [0843] Dr. Andrew **Musculus** subscribed
SD : 1 2 :040(636) [1103] Dr. Andrew **Musculus**, subscribed

Musical (1)
SD : 0 7 :100(586) [1007] or vacate any space; a **musical** sound or tone passes

Muster (2)
S 3 : 0 3 :016(305) [0483] much contrition he had to **muster** in order to avail before
SD : 1 1 :009(618) [1065] held a sort of military **muster**: This one shall be saved,

Mutably (1)
SD : 0 1 :055(518) [0877] present in another thing **mutably**, is not a substance (that

Mutation (1)
AL : 2 8 :061(091) [0093] concerning the **mutation** of the law, concerning

Mutilate (1), Mutilated (1)
AP : 2 4 :016(252) [0389] these instructions and **mutilate** the various members of
AP : 2 7 :048(277) [0437] to the text when they quote it in a **mutilated** form.

Mutual (11), Mutually (3)
AP : 0 4 :232(139) [0185] should be nurtured by **mutual** aid, for it is not possible to
AP : 0 4 :235(140) [0185] put up with many things for the sake of **mutual** peace.
AP : 0 4 :238(140) [0187] this statement with the commandment of **mutual** love.
AP : 1 2 :109(198) [0283] other, for it commands that the confession be **mutual**.
AP : 2 4 :068(262) [0407] a meal symbolizing the **mutual** union and friendship
S 3 : 0 4 :000(310) [0491] and finally, through the **mutual** conversation and
LC : 0 1 :275(402) [0659] good friends are under **mutual** obligation to reprove evil
EP : 0 3 :001(473) [0791] Two false and **mutually** contradictory teachings have
EP : 1 0 :007(493) [0831] God, as long as there is **mutual** agreement in doctrine and
EP : 1 1 :022(497) [0837] discussing and teaching in **mutually** contradictory terms.
SD : PR :002(503) [0851] our mouths declared in **mutual** agreement that we shall
SD : PR :015(506) [0857] have reached a basic and **mutual** agreement that we shall
SD : PR :016(507) [0857] to a clear and express **mutual** agreement concerning the
SD : 0 7 :113(589) [1011] opinions and **mutually** contradictory views, no matter

Muzzle (1)
SC : 0 9 :003(354) [0561] says, 'You shall not **muzzle** an ox when it is treading out

Myconius (2)
S 3 : 1 5 :005(317) [0501] I, Frederick **Myconius**, pastor of the church in Gotha,
TR : 0 0 :082(335) [0529] Frederick **Myconius** subscribed for himself and for Justus

Myself (15)
AP : 0 4 :030(111) [0129] Why then may I not **myself** exclaim, too—yes, I will
AP : 0 4 :168(130) [0169] Again (Rom. 7:25), "I of **myself** serve the law of God with
AP : 0 4 :236(140) [0185] as the poet writes, "I forgive **myself**, says Maenius."
AP : 0 4 :327(158) [0211] vv. 30-31, "If I wash **myself** with snow, and cleanse my
S 2 : 0 2 :010(294) [0465] God's help I would suffer **myself** to be burned to ashes
S 3 : 0 3 :028(308) [0487] I and others like **myself** who wished to be monks and
S 3 : 0 7 :003(312) [0493] of anything against **myself**, but I am not thereby
LC : PR :007(359) [0569] As for **myself**, let me say that I, too, am a doctor and a
LC : 0 1 :072(374) [0601] I have tried it **myself** and learned by experience that often
LC : 0 4 :056(443) [0747] I **myself**, and all who are baptized, must say before God:
EP : 0 1 :010(467) [0781] God; him I shall see for **myself**, and mine eyes shall
SD : 0 2 :064(533) [0907] Again, "So then, I of **myself** serve the law of God with my
SD : 0 6 :009(565) [0965] preaching to others I **myself** should be disqualified"
SD : 0 6 :021(567) [0969] of anything against **myself**, but I am not thereby
SD : 1 1 :010(618) [1067] and do not concern **myself** with repentance, faith, prayer,

Mystery (16), Mysteries (4)
PR : PR :021(011) [0019] of the personal union, which is an inscrutable **mystery**.
AP : 1 2 :012(184) [0257] is really what is called "departing before the **mysteries**."
AP : 2 2 :013(238) [0361] people, but there is no **mystery** as to why they defend this
EP : 0 7 :041(486) [0817] the supernatural and celestial **mysteries** of this sacrament.
EP : 0 7 :042(486) [0817] also, and accept this **mystery** in no other way than by
EP : 0 8 :018(489) [0823] Trinity this is the highest **mystery**, as the apostles
EP : 1 1 :003(494) [0833] in heaven who reveals **mysteries**, and he has made known
EP : 1 1 :011(496) [0835] does he speak of the **mystery** of God's eternal election.
SD : 0 7 :127(591) [1015] the supernatural and heavenly **mysteries** of this Supper.
SD : 0 8 :022(595) [1023] in expounding this **mystery** and have explained the one
SD : 0 8 :033(597) [1027] holy Trinity, the greatest **mystery** in heaven and on earth
SD : 0 8 :033(597) [1027] "Great indeed is the **mystery** of our religion: God was
SD : 0 8 :034(597) [1027] because of this exalted **mystery**, "become partakers of the
SD : 0 8 :096(609) [1049] Scriptures call Christ a **mystery** over which all heretics
SD : 0 8 :096(609) [1049] presumptuously into this **mystery** with their reason, but
SD : 1 1 :026(620) [1071] "made known to us the **mystery** of his will" and has
SD : 1 1 :043(623) [1077] far God has revealed the **mystery** of foreknowledge to us
SD : 1 1 :052(625) [1081] are many points in this **mystery** about which God has
SD : 1 1 :055(625) [1081] God has reserved this **mystery** to his own wisdom and
SD : 1 1 :064(626) [1083] shows how much of this **mystery** God has reserved for his

Mystical (1)
AP : 1 0 :003(179) [0247] we do not know the power of the **mystical** benediction?

Mythology (1), Myths (2)
AG : 2 8 :046(088) [0089] giving heed to Jewish **myths** or to commands of men who
AL : 2 8 :046(088) [0089] giving heed to Jewish **myths** or to commands of men who
AP : 0 7 :027(173) [0237] and regard the rest as **mythology**, like the tragedies of the

Naked (3)
AP : 0 4 :352(161) [0217] so that by putting it on we may not be found **naked**."
LC : 0 1 :190(391) [0635] you send a person away **naked** when you could clothe
LC : 0 1 :191(391) [0635] not welcome me, I was **naked** and you did not clothe me,

Name (193), Named (6), Names (13), Naming (3)
PR : PR :001(003) [0007] German Nation who are **named** below, tender our due
PR : PR :009(006) [0011] that, under the **name** of the frequently mentioned
PR : PR :027(014) [0025] and heart subscribed our **names** hereto and ordered our
AG : 0 0 :001(047) [0059] God by misusing his **name** or Word, nor should we wish
AL : 2 4 :019(058) [0067] will not hold him guiltless who takes his **name** in vain."
AP : PR :010(099) [0101] Therefore I am giving my **name**, so no one can complain
AP : 0 2 :006(101) [0107] the best of intentions we **named** it and explained it as a
AP : 0 2 :023(103) [0111] ourselves clear, we are **naming** these gifts knowledge of
AP : 0 4 :062(115) [0139] and forgiveness of sins should be preached in his **name**.
AP : 0 4 :083(118) [0145] in him receives forgiveness of sins through his **name**."
AP : 0 4 :083(118) [0145] sins, he says, through his **name**, that is, for his sake:
AP : 0 4 :083(119) [0145] We cannot take hold of the **name** of Christ except by

Continued ▶

A P : 0 4 :094(120) [0149] all who believed in his **name**, he gave power to become
A P : 0 4 :098(121) [0149] else, for there is no other **name** under heaven given
A P : 0 4 :098(121) [0149] But only faith takes hold of the **name** of Christ.
A P : 0 4 :098(121) [0151] are saved by trust in the **name** of Christ, not in our
A P : 0 4 :098(121) [0151] For "**name**" here means that which is cited as the cause of
A P : 0 4 :098(121) [0151] To cite the **name** of Christ is to trust in the name of
A P : 0 4 :098(121) [0151] of Christ is to trust in the **name** of Christ as the cause or
A P : 0 4 :273(148) [0199] in him receives forgiveness of sins through his **name**."
A P : 0 4 :331(158) [0211] because thy city and thy people are called by thy **name**."
A P : 0 4 :333(158) [0211] anything of the Father, he will give it to you in my **name**."
A P : 0 4 :333(158) [0211] "In my **name**," he says, because without the high priest we
A P : 0 4 :400(168) [0227] arrogate to themselves the **name** of the church, therefore,
A P : 0 7 :010(170) [0229] part of the church only in **name** and not in fact, while the
A P : 0 7 :010(170) [0229] godly are part of the church in fact as well as in **name**.
A P : 0 7 :012(170) [0231] of Christ and is the church in fact as well as in **name**.
A P : 1 2 :030(186) [0259] of sins should be preached in my **name** to all nations."
A P : 1 2 :045(188) [0263] us it is enough that he **names** contrition and faith as the
A P : 1 2 :046(188) [0263] he almost always **names** these two parts, mortifying and
A P : 1 2 :065(191) [0271] in him receives forgiveness of sins through his **name**."
A P : 1 2 :065(191) [0271] more clearly: "through his **name**," and he adds: "every one
A P : 1 2 :065(191) [0271] only through the **name** of Christ, that is, because of him
A P : 1 2 :066(191) [0271] in him receives forgiveness of sins through his **name**," etc.
A P : 1 2 :175(210) [0307] Still the **name** indulgences remains.
A P : 2 0 :002(227) [0339] in him receives forgiveness of sins through his **name**."
A P : 2 1 :017(231) [0347] anything of the Father, he will give it to you in my **name**."
A P : 2 1 :044(236) [0357] honors kings with his own **name** and calls them gods
A P : 2 2 :007(237) [0359] usage of language, **naming** one part also signifies the
A P : 2 4 :026(254) [0393] "that is, the fruit of lips that acknowledge his **name**."
A P : 2 4 :029(255) [0393] of thanksgiving and call on the **name** of the Lord."
A P : 2 4 :031(255) [0395] the sun to its setting my **name** is great among the nations,
A P : 2 4 :031(255) [0395] place incense is offered to my **name**, and a pure offering."
A P : 2 4 :032(255) [0395] They say, first, that the **name** of the Lord will be great.
A P : 2 4 :032(255) [0395] which makes known the **name** of Christ and the Father's
A P : 2 4 :032(255) [0395] This is how the **name** of the Lord becomes great among
A P : 2 4 :032(255) [0395] through which the **name** of the Lord becomes great, like
A P : 2 4 :033(256) [0395] of the heart, by which the **name** of the Lord really
A P : 2 4 :078(263) [0411] From the **names** for the Mass they take arguments which
A P : 2 4 :086(265) [0413] kept the term "Mass" as the **name** for the contributions.
A P : 2 4 :089(266) [0415] This is an abuse of the **name** of God in violation of the
A P : 2 7 :001(268) [0419] of Eisenach, there was a Franciscan **named** John Hilten.
A P : 2 7 :044(277) [0435] men, and doing so under the pretext of the divine **name**.
S 1 : P R :004(289) [0457] my labor and thus mislead the poor people in my **name**.
S 2 : 0 1 :005(292) [0463] says, "There is no other **name** under heaven given among
S 2 : 0 4 :012(300) [0475] to do even if we have to die for it in God's **name**.
S 3 : 0 1 :002(302) [0477] lying, swearing by God's **name**, failure to pray and call
S 3 : 0 3 :006(304) [0481] of sins should be preached in his **name** to all nations."
S 3 : 0 6 :004(311) [0493] and curse in God's **name** those who not only omit both
S 3 : 1 2 :002(315) [0499] command or forbid in the **name** of the church, for, thank
S 3 : 1 5 :005(317) [0501] subscribe in my own **name** and in the name of my
S 3 : 1 5 :005(317) [0501] my own name and in the **name** of my brethren and of the
S 3 : 1 5 :005(317) [0501] again subscribe in the **name** of Master John Brenz, who
S 3 : 1 5 :005(317) [0501] subscribe in my own **name** and in that of JUSTUS
S 3 : 1 5 :005(318) [0501] in Erfurt, in my own **name** and in the names of my other
S 3 : 1 5 :005(318) [0501] my own name and in the **names** of my other co-workers
T R : 0 0 :062(331) [0523] one who is known to be active and **name** him archdeacon.
T R : 0 0 :068(331) [0523] three are gathered in my **name**, there am I in the midst of
T R : 0 0 :082(334) [0529] Accordingly they subscribe their **names**.
T R : 0 0 :082(335) [0529] again subscribe in the **name** of Master John Brenz, as he
T R : 0 0 :082(335) [0529] his own hand both in his **name** and in that of Adam of
T R : 0 0 :082(000) [0529] courtesy may add my **name**, if it be necessary, to all that I
S C : 0 1 :003(342) [0539] *"You shall not take the **name** of the Lord your God in*
S C : 0 1 :004(342) [0539] so we should not use his **name** to curse, swear, practice
S C : 0 3 :003(346) [0547] *"Hallowed be thy **name**."*
S C : 0 3 :004(346) [0547] Answer: To be sure, God's **name** is holy in itself, but we
S C : 0 3 :005(346) [0547] of God teaches, profanes the **name** of God among us.
S C : 0 3 :011(347) [0547] us from hallowing his **name** and prevent the coming of
S C : 0 4 :004(348) [0551] baptizing them in the **name** of the Father and of the Son
S C : 0 5 :028(351) [0555] you your sins in the **name** of the Father and of the Son
S C : 0 7 :001(352) [0557] the cross and say, "In the **name** of God, the Father, the
S C : 0 7 :004(353) [0559] the cross and say, "In the **name** of God, the Father, the
L C : P R :009(359) [0569] three are gathered in my **name**, there am I in the midst of
L C : S P :006(362) [0575] in fact as well as in **name**, both young and old, may be
L C : S P :002(362) [0575] 2. You shall not take the **name** of God in vain.
L C : S P :014(363) [0577] Our Father who art in heaven, hallowed be thy **name**.
L C : S P :021(364) [0579] and baptize them in the **name** of the Father and of the
L C : 0 1 :006(365) [0581] has a god — mammon by **name**, that is, money and
L C : 0 1 :025(368) [0587] have called God by a **name** more elegant and worthy than
L C : 0 1 :025(368) [0587] in other languages, a **name** derived from the word "good"
L C : 0 1 :025(368) [0587] and pours forth all that is good in **name** and in fact.
L C : 0 1 :049(371) [0593] *"You shall not take the **name** of God in vain."*
L C : 0 1 :051(371) [0595] mean to misuse or take the **name** of God in vain?" you
L C : 0 1 :051(371) [0595] "It is a misuse of God's **name** if we call upon the Lord
L C : 0 1 :051(371) [0595] is appealing to God's **name** falsely or taking his name
L C : 0 1 :051(371) [0595] name falsely or taking his **name** upon our lips when our
L C : 0 1 :052(371) [0595] God's **name** cannot be more grievously abused than for
L C : 0 1 :053(371) [0595] in how many ways God's **name** is abused, though it is
L C : 0 1 :053(371) [0595] misuse of the divine **name** occurs most obviously in
L C : 0 1 :053(372) [0595] himself, swearing by God's **name** or by his own soul.
L C : 0 1 :055(372) [0595] yourself with God's **name** or to put up a good front and
L C : 0 1 :055(372) [0595] and who disgrace God's **name** unabashedly (these belong
L C : 0 1 :056(372) [0595] every misuse of the holy **name** as the greatest sin that can
L C : 0 1 :056(372) [0597] it by invoking God's **name** and using it as a cloak to
L C : 0 1 :057(372) [0597] will not hold him guiltless who takes his **name** in vain."
L C : 0 1 :057(372) [0597] so little will he permit his **name** to be used to gloss over a
L C : 0 1 :058(372) [0597] few who do not use the **name** of God for lies and all
L C : 0 1 :059(372) [0597] denounced, God and his **name** have to be dragged in to
L C : 0 1 :062(373) [0597] understand what it means to take God's **name** in vain.
L C : 0 1 :062(373) [0597] to lie and assert under his **name** something that is not so,
L C : 0 1 :063(373) [0597] you must also know how to use the **name** of God aright.
L C : 0 1 :063(373) [0599] "You shall not take the **name** of God in vain," God at the
L C : 0 1 :063(373) [0599] that we are to use his **name** properly, for it has been
L C : 0 1 :064(373) [0599] here to use the holy **name** in support of falsehood or
L C : 0 1 :064(373) [0599] again, when we call on his **name** in time of need, or praise
L C : 0 1 :064(373) [0599] mean by calling upon his **name** in service of truth and
L C : 0 1 :064(373) [0599] Thus his **name** is hallowed, as we pray in the Lord's
L C : 0 1 :069(374) [0599] to avoid calling upon God's **name** in its support.
L C : 0 1 :070(374) [0601] to honor God's **name** and keep it constantly upon their
L C : 0 1 :070(374) [0601] for true honor to God's **name** consists of looking to it for
L C : 0 1 :071(374) [0601] He hates to hear God's **name** and cannot long remain
L C : 0 1 :072(374) [0601] did not preserve us through our calling upon his **name**.
L C : 0 1 :072(374) [0601] always keep the holy **name** on our lips so that he may not
L C : 0 1 :077(375) [0603] the misuse of the divine **name** and taught that its right use
L C : 0 1 :077(375) [0603] with the right use of his **name** and will as richly reward it,
L C : 0 1 :103(379) [0611] not misuse his holy **name** in support of lies or any evil
L C : 0 1 :138(384) [0621] be cut off: and may their **name** be cut off in one
L C : 0 1 :144(385) [0623] ran in the devil's **name** into monasteries, on pilgrimages,
L C : 0 1 :150(385) [0625] since they bear this **name** and title with all honor as their
L C : 0 1 :158(387) [0627] For the **name** spiritual father belongs only to those who
L C : 0 1 :161(387) [0627] who would bear the **name** of Christians owe it to God
L C : 0 1 :255(399) [0653] our honor and good **name**, for it is intolerable to live
L C : 0 1 :270(401) [0657] of his honor and good **name** unless these have first been
L C : 0 1 :273(401) [0659] For honor and good **name** are easily taken away, but not
L C : 0 1 :326(409) [0675] fear God and not take his **name** in vain by cursing, lying,
L C : 0 1 :326(409) [0675] wickedness, but to use his **name** properly by calling upon
L C : 0 2 :040(416) [0689] that the Holy Spirit makes me holy, as his **name** implies."
L C : 0 2 :048(416) [0691] and give the house its **name** by virtue of the assembly.
L C : 0 3 :005(420) [0699] Commandment, "You shall not take God's **name** in vain."
L C : 0 3 :005(420) [0699] to praise the holy **name** and pray or call upon it in every
L C : 0 3 :008(421) [0699] and prayer the **name** of God is glorified and used to good
L C : 0 3 :014(422) [0701] be taught, in the devil's **name**, in such a way that no one
L C : 0 3 :024(423) [0705] must present a petition, **naming** and asking for something
L C : 0 3 :035(425) [0707] *"Hallowed be thy **name**."*
L C : 0 3 :036(425) [0707] Father, grant that thy **name** alone may be holy."
L C : 0 3 :037(425) [0707] But what is it to pray that his **name** may become holy?
L C : 0 3 :037(425) [0707] God's **name** was given to us when we became Christians
L C : 0 3 :038(425) [0707] of duly honoring his **name** and keeping it holy and
L C : 0 3 :038(425) [0709] as good children, that his **name**, which is already holy in
L C : 0 3 :040(425) [0709] Now, the **name** of God is profaned by us either in words
L C : 0 3 :041(425) [0709] teach, and speak in God's **name** anything that is false and
L C : 0 3 :041(425) [0709] and deceptive, using his **name** to cloak lies and make them
L C : 0 3 :041(425) [0709] the worst profanation and dishonor of the divine **name**.
L C : 0 3 :042(425) [0709] grossly misuse the divine **name** as a cloak for their
L C : 0 3 :042(425) [0709] Here again God's **name** must be profaned and
L C : 0 3 :044(425) [0709] we who are called by his **name** and enjoy his manifold
L C : 0 3 :045(426) [0709] Commandment: that his **name** should not be taken in
L C : 0 3 :045(426) [0709] Whoever uses God's **name** for any sort of wrong profanes
L C : 0 3 :045(426) [0709] and desecrates this holy **name**, as in the past a church was
L C : 0 3 :047(426) [0711] all of whom wear the holy **name** as a cloak and warrant
L C : 0 3 :049(426) [0711] from using his glory and **name** to cloak its lies and
L C : 0 3 :049(426) [0711] would rather keep God's **name** sacred and holy in both
L C : 0 3 :050(426) [0711] Just as God's **name** is holy in itself and yet we pray that it
L C : 0 3 :050(426) [0711] of those among whom his **name** is hallowed and his
L C : 0 3 :052(427) [0711] in us and that God's **name** may be praised through his
L C : 0 3 :060(428) [0715] we have prayed that God's **name** may be hallowed by us
L C : 0 3 :062(428) [0715] pretexts of God's **name**, are disclosed and exposed in all
L C : 0 3 :068(429) [0717] As God's **name** must be hallowed and his kingdom must
L C : 0 3 :070(429) [0717] God could not abide on earth nor his **name** be hallowed.
L C : 0 3 :113(435) [0729] that we pray for: God's **name** or glory, God's kingdom
L C : 0 3 :118(436) [0731] delivered from all evil, his **name** must first be hallowed in
L C : 0 4 :004(437) [0733] *baptizing them in the **name** of the Father and of the Son*
L C : 0 4 :009(437) [0735] it and, what is more, it is performed in his **name**.
L C : 0 4 :009(437) [0735] "Go, baptize," not in your **name** but "in God's name."
L C : 0 4 :009(437) [0735] "Go, baptize," not in your name but "in God's **name**."
L C : 0 4 :010(437) [0735] To be baptized in God's **name** is to be baptized not by
L C : 0 4 :016(438) [0735] commandment and God's **name**, and this is a treasure
L C : 0 4 :026(440) [0739] It shows also (as we said above) that God's **name** is in it.
L C : 0 4 :027(440) [0739] And where God's **name** is, there must also be life and
L C : 0 4 :029(440) [0739] Word and ordinance and the joining of his **name** to it.
L C : 0 4 :036(441) [0741] so that, baptized in the **name** of God, you may receive in
L C : 0 5 :059(453) [0767] that he has forfeited the **name** of Christian and has to be
E P : R N :002(465) [0777] teachers, whatever their **names**, should not be put on a
E P : 0 7 :001(481) [0809] their errors under the **name** of this Christian Confession,
E P : 0 8 :003(487) [0817] of the other but have in common only the **name**.
E P : 0 8 :003(487) [0819] union makes merely the **names** common," so that God is
E P : 0 8 :011(488) [0821] in truth) shared only the **name** of God with the divine
E P : 0 8 :024(490) [0823] personal union achieves only common **names** and titles.
S D : P R :001(503) [0851] and accepted in the **name** of those churches which
S D : P R :006(504) [0853] possibility that under the **name** of the Augsburg
S D : P R :007(505) [0853] for presentation, in the **name** of the illustrious and most
S D : 0 1 :045(516) [0873] sin is baptized in the **name** of the holy Trinity, is
S D : 0 2 :051(531) [0901] concerning all who in his **name** preach repentance and the
S D : 0 2 :057(532) [0903] gathered together in his **name** and occupy themselves with
S D : 0 3 :039(546) [0929] kind of pretense, title, or **name** are they to be mingled
S D : 0 3 :044(547) [0933] to the errors already **named** we must criticize, expose, and
S D : 0 5 :004(559) [0953] should be preached in his **name** to all nations" (Luke
S D : 0 7 :123(590) [1013] who only bear the **name** of Christ but do not have a
S D : 0 7 :128(591) [1015] and identified by **name** from the foregoing exposition, for
S D : 0 8 :012(593) [1019] and might over every **name** that is named not only in this
S D : 0 8 :012(593) [1019] over every name that is **named** not only in this age but
S D : 0 8 :016(594) [1021] the heretic Manes by the **name** of Paul, a native of
S D : 0 8 :031(597) [1025] that they not only have **names** in common but also in
S D : 0 8 :051(601) [1033] and might above every **name** that is named, not only in
S D : 0 8 :051(601) [1033] above every name that is **named**, not only in this age but
S D : 0 8 :063(603) [1037] all only a mode of speech, mere words, titles, and **names**.
S D : 0 8 :067(604) [1039] the bare titles and the **names** in words alone, while in
S D : 0 8 :076(606) [1043] three are gathered in my **name**, there am I in the midst of
S D : 0 8 :095(609) [1049] but has only the bare title and **name** in common with it.
S D : 1 0 :005(611) [1053] though they go under the **name** and guise of external
S D : 1 0 :019(614) [1059] command or forbid in the **name** of the church, for, thank
S D : 1 1 :006(617) [1065] to the glory of his divine **name** and the salvation of his
S D : 1 1 :025(620) [1071] only the elect "whose **names** are written in the book of
S D : 1 1 :028(620) [1071] and forgiveness of sins in his **name** among all nations."
S D : 1 1 :084(630) [1091] you my power, so that my **name** may be declared

Narrative (1)
A P : 0 4 :267(146) [0197] but about faith as well, as the **narrative** in the text shows.

Narrow (3), Narrowly (1)
LC : 01 :081(375) [0603] this commandment too **narrowly** and grossly misused it.
LC : 01 :086(376) [0605] of rest should not be so **narrow** as to forbid incidental
LC : 01 :250(399) [0651] not to be confined to **narrow** limits but must extend to
SD : 11 :033(621) [1073] "Strive to enter by the **narrow** door" (Luke 13:23, 24).

Nathan (1)
AP : 12 :056(189) [0267] David is rebuked by **Nathan**, and in his terror he says

Nation (8), Nations (30)
PR : PR :001(003) [0007] Empire of the German **Nation** who are named below,
PR : PR :002(003) [0007] fatherland, the German **nation**, and to light its way out of
PR : PR :022(011) [0019] inside or outside the Holy Empire of the German **Nation**.
AP : PR :015(099) [0101] to testify to all **nations** that we hold to the Gospel of
AP : 04 :262(145) [0195] was promised not only to the Israelites but to all **nations**.
AP : 07 :010(170) [0229] it to mean an outward government of certain **nations**.
AP : 07 :014(170) [0231] descendants from other **nations** by certain outward
AP : 07 :019(171) [0233] about the whole Jewish **nation** and says that the true
AP : 07 :042(176) [0241] of Nicaea, certain **nations** held tenaciously to the custom
AP : 09 :002(178) [0245] to Christ's command (Matt. 28:19), "Baptize all **nations**."
AP : 12 :030(186) [0259] of sins should be preached in my name to all **nations**."
AP : 12 :125(201) [0289] thinks it is right for all **nations** to recognize her as the
AP : 12 :129(202) [0291] the silent desires of all **nations**; they certainly demand
AP : 12 :129(202) [0291] you can bind all **nations** to yourself; for men of discretion
AP : 14 :005(215) [0315] God and among all **nations**, present and future, against
AP : 16 :002(222) [0331] ordinances of the **nation** in which we live, just as it lets us
AP : 21 :018(231) [0347] as an ensign to the peoples; him shall the **nations** seek."
AP : 23 :003(239) [0363] divine law, the law of the **nations**, and the canons of the
AP : 24 :031(255) [0395] name is great among the **nations**, and in every place
AP : 24 :032(255) [0395] the name of the Lord becomes great among the **nations**.
S3 : 03 :006(304) [0481] of sins should be preached in his name to all **nations**."
TR : 00 :035(326) [0513] kings of almost all the **nations** of Europe, but especially
TR : 00 :039(327) [0515] and not of the kings of **nations**, and he calls that man "an
TR : 00 :042(328) [0517] consensus of so many **nations** and to be called
SC : 04 :004(348) [0551] and make disciples of all **nations**, baptizing them in the
LC : SP :021(364) [0579] "Go and teach all **nations**, and baptize them in the name
LC : 01 :158(387) [0627] blood, fathers of a household, and fathers of the **nation**.
LC : 01 :175(388) [0631] who would be a benefit to the **nation** and the people.
LC : 01 :258(399) [0653] That **nation** had an excellent, orderly government, and
LC : 04 :004(437) [0733] *the world, and teach all **nations**, baptizing them in the*
SD : 05 :004(559) [0953] be preached in his name to all **nations**" (Luke 24:46, 47).
SD : 05 :023(562) [0959] Abraham, but whom all **nations** should be blessed;
SD : 05 :023(562) [0959] and be a light to the **nations**, "who was wounded for our
SD : 07 :051(578) [0991] them to teach all **nations** to observe all that he had
SD : 10 :023(615) [1061] consensus of so many **nations** and to be called
SD : 11 :028(620) [1071] and forgiveness of sins in his name among all **nations**."
SD : 11 :059(626) [1081] in the history of some **nations** and some persons God
SD : 11 :060(626) [1083] over certain lands, **nations**, and people so that, as we

Nationalities (1)
S2 : 04 :004(299) [0473] and of many other **nationalities** have never been under

Native (2)
SD : 02 :007(521) [0883] man cannot by any **native** or natural powers in any way
SD : 08 :016(594) [1021] by the name of Paul, a **native** of Samosata who had

Natural (115), Naturally (12)
AG : 02 :003(029) [0045] is sin, for they hold that **natural** man is made righteous by
AG : 18 :003(039) [0051] Paul says in I Cor. 2:14, "**Natural** man does not receive
AG : 18 :004(039) [0051] a free will, for all have a **natural**, innate understanding
AG : 23 :013(053) [0063] contrary to all divine, **natural**, and civil law, but was also
AG : 27 :054(079) [0083] not to take revenge, it is **natural** that some should
AL : 18 :002(039) [0051] righteousness — because **natural** man does not perceive
AL : 28 :041(087) [0089] is privative and not **natural** is a work that appeases God,
AP : 02 :014(102) [0109] and denied to man's **natural** powers the fear and trust of
AP : 02 :023(103) [0111] we do when we deny to **natural** man not only fear and
AP : 04 :007(108) [0121] extent human reason **naturally** understands the law since
AP : 04 :007(108) [0121] it has the same judgment **naturally** written in the mind.
AP : 04 :010(108) [0123] Because this view **naturally** flatters men, it has produced
AP : 04 :014(109) [0123] Aristotle wrote so well on **natural** ethics that nothing
AP : 04 :020(110) [0125] is there, because men **naturally** trust their own
AP : 04 :023(110) [0127] often overwhelmed by its **natural** weakness and by the
AP : 04 :029(111) [0129] *and Grace* he says: "If **natural** capacity, with the help of
AP : 04 :265(146) [0197] Human reason **naturally** admires them; because it sees
AP : 04 :391(167) [0225] can love God above all things by purely **natural** powers.
AP : 10 :003(179) [0247] as love, but also by a **natural** participation," etc.
AP : 12 :046(188) [0263] because in these troubles our **natural** lust is purged away.
AP : 15 :022(218) [0321] righteousness of faith, it **naturally** supposes that such
AP : 18 :007(226) [0337] says (I Cor. 2:14), "The **natural** man," that is, the man
AP : 18 :007(226) [0337] man who uses only his **natural** powers, "does not perceive
AP : 23 :006(240) [0365] clashes with divine and **natural** law and conflicts with the
AP : 23 :007(240) [0365] lust but about so-called "**natural** love," the desire which
AP : 23 :009(240) [0367] ordinance in man is a **natural** right, the jurists have said
AP : 23 :009(240) [0367] that the union of man and woman is by **natural** right.
AP : 23 :009(240) [0367] Now, since **natural** right is unchangeable, the right to
AP : 23 :010(241) [0367] they were born with a **natural** right and now they are not.
AP : 23 :010(241) [0367] thought up in order to circumvent the **natural** law.
AP : 23 :011(241) [0367] jurists: The union of man and woman is by **natural** right.
AP : 23 :012(241) [0367] **Natural** right is really divine right, because it is an
AP : 23 :012(241) [0367] For the **natural** desire of one sex for the other is an
AP : 23 :013(241) [0367] desire which is called "**natural** love," which lust did not
AP : 23 :016(241) [0369] Ever since man sinned, **natural** desire and the lust that
AP : 23 :060(247) [0379] conflicts with divine and **natural** law; it disagrees even
S3 : 01 :004(302) [0477] the fall of Adam the **natural** powers of man have
S3 : 01 :006(302) [0477] that man is able by his **natural** powers to observe and
S3 : 01 :007(302) [0477] that man is able by his **natural** powers to love God above
S3 : 03 :010(305) [0481] sin but asserted that the **natural** powers of man have
S3 : 06 :005(311) [0493] surrender or lose their **natural** substance and retain only
LC : 01 :137(384) [0619] that such wicked people die a **natural** and timely death.
LC : 01 :212(393) [0641] flesh and blood, and the **natural** inclinations and
LC : 04 :017(438) [0735] not by virtue of the **natural** substance but because here
LC : 04 :017(438) [0737] it is not simply a **natural** water, but a divine, heavenly,
LC : 04 :018(438) [0737] to the element or the **natural** substance, it becomes a
EP : 01 :013(467) [0783] in spiritual things its **natural** powers remained wholly
EP : 01 :015(468) [0783] but does not remove the **natural** powers of the magnet;
EP : 01 :018(468) [0783] that it is not the **natural** man himself who commits sin
EP : 02 :011(471) [0789] able by its own **natural** powers to add something (though
EP : 02 :016(472) [0791] to confirm the role of **natural** free will in conversion
EP : 07 :011(483) [0811] Christ is true, essential, **natural**, complete God and man
EP : 07 :022(484) [0813] lose their substance and **natural** essence and are thus
EP : 08 :007(487) [0819] and (according to its **natural** property, by itself)
EP : 08 :022(490) [0823] That Christ is not true, **natural**, and eternal God, as
EP : 12 :028(500) [0843] is not a true, essential, **natural** God, of one divine essence
SD : 01 :012(510) [0863] True, in **natural** and external things which are subject to
SD : 01 :020(511) [0865] matters it is good, pure, and in its **natural** powers perfect.
SD : 01 :022(512) [0865] not destroy the magnet's **natural** power but only impedes
SD : 01 :023(512) [0865] has of and from man's **natural** birth something that is
SD : 01 :027(513) [0867] and born in the **natural** way from a father and a mother,
SD : 01 :030(513) [0867] human being born in the **natural** way from a father and a
SD : 02 :003(520) [0881] still has so much of his **natural** powers prior to his
SD : 02 :007(521) [0883] cannot by any native or **natural** powers in any way
SD : 02 :007(521) [0883] and nature the **natural** free will is mighty and active only
SD : 02 :009(521) [0883] man's reason or **natural** intellect still has a dim spark of
SD : 02 :010(522) [0885] way Scripture calls the **natural** man simply "darkness" in
SD : 02 :012(522) [0885] heart, and will of the **natural** man every capacity,
SD : 02 :013(523) [0885] is set on the flesh (the **natural** man's understanding) "is
SD : 02 :015(523) [0887] of God they cannot obtain by their own **natural** powers.
SD : 02 :017(523) [0887] heart, and will of a **natural**, unregenerated man is not
SD : 02 :018(524) [0887] If the **natural** or carnal free will of St. Paul and other
SD : 02 :018(524) [0887] the free will by its own **natural** powers can do nothing for
SD : 02 :022(525) [0889] life, not by its own **natural** and efficient aptitude,
SD : 02 :025(526) [0891] the human powers of the **natural** free will, be it entirely
SD : 02 :046(530) [0899] the wickedness of our **natural** free will, as well as the
SD : 02 :046(530) [0899] themselves by their own **natural** powers, they will
SD : 02 :065(534) [0907] from our carnal and **natural** powers, but from the new
SD : 02 :071(535) [0909] answers this way: Man's **natural** powers cannot
SD : 02 :075(536) [0909] that by his own **natural** powers, without the Holy Spirit,
SD : 02 :076(536) [0911] who taught that by his **natural** powers man can start out
SD : 02 :076(536) [0911] of the good work which man began by his **natural** powers.
SD : 02 :077(536) [0911] the free will by its own **natural** powers can meet God and
SD : 02 :078(536) [0911] that such a capacity **naturally** to prepare oneself for grace
SD : 02 :078(536) [0911] come from man's own **natural** powers but solely through
SD : 02 :086(538) [0913] the view that man's **naturally** free will cooperates in his
SD : 02 :089(538) [0915] man of himself or by his **natural** powers is unable to do
SD : 03 :002(539) [0917] Christ himself as the true, **natural**, essential Son of God,
SD : 04 :007(552) [0941] done by a person's own **natural** powers but only after a
SD : 05 :022(562) [0959] the law, since from the **natural** law even the heathen had
SD : 07 :033(575) [0983] in the Supper is his true, **natural** body, which the godless
SD : 07 :037(575) [0985] the two essences, the **natural** bread and the true natural
SD : 07 :037(575) [0985] bread and the true **natural** body of Christ, are present
SD : 07 :046(577) [0987] reason and to divine and **natural** law but also to the
SD : 07 :048(578) [0989] he was speaking of true, **natural** bread and natural wine
SD : 07 :048(578) [0989] true, natural bread and **natural** wine as well as of oral
SD : 07 :064(581) [0995] he handed his disciples **natural** bread and natural wine,
SD : 07 :064(581) [0995] natural bread and **natural** wine, which he called his true
SD : 07 :091(585) [1003] the essential and **natural** properties of the human body,
SD : 07 :094(586) [1005] Jesus Christ is essential, **natural**, true, complete God and
SD : 07 :108(588) [1009] they allege has lost its **natural** substance and is no longer
SD : 08 :004(592) [1017] or contravenes its **natural**, essential properties, and they
SD : 08 :008(593) [1017] so that each retains its **natural** properties and throughout
SD : 08 :009(593) [1017] at the same time **naturally** (that is, according to the
SD : 08 :009(593) [1019] of the nature and of its **natural** essence), to be intrinsically
SD : 08 :011(593) [1019] natures, each with its **natural** essence and properties, are
SD : 08 :012(593) [1019] possesses and retains its **natural**, essential properties but
SD : 08 :036(598) [1027] and unblended in their **natural** essence and properties,
SD : 08 :048(600) [1031] more than their own **natural** and essential properties
SD : 08 :050(600) [1031] more than its own **natural** essential properties alone,
SD : 08 :050(600) [1031] or contravenes its **natural** properties, even though the
SD : 08 :051(600) [1033] in addition to its **natural**, essential, and abiding
SD : 08 :051(601) [1033] and according to its **natural** and essential properties, or
SD : 08 :053(601) [1033] over and above its **natural** properties without being
SD : 08 :060(602) [1035] and since each retains its **natural** and essential properties
SD : 08 :062(603) [1037] through an essential or **natural** outpouring of the
SD : 08 :062(603) [1037] completely laid aside its **natural** and essential properties
SD : 08 :062(603) [1037] in such a way that the **natural**, essential properties and
SD : 08 :063(603) [1037] to describe any essential, **natural** exchange or transfusion
SD : 08 :066(604) [1039] transformation of the **natural** properties of either the fire
SD : 08 :082(607) [1045] his deity, he is there as a **natural** divine person and is also
SD : 08 :082(607) [1045] person and is also **naturally** and personally there, as his
SD : 08 :082(607) [1045] be in his mother's womb **naturally** and personally and
SD : 08 :082(607) [1045] But if he is present **naturally** and personally wherever he
SD : 11 :044(623) [1077] about the powers of our **natural** will, for in his counsel
SD : 12 :006(633) [1097] abide by the true, simple, **natural**, and proper meaning of
SD : 12 :036(635) [1101] not a true, essential, and **natural** God, of one eternal,

Nature (483)
PR : PR :021(010) [0019] majesty of the human **nature** in the person of Christ, in
PR : PR :021(011) [0019] ascribed to the human **nature** of Christ outside the
PR : PR :021(011) [0019] together and the human **nature** according to its essence
PR : PR :021(011) [0019] is equalized with the divine **nature** and is thus negated.
AG : 02 :001(029) [0043] to the course of **nature** are conceived and born in sin.
AG : 02 :001(029) [0043] wombs and are unable by **nature** to have true fear of God
AG : 18 :005(040) [0051] they are capable of by **nature**: whether or not to labor in
AG : 19 :000(040) [0053] and still preserves **nature**, yet sin is caused in all wicked
AG : 19 :000(041) [0053] the devil lies, he speaks according to his own **nature**."
AG : 20 :036(046) [0057] without Christ human **nature** and human strength are
AG : 23 :005(052) [0061] of living in celibacy, and he certainly knew man's **nature**.
AG : 25 :008(062) [0069] Our wretched human **nature** is so deeply submerged in
AG : 27 :016(073) [0077] monastic life is of such a **nature** that thereby God's grace
AG : 27 :030(075) [0079] it belongs to the very **nature** and character of a vow that
AL : 02 :001(029) [0043] who are propagated according to **nature** are born in sin.
AL : 03 :001(029) [0045] of God — took on man's **nature** in the womb of the
AL : 18 :005(040) [0051] spring from the good in **nature**, that is, to will to labor in
AL : 18 :008(040) [0053] Spirit, by the power of **nature** alone, we are able to love
AL : 18 :009(040) [0053] Although **nature** is able in some measure to perform the
AL : 19 :000(040) [0053] God creates and preserves **nature**, the cause of sin is the

Continued ▶

A L : 1 9 :000(041) [0053] the devil lies, he speaks according to his own **nature**."
A L : 2 0 :036(046) [0057] For without faith human **nature** cannot possibly do the
A L : 2 3 :014(053) [0063] is growing old and man's **nature** is becoming weaker, it is
A L : 2 7 :027(075) [0079] silent concerning the **nature** of a vow, which ought to be
A L : 2 7 :030(075) [0079] that it is contrary to the **nature** of a vow to make a
A P : 0 2 :002(100) [0105] to the course of **nature** are conceived and born in sin.
A P : 0 2 :002(100) [0105] wombs and are unable by **nature** to have true fear of God
A P : 0 2 :003(101) [0105] denies that human **nature** has the gift and capacity to
A P : 0 2 :003(101) [0105] its acts or fruits, but the continual inclination of **nature**.
A P : 0 2 :005(101) [0107] or corruption in human **nature**, but only the subjection to
A P : 0 2 :006(101) [0107] as a disease since human **nature** is born full of corruption
A P : 0 2 :008(101) [0107] serious faults of human **nature**, namely, ignoring God,
A P : 0 2 :008(101) [0107] even attribute to human **nature** unimpaired power to love
A P : 0 2 :010(102) [0107] If human **nature** has such powers that by itself it can love
A P : 0 2 :011(102) [0109] minor faults in human **nature** and ignore the major ones.
A P : 0 2 :012(102) [0109] about the perfection of **nature** and attributed more than
A P : 0 2 :012(102) [0109] they failed to see the inner uncleanness of human **nature**.
A P : 0 2 :014(102) [0109] the chief flaws in human **nature**, transgressing as they do
A P : 0 2 :024(103) [0111] Since **nature** in its weakness cannot fear and love God or
A P : 0 2 :031(104) [0113] but an abiding deficiency in an unrenewed human **nature**.
A P : 0 2 :040(105) [0115] clearly call lust sin, by **nature** worthy of death if it is not
A P : 0 2 :043(106) [0117] It is no wiser to say that **nature** is not evil.
A P : 0 2 :045(106) [0117] in man are not in their **nature** neutral, but they need the
A P : 0 2 :046(106) [0117] There human **nature** is subjected not only to death and
A P : 0 2 :047(106) [0119] Human **nature** is enslaved and held prisoner by the devil,
A P : 0 3 :001(107) [0119] Word assumed the human **nature** into the unity of his
A P : 0 4 :024(110) [0127] credit; for our corrupt **nature** has no greater good than
A P : 0 4 :029(111) [0129] In ***Nature** and Grace* he says: "If natural capacity, with the
A P : 0 4 :030(111) [0129] of man's corrupted **nature**, for righteousness to 'every one
A P : 0 4 :036(112) [0131] eternal death, human **nature** cannot bring itself to love a
A P : 0 4 :068(116) [0139] of regeneration and the **nature** of the faith we have been
A P : 0 4 :084(119) [0145] Based upon the **nature** of a promise, this is Paul's chief
A P : 0 4 :138(126) [0161] For human **nature** is far too weak to be able by its own
A P : 0 4 :145(127) [0163] do not and cannot say what the **nature** of this love is.
A P : 0 4 :146(127) [0163] because our unspiritual **nature** continually brings forth
A P : 0 4 :153(128) [0163] this is faith, he utterly misunderstands the **nature** of faith.
A P : 0 4 :251(143) [0191] but only the **nature** of the just who have already been
A P : 0 4 :265(146) [0197] opinion clings by **nature** to the minds of men, and it
A P : 0 4 :297(152) [0205] the law because human **nature** cannot keep the law of
A P : 0 4 :301(153) [0205] who visits on human **nature** so many terrible evils,
A P : 0 4 :312(155) [0207] against us, human **nature** flees his wrath and judgment.
A P : 0 4 :313(155) [0207] hope that from this the **nature** of faith will be clearly
A P : 0 4 :340(159) [0215] is to be recognized, but **nature** is not to be ignored."
A P : 0 4 :341(159) [0215] We should trust the promise of grace, not our own **nature**.
A P : 0 4 :350(161) [0217] our old or new sins or the uncleanness of our **nature**!
A P : 0 4 :369(163) [0221] "reward," based on the **nature** of the law, but since it
A P : 0 4 :393(167) [0225] By **nature** men judge that God ought to be appeased by
A P : 1 2 :032(186) [0259] wrath, for human **nature** cannot bear it unless it is
A P : 1 2 :046(188) [0263] those of the dying, which **nature** could not bear without
A P : 1 2 :052(189) [0265] We cannot see how the **nature** of penitence could be
A P : 1 2 :097(196) [0281] understand neither the **nature** of penitence nor the
A P : 1 2 :142(204) [0295] 6:5) and condemns every aspect of lust in human **nature**.
A P : 1 8 :004(225) [0335] Since human **nature** still has reason and judgment about
A P : 1 8 :004(225) [0335] which the carnal **nature** — that is, the reason — can
A P : 1 8 :005(225) [0335] never stops inciting this feeble **nature** to various offenses.
A P : 1 9 :001(226) [0337] has established all of **nature** and preserves everything that
A P : 1 9 :001(226) [0337] "When he lies, he speaks according to his own **nature**."
A P : 2 3 :007(240) [0365] the desire which was meant to be in uncorrupted **nature**.
A P : 2 3 :008(240) [0365] of God did not form the **nature** of men to be fruitful only
A P : 2 3 :008(240) [0367] it still does as long as this physical **nature** of ours exists.
A P : 2 3 :008(240) [0367] cannot change the **nature** of the earth, so neither vows
A P : 2 3 :008(240) [0367] can change the **nature** of man without an extraordinary
A P : 2 3 :009(241) [0367] Where **nature** does not change, there must remain that
A P : 2 3 :009(241) [0367] which God has built into **nature**, and human regulations
A P : 2 3 :012(241) [0367] because it is an ordinance divinely stamped on **nature**.
A P : 2 3 :013(241) [0367] which lust did not remove from **nature** but only inflamed.
A P : 2 3 :015(241) [0367] applies to human **nature** in general, applies to priests as
A P : 2 3 :016(241) [0369] cannot abolish either **nature** or lust, they cannot abolish
A P : 2 3 :019(242) [0369] use the universal law of **nature** which he has instituted,
A P : 2 3 :053(246) [0379] **Nature** is growing older and progressively weaker, so that
A P : 2 4 :014(251) [0389] to do this we must first set down the **nature** of a sacrifice.
A P : 2 4 :015(252) [0389] Sacrifice, Its **Nature** and Types
A P : 2 4 :075(263) [0411] of these belongs to the **nature** of the sacrament, and the
A P : 2 7 :001(268) [0419] and from them the **nature** of his teaching can be well
A P : 2 7 :051(278) [0437] of priests that the law of **nature** in men cannot be
S 1 : 0 1 :000(291) [0461] in one divine essence and **nature**, are one God, who
S 3 : 0 1 :003(302) [0477] so deep a corruption of **nature** that reason cannot
S 3 : 0 1 :004(302) [0477] and that man by **nature** possesses a right understanding
S 3 : 0 1 :009(302) [0477] is the goodness of man's **nature** and such is the power of
S 3 : 0 2 :004(303) [0479] to what utter depths his **nature** has fallen and how
S 3 : 0 3 :028(308) [0487] born in us did what is its **nature** to do, sometimes while
L C : 0 1 :009(366) [0583] clings and cleaves to our **nature** all the way to the grave.
L C : 0 1 :013(366) [0583] can easily understand the **nature** and scope of this
L C : 0 1 :059(372) [0597] By **nature** we all have this beautiful virtue that whenever
L C : 0 1 :083(376) [0603] **Nature** teaches and demands that the common people —
L C : 0 1 :167(388) [0629] preach to parents on the **nature** of their office, how they
L C : 0 1 :212(393) [0641] Where **nature** has its way, as God implanted it, it is not
L C : 0 1 :250(398) [0651] Enough has been said concerning the **nature** of stealing.
L C : 0 1 :262(400) [0655] it is the blind world's **nature** to condemn and persecute
L C : 0 1 :264(400) [0655] a common vice of human **nature** that everyone would
L C : 0 1 :287(403) [0663] Even **nature** teaches the same thing in our own bodies, as
L C : 0 1 :297(405) [0665] Such is **nature** that we all begrudge another's having as
L C : 0 2 :010(411) [0679] of God the Father, his **nature**, his will, and his work.
L C : 0 3 :010(421) [0699] the human heart is by **nature** so desperately wicked that
L C : 0 3 :089(432) [0723] we daily live is of such a **nature** that it does not trust and
L C : 0 3 :102(434) [0727] of evil lusts which by **nature** cling to us and to which we
L C : 0 4 :018(438) [0737] the Word it derives its **nature** as a sacrament, as St.
L C : 0 4 :022(439) [0737] to be emphasized: the **nature** and dignity of this holy
L C : 0 4 :042(442) [0743] so boundless that if timid **nature** considers them, it may
L C : 0 4 :046(442) [0743] suffice concerning the **nature**, benefits, and use of Baptism
L C : 0 4 :066(445) [0749] with all vices and by **nature** has nothing good in him.
L C : 0 4 :071(445) [0749] the inclinations of his **nature** if he is not restrained and
L C : 0 5 :005(447) [0755] the Creed retain their **nature** and value even if we never
L C : 0 5 :056(453) [0767] Then **nature** and reason begin to contrast our
L C : 0 5 :056(453) [0767] Because **nature** and reason see this, such people refuse to
L C : 0 5 :063(454) [0767] **Nature** would like to act in such a way that it may rest
E P : 0 1 :001(466) [0779] sin is man's corrupted **nature**, substance, and essence, or
E P : 0 1 :001(466) [0779] between man's substance, **nature**, essence, body, and soul
E P : 0 1 :001(466) [0779] other hand, so that man's **nature** is one thing and original
E P : 0 1 :001(466) [0779] inheres in the corrupted **nature** and corrupts it, is
E P : 0 1 :002(466) [0779] distinction between man's **nature** and original sin, not
E P : 0 1 :002(466) [0779] sin, but also as we now have our **nature** after the Fall.
E P : 0 1 :002(466) [0779] Even after the fall our **nature** is and remains a creature of
E P : 0 1 :002(466) [0779] distinction between our **nature** and original sin is as great
E P : 0 1 :003(466) [0779] our corrupted human **nature** and original sin militates
E P : 0 1 :005(466) [0781] person this same human **nature**, though without sin, and
E P : 0 1 :005(466) [0781] blood, he himself likewise partook of the same **nature**....
E P : 0 1 :006(466) [0781] Christ has redeemed our **nature** as his creation, sanctifies
E P : 0 1 :007(467) [0781] between the corrupted **nature** itself and the corruption
E P : 0 1 :007(467) [0781] which is in the **nature** and which has corrupted the
E P : 0 1 :007(467) [0781] which is in the nature and which has corrupted the **nature**.
E P : 0 1 :008(467) [0781] corruption of human **nature**, but that it is so deep a
E P : 0 1 :008(467) [0781] Adam's fall man's **nature** and essence are all corrupt."
E P : 0 1 :010(467) [0781] the corruption of our **nature** from the nature itself.
E P : 0 1 :010(467) [0781] the corruption of our nature from the **nature** itself.
E P : 0 1 :010(467) [0781] Then the **nature** which we now bear will arise and live
E P : 0 1 :011(467) [0781] without any kind of corruption of our own **nature**.
E P : 0 1 :012(467) [0781] properties of human **nature**, or the teaching that the cited
E P : 0 1 :013(467) [0783] which asserts that man's **nature** is uncorrupted even after
E P : 0 1 :014(468) [0783] that underneath man's **nature** has retained unimpaired its
E P : 0 1 :016(468) [0783] that the human **nature** and essence in man is not entirely
E P : 0 1 :017(468) [0783] and mingled with human **nature**, as when poison and
E P : 0 1 :018(468) [0783] that therefore not the **nature** of man but only the original
E P : 0 1 :018(468) [0783] the original sin which is in the **nature** is being accused.
E P : 0 1 :019(468) [0783] man's substance, **nature**, and essence, so that no
E P : 0 1 :019(468) [0783] the mind, between man's **nature** itself after the Fall and
E P : 0 1 :020(468) [0783] Luther calls original sin "**nature**-sin," "person-sin,"
E P : 0 1 :020(468) [0783] any distinction man's **nature**, person, or essence itself with
E P : 0 1 :020(468) [0783] which inheres in human **nature**, and the other so-called
E P : 0 1 :021(468) [0783] commits; it inheres in the **nature**, substance, and essence
E P : 0 1 :021(468) [0783] place, nevertheless man's **nature** is corrupted through
E P : 0 1 :022(469) [0785] to observe that the word "**nature**" has several meanings.
E P : 0 1 :022(469) [0785] as when we say, "God has created human **nature**."
E P : 0 1 :022(469) [0785] which inheres in the **nature** or essence of a thing, as when
E P : 0 1 :022(469) [0785] as when we say, "It is the **nature** of a serpent to sting,"
E P : 0 1 :022(469) [0785] to sting," and, "It is the **nature** or quality of a man to
E P : 0 1 :022(469) [0785] or quality of a man to sin," or, "Man's **nature** is sin."
E P : 0 1 :022(469) [0785] Here the word "**nature**" does not mean the substance of
E P : 0 1 :022(469) [0785] but something which inheres in the **nature** or substance.
E P : 0 3 :001(472) [0791] According to which **nature** is Christ our righteousness?
E P : 0 3 :002(473) [0793] before God only according to the human **nature**.
E P : 0 3 :003(473) [0793] according to the divine **nature** alone nor according to the
E P : 0 3 :003(473) [0793] nature alone nor according to the human **nature** alone.
E P : 0 3 :013(474) [0795] our righteousness only according to the divine **nature**, etc.
E P : 0 3 :014(474) [0795] righteousness only according to the human **nature**, etc.
E P : 0 3 :016(475) [0795] but also to his divine **nature** (in so far as it dwells and
E P : 0 5 :008(479) [0803] they fail to learn the true **nature** of sin from the law, and
E P : 0 5 :008(479) [0803] for the first time the real **nature** of their sin, and
E P : 0 6 :004(480) [0805] (that is, their corrupt **nature** and kind), which clings to
E P : 0 7 :012(483) [0811] according to his human **nature**, rules presently and has in
E P : 0 7 :033(485) [0815] such a promise, since the **nature** and properties of his
E P : 0 7 :033(485) [0815] of his assumed human **nature** could neither permit nor
E P : 0 8 :006(487) [0819] divine and the human **nature** are not fused into one
E P : 0 8 :006(487) [0819] that they never become the properties of the other **nature**.
E P : 0 8 :007(487) [0819] properties of the divine **nature** are omnipotence, eternity,
E P : 0 8 :007(487) [0819] etc., which never become properties of the human **nature**.
E P : 0 8 :008(487) [0819] attributes of the human **nature** are to be a corporeal
E P : 0 8 :008(487) [0819] which never become the properties of the divine **nature**.
E P : 0 8 :009(487) [0819] such a kind that neither **nature** has anything in common
E P : 0 8 :011(488) [0821] shared only the name of God with the divine **nature**?
E P : 0 8 :013(488) [0821] but a man whose human **nature** has such a profound and
E P : 0 8 :014(488) [0821] property of the human **nature** which he assumed into the
E P : 0 8 :015(488) [0821] according to his human **nature** is really (that is, in deed
E P : 0 8 :015(488) [0821] womb and his human **nature** was personally united with
E P : 0 8 :016(489) [0821] of a slave (not the human **nature**) and was established in
E P : 0 8 :017(489) [0823] *or property of the human **nature*** but *according to the*
E P : 0 8 :018(489) [0823] or abolish the human **nature** in the person of Christ, or
E P : 0 8 :018(489) [0823] person of Christ, or change the one **nature** into the other.
E P : 0 8 :021(490) [0823] and that the human **nature** has been changed into the
E P : 0 8 :023(490) [0823] not have a true human **nature** with a body and a soul, as
E P : 0 8 :027(490) [0823] 8. That Christ's human **nature** has become an infinite
E P : 0 8 :027(490) [0823] essence, like the divine **nature**; that it is omnipresent in
E P : 0 8 :027(490) [0825] manner as the divine **nature**, because this essential power
E P : 0 8 :027(490) [0825] and communicated to and infused into the human **nature**.
E P : 0 8 :028(490) [0825] 9. That the human **nature** has been raised to the level of,
E P : 0 8 :028(490) [0825] equal to, the divine **nature** in its substance and essence, or
E P : 0 8 :029(490) [0825] 10. That the human **nature** of Christ is locally extended to
E P : 0 8 :029(490) [0825] (something that is not true of the divine **nature** either).
E P : 0 8 :030(490) [0825] property of the human **nature** it is impossible for Christ
E P : 0 8 :031(491) [0825] with the human **nature** in fact, as though it did not
E P : 0 8 :032(491) [0825] at all concern his human **nature**; and that after Christ had
E P : 0 8 :032(491) [0825] anything to do with us according to his human **nature**.
E P : 0 8 :033(491) [0825] who assumed the human **nature**, after he laid aside the
E P : 0 8 :033(491) [0825] and with his human **nature**, but only a few and only at
E P : 0 8 :033(491) [0825] at the place where the human **nature** is locally present.
E P : 0 8 :034(491) [0825] according to the human **nature**, is wholly incapable of
E P : 0 8 :034(491) [0825] of omnipotence and other properties of the divine **nature**.
E P : 0 8 :035(491) [0825] according to his human **nature** Christ has indeed been
E P : 0 8 :035(491) [0825] the exaltation the human **nature** of Christ received a
E P : 0 8 :039(491) [0827] according to the divine **nature**, as though in the state of
S D : P R :009(503) [0849] and they are of such a **nature** that the opinions of the
S D : 0 1 :001(508) [0859] contended that "man's **nature** and essence are wholly
S D : 0 1 :001(508) [0859] ever since the Fall the **nature**, substance, and essence of
S D : 0 1 :001(508) [0859] which has been called "**nature**-sin" or "person-sin"
S D : 0 1 :001(508) [0859] or a deed but the very **nature** itself out of which, as the
S D : 0 1 :001(508) [0859] between man's **nature** or essence and original sin.

Continued ▶

SD : 0 1 :002(508) [0859] speaking, is not man's **nature**, substance, or essence (that
SD : 0 1 :002(508) [0859] sin is something in man's **nature**, in his body, soul, and
SD : 0 1 :002(509) [0859] sin which inheres in his **nature**, all actual sins flow out of
SD : 0 1 :002(509) [0859] distinction between the **nature** and essence of fallen man
SD : 0 1 :002(509) [0859] the devil by which man's **nature** has become corrupted).
SD : 0 1 :003(509) [0861] from the devil's work, the corruption of human **nature**.
SD : 0 1 :005(509) [0861] inherited disease which has corrupted our entire **nature**.
SD : 0 1 :006(509) [0861] Dr. Luther calls this sin "**nature**-sin" or "person-sin" in
SD : 0 1 :006(509) [0861] impossible for human **nature** in this life — nevertheless
SD : 0 1 :006(509) [0861] life — nevertheless man's **nature** and person would still be
SD : 0 1 :006(509) [0861] and entirely poisoned and corrupted human **nature**.
SD : 0 1 :006(509) [0861] fall of the first man, our **nature** or person is under the
SD : 0 1 :006(509) [0861] God, so that we are "by **nature** the children of wrath," of
SD : 0 1 :007(510) [0861] Rather, along with the **nature** which God still creates and
SD : 0 1 :008(510) [0861] and understand the true **nature** of this inherited damage.
SD : 0 1 :009(510) [0861] are children of wrath by **nature**, as St. Paul says
SD : 0 1 :010(510) [0863] to unrenewed human **nature** the gifts and the power, or
SD : 0 1 :011(510) [0863] original sin in human **nature** is not only a total lack of
SD : 0 1 :011(510) [0863] corruption of his entire **nature** in all its powers, especially
SD : 0 1 :011(510) [0863] By **nature** every one of us inherits from Adam a heart,
SD : 0 1 :011(510) [0863] the light of reason, is by **nature** diametrically opposed to
SD : 0 1 :013(511) [0863] the devil, so that human **nature** is subject to the devil's
SD : 0 1 :014(511) [0863] can heal man's **nature**, which original sin has perverted
SD : 0 1 :017(511) [0865] else's action without any corruption of our own **nature**.
SD : 0 1 :018(511) [0865] but concreated and essential attributes of man's **nature**.
SD : 0 1 :020(511) [0865] That human **nature** even after the Fall is incorrupt and,
SD : 0 1 :021(512) [0865] elements in human **nature**, in spite of which and beneath
SD : 0 1 :021(512) [0865] beneath which human **nature** has and retains its goodness
SD : 0 1 :023(512) [0865] teach that, though man's **nature** has been greatly
SD : 0 1 :023(512) [0865] Adam's fall man's **nature** and being are wholly
SD : 0 1 :023(512) [0865] that human **nature** has of and from man's natural birth
SD : 0 1 :025(512) [0867] that man's corrupted **nature** can of and by itself do no
SD : 0 1 :026(512) [0867] since the Fall, human **nature** is initially created perfect
SD : 0 1 :026(512) [0867] essential) into man's **nature**, as when poison is blended
SD : 0 1 :027(512) [0867] of Adam and Eve man's **nature** was originally created
SD : 0 1 :027(512) [0867] sin did not invade their **nature** in such a way that Satan
SD : 0 1 :027(513) [0867] blended this with their **nature**, as the Manichaeans
SD : 0 1 :027(513) [0867] and corrupted human **nature** (as was indicated above)
SD : 0 1 :027(513) [0867] a mother, now inherit a **nature** with the same lack and
SD : 0 1 :028(513) [0867] For since the Fall human **nature** is not at first created
SD : 0 1 :028(513) [0867] from man's corrupted **nature**, just as it is not itself the
SD : 0 1 :029(513) [0867] sin and the human **nature** that has been thereby corrupted
SD : 0 1 :029(513) [0867] in such a way that man's **nature** is allegedly pure, holy,
SD : 0 1 :030(513) [0867] and condemn man's **nature**, corrupted by sin, but only
SD : 0 1 :030(513) [0867] of original sin, the whole **nature** of every human being
SD : 0 1 :030(513) [0867] imparted at creation to our **nature** in paradise.
SD : 0 1 :030(513) [0867] not mean that human **nature** has been totally destroyed,
SD : 0 1 :030(513) [0867] different from our **nature** and accordingly not coessential
SD : 0 1 :031(513) [0869] man's entire corrupted **nature** unless the sin is forgiven
SD : 0 1 :032(513) [0869] and condemns our **nature**, not because we are human
SD : 0 1 :032(513) [0869] and in so far as our **nature** and essence are the work, the
SD : 0 1 :032(513) [0869] and in so far as our **nature** has been poisoned and
SD : 0 1 :033(514) [0869] corrupted man's whole **nature** that within the corrupted
SD : 0 1 :033(514) [0869] that within the corrupted **nature** we are not able to point
SD : 0 1 :033(514) [0869] point out and expose the **nature** by itself and original sin
SD : 0 1 :033(514) [0869] our corrupted **nature** or the essence of corrupted man,
SD : 0 1 :033(514) [0869] original sin, by which the **nature**, essence, or total man is
SD : 0 1 :033(514) [0869] (which dwells in man's **nature** or essence and corrupts it).
SD : 0 1 :033(514) [0869] between (a) our **nature** as it is created and preserved by
SD : 0 1 :033(514) [0869] and (b) original sin itself which dwells in the **nature**.
SD : 0 1 :034(514) [0869] that God created human **nature** before the Fall, but also
SD : 0 1 :034(514) [0869] that after the Fall human **nature** is God's creature and
SD : 0 1 :039(515) [0871] our present human **nature**, which is so miserably
SD : 0 1 :041(515) [0871] whatever between the **nature** and essence of our body and
SD : 0 1 :041(515) [0871] sin itself (by which our **nature** is corrupted), we should be
SD : 0 1 :041(515) [0871] is the creator of this our **nature**, he has created and made
SD : 0 1 :041(515) [0871] is the creator of our **nature**, our body and soul, which
SD : 0 1 :041(515) [0871] creature if our corrupted **nature** were unqualifiedly
SD : 0 1 :042(515) [0873] But the fact that our **nature** is corrupted, that our
SD : 0 1 :043(515) [0873] God's Son assumed our **nature**, though without sin, so
SD : 0 1 :043(516) [0873] to his assumed human **nature** Christ is of one and the
SD : 0 1 :043(516) [0873] because the human **nature** which he assumed is in its
SD : 0 1 :044(516) [0873] no difference between the **nature** or essence of corrupted
SD : 0 1 :044(516) [0873] either did not assume our **nature** inasmuch as he did not
SD : 0 1 :044(516) [0873] Christ assumed sin inasmuch as he assumed our **nature**.
SD : 0 1 :044(516) [0873] God's Son assumed our **nature**, but not original sin, it is
SD : 0 1 :044(516) [0873] after the Fall human **nature** and original sin are not
SD : 0 1 :048(516) [0875] original sin is the very **nature** of corrupted man, its
SD : 0 1 :048(517) [0875] between our corrupted **nature** or substance or being and
SD : 0 1 :048(517) [0875] a distinction between the **nature** or substance of man,
SD : 0 1 :051(517) [0875] "God creates man's **nature**," the word "nature" means
SD : 0 1 :051(517) [0875] man's nature," the word "**nature**" means man's essence,
SD : 0 1 :051(517) [0875] "It is the serpent's **nature** to bite and poison," the term
SD : 0 1 :051(517) [0875] and poison," the term "**nature**" means — as it often does
SD : 0 1 :051(517) [0875] that sin and sinning are man's disposition and **nature**.
SD : 0 1 :052(517) [0875] deep corruption of our **nature** as it is described in the
SD : 0 1 :052(517) [0875] say, "Your birth, your **nature**, your entire essence is sin,
SD : 0 1 :053(517) [0875] that he uses the terms "**nature**-sin," "person-sin,"
SD : 0 1 :053(517) [0877] are sin but that the entire **nature**, person, and essence of
SD : 0 1 :055(518) [0877] statement, "Original sin is the **nature** or essence of man."
SD : 0 1 :056(518) [0877] Original sin is not man's **nature** itself, but an accidental
SD : 0 1 :056(518) [0877] itself, but an accidental defect and damage in the **nature**.
SD : 0 1 :060(519) [0879] a corruption of human **nature** that nothing pure nor good
SD : 0 1 :061(519) [0879] God's handiwork, our **nature** in spite of its being
SD : 0 1 :062(519) [0879] not simply sully human **nature** but corrupted it so deeply
SD : 0 1 :062(519) [0879] head, inasmuch as this befell a hitherto perfect **nature**."
SD : 0 2 :005(521) [0881] and salvation, he is by **nature** blind and does not and
SD : 0 2 :007(521) [0883] perverse disposition and **nature** the natural free will is
SD : 0 2 :017(524) [0887] that by disposition and **nature** he is thoroughly wicked,
SD : 0 2 :022(525) [0889] and corrupted human **nature** should again become and be
SD : 0 2 :022(525) [0889] capability — our human **nature** is in recalcitrant enmity
SD : 0 3 :003(539) [0917] is our righteousness only according to his human **nature**.
SD : 0 3 :004(540) [0917] according to the divine **nature** alone or according to the
SD : 0 3 :004(540) [0917] according to the human **nature** alone but according to
SD : 0 3 :022(543) [0923] sins which throughout this life still inhere in our **nature**.
SD : 0 3 :022(543) [0923] of their corrupted **nature**, they are still sinners and remain
SD : 0 3 :029(544) [0925] works, since the very **nature** of this article cannot admit
SD : 0 3 :055(549) [0935] neither upon his divine **nature** nor upon his human
SD : 0 3 :055(549) [0935] nor upon his human **nature** but upon the entire person of
SD : 0 3 :056(549) [0935] and had in his human **nature** alone fulfilled all
SD : 0 3 :056(549) [0935] passion of the human **nature** could not be reckoned to us
SD : 0 3 :056(549) [0935] become man, the divine **nature** alone could not have been
SD : 0 3 :056(549) [0935] the passion of the human **nature** alone, without the divine
SD : 0 3 :056(549) [0935] alone, without the divine **nature**, could render satisfaction
SD : 0 3 :058(550) [0937] the divine nor the human **nature** of Christ by itself is
SD : 0 3 :058(550) [0937] which inheres in our **nature**, in its thoughts, words, and
SD : 0 3 :060(550) [0937] before God only according to his divine **nature**;
SD : 0 3 :061(550) [0937] is our righteousness only according to his human **nature**.
SD : 0 3 :063(550) [0937] but also to his divine **nature** in so far as it dwells and
SD : 0 4 :008(552) [0941] because of our corrupted **nature** and because the person
SD : 0 5 :017(561) [0957] to be disposed in his **nature**, thoughts, words, and deeds
SD : 0 5 :020(561) [0959] it, his corrupted **nature**, thoughts, words, and deeds war
SD : 0 6 :006(564) [0965] such a way that in their **nature** and all its powers they
SD : 0 6 :007(565) [0965] Adam still clings to their **nature** and to all its internal and
SD : 0 7 :004(569) [0973] according to his divine **nature**, but not with his body and
SD : 0 7 :006(570) [0973] according to his divine **nature** and is not true of his body
SD : 0 7 :036(575) [0985] into the human **nature** but that both untransformed
SD : 0 7 :076(583) [0999] but are ever efficacious in **nature** and make things grow
SD : 0 7 :102(587) [1007] not know; it transcends **nature** and reason, even the
SD : 0 7 :119(590) [1013] can or wills to be with us on earth with his human **nature**.
SD : 0 7 :120(590) [1013] the Supper because the **nature** and properties of his
SD : 0 7 :120(590) [1013] of his assumed human **nature** neither permit nor allow
SD : 0 8 :004(592) [1017] attributed to the human **nature** in the person of Christ
SD : 0 8 :006(592) [1017] come, he took the human **nature** into the unity of his
SD : 0 8 :007(592) [1017] Christ each remains in its **nature** and essence through all
SD : 0 8 :008(593) [1017] and confess that in their **nature** and essence the two
SD : 0 8 :008(593) [1017] properties of the one **nature** ever become the essential
SD : 0 8 :009(593) [1017] to the property of the **nature** and of its natural essence),
SD : 0 8 :009(593) [1019] properties of the divine **nature**, which throughout eternity
SD : 0 8 :009(593) [1019] become the essential properties of the human **nature**.
SD : 0 8 :010(593) [1019] properties of the human **nature**, which never will become
SD : 0 8 :010(593) [1019] which never will become properties of the divine **nature**.
SD : 0 8 :011(593) [1019] the incarnation neither **nature** in Christ henceforth
SD : 0 8 :011(593) [1019] and the assumed human **nature**, so that after the
SD : 0 8 :011(593) [1019] not only his divine **nature** but also his assumed human
SD : 0 8 :011(593) [1019] also his assumed human **nature** belong to the total person
SD : 0 8 :012(593) [1019] that the assumed human **nature** in Christ not only
SD : 0 8 :013(594) [1019] when the divine and human **nature** were personally united
SD : 0 8 :019(595) [1021] divine and the human **nature** in the person of Christ is far
SD : 0 8 :019(595) [1021] on the contrary, each **nature** retains its essence and
SD : 0 8 :020(595) [1021] not only the bare human **nature** (whose property it is to
SD : 0 8 :020(595) [1021] to the assumed human **nature**) and, in the words of our
SD : 0 8 :020(595) [1021] died, although the divine **nature** can neither suffer nor
SD : 0 8 :021(595) [1023] who taught that one **nature** must be taken and
SD : 0 8 :023(595) [1023] according to his human **nature** at the right hand of the
SD : 0 8 :025(596) [1023] The human **nature** could not have accomplished this if it
SD : 0 8 :025(596) [1023] united with the divine **nature** and had communion with
SD : 0 8 :026(596) [1023] Hence also the human **nature** has, after the resurrection
SD : 0 8 :026(596) [1023] laying aside the human **nature**, which he retains
SD : 0 8 :026(596) [1023] divine majesty according to the assumed human **nature**.
SD : 0 8 :029(597) [1025] manner with the divine **nature** and installed in the
SD : 0 8 :032(597) [1025] Since it is true that each **nature** retains its essential
SD : 0 8 :032(597) [1025] not separated from one **nature** and poured into the other
SD : 0 8 :032(597) [1025] poured into the other **nature**, the way water is poured
SD : 0 8 :034(597) [1027] partakers of the divine **nature**" (II Pet. 1:4), what kind of
SD : 0 8 :034(597) [1027] in the divine **nature** must that be of which the apostle
SD : 0 8 :036(598) [1027] not only to the respective **nature** as something separate
SD : 0 8 :037(598) [1027] according to which **nature** the property in question is
SD : 0 8 :038(598) [1027] *is the property of one* ***nature*** (for while they mention the
SD : 0 8 :038(598) [1027] by that only the one **nature** and wholly eliminate the
SD : 0 8 :038(598) [1027] wholly eliminate the other **nature**, as if, for instance, only
SD : 0 8 :038(598) [1027] instance, only the human **nature** had suffered for us) and
SD : 0 8 :039(598) [1029] trick and substitutes the human **nature** for Christ.
SD : 0 8 :040(598) [1029] that only the human **nature** suffered for me, then Christ
SD : 0 8 :043(599) [1029] only to the human **nature** and completely excludes them
SD : 0 8 :043(599) [1029] and completely excludes them from the divine **nature**.
SD : 0 8 :043(599) [1029] thing according to this **nature** and the other thing
SD : 0 8 :043(599) [1029] according to the other **nature**, all of which scholars know
SD : 0 8 :044(599) [1031] According to his **nature** God cannot die, but since God
SD : 0 8 :046(600) [1031] or *according to* one **nature** only, but *in, according to,*
SD : 0 8 :046(600) [1031] Chalcedon declares, each **nature** according to its own
SD : 0 8 :047(600) [1031] not only according to one **nature** only, either the divine
SD : 0 8 :049(600) [1031] properties of the divine **nature** in Christ through the
SD : 0 8 :049(600) [1031] nor was the divine **nature** intrinsically diminished or
SD : 0 8 :050(600) [1031] as the assumed human **nature** in the person of Christ is
SD : 0 8 :050(600) [1031] with the deity the human **nature** has nothing else and
SD : 0 8 :050(600) [1031] be ascribed to the human **nature** in Christ which
SD : 0 8 :051(600) [1031] that, because the human **nature** in Christ is personally
SD : 0 8 :051(600) [1031] united with the divine **nature** in Christ, the former (when
SD : 0 8 :051(601) [1033] Christ's office, the human **nature** in Christ is employed
SD : 0 8 :051(601) [1033] might which the human **nature** has received through the
SD : 0 8 :052(601) [1033] with which the human **nature** in Christ is endowed and
SD : 0 8 :052(601) [1033] limit of what the human **nature** in Christ could or should
SD : 0 8 :053(601) [1033] to his assumed human **nature** and of what his assumed
SD : 0 8 :053(601) [1033] what his assumed human **nature** is capable over and
SD : 0 8 :053(601) [1033] not argue that the human **nature** in Christ is not capable
SD : 0 8 :054(601) [1033] true that Christ's human **nature** in and by itself possesses
SD : 0 8 :054(601) [1033] ascribe to the assumed human **nature** in Christ.
SD : 0 8 :056(601) [1035] according to the divine **nature** but also according to the
SD : 0 8 :056(601) [1035] nature but also according to the assumed human **nature**.
SD : 0 8 :057(602) [1035] according to his divine **nature** (according to which he has
SD : 0 8 :057(602) [1035] this in time according to the assumed human **nature**.
SD : 0 8 :059(602) [1035] to his assumed human **nature** when it states, "The blood
SD : 0 8 :059(602) [1035] not only the divine **nature** in Christ but also his blood
SD : 0 8 :060(602) [1035] according to his human **nature** and that it was all given
SD : 0 8 :060(602) [1035] communicated to the assumed human **nature** in Christ.

Continued ▶

SD : 08 :060(602) [1035] the properties of the one **nature** never become the
SD : 08 :060(602) [1035] properties of the other **nature**, we must correctly explain
SD : 08 :061(602) [1035] Christ's assumed human **nature** in the same way in which
SD : 08 :061(602) [1035] according to the divine **nature** so that he is of one essence
SD : 08 :061(602) [1035] according to the divine **nature** is Christ equal with the
SD : 08 :061(602) [1035] according to the assumed human **nature** he is below God.
SD : 08 :061(603) [1037] the way it is in his divine **nature**, that is, as an essential
SD : 08 :062(603) [1037] properties of the divine **nature** into the human nature in
SD : 08 :062(603) [1037] nature into the human **nature** in such a way that the
SD : 08 :062(603) [1037] a way that the human **nature** in Christ has completely laid
SD : 08 :064(603) [1037] Scripture, that the human **nature** in Christ has received
SD : 08 :064(603) [1037] efficacy in the assumed **nature**, spontaneously and when
SD : 08 :066(604) [1039] glory, which is the property of the divine **nature** alone.
SD : 08 :066(604) [1039] *and through* the assumed exalted human **nature** of Christ.
SD : 08 :067(604) [1039] to which the human **nature** of Christ has been exalted
SD : 08 :067(604) [1039] property of the divine **nature** of the Son of God, is to be
SD : 08 :067(604) [1039] according to his divine **nature**, or as if this majesty is in
SD : 08 :067(604) [1039] is in Christ's human **nature** only in such a way that it
SD : 08 :067(604) [1039] and in truth the human **nature** has no share in the divine
SD : 08 :069(604) [1039] according to his human **nature** and other holy people, and
SD : 08 :069(604) [1039] according to his human **nature** he has received above all
SD : 08 :070(605) [1041] according to the human **nature**, "All authority in heaven
SD : 08 :071(605) [1041] into the human **nature** of Christ of such a kind that
SD : 08 :071(605) [1041] that thereby the divine **nature** is weakened or surrenders
SD : 08 :071(605) [1041] and essence the human **nature** allegedly received equal
SD : 08 :071(605) [1041] or divided from the **nature** and essence of the Son of
SD : 08 :071(605) [1041] For the human **nature**, like every other creature in heaven
SD : 08 :071(605) [1041] Thereby Christ's human **nature** would be denied and
SD : 08 :072(605) [1041] to the assumed human **nature** (whence he is called
SD : 08 :072(605) [1041] to his assumed human **nature** (according to the deity he is
SD : 08 :074(606) [1041] with all power in, with, and through the human **nature**.
SD : 08 :075(606) [1043] to his assumed human **nature** many things are unknown
SD : 08 :076(606) [1043] the flesh, according to its **nature** and essence outside of
SD : 08 :078(606) [1043] same assumed human **nature** of his, Christ can be and is
SD : 08 :078(607) [1043] with his assumed human **nature**, according to which he is
SD : 08 :079(607) [1045] in us according to that **nature**, too, according to which he
SD : 08 :080(607) [1045] the majesty of Christ according to the human **nature**.
SD : 08 :087(608) [1047] in his assumed human **nature**, and who can therefore
SD : 08 :087(608) [1047] also according to that **nature** by which he is our brother
SD : 08 :089(609) [1047] union the human **nature** has allegedly been blended with
SD : 08 :090(609) [1047] Likewise, that the human **nature** in Christ is everywhere
SD : 08 :090(609) [1047] through an essential power or property of its **nature**.
SD : 08 :091(609) [1049] Likewise, that the human **nature** in Christ has been
SD : 08 :091(609) [1049] equal to the divine **nature** in its substance and essence or
SD : 08 :092(609) [1049] his true human **nature**, Christ's omnipotence and wisdom
SD : 08 :093(609) [1049] that the mere human **nature** of Christ alone, with which
SD : 08 :094(609) [1049] involve his assumed human **nature** in any way whatever.
SD : 08 :095(609) [1049] that the assumed human **nature** in Christ does not share
SD : 10 :014(613) [1057] adiaphora which in their **nature** and essence are and
SD : 11 :060(626) [1083] Since our **nature** is corrupted by sin and is worthy and
SD : 12 :029(635) [1101] to his assumed human **nature** Christ is a creature.

Natures (69)
PR : PR :020(010) [0017] union of the two **natures** in Christ, our theologians clearly
PR : PR :021(011) [0019] the divine and human **natures**, together with their
AG : 03 :002(029) [0045] Mary, and that the two **natures**, divine and human, are so
AL : 03 :002(029) [0045] So there are two **natures**, divine and human, inseparably
AP : 03 :001(107) [0119] that there are two **natures** in Christ, namely, that the
EP : 03 :001(472) [0791] the divine and human **natures** are personally united to
EP : 03 :003(473) [0793] Christ according to both **natures** is our righteousness
EP : 08 :001(486) [0817] person of Christ, the two **natures** in Christ, and their
EP : 08 :002(487) [0817] do the divine and human **natures**, together with their
EP : 08 :003(487) [0817] the divine and human **natures** are personally united in
EP : 08 :005(487) [0819] divine and human **natures** are personally united in
EP : 08 :009(487) [0819] 5. Since both **natures** are united personally (that is, in one
EP : 08 :009(488) [0819] union and sharing of the **natures** by the analogy of
EP : 08 :010(488) [0819] if the divine and human **natures** did not have a real and
EP : 08 :018(489) [0823] the properties of the two **natures** in Christ and thus he
EP : 08 :018(489) [0823] Nor do we mingle the **natures** and their properties
EP : 08 :021(490) [0823] the divine and human **natures** are mingled into one
EP : 12 :021(499) [0841] and that now both **natures** in Christ possess only one
SD : 03 :004(540) [0917] but according to both **natures**; as God and man he has by
SD : 07 :036(575) [0985] that both untransformed **natures** are personally united.
SD : 07 :037(575) [0985] and untransformed **natures** are indivisibly united, so in
SD : 07 :038(576) [0985] like that of the two **natures** in Christ, but a sacramental
SD : 08 :007(592) [1017] there are two distinct **natures**: the divine, which is from
SD : 08 :007(592) [1017] These two **natures** in the person of Christ will henceforth
SD : 08 :008(593) [1017] and essence the two **natures** referred to remain unmingled
SD : 08 :011(593) [1019] person, but that the two **natures** are united in such a way
SD : 08 :011(593) [1019] the fact that two distinct **natures**, each with its natural
SD : 08 :014(594) [1019] explained it, as if both **natures**, the divine and the
SD : 08 :014(594) [1019] deed and truth the two **natures** allegedly have no
SD : 08 :015(594) [1019] taught that the two **natures** have no communion
SD : 08 :015(594) [1019] would separate the two **natures** from each other and thus
SD : 08 :016(594) [1021] the divine and human **natures** are separated and distinct
SD : 08 :017(594) [1021] the divine and human **natures** in the person of Christ are
SD : 08 :017(594) [1021] each other, by which the **natures** are not blended into one
SD : 08 :019(594) [1021] or equalization of the **natures**, as mead is made out of
SD : 08 :019(595) [1021] of the divine and human **natures** in the person of Christ is
SD : 08 :019(595) [1021] thereby blending the **natures** or their properties; on the
SD : 08 :020(595) [1021] a true communion of the **natures** is unthinkable and
SD : 08 :023(595) [1023] of the divine and human **natures** in Christ, according to
SD : 08 :023(595) [1023] and communion of the **natures** in the person of Christ did
SD : 08 :024(595) [1023] and communion of the **natures**, Mary, the most blessed
SD : 08 :028(596) [1025] equalization of the two **natures** in their essence and
SD : 08 :029(597) [1025] personal union of both **natures** in Christ, the way Jesus,
SD : 08 :030(597) [1025] the divine and human **natures** are personally united in
SD : 08 :031(597) [1025] of the properties of the **natures**) likewise flows from this
SD : 08 :031(597) [1025] the divine and human **natures** are united with each other
SD : 08 :031(597) [1025] blending or equalization of the **natures** in their essence).
SD : 08 :032(597) [1027] union or communion of **natures** in the person of Christ
SD : 08 :035(597) [1027] between the two **natures** be treated and explained with
SD : 08 :035(597) [1027] the person of Christ, its **natures**, and their properties are
SD : 08 :036(598) [1027] in Christ two distinct **natures** are and remain unchanged
SD : 08 :036(598) [1027] and since both **natures** constitute only one person,
SD : 08 :036(598) [1027] only to one of the **natures**, is ascribed not only to the
SD : 08 :037(598) [1027] person is simultaneously the property of both **natures**.
SD : 08 :043(599) [1029] are not ascribed to the **natures** but to the person.
SD : 08 :043(599) [1029] neither confounding the **natures** nor dividing the person."
SD : 08 :046(600) [1031] *with*, and *through* both **natures**, or as the Council of
SD : 08 :047(600) [1031] but according to both **natures**, as we presented this
SD : 08 :048(600) [1031] discussion is this: Do the **natures** in the personal union
SD : 08 :060(602) [1035] we said above, since both **natures** in Christ are united in
SD : 08 :061(603) [1037] we do not confuse, equalize, or abolish the **natures** in
SD : 08 :062(603) [1037] and acts of both **natures** are henceforth of the same kind
SD : 08 :062(603) [1037] or equalization of the **natures** in Christ or of their
SD : 08 :063(603) [1037] which would blend the **natures** in their essence and in
SD : 08 :063(603) [1037] any blending of the **natures** and of their essential
SD : 08 :076(606) [1043] the divine and human **natures** have with each other in
SD : 08 :078(607) [1043] person to which both **natures**, the divine and the human,
SD : 08 :083(607) [1045] had separated the two **natures** from one another and thus
SD : 12 :029(635) [1101] Word, so that the two **natures** of Christ have but one kind

Naught (2)
AL : 20 :040(046) [0057] Thou art not, man hath **naught**, Nothing good in deed or
LC : 03 :070(429) [0717] must fail and come to **naught**, no matter how proud,

Naumburg (4)
PR : PR :008(005) [0009] and some of us gathered at **Naumburg**, in Thuringia.
PR : PR :017(008) [0015] and at **Naumburg** failed to accomplish the desired end of
PR : PR :017(008) [0015] discussions at **Naumburg** reserved to ourselves the right
PR : PR :019(009) [0017] referred to in the **Naumburg** discussions, is concerned, it

Nazareth (1)
SD : 08 :085(608) [1047] To me, Jesus of **Nazareth**, Mary's son, born a human

Nazarites (4)
AP : 27 :058(279) [0439] us the example of the **Nazarites** from the Old Testament.
AP : 27 :058(279) [0439] The ritual of the **Nazarites** was intended to exercise or
AP : 27 :058(279) [0439] now, so the ritual of the **Nazarites** should not be proposed
AP : 27 :058(279) [0439] with the ritual of the **Nazarites**, which had a Word of God

Nazianzus (1)
AP : 16 :006(223) [0331] disturbing to Origen, **Nazianzus**, and others, though they

Near (5), Nearest (1), Nearly (1)
AP : 04 :082(118) [0145] great high priest,...let us then with confidence draw **near**."
AP : 04 :082(118) [0145] By bidding us draw **near** to God with trust not in our
AP : 04 :333(158) [0211] without the high priest we cannot draw **near** to the Father
LC : 01 :200(392) [0637] proceed to the person **nearest** and dearest to him,
LC : 04 :043(442) [0743] crowd of rich men no one else could get **near** him.
SD : 05 :022(562) [0959] urged this distinction in **nearly** all his writings and showed
SD : 07 :101(587) [1007] it again as deep and as **near** in all creatures as God is

Neat (1)
AP : 12 :106(197) [0283] interpretation surely is a **neat** one, worthy of these men

Nebuchadnezzar (1)
EP : 11 :003(494) [0833] made known to King **Nebuchadnezzar** what will be in the

Necessarily (25)
AG : 01 :006(028) [0043] Holy Spirit, are not **necessarily** distinct persons but that
AL : 16 :006(038) [0051] Christians are **necessarily** bound to obey their magistrates
AP : 04 :019(110) [0125] For if God **necessarily** gives grace for the merit of
AP : 04 :114(123) [0155] and keep the law, although love must **necessarily** follow.
AP : 04 :159(129) [0167] From this it **necessarily** follows that we are justified by
AP : 04 :189(133) [0175] For these reasons good works must **necessarily** be done.
AP : 04 :214(136) [0179] that good works must **necessarily** be done since our
AP : 04 :250(143) [0191] faith is a new life, it **necessarily** produces new impulses
AP : 04 :267(146) [0197] sets forth a promise, he **necessarily** requires faith, which
AP : 04 :272(148) [0199] the forgiveness of sins, it **necessarily** requires faith.
AP : 04 :297(153) [0205] that justification must **necessarily** be attributed to faith.
AP : 04 :298(153) [0205] justification must **necessarily** be ascribed to faith.
AP : 07 :017(171) [0231] kingdom of the devil, it **necessarily** follows that since the
AP : 12 :061(190) [0269] of the forgiveness of sins, it **necessarily** requires faith.
AP : 12 :136(203) [0293] Since this **necessarily** follows from our opponents'
AP : 16 :006(223) [0331] to them, just as we are **necessarily** subjected to the laws
AP : 20 :015(229) [0343] conviction that good works must **necessarily** follow faith.
AP : 20 :015(229) [0343] the keeping of the law **necessarily** follows, by which love,
AP : 23 :012(241) [0367] right, the right to contract marriage **necessarily** remains.
AP : 23 :035(244) [0373] Therefore celibacy is not **necessarily** pure.
AP : 24 :090(266) [0415] forgiveness of sins, which **necessarily** implies real guilt.
SD : 01 :019(511) [0865] on that account is **necessarily** a child of wrath and of
SD : 01 :041(515) [0871] soul, which would also **necessarily** have to be Satan's
SD : 03 :027(543) [0923] a fruit which certainly and **necessarily** follows true faith.
SD : 04 :014(553) [0943] works because they **necessarily** follow faith and

Necessary (266)
PR : PR :013(007) [0013] that pertains to and is **necessary** for this end and put it
PR : PR :014(007) [0013] all kinds of Christian, **necessary**, and useful memoranda
PR : PR :017(008) [0015] one or if at any time it might become **necessary** to do so.
PR : PR :024(013) [0023] this salutary and most **necessary** effort toward concord
PR : PR :024(013) [0023] in this salutary, most **necessary**, and Christian effort and
AG : 07 :003(032) [0047] It is not **necessary** for the true unity of the Christian
AG : 09 :001(033) [0047] us that Baptism is **necessary** and that grace is offered
AG : 11 :001(034) [0047] in confession it is not **necessary** to enumerate all
AG : 15 :002(036) [0049] by the notion that such things are **necessary** for salvation.
AG : 20 :022(044) [0055] It was therefore **necessary** to preach this doctrine about
AG : 23 :014(053) [0063] Therefore it is most **necessary**, profitable, and Christian
AG : 23 :016(054) [0063] that it is sometimes **necessary** to relax severity and rigor
AG : 23 :016(054) [0063] would certainly be both Christian and very **necessary**.
AG : 25 :004(062) [0069] how comforting and **necessary** it is for terrified
AG : 25 :005(062) [0069] a word concerning these **necessary** matters but only
AG : 26 :002(064) [0071] as if these were a **necessary** service of God by means of
AG : 26 :010(065) [0071] the other hand, other **necessary** good works were
AG : 26 :012(066) [0073] of the opinion that they were a **necessary** service of God.

Continued ▶

A G : 2 6 :017(066) [0073] they were not to be considered **necessary** observances.
A G : 2 6 :021(067) [0073] they should not be made into a **necessary** service of God.
A G : 2 6 :023(067) [0073] he calls them vain service, they must not be **necessary**.
A G : 2 6 :039(069) [0075] is rejected is making a **necessary** service of fasts on
A G : 2 6 :043(070) [0075] by others that it was not **necessary** to maintain uniformity
A G : 2 7 :001(070) [0075] monastic vows it is **necessary** to begin by considering
A G : 2 7 :059(080) [0083] such matters it was **necessary** to give the people proper
A G : 2 8 :043(088) [0089] God's grace or as if they were **necessary** for salvation.
A G : 2 8 :050(089) [0091] have been instituted as **necessary** to propitiate God and
A G : 2 8 :051(089) [0091] It is **necessary** to preserve the teaching of Christian liberty
A G : 2 8 :051(089) [0091] to the law is not **necessary** for justification, as St. Paul
A G : 2 8 :053(090) [0091] considering these things **necessary** services of God and
A G : 2 8 :056(090) [0091] that such things are **necessary** for salvation or that it is a
A G : 2 8 :058(091) [0091] of the Sabbath as a **necessary** institution are very much
A G : 2 8 :060(091) [0091] because it was **necessary** to appoint a certain day so that
A G : 2 8 :060(091) [0093] neither of the Sabbath nor of any other day is **necessary**.
A G : 2 8 :061(091) [0093] new ceremonies which would be **necessary** for salvation.
A G : 2 8 :064(092) [0093] remains and prevails that their observance is **necessary**.
A G : 2 8 :068(093) [0093] are not to be deemed **necessary** and that disregard of them
A G : 0 0 :005(095) [0095] we have considered it **necessary** to adduce and mention in
A L : 0 6 :001(031) [0045] good fruits and that it is **necessary** to do the good works
A L : 0 7 :003(032) [0047] It is not **necessary** that human traditions or rites and
A L : 0 9 :001(033) [0047] teach that Baptism is **necessary** for salvation, that the
A L : 1 1 :001(034) [0047] of all sins is not **necessary**, for this is not possible
A L : 1 5 :002(036) [0049] as if observances of this kind were **necessary** for salvation.
A L : 2 0 :027(045) [0057] in addition that it is **necessary** to do good works, not that
A L : 2 5 :007(062) [0069] of sins is not **necessary** and that consciences should not
A L : 2 5 :010(063) [0069] an enumeration is not **necessary**, for Chrysostom is
A L : 2 6 :002(064) [0071] these works as a service **necessary** to merit grace and
A L : 2 6 :006(064) [0071] the opinion that it is **necessary** to merit grace and
A L : 2 6 :012(065) [0073] judged these observances to be **necessary** acts of worship.
A L : 2 6 :021(067) [0073] are not to be thought of as **necessary** acts of worship.
A L : 2 6 :039(069) [0075] as if works of this sort were **necessary** acts of worship.
A L : 2 7 :059(080) [0083] Concerning such things it was **necessary** to admonish men
A L : 2 8 :043(088) [0089] appeasing God or as if they were **necessary** for salvation.
A L : 2 8 :050(089) [0091] have been instituted as **necessary** or instituted with the
A L : 2 8 :050(089) [0091] to institute such services or require them as **necessary**.
A L : 2 8 :051(089) [0091] It is **necessary** to preserve the doctrine of Christian liberty
A L : 2 8 :051(089) [0091] to the law is not **necessary** for justification, as it is written
A L : 2 8 :052(089) [0091] It is **necessary** to preserve the chief article of the Gospel,
A L : 2 8 :053(090) [0091] are bound so as to regard these as **necessary** services.
A L : 2 8 :056(090) [0091] suggesting that they are **necessary** for salvation or by
A L : 2 8 :058(091) [0091] the church's authority as a **necessary** thing are mistaken.
A L : 2 8 :060(091) [0091] because it was **necessary** to appoint a certain day so that
A L : 2 8 :060(091) [0093] neither of the Sabbath nor of any other day is **necessary**.
A L : 2 8 :061(091) [0093] new ceremonies which would be **necessary** for salvation.
A L : 2 8 :064(092) [0093] as the opinion remains that their observance is **necessary**.
A L : 2 8 :068(093) [0093] holding them to be **necessary** and that no harm is done to
A L : 0 0 :005(095) [0095] which it seemed **necessary** to say in order that it may be
A P : P R :016(099) [0103] truth that is so clear and **necessary** for the church.
A P : 0 4 :043(113) [0133] Otherwise, why would a promise be **necessary**?
A P : 0 4 :070(116) [0141] promise of Christ is **necessary** over and above the law,"
A P : 0 4 :070(116) [0141] we must maintain that the promise of Christ is **necessary**.
A P : 0 4 :075(117) [0143] forgiveness of sins is supremely **necessary** in justification.
A P : 0 4 :118(123) [0155] One can easily see how **necessary** it is to understand this
A P : 0 4 :184(132) [0173] we must add that faith is **necessary**, and that they are
A P : 0 4 :222(137) [0181] anything more from this text than that love is **necessary**.
A P : 0 4 :222(137) [0181] It is also **necessary** not to steal.
A P : 0 4 :222(137) [0181] reason that because it is **necessary** not to steal, therefore
A P : 0 4 :224(138) [0181] Even though these are **necessary**, it would be a foolish
A P : 0 4 :243(141) [0189] This virtue is **necessary** for the preservation of domestic
A P : 0 4 :257(144) [0193] by itself, why would Christ and the Gospel be **necessary**?
A P : 0 4 :257(144) [0193] Therefore it is **necessary** to add the Gospel promise, that
A P : 0 4 :258(144) [0193] he commands these works as **necessary** to the new life.
A P : 0 4 :259(144) [0193] but he requires a new life, which is certainly **necessary**.
A P : 0 4 :280(149) [0201] It is **necessary** to consider passages in their context,
A P : 0 4 :348(160) [0217] Of course, good works are **necessary**.
A P : 0 4 :365(163) [0219] proclamation of rewards and punishments is **necessary**.
A P : 0 4 :397(167) [0227] has condemned a very **necessary** doctrine that all
A P : 0 7 :009(169) [0229] We set forth this doctrine for a very **necessary** reason.
A P : 0 7 :021(172) [0233] why will faith be **necessary** if sacraments justify *ex opere*
A P : 0 7 :030(174) [0237] It is not **necessary** that human traditions or rites and
A P : 0 7 :031(174) [0237] rites, whether universal or particular, is not **necessary**.
A P : 0 7 :032(174) [0239] traditions are devotions **necessary** for meriting
A P : 0 7 :034(175) [0239] is an act of worship **necessary** for righteousness before
A P : 0 7 :034(175) [0239] we decide whether it is **necessary** for the true unity of the
A P : 0 7 :034(175) [0239] are not acts of worship **necessary** for righteousness before
A P : 0 7 :034(175) [0239] not a devotion to God **necessary** for righteousness before
A P : 0 7 :036(175) [0241] not believe that they are **necessary** for righteousness
A P : 0 7 :037(175) [0241] But it is not **necessary** to cite a great deal of evidence
A P : 0 7 :037(175) [0241] are acts of devotion **necessary** for righteousness before
A P : 0 7 :039(176) [0241] or that such rites are **necessary** for righteousness before
A P : 0 7 :040(176) [0241] such observance was **necessary** for justification but to let
A P : 0 7 :041(176) [0241] as something **necessary** for justification, why did the
A P : 0 7 :045(177) [0243] of God if they regard as **necessary** a uniformity of
A P : 0 7 :046(177) [0243] universal ordinances are **necessary**, why do they change
A P : 0 9 :001(178) [0245] confess that Baptism is **necessary** for salvation; children
A P : 0 9 :001(178) [0245] is not useless but is **necessary** and efficacious for
A P : 0 9 :002(178) [0245] Therefore it is **necessary** to baptize children, so that the
A P : 1 1 :006(181) [0251] are discussing what is **necessary** according to divine law.
A P : 1 1 :006(181) [0251] enumeration of sins is **necessary** to obtain their
A P : 1 1 :008(181) [0251] is not an act of worship **necessary** for justification.
A P : 1 1 :010(182) [0253] enumeration of sins was **necessary** by divine law and yet
A P : 1 2 :003(182) [0253] godly, salutary, and **necessary** for the universal church of
A P : 1 2 :023(185) [0257] our opponents command it, is **necessary** by divine right.
A P : 1 2 :024(185) [0257] satisfactions are **necessary** to redeem the punishment of
A P : 1 2 :060(190) [0269] that this faith is really **necessary** for the forgiveness of
A P : 1 2 :080(194) [0275] Therefore it is **necessary** for the contrite by faith to take
A P : 1 2 :102(197) [0281] that we do not believe that it is **necessary** by divine right.
A P : 1 2 :110(198) [0285] of sins in confession is **necessary** by divine right, they will
A P : 1 2 :111(198) [0285] complete confession is **necessary** for salvation; this is
A P : 1 2 :113(199) [0285] because they are not **necessary** for the forgiveness of sins
A P : 1 2 :116(199) [0285] satisfactions are not **necessary** by divine law for the
A P : 1 2 :116(199) [0287] penitence were not **necessary** by divine law for the
A P : 1 2 :147(205) [0297] satisfactions are not **necessary** by divine law to remit
A P : 1 2 :148(205) [0297] or punishment is **necessary** for penitence because
A P : 1 2 :148(205) [0299] or punishment is **necessary** for penitence, but not as a
A P : 1 2 :167(208) [0303] that this discipline was **necessary** for the remission either
A P : 1 2 :169(209) [0305] Civil restitution is **necessary**, as it is written (Eph. 4:28),
A P : 1 2 :171(209) [0305] regard these canons as **necessary** for the forgiveness of
A P : 1 3 :006(212) [0309] does not require as **necessary** for salvation since they do
A P : 1 3 :018(213) [0313] It is much more **necessary** to know how to use the
A P : 1 5 :018(217) [0319] justification such rites are not only useful but **necessary**.
A P : 1 5 :018(217) [0319] of the church it is not **necessary** that rites instituted by
A P : 1 5 :020(218) [0321] not regard them as useful or **necessary** for justification.
A P : 1 5 :022(218) [0321] is very becoming in the church and is therefore **necessary**.
A P : 1 5 :027(219) [0323] such observances are **necessary** for justification,
A P : 1 5 :029(219) [0323] God, and that they are not **necessary** for justification.
A P : 1 5 :031(219) [0323] though they justified or were **necessary** for justification.
A P : 1 5 :032(219) [0323] Testament ceremonies were **necessary** for the time being.
A P : 1 5 :032(220) [0323] of the law or traditions be regarded as **necessary**.
A P : 1 5 :032(220) [0325] merit justification or are **necessary** for justification, they
A P : 1 5 :034(220) [0325] that they are not **necessary** for justification; that no one
A P : 1 5 :046(221) [0327] the cross, a voluntary kind of exercise is also **necessary**.
A P : 1 5 :049(221) [0329] they are required as **necessary**, they bring exquisite
A P : 1 5 :050(222) [0329] so-called "universal rites" as **necessary** for salvation.
A P : 1 5 :050(222) [0329] neither justify nor are **necessary** over and above the
A P : 2 1 :001(229) [0343] the invocation of the departed saints were also **necessary**.
A P : 2 3 :006(240) [0365] that no discussion is **necessary**, only the judgment of any
A P : 2 3 :013(241) [0367] more, and marriage is **necessary** for a remedy as well as
A P : 2 3 :016(241) [0369] marriage is more **necessary** now than in the state of
A P : 2 3 :041(245) [0375] this does not make it **necessary** to impose perpetual
A P : 2 3 :048(246) [0377] that discipline and restraint of the body are **necessary**.
A P : 2 8 :015(283) [0447] that they must not be **necessary** acts of worship but a
A P : 2 8 :015(283) [0447] though they were commanding **necessary** acts of worship.
A P : 2 8 :016(283) [0447] that they be not regarded as **necessary** acts of worship.
A P : 2 8 :016(283) [0449] the idea that human rites are **necessary** acts of worship.
A P : 2 8 :017(283) [0449] know that they are not **necessary** acts of worship, and yet
A P : 2 8 :018(284) [0449] to assure us, as was **necessary**, that the Word is
A P : 2 8 :021(284) [0449] of God; that they are **necessary** acts of worship; that they
S 1 : P R :012(290) [0459] Besides such **necessary** concerns of the church, there are
S 1 : 0 1 :000(292) [0461] Therefore, it is not **necessary** to treat them at greater
S 2 : 0 2 :006(293) [0463] can obtain what is more **necessary**, more useful, and more
S 2 : 0 2 :018(296) [0467] nor are they **necessary**, because we may obtain
S 2 : 0 3 :001(298) [0471] church, others who are **necessary** for secular government
S 2 : 0 4 :007(299) [0473] suppose that it were **necessary** to have a head, to whom
S 3 : 0 1 :010(303) [0479] Spirit and his gifts are **necessary** for the performance of a
S 3 : 0 3 :043(310) [0491] It is therefore **necessary** to know and to teach that when
T R : 0 0 :002(320) [0503] he declares that it is **necessary** for salvation to believe
T R : 0 0 :006(320) [0505] is that he adds that it is **necessary** to salvation to believe
T R : 0 0 :021(323) [0509] nor would a decree of the emperor have been **necessary**.
T R : 0 0 :024(324) [0511] In addition, it is **necessary** to acknowledge that the keys
T R : 0 0 :024(324) [0511] So it is **necessary** in these passages to regard Peter as the
T R : 0 0 :036(326) [0515] by asserting that it is **necessary** for salvation to believe
T R : 0 0 :057(330) [0521] On the contrary, it is **necessary** to resist him as
T R : 0 0 :067(331) [0523] Wherefore it is **necessary** for the church to retain the
T R : 0 0 :073(332) [0525] Nor is it **necessary** to speak about confirmation or the
T R : 0 0 :077(333) [0527] Wherefore it is not **necessary** to obey the bishops on
T R : 0 0 :082(000) [0529] add my name, if it be **necessary**, to all that I have above
S C : P R :016(340) [0535] ample time, for it is not **necessary** to take up all the parts
S C : P R :020(340) [0537] It is **necessary** to preach about such things.
S C : P R :023(341) [0539] It is not **necessary** to compel him by any law to receive
L C : S P :015(363) [0577] These are the most **necessary** parts of Christian
L C : S P :028(365) [0581] possible manner say about them as much as is **necessary**.
L C : 0 1 :064(373) [0599] we swear properly where it is **necessary** and required.
L C : 0 1 :140(384) [0621] no one will believe how **necessary** is this commandment,
L C : 0 1 :171(388) [0629] it recognized how very **necessary** it is to devote serious
L C : 0 1 :211(393) [0641] estate but also a **necessary** one, and it is solemnly
L C : 0 1 :232(396) [0647] It is **necessary**, therefore, to emphasize and explain it to
L C : 0 1 :275(402) [0659] to reprove evil where it is **necessary** and beneficial.
L C : 0 1 :330(410) [0677] It is useful and **necessary** always to teach, admonish, and
L C : 0 2 :002(411) [0679] Therefore it is as **necessary** to learn this part as it is the
L C : 0 2 :012(412) [0681] to indicate the most **necessary** points, namely, as we have
L C : 0 3 :002(420) [0697] nothing is so **necessary** as to call upon God incessantly
L C : 0 3 :004(420) [0699] part by part, it is very **necessary** to exhort and draw
L C : 0 3 :072(430) [0719] for everything that is **necessary** in order to have and enjoy
L C : 0 3 :089(432) [0723] Therefore it is **necessary** constantly to turn to this petition
L C : 0 3 :093(433) [0725] Meanwhile, a **necessary** but comforting clause is added,
L C : 0 4 :002(436) [0733] ourselves to that which is **necessary** for us to know.
L C : 0 4 :035(441) [0741] are salutary and **necessary** for salvation, and they do not
L C : 0 4 :037(441) [0741] on faith alone as so **necessary** that without it nothing can
L C : 0 5 :014(448) [0755] remain, as is right and **necessary**, then in virtue of them
L C : 0 5 :020(449) [0757] instituted, for it is most **necessary** that we know what we
L C : 0 6 :013(458) [0000] this public, daily, and **necessary** confession, there is also
L C : 0 6 :016(459) [0000] nor preached the very **necessary** second part; it was just
E P : 0 3 :023(475) [0797] way that good works are **necessary** for righteousness and
E P : 0 4 :002(475) [0797] that good works are **necessary** to salvation; that it is
E P : 0 4 :003(476) [0797] concerning the use of the words **"necessary"** and "free."
E P : 0 4 :003(476) [0797] not use the word **"necessary"** when speaking of the new
E P : 0 4 :003(476) [0797] reference to the word **"necessary"** that the new obedience
E P : 0 4 :009(476) [0799] In this sense the words **"necessary,"** "ought," and "must"
E P : 0 4 :010(476) [0799] words "necessity" and **"necessary"** are to be understood as
E P : 0 4 :016(477) [0801] that good works are **necessary** to salvation; likewise, that
E P : 0 4 :018(477) [0801] last times, it is just as **necessary** to exhort people to
E P : 0 4 :018(477) [0801] to remind them how **necessary** it is that they exercise
E P : 0 6 :004(480) [0807] all their powers, it is **necessary** for the law of God
E P : 0 6 :004(480) [0807] This is further **necessary** lest the Old Adam go his own
E P : 0 7 :001(481) [0809] to report as far as **necessary** concerning this controversy
E P : 0 7 :003(482) [0809] this controversy, it is **necessary** to mention, first of all,
E P : 0 8 :036(491) [0825] more than is fitting and **necessary** to perform his office as
E P : 1 0 :010(494) [0831] community of God as **necessary** things, in violation of the
S D : P R :007(505) [0853] reasons are set forth at **necessary** length for renouncing
S D : P R :009(505) [0853] writings, but in the **necessary** and Christian terms and
S D : P R :015(507) [0857] disturb the church) and **necessary** controversy (dissension
S D : P R :020(507) [0857] pious reader, as far as is **necessary**, to compare our
S D : 0 1 :051(517) [0875] about words, it is **necessary** to explain carefully and

Continued ▶

SD : 0 2 :033(527) [0893] Holy Spirit and his grace are **necessary** for good works."
SD : 0 3 :018(542) [0921] of "justification," it is **necessary** to explain the term
SD : 0 3 :024(543) [0923] as if it were a **necessary** or component part of this article,
SD : 0 3 :025(543) [0923] The only essential and **necessary** elements of justification
SD : 0 3 :029(544) [0925] and place where it is **necessary**, namely, when we deal
SD : 0 3 :039(546) [0929] the article of justification as pertinent or **necessary** to it.
SD : 0 3 :043(547) [0931] works along with faith is **necessary** if men are to be
SD : 0 3 :043(547) [0931] of good works is **necessary** in the article of justification,
SD : 0 3 :067(551) [0937] anything more as **necessary** by way of a detailed
SD : 0 4 :001(551) [0939] as "Good works are **necessary** to salvation," and "It is
SD : 0 4 :002(551) [0939] good works are indeed **necessary** — not for salvation,
SD : 0 4 :003(551) [0939] good works are not **necessary** but spontaneous, since they
SD : 0 4 :003(551) [0939] took the contrary view that good works are **necessary**.
SD : 0 4 :004(551) [0939] arose about the words "**necessary**" and "free," especially
SD : 0 4 :004(551) [0939] "necessary" and "free," especially the word "**necessary**."
SD : 0 4 :005(552) [0939] above, new obedience is not **necessary** in the regenerated.
SD : 0 4 :014(553) [0943] whether good works are **necessary** or free, both the
SD : 0 4 :014(553) [0943] these: "Good works are **necessary**"; again, "It is necessary
SD : 0 4 :014(553) [0943] necessary"; again, "It is **necessary** to do good works
SD : 0 4 :014(553) [0943] words like "necessity," "**necessary**," "needful," "should,"
SD : 0 4 :016(554) [0943] Here, however, it is **necessary** to keep a distinction in
SD : 0 4 :016(554) [0943] that when the word "**necessary**" is used in this context, it
SD : 0 4 :021(554) [0943] that good works are **necessary** we must also explain why
SD : 0 4 :021(554) [0945] what causes they are **necessary**, as the Augsburg
SD : 0 4 :022(554) [0945] that good works are **necessary** for the believers' salvation,
SD : 0 4 :027(555) [0945] have them as something **necessary** for salvation;
SD : 0 4 :028(555) [0947] require good works as **necessary** to salvation, we
SD : 0 4 :030(555) [0947] salvation or are **necessary** to preserve faith,
SD : 0 5 :027(563) [0961] to the other, it is **necessary** to urge and to maintain with
SD : 0 6 :004(564) [0963] It is **necessary** to hold this constantly before believers'
SD : 0 6 :010(565) [0965] It is also **necessary** to set forth distinctly what the Gospel
SD : 0 7 :061(580) [0995] useful, salutary, and **necessary** to salvation for all
SD : 0 7 :088(585) [1003] pervert this useful and **necessary** rule and interpret it as
SD : 0 8 :018(594) [1021] the Fathers, if it were **necessary**, and have frequently
SD : 0 8 :039(598) [1027] example, 'Was it not **necessary** that the Christ should
SD : 1 0 :012(613) [1057] works of the law are **necessary** for righteousness and
SD : 1 0 :013(613) [1057] on consciences as **necessary**, even in matters that were in
SD : 1 0 :015(613) [1057] on the church as **necessary** and as though their omission
SD : 1 0 :027(615) [1061] imposed by force on the community of God as **necessary**.
SD : 1 1 :025(620) [1071] following question is **necessary** for the further exposition
SD : 1 1 :036(622) [1075] destroy for us the **necessary** and comforting foundation,
SD : 1 1 :052(625) [1081] This admonition is eminently **necessary**.

Necessity (29), Necessities (7)
PR : PR :024(013) [0021] most acute and urgent **necessity** demands that in the
AG : 2 4 :024(058) [0067] without doubt by the **necessity** of such circumstances,
AG : 2 7 :026(075) [0079] dispensations be granted for **necessities** of men's souls!
AL : 2 7 :034(076) [0081] seems not to follow of **necessity** that the marriages of
AP : 0 2 :033(104) [0113] of original sin is a **necessity**, nor can we know the
AP : 0 4 :011(108) [0123] have declared that by **necessity**—the necessity of
AP : 0 4 :011(108) [0123] that by necessity—the **necessity** of unchanging order, not
AP : 0 4 :275(148) [0199] fruits ought to follow of **necessity**, and so he warns that
AP : 0 7 :044(177) [0243] liberty nor to impose a **necessity** upon consciences, since
AP : 1 2 :175(210) [0307] observance cannot be a **necessity** commanded by divine
AP : 2 4 :012(251) [0387] our works and by the **necessity** of faith to conquer the
S 2 : 0 2 :027(297) [0469] me, not in one particular **necessity** only, but in every kind
S 3 : 1 0 :001(314) [0497] and unity, but not of **necessity**) to ordain and confirm us
TR : 0 0 :067(331) [0523] electing and ordaining ministers must of **necessity** also be.
SC : 0 1 :010(343) [0541] harm, but help and befriend him in every **necessity** of life.
SC : 0 2 :002(345) [0543] abundantly with all the **necessities** of life, protects me
LC : 0 1 :275(402) [0659] **Necessity** requires one to report evil, to prefer charges, to
LC : 0 2 :004(411) [0679] the advantage and **necessity** of the Creed, it is sufficient,
LC : 0 2 :014(412) [0681] the comforts and **necessities** of life — sun, moon, and
LC : 0 3 :038(425) [0707] we are under the great **necessity** of duly honoring his
LC : 0 3 :073(430) [0719] and clothing and other **necessities** for our body, but also
LC : 0 3 :073(430) [0719] properly, there the **necessities** of life are also interfered
LC : 0 5 :041(451) [0763] matter of liberty, not of **necessity**, and that it is enough if
EP : 0 4 :003(476) [0797] it does not flow from **necessity** or coercion but from a
EP : 0 4 :010(476) [0799] regenerated the words "**necessity**" and "necessary" are to
EP : 0 8 :032(491) [0825] and in all our **necessities** only according to his deity, and
SD : PR :010(503) [0849] For that reason **necessity** requires that such controverted
SD : 0 1 :054(518) [0877] of the church, under the **necessity** of explaining this
SD : 0 1 :057(518) [0879] or subsist by itself), then **necessity** compels us to answer
SD : 0 2 :044(529) [0897] question of "absolute **necessity**"), indicates how he
SD : 0 4 :014(553) [0943] "We should and must of **necessity** do good works that
SD : 0 4 :014(553) [0943] itself uses words like "**necessity**," "necessary," "needful,"
SD : 0 4 :017(554) [0943] and I Pet. 5:2, "**necessity**" is used with reference to
SD : 0 6 :006(565) [0965] coercion, or **necessity**, and as the holy angels render God
SD : 1 0 :019(614) [1059] and unity, but not of **necessity**) to ordain and confirm us
SD : 1 1 :048(624) [1079] will assist us in all our **necessities**, grant us patience, give

Neck (8), Necked (1), Necks (2)
PR : PR :022(011) [0019] doctrines and their stiff-**necked** proponents and
AG : 2 6 :027(068) [0073] putting a yoke upon the **neck** of the disciples which
AG : 2 8 :042(088) [0089] Peter forbids putting a yoke on the **neck** of the disciples.
AL : 2 6 :027(068) [0073] putting a yoke upon the **neck** of the disciples which
LC : 0 1 :239(397) [0649] by the scruff of the **neck** so that others took warning.
LC : 0 3 :102(434) [0727] Adam hanging around our **necks**; he goes to work and
LC : 0 3 :115(435) [0731] He breaks many a man's **neck** and drives others to
LC : 0 4 :020(439) [0737] golden chain about his **neck**, yes, the crown on his head,
LC : 0 4 :086(446) [0753] is, as long as we carry the old Adam about our **necks**.
LC : 0 5 :071(454) [0769] which hangs around your **neck** and which is the very
SD : 1 0 :016(613) [1059] fastened around his **neck** and to be drowned in the depth

Need (146), Needed (11), Needful (2), Needing (2), Needless (4), Needs (30), Needy (1)
PR : PR :024(013) [0023] and churches, and to the **needed** consolation and
AG : 2 1 :003(047) [0059] call upon this same Jesus Christ in every time of **need**.
AG : 0 1 :003(056) [0065] to teach the people what they **need** to know about Christ.
AG : 2 4 :023(058) [0067] men expected to get everything they **needed** from God.
AG : 2 5 :009(063) [0069] On this account there is no **need** to compel people to give
AG : 2 6 :019(067) [0073] authority, but dire **need** has compelled them to give
AG : 2 7 :049(079) [0083] things of which we have **need**, and confidently expect help
AG : 2 8 :071(093) [0093] do this, too, in the case of **need**), but they ask only that
AL : 2 0 :003(041) [0053] they urged childish and **needless** works, such as particular
AL : 2 0 :022(044) [0055] Hence there was very great **need** to treat of and to restore
AL : 2 4 :003(056) [0065] for ceremonies are **needed** especially in order that the
AL : 2 4 :033(060) [0067] is administered to those who have **need** of consolation.
AL : 2 6 :019(067) [0073] There was great **need** to warn the churches of these errors
AL : 2 6 :043(070) [0075] by others that such customs **need** not be alike everywhere.
AL : 2 7 :015(073) [0077] is different, and it is **needless** to rehearse what is well
AP : PR :017(099) [0103] articles of Christian doctrine that the church sorely **needs**.
AP : PR :017(099) [0103] We **need** not describe here how they lay hidden under all
AP : 0 2 :010(102) [0107] What **need** is there for the grace of Christ if we can
AP : 0 2 :010(102) [0109] What **need** is there for the Holy Spirit if human powers
AP : 0 2 :031(104) [0113] but on so clear an issue there is no **need** of evidence.
AP : 0 2 :045(106) [0117] nature neutral, but they **need** the grace of Christ to be
AP : 0 4 :002(107) [0121] consciences the abundant consolation that they **need**.
AP : 0 4 :012(109) [0123] and its works, what **need** is there of Christ or of
AP : 0 4 :014(109) [0123] on natural ethics that nothing further **needs** to be added.
AP : 0 4 :033(111) [0129] so clear that they do not **need** an acute understanding but
AP : 0 4 :087(120) [0147] there would be no **need** for Christ and the promise, and
AP : 0 4 :119(123) [0155] And there must **needs** be a proclamation in the church
AP : 0 4 :139(126) [0161] than Christ's power is **needed** for our conflict with the
AP : 0 4 :166(130) [0169] Again, what **need** is there for a long argument?
AP : 0 4 :174(131) [0171] of the law, therefore, we **need** a faith which is sure that
AP : 0 4 :185(132) [0173] "Being sick in itself, an unjust cause **needs** wise remedies."
AP : 0 4 :220(137) [0181] upon being justified, **needed** urging to bear good fruits
AP : 0 4 :221(137) [0181] add the correction: We **need** the faith that we are
AP : 0 4 :232(140) [0185] harmony, to bear, if **need** be, with the crude behavior of
AP : 0 4 :244(142) [0189] excellence; that we do not **need** mercy and Christ, the
AP : 0 4 :253(143) [0193] that works do not **need** Christ, the propitiator.
AP : 0 4 :260(145) [0193] Otherwise what **need** would there be of Christ, what need
AP : 0 4 :260(145) [0193] need would there be of Christ, what **need** of the Gospel?
AP : 0 4 :275(148) [0199] other reason is that we **need** external signs of this
AP : 0 4 :275(148) [0199] since a terrified conscience **needs** manifold consolations.
AP : 0 4 :316(156) [0209] earns eternal life without **needing** Christ, the mediator.
AP : 0 4 :323(157) [0209] that even if we have good works we **need** mercy in them.
AP : 0 4 :325(157) [0211] down the doctrine that we **need** mercy even in our good
AP : 0 4 :357(162) [0219] and eternal life without **needing** mercy or the mediator
AP : 0 4 :358(162) [0219] "reward": therefore we **need** neither Christ the mediator
AP : 0 4 :387(166) [0225] Christians **need** to understand this faith, for it brings the
AP : 0 7 :003(168) [0227] Thus we do not **need** to defend ourselves at any length
AP : 1 2 :006(183) [0255] of contrition, what is the **need** of absolution and what
AP : 1 2 :049(188) [0265] But what **need** is there to cite passages since there are so
AP : 1 2 :074(192) [0273] What more do our opponents **need**?
AP : 1 2 :075(193) [0273] the forgiveness of sins, what **need** is there of the Gospel?
AP : 1 2 :075(193) [0273] What **need** is there of Christ if by our work we achieve
AP : 1 2 :105(197) [0283] consoling consciences, does not **need** an investigation.
AP : 1 2 :113(199) [0285] become antiquated, nor **need** we bring them back because
AP : 1 2 :174(210) [0307] possible generosity to the **needy**, restraint and
AP : 1 3 :007(212) [0311] the new covenant **needed** a priesthood like the Levitical to
AP : 1 3 :008(212) [0311] world and that there is no **need** for additional sacrifices
AP : 1 5 :008(216) [0317] you, for why does anyone **need** Christ if he believes he is
AP : 1 5 :013(216) [0319] What **need** is there of a long discussion?
AP : 1 5 :018(217) [0319] What **need** is there for words in a matter so clear?
AP : 1 8 :009(226) [0337] Holy Spirit; and it points out the **need** for the Holy Spirit
AP : 2 0 :005(227) [0339] There is no **need** for proofs to anyone who knows that
AP : 2 3 :013(241) [0367] Now it **needs** a remedy even more, and marriage is
AP : 2 3 :061(247) [0381] marriage for those who **need** it, but it does not force
AP : 2 4 :013(251) [0387] secure whatever they **need** in this life, and even free the
AP : 2 4 :028(254) [0393] mercy and help you, for I do not **need** your sacrifices.
AP : 2 4 :082(264) [0411] supplies what the saints **need** but also causes many to
AP : 2 4 :082(264) [0411] a "minister to my **need**," which surely does not mean a
AP : 2 4 :092(266) [0417] There is no **need** here of a very lengthy discussion.
AP : 2 4 :092(266) [0417] If the **need** ever arises, we shall discuss this whole issue
AP : 2 7 :034(275) [0431] Although they **need** mercy themselves, they wickedly
AP : 2 8 :024(285) [0451] truth which the church **needs**, nor can we agree with our
S 1 : PR :010(290) [0457] Not that we ourselves **need** such a council, for by God's
S 1 : PR :012(290) [0459] there are countless temporal matters that **need** reform.
S 2 : 0 2 :009(294) [0465] to meet his own private **need** and thus trifle with it
S 2 : 0 2 :026(297) [0469] them as helpers in time of **need**, and attribute all sorts of
S 2 : 0 2 :027(297) [0469] one particular necessity only, but in every kind of **need**.
S 2 : 0 3 :002(298) [0471] it causes dangerous and **needless** effort, and accordingly
S 2 : 0 4 :004(299) [0473] have everything that is **needful** for salvation, this is
S 3 : 0 1 :009(302) [0477] the sacrament there is no **need** of a good intention to do
S 3 : 0 3 :028(308) [0487] that they were more than we ourselves **needed** for heaven.
S 3 : 0 3 :029(308) [0487] Such persons did not **need** to repent, for what were they
S 3 : 0 3 :031(308) [0487] there are others who suppose, "We **need** no repentance."
S 3 : 0 3 :032(308) [0487] Both of you **need** the forgiveness of sins, for neither of
S 3 : 0 3 :032(308) [0489] who think you do not **need** to repent, you brood of
S 3 : 0 3 :036(309) [0489] We **need** not spend our time weighing, distinguishing,
S 3 : 0 6 :002(311) [0493] We **need** not resort to the specious learning of the
S 3 : 0 8 :001(312) [0495] young people who **need** to be examined and instructed in
TR : 0 0 :073(332) [0525] There is no **need**, therefore, for discussion of the other
TR : 0 0 :076(333) [0525] abused it, there is no **need**, on account of this
TR : 0 0 :080(334) [0527] defraud the church, which **needs** these means for the
SC : PR :021(340) [0537] Here, too, there is **need** of exhortation, but with this
SC : PR :023(341) [0539] hand, he suggests that he **needs** no grace, no life, no
SC : PR :023(341) [0539] that is evil and was in **need** of so much that is good, he
SC : PR :024(341) [0539] All you **need** to do is clearly to set forth the advantage
SC : PR :024(341) [0539] acknowledge their great **need** and God's gracious help
SC : 0 1 :004(342) [0539] but in every time of **need** call upon him, pray to him,
SC : 0 3 :014(347) [0547] to satisfy our bodily **needs**, such as food and clothing,
LC : PR :008(359) [0569] They **need** not fear a fall, for they have already fallen all
LC : PR :008(359) [0569] What they **need** is to become children and begin learning
LC : PR :013(360) [0571] Not only do we **need** God's Word daily as we need our
LC : PR :013(360) [0571] God's Word daily as we **need** our daily bread; we also
LC : PR :014(360) [0571] He knows our danger and **need**.
LC : PR :016(361) [0573] that we know it all and **need** not read or study it any
LC : 0 1 :002(365) [0581] good and in which we find refuge in every time of **need**.
LC : 0 1 :004(365) [0581] one who will satisfy you and help you out of every **need**.
LC : 0 1 :005(365) [0581] God and everything he **needs** when he has money and
LC : 0 1 :011(366) [0583] saint and worshiped and invoked him in time of **need**.
LC : 0 1 :041(370) [0591] blessing and will protect and help you in every **need**?
LC : 0 1 :047(371) [0593] of an inn, food, and bed (only for his temporal **need**).
LC : 0 1 :055(372) [0595] Of this there is no **need** to speak further.

Continued ▶

LC : 0 1 :064(373) [0599] on his name in time of **need**, or praise and thank him in
LC : 0 1 :073(374) [0601] have — for his protection against every conceivable **need**.
LC : 0 1 :083(376) [0603] well informed Christians, for these have no **need** of them.
LC : 0 1 :083(376) [0603] We keep them, first, for the sake of bodily **need**.
LC : 0 1 :087(376) [0605] In itself the day **needs** no sanctification, for it was created
LC : 0 1 :099(378) [0609] feel that they know it all and **need** no more instruction.
LC : 0 1 :102(379) [0609] if no other interest or **need** drove us to the Word, yet
LC : 0 1 :112(380) [0613] there would have been no **need** to institute monasticism
LC : 0 1 :161(387) [0627] Yet there is **need** to impress upon the common people
LC : 0 1 :173(388) [0629] otherwise God would have no **need** of father and mother.
LC : 0 1 :174(388) [0631] so that they may be of service wherever they are **needed**.
LC : 0 1 :183(389) [0631] The occasion and **need** for this commandment is that, as
LC : 0 1 :191(391) [0635] counsel and aid to men in **need** and in peril of body and
LC : 0 1 :203(392) [0639] he is in danger or **need**, and on the contrary to aid and
LC : 0 1 :248(398) [0651] But it **needs** to be impressed upon the young people so
LC : 0 1 :253(399) [0653] he is sufficient for your **needs** and will let you lack or
LC : 0 1 :287(403) [0663] and mouth; we do not **need** to, for they are our most
LC : 0 1 :294(404) [0665] these commandments **needed** because under the Jewish
LC : 0 1 :332(410) [0677] Commandments, and no one **need** search far for them.
LC : 0 2 :003(411) [0679] to be kept, we would **need** neither the Creed nor the
LC : 0 2 :024(413) [0683] is all that ordinary people **need** to learn at first, both
LC : 0 2 :031(414) [0687] of these things for himself, nor had he any **need** of them.
LC : 0 2 :054(417) [0693] Forgiveness is **needed** constantly, for although God's
LC : 0 3 :005(420) [0699] the holy name and pray or call upon it in every **need**.
LC : 0 3 :006(421) [0699] prayers we teach that there is no duty or **need** to pray.
LC : 0 3 :008(421) [0699] Commandment teaches, is to call upon God in every **need**
LC : 0 3 :022(423) [0703] he is concerned over our **needs**, and we shall never doubt
LC : 0 3 :024(423) [0703] we should reflect on our **needs**, which ought to drive and
LC : 0 3 :025(423) [0705] in his promise, or out of consideration for his own **needs**.
LC : 0 3 :026(424) [0705] We must feel our **need**, the distress that impels and drives
LC : 0 3 :026(424) [0705] should, and we shall not **need** to be taught how to
LC : 0 3 :027(424) [0705] The **need** which ought to be the concern of both ourselves
LC : 0 3 :027(424) [0705] We all have **needs** enough, but the trouble is that we do
LC : 0 3 :027(424) [0705] lament and express your **needs** and wants, not because he
LC : 0 3 :028(424) [0705] up to pray daily for all his **needs**, whenever he is aware of
LC : 0 3 :034(425) [0707] are comprehended all the **needs** that continually beset us,
LC : 0 3 :047(426) [0709] See, then, what a great **need** there is for this kind of
LC : 0 3 :060(428) [0715] But there is just as great **need** that we keep firm hold of
LC : 0 3 :061(428) [0715] good government there is **need** not only for good builders
LC : 0 3 :067(429) [0717] there is just as much **need** in this case as in every other
LC : 0 3 :072(430) [0717] poor bread-basket — the **needs** of our body and our life
LC : 0 3 :073(430) [0717] in this world; only for its sake do we **need** daily bread.
LC : 0 3 :074(430) [0719] Indeed, the greatest **need** of all is to pray for our civil
LC : 0 3 :082(431) [0721] he cares for us in all our **needs** and faithfully provides for
LC : 0 3 :088(432) [0723] Here again there is great **need** to call upon God and pray,
LC : 0 3 :091(432) [0723] reach the point where he does not **need** this forgiveness.
LC : 0 4 :078(446) [0751] But we **need** not again have the water poured over us.
LC : 0 5 :039(451) [0761] sacrament, there is great **need** also of an admonition and
LC : 0 5 :040(451) [0763] were such strong Christians that they have no **need** of it.
LC : 0 5 :043(451) [0763] to see the reason and the **need** for receiving the
LC : 0 5 :047(452) [0765] opportunity and **need**, being bound to no special place or
LC : 0 5 :049(452) [0765] be a Christian; then you **need** not believe or pray, for the
LC : 0 5 :052(452) [0765] nor compel anyone, nor **need** anyone partake of the
LC : 0 5 :071(454) [0769] be impelled by your own **need**, which hangs around your
LC : 0 5 :071(455) [0769] who are well have no **need** of a physician, but those who
LC : 0 5 :074(455) [0771] and upright, you have no **need** of me and I have no need
LC : 0 5 :074(455) [0771] you have no need of me and I have no **need** of you."
LC : 0 5 :075(455) [0771] I do if I cannot feel this **need** or experience hunger and
LC : 0 5 :076(455) [0771] If you cannot feel the **need**, therefore, at least believe the
LC : 0 5 :079(455) [0771] do not think that there will be any lack of sins and **needs**.
LC : 0 5 :081(456) [0773] making you unable to feel your **needs** or come to Christ.
LC : 0 5 :083(456) [0773] you have all the more **need** to lament both to God and to
LC : 0 5 :084(456) [0773] Then your **need** will become apparent, and you will
LC : 0 5 :084(456) [0773] sinner and are much in **need** of the sacrament to combat
LC : 0 6 :005(457) [0000] acting as if they will never **need** or desire to go to
LC : 0 6 :011(458) [0000] provoked another to anger and **needs** to beg his pardon.
LC : 0 6 :014(458) [0000] two but is left to everyone to use whenever he **needs** it.
LC : 0 6 :019(459) [0000] must do is to lament your **need** and allow yourself to be
LC : 0 6 :021(459) [0000] and coercion since we have no **need** of them.
LC : 0 6 :022(459) [0000] confess and express your **needs**, not for the purpose of
LC : 0 6 :023(459) [0000] and meanwhile if the **needs** which ought to move and
LC : 0 6 :023(459) [0000] indicated, there would be no **need** of coercion and force.
LC : 0 6 :023(460) [0000] a certain place; he would **need** no bailiff to drive and beat
LC : 0 6 :027(460) [0000] who feels his misery and **need** will develop such a desire
LC : 0 6 :028(460) [0000] be despised, especially when we consider our great **need**.
LC : 0 6 :028(460) [0000] you are a Christian, you **need** neither my compulsion nor
EP : 1 2 :006(498) [0839] Baptism (which according to this view they do not **need**).
SD : PR :015(506) [0857] distinction between **needless** and unprofitable contentions
SD : 0 2 :020(524) [0889] affecting the nurture and **needs** of the body, man is indeed
SD : 0 4 :014(553) [0943] "necessity," "necessary," "**needful**," "should," and "must"
SD : 0 7 :070(582) [0997] who are well have no **need** of a physician, but those who
SD : 0 8 :040(599) [1029] Saviour for me, in fact, he himself would **need** a Saviour.
SD : 0 8 :053(601) [1033] to us as much as we **need** to know in this life, and
SD : 1 1 :080(629) [1089] his will, he would not have **needed** any long-suffering.
SD : 1 2 :011(634) [1099] will be saved without Baptism, which they do not **need**.

Needle (1)
LC : 0 1 :047(371) [0593] as a cobbler uses his **needle**, awl, and thread (for work,

Nefarious (1)
TR : 0 0 :036(326) [0515] to these impious and **nefarious** opinions by asserting that

Negated (1), Negates (1)
PR : PR :021(011) [0019] is equalized with the divine nature and is thus **negated**.
AP : 2 4 :057(260) [0405] This notion completely **negates** the merit of Christ's

Neglect (11), Neglected (13), Neglecting (1), Neglects (3)
AG : 2 0 :008(042) [0053] Christian life, has been **neglected** so long (as all must
AG : 2 6 :015(066) [0073] such efforts that they **neglected** all wholesome Christian
AL : 2 0 :008(042) [0053] has so long been **neglected** (for everybody must grant
AP : 0 4 :377(165) [0223] of faith dare not be **neglected** in the church of Christ;
AP : 1 2 :106(197) [0283] of his holdings that he **neglects** the fear of God or faith or
AP : 1 2 :163(208) [0303] the penalty for their **neglect** of grammar when they
AP : 1 2 :178(211) [0307] our opponents have **neglected** to teach the faith that
AP : 1 3 :002(211) [0309] we have the duty not to **neglect** any of the rites and
AP : 2 8 :003(281) [0443] Meanwhile they **neglect** the state of the churches, and
S1 : PR :006(289) [0457] not, many souls that might have been saved are **neglected**.
S2 : 0 2 :018(296) [0467] Why do they **neglect** their own parishes, the Word of
S3 : 0 1 :002(302) [0477] pray and call upon God, **neglect** of God's Word,
S3 : 0 8 :002(312) [0495] keys, it should not be **neglected**; on the contrary, it should
TR : 0 0 :034(325) [0513] The ministry of the Gospel was **neglected**.
TR : 0 0 :082(334) [0527] the churches for luxuries and would **neglect** the ministry.
SC : PR :004(338) [0533] you have so shamefully **neglected** the people and paid no
SC : PR :019(340) [0537] do not do so, for by such **neglect** they undermine and lay
SC : PR :023(341) [0539] is good, he would not **neglect** the sacrament in which aid
SC : 0 5 :020(350) [0553] you have stolen, **neglected**, or wasted anything, or done
SC : 0 5 :022(350) [0553] caused him to curse, **neglected** to do my duty, and caused
SC : 0 5 :024(350) [0555] And I **neglected** this or that," etc.
LC : 0 1 :096(378) [0607] in their greed or frivolity **neglect** to hear God's Word or
LC : 0 1 :140(384) [0621] he makes God when he **neglects** this commandment, and
LC : 0 1 :144(385) [0623] in the past have been **neglected** and despised; instead,
LC : 0 1 :171(388) [0629] and punish us for its **neglect**, nor is it recognized how
LC : 0 1 :225(395) [0645] a servant wastes and **neglects** things to the vexation and
LC : 0 1 :312(407) [0671] fashioned while they **neglect** these commandments as if
LC : 0 5 :067(454) [0769] so distantly toward it, **neglecting** it so long that we grow

Negligent (8), Negligence (2)
AG : 2 8 :029(085) [0087] when bishops are **negligent** in the performance of such
AL : 2 4 :015(057) [0065] By their own **negligence** they let many corruptions creep
AL : 2 8 :029(085) [0087] When the bishops are **negligent** in the performance of
AP : 2 1 :040(235) [0355] that the ignorance and **negligence** of the pastors permitted
TR : 0 0 :077(333) [0527] to make these decisions if the bishops are **negligent**.
SC : PR :025(341) [0539] can they be other than **negligent** if you fail to do your
LC : PR :001(358) [0567] and preachers are very **negligent** in this respect and
LC : 0 1 :176(389) [0631] you do when you are **negligent** in this respect and fail to
LC : 0 3 :027(424) [0705] impress upon us not to become **negligent** about praying.
SD : 0 6 :012(566) [0967] of the flesh they are lazy, **negligent**, and recalcitrant, the

Negotiations (3)
AG : PR :012(026) [0041] and charitable **negotiations** take place between us, and if
AG : PR :023(027) [0043] these or any following **negotiations** (unless the matters in
AP : PR :003(098) [0099] During the **negotiations** that followed, it was clear that

Neighbor (93), Neighboring (3), Neighbors (16)
AG : 2 0 :037(046) [0057] in suffering, love one's **neighbor**, diligently engage in
AP : 0 4 :125(124) [0157] we also begin to love our **neighbor** because our hearts
AP : 0 4 :167(130) [0169] Who loves his **neighbor** as himself?
AP : 0 4 :226(138) [0183] about love to our **neighbor**, and he indicates that love is
AP : 0 4 :226(138) [0183] the love of God and **neighbor** is the greatest virtue
AP : 0 4 :231(139) [0183] He is obviously discussing love of our **neighbor**.
AP : 0 4 :238(140) [0187] here about love to the **neighbor**, for he connects this
AP : 0 4 :289(151) [0203] and "You shall love your **neighbor**" (Lev. 19:18).
AP : 0 4 :293(152) [0203] practice chastity, love toward our **neighbor**, and so forth.
AP : 0 7 :031(174) [0239] of God, the love of our **neighbor**, and the works of love.
AP : 0 7 :036(175) [0241] Holy Spirit (like love of **neighbor**, chastity, etc.), and are
AP : 2 7 :037(275) [0433] in the love of their **neighbor**, and similar spiritual virtues.
S3 : 0 1 :007(302) [0477] to love God above all things and his **neighbor** as himself.
TR : 0 0 :013(322) [0507] in the presence of one or more **neighboring** bishops.
TR : 0 0 :014(322) [0507] of ordinations the **neighboring** bishops of the same
TR : 0 0 :070(332) [0525] of that church or of a **neighboring** church, was brought in
SC : 0 1 :010(343) [0541] not endanger our **neighbor**'s life, nor cause him any
SC : 0 1 :014(343) [0541] we should not rob our **neighbor** of his money or
SC : 0 1 :015(343) [0541] *"You shall not bear false witness against your* ***neighbor****."*
SC : 0 1 :016(343) [0541] not tell lies about our **neighbor**, nor betray, slander, or
SC : 0 1 :017(343) [0541] *"You shall not covet your* ***neighbor's*** *house."*
SC : 0 1 :018(344) [0541] gain possession of our **neighbor**'s inheritance or home,
SC : 0 1 :019(344) [0543] *shall not covet your* ***neighbor's*** *wife, or his manservant,*
SC : 0 1 :019(344) [0543] *or his ox, or his ass, or anything that is your* ***neighbor's****."*
SC : 0 1 :020(344) [0543] or entice away our **neighbor**'s wife, servants, or cattle,
SC : 0 3 :014(347) [0549] and honor; true friends, faithful **neighbors**, and the like.
SC : 0 5 :023(350) [0553] I have injured my **neighbor** by speaking evil of him,
SC : 0 9 :014(356) [0563] 'You shall love your **neighbor** as yourself'" (Rom. 13:9).
LC : SP :008(362) [0575] 8. You shall not bear false witness against your **neighbor**.
LC : SP :009(363) [0577] 9. You shall not covet your **neighbor**'s house.
LC : 0 1 :026(368) [0587] in the position of **neighbors** — have received the command
LC : 0 1 :066(373) [0599] and for the advantage of our **neighbor** we are to swear.
LC : 0 1 :103(379) [0611] the benefit and salvation of our **neighbor** and ourselves.
LC : 0 1 :103(379) [0611] Now follow the other seven, which relate to our **neighbor**.
LC : 0 1 :105(379) [0611] to brothers, sisters, and **neighbors** in general he
LC : 0 1 :126(382) [0617] and all other works for our **neighbor** are not equal to this.
LC : 0 1 :141(384) [0621] help of his friends and **neighbors**; if he passes away, he
LC : 0 1 :151(386) [0625] out badly; servants, **neighbors**, or strangers and tyrants
LC : 0 1 :180(389) [0631] and go out among our **neighbors** to learn how we should
LC : 0 1 :184(390) [0633] For instance, a **neighbor**, envious that you have received
LC : 0 1 :185(390) [0633] and refuge about our **neighbor** so that no one may do him
LC : 0 1 :187(390) [0633] root and source of this bitterness toward our **neighbor**.
LC : 0 1 :189(390) [0635] fails to do good to his **neighbor**, or, though he has the
LC : 0 1 :192(391) [0635] permitted your **neighbor** to languish and perish in his
LC : 0 1 :200(392) [0637] us to guard against harming our **neighbor** in any way.
LC : 0 1 :200(392) [0637] First they deal with our **neighbor**'s person.
LC : 0 1 :203(392) [0639] protect, and rescue your **neighbor** whenever he is in
LC : 0 1 :205(393) [0639] chastely himself and to help his **neighbor** do the same.
LC : 0 1 :223(395) [0643] us to rob or pilfer the possessions of our **neighbor**.
LC : 0 1 :224(395) [0643] taking advantage of our **neighbor** in any sort of dealing
LC : 0 1 :224(395) [0643] takes advantage of his **neighbor** at the market, in a
LC : 0 1 :226(395) [0645] For these are my **neighbors**, my good friends, my own
LC : 0 1 :233(396) [0647] not to harm his **neighbor**, take advantage of him, or
LC : 0 1 :233(396) [0647] faithfully to protect his **neighbor**'s property and further
LC : 0 1 :250(399) [0651] but must extend to all our relations with our **neighbors**.
LC : 0 1 :250(399) [0651] are forbidden to do our **neighbor** any injury or wrong in
LC : 0 1 :251(399) [0651] promote and further our **neighbor**'s interests, and when
LC : 0 1 :252(399) [0651] kindness we show to our **neighbor**, as King Solomon
LC : 0 1 :254(399) [0653] *"You shall not bear false witness against your* ***neighbor****."*
LC : 0 1 :256(399) [0653] God will not have our **neighbor** deprived of his
LC : 0 1 :256(399) [0653] before his wife, children, servants, and **neighbors**.
LC : 0 1 :259(400) [0655] good friends, relatives, **neighbors**, and the rich and

Continued ▶

LC : 01 :260(400) [0655] everyone should help his **neighbor** maintain his rights.
LC : 01 :262(400) [0655] too, everyone bears false witness against his **neighbor**.
LC : 01 :263(400) [0655] tongue by which we may injure or offend our **neighbor**.
LC : 01 :263(400) [0655] the tongue against a **neighbor**, then, is forbidden by God.
LC : 01 :264(400) [0655] would rather hear evil than good about his **neighbor**.
LC : 01 :265(400) [0657] judge and reprove his **neighbor** publicly, even when he
LC : 01 :266(401) [0657] see and hear that my **neighbor** sins, but to make him the
LC : 01 :268(401) [0657] ventures to accuse his **neighbor** of such guilt assumes as
LC : 01 :268(401) [0657] tongue to the disgrace and harm of your **neighbor**.
LC : 01 :274(401) [0659] we are absolutely forbidden to speak evil of our **neighbor**.
LC : 01 :274(402) [0659] office he does not do his **neighbor** good but only harm
LC : 01 :276(402) [0659] and gossip about your **neighbor** but admonish him
LC : 01 :277(402) [0659] to complain to his **neighbors**, he would no doubt be told:
LC : 01 :278(402) [0661] would be corrected and the **neighbor**'s honor maintained.
LC : 01 :283(403) [0661] were acting for your **neighbor**'s improvement or from the
LC : 01 :285(403) [0661] No one shall harm his **neighbor**, whether friend or foe,
LC : 01 :285(403) [0663] of everyone, to cover his **neighbor**'s sins and infirmities,
LC : 01 :286(403) [0663] concerning our **neighbor**, "Whatever you wish that men
LC : 01 :288(404) [0663] we find in our **neighbor**, doing our utmost to serve and
LC : 01 :289(404) [0663] we may hear about our **neighbor**, as long as it is not a
LC : 01 :289(404) [0663] to criticize in their **neighbor**, misconstruing and twisting
LC : 01 :292(404) [0663] *"You shall not covet your **neighbor**'s house."*
LC : 01 :293(404) [0665] forbidden to covet our **neighbor**'s wife or property, or to
LC : 01 :295(404) [0665] to dismiss his servants or entice his **neighbor**'s from him.
LC : 01 :296(405) [0665] or scheme to despoil his **neighbor** of what belongs to
LC : 01 :296(405) [0665] away from your **neighbor**, even though in the eyes of the
LC : 01 :299(405) [0665] without regard for equity or for our **neighbor**'s plight.
LC : 01 :301(405) [0667] out to gain and squeeze something out of his **neighbor**.
LC : 01 :304(406) [0667] it does not see that the **neighbor** is being taken advantage
LC : 01 :307(406) [0669] wish you to deprive your **neighbor** of anything that is his,
LC : 01 :307(406) [0669] no one, you have trespassed on your **neighbor**'s rights.
LC : 01 :307(406) [0669] designs upon your **neighbor**'s property, luring it away
LC : 01 :309(407) [0669] to desire harm to our **neighbor**, nor become accessory to
LC : 01 :310(407) [0669] all the roots and causes of our injuries to our **neighbors**.
LC : 01 :313(407) [0671] domestic duties of one **neighbor** toward another, with no
LC : 01 :327(409) [0675] which concern our **neighbor**, everything proceeds from
LC : 01 :328(410) [0675] you are to do your **neighbor** no harm, injury, or violence,
LC : 01 :332(410) [0677] and abroad among his **neighbors**, he will find occasion
LC : 03 :028(424) [0705] preachers, magistrates, **neighbors**, servants; and, as we
LC : 03 :076(431) [0721] to grant us faithful **neighbors** and good friends, etc.
LC : 03 :093(433) [0725] yet on the condition that we also forgive our **neighbor**.
LC : 03 :094(433) [0725] must always forgive our **neighbor** who does us harm,
LC : 03 :102(434) [0727] deception against our **neighbor** — in short, into all kinds
LC : 04 :057(444) [0747] My **neighbor** and I — in short, all men — may err and
LC : 05 :079(455) [0771] If you do not know, ask your **neighbors** about it.
LC : 06 :008(458) [0000] to God alone or to our **neighbor** alone, begging for
LC : 06 :010(458) [0000] makes toward his **neighbor**, is included in the Lord's
LC : 06 :011(458) [0000] all"; no one does to God or his **neighbor** what he ought.
LC : 06 :012(458) [0000] both to God and to our **neighbor** are forgiven when we
LC : 06 :012(458) [0000] when we forgive our **neighbor** and become reconciled

Neither (167)

PR : PR :009(006) [0011] confession and that **neither** we nor our churches were
PR : PR :009(006) [0011] much and so often that **neither** we nor our theologians
AG : 23 :024(055) [0065] a command of God, **neither** can any vow alter a
AG : 26 :027(068) [0073] of the disciples which **neither** our fathers nor we have
AG : 28 :060(091) [0093] know that the keeping **neither** of the Sabbath nor of any
AL : 25 :009(063) [0069] peace, for many sins can **neither** be perceived nor
AL : 26 :027(068) [0073] of the disciples which **neither** our fathers nor we have
AL : 26 :033(069) [0075] exercises and labors, that **neither** plenty nor idleness may
AL : 28 :060(091) [0093] know that the keeping **neither** of the Sabbath nor of any
AP : PR :012(099) [0101] that they are after **neither** truth no harmony, but our
AP : 02 :043(106) [0117] of our emotions we are **neither** good nor bad, neither to
AP : 02 :043(106) [0117] neither good nor bad, **neither** to be praised nor
AP : 04 :003(107) [0121] since they understand **neither** the forgiveness of sins nor
AP : 04 :018(109) [0125] works and meanwhile **neither** fears God nor truly believes
AP : 04 :018(109) [0125] of faith man can **neither** have nor understand the love of
AP : 04 :024(110) [0127] Aristotle correctly says, "**Neither** the evening star nor the
AP : 04 :110(123) [0153] For men can **neither** render nor understand this love
AP : 04 :111(123) [0155] says, "In Christ Jesus **neither** circumcision nor
AP : 04 :181(132) [0171] does not justify; that is, it **neither** reconciles nor
AP : 04 :224(138) [0181] own, for they understand **neither** what justification is nor
AP : 04 :227(138) [0183] law does not justify, **neither** does the greatest virtue of the
AP : 04 :265(146) [0197] it sees only works and **neither** looks at nor understands
AP : 04 :287(150) [0203] based upon the law, **neither** one based upon the Gospel
AP : 04 :291(152) [0203] that we are justified **neither** by reason nor by the law.
AP : 04 :303(154) [0205] Therefore **neither** wicked people nor demons can have the
AP : 04 :348(160) [0217] to the flesh can retain **neither** faith nor righteousness.
AP : 04 :358(162) [0219] therefore we need **neither** Christ the mediator nor the
AP : 04 :368(163) [0221] We **neither** do nor can keep the law before we have been
AP : 07 :044(177) [0243] admonished the reader **neither** to destroy evangelical
AP : 09 :002(178) [0245] church, where there is **neither** Word nor sacrament,
AP : 11 :008(181) [0251] It is certain that we **neither** remember nor understand
AP : 12 :005(183) [0253] The people could grasp **neither** the sum of the matter nor
AP : 12 :048(188) [0265] this seriously, for they **neither** see nor read the sentence
AP : 12 :066(191) [0271] **Neither** to the pope nor to the church do we grant the
AP : 12 :078(193) [0275] and works are present, **neither** love nor works can be a
AP : 12 :097(196) [0281] opponents understand **neither** the nature of penitence nor
AP : 12 :101(197) [0281] absolution understand **neither** the forgiveness of sins nor
AP : 12 :156(207) [0301] because the keys can **neither** impose nor remit them; God
AP : 12 :178(211) [0309] and that these touch **neither** earth nor heaven and they
AP : 15 :029(219) [0323] us know that they merit **neither** the forgiveness of sins
AP : 15 :050(222) [0329] that these observances **neither** justify nor are necessary
AP : 18 :006(225) [0335] Spirit human hearts have **neither** the fear of God nor
AP : 21 :010(230) [0345] **Neither** a command nor a promise nor an example can be
AP : 21 :021(232) [0349] saints, though they have **neither** God's promise nor a
AP : 21 :031(233) [0351] saints, though they have **neither** a Word of God nor an
AP : 21 :043(235) [0357] way of doing things helps **neither** their position nor the
AP : 23 :007(240) [0365] of God, it follows that **neither** regulations nor vows can
AP : 23 :008(240) [0367] nature of the earth, so **neither** vows nor human
AP : 23 :036(244) [0373] **Neither** by virginity nor by marriage are we justified, but
AP : 23 :040(244) [0375] **Neither** Christ nor Paul commends virginity because it
AP : 23 :069(249) [0383] on the same level, but **neither** virginity nor marriage
AP : 24 :043(258) [0399] questions, which **neither** they nor the people understand.
AP : 24 :050(259) [0401] hold an audience, but **neither** the people nor the clergy
AP : 24 :087(265) [0413] But **neither** ceremonies nor prayers provide an advantage
AP : 24 :092(267) [0417] the meaning of **neither** sacrifice nor sacrament nor
AP : 27 :002(269) [0419] sake inasmuch as he had **neither** written nor taught
AP : 27 :020(272) [0427] tradition, which has **neither** a command of God nor a
AP : 27 :026(273) [0429] Hence they are **neither** justifying services nor perfection.
AP : 27 :046(277) [0435] of property is **neither** commanded nor advised in the
AP : 27 :054(278) [0437] Meanwhile they **neither** hear nor preach the Gospel
AP : 27 :059(279) [0439] as Jeremiah writes (35:6), **neither** had any possessions nor
AP : 28 :007(282) [0445] and that therefore **neither** sin nor righteousness depends
S1 : PR :010(290) [0457] Yet **neither** the bishops nor the canons care how the poor
S1 : PR :014(291) [0459] commanded by God, are **neither** regarded nor observed?
S1 : 01 :000(291) [0461] Son became man, and **neither** the Father nor the Holy
S2 : 02 :022(296) [0469] They are **neither** commanded nor commended.
S2 : 02 :025(297) [0469] It is **neither** commanded nor recommended, nor does it
S2 : 04 :002(298) [0471] This we **neither** will nor should nor can take upon our
S2 : 04 :010(300) [0475] to nothing since it is **neither** established nor commanded
S2 : 04 :011(300) [0475] **Neither** the Turks nor the Tartars, great as is their enmity
S2 : 04 :015(301) [0475] in the council, for they **neither** can nor will concede to us
S3 : 02 :004(303) [0479] law must tell him that he **neither** has nor cares for God or
S3 : 03 :016(305) [0483] They understood **neither** of these terms, and to this day
S3 : 03 :019(306) [0485] Here, again, there was **neither** faith nor Christ.
S3 : 03 :023(306) [0485] been placed in it, and **neither** faith nor Christ would have
S3 : 03 :032(308) [0487] forgiveness of sins, for **neither** of you knows what sin
S3 : 10 :001(314) [0497] However, they **neither** are nor wish to be true bishops.
S3 : 11 :001(314) [0499] The papists had **neither** authority nor right to prohibit
TR : 00 :008(321) [0505] ministers, just as a child **neither** seeks nor takes
TR : 00 :010(321) [0505] asserts that he was **neither** ordained nor confirmed by
TR : 00 :011(321) [0507] This is to say that **neither** Peter nor the other ministers
TR : 00 :015(322) [0509] Since, therefore, **neither** ordination nor confirmation
TR : 00 :050(329) [0519] for the judge is judged **neither** by the emperor, nor by all
SC : 03 :016(347) [0549] deny our prayers, for we **neither** merit nor deserve those
LC : 01 :012(366) [0583] They **neither** expect nor seek anything from him.
LC : 01 :021(367) [0585] It **neither** cares for God nor expects good things from him
LC : 01 :042(370) [0591] They have **neither** money, prestige, nor honor, and can
LC : 01 :042(370) [0591] and learn that they **neither** lie nor deceive but will yet
LC : 01 :090(377) [0607] holy day because they **neither** preach nor practice God's
LC : 01 :100(378) [0609] of the devil, who **neither** day nor night relaxes his effort
LC : 01 :124(382) [0617] **Neither** can parents, as a rule, do very much; one fool
LC : 01 :134(383) [0619] which this life can **neither** be heartily enjoyed nor long
LC : 01 :140(384) [0621] which in the past was **neither** heeded nor taught under the
LC : 01 :180(389) [0631] Therefore **neither** God nor the government is included in
LC : 01 :188(390) [0635] anyone; again, we should **neither** use nor sanction any
LC : 01 :201(392) [0637] was not commended, **neither** were public prostitution and
LC : 01 :238(397) [0647] They will **neither** prosper nor gain anything their whole
LC : 01 :318(408) [0673] much to do that you will **neither** seek nor pay attention to
LC : 01 :324(409) [0675] heaven and on earth will keep **neither** this nor any other.
LC : 02 :003(411) [0679] be kept, we would need **neither** the Creed nor the Lord's
LC : 02 :020(412) [0683] it, and recite it, but we **neither** see nor consider what the
LC : 02 :038(415) [0689] **Neither** you nor I could ever know anything of Christ, or
LC : 02 :049(417) [0691] us, who understand **neither** Latin nor German, have
LC : 02 :065(419) [0695] But **neither** could we know anything of Christ, had it not
LC : 03 :010(421) [0699] God, thinking that he **neither** wants nor cares for our
LC : 03 :108(435) [0729] is to give it free rein and **neither** resist it nor pray for help
LC : 04 :061(444) [0747] And because they see **neither** faith nor obedience, they
LC : 05 :052(452) [0765] But we **neither** force nor compel anyone, nor need anyone
LC : 05 :074(455) [0771] alone are unworthy who **neither** feel their infirmities nor
LC : 05 :082(456) [0773] and heedlessly is that we **neither** acknowledge nor believe
LC : 06 :009(458) [0000] but a confession that we **neither** have nor do what we
LC : 06 :016(459) [0000] We **neither** noticed nor preached the very necessary
LC : 06 :028(460) [0000] are a Christian, you need **neither** my compulsion nor the
EP : 03 :003(473) [0793] is our righteousness **neither** according to the divine nature
EP : 07 :033(485) [0815] human nature could **neither** permit nor admit this.
EP : 08 :003(487) [0817] united in such a way that **neither** of the two *really* (that
EP : 08 :009(487) [0819] of such a kind that **neither** nature has anything in
EP : 08 :009(487) [0819] are glued together and **neither** gives anything to or takes
EP : 10 :001(492) [0829] church usages which are **neither** commanded nor
EP : 10 :002(493) [0829] things and are **neither** commanded nor forbidden by
EP : 10 :003(493) [0829] church usages which are **neither** commanded nor
EP : 11 :004(495) [0833] **Neither** is it the cause of man's perdition; for this man
EP : 12 :008(498) [0839] too, the Anabaptists **neither** think highly of infant Baptism
EP : 12 :031(500) [0843] Christ, and that we shall **neither** secretly nor publicly say
SD : PR :002(503) [0851] agreement that we shall **neither** prepare nor accept a
SD : PR :007(505) [0853] with the papists, and for **neither** expecting nor planning
SD : 01 :016(511) [0865] such a way that we fall **neither** into Pelagian nor into
SD : 01 :040(515) [0871] **Neither** is original sin the creature or handiwork of God;
SD : 02 :010(522) [0885] dark, blind world which **neither** knows nor regards God)
SD : 02 :020(525) [0889] lifeless statue which uses **neither** mouth nor eyes nor
SD : 02 :055(532) [0903] On the other hand, **neither** the preacher nor the hearer
SD : 02 :057(532) [0903] in his sins, he can **neither** comfort himself with God's
SD : 02 :059(532) [0905] the person who moves it, **neither** does it understand or
SD : 03 :027(543) [0925] he indicates thereby that **neither** the preceding contrition
SD : 03 :030(544) [0925] before God faith trusts **neither** in contrition nor in love
SD : 03 :031(544) [0925] **Neither** is contrition nor love nor any other virtue the
SD : 03 :039(546) [0929] 3. That **neither** renewal, sanctification, virtues, nor other
SD : 03 :055(549) [0935] Our righteousness rests **neither** upon his divine nature
SD : 03 :056(549) [0935] For **neither** the obedience nor the passion of the human
SD : 03 :058(550) [0937] For this reason **neither** the divine nor the human nature
SD : 04 :008(552) [0941] **Neither** is there a controversy among us as to how and
SD : 04 :032(556) [0947] Do not be deceived; **neither** the immoral, nor idolaters,
SD : 05 :012(560) [0955] case of those who as yet **neither** know their sins nor are
SD : 05 :022(562) [0959] of God, although they **neither** understood nor honored
SD : 07 :001(569) [0971] Hence we **neither** could nor should refrain from giving
SD : 07 :089(585) [1003] and which are **neither** abrogated nor rendered impotent
SD : 07 :100(586) [1005] according to which he **neither** occupies nor vacates space
SD : 07 :100(586) [1007] a board and a wall and **neither** occupies nor vacates
SD : 07 :119(590) [1013] in heaven that he is **neither** able nor willing to be truly
SD : 07 :120(590) [1013] his assumed human nature **neither** permit nor allow this.
SD : 08 :011(593) [1019] after the incarnation **neither** nature in Christ henceforth
SD : 08 :020(595) [1021] although the divine nature can **neither** suffer nor die.
SD : 08 :043(599) [1029] and man in one person, **neither** confounding the natures
SD : 09 :003(610) [1053] from it the comfort that **neither** hell nor the devil can

Continued ▶

SD : 1 0 :001(610) [1053] church rites which are **neither** commanded nor forbidden
SD : 1 0 :002(611) [1053] indifference and that are **neither** commanded nor
SD : 1 0 :007(611) [1055] **Neither** are useless and foolish spectacles, which serve
SD : 1 0 :007(611) [1055] spectacles, which serve **neither** good order, Christian
SD : 1 0 :019(614) [1059] However, they **neither** are nor wish to be true bishops.
SD : 1 1 :002(616) [1063] example it provides, it **neither** can nor should be
SD : 1 1 :007(617) [1065] (since God **neither** creates nor works evil, nor does he
SD : 1 1 :026(620) [1071] **Neither** should we permit ourselves to try to explore the
SD : 1 1 :049(624) [1079] conclusion that **neither** "tribulation nor anguish, neither
SD : 1 1 :049(624) [1079] "tribulation nor anguish, **neither** death nor life, etc. can
SD : 1 1 :060(626) [1083] damnation, God owes us **neither** his Word, nor his Spirit,
SD : 1 2 :008(633) [1097] holy Gospel was allowed **neither** room nor scope, where
SD : 1 2 :016(634) [1099] of the Anabaptists; **neither** may one serve them or work

Nestorius (3)
EP : 0 8 :018(489) [0823] do not divide the person of Christ, as **Nestorius** did.
EP : 0 8 :020(490) [0823] the Son of man another, as **Nestorius** foolishly asserted.
SD : 0 8 :015(594) [1019] the error and heresy of **Nestorius** and the Samosatenes,

Net (4), Nets (1)
AP : 0 7 :001(168) [0227] Christ compared it to a **net** in which there are both good
AP : 0 7 :019(171) [0233] kingdom of God is like a **net** (Matt. 13:47) or like ten
LC : 0 3 :104(434) [0727] These are snares and **nets**; indeed, they are the real
SD : 1 1 :003(616) [1063] Accordingly, the **net** total and content of the teaching on
SD : 1 1 :076(629) [1089] divine Word, as with a **net** by which he snatches the elect

Neuburg (1)
PR : PR :027(014) [0025] Philip Louis, palsgrave [of Pfalz-**Neuburg**]

Neutral (4)
AP : 0 2 :041(105) [0115] lust is not a fault but is a **neutral** thing, like the color of
AP : 0 2 :042(105) [0115] inclination to evil is a **neutral** thing, not only will many
AP : 0 2 :042(105) [0117] attitudes as these are a **neutral** thing — doubt about God's
AP : 0 2 :045(106) [0117] are not in their nature **neutral**, but they need the grace of

New (237)
PR : PR :008(005) [0009] to defend, or to spread a different or a **new** doctrine.
PR : PR :017(008) [0015] palliate, or confirm any **new**, false, or erroneous doctrine
PR : PR :018(009) [0017] reason allegedly make a **new** confession almost every year
PR : PR :023(012) [0021] articles we have made no **new** or different confession from
PR : PR :025(013) [0023] to manufacture anything **new** by this work of agreement
PR : PR :026(014) [0025] should continue or **new** ones arise, we shall see to it that
AG : 0 1 :006(028) [0043] the Samosatenes, old and **new**, who hold that there is
AG : 0 6 :000(031) [0045] VI. [The **New** Obedience]
AG : 2 0 :012(042) [0055] That no **new** interpretation is here introduced can be
AG : 2 3 :012(052) [0063] who had published the **new** papal decree was almost
AG : 2 6 :002(064) [0071] For this reason **new** fasts, new ceremonies, new orders,
AG : 2 6 :002(064) [0071] For this reason new fasts, **new** ceremonies, new orders,
AG : 2 6 :002(064) [0071] new fasts, new ceremonies, **new** orders, and the like were
AG : 2 8 :002(081) [0083] have not only introduced **new** forms of worship and
AG : 2 8 :037(086) [0089] Almost every day **new** holy days and new fasts have been
AG : 2 8 :037(087) [0089] day new holy days and **new** fasts have been prescribed,
AG : 2 8 :037(087) [0089] have been prescribed, **new** ceremonies and new
AG : 2 8 :037(087) [0089] new ceremonies and **new** venerations of saints have been
AG : 2 8 :044(088) [0089] or with regard to a festival or a **new** moon or a sabbath.
AG : 2 8 :061(091) [0093] of the ceremonies of the **New** Testament, and of the
AG : 2 8 :061(091) [0093] and bishops to devise **new** ceremonies which would be
AG : 0 0 :005(095) [0095] God's help prevented any **new** and godless teaching from
AL : 0 1 :006(028) [0043] the Samosatenes, old and **new**, who contend that there is
AL : 0 6 :000(031) [0045] VI. [The **New** Obedience]
AL : 2 0 :012(043) [0055] that we have invented a **new** interpretation of Paul, this
AL : 2 0 :029(045) [0057] and endowed with **new** affections as to be able to bring
AL : 0 0 :001(048) [0059] few abuses which are **new** and have been adopted by the
AL : 2 4 :035(060) [0067] Nor is this custom **new** in the church, for before the time
AL : 2 6 :002(064) [0071] evident from the fact that **new** ceremonies, new orders,
AL : 2 6 :002(064) [0071] fact that new ceremonies, **new** orders, new holy days, and
AL : 2 6 :002(064) [0071] ceremonies, new orders, **new** holy days, and new fasts
AL : 2 6 :002(064) [0071] orders, new holy days, and **new** fasts were daily
AL : 2 8 :002(081) [0083] not only have instituted **new** forms of worship and
AL : 2 8 :037(086) [0089] more fasts prescribed, and **new** ceremonies and new
AL : 2 8 :037(086) [0089] and new ceremonies and **new** orders instituted because
AL : 2 8 :044(088) [0089] or with regard to a festival or a **new** moon or a sabbath."
AL : 2 8 :061(091) [0093] ceremonies of the **new** law, concerning the change of the
AL : 2 8 :061(091) [0093] and bishops to devise **new** ceremonies which would be
AL : 2 8 :072(093) [0093] unjust burdens which are **new** and were introduced
AL : 0 0 :005(095) [0095] into our churches of any **new** and ungodly doctrines.
AP : 0 2 :015(102) [0109] We have said nothing **new**.
AP : 0 2 :035(105) [0115] begins to mortify lust and to create **new** impulses in man.
AP : 0 4 :005(108) [0121] his sake, or when, in the **New** Testament, the Christ who
AP : 0 4 :057(115) [0137] of sins by faith, just as the saints in the **New** Testament.
AP : 0 4 :062(115) [0139] For this consolation is a **new** and spiritual life.
AP : 0 4 :064(116) [0139] from death, brings forth a **new** life in our hearts, and is a
AP : 0 4 :125(124) [0157] Holy Spirit and produces a **new** life in our hearts, it must
AP : 0 4 :132(125) [0159] in us eternal righteousness and a **new** and eternal life.
AP : 0 4 :170(130) [0171] and destroy them and to give us **new** spiritual impulses.
AP : 0 4 :208(135) [0177] rest, they kept thinking up **new** works beyond God's
AP : 0 4 :212(136) [0179] other works, make up **new** devotions, new vows, and new
AP : 0 4 :212(136) [0179] make up new devotions, **new** vows, and new monastic
AP : 0 4 :212(136) [0179] devotions, new vows, and **new** monastic orders beyond
AP : 0 4 :250(143) [0191] Since this faith is a **new** life, it necessarily produces new
AP : 0 4 :250(143) [0191] life, it necessarily produces **new** impulses and new works.
AP : 0 4 :250(143) [0191] life, it necessarily produces new impulses and **new** works.
AP : 0 4 :258(144) [0193] he commands these works as necessary to the **new** life.
AP : 0 4 :259(144) [0193] *operato*, but he requires a **new** life, which is certainly
AP : 0 4 :259(145) [0193] your bread with the hungry," he requires the **new** life.
AP : 0 4 :261(145) [0195] One part instructs about the **new** life and its works.
AP : 0 4 :272(148) [0199] not only demands **new** works but also promises the
AP : 0 4 :274(148) [0199] works are required, since a **new** life is certainly required;
AP : 0 4 :325(157) [0211] we are teaching anything **new** in this regard when the
AP : 0 4 :349(160) [0217] the Holy Spirit, that this **new** life might have new works
AP : 0 4 :349(160) [0217] this new life might have **new** works and new impulses, the
AP : 0 4 :349(160) [0217] might have new works and **new** impulses, the fear and
AP : 0 4 :350(161) [0217] when it shows our old or **new** sins or the uncleanness of
AP : 0 4 :357(162) [0219] Such logic is completely **new**.
AP : 0 4 :366(163) [0221] promise of grace, receives justification and **new** life gratis.
AP : 0 4 :374(164) [0223] and to show that a **new** life and new birth are required,
AP : 0 4 :374(164) [0223] show that a new life and **new** birth are required, not
AP : 0 4 :374(164) [0223] Such a **new** birth comes by faith amid penitence.
AP : 0 4 :392(167) [0225] through our works and **new** devotions, obscuring the
AP : 0 7 :007(169) [0229] We have not said anything **new**.
AP : 0 7 :035(175) [0239] or with regard to a festival or a **new** moon or a sabbath.
AP : 1 2 :022(185) [0257] consciences, to institute **new** acts of devotion, and to
AP : 1 2 :042(187) [0261] These are signs of the **new** testament, that is, signs of the
AP : 1 2 :042(187) [0263] This cup is the **new** testament" (Luke 22:19, 20).
AP : 1 2 :045(188) [0263] Christ also includes the fruits of penitence or the **new** life.
AP : 1 2 :048(188) [0265] This **new** sentence is faith, abolishing the earlier sentence
AP : 1 2 :060(190) [0269] and brings forth peace, joy, and a **new** life in the heart.
AP : 1 2 :136(203) [0293] these passages will have to be interpreted in a **new** way.
AP : 1 3 :004(211) [0309] of grace, which is the heart of the **New** Testament.
AP : 1 3 :007(212) [0311] to sacrifice, as though the **new** covenant needed a
AP : 1 3 :014(213) [0311] first instituted not in the **New** Testament but in the very
AP : 1 3 :014(213) [0311] to physical life and not strictly to the **New** Testament.
AP : 1 3 :014(213) [0311] strict sense, "signs of the **New** Testament," testimonies of
AP : 1 3 :020(213) [0313] this is a sacrament of the **New** Testament, as Christ clearly
AP : 1 3 :020(213) [0313] of sins, promised in the **New** Testament, is being offered
AP : 1 3 :020(214) [0313] as though God, by a **new** miracle, promised his will to
AP : 1 5 :015(217) [0319] are allowed to establish **new** rites and if by such rites they
AP : 1 5 :018(217) [0319] kingdom of Antichrist is a **new** kind of worship of God,
AP : 1 5 :030(219) [0323] or with regard to a festival or a **new** moon or a sabbath.
AP : 1 6 :003(223) [0331] does not introduce any **new** laws about the civil estate,
AP : 1 6 :008(223) [0333] is something external, a **new** and monastic form of
AP : 2 1 :043(235) [0357] They defend obvious abuses with **new** and illegal cruelty.
AP : 2 3 :023(242) [0369] These **new** canons do not represent the decision of the
AP : 2 3 :025(243) [0371] celibacy is peculiar to this **new** pontifical tyranny, and
AP : 2 3 :027(243) [0371] since the priests of the **New** Testament must pray
AP : 2 3 :067(248) [0383] This is a **new** charge, that marriage is a heresy!
AP : 2 4 :026(254) [0391] The sacrifices of the **New** Testament are of this type, as
AP : 2 4 :027(254) [0393] short, the worship of the **New** Testament is spiritual; it is
AP : 2 4 :030(255) [0395] of Levitical worship, the **New** Testament teaches that
AP : 2 4 :030(255) [0395] that there should be a **new** and pure sacrifice; this is
AP : 2 4 :033(256) [0395] all the worship of the **New** Testament, not only about the
AP : 2 4 :034(256) [0395] of those who teach in the **New** Testament) are the
AP : 2 4 :034(256) [0397] kill this old flesh and begin a **new** and eternal life in us.
AP : 2 4 :034(256) [0397] The **New** Testament requires sacrifices of the heart, not
AP : 2 4 :035(256) [0397] Mass ought to be the daily sacrifice of the **New** Testament
AP : 2 4 :035(256) [0397] the daily sacrifice of the **New** Testament; the ceremony
AP : 2 4 :036(257) [0397] Christ and the whole worship of the **New** Testament.
AP : 2 4 :037(257) [0397] Old Testament, so in the **New** we should look for what it
AP : 2 4 :039(257) [0399] of the heart, for in the **New** Testament we should look for
AP : 2 4 :041(257) [0399] and they have instituted **new** worship in the church.
AP : 2 4 :052(259) [0403] conclude that since the **New** Testament has priests and
AP : 2 4 :055(259) [0403] Old Testament as in the **New**, the saints had to be justified
AP : 2 4 :056(260) [0405] such sacrifice left in the **New** Testament except the one
AP : 2 4 :057(260) [0405] must be sacrifices in the **New** Testament besides the death
AP : 2 4 :057(260) [0405] of both the Old and the **New** Testament, and it replaces
AP : 2 4 :058(260) [0405] argues, therefore, that the **New** Testament must have a
AP : 2 4 :059(260) [0405] Since the priesthood of the **New** Testament is a ministry
AP : 2 4 :059(260) [0405] when he does work to give them **new** birth and life.
AP : 2 4 :069(262) [0409] it is correct to define the **New** Testament sacraments as
AP : 2 4 :069(262) [0409] In the **New** Testament, the Word is the added promise of
AP : 2 4 :069(262) [0409] The promise of the **New** Testament is the promise of the
AP : 2 4 :069(262) [0409] "this is the cup of the **new** testament with my blood,
AP : 2 4 :071(262) [0409] is the worship of the **New** Testament, because what
AP : 2 4 :071(262) [0409] what matters in the **New** Testament is the spiritual
AP : 2 7 :004(269) [0421] sermons and in thinking up **new** ways of making money.
AP : 2 8 :014(283) [0447] bishops may institute **new** acts of worship, for worship
S3 : 0 3 :001(303) [0479] of the law is retained and taught by the **New** Testament.
S3 : 0 3 :004(304) [0481] this office of the law the **New** Testament immediately
S3 : 0 3 :035(309) [0489] that we must become altogether **new** and different men.
S3 : 1 3 :001(315) [0499] (as St. Peter says) we get a **new** and clean heart and that
TR : 0 0 :026(324) [0511] Besides, the ministry of the **New** Testament is not bound
TR : 0 0 :071(332) [0525] Later on **new** ceremonies were added, many of which
SC : 0 4 :012(349) [0551] put to death, and that the **new** man should come forth
SC : 0 6 :004(351) [0557] This cup is the **new** covenant in my blood, which is
LC : PR :003(358) [0567] the Prayer Book, the **New** Testament, or something else
LC : PR :009(359) [0569] present and bestows ever **new** and greater light and
LC : PR :016(361) [0573] thing without varying it with anything **new** or different.
LC : PR :019(361) [0573] Vain imaginations, like **new** cloth, suffer shrinkage!
LC : SP :023(364) [0579] saying, 'This cup is the **new** testament in my blood, which
LC : 0 1 :101(379) [0609] It always awakens **new** understanding, new pleasure, and
LC : 0 1 :101(379) [0609] new understanding, **new** pleasure, and a new spirit of
LC : 0 1 :101(379) [0609] new pleasure, and a **new** spirit of devotion, and it
LC : 0 1 :240(397) [0649] **New** burdens and high prices are imposed.
LC : 0 1 :306(406) [0669] from another, for in the **New** Testament married people
LC : 0 2 :057(418) [0693] to complete and perfect holiness in a **new**, eternal life.
LC : 0 2 :058(418) [0693] and all evil, living in **new**, immortal and glorified bodies.
LC : 0 3 :109(435) [0729] weary; when one attack ceases, **new** ones always arise.
LC : 0 4 :006(437) [0733] indifferent matter, then, like putting on a **new** red coat.
LC : 0 4 :015(438) [0735] blasphemy when our **new** spirits, in order to slander
LC : 0 4 :028(440) [0739] Our know-it-alls, the **new** spirits, assert that faith alone
LC : 0 4 :065(445) [0749] and the resurrection of the **new** man, both of which
LC : 0 4 :065(445) [0749] that whatever belongs to the **new** man may come forth.
LC : 0 4 :075(445) [0751] attack on the old man and an entering upon a **new** life?
LC : 0 4 :075(445) [0751] not only announces this **new** life but also produces,
LC : 0 4 :076(446) [0751] the old man so that the **new** may come forth and grow
LC : 0 4 :083(446) [0751] and daily strengthens the **new** man, always remains until
LC : 0 4 :084(446) [0753] be suppressing the old man and growing up in the **new**.
LC : 0 5 :003(447) [0753] *saying, 'This cup is the* ***new*** *testament in my blood, which*
LC : 0 5 :013(448) [0755] of it, all of you, this is the **new** covenant in my blood,'
LC : 0 5 :023(449) [0757] the soul since it nourishes and strengthens the **new** man.
LC : 0 5 :025(449) [0759] For the **new** life should be one that continually develops
LC : 0 5 :027(449) [0759] Supper is given to bring us **new** strength and
LC : 0 5 :042(451) [0763] or compelled, lest we institute a **new** slaughter of souls.
EP : RN :001(464) [0777] writings of the Old and **New** Testaments are the only rule
EP : RN :007(465) [0779] Scripture of the Old and **New** Testaments and all other
EP : 0 2 :014(471) [0789] he creates out of nothing a **new** essence of the soul.

Continued ▶

E P : 0 2 :018(472) [0791] of divine grace in kindling **new** movements within the
E P : 0 2 :018(472) [0791] of man's will and works the **new** birth and conversion.
E P : 0 2 :018(472) [0791] *power and activity*, man's **new** will becomes an
E P : 0 3 :021(475) [0797] them and by the incipient **new** obedience, or in part by
E P : 0 3 :021(475) [0797] righteousness and in part by our incipient **new** obedience.
E P : 0 4 :003(476) [0797] when speaking of the **new** obedience, since it does not
E P : 0 4 :003(476) [0797] word "necessary" that the **new** obedience is not a matter
E P : 1 2 :005(498) [0839] which in fact is nothing else but a **new** kind of monkery.
E P : 1 2 :012(499) [0841] is not a God-pleasing estate in the **New** Testament.
E P : 1 2 :016(499) [0841] 5. That in the **New** Testament the government cannot with
E P : 1 2 :022(499) [0841] Christ, conversion, repentance, faith, and **new** obedience.
E P : 1 2 :027(500) [0843] Errors of the **New** Arians
E P : 1 2 :029(500) [0843] This is an entirely **new** sect, unknown in Christendom
S D : P R :002(501) [0847] pious reformation as a **new** doctrine and as wholly
S D : P R :005(502) [0847] Confession or to set up a different and **new** confession.
S D : P R :002(503) [0851] nor accept a different or a **new** confession of our faith.
S D : P R :003(503) [0851] writings of the Old and **New** Testaments as the pure and
S D : 0 1 :017(511) [0865] opposition to both old and **new** Pelagians, we condemn
S D : 0 2 :026(526) [0891] to receive inwardly a **new** heart, mind, and spirit, is solely
S D : 0 2 :026(526) [0891] stony heart and bestows a **new** and tender heart of flesh
S D : 0 2 :026(526) [0891] (Eph. 2:10); and makes us **new** creatures (II Cor. 5:17;
S D : 0 2 :044(529) [0897] God himself must draw man and give him **new** birth.
S D : 0 2 :048(530) [0901] true repentance, faith, and **new** spiritual power and ability
S D : 0 2 :060(533) [0905] This the Scriptures call the creation of a **new** heart.
S D : 0 2 :063(533) [0905] so far as he is reborn or a **new** man, and he delights in the
S D : 0 2 :065(534) [0907] powers, but from the **new** powers and gifts which the
S D : 0 2 :070(534) [0909] be a change, there must be **new** activities and emotions in
S D : 0 2 :081(537) [0911] God creates a **new** heart and a new man in such a way
S D : 0 2 :081(537) [0911] creates a new heart and a **new** man in such a way that the
S D : 0 2 :081(537) [0911] destroyed and a **new** substance of the soul is created out
S D : 0 2 :081(537) [0911] old man and put on the **new** man by adding, 'Therefore
S D : 0 2 :081(537) [0913] is laying off the old man and putting on the **new** man."
S D : 0 2 :089(538) [0915] Holy Spirit engenders no **new** impulses and begins no
S D : 0 3 :017(542) [0921] the Holy Scriptures of the Old and the **New** Testaments.
S D : 0 3 :032(545) [0927] righteousness of the **new** obedience or of good works.
S D : 0 3 :035(545) [0927] and, because our **new** obedience is imperfect and impure,
S D : 0 3 :050(548) [0933] their own inchoate **new** obedience, or in part by the
S D : 0 3 :050(548) [0933] righteousness and in part by the inchoate **new** obedience.
S D : 0 4 :005(552) [0939] order referred to above, **new** obedience is not necessary in
S D : 0 4 :017(554) [0943] contrary, the people of the **New** Testament are to be a
S D : 0 5 :004(558) [0953] on earth and in the **New** Testament he ordered to be
S D : 0 5 :011(560) [0955] Thus, even in the **New** Testament, he must perform what
S D : 0 5 :014(560) [0957] Articles state: "The **New** Testament retains and performs
S D : 0 5 :024(562) [0961] that in the ministry of the **New** Testament the
S D : 0 6 :002(564) [0963] do not learn the **new** obedience (that is, in what good
S D : 0 6 :010(565) [0965] in connection with the **new** obedience of believers and
S D : 0 6 :011(565) [0965] that we should walk in the **new** life, but it does not give
S D : 0 7 :022(573) [0979] of it, all of you, this is the **new** covenant in my blood,'
S D : 0 7 :044(577) [0987] his blessings, a seal of the **new** covenant, a comfort for all
S D : 0 7 :044(577) [0987] "This is my blood of the **new** covenant which is shed for
S D : 0 7 :053(579) [0991] and Paul, "This cup is the **new** covenant in my blood"
S D : 0 7 :053(579) [0991] cup) is my blood of the **new** covenant, whereby I
S D : 0 7 :053(579) [0991] this my testament and **new** covenant, namely, the
S D : 0 7 :091(585) [1005] have advanced no **new** arguments since his death.
S D : 0 7 :113(589) [1011] are to be given a different, **new**, and strange sense.
S D : 0 8 :061(602) [1035] we have not developed a **new** doctrine of our own, but we
S D : 1 0 :013(613) [1057] regard to a festival or a **new** moon or a sabbath" (Col.
S D : 1 1 :096(632) [1095] strengthen him in his **new** obedience, and thus justify and
S D : 1 2 :001(632) [1095] Schwenkfelders, and the **New** Arians and
S D : 1 2 :010(634) [1097] and self-chosen spirituality as on a kind of **new** monkery.
S D : 1 2 :017(634) [1099] 8. That in the **New** Testament era government service is
S D : 1 2 :024(634) [1099] ways, and to enter into a **new** marriage with another
S D : 1 2 :027(635) [1101] as basically nothing else than a **new** kind of monkery.
S D : 1 2 :030(635) [1101] repentance, and faith or works **new** obedience in them.
S D : 1 2 :035(635) [1101] Erroneous Articles of the **New** Arians
S D : 1 2 :036(635) [1101] condemn the error of the **New** Arians who teach that
S D : 1 2 :036(636) [1101] Erroneous Articles of the **New** Anti-Trinitarians

Newness (4)

A P : 0 4 :278(149) [0199] almsgiving that it is the whole **newness** of life which saves.
A P : 1 2 :132(202) [0291] about total penitence and total **newness** of life and fruits.
A P : 1 2 :137(203) [0293] works, about the whole **newness** of life, and not about
S C : 0 4 :014(349) [0553] glory of the Father, we too might walk in **newness** of life."

Next (20)

A P : 2 1 :034(234) [0353] From invocation the **next** step was to images.
A P : 2 7 :038(275) [0433] The **next** day Anthony went into the city and came to the
L C : 0 1 :105(379) [0611] other persons on earth, and places them **next** to himself.
L C : 0 1 :107(379) [0611] them very highly and that **next** to God we give them the
L C : 0 1 :116(381) [0615] and commanded **next** to obedience to his own majesty.
L C : 0 1 :125(382) [0617] work that we can do, **next** to the sublime worship of God
L C : 0 1 :188(390) [0633] first, by hand or by deed; **next**, we should not use our
L C : 0 1 :223(395) [0643] **Next** to our own person and our spouse, our temporal
L C : 0 1 :262(400) [0655] **Next**, it extends much further when it is applied to
L C : 0 2 :050(417) [0691] uprooted, and it would be **next** to heresy to alter a word.
L C : 0 3 :042(425) [0709] In the **next** place, it is also profaned by an openly evil life
L C : 0 3 :103(434) [0727] **Next** comes the world, which assails us by word and deed
E P : 0 8 :018(489) [0823] **Next** to the holy Trinity this is the highest mystery, as the
S D : P R :004(502) [0847] Christians ought to accept **next** to the Word of God, just
S D : 0 1 :024(512) [0865] which are subject to human reason in the **next** article.
S D : 0 3 :041(546) [0929] justified, the Holy Spirit **next** renews and sanctifies him,
S D : 0 4 :009(552) [0941] that God will reward both in this and in the **next** world.
S D : 0 8 :033(597) [1027] **Next** to the article of the holy Trinity, the greatest mystery
S D : 1 1 :073(628) [1087] **Next**, since the Holy Spirit dwells in the elect who have
S D : 1 1 :074(628) [1087] join David in the **next** words, "But thou didst hear my

Nicaea (7)

A G : 0 1 :001(027) [0043] decree of the Council of **Nicaea**, that there is one divine
A L : 0 1 :001(027) [0043] decree of the Council of **Nicaea** concerning the unity of
A P : 0 7 :042(176) [0241] Before the Council of **Nicaea** some people celebrated
A P : 0 7 :042(176) [0241] so, after the Council of **Nicaea**, certain nations held
T R : 0 0 :012(321) [0507] 5. The Council of **Nicaea** decided that the bishop of
T R : 0 0 :013(322) [0507] 6. Again, the Council of **Nicaea** decided that bishops
T R : 0 0 :017(323) [0509] not preside — as the Council of **Nicaea** and many others.

Nice (1), Nicely (1)

L C : 0 1 :197(392) [0637] so that they might live a **nice**, soft life without the cross
S D : 0 5 :016(561) [0957] the entire matter **nicely** and clearly for the Christian

Nicene (7)

A G : 2 4 :038(060) [0067] for the words of the **Nicene** canon read, "After the priests
A L : 2 4 :037(060) [0067] him, for the words of the **Nicene** canon read, "In order,
A P : 0 3 :001(107) [0119] etc., according to the Apostles' and **Nicene** Creeds.
E P : R N :003(465) [0777] the Apostles' Creed, the **Nicene** Creed, and the Athanasian
S D : P R :004(504) [0851] Creeds, the Apostles'; the **Nicene**, and the Athanasian, as
S D : P R :005(504) [0853] to appeal and confess adherence to the **Nicene** Creed.
S D : 1 2 :037(636) [1101] approved symbols, the **Nicene** and Athanasian Creeds,

Nicholas (6)

S 3 : 1 5 :005(316) [0501] **Nicholas** Amsdorf, of Magdeburg, subscribed
S 3 : 1 5 :005(318) [0501] the Rev. **Nicholas** Faber
T R : 0 0 :082(334) [0529] **Nicholas** Amsdorf, of Magdeburg, subscribed
L C : 0 1 :074(374) [0601] to fast and pray to St. **Nicholas** and other saints, but the
E P : 1 2 :031(501) [0843] Dr. **Nicholas** Selnecker subscribed
S D : 1 2 :040(636) [1103] Dr. **Nicholas** Selnecker, subscribed

Nienburg (1)

P R : P R :027(015) [0025] Otto, count of Hoya [-**Nienburg**] and Burghausen

Night (16)

A P : 0 7 :033(174) [0239] length of day and **night** does not harm the unity of the
S C : 0 6 :004(351) [0555] Lord Jesus Christ, on the **night** when he was betrayed,
S C : 0 7 :002(352) [0557] protected me through the **night** from all harm and
S C : 0 7 :005(353) [0559] Graciously protect me during the coming **night**.
S C : 0 9 :013(356) [0563] supplications and prayers **night** and day; whereas she who
L C : P R :010(360) [0569] blessed who "meditate on God's law day and **night**."
L C : S P :016(363) [0577] and they go to bed at **night**; until they repeat them they
L C : S P :023(364) [0579] Lord Jesus Christ on the **night** when he was betrayed
L C : 0 1 :100(378) [0609] devil, who neither day nor **night** relaxes his effort to steal
L C : 0 1 :243(397) [0649] and scratch day and **night** and yet grow not a penny
L C : 0 2 :014(412) [0681] in the heavens, day and **night**, air, fire, water, the earth
L C : 0 3 :025(423) [0705] growl frightfully day and **night**; not one of them thinks of
L C : 0 3 :064(429) [0715] without rest day and **night**, using all the arts, tricks,
L C : 0 5 :003(447) [0753] *Lord Jesus Christ on the **night** when he was betrayed*
E P : 0 6 :002(480) [0805] exercise themselves day and **night** in the law (Ps. 119:1).
S D : 0 6 :004(564) [0963] law he meditates day and **night**" (Ps. 1:1, 2; 119:1, 35, 47,

Nineteenth (1)

S D : 0 6 :009(565) [0965] on the Epistle for the **Nineteenth** Sunday after Trinity.

Ninevites (1)

A P : 1 2 :166(208) [0303] Here the example of the **Ninevites** is a case in point.

Ninth (8)

A G : 2 8 :034(086) [0089] canon law throughout the whole of the **ninth** Distinction.
A P : 0 4 :322(157) [0209] In the **ninth** book of the *Confessions* he says, "Woe to the
A P : 0 9 :001(178) [0245] They approve the **ninth** article where we confess that
T R : 0 0 :050(329) [0519] The **ninth** question of the third canon states, "No one
S C : 0 1 :017(343) [0541] The **Ninth**
L C : 0 1 :291(404) [0663] The **Ninth** and Tenth Commandments
S D : 1 1 :027(620) [1071] third, at the sixth, at the **ninth**, and even at the eleventh
S D : 1 1 :033(622) [1075] and in tribulation, the **ninth**, tenth, and eleventh chapters

Noble (10), Nobleman (1), Noblemen (1), Nobler (7), Nobles (1), Noblest (2), Nobility (1)

L C : P R :006(359) [0569] Indeed, even among the **nobility** there are some louts and
L C : P R :020(361) [0573] themselves will make the **noble** confession that the longer
L C : 0 1 :113(380) [0613] commands must be much **nobler** than anything we
L C : 0 1 :116(381) [0615] work that is greater and **nobler** than obedience to father
L C : 0 1 :148(385) [0623] You are a true **nobleman** if you are upright and obedient.
L C : 0 1 :195(391) [0637] and urge us to true, **noble**, exalted deeds, such as
L C : 0 1 :210(393) [0641] most universal and the **noblest**, pervading all Christendom
L C : 0 1 :235(397) [0647] like a thief, and even expect to be revered like **noblemen**.
L C : 0 1 :289(404) [0663] It is a particularly fine, **noble** virtue always to put the
L C : 0 1 :300(405) [0667] to belong, as many great **nobles**, lords, and princes do
L C : 0 3 :023(423) [0703] Thus there is no **nobler** prayer to be found on earth, for
L C : 0 4 :012(438) [0735] they would not be as **noble** and good as if God were to
L C : 0 4 :012(438) [0735] the person performing the act is **nobler** and better.
L C : 0 4 :014(438) [0735] that the water in itself is **nobler** than other water but that
L C : 0 4 :016(438) [0735] is a treasure greater and **nobler** than heaven and earth.
L C : 0 4 :017(438) [0735] substance but because here something **nobler** is added.
L C : 0 6 :015(459) [0000] surpassingly grand and **noble** thing that makes confession
S D : 0 1 :001(508) [0859] at least the foremost and **noblest** part of his essence
S D : 0 7 :006(570) [0973] were deceived by the **noble** and plausible words of the
S D : 0 7 :059(580) [0993] explanation of the **noble** testimony in I Cor. 10:16.
S D : 0 7 :069(582) [0997] unworthy of this **noble** treasure and the benefits of Christ
S D : 0 8 :059(602) [1035] Many other **noble** testimonies of the ancient orthodox
S D : 1 1 :082(630) [1089] he will be a vessel for **noble** use, consecrated and useful to

Nobody (18)

A G : 1 4 :000(036) [0049] is taught among us that **nobody** should publicly teach or
A G : 2 2 :008(050) [0061] **Nobody** knows when or through whom this custom of
A G : 2 6 :029(068) [0075] or with the notion that **nobody** is a Christian unless he
A L : 1 4 :000(036) [0049] Our churches teach that **nobody** should preach publicly in
A P : 0 4 :157(128) [0165] for the sake of our love, **nobody** will have the forgiveness
A P : 2 7 :032(274) [0431] end Bernard adds: "Let **nobody** deceive himself; for if he
S 3 : 0 3 :015(305) [0483] was the situation: Since **nobody** could recall all his sins
S 3 : 0 3 :016(305) [0483] Moreover, since **nobody** knew how much contrition he
S 3 : 0 3 :021(306) [0485] more complicated, for **nobody** could know how much he
S 3 : 0 3 :027(307) [0487] Moreover, **nobody** knew which soul was in purgatory,
S 3 : 0 3 :027(307) [0487] was in purgatory, and **nobody** knew which of those in
T R : 0 0 :055(329) [0521] to his will and grants **nobody** the right to express an
T R : 0 0 :075(333) [0525] is a very serious charge, **nobody** should be condemned
L C : 0 1 :265(400) [0655] we should note that **nobody** has the right to judge and
L C : 0 1 :281(403) [0661] and root around in the filth, **nobody** will be reformed.
L C : 0 3 :065(429) [0715] Let **nobody** think that he will have peace; he must
L C : 0 6 :017(459) [0000] was impossible), and **nobody** could feel his conscience at
S D : 0 7 :007(570) [0975] manner, so that **nobody** will imagine that the reality is

Nod (1)
AP : 2 1 :034(234) [0353] puppet so that it seemed to **nod** Yes or No to the

Noerdlingen (1)
PR : PR :027(015) [0027] Mayor and Council of the City of **Noerdlingen**

Nomads (1)
AP : 2 7 :062(280) [0441] purpose: since they were **nomads** rather than Israelites,

Nomoclasts (2)
SD : 0 5 :015(561) [0957] the Antinomians or **nomoclasts** who cast the preaching of
SD : 0 5 :017(561) [0957] Luther says against the **nomoclasts**, "Everything that

Non (12)
AP : 1 2 :138(203) [0293] they quote do not say that **non**-obligatory works
AP : 1 2 :139(203) [0295] are we told that only **non**-obligatory works like the
AP : 1 2 :163(208) [0303] and the fruits that are due, not to "**non**-obligatory works."
AP : 1 2 :172(209) [0305] canonical satisfactions or **non**-obligatory works be done
AP : 1 2 :173(209) [0305] works of satisfaction are **non**-obligatory works, why cite
AP : 1 2 :173(209) [0305] in their satisfactions they impose **non**-obligatory works.
AP : 2 7 :021(272) [0427] are not impure **non**-obligatory forms of discipline.
TR : 0 0 :075(333) [0525] but in dealing with **non**-observance of fasts or festivals
LC : 0 1 :090(377) [0607] **Non**-Christians can spend a day in rest and idleness, too,
LC : 0 4 :059(444) [0747] The saying goes, *"Abusus **non** tollit, sed confirmat*
EP : 0 6 :008(481) [0807] but only upon unbelievers, **non**-Christians, and the
SD : 0 6 :026(568) [0971] but only upon unbelievers, **non**-Christians, and the

Nonsense (4)
S1 : PR :013(291) [0459] crosiers, and similar **nonsense** would soon be forgotten.
S2 : 0 2 :022(296) [0469] lies and so much **nonsense** has been invented about the
LC : 0 1 :054(372) [0595] arise and peddle their lying **nonsense** as the Word of God.
LC : 0 5 :040(451) [0761] now that the pope's **nonsense** has been abolished and we

Noon (1), Noonday (1), Noontide (1)
AP : 0 7 :029(173) [0237] clearer than the light of **noonday**; if our opponents still
AP : 1 2 :031(186) [0259] "I said, In the **noontide** of my days I must
LC : PR :003(358) [0567] be fine if every morning, **noon**, and evening they would

Noose (1)
LC : 0 1 :225(395) [0645] would be strangled with a **noose**, but the servant may

Norm (12)
PR : PR :000(001) [0004] Word of God as the Only **Norm**, of Several Articles about
PR : PR :019(010) [0017] are in agreement with the **norm** incorporated in the
PR : PR :020(010) [0017] Concord itself and in the **norm** comprehended therein
EP : RN :000(464) [0777] Summary, Rule, and **Norm** According to Which All
EP : RN :001(464) [0777] are the only rule and **norm** according to which all
EP : RN :007(465) [0779] the only judge, rule, and **norm** according to which as the
EP : 0 2 :007(470) [0787] errors as being contrary to the **norm** of the Word of God:
SD : RN :000(503) [0849] Basis, Rule, and **Norm**, Indicating How All Doctrines
SD : PR :003(504) [0851] which is the only true **norm** according to which all
SD : PR :009(505) [0855] remain the sole rule and **norm** of all doctrine, and that no
SD : 0 6 :003(564) [0963] which is a certain rule and **norm** for achieving a godly life
SD : 0 7 :085(584) [1001] following useful rule and **norm** has been derived from the

Northanus (2)
S3 : 1 5 :005(317) [0501] I, Brixius **Northanus**, minister of the church of Christ
TR : 0 0 :082(335) [0529] Brixius **Northanus**, minister in Soest

Northeim (1)
PR : PR :027(016) [0027] The Council of the City of **Northeim**

Nose (1), Noses (1)
LC : 0 1 :287(403) [0663] one covers his face, eyes, **nose**, and mouth; we do not
LC : 0 4 :020(439) [0737] with reference to their **noses**, eyes, skin and hair, flesh and

Notaries (1)
SC : PR :020(340) [0537] pastors, preachers, **notaries**, etc., and tell them that God

Note (12), Noted (4), Notes (1)
PR : PR :010(006) [0011] and learned theologians **noted** these developments, they
AG : 2 5 :012(063) [0071] The marginal **note** in *De poenitentia*, Dist. 5, also teaches
AL : 2 5 :012(063) [0071] The marginal **note** in *De poenitentia*, Dist. 5, in the
AP : PR :006(098) [0101] some of us had taken **notes** on the main points of its
AP : 0 4 :245(142) [0189] First, we must **note** that this text is more against our
AP : 2 3 :032(244) [0373] Let the reader **note** that he adds faith and does not praise
AP : 2 7 :061(279) [0441] therefore, we must **note** that they did not observe their
LC : 0 1 :094(378) [0607] **Note**, then, that the power and force of this
LC : 0 1 :206(393) [0639] speak of it, let us carefully **note**, first, how highly God
LC : 0 1 :265(400) [0655] vice, therefore, we should **note** that nobody has the right
LC : 0 1 :276(402) [0659] ought to be carefully **noted** if we are to avoid this
LC : 0 3 :008(421) [0699] This you should **note** above all, so that you may silence
LC : 0 4 :017(438) [0735] **Note** the distinction, then: Baptism is a very different
LC : 0 6 :015(458) [0000] **Note**, then, as I have often said, that confession consists
EP : 1 1 :002(494) [0831] and the eternal election of God is to be diligently **noted**.
SD : 0 8 :035(597) [1027] The following presentation should be **noted** diligently.
SD : 1 1 :004(616) [1063] outset we must carefully **note** the difference between

Nothing (250)
PR : PR :024(013) [0023] obscured and lost and **nothing** beyond uncertain opinions
PR : PR :024(013) [0023] effort and will allow **nothing** to stand in the way of this
AG : 0 8 :001(033) [0047] properly speaking, is **nothing** else than the assembly of
AG : 1 2 :003(034) [0049] true repentance is **nothing** else than to have contrition
AG : 2 0 :008(042) [0053] (as all must admit) while **nothing** but works was preached
AG : 2 0 :039(046) [0057] says in John 15:5, "Apart from me you can do **nothing**."
AG : 0 0 :002(048) [0059] Since, then, there is **nothing** unfounded or defective in the
AG : 0 0 :000(048) [0059] above it is manifest that **nothing** is taught in our churches
AG : 2 8 :019(084) [0087] Such authority has **nothing** at all to do with the office of
AG : 2 8 :041(087) [0089] fact that canon law says **nothing** of the reservation of
AG : 2 8 :049(089) [0091] that the Holy Spirit warned against them for **nothing**?
AG : 0 0 :005(095) [0095] that we have introduced **nothing**, either in doctrine or in
AL : 2 0 :018(043) [0055] Christian righteousness is **nothing** else than civil or
AL : 2 0 :039(046) [0057] from me you can do **nothing**" (John 15:5), and the church
AL : 2 0 :040(046) [0057] not, man hath naught, **Nothing** good in deed or thought,
AL : 2 0 :040(046) [0057] good in deed or thought, **Nothing** free from taint of ill."
AL : 0 0 :001(047) [0059] As can be seen, there is **nothing** here that departs from
AL : 0 0 :006(049) [0059] readily be judged that **nothing** contributes so much to the
AL : 2 4 :016(057) [0067] was brought about by **nothing** else than those abuses
AL : 2 4 :020(058) [0067] beginning of the world **nothing** of divine institution seems
AL : 2 5 :005(062) [0069] immoderately extolled, but **nothing** was said about faith.
AL : 0 0 :004(095) [0095] **Nothing** has here been said or related for the purpose of
AL : 0 0 :005(095) [0095] may be understood that **nothing** has been received among
AP : 0 2 :001(100) [0105] and distort a statement that has **nothing** wrong in it.
AP : 0 2 :015(102) [0109] We have said **nothing** new.
AP : 0 2 :032(104) [0113] So we teach **nothing** about original sin that is contrary to
AP : 0 2 :043(106) [0117] Or they say that **nothing** is sin unless it is voluntary.
AP : 0 4 :006(108) [0121] present we are saying **nothing** about the ceremonial and
AP : 0 4 :014(109) [0123] on natural ethics that **nothing** further needs to be added.
AP : 0 4 :021(110) [0127] our opponents teach **nothing** but the righteousness of
AP : 0 4 :048(113) [0135] And so they say **nothing** about faith by which, as Paul
AP : 0 4 :079(117) [0143] same thing, yet on this question they had **nothing** to say.
AP : 0 4 :084(119) [0145] **Nothing** one can devise or imagine will refute Paul's
AP : 0 4 :119(124) [0155] those who have heard **nothing** about this faith and who
AP : 0 4 :123(124) [0157] And again, "If I have not love, I am **nothing**" (I Cor. 13:2)
AP : 0 4 :131(125) [0157] the first table they care **nothing**, as though it were
AP : 0 4 :139(126) [0161] **Nothing** less than Christ's power is needed for our conflict
AP : 0 4 :154(128) [0163] **Nothing** greater could she ascribe to him.
AP : 0 4 :192(133) [0175] who is determined that **nothing** happen to the praise of
AP : 0 4 :218(137) [0179] "If I have all faith, etc., but have not love, I am **nothing**."
AP : 0 4 :222(138) [0181] justifies but that "I am **nothing**"; that is, faith is
AP : 0 4 :245(142) [0189] love and works but say **nothing** about the faith by which
AP : 0 4 :252(143) [0191] will be justified," contain **nothing** contrary to our
AP : 0 4 :255(143) [0193] passages would say **nothing** against us if our opponents
AP : 0 4 :256(144) [0193] says (John 15:5), "Apart from me you can do **nothing**."
AP : 0 4 :266(146) [0197] says (John 15:5), "Apart from me you can do **nothing**."
AP : 0 4 :268(147) [0197] this text proves **nothing** against us, because then they will
AP : 0 4 :269(147) [0197] from me you can do **nothing**" (John 15:5)—and that
AP : 0 4 :271(147) [0199] the scholastics have said **nothing** at all about faith in their
AP : 0 4 :315(156) [0207] says (John 15:5), "Apart from me you can do **nothing**."
AP : 0 4 :324(157) [0209] in such a way as to add **nothing** about this faith that
AP : 0 4 :324(157) [0211] since it teaches **nothing** about justifying faith and
AP : 0 4 :344(160) [0217] to salvation, there is **nothing** to distinguish those who are
AP : 0 4 :372(164) [0221] says, "Apart from me you can do **nothing**" (John 15:5).
AP : 0 4 :377(165) [0223] of justification is **nothing** more than the teaching of the
AP : 0 7 :002(168) [0227] **Nothing** can be said so carefully that it can avoid
AP : 0 7 :031(174) [0237] or particular, contribute **nothing**; nor are they wrought by
AP : 0 7 :043(177) [0243] and says that it contains **nothing** contrary to the faith or
AP : 1 1 :002(180) [0249] and monks teach **nothing** about faith and free
AP : 1 1 :009(182) [0251] They say **nothing** about Christ.
AP : 1 2 :034(186) [0261] our opponents say **nothing** about faith, but present only
AP : 1 2 :075(193) [0273] This is **nothing** but the teaching of the law, the
AP : 1 2 :084(194) [0277] Paul's sentences, for **nothing** can be said so simply that
AP : 1 2 :085(194) [0277] from me you can do **nothing**," and "I am the vine, you are
AP : 1 2 :089(195) [0277] Consciences do **nothing** from faith if they always doubt
AP : 1 2 :091(196) [0279] and the scholastics add **nothing** about faith in their
AP : 1 2 :098(197) [0281] thus far have written **nothing** about confession and
AP : 1 2 :131(202) [0291] by our opponents say **nothing** whatever about canonical
AP : 1 2 :150(206) [0299] measure; not in thy anger, lest thou bring me to **nothing**."
AP : 1 2 :156(207) [0301] These penalties have **nothing** to do with the power of the
AP : 1 2 :170(209) [0305] This proves **nothing** against us.
AP : 1 3 :013(213) [0311] corner doing and saying **nothing**, but only waiting for
AP : 1 5 :017(217) [0319] since we can affirm **nothing** about the will of God
AP : 1 5 :042(221) [0327] works, but they say **nothing** about the righteousness of
AP : 1 5 :048(221) [0329] and seasons contributes **nothing** to the subjection of the
AP : 1 5 :051(222) [0329] **Nothing** should be changed in the accustomed rites
AP : 2 1 :012(230) [0345] opponents can produce **nothing** against the argument
AP : 2 1 :026(232) [0349] doctor of theology, do **nothing** but urge this prayer upon
AP : 2 1 :037(234) [0355] are clowns who know **nothing** about either faith or public
AP : 2 4 :006(250) [0385] There is **nothing** contrary to the church catholic in our
AP : 2 4 :016(252) [0389] because without them **nothing** can be explained or
AP : 2 4 :031(255) [0395] The prophet says **nothing** about these shameless
AP : 2 4 :043(258) [0399] teach the law and say **nothing** about the righteousness of
AP : 2 4 :052(259) [0403] of the papal order are **nothing** but a misinterpretation of
AP : 2 7 :040(276) [0433] passage of Scripture has **nothing** to do with the monastic
AP : 2 7 :046(277) [0435] Such examples have **nothing** to do with Christian
S1 : PR :003(289) [0455] ever permit a free council, to say **nothing** of calling one.
S1 : PR :015(291) [0459] They will have **nothing** to do with Thee.
S2 : 0 1 :005(292) [0461] **Nothing** in this article can be given up or compromised,
S2 : 0 2 :007(293) [0463] The Mass is and can be **nothing** else than a human work,
S2 : 0 2 :012(295) [0465] it are to be regarded as **nothing** else than illusions of the
S2 : 0 2 :012(295) [0465] Besides, **nothing** has been commanded or enjoined upon
S2 : 0 2 :013(295) [0467] Now, this is **nothing** but a human opinion of certain
S2 : 0 4 :004(299) [0473] This is **nothing** less than to say, "Although you believe in
S2 : 0 4 :004(299) [0473] for salvation, this is **nothing** and all in vain unless you
S2 : 0 4 :010(300) [0475] which amounts to **nothing** since it is neither established
S3 : 0 1 :003(302) [0477] this article is therefore **nothing** but error and stupidity,
S3 : 0 3 :021(306) [0485] was to do for one single sin, to say **nothing** of all his sins.
S3 : 0 3 :022(306) [0485] Here, too, there was **nothing** but anguish and misery.
S3 : 0 3 :032(308) [0487] what sin really is, to say **nothing** of repenting and
S3 : 0 3 :032(308) [0489] Your repentance accomplishes **nothing**.
S3 : 0 3 :036(309) [0489] in such repentance, for **nothing** is left that we might
S3 : 0 3 :039(309) [0489] holy and beautiful, is **nothing** but deceitful falsehood and
S3 : 0 3 :041(309) [0491] theologians, the jurists, and all men understand **nothing**.
S3 : 0 5 :001(310) [0491] Baptism is **nothing** else than the Word of God in water,
S3 : 0 8 :004(312) [0495] The papacy, too, is **nothing** but enthusiasm, for the pope
TR : 0 0 :010(321) [0505] who were of repute added **nothing** to me" (Gal. 2:6).
TR : 0 0 :046(328) [0517] indulgences, which are **nothing** but lies devised for the
SC : PR :023(341) [0539] no heaven, no Christ, no God, **nothing** good at all.
SC : 0 3 :016(347) [0549] we sin daily and deserve **nothing** but punishment, we
SC : 0 9 :007(355) [0563] if you do right and let **nothing** terrify you" (I Pet. 3:1, 6).
LC : PR :001(358) [0567] bellies' sake and had **nothing** to do but live off the fat of
LC : PR :010(359) [0569] **Nothing** is so effectual against the devil, the world, the
LC : PR :016(361) [0573] it daily, for he knows of **nothing** better to teach, and he
LC : PR :016(361) [0573] All the saints know of **nothing** better or different to
LC : SP :005(362) [0575] ignorant that they knew **nothing** of these things — indeed
LC : 0 1 :002(365) [0581] To have a god is **nothing** else than to trust and believe him

Continued ▶

L C : 0 1 :008(365) [0583] other hand, he who has **nothing** doubts and despairs as if
L C : 0 1 :015(366) [0583] him with all our heart is **nothing** else than to entrust
L C : 0 1 :017(366) [0585] how the world practices **nothing** but false worship and
L C : 0 1 :020(367) [0585] into an idol and entrust themselves to an empty **nothing**.
L C : 0 1 :028(368) [0587] that expects from him **nothing** but good, especially in
L C : 0 1 :046(371) [0593] which indeed endures for a time but in the end is **nothing**!
L C : 0 1 :067(373) [0599] it may take a long time, **nothing** he does will in the end
L C : 0 1 :087(376) [0605] **Nothing** else than to devote it to holy words, holy works,
L C : 0 1 :105(379) [0611] in general he commands **nothing** higher than that we love
L C : 0 1 :116(381) [0615] first and observed, **nothing** ought to be considered more
L C : 0 1 :122(382) [0617] and lay up for themselves **nothing** but misfortune.
L C : 0 1 :123(382) [0617] or honor; they do **nothing** until they are driven with
L C : 0 1 :148(385) [0623] are not, you will have **nothing** but the wrath and
L C : 0 1 :154(386) [0625] from all authority, care **nothing** for anyone, and do
L C : 0 1 :155(386) [0625] is only fair that we have **nothing** but unhappiness without
L C : 0 1 :198(392) [0637] and filth, and it merits **nothing** but wrath and
L C : 0 1 :224(395) [0643] For to steal is **nothing** else than to acquire another's
L C : 0 1 :228(396) [0645] in all its conditions, it is **nothing** but a vast, wide stable
L C : 0 1 :253(399) [0653] for your needs and will let you lack or want for **nothing**.
L C : 0 1 :268(401) [0657] This is **nothing** else than usurping the judgment and
L C : 0 1 :291(404) [0663] There is **nothing** about a man or in a man that can do
L C : 0 1 :314(407) [0671] tapers and candles until **nothing** else can be seen or
L C : 0 1 :314(407) [0671] does what she is told, that is regarded as **nothing**.
L C : 0 2 :010(412) [0681] Thus the Creed is **nothing** else than a response and
L C : 0 2 :026(413) [0685] has completely given himself to us, withholding **nothing**.
L C : 0 2 :039(415) [0689] Therefore to sanctify is **nothing** else than to bring us to
L C : 0 2 :048(416) [0691] *(Kirche)* really means **nothing** else than a common
L C : 0 2 :049(417) [0691] It is **nothing** but a comment or interpretation by which
L C : 0 2 :052(417) [0691] of the devil, knowing **nothing** of God and of Christ.
L C : 0 2 :065(419) [0695] Apart from him we see **nothing** but an angry and terrible
L C : 0 3 :002(420) [0697] Consequently **nothing** is so necessary as to call upon God
L C : 0 3 :005(420) [0699] For to call upon it is **nothing** else than to pray.
L C : 0 3 :010(421) [0699] we are sinners and have merited **nothing** but wrath.
L C : 0 3 :013(422) [0701] prayer would amount to **nothing**; but it is important
L C : 0 3 :048(426) [0711] For there is **nothing** he would rather hear than to have
L C : 0 3 :056(427) [0713] He desires of us **nothing** more ardently than that we ask
L C : 0 3 :068(429) [0717] they may accomplish **nothing** and we may remain
L C : 0 3 :083(431) [0721] he withdraws his hand, **nothing** can prosper or last for
L C : 0 3 :088(432) [0723] Gospel, in which there is **nothing** but forgiveness, before
L C : 0 3 :103(434) [0727] In short, there is in it **nothing** but hatred and envy,
L C : 0 3 :116(435) [0731] Therefore there is **nothing** for us to do on earth but to
L C : 0 3 :120(436) [0731] This word is **nothing** else than an unquestioning
L C : 0 3 :123(436) [0731] Therefore they receive **nothing**, as St. James says, "If
L C : 0 4 :001(436) [0733] unfortunately in the past **nothing** was taught about them.
L C : 0 4 :014(438) [0735] It is **nothing** else than a divine water, not that the water in
L C : 0 4 :015(438) [0735] and ordinance, consider **nothing** but the water drawn
L C : 0 4 :025(439) [0739] To be saved, we know, is **nothing** else than to be delivered
L C : 0 4 :028(440) [0739] works and external things contribute **nothing** to this end.
L C : 0 4 :028(440) [0739] We answer: It is true, **nothing** that is in us does it but
L C : 0 4 :034(441) [0741] is not faith contributes **nothing** toward salvation, and
L C : 0 4 :034(441) [0741] nothing toward salvation, and receives **nothing**.
L C : 0 4 :037(441) [0741] necessary that without it **nothing** can be received or
L C : 0 4 :038(441) [0741] Just so, if we had **nothing** more than these words, "Go
L C : 0 4 :058(444) [0747] I might argue, "If I have no faith, then Christ is **nothing**."
L C : 0 4 :058(444) [0747] then father, mother, and magistrates are **nothing**."
L C : 0 4 :065(445) [0749] Thus a Christian life is **nothing** else than a daily Baptism,
L C : 0 4 :066(445) [0749] with all vices and by nature has **nothing** good in him.
L C : 0 4 :074(445) [0751] called Penance, which is really **nothing** else than Baptism.
L C : 0 4 :079(446) [0751] Repentance, therefore, is **nothing** else than a return and
L C : 0 5 :014(448) [0755] the Word, you have **nothing** but ordinary bread and
L C : 0 5 :035(450) [0761] who does not believe has **nothing**, for he lets this gracious
L C : 0 5 :049(452) [0765] When a person, with **nothing** to hinder him, lets a long
L C : 0 5 :057(453) [0767] toward the time when **nothing** will prick your conscience,
L C : 0 5 :069(454) [0769] To such people **nothing** can be good or wholesome, just
L C : 0 5 :076(455) [0771] "For I know that **nothing** good dwells within me,
L C : 0 5 :077(455) [0771] leprous flesh which feels **nothing** though the disease rages
L C : 0 5 :081(456) [0771] **Nothing** else than what the Scriptures call him, a liar and
L C : 0 5 :083(456) [0773] If even then you feel **nothing**, you have all the more need
L C : 0 6 :003(457) [0000] confession even though **nothing** was more hateful to
L C : 0 6 :006(457) [0000] Gospel's benefits but did **nothing** about it and paid
L C : 0 6 :006(457) [0000] benefits but did nothing about it and paid **nothing** for it?
L C : 0 6 :009(458) [0000] whole Lord's Prayer is **nothing** else than such a
L C : 0 6 :030(460) [0000] preaching, we shall have **nothing** to do with him, nor may
E P : 0 1 :008(467) [0781] deep a corruption that **nothing** sound or uncorrupted has
E P : 0 2 :002(470) [0787] and that he understands **nothing** by his own powers, as it
E P : 0 2 :006(470) [0787] Christ also states, "Apart from me you can do **nothing**."
E P : 0 2 :014(471) [0789] rebirth he creates out of **nothing** a new essence of the
E P : 0 2 :018(472) [0791] (that is, that it does **nothing** at all) must be understood as
E P : 0 5 :008(478) [0803] only the law and hear **nothing** about Christ, the veil of
E P : 0 7 :004(482) [0809] that in the Holy Supper **nothing** but bread and wine are
E P : 0 8 :003(487) [0819] deed and in truth) has **nothing** in common with the
E P : 0 8 :003(487) [0819] the humanity really has **nothing** in common with the
E P : 0 8 :025(490) [0823] is, in fact) the deity has **nothing** in common with the
E P : 1 1 :003(494) [0833] God's foreknowledge in **nothing** else than that God
E P : 1 2 :005(498) [0839] which in fact is **nothing** else but a new kind of monkery.
E P : 1 2 :011(498) [0841] 9. That one is to have **nothing** to do with clergyman who
S D : 0 1 :012(510) [0863] them that they amount to **nothing** in the sight of God.
S D : 0 1 :025(512) [0867] it can by and of itself do **nothing** but sin (Gen. 6:5; 8:21).
S D : 0 1 :060(519) [0879] of human nature that **nothing** pure nor good has
S D : 0 1 :062(519) [0879] it so deeply that **nothing** in it remained pure and
S D : 0 2 :003(520) [0881] he could accomplish **nothing** with these powers but would
S D : 0 2 :014(523) [0885] from me you can do **nothing**" (John 15:5), and what St.
S D : 0 2 :017(524) [0887] Paul says, "I know that **nothing** good dwells within me,
S D : 0 2 :018(524) [0887] natural powers can do **nothing** for man's conversion,
S D : 0 2 :024(525) [0891] Holy Spirit, he can do **nothing** in spiritual things of
S D : 0 2 :026(526) [0891] from me," says Christ, "you can do **nothing** (John 15:5).
S D : 0 2 :032(527) [0893] spiritual things our free will and reason can do **nothing**."
S D : 0 2 :035(528) [0895] These words say **nothing** at all about our will, nor do they
S D : 0 2 :046(530) [0899] Spirit and they can do **nothing** of themselves in these
S D : 0 2 :059(532) [0905] Yet he can do **nothing** whatsoever toward his conversion,
S D : 0 2 :073(535) [0909] Spirit, and if he does **nothing** at all, but merely suffers
S D : 0 2 :081(537) [0911] and a new substance of the soul is created out of **nothing**.
S D : 0 2 :087(538) [0913] corrupted will, which is **nothing** else but a resurrection of
S D : 0 2 :089(538) [0915] is, man does or works **nothing**; he only suffers — though
S D : 0 2 :090(539) [0915] is to be converted does **nothing**, but only lets God work in
S D : 0 3 :036(545) [0927] or as though believers must or dare do **nothing** good.
S D : 0 5 :008(559) [0953] phrase "to repent" means **nothing** more than truly to
S D : 0 5 :012(560) [0955] that shows and gives **nothing** but grace and forgiveness in
S D : 0 5 :016(561) [0957] that we are concealing **nothing** in this present controversy
S D : 0 6 :008(565) [0965] writes, "I know that **nothing** good dwells within me."
S D : 0 6 :018(567) [0969] of the Lord, and yet do **nothing** by the compulsion of the
S D : 0 7 :003(569) [0973] earth, and consequently **nothing** but bread and wine are
S D : 0 7 :004(569) [0973] Christians, and that **nothing** more than mere bread and
S D : 0 7 :018(572) [0979] is intended to mean **nothing** more than the spiritual
S D : 0 7 :023(573) [0979] Word, you then have **nothing** but ordinary bread and
S D : 0 7 :078(583) [1001] is the body of Christ,' **nothing** would happen, but when
S D : 0 7 :085(584) [1001] the words of institution: **Nothing** has the character of a
S D : 0 7 :108(588) [1009] For **nothing** can be a sacrament apart from God's
S D : 0 7 :116(589) [1011] 5. Or that they are **nothing** more than symbols and
S D : 0 8 :004(592) [1017] That is, they said that **nothing** is to be attributed to the
S D : 0 8 :023(595) [1023] truth, all of this would be **nothing**, nor could it even be.
S D : 0 8 :048(600) [1031] the personal union have **nothing** else and nothing more
S D : 0 8 :048(600) [1031] have nothing else and **nothing** more than their own
S D : 0 8 :049(600) [1031] with God (James 1:17), **nothing** was added to or detracted
S D : 0 8 :050(600) [1031] the human nature has **nothing** else and nothing more than
S D : 0 8 :050(600) [1031] has nothing else and **nothing** more than its own natural
S D : 0 8 :050(600) [1031] and that for this reason **nothing** should or can be ascribed
S D : 0 8 :070(605) [1041] to him, he left **nothing** outside his control" (Heb. 2:7, 8),
S D : 0 8 :084(607) [1045] he would have to be **nothing** more than a mere isolated
S D : 1 1 :009(617) [1065] no more and that **nothing** more is involved in it, or that
S D : 1 1 :009(617) [1065] is involved in it, or that **nothing** more is to be considered
S D : 1 2 :016(634) [1099] 7. That one is to have **nothing** to do with those ministers
S D : 1 2 :027(635) [1101] as basically **nothing** else than a new kind of monkery.

Nothings (2)
A P : 2 3 :002(239) [0363] of these good-for-**nothings** who say that marriage
A P : 2 7 :029(274) [0431] is the way these good-for-**nothings** quote the Scriptures.

Notice (4), Noticed (1)
P R : P R :017(008) [0015] the right and served **notice** that we would furnish further
A P : 1 2 :120(200) [0287] church, but they did not **notice** that these public
L C : 0 1 :010(366) [0583] **Notice**, again, how presumptuous, secure, and proud
L C : 0 1 :112(380) [0613] In the second place, **notice** what a great, good, and holy
L C : 0 6 :016(459) [0000] We neither **noticed** nor preached the very necessary

Notify (1), Notified (1)
A G : P R :018(026) [0041] things, informed and **notified** by Your Imperial Majesty's
S C : P R :012(339) [0535] and drink and should **notify** them that the prince is

Notion (30), Notions (9)
A G : 1 5 :002(036) [0049] not be burdened by the **notion** that such things are
A G : 2 6 :029(068) [0075] of sin or with the **notion** that nobody is a Christian unless
A G : 2 8 :037(086) [0089] that because of this **notion** human ordinances have
A L : 2 6 :029(068) [0075] through them or with the **notion** that Christian
A L : 2 8 :037(086) [0089] that as a result of this **notion** traditions have multiplied in
A L : 2 8 :061(091) [0093] have arisen from the false **notion** that there must be a
A P : 0 2 :044(106) [0117] These **notions** prevailed, feeding a trust in human powers
A P : 0 4 :207(135) [0177] these sacrifices with the **notion** that on account of them
A P : 0 4 :207(135) [0177] did away with faith in the **notion** that through these
A P : 0 7 :042(177) [0243] the people of the foolish **notion** of having to observe a set
A P : 1 2 :068(192) [0271] defend the false **notions** we have been discussing about
A P : 1 3 :018(213) [0313] this ungodly and wicked **notion** is taught with great
A P : 1 3 :023(214) [0313] which this fanatical **notion**, about the sacraments *ex*
A P : 1 5 :018(217) [0319] our opponents defend the **notion** that these human rites
A P : 1 5 :034(220) [0325] good, especially from the **notion** that they merit
A P : 1 8 :003(225) [0335] from these Pelagian **notions** which the schools teach with
A P : 1 8 :003(225) [0335] emphatic refutation of these **notions**, based on Paul.
A P : 2 0 :004(227) [0339] if they dare to smuggle such a **notion** into the church.
A P : 2 1 :032(233) [0351] Such **notions** are obviously of pagan origin.
A P : 2 4 :013(251) [0387] this pharisaic and pagan **notion** about the working of the
A P : 2 4 :013(251) [0387] Yet this **notion** has taken hold among the people and has
A P : 2 4 :013(251) [0387] have brought this pharisaic **notion** into the church.
A P : 2 4 :027(254) [0393] clearly condemns the **notion** that the sacrifices are valid
A P : 2 4 :028(254) [0393] condemn the popular **notion** of worship *ex opere*
A P : 2 4 :034(256) [0395] it does not support the **notion** of ceremonies *ex opere*
A P : 2 4 :057(260) [0405] This **notion** completely negates the merit of Christ's
A P : 2 4 :097(268) [0417] Testament had a similar **notion** that they merited the
A P : 2 4 :097(268) [0417] prophets condemn this **notion**, therefore, they are battling
A P : 2 4 :097(268) [0417] instituted by God with this wicked **notion** in mind.
A P : 2 4 :097(268) [0417] But this **notion** clings to the world, and always will, that
A P : 2 7 :009(270) [0421] Are vows made with these **notions** in mind legitimate?
A P : 2 7 :016(271) [0425] this wicked and fanatical **notion** they bury the blessing of
A P : 2 7 :023(272) [0427] But the **notion** that these observances are services because
A P : 2 7 :036(275) [0433] they are modifying the common **notion** about perfection.
A P : 2 8 :008(282) [0445] vigorously defend their traditions and wicked **notions**.
S 3 : 0 1 :011(303) [0479] Such and many similar **notions** have resulted from
T R : 0 0 :034(325) [0513] This **notion** has caused horrible darkness to descend over
L C : 0 4 :080(446) [0751] We have such a **notion** because we regard Baptism only in
S D : 0 6 :003(564) [0963] according to their own **notions** but according to his

Notoriety (1), Notorious (8)
A P : 1 2 :112(198) [0285] Because the lapsed or **notorious** sinners were not accepted
A P : 1 2 :113(199) [0285] accept the lapsed or the **notorious** sinners unless they had
A P : 1 2 :113(199) [0285] warns, and admitting **notorious** people to communion
A P : 2 1 :039(235) [0355] to compel us to approve of the most **notorious** abuses.
A P : 2 3 :001(239) [0363] Despite the **notoriety** of their defiled celibacy, our
A P : 2 7 :001(268) [0419] because he had condemned certain **notorious** abuses.
A P : 2 7 :002(269) [0419] estate but had only denounced certain **notorious** abuses.
T R : 0 0 :060(330) [0521] those who are guilty of **notorious** crimes and absolve
L C : 0 1 :289(404) [0663] as long as it is not a **notorious** evil, and to defend him

Nourish (1), Nourished (2), Nourishes (2), Nourishing (1), Nourishment (2)
A L : 2 4 :008(057) [0065] and such use of the sacrament **nourishes** devotion to God.
A P : 1 2 :042(187) [0261] Meanwhile this faith is **nourished** in many ways, amid
A P : 2 3 :019(242) [0369] just as he wants to **nourish** our life by using food and
A P : 2 7 :053(278) [0437] as stupid as it is wicked, **nourishing** a false confidence.

Continued ▶

L C : 0 1 :024(367) [0587] body, life, food, drink, **nourishment**, health, protection,
L C : 0 1 :026(368) [0587] the earth for man's **nourishment** — things which no
L C : 0 1 :129(383) [0617] and that he has been **nourished** and nurtured by them
L C : 0 5 :023(449) [0757] food of the soul since it **nourishes** and strengthens the new

Novatians (2)
A G : 1 2 :009(035) [0049] the other hand are the **Novatians** who denied absolution
A L : 1 2 :009(035) [0049] Also condemned are the **Novatians** who were unwilling to

Novel (2), Novelty (4)
A G : 1 8 :004(039) [0051] that this teaching is no **novelty**, the clear words of
A G : 2 4 :025(059) [0067] It is an unprecedented **novelty** in church doctrine that
A G : 2 4 :040(060) [0069] Since, therefore, no **novelty** has been introduced which
A L : 2 7 :060(080) [0083] and testified that it was a **novelty** in his day to say that
A P : 2 1 :013(230) [0345] church, we reply that this is a **novel** custom in the church.
A P : 2 1 :013(230) [0345] Besides, this **novel** invocation in the church is not the

Novellae (1)
T R : 0 0 :077(333) [0527] from the *Codex* and ***Novellae*** of Justinian that decisions

Nowhere (8)
A L : 2 3 :018(054) [0063] a marvelous thing that **nowhere** is greater cruelty
A P : 0 4 :063(115) [0139] **Nowhere** can our opponents say how the Holy Spirit is
A P : 1 2 :139(203) [0295] But **nowhere** in Holy Scripture are we told that only
A P : 2 1 :001(229) [0343] **Nowhere** else do they expend so much sophistry, but all
A P : 2 1 :040(235) [0355] **Nowhere** do they distinguish between their teachings and
T R : 0 0 :044(328) [0517] **Nowhere** do they teach that sins are forgiven freely for
L C : 0 1 :046(370) [0593] and persecuted, his life **nowhere** secure, yet inevitably he
S D : 0 7 :006(570) [0973] is now in heaven and **nowhere** else, and that with the

Nucleus (1)
L C : 0 4 :016(438) [0735] For the **nucleus** in the water is God's Word or

Null (5), Nullify (5)
A G : 2 7 :018(073) [0079] marry, for vows cannot **nullify** God's order and
A G : 2 7 :036(076) [0081] still more reasons why monastic vows are **null** and void.
A G : 2 7 :040(077) [0081] vow, made contrary to God's command, is **null** and void.
A G : 2 7 :062(080) [0083] useless, and invented, monastic vows are **null** and void.
A L : 2 3 :008(052) [0061] of man and no vow can **nullify** a commandment of God
A L : 2 3 :024(055) [0065] as no human law can **nullify** a command of God, so no
A L : 2 7 :018(073) [0079] marry, for vows can not **nullify** the command and
A L : 2 7 :062(080) [0083] since they are false and useless, make vows **null** and void.
A P : 0 4 :042(113) [0133] are to be the heirs, faith is **null** and the promise is void."
L C : 0 4 :062(444) [0749] in addition, pervert and **nullify** all God's work and

Number (34), Numbered (1), Numerous (3)
P R : P R :010(006) [0011] When a **number** of pious, irenic, and learned theologians
P R : P R :013(007) [0013] and princes, convoked a **number** of prominent,
P R : P R :013(007) [0013] sent to a considerable **number** of electors, princes, and
P R : P R :015(007) [0013] other estates not of our **number**, some of us have had this
P R : P R :020(010) [0017] even though a **number** of theologians, like Luther
A L : 2 4 :040(061) [0069] Only the **number** of Masses is different, and on account
A L : 2 4 :040(061) [0069] it would certainly be of advantage to reduce the **number**.
A L : 2 6 :028(068) [0073] of consciences with **numerous** rites, whether of Moses or
A P : P R :001(098) [0099] princes' Confession, a **number** of theologians and monks
A P : 0 7 :009(169) [0229] There is an infinite **number** of ungodly within the church
A P : 1 2 :069(192) [0271] be moved by this large **number** of quotations, it must be
A P : 1 2 :124(201) [0289] with such important, **numerous**, and varied subjects in
A P : 1 2 :143(204) [0297] same holds when a fixed **number** of prayers or certain
A P : 1 3 :000(211) [0309] [Article XIII.] The **Number** and Use of the Sacraments
A P : 1 3 :002(211) [0309] instituted in Scripture, whatever their **number**.
A P : 1 3 :017(213) [0313] will quibble about the **number** of sacraments or the
A P : 2 4 :081(264) [0411] shows: "Even though the **number** of children does not
A P : 2 7 :003(269) [0419] regime and this same **number** of years written down by
A P : 2 7 :069(280) [0443] We have run through a **number** of our arguments, and in
S 3 : 1 5 :005(316) [0501] which are without **number**, we commend for adoration to
T R : 0 0 :023(324) [0511] spoken in the singular **number** ("I will give you the keys"
T R : 0 0 :062(331) [0523] chose one of their **number**, set him in a higher place, and
T R : 0 0 :062(331) [0523] may choose from their **number** one who is known to be
T R : 0 0 :064(331) [0523] should ordain the ministers in a **number** of churches.
T R : 0 0 :079(333) [0527] there are sufficiently **numerous** and compelling reasons
T R : 0 0 :081(334) [0527] The variety and **number** of matrimonial disputes are so
T R : 0 0 :082(000) [0529] although in so great a **number** of most learned men who
L C : 0 1 :305(406) [0667] others and by any of a **number** of ways, to make her
E P : 0 0 :000(463) [0775] and Explanation of a **Number** of Articles of the Augsburg
E P : 0 7 :001(481) [0807] teachers cannot be **numbered** among the theologians
S D : 0 0 :000(501) [0845] and Exposition of a **Number** of Articles of the Augsburg
S D : P R :003(501) [0847] At that time a **number** of Christian electors, princes, and
S D : P R :005(504) [0851] V at Augsburg by a **number** of Christian electors,
S D : P R :019(507) [0857] past twenty-five years a **number** of divisions have
S D : 0 1 :001(508) [0859] been dissension among a **number** of theologians of the
S D : 0 2 :001(519) [0881] but also among a **number** of theologians of the Augsburg
S D : 0 2 :073(535) [0909] that for a considerable **number** of years have been
S D : 0 7 :001(568) [0971] however, in later years a **number** of theologians and

Nuns (3)
L C : 0 1 :118(381) [0615] Carthusian monks and **nuns** would pay if in the exercise
L C : 0 1 :213(394) [0641] priests, monks, and **nuns** resist God's order and
L C : 0 1 :314(407) [0671] Otherwise, why should monks and **nuns** go into cloisters?

Nuptiarum (2)
A G : 2 7 :035(076) [0081] Augustine says in his ***Nuptiarum***, Question 27, Chapter I,
A L : 2 7 :035(076) [0081] denies that they should be dissolved in ***Nuptiarum***,

Nuremberg (4)
A L : 0 0 :017(096) [0095] Senate and magistrate of **Nuremberg**
S 3 : 1 5 :005(317) [0501] I, Andrew Osiander, minister in **Nuremberg**, subscribe
S 3 : 1 5 :005(317) [0501] I, Master Veit Dietrich, minister in **Nuremberg**, subscribe
T R : 0 0 :082(334) [0529] Master Veit Dietrich, of **Nuremberg**, subscribes

Nuremburg (1)
A G : 0 0 :007(096) [0095] Mayor and council of **Nuremburg**

Nurture (1), Nurtured (2)
A P : 0 4 :232(139) [0185] harmony should be **nurtured** by mutual aid, for it is not
L C : 0 1 :129(383) [0617] has been nourished and **nurtured** by them when otherwise
S D : 0 2 :020(524) [0889] matters affecting the **nurture** and needs of the body, man

Nut (1)
L C : 0 4 :019(439) [0737] (as we see the shell of a **nut**) but as that in which God's

Nyssa (1)
S D : 0 8 :022(595) [1023] Basil and Gregory of **Nyssa**, in Theodoret; John

Oath (15), Oaths (5)
A G : 1 6 :002(037) [0051] and sell, take required **oaths**, possess property, be
A G : 2 7 :040(077) [0081] the canons teach that an **oath** should not be an obligation
A G : 2 8 :070(093) [0093] unless he first swears an **oath** that he will not preach this
A L : 1 6 :002(037) [0051] hold property, to swear **oaths** when required by
A P : 1 2 :094(196) [0281] dwelling especially on the **oath** in the prophet (Ez. 33:11),
A P : 1 2 :094(196) [0281] for us, but this promise is confirmed with an **oath**.
A P : 1 2 :094(196) [0281] invites us to salvation with an offer and even an **oath**.
A P : 1 2 :094(196) [0281] Oh, blessed are we for whose sake God swears an **oath**!
A P : 1 2 :094(196) [0281] we do not believe the Lord even when he swears an **oath**!"
A P : 1 6 :001(222) [0329] own property, take an **oath** when the government
T R : 0 0 :055(329) [0521] he has bound by horrible **oaths** and curses to defend his
L C : 0 1 :051(371) [0595] example, where men take **oaths** in court and one side lies
L C : 0 1 :053(372) [0595] to each other and afterward deny it under **oath**.
L C : 0 1 :065(373) [0599] and yet Christ, St. Paul, and other saints took **oaths**.
L C : 0 1 :067(373) [0599] he may gain by the false **oath** will slip through his fingers
E P : 1 1 :013(496) [0835] words, but also with his **oath**, and has sealed it with his
E P : 1 2 :015(499) [0841] Christian cannot swear an **oath** with a good conscience
E P : 1 2 :015(499) [0841] a good conscience nor pay **oath**-bound feudal homage to
S D : 1 2 :020(634) [1099] good conscience swear an **oath** before a court or pay
S D : 1 2 :020(634) [1099] oath before a court or pay **oath**-bound feudal homage to

Oats (1)
S 3 : 1 5 :005(316) [0501] are blessings of candles, palms, spices, **oats**, cakes, etc.

Obduracy (1), Obdurate (2)
S D : 1 1 :054(625) [1081] falling away will return and who will become **obdurate**.
S D : 1 1 :083(630) [1091] sins God punishes with **obduracy** and blindness those who
S D : 1 1 :085(630) [1091] and became the more **obdurate** the more he was

Obedience (138), Obedient (20)
A G : P R :008(025) [0039] Wherefore, in dutiful **obedience** to Your Imperial
A G : P R :010(025) [0041] we are prepared, in **obedience** to Your Imperial Majesty,
A G : P R :021(026) [0043] above, we offer in full **obedience**, even beyond what is
A G : 0 6 :000(031) [0045] VI. [The New **Obedience**]
A G : 2 0 :037(046) [0057] are commanded, render **obedience**, avoid evil lusts, etc.
A G : 2 8 :013(083) [0085] laws or undermine **obedience** to government, should not
A G : 2 8 :022(084) [0087] are bound to be **obedient** to the bishops according to the
A G : 2 8 :023(084) [0087] command not to be **obedient** in such cases, for Christ
A G : 2 8 :055(090) [0091] of love and peace, to be **obedient** to the bishops and
A G : 2 8 :069(093) [0093] might easily retain the **obedience** of men if they did not
A G : 0 0 :007(096) [0095] Your Imperial Majesty's most **obedient** servants:
A L : 0 6 :000(031) [0045] VI. [The New **Obedience**]
A L : 2 8 :013(083) [0085] nor abolish lawful **obedience**, nor interfere with
A L : 2 8 :022(084) [0087] by divine law to be **obedient** to the bishops according to
A L : 2 8 :023(084) [0087] of God that forbids **obedience**: "Beware of false prophets"
A L : 2 8 :069(093) [0093] easily retain the lawful **obedience** of men if they did not
A P : 0 2 :023(103) [0111] it not only denies the **obedience** of man's lower powers,
A P : 0 4 :008(108) [0121] Finally, it requires **obedience** to God in death and all
A P : 0 4 :151(127) [0163] patience, chastity, or **obedience** to the government, etc.),
A P : 0 4 :159(129) [0165] keeping of the law, and **obedience** to the law certainly is
A P : 0 4 :160(129) [0167] keeping of the law and **obedience** to the law is perfect, it
A P : 0 4 :181(132) [0171] And to that extent this **obedience** of the law justifies by
A P : 0 4 :197(134) [0175] not mean to say that **obedience** to parents justifies us
A P : 0 4 :228(139) [0183] This **obedience** toward God, this desire to receive the
A P : 0 4 :289(151) [0203] and that such **obedience** to the law is worthy of grace and
A P : 0 4 :308(155) [0207] truly righteousness because it is **obedience** to the Gospel.
A P : 0 4 :308(155) [0207] **Obedience** to the edict of a superior is obviously a kind of
A P : 0 4 :308(155) [0207] Our good works or **obedience** to the law can be pleasing
A P : 0 4 :308(155) [0207] God only because this **obedience** to the Gospel takes hold
A P : 0 4 :311(155) [0207] opponents talk about **obedience** to the law; they do not
A P : 0 4 :311(155) [0207] the law; they do not talk about **obedience** to the Gospel.
A P : 1 2 :160(208) [0303] sacrifices, to show our **obedience** but not to pay for
A P : 1 2 :164(208) [0303] If you are willing and **obedient**, you shall eat the good of
A P : 1 2 :174(210) [0307] teaching of the Gospel, **obedience** to parents and
A P : 1 6 :003(223) [0331] or by others, and in this **obedience** to practice love.
A P : 1 8 :010(226) [0337] to them out of regard for the merit of this **obedience**.
A P : 2 4 :036(257) [0397] by the Spirit for **obedience** to Jesus Christ and for
A P : 2 7 :016(271) [0425] poverty, chastity, and **obedience** — hypocrisies all, since
A P : 2 7 :016(271) [0425] They brag about **obedience** though no class of men has
A P : 2 7 :021(272) [0427] Second, **obedience**, poverty, and celibacy, provided they
A P : 2 7 :049(277) [0437] This sets forth the example of **obedience** in a calling.
A P : 2 7 :049(277) [0437] and persons; but the example of **obedience** is universal.
A P : 2 7 :061(280) [0441] are praised for their **obedience**, which God commanded
A P : 2 8 :020(284) [0449] This statement requires **obedience** to the Gospel; it does
S 2 : 0 4 :004(299) [0473] can be saved unless he is **obedient** to the pope and
S 2 : 0 4 :004(299) [0473] me your god and are **obedient** and subject to me."
S 2 : 0 4 :011(300) [0475] receive bodily tribute and **obedience** from Christians.
S 2 : 0 4 :012(300) [0475] asserts that one must be **obedient** to him in order to be
T R : 0 0 :038(326) [0515] by divine right, **obedience** would still not be owing to
S C : P R :018(340) [0537] to be orderly, faithful, **obedient**, and peaceful.
S C : 0 9 :005(355) [0561] and authorities, to be **obedient**, to be ready for any
S C : 0 9 :010(356) [0563] "Be **obedient** to those who are your earthly masters, with
L C : 0 1 :066(373) [0599] people are reconciled, **obedience** is rendered, and quarrels
L C : 0 1 :069(374) [0599] is no government, no **obedience**, no fidelity, no faith —
L C : 0 1 :112(380) [0613] to show all honor and **obedience** to my parents, since God
L C : 0 1 :114(380) [0613] remained at home in **obedience** and service to their
L C : 0 1 :116(381) [0615] greater and nobler than **obedience** to father and mother,
L C : 0 1 :116(381) [0615] and commanded next to **obedience** to his own majesty.
L C : 0 1 :116(381) [0615] are subordinated to **obedience** toward God and are not
L C : 0 1 :125(382) [0617] should we be happy to show them honor and **obedience**.

Continued ▶

LC : 0 1 :136(383) [0619] will have it: render him **obedience** and love and service,
LC : 0 1 :137(384) [0621] The godly and the **obedient**, however, are blessed.
LC : 0 1 :139(384) [0621] God considers **obedience**, since he so highly exalts it, so
LC : 0 1 :141(384) [0621] the various kinds of **obedience** due to our superiors,
LC : 0 1 :148(385) [0623] You are a true nobleman if you are upright and **obedient**.
LC : 0 1 :149(385) [0623] God speaks to you and demands **obedience**.
LC : 0 1 :150(385) [0623] same may be said of **obedience** to the civil government,
LC : 0 1 :151(386) [0625] He who is **obedient**, willing, ready to serve, and cheerfully
LC : 0 1 :152(386) [0625] that works of **obedience** are so pleasing to God and have
LC : 0 1 :168(388) [0629] consider that they owe **obedience** to God, and that, above
LC : 0 1 :180(389) [0631] that is, divine and paternal authority and **obedience**.
LC : 0 1 :327(409) [0675] being submissive and **obedient** to them not on their own
LC : 0 3 :002(420) [0697] increase in us faith and **obedience** to the Ten
LC : 0 3 :009(421) [0699] to say to his father: "What is the use of being **obedient**?
LC : 0 3 :013(422) [0701] should never despise **obedience** to his father and mother,
LC : 0 3 :013(422) [0701] "This is a work of **obedience**, and what I do has no other
LC : 0 3 :013(422) [0701] than that it befits **obedience** and the commandment of
LC : 0 3 :013(422) [0701] as demanded by God and done in **obedience** to him.
LC : 0 3 :013(422) [0701] always approach God in **obedience** to this commandment.
LC : 0 3 :016(422) [0701] on account of his Word and the **obedience** accorded it.
LC : 0 3 :017(422) [0703] must be based on **obedience** to God, regardless of our
LC : 0 3 :025(423) [0705] to pray out of **obedience** to God and faith in his promise,
LC : 0 3 :077(431) [0721] at large to live together in **obedience**, peace, and concord.
LC : 0 4 :058(444) [0747] Or again, "If I am not **obedient**, then father, mother, and
LC : 0 4 :061(444) [0747] see neither faith nor **obedience**, they conclude that these
EP : 0 3 :003(473) [0793] solely in his **obedience** which as God and man he
EP : 0 3 :003(473) [0793] so by *one man's **obedience*** many will be made righteous"
EP : 0 3 :004(473) [0793] of Christ's **obedience**, on account of which righteousness
EP : 0 3 :006(473) [0793] solely because of his **obedience**, by grace, we have
EP : 0 3 :016(475) [0795] look alone to Christ's **obedience**, but also to his divine
EP : 0 3 :017(475) [0795] is a kind of trust in the **obedience** of Christ that can exist
EP : 0 3 :021(475) [0797] by the incipient new **obedience**, or in part by the
EP : 0 3 :021(475) [0797] righteousness and in part by our incipient new **obedience**.
EP : 0 4 :003(476) [0797] speaking of the new **obedience**, since it does not flow from
EP : 0 4 :003(476) [0797] that the new **obedience** is not a matter of our choice but
EP : 0 4 :003(476) [0797] regenerated persons are bound to render such **obedience**.
EP : 0 4 :010(476) [0799] coercion but the due **obedience** which genuine believers,
EP : 0 6 :007(481) [0807] The difference, as far as **obedience** is concerned, rests
EP : 0 7 :020(484) [0813] alone in the most holy **obedience** and complete merit of
EP : 0 7 :042(486) [0817] our intellect captive in **obedience** to Christ, as we do in
EP : 1 2 :022(499) [0841] Christ, conversion, repentance, faith, and new **obedience**.
SD : 0 2 :024(526) [0891] and other God-pleasing virtues and **obedience** in him.
SD : 0 2 :047(530) [0901] ardent faith and cordial **obedience** but only weakness and
SD : 0 2 :060(533) [0905] one and his resisting will becomes an **obedient** will.
SD : 0 2 :066(534) [0907] man could not remain in **obedience** to God for one
SD : 0 2 :075(536) [0911] by this spontaneous **obedience** earn the forgiveness of sin
SD : 0 2 :079(536) [0911] life and by such perfect **obedience** of the law merit
SD : 0 3 :004(540) [0917] he has by his perfect **obedience** redeemed us from our
SD : 0 3 :004(540) [0917] on account of the **obedience** of Christ, which, through
SD : 0 3 :004(540) [0917] from all their unrighteousness because of this **obedience**.
SD : 0 3 :009(541) [0919] the merit of the total **obedience**, the bitter passion, the
SD : 0 3 :009(541) [0919] Christ, our Lord, whose **obedience** is reckoned to us as
SD : 0 3 :011(541) [0919] for the sake of his **obedience** we have forgiveness of sins
SD : 0 3 :012(541) [0919] we are justified by the **obedience** of Christ, our only
SD : 0 3 :014(541) [0919] or to the believers is the **obedience**, the passion, and the
SD : 0 3 :015(541) [0919] Therefore his **obedience** consists not only in his suffering
SD : 0 3 :015(541) [0919] account of this entire **obedience** which, by doing and
SD : 0 3 :022(543) [0923] Christ with his perfect **obedience** covers all our sins which
SD : 0 3 :022(543) [0923] for the sake of Christ's **obedience**, which Christ rendered
SD : 0 3 :030(544) [0925] (in him) in his perfect **obedience** with which he fulfilled
SD : 0 3 :032(545) [0927] righteousness of the new **obedience** or of good works.
SD : 0 3 :032(545) [0927] the righteousness of the **obedience**, passion, and death of
SD : 0 3 :032(545) [0927] of eternal life only on account of Christ's **obedience**.
SD : 0 3 :035(545) [0927] and, because our new **obedience** is imperfect and impure,
SD : 0 3 :050(548) [0933] their own inchoate new **obedience**, or in part by the
SD : 0 3 :050(548) [0933] righteousness and in part by the inchoate new **obedience**.
SD : 0 3 :054(549) [0935] sinners on account of the **obedience** and merit of Christ.
SD : 0 3 :055(549) [0935] his sole, total, and perfect **obedience** is our righteousness.
SD : 0 3 :056(549) [0935] true, eternal God, the **obedience** and passion of the
SD : 0 3 :056(549) [0935] confess that the total **obedience** of Christ's total person,
SD : 0 3 :056(549) [0935] For neither the **obedience** nor the passion of the human
SD : 0 3 :057(549) [0935] above, it is the **obedience** of the entire person, therefore it
SD : 0 3 :057(549) [0935] This **obedience** is our righteousness which avails before
SD : 0 3 :057(550) [0935] so by one man's **obedience** many will be made righteous"
SD : 0 3 :058(550) [0937] but only the **obedience** of the person who is God and man
SD : 0 3 :058(550) [0937] Father entire, perfect **obedience** from his holy birth to his
SD : 0 3 :063(550) [0937] not look solely to the **obedience** of Christ, but also to his
SD : 0 3 :064(550) [0937] a kind of trust in the **obedience** of Christ that can exist
SD : 0 4 :004(551) [0939] and binds all men to be **obedient** to God, but at times it
SD : 0 4 :005(552) [0939] referred to above, new **obedience** is not necessary in the
SD : 0 4 :017(554) [0943] compulsion but with **obedience** from the heart (II Cor.
SD : 0 5 :022(562) [0959] and whose **obedience** is reckoned to us as righteousness in
SD : 0 6 :002(564) [0963] do not learn the new **obedience** (that is, in what good
SD : 0 6 :006(565) [0965] angels render God a completely spontaneous **obedience**.
SD : 0 6 :007(565) [0965] up through the perfect **obedience** of Christ, so that they
SD : 0 6 :010(565) [0965] with the new **obedience** of believers and what function the
SD : 0 6 :019(567) [0969] driven and coerced into **obedience** by the threats of the
SD : 0 6 :022(567) [0969] a perfect and pure **obedience** if it is to please God.
SD : 0 6 :024(568) [0969] must be coerced into the **obedience** of Christ, not only
SD : 0 7 :044(577) [0987] with great reverence and **obedience** until the end of the
SD : 0 7 :045(577) [0987] in simple faith and due **obedience** in their strict and clear
SD : 0 7 :047(578) [0989] in all humility and **obedience** the explicit, certain, clear,
SD : 0 7 :069(582) [0997] a stronger and more cheerful faith and a purer **obedience**.
SD : 0 7 :080(584) [1001] Thereby we render **obedience** to the command of Christ,
SD : 1 1 :015(619) [1069] that by his innocent **obedience**, suffering, and death
SD : 1 1 :096(632) [1095] him in his new **obedience**, and thus justify and save him
SD : 1 2 :010(633) [1097] alone on the sole **obedience** and merit of Christ but in
SD : 1 2 :030(635) [1101] repentance, and faith or works new **obedience** in them.

Obey (74), Obeyed (7), Obeying (1), Obeys (1)

AG : 1 6 :006(038) [0051] to civil authority and **obey** its commands and laws in all
AG : 1 6 :007(038) [0051] civil authority cannot be **obeyed** without sin, we must
AG : 1 6 :007(038) [0051] without sin, we must **obey** God rather than men (Acts
AG : 2 5 :011(063) [0069] yourself before others, but **obey** the prophet who says,
AG : 2 8 :028(085) [0087] that one should not **obey** even regularly elected bishops if
AG : 2 8 :075(094) [0095] rule which commands us to **obey** God rather than men.
AL : 1 6 :006(038) [0051] are necessarily bound to **obey** their magistrates and laws
AL : 1 6 :007(038) [0051] sin, for then they ought to **obey** God rather than men
AL : 2 5 :011(063) [0069] others, but I wish you to **obey** the prophet who says,
AL : 2 7 :021(074) [0079] Therefore those who **obey** this command and institution
AL : 2 8 :028(085) [0087] bishops are to be **obeyed** if they should happen to err or
AL : 2 8 :075(094) [0095] which commands us to **obey** God rather than men.
AP : 0 2 :008(102) [0107] above all things and to **obey** his commandments
AP : 0 2 :009(102) [0107] one's own power and to **obey** his commandments, what
AP : 0 2 :010(102) [0109] love God above all things and **obey** his commandments?
AP : 0 2 :046(106) [0117] they teach that man can **obey** the commandments of God
AP : 0 4 :027(111) [0127] he hears prayer, willingly **obey** him in death and in his
AP : 0 4 :035(112) [0131] So it does not **obey** the first table.
AP : 0 4 :045(113) [0133] so that we can finally **obey** God's law, love him, truly fear
AP : 0 4 :045(113) [0133] be sure that he hears us, and **obey** him in all afflictions.
AP : 0 4 :143(126) [0161] the flesh, who take pleasure in their lusts and **obey** them.
AP : 0 4 :144(127) [0161] not remain in those who **obey** their lusts, nor does it exist
AP : 0 4 :289(151) [0203] help of this disposition we **obey** the law of God both
AP : 0 4 :293(152) [0203] love God and his Word, **obey** God in the midst of
AP : 0 4 :309(155) [0207] what is properly his; it **obeys** him by accepting his
AP : 0 4 :311(155) [0207] Yet we cannot **obey** the law unless we have been reborn
AP : 0 4 :348(160) [0217] we might begin to do good works and **obey** God's law.
AP : 1 2 :151(206) [0299] will be the end of those who do not **obey** the gospel?"
AP : 1 5 :045(221) [0327] When this comes, we must **obey** God's will, as Paul says
AP : 1 6 :003(223) [0331] but commands us to **obey** the existing laws, whether they
AP : 1 6 :005(223) [0331] and it commands us to **obey** them as divine ordinances
AP : 1 8 :004(225) [0335] It can **obey** rulers and parents.
AP : 1 8 :005(225) [0335] of concupiscence that men **obey** their evil impulses more
AP : 1 8 :010(226) [0337] who dream that men can **obey** the law of God without the
AP : 2 4 :028(254) [0393] command I gave them, '**Obey** my voice, and I will be your
AP : 2 4 :028(254) [0393] "**Obey** me," that is, "Believe that I am your God and that
AP : 2 7 :039(276) [0433] are unmarried, and **obey** the rule in trifles like clothing
AP : 2 7 :050(277) [0437] for this young man to believe and **obey** this calling.
AP : 2 7 :050(277) [0437] for each of us with true faith to **obey** his own calling.
AP : 2 8 :020(284) [0449] quote the statement (Heb. 13:17), "**Obey** your leaders."
AP : 2 8 :020(284) [0449] do so, we are forbidden to **obey** them by the statement
AP : 2 8 :021(284) [0449] commands that we must **obey** God rather than men.
AP : 2 8 :025(285) [0451] For we must **obey** God rather than men (Acts 5:29).
TR : 0 0 :038(326) [0515] written in Acts, "We must **obey** God rather than men"
TR : 0 0 :038(326) [0515] clearly teach that a heretical pope is not to be **obeyed**.
TR : 0 0 :038(327) [0515] nevertheless, godless high priests were not to be **obeyed**.
TR : 0 0 :038(327) [0515] Caiaphas and were under no obligation to **obey** him.
TR : 0 0 :057(330) [0521] right, he should not be **obeyed** inasmuch as he defends
TR : 0 0 :076(333) [0525] need, on account of this jurisdiction, to **obey** the bishops.
TR : 0 0 :076(333) [0527] have good reason for not **obeying**, it is right to restore
TR : 0 0 :077(333) [0527] it is not necessary to **obey** the bishops on account of this
SC : 0 1 :008(343) [0541] to anger, but honor, serve, **obey**, love, and esteem them.
SC : 0 2 :002(345) [0543] of this I am bound to thank, praise, serve, and **obey** him.
SC : 0 9 :003(355) [0561] "**Obey** your leaders and submit to them; for they are
SC : 0 9 :007(355) [0563] your husbands, as Sarah **obeyed** Abraham, calling him
SC : 0 9 :009(356) [0563] "Children, **obey** your parents in the Lord, for this is
LC : 0 1 :108(380) [0611] you to be careful to **obey** me as your father and to
LC : 0 1 :135(383) [0619] If you are unwilling to **obey** father and mother or to
LC : 0 1 :135(383) [0619] or to submit to them, then **obey** the hangman; and if you
LC : 0 1 :135(383) [0619] and if you will not **obey** him, then obey the grim reaper,
LC : 0 1 :135(383) [0619] you will not obey him, then **obey** the grim reaper, Death!
LC : 0 1 :143(385) [0623] take care not only to **obey** their masters and mistresses,
LC : 0 1 :149(385) [0623] If you **obey** him you are his dear child; if you despise this
LC : 0 1 :293(404) [0663] when they **obeyed** the injunctions and prohibitions
LC : 0 2 :022(413) [0683] in duty bound to serve and **obey** him for all these things.
LC : 0 3 :008(421) [0699] our duty and obligation to **obey** our fathers and mothers
LC : 0 3 :009(421) [0699] stands the commandment, "You shall and must **obey**!"
LC : 0 3 :086(432) [0723] and believe, although we **obey** and submit to his will and
LC : 0 5 :045(452) [0763] coerced by men, but to **obey** and please the Lord Christ.
LC : 0 5 :049(452) [0765] from time to time satisfy and **obey** this commandment.
LC : 0 6 :006(457) [0000] The rabble who will not **obey** the Gospel deserve just such
EP : 0 2 :009(471) [0789] Gospel, whole-heartedly **obey** God's law, and thus merit
EP : 0 2 :011(471) [0789] God, and whole-heartedly **obey** God's law by his own
EP : 1 1 :011(496) [0835] believe in Christ, and to **obey** God, and only then does he
SD : 0 2 :018(524) [0889] cooperate, and cannot **obey**, believe, and give assent when
SD : 0 2 :075(536) [0911] believe the Gospel, and **obey** the law of God from the
SD : 0 2 :077(536) [0911] itself to God and to **obey** the law of God from the heart.
SD : 0 4 :016(554) [0943] indicates when it enjoins the creature to **obey** its Creator.
SD : 0 8 :096(609) [1049] their intellect captive to **obey** Christ, comfort themselves
SD : 1 1 :029(621) [1073] will that we should accept the Word, believe and **obey** it.
SD : 1 1 :041(623) [1077] few accept the Word and **obey** it; the majority despise the
SD : 1 1 :056(625) [1081] this to us, we must **obey** his command and operate
SD : 1 1 :073(628) [1087] in them but urges them to **obey** the commandments of

Object (24), Objected (2), Objection (10), Objections (8), Objects (2)

AG : 2 7 :022(074) [0079] What **objection** may be raised to this?
AL : 2 0 :012(042) [0055] anyone should captiously **object** that we have invented a
AL : 2 2 :003(049) [0059] should captiously **object** that this refers only to priests,
AL : 2 7 :022(074) [0079] What **objection** can be raised to this?
AP : P R :005(098) [0101] the opponents' **objections** and explaining to His Imperial
AP : 0 2 :043(106) [0117] In its place we do not **object** to this statement, but it is
AP : 0 4 :004(108) [0121] and to refute the **objections** of our opponents, we shall
AP : 0 4 :055(114) [0137] we are also thinking of its **object**, the promised mercy.
AP : 0 4 :061(115) [0139] means, and we shall answer our opponents' **objections**.
AP : 0 4 :129(125) [0157] Only then does he become an **object** that can be loved.
AP : 0 4 :159(129) [0165] Now let us reply to the **objection** of the opponents
AP : 0 4 :183(132) [0173] Gospel) it will be easy to refute the opponents' **objections**.
AP : 0 4 :225(138) [0183] They **object** that love is preferred to faith and hope since
AP : 0 4 :312(155) [0207] anyway, we say that the **object** of hope is properly a
AP : 0 4 :339(159) [0215] since the causes and **objects** of trust in the first are unlike
AP : 0 4 :388(166) [0225] issues on which our opponents had raised **objections**.
AP : 1 2 :028(185) [0259] whole life and character a third part, we shall not **object**.
AP : 1 2 :103(197) [0281] When someone **objects** that a judge must hear a case
AP : 1 2 :148(205) [0297] Our opponents **object** that revenge or punishment is
AP : 1 2 :150(206) [0299] They **object** that it is in accord with God's justice to
AP : 1 2 :175(210) [0307] and that without **objection** from the bishops, there is no

Continued ▶

A P : 1 3 :012(212) [0311] this way, we shall not **object** either to calling the laying on
A P : 2 2 :007(237) [0359] We do not seriously **object** if someone takes these
A P : 2 3 :021(242) [0369] If someone raises the **objection** here that Christ
A P : 2 3 :024(243) [0371] We do not **object** to the councils, for they do allow
A P : 2 3 :024(243) [0371] circumstances; but we do **object** to the regulations which
A P : 2 3 :036(244) [0373] more than marriage does, we shall really **object**.
A P : 2 4 :009(251) [0387] all our opponents' **objections**, both here in the
A P : 2 4 :096(267) [0417] wicked to whom it is applied, if they make no **objection**.
A P : 2 7 :069(280) [0443] passing we have refuted the **objections** of our opponents.
A P : 2 8 :012(283) [0447] according to canonical polity, to which we do not **object**.
A P : 2 8 :018(284) [0449] We do not see what possible **objection** there can be to this
A P : 2 8 :022(284) [0451] They also raise an **objection** on the basis of the public
T R : 0 0 :019(323) [0509] of Alexandria, Gregory **objected** to having himself
T R : 0 0 :039(327) [0515] every so-called god or **object** of worship, so that he takes
L C : 0 1 :047(371) [0593] and no trust in any other **object**; he makes no greater
L C : 0 1 :114(380) [0613] we should have had an **object** lesson in goodness and
L C : 0 1 :132(383) [0619] that it is not only an **object** of pleasure and delight to
L C : 0 1 :208(393) [0639] institution and an **object** of God's serious concern.
L C : 0 4 :030(440) [0739] to separate faith from the **object** to which faith is attached
L C : 0 4 :030(440) [0739] on the ground that the **object** is something external.
L C : 0 4 :035(441) [0741] However, it is often **objected**, "If Baptism is itself a work,
L C : 0 4 :055(443) [0745] So you see that the **objection** of the sectarians is absurd.
S D : P R :012(506) [0855] the Augsburg Confession **object** to these documents but
S D : 0 7 :045(577) [0987] Nor dare we permit any **objection** or human
S D : 0 7 :106(588) [1009] counter-arguments and **objections** of the

Oblation (3)
A L : 2 4 :021(058) [0067] the Mass in which an **oblation** should be made for daily
A L : 2 4 :025(058) [0067] passion of Christ was an **oblation** and satisfaction not
A P : 2 4 :021(253) [0391] sacrifices were the **oblation**, the drink offerings, the thank

Obligated (7), Obligates (2), Obligation (31), Obligations (1), Obligatory (18), Obliged (16)
P R : P R :024(013) [0023] mindful of the **obligation** that we have by divine precept,
A G : 1 6 :006(038) [0051] Christians are **obliged** to be subject to civil authority and
A G : 0 0 :000(049) [0059] with violence), we are **obliged** by our circumstances to
A G : 2 6 :010(065) [0071] works which everybody is **obliged** to do according to his
A G : 2 6 :031(068) [0075] cross that Christians are **obliged** to suffer, and this is true
A G : 2 6 :033(069) [0075] everybody is under **obligation** to conduct himself, with
A G : 2 7 :022(074) [0079] extols the vow and the **obligation**, no matter how highly
A G : 2 7 :023(074) [0079] much less must be their **obligation**, lawfulness, and power
A G : 2 7 :024(074) [0079] annulment of the **obligation** of a vow, the popes could
A G : 2 7 :024(074) [0079] released men from such **obligation**, for no man has the
A G : 2 7 :024(074) [0079] the right to cancel an **obligation** which is derived from
A G : 2 7 :025(074) [0079] in connection with this **obligation** and have often given
A G : 2 7 :030(075) [0079] insistently about the **obligation** of vows inasmuch as it is
A G : 2 7 :040(077) [0081] teach that an oath should not be an **obligation** to sin.
A G : 2 7 :061(080) [0083] which we are not **obligated** to render to God.
A G : 2 8 :029(085) [0087] duties, the princes are **obliged**, whether they like to or
A G : 2 8 :063(092) [0093] not be kept as of divine **obligation**, it must nevertheless
A G : 2 8 :063(092) [0093] kept as almost of divine **obligation**, and they prescribe the
A G : 2 8 :074(094) [0093] into disuse and are not **obligatory**, as papal law itself
A L : 2 4 :018(058) [0067] able to correct them and were under **obligation** to do so.
A L : 2 6 :031(068) [0075] the cross that Christians are **obliged** to suffer afflictions.
A L : 2 7 :022(074) [0079] Exaggerate the **obligation** of a vow as much as one
A L : 2 7 :024(074) [0079] If the **obligation** of vows could not be changed for any
A L : 2 7 :024(074) [0079] for a man to annul an **obligation** which is plainly derived
A L : 2 7 :025(074) [0079] should be observed in connection with this **obligation**.
A L : 2 7 :027(075) [0079] exaggerate the **obligation** or effect of a vow while they
A L : 2 7 :030(075) [0079] so insistently about the **obligation** inasmuch as it is
A L : 2 8 :063(092) [0093] is not *indeed* of divine **obligation** but is *as it were* of
A L : 2 8 :063(092) [0093] is *as it were* of divine **obligation**, and they prescribe the
A P : 0 4 :263(145) [0195] penitence, that is, the **obligation** or debt is removed
A P : 0 4 :264(146) [0195] be redeemed, that the **obligation** or debt can be removed,
A P : 0 4 :291(152) [0203] We are therefore **obliged** to disagree with our opponents
A P : 0 4 :342(159) [0215] worthiness whereby God **obligates** himself to bestow his
A P : 0 4 :377(165) [0223] We are therefore **obliged** to hold fast to the Gospel and
A P : 1 2 :133(202) [0293] are works that are not **obligatory**, but in these passages
A P : 1 2 :133(202) [0293] passages Scripture requires works that are **obligatory**.
A P : 1 2 :137(203) [0293] is speaking about **obligatory** works, about the whole
A P : 1 2 :137(203) [0293] and works that are not **obligatory** such as our opponents
A P : 1 2 :138(203) [0293] do not say that non-**obligatory** works compensate for
A P : 1 2 :139(203) [0295] we told that only non-**obligatory** works like the
A P : 1 2 :147(205) [0297] of satisfaction are not **obligatory** works but works of
A P : 1 2 :163(208) [0303] and the fruits that are due, not to "non-**obligatory** works."
A P : 1 2 :165(208) [0303] of penitence and **obligatory** works commanded by God
A P : 1 2 :172(209) [0305] satisfactions or non-**obligatory** works be done to
A P : 1 2 :173(209) [0305] of satisfaction are non-**obligatory** works, why cite the
A P : 1 2 :173(209) [0305] by such works, then they would certainly be **obligatory**.
A P : 1 2 :173(209) [0305] passages dealing with **obligatory** works, though in their
A P : 1 2 :173(209) [0305] in their satisfactions they impose non-**obligatory** works.
A P : 1 3 :011(212) [0311] the Word, we have no **obligation** to calling ordination a
A P : 2 3 :020(242) [0369] not commanded; it is voluntary rather than **obligatory**."
A P : 2 7 :021(272) [0427] are not impure, are non-**obligatory** forms of discipline.
S 2 : 0 2 :021(296) [0467] and vicars have **obligated** themselves to transfer (by legal
S 3 : 0 3 :018(306) [0483] The person involved was **obliged** to grieve, but he would
T R : 0 0 :038(327) [0515] Caiaphas and were under no **obligation** to obey him.
S C : P R :017(340) [0537] out their respective **obligations**, benefits, dangers,
S C : P R :019(340) [0537] be shown that they are **obliged** to do so, and that they are
L C : 0 1 :114(380) [0613] men did not feel **obliged** to set forth God's
L C : 0 1 :157(386) [0625] All this I have been **obliged** to set forth with such a
L C : 0 1 :201(392) [0637] among the Jewish people marriage was **obligatory**.
L C : 0 1 :233(396) [0647] than that, he is under **obligation** faithfully to protect his
L C : 0 1 :237(397) [0647] from whom we are **obliged** to suffer such intolerable
L C : 0 1 :275(402) [0659] are under mutual **obligation** to reprove evil where it is
L C : 0 1 :305(406) [0667] that her husband was **obliged** to dismiss her and leave her
L C : 0 3 :008(421) [0699] It is our duty and **obligation** to pray if we want to be
L C : 0 3 :008(421) [0699] as it is our duty and **obligation** to obey our fathers and
L C : 0 3 :009(421) [0699] but it is my duty and **obligation** [on pain of God's wrath
L C : 0 5 :047(452) [0763] which the Jews were **obliged** to eat only once a year,
E P : 0 4 :008(476) [0799] by the Holy Spirit, are **obligated** to do good works.
S D : 0 1 :017(511) [0865] original sin is only an **obligation** resulting from someone
S D : 0 3 :015(541) [0919] of the law — as he was **obligated** to suffer and die for his
S D : 0 4 :004(551) [0939] immutable order which **obligates** and binds all men to be
S D : 0 6 :006(565) [0965] would do what they are **obligated** to do according to the
S D : 1 0 :010(612) [1055] community of God, are **obligated** to confess openly, not
S D : 1 0 :016(613) [1057] every Christian is **obligated** to avoid both, as it is written,
S D : 1 2 :022(634) [1099] private property but is **obliged** to give his property to the

Obnoxious (1)
E P : 0 7 :042(486) [0817] in order to make our teaching **obnoxious** to their hearers.

Obscure (15), Obscured (20), Obscures (6), Obscuring (2)
P R : P R :024(013) [0023] doctrine will be entirely **obscured** and lost and nothing
A G : 2 6 :004(064) [0071] faith are thereby **obscured**, and yet the Gospel earnestly
A G : 2 6 :008(065) [0071] traditions have also **obscured** the commands of God, for
A G : 2 7 :048(078) [0081] the Christian church, is **obscured** when man's eyes are
A G : 2 7 :049(078) [0083] service of God are **obscured** when people are told that
A L : 0 2 :003(029) [0045] of origin is sin and who **obscure** the glory of Christ's
A L : 2 6 :004(064) [0071] In the first place, it has **obscured** the doctrine concerning
A L : 2 6 :008(065) [0071] place, these precepts **obscured** the commands of God, for
A L : 2 7 :038(077) [0081] the glory of Christ and **obscure** and deny the
A L : 2 7 :048(078) [0081] taught in the church, is **obscured** when the eyes of men
A L : 2 7 :049(078) [0083] true service of God are **obscured** when men hear that only
A P : 0 2 :032(104) [0113] Fathers that had been **obscured** by the sophistic
A P : 0 2 :044(106) [0117] in human powers and **obscuring** the knowledge of the
A P : 0 4 :003(107) [0121] doctrine miserably, they **obscure** the glory and the
A P : 0 4 :204(135) [0177] First, it **obscures** the glory of Christ when men offer these
A P : 0 4 :324(157) [0211] justifying faith and **obscures** Christ's glory and
A P : 0 4 :361(162) [0219] of Christ and the righteousness of faith are **obscured**.
A P : 0 4 :392(167) [0225] and new devotions, **obscuring** the work of Christ and
A P : 0 4 :393(167) [0225] teaching of works would **obscure** the righteousness of
A P : 1 2 :010(184) [0255] error and hypocrisy; it **obscures** the blessing of Christ, the
A P : 1 2 :091(195) [0279] our opponents quote in a distorted form to **obscure** faith.
A P : 1 2 :116(199) [0287] of faith be **obscured** or people think that because of these
A P : 1 2 :145(205) [0297] In this way they **obscure** the law of God in two ways:
A P : 1 2 :146(205) [0297] In addition, they **obscure** penitence and grace.
A P : 1 5 :004(215) [0315] This **obscures** the Gospel, the blessing of Christ, and
A P : 1 5 :010(216) [0317] God and therefore they **obscured** the work of Christ and
A P : 1 5 :020(218) [0321] They did not **obscure** the glory or work of Christ but
A P : 1 5 :025(218) [0321] of faith in Christ is **obscured** and replaced by a vain trust
A P : 1 5 :025(218) [0321] of God are **obscured**; for when men regard these works as
A P : 1 5 :032(220) [0325] for justification, they **obscure** the righteousness of faith.
A P : 1 6 :004(223) [0331] These ideas seriously **obscure** the Gospel and the spiritual
A P : 1 6 :013(224) [0333] of this had been **obscured** by foolish monastic theories
A P : 2 1 :015(231) [0347] put it mildly, even this **obscures** the work of Christ and
A P : 2 3 :046(246) [0377] It **obscures** the recognition of God's commands and gifts,
A P : 2 4 :098(268) [0419] God's command to **obscure** the glory of Christ and the
A P : 2 7 :054(278) [0439] or on ceremonial traditions that **obscure** Christ.
T R : 0 0 :037(326) [0515] these monstrous errors **obscure** faith and the kingdom of
T R : 0 0 :044(328) [0517] Thus they **obscure** the glory of Christ, deprive
T R : 0 0 :045(328) [0517] They have **obscured** the teaching concerning sin and have
T R : 0 0 :045(328) [0517] of which they have further **obscured** the benefit of Christ.
L C : 0 3 :036(425) [0707] This is rather **obscure**.
E P : 0 5 :011(479) [0805] the Holy Scriptures are **obscured**, Christians are robbed
S D : P R :001(501) [0847] had been hideously **obscured** by human doctrines and

Observe (48), Observed (45), Observes (9), Observance (41), Observances (61), Observation (2), Observing (13)
A G : 0 7 :003(032) [0047] by men, should be **observed** uniformly in all places.
A G : 1 5 :001(036) [0049] those usages are to be **observed** which may be observed
A G : 1 5 :001(036) [0049] observed which may be **observed** without sin and which
A G : 1 5 :002(036) [0049] we accompany these **observances** with instruction so that
A G : 2 2 :011(050) [0061] of those who desire to **observe** the sacrament according to
A G : 2 3 :018(054) [0063] As we have **observed**, the assertion that priests and
A G : 0 1 :009(056) [0065] manifest that the Mass is **observed** among us with greater
A G : 2 4 :010(057) [0065] and selling it, and by **observing** it in almost all churches
A G : 2 4 :034(060) [0067] for themselves, it is **observed** among us in the following
A G : 2 4 :035(060) [0067] use which was formerly **observed** in the church and which
A G : 2 6 :002(064) [0071] be earned if they were **observed** and a great sin committed
A G : 2 6 :009(065) [0071] Christian life: whoever **observed** festivals in this way,
A G : 2 6 :017(066) [0073] they were not to be considered necessary **observances**.
A G : 2 6 :021(067) [0073] cannot be atoned for by **observing** the said human
A G : 2 6 :022(067) [0073] the apostles for not **observing** the customary traditions,
A G : 2 6 :041(070) [0075] and that they are to be **observed** without burdening
A G : 2 6 :045(070) [0075] profitable Christian **observation**, "It was not the intention
A G : 2 7 :001(071) [0077] how many of the daily **observances** in them were contrary
A G : 2 7 :044(078) [0081] by their vows and their monastic life and **observances**.
A G : 2 7 :057(080) [0083] one is to serve God by **observing** the commands God has
A G : 2 8 :035(086) [0089] to require that they be **observed** in order to make
A G : 2 8 :053(090) [0091] it a sin to omit their **observance** even when this is done
A G : 2 8 :055(090) [0091] in such matters, and to **observe** the regulations in such a
A G : 2 8 :057(091) [0091] Of like character is the **observance** of Sunday, Easter,
A G : 2 8 :064(092) [0093] remains and prevails that their **observance** is necessary.
A G : 2 8 :065(092) [0093] Who **observes** this prohibition now?
A G : 2 8 :065(092) [0093] Those who do not **observe** it commit no sin, for the
A G : 2 8 :067(092) [0093] the ancient canons are **observed** according to the letter,
A G : 2 8 :067(093) [0093] even among those who **observe** such ordinance most
A G : 2 8 :069(093) [0093] did not insist on the **observance** of regulations which
A G : 2 8 :075(094) [0095] which are not to be **observed** without sin, we are bound to
A L : 1 5 :001(036) [0049] those rites should be **observed** which can be observed
A L : 1 5 :001(036) [0049] observed which can be **observed** without sin and which
A L : 1 5 :002(036) [0049] with such things, as if **observances** of this kind were
A L : 0 0 :004(048) [0059] the most part diligently **observed**, for it is false and
A L : 0 0 :001(049) [0059] may not be compelled to **observe** these abuses against
A L : 0 0 :004(049) [0059] and of ceremonies **observed** among us are not so
A L : 0 0 :006(049) [0059] people as the proper **observance** of ceremonies in the
A L : 2 4 :009(057) [0065] appear that the Mass is **observed** with more devotion
A L : 2 4 :034(060) [0067] one common Mass is **observed** among us on every holy
A L : 2 6 :008(065) [0071] consist wholly in the **observance** of certain holy days,
A L : 2 6 :009(065) [0071] Such **observances** claimed for themselves the glamorous
A L : 2 6 :010(065) [0071] works, far inferior to those glittering **observances**.
A L : 2 6 :011(065) [0071] imagining that the **observances** of such men were more
A L : 2 6 :012(065) [0071] yet men judged these **observances** to be necessary acts of
A L : 2 6 :017(066) [0073] consciences with such **observances** and prudently
A L : 2 6 :020(067) [0073] that they merit grace by **observances** of their own choice.
A L : 2 6 :021(067) [0073] for sins by the **observance** of human traditions.

Continued ▸

A L : 2 6 :021(067) [0073] Hence **observances** of this kind are not to be thought of
A L : 2 6 :022(067) [0073] the apostles for not **observing** the customary tradition, a
A L : 2 6 :041(070) [0075] are warned that such **observances** do not justify before
A L : 2 7 :003(071) [0077] Many other **observances** were gradually added in addition
A L : 2 7 :012(072) [0077] more, for it was an **observance** not only of the precepts
A L : 2 7 :013(073) [0077] without man-made **observances**, serve their calling in
A L : 2 7 :025(074) [0079] that leniency should be **observed** in connection with this
A L : 2 7 :037(077) [0081] not to be sought for in **observances** and services devised
A L : 2 7 :038(077) [0081] that their invented **observances** make satisfaction for sins
A L : 2 7 :044(078) [0081] merited forgiveness of sins by their vows and **observances**.
A L : 2 7 :046(078) [0081] men that their invented **observances** were a state of
A L : 2 7 :048(078) [0081] remarkable angelic **observances** and this pretense of
A L : 2 7 :057(080) [0083] God is to be served by **observing** the commands he has
A L : 2 7 :061(080) [0083] that the monks **observe** both the counsels and the
A L : 2 8 :035(086) [0089] to require the **observances** of traditions for the purpose
A L : 2 8 :036(086) [0089] we suppose that we are justified by such **observances**.
A L : 2 8 :052(089) [0091] not through certain **observances** or acts of worship
A L : 2 8 :057(091) [0091] Of the same sort is the **observance** of Sunday, Easter,
A L : 2 8 :058(091) [0091] who hold that the **observance** of the Lord's Day in place
A L : 2 8 :063(092) [0093] Some argue that the **observance** of the Lord's Day is not
A L : 2 8 :064(092) [0093] as the opinion remains that their **observance** is necessary.
A L : 2 8 :065(092) [0093] Who **observes** this prohibition now?
A L : 2 8 :065(092) [0093] Those who do not **observe** it commit no sin, for the
A L : 2 8 :067(092) [0093] any of the canons are **observed** according to the letter,
A L : 2 8 :069(093) [0093] did not insist on the **observance** of traditions which
A L : 2 8 :075(094) [0095] obtain a relaxation of **observances** which cannot be kept
A L : 2 8 :077(094) [0095] they relax some few **observances** which cannot be kept
A P : 0 4 :207(135) [0177] as outward **observances** in the state, but they do condemn
A P : 0 4 :288(151) [0203] the austerity of their **observances** to counteract the
A P : 0 4 :326(158) [0211] judgment of God if he **observes** our sins, "If thou, O
A P : 0 4 :330(158) [0211] who forsake mercy **observe** lying vanities"; that is, all
A P : 0 7 :013(170) [0231] it as only the outward **observance** of certain devotions
A P : 0 7 :032(174) [0239] ways, as though these **observances** were really acts of
A P : 0 7 :032(174) [0239] such traditions as the **observance** of Easter, the use of
A P : 0 7 :032(174) [0239] of the heart before God without these **observances**.
A P : 0 7 :033(174) [0239] when universal rites are **observed** for the sake of
A P : 0 7 :033(174) [0239] churches we willingly **observe** the order of the Mass, the
A P : 0 7 :034(175) [0239] whether it is profitable to **observe** them for the sake of
A P : 0 7 :034(175) [0239] question is whether the **observance** of human traditions is
A P : 0 7 :034(175) [0239] God even if he does not **observe** traditions that have been
A P : 0 7 :038(175) [0241] traditions should be **observed** because they are supposed
A P : 0 7 :039(176) [0241] nor to make the **observance** of days, food, and the like a
A P : 0 7 :040(176) [0241] They **observed** certain days, not because such observance
A P : 0 7 :040(176) [0241] days, not because such **observance** was necessary for
A P : 0 7 :040(176) [0241] assembled, they also **observed** other rites and a sequence
A P : 0 7 :040(176) [0241] the people continued to **observe** certain Old Testament
A P : 0 7 :042(177) [0243] notion of having to **observe** a set time, since they tell them
A P : 0 7 :045(177) [0243] a difference in human **observances** does not harm the
A P : 0 7 :045(177) [0243] a uniformity of **observances** in food, days, clothing, and
A P : 1 1 :001(180) [0249] *utriusque* should be **observed**, that confession should be
A P : 1 2 :014(184) [0257] these consist of stupid **observances** like pilgrimages,
A P : 1 2 :014(184) [0257] rosaries, or similar **observances** that do not have divine
A P : 1 2 :121(200) [0287] times that these **observances** were instituted for the sake
A P : 1 2 :137(203) [0293] of life, and not about **observances** and works that are not
A P : 1 2 :137(203) [0293] of Masses, and endless **observances** which make
A P : 1 2 :142(204) [0295] which man is bound to **observe**, namely, the
A P : 1 2 :174(210) [0307] not teach that only the **observance** of certain traditions
A P : 1 2 :175(210) [0307] and penalties, this **observance** cannot be a necessity
A P : 1 5 :001(215) [0315] we say that we should **observe** those ecclesiastical rites
A P : 1 5 :001(215) [0315] rites which can be **observed** without sin and which are
A P : 1 5 :003(215) [0315] of sins by the **observance** of human traditions.
A P : 1 5 :007(216) [0317] merit the forgiveness of sins by these human **observances**.
A P : 1 5 :008(216) [0317] That is, if by the **observance** of the law you think you
A P : 1 5 :008(216) [0317] believes he is righteous by his own **observance** of the law?
A P : 1 5 :011(216) [0317] we merit the forgiveness of sins by these **observances**.
A P : 1 5 :012(216) [0317] justified do merit grace by **observing** these traditions.
A P : 1 5 :012(216) [0317] his sake but must first merit this by other **observances**.
A P : 1 5 :012(216) [0317] acceptance and justification through these **observances**.
A P : 1 5 :014(217) [0319] of your fathers, nor **observe** their ordinances, nor defile
A P : 1 5 :014(217) [0319] in my statutes, and be careful to **observe** my ordinances."
A P : 1 5 :020(218) [0321] They **observed** these human rites because they were
A P : 1 5 :021(218) [0321] innumerable similar **observances** in the human traditions.
A P : 1 5 :026(219) [0323] they regarded these **observances** as better and holier.
A P : 1 5 :027(219) [0323] with the idea that such **observances** are necessary for
A P : 1 5 :032(220) [0323] in the church, lest the **observances** of the law or traditions
A P : 1 5 :032(220) [0325] men believe that these **observances** merit justification or
A P : 1 5 :035(220) [0325] Then if anybody **observes** them, let him do so without
A P : ! 5 :035(220) [0325] no value before God in **observing** secular customs, if
A P : 1 5 :048(221) [0329] opponents do not even **observe** the canonical
A P : 1 5 :049(221) [0329] to a conscience that has omitted some **observance**.
A P : 1 5 :050(222) [0329] he insists that these **observances** neither justify nor are
A P : 1 5 :052(222) [0329] of our willingness to **observe** adiaphora with others, even
A P : 2 1 :041(235) [0355] the trust in monastic **observances**, the mercenary worship
A P : 2 3 :020(242) [0369] Ambrose correctly **observes**, "Virginity is something that
A P : 2 3 :026(243) [0371] see that it is not being **observed**, still they cloak it with
A P : 2 3 :042(245) [0375] with these Levitical **observances**, we must definitely resist
A P : 2 3 :048(246) [0377] one should trust in certain **observances** for righteousness.
A P : 2 3 :049(246) [0377] of Epiphanius, such **observances** should be praised "for
A P : 2 4 :003(250) [0385] The purpose of **observing** ceremonies is that men may
A P : 2 4 :005(250) [0385] simply *ex opere operato*, by the mere doing or **observing**.
A P : 2 4 :049(258) [0401] could lay more claim to **observing** it than our opponents
A P : 2 7 :009(270) [0421] Are they the **observance** of commandments and counsels?
A P : 2 7 :009(270) [0421] weakness prevents their **observance** or because the
A P : 2 7 :012(270) [0423] they add that the monks **observe** everything for Christ's
A P : 2 7 :014(271) [0425] much less do these silly **observances** merit the forgiveness
A P : 2 7 :016(271) [0425] that among those who **observe** this law of Christ, the
A P : 2 7 :016(271) [0425] come closer in their **observance** than do others because of
A P : 2 7 :022(272) [0427] Word who follow these **observances** without wicked
A P : 2 7 :023(272) [0427] the notion that these **observances** are services because of
A P : 2 7 :024(273) [0427] they teach that these **observances** are services that justify.
A P : 2 7 :024(273) [0427] They imagine that they **observe** both precepts and
A P : 2 7 :025(273) [0429] monks to boast that the **observance** of a monastic life
A P : 2 7 :026(273) [0429] false that monastic **observances** are the works of the
A P : 2 7 :027(273) [0429] is it to be found in the **observance** of other things which
A P : 2 7 :027(274) [0429] life, in these silly **observances** of vestments and similar
A P : 2 7 :028(274) [0429] is maintained by a due **observance**, as by the grace of God
A P : 2 7 :033(275) [0431] much less do monastic **observances**, mere human
A P : 2 7 :034(275) [0431] to their own foolish **observances** the trust that is due
A P : 2 7 :039(276) [0433] the pretext that they **observe** both precepts and counsels.
A P : 2 7 :061(279) [0441] a sure thing that our **observances** do not merit the
A P : 2 7 :061(279) [0441] note that they did not **observe** their way of life out of the
A P : 2 7 :065(280) [0441] all works, if they are **observed** in order to merit the
A P : 2 7 :069(281) [0443] themselves and the **observance** of foods, lessons, chants,
A P : 2 7 :069(281) [0443] pharisaism: that these **observances** merit the forgiveness
A P : 2 7 :070(281) [0443] any confidence in such **observances**, learning that they
A P : 2 8 :003(281) [0445] greater strictness in the **observance** of their traditions than
A P : 2 8 :017(283) [0449] and yet we should **observe** them in their place and
A P : 2 8 :021(284) [0449] passage (Matt. 23:3), "**Observe** whatever they tell you."
A P : 2 8 :021(284) [0449] that we are to **observe** everything, for elsewhere (Acts
S 1 : P R :014(291) [0459] commanded by God, are neither regarded nor **observed**?
S 2 : 0 2 :005(293) [0463] will be damned for not **observing** it, and that one can be
S 2 : 0 2 :007(294) [0465] It is **observed** for this purpose when it is best observed.
S 2 : 0 2 :007(294) [0465] It is observed for this purpose when it is best **observed**.
S 3 : 0 1 :006(302) [0477] by his natural powers to **observe** and keep all the
T R : 0 0 :011(321) [0507] time, however, they reasoned thus: "Cephas **observes** this.
T R : 0 0 :011(321) [0507] Therefore Paul and the others ought to **observe** this."
T R : 0 0 :014(322) [0507] This was also **observed** in the West and in the Latin
T R : 0 0 :014(322) [0507] you must diligently **observe** and practice, according to
T R : 0 0 :014(322) [0507] apostolic usage, what is **observed** by us and in almost all
T R : 0 0 :015(322) [0509] he asserts that it was **observed** in almost all provinces.
T R : 0 0 :031(325) [0513] and teach them to **observe** all that I have commanded
T R : 0 0 :040(327) [0517] to have his own doctrine and worship **observed** as divine.
T R : 0 0 :062(330) [0523] And Jerome **observes**: "One man was chosen over the rest
T R : 0 0 :075(333) [0525] but in dealing with non-**observance** of fasts or festivals
T R : 0 0 :079(333) [0527] and since, finally, they **observe** unjust laws in
S C : P R :005(338) [0533] and insist on the **observance** of human laws, yet you do
S C : P R :013(339) [0535] is bound to know and **observe** the laws under whose
S C : 0 8 :008(353) [0559] (It is to be **observed** that "satisfying the desire of every
L C : 0 1 :005(365) [0581] examples of failure to **observe** this commandment.
L C : 0 1 :038(369) [0591] We **observe** this every day in the case of bishops and
L C : 0 1 :079(375) [0603] work" literally means "**observing** a holy day or holiday."
L C : 0 1 :080(375) [0603] As far as outward **observance** is concerned, the
L C : 0 1 :086(376) [0605] commandment: Since we **observe** holidays anyhow, we
L C : 0 1 :086(376) [0605] we should devote their **observance** to learning God's
L C : 0 1 :086(376) [0605] However, the **observance** of rest should not be so narrow
L C : 0 1 :095(378) [0607] insists upon a strict **observance** of this commandment and
L C : 0 1 :116(381) [0615] will are placed first and **observed**, nothing ought to be
L C : 0 1 :140(384) [0621] and acceptable a work he does when he **observes** it.
L C : 0 1 :212(393) [0641] as everyone's **observation** and experience testify.
L C : 0 1 :276(402) [0659] this matter would be to **observe** the order laid down by
L C : 0 3 :068(429) [0717] **Observe** that in these three petitions interests which
L C : 0 4 :006(437) [0733] **Observe**, first, that these words contain God's
L C : 0 4 :032(440) [0739] power of Baptism, let us **observe** further who receives
L C : 0 4 :038(441) [0741] still have to accept and **observe** Baptism as an ordinance
L C : 0 4 :064(444) [0749] this sign and external **observance** for the sacrament by
L C : 0 4 :065(444) [0749] This act or **observance** consists in being dipped into the
L C : 0 5 :040(451) [0761] men are becoming listless and lazy about its **observance**.
E P : 0 1 :022(469) [0785] It is important to **observe** that the word "nature" has
E P : 0 7 :032(485) [0815] still less in all places, where his Holy Supper is **observed**.
E P : 1 1 :011(495) [0835] will of God and **observes** the order which St. Paul follows
S D : 0 5 :001(558) [0951] We must therefore **observe** this distinction with particular
S D : 0 5 :004(558) [0953] and in the New Testament he ordered to be **observed**.
S D : 0 6 :015(566) [0967] of the Spirit, we must **observe** with special diligence that
S D : 0 7 :016(572) [0977] and command are **observed**, the body and blood of
S D : 0 7 :044(577) [0987] which was to be **observed** with great reverence and
S D : 0 7 :051(578) [0991] to teach all nations to **observe** all that he had commanded
S D : 0 7 :075(583) [0999] where the Supper is **observed** according to Christ's
S D : 0 7 :075(583) [0999] For wherever we **observe** his institution and speak his
S D : 0 7 :083(584) [1001] Christ ordained it is not **observed** (if, for instance, the
S D : 0 7 :085(584) [1001] (that is, if one does not **observe** Christ's institution as he
S D : 1 1 :057(625) [1081] same applies when we **observe** that God gives his Word

Obsessed (1)

A P : 1 5 :027(219) [0323] When minds are **obsessed** with the idea that such

Obsolete (3)

A L : 2 8 :067(092) [0093] many of them become **obsolete** from day to day even
A P : 1 2 :115(199) [0285] the practice has become **obsolete**, the word "satisfaction"
A P : 1 2 :175(210) [0307] itself has now become **obsolete**, and that without

Obstacle (5), Obstruct (1), Obstructs (3)

A G : 2 8 :017(083) [0085] and every proud **obstacle** to the knowledge of God."
A P : 1 2 :177(210) [0307] of cases should not be an **obstacle** to absolution.
A P : 1 3 :018(213) [0313] that unless there is some **obstacle**, the sacraments confer
A P : 2 4 :063(261) [0405] wicked people, if they do not put an **obstacle** in its way.
T R : 0 0 :056(330) [0521] when he evades and **obstructs** true understanding and
L C : 0 3 :062(428) [0715] how the devil opposes and **obstructs** their fulfillment.
L C : 0 3 :080(431) [0721] He is not satisfied to **obstruct** and overthrow spiritual
L C : 0 3 :113(435) [0729] It is he who **obstructs** everything that we pray for: God's
L C : 0 5 :063(454) [0767] for we always have this **obstacle** and hindrance to contend

Obstinate (3), Obstinately (1), Obstinacy (2)

A G : 2 8 :078(094) [0095] inasmuch as by their **obstinacy** they offer occasion for
A L : 2 8 :078(094) [0095] God that by their **obstinacy** they offer occasion for
L C : 0 1 :122(382) [0615] hand, when they are **obstinate** and never do their duty
S D : 0 2 :018(524) [0887] will be much more **obstinately** opposed and hostile to
S D : 0 2 :018(524) [0889] of the wicked and **obstinate** disposition with which he
S D : 0 2 :060(533) [0905] as Stephen describes the **obstinate** Jews (Acts 7:51), will

Obtain (76), Obtained (26), Obtaining (3), Obtains (12)

A G : 0 4 :001(030) [0045] among us that we cannot **obtain** forgiveness of sin and
A G : 0 5 :001(031) [0045] To **obtain** such faith God instituted the office of the
A G : 1 2 :005(035) [0049] and grace has been **obtained** through Christ), and this
A G : 1 2 :010(035) [0049] forgiveness of sin is not **obtained** through faith but
A G : 2 0 :009(042) [0053] reconcile us with God or **obtain** grace for us, for this
A G : 2 0 :013(043) [0055] thing, namely, that we **obtain** grace and are justified

Continued ▶

AG : 20 :022(044) [0055] discovered that they did not **obtain** peace by such means.
AG : 24 :028(059) [0067] St. Paul taught that we **obtain** grace before God through
AG : 24 :029(059) [0067] who think that grace is **obtained** through the performance
AG : 24 :029(059) [0067] used to remove sin and **obtain** grace and all sorts of
AG : 25 :004(062) [0069] that through such faith we **obtain** forgiveness of sins.
AG : 26 :005(064) [0071] faith in Christ that we **obtain** grace for Christ's sake.
AG : 27 :013(072) [0077] more merit could be **obtained** by monastic life than by all
AG : 27 :036(076) [0081] and instituted by men to **obtain** righteousness and God's
AG : 27 :038(077) [0081] satisfaction for sin and **obtains** God's grace and
AG : 28 :009(082) [0085] These gifts cannot be **obtained** except through the office
AG : 28 :035(086) [0089] satisfaction for sins and **obtain** grace, for the glory of
AG : 28 :052(089) [0091] namely, that we **obtain** the grace of God through faith in
AG : 28 :053(090) [0091] but not as a means of **obtaining** God's grace or making
AL : 05 :001(031) [0045] In order that we may **obtain** this faith, the ministry of
AL : 20 :009(042) [0053] and grace but that we **obtain** forgiveness and grace only
AL : 25 :004(062) [0069] that such faith truly **obtains** and receives the forgiveness
AL : 28 :052(089) [0091] Gospel, namely, that we **obtain** grace through faith in
AL : 28 :075(094) [0095] if it is impossible to **obtain** a relaxation of observances
AP : PR :002(098) [0099] But we could have **obtained** it only on terms so risky that
AP : 04 :042(113) [0133] that we would never **obtain** the promise of reconciliation.
AP : 04 :043(113) [0133] Since we **obtain** justification through a free promise,
AP : 04 :045(113) [0133] Christ, this personal faith **obtains** the forgiveness of sins
AP : 04 :074(117) [0143] We **Obtain** the Forgiveness of Sins Only by Faith in
AP : 04 :077(117) [0143] We **obtain** the forgiveness of sins only by faith in Christ,
AP : 04 :080(118) [0143] faith alone, therefore, we **obtain** the forgiveness of sins
AP : 04 :081(118) [0143] "Through him we have **obtained** access" to the Father,
AP : 04 :106(122) [0153] Justification is **obtained** by faith."
AP : 04 :106(122) [0153] by faith and that justification is **obtained** by faith.
AP : 04 :150(127) [0163] believes that he **obtains** the forgiveness of sins because he
AP : 04 :194(133) [0175] or justification (for we **obtain** these only by faith) but for
AP : 04 :195(134) [0175] Through him we have **obtained** access by faith."
AP : 04 :196(134) [0175] It is faith that **obtains** this because it justifies us and has a
AP : 04 :208(135) [0177] who hope that by similar actions they can **obtain** grace.
AP : 04 :246(142) [0189] and accepted and have **obtained** the forgiveness of sins.
AP : 04 :255(143) [0193] "Blessed are the merciful, for they shall **obtain** mercy."
AP : 04 :257(144) [0193] that by faith in Christ we **obtain** the forgiveness of sins.
AP : 04 :269(147) [0197] "Through him we have **obtained** access" to the Father
AP : 04 :274(148) [0199] of the Gospel, that we **obtain** forgiveness of sins by faith
AP : 04 :297(153) [0205] "Through him we have **obtained** access" to God, adding,
AP : 04 :314(156) [0207] Christ we have **obtained** access to God by faith."
AP : 04 :354(161) [0217] of your faith you **obtain** the salvation of your souls."
AP : 04 :384(166) [0225] show what kind of faith **obtains** eternal life, a faith that is
AP : 04 :398(167) [0227] of penance, by which we **obtain** forgiveness of sin,
AP : 04 :398(167) [0227] doctrine—that by faith we **obtain** the forgiveness of sin—is
AP : 07 :025(173) [0235] of Christ, that we **obtain** forgiveness of sins through faith
AP : 11 :006(181) [0251] of sins is necessary to **obtain** their forgiveness.
AP : 11 :009(182) [0251] Now, on this faith which **obtains** the forgiveness of sins
AP : 12 :001(182) [0253] fallen after Baptism can **obtain** the forgiveness of sins
AP : 12 :002(182) [0253] Gospel, that by faith we **obtain** the forgiveness of sins.
AP : 12 :002(182) [0253] we deny that by faith we **obtain** the forgiveness of sins,
AP : 12 :025(185) [0259] sacrament of penitence **obtains** grace *ex opere operato,*
AP : 12 :036(186) [0261] This faith **obtains** the forgiveness of sins.
AP : 12 :037(186) [0261] (Rom. 5:2), "Through him we have **obtained** access."
AP : 12 :059(190) [0267] our statement that men **obtain** the forgiveness of sins by
AP : 12 :063(191) [0269] "Through him we have **obtained** access by faith to this
AP : 12 :067(191) [0271] this teaching that we **obtain** the forgiveness of sins by
AP : 12 :074(193) [0273] still dare to deny that we **obtain** the forgiveness of sins by
AP : 12 :075(193) [0273] us to believe that we **obtain** the forgiveness of sins
AP : 12 :076(193) [0273] we must believe that we **obtain** the forgiveness of sins not
AP : 12 :077(193) [0275] if we believe that we **obtain** the forgiveness of sins
AP : 12 :078(193) [0275] doctrine that men **obtain** the forgiveness of sins by their
AP : 12 :079(194) [0275] the promise or if we **obtained** the forgiveness of sins
AP : 12 :096(196) [0281] from faith just as faith **obtains** it from the written
AP : 12 :110(198) [0285] suppose that they cannot **obtain** the forgiveness of sins
AP : 12 :116(199) [0287] doctrine that by faith we **obtain** the forgiveness of sins
AP : 12 :116(199) [0287] because of these works they **obtain** the forgiveness of sins.
AP : 12 :157(207) [0301] teaches that we **obtain** the forgiveness of sins freely
AP : 12 :161(208) [0303] prevent the man from **obtaining** eternal life, but the lesson
AP : 14 :005(215) [0315] unjust cruelty of the bishops, we could not **obtain** justice.
AP : 20 :011(228) [0341] our doctrine that we **obtain** the forgiveness of sins not on
AP : 21 :029(233) [0351] We **obtain** the forgiveness of sins only by Christ's merits
AP : 22 :016(238) [0361] because it could not **obtain** both parts; but we do blame
AP : 23 :039(244) [0375] that for Christ's sake he **obtains** the forgiveness of sins
AP : 24 :012(251) [0387] the impossibility of our **obtaining** the forgiveness of sins
AP : 28 :023(284) [0451] that by faith we freely **obtain** the forgiveness of sins for
S2 : 01 :004(292) [0461] believed and cannot be **obtained** or apprehended by any
S2 : 02 :006(293) [0463] and when we can **obtain** what is more necessary, more
S2 : 02 :007(294) [0465] and others to God and **obtain** and merit grace and the
S2 : 02 :018(296) [0467] because we may **obtain** forgiveness and grace in a better
S2 : 02 :024(296) [0469] the merits of Christ are **obtained** by grace, through faith,
TR : 00 :044(328) [0517] they bid us to doubt whether forgiveness is **obtained**.
TR : 00 :044(328) [0517] and that by this faith we **obtain** the remission of sins.
SC : 01 :018(344) [0541] or home, nor to **obtain** them under pretext of legal right,
LC : PR :011(360) [0571] blessing and benefit you **obtain** from it is to rout the
LC : 01 :157(387) [0627] we could learn how to **obtain** an abundance of joy,
LC : 01 :166(387) [0629] be willing to run to the ends of the world to **obtain** them.
LC : 02 :002(411) [0679] may know where and how to **obtain** strength for this task.
LC : 02 :037(415) [0687] Answer: Just as the Son **obtains** dominion by purchasing
LC : 02 :039(416) [0689] this blessing, which we could not **obtain** by ourselves.
LC : 02 :044(416) [0689] were, teaching us to **obtain** grace and be saved by our
LC : 02 :055(418) [0693] that we may daily **obtain** full forgiveness of sins through
LC : 04 :026(439) [0739] as being, for in it we **obtain** such an inexpressible
LC : 04 :046(442) [0743] for through it we **obtain** perfect holiness and salvation,
LC : 04 :086(446) [0753] As we have once **obtained** forgiveness of sins in Baptism,
LC : 05 :020(449) [0757] that we know what we should seek and **obtain** there.
LC : 05 :022(449) [0757] through and in which we **obtain** the forgiveness of sins.
LC : 05 :028(449) [0759] are the treasure through which forgiveness is **obtained**.
LC : 06 :020(459) [0000] faithful advice to go and **obtain** this precious treasure.
EP : 03 :005(473) [0793] Christ and in Christ **obtain** the "righteousness which
EP : 03 :015(475) [0795] absolved from sin and to **obtain** the forgiveness of sins,
EP : 05 :005(478) [0803] without man's merit has **obtained** and won for him
SD : 02 :011(522) [0885] by his own power to **obtain** spiritual and heavenly
SD : 02 :015(523) [0885] ask of God they cannot **obtain** by their own natural
SD : 02 :057(532) [0903] himself with God's eternal election nor **obtain** his mercy.
SD : 03 :025(543) [0923] to us and by which we **obtain** the forgiveness of sins,
SD : 03 :043(547) [0931] with God, and who have **obtained** forgiveness of sins
SD : 03 :052(548) [0933] or that salvation cannot be **obtained** without works.
SD : 04 :034(557) [0949] of your faith, you **obtain** the salvation of your souls"
SD : 05 :011(560) [0955] To this end Christ has **obtained** and sent us the Spirit,
SD : 05 :020(561) [0959] believe in order to **obtain** the forgiveness of sins from
SD : 05 :020(561) [0959] the good graces of God, **obtain** forgiveness of sins

Obviate (1), Obviated (1)
PR : PR :026(014) [0025] in order that all kinds of scandal might be **obviated**.
SD : 07 :085(584) [1001] the Holy Supper and to **obviate** and eliminate many

Obvious (18), Obviously (16)
AP : 02 :002(100) [0105] These quibbles have **obviously** come from the schools,
AP : 02 :035(105) [0115] Imperial Majesty will recognize an **obvious** slander here.
AP : 04 :171(130) [0171] subject, though they are **obvious** throughout not only the
AP : 04 :231(139) [0183] He is **obviously** discussing love of our neighbor.
AP : 04 :238(140) [0187] **Obviously** Peter, too, is talking here about love to the
AP : 04 :289(151) [0203] This is **obviously** a doctrine of the law.
AP : 04 :290(151) [0203] ungodliness of the first is **obvious** because it teaches that
AP : 04 :298(153) [0205] The proof is **obvious**: Since we are not justified before
AP : 04 :308(155) [0207] edict of a superior is **obviously** a kind of distributive
AP : 04 :342(159) [0215] It is **obviously** a childish quibble to interpret "unworthy
AP : 04 :376(164) [0223] This error **obviously** destroys the righteousness of faith,
AP : 04 :390(166) [0225] their own authority is **obviously** more important than the
AP : 04 :390(166) [0225] It is also **obvious** that the theologians have mingled more
AP : 04 :391(167) [0225] Despite its **obvious** falsehood, this teaching has spawned
AP : 07 :017(171) [0231] But why belabor the **obvious**?
AP : 07 :037(175) [0241] of evidence since it is **obvious** throughout the Scriptures
AP : 12 :083(194) [0275] passages if they were not **obvious** to every devout reader
AP : 12 :092(196) [0279] For there is **obvious** danger in these statements, requiring
AP : 12 :131(202) [0291] scholastics because these are **obviously** later inventions.
AP : 12 :172(209) [0305] This is **obvious** from the subject-matter itself.
AP : 16 :011(224) [0333] Wycliffe was **obviously** out of his mind in claiming that
AP : 20 :006(227) [0339] are condemning the **obvious** truth — truth which the
AP : 21 :014(231) [0347] of redemption, they **obviously** make the saints mediators
AP : 21 :032(233) [0351] Such notions are **obviously** of pagan origin.
AP : 21 :039(235) [0355] ignore even the **obvious** offenses, as though they
AP : 21 :040(235) [0355] distinguish between their teachings and **obvious** abuses.
AP : 21 :043(235) [0357] They defend **obvious** abuses with new and illegal cruelty.
AP : 22 :010(237) [0361] Our opponents are **obviously** clowning when they apply
AP : 23 :006(240) [0365] It **obviously** endangers religion and morality, for it
AP : 23 :056(247) [0379] inexorable, though it is **obviously** a matter of simple
AP : 24 :043(258) [0399] Despite the **obvious** wickedness of some of this, they
AP : 24 :095(267) [0417] twisted to support the **obvious** lies which our opponents
LC : 01 :053(371) [0595] name occurs most **obviously** in worldly business and in
LC : 01 :333(410) [0677] From all this it is **obvious** once again how highly these

Occasion (34), Occasionally (2), Occasioned (3), Occasions (2)
PR : PR :004(004) [0007] of divine truth took **occasion** to discredit us and our
PR : PR :007(004) [0009] on the **occasion** of a meeting of the electors in the year
PR : PR :022(012) [0021] and purpose to give **occasion** by this Christian agreement
AG : 23 :013(053) [0063] good but rather gave **occasion** for many great and evil
AG : 23 :025(055) [0065] not give their brothers and sisters **occasion** for offense."
AG : 26 :033(069) [0075] so that he does not give **occasion** to sin, but not as if he
AG : 28 :078(094) [0095] obstinacy they offer **occasion** for division and schism,
AG : 00 :002(095) [0095] sermons on special **occasions**, and about countless other
AL : 00 :003(049) [0059] men, they first gave **occasion** to this controversy, and now
AL : 28 :078(094) [0095] God that by their obstinacy they offer **occasion** for schism
AP : 12 :168(209) [0305] **Occasionally** the Fathers take the word "satisfaction"
S3 : 11 :001(314) [0499] and thereby they gave **occasion** for all sorts of horrible,
TR : 00 :072(332) [0525] of the bishops that give **occasion** to schism and discord,
SC : 05 :024(350) [0555] On one **occasion** I also spoke indecently.
LC : 01 :178(389) [0631] explanation will have to await another **occasion**.
LC : 01 :183(389) [0631] The **occasion** and need for this commandment is that, as
LC : 01 :187(390) [0633] those who have given us **occasion** for anger, namely, our
LC : 01 :202(392) [0639] chaste and to afford no **occasion**, aid, or encouragement
LC : 01 :206(393) [0639] of marriage and gives **occasion** to speak of it, let us
LC : 01 :309(407) [0669] accessory to it, nor give **occasion** for it; we are willingly to
LC : 01 :328(410) [0677] the opportunity and **occasion** to do so and no man may
LC : 01 :332(410) [0677] neighbors, he will find **occasion** enough to practice the
LC : 03 :086(432) [0723] vex us and give us **occasion** for impatience, wrath,
LC : 05 :004(447) [0753] We have no wish on this **occasion** to quarrel and dispute
LC : 05 :038(451) [0761] What may be further said belongs to another **occasion**.
LC : 05 :079(455) [0771] injure you and give you **occasion** for sin and
EP : 04 :002(475) [0797] some theologians was **occasioned** when one party asserted
EP : 05 :006(478) [0803] and this was the original **occasion** of the controversy.
EP : 11 :015(496) [0835] ever give anyone **occasion** either to despair or to lead a
EP : 12 :014(499) [0841] 3. That as **occasion** arises no Christian, without violating
SD : PR :020(508) [0859] afterward expounded as **occasion** demanded and what we
SD : 03 :005(540) [0917] of justification were **occasioned** and evoked by the Interim
SD : 03 :041(546) [0929] a way as though on **occasion** true faith could coexist and
SD : 04 :023(555) [0945] of the Gospel, give **occasion** for doubt, are dangerous in
SD : 05 :003(558) [0953] find that it was chiefly **occasioned** by the fact that the
SD : 05 :027(563) [0961] anything that might give **occasion** for a confusion
SD : 05 :027(563) [0961] a usage that we find **occasionally** in the Apology too, the
SD : 07 :046(577) [0987] But as on the previous **occasion** when Abraham received
SD : 11 :001(616) [1063] article has become the **occasion** of very serious
SD : 11 :089(631) [1093] this doctrine never **occasions** either despondency or a
SD : 12 :019(634) [1099] wicked persons as **occasion** may arise, nor may a subject

Occupation (2), Occupations (2)
AL : 26 :011(065) [0071] or in other civil **occupations** — and admired the monks
AP : 04 :192(133) [0175] done in the most humble **occupation** and in private life.
LC : 01 :094(378) [0607] Other trades and **occupations** are not properly called holy
LC : 03 :076(431) [0721] our work, craft, or **occupation**, whatever it may be, to

Occupy (9), Occupied (5), Occupies (2), Occupying (1)
AG : 16 :002(037) [0051] may without sin **occupy** civil offices or serve as princes
AG : 26 :015(066) [0073] but they were so **occupied** with such efforts that they
AP : 23 :043(245) [0375] especially when they are **occupied** with public service,
S2 : 02 :012(294) [0465] They were so **occupied** with requiem Masses, with vigils,

Continued ▶

TR : 00 :035(326) [0513] sometimes in order to **occupy** Italian cities and sometimes
LC : PR :010(359) [0569] all evil thoughts as to **occupy** oneself with the Word of
LC : PR :010(360) [0571] against the devil than to **occupy** yourself with God's
LC : 01 :088(377) [0605] has been said, when we **occupy** ourselves with God's
LC : 01 :089(377) [0605] holy activities — that is, **occupy** ourselves daily with
LC : 01 :115(381) [0613] the face of all who are **occupied** with works of their own
LC : 01 :182(389) [0631] said, to persons who **occupy** the place of God, that is,
SD : 02 :057(532) [0903] together in his name and **occupy** themselves with his holy
SD : 07 :099(586) [1005] on earth and vacated or **occupied** space according to his
SD : 07 :100(586) [1005] to which he neither **occupies** nor vacates space but
SD : 07 :100(586) [1007] or water and does not **occupy** or vacate any space; a
SD : 07 :100(586) [1007] and a wall and neither **occupies** nor vacates space;
SD : 07 :100(586) [1007] and exist without **occupying** or vacating space, and many

Occur (4), Occurred (8), Occurs (9)
PR : PR :011(006) [0011] the differences that had **occurred** were to be decided in a
AG : 27 :045(078) [0081] are now ashamed of and wish had never **occurred**!
AP : 04 :242(141) [0187] though these offenses **occur**, love covers them up,
AP : 24 :085(265) [0413] etymology when the term **occurs** in Deut. 16:10, where it
TR : 00 :021(323) [0509] dispute could not have **occurred**, nor would a decree of
LC : 01 :053(371) [0595] misuse of the divine name **occurs** most obviously in
LC : 01 :054(372) [0595] greatest abuse, however, **occurs** in spiritual matters, which
LC : 01 :258(399) [0653] is such a government, instances of this sin still **occur**.
LC : 01 :301(405) [0667] This situation **occurs** most frequently in lawsuits in which
EP : RN :004(465) [0777] of faith which has **occurred** in our times, we regard, as
EP : 05 :006(478) [0803] of this meaning **occur** in Mark 1:15 and Acts 20:24), then
EP : 07 :009(483) [0811] This blessing **occurs** through the recitation of the words
EP : 09 :001(492) [0827] Did it **occur** only according to the soul, or only according
SD : PR :008(502) [0849] the schisms which have **occurred** among us, in the
SD : PR :019(507) [0857] of divisions have **occurred** among some of the
SD : 07 :061(580) [0995] This **occurs**, in no other way than with the spirit and
SD : 07 :066(581) [0997] through faith, which **occurs** outside of the sacrament too,
SD : 07 :102(587) [1007] But who can explain or even conceive how this **occurs**?
SD : 07 :105(588) [1009] for although such eating **occurs** with the mouth, the mode
SD : 08 :063(603) [1037] such an exchange has **occurred** in deed and in truth but
SD : 09 :003(610) [1051] exalted and acute speculations about how this **occurred**.

Ocean (2)
EP : 03 :002(473) [0793] like a drop of water over against the immense **ocean**.
SD : 03 :002(539) [0917] are like a drop of water compared to the mighty **ocean**.

Odious (2)
AL : 27 :017(073) [0077] these things without **odious** exaggeration in order that
SC : PR :025(341) [0539] or if you adopt **odious** laws on the subject, it is your own

Oemcken (2)
S3 : 15 :005(317) [0501] Gerard **Oemcken**, superintendent of the church in
TR : 00 :082(334) [0529] Gerard **Oemcken**, minister of the church in Minden

Oettingen (1)
PR : PR :027(015) [0025] Godfrey, count of **Oettingen**

Oettinger (2)
S3 : 15 :005(317) [0501] Conrad **Oettinger**, preacher of Duke Ulric of Pforzheim
TR : 00 :082(335) [0529] Conrad **Oettinger**, of Pforzheim, preacher of Ulric, duke

Off (32)
PR : PR :019(009) [0017] have tried to palm them **off** on simple folk in spite of the
AP : 04 :198(134) [0175] ways and often puts **off** the rewards for the righteousness
AP : 12 :015(184) [0257] As they buy **off** purgatory with satisfactions, so later on a
AP : 12 :015(184) [0257] profitable way of buying **off** satisfactions was invented.
AP : 12 :015(184) [0257] They buy **off** the satisfactions of the dead not only by
AP : 12 :046(188) [0263] without hands, by putting **off** the body of the sins of the
AP : 12 :046(188) [0263] The one is putting **off** the body of sins, the other is being
AP : 12 :046(188) [0263] quickening, putting **off** the body of sins, being raised —
AP : 12 :046(188) [0263] Paul calls "putting **off** the body of sins" because in these
AP : 12 :118(199) [0287] the keys, and the rest must be bought **off** by satisfactions.
AP : 12 :123(200) [0289] therefore satisfactions buy **off** the punishments of
AP : 12 :162(208) [0303] even those in mortal sin can buy **off** their punishments.
AP : 12 :168(209) [0305] satisfaction means cutting **off** the causes of sin, that is,
AP : 12 :173(209) [0305] commanded us to buy **off** punishment by such works,
AP : 12 :174(210) [0307] truthfulness — not to buy **off** eternal punishment but to
AP : 21 :032(233) [0351] riches, Sebastian wards **off** pestilence, Valentine heals
AP : 21 :032(233) [0351] riches, Febris warded **off** fever, and Castor and Pollux
AP : 24 :010(251) [0387] at issue and not wander **off** into side issues, like wrestlers
AP : 24 :085(264) [0413] except perhaps to show **off** their knowledge of Hebrew?
AP : 27 :045(277) [0435] consists in casting **off** possessions and the control of
LC : PR :001(358) [0567] had nothing to do but live **off** the fat of the land all their
LC : 01 :138(384) [0621] "May his posterity be cut **off**: and may their name be cut
LC : 01 :138(384) [0621] cut off: and may their name be cut **off** in one generation."
LC : 02 :017(412) [0681] and misfortune, warding **off** all sorts of danger and
SD : 01 :022(512) [0865] of can easily be washed **off**, like a smudge of dirt from
SD : 02 :081(537) [0911] St. Paul's words, "Put **off** the old man," as follows: "Lest
SD : 02 :081(537) [0911] what it means to lay **off** the old man and put on the new
SD : 02 :081(537) [0913] Behold, this is laying **off** the old man and putting on the
SD : 03 :029(544) [0925] reason we summarily cut **off** every reference to the law
SD : 04 :034(556) [0949] he says, "They were broken **off** because of their unbelief,
SD : 06 :024(568) [0971] until the flesh of sin is put **off** entirely and man is
SD : 11 :064(626) [1083] commands silence and cuts **off** further discussion with the

Offend (5), Offended (7), Offenders (1), Offending (1), Offends (1)
AL : 28 :055(090) [0091] in so far as one does not **offend** another, so that
AP : 04 :073(117) [0141] The particle "alone" **offends** some people, even though
AP : 07 :019(171) [0233] stumbling block may not **offend** the faithful and so that
AP : 07 :028(173) [0237] that we may not be **offended** by the unworthiness of
AP : 07 :049(178) [0245] that when we are **offended** by the personal conduct of
AP : 12 :174(210) [0307] surrendering to the devil or **offending** the Holy Spirit.
AP : 15 :051(222) [0329] lest the weak be **offended** and become more hostile to the
AP : 27 :036(275) [0433] that wise men were **offended** by the immoderate praises
S1 : PR :003(289) [0455] They are deeply **offended**, as well they might be, and are
LC : 01 :239(397) [0649] promptly took such **offenders** by the scruff of the neck so
LC : 01 :258(399) [0653] course of the world, men are loathe to **offend** anyone.
LC : 01 :259(400) [0655] in all cases will often **offend** good friends, relatives,
LC : 01 :263(400) [0655] tongue by which we may injure or **offend** our neighbor.
LC : 01 :300(405) [0667] because they have not **offended** against the preceding
SD : 11 :050(624) [1079] church is, lest we be **offended** by the outward prestige of

Offense (25), Offenses (23)
AG : 23 :003(051) [0061] avoid such unbecoming **offense**, adultery, and other
AG : 23 :016(054) [0063] weakness and to prevent and avoid greater **offense**.
AG : 23 :018(054) [0063] frightful and unchristian **offense**, so much adultery, and
AG : 23 :025(055) [0065] not give their brothers and sisters occasion for **offense**."
AG : 27 :048(078) [0081] Now, it is no small **offense** in the Christian church that
AG : 28 :041(087) [0089] when it does not give **offense** to others), that it is a
AG : 28 :053(090) [0091] their observance even when this is done without **offense**.
AG : 28 :055(090) [0091] that one does not give **offense** to another and so that
AG : 28 :056(090) [0091] omit them, even when no **offense** is given to others, just
AG : 28 :056(090) [0091] commits a sin if without **offense** to others she goes out
AG : 28 :065(092) [0093] but forbade such eating for a time to avoid **offense**.
AL : 22 :011(050) [0061] been compelled, with **offense** to their consciences, to do
AL : 23 :025(055) [0065] least they should give no **offense** to their brothers and
AL : 27 :048(078) [0081] It is no light **offense** in the church to recommend to the
AL : 28 :041(087) [0089] even when it gives no **offense** to others, that certain foods
AL : 28 :056(090) [0091] who omit them without **offense** to others commit a sin,
AL : 28 :056(090) [0091] with her head uncovered, provided no **offense** is given.
AL : 28 :065(092) [0093] but forbade such eating for a time to avoid **offense**.
AP : 04 :240(141) [0187] means: "Hatred stirs up strife, but love covers all **offenses**."
AP : 04 :241(141) [0187] greatest tragedies come from the most trifling **offenses**.
AP : 04 :242(141) [0187] it says, "Love covers all **offenses**," namely, other people's
AP : 04 :242(141) [0187] namely, other people's **offenses** and offenses between
AP : 04 :242(141) [0187] other people's offenses and **offenses** between people.
AP : 04 :242(141) [0187] Even though these **offenses** occur, love covers them up,
AP : 04 :263(146) [0195] "Behold, there will be a healing of your **offenses**."
AP : 12 :112(198) [0285] that these satisfactions might be suited to their **offenses**.
AP : 12 :112(198) [0285] prescribed without knowing the character of the **offense**.
AP : 12 :112(198) [0285] Different **offenses** had different canons.
AP : 12 :178(211) [0309] endless enumeration of **offenses**, and satisfactions, and
AP : 15 :052(222) [0329] public harmony, without **offense** to consciences, should
AP : 18 :005(225) [0335] never stops inciting this feeble nature to various **offenses**.
AP : 21 :039(235) [0355] ignore even the obvious **offenses**, as though they
AP : 24 :062(260) [0405] on the altar for daily **offenses** so that in this the church
AP : 28 :013(283) [0447] who are guilty of public **offenses** or to absolve them if
AP : 28 :016(283) [0447] to be left free, only that **offenses** should be avoided and
AP : 28 :017(284) [0449] place and without superstition, in order to avoid **offenses**.
AP : 28 :022(284) [0451] the basis of the public **offenses** and commotions which
AP : 28 :023(284) [0451] If all the **offenses** are put together, still the one doctrine
AP : 28 :025(285) [0451] Besides, are there no **offenses** among our opponents?
TR : 00 :075(333) [0525] Not in punishing real **offenses**, but in dealing with
LC : 01 :183(389) [0633] There are many **offenses** against this commandment, as
LC : 01 :226(395) [0645] deal with them so that they will not repeat the **offense**.
LC : 01 :231(396) [0647] who have committed one **offense** must bear disgrace and
EP : 10 :005(493) [0829] matter all frivolity and **offenses** are to be avoided, and
EP : 10 :006(493) [0831] as well as preventing **offense** to the weak in faith.
SD : PR :007(502) [0849] would involve serious **offense** for both the unbelievers and
SD : 04 :036(557) [0949] wrangling and preserve the church from many **offenses**.
SD : 10 :009(612) [1055] so without frivolity and **offense** but in an orderly and

Offensive (11), Offensively (1)
PR : PR :011(006) [0011] how the aforementioned **offensive** differences might be
AP : 04 :185(132) [0173] the sources, will correct everything that seems **offensive**.
AP : 04 :242(141) [0187] even on the more **offensive** actions of others, as the
AP : 24 :088(265) [0413] Properly understood, this is not **offensive**.
EP : 04 :017(477) [0801] reject and condemn as **offensive** and as subversive of
EP : 07 :041(486) [0817] blasphemously and **offensively** in a coarse, carnal,
EP : 11 :001(494) [0831] lest as some future date **offensive** dissension concerning it
EP : 11 :022(497) [0837] In this way the **offensive** controversies that have
SD : 01 :059(519) [0879] Really to settle this **offensive** and highly detrimental
SD : 04 :036(557) [0949] point which led to many **offensive** exaggerations, it is
SD : 04 :039(557) [0951] it is false and **offensive**, might weaken discipline and
SD : 11 :002(616) [1063] unnecessary, still less **offensive** and detrimental, because

Offer (52), Offered (74), Offering (36), Offerings (11), Offers (42)
AG : PR :008(025) [0039] Your Imperial Majesty, we **offer** and present a confession
AG : PR :020(026) [0041] Majesty graciously **offered** to promote and bring about
AG : PR :021(026) [0043] we mentioned above, we **offer** in full obedience, even
AG : 09 :001(033) [0047] Baptism is necessary and that grace is **offered** through it.
AG : 20 :007(042) [0053] This teaching may **offer** a little more comfort than the
AG : 20 :035(046) [0057] are to be done and for **offering** help as to how they may
AG : 00 :002(048) [0059] although we hope to **offer** firm grounds and reasons why
AG : 23 :025(055) [0065] St. Cyprian therefore **offered** the counsel that women who
AG : 24 :027(059) [0067] the Hebrews that Christ **offered** himself once and by this
AG : 24 :027(059) [0067] himself once and by this **offering** made satisfaction for all
AG : 27 :036(076) [0081] vows, our teachers **offer** still more reasons why monastic
AG : 28 :078(094) [0095] as by their obstinacy they **offer** occasion for division and
AL : 09 :001(033) [0047] that the grace of God is **offered** through Baptism, and
AL : 09 :002(033) [0047] be baptized, for being **offered** to God through Baptism
AL : 13 :002(035) [0049] the promises that are set forth and **offered**, is added.
AL : 20 :015(043) [0055] find by experience that it **offers** the greatest consolation
AL : 23 :012(052) [0063] In fact, they **offered** such resistance that the archbishop
AL : 24 :007(056) [0065] the great consolation it **offers** to anxious consciences,
AL : 24 :026(059) [0067] sanctified through the **offering** of the body of Jesus
AL : 24 :027(059) [0067] and again, "By a single **offering** he has perfected for all
AL : 24 :031(059) [0067] realize that they are truly **offered** to us; and it is not
AL : 27 :036(076) [0081] their vows, our teachers **offer** still another reason to show
AL : 28 :078(094) [0095] God that by their obstinacy they **offer** occasion for schism.
AP : PR :007(098) [0101] They finally **offered** the apology to His Imperial Majesty,
AP : 04 :003(107) [0121] consciences of the consolation **offered** them in Christ.
AP : 04 :041(113) [0133] upon our merits but **offers** the forgiveness of sins and
AP : 04 :041(113) [0133] that is, the forgiveness of sins is **offered** freely.
AP : 04 :044(113) [0133] death, the promise freely **offers** reconciliation for Christ's
AP : 04 :048(114) [0135] firm acceptance of God's **offer** promising forgiveness of
AP : 04 :048(114) [0135] to accept the promised **offer** of forgiveness of sins and
AP : 04 :049(114) [0135] which receives God's **offered** blessing; the righteousness
AP : 04 :049(114) [0135] the law is that worship which **offers** God our own merits.
AP : 04 :049(114) [0135] that we receive from him what he promises and **offers**.
AP : 04 :052(114) [0135] why did Christ have to be **offered** for our sins if our

Continued ▶

AP : 04 :053(114) [0137] shows that the blessing is **offered** only by mercy; the
AP : 04 :062(115) [0139] For Christ's sake it **offers** forgiveness of sins and
AP : 04 :168(130) [0169] let every one who is godly **offer** prayer to thee" (Ps. 32:6).
AP : 04 :194(133) [0175] that rewards have been **offered** and promised to the
AP : 04 :195(134) [0175] as Christ is one, and it is **offered** freely to all who believe
AP : 04 :202(134) [0175] By faith Abel **offered** a more acceptable sacrifice (Heb.
AP : 04 :204(135) [0177] glory of Christ when men **offer** these works to God as a
AP : 04 :207(135) [0177] "I did not command concerning burnt **offerings**."
AP : 04 :209(135) [0177] The people heard that Abraham had **offered** up his son.
AP : 04 :209(136) [0179] But Abraham did not **offer** up his son with the idea that
AP : 04 :210(136) [0179] in those for whom it is **offered**, as Gabriel Biel writes.
AP : 04 :227(139) [0183] accept and grasp what is **offered** in the promise of Christ.
AP : 04 :228(139) [0183] this desire to receive the **offered** promise, is no less an act
AP : 04 :285(150) [0201] This **offers** the greatest consolation to faithful consciences
AP : 04 :299(153) [0205] see the most complete consolation **offered** them.
AP : 04 :304(154) [0205] accept what the promise **offers** — reconciliation and
AP : 04 :310(155) [0207] worship of the law is to **offer** and present our goods to
AP : 04 :310(155) [0207] We cannot **offer** anything to God unless we have first
AP : 04 :312(155) [0207] for what the promise **offers**, then the dispositions of faith
AP : 04 :312(155) [0207] the present forgiveness of sins that the promise **offers**.
AP : 04 :339(159) [0215] does not denounce the promise that **offers** mercy gratis.
AP : 04 :365(163) [0219] Just so they sometimes **offer** grace with other rewards, as
AP : 04 :366(163) [0221] law, in which a reward is **offered** and owed, not gratis but
AP : 04 :367(163) [0221] though the Gospel **offers** justification freely because of
AP : 04 :367(163) [0221] as in these passages a reward is **offered** for works.
AP : 04 :367(163) [0221] here, too, the law **offers** a reward for a certain
AP : 04 :368(163) [0221] that the Gospel **offers** justification freely for Christ's
AP : 04 :388(166) [0225] but by the Gospel, the promise of grace **offered** in Christ.
AP : 07 :009(170) [0229] The Creed **offers** us these consolations that we may not
AP : 07 :028(173) [0237] When they **offer** the Word of Christ or the sacraments,
AP : 09 :002(178) [0245] Just as there salvation is **offered** to all, so Baptism is
AP : 09 :002(178) [0245] to all, so Baptism is **offered** to all — men, women,
AP : 09 :002(178) [0245] be baptized because salvation is **offered** with Baptism.
AP : 10 :001(179) [0247] present and are truly **offered** with those things that are
AP : 10 :003(179) [0247] teaches that Christ is **offered** to us bodily in the Supper.
AP : 10 :004(179) [0247] present and are truly **offered** with those things that are
AP : 12 :029(185) [0259] is to denounce sin, to **offer** the forgiveness of sins and
AP : 12 :039(187) [0261] the keys administers and **offers** the Gospel through
AP : 12 :042(187) [0261] Therefore they **offer** the forgiveness of sins, as the words
AP : 12 :049(188) [0265] in contrition by the Word of God which **offers** us grace.
AP : 12 :055(189) [0267] and sin! this was the **offer** of the forgiveness of sins.
AP : 12 :086(194) [0277] justified by the law and to **offer** our works to God before
AP : 12 :094(196) [0281] invites us to salvation with an **offer** and even an oath.
AP : 13 :007(212) [0311] like the Levitical to **offer** sacrifices and merit the
AP : 13 :019(213) [0313] that which is promised and **offered** in the sacrament.
AP : 13 :020(213) [0313] promised in the New Testament, is being **offered** to him.
AP : 13 :021(214) [0313] of sins is actually being **offered**, not about a faith which
AP : 20 :009(228) [0341] which this article of ours **offers** to the universal church.
AP : 22 :010(237) [0361] with the one part **offered** by the priest, that is, with one
AP : 23 :019(242) [0369] by using the remedy he **offers**, just as he wants to nourish
AP : 24 :001(249) [0385] when the sacrament is **offered** to those who wish for it
AP : 24 :018(252) [0389] or act in which God **offers** us the content of the promise
AP : 24 :018(252) [0389] is not an act which we **offer** to God but one in which God
AP : 24 :018(252) [0389] Here God **offers** and presents the forgiveness of sins
AP : 24 :021(252) [0391] for whom they were **offered** did not have to be excluded
AP : 24 :021(253) [0391] sacrifices for sin or burnt **offerings** for trespasses.
AP : 24 :021(253) [0391] the oblation, the drink **offerings**, the thank offering, the
AP : 24 :021(253) [0391] offerings, the thank **offering**, the first fruits, and the
AP : 24 :022(253) [0391] sanctified through the **offering** of the body of Jesus
AP : 24 :023(253) [0391] he makes himself an **offering** for sin, he shall see his
AP : 24 :023(253) [0391] in Rom. 8:3, "As a sin **offering** he condemned sin," that
AP : 24 :023(253) [0391] he condemned sin," that is, through an **offering** for sin.
AP : 24 :023(253) [0391] The Latins **offered** a sacrificial victim to placate the wrath
AP : 24 :023(253) [0391] to be unusually severe; this they called a trespass **offering**.
AP : 24 :023(253) [0391] Sometimes they **offered** up human sacrifices, perhaps
AP : 24 :023(253) [0391] victim or trespass **offering** to reconcile God by his merits
AP : 24 :024(253) [0391] were so called only as symbols of a future **offering**.
AP : 24 :026(254) [0391] "A holy priesthood, to **offer** spiritual sacrifices."
AP : 24 :026(254) [0391] also with human works **offered** *ex opere operato*, for
AP : 24 :026(254) [0391] men suppose they are **offering** God a work *ex opere*
AP : 24 :026(254) [0391] him let us continually **offer** up a sacrifice of praise to
AP : 24 :026(254) [0393] He commands them to **offer** praises, that is, prayer,
AP : 24 :026(254) [0393] "Through him let us **offer**," namely, through faith in
AP : 24 :028(254) [0393] command them concerning burnt **offerings** and sacrifices.
AP : 24 :028(254) [0393] concerning burnt **offerings** and sacrifices, but what
AP : 24 :029(255) [0393] says, "Sacrifice and **offering** thou dost not desire;
AP : 24 :029(255) [0393] That is, "Thou has **offered** me thy Word to hear, and
AP : 24 :029(255) [0393] Ps. 51:16, 17 says, "Thou hast no delight in burnt **offering**.
AP : 24 :029(255) [0393] So also Ps. 4:5, "**Offer** right sacrifices, and put your trust
AP : 24 :029(255) [0393] And Ps. 116:17, "I will **offer** to thee sacrifices of
AP : 24 :031(255) [0395] in every place incense is **offered** to my name, and a pure
AP : 24 :031(255) [0395] place incense is offered to my name, and a pure **offering**."
AP : 24 :032(255) [0395] "incense" and "a pure **offering**" do not refer to a ceremony
AP : 24 :034(256) [0395] and silver, till they present right **offerings** to the Lord."
AP : 24 :034(256) [0395] clearly requires the **offerings** of the righteous; therefore it
AP : 24 :034(256) [0395] The **offerings** of the sons of Levi (that is, of those who
AP : 24 :034(256) [0395] of God, so that the **offering** of the Gentiles may be
AP : 24 :034(256) [0397] Gentiles may become **offerings** acceptable to God through
AP : 24 :034(256) [0397] sacrifices for sin **offered** by a Levitical priesthood.
AP : 24 :036(257) [0397] of the lamb, the drink **offering**, and the offering of flour.
AP : 24 :036(257) [0397] of the lamb, the drink offering, and the **offering** of flour.
AP : 24 :036(257) [0397] The drink **offering** symbolizes the sprinkling, that is, the
AP : 24 :036(257) [0397] The **offering** of flour symbolizes faith, prayer, and
AP : 24 :038(257) [0399] There must be a drink **offering**, namely, the effect of the
AP : 24 :038(257) [0399] There must also be an **offering** in thanksgiving,
AP : 24 :052(259) [0403] men in relation to God, to **offer** gifts and sacrifices for
AP : 24 :053(259) [0403] "every high priest is appointed to **offer** sacrifices for sins."
AP : 24 :055(259) [0403] that Christ would be the **offering** and the satisfaction for
AP : 24 :055(259) [0403] teaches, "When he makes himself an **offering** for sin."
AP : 24 :059(260) [0405] *ex opere operato;* but it **offers** to others the Gospel and
AP : 24 :062(260) [0405] body of the Lord, once **offered** on the cross for the
AP : 24 :062(260) [0405] the original debt, is daily **offered** on the altar for daily
AP : 24 :070(262) [0409] Therefore the Word **offers** the forgiveness of sins, while
AP : 24 :070(262) [0409] believes that the forgiveness of sins is being **offered** here.
AP : 24 :075(263) [0411] proves that the sacrament **offers** the forgiveness of sins
AP : 24 :085(265) [0413] gifts of the people rather than the **offering** of the priest?
AP : 24 :087(265) [0413] the Mass is called an **offering**, what does that term have
AP : 24 :087(265) [0413] It can be called an **offering**, as it is called a eucharist,
AP : 24 :087(265) [0413] thanksgivings, and the whole worship are **offered** there.
AP : 24 :088(265) [0413] also says much about an **offering**; but it clearly shows
AP : 24 :088(265) [0413] make us worthy to come to **offer** Thee entreaties and
AP : 24 :088(265) [0413] might be made worthy to **offer** prayers and supplications
AP : 24 :088(265) [0413] it says a little later: "We **offer** Thee this reasonable and
AP : 24 :090(266) [0415] For it **offers** the forgiveness of sins, which necessarily
AP : 24 :093(267) [0417] does not apply the **offering** as a satisfaction for the dead
AP : 24 :093(267) [0417] it seems that the Greeks **offer** it only as a thanksgiving
AP : 24 :093(267) [0417] they speak not only of **offering** the body and blood of the
AP : 24 :093(267) [0417] Then they add, "Yet we **offer** Thee this reasonable service
AP : 24 :094(267) [0417] opponents quote the Fathers on **offerings** for the dead.
AP : 24 :096(267) [0417] the Mass there was an **offering** for the living and the
S2 : 02 :001(293) [0463] of the Mass (even when **offered** by an evil scoundrel)
S2 : 02 :014(295) [0467] in Masses which are **offered** for souls in purgatory, etc.
S2 : 02 :024(296) [0469] They are **offered** to us without our money or merit, not
S2 : 02 :026(297) [0469] for them, say Masses and **offer** sacrifices to them,
S2 : 02 :027(297) [0469] and say Masses and **offer** sacrifices in your honor, or
S3 : 02 :001(303) [0479] and by the promise and **offer** of grace and favor.
S3 : 03 :008(304) [0481] Moreover, the Gospel **offers** consolation and forgiveness
S3 : 03 :016(305) [0483] God, this consolation was **offered**: If anybody could not
S3 : 03 :026(307) [0487] dead and afterwards by **offering** indulgences for the dead
S3 : 04 :000(310) [0491] to the Gospel, which **offers** council and help against sin in
TR : 00 :019(323) [0509] the primacy was **offered** to the bishop of Rome but he did
TR : 00 :040(327) [0515] church and the ministry, **offering** as pretext these words,
SC : 08 :006(353) [0559] *teach his household to* ***offer*** *blessing and thanksgiving at*
LC : PR :010(360) [0569] You will never **offer** up any incense or other savor more
LC : 01 :040(370) [0591] to us with so gracious an **offer**, so cordial an invitation,
LC : 01 :083(376) [0603] To **offer** ordinary people a Christian interpretation of
LC : 01 :118(381) [0615] lives they are not worthy to **offer** him a cup of water?
LC : 01 :191(391) [0635] murderers who do not **offer** counsel and aid to men in
LC : 01 :323(409) [0675] himself a kind father and **offers** us every grace and
LC : 02 :038(415) [0689] unless these were first **offered** to us and bestowed on our
LC : 02 :038(415) [0689] given the Holy Spirit to **offer** and apply to us this
LC : 03 :016(422) [0701] should say: "The prayer I **offer** is just as precious, holy,
LC : 03 :057(428) [0713] to God if we, to whom he **offers** and pledges so many
LC : 04 :029(440) [0739] external ordinance and **offered** it to us so that we may
LC : 04 :033(440) [0741] Since these blessings are **offered** and promised in the
LC : 04 :037(441) [0741] comprehended and **offered** to us in the Word and received
LC : 05 :030(450) [0759] in the Word and **offered** to us through the Word,
LC : 05 :031(450) [0759] been accomplished and **offered** to us if it were not
LC : 05 :032(450) [0759] in this sacrament and **offered** to us through the Word.
LC : 05 :034(450) [0761] And because he **offers** and promises forgiveness of sins, it
LC : 05 :035(450) [0761] this gracious blessing be **offered** to him in vain and
LC : 05 :036(450) [0761] Since this treasure is fully **offered** in the words, it can be
LC : 05 :066(454) [0769] In this sacrament he **offers** us all the treasure he brought
LC : 06 :007(458) [0000] precious and comforting treasure which the Gospel **offers**.
LC : 06 :030(460) [0000] but rather coming and compelling us to **offer** it.
EP : 02 :001(469) [0785] accept the grace of God **offered** in the Word and the holy
EP : 02 :011(471) [0789] of the Word and in it has **offered** his grace, man's will is
EP : 11 :008(495) [0833] To these he **offers** himself in his Word, and it is his will
SD : 02 :002(520) [0881] God is preached and the grace of God is **offered** to him.
SD : 02 :018(524) [0889] when the Holy Spirit **offers** the grace of God and
SD : 02 :057(532) [0903] in whom we are elected, **offers** his grace to all men in the
SD : 02 :064(533) [0905] says, "Your people will **offer** themselves freely on the day
SD : 02 :077(536) [0911] us by the Gospel and **offers** his grace, the forgiveness of
SD : 02 :083(537) [0913] of the Holy Spirit is able to accept the **offered** grace.
SD : 03 :010(541) [0919] The Holy Spirit **offers** these treasures to us in the promise
SD : 03 :016(541) [0921] This righteousness is **offered** to us by the Holy Spirit
SD : 03 :031(544) [0925] the forgiveness of sins **offered** to us in the promise of the
SD : 03 :039(546) [0929] merit, which treasures are **offered** to us in the promise of
SD : 04 :017(554) [0943] are to be a people who **offer** themselves freely (Ps. 110:3),
SD : 04 :017(554) [0943] who bring free-will **offerings** (Ps. 54:6), not reluctantly or
SD : 04 :033(556) [0947] The Apology **offers** a fine example as to when and how,
SD : 05 :009(559) [0955] of the holy Gospel **offers** to all penitent sinners who have
SD : 05 :021(562) [0959] which comforts and which **offers** the mercy and grace of
SD : 07 :011(571) [0975] present and are truly **offered** with the visible elements, the
SD : 07 :046(577) [0987] God's words about **offering** up his son, because these
SD : 07 :083(584) [1001] eaten but is locked up, **offered** up, or carried about), does
SD : 07 :087(585) [1003] is not distributed but is **offered** up, or locked up, or
SD : 10 :004(611) [1053] by the grace of God, we **offer** the Christian reader the
SD : 11 :016(619) [1069] of Christ are to be **offered**, given, and distributed to us
SD : 11 :037(622) [1075] promises of the Gospel **offered** not only in general but
SD : 11 :041(623) [1077] Holy Spirit which God **offers** to him through the call and

Office (69), Offices (5)

PR : PR :006(004) [0009] Mindful of the **office** which God has committed to us and
PR : PR :012(007) [0013] and zeal in view of the **office** that we bear and that God
PR : PR :024(013) [0023] precept, on account of the **office** we bear, over against the
AG : 05 :000(031) [0045] V. [The **Office** of the Ministry]
AG : 05 :001(031) [0045] faith God instituted the **office** of the ministry, that is,
AG : 16 :002(037) [0051] without sin occupy civil **offices** or serve as princes and
AG : 21 :001(046) [0057] are incumbents of a royal **office** which demands the
AG : 27 :013(073) [0077] by God — whether the **office** of pastor and preacher, of
AG : 27 :054(079) [0083] to take revenge outside of the exercise of their **office**.
AG : 27 :056(080) [0083] child, and also their civil **office**, to take shelter in a
AG : 28 :009(082) [0085] except through the **office** of preaching and of
AG : 28 :010(082) [0085] only through the **office** of preaching, it does not interfere
AG : 28 :019(084) [0087] has nothing at all to do with the **office** of the Gospel.
AG : 28 :021(084) [0087] right, therefore, it is the **office** of the bishop to preach the
AL : 16 :002(037) [0051] Christians to hold civil **office**, to sit as judges, to decide
AL : 27 :055(079) [0083] magistracy and all civil **offices** are unworthy of Christians
AP : 07 :004(169) [0227] that is, that he will rule and hold **office** in the church.
AP : 07 :017(171) [0233] are mingled with the church and hold **office** in the church.
AP : 07 :028(173) [0237] outward marks, and therefore hold **office** in the church.
AP : 13 :015(213) [0311] many other states or **offices** might also be called
AP : 16 :001(222) [0329] legitimately hold public **office**, render verdicts according
AP : 23 :023(242) [0369] from the public ministry who married while in **office**.
AP : 23 :057(247) [0379] suspend them all right — not from **office** but from trees!

Continued ▶

S 2 : 0 0 :000(292) [0461] which pertain to the **office** and work of Jesus Christ, or to
S 2 : 0 3 :002(298) [0471] Christian life and to the **offices** and callings established by
S 2 : 0 4 :006(299) [0473] use to the church because it exercises no Christian **office**.
S 2 : 0 4 :008(300) [0473] God would raise up a man fitted for such an **office**.
S 2 : 0 4 :009(300) [0473] all the bishops equal in **office** (however they may differ in
S 3 : 0 3 :004(304) [0481] To this **office** of the law the New Testament immediately
S 3 : 0 3 :007(304) [0481] where the law exercises its **office** alone, without the
S 3 : 0 8 :002(312) [0495] is derived from the **office** of the keys, it should not be
S 3 : 1 0 :002(314) [0497] or discharge any **office** or work in the church.
S 3 : 1 0 :003(314) [0497] and ought ourselves ordain suitable persons to this **office**.
T R : 0 0 :080(334) [0527] rule states, "The benefice is given because of the **office**."
S C : P R :004(338) [0533] and paid no attention at all to the duties of your **office**?
S C : P R :006(338) [0533] take the duties of your **office** seriously, that you have pity
S C : P R :026(341) [0539] Our **office** has become something different from what it
L C : P R :001(358) [0567] and despise both their **office** and this teaching itself.
L C : P R :008(359) [0569] they despise both their **office** and the people's souls, yes,
L C : 0 1 :086(376) [0605] The special **office** of this day, therefore, should be the
L C : 0 1 :158(387) [0627] this title to themselves but performed no fatherly **office**.
L C : 0 1 :167(388) [0629] on the nature of their **office**, how they should treat those
L C : 0 1 :168(388) [0629] knaves or tyrants in this **office** and responsibility; nor
L C : 0 1 :168(388) [0629] the duties of their **office**, not only to provide for the
L C : 0 1 :169(388) [0629] imagine that the parental **office** is a matter of your
L C : 0 1 :229(396) [0645] a cash box, they sit in **office** chairs and are called great
L C : 0 1 :266(401) [0657] to administer punishment by virtue of your **office**.
L C : 0 1 :268(401) [0657] the judgment and **office** of God, pronouncing the severest
L C : 0 1 :274(402) [0659] By virtue of his **office** he does not do his neighbor good
L C : 0 1 :274(402) [0659] own accord instituted that **office**, and as he warns in the
L C : 0 2 :035(415) [0687] the Holy Spirit and his **office**, which is that he makes us
L C : 0 2 :059(418) [0693] All this, then, is the **office** and work of the Holy Spirit, to
L C : 0 3 :075(430) [0719] subjects that through the **office** of the princes we enjoy
L C : 0 5 :086(456) [0773] us and succeed us in our **office** and work, so that they in
E P : 0 5 :010(479) [0803] he comes to his proper **office** — namely, to preach grace,
E P : 0 8 :036(491) [0825] is fitting and necessary to perform his **office** as judge.
E P : 1 2 :013(499) [0841] or function in any civic **office** with a good and clear
E P : 1 2 :014(499) [0841] conscience, may use an **office** of the government against
S D : 0 2 :056(532) [0903] heard and preached is an **office** and work of the Holy
S D : 0 3 :038(546) [0929] 2. That faith's sole **office** and property is to serve as the
S D : 0 3 :038(546) [0929] From this **office** and property of application and
S D : 0 5 :011(560) [0955] comfort but, through the **office** of the law, must also
S D : 0 5 :014(560) [0957] retains and performs the **office** of the law, which reveals
S D : 0 5 :014(560) [0957] God's wrath, but to this **office** it immediately adds the
S D : 0 5 :019(561) [0957] Holy Spirit through the **office** of the law rebukes the
S D : 0 5 :022(562) [0959] explained, is an **office** which kills through the letter and is
S D : 0 6 :012(566) [0967] performs both **offices**, "he kills and brings to life, he
S D : 0 6 :012(566) [0967] His **office** is not alone to comfort but also to rebuke, as it
S D : 0 7 :077(583) [0999] are daily distributed through our ministry and **office**."
S D : 0 8 :046(600) [1031] the discharge of Christ's **office** is concerned, the person
S D : 0 8 :051(601) [1033] the exercise of Christ's **office**, the human nature in Christ
S D : 1 0 :019(614) [1059] or discharge any **office** or work in the church.
S D : 1 2 :018(634) [1099] no Christian can hold an **office** in the government with an
S D : 1 2 :019(634) [1099] conscience use an **office** of the government against wicked

Officers (1)
T R : 0 0 :074(332) [0525] tyranny it is for civil **officers** to have the power to ban

Officials (5)
A P : 1 2 :069(192) [0271] but like petty public **officials** they quietly approved the
A P : 2 3 :055(247) [0379] This is the duty of public **officials**, who ought to maintain
T R : 0 0 :074(332) [0525] For it is evident that the **officials** (as they are called) have
S C : P R :011(339) [0535] over to the pope and his **officials**, and even to the devil
L C : 0 3 :077(431) [0721] magistrates, and **officials**, with wisdom, strength, and

Officiated (1)
A G : 2 4 :037(060) [0067] indicate that one man **officiated** and communicated the

Offscouring (2)
A P : 2 4 :023(253) [0391] The Greeks called them either "refuse" or "**offscouring**."
L C : 0 1 :160(387) [0627] be "the refuse of the world, and every man's **offscouring**."

Offspring (1)
A P : 2 4 :023(253) [0391] for sin, he shall see his **offspring**, he shall prolong his

Oft (1)
S D : 0 7 :105(588) [1009] in spite of our public and **oft**-repeated testimony to the

Oh (4)
A P : 1 2 :094(196) [0281] **Oh**, blessed are we for whose sake God swears an oath!
A P : 1 2 :094(196) [0281] **Oh**, most miserable are we if we do not believe the Lord
L C : 0 1 :270(401) [0657] "**Oh**, I cannot prove it publicly; I might be called a liar
S D : 0 4 :010(552) [0941] **Oh**, faith is a living, busy, active, mighty thing, so that it

Oil (3)
A P : 2 1 :030(233) [0351] extinguished, they begged the wise ones to lend them **oil**.
A P : 2 1 :030(233) [0351] of others, for everyone must buy **oil** for his own lamp."
S D : 0 8 :071(605) [1041] as when water, wine, or **oil** is poured from one container

Old (106), Older (2)
A G : 0 1 :006(028) [0043] that of the Samosatenes, **old** and new, who hold that
A G : 2 3 :016(054) [0063] The **old** canons also state that it is sometimes necessary to
A G : 2 8 :059(091) [0091] the Gospel all ceremonies of the **old** law may be omitted.
A L : 0 1 :006(028) [0043] condemn the Samosatenes, **old** and new, who contend
A L : 2 0 :007(042) [0053] it can afford more consolation than their **old** teaching.
A L : 0 0 :004(048) [0059] that all ceremonies and all **old** ordinances are abolished in
A L : 2 3 :014(053) [0063] as the world is growing **old** and man's nature is becoming
A L : 2 3 :016(054) [0063] state that in later times the **old** rigor should be relaxed
A P : 0 2 :015(102) [0109] Properly understood, the **old** definition says exactly the
A P : 0 4 :207(135) [0177] The people of the **Old** Testament imitated these sacrifices
A P : 0 4 :350(161) [0217] despair when it shows our **old** or new sins or the
A P : 0 7 :014(170) [0231] be between the church and the **Old** Testament people?
A P : 0 7 :014(170) [0231] the church from the **Old** Testament people by the fact
A P : 0 7 :014(170) [0231] Among the **Old** Testament people, those born according
A P : 0 7 :016(171) [0231] with the saints among the **Old** Testament people), for they
A P : 0 7 :040(176) [0241] to observe certain **Old** Testament customs, which the
A P : 1 2 :148(205) [0299] itself takes place by constantly mortifying the **old** life.
A P : 1 3 :009(212) [0311] for the people, as in the **Old** Testament, but they are called
A P : 1 5 :032(219) [0323] True, in the **Old** Testament ceremonies were necessary for
A P : 1 5 :038(220) [0325] We gladly keep the **old** traditions set up in the church
A P : 2 3 :027(243) [0371] the priests of the **Old** Testament were to be separated from
A P : 2 3 :053(246) [0379] Nature is growing **older** and progressively weaker, so that
A P : 2 3 :064(248) [0381] and purity laws of the **Old** Testament do not apply here
A P : 2 4 :021(252) [0389] The **Old** Testament called certain sacrifices propitiatory
A P : 2 4 :023(253) [0391] In the **Old** Testament this meant that a victim was to
A P : 2 4 :028(254) [0393] The **Old** Testament prophets also condemn the popular
A P : 2 4 :034(256) [0397] slaughter of animals in the **Old** Testament symbolized
A P : 2 4 :034(256) [0397] which should kill this **old** flesh and begin a new and
A P : 2 4 :035(256) [0397] was a daily sacrifice in the **Old** Testament, so the Mass
A P : 2 4 :036(257) [0397] The **Old** Testament had pictures or shadows of what was
A P : 2 4 :037(257) [0397] discern the shadow in the **Old** Testament, so in the New
A P : 2 4 :052(259) [0403] when the pomp of the **Old** Testament priesthood and
A P : 2 4 :052(259) [0403] or sacrifice for sins, just as the **Old** Testament did.
A P : 2 4 :055(259) [0403] In the **Old** Testament as in the New, the saints had to be
A P : 2 4 :056(259) [0403] The **Old** Testament sacrifices, therefore, did not merit
A P : 2 4 :057(260) [0405] the teaching of both the **Old** and the New Testament, and
A P : 2 4 :079(264) [0411] do they not mention the **old** term "communion," which
A P : 2 4 :081(264) [0411] It is an **old** word, ordinarily used in public law.
A P : 2 4 :097(268) [0417] The wicked people in the **Old** Testament had a similar
A P : 2 7 :001(269) [0419] testify that he was a mild **old** man, serious but not
A P : 2 7 :009(270) [0421] or from those who are not **old** enough to make up their
A P : 2 7 :058(279) [0439] us the example of the Nazarites from the **Old** Testament.
A P : 2 7 :058(279) [0439] exercise like the other ceremonies of the **Old** Testament.
A P : 2 7 :058(279) [0439] be said about other vows described in the **Old** Testament.
A P : 2 8 :013(283) [0447] We like the **old** division of power into the power of the
S 3 : 0 8 :005(312) [0495] All this is the **old** devil and the old serpent who made
S 3 : 0 8 :005(312) [0495] this is the old devil and the **old** serpent who made
S 3 : 0 8 :009(313) [0497] inoculated in man by the **old** dragon, and it is the source,
S 3 : 1 2 :002(315) [0499] thank God, a seven-year-**old** child knows what the church
S C : 0 4 :012(349) [0551] Answer: It signifies that the **old** Adam in us, together with
L C : P R :002(358) [0567] are in reality what the **old** manuals claimed in their titles
L C : S P :005(362) [0575] the time when there were **old** people who were so
L C : S P :006(362) [0575] in name, both young and **old**, may be well-trained in them
L C : 0 1 :080(375) [0603] In the **Old** Testament God set apart the seventh day and
L C : 0 1 :082(376) [0603] the other ordinances of the **Old** Testament connected with
L C : 0 1 :111(380) [0613] for them when they are **old**, sick, feeble, or poor; all this
L C : 0 1 :123(382) [0617] But young and **old** are altogether wayward and unruly;
L C : 0 1 :130(383) [0619] The wise men of **old** were right when they said, "God,
L C : 0 1 :134(383) [0619] means not merely to grow **old** but to have everything that
L C : 0 1 :138(384) [0621] where there are fine **old** families who prosper and have
L C : 0 1 :248(398) [0651] guard and not follow the **old**, wayward crowd, but may
L C : 0 1 :331(410) [0677] not without reason that the **Old** Testament commands
L C : 0 3 :066(429) [0717] grieves our flesh and the **old** Adam, for it means that we
L C : 0 3 :102(434) [0727] the flesh and we have the **old** Adam hanging around our
L C : 0 3 :107(434) [0729] chiefly by the flesh; **older** people are tempted by the
L C : 0 4 :065(445) [0749] is simply the slaying of the **old** Adam and the resurrection
L C : 0 4 :065(445) [0749] whatever pertains to the **old** Adam, so that whatever
L C : 0 4 :066(445) [0749] What is the **old** man?
L C : 0 4 :068(445) [0749] does not take place but the **old** man is given free rein and
L C : 0 4 :071(445) [0749] The **old** man therefore follows unchecked the inclinations
L C : 0 4 :071(445) [0749] we become Christians, the **old** man daily decreases until
L C : 0 4 :075(445) [0751] an earnest attack on the **old** man and an entering upon a
L C : 0 4 :076(446) [0751] and power to suppress the **old** man so that the new may
L C : 0 4 :077(446) [0751] access to it so that we may again subdue the **old** man.
L C : 0 4 :084(446) [0753] should be suppressing the **old** man and growing up in the
L C : 0 4 :086(446) [0753] is, as long as we carry the **old** Adam about our necks.
L C : 0 5 :023(449) [0757] our human flesh and blood have not lost their **old** skin.
L C : 0 5 :026(449) [0759] resist him and attack the **old** man, and when he cannot
L C : 0 5 :055(453) [0765] inherited from the **old** order under the pope when we
L C : 0 5 :086(456) [0773] For it is clearly useless to try to change **old** people.
E P : R N :001(464) [0777] apostolic writings of the **Old** and New Testaments are the
E P : R N :007(465) [0779] the Holy Scripture of the **Old** and New Testaments and
E P : 0 2 :014(471) [0789] and essence of the **Old** Adam, especially the rational soul,
E P : 0 6 :004(480) [0805] On account of this **Old** Adam, who inheres in people's
E P : 0 6 :004(480) [0807] further necessary lest the **Old** Adam go his own self-willed
S D : P R :003(503) [0851] apostolic writings of the **Old** and New Testaments as the
S D : 0 1 :017(511) [0865] First, in opposition to both **old** and new Pelagians, we
S D : 0 2 :081(537) [0911] and essence of the **Old** Adam, and especially the rational
S D : 0 2 :081(537) [0911] Paul's words, "Put off the **old** man," as follows: "Lest
S D : 0 2 :081(537) [0911] what it means to lay off the **old** man and put on the new
S D : 0 2 :081(537) [0913] this is laying off the **old** man and putting on the new
S D : 0 3 :017(542) [0921] the Holy Scriptures of the **Old** and the New Testaments.
S D : 0 4 :010(552) [0941] anew from God, kills the **Old** Adam, makes us entirely
S D : 0 6 :007(565) [0965] the mortification of the **Old** Adam and their renewal in
S D : 0 6 :007(565) [0965] minds, nevertheless the **Old** Adam still clings to their
S D : 0 6 :012(566) [0967] the world (to which the **Old** Adam belongs) of sin and of
S D : 0 6 :018(567) [0967] renewed in this life but the **Old** Adam clings to them down
S D : 0 6 :019(567) [0969] As far as the **Old** Adam who still adheres to them is
S D : 0 6 :023(568) [0969] continue in a constant conflict against the **Old** Adam.
S D : 0 6 :024(568) [0969] For the **Old** Adam, like an unmanageable and recalcitrant
S D : 0 7 :050(578) [0989] kinds of sacrifice in the **Old** Testament, and holy
S D : 0 8 :004(592) [1017] with accusations of almost all the monstrous **old** heresies.
S D : 0 8 :025(596) [1023] when he was twelve years **old**, among the teachers, again
S D : 0 8 :041(599) [1029] thereafter he states: "If the **old** witch, Dame Reason, the
S D : 0 8 :085(608) [1047] Jesus the son of Mary is 1543 years **old** this year.
S D : 1 0 :019(614) [1059] thank God, a seven-year-**old** child knows what the church
S D : 1 1 :075(628) [1087] will always show the same **old** fatherly heart to all who
S D : 1 2 :037(636) [1101] reject and condemn the **old**, approved symbols, the

Oldenburg (1)
P R : P R :027(015) [0025] John, count of **Oldenburg** and Delmenhorst

Omission (3)
A P : 2 8 :011(283) [0447] consciences so that their **omission** is judged to be a sin.
L C : 0 3 :089(432) [0723] in word and deed, in acts of commission and **omission**.
S D : 1 0 :015(613) [1057] and as though their **omission** were wrong and sinful, the

Omit (24), Omitted (17), Omitting (3)
A G : P R :013(026) [0041] we on our part shall not **omit** doing anything, in so far as

Continued ▶

AG : 2 2 :012(051) [0061] of the sacrament in processions is also **omitted** by us.
AG : 2 6 :002(064) [0071] observed and a great sin committed if they were **omitted**.
AG : 2 6 :041(070) [0075] say that it is not a sin to **omit** them if this is done without
AG : 2 8 :041(087) [0089] that it is a mortal sin to **omit** the seven hours, that some
AG : 2 8 :053(090) [0091] and counting it a sin to **omit** their observance even when
AG : 2 8 :056(090) [0091] or that it is a sin to **omit** them, even when no offense is
AG : 2 8 :059(091) [0091] the Gospel all ceremonies of the old law may be **omitted**.
AL : 0 0 :001(048) [0059] no article of faith but only **omit** some few abuses which
AL : 2 2 :012(051) [0061] which were hitherto held are also **omitted** among us.
AL : 2 6 :002(064) [0071] the consciences of those who **omitted** any of them.
AL : 2 6 :041(070) [0075] no sin is committed if they are **omitted** without scandal.
AL : 2 8 :041(087) [0089] that it is a mortal sin to **omit** the canonical hours, that in
AL : 2 8 :056(090) [0091] by judging that those who **omit** them without offense to
AL : 2 8 :059(091) [0091] Gospel all ceremonies of the Mosaic law can be **omitted**.
AP : 0 4 :183(132) [0173] about law and works but **omit** passages about the
AP : 0 4 :221(137) [0181] about the fruits, and they **omit** the many other texts in
AP : 0 4 :245(142) [0189] For he does not **omit** faith nor exalt love in preference to
AP : 0 4 :264(146) [0195] Everywhere our opponents **omit** the promises and look
AP : 0 4 :286(150) [0201] They **omit** the clearest scriptural passages on faith, select
AP : 0 4 :357(161) [0217] But they are not fair judges, for they **omit** the word "gift."
AP : 0 4 :357(161) [0217] They also **omit** the central thought of the discussion; they
AP : 0 4 :378(165) [0223] eternal life by works, **omitting** the faith that takes hold of
AP : 0 4 :382(165) [0225] If the doctrine of faith is **omitted**, it is vain to say that
AP : 1 2 :097(197) [0281] the sayings elsewhere about faith, they **omit** them.
AP : 1 2 :143(204) [0297] command: and where they do, it is a sin to **omit** them.
AP : 1 5 :049(221) [0329] to a conscience that has **omitted** some observance.
AP : 2 4 :034(256) [0397] They **omit** the proclamation of the Gospel, faith, prayer,
AP : 2 7 :002(269) [0419] Then with a sigh Hilten **omitted** all mention of his illness
AP : 2 8 :008(282) [0445] such traditions so that it would be a sin to **omit** them.
S2 : 0 2 :003(293) [0463] and so it can be **omitted** without sin and danger.
S2 : 0 2 :005(293) [0463] as trumpery, can be **omitted** without sin, that no one will
S2 : 0 2 :018(296) [0467] in a better way and may **omit** pilgrimages without sin and
S3 : 0 3 :037(309) [0489] his confession without **omitting** or forgetting a single
S3 : 0 6 :004(311) [0493] name those who not only **omit** both forms but even go so
SC : PR :022(341) [0537] Christ did not say, **"Omit** this," or "Despise this," but he
SC : PR :022(341) [0537] that this be done and not that it be **omitted** and despised.
LC : 0 1 :327(409) [0675] wrongly, doing or **omitting** to do things simply in order to
LC : 0 1 :327(410) [0675] If you **omit** that, you have an angry judge; otherwise, you
EP : 0 7 :009(483) [0811] no circumstances be **omitted**, but should be spoken
SD : 0 7 :079(584) [1001] and are under no circumstances to be **omitted**.
SD : 0 7 :121(590) [1013] Holy Supper, whence some **omit** the words of institution
SD : 0 7 :121(590) [1013] not in any case be **omitted** in the administration of the
SD : 1 1 :024(620) [1069] never be excluded or **omitted** when we speak of the

Omnes (1)
TR : 0 0 :033(325) [0513] of the chapter **"Omnes,"** and other similar statements

Omnipotence (16), Omnipotent (6)
EP : 0 7 :034(485) [0815] God, even with all his **omnipotence**, is unable (a dreadful
EP : 0 7 :035(485) [0815] That faith, and not the **omnipotent** words of Christ's
EP : 0 8 :007(487) [0819] the divine nature are **omnipotence**, eternity, infinity, and
EP : 0 8 :013(488) [0821] to the majesty and **omnipotent** power of God, but a man
EP : 0 8 :015(488) [0821] the right hand of the **omnipotent** majesty and power of
EP : 0 8 :033(491) [0825] all works of his **omnipotence** in, through, and with his
EP : 0 8 :034(491) [0825] is wholly incapable of **omnipotence** and other properties
EP : 0 8 :035(491) [0825] does not share in the **omnipotence** of God, and that this
EP : 0 8 :035(491) [0825] between God's **omnipotence** and the power of other
EP : 0 8 :035(491) [0825] is less than God's **omnipotence** but greater than the
SD : 0 7 :046(577) [0989] entire matter to God's **omnipotence** and wisdom,
SD : 0 7 :089(585) [1003] through our faith, but solely through his **omnipotence**.
SD : 0 7 :090(585) [1003] than ascribe it to the **omnipotence** of our Lord and
SD : 0 7 :106(588) [1009] upon the truth and **omnipotence** of the true and eternal
SD : 0 7 :121(590) [1013] not the words and the **omnipotence** of Christ but faith
SD : 0 8 :029(597) [1025] exercise of the divine, **omnipotent** majesty and power
SD : 0 8 :066(604) [1039] only a single divine **omnipotence**, power, majesty, and
SD : 0 8 :071(605) [1041] is not capable of the **omnipotence** of God in such a way
SD : 0 8 :071(605) [1041] it would become an **omnipotent** essence intrinsically or
SD : 0 8 :071(605) [1041] intrinsically or have **omnipotent** properties intrinsically.
SD : 0 8 :092(609) [1049] nature, Christ's **omnipotence** and wisdom can readily
SD : 0 8 :092(609) [1049] through his divine **omnipotence** Christ can be present

Omnipresence (1), Omnipresent (1), Omnipresently (1)
EP : 0 8 :007(487) [0819] property, by itself) **omnipresence**, omniscience, etc., which
EP : 0 8 :016(489) [0821] his power everywhere **omnipresently**, he can do
EP : 0 8 :027(490) [0823] divine nature; that it is **omnipresent** in the same manner

Omnis (3)
AP : 1 1 :001(180) [0249] that the regulation ***Omnis*** *utriusque* should be observed,
AP : 1 1 :006(181) [0251] against us the regulation ***Omnis*** *utriusque;* we are aware
AP : 1 1 :008(181) [0251] the regulation ***Omnis*** *utriusque*, for we judge that it, like

Omniscience (1)
EP : 0 8 :007(487) [0819] itself) omnipresence, **omniscience**, etc., which never

Onerous (1)
PR : PR :018(009) [0017] and their ministers the **onerous** burden of their pretense

Ones (23)
PR : PR :026(014) [0025] should continue or new **ones** arise, we shall see to it that
AG : 0 0 :001(095) [0095] undue length we have indicated only the principal **ones**.
AL : 0 0 :001(095) [0095] undue length we have discussed only the principle **ones**.
AP : 0 2 :011(102) [0109] minor faults in human nature and ignore the major **ones**.
AP : 0 2 :027(103) [0111] but even the more recent **ones** . at least the more sensible
AP : 1 2 :007(183) [0255] but only changes eternal punishments into temporal **ones**.
AP : 1 2 :069(192) [0271] them from earlier **ones** and transferred these opinions
AP : 1 3 :006(212) [0311] these from the earlier **ones** which have an express
AP : 1 3 :014(213) [0311] it from the preceding **ones** which are, in the strict sense,
AP : 1 5 :042(221) [0327] A few of the better **ones** are now beginning to talk about
AP : 2 1 :030(233) [0351] extinguished, they begged the wise **ones** to lend them oil.
AP : 2 1 :041(235) [0355] than the more recent **ones**, so their theology has steadily
AP : 2 4 :043(258) [0399] The better **ones** teach the law and say nothing about the
AP : 2 4 :073(262) [0409] consciences are the **ones** worthy of it, and how they
AP : 2 4 :091(266) [0415] These are the **ones** who, Paul said (I Cor. 11:27), are
AP : 2 7 :067(280) [0441] commands the younger **ones** to marry, v. 14), but because
LC : 0 1 :055(372) [0595] not only the very crass **ones** who are well known to
LC : 0 1 :298(405) [0665] tricks (better and better **ones** are being devised daily)
LC : 0 3 :109(435) [0729] weary; when one attack ceases, new **ones** always arise.
EP : 0 2 :015(471) [0789] out of unwilling people and dwells in the willing **ones**.
EP : 0 4 :019(477) [0801] sin, but that the holy **ones** and the elect retain the Holy
SD : 0 7 :093(586) [1005] are these (the same **ones** that Dr. Luther advanced
SD : 1 0 :016(613) [1059] causes one of these little **ones** who believe in me to sin, it

Oneself (6)
AL : 1 8 :005(040) [0051] a friend, will to clothe **oneself**, will to build a house, will
AP : 2 7 :039(276) [0433] If this is not arrogating perfection to **oneself**, what is?
S2 : 0 4 :011(300) [0475] what St. Paul calls exalting **oneself** over and against God.
LC : PR :010(359) [0569] thoughts as to occupy **oneself** with the Word of God, talk
SD : 0 2 :078(536) [0911] naturally to prepare **oneself** for grace does not come from
SD : 1 0 :002(611) [1053] may justifiably conform **oneself** to them in such

Open (25), Opened (7), Openest (1), Opening (2), Openly (18), Opens (4)
PR : PR :019(009) [0017] edition and in their **open** writings and in public print have
PR : PR :024(013) [0021] may not be left free and **open** to restless, contentious
AG : 0 3 :006(030) [0045] Lord Christ will return **openly** to judge the living and the
AG : 0 8 :001(033) [0047] hypocrites, and even **open** sinners remain among the
AG : 2 0 :033(045) [0057] this, and instead fell into many great and **open** sins.
AL : 0 3 :006(030) [0045] The same Christ will **openly** come again to judge the
AL : 2 3 :003(051) [0061] us desired to avoid such **open** scandals, they took wives
AL : 2 4 :010(057) [0065] a long time there has been **open** and very grievous
AP : 0 2 :036(105) [0115] Here he **openly** attests that sin is — that is, remains —
AP : 0 4 :023(110) [0127] weakness and by the devil, who drives it to **open** crimes.
AP : 0 4 :168(130) [0169] Here he **openly** says that he serves the law of sin.
AP : 0 4 :236(140) [0185] they even intimate their disapproval of some **open** abuse.
AP : 0 4 :390(166) [0225] knows that most of them are **openly** Epicureans.
AP : 0 4 :396(167) [0227] and clear that their ungodliness comes out into the **open**.
AP : 0 7 :021(172) [0233] It is also an **open** and wicked error when our opponents
AP : 0 7 :027(173) [0235] Many **openly** ridicule all religions, or if they accept
AP : 1 1 :004(180) [0249] The **openly** wicked and the despisers of the sacraments
AP : 1 2 :067(191) [0271] Leo quite **openly** condemns this doctrine of the
AP : 1 2 :090(195) [0279] since they condemn the **open** truth, it is not right for us to
AP : 1 2 :129(202) [0291] and so, of course, can **open** heaven for themselves
AP : 1 5 :004(215) [0315] Here our opponents are **openly** Judaizing; they are openly
AP : 1 5 :004(215) [0315] Judaizing; they are **openly** replacing the Gospel with
AP : 2 3 :005(239) [0365] or act honestly, frankly, or **openly** in this whole business.
AP : 2 3 :023(242) [0371] contracted, and all this in **open** defiance of Christ's
AP : 2 3 :059(247) [0379] we are laying ourselves **open** to the charge of schism
AP : 2 4 :029(255) [0393] dost not desire; but thou hast given me an **open** ear."
AP : 2 7 :009(270) [0421] vows legitimate if they **openly** point to an evil end, either
AP : 2 7 :011(270) [0423] This idea is an **open** insult to the Gospel, which teaches
S2 : 0 2 :005(293) [0463] "Let the people be told **openly** that the Mass, as
S2 : 0 2 :021(296) [0467] to transfer (by legal and **open** sale) all Masses, good
S3 : 0 3 :002(304) [0479] with one blow destroys both **open** sinners and false saints.
S3 : 0 3 :043(310) [0491] strive against it, fall into **open** sin (as David fell into
SC : 0 8 :007(353) [0559] Thou **openest** thy hand; Thou satisfiest the desire of every
LC : 0 1 :121(382) [0615] be very glad if we were to **open** our eyes and ears and
LC : 0 1 :214(394) [0641] and either indulge in **open** and shameless fornication or
LC : 0 1 :227(396) [0645] One person **openly** cheats another with defective
LC : 0 1 :231(396) [0647] who can steal and rob **openly** are safe and free,
LC : 0 1 :249(398) [0651] To restrain **open** lawlessness is the responsibility of
LC : 0 1 :308(406) [0669] take a yard, and at length **open** injustice and violence
LC : 0 2 :064(419) [0695] himself has revealed and **opened** to us the most profound
LC : 0 3 :042(425) [0709] it is also profaned by an **openly** evil life and wicked
LC : 0 3 :111(435) [0729] make the matter worse and give the devil a better **opening**.
LC : 0 3 :111(435) [0729] head; if it finds an **opening** into which it can slip, the
LC : 0 4 :021(439) [0737] a jest that the heavens **opened** when Christ allowed
LC : 0 5 :035(450) [0761] The treasure is **opened** and placed at everyone's door,
EP : 0 2 :004(470) [0787] with this Word and **opens** hearts so that, like Lydia in
EP : 0 5 :011(479) [0805] comfort, and the doors are again **opened** to the papacy.
EP : 0 8 :039(491) [0827] Christ's testament, but it **opens** a way for the accursed
EP : 1 1 :013(496) [0835] the Holy Gospel, Christ **opens** and reveals this book for
SD : 0 2 :026(526) [0891] He **opens** the intellect and the heart to understand the
SD : 0 2 :026(526) [0891] in Luke 24:45, "Then he **opened** their minds to
SD : 0 2 :026(526) [0891] heard us; the Lord **opened** her heart to give heed to what
SD : 0 7 :001(568) [0971] secretly but in part **openly** approved the
SD : 0 8 :038(598) [1027] But since secret as well as **open** Sacramentarians hide
SD : 1 0 :010(612) [1055] are obligated to confess **openly**, not only by words but
SD : 1 0 :015(613) [1057] sinful, the door has been **opened** to idolatry, and
SD : 1 2 :008(633) [1097] into contact with the **open** idolatry and false beliefs of the

Operate (2), Operates (3), Operation (14), Operations (3)
AP : 1 8 :009(226) [0337] will and the latter to the **operation** of the Holy Spirit in
AP : 2 4 :026(254) [0391] "spiritual" refers to the **operation** of the Holy Spirit
EP : 0 2 :019(472) [0791] solely by the grace and **operation** of God the Holy Spirit.
EP : 0 7 :031(485) [0815] Supper only the power, **operation**, and merit of the
EP : 1 1 :008(495) [0833] promises the power and **operation** of the Holy Spirit and
SD : 0 2 :025(526) [0891] and alone to the divine **operation** and the Holy Spirit, as
SD : 0 2 :034(528) [0895] the remaining sin and **operates** to make man truly pure
SD : 0 2 :055(531) [0903] added the power and **operation** of the Holy Spirit, who
SD : 0 2 :055(532) [0903] question this grace and **operation** of the Holy Spirit, but
SD : 0 2 :056(532) [0903] Holy Spirit's presence, **operations**, and gifts merely on the
SD : 0 2 :062(533) [0905] the question how God **operates** in man, it is correct to say
SD : 0 2 :072(535) [0909] is to hinder and resist such **operations** of the Holy Spirit.
SD : 0 2 :078(536) [0911] but solely through the **operation** of the Holy Spirit.
SD : 0 2 :089(538) [0915] no new impulses and begins no spiritual **operations** in us.
SD : 0 2 :089(538) [0915] part, but entirely, the **operation**, gift, endowment, and
SD : 0 7 :005(570) [0973] according to its power, **operation**, and benefits, by faith).
SD : 0 7 :055(579) [0991] to its virtue and **operation**, then the bread could not be
SD : 0 7 :117(589) [1013] to faith only the virtue, **operation**, and merit of the
SD : 0 8 :004(592) [1017] Supper of the Lord, did **operate** with and use the same
SD : 1 1 :006(617) [1065] God's foreknowledge **operates** in such a way that God
SD : 1 1 :056(625) [1081] obey his command and **operate** constantly with the
SD : 1 1 :082(630) [1089] that God's power and **operation** can transform the vessels

Operato (63)
AP : 0 4 :063(115) [0139] the Holy Spirit *ex opere* ***operato*** without the proper
AP : 0 4 :134(125) [0159] sacrifice and ritual justify before God *ex opere* ***operato***.

Continued ▶

AP : 04 :207(135) [0177] they had a gracious God, so to say, *ex opere* ***operato***.
AP : 04 :210(136) [0179] that justifies *ex opere* ***operato*** and removes the burden of
AP : 04 :258(144) [0193] of sins *ex opere* ***operato***, but he commands these works
AP : 04 :259(144) [0193] of sins *ex opere* ***operato***, but he requires a new life, which
AP : 04 :276(148) [0199] does not justify *ex opere* ***operato*** without faith, so
AP : 04 :276(148) [0199] does not justify *ex opere* ***operato*** without faith.
AP : 04 :278(149) [0199] does not free from sin and death *ex opere* ***operato***.
AP : 04 :288(151) [0203] seek righteousness, grace, and salvation *ex opere* ***operato***.
AP : 07 :021(172) [0233] justify *ex opere* ***operato***, without a good attitude in the
AP : 12 :012(184) [0257] grants grace *ex opere* ***operato***, without a right attitude in
AP : 12 :025(185) [0259] obtains grace *ex opere* ***operato***, without the proper
AP : 12 :059(190) [0267] does not come *ex opere* ***operato*** because of contrition,
AP : 12 :060(190) [0269] contrition, confession, and satisfaction *ex opere* ***operato***.
AP : 12 :143(204) [0297] worship which *ex opere* ***operato*** pay homage to God and
AP : 12 :162(208) [0303] they say avails *ex opere* ***operato*** so that even those in
AP : 13 :018(213) [0313] confer grace *ex opere* ***operato***, without a good disposition
AP : 13 :023(214) [0313] the sacraments *ex opere* ***operato*** without a good
AP : 24 :005(250) [0385] simply *ex opere* ***operato***, by the mere doing or observing.
AP : 24 :009(251) [0387] confer grace *ex opere* ***operato***, nor merit for others the
AP : 24 :011(251) [0387] not grant grace *ex opere* ***operato*** and does not merit for
AP : 24 :011(251) [0387] forgiveness of sins or of punishment *ex opere* ***operato***.
AP : 24 :012(251) [0387] of sins *ex opere* ***operato*** through our works and by the
AP : 24 :013(251) [0387] notion about the working of the Mass *ex opere* ***operato***.
AP : 24 :025(254) [0391] of sins or reconciliation for others *ex opere* ***operato***.
AP : 24 :026(254) [0391] works offered *ex opere* ***operato***, for "spiritual" refers to
AP : 24 :026(254) [0391] suppose they are offering God a work *ex opere* ***operato***.
AP : 24 :026(254) [0393] These are valid, not *ex opere* ***operato*** but because of faith.
AP : 24 :027(254) [0393] are valid *ex opere* ***operato***, and it teaches that worship
AP : 24 :028(254) [0393] of worship *ex opere* ***operato*** and teach spiritual
AP : 24 :028(254) [0393] namely, that such worship pleased him *ex opere* ***operato***.
AP : 24 :029(255) [0393] also condemns the idea of sacrifices *ex opere* ***operato***.
AP : 24 :030(255) [0395] that sacrifices do not reconcile God *ex opere* ***operato***.
AP : 24 :031(255) [0395] Mass justifies *ex opere* ***operato*** or that it merits the
AP : 24 :032(255) [0395] to a ceremony *ex opere* ***operato*** but to all those sacrifices
AP : 24 :033(255) [0395] by itself, or *ex opere* ***operato***, the ceremony is beneficial.
AP : 24 :033(256) [0395] does not justify *ex opere* ***operato*** or merit the forgiveness
AP : 24 :033(256) [0395] of ceremonies *ex opere* ***operato***; therefore he does not
AP : 24 :034(256) [0395] not support the notion of ceremonies *ex opere* ***operato***.
AP : 24 :035(256) [0397] that justifies *ex opere* ***operato*** or that merits the
AP : 24 :039(257) [0399] work *ex opere* ***operato***, we can see that their real meaning
AP : 24 :059(260) [0405] to others *ex opere* ***operato***; but it offers to others the
AP : 24 :059(260) [0405] the Spirit contradicts any such transfer *ex opere* ***operato***.
AP : 24 :059(260) [0405] transfer of one man's work to another *ex opere* ***operato***.
AP : 24 :060(260) [0405] Mass justifies *ex opere* ***operato*** or that it merits the
AP : 24 :061(260) [0405] wicked idea that the Mass justifies *ex opere* ***operato***.
AP : 24 :063(260) [0405] confers grace *ex opere* ***operato*** on one who uses it, or
AP : 24 :066(261) [0407] confers grace *ex opere* ***operato*** or that it merits the
AP : 24 :067(261) [0407] about merit *ex opere* ***operato*** is not to be found anywhere
AP : 24 :075(263) [0411] work *ex opere* ***operato*** and can be transferred to others;
AP : 24 :077(263) [0411] to others *ex opere* ***operato*** to merit the forgiveness of sins
AP : 24 :078(263) [0411] it grants grace *ex opere* ***operato*** or that it merits the
AP : 24 :087(265) [0413] of the act *ex opere* ***operato*** and its supposed applicability
AP : 24 :087(265) [0413] provide an advantage *ex opere* ***operato*** without faith.
AP : 24 :088(265) [0413] the like, in opposition to a theory of *ex opere* ***operato***.
AP : 24 :089(266) [0415] without faith, *ex opere* ***operato***, a ceremony is a sacrifice
AP : 24 :092(266) [0415] or guilt, *ex opere* ***operato*** and without faith, it follows
AP : 24 :094(267) [0417] of the Lord's Supper to the dead *ex opere* ***operato***.
AP : 24 :094(267) [0417] the opponents' idea of the transfer *ex opere* ***operato***.
AP : 24 :095(267) [0417] about transfer *ex opere* ***operato***, they would express
AP : 24 :096(267) [0417] Mass justifies *ex opere* ***operato*** and that it merits the
AP : 24 :097(268) [0417] by sacrifices *ex opere* ***operato*** rather than receiving it

Operators (1)
LC : 01 :229(396) [0645] men are called gentlemen swindlers or big **operators**.

Opere (63)
AP : 04 :063(115) [0139] bestow the Holy Spirit *ex* ***opere*** *operato* without the
AP : 04 :134(125) [0159] sacrifice and ritual justify before God *ex* ***opere*** *operato*.
AP : 04 :207(135) [0177] they had a gracious God, so to say, *ex* ***opere*** *operato*.
AP : 04 :210(136) [0179] is a work that justifies *ex* ***opere*** *operato* and removes the
AP : 04 :258(144) [0193] the forgiveness of sins *ex* ***opere*** *operato*, but he
AP : 04 :259(144) [0193] the forgiveness of sins *ex* ***opere*** *operato*, but he requires a
AP : 04 :276(148) [0199] Supper does not justify *ex* ***opere*** *operato* without faith, so
AP : 04 :276(148) [0199] does not justify *ex* ***opere*** *operato* without faith.
AP : 04 :278(149) [0199] does not free from sin and death *ex* ***opere*** *operato*.
AP : 04 :288(151) [0203] seek righteousness, grace, and salvation *ex* ***opere*** *operato*.
AP : 07 :021(172) [0233] if sacraments justify *ex* ***opere*** *operato*, without a good
AP : 12 :012(184) [0257] sacrament grants grace *ex* ***opere*** *operato*, without a right
AP : 12 :025(185) [0259] penitence obtains grace *ex* ***opere*** *operato*, without the
AP : 12 :059(190) [0267] of sins does not come *ex* ***opere*** *operato* because of
AP : 12 :060(190) [0269] contrition, confession, and satisfaction *ex* ***opere*** *operato*.
AP : 12 :143(204) [0297] acts of worship which *ex* ***opere*** *operato* pay homage to
AP : 12 :162(208) [0303] which they say avails *ex* ***opere*** *operato* so that even those
AP : 13 :018(213) [0313] confer grace *ex* ***opere*** *operato*, without a good disposition
AP : 13 :023(214) [0313] about the sacraments *ex* ***opere*** *operato* without a good
AP : 24 :005(250) [0385] or admonish, simply *ex* ***opere*** *operato*, by the mere doing
AP : 24 :009(251) [0387] does not confer grace *ex* ***opere*** *operato*, nor merit for
AP : 24 :011(251) [0387] does not grant grace *ex* ***opere*** *operato* and does not merit
AP : 24 :011(251) [0387] forgiveness of sins or of punishment *ex* ***opere*** *operato*.
AP : 24 :012(251) [0387] the forgiveness of sins *ex* ***opere*** *operato* through our
AP : 24 :013(251) [0387] notion about the working of the Mass *ex* ***opere*** *operato*.
AP : 24 :025(254) [0391] of sins or reconciliation for others *ex* ***opere*** *operato*.
AP : 24 :026(254) [0391] human works offered *ex* ***opere*** *operato*, for "spiritual"
AP : 24 :026(254) [0391] suppose they are offering God a work *ex* ***opere*** *operato*.
AP : 24 :026(254) [0393] These are valid, not *ex* ***opere*** *operato* but because of
AP : 24 :027(254) [0393] the sacrifices are valid *ex* ***opere*** *operato*, and it teaches
AP : 24 :028(254) [0393] notion of worship *ex* ***opere*** *operato* and teach spiritual
AP : 24 :028(254) [0393] namely, that such worship pleased him *ex* ***opere*** *operato*.
AP : 24 :029(255) [0393] also condemns the idea of sacrifices *ex* ***opere*** *operato*.
AP : 24 :030(255) [0395] that sacrifices do not reconcile God *ex* ***opere*** *operato*.
AP : 24 :031(255) [0395] that the Mass justifies *ex* ***opere*** *operato* or that it merits
AP : 24 :032(255) [0395] refer to a ceremony *ex* ***opere*** *operato* but to all those
AP : 24 :033(255) [0395] mean that by itself, or *ex* ***opere*** *operato*, the ceremony is
AP : 24 :033(256) [0395] but it does not justify *ex* ***opere*** *operato* or merit the
AP : 24 :033(256) [0395] idea of ceremonies *ex* ***opere*** *operato*; therefore he does
AP : 24 :034(256) [0395] not support the notion of ceremonies *ex* ***opere*** *operato*.
AP : 24 :035(256) [0397] ceremony that justifies *ex* ***opere*** *operato* or that merits
AP : 24 :039(257) [0399] that ceremonies work *ex* ***opere*** *operato*, we can see that
AP : 24 :059(260) [0405] transferred to others *ex* ***opere*** *operato*; but it offers to
AP : 24 :059(260) [0405] the Spirit contradicts any such transfer *ex* ***opere*** *operato*.
AP : 24 :059(260) [0405] transfer of one man's work to another *ex* ***opere*** *operato*.
AP : 24 :060(260) [0405] that the Mass justifies *ex* ***opere*** *operato* or that it merits
AP : 24 :061(260) [0405] wicked idea that the Mass justifies *ex* ***opere*** *operato*.
AP : 24 :063(260) [0405] the Mass confers grace *ex* ***opere*** *operato* on one who uses
AP : 24 :066(261) [0407] the Mass confers grace *ex* ***opere*** *operato* or that it merits
AP : 24 :067(261) [0407] fiction about merit *ex* ***opere*** *operato* is not to be found
AP : 24 :075(263) [0411] that sacraments work *ex* ***opere*** *operato* and can be
AP : 24 :077(263) [0411] transferred to others *ex* ***opere*** *operato* to merit the
AP : 24 :078(263) [0411] that it grants grace *ex* ***opere*** *operato* or that it merits the
AP : 24 :087(265) [0413] the efficacy of the act *ex* ***opere*** *operato* and its supposed
AP : 24 :087(265) [0413] provide an advantage *ex* ***opere*** *operato* without faith.
AP : 24 :088(265) [0413] the like, in opposition to a theory of *ex* ***opere*** *operato*.
AP : 24 :089(266) [0415] that without faith, *ex* ***opere*** *operato*, a ceremony is a
AP : 24 :092(266) [0415] punishment or guilt, *ex* ***opere*** *operato* and without faith,
AP : 24 :094(267) [0417] of the Lord's Supper to the dead *ex* ***opere*** *operato*.
AP : 24 :094(267) [0417] the opponents' idea of the transfer *ex* ***opere*** *operato*.
AP : 24 :095(267) [0417] teach about transfer *ex* ***opere*** *operato*, they would
AP : 24 :096(267) [0417] that the Mass justifies *ex* ***opere*** *operato* and that it merits
AP : 24 :097(268) [0417] of sins by sacrifices *ex* ***opere*** *operato* rather than receiving

Opinion (43), Opinions (60)
PR : PR :009(006) [0011] adherents of erroneous **opinions** which are opposed to us
PR : PR :009(006) [0011] and other erroneous **opinions** were now and again
PR : PR :013(007) [0013] all its aspects, have their **opinions** and criticisms reduced
PR : PR :024(013) [0023] beyond uncertain **opinions** and dubious, disputable
AG : PR :002(025) [0039] weigh the judgments, **opinions**, and beliefs of the several
AG : PR :006(025) [0039] Latin, his judgments, **opinions**, and beliefs with reference
AG : PR :009(025) [0041] of their judgments and **opinions**, in Latin and German,
AG : 17 :005(038) [0051] too, are certain Jewish **opinions** which are even now
AG : 23 :013(053) [0063] have expressed similar **opinions** and the misgiving that
AG : 26 :012(065) [0071] the people were of the **opinion** that they were a necessary
AG : 27 :001(071) [0075] by considering what **opinions** have hitherto been held
AG : 27 :061(080) [0083] there are many godless **opinions** and errors associated
AG : 28 :035(086) [0089] to make laws out of **opinions** or to require that they be
AG : 28 :061(091) [0093] the false and erroneous **opinion** that in Christendom one
AG : 28 :064(092) [0093] mitigation as long as the **opinion** remains and prevails
AG : 28 :064(092) [0093] And this **opinion** will remain as long as there is no
AL : 17 :005(038) [0051] now spreading Jewish **opinions** to the effect that before
AL : 20 :032(045) [0057] to various sins, impious **opinions**, and manifest crimes.
AL : 24 :021(058) [0067] To all this was added an **opinion** which infinitely
AL : 24 :022(058) [0067] has come the common **opinion** that the Mass is a work by
AL : 24 :024(058) [0067] Concerning these **opinions** our teachers have warned that
AL : 26 :001(063) [0071] It has been the common **opinion** not only of the people
AL : 26 :003(064) [0071] From this **opinion** concerning traditions much harm has
AL : 26 :006(064) [0071] which have produced the **opinion** that it is necessary to
AL : 27 :061(080) [0083] there are many impious **opinions** which are associated
AL : 28 :064(092) [0093] achieved as long as the **opinion** remains that their
AL : 28 :064(092) [0093] And this **opinion** must remain where there is no
AP : PR :017(099) [0103] all sorts of dangerous **opinions** in the writings of the
AP : 02 :022(103) [0111] We cite the **opinions** of the ancients, with which
AP : 02 :030(104) [0113] These **opinions** agree with the Scriptures.
AP : 02 :041(105) [0115] Augustine refutes the **opinion** that human lust is not a
AP : 02 :047(106) [0119] deludes it with wicked **opinions** and errors and incites it
AP : 02 :051(107) [0119] familiar phrases, the **opinions** of the holy Fathers, which
AP : 04 :013(109) [0123] On the basis of these **opinions**, things have come to such
AP : 04 :134(125) [0159] Paul means human **opinion** about the entire law, both the
AP : 04 :224(138) [0181] they read their own **opinions** into them instead of
AP : 04 :244(142) [0189] not read into them their **opinion** about the merit of
AP : 04 :244(142) [0189] falsely add their wicked **opinions** that by good works we
AP : 04 :253(143) [0193] them by reading into them their own wicked **opinions**.
AP : 04 :265(146) [0197] This legalistic **opinion** clings by nature to the minds of
AP : 04 :266(146) [0197] be turned from such fleshly **opinions** to the Word of God.
AP : 04 :280(149) [0201] Then they add something from their own **opinions**.
AP : 04 :282(149) [0201] Such were the **opinions** of the Pharisees, too.
AP : 04 :286(150) [0201] maliciously twist the Scriptures to fit their own **opinions**.
AP : 04 :286(150) [0201] they add human **opinions** to what the words of Scripture
AP : 04 :395(167) [0225] condemned this **opinion** and taught the righteousness of
AP : 04 :399(168) [0227] this assembly that when **opinions** were being expressed
AP : 04 :400(168) [0227] who defend wicked **opinions** against the Gospel, as the
AP : 04 :400(168) [0227] they defend human **opinions** contrary to the Gospel,
AP : 07 :020(172) [0233] structures of stubble, that is, unprofitable **opinions**.
AP : 07 :032(174) [0239] clear that many foolish **opinions** about traditions have
AP : 07 :040(176) [0241] In fact, Paul calls such **opinions** "doctrines of demons."
AP : 09 :003(178) [0245] the ungodly and fanatical **opinions** of the Anabaptists.
AP : 12 :003(183) [0253] which through the **opinions** of the scholastics and
AP : 12 :060(190) [0267] it in opposition to the **opinion** that bids us trust not in the
AP : 12 :069(192) [0271] and transferred these **opinions** from one book to another.
AP : 12 :085(194) [0277] we reject the Pharisaic **opinions** of our opponents that we
AP : 12 :093(196) [0279] select and combine their **opinions** not only about one but
AP : 12 :131(202) [0291] satisfactions or the **opinions** of the scholastics because
AP : 12 :131(202) [0291] and a distortion of the Scriptures to suit their **opinions**.
AP : 12 :141(204) [0295] to have to list these silly **opinions** of our opponents,
AP : 15 :038(220) [0325] way, excluding the **opinion** which holds that they justify.
AP : 20 :014(228) [0343] Finally they say that our **opinion** was condemned a
AP : 21 :040(235) [0355] contain many false **opinions** and that the ignorance and
AP : 23 :004(239) [0365] set against them their own foolish and vain **opinions**.
AP : 27 :008(269) [0421] who have a moderate **opinion** of human and "factitious"
AP : 27 :020(272) [0425] the wickedness of the **opinion** that we attain to the
AP : 27 :056(278) [0439] whole monastic life is full of hypocrisy and false **opinions**.
AP : 27 :057(279) [0439] a way of life so full of hypocrisy and false **opinions**.
AP : 27 :058(279) [0439] their vows with the **opinions** which, as we have said, we
S2 : 02 :008(294) [0465] he follows a false human **opinion** and imagination
S2 : 02 :013(295) [0467] that would constrain him to adopt such an **opinion**.
S2 : 02 :013(295) [0467] is nothing but a human **opinion** of certain individuals and
S2 : 02 :014(295) [0467] make use of such human **opinions** to make men believe
TR : 00 :036(326) [0515] impious and nefarious **opinions** by asserting that it is

Continued ▶

TR : 00 :055(329) [0521] the right to express an **opinion**, except his followers,
TR : 00 :059(330) [0521] and blasphemous **opinions**, make themselves guilty of the
TR : 00 :082(000) [0529] And in my humble **opinion** I judge that all these agree
LC : 04 :080(446) [0751] I say this to correct the **opinion**, which has long prevailed
EP : 07 :004(482) [0809] retain the former crass **opinion** that in the Holy Supper
EP : 07 :005(482) [0809] or way, since in their **opinion** it is confined to the highest
EP : 09 :002(492) [0827] it is our unanimous **opinion** that we should not engage in
EP : 11 :013(496) [0835] should banish all other **opinions** since they do not
SD : PR :009(503) [0849] of such a nature that the **opinions** of the erring party
SD : PR :010(503) [0849] can see which **opinion** in the controverted issues agrees
SD : 01 :017(511) [0865] and reject as false the **opinion** and doctrine that original
SD : 02 :027(526) [0891] his former erroneous **opinion** as he had set it forth in his
SD : 02 :085(537) [0913] and teach the correct **opinion** in this matter thoroughly,
SD : 04 :007(552) [0941] according to his own **opinion** or that are based on human
SD : 04 :035(557) [0949] tends toward the same **opinion**, namely, that our good
SD : 07 :001(568) [0971] It may be that in the **opinion** of some an explanation of
SD : 07 :006(570) [0973] that they hold no other **opinion** than that the Lord Christ
SD : 07 :013(571) [0977] Bucer has explained his **opinion**, and that of the other
SD : 07 :092(586) [1005] any clever human **opinions**, no matter what appearance
SD : 07 :112(589) [1011] all Sacramentarian **opinions** and doctrines when are
SD : 07 :113(589) [1011] all such Sacramentarian **opinions** and mutually
SD : 07 :128(591) [1015] additional condemnable **opinions** or erroneous views
SD : 08 :051(600) [1031] of God's Word that this **opinion** is erroneous and false,
SD : 10 :024(615) [1061] In a special **opinion** Dr. Luther exhaustively instructs the
SD : 10 :028(615) [1061] as wrongful the **opinion** of those who hold that in a
SD : 11 :010(618) [1065] and pernicious **opinions** and causes and fortifies in
SD : 11 :044(623) [1077] refutes all false **opinions** and erroneous doctrines about
SD : 12 :004(633) [1097] declare our unanimous **opinion** with a few bare words or

Opponents (344)

AG : 20 :004(041) [0053] Our **opponents** no longer praise these useless works so
AG : 00 :001(047) [0059] we think that our **opponents** cannot disagree with us in
AG : 01 :009(056) [0065] and more earnestness than among our **opponents**.
AG : 25 :006(062) [0069] Many of our **opponents** themselves acknowledge that we
AG : 27 :027(075) [0079] Why, then, do our **opponents** insist so strongly that vows
AP : PR :002(098) [0099] To see what our **opponents** condemned and to refute
AP : PR :002(098) [0099] we assumed that the **opponents** would produce the
AP : PR :004(098) [0099] But our **opponents** stubbornly insisted that we sanction
AP : PR :004(098) [0099] could not give in to the **opponents'** point of view with a
AP : PR :005(098) [0101] answering the **opponents'** objections and explaining to
AP : PR :008(098) [0101] a decree in which our **opponents** brag that they have
AP : PR :009(098) [0101] will show you what our **opponents** have judged, as we
AP : PR :011(099) [0101] contemporaries still further from the **opponents'** position.
AP : PR :012(099) [0101] But our **opponents** show by their actions that they are
AP : PR :016(099) [0103] evident from the bitter hatred inflaming our **opponents**.
AP : PR :018(099) [0103] which appears everywhere in our **opponents'** writings.
AP : 01 :001(100) [0103] Our **opponents** approve Article I of our Confession.
AP : 02 :001(100) [0105] The **opponents** approve Article II, "Original Sin," but
AP : 02 :004(101) [0105] Our scholastic **opponents** admit that concupiscence is the
AP : 02 :011(102) [0109] cannot see the foolishness of our **opponents'** position?
AP : 02 :035(104) [0113] Here our **opponents** lash out at Luther because he wrote
AP : 02 :035(105) [0115] Our **opponents** know what Luther meant by this
AP : 02 :037(105) [0115] Our **opponents** know that this is what Luther believes and
AP : 02 :042(105) [0115] If our **opponents** claim that the inclination to evil is a
AP : 02 :051(107) [0119] with which our **opponents** have slandered our article.
AP : 02 :051(107) [0119] If our **opponents** reopen the controversy, we shall not
AP : 02 :051(107) [0119] for in this case our **opponents** frequently do not know
AP : 03 :001(107) [0119] The **opponents** approve our third article, in which we
AP : 04 :003(107) [0121] nor righteousness, our **opponents** confuse this doctrine
AP : 04 :004(108) [0121] the objections of our **opponents**, we shall have to say a
AP : 04 :004(108) [0121] kinds of doctrine, the **opponents'** and our own, might be
AP : 04 :007(108) [0121] these two doctrines our **opponents** select the law and by
AP : 04 :014(109) [0123] If the **opponents'** ideas are correct, this was perfectly
AP : 04 :016(109) [0123] this teaching of the **opponents** that we merit forgiveness
AP : 04 :017(109) [0125] Christ altogether, our **opponents** require a knowledge of
AP : 04 :021(110) [0127] Thus our **opponents** teach nothing but the righteousness
AP : 04 :034(111) [0129] Our **opponents** concentrate on the commandments of the
AP : 04 :036(112) [0131] was very foolish of our **opponents** to write that men who
AP : 04 :039(112) [0131] of law or of reason which our **opponents** teach.
AP : 04 :039(112) [0131] those errors of our **opponents** that we have been
AP : 04 :047(113) [0133] there is not a syllable in the teaching of our **opponents**.
AP : 04 :047(113) [0133] we condemn our **opponents** for teaching the
AP : 04 :048(113) [0135] Our **opponents** imagine that faith is only historical
AP : 04 :059(115) [0137] It is strange that our **opponents** make so little of faith
AP : 04 :060(115) [0137] all afflictions, and our **opponents** take it away when they
AP : 04 :061(115) [0139] means, and we shall answer our **opponents'** objections.
AP : 04 :063(115) [0139] Nowhere can our **opponents** say how the Holy Spirit is
AP : 04 :073(117) [0141] or the sacraments, as our **opponents** slanderously claim.
AP : 04 :075(117) [0143] Even our **opponents** will grant, we suppose, that the
AP : 04 :079(117) [0143] Our idle **opponents** quibble as to whether the forgiveness
AP : 04 :081(118) [0143] Our **opponents** suppose that Christ is the mediator and
AP : 04 :087(120) [0147] This our **opponents** interpret as referring to Levitical
AP : 04 :107(122) [0153] amazing that our **opponents** are unmoved by the many
AP : 04 :110(123) [0153] If our **opponents** require us to trust in our own love for
AP : 04 :119(123) [0155] Our **opponents** give men bad advice when they bid them
AP : 04 :121(124) [0155] rejecting this faith, our **opponents** fail to see that thereby
AP : 04 :122(124) [0157] Here our **opponents** urge against us the texts, "If you
AP : 04 :131(125) [0157] But our **opponents** are fine theologians!
AP : 04 :136(126) [0159] Our **opponents** slanderously claim that we do not require
AP : 04 :145(127) [0161] effects of faith, our **opponents** teach that love justifies.
AP : 04 :159(129) [0165] reply to the objection of the **opponents** referred to above.
AP : 04 :182(132) [0173] Reply to the **Opponents'** Arguments
AP : 04 :183(132) [0173] Gospel) it will be easy to refute the **opponents'** objections.
AP : 04 :186(132) [0173] and reconciliation, our **opponents** simply abolish this free
AP : 04 :210(136) [0179] But our **opponents** claim that the Mass is a work that
AP : 04 :213(136) [0179] Our **opponents** maintain these wicked and unscriptural
AP : 04 :218(137) [0179] the texts that our **opponents** quote to prove that we are
AP : 04 :221(137) [0181] Our **opponents** proceed in reverse order.
AP : 04 :221(137) [0181] Thus our **opponents** exclude Christ from justification and
AP : 04 :222(137) [0181] not against us; only our **opponents** should not add their
AP : 04 :223(138) [0181] Let our **opponents** remove the promise about Christ, let
AP : 04 :224(138) [0181] Our **opponents** twist many texts because they read their
AP : 04 :224(138) [0181] interpretation that our **opponents** add to it on their own,
AP : 04 :226(138) [0183] we concede to our **opponents** that the love of God and
AP : 04 :229(139) [0183] Our **opponents** attribute justification to love because
AP : 04 :231(139) [0183] In the Confutation our **opponents** have also cited against
AP : 04 :235(140) [0185] make sense when our **opponents** argue on the basis of the
AP : 04 :236(140) [0185] in poor grace for our **opponents** to talk so much about
AP : 04 :236(140) [0185] praises of love; if our **opponents** lived up to them, they
AP : 04 :236(140) [0185] would die down if our **opponents** did not insist so bitterly
AP : 04 :244(142) [0189] cause no trouble if our **opponents** do not read into them
AP : 04 :244(142) [0189] are mentioned, our **opponents** falsely add their wicked
AP : 04 :244(142) [0189] mind, though our **opponents** uphold it under the pretext
AP : 04 :245(142) [0189] this text is more against our **opponents** than against us.
AP : 04 :246(142) [0189] fallacious for our **opponents** to argue from this text that
AP : 04 :250(143) [0191] an easy thing, as our **opponents** imagine; nor is it a
AP : 04 :253(143) [0191] no error, but our **opponents** twist them by reading into
AP : 04 :253(143) [0193] none of this, which our **opponents** shamelessly infer from
AP : 04 :255(143) [0193] against us if our **opponents** did not read something false
AP : 04 :257(144) [0193] If our **opponents** exclude the Gospel of Christ from the
AP : 04 :264(146) [0195] Everywhere our **opponents** omit the promises and look
AP : 04 :266(146) [0197] sins by penitence," our **opponents** would have passed
AP : 04 :266(146) [0197] same thought, and our **opponents** immediately twist his
AP : 04 :268(147) [0197] If our **opponents** understand Daniel as referring only to
AP : 04 :269(147) [0197] Cursed be our **opponents**, those Pharisees, who interpret
AP : 04 :271(148) [0199] think that none of our **opponents** is so mad as to deny
AP : 04 :274(148) [0199] Our **opponents** try to silence this proclamation of the
AP : 04 :274(148) [0199] required; but here our **opponents** maliciously maintain
AP : 04 :280(149) [0199] But our **opponents**, clever men that they are, pick out
AP : 04 :281(149) [0201] Our **opponents** must be deaf.
AP : 04 :283(149) [0201] Our **opponents** misinterpret the universal particle "all."
AP : 04 :283(150) [0201] Our **opponents** twist his meaning by sophistically
AP : 04 :285(150) [0201] our readers that our **opponents** counsel pious consciences
AP : 04 :286(150) [0201] passages which our **opponents** quote against us in arguing
AP : 04 :286(150) [0201] Our **opponents** maliciously twist the Scriptures to fit their
AP : 04 :287(150) [0203] The **opponents'** whole system is derived either from
AP : 04 :291(152) [0203] obliged to disagree with our **opponents** on justification.
AP : 04 :298(153) [0205] to see how furiously our **opponents** deny them.
AP : 04 :300(153) [0205] great blessings our **opponents** take from the church in
AP : 04 :300(153) [0205] Our **opponents'** teaching does not mention how we must
AP : 04 :301(153) [0205] this love at all, as our **opponents** admit, or surely they
AP : 04 :302(153) [0205] Let any of our **opponents** come forth to describe the love
AP : 04 :303(154) [0205] In answer to our **opponents'** quibble that many wicked
AP : 04 :311(155) [0207] Our **opponents** talk about obedience to the law; they do
AP : 04 :314(156) [0207] not only to refute the **opponents'** teaching that we come
AP : 04 :316(156) [0209] why we reject our **opponents'** teaching on the merit of
AP : 04 :318(156) [0209] highly absurd when our **opponents** teach that good works
AP : 04 :319(156) [0209] Second, the **opponents'** teaching leaves consciences in
AP : 04 :321(157) [0209] short, everything our **opponents** teach on this question is
AP : 04 :324(157) [0209] Our **opponents** teach wrongly when they praise merits in
AP : 04 :332(158) [0211] We wonder what our **opponents** do when they pray, if
AP : 04 :335(159) [0215] At this point our **opponents** make a marvelous play on
AP : 04 :336(159) [0215] Look how this childish sophistry delights our **opponents**!
AP : 04 :337(159) [0215] For one thing, our **opponents** are deceived with regard to
AP : 04 :341(159) [0215] As usual, our **opponents** twist against faith statements
AP : 04 :343(160) [0215] petty quibblings of our **opponents** which intelligent men
AP : 04 :348(160) [0217] Here our **opponents** will raise the cry that good works are
AP : 04 :353(161) [0217] better than what our **opponents** teach about
AP : 04 :354(161) [0217] Our **opponents** grant that the justified are children of God
AP : 04 :356(161) [0217] Here our **opponents** reply that eternal life is called a
AP : 04 :356(161) [0217] passages seem to our **opponents** to be in conflict, let them
AP : 04 :360(162) [0219] Not only do our **opponents** attribute to works a
AP : 04 :362(162) [0219] If our **opponents** will grant that we are accounted
AP : 04 :367(163) [0221] merit is discussed, our **opponents** immediately apply it
AP : 04 :370(163) [0221] Our **opponents** urge that good works properly merit
AP : 04 :375(164) [0223] its fruits, if only our **opponents** would grant that the
AP : 04 :376(164) [0223] we condemn in our **opponents'** position, that by
AP : 04 :378(165) [0223] about which we are arguing here with our **opponents**.
AP : 04 :384(166) [0225] Here we think that our **opponents** will grant that the
AP : 04 :388(166) [0225] issues on which our **opponents** had raised objections.
AP : 04 :400(168) [0227] Although our **opponents** arrogate to themselves the name
AP : 04 :400(168) [0227] The judgments of our **opponents** will not bother us since
AP : 07 :005(169) [0227] This much our **opponents** also admit, that the wicked are
AP : 07 :019(171) [0233] is more against our **opponents** than for them since it
AP : 07 :021(172) [0233] Most of what our **opponents** maintain, on the other
AP : 07 :021(172) [0233] wicked error when our **opponents** teach that men merit
AP : 07 :023(172) [0235] Perhaps our **opponents** demand some such definition of
AP : 07 :029(173) [0237] of noonday; if our **opponents** still continue to twist it, we
AP : 07 :030(173) [0237] Our **opponents** also condemn the part of the seventh
AP : 07 :031(174) [0237] We do not quite understand what our **opponents** mean.
AP : 07 :038(175) [0241] Our **opponents** say that universal traditions should be
AP : 07 :045(177) [0243] Our **opponents** completely misunderstand the meaning of
AP : 07 :046(177) [0243] But see what religious men our **opponents** are!
AP : 11 :003(180) [0249] many things which our **opponents**, if they are but honest,
AP : 11 :006(181) [0251] Therefore our **opponents** ought not cite against us the
AP : 11 :010(182) [0253] In our **opponents'** teaching on penitence there are other
AP : 12 :006(183) [0255] Let any one of our **opponents** step forward and tell us
AP : 12 :008(183) [0255] But our **opponents** give the legalistic reply that Judas did
AP : 12 :010(184) [0255] confess that our **opponents'** discussions are very confused
AP : 12 :010(184) [0255] Our **opponents'** whole teaching on the questions we have
AP : 12 :023(185) [0257] in confession, as our **opponents** command it, is necessary
AP : 12 :034(186) [0261] In these terrors our **opponents** say nothing about faith,
AP : 12 :059(190) [0267] Our **opponents** expressly condemn our statement that
AP : 12 :059(190) [0267] which we clash with our **opponents** and which we believe
AP : 12 :060(190) [0267] When our **opponents** talk about faith and say that it
AP : 12 :060(190) [0269] the same, in spite of our **opponents'** cries to the contrary.
AP : 12 :061(190) [0269] First, we ask our **opponents** whether the reception of
AP : 12 :063(191) [0269] we suppose our **opponents** will grant that the forgiveness
AP : 12 :066(191) [0271] Our **opponents** cry out that they are the church and follow
AP : 12 :067(191) [0271] sins in his bull, and our **opponents** condemn it in their
AP : 12 :074(192) [0273] What more do our **opponents** need?
AP : 12 :075(193) [0273] Third, our **opponents** say that sins are forgiven in this
AP : 12 :078(193) [0275] Our **opponents'** doctrine that men obtain the forgiveness
AP : 12 :084(194) [0277] devout minds if our **opponents** twist Paul's sentences, for
AP : 12 :085(194) [0277] opinions of our **opponents** that we do not receive the
AP : 12 :086(194) [0277] But our **opponents** imagine that we are members of

Continued ▶

AP : 12 :088(195) [0277] In the *Sentences* our **opponents** ask the same question.
AP : 12 :088(195) [0277] in the Gospel; our **opponents** leave consciences wavering
AP : 12 :089(195) [0279] Such is our **opponents'** doctrine — a doctrine of the law,
AP : 12 :090(195) [0279] our teaching or our **opponents'** teaching is more godly
AP : 12 :090(195) [0279] disagreeing with our **opponents**, we would very gladly
AP : 12 :091(195) [0279] Fathers and which our **opponents** quote in a distorted
AP : 12 :097(196) [0281] But since our **opponents** understand neither the nature of
AP : 12 :106(197) [0283] transformation, our **opponents** make passages of
AP : 12 :110(198) [0285] If our **opponents** contend that the enumeration of sins in
AP : 12 :111(198) [0285] In the Confutation our **opponents** have maintained that
AP : 12 :118(199) [0287] Still our **opponents** admit that satisfactions do not
AP : 12 :122(200) [0287] Look how our **opponents** prove these fictions of theirs in
AP : 12 :131(202) [0291] passages quoted by our **opponents** say nothing whatever
AP : 12 :134(202) [0293] Secondly, our **opponents** write that if a penitent refuses to
AP : 12 :136(203) [0293] follows from our **opponents'** position, these passages will
AP : 12 :137(203) [0293] words in refuting these silly arguments of our **opponents**.
AP : 12 :137(203) [0293] are not obligatory such as our **opponents** are discussing.
AP : 12 :139(204) [0295] This our **opponents** would have to prove.
AP : 12 :141(204) [0295] silly opinions of our **opponents**, which must enrage
AP : 12 :144(205) [0297] to placate God's displeasure, as our **opponents** claim.
AP : 12 :147(205) [0297] Our **opponents** carry on idle speculations about the
AP : 12 :147(205) [0297] death of Christ; our **opponents** admit that the works of
AP : 12 :148(205) [0297] Our **opponents** object that revenge or punishment is
AP : 12 :148(205) [0299] a merit or price, as our **opponents** imagine satisfactions to
AP : 12 :149(205) [0299] Our **opponents** are badly mistaken if they think that
AP : 12 :150(206) [0299] Our **opponents** admit that contrition can be so great as to
AP : 12 :154(206) [0299] because our **opponents** say that the power of the keys
AP : 12 :163(208) [0303] Our **opponents** are paying the penalty for their neglect of
AP : 12 :177(210) [0307] Thus our **opponents** are right in their judgment when they
AP : 12 :178(211) [0307] discussions of our **opponents**, they will see that our
AP : 12 :178(211) [0307] they will see that our **opponents** have neglected to teach
AP : 12 :178(211) [0309] will see, too, that our **opponents** have made up a great
AP : 13 :001(211) [0309] In Article XIII our **opponents** approve the statement that
AP : 13 :007(212) [0311] Our **opponents** do not interpret the priesthood in
AP : 15 :003(215) [0315] We expected our **opponents** to defend human traditions
AP : 15 :004(215) [0315] Here our **opponents** are openly Judaizing; they are openly
AP : 15 :005(215) [0317] Our **opponents**, on the other hand, set up these traditions
AP : 15 :017(217) [0319] How, then, can our **opponents** maintain that they justify?
AP : 15 :018(217) [0319] If our **opponents** defend the notion that these human
AP : 15 :021(218) [0321] are amazed when our **opponents** maintain that traditions
AP : 15 :030(219) [0323] of men, so that our **opponents** cannot use their customary
AP : 15 :030(219) [0323] Our **opponents** do not know what they are talking about.
AP : 15 :039(220) [0325] are more faithful to the canons than our **opponents** are.
AP : 15 :040(220) [0325] Among our **opponents**, unwilling celebrants and hirelings
AP : 15 :041(220) [0325] Among our **opponents** there is no catechization of the
AP : 15 :042(220) [0325] Among our **opponents**, there are many regions where no
AP : 15 :042(221) [0327] When our **opponents** do preach, they talk about human
AP : 15 :048(221) [0329] others' feasts, and our **opponents** do not even observe the
AP : 15 :050(222) [0329] and simple because our **opponents** condemn us for
AP : 16 :001(222) [0329] Our **opponents** approve Article XVI without exception.
AP : 17 :001(224) [0335] Our **opponents** accept Article XVII without exception.
AP : 18 :001(224) [0335] Our **opponents** accept Article XVIII on free will, but they
AP : 18 :002(225) [0335] the Pelagians and our **opponents**, since both believe that
AP : 19 :001(226) [0337] Our **opponents** accept Article XIX.
AP : 20 :005(227) [0339] Our **opponents**, on the other hand, teach that God has
AP : 20 :006(227) [0339] our conscience that our **opponents** are condemning the
AP : 20 :009(227) [0341] Confession, when our **opponents** use their terrors,
AP : 20 :011(228) [0341] way in which our **opponents** have treated this issue has
AP : 20 :012(228) [0341] Our **opponents** quote many Scripture passages to show
AP : 20 :012(228) [0341] dear reader, that our **opponents** have indeed got the most
AP : 21 :002(229) [0343] So our **opponents** state a triumph as though the war were
AP : 21 :003(229) [0343] with the theories our **opponents** now hold about the
AP : 21 :007(230) [0345] Our **opponents** do not require these real honors; they
AP : 21 :012(230) [0345] Our **opponents** can produce nothing against the
AP : 21 :013(230) [0345] Therefore our **opponents** should not coerce us to adopt
AP : 21 :014(230) [0345] Not only do our **opponents** require invocation in the
AP : 21 :018(231) [0347] or example can our **opponents** produce from Scripture
AP : 21 :021(232) [0349] Our **opponents** tell us, first of all, to invoke the saints,
AP : 21 :023(232) [0349] Here and there in our **opponents'** books and sermons
AP : 21 :031(233) [0351] Our **opponents** teach that we should put our trust in the
AP : 21 :039(235) [0355] in the Confutation our **opponents** completely ignore even
AP : 21 :042(235) [0355] it was dishonest of our **opponents** to ignore abuses when
AP : 21 :042(235) [0357] of the emperor, our **opponents** are doing everything to
AP : 21 :043(235) [0357] will arise whom our **opponents** will be unable to restrain.
AP : 21 :044(236) [0357] violent counsels of our **opponents** but to find other
AP : 22 :001(236) [0357] as we suppose our **opponents** admit, all of the church
AP : 22 :006(236) [0359] In the Confutation our **opponents** do not even try to
AP : 22 :008(237) [0359] Our **opponents** know this very well, but they throw sand
AP : 22 :010(237) [0361] Our **opponents** are obviously clowning when they apply
AP : 22 :010(238) [0361] Our **opponents** argue that the laity has been kept from
AP : 22 :013(238) [0361] from agreeing with our **opponents**, even though otherwise
AP : 23 :001(239) [0363] defiled celibacy, our **opponents** not only use the wicked
AP : 23 :002(239) [0363] read of greater brazenness than that of our **opponents**?
AP : 23 :004(239) [0365] Word of God, while our **opponents** set against them their
AP : 23 :005(239) [0365] Our **opponents** will not speak, write, or act honestly,
AP : 23 :006(240) [0365] put forth by our **opponents** because it clashes with divine
AP : 23 :006(240) [0365] we have advanced, our **opponents** have thought up some
AP : 23 :008(240) [0365] Our **opponents** reply with the silly argument that
AP : 23 :010(241) [0367] it is ridiculous for our **opponents** to say that originally
AP : 23 :015(241) [0367] Our **opponents** demand to be shown a command
AP : 23 :018(242) [0369] As we said before, our **opponents** are only clowning; they
AP : 23 :024(242) [0371] In the Confutation our **opponents** shriek that the councils
AP : 23 :026(243) [0371] *Fifth,* although our **opponents** do not defend this
AP : 23 :028(243) [0371] In the first place, our **opponents** must admit that for
AP : 23 :032(243) [0373] If our **opponents** could produce a passage like that about
AP : 23 :050(246) [0377] Our **opponents** do not demand celibacy for religious
AP : 23 :059(247) [0379] that to satisfy our **opponents** we would have to reject the
AP : 23 :059(247) [0379] to go along with our **opponents** in the defense of this
AP : 23 :059(247) [0379] our lack of an alliance with such murderous **opponents**.
AP : 23 :060(247) [0379] agree with our **opponents** in their defense of the
AP : 23 :062(247) [0381] and refuted the silly counter-arguments of our **opponents**.
AP : 23 :064(248) [0381] argument of our **opponents** is that priests should be pure,
AP : 23 :068(248) [0383] statements show our **opponents'** purpose in writing the
AP : 23 :070(249) [0383] the emptiness of our **opponents'** arguments and
AP : 24 :002(249) [0385] in the Mass, our clever **opponents** quibble about how a
AP : 24 :009(250) [0387] Our **opponents** have collected many statements to prove
AP : 24 :009(251) [0387] answer refutes all our **opponents'** objections, both here in
AP : 24 :010(251) [0387] In the same way our **opponents** should be forced to
AP : 24 :014(251) [0387] because of the way our **opponents** have twisted many
AP : 24 :015(251) [0389] the last ten years our **opponents** have been publishing
AP : 24 :016(252) [0389] would really call our **opponents** "poor cooks," for they
AP : 24 :031(255) [0395] Our **opponents** misinterpret this passage and apply it to
AP : 24 :034(256) [0397] But our **opponents** always apply the term "sacrifice" only
AP : 24 :035(256) [0397] Our **opponents** will really achieve something if we let them
AP : 24 :040(257) [0399] Our **opponents** imagine that it symbolizes the ceremony
AP : 24 :042(257) [0399] For in the Mass our **opponents** keep only the ceremony,
AP : 24 :044(258) [0399] In the Confutation our **opponents** wring their hands over
AP : 24 :046(258) [0401] ever understood our **opponents'** doctrine of penitence?
AP : 24 :046(258) [0401] Our **opponents** never mentioned faith, by which we freely
AP : 24 :049(258) [0401] observing it than our **opponents** because in their churches
AP : 24 :050(259) [0401] the clergy have ever understood our **opponents'** teaching.
AP : 24 :051(259) [0403] If our **opponents** center their worship in such things
AP : 24 :053(259) [0403] to the Hebrews, our **opponents** twist passages from this
AP : 24 :061(260) [0405] give no support to our **opponents'** wicked idea that the
AP : 24 :065(261) [0407] Our **opponents** cannot produce a syllable from the
AP : 24 :067(261) [0407] a general reply to our **opponents** regarding what the
AP : 24 :075(263) [0411] all of which our **opponents** twist in support of their idea
AP : 24 :078(263) [0411] Our **opponents** also refer us to philology.
AP : 24 :087(265) [0413] It is silly for our **opponents** to raise such quibbles about
AP : 24 :089(265) [0413] Our **opponents** defend the application of the ceremony to
AP : 24 :090(266) [0415] the sort of proofs our **opponents** have for purgatory, the
AP : 24 :091(266) [0415] be careful not to support the abuses of our **opponents**.
AP : 24 :092(267) [0417] we wrangle with our **opponents** who understand the
AP : 24 :094(267) [0417] Our **opponents** quote the Fathers on offerings for the
AP : 24 :094(267) [0417] do not support the **opponents'** idea of the transfer *ex*
AP : 24 :095(267) [0417] obvious lies which our **opponents** teach about transfer *ex*
AP : 24 :096(267) [0417] Our **opponents** also misapply against us the
AP : 24 :099(268) [0419] most valid reasons for disagreeing with our **opponents**.
AP : 24 :099(268) [0419] warned not to help our **opponents** in defending their
AP : 24 :099(268) [0419] But if our **opponents** make us compile all kinds of abuses
AP : 27 :010(270) [0423] But still our **opponents** demand the rejection of
AP : 27 :010(270) [0423] we shall refute our **opponents'** quibbles against them.
AP : 27 :015(271) [0425] Our **opponents** pretend that Paul abolished the law of
AP : 27 :018(272) [0425] How impudent our **opponents** are!
AP : 27 :024(273) [0427] But look at the impudence of our **opponents**!
AP : 27 :029(274) [0429] These are our **opponents'** words in which, first of all, they
AP : 27 :029(274) [0431] That is the way our **opponents** argue their case; that is the
AP : 27 :036(275) [0433] But our **opponents** slyly seek to give the impression that
AP : 27 :039(276) [0433] Although our **opponents** are now modifying their praises
AP : 27 :052(278) [0437] their very eyes, our **opponents** should defend their
AP : 27 :066(280) [0441] If our **opponents** insist upon misapplying this passage to
AP : 27 :069(280) [0443] passing we have refuted the objections of our **opponents**.
AP : 27 :069(280) [0443] only for the sake of our **opponents**, but even more for the
AP : 28 :001(281) [0443] Here our **opponents** rant about the privileges and the
AP : 28 :003(281) [0443] But if our **opponents** would only listen to the complaints
AP : 28 :003(281) [0443] Our **opponents** valiantly defend their own position and
AP : 28 :006(282) [0445] But our **opponents'** only reply is that bishops have the
AP : 28 :006(282) [0445] by which our **opponents** inform us that bishops have the
AP : 28 :008(282) [0445] does not scare our **opponents**, who vigorously defend
AP : 28 :010(282) [0447] So let our **opponents** explain how traditions are
AP : 28 :011(283) [0447] Therefore our **opponents** will never be able to show that
AP : 28 :024(285) [0451] nor can we agree with our **opponents** who condemn it.
AP : 28 :025(285) [0451] Besides, are there no offenses among our **opponents**?
AP : 28 :027(285) [0451] people whether our **opponents** are right in boasting that
TR : 00 :021(323) [0509] [Arguments of **Opponents** Refuted]
LC : 05 :032(450) [0761] Our **opponents** must still confess that these are the very
SD : PR :002(501) [0847] The **opponents**, however, regarded this pious reformation
SD : 08 :063(603) [1037] Some of our **opponents**, against their own conscience,

Opportunity (10)

AG : PR :020(026) [0041] Majesty, at the earliest **opportunity** and to allow no
AP : 23 :043(245) [0375] must withdraw to have **opportunity** for prayer, but Paul
S3 : 02 :002(303) [0479] people who do evil whenever they have **opportunity**.
LC : 01 :084(376) [0605] may have time and **opportunity**, which otherwise would
LC : 01 :174(388) [0631] are gifted to give them **opportunity** to learn and study so
LC : 01 :189(390) [0635] or, though he has the **opportunity**, fails to prevent,
LC : 01 :252(399) [0651] will here find ample **opportunity** to do things which are
LC : 01 :303(405) [0667] Or, seeing an **opportunity** for profit — let us say, when a
LC : 01 :328(410) [0677] though you have the **opportunity** and occasion to do so
LC : 05 :047(452) [0765] to everyone's **opportunity** and need, being bound to no

Oppose (7), Opposed (26), Opposes (5), Opposing (2)

PR : PR :009(006) [0011] opinions which are **opposed** to us and to our Christian
AG : 00 :001(047) [0059] and is not contrary or **opposed** to that of the universal
AG : 23 :013(053) [0063] but was also utterly **opposed** and contrary to the canons
AG : 26 :029(068) [0075] for it is diametrically **opposed** to the Gospel to institute
AG : 27 :036(076) [0081] and authority of God is **opposed** to God and the holy
AL : 15 :003(037) [0049] satisfaction for sins are **opposed** to the Gospel and the
AP : 04 :260(145) [0195] In this way we can **oppose** those who reject Christ,
AP : 12 :070(192) [0271] not hesitate, therefore, to **oppose** this statement of Peter,
AP : 12 :079(193) [0275] by the law; to the law he **opposes** the promise of the
AP : 15 :034(220) [0325] example the apostles compel us to **oppose** this teaching.
AP : 16 :006(223) [0331] Celsus, and many others **opposed** the Christians on the
AP : 27 :014(271) [0425] the forgiveness of sins, **opposed** as they are to the
AP : 28 :024(285) [0451] good will but that of many who are now **opposed** to us.
S2 : 02 :010(294) [0465] eternally divided and **opposed** the one to the other.
TR : 00 :039(327) [0515] adversary of Christ who **opposes** and exalts himself
SC : 09 :012(356) [0563] one another, for 'God **opposes** the proud, but gives grace
LC : 01 :042(370) [0591] grief and want and are **opposed** and attacked by the
LC : 03 :062(428) [0715] how the devil **opposes** and obstructs their fulfillment.
EP : RN :006(465) [0779] and condemned as **opposed** to the unanimous declaration
EP : 02 :003(470) [0787] that which is evil and **opposed** to God, as it is written,
EP : 05 :007(478) [0803] the law and Gospel are **opposed** to each other, as when
SD : PR :019(507) [0857] theses and antitheses, **opposing** the true doctrine to the
SD : 01 :011(510) [0863] by nature diametrically **opposed** to God and his highest
SD : 02 :017(524) [0887] he is thoroughly wicked, **opposed** and hostile to God, and

Continued ▶

S D : 0 2 :017(524) [0887] the Spirit, and these are **opposed** to each other" (Gal.
S D : 0 2 :018(524) [0887] much more obstinately **opposed** and hostile to God's law
S D : 0 2 :060(533) [0905] the Holy Spirit and **oppose** and constantly rebel against
S D : 0 2 :064(533) [0907] the flesh; for these are **opposed** to each other, to prevent
S D : 0 2 :086(538) [0913] doctrine but rather **opposes** it and therefore is rightly to
S D : 0 3 :053(548) [0933] it is diametrically **opposed** to Paul's statement that
S D : 0 4 :002(551) [0939] as well as formerly, to **oppose** that article of our Christian
S D : 0 4 :022(554) [0945] they are diametrically **opposed** to St. Paul's words which
S D : 0 6 :008(565) [0965] the flesh, for these are **opposed** to each other, to prevent
S D : 0 7 :107(588) [1009] is inconsistent with or **opposed** and contrary to the
S D : 0 7 :112(589) [1011] are inconsistent with, **opposed** to, or contrary to the
S D : 0 7 :128(591) [1015] with, contrary to, or **opposed** to the doctrine set forth
S D : 1 0 :005(611) [1053] of the papists, or that we are not seriously **opposed** to it.
S D : 1 0 :005(611) [1053] that these two **opposing** religions have been brought into
S D : 1 1 :012(618) [1067] We must **oppose** such false imagining and thoughts with
S D : 1 1 :073(628) [1087] not be idle, still less **oppose** the urgings of the Spirit of

Opposite (6)
A P : 0 4 :266(146) [0197] words to mean the very **opposite** of the teaching of grace
A P : 0 7 :016(170) [0231] kingdom of Christ, the **opposite** of the kingdom of the
A P : 1 3 :023(214) [0313] fact, Augustine says the **opposite**: that faith in the
E P : 0 8 :003(487) [0819] have contended for the **opposite** view against the
S D : 0 1 :004(509) [0861] the true doctrine and its **opposite** in theses and
S D : 0 8 :044(599) [1029] and God dead lie in the **opposite** scale, then his side goes

Opposition (17)
A L : 2 3 :018(054) [0063] exercised than in **opposition** to the marriage of priests.
A P : P R :009(099) [0101] several articles in **opposition** to the clear Scripture of the
A P : 0 4 :146(127) [0163] In **opposition** to the judgment of God they set a trust in
A P : 1 2 :060(190) [0267] faith, and we set it in **opposition** to the opinion that bids
A P : 1 3 :013(212) [0311] kind of praise in **opposition** to the fanatics who dream
A P : 1 3 :019(213) [0313] In **opposition** to this, Paul denies that Abraham was
A P : 1 5 :018(217) [0319] God, devised by human authority in **opposition** to Christ.
A P : 2 3 :003(239) [0363] In **opposition** to divine law, the law of the nations, and
A P : 2 4 :088(265) [0413] and the like, in **opposition** to a theory of *ex opere*
A P : 2 8 :004(281) [0445] unless they act in clear **opposition** to God's commands.
L C : 0 1 :116(381) [0615] and are not set into **opposition** to the preceding
L C : 0 5 :026(449) [0759] Meanwhile it must suffer much **opposition**.
E P : 0 3 :003(473) [0793] 1. In **opposition** to these two errors just recounted, we
S D : 0 1 :017(511) [0865] 1. First, in **opposition** to both old and new Pelagians, we
S D : 0 8 :017(594) [1021] In **opposition** to this condemned heresy the Christian
S D : 0 8 :063(603) [1037] this term merely in **opposition** to a "verbal exchange," the
S D : 1 0 :029(615) [1061] Gospel contrary and in **opposition** to the Christian

Oppress (5), Oppressed (7), Oppression (4), Oppressive (1), Oppressors (1)
P R : P R :022(012) [0021] and persecution of poor, **oppressed** Christians.
A P : 0 4 :044(113) [0133] But to us, **oppressed** by sin and death, the promise freely
A P : 0 4 :258(144) [0193] seek justice, correct **oppression**; defend the fatherless,
A P : 0 4 :258(144) [0193] at these works: "correct **oppression**, defend the
A P : 0 4 :258(144) [0193] these works—"correct **oppression**, defend the
A P : 0 4 :261(145) [0195] showing mercy to the **oppressed**," that is, redeem your
A P : 0 7 :009(169) [0229] number of ungodly within the church who **oppress** it.
S 1 : P R :014(291) [0459] But our sins **oppress** us and keep God from being
L C : 0 1 :249(398) [0651] not be burdened and **oppressed** and in order that they
L C : 0 1 :258(399) [0653] poor man is inevitably **oppressed**, loses his case, and
L C : 0 3 :084(431) [0723] of those who wantonly **oppress** the poor and deprive them
L C : 0 3 :084(432) [0723] but let exploiters and **oppressors** beware lest they lose the
L C : 0 4 :044(442) [0743] our sins or conscience **oppress** us, and we must retort,
L C : 0 5 :040(451) [0763] we are freed from his **oppression** and authority, let a
L C : 0 6 :001(457) [0000] been no law quite so **oppressive** as that which forced
L C : 0 6 :020(459) [0000] Further, no one dare **oppress** you with requirements.
S D : 0 5 :009(559) [0955] hearts, but to the "**oppressed**" or penitent (Luke 4:18).
S D : 1 1 :085(630) [1091] tyranny with which he **oppressed** the children of Israel by

Option (2), Optional (1)
L C : 0 1 :098(378) [0609] Do not regard it as an **optional** or unimportant matter.
E P : 0 4 :011(477) [0799] the regenerated person's **option** whether to do or not to
S D : 0 4 :020(554) [0945] it lies within their free **option** if they may or want to do

Oracles (1)
A P : 2 7 :004(269) [0421] signs, no less sure than **oracles**, which threaten a change

Oral (15), Orally (14)
S 3 : 1 5 :005(317) [0501] Smalcald directed me **orally** and by a letter which I have
L C : 0 4 :030(440) [0739] as the entire Gospel is an external, **oral** proclamation.
L C : 0 5 :031(450) [0759] if it were not proclaimed by preaching, by the **oral** Word?
E P : 0 7 :002(481) [0809] and if they are received **orally** by all those who use the
E P : 0 7 :003(482) [0809] and wine are present, distributed, and received **orally**.
E P : 0 7 :015(483) [0811] by faith, but also **orally** — however, not in a Capernaitic
E P : 0 7 :026(485) [0815] of Christ is not received **orally** with the bread, but that
S D : 0 2 :048(530) [0901] what means (namely, the **oral** Word and the holy
S D : 0 7 :003(569) [0973] but bread and wine are **orally** received in the Supper.
S D : 0 7 :006(570) [0975] by faith but not to receive it **orally** with the mouth.
S D : 0 7 :008(570) [0975] and impalpably, and is **orally** received with the blessed
S D : 0 7 :033(575) [0983] godless or Judas receive **orally** as well as St. Peter and all
S D : 0 7 :048(578) [0989] and natural wine as well as of **oral** eating and drinking.
S D : 0 7 :056(579) [0991] but of a sacramental or **oral** eating of the body of Christ
S D : 0 7 :060(580) [0993] body and blood of Christ **orally** in the sacrament, but also
S D : 0 7 :061(581) [0995] even the sacramental or **oral** eating in the Supper is not
S D : 0 7 :063(581) [0995] of the body of Christ is **oral** or sacramental, when all who
S D : 0 7 :063(581) [0995] of the true, essential body and blood of Christ **orally**.
S D : 0 7 :063(581) [0995] unbelievers receive it **orally**, too, but to their judgment
S D : 0 7 :064(581) [0995] as referring precisely to **oral** eating and drinking — not,
S D : 0 7 :065(581) [0995] and in addition to the **oral** eating he ordains the spiritual
S D : 0 7 :066(581) [0997] sacrament too, but also **orally**, and this by unworthy,
S D : 0 7 :067(582) [0997] church when they call **oral** eating and eating on the part
S D : 0 7 :068(582) [0997] who by their unworthy **oral** eating of the body of Christ
S D : 0 7 :072(582) [0997] faith spiritually, the other **orally**, which happens in the
S D : 0 7 :086(584) [1003] mean faith, or the **oral** eating alone, but the entire
S D : 0 7 :086(584) [1003] and reception, or the **oral** eating of the blessed bread and
S D : 0 7 :088(585) [1003] essential presence and the **oral** eating of the body of
S D : 0 7 :114(589) [1011] Likewise, the denial of an **oral** eating of the body and

Oration (1), Orator (2)
A G : P R :018(026) [0041] Your Imperial Majesty's **orator** and appointed
A P : 2 3 :039(244) [0375] does not make an **orator** more righteous before God than
A P : 2 4 :081(264) [0411] As Demosthenes' **oration** *Leptines* shows, it is completely

Ordain (9), Ordained (34), Ordaining (5), Ordains (2)
P R : P R :020(010) [0017] accomplish what he has **ordained** and promised in his
A G : 0 6 :003(032) [0047] for Ambrose says, "It is **ordained** of God that whoever
A G : 1 6 :001(037) [0051] were instituted and **ordained** by God for the sake of good
A L : 0 6 :003(032) [0047] for Ambrose says, "It is **ordained** of God that whoever
A L : 2 0 :009(042) [0053] who alone has been **ordained** to be the mediator and
A L : 2 8 :023(084) [0087] when bishops teach or **ordain** anything contrary to the
A L : 2 8 :054(090) [0091] So Paul **ordained** that women should cover their heads in
A P : 2 8 :016(283) [0449] Thus even the apostles **ordained** many things that were
S 3 : 1 0 :001(314) [0497] but not of necessity) to **ordain** and confirm us and our
S 3 : 1 0 :003(314) [0497] shall and ought ourselves **ordain** suitable persons to this
S 3 : 1 0 :003(314) [0497] state that those who are **ordained** by heretics shall also be
S 3 : 1 0 :003(314) [0497] heretics shall also be regarded as **ordained** and remain so.
S 3 : 1 1 :003(315) [0499] to be free, as God **ordained** and instituted it, and we shall
T R : 0 0 :005(320) [0505] he has the right to elect, **ordain**, confirm, and depose all
T R : 0 0 :010(321) [0505] that he was neither **ordained** nor confirmed by Peter, nor
T R : 0 0 :014(322) [0507] whom a head is to be **ordained**, and a bishop should be
T R : 0 0 :048(328) [0519] performed in callings which God requires and **ordained**.
T R : 0 0 :064(331) [0523] that one bishop should **ordain** the ministers in a number
T R : 0 0 :066(331) [0523] the churches retain the right to **ordain** for themselves.
T R : 0 0 :067(331) [0523] the right of calling, electing, and **ordaining** ministers.
T R : 0 0 :067(331) [0523] right of electing and **ordaining** ministers must of necessity
T R : 0 0 :069(331) [0525] certainly has the right of electing and **ordaining** ministers.
T R : 0 0 :072(332) [0525] retains the right of electing and **ordaining** ministers.
T R : 0 0 :072(332) [0525] divine right compelled to **ordain** pastors and ministers for
T R : 0 0 :079(333) [0527] of worship and do not **ordain** godly teachers but rather
L C : 0 1 :108(380) [0611] who has created and **ordained** them to be our parents.
L C : 0 4 :019(439) [0737] all the external things **ordained** and instituted by God
L C : 0 4 :039(441) [0743] has commanded and **ordained**; in short, it is so full of
L C : 0 4 :064(444) [0749] signifies and why God **ordained** just this sign and
E P : 1 1 :005(495) [0833] alone brings it about and **ordains** everything that belongs
S D : 0 5 :012(560) [0957] and Christ are not **ordained** and given us to terrify or to
S D : 0 7 :044(577) [0987] deliberation and care in **ordaining** and instituting this
S D : 0 7 :065(581) [0995] to the oral eating he **ordains** the spiritual eating, when he
S D : 0 7 :070(582) [0997] was instituted and **ordained** primarily for communicants
S D : 0 7 :083(584) [1001] Lord's Supper as Christ **ordained** it is not observed (if,
S D : 0 7 :085(584) [1003] Christ's institution as he **ordained** it, it is no sacrament).
S D : 0 7 :086(584) [1003] action of the Supper as **ordained** by Christ: the
S D : 0 7 :108(588) [1009] God's command and the **ordained** use for which it is
S D : 1 0 :019(614) [1059] but not of necessity) to **ordain** and confirm us and our
S D : 1 1 :008(617) [1065] again, "As many as were **ordained** to eternal life believed"
S D : 1 1 :014(619) [1069] his purpose and counsel God had **ordained** the following:
S D : 1 1 :023(619) [1069] Christ, and also **ordained** that in the manner just
S D : 1 1 :040(623) [1077] contrary, as God has **ordained** in his counsel that the
S D : 1 1 :040(623) [1077] faith, so he has also **ordained** in his counsel that he would
S D : 1 1 :045(624) [1079] he held counsel and **ordained** "according to his purpose"
S D : 1 1 :046(624) [1079] our hands — that he **ordained** my salvation in his eternal
S D : 1 1 :049(624) [1079] the world began God **ordained** in his counsel through
S D : 1 1 :070(627) [1085] of God, if he has been elected and **ordained** to eternal life.
S D : 1 1 :076(628) [1087] means, and he has **ordained** Word and sacraments as the
S D : 1 1 :086(631) [1091] secret counsel God had **ordained** him to eternal

Order (246), Ordered (13), Ordering (2), Orderly (5), Orders (19)
P R : P R :000(001) [0004] Agreement and **Order** of the aforementioned Electors,
P R : P R :004(003) [0007] the disruption of well-**ordered** government the foe of
P R : P R :008(005) [0009] of the divine Word, in **order** thereby to warn and, as far
P R : P R :013(007) [0013] brought together in good **order**, by the singular grace of
P R : P R :018(008) [0015] Confession, and in **order** that our contemporaries as well
P R : P R :018(009) [0015] likewise, we have **ordered** the incorporation of the
P R : P R :022(011) [0019] controverted articles in **order** that everybody may know
P R : P R :026(014) [0025] widespread in **order** that all kinds of scandal might be
P R : P R :027(014) [0025] our names hereto and **ordered** our privy seals impressed
A G : 0 3 :003(030) [0045] and was buried in **order** to be a sacrifice not only for
A G : 1 4 :000(036) [0049] XIV. **Order** in the Church
A G : 1 5 :001(036) [0049] to peace and good **order** in the church, among them being
A G : 1 6 :001(037) [0051] God for the sake of good **order**, and that Christians may
A G : 1 6 :005(038) [0051] all these be kept as true **orders** of God and that everyone,
A G : 1 8 :004(039) [0051] In **order** that it may be evident that this teaching is no
A G : 2 0 :022(044) [0055] diligently to apply it in **order** that men may know that the
A G : 0 0 :000(049) [0059] changes in these cases in **order** that Your Imperial
A G : 2 2 :001(049) [0059] is a clear command and **order** of Christ, "Drink of it, all
A G : 2 2 :003(049) [0059] In **order** that no one might question these words and
A G : 2 2 :007(050) [0061] Pope Gelasius himself **ordered** that the sacrament was
A G : 2 3 :003(051) [0061] In **order** to avoid such unbecoming offense, adultery, and
A G : 2 3 :014(053) [0063] to recognize this fact in **order** that the prohibition of
A G : 0 1 :007(056) [0065] terrified consciences) in **order** that the people may be
A G : 2 4 :038(060) [0069] receive the sacrament in **order** from the bishop or priest."
A G : 2 6 :002(064) [0071] new ceremonies, new **orders**, and the like were invented
A G : 2 6 :040(069) [0075] and the like) which serve to preserve **order** in the church.
A G : 2 7 :017(073) [0077] misrepresentation, in **order** that one may better grasp and
A G : 2 7 :018(073) [0079] marry, for vows cannot nullify God's **order** and command.
A G : 2 7 :020(074) [0079] but God's creation and **order** also direct all to marriage
A G : 2 7 :031(076) [0079] determine or arrange the **order** of one's whole future life.
A G : 2 7 :046(078) [0081] spiritual estate of the **orders** was Christian perfection.
A G : 2 8 :030(085) [0087] foods, holy days, and the different **orders** of the clergy.
A G : 2 8 :035(086) [0089] that they be observed in **order** to make satisfaction for
A G : 2 8 :037(087) [0089] have been instituted in **order** that by such works grace
A G : 2 8 :039(087) [0089] of the law, as if in **order** to earn God's grace there had to
A G : 2 8 :053(090) [0091] churches is done in good **order**, but not as a means of
A G : 2 8 :053(090) [0091] for sins, nor in **order** to bind men's consciences by
A G : 2 8 :054(090) [0091] not all speak at once, but one after another, in **order**.
A G : 2 8 :060(091) [0091] and pleased to do this in **order** that the people might have
A G : 0 0 :003(095) [0095] for the common good in **order** that the chief points at
A G : 0 0 :005(095) [0095] to adduce and mention in **order** that it may be made very
A L : 0 5 :001(031) [0045] In **order** that we may obtain this faith, the ministry of
A L : 1 4 :000(036) [0049] XIV. Ecclesiastical **Order**
A L : 1 5 :001(036) [0049] which contribute to peace and good **order** in the church.

Continued ▶

A L : 2 0 :022(044) [0055] faith in Christ in **order** that anxious consciences should
A L : 0 0 :001(049) [0059] for such changes are in **order** that the people may not be
A L : 0 0 :002(049) [0059] among the people in **order** to inflame the hatred of men
A L : 2 3 :020(055) [0063] The laws of all well-**ordered** states, even among the
A L : 2 4 :003(056) [0065] are needed especially in **order** that the unlearned may be
A L : 2 4 :038(060) [0067] Nicene canon read, "In **order**, after the presbyters, let the
A L : 2 4 :039(060) [0069] one wait for another in **order** that there may be a
A L : 2 6 :002(064) [0071] new ceremonies, new **orders**, new holy days, and new
A L : 2 6 :005(064) [0071] and human traditions in **order** to show that the
A L : 2 6 :033(069) [0075] him to sin, but not in **order** to merit forgiveness of sins or
A L : 2 6 :040(069) [0075] among us (such as the **order** of lessons in the Mass, holy
A L : 2 6 :040(069) [0075] are profitable for maintaining good **order** in the church.
A L : 2 7 :017(073) [0077] odious exaggeration in **order** that our teaching on this
A L : 2 8 :030(085) [0087] foods, holy days, grades or **orders** of ministers, etc.
A L : 2 8 :037(086) [0089] new ceremonies and new **orders** instituted because the
A L : 2 8 :039(087) [0089] of the law, as if in **order** to merit justification there had to
A L : 2 8 :053(090) [0091] may be done in good **order**, but not that by means of
A L : 2 8 :055(090) [0091] churches may be done in **order** and without confusion.
A L : 0 0 :005(095) [0095] necessary to say in **order** that it may be understood that
A L : 0 0 :006(095) [0095] the above articles in **order** that our confession may be
A P : P R :001(098) [0099] of the princes, and he **ordered** our princes to accept this
A P : P R :004(098) [0099] Imperial Majesty again **ordered** our princes to accept the
A P : P R :011(099) [0101] doctrinal formulas in **order** to foster the attainment of
A P : 0 2 :037(105) [0115] they twist his words in **order** by this device to crush an
A P : 0 2 :043(106) [0117] it is not right to twist it in **order** to minimize original sin.
A P : 0 4 :011(108) [0123] necessity of unchanging **order**, not of compulsion—God
A P : 0 4 :017(109) [0125] In **order** not to by-pass Christ altogether, our opponents
A P : 0 4 :019(109) [0125] they are only playing in **order** to avoid the impression
A P : 0 4 :050(114) [0135] why it depends on faith, in **order** that the promise may be
A P : 0 4 :084(119) [0145] why it depends on faith, in **order** that the promise may be
A P : 0 4 :093(120) [0149] in Christ Jesus, in **order** to be justified by faith in Christ,
A P : 0 4 :170(130) [0171] against such feelings in **order** to suppress and destroy
A P : 0 4 :189(133) [0175] commanded them and in **order** to exercise our faith, to
A P : 0 4 :189(133) [0175] And in **order** to keep the Gospel among men, he visibly
A P : 0 4 :201(134) [0175] receive circumcision in **order** to be justified
A P : 0 4 :208(135) [0177] to copy this action in **order** thereby to merit grace,
A P : 0 4 :209(135) [0177] put their sons to death in **order** by this cruel and painful
A P : 0 4 :211(136) [0179] without their faith in **order** by such works to merit the
A P : 0 4 :212(136) [0179] vows, and new monastic **orders** beyond God's
A P : 0 4 :221(137) [0181] Our opponents proceed in reverse **order**.
A P : 0 4 :288(151) [0203] men thought up monastic **orders**, which competed in the
A P : 0 4 :288(151) [0203] tranquillity there should be some **order** in the church.
A P : 0 4 :345(160) [0217] Precisely in **order** to make hope sure and to distinguish
A P : 0 4 :360(162) [0219] as when monks sell the merits of their **orders** to others.
A P : 0 4 :384(166) [0225] that confession saves in **order** to show what kind of faith
A P : 0 7 :007(169) [0229] saying that it should be purified in **order** to be holy.
A P : 0 7 :028(173) [0237] teaches us this in **order** that we may not be offended by
A P : 0 7 :033(174) [0239] we willingly observe the **order** of the Mass, the Lord's
A P : 1 2 :028(185) [0259] In **order** to deliver pious consciences from these
A P : 1 2 :058(190) [0267] put in these two parts in **order** to emphasize the faith that
A P : 1 2 :081(194) [0275] why it depends on faith, in **order** that the promise may
A P : 1 2 :083(194) [0275] to avoid being lengthy in **order** to make our case more
A P : 1 2 :092(196) [0279] the parts of penitence in **order** to make it more
A P : 1 2 :093(196) [0279] it would have been in **order** to select and combine their
A P : 1 2 :129(202) [0291] and settled now in **order** to heal devout minds and free
A P : 1 2 :137(203) [0293] they defend monastic **orders**, the sale of Masses, and
A P : 1 2 :158(207) [0301] is doing his alien work in **order** to do his proper work, as
A P : 1 4 :000(214) [0315] [Article XIV. Ecclesiastical **Order**]
A P : 1 5 :001(215) [0315] conducive to tranquillity and good **order** in the church.
A P : 1 5 :013(216) [0319] them for the sake of good **order** and tranquility in the
A P : 1 5 :020(218) [0321] were profitable for good **order**, because they gave the
A P : 1 5 :020(218) [0321] be done decently and in **order** in the churches, and finally
A P : 1 5 :022(218) [0321] This good **order** is very becoming in the church and is
A P : 1 5 :040(220) [0325] chant the Psalms in **order** to learn; the people sing, too, in
A P : 1 5 :040(220) [0325] the people sing, too, in **order** to learn or to worship.
A P : 1 6 :000(222) [0329] [Article XVI. Political **Order**]
A P : 2 0 :010(228) [0341] as a gift" (Rom. 3:24) "in **order** that the promise may be
A P : 2 0 :013(228) [0341] they should be done in **order** to confirm their call, that is,
A P : 2 1 :023(232) [0349] "It is a divinely instituted **order** that we should take
A P : 2 1 :024(232) [0349] is the "divinely instituted **order** that we should take refuge
A P : 2 1 :024(232) [0349] Perhaps they derive this "**order**" from the usage at royal
A P : 2 1 :029(233) [0351] like the monks who peddle the merits of their **orders**.
A P : 2 1 :038(235) [0355] the worship of saints in **order** to emphasize the honor and
A P : 2 2 :013(238) [0361] to make a distinction of **orders**, this in itself should keep
A P : 2 2 :013(238) [0361] are other distinctions of **order** between priest and people,
A P : 2 2 :013(238) [0361] the real dignity of the **order**, we shall not say anything
A P : 2 3 :010(241) [0367] thought up in **order** to circumvent the natural law.
A P : 2 3 :018(242) [0369] Here they **order** men to pray God for continence and to
A P : 2 3 :042(245) [0375] the law of celibacy in **order** to burden consciences with
A P : 2 3 :055(247) [0379] of public officials, who ought to maintain public **order**.
A P : 2 3 :066(248) [0381] continent in celibacy should marry in **order** to be pure.
A P : 2 4 :001(249) [0385] forms, such as the **order** of the lessons, prayers,
A P : 2 4 :003(250) [0385] this only in passing in **order** to point out that our
A P : 2 4 :024(253) [0391] Gospel was promised in **order** to set forth a propitiation.
A P : 2 4 :052(259) [0403] and the rest of the papal **order** are nothing but a
A P : 2 4 :052(259) [0403] are nothing but a misinterpretation of the Levitical **order**.
A P : 2 4 :098(268) [0417] Mass, which they apply in **order** by it to merit the
A P : 2 7 :001(268) [0419] thrown into prison by his **order** because he had
A P : 2 7 :009(270) [0423] the members of these **orders** are forced to approve and
A P : 2 7 :012(270) [0423] according to the Gospel in **order** to merit eternal life.
A P : 2 7 :040(276) [0433] parents or or his wife in **order** by this act to merit the
A P : 2 7 :047(277) [0437] praises upon something that conflicts with political **order**.
A P : 2 7 :055(278) [0439] If they undertook them in **order** to teach and exhort the
A P : 2 7 :065(280) [0441] if they are observed in **order** to merit the forgiveness of
A P : 2 8 :004(281) [0445] want instruction in **order** to have a sure way to go.
A P : 2 8 :006(282) [0445] and to correct by force in **order** to guide their subjects
A P : 2 8 :013(283) [0447] into the power of the **order** and the power of jurisdiction.
A P : 2 8 :013(283) [0447] has the power of the **order**, namely, the ministry of Word
A P : 2 8 :015(283) [0447] but a means of preserving **order** in the church, for the
A P : 2 8 :017(284) [0449] place and without superstition, in **order** to avoid offenses.
S 1 : P R :010(290) [0457] a true council assemble in **order** that many things and
S 2 : 0 2 :006(293) [0463] it be discontinued in **order** to guard forever against such
S 2 : 0 2 :009(294) [0465] if everything else is in **order**) for anyone to use the
S 2 : 0 2 :019(296) [0467] of these practices in **order** that great multitudes of people
S 2 : 0 2 :029(297) [0471] and its consequences in **order** that we may retain the holy
S 2 : 0 3 :001(297) [0471] to such purposes in **order** that we may have pastors,
S 2 : 0 4 :007(299) [0473] others should adhere, in **order** that the unity of
S 2 : 0 4 :012(300) [0475] that one must be obedient to him in **order** to be saved.
S 2 : 0 4 :013(300) [0475] even presumed to issue **orders** to the angels in heaven.
S 3 : 0 3 :005(304) [0481] that they were sinners in **order** that they might know how
S 3 : 0 3 :016(305) [0483] he had to muster in **order** to avail before God, this
S 3 : 0 6 :003(311) [0493] one form is not the whole **order** and institution as it was
T R : 0 0 :005(320) [0503] In **order** that the ground of this our assertion may be
T R : 0 0 :014(322) [0509] our colleague Sabinus) in **order** that by the votes of all
T R : 0 0 :035(326) [0513] and wars, sometimes in **order** to occupy Italian cities and
T R : 0 0 :035(326) [0513] cities and sometimes in **order** to make the German
S C : P R :018(340) [0537] the common people in **order** that they may be encouraged
S C : P R :018(340) [0537] may be encouraged to be **orderly**, faithful, obedient, and
S C : 0 2 :004(345) [0545] sufferings and death, in **order** that I may be his, live
S C : 0 3 :002(346) [0545] we are truly his children in **order** that we may approach
S C : 0 3 :014(347) [0549] weather, peace and health, **order** and honor; true friends,
S C : 0 9 :006(355) [0561] of the grace of life, in **order** that your prayers may not be
L C : 0 1 :012(366) [0583] a pact with the devil in **order** that he may give them
L C : 0 1 :022(367) [0585] Upon it all the religious **orders** are founded.
L C : 0 1 :029(368) [0589] Consequently, in **order** to show that God will not have
L C : 0 1 :047(371) [0593] in life according to God's **order**, allowing none of these
L C : 0 1 :085(376) [0605] In this way a common **order** will prevail and no one will
L C : 0 1 :094(378) [0607] and the entire outward **order** of worship are therefore
L C : 0 1 :094(378) [0607] and appointed in **order** that God's Word may exert its
L C : 0 1 :144(385) [0623] masters and mistresses in **order** to have such joyful
L C : 0 1 :177(389) [0631] is no longer any civil **order**, peace, or respect for
L C : 0 1 :208(393) [0639] everything in the world in **order** that this estate might be
L C : 0 1 :213(394) [0641] and nuns resist God's **order** and commandment when
L C : 0 1 :217(394) [0641] I say these things in **order** that our young people may be
L C : 0 1 :230(396) [0645] various petty thieves in **order** to launch an attack against
L C : 0 1 :232(396) [0647] to the common people in **order** that they may be
L C : 0 1 :249(398) [0651] to establish and maintain **order** in all areas of trade and
L C : 0 1 :249(398) [0651] of trade and commerce in **order** that the poor may not be
L C : 0 1 :249(398) [0651] and oppressed and in **order** that they may not themselves
L C : 0 1 :258(399) [0653] nation had an excellent, **orderly** government, and even
L C : 0 1 :276(402) [0659] would be to observe the **order** laid down by the Gospel,
L C : 0 1 :278(402) [0661] Let all monks and holy **orders** step forth, with all their
L C : 0 1 :312(407) [0671] boast of their spiritual **orders** and the great, difficult
L C : 0 1 :317(408) [0673] All this I say and repeat in **order** that men may get rid of
L C : 0 1 :317(408) [0673] a doctrine or social **order** equal to that of the Ten
L C : 0 1 :319(408) [0673] First Commandment in **order** to show how much effort
L C : 0 1 :326(409) [0675] In **order** that this may be constantly repeated and never
L C : 0 1 :327(409) [0675] or omitting to do things simply in **order** to please them.
L C : 0 1 :328(410) [0675] are commanded in that **order**, even though you have the
L C : 0 1 :328(410) [0677] out of love to God and in **order** to please him, in the
L C : 0 1 :333(410) [0677] and extolled above all **orders**, commands, and works
L C : 0 2 :002(411) [0679] It is given in **order** to help us do what the Ten
L C : 0 2 :026(413) [0685] and far-reaching, but in **order** to treat it briefly and
L C : 0 2 :030(414) [0685] under his protection, in **order** that he may rule us by his
L C : 0 2 :031(414) [0685] what he paid and risked in **order** to win us and bring us
L C : 0 2 :031(414) [0687] All this in **order** to become my Lord.
L C : 0 2 :038(415) [0689] In **order** that this treasure might not be buried but put to
L C : 0 2 :050(417) [0691] This I say in **order** that the expression may be
L C : 0 2 :055(418) [0693] Christian church is so **ordered** that we may daily obtain
L C : 0 3 :018(423) [0703] you, he would not have **ordered** you to pray and backed
L C : 0 3 :027(424) [0705] unaware of them, but in **order** that you may kindle your
L C : 0 3 :030(424) [0707] to arm themselves in **order** to stand against the devil.
L C : 0 3 :033(424) [0707] said as an admonition in **order** that men may learn above
L C : 0 3 :052(427) [0711] This we ask, both in **order** that we who have accepted it
L C : 0 3 :052(427) [0711] grow daily in it and in **order** that it may gain recognition
L C : 0 3 :063(428) [0715] and feeding the flames, in **order** to hinder us, put us to
L C : 0 3 :072(430) [0719] that is necessary in **order** to have and enjoy daily bread
L C : 0 3 :080(431) [0721] and overthrow spiritual **order**, so that he may deceive
L C : 0 3 :113(435) [0729] as the sum of all evil in **order** that the entire substance of
L C : 0 3 :119(436) [0731] that may ever beset us in **order** that we may never have an
L C : 0 4 :002(436) [0733] In **order** that it may be readily understood, we shall treat
L C : 0 4 :015(438) [0735] when our new spirits, in **order** to slander Baptism, ignore
L C : 0 4 :024(439) [0737] No one is baptized in **order** to become a prince, but as the
L C : 0 5 :006(447) [0755] as God has created and **ordered** them, regardless of how
L C : 0 5 :022(449) [0757] bids me eat and drink in **order** that the sacrament may be
L C : 0 5 :043(451) [0763] However, in **order** that the common people and the
L C : 0 5 :055(453) [0765] inherited from the old **order** under the pope when we
L C : 0 5 :073(455) [0771] are rid of your burden in **order** to come to the sacrament
E P : 0 1 :020(468) [0783] "essential sin," not in **order** to identify without any
E P : 0 4 :005(476) [0797] In **order** to explain this controversy from the ground up
E P : 0 7 :003(482) [0809] In **order** to explicate this controversy, it is necessary to
E P : 0 7 :042(486) [0817] our many protests, in **order** to make our teaching
E P : 1 0 :001(492) [0829] in the interest of good **order** and the general welfare.
E P : 1 0 :003(493) [0829] for the sake of good **order** and the general welfare, are in
E P : 1 1 :011(495) [0835] of God and observes the **order** which St. Paul follows in
E P : 1 2 :026(500) [0843] public expulsion and the **orderly** process of
S D : P R :003(501) [0847] to the Word of God, **ordered** the preparation of a
S D : P R :014(506) [0855] In **order** to preserve the pure doctrine and to maintain a
S D : P R :015(507) [0857] error must be refuted in **order** to preserve the truth).
S D : 0 1 :004(509) [0861] Hence, in **order** to explain this controversy in a Christian
S D : 0 1 :006(509) [0861] or "person-sin" in **order** to indicate that even though a
S D : 0 1 :039(515) [0871] corrupted by sin, in **order** that through his beloved Son
S D : 0 1 :042(515) [0871] For that reason and in **order** to distinguish God's creature
S D : 0 1 :051(517) [0875] In **order** to avoid all contentions about words, it is
S D : 0 2 :006(521) [0883] In **order** to settle this controversy in a Christian way
S D : 0 2 :015(523) [0887] God, but were written in **order** that above all things we
S D : 0 3 :007(540) [0917] terms with such zeal in **order** to indicate how very
S D : 0 3 :030(544) [0925] this account but also in **order** to afford saddened
S D : 0 3 :035(545) [0927] before God, in **order** to preserve the glory due to Christ,
S D : 0 3 :035(545) [0927] imperfect and impure, in **order** to supply tempted
S D : 0 3 :040(546) [0929] this way, too, the proper **order** between faith and good
S D : 0 3 :041(546) [0931] but this merely shows the **order** in which one thing
S D : 0 4 :002(551) [0939] be diminished and in **order** to retain for believers the firm
S D : 0 4 :004(551) [0939] refer to the immutable **order** which obligates and binds
S D : 0 4 :005(552) [0939] because of the divine **order** referred to above, new
S D : 0 4 :006(552) [0939] In **order** to explain this disagreement in a Christian way

Continued ▶

SD : 04 :016(554) [0943] only as referring to the **order** of God's immutable will,
SD : 04 :034(556) [0949] On the contrary, in **order** that the promise that we shall
SD : 04 :037(557) [0949] on good works in **order** to merit the grace of God and to
SD : 05 :004(558) [0953] and in the New Testament he **ordered** to be observed.
SD : 05 :009(559) [0955] And in **order** that contrition or the terrors of the law may
SD : 05 :015(561) [0957] by side, but in proper **order** and with the correct
SD : 05 :016(561) [0957] But in **order** that everyone may see that we are concealing
SD : 05 :017(561) [0957] words, and deeds in **order** to be pleasing and acceptable
SD : 05 :020(561) [0959] a man should believe in **order** to obtain the forgiveness of
SD : 05 :027(563) [0961] For this reason and in **order** that both doctrines, law and
SD : 06 :004(564) [0963] In **order** to explain and definitively to settle this
SD : 06 :006(565) [0965] courses according to the **order** which God instituted for
SD : 06 :015(566) [0967] In **order** as far as possible to avoid all
SD : 06 :016(566) [0967] Such people are saints after the **order** of Cain.
SD : 07 :037(576) [0985] here on earth in the **ordered** action of the sacrament,
SD : 07 :088(585) [1003] internal use of faith in **order** to deny the true, essential
SD : 08 :005(592) [1017] In **order** to explain this controversy in a Christian way
SD : 08 :063(603) [1037] in this direction in **order** to cast suspicion on the pure
SD : 08 :063(603) [1037] of a "real exchange" in **order** to indicate thereby that such
SD : 10 :001(610) [1053] for the sake of good **order** and decorum or else to
SD : 10 :007(611) [1055] which serve neither good **order**, Christian discipline, nor
SD : 10 :009(612) [1055] and offense but in an **orderly** and appropriate way, as at
SD : 10 :009(612) [1055] and salutary for good **order**, Christian discipline,
SD : 10 :010(612) [1055] on us by adversaries in **order** to undermine the genuine
SD : 11 :001(616) [1063] Therefore, in **order** by God's grace to prevent, as far as
SD : 11 :003(616) [1063] the contrary, precisely in **order** to avert such misuse and
SD : 11 :009(617) [1065] election or divine **ordering** to eternal life only in the
SD : 11 :012(618) [1067] us to despair but in **order** that "by steadfastness, by the
SD : 11 :013(618) [1067] the predestination and **ordering** of the children of God to
SD : 11 :033(621) [1073] it this way: "Follow the **order** in the Epistle to the
SD : 11 :069(627) [1085] In **order** that we may come to Christ, the Holy Spirit
SD : 11 :072(627) [1085] And in **order** that we may see it through and abide and
SD : 11 :079(629) [1089] fitted for damnation in **order** to make known the riches
SD : 11 :088(631) [1093] elected us in Christ — "in **order** that God's purpose of
SD : 12 :034(635) [1101] public expulsion or **orderly** process of excommunication

Ordinance (51), Ordinances (45)
PR : PR :025(014) [0023] to the content of the **ordinances** of the Holy Empire and
AG : 15 :003(036) [0049] it is taught that all **ordinances** and traditions instituted by
AG : 26 :044(070) [0075] disagreement in human **ordinances** is not in conflict with
AG : 28 :036(086) [0089] when we presume to earn grace by such **ordinances**.
AG : 28 :037(086) [0089] of this notion human **ordinances** have multiplied beyond
AG : 28 :039(087) [0089] who institute human **ordinances** also act contrary to
AG : 28 :047(088) [0089] those who urge human **ordinances** on people, "Let them
AG : 28 :053(090) [0091] and other similar church **ordinances** and ceremonies?
AG : 28 :055(090) [0091] assembly to keep such **ordinances** for the sake of love and
AG : 28 :067(093) [0093] among those who observe such **ordinance** most jealously.
AL : 16 :001(037) [0051] teach that lawful civil **ordinances** are good works of God
AL : 16 :005(038) [0051] their preservation as **ordinance** of God and the exercise
AL : 16 :005(038) [0051] of God and the exercise of love in these **ordinance**.
AL : 00 :004(048) [0059] ceremonies and all old **ordinances** are abolished in our
AL : 28 :013(083) [0085] concerning any civil **ordinances** or contracts, nor
AL : 28 :050(089) [0091] Inasmuch as **ordinances** which have been instituted as
AL : 28 :055(090) [0091] comply with such **ordinances** for the sake of love and
AL : 28 :073(093) [0093] reasons for these **ordinances** when they were introduced,
AP : 04 :307(154) [0207] God's imputation and **ordinances**, as Paul says
AP : 07 :014(170) [0231] nations by certain outward **ordinances** and promises.
AP : 07 :033(175) [0239] the useful and ancient **ordinances**, especially when they
AP : 07 :042(176) [0243] did not want to impose an **ordinance** on the churches.
AP : 07 :046(177) [0243] have changed the **ordinance** of Christ in the use of the
AP : 07 :046(177) [0243] which certainly was previously a universal **ordinance**.
AP : 07 :046(177) [0243] But if universal **ordinances** are necessary, why do they
AP : 07 :046(177) [0243] why do they change the **ordinance** of Christ's Supper,
AP : 07 :050(178) [0245] The right to hold property is a civil **ordinance**.
AP : 07 :050(178) [0245] Christians to use civil **ordinances** just as it is legitimate
AP : 07 :050(178) [0245] of the stars are truly **ordinances** of God and are preserved
AP : 07 :050(178) [0245] governments are **ordinances** of God and are preserved
AP : 15 :014(217) [0319] nor observe their **ordinances**, nor defile yourselves with
AP : 15 :014(217) [0319] in my statutes, and be careful to observe my **ordinances**."
AP : 15 :039(220) [0325] us of abolishing good **ordinances** and church discipline.
AP : 15 :043(221) [0327] rulers and for all civil **ordinances**, the distinction between
AP : 16 :001(222) [0329] short, that lawful civil **ordinances** are God's good
AP : 16 :001(222) [0329] creatures and divine **ordinances** in which a Christian may
AP : 16 :002(222) [0331] the legitimate political **ordinances** of the nation in which
AP : 16 :005(223) [0331] to obey them as divine **ordinances** not only from fear of
AP : 16 :006(223) [0331] the change of winter and summer as **ordinances** of God.
AP : 16 :009(224) [0333] not contempt of civil **ordinances** but attitudes of the
AP : 16 :012(224) [0333] may legitimately make use of civil **ordinances** and laws.
AP : 16 :013(224) [0333] of magistrates and the value of civil **ordinances** generally.
AP : 22 :002(236) [0357] Why is Christ's **ordinance** changed, especially since he
AP : 22 :005(236) [0359] decide what he should believe about a divine **ordinance**.
AP : 22 :014(238) [0361] which are not cogent enough to change Christ's **ordinance**.
AP : 22 :015(238) [0361] to call Christ's **ordinances** matters of indifference.
AP : 23 :007(240) [0365] love of one sex for the other is truly a divine **ordinance**.
AP : 23 :007(240) [0365] Since this **ordinance** of God cannot be suspended without
AP : 23 :008(240) [0367] Because of this **ordinance**, the earth did not begin to
AP : 23 :009(240) [0367] this creation or divine **ordinance** in man is a natural
AP : 23 :009(241) [0367] there must remain that **ordinance** which God has built
AP : 23 :012(241) [0367] right, because it is an **ordinance** divinely stamped on
AP : 23 :012(241) [0367] sex for the other is an **ordinance** of God, and therefore it
AP : 23 :019(242) [0369] does not want us to despise his **ordinances**, his creatures.
AP : 23 :053(246) [0377] who despise his gift and **ordinance** and forbid marriage.
AP : 27 :020(272) [0427] the same level with an **ordinance** of Christ which has both
AP : 27 :030(274) [0431] were not good and **ordinances** by which they could not
AP : 27 :046(277) [0435] of property are civil **ordinances**, approved by the Word
AP : 28 :002(281) [0443] not criticize political **ordinances** nor the gifts and
AP : 28 :016(283) [0447] the use of such **ordinances** ought to be left free, only that
LC : 01 :026(368) [0587] it all from God through his command and **ordinance**.
LC : 01 :082(376) [0603] matter, like the other **ordinances** of the Old Testament
LC : 04 :006(437) [0733] these words contain God's commandment and **ordinance**.
LC : 04 :015(438) [0735] God's Word and **ordinance**, consider nothing but the
LC : 04 :016(438) [0735] tamper thus with God's **ordinance** and tear from it the
LC : 04 :016(438) [0735] which he does not wish his **ordinance** to be separated?
LC : 04 :022(439) [0737] according to God's **ordinance**, Baptism is a sacrament,
LC : 04 :029(440) [0739] with God's Word and **ordinance** and the joining of his
LC : 04 :029(440) [0739] Word in this external **ordinance** and offered it to us so
LC : 04 :030(440) [0739] effects in us he does through such external **ordinances**.
LC : 04 :031(440) [0739] that is, the water comprehended in God's **ordinance**?
LC : 04 :036(441) [0741] as God's command and **ordinance**, so that, baptized in
LC : 04 :038(441) [0741] that it is God's **ordinance** and is to be held in all honor.
LC : 04 :038(441) [0741] to accept and observe Baptism as an **ordinance** of God.
LC : 04 :055(443) [0747] that God's Word and **ordinance** should be wrong and
LC : 04 :060(444) [0747] For God's **ordinance** and Word cannot be changed or
LC : 04 :061(444) [0749] conclude that these **ordinances** are in themselves invalid.
LC : 04 :062(444) [0749] pervert and nullify all God's work and **ordinances**.
LC : 04 :082(446) [0751] as we said, it is God's **ordinance** and not a work of ours.
LC : 05 :004(447) [0753] God's Word and **ordinance** or command, which is the
LC : 05 :006(447) [0755] that he would permit them to affect his **ordinance**?
LC : 05 :011(448) [0755] is not the word and **ordinance** of a prince or emperor,
LC : 06 :014(458) [0000] Thus by divine **ordinance** Christ himself has entrusted
SD : PR :001(501) [0847] human doctrines and **ordinances** under the papacy) was
SD : 04 :007(552) [0939] That it is God's will, **ordinance**, and command that
SD : 04 :014(553) [0943] to do because of God's **ordinance**, commandment, and
SD : 07 :032(574) [0983] but on the Word and **ordinance** of God — unless they
SD : 07 :032(574) [0983] God's Word and **ordinance** and misinterpret them, as the
SD : 07 :032(575) [0983] Word and instituted **ordinance** of God but have perverted
SD : 07 :074(583) [0999] Word, institution, and **ordinance** of our Lord Jesus
SD : 07 :077(583) [0999] but the command and **ordinance** of Christ that, from the
SD : 11 :013(619) [1067] counsel, purpose, and **ordinance** of God in Christ Jesus,
SD : 11 :014(619) [1069] counsel, will, and **ordinance** concerning our redemption,
SD : 11 :023(619) [1069] counsel, purpose, and **ordinance** God has not only
SD : 11 :024(620) [1069] election, and **ordinance** of God to eternal salvation.
SD : 11 :076(629) [1089] to his common **ordinance** he does this through the

Ordinarily (1), Ordinary (33)
AL : 00 :005(048) [0059] that certain abuses were connected with **ordinary** rites.
AP : 22 :007(237) [0359] was given; for by the **ordinary** usage of language, naming
AP : 24 :081(264) [0411] It is an old word, **ordinarily** used in public law.
S2 : 03 :002(298) [0471] to be superior to the **ordinary** Christian life and to the
S3 : 14 :001(316) [0501] better than that of the **ordinary** Christian and proposes
SC : 00 :000(337) [0531] of Dr. Martin Luther for **Ordinary** Pastors and Preachers
SC : 05 :029(351) [0555] is intended simply as an **ordinary** form of confession for
LC : SP :022(364) [0579] It is enough for an **ordinary** person to know this much
LC : 01 :024(367) [0587] should be said to **ordinary** people so that they may mark
LC : 01 :055(372) [0595] yourself, whether in **ordinary** worldly affairs or in
LC : 01 :083(376) [0603] To offer **ordinary** people a Christian interpretation of
LC : 01 :194(391) [0635] to our friends is but an **ordinary** heathen virtue, as Christ
LC : 01 :197(392) [0637] For in this teaching the **ordinary** Christian life would be
LC : 01 :303(405) [0667] same thing happens in **ordinary** business affairs, where
LC : 01 :315(408) [0671] is a simple life for the **ordinary** man, whereas theirs is for
LC : 02 :024(413) [0683] It is all that **ordinary** people need to learn at first, both
LC : 04 :026(439) [0739] that it is not simple, **ordinary** water, for ordinary water
LC : 04 :026(439) [0739] ordinary water, for **ordinary** water could not have such
LC : 04 :061(444) [0747] or in the pot, and magistrates only as **ordinary** people.
LC : 05 :014(448) [0755] Word, you have nothing but **ordinary** bread and wine.
LC : 05 :038(451) [0761] been said now for all **ordinary** instruction on the
EP : 08 :012(488) [0821] bore not only a plain, **ordinary**, mere man but the
EP : 08 :013(488) [0821] that it was not a plain, **ordinary**, mere man who for us
EP : 11 :012(496) [0835] hearts, and thus bar the **ordinary** way for the Holy Spirit,
SD : PR :008(505) [0853] matters also concern **ordinary** people and laymen who for
SD : PR :008(505) [0853] basis of God's Word for **ordinary** laymen in a most
SD : 02 :090(539) [0915] of his holy Word as his **ordinary** means and instrument.
SD : 07 :023(573) [0979] you then have nothing but **ordinary** bread and wine.
SD : 07 :039(576) [0985] "We receive this not as **ordinary** bread or an ordinary
SD : 07 :039(576) [0985] as ordinary bread or an **ordinary** beverage, but we believe
SD : 07 :077(583) [0999] distribute and receive **ordinary** bread and wine but his
SD : 08 :024(595) [1023] did not conceive a mere, **ordinary** human being, but a
SD : 08 :040(598) [1029] in his passion and death than any other **ordinary** saint.
SD : 11 :076(628) [1087] and sacraments as the **ordinary** means or instruments to

Ordination (19), Ordinations (1)
AP : 13 :011(212) [0311] If **ordination** is interpreted in relation to the ministry of
AP : 13 :011(212) [0311] we have no obligation to calling **ordination** a sacrament.
AP : 13 :012(212) [0311] If **ordination** is interpreted this way, we shall not object
AP : 14 :001(214) [0315] we employ canonical **ordination**, they accept Article
S3 : 10 :000(314) [0497] X. **Ordination** and Vocation
TR : 00 :005(320) [0505] world should seek **ordination** and confirmation from him
TR : 00 :010(321) [0507] other apostles, and that **ordination** or confirmation was
TR : 00 :012(322) [0507] forever have sought **ordination** and confirmation from
TR : 00 :014(322) [0507] proper celebration of **ordinations** the neighboring bishops
TR : 00 :014(322) [0509] done among you in the **ordination** of our colleague
TR : 00 :015(322) [0509] therefore, neither **ordination** nor confirmation were
TR : 00 :016(322) [0509] in remote places to seek **ordination** from him alone.
TR : 00 :016(322) [0509] which do not seek **ordination** or confirmation from the
TR : 00 :062(331) [0523] For, apart from **ordination**, what does a bishop do that a
TR : 00 :064(331) [0523] pastors, and this was **ordination**, for it was decided that
TR : 00 :065(331) [0523] it is manifest that **ordination** administered by a pastor in
TR : 00 :066(331) [0523] unwilling to administer **ordination**, the churches retain
TR : 00 :070(332) [0525] on of hands; nor was **ordination** anything more than such
TR : 00 :072(332) [0525] or refuse to administer **ordination**, the churches are by
TR : 00 :073(332) [0525] We have spoken of **ordination**, which is the one thing (as

Organization (2), Organize (1)
AP : 07 :013(170) [0231] as only an outward **organization** embracing both the good
AP : 21 :043(235) [0357] overthrow the whole **organization** of the church, which
SD : 11 :024(620) [1071] the Scriptures and **organize** our thinking about this

Orient (1)
SD : 11 :024(620) [1071] we can by the grace of God easily **orient** ourselves in it.

Origen (2)
AP : 16 :006(223) [0331] were very disturbing to **Origen**, Nazianzus, and others,
TR : 00 :027(324) [0511] the holy Fathers (such as **Origen**, Ambrose, Cyprian,

Origin (9), Original (145), Originally (17), Originated (1), Originator (1), Origins (1)
PR : PR :009(006) [0011] was the true and **originally** submitted Augsburg

Continued ▶

Outbreak (2)
SD : PR :002(503) [0851] Confession before the **outbreak** of the several
SD : 0 7 :093(586) [1005] consistently from the **outbreak** of this controversy, are

Outcome (4)
AG : PR :021(026) [0043] If the **outcome** should be such as we mentioned above, we
AP : 0 4 :354(161) [0217] says (I Pet. 1:9), "As the **outcome** of your faith you obtain
AP : 2 1 :043(235) [0357] the church, and good men can easily gauge its **outcome**.
SD : 0 4 :034(557) [0949] and again, "As the **outcome** of your faith, you obtain the

Outcry (1)
AP : 2 3 :037(244) [0373] But no such **outcry** will make us surrender the truth of

Outgrown (1)
LC : PR :008(359) [0569] ABC's, which they think they have **outgrown** long ago.

Outline (1)
LC : 0 3 :076(431) [0719] Let us **outline** very briefly how comprehensively this

Outpouring (2)
SD : 0 8 :062(603) [1037] an essential or natural **outpouring** of the properties of the
SD : 0 8 :071(605) [1041] teach, and confess an **outpouring** of the majesty of God

Outrage (3)
AG : 2 8 :003(081) [0085] Such **outrage** has long since been condemned by learned
LC : 0 1 :244(398) [0649] house and home and **outrage** and kill wife and children.
SD : 1 1 :083(630) [1091] (Luke 11:24, 25), and **outrage** the Holy Spirit

Outright (1)
AP : 0 4 :019(110) [0125] to avoid the impression that they are **outright** Pelagians.

Outset (6)
AP : 0 2 :001(100) [0105] Here at the very **outset** His Imperial Majesty will see that
AP : 2 1 :041(235) [0355] with Luther from the **outset** did so because they saw that
TR : 0 0 :005(320) [0503] we must at the **outset** define what the papists mean when
LC : 0 3 :052(427) [0711] We pray here at the **outset** that all this may be realized in
EP : 0 7 :001(481) [0807] the latter at the very **outset** when the Augsburg
SD : 1 1 :004(616) [1063] At the very **outset** we must carefully note the difference

Outside (25)
PR : PR :021(011) [0019] human nature of Christ **outside** the personal union, or in
PR : PR :022(011) [0019] entire churches inside or **outside** the Holy Empire of the
AG : 2 7 :054(079) [0083] not sinful to take revenge **outside** of the exercise of their
AP : 0 4 :028(111) [0129] commandments of God **outside** a state of grace do not
AP : 0 4 :297(153) [0205] before the law and **outside** the law from the very
AP : 0 9 :002(178) [0245] apply to those who are **outside** of Christ's church, where
AP : 1 6 :013(224) [0333] here so that those **outside** our group may understand that
AP : 1 8 :006(225) [0335] a man does not sin if, **outside** the state of grace, he does
LC : 0 1 :211(393) [0641] so that they can maintain chastity **outside** of marriage.
LC : 0 1 :212(393) [0641] possible to remain chaste **outside** of marriage; for flesh
LC : 0 1 :263(400) [0655] court and their lying and malicious talk **outside** of court.
LC : 0 2 :045(416) [0689] Christian church, and **outside** it no one can come to the
LC : 0 2 :056(418) [0693] But **outside** the Christian church (that is, where the
LC : 0 2 :066(419) [0697] All who are **outside** the Christian church, whether
LC : 0 4 :069(445) [0749] Those who are **outside** of Christ can only grow worse day
EP : 0 1 :012(467) [0783] on account of which man **outside** of Christ is a child of
SD : 0 2 :029(527) [0893] declares: "People **outside** of Christ and without faith and
SD : 0 2 :043(529) [0897] **Outside** of Christ death and sin are our masters and the
SD : 0 6 :002(564) [0963] course without any **outside** impulse, they, too, through
SD : 0 7 :066(581) [0997] faith, which occurs **outside** of the sacrament too, but also
SD : 0 8 :070(605) [1041] to him, he left nothing **outside** his control" (Heb. 2:7, 8),
SD : 0 8 :076(606) [1043] to its nature and essence **outside** of this union, cannot
SD : 1 1 :039(623) [1077] and salvation **outside** of Christ (Rom. 9:31).
SD : 1 1 :064(626) [1083] of the Lord?" — that is, **outside** and beyond what he has
SD : 1 1 :065(627) [1083] in Christ, and not **outside** of or apart from Christ.

Outstanding (1)
AP : 2 1 :041(235) [0355] were many learned and **outstanding** men who deplored

Outward (67), Outwardly (7)
AG : 1 3 :001(035) [0049] might be identified **outwardly** as Christians, but that they
AG : 1 6 :004(038) [0051] Gospel does not teach an **outward** and temporal but an
AG : 1 8 :001(039) [0051] enables him to live an **outwardly** honorable life and to
AG : 1 8 :004(040) [0051] him), for it is only in the **outward** acts of this life that
AG : 2 6 :028(068) [0073] with additional **outward** ceremonies, whether of Moses or
AG : 2 6 :041(070) [0075] are instructed that such **outward** forms of service do not
AG : 2 6 :042(070) [0075] liberty with respect to **outward** ceremonies, for in the
AL : 1 3 :003(036) [0049] justify by the **outward** act and who do not teach that
AL : 1 8 :009(040) [0053] measure to perform the **outward** works (for it can keep
AL : 2 4 :029(059) [0067] by a performance of the **outward** act, justification comes
AP : 0 4 :033(111) [0129] the flesh sins even when it performs **outward** civil works.
AP : 0 4 :130(125) [0157] civil works, that is, the **outward** works of the law,
AP : 0 4 :131(125) [0159] or at best they require only **outward** acts of worship.
AP : 0 4 :134(125) [0159] is, hypocrites think that **outward** and civil works satisfy
AP : 0 4 :136(126) [0159] inward spiritual impulses and the **outward** good works.
AP : 0 4 :154(128) [0165] he did show him the **outward** courtesies due a guest and a
AP : 0 4 :193(133) [0175] be to disparage the **outward** administration of Christ's
AP : 0 4 :207(135) [0177] surely commanded as **outward** observances in the state,
AP : 0 4 :256(144) [0193] can at most do certain **outward** works, this universal
AP : 0 4 :282(149) [0201] adds concerning the **outward** cleanness, "Give alms from
AP : 0 4 :283(150) [0201] He means that **outward** cleanness is to be sought in
AP : 0 4 :284(150) [0201] are clean and then the **outward** giving of alms is added
AP : 0 4 :284(150) [0201] men are completely clean, **outwardly** as well as inwardly.
AP : 0 4 :288(151) [0203] and is preoccupied with **outward** works, it can be
AP : 0 4 :289(151) [0203] the law of God both **outwardly** and inwardly, and that
AP : 0 4 :371(164) [0221] taken to mean not only **outward** works but also the faith
AP : 0 4 :373(164) [0221] understand not merely **outward** works but the entire
AP : 0 4 :394(167) [0225] who taught only this **outward** righteousness to the
AP : 0 7 :003(168) [0227] and hypocrites from the **outward** fellowship of the church
AP : 0 7 :003(169) [0227] church according to the **outward** associations of the
AP : 0 7 :005(169) [0227] merely an association of **outward** ties and rites like other
AP : 0 7 :005(169) [0227] this association has **outward** marks, the pure teaching of
AP : 0 7 :007(169) [0229] He also added the **outward** marks, the Word and the
AP : 0 7 :010(170) [0229] we take it to mean an **outward** government of certain
AP : 0 7 :012(170) [0231] the true church as far as **outward** ceremonies are
AP : 0 7 :013(170) [0231] the church as only an **outward** organization embracing
AP : 0 7 :013(170) [0231] think of it as only the **outward** observance of certain
AP : 0 7 :014(170) [0231] other nations by certain **outward** ordinances and
AP : 0 7 :016(171) [0231] the Pharisees had an **outward** affiliation with the church
AP : 0 7 :019(171) [0233] is talking about the **outward** appearance of the church
AP : 0 7 :019(171) [0233] men participate in the **outward** marks, still they are not
AP : 0 7 :023(172) [0235] It is the supreme **outward** monarchy of the whole world
AP : 0 7 :028(173) [0237] an association in the **outward** marks, are members of the
AP : 0 7 :028(173) [0237] to this association in the **outward** marks, and therefore
AP : 0 7 :032(174) [0239] of devotion rather than **outward** rules of discipline,
AP : 1 2 :106(197) [0283] of conscience and not **outward** conduct, and "flocks"
AP : 1 2 :106(197) [0283] surely interpret "condition" as meaning **outward** conduct.
AP : 1 2 :131(202) [0291] which does not produce **outwardly** the punishing of the
AP : 1 2 :145(205) [0297] because they think that **outward** and civil works satisfy
AP : 1 2 :148(205) [0299] Nor do we exclude here **outward** mortification of the
AP : 1 5 :024(218) [0321] them, they copy their **outward** behavior without copying
AP : 1 6 :002(222) [0331] time it lets us make **outward** use of the legitimate
AP : 1 6 :010(224) [0333] impressed men with this **outward** hypocrisy and blinded
AP : 1 8 :004(225) [0335] God and express its worship of him in **outward** works.
AP : 1 8 :007(225) [0337] and ability to do the **outward** works of the law, we do
AP : 1 8 :009(226) [0337] This safeguards **outward** discipline, because all men
AP : 2 3 :064(248) [0381] have also said that the **outward** ceremonies and purity
AP : 2 4 :050(259) [0401] And as for **outward** appearances, our church attendance
AP : 2 7 :058(279) [0439] of sins but to be an **outward** exercise like the other
LC : 0 1 :050(371) [0593] commandment leads us **outward** and directs the lips and
LC : 0 1 :056(372) [0595] name as the greatest sin that can be committed **outwardly**.
LC : 0 1 :080(375) [0603] As far as **outward** observance is concerned, the
LC : 0 1 :082(376) [0603] according to its literal, **outward** sense, this
LC : 0 1 :094(378) [0607] persons, and the entire **outward** order of worship are
LC : 0 3 :098(433) [0725] which are appointed as **outward** signs, this sign also can
EP : 0 1 :008(467) [0781] in man's body or soul, in his inward our **outward** powers.
EP : 0 7 :038(486) [0817] Christ, but also depends on people's **outward** preparation.
SD : 0 2 :019(524) [0889] divine Word, or that in **outward** or external secular
SD : 0 2 :026(526) [0891] and free will are able to lead an **outwardly** virtuous life.
SD : 0 4 :008(552) [0941] to the maintenance of **outward** discipline and which
SD : 1 1 :026(620) [1071] of the law, or on the basis of some **outward** appearance.
SD : 1 1 :039(623) [1077] make only an **outward** pretense (Matt. 7:15;
SD : 1 1 :050(624) [1079] we be offended by the **outward** prestige of the false
SD : 1 1 :095(632) [1095] of temporal peace, tranquility, and **outward** harmony.

Oven (2)
LC : 0 3 :072(430) [0719] to include not only the **oven** or the flour bin, but also the
LC : 0 3 :072(430) [0719] take a loaf of bread from the **oven** to set on the table.

Overburdening (1)
LC : 0 2 :070(420) [0697] for the common people without **overburdening** them.

Overcharge (1), Overcharging (1)
SC : 0 5 :023(350) [0555] speaking evil of him, **overcharging** him, giving him
LC : 0 1 :226(395) [0645] know enough ways to **overcharge** people and yet are

Overcome (13), Overcomes (5), Overcoming (1)
AP : 0 4 :214(136) [0179] Our works cannot **overcome** the terrors of sin, but faith
AP : 0 4 :214(136) [0179] the terrors of sin, but faith alone can **overcome** them.
AP : 0 4 :250(143) [0191] us alive and enables us to **overcome** death and the devil.
AP : 0 4 :250(143) [0191] faith is efficacious and **overcomes** death (Col. 2:12), "in
AP : 0 4 :278(149) [0199] forgiveness of sins and **overcomes** death as it becomes
AP : 0 4 :290(151) [0203] by faith in Christ we **overcome** the terrors of sin and
AP : 0 4 :300(153) [0205] as though we could **overcome** the wrath of God with our
AP : 0 4 :314(155) [0207] love but with faith we **overcome** the terrors of sin and
AP : 1 2 :060(190) [0269] follows on our terrors, **overcoming** them and restoring
AP : 1 2 :146(205) [0297] Faith in Christ **overcomes** death, just as it overcomes the
AP : 1 2 :146(205) [0297] overcomes death, just as it **overcomes** the wrath of God.
AP : 1 2 :153(206) [0299] now, once his faith has **overcome** its terrors, there is no
AP : 1 5 :047(221) [0327] on our flesh, lest we be **overcome** by satiety and become
AP : 2 1 :027(232) [0349] souls in death, does she **overcome** death, does she give
AP : 2 4 :089(266) [0415] of purgatory cannot be **overcome** by the application of
S 3 : 0 3 :014(305) [0483] by their own works to **overcome** and blot out their sins
LC : 0 3 :067(429) [0717] may patiently bear and **overcome**, so that our poor flesh
LC : 0 3 :105(434) [0727] it is impossible to **overcome** even the least temptation.
LC : 0 4 :083(446) [0751] makes God our own, **overcomes** and takes away sin and

Overflows (2)
LC : 0 1 :025(368) [0587] eternal fountain which **overflows** with sheer goodness and
LC : 0 3 :056(427) [0713] more it gushes forth and **overflows**, the more it continues

Overlook (3), Overlooked (1)
AP : 0 4 :131(125) [0159] They utterly **overlook** that eternal law, far beyond the
AP : 0 4 :243(141) [0189] pastors and churches **overlook** and forgive many things.
TR : 0 0 :048(328) [0519] Accordingly they cannot be **overlooked**.
LC : 0 1 :285(403) [0663] sins and infirmities, to **overlook** them, and to cloak and

Overlord (1), Overlords (1)
S 2 : 0 4 :001(298) [0471] under him as under an **overlord** but chose to stand beside
LC : 0 1 :142(384) [0621] Again, their princes and **overlords** were called *patres*

Overly (2)
AP : 0 4 :375(164) [0223] We are not trying to be **overly** subtle here in
AP : 0 4 :378(165) [0223] We are not trying to be **overly** subtle when we condemn

Overseer (1)
TR : 0 0 :016(322) [0509] for one bishop to be the **overseer** of all the churches in

Overtake (1), Overtaken (1)
LC : PR :005(359) [0567] plague of security and boredom has **overtaken** us.
LC : 0 1 :240(397) [0649] The same fate will **overtake** those who turn the free

Overthrow (15), Overthrown (3), Overthrows (1)
AG : 1 6 :005(038) [0051] The Gospel does not **overthrow** civil authority, the state,
AP : 0 2 :040(105) [0115] No quibbling can **overthrow** these proofs.
AP : 0 4 :087(120) [0147] that Paul says about the promise would be **overthrown**.

Continued ▶

A P : 0 4 :123(124) [0157] says that faith does not **overthrow** but upholds the law.
A P : 0 4 :132(125) [0159] says that faith does not **overthrow** but upholds the law
A P : 0 4 :260(145) [0193] and no gates of hell can **overthrow** it (Matt. 16:18), that
A P : 0 7 :020(172) [0233] But because they do not **overthrow** the foundation, these
A P : 0 7 :021(172) [0233] the foundation but that this did not **overthrow** their faith.
A P : 0 7 :021(172) [0233] on the other hand, does **overthrow** faith, as when they
A P : 2 0 :015(229) [0343] We do not **overthrow** the law, Paul says (Rom. 3:31), but
A P : 2 1 :043(235) [0357] godless teachings and **overthrow** the whole organization
S 2 : 0 4 :007(299) [0473] would have to suffer the **overthrow** and destruction of his
S 3 : 0 3 :039(309) [0489] With this repentance we **overthrow** the pope and
L C : 0 1 :035(369) [0589] just so in our day he **overthrows** all false worship so that
L C : 0 3 :054(427) [0713] kingdom may be **overthrown** and he may have no right
L C : 0 3 :080(431) [0721] to obstruct and **overthrow** spiritual order, so that he may
L C : 0 4 :051(443) [0745] one can take from us or **overthrow** this article, "I believe
S D : 0 7 :106(588) [1009] other hand they will **overthrow** and refute all the
S D : 1 1 :046(624) [1079] which cannot fail or be **overthrown**, and put it for

Overturn (1)
S D : 1 1 :039(622) [1075] This would also **overturn** and destroy for us the

Overwhelmed (5), Overwhelming (1)
A P : 0 4 :023(110) [0127] though it is often **overwhelmed** by its natural weakness
A P : 0 4 :128(125) [0157] terrible wrath he is **overwhelming** us with temporal and
A P : 1 2 :003(183) [0253] and canonists had **overwhelmed** the doctrine of
S C : P R :016(340) [0535] they will be so **overwhelmed** that they will hardly
L C : 0 1 :152(386) [0625] we shall be simply **overwhelmed** with our blessings and
L C : 0 3 :106(434) [0729] we may not fall into them and be **overwhelmed** by them.

Oves (2)
A G : 2 8 :027(085) [0087] II, Question 7, in the chapters "Sacerdotes" and "**Oves.**"
A L : 2 8 :027(085) [0087] (II, question 7, in chapters "Sacerdotes" and "**Oves**").

Owe (8), Owed (4), Owes (4), Owing (1)
A P : 0 4 :334(159) [0215] as a payment which he **owes** to us for our good works.
A P : 0 4 :362(162) [0219] it is something that is **owed** — not because of our merits
A P : 0 4 :363(162) [0219] The crown is **owed** to the justified because of the
A P : 0 4 :366(163) [0221] a reward is offered and **owed**, not gratis but for our
T R : 0 0 :038(326) [0515] would still not be **owing** to those pontiffs who defend
S C : 0 9 :003(354) [0561] Duties Christians **Owe** Their Teachers and Pastors
S C : 0 9 :005(355) [0561] Duties Subjects **Owe** to Governing Authorities
L C : 0 1 :143(385) [0621] What a child **owes** to father and mother, the entire
L C : 0 1 :143(385) [0621] and mother, the entire household **owes** them likewise.
L C : 0 1 :161(387) [0627] the name of Christians **owe** it to God to show "double
L C : 0 1 :166(387) [0627] toward those to whom we **owe** honor that we lift our
L C : 0 1 :168(388) [0629] should consider that they **owe** obedience to God, and
L C : 0 2 :024(413) [0683] receive from God and about what we **owe** him in return.
L C : 0 2 :031(414) [0687] for me and pay what I **owed**, not with silver and gold but
L C : 0 3 :075(430) [0719] render them the duties we **owe** and do all we can for
E P : 0 1 :011(467) [0781] is only a debt which we **owe** because of someone else's
S D : 1 1 :060(626) [1083] and damnation, God **owes** us neither his Word, nor his

Owner (1), Ownership (2)
A P : 1 6 :011(224) [0333] recognizes the right of **ownership** and commands
A P : 2 7 :047(277) [0437] that renouncing the **ownership** of everything for God is
L C : 0 1 :302(405) [0667] is taken away from the **owner** and legally awarded to him

Ox (2)
S C : 0 1 :019(344) [0543] *or his maidservant, or his* **ox**, *or his ass, or anything that*
S C : 0 9 :003(354) [0561] 'You shall not muzzle an **ox** when it is treading out the

Pacified (2), Pacify (2)
A L : 2 0 :015(043) [0055] of men cannot be **pacified** by any work but only by faith
A P : 0 4 :180(132) [0171] Thus works can never **pacify** the conscience; only the
A P : 0 4 :212(136) [0179] But because works cannot **pacify** the conscience, men
A P : 0 4 :301(153) [0205] be at rest, therefore, and when will it be **pacified**?

Pact (1)
L C : 0 1 :012(366) [0583] who go so far as to make a **pact** with the devil in order

Pagan (6)
A P : 2 1 :032(233) [0351] Such notions are obviously of **pagan** origin.
A P : 2 1 :034(234) [0351] with abuses that were enormous and worse than **pagan**.
A P : 2 4 :013(251) [0387] this pharisaic and **pagan** notion about the working of the
S 2 : 0 4 :014(301) [0475] taken from the imperial, **pagan** law and is a teaching
S 3 : 0 1 :011(303) [0479] They are thoroughly **pagan** doctrines, and we cannot
S D : 0 7 :057(579) [0993] and participating in **pagan** devil-worship and who

Page (1)
L C : P R :003(358) [0567] read, instead, at least a **page** or two from the Catechism,

Pain (5), Painful (2), Pains (4)
A G : 1 7 :004(038) [0051] condemned men will not suffer eternal **pain** and torment.
A P : 0 4 :209(135) [0177] order by this cruel and **painful** deed to placate the wrath
A P : 0 4 :288(151) [0203] undertook many other **painful** works to appease the
S 1 : P R :003(289) [0455] day take such wretched **pains** to postpone and prevent the
S 3 : 0 3 :002(304) [0479] (true sorrow of the heart, suffering, and **pain** of death).
S C : P R :019(340) [0537] You should also take **pains** to urge governing authorities
L C : 0 1 :174(388) [0629] that it is his chief duty, on **pain** of losing divine grace, to
L C : 0 3 :009(421) [0699] duty and obligation [on **pain** of God's wrath and
L C : 0 3 :062(428) [0715] It **pains** him beyond measure when his lies and
L C : 0 3 :081(431) [0721] In short, it **pains** him that anyone receives a morsel of
L C : 0 6 :001(457) [0000] to make confession on **pain** of the gravest mortal sin.

Painstakingly (1)
L C : 0 2 :063(419) [0695] world has sought **painstakingly** to learn what God is and

Paint (1), Painted (1)
A P : 2 1 :035(234) [0353] Some smart person **painted** Christopher in such a way as
S D : 0 1 :022(512) [0865] a smudge of dirt from one's face or **paint** from the wall.

Palaces (1)
A P : 2 7 :059(279) [0441] are fancier than kings' **palaces** and who live most

Palatine (1)
P R : P R :027(014) [0025] Louis, count **palatine** on the Rhine, elector.

Palliate (3)
P R : P R :004(004) [0009] and churches so as to **palliate** their own errors, to divert
P R : P R :017(008) [0015] to want to introduce, **palliate**, or confirm any new, false,
P R : P R :019(009) [0017] purpose and intention to **palliate**, to extenuate, or to

Palm (1), Palms (1)
P R : P R :019(009) [0017] public print have tried to **palm** them off on simple folk in
S 3 : 1 5 :005(316) [0501] are blessings of candles, **palms**, spices, oats, cakes, etc.

Palsgrave (1)
P R : P R :027(014) [0025] Philip Louis, **palsgrave** [of Pfalz-Neuburg]

Pamper (1)
A P : 1 5 :047(221) [0327] that we indulge and **pamper** the desires of our flesh.

Pan (3)
S D : 0 8 :044(599) [1031] goes down and we go upward like a light and empty **pan**.
S D : 0 8 :044(599) [1031] Of course, he can also go up again or jump out of his **pan**.
S D : 0 8 :044(599) [1031] could never have sat in the **pan** unless he had become a

Panormitanus (1)
A P : 1 1 :008(181) [0251] was approved by **Panormitanus** and other learned in the

Papacy (34)
P R : P R :003(003) [0007] over against both the **papacy** and all sorts of factions.
A P : 1 5 :018(217) [0319] So the **papacy** will also be a part of the kingdom of
S 2 : 0 2 :001(293) [0463] The Mass in the **papacy** must be regarded as the greatest
S 2 : 0 2 :010(294) [0465] aware that if the Mass falls, the **papacy** will fall with it.
S 2 : 0 4 :000(298) [0471] Article IV. [The **Papacy**]
S 2 : 0 4 :005(299) [0473] been said often) the **papacy** is a human invention, and it
S 2 : 0 4 :006(299) [0473] The **papacy** is of no use to the church because it exercises
S 2 : 0 4 :014(301) [0475] are the essence of the **papacy**) in contradiction to God,
S 3 : 0 8 :004(312) [0495] The **papacy**, too, is nothing but enthusiasm, for the pope
S 3 : 0 8 :009(313) [0497] including that of the **papacy** and Mohammedanism.
T R : 0 0 :082(334) [0529] article concerning the **papacy** presented to the princes in
T R : 0 0 :082(000) [0529] the tract concerning the **Papacy** and the Power and
L C : P R :001(358) [0567] land all their days, as they used to do under the **papacy**.
L C : P R :004(359) [0567] are sluggish and lazy, as we used to be under the **papacy**?
L C : 0 1 :011(366) [0583] what we used to do in our blindness under the **papacy**.
L C : 0 1 :140(384) [0621] the past was neither heeded nor taught under the **papacy**.
L C : 0 1 :158(387) [0627] — not like those in the **papacy** who applied this title to
L C : 0 2 :043(416) [0689] was the case under the **papacy**, where faith was entirely
L C : 0 5 :051(452) [0765] we were under the **papacy** when we attended the
E P : R N :004(465) [0777] and superstition of the **papacy** and against other sects,
E P : 0 5 :011(479) [0805] comfort, and the doors are again opened to the **papacy**.
E P : 0 7 :022(484) [0813] when it is taught in the **papacy** that the bread and wine in
S D : P R :001(501) [0847] and ordinances under the **papacy**) was once more clearly
S D : P R :005(504) [0851] darkness of the **papacy** through the faithful ministry of
S D : P R :005(504) [0851] against the aberrations of the **papacy** and of other sects.
S D : P R :005(504) [0851] churches from the **papacy** and from other condemned
S D : P R :006(504) [0853] the doctrines against the **papacy** more clearly and
S D : P R :009(505) [0853] established against the **papacy** and other sects.
S D : 0 5 :027(563) [0961] law, as happened in the **papacy**, and thus rob Christians
S D : 0 5 :027(563) [0961] and reopen the door to the **papacy** in the church of God.
S D : 0 7 :015(572) [0977] and exposed in procession, as happens in the **papacy**.
S D : 1 0 :005(611) [1053] or that a return to the **papacy** and an apostasy from the
S D : 1 2 :008(633) [1097] profound darkness of the **papacy** still reigned, and where
S D : 1 2 :008(633) [1097] and false beliefs of the **papacy**, unfortunately accepted in

Papal (20), Papist (2), Papistic (15), Papists (28)
P R : P R :002(003) [0007] to light its way out of **papistic** superstition and darkness.
P R : P R :004(004) [0009] in submitting to the **papal** yoke as well as in embracing
A G : 2 3 :012(052) [0063] had published the new **papal** decree was almost killed
A G : 2 7 :001(071) [0077] not only to the Word of God but also to **papal** canons.
A G : 2 7 :006(071) [0077] of the fact that even the **papal** canons might have set
A G : 2 7 :023(074) [0079] that a vow made contrary to **papal** canons is not binding.
A G : 2 7 :031(075) [0079] Several canons and **papal** regulations annul vows that are
A G : 2 8 :074(094) [0095] disuse and are not obligatory, as **papal** law itself testifies.
A P : 0 7 :024(172) [0235] Now, this definition of the **papal** kingdom rather than of
A P : 0 7 :026(173) [0235] define the church as anything but such a **papal** kingdom.
A P : 1 3 :018(213) [0313] taught with great authority throughout the **papal** realm.
A P : 2 4 :052(259) [0403] Mass and the rest of the **papal** order are nothing but a
A P : 2 4 :098(268) [0419] So in the **papal** realm the worship of Baal clings —
A P : 2 4 :098(268) [0419] endure together with the **papal** realm until Christ comes
A P : 2 7 :010(270) [0423] about such vows, which even the **papal** canons condemn.
S 1 : P R :001(288) [0455] and able to yield to the **papists** and, on the other hand,
S 1 : P R :010(290) [0457] But in the dioceses of the **papists** we see so many vacant
S 2 : 0 2 :001(293) [0463] and most precious of the **papal** idolatries, for it is held
S 2 : 0 2 :002(293) [0463] If there were reasonable **papists**, one would speak to them
S 2 : 0 2 :010(294) [0465] if it were possible for the **papists** to make concessions to
S 2 : 0 2 :010(294) [0465] The **papists** are well aware that if the Mass falls, the
S 2 : 0 2 :013(295) [0465] The **papists** here adduce passages from Augustine and
S 2 : 0 2 :014(295) [0467] But our **papists** make use of such human opinions to
S 2 : 0 2 :026(297) [0469] them a special function, as the **papists** teach and practice.
S 2 : 0 4 :014(301) [0475] transactions and judgments, as the **papal** decretals show.
S 2 : 0 4 :014(301) [0475] are characteristic of his **papal** government, as I have
S 3 : 0 3 :009(304) [0481] The False Repentance of the **Papists**
S 3 : 1 0 :003(314) [0497] The **papists** have no right to forbid or prevent us, not
S 3 : 1 1 :001(314) [0499] The **papists** had neither authority nor right to prohibit
S 3 : 1 2 :001(315) [0499] We do not concede to the **papists** that they are the
S 3 : 1 5 :001(316) [0501] The assertion of the **papists** that human traditions effect
S 3 : 1 5 :002(316) [0501] When the **papists** say that it is a mortal sin to break such
T R : 0 0 :005(320) [0503] outset define what the **papists** mean when they say that
T R : 0 0 :078(333) [0527] there are many unjust **papal** laws on matrimonial
L C : 0 1 :213(394) [0641] From this you see how the **papal** rabble, priests, monks,
L C : 0 6 :034(461) [0000] We shall let the **papists** torment and torture themselves
E P : 0 4 :018(477) [0801] people as much as a **papistic** and Pharisaic confidence in
E P : 0 7 :022(484) [0813] 1. The **papistic** transubstantiation, when it is taught in the
E P : 0 7 :023(484) [0815] 2. The **papistic** sacrifice of the Mass for the sins of the

Continued ▶

E P : 1 2 :010(498) [0839] temples where formerly **papistic** Masses were read and
S D : P R :006(502) [0847] for the charges of the **papists** — it can nevertheless not be
S D : P R :008(502) [0849] time our adversaries, the **papists**, rejoice over the schisms
S D : P R :007(505) [0853] for renouncing the **papistic** errors and idolatries, for
S D : P R :007(505) [0853] no communion with the **papists**, and for neither expecting
S D : 0 1 :060(519) [0879] No philosopher, no **papist**, no sophist, indeed, no human
S D : 0 2 :001(519) [0881] will, not only between the **papists** and our theologians
S D : 0 2 :076(536) [0911] 3. The error of the **papists** and scholastics, whose doctrine
S D : 0 2 :079(536) [0911] the teachings of the **papists** and the monks that man after
S D : 0 4 :002(551) [0939] have been used by the **papists**, now as well as formerly, to
S D : 0 4 :023(555) [0945] and are adopted by the **papists** and used to their own
S D : 0 4 :026(555) [0945] 2. In his writings against the **papists** at many places;
S D : 0 4 :036(557) [0949] error of the **papists**, yet, since a controversy subsequently
S D : 0 7 :035(575) [0983] We do this to reject the **papistic** transubstantiation and to
S D : 0 7 :087(585) [1003] as when in the **papistic** Mass the bread is not distributed
S D : 0 7 :087(585) [1003] It was against such **papistic** abuses that this rule was first
S D : 0 7 :108(588) [1009] First, **papistic** transubstantiation, when they teach that
S D : 0 7 :109(588) [1011] and condemn all other **papistic** abuses of this sacrament,
S D : 0 7 :110(588) [1011] These **papistic** abuses have been refuted at length in the
S D : 0 7 :121(590) [1013] and condemn the **papistic** consecration which ascribes to
S D : 1 0 :005(611) [1053] greatly from that of the **papists**, or that we are not
S D : 1 0 :019(614) [1059] do not concede to the **papists** (the papist bishops) that
S D : 1 0 :019(614) [1059] to the papists (the **papist** bishops) that they are the
S D : 1 0 :020(614) [1059] body and soul are characteristic of his **papal** government."
S D : 1 2 :008(633) [1097] what called itself evangelical and was not **papistic**.
S D : 1 2 :015(634) [1099] temples in which the **papistic** Mass had formerly been

Paper (1)
L C : P R :012(360) [0571] Time and **paper** would fail me if I were to recount all the

Par (4)
A P : 2 4 :090(266) [0415] the Mass would be on a **par** with the death of Christ.
E P : R N :002(465) [0777] names, should not be put on a **par** with Holy Scripture.
S D : P R :009(505) [0855] writings dare be put on a **par** with it, but that everything
S D : 1 0 :015(613) [1057] worship not only on a **par** with God's commandments,

Parable (2), Parables (3)
A P : 0 7 :019(171) [0233] Christ's **parables** agree with this.
A P : 0 7 :049(178) [0245] has also warned us in his **parables** on the church that
T R : 0 0 :008(321) [0505] thing is taught by a **parable** when, in a similar dispute
S D : 0 7 :115(589) [1011] they are only figures, **parables**, and types of the
S D : 1 1 :014(619) [1069] likewise does in the **parable** (Matt. 20:2-14), namely, that

Paraclete (1)
S D : 0 5 :011(560) [0955] the latter is called the **Paraclete**, as Luther explains it in

Paradise (5)
S C : P R :023(341) [0539] no grace, no life, no **paradise**, no heaven, no Christ, no
L C : 0 1 :007(365) [0583] fearless, as if he were sitting in the midst of **paradise**.
S D : 0 1 :010(510) [0863] righteousness of **paradise** or of the image of God
S D : 0 1 :030(513) [0867] imparted at creation to our nature in **paradise**.
S D : 1 1 :090(631) [1093] Adam and Eve did in **paradise** — yes, would be losing it

Parallel (1)
A P : 2 7 :059(279) [0439] Rechabites is a beautiful **parallel** to our monks, whose

Pardon (2), Pardoned (6)
A P : 1 2 :096(196) [0281] and that we shall be **pardoned**, in such a way that we
A P : 1 2 :096(196) [0281] a way that we hope for **pardon** from faith just as faith
A P : 2 0 :012(228) [0341] to die and then **pardoned**, "The magistrate commands
A P : 2 0 :012(228) [0341] on you steal no more, and therefore you are **pardoned**."
S 3 : 0 3 :019(306) [0483] had been forgotten were **pardoned** only when a man
L C : 0 3 :093(433) [0725] is forgiven and **pardoned**, yet on the condition that we
L C : 0 6 :011(458) [0000] provoked another to anger and needs to beg his **pardon**.
S D : 0 5 :002(558) [0953] law of God reproved, has been **pardoned** and forgiven.

Parental (3)
L C : 0 1 :115(381) [0613] or to those who have **parental** authority over them.
L C : 0 1 :169(388) [0629] do not imagine that the **parental** office is a matter of your
L C : 0 4 :020(439) [0737] way we speak about the **parental** estate and civil

Parents (58)
A P : 0 4 :197(134) [0175] to honor our **parents** by referring to the reward that is
A P : 0 4 :197(134) [0175] to say that obedience to **parents** justifies us before God,
A P : 1 2 :174(210) [0307] the Gospel, obedience to **parents** and magistrates,
A P : 1 8 :004(225) [0335] It can obey rulers and **parents**.
A P : 2 4 :081(264) [0411] of children does not excuse **parents** from public duties."
A P : 2 7 :009(270) [0421] their way of life, whom **parents** or friends pushed into the
A P : 2 7 :040(276) [0433] mean to say that leaving **parents** or wife or brothers is a
A P : 2 7 :040(276) [0433] for if someone leaves his **parents** or or his wife in order by
A P : 2 7 :061(280) [0441] a command from their **parents**, they are praised for their
S 3 : 0 1 :002(302) [0477] Word, disobedience to **parents**, murder, unchastity, theft,
T R : 0 0 :078(333) [0527] betrothals in violation of the right of **parents**.
S C : P R :012(339) [0535] In addition, **parents** and employers should refuse to
S C : P R :019(340) [0537] authorities and **parents** to rule wisely and educate their
S C : P R :020(340) [0537] The extent to which **parents** and governing authorities sin
S C : 0 1 :008(343) [0541] should not despise our **parents** and superiors, nor
S C : 0 9 :008(356) [0563] **Parents**
S C : 0 9 :009(356) [0563] "Children, obey your **parents** in the Lord, for this is
L C : 0 1 :026(368) [0587] Our **parents** and all authorities — in short, all people
L C : 0 1 :105(379) [0611] us not simply to love our **parents** but also to honor them.
L C : 0 1 :108(379) [0611] be taught to revere their **parents** as God's representatives,
L C : 0 1 :108(380) [0611] who has created and ordained them to be our **parents**.
L C : 0 1 :109(380) [0611] this commandment requires concerning honor to **parents**.
L C : 0 1 :111(380) [0613] right attitude toward his **parents** will not allow them to
L C : 0 1 :112(380) [0613] and obedience to my **parents**, since God himself has
L C : 0 1 :114(380) [0613] and service to their **parents**, and we should have had an
L C : 0 1 :116(381) [0615] the will and word of our **parents**, provided that these,
L C : 0 1 :121(382) [0615] Then all would be well; **parents** would have more
L C : 0 1 :121(382) [0615] and children would win their **parents**' hearts completely.
L C : 0 1 :122(382) [0617] on their backs, they anger both God and their **parents**.
L C : 0 1 :124(382) [0617] Neither can **parents**, as a rule, do very much; one fool
L C : 0 1 :125(382) [0617] he has given us living **parents**, should we be happy to
L C : 0 1 :126(382) [0617] has exalted this estate of **parents** above all others; indeed,
L C : 0 1 :127(382) [0617] all the good things we have received from our **parents**.
L C : 0 1 :128(382) [0617] children forget their **parents**, as we all forget God, and no
L C : 0 1 :128(383) [0617] so we act toward our **parents**, and there is no child that
L C : 0 1 :129(383) [0617] everyone to consider what his **parents** have done for him.
L C : 0 1 :130(383) [0619] when they said, "God, **parents**, and teachers can never be
L C : 0 1 :130(383) [0619] give all honor to his **parents** and esteem them as those
L C : 0 1 :138(384) [0621] of them were brought up well and revered their **parents**.
L C : 0 1 :141(384) [0621] Out of the authority of **parents** all other authority is
L C : 0 1 :142(384) [0621] stand in the place of **parents** and derive from them their
L C : 0 1 :143(385) [0623] honor them as their own **parents** and do everything that
L C : 0 1 :150(385) [0623] as through our own **parents**, God gives us food, house
L C : 0 1 :167(388) [0629] be well to preach to **parents** on the nature of their office,
L C : 0 1 :168(388) [0629] **Parents** should consider that they owe obedience to God,
L C : 0 1 :181(389) [0631] magistrates in place of **parents**; in early times, as we read
L C : 0 1 :181(389) [0631] as we read in Moses, **parents** had to bring their own
L C : 0 1 :182(389) [0631] who occupy the place of God, that is, **parents** and rulers.
L C : 0 1 :218(394) [0643] Therefore **parents** and magistrates have the duty of so
L C : 0 1 :274(402) [0659] preachers, and **parents**, for we must interpret this
L C : 0 1 :275(402) [0659] Just so, magistrates, **parents**, even brothers and sisters
E P : 0 2 :001(469) [0785] after the fall of our first **parents** and before his
E P : 0 6 :002(480) [0805] In the same way our first **parents** even before the Fall did
E P : 1 2 :008(498) [0839] the children of Christian **parents** are holy and the children
E P : 1 2 :008(498) [0839] by virtue of their birth from Christian and pious **parents**.
S D : 0 1 :006(509) [0861] after the Fall of our first **parents** is of course impossible
S D : 0 2 :005(521) [0881] the fall of our first **parents** man is so corrupted that in
S D : 1 2 :013(634) [1099] Christian and believing **parents**, are holy and children of

Paris (1)
A P : 1 8 :010(226) [0337] more recently William of **Paris** has discussed it very well.

Parish (4), Parishes (5), Parishioners (1)
A G : 2 8 :022(084) [0087] On this account **parish** ministers and churches are bound
A G : 2 8 :055(090) [0091] to the bishops and **parish** ministers in such matters, and
A G : 0 0 :002(095) [0095] **Parish** ministers also had endless quarrels with monks
A L : 0 0 :002(095) [0095] **Parishes** have been troubled in many ways by indulgence
A L : 0 0 :002(095) [0095] endless quarrels between **parish** ministers and monks
A P : 2 4 :006(250) [0385] Even today, Greek **parishes** have no private Masses but
S 1 : P R :010(290) [0457] vacant and desolate **parishes** everywhere that our hearts
S 2 : 0 2 :018(296) [0467] they neglect their own **parishes**, the Word of God, their
L C : P R :003(358) [0567] the Lord's Prayer for themselves and their **parishioners**.
L C : P R :006(359) [0569] So they blithely let **parishes** fall into decay, and brazenly

Parochial (2)
A G : 2 4 :040(061) [0069] held in addition to the **parochial** Mass, probably through
A L : 0 0 :002(095) [0095] and monks about **parochial** rights, confessions, burials,

Parry (1), Parrying (1)
L C : 0 3 :031(424) [0707] great results in the past, **parrying** the counsels and plots
L C : 0 3 :109(435) [0729] us but shall at all times expect his blows and **parry** them.

Part (157), Parts (64)
P R : P R :009(006) [0011] without distress on our **part**, that little account was taken
P R : P R :013(007) [0013] their considered judgment concerning every **part** of it.
A G : P R :013(026) [0041] nevertheless we on our **part** shall not omit doing
A G : 0 1 :004(028) [0043] this connection, not as a **part** or a property of another
A G : 2 0 :003(041) [0053] times, when for the most **part** sermons were concerned
A G : 2 5 :013(063) [0071] chief and most important **part**), for the consolation of
A G : 2 6 :040(069) [0075] We on our **part** also retain many ceremonies and
A G : 2 8 :027(085) [0087] law requires the same in **Part** II, Question 7, in the
A G : 2 8 :033(086) [0087] from and altered **part** of the Ten Commandments.
A L : 0 1 :004(028) [0043] to signify not a **part** or a quality in another but that which
A L : 1 2 :003(034) [0049] consists of these two **parts**: one is contrition, that is,
A L : 0 0 :004(048) [0059] rites are for the most **part** diligently observed, for it is
A L : 2 4 :002(056) [0065] here and there among the **parts** sung in Latin.
A L : 2 4 :030(059) [0067] instituted that faith on the **part** of those who use the
A L : 2 4 :040(061) [0069] public ceremonies are for the most **part** retained.
A L : 2 6 :004(064) [0071] of faith, which is the chief **part** of the Gospel and ought
A P : 0 2 :027(104) [0113] this, the inordinate disposition of the **parts** of the soul.
A P : 0 2 :031(104) [0113] many passages on both **parts** of our definition, but on so
A P : 0 2 :051(107) [0119] For our **part**, we have been reluctant to enter upon their
A P : 0 4 :022(110) [0127] We for our **part** maintain that God requires the
A P : 0 4 :230(139) [0183] We for our **part** preach the foolishness of the Gospel,
A P : 0 4 :235(140) [0185] perfect or whole when all its **parts** fit together properly."
A P : 0 4 :251(143) [0191] our propitiation is due in **part** to Christ and in part to
A P : 0 4 :251(143) [0191] is due in part to Christ and in **part** to our works.
A P : 0 4 :261(145) [0195] Daniel's sermon contains two **parts**.
A P : 0 4 :261(145) [0195] One **part** instructs about the new life and its works.
A P : 0 4 :261(145) [0195] In the other **part** Daniel promises the king forgiveness of
A P : 0 4 :283(150) [0201] particle to a single **part**: "All things will be clean when
A P : 0 4 :284(150) [0201] The admonition has many **parts**, some of which command
A P : 0 4 :398(167) [0227] words for saying faith is **part** of penance, by which we
A P : 0 7 :010(170) [0229] and that the wicked are **part** of the church only in name
A P : 0 7 :010(170) [0229] fact, while the godly are **part** of the church in fact as well
A P : 0 7 :011(170) [0229] any spot cannot be called **part** of the church of Christ,
A P : 0 7 :030(173) [0237] also condemn the **part** of the seventh article in which we
A P : 0 7 :037(175) [0241] assembled much of it in the latter **part** of our Confession.
A P : 1 1 :007(181) [0251] have been ensnared by the **part** of the regulation that
A P : 1 1 :009(182) [0253] The greater **part** deals with sins against human traditions,
A P : 1 2 :001(182) [0253] they approve the first **part**, where we explain that those
A P : 1 2 :001(182) [0253] They condemn the second **part**, in which we say that
A P : 1 2 :001(182) [0253] and faith are the **parts** of penitence, and they deny that
A P : 1 2 :001(182) [0253] and they deny that faith is the second **part** of penitence.
A P : 1 2 :013(184) [0257] that of these one **part** is forgiven by the power of the keys
A P : 1 2 :013(184) [0257] of the keys and another **part** is redeemed by satisfactions.
A P : 1 2 :028(185) [0259] have given penitence two **parts**, namely, contrition and
A P : 1 2 :028(185) [0259] whole life and character a third **part**, we shall not object.
A P : 1 2 :035(186) [0261] As the second **part** of our consideration of penitence, we
A P : 1 2 :044(187) [0263] us for assigning these two **parts** to penitence, we must
A P : 1 2 :044(187) [0263] makes them the chief **parts** in the penitence or conversion
A P : 1 2 :044(187) [0263] There are two **parts** here.
A P : 1 2 :045(187) [0263] There are, then, two chief **parts** here, contrition and
A P : 1 2 :045(187) [0263] In the first **part** he denounces our sins, in the latter part

Continued ▶

A P : 1 2 :045(187) [0263] our sins, in the latter **part** he consoles us and shows us the
A P : 1 2 :045(188) [0263] see that here, too, the two **parts** are combined: contrition,
A P : 1 2 :045(188) [0263] names contrition and faith as the chief **parts** of penitence.
A P : 1 2 :046(188) [0263] always names these two **parts**, mortifying and
A P : 1 2 :046(188) [0263] These are two **parts** here.
A P : 1 2 :047(188) [0263] There are therefore two **parts** here, contrition and faith.
A P : 1 2 :048(188) [0265] Here, too, there are two **parts**, the bond and the
A P : 1 2 :049(188) [0265] Here the first **part** contains contrition, while the second
A P : 1 2 :050(189) [0265] of these sentences the first **part** means contrition, the
A P : 1 2 :052(189) [0265] that these are the chief **parts** of penitence, contrition and
A P : 1 2 :053(189) [0265] One **part** is the law, which reveals, denounces, and
A P : 1 2 :053(189) [0265] The other **part** is the Gospel, that is, the promise of grace
A P : 1 2 :055(189) [0265] These two **parts** also appear in the lives of the saints.
A P : 1 2 :055(189) [0267] These are the chief **parts**.
A P : 1 2 :057(189) [0267] This was the second **part** of her penance, the faith that
A P : 1 2 :058(190) [0267] we put into penitence the **parts** that properly belong to it
A P : 1 2 :058(190) [0267] We have put in these two **parts** in order to emphasize the
A P : 1 2 :060(190) [0269] and therefore we put it in as one of the **parts** of penitence.
A P : 1 2 :061(190) [0269] the reception of absolution is **part** of penitence or not.
A P : 1 2 :061(190) [0269] must maintain that faith is **part** of penitence since only
A P : 1 2 :063(191) [0269] of sins is either a **part** of penitence or its goal — the
A P : 1 2 :063(191) [0269] properly be included as one of the **parts** of penitence.
A P : 1 2 :074(193) [0273] of sins by faith, or that faith is **part** of penitence?
A P : 1 2 :091(195) [0279] forth contrition and faith as the two **parts** of penitence.
A P : 1 2 :092(196) [0279] of faith among the **parts** of penitence in order to make it
A P : 1 2 :093(196) [0279] discuss sometimes one **part**, sometimes another part of
A P : 1 2 :093(196) [0279] part, sometimes another **part** of penitence, it would have
A P : 1 2 :093(196) [0279] only about one but about both **parts**, contrition and faith.
A P : 1 2 :097(196) [0281] they select sayings about a **part** of penitence, namely
A P : 1 2 :098(197) [0281] and faith, the two **parts** of penitence we have discussed
A P : 1 2 :118(199) [0287] They add further that **part** of this temporal punishment is
A P : 1 2 :118(199) [0287] keys, unless they say that **part** of the punishments of
A P : 1 2 :123(200) [0289] the command to remit **part** of the punishments of
A P : 1 2 :138(203) [0293] certain punishments or to remit **part** of the punishments.
A P : 1 2 :139(203) [0295] statement about remitting **part** of the punishments
A P : 1 2 :139(203) [0295] to canonical penalties, **part** of which the pastors remitted.
A P : 1 2 :139(204) [0295] command to commute penalties or to remit them in **part**.
A P : 1 2 :148(205) [0299] a formal sense revenge is **part** of penitence because
A P : 1 2 :154(206) [0301] that the power of the keys remits **part** of the punishment.
A P : 1 5 :001(215) [0315] XV they accept the first **part**, where we say that we should
A P : 1 5 :001(215) [0315] condemn the second **part**, where we say that human
A P : 1 5 :018(217) [0319] the papacy will also be a **part** of the kingdom of
A P : 1 5 :042(221) [0327] they even attack this most salutary **part** of the Gospel.
A P : 1 6 :001(222) [0329] ordinances in which a Christian may safely take **part**.
A P : 2 2 :001(236) [0357] he did not do so only for **part** of the church, but for all of
A P : 2 2 :002(236) [0357] one kind taken away from **part** of the church and its use
A P : 2 2 :006(237) [0359] to the church why one **part** of the sacrament has been
A P : 2 2 :006(237) [0359] that it is right to deny one **part**, and they refuse to grant
A P : 2 2 :007(237) [0359] was customary in some places to administer only one **part**.
A P : 2 2 :007(237) [0359] not follow that only one **part** was given; for by the
A P : 2 2 :007(237) [0359] of language, naming one **part** also signifies the other.
A P : 2 2 :008(237) [0359] custom of giving the laity only a **part** of the sacrament.
A P : 2 2 :009(237) [0359] the denial of one **part**: to elevate the position of the clergy
A P : 2 2 :010(237) [0359] to ask for the one **part** that belonged to the priests
A P : 2 2 :010(237) [0361] be satisfied with the one **part** offered by the priest, that
A P : 2 2 :012(238) [0361] those who withhold a **part** of the sacrament and rage
A P : 2 2 :016(238) [0361] it could not obtain both **parts**; but we do blame the
A P : 2 4 :036(257) [0397] Num. 28:4ff. lists three **parts** of this daily sacrifice, the
A P : 2 4 :054(259) [0403] Therefore a large **part** of the epistle is devoted to the
A P : 2 4 :069(262) [0409] There are two **parts** to a sacrament, the sign and the
A P : 2 4 :086(265) [0413] **Part** of this was taken to be consecrated, the rest was
A P : 2 4 :093(267) [0417] Lord, but about the other **parts** of the Mass, namely,
S 1 : P R :012(290) [0459] in every trade and on the **part** of peasants — who can
S 1 : 0 1 :000(291) [0461] **[Part I]**
S 1 : 0 1 :000(291) [0461] The first **part** of the Articles treats the sublime articles of
S 2 : 0 0 :000(292) [0461] **[Part II]**
S 2 : 0 0 :000(292) [0461] The second **part** treats the articles which pertain to the
S 3 : 0 0 :000(302) [0477] **[Part III]**
S 3 : 0 3 :012(305) [0481] divided into three **parts** — contrition, confession, and
T R : 0 0 :015(322) [0509] of Rome in the greater **part** of the world, whether in
T R : 0 0 :016(323) [0509] the churches in the greater **part** of the world never
T R : 0 0 :056(330) [0521] and true judgment on the **part** of the church.
S C : P R :005(338) [0533] Commandments, or a single **part** of the Word of God.
S C : P R :016(340) [0535] for it is not necessary to take up all the **parts** at once.
S C : P R :017(340) [0537] petition, and **part**, pointing out their respective
S C : P R :018(340) [0537] commandments or other **parts** which seem to require
S C : P R :024(341) [0539] their own accord and without compulsion on your **part**.
S C : 0 2 :002(345) [0543] and mercy, without any merit or worthiness on my **part**.
S C : 0 3 :016(347) [0549] And assuredly we on our **part** will heartily forgive and
S C : 0 5 :016(349) [0553] Answer: Confession consists of two **parts**.
L C : P R :009(359) [0569] they have learned these **parts** of the Catechism perfectly,
L C : S P :003(362) [0575] instructed in the various **parts** of the Catechism or
L C : S P :006(362) [0575] if they learned the three **parts** which have been heritage
L C : S P :015(363) [0577] are the most necessary **parts** of Christian instruction.
L C : S P :018(363) [0577] to learn these three **parts** in which everything contained in
L C : S P :020(364) [0579] When these three **parts** are understood, we ought also to
L C : S P :024(364) [0579] Thus we have, in all, five **parts** covering the whole of
L C : S P :025(364) [0579] When these **parts** have been well learned, you may assign
L C : S P :026(364) [0579] for them simply to learn and repeat these **parts** verbatim.
L C : S P :026(364) [0581] it explained and may learn the meaning of every **part**.
L C : S P :028(365) [0581] up the above-mentioned **parts** one by one and in the
L C : 0 1 :000(365) [0581] [First **Part**: The Ten Commandments]
L C : 0 1 :275(402) [0659] compelled to examine and handle his private **parts**.
L C : 0 1 :287(403) [0663] in I Cor. 12:22, 23, "The **parts** of the body which seem to
L C : 0 1 :287(403) [0663] indispensable, and those **parts** of the body which we think
L C : 0 1 :287(403) [0663] and our unpresentable **parts** are treated with greater
L C : 0 1 :293(404) [0663] to the Jews; nevertheless, in **part** they also apply to us.
L C : 0 1 :315(408) [0671] presumption on the **part** of those desperate saints to dare
L C : 0 1 :319(408) [0673] suffice concerning the first **part**, both for instruction and
L C : 0 2 :000(411) [0679] Second **Part**: The Creed
L C : 0 2 :001(411) [0679] far we have heard the first **part** of Christian doctrine.
L C : 0 2 :002(411) [0679] as necessary to learn this **part** as it is the other so that we
L C : 0 2 :012(412) [0681] fully and divided into as many **parts** as there are words.
L C : 0 2 :018(412) [0681] belongs in the other two **parts** of this article, where we
L C : 0 2 :031(414) [0685] The remaining **parts** of this article simply serve to clarify
L C : 0 2 :052(417) [0691] community I also am a **part** and member, a participant
L C : 0 2 :059(418) [0695] us in it by means of the last two **parts** of this article.
L C : 0 3 :000(420) [0697] Third **Part**: The Lord's Prayer
L C : 0 3 :001(420) [0697] Now follows the third **part**, how we are to pray.
L C : 0 3 :004(420) [0699] explain the Lord's Prayer **part** by part, it is very necessary
L C : 0 3 :004(420) [0699] the Lord's Prayer part by **part**, it is very necessary to
L C : 0 3 :050(426) [0711] us, so that we may be a **part** of those among whom his
L C : 0 3 :084(431) [0723] trading, and labor on the **part** of those who wantonly
L C : 0 3 :120(436) [0731] affirmation of faith on the **part** of one who does not pray
L C : 0 4 :000(436) [0733] Fourth **Part**: Baptism
L C : 0 4 :001(436) [0733] with the three chief **parts** of our common Christian
L C : 0 4 :050(443) [0745] the Holy Spirit nor any **part** of him; in short, all this time
L C : 0 4 :065(444) [0749] These two **parts**, being dipped under the water and
L C : 0 5 :000(447) [0753] [Fifth **Part**:] The Sacrament of the Altar
L C : 0 5 :020(449) [0757] briefly considered the first **part**, namely, the essence of
L C : 0 5 :071(454) [0769] Thus you have on God's **part** both the commandment and
L C : 0 5 :071(454) [0769] Meanwhile, on your **part**, you ought to be impelled by
L C : 0 6 :005(457) [0000] in the presence of the Gospel or to have any **part** of it.
L C : 0 6 :006(457) [0000] to share and enjoy any **part** of our liberty, but we shall let
L C : 0 6 :015(458) [0000] as I have often said, that confession consists of two **parts**.
L C : 0 6 :016(459) [0000] the very necessary second **part**; it was just as if our
L C : 0 6 :018(459) [0000] therefore take care to keep the two **parts** clearly separate.
E P : 0 0 :000(464) [0775] **[Part** I: Epitome]
E P : 0 1 :001(466) [0779] the principal and best **part** of his being (that is, his
E P : 0 3 :021(475) [0797] new obedience, or in **part** by the reckoning to them of
E P : 0 3 :021(475) [0797] righteousness and in **part** by our incipient new obedience.
E P : 0 7 :004(482) [0809] most harmful kind, who in **part** talk our language very
E P : 1 0 :003(493) [0829] and for themselves no divine worship or even a **part** of it.
E P : 1 0 :009(494) [0831] regarded as in themselves divine worship or a **part** of it.
E P : 1 2 :005(498) [0839] For the most **part** this piety is built on one's own
S D : 0 0 :000(501) [0845] **[Part** II. Solid Declaration]
S D : P R :015(507) [0857] of the Creed or the chief **parts** of our Christian doctrine,
S D : 0 1 :001(508) [0859] the foremost and noblest **part** of his essence (namely, his
S D : 0 1 :030(513) [0867] end, down to the ultimate **part** involving and affecting the
S D : 0 1 :055(518) [0877] by itself and is not a **part** of another self-subsisting
S D : 0 2 :005(521) [0881] any cooperation on his **part**, he is converted, becomes a
S D : 0 2 :025(526) [0891] or the least and tiniest **part**, but altogether and alone to
S D : 0 2 :036(528) [0895] Luther writes: "I am also a **part** and member of this
S D : 0 2 :044(529) [0897] no cooperation on the **part** of our will in man's
S D : 0 2 :089(538) [0915] conversion is not only in **part**, but entirely, the operation,
S D : 0 3 :009(541) [0919] merit or worthiness on our **part**, and without any
S D : 0 3 :024(543) [0923] a necessary or component **part** of this article, since we
S D : 0 3 :025(543) [0923] conversion is simultaneously also a **part** of justification.
S D : 0 3 :039(546) [0929] made and posited to be a **part** or a cause of our
S D : 0 3 :045(547) [0933] of our justification before God, either entirely or in **part**.
S D : 0 3 :048(548) [0933] consists of two pieces or **parts**, namely, the gracious
S D : 0 3 :050(548) [0933] new obedience, or in **part** by the reckoning of Christ's
S D : 0 3 :050(548) [0933] righteousness and in **part** by the inchoate new obedience.
S D : 0 4 :035(557) [0949] works either entirely or in **part** sustain and preserve either
S D : 0 5 :004(559) [0953] thereafter the chief **parts** are announced, namely,
S D : 0 6 :024(568) [0969] donkey, is still a **part** of them and must be coerced into
S D : 0 7 :001(568) [0971] no longer secretly but in **part** openly approved the
S D : 0 7 :017(572) [0977] assembled from all **parts** of Germany in Smalcald to
S D : 0 7 :053(579) [0991] no doubt that in the other **part** of the sacrament the
S D : 0 7 :067(582) [0997] eating and eating on the **part** of the unworthy "two hairs
S D : 0 8 :042(599) [1029] so to speak, the one **part** (namely, the deity) does not
S D : 0 8 :042(599) [1029] God suffers in the other **part** (namely, in the humanity).
S D : 0 8 :078(607) [1043] Not **part** or only one-half of the person of Christ, but the
S D : 1 0 :008(612) [1055] worship of God or even a **part** of it, but that we should
S D : 1 0 :026(615) [1061] as of themselves worship of God or a **part** thereof.
S D : 1 1 :062(626) [1083] is help for you is pure grace on my **part**" (Hos. 13:9).
S D : 1 1 :095(632) [1095] and determined on our **part** to do everything in our
S D : 1 2 :008(633) [1097] For the most **part** they insinuated themselves secretly,
S D : 1 2 :008(633) [1097] that we have no **part** or share in their errors, be they few
S D : 1 2 :010(634) [1097] piety rests for the greater **part** on their own peculiar

Partake (12), Partaken (2), Partaker (2), Partakers (2), Partakes (3), Partaking (1), Partook (2)
A P : 1 0 :003(179) [0247] are one body, for we all **partake** of the same loaf'
L C : 0 3 :052(427) [0711] of grace and become **partakers** of salvation, so that we
L C : 0 4 :045(443) [0745] Similarly, those who **partake** unworthily of the Lord's
L C : 0 5 :045(452) [0763] all who would be Christians to **partake** of the sacrament.
L C : 0 5 :047(452) [0763] is true, but it does not say that we should never **partake**.
L C : 0 5 :052(452) [0765] anyone, nor need anyone **partake** of the sacrament to
E P : 0 1 :005(466) [0781] blood, he himself likewise **partook** of the same nature....
E P : 0 7 :029(485) [0815] into heaven, it there **partakes** of the body and blood of
S D : 0 2 :022(525) [0889] and be capable of and a **partaker** in conversion, in the
S D : 0 2 :036(528) [0895] a shareholder and **partaker** in it of all the goods which it
S D : 0 7 :003(569) [0973] and receives and **partakes** truly and essentially, but still
S D : 0 7 :008(570) [0975] just so certainly do they **partake** spiritually by faith also
S D : 0 7 :054(579) [0991] the cup truly receive and **partake** of the true body and
S D : 0 7 :056(579) [0991] the blessed bread also **partake** of the body of Christ.
S D : 0 7 :057(579) [0993] table of the Lord and **partaking** of the body and blood of
S D : 0 7 :057(579) [0993] he said that all who **partake** of the blessed and broken
S D : 0 7 :063(581) [0995] Supper receive and **partake** of the true, essential body and
S D : 0 7 :071(582) [0997] weak faith (Mark 9:24) **partook** no less than Abraham,
S D : 0 7 :114(589) [1011] the body of Christ is **partaken** of only spiritually through
S D : 0 7 :116(589) [1011] rises above all heavens, **partakes** up there of the body and
S D : 0 7 :117(589) [1013] Christ, and that in this way we **partake** of his absent body.
S D : 0 7 :118(590) [1013] are only received and **partaken** of through faith,
S D : 0 7 :122(590) [1013] is present with his body and there to **partake** of him.
S D : 0 8 :034(597) [1027] mystery, "become **partakers** of the divine nature"

Partial (2), Partially (1)
S 3 : 0 3 :016(305) [0483] (which I might call half-way or **partially** repentant).
S 3 : 0 3 :036(309) [0489] This repentance is not **partial** and fragmentary like
S 3 : 0 3 :037(309) [0489] be false, uncertain, or **partial**, for a person who confesses

Partiality (1)
S C : 0 9 :011(356) [0563] and that there is no **partiality** with him" (Eph. 6:9).

Participant (1), Participants (2), Participate (7), Participated (1), Participating (1), Participation (20)

AG : PR :021(026) [0043] what is required, to **participate** in such a general, free, and
AL : 2 4 :039(060) [0069] in order that there may be a common **participation**.
AP : 0 7 :019(171) [0233] these wicked men **participate** in the outward marks, still
AP : 1 0 :001(179) [0247] that the bread is "a **participation** in the Lord's body," it
AP : 1 0 :001(179) [0247] bread would not be a **participation** in the body of Christ
AP : 1 0 :003(179) [0247] as love, but also by a natural **participation**," etc.
TR : 0 0 :041(327) [0517] beware of becoming **participants** in the impious
SC : PR :011(339) [0535] or be allowed to **participate** in any Christian privileges.
LC : 0 1 :084(376) [0605] not be available, to **participate** in public worship, that is,
LC : 0 2 :052(417) [0691] a part and member, a **participant** and co-partner in all the
EP : 0 7 :015(483) [0813] we break, is it not a **participation** in the body of Christ?"
SD : 0 6 :009(565) [0965] in which all have **participated**, then you are illegitimate
SD : 0 7 :011(571) [0975] which we break is a **participation** in the body of Christ,
SD : 0 7 :011(571) [0975] that the bread is a **participation** not in the body but in the
SD : 0 7 :035(575) [0983] body of Christ" or "a **participation** in the body of
SD : 0 7 :054(579) [0991] we bless, is it not a **participation** in the blood of Christ?
SD : 0 7 :054(579) [0991] we bread, is it not a **participation** in the body of Christ?")
SD : 0 7 :054(579) [0991] we break and bless is **participation** in the body and blood
SD : 0 7 :055(579) [0991] could not be called **participation** in the body but in the
SD : 0 7 :056(579) [0991] only of a spiritual **participation** in the body of Christ
SD : 0 7 :056(579) [0991] the spirit or faith is **participation** in the body of Christ.
SD : 0 7 :056(579) [0991] says that the bread is **participation** in the body of Christ,
SD : 0 7 :056(579) [0991] Christ in which both the godly and the godless **participate**.
SD : 0 7 :057(579) [0993] idol-sacrifices and **participating** in pagan devil-worship
SD : 0 7 :057(579) [0993] bread in the Supper **participate** in the body of Christ, St.
SD : 0 7 :059(580) [0993] follows: "The bread is **participation** in the body of Christ
SD : 0 7 :059(580) [0993] that whereby we have **participation** in the body of Christ,
SD : 0 7 :061(580) [0995] Without this spiritual **participation**, even the sacramental
SD : 0 7 :072(582) [0997] and the twofold **participation** in the body and blood of
SD : 0 7 :088(585) [1003] earth both the worthy and the unworthy alike **participate**.
SD : 0 8 :034(597) [1027] what kind of **participation** in the divine nature must that
SD : 1 0 :022(615) [1061] beware of becoming **participants** in the impious

Particle (5)

AP : 0 4 :073(117) [0141] The **particle** "alone" offends some people, even though
AP : 0 4 :073(117) [0141] they dislike the exclusive **particle** "alone," let them
AP : 0 4 :264(146) [0195] adds an extraneous **particle** expressing doubt, and in his
AP : 0 4 :283(149) [0201] Our opponents misinterpret the universal **particle** "all."
AP : 0 4 :283(150) [0201] the universal **particle** to a single part: "All things will be

Particular (36), Particularly (12)

PR : PR :013(007) [0013] peruse it with **particular** earnestness and Christian zeal,
PR : PR :023(012) [0021] We desire **particularly** that the young men who are being
PR : PR :024(013) [0023] of Christian concord and have a **particular** longing for it.
AG : 2 7 :049(079) [0083] connected with our **particular** calling and station in life;
AL : 2 0 :003(041) [0053] needless works, such as **particular** holy days, prescribed
AP : 0 4 :222(137) [0181] is not the approval of a **particular** act but of the total
AP : 0 7 :030(174) [0237] If we mean "**particular** rites" they approve our article, but
AP : 0 7 :031(174) [0237] rites, whether universal or **particular**, is not necessary.
AP : 0 7 :031(174) [0237] whether universal or **particular**, contribute nothing; nor
AP : 1 2 :116(199) [0287] satisfactions in **particular**, lest by their adoption the
AP : 1 2 :155(207) [0301] temporal punishments corresponding to **particular** sins.
AP : 1 2 :156(207) [0301] From the **particular** penalty imposed on David it does
AP : 1 2 :156(207) [0301] in purgatory, where the **particular** punishment fits the
AP : 1 2 :156(207) [0301] where the particular punishment fits the **particular** crime.
AP : 2 1 :034(234) [0353] horoscopes carved at a **particular** time contain power.
AP : 2 3 :032(244) [0373] of the tasks of a **particular** calling should follow
AP : 2 4 :068(261) [0407] of hood is the mark of a **particular** monastic profession.
AP : 2 4 :088(265) [0413] blood of the Lord in **particular**, but about the whole
S 2 : 0 2 :027(297) [0469] pray for me, not in one **particular** necessity only, but in
TR : 0 0 :024(324) [0511] to the person of one **particular** individual but to the
SC : 0 5 :022(350) [0553] In **particular** I confess in your presence that, as a
SC : 0 5 :023(350) [0553] or mistress may say: "In **particular** I confess in your
SC : 0 5 :024(350) [0555] For example, "In **particular** I confess that I once cursed.
SC : 0 5 :025(350) [0555] should mention none in **particular**, but receive
LC : 0 1 :082(376) [0603] connected with **particular** customs, persons, times, and
LC : 0 1 :085(376) [0605] is not restricted to a **particular** time, as it was among the
LC : 0 1 :094(378) [0607] so that this day should have its own **particular** holy work.
LC : 0 1 :201(392) [0637] Adultery is **particularly** mentioned because among the
LC : 0 1 :219(394) [0643] word, and deed in his **particular** situation (that is,
LC : 0 1 :264(400) [0655] It applies **particularly** to the detestable, shameful vice of
LC : 0 1 :289(404) [0663] It is a **particularly** fine, noble virtue always to put the
LC : 0 1 :325(409) [0675] The prophet David **particularly** teaches it throughout the
LC : 0 4 :020(439) [0737] and why I should honor this **particular** flesh and blood.
LC : 0 4 :070(445) [0749] child, who has no **particular** vice, becomes vicious and
LC : 0 6 :011(458) [0000] guilt there is also a **particular** one, when a person has
EP : RN :004(465) [0777] of our Christian faith, **particularly** against the false
EP : 0 1 :024(469) [0785] the essence of a **particular** thing and that which pertains
EP : 0 7 :019(484) [0813] instituted this Supper **particularly** for Christians who are
EP : 1 0 :005(493) [0829] are to be avoided, and **particularly** the weak in faith are
SD : 0 2 :022(525) [0889] willed, out of **particular** and pure grace, that our poor,
SD : 0 2 :027(526) [0891] It was this passage in **particular** which, by St. Augustine's
SD : 0 2 :090(538) [0915] conversion to God, **particularly** as to the manner in which
SD : 0 4 :029(555) [0947] when it was **particularly** important to have a clear and
SD : 0 5 :001(558) [0951] this distinction with **particular** diligence lest we confuse
SD : 0 8 :078(607) [1043] he wills, and in **particular** that he is present with his
SD : 1 0 :017(614) [1059] We are to be **particularly** mindful that Christ says, "So
SD : 1 0 :024(615) [1061] in general and matters of indifference in **particular**.
SD : 1 0 :025(615) [1061] Christian, and **particularly** the preachers may or may not

Partly (2)

AP : 0 4 :189(133) [0175] place in a flesh that is **partly** unregenerate and hinders
AP : 1 2 :118(199) [0287] which punishments are **partly** forgiven by the power of

Partner (1), Partnership (1)

LC : 0 2 :052(417) [0691] a participant and co-**partner** in all the blessings it
SD : 1 0 :006(611) [1055] For what **partnership** have righteousness and iniquity, or

Party (35), Parties (9)

AG : PR :002(025) [0039] and beliefs of the several **parties** among us to unite the
AG : PR :012(026) [0041] and estates of the other **party** do not comply with the
AP : PR :002(098) [0099] their arguments, our **party** requested a copy of the
AP : 2 1 :040(235) [0355] Yet anyone in their **party** with a little sense would admit
AP : 2 4 :010(251) [0387] the Jews that both **parties** in a controversy must deal only
S 1 : 0 0 :000(287) [0453] been presented by our **party** at the council in Mantua, or
S 1 : PR :003(289) [0455] Even adherents of that **party** have lost hope that the
S 1 : PR :004(289) [0455] to be adherents of our **party** — that they dare to cite my
S 1 : 0 1 :000(292) [0461] of dispute or contention, for both **parties** confess them.
LC : 0 1 :067(373) [0599] If one **party** in a dispute swears falsely, he will not escape
LC : 0 5 :075(455) [0771] selfishness, dissension, **party** spirit, envy, murder,
EP : 0 3 :002(473) [0791] One **party** has held that Christ is our righteousness only
EP : 0 4 :002(475) [0797] was occasioned when one **party** asserted that good works
EP : 0 4 :002(475) [0797] The other **party** asserted that good works are detrimental
EP : 0 4 :003(476) [0797] The one **party** contended that we should not use the word
EP : 0 4 :003(476) [0797] The other **party** held with reference to the word
EP : 0 4 :004(476) [0797] The one **party** contended that the law should not be
EP : 0 4 :004(476) [0797] This the other **party** denied.
EP : 0 6 :001(480) [0805] One **party** said Yes, the other says No.
EP : 1 0 :002(493) [0829] One **party** said Yes to this, the other party said No.
EP : 1 0 :002(493) [0829] One party said Yes to this, the other **party** said No.
SD : PR :008(502) [0849] which of the contending **parties** they should support.
SD : PR :009(503) [0849] about words, with one **party** talking past the other, so
SD : PR :009(503) [0849] the opinions of the erring **party** cannot be tolerated in the
SD : PR :012(506) [0855] as impartial, none of the **parties** in the various
SD : 0 1 :002(508) [0859] The other **party**, however, took a contrary view and
SD : 0 2 :003(520) [0881] The one **party** held and taught that, although by his own
SD : 0 2 :005(520) [0881] Against both of these **parties** the pure teachers of the
SD : 0 3 :002(539) [0917] The one **party** contended that the righteousness of faith,
SD : 0 3 :004(539) [0917] Against both **parties** the other teachers of the Augsburg
SD : 0 4 :001(551) [0939] One **party** employed such words and formulas as "Good
SD : 0 4 :002(551) [0939] The other **party** contended on the contrary that good
SD : 0 4 :003(551) [0939] Another **party** took the contrary view that good works
SD : 0 5 :002(558) [0951] The one **party** claimed that, strictly speaking, the Gospel
SD : 0 5 :002(558) [0951] The other **party**, however, maintained and contended
SD : 0 6 :002(564) [0963] This one **party** taught and held that the regenerated do
SD : 0 6 :003(564) [0963] The other **party** taught that although true believers are
SD : 0 7 :012(571) [0977] Luther and other theologians of both **parties** signed them:
SD : 1 0 :002(610) [1053] The one **party** held that even in a period of persecution
SD : 1 0 :003(611) [1053] The other **party**, however, contended that under no
SD : 1 1 :078(629) [1089] with the Pharisees and their **party** at the time of Christ.
SD : 1 2 :027(635) [1101] are divided into many **parties** among themselves, with one
SD : 1 2 :027(635) [1101] themselves, with one **party** holding more and another
SD : 1 2 :027(635) [1101] holding more and another **party** holding fewer errors.

Pass (29), Passed (4), Passes (4), Passing (7)

PR : PR :010(006) [0011] expanding with each **passing** day than, on the basis of
AG : 1 6 :002(037) [0051] render decisions and **pass** sentence according to imperial
AG : 2 6 :025(067) [0073] he says, "Let no one **pass** judgment on you in
AG : 2 8 :044(088) [0089] in Col. 2:16, "Let no one **pass** judgment on you in
AG : 2 8 :074(094) [0093] by men have with the **passing** of time fallen into disuse
AG : 0 0 :003(095) [0095] things we have discreetly **passed** over for the common
AL : 2 6 :025(067) [0073] in Col. 2:16, "Let no one **pass** judgment on you in
AL : 2 8 :044(088) [0089] Paul says, "Let no one **pass** judgment on you in
AL : 2 8 :074(094) [0093] been changed with the **passing** of time, as the canons
AL : 0 0 :003(095) [0095] We have **passed** over matters of this sort so that the chief
AP : 0 4 :013(109) [0123] have come to such a **pass** that many people ridicule us for
AP : 0 4 :017(109) [0125] In order not to by-**pass** Christ altogether, our opponents
AP : 0 4 :266(146) [0197] our opponents would have **passed** over this passage.
AP : 0 7 :035(175) [0239] (2:16, 17): "Let no one **pass** judgment on you in questions
AP : 1 3 :017(213) [0313] But let us **pass** over all this.
AP : 1 5 :030(219) [0323] he says: "Let no one **pass** judgment on you in
AP : 2 1 :016(231) [0347] As to the rest even the uninitiated can **pass** judgment.
AP : 2 4 :003(250) [0385] We mention this only in **passing** in order to point out
AP : 2 4 :087(265) [0413] But let us **pass** over these trifles.
AP : 2 4 :090(266) [0415] Now we shall **pass** over the sort of proofs our opponents
AP : 2 7 :010(270) [0423] of our arguments, and in **passing** we shall refute our
AP : 2 7 :069(280) [0443] of our arguments, and in **passing** we have refuted the
LC : 0 1 :140(384) [0621] So he **passes** over them lightly, fastens his attention on
LC : 0 1 :141(384) [0621] and neighbors; if he **passes** away, he confers and
LC : 0 1 :145(385) [0623] a treasure such as all who **pass** for the greatest saints do
LC : 0 1 :191(391) [0635] He will **pass** a most terrible sentence upon them in the
LC : 0 1 :243(398) [0649] that they can never enjoy it or **pass** it on to their children.
LC : 0 1 :262(400) [0655] But let this **pass**; it is the blind world's nature to condemn
LC : 0 1 :266(401) [0657] If I interfere and **pass** sentence on him, I fall into a
LC : 0 2 :020(412) [0683] We all **pass** over it, hear it, and recite it, but we neither
LC : 0 2 :059(418) [0695] Then, when we **pass** from this life, he will instantly
LC : 0 3 :007(421) [0699] and bellowing that used to **pass** for prayers in the church
LC : 0 4 :083(446) [0751] always remains until we **pass** from this present misery to
LC : 0 5 :039(451) [0761] among Christians, may not be heedlessly **passed** by .
LC : 0 5 :056(453) [0767] prepared, until one week **passes** into another and one half
SD : 0 2 :056(532) [0903] We should not and cannot **pass** judgment on the Holy
SD : 0 7 :043(577) [0987] "Heaven and earth shall **pass** away, but my words will
SD : 0 7 :043(577) [0987] but my words will not **pass** away," and again, "All
SD : 0 7 :047(578) [0989] accomplish and bring to **pass** whatever he promises.
SD : 0 7 :100(586) [1007] a musical sound or tone **passes** through air or water or a
SD : 1 0 :013(613) [1057] "Therefore let no one **pass** judgment on you in questions
SD : 1 1 :002(616) [1063] once, and as it were in **passing**, but discuss and present it
SD : 1 1 :003(616) [1063] way, one must not by-**pass** or reject a teaching of the
SD : 1 1 :026(620) [1071] We should not **pass** judgment on the basis of our reason,

Passage (50), Passages (85)

AG : 2 0 :011(042) [0055] treated by Paul in many **passages**, especially in Eph. 2:8,
AG : 2 8 :043(088) [0089] Yet there are clear **passages** of divine Scripture which
AL : 2 8 :031(085) [0087] cite as evidence the **passage**, "I have yet many things to
AP : 0 2 :003(101) [0105] This **passage** testifies that in those who are born
AP : 0 2 :031(104) [0113] We could quote many **passages** on both parts of our
AP : 0 2 :042(105) [0115] not only will many **passages** of the Scripture contradict
AP : 0 4 :083(119) [0145] But we shall discuss this **passage** later on in considering
AP : 0 4 :107(122) [0153] unmoved by the many **passages** in the Scriptures that
AP : 0 4 :122(124) [0157] and many similar **passages** regarding the law and
AP : 0 4 :124(124) [0157] These and similar **passages** assert that we should begin to
AP : 0 4 :155(128) [0165] we shall take up similar **passages**, like Luke 11:41, "Give
AP : 0 4 :183(132) [0173] For they quote **passages** about law and works but omit
AP : 0 4 :183(132) [0173] law and works but omit **passages** about the promises.

Continued ▶

A P : 0 4 :185(132) [0173] stated interprets all the **passages** they quote on law and
A P : 0 4 :207(135) [0177] Such **passages** do not condemn the sacrifices that God
A P : 0 4 :222(137) [0181] Hence this **passage** from Paul is not against us; only our
A P : 0 4 :226(138) [0183] In this **passage**, however, Paul speaks specifically about
A P : 0 4 :244(141) [0189] No other **passage** is supposed to contradict our position
A P : 0 4 :252(143) [0191] way, just as in the **passage** (Rom. 2:13), "the doers of the
A P : 0 4 :255(143) [0193] But these **passages** would say nothing against us if our
A P : 0 4 :259(144) [0193] We must interpret all similar **passages** in the same way.
A P : 0 4 :266(146) [0197] our opponents would have passed over this **passage**.
A P : 0 4 :272(148) [0199] In **passages** about penitence we should understand that
A P : 0 4 :273(148) [0199] Why recite **passages**?
A P : 0 4 :274(148) [0199] Gospel by twisting those **passages** which teach about the
A P : 0 4 :280(149) [0201] is necessary to consider **passages** in their context, because
A P : 0 4 :280(149) [0201] or reply to a single **passage** without taking the whole law
A P : 0 4 :280(149) [0201] When **passages** are considered in their own context, they
A P : 0 4 :282(149) [0201] of the whole **passage** shows that it requires faith.
A P : 0 4 :284(150) [0201] A study of the whole **passage** shows its agreement with
A P : 0 4 :284(150) [0201] about works and skip the **passages** about faith.
A P : 0 4 :286(150) [0201] have reviewed the main **passages** which our opponents
A P : 0 4 :286(150) [0201] These **passages** do not conflict with our position.
A P : 0 4 :286(150) [0201] They quote many **passages** in a garbled form.
A P : 0 4 :286(150) [0201] the clearest scriptural **passages** on faith, select the
A P : 0 4 :286(150) [0201] on faith, select the **passages** on works, and even distort
A P : 0 4 :305(154) [0205] In this **passage** "justify" is used in a judicial way to mean
A P : 0 4 :306(154) [0207] Since in this **passage** our righteousness is the imputation
A P : 0 4 :343(160) [0217] can see that this **passage** condemns trust in our own
A P : 0 4 :356(161) [0217] If these **passages** seem to our opponents to be in conflict,
A P : 0 4 :367(163) [0221] rewards, as in these **passages** a reward is offered for
A P : 0 4 :371(164) [0221] These **passages** and all others like them where works are
A P : 0 4 :372(164) [0221] we have said earlier, all **passages** on works can be
A P : 0 4 :376(164) [0223] by interpreting such **passages** of the Scriptures in either a
A P : 0 4 :376(164) [0223] From these **passages** they reason that works merit grace
A P : 0 4 :388(166) [0225] remember, whenever a **passage** on love or works is
A P : 0 7 :019(171) [0233] Therefore this **passage** is more against our opponents
A P : 1 2 :036(186) [0261] contrite according to the **passage** (Rom. 5:1), "Since we
A P : 1 2 :036(186) [0261] before God, as the same **passage** attests, "We are justified
A P : 1 2 :037(186) [0261] Christ, according to the **passage** (Rom. 5:2), "Through
A P : 1 2 :049(188) [0265] what need is there to cite **passages** since there are so many
A P : 1 2 :058(189) [0267] From all these **passages** godly readers can see that we put
A P : 1 2 :078(193) [0275] of God, according to the **passage** (Ps. 143:2), "Enter not
A P : 1 2 :083(194) [0275] We would cite more **passages** if they were not obvious to
A P : 1 2 :106(197) [0283] our opponents make **passages** of Scripture mean
A P : 1 2 :122(200) [0287] quote many Scripture **passages** to give the inexperienced
A P : 1 2 :122(200) [0289] These are **passages** they quote: "Bear fruit that befits
A P : 1 2 :131(202) [0291] The Scripture **passages** quoted by our opponents say
A P : 1 2 :133(202) [0293] to prove that these **passages** of Scripture apply in no way
A P : 1 2 :133(202) [0293] obligatory, but in these **passages** Scripture requires works
A P : 1 2 :134(203) [0293] Now, these **passages** are unquestionably commandments
A P : 1 2 :134(203) [0293] These **passages** cannot be applied to satisfactions that one
A P : 1 2 :135(203) [0293] distortion to apply these **passages** to canonical
A P : 1 2 :136(203) [0293] of purgatory, do these **passages** command that souls
A P : 1 2 :136(203) [0293] position, these **passages** will have to be interpreted in a
A P : 1 2 :138(203) [0293] The Scripture **passages** they quote do not say that
A P : 1 2 :140(204) [0295] death, according to the **passage** (Hos. 13:14), "O Death, I
A P : 1 2 :173(209) [0305] They quote **passages** dealing with obligatory works,
A P : 2 0 :005(227) [0339] we could quote endless **passages** from Scripture and the
A P : 2 0 :010(228) [0341] looks will find many **passages** in Scripture to set his mind
A P : 2 0 :012(228) [0341] quote many Scripture **passages** to show why they have
A P : 2 1 :009(230) [0345] Nevertheless, there is no **passage** in Scripture about the
A P : 2 2 :007(237) [0359] They quote **passages** that mention bread, like Luke 24:35,
A P : 2 2 :007(237) [0359] They quote other **passages** that talk about the breaking
A P : 2 2 :007(237) [0359] if someone takes these **passages** as referring to the
A P : 2 3 :032(243) [0373] could produce a **passage** like that about celibacy, they
A P : 2 3 :033(244) [0373] These **passages** teach that marriage is a lawful thing.
A P : 2 3 :063(248) [0381] it conflicts with clear **passages** of Scripture commanding
A P : 2 4 :014(251) [0387] have twisted many **passages** of Scripture in defense of
A P : 2 4 :014(251) [0389] Now we shall explain the **passages** of Scripture which
A P : 2 4 :027(254) [0393] This **passage** clearly condemns the notion that the
A P : 2 4 :030(255) [0395] Scripture is full of such **passages** which teach that
A P : 2 4 :031(255) [0395] misinterpret this **passage** and apply it to the Mass, and
A P : 2 4 :034(256) [0395] They quote another **passage** from Malachi (3:3), "And he
A P : 2 4 :034(256) [0395] This **passage** clearly requires the offerings of the
A P : 2 4 :053(259) [0403] our opponents twist **passages** from this very epistle
A P : 2 4 :061(260) [0405] that the Scripture **passages** quoted against us give no
A P : 2 4 :066(261) [0407] explained the Scripture **passages** that they quote against
A P : 2 4 :094(267) [0417] against the clearest and surest **passages** of Scripture.
A P : 2 7 :003(269) [0419] in the commentaries he left on certain **passages** in Daniel.
A P : 2 7 :012(270) [0423] They apply the **passage** in Paul only to the law of Moses.
A P : 2 7 :019(272) [0425] had been told about this **passage**, you would have seen to
A P : 2 7 :040(276) [0433] life, and it quotes the **passage** (Matt. 19:29), "Every one
A P : 2 7 :040(276) [0433] But this **passage** of Scripture has nothing to do with the
A P : 2 7 :044(277) [0435] so they quote **passages** of Scripture under false pretenses.
A P : 2 7 :045(277) [0435] They quote another **passage** on perfection (Matt. 19:21),
A P : 2 7 :045(277) [0435] This **passage** has exercised many people because they
A P : 2 7 :060(279) [0441] to the sure and clear **passages** of Scripture, not against
A P : 2 7 :060(279) [0441] passages of Scripture, not against the rule or the **passages**.
A P : 2 7 :065(280) [0441] here about vows, this **passage** does not support monastic
A P : 2 7 :066(280) [0441] upon misapplying this **passage** to vows, they must also
A P : 2 8 :008(282) [0445] is taught by that one **passage** in Acts (15:9), where the
A P : 2 8 :021(284) [0449] the same response to the **passage** (Matt. 23:3), "Observe
S 2 : 0 2 :013(295) [0465] The papists here adduce **passages** from Augustine and
S 2 : 0 2 :013(295) [0465] and to what end the authors wrote these **passages**.
S 2 : 0 2 :013(295) [0467] nor does he cite any **passage** of the Scriptures that would
T R : 0 0 :022(323) [0511] Here certain **passages** are quoted against us: "You are
T R : 0 0 :022(323) [0511] my sheep" (John 21:17), and certain other **passages**.
T R : 0 0 :023(324) [0511] In all these **passages** Peter is representative of the entire
T R : 0 0 :024(324) [0511] it is necessary in these **passages** to regard Peter as the
T R : 0 0 :024(324) [0511] on which account these **passages** do not ascribe to Peter
T R : 0 0 :030(325) [0513] As to the **passages** "Feed my sheep" (John 21:17) and "Do
S C : 0 5 :029(351) [0555] will know additional **passages** of the Scriptures with
S C : 0 9 :001(354) [0561] *consisting of certain **passages** of the Scriptures, selected*
L C : 0 1 :167(388) [0629] dealt with in many other **passages** of Scripture, and God
L C : 0 1 :278(402) [0661] himself says in the same **passage**, "If he listens to you, you
E P : 0 7 :025(485) [0815] whose meaning must first be sought in other **passages**.
E P : 1 1 :012(496) [0835] 11. The **passage**, "Many are called, but few are chosen,"
S D : 0 1 :038(514) [0871] These **passages** indicate clearly that even after the Fall
S D : 0 2 :014(523) [0885] This appealing **passage** is of very great comfort to all
S D : 0 2 :015(523) [0887] such prayers and **passages** about our ignorance and
S D : 0 2 :027(526) [0891] It was this **passage** in particular which, by St. Augustine's
S D : 0 2 :087(538) [0915] above from clear **passages** of Holy Scripture.
S D : 0 4 :024(555) [0945] words, like the Scripture **passage** which ascribes the bliss
S D : 0 5 :007(559) [0953] In some **passages** of Holy Writ the word is used and
S D : 0 5 :008(559) [0953] But in the cited **passage** in Mark 1:15, and in other places
S D : 0 7 :029(574) [0981] proportionately with the **passage** of time, and that there
S D : 0 7 :056(579) [0991] pervert this **passage**, he would not say that the bread but
S D : 0 7 :058(580) [0993] explained this **passage** of Paul in words which agree in
S D : 0 7 :059(580) [0993] that they now cite this **passage**, which they formerly
S D : 0 7 :060(580) [0995] understood and explained this **passage** in this way.
S D : 0 7 :099(586) [1005] The **passages** which the enthusiasts adduce concerning
S D : 0 8 :059(602) [1035] John is saying in this **passage** that in the work or matter
S D : 0 8 :061(602) [1035] on the basis of sound **passages** of the Holy Scriptures,
S D : 0 8 :078(606) [1043] We believe that the cited **passages** illustrate the majesty

Passion (27), Passions (3)
A G : 2 3 :004(051) [0061] to marry than to be aflame with **passion**" (I Cor. 7:9).
A L : 2 3 :004(051) [0061] to marry than to be aflame with **passion**" (I Cor. 7:9).
A L : 2 4 :021(058) [0067] that Christ had by his **passion** made satisfaction for
A L : 2 4 :024(058) [0067] the glory of Christ's **passion**, for the passion of Christ
A L : 2 4 :025(058) [0067] Christ's passion, for the **passion** of Christ was an oblation
A P : 2 1 :025(232) [0349] absolution is used: "The **passion** of our Lord Jesus Christ
A P : 2 3 :016(241) [0369] "It is better to marry than to be aflame with **passion**."
A P : 2 3 :016(241) [0369] and commands it because of these flaming **passions**.
A P : 2 3 :016(241) [0369] "It is better to marry than to be aflame with **passion**."
T R : 0 0 :008(320) [0505] when Christ spoke of his **passion**: Who was to be the
T R : 0 0 :032(325) [0513] That Christ in his **passion** was crowned with thorns and
L C : 0 1 :215(394) [0641] ragings of secret **passion**, which can be avoided in married
L C : 0 2 :032(415) [0687] such articles as the birth, **passion**, resurrection, and
E P : 0 5 :010(479) [0803] as all this — namely, the **passion** and death of Christ —
E P : 0 8 :031(491) [0825] us, and that in the **passion** the Son of God had no
S D : 0 2 :084(537) [0913] and likewise that the **passions** of the flesh wage war
S D : 0 3 :009(541) [0919] obedience, the bitter **passion**, the death, and the
S D : 0 3 :014(541) [0919] is the obedience, the **passion**, and the resurrection of
S D : 0 3 :032(545) [0927] of the obedience, **passion**, and death of Christ which is
S D : 0 3 :056(549) [0935] God, the obedience and **passion** of the human nature
S D : 0 3 :056(549) [0935] the obedience nor the **passion** of the human nature alone,
S D : 0 4 :019(554) [0945] killed) their flesh with its **passions**, desires, and deeds
S D : 0 5 :012(560) [0955] wrath over sin than the **passion** and death of Christ, his
S D : 0 7 :044(577) [0987] about to begin his bitter **passion** and death for our sin, in
S D : 0 7 :044(577) [0987] memorial of his bitter **passion** and death and all of his
S D : 0 7 :076(583) [0999] in his *Sermon on the **Passion***: "Christ himself prepares
S D : 0 8 :040(598) [1029] and does no more in his **passion** and death than any
S D : 0 8 :043(599) [1029] the texts concerning the **passion** only to the human
S D : 0 8 :044(599) [1031] be said: God dead, God's **passion**, God's blood, God's
S D : 0 8 :093(609) [1049] whatever in the **passion**, suffered for us and redeemed us.

Passiva (1)
S 3 : 0 3 :002(304) [0479] (artificial remorse), but ***passiva** contritio* (true sorrow of

Passive (1), Passively (1)
E P : 0 2 :018(472) [0791] behaves "altogether **passively**" (that is, that it does
S D : 0 2 :089(538) [0915] man behaves in a purely **passive** way in his conversion

Passover (8)
A P : 0 7 :040(176) [0241] Gospel history, like the **Passover** and Pentecost, so that
A P : 0 7 :042(176) [0241] by which our **Passover** falls at a different time from the
A P : 0 7 :042(176) [0241] falls at a different time from the Jewish **Passover**.
A P : 0 7 :042(176) [0241] to celebrate the **Passover** with the brethren who had been
A P : 0 7 :043(177) [0243] this apostolic decree the **Passover** should be celebrated
A P : 2 4 :085(265) [0413] to the celebration of the **Passover** had to bring some gift
L C : 0 5 :047(452) [0763] to a special time like the **Passover**, which the Jews were
L C : 0 5 :047(452) [0765] to say: "I institute a **Passover** or Supper for you, which

Past (21)
P R : P R :025(013) [0023] and confessed in the **past**, for our agreement is based on
A G : P R :015(026) [0041] In the **past** Your Imperial Majesty graciously gave
A G : 2 4 :041(061) [0069] In times **past**, even in large churches where there were
A G : 2 7 :008(072) [0077] many devout people in the **past**, for they must have seen
A G : 0 0 :002(095) [0095] In the **past** there have been grave complaints about
A P : 1 2 :091(195) [0279] means to lament **past** evils and not to commit again deeds
A P : 1 2 :158(207) [0301] were not imposed on him because of his **past** misdeeds.
A P : 1 2 :160(207) [0301] penalties for certain **past** deeds, but works of God,
L C : 0 1 :043(370) [0591] Reflect on the **past**, search it out, and tell me, When men
L C : 0 1 :140(384) [0621] which in the **past** was neither heeded nor taught under the
L C : 0 1 :144(385) [0623] These works in the **past** have been neglected and
L C : 0 1 :162(387) [0627] preacher although in the **past** they filled ten fat paunches.
L C : 0 2 :061(419) [0695] Creation is **past** and redemption is accomplished, but the
L C : 0 3 :031(424) [0707] such great results in the **past**, parrying the counsels and
L C : 0 3 :045(426) [0709] this holy name, as in the **past** a church was said to be
L C : 0 4 :001(436) [0733] unfortunately in the **past** nothing was taught about them.
L C : 0 4 :080(446) [0751] our Baptism is something **past** which we can no longer
L C : 0 6 :016(459) [0000] In the **past** we placed all the emphasis on our work alone,
L C : 0 6 :025(460) [0000] preachers have in the **past** kept silence about this
S D : P R :009(503) [0849] with one party talking **past** the other, so that the strife
S D : P R :019(507) [0857] place, since within the **past** twenty-five years a number of

Pastor (15), Pastors (46)
A G : P R :008(025) [0039] a confession of our **pastors**' and preachers' teaching and
A G : 2 3 :016(054) [0063] and especially of the **pastors** and others who are to
A G : 2 3 :017(054) [0063] may be a shortage of priests and **pastors** in the future.
A G : 2 7 :013(073) [0077] — whether the office of **pastor** and preacher, of ruler,
A G : 2 7 :015(073) [0077] Christian church, so that **pastors** and bishops were taken
A G : 2 8 :053(090) [0091] reply that bishops or **pastors** may make regulations so
A L : 2 3 :017(054) [0063] will soon be lacking in **pastors** if marriage continues to be
A L : 2 7 :013(072) [0077] the life of magistrates, **pastors**, and the like who, without
A L : 2 7 :015(073) [0077] to the church, and **pastors** and bishops were taken from
A L : 2 8 :030(085) [0087] whether bishops or **pastors** have the right to introduce

Continued ▶

AL : 28 :053(090) [0091] is lawful for bishops or **pastors** to make regulations so
AL : 28 :071(093) [0093] (which, however, good **pastors** ought to do), but ask only
AP : 04 :243(141) [0189] cannot endure unless **pastors** and churches overlook and
AP : 11 :005(181) [0251] Therefore our **pastors** do not force those who are not
AP : 11 :009(181) [0251] Good **pastors** know how profitable it is to examine the
AP : 12 :106(197) [0283] given a father to the **pastor** of a church, he should surely
AP : 12 :139(203) [0295] to canonical penalties, part of which the **pastors** remitted.
AP : 15 :041(220) [0325] In our circles the **pastors** and ministers of the churches
AP : 21 :040(235) [0355] and negligence of the **pastors** permitted many abuses to
AP : 22 :017(238) [0361] about bishops and **pastors** in the words of Ezekiel (7:26),
S2 : 03 :001(297) [0471] order that we may have **pastors**, preachers, and other
S2 : 04 :001(298) [0471] is only the bishop and **pastor** of the churches in Rome
S3 : 15 :005(317) [0501] Simon Schneeweiss, **pastor** of the church in Crailsheim
S3 : 15 :005(317) [0501] I, John Schlagenhaufen, **pastor** of the church in Koethen,
S3 : 15 :005(317) [0501] Wendal Faber, **pastor** of Seeburg in Mansfeld
S3 : 15 :005(317) [0501] I, Frederick Myconius, **pastor** of the church in Gotha,
TR : 00 :001(320) [0503] that he is by divine right above all bishops and **pastors**.
TR : 00 :005(320) [0503] That is, all bishops and **pastors** throughout the whole
TR : 00 :007(320) [0505] is not by divine right above all other bishops and **pastors**.
TR : 00 :026(324) [0511] God gives his gifts, apostles, prophets, **pastors**, teachers.
TR : 00 :061(330) [0521] whether they are called **pastors**, presbyters, or bishops.
TR : 00 :063(331) [0523] bishop and presbyter (or **pastor**) is by human authority.
TR : 00 :064(331) [0523] between bishops and **pastors**, and this was ordination, for
TR : 00 :065(331) [0523] between bishop and **pastor** is not by divine right, it is
TR : 00 :065(331) [0523] administered by a **pastor** in his own church is valid by
TR : 00 :067(331) [0523] He enumerates **pastors** and teachers among the gifts
TR : 00 :067(331) [0523] absolves and becomes the minister and **pastor** of another.
TR : 00 :070(332) [0525] was a time when the people elected **pastors** and bishops.
TR : 00 :072(332) [0525] compelled to ordain **pastors** and ministers for themselves.
TR : 00 :074(332) [0525] who are guilty of manifest crimes belongs to all **pastors**.
TR : 00 :076(333) [0527] this jurisdiction to godly **pastors** and see to it that it is
TR : 00 :079(333) [0527] jurisdiction from the **pastors** and tyrannically exercise it
TR : 00 :082(335) [0529] Simon Schneeweiss, **pastor** at Crailsheim
TR : 00 :082(335) [0529] Wendel Faber, **pastor** of Seeburg in Mansfeld
SC : 00 :000(337) [0531] of Dr. Martin Luther for Ordinary **Pastors** and Preachers
SC : PR :000(338) [0533] Martin Luther to all faithful, godly **pastors** and preachers.
SC : PR :002(338) [0533] and unfortunately many **pastors** are quite incompetent
SC : PR :006(338) [0533] brethren who are **pastors** and preachers, that you take the
SC : PR :020(340) [0537] of children to become **pastors**, preachers, notaries, etc.,
SC : PR :022(341) [0537] as it were, compel us **pastors** to administer it to them.
SC : PR :025(341) [0539] So it is up to you, dear **pastor** and preacher!
SC : 05 :021(350) [0553] to the confessor: "Dear **Pastor**, please hear my confession
SC : 09 :002(354) [0561] Bishops, **Pastors**, and Preachers
SC : 09 :003(354) [0561] Duties Christians Owe Their Teachers and **Pastors**
LC : PR :001(358) [0567] to our sorrow that many **pastors** and preachers are very
LC : PR :001(358) [0567] matter as if they were **pastors** or preachers for their
LC : PR :002(358) [0567] or dogkeepers than spiritual guides or **pastors**.
LC : PR :006(359) [0569] that we can do without **pastors** and preachers from now
LC : PR :006(359) [0569] and brazenly allow both **pastors** and preachers to suffer
LC : PR :013(360) [0571] — especially we who would be **pastors** and preachers?
LC : PR :019(361) [0573] all Christians, especially **pastors** and preachers, not to try

Pasture (2)
TR : 00 :030(325) [0513] for Christ bids Peter to **pasture** the sheep, that is, to
SD : PR :014(506) [0855] Luther states, "must both **pasture** or feed the lambs and

Patent (3), Patently (2)
PR : PR :004(003) [0007] of common knowledge, **patent** and unconcealed, what
AG : 28 :035(086) [0089] It is **patently** contrary to God's command and Word to
LC : 01 :302(405) [0667] to him with letters **patent** and the seal of the prince
SD : 01 :043(516) [0873] they also rejected the contrary doctrine as **patent** heresy.
SD : 07 :046(577) [0987] these words were **patently** contrary not only to reason and

Paternal (1)
LC : 01 :180(389) [0631] that is, divine and **paternal** authority and obedience.

Path (4)
LC : 01 :047(371) [0593] we shall be on the right **path** and walk straight ahead,
EP : RN :001(464) [0777] "Thy word is a lamp to my feet and a light to my **path**."
SD : 03 :058(550) [0937] us, bore our sin, and in his **path** to the Father rendered to
SD : 11 :062(626) [1083] we will remain on the right **path**, as it is written, "O

Patience (13), Patient (4), Patiently (4)
AG : 20 :037(046) [0057] call upon God, have **patience** in suffering, love one's
AL : 18 :009(040) [0053] such as fear of God, trust in God, **patience**, etc.]
AP : 04 :151(127) [0163] of them (whether **patience**, chastity, or obedience to the
AP : 04 :167(130) [0169] Who endures **patiently** enough the afflictions that God
AP : 07 :031(174) [0239] Spirit, as are chastity, **patience**, the fear of God, the love
AP : 12 :003(182) [0253] Charles, to hear us out **patiently** and to consider carefully
AP : 20 :015(229) [0343] follows, by which love, **patience**, chastity, and other fruits
LC : 01 :187(390) [0633] our anger and have a **patient**, gentle heart, especially
LC : 01 :195(391) [0637] such as gentleness, **patience**, and, in short, love and
LC : 01 :275(402) [0659] physician who, to cure a **patient**, is sometimes compelled
LC : 01 :313(407) [0671] practicing gentleness, **patience**, love toward enemies,
LC : 03 :066(429) [0717] remain steadfast, suffer **patiently** whatever befalls us, and
LC : 03 :067(429) [0717] on its account, we may **patiently** bear and overcome, so
LC : 03 :109(435) [0729] if at present I am chaste, **patient**, kind, and firm in faith,
LC : 04 :067(445) [0749] we live the more gentle, **patient**, and meek we become,
LC : 05 :044(451) [0763] to faith, love, and **patience** it is not enough simply to
SD : 11 :030(621) [1073] in love, have hope, **patience**, and comfort in afflictions
SD : 11 :048(624) [1079] our necessities, grant us **patience**, give us comfort, create
SD : 11 :073(628) [1087] modesty, temperance, **patience**, and brotherly love, and
SD : 11 :079(629) [1089] endured with much **patience** the vessels of wrath fitted for
SD : 11 :080(629) [1089] God "endured the vessels of wrath with much **patience**."

Patres (2)
LC : 01 :142(384) [0621] of the household ***patres*** *et matres familias* (that is,
LC : 01 :142(384) [0621] and overlords were called ***patres*** *patriae* (that is, fathers

Patriae (1)
LC : 01 :142(384) [0621] were called *patres* ***patriae*** (that is, fathers of the country)

Patriarch (1), Patriarchal (1), Patriarchs (8)
AP : 04 :057(114) [0137] forgiveness of sins, the **patriarchs** knew the promise of the
AP : 04 :059(115) [0137] Therefore the **patriarchs**, too, were justified not by the
AP : 04 :206(135) [0177] had sacrifices which they took over from the **patriarchs**.
AP : 12 :053(189) [0265] to Adam, later to the **patriarchs**, then illumined by the
AP : 24 :023(253) [0391] from their misinterpretation of the **patriarchal** tradition.
AP : 24 :093(267) [0417] to all the blessed **patriarchs**, prophets, and apostles.
AP : 24 :093(267) [0417] in faith, forefathers, fathers, **patriarchs**, prophets," etc.
TR : 00 :019(323) [0509] 10. When writing to the **patriarch** of Alexandria, Gregory
SD : 05 :023(562) [0959] descendants of the holy **patriarchs**, like the patriarchs
SD : 05 :023(562) [0959] holy patriarchs, like the **patriarchs** themselves, constantly

Patrimony (1)
AP : 27 :009(270) [0421] expense without the loss of their private **patrimony**?

Patristic (5)
AP : 02 :007(101) [0107] misunderstand the **patristic** definition of original sin and
AP : 12 :068(192) [0271] the like in addition to **patristic** statements which the
AP : 12 :167(208) [0303] we have said before, the **patristic** discussions and
AP : 24 :031(255) [0395] it to the Mass, and for this they quote **patristic** authority.
AP : 24 :065(261) [0407] **Patristic** Teaching on Sacrifice

Patron (1)
LC : 01 :011(366) [0583] St. Lawrence as his **patron**; if he feared the plague, he

Pattern (11), Patterns (1)
AP : 27 :017(271) [0425] to be sure, the monks "**pattern** their lives more closely
AP : 27 :039(276) [0433] say that monks try to **pattern** their lives more closely with
AP : 27 :039(276) [0433] if they say that monks **pattern** their lives more closely
EP : 04 :009(476) [0799] no way contrary to the **pattern** of sound words and
EP : 06 :001(479) [0805] to which they should **pattern** and regulate their entire
SD : PR :001(503) [0849] a summary formula and **pattern**, unanimously approved,
SD : PR :009(505) [0853] as the sum and **pattern** of the doctrine which Dr. Luther
SD : PR :010(506) [0855] with the aforementioned **pattern** of doctrine they are to
SD : 01 :050(517) [0875] is to use and keep the **pattern** of sound words, as the
SD : 04 :024(555) [0945] they are contrary to the **pattern** of sound words, like the
SD : 04 :036(557) [0949] St. Paul to maintain the **pattern** of sound words as well
SD : 07 :002(569) [0971] the formulas and speech-**patterns** of the Augsburg

Paul (399)
AG : 04 :003(030) [0045] faith as righteousness, as **Paul** says in Romans 3:21-26
AG : 07 :004(032) [0047] It is as **Paul** says in Eph. 4:4, 5, "There is one body and
AG : 18 :003(039) [0051] the Word of God, for **Paul** says in I Cor. 2:14, "Natural
AG : 20 :011(042) [0055] and clearly treated by **Paul** in many passages, especially in
AG : 20 :016(043) [0055] it has a gracious God, as **Paul** says in Rom. 5:1, "Since we
AG : 22 :003(049) [0059] if they apply only to priests, **Paul** shows in I Cor. 11:20ff.
AG : 23 :004(051) [0061] to avoid immorality, for **Paul** says, "Because of the
AG : 23 :011(052) [0061] **Paul** therefore said in I Tim. 3:2, "A bishop must be
AG : 23 :022(055) [0063] I Tim. 4:1, 3 the apostle **Paul** calls the teaching that
AG : 24 :028(059) [0067] In the second place, St. **Paul** taught that we obtain grace
AG : 24 :035(060) [0067] which can be proved by St. **Paul's** statement in
AG : 26 :005(064) [0071] On this account St. **Paul** contended mightily against the
AG : 26 :024(067) [0073] **Paul** also says in Rom. 14:17, "The kingdom of God does
AG : 26 :037(069) [0075] **Paul** said that he pommeled his body and subdued it, and
AG : 27 :037(077) [0081] St. **Paul** also teaches everywhere that one is not to seek
AG : 27 :041(077) [0081] St. **Paul** says in Gal. 5:4, "You are severed from Christ,
AG : 28 :009(082) [0085] holy sacraments, for St. **Paul** says, "The gospel is the
AG : 28 :016(083) [0085] **Paul** also wrote in Phil. 3:20, "Our commonwealth is in
AG : 28 :024(084) [0087] St. **Paul** also writes in Gal. 1:8, "Even if we, or an angel
AG : 28 :026(084) [0087] Again **Paul** refers to "the authority which the Lord has
AG : 28 :042(088) [0089] And St. **Paul** said in II Cor. 10:8 that authority was given
AG : 28 :044(088) [0089] Thus St. **Paul** says in Col. 2:16, "Let no one pass
AG : 28 :046(088) [0089] In Tit. 1:14 St. **Paul** also forbids giving heed to Jewish
AG : 28 :052(089) [0091] for justification, as St. **Paul** writes in Gal. 5:1, "For
AG : 28 :054(090) [0091] So St. **Paul** directed in I Cor. 11:5 that women should
AL : 07 :004(032) [0047] It is as **Paul** says, "One faith, one baptism, one God and
AL : 20 :011(042) [0055] is everywhere treated in **Paul**, as in Eph. 2:8, "For by
AL : 20 :012(043) [0055] a new interpretation of **Paul**, this whole matter is
AL : 20 :016(043) [0055] It is as **Paul** teaches in Rom. 5:1, "Since we are justified
AL : 22 :003(049) [0059] this refers only to priests, **Paul** in I Cor. 11:20ff. cites an
AL : 23 :004(051) [0061] this was done because **Paul** says, "Because of the
AL : 23 :011(052) [0061] **Paul** said that a married man should be chosen to be
AL : 23 :022(055) [0063] is called a doctrine of demons by **Paul** in I Tim. 4:3.
AL : 24 :004(056) [0065] **Paul** prescribed that in church a language should be used
AL : 24 :012(057) [0065] But **Paul** severely threatened those who dealt unworthily
AL : 24 :039(060) [0069] **Paul** also commands concerning Communion that one
AL : 26 :005(064) [0071] **Paul** therefore lays the greatest weight on this article and
AL : 26 :006(064) [0071] This teaching of **Paul** has been almost wholly smothered
AL : 26 :029(068) [0075] And in I Tim. 4:1, 3 **Paul** calls the prohibition of foods a
AL : 26 :037(069) [0075] **Paul** also said, "I pommel my body and subdue it."
AL : 27 :037(077) [0081] **Paul** also teaches everywhere that righteousness is not to
AL : 27 :041(077) [0081] **Paul** says, "You are severed from Christ, you who would
AL : 28 :009(082) [0085] Word and sacraments, for **Paul** says, "The gospel is the
AL : 28 :016(083) [0085] **Paul** also wrote in Phil. 3:20, "Our commonwealth is in
AL : 28 :042(088) [0089] yoke on the disciples and **Paul** says that authority was
AL : 28 :044(088) [0089] In Col. 2 **Paul** says, "Let no one pass judgment on you in
AL : 28 :046(088) [0089] In Tit. 1 **Paul** also says, "Not giving heed to Jewish myths
AL : 28 :054(090) [0091] So **Paul** ordained that women should cover their heads in
AP : 02 :020(103) [0111] In Eph. 5:9 and Col. 3:10 **Paul** shows that the image of
AP : 02 :030(104) [0113] For **Paul** sometimes mentions the deficiency, as in
AP : 02 :039(105) [0115] Besides, **Paul** says (Rom. 7:7), "I should not have known
AP : 04 :038(112) [0131] **Paul** says (Rom. 4:15), "The law brings wrath."
AP : 04 :041(113) [0133] As **Paul** says (Rom. 11:6), "If it is by works, it is no
AP : 04 :042(113) [0133] So **Paul** reasons in Rom. 4:14, "If it is the adherents of
AP : 04 :048(113) [0135] about faith by which, as **Paul** says so often, men are
AP : 04 :050(114) [0135] **Paul** clearly shows that faith does not simply mean
AP : 04 :067(116) [0139] through the Word, as **Paul** says (Rom. 1:16), "The Gospel
AP : 04 :073(117) [0141] some people, even though **Paul** says (Rom. 3:28), "We
AP : 04 :073(117) [0141] other exclusive terms from **Paul**, too, like "freely," "not of
AP : 04 :079(118) [0143] in our hearts, as **Paul** says in I Cor. 15:56, 57: "The sting
AP : 04 :081(118) [0143] Thus **Paul** says in Rom. 5:2, "Through him we have
AP : 04 :081(118) [0145] **Paul**, on the other hand, teaches that we have access (that
AP : 04 :082(118) [0145] as an expiation," and **Paul** adds, "to be received by faith."
AP : 04 :084(119) [0145] In Rom. 4:16 **Paul** says, "That is why it depends on faith,

Continued ▶

Continued ▶

SC : 04 :010(349) [0551] in the Holy Spirit, as St. **Paul** wrote to Titus (3:5-8), "He
SC : 04 :014(349) [0553] In Romans 6:4, St. **Paul** wrote, "We were buried therefore
SC : 06 :004(351) [0555] and Luke, and also St. **Paul**, write thus: "Our Lord Jesus
LC : PR :011(360) [0571] Dietrich of Bern, but as St. **Paul** says in Rom. 1:16, it is
LC : SP :022(364) [0579] in short, simple words according to the text of St. **Paul**.
LC : 01 :065(373) [0599] Gospel, and yet Christ, St. **Paul**, and other saints took
LC : 01 :133(383) [0619] St. **Paul** also highly exalts and praises this
LC : 01 :159(387) [0627] St. **Paul** boasts that he is a father in I Cor. 4:15, where he
LC : 01 :160(387) [0627] In short, as St. **Paul** says, they must be "the refuse of the
LC : 01 :220(394) [0643] This is why St. **Paul** so urgently admonishes husbands
LC : 01 :287(403) [0663] in our own bodies, as St. **Paul** says in I Cor. 12:22, 23,
LC : 03 :015(422) [0701] and holy as St. Peter or St. **Paul**, then I would pray."
LC : 03 :015(422) [0701] commandment that applied to St. **Paul** applies also to me.
LC : 03 :016(422) [0701] to God as those of St. **Paul** and the holiest of saints.
LC : 04 :027(440) [0739] "washing of regeneration," as St. **Paul** calls it in Titus 3:5.
LC : 05 :075(455) [0771] your own good turn to St. **Paul**'s Epistle to the Galatians
LC : 05 :076(455) [0771] Yes, and St. **Paul** concludes in Rom. 7:18, "For I know
LC : 05 :076(455) [0771] If St. **Paul** can speak thus of his flesh, let us not pretend
EP : RN :001(464) [0777] And St. **Paul** says in Gal. 1:8, "Even if an angel from
EP : 03 :010(474) [0795] words of the holy apostle **Paul** which separate the merit
EP : 03 :010(474) [0795] Thus the holy apostle **Paul** uses such expressions as *"by*
EP : 04 :013(477) [0799] much weakness, as St. **Paul** complains of himself in
EP : 05 :002(478) [0801] so that, according to St. **Paul**'s admonition, the Word of
EP : 06 :006(481) [0807] In his epistles St. **Paul** calls it the law of Christ and the
EP : 07 :015(483) [0813] Likewise, St. **Paul** says, "The bread which we break, is it
EP : 08 :016(489) [0821] given to me," and as St. **Paul** states, He ascended "far
EP : 08 :034(491) [0825] been given to me," and St. **Paul**'s statement, "In him
EP : 10 :006(493) [0829] things, as the apostle **Paul** writes, "For freedom Christ
EP : 11 :011(495) [0835] the order which St. **Paul** follows in the Epistle to the
EP : 11 :016(497) [0837] in Scripture, as St. **Paul** testifies, was written for our
SD : 01 :009(510) [0861] children of wrath by nature, as St. **Paul** says (Rom. 5:12).
SD : 02 :010(522) [0883] It is as St. **Paul** says in I Cor. 2:14, "The unspiritual man
SD : 02 :014(523) [0885] (John 15:5), and what St. **Paul** says is also true, "For God
SD : 02 :015(523) [0887] find similar prayers in St. **Paul**'s letters (Eph. 1:17, 18;
SD : 02 :017(524) [0887] St. **Paul** explains this text: "The mind that is set on the
SD : 02 :017(524) [0887] and shortly thereafter St. **Paul** says, "I know that nothing
SD : 02 :018(524) [0887] or carnal free will of St. **Paul** and other regenerated
SD : 02 :026(526) [0891] heart to give heed to what was said by **Paul**" (Acts 16:14).
SD : 02 :034(528) [0895] throughout life, as St. **Paul** says in Rom. 7:23, that he
SD : 02 :039(528) [0895] but the Holy Spirit, as St. **Paul** says, creates such willing
SD : 02 :063(533) [0905] motivates him, as St. **Paul** says, "For all who are led by
SD : 02 :064(533) [0905] the words of St. **Paul** apply also to the regenerated, "For
SD : 02 :066(534) [0907] in us in conversion, as St. **Paul** expressly and earnestly
SD : 02 :067(534) [0907] to the teaching of St. **Paul**, "all who have been baptized
SD : 02 :081(537) [0911] adduces and explains St. **Paul**'s words, "Put off the old
SD : 03 :002(539) [0917] of faith, which St. **Paul** calls the righteousness of God, is
SD : 03 :007(540) [0917] And St. **Paul** says specifically of this doctrine that a little
SD : 03 :012(541) [0919] statements of St. **Paul** are to be considered and taken as
SD : 03 :019(542) [0921] is regeneration, just as St. **Paul** uses the terms
SD : 03 :027(543) [0923] But when St. **Paul** says, "We are justified by faith apart
SD : 03 :029(544) [0925] then we answer with St. **Paul** that we are justified alone
SD : 03 :033(545) [0927] At this point St. **Paul**'s statement concerning Abraham is
SD : 03 :033(545) [0927] And St. **Paul** raises this question (Rom. 4:1): On what did
SD : 03 :036(545) [0927] And this is St. **Paul**'s intention when in this article he so
SD : 03 :042(547) [0931] faith justifies, it is St. **Paul**'s doctrine that faith alone
SD : 03 :043(547) [0931] exclusive terms which St. **Paul** employs, such as "apart
SD : 03 :053(548) [0933] diametrically opposed to **Paul**'s statement that salvation
SD : 03 :053(548) [0933] **Paul**'s reason is that we receive both our righteousness
SD : 03 :053(548) [0933] For this reason **Paul** uses and urges exclusive terms (that
SD : 03 :054(549) [0935] of faith of which St. **Paul** speaks and which he calls the
SD : 03 :067(551) [0937] splendid exposition of St. **Paul**'s Epistle to the Galatians.
SD : 04 :007(552) [0941] the Holy Spirit, or, as St. **Paul** says, "has been created in
SD : 04 :009(552) [0941] For this reason St. **Paul** calls them fruits of faith or of the
SD : 04 :010(552) [0941] to the Epistle of St. **Paul** to the Romans, "Faith is a
SD : 04 :019(554) [0945] to the distinction which **Paul** makes when he says on the
SD : 04 :019(554) [0945] and recalcitrant flesh, **Paul** says, "I pommel my body and
SD : 04 :022(554) [0945] opposed to St. **Paul**'s words which exclude our works and
SD : 04 :034(556) [0949] may be very certain to us, **Paul** ascribes to faith not only
SD : 04 :036(557) [0949] to follow the advice of St. **Paul** to maintain the pattern of
SD : 04 :037(557) [0949] thereby, it is not we, but **Paul** himself, who declares no
SD : 05 :004(559) [0953] Likewise, **Paul** calls his entire teaching "Gospel"
SD : 05 :010(560) [0955] For **Paul** testifies that although "Moses is read," the veil
SD : 05 :026(563) [0961] and mightily set forth by St. **Paul** in II Cor. 3:7-9.
SD : 06 :005(564) [0963] down for the just, as St. **Paul** says (I Tim. 1:9), but for the
SD : 06 :005(564) [0963] On the contrary, it is St. **Paul**'s intention that the law
SD : 06 :014(566) [0967] to the law of God, and St. **Paul** says, "All Scripture is
SD : 06 :016(566) [0967] St. **Paul** calls the works of such a man "works of the law"
SD : 06 :017(567) [0967] of the Spirit, or, as St. **Paul** calls them, the law of the
SD : 06 :017(567) [0967] According to St. **Paul**, such people are no longer under
SD : 06 :021(567) [0969] that we must say with St. **Paul**, "I am not aware of
SD : 06 :021(567) [0969] Thus, when **Paul** admonishes those who have been born
SD : 07 :011(571) [0975] there with the words of **Paul** in I Cor. 10:16 and with a
SD : 07 :011(571) [0975] Holy Spirit, then when **Paul** says that the bread which we
SD : 07 :016(572) [0977] receives it, since, as St. **Paul** says, the unworthy receive
SD : 07 :016(572) [0977] it for judgment, as St. **Paul** says, for they misuse the holy
SD : 07 :035(575) [0983] words of Christ and of St. **Paul** (the bread in the Lord's
SD : 07 :052(578) [0991] Luke (22:19), as well as St. **Paul** who received the same
SD : 07 :053(579) [0991] the words of Luke and **Paul**, "This cup is the new
SD : 07 :054(579) [0991] words of Christ which St. **Paul** gives us in I Cor. 10:16
SD : 07 :056(579) [0991] If **Paul** were speaking only of a spiritual participation in
SD : 07 :057(579) [0993] purpose and context of St. **Paul**'s entire discourse prove,
SD : 07 :057(579) [0993] in the body of Christ, St. **Paul** certainly could not be
SD : 07 :058(580) [0993] explained this passage of **Paul** in words which agree in the
SD : 07 :060(580) [0993] But St. **Paul** teaches expressly that not only godly, pious,
SD : 07 :060(580) [0993] St. **Paul** says, "Who eats the bread or drinks the cup of
SD : 07 :066(581) [0995] Christ's institution and St. **Paul**'s exposition of them, all
SD : 07 :067(582) [0997] the Lord Christ, St. **Paul**, and the entire church when they
SD : 07 :071(582) [0997] no less than Abraham, **Paul**, and others who had a
SD : 07 :082(584) [1001] us to eat and to drink, as **Paul** says, "The cup of blessing
SD : 07 :084(584) [1001] and inviolately, just as St. **Paul** sets the whole action of
SD : 07 :099(586) [1005] on the Last Day, as St. **Paul** says, "This will be made
SD : 08 :016(594) [1021] Manes by the name of **Paul**, a native of Samosata who
SD : 08 :033(597) [1027] is the personal union, as **Paul** says, "Great indeed is the
SD : 08 :077(606) [1043] If that were true, Peter, **Paul**, and all the saints in heaven
SD : 08 :085(608) [1047] and demonstrated, as St. **Paul** says, 'He is designated the
SD : 10 :006(611) [1055] In this case the words of **Paul** must be heeded: "Do not be
SD : 10 :009(612) [1055] **Paul** instructs us how we can with a good conscience give
SD : 10 :012(612) [1057] **Paul** is here speaking of circumcision, which at that time
SD : 10 :012(613) [1057] and salvation, **Paul** said that he would not yield, not even
SD : 10 :013(613) [1057] Thus **Paul** yielded and gave in to the weak as far as
SD : 10 :013(613) [1057] yielded to a certain extent, **Paul** criticized them publicly
SD : 10 :022(615) [1061] **Paul** also commanded that ungodly teachers should be
SD : 11 :005(617) [1065] the world was laid," as St. **Paul** says, "Even as he chose us
SD : 11 :014(619) [1069] and salvation, as **Paul** treats and explains this article
SD : 11 :019(619) [1069] love all who are thus justified, as St. **Paul** says (Eph. 1:4).
SD : 11 :027(620) [1071] to us, however, as **Paul** says, "Those whom God has
SD : 11 :027(620) [1071] St. **Paul** testified to the same effect when he wrote, "We
SD : 11 :033(622) [1073] warfare against sin as **Paul** teaches from the first to the
SD : 11 :042(623) [1077] This would contradict St. **Paul** in Phil. 1:6.
SD : 11 :047(624) [1079] For this reason, too, **Paul** asks, Since we are called
SD : 11 :049(624) [1079] Again, **Paul** presents this in a most comforting manner
SD : 11 :049(624) [1079] From this **Paul** draws the certain and indubitable
SD : 11 :058(625) [1081] **Paul** sets a definite limit for us as to how far we should go
SD : 11 :063(626) [1083] these limits, we must with **Paul** place our finger to our
SD : 11 :064(626) [1083] The great apostle **Paul** shows us that we cannot and
SD : 11 :064(626) [1083] his own hidden wisdom, **Paul** immediately commands
SD : 11 :065(627) [1083] For according to St. **Paul**'s testimony we have been
SD : 11 :079(629) [1089] Hence **Paul** very carefully distinguishes between the work
SD : 11 :082(630) [1089] And St. **Paul** testifies with clear words that God's power

Paunches (1)

LC : 01 :162(387) [0627] preacher although in the past they filled ten fat **paunches**.

Pay (35), Paying (1), Payment (10), Pays (1), Paid (12)

PR : PR :022(012) [0021] **Payment** for it will without doubt be required of the
AG : 28 :066(092) [0093] One must **pay** attention to the chief article of Christian
AP : 02 :032(104) [0113] have evidently not **paid** attention to what the Fathers
AP : 04 :051(114) [0135] what faith is if we **pay** attention to the article of the Creed
AP : 04 :057(114) [0137] they knew that our works could not **pay** so high a price.
AP : 04 :334(159) [0215] of his promise, not as a **payment** which he owes to us for
AP : 12 :024(185) [0257] of purgatory, or they profit as a **payment** to blot out guilt.
AP : 12 :106(197) [0283] a household, telling him to **pay** diligent attention to his
AP : 12 :128(201) [0291] You do not **pay** enough attention to the importance of
AP : 12 :132(202) [0293] imagine avail as a **payment** for the punishments of
AP : 12 :134(203) [0293] not sin but will have to **pay** the penalties in purgatory.
AP : 12 :143(204) [0297] but, as Scotus says, to **pay** homage to God and to
AP : 12 :143(204) [0297] which *ex opere operato* **pay** homage to God and
AP : 12 :144(205) [0297] the honor of being a price **paid** in lieu of eternal death.
AP : 12 :146(205) [0297] This **payment** of works does not atone for eternal death
AP : 12 :157(207) [0301] death only by the **payment** of certain penalties over and
AP : 12 :157(207) [0301] of present sin, not as a **payment** for or a ransom from
AP : 12 :160(208) [0303] our obedience but not to **pay** for eternal death; for this
AP : 12 :163(208) [0303] Our opponents are **paying** the penalty for their neglect of
AP : 12 :167(209) [0305] they did not mean a **payment** for eternal punishment, or a
AP : 12 :168(209) [0305] the flesh, not to **pay** for eternal punishments but to keep
AP : 12 :175(210) [0307] to civil discipline but to **payment** for penalties; so also
AP : 21 :019(231) [0347] If one **pays** a debt for one's friend, the debtor is freed by
AP : 24 :048(258) [0401] the priests in our churches **pay** attention to the ministry
AP : 24 :081(264) [0411] "liturgy" is a kind of tax to **pay** for the games, ships, care
AP : 24 :091(266) [0415] Some day they will **pay** the penalty for this sacrilege.
AP : 27 :038(275) [0433] for the whole city and then **paid** attention to his business.
S1 : PR :005(289) [0457] all poisoned) who do not **pay** attention to what I write
S3 : 03 :012(305) [0481] merited forgiveness and has **paid** for his sins before God.
S3 : 03 :027(307) [0487] year must be contrite, make confession, and **pay** money."
S3 : 03 :036(309) [0489] we might imagine to be good enough to **pay** for our sin.
S3 : 12 :002(315) [0499] Nor shall we **pay** any attention to what they command or
TR : 00 :082(334) [0527] know that God will require them to **pay** for their crime.
SC : PR :004(338) [0533] neglected the people and **paid** no attention at all to the
SC : 09 :005(355) [0561] the same reason you also **pay** taxes, for the authorities
SC : 09 :005(355) [0561] **Pay** all of them their dues, taxes to whom taxes are due,
LC : 01 :118(381) [0615] monks and nuns would **pay** if in the exercise of their
LC : 01 :144(385) [0623] ought even to be willing to **pay** for the privilege of service
LC : 01 :151(386) [0625] we seek and deserve, then, is **paid** back to us in retaliation
LC : 01 :152(386) [0625] difficult do you think it will be for him to **pay** you back?
LC : 01 :224(395) [0643] common vice, but people **pay** so little attention to it that
LC : 01 :236(397) [0647] you have done you will have to **pay** back thirty-fold.
LC : 01 :238(397) [0647] He will **pay** them what they deserve.
LC : 01 :316(408) [0671] a single groschen to **pay**, but I promise to pay ten
LC : 01 :316(408) [0671] single groschen to pay, but I promise to **pay** ten gulden."
LC : 01 :318(408) [0673] you will neither seek nor **pay** attention to any other
LC : 02 :031(414) [0685] it cost Christ and what he **paid** and risked in order to win
LC : 02 :031(414) [0687] satisfaction for me and **pay** what I owed, not with silver
LC : 03 :014(422) [0701] in such a way that no one **paid** any attention to it, and
LC : 03 :025(423) [0705] doing a good work as a **payment** to God, not willing to
LC : 03 :121(436) [0731] delusion when people **pay** in such a way that they dare
LC : 06 :006(457) [0000] benefits but did nothing about it and **paid** nothing for it?
EP : 05 :005(478) [0803] Christ has satisfied and **paid** for all guilt and without
EP : 11 :012(496) [0835] Word, they cast it to the wind and **pay** no attention to it.
EP : 12 :015(499) [0841] with a good conscience nor **pay** oath-bound feudal
SD : 03 :014(541) [0919] when he satisfied the law for us and **paid** for our sin.
SD : 05 :020(561) [0959] the law and expiated and **paid** for all our sins, that
SD : 10 :019(614) [1059] Nor shall we **pay** any attention to what they command or
SD : 12 :020(634) [1099] an oath before a court or **pay** oath-bound feudal homage

Peace (80), Peaceable (2), Peaceful (3)

PR : PR :024(013) [0023] to the tranquillity and **peace** of Christian schools and
PR : PR :025(014) [0023] purpose to live in genuine **peace** and concord with our
AG : 15 :001(036) [0049] and which contribute to **peace** and good order in the
AG : 20 :015(043) [0055] cannot come to rest and **peace** through works, but only
AG : 20 :016(043) [0055] "Since we are justified by faith, we have **peace** with God."
AG : 20 :022(044) [0055] discovered that they did not obtain **peace** by such means.
AG : 28 :029(085) [0087] subjects for the sake of **peace** and to prevent discord and
AG : 28 :055(090) [0091] for the sake of love and **peace**, to be obedient to the
AG : 28 :071(093) [0093] bishops should restore **peace** and unity at the expense of
AL : 15 :001(036) [0049] and which contribute to **peace** and good order in the
AL : 20 :016(043) [0055] "Since we are justified by faith, we have **peace** with God."

Continued ▶

AL : 2 5 :009(063) [0069] would never find **peace**, for many sins can neither be
AL : 2 8 :029(085) [0087] to their subjects for the sake of maintaining public **peace**.
AP : 0 4 :020(110) [0125] doubt and then seek to pile up other works to find **peace**.
AP : 0 4 :062(115) [0139] fears this faith brings **peace** of mind, consoles us, receives
AP : 0 4 :091(120) [0149] justified by faith, we have **peace** with God," that is, our
AP : 0 4 :100(121) [0151] because it brings forth **peace**, joy, and eternal life in the
AP : 0 4 :176(131) [0171] our conscience to be at **peace** we must seek justification
AP : 0 4 :181(132) [0171] to seek justification and **peace** of conscience elsewhere
AP : 0 4 :195(134) [0175] justified by faith, we have **peace** with God through our
AP : 0 4 :204(135) [0177] they still do not find **peace** of conscience in these works,
AP : 0 4 :216(137) [0179] by which we take hold of grace and **peace** of conscience.
AP : 0 4 :217(137) [0179] conscience cannot find **peace** before God except by faith
AP : 0 4 :217(137) [0179] "Since we are justified by faith, we have **peace**."
AP : 0 4 :224(138) [0181] must be stilled and the conscience find **peace** before him.
AP : 0 4 :227(139) [0183] merits and, through them, grace and **peace** from God.
AP : 0 4 :235(140) [0185] put up with many things for the sake of mutual **peace**.
AP : 0 4 :235(140) [0185] when Paul is speaking of unity and **peace** in the church.
AP : 0 4 :236(140) [0185] them, they would bring **peace** to both church and state.
AP : 0 4 :257(144) [0193] Consciences cannot find **peace** unless they hear the voice
AP : 0 4 :270(147) [0197] mediator, the heart is at **peace** and begins to love God
AP : 0 4 :285(150) [0201] him we might have grace, righteousness, and **peace**.
AP : 0 4 :304(154) [0205] justified by faith, we have **peace** with God" (Rom. 5:1).
AP : 0 4 :319(156) [0209] because of Christ, how will it have **peace** without faith?
AP : 0 4 :320(156) [0209] justified by faith, we have **peace** with God"; we ought to
AP : 0 4 :370(164) [0221] 10, "Glory and honor and **peace** for every one who does
AP : 0 4 :398(167) [0227] the terrors of sin, and receive **peace** for our conscience.
AP : 0 7 :036(175) [0241] but righteousness and **peace** and joy in the Holy Spirit."
AP : 1 2 :005(183) [0253] of penitence nor the source of the **peace** of conscience.
AP : 1 2 :007(183) [0255] is there that will finally bring **peace** to the conscience?
AP : 1 2 :036(186) [0261] "Since we are justified by faith, we have **peace** with God."
AP : 1 2 :047(188) [0263] Because there is no **peace** for the conscience except by
AP : 1 2 :048(188) [0265] earlier sentence and restoring **peace** and life to the heart.
AP : 1 2 :057(189) [0267] Your faith has saved you; go in **peace**."
AP : 1 2 :060(190) [0269] overcoming them and restoring **peace** to the conscience.
AP : 1 2 :060(190) [0269] terrors and brings forth **peace**, joy, and a new life in the
AP : 1 2 :064(191) [0269] wrath of God, but it finds **peace** only when it takes hold
AP : 1 2 :064(191) [0269] that the heart can find **peace** without faith in Christ do
AP : 1 2 :074(192) [0273] our hearts and the Holy Spirit grants them **peace**.
AP : 1 2 :088(195) [0277] will the conscience find **peace** if we receive the forgiveness
AP : 1 2 :174(210) [0307] to one's calling, **peaceable** conduct instead of murder and
AP : 2 4 :012(251) [0387] we are justified by faith, we have **peace**" (Rom. 5:1).
AP : 2 4 :060(260) [0405] "Since we are justified by faith, we have **peace**."
AP : 2 4 :089(266) [0415] (Rom. 5:1), "Being justified by faith, we have **peace**."
AP : 2 8 :015(283) [0447] of preserving order in the church, for the sake of **peace**.
S 3 : 1 5 :005(317) [0501] concession for the sake of **peace** and general unity among
SC : PR :000(338) [0533] Grace, mercy, and **peace** in Jesus Christ, our Lord, from
SC : PR :018(340) [0537] to be orderly, faithful, obedient, and **peaceful**.
SC : 0 3 :014(347) [0549] seasonable weather, **peace** and health, order and honor;
SC : 0 5 :028(351) [0555] Go in **peace**."
SC : 0 7 :005(353) [0559] Then quickly lie down and sleep in **peace**.
SC : 0 9 :003(355) [0561] Be at **peace** among yourselves" (I Thess. 5:12, 13).
SC : 0 9 :005(355) [0561] we may lead a quiet and **peaceable** life, godly and
LC : 0 1 :024(367) [0587] health, protection, **peace**, and all temporal and eternal
LC : 0 1 :134(383) [0619] wife and child, livelihood, **peace**, good government, etc.,
LC : 0 1 :137(384) [0621] They live long in **peace** and quietness.
LC : 0 1 :148(385) [0623] of God; there will be no **peace** in your heart, and
LC : 0 1 :153(386) [0625] better with God's favor, **peace**, and blessing than you will
LC : 0 1 :164(387) [0627] long life, sustenance, and **peace**, and afterwards
LC : 0 1 :177(389) [0631] no longer any civil order, **peace**, or respect for authority.
LC : 0 2 :015(412) [0681] temporal blessings — good government, **peace**, security.
LC : 0 3 :065(429) [0715] think that he will have **peace**; he must sacrifice all he has
LC : 0 3 :073(430) [0719] for our body, but also **peace** and concord in our daily
LC : 0 3 :074(430) [0719] unless he gives us a stable, **peaceful** government.
LC : 0 3 :075(430) [0719] we enjoy protection and **peace** and that without them we
LC : 0 3 :075(430) [0719] enjoy our possessions in **peace** and quietness, since
LC : 0 3 :077(431) [0721] at large to live together in obedience, **peace**, and concord.
LC : 0 3 :080(431) [0721] government or honorable and **peaceful** relations on earth.
LC : 0 3 :081(431) [0721] receives a morsel of bread from God and eats it in **peace**.
LC : 0 6 :017(459) [0000] feel his conscience at **peace** or have confidence in his
SD : 0 1 :058(519) [0879] will never attain abiding **peace** in this controversy but, on
SD : 0 2 :018(524) [0889] righteousness, **peace**, and salvation, cannot cooperate,
SD : 0 7 :034(575) [0983] who loves truth and **peace** can understand beyond all
SD : 1 1 :095(632) [1095] for the sake of temporal **peace**, tranquility, and outward
SD : 1 1 :095(632) [1095] Nor would such **peace** and harmony last, because it would

Peasants (1)
S 1 : PR :012(290) [0459] trade and on the part of **peasants** — who can enumerate

Peccadillo (1)
AP : 2 4 :089(265) [0413] It is no mere **peccadillo** to establish such services in the

Peculiar (6)
AP : 0 4 :381(165) [0223] Yet it is **peculiar** that they advise us to trust our love
AP : 2 3 :025(243) [0371] perpetual celibacy is **peculiar** to this new pontifical
AP : 2 4 :051(259) [0403] but they are not the **peculiar** adornment of the church.
S 3 : 0 4 :000(310) [0491] forgiveness of sin (the **peculiar** function of the Gospel) is
SD : 0 8 :075(606) [1043] Valens there was a **peculiar** sect among the Arians, called
SD : 1 2 :010(634) [1097] part on their own **peculiar** precepts and self-chosen

Peddle (3), Peddler (1)
AP : 2 1 :029(233) [0351] like the monks who **peddle** the merits of their orders.
AP : 2 4 :057(260) [0405] and sacrificers who daily **peddle** their wares in the
LC : 0 1 :054(372) [0595] false preachers arise and **peddle** their lying nonsense as
LC : 0 1 :152(386) [0625] are despised, as if they came from some loutish **peddler**.

Peevish (1)
AP : 0 4 :242(141) [0187] human relations it is not **peevish**, harsh, or implacable;

Pelagian (5), Pelagianism (1), Pelagians (13)
AG : 0 2 :003(029) [0045] this connection are the **Pelagians** and others who deny
AL : 0 2 :003(029) [0045] churches condemn the **Pelagians** and others who deny
AL : 1 8 :008(040) [0053] churches condemn the **Pelagians** and others who teach
AP : 0 4 :019(110) [0125] to avoid the impression that they are outright **Pelagians**.
AP : 0 4 :029(111) [0129] Against the **Pelagians**, Augustine maintains at length that
AP : 0 4 :106(122) [0153] writes many things in the same vein against the **Pelagians**.
AP : 0 4 :173(131) [0171] Against the **Pelagians**, Jerome writes, "We are righteous,
AP : 1 8 :001(225) [0335] to free will, as in **Pelagianism**, or all liberty be denied it,
AP : 1 8 :002(225) [0335] difference between the **Pelagians** and our opponents, since
AP : 1 8 :003(225) [0335] follow from these **Pelagian** notions which the schools
AP : 2 0 :014(228) [0343] sins is free; in fact, the **Pelagians** were condemned for
EP : 0 1 :013(467) [0783] 3. We likewise reject the **Pelagian** error which asserts that
EP : 0 2 :009(471) [0789] the error of the crass **Pelagians** who taught that by his
EP : 0 2 :010(471) [0789] the error of the Semi-**Pelagians** who teach that man by
SD : 0 1 :003(509) [0861] God and is purged of all **Pelagian** and Manichaean
SD : 0 1 :016(511) [0865] that we fall neither into **Pelagian** nor into Manichaean
SD : 0 1 :017(511) [0865] to both old and new **Pelagians**, we condemn and reject as
SD : 0 1 :020(511) [0865] and condemn the following and related **Pelagian** errors:
SD : 0 2 :075(536) [0909] The error of the coarse **Pelagians**, that by his own natural

Pelted (1)
LC : PR :013(360) [0571] but also to be chased out by dogs and **pelted** with dung.

Penalty (17), Penalties (30)
AG : 2 8 :011(082) [0085] the sword and physical **penalties** it protects body and
AG : 2 8 :041(087) [0089] only about the reservation of ecclesiastical **penalties**.
AL : 2 3 :023(055) [0063] of marriage is maintained by means of such **penalties**.
AL : 2 8 :011(082) [0085] the sword and physical **penalties**, while the Gospel
AL : 2 8 :041(087) [0089] reserving ecclesiastical **penalties** and not of reserving
AP : 0 2 :038(105) [0115] that concupiscence is a **penalty** and not a sin, while
AP : 0 2 :046(106) [0117] minimize both sin and its **penalty** when they teach that
AP : 0 2 :046(106) [0117] powers, Genesis describes another **penalty** for original sin.
AP : 0 2 :047(106) [0119] are sin as well as **penalty**; death, other physical ills, and
AP : 0 2 :047(106) [0119] tyranny of the devil are, in the precise sense, **penalties**.
AP : 0 2 :050(106) [0119] us to bear both sin and **penalty** and to destroy the rule of
AP : 0 4 :022(110) [0127] laws, learning, teaching, governments, and **penalties**.
AP : 1 2 :134(203) [0293] not sin but will have to pay the **penalties** in purgatory.
AP : 1 2 :136(203) [0293] If the **penalties** of purgatory are satisfactions, or rather
AP : 1 2 :136(203) [0293] a redemption from the **penalties** of purgatory, do these
AP : 1 2 :136(203) [0293] will mean "Suffer the **penalties** of purgatory after this
AP : 1 2 :138(203) [0295] bind" refer to imposing **penalties** but to retaining the sins
AP : 1 2 :139(203) [0295] referred to canonical **penalties**, part of which the pastors
AP : 1 2 :139(204) [0295] command to commute **penalties** or to remit them in part.
AP : 1 2 :140(204) [0295] our guilt but our **penalties** redeem us from eternal death!
AP : 1 2 :147(205) [0297] guilt or eternal punishment or the **penalties** of purgatory.
AP : 1 2 :154(206) [0301] the satisfactions and the **penalties** on account of which
AP : 1 2 :156(207) [0301] that the saints suffer **penalties** which are the work of
AP : 1 2 :156(207) [0301] Some of them suffer **penalties** which God imposes only
AP : 1 2 :156(207) [0301] These **penalties** have nothing to do with the power of the
AP : 1 2 :156(207) [0301] From the particular **penalty** imposed on David it does
AP : 1 2 :156(207) [0301] there is a special **penalty** in purgatory, where the
AP : 1 2 :157(207) [0301] the payment of certain **penalties** over and above our
AP : 1 2 :160(207) [0301] troubles are not always **penalties** for certain past deeds,
AP : 1 2 :163(208) [0303] opponents are paying the **penalty** for their neglect of
AP : 1 2 :174(210) [0307] traditions and the **penalties** of purgatory can remit
AP : 1 2 :175(210) [0307] remit satisfactions and **penalties**, this observance cannot
AP : 1 2 :175(210) [0307] but to payment for **penalties**; so also "indulgence" has
AP : 1 2 :176(210) [0307] the power to impose **penalties** or to institute forms of
AP : 1 2 :177(210) [0307] reservation of canonical **penalties**, not the reservation of
AP : 2 4 :089(266) [0415] Therefore the **penalty** of purgatory cannot be overcome
AP : 2 4 :090(266) [0415] purgatory, the sort of **penalties** they suppose purgatory
AP : 2 4 :091(266) [0415] transferred to the dead and to satisfaction for **penalties**.
AP : 2 4 :091(266) [0415] Some day they will pay the **penalty** for this sacrilege.
AP : 2 4 :093(267) [0417] and do not apply it as a satisfaction for **penalties**.
S 3 : 0 3 :025(307) [0485] called remission of all **penalty** and guilt, and the people
S 3 : 0 9 :000(314) [0497] it, to be merely a civil **penalty** which does not concern us
S 3 : 0 9 :000(314) [0497] with this spiritual **penalty** or excommunication.
LC : 0 1 :016(366) [0585] he commands under **penalty** of eternal wrath, namely,
LC : 0 1 :134(383) [0619] On the other hand, the **penalty** for him who disobeys it is
SD : 0 1 :013(511) [0863] 4. The punishment and **penalty** of original sin which God
SD : 1 2 :021(634) [1099] conscience impose the death **penalty** on evil-doers.

Penance (11)
AP : 0 4 :398(167) [0227] saying faith is part of **penance**, by which we obtain
AP : 1 2 :057(189) [0267] the second part of her **penance**, the faith that encouraged
AP : 2 7 :035(275) [0431] about justification, **penance**, and human traditions, it is
S 3 : 0 3 :011(305) [0481] follows that people did **penance** only for actual sins, such
S 3 : 0 3 :012(305) [0483] In their teaching of **penance** the sophists thus instructed
S 3 : 0 3 :021(306) [0485] For the **penance** that was still lacking man was referred to
S 3 : 0 3 :022(306) [0485] canons, seven years of **penance** were required for a single
S 3 : 0 3 :023(307) [0485] Even if one had done **penance** in this way for a hundred
S 3 : 0 3 :023(307) [0485] a case of always doing **penance** but never coming to
S 3 : 0 3 :030(308) [0487] "We have already done **penance**," and on the other hand
LC : 0 4 :074(445) [0751] formerly called **Penance**, which is really nothing else than

Pence (1)
S 3 : 0 3 :026(307) [0487] be so cheap that they were released at six **pence** a head.

Pending (1)
AP : 2 7 :002(269) [0419] have already happened, and others seem to be **pending**.

Penetrable (1), Penetrate (2), Penetrates (2), Penetrating (1)
LC : SP :027(364) [0581] simply, so that it may **penetrate** deeply into their minds
LC : 0 1 :321(408) [0673] commandment, **penetrating** and pervading them all.
SD : 0 7 :100(586) [1005] nor vacates space but **penetrates** every creature, wherever
SD : 0 7 :100(586) [1007] illustrations, my vision **penetrates** air, light, or water and
SD : 0 7 :101(587) [1007] are indeed much more **penetrable** and present to him than
SD : 0 7 :111(589) [1011] had the effrontery to **penetrate** our churches as adherents

Penig (1)
PR : PR :027(015) [0025] Wolf, baron of Schoenburg [-**Penig**-Remissa]

Penitence (137)
AP : 0 4 :045(113) [0133] In **penitence** and the terrors of conscience it consoles and
AP : 0 4 :062(115) [0139] Christ commands that **penitence** and forgiveness of sins
AP : 0 4 :062(115) [0139] the preaching of **penitence** terrifies our consciences with
AP : 0 4 :083(119) [0145] discuss this passage later on in considering **penitence**.

Continued ▶

AP : 04 :142(126) [0161] has its existence in **penitence**; that is, it is conceived in the
AP : 04 :200(134) [0175] time the doctrine of **penitence** is preached to the wicked,
AP : 04 :255(144) [0193] of the law or of **penitence**, which condemns wrongdoers
AP : 04 :257(144) [0193] Thus in the preaching of **penitence** it is not enough to
AP : 04 :257(144) [0193] from the preaching of **penitence**, they deserve to be
AP : 04 :258(144) [0193] in Isaiah's preaching of **penitence**: "Cease to do evil, learn
AP : 04 :258(144) [0193] Thus the prophet urges **penitence** and adds a promise.
AP : 04 :259(144) [0193] Christ is preaching **penitence** when he says, "Forgive,"
AP : 04 :259(145) [0193] work alone, but of all of **penitence**, as the text indicates;
AP : 04 :260(145) [0193] that in the preaching of **penitence** the preaching of the law
AP : 04 :261(145) [0195] but he includes all of **penitence** when he says, "Redeem
AP : 04 :262(145) [0195] clearly about complete **penitence** and bring out the
AP : 04 :262(145) [0195] These words deal with the total scope of **penitence**.
AP : 04 :263(145) [0195] Sins are redeemed by **penitence**, that is, the obligation or
AP : 04 :263(146) [0195] forth fruits worthy of **penitence**, as John the Baptist says
AP : 04 :266(146) [0197] "Redeem your sins by **penitence**," our opponents would
AP : 04 :267(146) [0197] Since he is preaching **penitence** he is teaching not only
AP : 04 :267(146) [0197] in connection with **penitence**, therefore, Daniel does not
AP : 04 :268(147) [0197] indeed by our complete **penitence**, according to the
AP : 04 :271(147) [0199] In this way we must view the preaching of **penitence**.
AP : 04 :271(147) [0199] of the doctrine of **penitence**, yet we think that none of
AP : 04 :272(148) [0199] Because the doctrine of **penitence** not only demands new
AP : 04 :272(148) [0199] In passages about **penitence** we should understand that
AP : 04 :274(148) [0199] is true that in teaching **penitence** works are required,
AP : 04 :275(148) [0199] and so he warns that **penitence** is hypocritical and false if
AP : 04 :278(149) [0199] As we said earlier that in **penitence** we must consider faith
AP : 04 :278(149) [0199] as we said a little earlier about **penitence** in general.
AP : 04 :292(152) [0203] by the preaching of **penitence**, he takes heart and believes
AP : 04 :349(160) [0217] The faith we speak of has its existence in **penitence**.
AP : 04 :353(161) [0217] that this faith arises in **penitence** and ought to grow
AP : 04 :353(161) [0217] in penitence and ought to grow continually in **penitence**.
AP : 04 :353(161) [0217] spiritual perfection, if **penitence** and faith amid penitence
AP : 04 :353(161) [0217] if penitence and faith amid **penitence** grow together.
AP : 04 :365(163) [0219] and hence this belongs to the preaching of **penitence**.
AP : 04 :374(164) [0223] Such a new birth comes by faith amid **penitence**.
AP : 11 :001(180) [0249] later when we explain our whole teaching on **penitence**.
AP : 11 :005(181) [0251] If they still do not commune, let them come to **penitence**.
AP : 11 :010(182) [0253] opponents' teaching on **penitence** there are other major
AP : 12 :000(182) [0253] [Article XII. **Penitence**]
AP : 12 :001(182) [0253] faith are the parts of **penitence**, and they deny that faith
AP : 12 :001(182) [0253] and they deny that faith is the second part of **penitence**.
AP : 12 :003(183) [0253] and canonists had overwhelmed the doctrine of **penitence**.
AP : 12 :004(183) [0253] writings the doctrine of **penitence** was very confused.
AP : 12 :005(183) [0253] chief requirements of **penitence** nor the source of the
AP : 12 :016(184) [0257] to reject the doctrine of **penitence** as taught by the
AP : 12 :025(185) [0259] of the sacrament of **penitence** obtains grace *ex opere*
AP : 12 :028(185) [0259] we have given **penitence** two parts, namely, contrition and
AP : 12 :028(185) [0259] to call fruits worthy of **penitence** (Matt. 3:8) and an
AP : 12 :030(186) [0259] of Luke (24:47), "That **penitence** and forgiveness of sins
AP : 12 :035(186) [0261] of our consideration of **penitence**, we therefore add faith
AP : 12 :041(187) [0261] be called a sacrament of **penitence**, as even the more
AP : 12 :043(187) [0263] This understanding of **penitence** is plain and clear, it adds
AP : 12 :044(187) [0263] these two parts to **penitence**, we must show that Scripture
AP : 12 :044(187) [0263] the chief parts in the **penitence** or conversion of the
AP : 12 :045(188) [0263] Christ also includes the fruits of **penitence** or the new life.
AP : 12 :045(188) [0263] names contrition and faith as the chief parts of **penitence**.
AP : 12 :052(189) [0265] are the chief parts of **penitence**, contrition and the faith
AP : 12 :052(189) [0265] see how the nature of **penitence** could be presented more
AP : 12 :057(189) [0267] faith there must always be in **penitence**, as in Luke 7:37ff.
AP : 12 :058(189) [0267] can see that we put into **penitence** the parts that properly
AP : 12 :058(190) [0267] order to emphasize the faith that we require in **penitence**.
AP : 12 :059(190) [0267] For the doctrine of **penitence** and the doctrine of
AP : 12 :060(190) [0267] and say that it precedes **penitence**, they do not mean
AP : 12 :060(190) [0269] and therefore we put it in as one of the parts of **penitence**.
AP : 12 :061(190) [0269] the reception of absolution is part of **penitence** or not.
AP : 12 :061(190) [0269] that faith is part of **penitence** since only faith can accept
AP : 12 :063(191) [0269] of sins is either a part of **penitence** or its goal — the
AP : 12 :063(191) [0269] properly be included as one of the parts of **penitence**.
AP : 12 :074(193) [0273] of sins by faith, or that faith is part of **penitence**?
AP : 12 :088(195) [0277] asks in connection with **penitence**, "How do we become
AP : 12 :090(195) [0279] On this doctrine of **penitence**, which is quite clear, we are
AP : 12 :091(195) [0279] forth contrition and faith as the two parts of **penitence**.
AP : 12 :091(195) [0279] many statements about **penitence** are circulating which
AP : 12 :091(195) [0279] For example, "**Penitence** means to lament past evils and
AP : 12 :091(196) [0279] Again, "**Penitence** is a sort of revenge by a person who is
AP : 12 :092(196) [0279] among the parts of **penitence** in order to make it more
AP : 12 :093(196) [0279] another part of **penitence**, it would have been in order to
AP : 12 :096(196) [0281] clear statement about **penitence**: "We should believe both
AP : 12 :097(196) [0281] neither the nature of **penitence** nor the language of the
AP : 12 :097(196) [0281] select sayings about a part of **penitence**, namely works.
AP : 12 :098(197) [0281] faith, the two parts of **penitence** we have discussed above.
AP : 12 :112(198) [0285] about the public rite of **penitence**, not about this
AP : 12 :113(199) [0285] "satisfaction" is a relic from this rite of public **penitence**.
AP : 12 :113(199) [0285] public evidence of their **penitence**, as far as was possible.
AP : 12 :116(199) [0285] of satisfaction in public **penitence** were not necessary by
AP : 12 :122(200) [0289] "Bear fruit that befits **penitence**" (Matt. 3:8); "Yield your
AP : 12 :122(200) [0289] Christ's preaching of **penitence** (Matt. 4:17), "Be
AP : 12 :122(200) [0289] (Luke 24:47) "that **penitence** should be preached"; Peter's
AP : 12 :122(200) [0289] be preached"; Peter's preaching of **penitence** (Acts 2:38).
AP : 12 :122(200) [0289] perform the prescribed **penitence**, following the statement
AP : 12 :123(200) [0289] Christ says, "Be penitent"; the apostles preach **penitence**.
AP : 12 :123(201) [0289] hear this they will conclude that we deny all **penitence**.
AP : 12 :123(201) [0289] heretics, who reject **penitence**, should be removed from
AP : 12 :131(202) [0291] We say that after **penitence** (that is, conversion or
AP : 12 :131(202) [0291] In a word, there is no **penitence** inwardly which does not
AP : 12 :132(202) [0291] "Bear fruit that befits **penitence**," and Paul when he says
AP : 12 :132(202) [0291] talking about total **penitence** and total newness of life and
AP : 12 :134(203) [0293] "Bear fruit that befits **penitence**," "Yield your members to
AP : 12 :135(203) [0293] as the chapter on "**Penitence** and Remission" teaches.
AP : 12 :135(203) [0293] like "Be penitent" and "Bear fruit that befits **penitence**."
AP : 12 :136(203) [0293] "Bear fruit that befits **penitence**" and "Be penitent" will
AP : 12 :139(203) [0295] and command require **penitence** to produce good fruits,
AP : 12 :141(204) [0295] of law and Gospel, **penitence** and quickening, and the
AP : 12 :146(205) [0297] In addition, they obscure **penitence** and grace.
AP : 12 :148(205) [0297] is necessary for **penitence** because Augustine says that
AP : 12 :148(205) [0299] Augustine says that "**penitence** is revenge punishing," etc.
AP : 12 :148(205) [0299] is necessary for **penitence**, but not as a merit or price, as
AP : 12 :148(205) [0299] sense revenge is part of **penitence** because regeneration
AP : 12 :148(205) [0299] may be beautiful, that **penitence** is so called because it
AP : 12 :149(206) [0299] comes over even the simplest people in true **penitence**?
AP : 12 :163(208) [0303] to the whole process of **penitence** and the fruits that are
AP : 12 :163(208) [0303] "Judge" means all of **penitence**; it means to "condemn
AP : 12 :164(208) [0303] The whole process of **penitence** — contrition, faith, and
AP : 12 :165(208) [0303] to the whole process of **penitence** and obligatory works
AP : 12 :165(208) [0303] are mitigated by our **penitence** and its true fruits, good
AP : 12 :166(208) [0303] By their **penitence** — we mean the whole process of
AP : 12 :166(208) [0303] the whole process of **penitence** — they were reconciled to
AP : 12 :169(209) [0305] about restitution that **penitence** is false if it does not
AP : 12 :170(209) [0305] works ought to follow **penitence**, and penitence ought to
AP : 12 :170(209) [0305] follow penitence, and **penitence** ought to be not a fraud
AP : 12 :171(209) [0305] sort of public or formal **penitence** described by the
AP : 12 :171(209) [0305] for they often say that **penitence** should be shown in
AP : 12 :174(210) [0305] often enough that **penitence** ought to produce good
AP : 12 :175(210) [0307] the remission of public **penitence** so as not to burden men
AP : 12 :178(211) [0307] of our doctrine on **penitence**; we are certain that it is
AP : 13 :004(211) [0309] is the sacrament of **penitence**), for these rites have the
AP : 15 :043(221) [0327] with topics like these: **penitence**, the fear of God, faith in
AP : 20 :013(228) [0343] Holy Spirit and reject **penitence**; as we have said before,
AP : 20 :013(228) [0343] as we have said before, faith has its existence in **penitence**.
AP : 21 :041(235) [0355] in the doctrine of **penitence** which ought to be as clear
AP : 23 :064(248) [0381] be taken to mean purity of the heart and total **penitence**.
AP : 24 :046(258) [0401] ever understood our opponents' doctrine of **penitence**?
AP : 27 :054(278) [0437] of faith, about true **penitence**, about works that have the

Penitent (15), Penitential (2), Penitently (1), Penitents (1)
AL : 28 :038(087) [0089] So the **penitential** canons formerly increased, and we can
AP : 04 :263(145) [0195] forgives those who are **penitent**, as is written in Ezek.
AP : 04 :386(166) [0225] reborn by a faith that **penitently** grasps the promise of
AP : 11 :009(182) [0251] of constitutions, glosses, summae, and **penitential** letters.
AP : 12 :096(196) [0281] both that we should be **penitent** and that we shall be
AP : 12 :122(200) [0289] (Matt. 4:17), "Be **penitent**"; Christ's command to the
AP : 12 :123(200) [0289] Christ says, "Be **penitent**"; the apostles preach penitence.
AP : 12 :123(201) [0289] quote the word, "Be **penitent**," against us so that when
AP : 12 :132(202) [0291] says (Matt. 4:17), "Be **penitent**," he is surely talking about
AP : 12 :133(202) [0293] this word of Christ is a word of command, "Be **penitent**."
AP : 12 :134(202) [0293] opponents write that if a **penitent** refuses to assume the
AP : 12 :134(203) [0293] referring to this life: "Be **penitent**," "Bear fruit that befits
AP : 12 :135(203) [0293] commandments like "Be **penitent**" and "Bear fruit that
AP : 12 :136(203) [0293] befits penitence" and "Be **penitent**" will mean "Suffer the
S3 : 03 :032(308) [0487] former group are false **penitents**, and those of you in the
EP : 06 :007(481) [0807] 6. Therefore both for the **penitent** and impenitent, for
SD : 05 :009(559) [0955] holy Gospel offers to all **penitent** sinners who have been
SD : 05 :009(559) [0955] hearts, but to the "oppressed" or **penitent** (Luke 4:18).
SD : 05 :022(562) [0959] Accordingly every **penitent** sinner must believe — that is,

Penny (8), Pennies (1)
S2 : 02 :024(296) [0469] by grace, through faith, without our work or **pennies**.
LC : 01 :156(386) [0625] we would not have a **penny** in the house or a straw in the
LC : 01 :236(397) [0647] for every **penny** you have taken and for every penny's
LC : 01 :236(397) [0647] have taken and for every **penny**'s damage you have done
LC : 01 :243(397) [0649] scratch day and night and yet grow not a **penny** richer!
LC : 01 :244(398) [0649] purse down to the last **penny**, and then by way of thanks
LC : 03 :075(430) [0719] and quietness, since otherwise we could not keep a **penny**.
LC : 03 :081(431) [0721] a straw in the field, a **penny** in the house, or even our life
SD : 11 :004(617) [1063] as it is written, "Are not two sparrows sold for a **penny**?

Pentecost (3)
AG : 28 :057(091) [0091] of Sunday, Easter, **Pentecost**, and similar holy days and
AL : 28 :057(091) [0091] of Sunday, Easter, **Pentecost**, and similar festivals and
AP : 07 :040(176) [0241] like the Passover and **Pentecost**, so that by these

People (380)
PR : PR :008(005) [0011] that other good-hearted **people** would have been
PR : PR :022(011) [0019] Besides, pious **people** should be warned against them.
PR : PR :022(011) [0019] many pious, innocent **people** even in those churches
PR : PR :022(011) [0019] These **people** go their way in the simplicity of their
PR : PR :024(013) [0023] doubt that all pious **people** who have an upright love for
AG : 13 :001(035) [0049] only to be signs by which **people** might be identified
AG : 20 :008(042) [0053] preached everywhere, our **people** have been instructed as
AG : 20 :015(043) [0055] contempt among untried **people**, yet it is a matter of
AG : 22 :006(050) [0061] sacrament distributed the blood of Christ to the **people**.
AG : 23 :001(051) [0061] Among all **people**, both of high and of low degree, there
AG : 23 :005(052) [0061] he indicated that few **people** have the gift of living in
AG : 23 :013(053) [0063] devout and intelligent **people** in high station have
AG : 23 :021(055) [0063] to persecute innocent **people** simply because they are
AG : 01 :007(056) [0065] Moreover, the **people** are instructed often and with great
AG : 01 :007(056) [0065] in order that the **people** may be drawn to the Communion
AG : 01 :007(056) [0065] The **people** are also given instruction about other false
AG : 01 :002(056) [0065] responses for the instruction and exercise of the **people**.
AG : 01 :003(056) [0065] is to teach the **people** what they need to know about
AG : 24 :023(058) [0067] one Mass held for many **people** merited as much as a
AG : 24 :024(058) [0067] was given so that our **people** might know how the
AG : 24 :041(061) [0069] where there were many **people**, Mass was not held on
AG : 24 :041(061) [0069] on every day that the **people** assembled, for according to
AG : 25 :002(061) [0069] At the same time the **people** are carefully instructed
AG : 25 :009(063) [0069] is no need to compel **people** to give a detailed account of
AG : 26 :010(065) [0071] and magistrates should govern land and **people**, etc.
AG : 26 :012(065) [0071] traditions, and yet the **people** were of the opinion that
AG : 26 :016(066) [0073] Many devout and learned **people** before our time have
AG : 26 :016(066) [0073] in the church that godly **people** were thereby hindered
AG : 26 :041(070) [0075] same time, however, the **people** are instructed that such
AG : 27 :008(072) [0077] displeased many devout **people** in the past, for they must
AG : 27 :009(072) [0077] Many **people** complained that in such a momentous
AG : 27 :016(073) [0077] In former times **people** gathered and adopted monastic
AG : 27 :046(078) [0081] this, they persuaded the **people** that the invented spiritual
AG : 27 :048(078) [0081] Christian church that the **people** should be presented with

Continued ▶

AG : 27 :049(078) [0083] God are obscured when **people** are told that monks alone
AG : 27 :051(079) [0083] However, the common **people**, hearing the state of
AG : 27 :054(079) [0083] When the **people** hear that it is only a counsel not to take
AG : 27 :059(080) [0083] it was necessary to give the **people** proper instruction.
AG : 28 :003(081) [0085] by learned and devout **people** in Christendom.
AG : 28 :047(088) [0089] human ordinances on **people**, "Let them alone; they are
AG : 28 :060(091) [0091] a certain day so that the **people** might know when they
AG : 28 :060(091) [0091] do this in order that the **people** might have an example of
AL : 00 :001(049) [0059] are in order that the **people** may not be compelled to
AL : 00 :002(049) [0059] slanders among the **people** in order to inflame the hatred
AL : 00 :006(049) [0059] and devotion among the **people** as the proper observance
AL : 22 :005(050) [0061] places testifies that the blood was given to the **people**.
AL : 22 :006(050) [0061] and distribute the blood of Christ to the **people**."
AL : 22 :011(050) [0061] Consequently, if any **people** preferred to use both kinds in
AL : 24 :002(056) [0065] for the instruction of the **people**, for ceremonies are
AL : 24 :004(056) [0065] should be used which is understood by the **people**.
AL : 24 :005(056) [0065] The **people** are accustomed to receive the sacrament
AL : 24 :007(056) [0065] The **people** are also admonished concerning the value and
AL : 24 :023(058) [0067] one Mass said for many **people** is worth as much as a
AL : 25 :002(061) [0069] The **people** are very diligently taught concerning faith in
AL : 25 :003(061) [0069] Our **people** are taught to esteem absolution highly
AL : 25 :004(062) [0069] of keys is praised, and **people** are reminded of the great
AL : 26 :001(063) [0071] opinion not only of the **people** but also of those who
AL : 26 :011(065) [0071] consciences of devout **people** who grieved that they were
AL : 27 :015(073) [0077] What happened after such **people** had entered
AL : 27 :016(073) [0077] Formerly **people** came together in monasteries to learn.
AL : 27 :048(078) [0081] to recommend to the **people** a certain service invented by
AL : 27 :051(079) [0083] The **people** draw many pernicious conclusions from such
AL : 28 :060(091) [0091] a certain day so that the **people** may know when they
AP : 02 :042(106) [0117] fretting because bad **people** are more fortunate than good
AP : 02 :042(106) [0117] more fortunate than good **people**; yielding to anger,
AP : 02 :044(106) [0117] purely academic, but moved out among the **people**.
AP : 04 :013(109) [0123] to such a pass that many **people** ridicule us for teaching
AP : 04 :035(112) [0131] Such **people** despise God when they do these things, as
AP : 04 :073(117) [0141] "alone" offends some **people**, even though Paul says
AP : 04 :191(133) [0175] of God to defend the **people** who had God's Word
AP : 04 :204(135) [0177] Thirdly, such **people** never attain the knowledge of God,
AP : 04 :207(135) [0177] The **people** of the Old Testament imitated these sacrifices
AP : 04 :207(135) [0177] we see how vehemently the prophets rebuke the **people**.
AP : 04 :208(135) [0177] The **people** of Israel had seen the prophets sacrifice on
AP : 04 :208(135) [0177] Therefore the **people** began zealously to copy this action
AP : 04 :209(135) [0177] The **people** heard that Abraham had offered up his son.
AP : 04 :220(137) [0181] He is writing to **people** who, upon being justified, needed
AP : 04 :233(140) [0185] heavy burdens on the **people** or have no regard for their
AP : 04 :233(140) [0185] also arise when the **people** judge their clergy's behavior
AP : 04 :234(140) [0185] with the weak, when the **people** put the best construction
AP : 04 :234(140) [0185] the bishops take into account the weakness of the **people**.
AP : 04 :242(141) [0187] own sins but of other **people**'s when it says, "Love covers
AP : 04 :242(141) [0187] offenses," namely, other **people**'s offenses and offenses
AP : 04 :242(141) [0187] other people's offenses and offenses between **people**.
AP : 04 :282(149) [0201] and cleanses the **people**," and the gloss says that it
AP : 04 :303(154) [0205] that many wicked **people** and demons also believe (James
AP : 04 :303(154) [0205] Sensible **people** can easily see that a faith which believes
AP : 04 :303(154) [0205] Therefore neither wicked **people** nor demons can have the
AP : 04 :331(158) [0211] because thy city and thy **people** are called by thy name."
AP : 04 :395(167) [0225] The same thing happened among the **people** of Israel.
AP : 04 :395(167) [0225] The majority of the **people** believed that they merited the
AP : 04 :395(167) [0225] The history of the **people** of Israel is a type of what was
AP : 07 :014(170) [0231] be between the church and the Old Testament **people**?
AP : 07 :014(170) [0231] from the Old Testament **people** by the fact that the
AP : 07 :014(170) [0231] the church is a spiritual **people**, separated from the
AP : 07 :014(170) [0231] but by being God's true **people**, reborn by the Holy
AP : 07 :014(170) [0231] the Old Testament **people**, those born according to the
AP : 07 :014(170) [0231] them were called the **people** of God inasmuch as God had
AP : 07 :014(170) [0231] Nevertheless, these evil **people** did not please God.
AP : 07 :016(170) [0231] only those are the true **people** who accept this promise of
AP : 07 :016(171) [0231] the Old Testament **people**), for they held high positions
AP : 07 :019(171) [0233] the true and spiritual **people** will be separated from the
AP : 07 :019(171) [0233] people will be separated from the physical **people**.
AP : 07 :020(171) [0233] are also many weak **people** in it who build on this
AP : 07 :033(175) [0239] to educate and instruct the **people** and the inexperienced.
AP : 07 :040(176) [0241] justification but to let the **people** know when to assemble.
AP : 07 :040(176) [0241] Frequently the **people** continued to observe certain Old
AP : 07 :042(176) [0241] Council of Nicaea some **people** celebrated Easter at one
AP : 07 :042(177) [0243] wanted to disabuse the **people** of the foolish notion of
AP : 07 :049(178) [0245] conduct of priests or **people**, we should not incite
AP : 09 :002(178) [0245] in our churches since our **people** have been armed by
AP : 11 :003(180) [0249] it is certain that most **people** in our churches use the
AP : 11 :003(180) [0249] Our clergy instruct the **people** about the worth and fruits
AP : 11 :005(181) [0249] in at the same time, the **people** could not be heard and
AP : 11 :008(181) [0251] want to impose on our **people**'s consciences the regulation
AP : 12 :005(183) [0253] The **people** could grasp neither the sum of the matter nor
AP : 12 :024(185) [0257] This is how uninformed **people** understand it.
AP : 12 :106(197) [0283] property and leave other **people**'s alone, but warning him
AP : 12 :113(199) [0285] and admitting notorious **people** to communion
AP : 12 :116(199) [0287] of faith be obscured or **people** think that because of these
AP : 12 :122(200) [0289] and to purify himself a **people** of his own who are zealous
AP : 12 :130(202) [0291] there are probably many **people** in many places who are
AP : 12 :149(206) [0299] comes over even the simplest **people** in true penitence?
AP : 13 :007(212) [0311] sacrifices and merit the forgiveness of sins for the **people**.
AP : 13 :009(212) [0311] of sins for the **people**, as in the Old Testament, but they
AP : 13 :009(212) [0311] the Gospel and administer the sacraments to the **people**.
AP : 15 :020(218) [0321] because they gave the **people** a set time to assemble,
AP : 15 :023(218) [0321] delusion the common **people** among the Israelites
AP : 15 :037(220) [0325] If our **people** drop certain useless traditions, they have
AP : 15 :040(220) [0325] in order to learn; the **people** sing, too, in order to learn or
AP : 15 :042(221) [0327] This the **people** rightly despise and walk out on them
AP : 21 :016(231) [0347] among the common **people** but discuss only the views of
AP : 21 :018(231) [0347] "The richest of the **people** will sue your favor."
AP : 21 :035(234) [0353] foolish monks taught the **people** to call on Christopher,
AP : 21 :043(235) [0357] a summary of the doctrines of the church for the **people**.
AP : 22 :004(236) [0359] and distribute the blood of the Lord to the **people**."
AP : 22 :013(238) [0361] order between priest and **people**, but there is no mystery
AP : 23 :005(239) [0365] false prophets would deceive **people** with their fictions.
AP : 24 :003(250) [0385] to give the common **people** something to learn that will
AP : 24 :004(250) [0385] almost everywhere the **people** sang in their own language.
AP : 24 :013(251) [0387] taken hold among the **people** and has infinitely multiplied
AP : 24 :043(258) [0399] questions, which neither they nor the **people** understand.
AP : 24 :045(258) [0401] The **people** were swamped by the many different
AP : 24 :046(258) [0401] Who among the **people** has ever understood our
AP : 24 :049(258) [0401] It is the **people** who use it, and this only when they have
AP : 24 :050(259) [0401] audience, but neither the **people** nor the clergy have ever
AP : 24 :059(260) [0405] this ministry benefits **people** when he does work to give
AP : 24 :063(261) [0405] even for wicked **people**, if they do not put an obstacle in
AP : 24 :064(261) [0407] without faith the Mass does not even benefit living **people**
AP : 24 :068(261) [0407] Some clever **people** imagine that the Lord's Supper was
AP : 24 :080(264) [0411] blood of the Lord to the **people**, just as a minister who
AP : 24 :080(264) [0411] forth the gospel to the **people**, as Paul says (I Cor. 4:1),
AP : 24 :085(265) [0413] collection or gifts of the **people** rather than the offering
AP : 24 :088(265) [0413] supplications and bloodless sacrifices for all the **people**."
AP : 24 :088(265) [0413] and supplications and bloodless sacrifices for the **people**.
AP : 24 :097(268) [0417] The wicked **people** in the Old Testament had a similar
AP : 27 :045(277) [0435] has exercised many **people** because they imagined that
AP : 27 :068(280) [0443] does not attribute faith to **people** who have a mortal sin;
AP : 28 :003(281) [0445] They admit all kinds of **people** to the priesthood quite
AP : 28 :004(281) [0445] difficult controversies the **people** desperately want
AP : 28 :027(285) [0451] the judgment of all pious **people** whether our opponents
S1 : PR :004(289) [0457] my labor and thus mislead the poor **people** in my name.
S1 : PR :007(289) [0457] by their lies to keep the **people** on their side, God has
S1 : PR :010(290) [0457] many things and many **people** might derive benefit from
S1 : PR :010(290) [0457] care how the poor **people** live or die, although Christ died
S1 : PR :010(290) [0457] Those **people** cannot hear Christ speak to them as the
S2 : 02 :005(293) [0463] "Let the **people** be told openly that the Mass, as
S2 : 02 :005(293) [0463] sensible, God-fearing **people** — especially if they hear that
S2 : 02 :019(296) [0467] that great multitudes of **people** may turn aside from
S2 : 04 :003(298) [0471] much good to come to a **people** through a tyrant or
S3 : 02 :002(303) [0479] are the rude and wicked **people** who do evil whenever
S3 : 03 :011(305) [0481] From this it follows that **people** did penance only for
S3 : 03 :012(305) [0483] thus instructed the **people** to place their confidence in
S3 : 03 :013(305) [0483] was recited to the **people**: "Prolong my life, Lord God,
S3 : 03 :016(305) [0483] substitute for contrition when **people** went to confession.
S3 : 03 :025(307) [0485] penalty and guilt, and the **people** came running, for
S3 : 03 :027(307) [0487] the pope taught the **people** to rely on and trust in such
S3 : 03 :027(307) [0487] practiced by these **people**, as we have heard above, are
S3 : 03 :027(307) [0487] the money, consoled the **people** with his power and
S3 : 03 :042(310) [0491] many foolish **people** like this and I fear that such a devil
S3 : 03 :043(310) [0491] to teach that when holy **people**, aside from the fact that
S3 : 08 :001(312) [0493] sake of untrained young **people** who need to be examined
S3 : 08 :006(312) [0495] himself comes to the **people** without and before their
S3 : 14 :001(316) [0501] of their St. Thomas, such **people** boast that a monastic
TR : 00 :014(322) [0507] should assemble with the **people** for whom a head is to be
TR : 00 :014(322) [0507] in the presence of the **people** who are thoroughly
TR : 00 :050(329) [0519] nor by all the clergy, nor by kings, nor by the **people**."
TR : 00 :070(332) [0525] was a time when the **people** elected pastors and bishops.
SC : PR :002(338) [0533] The common **people**, especially those who live in the
SC : PR :003(338) [0533] Although the **people** are supposed to be Christian, are
SC : PR :004(338) [0533] shamefully neglected the **people** and paid no attention at
SC : PR :005(338) [0533] interest in teaching the **people** the Lord's Prayer, the
SC : PR :006(338) [0533] that you have pity on the **people** who are entrusted to
SC : PR :006(338) [0533] the catechism to the **people**, especially those who are
SC : PR :006(338) [0533] and read them to the **people** word for word in this
SC : PR :007(339) [0533] Young and inexperienced **people** must be instructed on
SC : PR :009(339) [0535] intelligent and educated **people**, you are at liberty to
SC : PR :012(339) [0535] is disposed to banish such rude **people** from his land.
SC : PR :013(339) [0535] insist that the **people** learn to know how to distinguish
SC : PR :014(339) [0535] second place, after the **people** have become familiar with
SC : PR :017(340) [0535] catechism so that the **people** may have a richer and fuller
SC : PR :018(340) [0537] require special attention among the **people** where you are.
SC : PR :018(340) [0537] and the common **people** in order that they may be
SC : PR :021(340) [0537] Finally, now that the **people** are freed from the tyranny
SC : PR :022(341) [0537] and without any law, the **people** will desire the sacrament
SC : PR :024(341) [0539] Then the **people** will come of their own accord and
SC : PR :025(341) [0539] it is your own fault if the **people** treat the sacrament with
SC : 05 :015(349) [0553] *How Plain **People** Are to Be Taught to Confess*
SC : 05 :029(351) [0555] as an ordinary form of confession for plain **people**.
LC : PR :004(359) [0567] As it is, the common **people** take the Gospel altogether
LC : PR :006(359) [0569] have such disgraceful **people** among us and must put up
LC : PR :008(359) [0569] both their office and the **people**'s souls, yes, even God and
LC : SP :001(362) [0575] for the instruction of children and uneducated **people**.
LC : SP :003(362) [0575] For this reason young **people** should be thoroughly
LC : SP :005(362) [0575] time when there were old **people** who were so ignorant
LC : SP :006(362) [0575] As for the common **people**, however, we should be
LC : SP :024(364) [0579] teach and require young **people** to recite word for word.
LC : SP :026(364) [0579] The young **people** should also attend preaching, especially
LC : 01 :010(366) [0583] secure, and proud **people** become because of such
LC : 01 :017(367) [0585] There has never been a **people** so wicked that it did not
LC : 01 :024(367) [0587] be said to ordinary **people** so that they may mark well
LC : 01 :026(368) [0587] authorities — in short, all **people** placed in the position of
LC : 01 :029(368) [0589] impressed upon young **people** so that they may take them
LC : 01 :038(369) [0591] These are also the **people** he means when he says, "who
LC : 01 :044(370) [0593] and in the recollections of elderly and experienced **people**.
LC : 01 :061(372) [0597] therefore, our young **people** should be strictly required
LC : 01 :066(373) [0599] falsehood is refuted, **people** are reconciled, obedience is
LC : 01 :083(376) [0603] To offer ordinary **people** a Christian interpretation of
LC : 01 :083(376) [0603] that the common **people** — man-servants and
LC : 01 :084(376) [0605] we keep holy days so that **people** may have time and
LC : 01 :085(376) [0605] more than the common **people** can do, at least one day in
LC : 01 :086(376) [0605] for the sake of the young and the poor common **people**.
LC : 01 :089(377) [0605] as we have said, since all **people** do not have this much
LC : 01 :108(379) [0611] Young **people** must therefore be taught to revere their
LC : 01 :115(381) [0613] us at last teach our young **people** to banish all other
LC : 01 :118(381) [0615] of these poor wretched **people** when, standing before God
LC : 01 :137(384) [0619] happens that such wicked **people** die a natural and timely
LC : 01 :140(384) [0621] upon the young **people**, for no one will believe how
LC : 01 :142(384) [0621] and ought to have fatherly hearts toward their **people**.
LC : 01 :145(385) [0623] impressed upon the poor **people**, a servant girl would

Continued ▶

L C : 0 1 :147(385) [0623] faith alone serves him, while our works serve the **people**.
L C : 0 1 :150(385) [0623] family, but of as many **people** as he has inhabitants,
L C : 0 1 :156(386) [0625] must still be some godly **people**, or else God would not
L C : 0 1 :161(387) [0627] upon the common **people** that they who would bear the
L C : 0 1 :175(389) [0631] who would be a benefit to the nation and the **people**.
L C : 0 1 :183(390) [0633] We must live among many **people** who do us harm, and
L C : 0 1 :184(390) [0633] When we see such **people**, our hearts in turn rage and we
L C : 0 1 :185(390) [0633] he wishes to have all **people** defended, delivered, and
L C : 0 1 :188(390) [0633] upon the common **people**, the import of the
L C : 0 1 :188(390) [0635] be blameless toward all **people** in body and soul,
L C : 0 1 :196(391) [0637] thoroughly impressed on **people**'s minds, we would have
L C : 0 1 :201(392) [0637] among the Jewish **people** marriage was obligatory.
L C : 0 1 :209(393) [0641] themselves and allow all **people** to enter the estate of
L C : 0 1 :213(394) [0641] they deceive the common **people** with lying words and
L C : 0 1 :217(394) [0641] in order that our young **people** may be led to acquire a
L C : 0 1 :224(395) [0643] common vice, but **people** pay so little attention to it that
L C : 0 1 :225(395) [0643] clearer for the common **people** so that we may see how
L C : 0 1 :226(395) [0645] ways to overcharge **people** and yet are careless and
L C : 0 1 :232(396) [0647] explain it to the common **people** in order that they may
L C : 0 1 :238(397) [0647] them keep on boldly fleecing **people** as long as they can.
L C : 0 1 :243(397) [0649] How many **people** scrape and scratch day and night and
L C : 0 1 :248(398) [0651] upon the young **people** so that they may be on their guard
L C : 0 1 :300(405) [0665] to the most upright — to **people** who wish to be
L C : 0 1 :301(405) [0667] For example, when **people** wrangle and wrestle over a
L C : 0 1 :306(406) [0669] New Testament married **people** are forbidden to be
L C : 0 1 :316(408) [0671] these miserable, blind **people**, that no man can achieve so
L C : 0 1 :330(410) [0677] and remind young **people** of all this so that they may be
L C : 0 2 :020(412) [0681] to describe in detail how few **people** believe this article.
L C : 0 2 :024(413) [0683] It is all that ordinary **people** need to learn at first, both
L C : 0 2 :046(416) [0689] clear to the common **people**, we shall run through them
L C : 0 2 :048(416) [0691] not a group of **people** but a consecrated house or
L C : 0 2 :048(416) [0691] single reason that the group of **people** assembles there.
L C : 0 2 :048(417) [0691] or best and most clearly of all, "a holy Christian **people**."
L C : 0 2 :053(417) [0693] remains with the holy community or Christian **people**.
L C : 0 2 :058(418) [0693] perfectly pure and holy **people**, full of goodness and
L C : 0 2 :062(419) [0695] together all his Christian **people**, nor has he completed
L C : 0 2 :066(419) [0697] distinguish us Christians from all other **people** on earth.
L C : 0 2 :070(420) [0697] for the common **people** without overburdening them.
L C : 0 3 :004(420) [0699] to exhort and draw **people** to prayer, as Christ and the
L C : 0 3 :006(421) [0699] I pray or not, as vulgar **people** do who say in their
L C : 0 3 :028(424) [0705] that affects him or other **people** around him, such as
L C : 0 3 :029(424) [0705] I would like to see the **people** brought again to pray
L C : 0 3 :042(425) [0709] Christians and God's **people** are adulterers, drunkards,
L C : 0 3 :052(427) [0711] followers among other **people** and advance with power
L C : 0 3 :073(430) [0719] description with the **people** among whom we live and
L C : 0 3 :077(431) [0721] their subjects and the **people** at large to live together in
L C : 0 3 :079(431) [0721] upon the common **people** that all these things come from
L C : 0 3 :086(432) [0723] live in the world among **people** who sorely vex us and
L C : 0 3 :102(434) [0727] and example of other **people** and by things we hear and
L C : 0 3 :107(434) [0729] chiefly by the flesh; older **people** are tempted by the
L C : 0 3 :121(436) [0731] pernicious delusion when **people** pay in such a way that
L C : 0 4 :009(437) [0733] If **people** used to consider it a great thing when the pope
L C : 0 4 :030(440) [0739] Now, these **people** are so foolish as to separate faith from
L C : 0 4 :043(442) [0743] who had such skill that **people** would not die, or even
L C : 0 4 :056(444) [0747] fact that I believe and many **people** are praying for me.
L C : 0 4 :061(444) [0747] or in the pot, and magistrates only as ordinary **people**.
L C : 0 5 :040(451) [0761] A lot of **people** who heard the Gospel, now that the
L C : 0 5 :042(451) [0763] let it be understood that **people** who abstain and absent
L C : 0 5 :043(451) [0763] order that the common **people** and the weak, who also
L C : 0 5 :044(451) [0763] in preaching, lest **people** become indifferent and bored.
L C : 0 5 :044(451) [0763] hounding and driving **people** from it as much as he can.
L C : 0 5 :056(453) [0767] and reason see this, such **people** refuse to go to the
L C : 0 5 :061(453) [0767] **People** with such misgivings must learn that it is the
L C : 0 5 :069(454) [0769] To such **people** nothing can be good or wholesome, just
L C : 0 5 :085(456) [0773] but also for the young **people** who ought to be brought
L C : 0 5 :086(456) [0773] For it is clearly useless to try to change old **people**.
L C : 0 5 :086(456) [0773] unless we train the **people** who come after us and succeed
L C : 0 6 :003(457) [0000] a hellish torture since **people** had to make confession even
L C : 0 6 :006(457) [0000] For such **people** we shall provide no preaching, nor will
L C : 0 6 :017(459) [0000] Thereby the **people** were driven to the point that everyone
L C : 0 6 :025(460) [0000] just to show what impure and filthy **people** they were.
L C : 0 6 :034(461) [0000] it would be aroused that **people** would come running
L C : 0 6 :034(461) [0000] themselves and other **people** who ignore such a treasure
E P : 0 1 :022(469) [0785] to conceal their error and to mislead many simple **people**.
E P : 0 1 :023(469) [0785] to common, unlearned **people**, but simple folk should be
E P : 0 2 :015(471) [0789] God makes willing **people** out of unwilling people and
E P : 0 2 :015(471) [0789] people out of unwilling **people** and dwells in the willing
E P : 0 2 :017(472) [0791] stubborn and unwilling **people** into willing people, and
E P : 0 2 :017(472) [0791] people into willing **people**, and that after conversion, in
E P : 0 4 :004(476) [0797] all to Christians but that **people** should be admonished to
E P : 0 4 :018(477) [0801] as necessary to exhort **people** to Christian discipline and
E P : 0 4 :018(477) [0801] faith can damn **people** as much as a papistic and
E P : 0 5 :009(479) [0803] wrath which really directs **people** into the law, after the
E P : 0 5 :010(479) [0803] God's wrath and terrifies **people**, it is not, strictly
E P : 0 6 :002(480) [0805] confess that although **people** who genuinely believe and
E P : 0 6 :003(480) [0805] impenitent but also to **people** who are genuinely
E P : 0 6 :004(480) [0805] Adam, who inheres in **people**'s intellect, will, and all their
E P : 0 6 :005(480) [0807] as they are extorted from **people** only under the coercion
E P : 0 6 :007(481) [0807] and unregenerated **people** the law is and remains one and
E P : 0 7 :038(486) [0817] Christ, but also depends on **people**'s outward preparation.
E P : 1 1 :004(494) [0833] extends alike over good **people** and evil people.
E P : 1 1 :004(494) [0833] extends alike over good people and evil **people**.
E P : 1 1 :019(497) [0837] has predestined certain **people** to damnation so that they
E P : 1 2 :014(499) [0841] against wicked **people**, and that subjects may not call
E P : 1 2 :019(499) [0841] ground for married **people** to divorce one another, each
E P : 1 2 :022(499) [0841] the Holy Spirit teaches **people** and creates in them the
E P : 1 2 :029(500) [0843] like any three individual **people** who are essentially
S D : P R :002(503) [0851] during that period when **people** were everywhere and
S D : P R :008(505) [0853] also concern ordinary **people** and laymen who for their
S D : 0 1 :045(516) [0873] him and that Christ has saved his **people** from their sins.
S D : 0 1 :045(516) [0873] the uninstructed **people** although they are found in the
S D : 0 1 :055(518) [0877] scholars and intelligent **people** have always held that
S D : 0 2 :009(521) [0883] and the most educated **people** on earth read or hear the
S D : 0 2 :029(527) [0893] Confession declares: "**People** outside of Christ and
S D : 0 2 :046(530) [0899] of their statements many **people** have become dissolute
S D : 0 2 :055(532) [0903] and will, and when the **people** diligently and earnestly
S D : 0 2 :064(533) [0905] as David says, "Your **people** will offer themselves freely
S D : 0 2 :067(534) [0907] between baptized **people** and unbaptized people because,
S D : 0 2 :067(534) [0907] people and unbaptized **people** because, according to the
S D : 0 2 :088(538) [0915] Spirit, God makes willing **people** out of resisting and
S D : 0 2 :088(538) [0915] of resisting and unwilling **people**, and that after such
S D : 0 4 :010(552) [0941] makes us entirely different **people** in heart, spirit, mind,
S D : 0 4 :015(553) [0943] delusion, since many **people** dream up for themselves a
S D : 0 4 :017(554) [0943] On the contrary, the **people** of the New Testament are to
S D : 0 4 :017(554) [0943] Testament are to be a **people** who offer themselves freely
S D : 0 4 :028(555) [0947] nevertheless do not teach **people** to put their trust in their
S D : 0 5 :010(559) [0955] produces presumptuous **people**, who believe that they can
S D : 0 6 :001(563) [0963] dissolute and disobedient **people**, (2) and to bring people
S D : 0 6 :001(563) [0963] people, (2) and to bring **people** to a knowledge of their sin
S D : 0 6 :016(566) [0967] Such **people** are saints after the order of Cain.
S D : 0 6 :017(567) [0967] to St. Paul, such **people** are no longer under law but
S D : 0 7 :006(570) [0973] a result many important **people** were deceived by the
S D : 0 7 :024(573) [0979] which now trouble **people** — for example, whether even a
S D : 0 7 :053(579) [0991] and confirm with you **people** this my testament and new
S D : 0 7 :100(587) [1007] Lord's Supper, and, as **people** believe, when he was born
S D : 0 8 :063(603) [1037] the doctrine which these **people** advance, namely, that it
S D : 0 8 :069(604) [1039] nature and other holy **people**, and thus Christ would be
S D : 1 1 :001(616) [1063] at other places and has involved our **people** also.
S D : 1 1 :003(616) [1063] Word because some **people** misuse and misunderstand it;
S D : 1 1 :010(618) [1065] causes and fortifies in **people**'s minds either false security
S D : 1 1 :058(626) [1081] punishes a land or a **people** for contempt of his Word
S D : 1 1 :059(626) [1081] God shows his own **people** what all of us would rightfully
S D : 1 1 :060(626) [1083] lands, nations, and **people** so that, as we compare
S D : 1 1 :083(630) [1091] gracious will that such **people** should come to the
S D : 1 1 :089(631) [1093] Moreover, when **people** are taught to seek their eternal
S D : 1 1 :090(631) [1093] sorrowing and tempted **people** the permanently abiding
S D : 1 2 :008(633) [1097] where the poor, simple **people**, who were forced into
S D : 1 2 :016(634) [1099] to flee and avoid them as **people** who pervert the Word
S D : 1 2 :024(634) [1099] ground for married **people** to divorce each other, to go
S D : 1 2 :026(635) [1099] more and greater gifts and glory than other **people**.

Peoples (3)
A P : 2 1 :018(231) [0347] stand as an ensign to the **peoples**; him shall the nations
S 1 : P R :009(290) [0457] the king and foreign **peoples** as if they were the
L C : 0 1 :142(384) [0621] the Romans and other **peoples** called the masters and

Perceive (17), Perceived (5), Perceives (2), Perceptibly (1)
P R : P R :004(004) [0007] way hold back and **perceptibly** impede the course of the
A G : 0 0 :000(049) [0059] Imperial Majesty may **perceive** that we have not acted in
A G : 2 4 :030(059) [0067] our consciences when we **perceive** that through the
A G : 2 5 :008(062) [0069] sins that it is unable to **perceive** or know them all, and if
A G : 0 0 :003(095) [0095] that the chief points at issue may better be **perceived**.
A L : 1 8 :002(039) [0051] natural man does not **perceive** the gifts of the Spirit of
A L : 2 5 :009(063) [0069] for many sins can neither be **perceived** nor remembered.
A L : 2 6 :030(068) [0075] different may be **perceived** in the writings of our teachers,
A L : 2 7 :057(080) [0083] They did not **perceive** that God is to be served by
A P : 1 8 :007(226) [0337] his natural powers, "does not **perceive** the things of God."
A P : 2 1 :011(230) [0345] the saints, the power to **perceive** the unspoken thought of
S 1 : P R :003(289) [0455] on this account, for they **perceive** that the pope prefers to
S 3 : 0 7 :001(311) [0493] are subtle and secret and which God alone **perceives**.
L C : 0 1 :140(384) [0621] other things, and fails to **perceive** and believe how angry
L C : 0 1 :170(388) [0629] The trouble is that no one **perceives** or heeds this.
L C : 0 4 :030(440) [0739] so that it can be **perceived** and grasped by the senses and
L C : 0 4 :050(443) [0745] Holy Spirit, as we have **perceived** in some of the fathers,
L C : 0 5 :084(456) [0773] apparent, and you will **perceive** that you have sunk twice
S D : 0 2 :009(522) [0883] by their own powers **perceive** this, comprehend it,
S D : 0 2 :014(523) [0885] devout Christians who **perceive** and discover a little spark
S D : 0 2 :046(530) [0899] actually to feel and to **perceive** that God has truly
S D : 0 2 :056(532) [0903] of our feeling, how and when we **perceive** it in our hearts.
S D : 0 2 :059(532) [0905] does it understand or **perceive** what is being done to it, as
S D : 0 2 :089(538) [0915] what is going on or **perceive** or will anything in
S D : 0 7 :069(582) [0997] great impurity, and who **perceive** their weakness in faith,

Perchance (2)
S 3 : 0 3 :018(306) [0483] than wept, unless **perchance** he was really smitten by the
S D : 1 1 :074(628) [1087] And if **perchance** they should fall into such grave

Perdition (1)
E P : 1 1 :004(495) [0833] is it the cause of man's **perdition**; for this man himself is

Perfect (47), Perfected (1), Perfection (68), Perfectly (20)
A G : 1 6 :004(037) [0051] teach that Christian **perfection** requires the forsaking of
A G : 1 6 :004(037) [0051] Actually, true **perfection** consists alone of proper fear of
A G : 2 6 :011(065) [0071] glamorous title of alone being holy and **perfect** works.
A G : 2 7 :016(073) [0077] it is called a state of **perfection** and is regarded as far
A G : 2 7 :046(078) [0081] spiritual estate of the orders was Christian **perfection**.
A G : 2 7 :049(078) [0083] are told that monks alone are in a state of **perfection**.
A G : 2 7 :049(078) [0083] For this is Christian **perfection**: that we fear God honestly
A G : 2 7 :050(079) [0083] True **perfection** and right service of God consist of these
A G : 2 7 :053(079) [0083] that only mendicants are **perfect**, he is uncertain whether
A G : 2 7 :058(080) [0083] That is a good and **perfect** state of life which has God's
A G : 2 7 :060(080) [0083] the monks concerning **perfection** and indicated that it
A G : 2 7 :060(080) [0083] his time to speak of monastic life as a state of **perfection**.
A G : 2 7 :061(080) [0083] constitute Christian **perfection**, that they are the means of
A L : 1 2 :008(035) [0049] some may attain such **perfection** in this life that they
A L : 1 6 :004(038) [0051] those who place the **perfection** of the Gospel not in the
A L : 2 4 :027(059) [0067] a single offering he has **perfected** for all time those who
A L : 2 6 :009(065) [0071] title of comprising the spiritual life and the **perfect** life.
A L : 2 7 :016(073) [0077] that it is a state of **perfection**, and they put it far above
A L : 2 7 :046(078) [0081] invented observances were a state of Christian **perfection**.
A L : 2 7 :049(078) [0083] men hear that only monks are in a state of **perfection**.
A L : 2 7 :049(078) [0083] For this is Christian **perfection**: honestly to fear God and
A L : 2 7 :050(079) [0083] True **perfection** and true service of God consist of these
A L : 2 7 :053(079) [0083] that only mendicants are **perfect**, and therefore they have
A L : 2 7 :058(080) [0083] A good and **perfect** kind of life is one which has God's
A L : 2 7 :060(080) [0083] the monks concerning **perfection** and testified that it was

Continued ▶

A L : 2 7 :060(080) [0083] in his day to say that monastic life is a state of **perfection**.
A L : 2 7 :061(080) [0083] constitute Christian **perfection**, that the monks observe
A P : 0 2 :012(102) [0109] views about the **perfection** of nature and attributed more
A P : 0 4 :014(109) [0123] are correct, this was **perfectly** proper, for Aristotle wrote
A P : 0 4 :044(113) [0133] the law requires our own works and our own **perfection**.
A P : 0 4 :160(129) [0167] obedience to the law is **perfect**, it is indeed righteousness;
A P : 0 4 :161(129) [0167] before God by our own **perfection** and keeping of the
A P : 0 4 :175(131) [0171] realize how far we are from the **perfection** of the law.
A P : 0 4 :179(131) [0171] still far away from the **perfection** of the law, still the
A P : 0 4 :231(139) [0183] us Col. 3:14, "love, which is the bond of **perfection**."
A P : 0 4 :231(139) [0183] they argue that love justifies since it makes men **perfect**.
A P : 0 4 :231(139) [0183] many answers about **perfection**, we shall simply present
A P : 0 4 :231(139) [0183] either justification or **perfection** before God to the works
A P : 0 4 :231(139) [0183] it is love that makes men **perfect**, Christ, the propitiator,
A P : 0 4 :232(139) [0185] not about personal **perfection** but about fellowship in the
A P : 0 4 :234(140) [0185] On the other hand, **perfection** (that is, the integrity of the
A P : 0 4 :235(140) [0185] the basis of the word "**perfection**" that love justifies, when
A P : 0 4 :235(140) [0185] as a building is said to be **perfect** or whole when all its
A P : 0 4 :270(147) [0199] keeping of the law is impure and far from **perfect**.
A P : 0 4 :293(152) [0203] are a long way from the **perfection** of the law, these
A P : 0 4 :353(161) [0217] Christian and spiritual **perfection**, if penitence and faith
A P : 0 4 :353(161) [0217] our opponents teach about contemplation or **perfection**.
A P : 1 2 :142(204) [0295] we are far away from the **perfection** that the law requires.
A P : 1 2 :160(207) [0303] power of God is made **perfect** in weakness" (II Cor. 12:9).
A P : 1 5 :025(219) [0321] regard these works as **perfect** and spiritual, they will
A P : 1 5 :030(219) [0323] He makes it **perfectly** clear that he is talking about human
A P : 1 6 :009(224) [0333] to claim that Christian **perfection** consists in not holding
A P : 1 6 :009(224) [0333] makes for Christian **perfection** is not contempt of civil
A P : 1 6 :009(224) [0333] David, and Daniel were no less **perfect** than any hermit.
A P : 1 6 :010(224) [0333] and blinded them to the essence of real **perfection**.
A P : 2 4 :035(256) [0397] We are **perfectly** willing for the Mass to be understood as
A P : 2 7 :009(270) [0421] Are they "evangelical **perfection**"?
A P : 2 7 :024(273) [0427] say that they are more **perfect** services than other ways of
A P : 2 7 :026(273) [0429] Hence they are neither justifying services nor **perfection**.
A P : 2 7 :027(273) [0429] believe that evangelical **perfection** is to be found in
A P : 2 7 :027(273) [0429] could boast that they have evangelical **perfection**.
A P : 2 7 :027(273) [0429] in the heart, therefore **perfection** means to grow in the
A P : 2 7 :027(273) [0429] Paul also describes **perfection** (II Cor. 3:18) thus: "We are
A P : 2 7 :027(274) [0429] the church, finding the **perfection** of the Gospel and of
A P : 2 7 :035(275) [0431] services," they are not evangelical **perfection** at all.
A P : 2 7 :036(275) [0433] they are modifying the common notion about **perfection**.
A P : 2 7 :036(275) [0433] that the monastic life is **perfection**, but they say that it is a
A P : 2 7 :036(275) [0433] but they say that it is a state for acquiring **perfection**.
A P : 2 7 :036(275) [0433] to deny it the claim of **perfection** altogether, they added
A P : 2 7 :036(275) [0433] this correction, that it is a state for acquiring **perfection**.
A P : 2 7 :037(275) [0433] be no more a state of **perfection** than the life of a farmer
A P : 2 7 :037(275) [0433] These, too, are states for acquiring **perfection**.
A P : 2 7 :037(275) [0433] calling, ought to seek **perfection**, that is, growth in the
A P : 2 7 :039(276) [0433] their praises about **perfection**, they really believe
A P : 2 7 :039(276) [0433] If this is not arrogating **perfection** to oneself, what is?
A P : 2 7 :039(276) [0433] They are ascribing **perfection** to human traditions if they
A P : 2 7 :040(276) [0433] say, here, too, it claims **perfection** for artificial religious
A P : 2 7 :045(277) [0435] another passage on **perfection** (Matt. 19:21), "If you
A P : 2 7 :045(277) [0435] "If you would be **perfect**, go, sell what you possess
A P : 2 7 :045(277) [0435] they imagined that **perfection** consists in casting off
A P : 2 7 :046(277) [0435] examples have nothing to do with Christian **perfection**.
A P : 2 7 :047(277) [0437] God is meritorious and holy and the way of **perfection**.
A P : 2 7 :048(277) [0437] Yet Christ calls it **perfection** here!
A P : 2 7 :048(277) [0437] **Perfection** consists in that which Christ adds, "Follow
A P : 2 7 :050(277) [0437] It would have been **perfection** for this young man to
A P : 2 7 :050(277) [0437] So it is **perfection** for each of us with true faith to obey
S 3 : 0 3 :023(306) [0485] could have been **perfect**, full confidence would have been
T R : 0 0 :048(328) [0519] are services of God and **perfection**, and they have
L C : P R :009(359) [0569] parts of the Catechism **perfectly**, or at least sufficiently,
L C : P R :009(359) [0569] of Catechism were **perfect** (though that is impossible in
L C : P R :016(361) [0573] to learn, though they cannot learn it to **perfection**.
L C : P R :017(361) [0573] Ten Commandments **perfectly** knows the entire
L C : 0 1 :040(370) [0591] hearts upon God with **perfect** confidence since the divine
L C : 0 1 :100(378) [0609] you know the Word **perfectly** and have already mastered
L C : 0 1 :197(392) [0637] and works as "the most **perfect** life," so that they might
L C : 0 1 :219(394) [0643] each other whole-heartedly and with **perfect** fidelity.
L C : 0 1 :261(400) [0655] a goal set for our jurists: **perfect** justice and equity in
L C : 0 1 :315(408) [0671] man, whereas theirs is for the saints and the **perfect**.
L C : 0 2 :001(411) [0679] from God; in brief, it teaches us to know him **perfectly**.
L C : 0 2 :057(418) [0693] arise to complete and **perfect** holiness in a new, eternal
L C : 0 2 :058(418) [0693] In that life are only **perfectly** pure and holy people, full of
L C : 0 2 :059(418) [0695] this life, he will instantly **perfect** our holiness and will
L C : 0 2 :062(419) [0695] evil, he will finally make us **perfectly** and eternally holy.
L C : 0 3 :002(420) [0697] Ten Commandments **perfectly**, even though he has begun
L C : 0 3 :054(427) [0713] we may live forever in **perfect** righteousness and
L C : 0 4 :046(442) [0743] for through it we obtain **perfect** holiness and salvation,
L C : 0 5 :055(453) [0767] ourselves to become so **perfectly** pure that God might not
L C : 0 6 :016(459) [0000] was not made **perfectly** and in complete detail, we were
E P : 0 2 :012(471) [0789] to keep the law of God **perfectly** and entirely and that
E P : 0 4 :013(477) [0799] this spontaneity is not **perfect**, but they are still
E P : 0 8 :037(491) [0825] does not as yet have a **perfect** knowledge of God and all
E P : 1 2 :025(500) [0843] the Spirit of God can **perfectly** keep and fulfill the law of
S D : 0 1 :020(511) [0865] matters it is good, pure, and in its natural powers **perfect**.
S D : 0 1 :026(512) [0867] nature is initially created **perfect** and pure, and that
S D : 0 1 :054(518) [0877] use them in the sense of a **perfect** dichotomy (that is, a
S D : 0 1 :062(519) [0879] head, inasmuch as this befell a hitherto **perfect** nature."
S D : 0 2 :068(534) [0907] regeneration is not as yet **perfect** but has only been begun
S D : 0 2 :079(536) [0911] can keep the law of God **perfectly** in this life and by such
S D : 0 2 :079(536) [0911] in this life and by such **perfect** obedience of the law merit
S D : 0 3 :004(540) [0917] and man he has by his **perfect** obedience redeemed us
S D : 0 3 :015(541) [0919] keeping of the law in so **perfect** a fashion that, reckoning
S D : 0 3 :022(543) [0923] hold that Christ with his **perfect** obedience covers all our
S D : 0 3 :028(544) [0925] is never wholly pure and **perfect** on account of our
S D : 0 3 :030(544) [0925] Christ and (in him) in his **perfect** obedience with which he
S D : 0 3 :055(549) [0935] man in his sole, total, and **perfect** obedience is our
S D : 0 3 :057(549) [0935] person, therefore it is a **perfect** satisfaction and
S D : 0 3 :058(550) [0937] to his Father entire, **perfect** obedience from his holy birth
S D : 0 6 :006(564) [0963] children of God were **perfectly** renewed in this life
S D : 0 6 :007(565) [0965] life Christians are not renewed **perfectly** and completely.
S D : 0 6 :007(565) [0965] covered up through the **perfect** obedience of Christ, so
S D : 0 6 :021(567) [0969] that their works and life are **perfectly** pure and holy.
S D : 0 6 :022(567) [0969] The law demands a **perfect** and pure obedience if it is to
S D : 0 6 :025(568) [0971] coercion, unhindered, **perfectly**, completely, and with
S D : 0 7 :070(582) [0997] "The power of God is made **perfect** in weakness."
S D : 0 8 :006(592) [1017] true, essential, and **perfect** God with the Father and the
S D : 1 2 :033(635) [1101] to keep and fulfill the law of God **perfectly** in this life.

Perfidy (2)

L C : 0 1 :253(399) [0653] than you could scrape together by **perfidy** and injustice.
L C : 0 3 :103(434) [0727] violence and injustice, **perfidy**, vengeance, cursing,

Perform (22), Performance (14), Performances (1), Performed (15), Performing (5), Performs (10)

A G : 2 4 :023(058) [0067] of Masses, by the **performance** of which men expected to
A G : 2 4 :029(059) [0067] obtained through the **performance** of this work, for it is
A G : 2 6 :029(068) [0075] nobody is a Christian unless he **performs** such services.
A G : 2 6 :038(069) [0075] a condition that one can **perform** the duties required by
A G : 2 8 :029(085) [0087] are negligent in the **performance** of such duties, the
A L : 1 8 :009(040) [0053] able in some measure to **perform** the outward works (for
A L : 2 4 :022(058) [0067] is a work by which its **performance** takes away the sins of
A L : 2 4 :029(059) [0067] and the dead by a **performance** of the outward act,
A L : 2 7 :049(079) [0083] to be diligent in the **performance** of good works for
A L : 2 8 :029(085) [0087] are negligent in the **performance** of their duties, princes
A P : 0 4 :008(108) [0121] external works that reason can somehow **perform**.
A P : 0 4 :018(109) [0125] satisfied, that reason **performs** only certain external
A P : 0 4 :022(110) [0127] Decalogue should be **performed**, according to Gal. 3:24,
A P : 0 4 :033(111) [0129] the flesh sins even when it **performs** outward civil works.
A P : 0 4 :106(122) [0153] a good work by the **performance** of which he can live.
A P : 0 4 :321(156) [0209] when a work has been **performed** under the influence of
A P : 0 4 :321(157) [0209] intention of the one **performing** the work does not
A P : 0 4 :322(157) [0209] of the works that saints **perform** after justification,
A P : 1 2 :118(200) [0287] even when they are **performed** by those who have relapsed
A P : 1 2 :122(200) [0289] by the priest should **perform** the prescribed penitence,
A P : 1 2 :143(204) [0297] acts of charity are **performed** as acts of worship which *ex*
A P : 1 2 :143(204) [0297] to the mere **performance** of these acts, for they teach that
A P : 1 2 :162(208) [0303] The **performance** of canonical satisfactions does not do
A P : 1 2 :162(208) [0303] to man — that is, the **performance** of human traditions
A P : 1 2 :163(208) [0303] St. James dressed in armor or to **perform** similar works."
A P : 1 2 :165(208) [0303] to the satisfaction and **performance** of human traditions.
A P : 1 5 :026(219) [0323] profane, so that many **perform** them with scruples of
A P : 1 5 :027(219) [0323] the good works to be **performed** in one's calling, but only
A P : 1 5 :040(220) [0325] celebrants and hirelings **perform** Mass, and they often do
A P : 1 8 :002(225) [0335] men can love God and **perform** "the essence of the acts"
A P : 1 8 :007(226) [0337] the human heart cannot **perform** without the Holy Spirit.
A P : 2 3 :032(244) [0373] task of her calling, as **performance** of the tasks of a
A P : 2 3 :039(244) [0375] married person does by **performing** the duties of
A P : 2 3 :045(245) [0377] would merit grace by **performing** these works and
A P : 2 4 :097(268) [0417] other priests who **perform** the sacrifices instituted by God
A P : 2 8 :012(283) [0447] are now bishops do not **perform** the duties of bishops
S 3 : 0 1 :010(303) [0479] gifts are necessary for the **performance** of a good work.
T R : 0 0 :048(328) [0519] these to works **performed** in callings which God requires
L C : 0 1 :094(378) [0607] here a work must be **performed** by which the doer
L C : 0 1 :113(380) [0613] should do if we wish to **perform** truly good works, and by
L C : 0 1 :117(381) [0615] chosen and fitted you to **perform** a task so precious and
L C : 0 1 :158(387) [0627] this title to themselves but **performed** no fatherly office.
L C : 0 3 :014(422) [0701] enough if the act was **performed**, whether God heard it or
L C : 0 4 :009(437) [0735] it and, what is more, it is **performed** in his name.
L C : 0 4 :010(437) [0735] Although it is **performed** by men's hands, it is
L C : 0 4 :012(438) [0735] Because the person **performing** the act is nobler and
L C : 0 4 :080(446) [0751] only in the light of a work **performed** once for all.
L C : 0 5 :007(447) [0755] contrary to the Word of God, as human **performances**.
L C : 0 6 :018(459) [0000] act as if we wanted to **perform** a magnificent work to
L C : 0 6 :022(459) [0000] not for the purpose of **performing** a work but to hear
E P : 0 2 :017(472) [0791] all the works which the Holy Spirit **performs** through us.
E P : 0 2 :018(472) [0791] the Holy Spirit has **performed** and accomplished this and
E P : 0 6 :006(481) [0807] which the regenerated **perform** in so far as they are reborn
E P : 0 8 :033(491) [0825] of a slave, does not **perform** all works of his omnipotence
E P : 0 8 :036(491) [0825] is fitting and necessary to **perform** his office as judge.
S D : 0 2 :032(527) [0893] lies within our power to **perform** such external works, we
S D : 0 2 :044(529) [0897] blind and captive man **performs** only the devil's will and
S D : 0 2 :089(538) [0915] who accomplishes and **performs** it by his power and
S D : 0 4 :008(552) [0941] also able and require to **perform**, are indeed praiseworthy
S D : 0 4 :011(553) [0941] Whoever does not **perform** such good works is a faithless
S D : 0 5 :011(560) [0955] New Testament, he must **perform** what the prophet calls
S D : 0 5 :014(560) [0957] Testament retains and **performs** the office of the law,
S D : 0 6 :010(565) [0965] what function the law **performs** in this matter, as far as
S D : 0 6 :012(566) [0967] Spirit simultaneously **performs** both offices, "he kills and
S D : 0 7 :016(572) [0977] of this sacrament, **performed** by Christ, that makes it
S D : 0 8 :025(596) [1023] basis, likewise, Christ **performed** all his miracles and
S D : 0 8 :039(598) [1029] Here Zwingli **performs** a sleight-of-hand trick and

Perhaps (14)

A G : 2 8 :073(093) [0093] **Perhaps** there was some reason for introducing them, but
A L : 2 4 :018(057) [0067] **Perhaps** the world is being punished for such long
A L : 2 8 :073(093) [0093] **Perhaps** there were acceptable reasons for these
A P : 0 7 :023(172) [0235] **Perhaps** our opponents demand some such definition of
A P : 1 0 :003(179) [0247] Does he think **perhaps** that we do not know the power of
A P : 2 1 :011(230) [0345] and evening knowledge, **perhaps** because they are not
A P : 2 1 :024(232) [0349] **Perhaps** they derive this "order" from the usage at royal
A P : 2 4 :023(253) [0391] up human sacrifices, **perhaps** because they had heard that
A P : 2 4 :085(264) [0413] etymology, except **perhaps** to show off their knowledge
A P : 2 7 :043(276) [0435] to monastic life, unless **perhaps** the statement that they
S 2 : 0 2 :026(297) [0469] saints on earth, and **perhaps** also in heaven, do likewise,
S 3 : 0 3 :042(309) [0491] may appear (and **perhaps** they are already present, such
S C : P R :007(339) [0533] now and another form — **perhaps** with the intention of
L C : 0 4 :053(443) [0745] This, **perhaps**, is a rather subtle point, but it is based

Peril (6), Perilous (2), Perils (2)

P R : P R :004(003) [0007] unconcealed, what very **perilous** events and troublesome
P R : P R :014(007) [0013] God against all sorts of **perilous** misunderstanding, so
A G : 0 0 :001(047) [0059] and consciences in grave **peril** before God by misusing his

Continued ▶

AL : 2 6 :039(069) [0075] but traditions which with **peril** to conscience prescribe
AP : 0 4 :278(149) [0199] a defense for us in the **perils** of sin and death, as we said a
AP : 0 4 :288(151) [0203] but when men are in great **peril** they add other forms of
S 3 : 1 5 :003(316) [0501] let him do so at the **peril** of his own conscience.
LC : 0 1 :190(391) [0635] to death or in similar **peril** and do not save him although
LC : 0 1 :191(391) [0635] and aid to men in need and in **peril** of body and life.
LC : 0 3 :105(434) [0727] are the great, grievous **perils** and temptations which every

Period (10)
AP : 2 3 :027(243) [0371] that during the **period** of their ministration the priests of
AP : 2 3 :027(243) [0371] is forbidden only during the **period** of ministration.
LC : 0 5 :042(451) [0763] sacrament over a long **period** of time are not to be
LC : 0 5 :049(452) [0765] to hinder him, lets a long **period** of time elapse without
SD : PR :002(503) [0851] kept and used during that **period** when people were
SD : 1 0 :002(610) [1053] party held that even in a **period** of persecution and a case
SD : 1 0 :003(611) [1053] are concerned, in a **period** of persecution and a case of
SD : 1 0 :025(615) [1061] especially in a **period** of confession, so that they do not
SD : 1 0 :028(615) [1061] those who hold that in a **period** of persecution we may
SD : 1 0 :029(615) [1061] a culpable sin when in a **period** of persecution anything is

Perish (19), Perishable (1), Perished (4), Perishes (2), Perishing (1)
AG : 2 8 :045(088) [0089] to things which all **perish** as they are used), according to
AL : 2 8 :045(088) [0089] to things which all **perish** as they are used), according to
AP : 0 4 :191(133) [0175] of God might not **perish** utterly from the earth.
AP : 0 4 :322(157) [0209] extolling himself should **perish** even more, he is instructed
AP : 0 7 :020(172) [0233] build on this foundation **perishing** structures of stubble,
AP : 0 7 :035(175) [0241] to things which all **perish** as they are used), according to
AP : 0 7 :036(175) [0241] do not pertain to the heart and "**perish** as they are used."
AP : 2 2 :017(238) [0361] of Ezekiel (7:26), "The law **perishes** from the priest."
AP : 2 8 :010(282) [0447] and the like are things which **perish** as they are used.
LC : 0 1 :035(369) [0589] so that all who persist in it must ultimately **perish**.
LC : 0 1 :036(369) [0589] just as all others have **perished** who thought themselves to
LC : 0 1 :045(370) [0593] and power, he inevitably **perished** with all that he had;
LC : 0 1 :068(374) [0599] and thus they miserably **perished**, body, soul, and
LC : 0 1 :129(383) [0617] otherwise he would have **perished** a hundred times in his
LC : 0 1 :134(383) [0619] disobeys it is that he will **perish** sooner and never be
LC : 0 1 :151(386) [0625] to the hangman, or **perish** through war, pestilence, or
LC : 0 1 :191(391) [0635] by wild beasts, to rot in prison or **perish** from want."
LC : 0 1 :192(391) [0635] your neighbor to languish and **perish** in his misfortune.
LC : 0 3 :055(427) [0713] or for a temporal, **perishable** blessing, but for an eternal,
EP : 1 1 :010(495) [0833] does not want anyone to **perish** (Ezek. 33:11; 18:23), but
SD : 0 2 :049(530) [0901] believes on him should not **perish** but have eternal life."
SD : 0 2 :057(532) [0903] in this condition, and **perishes** in his sins, he can neither
SD : 0 5 :007(559) [0953] you will all likewise **perish**," and in Luke 15:7, "Even so,
SD : 1 1 :028(621) [1071] wishing that any should **perish**, but that all should turn to
SD : 1 1 :081(629) [1089] not will that "any should **perish**, but that all should reach
SD : 1 1 :084(630) [1091] all the earth") did not **perish** because God did not want to
SD : 1 1 :084(630) [1091] wishing that any should **perish**," nor has he any "pleasure

Perjures (1)
LC : 0 1 :053(372) [0595] when a person **perjures** himself, swearing by God's name

Permanent (1), Permanently (4)
AP : 1 1 :005(181) [0251] If they commune, let them not be **permanently** expelled.
SD : PR :001(503) [0849] for basic and **permanent** concord within the church is a
SD : 0 7 :014(571) [0977] are in some other way **permanently** united with it apart
SD : 1 1 :090(631) [1093] tempted people the **permanently** abiding comfort of
SD : 1 1 :093(632) [1093] exposition which is **permanently** and well grounded in

Permit (22), Permits (5), Permitted (16), Permitting (2)
PR : PR :002(003) [0007] toward mankind has **permitted** the pure, unalloyed, and
PR : PR :018(009) [0015] we were not minded to **permit** any doctrine in our lands,
PR : PR :023(012) [0021] and that no doctrine be **permitted** entrance which is
AG : 0 0 :000(049) [0059] our reasons for **permitting** changes in these cases in order
AG : 2 3 :002(053) [0063] and weightier reasons for **permitting** them to be married.
AP : 0 4 :231(139) [0185] Paul would never **permit** Christ, the propitiator, to be
AP : 0 4 :256(144) [0193] statement must be **permitted** to interpret the entire law
AP : 1 2 :131(202) [0291] of the soul do not **permit** the indulgence of the body in
AP : 1 5 :015(217) [0319] If we are **permitted** to establish rites that serve to merit
AP : 1 6 :013(224) [0333] whether the Gospel **permitted** such public and private
AP : 2 1 :040(235) [0355] of the pastors **permitted** many abuses to creep into the
AP : 2 2 :006(237) [0359] those who were not **permitted** to receive the entire
AP : 2 2 :008(237) [0359] and were no longer **permitted** to consecrate the elements.
AP : 2 3 :027(243) [0371] analogy marriage is **permitted** and intercourse is
AP : 2 3 :028(243) [0371] which the Word of God **permits** and approves, as the
AP : 2 3 :061(247) [0381] The Gospel **permits** marriage for those who need it, but it
AP : 2 4 :020(252) [0389] the limits of this book **permitted**, we would enumerate the
S 1 : PR :003(289) [0455] Roman court will ever **permit** a free council, to say
S 2 : 0 2 :001(293) [0463] this article either, for the first article does not **permit** it.
S 2 : 0 2 :010(294) [0465] Before they would **permit** this to happen, they would put
S 2 : 0 4 :003(298) [0471] where God sometimes **permits** much good to come to a
S 2 : 0 4 :010(300) [0475] for the pope will not **permit** Christians to be saved except
S 2 : 0 4 :012(300) [0475] the pope will not **permit** such faith but asserts that one
S 3 : 0 3 :044(310) [0491] the Holy Spirit does not **permit** sin to rule and gain the
S 3 : 1 0 :001(314) [0497] Gospel, they might be **permitted** (for the sake of love and
TR : 0 0 :055(329) [0521] as the pope does not **permit** anything to be decreed
TR : 0 0 :082(000) [0529] least, yet, as I am not **permitted** to await the end of the
LC : 0 1 :057(372) [0597] As little as God will **permit** the heart that turns away
LC : 0 1 :057(372) [0597] so little will he **permit** his name to be used to gloss over a
LC : 0 1 :081(375) [0603] Christ and would not **permit** him to do what they
LC : 0 1 :097(378) [0609] of the holy day, for we **permit** ourselves to be preached to
LC : 0 1 :191(391) [0635] say, "You would have **permitted** me and my followers to
LC : 0 1 :192(391) [0635] you have nevertheless **permitted** your neighbor to
LC : 0 1 :225(395) [0643] duty and does damage or **permits** damage to happen
LC : 0 1 :250(399) [0651] not even to consent to or **permit** such a thing, but are
LC : 0 4 :055(443) [0745] and he would not be **permitted** on account of that abuse
LC : 0 5 :006(447) [0755] conduct that he would **permit** them to affect his
EP : 0 7 :033(485) [0815] human nature could neither **permit** nor admit this.
SD : 0 2 :069(534) [0907] to their conscience and **permit** sin to rule in themselves
SD : 0 7 :045(577) [0987] Nor dare we **permit** any objection or human
SD : 0 7 :092(586) [1005] can not, and should not **permit** any clever human
SD : 0 7 :120(590) [1013] his assumed human nature neither **permit** nor allow this.
SD : 1 0 :019(614) [1059] Gospel, they might be **permitted** (for the sake of love and
SD : 1 1 :026(620) [1071] Neither should we **permit** ourselves to try to explore the
SD : 1 1 :060(626) [1083] But God **permits** us to behold his righteous and well

Permissible (2)
AP : 2 3 :031(243) [0371] the use of marriage is **permissible** and holy through faith
AP : 2 3 :031(243) [0373] faith in Christ just as the use of food, etc. is **permissible**.

Permission (3)
AP : 2 3 :033(244) [0373] something has God's **permission** and approval, then
LC : 0 6 :006(457) [0000] nor will they have our **permission** to share and enjoy any
EP : 0 1 :025(469) [0785] he can only, with God's **permission**, corrupt accidentally

Pernicious (13)
AL : 2 7 :051(079) [0083] The people draw many **pernicious** conclusions from such
LC : PR :003(359) [0567] Gospel than this rotten, **pernicious**, shameful, carnal
LC : 0 1 :099(378) [0609] satiety — a malignant, **pernicious** plague with which the
LC : 0 1 :317(408) [0673] men may get rid of the **pernicious** abuse which has
LC : 0 3 :121(436) [0731] It is therefore a **pernicious** delusion when people pay in
SD : 0 6 :026(568) [0971] reject and condemn, as **pernicious** and contrary to
SD : 0 7 :001(569) [0971] Christians against this **pernicious** error which is
SD : 0 7 :061(581) [0995] is not only salutary but actually **pernicious** and damning.
SD : 0 7 :090(585) [1003] It is therefore a **pernicious**, impudent error when some by
SD : 0 8 :038(598) [1027] hide their **pernicious** error under the words of the formula
SD : 0 8 :087(608) [1047] Hence we consider it a **pernicious** error to deprive Christ
SD : 0 8 :096(610) [1049] and will be well protected against **pernicious** errors.
SD : 1 1 :010(618) [1065] dangerous, and **pernicious** opinions and causes and

Perpetual (14), Perpetuate (1), Perpetuated (1)
PR : PR :023(012) [0021] may be preserved and **perpetuated** among our posterity
AG : 2 7 :028(075) [0079] to what an extent **perpetual** chastity lies within human
AL : 2 7 :028(075) [0079] to what an extent **perpetual** chastity lies in man's power.
AL : 2 8 :066(092) [0093] must consider what the **perpetual** aim of the Gospel is.
AP : 2 3 :025(243) [0371] the regulation about **perpetual** celibacy is peculiar to this
AP : 2 3 :027(243) [0371] continually, they must also preserve **perpetual** continence.
AP : 2 3 :027(243) [0371] as a proof to force **perpetual** celibacy on priests, though
AP : 2 3 :041(245) [0375] make it necessary to impose **perpetual** celibacy on priests.
AP : 2 3 :043(245) [0375] but Paul does not want this to be **perpetual** (I Cor. 7:5).
AP : 2 3 :051(246) [0377] many reasons for rejecting the law of **perpetual** celibacy.
AP : 2 3 :060(247) [0379] their defense of the pontifical law of **perpetual** celibacy.
AP : 2 3 :063(248) [0381] for the law of **perpetual** celibacy, though it conflicts with
AP : 2 3 :067(248) [0383] the world still did not know the law of **perpetual** celibacy.
S 3 : 1 1 :001(314) [0499] burden the divine estate of priests with **perpetual** celibacy.
LC : 0 1 :213(394) [0641] that they will maintain **perpetual** chastity while they
LC : 0 5 :086(456) [0773] We cannot **perpetuate** these and other teachings unless we

Persecute (12), Persecuted (3), Persecutes (1), Persecuting (1), Persecution (12), Persecutors (4)
PR : PR :022(012) [0021] any molestation and **persecution** of poor, oppressed
PR : PR :022(012) [0021] a cordial disapproval of the raging of their **persecutors**.
PR : PR :022(012) [0021] be required of the **persecutors** on the great day of the
AG : 2 3 :021(055) [0063] time does one begin to **persecute** innocent people simply
AP : 0 4 :167(130) [0169] the devout, because the wicked **persecute** the devout?
AP : 0 4 :198(134) [0175] are those who are **persecuted** for righteousness' sake, for
AP : 0 4 :326(158) [0211] of his cause against the **persecutors** of God's Word, not
AP : 1 4 :003(214) [0315] cruelty of those who **persecute** this teaching, for we know
AP : 2 1 :044(236) [0357] faithful consciences nor **persecute** innocent men, as has
AP : 2 2 :016(238) [0361] and violently **persecute** anyone that uses the entire
AP : 2 7 :056(278) [0439] are forced to agree with the **persecutors** of the truth.
AP : 2 8 :025(285) [0451] are now most cruelly **persecuting** it, will give an account
S 3 : 0 8 :008(313) [0497] Messiah and not deny or **persecute** him as the Jews did.
S 3 : 1 0 :002(314) [0497] than that, they expel, **persecute**, and condemn those who
TR : 0 0 :059(330) [0521] godly whom the pope **persecutes**, detract from the glory
LC : 0 1 :046(370) [0593] man, hunted down and **persecuted**, his life nowhere
LC : 0 1 :262(400) [0655] shameful and spiteful **persecution** and blasphemy; it is
LC : 0 1 :262(400) [0655] nature to condemn and **persecute** the truth and the
LC : 0 3 :047(426) [0711] those who attack and **persecute** our Gospel and pure
LC : 0 3 :067(429) [0717] nor of those who would **persecute** and suppress thy holy
LC : 0 3 :068(429) [0717] of all violence and **persecution**, submitting to the will of
EP : 1 0 :002(492) [0829] has been, In times of **persecution**, when a confession is
EP : 1 0 :006(493) [0829] confess that in time of **persecution**, when a clear-cut
EP : 1 0 :011(494) [0831] 3. That in a time of **persecution** and when a public
SD : 0 4 :029(555) [0947] which in times of **persecution**, when it was particularly
SD : 1 0 :002(611) [1053] even in a period of **persecution** and a case of confession,
SD : 1 0 :003(611) [1053] in a period of **persecution** and a case of confession,
SD : 1 0 :005(611) [1053] which give or (to avoid **persecution**) are designed to give
SD : 1 0 :019(614) [1059] than that, they expel, **persecute**, and condemn those who
SD : 1 0 :028(615) [1061] hold that in a period of **persecution** we may yield to
SD : 1 0 :029(615) [1061] sin when in a period of **persecution** anything is done in
SD : 1 1 :039(622) [1075] reject, blaspheme, and **persecute** it (Matt. 22:5, 6;
SD : 1 2 :008(633) [1097] the Gospel were being **persecuted**, where the profound

Perseverance (1), Persevere (14), Perseveringly (1)
AL : 2 3 :025(055) [0065] unwilling or unable to **persevere**, it is better for them to
AP : 2 0 :013(228) [0341] Do good works to **persevere** in your call and not to lose
S 1 : PR :001(288) [0455] hand, what we intended to hold fast to and **persevere** in.
S 3 : 0 3 :042(309) [0491] believers, they will **persevere** in faith even if they sin
LC : 0 2 :042(416) [0689] they grasp and accept it, cling to it, and **persevere** in it.
LC : 0 3 :031(424) [0707] for the devil, if we only **persevere** diligently and do not
LC : 0 3 :100(433) [0725] required to retain and **persevere** in all the gifts for which
SD : 0 2 :083(537) [0913] who stubbornly and **perseveringly** resist the Holy Spirit's
SD : 1 1 :009(618) [1065] damned, this one shall **persevere**, that one shall not
SD : 1 1 :009(618) [1065] this one shall persevere, that one shall not **persevere**.
SD : 1 1 :011(618) [1067] of such as did not **persevere** but fell away again, they may
SD : 1 1 :021(619) [1069] Word, pray diligently, **persevere** in the grace of God, and
SD : 1 1 :042(623) [1077] to impart the grace of **perseverance** to those in whom he
SD : 1 1 :054(625) [1081] of the converted will **persevere** and who will not
SD : 1 1 :054(625) [1081] and who will not **persevere**; and who after falling away
SD : 1 1 :072(628) [1085] through and abide and **persevere** in it, we should implore

Persist (8), Persistent (1), Persistently (2)
PR : PR :008(006) [0011] welfare to abide by it and **persist** in it in a Christian way
PR : PR :018(009) [0015] grace we, too, intend to **persist** in this confession until
LC : 0 1 :035(369) [0589] worship so that all who **persist** in it must ultimately

Continued ▶

LC : 0 1 :038(369) [0591] me," that is, those who **persist** in their stubbornness and
LC : 0 5 :044(451) [0763] this subject we must be **persistent** in preaching, lest
EP : 0 2 :015(471) [0789] is given to such as resist him purposely and **persistently**.
EP : 0 3 :011(474) [0795] that could coexist and co-**persist** with a wicked intention
EP : 0 4 :011(477) [0799] keep his faith even if he deliberately were to **persist** in sin.
EP : 0 4 :019(477) [0801] they fall into adultery and other sins and **persist** in them.
SD : 0 4 :015(553) [0943] even though he were to **persist** in sins against conscience
SD : 1 1 :040(623) [1077] spurn the Word and **persistently** resist the Holy Spirit

Person (233)

PR : PR :004(003) [0007] enlightened and pious **person**, Dr. Martin Luther, and
PR : PR :021(010) [0019] the human nature in the **person** of Christ, in that it is
PR : PR :022(012) [0021] against it, lest one blind **person** let himself be misled by
AG : 0 1 :004(028) [0043] The word "**person**" is to be understood as the Fathers
AG : 0 1 :006(028) [0043] that there is only one **person** and sophistically assert that
AG : 0 3 :002(029) [0045] united in one **person** that there is one Christ, true God
AG : 2 8 :041(087) [0089] is secured from the **person** for whom the case is reserved,
AL : 0 1 :004(028) [0043] And the term "**person**" is used, as the ancient Fathers
AL : 0 1 :006(028) [0043] that there is only one **person** and craftily and impiously
AL : 0 3 :002(029) [0045] in the unity of his **person**, one Christ, true God and true
AL : 2 4 :037(060) [0067] canons that some one **person** or other celebrated Mass
AL : 2 7 :031(075) [0079] that before that age a **person** does not seem to have
AL : 2 8 :041(087) [0089] by the authority of the **person** who reserved the case,
AP : 0 3 :001(107) [0119] into the unity of his **person**; that this same Christ suffered
AP : 0 4 :203(135) [0177] When such a **person** sees the works of the saints, he
AP : 0 4 :222(137) [0181] the approval of a particular act but of the total **person**.
AP : 0 7 :028(173) [0237] own persons but the **person** of Christ, because of the
AP : 1 2 :075(193) [0273] in this way: Because a **person** who has attrition or
AP : 1 2 :091(196) [0279] is a sort of revenge by a **person** who is sorry, punishing in
AP : 1 3 :017(213) [0313] No intelligent **person** will quibble about the number of
AP : 2 1 :035(234) [0353] Some smart **person** painted Christopher in such a way as
AP : 2 3 :039(244) [0375] more than the married **person** does by performing the
AP : 2 4 :013(251) [0387] No sane **person** can approve this pharisaic and pagan
AP : 2 4 :016(252) [0389] He tells the **person** making the distinctions to cut the
AP : 2 7 :049(277) [0437] but only for the **person** with whom Christ is talking here.
S3 : 0 3 :017(305) [0483] or the like), such a **person** was asked if he did not wish or
S3 : 0 3 :018(306) [0483] The **person** involved was obliged to grieve, but he would
S3 : 0 3 :037(309) [0489] or partial, for a **person** who confesses that he is
S3 : 1 3 :002(315) [0499] in respect both of his **person** and of his works, shall be
TR : 0 0 :024(324) [0511] keys do not belong to the **person** of one particular
TR : 0 0 :027(325) [0511] and not as applying to the **person** or superiority of Peter.
TR : 0 0 :078(333) [0527] which forbids an innocent **person** to marry after divorce.
SC : 0 9 :004(355) [0561] "Let every **person** be subject to the governing authorities.
SC : 0 9 :005(355) [0561] "Let every **person** be subject to the governing authorities.
LC : SP :018(363) [0577] circumstances should a **person** be tolerated if he is so
LC : SP :022(364) [0579] enough for an ordinary **person** to know this much about
LC : 0 1 :005(365) [0581] Many a **person** thinks he has God and everything he
LC : 0 1 :011(366) [0583] abominations, and every **person** selected his own saint
LC : 0 1 :047(371) [0593] Let each **person** be in his station in life according to
LC : 0 1 :053(372) [0595] or elsewhere, when a **person** perjures himself, swearing by
LC : 0 1 :092(377) [0607] or pondered, there the **person**, the day, and the work are
LC : 0 1 :147(385) [0623] really faith that makes a **person** holy; faith alone serves
LC : 0 1 :154(386) [0625] your master, another **person** comes along and treats you
LC : 0 1 :160(387) [0627] Since such **person** are fathers, they are entitled to honor,
LC : 0 1 :189(390) [0635] violated not only when a **person** actually does evil, but
LC : 0 1 :190(391) [0635] If you send a **person** away naked when you could clothe
LC : 0 1 :200(392) [0637] First they deal with our neighbor's **person**.
LC : 0 1 :200(392) [0637] Then they proceed to the **person** nearest and dearest to
LC : 0 1 :223(395) [0643] Next to our own **person** and our spouse, our temporal
LC : 0 1 :224(395) [0643] As I have just said, a **person** steals not only when he robs
LC : 0 1 :227(396) [0645] One **person** openly cheats another with defective
LC : 0 1 :234(397) [0647] A **person** who willfully disregards this commandment
LC : 0 1 :274(402) [0659] no one has in his own **person** the right to judge and
LC : 0 1 :276(402) [0659] to you what this or that **person** has done, teach him, if he
LC : 0 1 :280(403) [0661] procedure for restraining and reforming a wicked **person**.
LC : 0 1 :284(403) [0661] sin shun and avoid the **person** as one who has brought
LC : 0 1 :285(403) [0663] A **person** should use his tongue to speak only good of
LC : 0 1 :306(406) [0669] among us for a **person** to lure away another's
LC : 0 1 :328(410) [0675] molest him, either in his **person**, his wife, his property, his
LC : 0 2 :026(413) [0685] to know the second **person** of the Godhead, and we see
LC : 0 3 :016(422) [0701] is holier in respect to his **person**, but not on account of
LC : 0 3 :016(422) [0701] prayer on account of the **person**, but on account of his
LC : 0 3 :017(422) [0703] to God, regardless of our **person**, whether we be sinners
LC : 0 3 :024(423) [0705] A **person** who wants to pray must present a petition,
LC : 0 3 :123(436) [0731] For that **person** must not suppose that he will receive
LC : 0 4 :012(438) [0735] Because the **person** performing the act is nobler and
LC : 0 4 :012(438) [0735] we must evaluate not the **person** according to the works,
LC : 0 4 :012(438) [0735] works according to the **person**, from whom they must
LC : 0 4 :020(439) [0737] "Why should I think more of this **person** than of others?"
LC : 0 4 :033(440) [0741] is, faith alone makes the **person** worthy to receive the
LC : 0 4 :052(443) [0745] whether the baptized **person** believes or not, for in the
LC : 0 4 :060(444) [0747] even if only one **person** were baptized and he, moreover,
LC : 0 5 :049(452) [0765] When a **person**, with nothing to hinder him, lets a long
LC : 0 5 :053(453) [0765] in his own case, that if a **person** stays away from the
LC : 0 5 :054(453) [0765] conscience and act like a **person** who really desires to be
LC : 0 5 :061(453) [0767] The only exception is the **person** who desires no grace and
LC : 0 5 :069(454) [0769] just as when a sick **person** willfully eats and drinks what
LC : 0 6 :011(458) [0000] a particular one, when a **person** has provoked another to
EP : 0 1 :005(466) [0781] into the unity of his **person** this same human nature,
EP : 0 1 :020(468) [0783] original sin "nature-sin," "**person**-sin," "essential sin," not
EP : 0 1 :020(468) [0783] distinction man's nature, **person**, or essence itself with
EP : 0 2 :016(472) [0789] draws, but draws the **person** who is willing," or, "Man's
EP : 0 3 :011(474) [0795] On the contrary, after a **person** has been justified by
EP : 0 3 :017(475) [0795] can exist and remain in a **person** though he does not truly
EP : 0 3 :023(475) [0797] that unless they are present a **person** cannot be justified.
EP : 0 4 :011(477) [0799] left to the regenerated **person**'s option whether to do or
EP : 0 7 :011(483) [0811] God and man in one **person**, inseparable and undivided.
EP : 0 8 :000(486) [0817] VIII. The **Person** of Christ
EP : 0 8 :001(486) [0817] also) concerning the **person** of Christ, the two natures in
EP : 0 8 :002(487) [0817] of personal union in the **person** of Christ, do the divine
EP : 0 8 :003(487) [0819] *of the Christian Church concerning the* ***Person*** *of Christ*
EP : 0 8 :009(487) [0819] personally (that is, in one **person**) we believe, teach, and
EP : 0 8 :013(488) [0821] the Son of God that it has become one **person** with him.
EP : 0 8 :014(488) [0821] the unity of his divine **person** and made his own, so that
EP : 0 8 :018(489) [0823] do not divide the **person** of Christ, as Nestorius did.
EP : 0 8 :018(489) [0823] he actually divided the **person**, as Luther explains it in his
EP : 0 8 :018(489) [0823] the human nature in the **person** of Christ, or change the
EP : 0 8 :018(489) [0823] to all eternity, God and man in one indivisible **person**.
EP : 0 8 :018(490) [0823] *Contrary False Doctrine concerning the* ***Person*** *of Christ*
EP : 0 8 :020(490) [0823] God and man are not one **person**, but that the Son of
EP : 0 8 :020(490) [0823] the Son of God is one **person** and the Son of man
EP : 1 1 :011(495) [0835] and comforting to the **person** who concerns himself with
EP : 1 2 :004(498) [0839] more gifts of the Holy Spirit than any other holy **person**.
EP : 1 2 :029(500) [0843] distinct persons, so each **person** has its distinct divine
SD : 0 1 :001(508) [0859] called "nature-sin" or "**person**-sin" because it is not a
SD : 0 1 :006(509) [0861] this sin "nature-sin" or "**person**-sin" in order to indicate
SD : 0 1 :006(509) [0861] nevertheless man's nature and **person** would still be sinful.
SD : 0 1 :006(509) [0861] first man, our nature or **person** is under the accusation
SD : 0 1 :019(511) [0865] apart from Christ every **person** on that account is
SD : 0 1 :052(517) [0875] to include the concrete **person** or subject (that is, man
SD : 0 1 :053(517) [0875] the terms "nature-sin," "**person**-sin," "essential sin" to
SD : 0 1 :053(517) [0877] that the entire nature, **person**, and essence of man is
SD : 0 1 :057(518) [0877] by any really intelligent **person** that every existing thing is
SD : 0 2 :011(522) [0885] Just as little as a **person** who is physically dead can by his
SD : 0 2 :053(531) [0903] The **person** who is not yet converted to God and
SD : 0 2 :057(532) [0903] If a **person** will not hear preaching or read the Word of
SD : 0 2 :058(532) [0903] But if such a **person** despises the instruments of the Holy
SD : 0 2 :059(532) [0905] block does not resist the **person** who moves it, neither
SD : 0 2 :060(533) [0905] the Lord God draws the **person** whom he wills to
SD : 0 2 :086(537) [0913] draws, but he draws the **person** who wills," were
SD : 0 2 :090(539) [0915] this work the will of the **person** who is to be converted
SD : 0 3 :015(541) [0919] man in one undivided **person**, he was as little under the
SD : 0 3 :015(541) [0919] — as he was obligated to suffer and die for his **person**.
SD : 0 3 :020(542) [0921] Holy Spirit has brought a **person** to faith and has justified
SD : 0 3 :027(543) [0923] For if a **person** does not love, this indicates certainly that
SD : 0 3 :027(544) [0923] they follow it, since a **person** must first be righteous
SD : 0 3 :029(544) [0925] to do is not whether a **person** should also do good works
SD : 0 3 :029(544) [0925] and love, but how a **person** may be justified before God
SD : 0 3 :032(545) [0927] the best kind of life, a **person** is pleasing and acceptable to
SD : 0 3 :034(545) [0927] belongs solely to that **person** to whom God reckons
SD : 0 3 :041(546) [0929] the grace of God in Christ whereby the **person** is justified.
SD : 0 3 :041(546) [0929] After the **person** is justified, the Holy Spirit next renews
SD : 0 3 :043(547) [0931] a cause without which a **person** cannot be justified, and
SD : 0 3 :055(549) [0935] but upon the entire **person** of Christ, who as God and
SD : 0 3 :056(549) [0935] of Christ's total **person**, which he rendered to his heavenly
SD : 0 3 :057(549) [0935] obedience of the entire **person**, therefore it is a perfect
SD : 0 3 :058(550) [0937] only the obedience of the **person** who is God and man at
SD : 0 3 :058(550) [0937] Faith thus looks at the **person** of Christ, how this person
SD : 0 3 :058(550) [0937] of Christ, how this **person** was placed under the law for
SD : 0 3 :064(550) [0937] it can be and remain in a **person** who has no true
SD : 0 4 :007(552) [0941] works are not done by a **person**'s own natural powers but
SD : 0 4 :007(552) [0941] powers but only after a **person** has been reconciled to
SD : 0 4 :008(552) [0941] through faith, because the **person** is acceptable to God.
SD : 0 4 :008(552) [0941] nature and because the **person** is not reconciled with
SD : 0 4 :008(552) [0941] The **person** must first be pleasing to God — and that
SD : 0 4 :008(552) [0941] Christ's sake — before that **person**'s works are pleasing.
SD : 0 4 :015(553) [0943] Or as if a **person** could have and retain true faith,
SD : 0 4 :017(554) [0943] which is extorted from a **person** against his will, by
SD : 0 4 :037(557) [0951] an impediment to such a **person** but are actually harmful.
SD : 0 5 :019(561) [0957] rebukes unbelief, when a **person** does not believe the
SD : 0 6 :016(566) [0967] For as long as a **person** is not reborn, lives according to
SD : 0 6 :017(566) [0967] But when a **person** is born anew by the Spirit of God and
SD : 0 7 :025(573) [0981] rendered false because an individual's **person** or unbelief.
SD : 0 7 :034(575) [0983] every intelligent **person** who loves truth and peace can
SD : 0 7 :041(576) [0985] Confession and as the **person** whose entire doctrine in
SD : 0 7 :060(580) [0993] Such a **person** dishonors, abuses, and desecrates him who
SD : 0 7 :094(586) [1005] God and man in one **person**, undivided and inseparable.
SD : 0 7 :101(587) [1007] Thirdly, since he is one **person** with God, the divine,
SD : 0 7 :101(587) [1007] of Christ since he is one **person** with God, very far beyond
SD : 0 7 :101(587) [1007] For he is one indivisible **person** with God, and wherever
SD : 0 7 :102(587) [1007] in God beyond all creatures and is one **person** with God.
SD : 0 8 :000(591) [1015] VIII. The **Person** of Christ
SD : 0 8 :001(591) [1015] Augsburg Confession concerning the **person** of Christ.
SD : 0 8 :004(592) [1017] arguments about the **person** of Christ with which the
SD : 0 8 :004(592) [1017] the human nature in the **person** of Christ that transcends
SD : 0 8 :006(592) [1017] and complete divine **person** and therefore has been from
SD : 0 8 :006(592) [1017] into the unity of his **person**, not in such a manner that
SD : 0 8 :006(592) [1017] is henceforth in *one* **person** simultaneously true eternal
SD : 0 8 :007(592) [1017] in this single undivided **person** there are two distinct
SD : 0 8 :007(592) [1017] in time into the unity of the **person** of the Son of God.
SD : 0 8 :007(592) [1017] These two natures in the **person** of Christ will henceforth
SD : 0 8 :007(592) [1017] into the other, but in the **person** of Christ each remains in
SD : 0 8 :011(593) [1019] be or constitute a distinct **person**, but that the two
SD : 0 8 :011(593) [1019] they constitute a single **person** in which there are and
SD : 0 8 :011(593) [1019] nature belong to the total **person** of Christ; and that
SD : 0 8 :011(593) [1019] without his deity the **person** of Christ, or the Son of God
SD : 0 8 :011(593) [1019] persons, but one single **person**, in spite of the fact that
SD : 0 8 :015(594) [1019] so that Christ is one **person** and God the Word who
SD : 0 8 :017(594) [1021] human natures in the **person** of Christ are united in such
SD : 0 8 :017(594) [1021] one essence but, as Dr. Luther writes, into one **person**.
SD : 0 8 :019(595) [1021] human natures in the **person** of Christ is far different
SD : 0 8 :019(595) [1021] the human nature in the **person** of Christ is far different,
SD : 0 8 :023(595) [1023] of the natures in the **person** of Christ did not exist in deed
SD : 0 8 :032(597) [1027] of natures in the **person** of Christ did not truly exist.
SD : 0 8 :034(597) [1027] in such a way that God and man are a single **person**!
SD : 0 8 :035(597) [1027] that we make about the **person** of Christ, its natures, and
SD : 0 8 :036(598) [1027] constitute only one **person**, therefore any property,
SD : 0 8 :036(598) [1027] separate but to the entire **person** who is simultaneously
SD : 0 8 :037(598) [1027] is ascribed to the **person** is simultaneously the property of
SD : 0 8 :037(598) [1027] the property in question is being ascribed to the **person**.
SD : 0 8 :038(598) [1027] *to ascribe to the entire person what is the property of one*
SD : 0 8 :038(598) [1027] they mention the entire **person**, they nevertheless
SD : 0 8 :041(599) [1029] and humanity are one **person** in Christ, the Scriptures
SD : 0 8 :042(599) [1029] for you must say that the **person** (pointing to Christ)
SD : 0 8 :042(599) [1029] But this **person** is truly God, and therefore it is correct to
SD : 0 8 :042(599) [1029] suffer, nevertheless the **person** who is true God suffers in

Continued ▶

SD : 0 8 :042(599) [1029] for us — that is, this **person** who is God, for that is what
SD : 0 8 :042(599) [1029] that is what he is — this **person**, I say, is crucified
SD : 0 8 :043(599) [1029] and the other a human **person**, since Zwingli applies all
SD : 0 8 :043(599) [1029] and separated, the **person** will also have to be separated,
SD : 0 8 :043(599) [1029] are not ascribed to the natures but to the **person**.
SD : 0 8 :043(599) [1029] It is the **person** who does and suffers everything, the one
SD : 0 8 :043(599) [1029] as God and man in one **person**, neither confounding the
SD : 0 8 :043(599) [1029] neither confounding the natures nor dividing the **person**."
SD : 0 8 :044(599) [1031] man are united in one **person**, it is correct to talk about
SD : 0 8 :044(599) [1031] that man dies who is one thing or one **person** with God."
SD : 0 8 :046(600) [1031] office is concerned, the **person** does not act *in, with,*
SD : 0 8 :050(600) [1031] human nature in the **person** of Christ is concerned, some
SD : 0 8 :056(601) [1033] to be understood of the **person** not only according to the
SD : 0 8 :057(602) [1035] all eternity) but that the **person** received this in time
SD : 0 8 :059(602) [1035] in general terms of the **person** of the Son of Man, but
SD : 0 8 :067(604) [1039] is to be ascribed in the **person** of the Son of Man only
SD : 0 8 :073(605) [1041] Godhead is the second **person** in the holy Trinity and the
SD : 0 8 :076(606) [1043] in deed and truth in the **person** of Christ, things are
SD : 0 8 :078(607) [1043] or only one-half of the **person** of Christ, but the entire
SD : 0 8 :078(607) [1043] of Christ, but the entire **person** to which both natures, the
SD : 0 8 :081(607) [1045] he writes about the **person** of Christ: "Since he is a man
SD : 0 8 :082(607) [1045] there as a natural divine **person** and is also naturally and
SD : 0 8 :082(607) [1045] since he is not two separate persons but a single **person**.
SD : 0 8 :082(607) [1045] Wherever this **person** is, it is the single, indivisible
SD : 0 8 :082(607) [1045] is the single, indivisible **person**, and if you can say, 'Here
SD : 0 8 :082(607) [1045] not the man, then the **person** is already divided and I
SD : 0 8 :083(607) [1045] and thus had divided the **person**, even though death and
SD : 0 8 :084(607) [1045] as a divine and human **person**, and if at all other places
SD : 0 8 :084(607) [1045] isolated God and a divine **person** without the humanity.
SD : 0 8 :084(608) [1045] He has become one **person** and never separates the
SD : 0 8 :085(608) [1047] were united in one **person** this man, Mary's son, is and is
SD : 0 8 :085(608) [1047] because he is one **person** with the deity and is true God.
SD : 0 9 :002(610) [1051] after the burial the entire **person**, God and man,
SD : 1 1 :056(625) [1081] has determined for each **person** the time and hour of his
SD : 1 1 :086(631) [1091] Pharaoh or any other **person** eternal life, or that in his
SD : 1 2 :024(634) [1099] a new marriage with another **person** of the same faith.
SD : 1 2 :037(636) [1103] Holy Spirit, so also each **person** has a distinct essence

Persons (68)

PR : PR :016(008) [0013] Confession as well, the **persons** to whom it had been
PR : PR :018(009) [0015] by well-certified **persons** with the actual original that was
PR : PR :022(011) [0019] to mean thereby those **persons** who err ingenuously and
PR : PR :024(013) [0023] good-hearted Christian **persons**, of high station and low,
AG : 0 1 :002(027) [0043] and that there are three **persons** in this one divine
AG : 0 1 :006(028) [0043] not necessarily distinct **persons** but that the Word
AG : 1 2 :007(035) [0049] are those who teach that **persons** who have once become
AG : 2 7 :005(071) [0077] Many **persons** also entered monastic life ignorantly, for
AG : 2 8 :008(082) [0085] the sacraments (to many **persons** or to individuals,
AL : 0 1 :001(027) [0043] and concerning the three **persons** is true and should be
AL : 0 1 :003(027) [0043] Yet there are three **persons**, of the same essence and
AL : 0 1 :006(028) [0043] Spirit are not distinct **persons** since "Word" signifies a
AL : 0 8 :001(033) [0047] many hypocrites and evil **persons** are mingled with
AL : 2 0 :020(043) [0055] Some **persons** were by their consciences driven into the
AL : 2 7 :034(076) [0081] that the marriages of **persons** who violated them ought to
AL : 2 8 :021(084) [0087] of the church ungodly **persons** whose wickedness is
AP : 0 1 :001(100) [0103] distinct and coeternal **persons** of the same divine essence,
AP : 0 7 :022(172) [0235] is made up of those **persons** in whom there is true
AP : 0 7 :028(173) [0237] not represent their own **persons** but the person of Christ,
AP : 0 7 :047(177) [0243] not represent their own **persons**, according to the word
AP : 2 7 :049(277) [0437] vary with times and **persons**; but the example of
S 1 : PR :006(289) [0457] However, what such **persons** accomplish is manifest.
S 1 : 0 1 :000(291) [0461] Holy Spirit, three distinct **persons** in one divine essence
S 3 : 0 3 :029(308) [0487] Such **persons** did not need to repent, for what were they
S 3 : 1 0 :003(314) [0497] and ought ourselves ordain suitable **persons** to this office.
TR : 0 0 :026(324) [0511] not bound to places and **persons**, as the Levitical
TR : 0 0 :062(330) [0521] schism, lest several **persons**, by gathering separate
TR : 0 0 :075(333) [0525] sometimes punished **persons** involved in adultery, but in
SC : 0 9 :012(356) [0563] Young **Persons** in General
LC : PR :017(361) [0573] all doctrines, estates, **persons**, laws, and everything else in
LC : 0 1 :053(372) [0595] matters when two **persons** secretly betroth themselves to
LC : 0 1 :082(376) [0603] with particular customs, **persons**, times, and places, from
LC : 0 1 :094(378) [0607] Places, times, **persons**, and the entire outward order of
LC : 0 1 :105(379) [0611] mother above all other **persons** on earth, and places them
LC : 0 1 :108(379) [0611] are not to think of their **persons**, whatever they are, but
LC : 0 1 :141(384) [0621] due to our superiors, **persons** whose duty it is to
LC : 0 1 :182(389) [0631] as we have said, to **persons** who occupy the place of God,
LC : 0 1 :186(390) [0633] Many **persons**, though they may not actually commit
LC : 0 1 :191(391) [0635] God rightly calls all **persons** murderers who do not offer
LC : 0 1 :192(391) [0635] but to reproach such **persons** as murderers and
LC : 0 1 :208(393) [0639] importance to him that **persons** be brought up to serve
LC : 0 1 :241(397) [0649] stand by and let such **persons** fleece, grab, and hoard.
LC : 0 2 :004(411) [0679] step, for very simple **persons** to learn to understand the
LC : 0 2 :006(411) [0679] according to the three **persons** of the Godhead, to whom
LC : 0 2 :007(411) [0679] and one faith, but three **persons**, and therefore three
LC : 0 3 :042(425) [0709] drunkards, gluttons, jealous **persons**, and slanderers.
LC : 0 4 :020(439) [0737] If we regard these **persons** with reference to their noses,
LC : 0 4 :058(444) [0747] and stupid **persons** draw the conclusion that where there
LC : 0 5 :075(455) [0771] Answer: For **persons** in such a state of mind that they
EP : 0 3 :009(474) [0793] and truly regenerated **persons** retain much weakness and
EP : 0 4 :003(476) [0797] but that regenerated **persons** are bound to render such
EP : 1 2 :029(500) [0843] Spirit are three distinct **persons**, so each person has its
EP : 1 2 :029(500) [0843] essence, separate from the other **persons** of the Deity.
SD : 0 1 :054(518) [0877] or in the company of **persons** to whom these words are
SD : 0 2 :018(524) [0887] and other regenerated **persons** wars against the law of
SD : 0 3 :035(545) [0927] that although converted **persons** and believers possess the
SD : 0 6 :023(567) [0969] grace because their **persons** have been freed from the
SD : 0 7 :029(574) [0981] Hence lest any **persons** during my lifetime or after my
SD : 0 8 :006(592) [1017] that there are now two **persons** or two Christs, but in such
SD : 0 8 :011(593) [1019] is not two different **persons**, but one single person, in
SD : 0 8 :043(599) [1029] will have to be two **persons**, one a divine and the other a
SD : 0 8 :082(607) [1045] since he is not two separate **persons** but a single person.
SD : 1 1 :059(626) [1081] some nations and some **persons** God shows his own
SD : 1 2 :019(634) [1099] against wicked **persons** as occasion may arise, nor may a
SD : 1 2 :037(636) [1103] as there are three distinct **persons**, Father, Son, and Holy
SD : 1 2 :037(636) [1103] Some teach that all three **persons** in the Trinity, like any
SD : 1 2 :037(636) [1103] separate human **persons**, have the same power, wisdom,
SD : 1 2 :037(636) [1103] teach that the three **persons** in the Trinity are unequal in

Personal (46), Personally (25)

PR : PR :020(010) [0017] into a discussion of the **personal** union of the two natures
PR : PR :021(011) [0019] of Christ outside the **personal** union, or in such a way
PR : PR :021(011) [0019] a way that even in the **personal** union it is alleged to have
PR : PR :021(011) [0019] place on account of the **personal** union, which is an
AP : 0 4 :045(113) [0133] because of Christ, this **personal** faith obtains the
AP : 0 4 :232(139) [0185] he is talking not about **personal** perfection but about
AP : 0 4 :326(158) [0211] persecutors of God's Word, not of his **personal** purity.
AP : 0 7 :049(178) [0245] we are offended by the **personal** conduct of priests or
AP : 1 2 :059(190) [0267] contrition, but by that **personal** faith by which each
AP : 1 2 :060(190) [0267] are contending for this **personal** faith, and we set it in
AP : 1 2 :074(192) [0273] but he bids us add the **personal** faith that they are
AP : 1 2 :088(195) [0277] not doubting that they are forgiven them **personally**.
AP : 1 3 :021(214) [0313] we are talking about **personal** faith, which accepts the
AP : 2 7 :049(277) [0437] Callings are **personal**, just as matters of business
LC : 0 1 :276(402) [0659] and reprove the man **personally**, otherwise to hold his
LC : 0 1 :277(402) [0659] failing to do his duty, he takes him to task **personally**.
LC : 0 1 :279(403) [0661] is to be dealt with **personally** and not gossiped about
LC : 0 1 :305(406) [0667] he managed, either **personally** or through others and by
LC : 0 5 :065(454) [0769] and include yourself **personally** in the "you" so that he
EP : 0 3 :001(472) [0791] and human natures are **personally** united to one another
EP : 0 5 :006(478) [0803] which he proclaimed **personally** in his teaching ministry
EP : 0 8 :002(487) [0817] has been, Because of **personal** union in the person of
EP : 0 8 :003(487) [0817] and human natures are **personally** united in such a way
EP : 0 8 :003(487) [0819] declare boldly that the "**personal** union makes merely the
EP : 0 8 :005(487) [0819] the human natures are **personally** united in Christ in such
EP : 0 8 :009(487) [0819] both natures are united **personally** (that is, in one person)
EP : 0 8 :009(487) [0819] and confess that this **personal** union is not a combination
EP : 0 8 :009(487) [0819] common with the other **personally** (that is, on account of
EP : 0 8 :009(487) [0819] is, on account of the **personal** union), as when two boards
EP : 0 8 :009(488) [0819] Out of this **personal** union and the resultant exalted and
EP : 0 8 :011(488) [0821] his humanity were not **personally** and truly united with
EP : 0 8 :015(488) [0821] his human nature was **personally** united with the Son of
EP : 0 8 :016(488) [0821] 11. According to the **personal** union he always possessed
EP : 0 8 :024(490) [0823] 5. That **personal** union achieves only common names and
EP : 1 2 :007(498) [0839] the use of reason and can confess their faith **personally**.
SD : 0 7 :036(575) [0985] that both untransformed natures are **personally** united.
SD : 0 7 :037(575) [0985] others, have cited the **personal** union as an analogy to the
SD : 0 7 :038(576) [0985] bread and wine is not a **personal** union, like that of the
SD : 0 8 :012(593) [1019] thereto, through the **personal** union with the deity and
SD : 0 8 :013(594) [1019] when the divine and human nature were **personally** united
SD : 0 8 :014(594) [1019] 9. But this **personal** union is not to be understood, as
SD : 0 8 :018(594) [1021] On account of this **personal** union and communion, the
SD : 0 8 :018(594) [1021] further illustrated the **personal** union and communion by
SD : 0 8 :020(595) [1021] On account of this **personal** union, without which such a
SD : 0 8 :023(595) [1023] Because of this **personal** union and communion of the
SD : 0 8 :023(595) [1023] If the **personal** union and communion of the natures in
SD : 0 8 :024(595) [1023] On account of this **personal** union and communion of the
SD : 0 8 :025(596) [1023] this if it had not been **personally** united with the divine
SD : 0 8 :029(597) [1025] through and in the **personal** union of both natures in
SD : 0 8 :030(597) [1025] and human natures are **personally** united in such a way
SD : 0 8 :030(597) [1025] (Col. 2:9), and in this **personal** union they have such an
SD : 0 8 :031(597) [1025] we have explained the **personal** union (that is, the fact
SD : 0 8 :032(597) [1025] place or continue if the **personal** union or communion of
SD : 0 8 :033(597) [1027] and on earth is the **personal** union, as Paul says, "Great
SD : 0 8 :041(599) [1029] deity, because of this **personal** union, all that happens to
SD : 0 8 :048(600) [1031] Do the natures in the **personal** union have nothing else
SD : 0 8 :050(600) [1031] contend that even in the **personal** union with the deity the
SD : 0 8 :051(600) [1031] nature in Christ is **personally** united with the divine
SD : 0 8 :051(601) [1033] has received through the **personal** union, glorification,
SD : 0 8 :053(601) [1033] has received through the **personal** union, glorification, or
SD : 0 8 :064(603) [1037] to the manner of the **personal** union, that is, because the
SD : 0 8 :070(604) [1041] do so bodily nor is he **personally** united with them as in
SD : 0 8 :070(605) [1041] It is because of the **personal** union that Christ says, also
SD : 0 8 :073(605) [1041] it follows that through **personal** union the entire fullness
SD : 0 8 :073(605) [1041] to the flesh that is **personally** united with the Son of God.
SD : 0 8 :074(606) [1043] as a man, through the **personal** union, he really and truly
SD : 0 8 :076(606) [1043] Because of this **personal** union and the resultant
SD : 0 8 :082(607) [1045] is also naturally and **personally** there, as his conception in
SD : 0 8 :082(607) [1045] mother's womb naturally and **personally** and become man
SD : 0 8 :082(607) [1045] present naturally and **personally** wherever he is, then he
SD : 0 8 :089(609) [1047] that because of the **personal** union the human nature has

Personnel (1)

S 2 : 0 4 :014(301) [0475] vestments, food, **personnel**, and countless other

Persuade (1), Persuaded (8), Persuading (1)

AG : 2 7 :029(075) [0079] they were **persuaded** to take monastic vows, and
AG : 2 7 :046(078) [0081] Besides all this, they **persuaded** the people that the
AG : 2 8 :075(094) [0095] and they cannot be **persuaded** to mitigate or abrogate
AL : 2 7 :029(075) [0079] boys and girls are **persuaded**, and sometimes even
AL : 2 7 :046(078) [0081] Besides all this, they **persuaded** men that their invented
AP : 2 3 :070(249) [0383] reasons like these they **persuade** the princes to take a
S 1 : PR :008(290) [0457] that his king had been **persuaded** beyond a doubt that
LC : 0 1 :152(386) [0625] we ever let ourselves be **persuaded** that works of
LC : 0 6 :007(457) [0000] encouraging, and **persuading** them not to lose this
SD : 0 2 :027(526) [0891] own statement, **persuaded** him to recant his former

Pertain (6), Pertaining (8), Pertains (15)

PR : PR :013(007) [0013] Spirit, everything that **pertains** to and is necessary for this
PR : PR :020(010) [0017] Creed (especially those **pertaining** to the incarnation of
AG : PR :001(024) [0039] concerning matters **pertaining** to the Turk, that
AG : PR :006(025) [0039] with the matter **pertaining** to the faith and in conformity
AG : PR :016(026) [0041] decisions in matters **pertaining** to our holy faith but
AG : 1 8 :004(039) [0051] them to act in matters **pertaining** to God (such as loving
AL : 1 8 :004(039) [0051] in those things which **pertain** to God, for it is only in acts
AL : 1 8 :005(040) [0053] arts, or will to do whatever good **pertains** to this life.
AL : 2 6 :010(065) [0071] the commands of God **pertaining** to callings were without

Continued ▶

A L : 2 8 :029(085) [0087] cases (for example, **pertaining** to matrimony, tithes, etc.),
A P : 0 7 :036(175) [0241] are customs that do not **pertain** to the heart and "perish
S 2 : 0 0 :000(292) [0461] treats the articles which **pertain** to the office and work of
S 2 : 0 4 :003(298) [0471] and deeds (except what **pertains** to secular government,
S 3 : 0 3 :018(306) [0483] about in matters which **pertain** to God, seeking
T R : 0 0 :077(333) [0527] according to canon law **pertain** to ecclesiastical courts (as
L C : 0 1 :054(372) [0595] spiritual matters, which **pertain** to the conscience, when
L C : 0 1 :134(383) [0619] to have everything that **pertains** to long life — health,
L C : 0 1 :257(399) [0653] this commandment **pertains** to public courts of justice,
L C : 0 3 :060(428) [0715] points embrace all that **pertains** to God's glory and to our
L C : 0 3 :073(430) [0719] in short, everything that **pertains** to the regulation of our
L C : 0 4 :065(445) [0749] purging out whatever **pertains** to the old Adam, so that
L C : 0 5 :044(451) [0763] As in other matters **pertaining** to faith, love, and patience
E P : 0 1 :024(469) [0785] thing and that which **pertains** to it only accidentally.
E P : 0 4 :007(476) [0799] declares that salvation **pertains** only to the man to whom
E P : 1 2 :006(498) [0839] doctrine of original sin and everything that **pertains** to it.
S D : 1 0 :010(612) [1055] doctrine and all that **pertains** to it, according to the Word
S D : 1 0 :029(615) [1061] in doctrine, or in whatever else **pertains** to religion.
S D : 1 1 :008(617) [1065] and furthers our salvation and whatever **pertains** to it.
S D : 1 2 :011(634) [1099] teaching of original sin and all that **pertains** thereto.

Pertinax (1)
A P : 2 4 :081(264) [0411] as the rescript of **Pertinax** on the law of immunity shows:

Pertinent (1)
S D : 0 3 :039(546) [0929] the article of justification as **pertinent** or necessary to it.

Perturbed (1)
S D : 0 7 :069(582) [0997] hand, are those timid, **perturbed** Christians, weak in

Peruse (1)
P R : P R :013(007) [0013] their chief theologians **peruse** it with particular

Pervading (2)
L C : 0 1 :210(393) [0641] and the noblest, **pervading** all Christendom and even
L C : 0 1 :321(408) [0673] commandment, penetrating and **pervading** them all.

Perverse (11), Perversion (3), Perversity (2), Pervert (9), Perverted (13), Perverters (1), Perverting (1), Perverts (3)
P R : P R :005(004) [0009] teachers insinuated **perverted** teachings into the churches
A G : 1 9 :000(041) [0053] wicked men and despisers of God by the **perverted** will.
A P : 1 2 :084(194) [0277] be said so simply that some quibbler cannot **pervert** it.
A P : 2 3 :070(249) [0383] judgment of God no **perversion** of God's Word will
S 1 : P R :006(289) [0457] at once to poison and **pervert** everything by wagging
L C : 0 1 :069(374) [0601] fidelity, no faith — only **perverse**, unbridled men whom
L C : 0 1 :119(381) [0615] right for their devilish **perversity** in trampling God's
L C : 0 1 :129(383) [0617] The **perversity** of the world God knows very well.
L C : 0 1 :261(400) [0655] right remain right, nor **perverting** or concealing or
L C : 0 1 :262(400) [0655] it is contradicted, **perverted**, misused, and misinterpreted.
L C : 0 2 :021(413) [0683] is the way the wretched, **perverse** world acts, drowned in
L C : 0 3 :063(428) [0715] The world, too, is **perverse** and wicked.
L C : 0 4 :062(444) [0749] and would, in addition, **pervert** and nullify all God's work
L C : 0 5 :048(452) [0765] the pope afterward **perverted** it and turned it back into a
E P : 0 8 :039(491) [0827] and blasphemously **pervert** the words of Christ, "All
E P : 0 8 :039(491) [0827] This doctrine not only **perverts** the words of Christ's
E P : 1 1 :004(495) [0833] of this is the devil and man's wicked and **perverse** will.
E P : 1 2 :011(499) [0841] way, but flee and avoid them as **perverters** of God's Word
S D : 0 1 :014(511) [0863] nature, which original sin has **perverted** and corrupted.
S D : 0 1 :027(513) [0867] about, this loss has so **perverted** and corrupted human
S D : 0 1 :030(513) [0867] mother is corrupted and **perverted** by original sin in body
S D : 0 1 :038(515) [0871] has been corrupted and **perverted** in Adam and is
S D : 0 1 :039(515) [0871] cast this corrupted, **perverted**, and sinful dough into
S D : 0 2 :007(521) [0883] Hence according to its **perverse** disposition and nature
S D : 0 2 :008(521) [0883] that "the wisdom of this **perverse** world is folly with God"
S D : 0 2 :009(521) [0883] so ignorant, blind, and **perverse** that when even the most
S D : 0 2 :017(523) [0887] but is also turned and **perverted** against God and toward
S D : 0 2 :017(524) [0887] sin he is so miserably **perverted**, poisoned, and corrupted
S D : 0 2 :017(524) [0887] wicked," that is, is so **perverted** and full of misery that no
S D : 0 7 :001(568) [0971] forcibly to adduce and **pervert** the Augsburg Confession
S D : 0 7 :031(574) [0983] If he can twist and **pervert** the Word of God, what will he
S D : 0 7 :032(575) [0983] of God but have **perverted** and changed it according to
S D : 0 7 :056(579) [0991] as the Sacramentarians **pervert** this passage, he would
S D : 0 7 :085(584) [1001] idolatrous misuse and **perversion** of this testament, the
S D : 0 7 :088(585) [1003] and maliciously **pervert** this useful and necessary rule and
S D : 0 7 :090(585) [1003] when some by a subtle **perversion** of this common rule
S D : 1 0 :014(613) [1057] darkens and **perverts** this article because the adversaries
S D : 1 1 :006(617) [1065] beforehand whatever the **perverse** and wicked will of the
S D : 1 1 :007(617) [1065] rather the wicked and **perverse** will of the devil and of
S D : 1 1 :041(623) [1077] but man's own **perverse** will, which rejects or perverts the
S D : 1 1 :041(623) [1077] will, which rejects or **perverts** the means and instrument
S D : 1 1 :057(625) [1081] and is given over to a **perverse** mind while another in
S D : 1 2 :016(634) [1099] and avoid them as people who **pervert** the Word of God.

Pestilence (3)
A P : 2 1 :032(233) [0351] Sebastian wards off **pestilence**, Valentine heals epilepsy,
L C : 0 1 :151(386) [0625] or perish through war, **pestilence**, or famine, or his
L C : 0 3 :078(431) [0721] and flood; from poison, **pestilence**, and cattle-plague;

Peter (90)
P R : P R :027(015) [0025] **Peter** Ernest the Younger, count of Mansfeld [-Eisleben].
A G : 2 6 :027(068) [0073] In Acts 15:10, 11 **Peter** says, "Why do you make trial of
A G : 2 6 :028(068) [0073] Here **Peter** forbids the burdening of consciences with
A G : 2 8 :042(088) [0089] In Acts 15:10 St. **Peter** forbids putting a yoke on the neck
A G : 2 8 :076(094) [0095] St. **Peter** forbids the bishops to exercise lordship as if they
A L : 2 6 :027(068) [0073] In Acts 15:10, 11 **Peter** says, "Why do you make trial of
A L : 2 6 :028(068) [0073] Here **Peter** forbids the burdening of consciences with
A L : 2 8 :042(088) [0089] ensnare consciences when **Peter** forbids putting a yoke on
A L : 2 8 :076(094) [0095] **Peter** forbids the bishops to be domineering and to coerce
A P : 0 2 :021(103) [0111] **Peter** Lombard is not afraid to say that original
A P : 0 4 :083(118) [0145] Third, in Acts 10:43, **Peter** says, "To him all the prophets
A P : 0 4 :238(140) [0187] From **Peter** they quote this statement (I Pet. 4:8), "Love
A P : 0 4 :238(140) [0187] Obviously **Peter**, too, is talking here about love to the
A P : 0 4 :239(141) [0187] little earlier (I Pet. 2:4, 5) **Peter** commands us to come to
A P : 0 4 :242(141) [0187] **Peter** does not mean that love merits the forgiveness of
A P : 0 4 :284(150) [0201] Yet **Peter** says (Acts 15:9) that hearts are purified by
A P : 0 4 :354(161) [0217] As **Peter** says (I Pet. 1:9), "As the outcome of your faith
A P : 0 4 :386(166) [0225] Through this faith, **Peter** says (I Pet. 1:5), we are "guarded
A P : 1 2 :008(183) [0255] between the contrition of Judas and that of **Peter**.
A P : 1 2 :036(186) [0261] the one hand and that of **Peter** and David on the other.
A P : 1 2 :036(186) [0261] contrition of David and **Peter** did avail because it had the
A P : 1 2 :065(191) [0269] **Peter** (I Pet. 2:6) quotes the words from Isaiah (28:16),
A P : 1 2 :065(191) [0271] **Peter** also says in Acts 10:43, "To him all the prophets
A P : 1 2 :066(191) [0271] But here **Peter** cites the consensus of the church in
A P : 1 2 :070(192) [0271] oppose this statement of **Peter**, citing the consensus of the
A P : 1 2 :071(192) [0271] added to this statement of **Peter**, for the text says
A P : 1 2 :071(192) [0271] says (Acts 10:44), "While **Peter** was still saying this, the
A P : 1 2 :073(192) [0273] **Peter** clearly cites the consensus of the prophets; the
A P : 1 2 :119(200) [0287] Not even **Peter** Lombard speaks this way about
A P : 1 2 :122(200) [0287] though it was unknown in the time of **Peter** Lombard.
A P : 1 2 :122(200) [0289] should be preached"; **Peter's** preaching of penitence
A P : 1 2 :139(203) [0295] **Peter** Lombard's statement about remitting part of the
A P : 1 2 :149(206) [0299] or the basilica of St. **Peter** rather than undergo the
A P : 1 2 :151(206) [0299] the common troubles, as **Peter** says (I Pet. 4:17), "For the
A P : 1 5 :031(219) [0323] by putting a yoke," etc., **Peter** charges that to put this
A P : 2 0 :002(227) [0339] As **Peter** says (Acts 10:43), "To him all the prophets bear
A P : 2 0 :012(228) [0341] From **Peter** they quote (II Pet. 1:10), "Be zealous to
A P : 2 0 :013(228) [0341] **Peter** is talking about the works that follow the
A P : 2 1 :005(229) [0345] of our faith: when we see **Peter** forgiven after his denial,
A P : 2 1 :036(234) [0353] **Peter** was forgiven for denying Christ; Cyprian was
A P : 2 3 :005(239) [0365] we see the correctness of **Peter's** warning (II Pet. 2:1) that
A P : 2 4 :026(254) [0391] are of this type, as **Peter** teaches in I Pet. 2:5, "A holy
A P : 2 4 :036(257) [0397] of the Gospel, as **Peter** says (I Pet. 1:2); "Sanctified by the
S 2 : 0 1 :005(292) [0461] For as St. **Peter** says, "There is no other name under
S 3 : 0 8 :008(313) [0495] However, St. **Peter** had to reveal to him that the Messiah,
S 3 : 0 8 :013(313) [0497] St. **Peter** says that when the prophets spoke, they did not
S 3 : 0 8 :013(313) [0497] They were holy, St. **Peter** says, because the Holy Spirit
S 3 : 1 3 :001(315) [0499] that by faith (as St. **Peter** says) we get a new and clean
S 3 : 1 5 :005(317) [0501] Master **Peter** Geltner, preacher in Frankfurt, subscribed
T R : 0 0 :010(321) [0505] nor confirmed by **Peter**, nor does he acknowledge Peter
T R : 0 0 :010(321) [0505] nor does he acknowledge **Peter** as one from whom
T R : 0 0 :010(321) [0505] that his call did not depend on the authority of **Peter**.
T R : 0 0 :010(321) [0505] have acknowledged **Peter** as his superior if Peter had been
T R : 0 0 :010(321) [0505] Peter as his superior if **Peter** had been his superior by
T R : 0 0 :010(321) [0505] he at once preached the Gospel without consulting **Peter**.
T R : 0 0 :010(321) [0507] seek confirmation from **Peter**, even after he had come to
T R : 0 0 :010(321) [0507] on the Word of God, that **Peter** was not superior to the
T R : 0 0 :010(321) [0507] or confirmation was not to be sought from **Peter** alone.
T R : 0 0 :011(321) [0507] he does not attribute to **Peter** superiority or authority
T R : 0 0 :011(321) [0507] This is to say that neither **Peter** nor the other ministers
T R : 0 0 :011(321) [0507] Paul deprives **Peter** of this pretext and denies that Peter's
T R : 0 0 :011(321) [0507] pretext and denies that **Peter's** authority is superior to
T R : 0 0 :011(321) [0507] and of the church, I **Peter** 5:3, "Not domineering over the
T R : 0 0 :022(323) [0511] against us: "You are **Peter**, and on this rock I will build
T R : 0 0 :023(324) [0511] In all these passages **Peter** is representative of the entire
T R : 0 0 :023(324) [0511] Christ did not question **Peter** alone but asked, "Who do
T R : 0 0 :024(324) [0511] these passages to regard **Peter** as the representative of the
T R : 0 0 :024(324) [0511] passages do not ascribe to **Peter** any special prerogative,
T R : 0 0 :025(324) [0511] of the confession which **Peter** made when he declared
T R : 0 0 :025(324) [0511] Therefore Christ addresses **Peter** as a minister and says,
T R : 0 0 :027(325) [0511] and not as applying to the person or superiority of **Peter**.
T R : 0 0 :028(325) [0511] this rock" and not "on **Peter**," for he built his church not
T R : 0 0 :028(325) [0511] man but on the faith of **Peter**; and what was this faith
T R : 0 0 :029(325) [0513] "The Father revealed to **Peter** that he should say, 'You are
T R : 0 0 :030(325) [0513] a special authority on **Peter**, for Christ bids Peter to
T R : 0 0 :030(325) [0513] on Peter, for Christ bids **Peter** to pasture the sheep, that
T R : 0 0 :030(325) [0513] This commission **Peter** holds in common with the rest of
T R : 0 0 :062(330) [0523] Again, **Peter** and John call themselves presbyters.
T R : 0 0 :069(331) [0523] by the declaration of **Peter**, "You are a royal priesthood"
T R : 0 0 :082(334) [0527] **Peter** predicted that there would be wicked bishops in the
T R : 0 0 :082(335) [0529] **Peter** Geltner, preacher in the church in Frankfurt
L C : 0 3 :015(422) [0701] as godly and holy as St. **Peter** or St. Paul, then I would
E P : 1 1 :014(496) [0835] will of God and "to confirm our call," as St. **Peter** says.
S D : 0 2 :051(531) [0901] "**Peter** will declare to you a message by which you will be
S D : 0 4 :033(556) [0947] states in Article XX: "**Peter** teaches why we should do
S D : 0 7 :033(575) [0983] Judas receive orally as well as St. **Peter** and all the saints.
S D : 0 8 :030(597) [1025] joy in looking into it, as St. **Peter** testifies (I Pet. 1:12).
S D : 0 8 :034(597) [1027] Since St. **Peter** testifies with clear words that even we, in
S D : 0 8 :077(606) [1043] If that were true, **Peter**, Paul, and all the saints in heaven
S D : 1 0 :013(613) [1057] When **Peter** and Barnabas in a similar situation yielded to

Petilian (2)
A G : 2 8 :028(085) [0087] his reply to the letters of **Petilian** that one should not obey
A L : 2 8 :028(085) [0087] in reply to the letters of **Petilian** that not even catholic

Petition (46), Petitioned (1), Petitioners (1), Petitions (7)
P R : P R :005(004) [0009] and we besought and **petitioned** the Almighty, that our
A G : 2 8 :078(094) [0095] do this and ignore our **petition**, let them consider how
A P : 2 1 :034(234) [0353] so that it seemed to nod Yes or No to the **petitioners**.
S C : P R :017(340) [0535] every commandment, **petition**, and part, pointing out
S C : 0 3 :003(346) [0547] The First **Petition**
S C : 0 3 :004(346) [0547] but we pray in this **petition** that it may also be holy for
S C : 0 3 :006(346) [0547] The Second **Petition**
S C : 0 3 :007(346) [0547] but we pray in this **petition** that it may also come to us.
S C : 0 3 :009(347) [0547] The Third **Petition**
S C : 0 3 :010(347) [0547] but we pray in this **petition** that it may also be done by
S C : 0 3 :012(347) [0547] The Fourth **Petition**
S C : 0 3 :013(347) [0547] but we pray in this **petition** that God may make us aware
S C : 0 3 :015(347) [0549] The Fifth **Petition**
S C : 0 3 :016(347) [0549] Answer: We pray in this **petition** that our heavenly
S C : 0 3 :017(347) [0549] The Sixth **Petition**
S C : 0 3 :018(347) [0549] sin, but we pray in this **petition** that God may so guard
S C : 0 3 :019(348) [0549] The Seventh **Petition**
S C : 0 3 :020(348) [0549] Answer: We pray in this **petition**, as in a summary, that
S C : 0 3 :021(348) [0549] be assured that such **petitions** are acceptable to our
L C : 0 3 :024(423) [0705] to pray must present a **petition**, naming and asking for
L C : 0 3 :034(425) [0707] successive articles or **petitions** are comprehended all the

Continued ▶

L C : 0 3 :034(425) [0707] The First **Petition**
L C : 0 3 :045(426) [0709] So you see that in this **petition** we pray for exactly the
L C : 0 3 :046(426) [0709] This **petition**, then, is simple and clear as soon as we
L C : 0 3 :047(426) [0711] Likewise, this **petition** is for ourselves who have the Word
L C : 0 3 :048(426) [0711] If you pray the **petition** whole-heartedly, you can be sure
L C : 0 3 :048(426) [0711] The Second **Petition**
L C : 0 3 :049(426) [0711] We prayed in the first **petition** that God would prevent
L C : 0 3 :058(428) [0715] The Third **Petition**
L C : 0 3 :061(428) [0715] hinder and thwart the fulfillment of the first two **petitions**.
L C : 0 3 :068(429) [0717] that in these three **petitions** interests which concern God
L C : 0 3 :069(429) [0717] armed with this single **petition**, shall be our bulwark,
L C : 0 3 :070(430) [0717] The Fourth **Petition**
L C : 0 3 :073(430) [0719] To put it briefly, this **petition** includes everything that
L C : 0 3 :076(431) [0719] comprehensively this **petition** covers all kinds of relations
L C : 0 3 :080(431) [0721] But especially is this **petition** directed against our chief
L C : 0 3 :084(432) [0723] them take care lest this **petition** of the Lord's Prayer be
L C : 0 3 :084(432) [0723] The Fifth **Petition**
L C : 0 3 :086(432) [0723] This **petition** has to do with our poor, miserable life.
L C : 0 3 :087(432) [0723] against all the previous **petitions**, so that it is not possible
L C : 0 3 :089(432) [0723] constantly to turn to this **petition** for the comfort that
L C : 0 3 :090(432) [0723] he should examine himself in the light of this **petition**.
L C : 0 3 :092(432) [0723] Thus this **petition** is really an appeal to God not to regard
L C : 0 3 :096(433) [0725] is in agreement with this **petition**, Luke 6:37, "Forgive,
L C : 0 3 :097(433) [0725] sign is attached to the **petition**, therefore, that when we
L C : 0 3 :098(433) [0725] The Sixth **Petition**
L C : 0 3 :111(435) [0729] The Last **Petition**
L C : 0 3 :113(435) [0729] In the Greek this **petition** reads, "Deliver or keep us from
L C : 0 3 :113(435) [0729] The **petition** seems to be speaking of the devil as the sum
L C : 0 3 :115(435) [0729] Nevertheless, this **petition** includes all the evil that may
L C : 0 3 :118(436) [0731] But this **petition** he has put last, for if we are to be
S D : 0 2 :015(523) [0885] Here, too, belong all the **petitions** of the saints for divine
S D : 0 2 :015(523) [0885] By these **petitions** they indicate that what they ask of God
S D : 0 2 :016(523) [0887] and faith, we ought to **petition** him incessantly that by the
S D : 0 2 :041(529) [0897] exposition of the second **petition** of the Lord's Prayer

Petty (4)
A P : 0 4 :343(160) [0215] us have done with these **petty** quibblings of our
A P : 1 2 :069(192) [0271] no judgment, but like **petty** public officials they quietly
A P : 1 2 :128(201) [0291] the doctrinal doubts of good men are mere **petty** anxiety.
L C : 0 1 :230(396) [0645] quiet here about various **petty** thieves in order to launch

Pfalz (1)
P R : P R :027(014) [0025] Philip Louis, palsgrave [of **Pfalz**-Neuburg]

Pforzheim (2)
S 3 : 1 5 :005(317) [0501] Conrad Oettinger, preacher of Duke Ulric of **Pforzheim**
T R : 0 0 :082(335) [0529] Conrad Oettinger, of **Pforzheim**, preacher of Ulric, duke

Phaedrus (1)
A P : 2 4 :016(252) [0389] In Plato's ***Phaedrus***, Socrates says that he is very fond of

Phalaris (1)
A P : 0 4 :399(168) [0227] What would **Phalaris** say that was more cruel?

Pharaoh (6)
S D : 1 1 :084(630) [1091] Hence **Pharaoh** (of whom we read, "For this purpose
S D : 1 1 :085(630) [1091] But that God hardened **Pharaoh**'s heart so that Pharaoh
S D : 1 1 :085(630) [1091] Pharaoh's heart so that **Pharaoh** continued to sin and
S D : 1 1 :085(630) [1091] and his will revealed to **Pharaoh**, and he deliberately
S D : 1 1 :086(631) [1091] holy apostle adduces **Pharaoh**'s example for the sole
S D : 1 1 :086(631) [1091] had not wanted to grant **Pharaoh** or any other person

Pharisaic (7), Pharisaical (3), Pharisaism (1)
A P : 0 4 :016(109) [0123] philosophical or **Pharisaic** righteousness and Christian
A P : 1 2 :085(194) [0277] Therefore we reject the **Pharisaic** opinions of our
A P : 2 4 :005(250) [0385] Out with such **pharisaic** ideas!
A P : 2 4 :013(251) [0387] person can approve this **pharisaic** and pagan notion
A P : 2 4 :013(251) [0387] have brought this **pharisaic** notion into the church.
A P : 2 4 :033(256) [0395] does not propound the **pharisaic** idea of ceremonies *ex*
A P : 2 7 :002(269) [0419] Inflamed with a **pharisaical** hatred, the guardian began to
A P : 2 7 :025(273) [0427] All this is full of **pharisaical** vanity.
A P : 2 7 :027(274) [0429] to read and hear such **pharisaical** and even Mohammedan
A P : 2 7 :069(281) [0443] are plain, damnable **pharisaism**: that these observances
E P : 0 4 :018(477) [0801] much as a papistic and **Pharisaic** confidence in one's own

Pharisee (5), Pharisees (13)
A G : 0 8 :001(033) [0047] himself indicated, "The **Pharisees** sit on Moses' seat"
A L : 0 8 :001(033) [0047] Christ, "The scribes and **Pharisees** sit on Moses' seat,"
A P : 0 4 :154(128) [0163] woman but against the **Pharisee**, because Christ
A P : 0 4 :154(128) [0163] act of reverence of the **Pharisee** with that of the woman.
A P : 0 4 :154(128) [0165] He chides the **Pharisee** for not acknowledging him as the
A P : 0 4 :154(128) [0165] Christ to chide the **Pharisee**, this wise and honest but
A P : 0 4 :229(139) [0183] veiled face, just as the **Pharisees**, philosophers, and
A P : 0 4 :269(147) [0197] be our opponents, those **Pharisees**, who interpret the law
A P : 0 4 :282(149) [0201] Christ is upbraiding the **Pharisees** for thinking that they
A P : 0 4 :282(149) [0201] Such were the opinions of the **Pharisees**, too.
A P : 0 4 :332(158) [0211] then they pray like the **Pharisee** in Luke 18:11 who says,
A P : 0 7 :016(171) [0231] Certainly the **Pharisees** had an outward affiliation with
A P : 1 5 :036(220) [0325] as an example to the **Pharisees** of the uselessness of these
A P : 2 7 :052(278) [0437] of Christ upbraiding the **Pharisees** for setting up
S 3 : 0 3 :029(308) [0487] The scribes and **Pharisees** in Christ's time were just such
E P : 0 5 :008(479) [0803] hypocrites, like the **Pharisees**, or they despair, as Judas
S D : 0 2 :024(526) [0891] even talk about it, as **Pharisees** and hypocrites do, yet he
S D : 1 1 :078(629) [1089] as was the case with the **Pharisees** and their party at the

Phase (1)
A P : 1 2 :131(202) [0291] come good fruits and good works in every **phase** of life.

Philip (8)
P R : P R :019(009) [0017] writings of Master **Philip** Melanchthon or of [John]
P R : P R :027(014) [0025] **Philip** Louis, palsgrave [of Pfalz-Neuburg]
P R : P R :027(015) [0025] **Philip**, count of Hanau [-Lichtenburg]
A G : 0 0 :007(096) [0095] **Philip**, landgrave of Hesse
A L : 0 0 :017(096) [0095] **Philip**, landgrave of Hesse, subscribes
A P : P R :000(098) [0099] Greetings from **Philip** Melanchthon to the reader.
S 3 : 1 5 :005(316) [0501] I, **Philip** Melanchthon, regard the above articles as right
T R : 0 0 :082(335) [0529] **Philip** Melanchthon subscribes with his own hand

Philologists (1), Philology (1)
A P : 2 4 :078(263) [0411] Our opponents also refer us to **philology**.
A P : 2 4 :083(264) [0413] of the diphthong, **philologists** do not derive it from *lite*,

Philosopher (1), Philosophers (12)
A G : 2 0 :033(045) [0057] We see this in the **philosophers** who undertook to lead
A L : 2 0 :033(045) [0057] This we may see in the **philosophers**, who, although they
A P : 0 2 :043(106) [0117] The **philosophers** said this about the civil courts, not
A P : 0 4 :009(108) [0123] Here the scholastics have followed the **philosophers**.
A P : 0 4 :229(139) [0183] just as the Pharisees, **philosophers**, and Mohammedans.
A P : 0 4 :243(141) [0189] this duty of love which the **philosophers** call "leniency."
A P : 1 8 :005(225) [0335] the fact that even **philosophers** who seem to have wanted
A P : 2 7 :046(277) [0435] Let the **philosophers** praise Aristippus for throwing a
S 3 : 0 1 :004(302) [0477] understanding and a good will, as the **philosophers** teach.
E P : 0 2 :008(470) [0787] of the so-called Stoic **philosophers** and of Manichaeans
E P : 0 7 :014(483) [0811] single mode which the **philosophers** call *local* or spatial."
S D : 0 1 :060(519) [0879] No **philosopher**, no papist, no sophist, indeed, no human
S D : 0 7 :097(586) [1005] the one which the **philosophers** call local or spatial.

Philosophical (14), Philosophize (1), Philosophy (4)
A L : 2 0 :018(043) [0055] else than civil or **philosophical** righteousness, have bad
A P : 0 2 :004(101) [0105] now when so many **philosophize** about it irreligiously.
A P : 0 2 :012(102) [0109] doctrine with **philosophical** views about the perfection of
A P : 0 2 :012(102) [0109] before God by **philosophical** or civic righteousness, which
A P : 0 2 :015(102) [0109] quibble about **philosophical** questions and do not explain
A P : 0 2 :043(106) [0117] have taken over from **philosophy** the totally foreign idea
A P : 0 2 :043(106) [0117] improperly mingle **philosophical** and civil ethics with the
A P : 0 4 :012(109) [0123] is there between **philosophy** and the teaching of Christ?
A P : 0 4 :012(109) [0123] to seek some righteousness beyond the **philosophical**.
A P : 0 4 :016(109) [0123] no difference between **philosophical** or Pharisaic
A P : 0 4 :037(112) [0131] how vain these **philosophical** speculations are.
A P : 0 4 :306(154) [0207] way here from the **philosophical** or judicial investigation
A P : 0 4 :376(164) [0223] Scriptures in either a **philosophical** or a Jewish manner
A P : 0 4 :390(166) [0225] more than enough **philosophy** with Christian doctrine.
A P : 1 8 :009(226) [0337] between **philosophical** teaching and the teaching of the
A P : 2 1 :041(235) [0355] because it leads to **philosophical** disputes rather than to
A P : 2 4 :043(258) [0399] more learned take up **philosophical** questions, which
A P : 2 7 :054(278) [0439] their time either on **philosophical** discussions or on
S D : 0 2 :008(521) [0883] to proud reason and **philosophy**, but we also know that

Phocas (1)
T R : 0 0 :021(323) [0509] the primacy, Emperor **Phocas** had finally decided that the

Phrase (12), Phraseology (1), Phrases (3)
A P : 0 2 :051(107) [0119] list, in the usual familiar **phrases**, the opinions of the holy
A P : 0 4 :152(127) [0163] sometimes combine cause and effect in the same **phrase**.
A P : 0 4 :155(128) [0165] often do when they include many things in one **phrase**.
A P : 0 4 :385(166) [0225] prayer closes with this **phrase**: "through Christ our Lord."
A P : 0 7 :008(169) [0229] The following **phrase**, "the communion of saints," seems
A P : 2 2 :008(237) [0359] who when they hear the **phrase** "lay communion"
A P : 2 3 :026(243) [0371] it with pious-sounding **phrases** to give it a religious front.
A P : 2 3 :049(246) [0377] In the excellent **phrase** of Epiphanius, such observances
A P : 2 4 :026(254) [0393] We see this from the **phrase**, "Through him let us offer,"
A P : 2 7 :041(276) [0435] He adds the **phrase** "for the Gospel" (Mark 10:29) to
L C : 0 2 :026(413) [0685] we shall take up one **phrase** which contains the substance
L C : 0 2 :047(416) [0691] In early times the latter **phrase** was missing, and it is
L C : 0 2 :051(417) [0691] and substance of this **phrase**: I believe that there is on
S D : 0 1 :050(517) [0875] to vocabulary and **phraseology**, however, the best and
S D : 0 5 :008(559) [0953] from one another, the **phrase** "to repent" means nothing
S D : 0 7 :036(575) [0985] with such equivalent **phrases** as, "The Word dwelt in us,"

Physical (19), Physically (2)
A G : 0 1 :006(028) [0043] the Word signifies a **physical** word or voice and that the
A G : 2 8 :011(082) [0085] but with the sword and **physical** penalties it protects body
A L : 2 8 :011(082) [0085] men with the sword and **physical** penalties, while the
A P : 0 2 :017(102) [0109] not only a balanced **physical** constitution, but these gifts
A P : 0 2 :025(103) [0111] a corruption of the **physical** constitution, but the evil
A P : 0 2 :046(106) [0117] only to death and other **physical** ills, but also to the rule
A P : 0 2 :047(106) [0119] as penalty; death, other **physical** ills, and the tyranny of
A P : 0 4 :194(133) [0175] by faith) but for other **physical** and spiritual rewards in
A P : 0 7 :014(170) [0231] had promises about **physical** well-being, political affairs,
A P : 0 7 :014(170) [0231] God had separated these **physical** descendants from other
A P : 0 7 :019(171) [0233] people will be separated from the **physical** people.
A P : 1 2 :161(208) [0303] Thus God imposed **physical** death on man because of sin,
A P : 1 3 :014(213) [0311] but these apply to **physical** life and not strictly to the New
A P : 2 3 :008(240) [0367] it still does as long as this **physical** nature of ours exists.
A P : 2 7 :021(272) [0427] They used them for their **physical** advantage, to have
S 2 : 0 2 :028(297) [0469] When spiritual and **physical** benefit and help are no
T R : 0 0 :031(325) [0513] excommunicate the godless without **physical** violence.
L C : 0 1 :184(390) [0633] you even the least good, whether **physical** or spiritual.
L C : 0 1 :274(402) [0659] us to injure anyone **physically**, and yet an exception is
L C : 0 2 :015(412) [0681] Moreover, he gives all **physical** and temporal blessings —
S D : 0 2 :011(522) [0885] little as a person who is **physically** dead can by his own

Physician (5)
L C : 0 1 :275(402) [0659] the situation of the **physician** who, to cure a patient, is
L C : 0 4 :043(442) [0743] Suppose there were a **physician** who had such skill that
L C : 0 5 :069(454) [0769] eats and drinks what is forbidden him by the **physician**.
L C : 0 5 :071(455) [0769] well have no need of a **physician**, but those who are sick,"
S D : 0 7 :070(582) [0997] well have no need of a **physician**, but those who are sick."

Pick (4)
A P : 0 4 :280(149) [0201] clever men that they are, **pick** out garbled sentences to
A P : 0 4 :284(150) [0201] honest reader would not **pick** out the commands about
A P : 0 4 :357(161) [0217] central thought of the discussion; they **pick** out the word
L C : 0 4 :012(438) [0735] be as noble and good as if God were to **pick** up a straw.

Picklocks (1)
L C : 0 1 :229(396) [0645] Far from being **picklocks** and sneak-thieves who loot a

Picture (6), Pictured (1), Pictures (2)
A G : 2 7 :015(073) [0077] But now the **picture** is changed.
A P : 0 4 :276(148) [0199] promise is written and **pictured** in good works, which
A P : 1 3 :005(212) [0309] the eyes and is a sort of **picture** of the Word, signifying
A P : 2 1 :035(234) [0353] tales about statues and **pictures** do not even compare with
A P : 2 3 :054(247) [0379] This has given us a **picture** of the times that will precede
A P : 2 4 :036(257) [0397] The Old Testament had **pictures** or shadows of what was
A P : 2 4 :053(259) [0403] and say that it was a **picture** of Christ's priesthood.
A P : 2 4 :053(259) [0403] said, they were merely a **picture** of the sacrifice of Christ
A P : 2 4 :070(262) [0409] the ceremony is a sort of **picture** or "seal," as Paul calls it

Piece (2), Pieces (5)
A P : 0 4 :109(123) [0153] they have thought up a **piece** of sophistry to evade them.
S 2 : 0 2 :010(294) [0465] himself to be torn to **pieces** before he would give up the
S 3 : 0 3 :002(304) [0479] a hammer which breaks the rock in **pieces**?" (Jer. 23:29).
L C : 0 1 :160(387) [0627] the country and grudge them as much as a **piece** of bread.
L C : 0 1 :191(391) [0635] and cold, to be torn to **pieces** by wild beasts, to rot in
L C : 0 3 :069(429) [0717] against which the others shall dash themselves to **pieces**.
S D : 0 3 :048(548) [0933] God consists of two **pieces** or parts, namely, the gracious

Piety (15)
A L : 2 6 :045(070) [0075] holy days but to preach **piety** toward God and good
A P : 0 4 :236(140) [0185] which have no value for **piety** and most of which are not
A P : 1 2 :161(208) [0303] through humiliation his **piety** might be exercised and
A P : 2 1 :041(235) [0355] it leads to philosophical disputes rather than to **piety**.
A P : 2 4 :007(250) [0385] daily Mass, reasons of **piety** or of profit later changed
A P : 2 4 :076(263) [0411] the godly communicant, "**Piety** distinguishes between
A P : 2 4 :076(263) [0411] That is, **piety** looks at what is given and what is forgiven;
L C : 0 1 :176(389) [0631] and fail to bring up your children to usefulness and **piety**.
E P : 0 6 :008(481) [0807] discipline and true **piety** the erroneous teaching that the
E P : 1 2 :005(498) [0839] For the most part this **piety** is built on one's own
S D : 0 2 :060(532) [0905] does not coerce anyone to **piety**, for those who always
S D : 0 6 :020(567) [0969] on their own holiness and **piety** and under the pretext of
S D : 1 1 :075(628) [1087] life does not rest on our **piety** or virtue but solely on the
S D : 1 2 :010(634) [1097] renewal and in our own **piety**, in which we walk before
S D : 1 2 :010(634) [1097] But this **piety** rests for the greater part on their own

Pigs (4)
S C : P R :003(338) [0533] they live as if they were **pigs** and irrational beasts, and
L C : P R :003(358) [0567] a little shame because, like **pigs** and dogs, they remember
L C : 0 1 :267(401) [0657] and delighting in it like **pigs** that roll in the mud and root
L C : 0 6 :005(457) [0000] But such **pigs**, as I have said, are unworthy to appear in

Pilate (3)
S C : 0 2 :003(345) [0545] *suffered under Pontius **Pilate**, was crucified, dead, and*
L C : S P :012(363) [0577] suffered under Pontius **Pilate**, was crucified, dead, and
L C : 0 2 :025(413) [0683] *suffered under Pontius **Pilate**, was crucified, dead, and*

Pile (3), Piled (1)
A P : 0 4 :020(110) [0125] doubt and then seek to **pile** up other works to find peace.
A P : 0 4 :105(122) [0153] If you **pile** up all the commentators on the *Sentences* with
A P : 0 4 :204(135) [0177] but in real terror they **pile** up works and ultimately
L C : 0 4 :012(438) [0735] Scriptures teach that if we **piled** together all the works of

Pilfer (1)
L C : 0 1 :223(395) [0643] has forbidden us to rob or **pilfer** the possessions of our

Pilgrimage (1), Pilgrimages (12)
A G : 2 0 :003(041) [0053] of saints, monasticism, **pilgrimages**, appointed fasts, holy
A G : 2 5 :005(062) [0069] with indulgences, with **pilgrimages** and the like.
A G : 0 0 :002(095) [0095] about indulgences, **pilgrimages**, and misuse of the ban.
A L : 2 0 :003(041) [0053] fasts, brotherhoods, **pilgrimages**, services in honor of
A L : 0 0 :002(095) [0095] about indulgences, **pilgrimages**, and misuse of
A P : 1 2 :014(184) [0257] observances like **pilgrimages**, rosaries, or similar
A P : 1 2 :144(204) [0297] Some works, like **pilgrimages**, depart even further from
A P : 1 2 :163(208) [0303] "judge" as "to make a **pilgrimage** to St. James dressed in
S 2 : 0 2 :016(295) [0467] of demanding Masses, vigils, **pilgrimages**, and other alms.
S 2 : 0 2 :018(296) [0467] The third are **pilgrimages**.
S 2 : 0 2 :018(296) [0467] commanded to make **pilgrimages**, nor are they necessary,
S 2 : 0 2 :018(296) [0467] way and may omit **pilgrimages** without sin and danger.
L C : 0 1 :144(385) [0623] into monasteries, on **pilgrimages**, and after indulgences,

Pillar (2), Pillars (1)
A P : 0 7 :020(171) [0233] is properly called "the **pillar** of truth" (I Tim. 3:15), for it
A P : 0 7 :027(173) [0235] true church: that they are **pillars** of the truth and that
S D : 0 2 :020(525) [0889] of his soul, man is like a **pillar** of salt, like Lot's wife, yes,

Pin (1)
S 3 : 0 3 :036(309) [0489] thing is sure: We cannot **pin** our hope on anything that

Pindar (1)
A P : 2 8 :024(285) [0451] good will ceases, and mortals are forgetful," said **Pindar**.

Pious (48)
P R : P R :002(003) [0007] Latin languages by our **pious** and Christian predecessors
P R : P R :004(003) [0007] of that enlightened and **pious** person, Dr. Martin Luther,
P R : P R :009(006) [0011] allegation many **pious** hearts were frightened away and
P R : P R :010(006) [0011] When a number of **pious**, irenic, and learned theologians
P R : P R :010(006) [0011] provided for simple and **pious** hearts, so that they might
P R : P R :022(011) [0019] Besides, **pious** people should be warned against them.
P R : P R :022(011) [0019] that one can find many **pious**, innocent people even in
P R : P R :024(013) [0023] slightest doubt that all **pious** people who have an upright
P R : P R :025(013) [0023] the divine truth that our **pious** forebears and we have
A P : 0 2 :043(106) [0117] **Pious** men have confessed to these things, as the Psalms
A P : 0 4 :002(107) [0121] of Christ and brings to **pious** consciences the abundant
A P : 0 4 :003(107) [0121] of Christ, and they rob **pious** consciences of the
A P : 0 4 :085(119) [0147] So **pious** men should not let themselves be diverted from
A P : 0 4 :156(128) [0165] and firm consolation for **pious** minds—whether we should
A P : 0 4 :285(150) [0201] our opponents counsel **pious** consciences very badly when
A P : 0 4 :286(150) [0203] shown all this to the satisfaction of **pious** consciences.
A P : 0 4 :303(154) [0205] We hope that **pious** minds will easily understand our
A P : 0 4 :396(167) [0225] Therefore let not **pious** minds be troubled by the crowd
A P : 0 4 :400(168) [0227] Fathers, and contrary to the testimony of **pious** minds.
A P : 1 1 :007(181) [0251] What great tortures for the most **pious** minds!
A P : 1 2 :028(185) [0259] In order to deliver **pious** consciences from these
A P : 1 2 :072(192) [0271] Let **pious** consciences know, therefore, that God
A P : 1 5 :044(221) [0327] church discipline, **pious** ceremonies, and the good
A P : 2 0 :008(227) [0339] **Pious** consciences will have no sure foundation when sin
A P : 2 3 :026(243) [0371] still they cloak it with **pious**-sounding phrases to give it a
A P : 2 7 :021(272) [0427] for teaching and other **pious** duties, not because the
A P : 2 7 :069(281) [0443] for the sake of showing **pious** hearts why they should
A P : 2 7 :069(281) [0443] And let every **pious** heart know and be sure that such
A P : 2 8 :003(281) [0443] listen to the complaints of churches and **pious** hearts!
A P : 2 8 :027(285) [0451] it to the judgment of all **pious** people whether our
S C : 0 3 :014(347) [0547] money and property; a **pious** spouse and good children,
E P : 1 1 :005(495) [0833] concerned only with the **pious** children of God in whom
E P : 1 2 :005(498) [0839] of Christ, but in renewal and in our own **pious** behavior.
E P : 1 2 :008(498) [0839] by virtue of their birth from Christian and **pious** parents.
E P : 1 2 :027(500) [0843] unless he is himself truly reborn, righteous, and **pious**.
E P : 1 2 :030(500) [0843] All **pious** Christians, of high degree and low, must guard
S D : P R :002(501) [0847] however, regarded this **pious** reformation as a new
S D : P R :020(507) [0857] will enable the **pious** reader, as far as is necessary, to
S D : 0 2 :035(528) [0895] daily makes man more **pious** and holy, to the complete
S D : 0 7 :001(569) [0971] our hearers and other **pious** Christians against this
S D : 0 7 :008(570) [0975] certainly as believing and **pious** Christians eat the bread
S D : 0 7 :060(580) [0993] that not only godly, **pious**, and believing Christians
S D : 0 7 :066(581) [0997] and wicked Christians as well as by the godly and **pious**.
S D : 0 7 :067(582) [0997] are so terrible that a **pious** Christian should be ashamed
S D : 1 1 :011(618) [1067] may well come to **pious** hearts, too, even though by the
S D : 1 1 :070(627) [1085] adversary is accustomed to tempt and vex **pious** hearts.
S D : 1 2 :035(635) [1101] renewed, righteous, and **pious** cannot teach profitably
S D : 1 2 :039(636) [1103] All **pious** Christians will and should avoid these as dearly

Pit (4), Pits (1)
A P : 0 4 :189(133) [0175] among men, he visibly **pits** the witness of the saints
A P : 0 4 :214(136) [0179] We cannot **pit** our works against the wrath and judgment
A P : 0 4 :327(158) [0211] my hands with lye, yet thou wilt plunge me into a **pit**."
A P : 1 2 :064(191) [0269] terrified conscience cannot **pit** our works or our love
L C : 0 1 :240(397) [0649] free public market into a carrion-**pit** and a robbers' den.

Pitted (1)
A P : 0 4 :214(136) [0179] the mediator, can be **pitted** against God's wrath and

Pitiful (1), Pity (1)
A P : 2 8 :005(281) [0445] the sufferers and hear the **pitiful** complaints of many good
S C : P R :006(338) [0533] seriously, that you have **pity** on the people who are

Pius (3)
A G : 2 3 :002(053) [0063] even one of the popes, **Pius** II, often said and allowed
A G : 2 3 :002(053) [0063] is no doubt that Pope **Pius**, as a prudent and intelligent
A L : 2 3 :002(051) [0061] On this account Pope **Pius** is reported to have said that

Placate (8), Placated (2), Placates (1), Placating (1)
A P : 0 4 :207(135) [0177] that through these works they **placated** the wrath of God.
A P : 0 4 :209(136) [0177] this cruel and painful deed to **placate** the wrath of God.
A P : 1 2 :107(198) [0283] wrathful and cannot be **placated** by our works, and yet
A P : 1 2 :117(199) [0287] they say that it is done to **placate** the divine displeasure.
A P : 1 2 :118(200) [0287] who are in mortal sin could **placate** the divine displeasure.
A P : 1 2 :120(200) [0287] not for discipline in the church, but for **placating** God.
A P : 1 2 :144(205) [0297] so they do not serve to **placate** God's displeasure, as our
A P : 2 0 :010(228) [0341] that it thought adequate to **placate** the wrath of God?
A P : 2 4 :013(251) [0387] they think they can **placate** God's wrath, gain the
A P : 2 4 :019(252) [0389] that reconciles God or **placates** his wrath or merits the
A P : 2 4 :023(253) [0391] a sacrificial victim to **placate** the wrath of God when,
A P : 2 4 :023(253) [0391] victim was going to **placate** God for the whole human

Place (179), Placed (18), Places (43), Placing (2)
P R : P R :004(003) [0007] disturbances took **place** in our beloved German
P R : P R :021(011) [0019] church put it, it takes **place** on account of the personal
A G : P R :012(026) [0041] negotiations take **place** between us, and if no results are
A G : 0 6 :001(032) [0045] for God's sake and not **place** our trust in them as if
A G : 0 7 :003(032) [0047] by men, should be observed uniformly in all **places**.
A G : 2 2 :005(050) [0061] In several **places** Cyprian mentions that the cup was given
A G : 2 3 :018(054) [0063] but has in many **places** been swiftly punished, as if it were
A G : 0 1 :002(056) [0065] except that in certain **places** German hymns are sung in
A G : 2 4 :026(058) [0067] Scriptures show in many **places** that there is no sacrifice
A G : 2 4 :028(059) [0067] In the second **place**, St. Paul taught that we obtain grace
A G : 2 4 :030(059) [0067] In the third **place**, the holy sacrament was not instituted
A G : 2 4 :030(059) [0067] has already taken **place** — but to awaken our faith and
A G : 2 6 :004(064) [0071] In the first **place**, the grace of Christ and the teaching
A G : 2 6 :008(065) [0071] In the second **place**, such traditions have also obscured
A G : 2 6 :012(065) [0071] In the third **place**, such traditions have turned out to be a
A G : 2 8 :058(091) [0091] appointment of Sunday in **place** of the Sabbath as a
A L : 1 6 :004(037) [0051] also condemn those who **place** the perfection of the
A L : 2 2 :005(050) [0061] Cyprian in several **places** testifies that the blood was given
A L : 2 3 :004(051) [0061] In the first **place**, this was done because Paul says,
A L : 2 3 :005(051) [0061] In the second **place**, Christ said, "Not all men can receive
A L : 2 6 :004(064) [0071] In the first **place**, it has obscured the doctrine concerning
A L : 2 6 :008(065) [0071] In the second **place**, these precepts obscured the
A L : 2 6 :012(065) [0071] In the third **place**, traditions brought great dangers to
A L : 2 7 :008(072) [0077] were created, what snares were **placed** on consciences.
A L : 2 7 :018(073) [0077] In the first **place**, we teach concerning those who contract
A L : 2 7 :027(075) [0079] In the second **place**, why do our adversaries exaggerate
A L : 2 8 :058(091) [0091] of the Lord's Day in **place** of the Sabbath was instituted
A P : P R :014(099) [0101] slanderously that in some **places** it could deceive even the
A P : 0 2 :043(106) [0117] In its **place** we do not object to this statement, but it is
A P : 0 4 :005(108) [0121] In some **places** it presents the law.
A P : 0 4 :020(110) [0125] forgiveness of sins takes **place**, or how the judgment of
A P : 0 4 :065(116) [0139] on the *Sentences* that tells how regeneration takes **place**.
A P : 0 4 :067(116) [0139] justification takes **place** through the Word, as Paul says
A P : 0 4 :067(116) [0139] For if justification takes **place** only through the Word,
A P : 0 4 :069(116) [0141] In the first **place**, we would remind our readers that if we
A P : 0 4 :079(117) [0143] if we know how the forgiveness of sins takes **place**.
A P : 0 4 :102(121) [0151] In some **places** it teaches the law; in others it teaches the
A P : 0 4 :178(131) [0171] the law itself—should be **placed** the death and satisfaction
A P : 0 4 :186(132) [0173] we concede that in some **places** the Scripture presents the

Continued ▶

A P : 0 4 :189(133) [0175] They take **place** in a flesh that is partly unregenerate and
A P : 0 4 :197(134) [0175] rather that when it takes **place** in the justified it merits
A P : 0 4 :208(135) [0177] Israel had seen the prophets sacrifice on the high **places**.
A P : 0 4 :208(135) [0177] not sacrifice on the high **places** to merit grace and
A P : 0 4 :208(135) [0177] were teaching in these **places** and thus gave evidence of
A P : 0 4 :238(140) [0187] sin and death; or that in **place** of Christ, the mediator,
A P : 0 4 :242(141) [0187] relation to God; that in **place** of Christ the mediator it is
A P : 0 4 :247(142) [0191] said that regeneration takes **place** through the Gospel.
A P : 0 4 :273(148) [0199] So the Scriptures testify in many other **places**.
A P : 0 4 :282(149) [0201] Christ rejects, and in **place** of this false cleansing he puts a
A P : 0 4 :342(160) [0215] us, though it is out of **place** here to discuss what is worthy
A P : 0 4 :361(162) [0219] as when a monk's hood is **placed** on a dead man.
A P : 0 4 :365(163) [0219] as in Isa. 58:8, 9 and often in other **places** in the prophets.
A P : 0 4 :381(165) [0223] that therefore we must **place** our confidence in God's
A P : 0 4 :393(167) [0225] there were some who in **place** of the righteousness of faith
A P : 0 7 :011(170) [0229] The Fathers say the same thing in many **places**.
A P : 0 7 :028(173) [0237] or the sacraments, they do so in Christ's **place** and stead.
A P : 0 7 :048(177) [0245] no longer function in the **place** of Christ, but are
A P : 1 2 :006(183) [0255] and tell us when the forgiveness of sins takes **place**.
A P : 1 2 :006(183) [0255] forgiveness of sins takes **place** in attrition or in
A P : 1 2 :006(183) [0255] If it takes **place** because of contrition, what is the need of
A P : 1 2 :029(185) [0259] This contrition takes **place** when the Word of God
A P : 1 2 :075(193) [0273] What is this but to **place** our trust in our own works
A P : 1 2 :127(201) [0289] think there are in these **places** who have begun to doubt
A P : 1 2 :130(202) [0291] many people in many **places** who are in doubt about
A P : 1 2 :148(205) [0299] regeneration itself takes **place** by constantly mortifying
A P : 1 3 :016(213) [0311] If it were **placed** among the sacraments and thus given, so
A P : 1 4 :002(214) [0315] government in some **places**, despite our earnest desire to
A P : 2 1 :017(231) [0347] In the first **place**, there must be a Word of God to assure
A P : 2 1 :025(232) [0349] In some **places** this form of absolution is used: "The
A P : 2 2 :007(237) [0359] it was customary in some **places** to administer only one
A P : 2 3 :028(243) [0371] In the first **place**, our opponents must admit that for
A P : 2 3 :035(244) [0373] In the second **place**, the proper contrast is between lust
A P : 2 4 :016(252) [0389] unskilled cook he sever the member at the wrong **place**.
A P : 2 4 :018(252) [0389] baptizes us through a minister functioning in his **place**.
A P : 2 4 :031(255) [0395] the nations, and in every **place** incense is offered to my
A P : 2 4 :032(255) [0395] This takes **place** through the proclamation of the Gospel,
A P : 2 4 :068(261) [0407] In the second **place**, Christ was supposed to be very
A P : 2 4 :086(265) [0413] was called *agape* in some **places**, unless some one prefers
A P : 2 7 :015(271) [0425] and that Christ took its **place**, so that he does not give the
A P : 2 7 :017(271) [0425] Christ takes Moses' **place**, not by forgiving sins on
A P : 2 7 :031(274) [0431] In the first **place**, it is sure that the monastic life does not
A P : 2 7 :032(274) [0431] In the second **place**, eternal life is given by mercy for
A P : 2 7 :053(278) [0437] fault: it arrogates Christ's **place** to the saints, and it
A P : 2 8 :017(284) [0449] observe them in their **place** and without superstition, in
S 1 : P R :003(289) [0455] a little and allow limitations to be **placed** on his tyranny.
S 2 : 0 2 :024(296) [0469] The sixth **place** belongs to the precious indulgences,
S 2 : 0 4 :008(300) [0473] Rome or some other fixed **place**, but it could be
S 3 : 0 3 :012(305) [0483] instructed the people to **place** their confidence in their
S 3 : 0 3 :020(306) [0485] But this is not the **place** to recount the torture, rascality,
S 3 : 0 3 :023(306) [0485] confidence was **placed** in man's own works of
S 3 : 0 3 :023(306) [0485] would have been **placed** in it, and neither faith nor Christ
S 3 : 0 5 :003(311) [0493] as if the washing takes **place** only through God's will and
T R : 0 0 :011(321) [0507] 4. In I Cor. 3:4-8 Paul **places** ministers on an equality and
T R : 0 0 :016(322) [0509] situated in remote **places** to seek ordination from him
T R : 0 0 :026(324) [0511] is not bound to **places** and persons, as the Levitical
T R : 0 0 :052(329) [0519] should know, in the first **place**, that these errors must be
T R : 0 0 :053(329) [0519] Then, in the second **place**, they should also know how
T R : 0 0 :062(331) [0523] number, set him in a higher **place**, and called him bishop.
S C : P R :007(338) [0533] In the first **place**, the preacher should take the utmost
S C : P R :014(339) [0535] In the second **place**, after the people have become
S C : P R :017(340) [0535] In the third **place**, after you have thus taught this brief
S C : P R :021(340) [0537] it, and no time or **place** should be appointed for it.
L C : 0 1 :013(366) [0583] heart and confidence be **placed** in God alone, and in no
L C : 0 1 :026(368) [0587] — in short, all people **placed** in the position of neighbors
L C : 0 1 :045(370) [0593] heart depart from God, **placing** his confidence in his
L C : 0 1 :082(376) [0603] persons, times, and **places**, from all of which we are now
L C : 0 1 :088(377) [0605] How does this sanctifying take **place**?
L C : 0 1 :094(378) [0607] as we have heard, takes **place** only through God's Word.
L C : 0 1 :094(378) [0607] **Places**, times, persons, and the entire outward order of
L C : 0 1 :105(379) [0611] other persons on earth, and **places** them next to himself.
L C : 0 1 :107(379) [0611] and that next to God we give them the very highest **place**.
L C : 0 1 :111(380) [0613] want or hunger, but will **place** them above himself and at
L C : 0 1 :112(380) [0613] In the second **place**, notice what a great, good, and holy
L C : 0 1 :115(381) [0613] from sight and give first **place** to this commandment.
L C : 0 1 :115(381) [0613] does this has, in the first **place**, the great comfort of being
L C : 0 1 :116(381) [0615] God's Word and will are **placed** first and observed,
L C : 0 1 :117(381) [0615] but because it has its **place** within that jewel and holy
L C : 0 1 :142(384) [0621] masters stand in the **place** of parents and derive from
L C : 0 1 :181(389) [0631] to civil magistrates in **place** of parents; in early times, as
L C : 0 1 :182(389) [0631] persons who occupy the **place** of God, that is, parents and
L C : 0 1 :183(389) [0633] He has therefore **placed** this and the other
L C : 0 1 :188(390) [0633] killing is this: In the first **place**, we should not harm
L C : 0 1 :189(390) [0635] In the second **place**, this commandment is violated not
L C : 0 1 :209(393) [0639] It is not an estate to be **placed** on a level with the others;
L C : 0 1 :211(393) [0641] In the second **place**, remember that it is not only an
L C : 0 1 :261(400) [0655] plainest meaning, applying to all that takes **place** in court.
L C : 0 1 :313(407) [0671] to special times, **places**, rites, and ceremonies, but are
L C : 0 2 :005(411) [0679] In the first **place**, the Creed used to be divided into twelve
L C : 0 2 :030(414) [0685] been routed, and their **place** has been taken by Jesus
L C : 0 2 :032(414) [0687] But the proper **place** to explain all these different points
L C : 0 2 :037(415) [0687] How does this sanctifying take **place**?
L C : 0 2 :037(415) [0687] his holy community, **placing** us upon the bosom of the
L C : 0 2 :042(416) [0689] In the first **place**, he has a unique community in the
L C : 0 2 :048(416) [0691] assemble select a special **place** and give the house its
L C : 0 3 :019(423) [0703] In the second **place**, we should be all the more urged and
L C : 0 3 :041(425) [0709] In the first **place**, then, it is profaned when men preach,
L C : 0 3 :042(425) [0709] In the next **place**, it is also profaned by an openly evil life
L C : 0 4 :003(437) [0733] In the first **place**, we must above all be familiar with the
L C : 0 4 :023(439) [0737] In the second **place**, since we now know what Baptism is
L C : 0 4 :032(440) [0739] In the third **place**, having learned the great benefit and
L C : 0 4 :068(445) [0749] of life does not take **place** but the old man is given free
L C : 0 5 :033(450) [0761] and in many other **places**, the answer is: It is he who
L C : 0 5 :035(450) [0761] treasure is opened and **placed** at everyone's door, yes,
L C : 0 5 :037(450) [0761] the like may have their **place** as an external preparation
L C : 0 5 :045(451) [0763] In the first **place**, we have a clear text in the words of
L C : 0 5 :047(452) [0765] being bound to no special **place** or time" (although the
L C : 0 5 :064(454) [0769] In the second **place**, a promise is attached to the
L C : 0 5 :066(454) [0769] invites us in other **places**, as when he says in Matt. 11:28,
L C : 0 6 :009(458) [0000] should and must take **place** incessantly as long as we live.
L C : 0 6 :013(458) [0000] confession which takes **place** privately before a single
L C : 0 6 :015(459) [0000] of my sins through a word **placed** in the mouth of a man.
L C : 0 6 :016(459) [0000] In the past we **placed** all the emphasis on our work alone,
L C : 0 6 :023(460) [0000] be given out at a certain **place**; he would need no bailiff to
L C : 0 6 :024(460) [0000] beggars should run to the **place**, no reason being given
E P : 0 1 :010(467) [0781] This will take **place** wholly by way of death in the
E P : 0 1 :021(468) [0785] wicked act or deed took **place**, nevertheless man's nature
E P : 0 3 :008(474) [0793] (making alive) are used in **place** of justification, and then
E P : 0 7 :004(482) [0809] Supper but assert that this takes **place** spiritually by faith.
E P : 0 7 :014(483) [0811] modes of being at a given **place**, and not only the single
E P : 0 7 :015(483) [0813] drink, all of which took **place** in the case of the apostles,
E P : 0 7 :032(485) [0815] and the same time in may **places**, still less in all places,
E P : 0 7 :032(485) [0815] may places, still less in all **places**, where his Holy Supper
E P : 0 7 :034(485) [0815] present at more than one **place** at a single given time.
E P : 0 8 :008(487) [0819] to descend, to move from **place** to place, to endure
E P : 0 8 :008(487) [0819] to move from place to **place**, to endure hunger, thirst,
E P : 0 8 :029(490) [0825] locally extended to every **place** in heaven and earth
E P : 0 8 :030(490) [0825] time at more than one **place**, still less to be present with
E P : 0 8 :033(491) [0825] only a few and only at the **place** where the human nature
E P : 0 8 :038(491) [0827] everywhere today, nor what will yet take **place** in eternity.
E P : 0 9 :004(492) [0827] How this took **place** is something that we should
E P : 1 2 :026(500) [0843] orderly process of excommunication do not take **place**.
S D : P R :002(503) [0851] at all times and in all **places** been accepted in all the
S D : P R :007(505) [0853] 5. In the fifth **place**, we also commit ourselves to the
S D : P R :017(507) [0857] 1. In the first **place**, we reject and condemn all heresies
S D : P R :018(507) [0857] 2. In the second **place**, we reject and condemn all the
S D : P R :019(507) [0857] 3. In the third **place**, since within the past twenty-five
S D : 0 1 :001(508) [0859] In the first **place**, there has been dissension among a
S D : 0 1 :005(509) [0861] In the first **place**, it is an established truth that Christians
S D : 0 1 :007(510) [0861] In the second **place**, it is also a clearly established truth,
S D : 0 1 :034(514) [0869] In the first **place**, in the article of creation Scripture
S D : 0 2 :009(521) [0883] In the first **place**, although man's reason or natural
S D : 0 2 :012(522) [0885] "My Word finds no **place** in you" (John 8:37).
S D : 0 2 :017(523) [0887] In the second **place**, the Word of God testifies that in
S D : 0 2 :025(526) [0891] In the third **place**, Holy Scriptures ascribe conversion,
S D : 0 2 :070(535) [0909] none of these things takes **place** or exists, there is no true
S D : 0 2 :083(537) [0913] the Word, conversion does not and cannot take **place**.
S D : 0 2 :083(537) [0913] and impulses, which take **place** through the Word, do not
S D : 0 2 :089(538) [0915] that conversion takes **place** without the preaching and the
S D : 0 3 :018(542) [0921] is sometimes used in **place** of "justification," it is necessary
S D : 0 3 :019(542) [0921] is used, in the first **place**, to include both the forgiveness
S D : 0 3 :020(542) [0921] has indeed taken **place** because he has transformed a child
S D : 0 3 :029(544) [0925] be done at the time and **place** where it is necessary,
S D : 0 3 :058(550) [0937] how this person was **placed** under the law for us, bore
S D : 0 4 :014(553) [0943] In the first **place**, it is evident that in discussing the
S D : 0 4 :026(555) [0945] 2. In his writings against the papists at many **places**;
S D : 0 4 :030(555) [0947] In the third **place**, a disputation has arisen as to whether
S D : 0 4 :037(557) [0949] In the fourth **place**, concerning the proposition that good
S D : 0 4 :037(557) [0951] express Word of God, is being **placed** upon good works.
S D : 0 5 :008(559) [0953] Mark 1:15, and in other **places** where repentance and
S D : 0 7 :003(569) [0973] of Christ not as taking **place** here on earth but only in
S D : 0 7 :075(583) [0999] efficacious power in all **places** where the Supper is
S D : 0 7 :088(585) [1003] the body of Christ takes **place** only spiritually through
S D : 0 7 :097(586) [1005] to be present at a certain **place**, not only, as the
S D : 0 7 :098(586) [1005] modes, or all three modes, of being at any given **place**.
S D : 0 7 :099(586) [1005] spirit dreams, for God is not a corporeal space or **place**.
S D : 0 7 :103(587) [1007] simultaneously in many **places**, even in a corporeal and
S D : 0 7 :116(589) [1013] the Supper allegedly take **place** not through the true
S D : 0 7 :122(590) [1013] their faith to look to that **place** in heaven where Christ is
S D : 0 7 :126(591) [1015] spirit and in truth in all **places** but especially where his
S D : 0 8 :010(593) [1019] to move from one **place** to another, to suffer hunger,
S D : 0 8 :028(596) [1025] Yet, this does not take **place** in a mundane way, but as
S D : 0 8 :028(596) [1025] which is not a specific **place** in heaven, as the
S D : 0 8 :032(597) [1025] properties could not take **place** or continue if the
S D : 0 8 :036(598) [1027] In the first **place**, since in Christ two distinct natures are
S D : 0 8 :046(600) [1031] In the second **place**, as far as the discharge of Christ's
S D : 0 8 :048(600) [1031] matter when, in the third **place**, the question being treated
S D : 0 8 :057(602) [1035] 1. In the first **place**, it is a unanimously accepted rule of
S D : 0 8 :058(602) [1035] 2. In the second **place**, Scripture testifies clearly
S D : 0 8 :059(602) [1035] 3. In the third **place**, Scripture not only speaks in general
S D : 0 8 :062(603) [1037] did not take **place** through an essential or natural
S D : 0 8 :063(603) [1037] or exchange that takes **place** in deed and in truth — to
S D : 0 8 :065(604) [1039] been laid aside, it takes **place** fully, mightily, and publicly
S D : 0 8 :082(607) [1045] if you could show me one **place** where God is and not the
S D : 0 8 :083(607) [1045] from this that space and **place** had separated the two
S D : 0 8 :084(607) [1045] present only at one single **place** as a divine and human
S D : 0 8 :084(607) [1045] person, and if at all other **places** he would have to be
S D : 0 8 :092(609) [1049] extended into every **place** in heaven and earth, something
S D : 0 8 :092(609) [1049] his body, which he has **placed** at the right hand of the
S D : 1 0 :005(611) [1055] true religion has taken **place** or will allegedly result little
S D : 1 0 :009(612) [1055] of God in every **place** and at every time has the right,
S D : 1 0 :030(616) [1061] at any time and **place**, according to its circumstances, as
S D : 1 1 :001(616) [1063] controversies at other **places** and has involved our people
S D : 1 1 :002(616) [1063] but discuss and present it in detail in many **places**.
S D : 1 1 :029(621) [1073] call of God which takes **place** through the preaching of
S D : 1 1 :034(622) [1075] in his call, which takes **place** through the Word, God
S D : 1 1 :057(625) [1081] God gives his Word at one **place** and not at another; that
S D : 1 1 :057(625) [1081] he removes it from one **place** but lets it remain at
S D : 1 1 :063(626) [1083] limits, we must with Paul **place** our finger to our lips and
S D : 1 1 :096(632) [1095] Gospel, that will not give **place** to the smallest error but
S D : 1 2 :008(633) [1097] of these spirits, into those **places** and especially at those
S D : 1 2 :029(635) [1101] 1. In the first **place**, that no one has a true knowledge of
S D : 1 2 :034(635) [1101] does not take **place** is not a true Christian congregation.

Plague (6), Plagued (1), Plagues (2)

A L : 2 0 :019(043) [0055] Consciences used to be **plagued** by the doctrine of works

Continued ▶

S 2 : 0 4 :014(301) [0475] and to damn, slay, and **plague** all Christians who do not
T R : 0 0 :037(326) [0515] that they have been great **plagues** in the church.
L C : P R :005(359) [0567] a shameful and insidious **plague** of security and boredom
L C : 0 1 :011(366) [0583] patron; if he feared the **plague**, he made a vow to St.
L C : 0 1 :060(372) [0597] we get what we deserve: **plague**, war, famine, fire, flood,
L C : 0 1 :099(378) [0609] a malignant, pernicious **plague** with which the devil
L C : 0 3 :078(431) [0721] pestilence, and cattle-**plague**; from war and bloodshed,
E P : 0 6 :004(480) [0807] by its punishments and **plagues**, to follow the Spirit and

Plain (30), Plainest (3), Plainly (10)
P R : P R :020(010) [0017] faith they are to stay with the **plain** words of Christ.
A G : 2 0 :011(042) [0055] teaching about faith is **plainly** and clearly treated by Paul
A L : 2 7 :024(074) [0079] an obligation which is **plainly** derived from divine law.
A P : 0 4 :063(115) [0139] This is **plain** and clear, the faithful can grasp it, and it has
A P : 0 4 :083(118) [0145] How could he say it any more **plainly**?
A P : 0 4 :293(152) [0203] These things are **plain** and in conformity with the Gospel,
A P : 1 2 :043(187) [0263] of penitence is **plain** and clear, it adds to the honor of the
A P : 1 5 :050(222) [0329] But our case is **plain** and simple because our opponents
A P : 2 1 :041(235) [0355] ought to be as clear and **plain** as possible in the church.
A P : 2 7 :069(281) [0443] that such ideas as this are **plain**, damnable pharisaism:
T R : 0 0 :010(321) [0505] 3. In Gal. 2:2, 6 Paul **plainly** asserts that he was neither
T R : 0 0 :039(327) [0515] of worship, and it is **plain** that the marks of the
S C : P R :020(340) [0537] Make very **plain** to them the shocking evils they
S C : 0 1 :000(342) [0539] Commandments *in the **plain** form in which the head of*
S C : 0 2 :000(344) [0543] [II] The Creed *in the **plain** form in which the head of the*
S C : 0 3 :000(346) [0545] The Lord's Prayer *in the **plain** form in which the head of*
S C : 0 4 :000(348) [0551] *in the **plain** form in which the head of the family shall*
S C : 0 5 :015(349) [0553] *How **Plain** People Are to Be Taught to Confess*
S C : 0 5 :029(351) [0555] as an ordinary form of confession for **plain** people.
S C : 0 6 :000(351) [0555] of the Altar *in the **plain** form in which the head of the*
L C : S P :018(363) [0577] is comprehended in short, **plain**, and simple terms, for the
L C : S P :028(365) [0581] one by one and in the **plainest** possible manner say about
L C : 0 1 :005(365) [0581] must explain a little more **plainly**, so that it may be
L C : 0 1 :052(371) [0595] Let this stand as the **plain** and simple meaning of this
L C : 0 1 :077(375) [0603] This I say **plainly** for the sake of the young, so that it may
L C : 0 1 :086(376) [0605] This, then, is the **plain** meaning of this commandment:
L C : 0 1 :133(383) [0619] implied, yet in none is it so **plainly** and explicitly stated.
L C : 0 1 :140(384) [0621] These are **plain** and simple words, and everyone thinks he
L C : 0 1 :261(400) [0655] commandment, and its **plainest** meaning, applying to all
L C : 0 1 :310(407) [0669] he sets it forth in **plain** words: "You shall not covet," etc.
L C : 0 3 :039(425) [0709] The **plainest** answer is: When both our teaching and our
L C : 0 4 :037(441) [0741] Thus you see **plainly** that Baptism is not a work which we
L C : 0 5 :021(449) [0757] This is **plainly** evident from the words just quoted, "This
L C : 0 5 :075(455) [0771] works of the flesh are **plain**: adultery, immorality,
E P : 0 8 :012(488) [0821] and bore not only a **plain**, ordinary, mere man but the
E P : 0 8 :013(488) [0821] confess that it was not a **plain**, ordinary, mere man who
E P : 1 1 :022(497) [0837] the Word of God and the **plain** Catechism, every simple
S D : P R :004(502) [0847] and we abide by the **plain**, clear, and pure meaning of its
S D : 0 7 :046(577) [0989] and command of God **plainly** and simply, as the words
S D : 0 8 :005(592) [1017] in accordance with our **plain** Christian creed, and to settle
S D : 0 8 :020(595) [1021] and, in the words of our **plain** Christian Creed, has truly
S D : 0 8 :023(595) [1023] Christ, according to our **plain** Christian Creed we
S D : 0 8 :045(600) [1031] For our **plain** Christian Creed teaches us that the Son of

Plan (3), Planned (1), Planning (1)
P R : P R :015(007) [0013] able to undertake such a **plan** because special
A L : 2 7 :002(071) [0077] of restoring discipline, as in a carefully **planned** prison.
A P : 0 4 :399(168) [0227] father said that no **plan** seemed better to him than to give
L C : 0 3 :069(429) [0717] worst, let them plot and **plan** how to suppress and
S D : P R :007(505) [0853] neither expecting nor **planning** to come to an

Plane (1)
L C : 0 2 :002(411) [0679] they are set on so high a **plane** that all human ability is

Plank (1)
L C : 0 4 :081(446) [0751] is the second **plank** on which we must swim ashore after

Plant (2), Planted (3), Planting (2), Plants (2)
P R : P R :005(004) [0009] apostles themselves had **planted** the pure, unadulterated
A G : 2 8 :048(089) [0091] of God and says, "Every **plant** which my heavenly Father
A G : 2 8 :048(089) [0091] heavenly Father has not **planted** will be rooted up"
A L : 2 8 :048(089) [0091] services and says, "Every **plant** which my heavenly Father
A L : 2 8 :048(089) [0091] my heavenly Father has not **planted** will be rooted up."
A P : 2 3 :008(240) [0367] "Let the earth put forth vegetation, **plants** yielding seed."
A P : 2 3 :008(240) [0367] not begin to bring forth **plants** only at the beginning, but
E P : 0 2 :006(470) [0787] our "will and effort," our **planting**, sowing, and watering
S D : 0 2 :055(531) [0903] that both the preacher's **planting** and watering and the

Platina (1)
A L : 2 3 :002(051) [0061] **Platina** writes to this effect.

Plato (3)
A P : 2 4 :016(252) [0389] In **Plato**'s *Phaedrus*, Socrates says that he is very fond of
A P : 2 4 :016(252) [0389] **Plato** would really call our opponents "poor cooks," for
A P : 2 7 :005(269) [0421] into bad harmonies which, **Plato** says, cause destruction.

Platonic (5)
A P : 0 7 :020(171) [0233] dreaming about some **Platonic** republic, as has been
A P : 1 2 :046(188) [0263] these terms in a **Platonic** sense as counterfeit changes; but
A P : 1 2 :046(188) [0263] not be understood as a **Platonic** figment but as
A P : 1 6 :013(224) [0333] command while the **Platonic** commune does not have
A P : 2 7 :005(269) [0421] to an iron age, or as the **Platonic** cube degenerates into

Platz (1)
S 3 : 1 5 :005(318) [0501] the Rev. Licentiate Louis **Platz**, of Melsungen

Plausible (3), Plausibly (1)
A P : 0 4 :230(139) [0183] law about love is more **plausible**; for this is human
E P : 0 7 :004(482) [0809] talk our language very **plausibly** and claim to believe a
E P : 0 7 :004(482) [0809] But under this **plausible** terminology they really retain the
S D : 0 7 :006(570) [0973] by the noble and **plausible** words of the Sacramentarians

Play (3), Played (1), Playful (1), Playing (1), Plays (2), Plaything (1)
A P : 0 4 :019(109) [0125] condignity, they are only **playing** in order to avoid the
A P : 0 4 :335(159) [0215] our opponents make a marvelous **play** on Christ's words.
A P : 1 2 :107(198) [0283] from the heart and not just from the voice, as in a **play**.
A P : 2 2 :011(238) [0361] Like some tyrant in a **play**, he commands, "Whether they
A P : 2 4 :072(262) [0409] sake of example, the way **plays** celebrate the memory of
L C : 0 1 :075(375) [0601] With childish and **playful** methods like these we may
L C : 0 1 :245(398) [0649] must put up with another who **plays** the same game.
L C : 0 4 :006(437) [0733] Baptism is no human **plaything** but is instituted by God
S D : 1 1 :075(628) [1087] You have **played** the harlot with many lovers; yet return

Plea (1), Plead (2), Pleas (2)
A P : 0 4 :054(114) [0137] Scripture contains many **pleas** for mercy, and the holy
A P : 0 4 :258(144) [0193] oppression; defend the fatherless, **plead** for the widow.
L C : 0 1 :190(391) [0635] It will do you no good to **plead** that you did not
L C : 0 6 :009(458) [0000] do what we ought and a **plea** for grace and a happy
S D : 0 2 :021(525) [0889] All **pleas**, all appeals, all admonitions are in vain.

Pleasant (2)
L C : 0 1 :076(375) [0603] be trained with kind and **pleasant** methods, for those who
L C : 0 1 :132(383) [0619] welfare, to lead us to a quiet, **pleasant**, and blessed life.

Please (53), Pleased (21), Pleasers (1), Pleases (18), Pleasing (49)
P R : P R :024(013) [0023] and for Christian, God-**pleasing** concord will, together
A G : 0 5 :002(031) [0045] when and where he **pleases**, in those who hear the
A G : 2 7 :057(080) [0083] and seeking a life more **pleasing** to God than the other.
A G : 2 8 :060(091) [0091] the more inclined and **pleased** to do this in order that the
A L : 0 5 :002(031) [0045] faith, where and when it **pleases** God, in those who hear
A L : 2 0 :002(041) [0053] what kinds of work are **pleasing** to God in the several
A L : 2 4 :008(056) [0065] Such worship **pleases** God, and such use of the sacrament
A L : 2 6 :011(065) [0071] the observances of such men were more **pleasing** to God.
A L : 2 7 :022(074) [0079] of a vow as much as one **pleases**, it cannot be brought
A L : 2 8 :060(091) [0091] the church was the more **pleased** to do this for the
A P : 0 2 :036(105) [0115] This view **pleased** later generations so much that they
A P : 0 4 :032(111) [0129] and those who are in the flesh cannot **please** God."
A P : 0 4 :140(126) [0161] but also that God is **pleased** when we keep it—not because
A P : 0 4 :160(129) [0167] Therefore it does not **please** God for its own sake, and it
A P : 0 4 :162(129) [0169] and that afterward we **please** God and merit eternal life
A P : 0 4 :164(129) [0169] conscience be sure that it **pleases** God, since we never
A P : 0 4 :166(130) [0169] of the law does not **please** God for its own sake, but for
A P : 0 4 :172(130) [0171] that for Christ's sake we **please** God and that the works in
A P : 0 4 :172(131) [0171] works in themselves do not have the value to **please** God.
A P : 0 4 :177(131) [0171] keeping of the law **pleases** God because of faith; because
A P : 0 4 :184(132) [0173] works are done without Christ they do not **please** God.
A P : 0 4 :252(143) [0191] the saints are righteous and **please** God because of faith.
A P : 0 4 :252(143) [0191] have good fruits, which **please** him because of faith and
A P : 0 4 :253(143) [0193] a propitiation; that works **please** God without Christ, the
A P : 0 4 :256(144) [0193] "Without faith it is impossible to **please** God."
A P : 0 4 :266(146) [0197] that our works may be **pleasing** to God, as Christ says
A P : 0 4 :269(147) [0197] "without faith it is impossible to **please** God" (Heb. 11:6).
A P : 0 4 :269(147) [0197] works are praised for **pleasing** God on account of faith,
A P : 0 4 :269(147) [0197] of faith, since they do not **please** him without Christ, the
A P : 0 4 :270(147) [0197] keep the commandments or **please** God without Christ.
A P : 0 4 :270(147) [0197] It knows that now it is **pleasing** to God for the sake of
A P : 0 4 :278(149) [0199] Thus God is **pleased** by that almsgiving which follows
A P : 0 4 :281(149) [0201] of the law, that for his sake good works **please** God.
A P : 0 4 :288(151) [0203] reason thinks that it **pleases** God if it does good, but when
A P : 0 4 :293(152) [0203] of the law, these works **please** God on account of the
A P : 0 4 :308(155) [0207] to the law can be **pleasing** to God only because this
A P : 0 4 :310(155) [0207] beloved Son, with whom I am well **pleased**; listen to him."
A P : 0 4 :316(156) [0209] or the fact that for Christ's sake we **please** God by faith.
A P : 0 4 :316(156) [0209] worthy righteousness that **pleases** God of itself and earns
A P : 0 4 :317(156) [0209] If we want to **please** God because of our works and not
A P : 0 4 :319(156) [0209] that it ought to be **pleasing** to God because of its own
A P : 0 4 :355(161) [0217] spiritual rewards because they **please** God through faith.
A P : 0 4 :359(162) [0219] life or whether they **please** God only because of the faith
A P : 0 4 :360(162) [0219] a reward; therefore works **please** God for their own sake,
A P : 0 4 :362(162) [0219] and that good works are **pleasing** to God because of
A P : 0 4 :368(163) [0221] of the law would not **please** God unless we had been
A P : 0 4 :368(163) [0221] keeping of the law **pleases** God and has its reward, both
A P : 0 4 :372(164) [0221] nor can good works **please** God without the mediator
A P : 0 4 :372(164) [0221] Heb. 11:6, "Without faith it is impossible to **please** God."
A P : 0 4 :375(164) [0223] would grant that the fruits **please** God because of faith
A P : 0 4 :381(165) [0223] schools that good works **please** God because of grace and
A P : 0 4 :381(165) [0223] and that good works **please** God because of grace; for
A P : 0 4 :385(166) [0225] Thus other good works **please** God because of faith, as
A P : 0 7 :014(170) [0231] Nevertheless, these evil people did not **please** God.
A P : 0 7 :023(172) [0235] enact whatever laws he **pleases**, excuse and exempt men
A P : 1 5 :014(216) [0319] he know that these works **please** God since they do not
A P : 1 5 :017(217) [0319] God, the conscience must doubt whether they **please** God.
A P : 1 8 :006(225) [0335] "without faith it is impossible to **please**" God (Heb. 11:6).
A P : 2 3 :022(242) [0369] Impure continence does not **please** Christ.
A P : 2 3 :032(244) [0373] follow everyone's faith, **pleasing** God because of faith.
A P : 2 3 :032(244) [0373] So a woman's duties **please** God because of faith, and a
A P : 2 3 :045(245) [0377] and unclean and hardly **pleasing** to God, even though it
A P : 2 4 :028(254) [0393] namely, that such worship **pleased** him *ex opere operato.*
A P : 2 4 :068(262) [0407] was supposed to be very **pleased** with a mark that took
A P : 2 7 :070(281) [0443] services, and that God is **pleased** only with services
A P : 2 8 :008(282) [0445] were acts of worship that **pleased** God as righteousness.
A P : 2 8 :009(282) [0445] they acts of worship which **please** God as righteousness?
A P : 2 8 :011(283) [0447] to be acts of worship that **please** God as righteousness or
S 1 : P R :008(290) [0457] like cattle and everybody does what he **pleases**.
S C : P R :008(339) [0535] Choose the form that **pleases** you, therefore, and adhere
S C : 0 5 :021(350) [0553] **Please** give me a brief form of confession.
S C : 0 5 :021(350) [0553] confessor: "Dear Pastor, **please** hear my confession and
S C : 0 7 :002(352) [0557] in all my thoughts, words, and deeds I may **please** Thee.
S C : 0 9 :010(356) [0563] of eye-service, as men-**pleasers**, but as servants of Christ,
L C : 0 1 :016(366) [0585] the true worship which **please** God and which he
L C : 0 1 :069(374) [0599] are allowed to do as they **please**, no good will come of it.
L C : 0 1 :074(375) [0601] practices would be more **pleasing** and acceptable to God
L C : 0 1 :077(375) [0603] to know that God is well **pleased** with the right use of his
L C : 0 1 :092(377) [0607] by God's Word if they are to be God-**pleasing** or holy.
L C : 0 1 :102(379) [0609] and God is more **pleased** than by any work of hypocrisy,
L C : 0 1 :113(380) [0613] them he shows that he is well **pleased** with them.

Continued ▶

L C : 0 1 :115(381) [0613] they must do what is **pleasing** to their fathers and
L C : 0 1 :115(381) [0615] "See, this work is well **pleasing** to my God in heaven; this
L C : 0 1 :117(381) [0615] you to perform a task so precious and **pleasing** to him.
L C : 0 1 :118(381) [0615] "Now I know that this work is well **pleasing** to Thee!"
L C : 0 1 :125(382) [0617] we know that it is highly **pleasing** to the divine Majesty
L C : 0 1 :143(385) [0623] and is more **pleasing** to him than all other works.
L C : 0 1 :151(386) [0625] it is due, knows that he **pleases** God and receives joy and
L C : 0 1 :152(386) [0625] of obedience are so **pleasing** to God and have so rich a
L C : 0 1 :154(386) [0625] care nothing for anyone, and do whatever he **pleases**.
L C : 0 1 :170(388) [0629] to treat them as we **please**, as if it were no concern of
L C : 0 1 :217(394) [0641] life and know that it is a blessed and God-**pleasing** estate.
L C : 0 1 :240(397) [0649] his goods as dearly as he **pleases** without a word of
L C : 0 1 :252(399) [0651] things which are heartily acceptable and **pleasing** to God.
L C : 0 1 :290(404) [0663] of good works which **please** God most highly and bring
L C : 0 1 :311(407) [0669] what we are to do to make our whole life **pleasing** to God.
L C : 0 1 :311(407) [0671] conduct can be good or **pleasing** to God, no matter how
L C : 0 1 :327(409) [0675] or omitting to do things simply in order to **please** them.
L C : 0 1 :328(410) [0677] to God and in order to **please** him, in the confidence that
L C : 0 2 :068(420) [0697] pure grace and makes us upright and **pleasing** to God.
L C : 0 3 :009(421) [0699] I will go and do as I **please**; what difference does it
L C : 0 3 :016(422) [0701] as precious, holy, and **pleasing** to God as those of St.
L C : 0 3 :020(423) [0703] our prayer is heartily **pleasing** to him and will assuredly
L C : 0 3 :022(423) [0703] doubt that our prayer **pleases** him and will assuredly be
L C : 0 3 :023(423) [0703] who knows whether it **pleased** him, or whether I have hit
L C : 0 3 :048(426) [0711] whole-heartedly, you can be sure that God is **pleased**.
L C : 0 4 :049(442) [0743] the Baptism of infants is **pleasing** to Christ is sufficiently
L C : 0 4 :050(443) [0745] must acknowledge that infant Baptism is **pleasing** to God.
L C : 0 5 :045(452) [0763] coerced by men, but to obey and **please** the Lord Christ.
L C : 0 5 :052(452) [0765] anyone partake of the sacrament to serve or **please** us.
L C : 0 5 :052(452) [0765] you is the fact that Christ desires it, and it **pleases** him.
L C : 0 6 :005(457) [0000] they do whatever they **please** and take advantage of their
E P : 0 5 :003(478) [0801] what is right and God-**pleasing** and which condemns
E P : 0 8 :016(489) [0821] disclose this majesty, but only when it **pleased** him.
E P : 1 1 :005(495) [0833] with the pious children of God in whom he is well **pleased**.
E P : 1 1 :022(497) [0837] abide in this Christian and God-**pleasing** concord.
E P : 1 2 :012(499) [0841] is not a God-**pleasing** estate in the New Testament.
S D : P R :014(506) [0855] lasting, and God-**pleasing** concord within the church, it is
S D : 0 2 :010(522) [0883] through its wisdom, it **pleased** God through the folly of
S D : 0 2 :016(523) [0887] and learn anything **pleasing** to him and beneficial to us
S D : 0 2 :024(526) [0891] faith and other God-**pleasing** virtues and obedience in
S D : 0 2 :032(527) [0893] bear good fruit, and without faith no one can **please** God.
S D : 0 2 :043(529) [0897] to do and to think what **pleases** them and what is
S D : 0 2 :051(531) [0901] God through wisdom, it **pleased** God through the folly of
S D : 0 2 :071(535) [0909] faith and other God-**pleasing** virtues in us, so that they
S D : 0 2 :090(539) [0915] by doing that which is **pleasing** to God, in the manner and
S D : 0 3 :013(541) [0919] a work and so God-**pleasing** a virtue, but because it lays
S D : 0 3 :032(545) [0927] kind of life, a person is **pleasing** and acceptable to God
S D : 0 3 :033(545) [0927] a gracious God and was **pleasing** and acceptable to him to
S D : 0 4 :008(552) [0941] works of believers are **pleasing** and acceptable to God,
S D : 0 4 :008(552) [0941] The person must first be **pleasing** to God — and that
S D : 0 4 :008(552) [0941] Christ's sake — before that person's works are **pleasing**.
S D : 0 4 :009(552) [0941] the truly good and God-**pleasing** works that God will
S D : 0 4 :038(557) [0951] and God is willing to be **pleased** with them for Christ's
S D : 0 5 :017(561) [0957] and deeds in order to be **pleasing** and acceptable to God,
S D : 0 6 :004(564) [0963] will of God and what is **pleasing** to him is correctly
S D : 0 6 :022(567) [0969] a perfect and pure obedience if it is to **please** God.
S D : 0 6 :022(567) [0969] works of believers are **pleasing** to God, even though in
S D : 0 6 :023(568) [0969] self they do what is **pleasing** to God not by coercion of
S D : 0 7 :033(575) [0983] will not believe this, will **please** let me alone and expect
S D : 1 0 :029(615) [1061] done in deed or action to **please** enemies of the holy
S D : 1 1 :065(627) [1083] with whom I am well **pleased**; listen to him" (Luke 3:22).

Pleasure (32)

P R : P R :022(011) [0019] the issues, and take no **pleasure** in blasphemies against
P R : P R :024(013) [0023] with us, take Christian **pleasure** in this salutary, most
A G : 2 8 :002(081) [0085] depose kings and emperors according to their **pleasure**.
A P : P R :016(099) [0101] We take no **pleasure** in discord, nor are we indifferent to
A P : 0 4 :143(126) [0161] to the flesh, who take **pleasure** in their lusts and obey
A P : 1 2 :090(195) [0279] certainly give us no **pleasure**; therefore if we did not have
A P : 1 2 :094(196) [0281] Lord God, I have no **pleasure** in the death of the wicked,
A P : 1 2 :094(196) [0281] swearing that he has no **pleasure** in the death of the
A P : 2 8 :003(281) [0445] as though they took **pleasure** in the destruction of their
S 2 : 0 2 :009(294) [0465] it according to his own **pleasure** apart from the fellowship
S 2 : 0 4 :008(299) [0473] depend on the good **pleasure** of men rather than on a
S 3 : 0 8 :003(312) [0495] Scriptures or spoken Word according to their **pleasure**.
S C : 0 8 :010(354) [0559] of the horse, nor his **pleasure** in the legs of a man; but the
S C : 0 8 :010(354) [0559] man; but the Lord takes **pleasure** in those who fear him,
L C : 0 1 :018(367) [0585] for riches, happiness, **pleasure**, and a life of ease
L C : 0 1 :101(379) [0609] new understanding, new **pleasure**, and a new spirit of
L C : 0 1 :126(382) [0617] This will and **pleasure** of God ought to provide us
L C : 0 1 :132(383) [0619] is not only an object of **pleasure** and delight to himself,
L C : 0 1 :169(388) [0629] the parental office is a matter of your **pleasure** and whim.
L C : 0 1 :170(388) [0629] gave us children for our **pleasure** and amusement, gave us
L C : 0 1 :325(409) [0675] he says, "The Lord takes **pleasure** in those who fear him,
L C : 0 1 :325(409) [0675] to say, "The Lord takes **pleasure** in those who have no
L C : 0 2 :021(413) [0683] its own pride and greed, **pleasure** and enjoyment, and
S D : 0 2 :014(523) [0885] to will and to work for his good **pleasure**" (Phil. 2:13).
S D : 0 2 :049(530) [0901] "As I live, I have no **pleasure** in the death of the wicked,
S D : 0 8 :025(596) [1023] according to his good **pleasure**, when and how he wanted
S D : 1 1 :008(617) [1065] God's gracious will and **pleasure** in Christ Jesus it is also
S D : 1 1 :081(629) [1089] not will sin and has no **pleasure** in sin, so he also does
S D : 1 1 :081(629) [1089] death of a sinner and has no **pleasure** in his damnation.
S D : 1 1 :081(629) [1089] Lord God, I have no **pleasure** in the death of the wicked,
S D : 1 1 :084(630) [1091] it was God's good **pleasure** that he should be damned and
S D : 1 1 :084(630) [1091] perish," nor has he any "**pleasure** in the death of the

Pledge (8), Pledged (1), Pledges (2)

L C : 0 3 :057(428) [0713] to whom he offers and **pledges** so many inexpressible
L C : 0 5 :022(449) [0757] blessing to me as a sure **pledge** and sign — indeed, as the
E P : R N :003(465) [0777] We **pledge** ourselves to these, and we hereby reject all
E P : 0 7 :029(485) [0815] reminders, seals, and **pledges** to assure us that when our
S D : P R :004(502) [0847] teachers and hearers **pledged** themselves to these symbols
S D : P R :002(503) [0851] Rather, we **pledge** ourselves again to those public and
S D : P R :003(503) [0851] 1. We **pledge** ourselves to the prophetic and apostolic
S D : P R :004(504) [0851] of heretics, we further **pledge** allegiance to the three
S D : P R :006(504) [0853] We therefore unanimously **pledge** our adherence to this
S D : 0 7 :063(581) [0995] receive it as a certain **pledge** and assurance that their sins
S D : 0 7 :116(589) [1011] as through an external **pledge**, we are assured that our

Plenary (1)

A P : 0 7 :023(172) [0235] He must have **plenary** power in both the temporal and

Plenteous (1), Plenty (2)

A L : 2 6 :033(069) [0075] and labors, that neither **plenty** nor idleness may tempt
S 3 : 0 3 :008(304) [0481] for with God there is **plenteous** redemption (as Ps. 130:7
L C : 0 1 :012(366) [0583] that he may give them **plenty** of money, help them in love

Plight (3)

L C : 0 1 :120(382) [0615] This is the **plight** and the miserable blindness of the world
L C : 0 1 :299(405) [0665] without regard for equity or for our neighbor's **plight**.
L C : 0 3 :011(421) [0701] lament our misery and **plight**, and pray for grace and

Plot (1), Plots (1)

L C : 0 3 :031(424) [0707] parrying the counsels and **plots** of our enemies and
L C : 0 3 :069(429) [0717] do their worst, let them **plot** and plan how to suppress

Pluck (3)

E P : 1 1 :013(496) [0835] of our own, and that no one can **pluck** us out of his hand.
S D : 1 1 :046(624) [1079] Christ, out of which no one can **pluck** us (John 10:28).
S D : 1 1 :090(631) [1093] whose hand "no one can **pluck**" us (John 10:28;

Plunder (1), Plundered (1)

L C : 0 1 :230(396) [0645] and princes and daily **plunder** not only a city or two, but
L C : 0 1 :230(396) [0645] its retinue, which has **plundered** and stolen the treasures

Plunge (3), Plunged (2)

A P : 0 4 :157(128) [0165] vain and our consciences will then **plunge** into despair.
A P : 0 4 :327(158) [0211] my hands with lye, yet thou wilt **plunge** me into a pit."
L C : 0 4 :071(445) [0751] This is what it means to **plunge** into Baptism and daily
S D : 0 5 :023(562) [0959] all his descendants, and **plunged** them into death and
S D : 1 1 :007(617) [1065] "Israel, thou hast **plunged** thyself into misfortune, but in

Plural (1)

T R : 0 0 :023(324) [0511] is elsewhere given in the **plural** ("Whatever you bind"),

Pocket (1)

L C : 0 1 :224(395) [0643] a man's strongbox or his **pocket**, but also when he takes

Poenitentia (3)

A G : 2 5 :010(063) [0069] be seen in Dist. I, *De* ***poenitentia***, where these words of
A G : 2 5 :012(063) [0071] marginal note in *De* ***poenitentia***, Dist. 5, also teaches that
A L : 2 5 :012(063) [0071] marginal note in *De* ***poenitentia***, Dist. 5, in the chapter

Poet (2), Poets (1)

A P : 0 4 :185(132) [0173] the word of the ancient **poet** is true, "Being sick in itself,
A P : 0 4 :236(140) [0185] but not for others, as the **poet** writes, "I forgive myself,
A P : 0 7 :027(173) [0237] the rest as mythology, like the tragedies of the **poets**.

Point (58), Pointed (6), Pointing (3), Points (28)

P R : P R :017(008) [0015] doctrine or in the least **point** to depart from the Augsburg
A G : 2 8 :004(081) [0085] consciences, to **point** out the difference between spiritual
A G : 0 0 :003(095) [0095] in order that the chief **points** at issue may better be
A L : 2 5 :005(062) [0069] with our churches on this **point**, for even our adversaries
A L : 2 8 :034(086) [0087] assert, as has been **pointed** out above, that bishops do
A L : 0 0 :003(095) [0095] this sort so that the chief **points** at issue, being briefly set
A P : P R :004(098) [0099] give in to the opponents' **point** of view with a clear
A P : P R :006(098) [0101] had taken notes on the main **points** of its argumentation.
A P : P R :011(099) [0101] I have always made it a **point** to stick as closely as
A P : P R :018(099) [0103] blessing, that on many **points** our Confession's teaching is
A P : 0 2 :002(100) [0105] that our teaching on this **point** is not absurd, we ask them
A P : 0 4 :012(108) [0123] In this **point** of view there are many vicious errors that
A P : 0 4 :064(116) [0139] it brings forth good fruits, as we shall **point** out later.
A P : 0 4 :154(128) [0165] He **points** to the woman and praises her reverence, her
A P : 0 4 :323(157) [0209] But the **point** is well known and has many clear
A P : 0 4 :335(159) [0215] At this **point** our opponents make a marvelous play on
A P : 0 4 :344(160) [0217] At this **point** someone may say, "Hope will be uncertain
A P : 0 4 :388(166) [0225] possible here, we have **pointed** out the sources of this
A P : 0 9 :003(178) [0245] This **point** by itself can effectually confirm good and
A P : 1 2 :059(190) [0267] enough about this earlier, we shall be briefer at this **point**.
A P : 1 2 :166(208) [0303] Here the example of the Ninevites is a case in **point**.
A P : 1 2 :175(210) [0307] from the bishops, there is no **point** in such remissions.
A P : 1 4 :005(215) [0315] we want at this **point** to declare our willingness to keep
A P : 1 5 :010(216) [0317] From this **point** of view there is no difference between
A P : 1 8 :009(226) [0337] of the Holy Spirit; and it **points** out the need for the Holy
A P : 2 0 :011(228) [0341] rather than compose a **point**-by-point refutation.
A P : 2 0 :011(228) [0341] rather than compose a point-by-**point** refutation.
A P : 2 1 :037(234) [0355] There is no **point** in listing here the miracles they have
A P : 2 1 :040(235) [0355] At this **point**, and almost everywhere else, the
A P : 2 1 :042(235) [0355] the church at heart at this **point**, they would ask that our
A P : 2 3 :063(248) [0381] Paul **points** out the real author of such a law when he
A P : 2 4 :003(250) [0385] not want to belabor this **point**, but we leave it up to the
A P : 2 4 :003(250) [0385] only in passing in order to **point** out that our churches
A P : 2 4 :010(251) [0387] must deal only with the **point** at issue and not wander off
A P : 2 4 :010(251) [0387] opponents should be forced to discuss the **point** at issue.
A P : 2 4 :043(257) [0399] or console consciences or **point** out that sins are freely
A P : 2 7 :009(270) [0421] legitimate if they openly **point** to an evil end, either
A P : 2 7 :038(275) [0433] in his way of life, God **pointed** in a dream to a certain
A P : 2 7 :055(278) [0439] the hearers, brief and **pointed** lessons would be more
T R : 0 0 :062(330) [0523] in every town," and **points** out that these words are
T R : 0 0 :078(333) [0527] It is enough to have **pointed** out that there are many
S C : P R :017(340) [0537] petition, and part, **pointing** out their respective
L C : 0 1 :083(376) [0603] in this commandment, we **point** out that we keep holy
L C : 0 2 :012(412) [0681] the most necessary **points**, namely, as we have said, that
L C : 0 2 :032(414) [0687] explain all these different **points** is not the brief children's
L C : 0 2 :046(416) [0689] But since various **points** in it are not quite clear to the
L C : 0 3 :017(422) [0703] first and most important **point**, that all our prayers must

Continued ▶

LC : 0 3 :060(428) [0715] These two **points** embrace all that pertains to God's glory
LC : 0 3 :088(432) [0723] But the **point** here is for us to recognize and accept this
LC : 0 3 :091(432) [0723] ever in this life reach the **point** where he does not need
LC : 0 4 :022(439) [0737] This is the first **point** to be emphasized: the nature and
LC : 0 4 :053(443) [0745] perhaps, is a rather subtle **point**, but it is based upon
LC : 0 5 :043(451) [0763] sacrament, we shall devote a little attention to this **point**.
LC : 0 5 :053(453) [0765] This is the first **point**, especially for the benefit of the cold
LC : 0 5 :063(454) [0767] Let this suffice for the first **point**.
LC : 0 6 :017(459) [0000] people were driven to the **point** that everyone inevitably
LC : 0 6 :028(460) [0000] pope's command at any **point**, but you will compel
LC : 0 6 :032(460) [0000] If I bring you to this **point**, I have also brought you to
EP : 0 1 :007(467) [0781] These **points** clearly set forth the distinction between the
EP : 0 9 :004(492) [0827] to us not only this **point**, but many others as well, which
SD : PR :015(506) [0857] On this **point** we have reached a basic and mutual
SD : 0 1 :008(510) [0861] As the Smalcald Articles **point** out, it is something that
SD : 0 1 :015(511) [0863] These **points**, which we have given in summary form, are
SD : 0 1 :033(514) [0869] nature we are not able to **point** out and expose the nature
SD : 0 1 :039(515) [0871] At this **point** all Christian hearts may well ponder God's
SD : 0 1 :049(517) [0875] as far as the chief **points** in this controversy are
SD : 0 1 :049(517) [0875] but are treating only the chief **points** in summary fashion.
SD : 0 2 :018(524) [0887] it is evident, as we have **pointed** out at greater length in
SD : 0 2 :029(527) [0893] Spirit is given, and by **pointing** out that Christ helps us
SD : 0 2 :039(528) [0895] still in this life, reach the **point** where they desire to do
SD : 0 2 :044(529) [0897] takes up several disputed **points** which Erasmus raised
SD : 0 3 :029(544) [0925] At this **point** the main question with which we have to do
SD : 0 3 :033(545) [0927] At this **point** St. Paul's statement concerning Abraham is
SD : 0 3 :036(545) [0927] The **point** is that good works are excluded from the
SD : 0 3 :036(546) [0929] The same **points** should be urged with all diligence and
SD : 0 4 :007(552) [0939] concerning the following **points**: That it is God's will,
SD : 0 4 :013(553) [0943] But since on these **points** there has been no controversy
SD : 0 4 :013(553) [0943] explain only the controverted **points** simply and clearly.
SD : 0 4 :036(557) [0949] arose on this **point** which led to many offensive
SD : 0 5 :002(558) [0951] On this **point**, too, there has been a controversy among
SD : 0 5 :024(563) [0961] (Gal. 3:24), and hence **points** and leads not away from
SD : 0 7 :029(574) [0981] my faith before God and all the world, **point** by point.
SD : 0 7 :029(574) [0981] my faith before God and all the world, point by **point**.
SD : 0 7 :088(585) [1003] We must, however, also **point** out that the
SD : 0 7 :128(591) [1015] brevity we have not wanted to repeat them at this **point**.
SD : 0 8 :018(594) [1021] many testimonies on this **point** from the Fathers, if it
SD : 0 8 :035(598) [1027] it can be comprehended under three main **points**.
SD : 0 8 :042(599) [1029] must say that the person (**pointing** to Christ) suffers, dies.
SD : 0 8 :050(600) [1031] the testimony of the Scripture **points** in that direction.
SD : 0 8 :059(602) [1035] of Man, but expressly **points** to his assumed human
SD : 0 8 :079(607) [1045] doubly sure on this **point**, he instituted his Holy Supper
SD : 1 1 :003(616) [1063] teaching on this article consists of the following **points**:
SD : 1 1 :049(624) [1079] manner when he **points** out that before the world began
SD : 1 1 :052(625) [1081] thus far, there are many **points** in this mystery about
SD : 1 1 :064(626) [1083] soon as he comes to the **point** where he shows how much

Poison (11), Poisoned (8), Poisonous (2), Poisonously (1), Poisons (1)
S1 : PR :005(289) [0457] those (for they are all **poisoned**) who do not pay attention
S1 : PR :006(289) [0457] devil appears at once to **poison** and pervert everything by
S2 : 0 2 :011(294) [0465] a brood of vermin and the **poison** of manifold idolatries.
S3 : 0 8 :009(313) [0497] It is a **poison** implanted and inoculated in man by the old
LC : PR :014(360) [0571] a good antidote against their evil infection and **poison**.
LC : PR :019(361) [0573] diligence against the **poisonous** infection of such security
LC : 0 1 :289(404) [0663] defend him against the **poisonous** tongues of those who
LC : 0 3 :078(431) [0721] hail, fire, and flood; from **poison**, pestilence, and
LC : 0 3 :080(431) [0721] to destroy crops and cattle, why he **poisons** the air, etc.
LC : 0 5 :068(454) [0769] if the sacrament were a **poison** which would kill us if we
LC : 0 5 :070(454) [0769] as a precious antidote against the **poison** in their systems.
EP : 0 1 :017(468) [0783] with human nature, as when **poison** and wine are mixed.
SD : 0 1 :006(509) [0861] thoroughly and entirely **poisoned** and corrupted human
SD : 0 1 :012(510) [0863] inherited malady has so **poisoned** and tainted them that
SD : 0 1 :026(512) [0867] into man's nature, as when **poison** is blended with water.
SD : 0 1 :032(513) [0869] far as our nature has been **poisoned** and corrupted by sin.
SD : 0 1 :033(514) [0869] sin, like a spiritual **poison** and leprosy, has so poisoned
SD : 0 1 :033(514) [0869] and leprosy, has so **poisoned** and corrupted man's whole
SD : 0 1 :051(517) [0875] nature to bite and **poison**," the term "nature" means — as
SD : 0 1 :052(517) [0875] through sin man is corrupted, **poisoned**, and sinful.
SD : 0 1 :062(519) [0879] of original sin has **poisoned** us from the soles of our feet
SD : 0 2 :017(524) [0887] so miserably perverted, **poisoned**, and corrupted that by
SD : 0 7 :067(581) [0997] how unjustly and **poisonously** the Sacramentarian

Polemical (4), Polemics (1)
AP : 1 5 :042(221) [0327] In their **polemics** they even attack this most salutary part
SD : PR :009(505) [0853] in his doctrinal and **polemical** writings, but in the
SD : 0 7 :041(576) [0985] than from Dr. Luther's doctrinal and **polemical** writings.
SD : 0 7 :091(585) [1005] by Dr. Luther in his **polemical** writings, *Against the*
SD : 0 8 :003(592) [1017] as his doctrinal and **polemical** writings concerning the

Politic (3), Political (11), Politics (1)
AP : 0 4 :131(125) [0157] at the second table and **political** works; about the first
AP : 0 7 :014(170) [0231] physical well-being, **political** affairs, etc. in addition to
AP : 1 5 :043(221) [0327] spiritual kingdom) and **political** affairs, marriage, the
AP : 1 6 :000(222) [0329] [Article XVI. **Political** Order]
AP : 1 6 :002(222) [0329] between Christ's kingdom and a **political** kingdom.
AP : 1 6 :002(222) [0331] use of the legitimate **political** ordinances of the nation in
AP : 1 6 :013(224) [0333] this whole matter of **political** affairs so clearly that many
AP : 1 6 :013(224) [0333] good men involved in **politics** and in business have
AP : 2 7 :047(277) [0437] praises upon something that conflicts with **political** order.
AP : 2 8 :002(281) [0443] that we do not criticize **political** ordinances nor the gifts
S1 : PR :012(290) [0459] There is discord among princes and **political** estates.
LC : 0 3 :073(430) [0719] of our domestic and our civil or **political** affairs.
EP : 1 2 :002(498) [0839] church, or in the body **politic** and secular administration,
EP : 1 2 :011(499) [0841] *Intolerable Articles in the Body* ***Politic***
SD : 1 2 :009(633) [1097] the churches or in the body **politic** or in domestic society.

Polity (3)
AP : 1 4 :001(214) [0315] to maintain the church **polity** and various ranks of the
AP : 1 4 :005(215) [0315] and canonical **polity**, provided that the bishops stop
AP : 2 8 :012(283) [0447] according to canonical **polity**, to which we do not object.

Polluted (1)
SD : 1 1 :075(628) [1087] Would not that land be greatly **polluted**?

Pollux (1)
AP : 2 1 :032(233) [0351] off fever, and Castor and **Pollux** protected knights.

Polygamists (1)
AP : 2 3 :064(248) [0381] and Jacob, who were **polygamists**, was purer and less

Polyphemus (1)
AP : 2 1 :035(234) [0353] as though there had really been such a **Polyphemus**.

Pomerania (4)
PR : PR :019(009) [0017] [John Bugenhagen] of **Pomerania**, and others in so far as
S3 : 1 5 :005(316) [0501] Dr. John Bugenhagen, of **Pomerania**, subscribed
S3 : 1 5 :005(317) [0501] John Bugenhagen of **Pomerania**, again subscribe in the
TR : 0 0 :082(334) [0529] John Bugenhagen, of **Pomerania**, subscribe the articles of

Pomeranus (1)
TR : 0 0 :082(335) [0529] I, **Pomeranus**, again subscribe in the name of Master

Pommel (4), Pommeled (2)
AG : 2 6 :037(069) [0075] Paul said that he **pommeled** his body and subdued it, and
AL : 2 6 :037(069) [0075] Paul also said, "I **pommel** my body and subdue it."
AL : 2 6 :038(069) [0075] he clearly shows that he **pommeled** his body not to merit
AP : 1 5 :046(221) [0327] says (I Cor. 9:27), "I **pommel** my body and subdue it."
SD : 0 4 :019(554) [0945] flesh, Paul says, "I **pommel** my body and subdue it"
SD : 0 6 :009(565) [0965] And again, "I **pommel** my body and subdue it, lest after

Pomp (3), Pompous (2)
AP : 0 4 :283(150) [0201] the distinctions of foods, and similar **pompous** acts.
AP : 2 4 :052(259) [0403] especially when the **pomp** of the Old Testament
S2 : 0 2 :012(295) [0465] purgatory and all the **pomp**, services, and business
LC : 0 1 :313(407) [0671] are not unusual and **pompous**, restricted to special times,
LC : 0 1 :314(407) [0671] Aided by great **pomp**, splendor, and magnificent

Pompey (1)
AP : 0 4 :241(141) [0187] Gaius Caesar and **Pompey** certain minor disagreements

Ponder (7), Pondered (1)
AP : 2 4 :091(266) [0415] all the faithful if they **ponder** the fact that the Mass has
LC : PR :011(360) [0571] eagerly read, recite, **ponder**, and practice the Catechism,
LC : PR :019(361) [0573] to read and teach, to learn and meditate and **ponder**.
LC : 0 1 :044(370) [0593] Just **ponder** and heed them.
LC : 0 1 :092(377) [0607] heard, read, or **pondered**, there the person, the day, and
LC : 0 1 :101(379) [0609] hand, when we seriously **ponder** the Word, hear it, and
LC : 0 5 :065(454) [0769] **Ponder**, then, and include yourself personally in the "you"
SD : 0 1 :039(515) [0871] Christian hearts may well **ponder** God's inexpressible

Pontifex (1)
TR : 0 0 :038(326) [0515] priest was the supreme **pontifex** by divine right;

Pontiff (4), Pontiffs (15), Pontifical (4)
AL : 2 3 :012(052) [0063] to publish the Roman **pontiff**'s edict on this matter, was
AL : 2 7 :024(074) [0079] reason at all, the Roman **pontiffs** would not have granted
AL : 2 7 :025(074) [0079] But the Roman **pontiffs** have prudently judged that
AL : 2 8 :002(081) [0083] have resulted, while the **pontiffs**, relying on the power of
AL : 2 8 :040(087) [0089] have written, and the **pontiffs** seem in some measure to
AP : 0 7 :022(172) [0235] princes and supreme **pontiffs** as well as those in lesser
AP : 0 7 :023(172) [0235] in which the Roman **pontiff** must have unlimited power
AP : 1 2 :124(201) [0289] The Roman **pontiff** did not add anything to his dignity in
AP : 2 2 :017(238) [0361] or accepts whatever the **pontiffs** decide, especially when
AP : 2 3 :001(239) [0363] defense of the **pontifical** law, but they even urge the
AP : 2 3 :023(242) [0369] *Fourth*, the **pontifical** regulation also disagrees with the
AP : 2 3 :024(243) [0371] which the Roman **pontiffs** have set up since the ancient
AP : 2 3 :024(243) [0371] The **pontiffs** show contempt for the authority of the
AP : 2 3 :025(243) [0371] is peculiar to this new **pontifical** tyranny, and with good
AP : 2 3 :056(247) [0379] Daily the **pontiffs** dispense and change other good laws;
AP : 2 3 :060(247) [0379] in their defense of the **pontifical** law of perpetual
TR : 0 0 :021(323) [0509] primacy of the Roman **pontiff**, this dispute could not
TR : 0 0 :038(326) [0515] not be owing to those **pontiffs** who defend godless forms
TR : 0 0 :038(326) [0515] On the contrary, such **pontiffs** and such government
TR : 0 0 :039(327) [0515] manifest that the Roman **pontiffs** and their adherents
TR : 0 0 :049(329) [0519] much more impudently by the **pontiffs**, as examples show.
TR : 0 0 :056(329) [0521] church and not of the **pontiffs**, it is especially incumbent
TR : 0 0 :056(329) [0521] the license of the **pontiffs** and see to it that the church is

Pontius (3)
SC : 0 2 :003(345) [0545] *Mary, suffered under* ***Pontius*** *Pilate, was crucified, dead,*
LC : SP :012(363) [0577] Mary, suffered under **Pontius** Pilate, was crucified, dead,
LC : 0 2 :025(413) [0683] *Mary, suffered under* ***Pontius*** *Pilate, was crucified, dead,*

Poor (70)
PR : PR :004(004) [0009] their own errors, to divert **poor**, erring consciences from
PR : PR :022(012) [0021] and persecution of **poor**, oppressed Christians.
PR : PR :024(013) [0023] and instruction of **poor**, misguided consciences.
AG : 2 0 :019(043) [0055] heard in preaching, but **poor** consciences were driven to
AG : 2 0 :032(045) [0057] of the devil, who drives **poor** human beings into many
AP : 0 4 :236(140) [0185] Moreover, it comes in **poor** grace for our opponents to
AP : 0 4 :254(143) [0193] Matt. 5:3, "Blessed are the **poor** in spirit, for theirs is the
AP : 0 4 :262(145) [0195] righteousness and your iniquities by favor to the **poor**."
AP : 0 4 :262(145) [0195] do good and to defend the **poor** against injustice, as was
AP : 1 6 :008(223) [0331] How **poor** the judgment of many writers in these matters
AP : 2 3 :059(247) [0379] submit, and the exile of **poor** women and orphaned
AP : 2 4 :016(252) [0389] really call our opponents "**poor** cooks," for they despise
AP : 2 4 :086(265) [0413] to be consecrated, the rest was distributed to the **poor**.
AP : 2 7 :045(277) [0435] you possess and give to the **poor**; and come, follow me."
AP : 2 7 :046(277) [0435] Thus David was **poor** in a very rich kingdom.
AP : 2 7 :059(279) [0441] Though they were **poor** in everything, the Rechabites
S1 : PR :004(289) [0457] my labor and thus mislead the **poor** people in my name.
S1 : PR :010(290) [0457] the canons care how the **poor** people live or die, although
S1 : PR :015(291) [0459] But help us, **poor** and wretched souls who cry unto Thee

Continued ▶

S 3 : 0 3 :018(306) [0483] A **poor** sinner who reflected on his lust or revenge in this
S 3 : 0 3 :024(307) [0485] came to the aid of the **poor** church and invented
S 3 : 0 3 :029(308) [0487] sell their superfluous righteousness to other **poor** sinners?
S 3 : 0 8 :002(312) [0495] not be untruthful if we say, "I am a **poor** man, full of sin.
T R : 0 0 :080(334) [0527] education, the care of the **poor**, and the establishment of
S C : 0 5 :022(350) [0553] "I, a **poor** sinner, confess before God that I am guilty of
L C : 0 1 :046(370) [0593] on the other hand, was a **poor**, despised man, hunted
L C : 0 1 :086(376) [0605] for the sake of the young and the **poor** common people.
L C : 0 1 :108(379) [0611] that, however lowly, **poor**, feeble, and eccentric they may
L C : 0 1 :111(380) [0613] are old, sick, feeble, or **poor**; all this you should do not
L C : 0 1 :118(381) [0615] What will become of these **poor** wretched people when,
L C : 0 1 :145(385) [0623] be impressed upon the **poor** people, a servant girl would
L C : 0 1 :216(394) [0641] indeed, all **poor**, captive consciences deceived by their
L C : 0 1 :240(397) [0649] Daily the **poor** are defrauded.
L C : 0 1 :246(398) [0651] how you deal with the **poor**, of whom there are many
L C : 0 1 :247(398) [0651] If, when you meet a **poor** man who must live from hand
L C : 0 1 :247(398) [0651] God, who watches over **poor**, sorrowful hearts, and he
L C : 0 1 :249(398) [0651] in order that the **poor** may not be burdened and
L C : 0 1 :252(399) [0653] "He who is kind to the **poor** lends to the Lord, and he
L C : 0 1 :257(399) [0653] courts of justice, where a **poor**, innocent man is accused
L C : 0 1 :258(399) [0653] Consequently, a **poor** man is inevitably oppressed, loses
L C : 0 1 :273(401) [0659] would bring some **poor** man into disgrace, from which he
L C : 0 1 :314(407) [0671] But when a **poor** girl tends a little child, or faithfully does
L C : 0 2 :030(414) [0685] He has snatched us, **poor** lost creatures, from the jaws of
L C : 0 3 :057(427) [0713] emperor who bade a **poor** beggar to ask for whatever he
L C : 0 3 :067(429) [0717] and overcome, so that our **poor** flesh may not yield or
L C : 0 3 :072(430) [0717] Here we consider the **poor** bread-basket — the needs of
L C : 0 3 :084(431) [0723] who wantonly oppress the **poor** and deprive them of their
L C : 0 3 :086(432) [0723] This petition has to do with our **poor**, miserable life.
L C : 0 3 :121(436) [0731] I am only a **poor** sinner," etc.
L C : 0 5 :061(453) [0767] the contrary, we come as **poor**, miserable men, precisely
L C : 0 5 :084(456) [0773] twice as low as any other **poor** sinner and are much in
L C : 0 6 :023(459) [0000] rejoice and act like a **poor** miserable beggar who hears
L C : 0 6 :024(460) [0000] just letting everyone see how **poor** and miserable he is?
L C : 0 6 :026(460) [0000] we advise: If you are **poor** and miserable, then go and
E P : 0 3 :001(472) [0791] Confession that we **poor** sinners are justified before God
S D : 0 1 :023(512) [0865] only a small, limited, and **poor** degree — such as the
S D : 0 2 :022(525) [0889] and pure grace, that our **poor**, fallen, and corrupted
S D : 0 3 :001(539) [0917] through faith reckons to **poor** sinners as righteousness.
S D : 0 3 :006(540) [0917] "without which no **poor** conscience can have any abiding
S D : 0 3 :009(540) [0919] described above, that a **poor** sinner is justified before God
S D : 0 3 :036(545) [0927] of the justification of **poor** sinners before God they should
S D : 0 3 :054(549) [0935] gracious acceptance of **poor** sinners on account of the
S D : 0 3 :058(550) [0937] his death in the stead of us **poor** sinners, and thus covered
S D : 0 8 :040(599) [1029] me, then Christ would be a **poor** Saviour for me, in fact,
S D : 0 8 :084(607) [1045] And he would remain a **poor** Christ for me if he were
S D : 0 8 :087(608) [1047] unveiled deity, which to us **poor** sinners is like a
S D : 1 1 :077(629) [1089] Every **poor** sinner must therefore attend on it, hear it with
S D : 1 1 :089(631) [1093] but invites and calls all **poor**, burdened, and heavy-laden
S D : 1 1 :096(632) [1095] error but will lead the **poor** sinner to true and sincere
S D : 1 2 :008(633) [1097] reigned, and where the **poor**, simple people, who were

Pope (114), Popes (12)
A G : P R :016(026) [0041] would diligently urge it upon the **pope** to call a council.
A G : P R :019(026) [0041] Imperial Majesty and the **pope** were improving and were
A G : P R :019(026) [0041] Majesty was sure that the **pope** would not refuse to call a
A G : P R :020(026) [0041] a general council by the **pope**, along with Your Imperial
A G : 2 2 :007(050) [0061] **Pope** Gelasius himself ordered that the sacrament was not
A G : 2 3 :012(053) [0063] and indecently that the **pope** at the time not only forbade
A G : 2 3 :013(053) [0063] to the canons which the **popes** had themselves made and
A G : 2 3 :002(053) [0063] shows, even one of the **popes**, Pius II, often said and
A G : 2 3 :002(053) [0063] There is no doubt that **Pope** Pius, as a prudent and
A G : 2 7 :024(074) [0079] obligation of a vow, the **popes** could not have dispensed
A G : 2 7 :025(074) [0079] Consequently the **popes** were well aware that some
A L : 2 2 :007(050) [0061] In fact, **Pope** Gelasius commanded that the sacrament
A L : 2 3 :002(051) [0061] On this account **Pope** Pius is reported to have said that
A L : 2 3 :013(053) [0063] both those made by the **popes** and those made by the
A L : 2 6 :044(070) [0075] unity in faith," and **Pope** Gregory indicates in Dist. 12
A P : 0 4 :282(149) [0201] Just so some **pope** — I am not sure which — said that
A P : 0 4 :390(166) [0225] everything that the **pope** or cardinals or bishops or some
A P : 0 7 :023(172) [0235] him, so now this right has been transferred to the **pope**.
A P : 0 7 :023(172) [0235] Therefore the **pope** must be lord of the whole world, of
A P : 0 7 :025(173) [0235] the power of the Roman **pope** for which no one has ever
A P : 0 7 :025(173) [0235] in him and not through devotions invented by the **pope**.
A P : 0 7 :027(173) [0235] that be transferred to the **popes** which is the prerogative
A P : 1 2 :066(191) [0271] Neither to the **pope** nor to the church do we grant the
A P : 2 3 :023(242) [0369] of the synods but the private judgment of the **popes**.
A P : 2 3 :052(246) [0377] danger, but none of the **popes** listened to these
S 1 : P R :001(288) [0455] **Pope** Paul III called a council to meet in Mantua last
S 1 : P R :002(288) [0455] of our faith if the **pope** and his adherents ever became so
S 1 : P R :002(289) [0455] free council, as indeed the **pope** is in duty bound to do.
S 1 : P R :003(289) [0455] for they perceive that the **pope** prefers to see all
S 1 : P R :015(291) [0459] The **pope** and his adherents are lost.
S 2 : 0 1 :005(292) [0463] and practice against the **pope**, the devil, and the world.
S 2 : 0 1 :005(292) [0463] all is lost, and the **pope**, the devil, and all our adversaries
S 2 : 0 2 :017(296) [0467] Moreover, the **pope** gave his approval to these things as
S 2 : 0 2 :019(296) [0467] devil has possessed the **pope** to praise and approve of
S 2 : 0 2 :024(296) [0469] money) and by which the **pope** sells the merits of Christ
S 2 : 0 2 :024(296) [0469] not by the power of the **pope** but by the preaching of
S 2 : 0 4 :001(298) [0471] The **pope** is not the head of all Christendom by divine
S 2 : 0 4 :001(298) [0471] The **pope** is only the bishop and pastor of the churches in
S 2 : 0 4 :002(298) [0471] no bishop dares to call the **pope** "brother," as was then
S 2 : 0 4 :003(298) [0471] that all the things that the **pope** has undertaken and done
S 2 : 0 4 :004(298) [0473] All the **pope**'s bulls and books, in which he roars like a
S 2 : 0 4 :004(299) [0473] he is obedient to the **pope** and submits to him in all that
S 2 : 0 4 :004(299) [0473] holy church was without a **pope** for more that five
S 2 : 0 4 :004(299) [0473] have never been under the **pope** and are not at the
S 2 : 0 4 :006(299) [0473] the church must continue to exist without the **pope**.
S 2 : 0 4 :007(299) [0473] Suppose that the **pope** would renounce the claim that he
S 2 : 0 4 :007(299) [0473] with reference to the **popes** when it deposed three and
S 2 : 0 4 :007(299) [0473] If, I say, the **pope** and the see of Rome were to concede
S 2 : 0 4 :009(300) [0475] Christendom, until the **pope** raised his head over them
S 2 : 0 4 :010(300) [0475] demonstration that the **pope** is the real Antichrist who
S 2 : 0 4 :010(300) [0475] against Christ, for the **pope** will not permit Christians to
S 2 : 0 4 :012(300) [0475] However, the **pope** will not permit such faith but asserts
S 2 : 0 4 :014(301) [0475] When the teaching of the **pope** is distinguished from that
S 2 : 0 4 :014(301) [0475] best, the teaching of the **pope** has been taken from the
S 2 : 0 4 :014(301) [0475] is most diabolical for the **pope** to promote his lies about
S 2 : 0 4 :014(301) [0475] suffer his apostle, the **pope** or Antichrist, to govern us as
S 2 : 0 4 :016(301) [0477] we shall stand before the **pope** and the devil himself, who
S 3 : 0 0 :000(302) [0477] The **pope** and his court do not care much about these
S 3 : 0 3 :024(307) [0485] a hundred days, but the **pope** reserved for himself alone
S 3 : 0 3 :025(307) [0485] became profitable, the **pope** invented the jubilee year and
S 3 : 0 3 :025(307) [0485] The **popes** went further and quickly multiplied the jubilee
S 3 : 0 3 :026(307) [0485] Finally the **popes** forced their way into purgatory, first by
S 3 : 0 3 :027(307) [0487] however, for although the **pope** taught the people to rely
S 3 : 0 3 :027(307) [0487] So the **pope** took the money, consoled the people with his
S 3 : 0 3 :039(309) [0489] we overthrow the **pope** and everything that is built on our
S 3 : 0 3 :041(309) [0491] about which the **pope**, the theologians, the jurists, and all
S 3 : 0 8 :004(312) [0495] but enthusiasm, for the **pope** boasts that "all laws are in
S 3 : 0 9 :000(314) [0497] excommunication, as the **pope** calls it, to be merely a
S 3 : 1 5 :004(316) [0501] Finally, there remains the **pope**'s bag of magic tricks
S 3 : 1 5 :005(316) [0501] However, concerning the **pope** I hold that, if he would
T R : 0 0 :000(319) [0503] Treatise on the Power and Primacy of the **Pope**
T R : 0 0 :005(320) [0503] They mean that the **pope** is the universal bishop or, as
T R : 0 0 :020(323) [0509] 11. Finally, how can the **pope** be over the whole church
T R : 0 0 :033(325) [0513] which claim that the **pope** is by divine right lord of the
T R : 0 0 :034(325) [0513] be that external government which the **pope** had set up.
T R : 0 0 :035(325) [0513] Then the **popes** began to seize kingdoms for themselves,
T R : 0 0 :035(326) [0513] throne is vacant, the **pope** is the legitimate successor."
T R : 0 0 :036(326) [0515] So the **pope** not only usurped dominion contrary to the
T R : 0 0 :036(326) [0515] that such dominion belongs to the **pope** by divine right.
T R : 0 0 :038(326) [0515] clearly teach that a heretical **pope** is not to be obeyed.
T R : 0 0 :039(327) [0515] coincide with those of the **pope**'s kingdom and his
T R : 0 0 :040(327) [0515] it is manifest that the **pope** rules in the church and that he
T R : 0 0 :040(327) [0515] hand, the doctrine of the **pope** conflicts in many ways
T R : 0 0 :040(327) [0515] with the Gospel, and the **pope** arrogates to himself a
T R : 0 0 :040(327) [0517] Third, because the **pope** is unwilling to be judged by the
T R : 0 0 :041(327) [0517] doctrines, blasphemies, and unjust cruelties of the **pope**.
T R : 0 0 :041(327) [0517] abandon and execrate the **pope** and his adherents as the
T R : 0 0 :042(328) [0517] The errors of the **pope**'s kingdom are manifest, and the
T R : 0 0 :044(328) [0517] corrupted by the **pope** and his adherents, who teach that
T R : 0 0 :049(328) [0519] The first is that the **pope** defends these errors with savage
T R : 0 0 :049(328) [0519] The other is that the **pope** wrests judgment from the
T R : 0 0 :051(329) [0519] Thus the **pope** exercises a twofold tyranny: he defends his
T R : 0 0 :052(329) [0519] enormous errors of the **pope**'s kingdom and his tyranny.
T R : 0 0 :055(329) [0521] Even if the **pope** should hold synods, how can the church
T R : 0 0 :055(329) [0521] be purified as long as the **pope** does not permit anything
T R : 0 0 :056(330) [0521] to censure the rest of the **pope**'s errors, so they ought also
T R : 0 0 :056(330) [0521] ought also to rebuke the **pope** when he evades and
T R : 0 0 :058(330) [0521] The errors of the **pope** are manifest, and they are not
T R : 0 0 :058(330) [0521] for not submitting to the **pope**, and these urgent reasons
T R : 0 0 :059(330) [0521] those who agree with the **pope** and defend his doctrines
T R : 0 0 :059(330) [0521] of the godly whom the **pope** persecutes, detract from the
T R : 0 0 :079(333) [0527] who are adherents of the **pope** defend impious doctrines
T R : 0 0 :079(333) [0527] support the cruelty of the **pope**; since, in addition, they
T R : 0 0 :082(334) [0529] the primacy of the **pope** and the power and jurisdiction
S C : P R :011(339) [0535] be turned over to the **pope** and his officials, and even to
S C : P R :021(340) [0537] from the tyranny of the **pope**, they are unwilling to
S C : P R :024(341) [0539] you are not to make a law of this, as the **pope** has done.
S C : P R :026(341) [0539] something different from what it was under the **pope**.
L C : 0 1 :284(403) [0661] we now censure the **pope** and his teaching, which is
L C : 0 4 :009(437) [0733] it a great thing when the **pope** dispensed indulgences with
L C : 0 5 :040(451) [0761] the Gospel, now that the **pope**'s nonsense has been
L C : 0 5 :048(452) [0765] or time" (although the **pope** afterward perverted it and
L C : 0 5 :055(453) [0765] the old order under the **pope** when we tortured ourselves
L C : 0 6 :001(457) [0000] it should be voluntary and purged of the **pope**'s tyranny.
L C : 0 6 :005(457) [0000] ought to remain under the **pope** and submit to being
L C : 0 6 :006(457) [0000] but we shall let the **pope** or his like bring them back into
L C : 0 6 :021(459) [0000] Hereby we abolish the **pope**'s tyranny, commandments,
L C : 0 6 :025(460) [0000] In the same way the **pope**'s preachers have in the past
L C : 0 6 :028(460) [0000] my compulsion nor the **pope**'s command at any point,
S D : P R :003(502) [0847] in controversy between them and the **pope**'s adherents.
S D : P R :007(505) [0853] to an understanding with the **pope** about these matters.
S D : 1 0 :020(614) [1059] primacy or lordship of the **pope**, the Smalcald Articles
S D : 1 0 :020(614) [1059] suffer his apostle, the **pope** or Antichrist, to govern us as
S D : 1 0 :021(614) [1059] Power and Primacy of the **Pope**, which constitutes an
S D : 1 0 :022(615) [1061] doctrines, blasphemies, and unjust cruelties of the **pope**.
S D : 1 0 :022(615) [1061] abandon and execrate the **pope** and his adherents as the

Popish (1)
S D : P R :001(501) [0847] holy memory, and the **popish** errors, abuses, and idolatry

Popular (2)
A P : 2 1 :028(232) [0351] of the matter is that in **popular** estimation the blessed
A P : 2 4 :028(254) [0393] also condemn the **popular** notion of worship *ex opere*

Portion (2)
L C : 0 1 :212(394) [0641] may have his allotted **portion** and be satisfied with it —
S D : 0 6 :009(565) [0965] length in the summer **portion** of the Church Postil, on the

Portray (1), Portrayed (2)
L C : 0 2 :010(412) [0679] How can we praise or **portray** or describe him in such a
L C : 0 2 :035(415) [0687] In it is expressed and **portrayed** the Holy Spirit and his
S D : 0 6 :004(564) [0963] of God and what is pleasing to him is correctly **portrayed**.

Posed (1)
L C : 0 1 :305(406) [0669] was still living, and yet **posed** as an honorable, upright

Posit (2), Posited (2)
A L : 0 1 :005(028) [0043] of the Manichaeans, who **posited** two principles, one
S D : 0 3 :039(546) [0929] are they to be made and **posited** to be a part or a cause of
S D : 0 7 :101(587) [1007] You must **posit** this essence of Christ since he is one
S D : 0 7 :101(587) [1007] them, and you must **posit** it again as deep and as near in

Position (45), Positions (4)
A G : P R :023(027) [0043] be turned aside from our **position** by these or any

Continued ▶

A P : P R :011(099) [0101] contemporaries still further from the opponents' **position**.
A P : 0 2 :011(102) [0109] cannot see the foolishness of our opponents' **position**?
A P : 0 2 :038(105) [0115] argue with Augustine if this **position** displeases them!
A P : 0 4 :029(111) [0129] We have proof for this **position** of ours not only in the
A P : 0 4 :104(122) [0151] clearly support our **position**; he denies justification to
A P : 0 4 :244(141) [0189] to contradict our **position** more, but the answer is easy
A P : 0 4 :252(143) [0191] nothing contrary to our **position**, so we maintain the
A P : 0 4 :286(150) [0201] These passages do not conflict with our **position**.
A P : 0 4 :376(164) [0223] in our opponents' **position**, that by interpreting such
A P : 0 7 :016(171) [0231] for they held high **positions** and they sacrificed and
A P : 0 7 :022(172) [0235] reason of their power or **position**, whether ecclesiastical
A P : 1 0 :002(179) [0247] the Greek Church has taken and still takes this **position**.
A P : 1 2 :004(183) [0253] the defense of our **position**, we must say something by
A P : 1 2 :066(191) [0271] church in support of our **position**: "To him all the
A P : 1 2 :084(194) [0277] doubt that this is Paul's **position** that we are defending:
A P : 1 2 :084(194) [0277] means; we know that this **position** of ours brings devout
A P : 1 2 :136(203) [0293] from our opponents' **position**, these passages will have to
A P : 1 3 :016(213) [0311] to speak, a more exalted **position**, this would move men
A P : 1 5 :026(219) [0323] up their administrative **positions** in the government and
A P : 1 6 :009(224) [0333] wealthy and held high **positions**, Abraham, David, and
A P : 1 6 :013(224) [0333] We have repeated our **position** here so that those outside
A P : 2 1 :043(235) [0357] helps neither their **position** nor the church, and good men
A P : 2 2 :009(237) [0359] one part: to elevate the **position** of the clergy by a
A P : 2 3 :004(239) [0365] you learn that for our **position** we have the most serious
A P : 2 3 :006(240) [0365] have thought up some subterfuges to satirize our **position**.
A P : 2 3 :069(249) [0383] previously stated our **position** in the Jovinian controversy
A P : 2 3 :070(249) [0383] the princes to take a **position** contrary to the judgment of
A P : 2 4 :010(251) [0387] into side issues, like wrestlers fighting for their **position**.
A P : 2 4 :011(251) [0387] we have stated our **position** that the Lord's Supper does
A P : 2 4 :012(251) [0387] This **position** is established and proved by the
A P : 2 4 :033(256) [0395] therefore he does not refute our **position** but supports it.
A P : 2 4 :053(259) [0403] the main proofs for our **position** are in the Epistle to the
A P : 2 4 :080(264) [0411] Thus it squares with our **position** that a minister who
A P : 2 4 :096(267) [0417] comparing them with our **position** they try to crush us.
A P : 2 8 :003(281) [0443] opponents valiantly defend their own **position** and wealth.
A P : 2 8 :019(284) [0449] that supports our **position** and contains the deepest kind
S 2 : 0 4 :001(298) [0471] to God's Word, for this **position** belongs only to one,
S C : 0 9 :005(355) [0561] and all who are in high **positions**, that we may lead a
L C : 0 1 :026(368) [0587] all people placed in the **position** of neighbors — have
L C : 0 1 :259(400) [0655] and powerful who are in a **position** to help or harm him.
S D : P R :013(506) [0855] for just as we base our **position** on the Word of God as
S D : P R :020(507) [0857] to compare our present **position** with the aforementioned
S D : 0 2 :033(527) [0893] scriptural basis for the **position** that the Holy Spirit and
S D : 0 2 :086(538) [0913] discussion that this **position** does not conform to the form
S D : 0 7 :001(568) [0971] the Sacramentarians' **position** and against their own
S D : 0 7 :020(572) [0979] and confirms this **position** at greater length from the
S D : 0 7 :042(576) [0985] Thus the **position** set forth above rests on a unique, firm,
S D : 1 2 :006(633) [1097] wanted to set forth our **position** so clearly that our very

Possess (24), Possessed (4), Possesses (16), Possessing (1), Possession (10), Possessions (20)
P R : P R :018(008) [0015] informed and **possess** final certainty as to which Christian
A G : 1 6 :002(037) [0051] sell, take required oaths, **possess** property, be married,
A G : 1 7 :005(039) [0051] and godly men will **possess** a worldly kingdom and
A G : 1 8 :001(039) [0051] among us that man **possesses** some measure of freedom of
A G : 2 0 :023(044) [0055] spoken of is not that **possessed** by the devil and the
A G : 2 0 :025(044) [0057] it such knowledge as the devil and ungodly men **possess**.
A G : 2 0 :026(045) [0057] knowledge of historical events as the devil also **possesses**.
A G : 2 7 :031(076) [0079] this age one does not **possess** sufficient understanding to
A G : 2 7 :053(079) [0083] he can keep his **possessions** and engage in business
A G : 2 8 :019(083) [0087] In cases where bishops **possess** temporal authority and
A G : 2 8 :019(083) [0087] and the sword, they **possess** it not as bishops by divine
A L : 1 7 :005(039) [0051] dead the godly will take **possession** of the kingdom of the
A L : 2 7 :053(079) [0083] when they keep their **possessions** or engage in business.
A P : 0 7 :050(178) [0245] to priests the right to hold property or other **possessions**.
A P : 1 6 :011(224) [0333] of ownership and commands everyone to **possess** his own.
A P : 2 3 :043(245) [0375] commands each one to **possess** his vessel in holiness
A P : 2 3 :065(248) [0381] and of what Paul calls **possessing** one's vessel in holiness
A P : 2 7 :042(276) [0435] service to God to leave **possessions**, friends, wife, and
A P : 2 7 :045(277) [0435] perfect, go, sell what you **possess** and give to the poor;
A P : 2 7 :045(277) [0435] consists in casting off **possessions** and the control of
A P : 2 7 :046(277) [0435] control, and **possession** of property are civil ordinances,
A P : 2 7 :059(279) [0439] neither had any **possessions** nor drank any wine.
S 2 : 0 2 :006(293) [0463] even if it actually **possessed** some value in and of itself.
S 2 : 0 2 :009(294) [0465] which is the common **possession** of the church, to meet
S 2 : 0 2 :019(296) [0467] because the devil has **possessed** the pope to praise and
S 3 : 0 1 :004(302) [0477] and that man by nature **possesses** a right understanding
S 3 : 0 3 :043(310) [0491] the fact that they still **possess** and feel original sin and
S 3 : 0 8 :003(312) [0495] who boast that they **possess** the Spirit without and before
S 3 : 1 5 :005(316) [0501] the bishops which he **possesses** by human right, making
T R : 0 0 :002(320) [0503] that by divine right he **possesses** both swords, that is, the
T R : 0 0 :024(324) [0511] the church especially **possesses** the right of vocation.
T R : 0 0 :031(325) [0513] right to establish, take **possession** of, or transfer the
T R : 0 0 :031(325) [0513] sent to wield a sword or **possess** a worldly kingdom, for
T R : 0 0 :038(326) [0515] bishop of Rome should **possess** primacy and superiority
T R : 0 0 :057(330) [0521] the bishop of Rome did **possess** the primacy by divine
T R : 0 0 :069(331) [0525] which, since it alone **possesses** the priesthood, certainly
T R : 0 0 :080(334) [0527] Wherefore they cannot **possess** these alms with a good
S C : 0 1 :014(343) [0541] nor bring them into our **possession** by dishonest trade or
S C : 0 1 :018(344) [0541] by craftiness to gain **possession** of our neighbor's
L C : S P :002(362) [0575] Whoever does not **possess** it should not be reckoned
L C : 0 1 :006(365) [0581] that is, money and **possessions** — on which he fixes his
L C : 0 1 :010(366) [0583] because of such **possessions**, and how despondent when
L C : 0 1 :012(366) [0583] cattle, recover lost **possessions**, etc., as magicians and
L C : 0 1 :068(374) [0599] they miserably perished, body, soul, and **possessions**.
L C : 0 1 :111(380) [0613] is, with your body and **possessions**), serving them, helping
L C : 0 1 :200(392) [0637] In no **possession** of his can we inflict a greater injury
L C : 0 1 :223(395) [0643] us to rob or pilfer the **possessions** of our neighbor.
L C : 0 1 :237(397) [0647] were lords over others' **possessions** and entitled to
L C : 0 1 :243(397) [0649] every day that no stolen or ill-gotten **possession** thrives.
L C : 0 1 :250(399) [0651] or interfering with his **possessions** and property.
L C : 0 1 :256(399) [0653] than of his money and **possessions**; he would have every
L C : 0 1 :294(404) [0665] property, the same as his cattle and other **possessions**.
L C : 0 1 :296(405) [0665] withholding another's **possessions** to which you have no
L C : 0 1 :300(405) [0667] honor and right when it comes to acquiring **possessions**.
L C : 0 1 :308(406) [0669] have to leave you in **possession** of it, but God will not,
L C : 0 2 :019(412) [0681] since everything we **possess**, and everything in heaven and
L C : 0 2 :051(417) [0691] It **possesses** a variety of gifts, yet is united in love without
L C : 0 2 :052(417) [0691] participant and co-partner in all the blessings it **possesses**.
L C : 0 3 :055(427) [0713] treasure and everything that God himself **possesses**.
L C : 0 3 :065(429) [0717] all he has on earth — **possessions**, honor, house and
L C : 0 3 :075(430) [0719] whom we enjoy our **possessions** in peace and quietness,
E P : 0 2 :001(469) [0785] What powers does man **possess** in spiritual matters after
E P : 0 8 :016(488) [0821] to the personal union he always **possessed** this majesty.
E P : 1 2 :014(499) [0841] to use the power that it **possesses** and that it has received
E P : 1 2 :017(499) [0841] good conscience hold or **possess** private property but is in
E P : 1 2 :021(499) [0841] both natures in Christ **possess** only one divine essence,
S D : 0 1 :012(510) [0863] to reason man still **possesses** a measure of reason, power,
S D : 0 2 :036(528) [0895] and partaker in it of all the goods which it **possesses**.
S D : 0 3 :032(544) [0927] Christ have been justified **possess** in this life, first, the
S D : 0 3 :035(545) [0927] persons and believers **possess** the beginning of renewal,
S D : 0 7 :119(590) [1013] "Christ must take **possession** of heaven," to read
S D : 0 8 :012(593) [1019] in Christ not only **possesses** and retains its natural,
S D : 0 8 :054(601) [1033] nature in and by itself **possesses** all the created gifts which
S D : 1 2 :022(634) [1099] good conscience hold or **possess** private property but is
S D : 1 2 :026(635) [1099] essentially God but only **possesses** more and greater gifts

Possible (41), Possibly (3), Possibility (2)
P R : P R :024(013) [0023] errors, the only **possible** consequence of which is that
A G : 2 6 :012(065) [0071] for it was not **possible** to keep all the traditions, and yet
A G : 2 7 :027(075) [0079] must involve what is **possible** and voluntary and must be
A G : 2 8 :049(089) [0091] Is it **possible** that the Holy Spirit warned against them for
A L : 1 1 :002(034) [0047] necessary, for this is not **possible** according to the Psalm,
A L : 2 0 :036(046) [0057] human nature cannot **possibly** do the works of the First
A L : 2 8 :068(093) [0093] It is not **possible** to counsel consciences unless this
A P : P R :011(099) [0101] to stick as closely as **possible** to traditional doctrinal
A P : 0 2 :003(101) [0105] in God but also of the **possibility** and gift to produce it.
A P : 0 4 :130(125) [0157] Although it is somewhat **possible** to do civil works, that
A P : 0 4 :232(139) [0185] mutual aid, for it is not **possible** to preserve tranquility
A P : 0 4 :264(146) [0195] the forgiveness of sins is **possible**, that sins can be
A P : 0 4 :298(153) [0205] argument can anybody **possibly** bring against this proof
A P : 0 4 :310(155) [0207] and reborn. The greatest **possible** comfort comes from
A P : 0 4 :388(166) [0225] As much as was **possible** here, we have pointed out the
A P : 1 2 :009(183) [0255] these two motives is **possible**, but in fact they are not so
A P : 1 2 :113(199) [0285] public evidence of their penitence, as far as was **possible**.
A P : 1 2 :174(210) [0307] and hatred, the greatest **possible** generosity to the needy,
A P : 1 3 :013(212) [0311] of the Word with every **possible** kind of praise in
A P : 1 5 :052(222) [0329] believed that the greatest **possible** public harmony,
A P : 2 1 :041(235) [0355] ought to be as clear and plain as **possible** in the church.
A P : 2 2 :009(237) [0359] To put it as mildly as **possible**, this is a human device and
A P : 2 3 :019(242) [0369] If continence were **possible** for everyone, it would not
A P : 2 3 :064(248) [0381] It is **possible** that the heart of married men like Abraham
A P : 2 4 :067(261) [0407] whole matter as clear as **possible**, we shall say about the
A P : 2 8 :018(284) [0449] We do not see what **possible** objection there can be to
S 1 : P R :001(288) [0455] to serve as a basis for **possible** deliberations and to
S 2 : 0 2 :010(294) [0465] Even if it were **possible** for the papists to make
S 2 : 0 2 :010(294) [0465] articles, it would not be **possible** for them to yield on this
T R : 0 0 :016(322) [0509] impossible, for it is not **possible** for one bishop to be the
S C : 0 7 :003(352) [0557] After singing a hymn (**possibly** a hymn on the Ten
L C : S P :028(365) [0581] one and in the plainest **possible** manner say about them
L C : 0 1 :201(392) [0637] Youths were married at the earliest age **possible**.
L C : 0 1 :212(393) [0641] implanted it, it is not **possible** to remain chaste outside of
L C : 0 2 :040(416) [0689] Learn this article, then, as clearly as **possible**.
L C : 0 3 :065(429) [0715] on their inflicting every **possible** misfortune and grief
L C : 0 3 :087(432) [0723] petitions, so that it is not **possible** always to stand firm in
L C : 0 5 :082(456) [0773] be glad to come to the sacrament as often as **possible**.
S D : P R :006(504) [0853] and to forestalling the **possibility** that under the name of
S D : 0 2 :073(535) [0909] doctrine of free will it is **possible** to decide the questions
S D : 0 6 :015(566) [0967] In order as far as **possible** to avoid all
S D : 0 7 :002(569) [0971] which is as close as **possible** to the formulas and
S D : 0 7 :047(578) [0989] is to be reconciled with our reason or how it is **possible**.
S D : 0 7 :058(580) [0993] which agree in the best **possible** way with the words of
S D : 0 8 :038(598) [1027] be forearmed in the best **possible** way against this error.
S D : 1 1 :051(625) [1079] Thus it is **possible** to use the teaching in this article in a

Post (1)
E P : R N :002(465) [0777] and apostles was preserved in **post**-apostolic times.

Posterity (14)
P R : P R :008(005) [0009] we might, to secure our **posterity** in the future against
P R : P R :014(007) [0013] of the truth might be transmitted to our **posterity** as well.
P R : P R :018(008) [0015] as well as our beloved **posterity** may be clearly and
P R : P R :023(012) [0021] perpetuated among our **posterity** through the help and
A G : 0 0 :001(047) [0059] to our children and **posterity** any other teaching than that
A P : P R :016(099) [0103] and we hope that **posterity** will judge us more equitably.
A P : 0 7 :040(176) [0241] they might transmit to **posterity** the memory of these
A P : 1 2 :125(201) [0289] What will **posterity** think about these slanderous
T R : 0 0 :059(330) [0521] and other crimes as to impose them on all **posterity**.
L C : 0 1 :138(384) [0621] in Ps. 109:13, "May his **posterity** be cut off: and may their
S D : P R :016(507) [0857] but also to our **posterity**, of that which our churches
S D : 1 1 :001(616) [1063] this article among our **posterity**, we have determined to
S D : 1 1 :058(626) [1081] extends also to their **posterity**, as with the Jews.
S D : 1 2 :040(636) [1103] contemporaries and our **posterity**, we wish to have

Postil (1)
S D : 0 6 :009(565) [0965] portion of the Church **Postil**, on the Epistle for the

Postpone (3)
P R : P R :024(013) [0023] we ought not suspend or **postpone** its printing and
S 1 : P R :003(289) [0455] such wretched pains to **postpone** and prevent the
E P : 0 9 :004(492) [0827] that we should **postpone** until the other world, where

Pot (2)
L C : 0 1 :036(369) [0589] proud, powerful, and rich **pot**-bellies who, not caring
L C : 0 4 :061(444) [0747] water in the brook or in the **pot**, and magistrates only as

Potency (1), Potent (4), Potentates (1)
P R : P R :025(014) [0023] with other Christian **potentates**, according to the content

Continued ▶

L C : P R :010(360) [0569] or other savor more **potent** against the devil than to
L C : 0 4 :034(440) [0741] "He who believes," is so **potent** that it excludes and
L C : 0 4 :070(445) [0749] the real vices become more and more **potent** day by day.
S D : 0 2 :056(532) [0903] whereby he assuredly is **potent** and active in our hearts
S D : 0 7 :075(583) [0999] by the virtue and **potency** of the same words which Christ

Pounce (1)
L C : 0 1 :289(404) [0663] they can pry out and **pounce** on something to criticize in

Pour (1), Poured (18), Pours (2)
A P : 2 4 :069(262) [0409] with my blood, which is **poured** out for many for the
S 3 : 1 3 :002(315) [0499] mercy which have been **poured** out upon us so
S C : 0 4 :010(349) [0551] Holy Spirit, which he **poured** out upon us richly through
S C : 0 6 :004(351) [0557] in my blood, which is **poured** out for many for the
L C : 0 1 :025(368) [0587] with sheer goodness and **pours** forth all that is good in
L C : 0 4 :036(441) [0741] allowing the water to be **poured** over you, you do not
L C : 0 4 :045(442) [0743] the body has water **poured** over it, though it cannot
L C : 0 4 :078(446) [0751] But we need not again have the water **poured** over us.
L C : 0 5 :003(447) [0753] *in my blood, which is* **poured** *out for you for the*
L C : 0 5 :021(449) [0757] and blood, given and **poured** out *for you* for the
L C : 0 5 :029(449) [0759] than through the words, "given and **poured** out for you."
L C : 0 5 :031(450) [0759] blood are not given and **poured** out for us in the Lord's
L C : 0 5 :034(450) [0761] "Given *for you*" and "**poured** out *for you*," as if he said,
L C : 0 5 :064(454) [0769] *you*," "This is my blood, **poured** out *for you* for the
S D : 0 1 :035(514) [0869] Didst thou not **pour** me out like milk and curdle me like
S D : 0 2 :046(530) [0899] but will wait until God **pours** his gifts into them out of
S D : 0 3 :062(550) [0937] and virtues which are **poured** into them by the Holy
S D : 0 8 :032(597) [1025] from one nature and **poured** into the other nature, the
S D : 0 8 :032(597) [1025] nature, the way water is **poured** from one container into
S D : 0 8 :071(605) [1041] water, wine, or oil is **poured** from one container into
S D : 0 8 :074(606) [1043] The Father **poured** out upon him without measure the

Poverty (9)
A G : 2 7 :048(078) [0081] spirituality and sham of **poverty**, humility, and chastity.
A L : 2 7 :048(078) [0081] and this pretense of **poverty**, humility, and chastity.
A P : 1 6 :013(224) [0333] which put a hypocritical **poverty** and humility far above
A P : 2 7 :016(271) [0425] others because of their **poverty**, chastity, and obedience
A P : 2 7 :016(271) [0425] They brag about **poverty** amid a bounty of everything.
A P : 2 7 :021(272) [0427] Second, obedience, **poverty**, and celibacy, provided they
A P : 2 7 :046(277) [0435] The **poverty** of the Gospel (Matt. 5:3) does not consist in
T R : 0 0 :018(323) [0509] riches or the humility of **poverty** that makes a bishop
L C : 0 3 :115(435) [0731] the devil's kingdom: **poverty**, shame, death, and, in short,

Power (333), Powers (87)
P R : P R :020(010) [0017] hand of God's almighty **power** and majesty) and hence
A G : 0 1 :002(027) [0043] this one divine essence, equal in **power** and alike eternal:
A G : 0 1 :003(027) [0043] without end, of infinite **power**, wisdom, and goodness,
A G : 0 2 :003(029) [0045] righteous by his own **powers**, thus disparaging the
A G : 2 0 :032(045) [0057] Moreover, it is in the **power** of the devil, who drives poor
A G : 2 3 :006(052) [0061] or not it lies in human **power** and ability to improve or
A G : 2 5 :004(062) [0069] about this command and **power** of keys and how
A G : 2 7 :018(073) [0079] for celibacy have the **power**, right, and authority to
A G : 2 7 :023(074) [0079] lawfulness, and **power** when they are contrary to God's
A G : 2 7 :028(075) [0079] lies within human **power** and ability, and there are few,
A G : 2 8 :000(081) [0083] XXVIII. The **Power** of Bishops
A G : 2 8 :001(081) [0083] former times about the **power** of bishops, and some have
A G : 2 8 :001(081) [0083] improperly confused the **power** of bishops with the
A G : 2 8 :002(081) [0083] under pretext of the **power** given them by Christ, have
A G : 2 8 :004(081) [0085] spiritual and temporal **power**, sword, and authority, and
A G : 2 8 :004(081) [0085] both authorities and **powers** are to be honored and
A G : 2 8 :005(081) [0085] to the Gospel the **power** of keys or the power of bishops
A G : 2 8 :005(081) [0085] the power of keys or the **power** of bishops is a power and
A G : 2 8 :005(081) [0085] the power of bishops is a **power** and command of God to
A G : 2 8 :008(082) [0085] This **power** of keys or of bishops is used and exercised
A G : 2 8 :009(082) [0085] says, "The gospel is the **power** of God for salvation to
A G : 2 8 :010(082) [0085] Inasmuch as the **power** of the church or of bishops
A G : 2 8 :011(082) [0085] Temporal **power** does not protect the soul, but with the
A G : 2 8 :011(082) [0085] it protects body and goods from the **power** of others.
A G : 2 8 :012(083) [0085] for the spiritual **power** has its commission to preach the
A G : 2 8 :013(083) [0085] prescribe to the temporal **power** laws concerning worldly
A G : 2 8 :017(083) [0085] worldly but have divine **power** to destroy strongholds and
A G : 2 8 :018(083) [0085] the functions of the two **powers**, directing that both be
A G : 2 8 :021(084) [0087] to be done not by human **power** but by God's Word
A G : 2 8 :029(085) [0087] Whatever other **power** and jurisdiction bishops may have
A G : 2 8 :030(085) [0087] whether bishops have the **power** to introduce ceremonies
A G : 2 8 :031(085) [0087] Those who attribute such **power** to bishops cite Christ's
A G : 2 8 :033(086) [0087] wish to maintain that the **power** of the church is indeed
A G : 2 8 :034(086) [0087] that bishops do not have **power** to institute or establish
A G : 2 8 :042(088) [0089] bishops get the right and **power** to impose such
A G : 2 8 :049(089) [0091] If, then, bishops have the **power** to burden the churches
A G : 2 8 :076(094) [0095] lordship as if they had **power** to coerce the churches
A G : 2 8 :077(094) [0095] of reducing the bishops' **power**, but we desire and pray
A L : 0 1 :002(027) [0043] indivisible, of infinite **power**, wisdom, and goodness, the
A L : 0 1 :003(028) [0043] of the same essence and **power**, who are also coeternal:
A L : 0 3 :005(030) [0045] and defend them against the devil and the **power** of sin.
A L : 1 8 :002(039) [0051] it does not have the **power**, without the Holy Spirit, to
A L : 1 8 :008(040) [0053] the Holy Spirit, by the **power** of nature alone, we are able
A L : 2 0 :031(045) [0057] the Holy Spirit man's **powers** are full of ungodly
A L : 2 0 :032(045) [0057] Besides, they are in the **power** of the devil, who impels
A L : 2 3 :006(052) [0061] it is not in man's **power** to alter his creation without a
A L : 2 5 :004(062) [0069] The **power** of keys is praised, and people are reminded of
A L : 2 7 :028(075) [0079] to what an extent perpetual chastity lies in man's **power**.
A L : 2 8 :000(081) [0083] XXVIII. Ecclesiastical **Power**
A L : 2 8 :001(081) [0083] controversy about the **power** of bishops, and some have
A L : 2 8 :001(081) [0083] improperly confused the **power** of the church with the
A L : 2 8 :001(081) [0083] the power of the church with the **power** of the sword.
A L : 2 8 :002(081) [0083] pontiffs, relying on the **power** of the keys, not only have
A L : 2 8 :002(081) [0085] of this world and take away the imperial **power**.
A L : 2 8 :004(081) [0085] difference between the **power** of the church and the
A L : 2 8 :004(081) [0085] of the church and the **power** of the sword, and they have
A L : 2 8 :005(081) [0085] to the Gospel the **power** of keys or the power of bishops
A L : 2 8 :005(081) [0085] the power of keys or the **power** of bishops is a power or
A L : 2 8 :005(081) [0085] the power of bishops is a **power** or command of God to
A L : 2 8 :008(082) [0085] This **power** is exercised only by teaching or preaching the
A L : 2 8 :009(082) [0085] says, "The gospel is the **power** of God for salvation to
A L : 2 8 :010(082) [0085] Inasmuch as the **power** of the church bestows eternal
A L : 2 8 :012(083) [0085] ecclesiastical and civil **power** are not to be confused.
A L : 2 8 :012(083) [0085] The **power** of the church has its own commission to
A L : 2 8 :017(083) [0085] worldly but have divine **power** to destroy arguments,"
A L : 2 8 :018(083) [0085] the functions of the two **powers**, and they command that
A L : 2 8 :019(083) [0087] If bishops have any **power** of the sword, they have this
A L : 2 8 :021(084) [0087] doing all this without human **power**, simply by the Word.
A L : 2 8 :029(085) [0087] If they have any other **power** or jurisdiction to decide
A L : 2 8 :033(086) [0087] Great, they say, is the **power** of the church, for it
A L : 2 8 :034(086) [0087] that bishops do not have **power** to institute anything
A L : 2 8 :077(094) [0095] the bishops give up their **power** to govern, but we ask for
A P : 0 2 :008(101) [0107] nature unimpaired **power** to love God above all things
A P : 0 2 :009(102) [0107] all things by one's own **power** and to obey his
A P : 0 2 :010(102) [0107] human nature has such **powers** that by itself it can love
A P : 0 2 :010(102) [0109] the Holy Spirit if human **powers** by themselves can love
A P : 0 2 :012(102) [0109] we agree is subject to reason and somewhat in our **power**.
A P : 0 2 :014(102) [0109] denied to man's natural **powers** the fear and trust of God.
A P : 0 2 :017(102) [0109] or at least the inclination and **power** to do these things.
A P : 0 2 :023(103) [0111] obedience of man's lower **powers**, but also denies that he
A P : 0 2 :023(103) [0111] love of God, or surely the **power** to produce these things.
A P : 0 2 :023(103) [0111] of God but also the gifts and **power** to produce them.
A P : 0 2 :044(106) [0117] feeding a trust in human **powers** and obscuring the
A P : 0 2 :046(106) [0117] of God by his own **powers**, Genesis describes another
A P : 0 2 :049(106) [0119] history itself shows the great **power** of the devil's rule.
A P : 0 4 :067(116) [0139] "The Gospel is the **power** of God for salvation to
A P : 0 4 :079(118) [0143] "The sting of death is sin, and the **power** of sin is law.
A P : 0 4 :094(120) [0149] in his name, he gave **power** to become children of God;
A P : 0 4 :139(126) [0161] Nothing less than Christ's **power** is needed for our
A P : 0 4 :250(143) [0191] nor is it a human **power**, but a divine power that makes
A P : 0 4 :250(143) [0191] power, but a divine **power** that makes us alive and
A P : 0 4 :250(143) [0191] says that through the **power** of God faith is efficacious
A P : 0 4 :383(165) [0225] or of dogmas, not as the **power** that grasps the promise
A P : 0 4 :391(167) [0225] can love God above all things by purely natural **powers**.
A P : 0 7 :016(170) [0231] that the wicked are in the **power** of the devil and are
A P : 0 7 :022(172) [0235] of men by reason of their **power** or position, whether
A P : 0 7 :023(172) [0235] must have unlimited **power** beyond question or censure.
A P : 0 7 :023(172) [0235] kings have received their **power** and right to rule, and this
A P : 0 7 :023(172) [0235] He must have plenary **power** in both the temporal and
A P : 0 7 :025(173) [0235] wicked writings about the **power** of the Roman pope for
A P : 1 0 :003(179) [0247] that we do not know the **power** of the mystical
A P : 1 1 :002(180) [0249] of absolution and the **power** of the keys that many
A P : 1 1 :002(180) [0249] Previously the whole **power** of absolution had been
A P : 1 2 :006(183) [0255] and what does the **power** of the keys accomplish if the sin
A P : 1 2 :006(183) [0255] still more and wickedly minimize the **power** of the keys.
A P : 1 2 :007(183) [0255] of them imagine that the **power** of the keys does not
A P : 1 2 :007(183) [0255] Then the salutary **power** of the keys would be a ministry
A P : 1 2 :007(183) [0255] and suppose that the **power** of the keys forgives sins
A P : 1 2 :007(183) [0255] For if the **power** of the keys does not console us before
A P : 1 2 :010(184) [0255] blessing of Christ, the **power** of the keys, and the
A P : 1 2 :013(184) [0257] part is forgiven by the **power** of the keys and another
A P : 1 2 :021(185) [0257] 5. The **power** of the keys has validity for the forgiveness
A P : 1 2 :022(185) [0257] 6. The **power** of the keys does not forgive sins before
A P : 1 2 :026(185) [0259] 10. By the **power** of the keys, through indulgences, souls
A P : 1 2 :039(187) [0261] The **power** of the keys administers and offers the Gospel
A P : 1 2 :043(187) [0263] adds to the honor of the **power** of the keys and the
A P : 1 2 :099(197) [0281] Word of God that the **power** of the keys proclaims to
A P : 1 2 :101(197) [0281] neither the forgiveness of sins nor the **power** of the keys.
A P : 1 2 :118(199) [0287] is forgiven by the **power** of the keys, and the rest must be
A P : 1 2 :118(199) [0287] are partly forgiven by the **power** of the keys, unless they
A P : 1 2 :139(203) [0295] punishments, or that the **power** of the keys carries with it
A P : 1 2 :149(206) [0299] undergo the unspeakable **power** of the grief that comes
A P : 1 2 :153(206) [0299] sting of death is sin, and the **power** of sin is the law."
A P : 1 2 :153(206) [0299] This **power** of sin, this sense of wrath, is a real
A P : 1 2 :154(206) [0301] opponents say that the **power** of the keys remits part of
A P : 1 2 :154(206) [0301] Clearly the **power** of the keys does not remove these
A P : 1 2 :156(207) [0301] nothing to do with the **power** of the keys because the keys
A P : 1 2 :160(207) [0301] for our profit, that the **power** of God might be made
A P : 1 2 :160(207) [0303] Thus Paul says, "The **power** of God is made perfect in
A P : 1 2 :176(210) [0307] that the keys have the **power** to bind and loose, according
A P : 1 2 :176(210) [0307] the keys do not have the **power** to impose penalties or to
A P : 1 3 :011(212) [0311] "The Gospel is the **power** of God for salvation to every
A P : 1 5 :031(219) [0323] Nor do bishops have the **power** to institute rites as though
A P : 1 8 :005(225) [0335] But so great is the **power** of concupiscence that men obey
A P : 1 8 :007(226) [0337] who uses only his natural **powers**, "does not perceive the
A P : 2 1 :011(230) [0345] divinity to the saints, the **power** to perceive the unspoken
A P : 2 1 :034(234) [0353] some sort of magical **power**, just as sorcerers imagine
A P : 2 1 :034(234) [0353] horoscopes carved at a particular time contain **power**.
A P : 2 1 :036(234) [0353] Augustine experienced the **power** of faith in sickness and
A P : 2 8 :000(281) [0443] [Article XXVIII.] Ecclesiastical **Power**
A P : 2 8 :006(282) [0445] is that bishops have the **power** to rule and to correct by
A P : 2 8 :006(282) [0445] eternal bliss, and that the **power** to rule requires the
A P : 2 8 :006(282) [0445] power to rule requires the **power** to judge, define,
A P : 2 8 :011(283) [0447] that bishops have the **power** to institute such acts of
A P : 2 8 :012(283) [0447] we have said what **power** the Gospel grants to bishops.
A P : 2 8 :013(283) [0447] We like the old division of **power** into the power of the
A P : 2 8 :013(283) [0447] division of power into the **power** of the order and the
A P : 2 8 :013(283) [0447] into the power of the order and the **power** of jurisdiction.
A P : 2 8 :013(283) [0447] a bishop has the **power** of the order, namely, the ministry
A P : 2 8 :013(283) [0447] He also has the **power** of jurisdiction, namely, the
A P : 2 8 :014(283) [0447] bishops does not have the **power** of a tyrant to act
S 2 : 0 2 :024(296) [0469] or merit, not by the **power** of the pope but by the
S 2 : 0 4 :003(298) [0473] so far as this lies in his **power**) and come into conflict with
S 2 : 0 4 :007(299) [0473] and it remained in their **power** and choice to change or
S 2 : 0 4 :010(300) [0475] saved except by his own **power**, which amounts to
S 3 : 0 0 :000(302) [0477] of conscience but only about money, honor, and **power**.
S 3 : 0 1 :004(302) [0477] fall of Adam the natural **powers** of man have remained
S 3 : 0 1 :006(302) [0477] man is able by his natural **powers** to observe and keep all
S 3 : 0 1 :007(302) [0477] man is able by his natural **powers** to love God above all
S 3 : 0 1 :009(302) [0477] of man's nature and such is the **power** of the sacrament.
S 3 : 0 2 :003(303) [0479] the law by their own **powers**, as was just said above
S 3 : 0 2 :004(303) [0479] the chief function or **power** of the law is to make original

Continued ▶

S 3 : 0 3 :010(305) [0481] asserted that the natural **powers** of man have remained
S 3 : 0 3 :018(306) [0483] evolved by man's own **powers** without faith and without
S 3 : 0 3 :020(306) [0485] not become aware of the **power** of absolution, for his
S 3 : 0 3 :027(308) [0487] the people with his **power** and indulgences, and once
S 3 : 0 3 :040(309) [0489] this not with his own **powers** but with the gift of the Holy
S 3 : 0 4 :000(310) [0491] Altar; fourth, through the **power** of the keys; and finally,
S 3 : 0 5 :002(310) [0491] to the water a spiritual **power** which, through the water,
S 3 : 0 7 :001(311) [0493] keys are a function and **power** given to the church by
S 3 : 0 7 :002(311) [0493] It is not in our **power** but in God's alone to judge which,
S 3 : 0 8 :001(312) [0493] Since absolution or the **power** of the keys, which was
S 3 : 0 8 :009(313) [0497] the source, strength, and **power** of all heresy, including
S 3 : 1 1 :002(314) [0499] As little as the **power** has been given to us or to them to
S 3 : 1 1 :002(314) [0499] little have they had the **power** to separate such creatures
T R : 0 0 :000(319) [0503] Treatise on the **Power** and Primacy of the Pope
T R : 0 0 :006(320) [0505] because he holds that his **power** is by divine right and is
T R : 0 0 :018(323) [0509] It is the **power** of riches or the humility of poverty that
T R : 0 0 :024(324) [0511] to Peter any special prerogative, superiority, or **power**.
T R : 0 0 :031(325) [0513] apostles only spiritual **power**, that is, the command to
T R : 0 0 :031(325) [0513] He did not give them the **power** of the sword or the right
T R : 0 0 :032(325) [0513] would be set up on the pretext of ecclesiastical **power**.
T R : 0 0 :035(326) [0513] bishops subject to their **power** and deprive the emperors
T R : 0 0 :040(327) [0517] for himself not only the **power** to loose and bind in this
T R : 0 0 :054(329) [0519] use their authority and **power** for the support of idolatry
T R : 0 0 :056(329) [0521] is not deprived of the **power** of making judgments and
T R : 0 0 :059(330) [0521] The **Power** and Jurisdiction of Bishops
T R : 0 0 :059(330) [0521] terms what we have to say about ecclesiastical **power**.
T R : 0 0 :061(330) [0521] it is evident that this **power** belongs by divine right to all
T R : 0 0 :063(331) [0523] witness to this, for the **power** is the same, as I have
T R : 0 0 :071(332) [0525] words, "I give thee the **power** to sacrifice for the living
T R : 0 0 :074(332) [0525] civil officers to have the **power** to ban men arbitrarily
T R : 0 0 :075(333) [0525] And in what kinds of cases they have abused this **power**!
T R : 0 0 :082(334) [0529] of the pope and the **power** and jurisdiction of the bishops
T R : 0 0 :082(000) [0529] the Papacy and the **Power** and Jurisdiction of Bishops.
S C : 0 2 :004(345) [0545] from death, and from the **power** of the devil, not with
S C : 0 7 :002(352) [0557] of me, that the wicked one may have no **power** over me.
S C : 0 7 :005(353) [0559] of me, that the wicked one may have no **power** over me.
L C : P R :011(360) [0571] in Rom. 1:16, it is "the **power** of God," indeed, the power
L C : P R :011(360) [0571] of God," indeed, the **power** of God which burns the devil
L C : P R :013(360) [0571] this might, blessing, **power**, and fruit — especially we who
L C : S P :014(363) [0577] is the kingdom and the **power** and the glory, forever.
L C : 0 1 :010(366) [0583] great learning, wisdom, **power**, prestige, family, and
L C : 0 1 :018(367) [0585] who put their trust in **power** and dominion exalted
L C : 0 1 :042(370) [0591] who serve mammon have **power**, prestige, honor, wealth,
L C : 0 1 :045(370) [0593] in his crown and **power**, he inevitably perished with all
L C : 0 1 :094(378) [0607] Note, then, that the **power** and force of this
L C : 0 1 :094(378) [0607] in order that God's Word may exert its **power** publicly.
L C : 0 1 :101(379) [0609] put it to use, such is its **power** that it never departs
L C : 0 1 :142(384) [0621] derive from them their **power** and authority to govern.
L C : 0 1 :168(388) [0629] them this honor (that is, **power** and authority to govern)
L C : 0 1 :216(394) [0641] yet it is not in their **power** to maintain chastity, and if
L C : 0 1 :261(400) [0655] account of anyone's money, property, honor, or **power**.
L C : 0 1 :295(404) [0665] Moreover, every man had **power** to dismiss his wife
L C : 0 1 :317(408) [0673] for they are beyond human **power** to fulfill.
L C : 0 2 :021(413) [0683] as if we had life, riches, **power**, honor, and such things of
L C : 0 2 :027(414) [0685] and King but was captive under the **power** of the devil.
L C : 0 2 :030(414) [0685] his righteousness, wisdom, **power**, life, and blessedness.
L C : 0 2 :031(414) [0687] The devil and all **powers**, therefore, must be subject to
L C : 0 2 :069(420) [0697] with all his gifts and his **power**, to help us keep the Ten
L C : 0 3 :002(420) [0697] world and our flesh, resists our efforts with all his **power**.
L C : 0 3 :051(426) [0711] and deliver us from the **power** of the devil and to bring us
L C : 0 3 :051(427) [0711] and to enlighten and strengthen us in faith by his **power**.
L C : 0 3 :052(427) [0711] people and advance with **power** throughout the world.
L C : 0 3 :054(427) [0713] the Word and the **power** of the Holy Spirit, that the
L C : 0 3 :054(427) [0713] he may have no right or **power** over us, until finally the
L C : 0 3 :061(428) [0715] been redeemed from the **power** of the devil — we must
L C : 0 3 :062(428) [0715] and rages with all his **power** and might, marshaling all his
L C : 0 3 :063(428) [0715] cut us down, and bring us once more under his **power**.
L C : 0 3 :080(431) [0721] and bring them under his **power**, but he also prevents and
L C : 0 3 :081(431) [0721] If it were in his **power**, and our prayer to God did not
L C : 0 3 :103(434) [0727] along with fondness for luxury, honor, fame, and **power**.
L C : 0 3 :106(434) [0727] when God gives us **power** and strength to resist, even
L C : 0 4 :017(438) [0735] himself stakes his honor, his **power**, and his might on it.
L C : 0 4 :024(439) [0737] To put it most simply, the **power**, effect, benefit, fruit,
L C : 0 4 :027(440) [0739] Word Baptism receives the **power** to become the "washing
L C : 0 4 :032(440) [0739] the great benefit and **power** of Baptism, let us observe
L C : 0 4 :049(442) [0745] we have been given the **power** to interpret the Scriptures
L C : 0 4 :065(444) [0749] from it, indicate the **power** and effect of Baptism, which
L C : 0 4 :071(445) [0749] not restrained and suppressed by the **power** of Baptism.
L C : 0 4 :074(445) [0751] that Baptism, both by its **power** and by its signification,
L C : 0 4 :076(446) [0751] the grace, Spirit, and **power** to suppress the old man so
L C : 0 5 :020(449) [0757] Now we come to its **power** and benefit, the purpose for
L C : 0 5 :033(450) [0761] to consider who it is that receives this **power** and benefit.
L C : 0 5 :070(454) [0769] protection, defense, and **power** against death and the
L C : 0 6 :020(459) [0000] no such comfort, we shall leave you to another's **power**.
E P : 0 1 :001(466) [0779] (that is, his rational soul in its highest form and **powers**).
E P : 0 1 :008(467) [0781] in man's body or soul, in his inward or outward **powers**.
E P : 0 1 :013(467) [0783] things its natural **powers** remained wholly good and
E P : 0 1 :014(468) [0783] retained unimpaired its **powers** for good even in spiritual
E P : 0 1 :015(468) [0783] to man's good spiritual **powers** and not the complete
E P : 0 1 :015(468) [0783] not remove the natural **powers** of the magnet; likewise the
E P : 0 1 :016(468) [0783] skill, capability, or **power** to initiate, to effect, or to
E P : 0 2 :001(469) [0785] The question is, What **powers** does man possess in
E P : 0 2 :001(469) [0785] Can man by his own **powers**, before he is reborn through
E P : 0 2 :002(470) [0787] nothing by his own **powers**, as it is written in I Cor. 2:14,
E P : 0 2 :004(470) [0787] that the Gospel is a "**power** of God" for salvation;
E P : 0 2 :004(470) [0787] through the grace and **power** of the Holy Spirit, for
E P : 0 2 :006(470) [0787] few words he denies all **power** to free will and ascribes
E P : 0 2 :009(471) [0789] taught that by his own **powers**, without the grace of the
E P : 0 2 :010(471) [0789] man by virtue of his own **powers** could make a beginning
E P : 0 2 :011(471) [0789] God's law by his own **powers**, yet after the Holy Spirit
E P : 0 2 :011(471) [0789] able by its own natural **powers** to add something (though
E P : 0 2 :018(472) [0791] renewed *solely by God's* **power** *and activity,* man's new
E P : 0 2 :019(472) [0791] and accept it by his own **powers** but solely by the grace
E P : 0 6 :004(480) [0807] will, and all their **powers**, it is necessary for the law of
E P : 0 7 :005(482) [0809] of Christ's spirit, or the **power** of Christ's absent body, or
E P : 0 7 :008(482) [0811] and alone to the almighty **power** of our Lord Jesus
E P : 0 7 :031(485) [0815] the Holy Supper only the **power**, operation, and merit of
E P : 0 8 :013(488) [0821] majesty and omnipotent **power** of God, but a man whose
E P : 0 8 :015(488) [0821] omnipotent majesty and **power** of God, because he was
E P : 0 8 :016(489) [0821] He exercises his **power** everywhere omnipresently, he can
E P : 0 8 :027(490) [0825] because this essential **power** and property has been
E P : 0 8 :035(491) [0825] been given greater **power** in heaven and on earth, that is,
E P : 0 8 :035(491) [0825] invent an intermediate **power** (that is, a power that lies
E P : 0 8 :035(491) [0825] power (that is, a **power** that lies somewhere between
E P : 0 8 :035(491) [0825] omnipotence and the **power** of other creatures) and they
E P : 0 8 :035(491) [0825] of Christ received a **power** which is less than God's
E P : 0 8 :035(491) [0825] but greater than the **power** of other creatures.
E P : 0 8 :039(491) [0827] and his ascension all **power** in heaven and on earth was
E P : 0 9 :004(492) [0827] redeemed them from the **power** of death, of the devil, and
E P : 1 1 :008(495) [0833] addition he promises the **power** and operation of the
E P : 1 2 :014(499) [0841] government to use the **power** that it possesses and that it
E P : 1 2 :021(499) [0841] Word as far as might, **power**, majesty, and glory are
E P : 1 2 :029(500) [0843] of the three has the same **power**, wisdom, majesty, and
S D : 0 1 :001(508) [0859] degree and foremost **powers**) is original sin itself, which
S D : 0 1 :002(508) [0859] his body, soul, and all his **powers**, and that it is an
S D : 0 1 :010(510) [0863] nature the gifts and the **power**, or the faculty and the
S D : 0 1 :011(510) [0863] his entire nature in all its **powers**, especially of the highest
S D : 0 1 :011(510) [0863] the highest and foremost **powers** of the soul in mind,
S D : 0 1 :011(510) [0863] which, in its highest **powers** and the light of reason, is by
S D : 0 1 :012(510) [0863] a measure of reason, **power**, and ability, although greatly
S D : 0 1 :013(511) [0863] abandoned to his **power**, and held captive in his
S D : 0 1 :020(511) [0865] matters it is good, pure, and in its natural **powers** perfect.
S D : 0 1 :021(512) [0865] retains its goodness and **powers** also in spiritual matters.
S D : 0 1 :022(512) [0865] of man's spiritual good **powers**, but only an external
S D : 0 1 :022(512) [0865] the magnet's natural **power** but only impedes it; or that
S D : 0 1 :030(513) [0867] and in soul, in all its **powers** from beginning to end, down
S D : 0 1 :060(519) [0879] its internal and external **powers**, but that it is altogether
S D : 0 1 :060(519) [0879] lifeless and with all his **powers** dead indeed to that which
S D : 0 2 :000(519) [0881] II. Free Will or Human **Powers**
S D : 0 2 :002(520) [0881] regeneration, by those **powers** of his own that have
S D : 0 2 :003(520) [0881] although by his own **powers** and without the gift of the
S D : 0 2 :003(520) [0881] so much of his natural **powers** prior to his conversion
S D : 0 2 :003(520) [0881] nothing with these **powers** but would succumb in the
S D : 0 2 :005(521) [0881] of God until by the **power** of the Holy Spirit, through the
S D : 0 2 :007(521) [0883] by any native or natural **powers** in any way understand,
S D : 0 2 :007(521) [0883] not a spark of spiritual **powers** has remained or exists in
S D : 0 2 :007(521) [0883] conversion by his own **powers**, either altogether or
S D : 0 2 :009(522) [0883] they cannot by their own **powers** perceive this,
S D : 0 2 :011(522) [0885] dead can by his own **powers** prepare or accommodate
S D : 0 2 :011(522) [0885] himself by his own **power** to obtain spiritual and heavenly
S D : 0 2 :015(523) [0887] of God they cannot obtain by their own natural **powers**.
S D : 0 2 :018(524) [0887] will by its own natural **powers** can do nothing for man's
S D : 0 2 :024(525) [0891] in spiritual things of himself and by his own **powers**.
S D : 0 2 :025(526) [0891] in no way to the human **powers** of the natural free will,
S D : 0 2 :027(527) [0893] is our own work and lies within our own **power**."
S D : 0 2 :027(527) [0893] that it lies within our **power** to believe and to will, but
S D : 0 2 :029(527) [0893] faith and the Holy Spirit are in the **power** of the devil.
S D : 0 2 :029(527) [0893] that "human reason and **power** without Christ is much
S D : 0 2 :030(527) [0893] how can man by his own **powers** turn to the Gospel or to
S D : 0 2 :032(527) [0893] that it lies within our **power** to perform such external
S D : 0 2 :034(528) [0895] does so not by his own **powers** but through the gift of the
S D : 0 2 :035(528) [0895] and holy, to the complete exclusion of our own **powers**.
S D : 0 2 :039(528) [0895] not of our own will and **power**, but the Holy Spirit, as
S D : 0 2 :042(529) [0897] we cannot by our own **powers** come to Christ, but that
S D : 0 2 :043(529) [0897] and lord, and there is no **power** or ability, no cleverness
S D : 0 2 :044(529) [0897] grants our free will no **power** of its own to prepare itself
S D : 0 2 :045(530) [0899] man still has enough **powers** to want to accept the Gospel
S D : 0 2 :046(530) [0899] exclusively the work of God and not of our own **powers**.
S D : 0 2 :046(530) [0899] by their own natural **powers**, they will continue wholly to
S D : 0 2 :048(530) [0901] faith, and new spiritual **power** and ability for good in our
S D : 0 2 :055(531) [0903] there were not added the **power** and operation of the
S D : 0 2 :055(532) [0903] what man is unable by his own **powers** to take or to give.
S D : 0 2 :061(533) [0905] there can be in him no **power** to do something good in
S D : 0 2 :065(534) [0907] must cooperate by the **power** of the Holy Spirit, even
S D : 0 2 :065(534) [0907] our carnal and natural **powers**, but from the new powers
S D : 0 2 :065(534) [0907] but from the new **powers** and gifts which the Holy Spirit
S D : 0 2 :071(535) [0909] this way: Man's natural **powers** cannot contribute
S D : 0 2 :074(535) [0909] will has no freedom or **power** whatever to achieve a
S D : 0 2 :075(536) [0911] that by his own natural **powers**, without the Holy Spirit,
S D : 0 2 :076(536) [0911] that by his natural **powers** man can start out toward that
S D : 0 2 :076(536) [0911] of the good work which man began by his natural **powers**.
S D : 0 2 :077(536) [0911] beginning and by its own **powers** to convert itself to God
S D : 0 2 :077(536) [0911] will by its own natural **powers** can meet God and to some
S D : 0 2 :077(536) [0911] Gospel, and by its own **powers** cooperate with the Holy
S D : 0 2 :078(536) [0911] from man's own natural **powers** but solely through the
S D : 0 2 :089(538) [0915] himself or by his natural **powers** is unable to do anything
S D : 0 2 :089(538) [0915] and performs it by his **power** and might through the
S D : 0 3 :043(547) [0931] ask where faith gets the **power** to justify and save, and
S D : 0 3 :043(547) [0931] account of which love the **power** to justify is ascribed to
S D : 0 4 :007(552) [0941] a person's own natural **powers** but only after a person has
S D : 0 4 :010(552) [0941] spirit, mind, and all our **powers**, and brings the Holy
S D : 0 4 :034(557) [0949] "By God's **power** we are guarded through faith for a
S D : 0 5 :022(562) [0959] but the Gospel is "the **power** of God for salvation to
S D : 0 6 :006(564) [0965] in their nature and all its **powers** they would be totally
S D : 0 6 :007(565) [0965] to their nature and to all its internal and external **powers**.
S D : 0 6 :011(565) [0965] but it does not give the **power** and ability to begin it or to
S D : 0 7 :005(570) [0973] (that is, according to its **power**, operation, and benefits,
S D : 0 7 :070(582) [0997] Likewise, "The **power** of God is made perfect in
S D : 0 7 :074(583) [0999] only to the almighty **power** of God and the Word,
S D : 0 7 :075(583) [0999] validity and efficacious **power** in all places where the
S D : 0 7 :076(583) [0999] the priest, but by God's **power** and grace through the
S D : 0 7 :090(585) [1003] ascribe to our faith the **power** to achieve the presence of
S D : 0 7 :103(587) [1007] in any way that God's **power** is able to make a body be
S D : 0 7 :103(587) [1009] Who has seen the limits of his **power**?
S D : 0 7 :121(590) [1013] work of the priest the **power** allegedly to effect a
S D : 0 8 :012(593) [1019] right hand of majesty, **power**, and might over every name

Continued ▶

SD : 08 :023(595) [1023] hand of the almighty **power** of God, and everything that
SD : 08 :028(596) [1025] is precisely the almighty **power** of God which fills heaven
SD : 08 :029(596) [1025] of this communicated **power** he can be and is truly
SD : 08 :029(597) [1025] omnipotent majesty and **power** through and in the
SD : 08 :051(600) [1031] hand of the majesty and **power** of God, after the form of
SD : 08 :051(601) [1033] in majesty, glory, **power**, and might above every name
SD : 08 :051(601) [1033] with the other, and has its **power** and efficacy not only
SD : 08 :051(601) [1033] to the majesty, glory, **power**, and might which the human
SD : 08 :058(602) [1035] execute that the **power** to make the dead alive and to
SD : 08 :059(602) [1035] decreed that the flesh of Christ has the **power** to give life.
SD : 08 :061(602) [1035] namely, that such divine **power**, life, might, majesty, and
SD : 08 :061(603) [1037] Thus also the **power** to give life is not in the flesh of
SD : 08 :064(603) [1037] forth with all its majesty, **power**, glory, and efficacy in the
SD : 08 :064(603) [1039] and exercises his divine **power**, glory, and efficacy, as the
SD : 08 :066(604) [1039] divine omnipotence, **power**, majesty, and glory, which is
SD : 08 :066(604) [1039] iron there are not two **powers** of illumination and
SD : 08 :066(604) [1039] and combustion — the **power** of illumination and
SD : 08 :066(604) [1039] and manifests its **power** of illumination and combustion
SD : 08 :066(604) [1039] the glowing iron has the **power** of illumination and
SD : 08 :068(604) [1039] for the Spirit, who has all **power**, has been given to them.
SD : 08 :074(606) [1041] and with all **power** in, with, and through the human
SD : 08 :074(606) [1043] the Spirit of wisdom and **power**, so that as a man,
SD : 08 :074(606) [1043] really and truly has received all knowledge and all **power**.
SD : 08 :074(606) [1043] to the right hand of the majesty and **power** of God.
SD : 08 :078(606) [1043] hand of the majesty and **power** of God, so that, also
SD : 08 :085(608) [1045] human birth, the eternal **power** of God is also given to
SD : 08 :085(608) [1047] of qualities has eternal **power** and has created and
SD : 08 :085(608) [1047] the Son of God in **power**' (Rom. 1:4), and John calls it
SD : 08 :090(609) [1047] through an essential **power** or property of its nature.
SD : 08 :092(609) [1049] hand of the majesty and **power** of God, wherever he
SD : 08 :095(609) [1049] deed and truth the divine **power**, might, wisdom, majesty,
SD : 08 :096(610) [1049] right hand of the majesty and almighty **power** of God.
SD : 09 :002(610) [1051] the devil, destroyed hell's **power**, and took from the devil
SD : 09 :003(610) [1051] right hand of the almighty **power** and majesty of God.
SD : 10 :009(612) [1055] the right, authority, and **power** to change, to reduce, or to
SD : 10 :021(614) [1059] In the Treatise on the **Power** and Primacy of the Pope,
SD : 11 :029(621) [1073] (II Cor. 3:8) and a "**power** of God" to save (Rom. 1:16).
SD : 11 :029(621) [1073] us, and to give us **power** and ability, it is God's will that
SD : 11 :033(621) [1073] Holy Spirit gives grace, **power**, and ability through the
SD : 11 :044(623) [1077] doctrines about the **powers** of our natural will, for in his
SD : 11 :044(624) [1077] world began that by the **power** of his Holy Spirit through
SD : 11 :046(624) [1079] through the deceit and **power** of the devil and the world
SD : 11 :071(627) [1085] to do this by our own **powers**, the Holy Spirit wills to
SD : 11 :073(628) [1087] more they experience the **power** and might of the Spirit
SD : 11 :074(628) [1087] longer experiencing any **power** whatever of the indwelling
SD : 11 :076(629) [1087] indeed draws by the **power** of the Holy Spirit, but
SD : 11 :077(629) [1089] the Word and to be efficacious with his **power** through it.
SD : 11 :082(630) [1089] clear words that God's **power** and operation can transform
SD : 11 :084(630) [1091] you live to show you my **power**, so that my name may be
SD : 11 :095(632) [1095] part to do everything in our **power** to further the same.
SD : 12 :029(635) [1101] a way that in might, in **power**, in majesty, and in glory he
SD : 12 :037(636) [1103] persons, have the same **power**, wisdom, majesty, and

Powerful (8), Powerfully (3)
AP : 04 :149(127) [0163] sin (Rom. 5:20), that mercy is more **powerful** than sin.
AP : 04 :154(128) [0165] reason that this truly **powerful** example moved Christ to
AP : 27 :032(274) [0431] Bernard also says very **powerfully**, "First of all, you must
S2 : 04 :010(300) [0475] This is a **powerful** demonstration that the pope is the real
TR : 00 :024(324) [0511] by many clear and **powerful** arguments, for after speaking
LC : 01 :036(369) [0589] now there are proud, **powerful**, and rich pot-bellies who,
LC : 01 :230(396) [0645] attack against the great, **powerful** arch-thieves who
LC : 01 :259(400) [0655] and the rich and **powerful** who are in a position to help
LC : 03 :070(429) [0717] how proud, secure, and **powerful** they think they are.
LC : 05 :064(454) [0769] above, which should most **powerfully** draw and impel us.
SD : 01 :048(517) [0875] Christian faith show **powerfully** and mightily why we

Practical (3), Practically (2)
AG : PR :010(025) [0041] honorably be done, such **practical** and equitable ways as
AP : 24 :050(259) [0401] **Practical** and clear sermons hold an audience, but neither
AP : 24 :051(259) [0401] of the churches is godly, **practical**, and clear teaching, the
LC : 01 :197(391) [0637] It would be **practically** the same as forbidding their good
SD : PR :006(502) [0847] has remained **practically** unchallenged — except for the

Practice (40), Practiced (7), Practices (9), Practicing (1)
AG : 26 :029(068) [0075] Gospel to institute or **practice** such works for the purpose
AG : 26 :034(069) [0075] certain specified days but should be **practiced** continually.
AG : 27 :007(071) [0077] The **practice** was stricter in women's convents than in
AG : 28 :068(093) [0093] unless this mitigation is **practiced**, that one recognizes
AL : 26 :029(068) [0075] Gospel to institute or **practice** such works for the purpose
AL : 28 :068(093) [0093] unless this mitigation is **practiced**, that one recognizes
AP : 04 :293(152) [0203] midst of afflictions, and **practice** chastity, love toward
AP : 11 :006(181) [0251] It is, of course, a good **practice** to accustom the unlearned
AP : 12 :052(189) [0265] way Scripture makes a **practice** of joining these two,
AP : 12 :113(199) [0285] These **practices** have long since become antiquated, nor
AP : 12 :114(199) [0285] not believe that by such **practices** or such works men
AP : 12 :115(199) [0285] But now that the **practice** has become obsolete, the word
AP : 16 :003(223) [0331] or by others, and in this obedience to **practice** love.
AP : 21 :031(233) [0351] venerating the saints or their **practice** of praying to them.
AP : 22 :004(236) [0359] the Greek churches this **practice** still remains, and once it
AP : 22 :013(238) [0361] otherwise we might want to maintain their **practice**.
AP : 23 :005(239) [0365] good and well how few **practice** chastity, but they use
AP : 24 :006(250) [0385] are remnants of ancient **practice**, for the Fathers of the
AP : 24 :008(250) [0385] a week, and that this **practice** came from the apostles.
AP : 24 :068(262) [0409] It talks only about the **practice** of love, which even
AP : 24 :085(265) [0413] Originally the Christians kept this **practice**.
AP : 24 :086(265) [0413] With this **practice** they also kept the term "Mass" as the
S2 : 01 :005(292) [0463] all that we teach and **practice** against the pope, the devil,
S2 : 02 :019(296) [0467] and approve of these **practices** in order that great
S2 : 02 :025(297) [0469] of saints were a precious **practice** (which it is not), we
S2 : 02 :026(297) [0469] them a special function, as the papists teach and **practice**.
S3 : 03 :027(307) [0487] and confession **practiced** by these people, as we have
TR : 00 :014(322) [0507] diligently observe and **practice**, according to divine
SC : 01 :004(342) [0539] his name to curse, swear, **practice** magic, lie, or deceive,
LC : PR :011(360) [0571] read, recite, ponder, and **practice** the Catechism, even if
LC : PR :019(361) [0573] constantly put it into **practice**, guarding themselves with
LC : SP :002(362) [0575] not know the rules and **practices** of his craft is rejected
LC : SP :003(362) [0575] children's sermons and diligently drilled in their **practice**.
LC : 01 :017(366) [0585] judge how the world **practices** nothing but false worship
LC : 01 :022(367) [0585] idolatry that has been **practiced** up to now, and it is still
LC : 01 :062(373) [0597] conjure, and, in short, to **practice** wickedness of any sort.
LC : 01 :074(375) [0601] saints, but the other **practices** would be more pleasing and
LC : 01 :075(375) [0601] may become familiar and be constantly **practiced**.
LC : 01 :077(375) [0603] consists not only of words but also of **practice** and life.
LC : 01 :090(377) [0605] Wherever this **practice** is in force, a holy day is truly
LC : 01 :090(377) [0607] they neither preach nor **practice** God's Word but teach
LC : 01 :227(396) [0645] tricks and sharp **practices** and crafty dealing.
LC : 01 :302(405) [0667] or other great estate, he **practices** bribery, through
LC : 01 :313(407) [0671] these commandments, **practicing** gentleness, patience,
LC : 01 :319(408) [0673] how to teach and **practice** the Ten Commandments.
LC : 01 :331(410) [0677] in our memory, and **practice** them in all our works and
LC : 01 :332(410) [0677] find occasion enough to **practice** the Ten
LC : 01 :333(410) [0677] works which are taught and **practiced** apart from them.
LC : 03 :098(433) [0725] for us to use and **practice** every hour, keeping it with us
LC : 04 :041(441) [0743] Christian has enough to study and to **practice** all his life.
LC : 04 :079(446) [0751] Baptism, to resume and **practice** what had earlier been
LC : 04 :085(446) [0753] be Christians, we must **practice** the work that makes us
LC : 05 :083(456) [0773] Try this, therefore, and **practice** it well.
LC : 05 :085(456) [0773] with joy and earnestness, **practice** them from their youth,
LC : 06 :008(458) [0000] I refer to the **practice** of confessing to God alone or to
SD : 02 :016(523) [0887] Word and putting it into **practice**, he would preserve faith
SD : 10 :028(615) [1061] or conform to their **practices**, since this serves to imperil

Praescientia (1)
SD : 11 :006(617) [1065] God's foreknowledge (*praescientia*) sees and knows in

Praise (51), Praised (23), Praises (12), Praiseworthy (6), Praising (1)
PR : PR :002(003) [0007] Charles V, of most **praiseworthy** memory, at the Diet of
PR : PR :007(004) [0009] and to this end our **praiseworthy** predecessors, and also
PR : PR :013(007) [0013] almighty God to his **praise** and glory and after mature
PR : PR :017(008) [0015] reached by our **praiseworthy** predecessors and by
PR : PR :024(013) [0023] and expansion of God's **praise** and glory, to the
AG : 20 :004(041) [0053] Our opponents no longer **praise** these useless works so
AG : 20 :035(046) [0057] works but is rather to be **praised** for teaching that good
AG : 23 :020(055) [0063] has also been highly **praised** in the imperial laws and in
AG : 27 :013(072) [0077] so monastic vows were **praised** more highly than
AG : 27 :051(079) [0083] the state of celibacy **praised** above all measure, draw
AL : 23 :020(055) [0063] heathen, have adorned marriage with the greatest **praise**.
AL : 25 :004(062) [0069] The power of keys is **praised**, and people are reminded of
AL : 27 :052(079) [0083] They hear celibacy **praised** above measure, and therefore
AP : 02 :043(106) [0117] good nor bad, neither to be **praised** nor condemned.
AP : 04 :024(110) [0127] it ought not be **praised** at the expense of Christ.
AP : 04 :033(111) [0129] deeds that are excellent and **praiseworthy** in human eyes.
AP : 04 :057(114) [0137] and worship is especially **praised** throughout the prophets
AP : 04 :059(115) [0137] of faith when they see it **praised** everywhere as the
AP : 04 :072(116) [0141] They imagine faith is **praised** so highly because it is this
AP : 04 :073(117) [0141] and we give the highest **praise** to the ministry of the
AP : 04 :125(124) [0157] from him, to thank and **praise** him, and to submit to him
AP : 04 :154(128) [0165] points to the woman and **praises** her reverence, her
AP : 04 :155(128) [0165] In this way, therefore, he **praises** her entire act of
AP : 04 :188(133) [0173] For they **praise** works in such a way as not to remove the
AP : 04 :192(133) [0175] is determined that nothing happen to the **praise** of God.
AP : 04 :199(134) [0175] Such **praise** undoubtedly moves the faithful to good
AP : 04 :200(134) [0175] Therefore we **praise** good works and require them, and
AP : 04 :236(140) [0185] fit very well with their **praises** of love; if our opponents
AP : 04 :237(140) [0185] different from those **praises** of love which they recite from
AP : 04 :269(147) [0197] Whenever good works are **praised** and the law preached,
AP : 04 :269(147) [0197] therefore, that works are **praised** for pleasing God on
AP : 04 :322(157) [0209] life of men, however **praiseworthy**, if it is to be judged
AP : 04 :324(157) [0209] teach wrongly when they **praise** merits in such a way as to
AP : 04 :371(164) [0221] them where works are **praised** in the Scriptures must be
AP : 07 :043(177) [0243] of them Epiphanius **praises** the decree and says that it
AP : 11 :002(180) [0249] Luther the highest **praise** of all good men, since it
AP : 11 :003(180) [0249] they are but honest, will undoubtedly approve and **praise**.
AP : 13 :013(212) [0311] every possible kind of **praise** in opposition to the fanatics
AP : 16 :010(224) [0333] How they have **praised** the theory that the Gospel
AP : 16 :011(224) [0333] Such **praise** is dangerous, especially because it is so out of
AP : 21 :004(229) [0343] highly; we should also **praise** the saints themselves for
AP : 21 :004(229) [0343] these gifts, just as Christ **praises** faithful businessmen
AP : 23 :021(242) [0369] remember that Christ is **praising** those who have the gift
AP : 23 :032(244) [0373] adds faith and does not **praise** domestic duties apart from
AP : 23 :047(246) [0377] is the exaggerated way the monks have **praised** celibacy.
AP : 23 :049(246) [0377] observances should be **praised** "for the sake of discipline
AP : 24 :025(253) [0391] called "sacrifices of **praise**": the proclamation of the
AP : 24 :026(254) [0393] offer up a sacrifice of **praise** to God," with the
AP : 24 :026(254) [0393] commands them to offer **praises**, that is, prayer,
AP : 24 :033(255) [0395] Among the **praises** of God or sacrifices of praise we
AP : 24 :033(256) [0395] of God or sacrifices of **praise** we include the proclamation
AP : 24 :033(256) [0395] Supper itself can be **praise** or thanksgiving, but it does
AP : 24 :074(263) [0411] the ceremony itself as **praise** to God, as a demonstration
AP : 24 :074(263) [0411] Thus the ceremony becomes a sacrifice of **praise**.
AP : 24 :075(263) [0411] and of thanksgiving or **praise**; the first of these belongs to
AP : 27 :036(275) [0433] by the immoderate **praises** of the monastic life; but since
AP : 27 :039(276) [0433] are now modifying their **praises** about perfection, they
AP : 27 :046(277) [0435] Let the philosophers **praise** Aristippus for throwing a
AP : 27 :047(277) [0437] It is an exaggeration to **praise** it the way the *Extravagant*
AP : 27 :047(277) [0437] to heap such extravagant **praises** upon something that
AP : 27 :061(279) [0441] When the Rechabites are **praised**, therefore, we must note
AP : 27 :061(280) [0441] their parents, they are **praised** for their obedience, which
S2 : 02 :019(296) [0467] has possessed the pope to **praise** and approve of these
SC : PR :027(341) [0539] To him be **praise** and thanks forever, through Christ, our
SC : 01 :004(342) [0539] upon him, pray to him, **praise** him, and give him thanks.
SC : 02 :002(345) [0543] of this I am bound to thank, **praise**, serve, and obey him.
SC : 09 :005(355) [0561] who do wrong and to **praise** those who do right"
LC : 01 :064(373) [0599] name in time of need, or **praise** and thank him in time of
LC : 01 :066(373) [0599] work by which God is **praised**, truth and justice are
LC : 01 :074(374) [0601] he may say, "God be **praised** and thanked!" "This God

Continued ▶

LC : 01 :084(376) [0605] God's Word and then **praise** God with song and prayer.
LC : 01 :103(379) [0611] but use it for the **praise** of God and the benefit and
LC : 01 :133(383) [0619] also highly exalts and **praises** this commandment, saying
LC : 01 :145(385) [0623] would dance for joy and **praise** and thank God; and with
LC : 01 :168(388) [0629] to bring them up to the **praise** and honor of God.
LC : 01 :326(409) [0675] upon him in prayer, **praise**, and thanksgiving, which
LC : 02 :010(412) [0679] How can we **praise** or portray or describe him in such a
LC : 02 :019(412) [0681] in duty bound to love, **praise**, and thank him without
LC : 02 :023(413) [0683] a desire to use all these blessings to his glory and **praise**.
LC : 03 :005(420) [0699] we are required to **praise** the holy name and pray or call
LC : 03 :039(425) [0709] he may receive from us not shame but honor and **praise**.
LC : 03 :045(426) [0709] etc., but used rightly to the **praise** and glory of God.
LC : 03 :046(426) [0709] same as in our idiom "to **praise**, extol, and honor" in
LC : 03 :048(426) [0711] to have his glory and **praise** exalted above everything else
LC : 03 :049(426) [0711] and life so that he may be **praised** and exalted is us.
LC : 03 :052(427) [0711] that God's name may be **praised** through his holy Word
LC : 04 :017(438) [0737] holy, and blessed water — **praise** it in any other terms
LC : 06 :022(459) [0000] treasure to be accepted with all **praise** and gratitude.
LC : 06 :035(461) [0000] let us lift up our hands in **praise** and thanks to God that
SD : 01 :036(514) [0869] David says: "I will **praise** thee, for I am wonderfully
SD : 04 :008(552) [0941] perform, are indeed **praiseworthy** in the sight of the
SD : 11 :060(626) [1083] to recognize and **praise** God's pure and unmerited grace
SD : 11 :087(631) [1093] of his will, and to the **praise** of his glorious grace which

Pray (122), Prayed (13), Praying (16), Prays (11)
AG : 26 :009(065) [0071] festivals in this way, **prayed** in this way, fasted in this
AG : 27 :049(079) [0083] may and should ask and **pray** God for those things of
AG : 28 :077(094) [0095] power, but we desire and **pray** that they may not coerce
AL : 21 :002(047) [0057] do not teach us to **pray** to the saints or seek their help,
AL : 21 :003(047) [0057] He is to be **prayed** to, and he has promised to hear our
AL : 00 :001(049) [0059] intent of the canons, we **pray** that Your Imperial Majesty
AP : 04 :125(124) [0157] to fear and love God, to **pray** and expect help from him,
AP : 04 :139(126) [0161] And therefore we **pray** that the Holy Spirit may govern
AP : 04 :168(130) [0169] Even this servant of God **prays** God to avert his
AP : 04 :168(130) [0169] that even the godly must **pray** for the forgiveness of sins.
AP : 04 :322(157) [0209] daily, since he is commanded to **pray** daily for his sins."
AP : 04 :326(158) [0211] He **prays** for the defense of God's cause and his glory, as
AP : 04 :328(158) [0211] Lord's Prayer the saints **pray** for the forgiveness of sins;
AP : 04 :331(158) [0211] Therefore Daniel **prays** (9:18, 19), "For we do not present
AP : 04 :331(158) [0211] hold of mercy when we **pray**, that is, to trust the mercy of
AP : 04 :332(158) [0211] opponents do when they **pray**, if indeed these profane
AP : 04 :332(158) [0211] had earned it, then they **pray** like the Pharisee in Luke
AP : 10 :002(179) [0247] in which the priest clearly **prays** that the bread may be
AP : 12 :150(206) [0299] attests to this when he **prays** (Ps. 6:1), "O Lord, rebuke
AP : 13 :016(213) [0313] a more exalted position, this would move men to **pray**.
AP : 15 :040(220) [0325] it is not to learn or **pray** but for the sake of the rite, as if
AP : 21 :001(229) [0343] honored and that the living saints should **pray** for others.
AP : 21 :002(229) [0343] while he was still alive, to **pray** for his brothers after his
AP : 21 :008(230) [0345] Besides, we grant that the angels **pray** for us.
AP : 21 :008(230) [0345] where the angel **prays**, "O Lord of hosts, how long
AP : 21 :009(230) [0345] that the saints in heaven **pray** for the church in general,
AP : 21 :009(230) [0345] in general, as they **prayed** for the church universal while
AP : 21 :009(230) [0345] Scripture about the dead **praying**, except for the dream
AP : 21 :010(230) [0345] Even if the saints do **pray** fervently for the church, it does
AP : 21 :018(231) [0347] In II Thess. 2:16, 17 Paul **prays**, "May our Lord Jesus
AP : 21 :027(232) [0349] Granted that blessed Mary **prays** for the church, does she
AP : 21 :031(233) [0351] venerating the saints or their practice of **praying** to them.
AP : 23 :018(242) [0369] Here they order men to **pray** God for continence and to
AP : 23 :027(243) [0371] the New Testament must **pray** continually, they must also
AP : 23 :027(243) [0371] The saints **prayed** even when they were not carrying on
AP : 23 :027(243) [0371] and marital intercourse did not keep them from **praying**.
AP : 23 :040(244) [0375] it gives more time for **praying**, teaching, and serving and
AP : 24 :003(250) [0385] Word may receive faith and fear and so may also **pray**.
AP : 24 :088(265) [0413] It **prays** that we might be made worthy to offer prayers
AP : 24 :093(267) [0417] after the consecration they **pray** that it may benefit the
AP : 27 :038(275) [0433] that in the morning he **prayed** in a few words for the
S2 : 02 :026(297) [0469] Although angels in heaven **pray** for us (as Christ himself
S2 : 02 :026(297) [0469] invoke angels and saints, **pray** to them, keep fasts and
S2 : 02 :027(297) [0469] a saint on earth, you can **pray** for me, not in one
S2 : 02 :027(297) [0469] not on this account **pray** to you, invoke you, keep fasts
S3 : 01 :002(302) [0477] by God's name, failure to **pray** and call upon God,
S3 : 12 :003(315) [0499] So children **pray**, "I believe in one holy Christian
SC : 01 :004(342) [0539] of need call upon him, **pray** to him, praise him, and give
SC : 03 :004(346) [0547] is holy in itself, but we **pray** in this petition that it may
SC : 03 :007(346) [0547] without our prayer, but we **pray** in this petition that it
SC : 03 :010(347) [0547] without our prayer, but we **pray** in this petition that it
SC : 03 :013(347) [0547] without our prayer, but we **pray** in this petition that God
SC : 03 :016(347) [0549] Answer: We **pray** in this petition that our heavenly
SC : 03 :016(347) [0549] neither merit nor deserve those things for which we **pray**.
SC : 03 :016(347) [0549] we nevertheless **pray** that God may grant us all things by
SC : 03 :018(347) [0549] no one to sin, but we **pray** in this petition that God may
SC : 03 :020(348) [0549] Answer: We **pray** in this petition, as in a summary, that
SC : 03 :021(348) [0549] himself commanded us to **pray** like this and promised to
SC : 05 :022(350) [0553] For all this I am sorry and **pray** for grace.
LC : PR :003(358) [0567] from the Bible and would **pray** the Lord's Prayer for
LC : 01 :021(367) [0585] not consist merely of erecting an image and **praying** to it.
LC : 01 :064(373) [0599] his name is hallowed, as we **pray** in the Lord's Prayer.
LC : 01 :074(374) [0601] to be trained to fast and **pray** to St. Nicholas and other
LC : 01 :120(381) [0615] with fasting and **pray** on their knees without ceasing"?
LC : 01 :316(408) [0671] them we must seek and **pray** for help and receive it
LC : 03 :001(420) [0697] Now follows the third part, how we are to **pray**.
LC : 03 :003(420) [0697] know what and how to **pray**, our Lord Christ himself has
LC : 03 :005(420) [0699] is this: It is our duty to **pray** because God has
LC : 03 :005(420) [0699] praise the holy name and **pray** or call upon it in every
LC : 03 :005(420) [0699] For to call upon it is nothing else than to **pray**.
LC : 03 :006(421) [0699] no difference whether I **pray** or not, as vulgar people do
LC : 03 :006(421) [0699] people do who say in their delusion: "Why should I **pray**?
LC : 03 :006(421) [0699] If I do not **pray**, someone else will."
LC : 03 :006(421) [0699] into the habit of never **praying**, alleging that since we
LC : 03 :006(421) [0699] prayers we teach that there is no duty or need to **pray**.
LC : 03 :008(421) [0699] To **pray**, as the Second Commandment teaches, is to call
LC : 03 :008(421) [0699] our duty and obligation to **pray** if we want to be
LC : 03 :008(421) [0699] thoughts that would prevent or deter us from **praying**.
LC : 03 :009(421) [0699] my choice here whether to **pray** or not, but it is my duty
LC : 03 :010(421) [0699] prevent or deter us from **praying**, as though it made no
LC : 03 :010(421) [0699] difference if we do not **pray**, or as though prayer were
LC : 03 :011(421) [0701] our misery and plight, and **pray** for grace and help.
LC : 03 :013(422) [0701] What we shall **pray**, and for what, we should regard as
LC : 03 :013(422) [0701] no matter what he has to **pray** for, everybody should
LC : 03 :015(422) [0701] and holy as St. Peter or St. Paul, then I would **pray**."
LC : 03 :016(422) [0703] Moreover, I **pray** for the same thing for which they all
LC : 03 :016(422) [0703] same thing for which they all **pray**, or ever have prayed."
LC : 03 :016(422) [0703] same thing for which they all pray, or ever have **prayed**."
LC : 03 :018(422) [0703] and punish us if we do not **pray**, just as he punishes all
LC : 03 :018(423) [0703] not have ordered you to **pray** and backed it up with such
LC : 03 :019(423) [0703] urged and encouraged to **pray** because God has promised
LC : 03 :020(423) [0703] awaken and kindle in our hearts a desire and love to **pray**.
LC : 03 :020(423) [0703] that we may not despise or disdain it or **pray** uncertainly.
LC : 03 :021(423) [0703] to Thee, dear Father, and **pray** not of my own accord or
LC : 03 :022(423) [0703] encouraged and drawn to **pray** because, in addition to
LC : 03 :023(423) [0703] in doubt, saying, "I have **prayed**, but who knows whether
LC : 03 :024(423) [0705] ought to drive and impel us to **pray** without ceasing.
LC : 03 :024(423) [0705] A person who wants to **pray** must present a petition,
LC : 03 :025(423) [0705] confess that they never **prayed** whole-heartedly for so
LC : 03 :025(423) [0705] has ever undertaken to **pray** out of obedience to God and
LC : 03 :027(424) [0705] impress upon us not to become negligent about **praying**.
LC : 03 :028(424) [0705] habit from his youth up to **pray** daily for all his needs,
LC : 03 :029(424) [0705] people brought again to **pray** rightly and not act so
LC : 03 :029(424) [0705] and coldly that they become daily more inept at **praying**.
LC : 03 :032(424) [0707] a good Christian **prays**, "Dear Father, thy will be done,"
LC : 03 :033(424) [0707] vain babbling and **praying** for something definite.
LC : 03 :034(425) [0707] that it should impel us to keep **praying** for it all our lives.
LC : 03 :037(425) [0707] But what is it to **pray** that his name may become holy?
LC : 03 :038(425) [0709] thing we have, and **praying**, as good children, that his
LC : 03 :045(426) [0709] see that in this petition we **pray** for exactly the same thing
LC : 03 :048(426) [0711] If you **pray** the petition whole-heartedly, you can be sure
LC : 03 :049(426) [0711] We **prayed** in the first petition that God would prevent
LC : 03 :050(426) [0711] is holy in itself and yet we **pray** that it may be holy among
LC : 03 :050(426) [0711] our prayer and yet we **pray** that it may come to us.
LC : 03 :052(427) [0711] We **pray** here at the outset that all this may be realized in
LC : 03 :052(427) [0711] So we **pray** that, led by the Holy Spirit, many may come
LC : 03 :053(427) [0713] Now, we **pray** for both of these, that it may come to those
LC : 03 :054(427) [0713] to say: "Dear Father, we **pray** Thee, give us thy Word,
LC : 03 :054(427) [0713] So we **pray** that thy kingdom may prevail among us
LC : 03 :055(427) [0713] You see that we are **praying** here not for a crust of bread
LC : 03 :058(428) [0713] the kingdom of God be the first thing for which we **pray**.
LC : 03 :060(428) [0715] Thus far we have **prayed** that God's name may be
LC : 03 :061(428) [0715] also; although we have **prayed** for what is most essential
LC : 03 :061(428) [0715] the devil — we must also **pray** that God's will may be
LC : 03 :067(429) [0717] as in every other case to **pray** without ceasing: "Thy will
LC : 03 :068(429) [0717] simply expressed, yet we have **prayed** in our own behalf.
LC : 03 :068(429) [0717] What we **pray** for concerns only ourselves when we ask
LC : 03 :068(429) [0717] for our own sake we must **pray** that his will may be done
LC : 03 :072(430) [0719] When you **pray** for "daily bread" you pray for everything
LC : 03 :072(430) [0719] pray for "daily bread" you **pray** for everything that is
LC : 03 :074(430) [0719] greatest need of all is to **pray** for our civil authorities and
LC : 03 :075(430) [0719] Moreover, we should **pray** for them, that through them
LC : 03 :079(431) [0721] things come from God and that we must **pray** for them.
LC : 03 :083(431) [0721] rogues, yet he wishes us to **pray** for them so we may
LC : 03 :088(432) [0723] need to call upon God and **pray**, "Dear Father, forgive us
LC : 03 :088(432) [0723] but forgiveness, before we **prayed** or even thought of it.
LC : 03 :092(433) [0725] cannot achieve such confidence, it will never dare to **pray**.
LC : 03 :097(433) [0725] therefore, that when we **pray** we may recall the promise
LC : 03 :097(433) [0725] Father, I come to Thee **praying** for forgiveness, not
LC : 03 :100(433) [0725] to retain and persevere in all the gifts for which we **pray**.
LC : 03 :100(433) [0727] good conscience, we must **pray** again that he will not
LC : 03 :105(434) [0727] constrained to cry out and **pray** every hour that God may
LC : 03 :106(434) [0729] entangled in them, but we **pray** here that we may not fall
LC : 03 :108(435) [0729] free rein and neither resist it nor **pray** for help against it.
LC : 03 :110(435) [0729] hast commanded me to **pray**; let me not fall because of
LC : 03 :113(435) [0729] everything that we **pray** for: God's name or glory, God's
LC : 03 :116(435) [0731] us to do on earth but to **pray** constantly against this
LC : 03 :117(436) [0731] see how God wants us to **pray** to him for everything that
LC : 03 :119(436) [0731] that we may never have an an excuse for failing to **pray**.
LC : 03 :120(436) [0731] part of one who does not **pray** as a matter of chance but
LC : 03 :123(436) [0731] St. James says, "If anyone **prays**, let him ask in faith, with
LC : 03 :124(436) [0731] certain that we do not **pray** in vain and that we must not
LC : 04 :056(444) [0747] fact that I believe and many people are **praying** for me.
LC : 04 :057(444) [0747] that he may believe, and we **pray** God to grant him faith.
LC : 05 :005(447) [0755] even if we never keep, **pray**, or believe them, so also does
LC : 05 :049(452) [0765] you need not believe or **pray**, for the one is just as much
LC : 05 :087(457) [0773] help us to believe, to love, to **pray**, and to fight the devil.
LC : 06 :009(458) [0000] to acknowledge that we are sinners and to **pray** for grace.
SD : 02 :051(531) [0901] I **pray** for those who are to believe in me through their
SD : 11 :021(619) [1069] they cling to God's Word, **pray** diligently, persevere in the
SD : 11 :030(621) [1073] Gospel, believe on Christ, **pray** and give thanks, are
SD : 11 :031(621) [1073] they "do not know how to **pray** as we ought," he

Prayer (139), Prayers (45)
AG : 21 :002(047) [0057] He alone has promised to hear our **prayers**.
AG : 25 :011(063) [0071] the true judge, in your **prayer**, telling him of your sins not
AG : 26 :036(069) [0075] cannot be driven out by anything but fasting and **prayer**."
AL : 21 :003(047) [0057] to be prayed to, and he has promised to hear our **prayers**.
AL : 25 :011(063) [0071] confess your sins to God, the true judge, in your **prayer**.
AL : 26 :036(069) [0075] cannot be driven out by anything but fasting and **prayer**."
AP : 04 :008(108) [0121] true love of God, true **prayer** to God, true conviction that
AP : 04 :008(108) [0121] that God hears **prayer**, and the expectation of God's help
AP : 04 :027(111) [0127] believe that he hears **prayer**, willingly obey him in death
AP : 04 :168(130) [0169] let every one who is godly offer **prayer** to thee" (Ps. 32:6).
AP : 04 :268(147) [0197] us are lightened by our **prayers** and good works, indeed
AP : 04 :322(157) [0209] on the Lord's **Prayer**: "Lest anybody should flatter
AP : 04 :328(158) [0211] And in the Lord's **Prayer** the saints pray for the
AP : 04 :332(158) [0211] Such **prayer**, which relies on its own righteousness and
AP : 04 :333(158) [0211] Therefore **prayer** relies upon the mercy of God when we
AP : 04 :385(166) [0225] because of faith, as the **prayers** of the church ask that
AP : 04 :385(166) [0225] is well known that every **prayer** closes with this phrase:

Continued ▶

A P : 0 7 :009(170) [0229] of sins, answer to **prayer**, and the gift of the Holy Spirit.
A P : 1 2 :139(203) [0295] fruits like true fasting, **prayer**, and charity have his
A P : 1 2 :143(204) [0295] True **prayer**, charity, and fasting have God's command:
A P : 1 2 :143(204) [0297] when a fixed number of **prayers** or certain acts of charity
A P : 1 2 :174(210) [0307] the commandments — **prayer**, thanksgiving, the
A P : 1 3 :016(213) [0311] to them, then why not **prayer**, which can most truly be
A P : 1 5 :043(221) [0327] the exercise of faith, **prayer** and our assurance that it is
A P : 2 1 :010(230) [0345] Since **prayer** ought to come from faith, how do we know
A P : 2 1 :010(230) [0345] Scripture, that the saints hear the individual's **prayers**?
A P : 2 1 :013(230) [0345] something uncertain, for **prayer** without faith is not
A P : 2 1 :013(230) [0345] uncertain, for prayer without faith is not **prayer**.
A P : 2 1 :013(230) [0345] The ancient **prayers** mention the saints, but they do not
A P : 2 1 :018(231) [0347] May **prayer** be made for him continually!"
A P : 2 1 :020(232) [0349] promise and Christ's merits must be the basis for **prayer**.
A P : 2 1 :026(232) [0349] do nothing but urge this **prayer** upon the dying man,
A P : 2 1 :034(233) [0353] as in the ancient **prayers**, this was not done in a
A P : 2 1 :036(234) [0353] affirmed that God hears the **prayers** of believers.
A P : 2 1 :037(234) [0353] examples of certain **prayers**, fasts, and other profitable
A P : 2 3 :027(243) [0371] Besides, **prayer** is one thing and ministration another.
A P : 2 3 :030(243) [0371] by the word of God and **prayer**" (I Tim. 4:5): by the Word
A P : 2 3 :030(243) [0371] God approves, and by **prayer**, that is, by faith which uses
A P : 2 3 :043(245) [0375] to have opportunity for **prayer**, but Paul does not want
A P : 2 4 :001(249) [0385] such as the order of the lessons, **prayers**, vestments, etc.
A P : 2 4 :003(250) [0385] out that our churches keep the Latin lessons and **prayers**.
A P : 2 4 :025(253) [0391] of the Gospel, faith, **prayer**, thanksgiving, confession, the
A P : 2 4 :026(254) [0393] to offer praises, that is, **prayer**, thanksgiving, confession,
A P : 2 4 :029(255) [0393] victims and requires **prayer**: "Do I eat the flesh of bulls?
A P : 2 4 :029(255) [0393] **Prayer** is called a sacrifice of thanksgiving.
A P : 2 4 :030(255) [0395] sacrifice; this is faith, **prayer**, thanksgiving, confession,
A P : 2 4 :032(255) [0395] becomes great, like faith, **prayer**, proclamation of the
A P : 2 4 :034(256) [0397] of the Gospel, faith, **prayer**, and things like that, though
A P : 2 4 :035(256) [0397] of the Gospel, faith, **prayer**, and thanksgiving.
A P : 2 4 :036(257) [0397] of flour symbolizes faith, **prayer**, and thanksgiving in the
A P : 2 4 :051(259) [0401] godly use of the sacraments, ardent **prayer**, and the like.
A P : 2 4 :083(264) [0413] from *lite*, which means **prayers**, but from *leita*, which
A P : 2 4 :087(265) [0413] a eucharist, because **prayers**, thanksgivings, and the
A P : 2 4 :087(265) [0413] neither ceremonies nor **prayers** provide an advantage *ex*
A P : 2 4 :087(265) [0413] arguing here not about **prayers**, but really about the
A P : 2 4 :088(265) [0413] the whole service, about the **prayers** and thanksgivings.
A P : 2 4 :088(265) [0413] be made worthy to offer **prayers** and supplications and
A P : 2 4 :088(265) [0413] It calls even **prayers** "bloodless sacrifices."
A P : 2 4 :088(265) [0413] of the mind, fear, faith, **prayer**, thanksgiving, and the
A P : 2 4 :093(267) [0417] parts of the Mass, namely, **prayers** and thanksgivings.
A P : 2 4 :093(267) [0417] the host itself but the **prayers** and everything that goes on
A P : 2 4 :094(267) [0417] We know that the ancients spoke of **prayer** for the dead.
A P : 2 4 :096(267) [0417] that Aerius believed that **prayers** for the dead were
S 2 : 0 4 :009(300) [0473] of doctrine, faith, sacraments, **prayer**, works of love, etc.
S 3 : 0 3 :028(308) [0487] by fasting, vigils, **prayers**, Masses, coarse clothing, and
S 3 : 0 8 :008(313) [0495] before God, and his **prayers** and alms were acceptable to
S C : P R :003(338) [0533] do not know the Lord's **Prayer**, the Creed, or the Ten
S C : P R :005(338) [0533] the people the Lord's **Prayer**, the Creed, the Ten
S C : P R :007(339) [0533] the Creed, the Lord's **Prayer**, the sacraments, etc.
S C : P R :008(339) [0535] in teaching the Lord's **Prayer**, the Creed, and the Ten
S C : P R :010(339) [0535] the Creed, the Lord's **Prayer**, etc., following the text word
S C : 0 3 :000(346) [0545] [III] The Lord's **Prayer** *in the plain form in which the*
S C : 0 3 :002(346) [0545] boldly and confidently in **prayer**, even as beloved children
S C : 0 3 :007(346) [0547] of itself, without our **prayer**, but we pray in this petition
S C : 0 3 :010(347) [0547] God is done without our **prayer**, but we pray in this
S C : 0 3 :013(347) [0547] the wicked, without our **prayer**, but we pray in this
S C : 0 3 :016(347) [0549] their account deny our **prayers**, for we neither merit nor
S C : 0 5 :018(350) [0553] of which we are not aware, as we do in the Lord's **Prayer**.
S C : 0 7 :000(352) [0557] [Morning and Evening **Prayers**]
S C : 0 7 :000(352) [0557] *teach his household to say morning and evening* ***prayers***
S C : 0 7 :002(352) [0557] standing, say the Apostles' Creed and the Lord's **Prayer**.
S C : 0 7 :002(352) [0557] Then you may say this **prayer**:
S C : 0 7 :005(353) [0559] standing, say the Apostles' Creed and the Lord's **Prayer**.
S C : 0 7 :005(353) [0559] Then you may say this **prayer**:
S C : 0 8 :009(353) [0559] Then the Lord's **Prayer** should be said, and afterwards
S C : 0 8 :009(353) [0559] Lord's Prayer should be said, and afterwards this **prayer**:
S C : 0 8 :011(354) [0559] Then the Lord's **Prayer** should be said, and afterwards
S C : 0 8 :011(354) [0559] Lord's Prayer should be said, and afterwards this **prayer**:
S C : 0 9 :005(355) [0561] urge that supplications, **prayers**, intercessions, and
S C : 0 9 :006(355) [0561] of life, in order that your **prayers** may not be hindered"
S C : 0 9 :013(356) [0563] in supplications and **prayers** night and day; whereas she
S C : 0 9 :014(356) [0563] urge that supplications, **prayers**, intercessions, and
L C : P R :003(358) [0567] from the Catechism, the **Prayer** Book, the New
L C : P R :003(358) [0567] would pray the Lord's **Prayer** for themselves and their
L C : P R :007(359) [0569] word for word the Lord's **Prayer**, the Ten
L C : S P :013(363) [0577] III. The **Prayer**, or Our Father, Which Christ Taught
L C : 0 1 :064(373) [0599] his name is hallowed, as we pray in the Lord's **Prayer**.
L C : 0 1 :073(374) [0601] meals and saying other **prayers** for both morning and
L C : 0 1 :084(376) [0605] God's Word and then praise God with song and **prayer**.
L C : 0 1 :089(377) [0605] Ten Commandments, the Creed, and the Lord's **Prayer**.
L C : 0 1 :187(390) [0633] hearty confidence and **prayer** commit to him whatever
L C : 0 1 :246(398) [0651] show forgiveness and mercy, as the Lord's **Prayer** teaches.
L C : 0 1 :316(408) [0671] the Creed and the Lord's **Prayer** must help us, as we shall
L C : 0 1 :326(409) [0675] by calling upon him in **prayer**, praise, and thanksgiving,
L C : 0 2 :003(411) [0679] we would need neither the Creed nor the Lord's **Prayer**.
L C : 0 3 :000(420) [0697] Third Part: The Lord's **Prayer**
L C : 0 3 :002(420) [0697] drum into his ears our **prayer** that he may give, preserve,
L C : 0 3 :004(420) [0699] we explain the Lord's **Prayer** part by part, it is very
L C : 0 3 :004(420) [0699] and draw people to **prayer**, as Christ and the apostles also
L C : 0 3 :006(420) [0699] **Prayer**, therefore, is as strictly and solemnly commanded
L C : 0 3 :006(421) [0699] knows whether God heeds my **prayer** or cares to hear it?
L C : 0 3 :006(421) [0699] false and hypocritical **prayers** we teach that there is no
L C : 0 3 :007(421) [0699] that used to pass for **prayers** in the church was not really
L C : 0 3 :007(421) [0699] to pass for prayers in the church was not really **prayer**.
L C : 0 3 :007(421) [0699] called singing or reading exercise, it is not really **prayer**.
L C : 0 3 :008(421) [0699] By invocation and **prayer** the name of God is glorified
L C : 0 3 :010(421) [0699] do not pray, or as though **prayer** were commanded for
L C : 0 3 :010(421) [0699] wants nor cares for our **prayers** because we are sinners
L C : 0 3 :011(421) [0701] and assuage his wrath and seek grace by their **prayers**.]
L C : 0 3 :012(422) [0701] From the fact that **prayer** is so urgently commanded, we
L C : 0 3 :012(422) [0701] by no means despise our **prayers**, but rather prize them
L C : 0 3 :013(422) [0701] "On my account this **prayer** would amount to nothing;
L C : 0 3 :014(422) [0701] these words to heart and in no case to despise **prayer**.
L C : 0 3 :014(422) [0701] **Prayer** used to be taught, in the devil's name, in such a
L C : 0 3 :014(422) [0701] But that is to stake **prayer** on luck and to mumble
L C : 0 3 :014(422) [0701] Such a **prayer** is worthless.
L C : 0 3 :016(422) [0701] you should say: "The **prayer** I offer is just as precious,
L C : 0 3 :016(422) [0701] God does not regard **prayer** on account of the person,
L C : 0 3 :016(422) [0703] which all the saints base their **prayer**, I, too, base mine.
L C : 0 3 :017(422) [0703] point, that all our **prayers** must be based on obedience to
L C : 0 3 :018(422) [0703] Nor will he allow our **prayers** to be frustrated or lost, for
L C : 0 3 :019(423) [0703] has promised that our **prayer** will surely be answered, as
L C : 0 3 :020(423) [0703] God testifies that our **prayer** is heartily pleasing to him
L C : 0 3 :022(423) [0703] never doubt that our **prayer** pleases him and will
L C : 0 3 :023(423) [0703] So this **prayer** is far superior to all others that we might
L C : 0 3 :023(423) [0703] Thus there is no nobler **prayer** to be found on earth, for
L C : 0 3 :024(423) [0705] which he desires; otherwise it cannot be called a **prayer**.
L C : 0 3 :025(423) [0705] have rightly rejected the **prayers** of monks and priests,
L C : 0 3 :026(423) [0705] But where there is true **prayer** there must be earnestness.
L C : 0 3 :026(424) [0705] Then **prayer** will come spontaneously, as it should, and
L C : 0 3 :027(424) [0705] and others is quite amply indicated in the Lord's **Prayer**.
L C : 0 3 :029(424) [0705] damage and harm he suffers when **prayer** is in proper use.
L C : 0 3 :030(424) [0705] that all our safety and protection consist in **prayer** alone.
L C : 0 3 :031(424) [0707] as well, except that the **prayers** of a few godly men
L C : 0 3 :031(424) [0707] But by **prayer** alone we shall be a match both for them
L C : 0 3 :033(424) [0707] learn above all to value **prayer** as a great and precious
L C : 0 3 :033(424) [0707] We by no means reject **prayer**, but we do denounce the
L C : 0 3 :034(425) [0707] we shall treat the Lord's **Prayer** very briefly and clearly.
L C : 0 3 :039(425) [0709] Since in this **prayer** we call God our Father, it is our duty
L C : 0 3 :047(426) [0709] then, what a great need there is for this kind of **prayer**!
L C : 0 3 :050(426) [0711] of itself without our **prayer** and yet we pray that it may
L C : 0 3 :068(429) [0717] come even without our **prayer**, so must his will be done
L C : 0 3 :069(429) [0717] Such **prayer** must be our protection and defense now to
L C : 0 3 :076(431) [0719] it one might make a long **prayer**, enumerating with many
L C : 0 3 :081(431) [0721] in his power, and our **prayer** to God did not restrain him,
L C : 0 3 :084(432) [0723] this petition of the Lord's **Prayer** be turned against them.
L C : 0 3 :088(432) [0723] without and before our **prayer**; and he gave us the
L C : 0 3 :092(432) [0725] and cheerful conscience to stand before him in **prayer**.
L C : 0 3 :096(433) [0725] after the Lord's **Prayer** in Matt. 6:14, saying, "If you
L C : 0 3 :110(435) [0729] take refuge in the Lord's **Prayer** and to appeal to God
L C : 0 3 :111(435) [0729] But **prayer** can resist him and drive him back.
L C : 0 3 :113(435) [0729] entire substance of our **prayer** may be directed against
L C : 0 3 :119(436) [0731] But the efficacy of **prayer** consists in our learning also to
L C : 0 3 :119(436) [0731] is, not to doubt that our **prayer** is surely heard and will be
L C : 0 3 :120(436) [0731] Where such faith is wanting, there can be no true **prayer**.
L C : 0 3 :121(436) [0731] that God hears their **prayer** but remain in doubt, saying,
L C : 0 3 :121(436) [0731] I be so bold as to boast that God hears my **prayer**?
L C : 0 3 :124(436) [0731] vain and that we must not in any way despise our **prayers**.
L C : 0 4 :006(437) [0733] Creed, and the Lord's **Prayer** are not spun out of any
L C : 0 5 :005(447) [0755] the Lord's **Prayer**, and the Creed retain their nature and
L C : 0 5 :037(450) [0761] Fasting and **prayer** and the like may have their place as
L C : 0 5 :083(456) [0773] advice and seek their **prayers**, and never give up until the
L C : 0 5 :085(456) [0773] Creed, and the Lord's **Prayer** into the young so that they
L C : 0 6 :008(458) [0000] expressed in the Lord's **Prayer** when we say, "Forgive us
L C : 0 6 :009(458) [0000] Indeed, the whole Lord's **Prayer** is nothing else than such
L C : 0 6 :009(458) [0000] For what is our **prayer** but a confession that we neither
L C : 0 6 :010(458) [0000] toward his neighbor, is included in the Lord's **prayer**.
L C : 0 6 :012(458) [0000] we have in the Lord's **Prayer** a twofold absolution: our
S D : 0 2 :015(523) [0887] We find similar **prayers** in St. Paul's letters (Eph. 1:17,
S D : 0 2 :015(523) [0887] Of course, such **prayers** and passages about our ignorance
S D : 0 2 :041(529) [0897] petition of the Lord's **Prayer** Luther answers the
S D : 0 2 :046(530) [0899] Christian exercises as **prayer**, reading, and Christian
S D : 0 7 :039(576) [0985] through the Word and **prayer** is the true flesh and blood
S D : 1 1 :010(618) [1067] myself with repentance, faith, **prayer**, and godliness.

Preach (61), Preached (56), Preaches (8), Preaching (82)

A G : P R :008(025) [0039] these things are **preached**, taught, communicated, and
A G : 0 7 :001(032) [0047] who the Gospel is **preached** in its purity and the holy
A G : 0 7 :002(032) [0047] that the Gospel be **preached** in conformity with a pure
A G : 1 4 :000(036) [0049] should publicly teach or **preach** or administer the
A G : 2 0 :005(041) [0053] about which they did not **preach** at all in former times.
A G : 2 0 :008(042) [0053] nothing but works was **preached** everywhere, our people
A G : 2 0 :019(043) [0055] was not heard in **preaching**, but poor consciences were
A G : 2 0 :022(044) [0055] therefore necessary to **preach** this doctrine about faith in
A G : 0 0 :001(047) [0059] of the doctrines that are **preached** and taught in our
A G : 2 4 :012(057) [0065] when our preachers **preached** about these things and the
A G : 2 6 :001(063) [0071] times men taught, **preached**, and wrote that distinctions
A G : 2 7 :017(073) [0077] and understand what our teachers teach and **preach**.
A G : 2 7 :038(077) [0081] monks have taught and **preached** that their invented
A G : 2 7 :044(078) [0081] monks have taught and **preached** that they were justified
A G : 2 8 :005(081) [0085] and command of God to **preach** the Gospel, to forgive
A G : 2 8 :008(082) [0085] only by teaching and **preaching** the Word of God and by
A G : 2 8 :009(082) [0085] through the office of **preaching** and of administering the
A G : 2 8 :010(082) [0085] through the office of **preaching**, it does not interfere at all
A G : 2 8 :012(083) [0085] has its commission to **preach** the Gospel and administer
A G : 2 8 :021(084) [0087] office of the bishop to **preach** the Gospel, forgive sins,
A G : 2 8 :024(084) [0087] from heaven, should **preach** to you a gospel contrary to
A G : 2 8 :024(084) [0087] to that which we **preached** to you, let him be accursed,"
A G : 2 8 :062(092) [0093] no longer taught and **preached** with clarity and purity.
A G : 2 8 :070(093) [0093] an oath that he will not **preach** this doctrine, although
A L : 1 4 :000(036) [0049] that nobody should **preach** publicly in the church or
A L : 2 0 :004(041) [0053] them and do not **preach** about such unprofitable works
A L : 2 6 :045(070) [0075] to holy days but to **preach** piety toward God and good
A L : 2 8 :005(081) [0085] or command of God to **preach** the Gospel, to remit and
A L : 2 8 :007(082) [0085] he also said, "Go and **preach** the gospel to the whole
A L : 2 8 :008(082) [0085] only by teaching or **preaching** the Gospel and by
A L : 2 8 :012(083) [0085] its own commission to **preach** the Gospel and administer
A L : 2 8 :024(084) [0087] from heaven should **preach** any other Gospel, let him be
A P : 0 4 :062(115) [0139] and forgiveness of sins should be **preached** in his name.
A P : 0 4 :062(115) [0139] By its accusations, the **preaching** of penitence terrifies our
A P : 0 4 :200(134) [0175] doctrine of penitence is **preached** to the wicked, whose
A P : 0 4 :230(139) [0181] We for our part **preach** the foolishness of the Gospel,
A P : 0 4 :252(143) [0191] James **preaches** only the works that faith produces, as he

Continued ▶

A P : 0 4 :256(144) [0193] In the **preaching** of the law there are two things we must
A P : 0 4 :257(144) [0193] Otherwise, if the **preaching** of the law were enough by
A P : 0 4 :257(144) [0193] Thus in the **preaching** of penitence it is not enough to
A P : 0 4 :257(144) [0193] it is not enough to **preach** the law, the Word that convicts
A P : 0 4 :257(144) [0193] of Christ from the **preaching** of penitence, they deserve to
A P : 0 4 :258(144) [0193] is evident in Isaiah's **preaching** of penitence: "Cease to do
A P : 0 4 :259(144) [0193] Christ is **preaching** penitence when he says, "Forgive,"
A P : 0 4 :260(145) [0193] that in the **preaching** of penitence the preaching of
A P : 0 4 :260(145) [0193] of penitence the **preaching** of the law is not enough
A P : 0 4 :260(145) [0193] The **preaching** of the Gospel must be added, that is, that
A P : 0 4 :261(145) [0195] of sins is not the **preaching** of the law, but a truly
A P : 0 4 :266(146) [0197] Christ when the law is **preached** and works are enjoined.
A P : 0 4 :267(146) [0197] of Daniel: Since he is **preaching** penitence he is teaching
A P : 0 4 :269(147) [0197] are praised and the law **preached**, therefore, we must hold
A P : 0 4 :271(147) [0199] In this way we must view the **preaching** of penitence.
A P : 0 4 :281(149) [0201] must be added to the **preaching** of the law, that for his
A P : 0 4 :292(152) [0203] terrified by the **preaching** of penitence, he takes heart and
A P : 0 4 :365(163) [0219] and hence this belongs to the **preaching** of penitence.
A P : 0 7 :025(173) [0235] are accused, because we **preach** the blessing of Christ,
A P : 0 7 :048(177) [0245] (Gal 1:9), "If anyone is **preaching** to you a gospel contrary
A P : 1 2 :030(186) [0259] of sins should be **preached** in my name to all nations."
A P : 1 2 :122(200) [0289] (Rom. 6:19); Christ's **preaching** of penitence (Matt. 4:17),
A P : 1 2 :122(200) [0289] penitence should be **preached**"; Peter's preaching of
A P : 1 2 :122(200) [0289] be preached"; Peter's **preaching** of penitence (Acts 2:38).
A P : 1 2 :123(200) [0289] Christ says, "Be penitent"; the apostles **preach** penitence.
A P : 1 3 :009(212) [0311] but they are called to **preach** the Gospel and administer
A P : 1 5 :042(220) [0325] where no sermons are **preached** during the whole year,
A P : 1 5 :042(221) [0327] the chief worship of God is the **preaching** of the Gospel.
A P : 1 5 :042(221) [0327] When our opponents do **preach**, they talk about human
A P : 2 4 :040(257) [0399] alone and not **preaching** the Gospel, being put to death
A P : 2 4 :041(257) [0399] regard for religion and the **preaching** of the Gospel.
A P : 2 4 :043(257) [0399] sermons they do not **preach** the Gospel or console
A P : 2 4 :080(264) [0411] just as a minister who **preaches** shows forth the gospel to
A P : 2 4 :089(266) [0415] for commemoration and **preaching** among the living.
A P : 2 7 :054(278) [0437] they neither hear nor **preach** the Gospel about the free
A P : 2 8 :003(281) [0443] it that there is proper **preaching** and administration of the
A P : 2 8 :020(284) [0449] (Gal. 1:8), "If anyone **preaches** another Gospel, let him be
S 1 : P R :004(289) [0455] I am still writing, **preaching**, and lecturing every day.
S 2 : 0 2 :024(296) [0469] power of the pope but by the **preaching** of God's Word.
S 3 : 0 3 :006(304) [0481] of sins should be **preached** in his name to all nations."
S 3 : 0 3 :039(309) [0489] repentance which John **preaches**, which Christ
S 3 : 0 3 :039(309) [0489] Christ subsequently **preaches** in the Gospel, and which we
S 3 : 0 3 :039(309) [0489] preaches in the Gospel, and which we also **preach**.
S 3 : 0 4 :000(310) [0491] of the Gospel) is **preached** to the whole world; second,
S 3 : 0 8 :006(312) [0495] Why do they not stop **preaching** and writing until the
S 3 : 1 0 :002(314) [0497] who are unwilling to **preach** or teach or baptize or
S 3 : 1 5 :005(317) [0501] believed and am still **preaching** and firmly believing as
T R : 0 0 :010(321) [0505] however, that he at once **preached** the Gospel without
T R : 0 0 :030(325) [0513] the sheep, that is, to **preach** the Word or govern the
T R : 0 0 :031(325) [0513] that is, the command to **preach** the Gospel, proclaim the
T R : 0 0 :038(326) [0515] from heaven should **preach** to you a gospel contrary to
T R : 0 0 :038(326) [0515] to that which we **preached** to you, let him be accursed"
T R : 0 0 :060(330) [0521] the churches that they **preach** the Gospel, remit sins,
S C : P R :009(339) [0535] When you **preach** to intelligent and educated people, you
S C : P R :020(340) [0537] It is necessary to **preach** about such things.
S C : P R :022(341) [0537] We should so **preach** that, of their own accord and
S C : 0 1 :006(342) [0541] his Word and the **preaching** of the same, but deem it holy
S C : 0 9 :003(354) [0561] those who labor in **preaching** and teaching; for the
L C : P R :002(358) [0567] they are to teach and **preach** is now available to them in
L C : P R :002(358) [0567] to be: "Sermons That **Preach** Themselves," "Sleep
L C : S P :026(364) [0579] should also attend **preaching**, especially at the time
L C : S P :026(364) [0581] and thus the **preaching** will not be without benefit and
L C : S P :027(364) [0581] we take such care to **preach** on the Catechism frequently
L C : 0 1 :038(369) [0591] They refuse to hear what is **preached** or spoken to them.
L C : 0 1 :077(375) [0603] their minds, for when we **preach** to children, we must also
L C : 0 1 :090(377) [0607] day because they neither **preach** nor practice God's Word
L C : 0 1 :092(377) [0607] God's Word is taught, **preached**, heard, read, or
L C : 0 1 :096(378) [0609] of habit go to hear **preaching** and depart again with as
L C : 0 1 :097(378) [0609] permit ourselves to be **preached** to and admonished but
L C : 0 1 :167(388) [0629] it would be well to **preach** to parents on the nature of
L C : 0 1 :197(391) [0637] But this would be no **preaching** for monks.
L C : 0 1 :232(396) [0647] For we must **preach** this not to Christians but chiefly to
L C : 0 1 :232(396) [0647] if the judge, the jailer, or the hangman did the **preaching**.
L C : 0 2 :033(415) [0687] the entire Gospel that we **preach** depends on the proper
L C : 0 2 :037(415) [0687] of the church, where he **preaches** to us and brings us to
L C : 0 2 :038(415) [0689] our hearts through the **preaching** of the Gospel by the
L C : 0 2 :042(416) [0689] Holy Spirit reveals and **preaches** that Word, and by it he
L C : 0 2 :043(416) [0689] cause the Word to be **preached** and does not awaken
L C : 0 2 :044(416) [0689] Spirit present to reveal this truth and have it **preached**.
L C : 0 2 :045(416) [0689] For where Christ is not **preached**, there is no Holy Spirit
L C : 0 2 :053(417) [0693] it he gathers us, using it to teach and **preach** the Word.
L C : 0 2 :054(417) [0693] everything that is to be **preached** concerning the
L C : 0 2 :070(420) [0697] we shall have enough to **preach** and learn on the subject
L C : 0 3 :041(425) [0709] it is profaned when men **preach**, teach, and speak in
L C : 0 3 :047(426) [0711] cry out against all who **preach** and believe falsely and
L C : 0 3 :054(427) [0713] Gospel may be sincerely **preached** throughout the world
L C : 0 3 :065(429) [0715] where God's Word is **preached**, accepted or believed, and
L C : 0 4 :037(441) [0741] they cry out against us as though we **preach** against faith.
L C : 0 5 :031(450) [0759] if it were not proclaimed by **preaching**, by the oral Word?
L C : 0 5 :033(450) [0761] they are not spoken or **preached** to stone and wood but to
L C : 0 5 :044(451) [0763] we must be persistent in **preaching**, lest people become
L C : 0 5 :065(454) [0769] I have said, are not **preached** to wood or stone but to you
L C : 0 6 :006(457) [0000] we shall provide no **preaching**, nor will they have our
L C : 0 6 :007(457) [0000] gladly, however, we must **preach**, exhorting,
L C : 0 6 :016(459) [0000] We neither noticed nor **preached** the very necessary
L C : 0 6 :030(460) [0000] heed the warning of our **preaching**, we shall have nothing
L C : 0 6 :031(460) [0000] as we are compelled to **preach** and administer the
E P : R N :001(464) [0777] from heaven should **preach** to you a gospel contrary to
E P : R N :001(464) [0777] to that which we **preached** to you, let him be accursed."
E P : 0 2 :004(470) [0787] employs to this end the **preaching** and the hearing of
E P : 0 2 :011(471) [0789] beginning through the **preaching** of the Word and in it
E P : 0 4 :004(476) [0797] the law should not be **preached** at all to Christians but
E P : 0 5 :001(477) [0801] has been, Is the **preaching** of the Holy Gospel strictly
E P : 0 5 :001(477) [0801] strictly speaking only a **preaching** of grace which
E P : 0 5 :001(478) [0801] of sins, or is it also a **preaching** of repentance and reproof
E P : 0 5 :009(479) [0803] earnest and terrifying **preaching** and advertisement of
E P : 0 5 :010(479) [0803] strictly speaking, the **preaching** of the Gospel but the
E P : 0 5 :010(479) [0803] of the Gospel but the **preaching** of Moses and the law,
E P : 0 5 :010(479) [0803] office — namely, to **preach** grace, to comfort, to make
E P : 0 5 :010(479) [0803] And this is the **preaching** of the Gospel, strictly speaking.
E P : 0 6 :003(480) [0805] and confess that the **preaching** of the law is to be
E P : 0 9 :003(492) [0827] taught in his sermon **preached** at Torgau in the year
E P : 1 2 :011(498) [0841] do with clergyman who **preach** the Gospel according to
E P : 1 2 :011(499) [0841] and reprove the **preaching** and the errors of the
E P : 1 2 :022(499) [0841] the church — the Word **preached** and heard — is not a
S D : 0 2 :002(520) [0881] the Word of God is **preached** and the grace of God is
S D : 0 2 :004(520) [0881] is, without the external **preaching** and hearing of the
S D : 0 2 :005(521) [0881] Word of God when it is **preached**, but considers it
S D : 0 2 :005(521) [0881] the Word which is **preached** and heard, purely out of
S D : 0 2 :010(522) [0883] of the Gospel that we **preach** to save those who believe"
S D : 0 2 :021(525) [0889] or even to teach and **preach**" until the Holy Spirit
S D : 0 2 :027(527) [0891] in this, that God in the **preaching** of the truth reveals his
S D : 0 2 :027(527) [0891] this Gospel when it is **preached** is our own work and lies
S D : 0 2 :050(531) [0901] Word (when one hears it **preached** or reads it) and the
S D : 0 2 :051(531) [0901] the folly of what we **preach** to save those who believe"
S D : 0 2 :051(531) [0901] is heard comes by the **preaching** of Christ" (Rom. 10:17).
S D : 0 2 :051(531) [0901] all who in his name **preach** repentance and the remission
S D : 0 2 :052(531) [0901] be saved must hear this **preaching**, for the preaching and
S D : 0 2 :052(531) [0901] this preaching, for the **preaching** and the hearing of God's
S D : 0 2 :054(531) [0903] this means (namely, the **preaching** and the hearing of his
S D : 0 2 :054(531) [0903] so that through the **preaching** of the law man learns to
S D : 0 2 :054(531) [0903] heart, and through the **preaching** of and meditation upon
S D : 0 2 :055(531) [0903] who through the Word **preached** and heard illuminates
S D : 0 2 :055(532) [0903] the Word of God is **preached**, pure and unalloyed
S D : 0 2 :056(532) [0903] Word which is heard and **preached** is an office and work
S D : 0 2 :057(532) [0903] a person will not hear **preaching** or read the Word of
S D : 0 2 :071(535) [0909] and has his holy Gospel **preached** to us, through which
S D : 0 2 :071(535) [0909] in us, and through the **preaching** of his Word and our
S D : 0 2 :089(538) [0915] takes place without the **preaching** and the hearing of the
S D : 0 2 :090(538) [0915] three (the Word of God **preached** and heard, the Holy
S D : 0 2 :090(539) [0915] for which he uses the **preaching** and the hearing of his
S D : 0 5 :001(558) [0951] holy Gospel when it is **preached** purely and without
S D : 0 5 :004(559) [0953] his apostles to **preach** the Gospel in all the world
S D : 0 5 :004(559) [0953] of sin should be **preached** in his name to all nations"
S D : 0 5 :005(559) [0953] apostles began in their **preaching** with repentance and
S D : 0 5 :006(559) [0953] of repentance but solely the **preaching** of God's grace.
S D : 0 5 :009(559) [0955] For the Gospel does not **preach** the forgiveness of sin to
S D : 0 5 :010(559) [0955] The mere **preaching** of the law without Christ either
S D : 0 5 :011(560) [0955] own work (that is, to comfort and to **preach** about grace).
S D : 0 5 :012(560) [0955] states: "Everything that **preaches** about our sin and the
S D : 0 5 :012(560) [0955] terrible revelation and **preaching** of God's wrath over sin
S D : 0 5 :015(561) [0957] the Apology says: "The **preaching** of the law is not
S D : 0 5 :015(561) [0957] who cast the **preaching** of the law out of the churches and
S D : 0 6 :009(565) [0965] and subdue it, lest after **preaching** to others I myself
S D : 0 6 :011(566) [0965] the law but through the **preaching** of the Gospel
S D : 0 6 :014(566) [0967] and comforts them with the **preaching** of the holy Gospel.
S D : 0 6 :024(568) [0971] require either the **preaching** of the law or its threats and
S D : 0 7 :003(569) [0973] the same way as by the **preached** Word, lifts itself up and
S D : 0 7 :061(580) [0995] spirit and faith, in the **preaching** and contemplation of
S D : 0 8 :094(609) [1049] 6. Likewise, that in the **preached** Word and in the right
S D : 1 0 :019(614) [1059] who are unwilling to **preach** or teach or baptize or
S D : 1 1 :017(619) [1069] the Word when it is **preached**, heard, and meditated on,
S D : 1 1 :026(620) [1071] so that it should be **preached** (Eph. 1:9, 10;
S D : 1 1 :027(620) [1071] he has commanded the **preaching** of repentance and
S D : 1 1 :028(620) [1071] Christ has commanded to **preach** "repentance and
S D : 1 1 :028(621) [1073] to whom repentance is **preached** should also have this
S D : 1 1 :029(621) [1073] takes place through the **preaching** of the Word as a
S D : 1 1 :069(627) [1085] (Rom. 10:17) when it is **preached** in sincerity and purity.
S D : 1 1 :076(629) [1087] or should despise the **preaching** of his Word and should
S D : 1 2 :016(634) [1099] of the church who **preach** the Gospel according to the

Preacher (20), Preachers (42)

A G : P R :008(025) [0039] of our pastors' and **preachers'** teaching and of our own
A G : 2 4 :012(057) [0065] Then when our **preachers** preached about these things and
A G : 2 5 :001(061) [0069] has not been abolished by the **preachers** on our side.
A G : 2 5 :005(062) [0069] In former times the **preachers** who taught much about
A G : 2 5 :013(063) [0071] Yet the **preachers** on our side diligently teach that
A G : 2 7 :013(073) [0077] the office of pastor and **preacher**, of ruler, prince, lord, or
A G : 2 8 :054(090) [0091] that in the assembly **preachers** should not all speak at
A G : 0 0 :006(096) [0095] of our confession and the teaching of our **preachers**.
A L : 2 0 :003(041) [0053] Concerning such things **preachers** used to teach little.
A P : 0 2 :050(106) [0119] Therefore our **preachers** have stressed this in their
A P : 2 1 :039(235) [0355] their authority and the **preachers** do their duty in
A P : 2 3 :055(247) [0379] Meanwhile, **preachers** of the Gospel should exhort the
A P : 2 4 :043(258) [0399] The **preachers** who want to look more learned take up
S 2 : 0 3 :001(297) [0471] we may have pastors, **preachers**, and other ministers in
S 3 : 0 3 :005(304) [0481] Christ, is called a **preacher** of repentance — but for the
S 3 : 0 3 :030(308) [0487] fiery angel St. John, the **preacher** of true repentance,
S 3 : 0 9 :000(314) [0497] **Preachers** should not mingle civil punishments with this
S 3 : 1 0 :001(314) [0497] and confirm us and our **preachers**, provided this could be
S 3 : 1 0 :003(314) [0497] without bishops by priests and **preachers** in common.
S 3 : 1 5 :005(317) [0501] I, Erhard Schnepf, **preacher** in Stuttgart, subscribe
S 3 : 1 5 :005(317) [0501] Conrad Oettinger, **preacher** of Duke Ulric of Pforzheim
S 3 : 1 5 :005(317) [0501] Master Adam of Fulda, **preacher** in Hesse
S 3 : 1 5 :005(317) [0501] Michael Caelius, **preacher** in Mansfeld, subscribed
S 3 : 1 5 :005(317) [0501] Master Peter Geltner, **preacher** in Frankfurt, subscribed
S 3 : 1 5 :005(318) [0501] I, Dr. John Lang, **preacher** of the church in Erfurt, in my
T R : 0 0 :082(334) [0529] List of the Doctors and **Preachers** Who Subscribed the
T R : 0 0 :082(334) [0529] favor of God, all the **preachers** who have been present in
T R : 0 0 :082(334) [0529] Paul Rhode, **preacher** in Stettin
T R : 0 0 :082(335) [0529] Michael Caelius, **preacher** in Mansfeld
T R : 0 0 :082(335) [0529] Peter Geltner, **preacher** in the church in Frankfurt
T R : 0 0 :082(335) [0529] Oettinger, of Pforzheim, **preacher** of Ulric, duke of
S C : 0 0 :000(337) [0531] of Dr. Martin Luther for Ordinary Pastors and **Preachers**
S C : P R :000(338) [0533] Martin Luther to all faithful, godly pastors and **preachers**.
S C : P R :006(338) [0533] who are pastors and **preachers**, that you take the duties

Continued ▸

S C : P R :007(338) [0533] In the first place, the **preacher** should take the utmost
S C : P R :020(340) [0537] to become pastors, **preachers**, notaries, etc., and tell them
S C : P R :025(341) [0539] So it is up to you, dear pastor and **preacher**!
S C : 0 9 :002(354) [0561] Bishops, Pastors, and **Preachers**
L C : P R :001(358) [0567] that many pastors and **preachers** are very negligent in this
L C : P R :001(358) [0567] if they were pastors or **preachers** for their bellies' sake and
L C : P R :006(359) [0569] do without pastors and **preachers** from now on because
L C : P R :006(359) [0569] allow both pastors and **preachers** to suffer distress and
L C : P R :007(359) [0569] too, am a doctor and a **preacher** — yes, and as learned
L C : P R :013(360) [0571] — especially we who would be pastors and **preachers**?
L C : P R :019(361) [0573] especially pastors and **preachers**, not to try to be doctors
L C : 0 1 :054(372) [0595] conscience, when false **preachers** arise and peddle their
L C : 0 1 :162(387) [0627] now support one good **preacher** although in the past they
L C : 0 1 :163(387) [0627] and once again allow **preachers** of lies to arise and lead us
L C : 0 1 :262(400) [0655] Wherever there are godly **preachers** and Christians, they
L C : 0 1 :263(400) [0655] This applies to false **preachers** with their corrupt teaching
L C : 0 1 :274(402) [0659] of civil magistrates, **preachers**, and parents, for we must
L C : 0 1 :289(404) [0663] especially to the precious Word of God and its **preachers**.
L C : 0 3 :028(424) [0705] around him, such as **preachers**, magistrates, neighbors,
L C : 0 6 :025(460) [0000] same way the pope's **preachers** have in the past kept
E P : 0 5 :007(478) [0803] contrast to Christ as a **preacher** of the Gospel, then we
S D : 0 2 :055(531) [0903] it is true that both the **preacher**'s planting and watering
S D : 0 2 :055(532) [0903] other hand, neither the **preacher** nor the hearer should
S D : 0 5 :012(560) [0955] the apostles and the **preachers** of the Gospel, just as
S D : 0 7 :013(571) [0977] and that of the other **preachers** who came with him from
S D : 1 0 :019(614) [1059] and confirm us and our **preachers**, provided this could be
S D : 1 0 :025(615) [1061] and particularly the **preachers** may or may not do with a
S D : 1 2 :003(633) [1095] there are not two **preachers** who are agreed in each and

Precautions (1)
A L : 2 3 :014(053) [0063] it is also well to take **precautions** against the introduction

Precede (4), Preceded (4), Precedes (10), Preceding (21)
A P : 0 4 :017(109) [0125] bid us merit this first disposition by our **preceding** merits.
A P : 0 4 :046(113) [0133] regenerates our hearts, it **precedes** our keeping of the law.
A P : 0 4 :141(126) [0161] So he indicates that faith **precedes** while love follows.
A P : 0 4 :278(149) [0199] or reconciliation, not by that which **precedes**.
A P : 0 4 :290(151) [0203] the forgiveness of sins **precedes** our love, but it imagines
A P : 1 2 :060(190) [0267] faith and say that it **precedes** penitence, they do not mean
A P : 1 2 :116(199) [0287] not because of our works, either **preceding** or following.
A P : 1 3 :014(213) [0311] distinguish it from the **preceding** ones which are, in the
A P : 2 3 :054(246) [0379] Similar vices have **preceded** the fall of many other cities,
A P : 2 3 :054(247) [0379] picture of the times that will **precede** the end of all things.
A P : 2 4 :053(259) [0403] The **preceding** words talk about the Levitical priesthood
S 3 : 0 3 :005(304) [0481] John, who **preceded** Christ, is called a preacher of
S 3 : 0 8 :007(313) [0495] to their faith through the external Word which **preceded**.
S 3 : 0 8 :008(313) [0495] if the Word and his hearing of it had not **preceded**.
S 3 : 0 8 :012(313) [0497] conceived without the **preceding** word of Gabriel, nor did
L C : 0 1 :116(381) [0615] not set into opposition to the **preceding** commandments.
L C : 0 1 :200(392) [0637] are easily understood from the **preceding** one.
L C : 0 1 :209(393) [0639] a level with the others; it **precedes** and surpasses them all,
L C : 0 1 :300(405) [0667] have not offended against the **preceding** commandments.
E P : 0 3 :004(473) [0793] his grace, without any **preceding**, present, or subsequent
E P : 0 3 :011(474) [0795] that the contrition that **precedes** justification and the
E P : 0 9 :002(492) [0827] This article, like the **preceding** one, cannot be
E P : 1 2 :001(498) [0839] In the **preceding** explanation we have made no mention
S D : 0 2 :086(538) [0913] It is evident from the **preceding** discussion that this
S D : 0 3 :009(541) [0919] part, and without any **preceding**, present, or subsequent
S D : 0 3 :022(543) [0923] For genuine contrition must **precede**.
S D : 0 3 :024(543) [0923] or insert that which **precedes** faith or follows faith into
S D : 0 3 :026(543) [0923] sin, for true contrition **precedes** and genuine faith exists
S D : 0 3 :027(543) [0925] thereby that neither the **preceding** contrition nor the
S D : 0 3 :027(544) [0925] For good works do not **precede** justification; rather they
S D : 0 3 :041(546) [0929] For good works do not **precede** faith, nor is sanctification
S D : 0 3 :041(546) [0931] order in which one thing **precedes** or follows the other.
S D : 0 3 :044(547) [0933] similar errors as contrary to the **preceding** explanation:
S D : 0 3 :054(549) [0935] indwelling follows the **preceding** righteousness of faith,
S D : 0 4 :002(551) [0939] held that therefore the **preceding** propositions and
S D : 0 4 :022(555) [0945] merit of Christ, as was explained in the **preceding** article).
S D : 0 4 :033(556) [0947] how, on the basis of the **preceding**, the exhortation to do
S D : 0 9 :003(610) [1051] any more than the **preceding** one, how Christ has been
S D : 1 1 :085(630) [1091] a punishment for his **preceding** sin and his horrible

Precedent (2)
A P : 2 1 :033(233) [0351] great moderation, the **precedent** still would be dangerous.
S 2 : 0 2 :025(297) [0469] nor does it have any **precedent** in the Scriptures.

Precept (11), Precepts (32)
P R : P R :024(013) [0023] that we have by divine **precept**, on account of the office
A G : 2 3 :005(051) [0061] all men can receive this **precept**," he indicated that few
A G : 2 6 :022(067) [0073] teaching as doctrines the **precepts** of men" (Matt. 15:9).
A G : 2 7 :012(072) [0077] of this life both the **precepts** and the counsels included in
A G : 2 7 :036(077) [0081] worship me, teaching as doctrines the **precepts** of men."
A G : 2 7 :037(077) [0081] for righteousness in the **precepts** and services invented by
A G : 2 7 :061(080) [0083] evangelical counsels and **precepts**, and that they furnish
A G : 2 8 :045(088) [0089] are used), according to human **precepts** and doctrines?
A L : 2 3 :005(051) [0061] all men can receive this **precept**" (Matt. 19:11), by which
A L : 2 6 :008(065) [0071] the second place, these **precepts** obscured the commands
A L : 2 6 :022(067) [0073] "In vain do they worship me with the **precepts** of men."
A L : 2 7 :012(072) [0077] not only of the **precepts** but also of the counsels of the
A L : 2 7 :036(077) [0081] "In vain do they worship me with the **precepts** of men."
A L : 2 7 :054(079) [0083] that this is prohibited by a counsel and not by a **precept**.
A L : 2 7 :061(080) [0083] the counsels and the **precepts**, and that monks do works
A L : 2 8 :045(088) [0089] are used), according to human **precepts** and doctrines?
A P : 0 4 :087(120) [0147] is not justified by the **precepts** of a good life, but through
A P : 0 7 :035(175) [0241] are used), according to human **precepts** and doctrines?
A P : 1 2 :143(204) [0297] "In vain do they worship me with the **precepts** of men."
A P : 1 5 :005(215) [0317] "In vain do they worship me with the **precepts** of men."
A P : 1 5 :028(219) [0323] and limitations of these **precepts** and cannot fix the
A P : 1 5 :034(220) [0325] By **precept** and example the apostles compel us to oppose
A P : 2 1 :018(231) [0347] But what **precept** or example can our opponents produce
A P : 2 1 :024(232) [0349] Let him produce one example or **precept** from Scripture.
A P : 2 3 :016(241) [0369] all men can receive this **precept**, but only those to whom
A P : 2 7 :023(273) [0427] "In vain do they worship me with the **precepts** of men."
A P : 2 7 :024(273) [0427] imagine that they observe both **precepts** and counsels.
A P : 2 7 :039(276) [0433] the pretext that they observe both **precepts** and counsels.
A P : 2 7 :069(281) [0443] "In vain do they worship me with the **precepts** of men."
S 1 : P R :013(291) [0459] God's commands and **precepts** in the spiritual and
S 2 : 0 2 :002(293) [0463] teaching as doctrines the **precepts** of men' (Matt. 15:9).
S 3 : 1 5 :001(316) [0501] as doctrines the **precepts** of men" (Matt. 15:9), and it is
S 3 : 1 5 :002(316) [0501] mortal sin to break such **precepts** of men, this, too, is
L C : P R :014(360) [0571] meditate upon his **precepts** whether sitting, walking,
L C : 0 1 :112(380) [0613] as God's command or as a holy, divine word and **precept**.
L C : 0 1 :276(402) [0659] you have a fine, precious **precept** for governing the
L C : 0 1 :317(408) [0673] themselves to look only to these **precepts** and heed them.
L C : 0 5 :045(451) [0763] These are words of **precept** and command, enjoining all
E P : 1 0 :003(493) [0829] teaching as doctrines the **precepts** of men" (Matt. 15:9).
E P : 1 0 :009(494) [0831] 1. That human **precepts** and institutions in the church are
E P : 1 0 :010(494) [0831] When such ceremonies, **precepts**, and institutions are
S D : 1 0 :008(612) [1055] teaching for doctrines the **precepts** of men" (Matt. 15:9).
S D : 1 2 :010(634) [1097] on their own peculiar **precepts** and self-chosen spirituality

Preceptor (1)
T R : 0 0 :082(000) [0529] our most revered **preceptor**, and the tract concerning the

Precious (37)
A G : 2 5 :002(061) [0069] they may esteem absolution as a great and **precious** thing.
A G : 2 6 :004(064) [0071] as something great and **precious** and know that faith in
A P : 0 4 :357(162) [0219] ought to be counted so **precious** that eternal life is their
A P : 0 4 :360(162) [0219] we have works that are **precious** enough to earn a
A P : 1 5 :019(218) [0319] with gold and silver, with **precious** stones and costly gifts."
A P : 1 5 :021(218) [0321] gold and silver and **precious** stones," believing that he is
S 2 : 0 2 :001(293) [0463] the supreme and most **precious** of the papal idolatries, for
S 2 : 0 2 :024(296) [0469] place belongs to the **precious** indulgences, which are
S 2 : 0 2 :025(297) [0469] of saints were a **precious** practice (which it is not), we
S C : 0 2 :004(345) [0545] but with his holy and **precious** blood and with his
L C : 0 1 :109(380) [0611] and prize them as the most **precious** treasure on earth.
L C : 0 1 :117(381) [0615] you to perform a task so **precious** and pleasing to him.
L C : 0 1 :117(381) [0615] regard it as great and **precious**, not on account of your
L C : 0 1 :140(384) [0621] and how **precious** and acceptable a work he does when he
L C : 0 1 :150(386) [0625] them as the most **precious** treasure and jewel on earth.
L C : 0 1 :221(395) [0643] Here you have another **precious** good work — indeed,
L C : 0 1 :276(402) [0659] Here you have a fine, **precious** precept for governing the
L C : 0 1 :289(404) [0663] now especially to the **precious** Word of God and its
L C : 0 1 :311(407) [0671] no matter how great or **precious** it may be in the eyes of
L C : 0 1 :314(407) [0671] this is considered a **precious** work that cannot be
L C : 0 2 :031(414) [0687] not with silver and gold but with his own **precious** blood.
L C : 0 3 :016(422) [0701] prayer I offer is just as **precious**, holy, and pleasing to
L C : 0 3 :033(424) [0707] prayer as a great and **precious** thing and may clearly
L C : 0 4 :008(437) [0733] It is a most **precious** thing, even though to all
L C : 0 4 :009(437) [0735] much greater and more **precious** because God has
L C : 0 4 :012(438) [0735] monks, no matter how **precious** and dazzling they might
L C : 0 4 :016(438) [0735] and tear from it the **precious** jeweled clasp with which
L C : 0 4 :026(439) [0739] Here you see again how **precious** and important a thing
L C : 0 5 :056(453) [0767] with this great and **precious** blessing, and it appears like a
L C : 0 5 :070(454) [0769] use the sacrament as a **precious** antidote against the
L C : 0 6 :007(458) [0000] them not to lose this **precious** and comforting treasure
L C : 0 6 :017(459) [0000] Thus the **precious** confession was not only made useless
L C : 0 6 :020(459) [0000] faithful advice to go and obtain this **precious** treasure.
L C : 0 6 :028(460) [0000] teach what a wonderful, **precious**, and comforting thing
L C : 0 6 :028(460) [0000] and we urge that such a **precious** blessing should not be
S D : P R :014(506) [0857] voices and separate the **precious** from the vile"
S D : 0 1 :003(509) [0861] Christ's benefits, his **precious** merits, and the Holy

Precise (2), Precisely (28)
A P : 0 2 :024(103) [0111] This is **precisely** the intention of Augustine's definition
A P : 0 2 :047(106) [0119] tyranny of the devil are, in the **precise** sense, penalties.
A P : 0 4 :345(160) [0217] **Precisely** in order to make hope sure and to distinguish
A P : 0 7 :016(171) [0231] kingdom of Christ, is, **precisely** speaking, the
A P : 1 2 :080(194) [0275] Christ revealed to us **precisely** because we cannot keep
A P : 1 5 :016(217) [0319] were condemned **precisely** because, in their ignorance of
L C : 0 1 :031(369) [0589] yet they are attached **precisely** to this one which stands at
L C : 0 1 :063(373) [0599] revealed and given to us **precisely** for our use and benefit.
L C : 0 1 :085(376) [0605] Jews, when it had to be **precisely** this or that day, for in
L C : 0 1 :099(378) [0609] This is **precisely** the sin that used to be classed among the
L C : 0 1 :300(405) [0665] wicked rogues, but **precisely** to the most upright — to
L C : 0 2 :035(415) [0687] Spirit," because it is so **precise** that we can find no
L C : 0 4 :059(444) [0747] argument and conclude, **Precisely** because Baptism has
L C : 0 5 :047(452) [0763] to eat only once a year, **precisely** on the evening of the
L C : 0 5 :061(453) [0767] as poor, miserable men, **precisely** because we are
E P : 0 5 :007(478) [0803] but is, strictly speaking, **precisely** a comforting and joyful
E P : 0 6 :002(480) [0805] by the Son of God **precisely** that they should exercise
S D : 0 1 :046(516) [0873] Scripture testifies that **precisely** the substance of this our
S D : 0 1 :046(516) [0873] we shall have and keep **precisely** this soul, although
S D : 0 3 :054(549) [0935] of faith, which is **precisely** the forgiveness of sins and the
S D : 0 6 :021(567) [0969] he holds up before them **precisely** the Ten
S D : 0 7 :017(572) [0979] is set forth briefly and **precisely** in words which agree in
S D : 0 7 :018(572) [0979] with the bread in **precisely** the same way as with the Word
S D : 0 7 :062(581) [0995] eating, however, is **precisely** faith — namely, that we hear,
S D : 0 7 :064(581) [0995] understood as referring **precisely** to oral eating and
S D : 0 7 :082(584) [1001] we bless," which happens **precisely** through the repetition
S D : 0 7 :104(587) [1009] word "spiritual" means **precisely** that spiritual communion
S D : 0 8 :026(596) [1023] This is **precisely** that he has laid aside completely and
S D : 0 8 :028(596) [1025] The right hand of God is **precisely** the almighty power of
S D : 1 1 :003(616) [1063] it; on the contrary, **precisely** in order to avert such misuse

Precluded (1)
S D : 0 7 :049(578) [0989] Christ himself likewise **precluded** a metonymy (that is, a

Predecessors (5)
P R : P R :002(003) [0007] pious and Christian **predecessors** to the then Emperor
P R : P R :007(004) [0009] end our praiseworthy **predecessors**, and also some of us,
P R : P R :008(005) [0009] later date our sainted **predecessors** and some of us
P R : P R :017(008) [0015] by our praiseworthy **predecessors** and by ourselves at
S D : P R :013(506) [0855] understanding of our **predecessors** who remained

Predestination (5), Predestined (3)
E P : 1 1 :005(495) [0833] 4. **Predestination** or the eternal election of God, however,

Continued ▶

E P : 1 1 :006(495) [0833] not to investigate this **predestination** in the secret counsel
E P : 1 1 :013(496) [0835] us, as it is written, "Those he **predestined**, he also called."
E P : 1 1 :019(497) [0837] for their sin, God has **predestined** certain people to
S D : 0 2 :027(526) [0891] treatise *Concerning **Predestination***, "The grace of God
S D : 1 1 :005(617) [1065] of God or God's **predestination** to salvation does not
S D : 1 1 :005(617) [1065] have been elected and **predestined** to eternal life "before
S D : 1 1 :013(618) [1067] election or about the **predestination** and ordering of the

Predication (1)
S D : 0 7 :038(576) [0985] to do with a figurative **predication**, but with an unusual

Predicted (4), Predicts (1)
A P : 0 4 :393(167) [0225] Moreover, the Scriptures **predicted** that human traditions
A P : 0 7 :004(169) [0227] Paul also **predicts** that Antichrist will "take his seat in the
A P : 1 2 :126(201) [0289] times, in which Christ **predicted** there would be the
A P : 2 7 :002(269) [0419] He **predicted** many things.
T R : 0 0 :082(334) [0527] Peter **predicted** that there would be wicked bishops in the

Pre-eminence (1), Preeminence (1), Preeminently (1)
A L : 2 0 :014(043) [0055] of little value and the **preeminence** of human works would
T R : 0 0 :008(321) [0505] a child neither seeks nor takes **pre-eminence** for himself
S D : 0 7 :111(589) [1011] and recite the errors **preeminently** of the Sacramentarians

Preface (11)
P R : P R :000(001) [0004] **Preface** to the Book of Concord
P R : P R :000(003) [0005] **Preface** to the Christian Book of Concord
A G : P R :000(024) [0039] **Preface**
A P : 0 4 :004(108) [0121] a few things by way of **preface** so that the sources of both
A P : 1 2 :004(183) [0253] of our position, we must say something by way of **preface**.
S 1 : P R :000(288) [0455] **Preface** of Dr. Martin Luther
S C : P R :000(338) [0533] **[Preface]**
L C : P R :000(358) [0567] Martin Luther's **Preface**
L C : S P :000(362) [0575] **Preface**
S D : P R :009(505) [0853] refers to them in the **Preface** to the Latin edition of his
S D : 0 4 :010(552) [0941] as Luther writes in his **Preface** to the Epistle of St. Paul

Prefatory (1)
A P : 2 4 :001(249) [0383] with, we must repeat the **prefatory** statement that we do

Prefer (5), Preference (1), Preferred (6), Prefers (2)
P R : P R :005(004) [0009] We should have **preferred**, and we besought and
A L : 2 2 :011(050) [0061] if any people **preferred** to use both kinds in the
A P : 0 4 :225(138) [0183] They object that love is **preferred** to faith and hope since
A P : 0 4 :245(142) [0189] faith nor exalt love in **preference** to it, but keeps it, lest
A P : 1 5 :025(219) [0321] spiritual, they will vastly **prefer** them to the works that
A P : 1 5 :052(222) [0329] consciences, should be **preferred** to all other advantages,
A P : 2 4 :086(265) [0413] places, unless some one **prefers** to think it was called that
S 1 : P R :003(289) [0455] perceive that the pope **prefers** to see all Christendom lost
T R : 0 0 :006(320) [0505] right and is even to be **preferred** to the commandments of
T R : 0 0 :048(328) [0519] and they have **preferred** these to works performed in
S C : P R :014(340) [0535] which you may **prefer**, and adhere to them without
L C : 0 1 :059(372) [0597] We **prefer** to act in secret without anyone's being aware
L C : 0 1 :275(402) [0659] one to report evil, to **prefer** charges, to attest, examine,
L C : 0 3 :108(435) [0729] is contrary to our will and we would **prefer** to be rid of it.

Pregnant (1)
L C : 0 1 :018(367) [0585] Venus, or others, while **pregnant** women worshiped

Prejudice (1)
S D : 1 0 :003(611) [1053] conscience and without **prejudice** to the divine truth, even

Prelates (2)
A P : 0 4 :390(166) [0225] To the **prelates** their own authority is obviously more
A P : 0 4 :392(167) [0225] in spite of the fact that **prelates** and some theologians and

Prematurely (1)
L C : P R :019(361) [0573] to try to be doctors **prematurely** and to imagine that they

Premise (2)
A P : 0 4 :079(117) [0143] easy to state the minor **premise** if we know how the
A P : 0 4 :080(118) [0143] We prove the minor **premise** as follows.

Preoccupied (3)
A L : 2 6 :015(066) [0073] and sermons were so **preoccupied** with gathering
A P : 0 4 :288(151) [0203] is reasonable and is **preoccupied** with outward works, it
A P : 1 2 :106(197) [0283] him not to be so **preoccupied** with the increase of his

Prepare (18), Preparation (8), Preparations (4), Prepared (23), Prepares (4)
P R : P R :000(001) [0004] Death of Martin Luther, **Prepared** for Publication by the
A G : P R :010(025) [0041] and German, we are **prepared**, in obedience to Your
A G : 0 5 :004(031) [0045] us through our own **preparations**, thoughts, and works
A L : 0 5 :004(031) [0045] Word, through their own **preparations** and works.
A P : P R :001(098) [0099] of theologians and monks **prepared** a Confutation of it.
A P : P R :005(098) [0101] me and several others to **prepare** an apology of our
A P : 0 4 :071(116) [0141] the start of justification or a **preparation** for justification.
A P : 0 4 :072(117) [0141] of all the arts since it **prepares** for them, even though it is
A P : 1 3 :013(213) [0311] through the Word but because of their own **preparations**.
S 3 : 0 3 :005(304) [0481] this way they were to be **prepared** to receive grace from
S C : P R :001(338) [0533] visitor constrained me to **prepare** this brief and simple
S C : 0 6 :010(352) [0557] Fasting and bodily **preparation** are a good external
S C : 0 6 :010(352) [0557] is truly worthy and well **prepared** who believes these
L C : P R :002(358) [0567] "Sleep Soundly," "**Prepared**!" and "Treasury."
L C : 0 3 :026(424) [0705] need to be taught how to **prepare** for it or how to
L C : 0 3 :057(427) [0713] he might desire and was **prepared** to give great and
L C : 0 3 :109(435) [0729] must be armed and **prepared** for incessant attacks.
L C : 0 5 :036(450) [0761] This, now, is the **preparation** required of a Christian for
L C : 0 5 :037(451) [0761] place as an external **preparation** and children's exercise so
L C : 0 5 :039(451) [0761] to be Christians should **prepare** themselves to receive this
L C : 0 5 :056(453) [0767] wait until they become **prepared**, until one week passes
E P : 0 2 :001(469) [0785] Holy Spirit, dispose and **prepare** himself for the grace of
E P : 0 2 :011(471) [0789] to help, to cooperate, to **prepare** itself for grace, to
E P : 0 7 :020(484) [0813] own virtues or in our internal and external **preparations**.
E P : 0 7 :038(486) [0817] Christ, but also depends on people's outward **preparation**.
S D : P R :003(501) [0847] of God, ordered the **preparation** of a Christian
S D : P R :002(503) [0851] that we shall neither **prepare** nor accept a different or a
S D : P R :005(504) [0851] this confession was **prepared** by our theologians but
S D : P R :006(504) [0853] extensive Apology was **prepared** and published in 1531 to
S D : P R :007(505) [0853] to the Articles which we **prepared** in the great assembly
S D : P R :007(505) [0853] as it was initially **prepared** and published for
S D : P R :008(505) [0853] Large Catechisms, as he **prepared** them and incorporated
S D : P R :012(506) [0855] also because all were **prepared** and published before the
S D : 0 2 :002(520) [0881] Can man **prepare** himself for such grace, accept it and
S D : 0 2 :003(520) [0881] he can to some extent **prepare** himself for grace and give
S D : 0 2 :007(521) [0883] apply himself to it or **prepare** himself for it, or help, do,
S D : 0 2 :011(522) [0885] can by his own powers **prepare** or accommodate himself
S D : 0 2 :011(522) [0885] spiritually dead, in sin, **prepare** or address himself by his
S D : 0 2 :039(528) [0895] good works, which God **prepared** beforehand, that we
S D : 0 2 :043(529) [0897] with which we can **prepare** ourselves for righteousness
S D : 0 2 :044(529) [0897] no power of its own to **prepare** itself and to strive for
S D : 0 2 :077(536) [0911] help and cooperate and **prepare** itself for the grace of
S D : 0 2 :078(536) [0911] a capacity naturally to **prepare** oneself for grace does not
S D : 0 2 :083(537) [0913] the promise and is not **prepared** by God for grace, but
S D : 0 6 :012(566) [0967] works, which God has **prepared** beforehand, they should
S D : 0 7 :076(583) [0999] *Passion:* "Christ himself **prepares** this table and blesses it.
S D : 0 7 :124(591) [1015] in true faith alone but also in man's own **preparation**.
S D : 0 7 :125(591) [1015] standard of **preparation**, may receive this sacrament for
S D : 1 1 :023(619) [1069] God has not only **prepared** salvation in general, but he
S D : 1 1 :079(629) [1089] work of God, who alone **prepares** vessels of honor, and
S D : 1 1 :079(629) [1089] of mercy, which he has **prepared** beforehand for
S D : 1 1 :081(629) [1089] Everything which **prepares** and fits man for damnation
S D : 1 1 :081(629) [1089] to be damned, how could he **prepare** man for damnation?
S D : 1 1 :082(630) [1091] that the Lord himself "has **prepared** them unto glory."
S D : 1 1 :082(630) [1091] whom God has not **prepared** but who have prepared
S D : 1 1 :082(630) [1091] prepared but who have **prepared** themselves to be vessels
S D : 1 1 :083(630) [1091] this world (II Pet. 2:20), **prepare** their hearts for Satan

Prerogative (6), Prerogatives (2)
A P : 0 4 :277(148) [0199] glory of Christ, whose **prerogative** it is to free from sin
A P : 0 7 :027(173) [0235] the popes which is the **prerogative** of the true church:
S 2 : 0 2 :013(295) [0467] That is the **prerogative** of God alone.
T R : 0 0 :009(321) [0505] he granted to none a **prerogative** or lordship over the
T R : 0 0 :024(324) [0511] to Peter any special **prerogative**, superiority, or power.
L C : 0 1 :182(389) [0631] punishment are the **prerogatives** of God and his
L C : 0 3 :090(432) [0723] to himself this **prerogative**, that if anybody boasts of his
S D : 0 8 :051(601) [1033] ineffable, heavenly **prerogatives** and privileges in majesty,

Presbyter (5), Presbyters (8)
A L : 2 4 :037(060) [0067] Mass and the rest of the **presbyters** and deacons received
A L : 2 4 :038(060) [0067] "In order, after the **presbyters**, let the deacons receive
A L : 2 4 :038(060) [0069] Holy Communion from the bishop or from a **presbyter**."
T R : 0 0 :061(330) [0521] whether they are called pastors, **presbyters**, or bishops.
T R : 0 0 :062(330) [0521] over the churches are both bishops and **presbyters**.
T R : 0 0 :062(330) [0523] that you might appoint **presbyters** in every town," and
T R : 0 0 :062(330) [0523] Again, Peter and John call themselves **presbyters**.
T R : 0 0 :062(331) [0523] and Dionysius, the **presbyters** always chose one of their
T R : 0 0 :062(331) [0523] what does a bishop do that a **presbyter** does not do?"
T R : 0 0 :063(331) [0523] grades of bishop and **presbyter** (or pastor) is by human
T R : 0 0 :073(332) [0525] that distinguishes bishops from the rest of the **presbyters**.
S D : 0 8 :015(594) [1019] and Theodore, the **presbyter** of Rhaitu, taught that the
S D : 0 8 :016(594) [1019] Theodore the **Presbyter** wrote: "A contemporary of the

Prescribe (7), Prescribed (13), Prescribes (2), Prescribing (1), Prescription (1), Prescriptions (2)
A G : 2 6 :006(064) [0071] grace is to be earned by **prescribed** fasts, distinctions
A G : 2 6 :039(069) [0075] service of fasts on **prescribed** days and with specified
A G : 2 8 :013(083) [0085] should not make or **prescribe** to the temporal power laws
A G : 2 8 :037(087) [0089] new fasts have been **prescribed**, new ceremonies and new
A G : 2 8 :063(092) [0093] obligation, and they **prescribe** the kind and amount of
A L : 2 0 :003(041) [0053] as particular holy days, **prescribed** fasts, brotherhoods,
A L : 2 4 :004(056) [0065] Paul **prescribed** that in church a language should be used
A L : 2 6 :034(069) [0075] at all times, and not merely on a few **prescribed** days.
A L : 2 6 :039(069) [0075] with peril to conscience **prescribe** certain days and certain
A L : 2 8 :013(083) [0085] or contracts, nor **prescribe** to civil rulers laws about the
A L : 2 8 :037(086) [0089] appointed, more fasts **prescribed**, and new ceremonies
A L : 2 8 :063(092) [0093] obligation, and they **prescribe** the extent to which one is
A P : 1 1 :005(181) [0249] But we do not **prescribe** a set time because not everyone
A P : 1 2 :112(198) [0285] could not be **prescribed** without knowing the character of
A P : 1 2 :115(199) [0285] of the custom in **prescribing** certain satisfactions in
A P : 1 2 :122(200) [0289] should perform the **prescribed** penitence, following the
A P : 1 5 :041(220) [0325] at all, though even the canons give **prescriptions** about it.
A P : 1 5 :048(221) [0327] But their **prescription** of certain foods and seasons
A P : 1 5 :048(221) [0329] do not even observe the canonical **prescriptions**.
A P : 1 6 :001(222) [0329] other established laws, **prescribe** legal punishments,
A P : 1 8 :006(225) [0335] he does the works **prescribed** in the commandments; to
A P : 2 3 :027(243) [0371] the Mosaic law which **prescribed** that during the period
A P : 2 8 :018(284) [0449] about something **prescribed**," about a special
L C : 0 3 :024(423) [0703] It has been **prescribed** for this reason, also, that we should
S D : 0 4 :007(552) [0939] which God himself **prescribes** and commands in his
S D : 0 6 :021(567) [0969] But the law of God **prescribes** good works for faith in

Presence (61)
P R : P R :002(003) [0007] 1530, presented in the **presence** of all the estates of the
P R : P R :024(013) [0021] demands that in the **presence** of so many intrusive errors,
A P : 0 4 :205(135) [0177] gives assurance of God's **presence** when it is sure that he
A P : 1 0 :002(179) [0247] affirms the bodily **presence** of Christ, but that the Greek
A P : 1 0 :004(180) [0247] We are talking about the **presence** of the living Christ,
S 1 : P R :008(290) [0457] who reported in our **presence** that his king had been
T R : 0 0 :013(322) [0507] own churches in the **presence** of one or more neighboring
T R : 0 0 :014(322) [0507] should be elected in the **presence** of the people who are
T R : 0 0 :014(322) [0509] assembled in their **presence**, the episcopate might be
S C : 0 4 :012(349) [0551] cleansed and righteous, to live forever in God's **presence**.
S C : 0 5 :022(350) [0553] I confess in your **presence** that, as a manservant or
S C : 0 5 :023(350) [0553] I confess in your **presence** that I have not been faithful in
S C : 0 5 :025(351) [0555] which you make to God in the **presence** of the confessor.
L C : 0 1 :118(381) [0615] with a joyful heart in his **presence**, "Now I know that this
L C : 0 3 :057(427) [0713] command and was unworthy to come into his **presence**.
L C : 0 3 :090(432) [0723] than others, that in the **presence** of God all men must
L C : 0 6 :005(457) [0000] to appear in the **presence** of the Gospel or to have any

Continued ▶

LC : 0 6 :010(458) [0000] we come into God's **presence** to beg for forgiveness.
LC : 0 6 :010(458) [0000] publicly in everyone's **presence**, no one being afraid of
EP : 0 2 :006(470) [0787] no one might boast in the **presence** of God (I Cor. 9:16).
EP : 0 4 :015(477) [0799] testimonies of the Holy Spirit's **presence** and indwelling.
EP : 0 7 :004(482) [0809] claim to believe a true **presence** of the true, essential, and
EP : 0 7 :005(482) [0809] means no more than the **presence** of Christ's spirit, or the
EP : 0 7 :008(482) [0811] the minister effect this **presence** of the body and blood of
EP : 0 7 :035(485) [0815] effect and cause this **presence** of the body and blood of
EP : 0 8 :017(489) [0823] This **presence** is not mundane or Capernaitic although it
EP : 0 8 :032(491) [0825] his deity, and that this **presence** does not at all concern
SD : 0 2 :056(532) [0903] on the Holy Spirit's **presence**, operations, and gifts merely
SD : 0 3 :043(547) [0931] ascribed to faith; or, the **presence** of good works along
SD : 0 3 :043(547) [0931] by it before God; or, the **presence** of good works is
SD : 0 7 :003(569) [0973] they understand this **presence** of the body of Christ not as
SD : 0 7 :011(571) [0975] has taught the bodily **presence** of Christ in the Holy
SD : 0 7 :018(572) [0979] more than the spiritual **presence** of the body of the Lord
SD : 0 7 :027(574) [0981] establishes the true **presence** of the body and blood of
SD : 0 7 :054(579) [0991] to the true and essential **presence** and distribution of the
SD : 0 7 :072(582) [0997] concerning the true **presence** and the twofold
SD : 0 7 :074(583) [0999] can effect the true **presence** of the body and blood of
SD : 0 7 :081(584) [1001] of this sacrament (the **presence** of the body and blood of
SD : 0 7 :088(585) [1003] deny the true, essential **presence** and the oral eating of the
SD : 0 7 :088(585) [1003] or that faith effects the **presence** of Christ's body in the
SD : 0 7 :090(585) [1003] power to achieve the **presence** of the body of Christ and
SD : 0 7 :099(586) [1005] corporeal mode of **presence**, as when he walked bodily on
SD : 0 7 :099(586) [1005] employ this mode of **presence** when he wills to do so, as
SD : 0 7 :099(586) [1005] and going to the Father speak of this mode of **presence**.
SD : 0 7 :100(586) [1005] spiritual mode of **presence** according to which he neither
SD : 0 7 :100(586) [1007] employed this mode of **presence** when he left the closed
SD : 0 7 :103(587) [1007] comprehensible mode of **presence** to the body of Christ
SD : 0 7 :105(588) [1009] of a gross, carnal **presence** which the Sacramentarians
SD : 0 7 :106(588) [1009] concerning the true **presence** of the body and blood of
SD : 0 7 :111(589) [1011] concerning the true **presence** of the body and blood of
SD : 0 7 :113(589) [1011] the true essential **presence** of the body and blood of
SD : 0 7 :120(590) [1013] the true, essential **presence** of his body and blood in the
SD : 0 7 :121(590) [1013] faith that achieves the **presence** of the body of Christ in
SD : 0 8 :002(591) [1015] the true, essential **presence** of the body and blood of
SD : 0 8 :004(592) [1017] the true, essential **presence** of the body and blood of
SD : 0 8 :077(606) [1043] and that this **presence** of Christ in no way involves his
SD : 0 8 :077(606) [1043] Scriptures ascribe such **presence** only to Christ, and to no
SD : 0 8 :087(608) [1047] cited promises of the **presence** and indwelling of their
SD : 0 8 :092(609) [1049] he has promised his **presence** in his Word, as in the Holy
SD : 0 8 :094(609) [1049] his deity, and that this **presence** does not involve his
SD : 1 2 :040(636) [1103] Therefore, in the **presence** of God and of all Christendom

Present (154), Presentation (4), Presented (23), Presenting (5), Presently (2), Presents (10)

PR : PR :002(003) [0007] in the year 1530, **presented** in the presence of all the
PR : PR :016(008) [0013] to whom it had been **presented**, as indicated above, gladly
PR : PR :017(008) [0015] Those of us who were **present** at the above-mentioned
PR : PR :023(012) [0021] To this end the **present** agreement was proposed,
PR : PR :023(012) [0021] repeatedly mentioned **present** explanation of the
AG : 0 0 :000(023) [0037] A Confession of Faith **Presented** in Augsburg by certain
AG : PR :006(025) [0039] commit to writing and **present**, in German and Latin, his
AG : PR :007(025) [0039] Majesty's wish, we should **present** our case in German
AG : PR :008(025) [0039] Majesty, we offer and **present** a confession of our
AG : PR :010(025) [0041] between us may be **presented** in writing on both sides,
AG : 1 0 :001(034) [0047] blood of Christ are really **present** in the Supper of our
AG : 2 4 :034(060) [0067] when communicants are **present**, Mass is held and those
AG : 2 7 :048(078) [0081] the people should be **presented** with such a service of
AG : 0 0 :006(095) [0095] we have desired to **present** the above articles as a
AG : 0 0 :007(096) [0095] respect, we are ready to **present** further information on
AL : 1 0 :001(034) [0047] blood of Christ are truly **present** and are distributed to
AL : 0 0 :006(095) [0095] we have desired to **present** the above articles in order that
AL : 0 0 :017(096) [0095] ready, God willing, to **present** ampler information
AP : 0 2 :019(103) [0111] in the image of God in which God is not always **present**."
AP : 0 4 :005(108) [0121] In some places it **presents** the law.
AP : 0 4 :005(108) [0121] In others it **presents** the promise of Christ; this it does
AP : 0 4 :006(108) [0121] For the **present** we are saying nothing about the
AP : 0 4 :019(110) [0125] have him doubt whether the disposition is truly **present**.
AP : 0 4 :066(116) [0139] Like the **present**-day Anabaptists, they deny that it is
AP : 0 4 :168(130) [0169] Therefore in our **present** weakness there is always sin that
AP : 0 4 :186(132) [0173] places the Scripture **presents** the law, while in others it
AP : 0 4 :186(132) [0173] law, while in others it **presents** the Gospel, the free
AP : 0 4 :231(139) [0183] about perfection, we shall simply **present** Paul's meaning.
AP : 0 4 :245(142) [0189] faith and love in **presenting** a summary of the Christian
AP : 0 4 :266(146) [0197] the Gospel and the promise of Christ are **presented** to us.
AP : 0 4 :284(150) [0201] Moreover, why do they not **present** the whole sermon?
AP : 0 4 :310(155) [0207] of the law is to offer and **present** our goods to God.
AP : 0 4 :312(155) [0207] with both future and **present** things and receives in the
AP : 0 4 :312(155) [0207] and receives in the **present** the forgiveness of sins that the
AP : 0 4 :331(158) [0211] "For we do not **present** our supplications before thee
AP : 0 4 :337(159) [0215] above, "For we do not **present** our supplications before
AP : 0 4 :381(165) [0223] they teach that we cannot know whether it is **present**.
AP : 0 7 :007(169) [0229] the church might be **presented** before him in splendor,
AP : 0 7 :032(174) [0239] had weighty reasons for **presenting** this article, for it is
AP : 1 0 :001(179) [0247] truly and substantially **present** and are truly offered with
AP : 1 0 :001(179) [0247] only in his spirit if the Lord's body were not truly **present**.
AP : 1 0 :004(179) [0247] truly and substantially **present** and are truly offered with
AP : 1 1 :010(182) [0253] other major faults, and these we shall **presently** discuss.
AP : 1 2 :034(186) [0261] nothing about faith, but **present** only the Word that
AP : 1 2 :037(186) [0261] Nor is love **present** before faith has effected the
AP : 1 2 :052(189) [0265] of penitence could be **presented** more clearly and simply.
AP : 1 2 :078(193) [0275] that love and works are **present**, neither love nor works
AP : 1 2 :132(202) [0291] elsewhere (Rom. 12:1), "**Present** your bodies as a living
AP : 1 2 :152(206) [0299] inflicted on account of **present** sin because in the saints
AP : 1 2 :152(206) [0299] because of the sin still **present** and remaining in the flesh.
AP : 1 2 :153(206) [0299] as long as it is **present**; without this sense of wrath death
AP : 1 2 :157(207) [0301] as the mortification of **present** sin, not as a payment for
AP : 1 3 :012(212) [0311] know that God approves this ministry and is **present** in it.
AP : 1 3 :021(214) [0313] accepts the promise as a **present** reality and believes that
AP : 1 4 :004(214) [0315] know that the church is **present** among those who rightly
AP : 1 4 :004(215) [0315] It is not **present** among those who seek to destroy the
AP : 1 4 :005(215) [0315] and among all nations, **present** and future, against the
AP : 1 5 :045(221) [0327] Paul says (Rom. 12:1), "**Present** your bodies as a
AP : 2 1 :001(229) [0343] They **present** this as though on this account the
AP : 2 1 :016(231) [0347] For the **present** we shall not list the abuses among the
AP : 2 1 :017(231) [0347] qualifications must be **present** if one is to be a
AP : 2 2 :008(237) [0359] that it means our **present** custom of giving the laity only a
AP : 2 3 :027(243) [0371] This clumsy analogy is **presented** as a proof to force
AP : 2 3 :062(247) [0381] In **presenting** our own arguments, we have incidentally
AP : 2 4 :007(250) [0385] For the **present**, we forego any discussion of their origins.
AP : 2 4 :010(251) [0387] easy to evaluate the arguments both sides have **presented**.
AP : 2 4 :018(252) [0389] Here God offers and **presents** the forgiveness of sins
AP : 2 4 :026(254) [0391] the same in Rom. 12:1, "**Present** your bodies as a living
AP : 2 4 :034(256) [0395] gold and silver, till they **present** right offerings to the
AP : 2 4 :070(262) [0409] the heart to believe through what it **presents** to the eyes.
AP : 2 7 :063(280) [0441] the other evils inherent in **present**-day monasticism.
AP : 2 8 :001(281) [0443] is false that the **present** article states about the immunity
S 1 : 0 0 :000(287) [0453] which were to have been **presented** by our party at the
S 1 : PR :002(288) [0455] these articles should be **presented** publicly as the
S 2 : 0 4 :004(299) [0473] been under the pope and are not at the **present** time.
S 3 : 0 3 :032(308) [0487] For he is here **present**, and from his fullness have we all
S 3 : 0 3 :042(309) [0491] perhaps they are already **present**, such as I saw with my
S 3 : 0 3 :044(310) [0491] Spirit and faith are not **present**, for St. John says, "No
S 3 : 0 8 :008(313) [0497] had to be saved by the **present** Messiah and not deny or
TR : 0 0 :082(334) [0529] of the Confession **presented** to the emperor in the diet of
TR : 0 0 :082(334) [0529] preachers who have been **present** in this assembly in
TR : 0 0 :082(334) [0529] the bishops which was **presented** to the princes here in
TR : 0 0 :082(334) [0529] concerning the papacy **presented** to the princes in
TR : 0 0 :082(000) [0529] and Apology **presented** at Augsburg by the Most
SC : PR :016(340) [0535] They can be **presented** one at a time.
LC : PR :009(359) [0569] the Holy Spirit is **present** and bestows ever new and
LC : 0 1 :158(387) [0627] three kinds of fathers **presented** in this commandment:
LC : 0 1 :258(399) [0653] us only a little at **present**, but among the Jews it was
LC : 0 1 :259(400) [0655] but the evidence **presented**, and make his decision
LC : 0 1 :325(409) [0675] have proclaimed and **presented** this commandment
LC : 0 2 :044(416) [0689] There was no Holy Spirit **present** to reveal this truth and
LC : 0 2 :070(420) [0697] For the **present** this is enough concerning the Creed to lay
LC : 0 3 :024(423) [0705] who wants to pray must **present** a petition, naming and
LC : 0 3 :100(433) [0727] even though at **present** we are upright and stand before
LC : 0 3 :109(435) [0729] Even if at **present** I am chaste, patient, kind, and firm in
LC : 0 4 :022(439) [0737] But when the Word is **present** according to God's
LC : 0 4 :046(442) [0743] and use of Baptism as answering the **present** purpose.
LC : 0 4 :050(443) [0745] all this time down to the **present** day no man on earth
LC : 0 4 :073(445) [0751] Where faith is **present** with its fruits, there Baptism is no
LC : 0 4 :083(446) [0751] until we pass from this **present** misery to eternal glory.
LC : 0 6 :018(459) [0000] a magnificent work to **present** to him, but simply to
EP : 0 2 :004(470) [0787] The Holy Spirit is **present** with this Word and opens
EP : 0 3 :004(473) [0793] without any preceding, **present**, or subsequent work,
EP : 0 3 :023(475) [0797] and that unless they are **present** a person cannot be
EP : 0 7 :002(481) [0809] truly and essentially **present** if they are distributed with
EP : 0 7 :003(482) [0809] only bread and wine are **present**, distributed, and received
EP : 0 7 :004(482) [0809] but bread and wine are **present** and received with the
EP : 0 7 :005(482) [0809] the body of Christ is **present** in any manner or way, since
EP : 0 7 :006(482) [0809] are truly and essentially **present** and are truly distributed
EP : 0 7 :012(483) [0811] his human nature, rules **presently** and has in his hands
EP : 0 7 :017(484) [0813] He is just as much **present** to exercise and manifest his
EP : 0 7 :030(485) [0815] wine and not by the truly **present** body and blood of
EP : 0 7 :032(485) [0815] that it can in no way be **present** at one and the same time
EP : 0 7 :033(485) [0815] would be essentially **present** in the Holy Supper, nor
EP : 0 7 :034(485) [0815] his body to be essentially **present** at more than one place
EP : 0 8 :016(489) [0821] can do all things, is **present** to all creatures, and has all
EP : 0 8 :017(489) [0823] and blood which are **present** in the Holy Supper, *not*
EP : 0 8 :030(490) [0825] for Christ to be **present** at the same time at more than
EP : 0 8 :030(490) [0825] one place, still less to be **present** with his body
EP : 0 8 :032(491) [0825] 13. That Christ is **present** with us on earth in the Word, in
EP : 0 8 :033(491) [0825] at the place where the human nature is locally **present**.
SD : PR :008(502) [0849] Similarly at the **present** time our adversaries, the papists,
SD : PR :006(504) [0853] with a view both to **presenting** the doctrines against the
SD : PR :007(505) [0853] and published for **presentation**, in the name of the
SD : PR :014(506) [0855] it is essential not only to **present** the true and wholesome
SD : PR :020(507) [0857] to compare our **present** position with the aforementioned
SD : 0 1 :003(509) [0859] the contrary, when it is **presented** clearly from and
SD : 0 1 :007(510) [0861] creates and makes at the **present** time, original sin is
SD : 0 1 :039(515) [0871] makes and fashions our **present** human nature, which is
SD : 0 1 :055(518) [0877] essence, but is **present** in another thing mutably, is not a
SD : 0 2 :044(529) [0897] and in great detail **presents** and demonstrates his case.
SD : 0 2 :055(532) [0903] on it, God is certainly **present** with his grace and gives
SD : 0 2 :073(535) [0909] basis of this thorough **presentation** of the entire doctrine
SD : 0 3 :009(541) [0919] without any preceding, **present**, or subsequent works, by
SD : 0 4 :034(556) [0949] into grace but also our **present** state of grace and our
SD : 0 4 :034(557) [0949] "He will **present** you holy and blameless and
SD : 0 5 :016(561) [0957] nothing in this **present** controversy but are presenting the
SD : 0 5 :016(561) [0957] controversy but are **presenting** the entire matter nicely
SD : 0 7 :004(569) [0973] the Lord Christ is truly **present** in the Supper, namely,
SD : 0 7 :005(570) [0973] the body of Christ is **present** in the Supper, they still did
SD : 0 7 :006(570) [0973] that the Lord Christ is **present** in his Supper truly,
SD : 0 7 :007(570) [0973] Christ's body is even now **present** on earth in some
SD : 0 7 :008(570) [0975] of Christ is essentially **present** here on earth in the Lord's
SD : 0 7 :009(570) [0975] blood of Christ are really **present** in the Holy Supper
SD : 0 7 :009(571) [0975] not truly and essentially **present** here on earth in the
SD : 0 7 :010(571) [0975] Dr. Luther clearly **presents** the same view in the Small
SD : 0 7 :011(571) [0975] are truly and essentially **present** and are truly offered with
SD : 0 7 :011(571) [0975] of Christ were not truly **present**, but only the Holy Spirit,
SD : 0 7 :014(571) [0977] are truly and essentially **present**, distributed, and
SD : 0 7 :015(572) [0977] the body of Christ is **present** apart from the use, as when
SD : 0 7 :032(574) [0983] as the enemies of the sacrament do at the **present** time.
SD : 0 7 :037(575) [0985] body of Christ, are **present** together here on earth in the
SD : 0 7 :055(579) [0991] not truly and essentially **present** and were received only
SD : 0 7 :060(580) [0993] him who is there **present** as certainly as did the Jews when
SD : 0 7 :062(581) [0995] and everlasting life), is **presented** — and that we rest
SD : 0 7 :075(583) [0999] blood of Christ are truly **present**, distributed, and received
SD : 0 7 :076(583) [0999] true body and blood are **present** in the church's Supper."
SD : 0 7 :088(585) [1003] the body of Christ because it is not **present** to them.
SD : 0 7 :097(586) [1005] various ways to be **present** at a certain place, not only, as
SD : 0 7 :101(587) [1007] more penetrable and **present** to him than they are

Continued ▶

SD : 0 7 :101(587) [1007] second mode he can be **present** in and with creatures in
SD : 0 7 :101(587) [1007] marvelously will he be **present** in all creatures according
SD : 0 7 :101(587) [1007] but where he has them **present** to himself, measures and
SD : 0 7 :105(588) [1009] to which Christ is **present** in the Holy Supper, not only to
SD : 0 7 :108(588) [1009] the body of Christ is **present** even apart from the action
SD : 0 7 :116(589) [1013] not through the true **present** body and blood of Christ,
SD : 0 7 :119(590) [1013] be truly and essentially **present** with us in the Supper,
SD : 0 7 :122(590) [1013] heaven where Christ is **present** with his body and there to
SD : 0 7 :126(591) [1015] is truly and essentially **present** in the Supper when it is
SD : 0 8 :002(591) [1015] human body if it were **present** at the same time in heaven
SD : 0 8 :009(593) [1019] to be intrinsically **present**, and to know everything are
SD : 0 8 :027(596) [1025] things, he is everywhere **present** to rule, not only as God
SD : 0 8 :029(596) [1025] he can be and is truly **present** with his body and blood in
SD : 0 8 :035(597) [1027] The following **presentation** should be noted diligently.
SD : 0 8 :035(598) [1027] a better and simpler **presentation** it can be comprehended
SD : 0 8 :047(600) [1031] to both natures, as we **presented** this matter previously.
SD : 0 8 :068(604) [1039] is therefore everywhere **present** in all creatures, and since
SD : 0 8 :077(606) [1043] only the deity of Christ is **present** with us in the Christian
SD : 0 8 :078(606) [1043] his, Christ can be and is **present** wherever he wills, and in
SD : 0 8 :078(607) [1043] in particular that he is **present** with his church and
SD : 0 8 :078(607) [1043] both natures, the divine and the human, belong is **present**.
SD : 0 8 :078(607) [1043] He is **present** not only according to his deity, but also
SD : 0 8 :079(607) [1045] Supper that he might be **present** with us, dwell in us,
SD : 0 8 :082(607) [1045] But if he is **present** naturally and personally wherever he
SD : 0 8 :082(607) [1045] then you must also say, 'Christ the man is **present** too.'
SD : 0 8 :084(607) [1045] Christ for me if he were **present** only at one single place
SD : 0 8 :090(609) [1047] in Christ is everywhere **present** in the same way as the
SD : 0 8 :092(609) [1049] Christ can be **present** with his body, which he has placed
SD : 0 8 :094(609) [1049] holy sacraments Christ is **present** with us on earth only
SD : 1 1 :002(616) [1063] passing, but discuss and **present** it in detail in many
SD : 1 1 :004(617) [1063] and evil, since all things, **present** or future, are manifest
SD : 1 1 :004(617) [1063] future, are manifest and **present** to God, as it is written,
SD : 1 1 :012(618) [1067] So, too, Scripture **presents** this doctrine in no other way
SD : 1 1 :039(622) [1075] wills to be certainly **present** with and efficacious and
SD : 1 1 :049(624) [1079] Again, Paul **presents** this in a most comforting manner
SD : 1 1 :077(629) [1089] Holy Spirit wills to be **present** in the Word and to be
SD : 1 2 :004(633) [1097] or our signatures, but to **present** a clear, lucid, and
SD : 1 2 :040(636) [1103] to have testified that the **present** explanation of all the

Preservation (3), Preserve (40), Preserved (25), Preserver (2), Preserves (10), Preserving (2)
PR : PR :005(004) [0009] might have been **preserved** in the teaching of God's Word
PR : PR :006(004) [0009] our subjects might be **preserved** from straying from the
PR : PR :010(006) [0011] grace they might be **preserved** from false doctrine in the
PR : PR :023(012) [0021] of the faith may be **preserved** and perpetuated among our
AG : 0 1 :003(028) [0043] one creator and **preserver** of all things visible and
AG : 1 9 :000(040) [0053] God has created and still **preserves** nature, yet sin is
AG : 2 4 :035(060) [0067] Thus the Mass is **preserved** among us in its proper use,
AG : 2 6 :040(069) [0075] and the like) which serve to **preserve** order in the church.
AG : 2 8 :051(089) [0091] It is necessary to **preserve** the teaching of Christian liberty
AL : 0 1 :002(027) [0043] the maker and **preserver** of all things, visible and
AL : 1 6 :005(038) [0051] requires their **preservation** as ordinance of God and the
AL : 1 9 :000(040) [0053] God creates and **preserves** nature, the cause of sin is the
AL : 2 8 :051(089) [0091] It is necessary to **preserve** the doctrine of Christian liberty
AL : 2 8 :052(089) [0091] It is necessary to **preserve** the chief article of the Gospel,
AP : 0 4 :022(110) [0127] the unspiritual, and to **preserve** it he has given laws,
AP : 0 4 :232(139) [0185] for it is not possible to **preserve** tranquility unless men
AP : 0 4 :232(140) [0185] be love in the church to **preserve** harmony, to bear, if
AP : 0 4 :234(140) [0185] of the church) is **preserved** when the strong bear with the
AP : 0 4 :243(141) [0189] is necessary for the **preservation** of domestic tranquillity,
AP : 0 7 :042(176) [0243] The text of the decree is **preserved** in Epiphanius: "Do
AP : 0 7 :050(178) [0245] of God and are **preserved** by God, so lawful governments
AP : 0 7 :050(178) [0245] of God and are **preserved** and defended by God against
AP : 1 2 :098(197) [0281] great importance of **preserving** the true teaching about
AP : 1 3 :002(211) [0309] provided what is handed down in Scripture is **preserved**.
AP : 1 9 :001(226) [0337] all of nature and **preserves** everything that exists.
AP : 2 3 :027(243) [0371] continually, they must also **preserve** perpetual continence.
AP : 2 4 :099(268) [0419] that we most zealously **preserve** the dignity of the Mass,
AP : 2 8 :015(283) [0447] worship but a means of **preserving** order in the church,
S 2 : 0 3 :002(298) [0471] them down rather than **preserve** them with their
S 2 : 0 4 :007(299) [0473] might better be **preserved** against the attacks of sects and
SC : 0 2 :002(345) [0543] me from all danger, and **preserves** me from all evil.
SC : 0 2 :006(345) [0545] gifts, and sanctified and **preserved** me in true faith, just as
SC : 0 2 :006(345) [0545] church on earth and **preserves** it in union with Jesus
SC : 0 3 :005(346) [0547] From this **preserve** us, heavenly Father!
SC : 0 3 :018(347) [0549] God may so guard and **preserve** us that the devil, the
LC : 0 1 :072(374) [0601] befall us if God did not **preserve** us through our calling
LC : 0 2 :016(412) [0681] nor can he by himself **preserve** any of them, however
LC : 0 2 :059(418) [0695] and will eternally **preserve** us in it by means of the last
LC : 0 3 :002(420) [0697] prayer that he may give, **preserve**, and increase in us faith
LC : 0 3 :072(430) [0719] and did not bless and **preserve** it in the field, we could
LC : 0 3 :076(431) [0721] well and give and **preserve** to us a good wife, children,
LC : 0 3 :118(436) [0731] Then he will **preserve** us from sin and shame and from
LC : 0 5 :086(456) [0773] Word of God and the Christian church will be **preserved**.
EP : RN :002(465) [0777] and apostles was **preserved** in post-apostolic times.
EP : 0 1 :003(466) [0779] confess that we must **preserve** this distinction most
EP : 0 3 :010(474) [0795] confess that if we would **preserve** the pure doctrine
EP : 0 4 :015(477) [0799] working through faith, **preserves** faith and salvation in
EP : 1 0 :006(493) [0829] of the Gospel might be **preserved** for you" (Gal. 2:5).
SD : PR :014(506) [0855] In order to **preserve** the pure doctrine and to maintain a
SD : PR :015(507) [0857] error must be refuted in order to **preserve** the truth).
SD : 0 1 :002(509) [0859] Hence, they say, we must **preserve** the distinction between
SD : 0 1 :004(509) [0861] the Word of God and to **preserve** the true and correct
SD : 0 1 :016(511) [0865] upon us to maintain and **preserve** this doctrine in such a
SD : 0 1 :033(514) [0869] as it is created and **preserved** by God and in which sin
SD : 0 1 :035(514) [0869] love; and thy care has **preserved** my spirit" (Job 10:8-12).
SD : 0 2 :016(523) [0887] into practice, he would **preserve** faith and his heavenly
SD : 0 2 :040(528) [0895] gifts, and sanctified and **preserved** me in true faith, just as
SD : 0 2 :040(528) [0895] church on earth and **preserves** it in union with Jesus
SD : 0 2 :072(535) [0909] reminds us also how he **preserves**, strengthens, and
SD : 0 2 :077(536) [0911] the continuation and **preservation** of this work within us.
SD : 0 3 :035(545) [0927] before God, in order to **preserve** the glory due to Christ,
SD : 0 3 :040(546) [0929] to be maintained and **preserved**, as well as between
SD : 0 4 :030(555) [0947] to whether good works **preserve** salvation or are
SD : 0 4 :030(555) [0947] or are necessary to **preserve** faith, righteousness, and
SD : 0 4 :030(556) [0947] and salvation are **preserved** in us so that we do not lose
SD : 0 4 :034(556) [0949] works should henceforth **preserve** faith, the righteousness
SD : 0 4 :035(557) [0949] only received but also **preserved** by God, we rightly reject
SD : 0 4 :035(557) [0949] that our good works **preserve** salvation, or that our
SD : 0 4 :035(557) [0949] or in part sustain and **preserve** either the righteousness of
SD : 0 4 :036(557) [0949] useless wrangling and **preserve** the church from many
SD : 0 7 :001(569) [0971] do everything we can to **preserve** it for our descendants
SD : 0 8 :085(608) [1047] and has created and **preserved** everything because he is
SD : 1 0 :001(610) [1053] and decorum or else to **preserve** Christian discipline.
SD : 1 0 :011(612) [1057] of the gospel might be **preserved** for you" (Gal. 2:4, 5).
SD : 1 0 :012(613) [1057] so that the truth of the Gospel might be **preserved**.
SD : 1 0 :014(613) [1057] the truth of the Gospel might be **preserved** (Gal. 2:5).
SD : 1 0 :015(613) [1057] the church to **preserve**, as we have just heard.
SD : 1 1 :020(619) [1069] and comfort and **preserve** them in tribulation and
SD : 1 1 :021(619) [1069] which he has begun, and **preserve** them unto the end, if
SD : 1 1 :023(619) [1069] help, further, strengthen, and **preserve** them to this end.
SD : 1 1 :059(626) [1083] to whom he gives and **preserves** his Word and whom he
SD : 1 1 :061(626) [1083] to whom God gives and **preserves** his Word, whereby he

Preside (5)
TR : 0 0 :017(323) [0509] bishop of Rome did not **preside** — as the Council of
TR : 0 0 :060(330) [0521] requires of those who **preside** over the churches that they
TR : 0 0 :061(330) [0521] by divine right to all who **preside** over the churches,
TR : 0 0 :062(330) [0521] apostolic letters all who **preside** over the churches are
LC : 0 1 :258(400) [0653] that men of integrity seldom **preside** in courts of justice.

Press (2), Pressed (2), Pressing (1)
AG : 2 7 :006(071) [0077] and entangled were **pressed** and compelled to remain, in
AP : PR :010(099) [0101] but as it was going through the **press** I added some things.
LC : 0 4 :043(442) [0743] Because of the **pressing** crowd of rich men no one else
LC : 0 5 :027(449) [0759] our heart feels too sorely **pressed**, this comfort of the
SD : 0 7 :002(569) [0973] Yet when we **press** them to set forth their meaning

Pressure (1)
EP : 1 0 :002(493) [0829] conscience yield to their **pressure** and demands,

Prestige (6)
AP : 1 2 :125(201) [0289] might tend to diminish the **prestige** of the Roman See.
LC : 0 1 :010(366) [0583] wisdom, power, **prestige**, family, and honor, and trusts in
LC : 0 1 :042(370) [0591] have neither money, **prestige**, nor honor, and can scarcely
LC : 0 1 :042(370) [0591] mammon have power, **prestige**, honor, wealth, and every
SD : 0 7 :092(586) [1005] what appearance or **prestige** they may have, to lead us
SD : 1 1 :050(624) [1079] offended by the outward **prestige** of the false church

Presume (3), Presumed (2), Presumes (1), Presumption (5), Presumptuous (10), Presumptuously (1)
AG : 0 0 :001(048) [0059] Therefore, those who **presume** to reject, avoid, and
AG : 2 8 :002(081) [0083] the ban, but have also **presumed** to set up and depose
AG : 2 8 :036(086) [0089] is blasphemed when we **presume** to earn grace by such
AP : 0 4 :021(110) [0127] the law, they arouse **presumption**, a vain trust in works
S 2 : 0 4 :013(300) [0475] an earthly god and even **presumed** to issue orders to the
S 3 : 0 1 :002(302) [0477] the fear of God, **presumption**, despair, blindness — in
S 3 : 0 2 :003(303) [0479] become blind and **presumptuous**, imagining that they can
LC : PR :009(359) [0569] these lazy-bellies and **presumptuous** saints, for God's
LC : PR :016(361) [0571] Look at these bored, **presumptuous** saints who will not or
LC : PR :018(361) [0573] such lazy-bellies and **presumptuous** fellows do not
LC : 0 1 :010(366) [0583] Notice, again, how **presumptuous**, secure, and proud
LC : 0 1 :022(367) [0585] in its own works and **presumes** to wrest heaven from
LC : 0 1 :027(368) [0587] one, therefore, should **presume** to take or give anything
LC : 0 1 :047(371) [0593] God will tolerate no **presumption** and no trust in any
LC : 0 1 :315(408) [0671] is it not a devilish **presumption** on the part of those
LC : 0 4 :058(444) [0747] Therefore only **presumptuous** and stupid persons draw
EP : 0 7 :041(486) [0817] judgment of God all **presumptuous**, sarcastic, and
SD : 0 4 :023(555) [0945] many ways, confirm **presumptuous** trust in one's own
SD : 0 5 :010(559) [0955] Christ either produces **presumptuous** people, who believe
SD : 0 7 :127(591) [1015] and condemn all **presumptuous**, scoffing, and
SD : 0 8 :096(609) [1049] Christians not to pry **presumptuously** into this mystery
SD : 1 1 :053(625) [1081] In our **presumption** we take much greater delight in

Presupposes (1)
AP : 0 4 :261(145) [0195] This **presupposes** faith.

Pretend (12), Pretended (2)
AL : 2 7 :016(073) [0077] Now they **pretend** that this kind of life was instituted to
AP : 0 4 :066(116) [0139] disposition of love, they **pretend** that one merits it by
AP : 1 2 :012(184) [0255] They **pretend** that the sacrament grants grace *ex opere*
AP : 2 7 :015(271) [0425] Our opponents **pretend** that Paul abolished the law of
AP : 2 7 :016(271) [0425] Then they **pretend** that among those who observe this law
TR : 0 0 :048(328) [0519] They have **pretended** that the most trivial traditions are
LC : PR :018(361) [0573] Scriptures, yet they **pretend** to know and despise the
LC : 0 1 :298(405) [0665] Yet we all **pretend** to be upright.
LC : 0 1 :315(408) [0671] They **pretend**, as we have said, that this is a simple life for
LC : 0 5 :041(451) [0763] Some **pretend** that it is a matter of liberty, not of
LC : 0 5 :076(455) [0771] of his flesh, let us not **pretend** to be better or more holy.
SD : PR :007(502) [0849] arose among those who **pretended** to be Christians and
SD : 0 2 :045(530) [0899] teach wrongly when they **pretend** that unregenerated man
SD : 1 2 :003(632) [1095] had the effrontery to **pretend** and proclaim to the whole

Pretense (10), Pretenses (1), Pretensions (1)
PR : PR :018(009) [0017] onerous burden of their **pretense** that we are uncertain of
AL : 2 7 :048(078) [0081] observances and this **pretense** of poverty, humility, and
AP : 2 3 :005(240) [0365] are trying to fortify it with a wicked **pretense** of godliness.
AP : 2 7 :044(277) [0435] so they quote passages of Scripture under false **pretenses**.
S 2 : 0 4 :007(299) [0473] and estate, together with all his rights and **pretensions**.
S 3 : 1 0 :001(314) [0497] could be done without **pretense**, humbug, and unchristian
SD : 0 3 :039(546) [0929] nor under any kind of **pretense**, title, or name are they to
SD : 0 4 :017(554) [0943] he does externally, for a **pretense**, something that is really
SD : 0 4 :017(554) [0943] Such works of **pretense** God does not want.
SD : 1 0 :019(614) [1059] could be done without **pretense**, humbug, and
SD : 1 1 :039(623) [1077] make only an outward **pretense** (Matt. 7:15; 22:12), or
SD : 1 2 :005(633) [1097] was not a mere **pretense** but that we wanted to help

Pretext (23), Pretexts (4)
PR : PR :011(006) [0011] and in this way the **pretext** and basis for slander that the
AG : 2 8 :002(081) [0083] the bishops, under **pretext** of the power given them by
AP : 0 4 :244(142) [0189] uphold it under the **pretext** that this is what James
AP : 1 2 :012(184) [0255] enumeration under the **pretext** that it is by divine right,
AP : 2 3 :001(239) [0363] use the wicked and false **pretext** of divine authority for
AP : 2 3 :005(239) [0365] but they use religion as a **pretext** to maintain their
AP : 2 3 :050(246) [0377] They use religion as a **pretext** to put something over on
AP : 2 3 :050(246) [0377] These Epicureans purposely use religion as a **pretext**.
AP : 2 3 :060(247) [0381] domination, for which religion is just a wicked **pretext**.
AP : 2 4 :041(257) [0399] Under the **pretext** of religion they usurp the kingdom of
AP : 2 4 :091(266) [0415] of faith, and under the **pretext** of satisfactions they have
AP : 2 7 :009(270) [0421] have been taken with the **pretext** of religion, but actually
AP : 2 7 :039(276) [0433] them to others under the **pretext** that they observe both
AP : 2 7 :044(277) [0435] men, and doing so under the **pretext** of the divine name.
AP : 2 8 :022(284) [0451] which have arisen under the **pretext** of our teaching.
TR : 0 0 :011(321) [0507] deprives Peter of this **pretext** and denies that Peter's
TR : 0 0 :032(325) [0513] would be set up on the **pretext** of ecclesiastical power.
TR : 0 0 :036(326) [0515] deplored so much as the **pretext** is to be censured that he
TR : 0 0 :040(327) [0515] for himself on the **pretext** of the authority of the church
TR : 0 0 :040(327) [0515] the ministry, offering as **pretext** these words, "I will give
SC : 0 1 :018(344) [0541] nor to obtain them under **pretext** of legal right, but be of
LC : 0 1 :296(405) [0665] even with a specious **pretext**, to covet or scheme to
LC : 0 1 :299(405) [0665] and using them for **pretexts**, without regard for equity or
LC : 0 1 :304(406) [0667] how much he can acquire by such specious **pretexts**?
LC : 0 1 :304(406) [0667] this it is clear that all these **pretexts** and shams are false.
LC : 0 3 :062(428) [0715] under the most specious **pretexts** of God's name, are
SD : 0 6 :020(567) [0969] and piety and under the **pretext** of the Holy Spirit's

Prevail (11), Prevailed (4), Prevails (2)
AG : 2 3 :014(054) [0063] disgraceful lewdness and vice to **prevail** in German lands.
AG : 2 8 :064(092) [0093] the opinion remains and **prevails** that their observance is
AP : 0 2 :044(106) [0117] These notions **prevailed**, feeding a trust in human powers
AP : 2 2 :004(236) [0359] remains, and once it **prevailed** in the Latin church, as
AP : 2 4 :012(251) [0387] firm and sure that it can **prevail** against all the gates of
TR : 0 0 :020(323) [0509] the custom gradually **prevailed** that the bishops of Rome
SC : 0 3 :018(348) [0549] so tempted, we may finally **prevail** and gain the victory.
LC : 0 1 :085(376) [0605] way a common order will **prevail** and no one will create
LC : 0 1 :227(396) [0645] everyday business the same fraud **prevails** in full force.
LC : 0 3 :050(426) [0711] is, we ask that it may **prevail** among us and with us, so
LC : 0 3 :054(427) [0713] that thy kingdom may **prevail** among us through the
LC : 0 3 :060(428) [0715] by us and that his kingdom may **prevail** among us.
LC : 0 3 :068(429) [0717] must his will be done and **prevail** even though the devil
LC : 0 3 :069(429) [0717] exterminate us so that their will and scheme may **prevail**.
LC : 0 3 :074(430) [0719] strife, and war **prevail**, there our daily bread is taken
LC : 0 4 :080(446) [0751] opinion, which has long **prevailed** among us, that our
EP : 1 1 :005(495) [0833] "gates of Hades cannot **prevail** against" it (John 10:28;

Prevalence (2), Prevalent (2)
AG : 2 3 :018(054) [0063] their abomination and **prevalence**, arouse the wrath of
AP : 2 4 :007(250) [0385] But is is clear that the **prevalence** of the mendicant friars
LC : 0 1 :022(367) [0585] practiced up to now, and it is still **prevalent** in the world.
LC : 0 1 :305(406) [0667] undoubtedly was quite **prevalent** in the time of the law,

Prevent (23), Prevented (4), Preventing (1), Prevents (2)
AG : 2 3 :015(054) [0063] marriage to aid human infirmity and **prevent** unchastity.
AG : 2 3 :016(054) [0063] human weakness and to **prevent** and avoid greater
AG : 2 8 :029(085) [0087] the sake of peace and to **prevent** discord and great
AG : 2 8 :078(094) [0095] and schism, which they should in truth help to **prevent**.
AG : 0 0 :005(095) [0095] and with God's help **prevented** any new and godless
AP : PR :007(098) [0101] very weighty reasons **prevented** us from approving the
AP : 1 2 :161(208) [0303] was forgiven so as not to **prevent** the man from obtaining
AP : 1 5 :024(218) [0321] writes, "Fasting avails to destroy and **prevent** guilt."
AP : 2 4 :024(253) [0391] the ceremonial law and **prevented** the exclusion of the
AP : 2 7 :009(270) [0421] either because weakness **prevents** their observance or
S 1 : PR :003(289) [0455] pains to postpone and **prevent** the council), those who
S 3 : 1 0 :003(314) [0497] no right to forbid or **prevent** us, not even according to
TR : 0 0 :062(330) [0523] chosen over the rest to **prevent** schism, lest several
SC : 0 3 :011(347) [0547] hallowing his name and **prevent** the coming of his
SC : 0 8 :008(353) [0559] Greed and anxiety about food **prevent** such satisfaction.)
LC : 0 1 :189(390) [0635] the opportunity, fails to **prevent**, protect, and save him
LC : 0 1 :204(392) [0639] this (though you could **prevent** a wrong) or wink at it as
LC : 0 1 :250(399) [0651] permit such a thing, but are rather to avert and **prevent** it.
LC : 0 1 :288(404) [0663] other hand, we should **prevent** everything that tends to
LC : 0 1 :303(405) [0667] another's hand so that the victim is helpless to **prevent** it.
LC : 0 3 :008(421) [0699] any thoughts that would **prevent** or deter us from
LC : 0 3 :010(421) [0699] thoughts which would **prevent** or deter us from praying,
LC : 0 3 :049(426) [0711] petition that God would **prevent** the world from using his
LC : 0 3 :067(429) [0717] thy holy Word or **prevent** thy kingdom from coming; and
LC : 0 3 :073(430) [0719] are interfered with and **prevented** from functioning
LC : 0 3 :080(431) [0721] his power, but he also **prevents** and hinders the
EP : 1 0 :006(493) [0831] idolatry, as well as **preventing** offense to the weak in
SD : 0 2 :064(533) [0907] to each other, to **prevent** you from doing what you
SD : 0 6 :008(565) [0965] to each other, to **prevent** you from doing what you
SD : 1 1 :001(616) [1063] order by God's grace to **prevent**, as far as we can, disunity

Previous (11), Previously (17)
PR : PR :009(006) [0011] and repetition of our **previous** Christian confession and
PR : PR :023(012) [0021] from the one that was **previously** submitted at Augsburg
AG : 2 5 :001(061) [0069] to those who have not **previously** been examined and
AL : 2 5 :001(061) [0069] those who have been **previously** examined and absolved.
AP : 0 7 :018(171) [0233] is the same, whether now glorified or **previously** afflicted.
AP : 0 7 :046(177) [0243] which certainly was **previously** a universal ordinance.
AP : 1 1 :002(180) [0249] **Previously** the whole power of absolution had been
AP : 1 5 :006(215) [0317] We have **previously** shown at length that men are justified
AP : 2 2 :003(236) [0359] the sacrament; **previously** he had said that those who
AP : 2 3 :068(249) [0383] and convicted by many **previous** tribunals of the church.
AP : 2 3 :069(249) [0383] We have **previously** stated our position in the Jovinian
S 1 : PR :003(289) [0455] which I have **previously** given) to show where I have
S 3 : 0 8 :008(313) [0495] whose coming he had **previously** believed, had already
LC : 0 1 :125(382) [0617] worship of God described in the **previous** commandments.
LC : 0 1 :250(399) [0651] as we have done in the **previous** commandments: On one
LC : 0 3 :087(432) [0723] attacks against all the **previous** petitions, so that it is not
SD : PR :016(507) [0857] Word will find in the **previously** mentioned writings what
SD : 0 2 :073(535) [0909] In the light of the **previous** discussion one can readily
SD : 0 2 :090(539) [0915] From the **previous** explanation it is evident that
SD : 0 3 :044(547) [0931] set forth in detail in the **previously** mentioned writings.
SD : 0 3 :059(550) [0937] in addition to the **previously** mentioned errors, the
SD : 0 5 :022(562) [0959] Thus the law, as **previously** explained, is an office which
SD : 0 7 :018(572) [0979] adopted in the **previous** year, to their own advantage,
SD : 0 7 :046(577) [0987] But as on the **previous** occasion when Abraham received
SD : 0 7 :121(590) [1013] of the Supper, as shown above in a **previous** exposition.
SD : 0 8 :047(600) [1031] to both natures, as we presented this matter **previously**.
SD : 0 8 :086(608) [1047] the Holy Supper in connection with the **previous** article.
SD : 1 0 :016(613) [1057] in doctrine has not **previously** been achieved, will support

Price (17), Priceless (2), Prices (1)
AP : 0 4 :053(114) [0137] and the merits of Christ as the **price** and propitiation.
AP : 0 4 :053(114) [0137] merits of Christ are the **price** because there must be a
AP : 0 4 :057(114) [0137] the Christ would be the **price** for our sins, they knew that
AP : 0 4 :057(114) [0137] they knew that our works could not pay so high a **price**.
AP : 0 4 :098(121) [0151] of Christ as the cause or **price** on account of which we are
AP : 0 4 :155(128) [0165] that these fruits are the **price** of propitiation which earns
AP : 0 4 :204(135) [0177] these works to God as a **price** and propitiation, thus
AP : 0 4 :206(135) [0177] were a propitiation and **price** that reconciled God to
AP : 0 4 :209(136) [0179] idea that this work was a **price** or propitiation for which
AP : 0 4 :212(136) [0179] God is appeased and a **price** because of which we are
AP : 0 4 :244(142) [0189] are a propitiation and **price** that reconciles God to us;
AP : 1 2 :144(205) [0297] them the honor of being a **price** paid in lieu of eternal
AP : 1 2 :148(205) [0299] but not as a merit or **price**, as our opponents imagine
AP : 1 2 :160(208) [0303] for this God has another **price**, the death of his Son.
AP : 2 4 :064(261) [0407] They sell the Mass as a **price** for success, to merchants for
AP : 2 7 :035(275) [0431] monastic vows are not a **price** for which the forgiveness
LC : 0 1 :118(381) [0615] O how great a **price** all the Carthusian monks and nuns
LC : 0 1 :240(397) [0649] New burdens and high **prices** are imposed.
LC : 0 3 :055(427) [0713] but for an eternal, **priceless** treasure and everything that
LC : 0 4 :043(442) [0743] man's door just such a **priceless** medicine which swallows

Prick (1)
LC : 0 5 :057(453) [0767] time when nothing will **prick** your conscience, you will

Pride (6)
AP : 0 4 :302(154) [0205] works; it leads consciences into either **pride** or despair.
LC : 0 1 :038(369) [0591] that is, those who persist in their stubbornness and **pride**.
LC : 0 2 :021(413) [0683] of God solely for its own **pride** and greed, pleasure and
LC : 0 3 :090(432) [0723] God's purpose to break our **pride** and keep us humble.
LC : 0 3 :103(434) [0727] slander, arrogance, and **pride**, along with fondness for
LC : 0 4 :067(445) [0749] and the more free from greed, hatred, envy, and **pride**.

Priest (35), Priesthood (16), Priestly (2), Priests (86)
AG : 0 8 :001(033) [0047] are efficacious even if the **priests** who administer them are
AG : 2 2 :003(049) [0059] as if they apply only to **priests**, Paul shows in I Cor.
AG : 2 2 :006(050) [0061] also states that the **priests** who administered the
AG : 2 3 :000(051) [0061] XXIII. The Marriage of **Priests**
AG : 2 3 :001(051) [0061] and the dissolute life of **priests** who were not able to
AG : 2 3 :003(051) [0061] lechery, some of our **priests** have entered the married
AG : 2 3 :009(052) [0061] human vows or laws, our **priests** and other clergy have
AG : 2 3 :010(052) [0061] that it was customary for **priests** and deacons to marry in
AG : 2 3 :012(052) [0063] years ago that the **priests** in Germany were compelled by
AG : 2 3 :012(053) [0063] during an uprising of the entire body of **priests**.
AG : 2 3 :012(053) [0063] future marriages of **priests** but also broke up the
AG : 2 3 :016(054) [0063] would the marriage of **priests** and the clergy, and
AG : 2 3 :017(054) [0063] may be a shortage of **priests** and pastors in the future.
AG : 2 3 :018(054) [0063] the assertion that **priests** and clergymen may marry is
AG : 2 3 :018(054) [0063] demonstrates both that **priests** were married and that the
AG : 2 3 :021(055) [0063] married — and especially **priests**, who above all others
AG : 2 3 :026(056) [0063] youth — and most of the **priests** and monks entered into
AG : 2 4 :012(057) [0065] these things and the **priests** were reminded of the terrible
AG : 2 4 :029(059) [0067] God, not only for the **priest** himself but also for the whole
AG : 2 4 :034(060) [0067] Communion in which the **priest** and others receive the
AG : 2 4 :036(060) [0067] reports how the **priest** stood every day, inviting some to
AG : 2 4 :037(060) [0067] and communicated the other **priests** and deacons,
AG : 2 4 :038(060) [0067] canon read, "After the **priests** the deacons shall receive
AG : 2 4 :038(060) [0069] receive the sacrament in order from the bishop or **priest**."
AL : 2 2 :003(049) [0059] that this refers only to **priests**, Paul in I Cor. 11:20ff. cites
AL : 2 2 :006(050) [0061] Jerome, who said, "The **priests** administer the Eucharist
AL : 2 3 :000(051) [0061] XXIII. The Marriage of **Priests**
AL : 2 3 :001(051) [0061] complaint concerning **priests** who have not been
AL : 2 3 :002(051) [0061] were some reasons why **priests** were forbidden to marry
AL : 2 3 :003(051) [0061] Since **priests** among us desired to avoid such open
AL : 2 3 :009(052) [0061] For these reasons our **priests** teach that it is lawful for
AL : 2 3 :010(052) [0061] that in the ancient church **priests** were married men.
AL : 2 3 :012(052) [0063] hundred years ago were **priests** in Germany compelled by
AL : 2 3 :012(053) [0063] was almost killed by the enraged **priests** in an uprising.
AL : 2 3 :018(054) [0063] exercised than in opposition to the marriage of **priests**.
AL : 2 3 :021(055) [0063] But now men, and even **priests**, are cruelly put to death,
AL : 2 4 :013(057) [0065] Accordingly when our **priests** were admonished
AL : 2 4 :036(060) [0067] Chrysostom says that the **priest** stands daily at the altar,
AP : 0 4 :082(118) [0145] then we have a great high **priest**,...let us then with
AP : 0 4 :082(118) [0145] but in Christ, the high **priest**, this statement requires
AP : 0 4 :165(130) [0169] because of Christ's promise, he insults this high **priest**.
AP : 0 4 :236(140) [0185] They are slaughtering **priests** and other good men if they
AP : 0 4 :332(158) [0211] insults Christ, who intercedes for us as our high **priest**.
AP : 0 4 :333(158) [0211] because of Christ the high **priest**, as he himself says
AP : 0 4 :333(158) [0211] because without the high **priest** we cannot draw near to
AP : 0 4 :376(165) [0223] and that through his **priestly** mediation we are led to the
AP : 0 7 :049(178) [0245] the personal conduct of **priests** or people, we should not
AP : 0 7 :050(178) [0245] because they denied to **priests** the right to hold property
AP : 1 0 :002(179) [0247] of the Mass, in which the **priest** clearly prays that the
AP : 1 1 :008(181) [0251] of who was the proper **priest**, when brothers did not act
AP : 1 2 :109(198) [0283] confession to be made to **priests** but of the reconciliation
AP : 1 2 :112(198) [0285] made confession to the **priests** so that these satisfactions
AP : 1 2 :122(200) [0289] have been absolved by the **priest** should perform the
AP : 1 3 :007(212) [0311] do not interpret the **priesthood** in reference to the
AP : 1 3 :007(212) [0311] new covenant needed a **priesthood** like the Levitical to
AP : 1 3 :009(212) [0311] Thus **priests** are not called to make sacrifices that merit

Continued ▶

AP : 13 :010(212) [0311] enough, we do not have a **priesthood** like the Levitical.
AP : 14 :002(214) [0315] bishops either force our **priests** to forsake and condemn
AP : 14 :002(214) [0315] This keeps our **priests** from acknowledging such bishops.
AP : 16 :011(224) [0333] his mind in claiming that **priests** were not allowed to own
AP : 21 :024(232) [0349] as our intercessor and high **priest**, why seek others?
AP : 22 :001(236) [0357] all of the church uses the sacrament, not only the **priests**.
AP : 22 :004(236) [0359] Jerome says, "The **priests** who serve the Eucharist and
AP : 22 :008(237) [0359] When **priests** were commanded to use lay communion,
AP : 22 :010(237) [0359] the loss of the high **priesthood**, they were supposed to ask
AP : 22 :010(237) [0359] the one part that belonged to the **priests** (I Sam. 2:36).
AP : 22 :010(237) [0361] the one part offered by the **priest**, that is, with one kind."
AP : 22 :013(238) [0361] of order between **priest** and people, but there is no
AP : 22 :017(238) [0361] of Ezekiel (7:26), "The law perishes from the **priest**."
AP : 23 :000(239) [0363] [Article XXIII. The Marriage of **Priests**]
AP : 23 :001(239) [0363] be disgraced and shamed by the marriage of **priests**.
AP : 23 :003(239) [0363] punishments, slaughter **priests** whom even the barbarians
AP : 23 :015(241) [0367] command requiring that **priests** should marry — as
AP : 23 :015(241) [0367] should marry — as though **priests** were not human beings.
AP : 23 :015(241) [0369] to human nature in general, applies to **priests** as well.
AP : 23 :027(243) [0371] of their ministration the **priests** of the Old Testament
AP : 23 :027(243) [0371] their wives; since the **priests** of the New Testament must
AP : 23 :027(243) [0371] perpetual celibacy on **priests**, though in this very analogy
AP : 23 :041(245) [0375] with the Levitical **priests**, we have already answered that
AP : 23 :041(245) [0375] make it necessary to impose perpetual celibacy on **priests**.
AP : 23 :044(245) [0375] the great crowd of lazy **priests** in the confraternities,
AP : 23 :057(247) [0379] canon commands that **priests** be suspended; our canonists
AP : 23 :059(247) [0379] marriages, the murder of **priests** who refuse to submit,
AP : 23 :061(247) [0381] We believe that **priests** should have this same freedom; we
AP : 23 :064(248) [0381] of our opponents is that **priests** should be pure, according
AP : 23 :067(248) [0383] is horrible: the marriage of **priests** is the Jovinian heresy.
AP : 23 :067(248) [0383] say that the marriage of **priests** is the Jovinian heresy or
AP : 23 :070(249) [0383] breaking up marriages and torturing and killing **priests**.
AP : 23 :071(249) [0383] Even if the **priests** had done wrong in marrying, it is
AP : 24 :026(254) [0391] in I Pet. 2:5, "A holy **priesthood**, to offer spiritual
AP : 24 :034(256) [0395] in Rom. 15:16 of "the **priestly** service of the gospel of
AP : 24 :034(256) [0397] sacrifices for sin offered by a Levitical **priesthood**.
AP : 24 :048(258) [0401] the blessing of God, the **priests** in our churches pay
AP : 24 :049(258) [0401] in their churches mercenary **priests** use the sacrament.
AP : 24 :052(259) [0403] Hebrews (5:1), "Every high **priest** chosen from among
AP : 24 :052(259) [0403] the New Testament has **priests** and high priests, it must
AP : 24 :052(259) [0403] has priests and high **priests**, it must also have some sort
AP : 24 :052(259) [0403] of the Old Testament **priesthood** and sacrifices is spread
AP : 24 :053(259) [0403] says that "every high **priest** is appointed to offer sacrifices
AP : 24 :053(259) [0403] itself adds immediately that Christ is the high **priest**.
AP : 24 :053(259) [0403] about the Levitical **priesthood** and say that it was a
AP : 24 :053(259) [0403] and say that it was a picture of Christ's **priesthood**.
AP : 24 :054(259) [0403] theme that the ancient **priesthood** and the ancient
AP : 24 :057(260) [0405] and propitiator with **priests** and sacrificers who daily
AP : 24 :058(260) [0405] Testament must have a **priest** who sacrifices for sin, this
AP : 24 :059(260) [0405] Since the **priesthood** of the New Testament is a ministry
AP : 24 :085(265) [0413] gifts of the people rather than the offering of the **priest**?
AP : 24 :089(266) [0415] as much to the work of a **priest** as to the death of Christ.
AP : 24 :097(268) [0417] but also against other **priests** who perform the sacrifices
AP : 24 :098(268) [0417] clung to the wicked **priests** in Judah, and in Israel the
AP : 27 :051(277) [0437] with the marriage of **priests** that the law of nature in men
AP : 28 :001(281) [0443] article states about the immunity of churches and **priests**."
AP : 28 :003(281) [0445] kinds of people to the **priesthood** quite indiscriminately.
S2 : 04 :009(300) [0473] St. Jerome writes that the **priests** of Alexandria governed
S3 : 03 :014(305) [0483] we, too, became **priests** and monks, that we might set
S3 : 03 :019(306) [0485] abased himself before the **priest**, the sooner and the better
S3 : 03 :028(308) [0487] wished to be monks and **priests** in monasteries and
S3 : 10 :003(314) [0497] without bishops by **priests** and preachers in common.
S3 : 11 :000(314) [0499] XI. The Marriage of **Priests**
S3 : 11 :001(314) [0499] burden the divine estate of **priests** with perpetual celibacy.
TR : 00 :018(323) [0509] or Alexandria — he is of the same dignity and **priesthood**.
TR : 00 :026(324) [0511] as the Levitical **priesthood** is, but is spread abroad
TR : 00 :038(326) [0515] The Levitical high **priest** was the supreme pontifex by
TR : 00 :038(327) [0515] nevertheless, godless high **priests** were not to be obeyed.
TR : 00 :069(331) [0523] of Peter, "You are a royal **priesthood**" (I Pet. 2:9).
TR : 00 :069(331) [0525] it alone possesses the **priesthood**, certainly has the right
TR : 00 :078(333) [0527] law concerning the celibacy of **priests** is likewise unjust.
LC : 01 :213(394) [0641] see how the papal rabble, **priests**, monks, and nuns resist
LC : 01 :314(407) [0671] For when a **priest** stands in a gold-embroidered chasuble
LC : 03 :025(423) [0705] prayers of monks and **priests**, who howl and growl
LC : 05 :015(448) [0757] whether even a wicked **priest** can administer the
EP : 08 :014(488) [0821] suffer and be our high **priest** for our reconciliation with
SD : 07 :024(573) [0979] whether even a wicked **priest** can administer and give the
SD : 07 :032(574) [0983] and wine, though the **priests** who distribute them or those
SD : 07 :076(583) [0999] by the mouth of the **priest**, but by God's power and grace
SD : 07 :121(590) [1013] the word and work of the **priest** the power allegedly to
SD : 08 :047(600) [1031] redeemer, king, high **priest**, head, shepherd, and so forth,
SD : 08 :078(607) [1043] on earth as mediator, head, king, and high **priest**.
SD : 08 :087(608) [1047] their head, king, and high **priest**, who has promised that

Primacy (12)
TR : 00 :000(319) [0503] Treatise on the Power and **Primacy** of the Pope
TR : 00 :008(321) [0505] that there was to be no **primacy** among ministers, just as
TR : 00 :017(323) [0509] then acknowledge the **primacy** or superiority of the
TR : 00 :019(323) [0509] of Chalcedon the **primacy** was offered to the bishop of
TR : 00 :021(323) [0509] Constantinople over the **primacy**, Emperor Phocas had
TR : 00 :021(323) [0509] finally decided that the **primacy** should be assigned to the
TR : 00 :021(323) [0509] had acknowledged the **primacy** of the Roman pontiff,
TR : 00 :038(326) [0515] of Rome should possess **primacy** and superiority by
TR : 00 :057(330) [0521] of Rome did possess the **primacy** by divine right, he
TR : 00 :082(334) [0529] article concerning the **primacy** of the pope and the power
SD : 10 :020(614) [1059] Under the article on the **primacy** or lordship of the pope,
SD : 10 :021(614) [1059] on the Power and **Primacy** of the Pope, which constitutes

Primarily (9)
LC : 01 :021(367) [0585] It is **primarily** in the heart, which pursues other things
LC : 01 :321(408) [0673] Although **primarily** attached to the First Commandment,
LC : 04 :052(443) [0745] Further, we are not **primarily** concerned whether the
SD : 01 :005(509) [0861] but also, and **primarily**, the abominable and dreadful
SD : 07 :070(582) [0997] instituted and ordained **primarily** for communicants like
SD : 07 :086(584) [1003] or "action" does not **primarily** mean faith, or the oral
SD : 07 :111(589) [1011] intended to set forth **primarily** our confession and
SD : 08 :051(601) [1033] capacity extends, but **primarily** from and according to the
SD : 10 :014(613) [1057] Here we are dealing **primarily** with the chief article of our

Primary (4)
S1 : PR :014(291) [0459] especially when the **primary** things, which are
EP : 02 :001(469) [0785] In this controversy the **primary** question revolves
EP : 03 :020(475) [0797] indeed as if it were the **primary** cause of our
SD : PR :001(503) [0849] The **primary** requirement for basic and permanent

Primitive (1)
SD : PR :017(507) [0857] and errors which the **primitive**, ancient, orthodox church

Prince (13), Princely (1), Princes (56)
PR : PR :000(001) [0004] undersigned Electors, **Princes**, and Estates who Embrace
PR : PR :000(001) [0004] aforementioned Electors, **Princes**, and Estates for the
PR : PR :001(003) [0007] comes, we, the electors, **princes**, and estates in the Holy
PR : PR :013(007) [0013] among the electors and **princes**, convoked a number of
PR : PR :013(007) [0013] number of electors, **princes**, and estates adhering to the
PR : PR :018(009) [0015] year 1530 by the electors, **princes**, and estates referred to
AG : 00 :000(023) [0037] in Augsburg by certain **Princes** and Cities to His Imperial
AG : PR :005(025) [0039] undersigned elector and **princes** and our associates, have
AG : PR :005(025) [0039] with other electors, **princes**, and estates, we have complied
AG : PR :006(025) [0039] that each of the electors, **princes**, and estates should
AG : PR :009(025) [0039] If the other electors, **princes**, and estates also submit a
AG : PR :012(026) [0041] represent the electors, **princes**, and estates of the other
AG : PR :014(026) [0041] friends (the electors, **princes**, and estates), and every lover
AG : PR :015(026) [0041] assurance to the electors, **princes**, and estates of the
AG : PR :018(026) [0041] a year ago, the electors, **princes**, and estates of the empire
AG : PR :018(026) [0041] with the absent electors, **princes**, and representatives of
AG : PR :021(027) [0043] council as the electors, **princes**, and estates have with the
AG : 16 :002(037) [0051] civil offices or serve as **princes** and judges, render
AG : 26 :010(065) [0071] and care for them, that a **prince** and magistrates should
AG : 27 :013(073) [0077] and preacher, of ruler, **prince**, lord, or the like, all of
AG : 28 :029(085) [0087] of such duties, the **princes** are obliged, whether they like
AG : 00 :007(096) [0095] Wolfgang, **prince** of Anhalt
AL : 26 :010(065) [0071] bear children, that a **prince** should govern his country.
AL : 28 :029(085) [0087] of their duties, **princes** are bound, even against their will,
AL : 00 :017(096) [0095] Wolfgang, **prince** of Anhalt
AP : PR :001(098) [0099] a public reading of our **princes**' Confession, a number of
AP : PR :001(098) [0099] the assembly of the **princes**, and he ordered our princes to
AP : PR :001(098) [0099] and he ordered our **princes** to accept this Confutation.
AP : PR :004(098) [0099] Majesty again ordered our **princes** to accept the
AP : PR :013(099) [0101] with the emperor or the **princes**, whom I hold in due
AP : 04 :236(140) [0185] this most clement **prince**, that these laws should be
AP : 04 :399(168) [0227] Some of the **princes** regarded this expression as unworthy
AP : 07 :022(172) [0235] or secular, because **princes** and supreme pontiffs as well
AP : 20 :004(227) [0339] Majesty and many of the **princes** would have refused to
AP : 23 :001(239) [0363] urge the emperor and the **princes** not to let the Roman
AP : 23 :070(249) [0383] these they persuade the **princes** to take a position
AP : 23 :071(249) [0383] Whatever happens, our **princes** can have a clear
AP : 23 :071(249) [0383] Our **princes** do not delight in change for its own sake, but
AP : 27 :018(272) [0425] Emperor Charles; look, **princes**; look, all you estates!
AP : 28 :002(281) [0443] political ordinances nor the gifts and privileges of **princes**.
S1 : PR :012(290) [0459] There is discord among **princes** and political estates.
S3 : 10 :002(314) [0497] are temporal lords and **princes** who are unwilling to
TR : 00 :054(329) [0519] church, the kings and the **princes**, to have regard for the
TR : 00 :082(334) [0529] of the most illustrious **princes** and of the estates and cities
TR : 00 :082(334) [0529] was presented to the **princes** here in this assembly in
TR : 00 :082(334) [0529] the papacy presented to the **princes** in Smalcald
TR : 00 :082(000) [0529] by the Most Illustrious **Prince**, the Elector of Saxony, and
TR : 00 :082(000) [0529] Saxony, and by the other **princes** and estates of the
SC : PR :012(339) [0535] notify them that the **prince** is disposed to banish such
LC : 01 :038(369) [0591] observe this every day in the case of bishops and **princes**.
LC : 01 :142(384) [0621] Again, their **princes** and overlords were called *patres*
LC : 01 :209(393) [0641] those of emperor, **princes**, bishops, or anyone else.
LC : 01 :230(396) [0645] consort with lords and **princes** and daily plunder not only
LC : 01 :249(398) [0651] is the responsibility of **princes** and magistrates.
LC : 01 :258(399) [0653] Where judges, mayors, **princes**, or others in authority sit
LC : 01 :300(405) [0667] belong, as many great nobles, lords, and **princes** do now.
LC : 01 :302(405) [0667] patent and the seal of the **prince** attesting that it was
LC : 03 :057(427) [0713] to give great and **princely** gifts, and the fool asked only
LC : 03 :075(430) [0719] of every upright **prince** were emblazoned with a loaf of
LC : 03 :075(430) [0719] on coins, to remind both **princes** and subjects that
LC : 03 :075(430) [0719] through the office of the **princes** we enjoy protection and
LC : 03 :077(431) [0721] men, and especially our **princes**, counselors, magistrates,
LC : 04 :024(439) [0737] in order to become a **prince**, but as the words say, to "be
LC : 05 :011(448) [0755] word and ordinance of a **prince** or emperor, but of the
SD : PR :003(501) [0847] of Christian electors, **princes**, and estates who had then
SD : PR :005(504) [0851] of Christian electors, **princes**, and estates of the Roman
SD : PR :007(505) [0853] most illustrious electors, **princes**, and estates, before the
SD : PR :007(505) [0853] to which the electors, **princes**, and estates were resolved
SD : 10 :019(614) [1059] are temporal lords and **princes** who are unwilling to
SD : 12 :020(634) [1099] pay oath-bound feudal homage to his **prince** or liege lord.

Principal (7)
AG : 00 :002(048) [0059] or defective in the **principal** articles and since this our
AG : 00 :001(095) [0095] undue length we have indicated only the **principal** ones.
AP : 24 :046(258) [0401] Yet this is the **principal** doctrine of the Christian faith.
AP : 24 :073(262) [0409] The **principal** use of the sacrament is to make clear that
EP : 01 :001(466) [0779] The **principal** question in this controversy is if, strictly
EP : 01 :001(466) [0779] essence, or indeed the **principal** and best part of his being
SD : 03 :049(548) [0933] that they are not the **principal** cause but that our

Principalities (1)
AG : PR :008(025) [0039] in our lands, **principalities**, dominions, cities and

Principle (4), Principles (1)
AL : 01 :005(028) [0043] who posited two **principles**, one good and the other evil,
AL : 00 :001(095) [0095] undue length we have discussed only the **principle** ones.
AP : 02 :037(105) [0115] they cannot refute the **principle**, they twist his words in
SD : 03 :055(549) [0935] Confession accept the **principle** that we must seek our
SD : 04 :003(551) [0939] proposition or **principle** "that good works are detrimental

Print (1), Printed (1), Printers (1), Printing (1)
P R : P R :019(009) [0017] writings and in public **print** have tried to palm them off
P R : P R :024(013) [0023] suspend or postpone its **printing** and publication any
P R : P R :026(014) [0025] the supervision of **printers**, and other salutary means.
E P : R N :005(465) [0777] as both of them are contained in his **printed** works.

Prior (14), Priority (1)
A P : 0 4 :344(160) [0217] through mercy and if, **prior** to salvation, there is nothing
E P : 0 2 :019(472) [0791] **Prior** to man's conversion there are only two efficient
E P : 1 2 :008(498) [0839] 6. That without and **prior** to Baptism the children of
S D : 0 1 :056(518) [0877] In the same way, **prior** to this controversy, the
S D : 0 2 :002(520) [0881] man after the Fall and **prior** to his conversion can do in
S D : 0 2 :003(520) [0881] of his natural powers **prior** to his conversion that he can
S D : 0 2 :007(521) [0883] that after the Fall and **prior** to his conversion not a spark
S D : 0 2 :018(524) [0887] the will of man **prior** to his conversion will be much more
S D : 0 2 :059(532) [0905] And it is equally true that **prior** to his conversion man is
S D : 0 2 :061(533) [0905] **Prior** to his conversion man is dead in sin (Eph. 2:5);
S D : 0 2 :062(533) [0905] one cannot ascribe to man **prior** to his conversion any
S D : 0 3 :041(546) [0929] precede faith, nor is sanctification **prior** to justification.
S D : 0 3 :049(548) [0933] by faith, or that faith has **priority** in justification but that
S D : 0 4 :036(557) [0949] For although, **prior** to this controversy, not a few
S D : 1 2 :013(634) [1099] and children of God even without and **prior** to Baptism.

Prison (6), Prisoner (1)
A G : 2 7 :002(071) [0077] by means of these vows as if in a well-conceived **prison**.
A L : 2 7 :002(071) [0077] of restoring discipline, as in a carefully planned **prison**.
A P : 0 2 :047(106) [0119] is enslaved and held **prisoner** by the devil, who deludes it
A P : 2 7 :001(268) [0419] He was thrown into **prison** by his order because he had
A P : 2 7 :002(269) [0419] account of the filth of the **prison**, he sent for the guardian
L C : 0 1 :191(391) [0635] me, I was sick and in **prison** and you did not visit me."
L C : 0 1 :191(391) [0635] by wild beasts, to rot in **prison** or perish from want."

Private (30), Privately (3)
A G : 1 1 :001(034) [0047] is taught among us that **private** absolution should be
A G : 2 4 :013(057) [0065] mercenary Masses and **private** Masses, which had
A L : 1 1 :001(034) [0047] Our churches teach that **private** absolution should be
A L : 2 4 :013(057) [0065] concerning this sin, **private** Masses were discontinued
A L : 2 4 :013(057) [0065] inasmuch as hardly any **private** Masses were held except
A L : 2 4 :021(058) [0067] which infinitely increased **private** Masses, namely, that
A L : 2 4 :035(060) [0067] ancients do not mention **private** Masses but speak often
A L : 2 7 :054(079) [0083] take vengeance in their **private** life since they are told that
A P : 0 4 :192(133) [0175] done in the most humble occupation and in **private** life.
A P : 0 7 :023(172) [0235] of the world, and of all public and **private** affairs.
A P : 1 2 :100(197) [0281] be wicked to remove **private** absolution from the church.
A P : 1 2 :101(197) [0281] And those who despise **private** absolution understand
A P : 1 2 :164(208) [0303] mitigation of public and **private** punishments and
A P : 1 6 :007(223) [0331] The Gospel forbids **private** revenge, and Christ stresses
A P : 1 6 :007(223) [0331] Thus **private** revenge is forbidden not as an evangelical
A P : 1 6 :013(224) [0333] the Gospel permitted such public and **private** business.
A P : 2 1 :036(234) [0353] to men in their public or **private** life, as a means of
A P : 2 3 :023(242) [0369] of the synods but the **private** judgment of the popes.
A P : 2 3 :051(246) [0377] dangerous to public and **private** morals; this alone should
A P : 2 4 :006(250) [0385] Greek parishes have no **private** Masses but only one
A P : 2 4 :006(250) [0385] before Gregory make no mention of **private** Masses.
A P : 2 4 :007(250) [0385] on the multiplication of **private** Masses; so superstitious
A P : 2 7 :009(270) [0421] expense without the loss of their **private** patrimony?
S 2 : 0 2 :009(294) [0465] church, to meet his own **private** need and thus trifle with
S 3 : 0 8 :002(312) [0495] Although **private** absolution is derived from the office of
L C : 0 1 :181(389) [0631] forbidden here applies to **private** individuals, not to
L C : 0 1 :275(402) [0659] compelled to examine and handle his **private** parts.
L C : 0 1 :276(402) [0659] but admonish him **privately** so that he may amend.
L C : 0 6 :013(458) [0000] which takes place **privately** before a single brother.
E P : 1 2 :017(499) [0841] hold or possess **private** property but is in conscience
S D : P R :001(503) [0851] based these not on mere **private** writings, but on such
S D : 1 2 :022(634) [1099] hold or possess **private** property but is obliged to give his
S D : 1 2 :040(636) [1103] speak or write anything, **privately** or publicly, contrary to

Privation (2)
A P : 0 2 :027(104) [0113] sin denotes the **privation** of original justice, and besides
A P : 0 2 :027(104) [0113] it is not a pure **privation**, but also a corrupt habit."

Privative (1)
A L : 2 8 :041(087) [0089] that fasting which is **privative** and not natural is a work

Privilege (4), Privileges (4)
A P : 1 5 :015(217) [0319] did not the heathen and Israelites have the same **privilege**?
A P : 2 8 :001(281) [0443] rant about the **privileges** and the ecclesiastical estate, and
A P : 2 8 :002(281) [0443] political ordinances nor the gifts and **privileges** of princes.
S C : P R :011(339) [0535] or be allowed to participate in any Christian **privileges**.
L C : 0 1 :144(385) [0623] be willing to pay for the **privilege** of service and be glad to
L C : 0 1 :240(397) [0649] if it were his right and **privilege** to sell his goods as dearly
L C : 0 6 :028(460) [0000] yourself and beg me for the **privilege** of sharing in it.
S D : 0 8 :051(601) [1033] prerogatives and **privileges** in majesty, glory, power, and

Privy (1)
P R : P R :027(014) [0025] hereto and ordered our **privy** seals impressed hereon.

Prize (4)
L C : 0 1 :109(380) [0611] You are to esteem and **prize** them as the most precious
L C : 0 1 :322(409) [0673] good things on those who **prize** them and gladly act and
L C : 0 1 :333(411) [0677] Therefore we should **prize** and value them above all other
L C : 0 3 :012(422) [0701] means despise our prayers, but rather **prize** them highly.

Probably (4)
A G : 2 4 :040(061) [0069] to the parochial Mass, **probably** through abuse, have been
A P : 0 7 :025(172) [0235] church that way, we would **probably** have fairer judges.
A P : 1 2 :130(202) [0291] But there are **probably** many people in many places who
L C : 0 1 :281(403) [0661] to witness, you will **probably** deny having said anything.

Problem (7), Problems (2)
A P : 0 4 :224(138) [0181] There is no **problem** in this text if we remove the
A P : 0 4 :345(160) [0217] This can be a great **problem** to the human mind.
A P : 1 5 :049(222) [0329] abrogation involves its own difficulties and **problems**.
A P : 2 3 :043(245) [0375] good men that domestic **problems** are excluded from
A P : 2 4 :013(251) [0387] If this were the whole **problem**, the case would be settled.
L C : 0 1 :258(399) [0653] This **problem** appears to concern us only a little at
L C : 0 6 :013(458) [0000] When some **problem** or quarrel sets us at one another's
S D : P R :009(503) [0849] reflects a mere semantic **problem** of little or no
S D : 0 4 :005(551) [0939] to be only a semantic **problem** and became a vehemently

Procedure (6), Proceed (16), Proceeded (2), Proceeds (3)
A G : P R :012(026) [0041] do not comply with the **procedure** intended by Your
A G : P R :022(027) [0043] matters, and have done so in legal form and **procedure**.
A P : 0 4 :035(112) [0131] "whatever does not **proceed** from faith is sin."
A P : 0 4 :221(137) [0181] Our opponents **proceed** in reverse order.
A P : 1 2 :089(195) [0279] "Whatever does not **proceed** from faith is sin."
A P : 1 5 :017(217) [0319] "Whatever does not **proceed** from faith is sin."
A P : 2 7 :023(273) [0427] "Whatever does not **proceed** from faith is sin."
S 1 : 0 1 :000(291) [0461] and the Holy Spirit **proceeded** from the Father and the
S C : P R :016(340) [0535] First Commandment, **proceed** to the Second
S C : 0 5 :021(350) [0553] **"Proceed."**
L C : 0 1 :200(392) [0637] Then they **proceed** to the person nearest and dearest to
L C : 0 1 :280(403) [0661] This is the right **procedure** for restraining and reforming a
L C : 0 1 :323(409) [0673] that all our actions **proceed** from a heart that fears and
L C : 0 1 :324(409) [0675] chief commandment, from which all the others **proceed**.
L C : 0 1 :327(409) [0675] neighbor, everything **proceeds** from the force of the First
L C : 0 1 :329(410) [0677] which all the others **proceed**; again, to it they all return
L C : 0 5 :063(454) [0767] than upon the words that **proceed** from Christ's lips.
E P : 1 1 :013(496) [0835] since they do not **proceed** from God but are inspired by
S D : 0 1 :001(508) [0859] of which, as the root and source, all other sins **proceed**.
S D : 0 1 :050(517) [0875] the best and safest **procedure** is to use and keep the
S D : 0 2 :065(534) [0907] cooperation does not **proceed** from our carnal and
S D : 0 4 :008(552) [0941] "Whatsoever does not **proceed** from faith is sin"
S D : 0 4 :031(556) [0947] Spirit, and deliberately **proceeds** to sin against his
S D : 0 8 :001(591) [1015] them, however, but **proceeded** originally from the
S D : 0 8 :073(605) [1041] and the Holy Spirit **proceeds** from him as well as from
S D : 1 0 :027(615) [1061] as wrongful the **procedure** whereby such commandments
S D : 1 0 :030(615) [1061] reject and condemn the **procedure** whereby matters of

Process (14)
A P : 0 4 :285(150) [0201] Describing this **process** in Rom. 4:5 ff., Paul proves that
A P : 1 2 :163(208) [0303] refers to the whole **process** of penitence and the fruits
A P : 1 2 :164(208) [0303] The whole **process** of penitence — contrition, faith, and
A P : 1 2 :165(208) [0303] with regard to the whole **process** of penitence and
A P : 1 2 :166(208) [0303] — we mean the whole **process** of penitence — they were
A P : 2 7 :055(278) [0439] the listeners and, in the **process** of teaching, prompting
T R : 0 0 :051(329) [0519] for when proper judicial **process** has been taken away, the
T R : 0 0 :074(332) [0525] and excommunicated them without due **process** of law.
T R : 0 0 :074(332) [0525] power to ban men arbitrarily without due **process** of law!
T R : 0 0 :075(333) [0525] nobody should be condemned without due **process** of law.
E P : 0 1 :009(467) [0781] recognized by a rational **process**, but only from God's
E P : 1 2 :026(500) [0843] and the orderly **process** of excommunication do not take
S D : 0 1 :014(511) [0863] Of course, this **process** is only begun in this life, not to be
S D : 1 2 :034(635) [1101] expulsion or orderly **process** of excommunication does

Procession (1), Processions (2)
A G : 2 2 :012(051) [0061] of the sacrament in **processions** is also omitted by us.
A L : 2 2 :012(051) [0061] of Christ, the **processions** which were hitherto held are
S D : 0 7 :015(572) [0977] about and exposed in **procession**, as happens in the

Proclaim (10), Proclaimed (16), Proclaiming (1), Proclaims (6), Proclamation (57), Proclamations (1)
P R : P R :002(003) [0007] and published and **proclaimed** in all of Christendom
A P : 0 4 :043(113) [0133] by faith, the Gospel **proclaims** the righteousness of faith
A P : 0 4 :047(113) [0133] of the Gospel, which **proclaims** the righteousness of faith
A P : 0 4 :097(121) [0149] forgiveness of sins is **proclaimed** to you, and by him every
A P : 0 4 :119(123) [0155] there must needs be a **proclamation** in the church from
A P : 0 4 :166(130) [0169] and the church **proclaim** that the law cannot be satisfied.
A P : 0 4 :210(136) [0179] "As often as you do this, you **proclaim** the Lord's death."
A P : 0 4 :229(139) [0183] and learned scholastics **proclaimed** the highest work of
A P : 0 4 :255(144) [0193] One is the **proclamation** of the law or of penitence, which
A P : 0 4 :261(145) [0195] Daniel **proclaimed** many things to the king about the one
A P : 0 4 :274(148) [0199] This is the essential **proclamation** of the Gospel, that we
A P : 0 4 :274(148) [0199] try to silence this **proclamation** of the Gospel by twisting
A P : 0 4 :365(163) [0219] Yet the **proclamation** of rewards and punishments is
A P : 0 4 :365(163) [0219] In the **proclamation** of punishments the wrath of God is
A P : 0 4 :365(163) [0219] In the **proclamation** of rewards grace is displayed.
A P : 1 2 :029(185) [0259] For the sum of the **proclamation** of the Gospel is to
A P : 1 2 :042(187) [0261] through the **proclamation** of the Gospel and the use of
A P : 1 2 :053(189) [0265] prophets, and finally **proclaimed** and revealed by Christ
A P : 1 2 :058(190) [0267] to understand the faith **proclaimed** by the Gospel when it
A P : 1 2 :099(197) [0281] the power of the keys **proclaims** to individuals by divine
A P : 2 4 :025(253) [0391] of praise": the **proclamation** of the Gospel, faith, prayer,
A P : 2 4 :030(255) [0395] confession, and **proclamation** of the Gospel, suffering
A P : 2 4 :032(255) [0395] place through the **proclamation** of the Gospel, which
A P : 2 4 :032(255) [0395] The **proclamation** of the Gospel produces faith in those
A P : 2 4 :032(255) [0395] like faith, prayer, **proclamation** of the Gospel,
A P : 2 4 :033(256) [0395] of praise we include the **proclamation** of the Word.
A P : 2 4 :034(256) [0395] Testament) are the **proclamation** of the Gospel and its
A P : 2 4 :034(256) [0397] of Christ and the **proclamation** of the Gospel, which
A P : 2 4 :034(256) [0397] They omit the **proclamation** of the Gospel, faith, prayer,
A P : 2 4 :035(256) [0397] and also the **proclamation** of the Gospel, faith, prayer,
A P : 2 4 :035(256) [0397] bread and drink the cup, you **proclaim** the Lord's death."
A P : 2 4 :036(256) [0397] only the ceremony but the **proclamation** of the Gospel.
A P : 2 4 :036(257) [0397] of the lamb, by the **proclamation** of the Gospel, as Peter
A P : 2 4 :038(257) [0399] daily sacrifice, the **proclamation** of the faith which truly
A P : 2 4 :038(257) [0399] the effect of the **proclamation**, as we are sanctified, put to
A P : 2 4 :049(258) [0401] we keep both the **proclamation** of the Gospel and the
A P : 2 4 :051(259) [0403] rather than in the **proclamation** of the Gospel, in faith,
S 2 : 0 2 :013(300) [0475] and above Christ and to **proclaim** himself the head, and
T R : 0 0 :031(325) [0513] to preach the Gospel, **proclaim** the forgiveness of sins,
T R : 0 0 :039(327) [0515] in the temple of God, **proclaiming** himself to be God"
S C : 0 9 :003(354) [0561] that those who **proclaim** the gospel should get their living
L C : 0 1 :325(409) [0675] entire Scriptures have **proclaimed** and presented this
L C : 0 2 :038(415) [0689] to be published and **proclaimed**, in which he has given the
L C : 0 4 :007(437) [0733] now is full of sects who **proclaim** that Baptism is an

Continued ▶

LC : 0 4 :030(440) [0739] as the entire Gospel is an external, oral **proclamation**.
LC : 0 5 :031(450) [0759] to us if it were not **proclaimed** by preaching, by the oral
EP : 0 5 :001(477) [0801] of grace which **proclaims** the forgiveness of sins, or is it
EP : 0 5 :004(478) [0801] sin is and belongs to the **proclamation** of the law.
EP : 0 5 :006(478) [0803] of Christ which he **proclaimed** personally in his teaching
EP : 0 5 :006(478) [0803] that the Gospel is a **proclamation** both of repentance and
EP : 0 5 :007(478) [0803] the Gospel is not a **proclamation** of contrition and
EP : 0 5 :007(478) [0803] by the delightful **proclamation** of God's grace and favor
EP : 0 5 :009(479) [0803] Therefore the **proclamation** of the suffering and death of
EP : 0 5 :010(479) [0803] and death of Christ — **proclaims** God's wrath and terrifies
EP : 0 5 :011(479) [0805] strictly speaking, is a **proclamation** of conviction and
EP : 0 5 :011(479) [0805] and reproof and not exclusively a **proclamation** of grace.
EP : 1 1 :013(496) [0835] Through the **proclamation** of the Holy Gospel, Christ
SD : 0 2 :037(528) [0895] us and which he uses to **proclaim** and propagate his
SD : 0 2 :050(530) [0901] for the public **proclamation** of his divine, eternal law and
SD : 0 5 :002(558) [0951] Gospel is not only a **proclamation** of grace but also at the
SD : 0 5 :002(558) [0951] at the same time a **proclamation** of repentance, which
SD : 0 5 :002(558) [0951] the Gospel is not a **proclamation** of repentance or
SD : 0 5 :002(558) [0953] in its strict sense is a **proclamation** of the grace and mercy
SD : 0 5 :002(558) [0953] Christ's sake, which **proclamation** assures those who have
SD : 0 5 :004(559) [0953] of the law and the **proclamation** of the mercy and grace
SD : 0 5 :005(559) [0953] define the word as the **proclamation** of both repentance
SD : 0 5 :006(559) [0953] does not include the **proclamation** of repentance but
SD : 0 5 :009(559) [0955] merit the comforting **proclamation** of the holy Gospel
SD : 0 5 :009(559) [0955] who have been terrified by the **proclamation** of the law.
SD : 0 5 :009(559) [0955] end in despair, the **proclamation** of the Gospel must be
SD : 0 5 :012(560) [0955] how or when it happens, is the **proclamation** of the law.
SD : 0 5 :012(560) [0955] hand, the Gospel is a **proclamation** that shows and gives
SD : 0 5 :012(560) [0955] did, confirm the **proclamation** of the law and begin with
SD : 0 5 :012(560) [0955] But as long as all this **proclaims** the wrath of God and
SD : 0 5 :012(560) [0955] nor Christ's own **proclamation**, but it is Moses and the
SD : 0 5 :023(562) [0959] the world these two **proclamations** have continually been
SD : 0 5 :023(562) [0959] themselves with the **proclamation** of the woman's seed,
SD : 0 5 :024(562) [0961] New Testament the **proclamation** of the law and its
SD : 0 5 :025(563) [0961] law (Rom. 10:4), the **proclamation** of the Gospel of our
SD : 0 5 :027(563) [0961] from the law, a **proclamation** of repentance and
SD : 0 5 :027(563) [0961] too, the Gospel is a **proclamation** both of repentance and
SD : 0 7 :084(584) [1001] drink it, and therewith **proclaim** the Lord's death), must
SD : 1 1 :028(620) [1071] to the fact that as the **proclamation** of repentance extends
SD : 1 1 :028(621) [1073] promise of the Gospel **proclaimed** to them (Luke 24:47;
SD : 1 1 :039(622) [1075] the Word when it is **proclaimed**, heard, and meditated
SD : 1 1 :065(627) [1083] heaven through the **proclaimed** Word when the Father
SD : 1 1 :067(627) [1085] (John 1:18), has **proclaimed** the Father's will and thereby
SD : 1 1 :068(627) [1085] men should hear this **proclamation** and come to Christ,
SD : 1 1 :085(630) [1091] to have his Word **proclaimed** and his will revealed to
SD : 1 2 :003(632) [1095] to pretend and **proclaim** to the whole world that among
SD : 1 2 :030(635) [1101] the church, the Word **proclaimed** and heard, is not a

Procreation (2)
AL : 2 3 :005(052) [0061] because God created man for **procreation** (Gen. 1:28).
AP : 2 3 :013(241) [0367] is necessary for a remedy as well as for **procreation**.

Produce (37), Produced (12), Produces (15), Producing (2)
PR : PR :011(006) [0011] in the fear of God, and **produced** a document in which
AG : 0 6 :001(031) [0045] us that such faith should **produce** good fruits and goods
AG : 2 3 :013(053) [0063] left free to man) never **produced** any good but rather gave
AL : 0 1 :006(028) [0043] "Spirit" signifies a movement which is **produced** in things.
AL : 0 5 :002(031) [0045] and the Holy Spirit **produces** faith, where and when it
AL : 1 8 :009(040) [0053] murder), yet it cannot **produce** the inward affections, such
AL : 2 4 :023(058) [0067] for individuals, and this **produced** that infinite
AL : 2 6 :006(064) [0071] traditions which have **produced** the opinion that it is
AP : PR :002(098) [0099] the opponents would **produce** the document without
AP : 0 2 :003(101) [0105] in God but also of the possibility and gift to **produce** it.
AP : 0 2 :003(101) [0105] and cannot **produce** true fear and trust in God.
AP : 0 2 :003(101) [0105] the gift and capacity to **produce** the fear and trust of
AP : 0 2 :003(101) [0105] trust of God, and it denies that adults actually **produce** it.
AP : 0 2 :023(103) [0111] love of God, or surely the power to **produce** these things.
AP : 0 2 :023(103) [0111] these things cannot be **produced** without certain gifts and
AP : 0 2 :023(103) [0111] of God but also the gifts and power to **produce** them.
AP : 0 4 :010(108) [0123] flatters men, it has **produced** and increased many types of
AP : 0 4 :023(110) [0127] some extent, reason can **produce** this righteousness by its
AP : 0 4 :027(111) [0127] But reason can **produce** civil works.
AP : 0 4 :033(111) [0129] sinning even when it **produces** deeds that are excellent
AP : 0 4 :065(116) [0139] of writers, let them **produce** one commentary on the
AP : 0 4 :072(117) [0141] can say that grammar **produces** the teachers of all the arts
AP : 0 4 :125(124) [0157] the Holy Spirit and **produces** a new life in our hearts, it
AP : 0 4 :125(124) [0157] our hearts, it must also **produce** spiritual impulses in our
AP : 0 4 :185(132) [0173] and dangerous issues **produce** many and varied solutions.
AP : 0 4 :249(142) [0191] a faith which does not **produce** good works is dead, but it
AP : 0 4 :250(143) [0191] a new life, it necessarily **produces** new impulses and new
AP : 0 4 :252(143) [0191] the works that faith **produces**, as he shows when he says
AP : 0 4 :290(151) [0203] but it imagines that we **produce** an act of love whereby
AP : 0 4 :346(160) [0217] This faith **produces** a sure hope, for it rests on the Word
AP : 1 2 :069(192) [0271] theologians who did not **produce** their own books but
AP : 1 2 :128(201) [0291] Such doubt cannot help **producing** the most bitter hatred
AP : 1 2 :131(202) [0291] which does not **produce** outwardly the punishing of the
AP : 1 2 :139(203) [0295] require penitence to **produce** good fruits, and that good
AP : 1 2 :174(210) [0305] often enough that penitence ought to **produce** good fruits.
AP : 1 3 :023(214) [0313] No one can **produce** a single word from the Fathers that
AP : 1 5 :041(220) [0325] youth publicly, a custom that **produces** very good results.
AP : 1 8 :002(225) [0335] justification by works that reason **produces** on its own?
AP : 2 1 :012(230) [0345] Our opponents can **produce** nothing against the
AP : 2 1 :018(231) [0347] can our opponents **produce** from Scripture for the
AP : 2 1 :024(232) [0349] Let him **produce** one example or precept from Scripture.
AP : 2 2 :007(237) [0359] They cannot **produce** any ancient examples to prove their
AP : 2 3 :006(240) [0365] and morality, for it **produces** endless scandals, sins, and
AP : 2 3 :032(243) [0373] If our opponents could **produce** a passage like that about
AP : 2 4 :032(255) [0395] of the Gospel **produces** faith in those who accept it.
AP : 2 4 :065(261) [0407] Our opponents cannot **produce** a syllable from the
AP : 2 7 :010(270) [0423] everything that we have **produced**; these are the very
S 3 : 0 2 :003(303) [0479] Hypocrites and false saints are **produced** in this way.
S 3 : 0 3 :020(306) [0485] and idolatry which such confession has **produced**.
TR : 0 0 :045(328) [0517] of sins which has **produced** many errors and introduced
TR : 0 0 :047(328) [0519] many abuses and what horrible idolatry it has **produced**!
TR : 0 0 :048(328) [0519] have feigned that vows **produce** righteousness before God
SC : 0 4 :009(349) [0551] How can water **produce** such great effects?
SC : 0 4 :010(349) [0551] It is not the water that **produces** these effects, but the
SC : 0 6 :007(352) [0557] bodily eating and drinking **produce** such great effects?
SC : 0 6 :008(352) [0557] do not in themselves **produce** them, but the words "for
LC : 0 1 :026(368) [0587] — things which no creature could **produce** by himself.
LC : 0 1 :116(381) [0615] see whether they can **produce** a single work that is greater
LC : 0 1 :317(408) [0673] a long time before men **produce** a doctrine or social order
LC : 0 1 :333(410) [0677] saints step forward and **produce**, if they can, any work
LC : 0 2 :014(412) [0681] birds and fish, beasts, grain and all kinds of **produce**.
LC : 0 3 :072(430) [0719] the whole land which **produce** and provide for us our
LC : 0 4 :075(445) [0751] this new life but also **produces**, begins, and promotes it.
SD : 0 1 :025(512) [0867] thing (such as, for example, **producing** a good thought).
SD : 0 2 :083(537) [0913] Holy Spirit's activity **produces** no change at all for the
SD : 0 5 :010(559) [0955] without Christ either **produces** presumptuous people, who

Product (2), Productive (1)
AP : 2 3 :052(246) [0377] public morals and how **productive** of vices and shameful
SD : 0 1 :032(513) [0869] essence are the work, the **product**, and the creature of
SD : 0 1 :055(518) [0877] is either God himself or a **product** and creature of God.

Profanation (2), Profanations (1), Profane (7), Profaned (7), Profanes (2), Profaning (2)
AL : 2 0 :018(043) [0055] inexperienced and **profane** men, who dream that
AL : 2 4 :010(057) [0065] were being shamefully **profaned** and applied to purposes
AL : 2 4 :012(057) [0065] manner will be guilty of **profaning** the body and blood of
AL : 2 4 :018(058) [0067] such long continued **profanations** of the Mass as have
AP : 0 4 :332(158) [0211] pray, if indeed these **profane** men ever ask God for
AP : 1 1 :007(181) [0251] terrors made no impression on wild and **profane** men.
AP : 1 5 :026(219) [0323] such tasks seem **profane**, so that many perform them with
AP : 2 3 :045(245) [0377] marriage, which seemed **profane** and unclean and hardly
AP : 2 4 :047(258) [0401] addition, they horribly **profaned** the Mass and introduced
AP : 2 4 :068(262) [0409] of love, which even **profane** and secular men understand;
TR : 0 0 :043(328) [0517] The idolatry in the **profanation** of Masses is manifest, for
SC : 0 3 :005(346) [0547] Word of God teaches, **profanes** the name of God among
LC : 0 3 :040(425) [0709] the name of God is **profaned** by us either in words or in
LC : 0 3 :041(425) [0709] first place, then, it is **profaned** when men preach, teach,
LC : 0 3 :041(425) [0709] this is the worst **profanation** and dishonor of the divine
LC : 0 3 :042(425) [0709] the next place, it is also **profaned** by an openly evil life
LC : 0 3 :042(425) [0709] God's name must be **profaned** and blasphemed because
LC : 0 3 :045(426) [0709] for any sort of wrong **profanes** and desecrates this holy
LC : 0 3 :045(426) [0709] or a relic was **profaned**, thus rendering unholy by misuse
SD : 0 7 :060(580) [0993] but becomes guilty of **profaning** the body and blood of
SD : 0 7 :068(582) [0997] punishments) and **profane** the body and blood of Christ.

Profess (3), Professed (1), Professing (1)
S 1 : PR :004(289) [0455] among those who **profess** to be adherents of our party —
TR : 0 0 :082(334) [0529] of the estates and cities **professing** the doctrine of the
EP : 1 2 :002(498) [0839] But in general they **profess** doctrines of a kind that
SD : 0 7 :001(568) [0971] and others who **professed** adherence to the Augsburg
SD : 0 8 :003(592) [1017] we herewith publicly **profess** our adherence, clearly

Profession (6)
AL : 1 3 :001(035) [0049] merely to be marks of **profession** among men but
AL : 2 7 :013(072) [0077] that the monastic **profession** was far better than Baptism,
AP : 1 3 :001(211) [0309] are no mere marks of **profession** among men, as some
AP : 2 4 :068(261) [0407] a mark and witness of **profession**, just as a certain type of
AP : 2 4 :068(261) [0407] of hood is the mark of a particular monastic **profession**.
AP : 2 7 :020(272) [0427] says that a monastic **profession** is equal to Baptism.

Professor (1)
S 3 : 1 5 :005(317) [0501] Also I, John Drach, **professor** and minister in Marburg,

Proffered (3)
SD : 0 2 :007(521) [0883] of God or to accept the **proffered** grace, nor that he has
SD : 0 7 :044(577) [0987] said of the blessed and **proffered** bread, "Take, eat, this is
SD : 0 7 :052(578) [0991] to the blessed and **proffered** bread without any

Profit (10), Profitable (27), Profitably (9), Profits (2)
PR : PR :019(009) [0017] condemned any other **profitable** writings of Master Philip
PR : PR :024(013) [0023] that is useful and **profitable** to the increase and expansion
AG : PR :019(026) [0041] that it would be **profitable** to have such a council called.
AG : 1 8 :005(040) [0053] a trade, or do whatever else may be good and **profitable**.
AG : 2 0 :002(041) [0053] have given good and **profitable** accounts and instructions
AG : 2 3 :014(053) [0063] it is most necessary, **profitable**, and Christian to recognize
AG : 2 6 :045(070) [0075] usages and adds the **profitable** Christian observation, "It
AG : 2 7 :015(073) [0077] of learning which are **profitable** to the Christian church,
AL : 2 6 :001(064) [0071] are works which are **profitable** to merit grace and make
AL : 2 6 :015(066) [0073] and seek for the more **profitable** teachings concerning
AL : 2 6 :040(069) [0075] days, etc.) which are **profitable** for maintaining good
AL : 2 7 :015(073) [0077] of learning which were **profitable** to the church, and
AP : 0 7 :034(175) [0239] discussing whether it is **profitable** to observe them for the
AP : 0 7 :034(175) [0239] observe them for the sake of tranquility or bodily **profit**.
AP : 1 1 :009(181) [0251] Good pastors know how **profitable** it is to examine the
AP : 1 2 :015(184) [0257] so later on a most **profitable** way of buying off
AP : 1 2 :024(185) [0257] of purgatory, or they **profit** as a payment to blot out
AP : 1 2 :160(207) [0301] of God, intended for our **profit**, that the power of God
AP : 1 5 :020(218) [0321] rites because they were **profitable** for good order, because
AP : 1 6 :002(222) [0329] of our theologians have **profitably** illumined this whole
AP : 1 8 :009(226) [0337] Therefore we may **profitably** distinguish between civil
AP : 2 1 :037(234) [0355] prayers, fasts, and other **profitable** ceremonies, are
AP : 2 1 :041(235) [0355] and was teaching things **profitable** for godliness.
AP : 2 4 :007(250) [0385] Mass, reasons of piety or of **profit** later changed this.
AP : 2 4 :089(265) [0413] souls of the dead, from which they make infinite **profits**.
AP : 2 4 :091(266) [0415] and blood of the Lord for their own sacrilegious **profit**.
AP : 2 7 :053(278) [0437] Mass by its application to the dead for the sake of **profit**.
AP : 2 7 :053(278) [0437] This wickedness, too, is used only for the sake of **profit**.
AP : 2 8 :026(285) [0451] is in the sacrilegious desecration of the Mass for **profit**!
S 3 : 0 3 :025(307) [0485] the bull market became **profitable**, the pope invented the
TR : 0 0 :043(328) [0517] are shamelessly employed to secure disgraceful **profits**.
TR : 0 0 :078(333) [0527] but it would not be **profitable** to enumerate all of them
TR : 0 0 :080(334) [0527] the administration and **profit** of the churches, as the rule
LC : PR :009(359) [0569] this life), yet it is highly **profitable** and fruitful daily to

Continued ▶

LC : 0 1 :303(405) [0667] seeing an opportunity for **profit** — let us say, when a man
LC : 0 1 :309(407) [0669] whatever may be **profitable** and serviceable to him, as we
LC : 0 4 :033(440) [0741] worthy to receive the salutary, divine water **profitably**.
EP : 0 1 :024(469) [0785] circles these words can **profitably** be retained in the
EP : 1 0 :004(493) [0829] as it may be most **profitable** and edifying to the
EP : 1 1 :011(495) [0835] God's eternal election is **profitable** and comforting to the
EP : 1 2 :027(500) [0843] church cannot teach **profitably** or administer true and
SD : 0 6 :014(566) [0967] is inspired by God and **profitable** for teaching, for
SD : 0 7 :085(584) [1003] it can and should be **profitably** urged and retained in the
SD : 1 0 :009(612) [1055] may seem to be most **profitable**, beneficial, and salutary
SD : 1 1 :013(618) [1067] or speak correctly and **profitably** about eternal election
SD : 1 1 :028(620) [1071] election to salvation **profitably**, we must by all means
SD : 1 1 :051(625) [1079] in this article in a **profitable**, comforting, and salutary
SD : 1 2 :035(635) [1101] and pious cannot teach **profitably** nor administer genuine

Profligate (1)
TR : 0 0 :048(328) [0519] How many **profligate** acts have sprung from the tradition

Profound (5), Profoundly (1)
AL : 2 0 :008(042) [0053] that there has been **profound** silence concerning the
AL : 2 5 :002(061) [0069] which there has been **profound** silence before this time.
LC : 0 2 :064(419) [0695] opened to us the most **profound** depths of his fatherly
EP : 0 8 :013(488) [0821] nature has such a **profound** and ineffable union and
SD : 0 1 :061(519) [0879] inheres in and most **profoundly** and inexpressibly
SD : 1 2 :008(633) [1097] persecuted, where the **profound** darkness of the papacy

Profusion (1)
LC : 0 1 :157(386) [0625] to set forth with such a **profusion** of words in the hope

Progress (3), Progresses (1), Progressing (1), Progressively (1)
AG : PR :019(026) [0041] improving and were **progressing** toward a good, Christian
AP : 2 3 :053(246) [0379] is growing older and **progressively** weaker, so that we
AP : 2 7 :038(275) [0433] God to show him what **progress** he was making in his way
LC : SP :025(364) [0579] will be led into the Scriptures so they make **progress** daily
LC : 0 5 :025(449) [0759] should be one that continually develops and **progresses**.
LC : 0 5 :060(453) [0767] No one will make such **progress** that he does not retain

Prohibit (6), Prohibited (3), Prohibiting (1), Prohibition (10), Prohibitions (3), Prohibits (2)
AG : 2 3 :013(053) [0063] celibacy and such **prohibition** of marriage (which God
AG : 2 3 :002(053) [0063] been some reasons for **prohibiting** the marriage of
AG : 2 3 :014(053) [0063] fact in order that the **prohibition** of marriage may not
AG : 2 3 :017(054) [0063] If this hard **prohibition** of marriage is to continue longer,
AG : 2 6 :029(068) [0075] In I Tim. 4:1, 3 such **prohibitions** as forbid food or
AG : 2 7 :032(076) [0079] to human frailty, for it **prohibits** the taking of monastic
AG : 2 8 :065(092) [0093] Who observes this **prohibition** now?
AG : 2 8 :070(093) [0093] in one kind and **prohibit** administration in both kinds.
AL : 2 3 :013(053) [0063] were future marriages **prohibited** but existing marriages
AL : 2 3 :022(055) [0063] To **prohibit** marriage is called a doctrine of demons by
AL : 2 3 :023(055) [0063] now that the **prohibition** of marriage is maintained by
AL : 2 6 :029(068) [0075] 4:1, 3 Paul calls the **prohibition** of foods a doctrine of
AL : 2 7 :054(079) [0083] are told that this is **prohibited** by a counsel and not by a
AL : 2 8 :043(088) [0089] clear testimonies which **prohibit** the making of traditions
AL : 2 8 :049(089) [0091] does Scripture so often **prohibit** the making of traditions?
AL : 2 8 :065(092) [0093] Who observes this **prohibition** now?
AP : 1 6 :006(223) [0331] commonwealth by its **prohibition** of legal redress and by
AP : 2 2 :002(236) [0357] taken away from part of the church and its use **prohibited**
AP : 2 3 :071(249) [0383] up marriages and to issue savage and cruel **prohibitions**.
S3 : 0 6 :004(311) [0493] far as autocratically to **prohibit**, condemn, and slander
S3 : 1 1 :001(314) [0499] authority nor right to **prohibit** marriage and burden the
LC : 0 1 :269(401) [0657] the more urgent is the **prohibition** if you are not sure but
LC : 0 1 :293(404) [0665] the injunctions and **prohibitions** contained in them.
LC : 0 1 :296(405) [0665] seventh commandment **prohibits** seizing or withholding
SD : 1 0 :014(613) [1057] to a command or a **prohibition**, requiring us to use them

Proliferation (1)
AL : 2 4 :023(058) [0067] produced that infinite **proliferation** of Masses to which

Prolixity (1)
AG : 0 0 :001(095) [0095] and wrongs, to avoid **prolixity** and undue length we have

Prolong (2)
AP : 2 4 :023(253) [0391] sin, he shall see his offspring, he shall **prolong** his days."
S3 : 0 3 :013(305) [0483] recited to the people: "**Prolong** my life, Lord God, until I

Prominent (5)
PR : PR :013(007) [0013] convoked a number of **prominent**, trustworthy,
AL : 2 6 :004(064) [0071] the church, and to be **prominent** in it, so that the merit of
EP : 0 3 :020(475) [0797] indeed has the most **prominent** role in justification, but
SD : 0 1 :054(518) [0877] as well as many other **prominent** doctors of the church,
SD : 0 7 :037(575) [0985] Many **prominent** ancient teachers, like Justin, Cyprian,

Promiscuity (1), Promiscuously (1)
AP : 2 3 :035(244) [0373] that the law forbids, but lust, adultery, and **promiscuity**.
S1 : PR :008(290) [0457] but that all live **promiscuously** like cattle and everybody

Promise (256), Promised (62), Promises (59), Promising (3)
PR : PR :020(010) [0017] what he has ordained and **promised** in his Word.
AG : 2 0 :025(045) [0057] confidence in God and in the fulfillment of his **promises**.
AG : 2 1 :002(047) [0057] He alone has **promised** to hear our prayers.
AG : 2 4 :030(059) [0067] grace and forgiveness of sin are **promised** us by Christ.
AL : 0 5 :003(031) [0045] we might receive the **promise** of the Spirit through faith."
AL : 1 3 :002(035) [0049] faith, which believes the **promises** that are set forth and
AL : 2 1 :003(047) [0057] to be prayed to, and he has **promised** to hear our prayers.
AL : 2 3 :025(055) [0065] keep the chastity which they had **promised** should marry.
AL : 2 7 :030(075) [0079] of a vow to make a **promise** which is not spontaneous and
AP : 0 4 :005(108) [0121] into these two chief doctrines, the law and the **promises**.
AP : 0 4 :005(108) [0121] In others it presents the **promise** of Christ; this it does
AP : 0 4 :005(108) [0121] it does either when it **promises** that the Messiah will come
AP : 0 4 :005(108) [0121] Messiah will come and **promises** forgiveness of sins,
AP : 0 4 :005(108) [0121] the Christ who came **promises** forgiveness of sins,
AP : 0 4 :035(112) [0131] God and to doubt his Word with its threats and **promises**.
AP : 0 4 :040(112) [0131] sin or justify us, but the **promise** of the forgiveness of sins
AP : 0 4 :041(113) [0131] This **promise** is not conditional upon our merits but
AP : 0 4 :042(113) [0133] that we would never obtain the **promise** of reconciliation.
AP : 0 4 :042(113) [0133] are to be the heirs, faith is null and the **promise** is void."
AP : 0 4 :042(113) [0133] For if the **promise** were conditional upon our merits and
AP : 0 4 :042(113) [0133] we never keep, it would follow that the **promise** is useless.
AP : 0 4 :043(113) [0133] through a free **promise**, however, it follows that we
AP : 0 4 :043(113) [0133] Otherwise, why would a **promise** be necessary?
AP : 0 4 :043(113) [0133] is, strictly speaking, the **promise** of forgiveness of sins and
AP : 0 4 :043(113) [0133] Since we can accept this **promise** only by faith, the
AP : 0 4 :044(113) [0133] by sin and death, the **promise** freely offers reconciliation
AP : 0 4 :044(113) [0133] own merits, but only in the **promise** of mercy in Christ.
AP : 0 4 :048(114) [0135] of God's offer **promising** forgiveness of sins and
AP : 0 4 :048(114) [0135] want and to accept the **promised** offer of forgiveness of
AP : 0 4 :049(114) [0135] that we receive from him what he **promises** and offers.
AP : 0 4 :050(114) [0135] a firm acceptance of the **promise** (Rom. 4:16): "That is
AP : 0 4 :050(114) [0135] on faith, in order that the **promise** may be guaranteed."
AP : 0 4 :050(114) [0135] For he says that only faith can accept the **promise**.
AP : 0 4 :050(114) [0135] He therefore correlates and connects **promise** and faith.
AP : 0 4 :053(114) [0137] belong together: the **promise** itself, the fact that the
AP : 0 4 :053(114) [0137] itself, the fact that the **promise** is free, and the merits of
AP : 0 4 :053(114) [0137] The **promise** is accepted by faith; the fact that it is free
AP : 0 4 :055(114) [0137] this requires faith, which accepts the **promise** of mercy.
AP : 0 4 :055(114) [0137] we are also thinking of its object, the **promised** mercy.
AP : 0 4 :056(114) [0137] in itself, but only because it accepts the **promised** mercy.
AP : 0 4 :057(114) [0137] the patriarchs knew the **promise** of the Christ, that for his
AP : 0 4 :058(115) [0137] He quotes the **promise**: "My soul waits for his word, my
AP : 0 4 :058(115) [0137] is, because thou has **promised** the forgiveness of sins I am
AP : 0 4 :058(115) [0137] the forgiveness of sins I am sustained by thy **promise**.
AP : 0 4 :059(115) [0137] were justified not by the law but by the **promise** and faith.
AP : 0 4 :062(115) [0139] if they believe Christ's **promise** that for his sake we have
AP : 0 4 :070(116) [0141] the proposition, "The **promise** of Christ is necessary over
AP : 0 4 :070(116) [0141] we must maintain that the **promise** of Christ is necessary.
AP : 0 4 :079(118) [0143] by firm trust in the mercy **promised** because of Christ.
AP : 0 4 :080(118) [0143] hearts with trust in the mercy **promised** for Christ's sake.
AP : 0 4 :081(118) [0143] by trust in the mercy **promised** for Christ's sake.
AP : 0 4 :082(118) [0145] we receive the mercy **promised** in him and set it against
AP : 0 4 :084(119) [0145] forgiveness of sins is a thing **promised** for Christ's sake.
AP : 0 4 :084(119) [0145] only by faith, since a **promise** can be accepted only on
AP : 0 4 :084(119) [0145] faith, in order that the **promise** may rest on grace and be
AP : 0 4 :084(119) [0145] on our merits, the **promise** would be uncertain and
AP : 0 4 :084(119) [0145] to sin, that what was **promised** to faith in Jesus Christ
AP : 0 4 :084(119) [0145] Then he adds that the **promise** of the forgiveness of sins
AP : 0 4 :084(119) [0145] gift, and further that the **promise** can be accepted by
AP : 0 4 :084(119) [0145] upon the nature of a **promise**, this is Paul's chief
AP : 0 4 :086(119) [0147] because it receives God's **promise** that for Christ's sake he
AP : 0 4 :087(120) [0147] need for Christ and the **promise**, and everything that
AP : 0 4 :087(120) [0147] that Paul says about the **promise** would be overthrown.
AP : 0 4 :101(121) [0151] Christ's blessings, the **promises** which by the Gospel he
AP : 0 4 :101(121) [0151] accomplish what he has **promised** for Christ's sake.
AP : 0 4 :102(121) [0151] in others it teaches the **promises** of Christ, of the
AP : 0 4 :110(123) [0153] with the abolition of the **promise** and a return to the law?
AP : 0 4 :112(123) [0155] of the word—since the **promise** can be received only by
AP : 0 4 :113(123) [0155] use the word, is that which accepts the **promise**.
AP : 0 4 :120(124) [0155] the Gospel (that is, the **promise** that sins are forgiven
AP : 0 4 :121(124) [0155] they destroy the entire **promise** of the free forgiveness of
AP : 0 4 :127(125) [0157] we might receive the **promise** of the Spirit through faith."
AP : 0 4 :139(126) [0161] Christ's sake we have a gracious God and his **promise**.
AP : 0 4 :139(126) [0161] the devil and gave us his **promise** and the Holy Spirit, so
AP : 0 4 :148(127) [0163] alone, looking to the **promise** and believing with full
AP : 0 4 :149(127) [0163] than the death and **promise** of Christ, though Paul says
AP : 0 4 :163(129) [0169] of the righteousness of the Gospel is through the **promise**.
AP : 0 4 :164(129) [0169] Therefore we must always go back to the **promise**.
AP : 0 4 :165(130) [0169] than because of Christ's **promise**, he insults this high
AP : 0 4 :180(131) [0171] Because of his **promise**, because of Christ, God wishes to
AP : 0 4 :180(132) [0171] law or our works: this **promise** we must always keep in
AP : 0 4 :180(132) [0171] In this **promise** timid consciences should seek
AP : 0 4 :180(132) [0171] themselves with this **promise** and being sure that because
AP : 0 4 :180(132) [0171] of Christ and his **promise** they have a gracious God.
AP : 0 4 :180(132) [0171] never pacify the conscience; only the **promise** can do this.
AP : 0 4 :182(132) [0173] is something **promised** because of Christ, not because of
AP : 0 4 :183(132) [0173] between the law and the **promises** or Gospel) it will be
AP : 0 4 :183(132) [0173] law and works but omit passages about the **promises**.
AP : 0 4 :186(132) [0173] the Gospel, the free **promise** of the forgiveness of sins for
AP : 0 4 :186(133) [0173] our opponents simply abolish this free **promise**.
AP : 0 4 :187(133) [0173] completely unsure and the **promise** would be abolished.
AP : 0 4 :188(133) [0173] minds to consider the **promises**, and we teach them about
AP : 0 4 :188(133) [0173] ascribe to the law and what they ascribe to the **promises**.
AP : 0 4 :188(133) [0173] works in such a way as not to remove the free **promise**.
AP : 0 4 :194(133) [0175] have been offered and **promised** to the works of the
AP : 0 4 :210(136) [0179] sign reminds us of the **promises** of Christ, the
AP : 0 4 :217(137) [0179] something that is only **promised** freely because of Christ,
AP : 0 4 :222(138) [0181] our love we receive the **promised** forgiveness of sins —
AP : 0 4 :223(138) [0181] opponents remove the **promise** about Christ, let them
AP : 0 4 :227(139) [0183] accept and grasp what is offered in the **promise** of Christ.
AP : 0 4 :228(139) [0183] to receive the offered **promise**, is no less an act of worship
AP : 0 4 :238(141) [0187] of the Gospel which **promises** us reconciliation and
AP : 0 4 :247(142) [0191] that takes hold of the **promise** of Christ when we set it
AP : 0 4 :255(144) [0193] The other is a **promise** that is added.
AP : 0 4 :256(144) [0193] We must keep the Gospel **promise** that through Christ we
AP : 0 4 :257(144) [0193] voice of God, clearly **promising** the forgiveness of sins.
AP : 0 4 :257(144) [0193] to add the Gospel **promise**, that for Christ's sake sins are
AP : 0 4 :258(144) [0193] Thus the prophet urges penitence and adds a **promise**.
AP : 0 4 :258(144) [0193] of sins to be received by faith, and so he adds a **promise**.
AP : 0 4 :259(144) [0193] and he adds the **promise**, "You will be forgiven"
AP : 0 4 :261(145) [0195] In the other part Daniel **promises** the king forgiveness of
AP : 0 4 :261(145) [0195] This **promise** of the forgiveness of sins is not the
AP : 0 4 :262(145) [0195] of sins in the Christ was **promised** not only to the
AP : 0 4 :262(145) [0195] he could not have **promised** the king forgiveness of sins.
AP : 0 4 :262(145) [0195] and bring out the **promise**, "Redeem your sins by
AP : 0 4 :263(145) [0195] alms, but because of his **promise** he forgives those who
AP : 0 4 :263(145) [0195] promise he forgives those who take hold of that **promise**.
AP : 0 4 :263(146) [0195] The **promise** is therefore added (Dan. 4:27), "Behold,
AP : 0 4 :264(146) [0195] that the Gospel **promises** the forgiveness of sins with
AP : 0 4 :264(146) [0195] the forgiveness of sins must surely be given by a **promise**.

Continued ▶

AP : 04 :264(146) [0195] of this text, though the **promise** is involved even in the
AP : 04 :264(146) [0195] our opponents omit the **promises** and look only at the
AP : 04 :264(146) [0197] Wherever there is a **promise**, there faith is required.
AP : 04 :264(146) [0197] Only faith can accept a **promise**.
AP : 04 :266(146) [0197] that the Gospel and the **promise** of Christ are presented to
AP : 04 :266(146) [0197] We must not reject the **promise** of Christ when the law is
AP : 04 :266(146) [0197] first take hold of the **promise** so that we may be able to
AP : 04 :267(146) [0197] Daniel clearly sets forth a **promise**, he necessarily requires
AP : 04 :270(147) [0197] setting forth the most ample **promise** of the law.
AP : 04 :272(148) [0199] new works but also **promises** the forgiveness of sins, it
AP : 04 :272(148) [0199] a work is required and a **promise** of the forgiveness of
AP : 04 :275(148) [0199] frequently connects the **promise** of forgiveness of sins
AP : 04 :275(148) [0199] of this exceedingly great **promise**, since a terrified
AP : 04 :276(148) [0199] This same **promise** is written and pictured in good works,
AP : 04 :276(148) [0199] arouse themselves to believe but despise these **promises**.
AP : 04 :276(148) [0199] glad to have signs and testimonies of this great **promise**.
AP : 04 :285(150) [0201] Paul proves that the **promise** of righteousness does
AP : 04 :285(150) [0201] Thus the **promise** would be vain and unsure.
AP : 04 :285(150) [0201] but faith accepts the **promised** forgiveness of sins and
AP : 04 :287(150) [0203] one based upon the Gospel or the **promise** of Christ.
AP : 04 :291(152) [0203] Christ was not **promised**, revealed, born, crucified, and
AP : 04 :292(152) [0203] by the law but by the **promise**, in which the Father has
AP : 04 :292(152) [0203] This **promise** is received by faith alone, as Paul declares in
AP : 04 :294(152) [0203] by the law but by the **promise**, which is received by faith
AP : 04 :295(152) [0203] first take hold of the **promise** by faith, that for Christ's
AP : 04 :297(152) [0205] we are justified by the **promise**, in which reconciliation,
AP : 04 :297(153) [0205] Christ was not **promised**, revealed, born, crucified, and
AP : 04 :297(153) [0205] and raised in vain; the **promise** of grace in Christ was not
AP : 04 :297(153) [0205] The **promise** is to be accepted by faith, as John says
AP : 04 :297(153) [0205] therefore, we accept the **promise** of the forgiveness of sins
AP : 04 :298(153) [0205] by the law but by the **promise**, justification must
AP : 04 :303(154) [0205] truly and wholeheartedly accepts the **promise** of grace.
AP : 04 :304(154) [0205] and to accept what the **promise** offers — reconciliation
AP : 04 :309(155) [0207] is properly his; it obeys him by accepting his **promises**.
AP : 04 :309(155) [0207] waver concerning the **promise** of God, but he grew strong
AP : 04 :312(155) [0207] that wishes for what the **promise** offers, then the
AP : 04 :312(155) [0207] confused, since it is hope that expects what is **promised**.
AP : 04 :312(155) [0207] the present the forgiveness of sins that the **promise** offers.
AP : 04 :324(157) [0209] have said above that the **promise** and faith are correlative
AP : 04 :324(157) [0211] can take hold of the **promise**, so we say here that the
AP : 04 :324(157) [0211] so we say here that the **promised** mercy correlatively
AP : 04 :334(159) [0215] mercy and because of his **promise**, not as a payment
AP : 04 :337(159) [0215] but about trust in God's **promise** and in his mercy.
AP : 04 :337(159) [0215] This trust in the **promise** confesses that we are unworthy
AP : 04 :338(159) [0215] hold of mercy and the **promise** of grace, even though our
AP : 04 :339(159) [0215] believed everything, do not trust in the divine **promise**."
AP : 04 :339(159) [0215] works; in the second, trust is a trust in the divine **promise**.
AP : 04 :339(159) [0215] our own works; he does not condemn trust in his **promise**.
AP : 04 :339(159) [0215] does not denounce the **promise** that offers mercy gratis.
AP : 04 :341(159) [0215] We should trust the **promise** of grace, not our own
AP : 04 :345(160) [0217] has God's clear and certain **promise** and his command.
AP : 04 :346(160) [0217] mercy is spoken of, faith in the **promise** must be added.
AP : 04 :347(160) [0217] because eternal life is **promised** to the justified and it is
AP : 04 :348(160) [0217] We say that eternal life is **promised** to the justified, but
AP : 04 :362(162) [0219] — not because of our merits but because of the **promise**.
AP : 04 :362(162) [0219] is strictly a gift of God; it is a thing **promised**.
AP : 04 :362(162) [0219] To this gift the **promise** of eternal life has been added,
AP : 04 :363(162) [0219] The crown is owed to the justified because of the **promise**.
AP : 04 :363(162) [0219] This **promise** the saints must know.
AP : 04 :366(163) [0221] which deals with the **promise** of grace, receives
AP : 04 :377(165) [0223] and the teaching of the **promise** given for Christ's sake.
AP : 04 :383(165) [0225] power that grasps the **promise** of grace and
AP : 04 :386(166) [0225] penitently grasps the **promise** of grace, truly enlivens the
AP : 04 :387(166) [0225] propitiator, deny the **promise** of grace and the Gospel.
AP : 04 :388(166) [0225] but by the Gospel, the **promise** of grace offered in Christ.
AP : 07 :009(169) [0229] it with the gifts he has **promised** — the forgiveness of sins,
AP : 07 :014(170) [0231] to the flesh had **promises** about physical well-being,
AP : 07 :014(170) [0231] affairs, etc. in addition to the **promise** about Christ.
AP : 07 :014(170) [0231] Because of these **promises** even the wicked among them
AP : 07 :014(170) [0231] nations by certain outward ordinances and **promises**.
AP : 07 :016(170) [0231] are the true people who accept this **promise** of the Spirit.
AP : 07 :022(172) [0233] as the church has the **promise** that it will always have the
AP : 09 :002(178) [0245] is most certain that the **promise** of salvation also applies
AP : 09 :002(178) [0245] children, so that the **promise** of salvation might be
AP : 12 :008(183) [0255] himself with the Gospel and the **promise** of Christ.
AP : 12 :035(186) [0261] the Gospel which freely **promises** the forgiveness of sins
AP : 12 :053(189) [0265] the Gospel, that is, the **promise** of grace granted in
AP : 12 :053(189) [0265] This **promise** is repeated continually throughout
AP : 12 :054(189) [0265] justified by faith in this **promise**, not by their own
AP : 12 :055(189) [0267] Then God **promised** grace and said there would be a seed
AP : 12 :060(190) [0269] bids us trust not in the **promise** of Christ but in
AP : 12 :061(190) [0269] teaches in Rom. 4:16 that only faith accepts a **promise**.
AP : 12 :061(190) [0269] since absolution is the **promise** of the forgiveness of sins,
AP : 12 :062(190) [0269] it maintains that God's **promises** are uncertain and inane.
AP : 12 :064(191) [0269] mediator, and believes the **promises** given for his sake.
AP : 12 :075(193) [0273] of the Gospel, and the abolition of the **promise** of Christ.
AP : 12 :075(193) [0273] rather than in God's Word and the **promise** of Christ?
AP : 12 :076(193) [0273] works to trust in the **promise** and in Christ; for the
AP : 12 :076(193) [0273] shows us Christ and **promises** the forgiveness of sins
AP : 12 :076(193) [0273] This **promise** bids us trust that because of Christ we are
AP : 12 :079(193) [0275] the law he opposes the **promise** of the forgiveness of sins
AP : 12 :079(194) [0275] Paul calls us away from the law to this **promise**.
AP : 12 :079(194) [0275] He asks us to look at this **promise**, which would certainly
AP : 12 :079(194) [0275] by the law before the **promise** or if we obtained the
AP : 12 :080(194) [0275] But clearly the **promise** was given and Christ revealed to
AP : 12 :080(194) [0275] must be reconciled by the **promise** before we keep the
AP : 12 :080(194) [0275] Only faith accepts the **promise**.
AP : 12 :080(194) [0275] faith to take hold of the **promise** of the forgiveness of sins
AP : 12 :081(194) [0275] faith, in order that the **promise** may rest on grace and be
AP : 12 :081(194) [0275] to sin, that what was **promised** to faith in Jesus Christ
AP : 12 :081(194) [0275] hold through faith of the **promise** of the forgiveness of
AP : 12 :086(194) [0277] we must accept the **promise** that by faith we are
AP : 12 :087(195) [0277] We must take hold of the **promise** of the forgiveness of
AP : 12 :088(195) [0277] doubts, he makes the divine **promise** a lie, as John says.
AP : 12 :094(196) [0281] authority of the divine **promises** ought to be sufficient for
AP : 12 :094(196) [0281] sufficient for us, but this **promise** is confirmed with an
AP : 12 :095(196) [0281] Christ and because of his **promise**, not because of our
AP : 12 :107(198) [0283] and yet we seek mercy because of the **promise** of God.
AP : 13 :003(211) [0309] of God and to which the **promise** of grace has been
AP : 13 :003(211) [0309] since men do not have the authority to **promise** grace.
AP : 13 :004(211) [0309] of God and the **promise** of grace, which is the heart of the
AP : 13 :006(212) [0311] express command from God and a clear **promise** of grace.
AP : 13 :011(212) [0311] command and glorious **promises**: "The Gospel is the
AP : 13 :014(213) [0311] of God and also certain **promises**, but these apply to
AP : 13 :016(213) [0311] God's command and a **promise** added to them, then why
AP : 13 :016(213) [0311] It has both the command of God and many **promises**.
AP : 13 :017(213) [0313] themselves are signs to which God has added **promises**.
AP : 13 :017(213) [0313] are kept which have God's command and **promises**.
AP : 13 :019(213) [0313] which believes these **promises** and accepts that which is
AP : 13 :019(213) [0313] accepts that which is **promised** and offered in the
AP : 13 :020(213) [0313] A **promise** is useless unless faith accepts it.
AP : 13 :020(213) [0313] The sacraments are signs of the **promises**.
AP : 13 :020(213) [0313] free forgiveness of sins, **promised** in the New Testament,
AP : 13 :020(214) [0313] God, by a new miracle, **promised** his will to forgive.
AP : 13 :020(214) [0313] good would such miracles or **promises** do an unbeliever?
AP : 13 :021(214) [0313] faith, which accepts the **promise** as a present reality and
AP : 15 :010(216) [0317] of sins has been **promised**, not because of our works but
AP : 15 :010(216) [0317] we accept it by faith; for only faith can accept a **promise**.
AP : 15 :012(216) [0317] the covenant of God, **promising** that he will be gracious
AP : 20 :010(228) [0341] "in order that the **promise** may be guaranteed"
AP : 20 :010(228) [0341] That is, if the **promise** were conditional on our works, it
AP : 21 :010(230) [0345] a command nor a **promise** nor an example can be shown
AP : 21 :017(231) [0347] Christ there is such a **promise** (John 16:23), "If you ask
AP : 21 :017(231) [0347] saints there is no such **promise**, and hence consciences
AP : 21 :020(231) [0349] Both the **promise** and the bestowal of merits are therefore
AP : 21 :020(232) [0349] Such trust in God's **promise** and Christ's merits must be
AP : 21 :021(232) [0349] they have neither God's **promise** nor a command nor an
AP : 21 :031(233) [0351] of Christ because only this has God's **promise**.
AP : 24 :018(252) [0389] us the content of the **promise** joined to the ceremony;
AP : 24 :018(252) [0389] of sins according to the **promise** (Mark 16:16), "He who
AP : 24 :024(253) [0391] since the Gospel was **promised** in order to set forth a
AP : 24 :028(254) [0393] because of my Word and **promise**, not because of works.
AP : 24 :029(255) [0393] me to believe it and thy **promises** of willingness to show
AP : 24 :032(255) [0395] of Christ and the Father's mercy **promised** in Christ.
AP : 24 :055(259) [0403] justified by faith in the **promise** of the forgiveness of sins
AP : 24 :069(262) [0409] New Testament, the Word is the added **promise** of grace.
AP : 24 :069(262) [0409] The **promise** of the New Testament is the promise of the
AP : 24 :069(262) [0409] New Testament is the **promise** of the forgiveness of sins,
AP : 24 :070(262) [0409] as Paul calls it (Rom. 4:11), showing forth the **promise**.
AP : 24 :070(262) [0409] As the **promise** is useless unless faith accepts it, so the
AP : 24 :090(266) [0415] not a satisfaction but a **promise** and a sacrament
AP : 24 :091(266) [0415] transferred the blessed **promises** of the forgiveness of
AP : 27 :017(272) [0425] does this abolishes the **promise** of Christ, has cast Christ
AP : 27 :020(272) [0427] command of God nor a **promise**, on the same level with
AP : 27 :020(272) [0427] both a command and a **promise** of God, which contains a
AP : 27 :027(273) [0429] in trust in the mercy **promised** in Christ, and in devotion
AP : 27 :028(274) [0429] Indeed, Christ has **promised** this in abundance to those
AP : 27 :033(275) [0431] but must seek the mercy **promised** in Christ, much less do
AP : 27 :034(275) [0431] of sins and the **promised** mercy available in Christ and
AP : 27 :051(277) [0437] Third, in monastic vows chastity is **promised**.
AP : 27 :061(279) [0441] it — not because of the **promised** Seed, through the mercy
S3 : 02 :001(303) [0479] punishment and by the **promise** and offer of grace and
S3 : 03 :004(304) [0481] adds the consoling **promise** of grace in the Gospel.
S3 : 03 :004(304) [0481] different, do otherwise, and believe my **promise**."
S3 : 05 :004(311) [0493] too, are included in the **promise** of redemption which
SC : 01 :022(344) [0543] On the other hand, he **promises** grace and every blessing
SC : 03 :021(348) [0549] commanded us to pray like this and **promised** to hear us.
SC : 04 :006(349) [0551] all who believe, as the Word and **promise** of God declare.
SC : 04 :007(349) [0551] What is this Word and **promise** of God?
SC : 09 :009(356) [0563] commandment with a **promise**) 'that it may be well with
LC : PR :009(359) [0569] is according to Christ's **promise** in Matt. 18:20, "Where
LC : PR :020(361) [0573] such diligence, then I **promise** them — and their
LC : 01 :029(368) [0589] terrible threat and, then, a beautiful, comforting **promise**.
LC : 01 :039(370) [0591] is the comfort in the **promise** that assures mercy to those
LC : 01 :040(370) [0591] an offer, so cordial an invitation, and so rich a **promise**.
LC : 01 :041(370) [0591] than God's gracious **promise** that he will be yours with
LC : 01 :068(374) [0599] of many who broke their **promise** of marriage; they never
LC : 01 :131(383) [0619] attached to it a lovely **promise**, "That you may have long
LC : 01 :133(383) [0619] commandment with a **promise**: that it may be well with
LC : 01 :133(383) [0619] also have a **promise** implied, yet in none is it so plainly
LC : 01 :146(385) [0623] You have the **promise**, moreover, that you will prosper
LC : 01 :164(387) [0627] however, have the **promise** that they will be richly
LC : 01 :165(387) [0627] Since he has **promised** it, and has never yet lied, he will
LC : 01 :166(387) [0629] in joyful thanks to God for giving us such **promises**.
LC : 01 :316(408) [0671] single groschen to pay, but I **promise** to pay ten gulden."
LC : 01 :322(408) [0673] threat and a friendly **promise**, not only to terrify and
LC : 01 :333(410) [0677] he adds such glorious **promises** that he will shower us
LC : 03 :019(423) [0703] pray because God has **promised** that our prayer will
LC : 03 :020(423) [0703] Such **promises** certainly ought to awaken and kindle in
LC : 03 :021(423) [0703] thy commandment and **promise**, which cannot fail or
LC : 03 :021(423) [0703] does not believe this **promise** should realize once again
LC : 03 :022(423) [0703] this commandment and **promise**, God takes the initiative
LC : 03 :025(423) [0705] to God and faith in his **promise**, or out of consideration
LC : 03 :028(424) [0705] his commandment and **promise**, knowing that he will not
LC : 03 :058(428) [0713] things when he **promises** that which is eternal and
LC : 03 :092(432) [0725] us, forgive as he has **promised**, and thus grant us a happy
LC : 03 :093(433) [0725] God has **promised** us assurance that everything is forgiven
LC : 03 :096(433) [0725] grace, because he has **promised** it, as the Gospel teaches.
LC : 03 :096(433) [0725] as a sign along with the **promise** which is in agreement
LC : 03 :097(433) [0725] pray we may recall the **promise** and think, "Dear Father,
LC : 03 :097(433) [0725] Thou hast given the **promise** and hast set thy seal to it,
LC : 03 :120(436) [0731] does not lie since he has **promised** to grant his requests.
LC : 03 :122(436) [0731] their eye not on God's **promise** but on their own works
LC : 04 :033(440) [0741] are offered and **promised** in the words which accompany
LC : 04 :036(441) [0741] God, you may receive in the water the **promised** salvation.
LC : 04 :039(441) [0741] God's commandment and injunction, but also his **promise**

Continued ▶

LC : 04 :041(441) [0743] firmly what Baptism **promises** and brings — victory over
LC : 04 :044(442) [0743] am baptized, I have the **promise** that I shall be saved and
LC : 05 :034(450) [0761] because he offers and **promises** forgiveness of sins, it
LC : 05 :064(454) [0769] In the second place, a **promise** is attached to the
LC : 05 :071(454) [0769] the commandment and the **promise** of the Lord Christ.
LC : 05 :071(455) [0769] reason for this command and invitation and **promise**.
EP : 03 :009(474) [0795] sake, on the basis of the **promises** and the Word of the
EP : 03 :022(475) [0797] 10. That the **promise** of grace becomes our own by faith
EP : 07 :033(485) [0815] Christ could not have **promised** that his body and blood
EP : 07 :033(485) [0815] he have kept such a **promise**, since the nature and
EP : 11 :008(495) [0833] all sinners to himself and **promises** them refreshment.
EP : 11 :008(495) [0833] In addition he **promises** the power and operation of the
EP : 12 :008(498) [0839] expressed word of God's **promise** which extends only to
SD : 02 :009(522) [0883] Son of God and the **promise** of eternal salvation, they
SD : 02 :054(531) [0903] sake and comforts itself with the **promise** of the Gospel.
SD : 02 :056(532) [0903] and on the basis of his **promise**, that the Word which is
SD : 02 :057(532) [0903] that we hear it, and has **promised** that, where two or
SD : 02 :070(535) [0909] and accept the **promise** of grace in Christ, to have good
SD : 02 :083(537) [0913] in no way believes the **promise** and is not prepared by
SD : 03 :010(541) [0919] treasures to us in the **promise** of the Gospel, and faith is
SD : 03 :013(541) [0919] the merit of Christ in the **promise** of the holy Gospel.
SD : 03 :025(543) [0923] accepts these in the **promise** of the Gospel, whereby the
SD : 03 :030(544) [0925] we receive only by faith in the **promise** of the Gospel.
SD : 03 :031(544) [0925] sins offered to us in the **promise** of the Gospel, but only
SD : 03 :038(546) [0929] and the merit of Christ in the **promise** of the Gospel.
SD : 03 :039(546) [0929] are offered to us in the **promise** of the Gospel and
SD : 03 :043(547) [0931] and the merit of Christ in the **promise** of the Gospel.
SD : 03 :051(548) [0933] 7. Likewise that the **promise** of grace is made our own
SD : 04 :002(551) [0939] for believers the firm and certain **promise** of salvation.
SD : 04 :034(556) [0949] in order that the **promise** that we shall not only receive
SD : 04 :038(557) [0951] for Christ's sake and he **promises** to reward them
SD : 05 :005(559) [0953] not only the gracious **promises** of the forgiveness of sins
SD : 05 :014(560) [0957] it immediately adds the **promise** of God's grace through
SD : 05 :027(563) [0961] the Gospel is the **promise** of forgiveness of sins and
SD : 07 :043(577) [0987] what he speaks and **promises**, as he says, "Heaven and
SD : 07 :046(577) [0987] of faith concerning the **promised** seed, Christ, who was to
SD : 07 :046(577) [0989] Abraham received the **promise** of the blessed seed of
SD : 07 :046(577) [0989] his heart that what God **promised** he was also able to do.
SD : 07 :046(577) [0989] means of fulfilling the **promises** concerning the seed of
SD : 07 :047(578) [0989] accomplish and bring to pass whatever he **promises**.
SD : 07 :120(590) [1013] not or would not have **promised** or have been able to
SD : 08 :087(608) [1047] them in the cited **promises** of the presence and indwelling
SD : 08 :087(608) [1047] high priest, who has **promised** that not only his unveiled
SD : 08 :092(609) [1049] especially where he has **promised** his presence in his
SD : 11 :028(620) [1071] men (Luke 24:47), so also does the **promise** of the Gospel.
SD : 11 :028(621) [1073] should also have this **promise** of the Gospel proclaimed to
SD : 11 :032(621) [1073] such constancy he has **promised** his grace (I Cor. 1:8;
SD : 11 :036(622) [1075] us and what assures and **promises** it to us solely from his
SD : 11 :037(622) [1075] reason Christ has the **promises** of the Gospel offered not
SD : 11 :037(622) [1075] attached as a seal of the **promise** and by which he
SD : 11 :071(627) [1085] sin, repent, believe his **promise**, and trust in him
SD : 11 :072(628) [1085] doubt that according to his **promise** he will give it to us.
SD : 11 :089(631) [1093] to further in Christ and **promises** them the Holy Spirit to
SD : 12 :013(634) [1099] the express words of the **promise** which extends only to

Promote (11), Promoted (2), Promotes (1), Promoting (1), Promotion (3)

PR : PR :012(007) [0013] ourselves bound to **promote** it with Christian earnestness
PR : PR :013(007) [0013] the year 1576 for the **promotion** of concord among
PR : PR :024(013) [0023] of this cause and the **promotion** of God's glory and the
AG : PR :020(026) [0041] graciously offered to **promote** and bring about the calling
AG : 26 :002(064) [0071] ardently and urgently **promoted**, as if these were a
AP : 07 :035(175) [0241] of wisdom in **promoting** rigor of devotion and
AP : 15 :038(220) [0325] they are useful and **promote** tranquillity, and we interpret
S1 : PR :007(289) [0457] God has constantly **promoted** his work, has made their
S2 : 04 :014(301) [0475] for the pope to **promote** his lies about Masses, purgatory,
TR : 00 :080(334) [0527] of ministers, the **promotion** of education, the care of the
LC : 01 :208(393) [0639] up to serve the world, **promote** knowledge of God, godly
LC : 01 :251(399) [0651] we are commanded to **promote** and further our
LC : 01 :260(400) [0655] or distorted but should **promote** and resolutely guard
LC : 01 :288(404) [0663] our utmost to serve and help him to **promote** his honor.
LC : 01 :309(407) [0669] him what is his, and **promote** and protect whatever may
LC : 01 :328(410) [0677] all men, help them and **promote** their interests, however
LC : 04 :075(445) [0751] this new life but also produces, begins, and **promotes** it.
SD : 11 :007(617) [1065] he help it along and **promote** it), but rather the wicked

Prompted (1), Prompting (2), Promptly (1)

AP : 12 :016(184) [0257] and proper reasons **prompted** us to reject the doctrine of
AP : 27 :055(278) [0439] process of teaching, **prompting** some of them to fear or
LC : 01 :184(390) [0633] Thus by the devil's **prompting** you acquire many enemies
LC : 01 :239(397) [0649] Romans, for example, **promptly** took such offenders by

Promulgated (1)

AP : 04 :236(140) [0185] clement prince, that these laws should be **promulgated**.

Pronounce (6), Pronounced (8), Pronouncements (1), Pronounces (2), Pronouncing (2)

AL : 25 :003(062) [0069] the voice of God and is **pronounced** by God's command.
AP : 02 :046(106) [0119] this fearful sentence is **pronounced**, "I will put enmity
AP : 04 :072(117) [0141] them, as well as to be **pronounced** or accounted
AP : 04 :252(143) [0191] but that he is **pronounced** righteous in a forensic way,
AP : 04 :252(143) [0191] faith and good works are certainly **pronounced** righteous.
AP : 04 :252(143) [0191] justified"; that is, God **pronounces** righteous those who
AP : 04 :305(154) [0205] a guilty man and **pronounce** him righteous," and to do so
AP : 12 :103(197) [0281] hear a case before **pronouncing** sentence, that is
S1 : PR :009(290) [0457] I am sure that he will **pronounce** sentence upon them.
LC : 01 :242(397) [0649] for a long time, he will **pronounce** this kind of blessing
LC : 01 :268(401) [0657] and office of God, **pronouncing** the severest kind of
LC : 01 :268(401) [0657] verdict a judge can **pronounce** is to declare somebody a
LC : 03 :097(433) [0725] it as certain as an absolution **pronounced** by thyself."
LC : 05 :074(455) [0771] In such a case Christ **pronounces** the judgment, "If you
LC : 05 :078(455) [0771] the Scriptures, which **pronounce** this judgment upon you.
EP : 03 :007(473) [0793] in this article "absolve," that is, **pronounce** free from sin.
EP : 03 :015(475) [0795] is spoken of in the **pronouncements** of the prophets and
SD : 02 :008(521) [0883] that judgments on articles of faith are to be **pronounced**.
SD : 05 :012(560) [0957] is Moses and the law **pronounced** upon the unconverted.

Proof (12), Proofs (11) ***(See also "prove," etc., below)***

AP : 02 :040(105) [0115] No quibbling can overthrow these **proofs**.
AP : 04 :029(111) [0129] We have **proof** for this position of ours not only in the
AP : 04 :298(153) [0205] The **proof** is obvious: Since we are not justified before
AP : 04 :298(153) [0205] possibly bring against this **proof** unless he wants utterly to
AP : 12 :059(190) [0267] shall therefore add a few **proofs** to show that the
AP : 15 :030(219) [0323] already quoted some **proofs** for this, and Paul's letters
AP : 18 :001(224) [0335] will, but they add several **proofs** which are hardly
AP : 20 :005(227) [0339] There is no need for **proofs** to anyone who knows that
AP : 20 :011(228) [0341] The reader can find our **proofs** in our earlier discussion
AP : 20 :014(228) [0343] They add other **proofs** that are no more relevant.
AP : 21 :010(230) [0345] How do we know, without **proof** from Scripture, that the
AP : 21 :015(231) [0347] They do not even have **proof** from Scripture for calling
AP : 21 :033(233) [0351] if it has no command or **proof** in the Word of God?
AP : 21 :033(233) [0351] In fact, there is no **proof** for it either in the Fathers of the
AP : 23 :027(243) [0371] analogy is presented as a **proof** to force perpetual celibacy
AP : 24 :020(252) [0389] enumerate the many **proofs** for this distinction found in
AP : 24 :053(259) [0403] Though the main **proofs** for our position are in the
AP : 24 :083(264) [0411] But further **proofs** are unnecessary since anyone who
AP : 24 :089(265) [0413] But for this they have no scriptural **proof** or command.
AP : 24 :090(266) [0415] pass over the sort of **proofs** our opponents have for
AP : 27 :023(273) [0427] him when they have no **proof** for this from the Word of
LC : 04 :051(443) [0745] is the best and strongest **proof** for the simple and
SD : 08 :028(596) [1025] maintain without **proof** from the Holy Scriptures.

Propagate (3), Propagated (1), Propagation (1)

PR : PR :024(013) [0023] and glory, to the **propagation** of that Word of his that
AL : 02 :001(029) [0043] Adam all men who are **propagated** according to nature
AP : 21 :044(236) [0357] God to maintain and **propagate** sound doctrine and to
AP : 21 :044(236) [0357] care to maintain and **propagate** divine things on earth,
SD : 02 :037(528) [0895] he uses to proclaim and **propagate** his Word, whereby he

Proper (54), Properly (49)

AG : 08 :001(033) [0047] the Christian church, **properly** speaking, is nothing else
AG : 12 :003(034) [0049] **Properly** speaking, true repentance is nothing else than to
AG : 16 :004(037) [0051] consists alone of **proper** fear of God and real faith in
AG : 00 :001(047) [0059] in our churches for **proper** Christian instruction, the
AG : 22 :011(050) [0061] Accordingly it is not **proper** to burden the consciences of
AG : 24 :012(057) [0065] which should **properly** concern every Christian (namely,
AG : 24 :035(060) [0067] preserved among us in its **proper** use, the use which was
AG : 27 :027(075) [0079] first ascertaining whether a vow is of the **proper** sort?
AG : 27 :049(078) [0083] of God and true and **proper** service of God are obscured
AG : 27 :059(080) [0083] it was necessary to give the people **proper** instruction.
AG : 28 :050(089) [0091] Gospel, it is not at all **proper** for the bishops to require
AG : 28 :055(090) [0091] It is **proper** for the Christian assembly to keep such
AL : 08 :001(033) [0047] **Properly** speaking, the church is the assembly of saints
AL : 12 :003(034) [0049] **Properly** speaking, repentance consists of these two parts:
AL : 00 :002(047) [0059] have crept into the churches without **proper** authority.
AL : 00 :006(049) [0059] among the people as the **proper** observance of ceremonies
AL : 23 :026(056) [0065] vows before attaining a **proper** age, and as a rule vows
AL : 27 :043(077) [0081] their own works what **properly** belongs to the glory of
AL : 28 :055(090) [0091] It is **proper** that the churches comply with such
AP : 02 :012(102) [0109] attributed more than was **proper** to free will and to
AP : 02 :015(102) [0109] **Properly** understood, the old definition says exactly the
AP : 02 :028(104) [0113] to answer that it is the lack of **proper** righteousness.
AP : 02 :035(104) [0115] add that this doctrine was **properly** condemned by Leo X.
AP : 04 :002(107) [0121] is involved; when it is **properly** understood, it illumines
AP : 04 :014(109) [0123] this was perfectly **proper**, for Aristotle wrote so well on
AP : 04 :063(115) [0139] *operato* without the **proper** attitude in the recipient, as
AP : 04 :146(127) [0163] the law, though this glory **properly** belongs to Christ.
AP : 04 :155(128) [0165] that it is faith that **properly** accepts the forgiveness of
AP : 04 :235(140) [0185] perfect or whole when all its parts fit together **properly**."
AP : 04 :279(149) [0199] These actions **properly** belong to the kind of faith we
AP : 04 :309(155) [0207] God, gives him what is **properly** his; it obeys him by
AP : 04 :312(155) [0207] the object of hope is **properly** a future event, while faith
AP : 04 :324(157) [0211] **Properly**, then, do we reject the doctrine of the merit of
AP : 04 :345(160) [0217] **Properly** speaking, the Gospel is the command to believe
AP : 04 :368(163) [0221] a reward, since a reward **properly** belongs to the law, still
AP : 04 :370(163) [0221] urge that good works **properly** merit eternal life, since
AP : 07 :020(171) [0233] This church is **properly** called "the pillar of truth"
AP : 07 :022(172) [0235] But the church, **properly** speaking, is that which has the
AP : 07 :022(172) [0235] church, they are not, **properly** speaking, the kingdom of
AP : 07 :028(173) [0237] that the church in the **proper** sense is the assembly of
AP : 07 :029(173) [0237] since the church, **properly** so called, is termed the body of
AP : 11 :005(181) [0249] the people could not be heard and instructed **properly**.
AP : 11 :008(181) [0251] question of who was the **proper** priest, when brothers did
AP : 12 :016(184) [0257] therefore, that good and **proper** reasons prompted us to
AP : 12 :025(185) [0259] *operato*, without the **proper** attitude in the recipient, that
AP : 12 :041(187) [0261] Absolution may **properly** be called a sacrament of
AP : 12 :051(189) [0265] because God's own **proper** work is to quicken and
AP : 12 :058(190) [0267] penitence the parts that **properly** belong to it in
AP : 12 :063(191) [0269] of sins should **properly** be included as one of the parts of
AP : 12 :158(207) [0301] work in order to do his **proper** work, as Isaiah teaches in
AP : 23 :007(240) [0365] that one sex should have a **proper** desire for the other.
AP : 23 :035(244) [0373] In the second place, the **proper** contrast is between lust
AP : 24 :017(252) [0389] The theologians make a **proper** distinction between
AP : 24 :049(258) [0401] are instructed about the **proper** use of the sacrament as a
AP : 24 :049(258) [0401] of the Gospel and the **proper** use of the sacraments, we
AP : 24 :088(265) [0413] **Properly** understood, this is not offensive.
AP : 24 :099(268) [0419] Mass, that we show its **proper** use, and that we have most
AP : 27 :057(279) [0439] took their vows without **proper** judgment because they
AP : 27 :057(279) [0439] and that therefore it is **proper** to abandon a way of life so
AP : 28 :003(281) [0443] not see to it that there is **proper** preaching and
S2 : 02 :008(294) [0465] do so most fittingly and **properly** in the sacrament
S3 : 03 :012(305) [0481] that a man who **properly** repents, confesses, and makes
S3 : 03 :027(307) [0487] in purgatory had truly repented and **properly** confessed.
TR : 00 :014(322) [0507] namely, that for the **proper** celebration of ordinations the
TR : 00 :049(329) [0519] controversies to be decided in the **proper** manner.
TR : 00 :051(329) [0519] punishments, for when **proper** judicial process has been
TR : 00 :076(333) [0527] see to it that it is used **properly** for the reformation of
SC : PR :016(340) [0535] When the learners have a **proper** understanding of the
LC : 01 :010(366) [0583] I repeat, to have a God **properly** means to have

Continued ▶

L C : 0 1 :063(373) [0599] we are to use his name **properly**, for it has been revealed
L C : 0 1 :064(373) [0599] when we swear **properly** where it is necessary and
L C : 0 1 :064(373) [0599] So, also, when we teach **properly**; again, when we call on
L C : 0 1 :079(375) [0603] word "Sabbath," which **properly** means to rest, that is, to
L C : 0 1 :094(378) [0607] and occupations are not **properly** called holy work unless
L C : 0 1 :097(378) [0609] that Sunday had been **properly** hallowed if one heard a
L C : 0 1 :108(380) [0611] must be this sort of inequality and **proper** distinctions.
L C : 0 1 :114(380) [0613] have had godly children, **properly** taught, and reared in
L C : 0 1 :217(394) [0643] may in due time regain its **proper** honor, and there may
L C : 0 1 :270(401) [0657] your charges before the **proper** authorities, then hold
L C : 0 1 :285(403) [0661] unless it is done with **proper** authority or for his
L C : 0 1 :326(409) [0675] but to use his name **properly** by calling upon him in
L C : 0 2 :001(411) [0679] The Creed **properly** follows, setting forth all that we must
L C : 0 2 :032(414) [0687] But the **proper** place to explain all these different points
L C : 0 2 :033(415) [0687] we preach depends on the **proper** understanding of this
L C : 0 2 :047(416) [0691] The word *ecclesia* **properly** means an assembly.
L C : 0 3 :007(421) [0699] repetition, when **properly** used, may serve as an exercise
L C : 0 3 :029(424) [0705] damage and harm he suffers when prayer is in **proper** use.
L C : 0 3 :073(430) [0719] from functioning **properly**, there the necessities of life are
L C : 0 4 :014(438) [0735] how to answer **properly** the question, What is Baptism?
L C : 0 4 :016(438) [0735] know that water is water, if such a separation is **proper**?
L C : 0 4 :054(443) [0745] God's Word, even though he failed to receive it **properly**.
L C : 0 5 :037(451) [0761] one's body may behave **properly** and reverently toward
E P : 0 5 :010(479) [0803] by which he comes to his **proper** office — namely, to
S D : 0 1 :003(509) [0861] extolling God's honor **properly** when we carefully
S D : 0 1 :028(513) [0867] just as it is not itself the **proper** essence, body, or soul of
S D : 0 3 :040(546) [0929] In this way, too, the **proper** order between faith and good
S D : 0 4 :035(557) [0949] of God that faith is the **proper** and the only means
S D : 0 5 :015(561) [0957] urged side by side, but in **proper** order and with the
S D : 0 5 :017(561) [0957] belongs to the law, the **proper** function of which is to
S D : 0 5 :023(562) [0959] by side in the church of God with the **proper** distinction.
S D : 0 5 :027(563) [0961] all diligence the true and **proper** distinction between law
S D : 0 7 :099(586) [1005] be made manifest at the **proper** time by the blessed God"
S D : 1 2 :006(633) [1097] simple, natural, and **proper** meaning of the Augsburg

Property (75), Properties (68)
P R : P R :021(011) [0019] with their respective **properties**, are mixed together and
P R : P R :021(011) [0019] to its essence and **properties** is equalized with the divine
A G : 0 1 :004(028) [0043] not as a part or a **property** of another but as that which
A G : 1 6 :002(037) [0051] take required oaths, possess **property**, be married, etc.
A L : 1 6 :002(037) [0051] legal contracts, to hold **property**, to swear oaths when
A P : 0 7 :050(178) [0245] to priests the right to hold **property** or other possessions.
A P : 0 7 :050(178) [0245] The right to hold **property** is a civil ordinance.
A P : 1 2 :106(197) [0283] attention to his own **property** and leave other people's
A P : 1 2 :169(209) [0305] if it does not satisfy those whose **property** we have taken.
A P : 1 2 :169(209) [0305] as long as he unjustly holds on to another man's **property**.
A P : 1 6 :001(222) [0329] legal contracts, own **property**, take an oath when the
A P : 1 6 :004(223) [0331] evangelical state to hold **property** in common, and they
A P : 1 6 :004(223) [0331] counsel not to own **property** and not to go to court.
A P : 1 6 :009(224) [0333] Christian perfections consists in not holding **property**.
A P : 1 6 :010(224) [0333] that the Gospel requires us to hold **property** in common!
A P : 1 6 :011(224) [0333] not command holding **property** in common, but by its
A P : 1 6 :011(224) [0333] claiming that priests were not allowed to own **property**.
A P : 2 7 :026(273) [0429] among clothes or foods, nor the surrender of **property**.
A P : 2 7 :039(276) [0433] they do not have **property**, are unmarried, and obey the
A P : 2 7 :041(276) [0435] to bear the injury, to let **property**, wife, and children, even
A P : 2 7 :045(277) [0435] in casting off possessions and the control of **property**.
A P : 2 7 :046(277) [0435] and possession of **property** are civil ordinances, approved
A P : 2 7 :046(277) [0435] The abandonment of **property** is neither commanded nor
A P : 2 7 :046(277) [0435] in the abandonment of **property**, but in the absence of
A P : 2 7 :047(277) [0437] the abandonment of **property** is therefore merely a human
S C : 0 1 :014(343) [0541] of his money or **property**, nor bring them into our
S C : 0 1 :014(343) [0541] help him to improve and protect his income and **property**.
S C : 0 2 :002(345) [0543] and home, family and **property**; that he provides me daily
S C : 0 3 :014(347) [0547] and flocks, money and **property**; a pious spouse and good
S C : 0 3 :020(348) [0549] it affect body or soul, **property** or reputation, and that at
L C : 0 1 :005(365) [0581] when he has money and **property**; in them he trusts and
L C : 0 1 :007(365) [0583] He who has money and **property** feels secure, happy,
L C : 0 1 :053(372) [0595] matters involving money, **property**, and honor, whether
L C : 0 1 :172(388) [0629] not think only of amassing money and **property** for them.
L C : 0 1 :223(395) [0643] and our spouse, our temporal **property** is dearest to us.
L C : 0 1 :224(395) [0643] else than to acquire another's **property** by unjust means.
L C : 0 1 :233(396) [0647] to protect his neighbor's **property** and further his
L C : 0 1 :235(397) [0647] master's or mistress's **property**, which enables you to stuff
L C : 0 1 :236(397) [0647] When you come into **property** yourself and have a house
L C : 0 1 :250(399) [0651] or interfering with his possessions and **property**.
L C : 0 1 :255(399) [0653] and our temporal **property**, we have one more treasure
L C : 0 1 :257(399) [0653] consequently punished in his body, **property**, or honor.
L C : 0 1 :261(400) [0655] account of anyone's money, **property**, honor, or power.
L C : 0 1 :293(404) [0665] our neighbor's wife or **property**, or to have any designs on
L C : 0 1 :294(404) [0665] they were their master's **property**, the same as his cattle
L C : 0 1 :301(405) [0667] such secure title to the **property** as to put it beyond
L C : 0 1 :302(405) [0667] at his disposal, until the **property** is taken away from the
L C : 0 1 :303(406) [0667] cannot hold on to his **property**, nor yet sell it without loss
L C : 0 1 :307(406) [0669] of the world you might honorably retain the **property**.
L C : 0 1 :307(406) [0669] upon your neighbor's **property**, luring it away from him
L C : 0 1 :328(410) [0675] his person, his wife, his **property**, his honor or rights, as
L C : 0 2 :022(413) [0683] and soul, money and **property**, and with all that we have.
E P : 0 1 :012(467) [0781] and essential **properties** of human nature, or the teaching
E P : 0 7 :033(485) [0815] since the nature and **properties** of his assumed human
E P : 0 8 :001(486) [0817] of Christ, the two natures in Christ, and their **properties**.
E P : 0 8 :002(487) [0817] together with their **properties**, *really* (that is, in deed and
E P : 0 8 :003(487) [0817] in truth) shares in the **properties** of the other but have in
E P : 0 8 :003(487) [0819] in common with the deity, its majesty, and its **properties**.
E P : 0 8 :006(487) [0819] retains its essential **properties** and that they never become
E P : 0 8 :006(487) [0819] that they never become the **properties** of the other nature.
E P : 0 8 :007(487) [0819] 3. The **properties** of the divine nature are omnipotence,
E P : 0 8 :007(487) [0819] (according to its natural **property**, by itself)
E P : 0 8 :007(487) [0819] etc., which never become **properties** of the human nature.
E P : 0 8 :008(487) [0819] which never become the **properties** of the divine nature.
E P : 0 8 :014(488) [0821] us, but according to the **property** of the human nature
E P : 0 8 :017(489) [0823] *to the mode or **property** of the human nature* but
E P : 0 8 :017(489) [0823] *to the mode* and **property** of God's right hand, as Dr.
E P : 0 8 :018(489) [0823] genuine sharing of the **properties** of the two natures in
E P : 0 8 :018(489) [0823] the natures and their **properties** together in one essence,
E P : 0 8 :027(490) [0825] this essential power and **property** has been severed from
E P : 0 8 :028(490) [0825] in its substance and essence, or in its essential **properties**.
E P : 0 8 :030(490) [0825] 11. That because of the **property** of the human nature it is
E P : 0 8 :034(491) [0825] of omnipotence and other **properties** of the divine nature.
E P : 1 2 :017(499) [0841] hold or possess private **property** but is in conscience
E P : 1 2 :021(499) [0841] received all the divine **properties** in such a way that
E P : 1 2 :021(499) [0841] only one divine essence, **property**, will, and glory and
E P : 1 2 :029(500) [0843] unequal in essence and **properties** and that only the
S D : 0 2 :043(529) [0897] captives of sin and the **property** of the devil to do and to
S D : 0 3 :038(546) [0929] faith's sole office and **property** is to serve as the only and
S D : 0 3 :038(546) [0929] From this office and **property** of application and
S D : 0 7 :004(569) [0973] to the exchange of **properties** (that is, only according to
S D : 0 7 :091(585) [1003] essential and natural **properties** of the human body,
S D : 0 7 :120(590) [1013] because the nature and **properties** of his assumed human
S D : 0 8 :004(592) [1017] its natural, essential **properties**, and they went so far as to
S D : 0 8 :008(593) [1017] each retains its natural **properties** and throughout all
S D : 0 8 :008(593) [1017] nor do the essential **properties** of the one nature ever
S D : 0 8 :008(593) [1017] nature ever become the essential **properties** of the other.
S D : 0 8 :009(593) [1017] is, according to the **property** of the nature and of its
S D : 0 8 :009(593) [1019] everything are essential **properties** of the divine nature,
S D : 0 8 :009(593) [1019] become the essential **properties** of the human nature.
S D : 0 8 :010(593) [1019] and similar things are **properties** of the human nature,
S D : 0 8 :010(593) [1019] which never will become **properties** of the divine nature.
S D : 0 8 :011(593) [1019] its natural essence and **properties**, are found unblended in
S D : 0 8 :012(593) [1019] its natural, essential **properties** but that in addition
S D : 0 8 :019(595) [1021] the natures or their **properties**; on the contrary, each
S D : 0 8 :019(595) [1021] contrary, each nature retains its essence and **properties**.
S D : 0 8 :020(595) [1021] human nature (whose **property** it is to suffer and to die)
S D : 0 8 :028(596) [1025] the two natures in their essence and essential **properties**.
S D : 0 8 :031(597) [1025] of an exchange of **properties** (that is, of a true
S D : 0 8 :031(597) [1025] communication of the **properties** of the natures) likewise
S D : 0 8 :032(597) [1025] retains its essential **properties** and that these are not
S D : 0 8 :032(597) [1025] an exchange of **properties** could not take place or
S D : 0 8 :035(597) [1027] of the exchange of **properties** between the two natures be
S D : 0 8 :035(597) [1027] its natures, and their **properties** are not all of the same
S D : 0 8 :036(598) [1027] natural essence and **properties**, and since both natures
S D : 0 8 :036(598) [1027] person, therefore any **property**, though it belongs only to
S D : 0 8 :037(598) [1027] person is simultaneously the **property** of both natures.
S D : 0 8 :037(598) [1027] to which nature the **property** in question is being ascribed
S D : 0 8 :038(598) [1027] *entire person what is the **property** of one nature* (for
S D : 0 8 :046(600) [1031] according to its own **properties** acts in communion with
S D : 0 8 :048(600) [1031] natural and essential **properties** (which, as has been
S D : 0 8 :049(600) [1031] from the essence and **properties** of the divine nature in
S D : 0 8 :050(600) [1031] own natural essential **properties** alone, according to which
S D : 0 8 :050(600) [1031] contravenes its natural **properties**, even though the
S D : 0 8 :051(600) [1033] essential, and abiding **properties**, special, high, great,
S D : 0 8 :051(601) [1033] natural and essential **properties**, or only as far as their
S D : 0 8 :053(601) [1033] and above its natural **properties** without being destroyed.
S D : 0 8 :055(601) [1033] of the Scriptures these **properties** have been given and
S D : 0 8 :060(602) [1035] natural and essential **properties** in such a way that the
S D : 0 8 :060(602) [1035] in such a way that the **properties** of the one nature never
S D : 0 8 :060(602) [1035] never become the **properties** of the other nature, we must
S D : 0 8 :061(602) [1035] and all the divine **properties** from eternity to the Son
S D : 0 8 :061(603) [1037] it is in his divine nature, that is, as an essential **property**.
S D : 0 8 :062(603) [1037] outpouring of the **properties** of the divine nature into the
S D : 0 8 :062(603) [1037] natural and essential **properties** and is now either
S D : 0 8 :062(603) [1037] of these communicated **properties** has become
S D : 0 8 :062(603) [1037] the natural, essential **properties** and acts of both natures
S D : 0 8 :062(603) [1037] or of their essential **properties** be taught or conceded.
S D : 0 8 :063(603) [1037] natures in their essence and in their essential **properties**.
S D : 0 8 :063(603) [1037] blending of the natures and of their essential **properties**.
S D : 0 8 :066(604) [1039] and glory, which is the **property** of the divine nature
S D : 0 8 :066(604) [1039] and combustion is the **property** of fire — but since the fire
S D : 0 8 :066(604) [1039] of the natural **properties** of either the fire or the iron.
S D : 0 8 :067(604) [1039] majesty, which is the **property** of the divine nature of the
S D : 0 8 :071(605) [1041] of God and all its **properties** into the human nature of
S D : 0 8 :071(605) [1041] intrinsically or have omnipotent **properties** intrinsically.
S D : 0 8 :090(609) [1047] through an essential power or **property** of its nature.
S D : 0 8 :091(609) [1049] in its substance and essence or in its essential **properties**.
S D : 1 2 :022(634) [1099] hold or possess private **property** but is obliged to give his
S D : 1 2 :022(634) [1099] but is obliged to give his **property** to the community.
S D : 1 2 :029(635) [1101] assumed all the divine **properties** in such a way that in
S D : 1 2 :029(635) [1101] but one kind of essence, **property**, will, and glory and so
S D : 1 2 :037(636) [1103] in the Trinity are unequal in their essence and **properties**.

Prophecy (1), Prophecies (1), Prophesies (1), Prophesy (2)
A G : 2 3 :014(053) [0063] of which the Scriptures **prophesy**, the world is growing
A P : 2 2 :017(238) [0361] when Scripture **prophesies** about bishops and pastors in
A P : 2 3 :003(239) [0363] some of the ancient **prophecies** call the king with the
A P : 2 3 :038(244) [0373] Thus **prophecy** surpasses eloquence, military science
S 3 : 0 8 :013(313) [0497] spoke, they did not **prophesy** by the impulse of man but

Prophet (16), Prophets (53)
A G : 2 5 :011(063) [0069] others, but obey the **prophet** who says, 'Show your way to
A G : 2 8 :023(084) [0087] for Christ says in Matt. 7:15, "Beware of false **prophets**."
A L : 2 5 :011(063) [0069] I wish you to obey the **prophet** who says, 'Show your way
A L : 2 8 :023(084) [0087] "Beware of false **prophets**" (Matt. 7:15), "If an angel from
A P : 0 2 :011(102) [0109] us and of these that the **prophets** constantly complain,
A P : 0 2 :033(104) [0113] Thus the **prophet** says, "After I was instructed, I smote
A P : 0 2 :043(106) [0117] to these things, as the Psalms and the **prophets** show.
A P : 0 4 :057(114) [0137] praised throughout the **prophets** and the Psalms.
A P : 0 4 :058(115) [0137] in the Psalms and the **prophets** belong here; for example,
A P : 0 4 :083(118) [0145] says, "To him all the **prophets** bear witness that every one
A P : 0 4 :083(119) [0145] the consensus of all the **prophets**, which is really citing
A P : 0 4 :123(124) [0157] It is written in the **prophet** (Jer. 31:33), "I will put my law
A P : 0 4 :125(124) [0157] these impulses are, the **prophet** shows when he says
A P : 0 4 :207(135) [0177] we see how vehemently the **prophets** rebuke the people.
A P : 0 4 :208(135) [0177] of Israel had seen the **prophets** sacrifice on the high
A P : 0 4 :208(135) [0177] But the **prophets** did not sacrifice on the high places to
A P : 0 4 :258(144) [0193] Thus the **prophet** urges penitence and adds a promise.
A P : 0 4 :258(144) [0193] The **prophet** does not say that through these

Continued ▶

AP : 04 :259(145) [0193] Nor does the **prophet** speak of this one work alone, but
AP : 04 :273(148) [0199] "To him all the **prophets** bear witness that every
AP : 04 :365(163) [0219] as in Isa. 58:8, 9 and often in other places in the **prophets**.
AP : 04 :395(167) [0225] The **prophets**, on the contrary, condemned this opinion
AP : 07 :026(173) [0235] Christ, the **prophets**, and the apostles define the church
AP : 07 :048(177) [0245] 7:15), "Beware of false **prophets**"; Paul says (Gal 1:9), "If
AP : 12 :009(183) [0255] in the Psalms and the **prophets** and certainly experienced
AP : 12 :053(189) [0265] then illumined by the **prophets**, and finally proclaimed
AP : 12 :065(191) [0271] "To him all the **prophets** bear witness that every
AP : 12 :066(191) [0271] position: "To him all the **prophets** bear witness that every
AP : 12 :066(191) [0271] the consensus of the **prophets** should be interpreted as the
AP : 12 :066(191) [0271] issue decrees contrary to this consensus of the **prophets**.
AP : 12 :070(192) [0271] the consensus of the **prophets**, to the many legions of
AP : 12 :073(192) [0273] the consensus of the **prophets**; the writings of the apostles
AP : 12 :094(196) [0281] on the oath in the **prophet** (Ez. 33:11), "As I live, says the
AP : 12 :159(207) [0301] Thus the **prophets** were killed, and John the Baptist, and
AP : 15 :014(217) [0319] not God throughout the **prophets** forbid the
AP : 20 :002(227) [0339] 10:43), "To him all the **prophets** bear witness that every
AP : 20 :002(227) [0339] with this church of the **prophets** than with those
AP : 23 :005(239) [0365] (II Pet. 2:1) that false **prophets** would deceive people with
AP : 24 :028(254) [0393] The Old Testament **prophets** also condemn the popular
AP : 24 :031(255) [0395] The **prophet** says nothing about these shameless
AP : 24 :032(255) [0395] Besides, the **prophet**'s own words give us his meaning.
AP : 24 :093(267) [0417] to all the blessed patriarchs, **prophets**, and apostles.
AP : 24 :093(267) [0417] in faith, forefathers, fathers, patriarchs, **prophets**," etc.
AP : 24 :096(267) [0417] clearly conflicts with the **prophets**, apostles, and holy
AP : 24 :097(268) [0417] When the **prophets** condemn this notion, therefore, they
AP : 24 :099(268) [0419] to the work the the **prophet** Elijah in condemning the
AP : 27 :025(273) [0429] The **prophet** says (Ps. 116:11), "All men are liars"; that is,
S2 : 03 :002(298) [0471] and accordingly the **prophets** call such service of God
S3 : 08 :011(313) [0497] spoken word, and no **prophet**, whether Elijah or Elisha,
S3 : 08 :013(313) [0497] Peter says that when the **prophets** spoke, they did not
TR : 00 :026(324) [0511] God gives his gifts, apostles, **prophets**, pastors, teachers.
TR : 00 :038(327) [0515] So Jeremiah and other **prophets** dissented from them, and
TR : 00 :041(327) [0517] commanded, "Beware of false **prophets**" (Matt. 7:15).
LC : PR :016(361) [0573] than all his holy angels, **prophets**, apostles, and all
LC : PR :016(361) [0573] world to the end, and all **prophets** and saints have been
LC : 01 :325(409) [0675] The **prophet** David particularly teaches it throughout the
EP : RN :002(465) [0777] which the doctrine of the **prophets** and apostles was
EP : 03 :015(475) [0795] pronouncements of the **prophets** and apostles, the words
SD : 03 :059(550) [0937] God, the teaching of the **prophets** and apostles, and our
SD : 03 :062(550) [0937] 3. That when the **prophets** and the apostles speak of the
SD : 04 :025(555) [0945] 1. In the case of the false **prophets** among the Galatians;
SD : 05 :001(558) [0951] the writings of the holy **prophets** and apostles may be
SD : 05 :011(560) [0955] must perform what the **prophet** calls "a strange deed"
SD : 07 :091(585) [1005] *Against the Heavenly **Prophets**, That These Words "This*
SD : 08 :016(594) [1021] the Word of God dwelled just as in each of the **prophets**.
SD : 08 :027(596) [1025] ends of the earth, as the **prophets** foretell (Ps. 8:6; 93:1;
SD : 08 :096(609) [1049] the writings of the holy **prophets** and apostles, and our
SD : 10 :012(612) [1057] But when false **prophets** demanded circumcision and
SD : 10 :022(615) [1061] commanded, 'Beware of false **prophets**' (Matt. 7:15).

Prophetic (10)

PR : PR :002(003) [0007] out of the divine, **prophetic**, and apostolic Scriptures.
PR : PR :024(012) [0021] the basis of the divine, **prophetic**, and apostolic
PR : PR :025(013) [0023] is based on the **prophetic** and apostolic Scriptures and is
AP : 04 :261(145) [0195] of the law, but a truly **prophetic** and evangelical voice
AP : 04 :389(166) [0225] said agrees with the **prophetic** and apostolic Scriptures,
EP : RN :001(464) [0777] and confess that the **prophetic** and apostolic writings of
SD : PR :003(503) [0851] pledge ourselves to the **prophetic** and apostolic writings
SD : PR :016(507) [0857] faith, according to the **prophetic** and apostolic writings of
SD : 08 :071(605) [1041] Creed and to the entire **prophetic** and apostolic doctrine.
SD : 08 :088(609) [1047] forth as contrary to the **prophetic** and apostolic writings,

Propitiate (3), Propitiating (1), Propitiation (30), Propitiations (2), Propitiatory (7), Propitious (4)

AG : 03 :003(030) [0045] but also for all other sins and to **propitiate** God's wrath.
AG : 15 :003(036) [0049] men for the purpose of **propitiating** God and earning
AG : 28 :050(089) [0091] as necessary to **propitiate** God and merit grace are
AL : 15 :003(036) [0049] which are instituted to **propitiate** God, merit grace, and
AL : 20 :009(042) [0053] be the mediator and **propitiation** through whom the
AL : 21 :002(047) [0057] for the only mediator, **propitiation**, highpriest, and
AP : 04 :053(114) [0137] and the merits of Christ as the price and **propitiation**.
AP : 04 :053(114) [0137] because there must be a certain **propitiation** for our sins.
AP : 04 :086(119) [0147] sake he wishes to be **propitious** to believers in Christ and
AP : 04 :100(121) [0151] believes that God is **propitious**; and he adds that this
AP : 04 :155(128) [0165] fruits are the price of **propitiation** which earns the
AP : 04 :179(131) [0171] he himself is their **propitiation**, for whose sake they are
AP : 04 :204(135) [0177] to God as a price and **propitiation**, thus giving our works
AP : 04 :206(135) [0177] these works were a **propitiation** and price that reconciled
AP : 04 :209(136) [0179] work was a price or **propitiation** for which he would be
AP : 04 :212(136) [0179] works, that they are a **propitiation** by which God is
AP : 04 :213(136) [0179] our works with being a **propitiation** and to claim that
AP : 04 :238(140) [0187] mediator, love is the **propitiation** that reconciles God to
AP : 04 :242(141) [0187] the mediator it is our **propitiation**; or that it regenerates
AP : 04 :244(142) [0189] that good works are a **propitiation** and price that
AP : 04 :251(143) [0191] does he say that our **propitiation** is due in part to Christ
AP : 04 :253(143) [0193] that works are a **propitiation**; that works ple≀se God
AP : 04 :255(144) [0193] faith or that these works are themselves a **pr(pitiation**.
AP : 04 :269(147) [0197] and make of them a **propitiation** that merits the
AP : 04 :275(148) [0199] that good works are a **propitiation** — for they follow
AP : 04 :290(151) [0203] it teaches that our works are a **propitiation** for sin.
AP : 04 :379(165) [0223] that the Father is **propitious** to us for Christ's sake, there
AP : 04 :382(165) [0225] Christ is a **propitiation**, as Paul says, through faith
AP : 04 :386(166) [0225] God is reconciled and **propitious** to us because of Christ.
AP : 12 :078(193) [0275] neither love nor works can be a **propitiation** for sin.
AP : 20 :002(227) [0339] that not our works but Christ is the **propitiation** for sin?
AP : 20 :005(227) [0339] Christ was given to us to be a **propitiation** for our sins.
AP : 21 :031(233) [0351] know that the merits of Christ are our only **propitiation**.
AP : 24 :019(252) [0389] One is the **propitiatory** sacrifice; this is a work of
AP : 24 :021(252) [0389] certain sacrifices **propitiatory** because of what they
AP : 24 :021(252) [0391] were accordingly called **propitiatory** sacrifices for sin or
AP : 24 :022(253) [0391] really been only one **propitiatory** sacrifice in the world,
AP : 24 :023(253) [0391] the death of Christ is the only real **propitiatory** sacrifice.
AP : 24 :024(253) [0391] The Levitical **propitiatory** sacrifices were so called only as
AP : 24 :024(253) [0391] they were not really **propitiations**, since the Gospel was
AP : 24 :024(253) [0391] Gospel was promised in order to set forth a **propitiation**.
AP : 24 :053(259) [0403] of Christ which was to be the one **propitiatory** sacrifice.
AP : 24 :097(268) [0417] always will, that services and sacrifices are **propitiations**.
AP : 24 :097(268) [0417] only the sacrifice of Christ is honored as a **propitiation**.
AP : 27 :017(271) [0425] his merits and his **propitiation** against the wrath of God
AP : 27 :017(271) [0425] in addition to Christ's **propitiation**, against the wrath of
SD : 11 :028(620) [1071] his blood is "the **propitiation** for the whole world's"

Propitiator (46), Propitiators (4)

AP : 04 :040(112) [0131] has been appointed as the mediator and the **propitiator**.
AP : 04 :046(113) [0133] merits of love, but Christ the mediator and **propitiator**.
AP : 04 :080(118) [0143] is set forth to be the **propitiator**, through whom the
AP : 04 :081(118) [0143] is the mediator and **propitiator** because he merited for us
AP : 04 :082(118) [0145] because of Christ, the **propitiator**, according to
AP : 04 :082(118) [0145] So this **propitiator** benefits us when by faith we receive
AP : 04 :157(128) [0165] we rob Christ of his honor as mediator and **propitiator**.
AP : 04 :165(130) [0169] away with Christ, the **propitiator** and mediator, and then
AP : 04 :211(136) [0179] received these freely because of Christ, the **propitiator**.
AP : 04 :212(136) [0179] that Christ is the **propitiator**, or that freely by faith we
AP : 04 :213(136) [0179] to rob Christ of his honor as mediator and **propitiator**?
AP : 04 :215(137) [0179] been set forth as the **propitiator** through whom we have
AP : 04 :221(137) [0181] accounted righteous because of Christ, the **propitiator**.
AP : 04 :222(138) [0181] without Christ, the **propitiator**; that by our love we
AP : 04 :222(138) [0181] hold of Christ, the **propitiator**, and believe that for his
AP : 04 :222(138) [0181] even to be dreamed without Christ, the **propitiator**.
AP : 04 :223(138) [0181] and can have access to God without him as **propitiator**.
AP : 04 :230(139) [0183] because of Christ, the **propitiator**, we are accounted
AP : 04 :231(139) [0183] men perfect, Christ, the **propitiator**, will be unnecessary.
AP : 04 :231(139) [0183] Only faith takes hold of Christ, the **propitiator**.
AP : 04 :231(139) [0185] permit Christ, the **propitiator**, to be excluded, and hence
AP : 04 :238(141) [0187] the sake of Christ, the **propitiator**, the Father is gracious
AP : 04 :244(142) [0189] that we do not need mercy and Christ, the **propitiator**.
AP : 04 :245(142) [0189] the faith by which we take hold of Christ, the **propitiator**.
AP : 04 :245(142) [0189] keeps it, lest Christ, the **propitiator**, be excluded from
AP : 04 :246(142) [0189] we have access to God without Christ, the **propitiator**.
AP : 04 :253(143) [0193] God without Christ, the **propitiator**; that works do not
AP : 04 :253(143) [0193] that works do not need Christ, the **propitiator**.
AP : 04 :269(147) [0197] intended to abolish the Gospel of Christ, the **propitiator**.
AP : 04 :269(147) [0197] they do not please him without Christ, the **propitiator**.
AP : 04 :290(151) [0203] of the law and not through Christ, the **propitiator**.
AP : 04 :290(151) [0203] with[out] Christ, the **propitiator**, is a righteousness worthy
AP : 04 :291(152) [0203] him, the mediator and **propitiator**, against the wrath of
AP : 04 :299(153) [0205] men to make use of him as mediator and **propitiator**.
AP : 04 :308(155) [0207] hold of Christ, the **propitiator**, and is reckoned for
AP : 04 :387(166) [0225] is the mediator and **propitiator**, deny the promise of grace
AP : 04 :389(166) [0225] confesses that Christ is the **propitiator** and the justifier.
AP : 04 :392(167) [0225] making of him not the **propitiator** and justifier, but only a
AP : 12 :043(187) [0263] us to make use of Christ as our mediator and **propitiator**.
AP : 12 :076(193) [0273] for there is no other mediator or **propitiator** but Christ.
AP : 12 :076(193) [0275] works but because of Christ, the mediator and **propitiator**
AP : 21 :014(230) [0345] and make the saints **propitiators** as well as intercessors.
AP : 21 :014(230) [0347] It makes them mediators and **propitiators**.
AP : 21 :016(231) [0347] only intercessors but **propitiators**, that is, mediators of
AP : 21 :017(231) [0347] qualifications must be present if one is to be a **propitiator**.
AP : 21 :017(231) [0347] answer those who call upon him through this **propitiator**.
AP : 21 :019(231) [0347] qualification in a **propitiator** is this: His merits must be
AP : 21 :023(232) [0349] What is this if not to make the saints **propitiators**?
AP : 21 :028(233) [0351] though he were not a **propitiator** but only a terrible judge
AP : 24 :057(260) [0405] as our mediator and **propitiator** with priests and

Proponents (1)

PR : PR :022(011) [0019] and their stiff-necked **proponents** and blasphemers.

Proportionately (1)

SD : 07 :029(574) [0981] errors are increasing **proportionately** with the passage of

Proposal (1), Propose (2), Proposed (6), Proposes (1), Proposing (1)

PR : PR :023(012) [0021] present agreement was **proposed**, purposed, and
AG : PR :002(025) [0039] and to this end it was **proposed** to employ all diligence
AG : PR :018(026) [0041] had considered the **proposal** concerning a general council
AL : 26 :007(065) [0071] of satisfaction were **proposed**, and the whole of
AP : 23 :003(239) [0363] excellent Emperor, they **propose** laws which no
AP : 27 :026(273) [0429] Indeed, when they are **proposed** under the cover of these
AP : 27 :058(279) [0439] Nazarites should not be **proposed** as an act of worship
S3 : 14 :001(316) [0501] ordinary Christian and **proposes** by means of his work to
EP : 07 :010(483) [0811] those which Dr. Luther **proposed** in his *Great*
SD : 12 :005(633) [1097] to see that we were not **proposing** or hiding anything with
SD : 12 :006(633) [1097] is concerned, we do not **propose** to look on idly or stand

Proposition (12), Propositions (8)

AP : 04 :069(116) [0141] if we must hold to the **proposition**, "Christ is the
AP : 04 :069(116) [0141] then we must defend the **proposition**, "Faith justifies."
AP : 04 :070(116) [0141] if we must defend the **proposition**, "The promise of
AP : 04 :070(116) [0141] then we must defend the **proposition**, "Faith justifies."
AP : 12 :131(202) [0291] Let us return to the **proposition**.
SD : 04 :002(551) [0939] the preceding **propositions** and formulas are contrary to
SD : 04 :002(551) [0939] Hence, they held, these **propositions** should not be
SD : 04 :003(551) [0939] the provocative **proposition** or principle "that good works
SD : 04 :015(553) [0943] and reject the cited **propositions** and formulas when they
SD : 04 :018(554) [0943] many defended the **proposition** that good works are
SD : 04 :022(554) [0945] we correctly reject the **propositions** that good works are
SD : 04 :022(554) [0945] works, since such **propositions** are directly contrary to the
SD : 04 :023(555) [0945] Furthermore, these **propositions** deprive tempted and
SD : 04 :024(555) [0945] also has rejected and condemned these **propositions**:
SD : 04 :028(555) [0945] to explain the **proposition** by saying that, although we
SD : 04 :029(555) [0947] the aforementioned **propositions** are not to be taught,
SD : 04 :037(557) [0949] place, concerning the **proposition** that good works are
SD : 04 :039(557) [0951] and reject this **proposition**, too, because when asserted
SD : 04 :040(558) [0951] teach, or defend this **proposition**, unqualifiedly stated, in
SD : 07 :038(576) [0985] consider that in the **proposition** (that is, the words of

Propound (1)

AP : 24 :033(256) [0395] and he does not **propound** the pharisaic idea of

Prospects (1)
LC : 01 :258(399) [0653] an eye to gaining favor, money, **prospects**, or friendship.

Prosper (7), Prosperity (3)
AP : 13 :011(212) [0311] which I purpose, and **prosper** in the thing for which I
LC : 01 :064(373) [0599] need, or praise and thank him in time of **prosperity**, etc.
LC : 01 :134(383) [0619] will enjoy good days, happiness, and **prosperity**.
LC : 01 :138(384) [0621] are fine old families who **prosper** and have many
LC : 01 :146(385) [0623] moreover, that you will **prosper** and fare well in
LC : 01 :238(397) [0647] They will neither **prosper** nor gain anything their whole
LC : 01 :247(398) [0651] If you succeed and **prosper**, before all the world you may
LC : 03 :076(431) [0721] whatever it may be, to **prosper** and succeed; to grant us
LC : 03 :077(431) [0721] wisdom, strength, and **prosperity** to govern well and to be
LC : 03 :083(431) [0721] his hand, nothing can **prosper** or last for any length of

Prostitution (2)
LC : 01 :201(392) [0637] neither were public **prostitution** and lewdness tolerated as
LC : 01 :217(394) [0643] everywhere in public **prostitution** and other shameful

Protect (16), Protected (11), Protecting (2), Protection (14), Protector (1), Protectors (1), Protects (8)
AG : 03 :005(030) [0045] blessing, and that he may **protect** and defend them
AG : 21 :001(046) [0057] demands the defense and **protection** of their subjects.
AG : 28 :011(082) [0085] Temporal power does not **protect** the soul, but with the
AG : 28 :011(082) [0085] and physical penalties it **protects** body and goods from
AL : 28 :011(082) [0085] The state **protects** not souls but bodies and goods from
AL : 28 :011(082) [0085] while the Gospel **protects** souls from heresies, the devil,
AP : 21 :026(232) [0349] man, "Mother of grace, **protect** us from the enemy and
AP : 21 :032(233) [0351] Valentine heals epilepsy, and George **protects** knights.
AP : 21 :032(233) [0351] off fever, and Castor and Pollux **protected** knights.
S3 : 08 :003(312) [0495] Thus we shall be **protected** from the enthusiasts — that is,
SC : PR :013(339) [0535] the laws under whose **protection** he lives, no matter
SC : 01 :014(343) [0541] help him to improve and **protect** his income and
SC : 02 :002(345) [0543] all the necessities of life, **protects** me from all danger, and
SC : 07 :002(352) [0557] Christ, that Thou hast **protected** me through the night
SC : 07 :005(353) [0559] Christ, that Thou hast this day graciously **protected** me.
SC : 07 :005(353) [0559] Graciously **protect** me during the coming night.
LC : PR :014(360) [0571] to warn, equip, and **protect** us against them with good
LC : 01 :012(366) [0583] help them in love affairs, **protect** their cattle, recover lost
LC : 01 :024(367) [0587] nourishment, health, **protection**, peace, and all temporal
LC : 01 :024(367) [0587] It is he who **protects** us from evil, he who saves and
LC : 01 :041(370) [0591] every blessing and will **protect** and help you in every
LC : 01 :073(374) [0601] that we have — for his **protection** against every
LC : 01 :128(382) [0617] God feeds, guards, and **protects** us and how many
LC : 01 :148(385) [0623] is good — shelter and **protection** in the Lord and, what is
LC : 01 :150(385) [0625] gives us food, house and home, **protection** and security.
LC : 01 :185(390) [0633] defended, delivered, and **protected** from the wickedness
LC : 01 :189(390) [0635] fails to prevent, **protect**, and save him from suffering
LC : 01 :195(391) [0637] is, he wishes to help and **protect** us, so that he may
LC : 01 :203(392) [0639] you are to defend, **protect**, and rescue your neighbor
LC : 01 :205(393) [0639] husband or wife guarded and **protected** from any trespass
LC : 01 :206(393) [0639] life, sanctioning and **protecting** it by his commandment.
LC : 01 :206(393) [0639] but here, as I said, he has secured it and **protected** it.
LC : 01 :223(395) [0643] This, too, God wants to have **protected**.
LC : 01 :230(396) [0645] of the head and chief **protector** of all thieves, the Holy
LC : 01 :233(396) [0647] obligation faithfully to **protect** his neighbor's property
LC : 01 :235(397) [0647] them the favor and service of **protecting** them from loss.
LC : 01 :309(407) [0669] is his, and promote and **protect** whatever may be
LC : 02 :030(414) [0685] us as his own, under his **protection**, in order that he may
LC : 03 :030(424) [0705] that all our safety and **protection** consist in prayer alone.
LC : 03 :061(428) [0715] but also for defenders, **protectors**, and vigilant guardians.
LC : 03 :069(429) [0717] prayer must be our **protection** and defense now to repulse
LC : 03 :075(430) [0719] of the princes we enjoy **protection** and peace and that
LC : 03 :078(431) [0721] On the other hand, to **protect** us from all kinds of harm
LC : 03 :118(436) [0731] last, for if we are to be **protected** and delivered from all
LC : 05 :019(449) [0757] our whole argument, **protection**, and defense against all
LC : 05 :070(454) [0769] Spirit with all his gifts, **protection**, defense, and power
EP : 12 :014(499) [0841] it has received from God for their **protection** and defense.
SD : PR :010(503) [0849] know how to guard and **protect** themselves against the
SD : 01 :026(512) [0867] doctrine must also be **protected** against any Manichaean
SD : 02 :029(527) [0893] out that Christ helps us and **protects** us against the devil."
SD : 07 :026(573) [0981] our whole argument, **protection**, and defense against all
SD : 08 :096(610) [1049] and will be well **protected** against pernicious errors.
SD : 11 :020(619) [1069] 6. That he also would **protect** them in their great

Protest (1), Protestation (2), Protestations (1), Protests (1)
AG : PR :022(027) [0043] times made our **protestations** and appeals concerning
AP : 14 :005(215) [0315] read that, despite our **protest** against the unjust cruelty of
EP : 07 :042(486) [0817] over our many **protests**, in order to make our teaching
SD : 07 :029(574) [0981] the following **protestation** to his *Great Confession:* "I see
SD : 07 :032(574) [0983] Following this **protestation** Luther, of blessed memory,

Proud (9), Proudly (1)
AG : 28 :017(083) [0085] strongholds and every **proud** obstacle to the knowledge
SC : 09 :012(356) [0563] for 'God opposes the **proud**, but gives grace to the
LC : 01 :010(366) [0583] secure, and **proud** people become because of such
LC : 01 :036(369) [0589] Even now there are **proud**, powerful, and rich pot-bellies
LC : 01 :075(375) [0601] men may grow up of whom an entire land may be **proud**.
LC : 03 :070(429) [0717] naught, no matter how **proud**, secure, and powerful they
LC : 04 :066(445) [0749] unchaste, greedy, lazy, **proud**, yes, and unbelieving; he is
LC : 04 :070(445) [0749] If a year ago a man was **proud** and greedy, this year he is
LC : 06 :029(460) [0000] if you despise it and **proudly** stay away from confession,
SD : 02 :008(521) [0883] that they are contrary to **proud** reason and philosophy,

Prove (22), Proved (13), Proves (6)
PR : PR :019(009) [0017] a very different doctrine by far can be **proved** therefrom.
AG : 20 :013(043) [0055] His whole book, *De spiritu et litera,* **proves** this.
AG : 21 :002(047) [0057] However, it cannot be **proved** from the Scriptures that we
AG : 24 :035(060) [0067] church and which can be **proved** by St. Paul's statement
AP : 04 :067(116) [0139] From this we can **prove** that faith justifies.
AP : 04 :080(118) [0143] We **prove** the minor premise as follows.
AP : 04 :218(137) [0179] our opponents quote to **prove** that we are justified by
AP : 04 :268(147) [0197] of punishment, this text **proves** nothing against us,
AP : 04 :285(150) [0201] in Rom. 4:5 ff., Paul **proves** that the promise of
AP : 12 :061(190) [0269] the absolution can be **proved** from Paul, who teaches in
AP : 12 :122(200) [0287] Look how our opponents **prove** these fictions of theirs in
AP : 12 :133(202) [0293] could be assembled to **prove** that these passages of
AP : 12 :139(204) [0295] This our opponents would have to **prove**.
AP : 12 :170(209) [0305] This **proves** nothing against us.
AP : 21 :001(229) [0343] but all they manage to **prove** is that the saints should be
AP : 21 :002(229) [0343] They cite this example to **prove** the invocation of the
AP : 21 :012(230) [0345] invocation cannot be **proved** from the Word of God, we
AP : 21 :016(231) [0347] Now we shall **prove** that they actually make the saints
AP : 22 :007(237) [0359] any ancient examples to **prove** their fiction that in the
AP : 24 :009(250) [0387] many statements to **prove** that the Mass is a sacrifice.
AP : 24 :012(251) [0387] is established and **proved** by the impossibility of our
AP : 24 :035(256) [0397] that allegory does not **prove** or establish anything.
AP : 24 :075(263) [0411] This **proves** that the sacrament offers the forgiveness of
AP : 24 :092(266) [0417] to the dead cannot be **proved** from the Scriptures, and it
S2 : 04 :001(298) [0471] as the ancient councils and the time of Cyprian **prove**.
S3 : 01 :010(303) [0477] 7. That it cannot be **proved** from the Scriptures that the
LC : PR :019(361) [0573] stop until they have **proved** by experience that they have
LC : 01 :042(370) [0591] they neither lie nor deceive but will yet **prove** to be true.
LC : 01 :046(370) [0593] words must stand and **prove** to be true since God cannot
LC : 01 :214(394) [0641] mention, as unfortunately has been only too well **proved**.
LC : 01 :270(401) [0657] "Oh, I cannot **prove** it publicly; I might be called a liar
LC : 01 :270(401) [0657] a story that you cannot **prove**, even if it is true, you
LC : 01 :271(401) [0657] then, that cannot be adequately **proved** is false witness.
LC : 04 :049(442) [0743] to Christ is sufficiently **proved** from his own work.
LC : 04 :055(443) [0745] not the case, as we have **proved** — still their Baptism
SD : 07 :057(579) [0993] St. Paul's entire discourse **prove**, he had in mind those
SD : 07 :102(587) [1007] until we know how to **prove** certainly that the body of
SD : 07 :102(587) [1007] Let the enthusiasts **prove** it!
SD : 07 :103(587) [1007] they are unable to **prove** that even this mode is contrary
SD : 07 :103(587) [1007] For who wants to try to **prove** that God is unable to do
SD : 08 :082(607) [1045] his conception in his mother's womb **proves** conclusively.

Provide (15), Provided (16), Provides (9), Provision (4)
PR : PR :010(006) [0011] and direction might be **provided** for simple and pious
AG : 05 :001(031) [0045] of the ministry, that is, **provided** the Gospel and the
AG : 24 :030(059) [0067] not instituted to make **provision** for a sacrifice for sin —
AG : 27 :008(072) [0077] thrust into monasteries to **provide** for their maintenance.
AG : 27 :033(076) [0079] On the basis of this **provision** most monastics have excuse
AL : 28 :056(090) [0091] with her head uncovered, **provided** no offense is given.
AP : 04 :118(123) [0155] his blessings and it alone **provides** a sure and firm
AP : 13 :002(211) [0309] the enumeration varies, **provided** what is handed down in
AP : 14 :005(215) [0315] and canonical polity, **provided** that the bishops stop
AP : 15 :010(216) [0317] freely because of Christ, **provided** that we accept it by
AP : 15 :020(218) [0321] assemble, because they **provided** an example of how all
AP : 21 :043(235) [0357] They make no effort to **provide** a summary of the
AP : 23 :063(248) [0381] the many murders for which this law **provides** an excuse.
AP : 24 :007(250) [0385] to regulate this with the **provision** that each community
AP : 24 :035(256) [0397] as a daily sacrifice, **provided** this means the whole Mass,
AP : 24 :072(262) [0409] He **provides** food for those who fear him."
AP : 24 :087(265) [0413] ceremonies nor prayers **provide** an advantage *ex opere*
AP : 27 :021(272) [0427] poverty, and celibacy, **provided** they are not impure, are
AP : 27 :067(280) [0443] "If any one does not **provide** for his relatives, and
AP : 27 :068(280) [0443] that those who do not **provide** for their relatives have
S3 : 10 :001(314) [0497] us and our preachers, **provided** this could be done
SC : 02 :002(345) [0543] and property; that he **provides** me daily and abundantly
SC : 03 :013(347) [0547] Answer: To be sure, God **provides** daily bread, even to
SC : 09 :003(354) [0561] and drinking what they **provide**, for the laborer deserves
LC : 01 :116(381) [0615] word of our parents, **provided** that these, too, are
LC : 01 :126(382) [0617] pleasure of God ought to **provide** us sufficient reason and
LC : 01 :161(387) [0627] and to treat them well and make **provision** for them.
LC : 01 :165(387) [0627] how he will support you and **provide** for all your wants.
LC : 01 :168(388) [0629] their office, not only to **provide** for the material support
LC : 01 :173(388) [0629] God can **provide** for them and make them rich without
LC : 01 :208(393) [0639] that this estate might be **provided** for richly and
LC : 02 :014(412) [0681] makes all creation help **provide** the comforts and
LC : 02 :024(413) [0683] has abundantly **provided** for us in this life, and, further,
LC : 03 :072(430) [0719] land which produce and **provide** for us our daily bread
LC : 03 :074(430) [0719] through them does God **provide** us our daily bread and
LC : 03 :082(431) [0721] our needs and faithfully **provides** for our daily existence.
LC : 03 :083(431) [0721] Although he gives and **provides** these blessings
LC : 05 :022(449) [0757] as the very gift he has **provided** for me against my sins,
LC : 06 :006(457) [0000] For such people we shall **provide** no preaching, nor will
SD : 02 :050(530) [0901] and mercy, God **provides** for the public proclamation of
SD : 04 :034(557) [0949] before him, **provided** you continue in the faith"
SD : 08 :092(609) [1049] and wisdom can readily **provide** that through his divine
SD : 10 :019(614) [1059] us and our preachers, **provided** this could be done
SD : 11 :002(616) [1063] to the example it **provides**, it neither can nor should be

Providence (1), Providential (1)
AL : 18 :006(040) [0053] exists without the **providence** of God; indeed, it is from
AP : 04 :135(125) [0159] or truly believe in his **providential** care, but supposes that

Province (1), Provinces (3)
TR : 00 :012(322) [0507] is, those that were in the Roman **provinces** in the West.
TR : 00 :014(322) [0507] by us and in almost all **provinces**, namely, that for the
TR : 00 :014(322) [0507] bishops of the same **province** should assemble with the
TR : 00 :015(322) [0509] he asserts that it was observed in almost all **provinces**.

Proviso (1)
AP : 14 :001(214) [0315] With the **proviso** that we employ canonical ordination,

Provocative (1), Provoke (5), Provoked (2)
AP : 28 :025(285) [0451] give an account for the schism that has been **provoked**.
SC : 01 :008(343) [0541] and superiors, nor **provoke** them to anger, but honor,
SC : 09 :008(356) [0563] "Fathers, do not **provoke** your children to anger, lest they
LC : 01 :136(383) [0619] the other hand, if you **provoke** him to anger, he will send
LC : 03 :011(421) [0701] God so that we may not **provoke** his anger by such
LC : 06 :011(458) [0000] one, when a person has **provoked** another to anger and
SD : 04 :003(551) [0939] a very few asserted the **provocative** proposition or
SD : 10 :025(615) [1061] so that they do not **provoke** the wrath of God, violate

Prowling (1)
LC : 03 :106(434) [0727] we live in the flesh and have the devil **prowling** about us.

Prudent (3), Prudently (2)
AG : 2 3 :002(053) [0063] that Pope Pius, as a **prudent** and intelligent man, made
AL : 2 6 :017(066) [0073] such observances and **prudently** admonishes Januarius
AL : 2 7 :025(074) [0079] Roman pontiffs have **prudently** judged that leniency
AP : 2 2 :005(236) [0359] but we leave it to the **prudent** reader to decide what he
S 2 : 0 2 :006(293) [0463] of Masses, it would be **prudent** to do without the Mass

Pry (3)
LC : 0 1 :289(404) [0663] are busy wherever they can **pry** out and pounce on
SD : 0 8 :096(609) [1049] all Christians not to **pry** presumptuously into this mystery
SD : 1 1 :052(625) [1081] We are not to **pry** into these, nor are we to follow our

Psalmist (2)
AG : 2 5 :008(062) [0069] As the **psalmist** says, "Who can discern his errors?"
AP : 0 4 :058(115) [0137] Here the **psalmist** confesses his sins, but he does not lay

Psalms (10)
AP : 0 2 :043(106) [0117] to these things, as the **Psalms** and the prophets show.
AP : 0 4 :057(114) [0137] praised throughout the prophets and the **Psalms**.
AP : 0 4 :058(115) [0137] to mercy and faith in the **Psalms** and the prophets belong
AP : 0 4 :198(134) [0175] Many **Psalms** teach us this as they console us against the
AP : 1 2 :009(183) [0255] terrors described in the **Psalms** and the prophets and
AP : 1 2 :107(197) [0283] The **Psalms** mention confession from time to time; for
AP : 1 5 :040(220) [0325] When they chant the **Psalms**, it is not to learn or pray but
AP : 1 5 :040(220) [0325] The children chant the **Psalms** in order to learn; the
LC : P R :007(359) [0569] the Ten Commandments, the Creed, the **Psalms**, etc.
LC : S P :025(364) [0579] assign them also some **Psalms** and some hymns, based on

Psalter (3)
AP : 2 1 :035(234) [0353] one recited the whole **Psalter** every day while standing on
LC : P R :018(361) [0573] What is the whole **Psalter** but meditations and exercises
LC : 0 1 :325(409) [0675] teaches it throughout the **Psalter**, as when he says, "The

Public (93), Publicly (34)
PR : P R :016(008) [0013] Confession and **publicly** attested this with their hearts,
PR : P R :019(009) [0017] open writings and in **public** print have tried to palm them
PR : P R :019(009) [0017] to attest and affirm **publicly** that, then as now, it never
PR : P R :023(012) [0021] more to have witnessed **publicly** before God and all
AG : P R :015(026) [0041] empire, especially in a **public** instruction at the diet in
AG : P R :023(027) [0043] summons) as we herewith **publicly** witness and assert.
AG : 1 4 :000(036) [0049] us that nobody should **publicly** teach or preach or
AL : 1 4 :000(036) [0049] nobody should preach **publicly** in the church or
AG : 0 1 :002(056) [0065] have been made in the **public** ceremonies of the Mass,
AG : 2 4 :040(061) [0069] has been made in the **public** ceremonies of the Mass
AG : 2 5 :011(063) [0069] should expose yourself in **public** or should accuse
AL : 0 0 :006(049) [0059] maintenance of dignity in **public** worship and the
AL : 2 4 :006(056) [0065] and devotion of **public** worship, for none are admitted
AL : 2 4 :040(061) [0069] since the customary **public** ceremonies are for the most
AL : 2 5 :011(063) [0069] should expose yourself in **public** or should accuse
AL : 2 8 :029(085) [0087] to their subjects for the sake of maintaining **public** peace.
AL : 2 8 :056(090) [0091] sins by going out in **public** with her head uncovered,
AP : P R :001(098) [0099] After a **public** reading of our princes' Confession, a
AP : P R :018(099) [0103] good men have testified **publicly** and thanked God for
AP : 0 4 :210(136) [0179] our faith and we might **publicly** confess our faith and
AP : 0 7 :023(172) [0235] of the world, and of all **public** and private affairs.
AP : 1 2 :069(192) [0271] judgment, but like petty **public** officials they quietly
AP : 1 2 :112(198) [0285] are talking about the **public** rite of penitence, not about
AP : 1 2 :113(199) [0285] "satisfaction" is a relic from this rite of **public** penitence.
AP : 1 2 :113(199) [0285] unless they had given **public** evidence of their penitence,
AP : 1 2 :116(199) [0285] of satisfaction in **public** penitence were not necessary by
AP : 1 2 :120(200) [0287] did not notice that these **public** exhibitions had been
AP : 1 2 :164(208) [0303] about the mitigation of **public** and private punishments
AP : 1 2 :168(209) [0305] "satisfaction" from the **public** rite and use it to denote the
AP : 1 2 :171(209) [0305] was enough for the sort of **public** or formal penitence
AP : 1 2 :175(210) [0307] were the remission of **public** penitence so as not to burden
AP : 1 5 :025(219) [0323] the administration of **public** affairs, the administration of
AP : 1 5 :039(220) [0325] that in our churches the **public** liturgy is more decent than
AP : 1 5 :041(220) [0325] and examine the youth **publicly**, a custom that produces
AP : 1 5 :052(222) [0329] that the greatest possible **public** harmony, without offense
AP : 1 6 :001(222) [0329] might legitimately hold **public** office, render verdicts
AP : 1 6 :007(223) [0331] **Public** redress through a judge is not forbidden but
AP : 1 6 :007(223) [0331] Now the various kinds of **public** redress are court
AP : 1 6 :013(224) [0333] the Gospel permitted such **public** and private business.
AP : 2 1 :035(234) [0353] which are being taught in **public** on the highest authority.
AP : 2 1 :036(234) [0353] examples to men in their **public** or private life, as a means
AP : 2 1 :036(234) [0353] faith and as an incentive to imitate them in **public** affairs.
AP : 2 1 :036(234) [0353] The saints administered **public** affairs, underwent
AP : 2 1 :036(234) [0353] about faith or fear in the administration of **public** affairs.
AP : 2 1 :037(234) [0355] who know nothing about either faith or **public** affairs.
AP : 2 1 :041(235) [0355] Luther was not the first to complain about **public** abuses.
AP : 2 3 :002(239) [0363] were adorned by the **public** disgrace and the unnatural
AP : 2 3 :006(240) [0365] scandals, sins, and the corruption of **public** morals.
AP : 2 3 :023(242) [0369] remove those from the **public** ministry who married while
AP : 2 3 :027(243) [0371] were not carrying on their **public** ministry, and marital
AP : 2 3 :043(245) [0375] they are occupied with **public** service, which is often so
AP : 2 3 :049(246) [0377] of the body and for **public** morality), just as certain rites
AP : 2 3 :051(246) [0377] unjust, it is dangerous to **public** and private morals; this
AP : 2 3 :052(246) [0377] this law has been to **public** morals and how productive of
AP : 2 3 :055(247) [0379] This is the duty of **public** officials, who ought to maintain
AP : 2 3 :055(247) [0379] of public officials, who ought to maintain **public** order.
AP : 2 4 :006(250) [0385] catholic in our having only the **public** or common Mass.
AP : 2 4 :006(250) [0385] Masses but only one **public** Mass, and this only on
AP : 2 4 :006(250) [0385] The monasteries have **public**, though daily, Mass.
AP : 2 4 :042(257) [0399] which they put on in **public** as a money-making venture.
AP : 2 4 :080(264) [0411] It does not really mean a sacrifice but a **public** service.
AP : 2 4 :081(264) [0411] It is an old word, ordinarily used in **public** law.
AP : 2 4 :081(264) [0411] To the Greeks it meant "**public** duties," like the taxes
AP : 2 4 :081(264) [0411] completely taken up with **public** duties and immunities:
AP : 2 4 :081(264) [0411] have found an immunity and have avoided **public** duty."
AP : 2 4 :081(264) [0411] of children does not excuse parents from **public** duties."
AP : 2 4 :081(264) [0411] of the gymnasium, and similar **public** responsibilities.
AP : 2 4 :083(264) [0413] use of "liturgy" to mean **public** duties or ministrations.
AP : 2 4 :083(264) [0413] from *leita*, which means **public** goods; thus the verb
AP : 2 4 :083(264) [0413] the verb means to care for or to administer **public** goods.
AP : 2 7 :005(269) [0421] crowd that gorges itself on the **public** alms of the church.
AP : 2 7 :009(270) [0421] to be supported at **public** expense without the loss of
AP : 2 7 :014(271) [0425] of sins, opposed as they are to the customs of **public** life?
AP : 2 7 :064(280) [0441] and were supported from **public** funds, "They desire to
AP : 2 7 :067(280) [0441] being supported from **public** funds and thus lost the
AP : 2 8 :013(283) [0447] those who are guilty of **public** offenses or to absolve them
AP : 2 8 :022(284) [0451] on the basis of the **public** offenses and commotions which
S 1 : P R :002(288) [0455] should be presented **publicly** as the confession of our faith
S 1 : P R :006(289) [0457] doubted whether one ought to make good writings **public**.
LC : 0 1 :053(372) [0595] and honor, whether **publicly** in court or in the market or
LC : 0 1 :055(372) [0595] but also those who **publicly** slander the truth and God's
LC : 0 1 :084(376) [0605] to participate in **public** worship, that is, that they may
LC : 0 1 :094(378) [0607] in order that God's Word may exert its power **publicly**.
LC : 0 1 :201(392) [0637] commended, neither were **public** prostitution and
LC : 0 1 :217(394) [0643] rampant everywhere in **public** prostitution and other
LC : 0 1 :240(397) [0649] those who turn the free **public** market into a carrion-pit
LC : 0 1 :255(399) [0653] to live among men in **public** disgrace and contempt.
LC : 0 1 :257(399) [0653] pertains to **public** courts of justice, where a poor,
LC : 0 1 :265(400) [0657] reprove his neighbor **publicly**, even when he has seen a sin
LC : 0 1 :270(401) [0657] "Oh, I cannot prove it **publicly**; I might be called a liar
LC : 0 1 :270(401) [0657] unless these have first been taken away from him **publicly**.
LC : 0 1 :272(401) [0657] No one should **publicly** assert as truth what is not
LC : 0 1 :272(401) [0657] publicly assert as truth what is not **publicly** substantiated.
LC : 0 1 :280(403) [0661] the matter before the **public**, either before the civil or the
LC : 0 1 :284(403) [0661] But where the sin is so **public** that the judge and the
LC : 0 1 :284(403) [0661] himself, and you may testify **publicly** concerning him.
LC : 0 1 :284(403) [0661] his teaching, which is **publicly** set forth in books and
LC : 0 1 :284(403) [0661] Where the sin is **public**, the punishment ought to be
LC : 0 1 :284(403) [0661] punishment ought to be **public** so that everyone may
LC : 0 1 :295(404) [0665] power to dismiss his wife **publicly** by giving her a bill of
LC : 0 1 :308(406) [0669] The judge and the **public** may have to leave you in
LC : 0 3 :084(431) [0723] exploitation and usury in **public** business, trading, and
LC : 0 6 :010(458) [0000] and we may confess **publicly** in everyone's presence, no
LC : 0 6 :013(458) [0000] Besides this **public**, daily, and necessary confession, there
EP : 0 7 :009(483) [0811] but should be spoken **publicly**, as it is written, "the cup of
EP : 1 0 :006(493) [0831] and the sanctioning of **public** idolatry, as well as
EP : 1 0 :011(494) [0831] persecution and when a **public** confession is required, one
EP : 1 1 :001(494) [0831] No **public** dissension has developed among the
EP : 1 2 :026(500) [0843] congregation in which **public** expulsion and the orderly
EP : 1 2 :031(500) [0843] shall neither secretly nor **publicly** say or write anything
SD : P R :002(503) [0851] ourselves again to those **public** and well-known symbols
SD : P R :008(505) [0853] accepted and are used **publicly** in the churches, the
SD : P R :009(505) [0853] recognized these **publicly** and generally accepted
SD : P R :016(507) [0857] set forth as a certain and **public** testimony, not only to
SD : 0 2 :050(530) [0901] God provides for the **public** proclamation of his divine,
SD : 0 5 :004(558) [0953] our Lord, which in his **public** ministry on earth and in the
SD : 0 7 :105(588) [1009] churches in spite of our **public** and oft-repeated testimony
SD : 0 8 :003(592) [1017] to which we herewith **publicly** profess our adherence,
SD : 0 8 :004(592) [1017] to commit themselves **publicly** and explicitly to the
SD : 0 8 :065(604) [1039] place fully, mightily, and **publicly** before all the saints in
SD : 1 0 :013(613) [1057] Paul criticized them **publicly** because they had not been
SD : 1 0 :014(613) [1057] will forthwith **publicly** demand such matters of
SD : 1 1 :001(616) [1063] There has been no **public**, scandalous, and widespread
SD : 1 1 :095(632) [1095] of true doctrine or any **publicly** condemned errors.
SD : 1 2 :008(633) [1097] refrain from witnessing **publicly** before all Christendom
SD : 1 2 :034(635) [1101] a congregation in which **public** expulsion or orderly
SD : 1 2 :040(636) [1103] anything, privately or **publicly**, contrary to this

Publication (2), Publications (1), Publish (2), Published (8), Publishing (1)
PR : P R :000(001) [0004] Luther, Prepared for **Publication** by the Unanimous
PR : P R :002(003) [0007] of the empire, and **published** and proclaimed in all of
PR : P R :024(013) [0023] or postpone its printing and **publication** any longer.
AG : 2 3 :012(052) [0063] of Mayence who had **published** the new papal decree was
AL : 2 0 :002(041) [0053] Their **publications** on the Ten Commandments and
AL : 2 3 :012(052) [0063] Mayence, when about to **publish** the Roman pontiff's
AP : 1 2 :125(201) [0289] world evaluate the Confutation — if it is ever **published**?
AP : 2 4 :015(251) [0389] opponents have been **publishing** almost endless books
S 1 : P R :003(289) [0455] I have decided to **publish** these articles so that, if I should
LC : 0 2 :038(415) [0689] caused the Word to be **published** and proclaimed, in
SD : P R :006(504) [0853] was prepared and **published** in 1531 to set forth clearly
SD : P R :007(505) [0853] initially prepared and **published** for presentation, in the
SD : P R :008(505) [0853] them in his **published** works, since they have been
SD : P R :012(506) [0855] all were prepared and **published** before the dissensions

Puerilities (1)
S 2 : 0 4 :014(301) [0475] and countless other **puerilities**, fantasies, and follies

Pull (1)
LC : 0 1 :192(391) [0635] extend him my hand to **pull** him out and save him, and

Pulpit (1)
S 3 : 0 3 :013(305) [0483] the expression in the **pulpit** when the general confession

Punish (16), Punished (8), Punishes (9), Punishing (11)
AG : 1 6 :002(037) [0051] and other existing laws, **punish** evildoers with the sword,
AG : 2 3 :018(054) [0063] many places been swiftly **punished**, as if it were a great
AL : 2 4 :018(058) [0067] the world is being **punished** for such long continued
AP : 0 4 :036(112) [0131] bring itself to love a wrathful, judging, **punishing** God.
AP : 1 2 :091(196) [0279] a person who is sorry, **punishing** in himself what he is
AP : 1 2 :108(198) [0283] Thee to be justified in condemning and **punishing** us.
AP : 1 2 :108(198) [0283] to be unrighteous in **punishing** them or condemning those
AP : 1 2 :118(199) [0287] divine righteousness to **punish** sin, he commutes the
AP : 1 2 :131(202) [0291] does not produce outwardly the **punishing** of the flesh.
AP : 1 2 :136(203) [0293] command that souls should be **punished** in purgatory?
AP : 1 2 :148(205) [0299] Augustine says that "penitence is revenge **punishing**," etc.
AP : 1 2 :150(206) [0299] object that it is in accord with God's justice to **punish** sin.
AP : 1 2 :150(206) [0299] He is certainly **punishing** it when amid the terrors of
AP : 1 2 :155(207) [0301] Adam, and of David who was **punished** for his adultery.
TR : 0 0 :075(333) [0525] Not in **punishing** real offenses, but in dealing with
TR : 0 0 :075(333) [0525] be sure, they sometimes **punished** persons involved in
SC : P R :018(340) [0537] the Scriptures to show how God **punished** and blessed.
SC : 0 1 :022(344) [0543] Answer: God threatens to **punish** all who transgress these

Continued ▶

SC : 0 9 :005(355) [0561] as sent by him to **punish** those who do wrong and to
LC : 0 1 :037(369) [0591] he must strike and **punish** them so severely that he will
LC : 0 1 :077(375) [0603] richly reward it, even as he will terribly **punish** its misuse.
LC : 0 1 :095(378) [0607] commandment and will **punish** all who despise his Word
LC : 0 1 :123(382) [0617] God therefore **punishes** them so that they sink into all
LC : 0 1 :139(384) [0621] is so strict about **punishing** those who transgress it.
LC : 0 1 :154(386) [0625] So God **punishes** one knave by means of another.
LC : 0 1 :171(388) [0629] call us to account and **punish** us for its neglect, nor is it
LC : 0 1 :177(389) [0631] God terribly **punishes** the world; hence there is no longer
LC : 0 1 :181(389) [0631] his authority of **punishing** evil-doers to civil magistrates in
LC : 0 1 :231(396) [0647] thieves, and that he will **punish** them as they deserve.
LC : 0 1 :244(398) [0649] our business, God must **punish** us and teach us morals in
LC : 0 1 :245(398) [0649] steals from the other, he **punishes** one thief by means of
LC : 0 1 :257(399) [0653] and consequently **punished** in his body, property, or
LC : 0 1 :322(409) [0673] fearfully and terribly **punishing** all who despise and
LC : 0 3 :018(422) [0703] but will be angry and **punish** us if we do not pray, just as
LC : 0 3 :018(422) [0703] do not pray, just as he **punishes** all other kinds of
LC : 0 3 :092(432) [0723] to regard our sins and **punish** us as we daily deserve, but
SD : 0 5 :021(562) [0959] that God wills not to **punish** sins but to forgive them for
SD : 1 1 :006(617) [1065] and when and how he will interfere with it and **punish** it.
SD : 1 1 :035(622) [1075] Yet God himself **punishes** men for such wickedness when
SD : 1 1 :058(626) [1081] when God so severely **punishes** a land or a people for
SD : 1 1 :061(626) [1083] done to those who are **punished** and receive their "wages
SD : 1 1 :083(630) [1091] diligently that God **punishes** sin with sin, that is, because
SD : 1 1 :083(630) [1091] and deliberate sins God **punishes** with obduracy and
SD : 1 1 :083(630) [1091] second, that he would **punish** those who deliberately turn

Punishment (90), Punishments (60)

AG : 1 7 :003(038) [0051] men and the devil to hell and eternal **punishment**.
AL : 1 6 :002(037) [0051] laws, to award just **punishments**, to engage in just wars,
AL : 1 7 :004(038) [0051] will be an end to the **punishments** of condemned men and
AL : 2 3 :018(054) [0063] which deserve the **punishments** of just magistrates, yet it
AP : 0 4 :034(112) [0131] or in the midst of **punishment** it flees and hates his
AP : 0 4 :106(122) [0153] But to those who fear **punishment** grace is hidden;
AP : 0 4 :179(131) [0171] but by undergoing the **punishment** of sin and becoming a
AP : 0 4 :210(136) [0179] burden of guilt and **punishment** in those for whom it is
AP : 0 4 :267(147) [0197] about remission of **punishment** alone, because it is vain to
AP : 0 4 :267(147) [0197] to seek remission of **punishment** unless the heart first
AP : 0 4 :268(147) [0197] only to remission of **punishment**, this text proves nothing
AP : 0 4 :268(147) [0197] we readily admit, the **punishments** that chasten us are
AP : 0 4 :270(147) [0197] the judgment and **punishment** of the law, "for the law
AP : 0 4 :278(149) [0199] blessings, lighten our **punishments**, and merit a defense
AP : 0 4 :364(163) [0219] hear the mention of **punishments** and rewards in one
AP : 0 4 :365(163) [0219] proclamation of rewards and **punishments** is necessary.
AP : 0 4 :365(163) [0219] the proclamation of **punishments** the wrath of God is
AP : 1 2 :007(183) [0255] but only changes eternal **punishments** into temporal ones.
AP : 1 2 :007(183) [0255] life and of the Spirit, but only of wrath and **punishment**.
AP : 1 2 :008(183) [0255] that Judas did not love God but feared the **punishments**.
AP : 1 2 :009(183) [0255] away from eternal **punishments** — especially in those
AP : 1 2 :013(184) [0257] imagine that eternal **punishments** are changed into the
AP : 1 2 :013(184) [0257] are changed into the **punishments** of purgatory, that of
AP : 1 2 :022(185) [0257] eternal to temporal **punishments**, to impose certain
AP : 1 2 :024(185) [0257] to redeem the **punishment** of purgatory, or they profit as
AP : 1 2 :027(185) [0259] not only the canonical **punishment** but also the guilt
AP : 1 2 :029(185) [0259] we love God and when because we fear **punishment**.
AP : 1 2 :055(189) [0267] Even when **punishment** is still added afterwards, this
AP : 1 2 :055(189) [0267] added afterwards, this **punishment** does not merit the
AP : 1 2 :055(189) [0267] We shall discuss this form of **punishment** later.
AP : 1 2 :056(189) [0267] A **punishment** is also added here, but it does not merit
AP : 1 2 :057(189) [0267] Nor are special **punishments** always added, but contrition
AP : 1 2 :058(190) [0267] Worthy fruits as well as **punishments** follow regeneration
AP : 1 2 :060(190) [0267] that God exists, that **punishments** hang over the wicked,
AP : 1 2 :118(199) [0287] to the redemption of purgatorial and other **punishments**.
AP : 1 2 :118(199) [0287] commutes the eternal **punishment** to a temporal
AP : 1 2 :118(199) [0287] the eternal punishment to a temporal **punishment**.
AP : 1 2 :118(199) [0287] part of this temporal **punishment** is forgiven by the power
AP : 1 2 :118(199) [0287] understand which **punishments** are partly forgiven by the
AP : 1 2 :118(199) [0287] say that part of the **punishments** of purgatory is forgiven;
AP : 1 2 :118(200) [0287] would only be **punishments** redeeming from purgatory.
AP : 1 2 :123(200) [0289] Therefore the **punishments** of purgatory compensate for
AP : 1 2 :123(200) [0289] for eternal **punishments**; therefore the keys have the
AP : 1 2 :123(200) [0289] to remit part of the **punishments** of purgatory; therefore
AP : 1 2 :123(200) [0289] satisfactions buy off the **punishments** of purgatory.
AP : 1 2 :132(202) [0293] as a payment for the **punishments** of purgatory or other
AP : 1 2 :132(202) [0293] of purgatory or other **punishments** even when they come
AP : 1 2 :137(203) [0293] which make satisfaction for **punishment**, if not for guilt.
AP : 1 2 :138(203) [0293] for eternal **punishments**; it is rash for them to say,
AP : 1 2 :138(203) [0293] canonical satisfactions compensate for these **punishments**.
AP : 1 2 :138(203) [0293] to commute certain **punishments** or to remit part of the
AP : 1 2 :138(203) [0293] certain punishments or to remit part of the **punishments**.
AP : 1 2 :139(203) [0295] remitting part of the **punishments** referred to canonical
AP : 1 2 :139(203) [0295] works like the **punishments** of purgatory or canonical
AP : 1 2 :139(203) [0295] can remit eternal **punishments**, or that the power of the
AP : 1 2 :147(205) [0297] either guilt or eternal **punishment** or the penalties of
AP : 1 2 :148(205) [0297] object that revenge or **punishment** is necessary for
AP : 1 2 :148(205) [0299] grant that revenge or **punishment** is necessary for
AP : 1 2 :148(205) [0299] that penitence is so called because it holds **punishment**.
AP : 1 2 :148(205) [0299] But what **punishment** and revenge is Augustine
AP : 1 2 :148(205) [0299] Certainly true **punishment** and revenge, that is, contrition
AP : 1 2 :149(205) [0299] are more genuine **punishments** than are real terrors in the
AP : 1 2 :149(205) [0299] to apply the term "**punishments**" to those vain
AP : 1 2 :150(206) [0299] This certainly speaks of the most bitter **punishments**.
AP : 1 2 :150(206) [0299] is a more genuine **punishment** than is satisfaction.
AP : 1 2 :151(206) [0299] As a rule, these troubles are **punishments** for sin.
AP : 1 2 :153(206) [0299] of wrath, is a real **punishment** as long as it is present;
AP : 1 2 :153(206) [0299] this sense of wrath death is actually no **punishment** at all.
AP : 1 2 :154(206) [0299] do not apply to these **punishments** because our
AP : 1 2 :154(206) [0301] that the power of the keys remits part of the **punishment**.
AP : 1 2 :155(207) [0301] must be temporal **punishments** corresponding to
AP : 1 2 :156(207) [0301] where the particular **punishment** fits the particular crime.
AP : 1 2 :158(207) [0301] afflictions are not always **punishments** or signs of wrath.
AP : 1 2 :158(207) [0301] see only God's **punishment** and wrath, they should not
AP : 1 2 :161(208) [0303] Gregory interprets the **punishment** of David when he
AP : 1 2 :162(208) [0303] even those in mortal sin can buy off their **punishments**.
AP : 1 2 :164(208) [0303] of public and private **punishments** and calamities, as Isa.
AP : 1 2 :167(209) [0305] for the remission either of the guilt or of the **punishment**.
AP : 1 2 :167(209) [0305] a payment for eternal **punishment**, or a satisfaction, but
AP : 1 2 :168(209) [0305] not to pay for eternal **punishments** but to keep the flesh
AP : 1 2 :172(209) [0305] works be done to compensate for **punishment**.
AP : 1 2 :173(209) [0305] us to buy off **punishment** by such works, then they would
AP : 1 2 :174(210) [0307] not to buy off eternal **punishment** but to keep from
AP : 1 2 :174(210) [0307] the penalties of purgatory can remit eternal **punishments**.
AP : 1 6 :001(222) [0329] laws, prescribe legal **punishments**, engage in just wars,
AP : 1 6 :005(223) [0331] not only from fear of **punishment** but also "for the sake
AP : 1 6 :007(223) [0331] are court decisions, **punishments**, wars, military service.
AP : 2 0 :009(228) [0341] terrors, tortures, and **punishments** to try to drive you
AP : 2 2 :010(237) [0361] The story describes Eli's **punishment**.
AP : 2 2 :010(237) [0361] laity has been kept from the one kind as a **punishment**?
AP : 2 2 :010(238) [0361] laity has been kept from the one kind as a **punishment**.
AP : 2 3 :003(239) [0363] innocent men to cruel **punishments**, slaughter priests
AP : 2 4 :009(251) [0387] of venial or mortal sins, of guilt, or of **punishment**.
AP : 2 4 :011(251) [0387] forgiveness of sins or of **punishment** *ex opere operato.*
AP : 2 4 :013(251) [0387] remission of guilt and **punishment**, secure whatever they
AP : 2 4 :019(252) [0389] for guilt and **punishment** that reconciles God or placates
AP : 2 4 :063(261) [0405] of sins, guilt, and **punishment** for those to whom it is
AP : 2 4 :064(261) [0407] souls from purgatorial **punishment** by the application of
AP : 2 4 :066(261) [0407] of sins, of guilt, and of **punishment** for those to whom it
AP : 2 4 :092(266) [0415] a satisfaction for either **punishment** or guilt, *ex opere*
AP : 2 4 :096(267) [0417] of guilt and **punishment** even for the wicked to whom it is
AP : 2 4 :098(268) [0417] the forgiveness of guilt and **punishment** for the wicked.
AP : 2 8 :004(281) [0445] men with horrible **punishments** unless they act in clear
S3 : 0 2 :001(303) [0479] by threats and fear of **punishment** and by the promise and
S3 : 0 2 :002(303) [0479] are not restrained by **punishment**, they act against the law
S3 : 0 9 :000(314) [0497] not mingle civil **punishments** with this spiritual penalty or
TR : 0 0 :049(328) [0519] defends these errors with savage cruelty and **punishment**.
TR : 0 0 :051(329) [0519] more harm than all the **punishments**, for when proper
SC : P R :004(338) [0533] May you escape **punishment** for this!
SC : P R :020(340) [0537] God will inflict awful **punishments** on them for these
SC : 0 3 :016(347) [0549] deserve nothing but **punishment**, we nevertheless pray
LC : 0 1 :038(369) [0591] mend their ways before **punishment** descends, they
LC : 0 1 :061(373) [0597] up not merely with **punishment** but in the reverence and
LC : 0 1 :067(373) [0599] a dispute swears falsely, he will not escape **punishment**.
LC : 0 1 :069(374) [0599] threat, restraint and **punishment**, children be trained in
LC : 0 1 :069(374) [0601] men whom no teaching or **punishment** can help.
LC : 0 1 :069(374) [0601] is God's wrath and **punishment** upon such willful
LC : 0 1 :137(384) [0619] consequently, by the **punishment** of God they bring upon
LC : 0 1 :155(386) [0625] have roundly deserved **punishment** and that we are not
LC : 0 1 :182(389) [0631] Anger, reproof, and **punishment** are the prerogatives of
LC : 0 1 :231(396) [0647] must bear disgrace and **punishment** so as to make the
LC : 0 1 :234(397) [0647] but he will not escape God's wrath and **punishment**.
LC : 0 1 :248(398) [0651] lest his wrath and **punishment** come upon them too.
LC : 0 1 :258(399) [0653] oppressed, loses his case, and suffers **punishment**.
LC : 0 1 :266(401) [0657] to administer **punishment** by virtue of your office.
LC : 0 1 :274(402) [0659] he has reserved to himself the right of **punishment**.
LC : 0 1 :284(403) [0661] the sin is public, the **punishment** ought to be public so
LC : 0 1 :333(410) [0677] his greatest wrath and **punishment**, while at the same time
EP : 0 4 :012(477) [0799] not from a fear of **punishment**, like a slave, but out of a
EP : 0 6 :004(480) [0807] law, but also by its **punishments** and plagues, to follow
EP : 0 6 :005(480) [0807] under the coercion of **punishments** and the threat of
EP : 1 2 :016(499) [0841] conscience inflict capital **punishment** upon criminals.
SD : 0 1 :013(511) [0863] 4. The **punishment** and penalty of original sin which God
SD : 0 1 :027(513) [0867] man lost the concreated righteousness as a **punishment**.
SD : 0 3 :017(542) [0921] and from the eternal **punishment** of these sins on account
SD : 0 4 :003(551) [0939] extorted by fear and **punishment** of the law but flow from
SD : 0 4 :032(556) [0947] threats and earnest **punishments** and admonitions: "Do
SD : 0 5 :017(561) [0957] with God's wrath and temporal and eternal **punishment**.
SD : 0 5 :020(561) [0959] to temporal miseries, and to the **punishment** of hell-fire.
SD : 0 5 :020(561) [0959] death and all the **punishments** of sin, and are saved
SD : 0 5 :027(563) [0961] the law, a proclamation of repentance and **punishment**.
SD : 0 6 :009(565) [0965] but frequently the **punishment** of the law as well, to egg
SD : 0 6 :016(566) [0967] from fear of **punishment** or in hope of reward, he is still
SD : 0 6 :024(568) [0969] also with the club of **punishments** and miseries, until the
SD : 0 6 :024(568) [0971] law or its threats and **punishments**, just as he will no
SD : 0 7 :068(582) [0997] temporal and eternal **punishments**) and profane the body
SD : 1 1 :058(625) [1081] indeed a well deserved **punishment** for sin when God so
SD : 1 1 :058(626) [1081] of his Word that the **punishment** extends also to their
SD : 1 1 :081(629) [1089] sin, nor is he the cause of the **punishment**, the damnation.
SD : 1 1 :085(630) [1091] was admonished was a **punishment** for his preceding sin

Pupil (1), Pupils (4)

LC : P R :008(359) [0569] must remain a child and **pupil** of the Catechism, and I do
LC : P R :016(361) [0573] have always remained **pupils**, and must continue to do
LC : 0 1 :023(367) [0587] is a little too subtle to be understood by young **pupils**.
LC : 0 2 :012(412) [0681] But for young **pupils** it is enough to indicate the most
LC : 0 3 :007(421) [0699] for young children, **pupils**, and simple folk; while it may

Puppet (1)

AP : 2 1 :034(234) [0353] was manipulated like a **puppet** so that it seemed to nod

Purchase (1), Purchased (2), Purchasing (1)

AP : 0 4 :260(145) [0195] that by our works we **purchase** the forgiveness of sins.
LC : 0 1 :303(406) [0667] as illegally acquired, but rather as honestly **purchased**.
LC : 0 2 :037(415) [0687] obtains dominion by **purchasing** us through his birth,
EP : 0 8 :014(488) [0821] in Acts 20:28, We are **purchased** with God's own blood.

Pure (128), Purely (18), Purer (2)

PR : P R :002(003) [0007] mankind has permitted the **pure**, unalloyed, and
PR : P R :004(004) [0007] thereby adulterate the **pure** doctrine of God's Word, sever
PR : P R :004(004) [0009] from an understanding of **pure** evangelical doctrine, and
PR : P R :005(004) [0009] had planted the **pure**, unadulterated Word of God, so
PR : P R :008(005) [0011] thereby the adversaries of **pure** evangelical doctrine would
PR : P R :014(007) [0013] thereunder and that a **pure** declaration of the truth might
PR : P R :018(008) [0015] in accordance with the **pure**, infallible, and unalterable
PR : P R :023(012) [0021] therein, so that the **pure** teaching and confession of the
PR : P R :024(013) [0021] in God's Word so that **pure** doctrine can be recognized
PR : P R :024(013) [0021] to any certain formula of **pure** doctrine, to start

Continued ▶

AG : 07 :002(032) [0047] in conformity with a **pure** understanding of it and that
AG : 00 :001(047) [0059] that which agrees with the **pure** Word of God and
AL : 07 :001(032) [0047] the Gospel is taught **purely** and the sacraments are
AL : 28 :070(093) [0093] that he will not teach the **pure** doctrine of the Gospel.
AL : 28 :077(094) [0095] the Gospel to be taught **purely** and that they relax some
AP : 02 :027(104) [0113] Consequently it is not a **pure** privation, but also a
AP : 02 :044(106) [0117] ideas did not remain **purely** academic, but moved out
AP : 04 :204(135) [0177] despair because they cannot find works **pure** enough.
AP : 04 :245(142) [0189] is love that issues from a **pure** heart and a good
AP : 04 :327(158) [0211] 'I have made my heart clean, I am **pure** from my sin?"
AP : 04 :391(167) [0225] can love God above all things by **purely** natural powers.
AP : 07 :005(169) [0227] has outward marks, the **pure** teaching of the Gospel and
AP : 07 :020(171) [0233] And we add its marks, the **pure** teaching of the Gospel
AP : 07 :020(171) [0233] for it retains the **pure** Gospel and what Paul calls
AP : 09 :001(178) [0245] Among us, the Gospel is taught **purely** and diligently.
AP : 23 :026(243) [0371] celibacy because it is **pure**, as though marriage were
AP : 23 :028(243) [0371] for believers marriage is **pure** because it has been
AP : 23 :033(244) [0373] then marriages are **pure** since they are approved by the
AP : 23 :034(244) [0373] things (Tit. 1:15), "To the **pure** all things are pure," that
AP : 23 :034(244) [0373] "To the pure all things are **pure**," that is, to believers in
AP : 23 :034(244) [0373] therefore, so marriage is **pure** in the godly, through the
AP : 23 :035(244) [0373] Therefore celibacy is not necessarily **pure**.
AP : 23 :041(245) [0375] Paul says (Titus 1:15), "To the **pure** all things are pure."
AP : 23 :041(245) [0375] Paul says (Titus 1:15), "To the pure all things are **pure**."
AP : 23 :046(246) [0377] that through such hypocrisy they are **pure** and righteous.
AP : 23 :064(248) [0381] is that priests should be **pure**, according to the statement
AP : 23 :064(248) [0381] faith virginity is not **pure** in the sight of God, and that
AP : 23 :064(248) [0381] of faith marriage is **pure**, according to the statement
AP : 23 :064(248) [0381] statement (Titus 1:15), "To the **pure** all things are pure."
AP : 23 :064(248) [0381] statement (Titus 1:15), "To the pure all things are **pure**."
AP : 23 :064(248) [0381] were polygamists, was **purer** and less inflamed with lust
AP : 23 :066(248) [0381] Finally, since marriage is **pure**, it is right to say that those
AP : 23 :066(248) [0381] continent in celibacy should marry in order to be **pure**.
AP : 23 :066(248) [0381] requires impure celibates to become **pure** husbands.
AP : 24 :030(255) [0395] there should be a new and **pure** sacrifice; this is faith,
AP : 24 :031(255) [0395] place incense is offered to my name, and a **pure** offering."
AP : 24 :032(255) [0395] Therefore "incense" and "a **pure** offering" do not refer to
AP : 27 :016(271) [0425] Gerson indicates how **pure** this is in most of those who
S1 : PR :010(290) [0457] and supplied with the **pure** Word and the right use of the
S1 : 01 :000(292) [0461] of man, and was born of the **pure**, holy, and virgin Mary.
S2 : 02 :002(293) [0463] "1. After all, they are a **purely** human invention.
S2 : 04 :003(298) [0471] have been and still are **purely** diabolical transactions and
S3 : 03 :018(306) [0483] cases like this, such repentance surely was **pure** hypocrisy.
S3 : 03 :019(306) [0483] a sufficiently complete or a sufficiently **pure** confession.
S3 : 03 :040(309) [0489] remain and enables man to become truly **pure** and holy.
S3 : 13 :002(315) [0499] and holy through the **pure** grace and mercy which have
SC : 01 :012(343) [0541] should lead a chaste and **pure** life in word and deed, each
SC : 02 :002(345) [0543] All this he does out of his **pure**, fatherly, and divine
SC : 03 :005(346) [0547] God is taught clearly and **purely** and we, as children of
LC : 01 :121(382) [0615] be led astray from the **pure** Word of God to the lying
LC : 01 :212(394) [0641] too, God's grace is still required to keep the heart **pure**.
LC : 01 :310(407) [0669] he wants our hearts to be **pure**, even though as long as we
LC : 01 :328(410) [0677] and whenever you can, **purely** out of love to God and in
LC : 02 :017(412) [0681] All this he does out of **pure** love and goodness, without
LC : 02 :051(417) [0691] flock or community of **pure** saints under one head,
LC : 02 :058(418) [0693] Now we are only halfway **pure** and holy.
LC : 02 :058(418) [0693] that life are only perfectly **pure** and holy people, full of
LC : 02 :068(420) [0697] But the Creed brings **pure** grace and makes us upright
LC : 03 :047(426) [0711] persecute our Gospel and **pure** doctrine and try to
LC : 03 :096(433) [0725] it altogether freely, out of **pure** grace, because he has
LC : 05 :055(453) [0767] to become so perfectly **pure** that God might not find the
LC : 05 :057(453) [0767] your eye on how good and **pure** you are, to work toward
LC : 05 :061(453) [0767] do we come to confession **pure** and without sin; on the
LC : 05 :068(454) [0769] we should flee, but as a **pure**, wholesome, soothing
LC : 05 :073(455) [0771] to come to the sacrament **purely** and worthily, you must
LC : 05 :074(455) [0771] the judgment, "If you are **pure** and upright, you have no
LC : 06 :002(457) [0000] of sin that no one was able to confess **purely** enough.
LC : 06 :016(459) [0000] only concerned whether we had confessed **purely** enough.
LC : 06 :017(459) [0000] of confessing so **purely** (which was impossible), and
EP : 00 :000(463) [0775] A Thorough, **Pure**, Correct, and Final Restatement and
EP : 01 :001(466) [0779] *The **Pure** Doctrine, Faith, and Confession according to*
EP : 01 :002(466) [0779] when God created man **pure** and holy and without sin,
EP : 01 :013(467) [0783] things its natural powers remained wholly good and **pure**.
EP : 02 :001(470) [0787] *The **Pure** Teaching concerning this Article on the Basis of*
EP : 03 :002(473) [0793] *The **Pure** Doctrine of the Christian Church Against Both*
EP : 03 :004(473) [0793] God forgives us our sins **purely** by his grace, without any
EP : 03 :010(474) [0795] if we would preserve the **pure** doctrine concerning the
EP : 04 :004(476) [0797] *The **Pure** Doctrine of the Christian Church in this*
EP : 05 :001(478) [0801] *The **Pure** Doctrine of God's Word*
EP : 07 :005(482) [0809] *Confession of the **Pure** Doctrine of the Holy Supper*
EP : 08 :003(487) [0819] *The **Pure** Teaching of the Christian Church concerning*
EP : 11 :001(494) [0831] ***Pure** and True Doctrine concerning this Article*
EP : 11 :013(496) [0835] to eternal life out of **pure** grace in Christ without any
EP : 11 :015(496) [0835] because he out of **pure** grace alone, without any merit of
EP : 11 :022(497) [0837] have not only set forth the **pure** doctrine but have also
SD : 00 :000(501) [0845] A General, **Pure**, Correct, and Definitive Restatement
SD : PR :003(501) [0847] who had then accepted the **pure** doctrine of the holy
SD : PR :004(502) [0847] abide by the plain, clear, and **pure** meaning of its words.
SD : PR :008(502) [0849] will ultimately lead to the ruin of the **pure** doctrine.
SD : PR :008(502) [0849] some will doubt if the **pure** doctrine can coexist among us
SD : PR :001(503) [0851] by the churches of the **pure** Christian religion is drawn
SD : PR :002(503) [0851] faithful to the **pure** doctrine of the Word of God as Dr.
SD : PR :003(503) [0851] New Testaments as the **pure** and clear fountain of Israel,
SD : PR :009(505) [0853] The **pure** churches and schools have everywhere
SD : PR :010(506) [0855] other good, useful, and **pure** books, such as
SD : PR :013(506) [0855] who remained steadfastly in the **pure** doctrine.
SD : PR :014(506) [0855] In order to preserve the **pure** doctrine and to maintain a
SD : 01 :020(511) [0865] matters it is good, **pure**, and in its natural powers perfect.
SD : 01 :026(512) [0867] created perfect and **pure**, and that afterward Satan
SD : 01 :027(512) [0867] was originally created **pure**, good, and holy, sin did not
SD : 01 :028(513) [0867] is not at first created **pure** and holy and is corrupted only
SD : 01 :029(513) [0867] man's nature is allegedly **pure**, holy, righteous, and
SD : 01 :056(518) [0877] dependable teacher of our **pure** Evangelical churches.
SD : 01 :060(519) [0879] nature that nothing **pure** nor good has remained in itself
SD : 01 :062(519) [0879] deeply that nothing in it remained **pure** and uncorrupted.
SD : 02 :005(520) [0881] both of these parties the **pure** teachers of the Augsburg
SD : 02 :005(521) [0881] is preached and heard, **purely** out of grace and without
SD : 02 :022(525) [0889] out of particular and **pure** grace, that our poor, fallen,
SD : 02 :022(525) [0889] against God — but out of **pure** grace through the gracious
SD : 02 :034(528) [0895] sin and operates to make man truly **pure** and holy."
SD : 02 :055(532) [0903] Word of God is preached, **pure** and unalloyed according
SD : 02 :089(538) [0915] that man behaves in a **purely** passive way in his
SD : 03 :004(540) [0917] alone, is reckoned by **pure** grace to all true believers as
SD : 03 :005(540) [0917] enumeration of those who contradict the **pure** doctrine.
SD : 03 :006(540) [0917] this single article remains **pure**, Christendom will remain
SD : 03 :006(540) [0917] Christendom will remain **pure**, in beautiful harmony, and
SD : 03 :006(540) [0917] where it does not remain **pure**, it is impossible to repel
SD : 03 :024(543) [0923] justification is to remain **pure**, we must give especially
SD : 03 :028(544) [0925] is never wholly **pure** and perfect on account of our
SD : 03 :030(544) [0925] is bestowed upon us by **pure** grace because of the unique
SD : 04 :023(555) [0945] own advantage against the **pure** doctrine of salvation by
SD : 05 :001(558) [0951] when it is preached **purely** and without admixture, for by
SD : 05 :025(563) [0961] God's children, and out of **pure** grace, without any merit
SD : 06 :021(567) [0969] that their works and life are perfectly **pure** and holy.
SD : 06 :022(567) [0969] demands a perfect and **pure** obedience if it is to please
SD : 07 :058(580) [0993] like Luther and other **pure** teachers of the Augsburg
SD : 07 :069(582) [0997] a stronger and more cheerful faith and a **purer** obedience.
SD : 08 :063(603) [1037] direction in order to cast suspicion on the **pure** doctrine.
SD : 08 :096(609) [1049] as being contrary to the **pure** Word of God, the writings
SD : 10 :003(611) [1053] methods to suppress the **pure** doctrine and gradually to
SD : 10 :005(611) [1053] and an apostasy from the **pure** doctrine of the Gospel and
SD : 10 :010(612) [1055] God desire to suppress the **pure** doctrine of the holy
SD : 10 :014(613) [1057] and to suppress the **pure** doctrine and Christian liberty,
SD : 11 :043(623) [1077] our works and merit, **purely** by grace and solely for
SD : 11 :060(626) [1083] and praise God's **pure** and unmerited grace toward the
SD : 11 :061(626) [1083] them, God commends his **pure** and unmerited grace and
SD : 11 :062(626) [1083] there is help for you is **pure** grace on my part"
SD : 12 :008(633) [1097] at those times where the **pure** Word of the holy Gospel

Purgatorial (3), Purgatory (39)

AP : 12 :013(184) [0257] the punishments of **purgatory**, that of these one part is
AP : 12 :015(184) [0257] As they buy off **purgatory** with satisfactions, so later on a
AP : 12 :024(185) [0257] the punishment of **purgatory**, or they profit as a payment
AP : 12 :026(185) [0259] through indulgences, souls are delivered from **purgatory**.
AP : 12 :118(199) [0287] to the redemption of **purgatorial** and other punishments.
AP : 12 :118(199) [0287] of the punishments of **purgatory** is forgiven; in that case
AP : 12 :118(200) [0287] would only be punishments redeeming from **purgatory**.
AP : 12 :123(200) [0289] the punishments of **purgatory** compensate for eternal
AP : 12 :123(200) [0289] of the punishments of **purgatory**; therefore satisfactions
AP : 12 :123(200) [0289] satisfactions buy off the punishments of **purgatory**.
AP : 12 :132(202) [0293] for the punishments of **purgatory** or other punishments
AP : 12 :134(203) [0293] not sin but will have to pay the penalties in **purgatory**.
AP : 12 :136(203) [0293] If the penalties of **purgatory** are satisfactions, or rather
AP : 12 :136(203) [0293] from the penalties of **purgatory**, do these passages
AP : 12 :136(203) [0293] command that souls should be punished in **purgatory**?
AP : 12 :136(203) [0293] will mean "Suffer the penalties of **purgatory** after this life.
AP : 12 :139(203) [0295] like the punishments of **purgatory** or canonical
AP : 12 :147(205) [0297] guilt or eternal punishment or the penalties of **purgatory**.
AP : 12 :154(207) [0301] do they add that we must make satisfaction in **purgatory**?
AP : 12 :156(207) [0301] is a special penalty in **purgatory**, where the particular
AP : 12 :167(209) [0305] By their references to **purgatory** in this connection they
AP : 12 :174(210) [0307] and the penalties of **purgatory** can remit eternal
AP : 12 :175(210) [0307] misinterpreted as a liberation of souls from **purgatory**.
AP : 24 :064(261) [0407] and free souls from **purgatorial** punishment by the
AP : 24 :089(266) [0415] Therefore the penalty of **purgatory** cannot be overcome
AP : 24 :090(266) [0415] our opponents have for **purgatory**, the sort of penalties
AP : 24 :090(266) [0415] penalties they suppose **purgatory** has, the reasons they
S2 : 02 :001(293) [0463] this life and yonder in **purgatory**, although in reality this
S2 : 02 :012(294) [0465] The first is **purgatory**.
S2 : 02 :012(295) [0465] Consequently **purgatory** and all the pomp, services, and
S2 : 02 :012(295) [0465] of the devil, for **purgatory**, too, is contrary to the
S2 : 02 :013(295) [0465] Fathers who are said to have written about **purgatory**.
S2 : 02 :013(295) [0467] not write that there is a **purgatory**, nor does he cite any
S2 : 02 :013(295) [0467] whether or not there is a **purgatory** and merely mentions
S2 : 02 :014(295) [0467] in Masses which are offered for souls in **purgatory**, etc.
S2 : 02 :014(295) [0467] their traffic in **purgatorial** Masses (which St. Augustine
S2 : 04 :014(301) [0475] his lies about Masses, **purgatory**, monastic life, and
S3 : 03 :021(306) [0485] that was still lacking man was referred to **purgatory**.
S3 : 03 :022(306) [0485] would never get out of **purgatory** because, according to
S3 : 03 :026(307) [0485] forced their way into **purgatory**, first by instituting
S3 : 03 :027(307) [0487] knew which soul was in **purgatory**, and nobody knew
S3 : 03 :027(307) [0487] knew which of those in **purgatory** had truly repented and

Purged (3), Purging (1)

AP : 12 :046(188) [0263] because in these troubles our natural lust is **purged** away.
LC : 04 :065(445) [0749] at it incessantly, always **purging** out whatever pertains to
LC : 06 :001(457) [0000] it should be voluntary and **purged** of the pope's tyranny.
SD : 01 :003(509) [0859] the Word of God and is **purged** of all Pelagian and

Purify (7), Purifications (1), Purified (4), Purifies (4)

AG : 03 :004(030) [0045] Spirit he may sanctify, **purify**, strengthen, and comfort
AL : 26 :022(067) [0073] a relationship with the **purifications** of the law, and he
AP : 04 :284(150) [0201] Yet Peter says (Acts 15:9) that hearts are **purified** by faith.
AP : 07 :007(169) [0229] saying that it should be **purified** in order to be holy.
AP : 12 :122(200) [0289] from all iniquity and to **purify** himself a people of his own
AP : 23 :064(248) [0381] statement (Isa. 52:11), "**Purify** yourselves, you who bear
AP : 23 :064(248) [0381] Isaiah's words, "**Purify** yourselves, you who bear the
AP : 23 :066(248) [0381] Thus the same law, "**Purify** yourselves, you who bear the
AP : 24 :034(256) [0395] "And he will **purify** the sons of Levi and refine them
TR : 00 :055(329) [0521] how can the church be **purified** as long as the pope does
SD : PR :001(501) [0847] of the Word of God and **purified** by Dr. Luther, of
SD : 01 :045(516) [0873] cleanses man from sin, **purifies** him, and sanctifies him
SD : 02 :034(528) [0895] This gift **purifies** us and daily sweeps out the remaining
SD : 02 :035(528) [0895] of the Holy Spirit, who **purifies** and daily makes man
SD : 11 :082(630) [1089] he writes, "If any one **purifies** himself from what is
SD : 11 :082(630) [1089] He who is to **purify** himself must beforehand have been

Purity (18)
AG : 0 7 :001(032) [0047] Gospel is preached in its **purity** and the holy sacraments
AG : 2 8 :062(092) [0093] no longer taught and preached with clarity and **purity**.
AP : 0 4 :086(119) [0147] on account of their own **purity** but by mercy on account
AP : 0 4 :178(131) [0171] Far above our **purity**—yes, far above the law itself—
AP : 0 4 :326(158) [0211] persecutors of God's Word, not of his personal **purity**.
AP : 2 3 :016(241) [0369] marriage is more necessary now than in the state of **purity**
AP : 2 3 :033(244) [0373] If **purity** means that something has God's permission and
AP : 2 3 :035(244) [0373] is between lust and **purity** understood as the purity of the
AP : 2 3 :035(244) [0373] purity understood as the **purity** of the heart and the
AP : 2 3 :035(244) [0373] There may be greater **purity** of heart in a married man
AP : 2 3 :036(244) [0373] interpret celibacy as a **purity** that merits justification
AP : 2 3 :064(248) [0381] outward ceremonies and **purity** laws of the Old
AP : 2 3 :064(248) [0381] the Gospel requires **purity** of the heart and not
AP : 2 3 :064(248) [0381] must be taken to mean **purity** of the heart and total
S 2 : 0 2 :029(297) [0471] the holy sacrament in its **purity** and certainly according to
LC : 0 3 :048(426) [0711] his Word taught in its **purity** and cherished and
LC : 0 6 :021(459) [0000] goes about relying on the **purity** of his confession, let him
SD : 1 1 :069(627) [1085] (Rom. 10:17) when it is preached in sincerity and **purity**.

Purple (1)
TR : 0 0 :032(325) [0513] to be mocked in royal **purple** signified that the time would

Purpose (100), Purposed (2), Purposely (3), Purposes (10)
PR : PR :018(008) [0015] we have in what follows **purposed** to commit ourselves
PR : PR :019(009) [0017] as now, it never was our **purpose** and intention to
PR : PR :022(011) [0019] However, it is not our **purpose** and intention to mean
PR : PR :022(012) [0021] way our disposition and **purpose** to give occasion by this
PR : PR :023(012) [0021] was proposed, **purposed**, and undertaken, and we desire
PR : PR :025(014) [0023] we have resolved and **purpose** to live in genuine peace and
PR : PR :026(014) [0025] We likewise **purpose** to cooperate with one another in the
AG : PR :005(025) [0039] summoned for these **purposes**, together with other
AG : 1 3 :001(035) [0049] will toward us for the **purpose** of awakening and
AG : 1 3 :002(036) [0049] in faith and for the **purpose** of strengthening faith.
AG : 1 5 :003(036) [0049] by men for the **purpose** of propitiating God and earning
AG : 2 0 :021(044) [0055] other works for the **purpose** of earning grace and making
AG : 0 1 :003(056) [0065] After all, the chief **purpose** of all ceremonies is to teach
AG : 2 6 :029(068) [0075] such works for the **purpose** of earning forgiveness of sin
AG : 2 6 :038(069) [0075] that it is not the **purpose** of mortification to merit grace
AG : 2 7 :016(073) [0077] monastic life for the **purpose** of learning the Scriptures,
AG : 2 7 :045(078) [0081] all these claims for the **purpose** of casting them into their
AG : 2 8 :043(088) [0089] such regulations for the **purpose** of earning God's grace
AG : 2 8 :060(091) [0091] Sunday for this **purpose**, and it was the more inclined and
AG : 0 0 :004(095) [0095] out of hatred or for the **purpose** of injuring anybody, but
AL : 2 0 :002(041) [0053] have taught to **purpose** about all stations and duties
AL : 2 4 :010(057) [0065] shamefully profaned and applied to **purposes** of gain.
AL : 2 6 :029(068) [0075] such works for the **purpose** of meriting grace through
AL : 2 7 :002(071) [0077] vows were added for the **purpose** of restoring discipline,
AL : 2 8 :035(086) [0089] of traditions for the **purpose** of making satisfaction for
AL : 2 8 :043(088) [0089] of traditions for the **purpose** of appeasing God or as if
AL : 2 8 :060(091) [0091] the Lord's Day for this **purpose**, and it seems that the
AL : 0 0 :004(095) [0095] been said or related for the **purpose** of injuring anybody.
AP : 0 4 :029(111) [0129] then 'Christ died to no **purpose**' (Gal. 2:21), and therefore
AP : 0 4 :051(114) [0135] we add this article, the **purpose** of the history, "the
AP : 0 4 :348(160) [0217] are justified for this very **purpose**, that, being righteous,
AP : 0 4 :349(160) [0217] For this **purpose** we are reborn and receive the Holy
AP : 1 2 :151(206) [0299] have another and better **purpose**, that is, to exercise them
AP : 1 2 :153(206) [0299] itself serves this same **purpose**: to destroy this sinful flesh
AP : 1 2 :158(207) [0301] that troubles have other and more important **purposes**.
AP : 1 2 :158(207) [0301] and more important **purposes**, that God is doing his alien
AP : 1 3 :002(211) [0309] much difference if, for **purposes** of teaching, the
AP : 1 3 :011(212) [0311] accomplish that which I **purpose**, and prosper in the thing
AP : 1 5 :013(216) [0319] any traditions for the **purpose** of meriting the forgiveness
AP : 1 5 :021(218) [0321] traditions have another **purpose**, namely, to merit the
AP : 1 5 :024(218) [0321] Though their **purpose** is to restrain the flesh, reason
AP : 2 2 :009(237) [0359] this is a human device and its **purpose** is quite evident.
AP : 2 3 :050(246) [0377] These Epicureans **purposely** use religion as a pretext.
AP : 2 3 :060(247) [0381] The real **purpose** of the law is not religion but
AP : 2 3 :068(248) [0383] show our opponents' **purpose** in writing the Confutation.
AP : 2 4 :003(250) [0385] The **purpose** of observing ceremonies is that men may
AP : 2 4 :014(251) [0389] in our Confession we **purposely** avoided this term because
AP : 2 4 :074(262) [0409] a sacrifice, since one action can have several **purposes**.
AP : 2 7 :055(278) [0439] are in school, with the **purpose** of teaching the listeners
AP : 2 7 :062(280) [0441] had an immediate **purpose**: since they were nomads
AP : 2 7 :062(280) [0441] of faith and immortality — surely a lawful **purpose**.
AP : 2 7 :062(280) [0441] But vastly different **purposes** are set forth for
S 2 : 0 2 :007(294) [0465] It is observed for this **purpose** when it is best observed.
S 2 : 0 2 :007(294) [0465] What other **purpose** could it have?
S 2 : 0 2 :013(295) [0465] not understand for what **purpose** and to what end the
S 2 : 0 3 :001(297) [0471] be restored to such **purposes** in order that we may have
S 2 : 0 3 :002(298) [0471] unwilling to serve this **purpose**, it would be better to
S 2 : 0 4 :015(301) [0475] and will accomplish his **purpose** by his Spirit and his
S 3 : 0 2 :001(303) [0479] But this **purpose** failed because of the wickedness which
SC : PR :014(339) [0535] For this **purpose**, take the explanations in this booklet, or
SC : PR :017(340) [0537] at length in the many books written for this **purpose**.
SC : PR :020(340) [0537] The devil also has a horrible **purpose** in mind.
SC : 0 3 :011(347) [0547] every evil counsel and **purpose** of the devil, of the world,
LC : 0 1 :004(365) [0581] The **purpose** of this commandment, therefore, is to
LC : 0 1 :052(371) [0595] abused than for **purposes** of falsehood and deceit.
LC : 0 1 :073(374) [0601] For this **purpose** it also helps to form the habit of
LC : 0 1 :085(376) [0605] been appointed for this **purpose**, we should not change it.
LC : 0 1 :103(379) [0611] of lies or any evil **purpose** whatsoever, but use it for the
LC : 0 1 :141(384) [0621] and responsibility to others appointed for the **purpose**.
LC : 0 1 :299(405) [0665] the law to suit their **purpose**, straining words and using
LC : 0 1 :310(407) [0669] covetousness, God's **purpose** being to destroy all the
LC : 0 2 :061(419) [0695] For this **purpose** he has appointed a community on
LC : 0 2 :064(419) [0695] created us for this very **purpose**, to redeem and sanctify
LC : 0 3 :008(421) [0699] the name of God is glorified and used to good **purpose**.
LC : 0 3 :013(422) [0701] what I do has no other **purpose** than that it befits
LC : 0 3 :064(428) [0715] This is his only **purpose**, his desire and thought.
LC : 0 3 :070(429) [0717] boast that the will and **purpose** of the devil and of all our
LC : 0 3 :080(431) [0721] the devil, whose whole **purpose** and desire it is to take
LC : 0 3 :090(432) [0723] This should serve God's **purpose** to break our pride and
LC : 0 3 :104(434) [0727] His **purpose** is to make us scorn and despise both the
LC : 0 4 :023(439) [0737] must also learn for what **purpose** it was instituted, that is,
LC : 0 4 :024(439) [0737] effect, benefit, fruit, and **purpose** of Baptism is to save.
LC : 0 4 :030(440) [0739] no matter for what **purpose** or by what means he speaks
LC : 0 4 :046(442) [0743] and use of Baptism as answering the present **purpose**.
LC : 0 4 :054(443) [0745] and with an evil **purpose**, and we baptized him in all good
LC : 0 4 :055(443) [0745] it with an evil **purpose**, and he would not be permitted on
LC : 0 4 :057(444) [0747] bring the child with the **purpose** and hope that he may
LC : 0 5 :020(449) [0757] power and benefit, the **purpose** for which the sacrament
LC : 0 6 :022(459) [0000] your needs, not for the **purpose** of performing a work but
EP : 0 2 :015(471) [0789] is given to such as resist him **purposely** and persistently.
EP : 1 1 :015(496) [0835] of ours, saves us "according to the **purpose**" of his will.
EP : 1 1 :019(497) [0837] by an arbitrary counsel, **purpose**, and will, without regard
SD : PR :001(503) [0851] For this same **purpose** the ancient church always had its
SD : 0 2 :047(530) [0901] them and actually **purposes** through his Holy Spirit to
SD : 0 5 :001(558) [0951] light which serves the **purpose** that the Word of God may
SD : 0 7 :057(579) [0993] As the **purpose** and context of St. Paul's entire discourse
SD : 0 7 :103(587) [1007] My only **purpose** was to show what crass fools our
SD : 1 1 :012(618) [1067] down for us, not for the **purpose** of thereby driving us to
SD : 1 1 :013(619) [1067] consider the counsel, **purpose**, and ordinance of God in
SD : 1 1 :014(619) [1069] entire doctrine of God's **purpose**, counsel, will, and
SD : 1 1 :014(619) [1069] namely, that in his **purpose** and counsel God had
SD : 1 1 :023(619) [1069] this his eternal counsel, **purpose**, and ordinance God has
SD : 1 1 :024(620) [1069] when we speak of the **purpose**, foreknowledge, election,
SD : 1 1 :030(621) [1073] "according to God's **purpose**" to "the inheritance" hear
SD : 1 1 :043(623) [1077] "according to his **purpose**" by grace in Christ (Rom. 9:11;
SD : 1 1 :045(624) [1079] "according to his **purpose**" how he would bring me
SD : 1 1 :046(624) [1079] salvation in his eternal **purpose**, which cannot fail or be
SD : 1 1 :047(624) [1079] called according to the **purpose** of God, "who will
SD : 1 1 :049(624) [1079] good" since they are "called according to his **purpose**."
SD : 1 1 :084(630) [1091] whom we read, "For this **purpose** have I let you live to
SD : 1 1 :086(631) [1091] example for the sole **purpose** of thereby setting forth the
SD : 1 1 :087(631) [1093] us "according to the **purpose**" of his will through sheer
SD : 1 1 :087(631) [1093] Christ, according to the **purpose** of his will, and to the
SD : 1 1 :088(631) [1093] — "in order that God's **purpose** of election might
SD : 1 2 :004(633) [1097] Therefore it was our **purpose** not only to declare our

Purse (3)
LC : 0 1 :013(366) [0583] him, or put him into a **purse**, or shut him up in a chest.
LC : 0 1 :226(395) [0645] would ten times rather lose the money from one's **purse**.
LC : 0 1 :244(398) [0649] clean out our chests and **purse** down to the last penny,

Pursue (1), Pursues (3)
AP : 0 2 :026(103) [0111] concupiscence, which **pursues** carnal ends contrary to the
S 2 : 0 2 :018(296) [0467] an children, etc. and **pursue** these unnecessary, uncertain,
LC : 0 1 :021(367) [0585] in the heart, which **pursues** other things and seeks help
LC : 0 1 :234(397) [0647] Though he **pursues** his defiant and arrogant course for a

Pushed (1)
AP : 2 7 :009(270) [0421] whom parents or friends **pushed** into the monastery to be

Put (119), Puts (11), Putting (16)
PR : PR :013(007) [0013] and is necessary for this end and **put** it down in one book.
PR : PR :021(011) [0019] of the ancient church **put** it, it takes place on account of
PR : PR :024(013) [0023] from everyone's eyes, or to **put** the light of divine truth
AG : 0 0 :000(023) [0037] testimonies before kings, and shall not be **put** to shame."
AG : PR :003(025) [0039] on one Christian truth, to **put** aside whatever may not
AG : PR :020(026) [0041] and to allow no hindrance to be **put** in the way.
AG : 0 0 :001(047) [0059] we would not wish to **put** our own souls and consciences
AG : 2 6 :027(068) [0073] make trial of God by **putting** a yoke upon the neck of the
AG : 2 8 :042(088) [0089] 15:10 St. Peter forbids **putting** a yoke on the neck of the
AL : 2 3 :021(055) [0063] even priests, are cruelly **put** to death, contrary to the
AL : 2 6 :005(064) [0071] weight on this article and **puts** aside the law and human
AL : 2 6 :027(068) [0073] make trial of God by **putting** a yoke upon the neck of the
AL : 2 7 :016(073) [0077] of perfection, and they **put** it far above all other kinds of
AL : 2 8 :042(088) [0089] when Peter forbids **putting** a yoke on the disciples and
AP : PR :003(098) [0099] our side was willing to **put** up with anything, however
AP : 0 2 :021(103) [0111] is the very likeness of God which he **put** into man.
AP : 0 2 :046(106) [0119] is pronounced, "I will **put** enmity between you and the
AP : 0 4 :082(118) [0145] Rom. 3:25, "Whom God **put** forward as an expiation,"
AP : 0 4 :123(124) [0157] prophet (Jer. 31:33), "I will **put** my law upon their hearts."
AP : 0 4 :125(124) [0157] he says (Jer. 31:33), "I will **put** my law upon their hearts."
AP : 0 4 :143(127) [0161] die, but if by the Spirit you **put** to death the deeds of the
AP : 0 4 :156(128) [0165] minds—whether we should **put** our trust in Christ or in
AP : 0 4 :157(128) [0165] If we **put** it in our works, we rob Christ of his honor as
AP : 0 4 :198(134) [0175] different ways and often **puts** off the rewards for the
AP : 0 4 :203(135) [0175] But they are **put** to a different use by anyone who cannot
AP : 0 4 :208(135) [0177] Because no works can **put** the conscience at rest, they
AP : 0 4 :209(135) [0177] And so they **put** their sons to death in order by this cruel
AP : 0 4 :219(137) [0181] (Jer. 31:33), "I will **put** my law within their hearts."
AP : 0 4 :234(140) [0185] the weak, when the people **put** the best construction on
AP : 0 4 :235(140) [0185] in everyday life we should **put** up with many things for
AP : 0 4 :239(141) [0187] "He who believes in him will not be **put** to shame."
AP : 0 4 :242(141) [0187] of its friends; and that it **puts** the best construction even
AP : 0 4 :280(149) [0201] out garbled sentences to **put** something over on the
AP : 0 4 :282(149) [0201] of this false cleansing he **puts** a twofold cleanness, one
AP : 0 4 :352(161) [0217] Cor. 5:2, 3), "We long to **put** on our heavenly dwelling, so
AP : 0 4 :352(161) [0217] dwelling, so that by **putting** it on we may not be found
AP : 0 4 :362(162) [0219] We are not **putting** forward an empty quibble about the
AP : 0 4 :381(165) [0223] to say that we should **put** confidence in our love, which
AP : 0 4 :381(165) [0223] when they say that we must **put** our confidence in grace
AP : 1 2 :046(188) [0263] made without hands, by **putting** off the body of the sins
AP : 1 2 :046(188) [0263] The one is **putting** off the body of sins, the other is being
AP : 1 2 :046(188) [0263] Mortifying, quickening, **putting** off the body of sins,
AP : 1 2 :046(188) [0263] contrition Paul calls "**putting** off the body of sins"
AP : 1 2 :056(189) [0267] "The Lord has **put** away your sin; you shall not
AP : 1 2 :058(189) [0267] readers can see that we **put** into penitence the parts that
AP : 1 2 :058(190) [0267] We have **put** in these two parts in order to emphasize the
AP : 1 2 :060(190) [0269] of sins, and therefore we **put** it in as one of the parts of
AP : 1 2 :063(191) [0269] Rom. 3:25, "Whom God **put** forward as an expiation by
AP : 1 2 :065(191) [0271] "He who believes in him will not be **put** to shame."
AP : 1 2 :065(191) [0271] therefore must be **put** to shame, for they trust in their
AP : 1 2 :067(191) [0271] men who hold this faith be **put** to death with all sorts of

Continued ▶

Continued ▶

EP : 07 :002(481) [0809] The **question** is, In the Holy Communion are the true
EP : 07 :041(486) [0817] and blasphemous **questions** and statements, which
EP : 08 :001(487) [0817] The Chief **Question** at Issue in This Controversy
EP : 08 :002(487) [0817] The chief **question** has been, Because of personal union in
EP : 09 :000(492) [0827] The Chief **Question** at Issue in the Controversy about
EP : 09 :001(492) [0827] The **questions** raised were: When and how, according to
EP : 09 :003(492) [0827] all unnecessary **questions**, and admonishes all Christians
EP : 10 :001(492) [0829] The Chief **Question** at Issue in this Controversy
EP : 10 :002(492) [0829] The chief **question** has been, In times of persecution,
EP : 10 :006(493) [0829] a case it is no longer a **question** of indifferent things, but
SD : 01 :057(518) [0877] teachers, and never **questioned** by any really intelligent
SD : 01 :060(519) [0879] It involves another **question**, however, when someone
SD : 02 :002(520) [0881] In this controversy the **question** is not concerning the
SD : 02 :008(521) [0883] summary reply to the **questions** and issues stated at the
SD : 02 :041(529) [0897] Luther answers the **question**, "How does the kingdom of
SD : 02 :044(529) [0897] raised (for example, the **question** of "absolute necessity"),
SD : 02 :055(532) [0903] nor the hearer should **question** this grace and operation
SD : 02 :062(533) [0905] if one is discussing the **question** how God operates in
SD : 02 :071(535) [0909] But since the **question** is asked concerning the efficient
SD : 02 :073(535) [0909] is possible to decide the **questions** that for a considerable
SD : 03 :029(544) [0925] At this point the main **question** with which we have to do
SD : 03 :033(545) [0927] And St. Paul raises this **question** (Rom. 4:1): On what did
SD : 03 :042(547) [0931] When, however, the **question** is asked, how a Christian
SD : 04 :014(553) [0943] that in discussing the **question** whether good works are
SD : 04 :030(555) [0947] a serious and important **question** since only he who
SD : 07 :024(573) [0979] to answer all kinds of **questions** which now trouble
SD : 07 :024(573) [0979] administer and give the sacrament, and like **questions**.
SD : 07 :074(583) [0999] In this **question** we have reached the following fraternal
SD : 07 :127(591) [1015] and blasphemous **questions** and expressions which are
SD : 08 :037(598) [1027] nature the property in **question** is being ascribed to the
SD : 08 :048(600) [1031] in the third place, the **question** being treated in the
SD : 10 :013(613) [1057] judgment on you in **questions** of food and drink, or with
SD : 11 :025(620) [1071] answer to the following **question** is necessary for the
SD : 11 :033(621) [1073] as Christ answered the **question**, "Lord, will those who
SD : 11 :053(625) [1081] with those aspects of the **question** which God has revealed
SD : 11 :058(625) [1081] go in these and similar **questions** (Rom. 9:14ff.; 11:22ff.).
SD : 11 :093(632) [1095] abstruse and specious **questions** and disputations, and we
SD : 12 :006(633) [1097] confess that in all these **questions** we abide by the true,

Quibble (10), Quibbler (1), Quibbles (3), Quibbling (2), Quibblings (1)
AP : 02 :002(100) [0105] These **quibbles** have obviously come from the schools,
AP : 02 :015(102) [0109] Here the scholastics **quibble** about philosophical
AP : 02 :040(105) [0115] No **quibbling** can overthrow these proofs.
AP : 02 :051(107) [0119] the childish and trivial **quibbling** with which our
AP : 04 :079(117) [0143] Our idle opponents **quibble** as to whether the forgiveness
AP : 04 :303(154) [0205] to our opponents' **quibble** that many wicked people and
AP : 04 :304(154) [0205] Some sophist may **quibble** here that righteousness is in
AP : 04 :312(155) [0207] Someone may **quibble** that if it is faith that wishes for
AP : 04 :342(159) [0215] It is obviously a childish **quibble** to interpret "unworthy
AP : 04 :343(160) [0215] done with these petty **quibblings** of our opponents which
AP : 04 :362(162) [0219] forward an empty **quibble** about the term "reward."
AP : 12 :084(194) [0277] be said so simply that some **quibbler** cannot pervert it.
AP : 13 :017(213) [0313] No intelligent person will **quibble** about the number of
AP : 24 :002(249) [0385] our clever opponents **quibble** about how a hearer who is
AP : 24 :087(265) [0413] opponents to raise such **quibbles** about such an
AP : 27 :010(270) [0423] we shall refute our opponents' **quibbles** against them.
SD : 07 :038(576) [0985] as a figurative, flowery formula or **quibble** about words).

Quick (1), Quickly (7)
S2 : 02 :028(297) [0469] remains will do no harm and will **quickly** be forgotten.
S2 : 04 :008(299) [0473] he would very easily and **quickly** be despised and would
S3 : 03 :025(307) [0485] popes went further and **quickly** multiplied the jubilee
SC : 07 :005(353) [0559] Then **quickly** lie down and sleep in peace.
LC : PR :008(359) [0569] fellows would like **quickly**, with one reading, to become
LC : 01 :276(402) [0659] that you should not be **quick** to spread slander and gossip
LC : 05 :084(456) [0773] How **quickly** can he bring you into misery and distress
LC : 06 :005(457) [0000] We **quickly** understand whatever benefits us, and we

Quicken (6), Quickened (2), Quickening (9), Quickens (13)
AL : 03 :005(030) [0045] to rule, comfort, and **quicken** them and defend them
AP : 04 :062(115) [0139] receives the forgiveness of sins, justifies and **quickens** us.
AP : 04 :100(121) [0151] adds that this same faith **quickens** because it brings forth
AP : 04 :115(123) [0155] us from death, comforting and **quickening** terrified minds.
AP : 04 :293(152) [0203] heart is encouraged and **quickened** by faith in this way, it
AP : 04 :383(165) [0225] and righteousness, **quickening** the heart amid the terrors
AP : 07 :018(171) [0233] What he **quickens** by his Spirit is always the same
AP : 07 :031(174) [0237] of the heart is something that **quickens** the heart.
AP : 07 :031(174) [0237] To this **quickening** human traditions, whether universal
AP : 07 :036(175) [0241] of the heart is a spiritual thing that **quickens** men's hearts.
AP : 07 :036(175) [0241] human traditions do not **quicken** the heart, are not works
AP : 12 :036(186) [0261] sustains, and **quickens** the contrite according to the
AP : 12 :040(187) [0261] Because God truly **quickens** through the Word, the keys
AP : 12 :044(187) [0263] believe, the Holy Spirit **quickens** our hearts through the
AP : 12 :046(188) [0263] always names these two parts, mortifying and **quickening**.
AP : 12 :046(188) [0263] Mortifying, **quickening**, putting off the body of sins,
AP : 12 :046(188) [0263] And **quickening** should not be understood as a Platonic
AP : 12 :047(188) [0265] therefore faith alone **quickens**, according to the word
AP : 12 :049(189) [0265] This sustains and **quickens** the heart.
AP : 12 :051(189) [0265] God's own proper work is to **quicken** and console.
AP : 12 :051(189) [0265] for consolation and **quickening** because hearts that do
AP : 12 :053(189) [0265] in men, to terrify and to justify and **quicken** the terrified.
AP : 12 :056(189) [0267] David and by faith it sustains, justifies, and **quickens** him.
AP : 12 :141(204) [0295] Gospel, penitence and **quickening**, and the blessings of
LC : 05 :068(454) [0769] medicine which aids and **quickens** us in both soul and
EP : 01 :006(467) [0781] it as his creation, **quickens** it from the dead as his
EP : 01 :006(467) [0781] not sanctified it, will not **quicken** it in the elect, will not
EP : 02 :003(470) [0787] As little as a corpse can **quicken** itself to bodily, earthly
SD : 07 :003(569) [0973] our faith, reminded and **quickened** by the visible signs in
SD : 08 :076(606) [1043] and his blood truly a **quickening** beverage, as the two

Quiet (5), Quieted (2), Quietly (1), Quietness (2)
AP : 04 :241(141) [0187] arise they should be **quieted** and settled by calmness and
AP : 12 :069(192) [0271] petty public officials they **quietly** approved the errors of
AP : 12 :088(195) [0277] nor consciences **quieted** unless we know it is God's
AP : 12 :090(195) [0279] with our opponents, we would very gladly keep **quiet**.
SC : 09 :005(355) [0561] that we may lead a **quiet** and peaceable life, godly and
LC : 01 :132(383) [0619] welfare, to lead us to a **quiet**, pleasant, and blessed life.
LC : 01 :137(384) [0621] They live long in peace and **quietness**.
LC : 01 :230(396) [0645] Yes, we might well keep **quiet** here about various petty
LC : 03 :075(430) [0719] possessions in peace and **quietness**, since otherwise we
LC : 05 :065(454) [0769] just as well have kept **quiet** and not instituted a

Quite (30)
AG : 26 :030(068) [0075] discipline, their writings reveal something **quite** different.
AG : 27 :038(077) [0081] It is **quite** evident that the monks have taught and
AG : 28 :040(087) [0089] It is **quite** believable that some bishops were misled by the
AL : 22 :008(050) [0061] It is only a custom of **quite** recent times that holds
AP : 07 :031(174) [0237] We do not **quite** understand what our opponents mean.
AP : 12 :067(191) [0271] Leo **quite** openly condemns this doctrine of the
AP : 12 :090(195) [0279] of penitence, which is **quite** clear, we are happy to have
AP : 22 :009(237) [0359] this is a human device and its purpose is **quite** evident.
AP : 27 :035(275) [0431] human traditions, it is **quite** clear that monastic vows are
AP : 28 :003(281) [0445] kinds of people to the priesthood **quite** indiscriminately.
S2 : 01 :005(292) [0463] Therefore we must be **quite** certain and have no doubts
TR : 00 :015(322) [0509] or Latin churches, it is **quite** apparent that the churches
TR : 00 :016(323) [0509] in accordance with it, it is **quite** apparent that it was not
SC : PR :002(338) [0533] many pastors are **quite** incompetent and unfitted for
SC : 05 :025(350) [0555] of no sin at all (which is **quite** unlikely), you should
LC : 01 :259(400) [0655] He must therefore be **quite** blind, shutting his eyes and
LC : 01 :305(406) [0667] of thing undoubtedly was **quite** prevalent in the time of
LC : 01 :327(409) [0675] wants of you and what he will **quite** surely demand of you
LC : 02 :046(416) [0689] points in it are not **quite** clear to the common people, we
LC : 02 :047(416) [0691] idiomatically, we must express it **quite** differently.
LC : 03 :007(421) [0699] It is **quite** true that the kind of babbling and bellowing
LC : 03 :027(424) [0705] ourselves and others is **quite** amply indicated in the
LC : 03 :107(434) [0729] temptation, therefore, is **quite** a different thing from
LC : 04 :035(441) [0741] Christ's Baptism **quite** clearly from a bath-keeper's
LC : 05 :041(451) [0763] far that they have become **quite** barbarous, and ultimately
LC : 05 :067(454) [0769] it so long that we grow **quite** cold and callous and lose all
LC : 06 :001(457) [0000] there has been no law **quite** so oppressive as that which
SD : 02 :002(520) [0881] of the Augsburg Confession for **quite** a few years.
SD : 02 :061(533) [0905] this same reason it is not **quite** right to say that before his
SD : 08 :004(592) [1017] Augsburg Confession, not **quite** ready to commit

Quotation (2), Quotations (3)
AP : 12 :069(192) [0271] by this large number of **quotations**, it must be kept in
AP : 23 :064(248) [0381] They give many **quotations** to support this.
AP : 24 :009(250) [0387] But all the **quotations** from the Fathers and the
SD : 07 :011(571) [0975] I Cor. 10:16 and with a **quotation** from Cyril as follows:
SD : 07 :027(573) [0981] So far the **quotation** from the Large Catechism, which

Quote (41), Quoted (20), Quotes (5)
AG : 18 :004(039) [0051] on free will are here **quoted** from the third book of his
AG : 23 :002(053) [0063] allowed himself to be **quoted** as saying that while there
AG : 25 :011(063) [0069] words of Chrysostom are **quoted**: "I do not say that you
AL : 25 :011(063) [0069] for Chrysostom is **quoted** in the canons as saying, "I do
AP : 02 :031(104) [0113] We could **quote** many passages on both parts of our
AP : 04 :058(115) [0137] He **quotes** the promise: "My soul waits for his word, my
AP : 04 :087(120) [0147] For later on he **quotes** the Decalogue, "You shall not
AP : 04 :106(122) [0153] A little later we shall **quote** several other statements.
AP : 04 :183(132) [0173] For they **quote** passages about law and works but omit
AP : 04 :185(132) [0173] interprets all the passages they **quote** on law and works.
AP : 04 :218(137) [0179] texts that our opponents **quote** to prove that we are
AP : 04 :218(137) [0179] From I Cor. 13:2 they **quote**, "If I have all faith, etc., but
AP : 04 :221(137) [0181] They **quote** this one text in which Paul teaches about the
AP : 04 :238(140) [0187] From Peter they **quote** this statement (I Pet. 4:8), "Love
AP : 04 :244(141) [0189] From James they **quote** the text, "You see that a man is
AP : 04 :254(143) [0193] Other statements about works are also **quoted** against us.
AP : 04 :281(149) [0201] Luke 11:41 is also **quoted** in a garbled form: "Give alms;
AP : 04 :286(150) [0201] which our opponents **quote** against us in arguing that
AP : 04 :286(150) [0201] They **quote** many passages in a garbled form.
AP : 04 :380(165) [0223] as it were, and these they **quote** in a twisted way, boasting
AP : 04 :388(166) [0225] on love or works is **quoted**, that the law cannot be kept
AP : 10 :004(179) [0247] We have **quoted** all of this here, not to begin an
AP : 12 :065(191) [0271] Peter (I Pet. 2:6) **quotes** the words from Isaiah (28:16),
AP : 12 :068(192) [0271] statements which the decrees **quote** in garbled form.
AP : 12 :091(195) [0279] are circulating which are **quoted** in garbled form from the
AP : 12 :091(195) [0279] and which our opponents **quote** in a distorted form to
AP : 12 :109(198) [0283] Maybe someone will **quote** James 5:16, "Confess your
AP : 12 :122(200) [0287] They **quote** many Scripture passages to give the
AP : 12 :122(200) [0289] These are passages they **quote**: "Bear fruit that befits
AP : 12 :122(200) [0289] Then they **quote** certain statements from the Fathers and
AP : 12 :123(201) [0289] They **quote** the word, "Be penitent," against us so that
AP : 12 :131(202) [0291] The Scripture passages **quoted** by our opponents say
AP : 12 :138(203) [0293] Scripture passages they **quote** do not say that
AP : 12 :163(208) [0303] They **quote** Paul against us (I Cor. 11:31), "If we judged
AP : 12 :173(209) [0305] They **quote** passages dealing with obligatory works,
AP : 15 :030(219) [0323] We have already **quoted** some proofs for this, and Paul's
AP : 18 :003(225) [0335] article on justification we **quoted** Augustine's emphatic
AP : 20 :005(227) [0339] Here we could **quote** endless passages from Scripture and
AP : 20 :012(228) [0341] Our opponents **quote** many Scripture passages to show
AP : 20 :012(228) [0341] From Peter they **quote** (II Pet. 1:10), "Be zealous to
AP : 22 :007(237) [0359] They **quote** passages that mention bread, like Luke 24:35,
AP : 22 :007(237) [0359] They **quote** other passages that talk about the breaking
AP : 24 :008(250) [0385] of the Fathers and then **quote** the authority of the
AP : 24 :031(255) [0395] it to the Mass, and for this they **quote** patristic authority.
AP : 24 :034(256) [0395] They **quote** another passage from Malachi (3:3), "And he
AP : 24 :052(259) [0403] They also **quote** the Epistle to the Hebrews (5:1), "Every
AP : 24 :061(260) [0405] the Scripture passages **quoted** against us give no support
AP : 24 :066(261) [0407] passages that they **quote** against us, we must also discuss
AP : 24 :094(267) [0417] Our opponents **quote** the Fathers on offerings for the
AP : 27 :011(270) [0423] it was fitting for us to **quote** Paul's statement from
AP : 27 :018(272) [0425] Though we have **quoted** Paul's statement in support of
AP : 27 :029(274) [0431] is the way these good-for-nothings **quote** the Scriptures.
AP : 27 :032(274) [0431] We have **quoted** earlier the other things that follow this
AP : 27 :040(276) [0433] eternal life, and it **quotes** the passage (Matt. 19:29),

Continued ▶

AP : 27 :044(277) [0435] of counterfeits, so they **quote** passages of Scripture under
AP : 27 :045(277) [0435] They **quote** another passage on perfection (Matt. 19:21),
AP : 27 :048(277) [0437] to the text when they **quote** it in a mutilated form.
AP : 27 :058(279) [0439] Here they **quote** against us the example of the Nazarites
AP : 28 :020(284) [0449] They also **quote** the statement (Heb. 13:17), "Obey your
TR : 00 :022(323) [0511] Here certain passages are **quoted** against us: "You are
TR : 00 :062(330) [0521] He **quotes** from Titus, "This is why I left you in Crete,
LC : 04 :023(439) [0737] from the words of Christ **quoted** above, "He who believes
LC : 05 :021(449) [0757] from the words just **quoted**, "This is my body and blood,
SD : 07 :011(571) [0975] Cyril is **quoted** to the effect that Christ dwells bodily in
SD : 08 :018(594) [1021] and have frequently **quoted** them in our writings.
SD : 08 :038(598) [1027] *alloeosis,* we shall here **quote** Dr. Luther's own words, so

Rabble (3)
S2 : 02 :005(293) [0463] — not only for the rude **rabble**, but also for all godly,
LC : 01 :213(394) [0641] you see how the papal **rabble**, priests, monks, and nuns
LC : 06 :006(457) [0000] The **rabble** who will not obey the Gospel deserve just such

Race (6)
AP : 13 :014(213) [0311] in the very beginning, at the creation of the human **race**.
AP : 24 :023(253) [0391] was going to placate God for the whole human **race**.
SD : 02 :050(531) [0901] himself out of the human **race** and works in the hearts of
SD : 03 :057(549) [0935] of the human **race**, since it satisfied the eternal and
SD : 08 :006(592) [1017] as it is written, "Of their **race**, according to the flesh, is
SD : 11 :015(619) [1069] through Christ the human **race** has truly been redeemed

Rage (8), Rages (2), Raging (3), Ragings (1)
PR : PR :022(012) [0021] a cordial disapproval of the **raging** of their persecutors.
AP : 14 :005(215) [0315] that the bishops stop **raging** against our churches.
AP : 22 :012(238) [0361] part of the sacrament and **rage** against good men who use
AP : 23 :070(249) [0383] the many innocent victims of their **rage** will also cry out.
LC : 01 :128(382) [0617] an evil hour comes do we **rage** and grumble impatiently
LC : 01 :184(390) [0633] people, our hearts in turn **rage** and we are ready to shed
LC : 01 :187(390) [0633] to let our enemies rave and **rage** and do their worst.
LC : 01 :215(394) [0641] that they suffer incessant **ragings** of secret passion, which
LC : 03 :062(428) [0715] furious foe, he raves and **rages** with all his power and
LC : 03 :068(429) [0717] and all his host storm and **rage** furiously against it in
LC : 03 :069(429) [0717] Let them all **rage** and do their worst, let them plot and
LC : 05 :077(455) [0771] which feels nothing though the disease **rages** and rankles.
SD : 07 :029(574) [0981] and that there is no end to the **rage** and fury of Satan.
SD : 11 :004(617) [1065] and coming in, and your **raging** against me" (Isa. 37:28).

Rain (1)
LC : 04 :043(442) [0743] how the world would snow and **rain** money upon him!

Raise (14), Raised (23), Raises (8)
AG : 17 :001(038) [0051] day for judgment and will **raise** up all the dead, to give
AG : 27 :022(074) [0079] What objection may be **raised** to this?
AL : 17 :001(038) [0051] will appear for judgment and will **raise** up all the dead.
AL : 27 :022(074) [0079] What objection can be **raised** to this?
AP : 03 :001(107) [0119] to us; and that he was **raised** to rule, justify, and sanctify
AP : 04 :051(114) [0135] born, suffered, and was **raised** unless we add this article,
AP : 04 :250(143) [0191] "in which you were also **raised** with him through faith in
AP : 04 :291(152) [0203] promised, revealed, born, crucified, and **raised** in vain.
AP : 04 :297(153) [0205] born, crucified, and **raised** in vain; the promise of grace in
AP : 04 :348(160) [0217] Here our opponents will **raise** the cry that good works are
AP : 04 :388(166) [0225] issues on which our opponents had **raised** objections.
AP : 07 :037(175) [0241] Later on we must **raise** again and discuss more fully the
AP : 12 :046(188) [0263] later on, "You were also **raised** with him through faith in
AP : 12 :046(188) [0263] the body of sins, the other is being **raised** through faith.
AP : 12 :046(188) [0263] off the body of sins, being **raised** — we are not to
AP : 12 :050(189) [0265] and brings to life; he brings down to Sheol and **raises** up."
AP : 12 :151(206) [0299] us rely not on ourselves but on God who **raises** the dead."
AP : 17 :001(224) [0335] Christ will appear and **raise** all the dead, granting eternal
AP : 23 :021(242) [0369] If someone **raises** the objection here that Christ
AP : 23 :068(249) [0383] arouse the ignorant was to **raise** the cry of heresy against
AP : 24 :087(265) [0413] silly for our opponents to **raise** such quibbles about such
AP : 28 :022(284) [0451] They also **raise** an objection on the basis of the public
S2 : 01 :001(292) [0461] for our trespasses and **raised** again for our justification"
S2 : 04 :005(299) [0473] better if such a head had not been **raised** up by the devil.
S2 : 04 :008(300) [0473] church God would **raise** up a man fitted for such an
S2 : 04 :009(300) [0475] Christendom, until the pope **raised** his head over them all.
S2 : 04 :010(300) [0475] real Antichrist who has **raised** himself over and set
SC : 02 :006(345) [0545] and on the last day he will **raise** me and all the dead and
SC : 04 :014(349) [0553] so that as Christ was **raised** from the dead by the glory of
LC : 01 :166(388) [0629] add an hour to our life or **raise** from the earth a single
EP : 02 :003(470) [0787] sin is spiritually dead **raise** himself to spiritual life, as it is
EP : 05 :007(478) [0803] the merit of Christ, and **raises** them up again by the
EP : 08 :028(490) [0825] human nature has been **raised** to the level of, and has
EP : 09 :001(492) [0827] The questions **raised** were: When and how, according to
SD : PR :002(501) [0847] unwarrantedly), and **raised** no end of slanders and
SD : 01 :047(516) [0875] or else that sin would be **raised** and would be and remain
SD : 02 :044(529) [0897] points which Erasmus **raised** (for example, the question
SD : 02 :059(532) [0905] and will of God until God **raises** him from the death of
SD : 03 :033(545) [0927] And St. Paul **raises** this question (Rom. 4:1): On what did
SD : 04 :029(555) [0947] of justification, were **raised** again as a result of the
SD : 05 :022(562) [0959] for our trespasses and **raised** for our justification," who
SD : 06 :012(566) [0967] brings to life, he brings down into Sheol, and **raises** up."
SD : 06 :014(566) [0967] But the same Spirit **raises** them up again and comforts
SD : 11 :020(619) [1069] and lead them in his ways, **raise** them up again when they
SD : 11 :096(632) [1095] and sincere repentance, **raise** him up through faith,

Rampant (2)
AP : 07 :022(172) [0235] teachers may run **rampant** in the church, they are not,
LC : 01 :217(394) [0643] conduct which now is so **rampant** everywhere in public

Ran (1)
LC : 01 :144(385) [0623] instead, everybody **ran** in the devil's name into

Rank (5), Ranks (1)
AP : 12 :145(205) [0297] Thus they **rank** them above the works of God's
AP : 12 :145(205) [0297] whose works they **rank** above the works of the law.
AP : 14 :001(214) [0315] church polity and various **ranks** of the ecclesiastical
TR : 00 :011(321) [0507] He is an apostle of superior **rank**.
EP : 12 :021(499) [0841] as man is fully equal in **rank** and essential estates to the
SD : 12 :029(635) [1101] way equal in grade and **rank** of essence to the Father and

Rankles (1)
LC : 05 :077(455) [0771] which feels nothing though the disease rages and **rankles**.

Ransom (1)
AP : 12 :157(207) [0301] sin, not as a payment for or a **ransom** from eternal death.

Rant (1)
AP : 28 :001(281) [0443] Here our opponents **rant** about the privileges and the

Rare (2), Rarely (1)
AP : 04 :290(151) [0203] and feeble keeping of the law is **rare**, even among saints.
AP : 18 :005(225) [0335] even civil righteousness is **rare** among men, as we see from
LC : SP :006(362) [0575] times, though they were **rarely** taught and treated

Rascal (1), Rascality (3), Rascals (2)
AP : 23 :063(248) [0381] Just look at these impudent **rascals**!
AP : 27 :019(272) [0425] These **rascals** have the audacity to call this statement
S3 : 03 :020(306) [0485] to recount the torture, **rascality**, and idolatry which such
LC : 01 :298(405) [0665] know how to put up a fine front to conceal our **rascality**.
LC : 01 :298(405) [0665] it should be called not **rascality** but shrewdness and
SD : 07 :024(573) [0979] is that even though a **rascal** receives or gives the

Rash (2), Rashly (2)
AG : 27 :030(075) [0079] it is not right to argue so **rashly** and insistently about the
AL : 26 :018(067) [0073] taken up this matter **rashly** or out of hatred for the
AP : 12 :138(203) [0293] eternal punishments; it is **rash** for them to say, therefore,
SD : 07 :059(580) [0993] that some are so **rash** that they now cite this passage,

Rate (1)
LC : 01 :272(401) [0657] to remain secret, or at any **rate** be reproved in secret, as

Rather (105)
PR : PR :008(005) [0009] **Rather**, with divine assistance, it was our intention to
AG : 16 :007(038) [0051] sin, we must obey God **rather** than men (Acts 5:29).
AG : 20 :035(046) [0057] good works but is **rather** to be praised for teaching that
AG : 23 :013(053) [0063] produced any good but **rather** gave occasion for many
AG : 26 :032(068) [0075] and this is true and real **rather** than invented
AG : 28 :075(094) [0095] rule which commands us to obey God **rather** than men.
AL : 16 :007(038) [0051] then they ought to obey God **rather** than men (Acts 5:29).
AL : 20 :014(043) [0055] it would be a reward for works **rather** than a free gift."
AL : 20 :035(046) [0057] On the contrary, it should **rather** be commended for
AL : 26 :014(066) [0073] in releasing them but **rather** entangled consciences even
AL : 26 :032(068) [0075] Christ is true and real, **rather** than invented,
AL : 28 :008(082) [0085] that are thus given, but **rather** such eternal things as
AL : 28 :075(094) [0095] which commands us to obey God **rather** than men.
AP : PR :015(099) [0101] **Rather** I have assembled the main arguments, to testify to
AP : 02 :051(107) [0119] thought it worthwhile **rather** to list, in the usual familiar
AP : 04 :015(109) [0123] the forgiveness of sins **rather** than receiving it freely for
AP : 04 :060(115) [0137] because of his mercy **rather** than because of our own
AP : 04 :072(117) [0141] we maintain not this, but **rather** that because of Christ by
AP : 04 :116(123) [0155] us acceptable to God" **rather** than love, which is the effect
AP : 04 :165(130) [0169] own keeping of the law **rather** than because of Christ's
AP : 04 :197(134) [0175] us before God, but **rather** that when it takes place in the
AP : 04 :198(134) [0175] to seek the will of God **rather** than the rewards, as is
AP : 04 :213(136) [0179] God because of them **rather** than because of Christ by
AP : 04 :227(139) [0183] not merely knowledge but **rather** a desire to accept and
AP : 04 :231(139) [0183] to the works of the Second Table **rather** than the First.
AP : 04 :238(141) [0187] a righteousness of the law **rather** than of the Gospel which
AP : 04 :261(145) [0195] him not only to the giving of alms but **rather** to faith.
AP : 04 :264(146) [0197] The text does not say this, but **rather** requires faith.
AP : 04 :287(150) [0203] or from the teaching of the law **rather** than the Gospel.
AP : 04 :294(152) [0203] justification to faith **rather** than to love, though love
AP : 04 :314(156) [0207] Christ, the mediator, **rather** than by faith, but also to
AP : 04 :321(157) [0209] **Rather**, smug hypocrites simply believe that their works
AP : 07 :010(170) [0229] It is, **rather**, made up of men scattered throughout the
AP : 07 :024(172) [0235] of the papal kingdom **rather** than of the church of Christ
AP : 07 :032(174) [0239] really acts of devotion **rather** than outward rules of
AP : 07 :034(175) [0239] according to the French **rather** than the German style.
AP : 07 :036(175) [0241] **Rather**, they are customs that do not pertain to the heart
AP : 11 :006(181) [0251] They ought **rather** show from divine law that the
AP : 12 :075(193) [0273] trust in our own works **rather** than in God's Word and
AP : 12 :086(194) [0277] that we are members of Moses **rather** than of Christ.
AP : 12 :136(203) [0293] are satisfactions, or **rather** "satispassions," or if
AP : 12 :149(206) [0299] the basilica of St. Peter **rather** than undergo the
AP : 13 :001(211) [0309] as some imagine, but are **rather** signs and testimonies of
AP : 16 :005(223) [0331] state or the family but **rather** approves them, and it
AP : 16 :013(224) [0333] does not weaken but **rather** strengthens the authority of
AP : 20 :002(227) [0339] We would **rather** agree with this church of the prophets
AP : 20 :011(228) [0341] us to register a complaint **rather** than compose a
AP : 21 :041(235) [0355] it leads to philosophical disputes **rather** than to piety.
AP : 23 :020(242) [0369] not commanded; it is voluntary **rather** than obligatory."
AP : 24 :051(259) [0403] worship in such things **rather** than in the proclamation of
AP : 24 :072(262) [0409] It is **rather** the remembrance of Christ's blessings and the
AP : 24 :085(265) [0413] or gifts of the people **rather** than the offering of the
AP : 24 :094(267) [0417] We do not forbid this, but **rather** we reject the transfer of
AP : 24 :097(268) [0417] *ex opere operato* **rather** than receiving it freely through
AP : 27 :004(269) [0421] other vices, too, which we would **rather** not talk about.
AP : 27 :016(271) [0425] As for celibacy, we would **rather** not discuss it.
AP : 27 :041(276) [0435] we have the command **rather** to bear the injury, to let
AP : 27 :062(280) [0441] since they were nomads **rather** than Israelites, their father
AP : 27 :069(281) [0443] life because of them **rather** than because of Christ through
AP : 28 :018(284) [0449] to traditions but is **rather** directed against traditions.
AP : 28 :018(284) [0449] unlimited authority," but **rather** a "caution about
AP : 28 :018(284) [0449] basis of another's Word **rather** than on the basis of their
AP : 28 :021(284) [0449] commands that we must obey God **rather** than men.
AP : 28 :025(285) [0451] For we must obey God **rather** than men (Acts 5:29).
S1 : PR :003(289) [0455] lost and all souls damned **rather** than suffer himself and
S2 : 03 :002(298) [0471] them or tear them down **rather** than preserve them with
S2 : 04 :008(299) [0473] the good pleasure of men **rather** than on a divine

Continued ▶

S 2 : 0 4 :016(301) [0477] lord," but we ought **rather** speak as the angel spoke to the
S 3 : 0 3 :014(305) [0483] **Rather**, men hoped by their own works to overcome and
S 3 : 0 3 :018(306) [0483] to grieve, but he would **rather** have sinned if he had been
T R : 0 0 :008(320) [0505] But not so with you; **rather** let the greatest among you
T R : 0 0 :038(326) [0515] Acts, "We must obey God **rather** than men" (Acts 5:29).
T R : 0 0 :041(327) [0517] They ought **rather** to abandon and execrate the pope and
T R : 0 0 :079(333) [0527] ordain godly teachers but **rather** support the cruelty of
L C : 0 1 :226(395) [0645] One would ten times **rather** lose the money from one's
L C : 0 1 :250(399) [0651] permit such a thing, but are **rather** to avert and prevent it.
L C : 0 1 :264(400) [0655] that everyone would **rather** hear evil than good about his
L C : 0 1 :303(406) [0667] as illegally acquired, but **rather** as honestly purchased.
L C : 0 1 :327(409) [0675] **Rather**, ask what God wants of you and what he will quite
L C : 0 2 :032(415) [0687] children's sermons, but **rather** the longer sermons
L C : 0 2 :056(418) [0693] through their works **rather** than through the Gospel and
L C : 0 3 :011(421) [0701] we are sinners; he wishes **rather** to draw us to himself so
L C : 0 3 :012(422) [0701] means despise our prayers, but **rather** prize them highly.
L C : 0 3 :036(425) [0707] This is **rather** obscure.
L C : 0 3 :048(426) [0711] there is nothing he would **rather** hear than to have his
L C : 0 3 :049(426) [0711] wickedness, but would **rather** keep God's name sacred
L C : 0 4 :035(441) [0741] they do not exclude but **rather** demand faith, for without
L C : 0 4 :040(441) [0743] treasure that is lacking; **rather**, what is lacking is that it
L C : 0 4 :053(443) [0745] This, perhaps, is a **rather** subtle point, but it is based
L C : 0 4 :059(444) [0747] My friend, **rather** invert the argument and conclude,
L C : 0 6 :020(459) [0000] **Rather**, whoever is a Christian, or would like to be one,
L C : 0 6 :026(460) [0000] **Rather** we advise: If you are poor and miserable, then go
L C : 0 6 :030(460) [0000] not under compulsion but **rather** coming and compelling
S D : P R :002(503) [0851] **Rather**, we pledge ourselves again to those public and
S D : P R :015(507) [0857] since they destroy **rather** than edify, should never be
S D : 0 1 :007(510) [0861] **Rather**, along with the nature which God still creates and
S D : 0 2 :019(524) [0889] a hard stone which resists **rather** than yields in any way to
S D : 0 2 :086(538) [0913] of sound doctrine but **rather** opposes it and therefore is
S D : 0 3 :027(544) [0925] not precede justification; **rather** they follow it, since a
S D : 0 3 :028(544) [0925] before God; it **rather** follows justification, because in this
S D : 0 5 :024(563) [0961] **Rather**, since "the law was our custodian until Christ
S D : 0 7 :090(585) [1003] Christ and to receive it, **rather** than ascribe it to the
S D : 0 8 :073(605) [1041] **Rather**, since Christ according to the Godhead is the
S D : 1 0 :022(615) [1061] They ought **rather** abandon and execrate the pope and
S D : 1 1 :007(617) [1065] and promote it), but **rather** the wicked and perverse will

Rational (8)
E P : 0 1 :001(466) [0779] of his being (that is, his **rational** soul in its highest form
E P : 0 1 :009(467) [0781] not be recognized by a **rational** process, but only from
E P : 0 2 :014(471) [0789] Old Adam, especially the **rational** soul, and that in
S D : 0 1 :001(508) [0859] his essence (namely, his **rational** soul in its highest degree
S D : 0 2 :019(524) [0889] the Fall is no longer a **rational** creature, or that he is
S D : 0 2 :059(532) [0905] conversion man is still a **rational** creature with an
S D : 0 2 :062(533) [0905] of acting in man as a **rational** creature and another mode
S D : 0 2 :081(537) [0911] Adam, and especially the **rational** soul, are completely

Ratisbon (1)
A G : P R :018(026) [0041] at the diet convened in **Ratisbon** had considered the

Ravage (1)
L C : 0 1 :244(398) [0649] of thanks they burn and **ravage** house and home and

Rave (1), Raves (1)
L C : 0 1 :187(390) [0633] content to let our enemies **rave** and rage and do their
L C : 0 3 :062(428) [0715] like a furious foe, he **raves** and rages with all his power

Ravens (1)
S C : 0 8 :010(354) [0559] the beasts their food, and to the young **ravens** which cry.

Reach (6), Reached (7), Reaches (1), Reaching (2)
P R : P R :012(006) [0013] Christian undertaking **reached** some of us, we not only
P R : P R :017(008) [0015] well-intended agreements **reached** by our praiseworthy
P R : P R :017(008) [0015] therewith we have **reached** Christian unanimity and
A L : 2 7 :033(076) [0079] of them took vows before they **reached** such an age.
A P : 0 4 :008(108) [0121] works far beyond the **reach** of reason, like true fear of
S 3 : 0 3 :025(307) [0485] church and house was **reached** by jubilee indulgences.
L C : 0 1 :232(396) [0647] commandment is very far-**reaching**, as we have shown.
L C : 0 1 :247(398) [0651] to bear, for they will **reach** God, who watches over poor,
L C : 0 1 :310(407) [0669] though as long as we live here we cannot **reach** that ideal.
L C : 0 2 :026(413) [0685] is very rich and far-**reaching**, but in order to treat it
L C : 0 3 :091(432) [0723] he will ever in this life **reach** the point where he does not
L C : 0 4 :070(445) [0749] When he **reaches** full manhood, the real vices become
S D : P R :015(506) [0857] On this point we have **reached** a basic and mutual
S D : 0 2 :039(528) [0895] while still in this life, **reach** the point where they desire to
S D : 0 7 :074(583) [0999] In this question we have **reached** the following fraternal
S D : 1 1 :081(629) [1089] perish, but that all should **reach** repentance" (II Pet. 3:9).

Read (59), Reading (15), Reads (5)
P R : P R :015(007) [0013] us have had this document **read** article by article to each
A G : 2 4 :038(060) [0067] words of the Nicene canon **read**, "After the priests the
A G : 2 4 :041(061) [0069] Friday the Scriptures were **read** and expounded in
A G : 2 7 :019(073) [0079] command in I Cor. 7:2 **reads**, "Because of the temptation
A L : 2 4 :037(060) [0067] words of the Nicene canon **read**, "In order, after the
A L : 2 4 :041(061) [0069] the Scriptures are **read** and the doctors expound them on
A L : 2 7 :025(074) [0079] Therefore, we **read** that they often granted dispensation
A L : 2 7 :056(080) [0083] Cases can be **read** of men who, forsaking marriage and
A P : P R :001(098) [0099] After a public **reading** of our princes' Confession, a
A P : P R :001(098) [0099] Imperial Majesty had this **read** before the assembly of the
A P : P R :006(098) [0101] For during the **reading** some of us had taken notes on the
A P : 0 4 :105(122) [0153] and others "irrefutable" — **read** them and reread them,
A P : 0 4 :133(125) [0159] day whenever Moses is **read** a veil lies over their minds;
A P : 0 4 :224(138) [0181] many texts because they **read** their own opinions into
A P : 0 4 :244(142) [0189] if our opponents do not **read** into them their opinion
A P : 0 4 :253(143) [0193] opponents twist them by **reading** into them their own
A P : 0 4 :255(143) [0193] if our opponents did not **read** something false into them.
A P : 0 7 :027(173) [0235] care anything for the Gospel or think it worth **reading**?
A P : 1 2 :048(188) [0265] for they neither see nor **read** the sentence of the law
A P : 1 4 :005(215) [0315] Thus men may **read** that, despite our protest against the
A P : 1 5 :042(221) [0327] and walk out on them after the **reading** of the Gospel.
A P : 2 3 :002(239) [0363] in any history can one **read** of greater brazenness than
A P : 2 3 :052(246) [0377] In its satires Rome still **reads** and recognizes its own
A P : 2 4 :060(260) [0405] but faith in Christ, as we **read** (Rom. 5:1), "Since we are
A P : 2 4 :083(264) [0413] since anyone who **reads** the Greek authors can find
A P : 2 7 :027(274) [0429] It is terrible to **read** and hear such pharisaical and even
T R : 0 0 :082(000) [0529] [I have **read**, and again and again reread, the Confession
T R : 0 0 :082(000) [0529] I have also **read** the Formula of Concord concerning the
T R : 0 0 :082(000) [0529] I have also **read** the articles written at the Assembly at
S C : P R :006(338) [0533] and these forms and **read** them to the people word for
L C : P R :002(358) [0567] books, or if they have them, to examine and **read** them.
L C : P R :003(358) [0567] and evening they would **read**, instead, at least a page or
L C : P R :005(359) [0567] which they can absorb and master at one **reading**.
L C : P R :005(359) [0567] After **reading** it once they toss the book into a corner as
L C : P R :005(359) [0567] book into a corner as if they are ashamed to **read** it again.
L C : P R :007(359) [0569] else I have time, I **read** and recite word for word the
L C : P R :008(359) [0569] I must still **read** and study the Catechism daily, yet I
L C : P R :008(359) [0569] like quickly, with one **reading**, to become doctors above
L C : P R :009(359) [0569] and fruitful daily to **read** it and make it the subject of
L C : P R :009(359) [0569] In such **reading**, conversation, and meditation the Holy
L C : P R :011(360) [0571] alone you should eagerly **read**, recite, ponder, and
L C : P R :014(360) [0571] enough to admonish us to **read** the Catechism daily, there
L C : P R :016(361) [0571] who will not or cannot **read** and study the Catechism
L C : P R :016(361) [0573] if we imagine, after **reading** or hearing it once, that we
L C : P R :016(361) [0573] we know it all and need not **read** or study it any more?
L C : P R :019(361) [0573] Let them continue to **read** and teach, to learn and
L C : 0 1 :081(375) [0603] doing on that day, as we **read** in the Gospel — as if the
L C : 0 1 :092(377) [0607] taught, preached, heard, **read**, or pondered, there the
L C : 0 1 :097(378) [0609] one heard a Mass or the **reading** of the Gospel; no one
L C : 0 1 :181(389) [0631] in early times, as we **read** in Moses, parents had to bring
L C : 0 1 :305(406) [0669] the time of the law, for we **read** even in the Gospel that
L C : 0 3 :007(421) [0699] may be called singing or **reading** exercise, it is not really
L C : 0 3 :011(421) [0701] Therefore we **read** in the Scriptures that he is angry
L C : 0 3 :113(435) [0729] In the Greek this petition **reads**, "Deliver or keep us from
L C : 0 4 :009(437) [0735] So the words **read**, "Go, baptize," not in your name but
E P : 0 7 :025(484) [0815] their simple sense, as they **read**, but that they are dark
E P : 1 2 :010(498) [0839] where formerly papistic Masses were **read** and celebrated.
S D : 0 1 :037(514) [0871] And in Ecclesiastes we **read**, "And the dust returns to the
S D : 0 2 :009(521) [0883] educated people on earth **read** or hear the Gospel of the
S D : 0 2 :015(523) [0887] remiss and lazy in **reading**, hearing, and meditating on
S D : 0 2 :016(523) [0887] through daily exercise in **reading** his Word and putting it
S D : 0 2 :026(526) [0891] to heed the Word, as we **read** in Luke 24:45, "Then he
S D : 0 2 :040(528) [0895] Small Catechism we **read**: "I believe that by my own
S D : 0 2 :046(530) [0899] exercises as prayer, **reading**, and Christian meditation.
S D : 0 2 :046(530) [0899] refuse to heed, hear, or **read** the Word and the
S D : 0 2 :050(531) [0901] one hears it preached or **reads** it) and the sacraments
S D : 0 2 :053(531) [0903] regenerated can hear and **read** this Word externally
S D : 0 2 :057(532) [0903] will not hear preaching or **read** the Word of God, but
S D : 0 5 :010(560) [0955] that although "Moses is **read**," the veil which "he put over
S D : 0 7 :038(576) [0985] strict sense and as they **read**, and they do not consider
S D : 0 7 :045(577) [0987] obedience in their strict and clear sense, just as they **read**.
S D : 0 7 :046(577) [0989] and simply, as the words **read**, and committed the entire
S D : 0 7 :077(583) [0999] and blood, as his words **read**, 'This is my body,' etc.,
S D : 0 7 :092(586) [1005] from the way the letters **read**, but, as stated above, we
S D : 0 7 :113(589) [1011] their strict sense, as they **read**, concerning the true
S D : 0 7 :119(590) [1013] possession of heaven," to **read** "Christ must be received by
S D : 0 8 :038(598) [1027] His words **read**:
S D : 1 1 :084(630) [1091] Pharaoh (of whom we **read**, "For this purpose have I let
S D : 1 2 :015(634) [1099] in which the papistic Mass had formerly been **read**.

Reader (26), Readers (7)
P R : P R :001(003) [0007] To each and every **reader**, according to the requirements
A L : 2 0 :026(045) [0057] too, admonishes his **readers** in this way concerning the
A P : P R :000(098) [0099] Greetings from Philip Melanchthon to the **reader**.
A P : P R :009(098) [0101] And now, dear **reader**, you have our Apology.
A P : P R :014(099) [0101] in some places it could deceive even the cautious **reader**.
A P : 0 2 :031(104) [0113] The wise **reader** will easily be able to see that when the
A P : 0 4 :012(108) [0123] But let the intelligent **reader** just consider this.
A P : 0 4 :069(116) [0141] we would remind our **readers** that if we must hold to the
A P : 0 4 :284(150) [0201] An honest **reader** would not pick out the commands
A P : 0 4 :285(150) [0201] we would remind our **readers** that our opponents counsel
A P : 0 4 :353(161) [0217] the fair-minded **reader** can judge that we very definitely
A P : 0 4 :360(162) [0219] Look out, dear **reader**, you have not yet heard the whole
A P : 0 7 :042(176) [0243] from them the discerning **reader** can easily judge that the
A P : 0 7 :044(177) [0243] wisely admonished the **reader** neither to destroy
A P : 1 0 :004(179) [0247] to make clear to all our **readers** that we defend the
A P : 1 2 :058(189) [0267] all these passages godly **readers** can see that we put into
A P : 1 2 :083(194) [0275] obvious to every devout **reader** of Scripture, and we want
A P : 2 0 :011(228) [0341] The **reader** can find our proofs in our earlier discussion
A P : 2 0 :012(228) [0341] Now you see, dear **reader**, that our opponents have
A P : 2 2 :005(236) [0359] we leave it to the prudent **reader** to decide what he should
A P : 2 3 :002(239) [0363] First, let the intelligent **reader** consider the impudence of
A P : 2 3 :032(244) [0373] Let the **reader** note that he adds faith and does not praise
A P : 2 4 :003(250) [0385] point, but we leave it up to the judgment of the **reader**.
A P : 2 4 :010(251) [0387] We want to remind our **readers** of the real issue.
A P : 2 7 :020(272) [0425] From that the discerning **reader** will easily be able to
S D : P R :016(507) [0857] is true that the Christian **reader** who really delights in the
S D : P R :020(507) [0857] will enable the pious **reader**, as far as is necessary, to
S D : 0 5 :016(561) [0957] clearly for the Christian **reader**, we submit the following:
S D : 0 7 :066(581) [0997] we direct the Christian **reader** to our more extensive
S D : 0 7 :091(586) [1005] merely refer the Christian **reader** to these writings and
S D : 0 7 :111(589) [1011] thereby forewarn our **readers** so they can avoid and shun
S D : 0 8 :035(597) [1027] becomes tangled up and the simple **reader** is easily misled.
S D : 1 0 :004(611) [1053] we offer the Christian **reader** the following exposition:

Readily (14), Ready (12)
A G : 0 0 :001(095) [0095] The others can **readily** be weighed in the light of these.
A G : 0 0 :007(096) [0095] in some respect, we are **ready** to present further
A L : 2 0 :035(046) [0057] Hence it may **readily** be seen that this teaching is not to
A L : 0 0 :006(049) [0059] However, it can **readily** be judged that nothing
A L : 2 3 :023(055) [0063] This can be **readily** understood now that the prohibition
A L : 0 0 :003(095) [0095] being briefly set forth, may more **readily** be understood.
A L : 0 0 :017(096) [0095] in this confession, we are **ready**, God willing, to present
A P : 0 4 :084(119) [0145] Experienced consciences can **readily** understand this.
A P : 0 4 :268(147) [0197] Afterwards, as we **readily** admit, the punishments that

Continued ▶

A P : 0 4 :386(166) [0225] we are "guarded for a salvation **ready** to be revealed."
A P : 1 1 :005(181) [0249] because not everyone is **ready** in the same way at the
A P : 1 1 :005(181) [0251] not force those who are not **ready** to use the sacraments.
A P : 2 4 :023(253) [0391] of the word more **readily** if we look at the customs which
S 2 : 0 2 :014(295) [0467] dreamed of) shall we be **ready** to discuss with them
S C : 0 9 :005(355) [0561] to be obedient, to be **ready** for any honest work"
L C : 0 1 :053(371) [0595] From this everyone can **readily** infer when and in how
L C : 0 1 :151(386) [0625] who is obedient, willing, **ready** to serve, and cheerfully
L C : 0 1 :184(390) [0633] in turn rage and we are **ready** to shed blood and take
L C : 0 4 :002(436) [0733] In order that it may be **readily** understood, we shall treat
E P : 0 1 :015(468) [0783] may be removed as **readily** as a spot can be washed from
S D : 0 2 :007(521) [0883] he could make himself **ready** for the grace of God or to
S D : 0 2 :073(535) [0909] discussion one can **readily** recognize, expose, reject, and
S D : 0 8 :004(592) [1017] Confession, not quite **ready** to commit themselves
S D : 0 8 :092(609) [1049] and wisdom can **readily** provide that through his divine
S D : 1 1 :082(630) [1089] the master of the house, **ready** for any good work"
S D : 1 1 :090(631) [1093] they would lose it more **readily** than Adam and Eve did in

Real (43)
A G : 1 6 :004(037) [0051] of proper fear of God and **real** faith in God, for the
A G : 2 6 :032(068) [0075] suffer, and this is true and **real** rather than invented
A L : 2 6 :032(068) [0075] with Christ is true and **real**, rather than invented,
A P : 0 4 :062(115) [0139] terrifies our consciences with **real** and serious fears.
A P : 0 4 :204(135) [0177] in these works, but in **real** terror they pile up works and
A P : 1 2 :034(186) [0261] men love God amid such **real** terrors when they feel the
A P : 1 2 :149(205) [0299] genuine punishments than are **real** terrors in the heart.
A P : 1 2 :153(206) [0299] this sense of wrath, is a **real** punishment as long as it is
A P : 1 2 :168(209) [0305] the public rite and use it to denote the **real** mortification.
A P : 1 5 :049(221) [0329] experience that traditions are **real** snares for consciences.
A P : 1 6 :010(224) [0333] and blinded them to the essence of **real** perfection.
A P : 1 8 :007(226) [0337] These are the **real** works of the first table, which the
A P : 2 1 :007(230) [0345] do not require these **real** honors; they only argue about
A P : 2 2 :013(238) [0361] that we are minimizing the **real** dignity of the order, we
A P : 2 3 :060(247) [0381] The **real** purpose of the law is not religion but
A P : 2 3 :063(248) [0381] Paul points out the **real** author of such a law when he
A P : 2 3 :063(248) [0381] The **real** author is evident in the results, the many
A P : 2 4 :010(251) [0387] We want to remind our readers of the **real** issue.
A P : 2 4 :010(251) [0387] Once the **real** issue of the controversy is clear, it will be
A P : 2 4 :023(253) [0391] the death of Christ is a **real** satisfaction or expiation for
A P : 2 4 :023(253) [0391] the death of Christ is the only **real** propitiatory sacrifice.
A P : 2 4 :038(257) [0399] the commemoration is the **real** daily sacrifice, the
A P : 2 4 :039(257) [0399] we can see that their **real** meaning is spiritual worship and
A P : 2 4 :051(259) [0401] The **real** adornment of the churches is godly, practical,
A P : 2 4 :090(266) [0415] forgiveness of sins, which necessarily implies **real** guilt.
S 2 : 0 4 :010(300) [0475] that the pope is the **real** Antichrist who has raised himself
S 3 : 0 6 :005(311) [0493] without any longer being **real** bread, for that bread is and
T R : 0 0 :075(333) [0525] Not in punishing **real** offenses, but in dealing with
S C : 0 9 :013(356) [0563] "She who is a **real** widow, and is left all alone, has set her
L C : 0 1 :193(391) [0635] Therefore it is God's **real** intention that we should allow
L C : 0 1 :301(405) [0667] over a large inheritance, **real** estate, etc., they resort to
L C : 0 3 :104(434) [0727] nets; indeed, they are the **real** "flaming darts" which are
L C : 0 4 :070(445) [0749] reaches full manhood, the **real** vices become more and
E P : 0 4 :004(476) [0797] Later on, a **real** controversy developed.
E P : 0 5 :008(479) [0803] it for the first time the **real** nature of their sin, and
E P : 0 8 :010(488) [0819] natures did not have a **real** and true communion with
S D : 0 2 :001(520) [0881] first of all set forth the **real** issue in this controversy.
S D : 0 2 :025(526) [0891] that belongs to its **real** beginning and completion in no
S D : 0 3 :047(548) [0933] 3. That our **real** righteousness before God is our love or
S D : 0 6 :014(566) [0967] But to reprove is the **real** function of the law.
S D : 0 7 :034(575) [0983] the Augsburg Confession's **real** meaning and intention in
S D : 0 8 :063(603) [1037] understood the term "**real** exchange" — a communication
S D : 0 8 :063(603) [1037] we have spoken of a "**real** exchange" in order to indicate

Reality (5), Realization (1), Realize (13), Realized (2)
A L : 2 4 :031(059) [0067] his benefits and **realize** that they are truly offered to us;
A P : P R :014(099) [0101] I saw the Confutation, I **realized** it was written so cleverly
A P : 0 4 :175(131) [0171] be added that we should **realize** how far we are from the
A P : 0 4 :270(147) [0197] (Matt. 19:17), we must **realize** that no one can keep the
A P : 1 3 :021(214) [0313] the promise as a present **reality** and believes that the
S 2 : 0 2 :001(293) [0463] in purgatory, although in **reality** this can and must be
L C : P R :002(358) [0567] books which are in **reality** what the old manuals claimed
L C : 0 1 :047(371) [0593] commandment well and **realize** that God will tolerate no
L C : 0 1 :095(378) [0607] without it, we must **realize** that God insists upon a strict
L C : 0 1 :100(379) [0609] devil breaks in and does his damage before we **realize** it.
L C : 0 1 :102(379) [0609] be spurred on by the **realization** that in this way the devil
L C : 0 3 :021(423) [0703] this promise should **realize** once again that he angers
L C : 0 3 :038(425) [0707] So we should **realize** that we are under the great necessity
L C : 0 3 :052(427) [0711] that all this may be **realized** in us and that God's name
L C : 0 3 :083(431) [0721] pray for them so we may **realize** that we have received
L C : 0 5 :061(453) [0767] is the highest wisdom to **realize** that this sacrament does
S D : 0 1 :062(519) [0879] but that we do not even **realize** what we are suffering."
S D : 0 7 :007(570) [0975] will imagine that the **reality** is joined to the symbols in
S D : 0 7 :031(574) [0983] I am saying, and I well **realize** what this will mean for me
S D : 0 8 :045(600) [1031] merely empty words which do not correspond to **reality**.
S D : 0 8 :053(601) [1033] in this controversy is to **realize** that no one can know

Really (84)
A G : 1 0 :001(034) [0047] and blood of Christ are **really** present in the Supper of
A P : 0 4 :035(112) [0131] Therefore men **really** sin even when they do virtuous
A P : 0 4 :036(112) [0131] A heart that **really** feels God's wrath cannot love him
A P : 0 4 :083(119) [0145] all the prophets, which is **really** citing the authority of the
A P : 0 4 :179(131) [0171] them, even though they have not **really** satisfied the law.
A P : 0 4 :285(150) [0201] This is what Paul **really** and truly means.
A P : 0 4 :346(160) [0217] on works, then it would **really** be unsure since works
A P : 0 7 :032(174) [0239] these observances were **really** acts of devotion rather than
A P : 1 2 :012(184) [0255] coldly about absolution, which **really** is by divine right.
A P : 1 2 :012(184) [0257] This is **really** what is called "departing before the
A P : 1 2 :013(184) [0257] Here their discussions **really** become confused.
A P : 1 2 :060(190) [0269] We insist that this faith is **really** necessary for the
A P : 1 2 :084(194) [0277] we have said is what Paul **really** and truly means; we
A P : 1 2 :164(208) [0303] Such condemnation **really** happens in contrition and in a
A P : 1 2 :169(209) [0305] keeps on stealing is not **really** sorry that he has stolen or
A P : 1 3 :004(211) [0309] firmly believe that God **really** forgives us for Christ's
A P : 1 8 :008(226) [0337] God's will, whether they **really** believe that God regards
A P : 2 1 :034(233) [0353] Let us look at this as it **really** is.
A P : 2 1 :035(234) [0353] as though there had **really** been such a Polyphemus.
A P : 2 1 :042(235) [0355] If they **really** had the good of the church at heart at this
A P : 2 3 :012(241) [0367] Natural right is **really** divine right, because it is an
A P : 2 3 :036(244) [0373] more than marriage does, we shall **really** object.
A P : 2 3 :061(247) [0381] to remain continent, as long as he is **really** continent.
A P : 2 3 :064(248) [0381] lust than that of many celibates who are **really** continent.
A P : 2 4 :016(252) [0389] Plato would **really** call our opponents "poor cooks," for
A P : 2 4 :022(253) [0391] There has **really** been only one propitiatory sacrifice in
A P : 2 4 :024(253) [0391] therefore they were not **really** propitiations, since the
A P : 2 4 :029(255) [0393] that calling upon God is **really** worshiping and honoring
A P : 2 4 :033(256) [0395] by which the name of the Lord **really** becomes great.
A P : 2 4 :035(256) [0397] Our opponents will **really** achieve something if we let them
A P : 2 4 :048(258) [0401] This teaching **really** consoles consciences.
A P : 2 4 :049(258) [0401] to timid consciences **really** to trust and believe that their
A P : 2 4 :070(262) [0409] without the faith which **really** believes that the
A P : 2 4 :074(263) [0409] from terror, then it **really** gives thanks for the blessing of
A P : 2 4 :080(264) [0411] It does not **really** mean a sacrifice but a public service.
A P : 2 4 :087(265) [0413] not about prayers, but **really** about the Lord's Supper.
A P : 2 7 :009(270) [0421] Are vows **really** vows if they have been extorted from the
A P : 2 7 :039(276) [0433] praises about perfection, they **really** believe otherwise.
A P : 2 7 :039(276) [0433] Therefore they **really** believe that they have merits left
A P : 2 7 :057(279) [0439] even the canons maintain that such vows are **really** vows.
A P : 2 8 :027(285) [0451] boasting that they have **really** refuted our Confession with
S 2 : 0 2 :008(294) [0465] is not honest, for if he **really** desires to commune, he can
S 3 : 0 3 :010(304) [0481] repentance because they did not know what sin **really** is.
S 3 : 0 3 :016(305) [0483] not be contrite (that is, **really** repentant), he should at
S 3 : 0 3 :018(306) [0483] unless perchance he was **really** smitten by the law or
S 3 : 0 3 :032(308) [0487] of you knows what sin **really** is, to say nothing of
S 3 : 0 3 :042(310) [0491] and the Spirit, he never **really** had the Spirit and faith.
L C : P R :009(359) [0569] heads that they are not **really** and truly such learned and
L C : 0 1 :003(365) [0581] heart clings and entrusts itself is, I say, **really** your God.
L C : 0 1 :147(385) [0623] In the sight of God it is **really** faith that makes a person
L C : 0 1 :310(407) [0669] and shows just how upright we **really** are in God's sight.
L C : 0 2 :048(416) [0691] word "church" *(Kirche)* **really** means nothing else than a
L C : 0 3 :007(421) [0699] to pass for prayers in the church was not **really** prayer.
L C : 0 3 :007(421) [0699] called singing or reading exercise, it is not **really** prayer.
L C : 0 3 :092(432) [0723] Thus this petition is **really** an appeal to God not to regard
L C : 0 4 :055(443) [0747] hour, as if he had not **really** received the sacrament the
L C : 0 4 :074(445) [0751] called Penance, which is **really** nothing else than
L C : 0 5 :020(449) [0757] which the sacrament was **really** instituted, for it is most
L C : 0 5 :054(453) [0765] and act like a person who **really** desires to be right with
L C : 0 5 :062(454) [0767] him, saying, "I would **really** like to be worthy, but I come
L C : 0 6 :032(460) [0000] Those who **really** want to be good Christians, free from
E P : 0 5 :009(479) [0803] of God's wrath which **really** directs people into the law,
E P : 0 7 :004(482) [0809] terminology they **really** retain the former crass opinion
E P : 0 7 :012(483) [0811] Christ, **really** and truly set at this right hand of God
E P : 0 8 :002(487) [0817] with their properties, ***really*** (that is, in deed and truth)
E P : 0 8 :003(487) [0817] that neither of the two ***really*** (that is, in deed and in
E P : 0 8 :003(487) [0819] called God, but that God **really** (that is, in deed and in
E P : 0 8 :003(487) [0819] and that the humanity **really** has nothing in common with
E P : 0 8 :011(488) [0821] Son of God and hence **really** (that is, in deed and in
E P : 0 8 :015(488) [0821] to his human nature is **really** (that is, in deed and in
E P : 0 8 :025(490) [0823] man, man is God," since **really** (that is, in fact) the deity
S D : P R :010(503) [0849] Christians who are **really** concerned about the truth may
S D : P R :016(507) [0857] the Christian reader who **really** delights in the truth of
S D : 0 1 :019(511) [0865] damage allegedly are not **really** and truly such a sin in the
S D : 0 1 :057(518) [0877] never questioned by any **really** intelligent person that
S D : 0 1 :059(519) [0879] **Really** to settle this offensive and highly detrimental
S D : 0 2 :047(530) [0901] and wonder if God has **really** elected them and actually
S D : 0 3 :062(550) [0937] of sins," but to be made **really** and truly righteous on
S D : 0 4 :017(554) [0943] something that is **really** unwilled by him or even contrary
S D : 0 5 :010(560) [0955] to the law, and there he **really** learns to know his sin, an
S D : 0 7 :009(570) [0975] and blood of Christ are **really** present in the Holy Supper
S D : 0 8 :074(606) [1043] the personal union, he **really** and truly has received all
S D : 1 2 :003(633) [1097] the Augsburg Confession **really** is and what it really
S D : 1 2 :003(633) [1097] Augsburg Confession really is and what it **really** means.

Realm (4)
A P : 0 7 :023(172) [0235] and the spiritual **realm**, both swords, the temporal and
A P : 1 3 :018(213) [0313] taught with great authority throughout the papal **realm**.
A P : 2 4 :098(268) [0417] So in the papal **realm** the worship of Baal clings —
A P : 2 4 :098(268) [0419] together with the papal **realm** until Christ comes to judge

Reap (2), Reaper (2)
A P : 0 4 :367(163) [0221] sows sparingly will also **reap** sparingly, he who sows
A P : 0 4 :367(163) [0221] sows bountifully will also **reap** bountifully" (II Cor. 9:6);
L C : 0 1 :135(383) [0619] you will not obey him, then obey the grim **reaper**, Death!
L C : 0 1 :149(385) [0623] godliness, we deliver to the hangman and the grim **reaper**.

Reared (2), Rearing (1)
A P : 1 5 :025(219) [0323] of the household, married life, and the **rearing** of children.
L C : 0 1 :114(380) [0613] properly taught, and **reared** in true blessedness; they
L C : 0 1 :176(389) [0631] hell by the way you have **reared** your own children, no

Reason (203), Reasons (59)
P R : P R :018(009) [0015] For that **reason**, likewise, we have ordered the
P R : P R :018(009) [0017] of our faith and for that **reason** allegedly make a new
P R : P R :022(011) [0019] are also many other **reasons** why condemnations cannot
P R : P R :022(011) [0021] For this **reason** we desire to testify before the face of
A G : P R :016(026) [0041] Spires in 1526, that for **reasons** there stated Your
A G : 1 3 :002(036) [0049] For this **reason** they require faith, and they are rightly
A G : 1 8 :001(039) [0051] make choices among the things that **reason** comprehends.
A G : 1 8 :004(039) [0051] for all have a natural, innate understanding and **reason**.
A G : 0 0 :002(048) [0059] offer firm grounds and **reasons** why we have changed
A G : 0 0 :000(049) [0059] them and to indicate our **reasons** for permitting changes
A G : 2 2 :001(049) [0059] The **reason** is that there is a clear command and order of
A G : 2 3 :003(051) [0061] They have given as their **reason** that they have been
A G : 2 3 :009(052) [0061] to themselves for these and other **reasons** and causes.
A G : 2 3 :002(053) [0063] may well have been some **reasons** for prohibiting the
A G : 2 3 :002(053) [0063] better, and weightier **reasons** for permitting them to be
A G : 2 5 :013(063) [0071] of terrified consciences, and also for other **reasons**.

Continued ▶

AG : 2 6 :002(064) [0071] For this **reason** new fasts, new ceremonies, new orders,
AG : 2 6 :022(067) [0073] **Reasons** for this shall be cited from the Scriptures.
AG : 2 7 :024(074) [0079] If there were no **reasons** which allowed annulment of the
AG : 2 7 :033(076) [0079] have excuse and **reason** for leaving their monasteries
AG : 2 7 :036(076) [0081] teachers offer still more **reasons** why monastic vows are
AG : 2 8 :073(093) [0093] Perhaps there was some **reason** for introducing them, but
AL : 0 2 :003(029) [0045] be justified before God by his own strength and **reason**.
AL : 0 8 :002(033) [0047] Word are effectual by **reason** of the institution and
AL : 1 8 :001(039) [0051] and for the choice of things subject to **reason**.
AL : 1 8 :004(039) [0051] enables them to make judgments according to **reason**.
AL : 0 0 :001(049) [0059] changed and what our **reasons** for such changes are in
AL : 2 3 :002(051) [0061] that there were some **reasons** why priests were forbidden
AL : 2 3 :002(051) [0061] are now far weightier **reasons** why this right should be
AL : 2 3 :009(052) [0061] For these **reasons** our priests teach that it is lawful for
AL : 2 7 :024(074) [0079] not be changed for any **reason** at all, the Roman pontiffs
AL : 2 7 :036(076) [0081] offer still another **reason** to show that vows are void.
AL : 2 8 :060(091) [0091] do this for the additional **reason** that men would have an
AL : 2 8 :073(093) [0093] there were acceptable **reasons** for these ordinances when
AP : PR :007(098) [0101] him that very weighty **reasons** prevented us from
AP : 0 2 :012(102) [0109] we agree is subject to **reason** and somewhat in our power.
AP : 0 4 :007(108) [0121] to some extent human **reason** naturally understands the
AP : 0 4 :008(108) [0121] external works that **reason** can somehow perform.
AP : 0 4 :008(108) [0121] far beyond the reach of **reason**, like true fear of God, true
AP : 0 4 :009(108) [0123] only the righteousness of **reason**—that is, civil works—
AP : 0 4 :009(108) [0123] without the Holy Spirit **reason** can love God above all
AP : 0 4 :009(108) [0123] is within them, that is, if **reason** in its sorrow over sin
AP : 0 4 :012(109) [0123] If we can be justified by **reason** and its works, what need
AP : 0 4 :016(109) [0123] by the works of **reason**, there will be no difference
AP : 0 4 :018(109) [0125] is never satisfied, that **reason** performs only certain
AP : 0 4 :021(110) [0127] but the righteousness of **reason** or of law, at which they
AP : 0 4 :022(110) [0127] maintain that God requires the righteousness of **reason**.
AP : 0 4 :023(110) [0127] To some extent, **reason** can produce this righteousness by
AP : 0 4 :024(110) [0127] give this righteousness of **reason** its due credit; for our
AP : 0 4 :026(110) [0127] before God because of the righteousness of **reason**.
AP : 0 4 :027(111) [0127] that by its own strength **reason** can love God above all
AP : 0 4 :027(111) [0127] But **reason** can produce civil works.
AP : 0 4 :031(111) [0129] Therefore **reason** cannot free us from our sins or merit
AP : 0 4 :031(111) [0129] then the righteousness of **reason** does not justify us before
AP : 0 4 :034(111) [0129] contain the civil righteousness that **reason** understands.
AP : 0 4 :039(112) [0131] of law or of **reason** which our opponents teach.
AP : 0 4 :042(113) [0133] So Paul **reasons** in Rom. 4:14, "If it is the adherents of
AP : 0 4 :108(122) [0153] they suppose that this is repeated so often for no **reason**?
AP : 0 4 :139(126) [0161] And I John 3:8 says, "The **reason** the Son of God
AP : 0 4 :154(128) [0165] It was not without **reason** that this truly powerful
AP : 0 4 :189(133) [0175] For these **reasons** good works must necessarily be done.
AP : 0 4 :201(134) [0175] and we show many **reasons** why they should be done.
AP : 0 4 :222(137) [0181] It would be a fallacy to **reason** that because it is necessary
AP : 0 4 :230(139) [0183] is to the judgment of **reason** and law and that the
AP : 0 4 :243(141) [0189] It is not without **reason** that the apostles speak so often
AP : 0 4 :258(144) [0193] Come now, let us **reason** together, says the Lord: though
AP : 0 4 :263(145) [0195] We are not to **reason** from this that God forgives because
AP : 0 4 :265(146) [0197] Human **reason** naturally admires them; because it sees
AP : 0 4 :275(148) [0199] follow reconciliation — but he does so for two **reasons**.
AP : 0 4 :275(148) [0199] The other **reason** is that we need external signs of this
AP : 0 4 :287(150) [0203] either from human **reason** or from the teaching of the law
AP : 0 4 :287(150) [0203] one based upon **reason**, the other based upon the law,
AP : 0 4 :288(151) [0203] This mode is a doctrine of **reason**.
AP : 0 4 :288(151) [0203] uncleanness of the heart, **reason** thinks that it pleases God
AP : 0 4 :288(151) [0203] For this **reason** the canonists have twisted ecclesiastical
AP : 0 4 :291(152) [0203] that we are justified neither by **reason** nor by the law.
AP : 0 4 :296(152) [0205] Far away from human **reason**, far away from Moses, we
AP : 0 4 :297(153) [0205] not justified before God either by **reason** or by the law.
AP : 0 4 :313(155) [0207] as well as the **reasons** that compel us to hold that we are
AP : 0 4 :344(160) [0217] seems that for some such **reason** the scholastics invented
AP : 0 4 :373(164) [0221] and of faith, and for this **reason** eternal life is granted to
AP : 0 4 :376(164) [0223] From these passages they **reason** that works merit grace
AP : 0 4 :379(165) [0223] works, either done by the **reason** or at least wrought by
AP : 0 4 :387(166) [0225] justification derived either from **reason** or from the law.
AP : 0 4 :394(167) [0225] only righteousness that **reason** can see is the
AP : 0 7 :009(169) [0229] We set forth this doctrine for a very necessary **reason**.
AP : 0 7 :022(172) [0235] not made up of men by **reason** of their power or position,
AP : 0 7 :027(173) [0237] what agrees with human **reason** and regard the rest as
AP : 0 7 :032(174) [0239] We certainly had weighty **reasons** for presenting this
AP : 0 7 :032(174) [0239] For good and valid **reasons**, these vary according to the
AP : 1 2 :016(184) [0257] that good and proper **reasons** prompted us to reject the
AP : 1 2 :077(193) [0275] where we gave our **reasons** for declaring that men are
AP : 1 2 :079(193) [0275] For these **reasons** Paul contends that we are not justified
AP : 1 2 :090(195) [0279] grave and important **reasons** for disagreeing with our
AP : 1 2 :112(198) [0285] The **reason** for the confession was not that without it
AP : 1 2 :113(199) [0285] There seem to have been many **reasons** for this.
AP : 1 2 :116(199) [0287] For this **reason** we have discussed satisfactions in
AP : 1 2 :159(207) [0301] Christ replied that the **reason** for his blindness was not sin
AP : 1 3 :020(213) [0313] The **reason** for this is clear and well founded.
AP : 1 4 :001(214) [0315] had good and useful **reasons** for instituting ecclesiastical
AP : 1 4 :002(214) [0315] of the bishops is the **reason** for the abolition of canonical
AP : 1 5 :021(218) [0321] For these **reasons** the Fathers kept ceremonies, and for
AP : 1 5 :021(218) [0321] and for the same **reasons** we also believe in keeping
AP : 1 5 :022(218) [0321] But because human **reason** does not understand the
AP : 1 5 :024(218) [0321] This is how human **reason** interprets fasting and bodily
AP : 1 5 :024(218) [0321] is to restrain the flesh, **reason** imagines that they are to be
AP : 1 5 :051(222) [0329] rites without good **reason**, and to foster harmony those
AP : 1 8 :002(225) [0335] justification by works that **reason** produces on its own?
AP : 1 8 :004(225) [0335] the works and things which **reason** by itself can grasp.
AP : 1 8 :004(225) [0335] human nature still has **reason** and judgment about the
AP : 1 8 :004(225) [0335] nature — that is, the **reason** — can achieve on its own
AP : 1 8 :005(225) [0335] For these **reasons** even civil righteousness is rare among
AP : 2 2 :009(237) [0359] Among the **reasons** why both kinds are not given,
AP : 2 2 :009(237) [0359] This is no doubt the main **reason** for defending the denial
AP : 2 2 :011(238) [0361] They should not ask for a **reason**; but whatever the
AP : 2 2 :012(238) [0361] of God, will the **reasons** he gives exonerate those who
AP : 2 3 :004(239) [0365] have the most serious of **reasons**, taken from the Word of
AP : 2 3 :025(243) [0371] tyranny, and with good **reason**: Daniel says that it is
AP : 2 3 :026(243) [0371] regulation for religious **reasons**, since they see that it is
AP : 2 3 :050(246) [0377] celibacy for religious **reasons**, for they know that chastity
AP : 2 3 :051(246) [0377] *Sixth*, we have many **reasons** for rejecting the law of
AP : 2 3 :053(246) [0379] There are so many good **reasons** for changing it,
AP : 2 3 :070(249) [0383] With **reasons** like these they persuade the princes to take
AP : 2 4 :007(250) [0385] common daily Mass, **reasons** of piety or of profit later
AP : 2 4 :068(261) [0407] that the Lord's Supper was instituted for two **reasons**.
AP : 2 4 :090(266) [0415] purgatory has, the **reasons** they adduce in support of the
AP : 2 4 :099(268) [0419] that we have most valid **reasons** for disagreeing with our
AP : 2 7 :056(278) [0439] many serious and cogent **reasons** that release good men
S 1 : PR :001(288) [0455] In any case, we had **reason** to expect that we might be
S 1 : PR :010(290) [0457] sake, and we have no **reason** to hope or expect that a
S 2 : 0 2 :006(293) [0463] the Mass for no other **reason** than to curb such abuses,
S 3 : 0 1 :003(302) [0477] a corruption of nature that **reason** cannot understand it.
S 3 : 0 3 :010(305) [0481] and uncorrupted, that **reason** is capable of right
S 3 : 0 3 :018(306) [0483] Here we see how blind **reason** gropes about in matters
S 3 : 0 8 :007(313) [0495] have attained the age of **reason** must first have heard, "He
TR : 0 0 :002(320) [0503] things, and for such **reasons** the bishop of Rome calls
TR : 0 0 :024(324) [0511] church, and for the same **reason** the church especially
TR : 0 0 :058(330) [0521] compelling, and evident **reasons** for not submitting to the
TR : 0 0 :058(330) [0521] pope, and these urgent **reasons** are a comfort to the godly
TR : 0 0 :076(333) [0527] And since we have good **reason** for not obeying, it is
TR : 0 0 :078(333) [0527] courts, there is additional **reason** why other courts should
TR : 0 0 :079(333) [0527] and compelling **reasons** why the churches should not
SC : 0 2 :002(345) [0543] my limbs and senses, my **reason** and all the faculties of
SC : 0 2 :006(345) [0545] I believe that by my own **reason** or strength I cannot
SC : 0 9 :005(355) [0561] For the same **reason** you also pay taxes, for the
LC : PR :001(358) [0567] It is not for trivial **reasons** that we constantly treat the
LC : PR :011(360) [0571] For this **reason** alone you should eagerly read, recite,
LC : PR :014(360) [0571] and command this so solemnly without good **reason**.
LC : SP :003(362) [0575] For this **reason** young people should be thoroughly
LC : SP :027(364) [0581] The **reason** we take such care to preach on the Catechism
LC : 0 1 :125(382) [0617] be the first and strongest **reason** impelling us to keep this
LC : 0 1 :126(382) [0617] to provide us sufficient **reason** and incentive to do
LC : 0 1 :143(385) [0623] they should do it for the **reason** just mentioned, that it is
LC : 0 1 :183(390) [0633] us harm, and so we have **reason** to be at enmity with
LC : 0 1 :258(399) [0653] The **reason** is this: Where judges, mayors, princes, or
LC : 0 1 :286(403) [0663] Our chief **reason** for doing so should be the one which
LC : 0 1 :321(408) [0673] For this **reason** I said that we should keep it before the
LC : 0 1 :331(410) [0677] it is not without **reason** that the Old Testament
LC : 0 2 :013(412) [0681] faculties of my mind, my **reason** and understanding, and
LC : 0 2 :023(413) [0683] For this **reason** we ought daily to study this article and
LC : 0 2 :048(416) [0691] except for the single **reason** that the group of people
LC : 0 2 :063(419) [0695] all the wisdom, understanding, and **reason** of men.
LC : 0 3 :016(422) [0701] The **reason** is this: I freely admit that he is holier in
LC : 0 3 :024(423) [0703] been prescribed for this **reason**, also, that we should
LC : 0 4 :013(438) [0735] But mad **reason** rushes forth and, because Baptism is not
LC : 0 4 :045(442) [0743] This is the **reason** why these two things are done in
LC : 0 5 :043(451) [0763] may be induced to see the **reason** and the need for
LC : 0 5 :056(453) [0767] Then nature and **reason** begin to contrast our
LC : 0 5 :056(453) [0767] Because nature and **reason** see this, such people refuse to
LC : 0 5 :058(453) [0767] For this **reason** we must make a distinction among men.
LC : 0 5 :071(455) [0769] and which is the very **reason** for this command and
LC : 0 5 :078(455) [0771] and infirmities, the more **reason** you have to go to the
LC : 0 5 :082(456) [0773] The only **reason** we go about so securely and heedlessly is
LC : 0 6 :024(460) [0000] run to the place, no **reason** being given and no mention
EP : 0 2 :002(470) [0787] man's understanding and **reason** are blind and that he
EP : 0 3 :009(474) [0793] graves, they still have no **reason** to doubt either the
EP : 0 6 :001(479) [0805] given to men for three **reasons**: (1) to maintain external
EP : 0 7 :042(486) [0817] we cannot comprehend with our human sense or **reason**.
EP : 0 8 :012(488) [0821] Son of God; for this **reason** she is rightly called, and truly
EP : 0 9 :002(492) [0827] with our senses and **reason**, but must be apprehended by
EP : 0 9 :004(492) [0827] as well, which our blind **reason** cannot comprehend in
EP : 1 1 :009(495) [0833] to eternal life on the basis either of **reason** or God's law.
EP : 1 1 :009(495) [0833] long as men follow their **reason**, they can hardly escape
EP : 1 1 :016(497) [0837] but in accord with his **reason** and under the direction of
EP : 1 2 :006(498) [0839] not achieved the use of **reason** they will be saved in this
EP : 1 2 :007(498) [0839] have achieved the use of **reason** and can confess their
EP : 1 2 :008(498) [0839] For this **reason**, too, the Anabaptists neither think highly
SD : PR :010(503) [0849] For that **reason** necessity requires that such controverted
SD : PR :007(505) [0853] the grounds and **reasons** are set forth at necessary length
SD : PR :011(506) [0855] The **reason** why we have embodied the writings above
SD : PR :019(507) [0857] Interim and for other **reasons**, we wanted to set forth and
SD : 0 1 :001(508) [0859] For this **reason** there is now after the Fall allegedly no
SD : 0 1 :008(510) [0861] Thirdly, **reason** does not know and understand the true
SD : 0 1 :009(510) [0861] inherited damage is the **reason** why all of us, because of
SD : 0 1 :011(510) [0863] powers and the light of **reason**, is by nature diametrically
SD : 0 1 :012(510) [0863] which are subject to **reason** man still possesses a measure
SD : 0 1 :012(510) [0863] possesses a measure of **reason**, power, and ability,
SD : 0 1 :016(511) [0865] For this **reason** we shall briefly enumerate the contrary
SD : 0 1 :024(512) [0865] which are subject to human **reason** in the next article.
SD : 0 1 :026(512) [0867] For that **reason** the following and similar errors are
SD : 0 1 :038(515) [0871] ears, and all my members, my **reason** and all my senses."
SD : 0 1 :038(515) [0871] faculties of my mind, my **reason** and understanding," etc.
SD : 0 1 :042(515) [0871] For that **reason** and in order to distinguish God's creature
SD : 0 1 :056(518) [0877] suspicion, and for that **reason** without ever being
SD : 0 1 :058(519) [0879] For this **reason** the churches of God will never attain
SD : 0 1 :060(519) [0879] indeed, no human **reason**, be it ever so keen, can give the
SD : 0 2 :008(521) [0883] The following **reasons** from the Word of God support and
SD : 0 2 :008(521) [0883] are contrary to proud **reason** and philosophy, but we also
SD : 0 2 :009(521) [0883] place, although man's **reason** or natural intellect still has
SD : 0 2 :009(522) [0883] spiritual things with their **reason**, the less they understand
SD : 0 2 :019(524) [0889] For this **reason** the Holy Scriptures compare the heart of
SD : 0 2 :026(526) [0891] To some extent **reason** and free will are able to lead an
SD : 0 2 :029(527) [0893] For that **reason** we begin our teaching with faith, through
SD : 0 2 :029(527) [0893] article states that "human **reason** and power without
SD : 0 2 :031(527) [0893] also declare that to a certain extent **reason** has a free will.
SD : 0 2 :031(527) [0893] can be comprehended by **reason** we have a free will."
SD : 0 2 :032(527) [0893] spiritual things our free will and **reason** can do nothing."
SD : 0 2 :040(528) [0895] believe that by my own **reason** or strength I cannot
SD : 0 2 :043(529) [0897] ability, no cleverness or **reason**, with which we can
SD : 0 2 :060(533) [0905] way that man's darkened **reason** becomes an enlightened
SD : 0 2 :061(533) [0905] For this same **reason** it is not quite right to say that
SD : 0 2 :085(537) [0913] For that **reason** with the law of his mind he serves the law

Continued ▶

SD : 0 3 :029(544) [0925] For this **reason** we summarily cut off every reference to
SD : 0 3 :043(547) [0931] justifies solely for this **reason** and on this account, that as
SD : 0 3 :053(548) [0933] Paul's **reason** is that we receive both our righteousness
SD : 0 3 :053(548) [0933] For this **reason** Paul uses and urges exclusive terms (that
SD : 0 3 :058(550) [0937] For this **reason** neither the divine nor the human nature
SD : 0 4 :002(551) [0939] — not for salvation, however, but for other **reasons**.
SD : 0 4 :009(552) [0941] For this **reason** St. Paul calls them fruits of faith or of the
SD : 0 4 :029(555) [0947] Hence and for these **reasons** it is right for our churches to
SD : 0 4 :030(555) [0947] For this **reason** it is important to declare well and in
SD : 0 5 :011(560) [0955] us the Spirit, and for this **reason** the latter is called the
SD : 0 5 :027(563) [0961] For this **reason** and in order that both doctrines, law and
SD : 0 7 :045(577) [0987] as they appear to our **reason**, but we must accept them in
SD : 0 7 :045(577) [0987] spun out of human **reason**, to turn us away from these
SD : 0 7 :045(577) [0987] words, no matter how appealing our **reason** may find it.
SD : 0 7 :046(577) [0987] contrary not only to **reason** and to divine and natural law
SD : 0 7 :046(577) [0989] seemed impossible to his **reason**, he gave God the honor
SD : 0 7 :046(578) [0989] of Isaac than he could comprehend with his blind **reason**.
SD : 0 7 :047(578) [0989] is to be reconciled with our **reason** or how it is possible.
SD : 0 7 :091(585) [1003] All the imaginary **reasons** and futile counter-arguments
SD : 0 7 :102(587) [1007] it transcends nature and **reason**, even the comprehension
SD : 0 7 :106(588) [1009] they may appear to **reason**, and will enable a Christian
SD : 0 8 :022(595) [1023] For this **reason** the ancient teachers of the church have
SD : 0 8 :041(599) [1029] "If the old witch, Dame **Reason**, the grandmother of the
SD : 0 8 :050(600) [1031] and that for this **reason** nothing should or can be ascribed
SD : 0 8 :056(601) [1035] These **reasons** are the following:
SD : 0 8 :096(609) [1049] this mystery with their **reason**, but with the holy apostles
SD : 0 8 :096(609) [1049] believe, close the eyes of **reason**, take their intellect
SD : 0 9 :003(610) [1051] With our **reason** and five senses this article cannot be
SD : 1 1 :026(620) [1071] on the basis of our **reason**, or on the basis of the law, or
SD : 1 1 :034(622) [1075] The **reason** why "many are called and few are chosen" is
SD : 1 1 :037(622) [1075] For this **reason** Christ has the promises of the Gospel
SD : 1 1 :038(622) [1075] For that **reason** also, as the Augsburg Confession states in
SD : 1 1 :041(623) [1077] The **reason** for such contempt of the Word is not God's
SD : 1 1 :042(623) [1077] But the **reason** for this is not that God does not want to
SD : 1 1 :042(623) [1077] The **reason** is that they willfully turn away from the holy
SD : 1 1 :047(624) [1079] For this **reason**, too, Paul asks, Since we are called
SD : 1 1 :078(629) [1089] The **reason** why all who hear the Word do not come to
SD : 1 1 :091(632) [1093] of God but according to **reason** and the suggestion of the
SD : 1 2 :002(632) [1095] we had not for that **reason** intended to make special and
SD : 1 2 :012(634) [1099] have achieved the use of **reason** and are able to make

Reasonable (7)
AP : 0 4 :288(151) [0203] gaining justification is **reasonable** and is preoccupied with
AP : 2 4 :088(265) [0413] "We offer Thee this **reasonable** and bloodless service."
AP : 2 4 :088(265) [0413] to translate this as "**reasonable** victim" and apply it to the
AP : 2 4 :088(265) [0413] whole service; and by "**reasonable** service" (Rom. 12:1)
AP : 2 4 :093(267) [0417] "Yet we offer Thee this **reasonable** service for those who
AP : 2 4 :093(267) [0417] And "**reasonable** service" does not mean the host itself
S2 : 0 2 :002(293) [0463] If there were **reasonable** papists, one would speak to them

Reasoned (1), Reasoning (2)
PR : PR :010(006) [0011] be stopped by solid **reasoning**, and a correct explanation
TR : 0 0 :011(321) [0507] time, however, they **reasoned** thus: "Cephas observes this.
LC : 0 1 :023(367) [0587] This **reasoning**, however, is a little too subtle to be

Rebaptize (1)
LC : 0 4 :055(443) [0745] would be valid and no one should **rebaptize** them.

Rebel (1), Rebelled (1), Rebelliously (1), Rebels (1)
LC : 0 1 :151(386) [0625] love, but despises or **rebelliously** resists authority, let him
LC : 0 1 :162(387) [0627] everybody resists and **rebels**; all are afraid that their
SD : 0 2 :060(533) [0905] oppose and constantly **rebel** against acknowledged truth,
SD : 1 1 :085(630) [1091] and he deliberately **rebelled** against all the admonitions

Rebirth (5), Reborn (28), Reborne (1)
AP : 0 4 :251(143) [0191] of the just who have already been justified and **reborn**.
AP : 0 4 :256(144) [0193] law unless we have been **reborn** by faith in Christ, as
AP : 0 4 :263(146) [0195] **Reborn** in this way, they bring forth fruits worthy of
AP : 0 4 :310(155) [0207] first been reconciled and **reborn**. The greatest possible
AP : 0 4 :311(155) [0207] law unless we have been **reborn** through the Gospel, and
AP : 0 4 :313(155) [0207] justified, reconciled, and **reborn** by faith, if indeed we
AP : 0 4 :315(156) [0207] we can keep the law, our hearts must be **reborn** by faith.
AP : 0 4 :349(160) [0217] For this purpose we are **reborn** and receive the Holy
AP : 0 4 :352(161) [0217] This **rebirth** is, so to speak, the beginning of eternal life,
AP : 0 4 :368(163) [0221] we have been reconciled to God, justified, and **reborn**.
AP : 0 4 :386(166) [0225] reconciled to him, and **reborn** by a faith that penitently
AP : 0 7 :014(170) [0231] but by being God's true people, **reborn** by the Holy Spirit.
EP : 0 2 :001(469) [0785] own powers, before he is **reborn** through the Holy Spirit,
EP : 0 2 :014(471) [0789] that in conversion and **rebirth** God wholly destroys the
EP : 0 2 :014(471) [0789] that in conversion and **rebirth** he creates out of nothing a
EP : 0 2 :017(472) [0791] of repentance, the **reborn** will of man is not idle but
EP : 0 3 :008(474) [0793] the words *regeneratio* (**rebirth**) and *vivificatio* (making
EP : 0 4 :010(476) [0799] in so far as they are **reborn**, render not by coercion or
EP : 0 6 :001(479) [0805] sin, (3) after they are **reborn**, and although the flesh still
EP : 0 6 :001(480) [0805] whether or not the law is to be urged upon **reborn**
EP : 0 6 :004(480) [0805] although they are indeed **reborn** and have been renewed
EP : 0 6 :006(481) [0807] in so far as they are **reborn** and do them as spontaneously
EP : 0 6 :007(481) [0807] spirit, in so far as he is **reborn**, does what no threat of the
EP : 1 2 :023(500) [0841] God seals the adoption of children and effects **rebirth**.
EP : 1 2 :027(500) [0843] unless he is himself truly **reborn**, righteous, and pious.
SD : 0 2 :010(522) [0883] The others, who are not **reborn** through God's Spirit,
SD : 0 2 :015(523) [0887] his Son, and for having **reborne** and illuminated us
SD : 0 2 :024(525) [0891] illuminated, converted, **reborn**, renewed, and drawn by
SD : 0 2 :063(533) [0905] is good, in so far as he is **reborn** or a new man, and he
SD : 0 2 :068(534) [0907] the Spirit continues also in the elect and truly **reborn**.
SD : 0 2 :088(538) [0915] such conversion man's **reborn** will is not idle in the daily
SD : 0 3 :022(543) [0923] Holy Spirit's work we are **reborn** and justified, we do not
SD : 0 6 :009(565) [0965] truly believing, elect, and **reborn** children of God require
SD : 0 6 :016(566) [0967] as long as a person is not **reborn**, lives according to the

Rebuke (8), Rebuked (7), Rebukes (6)
AL : 2 7 :034(076) [0079] of vows might be **rebuked**, yet it seems not to follow of
AL : 2 7 :060(080) [0083] Before our times Gerson **rebuked** the error of the monks
AL : 2 8 :003(081) [0085] have long since been **rebuked** in the church by devout and
AL : 2 8 :048(089) [0091] He **rebukes** such services and says, "Every plant which my
AP : 0 4 :207(135) [0177] we see how vehemently the prophets **rebuke** the people.
AP : 1 2 :055(189) [0267] Adam was **rebuked** and terrified after his sin; this was
AP : 1 2 :056(189) [0267] Thus David is **rebuked** by Nathan, and in his terror he
AP : 1 2 :150(206) [0299] prays (Ps. 6:1), "O Lord, **rebuke** me not in thy anger"; and
S2 : 0 4 :016(301) [0477] in Zechariah, "The Lord **rebuke** you, O Satan"
TR : 0 0 :056(330) [0521] so they ought also to **rebuke** the pope when he evades and
LC : 0 1 :038(369) [0591] When they are **rebuked**, to bring them to their senses and
LC : 0 1 :273(401) [0659] and slanders someone, **rebuke** him straight to his face and
SD : 0 5 :002(558) [0951] of repentance, which **rebukes** the greatest sin, unbelief.
SD : 0 5 :011(560) [0955] strange deed" (that is, to **rebuke**) until he comes to his
SD : 0 5 :017(561) [0957] "Everything that **rebukes** sin is and belongs to the law,
SD : 0 5 :018(561) [0957] of the law remains, to **rebuke** sin and to give instruction
SD : 0 5 :019(561) [0957] way in which the law **rebukes** unbelief, when a person
SD : 0 5 :019(561) [0957] the office of the law **rebukes** the unbelief involved in
SD : 0 5 :027(563) [0961] the law is a message that **rebukes** and condemns sin.
SD : 0 6 :012(566) [0967] to comfort but also to **rebuke**, as it is written, "When the
SD : 0 6 :014(566) [0967] Christians trip, they are **rebuked** through the Spirit of

Rebuttal (1)
AP : 1 2 :155(207) [0301] In **rebuttal** they bring up the case of Adam, and of David

Recalcitrant (4)
SD : 0 2 :022(525) [0889] our human nature is in **recalcitrant** enmity against God —
SD : 0 4 :019(554) [0945] this unwilling and **recalcitrant** flesh, Paul says, "I
SD : 0 6 :012(566) [0967] are lazy, negligent, and **recalcitrant**, the Holy Spirit
SD : 0 6 :024(568) [0969] an unmanageable and **recalcitrant** donkey, is still a part

Recall (7), Recalled (2)
AL : 2 7 :001(071) [0075] better understood if it is **recalled** what the condition of
AL : 2 7 :026(075) [0079] of Aragon, who was **recalled** from a monastery, and there
AP : 1 1 :001(180) [0249] should diligently try to **recall** them and to enumerate
AP : 1 1 :001(180) [0249] try to recall them and to enumerate those one does **recall**.
AP : 2 1 :036(234) [0353] It would be useful to **recall** such examples as these which
S3 : 0 3 :015(305) [0483] Since nobody could **recall** all his sins (especially those
LC : 0 3 :097(433) [0725] when we pray we may **recall** the promise and think,
SD : 1 1 :065(627) [1085] me" (John 16:14) and **recall** everything to you that I have
SD : 1 1 :075(628) [1087] stumble, he arranges to **recall** them to repentance through

Recant (1)
SD : 0 2 :027(526) [0891] persuaded him to **recant** his former erroneous opinion as

Recapitulation (1)
EP : 0 0 :000(464) [0777] with God's Word in the **Recapitulation** Here Following

Recede (1)
LC : 0 4 :086(446) [0753] the mercy-seat, does not **recede** from us or forbid us to

Receive (204), Received (141), Receives (37), Receiving (14)
PR : PR :014(007) [0013] judgments had been **received** they were found to contain
AG : 0 4 :001(030) [0045] satisfactions, but that we **receive** forgiveness of sin and
AG : 0 6 :002(032) [0045] For we **receive** forgiveness of sin and righteousness
AG : 1 0 :001(034) [0047] of bread and wine and are there distributed and **received**.
AG : 1 2 :001(034) [0049] who sin after Baptism **receive** forgiveness of sin whenever
AG : 1 3 :002(036) [0049] used when they are **received** in faith and for the purpose
AG : 1 8 :003(039) [0051] "Natural man does not **receive** the gifts of the Spirit of
AG : 2 0 :023(044) [0055] faith as believes that we **receive** grace and forgiveness of
AG : 2 0 :025(044) [0057] upon him, and have no hope of **receiving** good from him.
AG : 2 1 :001(046) [0057] we see what grace they **received** and how they were
AG : 2 2 :003(050) [0059] of the congregation in Corinth **received** both kinds.
AG : 2 2 :008(050) [0061] whom this custom of **receiving** only one kind was
AG : 2 3 :005(051) [0061] "Not all men can **receive** this precept," he indicated
AG : 2 4 :034(060) [0067] the priest and others **receive** the sacrament for
AG : 2 4 :038(060) [0069] priests the deacons shall **receive** the sacrament in order
AG : 2 7 :037(077) [0081] we believe that God **receives** us into his favor for the sake
AG : 2 8 :006(082) [0085] **Receive** the Holy Spirit.
AL : 0 4 :002(030) [0045] believe that they are **received** into favor and that their
AL : 0 5 :003(031) [0045] who believe that they are **received** into favor for Christ's
AL : 0 5 :003(031) [0045] Gal. 3:14, "That we might **receive** the promise of the
AL : 0 6 :003(032) [0047] faith alone, and he shall **receive** forgiveness of sins by
AL : 0 9 :002(033) [0047] to God through Baptism they are **received** into his grace.
AL : 1 2 :001(034) [0049] fallen after Baptism can **receive** forgiveness of sins
AL : 1 8 :003(039) [0051] heart when the Holy Spirit is **received** through the Word.
AL : 2 0 :009(042) [0053] we believe that we are **received** into favor for Christ's
AL : 2 0 :029(045) [0057] faith the Holy Spirit is **received**, hearts are so renewed
AL : 2 3 :005(051) [0061] said, "Not all men can **receive** this precept" (Matt. 19:11),
AL : 2 4 :005(056) [0065] people are accustomed to **receive** the sacrament together,
AL : 2 4 :030(059) [0067] what benefits are **received** through Christ and should
AL : 2 4 :037(060) [0067] presbyters and deacons **received** the body of the Lord
AL : 2 4 :038(060) [0069] let the deacons **receive** Holy Communion from the bishop
AL : 2 5 :004(062) [0069] faith truly obtains and **receives** the forgiveness of sins.
AL : 2 6 :005(064) [0071] believes that for Christ's sake we are **received** into grace.
AL : 2 7 :037(077) [0081] who believe that they are **received** by God into favor for
AL : 2 8 :006(082) [0085] **Receive** the Holy Spirit.
AL : 0 0 :005(095) [0095] that nothing has been **received** among us, in doctrine or in
AP : PR :007(098) [0101] Confutation, but his Imperial Majesty did not **receive** it.
AP : 0 2 :018(103) [0111] him, that is, that man **received** gifts like the knowledge of
AP : 0 2 :030(104) [0113] unspiritual man does not **receive** the gifts of the Spirit of
AP : 0 4 :001(107) [0119] teaching that men do not **receive** the forgiveness of sins
AP : 0 4 :001(107) [0121] for denying that men **receive** the forgiveness of sins
AP : 0 4 :001(107) [0121] for affirming that men **receive** the forgiveness of sins by
AP : 0 4 :015(109) [0123] of sins rather than **receiving** it freely for his merits.
AP : 0 4 :018(109) [0125] for his sake they freely **receive** the forgiveness of sins and
AP : 0 4 :049(114) [0135] is that worship which **receives** God's offered blessing; the
AP : 0 4 :049(114) [0135] namely, that we **receive** from him what he promises and
AP : 0 4 :057(114) [0137] Therefore they **received** free mercy and the forgiveness of
AP : 0 4 :060(115) [0137] accept his blessings and **receive** them because of his mercy
AP : 0 4 :062(115) [0139] of sins and justification, which are **received** by faith.
AP : 0 4 :062(115) [0139] For these, our hearts must again **receive** consolation.
AP : 0 4 :062(115) [0139] of mind, consoles us, **receives** the forgiveness of sins,
AP : 0 4 :066(116) [0139] they deny that it is **received** through the Word.
AP : 0 4 :067(116) [0139] Word, and the Word is **received** only by faith, then it

Continued ▶

A P : 0 4 :070(116) [0141] keep the law unless we first **receive** the Holy Spirit.
A P : 0 4 :072(117) [0141] one, that is, that it **receives** the forgiveness of sins.
A P : 0 4 :081(118) [0143] to the Father and **receive** the forgiveness of sins when we
A P : 0 4 :081(118) [0145] for Christ's sake we **receive** the forgiveness of sins.
A P : 0 4 :082(118) [0145] as an expiation," and Paul adds, "to be **received** by faith."
A P : 0 4 :082(118) [0145] us when by faith we **receive** the mercy promised in him
A P : 0 4 :083(118) [0145] one who believes in him **receives** forgiveness of sins
A P : 0 4 :083(118) [0145] We **receive** the forgiveness of sins, he says, through his
A P : 0 4 :085(119) [0147] this declaration, that we **receive** the forgiveness of sins for
A P : 0 4 :086(119) [0147] alone justifies because we **receive** the forgiveness of sins
A P : 0 4 :086(119) [0147] in itself, but because it **receives** God's promise that for
A P : 0 4 :099(121) [0151] but a thing that **receives** the Holy Spirit and justifies us.
A P : 0 4 :106(122) [0153] terrified by the law but **receive** consolation by faith, and
A P : 0 4 :106(122) [0153] we try to keep the law we should **receive** mercy by faith.
A P : 0 4 :110(123) [0153] If faith **receives** the forgiveness of sins on account of
A P : 0 4 :110(123) [0153] they believe that the forgiveness of sins is **received** freely.
A P : 0 4 :112(123) [0155] think from this that we **receive** the forgiveness of sins by
A P : 0 4 :112(123) [0155] love, just as little as we **receive** the forgiveness of sins on
A P : 0 4 :112(123) [0155] the forgiveness of sins is **received** by faith alone—and we
A P : 0 4 :112(123) [0155] the word—since the promise can be **received** only by faith.
A P : 0 4 :114(123) [0155] And because it **receives** the forgiveness of sins and
A P : 0 4 :116(123) [0155] And since this faith alone **receives** the forgiveness of sins,
A P : 0 4 :117(123) [0155] that by faith alone we **receive** the forgiveness of sins for
A P : 0 4 :118(123) [0155] Christ's work and **receive** his blessings and it alone
A P : 0 4 :119(123) [0155] which the faithful may **receive** the sure hope of salvation.
A P : 0 4 :119(124) [0155] doubt whether they have **received** the forgiveness of sins.
A P : 0 4 :119(124) [0155] they should doubt about **receiving** the forgiveness of sins?
A P : 0 4 :126(124) [0157] justified and regenerated, we **receive** the Holy Spirit.
A P : 0 4 :127(125) [0157] But the Spirit is **received** by faith, according to Paul's
A P : 0 4 :127(125) [0157] "That we might **receive** the promise of the Spirit
A P : 0 4 :132(125) [0159] for his sake we might **receive** the gift of the forgiveness of
A P : 0 4 :132(125) [0159] the law unless by faith we have **received** the Holy Spirit.
A P : 0 4 :133(125) [0159] removed except by faith, which **receives** the Holy Spirit.
A P : 0 4 :135(125) [0159] forgiveness of sins, we **receive** the Holy Spirit, so that we
A P : 0 4 :141(126) [0161] the Father; and having **received** the forgiveness of sins,
A P : 0 4 :144(127) [0161] **Receiving** the forgiveness of sins for a heart terrified and
A P : 0 4 :145(127) [0163] teach that we must first **receive** the forgiveness of sins by
A P : 0 4 :147(127) [0163] of all, that we do not **receive** the forgiveness of sins
A P : 0 4 :151(127) [0163] We do not **receive** the forgiveness of sins by other virtues
A P : 0 4 :151(127) [0163] Just as little do we **receive** the forgiveness of sins on
A P : 0 4 :158(129) [0165] for it is sure that we **receive** the forgiveness of sins by
A P : 0 4 :159(129) [0167] by the law; but we **receive** the forgiveness of sins and
A P : 0 4 :163(129) [0169] This forgiveness is always **received** by faith.
A P : 0 4 :163(129) [0169] Therefore it is always **received** by faith; we must always
A P : 0 4 :175(131) [0171] been regenerated by faith **receive** the Holy Spirit and that
A P : 0 4 :182(132) [0173] since by faith alone we **receive** the forgiveness of sins and
A P : 0 4 :182(132) [0173] Therefore it is **received** by faith alone, though the keeping
A P : 0 4 :186(132) [0173] of our love and works we **receive** the forgiveness of sins
A P : 0 4 :194(133) [0175] (I Cor. 3:8), "Each shall **receive** his wages according to his
A P : 0 4 :195(134) [0175] sins and justification are **received** only by faith, not
A P : 0 4 :201(134) [0175] that Abraham did not **receive** circumcision in order to be
A P : 0 4 :211(136) [0179] did not believe that they **received** these freely because of
A P : 0 4 :217(137) [0179] therefore it is always **received** before God by faith alone.
A P : 0 4 :222(138) [0181] that by our love we **receive** the promised forgiveness of
A P : 0 4 :224(138) [0181] justified, the Corinthians **received** many excellent gifts.
A P : 0 4 :228(139) [0183] God, this desire to **receive** the offered promise, is no less
A P : 0 4 :258(144) [0193] forgiveness of sins to be **received** by faith, and so he adds
A P : 0 4 :259(144) [0193] he wants the forgiveness of sins to be **received** by faith.
A P : 0 4 :259(145) [0193] he wishes the forgiveness of sins to be **received** by faith.
A P : 0 4 :261(145) [0195] voice which Daniel surely wanted to be **received** by faith.
A P : 0 4 :267(147) [0197] unless the heart first **receives** remission of guilt.
A P : 0 4 :271(148) [0199] Absolution should be **received** by faith, to cheer the
A P : 0 4 :273(148) [0199] one who believes in him **receives** forgiveness of sins
A P : 0 4 :291(152) [0203] that by faith in Christ we **receive** the forgiveness of sins,
A P : 0 4 :292(152) [0203] This promise is **received** by faith alone, as Paul declares in
A P : 0 4 :293(152) [0203] quickened by faith in this way, it **receives** the Holy Spirit.
A P : 0 4 :294(152) [0203] law but by the promise, which is **received** by faith only.
A P : 0 4 :294(152) [0203] the mediator; nor do we **receive** forgiveness of sin because
A P : 0 4 :310(155) [0207] of the Gospel is to **receive** good things from God, while
A P : 0 4 :310(155) [0207] Gospel is the desire to **receive** forgiveness of sins, grace,
A P : 0 4 :311(155) [0207] love God unless we have **received** the forgiveness of sins.
A P : 0 4 :312(155) [0207] and present things and **receives** in the present the
A P : 0 4 :349(160) [0217] we are reborn and **receive** the Holy Spirit, that this new
A P : 0 4 :351(161) [0217] While we are **receiving** encouragement and comfort in the
A P : 0 4 :366(163) [0219] to I Cor. 3:8, "Each shall **receive** his wages according to
A P : 0 4 :366(163) [0221] the promise of grace, **receives** justification and new life
A P : 0 4 :398(167) [0227] the terrors of sin, and **receive** peace for our conscience.
A P : 0 7 :021(172) [0233] doctrine that the forgiveness of sins is **received** by faith.
A P : 0 7 :023(172) [0235] and all kings have **received** their power and right to rule,
A P : 0 7 :029(173) [0237] that men sinned if they **received** the sacraments from
A P : 0 7 :048(177) [0245] contrary to that which you **received**, let him be accursed."
A P : 0 9 :002(178) [0245] We have therefore **received** this fruit from it, by God's
A P : 1 0 :001(179) [0247] bread and the wine, to those who **receive** the sacrament.
A P : 1 0 :004(179) [0247] we defend the doctrine **received** in the whole church —
A P : 1 1 :002(180) [0249] consciences have **received** consolation from our teaching.
A P : 1 1 :005(181) [0251] that those who **receive** in an unworthy manner
A P : 1 1 :005(181) [0251] in an unworthy manner **receive** judgment upon
A P : 1 2 :020(185) [0257] 4. We **receive** the forgiveness of sins because of
A P : 1 2 :062(190) [0269] anyone can be said to **receive** absolution unless he
A P : 1 2 :063(191) [0269] by his blood, to be **received** by faith," and Rom. 5:2,
A P : 1 2 :065(191) [0271] works and not in Christ to **receive** the forgiveness of sins.
A P : 1 2 :065(191) [0271] one who believes in him **receives** forgiveness of sins
A P : 1 2 :065(191) [0271] We **receive** the forgiveness of sins, therefore, only through
A P : 1 2 :066(191) [0271] one who believes in him **receives** forgiveness of sins
A P : 1 2 :082(194) [0275] faith, for the regenerate **receive** the Holy Spirit and
A P : 1 2 :084(194) [0277] defending: by faith we **receive** the forgiveness of sins for
A P : 1 2 :085(194) [0277] opponents that we do not **receive** the forgiveness of sins
A P : 1 2 :088(195) [0277] find peace if we **receive** the forgiveness of sins because we
A P : 1 2 :117(199) [0287] Such errors **received** support from many statements of
A P : 1 2 :151(206) [0299] "We felt that we had **received** the sentence of death; but
A P : 1 3 :005(212) [0309] Word," for the rite is **received** by the eyes and is a sort of
A P : 1 3 :006(212) [0309] unction are rites **received** from the Fathers which even the
A P : 1 5 :005(215) [0317] Christ's sake, we freely **receive** the forgiveness of sins and
A P : 1 8 :008(226) [0337] terrified hearts hear the Gospel and **receive** consolation.
A P : 2 0 :002(227) [0339] one who believes in him **receives** forgiveness of sins
A P : 2 0 :003(227) [0339] not mean to say that we **receive** the forgiveness of sins
A P : 2 0 :007(227) [0339] of the article that we **receive** the forgiveness of sins freely
A P : 2 0 :015(229) [0343] it; for when we have **received** the Holy Spirit by faith, the
A P : 2 1 :026(232) [0349] us from the enemy and **receive** us in the hour of death."
A P : 2 1 :027(232) [0349] for the church, does she **receive** souls in death, does she
A P : 2 1 :029(233) [0351] (I Cor. 3:8), "Each shall **receive** his wages according to his
A P : 2 2 :003(236) [0357] that he had **received** from the Lord what he
A P : 2 2 :006(237) [0359] who were not permitted to **receive** the entire sacrament.
A P : 2 3 :016(241) [0369] "Not all men can **receive** this precept, but only
A P : 2 3 :021(242) [0369] adds, "He who is able to **receive** this, let him receive it."
A P : 2 3 :021(242) [0369] adds, "He who is able to receive this, let him **receive** it."
A P : 2 4 :003(250) [0385] by the Word may **receive** faith and fear and so may also
A P : 2 4 :019(252) [0389] for the forgiveness of sins and other blessings **received**.
A P : 2 4 :046(258) [0401] faith, by which we freely **receive** the forgiveness of sins.
A P : 2 4 :059(260) [0405] so that thereby they may **receive** faith and the Holy Spirit
A P : 2 4 :075(263) [0411] of sins and that it ought to be **received** by faith.
A P : 2 4 :097(268) [0417] *opere operato* rather than **receiving** it freely through faith.
A P : 2 7 :013(271) [0423] the forgiveness of sins is **received** freely for Christ's sake,
A P : 2 7 :013(271) [0423] of the Gospel that we **receive** the forgiveness of sins not
A P : 2 7 :027(274) [0429] say, "We are constantly **receiving** another hood or other
A P : 2 7 :031(274) [0431] of sins but that we **receive** this freely by faith, as has been
A P : 2 7 :043(277) [0435] statement that they will **receive** a hundredfold in this life
A P : 2 8 :007(282) [0445] this teaching, that we **receive** forgiveness of sins freely for
A P : 2 8 :014(283) [0447] to that Word which they have **received** from Christ.
S 2 : 0 2 :029(297) [0471] institution of Christ and may use and **receive** it in faith.
S 2 : 0 4 :011(300) [0475] in Christ, and they **receive** bodily tribute and obedience
S 3 : 0 3 :005(304) [0481] were to be prepared to **receive** grace from the Lord and to
S 3 : 0 3 :032(308) [0487] from his fullness have we all **received**, grace upon grace.
S 3 : 0 3 :042(309) [0491] hold that once they have **received** the Spirit or the
S 3 : 0 3 :042(310) [0491] anyone sins after he has **received** faith and the Spirit, he
S 3 : 0 6 :001(311) [0493] that these are given and **received** not only by godly but
S 3 : 0 8 :007(313) [0495] once believe and did not **receive** the Spirit and Baptism
S 3 : 0 8 :011(313) [0497] whether Elijah or Elisha, **received** the Spirit without the
S C : P R :003(338) [0533] are baptized, and **receive** the holy sacrament, they do not
S C : P R :011(339) [0535] If any refuse to **receive** your instructions, tell them that
S C : P R :021(340) [0537] they are unwilling to **receive** the sacrament and they treat
S C : P R :021(340) [0537] to believe or to **receive** the sacrament, no law is to be
S C : P R :022(341) [0537] who does not desire to **receive** the sacrament at least three
S C : P R :023(341) [0539] him by any law to **receive** the sacrament, for he will
S C : P R :023(341) [0539] he will feel constrained to **receive** it, he will insist that you
S C : 0 3 :013(347) [0547] his gifts and enable us to **receive** our daily bread with
S C : 0 5 :016(349) [0553] The other is that we **receive** absolution or forgiveness from
S C : 0 5 :025(350) [0555] none in particular, but **receive** forgiveness upon the
S C : 0 6 :009(352) [0557] Who, then, **receives** this sacrament worthily?
S C : 0 8 :008(353) [0559] means that all creatures **receive** enough to eat to make
S C : 0 9 :010(356) [0563] anyone does, he will **receive** the same again from the
L C : 0 1 :015(366) [0583] or what you hoped to **receive** from mammon or anything
L C : 0 1 :021(367) [0585] it believe that whatever good it **receives** comes from God.
L C : 0 1 :022(367) [0585] it boasts, unwilling to **receive** anything as a gift from
L C : 0 1 :024(368) [0587] repeated, from whom we **receive** all that is good and by
L C : 0 1 :026(368) [0587] to us from men, we **receive** it all from God through his
L C : 0 1 :026(368) [0587] of neighbors — have **received** the command to do us all
L C : 0 1 :026(368) [0587] So we **receive** our blessings not from them, but from God
L C : 0 1 :027(368) [0587] Therefore, this way of **receiving** good through God's
L C : 0 1 :027(368) [0587] for that would be not **receiving** our blessings from God
L C : 0 1 :028(368) [0587] from which it hopes to **receive** more good and help than
L C : 0 1 :038(369) [0591] and foolish that they justly merit the wrath they **receive**.
L C : 0 1 :127(382) [0617] all the good things we have **received** from our parents.
L C : 0 1 :128(382) [0617] all the blessings we have **received** throughout our life.
L C : 0 1 :129(383) [0617] recognizes that he has **received** his body and life from
L C : 0 1 :145(385) [0623] work, for which she **receives** sustenance and wages, she
L C : 0 1 :151(386) [0625] that he pleases God and **receives** joy and happiness for
L C : 0 1 :160(387) [0627] But they very seldom **receive** it, for the world's way of
L C : 0 1 :168(388) [0629] power and authority to govern) merely to **receive** homage.
L C : 0 1 :184(390) [0633] envious that you have **received** from God a better house
L C : 0 1 :316(408) [0671] we must seek and pray for help and **receive** it continually.
L C : 0 1 :322(409) [0673] therefore, ought to be **received** and esteemed as a serious
L C : 0 2 :001(411) [0679] that we must expect and **receive** from God; in brief, it
L C : 0 2 :024(413) [0683] about what we have and **receive** from God and about
L C : 0 2 :026(413) [0685] and we see what we **receive** from God over and above the
L C : 0 2 :028(414) [0685] God the Father, and had **received** from him all kinds of
L C : 0 2 :039(416) [0689] us to the Lord Christ to **receive** this blessing, which we
L C : 0 3 :019(423) [0703] "For every one who asks **receives**."
L C : 0 3 :025(423) [0705] to God, not willing to **receive** anything from him, but
L C : 0 3 :027(424) [0705] and spread your cloak wide to **receive** many things.
L C : 0 3 :039(425) [0709] children so that he may **receive** from us not shame but
L C : 0 3 :054(427) [0713] world and that it may be **received** by faith and may work
L C : 0 3 :057(428) [0713] confidence that we shall **receive** them and scarcely
L C : 0 3 :074(430) [0719] Although we have **received** from God all good things in
L C : 0 3 :080(431) [0721] away or interfere with all we have **received** from God.
L C : 0 3 :081(431) [0721] it pains him that anyone **receives** a morsel of bread from
L C : 0 3 :083(431) [0721] may realize that we have **received** them from his hand and
L C : 0 3 :123(436) [0731] Therefore they **receive** nothing, as St. James says, "If
L C : 0 3 :123(436) [0731] must not suppose that he will **receive** anything from God."
L C : 0 4 :002(436) [0733] which we are first **received** into the Christian community.
L C : 0 4 :027(440) [0739] the Word Baptism **receives** the power to become the
L C : 0 4 :032(440) [0739] us observe further who **receives** these gifts and benefits of
L C : 0 4 :033(440) [0741] the person worthy to **receive** the salutary, divine water
L C : 0 4 :033(440) [0741] water, they cannot be **received** unless we believe them
L C : 0 4 :034(441) [0741] nothing toward salvation, and **receives** nothing.
L C : 0 4 :036(441) [0741] over you, you do not **receive** Baptism in such a manner
L C : 0 4 :036(441) [0741] name of God, you may **receive** in the water the promised
L C : 0 4 :037(441) [0741] and offered to us in the Word and **received** by faith.
L C : 0 4 :037(441) [0741] that without it nothing can be **received** or enjoyed.
L C : 0 4 :045(442) [0743] over it, though it cannot **receive** anything but the water,
L C : 0 4 :053(443) [0745] For my faith does not constitute Baptism but **receives** it.
L C : 0 4 :053(443) [0745] even if it is wrongly **received** or used, for it is bound not
L C : 0 4 :054(443) [0745] God's Word, even though he failed to **receive** it properly.
L C : 0 4 :054(443) [0745] of the Lord's Supper **receive** the true sacrament even
L C : 0 4 :055(443) [0747] as if he had not really **received** the sacrament the first
L C : 0 4 :056(443) [0747] was right, but unfortunately I did not **receive** it rightly."

Continued ▶

LC : 0 4 :059(444) [0747] has been wrongly **received**, it has existence and value.
LC : 0 4 :064(444) [0749] by which we are first **received** into the Christian church.
LC : 0 5 :001(447) [0753] what it is, what its benefits are, and who is to **receive** it.
LC : 0 5 :016(448) [0757] though a knave should **receive** or administer it, it is the
LC : 0 5 :017(448) [0757] or if you are worthy, you **receive** my body and blood,"
LC : 0 5 :022(449) [0757] sacrament because we **receive** there a great treasure,
LC : 0 5 :033(450) [0761] to consider who it is that **receives** this power and benefit.
LC : 0 5 :034(450) [0761] forgiveness of sins, it cannot be **received** except by faith.
LC : 0 5 :036(450) [0761] of a Christian for **receiving** this sacrament worthily.
LC : 0 5 :039(451) [0761] prepare themselves to **receive** this blessed sacrament
LC : 0 5 :040(451) [0763] years go by without **receiving** the sacrament, as if they
LC : 0 5 :043(451) [0763] reason and the need for **receiving** the sacrament, we shall
LC : 0 5 :058(453) [0767] for they are not fit to **receive** the forgiveness of sins since
LC : 0 5 :069(454) [0769] and lead unchristian lives **receive** it to their harm and
LC : 0 5 :070(454) [0769] in the sacrament you **receive** from Christ's lips the
LC : 0 5 :072(455) [0769] to the sacrament and **receive** refreshment, comfort, and
LC : 0 5 :085(456) [0773] young so that they will **receive** them with joy and
LC : 0 5 :087(456) [0773] they are baptized and **received** into the Christian church,
LC : 0 6 :018(459) [0000] but simply to accept and **receive** something from him.
LC : 0 6 :024(460) [0000] and no mention of what they were to look for or **receive**.
LC : 0 6 :024(460) [0000] not expecting to **receive** anything but just letting everyone
LC : 0 6 :029(460) [0000] Christian and that you ought not **receive** the sacrament.
EP : RN :002(465) [0777] Scriptures and should be **received** in no other way and no
EP : 0 2 :002(470) [0787] unspiritual man does not **receive** the gifts of the Spirit of
EP : 0 7 :002(481) [0809] the wine and if they are **received** orally by all those who
EP : 0 7 :003(482) [0809] and wine are present, distributed, and **received** orally.
EP : 0 7 :004(482) [0809] bread and wine are present and **received** with the mouth.
EP : 0 7 :006(482) [0809] are truly distributed and **received** with the bread and
EP : 0 7 :015(483) [0811] and blood of Christ are **received** not only spiritually, by
EP : 0 7 :016(484) [0813] and the unbelievers **receive** the true body and blood of
EP : 0 7 :016(484) [0813] and do not repent, they **receive** them not to life and
EP : 0 7 :019(484) [0813] retains a living faith, will **receive** the Holy Supper to his
EP : 0 7 :026(485) [0815] the body of Christ is not **received** orally with the bread,
EP : 0 7 :026(485) [0815] that with the mouth we **receive** only bread and wine and
EP : 0 7 :026(485) [0815] and wine and that we **receive** the body of Christ only
EP : 0 7 :037(486) [0815] Christians do not **receive** the body and blood of Christ,
EP : 0 7 :039(486) [0817] faith in Christ, can also **receive** this sacrament to their
EP : 0 8 :035(491) [0825] human nature of Christ **received** a power which is less
EP : 1 1 :022(497) [0837] that have developed **receive** a basic settlement.
EP : 1 2 :014(499) [0841] possesses and that it has **received** from God for their
EP : 1 2 :021(499) [0841] glorification his flesh **received** all the divine properties in
SD : PR :011(506) [0855] that all Evangelical churches and schools **received** them.
SD : 0 1 :045(516) [0873] man himself, since God **receives** man for Christ's sake
SD : 0 2 :010(522) [0883] unspiritual man does not **receive** the gifts of the Spirit of
SD : 0 2 :012(522) [0885] unspiritual man does not **receive** (or, as the Greek word
SD : 0 2 :026(526) [0891] But to be born anew, to **receive** inwardly a new heart,
SD : 0 2 :026(526) [0891] "What have you that you did not **receive**?
SD : 0 2 :026(526) [0891] If then you **received** it, why do you boast as if it were not
SD : 0 2 :068(534) [0907] since in this life we have **received** only the first fruits of
SD : 0 2 :072(535) [0909] admonishes us not to **receive** this grace of God in vain
SD : 0 2 :083(537) [0913] the Word, do not **receive** the Holy Spirit but grieve and
SD : 0 3 :030(544) [0925] mediator, and which we **receive** only by faith in the
SD : 0 3 :031(544) [0925] through which we could **receive** and accept the grace of
SD : 0 3 :038(546) [0929] and through which we **receive**, grasp, accept, apply to
SD : 0 3 :039(546) [0929] of the Gospel and **received**, accepted, applied to us, and
SD : 0 3 :053(548) [0933] Paul's reason is that we **receive** both our righteousness
SD : 0 3 :053(548) [0933] faith we simultaneously **receive** adoption and the
SD : 0 3 :062(550) [0937] from sins" and "to **receive** forgiveness of sins," but to be
SD : 0 4 :031(556) [0947] once it has been **received**, through any sin, even a wanton
SD : 0 4 :033(556) [0949] which you have not **received** because of your subsequent
SD : 0 4 :034(556) [0949] the righteousness that has been **received**, and salvation.
SD : 0 4 :034(556) [0949] that we shall not only **receive** but also retain
SD : 0 4 :035(557) [0949] salvation are not only **received** but also preserved by
SD : 0 4 :035(557) [0949] of faith that we have **received** or even faith itself.
SD : 0 6 :005(564) [0963] after his creation **received** a law according to which he
SD : 0 6 :011(565) [0965] who is not given and **received** through the law but
SD : 0 7 :002(569) [0973] Supper the body of Christ is truly **received** by believers.
SD : 0 7 :003(569) [0973] above all heavens and **receives** and partakes truly and
SD : 0 7 :003(569) [0973] but bread and wine are orally **received** in the Supper.
SD : 0 7 :005(570) [0973] as something to be **received** spiritually (that is, according
SD : 0 7 :006(570) [0975] by faith but not to **receive** it orally with the mouth.
SD : 0 7 :008(570) [0975] and is orally **received** with the blessed bread even by
SD : 0 7 :009(570) [0975] they are distributed and **received**," and it condemns the
SD : 0 7 :011(571) [0975] bread and the wine, to those who **receive** the sacrament.
SD : 0 7 :014(571) [0977] are truly and essentially present, distributed, and **received**.
SD : 0 7 :016(572) [0977] or of him who **receives** it, since, as St. Paul says, the
SD : 0 7 :016(572) [0977] as St. Paul says, the unworthy **receive** the sacrament too.
SD : 0 7 :016(572) [0977] to the unworthy, too, and that they truly **receive** it.
SD : 0 7 :016(572) [0977] But they **receive** it for judgment, as St. Paul says, for they
SD : 0 7 :016(572) [0977] holy sacrament since they **receive** it without true
SD : 0 7 :016(572) [0977] faith in Christ there **receive** the grace and merits of
SD : 0 7 :019(572) [0979] which are given and **received** not only by godly but also
SD : 0 7 :024(573) [0979] even though a rascal **receives** or gives the sacrament, it is
SD : 0 7 :032(574) [0983] them or those who **receive** them do not believe or
SD : 0 7 :033(575) [0983] the godless or Judas **receive** orally as well as St. Peter and
SD : 0 7 :039(576) [0985] As Justin says, "We **receive** this not as ordinary bread or
SD : 0 7 :046(577) [0987] literally or if it was to **receive** a tolerable and loose
SD : 0 7 :046(577) [0987] occasion when Abraham **received** the promise of the
SD : 0 7 :052(578) [0991] as well as St. Paul who **received** the same information
SD : 0 7 :054(579) [0991] and drink the cup truly **receive** and partake of the true
SD : 0 7 :055(579) [0991] present and were **received** only according to its virtue and
SD : 0 7 :056(579) [0991] that means that all who **receive** the blessed bread also
SD : 0 7 :057(579) [0993] warning them against **receiving** the body and blood of
SD : 0 7 :058(580) [0993] distributed among those who **receive** the broken bread."
SD : 0 7 :059(580) [0993] Supper the body of Christ is **received** only spiritually.
SD : 0 7 :060(580) [0993] and believing Christians **receive** the true body and blood
SD : 0 7 :063(581) [0995] wine in the Lord's Supper **receive** and partake of the
SD : 0 7 :063(581) [0995] Believers **receive** it as a certain pledge and assurance that
SD : 0 7 :063(581) [0995] in them; unbelievers **receive** it orally, too, but to their
SD : 0 7 :066(581) [0997] the body of Christ is **received** not only spiritually through
SD : 0 7 :075(583) [0999] present, distributed, and **received** by the virtue and
SD : 0 7 :077(583) [0999] we do not distribute and **receive** ordinary bread and wine
SD : 0 7 :083(584) [1001] bread is not distributed, **received**, and eaten but is locked
SD : 0 7 :084(584) [1001] it, distribute it, **receive** it, eat and drink it, and therewith
SD : 0 7 :088(585) [1003] hypocrites do not **receive** the body of Christ because it is
SD : 0 7 :089(585) [1003] or the unbelief of him who **receives** the sacrament.
SD : 0 7 :089(585) [1003] so whether those who **receive** the sacrament believe or do
SD : 0 7 :090(585) [1003] body of Christ and to **receive** it, rather than ascribe it to
SD : 0 7 :105(588) [1009] in the Holy Supper are **received**, eaten, and drunk
SD : 0 7 :114(589) [1011] in the Supper our mouth **receives** only bread and wine.
SD : 0 7 :116(589) [1011] truly as in the Supper we **receive** the external sign with
SD : 0 7 :118(590) [1013] blood of Christ are only **received** and partaken of through
SD : 0 7 :119(590) [1013] to read "Christ must be **received** by heaven" — that is,
SD : 0 7 :123(590) [1013] living, and saving faith, **receive** only bread and wine in
SD : 0 7 :123(590) [1015] community of the church **receive** only bread and wine in
SD : 0 7 :125(591) [1015] of preparation, may **receive** this sacrament for judgment,
SD : 0 8 :013(593) [1019] 8. But Christ did not **receive** this majesty, to which he
SD : 0 8 :051(600) [1033] after the humiliation) **received**, in addition to its natural,
SD : 0 8 :051(601) [1033] the human nature has **received** through the personal
SD : 0 8 :053(601) [1033] himself what Christ has **received** through the personal
SD : 0 8 :057(602) [1035] testify that Christ **received** in time he received not
SD : 0 8 :057(602) [1035] received in time he **received** not according to his divine
SD : 0 8 :057(602) [1035] but that the person **received** this in time according to the
SD : 0 8 :060(602) [1035] must believe that Christ **received** all this according to his
SD : 0 8 :064(603) [1037] nature in Christ has **received** this majesty according to the
SD : 0 8 :069(604) [1039] to his human nature he has **received** above all creatures.
SD : 0 8 :071(605) [1041] human nature allegedly **received** equal majesty, separated
SD : 0 8 :072(605) [1041] in such a way that he **received** the Spirit's gifts not by
SD : 0 8 :074(606) [1043] he really and truly has **received** all knowledge and all
SD : 0 8 :078(606) [1043] man Christ, which Christ **received** according to his
SD : 0 8 :085(608) [1047] when I became man I **received** it in time according to the
SD : 1 1 :021(619) [1069] of God, and use faithfully the gifts they have **received**.
SD : 1 1 :042(623) [1077] In the same way many "**receive** the Word with joy," but
SD : 1 1 :061(626) [1083] those who are punished and **receive** their "wages of sin."
SD : 1 1 :075(628) [1087] becomes another man's wife, may he **receive** her again?
SD : 1 1 :078(629) [1089] to faith and therefore **receive** the greater damnation is
SD : 1 1 :083(630) [1091] First, that he would **receive** into grace all who repent and

Recent (9), Recently (3)
AL : 2 2 :008(050) [0061] is only a custom of quite **recent** times that holds
AP : PR :014(099) [0101] But **recently**, when I saw the Confutation, I realized it
AP : 0 2 :027(103) [0111] alone, but even the more **recent** ones — at least the more
AP : 1 2 :119(200) [0287] This whole theory is a **recent** fiction, without authority
AP : 1 8 :010(226) [0337] it too, and more **recently** William of Paris has discussed
AP : 2 1 :041(235) [0355] Scripture than the more **recent** ones, so their theology has
AP : 2 4 :063(261) [0405] These are the wicked and **recent** fictions of the ignorant
AP : 2 4 :094(267) [0417] Gregory and the more **recent** theologians, we set them
AP : 2 7 :029(274) [0431] that monasticism is a **recent** invention, they still cite the
TR : 0 0 :071(332) [0525] Still more **recent** writers added the words, "I give thee the
SC : PR :001(338) [0533] conditions which I **recently** encountered when I was a
SC : 0 9 :002(354) [0561] He must not be a **recent** convert," etc. (I Tim. 3:2-6).

Reception (8)
AG : 2 2 :008(050) [0061] be found which requires the **reception** of only one kind.
AP : 1 2 :025(185) [0259] 9. The **reception** of the sacrament of penitence obtains
AP : 1 2 :061(190) [0269] opponents whether the **reception** of absolution is part of
AP : 1 2 :061(190) [0269] do not separate the **reception** of absolution from
AP : 2 4 :033(256) [0395] In the same way, the **reception** of the Lord's Supper itself
SD : 0 7 :084(584) [1001] of the distribution and **reception**, before our eyes in
SD : 0 7 :086(584) [1003] the distribution and **reception**, or the oral eating of the
SD : 0 7 :088(585) [1003] sacrament, and that the **reception** of the body of Christ

Rechabites (5)
AP : 2 7 :059(279) [0439] also cite the case of the **Rechabites** who, as Jeremiah
AP : 2 7 :059(279) [0439] the example of the **Rechabites** is a beautiful parallel to our
AP : 2 7 :059(279) [0441] poor in everything, the **Rechabites** were married; though
AP : 2 7 :061(279) [0441] When the **Rechabites** are praised, therefore, we must note
AP : 2 7 :063(280) [0441] Thus the example of the **Rechabites** does not resemble

Recipient (3)
AP : 0 4 :063(115) [0139] proper attitude in the **recipient**, as though the gift of the
AP : 1 2 :012(184) [0257] a right attitude in the **recipient**, and they do not mention
AP : 1 2 :025(185) [0259] proper attitude in the **recipient**, that is, without faith in

Recite (11), Recited (3), Recitation (4)
AP : 0 4 :237(140) [0187] praises of love which they **recite** from Paul; they have no
AP : 0 4 :273(148) [0199] Why **recite** passages?
AP : 1 1 :009(182) [0251] They only **recite** lists of sins.
AP : 2 1 :035(234) [0353] Another one **recited** the whole Psalter every day while
AP : 2 3 :062(247) [0381] we have incidentally **recited** and refuted the silly
AP : 2 7 :002(269) [0419] We do not want to **recite** them here lest we give the
S3 : 0 3 :013(305) [0483] general confession was **recited** to the people: "Prolong my
SC : PR :008(339) [0535] alter a single syllable or **recite** the catechism differently
LC : PR :007(359) [0569] I have time, I read and **recite** word for word the Lord's
LC : PR :011(360) [0571] you should eagerly read, **recite**, ponder, and practice the
LC : SP :024(364) [0579] teach and require young people to **recite** word for word.
LC : 0 2 :020(412) [0683] pass over it, hear it, and **recite** it, but we neither see nor
EP : 0 7 :008(482) [0811] no man's work nor the **recitation** of the minister effect
EP : 0 7 :009(483) [0811] occurs through the **recitation** of the words of Christ.
EP : 0 7 :041(486) [0817] decency forbids us to **recite** and which the
SD : 0 7 :082(584) [1001] the repetition and **recitation** of the words of institution.
SD : 0 7 :083(584) [1001] But this blessing or **recitation** of Christ's words of
SD : 0 7 :111(589) [1011] therefore set forth and **recite** the errors preeminently of

Reciting (1)
LC : SP :016(363) [0577] be taught the habit of **reciting** them daily when they rise

Reckless (2)
EP : 1 1 :009(495) [0833] either lead us into a **reckless**, dissolute, Epicurean life, or
EP : 1 1 :015(496) [0835] either to despair or to lead a **reckless** and godless life.

Reckon (3), Reckoned (28), Reckoning (5), Reckons (8)
AG : 0 4 :003(030) [0045] For God will regard and **reckon** this faith as
AP : 0 4 :089(120) [0149] works, his wages are not **reckoned** as a gift but are his
AP : 0 4 :089(120) [0149] the ungodly, his faith is **reckoned** as righteousness."
AP : 0 4 :090(120) [0149] "We say that faith was **reckoned** to Abraham as

Continued ▶

AP : 04 :307(154) [0207] says (Rom. 4:5), “Faith is **reckoned** as righteousness.”
AP : 04 :308(155) [0207] Christ, the propitiator, and is **reckoned** for righteousness.
S3 : 03 :016(305) [0483] such attrition was **reckoned** as a substitute for contrition
S3 : 13 :002(315) [0499] these works will not be **reckoned** as sin or defect for the
LC : SP :002(362) [0575] possess it should not be **reckoned** among Christians nor
LC : 01 :236(397) [0647] — there will come a day of **reckoning** and retribution:
EP : 03 :004(473) [0793] merit, or worthiness, and **reckons** to us the righteousness
EP : 03 :005(473) [0793] sake such faith is **reckoned** for righteousness (Rom. 4:5).
EP : 03 :009(474) [0795] righteousness which is **reckoned** to them through faith or
EP : 03 :021(475) [0797] righteousness of Christ **reckoned** to them and by the
EP : 03 :021(475) [0797] or in part by the **reckoning** to them of Christ's
EP : 04 :007(476) [0799] the man to whom God **reckons** righteousness apart from
EP : 04 :014(477) [0799] sake the Lord does not **reckon** this weakness against his
SD : 03 :001(539) [0917] by grace through faith **reckons** to poor sinners as
SD : 03 :004(540) [0917] through faith alone, is **reckoned** by pure grace to all true
SD : 03 :009(541) [0919] Lord, whose obedience is **reckoned** to us as righteousness.
SD : 03 :012(541) [0919] (Rom. 3:28), or “faith is **reckoned** to us as righteousness”
SD : 03 :014(541) [0919] which by grace is **reckoned** to faith or to the believers is
SD : 03 :015(541) [0919] perfect a fashion that, **reckoning** it to us as righteousness,
SD : 03 :017(542) [0921] of Christ which God **reckons** to faith (Phil. 3:9).
SD : 03 :023(543) [0923] solely in the gracious **reckoning** of Christ's righteousness
SD : 03 :023(543) [0923] covered up and are not **reckoned** to our account
SD : 03 :025(543) [0923] of Christ is **reckoned** to us and by which we obtain the
SD : 03 :030(544) [0925] our stead and which is **reckoned** to the believers as
SD : 03 :032(544) [0927] in this life, first, the **reckoned** righteousness of faith and,
SD : 03 :032(545) [0927] death of Christ which is **reckoned** to faith can stand
SD : 03 :034(545) [0927] the ungodly, his faith is **reckoned** as righteousness”
SD : 03 :034(545) [0927] person to whom God **reckons** righteousness without the
SD : 03 :050(548) [0933] both through the **reckoned** righteousness of Christ and
SD : 03 :050(548) [0933] or in part by the **reckoning** of Christ's righteousness and
SD : 03 :053(548) [0933] that man to whom God **reckons** righteousness without
SD : 03 :056(549) [0935] nature could not be **reckoned** to us as righteousness.
SD : 03 :056(549) [0935] death of the cross, is **reckoned** to us as righteousness.
SD : 03 :057(549) [0935] God and which God **reckons** to faith, as it is written,
SD : 03 :058(550) [0937] of Christ by itself is **reckoned** to us as righteousness, but
SD : 03 :058(550) [0937] our disobedience is not **reckoned** to us for our damnation
SD : 04 :024(555) [0945] the man to whom God **reckons** righteousness apart from
SD : 05 :022(562) [0959] and whose obedience is **reckoned** to us as righteousness in
SD : 06 :007(565) [0965] so that they are not **reckoned** to believers for damnation,
SD : 07 :033(575) [0983] and wrote as follows: “I **reckon** them all as belonging

Recognize (25), Recognized (11), Recognizes (7), Recognition (3), Recognizable (1), Recognizing (2)

PR : PR :003(003) [0007] ancient symbols, **recognizing** the doctrine as the ancient
PR : PR :008(005) [0009] by the truth once **recognized** and confessed at Augsburg
PR : PR :024(013) [0021] pure doctrine can be **recognized** and distinguished from
AG : 23 :014(053) [0063] and Christian to **recognize** this fact in order that the
AG : 28 :068(093) [0093] is practiced, that one **recognizes** that such rules are not to
AL : 28 :068(093) [0093] is practiced, that one **recognizes** that canons are kept
AP : 02 :033(104) [0113] **Recognition** of original sin is a necessity, nor can we know
AP : 02 :035(105) [0115] Imperial Majesty will **recognize** an obvious slander here.
AP : 02 :050(106) [0119] we cannot know his blessings unless we **recognize** our evil.
AP : 04 :004(108) [0121] the opponents' and our own, might be **recognized**.
AP : 04 :103(121) [0151] is, by the law sin is **recognized** but its guilt is not relieved.
AP : 04 :106(122) [0153] will live in it, so that by **recognizing** his weakness one
AP : 04 :118(123) [0155] for through it alone we **recognize** Christ's work and
AP : 04 :135(125) [0159] Then we **recognize** how our flesh in its smugness and
AP : 04 :340(159) [0215] said, “Grace is to be **recognized**, but nature is not to be
AP : 07 :005(169) [0227] To make it **recognizable**, this association has outward
AP : 12 :125(201) [0289] right for all nations to **recognize** her as the mistress of the
AP : 16 :011(224) [0333] steal,” the Decalogue **recognizes** the right of ownership
AP : 22 :007(237) [0359] says that the disciples **recognized** Christ in the breaking
AP : 22 :011(238) [0361] We **recognize** these Thrasonian voices, and if we wanted
AP : 23 :046(246) [0377] It obscures the **recognition** of God's commands and gifts,
AP : 23 :052(246) [0377] its satires Rome still reads and **recognizes** its own morals.
S3 : 03 :003(304) [0481] stood before God and **recognize** themselves as lost men.
TR : 00 :016(323) [0509] part of the world never **recognized** or acted in accordance
TR : 00 :079(333) [0527] why the churches should not **recognize** them as bishops.
LC : 01 :042(370) [0591] this at all, and does not **recognize** it as God's Word.
LC : 01 :112(380) [0613] aside, and no one **recognizes** it as God's command or as a
LC : 01 :128(383) [0617] there is no child that **recognizes** and considers this, unless
LC : 01 :129(383) [0617] Then everybody **recognizes** that he has received his body
LC : 01 :171(388) [0629] for its neglect, nor is it **recognized** how very necessary it
LC : 01 :290(404) [0663] blind world and the false saints would **recognize** them.
LC : 02 :023(413) [0683] or danger, we should **recognize** that this is God's doing.
LC : 02 :043(416) [0689] the bench and no one **recognized** Christ as the Lord, or
LC : 02 :065(419) [0695] we could never come to **recognize** the Father's favor and
LC : 03 :052(427) [0711] order that it may gain **recognition** and followers among
LC : 03 :083(431) [0721] from his hand and may **recognize** in them his fatherly
LC : 03 :088(432) [0723] point here is for us to **recognize** and accept this
EP : 01 :009(467) [0781] that it may not be **recognized** by a rational process, but
EP : 03 :006(473) [0793] Word of the Gospel we **recognize** Christ aright as our
EP : 07 :027(485) [0815] tokens whereby Christians **recognize** each one another.
SD : PR :009(505) [0853] have everywhere **recognized** these publicly and generally
SD : 01 :005(509) [0861] must regard and **recognize** as sin not only the actual
SD : 02 :021(525) [0889] as man does not see or **recognize** the dreadful, cruel wrath
SD : 02 :030(527) [0893] does not in any way **recognize** the freedom of the human
SD : 02 :073(535) [0909] one can readily **recognize**, expose, reject, and condemn
SD : 05 :008(559) [0953] more than truly to **recognize** one's sins, to feel heartily
SD : 07 :115(589) [1011] badges whereby Christians **recognize** one another, or
SD : 11 :059(626) [1083] the fear of God and to **recognize** and glorify God's
SD : 11 :060(626) [1083] the more diligently to **recognize** and praise God's pure

Recollections (1)

LC : 01 :044(370) [0593] all histories and in the **recollections** of elderly and

Recommend (1), Recommended (3)

AL : 27 :048(078) [0081] in the church to **recommend** to the people a certain
AP : 23 :020(242) [0369] that can only be **recommended**, but not commanded; it is
AP : 27 :027(273) [0429] Virginity is **recommended** — but to those who have the
S2 : 02 :025(297) [0469] commanded nor **recommended**, nor does it have any

Recompense (1)

LC : 01 :161(387) [0627] God will adequately **recompense** those who do so and

Reconcile (10), Reconciled (65), Reconciles (11)

AG : PR :010(025) [0041] our differences may be **reconciled**, and we may be united
AG : 20 :009(042) [0053] that our works cannot **reconcile** us with God or obtain
AG : 20 :009(042) [0053] who alone is the mediator who **reconciles** the Father.
AG : 24 :022(058) [0067] of which sin was taken away and God was **reconciled**.
AG : 26 :021(067) [0073] earned, God cannot be **reconciled**, and sin cannot be
AG : 28 :041(087) [0089] a work by which God is **reconciled**, that in a reserved case
AL : 03 :003(030) [0045] buried, that he might **reconcile** the Father to us and be a
AL : 20 :009(042) [0053] that our works cannot **reconcile** God or merit forgiveness
AL : 20 :009(042) [0053] and propitiation through whom the Father is **reconciled**.
AL : 20 :024(044) [0055] that he has a Father **reconciled** to him through Christ
AP : 03 :001(107) [0119] suffered and died to **reconcile** the Father to us; and that
AP : 04 :036(112) [0131] wrath cannot love him unless it sees that he is **reconciled**.
AP : 04 :045(113) [0133] Christ and that God is **reconciled** and favorably disposed
AP : 04 :069(116) [0141] that because of him God wants to be **reconciled** to us.
AP : 04 :080(118) [0143] whom the Father is **reconciled** to us, we cannot appease
AP : 04 :081(118) [0143] In this way we are **reconciled** to the Father and receive
AP : 04 :086(119) [0147] The **reconciled** are accounted righteous and children of
AP : 04 :087(119) [0147] we believe that God is **reconciled** to us for Christ's sake
AP : 04 :097(121) [0149] we believe that God is **reconciled** to us because of him.
AP : 04 :106(122) [0153] He **reconciles** the justifier by faith, not by his own
AP : 04 :106(122) [0153] says that the justifier is **reconciled** by faith and that
AP : 04 :114(123) [0155] forgiveness of sins and **reconciles** us to God, we must be
AP : 04 :150(127) [0163] Therefore it must be faith that **reconciles** and justifies.
AP : 04 :155(128) [0165] earns the forgiveness of sins that **reconciles** us to God.
AP : 04 :177(131) [0171] therefore, that being **reconciled** by faith we are accounted
AP : 04 :181(132) [0171] that is, it neither **reconciles** nor regenerates nor of itself
AP : 04 :206(135) [0177] were a propitiation and price that **reconciled** God to them.
AP : 04 :217(137) [0179] it is sure that God is **reconciled** to us for Christ's sake,
AP : 04 :238(140) [0187] is the propitiation that **reconciles** God to us; or that love
AP : 04 :244(142) [0189] and price that **reconciles** God to us; that good works
AP : 04 :246(142) [0189] who have already been **reconciled** and accepted and have
AP : 04 :270(147) [0197] as he hears that God is **reconciled** to us for Christ's sake
AP : 04 :279(149) [0199] believes that God is **reconciled** on account of his mercy
AP : 04 :292(152) [0203] he wishes to forgive and to be **reconciled** for Christ's sake.
AP : 04 :295(152) [0203] for Christ's sake the Father is **reconciled** and forgiving.
AP : 04 :299(153) [0205] fact that they have a **reconciled** Father because of Christ,
AP : 04 :310(155) [0207] we have first been **reconciled** and reborn. The greatest
AP : 04 :313(155) [0207] that we are justified, **reconciled**, and reborn by faith, if
AP : 04 :368(163) [0221] before we have been **reconciled** to God, justified, and
AP : 04 :376(165) [0223] the Father and have a **reconciled** Father, as we have said
AP : 04 :382(165) [0225] and that God has been **reconciled** to us because of
AP : 04 :386(166) [0225] justified before God, **reconciled** to him, and reborn by a
AP : 04 :386(166) [0225] convinced that God is **reconciled** and propitious to us
AP : 04 :393(167) [0225] taught that men were **reconciled** to God and justified by
AP : 11 :002(180) [0249] be sure that by this faith we are truly **reconciled** to God.
AP : 12 :076(193) [0273] of Christ we are **reconciled** to the Father, not because of
AP : 12 :076(193) [0273] the law before we have been **reconciled** through Christ.
AP : 12 :080(194) [0275] therefore we must be **reconciled** by the promise before we
AP : 12 :085(194) [0277] by the law before being **reconciled** to God through
AP : 12 :086(194) [0277] to God before being **reconciled** to God and becoming the
AP : 12 :086(195) [0277] that by faith we are **reconciled** to God before we keep the
AP : 12 :114(199) [0285] sin by which they supposed they were **reconciled** to God.
AP : 12 :166(208) [0303] penitence — they were **reconciled** to God and saved their
AP : 15 :005(215) [0317] receive the forgiveness of sins and are **reconciled** to God.
AP : 15 :009(216) [0317] men believe that God is **reconciled** and gracious because
AP : 15 :021(218) [0321] believing that he is **reconciled** by a variety of vestments,
AP : 15 :022(218) [0321] supposes that such works justify men and **reconcile** God.
AP : 21 :025(232) [0349] of absolution, we are **reconciled** and accounted righteous
AP : 21 :029(233) [0351] us, as though God were **reconciled** to us or accounted us
AP : 24 :019(252) [0389] and punishment that **reconciles** God or placates his wrath
AP : 24 :019(252) [0389] it those who have been **reconciled** give thanks or show
AP : 24 :023(253) [0391] a victim was to come to **reconcile** God and make
AP : 24 :023(253) [0391] of another (namely, of Christ) to **reconcile** him to us.
AP : 24 :023(253) [0391] or trespass offering to **reconcile** God by his merits instead
AP : 24 :025(254) [0391] Those who bring them are already **reconciled**.
AP : 24 :030(255) [0395] that sacrifices do not **reconcile** God *ex opere operato.*
AP : 24 :038(257) [0399] that by the death of Christ God has been **reconciled**.
AP : 24 :058(260) [0405] that was valid for the sins of others and **reconciled** God.
AP : 24 :062(260) [0405] this the church might have a service that **reconciles** God.”
AP : 24 :067(261) [0407] but comes from the **reconciled**, just as afflictions do not
AP : 24 :067(261) [0407] eucharistic sacrifices when the **reconciled** endure them.
AP : 24 :080(264) [0411] We beseech you on behalf of Christ, be **reconciled** to God
AP : 24 :089(266) [0415] is a sacrifice that **reconciles** God and makes satisfaction
S2 : 02 :007(294) [0465] of the Mass men try to **reconcile** themselves and others to
LC : 01 :066(373) [0599] is refuted, people are **reconciled**, obedience is rendered,
LC : 06 :012(458) [0000] we forgive our neighbor and become **reconciled** with him.
EP : 00 :000(463) [0775] Resolved and **Reconciled** under the Guidance of the Word
SD : 03 :043(547) [0931] Christ, who are **reconciled** with God, and who have
SD : 03 :054(548) [0935] through Christ and **reconciled** with God, since all
SD : 04 :007(552) [0941] after a person has been **reconciled** to God through faith
SD : 04 :008(552) [0941] nature and because the person is not **reconciled** with God.
SD : 06 :005(564) [0963] Christ have been **reconciled** with God, nor may it torture
SD : 07 :047(578) [0989] as to how it is to be **reconciled** with our reason or how it
SD : 11 :015(619) [1069] been redeemed and **reconciled** with God and that by his
SD : 11 :027(620) [1071] you through us, ‘Be **reconciled** to God’” (II Cor. 5:20).
SD : 11 :038(622) [1075] we are as truly **reconciled** with God as if we had heard a

Reconciliation (40)

PR : PR :024(013) [0021] explanation and **reconciliation** of all of the disputes which
AP : 04 :018(109) [0125] of sins and **reconciliation**, but should dream that they
AP : 04 :041(113) [0133] **Reconciliation** does not depend upon our merits.
AP : 04 :042(113) [0133] our merits and if **reconciliation** were by the law, it would
AP : 04 :042(113) [0133] that we would never obtain the promise of **reconciliation**.
AP : 04 :044(113) [0133] promise freely offers **reconciliation** for Christ's sake,
AP : 04 :081(118) [0145] we have access (that is, **reconciliation**) through Christ.
AP : 04 :157(128) [0165] of sins and **reconciliation** do not come freely for Christ's
AP : 04 :158(129) [0165] Justification is **reconciliation** for Christ's sake.
AP : 04 :159(129) [0167] of sins and **reconciliation** by faith for Christ's sake, not

Continued ▶

A P : 0 4 :161(129) [0167] our renewal, but the **reconciliation** by which we are later
A P : 0 4 :179(131) [0171] have a firm and sure **reconciliation** through faith, though
A P : 0 4 :180(132) [0171] should seek **reconciliation** and justification, sustaining
A P : 0 4 :182(132) [0173] of sins and **reconciliation** for Christ's sake, and
A P : 0 4 :182(132) [0173] for Christ's sake, and **reconciliation** or justification is
A P : 0 4 :186(132) [0173] of sins and **reconciliation**, our opponents simply abolish
A P : 0 4 :188(133) [0173] of sins and the **reconciliation** that comes through faith in
A P : 0 4 :238(141) [0187] which promises us **reconciliation** and righteousness if we
A P : 0 4 :275(148) [0199] — for they follow **reconciliation** — but he does so for two
A P : 0 4 :278(149) [0199] justification or **reconciliation**, not by that which
A P : 0 4 :291(152) [0203] forgiveness of sins, **reconciliation**, and victory over the
A P : 0 4 :297(152) [0205] the promise, in which **reconciliation**, righteousness, and
A P : 0 4 :304(154) [0205] the promise offers — **reconciliation** and forgiveness of
A P : 0 4 :381(165) [0223] hold of God's mercy, **reconciliation**, and love toward us
A P : 1 2 :037(186) [0261] is love present before faith has effected the **reconciliation**.
A P : 1 2 :109(198) [0283] to priests but of the **reconciliation** of brethren to each
A P : 2 4 :019(252) [0389] forgiveness of sins or **reconciliation**, but by it those who
A P : 2 4 :025(254) [0391] forgiveness of sins or **reconciliation** for others *ex opere*
A P : 2 4 :054(259) [0403] forgiveness of sins or **reconciliation** before God, but only
A P : 2 4 :056(259) [0403] did not merit **reconciliation** — unless by analogy, since
A P : 2 4 :056(259) [0403] they merited civil **reconciliation** — but only symbolized
A P : 2 4 :067(261) [0407] does not merit **reconciliation** but comes from the
A P : 2 4 :067(261) [0407] do not merit **reconciliation** but are eucharistic sacrifices
E P : 0 8 :014(488) [0821] high priest for our **reconciliation** with God, as it is written
S D : 0 3 :004(540) [0917] is forgiveness of sins, **reconciliation** with God, and the
S D : 0 3 :016(541) [0921] thus believers have **reconciliation** with God, forgiveness
S D : 0 3 :025(543) [0923] forgiveness of sins, **reconciliation** with God, adoption,
S D : 0 3 :030(544) [0925] solely in a gracious **reconciliation** or the forgiveness of
S D : 0 3 :057(549) [0935] satisfaction and **reconciliation** of the human race, since it
S D : 0 4 :014(553) [0943] follow faith and **reconciliation**"; again, "We should and

Record (3), Recorded (6), Records (2)
A G : 2 7 :056(080) [0083] Many instances are also **recorded** of men who forsook
A P : 1 5 :026(219) [0323] It is a matter of **record** that many have given up their
A P : 2 0 :011(228) [0341] They have gone on **record** as rejecting our doctrine that
A P : 2 1 :009(230) [0345] except for the dream **recorded** in the Second Book of the
T R : 0 0 :019(323) [0509] And in the **records** he states that at the Council of
S C : 0 4 :004(348) [0551] Answer: As **recorded** in Matthew 28:19, our Lord Christ
S C : 0 4 :008(349) [0551] Answer: As **recorded** in Mark 16:16, our Lord Christ
L C : 0 1 :035(369) [0589] has witnessed in all the **records** of history, as Scripture
S D : 0 7 :042(576) [0987] the words of institution **recorded** in the holy Word of
S D : 0 8 :059(602) [1035] church concerning this article are **recorded** elsewhere.
S D : 0 8 :086(608) [1047] we here merely go on **record** as having appealed to these

Recount (4), Recounted (4)
A G : 2 5 :007(062) [0069] should be compelled to **recount** sins in detail, for this is
A L : 2 5 :007(062) [0069] of all sins because it is impossible to **recount** all of them.
A L : 2 5 :009(062) [0069] except those which are **recounted**, our consciences would
A L : 0 0 :005(095) [0095] those things have been **recounted** which it seemed
S 3 : 0 3 :020(306) [0485] this is not the place to **recount** the torture, rascality, and
L C : P R :012(360) [0571] would fail me if I were to **recount** all the blessings that
E P : 0 3 :003(473) [0793] to these two errors just **recounted**, we believe, teach, and
S D : 1 1 :023(619) [1069] that in the manner just **recounted** he wills by his grace,

Recover (1)
L C : 0 1 :012(366) [0583] protect their cattle, **recover** lost possessions, etc., as

Rector (1)
S 3 : 1 5 :005(316) [0501] Dr. Justus Jonas, **rector**, subscribed with his own hand

Red (1)
L C : 0 4 :006(437) [0733] indifferent matter, then, like putting on a new **red** coat.

Redeem (11), Redeemed (21), Redeeming (1), Redeems (1)
A P : 0 4 :179(131) [0171] in Gal. 3:13, "Christ **redeemed** us from the curse of the
A P : 0 4 :254(143) [0193] Dan. 4:27, "**Redeem** your sins by showing mercy."
A P : 0 4 :261(145) [0195] penitence when he says, "**Redeem** your iniquities by
A P : 0 4 :261(145) [0195] the oppressed," that is, **redeem** your sins by changing
A P : 0 4 :262(145) [0195] bring out the promise, "**Redeem** your sins by righteousness
A P : 0 4 :263(145) [0195] Sins are **redeemed** by penitence, that is, the obligation or
A P : 0 4 :264(146) [0195] the promise is involved even in the word "**redeem**."
A P : 0 4 :264(146) [0195] that sins can be **redeemed**, that the obligation or debt can
A P : 0 4 :266(146) [0197] If Daniel had said, "**Redeem** your sins by penitence," our
A P : 1 2 :013(184) [0257] of the keys and another part is **redeemed** by satisfactions.
A P : 1 2 :024(185) [0257] are necessary to **redeem** the punishment of purgatory, or
A P : 1 2 :118(200) [0287] would only be punishments **redeeming** from purgatory.
A P : 1 2 :122(200) [0289] gave himself for us to **redeem** us from all iniquity and to
A P : 1 2 :140(204) [0295] that Christ's satisfaction **redeems** our guilt but our
A P : 1 2 :140(204) [0295] our guilt but our penalties **redeem** us from eternal death!
A P : 1 3 :009(212) [0311] of Christ if they believe that it has **redeemed** them.
S C : 0 2 :004(345) [0545] is my Lord, who has **redeemed** me, a lost and condemned
L C : 0 2 :007(411) [0679] in God the Son, who **redeemed** me; I believe in the Holy
L C : 0 2 :026(414) [0685] of the article; from it we shall learn how we are **redeemed**.
L C : 0 2 :027(414) [0685] It means that he has **redeemed** me from sin, from the
L C : 0 2 :064(419) [0695] us for this very purpose, to **redeem** and sanctify us.
L C : 0 3 :051(426) [0711] Lord, into the world to **redeem** and deliver us from the
L C : 0 3 :061(428) [0715] us who have been **redeemed** from the power of the devil
E P : 0 1 :006(466) [0781] Thus Christ has **redeemed** our nature as his creation,
E P : 0 1 :006(467) [0781] not assumed it, has not **redeemed** it, has not sanctified it,
E P : 0 6 :002(480) [0805] they have been **redeemed** by the Son of God precisely
E P : 0 8 :031(490) [0825] suffered for us and **redeemed** us, and that in the passion
E P : 0 8 :032(491) [0825] that after Christ had **redeemed** us by his suffering and
E P : 0 9 :004(492) [0827] all believers, and has **redeemed** them from the power of
S D : 0 1 :006(509) [0861] unless we are **redeemed** from this state through Christ's
S D : 0 3 :004(540) [0917] by his perfect obedience **redeemed** us from our sins,
S D : 0 8 :045(600) [1031] suffered for us, died, and **redeemed** us with his blood.
S D : 0 8 :093(609) [1049] whatever in the passion, suffered for us and **redeemed** us.
S D : 1 1 :015(619) [1069] race has truly been **redeemed** and reconciled with God

Redeemer (13)
P R : P R :023(012) [0021] advent of our only **Redeemer** and Saviour Jesus Christ.
L C : 0 2 :031(414) [0685] means the same as **Redeemer**, that is, he who has brought
L C : 0 2 :036(415) [0687] and the Son is called **Redeemer**, so on account of his work
E P : 0 3 :006(473) [0793] Christ aright as our **redeemer** and trust in him, so that
E P : 0 7 :017(484) [0813] they reject Christ as a **redeemer**, they must accept him
S D : 0 2 :050(530) [0901] eternal Son, our only Saviour and **Redeemer**, Jesus Christ
S D : 0 3 :011(541) [0919] to know Christ as our **redeemer** in the Word of the
S D : 0 3 :035(545) [0927] glory due to Christ, the **redeemer**, and, because our new
S D : 0 4 :002(551) [0939] the merit of Christ, our **redeemer**, be diminished and in
S D : 0 7 :044(577) [0987] Lord, our Creator and **Redeemer** Jesus Christ, selected his
S D : 0 7 :045(577) [0987] our Lord, Creator, and **Redeemer**, not as flowery,
S D : 0 7 :047(578) [0989] of our Creator and **Redeemer**, without any doubts or
S D : 0 8 :047(600) [1031] Christ is our mediator, **redeemer**, king, high priest, head,

Redemption (25)
A L : 2 0 :014(043) [0055] *gentium* he says: "**Redemption** by the blood of Christ
A P : 0 4 :086(119) [0147] and sanctification and **redemption**" (I Cor. 1:30).
A P : 0 4 :273(148) [0199] "In him we have **redemption** through his blood, the
A P : 0 4 :306(154) [0207] our righteousness and sanctification and **redemption**."
A P : 1 2 :118(199) [0287] do contribute to the **redemption** of purgatorial and other
A P : 1 2 :136(203) [0293] or if satisfactions are a **redemption** from the penalties of
A P : 2 1 :014(230) [0347] and mediators of **redemption**, they obviously make the
A P : 2 1 :014(231) [0347] they obviously make the saints mediators of **redemption**.
A P : 2 1 :015(231) [0347] Thus they actually make them mediators of **redemption**.
A P : 2 1 :016(231) [0347] but propitiators, that is, mediators of **redemption**.
S 2 : 0 0 :000(292) [0461] office and work of Jesus Christ, or to our **redemption**.
S 2 : 0 1 :003(292) [0461] as a gift, through the **redemption** which is in Christ
S 2 : 0 2 :021(296) [0469] it is contrary to the first article, concerning **redemption**.
S 2 : 0 3 :002(298) [0471] article concerning **redemption** in Jesus Christ.
S 2 : 0 4 :003(298) [0473] which is concerned with **redemption** in Jesus Christ.
S 3 : 0 3 :008(304) [0481] God there is plenteous **redemption** (as Ps. 130:7 puts it)
S 3 : 0 5 :004(311) [0493] in the promise of **redemption** which Christ made, and the
S C : 0 2 :003(345) [0545] The Second Article: **Redemption**
L C : 0 2 :006(411) [0679] second, of the Son, **redemption**; the third, of the Holy
L C : 0 2 :031(414) [0685] by what means this **redemption** was accomplished — that
L C : 0 2 :061(419) [0695] Creation is past and **redemption** is accomplished, but the
E P : 0 1 :003(466) [0779] namely, creation, **redemption**, sanctification, and the
S D : 0 1 :043(515) [0873] in the article of our **redemption** we have the mighty
S D : 0 2 :050(530) [0901] concerning our **redemption**, namely, the holy and only
S D : 1 1 :014(619) [1069] concerning our **redemption**, call, justification, and

Redound (1)
S D : 1 1 :006(617) [1065] such a way that it must **redound** to the glory of his divine

Redress (3)
A P : 1 6 :006(223) [0331] by its prohibition of legal **redress** and by other teachings
A P : 1 6 :007(223) [0331] Public **redress** through a judge is not forbidden but
A P : 1 6 :007(223) [0331] various kinds of public **redress** are court decisions,

Reduce (2), Reduced (2), Reducing (1)
P R : P R :013(007) [0013] opinions and criticisms **reduced** to writing, and
A G : 2 8 :077(094) [0095] to find ways of **reducing** the bishops' power, but we desire
A L : 2 4 :040(061) [0069] it would certainly be of advantage to **reduce** the number.
L C : 0 3 :074(430) [0719] there our daily bread is taken away, or at least **reduced**.
S D : 1 0 :009(612) [1055] and power to change, to **reduce**, or to increase

Re-enter (1)
S D : 0 5 :020(561) [0959] through him alone we **re-enter** the good graces of God,

Refer (20), Referred (11), Referring (16), Refers (9), Reference (25), References (2)
P R : P R :003(003) [0007] They **referred** and appealed to it without either
P R : P R :010(006) [0011] that had arisen with **reference** to all the articles in
P R : P R :013(007) [0013] cited written agreement composed with **reference** thereto.
P R : P R :018(009) [0015] by the electors, princes, and estates **referred** to above.
P R : P R :019(009) [0017] Augsburg Confession, **referred** to in the Naumburg
P R : P R :021(010) [0019] speech employed with **reference** to the majesty of the
P R : P R :022(011) [0019] With **reference** to the condemnations, censures, and
A G : P R :006(025) [0039] and beliefs with **reference** to the said errors, dissensions,
A G : 2 6 :033(069) [0075] conduct himself, with **reference** to such bodily exercise as
A G : 2 8 :026(084) [0087] Again Paul **refers** to "the authority which the Lord has
A G : 2 8 :045(088) [0089] not taste, Do not touch' (**referring** to things which all
A L : 2 0 :017(043) [0055] whole teaching is to be **referred** to that conflict of the
A L : 2 2 :002(049) [0059] commanded with **reference** to the cup that all should
A L : 2 2 :003(049) [0059] captiously object that this **refers** only to priests, Paul in
A L : 2 4 :023(058) [0067] proliferation of Masses to which **reference** has been made.
A L : 2 8 :045(088) [0089] not taste, Do not touch' (**referring** to things which all
A P : 0 4 :058(115) [0137] The frequent **references** to mercy and faith in the Psalms
A P : 0 4 :071(116) [0141] some may think this **refers** to the beginning, as though
A P : 0 4 :087(120) [0147] opponents interpret as **referring** to Levitical ceremonies,
A P : 0 4 :109(123) [0153] so they say, as **referring** to "faith fashioned by love," that
A P : 0 4 :159(129) [0165] reply to the objection of the opponents **referred** to above.
A P : 0 4 :197(134) [0175] to honor our parents by **referring** to the reward that is
A P : 0 4 :221(137) [0181] be understood in **reference** to "faith formed by love."
A P : 0 4 :268(147) [0197] understand Daniel as **referring** only to remission of
A P : 0 4 :278(149) [0199] so here we say in **reference** to almsgiving that it is the
A P : 0 4 :337(159) [0215] the example of Daniel **referred** to above, "For we do not
A P : 0 7 :035(175) [0241] not taste, Do not touch' (**referring** to things which all
A P : 0 7 :043(177) [0243] did not intend it to **refer** to the time when Easter should
A P : 1 2 :008(183) [0255] the answer must be in **reference** to faith and the Gospel,
A P : 1 2 :134(203) [0293] commandments **referring** to this life: "Be penitent," "Bear
A P : 1 2 :138(203) [0293] "Whatever you bind" **refer** to imposing penalties but to
A P : 1 2 :139(203) [0295] part of the punishments **referred** to canonical penalties,
A P : 1 2 :163(208) [0303] but the word "judge" **refers** to the whole process of
A P : 1 2 :167(209) [0305] By their **references** to purgatory in this connection they
A P : 1 2 :175(210) [0307] "satisfaction" no longer **refers** to civil discipline but to
A P : 1 3 :007(212) [0311] the priesthood in **reference** to the ministry of the Word or
A P : 1 3 :007(212) [0311] to others, but in **reference** to sacrifice, as though the new
A P : 2 1 :002(229) [0343] They also **refer** to Jerome's controversy with Vigilantius
A P : 2 1 :013(230) [0345] Since they **refer** to the example of the church, we reply
A P : 2 2 :007(237) [0359] takes these passages as **referring** to the sacrament.
A P : 2 2 :008(237) [0359] They also **refer** to "lay communion."
A P : 2 2 :014(238) [0361] They also **refer** to the danger of spilling and similar
A P : 2 3 :027(243) [0371] For this they **refer** to the ceremonies of the Mosaic law
A P : 2 4 :026(254) [0391] *operato*, for "spiritual" **refers** to the operation of the Holy
A P : 2 4 :031(255) [0395] Even if this were a **reference** to the Mass, it would not
A P : 2 4 :032(255) [0395] "a pure offering" do not **refer** to a ceremony *ex opere*

Continued ▶

A P : 2 4 :035(256) [0397] They also **refer** to the daily sacrifice: as there was a daily
A P : 2 4 :078(263) [0411] Our opponents also **refer** us to philology.
A P : 2 8 :018(284) [0449] me" (Luke 10:16), is not **referring** to traditions but is
S 2 : 0 2 :012(295) [0465] or enjoined upon us with **reference** to the dead.
S 2 : 0 4 :007(299) [0473] of Constance acted with **reference** to the popes when it
S 3 : 0 3 :021(306) [0485] that was still lacking man was **referred** to purgatory.
T R : 0 0 :022(324) [0511] here once more, we **refer** to those writings and wish them
S C : P R :015(340) [0535] single syllable, as stated above with **reference** to the text.
L C : 0 1 :284(403) [0661] All this **refers** to secret sins.
L C : 0 1 :293(404) [0663] not interpret them as **referring** to unchastity or theft,
L C : 0 1 :321(408) [0673] of them as a whole ought to be **referred** and directed to it.
L C : 0 4 :020(439) [0737] these persons with **reference** to their noses, eyes, skin and
L C : 0 4 :031(440) [0739] To what do they **refer** but to Baptism, that is, the water
L C : 0 4 :038(441) [0741] your father and mother," **refers** only to human flesh and
L C : 0 4 :048(442) [0743] this question from their minds and **refer** it to the learned.
L C : 0 6 :008(458) [0000] I **refer** to the practice of confessing to God alone or to
E P : R N :004(465) [0777] 3. With **reference** to the schism in matters of faith which
E P : R N :008(465) [0779] the church of God with **reference** to controverted articles,
E P : 0 2 :018(472) [0791] must be understood as **referring** to the action of divine
E P : 0 3 :008(474) [0793] otherwise these terms **refer** to the renovation of man and
E P : 0 4 :003(476) [0797] other party held with **reference** to the word "necessary"
S D : P R :009(505) [0853] in which he himself **refers** to them in the Preface to the
S D : 0 1 :050(517) [0875] With specific **reference** to vocabulary and phraseology,
S D : 0 2 :018(524) [0887] sake of brevity we only **refer**), that the free will by its own
S D : 0 2 :044(529) [0897] hereby appeal to these writings and **refer** others to them.
S D : 0 3 :029(544) [0925] summarily cut off every **reference** to the law and the
S D : 0 4 :004(551) [0939] This word may **refer** to the immutable order which
S D : 0 4 :005(552) [0939] of the divine order **referred** to above, new obedience is
S D : 0 4 :016(554) [0943] compulsion but only as **referring** to the order of God's
S D : 0 4 :017(554) [0943] "necessity" is used with **reference** to that which is extorted
S D : 0 5 :027(563) [0961] generally understood as **referring** to the entire teaching, a
S D : 0 7 :027(574) [0981] not only with **reference** to believers and worthy
S D : 0 7 :064(581) [0995] only be understood as **referring** precisely to oral eating
S D : 0 7 :088(585) [1003] rule and interpret it as **referring** only to the spiritual and
S D : 0 7 :091(586) [1005] desirable brevity, merely **refer** the Christian reader to
S D : 0 8 :008(593) [1017] essence the two natures **referred** to remain unmingled and
S D : 0 8 :059(602) [1035] This does not **refer** only to the merit that was once

Refine (1)
A P : 2 4 :034(256) [0395] the sons of Levi and **refine** them like gold and silver, till

Reflect (7), Reflected (2), Reflection (1), Reflections (1), Reflects (3)
P R : P R :013(007) [0013] glory and after mature **reflection** and careful diligence,
A G : 0 0 :001(047) [0059] as the latter's teaching is **reflected** in the writings of the
A P : 0 2 :018(103) [0111] would grasp God and **reflect** him, that is, that man
A P : 0 4 :291(152) [0203] Whoever **reflects** on this will easily understand that we
A P : 0 4 :297(153) [0205] Whoever **reflects** on all this will easily understand that
S 3 : 0 3 :018(306) [0483] A poor sinner who **reflected** on his lust or revenge in this
S C : 0 5 :020(350) [0553] Answer: **Reflect** on your condition in the light of the Ten
L C : 0 1 :043(370) [0591] **Reflect** on the past, search it out, and tell me, When men
L C : 0 3 :013(422) [0701] mother, but should always **reflect**: "This is a work of
L C : 0 3 :024(423) [0703] also, that we should **reflect** on our needs, which ought to
L C : 0 5 :050(452) [0765] your inner life and **reflect**: "See what sort of Christian I
E P : 1 1 :009(495) [0833] can hardly escape such **reflections** as this: "If God has
S D : P R :009(503) [0849] other, so that the strife **reflects** a mere semantic problem
S D : 0 5 :003(558) [0953] When we rightly **reflect** on this controversy, we find that

Reform (2), Reformation (2), Reformed (5), Reforming (1)
S 1 : P R :003(289) [0455] and his adherents to be **reformed** a little and allow
S 1 : P R :012(290) [0459] there are countless temporal matters that need **reform**.
S 1 : P R :013(291) [0459] find enough time to **reform** the regulations concerning
T R : 0 0 :076(333) [0527] used properly for the **reformation** of morals and the glory
L C : 0 1 :280(403) [0661] procedure for restraining and **reforming** a wicked person.
L C : 0 1 :281(403) [0661] and root around in the filth, nobody will be **reformed**.
S D : P R :002(501) [0847] regarded this pious **reformation** as a new doctrine and as
S D : P R :003(501) [0847] their churches to be **reformed** according to the Word of
S D : P R :005(504) [0851] confession of the **reformed** churches) as our symbol in
S D : P R :005(504) [0851] distinguishes our **reformed** churches from the papacy and

Refrain (5), Refrained (1), Refraining (1), Refrains (1)
S 3 : 0 1 :005(302) [0477] either to do good and **refrain** from evil or to refrain from
S 3 : 0 1 :005(302) [0477] and refrain from evil or to **refrain** from good and do evil.
S 3 : 0 3 :029(308) [0487] should they confess when they **refrained** from evil words?
L C : 0 1 :037(369) [0589] imagine, when God **refrains** from disturbing their
L C : 0 1 :081(376) [0603] could be fulfilled by **refraining** from manual labor of any
L C : 0 1 :088(377) [0605] sit behind the stove and **refrain** from external work, or
S D : 0 7 :001(569) [0971] neither could nor should **refrain** from giving testimony to
S D : 1 2 :008(633) [1097] We have not been able to **refrain** from witnessing publicly

Refresh (2), Refreshed (2), Refreshment (4)
L C : 0 1 :080(375) [0603] man and beast might be **refreshed** and not be exhausted
L C : 0 1 :083(376) [0603] long — should retire for a day to rest and be **refreshed**.
L C : 0 5 :024(449) [0759] so that our faith may **refresh** and strengthen itself and
L C : 0 5 :027(449) [0759] Supper is given to bring us new strength and **refreshment**.
L C : 0 5 :066(454) [0769] who labor and are heavy-laden, and I will **refresh** you."
L C : 0 5 :072(455) [0769] sacrament and receive **refreshment**, comfort, and
E P : 1 1 :008(495) [0833] all sinners to himself and promises them **refreshment**.
S D : 1 1 :070(627) [1085] sin to come to him and find **refreshment** and be saved.

Refuge (6)
A P : 2 1 :023(232) [0349] order that we should take **refuge** in the help of the saints,
A P : 2 1 :024(232) [0349] order that we should take **refuge** in the help of the
L C : 0 1 :002(365) [0581] good and in which we find **refuge** in every time of need.
L C : 0 1 :185(390) [0633] as a wall, fortress, and **refuge** about our neighbor so that
L C : 0 3 :110(435) [0729] help or comfort is to take **refuge** in the Lord's Prayer and
L C : 0 6 :014(458) [0000] it has here a sure **refuge** when it hears in God's Word that

Refuse (24), Refused (3), Refuses (6), Refusal (1)
A G : P R :019(026) [0041] that the pope would not **refuse** to call a general council,
A P : P R :004(098) [0099] This they **refused** to do.
A P : 1 2 :062(190) [0269] What else is the **refusal** to believe absolution but the
A P : 1 2 :127(201) [0291] is there because you **refuse** to examine these questions
A P : 1 2 :128(202) [0291] be healing consciences, **refuse** to let the issue be
A P : 1 2 :134(202) [0293] write that if a penitent **refuses** to assume the satisfactions
A P : 1 2 :134(203) [0293] that one may **refuse**, for one may not refuse the
A P : 1 2 :134(203) [0293] refuse, for one may not **refuse** the commandments of
A P : 1 2 :176(210) [0307] and excommunicate those who **refuse** to be converted.
A P : 2 0 :004(227) [0339] the princes would have **refused** to let this statement of the
A P : 2 1 :038(234) [0355] And they **refuse** to tolerate us because we do not require
A P : 2 2 :006(237) [0359] to deny one part, and they **refuse** to grant both kinds.
A P : 2 3 :059(247) [0379] murder of priests who **refuse** to submit, and the exile of
A P : 2 3 :061(247) [0381] this same freedom; we **refuse** to force anyone into
A P : 2 3 :068(249) [0383] aware of this; hence they **refuse** to show us a copy of the
A P : 2 4 :023(253) [0391] The Greeks called them either "**refuse**" or "offscouring."
A P : 2 7 :014(271) [0423] forgiveness of sins, he **refuses** even more to give this
T R : 0 0 :072(332) [0525] bishops are heretics or **refuse** to administer ordination,
S C : P R :011(339) [0535] If any **refuse** to receive your instructions, tell them that
S C : P R :012(339) [0535] and employers should **refuse** to furnish them with food
S C : P R :020(340) [0537] they introduce when they **refuse** their aid in the training
S C : P R :024(341) [0539] But if they **refuse** to come, let them be, and tell them that
L C : P R :013(360) [0571] we deserve not only to be **refused** food but also to be
L C : S P :018(363) [0577] unruly that he **refuses** to learn these three parts in which
L C : 0 1 :038(369) [0591] They **refuse** to hear what is preached or spoken to them.
L C : 0 1 :095(378) [0607] who despise his Word and **refuse** to hear and learn it,
L C : 0 1 :160(387) [0627] says, they must be "the **refuse** of the world, and every
L C : 0 5 :035(450) [0761] blessing be offered to him in vain and **refuses** to enjoy it.
L C : 0 5 :056(453) [0767] see this, such people **refuse** to go to the sacrament and
L C : 0 5 :063(454) [0767] rely firmly upon itself; otherwise it **refuses** to take a step.
L C : 0 6 :030(460) [0000] However, if anyone **refuses** to hear and heed the warning
S D : 0 2 :046(530) [0899] matters, they will **refuse** to heed, hear, or read the Word
S D : 1 1 :041(623) [1077] despise the Word and **refuse** to come to the wedding.
S D : 1 1 :076(629) [1087] Son that any one should **refuse** to hear or should despise

Refute (14), Refuted (14), Refutes (3), Refutation (4), Refutations (1), Refuting (1)
A P : P R :002(098) [0099] condemned and to **refute** their arguments, our party
A P : P R :008(098) [0101] brag that they have **refuted** our Confession from the
A P : 0 2 :002(100) [0105] This sophistry is easy to **refute**.
A P : 0 2 :037(105) [0115] and since they cannot **refute** the principle, they twist his
A P : 0 2 :041(105) [0115] discussion Augustine **refutes** the opinion that human lust
A P : 0 4 :004(108) [0121] our Confession and to **refute** the objections of our
A P : 0 4 :039(112) [0131] this will also help **refute** those errors of our opponents
A P : 0 4 :084(119) [0147] one can devise or imagine will **refute** Paul's argument.
A P : 0 4 :183(132) [0173] Gospel) it will be easy to **refute** the opponents'
A P : 0 4 :314(156) [0207] it in mind, not only to **refute** the opponents' teaching that
A P : 0 4 :336(159) [0215] do not deserve a **refutation**, we shall nevertheless give a
A P : 0 4 :348(160) [0217] We have **refuted** this slander earlier.
A P : 0 7 :043(177) [0243] In his **refutation** of them Epiphanius praises the decree
A P : 1 2 :137(203) [0293] waste any more words in **refuting** these silly arguments of
A P : 1 8 :003(225) [0335] Augustine's emphatic **refutation** of these notions, based
A P : 2 0 :011(228) [0341] rather than compose a point-by-point **refutation**.
A P : 2 3 :062(247) [0381] incidentally recited and **refuted** the silly
A P : 2 3 :064(248) [0381] We have already **refuted** this very specious argument.
A P : 2 4 :009(251) [0387] This single answer **refutes** all our opponents' objections,
A P : 2 4 :033(256) [0395] therefore he does not **refute** our position but supports it.
A P : 2 4 :040(257) [0399] daily sacrifice does not **refute** but supports our stand
A P : 2 4 :090(266) [0415] doctrine of satisfaction, which we have **refuted** earlier.
A P : 2 7 :010(270) [0423] and in passing we shall **refute** our opponents' quibbles
A P : 2 7 :069(280) [0443] and in passing we have **refuted** the objections of our
A P : 2 8 :027(285) [0451] that they have really **refuted** our Confession with the
T R : 0 0 :021(323) [0509] [Arguments of Opponents **Refuted**]
L C : 0 1 :066(373) [0599] established, falsehood is **refuted**, people are reconciled,
L C : 0 5 :007(447) [0755] thus we can thoroughly **refute** all the babbling of the
E P : 0 8 :039(491) [0827] Hence, unless we **refute** these errors on the firm basis of
S D : P R :004(504) [0851] within the Christian church are clearly and solidly **refuted**.
S D : P R :010(506) [0855] of the Holy Scriptures, **refutations** of errors, and
S D : P R :015(507) [0857] contrary error must be **refuted** in order to preserve the
S D : 0 7 :091(585) [1005] and definitively **refuted** on the basis of God's Word by
S D : 0 7 :106(588) [1009] they will overthrow and **refute** all the counter-arguments
S D : 0 7 :110(588) [1011] papistic abuses have been **refuted** at length in the
S D : 0 8 :003(592) [1017] and mightily **refuted** this, as his doctrinal and polemical
S D : 1 1 :044(623) [1077] This also completely **refutes** all false opinions and

Regain (2)
L C : 0 1 :217(394) [0643] Thus it may in due time **regain** its proper honor, and
S D : 0 2 :011(522) [0885] accommodate himself to **regain** temporal life, so little can

Regard (67), Regarded (41), Regarding (8), Regardless (3), Regards (6)
P R : P R :012(006) [0013] by it but we also **regarded** ourselves bound to promote it
A G : 0 4 :003(030) [0045] For God will **regard** and reckon this faith as
A G : 1 5 :001(036) [0049] With **regard** to church usages that have been established
A G : 0 0 :002(048) [0059] some defect among us in **regard** to traditions, although
A G : 0 0 :000(049) [0059] (which is rightly to be **regarded** as above all custom) to
A G : 2 6 :004(064) [0071] strongly insists that we **regard** the merit of Christ as
A G : 2 6 :009(065) [0071] This also was **regarded** as Christian life: whoever
A G : 2 6 :011(065) [0071] by God, were to be **regarded** as secular and imperfect,
A G : 2 6 :025(068) [0073] of food and drink or with **regard** to a festival," etc.
A G : 2 6 :043(070) [0075] When some **regarded** this difference a divisive of the
A G : 2 7 :016(073) [0077] of perfection and is **regarded** as far superior to the other
A G : 2 7 :018(073) [0077] is taught among us with **regard** to those who desire to
A G : 2 8 :044(088) [0089] of food and drink or with **regard** to a festival or a new
A G : 0 0 :001(094) [0095] are the chief articles that are **regarded** as controversial.
A L : 0 0 :001(047) [0059] our teachers are to be **regarded** as heretics judge too
A L : 2 6 :010(065) [0071] These were **regarded** as secular and imperfect works, far
A L : 2 6 :025(067) [0073] of food and drink or with **regard** to a festival or a
A L : 2 8 :044(088) [0089] of food and drink or with **regard** to a festival or a new
A L : 2 8 :053(090) [0091] are bound so as to **regard** these as necessary services.
A L : 0 0 :001(094) [0095] the chief articles that are **regarded** as controversial.
A P : P R :019(099) [0103] We beseech him to **regard** his afflicted and scattered
A P : 0 4 :035(112) [0131] believe that God cared for him or **regarded** or heard him.
A P : 0 4 :072(117) [0141] **Regarding** faith we maintain not this, but rather that
A P : 0 4 :087(120) [0147] had God's command **regarding** circumcision
A P : 0 4 :122(124) [0157] and many similar passages **regarding** the law and works.
A P : 0 4 :233(140) [0185] on the people or have no **regard** for their weakness.
A P : 0 4 :257(144) [0193] they deserve to be **regarded** as blasphemers against
A P : 0 4 :325(157) [0211] anything new in this **regard** when the Church Fathers
A P : 0 4 :337(159) [0215] opponents are deceived with **regard** to the term "faith."

Continued ▶

A P : 0 4 :399(168) [0227] Some of the princes **regarded** this expression as unworthy
A P : 0 7 :027(173) [0237] with human reason and **regard** the rest as mythology, like
A P : 0 7 :035(175) [0239] of food and drink or with **regard** to a festival or a new
A P : 0 7 :045(177) [0243] kingdom of God if they **regard** as necessary a uniformity
A P : 0 7 :050(178) [0245] We **regard** as utterly seditious those who have incited
A P : 1 1 :003(180) [0249] With **regard** to the time, it is certain that most people in
A P : 1 1 :006(181) [0251] With **regard** to the enumeration of sins in confession we
A P : 1 2 :142(204) [0295] **Regarding** the law they say that in condescension to our
A P : 1 2 :165(208) [0303] and wholesome with **regard** to the whole process of
A P : 1 2 :171(209) [0305] is clear that they did not **regard** these canons as necessary
A P : 1 5 :020(218) [0321] traditions, they did not **regard** them as useful or necessary
A P : 1 5 :025(219) [0321] obscured; for when men **regard** these works as perfect and
A P : 1 5 :026(219) [0323] marriages because they **regarded** these observances as
A P : 1 5 :030(219) [0323] of food and drink or with **regard** to a festival or a new
A P : 1 5 :032(220) [0323] of the law or traditions be **regarded** as necessary.
A P : 1 5 :045(221) [0327] With **regard** to the mortifying of the body and the
A P : 1 8 :008(226) [0337] they really believe that God **regards** and hears them.
A P : 1 8 :010(226) [0337] is given to them out of **regard** for the merit of this
A P : 2 3 :059(247) [0379] from those who are **regarded** as the regular bishops.
A P : 2 4 :041(257) [0399] and they rule without **regard** for religion and the
A P : 2 4 :067(261) [0407] reply to our opponents **regarding** what the Fathers said.
A P : 2 4 :080(264) [0411] "This is how one should **regard** us, as ministers of Christ
A P : 2 7 :058(279) [0439] worship but should be **regarded** simply as a matter of
A P : 2 8 :016(283) [0447] and that they be not **regarded** as necessary acts of
S 1 : P R :014(291) [0459] commanded by God, are neither **regarded** nor observed?
S 2 : 0 2 :001(293) [0463] in the papacy must be **regarded** as the greatest and most
S 2 : 0 2 :012(295) [0465] with it are to be **regarded** as nothing else than illusions of
S 2 : 0 2 :026(297) [0469] them in still other ways, **regard** them as helpers in time of
S 3 : 0 6 :005(311) [0493] we have no **regard** for the subtle sophistry of those who
S 3 : 1 0 :003(314) [0497] by heretics shall also be **regarded** as ordained and remain
S 3 : 1 5 :005(316) [0501] I, Philip Melanchthon, **regard** the above articles as right
T R : 0 0 :006(320) [0505] and his laws to be **regarded** as articles of faith or
T R : 0 0 :022(324) [0511] those writings and wish them to be **regarded** as reiterated.
T R : 0 0 :024(324) [0511] in these passages to **regard** Peter as the representative of
T R : 0 0 :038(326) [0515] and such government ought to be **regarded** as accursed.
T R : 0 0 :054(329) [0519] and the princes, to have **regard** for the interests of the
T R : 0 0 :055(329) [0521] and wickedness without any **regard** for the Word of God?
T R : 0 0 :072(332) [0525] forms of worship should be **regarded** as anathema.
L C : P R :005(359) [0567] Many **regard** the Catechism as a simple, silly teaching
L C : 0 1 :001(365) [0581] That is, you shall **regard** me alone as your God.
L C : 0 1 :041(370) [0591] be careful not to **regard** this as if it were spoken by man.
L C : 0 1 :061(373) [0597] this as well as the other commandments in high **regard**.
L C : 0 1 :098(378) [0609] Do not **regard** it as an optional or unimportant matter.
L C : 0 1 :107(379) [0611] to honor, we must truly **regard** as high and great.
L C : 0 1 :112(380) [0613] For if we had **regarded** it as such, it would have been
L C : 0 1 :117(381) [0615] make sure that you **regard** it as great and precious, not on
L C : 0 1 :197(392) [0637] to the winds, **regarding** them as unnecessary, as if they
L C : 0 1 :299(405) [0665] for pretexts, without **regard** for equity or for our
L C : 0 1 :314(407) [0671] does what she is told, that is **regarded** as nothing.
L C : 0 1 :321(408) [0673] appendix ought to be **regarded** as attached to each
L C : 0 1 :323(409) [0673] a heart that fears and **regards** God alone and, because of
L C : 0 3 :013(422) [0701] and for what, we should **regard** as demanded by God and
L C : 0 3 :016(422) [0701] God does not **regard** prayer on account of the person,
L C : 0 3 :017(422) [0703] on obedience to God, **regardless** of our person, whether
L C : 0 3 :038(425) [0707] it holy and sacred, **regarding** it as the greatest treasure
L C : 0 3 :092(432) [0723] an appeal to God not to **regard** our sins and punish us as
L C : 0 4 :006(437) [0733] We are not to **regard** it as an indifferent matter, then, like
L C : 0 4 :007(437) [0733] importance that we **regard** Baptism as excellent, glorious,
L C : 0 4 :009(437) [0735] seals, then we ought to **regard** Baptism as much greater
L C : 0 4 :013(438) [0735] like the works which we do, **regards** it as worthless.
L C : 0 4 :019(439) [0737] by God should be **regarded** not according to the gross,
L C : 0 4 :020(439) [0737] If we **regard** these persons with reference to their noses,
L C : 0 4 :023(439) [0737] is and how it is to be **regarded**, we must also learn for
L C : 0 4 :026(439) [0739] Baptism should be **regarded** as being, for in it we obtain
L C : 0 4 :061(444) [0747] They **regard** Baptism only as water in the brook or in the
L C : 0 4 :063(444) [0749] aside from the Word, **regarding** Baptism merely as an
L C : 0 4 :080(446) [0751] such a notion because we **regard** Baptism only in the light
L C : 0 4 :084(446) [0753] Therefore let everybody **regard** his Baptism as the daily
L C : 0 5 :006(447) [0755] and ordered them, **regardless** of how we treat them.
L C : 0 5 :007(447) [0755] the seditious spirits who **regard** the sacraments, contrary
L C : 0 5 :051(452) [0765] love and even without **regard** for Christ's commandment.
L C : 0 5 :068(454) [0769] We must never **regard** the sacrament as a harmful thing
L C : 0 5 :070(454) [0769] it and desire help, should **regard** and use the sacrament as
L C : 0 6 :027(460) [0000] ought to know that we do not **regard** them as Christians.
E P : R N :004(465) [0777] occurred in our times, we **regard**, as the unanimous
E P : 0 3 :004(473) [0793] accepted by God into grace and are **regarded** as righteous.
E P : 0 3 :006(473) [0793] forgiveness of sins, are **regarded** as holy and righteous by
E P : 0 3 :009(474) [0795] souls, but they must **regard** it as certain that for Christ's
E P : 1 0 :009(494) [0831] in the church are to be **regarded** as in themselves divine
E P : 1 1 :019(497) [0837] and will, without **regard** for their sin, God has predestined
S D : P R :002(501) [0847] opponents, however, **regarded** this pious reformation as a
S D : P R :009(505) [0853] We also wish to be **regarded** as appealing to further
S D : P R :012(506) [0855] They are therefore **regarded** as impartial, none of the
S D : P R :019(507) [0857] be misled by the high **regard** in which these theologians
S D : 0 1 :005(509) [0861] that Christians must **regard** and recognize as sin not only
S D : 0 2 :010(522) [0885] which neither knows nor **regards** God) and the darkness
S D : 0 3 :022(543) [0923] Nevertheless, they are **regarded** as holy and righteous
S D : 0 3 :037(546) [0929] rely on them, or make or **regard** them as entirely or
S D : 0 3 :067(551) [0937] If anybody **regards** anything more as necessary by way of
S D : 0 4 :008(552) [0941] sight of God), and God **regards** them as sin and as impure
S D : 0 7 :041(576) [0985] Luther is rightly to be **regarded** as the most eminent
S D : 0 7 :054(579) [0991] of Christ?") are to be **regarded** diligently and earnestly as
S D : 0 8 :043(599) [1029] Therefore we **regard** our Lord Christ as God and man in
S D : 1 0 :013(613) [1057] food and drink, or with **regard** to a festival or a new
S D : 1 1 :029(621) [1073] And we should not **regard** this call of God which takes
S D : 1 1 :074(628) [1087] sight" (Ps. 31:22), then, **regardless** of what they

Regenerate (5), Regenerated (38), Regenerates (8), Regeneration (38)
A P : 0 2 :036(105) [0115] forgiven by spiritual **regeneration**, but it remains in the
A P : 0 2 :036(105) [0115] is absolved by the sacrament that **regenerates** the faithful.
A P : 0 4 :012(109) [0123] its works, what need is there of Christ or of **regeneration**?
A P : 0 4 :045(113) [0133] Thus it **regenerates** us and brings us the Holy Spirit, so
A P : 0 4 :046(113) [0133] it uses his blessings, it **regenerates** our hearts, it precedes
A P : 0 4 :065(116) [0139] conversion of the wicked or the manner of **regeneration**?
A P : 0 4 :065(116) [0139] on the *Sentences* that tells how **regeneration** takes place.
A P : 0 4 :068(116) [0139] show the manner of **regeneration** and the nature of the
A P : 0 4 :072(117) [0141] men righteous or to **regenerate** them, as well as to be
A P : 0 4 :078(117) [0143] unrighteous man righteous or effecting his **regeneration**.
A P : 0 4 :117(123) [0155] unrighteous we are made righteous and **regenerated** men.
A P : 0 4 :125(124) [0157] have been justified and **regenerated** by faith, therefore, we
A P : 0 4 :126(124) [0157] being justified and **regenerated**, we receive the Holy
A P : 0 4 :164(129) [0169] If those who are **regenerated** are supposed later to believe
A P : 0 4 :175(131) [0171] those who have been **regenerated** by faith receive the
A P : 0 4 :181(132) [0171] neither reconciles nor **regenerates** nor of itself makes us
A P : 0 4 :242(141) [0187] it is our propitiation; or that it **regenerates** and justifies.
A P : 0 4 :247(142) [0191] has just said that **regeneration** takes place through the
A P : 0 4 :247(142) [0191] says that we have been **regenerated** by the Gospel, he
A P : 0 4 :247(142) [0191] he teaches that we are **regenerated** and justified by faith.
A P : 0 4 :247(142) [0191] does not hold that we are **regenerated** by our works.
A P : 0 4 :251(143) [0191] does not mean that we are **regenerated** by works.
A P : 0 4 :253(143) [0193] of sins; that works **regenerate** our hearts; that works are a
A P : 0 4 :290(151) [0203] teach us to avail ourselves of Christ in our **regeneration**.
A P : 0 4 :292(152) [0203] accepts the forgiveness of sins, justifies, and **regenerates**.
A P : 0 9 :002(178) [0245] because Christ **regenerates** through Word and sacrament.
A P : 1 2 :029(186) [0259] eternal life, and to lead us as **regenerated** men to do good.
A P : 1 2 :058(190) [0267] to it in conversion or **regeneration** and the forgiveness of
A P : 1 2 :058(190) [0267] as punishments follow **regeneration** and the forgiveness
A P : 1 2 :060(190) [0269] justification and **regeneration**, for it frees us from our
A P : 1 2 :082(194) [0275] follows faith, for the **regenerate** receive the Holy Spirit
A P : 1 2 :131(202) [0291] (that is, conversion or **regeneration**) must come good
A P : 1 2 :148(205) [0299] of penitence because **regeneration** itself takes place by
A P : 1 8 :009(226) [0337] to the operation of the Holy Spirit in the **regenerate**.
S C : 0 4 :010(349) [0551] life and a washing of **regeneration** in the Holy Spirit, as
S C : 0 4 :010(349) [0551] us by the washing of **regeneration** and renewal in the
L C : 0 4 :027(440) [0739] the "washing of **regeneration**," as St. Paul calls it in Titus
E P : 0 2 :001(469) [0785] after the Fall, (3) after **regeneration**, (4) after the
E P : 0 2 :001(469) [0785] the fall of our first parents and before his **regeneration**?
E P : 0 3 :009(474) [0793] believing and truly **regenerated** persons retain much
E P : 0 4 :003(476) [0797] of our choice but that **regenerated** persons are bound to
E P : 0 4 :008(476) [0799] those who are **regenerated** and renewed by the Holy
E P : 0 4 :009(476) [0799] way applied to the **regenerated** and are in no way
E P : 0 4 :010(476) [0799] when applied to the **regenerated** the words "necessity" and
E P : 0 4 :011(477) [0799] the statement, "The **regenerated** do good works from a
E P : 0 4 :011(477) [0799] it were left to the **regenerated** person's option whether to
E P : 0 6 :003(480) [0805] truly converted, **regenerated**, and justified through faith.
E P : 0 6 :004(480) [0805] of their mind, such **regeneration** and renewal is
E P : 0 6 :006(481) [0807] works through the **regenerated**, and which the regenerated
E P : 0 6 :006(481) [0807] and which the **regenerated** perform in so far as they are
E P : 0 6 :007(481) [0807] and impenitent, for **regenerated** and unregenerated people
E P : 0 6 :007(481) [0807] man — just like the **regenerated** according to the flesh —
S D : 0 1 :014(511) [0863] only the Holy Spirit's **regeneration** and renovation can
S D : 0 2 :002(520) [0881] the Holy Spirit has **regenerated** him and rules him, nor
S D : 0 2 :002(520) [0881] in his conversion and **regeneration**, by those powers of
S D : 0 2 :005(521) [0881] becomes a believer, is **regenerated** and renewed.
S D : 0 2 :017(524) [0887] the Holy Spirit has **regenerated**), but I see in my members
S D : 0 2 :018(524) [0887] of St. Paul and other **regenerated** persons wars against
S D : 0 2 :018(524) [0887] of God even after their **regeneration**, the will of man
S D : 0 2 :021(525) [0889] converts, and **regenerates** man, a destiny for which only
S D : 0 2 :024(525) [0891] In his conversion or **regeneration** he can as little begin,
S D : 0 2 :025(526) [0891] faith in Christ, **regeneration**, renewal, and everything that
S D : 0 2 :026(526) [0891] Spirit is a Spirit "of **regeneration** and renewal" (Titus 3:5,
S D : 0 2 :035(528) [0895] say that even in the **regenerated** the will can do something
S D : 0 2 :039(528) [0895] Although the **regenerated**, while still in this life, reach the
S D : 0 2 :046(530) [0899] our conversion and **regeneration** are exclusively the work
S D : 0 2 :053(531) [0903] converted to God and **regenerated** can hear and read this
S D : 0 2 :064(533) [0905] Paul apply also to the **regenerated**, "For I delight in the
S D : 0 2 :065(534) [0907] initiated his work of **regeneration** and renewal in us
S D : 0 2 :068(534) [0907] of the Spirit, and **regeneration** is not as yet perfect but
S D : 0 2 :081(536) [0911] in conversion and **regeneration** God creates a new heart
S D : 0 2 :084(537) [0913] remains also in the **regenerated** a resistance, of which the
S D : 0 2 :085(537) [0913] But the **regenerated** man delights in the law of God
S D : 0 3 :018(542) [0921] Since the word "**regeneration**" is sometimes used in place
S D : 0 3 :019(542) [0921] The word "**regeneration**" is used, in the first place, to
S D : 0 3 :019(542) [0921] made, "Justification is **regeneration**," that is, justification
S D : 0 3 :019(542) [0921] before God is **regeneration**, just as St. Paul uses the terms
S D : 0 3 :019(542) [0921] us by the washing of **regeneration** and renewing in the
S D : 0 3 :020(542) [0921] has justified him, a **regeneration** has indeed taken place
S D : 0 3 :021(542) [0921] Frequently the word "**regeneration**" means the
S D : 0 3 :022(543) [0923] do not mean that after **regeneration** no unrighteousness in
S D : 0 3 :022(543) [0923] have been justified and **regenerated**, but we hold that
S D : 0 3 :023(543) [0923] even in the case of the **regenerated**, the righteousness of
S D : 0 4 :005(552) [0939] above, new obedience is not necessary in the **regenerated**.
S D : 0 4 :038(557) [0951] God demands of the **regenerated**), they are an indication
S D : 0 6 :002(564) [0963] and held that the **regenerated** do not learn the new
S D : 0 6 :005(564) [0963] nor may it torture the **regenerated** with its coercion, for
S D : 0 6 :012(566) [0967] the law to instruct the **regenerate** out of it and to show
S D : 1 2 :031(635) [1101] God seals the adoption of sons and works **regeneration**.

Regeneratio (1)
E P : 0 3 :008(474) [0793] Apology, the words ***regeneratio*** (rebirth) and *vivificatio*

Regensburg (1)
P R : P R :027(016) [0027] Chamberlain and Council of the City of **Regensburg**

Regenstein (2)
P R : P R :027(015) [0025] Ernest, count of **Regenstein**
P R : P R :027(015) [0025] Bodo, count of **Regenstein**

Regime (2)
A P : 2 7 :003(269) [0419] decline of the monastic **regime** and this same number of
A P : 2 7 :004(269) [0421] oracles, which threaten a change in the monastic **regime**.

Regions (1)
A P : 1 5 :042(220) [0325] there are many **regions** where no sermons are preached

Register (1)
A P : 2 0 :011(228) [0341] has compelled us to **register** a complaint rather than

Regret (1), Regretted (1)
AL : 2 7 :009(072) [0077] They **regretted** that in such a momentous matter the
AP : 2 3 :059(247) [0379] to God, we do not **regret** our lack of an alliance with such

Regular (6), Regularly (3)
AG : 1 4 :000(036) [0049] the sacraments in the church without a **regular** call.
AG : 2 8 :028(085) [0087] should not obey even **regularly** elected bishops if they err
AL : 1 4 :000(036) [0049] or administer the sacraments unless he is **regularly** called.
AP : 1 1 :008(181) [0251] the secular and the **regular** clergy over the question of
AP : 2 3 :059(247) [0379] from those who are regarded as the **regular** bishops.
TR : 0 0 :066(331) [0523] Consequently, when the **regular** bishops become enemies
LC : 0 1 :270(401) [0657] reply: "Why don't you bring it before the **regular** judge?"
SD : 0 6 :002(564) [0963] completes its **regular** course without any outside impulse,
SD : 0 6 :006(565) [0965] all the stars of heaven **regularly** run their courses

Regulate (4), Regulated (3)
PR : PR :025(014) [0023] of faith and to **regulate** all religious controversies and
AP : 2 4 :007(250) [0385] St. Francis sought to **regulate** this with the provision that
LC : 0 1 :089(377) [0605] Thus we may **regulate** our whole life and being according
LC : 0 1 :103(379) [0611] so that all our conduct and life may be **regulated** by it.
LC : 0 1 :239(397) [0649] government were well **regulated**, such insolence might
EP : 0 6 :001(480) [0805] to which they should pattern and **regulate** their entire life.
SD : PR :010(506) [0855] are to be approved and accepted, judged and **regulated**.

Regulation (11), Regulations (30)
AG : 2 7 :031(075) [0079] canons and papal **regulations** annul vows that are made
AG : 2 8 :030(085) [0087] the church or establish **regulations** concerning foods, holy
AG : 2 8 :041(087) [0089] was that countless **regulations** came into being — for
AG : 2 8 :043(088) [0089] establishment of such **regulations** for the purpose of
AG : 2 8 :045(088) [0089] Christ you died to the **regulations** of the world, why do
AG : 2 8 :045(088) [0089] Why do you submit to **regulations**, 'Do not handle, Do
AG : 2 8 :049(089) [0091] forbid the making and keeping of human **regulations**?
AG : 2 8 :050(089) [0091] Inasmuch as such **regulations** as have been instituted as
AG : 2 8 :053(090) [0091] or pastors may make **regulations** so that everything in the
AG : 2 8 :055(090) [0091] and to observe the **regulations** in such a way that one
AG : 2 8 :064(092) [0093] and mitigate human **regulations**, yet there can be no
AG : 2 8 :067(092) [0093] letter, and many of the **regulations** fall into disuse from
AG : 2 8 :069(093) [0093] on the observance of **regulations** which cannot be kept
AG : 2 8 :074(093) [0093] it be denied that some **regulations** were adopted from
AG : 2 8 :074(093) [0093] as to temper these **regulations** inasmuch as such changes
AG : 2 8 :074(094) [0093] For many **regulations** devised by men have with the
AG : 2 8 :075(094) [0095] or abrogate human **regulations** which are not to be
AL : 2 8 :045(088) [0089] Why do you submit to **regulations**, 'Do not handle, Do
AL : 2 8 :053(090) [0091] or pastors to make **regulations** so that things in the
AL : 2 8 :074(093) [0093] to mitigate these **regulations** now, for such change does
AP : 0 4 :288(151) [0203] the canonists have twisted ecclesiastical **regulations**.
AP : 0 7 :035(175) [0241] Why do you submit to **regulations**, 'Do not handle, Do
AP : 1 1 :001(180) [0249] the correction that the **regulation** *Omnis utriusque* should
AP : 1 1 :006(181) [0251] not cite against us the **regulation** *Omnis utriusque;* we are
AP : 1 1 :007(181) [0251] by the part of the **regulation** that requires all sins to be
AP : 1 1 :008(181) [0251] people's consciences the **regulation** *Omnis utriusque*, for
AP : 1 1 :008(181) [0251] This **regulation** commands the impossible, namely, that
AP : 2 3 :007(240) [0365] it follows that neither **regulations** nor vows can abolish
AP : 2 3 :008(240) [0367] Just as human **regulations** cannot change the nature of
AP : 2 3 :008(240) [0367] vows nor human **regulations** can change the nature of
AP : 2 3 :009(241) [0367] into nature, and human **regulations** cannot abolish it.
AP : 2 3 :016(241) [0369] human authority, **regulations**, and vows cannot abolish
AP : 2 3 :022(242) [0369] are arguing about the **regulation** and about those who do
AP : 2 3 :022(242) [0369] snares should be set for the weak through this **regulation**.
AP : 2 3 :023(242) [0369] *Fourth*, the pontifical **regulation** also disagrees with the
AP : 2 3 :024(243) [0371] but we do object to the **regulations** which the Roman
AP : 2 3 :025(243) [0371] Thus the **regulation** about perpetual celibacy is peculiar to
AP : 2 3 :026(243) [0371] do not defend this **regulation** for religious reasons, since
AP : 2 3 :041(245) [0375] frees us from these Levitical **regulations** about impurity.
S 1 : PR :013(291) [0459] time to reform the **regulations** concerning fasts,
LC : 0 3 :073(430) [0719] that pertains to the **regulation** of our domestic and our

Rehearse (1), Rehearsed (1)
AL : 2 7 :015(073) [0077] and it is needless to **rehearse** what is well known.
AL : 2 7 :017(073) [0077] We have **rehearsed** these things without odious

Reign (4), Reigned (1), Reigneth (1), Reigning (2), Reigns (2)
AG : PR :021(027) [0043] have been held during Your Imperial Majesty's **reign**.
AL : 0 3 :004(030) [0045] of the Father, forever **reign** and have dominion over all
AP : 0 4 :189(133) [0175] works, sacrifices, and the **reign** of Christ, whereby he
AP : 2 3 :003(239) [0363] you, "A man with a modest face will **reign** everywhere."
S 1 : PR :015(291) [0459] Thee and the Father liveth and **reigneth**, blessed forever.
SC : 0 2 :004(345) [0545] is risen from the dead and lives and **reigns** to all eternity.
SC : 0 8 :011(354) [0559] Jesus Christ our Lord, who lives and **reigns** forever.
EP : 1 2 :020(499) [0841] understanding of Christ as the **reigning** king of heaven.
SD : 1 2 :008(633) [1097] of the papacy still **reigned**, and where the poor, simple
SD : 1 2 :029(635) [1101] knowledge of Christ, the **reigning** king of heaven, who

Rein (2)
LC : 0 3 :108(435) [0729] to it is to give it free **rein** and neither resist it nor pray for
LC : 0 4 :068(445) [0749] the old man is given free **rein** and continually grows

Reinforces (1)
AP : 0 4 :088(120) [0149] inadvertently, he **reinforces** and confirms it with a long

Reintroduce (1)
EP : 1 0 :002(493) [0829] pressure and demands, **reintroduce** some ceremonies that

Reiterated (3), Reiterating (1)
PR : PR :000(001) [0004] Christian, **Reiterated**, and Unanimous Confession of the
PR : PR :008(005) [0011] stimulated by this our **reiterated** and repeated confession
AP : 2 7 :010(270) [0423] we want to be interpreted here as **reiterating** that book.
TR : 0 0 :022(324) [0511] those writings and wish them to be regarded as **reiterated**.

Reject (104), Rejected (39), Rejecting (4), Rejection (5), Rejections (1), Rejects (9)
PR : PR :010(006) [0011] to expose and to **reject** false doctrine, and clearly to
PR : PR :019(009) [0017] doctrine is expressly **rejected** in the confession submitted
PR : PR :019(009) [0017] Nor do we want to have **rejected** or condemned any other
PR : PR :022(011) [0019] censures, and **rejections** of false and adulterated doctrine,
AG : 0 1 :005(028) [0043] the heresies which are contrary to this article are **rejected**.
AG : 0 2 :003(029) [0045] **Rejected** in this connection are the Pelagians and others
AG : 0 9 :003(033) [0047] who teach that infant Baptism is not right are **rejected**.
AG : 1 0 :002(034) [0047] The contrary doctrine is therefore **rejected**.
AG : 1 2 :007(035) [0049] **Rejected** here are those who teach that persons who have
AG : 1 2 :010(035) [0049] **Rejected** also are those who teach that forgiveness of sin is
AG : 1 7 :004(038) [0051] **Rejected**, therefore, are the Anabaptists who teach that
AG : 1 7 :005(038) [0051] **Rejected**, too, are certain Jewish opinions which are even
AG : 0 0 :001(048) [0059] those who presume to **reject**, avoid, and separate from
AG : 2 6 :039(069) [0075] fasting in itself is not **rejected**, but what is rejected is
AG : 2 6 :039(069) [0075] not rejected, but what is **rejected** is making a necessary
AG : 2 8 :046(088) [0089] myths or to commands of men who **reject** the truth.
AG : 2 8 :048(089) [0091] He **rejects** such service of God and says, "Every plant
AL : 0 9 :003(033) [0047] the Anabaptists who **reject** the Baptism of children and
AL : 1 2 :010(035) [0049] **Rejected** also are those who do not teach that remission
AL : 2 8 :021(084) [0087] except to forgive sins, to **reject** doctrine which is contrary
AL : 2 8 :046(088) [0089] myths or to commands of men who **reject** the truth."
AP : 0 4 :098(121) [0149] is the stone which was **rejected** by you builders, but which
AP : 0 4 :121(124) [0155] In following them and **rejecting** this faith, our opponents
AP : 0 4 :260(145) [0195] we can oppose those who **reject** Christ, destroy the
AP : 0 4 :266(146) [0197] We must not **reject** the promise of Christ when the law is
AP : 0 4 :282(149) [0201] These Christ **rejects**, and in place of this false cleansing he
AP : 0 4 :290(151) [0203] both exclude Christ and therefore both are to be **rejected**.
AP : 0 4 :316(156) [0209] is understandable why we **reject** our opponents' teaching
AP : 0 4 :324(157) [0211] Properly, then, do we **reject** the doctrine of the merit of
AP : 1 2 :016(184) [0257] reasons prompted us to **reject** the doctrine of penitence as
AP : 1 2 :085(194) [0277] Therefore we **reject** the Pharisaic opinions of our
AP : 1 2 :123(201) [0289] terrible heretics, who **reject** penitence, should be removed
AP : 1 2 :158(207) [0301] not feel that God has **rejected** them but they should be
AP : 1 2 :173(210) [0305] their schools that it is not a sin to **reject** satisfactions.
AP : 2 0 :001(226) [0337] expressly state their **rejection** and condemnation of our
AP : 2 0 :001(226) [0337] This article they explicitly **reject** and condemn.
AP : 2 0 :011(228) [0341] have gone on record as **rejecting** our doctrine that we
AP : 2 0 :013(228) [0343] lose the Holy Spirit and **reject** penitence; as we have said
AP : 2 3 :051(246) [0377] have many reasons for **rejecting** the law of perpetual
AP : 2 3 :059(247) [0379] our opponents we would have to **reject** the clear truth.
AP : 2 4 :029(255) [0393] It **rejects** sacrificial victims and requires prayer: "Do I eat
AP : 2 4 :039(257) [0399] With the **rejection** of the idea that ceremonies work *ex*
AP : 2 4 :062(260) [0405] We therefore **reject** the error of Thomas when he writes,
AP : 2 4 :063(260) [0405] We also **reject** other common errors: that the Mass
AP : 2 4 :094(267) [0417] forbid this, but rather we **reject** the transfer of the Lord's
AP : 2 4 :096(267) [0417] This he **rejects**.
AP : 2 4 :096(267) [0417] We **reject** these wicked errors which rob Christ's suffering
AP : 2 4 :098(268) [0419] believe the Gospel should **reject** those wicked services
AP : 2 7 :010(270) [0423] opponents demand the **rejection** of everything that we
AP : 2 7 :068(280) [0443] do not provide for their relatives have **rejected** the faith.
AP : 2 7 :068(280) [0443] way he says that the wanton women had **rejected** the faith.
AP : 2 7 :069(281) [0443] hearts why they should **reject** the hypocrisy and the sham
AP : 2 7 :070(281) [0443] of life must have come to **reject** any confidence in such
S 3 : 1 5 :001(316) [0501] written in Titus 1:14, "They are men who **reject** the truth."
TR : 0 0 :052(329) [0519] these errors must be **rejected** and that the true teaching
LC : SP :002(362) [0575] practices of his craft is **rejected** and considered
LC : 0 3 :006(421) [0699] alleging that since we **reject** false and hypocritical prayers
LC : 0 3 :025(423) [0705] we have rightly **rejected** the prayers of monks and priests,
LC : 0 3 :033(424) [0707] We by no means **reject** prayer, but we do denounce the
LC : 0 3 :033(424) [0707] as Christ himself **rejects** and forbids great wordiness.
LC : 0 4 :031(440) [0739] it follows that whoever **rejects** Baptism rejects God's
LC : 0 4 :031(440) [0739] whoever rejects Baptism **rejects** God's Word, faith, and
LC : 0 4 :034(440) [0741] that it excludes and **rejects** all works that we may do with
EP : RN :003(465) [0777] to these, and we hereby **reject** all heresies and teachings
EP : RN :006(465) [0779] to them should be **rejected** and condemned as opposed to
EP : RN :008(465) [0779] how contrary teachings were **rejected** and condemned.
EP : 0 1 :010(467) [0781] ***Rejection** of the Contrary False Teaching*
EP : 0 1 :011(467) [0781] 1. Accordingly we **reject** and condemn the teaching that
EP : 0 1 :013(467) [0783] 3. We likewise **reject** the Pelagian error which asserts that
EP : 0 1 :017(468) [0783] 7. We also **reject** the Manichaean error that original sin is
EP : 0 1 :019(468) [0783] 9. We also **reject** and condemn as a Manichaean error the
EP : 0 2 :007(470) [0787] Accordingly we **reject** and condemn all the following
EP : 0 2 :009(471) [0789] 2. We also **reject** the error of the crass Pelagians who
EP : 0 2 :010(471) [0789] 3. We also **reject** the error of the Semi-Pelagians who
EP : 0 2 :013(471) [0789] 6. Likewise we **reject** and condemn the error of the
EP : 0 3 :011(474) [0795] ***Rejection** of the Contrary Doctrine*
EP : 0 3 :012(474) [0795] Accordingly we **reject** and condemn all the following
EP : 0 4 :016(477) [0801] 1. Accordingly we **reject** and condemn spoken and written
EP : 0 4 :017(477) [0801] 2. We also **reject** and condemn as offensive and as
EP : 0 4 :019(477) [0801] 3. We also **reject** and condemn the teaching that faith and
EP : 0 5 :010(479) [0805] ***Rejected** Contrary Doctrine*
EP : 0 5 :011(479) [0805] 1. Hence we **reject** and deem it as false and detrimental
EP : 0 7 :017(484) [0813] For although they **reject** Christ as a redeemer, they must
EP : 0 7 :021(484) [0813] side, we unanimously **reject** and condemn all the
EP : 0 8 :019(490) [0823] Accordingly we **reject** and condemn as contrary to the
EP : 1 0 :008(494) [0831] Therefore we **reject** and condemn as false and contrary to
EP : 1 1 :016(497) [0837] Therefore we **reject** the following errors:
EP : 1 2 :006(498) [0839] They thus **reject** the entire doctrine of original sin and
EP : 1 2 :030(500) [0843] and conclusions, we **reject** and condemn as wrong, false,
SD : PR :006(504) [0853] into the church errors that had already been **rejected**.
SD : PR :010(506) [0855] and expositions of doctrinal articles, should be **rejected**.
SD : PR :012(506) [0855] can or should **reject** them, nor can anyone who sincerely
SD : PR :016(507) [0857] Word, and what he should **reject**, flee, and avoid as false
SD : PR :017(507) [0857] 1. In the first place, we **reject** and condemn all heresies
SD : PR :017(507) [0857] orthodox church **rejected** and condemned on the certain
SD : PR :018(507) [0857] 2. In the second place, we **reject** and condemn all the
SD : PR :018(507) [0857] and heresies that are **rejected** in the aforementioned
SD : 0 1 :016(511) [0865] doctrines which are **rejected** and condemned in our
SD : 0 1 :017(511) [0865] we condemn and **reject** as false the opinion and doctrine
SD : 0 1 :020(511) [0865] 4. We likewise **reject** and condemn the following and
SD : 0 1 :023(512) [0865] 7. Likewise, we also **reject** and condemn those who teach
SD : 0 1 :025(512) [0865] We condemn and **reject** these and similar false doctrines
SD : 0 1 :026(512) [0867] that reason the following and similar errors are **rejected**:
SD : 0 1 :043(516) [0873] with ours; they also **rejected** the contrary doctrine as
SD : 0 1 :048(516) [0875] it is evident that we must **reject** this doctrine with all its
SD : 0 1 :055(518) [0877] condemned and **rejected** the statement, "Original sin is

Continued ▶

SD : 0 2 :033(527) [0893] The Smalcald Articles **reject** the following errors
SD : 0 2 :043(529) [0897] "I herewith **reject** and condemn as sheer error every
SD : 0 2 :073(535) [0909] readily recognize, expose, **reject**, and condemn such false
SD : 0 2 :079(536) [0911] 5. Likewise we **reject** the teachings of the papists and the
SD : 0 2 :082(537) [0913] 8. We also **reject** the following formulas if they are used
SD : 0 3 :029(544) [0925] as if we thereby utterly **rejected** works and love (as the
SD : 0 3 :029(544) [0925] article of justification, we **reject** and condemn works,
SD : 0 3 :044(547) [0933] must criticize, expose, and **reject** the following and
SD : 0 3 :059(550) [0937] we unanimously **reject** and condemn, in addition to the
SD : 0 3 :066(550) [0937] and all similar errors we **reject** unanimously as contrary
SD : 0 4 :015(553) [0943] therefore, to criticize and **reject** the cited propositions and
SD : 0 4 :015(553) [0943] and urged to criticize and **reject** a complacent Epicurean
SD : 0 4 :020(554) [0945] But we **reject** and condemn as false the view that good
SD : 0 4 :022(554) [0945] Therefore we correctly **reject** the propositions that good
SD : 0 4 :024(555) [0945] Luther also has **rejected** and condemned these
SD : 0 4 :029(555) [0947] are to be expelled and **rejected** by our churches as false
SD : 0 4 :031(556) [0947] earnestly criticizing and **rejecting** the false Epicurean
SD : 0 4 :033(556) [0949] a wicked life, lose the Holy Spirit, and **reject** repentance."'
SD : 0 4 :035(557) [0949] by God, we rightly **reject** the decree of the Council of
SD : 0 4 :039(557) [0951] churches condemn and **reject** this proposition, too,
SD : 0 6 :026(568) [0971] Hence we **reject** and condemn, as pernicious and contrary
SD : 0 7 :035(575) [0983] We do this to **reject** the papistic transubstantiation and to
SD : 0 7 :085(584) [1003] dare not in any way be **rejected**, but it can and should be
SD : 0 7 :105(588) [1009] Thus we **reject** the Capernaitic conception of a gross,
SD : 0 7 :107(588) [1009] Accordingly we **reject** and condemn with heart and mouth
SD : 0 7 :109(588) [1011] Secondly, we also **reject** and condemn all other papistic
SD : 0 7 :112(589) [1011] Therefore we **reject** and condemn with heart and mouth
SD : 0 7 :113(589) [1011] We **reject** all such Sacramentarian opinions and mutually
SD : 0 7 :123(590) [1013] 12. We also **reject** the doctrine that unbelieving,
SD : 0 7 :123(590) [1015] Therefore we **reject** the making of such a distinction
SD : 0 7 :124(591) [1015] 13. We also **reject** the doctrine that worthiness does not
SD : 0 7 :127(591) [1015] 16. We also **reject** and condemn all presumptuous,
SD : 0 7 :128(591) [1015] Additional antitheses and **rejected** erroneous views have
SD : 0 7 :128(591) [1015] have been criticized and **rejected** in the foregoing
SD : 0 7 :128(591) [1015] exposition, for we **reject** and condemn everything that is
SD : 0 8 :051(600) [1031] own co-religionists now criticize and **reject** this error.
SD : 0 8 :062(603) [1037] have been justly **rejected** and condemned in the ancient
SD : 0 8 :088(609) [1047] we unanimously **reject** and condemn with mouth and
SD : 0 8 :096(609) [1049] 8. We **reject** and condemn these errors and all others that
SD : 1 0 :026(615) [1061] 1. Therefore we **reject** and condemn as wrongful the view
SD : 1 0 :027(615) [1061] 2. We also **reject** and condemn as wrongful the procedure
SD : 1 0 :028(615) [1061] 3. We **reject** and condemn as wrongful the opinion of
SD : 1 0 :030(615) [1061] 5. We also **reject** and condemn the procedure whereby
SD : 1 1 :003(616) [1063] one must not by-pass or **reject** a teaching of the divine
SD : 1 1 :039(622) [1075] God's Word and who **reject**, blaspheme, and persecute it
SD : 1 1 :040(623) [1077] that he would harden, **reject**, and condemn all who, when
SD : 1 1 :041(623) [1077] own perverse will, which **rejects** or perverts the means and
SD : 1 1 :059(626) [1083] his Word and whom he does not harden and **reject**.
SD : 1 1 :093(632) [1095] and disputations, and we **reject** and condemn all those
SD : 1 2 :008(633) [1097] that on the contrary we **reject** and condemn all these
SD : 1 2 :009(633) [1097] We **reject** and condemn the erroneous and heretical
SD : 1 2 :011(634) [1099] Thus they deny and **reject** the entire teaching of original
SD : 1 2 :028(635) [1101] We **reject** and condemn these errors of the
SD : 1 2 :036(635) [1101] We **reject** and condemn the error of the New Arians who
SD : 1 2 :037(636) [1101] 1. Some Anti-Trinitarians **reject** and condemn the old,
SD : 1 2 :039(636) [1103] or follows from them, we **reject** and condemn as false,

Rejoice (5), Rejoices (1)
LC : 0 1 :117(381) [0615] You should **rejoice** heartily and thank God that he has
LC : 0 1 :198(392) [0637] and divine works in which he **rejoices** with all the angels.
LC : 0 6 :023(459) [0000] so anxious that he would **rejoice** and act like a poor
SD : PR :008(502) [0849] adversaries, the papists, **rejoice** over the schisms which
SD : 0 6 :025(568) [0971] and with sheer joy, and will **rejoice** therein forever.
SD : 0 8 :096(610) [1049] therewith, and **rejoice** constantly that our flesh and blood

Relapsed (1)
AP : 1 2 :118(200) [0287] by those who have **relapsed** into mortal sin, as though

Relate (2), Related (6), Relates (1), Relating (1)
AG : 0 0 :005(095) [0095] anybody, but we have **related** only matters which we have
AL : 0 0 :004(095) [0095] has here been said or **related** for the purpose of injuring
AP : 1 2 :059(190) [0267] and the doctrine of justification are very closely **related**.
TR : 0 0 :067(331) [0523] which Augustine **relates** of two Christians in a ship, one
LC : 0 1 :103(379) [0611] Now follow the other seven, which **relate** to our neighbor.
LC : 0 2 :006(411) [0679] of the Godhead, to whom all that we believe is **related**.
LC : 0 2 :070(420) [0697] initiative learn more, **relating** these teachings of the
LC : 0 4 :003(437) [0733] to which everything is **related** that is to be said on the
SD : 0 1 :020(511) [0865] and condemn the following and **related** Pelagian errors:
SD : 0 2 :048(530) [0901] hearts, and how we are to **relate** ourselves to and use

Relation (5), Relations (8)
AG : PR :019(026) [0041] Since the **relations** between Your Imperial Majesty and
AP : 0 4 :242(141) [0187] the forgiveness of sins in **relation** to God; that in place of
AP : 0 4 :242(141) [0187] He means that in human **relations** it is not peevish,
AP : 1 3 :011(212) [0311] is interpreted in **relation** to the ministry of the Word, we
AP : 2 4 :052(259) [0403] act on behalf of men in **relation** to God, to offer gifts and
LC : 0 1 :050(371) [0593] the lips and the tongue into the right **relation** to God.
LC : 0 1 :150(385) [0623] of fatherhood, the most comprehensive of all **relations**.
LC : 0 1 :250(399) [0651] but must extend to all our **relations** with our neighbors.
LC : 0 1 :288(403) [0663] Thus in our **relations** with one another, we should veil
LC : 0 3 :073(430) [0719] For where these two **relations** are interfered with and
LC : 0 3 :076(431) [0719] this petition covers all kinds of **relations** on earth.
LC : 0 3 :080(431) [0721] government or honorable and peaceful **relations** on earth.
SD : 0 7 :117(589) [1013] in terms of the **relation** between the sign and that which is

Relationship (2), Relationships (1)
AL : 2 6 :022(067) [0073] and to have a **relationship** with the purifications of the
AP : 1 6 :006(223) [0331] other teachings that were not suited to civil **relationships**.
TR : 0 0 :078(333) [0527] concerning spiritual **relationship** are unjust, and equally

Relative (1), Relatives (3)
AP : 2 3 :069(249) [0383] controversy on the **relative** value of marriage and
AP : 2 7 :067(280) [0443] does not provide for his **relatives**, and especially for his
AP : 2 7 :068(280) [0443] do not provide for their **relatives** have rejected the faith.
LC : 0 1 :259(400) [0655] offend good friends, **relatives**, neighbors, and the rich and

Relax (4), Relaxation (2), Relaxed (1), Relaxes (1)
AG : 2 3 :016(054) [0063] is sometimes necessary to **relax** severity and rigor for the
AG : 2 3 :016(054) [0063] In this case **relaxation** would certainly be both Christian
AG : 2 8 :072(093) [0093] ask only that the bishops **relax** certain unreasonable
AL : 2 3 :016(054) [0063] the old rigor should be **relaxed** now and then on account
AL : 2 8 :072(093) [0093] do), but ask only that they **relax** unjust burdens which are
AL : 2 8 :075(094) [0095] impossible to obtain a **relaxation** of observances which
AL : 2 8 :077(094) [0095] purely and that they **relax** some few observances which
LC : 0 1 :100(378) [0609] neither day nor night **relaxes** his effort to steal upon you

Release (3), Released (5), Releases (1), Releasing (1)
AG : 2 7 :024(074) [0079] not have dispensed and **released** men from such
AG : 2 7 :036(076) [0081] marriage frees and **releases** many from monastic vows,
AL : 2 6 :014(066) [0073] altogether succeed in **releasing** them but rather entangled
AP : 1 2 :135(203) [0293] But indulgences do not **release** us from commandments
AP : 2 7 :053(278) [0437] live in monasteries are **released** by such wicked
AP : 2 7 :056(278) [0439] and cogent reasons that **release** good men from this way
AP : 2 7 :057(279) [0439] the canons themselves **release** many who took their vows
S3 : 0 3 :026(307) [0487] be so cheap that they were **released** at six pence a head.
LC : 0 1 :211(393) [0641] and others whom he has **released** by a high supernatural
LC : 0 6 :004(457) [0000] or fear, and we are **released** from the torture of

Relevant (1)
AP : 2 0 :014(228) [0343] They add other proofs that are no more **relevant**.

Relic (2), Relics (5)
AP : 1 2 :113(199) [0285] word "satisfaction" is a **relic** from this rite of public
S2 : 0 2 :015(295) [0467] articles of faith — as has happened in the case of **relics**.
S2 : 0 2 :022(296) [0469] The fifth are **relics**.
S2 : 0 2 :022(296) [0469] were some good in them, **relics** should long since have
S2 : 0 2 :023(296) [0469] however, is the claim that **relics** effect indulgences and the
LC : 0 1 :093(377) [0607] covered with holy **relics**, as are the so-called spiritual
LC : 0 3 :045(426) [0709] or when a monstrance or a **relic** was profaned, thus

Relieve (2), Relieved (1)
AG : 2 6 :014(066) [0073] and sought mitigations to **relieve** consciences, but they
AL : 2 6 :014(066) [0073] and sought mitigations to **relieve** consciences; yet they did
AP : 0 4 :103(121) [0151] is, by the law sin is recognized but its guilt is not **relieved**.

Religion (29), Religions (2), Religious (18), Religiously (1)
PR : PR :009(006) [0011] us and to our Christian **religion** as if we were so uncertain
PR : PR :009(006) [0011] of the confession of our **religion** and had altered it so
PR : PR :010(006) [0011] calumnies and the **religious** controversies that were
PR : PR :025(014) [0023] faith and to regulate all **religious** controversies and their
PR : PR :026(014) [0025] about our Christian **religion** should continue or new ones
AG : PR :001(024) [0039] ours and of the Christian **religion**, and how with
AG : PR :002(025) [0039] faith and the Christian **religion**, and to this end it was
AG : PR :004(025) [0039] adhere to a single, true **religion** and live together in unity
AG : PR :010(025) [0041] be united in one, true **religion**, even as we are all under
AG : PR :014(026) [0041] lover of the Christian **religion** who is concerned about
AP : PR :002(098) [0099] Since **religion** and consciences are involved, we assumed
AP : PR :004(098) [0099] In a **religious** issue, how could they accept a document
AP : 0 7 :027(173) [0235] Many openly ridicule all **religions**, or if they accept
AP : 0 7 :046(177) [0243] But see what **religious** men our opponents are!
AP : 1 2 :125(201) [0289] and integrity do the investigating on **religious** questions.
AP : 1 2 :126(201) [0289] predicted there would be the greatest danger for **religion**.
AP : 1 2 :126(201) [0289] a watchtower to guide **religious** affairs, ought in such
AP : 1 2 :127(201) [0289] Men are demanding instruction in **religion**.
AP : 1 2 :128(201) [0291] to the importance of **religion** if you suppose that the
AP : 1 5 :004(215) [0315] someone teaches that **religious** rites are helpful in gaining
AP : 1 5 :015(217) [0319] have to approve the **religious** rites of all the heathen, as
AP : 1 5 :017(217) [0319] do we have that **religious** rites established by men
AP : 2 1 :011(230) [0345] up to honor the saints but to defend their **religious** traffic.
AP : 2 2 :006(237) [0359] This is what good **religious** men ought to do.
AP : 2 2 :009(237) [0359] to elevate the position of the clergy by a **religious** rite.
AP : 2 3 :005(239) [0365] chastity, but they use **religion** as a pretext to maintain
AP : 2 3 :006(240) [0365] It obviously endangers **religion** and morality, for it
AP : 2 3 :026(243) [0371] this regulation for **religious** reasons, since they see that it
AP : 2 3 :026(243) [0371] it with pious-sounding phrases to give it a **religious** front.
AP : 2 3 :050(246) [0377] not demand celibacy for **religious** reasons, for they know
AP : 2 3 :050(246) [0377] They use **religion** as a pretext to put something over on
AP : 2 3 :050(246) [0377] seem to have gone astray through some sort of **religion**.
AP : 2 3 :050(246) [0377] These Epicureans purposely use **religion** as a pretext.
AP : 2 3 :060(247) [0381] purpose of the law is not **religion** but domination, for
AP : 2 3 :060(247) [0381] domination, for which **religion** is just a wicked pretext.
AP : 2 4 :001(249) [0383] not abolish the Mass but **religiously** keep and defend it.
AP : 2 4 :041(257) [0399] Under the pretext of **religion** they usurp the kingdom of
AP : 2 4 :041(257) [0399] rule without regard for **religion** and the preaching of the
AP : 2 7 :009(270) [0421] taken with the pretext of **religion**, but actually for the
AP : 2 7 :040(276) [0433] here, too, it claims perfection for artificial **religious** acts.
LC : 0 1 :022(367) [0585] Upon it all the **religious** orders are founded.
LC : 0 1 :118(381) [0615] if in the exercise of their **religion** they could bring before
SD : PR :001(503) [0851] of the pure Christian **religion** is drawn together out of the
SD : PR :001(503) [0851] churches which confessed the same doctrine and **religion**.
SD : 0 8 :033(597) [1027] is the mystery of our **religion**: God was manifested in the
SD : 1 0 :005(611) [1053] the impression that our **religion** does not differ greatly
SD : 1 0 :005(611) [1053] that these two opposing **religions** have been brought into
SD : 1 0 :005(611) [1055] Gospel and from true **religion** has taken place or will
SD : 1 0 :029(615) [1061] in doctrine, or in whatever else pertains to **religion**.
SD : 1 1 :094(632) [1095] have erred and serious **religious** contentions have arisen.

Religionists (1)
SD : 0 8 :051(600) [1031] that even their own co-**religionists** now criticize and reject

Relish (2), Relishing (1)
LC : PR :009(359) [0569] so that day by day we **relish** and appreciate the Catechism
LC : PR :020(361) [0573] and thirsty, will they truly **relish** what now they cannot
LC : 0 1 :267(401) [0657] it into every corner, **relishing** and delighting in it like pigs

Reluctant (1), Reluctantly (2)
AP : 0 2 :051(107) [0119] our part, we have been **reluctant** to enter upon their
LC : 0 1 :143(385) [0623] from compulsion and **reluctantly** but gladly and
SD : 0 4 :017(554) [0943] offerings (Ps. 54:6), not **reluctantly** or under compulsion

Rely (13), Relying (2), Reliable (1), Relies (5)
AG : 2 0 :007(042) [0053] than the teaching that we are to **rely** solely on our works.
AG : 2 0 :019(043) [0055] consciences were driven to **rely** on their own efforts, and
AG : 2 0 :027(045) [0057] be done, not that we are to **rely** on them to earn grace
AL : 0 6 :001(032) [0045] will and not because we **rely** on such works to merit
AL : 2 8 :002(081) [0083] while the pontiffs, **relying** on the power of the keys, not
AP : 0 4 :299(153) [0205] taught to believe and to **rely** on the sure fact that they
AP : 0 4 :332(158) [0211] Such prayer, which **relies** on its own righteousness and
AP : 0 4 :333(158) [0211] Therefore prayer **relies** upon the mercy of God when we
AP : 1 2 :095(196) [0281] For if faith **relies** on these works, it immediately becomes
AP : 1 2 :151(206) [0299] but that was to make us **rely** not on ourselves but on God
S 2 : 0 4 :015(301) [0475] be certain, and we must **rely** on the hope that Christ, our
S 3 : 0 3 :027(307) [0487] pope taught the people to **rely** on and trust in such
SC : 0 4 :010(349) [0551] water, and our faith which **relies** on the Word of God
LC : 0 1 :022(367) [0585] On such things it **relies** and of them it boasts, unwilling to
LC : 0 1 :032(369) [0589] God is with those who **rely** on anything but himself, and
LC : 0 3 :013(422) [0701] On this I can **rely** and depend, and I can revere it highly,
LC : 0 5 :063(454) [0767] a way that it may rest and **rely** firmly upon itself;
LC : 0 6 :021(459) [0000] if anybody goes about **relying** on the purity of his
SD : 0 3 :030(544) [0925] dependable and **reliable** comfort and to give due honor to
SD : 0 3 :037(546) [0929] in this article or matter, or **rely** on them, or make or
SD : 0 7 :106(588) [1009] enable a Christian heart to **rely** on and trust in them with

Remain (83), Remained (23), Remaining (4), Remains (51)
PR : PR :008(005) [0009] it was our intention to **remain** and abide loyally by the
PR : PR :018(009) [0015] to the emperor and that **remained** in the custody of the
PR : PR :020(010) [0017] When they **remain** unattacked on this basis, theologians
PR : PR :025(014) [0023] Holy Spirit to abide and **remain** unanimously in this
AG : 0 7 :001(032) [0047] one holy Christian church will be and **remain** forever.
AG : 0 8 :001(033) [0047] and even open sinners **remain** among the godly, the
AG : 2 3 :001(051) [0061] who were not able to **remain** continent and who went so
AG : 2 7 :006(071) [0077] pressed and compelled to **remain**, in spite of the fact that
AG : 2 8 :064(092) [0093] as long as the opinion **remains** and prevails that their
AG : 2 8 :064(092) [0093] And this opinion will **remain** as long as there is no
AL : 2 7 :006(071) [0077] were compelled to **remain**, though some could have been
AL : 2 7 :027(075) [0079] of a vow while they **remain** silent concerning the nature
AL : 2 8 :064(092) [0093] as long as the opinion **remains** that their observance is
AL : 2 8 :064(092) [0093] And this opinion must **remain** where there is no
AP : 0 2 :035(104) [0115] he wrote that original sin **remains** after Baptism, and they
AP : 0 2 :035(105) [0115] by this statement that original sin **remains** after Baptism.
AP : 0 2 :035(105) [0115] though concupiscence **remains** — or, as they call it, the
AP : 0 2 :036(105) [0115] that sin is — that is, **remains** — even though it is not
AP : 0 2 :036(105) [0115] spiritual regeneration, but it **remains** in the mortal flesh.
AP : 0 2 :036(105) [0115] But it **remains** because there continue to work those
AP : 0 2 :044(106) [0117] these ideas did not **remain** purely academic, but moved
AP : 0 4 :144(127) [0161] such a faith does not **remain** in those who obey their
AP : 0 4 :163(129) [0169] Christ **remains** the mediator.
AP : 0 4 :392(167) [0225] knowledge of Christ has **remained** with some faithful
AP : 1 2 :013(184) [0257] There **remains** the third step, satisfaction.
AP : 1 2 :115(199) [0285] word "satisfaction" still **remains** together with a remnant
AP : 1 2 :152(206) [0299] because of the sin still present and **remaining** in the flesh.
AP : 1 2 :175(210) [0307] Still the name indulgences **remains**.
AP : 1 5 :032(220) [0323] that Christian liberty **remain** in the church, lest the
AP : 2 0 :013(228) [0343] Faith does not **remain** in those who lose the Holy Spirit
AP : 2 2 :004(236) [0359] this practice still **remains**, and once it prevailed in the
AP : 2 3 :009(240) [0367] the right to contract marriage must always **remain**.
AP : 2 3 :009(241) [0367] not change, there must **remain** that ordinance which God
AP : 2 3 :012(241) [0367] right, the right to contract marriage necessarily **remains**.
AP : 2 3 :061(247) [0381] on anyone who wants to **remain** continent, as long as he
S 2 : 0 2 :010(294) [0465] Accordingly we are and **remain** eternally divided and
S 2 : 0 2 :028(297) [0469] saints, the honor that **remains** will do no harm and will
S 2 : 0 4 :005(299) [0473] head, and it would have **remained** much better if such a
S 2 : 0 4 :007(299) [0473] be elected by men and it **remained** in their power and
S 3 : 0 1 :004(302) [0477] powers of man have **remained** whole and uncorrupted,
S 3 : 0 3 :010(305) [0481] powers of man have **remained** whole and uncorrupted,
S 3 : 0 3 :040(309) [0489] life it contends with the sins that **remain** in the flesh.
S 3 : 0 3 :040(309) [0489] and expels the sins that **remain** and enables man to
S 3 : 0 6 :005(311) [0493] for that bread is and **remains** there agrees better with the
S 3 : 0 8 :006(312) [0495] Word, yet they do not **remain** silent but fill the world with
S 3 : 1 0 :003(314) [0497] heretics shall also be regarded as ordained and **remain** so.
S 3 : 1 5 :004(316) [0501] Finally, there **remains** the pope's bag of magic tricks
TR : 0 0 :077(333) [0527] There **remains** jurisdiction in those cases which according
SC : PR :025(341) [0539] negligent if you fail to do your duty and **remain** silent.
SC : 0 1 :020(344) [0543] but encourage them to **remain** and discharge their duty to
SC : 0 9 :003(354) [0561] "**Remain** in the same house, eating and drinking what they
LC : PR :008(359) [0569] it as I wish, but must **remain** a child and pupil of the
LC : PR :016(361) [0573] it and have always **remained** pupils, and must continue to
LC : SP :027(364) [0581] into their minds and **remain** fixed in their memories.
LC : 0 1 :045(370) [0593] with all that he had; not one of his children **remained**.
LC : 0 1 :046(370) [0593] secure, yet inevitably he **remained** safe from Saul and
LC : 0 1 :071(374) [0601] name and cannot long **remain** when it is uttered and
LC : 0 1 :076(375) [0603] end; at best they will **remain** good only as long as the rod
LC : 0 1 :112(380) [0613] Every child would have **remained** faithful to this
LC : 0 1 :114(380) [0613] they would have **remained** at home in obedience and
LC : 0 1 :212(393) [0641] it, it is not possible to **remain** chaste outside of marriage;
LC : 0 1 :212(393) [0641] for flesh and blood **remain** flesh and blood, and the
LC : 0 1 :215(394) [0641] the act, yet their hearts **remain** so full of unchaste
LC : 0 1 :216(394) [0641] chastity, and if they **remain** they will inevitably sin more
LC : 0 1 :234(397) [0647] a long time, still he will **remain** a tramp and a beggar and
LC : 0 1 :261(400) [0655] They should let right **remain** right, nor perverting or
LC : 0 1 :272(401) [0657] should be allowed to **remain** secret, or at any rate be
LC : 0 1 :310(407) [0669] So this commandment **remains**, like all the rest, one that
LC : 0 1 :314(407) [0671] chasuble or a layman **remains** on his knees a whole day in
LC : 0 2 :031(414) [0685] The **remaining** parts of this article simply serve to clarify
LC : 0 2 :038(415) [0689] But if the work **remained** hidden and no one knew of it,
LC : 0 2 :053(417) [0691] last day the Holy Spirit **remains** with the holy community
LC : 0 2 :061(419) [0695] then, is the article which must always **remain** in force.
LC : 0 2 :066(419) [0697] Therefore they **remain** in eternal wrath and damnation,
LC : 0 2 :068(420) [0697] and displeasure still **remain** on us because we cannot
LC : 0 3 :052(427) [0711] who have accepted it may **remain** faithful and grow daily
LC : 0 3 :052(427) [0711] so that we may all **remain** together eternally in this
LC : 0 3 :066(429) [0717] it means that we must **remain** steadfast, suffer patiently
LC : 0 3 :068(429) [0717] nothing and we may **remain** steadfast in the face of all
LC : 0 3 :105(434) [0727] As long as we **remain** in this vile life in which we are
LC : 0 3 :121(436) [0731] hears their prayer but **remain** in doubt, saying, "Why
LC : 0 4 :001(436) [0733] It **remains** for us to speak of our two sacraments,
LC : 0 4 :059(444) [0747] Gold **remains** no less gold if a harlot wears it in sin and
LC : 0 4 :060(444) [0747] be that Baptism always **remains** valid and retains its
LC : 0 4 :073(445) [0751] where faith is lacking, it **remains** a mere unfruitful sign.
LC : 0 4 :077(446) [0751] Therefore Baptism **remains** forever.
LC : 0 4 :078(446) [0751] and signification of Baptism would continue and **remain**.
LC : 0 4 :083(446) [0751] the new man, always **remains** until we pass from this
LC : 0 4 :086(446) [0753] even though we sin, so all his treasures and gifts **remain**.
LC : 0 4 :086(446) [0753] Baptism, so forgiveness **remains** day by day as long as we
LC : 0 5 :005(447) [0755] this blessed sacrament **remain** unimpaired and inviolate
LC : 0 5 :006(447) [0755] No, all temporal things **remain** as God has created and
LC : 0 5 :010(448) [0755] a sacrament; otherwise it **remains** a mere element.
LC : 0 5 :014(448) [0755] But if the words **remain**, as is right and necessary, then in
LC : 0 5 :033(450) [0761] It **remains** for us to consider who it is that receives this
LC : 0 6 :005(457) [0000] They ought to **remain** under the pope and submit to being
EP : RN :007(465) [0779] and Holy Scripture **remains** the only judge, rule, and
EP : 0 1 :002(466) [0779] after the fall our nature is and **remains** a creature of God.
EP : 0 1 :013(467) [0783] things its natural powers **remained** wholly good and pure.
EP : 0 3 :017(475) [0795] Christ that can exist and **remain** in a person though he
EP : 0 6 :007(481) [0807] people the law is and **remains** one and the same law,
EP : 0 7 :022(484) [0813] of Christ and that only the exterior appearance **remains**.
EP : 0 8 :018(489) [0823] Christ is, and **remains** to all eternity, God and man in one
SD : PR :003(502) [0847] but, thank God, it has **remained** unrefuted and
SD : PR :006(502) [0847] in this Confession has **remained** practically unchallenged
SD : PR :007(505) [0853] estates were resolved by God's grace to **remain** faithful.
SD : PR :009(505) [0855] of God is and should **remain** the sole rule and norm of all
SD : PR :013(506) [0855] of our predecessors who **remained** steadfastly in the pure
SD : 0 1 :002(508) [0859] after the Fall are and **remain** God's handiwork and
SD : 0 1 :045(516) [0873] sake into his grace but **remains** the enemy of sin
SD : 0 1 :047(516) [0875] raised and would be and **remain** in the elect in eternal
SD : 0 1 :060(519) [0879] pure nor good has **remained** in itself and all its internal
SD : 0 1 :062(519) [0879] deeply that nothing in it **remained** pure and uncorrupted.
SD : 0 2 :002(520) [0881] of his own that have **remained** after the Fall, when the
SD : 0 2 :005(521) [0881] God, but he is and **remains** an enemy of God until by the
SD : 0 2 :007(521) [0883] of spiritual powers has **remained** or exists in man by
SD : 0 2 :014(523) [0885] the Son of God says **remains** eternally true, "Apart from
SD : 0 2 :014(523) [0885] and to help them to **remain** in true faith until their end.
SD : 0 2 :034(527) [0895] it contends with the sin **remaining** in the flesh throughout
SD : 0 2 :034(528) [0895] daily sweeps out the **remaining** sin and operates to make
SD : 0 2 :037(528) [0895] Day, the Holy Spirit **remains** with the holy community of
SD : 0 2 :043(529) [0897] On the contrary, we must **remain** the dupes and captives
SD : 0 2 :058(532) [0903] him but lets him **remain** in the darkness of his unbelief
SD : 0 2 :066(534) [0907] hand man could not **remain** in obedience to God for one
SD : 0 2 :084(537) [0913] Of course, there **remains** also in the regenerated a
SD : 0 3 :006(540) [0917] this single article **remains** pure, Christendom will remain
SD : 0 3 :006(540) [0917] pure, Christendom will **remain** pure, in beautiful
SD : 0 3 :006(540) [0917] But where it does not **remain** pure, it is impossible to
SD : 0 3 :022(543) [0923] they are still sinners and **remain** sinners until they die.
SD : 0 3 :023(543) [0923] of the inchoate renewal **remains** imperfect in this life and
SD : 0 3 :024(543) [0923] of justification is to **remain** pure, we must give especially
SD : 0 3 :026(543) [0923] a wicked intention to **remain** and abide in sin, for true
SD : 0 3 :041(546) [0931] excellent statement **remains** true: "There is a beautiful
SD : 0 3 :064(550) [0937] Christ that it can be and **remain** in a person who has no
SD : 0 3 :064(550) [0937] no love follows) but against his conscience **remains** in sin.
SD : 0 3 :066(550) [0937] by God's grace we shall **remain** steadfastly and constantly
SD : 0 4 :033(556) [0949] good works so that you **remain** in your heavenly calling,
SD : 0 4 :033(556) [0949] Faith, however, does not **remain** in those who lead a
SD : 0 5 :010(560) [0955] "he put over his face" **remains** unremoved, so that they do
SD : 0 5 :018(561) [0957] true function of the law **remains**, to rebuke sin and to
SD : 0 7 :023(573) [0979] But if the words **remain** with the elements, as they should
SD : 0 7 :033(575) [0983] better than any one else, **remained** by it steadfastly and
SD : 0 7 :089(585) [1003] Christ, which always **remain** efficacious in Christendom
SD : 0 7 :089(585) [1003] Just as the Gospel is and **remains** the true Gospel even
SD : 0 7 :089(585) [1003] Christ nonetheless **remains** truthful in his words when he
SD : 0 7 :108(588) [1009] and wine, or their accidents without a subject, **remain**.
SD : 0 8 :007(592) [1017] person of Christ each **remains** in its nature and essence
SD : 0 8 :008(593) [1017] two natures referred to **remain** unmingled and
SD : 0 8 :024(595) [1023] she is truly the mother of God and yet **remained** a virgin.
SD : 0 8 :036(598) [1027] distinct natures are and **remain** unchanged and unblended
SD : 0 8 :066(604) [1039] Thus there is and **remains** in Christ only a single divine
SD : 0 8 :073(605) [1041] (and therefore he is and **remains** to all eternity his and the
SD : 0 8 :084(607) [1045] And he would **remain** a poor Christ for me if he were
SD : 1 0 :014(613) [1057] and essence are and **remain** of themselves free and which
SD : 1 1 :034(622) [1075] but are to be and **remain** under condemnation, although I
SD : 1 1 :039(623) [1077] Holy Spirit (Acts 7:51), **remain** in sin without repentance
SD : 1 1 :050(624) [1079] of God shall exist and **remain** against all the "gates of
SD : 1 1 :052(625) [1081] about which God has **remained** silent and which he has
SD : 1 1 :057(625) [1081] from one place but lets it **remain** at another; or that one
SD : 1 1 :062(626) [1083] far in this article we will **remain** on the right path, as it is
SD : 1 2 :006(633) [1097] desire by God's grace to **remain** steadfastly in our

Remarkable (1)
AL : 2 7 :048(078) [0081] are blinded by these **remarkable** angelic observances and

Remedy (6), Remedies (2)
AL : 2 3 :015(054) [0063] marriage to be a **remedy** against human infirmity.
AP : 0 4 :185(132) [0173] "Being sick in itself, an unjust cause needs wise **remedies**."
AP : 2 3 :013(241) [0367] Now it needs a **remedy** even more, and marriage is
AP : 2 3 :013(241) [0367] is necessary for a **remedy** as well as for procreation.
AP : 2 3 :016(241) [0369] speaks of marriage as a **remedy** and commands it because
AP : 2 3 :019(242) [0369] to be chaste by using the **remedy** he offers, just as he
AP : 2 3 :053(246) [0379] so that we ought to use the **remedies** God has given us.
LC : 0 5 :078(455) [0771] you have to go to the sacrament and seek a **remedy**.

Remember (32), Rememberance (1), Remembered (6), Remembrance (15)
AG : 2 1 :001(046) [0057] should be kept in **rememberance** so that our faith may be
AL : 2 1 :001(046) [0057] teach that the **remembrance** of saints may be commended
AL : 2 4 :030(059) [0067] Christ commands us to do this in **remembrance** of him.
AL : 2 4 :030(059) [0067] the sacrament should **remember** what benefits are
AL : 2 4 :031(059) [0067] For to **remember** Christ is to remember his benefits and
AL : 2 4 :031(059) [0067] remember Christ is to **remember** his benefits and realize

Continued ▶

AL : 24 :032(059) [0067] and it is not enough to **remember** the history, for the
AL : 24 :032(059) [0067] for the Jews and the ungodly can also **remember** this.
AL : 24 :041(061) [0069] done except for the solemn **remembrance** of the sacrifice."
AL : 25 :009(063) [0069] for many sins can neither be perceived nor **remembered**.
AP : 04 :053(114) [0135] therefore, we must **remember** that these three elements
AP : 04 :055(114) [0137] of mercy we must **remember** that this requires faith,
AP : 04 :210(136) [0179] of Christ, the **remembrance** might strengthen our faith
AP : 04 :264(146) [0195] Let us **remember** that the Gospel promises the forgiveness
AP : 04 :368(163) [0221] the law, still we must **remember** that the Gospel offers
AP : 04 :388(166) [0225] men to evaluate if they **remember**, whenever a passage on
AP : 11 :008(181) [0251] certain that we neither **remember** nor understand most of
AP : 12 :105(197) [0283] those which we do not **remember**; therefore absolution,
AP : 23 :021(242) [0369] (Matt. 19:12), let him **remember** that Christ is praising
AP : 24 :071(262) [0409] (I Cor. 11:24), "Do this in **remembrance** of me."
AP : 24 :072(262) [0409] The **remembrance** of Christ is not the vain celebration of
AP : 24 :072(262) [0409] It is rather the **remembrance** of Christ's blessings and the
AP : 24 :072(262) [0409] wonderful works to be **remembered**; the Lord is gracious
AP : 27 :036(275) [0433] We **remember** that this correction is found in Gerson.
S2 : 02 :013(295) [0467] asked that she be **remembered** at the altar or sacrament.
S2 : 02 :028(297) [0471] for no one will long **remember**, esteem, or honor them
S3 : 03 :015(305) [0483] sin was afterwards **remembered**, it had also to be repented
S3 : 03 :019(306) [0483] only when a man **remembered** them and thereupon
TR : 00 :080(333) [0527] They themselves should **remember** that riches have been
SC : PR :016(340) [0535] that they will hardly **remember** anything at all.
SC : 01 :005(342) [0541] ***"Remember** the Sabbath day, to keep it holy."*
SC : 06 :004(351) [0555] Do this in **remembrance** of me.'
SC : 06 :004(351) [0557] Do this, as often as you drink it, in **remembrance** of me.'"
LC : PR :003(358) [0567] pigs and dogs, they **remember** no more of the Gospel than
LC : SP :005(362) [0575] I well **remember** the time when there were old people who
LC : SP :023(364) [0579] Do this in **remembrance** of me.'
LC : SP :023(364) [0579] as you drink it, in **remembrance** of me'" (I Cor. 11:23-25).
LC : 01 :005(365) [0581] be understood and **remembered**, by citing some common
LC : 01 :024(367) [0587] may mark well and **remember** the meaning of this
LC : 01 :029(368) [0589] so that they may take them to heart and **remember** them.
LC : 01 :098(378) [0609] **Remember**, then, that you must be concerned not only
LC : 01 :108(379) [0611] representatives, and to **remember** that, however lowly,
LC : 01 :149(385) [0623] who can take advice **remember** that God is not to be
LC : 01 :211(393) [0641] In the second place, **remember** that it is not only an
LC : 01 :321(408) [0673] that they learn and **remember** it so that we may see why
LC : 05 :003(447) [0753] *Do this in **remembrance** of me.'"*
LC : 05 :003(447) [0753] *Do this, as often as you drink it, in **remembrance** of me.'"*
LC : 05 :019(448) [0757] Mark this and **remember** it well.
LC : 05 :042(451) [0763] Christians to eat and drink and thereby **remember** him.
LC : 05 :045(451) [0763] in the words of Christ, *"Do this* in **remembrance** of me."
LC : 05 :087(456) [0773] head of a household **remember** that it is his duty, by
SD : 01 :035(514) [0869] **Remember** that thou hast made me of clay, and wilt thou
SD : 07 :026(573) [0981] Mark this and **remember** it well, for on these words rest
SD : 07 :065(581) [0995] eating, when he said, "Do this in **remembrance** of me."

Remind (14), Reminded (8), Reminders (3), Reminds (6)
PR : PR :008(005) [0011] people would have been **reminded** and stimulated by this
PR : PR :015(007) [0013] and have had them **reminded** and exhorted to consider
PR : PR :022(012) [0019] and ministers duly to **remind** even those who err
AG : 20 :026(045) [0057] Augustine also **reminds** us that we would understand the
AG : 24 :012(057) [0065] and the priests were **reminded** of the terrible
AL : 25 :004(062) [0069] praised, and people are **reminded** of the great consolation
AP : 04 :069(116) [0141] the first place, we would **remind** our readers that if we
AP : 04 :201(134) [0175] by which he might be **reminded** and grow in faith, and
AP : 04 :210(136) [0179] so that as this sign **reminds** us of the promises of Christ,
AP : 04 :285(150) [0201] Finally, we would **remind** our readers that our opponents
AP : 15 :020(218) [0321] and various rites serve as **reminders** for the common folk.
AP : 24 :010(251) [0387] We want to **remind** our readers of the real issue.
AP : 24 :010(251) [0387] Aeschines **reminded** the Jews that both parties in a
AP : 27 :062(280) [0441] marks he wanted to **remind** them of the teaching of faith
SC : 09 :005(355) [0561] "**Remind** them to be submissive to rulers and authorities,
LC : 01 :129(383) [0617] therefore, he **reminds** and impels everyone to consider
LC : 01 :195(391) [0637] He always wants to **remind** us to think back to the First
LC : 01 :330(410) [0677] to teach, admonish, and **remind** young people of all this
LC : 02 :023(413) [0683] every blessing that comes our way, should **remind** us of it.
LC : 03 :027(424) [0705] Therefore it may serve to **remind** us and impress upon us
LC : 03 :028(424) [0705] said, he should always **remind** God of his commandment
LC : 03 :075(430) [0719] stamped on coins, to **remind** both princes and subjects
EP : 04 :018(477) [0801] and good works, and to **remind** them how necessary it is
EP : 07 :029(485) [0815] wine are no more than **reminders**, seals, and pledges to
EP : 11 :013(496) [0835] of which we can **remind** ourselves and with which we can
SD : 02 :066(534) [0907] expressly and earnestly **reminds** us, "Working together
SD : 02 :072(535) [0909] and accomplish all this, **reminds** us also how he
SD : 05 :023(562) [0959] themselves, constantly **reminded** themselves not only how
SD : 07 :003(569) [0973] faith (that is, our faith, **reminded** and quickened by the
SD : 07 :116(589) [1011] more than symbols and **reminders** of the absent body of
SD : 11 :036(622) [1075] foundation, which daily **reminds** and admonishes us to

Remiss (1)
SD : 02 :015(523) [0887] so that we might become **remiss** and lazy in reading,

Remissa (1)
PR : PR :027(015) [0025] Wolf, baron of Schoenburg [-Penig-**Remissa**]

Remission (22), Remissions (1)
AL : 12 :010(035) [0049] who do not teach that **remission** of sins comes through
AP : 04 :267(147) [0197] is not speaking about **remission** of punishment alone,
AP : 04 :267(147) [0197] it is vain to seek **remission** of punishment unless the heart
AP : 04 :267(147) [0197] unless the heart first receives **remission** of guilt.
AP : 04 :268(147) [0197] as referring only to **remission** of punishment, this text
AP : 12 :015(184) [0257] they interpret as the **remission** of satisfactions, and
AP : 12 :118(199) [0287] do not contribute to the **remission** of guilt, though they
AP : 12 :135(203) [0293] as the chapter on "Penitence and **Remission**" teaches.
AP : 12 :138(203) [0293] is talking about the **remission** of sins when he says
AP : 12 :138(203) [0293] This **remission** removes eternal death and brings eternal
AP : 12 :147(205) [0297] carry on idle speculations about the **remission** of guilt.
AP : 12 :147(205) [0297] do not see how, in the **remission** of guilt, faith frees the
AP : 12 :167(208) [0303] was necessary for the **remission** either of the guilt or of
AP : 12 :175(210) [0307] indulgences were the **remission** of public penitence so as
AP : 12 :175(210) [0307] from the bishops, there is no point in such **remissions**.
AP : 24 :013(251) [0387] God's wrath, gain the **remission** of guilt and punishment,
AP : 24 :063(261) [0405] it, or that it merits the **remission** of sins, guilt, and
AP : 24 :066(261) [0407] or that it merits the **remission** of sins, of guilt, and of
S3 : 03 :005(304) [0481] a preacher of repentance — but for the **remission** of sins.
S3 : 03 :025(307) [0485] This was called **remission** of all penalty and guilt, and the
TR : 00 :044(328) [0517] and that by this faith we obtain the **remission** of sins.
SD : 02 :051(531) [0901] repentance and the **remission** of sins, "Listen to him"
SD : 07 :044(577) [0987] covenant which is shed for you for the **remission** of sins."

Remit (13), Remits (3), Remitted (3), Remitting (1)
AL : 28 :005(081) [0085] to preach the Gospel, to **remit** and retain sins, and to
AP : 12 :118(199) [0287] forgiveness of sin God **remits** the guilt, and yet, because it
AP : 12 :123(200) [0289] have the command to **remit** part of the punishments of
AP : 12 :135(203) [0293] that indulgences **remit**, as the chapter on "Penitence and
AP : 12 :138(203) [0293] certain punishments or to **remit** part of the punishments.
AP : 12 :139(203) [0295] statement about **remitting** part of the punishments
AP : 12 :139(203) [0295] to canonical penalties, part of which the pastors **remitted**.
AP : 12 :139(203) [0295] satisfactions can **remit** eternal punishments, or that the
AP : 12 :139(204) [0295] command to commute penalties or to **remit** them in part.
AP : 12 :147(205) [0297] necessary by divine law to **remit** either guilt or eternal
AP : 12 :154(206) [0301] that the power of the keys **remits** part of the punishment.
AP : 12 :154(206) [0301] also say that the keys **remit** both the satisfactions and the
AP : 12 :156(207) [0301] can neither impose nor **remit** them; God imposes and
AP : 12 :156(207) [0301] them; God imposes and **remits** them apart from the
AP : 12 :174(210) [0307] the penalties of purgatory can **remit** eternal punishments.
AP : 12 :175(210) [0307] if human authority can **remit** satisfactions and penalties,
S3 : 03 :024(307) [0485] these satisfaction was **remitted** and canceled, first for
S3 : 03 :024(307) [0485] for himself alone the right to **remit** the entire satisfaction.
TR : 00 :060(330) [0521] they preach the Gospel, **remit** sins, administer the
SD : 03 :058(550) [0937] but is forgiven and **remitted** by sheer grace for Christ's

Remlingen (1)
PR : PR :027(015) [0025] Henry, count and lord of Castell [-**Remlingen**]

Remnant (1), Remnants (3)
AP : 02 :045(106) [0117] he taught that the **remnants** of original sin in man are not
AP : 04 :179(131) [0171] of the law, still the **remnants** of your sin do not condemn
AP : 12 :115(199) [0285] remains together with a **remnant** of the custom in
AP : 24 :006(250) [0385] These are **remnants** of ancient practice, for the Fathers of

Remorse (1)
S3 : 03 :002(304) [0479] *contritio* (artificial **remorse**), but *passiva contritio* (true

Remote (1)
TR : 00 :016(322) [0509] for churches situated in **remote** places to seek ordination

Remove (17), Removed (19), Removes (6), Removal (2)
PR : PR :021(010) [0019] on this account will be **removed** inasmuch as the word
AG : 24 :029(059) [0067] that the Mass is used to **remove** sin and obtain grace and
AG : 24 :034(060) [0067] Mass is not a sacrifice to **remove** the sins of others,
AP : 02 :035(105) [0115] written that Baptism **removes** the guilt of original sin,
AP : 04 :029(111) [0129] of the cross has been **removed**' (Gal. 5:11).
AP : 04 :073(117) [0141] particle "alone," let them **remove** the other exclusive
AP : 04 :133(125) [0159] face of Moses cannot be **removed** except by faith, which
AP : 04 :133(125) [0159] but when a man turns to the Lord the veil is **removed**.
AP : 04 :135(125) [0159] But this veil is **removed** from us, and this error taken
AP : 04 :188(133) [0173] works in such a way as not to **remove** the free promise.
AP : 04 :210(136) [0179] *ex opere operato* and **removes** the burden of guilt and
AP : 04 :223(138) [0181] Let our opponents **remove** the promise about Christ, let
AP : 04 :224(138) [0181] problem in this text if we **remove** the interpretation that
AP : 04 :231(139) [0185] and hence this view is far **removed** from his intention.
AP : 04 :263(145) [0195] the obligation or debt is **removed** because God forgives
AP : 04 :264(146) [0195] or debt can be **removed**, that the wrath of God can be
AP : 07 :021(172) [0233] This, too, means to **remove** Christ as the foundation.
AP : 12 :007(183) [0255] of the keys does not **remove** guilt, but only changes
AP : 12 :048(188) [0265] of the bond is the **removal** of the sentence which declares
AP : 12 :100(197) [0281] therefore be wicked to **remove** private absolution from
AP : 12 :123(201) [0289] who reject penitence, should be **removed** from their midst.
AP : 12 :138(203) [0293] This remission **removes** eternal death and brings eternal
AP : 12 :154(206) [0301] of the keys does not **remove** these common troubles; but
AP : 15 :010(216) [0317] With the **removal** of the law and of the traditions, he
AP : 23 :013(241) [0367] love," which lust did not **remove** from nature but only
AP : 23 :023(242) [0369] contracted, though they **remove** those from the public
AP : 27 :019(272) [0425] that such blasphemy was **removed** from the Confutation.
S3 : 13 :001(315) [0499] has not been completely **removed** or eradicated, he will
TR : 00 :051(329) [0519] churches are not able to **remove** impious teachings and
TR : 00 :054(329) [0519] see to it that errors are **removed** and consciences are
LC : 01 :097(378) [0609] Word, we still fail to **remove** the abuse of the holy day,
LC : 01 :187(390) [0633] Therefore God wishes to **remove** the root and source of
LC : 03 :002(420) [0697] Ten Commandments and **remove** all that stands in our
LC : 03 :106(434) [0727] even though the tribulation is not **removed** or ended.
LC : 05 :083(456) [0773] never give up until the stone is **removed** from your heart.
LC : 06 :004(457) [0000] things have now been **removed** and made voluntary so
EP : 01 :010(467) [0781] separated and **removed** from it, as Job 19:26, 27 asserts,
EP : 01 :015(468) [0783] impedes but does not **remove** the natural powers of the
EP : 01 :015(468) [0783] this blemish may be **removed** as readily as a spot can be
EP : 05 :009(479) [0803] veil of Moses has been **removed** for them, so they now
SD : 02 :026(526) [0891] God **removes** the hard, stony heart and bestows a new
SD : 05 :010(560) [0955] turns to the Lord, the veil is **removed**" (II Cor. 3:13-15).
SD : 11 :057(625) [1081] not at another; that he **removes** it from one place but lets
SD : 11 :092(632) [1093] which weakens or even **removes** this comfort and hope is

Remuneration (1)
LC : 01 :233(396) [0647] especially when he takes **remuneration** for such services.

Rend (1), Render (23), Rendered (12), Rendering (2), Renders (1)
AG : PR :016(026) [0041] was not disposed to **render** decisions in matters pertaining
AG : 16 :002(037) [0051] as princes and judges, **render** decisions and pass sentence
AG : 20 :037(046) [0057] which are commanded, **render** obedience, avoid evil lusts,
AG : 27 :061(080) [0083] that they justify and **render** men righteous before God,
AG : 27 :061(080) [0083] which we are not obligated to **render** to God.
AP : 04 :110(123) [0153] For men can neither **render** nor understand this love

Continued ▶

AP : 04 :116(123) [0155] the forgiveness of sins, **renders** us acceptable to God, and
AP : 04 :189(133) [0175] our faith, to give testimony, and to **render** thanks.
AP : 04 :370(164) [0221] says (Rom. 2:6), "He will **render** to every man according
AP : 04 :373(164) [0221] When Paul says, "He will **render** to every man according
AP : 16 :001(222) [0329] hold public office, **render** verdicts according to imperial
AP : 16 :001(222) [0329] engage in just wars, **render** military service, enter into
AP : 24 :018(252) [0389] a ceremony or act which we **render** to God to honor him.
AP : 27 :028(274) [0429] verdict our judges have **rendered** in the Confutation.
S3 : 03 :021(306) [0485] which were easy to **render**, like saying five Our Fathers,
S3 : 03 :029(308) [0487] satisfaction should they **render** when they were innocent
TR : 00 :062(330) [0523] followings around themselves, **rend** the church of Christ.
SC : 09 :005(355) [0561] "**Render** therefore to Caesar the things that are Caesar's,
SC : 09 :010(356) [0563] of God from the heart, **rendering** service with a good will
LC : 01 :066(373) [0599] reconciled, obedience is **rendered**, and quarrels are
LC : 01 :136(383) [0619] the way God will have it: **render** him obedience and love
LC : 01 :164(387) [0627] and spiritual fathers, and for the honor they **render** them.
LC : 02 :047(416) [0691] If it is to be **rendered** idiomatically, we must express it
LC : 02 :049(417) [0691] Latin nor German, have **rendered** this "communion of
LC : 03 :045(426) [0709] relic was profaned, thus **rendering** unholy by misuse that
LC : 03 :075(430) [0719] all honor, and we should **render** them the duties we owe
LC : 05 :017(448) [0757] a sacrament is not **rendered** false because of an
EP : 03 :003(473) [0793] as God and man he **rendered** to his heavenly Father into
EP : 04 :003(476) [0797] regenerated persons are bound to **render** such obedience.
EP : 04 :010(476) [0799] so far as they are reborn, **render** not by coercion or
SD : 03 :015(541) [0921] life and in death, Christ **rendered** for us to his heavenly
SD : 03 :022(543) [0923] obedience, which Christ **rendered** to his Father from his
SD : 03 :056(549) [0935] total person, which he **rendered** to his heavenly Father
SD : 03 :056(549) [0935] the divine nature, could **render** satisfaction to the eternal
SD : 03 :058(550) [0937] his path to the Father **rendered** to his Father entire,
SD : 06 :006(565) [0965] and as the holy angels **render** God a completely
SD : 07 :025(573) [0981] a sacrament is not **rendered** false because an individual's
SD : 07 :080(584) [1001] Thereby we **render** obedience to the command of Christ,
SD : 07 :089(585) [1003] neither abrogated nor **rendered** impotent by either the

Renew (2), Renewal (34), Renewed (17), Renewing (1), Renews (6)

AL : 20 :029(045) [0057] is received, hearts are so **renewed** and endowed with new
AP : 04 :161(129) [0167] the beginning of our **renewal**, but the reconciliation by
AP : 04 :162(129) [0169] Christ does not stop being the mediator after our **renewal**.
AP : 04 :219(137) [0181] above that we should be **renewed** and begin to keep the
AP : 04 :293(152) [0203] Through his **renewal** we can keep the law, love God and
AP : 04 :351(161) [0217] We are **renewed**, as Paul says (Col. 3:10; II Cor. 3:18), "in
AP : 07 :005(169) [0227] of Christ, which Christ **renews**, consecrates, and governs
AP : 07 :008(169) [0229] same Holy spirit, who **renews**, consecrates, and governs
AP : 12 :046(188) [0263] describes conversion or **renewal**, he almost always names
AP : 12 :152(206) [0299] kill and wipe out lust so that the Spirit may **renew** them.
AP : 12 :153(206) [0299] this sinful flesh so that we may rise completely **renewed**.
S3 : 13 :002(315) [0499] Good works follow such faith, **renewal**, and forgiveness.
SC : 04 :010(349) [0551] of regeneration and **renewal** in the Holy Spirit, which he
EP : 02 :018(472) [0791] has been changed and **renewed** *solely by God's power and*
EP : 03 :019(475) [0795] there is begun in us the **renewal** which consists in love
EP : 03 :020(475) [0797] but that also **renewal** and love belong to our
EP : 03 :020(475) [0797] incomplete and imperfect without such love and **renewal**.
EP : 04 :008(476) [0799] who are regenerated and **renewed** by the Holy Spirit, are
EP : 06 :004(480) [0805] reborn and have been **renewed** in the spirit of their mind,
EP : 06 :004(480) [0805] such regeneration and **renewal** is incomplete in this
EP : 12 :005(498) [0839] merit of Christ, but in **renewal** and in our own pious
SD : 02 :005(521) [0881] becomes a believer, is regenerated and **renewed**.
SD : 02 :024(525) [0891] converted, reborn, **renewed**, and drawn by the Holy
SD : 02 :025(526) [0891] in Christ, regeneration, **renewal**, and everything that
SD : 02 :026(526) [0891] is a Spirit "of regeneration and **renewal**" (Titus 3:5, 6).
SD : 02 :059(532) [0905] from the death of sin, illuminates him, and **renews** him.
SD : 02 :063(533) [0905] and his will is **renewed**, then he wills that which is good,
SD : 02 :065(534) [0907] work of regeneration and **renewal** in us through the Word
SD : 02 :071(535) [0909] such conversion and **renewal** in us, and through the
SD : 02 :090(539) [0915] in whom the Holy Spirit works conversion and **renewal**.
SD : 03 :018(542) [0921] term strictly so that the **renewal** which follows
SD : 03 :019(542) [0921] sake and the subsequent **renewal** which the Holy Spirit
SD : 03 :019(542) [0921] of regeneration and **renewing** in the Holy Spirit" (Titus
SD : 03 :021(542) [0921] the sanctification or **renewal** which follows the
SD : 03 :023(543) [0923] the Holy Spirit, who **renews** and sanctifies them and
SD : 03 :023(543) [0923] because of the inchoate **renewal** remains imperfect in this
SD : 03 :028(544) [0925] Similarly, although **renewal** and sanctification are a
SD : 03 :032(545) [0927] righteousness or **renewal** in us is imperfect and impure in
SD : 03 :032(545) [0927] Hence even after his **renewal**, after he has done many
SD : 03 :033(545) [0927] the Holy Spirit had **renewed** and adorned him with many
SD : 03 :035(545) [0927] possess the beginning of **renewal**, sanctification, love,
SD : 03 :039(546) [0929] 3. That neither **renewal**, sanctification, virtues, nor other
SD : 03 :040(546) [0929] well as between justification and **renewal** or sanctification.
SD : 03 :041(546) [0929] the Holy Spirit next **renews** and sanctifies him, and from
SD : 03 :041(546) [0929] him, and from this **renewal** and sanctification the fruits
SD : 03 :047(548) [0933] God is our love or the **renewal** which the Holy Spirit
SD : 03 :048(548) [0933] sins and, as a second element, **renewal** or sanctification.
SD : 03 :049(548) [0933] in justification but that **renewal** and love likewise belong
SD : 03 :049(548) [0933] incomplete or imperfect without such love and **renewal**.
SD : 04 :007(552) [0941] God through faith and **renewed** through the Holy Spirit,
SD : 06 :006(564) [0963] of God were perfectly **renewed** in this life through the
SD : 06 :007(565) [0965] life Christians are not **renewed** perfectly and completely.
SD : 06 :007(565) [0965] the Old Adam and their **renewal** in the spirit of their
SD : 06 :011(566) [0965] of the Gospel (Gal. 3:2, 14), who **renews** the heart.
SD : 06 :018(567) [0967] believers are not fully **renewed** in this life but the Old
SD : 06 :023(568) [0969] from the heart by the **renewal** of the Holy Spirit.
SD : 06 :024(568) [0971] and man is completely **renewed** in the resurrection.
SD : 11 :089(631) [1093] promises them the Holy Spirit to cleanse and **renew** them.
SD : 12 :010(633) [1097] merit of Christ but in **renewal** and in our own piety, in
SD : 12 :035(635) [1101] who is himself not truly **renewed**, righteous, and pious

Renounce (2), Renounces (1), Renouncing (2)

AP : 27 :047(277) [0437] does, saying that **renouncing** the ownership of everything
S2 : 04 :007(299) [0473] that the pope would **renounce** the claim that he is the
LC : 01 :028(368) [0587] distress and want, and **renounces** and forsakes all that is
LC : 05 :026(449) [0759] us out so that we either **renounce** our faith or yield hand
SD : PR :007(505) [0853] at necessary length for **renouncing** the papistic errors and

Renovation (2)

EP : 03 :008(474) [0793] these terms refer to the **renovation** of man and distinguish
SD : 01 :014(511) [0863] regeneration and **renovation** can heal man's nature, which

Renowned (3)

AG : 23 :013(053) [0063] made and to the decisions of the most **renowned** councils.
AG : 23 :014(053) [0063] that, as a most **renowned** Christian emperor, Your
TR : 00 :082(000) [0529] I ask you, most **renowned** man, Dr. John Bugenhagen,

Rent (1)

EP : 07 :042(486) [0817] of Christ as though one **rent** Christ's flesh with one's teeth

Renunciation (1)

AG : 16 :004(037) [0051] wife and child, and the **renunciation** of such activities as

Reopen (2)

AP : 02 :051(107) [0119] If our opponents **reopen** the controversy, we shall not
SD : 05 :027(563) [0961] terrors of the law and **reopen** the door to the papacy in

Repay (1), Repaid (1)

LC : 01 :130(383) [0619] teachers can never be sufficiently thanked and **repaid**."
LC : 01 :252(399) [0653] lends to the Lord, and he will **repay** him for his deed."

Repealed (1)

AP : 27 :051(278) [0437] law of nature in men cannot be **repealed** by vows or laws.

Repeat (24), Repeated (11), Repeatedly (8), Repeating (1), Repeats (4)

PR : PR :003(003) [0007] many heresies and errors, and **repeatedly** affirmed.
PR : PR :008(005) [0009] We took up the **repeatedly** mentioned Augsburg
PR : PR :008(005) [0011] this our reiterated and **repeated** confession the more
PR : PR :023(012) [0021] mankind that with the **repeatedly** mentioned present
PR : PR :025(013) [0023] In conclusion, we **repeat** once again that we are not
AP : 04 :084(119) [0145] argument, which he often **repeats** (Rom. 4:16; Gal. 3:18).
AP : 04 :088(120) [0149] discussion in Rom. 4 and **repeats** it later in all his
AP : 04 :108(122) [0153] they suppose that this is **repeated** so often for no reason?
AP : 07 :007(169) [0229] We have **repeated** this statement almost verbatim in our
AP : 12 :053(189) [0265] This promise is **repeated** continually throughout
AP : 15 :002(215) [0315] of the Confession, we must **repeat** a few things here.
AP : 16 :013(224) [0333] We have **repeated** our position here so that those outside
AP : 24 :001(249) [0383] To begin with, we must **repeat** the prefatory statement
S2 : 04 :005(299) [0473] Manifestly (to **repeat** what has already been said often)
SC : PR :007(339) [0533] form, adhere to it, and use it **repeatedly** year after year.
SC : PR :010(339) [0535] so that the young may **repeat** these things after you and
LC : SP :015(363) [0577] We should learn to **repeat** them word for word.
LC : SP :016(363) [0577] bed at night; until they **repeat** them they should not be
LC : SP :026(364) [0579] for them simply to learn and **repeat** these parts verbatim.
LC : SP :026(364) [0581] they will also be able to **repeat** what they have heard and
LC : 01 :010(366) [0583] Therefore, I **repeat**, to have a God properly means to
LC : 01 :024(368) [0587] I have often enough **repeated**, from whom we receive all
LC : 01 :062(373) [0597] To **repeat** very briefly, it is either simply to lie and assert
LC : 01 :092(377) [0607] Accordingly, I constantly **repeat** that all our life and work
LC : 01 :121(382) [0615] Therefore, I **repeat**, I should be very glad if we were to
LC : 01 :226(395) [0645] deal with them so that they will not **repeat** the offense.
LC : 01 :247(398) [0651] Beware of this, I **repeat**, as of the devil himself.
LC : 01 :270(401) [0657] For when you **repeat** a story that you cannot prove, even
LC : 01 :317(408) [0673] All this I say and **repeat** in order that men may get rid of
LC : 01 :319(408) [0673] however, we must **repeat** the text which we have already
LC : 01 :326(409) [0675] this may be constantly **repeated** and never forgotten,
LC : 03 :096(433) [0725] Therefore Christ **repeats** it immediately after the Lord's
LC : 05 :042(451) [0763] Now it is true, we **repeat**, that no one should under any
EP : 12 :001(498) [0839] err and contradict our **repeatedly** cited Christian Creed
SD : PR :005(502) [0847] until our end by this **repeatedly** cited Christian
SD : PR :006(504) [0853] 4. After the **repeatedly** cited Augsburg Confession had
SD : PR :007(505) [0853] Augsburg Confession is **repeated**, several articles are
SD : PR :020(508) [0859] and what we now **repeat** in this document, but that it is
SD : 02 :044(529) [0897] of Chapter 26, he **repeats** and explicates the same
SD : 04 :032(556) [0947] diligence and earnestness, **repeat** and impress upon
SD : 07 :001(569) [0971] document and from **repeating** the true intention and the
SD : 07 :001(569) [0971] Confession and which has **repeatedly** been condemned.
SD : 07 :033(575) [0983] his last confession, he **repeated** his faith in this article with
SD : 07 :052(578) [0991] same words and syllables **repeat** these simple, clear,
SD : 07 :075(583) [0999] of the first institution, which he wants to be **repeated**.
SD : 07 :105(588) [1009] of our public and oft-**repeated** testimony to the contrary.
SD : 07 :128(591) [1015] brevity we have not wanted to **repeat** them at this point.
SD : 08 :061(602) [1035] own, but we accept and **repeat** the statements which the

Repel (3)

LC : 03 :008(421) [0699] that you may silence and **repel** any thoughts that would
LC : 03 :010(421) [0699] that you may silence and **repel** thoughts which would
SD : 03 :006(540) [0917] pure, it is impossible to **repel** any error or heretical spirit.

Repent (27), Repented (2), Repenting (1), Repents (2)

AP : 12 :045(187) [0263] Mark 1:15 Christ says, "**Repent**, and believe in the
S1 : PR :014(291) [0459] to us, for we do not **repent** and we even try to justify all
S3 : 03 :004(304) [0481] Christ says in Mark 1:15, "**Repent** and believe in the
S3 : 03 :012(305) [0481] that a man who properly **repents**, confesses, and makes
S3 : 03 :015(305) [0483] it had also to be **repented** of, confessed, etc., but
S3 : 03 :017(305) [0483] that he was unable to **repent** or be sorry for his sin (which
S3 : 03 :027(307) [0487] in purgatory had truly **repented** and properly confessed.
S3 : 03 :029(308) [0487] persons did not need to **repent**, for what were they to
S3 : 03 :029(308) [0487] for what were they to **repent** of when they did not
S3 : 03 :030(308) [0487] "**Repent**," he says.
S3 : 03 :032(308) [0487] But John says: "**Repent**, both of you.
S3 : 03 :032(308) [0487] sin really is, to say nothing of **repenting** and shunning sin.
S3 : 03 :032(308) [0489] Accordingly, if you would **repent**, repent rightly.
S3 : 03 :032(308) [0489] Accordingly, if you would repent, **repent** rightly.
S3 : 03 :032(308) [0489] think you do not need to **repent**, you brood of vipers,
S3 : 03 :034(309) [0489] "Now he commands all men everywhere to **repent**."
S3 : 03 :043(310) [0491] feel original sin and daily **repent** and strive against it, fall
TR : 00 :060(330) [0521] guilty of notorious crimes and absolve those who **repent**.
EP : 03 :017(475) [0795] though he does not truly **repent** and gives no evidence of
EP : 07 :016(484) [0813] not converted and do not **repent**, they receive them not to

Continued ▶

E P : 1 1 :010(495) [0833] but that everyone should **repent** and believe on the Lord
E P : 1 1 :011(496) [0835] there directs men first to **repent**, to acknowledge their
S D : 0 5 :006(559) [0953] Mark, where Christ said, "**Repent** and believe in the
S D : 0 5 :007(559) [0953] Luke 13:5, "Unless you **repent** you will all likewise
S D : 0 5 :007(559) [0953] there will be joy in heaven over one sinner who **repents**."
S D : 0 5 :008(559) [0953] another, the phrase "to **repent**" means nothing more than
S D : 0 7 :016(572) [0977] that those who truly **repent** and comfort themselves
S D : 1 1 :010(618) [1067] were to hold to the Word, **repent**, believe, etc., since I
S D : 1 1 :012(618) [1067] to admonish us to **repent** (II Tim. 3:16), to urge us to
S D : 1 1 :067(627) [1085] of God is at hand; **repent** and believe in the Gospel"
S D : 1 1 :071(627) [1085] are to desist from sin, **repent**, believe his promise, and
S D : 1 1 :083(630) [1091] receive into grace all who **repent** and believe in Christ;

Repentance (94)
A G : 1 2 :000(034) [0049] XII. **Repentance**
A G : 1 2 :001(034) [0049] whenever they come to **repentance**, and absolution should
A G : 1 2 :003(034) [0049] Properly speaking, true **repentance** is nothing else than to
A G : 1 2 :006(035) [0049] must be the fruits of **repentance**, as John says, "Bear fruit
A G : 1 2 :006(035) [0049] John says, "Bear fruit that befits **repentance**" (Matt. 3:8).
A G : 2 5 :006(062) [0069] of true Christian **repentance** in a more fitting fashion than
A L : 1 2 :000(034) [0049] XII. **Repentance**
A L : 1 2 :002(034) [0049] to impart absolution to those who return to **repentance**.
A L : 1 2 :003(034) [0049] Properly speaking, **repentance** consists of these two
A L : 1 2 :006(035) [0049] which are the fruits of **repentance**, are bound to follow.
A L : 1 2 :009(035) [0049] after Baptism although they returned to **repentance**.
A L : 2 5 :006(062) [0069] on the doctrine of **repentance** and have treated it with
A L : 2 6 :007(065) [0071] In treating of **repentance** no mention was made of faith;
A L : 2 6 :007(065) [0071] and the whole of **repentance** was thought to consist of
S 1 : P R :009(290) [0457] are capable of conversion and turn them to **repentance**!
S 3 : 0 3 :000(303) [0479] III. **Repentance**
S 3 : 0 3 :003(304) [0481] This is what the beginning of true **repentance** is like.
S 3 : 0 3 :005(304) [0481] is called a preacher of **repentance** — but for the remission
S 3 : 0 3 :006(304) [0481] this in Luke 24:47, "**Repentance** and the forgiveness of sins
S 3 : 0 3 :009(304) [0481] must compare the false **repentance** of the sophists with
S 3 : 0 3 :009(304) [0481] the sophists with true **repentance** so that both may be
S 3 : 0 3 :009(304) [0481] The False **Repentance** of the Papists
S 3 : 0 3 :010(304) [0481] teach correctly about **repentance** because they did not
S 3 : 0 3 :012(305) [0481] Such **repentance** the sophists divided into three parts —
S 3 : 0 3 :018(306) [0483] cases like this, such **repentance** surely was pure
S 3 : 0 3 :023(307) [0485] of always doing penance but never coming to **repentance**.
S 3 : 0 3 :030(308) [0487] St. John, the preacher of true **repentance**, intervenes.
S 3 : 0 3 :031(308) [0487] there are others who suppose, "We need no **repentance**."
S 3 : 0 3 :032(308) [0489] Your **repentance** accomplishes nothing.
S 3 : 0 3 :035(309) [0489] Such **repentance** teaches us to acknowledge sin — that is,
S 3 : 0 3 :036(309) [0489] This **repentance** is not partial and fragmentary like
S 3 : 0 3 :036(309) [0489] and fragmentary like **repentance** for actual sins, nor is it
S 3 : 0 3 :036(309) [0489] no uncertainty in such **repentance**, for nothing is left that
S 3 : 0 3 :037(309) [0489] And so our **repentance** cannot be false, uncertain, or
S 3 : 0 3 :039(309) [0489] This is the **repentance** which John preaches, which Christ
S 3 : 0 3 :039(309) [0489] With this **repentance** we overthrow the pope and
S 3 : 0 3 :040(309) [0489] of a Christian such **repentance** continues until death, for
T R : 0 0 :044(328) [0517] The doctrine of **repentance** has been completely corrupted
S C : 0 4 :012(349) [0551] by daily sorrow and **repentance** and be put to death, and
L C : 0 4 :075(445) [0751] What is **repentance** but an earnest attack on the old man
L C : 0 4 :075(445) [0751] If you live in **repentance**, therefore, you are walking in
L C : 0 4 :079(446) [0751] **Repentance**, therefore, is nothing else than a return and
L C : 0 4 :081(446) [0751] view, for he wrote, "**Repentance** is the second plank on
E P : 0 2 :017(472) [0791] in the daily exercise of **repentance**, the reborn will of man
E P : 0 5 :001(478) [0801] it also a preaching of **repentance** and reproof that
E P : 0 5 :006(478) [0803] a proclamation both of **repentance** and of forgiveness of
E P : 1 1 :017(497) [0837] all men to come to **repentance** and to believe the Gospel.
E P : 1 2 :022(499) [0841] of Christ, conversion, **repentance**, faith, and new
S D : 0 2 :026(526) [0891] God "gives the **repentance**" (Acts 5:51; II Tim. 2:25).
S D : 0 2 :034(527) [0895] state further: "This **repentance** continues in Christians
S D : 0 2 :048(530) [0901] and working true **repentance**, faith, and new spiritual
S D : 0 2 :050(531) [0901] the hearts of men true **repentance** and knowledge of their
S D : 0 2 :051(531) [0901] who in his name preach **repentance** and the remission of
S D : 0 2 :088(538) [0915] in the daily exercise of **repentance** but cooperates in all
S D : 0 3 :022(543) [0923] therein without **repentance**, conversion, and
S D : 0 3 :026(543) [0923] and genuine faith exists only in or with true **repentance**.
S D : 0 3 :064(550) [0937] person who has no true **repentance** (and upon which no
S D : 0 4 :015(553) [0943] or superstition, without **repentance** and without good
S D : 0 4 :033(556) [0949] a wicked life, lose the Holy Spirit, and reject **repentance**.'"
S D : 0 5 :002(558) [0951] time a proclamation of **repentance**, which rebukes the
S D : 0 5 :002(558) [0951] Gospel is not a proclamation of **repentance** or reproof.
S D : 0 5 :004(559) [0953] announced, namely, **repentance** and forgiveness of sins
S D : 0 5 :004(559) [0953] the dead, and that **repentance** and forgiveness of sin
S D : 0 5 :004(559) [0953] it under these heads: **repentance** to God and faith in
S D : 0 5 :005(559) [0953] proclamation of both **repentance** and the forgiveness of
S D : 0 5 :005(559) [0953] in their preaching with **repentance** and expounded and
S D : 0 5 :006(559) [0953] the proclamation of **repentance** but solely the preaching
S D : 0 5 :007(559) [0953] Again, the little word "**repentance**" is not used in a single
S D : 0 5 :008(559) [0953] in other places where **repentance** and faith in Christ
S D : 0 5 :008(559) [0953] Christ (Acts 20:21) or **repentance** and forgiveness of sins
S D : 0 5 :015(561) [0957] genuine and salutary **repentance**; the Gospel must also be
S D : 0 5 :024(563) [0961] of their sin and to **repentance**, but not in such a way that
S D : 0 5 :027(563) [0961] the law, a proclamation of **repentance** and punishment.
S D : 0 5 :027(563) [0961] a proclamation both of **repentance** and of forgiveness of
S D : 0 7 :016(572) [0977] they receive it without true **repentance** and without faith.
S D : 0 7 :060(580) [0993] table without true **repentance** and conversion to God, and
S D : 1 1 :010(618) [1067] of sin and vice without **repentance**, despise Word and
S D : 1 1 :010(618) [1067] concern myself with **repentance**, faith, prayer, and
S D : 1 1 :011(618) [1067] grace of God they have **repentance**, faith, and the good
S D : 1 1 :017(619) [1069] convert hearts to true **repentance**, and would enlighten
S D : 1 1 :018(619) [1069] life all who in sincere **repentance** and true faith accept
S D : 1 1 :027(620) [1071] the preaching of **repentance** and forgiveness of sin.
S D : 1 1 :028(620) [1071] as the proclamation of **repentance** extends over all men
S D : 1 1 :028(620) [1071] commanded to preach "**repentance** and forgiveness of sins
S D : 1 1 :028(621) [1071] but that all should turn to **repentance**" (II Pet. 3:9).
S D : 1 1 :028(621) [1073] in common to whom **repentance** is preached should also
S D : 1 1 :039(623) [1077] remain in sin without **repentance** (Luke 14:18, 24), do not
S D : 1 1 :071(627) [1085] wills to work such **repentance** and faith in us through the
S D : 1 1 :075(628) [1087] to recall them to **repentance** through the Word, and
S D : 1 1 :075(628) [1087] return to him in true **repentance** through a right faith, he
S D : 1 1 :081(629) [1089] perish, but that all should reach **repentance**" (II Pet. 3:9).
S D : 1 1 :089(631) [1093] heavy-laden sinners to **repentance**, to a knowledge of
S D : 1 1 :096(632) [1095] to true and sincere **repentance**, raise him up through
S D : 1 2 :030(635) [1101] of Christ, conversion, **repentance**, and faith or works new

Repentant (5)
S 3 : 0 3 :016(305) [0483] contrite (that is, really **repentant**), he should at least be
S 3 : 0 3 :016(305) [0483] (which I might call half-way or partially **repentant**).
S 3 : 0 3 :017(305) [0483] was asked if he did not wish or desire to be **repentant**.
E P : 0 7 :019(484) [0813] are weak in faith but **repentant**, to comfort them and to
S D : 1 1 :089(631) [1093] does not exclude any **repentant** sinner but invites and

Repetition (5)
P R : P R :009(006) [0011] of this explanation and **repetition** of our previous
P R : P R :017(008) [0015] Book of Concord and **repetition** of our Christian faith
L C : 0 3 :007(421) [0699] Such external **repetition**, when properly used, may serve
S D : 0 7 :054(579) [0991] Thus, too, the **repetition**, confirmation, and exposition of
S D : 0 7 :082(584) [1001] precisely through the **repetition** and recitation of the

Replaced (2), Replaces (2), Replacing (1)
A P : 1 5 :004(215) [0315] they are openly **replacing** the Gospel with doctrines of
A P : 1 5 :025(218) [0321] Christ is obscured and **replaced** by a vain trust in such
A P : 2 1 :028(233) [0351] the blessed Virgin has completely **replaced** Christ.
A P : 2 4 :057(260) [0405] New Testament, and it **replaces** Christ as our mediator
S D : 0 1 :011(510) [0863] that at the same time it **replaces** the lost image of God in

Replenish (1), Replenished (1)
A P : 2 3 :008(240) [0365] was a command to **replenish** the earth, but now that the
A P : 2 3 :008(240) [0365] that the earth has been **replenished** marriage is not

Reply (23), Replying (1), Replied (3), Replies (2)
A G : 2 8 :028(085) [0087] also writes in his **reply** to the letters of Petilian that one
A G : 2 8 :053(090) [0091] To this our teachers **reply** that bishops or pastors may
A L : 2 8 :028(085) [0087] Augustine also says in **reply** to the letters of Petilian that
A L : 2 8 :053(090) [0091] To this our teachers **reply** that it is lawful for bishops or
A P : 0 2 :051(107) [0119] we shall not lack men to **reply** in defense of the truth, for
A P : 0 4 :159(129) [0165] Now let us **reply** to the objection of the opponents
A P : 0 4 :182(132) [0173] **Reply** to the Opponents' Arguments
A P : 0 4 :267(146) [0197] This, then, is how we **reply** to the words of Daniel: Since
A P : 0 4 :280(149) [0201] an argument to judge or **reply** to a single passage without
A P : 0 4 :345(160) [0217] We shall therefore **reply** briefly.
A P : 0 4 :356(161) [0217] Here our opponents **reply** that eternal life is called a
A P : 0 7 :029(173) [0237] to twist it, we shall not mind **replying** more fully.
A P : 1 2 :008(183) [0255] give the legalistic **reply** that Judas did not love God but
A P : 1 2 :159(207) [0301] of the blind man, Christ **replied** that the reason for his
A P : 1 5 :012(216) [0317] To this Paul **replies** that Christ would be "an agent of
A P : 2 1 :013(230) [0345] example of the church, we **reply** that this is a novel custom
A P : 2 1 :030(233) [0351] These **replied** that they could not give it for fear that their
A P : 2 3 :008(240) [0365] Our opponents **reply** with the silly argument that
A P : 2 3 :028(243) [0371] We shall **reply** to these figments one by one.
A P : 2 4 :067(261) [0407] is enough of a general **reply** to our opponents regarding
A P : 2 4 :090(266) [0415] In **reply** we shall say only this much.
A P : 2 4 :099(268) [0419] and now we have **replied** without casting any reproach.
A P : 2 8 :006(282) [0445] But our opponents' only **reply** is that bishops have the
A P : 2 8 :026(285) [0451] time being we have made this **reply** to the Confutation.
S 1 : P R :005(289) [0457] I suppose I should **reply** to everything while I am still
L C : 0 1 :270(401) [0657] I **reply**: "Why don't you bring it before the regular
L C : 0 3 :032(424) [0707] thy will be done," God **replies** from on high, "Yes, dear
L C : 0 4 :048(442) [0743] To this we **reply** briefly: Let the simple dismiss this
S D : 0 2 :008(521) [0883] of and summary **reply** to the questions and issues stated

Report (3), Reported (4), Reports (1)
A G : 2 4 :036(060) [0067] For Chrysostom **reports** how the priest stood every day,
A L : 2 3 :002(051) [0061] account Pope Pius is **reported** to have said that there
A P : P R :009(098) [0101] have judged, as we have **reported** this faithfully; far from
S 1 : P R :008(290) [0457] sent from France, who **reported** in our presence that his
L C : 0 1 :271(401) [0657] Every **report**, then, that cannot be adequately proved is
L C : 0 1 :275(402) [0659] Necessity requires one to **report** evil, to prefer charges, to
E P : 0 7 :001(481) [0809] we have wished to **report** as far as necessary concerning
S D : 0 2 :069(534) [0907] as we have sufficiently **reported** above on this matter.

Reprehensible (1)
A P : 2 1 :034(233) [0353] ancient prayers, this was not done in a **reprehensible** way.

Represent (6), Representation (1), Representative (3), Representatives (4), Represents (1)
A G : P R :012(026) [0041] and associates who **represent** the electors, princes, and
A G : P R :018(026) [0041] electors, princes, and **representatives** of the estates) who
A L : 0 0 :004(049) [0059] as those ungodly and malicious men **represent**.
A P : 0 7 :028(173) [0237] For they do not **represent** their own persons but the
A P : 0 7 :047(177) [0243] stead and do not **represent** their own persons, according
A P : 2 3 :023(242) [0369] new canons do not **represent** the decision of the synods
A P : 2 4 :037(257) [0397] should look for what it **represents** and not for another
S 1 : P R :002(288) [0455] these articles and submitted them to our **representatives**.
T R : 0 0 :023(324) [0511] passages Peter is **representative** of the entire company of
T R : 0 0 :024(324) [0511] to regard Peter as the **representative** of the entire
L C : S P :002(362) [0575] Its contents **represent** the minimum of knowledge
L C : 0 1 :108(379) [0611] parents as God's **representatives**, and to remember that,
L C : 0 1 :126(382) [0617] he has appointed it to be his **representative** on earth.
L C : 0 1 :182(389) [0631] of God and his **representatives**, and they are to be
S D : 0 7 :049(578) [0989] of his body, or of a **representation** or of his body in a

Represses (1)
S 3 : 0 3 :044(310) [0491] but the Holy Spirit **represses** and restrains it so that it

Reproach (7), Reproached (1)
A G : 2 3 :011(052) [0063] "A bishop must be above **reproach**, married only once."
A P : 0 4 :028(111) [0129] It is false, too, and a **reproach** to Christ, that men who
A P : 2 4 :099(268) [0419] and now we have replied without casting any **reproach**.
T R : 0 0 :058(330) [0521] often happens, they are **reproached** for scandal, schism,
S C : 0 9 :002(354) [0561] bishop must be above **reproach**, married only once,
L C : 0 1 :192(391) [0635] What else is this but to **reproach** such persons as
L C : 0 3 :044(425) [0709] father suffers scorn and **reproach**, so God is dishonored if
L C : 0 3 :057(427) [0713] Just so, it is a great **reproach** and dishonor to God if we,

Reproduce (1)
S D : 0 7 :036(575) [0985] same thing when they **reproduce** and explain the

Reprove (10), Reproved (3), Reproves (4), Reproof (7)
A P : 0 4 :154(128) [0165] with irreverence and **reproves** him with the example of
A P : 0 4 :207(135) [0177] Ps. 50:8, "I do not **reprove** you for your sacrifices."
T R : 0 0 :008(320) [0505] Christ **reproved** the apostles for this error and taught
L C : 0 1 :182(389) [0631] Anger, **reproof**, and punishment are the prerogatives of
L C : 0 1 :249(398) [0651] is only to instruct and **reprove** by means of God's Word.
L C : 0 1 :265(400) [0657] the right to judge and **reprove** his neighbor publicly, even
L C : 0 1 :265(401) [0657] unless he has been authorized to judge and **reprove**.
L C : 0 1 :272(401) [0659] secret, or at any rate be **reproved** in secret, as we shall
L C : 0 1 :275(402) [0659] mutual obligation to **reprove** evil where it is necessary and
L C : 0 1 :276(402) [0659] wrongdoing, to go and **reprove** the man personally,
L C : 0 1 :328(410) [0677] and occasion to do so and no man may **reprove** you.
E P : 0 5 :001(478) [0801] of repentance and **reproof** that condemns unbelief, since
E P : 0 5 :007(478) [0803] of contrition and **reproof** but is, strictly speaking,
E P : 0 5 :007(478) [0803] message which does not **reprove** or terrify but comforts
E P : 0 5 :011(479) [0805] of conviction and **reproof** and not exclusively a
E P : 1 2 :011(499) [0841] Confession and **reprove** the preaching and the errors of
S D : 0 5 :002(558) [0951] Gospel is not a proclamation of repentance or **reproof**.
S D : 0 5 :002(558) [0951] the law of God, which **reproves** all sins, including
S D : 0 5 :002(558) [0953] which the law of God **reproved**, has been pardoned and
S D : 0 5 :017(561) [0957] of all culpable sin, the law **reproves** unbelief also.
S D : 0 6 :012(566) [0967] the Holy Spirit **reproves** them through the law.
S D : 0 6 :014(566) [0967] inspired by God and profitable for teaching, for **reproof**."
S D : 0 6 :014(566) [0967] But to **reprove** is the real function of the law.
S D : 1 1 :012(618) [1067] and impenitence but "to **reproof**, correction, and

Republic (1)
A P : 0 7 :020(171) [0233] about some Platonic **republic**, as has been slanderously

Repugnance (1)
L C : 0 6 :024(460) [0000] the beggar go but with **repugnance**, not expecting to

Repulse (1), Repulsive (1)
A P : 0 4 :230(139) [0183] We know how **repulsive** this teaching is to the judgment
L C : 0 3 :069(429) [0717] and defense now to **repulse** and beat down all that the

Reputation (5), Repute (1), Reputed (1)
A G : 2 7 :010(072) [0077] vows gained such a **reputation**, as is well known, that
A L : 2 7 :010(072) [0077] that vows had such a **reputation** that it was clearly
A P : 1 2 :068(192) [0271] theologians of great **reputation**, like Duns Scotus,
T R : 0 0 :010(321) [0505] they were who were **reputed** to be something," he says,
T R : 0 0 :010(321) [0505] "Those who were of **repute** added nothing to me"
S C : 0 3 :020(348) [0549] or soul, property or **reputation**, and that at last, when the
L C : 0 1 :256(399) [0653] deprived of his **reputation**, honor, and character any

Request (2), Requested (4), Requests (1)
P R : P R :013(007) [0013] Confession with the **request** that they and their chief
P R : P R :014(007) [0013] When the **requested** judgments had been received they
A G : P R :006(025) [0039] graciously and earnestly **requested** that each of the
A G : P R :021(027) [0043] and best motives **requested** in all the diets of the empire
A P : P R :002(098) [0099] arguments, our party **requested** a copy of the
A P : 0 4 :385(166) [0225] because of Christ and **request** everything because of
L C : 0 3 :120(436) [0731] does not lie since he has promised to grant his **requests**.

Requiem (1), Requiems (1)
S 2 : 0 2 :012(294) [0465] were so occupied with **requiem** Masses, with vigils, with
S 2 : 0 2 :012(294) [0465] yearly celebrations of **requiems**, with the common week,

Require (57), Required (37), Requirement (2), Requirements (11), Requires (64), Requiring (4)
P R : P R :001(003) [0007] according to the **requirements** of his station and dignity,
P R : P R :022(012) [0021] it will without doubt be **required** of the persecutors on the
A G : P R :021(026) [0043] even beyond what is **required**, to participate in such a
A G : 1 3 :002(036) [0049] For this reason they **require** faith, and they are rightly
A G : 1 6 :002(037) [0051] buy and sell, take **required** oaths, possess property, be
A G : 1 6 :004(037) [0051] Christian perfection **requires** the forsaking of house and
A G : 1 6 :005(038) [0051] state, and marriage but **requires** that all these be kept as
A G : 2 2 :008(050) [0061] can be found which **requires** the reception of only one
A G : 2 4 :030(059) [0067] the sacrament **requires** faith, and without faith it is used
A G : 2 5 :004(062) [0069] We also teach that God **requires** us to believe this
A G : 2 5 :011(063) [0071] Chrysostom does not **require** a detailed enumeration of
A G : 2 6 :038(069) [0075] that one can perform the duties **required** by one's calling.
A G : 2 7 :003(071) [0077] vows many other **requirements** were imposed, and such
A G : 2 8 :027(085) [0087] Canon law **requires** the same in Part II, Question 7, in the
A G : 2 8 :035(086) [0089] out of opinions or to **require** that they be observed in
A G : 2 8 :042(088) [0089] power to impose such **requirements** on Christendom to
A G : 2 8 :042(088) [0089] Why, then, do they multiply sins with such **requirements**?
A G : 2 8 :049(089) [0091] with countless **requirements** and thus ensnare
A G : 2 8 :050(089) [0091] all proper for the bishops to **require** such services of God.
A L : 1 3 :003(036) [0049] that sins are forgiven, is **required** in the use of the
A L : 1 6 :002(037) [0051] to swear oaths when **required** by magistrates, to marry, to
A L : 1 6 :005(038) [0051] contrary, it especially **requires** their preservation as
A L : 2 5 :004(062) [0069] are told that God **requires** faith to believe such absolution
A L : 2 6 :023(067) [0073] So he does not **require** an unprofitable act of worship.
A L : 2 8 :027(084) [0087] The canons **require** the same thing (II, question 7, in
A L : 2 8 :035(086) [0089] it is against Scripture to **require** the observances of
A L : 2 8 :047(088) [0089] concerning those who **require** traditions, "Let them
A L : 2 8 :050(089) [0091] to institute such services or **require** them as necessary.
A P : 0 4 :008(108) [0121] Decalogue does not only **require** external works that
A P : 0 4 :008(108) [0121] It also **requires** other works far beyond the reach of
A P : 0 4 :008(108) [0121] Finally, it **requires** obedience to God in death and all
A P : 0 4 :017(109) [0125] our opponents **require** a knowledge of the history about
A P : 0 4 :022(110) [0127] part maintain that God **requires** the righteousness of
A P : 0 4 :044(113) [0133] For the law **requires** our own works and our own
A P : 0 4 :055(114) [0137] must remember that this **requires** faith, which accepts the
A P : 0 4 :082(118) [0145] but in Christ, the high priest, this statement **requires** faith.
A P : 0 4 :083(119) [0145] Thus he **requires** faith.
A P : 0 4 :110(123) [0153] If our opponents **require** us to trust in our own love for
A P : 0 4 :131(125) [0157] or at best they **require** only outward acts of worship.
A P : 0 4 :136(126) [0159] claim that we do not **require** good works, whereas we not
A P : 0 4 :136(126) [0159] whereas we not only **require** them but show how they can
A P : 0 4 :140(126) [0161] So it is clear that we **require** good works.
A P : 0 4 :167(130) [0169] Who lives up to the **requirements** of his calling?
A P : 0 4 :172(130) [0171] even in good works he **requires** our faith that for Christ's
A P : 0 4 :200(134) [0175] praise good works and **require** them, and we show many
A P : 0 4 :219(137) [0179] In this text Paul **requires** love.
A P : 0 4 :219(137) [0179] We **require** it, too.
A P : 0 4 :229(139) [0183] they teach and **require** the righteousness of the law.
A P : 0 4 :258(144) [0193] evil," as he denounces ungodly hearts and **requires** faith.
A P : 0 4 :259(144) [0193] *opere operato*, but he **requires** a new life, which is
A P : 0 4 :259(145) [0193] your bread with the hungry," he **requires** the new life.
A P : 0 4 :261(145) [0195] Thus in Daniel's sermon (4:24) faith is **required**.
A P : 0 4 :264(146) [0197] The text does not say this, but rather **requires** faith.
A P : 0 4 :264(146) [0197] Wherever there is a promise, there faith is **required**.
A P : 0 4 :267(146) [0197] a promise, he necessarily **requires** faith, which believes
A P : 0 4 :272(148) [0199] the forgiveness of sins, it necessarily **requires** faith.
A P : 0 4 :272(148) [0199] understand that faith is **required**, not merely works, as in
A P : 0 4 :272(148) [0199] Here a work is **required** and a promise of the forgiveness
A P : 0 4 :274(148) [0199] penitence works are **required**, since a new life is certainly
A P : 0 4 :274(148) [0199] a new life is certainly **required**; but here our opponents
A P : 0 4 :279(149) [0199] shows that faith is **required** before almsgiving: "Have God
A P : 0 4 :282(149) [0201] of the whole passage shows that it **requires** faith.
A P : 0 4 :288(151) [0203] and, to some extent, its **requirements** can be met.
A P : 0 4 :324(157) [0211] mercy correlatively **requires** faith and that only faith can
A P : 0 4 :353(161) [0217] that we very definitely **require** good works, since we teach
A P : 0 4 :374(164) [0223] that a new life and new birth are **required**, not hypocrisy.
A P : 0 7 :046(177) [0243] They **require** uniform human ceremonies for the unity of
A P : 1 1 :007(181) [0251] of the regulation that **requires** all sins to be confessed.
A P : 1 1 :008(181) [0251] the enumeration of sins is not **required** by divine law.
A P : 1 2 :005(183) [0253] matter nor the chief **requirements** of penitence nor the
A P : 1 2 :058(190) [0267] order to emphasize the faith that we **require** in penitence.
A P : 1 2 :060(190) [0267] Beyond such "faith" we **require** everyone to believe that
A P : 1 2 :061(190) [0269] of the forgiveness of sins, it necessarily **requires** faith.
A P : 1 2 :074(192) [0273] He does not merely **require** that we believe in a general
A P : 1 2 :075(193) [0273] They **require** only the law and our works because the law
A P : 1 2 :088(195) [0277] a certainty of faith is **required** in the Gospel; our
A P : 1 2 :092(196) [0279] in these statements, **requiring** contrition or good works
A P : 1 2 :094(196) [0281] God shows that he **requires** the faith with which we
A P : 1 2 :111(198) [0285] What snares this **requirement** of complete confession has
A P : 1 2 :133(202) [0293] these passages Scripture **requires** works that are
A P : 1 2 :139(203) [0295] glory and command **require** penitence to produce good
A P : 1 2 :142(204) [0295] to do even more than it **requires**, but Scripture cries out
A P : 1 2 :142(204) [0295] we are far away from the perfection that the law **requires**.
A P : 1 2 :142(204) [0295] They do not see that it **requires** us to love God "with all
A P : 1 2 :142(204) [0295] does as much as the law **requires**, and it is foolish of them
A P : 1 2 :142(204) [0295] that God's law does not **require**, it is vain and wicked to
A P : 1 2 :171(209) [0305] besides this formal one **required** in the canons dealing
A P : 1 3 :006(212) [0309] even the church does not **require** as necessary for
A P : 1 5 :027(219) [0323] because they cannot keep the **requirements** in every detail.
A P : 1 5 :037(220) [0325] now that these are being **required** as a means of meriting
A P : 1 5 :041(220) [0325] of the churches are **required** to instruct and examine the
A P : 1 5 :049(221) [0329] When they are **required** as necessary, they bring exquisite
A P : 1 5 :050(222) [0329] of sins, and they **require** so-called "universal rites" as
A P : 1 6 :001(222) [0329] when the government **requires** it, or contract marriage —
A P : 1 6 :010(224) [0333] theory that the Gospel **requires** us to hold property in
A P : 1 8 :002(225) [0335] "the essence of the acts" **required** by his commandments
A P : 1 8 :009(226) [0337] ought to know that God **requires** this civil righteousness
A P : 2 0 :005(227) [0339] inclined to mention here the type of works they **require**.
A P : 2 1 :001(229) [0343] XXI because we do not **require** the invocation of the
A P : 2 1 :007(230) [0345] Our opponents do not **require** these real honors; they
A P : 2 1 :014(230) [0345] only do our opponents **require** invocation in the
A P : 2 1 :038(234) [0355] us because we do not **require** the invocation of saints and
A P : 2 1 :042(235) [0355] abuses when they **required** us to accept the Confutation.
A P : 2 3 :015(241) [0367] be shown a command **requiring** that priests should marry
A P : 2 3 :019(242) [0369] possible for everyone, it would not **require** a special gift.
A P : 2 3 :019(242) [0369] Christ shows that it does **require** a special gift; therefore,
A P : 2 3 :026(243) [0371] They claim that they **require** celibacy because it is pure,
A P : 2 3 :032(244) [0373] and above all he **requires** the faith by which a woman
A P : 2 3 :042(245) [0375] resisted those who **required** circumcision and tried to
A P : 2 3 :064(248) [0381] here because the Gospel **requires** purity of the heart and
A P : 2 3 :066(248) [0381] the vessels of the Lord," **requires** impure celibates to
A P : 2 4 :029(255) [0393] sacrificial victims and **requires** prayer: "Do I eat the flesh
A P : 2 4 :029(255) [0393] Word to hear, and dost **require** me to believe it and thy
A P : 2 4 :033(256) [0395] For he **requires** the worship of the heart, by which the
A P : 2 4 :034(256) [0395] This passage clearly **requires** the offerings of the
A P : 2 4 :034(256) [0397] The New Testament **requires** sacrifices of the heart, not
A P : 2 4 :040(257) [0399] our stand because we **require** all the actions that it
A P : 2 4 :075(263) [0411] but the Fathers clearly **require** faith and speak of the
A P : 2 4 :090(266) [0415] but a promise and a sacrament **requiring** faith.
A P : 2 8 :006(282) [0445] that the power to rule **requires** the power to judge,
A P : 2 8 :019(284) [0449] For Christ **requires** them to teach in such a way that he
A P : 2 8 :020(284) [0449] This statement **requires** obedience to the Gospel; it does
S 3 : 0 3 :022(306) [0485] years of penance were **required** for a single mortal sin.
T R : 0 0 :048(328) [0519] performed in callings which God **requires** and ordained.
T R : 0 0 :060(330) [0521] The Gospel **requires** of those who preside over the
T R : 0 0 :081(334) [0527] are so great that they **require** special courts, but these
T R : 0 0 :082(334) [0527] know that God will **require** them to pay for their crime.
S C : P R :018(340) [0537] parts which seem to **require** special attention among the
S C : 0 3 :014(347) [0547] Answer: Everything **required** to satisfy our bodily needs,
S C : 0 6 :010(352) [0557] for the words "for you" **require** truly believing hearts.
L C : P R :014(360) [0571] Certainly God did not **require** and command this so
L C : S P :002(362) [0575] the minimum of knowledge **required** of a Christian.
L C : S P :024(364) [0579] constantly teach and **require** young people to recite word
L C : 0 1 :004(365) [0581] therefore, is to **require** true faith and confidence of the
L C : 0 1 :013(366) [0583] It **requires** that man's whole heart and confidence be
L C : 0 1 :027(368) [0587] and thank him for them, as this commandment **requires**.
L C : 0 1 :061(373) [0597] people should be strictly **required** and trained to hold this
L C : 0 1 :064(373) [0599] we swear properly where it is necessary and **required**.
L C : 0 1 :083(376) [0603] of what God **requires** in this commandment, we point out
L C : 0 1 :098(378) [0609] of God, and he will **require** of you an accounting of how
L C : 0 1 :107(379) [0611] It **requires** us not only to address them affectionately and
L C : 0 1 :109(380) [0611] what this commandment **requires** concerning honor to
L C : 0 1 :205(393) [0639] In short, everyone is **required** both to live chastely
L C : 0 1 :212(394) [0641] too, God's grace is still **required** to keep the heart pure.

Continued ▶

LC : 0 1 :219(394) [0643] that this commandment **requires** everyone not only to live
LC : 0 1 :275(402) [0659] Necessity **requires** one to report evil, to prefer charges, to
LC : 0 1 :319(408) [0673] how much effort God **requires** us to devote to learning
LC : 0 1 :326(409) [0675] love and trust which the First Commandment **requires**.
LC : 0 1 :333(410) [0677] so earnestly **requires** and enjoins under threat of his
LC : 0 2 :002(411) [0679] help us do what the Ten Commandments **require** of us.
LC : 0 2 :019(412) [0681] to his service, as he has **required** and enjoined in the Ten
LC : 0 3 :005(420) [0699] Thereby we are **required** to praise the holy name and pray
LC : 0 3 :008(421) [0699] This God **requires** of us; he has not left it to our choice.
LC : 0 3 :073(430) [0719] Now, our life **requires** not only food and clothing and
LC : 0 3 :100(433) [0725] the trouble and effort **required** to retain and persevere in
LC : 0 5 :036(450) [0761] now, is the preparation **required** of a Christian for
LC : 0 6 :020(459) [0000] Further, no one dare oppress you with **requirements**.
EP : 1 0 :011(494) [0831] a public confession is **required**, one may make
SD : PR :010(503) [0849] For that reason necessity **requires** that such controverted
SD : PR :001(503) [0849] The primary **requirement** for basic and permanent
SD : 0 1 :059(519) [0879] and schools therefore **requires** that every one be rightly
SD : 0 3 :044(547) [0931] by faith, since it meets the **requirements** of this document.
SD : 0 4 :001(551) [0939] since good works are **required** of true believers as fruits
SD : 0 4 :008(552) [0941] are also able and **require** to perform, are indeed
SD : 0 4 :028(555) [0947] saying that, although we **require** good works as necessary
SD : 0 5 :010(560) [0955] or how much it **requires** of us, or how severely it curses
SD : 0 6 :002(564) [0963] Holy Spirit spontaneously do what God **requires** of them.
SD : 0 6 :006(564) [0965] free from sins, they would **require** no law, no driver.
SD : 0 6 :009(565) [0965] reborn children of God **require** in this life not only the
SD : 0 6 :020(567) [0969] Believers, furthermore, **require** the teaching of the law so
SD : 0 6 :021(567) [0969] Believers, furthermore, **require** the teaching of the law in
SD : 0 6 :024(568) [0971] There he will no longer **require** either the preaching of the
SD : 0 6 :024(568) [0971] punishments, just as he will no longer **require** the Gospel.
SD : 0 7 :065(581) [0995] In these words he **required** faith.
SD : 1 0 :014(613) [1057] or a prohibition, **requiring** us to use them or to

Reread (3)
AP : 0 4 :105(122) [0153] — read them and **reread** them, they contribute less to an
TR : 0 0 :082(334) [0529] of the Gospel, we have **reread** the articles of the
TR : 0 0 :082(000) [0529] and again and again **reread**, the Confession and Apology

Rescind (1)
TR : 0 0 :049(329) [0519] above councils and can **rescind** the decrees of councils, as

Rescript (1)
AP : 2 4 :081(264) [0411] of the Romans, as the **rescript** of Pertinax on the law of

Rescue (2)
AP : 0 4 :364(163) [0219] that it is the will of God to help, **rescue**, and save them.
LC : 0 1 :203(392) [0639] to defend, protect, and **rescue** your neighbor whenever he

Resemble (2)
AP : 2 1 :037(234) [0355] many things that **resemble** the "true stories" of Lucian.
AP : 2 7 :063(280) [0441] of the Rechabites does not **resemble** monasticism.

Reservation (7), Reserve (1), Reserved (17), Reserving (2)
PR : PR :013(007) [0013] to us without **reserve** their considered judgment
PR : PR :017(008) [0015] at Naumburg **reserved** to ourselves the right and served
AG : 2 8 :002(081) [0083] consciences with **reserved** cases and violent use of the
AG : 2 8 :041(087) [0089] is reconciled, that in a **reserved** case sin is not forgiven
AG : 2 8 :041(087) [0089] for whom the case is **reserved**, in spite of the fact that
AG : 2 8 :041(087) [0089] says nothing of the **reservation** of guilt but speaks only
AG : 2 8 :041(087) [0089] speaks only about the **reservation** of ecclesiastical
AL : 2 8 :002(081) [0083] consciences with **reservation** of cases and violent
AL : 2 8 :041(087) [0089] hours, that in a **reserved** case a sin cannot be forgiven
AL : 2 8 :041(087) [0089] of the person who **reserved** the case, although the canons
AL : 2 8 :041(087) [0089] speak only of **reserving** ecclesiastical penalties and not of
AL : 2 8 :041(087) [0089] ecclesiastical penalties and not of **reserving** guilt.
AP : 1 2 :027(185) [0259] 11. In **reserved** cases, not only the canonical punishment
AP : 1 2 :027(185) [0259] the guilt ought to be **reserved** in the case of someone who
AP : 1 2 :177(210) [0307] But the **reservation** of cases is a secular matter.
AP : 1 2 :177(210) [0307] It is the **reservation** of canonical penalties, not the
AP : 1 2 :177(210) [0307] penalties, not the **reservation** of guilt before God in the
AP : 1 2 :177(210) [0307] the hour of death the **reservation** of cases should not be
S3 : 0 3 :024(307) [0485] days, but the pope **reserved** for himself alone the right to
TR : 0 0 :074(332) [0525] have tyrannically **reserved** for themselves alone and have
TR : 0 0 :076(333) [0525] have tyrannically **reserved** this jurisdiction for themselves
LC : 0 1 :274(402) [0659] Commandment, he has **reserved** to himself the right of
LC : 0 3 :090(432) [0723] He has **reserved** to himself this prerogative, that if
SD : 0 7 :015(572) [0977] bread is laid aside or **reserved** in the tabernacle or carried
SD : 1 1 :052(625) [1081] revealed but has kept **reserved** solely to his own wisdom
SD : 1 1 :055(625) [1081] But because God has **reserved** this mystery to his own
SD : 1 1 :064(626) [1083] of this mystery God has **reserved** for his own hidden

Reside (1), Residence (1), Resides (1)
AP : 0 4 :306(154) [0207] own righteousness, which certainly **resides** in the will.
S2 : 0 4 :008(300) [0473] always have to have his **residence** in Rome or some other
SC : PR :013(339) [0535] anyone who desires to **reside** in a city is bound to know

Resist (20), Resistance (3), Resistant (1), Resisted (4), Resisting (2), Resists (18)
AG : PR :001(024) [0039] how with continuing help he might effectively be **resisted**.
AG : 2 3 :012(052) [0063] such serious and strong **resistance** that an archbishop of
AL : 2 3 :012(052) [0063] fact, they offered such **resistance** that the archbishop of
AP : 0 4 :138(126) [0161] by its own strength to **resist** the devil, who holds
AP : 0 4 :146(127) [0163] forth evil desires, though the Spirit in us **resists** them.
AP : 0 4 :249(143) [0191] but about a faith that **resists** the terrors of conscience and
AP : 2 3 :042(245) [0375] we must definitely **resist** him as the apostles in Acts 15
AP : 2 3 :042(245) [0375] as the apostles in Acts 15 **resisted** those who required
AP : 2 7 :003(269) [0419] He will destroy you, and you will be unable to **resist** him."
TR : 0 0 :057(330) [0521] On the contrary, it is necessary to **resist** him as Antichrist.
SC : 0 9 :004(355) [0561] Therefore he who **resists** the authorities resists what God
SC : 0 9 :004(355) [0561] who resists the authorities **resists** what God has
SC : 0 9 :004(355) [0561] has appointed, and those who **resist** will incur judgment.
LC : 0 1 :151(386) [0625] despises or rebelliously **resists** authority, let him know
LC : 0 1 :162(387) [0627] But here everybody **resists** and rebels; all are afraid that
LC : 0 1 :213(394) [0641] priests, monks, and nuns **resist** God's order and
LC : 0 3 :002(420) [0697] the world and our flesh, **resists** our efforts with all his
LC : 0 3 :106(434) [0727] us power and strength to **resist**, even though the
LC : 0 3 :108(435) [0729] it free rein and neither **resist** it nor pray for help against
LC : 0 3 :111(435) [0729] But prayer can **resist** him and drive him back.
LC : 0 4 :068(445) [0749] grows stronger, Baptism is not being used but **resisted**.
LC : 0 5 :026(449) [0759] when he sees that we **resist** him and attack the old man,
EP : 0 2 :015(471) [0789] in, and after conversion **resists** the Holy Spirit, and that
EP : 0 2 :015(471) [0789] Spirit is given to such as **resist** him purposely and
SD : 0 2 :018(524) [0889] he was born, he defiantly **resists** God and his will unless
SD : 0 2 :019(524) [0889] man to a hard stone which **resists** rather than yields in
SD : 0 2 :024(526) [0891] a block because he is **resistant** and hostile to the will of
SD : 0 2 :046(530) [0899] will continue wholly to **resist** God or wait until God
SD : 0 2 :059(532) [0905] stone or a block does not **resist** the person who moves it,
SD : 0 2 :059(532) [0905] does who with his will **resists** the Lord God until he is
SD : 0 2 :059(532) [0905] a stone or block, for he **resists** the Word and will of God
SD : 0 2 :060(533) [0905] for those who always **resist** the Holy Spirit and oppose
SD : 0 2 :060(533) [0905] enlightened one and his **resisting** will becomes an
SD : 0 2 :072(535) [0909] sin it is to hinder and **resist** such operations of the Holy
SD : 0 2 :073(535) [0909] or after his conversion **resists** the Holy Spirit, and if he
SD : 0 2 :073(535) [0909] Whether the Holy Spirit is given to those who **resist** him?
SD : 0 2 :082(537) [0913] in, and after conversion **resists** the Holy Spirit, and that
SD : 0 2 :082(537) [0913] and that the Holy Spirit is given to those who **resist** him.
SD : 0 2 :083(537) [0913] God for grace, but wholly **resists** the Word, conversion
SD : 0 2 :083(537) [0913] and perseveringly **resist** the Holy Spirit's activities and
SD : 0 2 :084(537) [0913] in the regenerated a **resistance**, of which the Scriptures
SD : 0 2 :085(537) [0913] the unregenerated man **resists** God entirely and is
SD : 0 2 :088(538) [0915] willing people out of **resisting** and unwilling people, and
SD : 0 4 :031(556) [0947] without fear and shame, **resists** the Holy Spirit, and
SD : 1 1 :039(623) [1075] they hear it (Heb. 4:2, 7), **resist** the Holy Spirit
SD : 1 1 :040(623) [1077] the Word and persistently **resist** the Holy Spirit who
SD : 1 1 :041(623) [1077] him through the call and **resists** the Holy Spirit who wills
SD : 1 1 :078(629) [1089] and ridicule it, and they **resisted** the Holy Spirit who

Resolute (1), Resolutely (1)
LC : 0 1 :249(398) [0651] They should be alert and **resolute** enough to establish and
LC : 0 1 :260(400) [0655] but should promote and **resolutely** guard them, whether

Resolutions (1)
AG : 2 3 :006(052) [0061] by means of human **resolutions** or vows without a special

Resolve (2), Resolved (5)
PR : PR :025(014) [0023] In addition, we have **resolved** and purpose to live in
S1 : PR :002(288) [0455] as their confession, and **resolved** that these articles should
EP : 0 0 :000(463) [0775] to this Confession, **Resolved** and Reconciled under the
EP : 0 4 :005(476) [0797] the ground up and to **resolve** it, this is our doctrine, faith,
SD : 0 0 :000(501) [0845] Theologians for a Time, **Resolved** and Settled According
SD : PR :007(505) [0853] princes, and estates were **resolved** by God's grace to
SD : 1 1 :011(618) [1067] faith, and the good **resolve** to lead a godly life.

Resort (2), Resorted (2)
S3 : 0 3 :015(305) [0483] following loophole was **resorted** to, namely, that when a
S3 : 0 3 :021(306) [0485] Here the expedient was **resorted** to of imposing small
S3 : 0 6 :002(311) [0493] We need not **resort** to the specious learning of the
LC : 0 1 :301(405) [0667] real estate, etc., they **resort** to whatever arguments have

Respect (28), Respectable (1), Respectful (3), Respectfully (1), Respective (4), Respects (3)
PR : PR :001(003) [0007] will, as well as our most **respectful**, humble, and willing
PR : PR :021(011) [0019] together with their **respective** properties, are mixed
AG : 2 6 :042(070) [0075] such liberty with **respect** to outward ceremonies, for in
AG : 0 0 :007(096) [0095] that it is lacking in some **respect**, we are ready to present
AL : 2 6 :045(070) [0075] enact binding laws with **respect** to holy days but to preach
AP : 1 5 :043(221) [0327] and is heard, the cross, **respect** for rulers and for all civil
AP : 2 3 :071(249) [0383] but they have greater **respect** for the Word of God than
S3 : 1 3 :002(315) [0499] The whole man, in **respect** both of his person and of his
SC : PR :017(340) [0537] part, pointing out their **respective** obligations, benefits,
SC : PR :020(340) [0537] governing authorities sin in this **respect** is beyond telling.
SC : 0 9 :001(354) [0561] *they may be admonished to do their **respective** duties*
SC : 0 9 :002(354) [0561] his children submissive and **respectful** in every way.
SC : 0 9 :003(354) [0561] beseech you, brethren, to **respect** those who labor among
SC : 0 9 :005(355) [0561] to whom revenue is due, **respect** to whom respect is due,
SC : 0 9 :005(355) [0561] is due, respect to whom **respect** is due, honor to whom
SC : 0 9 :005(355) [0561] life, godly and **respectful** in every way" (I Tim. 2:1-2).
LC : PR :001(358) [0567] are very negligent in this **respect** and despise both their
LC : 0 1 :105(379) [0611] With **respect** to brothers, sisters, and neighbors in general
LC : 0 1 :107(379) [0611] and of body, that we **respect** them very highly and that
LC : 0 1 :108(380) [0611] In other **respects**, indeed, we are all equal in the sight of
LC : 0 1 :110(380) [0611] you are to behave **respectfully** toward them, and not
LC : 0 1 :176(389) [0631] you are negligent in this **respect** and fail to bring up your
LC : 0 1 :176(389) [0631] matter how devout and holy you may be in other **respects**.
LC : 0 1 :177(389) [0631] no longer any civil order, peace, or **respect** for authority.
LC : 0 1 :218(394) [0643] up to decency and **respect** for authority and, when they
LC : 0 1 :231(396) [0647] so as to make the others look **respectable** and honorable.
LC : 0 1 :256(399) [0653] man maintain his self-**respect** before his wife, children,
LC : 0 1 :305(406) [0667] was also the case in ancient times with **respect** to wives.
LC : 0 1 :327(409) [0675] For you dare not **respect** or fear father or mother
LC : 0 3 :011(421) [0699] I say, we should **respect** this commandment and turn to
LC : 0 3 :016(422) [0701] admit that he is holier in **respect** to his person, but not on
LC : 0 5 :059(453) [0767] even though in other **respects** they are weak and frail.
EP : 0 1 :005(466) [0781] be made like his brethren in every **respect**," sin excepted.
SD : 0 1 :043(515) [0873] sin, so that in every **respect** he was made like us, his
SD : 0 2 :024(526) [0891] In this **respect** he is worse than a block because he is
SD : 0 2 :059(532) [0905] above, and in this **respect** is much worse than a stone or
SD : 0 6 :023(567) [0969] In this **respect** Christians are not under the law but under
SD : 0 7 :003(569) [0973] here on earth but only in **respect** to faith (that is, our
SD : 0 8 :036(598) [1027] ascribed not only to the **respective** nature as something
SD : 0 8 :050(600) [1031] to which it is in every **respect** made like its brethren, and

Resplendent (1)
SD : 0 3 :033(545) [0927] him with many **resplendent** good works (Rom. 4:3;

Respond (2), Responded (1), Response (2), Responses (1)
AG : 0 1 :002(056) [0065] in addition to the Latin **responses** for the instruction and
AP : 2 8 :021(284) [0449] We give the same **response** to the passage (Matt. 23:3),
AP : 2 8 :023(284) [0451] We shall **respond** to this in brief.

Continued ▶

S 2 : 0 4 :016(301) [0475] at Augsburg, where we **responded** to a gracious summons
T R : 0 0 :023(324) [0511] Nevertheless, we shall **respond** briefly by way of
L C : 0 2 :010(412) [0681] is nothing else than a **response** and confession of

Responsibility (10), Responsibilities (1), Responsible (3)
P R : P R :022(012) [0019] Consequently the **responsibility** devolves upon the
P R : P R :022(012) [0021] no share of the **responsibility** for this bloodshed.
A G : 2 4 :012(057) [0065] of the terrible **responsibility** which should properly
A P : 2 1 :044(236) [0357] It is your special **responsibility** before God to maintain
A P : 2 4 :081(264) [0411] of the gymnasium, and similar public **responsibilities**.
A P : 2 7 :007(269) [0421] sometimes they are **responsible** for murdering good men.
L C : 0 1 :141(384) [0621] his authority and **responsibility** to others appointed for
L C : 0 1 :142(384) [0621] because in their **responsibility** they act in the capacity of
L C : 0 1 :168(388) [0629] in this office and **responsibility**; nor does he assign them
L C : 0 1 :249(398) [0651] Our **responsibility** is only to instruct and reprove by
L C : 0 1 :249(398) [0651] lawlessness is the **responsibility** of princes and
L C : 0 4 :081(446) [0751] Indeed, St. Jerome is **responsible** for this view, for he
L C : 0 5 :035(450) [0761] but it is also your **responsibility** to take it and confidently
E P : 1 1 :004(495) [0833] of man's perdition; for this man himself is **responsible**.

Rest (55), Resting (1), Rests (9)
A G : 1 2 :005(035) [0049] this faith will comfort the heart and again set it at **rest**.
A G : 2 0 :015(043) [0055] conscience cannot come to **rest** and peace through works,
A G : 2 8 :063(092) [0093] and amount of work that may be done on the day of **rest**.
A L : 2 4 :037(060) [0067] celebrated Mass and the **rest** of the presbyters and
A L : 2 7 :031(076) [0079] judgment to make a decision involving the **rest** of his life.
A P : 0 4 :009(108) [0123] long as a man's mind is at **rest** and he does not feel God's
A P : 0 4 :051(114) [0135] The **rest** must be integrated with this article, namely, that
A P : 0 4 :084(119) [0145] that the promise may **rest** on grace and be guaranteed,"
A P : 0 4 :208(135) [0177] can put the conscience at **rest**, they kept thinking up new
A P : 0 4 :284(150) [0201] its agreement with the **rest** of the Scripture; for if hearts
A P : 0 4 :301(153) [0205] will the conscience be at **rest**, therefore, and when will it
A P : 0 4 :346(160) [0217] a sure hope, for it **rests** on the Word and commandment
A P : 0 4 :346(160) [0217] If our hope were to **rest** on works, then it would really be
A P : 0 7 :027(173) [0237] reason and regard the **rest** as mythology, like the
A P : 1 2 :044(187) [0263] who labor and are heavy-laden, and I will give you **rest**."
A P : 1 2 :081(194) [0275] that the promise may **rest** on grace and be guaranteed";
A P : 1 2 :110(198) [0285] for they will never be at **rest** if they suppose that they
A P : 1 2 :118(199) [0287] power of the keys, and the **rest** must be bought off by
A P : 1 2 :130(202) [0291] hear teachers capable of setting their consciences at **rest**.
A P : 2 1 :003(229) [0343] Nor do the **rest** of the ancient Fathers before Gregory
A P : 2 1 :016(231) [0347] As to the **rest** even the uninitiated can pass judgment.
A P : 2 3 :019(242) [0369] God wants the **rest** to use the universal law of nature
A P : 2 4 :025(253) [0391] The **rest** are eucharistic sacrifices, called "sacrifices of
A P : 2 4 :052(259) [0403] of the Mass and the **rest** of the papal order are nothing
A P : 2 4 :086(265) [0413] to be consecrated, the **rest** was distributed to the poor.
S 1 : P R :009(290) [0457] As for the **rest**, wretchedness and woe will be their lot
S 2 : 0 1 :005(292) [0463] On this article **rests** all that we teach and practice against
S 3 : 0 3 :020(306) [0485] consolation was made to **rest** on his enumeration of sins
T R : 0 0 :009(321) [0505] he granted to none a prerogative or lordship over the **rest**.
T R : 0 0 :030(325) [0513] Peter holds in common with the **rest** of the apostles.
T R : 0 0 :056(330) [0521] ought to censure the **rest** of the pope's errors, so they
T R : 0 0 :062(330) [0523] man was chosen over the **rest** to prevent schism, lest
T R : 0 0 :073(332) [0525] that distinguishes bishops from the **rest** of the presbyters.
L C : 0 1 :079(375) [0603] which properly means to **rest**, that is, to cease from
L C : 0 1 :080(375) [0603] day and appointed it for **rest** and he commanded it to be
L C : 0 1 :080(375) [0603] from hard work and to **rest**, so that both man and beast
L C : 0 1 :081(376) [0603] meant that we should sanctify the holy day or day of **rest**.
L C : 0 1 :083(376) [0603] long — should retire for a day to **rest** and be refreshed.
L C : 0 1 :086(376) [0605] However, the observance of **rest** should not be so narrow
L C : 0 1 :090(377) [0607] can spend a day in **rest** and idleness, too, and so can the
L C : 0 1 :094(378) [0607] consist not of the **resting** but of the sanctifying, so that
L C : 0 1 :103(379) [0611] on holy days or days of **rest** we should diligently devote
L C : 0 1 :310(407) [0669] remains, like all the **rest**, one that constantly accuses us
L C : 0 3 :064(429) [0715] this end he strives without **rest** day and night, using all
L C : 0 5 :019(449) [0757] For upon these words **rest** our whole argument,
L C : 0 5 :063(454) [0767] in such a way that it may **rest** and rely firmly upon itself;
E P : 0 6 :007(481) [0807] as obedience is concerned, **rests** exclusively with man, for
S D : 0 3 :033(545) [0927] was pleasing and acceptable to him to eternal life, **rest**?
S D : 0 3 :055(549) [0935] and that our righteousness **rests** solely and alone on the
S D : 0 3 :055(549) [0935] Our righteousness **rests** neither upon his divine nature
S D : 0 4 :037(557) [0949] article of justification and **rests** his righteousness or his
S D : 0 7 :026(573) [0981] it well, for on these words **rest** our whole argument,
S D : 0 7 :032(574) [0983] It does not **rest** on man's faith or unbelief but on the
S D : 0 7 :042(576) [0985] position set forth above **rests** on a unique, firm,
S D : 0 7 :062(581) [0995] is presented — and that we **rest** indomitably, with certain
S D : 0 7 :070(582) [0997] are heavy laden, and I will give you **rest**" (Matt. 11:28).
S D : 0 7 :093(586) [1005] "My grounds, on which I **rest** in this matter, are as
S D : 0 8 :072(605) [1041] (Isa. 11:2; 61:1) does not **rest** upon Christ the Lord
S D : 0 9 :001(610) [1051] Hence we let matters **rest** on the simple statement of our
S D : 1 1 :028(620) [1071] are heavy-laden, and I will give you **rest**" (Matt. 11:28).
S D : 1 1 :065(627) [1085] are heavy-laden, and I will give you **rest**" (Matt. 11:28).
S D : 1 1 :075(628) [1087] to eternal life does not **rest** on our piety or virtue but
S D : 1 1 :090(631) [1093] that their salvation does not **rest** in their own hands.
S D : 1 1 :090(631) [1093] Their salvation **rests** in the gracious election of God,
S D : 1 2 :010(634) [1097] But this piety **rests** for the greater part on their own

Restatement (2)
E P : 0 0 :000(463) [0775] Correct, and Final **Restatement** and Explanation of a
S D : 0 0 :000(501) [0845] Correct, and Definitive **Restatement** and Exposition of a

Restitution (2)
A P : 1 2 :169(209) [0305] Gregory says about **restitution** that penitence is false if it
A P : 1 2 :169(209) [0305] Civil **restitution** is necessary, as it is written (Eph. 4:28),

Restless (2)
P R : P R :024(013) [0021] be left free and open to **restless**, contentious individuals,
L C : 0 3 :089(432) [0723] our conscience becomes **restless**; it fears God's wrath and

Restoration (1), Restore (10), Restored (6), Restoring (3)
A G : P R :010(025) [0041] practical and equitable ways as may **restore** unity.
A G : 2 7 :002(071) [0077] the attempt was made to **restore** discipline by means of
A G : 2 8 :071(093) [0093] that the bishops should **restore** peace and unity at the
A L : 2 0 :022(044) [0055] need to treat of and to **restore** this teaching concerning
A L : 2 3 :002(051) [0061] far weightier reasons why this right should be **restored**.
A L : 2 7 :002(071) [0077] for the purpose of **restoring** discipline, as in a carefully
A L : 2 8 :071(093) [0093] not ask that the bishops **restore** concord at the expense of
A P : P R :019(099) [0103] churches and to **restore** them to a godly and abiding
A P : 1 2 :048(188) [0265] the earlier sentence and **restoring** peace and life to the
A P : 1 2 :060(190) [0269] overcoming them and **restoring** peace to the conscience.
S 2 : 0 3 :001(297) [0471] decent women should be **restored** to such purposes in
T R : 0 0 :076(333) [0527] not obeying, it is right to **restore** this jurisdiction to godly
S C : P R :003(338) [0533] the Gospel has been **restored** they have mastered the fine
L C : 0 1 :273(401) [0659] good name are easily taken away, but not easily **restored**.
L C : 0 2 :030(414) [0685] us, made us free, and **restored** us to the Father's favor and
L C : 0 3 :089(432) [0723] petition for the comfort that will **restore** our conscience.
L C : 0 6 :015(459) [0000] my sin and desire comfort and **restoration** for my soul.
E P : 0 8 :039(491) [0827] heaven and on earth was **restored** or again returned to
S D : 0 5 :023(562) [0959] David's son, who should **restore** the kingdom of Israel
S D : 1 0 :002(611) [1053] insistent demand, **restore** once more certain abrogated

Restrain (7), Restrained (5), Restraining (2), Restrains (1), Restraint (3), Restraints (1)
A P : 0 4 :022(110) [0127] this civil discipline to **restrain** the unspiritual, and to
A P : 0 4 :190(133) [0175] battles by which Christ **restrained** the devil and drove him
A P : 1 2 :168(209) [0305] that is, mortifying and **restraining** the flesh, not to pay
A P : 1 2 :174(210) [0307] generosity to the needy, **restraint** and chastisement of the
A P : 1 5 :024(218) [0321] their purpose is to **restrain** the flesh, reason imagines that
A P : 1 5 :047(221) [0327] that justify but as **restraints** on our flesh, lest we be
A P : 2 1 :043(235) [0357] will arise whom our opponents will be unable to **restrain**.
A P : 2 3 :048(246) [0377] that discipline and **restraint** of the body are necessary.
S 3 : 0 2 :001(303) [0479] by God first of all to **restrain** sins by threats and fear of
S 3 : 0 2 :002(303) [0479] so far as they are not **restrained** by punishment, they act
S 3 : 0 3 :044(310) [0491] Holy Spirit represses and **restrains** it so that it does not
T R : 0 0 :056(329) [0521] on the kings to **restrain** the license of the pontiffs and see
L C : 0 1 :069(374) [0599] of warning and threat, **restraint** and punishment, children
L C : 0 1 :232(396) [0647] order that they may be **restrained** in their wantonness and
L C : 0 1 :249(398) [0651] To **restrain** open lawlessness is the responsibility of
L C : 0 1 :280(403) [0661] the right procedure for **restraining** and reforming a
L C : 0 3 :081(431) [0721] prayer to God did not **restrain** him, surely we would not
L C : 0 4 :071(445) [0749] of his nature if he is not **restrained** and suppressed by the
S D : 0 8 :065(604) [1039] was concealed and **restrained**, but now, since the form of

Restricted (2)
L C : 0 1 :085(376) [0605] This, I say, is not **restricted** to a particular time, as it was
L C : 0 1 :313(407) [0671] unusual and pompous, **restricted** to special times, places,

Result (19), Resultant (2), Resulted (9), Resulting (5), Results (7)
A G : P R :012(026) [0041] between us, and if no **results** are attained, nevertheless we
A G : 2 3 :006(052) [0061] What good has **resulted**?
A G : 2 3 :006(052) [0061] honorable sort of conduct has **resulted** in many cases?
A G : 2 6 :003(064) [0071] Many harmful errors in the church have **resulted** from
A G : 2 7 :008(072) [0077] what scandals and burdened consciences **resulted**.
A G : 2 8 :002(081) [0083] and uprisings have **resulted** because the bishops, under
A G : 2 8 :041(087) [0089] The **result** was that countless regulations came into being
A L : 2 6 :003(064) [0071] traditions much harm has **resulted** in the church.
A L : 2 7 :008(072) [0077] saw what unfortunately **resulted** from this arrangement,
A L : 2 8 :002(081) [0083] wars and tumults have **resulted**, while the pontiffs, relying
A L : 2 8 :037(086) [0089] It is also evident that as a **result** of this notion traditions
A P : 0 4 :116(123) [0155] God" rather than love, which is the effect **resulting** from it
A P : 0 4 :137(126) [0159] The **results** show that hypocrites who try to keep the law
A P : 1 5 :025(218) [0321] As a **result**, the commandments of God are obscured; for
A P : 1 5 :041(220) [0325] youth publicly, a custom that produces very good **results**.
A P : 1 5 :047(221) [0327] and idle with the **result** that we indulge and pamper the
A P : 2 3 :063(248) [0381] author is evident in the **results**, the many unnatural lusts
S 3 : 0 1 :011(303) [0479] similar notions have **resulted** from misunderstanding and
L C : 0 1 :056(372) [0597] a single lie a double one **results** — indeed, manifold lies.
L C : 0 1 :217(394) [0643] other shameful vices **resulting** from contempt of married
L C : 0 1 :224(395) [0643] neighbor in any sort of dealing that **results** in loss to him.
L C : 0 3 :031(424) [0707] accomplished such great **results** in the past, parrying the
L C : 0 3 :044(425) [0709] word and deed with the **result** that on his account the
L C : 0 3 :044(426) [0709] heavenly children with the **result** that he must hear us
E P : 0 3 :015(475) [0795] Holy Spirit has infused and the works **resulting** therefrom
E P : 0 3 :017(475) [0795] and gives no evidence of **resulting** love, but continues to
E P : 0 5 :008(479) [0803] covers their eyes, as a **result** they fail to learn the true
E P : 0 8 :009(488) [0819] personal union and the **resultant** exalted and ineffable
E P : 1 2 :001(498) [0839] But lest as a **result** of our silence these errors be attributed
S D : 0 1 :001(508) [0859] are wholly corrupt as a **result** of the fall of Adam," so
S D : 0 1 :011(510) [0863] As a **result**, since the Fall man inherits an inborn wicked
S D : 0 1 :017(511) [0865] sin is only an obligation **resulting** from someone else's
S D : 0 2 :046(530) [0899] As a **result** of their statements many people have become
S D : 0 2 :067(534) [0907] As a **result**, they not only hear the Word of God but also
S D : 0 2 :077(536) [0911] As a **result**, his free will is too weak to make a beginning
S D : 0 4 :029(555) [0947] were raised again as a **result** of the Interim, flowed forth
S D : 0 7 :006(570) [0973] As a **result** many important people were deceived by the
S D : 0 8 :074(606) [1041] The **result** is not that he knows only certain things and
S D : 0 8 :076(606) [1043] personal union and the **resultant** communion that the
S D : 1 0 :005(611) [1055] place or will allegedly **result** little by little from these
S D : 1 1 :010(618) [1067] As a **result** they trouble themselves with burdensome
S D : 1 2 :007(633) [1097] Let no one as a **result** of our silence attribute to us the

Resume (1)
L C : 0 4 :079(446) [0751] approach to Baptism, to **resume** and practice what had

Resurrection (35)
A G : 1 7 :005(039) [0051] teach that, before the **resurrection** of the dead, saints and
A G : 2 0 :023(044) [0055] suffering and his **resurrection** from the dead, but we mean
A L : 1 7 :005(038) [0051] effect that before the **resurrection** of the dead the godly
A P : 0 4 :370(164) [0221] will come forth to the **resurrection** of life"; Matt. 25:35, "I
A P : 2 7 :013(271) [0423] death is a witness, thy **resurrection** is a witness, the Holy
S C : 0 2 :005(345) [0545] *forgiveness of sins, the* **resurrection** *of the body, and the*
L C : S P :013(363) [0577] forgiveness of sins, the **resurrection** of the body, and the
L C : 0 2 :032(415) [0687] as the birth, passion, **resurrection**, and ascension of
L C : 0 2 :034(415) [0687] *forgiveness of sins, the* **resurrection** *of the body, and the*
L C : 0 2 :037(415) [0687] his birth, death, and **resurrection**, etc., so the Holy Spirit
L C : 0 2 :037(415) [0687] forgiveness of sins, the **resurrection** of the body, and the
L C : 0 2 :038(415) [0689] for us by his sufferings, death, and **resurrection**, etc.

Continued ▶

LC : 0 2 :041(416) [0689] forgiveness of sins, the **resurrection** of the body, and the
LC : 0 2 :060(418) [0695] The term "**resurrection** of the flesh," however, is not well
LC : 0 2 :060(418) [0695] Idiomatically we would say "**resurrection** of the body."
LC : 0 4 :065(445) [0749] the old Adam and the **resurrection** of the new man, both
EP : 0 1 :003(466) [0779] sanctification, and the **resurrection** of our flesh.
EP : 0 1 :006(467) [0781] On the contrary, in the **resurrection** it will be utterly
EP : 0 1 :010(467) [0781] will take place wholly by way of death in the **resurrection**.
EP : 0 2 :001(469) [0785] after regeneration, (4) after the **resurrection** of the flesh.
EP : 0 8 :016(489) [0821] Finally, after his **resurrection** he laid aside completely the
EP : 0 8 :039(491) [0827] to mean that in the **resurrection** and his ascension all
SD : PR :007(502) [0849] some denied the **resurrection** of the dead (I Cor. 15:12)
SD : 0 1 :046(516) [0873] the doctrine of the **resurrection** Scripture testifies that
SD : 0 2 :087(538) [0913] is nothing else but a **resurrection** of the will from
SD : 0 2 :087(538) [0915] God, just as the bodily **resurrection** of the flesh is to be
SD : 0 3 :009(541) [0919] the death, and the **resurrection** of Christ, our Lord,
SD : 0 3 :014(541) [0919] the passion, and the **resurrection** of Christ when he
SD : 0 5 :004(559) [0953] when Christ after his **resurrection** commands his apostles
SD : 0 6 :024(568) [0971] and man is completely renewed in the **resurrection**.
SD : 0 7 :099(586) [1005] so, as he did after his **resurrection** and as he will on the
SD : 0 8 :013(593) [1019] only after his **resurrection** from the dead and his
SD : 0 8 :025(596) [1023] so not only after his **resurrection**, and ascension but also
SD : 0 8 :026(596) [1023] nature has, after the **resurrection** from the dead, its
SD : 0 8 :085(608) [1047] concealed it until my **resurrection** and ascension, when it

Retain (35), Retained (16), Retaining (3), Retains (15)
AG : 1 1 :001(034) [0047] absolution should be **retained** and not allowed to fall into
AG : 2 5 :001(061) [0069] The custom has been **retained** among us of not
AG : 2 5 :013(063) [0071] that confession is to be **retained** for the sake of absolution
AG : 2 6 :040(069) [0075] We on our part also **retain** many ceremonies and
AG : 2 8 :005(081) [0085] Gospel, to forgive and **retain** sins, and to administer and
AG : 2 8 :006(082) [0085] they are forgiven; if you **retain** the sins of any, they are
AG : 2 8 :006(082) [0085] retain the sins of any, they are **retained**" (John 20:21-23).
AG : 2 8 :069(093) [0093] The bishops might easily **retain** the obedience of men if
AL : 1 1 :001(034) [0047] private absolution should be **retained** in the churches.
AL : 2 4 :001(056) [0065] Actually, the Mass is **retained** among us and is celebrated
AL : 2 4 :002(056) [0065] ceremonies are also **retained**, except that German hymns
AL : 2 4 :040(061) [0069] public ceremonies are for the most part **retained**.
AL : 2 5 :013(063) [0071] confession is **retained** among us on account of the great
AL : 2 8 :005(081) [0085] the Gospel, to remit and **retain** sins, and to administer the
AL : 2 8 :006(082) [0085] they are forgiven; if you **retain** the sins of any, they are
AL : 2 8 :006(082) [0085] forgiven; if you retain the sins of any, they are **retained**."
AL : 2 8 :069(093) [0093] The bishops might easily **retain** the lawful obedience of
AP : 0 4 :120(124) [0155] freely for Christ's sake) must be **retained** in the church.
AP : 0 4 :348(160) [0217] according to the flesh can **retain** neither faith nor
AP : 0 7 :020(171) [0233] (I Tim. 3:15), for it **retains** the pure Gospel and what
AP : 1 1 :001(180) [0247] the eleventh article on **retaining** absolution in the church.
AP : 1 2 :138(203) [0295] penalties but to **retaining** the sins of the unconverted.
AP : 1 8 :004(225) [0335] senses can grasp, it also **retains** a choice in these things,
AP : 2 3 :016(241) [0369] Thus anyone who is aflame **retains** the right to marry.
S 2 : 0 2 :029(297) [0471] in order that we may **retain** the holy sacrament in its
S 3 : 0 3 :001(303) [0479] function of the law is **retained** and taught by the New
S 3 : 0 6 :005(311) [0493] natural substance and **retain** only the appearance and
TR : 0 0 :066(331) [0523] ordination, the churches **retain** the right to ordain for
TR : 0 0 :067(331) [0523] for the church to **retain** the right of calling, electing, and
TR : 0 0 :072(332) [0525] evident that the church **retains** the right of electing and
TR : 0 0 :073(332) [0525] almost the only things they have **retained** for themselves.
SC : PR :010(339) [0535] these things after you and **retain** them in their memory.
LC : SP :024(364) [0579] that they will learn and **retain** this teaching from sermons
LC : 0 1 :098(378) [0609] hearing the Word but also about learning and **retaining** it.
LC : 0 1 :203(392) [0639] to aid and assist him so that he may **retain** his honor.
LC : 0 1 :307(406) [0669] of the world you might honorably **retain** the property.
LC : 0 1 :309(406) [0669] commandments therefore **retain** their general application.
LC : 0 3 :074(430) [0719] in abundance, we cannot **retain** any of them or enjoy them
LC : 0 3 :100(433) [0725] and effort required to **retain** and persevere in all the gifts
LC : 0 4 :060(444) [0747] always remains valid and **retains** its integrity, even if only
LC : 0 5 :005(447) [0755] Prayer, and the Creed **retain** their nature and value even
LC : 0 5 :060(453) [0767] progress that he does not **retain** many common
EP : 0 1 :014(468) [0783] man's nature has **retained** unimpaired its powers for good
EP : 0 1 :024(469) [0785] words can profitably be **retained** in the discussion of
EP : 0 3 :009(474) [0793] truly regenerated persons **retain** much weakness and
EP : 0 4 :019(477) [0801] holy ones and the elect **retain** the Holy Spirit even though
EP : 0 7 :004(482) [0809] terminology they really **retain** the former crass opinion
EP : 0 7 :019(484) [0813] he may be, as long as he **retains** a living faith, will receive
EP : 0 8 :006(487) [0819] the other, but that each **retains** its essential properties and
SD : 0 1 :021(512) [0865] human nature has and **retains** its goodness and powers
SD : 0 4 :002(551) [0939] and in order to **retain** for believers the firm and certain
SD : 0 4 :015(553) [0943] a person could have and **retain** true faith, righteousness,
SD : 0 4 :020(554) [0945] and nonetheless still **retain** faith and God's mercy and his
SD : 0 4 :031(556) [0947] he can nevertheless **retain** faith, the grace of God,
SD : 0 4 :033(556) [0949] grace through Christ and which you **retain** through faith!
SD : 0 4 :034(556) [0949] not only receive but also **retain** righteousness and
SD : 0 5 :014(560) [0957] "The New Testament **retains** and performs the office of
SD : 0 7 :075(583) [0999] first Supper but they still **retain** their validity and
SD : 0 7 :085(584) [1003] be profitably urged and **retained** in the church of God.
SD : 0 7 :125(591) [1015] believers who have and **retain** a true, genuine, living
SD : 0 8 :008(593) [1017] unabolished, so that each **retains** its natural properties
SD : 0 8 :012(593) [1019] not only possesses and **retains** its natural, essential
SD : 0 8 :019(595) [1021] the contrary, each nature **retains** its essence and
SD : 0 8 :026(596) [1023] human nature, which he **retains** throughout eternity) and
SD : 0 8 :032(597) [1025] is true that each nature **retains** its essential properties and
SD : 0 8 :048(600) [1031] as has been indicated above, they have and **retain**)?
SD : 0 8 :060(602) [1035] the other, and since each **retains** its natural and essential
SD : 0 9 :003(610) [1053] Then we shall **retain** the heart of this article and derive
SD : 1 1 :038(622) [1075] states in Article XI, we **retain** individual absolution and

Retaliation (1)
LC : 0 1 :151(386) [0625] we seek and deserve, then, is paid back to us in **retaliation**.

Retinue (1)
LC : 0 1 :230(396) [0645] See at Rome, and all its **retinue**, which has plundered and

Retire (2)
SC : 0 7 :004(353) [0559] In the evening, when you **retire**, make the sign of the
LC : 0 1 :083(376) [0603] whole week long — should **retire** for a day to rest and be

Retort (1)
LC : 0 4 :044(442) [0743] oppress us, and we must **retort**, "But I am baptized!

Retribution (1)
LC : 0 1 :236(397) [0647] — there will come a day of reckoning and **retribution**:

Return (27), Returned (2), Returning (1), Returns (2)
AG : 0 3 :006(030) [0045] same Lord Christ will **return** openly to judge the living
AG : 1 7 :000(038) [0051] XVII. [The **Return** of Christ to Judgment]
AG : 1 7 :001(038) [0051] Lord Jesus Christ will **return** on the last day for
AL : 1 2 :002(034) [0049] to impart absolution to those who **return** to repentance.
AL : 1 2 :009(035) [0049] after Baptism although they **returned** to repentance.
AL : 1 7 :000(038) [0051] XVII. [The **Return** of Christ for Judgment]
AP : 0 4 :110(123) [0153] with the abolition of the promise and a **return** to the law?
AP : 0 4 :221(137) [0181] But let us **return** to Paul.
AP : 0 4 :268(147) [0197] you" (Jer. 15:19); "**Return** to me and I will return to you"
AP : 0 4 :268(147) [0197] "Return to me and I will **return** to you" (Zech. 1:3); "Call
AP : 1 2 :131(202) [0291] Let us **return** to the proposition.
AP : 1 3 :011(212) [0311] from my mouth shall not **return** to me empty, but it shall
AP : 1 7 :000(224) [0335] [Article XVII. Christ's **Return** to Judgment]
S 1 : PR :010(290) [0457] But let us **return** to the subject.
S 2 : 0 2 :028(297) [0471] them out of love when there is no expectation of **return**.
S 3 : 0 4 :000(310) [0491] We shall now **return** to the Gospel, which offers council
LC : 0 1 :073(374) [0601] of saying grace and **returning** thanks at meals and saying
LC : 0 1 :329(410) [0677] again, to it they all **return** and upon it they depend, so
LC : 0 2 :024(413) [0683] receive from God and about what we owe him in **return**.
LC : 0 3 :011(421) [0701] down for their sin did not **return** to him and assuage his
LC : 0 4 :079(446) [0751] is nothing else than a **return** and approach to Baptism, to
LC : 0 4 :086(446) [0753] anybody falls away from his Baptism let him **return** to it.
LC : 0 4 :086(446) [0753] from us or forbid us to **return** to him even though we sin,
EP : 0 8 :039(491) [0827] was restored or again **returned** to Christ according to the
SD : 0 1 :037(514) [0871] we read, "And the dust **returns** to the earth as it was, and
SD : 0 1 :037(514) [0871] as it was, and the spirit **returns** to God who gave it"
SD : 0 7 :076(583) [0999] this day, and until his **return** it brings about that his true
SD : 1 0 :005(611) [1053] one body, or that a **return** to the papacy and an apostasy
SD : 1 1 :054(625) [1081] after falling away will **return** and who will become
SD : 1 1 :075(628) [1087] If they **return** to him in true repentance through a right
SD : 1 1 :075(628) [1087] his Word and cordially **return** to him, as it is written, "If a
SD : 1 1 :075(628) [1087] with many lovers; yet **return** again to me, says the Lord"

Reutlingen (3)
PR : PR :027(015) [0027] The Council of the City of **Reutlingen**
AG : 0 0 :007(096) [0095] Mayor and council or **Reutlingen**
AL : 0 0 :017(096) [0095] Senate of **Reutlingen**

Reveal (5), Revealed (52), Revealing (1), Reveals (11)
AG : 2 6 :030(068) [0075] discipline, their writings **reveal** something quite different.
AP : 0 4 :200(134) [0175] and the wrath of God is **revealed**, threatening all the
AP : 0 4 :230(139) [0183] of the Gospel, which **reveals** another righteousness,
AP : 0 4 :291(152) [0203] Christ was not promised, **revealed**, born, crucified, and
AP : 0 4 :297(153) [0205] Christ was not promised, **revealed**, born, crucified, and
AP : 0 4 :386(166) [0225] we are "guarded for a salvation ready to be **revealed**."
AP : 0 7 :017(171) [0233] Christ has not yet been **revealed**, they are mingled with
AP : 0 7 :018(171) [0233] of Christ, whether it be **revealed** or hidden under the
AP : 1 2 :045(188) [0263] of sins has been granted us; this is **revealed** in the Gospel.
AP : 1 2 :053(189) [0265] One part is the law, which **reveals**, denounces, and
AP : 1 2 :053(189) [0265] finally proclaimed and **revealed** by Christ among the
AP : 1 2 :080(194) [0275] was given and Christ **revealed** to us precisely because we
AP : 1 2 :150(206) [0299] when amid the terrors of contrition he **reveals** his wrath.
AP : 2 1 :004(229) [0343] examples of his mercy, **revealing** his will to save men, and
AP : 2 3 :054(246) [0379] of Sodom and Gomorrah **reveal** God's wrath at human
AP : 2 3 :063(247) [0381] They say, first, that it was **revealed** by God.
AP : 2 7 :013(271) [0423] of the Father hast **revealed** to the world — then the charge
AP : 2 7 :014(271) [0423] which was divinely **revealed**, did not merit the forgiveness
S 3 : 0 3 :001(303) [0479] "The wrath of God is **revealed** from heaven against all
S 3 : 0 3 :041(309) [0491] a teaching from heaven, **revealed** in the Gospel, and yet it
S 3 : 0 8 :008(313) [0495] However, St. Peter had to **reveal** to him that the
TR : 0 0 :029(325) [0513] declares: "The Father **revealed** to Peter that he should
LC : 0 1 :063(373) [0599] properly, for it has been **revealed** and given to us precisely
LC : 0 2 :042(416) [0689] The Holy Spirit **reveals** and preaches that Word, and by
LC : 0 2 :044(416) [0689] no Holy Spirit present to **reveal** this truth and have it
LC : 0 2 :064(419) [0695] articles God himself has **revealed** and opened to us the
LC : 0 2 :065(419) [0695] of Christ, had it not been **revealed** by the Holy Spirit.
LC : 0 4 :006(437) [0733] man's imagination but **revealed** and given by God
EP : 0 5 :008(479) [0803] Then "God's wrath is **revealed** from heaven" over all
EP : 0 7 :042(486) [0817] other way than by faith and as it is **revealed** in the Word.
EP : 0 9 :004(492) [0827] where there will be **revealed** to us not only this point, but
EP : 1 1 :003(494) [0833] is a God in heaven who **reveals** mysteries, and he has
EP : 1 1 :006(495) [0833] is to be looked for in his Word, where he has **revealed** it.
EP : 1 1 :011(495) [0835] himself with the **revealed** will of God and observes the
EP : 1 1 :013(496) [0835] God only in so far as it is **revealed** in the Word of God,
EP : 1 1 :013(496) [0835] Gospel, Christ opens and **reveals** this book for us, as it is
EP : 1 1 :014(496) [0835] are we to abide by the **revealed** Word which cannot and
SD : 0 2 :026(526) [0891] to whom the Son chooses to **reveal** him" (Matt. 11:27).
SD : 0 2 :027(527) [0891] preaching of the truth **reveals** his will; but to assent to
SD : 0 3 :057(549) [0935] and immutable righteousness of God **revealed** in the law.
SD : 0 3 :057(549) [0935] avails before God and is **revealed** in the Gospel, upon
SD : 0 5 :010(560) [0955] Rom. 7:6, 14); thus he **reveals** his wrath from heaven over
SD : 0 5 :014(560) [0957] office of the law, which **reveals** sin and God's wrath, but
SD : 0 5 :017(561) [0957] a divine doctrine which **reveals** the righteousness and
SD : 0 8 :053(601) [1033] In his Word he has **revealed** to us as much as we need to
SD : 0 8 :085(608) [1047] when it was to have been **revealed** and demonstrated, as
SD : 1 1 :013(619) [1067] "book of life" as it is **revealed** to us through the Word.
SD : 1 1 :026(620) [1071] Instead we must heed the **revealed** will of God.
SD : 1 1 :026(620) [1071] For he has **revealed** and "made known to us the mystery
SD : 1 1 :027(620) [1071] This is **revealed** to us, however, as Paul says, "Those
SD : 1 1 :029(621) [1073] know certainly that God **reveals** his will in this way, and
SD : 1 1 :033(621) [1073] ourselves with this **revealed** will of God, follow it, and be
SD : 1 1 :043(623) [1077] Thus far God has **revealed** the mystery of foreknowledge
SD : 1 1 :052(625) [1081] what God has expressly **revealed** in his Word and what he
SD : 1 1 :052(625) [1081] revealed in his Word and what he has not **revealed**.
SD : 1 1 :052(625) [1081] matters which have been **revealed** in Christ and of which

Continued ▶

SD : 1 1 :052(625) [1081] and which he has not **revealed** but has kept reserved
SD : 1 1 :052(625) [1081] but we are to adhere exclusively to the **revealed** Word.
SD : 1 1 :053(625) [1081] of the question which God has **revealed** to us in his Word.
SD : 1 1 :055(625) [1081] his own wisdom and not **reveal** anything concerning it
SD : 1 1 :055(625) [1081] it, but cling solely to his **revealed** Word, to which he
SD : 1 1 :056(625) [1081] But since he has not **revealed** this to us, we must obey his
SD : 1 1 :064(626) [1083] on the basis of the **revealed** Word of God, as soon as he
SD : 1 1 :064(626) [1083] and beyond what he has **revealed** to us in his Word.
SD : 1 1 :065(627) [1083] This election is **revealed** from heaven through the
SD : 1 1 :083(630) [1091] God's **revealed** will involves both items: First, that he
SD : 1 1 :085(630) [1091] proclaimed and his will **revealed** to Pharaoh, and he
SD : 1 1 :090(631) [1093] of God, which he has **revealed** to us in Christ, out of
SD : 1 1 :093(632) [1095] well grounded in God's **revealed** will, we shall avoid and

Revelation (10)
AG : 2 8 :059(091) [0091] and teach that after the **revelation** of the Gospel all
AL : 2 8 :059(091) [0091] Sabbath, for after the **revelation** of the Gospel all
AP : 0 7 :018(171) [0233] The fact that the **revelation** has not yet come does not
AP : 2 3 :063(248) [0381] dare to claim divine **revelation** for the law of perpetual
AP : 2 4 :024(253) [0391] But after the **revelation** of the Gospel they had to stop;
S3 : 0 1 :003(302) [0477] believed because of the **revelation** in the Scriptures
LC : 0 3 :053(427) [0711] in eternity, it comes through the final **revelation**.
EP : 0 8 :016(489) [0821] in the full use, **revelation**, and manifestation of his divine
SD : 0 1 :008(510) [0861] and believed from the **revelation** of the Scriptures.
SD : 0 5 :012(560) [0955] earnest and terrible **revelation** and preaching of God's

Revenge (18)
AG : 2 7 :054(079) [0083] a counsel not to take **revenge**, it is natural that some
AG : 2 7 :054(079) [0083] it is not sinful to take **revenge** outside of the exercise of
AL : 2 7 :054(079) [0083] counsel not to take **revenge**, and therefore some are not
AP : 1 2 :091(196) [0279] "Penitence is a sort of **revenge** by a person who is sorry,
AP : 1 2 :148(205) [0297] opponents object that **revenge** or punishment is necessary
AP : 1 2 :148(205) [0299] Augustine says that "penitence is **revenge** punishing," etc.
AP : 1 2 :148(205) [0299] We grant that **revenge** or punishment is necessary for
AP : 1 2 :148(205) [0299] But in a formal sense **revenge** is part of penitence because
AP : 1 2 :148(205) [0299] what punishment and **revenge** is Augustine discussing?
AP : 1 2 :148(205) [0299] true punishment and **revenge**, that is, contrition and true
AP : 1 6 :007(223) [0331] Gospel forbids private **revenge**, and Christ stresses this so
AP : 1 6 :007(223) [0331] Thus private **revenge** is forbidden not as an evangelical
AP : 2 3 :053(246) [0377] So God takes **revenge** against those who despise his gift
S3 : 0 3 :017(305) [0483] let us say, in whoredom, **revenge**, or the like), such a
S3 : 0 3 :018(306) [0483] reflected on his lust or **revenge** in this fashion would
LC : 0 1 :184(390) [0633] rage and we are ready to shed blood and take **revenge**.
LC : 0 1 :187(390) [0633] This spirit or **revenge** clings to every one of us, and it is
LC : 0 1 :195(391) [0637] protect us, so that he may subdue our desire for **revenge**.

Revenue (3), Revenues (2)
AG : 2 4 :013(057) [0065] for the sake of **revenues** and stipends, were discontinued
AL : 2 4 :011(057) [0065] are celebrated only for **revenues** or stipends, and how
AP : 1 2 :015(184) [0257] and collect this **revenue** not only from the living but even
SC : 0 9 :005(355) [0561] to whom taxes are due, **revenue** to whom revenue is due,
SC : 0 9 :005(355) [0561] due, revenue to whom **revenue** is due, respect to whom

Revere (2), Revered (5), Reverence (12), Reverend (2), Reverently (5)
AG : 2 8 :004(081) [0085] and esteemed with all **reverence** as the two highest gifts of
AL : 0 0 :006(049) [0059] and the cultivation of **reverence** and devotion among the
AL : 2 4 :001(056) [0065] among us and is celebrated with the greatest **reverence**.
AL : 2 4 :006(056) [0065] likewise increases the **reverence** and devotion of public
AL : 2 8 :004(081) [0085] both are to be held in **reverence** and honor as the chief
AP : 0 4 :154(128) [0163] the whole act of **reverence** of the Pharisee with that of the
AP : 0 4 :154(128) [0165] woman and praises her **reverence**, her anointing and
AP : 0 4 :399(168) [0227] about our Confession, a **reverend** father said that no plan
AP : 2 3 :003(239) [0363] even the barbarians **reverently** spare, and banish deserted
S3 : 1 5 :005(317) [0501] the articles of the **reverend** father, Martin Luther, confess
TR : 0 0 :082(000) [0529] Martin Luther, our most **revered** preceptor, and the tract
TR : 0 0 :082(000) [0529] John Bugenhagen, most **revered** Father in Christ, that
SC : 0 8 :007(353) [0559] the table, they should **reverently** fold their hands and say:
SC : 0 8 :010(353) [0559] likewise, they should fold their hands **reverently** and say:
LC : 0 1 :061(373) [0597] with punishment but in the **reverence** and fear of God.
LC : 0 1 :107(379) [0611] them affectionately and **reverently**, but above all to show
LC : 0 1 :108(379) [0611] therefore be taught to **revere** their parents as God's
LC : 0 1 :111(380) [0613] but with humility and **reverence**, as in God's sight.
LC : 0 1 :138(384) [0621] of them were brought up well and **revered** their parents.
LC : 0 1 :235(397) [0647] like a thief, and even expect to be **revered** like noblemen.
LC : 0 1 :330(410) [0677] like cattle, but in the fear and **reverence** of God.
LC : 0 3 :013(422) [0701] and depend, and I can **revere** it highly, not because of my
LC : 0 5 :011(448) [0755] and should accept it with all **reverence**, fear, and humility.
LC : 0 5 :037(451) [0761] behave properly and **reverently** toward the body and
SD : 0 7 :044(577) [0987] be observed with great **reverence** and obedience until the
SD : 0 7 :058(580) [0993] Therefore our **revered** fathers and forebears, like Luther

Reverse (1)
AP : 0 4 :221(137) [0181] Our opponents proceed in **reverse** order.

Review (2), Reviewed (3)
AL : 0 0 :001(094) [0095] We have now **reviewed** the chief articles that are regarded
AP : 0 4 :286(150) [0201] So far we have **reviewed** the main passages which our
AP : 2 3 :002(239) [0363] We shall **review** their arguments in a moment.
AP : 2 3 :062(247) [0381] Now we shall briefly **review** their weighty arguments in
TR : 0 0 :022(323) [0511] all the details cannot be **reviewed** here once more, we

Reviling (1)
LC : 0 3 :103(434) [0727] vengeance, cursing, **reviling**, slander, arrogance, and

Revive (1), Revived (2)
AP : 1 2 :049(188) [0265] describes how we are **revived** in contrition by the Word
LC : 0 2 :055(418) [0693] appointed to comfort and **revive** our consciences as long
SD : 0 5 :023(562) [0959] damnation, but also **revived** their courage and comforted

Revolves (1)
EP : 0 2 :001(469) [0785] the primary question **revolves** exclusively about man's

Reward (44), Rewarded (2), Rewards (17)
AL : 2 0 :014(043) [0055] for then it would be a **reward** for works rather than a free
AP : 0 4 :024(110) [0127] God even honors it with material **rewards**.
AP : 0 4 :089(120) [0149] it could be accounted freely if it were a **reward** for works.
AP : 0 4 :193(133) [0175] Let us add a word here about **reward** and merit.
AP : 0 4 :194(133) [0175] We teach that **rewards** have been offered and promised to
AP : 0 4 :194(133) [0175] physical and spiritual **rewards** in this life and in that
AP : 0 4 :194(133) [0175] there will be different **rewards** for different labors.
AP : 0 4 :197(134) [0175] by referring to the **reward** that is connected to that
AP : 0 4 :197(134) [0175] it takes place in the justified it merits other great **rewards**.
AP : 0 4 :198(134) [0175] and often puts off the **rewards** for the righteousness of
AP : 0 4 :198(134) [0175] of God rather than the **rewards**, as is evident in Job, in
AP : 0 4 :355(161) [0217] bodily and spiritual **rewards** because they please God
AP : 0 4 :356(161) [0217] eternal life is called a **reward** and that therefore it is
AP : 0 4 :356(161) [0217] it is written, "Your **reward** is great in heaven."
AP : 0 4 :357(162) [0217] **"reward"** and in their explanation do violence not only to
AP : 0 4 :357(162) [0217] Because a **"reward"** is mentioned, they argue that our
AP : 0 4 :358(162) [0219] We hear the term **"reward"**: therefore we need neither
AP : 0 4 :359(162) [0219] We are not arguing about the term **"reward."**
AP : 0 4 :360(162) [0219] they hear this one word **"reward"**: "It is called a reward,
AP : 0 4 :360(162) [0219] "reward": "It is called a **reward**, therefore we have works
AP : 0 4 :360(162) [0219] enough to earn a **reward**; therefore works please God for
AP : 0 4 :362(162) [0219] forward an empty quibble about the term **"reward."**
AP : 0 4 :362(162) [0219] then we will not argue much about the term **"reward."**
AP : 0 4 :362(162) [0219] grant that eternal life is a **reward** because it is something
AP : 0 4 :364(163) [0219] of punishments and **rewards** in one way, and the weak in
AP : 0 4 :365(163) [0219] Yet the proclamation of **rewards** and punishments is
AP : 0 4 :365(163) [0219] In the proclamation of **rewards** grace is displayed.
AP : 0 4 :365(163) [0219] offer grace with other **rewards**, as in Isa. 58:8, 9 and often
AP : 0 4 :366(163) [0219] good works merit other **rewards**, both bodily and
AP : 0 4 :366(163) [0221] with the law, in which a **reward** is offered and owed, not
AP : 0 4 :367(163) [0221] apply it not to the other **rewards** but to justification,
AP : 0 4 :367(163) [0221] justification but other **rewards**, as in these passages a
AP : 0 4 :367(163) [0221] as in these passages a **reward** is offered for works.
AP : 0 4 :367(163) [0221] here the degree of the **reward** is evidently commensurate
AP : 0 4 :367(163) [0221] here, too, the law offers a **reward** for a certain work.
AP : 0 4 :368(163) [0221] the law thus merits a **reward**, since a reward properly
AP : 0 4 :368(163) [0221] merits a reward, since a **reward** properly belongs to the
AP : 0 4 :368(163) [0221] pleases God and has its **reward**, both here and hereafter.
AP : 0 4 :369(163) [0221] say more on the term **"reward,"** based on the nature of
AP : 1 2 :174(210) [0307] and because of his command, and they have their **reward**.
AP : 1 5 :040(220) [0325] were an act of worship or at least worth some **reward**.
AP : 2 1 :035(234) [0353] Barbara asks for a **reward** — that no one who calls upon
SC : PR :027(341) [0539] temptations, with little **reward** or gratitude from the
SC : PR :027(341) [0539] Christ himself will be our **reward** if we labor faithfully.
LC : 0 1 :077(375) [0603] name and will as richly **reward** it, even as he will terribly
LC : 0 1 :119(381) [0615] meanwhile have only scorn and trouble for their **reward**.
LC : 0 1 :134(383) [0619] then, is the fruit and the **reward**, that whoever keeps this
LC : 0 1 :136(383) [0619] and service, and he will **reward** you abundantly with
LC : 0 1 :139(384) [0621] delights in it, so richly **rewards** it, and besides is so strict
LC : 0 1 :148(385) [0623] and a gracious God who will **reward** you a hundredfold.
LC : 0 1 :149(385) [0623] then take shame, misery, and grief for your **reward**.
LC : 0 1 :151(386) [0625] God and receives joy and happiness for his **reward**.
LC : 0 1 :152(386) [0625] God and have so rich a **reward**, we shall be simply
LC : 0 1 :164(387) [0627] that they will be richly **rewarded** for all they contribute to
LC : 0 1 :252(399) [0653] We shall be richly **rewarded** for all the help and kindness
LC : 0 1 :322(409) [0673] again, how richly he will **reward**, bless, and bestow all
LC : 0 1 :328(410) [0677] that he will abundantly **reward** you for all you do.
LC : 0 1 :330(410) [0677] the contrary, abundantly **rewards** those who keep them.
EP : 0 6 :006(481) [0807] as if they knew of no command, threat, or **reward**.
SD : 0 4 :008(552) [0941] world, and even God will **reward** them with temporal
SD : 0 4 :009(552) [0941] works that God will **reward** both in this and in the next
SD : 0 4 :038(557) [0951] sake and he promises to **reward** them gloriously in this
SD : 0 6 :016(566) [0967] punishment or in hope of **reward**, he is still under the

Rhaitu (1)
SD : 0 8 :015(594) [1019] the presbyter of **Rhaitu**, taught that the two natures have

Rhegium (1)
TR : 0 0 :018(323) [0509] or Constantinople or **Rhegium** or Alexandria — he is of

Rhegius (3)
PR : PR :019(009) [0017] of [John] Brenz, Urban **Rhegius**, [John Bugenhagen] of
S3 : 1 5 :005(317) [0501] I, Dr. Urban **Rhegius**, superintendent of the churches in
TR : 0 0 :082(334) [0529] I also, Dr. Urban **Rhegius**, superintendent of the churches

Rhine (1)
PR : PR :027(014) [0025] Louis, count palatine on the **Rhine**, elector

Rhode (2)
S3 : 1 5 :005(317) [0501] Paul **Rhode**, superintendent of Stettin
TR : 0 0 :082(334) [0529] Paul **Rhode**, preacher in Stettin

Rich (17), Richer (3), Riches (12), Richest (3), Richly (11)
AP : 2 1 :018(231) [0347] Ps. 45:12, 13, "The **richest** of the people will sue your
AP : 2 1 :032(233) [0351] Thus Anne grants **riches**, Sebastian wards off pestilence,
AP : 2 1 :032(233) [0351] that Juno granted **riches**, Febris warded off fever, and
AP : 2 7 :005(269) [0421] Some of the **richest** monasteries just feed a lazy crowd
AP : 2 7 :043(277) [0435] of a slender inheritance they find the most ample **riches**.
AP : 2 7 :046(277) [0435] but in the absence of greed and of trust in **riches**.
AP : 2 7 :046(277) [0435] Thus David was poor in a very **rich** kingdom.
S3 : 0 4 :000(310) [0491] for God is surpassingly **rich** in his grace: First, through
TR : 0 0 :018(323) [0509] It is the power of **riches** or the humility of poverty that
TR : 0 0 :080(333) [0527] should remember that **riches** have been given to bishops
SC : PR :017(340) [0535] the people may have a **richer** and fuller understanding.
SC : 0 4 :010(349) [0551] he poured out upon us **richly** through Jesus Christ our
LC : 0 1 :015(366) [0585] to help you and to lavish all good upon you **richly**."
LC : 0 1 :018(367) [0585] Others who strove for **riches**, happiness, pleasure, and a
LC : 0 1 :036(369) [0589] are proud, powerful, and **rich** pot-bellies who, not caring
LC : 0 1 :040(370) [0591] an offer, so cordial an invitation, and so **rich** a promise.
LC : 0 1 :077(375) [0603] of his name and will as **richly** reward it, even as he will
LC : 0 1 :139(384) [0621] greatly delights in it, so **richly** rewards it, and besides is so
LC : 0 1 :152(386) [0625] to God and have so **rich** a reward, we shall be simply
LC : 0 1 :164(387) [0627] promise that they will be **richly** rewarded for all they

Continued ▶

L C : 0 1 :173(388) [0629] for them and make them **rich** without our help, as indeed
L C : 0 1 :175(388) [0631] were done, God would **richly** bless us and give us grace so
L C : 0 1 :208(393) [0639] God has therefore most **richly** blessed this estate above
L C : 0 1 :208(393) [0639] this estate might be provided for **richly** and adequately.
L C : 0 1 :243(397) [0649] scratch day and night and yet grow not a penny **richer**!
L C : 0 1 :252(399) [0653] blessing: We shall be **richly** rewarded for all the help and
L C : 0 1 :253(399) [0653] Here you have a **rich** Lord.
L C : 0 1 :259(400) [0655] neighbors, and the **rich** and powerful who are in a
L C : 0 1 :306(406) [0669] may by trickery entice a **rich** bride away from another,
L C : 0 1 :322(409) [0673] and again, how **richly** he will reward, bless, and bestow
L C : 0 2 :021(413) [0683] boast as if we had life, **riches**, power, honor, and such
L C : 0 2 :026(413) [0685] This article is very **rich** and far-reaching, but in order to
L C : 0 2 :033(415) [0687] are based, and it is so **rich** and broad that we can never
L C : 0 2 :063(419) [0695] his work exquisitely depicted in very short but **rich** words.
L C : 0 2 :063(419) [0695] But here you have everything in **richest** measure.
L C : 0 2 :070(420) [0697] and thus advance and grow **richer** in understanding.
L C : 0 3 :023(423) [0703] This we should not trade for all the **riches** in the world.
L C : 0 3 :057(427) [0713] Imagine a very **rich** and mighty emperor who bade a poor
L C : 0 3 :076(431) [0721] field to grow and yield **richly**; to help us manage our
L C : 0 4 :043(442) [0743] of the pressing crowd of **rich** men no one else could get
L C : 0 6 :023(459) [0000] beggar who hears that a **rich** gift, of money or clothes, is
L C : 0 6 :025(460) [0000] about this wonderful, **rich** alms and this indescribable
S D : 0 3 :006(540) [0917] or rightly understand the **riches** of the grace of Christ."
S D : 1 1 :028(621) [1071] one Lord of all, **rich** toward all who call upon him"
S D : 1 1 :064(626) [1083] words: "O the depth of the **riches** and wisdom and
S D : 1 1 :079(629) [1089] order to make known the **riches** of his glory in the vessels

Rid (6)
A P : 0 4 :288(151) [0203] forms of worship to get **rid** of the terrors of conscience.
L C : 0 1 :317(408) [0673] in order that men may get **rid** of the pernicious abuse
L C : 0 3 :108(435) [0729] is contrary to our will and we would prefer to be **rid** of it.
L C : 0 3 :114(435) [0729] "Dear Father, help us to get **rid** of all this misfortune."
L C : 0 5 :070(454) [0769] who are anxious to be **rid** of it and desire help, should
L C : 0 5 :073(455) [0771] If you wait until you are **rid** of your burden in order to

Rides (1)
L C : 0 1 :264(400) [0655] vice of back-biting or slander by which the devil **rides** us.

Ridicule (6), Ridiculous (1)
A P : 0 4 :013(109) [0123] a pass that many people **ridicule** us for teaching that men
A P : 0 7 :027(173) [0235] Many openly **ridicule** all religions, or if they accept
A P : 2 3 :010(241) [0367] So it is **ridiculous** for our opponents to say that originally
S 3 : 1 5 :004(316) [0501] Such baptizing is a **ridicule** and mockery of holy Baptism
L C : 0 3 :031(424) [0707] Now they may confidently **ridicule** and mock.
S D : 0 7 :067(582) [0997] enthusiasts **ridicule** the Lord Christ, St. Paul, and the
S D : 1 1 :078(629) [1089] despise, blaspheme, and **ridicule** it, and they resisted the

Right (235), Rights (7)
P R : P R :006(004) [0009] from straying from the **right** course of divine truth which
P R : P R :017(008) [0015] reserved to ourselves the **right** and served notice that we
P R : P R :020(010) [0017] and his session at the **right** hand of God's almighty power
P R : P R :021(010) [0019] in that it is seated at the **right** hand of God and is
A G : 0 3 :004(030) [0045] heaven, and sits on the **right** hand of God, that he may
A G : 0 9 :003(033) [0047] who teach that infant Baptism is not **right** are rejected.
A G : 2 6 :016(066) [0073] hindered from coming to a **right** knowledge of Christ.
A G : 2 7 :018(073) [0079] celibacy have the power, **right**, and authority to marry,
A G : 2 7 :024(074) [0079] for no man has the **right** to cancel an obligation which is
A G : 2 7 :029(075) [0079] Before they came to a **right** understanding they were
A G : 2 7 :030(075) [0079] Accordingly it is not **right** to argue so rashly and
A G : 2 7 :050(079) [0083] True perfection and **right** service of God consist of these
A G : 2 7 :055(079) [0083] others think that it is not **right** at all for Christians, even
A G : 2 8 :019(083) [0087] not as bishops by divine **right**, but by human, imperial
A G : 2 8 :019(083) [0087] but by human, imperial **right**, bestowed by Roman
A G : 2 8 :021(084) [0087] According to divine **right**, therefore, it is the office of the
A G : 2 8 :029(085) [0087] and in tithes), they have these by virtue of human **right**.
A G : 2 8 :042(088) [0089] did the bishops get the **right** and power to impose such
A L : 0 3 :004(030) [0045] into heaven to sit on the **right** hand of the Father, forever
A L : 1 6 :002(037) [0051] works of God and that it is **right** for Christians to hold
A L : 2 0 :030(045) [0057] "Faith is the mother of the good will and the **right** deed."
A L : 2 3 :002(051) [0061] far weightier reasons why this **right** should be restored.
A L : 2 5 :012(063) [0071] admits that such confession is of human **right**.
A L : 2 7 :023(074) [0079] state that every vow is subject to the **right** of a superior.
A L : 2 8 :019(083) [0087] the Gospel, but by human **right** granted by kings and
A L : 2 8 :021(084) [0087] (or, as they say, by divine **right**) no jurisdiction belongs to
A L : 2 8 :029(085) [0087] matrimony, tithes, etc.), bishops have this by human **right**.
A L : 2 8 :030(085) [0087] or pastors have the **right** to introduce ceremonies in the
A L : 2 8 :031(085) [0087] Those who attribute this **right** to bishops cite as evidence
A L : 2 8 :042(088) [0089] did the bishops get the **right** to impose such traditions on
A L : 2 8 :049(089) [0091] If bishops have the **right** to burden consciences with such
A L : 0 0 :002(095) [0095] monks about parochial **rights**, confessions, burials, and
A P : 0 2 :034(104) [0113] all liars," that is, they do not have the **right** view of God.
A P : 0 2 :042(106) [0117] deliver us from trouble **right** away; fretting because bad
A P : 0 2 :043(106) [0117] statement, but it is not **right** to twist it in order to
A P : 0 4 :159(129) [0165] They are **right** when they say that love is the keeping of
A P : 0 4 :165(129) [0169] of Christ, "who is at the **right** hand of God, who indeed
A P : 0 4 :179(131) [0171] Christ took away the **right** of the law to accuse and
A P : 0 4 :231(139) [0183] We have no **right** to suppose that Paul would ascribe
A P : 0 4 :255(144) [0193] condemns wrongdoers and commands that they do **right**.
A P : 0 4 :345(160) [0217] of human judgment a **right** or debt is certain, while mercy
A P : 0 7 :023(172) [0235] received their power and **right** to rule, and this at Christ's
A P : 0 7 :023(172) [0235] to him, so now this **right** has been transferred to the
A P : 0 7 :041(176) [0241] If they were of divine **right**, it was unlawful for men to
A P : 0 7 :041(176) [0241] was unlawful for men to assume the **right** to change them.
A P : 0 7 :050(178) [0245] they denied to priests the **right** to hold property or other
A P : 0 7 :050(178) [0245] The **right** to hold property is a civil ordinance.
A P : 1 2 :012(184) [0255] pretext that it is by divine **right**, they speak very coldly
A P : 1 2 :012(184) [0255] coldly about absolution, which really is by divine **right**.
A P : 1 2 :012(184) [0257] *opere operato,* without a **right** attitude in the recipient,
A P : 1 2 :023(185) [0257] our opponents command it, is necessary by divine **right**.
A P : 1 2 :068(192) [0271] authorities, they would be **right**; for there is a great crowd
A P : 1 2 :090(195) [0279] the open truth, it is not **right** for us to forsake the cause —
A P : 1 2 :102(197) [0281] that we do not believe that it is necessary by divine **right**.
A P : 1 2 :110(198) [0285] is necessary by divine **right**, they will be condemning
A P : 1 2 :125(201) [0289] Roman See thinks it is **right** for all nations to recognize
A P : 1 2 :177(210) [0307] Thus our opponents are **right** in their judgment when they
A P : 1 4 :004(215) [0315] who teaches what is **right** and true, though the canons
A P : 1 6 :011(224) [0333] Decalogue recognizes the **right** of ownership and
A P : 2 2 :006(237) [0359] men maintain that it is **right** to deny one part, and they
A P : 2 3 :003(239) [0363] of theirs with your chaste **right** hand, Emperor Charles —
A P : 2 3 :007(240) [0365] nor vows can abolish the **right** to contract marriage.
A P : 2 3 :009(240) [0367] in man is a natural **right**, the jurists have said wisely and
A P : 2 3 :009(240) [0367] that the union of man and woman is by natural **right**.
A P : 2 3 :009(240) [0367] Now, since natural **right** is unchangeable, the right to
A P : 2 3 :009(240) [0367] right is unchangeable, the **right** to contract marriage must
A P : 2 3 :010(241) [0367] they were born with a natural **right** and now they are not.
A P : 2 3 :011(241) [0367] jurists: The union of man and woman is by natural **right**.
A P : 2 3 :012(241) [0367] Natural **right** is really divine right, because it is an
A P : 2 3 :012(241) [0367] right is really divine **right**, because it is an ordinance
A P : 2 3 :012(241) [0367] of God can change this **right**, the right to contract
A P : 2 3 :012(241) [0367] can change this right, the **right** to contract marriage
A P : 2 3 :012(241) [0367] God, and therefore it is a **right**; otherwise, why would
A P : 2 3 :016(241) [0369] Thus anyone who is aflame retains the **right** to marry.
A P : 2 3 :056(247) [0379] though it is obviously a matter of simple human **right**.
A P : 2 3 :057(247) [0379] suspend them all **right** — not from office but from trees!
A P : 2 3 :066(248) [0381] marriage is pure, it is **right** to say that those who are not
A P : 2 4 :029(255) [0393] So also Ps. 4:5, "Offer **right** sacrifices, and put your trust
A P : 2 4 :029(255) [0393] and says that this is a **right** sacrifice, indicating that other
A P : 2 4 :029(255) [0393] indicating that other sacrifices are not true and **right**.
A P : 2 4 :034(256) [0395] and silver, till they present **right** offerings to the Lord."
A P : 2 7 :058(279) [0439] Hence it is not **right** to compare monasticism, thought up
A P : 2 8 :008(282) [0445] Thus bishops have no **right** to create traditions apart from
A P : 2 8 :008(282) [0445] do the bishops have the **right** to burden consciences with
A P : 2 8 :027(285) [0451] whether our opponents are **right** in boasting that they
S 1 : P R :010(290) [0457] the pure Word and the **right** use of the sacraments, with
S 1 : P R :012(290) [0459] twenty diets would not be able to set things **right** again.
S 1 : 0 1 :000(292) [0461] and he is seated at the **right** hand of God, will come to
S 2 : 0 2 :009(294) [0465] Nor is it **right** (even if everything else is in order) for
S 2 : 0 4 :001(298) [0471] all Christendom by divine **right** or according to God's
S 2 : 0 4 :007(299) [0473] of the church by divine **right** or by God's command;
S 2 : 0 4 :007(299) [0473] and estate, together with all his **rights** and pretensions.
S 2 : 0 4 :013(300) [0475] to be the head of the Christian church by divine **right**.
S 3 : 0 1 :004(302) [0477] man by nature possesses a **right** understanding and a
S 3 : 0 3 :010(305) [0481] they did not have the **right** teaching concerning original
S 3 : 0 3 :010(305) [0481] that reason is capable of **right** understanding and the will
S 3 : 0 3 :024(307) [0485] for himself alone the **right** to remit the entire satisfaction.
S 3 : 1 0 :003(314) [0497] The papists have no **right** to forbid or prevent us, not
S 3 : 1 1 :001(314) [0499] had neither authority nor **right** to prohibit marriage and
S 3 : 1 5 :005(316) [0501] regard the above articles as **right** and Christian.
S 3 : 1 5 :005(316) [0501] he possesses by human **right**, making this concession for
T R : 0 0 :001(320) [0503] claim that he is by divine **right** above all bishops and
T R : 0 0 :002(320) [0503] he adds that by divine **right** he possesses both swords,
T R : 0 0 :005(320) [0503] the Roman bishop is above all bishops by divine **right**.
T R : 0 0 :005(320) [0505] him because he has the **right** to elect, ordain, confirm, and
T R : 0 0 :006(320) [0505] his power is by divine **right** and is even to be preferred to
T R : 0 0 :007(320) [0505] bishop is not by divine **right** above all other bishops and
T R : 0 0 :010(321) [0505] his superior if Peter had been his superior by divine **right**.
T R : 0 0 :012(322) [0507] a council and is of human **right**, for if the bishop of
T R : 0 0 :012(322) [0507] his superiority by divine **right**, it would not have been
T R : 0 0 :012(322) [0507] council to withdraw any **right** from him and transfer it to
T R : 0 0 :020(323) [0509] whole church by divine **right** when the church elects him
T R : 0 0 :024(324) [0511] the church especially possesses the **right** of vocation.
T R : 0 0 :031(325) [0513] power of the sword or the **right** to establish, take
T R : 0 0 :033(325) [0513] that the pope is by divine **right** lord of the kingdoms of
T R : 0 0 :035(326) [0513] and deprive the emperors of the **right** to appoint bishops.
T R : 0 0 :036(326) [0515] that such dominion belongs to the pope by divine **right**.
T R : 0 0 :038(326) [0515] and superiority by divine **right**, obedience would still not
T R : 0 0 :038(327) [0515] pontifex by divine **right**; nevertheless, godless high priests
T R : 0 0 :040(327) [0515] he assumes for himself the **right** to change the doctrine of
T R : 0 0 :055(329) [0521] will and grants nobody the **right** to express an opinion,
T R : 0 0 :057(330) [0521] the primacy by divine **right**, he should not be obeyed
T R : 0 0 :061(330) [0521] power belongs by divine **right** to all who preside over the
T R : 0 0 :065(331) [0523] pastor is not by divine **right**, it is manifest that ordination
T R : 0 0 :065(331) [0523] by a pastor in his own church is valid by divine **right**.
T R : 0 0 :066(331) [0523] the churches retain the **right** to ordain for themselves.
T R : 0 0 :067(331) [0523] the church exists, the **right** to administer the Gospel also
T R : 0 0 :067(331) [0523] the church to retain the **right** of calling, electing, and
T R : 0 0 :067(331) [0523] This **right** is a gift given exclusively to the church, and no
T R : 0 0 :067(331) [0523] church is, therefore, the **right** of electing and ordaining
T R : 0 0 :069(331) [0525] certainly has the **right** of electing and ordaining
T R : 0 0 :072(332) [0525] the church retains the **right** of electing and ordaining
T R : 0 0 :072(332) [0525] the churches are by divine **right** compelled to ordain
T R : 0 0 :076(333) [0527] for not obeying, it is **right** to restore this jurisdiction to
T R : 0 0 :077(333) [0527] bishops have by human **right** only, and they have not had
T R : 0 0 :077(333) [0527] By divine **right** temporal magistrates are compelled to
T R : 0 0 :078(333) [0527] betrothals in violation of the **right** of parents.
S C : P R :013(339) [0535] to distinguish between **right** and wrong according to the
S C : 0 1 :018(344) [0541] under pretext of legal **right**, but be of service and help to
S C : 0 2 :003(345) [0545] *and is seated on the* **right** *hand of God, the Father*
S C : 0 9 :005(355) [0561] wrong and to praise those who do **right**" (I Pet. 2:13, 14).
S C : 0 9 :007(355) [0563] now her children if you do **right** and let nothing terrify
S C : 0 9 :009(356) [0563] "Children, obey your parents in the Lord, for this is **right**.
L C : S P :005(362) [0575] Altar and exercise all the **rights** of Christians, although
L C : S P :012(363) [0577] heaven, and sits on the **right** hand of God, the Father
L C : 0 1 :003(365) [0581] If your faith and trust are **right**, then your God is the true
L C : 0 1 :031(369) [0589] the utmost importance for a man to have the **right** head.
L C : 0 1 :031(369) [0589] For where the head is **right**, the whole life must be right,
L C : 0 1 :031(369) [0589] head is right, the whole life must be **right**, and vice versa.
L C : 0 1 :047(371) [0593] Then we shall be on the **right** path and walk straight
L C : 0 1 :048(371) [0593] before, where the heart is **right** with God and this
L C : 0 1 :050(371) [0593] the lips and the tongue into the **right** relation to God.
L C : 0 1 :066(373) [0599] intervenes and separates **right** from wrong, good from
L C : 0 1 :076(375) [0601] This would be the **right** way to bring up children, so long
L C : 0 1 :077(375) [0603] name and taught that its **right** use consists not only of
L C : 0 1 :077(375) [0603] is well pleased with the **right** use of his name and will as
L C : 0 1 :111(380) [0613] He who has the **right** attitude toward his parents will not
L C : 0 1 :112(380) [0613] able to set his conscience **right** toward God, saying: "If I

Continued ▶

LC : 0 1 :119(381) [0615] It serves them **right** for their devilish perversity in
LC : 0 1 :130(383) [0619] The wise men of old were **right** when they said, "God,
LC : 0 1 :180(389) [0631] commandment, yet their **right** to take human life is not
LC : 0 1 :240(397) [0649] way, as if it were his **right** and privilege to sell his goods
LC : 0 1 :247(398) [0651] you skin and scrape him **right** down to the bone, and you
LC : 0 1 :260(400) [0655] everyone should help his neighbor maintain his **rights**.
LC : 0 1 :260(400) [0655] He must not allow these **rights** to be thwarted or distorted
LC : 0 1 :261(400) [0655] They should let **right** remain right, nor perverting or
LC : 0 1 :261(400) [0655] should let right remain **right**, nor perverting or concealing
LC : 0 1 :265(400) [0655] note that nobody has the **right** to judge and reprove his
LC : 0 1 :266(401) [0657] Knowledge of sin does not entail the **right** to judge it.
LC : 0 1 :274(402) [0659] he has reserved to himself the **right** of punishment.
LC : 0 1 :274(402) [0659] has in his own person the **right** to judge and condemn
LC : 0 1 :276(402) [0659] But the **right** way to deal with this matter would be to
LC : 0 1 :280(403) [0661] This is the **right** procedure for restraining and reforming a
LC : 0 1 :282(403) [0661] would serve such gossips **right** to have their sport spoiled,
LC : 0 1 :296(405) [0665] another's possessions to which you have no **right**.
LC : 0 1 :300(405) [0667] questions of honor and **right** when it comes to acquiring
LC : 0 1 :301(405) [0667] the least semblance of **right**, so varnishing and garnishing
LC : 0 1 :307(406) [0669] no one, you have trespassed on your neighbor's **rights**.
LC : 0 1 :324(409) [0675] exactly the meaning and **right** interpretation of the first
LC : 0 1 :328(410) [0675] his property, his honor or **rights**, as these things are
LC : 0 2 :025(413) [0683] *and is seated on the **right** hand of God, the Father*
LC : 0 2 :031(414) [0687] and assumed dominion at the **right** hand of the Father.
LC : 0 3 :023(423) [0703] or whether I have hit upon the **right** form and mode?"
LC : 0 3 :054(427) [0713] and he may have no **right** or power over us, until finally
LC : 0 3 :092(432) [0725] Where the heart is not **right** with God and cannot achieve
LC : 0 4 :047(442) [0743] Do children also believe, and is it **right** to baptize them?
LC : 0 4 :056(443) [0747] "The Baptism indeed was **right**, but unfortunately I did
LC : 0 4 :068(445) [0749] This is the **right** use of Baptism among Christians,
LC : 0 5 :014(448) [0755] if the words remain, as is **right** and necessary, then in
LC : 0 5 :039(451) [0761] now that we have the **right** interpretation and doctrine of
LC : 0 5 :054(453) [0765] act like a person who really desires to be **right** with God.
LC : 0 5 :085(456) [0773] up in Christian doctrine and a **right** understanding of it.
LC : 0 6 :008(458) [0000] which have an even greater **right** to be called the
EP : R N :007(465) [0779] be understood and judged as good or evil, **right** or wrong.
EP : 0 5 :003(478) [0801] which teaches what is **right** and God-pleasing and which
EP : 0 7 :012(483) [0811] "The second ground is: "God's **right** hand is everywhere.
EP : 0 7 :012(483) [0811] really and truly set at this **right** hand of God according to
EP : 0 7 :012(483) [0811] Son, is so set down at the **right** hand of God, whence he
EP : 0 8 :015(488) [0821] in truth) exalted to the **right** hand of the omnipotent
EP : 0 8 :017(489) [0823] and property of God's **right** hand, as Dr. Luther says on
EP : 1 0 :007(493) [0831] articles as well as in the **right** use of the holy sacraments,
EP : 1 1 :022(497) [0837] can understand what is **right** and what is wrong, since we
EP : 1 2 :020(499) [0841] a creature do not have a **right** understanding of Christ as
SD : 0 1 :036(514) [0869] Thou knowest me **right** well; my frame was not hidden
SD : 0 1 :058(519) [0879] or an accident in the **right** and strict sense of the word.
SD : 0 1 :060(519) [0879] reason, be it ever so keen, can give the **right** answer.
SD : 0 1 :060(519) [0879] alone can lead to a **right** understanding and give a correct
SD : 0 2 :012(522) [0885] to think anything good or **right** in spiritual matters, to
SD : 0 2 :061(533) [0905] same reason it is not quite **right** to say that before his
SD : 0 3 :002(539) [0917] impels them to do what is **right**, and is in this way their
SD : 0 3 :017(542) [0921] a bribe, and deprive the innocent of his **right**" (Isa. 5:22).
SD : 0 3 :036(545) [0929] And the **right** understanding of the exclusive terms in the
SD : 0 4 :015(553) [0943] be in a single heart both a **right** faith and a wicked
SD : 0 4 :018(554) [0943] and in this sense it is **right** to say and teach that truly
SD : 0 4 :029(555) [0947] and for these reasons it is **right** for our churches to
SD : 0 4 :038(557) [0951] are done on account of **right** causes and for right ends
SD : 0 4 :038(557) [0951] of right causes and for **right** ends (that is, with the
SD : 0 5 :012(560) [0955] same time it is true and **right** that the apostles and the
SD : 0 6 :020(567) [0969] do every man whatever is **right** in his own eyes, but heed
SD : 0 7 :001(569) [0971] the true intention and the **right** understanding of the
SD : 0 7 :095(586) [1005] "2. The second is that the **right** hand of God is
SD : 0 7 :123(590) [1013] Christ but do not have a **right**, truthful, living, and saving
SD : 0 8 :012(593) [1019] it has been elevated to the **right** hand of majesty, power,
SD : 0 8 :018(594) [1021] "mixture" in a good sense and with the **right** distinction.
SD : 0 8 :023(595) [1023] his human nature at the **right** hand of the almighty power
SD : 0 8 :028(596) [1025] after the manner of the **right** hand of God, which is not a
SD : 0 8 :028(596) [1025] The **right** hand of God is precisely the almighty power of
SD : 0 8 :043(599) [1029] to the other nature, all of which scholars know **right** well.
SD : 0 8 :051(600) [1031] and exalted to the **right** hand of the majesty and power of
SD : 0 8 :074(606) [1043] and he is exalted to the **right** hand of the majesty and
SD : 0 8 :078(606) [1043] to his humanity at the **right** hand of the majesty and
SD : 0 8 :086(608) [1047] majesty of Christ at the **right** hand of God in connection
SD : 0 8 :092(609) [1049] which he has placed at the **right** hand of the majesty and
SD : 0 8 :094(609) [1049] preached Word and in the **right** use of the holy
SD : 0 8 :096(610) [1049] made to sit so high at the **right** hand of the majesty and
SD : 0 9 :003(610) [1051] has been made to sit at the **right** hand of the almighty
SD : 1 0 :009(612) [1055] and at every time has the **right**, authority, and power to
SD : 1 0 :031(616) [1063] also agreed concerning the **right** use of the holy
SD : 1 1 :012(618) [1067] true understanding or the **right** use of the teaching of
SD : 1 1 :054(625) [1081] world began God foresaw **right** well and with utter
SD : 1 1 :062(626) [1083] we will remain on the **right** path, as it is written, "O
SD : 1 1 :075(628) [1087] true repentance through a **right** faith, he will always show

Righteous (129)

AG : 0 2 :003(029) [0045] natural man is made **righteous** by his own powers, thus
AG : 0 4 :001(030) [0045] of sin and become **righteous** before God by grace, for
AG : 2 0 :006(041) [0053] now that we become **righteous** before God by our works
AG : 2 0 :006(042) [0053] say that faith and works make us **righteous** before God.
AG : 2 1 :004(047) [0059] with the Father, Jesus Christ the **righteous**" (I John 2:1).
AG : 2 6 :041(070) [0075] service do not make us **righteous** before God and that
AG : 2 7 :048(078) [0081] service would make men good and **righteous** before God.
AG : 2 7 :061(080) [0083] justify and render men **righteous** before God, that they
AP : 0 2 :010(102) [0107] Christ if we can become **righteous** by our own
AP : 0 2 :049(106) [0119] those who are wise and **righteous** in the eyes of the
AP : 0 4 :018(109) [0125] sins and are accounted **righteous** by they own keeping of
AP : 0 4 :026(110) [0127] that men are accounted **righteous** before God because of
AP : 0 4 :048(114) [0135] who are accounted **righteous** before God do not live in
AP : 0 4 :069(116) [0141] and believe that for his sake we are accounted **righteous**?
AP : 0 4 :072(117) [0141] we are truly accounted **righteous** or acceptable before
AP : 0 4 :072(117) [0141] make unrighteous men **righteous** or to regenerate them,
AP : 0 4 :072(117) [0141] as well as to be pronounced or accounted **righteous**.
AP : 0 4 :072(117) [0141] faith alone makes a **righteous** man out of an unrighteous
AP : 0 4 :078(117) [0143] an unrighteous man **righteous** or effecting his
AP : 0 4 :086(119) [0147] are accounted **righteous** and children of God not on
AP : 0 4 :086(119) [0147] Scriptures testify that we are accounted **righteous** by faith.
AP : 0 4 :086(119) [0147] by which we are accounted **righteous** before God.
AP : 0 4 :097(121) [0149] we are accounted **righteous** for Christ's sake when we
AP : 0 4 :100(121) [0151] Hab. 2:4, "The **righteous** shall live by his faith."
AP : 0 4 :100(121) [0151] says first that men are **righteous** by the faith which
AP : 0 4 :103(122) [0151] But he who is **righteous** has it as a gift because he was
AP : 0 4 :114(123) [0155] we must be accounted **righteous** by this faith for Christ's
AP : 0 4 :117(123) [0155] unrighteous we are made **righteous** and regenerated men.
AP : 0 4 :161(129) [0167] that we are accounted **righteous** before God by our own
AP : 0 4 :163(129) [0169] that he is accounted **righteous** by faith for Christ's sake,
AP : 0 4 :163(129) [0169] that we are accounted **righteous** by faith for the sake of
AP : 0 4 :165(129) [0169] that we are accounted **righteous** on account of Christ,
AP : 0 4 :165(129) [0169] anyone thinks that he is **righteous** and acceptable because
AP : 0 4 :165(130) [0169] and then imagine that he is **righteous** before God.
AP : 0 4 :168(130) [0169] thy servant; for no man living is **righteous** before thee."
AP : 0 4 :173(131) [0171] Jerome writes, "We are **righteous**, therefore, when we
AP : 0 4 :176(131) [0171] that we are accounted **righteous** before God on account
AP : 0 4 :176(131) [0171] and are angry at him, we are not **righteous** before him.
AP : 0 4 :177(131) [0171] faith we are accounted **righteous** because of Christ, not
AP : 0 4 :179(131) [0171] for whose sake they are now accounted **righteous**.
AP : 0 4 :179(131) [0171] when they are accounted **righteous**, the law cannot accuse
AP : 0 4 :202(134) [0175] Because he was **righteous** by faith, the sacrifice he made
AP : 0 4 :209(136) [0179] propitiation for which he would be accounted **righteous**.
AP : 0 4 :211(136) [0179] they were accounted **righteous** and had a gracious God
AP : 0 4 :212(136) [0179] and a price because of which we are accounted **righteous**.
AP : 0 4 :212(136) [0179] by faith we are accounted **righteous** for Christ's sake.
AP : 0 4 :213(136) [0179] that we are accounted **righteous** before God because of
AP : 0 4 :214(136) [0179] We are accounted **righteous** before God for Christ's sake
AP : 0 4 :214(136) [0179] We are not accounted **righteous** because of our works
AP : 0 4 :221(137) [0181] that we are accounted **righteous** because of Christ, the
AP : 0 4 :230(139) [0183] we are accounted **righteous** when we believe that for
AP : 0 4 :252(143) [0191] a wicked man is made **righteous** but that he is
AP : 0 4 :252(143) [0191] that he is pronounced **righteous** in a forensic way, just as
AP : 0 4 :252(143) [0191] faith and good works are certainly pronounced **righteous**.
AP : 0 4 :252(143) [0191] works of the saints are **righteous** and please God because
AP : 0 4 :252(143) [0191] is, God pronounces **righteous** those who believe him from
AP : 0 4 :262(145) [0195] him to become **righteous**, then to do good and to defend
AP : 0 4 :289(151) [0203] teaches that we are **righteous** through a certain
AP : 0 4 :296(152) [0205] we are not accounted **righteous** because of the law but
AP : 0 4 :305(154) [0205] man and pronounce him **righteous**," and to do so on
AP : 0 4 :321(157) [0209] to account them **righteous**, whereas terrified consciences
AP : 0 4 :326(157) [0211] thy servant, for no man living is **righteous** before thee."
AP : 0 4 :348(160) [0217] purpose, that, being **righteous**, we might begin to do good
AP : 0 4 :362(162) [0219] that we are accounted **righteous** by faith for Christ's sake
AP : 0 4 :363(162) [0219] which the Lord, the **righteous** judge, will give me," etc.
AP : 0 4 :373(164) [0221] for him who does good," namely, for the **righteous** man.
AP : 0 4 :379(165) [0223] we are acceptable and **righteous** because of our works,
AP : 0 7 :015(170) [0231] the righteousness by which we are **righteous** before God.
AP : 0 7 :020(171) [0233] up of true believers and **righteous** men scattered
AP : 0 7 :034(175) [0239] that somebody can be **righteous** and a child of God even
AP : 0 7 :034(175) [0239] follows that men can be **righteous**, children of God, and
AP : 1 2 :047(188) [0265] word (Hab. 2:4), "The **righteous** shall live by his faith."
AP : 1 2 :078(193) [0275] thy servant; for no man living is **righteous** before thee."
AP : 1 2 :108(198) [0283] justify us and account us **righteous** through Thy mercy."-
AP : 1 5 :008(216) [0317] deserve to be accounted **righteous** before God, then
AP : 1 5 :008(216) [0317] Christ if he believes he is **righteous** by his own observance
AP : 1 5 :012(216) [0317] we are not accounted **righteous** for his sake but must first
AP : 2 0 :003(227) [0339] of sins men are **righteous** before God not through faith
AP : 2 1 :019(231) [0347] we may be accounted **righteous** as though the merits were
AP : 2 1 :019(231) [0347] him we are accounted **righteous** by our trust in Christ's
AP : 2 1 :022(232) [0349] we were accounted **righteous** on account of them just as
AP : 2 1 :025(232) [0349] and accounted **righteous** not only by Christ's merits but
AP : 2 1 :029(233) [0351] to us or accounted us **righteous** or saved us on this
AP : 2 1 :031(233) [0351] them we are accounted **righteous** when we believe in him,
AP : 2 1 :031(233) [0351] that we are accounted **righteous** by the merits of the
AP : 2 3 :034(244) [0373] that is, to believers in Christ who are **righteous** by faith.
AP : 2 3 :039(244) [0375] make an orator more **righteous** before God than building
AP : 2 3 :039(244) [0375] that through faith he is accounted **righteous** before God.
AP : 2 3 :046(246) [0377] that through such hypocrisy they are pure and **righteous**.
AP : 2 4 :034(256) [0395] the offerings of the **righteous**; therefore it does not
AP : 2 7 :023(272) [0427] which we are accounted **righteous** before God and
AP : 2 7 :069(281) [0443] them we are accounted **righteous**; that we attain eternal
S 2 : 0 1 :004(292) [0461] he [God] himself is **righteous** and that he justifies him
S 3 : 0 3 :033(308) [0489] Rom. 3:10-12: "None is **righteous**, no, not one; no one
S 3 : 0 7 :002(312) [0493] for no man living is **righteous** before thee" (Ps. 143:2),
S 3 : 1 3 :001(315) [0499] account us altogether **righteous** and holy for the sake of
S 3 : 1 3 :002(315) [0499] accounted and shall be **righteous** and holy through the
SC : 0 4 :012(349) [0551] rise up, cleansed and **righteous**, to live forever in God's
EP : 0 3 :003(473) [0793] *man's obedience* many will be made **righteous**"
EP : 0 3 :004(473) [0793] accepted by God into grace and are regarded as **righteous**.
EP : 0 3 :006(473) [0793] regarded as holy and **righteous** by God the Father, and
EP : 0 3 :007(473) [0793] he who condemns the **righteous** are both alike an
EP : 0 3 :010(474) [0795] effect that we become **righteous** and are saved "alone by
EP : 0 3 :015(475) [0795] but mean to be made **righteous** in fact before God on
EP : 0 7 :041(486) [0817] we commend to the **righteous** judgment of God all
EP : 1 2 :006(498) [0839] are not sinners but are **righteous** and innocent, and that
EP : 1 2 :027(500) [0843] unless he is himself truly reborn, **righteous**, and pious.
EP : 1 2 :031(500) [0843] the Last Day before the **righteous** judge, our Lord Jesus
SD : P R :007(502) [0849] Some wanted to become **righteous** and to be saved by the
SD : 0 1 :029(513) [0867] is allegedly pure, holy, **righteous**, and incorrupt in the
SD : 0 2 :022(525) [0889] And while God in his **righteous** and severe judgment cast
SD : 0 3 :011(541) [0919] by grace, are accounted **righteous** and holy by God the
SD : 0 3 :015(541) [0919] accounts us holy and **righteous**, and saves us forever on
SD : 0 3 :017(541) [0921] here means to declare **righteous** and free from sins and
SD : 0 3 :017(542) [0921] he who condemns the **righteous** are both alike an
SD : 0 3 :020(542) [0921] "He who through faith is **righteous** shall live (Rom. 1:17).
SD : 0 3 :022(543) [0923] regarded as holy and **righteous** through faith and for the
SD : 0 3 :027(544) [0925] a person must first be **righteous** before he can do good
SD : 0 3 :043(547) [0931] faith justifies or makes **righteous** in so far as it is
SD : 0 3 :050(548) [0933] before God and are **righteous** both through the reckoned

Continued ▶

SD : 0 3 :057(550) [0935] many will be made **righteous**" (Rom. 5:19), and "the
SD : 0 3 :057(550) [0935] , and again, "The **righteous** shall live by his faith"
SD : 0 3 :062(550) [0937] be made really and truly **righteous** on account of the love
SD : 0 5 :023(562) [0959] beginning was created **righteous** and holy by God and
SD : 0 6 :005(564) [0963] as though the **righteous** should live without the law.
SD : 0 6 :021(567) [0969] for no man living is **righteous** before thee" (Ps. 143:2).
SD : 1 1 :060(626) [1083] permits us to behold his **righteous** and well deserved
SD : 1 2 :011(634) [1099] sinners before God but **righteous** and innocent, and hence
SD : 1 2 :035(635) [1101] not truly renewed, **righteous**, and pious cannot teach

Righteousness (426)
AG : 0 4 :001(030) [0045] forgiveness of sin and **righteousness** before God by our
AG : 0 4 :002(030) [0045] sin is forgiven and **righteousness** and eternal life are given
AG : 0 4 :003(030) [0045] reckon this faith as **righteousness**, as Paul says in
AG : 0 6 :002(032) [0045] forgiveness of sin and **righteousness** through faith in
AG : 1 6 :004(038) [0051] eternal mode of existence and **righteousness** of the heart.
AG : 2 7 :012(072) [0077] life not only earned **righteousness** and godliness, but also
AG : 2 7 :016(073) [0077] God's grace and **righteousness** before God are earned.
AG : 2 7 :036(076) [0081] by men to obtain **righteousness** and God's grace without
AG : 2 7 :037(077) [0081] one is not to seek for **righteousness** in the precepts and
AG : 2 7 :037(077) [0081] by men but that **righteousness** and godliness in God's
AG : 2 7 :038(077) [0081] for sin and obtains God's grace and **righteousness**.
AG : 2 7 :038(077) [0081] of the grace of Christ and deny the **righteousness** of faith?
AG : 2 7 :048(078) [0081] For **righteousness** of faith, which should be emphasized
AG : 2 8 :008(082) [0085] gifts, namely, eternal **righteousness**, the Holy Spirit, and
AG : 2 8 :037(086) [0089] concerning faith and **righteousness** of faith has almost
AG : 2 8 :062(092) [0093] Christendom when the **righteousness** of faith was no
AG : 2 8 :064(092) [0093] understanding of the **righteousness** of faith and Christian
AL : 0 4 :003(030) [0045] faith God imputes for **righteousness** in his sight
AL : 1 6 :004(038) [0051] teaches an eternal **righteousness** of the heart, but it does
AL : 1 8 :001(039) [0051] attainment of civil **righteousness** and for the choice of
AL : 1 8 :002(039) [0051] Spirit, to attain the **righteousness** of God — that is,
AL : 1 8 :002(039) [0051] — that is, spiritual **righteousness** — because natural man
AL : 1 8 :003(039) [0051] (I Cor. 2:14); but this **righteousness** is wrought in the
AL : 2 0 :008(042) [0053] silence concerning the **righteousness** of faith in sermons
AL : 2 0 :013(043) [0055] defends grace and the **righteousness** of faith against the
AL : 2 0 :018(043) [0055] dream that Christian **righteousness** is nothing else than
AL : 2 0 :018(043) [0055] civil or philosophical **righteousness**, have bad judgment
AL : 2 0 :023(044) [0055] that we have grace, **righteousness**, and forgiveness of sins
AL : 2 6 :004(064) [0071] grace and the **righteousness** of faith, which is the chief
AL : 2 6 :005(064) [0071] order to show that the **righteousness** of a Christian is
AL : 2 6 :006(065) [0071] to merit grace and **righteousness** by distinctions among
AL : 2 6 :013(066) [0073] the consolation of grace and of the **righteousness** of faith.
AL : 2 6 :020(067) [0073] grace and the **righteousness** of faith, and this cannot be
AL : 2 6 :029(068) [0075] notion that Christian **righteousness** cannot exist without
AL : 2 7 :012(072) [0077] life merited not only **righteousness** before God but even
AL : 2 7 :016(073) [0077] of life was instituted to merit grace and **righteousness**.
AL : 2 7 :037(077) [0081] everywhere that **righteousness** is not to be sought for in
AL : 2 7 :038(077) [0081] of Christ and obscure and deny the **righteousness** of faith?
AL : 2 7 :048(078) [0081] For **righteousness** of faith, which ought especially to be
AL : 2 8 :008(082) [0085] things as eternal **righteousness**, the Holy Spirit, and
AL : 2 8 :037(086) [0089] faith and the **righteousness** of faith has been suppressed,
AL : 2 8 :062(092) [0093] the church when the **righteousness** of faith was not taught
AL : 2 8 :064(092) [0093] understanding of the **righteousness** of faith and Christian
AP : 0 2 :009(102) [0107] what else is this but to have original **righteousness**?
AP : 0 2 :010(102) [0109] if we can become righteous by our own **righteousness**?
AP : 0 2 :012(102) [0109] philosophical or civic **righteousness**, which we agree is
AP : 0 2 :015(102) [0109] thing, "Original sin is the lack of original **righteousness**."
AP : 0 2 :015(102) [0109] But what is **righteousness**?
AP : 0 2 :015(102) [0109] and do not explain what original **righteousness** is.
AP : 0 2 :016(102) [0109] In the Scriptures **righteousness** contains not merely the
AP : 0 2 :017(102) [0109] So original **righteousness** was intended to involve not
AP : 0 2 :018(102) [0111] that a wisdom and **righteousness** was implanted in man
AP : 0 2 :020(103) [0111] of God is the knowledge of God, **righteousness**, and truth.
AP : 0 2 :021(103) [0111] to say that original **righteousness** is the very likeness of
AP : 0 2 :023(103) [0111] **righteousness**, it not only denies the obedience of man's
AP : 0 2 :024(103) [0111] It means that when **righteousness** is lost, concupiscence
AP : 0 2 :026(103) [0111] carnal wisdom and **righteousness** in which it trusts while
AP : 0 2 :028(104) [0113] to answer that it is the lack of proper **righteousness**.
AP : 0 2 :033(104) [0113] All the **righteousness** of man is mere hypocrisy before
AP : 0 4 :003(107) [0121] faith nor grace nor **righteousness**, our opponents confuse
AP : 0 4 :009(108) [0123] they teach only the **righteousness** of reason—that is, civil
AP : 0 4 :012(109) [0123] If this is Christian **righteousness**, what difference is there
AP : 0 4 :013(109) [0123] ought to seek some **righteousness** beyond the
AP : 0 4 :016(109) [0123] or Pharisaic **righteousness** and Christian righteousness.
AP : 0 4 :016(109) [0123] or Pharisaic righteousness and Christian **righteousness**.
AP : 0 4 :018(109) [0125] yet without the **righteousness** of faith man can neither
AP : 0 4 :020(110) [0125] because men naturally trust their own **righteousness**.
AP : 0 4 :020(110) [0125] the free forgiveness of sins and the **righteousness** of faith.
AP : 0 4 :021(110) [0127] teach nothing but the **righteousness** of reason or of law,
AP : 0 4 :022(110) [0127] maintain that God requires the **righteousness** of reason.
AP : 0 4 :023(110) [0127] can produce this **righteousness** by its own strength,
AP : 0 4 :024(110) [0127] We freely give this **righteousness** of reason its due credit;
AP : 0 4 :024(110) [0127] the morning star is more beautiful than **righteousness**."
AP : 0 4 :026(110) [0127] before God because of the **righteousness** of reason.
AP : 0 4 :030(111) [0129] 'being ignorant of the **righteousness** that comes from
AP : 0 4 :030(111) [0129] you did not submit to God's **righteousness**' (Rom. 10:3).
AP : 0 4 :030(111) [0129] corrupted nature, for **righteousness** to 'every one who has
AP : 0 4 :031(111) [0129] Holy Spirit, then the **righteousness** of reason does not
AP : 0 4 :032(111) [0129] lack the wisdom and **righteousness** of God which
AP : 0 4 :034(111) [0129] which contain the civil **righteousness** that reason
AP : 0 4 :039(112) [0131] enough about the **righteousness** of law or of reason which
AP : 0 4 :039(112) [0131] of our doctrine of the **righteousness** of faith, the subject
AP : 0 4 :041(113) [0133] he says, "Now, the **righteousness** of God has been
AP : 0 4 :043(113) [0133] Gospel proclaims the **righteousness** of faith in Christ,
AP : 0 4 :043(113) [0133] And this is not the **righteousness** of the law.
AP : 0 4 :047(113) [0133] for teaching the **righteousness** of the law instead of the
AP : 0 4 :047(113) [0133] the law instead of the **righteousness** of the Gospel, which
AP : 0 4 :047(113) [0133] which proclaims the **righteousness** of faith in Christ.
AP : 0 4 :049(114) [0135] between this faith and the **righteousness** of the law.
AP : 0 4 :049(114) [0135] offered blessing; the **righteousness** of the law is that
AP : 0 4 :086(119) [0147] that faith is the very **righteousness** by which we are
AP : 0 4 :086(119) [0147] our wisdom, our **righteousness** and sanctification and
AP : 0 4 :089(120) [0149] the ungodly, his faith is reckoned as **righteousness**."
AP : 0 4 :089(120) [0149] clearly says that faith itself is accounted for **righteousness**.
AP : 0 4 :089(120) [0149] God declares to be **righteousness**; he adds that it is
AP : 0 4 :089(120) [0149] would not be accounted for **righteousness** without works.
AP : 0 4 :090(120) [0149] that faith was reckoned to Abraham as **righteousness**."
AP : 0 4 :092(120) [0149] he declares that faith is the **righteousness** of the heart.
AP : 0 4 :106(122) [0153] *Letter* he says: "The **righteousness** of law is set forth in
AP : 0 4 :121(124) [0155] free forgiveness of sins and of the **righteousness** of Christ.
AP : 0 4 :132(125) [0159] forth in us eternal **righteousness** and a new and eternal
AP : 0 4 :147(127) [0163] Spirit and since it is **righteousness** because it is the
AP : 0 4 :150(127) [0163] this trust in his own **righteousness** was wicked and
AP : 0 4 :155(128) [0165] not only alms, but also the **righteousness** of faith.
AP : 0 4 :159(129) [0165] law, and obedience to the law certainly is **righteousness**.
AP : 0 4 :160(129) [0167] is perfect, it is indeed **righteousness**; but in us it is weak
AP : 0 4 :163(129) [0169] the imputation of the **righteousness** of the Gospel is
AP : 0 4 :173(131) [0171] are sinners; and our **righteousness** does not consist in our
AP : 0 4 :181(132) [0171] in keeping with the **righteousness** of the law, to the extent
AP : 0 4 :181(132) [0171] of the law justifies by the **righteousness** of the law.
AP : 0 4 :181(132) [0171] accepts this imperfect **righteousness** of the law only
AP : 0 4 :198(134) [0175] often puts off the rewards for the **righteousness** of works.
AP : 0 4 :198(134) [0175] to trust in their own **righteousness**, but to seek the will of
AP : 0 4 :198(134) [0175] are persecuted for **righteousness**' sake, for theirs is the
AP : 0 4 :208(135) [0177] to merit grace, **righteousness**, and the forgiveness of sins.
AP : 0 4 :211(136) [0179] to merit the forgiveness of sins, grace, and **righteousness**.
AP : 0 4 :214(136) [0179] of sins, grace, and **righteousness** through works.
AP : 0 4 :216(137) [0179] now about the **righteousness** by which we deal with God,
AP : 0 4 :221(137) [0181] justification and teach only the **righteousness** of the law.
AP : 0 4 :229(139) [0183] they teach and require the **righteousness** of the law.
AP : 0 4 :229(139) [0183] wisdom looks at the law and seeks **righteousness** in it.
AP : 0 4 :230(139) [0183] which reveals another **righteousness**, namely, that because
AP : 0 4 :238(141) [0187] to us; or that love is **righteousness** without Christ, the
AP : 0 4 :238(141) [0187] a love, it would be a **righteousness** of the law rather than
AP : 0 4 :238(141) [0187] us reconciliation and **righteousness** if we believe that for
AP : 0 4 :262(145) [0195] "Redeem your sins by **righteousness** and your iniquities
AP : 0 4 :263(145) [0195] **Righteousness** is faith in the heart.
AP : 0 4 :285(150) [0201] that the promise of **righteousness** does not depend upon
AP : 0 4 :285(150) [0201] promised forgiveness of sins and **righteousness** of faith.
AP : 0 4 :285(150) [0201] him we might have grace, **righteousness**, and peace.
AP : 0 4 :288(151) [0203] that we should seek **righteousness** through these works
AP : 0 4 :288(151) [0203] which they seek **righteousness**, grace, and salvation *ex*
AP : 0 4 :290(151) [0203] the propitiator, is a **righteousness** worthy of grace and
AP : 0 4 :292(152) [0203] Paul says, too, that **righteousness** is not by the law but by
AP : 0 4 :293(152) [0203] faith is accounted for **righteousness** before God
AP : 0 4 :297(153) [0205] which reconciliation, **righteousness**, and eternal life are
AP : 0 4 :297(153) [0205] the promise of the forgiveness of sins and **righteousness**.
AP : 0 4 :299(153) [0205] not because of our **righteousness** but because Christ still
AP : 0 4 :300(153) [0205] trying to destroy the doctrine of **righteousness** by faith.
AP : 0 4 :304(154) [0205] may quibble here that **righteousness** is in the will and
AP : 0 4 :305(154) [0205] of someone else's **righteousness**, namely, Christ's, which
AP : 0 4 :306(154) [0207] in this passage our **righteousness** is the imputation of
AP : 0 4 :306(154) [0207] of someone else's **righteousness**, we must speak of
AP : 0 4 :306(154) [0207] we must speak of **righteousness** in a different way here
AP : 0 4 :306(154) [0207] of a man's own **righteousness**, which certainly resides in
AP : 0 4 :306(154) [0207] made our wisdom, our **righteousness** and sanctification
AP : 0 4 :306(154) [0207] that in him we might become the **righteousness** of God."
AP : 0 4 :307(154) [0207] Because the **righteousness** of Christ is given to us through
AP : 0 4 :307(154) [0207] faith, therefore faith is **righteousness** in us by imputation.
AP : 0 4 :307(154) [0207] says (Rom. 4:5), "Faith is reckoned as **righteousness**."
AP : 0 4 :308(155) [0207] critics: faith is truly **righteousness** because it is obedience
AP : 0 4 :308(155) [0207] superior is obviously a kind of distributive **righteousness**.
AP : 0 4 :308(155) [0207] Christ, the propitiator, and is reckoned for **righteousness**.
AP : 0 4 :310(155) [0207] to receive forgiveness of sins, grace, and **righteousness**.
AP : 0 4 :313(155) [0207] we want to teach the **righteousness** of the Gospel and not
AP : 0 4 :313(155) [0207] by love teach the **righteousness** of the law, they do not
AP : 0 4 :316(156) [0209] of love, are a worthy **righteousness** that pleases God of
AP : 0 4 :317(156) [0209] must then seek his **righteousness** elsewhere, he thereby
AP : 0 4 :320(156) [0209] to be utterly sure that **righteousness** and eternal life are
AP : 0 4 :326(157) [0211] any glory in man's **righteousness**, even to all the saints
AP : 0 4 :326(157) [0211] boasts of his **righteousness**, he is speaking of his cause
AP : 0 4 :326(158) [0211] Lord, according to my **righteousness** and according to the
AP : 0 4 :329(158) [0211] is, the flesh and the **righteousness** of the flesh cannot
AP : 0 4 :331(158) [0211] on the ground of our **righteousness**, but on the ground of
AP : 0 4 :332(158) [0211] relies on its own **righteousness** and not on the mercy of
AP : 0 4 :337(159) [0215] before thee on the ground of our **righteousness**," etc.
AP : 0 4 :348(160) [0217] to the flesh can retain neither faith nor **righteousness**.
AP : 0 4 :352(161) [0217] of sin, your spirits are alive because of **righteousness**."
AP : 0 4 :356(161) [0217] because the **righteousness** bestowed on us for
AP : 0 4 :361(162) [0219] of Christ and the **righteousness** of faith are obscured.
AP : 0 4 :363(162) [0219] for me the crown of **righteousness**, which the Lord, the
AP : 0 4 :365(163) [0219] wish to include the **righteousness** of the heart with other
AP : 0 4 :366(163) [0221] The **righteousness** of the Gospel, which deals with the
AP : 0 4 :371(164) [0221] of hypocrisy but of **righteousness** in the heart and of its
AP : 0 4 :373(164) [0221] works but the entire **righteousness** or unrighteousness.
AP : 0 4 :373(164) [0221] and evidence of the **righteousness** of the heart and of
AP : 0 4 :373(164) [0221] and for this reason eternal life is granted to **righteousness**.
AP : 0 4 :374(164) [0221] lump together the **righteousness** of the heart and its fruit.
AP : 0 4 :375(164) [0223] in distinguishing the **righteousness** of the heart from its
AP : 0 4 :376(164) [0223] from them the **righteousness** of faith and Christ, the
AP : 0 4 :376(164) [0223] and because they are **righteousness** that they are worthy
AP : 0 4 :376(164) [0223] obviously destroys the **righteousness** of faith, which
AP : 0 4 :377(165) [0223] teaching about the **righteousness** of faith dare not be
AP : 0 4 :383(165) [0225] The scholastics do not teach the **righteousness** of faith.
AP : 0 4 :383(165) [0225] promise of grace and **righteousness**, quickening the heart
AP : 0 4 :392(167) [0225] of sins, grace, and **righteousness** through our works and
AP : 0 4 :393(167) [0225] would obscure the **righteousness** of faith in this way.
AP : 0 4 :393(167) [0225] who in place of the **righteousness** of faith taught that men
AP : 0 4 :394(167) [0225] The only **righteousness** that reason can see is the
AP : 0 4 :394(167) [0225] reason can see is the **righteousness** of the law, understood
AP : 0 4 :394(167) [0225] only this outward **righteousness** to the exclusion of the
AP : 0 4 :394(167) [0225] the exclusion of the **righteousness** of faith, and such
AP : 0 4 :395(167) [0225] this opinion and taught the **righteousness** of faith.
AP : 0 7 :013(170) [0231] of Christ is the **righteousness** of the heart and the gift of
AP : 0 7 :015(170) [0231] Holy Spirit and the **righteousness** by which we are

Continued ▶

A P : 0 7 :031(174) [0237] faith in the heart nor **righteousness** in the heart before
A P : 0 7 :031(174) [0237] The **righteousness** of faith is not a righteousness tied to
A P : 0 7 :031(174) [0237] of faith is not a **righteousness** tied to certain traditions, as
A P : 0 7 :031(174) [0237] traditions, as the **righteousness** of the law was tied to the
A P : 0 7 :031(174) [0237] because this **righteousness** of the heart is something that
A P : 0 7 :032(174) [0239] unrelated to the **righteousness** of the heart or the worship
A P : 0 7 :032(174) [0239] that there can be no **righteousness** of the heart before God
A P : 0 7 :034(175) [0239] an act of worship necessary for **righteousness** before God.
A P : 0 7 :034(175) [0239] worship necessary for **righteousness** before God, it
A P : 0 7 :034(175) [0239] to God necessary for **righteousness** before him, it follows
A P : 0 7 :036(175) [0241] The **righteousness** of the heart is a spiritual thing that
A P : 0 7 :036(175) [0241] that they are necessary for **righteousness** before God.
A P : 0 7 :036(175) [0241] food and drink but **righteousness** and peace and joy in
A P : 0 7 :037(175) [0241] acts of devotion necessary for **righteousness** before God.
A P : 0 7 :039(176) [0241] such rites are necessary for **righteousness** before God.
A P : 0 7 :039(176) [0241] food, and the like a matter of **righteousness** or of sin.
A P : 0 7 :045(177) [0243] the meaning of the **righteousness** of faith and of the
A P : 1 2 :010(184) [0255] the power of the keys, and the **righteousness** of faith.
A P : 1 2 :016(184) [0257] the doctrine of the **righteousness** of faith in Christ and of
A P : 1 2 :029(185) [0259] of sins and **righteousness** for Christ's sake, to grant the
A P : 1 2 :079(194) [0275] the forgiveness of sins because of our **righteousness**.
A P : 1 2 :108(198) [0283] and I cannot set my **righteousness** or my merits against
A P : 1 2 :116(199) [0287] by their adoption the **righteousness** of faith be obscured
A P : 1 2 :118(199) [0287] it is fitting for divine **righteousness** to punish sin, he
A P : 1 2 :122(200) [0289] your members to **righteousness**" (Rom. 6:19); Christ's
A P : 1 2 :132(202) [0291] your members to **righteousness**," and elsewhere
A P : 1 2 :134(203) [0293] befits penitence," "Yield your members to **righteousness**."
A P : 1 2 :142(204) [0295] that God's law deals with external, civil **righteousness**.
A P : 1 2 :161(208) [0303] it, for the sake of **righteousness**, that is, to exercise and
A P : 1 2 :161(208) [0303] exercise and test the **righteousness** of those who are
A P : 1 5 :004(215) [0315] Gospel, the blessing of Christ, and **righteousness** of faith.
A P : 1 5 :009(216) [0317] to us through him, not through our own **righteousness**.
A P : 1 5 :010(216) [0317] of as works meriting **righteousness** before God and
A P : 1 5 :010(216) [0317] the work of Christ and the **righteousness** of faith.
A P : 1 5 :013(216) [0319] of meriting the forgiveness of sins or **righteousness**.
A P : 1 5 :014(216) [0319] forgiveness of sins or **righteousness**, how will he know
A P : 1 5 :015(217) [0319] to merit grace or **righteousness**, why did not the heathen
A P : 1 5 :016(217) [0319] their ignorance of the **righteousness** of faith, they believed
A P : 1 5 :016(217) [0319] they merited the forgiveness of sins and **righteousness**.
A P : 1 5 :022(218) [0321] not understand the **righteousness** of faith, it naturally
A P : 1 5 :024(218) [0321] appearance of wisdom and **righteousness** in such works.
A P : 1 5 :025(218) [0321] of wisdom and **righteousness** has deceived men, all sorts
A P : 1 5 :025(218) [0321] The Gospel of the **righteousness** of faith in Christ is
A P : 1 5 :029(219) [0323] of wisdom and **righteousness** in human rites, let us
A P : 1 5 :032(220) [0325] for justification, they obscure the **righteousness** of faith.
A P : 1 5 :042(221) [0327] say nothing about the **righteousness** of faith or about
A P : 1 5 :043(221) [0327] faith in Christ, the **righteousness** of faith, comfort for the
A P : 1 5 :050(222) [0329] are necessary over and above the **righteousness** of faith.
A P : 1 6 :002(222) [0331] the beginning of eternal **righteousness** and eternal life.
A P : 1 6 :008(223) [0333] Gospel brings eternal **righteousness** to hearts, while it
A P : 1 8 :004(225) [0335] it can achieve civil **righteousness** or the righteousness of
A P : 1 8 :004(225) [0335] achieve civil righteousness or the **righteousness** of works.
A P : 1 8 :004(225) [0335] as the liberty and ability to achieve civil **righteousness**.
A P : 1 8 :004(225) [0335] This **righteousness** which the carnal nature — that is, the
A P : 1 8 :004(225) [0335] Holy Spirit, Scripture calls the **righteousness** of the flesh.
A P : 1 8 :005(225) [0335] reasons even civil **righteousness** is rare among men, as we
A P : 1 8 :005(225) [0335] seem to have wanted this **righteousness** did not achieve it.
A P : 1 8 :009(226) [0337] between civil **righteousness** and spiritual righteousness,
A P : 1 8 :009(226) [0337] and spiritual **righteousness**, attributing the former to the
A P : 1 8 :009(226) [0337] God requires this civil **righteousness** and that, to some
A P : 1 8 :009(226) [0337] between human **righteousness** and spiritual
A P : 1 8 :009(226) [0337] and spiritual **righteousness**, between philosophical
A P : 2 3 :037(244) [0373] the truth of the **righteousness** of faith, as we have
A P : 2 3 :048(246) [0377] one should trust in certain observances for **righteousness**.
A P : 2 4 :012(251) [0387] his merits and **righteousness** are bestowed upon us.
A P : 2 4 :023(253) [0391] not want our own **righteousness** but the merits of another
A P : 2 4 :024(253) [0391] since they gained the **righteousness** of the ceremonial law
A P : 2 4 :027(254) [0393] is spiritual; it is the **righteousness** of faith in the heart and
A P : 2 4 :028(254) [0393] *operato* and teach spiritual **righteousness** and sacrifice.
A P : 2 4 :043(258) [0399] the law and say nothing about the **righteousness** of faith.
A P : 2 4 :057(260) [0405] suffering and the **righteousness** of faith, it corrupts the
A P : 2 4 :060(260) [0405] conflict between the **righteousness** of faith and the idea
A P : 2 4 :063(261) [0405] glory of Christ's suffering and the **righteousness** of faith.
A P : 2 4 :077(263) [0411] else without faith conflicts with the **righteousness** of faith.
A P : 2 4 :096(268) [0417] and utterly destroy the doctrine of **righteousness** by faith.
A P : 2 4 :097(268) [0417] do not understand the **righteousness** of faith but give
A P : 2 4 :098(268) [0419] obscure the glory of Christ and the **righteousness** of faith.
A P : 2 7 :023(272) [0427] with the Gospel of the **righteousness** of faith, which
A P : 2 7 :023(272) [0427] that for Christ's sake **righteousness** and eternal life are
A P : 2 7 :023(273) [0427] God approves as **righteousness** before him when they
A P : 2 7 :027(273) [0429] kingdom of God is **righteousness** (Rom. 14:17) and life in
A P : 2 7 :054(278) [0437] sake, about the **righteousness** of faith, about true
A P : 2 8 :007(282) [0445] neither sin nor **righteousness** depends upon food, drink,
A P : 2 8 :008(282) [0445] were acts of worship that pleased God as **righteousness**.
A P : 2 8 :009(282) [0445] they acts of worship which please God as **righteousness**?
A P : 2 8 :010(282) [0447] avail for eternal **righteousness** and eternal life since food,
A P : 2 8 :011(283) [0447] that please God as **righteousness** or to burden consciences
S 3 : 0 3 :029(308) [0487] sell their superfluous **righteousness** to other poor sinners?
T R : 0 0 :034(325) [0513] Christian **righteousness** was thought to be that external
T R : 0 0 :048(328) [0519] that vows produce **righteousness** before God and merit
S C : 0 2 :004(345) [0545] him in everlasting **righteousness**, innocence, and
L C : 0 1 :059(372) [0597] turn the villainy into **righteousness** and the disgrace into
L C : 0 2 :030(414) [0685] the Lord of life and **righteousness** and every good and
L C : 0 2 :030(414) [0685] he may rule us by his **righteousness**, wisdom, power, life,
L C : 0 2 :031(414) [0685] to life, from sin to **righteousness**, and now keeps us safe
L C : 0 2 :058(418) [0693] full of goodness and **righteousness**, completely freed from
L C : 0 3 :051(426) [0711] rule us as a king of **righteousness**, life, and salvation
L C : 0 3 :054(427) [0713] may live forever in perfect **righteousness** and blessedness."
E P : 0 2 :012(471) [0789] constitutes our **righteousness** before God whereby we
E P : 0 3 :000(472) [0791] III. The **Righteousness** of Faith before God
E P : 0 3 :001(472) [0791] faith in Christ, so that Christ alone is our **righteousness**.
E P : 0 3 :001(473) [0791] According to which nature is Christ our **righteousness**?
E P : 0 3 :002(473) [0791] held that Christ is our **righteousness** only according to his
E P : 0 3 :002(473) [0793] held that Christ is our **righteousness** before God only
E P : 0 3 :003(473) [0793] that Christ is our **righteousness** neither according to the
E P : 0 3 :003(473) [0793] to both natures is our **righteousness** solely in his
E P : 0 3 :004(473) [0793] and confess that our **righteousness** before God consists in
E P : 0 3 :004(473) [0793] and reckons to us the **righteousness** of Christ's obedience,
E P : 0 3 :004(473) [0793] on account of which **righteousness** we are accepted by
E P : 0 3 :005(473) [0793] in Christ obtain the "**righteousness** which avails before
E P : 0 3 :005(473) [0793] sake such faith is reckoned for **righteousness** (Rom. 4:5).
E P : 0 3 :009(474) [0795] to doubt either the **righteousness** which is reckoned to
E P : 0 3 :010(474) [0795] concerning the **righteousness** of faith before God, we
E P : 0 3 :013(474) [0795] 1. That Christ is our **righteousness** only according to the
E P : 0 3 :014(474) [0795] 2. That Christ is our **righteousness** only according to the
E P : 0 3 :015(474) [0795] 3. That when the **righteousness** of faith is spoken of in the
E P : 0 3 :020(475) [0797] love belong to our **righteousness** before God, not indeed
E P : 0 3 :020(475) [0797] primary cause of our **righteousness**, but that nevertheless
E P : 0 3 :020(475) [0797] that nevertheless our **righteousness** before God is
E P : 0 3 :021(475) [0797] and saved both by the **righteousness** of Christ reckoned to
E P : 0 3 :021(475) [0797] to them of Christ's **righteousness** and in part by our
E P : 0 3 :023(475) [0797] are necessary for **righteousness** and that unless they are
E P : 0 4 :007(476) [0799] whom God reckons **righteousness** apart from works,
E P : 0 4 :012(477) [0799] but out of a love of **righteousness**, like a child
E P : 0 5 :005(478) [0803] of sins, the "**righteousness** that avails before God," and
E P : 0 5 :009(479) [0803] that we should now seek all our **righteousness** in Christ.
E P : 1 2 :005(498) [0839] 3. That our **righteousness** before God does not consist
S D : 0 1 :002(508) [0859] that man lacks the **righteousness** in which he was
S D : 0 1 :010(510) [0863] original concreated **righteousness** of paradise or of the
S D : 0 1 :010(510) [0863] truth, holiness, and **righteousness**, together with a
S D : 0 1 :027(513) [0867] man lost the concreated **righteousness** as a punishment.
S D : 0 1 :030(513) [0867] truth, holiness, and **righteousness** imparted at creation to
S D : 0 2 :011(522) [0885] and heavenly **righteousness** and life, unless the Son of
S D : 0 2 :018(524) [0889] for man's conversion, **righteousness**, peace, and
S D : 0 2 :043(529) [0897] prepare ourselves for **righteousness** and life or seek after
S D : 0 2 :044(529) [0897] of its own to prepare itself and to strive for **righteousness**.
S D : 0 2 :074(535) [0909] a measure of external **righteousness** and honorable
S D : 0 2 :079(536) [0911] of the law merit **righteousness** before God and eternal
S D : 0 3 :000(539) [0917] III. The **Righteousness** of Faith before God
S D : 0 3 :001(539) [0917] concerns the **righteousness** of Christ or of faith which
S D : 0 3 :001(539) [0917] through faith reckons to poor sinners as **righteousness**.
S D : 0 3 :002(539) [0917] contended that the **righteousness** of faith, which St. Paul
S D : 0 3 :002(539) [0917] St. Paul calls the **righteousness** of God, is the essential
S D : 0 3 :002(539) [0917] God, is the essential **righteousness** of God (namely,
S D : 0 3 :002(539) [0917] is in this way their **righteousness**), and that in comparison
S D : 0 3 :002(539) [0917] comparison with this **righteousness** the sins of all men are
S D : 0 3 :003(539) [0917] that Christ is our **righteousness** only according to his
S D : 0 3 :004(539) [0917] that Christ is our **righteousness**, not according to the
S D : 0 3 :004(540) [0917] maintained that the **righteousness** of faith is forgiveness
S D : 0 3 :004(540) [0917] to all true believers as **righteousness**, and that they are
S D : 0 3 :009(540) [0919] Concerning the **righteousness** of faith before God we
S D : 0 3 :009(541) [0919] Lord, whose obedience is reckoned to us as **righteousness**.
S D : 0 3 :012(541) [0919] is reckoned to us as **righteousness**" (Rom. 4:5), or when
S D : 0 3 :012(541) [0919] "one man's act of **righteousness** leads to acquittal and life
S D : 0 3 :014(541) [0919] Therefore the **righteousness** which by grace is reckoned to
S D : 0 3 :015(541) [0919] reckoning it to us as **righteousness**, God forgives us our
S D : 0 3 :016(541) [0921] This **righteousness** is offered to us by the Holy Spirit
S D : 0 3 :017(542) [0921] sins on account of the **righteousness** of Christ which God
S D : 0 3 :021(542) [0921] which follows the **righteousness** of faith, as Dr. Luther
S D : 0 3 :023(543) [0923] the regenerated, the **righteousness** of faith before God
S D : 0 3 :023(543) [0923] reckoning of Christ's **righteousness** to us, without the
S D : 0 3 :025(543) [0923] Gospel, whereby the **righteousness** of Christ is reckoned
S D : 0 3 :027(543) [0923] he has again lost the **righteousness** of faith, as St. John
S D : 0 3 :030(544) [0925] teaches that the **righteousness** of faith before God
S D : 0 3 :030(544) [0925] and which is reckoned to the believers as **righteousness**.
S D : 0 3 :032(544) [0927] first, the reckoned **righteousness** of faith and, second, also
S D : 0 3 :032(544) [0927] also the inchoate **righteousness** of the new obedience or
S D : 0 3 :032(545) [0927] because this inchoate **righteousness** or renewal in us is
S D : 0 3 :032(545) [0927] Only the **righteousness** of the obedience, passion, and
S D : 0 3 :033(545) [0927] On what did the **righteousness** of Abraham before
S D : 0 3 :034(545) [0927] faith is reckoned as **righteousness**" (Rom. 4:5,6), and
S D : 0 3 :034(545) [0927] whom God reckons **righteousness** without the addition of
S D : 0 3 :039(546) [0929] good works are our **righteousness** before God, nor are
S D : 0 3 :039(546) [0929] The **righteousness** of faith consists solely in the
S D : 0 3 :047(548) [0933] 3. That our real **righteousness** before God is our love or
S D : 0 3 :048(548) [0933] 4. That **righteousness** by faith before God consists of two
S D : 0 3 :049(548) [0933] justifies only because **righteousness** is begun in us by
S D : 0 3 :049(548) [0933] belong to our **righteousness** before God, in such a way,
S D : 0 3 :050(548) [0933] through the reckoned **righteousness** of Christ and through
S D : 0 3 :050(548) [0933] reckoning of Christ's **righteousness** and in part by the
S D : 0 3 :053(548) [0933] whom God reckons **righteousness** without works
S D : 0 3 :053(548) [0933] we receive both our **righteousness** and our salvation in
S D : 0 3 :054(548) [0933] the indwelling of God's essential **righteousness** in us.
S D : 0 3 :054(548) [0935] eternal and essential **righteousness**, dwells by faith in the
S D : 0 3 :054(549) [0935] of God is not the **righteousness** of faith of which St. Paul
S D : 0 3 :054(549) [0935] and which he calls the **righteousness** of God, on account
S D : 0 3 :054(549) [0935] follows the preceding **righteousness** of faith, which is
S D : 0 3 :055(549) [0935] must seek our entire **righteousness** apart from our own
S D : 0 3 :055(549) [0935] and that our **righteousness** rests solely and alone on the
S D : 0 3 :055(549) [0935] Christ is called our **righteousness** in this matter of
S D : 0 3 :055(549) [0935] of justification: Our **righteousness** rests neither upon his
S D : 0 3 :055(549) [0935] his sole, total, and perfect obedience is our **righteousness**.
S D : 0 3 :056(549) [0935] alone fulfilled all **righteousness** but had not been true,
S D : 0 3 :056(549) [0935] nature could not be reckoned to us as **righteousness**.
S D : 0 3 :056(549) [0935] nature alone could not have been our **righteousness**.
S D : 0 3 :056(549) [0935] death of the cross, is reckoned to us as **righteousness**.
S D : 0 3 :057(549) [0935] and immutable **righteousness** of God revealed in the law.
S D : 0 3 :057(549) [0935] This obedience is our **righteousness** which avails before
S D : 0 3 :058(550) [0937] is reckoned to us as **righteousness**, but only the obedience
S D : 0 3 :060(550) [0937] that Christ is our **righteousness** before God only
S D : 0 3 :061(550) [0937] 2. That Christ is our **righteousness** only according to his
S D : 0 3 :062(550) [0937] apostles speak of the **righteousness** of faith, the words, "to
S D : 0 4 :015(553) [0943] and retain true faith, **righteousness**, and salvation even
S D : 0 4 :023(555) [0945] trust in one's own **righteousness** and confidence in one's
S D : 0 4 :024(555) [0945] whom God reckons **righteousness** apart from works
S D : 0 4 :030(555) [0947] necessary to preserve faith, **righteousness**, and salvation.

Continued ▶

SD : 04 :030(556) [0947] well and in detail how **righteousness** and salvation are
SD : 04 :031(556) [0947] faith and the gift of **righteousness** and salvation, once it
SD : 04 :031(556) [0947] faith, the grace of God, **righteousness**, and salvation.
SD : 04 :034(556) [0949] that faith accepts **righteousness** and salvation only at the
SD : 04 :034(556) [0949] preserve faith, the **righteousness** that has been received,
SD : 04 :034(556) [0949] receive but also retain **righteousness** and salvation may be
SD : 04 :035(557) [0949] only means whereby **righteousness** and salvation are not
SD : 04 :035(557) [0949] preserve either the **righteousness** of faith that we have
SD : 04 :037(557) [0949] and rests his **righteousness** or his assurance of salvation
SD : 05 :017(561) [0957] which reveals the **righteousness** and immutable will of
SD : 05 :022(562) [0959] we might become the **righteousness** of God," who was
SD : 05 :022(562) [0959] who was "made our **righteousness**," and whose obedience
SD : 05 :022(562) [0959] is reckoned to us as **righteousness** in the strict judgment
SD : 05 :022(562) [0959] "a dispensation of **righteousness**" and "of the Spirit."
SD : 06 :012(566) [0967] belongs) of sin and of **righteousness** and of judgment."
SD : 07 :062(581) [0995] forgiveness of sins, **righteousness**, and everlasting life), is
SD : 10 :006(611) [1055] what partnership have **righteousness** and iniquity, or
SD : 10 :012(613) [1057] law are necessary for **righteousness** and salvation, Paul
SD : 11 :015(619) [1069] has earned for us "the **righteousness** which avails before
SD : 11 :028(621) [1071] **Righteousness** "comes through faith in Christ to all and
SD : 11 :030(621) [1073] hunger and thirst after **righteousness** (Matt. 5:6).
SD : 11 :039(623) [1077] or seek other ways to **righteousness** and salvation outside
SD : 11 :045(624) [1079] conversion, **righteousness**, and salvation and so faithfully
SD : 11 :086(631) [1091] setting forth the **righteousness** of God which God
SD : 12 :010(633) [1097] 1. That our **righteousness** before God does not depend

Rightfully (1), Rightly (42)
PR : PR :022(012) [0019] hoped that when they are **rightly** instructed in this
AG : PR :003(025) [0039] may not have been **rightly** interpreted or treated by either
AG : 13 :002(036) [0049] faith, and they are **rightly** used when they are received in
AG : 00 :000(049) [0059] God's command (which is **rightly** to be regarded as above
AG : 24 :024(058) [0067] might know how the sacrament is to be used **rightly**.
AL : 07 :001(032) [0047] purely and the sacraments are administered **rightly**.
AP : 04 :101(121) [0151] know these blessings is **rightly** and truly to believe in
AP : 04 :135(125) [0159] so that we can think **rightly** about God, fear him, and
AP : 12 :093(196) [0279] Discernment may **rightly** be demanded of those who have
AP : 12 :127(201) [0291] and adjudge them **rightly**, because you do not strengthen
AP : 14 :004(214) [0315] present among those who **rightly** teach the Word of God
AP : 14 :004(215) [0315] the Word of God and **rightly** administer the sacraments.
AP : 15 :042(221) [0327] This the people **rightly** despise and walk out on them
S3 : 03 :032(308) [0489] Accordingly, if you would repent, repent **rightly**.
LC : 01 :157(386) [0627] so deeply sunk and may **rightly** understand the Word and
LC : 01 :191(391) [0635] Therefore God **rightly** calls all persons murderers who do
LC : 02 :060(418) [0695] importance, as long as the words are **rightly** understood.
LC : 03 :025(423) [0705] Therefore we have **rightly** rejected the prayers of monks
LC : 03 :029(424) [0705] brought again to pray **rightly** and not act so crudely and
LC : 03 :045(426) [0709] deceiving, etc., but used **rightly** to the praise and glory of
LC : 03 :057(427) [0713] He would **rightly** be considered a rogue and a scoundrel
LC : 03 :062(428) [0715] He cannot bear to have anyone teach or believe **rightly**.
LC : 04 :056(443) [0747] was right, but unfortunately I did not receive it **rightly**."
LC : 05 :010(448) [0755] it a sacrament which is **rightly** called Christ's body and
LC : 06 :034(461) [0000] see, confession would be **rightly** taught, and such a desire
EP : 05 :002(478) [0801] admonition, the Word of God may be divided **rightly**.
EP : 08 :012(488) [0821] God; for this reason she is **rightly** called, and truly is, the
EP : 12 :029(500) [0843] and that only the Father is **rightly** and truly God.
SD : 01 :054(517) [0877] of the uninstructed ought **rightly** be spared these terms in
SD : 01 :059(519) [0879] that every one be **rightly** instructed in these issues.
SD : 02 :015(523) [0887] so that he might **rightly** comprehend and learn the divine
SD : 02 :086(538) [0913] it and therefore is **rightly** to be avoided in the discussion
SD : 03 :006(540) [0917] any abiding comfort or **rightly** understand the riches of
SD : 03 :011(541) [0919] a gift of God whereby we **rightly** learn to know Christ as
SD : 03 :054(549) [0935] Son, and Holy Spirit, who impels them to do **rightly**.
SD : 04 :015(553) [0943] They should **rightly** be used and urged to criticize and
SD : 04 :035(557) [0949] preserved by God, we **rightly** reject the decree of the
SD : 05 :001(558) [0951] the Word of God may be **rightly** divided and the writings
SD : 05 :003(558) [0953] When we **rightly** reflect on this controversy, we find that
SD : 05 :022(562) [0959] neither understood nor honored him **rightly** (Rom. 1:21).
SD : 07 :041(576) [0985] Since Dr. Luther is **rightly** to be regarded as the most
SD : 07 :126(591) [1015] in the Supper when it is **rightly** used, should be adored in
SD : 11 :059(626) [1081] what all of us would **rightfully** have deserved, earned, and

Rigidly (1)
SD : 11 :028(620) [1071] must by all means cling **rigidly** and firmly to the fact that

Rigor (5)
AG : 23 :016(054) [0063] to relax severity and **rigor** for the sake of human
AG : 27 :008(072) [0077] Such severity and **rigor** displeased many devout people in
AL : 23 :016(054) [0063] that in later times the old **rigor** should be relaxed now
AL : 27 :008(071) [0077] Such **rigor** displeased many good men before our time
AP : 07 :035(175) [0241] of wisdom in promoting **rigor** of devotion and

Ringing (2)
LC : 01 :090(377) [0607] churches, singing and **ringing** bells, without sanctifying
LC : 01 :314(407) [0671] of incense, singing and **ringing** of bells, lighting of tapers

Riotous (1)
SD : 11 :089(631) [1093] either despondency or a **riotous** and dissolute life.

Rise (6), Risen (2), Rises (1), Rising (2), Rose (8)
AG : 03 :004(030) [0045] descended into hell, truly **rose** from the dead on the third
AL : 03 :004(030) [0045] descended into hell, and on the third day truly **rose** again.
AP : 12 :153(206) [0299] this sinful flesh so that we may **rise** completely renewed.
AP : 24 :031(255) [0395] says (1:11), "From the **rising** of the sun to its setting my
S1 : 01 :000(292) [0461] buried, descended to hell, **rose** from the dead, and
SC : 02 :003(345) [0545] *into hell, the third day he* ***rose*** *from the dead, he ascended*
SC : 02 :004(345) [0545] blessedness, even as he is **risen** from the dead and lives
SC : 04 :012(349) [0551] come forth daily and **rise** up, cleansed and righteous, to
SC : 07 :001(352) [0557] In the morning, when you **rise**, make the sign of the cross
LC : PR :014(360) [0571] standing, lying down, or **rising**, and keep them before our
LC : SP :012(363) [0577] into hell, the third day he **rose** from the dead, he ascended
LC : SP :016(363) [0577] them daily when they **rise** in the morning, when they go to
LC : 02 :025(413) [0683] *into hell, the third day he* ***rose*** *from the dead, he ascended*
LC : 02 :031(414) [0687] Afterward he **rose** again from the dead, swallowed up and
EP : 08 :013(488) [0821] descended into hell, **rose** from the dead, ascended into
SD : 01 :047(516) [0875] that our flesh would not **rise** on Judgment Day and that
SD : 02 :002(520) [0881] is going to be like after he will have **risen** from the dead.
SD : 05 :004(559) [0953] suffer and on the third day **rise** from the dead, and that
SD : 07 :116(589) [1011] away from the Supper and **rises** above all heavens,

Risk (2), Risked (1), Risky (1)
AP : PR :002(098) [0099] it only on terms so **risky** that we could not accept them.
LC : 01 :016(366) [0585] him, but for him should **risk** and disregard everything else
LC : 01 :233(396) [0647] that it is his duty, at the **risk** of God's displeasure, not to
LC : 02 :031(414) [0685] and what he paid and **risked** in order to win us and bring

Rite (9), Rites (63)
AL : 07 :003(032) [0047] that human traditions or **rites** and ceremonies, instituted
AL : 15 :000(036) [0049] XV. Ecclesiastical **Rites**
AL : 15 :001(036) [0049] churches teach that those **rites** should be observed which
AL : 00 :002(048) [0059] severe as to demand that **rites** should be the same
AL : 00 :003(048) [0059] everywhere, nor have the **rites** of all the churches ever
AL : 00 :004(048) [0059] Among us the ancient **rites** are for the most part diligently
AL : 00 :005(048) [0059] that certain abuses were connected with ordinary **rites**.
AL : 26 :008(065) [0071] of certain holy days, **rites**, fasts, and vestments.
AL : 26 :028(068) [0073] with numerous **rites**, whether of Moses or of others.
AL : 26 :045(070) [0075] examples of dissimilar **rites** are gathered, and this
AL : 28 :053(090) [0091] about Sunday and about similar **rites** in our churches?
AL : 28 :057(091) [0091] Sunday, Easter, Pentecost, and similar festivals and **rites**.
AP : 07 :005(169) [0227] of outward ties and **rites** like other civic governments,
AP : 07 :014(170) [0231] the heathen not by civil **rites** but by being God's true
AP : 07 :030(174) [0237] that human traditions or **rites** and ceremonies, instituted
AP : 07 :030(174) [0237] If we mean "particular **rites**" they approve our article, but
AP : 07 :030(174) [0237] article, but if we mean "universal **rites**" they disapprove it.
AP : 07 :031(174) [0237] say, a similarity of human **rites**, whether universal or
AP : 07 :033(174) [0239] harmed by differences in **rites** instituted by men, although
AP : 07 :033(174) [0239] we like it when universal **rites** are observed for the sake
AP : 07 :038(176) [0241] Apostolic **rites** they want to keep, apostolic doctrine they
AP : 07 :039(176) [0241] We should interpret those **rites** just as the apostles
AP : 07 :039(176) [0241] we are justified by such **rites** or that such rites are
AP : 07 :039(176) [0241] by such rites or that such **rites** are necessary for
AP : 07 :040(176) [0241] they also observed other **rites** and a sequence of lessons.
AP : 12 :112(198) [0285] talking about the public **rite** of penitence, not about this
AP : 12 :113(199) [0285] "satisfaction" is a relic from this **rite** of public penitence.
AP : 12 :168(209) [0305] from the public **rite** and use it to denote the real
AP : 13 :002(211) [0309] not to neglect any of the **rites** and ceremonies instituted in
AP : 13 :003(211) [0309] we define sacraments as "**rites** which have the command
AP : 13 :003(211) [0309] By this definition, **rites** instituted by men are not
AP : 13 :004(211) [0309] of penitence), for these **rites** have the commandment of
AP : 13 :005(211) [0309] Through the Word and the **rite** God simultaneously
AP : 13 :005(212) [0309] to strike the heart, so the **rite** itself enters through the
AP : 13 :005(212) [0309] The Word and the **rite** have the same effect, as Augustine
AP : 13 :005(212) [0309] "the visible Word," for the **rite** is received by the eyes and
AP : 13 :006(212) [0309] and extreme unction are **rites** received from the Fathers
AP : 15 :001(215) [0315] observe those ecclesiastical **rites** which can be observed
AP : 15 :004(215) [0315] teaches that religious **rites** are helpful in gaining grace and
AP : 15 :015(217) [0319] allowed to establish new **rites** and if by such rites they
AP : 15 :015(217) [0319] new rites and if by such **rites** they merit grace, we shall
AP : 15 :015(217) [0319] to approve the religious **rites** of all the heathen, as well as
AP : 15 :015(217) [0319] the heathen, as well as the **rites** established by Jeroboam
AP : 15 :015(217) [0319] are permitted to establish **rites** that serve to merit grace
AP : 15 :016(217) [0319] Yet the **rites** of the heathen and the Israelites were
AP : 15 :017(217) [0319] do we have that religious **rites** established by men
AP : 15 :017(217) [0319] Since these **rites** have no testimony in the Word of God,
AP : 15 :018(217) [0319] notion that these human **rites** merit justification, grace,
AP : 15 :018(217) [0319] of Mohammed has **rites** and works by which it seeks to
AP : 15 :018(217) [0319] of Antichrist if it maintains that human **rites** justify.
AP : 15 :018(217) [0319] for his sake but by such **rites**, and especially when they
AP : 15 :018(217) [0319] that for justification such **rites** are not only useful but
AP : 15 :018(217) [0319] it is not necessary that **rites** instituted by men be
AP : 15 :019(217) [0319] the invention of human **rites** will be the very form and
AP : 15 :019(218) [0319] describing the invention of **rites**, for he says that a god
AP : 15 :020(218) [0321] Fathers themselves had **rites** and traditions, they did not
AP : 15 :020(218) [0321] for Christ's sake, not for the sake of these human **rites**.
AP : 15 :020(218) [0321] observed these human **rites** because they were profitable
AP : 15 :020(218) [0321] seasons and various **rites** serve as reminders for the
AP : 15 :024(218) [0321] that they are to be **rites** which justify, as Thomas writes,
AP : 15 :029(219) [0323] righteousness in human **rites**, let us therefore arm
AP : 15 :031(219) [0323] have the power to institute **rites** as though they justified
AP : 15 :040(220) [0325] pray but for the sake of the **rite**, as if this work were an
AP : 15 :050(222) [0329] so-called "universal **rites**" as necessary for salvation.
AP : 15 :051(222) [0329] in the accustomed **rites** without good reason, and to
AP : 22 :009(237) [0359] to elevate the position of the clergy by a religious **rite**.
AP : 23 :049(246) [0377] morality), just as certain **rites** were introduced as lessons
AP : 28 :016(283) [0449] from the idea that human **rites** are necessary acts of
LC : 01 :313(407) [0671] to special times, places, **rites**, and ceremonies, but are
SD : 10 :000(610) [1053] X. The Ecclesiastical **Rites** That Are Called Adiaphora or
SD : 10 :001(610) [1053] ceremonies and church **rites** which are neither
SD : 10 :005(611) [1053] Nor are such **rites** matters of indifference when these

Ritual (4), Rituals (1)
AP : 04 :134(125) [0159] God and that sacrifice and **ritual** justify before God *ex*
AP : 07 :013(170) [0231] the outward observance of certain devotions and **rituals**.
AP : 27 :058(279) [0439] The **ritual** of the Nazarites was intended to exercise or
AP : 27 :058(279) [0439] of worship now, so the **ritual** of the Nazarites should not
AP : 27 :058(279) [0439] and justification, with the **ritual** of the Nazarites, which

Roars (1)
S2 : 04 :004(298) [0473] and books, in which he **roars** like a lion (as the angel in

Roast (1)
LC : 01 :270(401) [0657] Ah, now do you smell the **roast**?

Rob (16), Robbed (4), Robber (1), Robbers (2), Robbery (2), Robs (4)
AG : 27 :043(077) [0081] from God's grace, for they **rob** Christ, who alone
AP : 04 :003(107) [0121] of Christ, and they **rob** pious consciences of the
AP : 04 :157(128) [0165] we put it in our works, we **rob** Christ of his honor as

Continued ▶

A P : 0 4 :213(136) [0179] faith — what is this but to **rob** Christ of his honor as
A P : 0 7 :028(173) [0237] unworthy men, this does not **rob** them of their efficacy.
A P : 0 9 :002(178) [0245] against the wicked and seditious faction of these **robbers**.
A P : 1 2 :169(209) [0305] that he has stolen or **robbed**, for he is still a thief and a
A P : 1 2 :169(209) [0305] he is still a thief and a **robber** as long as he unjustly holds
A P : 1 5 :009(216) [0317] Thus they **rob** Christ of his honor as the mediator.
A P : 2 4 :096(267) [0417] these wicked errors which **rob** Christ's suffering of its
S C : 0 1 :014(343) [0541] God, and so we should not **rob** our neighbor of his
L C : 0 1 :190(391) [0635] your love from him and **robbed** him of the service by
L C : 0 1 :223(395) [0643] He has forbidden us to **rob** or pilfer the possessions of
L C : 0 1 :224(395) [0643] steals not only when he **robs** a man's strongbox or his
L C : 0 1 :229(396) [0645] and yet with a great show of legality they **rob** and steal.
L C : 0 1 :231(396) [0647] Those who can steal and **rob** openly are safe and free,
L C : 0 1 :240(397) [0649] free public market into a carrion-pit and a **robbers'** den.
L C : 0 1 :245(398) [0649] Anyone who **robs** and takes things by violence and
L C : 0 1 :245(398) [0649] of this art; since everyone **robs** and steals from the other,
L C : 0 1 :246(398) [0651] with those of you who despise, defraud, steal, and **rob** us.
E P : 0 2 :008(471) [0789] and acts like fornication, **robbery**, murder, theft, and
E P : 0 5 :011(479) [0805] obscured, Christians are **robbed** of their true comfort, and
E P : 1 1 :013(496) [0835] to weaken for us or to **rob** us entirely of the glorious
E P : 1 1 :021(497) [0837] terrible errors, for they **rob** Christians of all the comfort
S D : 0 2 :074(536) [0909] doing such wicked acts as lechery, **robbery**, and murder.
S D : 0 5 :001(558) [0951] the merit of Christ and **rob** disturbed consciences of the
S D : 0 5 :027(563) [0961] in the papacy, and thus **rob** Christians of the true
S D : 0 8 :069(604) [1039] and thus Christ would be **robbed** of his majesty, which as
S D : 0 8 :087(608) [1047] To do so **robs** Christians of their highest comfort,

Roch (1)
L C : 0 1 :011(366) [0583] the plague, he made a vow to St. Sebastian or **Roch**.

Rock (8)
S 3 : 0 3 :002(304) [0479] a hammer which breaks the **rock** in pieces?" (Jer. 23:29).
T R : 0 0 :022(323) [0511] are Peter, and on this **rock** I will build my church"
T R : 0 0 :025(324) [0511] to the statement, "On this **rock** I will build my church"
T R : 0 0 :025(324) [0511] minister and says, "On this **rock**," that is, on this
T R : 0 0 :027(325) [0511] the statement "on this **rock**" in this way and not as
T R : 0 0 :028(325) [0511] that Christ says "on this **rock**" and not "on Peter," for he
T R : 0 0 :029(325) [0513] On this **rock** of confession, therefore, the church is built.
S D : 0 7 :042(576) [0985] and indubitable **rock** of truth in the words of institution

Rod (3), Rods (2)
L C : 0 1 :061(373) [0597] after them at once with the **rod**, confront them with the
L C : 0 1 :076(375) [0603] to be forced by means of **rods** and blows will come to no
L C : 0 1 :076(375) [0603] will remain good only as long as the **rod** is on their backs.
L C : 0 1 :077(375) [0603] that they fear God more than they do **rods** and clubs.
L C : 0 1 :122(382) [0615] never do their duty until a **rod** is laid on their backs, they

Rogue (1), Rogues (2)
L C : 0 1 :300(405) [0665] world considers wicked **rogues**, but precisely to the most
L C : 0 3 :057(427) [0713] rightly be considered a **rogue** and a scoundrel who had
L C : 0 3 :083(431) [0721] even for wicked men and **rogues**, yet he wishes us to pray

Role (2)
E P : 0 2 :016(472) [0789] introduced to confirm the **role** of natural free will in
E P : 0 3 :020(475) [0797] has the most prominent **role** in justification, but that also

Roll (1)
L C : 0 1 :267(401) [0657] in it like pigs that **roll** in the mud and root around in it

Roman (29)
P R : P R :008(005) [0009] most gracious lord, His **Roman** Imperial Majesty, and to
P R : P R :025(014) [0023] and estates in the Holy **Roman** Empire, and also with
A G : 0 0 :001(047) [0059] church, or even of the **Roman** church (in so far as the
A G : 2 8 :019(083) [0087] right, bestowed by **Roman** emperors and kings for the
A L : 2 3 :012(052) [0063] when about to publish the **Roman** pontiff's edict on this
A L : 2 7 :024(074) [0079] for any reason at all, the **Roman** pontiffs would not have
A L : 2 7 :025(074) [0079] But the **Roman** pontiffs have prudently judged that
A P : 0 7 :023(172) [0235] whole world in which the **Roman** pontiff must have
A P : 0 7 :025(173) [0235] about the power of the **Roman** pope for which no one has
A P : 1 0 :002(179) [0247] know that not only the **Roman** Church affirms the bodily
A P : 1 2 :124(201) [0289] The **Roman** pontiff did not add anything to his dignity in
A P : 1 2 :125(201) [0289] might tend to diminish the prestige of the **Roman** See.
A P : 1 2 :125(201) [0289] If the **Roman** See thinks it is right for all nations to
A P : 1 2 :126(201) [0289] take care, indicate a change in the Holy **Roman** Empire.
A P : 2 3 :001(239) [0363] the princes not to let the **Roman** Empire be disgraced and
A P : 2 3 :024(243) [0371] the regulations which the **Roman** pontiffs have set up
S 1 : P R :003(289) [0455] But the **Roman** court is dreadfully afraid of a free council
S 1 : P R :003(289) [0455] have lost hope that the **Roman** court will ever permit a
T R : 0 0 :001(320) [0503] The **Roman** bishop arrogates to himself the claim that he
T R : 0 0 :005(320) [0503] when they say that the **Roman** bishop is above all bishops
T R : 0 0 :007(320) [0505] from the Gospel that the **Roman** bishop is not by divine
T R : 0 0 :012(322) [0507] is, those that were in the **Roman** provinces in the West.
T R : 0 0 :012(322) [0507] the authority of the **Roman** bishop grew out of a decision
T R : 0 0 :012(322) [0507] ordination and confirmation from the **Roman** bishop.
T R : 0 0 :021(323) [0509] the primacy of the **Roman** pontiff, this dispute could not
T R : 0 0 :039(327) [0515] But it is manifest that the **Roman** pontiffs and their
T R : 0 0 :082(000) [0529] princes and estates of the **Roman** Empire, to his Imperial
S D : P R :005(504) [0851] princes, and estates of the **Roman** Empire as the common
S D : 0 7 :011(571) [0975] know that not only the **Roman** but also the Greek Church

Romans (12)
A G : 0 4 :003(030) [0045] as righteousness, as Paul says in **Romans** 3:21-26 and 4:5.
A L : 2 6 :043(070) [0075] of this difference the **Romans** accused the East of schism,
A P : 0 4 :087(119) [0147] In the Epistle to the **Romans**, especially, Paul deals with
A P : 2 1 :032(233) [0351] The **Romans** thought that Juno granted riches, Febris
A P : 2 4 :081(264) [0411] way in the time of the **Romans**, as the rescript of Pertinax
S 2 : 0 1 :004(292) [0461] us, as St. Paul says in **Romans** 3, "For we hold that a man
S C : 0 4 :014(349) [0553] Answer: In **Romans** 6:4, St. Paul wrote, "We were buried
L C : 0 1 :142(384) [0621] from ancient times the **Romans** and other peoples called
L C : 0 1 :239(397) [0649] The ancient **Romans**, for example, promptly took such
E P : 1 1 :011(496) [0835] order which St. Paul follows in the Epistle to the **Romans**.
S D : 0 4 :010(552) [0941] Epistle of St. Paul to the **Romans**, "Faith is a divine work
S D : 1 1 :033(621) [1073] this way: "Follow the order in the Epistle to the **Romans**.

Rome (29)
A G : 2 3 :018(054) [0063] some of the courtiers in **Rome** have often acknowledged
A G : 2 6 :043(070) [0075] they kept Easter at a time different from that in **Rome**.
A L : 0 0 :001(047) [0059] church or the church of **Rome**, in so far as the ancient
A L : 2 6 :043(070) [0075] different from that in **Rome**, and when on account of this
A P : 0 4 :390(166) [0225] that the church of **Rome** accepts everything that the pope
A P : 1 2 :127(201) [0289] France, Italy, even in **Rome** itself — how many do you
A P : 2 3 :052(246) [0377] In its satires **Rome** still reads and recognizes its own
A P : 2 3 :054(246) [0379] the fall of many other cities, like Sybaris and **Rome**.
S 2 : 0 4 :001(298) [0471] pastor of the churches in **Rome** and of such other
S 2 : 0 4 :007(299) [0473] the pope and the see of **Rome** were to concede and accept
S 2 : 0 4 :008(300) [0473] to have his residence in **Rome** or some other fixed place,
S 3 : 0 3 :024(307) [0485] Here the holy see in **Rome** came to the aid of the poor
S 3 : 0 3 :025(307) [0485] pope invented the jubilee year and attached it to **Rome**.
T R : 0 0 :002(320) [0503] reasons the bishop of **Rome** calls himself the vicar of
T R : 0 0 :012(321) [0507] East and the bishop of **Rome** should administer the
T R : 0 0 :012(322) [0507] right, for if the bishop of **Rome** had his superiority by
T R : 0 0 :015(322) [0509] sought from the bishop of **Rome** in the greater part of the
T R : 0 0 :015(322) [0509] attribute superiority and lordship to the bishop of **Rome**.
T R : 0 0 :016(322) [0509] seek ordination or confirmation from the bishop of **Rome**
T R : 0 0 :017(323) [0509] in which the bishop of **Rome** did not preside — as the
T R : 0 0 :017(323) [0509] the primacy or superiority of the bishop of **Rome**.
T R : 0 0 :018(323) [0509] is a bishop — whether in **Rome** or Eugubium or
T R : 0 0 :019(323) [0509] was offered to the bishop of **Rome** but he did not accept
T R : 0 0 :020(323) [0509] that the bishops of **Rome** were confirmed by the
T R : 0 0 :021(323) [0509] between the bishops of **Rome** and Constantinople over
T R : 0 0 :021(323) [0509] the primacy should be assigned to the bishop of **Rome**.
T R : 0 0 :038(326) [0515] Even if the bishop of **Rome** should possess primacy and
T R : 0 0 :057(330) [0521] even if the bishop of **Rome** did possess the primacy by
L C : 0 1 :230(396) [0645] thieves, the Holy See at **Rome**, and all its retinue, which

Room (3)
A P : 1 2 :051(189) [0265] terrifies, he says, to make **room** for consolation and
A P : 2 3 :040(245) [0375] that is, to make **room** for hearing or teaching the
S D : 1 2 :008(633) [1097] was allowed neither **room** nor scope, where the true

Root (10), Rooted (4), Roots (1)
A G : 2 8 :048(089) [0091] Father has not planted will be **rooted** up" (Matt. 15:13).
A L : 2 8 :048(089) [0091] my heavenly Father has not planted will be **rooted** up."
A P : 2 1 :018(231) [0347] "In that day the **root** of Jesse shall stand as an
S 3 : 0 1 :001(302) [0477] This is called original sin, or the **root** sin.
L C : 0 1 :035(369) [0589] he has completely **rooted** out all idolatry, and on that
L C : 0 1 :075(375) [0601] Then some good may take **root**, spring up, and bear
L C : 0 1 :077(375) [0603] kind of training takes such **root** in their hearts that they
L C : 0 1 :187(390) [0633] God wishes to remove the **root** and source of this
L C : 0 1 :267(401) [0657] that roll in the mud and **root** around in it with their
L C : 0 1 :281(403) [0661] in every corner and **root** around in the filth, nobody will
L C : 0 1 :310(407) [0669] being to destroy all the **roots** and causes of our injuries to
L C : 0 1 :317(408) [0673] has become so deeply **rooted** and still clings to every
S D : 0 1 :001(508) [0859] itself out of which, as the **root** and source, all other sins
S D : 0 1 :005(509) [0861] this as the chief sin, the **root** and fountain of all actual
S D : 0 5 :017(561) [0957] Since unbelief is a **root** and fountainhead of all culpable

Ropes (1)
L C : 0 1 :245(398) [0649] where would we find enough gallows and **ropes**?

Rosary (1), Rosaries (5)
A G : 2 0 :003(041) [0053] and useless works like **rosaries**, the cult of saints,
A L : 2 0 :003(041) [0053] in honor of saints, **rosaries**, monasticism, and the like.
A P : 1 2 :014(184) [0257] like pilgrimages, **rosaries**, or similar observances that do
A P : 2 1 :037(234) [0355] have invented about **rosaries** and similar ceremonies, or
A P : 2 1 :037(234) [0355] and the mirrors and the **rosaries**, all of which contain
A P : 2 7 :053(278) [0437] Dominicans made up the **rosary** of the blessed Virgin,

Rot (1), Rotten (2)
S 3 : 0 3 :039(309) [0489] on an unreal and **rotten** foundation which is called good
L C : P R :003(358) [0567] of the Gospel than this **rotten**, pernicious, shameful,
L C : 0 1 :191(391) [0635] to pieces by wild beasts, to **rot** in prison or perish from

Rothenburg (1)
P R : P R :027(015) [0027] Mayor and Council of **Rothenburg**-on-the-Tauber.

Round (2), Roundly (2)
L C : 0 1 :155(386) [0625] are knaves who have **roundly** deserved punishment and
E P : 0 1 :004(466) [0781] and made me, all that I am **round** about" (Job 10:8).
S D : 0 1 :035(514) [0869] and made me together **round** about, and thou dost
S D : 0 1 :057(518) [0879] us to answer simply and **roundly** that original sin is not a

Rout (2), Routed (1), Routs (2)
L C : P R :010(360) [0571] holy water, the sign which **routs** the devil and puts him to
L C : P R :011(360) [0571] you obtain from it is to **rout** the devil and evil thoughts.
L C : P R :012(360) [0571] call God's Word, which **routs** and destroys this master of
L C : 0 2 :030(414) [0685] jailers now have been **routed**, and their place has been
L C : 0 5 :026(449) [0759] man, and when he cannot **rout** us by force, he sneaks and

Royal (5)
A G : P R :018(026) [0041] Majesty's viceroy (His **Royal** Majesty of Hungary and
A G : 2 1 :001(046) [0057] both are incumbents of a **royal** office which demands the
A P : 2 1 :024(232) [0349] "order" from the usage at **royal** courts, where friends
T R : 0 0 :032(325) [0513] led forth to be mocked in **royal** purple signified that the
T R : 0 0 :069(331) [0523] of Peter, "You are a **royal** priesthood" (I Pet. 2:9).

Rude (4)
S 2 : 0 2 :005(293) [0463] of itself — not only for the **rude** rabble, but also for all
S 3 : 0 2 :002(303) [0479] These are the **rude** and wicked people who do evil
S C : P R :012(339) [0535] is disposed to banish such **rude** people from his land.
L C : S P :018(363) [0577] should a person be tolerated if he is so **rude** and

Rudolstadt (1)
P R : P R :027(015) [0025] Albert, count of Schwarzburg [-**Rudolstadt**]

Rue (1)
L C : 0 3 :075(430) [0719] of a lion or a wreath of **rue**, or if a loaf of bread were

Ruedenhausen (1)
PR : PR :027(015) [0025] George, count and lord of Castell [-**Ruedenhausen**]

Ruin (2)
AP : 0 7 :009(169) [0229] the infinite dangers that threaten the church with **ruin**.
SD : PR :008(502) [0849] will ultimately lead to the **ruin** of the pure doctrine.

Rule (60), Ruled (2), Ruler (1), Rulers (13), Rules (13)
AG : 0 3 :004(030) [0045] God, that he may eternally **rule** and have dominion over
AG : 1 6 :001(037) [0051] world and all established **rule** and laws were instituted
AG : 2 7 :013(073) [0077] of pastor and preacher, of **ruler**, prince, lord, or the like,
AG : 2 8 :068(093) [0093] one recognizes that such **rules** are not to be deemed
AG : 2 8 :075(094) [0095] to follow the apostolic **rule** which commands us to obey
AL : 0 3 :005(030) [0045] Spirit into their hearts to **rule**, comfort, and quicken them
AL : 2 0 :038(046) [0057] all manner of lusts and human devices **rule** in the heart.
AL : 2 3 :026(056) [0065] a proper age, and as a **rule** vows used to be so made in
AL : 2 8 :013(083) [0085] abrogate the laws of civil **rulers**, nor abolish lawful
AL : 2 8 :013(083) [0085] nor prescribe to civil **rulers** laws about the forms of
AP : 0 2 :046(106) [0117] and other physical ills, but also to the **rule** of the devil.
AP : 0 2 :049(106) [0119] history itself shows the great power of the devil's **rule**.
AP : 0 2 :050(106) [0119] penalty and to destroy the **rule** of the devil, sin, and
AP : 0 3 :001(107) [0119] and that he was raised to **rule**, justify, and sanctify the
AP : 0 4 :185(132) [0173] The **rule** I have just stated interprets all the passages they
AP : 0 4 :189(133) [0175] of Christ, whereby he shows his **rule** before the world.
AP : 0 4 :189(133) [0175] of the saints against the **rule** of the devil; in our weakness
AP : 0 4 :193(133) [0175] the outward administration of Christ's **rule** among men.
AP : 0 4 :269(147) [0197] we must hold fast to these **rules**: that the law is not kept
AP : 0 4 :277(148) [0199] We must come back to the **rule** that without Christ the
AP : 0 4 :280(149) [0201] according to the common **rule** it is improper in an
AP : 0 4 :372(164) [0221] By this **rule**, as we have said earlier, all passages on works
AP : 0 7 :004(169) [0227] that is, that he will **rule** and hold office in the
AP : 0 7 :016(171) [0231] The wicked are **ruled** by the devil and are his captives;
AP : 0 7 :016(171) [0231] are his captives; they are not **ruled** by the Spirit of Christ.
AP : 0 7 :023(172) [0235] their power and right to **rule**, and this at Christ's
AP : 0 7 :032(174) [0239] rather than outward **rules** of discipline, completely
AP : 0 7 :043(177) [0243] contrary to the faith or the **rule** of the church, and he
AP : 1 2 :151(206) [0299] As a **rule**, these troubles are punishments for sin.
AP : 1 2 :155(207) [0301] construct the universal **rule** that for the forgiveness of
AP : 1 2 :156(207) [0301] not follow as a universal **rule** that over and above our
AP : 1 5 :043(221) [0327] the cross, respect for **rulers** and for all civil ordinances,
AP : 1 6 :012(224) [0333] unless they keep the **rule** in mind, that a Christian may
AP : 1 6 :012(224) [0333] This **rule** safeguards consciences, for it teaches that if
AP : 1 8 :004(225) [0335] It can obey **rulers** and parents.
AP : 2 4 :041(257) [0399] Experience shows the sort of tyrants who **rule** the church.
AP : 2 4 :041(257) [0399] of the world, and they **rule** without regard for religion
AP : 2 7 :017(272) [0425] or of the Decalogue or the **rule** of Benedict or of the rule
AP : 2 7 :017(272) [0425] rule of Benedict or of the **rule** of Augustine or of other
AP : 2 7 :017(272) [0425] of Augustine or of other **rules** — whoever does this
AP : 2 7 :039(276) [0433] unmarried, and obey the **rule** in trifles like clothing and
AP : 2 7 :049(277) [0437] Thus the call of David to **rule**, or of Abraham to sacrifice
AP : 2 7 :060(279) [0441] according to the **rule**, that is, according to the sure and
AP : 2 7 :060(279) [0441] passages of Scripture, not against the **rule** or the passages.
AP : 2 8 :006(282) [0445] bishops have the power to **rule** and to correct by force in
AP : 2 8 :006(282) [0445] and that the power to **rule** requires the power to judge,
S 2 : 0 4 :007(299) [0473] destruction of his whole **rule** and estate, together with all
S 3 : 0 3 :044(310) [0491] does not permit sin to **rule** and gain the upper hand in
TR : 0 0 :039(327) [0515] therefore of one who **rules** in the church and not of the
TR : 0 0 :040(327) [0515] is manifest that the pope **rules** in the church and that he
TR : 0 0 :054(329) [0519] be wise; be warned, O **rulers** of the earth" (Ps. 2:10).
TR : 0 0 :080(334) [0527] of the churches, as the **rule** states, "The benefice is given
SC : PR :019(340) [0537] authorities and parents to **rule** wisely and educate their
SC : 0 3 :014(347) [0549] godly and faithful **rulers**, good government; seasonable
SC : 0 9 :003(354) [0561] "Let the elders who **rule** well be considered worthy of
SC : 0 9 :005(355) [0561] them to be submissive to **rulers** and authorities, to be
LC : SP :002(362) [0575] who does not know the **rules** and practices of his craft is
LC : 0 1 :124(382) [0617] Neither can parents, as a **rule**, do very much; one fool
LC : 0 1 :128(382) [0617] But here again the devil **rules** in the world; children
LC : 0 1 :142(385) [0621] who do not speak of our **rulers** in the same way, or at
LC : 0 1 :150(385) [0623] Through civil **rulers**, as through our own parents, God
LC : 0 1 :182(389) [0631] who occupy the place of God, that is, parents and **rulers**.
LC : 0 1 :276(402) [0659] Let this be your **rule**, then, that you should not be quick
LC : 0 2 :030(414) [0685] in order that he may **rule** us by his righteousness,
LC : 0 3 :051(426) [0711] to bring us to himself and **rule** us as a king of
LC : 0 3 :061(428) [0715] for good builders and **rulers**, but also for defenders,
LC : 0 3 :075(430) [0719] **Rulers** are worthy of all honor, and we should render
LC : 0 4 :062(444) [0749] the crown from the **rulers** and trample it under foot and
EP : RN :000(464) [0777] Comprehensive Summary, **Rule**, and Norm According to
EP : RN :001(464) [0777] Testaments are the only **rule** and norm according to
EP : RN :007(465) [0779] remains the only judge, **rule**, and norm according to
EP : 0 6 :001(479) [0805] on that account a definite **rule** according to which they
EP : 0 7 :012(483) [0811] to his human nature, **rules** presently and has in his hands
SD : RN :000(503) [0849] Formulation, Basis, **Rule**, and Norm, Indicating How All
SD : PR :009(505) [0855] and should remain the sole **rule** and norm of all doctrine,
SD : 0 1 :056(518) [0877] churches, following the **rules** of logic, used the same
SD : 0 2 :002(520) [0881] has regenerated him and **rules** him, nor what man's free
SD : 0 2 :018(524) [0889] his will unless the Holy Spirit illuminates and **rules** him.
SD : 0 2 :066(534) [0907] much and as long as God **rules** in him through his Holy
SD : 0 2 :069(534) [0907] and permit sin to **rule** in themselves and thus grieve the
SD : 0 6 :003(564) [0963] Word, which is a certain **rule** and norm for achieving a
SD : 0 7 :073(583) [0999] and the common **rule** that there is no sacrament apart
SD : 0 7 :085(584) [1001] the following useful **rule** and norm has been derived from
SD : 0 7 :085(584) [1003] This **rule** dare not in any way be rejected, but it can and
SD : 0 7 :087(585) [1003] papistic abuses that this **rule** was first formulated and
SD : 0 7 :088(585) [1003] this useful and necessary **rule** and interpret it as referring
SD : 0 7 :090(585) [1003] perversion of this common **rule** ascribe to our faith the
SD : 0 8 :027(596) [1025] he is everywhere present to **rule**, not only as God but also
SD : 0 8 :057(602) [1035] is a unanimously accepted **rule** of the entire ancient

Rumors (1)
AL : 0 0 :005(049) [0059] gathered from common **rumors** or the accusations of our

Run (13), Running (4), Runs (3)
AP : 0 4 :020(110) [0125] of condignity, and so they **run** headlong into despair,
AP : 0 4 :170(130) [0171] even defies God's will and **runs** away from afflictions that
AP : 0 7 :022(172) [0235] and ungodly teachers may **run** rampant in the church,
AP : 1 2 :009(183) [0255] for his own sake or is **running** away from eternal
AP : 2 7 :010(270) [0423] Therefore we shall briefly **run** through a few of our
AP : 2 7 :069(280) [0443] We have **run** through a number of our arguments, and in
S 2 : 0 2 :001(293) [0463] abomination because it **runs** into direct and violent
S 3 : 0 3 :025(307) [0485] and the people came **running**, for everyone was eager to
LC : 0 1 :166(387) [0629] We ought to be willing to **run** to the ends of the world to
LC : 0 1 :326(409) [0675] let these concluding words **run** through all the
LC : 0 2 :046(416) [0689] to the common people, we shall **run** through them also.
LC : 0 6 :023(460) [0000] and beat him but would **run** there as fast as he could so
LC : 0 6 :024(460) [0000] that all beggars should **run** to the place, no reason being
LC : 0 6 :027(460) [0000] a desire for confession that he will **run** toward it with joy.
LC : 0 6 :030(460) [0000] you should be glad to **run** more than a hundred miles for
LC : 0 6 :034(461) [0000] that people would come **running** after us to get it, more
SD : 0 2 :021(525) [0889] willingly — and thereby **runs** into a thousand dangers and
SD : 0 2 :055(531) [0903] watering and the hearer's **running** and willing would be in
SD : 0 6 :006(565) [0965] stars of heaven regularly **run** their courses according to
SD : 0 6 :021(567) [0969] David says, "I will **run** in the way of thy commandments"

Rush (3), Rushed (1), Rushes (1)
AP : 1 1 :005(181) [0249] In fact, if everyone **rushed** in at the same time, the people
AP : 1 2 :089(195) [0279] faith is, and so it is that at last they **rush** into despair.
LC : 0 1 :267(401) [0657] are not content just to know but **rush** ahead and judge.
LC : 0 4 :013(438) [0735] But mad reason **rushes** forth and, because Baptism is not
LC : 0 5 :012(448) [0755] with all the fanatics, **rush** forward and say, 'How can

Rust (1)
LC : 0 1 :242(397) [0649] hoard will be consumed by **rust** so that you will never

Sabbath (22)
AG : 2 8 :033(086) [0087] to the fact that the **Sabbath** was changed to Sunday —
AG : 2 8 :033(086) [0087] as the change of the **Sabbath**, for thereby they wish to
AG : 2 8 :044(088) [0089] or with regard to a festival or a new moon or a **sabbath**.
AG : 2 8 :058(091) [0091] of Sunday in place of the **Sabbath** as a necessary
AG : 2 8 :059(091) [0091] have abrogated the **Sabbath** and teach that after the
AG : 2 8 :060(091) [0093] keeping neither of the **Sabbath** nor of any other day is
AG : 2 8 :061(091) [0093] and of the change of the **Sabbath**, all of which have arisen
AL : 2 6 :025(068) [0073] food and drink or with regard to a festival or a **sabbath**."
AL : 2 8 :033(086) [0087] cite the change from the **Sabbath** to the Lord's Day —
AL : 2 8 :033(086) [0087] No case is made more of than this change of the **Sabbath**.
AL : 2 8 :044(088) [0089] or with regard to a festival or a new moon or a **sabbath**."
AL : 2 8 :058(091) [0091] Day in place of the **Sabbath** was instituted by the church's
AL : 2 8 :059(091) [0091] church, abrogated the **Sabbath**, for after the revelation of
AL : 2 8 :060(091) [0093] keeping neither of the **Sabbath** nor of any other day is
AL : 2 8 :061(091) [0093] the change of the **Sabbath**, all of which have arisen from
AP : 0 7 :035(175) [0239] or with regard to a festival or a new moon or a **sabbath**.
AP : 1 5 :030(219) [0323] or with regard to a festival or a new moon or a **sabbath**.
AP : 2 4 :008(250) [0385] on the fourth day, on **Sabbath** eve, and on the Lord's
SC : 0 1 :005(342) [0541] *"Remember the **Sabbath** day, to keep it holy."*
LC : SP :003(362) [0575] 3. You shall keep the **Sabbath** day holy.
LC : 0 1 :079(375) [0603] from the Hebrew word "**Sabbath**," which properly means
SD : 1 0 :013(613) [1057] to a festival or a new moon or a **sabbath**" (Col. 2:16).

Sabinus (1)
TR : 0 0 :014(322) [0509] of our colleague **Sabinus**) in order that by the votes of all

Sacerdotal (1), Sacerdotes (2)
AG : 2 8 :027(085) [0087] II, Question 7, in the chapters "**Sacerdotes**" and "Oves."
AL : 2 3 :016(054) [0063] that this be done in the case of **sacerdotal** marriage.
AL : 2 8 :027(085) [0087] (II, question 7, in chapters "**Sacerdotes**" and "Oves").

Sacrament (251)
PR : PR :009(006) [0011] doctrine about the holy **sacrament** of the body and the
AG : 2 2 :000(049) [0059] XXII. Both Kinds in the **Sacrament**
AG : 2 2 :001(049) [0059] us both kinds are given to laymen in the **sacrament**.
AG : 2 2 :006(050) [0061] who administered the **sacrament** distributed the blood of
AG : 2 2 :007(050) [0061] himself ordered that the **sacrament** was not to be divided.
AG : 2 2 :011(050) [0061] desire to observe the **sacrament** according to Christ's
AG : 2 2 :012(051) [0061] the division of the **sacrament** is contrary to the institution
AG : 2 2 :012(051) [0061] carrying about of the **sacrament** in processions is also
AG : 0 1 :007(056) [0065] concerning the holy **sacrament**, why it was instituted, and
AG : 0 1 :007(056) [0065] about other false teachings concerning the **sacrament**.
AG : 2 4 :012(057) [0065] that whoever uses the **sacrament** unworthily is guilty of
AG : 2 4 :024(058) [0067] might know how the **sacrament** is to be used rightly.
AG : 2 4 :030(059) [0067] third place, the holy **sacrament** was not instituted to
AG : 2 4 :030(059) [0067] that through the **sacrament** grace and forgiveness of sin
AG : 2 4 :030(059) [0067] Accordingly the **sacrament** requires faith, and without
AG : 2 4 :034(060) [0067] and others receive the **sacrament** for themselves, it is
AG : 2 4 :038(060) [0069] shall receive the **sacrament** in order from the bishop or
AG : 2 5 :001(061) [0069] not administering the **sacrament** to those who have not
AG : 2 8 :070(093) [0093] they administer the **sacrament** in one kind and prohibit
AL : 2 2 :001(049) [0059] In the **sacrament** of the Lord's Supper both kinds are
AL : 2 2 :007(050) [0061] commanded that the **sacrament** should not be divided.
AL : 2 2 :011(050) [0061] use both kinds in the **sacrament**, they should not have
AL : 2 2 :012(051) [0061] the division of the **sacrament** does not agree with the
AL : 2 4 :005(056) [0065] to receive the **sacrament** together, in so far as they are fit
AL : 2 4 :007(056) [0065] value and use of the **sacrament** and the great consolation
AL : 2 4 :008(057) [0065] and such use of the **sacrament** nourishes devotion to
AL : 2 4 :017(057) [0067] arisen concerning the Mass, concerning the **sacrament**.
AL : 2 4 :030(059) [0067] of those who use the **sacrament** should remember what
AL : 2 4 :033(060) [0067] to this end, that the **sacrament** is administered to those
AL : 2 4 :034(060) [0067] is such a giving of the **sacrament**, one common Mass is
AL : 2 4 :034(060) [0067] days, if any desire the **sacrament**, it is also administered to
AP : 0 2 :036(105) [0115] guilt is absolved by the **sacrament** that regenerates the
AP : 0 9 :002(178) [0245] is neither Word nor **sacrament**, because Christ
AP : 0 9 :002(178) [0245] because Christ regenerates through Word and **sacrament**.
AP : 1 0 :001(179) [0247] bread and the wine, to those who receive the **sacrament**.
AP : 1 2 :012(184) [0255] They pretend that the **sacrament** grants grace *ex opere*
AP : 1 2 :025(185) [0259] 9. The reception of the **sacrament** of penitence obtains
AP : 1 2 :041(187) [0261] may properly be called a **sacrament** of penitence, as even
AP : 1 3 :004(211) [0309] absolution (which is the **sacrament** of penitence), for
AP : 1 3 :005(212) [0309] well when he called the **sacrament** "the visible Word," for

Continued ▶

A P : 1 3 :011(212) [0311] we have no obligation to calling ordination a **sacrament**.
A P : 1 3 :012(212) [0311] either to calling the laying on of hands a **sacrament**.
A P : 1 3 :014(213) [0311] wants to call it a **sacrament**, he should distinguish it from
A P : 1 3 :015(213) [0311] should be called a **sacrament** because it has God's
A P : 1 3 :016(213) [0311] not prayer, which can most truly be called a **sacrament**?
A P : 1 3 :019(213) [0313] that which is promised and offered in the **sacrament**.
A P : 1 3 :020(213) [0313] Because this is a **sacrament** of the New Testament, as
A P : 1 3 :022(214) [0313] Such use of the **sacrament** comforts devout and troubled
A P : 1 3 :023(214) [0313] that faith in the **sacrament**, and not the sacrament,
A P : 1 3 :023(214) [0313] faith in the sacrament, and not the **sacrament**, justifies.
A P : 2 2 :001(236) [0357] all of the church uses the **sacrament**, not only the priests.
A P : 2 2 :003(236) [0359] him who instituted the **sacrament**; previously he had said
A P : 2 2 :004(236) [0359] that the entire **sacrament** was instituted for the whole
A P : 2 2 :006(237) [0359] church why one part of the **sacrament** has been withheld.
A P : 2 2 :006(237) [0359] who were not permitted to receive the entire **sacrament**.
A P : 2 2 :007(237) [0359] takes these passages as referring to the **sacrament**.
A P : 2 2 :008(237) [0359] custom of giving the laity only a part of the **sacrament**.
A P : 2 2 :010(237) [0361] when they apply the story of Eli's sons to the **sacrament**.
A P : 2 2 :010(237) [0361] The **sacrament** was instituted to console and strengthen
A P : 2 2 :012(238) [0361] withhold a part of the **sacrament** and rage against good
A P : 2 2 :012(238) [0361] and rage against good men who use the entire **sacrament**?
A P : 2 2 :016(238) [0361] both kinds in the **sacrament** and who even
A P : 2 2 :016(238) [0361] violently persecute anyone that uses the entire **sacrament**.
A P : 2 4 :001(249) [0385] festivals, when the **sacrament** is offered to those who wish
A P : 2 4 :017(252) [0389] a proper distinction between **sacrament** and sacrifice.
A P : 2 4 :018(252) [0389] A **sacrament** is a ceremony or act in which God offers us
A P : 2 4 :049(258) [0401] If the use of the **sacrament** were the daily sacrifice, we
A P : 2 4 :049(258) [0401] in their churches mercenary priests use the **sacrament**.
A P : 2 4 :049(258) [0401] the proper use of the **sacrament** as a seal and witness of
A P : 2 4 :064(261) [0407] the application of the **sacrament**, though without faith the
A P : 2 4 :067(261) [0407] about the use of the **sacrament** what actually agrees with
A P : 2 4 :067(261) [0407] Sacrifice and the Use of the **Sacrament**
A P : 2 4 :069(262) [0409] There are two parts to a **sacrament**, the sign and the
A P : 2 4 :070(262) [0409] arouse this faith, so the **sacrament** was instituted to move
A P : 2 4 :071(262) [0409] This use of the **sacrament**, when faith gives life to terrified
A P : 2 4 :073(262) [0409] The principal use of the **sacrament** is to make clear that
A P : 2 4 :075(263) [0411] to the nature of the **sacrament**, and the second to the
A P : 2 4 :075(263) [0411] This proves that the **sacrament** offers the forgiveness of
A P : 2 4 :090(266) [0415] but a promise and a **sacrament** requiring faith.
A P : 2 4 :092(267) [0417] of neither sacrifice nor **sacrament** nor forgiveness of sins
S 2 : 0 2 :004(293) [0463] "3. The **sacrament** can be had in a far better and more
S 2 : 0 2 :004(293) [0463] matter when the **sacrament** can be had in another and
S 2 : 0 2 :008(294) [0465] and properly in the **sacrament** administered according to
S 2 : 0 2 :009(294) [0465] for anyone to use the **sacrament**, which is the common
S 2 : 0 2 :012(295) [0465] Christ instituted the **sacrament** for the living alone.
S 2 : 0 2 :013(295) [0467] asked that she be remembered at the altar or **sacrament**.
S 2 : 0 2 :014(295) [0467] the dead are to be commemorated in the **sacrament**.
S 2 : 0 2 :029(297) [0471] we may retain the holy **sacrament** in its purity and
S 3 : 0 1 :009(302) [0477] when a man goes to the **sacrament** there is no need of a
S 3 : 0 1 :009(302) [0477] of man's nature and such is the power of the **sacrament**.
S 3 : 0 4 :000(310) [0491] third, through the holy **Sacrament** of the Altar; fourth,
S 3 : 0 5 :001(310) [0491] Word is added to the element and it becomes a **sacrament**.
S 3 : 0 6 :000(311) [0493] VI. The **Sacrament** of the Altar
S 3 : 0 8 :010(313) [0497] with us except through his external Word and **sacrament**.
S 3 : 0 8 :010(313) [0497] apart from such Word and **sacrament** is of the devil.
S 3 : 0 9 :000(314) [0497] sinners from the **sacrament** and other fellowship in the
T R : 0 0 :082(000) [0529] Concord concerning the **Sacrament**, made at Wittenberg
S C : P R :003(338) [0533] and receive the holy **sacrament**, they do not know the
S C : P R :011(339) [0535] not be admitted to the **sacrament**, be accepted as
S C : P R :021(340) [0537] unwilling to receive the **sacrament** and they treat it with
S C : P R :021(340) [0537] believe or to receive the **sacrament**, no law is to be made
S C : P R :022(341) [0537] people will desire the **sacrament** and, as it were, compel
S C : P R :022(341) [0537] not desire to receive the **sacrament** at least three or four
S C : P R :022(341) [0537] a year despises the **sacrament** and is no Christian, just as
S C : P R :023(341) [0537] not highly esteem the **sacrament** suggests thereby that he
S C : P R :023(341) [0539] would not neglect the **sacrament** in which aid is afforded
S C : P R :023(341) [0539] any law to receive the **sacrament**, for he will hasten to it
S C : P R :024(341) [0539] the blessing and danger connected with this **sacrament**.
S C : P R :025(341) [0539] own fault if the people treat the **sacrament** with contempt.
S C : 0 4 :000(348) [0551] [IV] The **Sacrament** of Holy Baptism
S C : 0 6 :000(351) [0555] The **Sacrament** of the Altar *in the plain form in which the*
S C : 0 6 :001(351) [0555] What is the **Sacrament** of the Altar?
S C : 0 6 :006(352) [0557] are given to us in the **sacrament**, for where there is
S C : 0 6 :008(352) [0557] the chief thing in the **sacrament**, and he who believes
S C : 0 6 :009(352) [0557] Who, then, receives this **sacrament** worthily?
L C : S P :002(362) [0575] nor admitted to a **sacrament**, just as a craftsman who
L C : S P :005(362) [0575] to Baptism and the **Sacrament** of the Altar and exercise
L C : S P :005(362) [0575] those who come to the **sacrament** ought to know more
L C : S P :022(364) [0579] The other **sacrament** may be dealt with similarly, in
L C : S P :023(364) [0579] The **Sacrament** [of the Altar]
L C : 0 4 :018(438) [0737] derives its nature as a **sacrament**, as St. Augustine
L C : 0 4 :018(438) [0737] substance, it becomes a **sacrament**, that is, a holy, divine
L C : 0 4 :022(439) [0737] ordinance, Baptism is a **sacrament**, and it is called
L C : 0 4 :022(439) [0737] the nature and dignity of this holy **sacrament**.
L C : 0 4 :038(441) [0741] be known about this **sacrament**, especially that it is God's
L C : 0 4 :054(443) [0745] Supper receive the true **sacrament** even though they do
L C : 0 4 :055(443) [0745] Similarly, the **Sacrament** of the Altar is not vitiated if
L C : 0 4 :055(443) [0747] he had not really received the **sacrament** the first time.
L C : 0 4 :055(443) [0747] blaspheme and desecrate the **sacrament** in the worst way.
L C : 0 4 :056(444) [0747] Just so, I go to the **Sacrament** of the Altar not on the
L C : 0 4 :064(444) [0749] observance for the **sacrament** by which we are first
L C : 0 4 :074(445) [0751] also the third **sacrament**, formerly called Penance, which
L C : 0 5 :000(447) [0753] [Fifth Part:] The **Sacrament** of the Altar
L C : 0 5 :001(447) [0753] deal with the second **sacrament** in the same way, stating
L C : 0 5 :002(447) [0753] Christian and go to the **sacrament** should be familiar with
L C : 0 5 :002(447) [0753] intend to admit to the **sacrament** and administer it to
L C : 0 5 :004(447) [0753] and desecrate this **sacrament**; but as in the case of
L C : 0 5 :005(447) [0755] also does this blessed **sacrament** remain unimpaired and
L C : 0 5 :008(447) [0755] Now, what is the **Sacrament** of the Altar?
L C : 0 5 :009(447) [0755] so we say here that the **sacrament** is bread and wine, but
L C : 0 5 :010(448) [0755] wine and constitutes it a **sacrament** which is rightly called
L C : 0 5 :010(448) [0755] joined to the external element, it becomes a **sacrament**."
L C : 0 5 :010(448) [0755] make the element a **sacrament**; otherwise it remains a
L C : 0 5 :015(448) [0757] priest can administer the **sacrament**, and like questions.
L C : 0 5 :016(448) [0757] it, it is the true **sacrament** (that is, Christ's body and
L C : 0 5 :016(448) [0757] can change or alter the **sacrament**, even if it is misused.
L C : 0 5 :017(448) [0757] it was constituted a **sacrament** is not rendered false
L C : 0 5 :020(449) [0757] the first part, namely, the essence of this **sacrament**.
L C : 0 5 :020(449) [0757] purpose for which the **sacrament** was really instituted, for
L C : 0 5 :022(449) [0757] words, we go to the **sacrament** because we receive there a
L C : 0 5 :022(449) [0757] drink in order that the **sacrament** may be mine and may
L C : 0 5 :031(450) [0759] that we cannot have forgiveness of sins in the **sacrament**.
L C : 0 5 :032(450) [0759] are embodied in this **sacrament** and offered to us through
L C : 0 5 :032(450) [0761] we allow this treasure to be torn out of the **sacrament**?
L C : 0 5 :032(450) [0761] that these words in the **sacrament** are of no value just as
L C : 0 5 :032(450) [0761] or Word of God apart from the **sacrament** is of no value.
L C : 0 5 :033(450) [0761] far we have treated the **sacrament** from the standpoint
L C : 0 5 :036(450) [0761] of a Christian for receiving this **sacrament** worthily.
L C : 0 5 :037(451) [0761] is given in and with the **sacrament** cannot be grasped and
L C : 0 5 :038(451) [0761] ordinary instruction on the essentials of this **sacrament**.
L C : 0 5 :039(451) [0761] and doctrine of the **sacrament**, there is great need also of
L C : 0 5 :039(451) [0761] themselves to receive this blessed **sacrament** frequently.
L C : 0 5 :040(451) [0763] without receiving the **sacrament**, as if they were such
L C : 0 5 :041(451) [0763] despise both the **sacrament** and the Word of God.
L C : 0 5 :042(451) [0763] themselves from the **sacrament** over a long period of time
L C : 0 5 :043(451) [0763] cherish and honor the **sacrament** will of their own accord
L C : 0 5 :043(451) [0763] need for receiving the **sacrament**, we shall devote a little
L C : 0 5 :045(452) [0763] all who would be Christians to partake of the **sacrament**.
L C : 0 5 :045(452) [0763] faithfully hold to this **sacrament**, not from compulsion,
L C : 0 5 :047(452) [0763] Christ wishes the **sacrament** to be free, not bound to a
L C : 0 5 :049(452) [0765] that we are not granted liberty to despise the **sacrament**.
L C : 0 5 :049(452) [0765] ever desiring the **sacrament**, I call that despising it.
L C : 0 5 :051(452) [0765] an aversion toward the **sacrament**, men can easily sense
L C : 0 5 :051(452) [0765] when we attended the **sacrament** merely from compulsion
L C : 0 5 :052(452) [0765] anyone partake of the **sacrament** to serve or please us.
L C : 0 5 :053(453) [0765] stays away from the **sacrament**, day by day he will
L C : 0 5 :056(453) [0767] refuse to go to the **sacrament** and wait until they become
L C : 0 5 :059(453) [0767] himself from the **sacrament**," lest he deprive himself of
L C : 0 5 :061(453) [0767] to realize that this **sacrament** does not depend upon our
L C : 0 5 :065(454) [0769] as well have kept quiet and not instituted a **sacrament**.
L C : 0 5 :066(454) [0769] In this **sacrament** he offers us all the treasure he brought
L C : 0 5 :068(454) [0769] must never regard the **sacrament** as a harmful thing from
L C : 0 5 :068(454) [0769] do we act as if the **sacrament** were a poison which would
L C : 0 5 :069(454) [0769] those who despise the **sacrament** and lead unchristian
L C : 0 5 :070(454) [0769] regard and use the **sacrament** as a precious antidote
L C : 0 5 :070(454) [0769] For here in the **sacrament** you receive from Christ's lips
L C : 0 5 :072(455) [0769] go joyfully to the **sacrament** and receive refreshment,
L C : 0 5 :073(455) [0771] in order to come to the **sacrament** purely and worthily,
L C : 0 5 :075(455) [0771] need or experience hunger and thirst for the **sacrament**?"
L C : 0 5 :078(455) [0771] you have to go to the **sacrament** and seek a remedy.
L C : 0 5 :082(456) [0773] be glad to come to the **sacrament** as often as possible.
L C : 0 5 :084(456) [0773] are much in need of the **sacrament** to combat your
L C : 0 5 :084(456) [0773] more sensitive to it and more hungry for the **sacrament**.
L C : 0 5 :087(456) [0773] this fellowship of the **sacrament** so that they may serve us
L C : 0 6 :029(460) [0000] Christian and that you ought not receive the **sacrament**.
L C : 0 6 :031(460) [0000] we are compelled to preach and administer the **sacrament**.
L C : 0 6 :033(461) [0000] tremble for God's Word, absolution, the **sacrament**, etc.
E P : 0 7 :002(481) [0809] by all those who use the **sacrament**, be they worthy or
E P : 0 7 :018(484) [0813] use of the holy **sacrament** increases, magnifies, and
E P : 0 7 :020(484) [0813] faith and of which we are assured through the **sacrament**.
E P : 0 7 :024(484) [0815] of only one kind of the **sacrament** to the laity and the
E P : 0 7 :026(485) [0815] 5. That in the holy **sacrament** the body of Christ is not
E P : 0 7 :039(486) [0817] can also receive this **sacrament** to their condemnation
E P : 0 7 :040(486) [0817] bread and wine in the holy **sacrament** should be adored.
E P : 0 7 :041(486) [0817] the supernatural and celestial mysteries of this **sacrament**.
S D : 0 7 :009(571) [0975] and essentially present here on earth in the **sacrament**).
S D : 0 7 :010(571) [0975] following words: "The **Sacrament** of the Altar, instituted
S D : 0 7 :011(571) [0975] bread and the wine, to those who receive the **sacrament**.
S D : 0 7 :013(571) [0977] concerning the holy **sacrament** of the body and blood of
S D : 0 7 :014(571) [0977] are two things in this **sacrament**, one heavenly and the
S D : 0 7 :014(571) [0977] from the use of the **sacrament**, they grant that through
S D : 0 7 :016(572) [0977] is the institution of this **sacrament**, performed by Christ,
S D : 0 7 :016(572) [0977] who distributes the **sacrament** or of him who receives it,
S D : 0 7 :016(572) [0977] as St. Paul says, the unworthy receive the **sacrament** too.
S D : 0 7 :016(572) [0977] they misuse the holy **sacrament** since they receive it
S D : 0 7 :020(573) [0979] he writes as follows: "What is the **Sacrament** of the Altar?
S D : 0 7 :021(573) [0979] say, is what makes this **sacrament** and so distinguishes it
S D : 0 7 :024(573) [0979] administer and give the **sacrament**, and like questions.
S D : 0 7 :024(573) [0979] receives or gives the **sacrament**, it is the true sacrament
S D : 0 7 :024(573) [0979] sacrament, it is the true **sacrament** (that is, Christ's body
S D : 0 7 :024(573) [0981] worthy manner, for the **sacrament** is not based on the
S D : 0 7 :024(573) [0981] alter or change the **sacrament**, even though it is misused.
S D : 0 7 :025(573) [0981] and has become a **sacrament** is not rendered false because
S D : 0 7 :030(574) [0983] as I have now defended the **Sacrament** of the Altar.
S D : 0 7 :032(574) [0983] and confess that in the **Sacrament** of the Altar the body
S D : 0 7 :032(574) [0983] them do not believe or otherwise misuse the **sacrament**.
S D : 0 7 :032(574) [0983] as the enemies of the **sacrament** do at the present time.
S D : 0 7 :037(576) [0985] ordered action of the **sacrament**, though the union of the
S D : 0 7 :044(577) [0987] this most venerable **sacrament**, which was to be observed
S D : 0 7 :053(579) [0991] in the other part of the **sacrament** the words of Luke and
S D : 0 7 :060(580) [0993] of Christ orally in the **sacrament**, but also the unworthy
S D : 0 7 :066(581) [0997] occurs outside of the **sacrament** too, but also orally, and
S D : 0 7 :068(582) [0997] those who go to this **sacrament** without true contrition
S D : 0 7 :070(582) [0997] This most venerable **sacrament** was instituted and
S D : 0 7 :073(583) [0999] rule that there is no **sacrament** apart from the instituted
S D : 0 7 :081(584) [1001] and benefits of this **sacrament** (the presence of the body
S D : 0 7 :083(584) [1001] offered up, or carried about), does not make a **sacrament**.
S D : 0 7 :084(584) [1001] administration of this **sacrament** (namely, that in a
S D : 0 7 :085(584) [1001] has the character of a **sacrament** apart from the use
S D : 0 7 :085(584) [1003] Christ's institution as he ordained it, it is no **sacrament**).
S D : 0 7 :087(585) [1003] it is not to be deemed a **sacrament**, as when in the
S D : 0 7 :087(585) [1003] baptismal water is no **sacrament** or Baptism if it should
S D : 0 7 :088(585) [1003] the unworthy it is no **sacrament**, and that the reception of
S D : 0 7 :089(585) [1003] faith which makes the **sacrament**, but solely the Word and
S D : 0 7 :089(585) [1003] or the unbelief of him who receives the **sacrament**.
S D : 0 7 :089(585) [1003] those who receive the **sacrament** believe or do not

Continued ▶

SD : 07 :108(588) [1009] from the action of the **sacrament** (when, for instance, the
SD : 07 :108(588) [1009] For nothing can be a **sacrament** apart from God's
SD : 07 :109(588) [1011] papistic abuses of this **sacrament**, such as the
SD : 07 :121(590) [1013] allegedly to effect a **sacrament**, the words of institution
SD : 07 :125(591) [1015] may receive this **sacrament** for judgment, just as

Sacraments (127)
AG : 05 :001(031) [0045] ministry, that is, provided the Gospel and the **sacraments**.
AG : 07 :001(032) [0047] its purity and the holy **sacraments** are administered
AG : 07 :002(032) [0047] of it and that the **sacraments** be administered in
AG : 08 :001(033) [0047] among the godly, the **sacraments** are efficacious even if
AG : 13 :000(035) [0049] XIII. The Use of the **Sacraments**
AG : 13 :001(035) [0049] among us that the **sacraments** were instituted not only to
AG : 14 :000(036) [0049] or administer the **sacraments** in the church without a
AG : 28 :005(081) [0085] sins, and to administer and distribute the **sacraments**.
AG : 28 :008(082) [0085] by administering the **sacraments** (to many persons or to
AG : 28 :009(082) [0085] administering the holy **sacraments**, for St. Paul says, "The
AG : 28 :012(083) [0085] to preach the Gospel and administer the **sacraments**.
AL : 05 :001(031) [0045] Gospel and administering the **sacraments** was instituted.
AL : 05 :002(031) [0045] the Word and the **sacraments**, as through instruments,
AL : 07 :001(032) [0047] taught purely and the **sacraments** are administered
AL : 07 :002(032) [0047] of the Gospel and the administration of the **sacraments**.
AL : 08 :001(033) [0047] is allowable to use the **sacraments** even when they are
AL : 08 :002(033) [0047] Both the **sacraments** and the Word are effectual by reason
AL : 13 :000(035) [0049] XIII. The Use of the **Sacraments**
AL : 13 :001(035) [0049] churches teach that the **sacraments** were instituted not
AL : 13 :002(035) [0049] Consequently the **sacraments** should be so used that
AL : 13 :003(036) [0049] who teach that the **sacraments** justify by the outward act
AL : 13 :003(036) [0049] are forgiven, is required in the use of the **sacraments**.]
AL : 14 :000(036) [0049] or administer the **sacraments** unless he is regularly called.
AL : 28 :005(081) [0085] remit and retain sins, and to administer the **sacraments**.
AL : 28 :008(082) [0085] by administering the **sacraments** either to many or to
AL : 28 :009(082) [0085] of the Word and **sacraments**, for Paul says, "The gospel is
AL : 28 :012(083) [0085] to preach the Gospel and administer the **sacraments**.
AL : 28 :021(084) [0087] of the Word and **sacraments**) except to forgive sins, to
AP : 04 :063(115) [0139] They imagine that the **sacraments** bestow the Holy Spirit
AP : 04 :073(117) [0141] not the Word or the **sacraments**, as our opponents
AP : 04 :288(151) [0203] have also distorted the **sacraments**, especially the Mass,
AP : 04 :361(162) [0219] We must add certain "**sacraments**" of this transfer, as
AP : 07 :003(168) [0227] or deny efficacy to the **sacraments** which evil men or
AP : 07 :003(169) [0227] Word, confession, and **sacraments** — especially if they
AP : 07 :003(169) [0227] The **sacraments** do not lose their efficacy when they are
AP : 07 :003(169) [0227] we may legitimately use **sacraments** that are administered
AP : 07 :005(169) [0227] administration of the **sacraments** in harmony with the
AP : 07 :007(169) [0229] added the outward marks, the Word and the **sacraments**.
AP : 07 :010(170) [0229] Spirit, and the same **sacraments**, whether they have the
AP : 07 :019(171) [0233] that the Word and the **sacraments** are efficacious even
AP : 07 :020(171) [0233] the pure teaching of the Gospel and the **sacraments**.
AP : 07 :021(172) [0233] faith be necessary if **sacraments** justify *ex opere operato*,
AP : 07 :028(173) [0237] When the **sacraments** are administered by unworthy men,
AP : 07 :028(173) [0237] Word of Christ or the **sacraments**, they do so in Christ's
AP : 07 :029(173) [0237] if they received the **sacraments** from unworthy men in the
AP : 07 :030(174) [0237] of the Gospel and the administration of the **sacraments**.
AP : 07 :036(175) [0241] believe (like the divinely instituted Word and **sacraments**).
AP : 07 :047(177) [0243] church and that the **sacraments** are efficacious even when
AP : 11 :003(180) [0249] our churches use the **sacraments**, absolution and the
AP : 11 :003(180) [0249] worth and fruits of the **sacraments** in such a way as to
AP : 11 :003(180) [0249] such a way as to invite them to use the **sacraments** often.
AP : 11 :004(180) [0249] and the despisers of the **sacraments** are excommunicated.
AP : 11 :005(181) [0251] not force those who are not ready to use the **sacraments**.
AP : 12 :042(187) [0261] proclamation of the Gospel and the use of the **sacraments**.
AP : 12 :043(187) [0263] of the keys and the **sacraments**, it illumines the blessing
AP : 13 :000(211) [0309] [Article XIII.] The Number and Use of the **Sacraments**
AP : 13 :001(211) [0309] the statement that the **sacraments** are no mere marks of
AP : 13 :001(211) [0309] But they insist that we enumerate seven **sacraments**.
AP : 13 :003(211) [0309] If we define **sacraments** as "rites which have the command
AP : 13 :003(211) [0309] easily determine which are **sacraments** in the strict sense.
AP : 13 :003(211) [0309] by men are not **sacraments** in the strict sense since men do
AP : 13 :004(211) [0309] The genuine **sacraments**, therefore, are Baptism, the
AP : 13 :007(212) [0311] administration of the **sacraments** to others, but in
AP : 13 :009(212) [0311] the Gospel and administer the **sacraments** to the people.
AP : 13 :015(213) [0311] might also be called **sacraments** because they have God's
AP : 13 :016(213) [0311] if we should list as **sacraments** all the things that have
AP : 13 :016(213) [0311] were placed among the **sacraments** and thus given, so to
AP : 13 :017(213) [0313] about the number of **sacraments** or the terminology, so
AP : 13 :018(213) [0313] much more necessary to know how to use the **sacraments**.
AP : 13 :018(213) [0313] is some obstacle, the **sacraments** confer grace *ex opere*
AP : 13 :019(213) [0313] teach that in using the **sacraments** there must be a faith
AP : 13 :020(213) [0313] The **sacraments** are signs of the promises.
AP : 13 :023(214) [0313] notion, about the **sacraments** *ex opere operato* without a
AP : 14 :001(214) [0315] the Word and the **sacraments** in the church unless he is
AP : 14 :004(215) [0315] the Word of God and rightly administer the **sacraments**.
AP : 24 :048(258) [0401] and they talk about the value and use of the **sacraments**.
AP : 24 :049(258) [0401] the proper use of the **sacraments**, we still have the daily
AP : 24 :051(259) [0401] the godly use of the **sacraments**, ardent prayer, and the
AP : 24 :059(260) [0405] the Gospel and the **sacraments** so that thereby they may
AP : 24 :069(262) [0409] The **sacraments** are not only signs among men, but signs
AP : 24 :070(262) [0409] Holy Spirit works through the Word and the **sacraments**.
AP : 24 :075(263) [0411] of their idea that **sacraments** work *ex opere operato* and
AP : 24 :080(264) [0411] and dispensers of the **sacraments** of God," that is, of the
AP : 24 :080(264) [0411] is, of the Word and **sacraments**; and II Cor. 5:20, "We are
AP : 24 :091(266) [0415] of the Gospel, a corruption of the use of the **sacraments**.
AP : 28 :003(281) [0443] and administration of the **sacraments** in the churches.
AP : 28 :013(283) [0447] the order, namely, the ministry of Word and **sacraments**.
S1 : PR :010(290) [0457] and the right use of the **sacraments**, with an
S2 : 04 :009(300) [0473] unity of doctrine, faith, **sacraments**, prayer, works of
S3 : 03 :008(304) [0481] through the Word, the **sacraments**, and the like, as we
TR : 00 :006(320) [0505] changes in the **sacraments**, and concerning doctrine.
TR : 00 :031(325) [0513] of sins, administer the **sacraments**, and excommunicate
TR : 00 :060(330) [0521] sins, administer the **sacraments**, and, in addition, exercise
SC : PR :007(339) [0533] the Creed, the Lord's Prayer, the **sacraments**, etc.
LC : SP :020(364) [0579] what to say about the **sacraments** which Christ himself
LC : 02 :054(417) [0693] through the holy **sacraments** and absolution as well as
LC : 02 :054(417) [0693] concerning the **sacraments** and, in short, the entire
LC : 03 :037(425) [0707] of God and enjoy the **sacraments**, through which he so
LC : 04 :001(436) [0733] us to speak of our two **sacraments**, instituted by Christ.
LC : 04 :019(438) [0737] teach that the **sacraments** and all the external things
LC : 05 :007(447) [0755] spirits who regard the **sacraments**, contrary to the Word
EP : 02 :001(469) [0785] of God offered in the Word and the holy **sacraments**?
EP : 02 :013(471) [0789] God's Word and without the use of the holy **sacraments**.
EP : 02 :018(472) [0791] the use of the holy **sacraments** takes hold of man's will
EP : 08 :032(491) [0825] in the Word, in the **sacraments**, and in all our necessities
EP : 10 :007(493) [0831] right use of the holy **sacraments**, according to the familiar
EP : 11 :013(496) [0835] sealed it with his holy **sacraments**, of which we can
EP : 11 :021(497) [0837] in the holy Gospel and in the use of the holy **sacraments**.
EP : 12 :027(500) [0843] true and genuine **sacraments** unless he is himself truly
SD : 02 :046(530) [0899] read the Word and the **sacraments** but will wait until God
SD : 02 :048(530) [0901] Word and the holy **sacraments**) the Holy Spirit wills to be
SD : 02 :050(531) [0901] or reads it) and the **sacraments** (when they are used
SD : 02 :057(532) [0903] the Word and the holy **sacraments**, earnestly wills that we
SD : 02 :065(534) [0907] the Word and the holy **sacraments**, it is certain that we
SD : 02 :080(536) [0911] the use of the holy **sacraments**, God draws man to
SD : 03 :016(541) [0921] the Gospel and in the **sacraments**, and is applied,
SD : 07 :050(578) [0989] and signs of grace or **sacraments**, such as circumcision,
SD : 08 :094(609) [1049] right use of the holy **sacraments** Christ is present with us
SD : 10 :031(616) [1063] right use of the holy **sacraments**, according to the
SD : 11 :010(618) [1067] despise Word and **sacraments**, and do not concern myself
SD : 11 :016(619) [1069] and distributed to us through his Word and **sacraments**.
SD : 11 :037(622) [1075] but also through the **sacraments**, which he has attached
SD : 11 :038(622) [1075] to us through the Word and through the **sacraments**.
SD : 11 :071(627) [1085] and faith in us through the Word and the **sacraments**.
SD : 11 :076(628) [1087] ordained Word and **sacraments** as the ordinary means or
SD : 11 :076(629) [1087] the Father to draw him without Word and **sacraments**.
SD : 12 :035(635) [1101] profitably nor administer genuine and true **sacraments**.

Sacramental (10)
EP : 07 :007(482) [0811] but that because of the **sacramental** union they are truly
EP : 07 :015(483) [0811] but because of the **sacramental** union in a supernatural
SD : 07 :014(572) [0977] grant that through **sacramental** union the bread is the
SD : 07 :018(572) [0979] Gospel, and that the **sacramental** union is intended to
SD : 07 :035(575) [0983] and to indicate the **sacramental** union between the
SD : 07 :038(576) [0985] in Christ, but a **sacramental** union, as Dr. Luther and our
SD : 07 :056(579) [0991] eating but of a **sacramental** or oral eating of the body of
SD : 07 :061(581) [0995] participation, even the **sacramental** or oral eating in the
SD : 07 :063(581) [0995] of Christ is oral or **sacramental**, when all who eat and
SD : 07 :117(589) [1013] Accordingly the term "**sacramental** union" is to be

Sacramentally (2)
SD : 07 :007(570) [0975] the word "is" **sacramentally** or in a figurative manner, so
SD : 07 :008(570) [0975] the body of Christ is **sacramentally** or symbolically united

Sacramentarian (4), Sacramentarians (37)
EP : 07 :001(481) [0809] Our Doctrine and the **Sacramentarian** Doctrine in This
EP : 07 :002(482) [0809] The **Sacramentarians** say No; we say Yes.
EP : 07 :003(482) [0809] first of all, that there are two kinds of **Sacramentarians**.
EP : 07 :003(482) [0809] Some are crass **Sacramentarians** who set forth in clear
EP : 07 :004(482) [0809] however, are subtle **Sacramentarians**, the most harmful
EP : 07 :005(482) [0809] *Doctrine of the Holy Supper Against the* ***Sacramentarians***
EP : 07 :010(483) [0811] controversy with the **Sacramentarians** are those which
EP : 07 :021(484) [0813] *and Condemned Doctrine of the* ***Sacramentarians***
EP : 07 :041(486) [0817] recite and which the **Sacramentarians** advance most
EP : 07 :042(486) [0817] The **Sacramentarians** deliberately insist on crediting us
EP : 08 :003(487) [0817] The **Sacramentarians** have asserted that in Christ the
EP : 08 :003(487) [0819] for the opposite view against the **Sacramentarians**.
SD : 07 :001(568) [0971] to the emperor, the **Sacramentarians** completely
SD : 07 :001(568) [0971] openly approved the **Sacramentarians'** position and
SD : 07 :001(569) [0971] with the teaching of the **Sacramentarians** in this article.
SD : 07 :001(569) [0971] Doctrine and That of the **Sacramentarians** in This Article
SD : 07 :002(569) [0971] Some **Sacramentarians** diligently endeavor to employ
SD : 07 :006(570) [0973] words of the **Sacramentarians** when they alleged and
SD : 07 :009(570) [0975] the doctrine of the **Sacramentarians**, who at the same time
SD : 07 :018(572) [0979] loop-hole which the **Sacramentarians** had employed to
SD : 07 :029(574) [0981] their error, as the **Sacramentarians** and Anabaptists are
SD : 07 :033(575) [0983] together (that is, as **Sacramentarians** and enthusiasts), for
SD : 07 :056(579) [0991] through faith, as the **Sacramentarians** pervert this
SD : 07 :059(580) [0993] against the **Sacramentarians**, as a basis for their error that
SD : 07 :067(581) [0997] and poisonously the **Sacramentarian** enthusiasts ridicule
SD : 07 :088(585) [1003] point out that the **Sacramentarians** dishonestly and
SD : 07 :091(585) [1003] of the **Sacramentarians** concerning the essential and
SD : 07 :093(586) [1005] against the **Sacramentarians** at the very beginning in the
SD : 07 :104(587) [1009] To the **Sacramentarians** this word "spiritual" means
SD : 07 :105(588) [1009] presence which the **Sacramentarians** ascribe to and force
SD : 07 :106(588) [1009] objections of the **Sacramentarians**, no matter how
SD : 07 :111(589) [1011] of Christ against the **Sacramentarians**, some of whom
SD : 07 :111(589) [1011] preeminently of the **Sacramentarians** and thereby
SD : 07 :112(589) [1011] and deceiving all **Sacramentarian** opinions and doctrines
SD : 07 :113(589) [1011] We reject all such **Sacramentarian** opinions and mutually
SD : 07 :119(590) [1013] of their error, some **Sacramentarians** have deliberately
SD : 08 :001(591) [1015] but proceeded originally from the **Sacramentarians**.
SD : 08 :004(592) [1017] and explicitly to the **Sacramentarians** in the doctrine of
SD : 08 :004(592) [1017] with which the **Sacramentarians** ventured to eliminate
SD : 08 :028(596) [1025] in heaven, as the **Sacramentarians** maintain without proof
SD : 08 :038(598) [1027] as well as open **Sacramentarians** hide their pernicious

Sacramentum (2)
LC : 04 :018(438) [0737] *"Accedat verbum ad elementum et fit* ***sacramentum***."
LC : 05 :010(448) [0755] *ad elementum et fit* ***sacramentum***," that is, "When the

Sacred (9)
AP : 10 :003(179) [0247] this would be completely foreign to the **sacred** Scriptures.
AP : 24 :017(252) [0389] common to both could be "ceremony" or "**sacred** act."
AP : 27 :028(274) [0429] "It has been stated in the **Sacred** Scriptures that the
AP : 27 :029(274) [0431] to the statement of the **Sacred** Scriptures the monastic life
AP : 27 :029(274) [0431] Where do the **Sacred** Scriptures talk about monastic life?
LC : 03 :038(425) [0707] and keeping it holy and **sacred**, regarding it as the
LC : 03 :038(425) [0707] treasure and most **sacred** thing we have, and praying, as
LC : 03 :049(426) [0711] rather keep God's name **sacred** and holy in both doctrine
SD : 02 :044(529) [0897] words Dr. Luther, of **sacred** and holy memory, grants our

Sacrifice (97), Sacrificed (4), Sacrifices (66)
A G : 0 3 :003(030) [0045] buried in order to be a **sacrifice** not only for original sin
A G : 2 4 :021(058) [0067] and had instituted the Mass as a **sacrifice** for other sins.
A G : 2 4 :022(058) [0067] the Mass into a **sacrifice** for the living and the dead, a
A G : 2 4 :022(058) [0067] living and the dead, a **sacrifice** by means of which sin was
A G : 2 4 :026(058) [0067] places that there is no **sacrifice** for original sin, or for any
A G : 2 4 :030(059) [0067] to make provision for a **sacrifice** for sin — for the sacrifice
A G : 2 4 :030(059) [0067] for sin — for the **sacrifice** has already taken place — but to
A G : 2 4 :034(060) [0067] as the Mass is not a **sacrifice** to remove the sins of others,
A L : 0 3 :003(030) [0045] Father to us and be a **sacrifice** not only for original guilt
A L : 2 4 :041(061) [0069] done except for the solemn remembrance of the **sacrifice**."
A P : 0 4 :134(125) [0159] the law of God and that **sacrifice** and ritual justify before
A P : 0 4 :179(131) [0171] of sin and becoming a **sacrifice** for us, the sinless Christ
A P : 0 4 :189(133) [0175] holy and divine works, **sacrifices**, and the reign of Christ,
A P : 0 4 :190(133) [0175] are holy works, true **sacrifices** acceptable to God, battles
A P : 0 4 :191(133) [0175] are holy works, true **sacrifices**, battles of God to defend
A P : 0 4 :192(133) [0175] work (I Cor. 16:1), a **sacrifice**, and a battle of Christ
A P : 0 4 :202(134) [0175] faith Abel offered a more acceptable **sacrifice** (Heb. 11:4).
A P : 0 4 :202(134) [0175] righteous by faith, the **sacrifice** he made was acceptable to
A P : 0 4 :206(135) [0177] The Gentiles had **sacrifices** which they took over from the
A P : 0 4 :207(135) [0177] imitated these **sacrifices** with the notion that on account
A P : 0 4 :207(135) [0177] Ps. 50:8, "I do not reprove you for your **sacrifices**."
A P : 0 4 :207(135) [0177] do not condemn the **sacrifices** that God surely
A P : 0 4 :208(135) [0177] Israel had seen the prophets **sacrifice** on the high places.
A P : 0 4 :208(135) [0177] But the prophets did not **sacrifice** on the high places to
A P : 0 4 :288(151) [0203] and the Israelites **sacrificed** human victims and undertook
A P : 0 4 :395(167) [0225] works, and so they multiplied **sacrifices** and devotions.
A P : 0 7 :016(171) [0231] they held high positions and they **sacrificed** and taught.
A P : 0 7 :023(172) [0235] institute devotions and **sacrifices**, enact whatever laws he
A P : 1 2 :015(184) [0257] only by indulgences but also by the **sacrifice** of the Mass.
A P : 1 2 :132(202) [0291] "Present your bodies as a living **sacrifice**, holy," etc.
A P : 1 2 :160(207) [0303] our bodies should be **sacrifices**, to show our obedience
A P : 1 3 :007(212) [0311] but in reference to **sacrifice**, as though the new covenant
A P : 1 3 :007(212) [0311] the Levitical to offer **sacrifices** and merit the forgiveness
A P : 1 3 :008(212) [0311] no need for additional **sacrifices** as though this were not
A P : 1 3 :009(212) [0311] because of any other **sacrifices**, but because of this one
A P : 1 3 :009(212) [0311] but because of this one **sacrifice** of Christ if they believe
A P : 1 3 :009(212) [0311] are not called to make **sacrifices** that merit forgiveness of
A P : 1 5 :045(221) [0327] says (Rom. 12:1), "Present your bodies as a **sacrifice**."
A P : 2 4 :009(250) [0387] many statements to prove that the Mass is a **sacrifice**.
A P : 2 4 :014(251) [0387] a great deal to say about **sacrifice**, though in our
A P : 2 4 :014(251) [0389] understanding of **sacrifice** among those whose abuses we
A P : 2 4 :014(251) [0389] to do this we must first set down the nature of a **sacrifice**.
A P : 2 4 :015(251) [0389] endless books about **sacrifice**, but none of them has
A P : 2 4 :015(251) [0389] They find the term "**sacrifice**" in either the Scriptures or
A P : 2 4 :015(252) [0389] **Sacrifice**, Its Nature and Types
A P : 2 4 :016(252) [0389] members of the concept "**sacrifice**," as our enumeration
A P : 2 4 :016(252) [0389] our enumeration of the types of **sacrifice** will make clear.
A P : 2 4 :017(252) [0389] a proper distinction between sacrament and **sacrifice**.
A P : 2 4 :018(252) [0389] By way of contrast, a **sacrifice** is a ceremony or act which
A P : 2 4 :019(252) [0389] There are two, and only two, basic types of **sacrifice**.
A P : 2 4 :019(252) [0389] One is the propitiatory **sacrifice**; this is a work of
A P : 2 4 :019(252) [0389] type is the eucharistic **sacrifice**; this does not merit the
A P : 2 4 :020(252) [0389] of these two types of **sacrifice** and be very careful not to
A P : 2 4 :021(252) [0389] All the Levitical **sacrifices** can be classified under one or
A P : 2 4 :021(252) [0389] Testament called certain **sacrifices** propitiatory because
A P : 2 4 :021(252) [0391] called propitiatory **sacrifices** for sin or burnt offerings for
A P : 2 4 :021(253) [0391] The eucharistic **sacrifices** were the oblation, the drink
A P : 2 4 :022(253) [0391] only one propitiatory **sacrifice** in the world, the death of
A P : 2 4 :023(253) [0391] here (*'asam*) means a victim **sacrificed** for transgression.
A P : 2 4 :023(253) [0391] they offered up human **sacrifices**, perhaps because they
A P : 2 4 :023(253) [0391] the death of Christ is the only real propitiatory **sacrifice**.
A P : 2 4 :024(253) [0391] Levitical propitiatory **sacrifices** were so called only as
A P : 2 4 :025(253) [0391] The rest are eucharistic **sacrifices**, called "sacrifices of
A P : 2 4 :025(253) [0391] sacrifices, called "**sacrifices** of praise": the proclamation
A P : 2 4 :025(253) [0391] These **sacrifices** are not satisfactions on behalf of those
A P : 2 4 :026(254) [0391] The **sacrifices** of the New Testament are of this type, as
A P : 2 4 :026(254) [0391] Pet. 2:5, "A holy priesthood, to offer spiritual **sacrifices**."
A P : 2 4 :026(254) [0391] Spiritual **sacrifices** are contrasted not only with the
A P : 2 4 :026(254) [0391] not only with the **sacrifices** of cattle but also with human
A P : 2 4 :026(254) [0391] your bodies as a living **sacrifice**, holy and acceptable to
A P : 2 4 :026(254) [0393] us continually offer up a **sacrifice** of praise to God," with
A P : 2 4 :027(254) [0393] the notion that the **sacrifices** are valid *ex opere operato*,
A P : 2 4 :028(254) [0393] *operato* and teach spiritual righteousness and **sacrifice**.
A P : 2 4 :028(254) [0393] command them concerning burnt offerings and **sacrifices**.
A P : 2 4 :028(254) [0393] burnt offerings and **sacrifices**, but what Jeremiah is
A P : 2 4 :028(254) [0393] is an idea of **sacrifices** that did not come from God,
A P : 2 4 :028(254) [0393] mercy and help you, for I do not need your **sacrifices**.
A P : 2 4 :029(255) [0393] also condemns the idea of **sacrifices** *ex opere operato*.
A P : 2 4 :029(255) [0393] Ps. 40:6 says, "**Sacrifice** and offering thou dost not desire;
A P : 2 4 :029(255) [0393] The **sacrifice** acceptable to God is a broken spirit; a
A P : 2 4 :029(255) [0393] also Ps. 4:5, "Offer right **sacrifices**, and put your trust in
A P : 2 4 :029(255) [0393] says that this is a right **sacrifice**, indicating that other
A P : 2 4 :029(255) [0393] indicating that other **sacrifices** are not true and right.
A P : 2 4 :029(255) [0393] "I will offer to thee **sacrifices** of thanksgiving and call on
A P : 2 4 :029(255) [0393] Prayer is called a **sacrifice** of thanksgiving.
A P : 2 4 :030(255) [0395] which teach that **sacrifices** do not reconcile God *ex opere*
A P : 2 4 :030(255) [0395] be a new and pure **sacrifice**; this is faith, prayer,
A P : 2 4 :031(255) [0395] About such **sacrifices** Malachi says (1:11), "From the
A P : 2 4 :032(255) [0395] *operato* but to all those **sacrifices** through which the
A P : 2 4 :033(256) [0395] the praises of God or **sacrifices** of praise we include the
A P : 2 4 :033(256) [0395] we shall explain how even a ceremony is a **sacrifice**.
A P : 2 4 :034(256) [0397] always apply the term "**sacrifice**" only to the ceremony.
A P : 2 4 :034(256) [0397] New Testament requires **sacrifices** of the heart, not the
A P : 2 4 :034(256) [0397] not the ceremonial **sacrifices** for sin offered by a Levitical
A P : 2 4 :035(256) [0397] also refer to the daily **sacrifice**: as there was a daily
A P : 2 4 :035(256) [0397] as there was a daily **sacrifice** in the Old Testament, so the
A P : 2 4 :035(256) [0397] Mass ought to be the daily **sacrifice** of the New Testament.
A P : 2 4 :035(256) [0397] be understood as a daily **sacrifice**, provided this means
A P : 2 4 :035(256) [0397] these are the daily **sacrifice** of the New Testament; the
A P : 2 4 :036(257) [0397] three parts of this daily **sacrifice**, the burning of the lamb,
A P : 2 4 :037(257) [0397] and not for another symbol that seems to be a **sacrifice**.
A P : 2 4 :038(257) [0399] it is not the daily **sacrifice** by itself; the commemoration is
A P : 2 4 :038(257) [0399] is the real daily **sacrifice**, the proclamation of the faith
A P : 2 4 :039(257) [0399] worship and the daily **sacrifice** of the heart, for in the New
A P : 2 4 :040(257) [0399] the analogy of the daily **sacrifice** does not refute but
A P : 2 4 :041(257) [0399] of the charge that we do away with the daily **sacrifice**.
A P : 2 4 :049(258) [0401] were the daily **sacrifice**, we could lay more claim to
A P : 2 4 :049(258) [0401] use of the sacraments, we still have the daily **sacrifice**.
A P : 2 4 :052(259) [0403] in relation to God, to offer gifts and **sacrifices** for sins."
A P : 2 4 :052(259) [0403] priests, it must also have some sort of **sacrifice** for sins.
A P : 2 4 :052(259) [0403] priesthood and **sacrifices** is spread before their eyes.
A P : 2 4 :052(259) [0403] have some ceremony or **sacrifice** for sins, just as the Old
A P : 2 4 :053(259) [0403] "every high priest is appointed to offer **sacrifices** for sins."
A P : 2 4 :053(259) [0403] The Levitical **sacrifices** for sin did not merit the
A P : 2 4 :053(259) [0403] merely a picture of the **sacrifice** of Christ which was to be
A P : 2 4 :053(259) [0403] of Christ which was to be the one propitiatory **sacrifice**.
A P : 2 4 :054(259) [0403] and the ancient **sacrifices** were not instituted to merit the
A P : 2 4 :056(259) [0403] The Old Testament **sacrifices**, therefore, did not merit
A P : 2 4 :056(259) [0403] reconciliation — but only symbolized the coming **sacrifice**.
A P : 2 4 :056(260) [0405] only the **sacrifice** of Christ can be valid for the sins of
A P : 2 4 :056(260) [0405] there is no other such **sacrifice** left in the New Testament
A P : 2 4 :056(260) [0405] Testament except the one **sacrifice** of Christ on the cross.
A P : 2 4 :057(260) [0405] that the Levitical **sacrifices** merited the forgiveness of sins
A P : 2 4 :057(260) [0405] analogy there must be **sacrifices** in the New Testament
A P : 2 4 :058(260) [0405] must have a priest who **sacrifices** for sin, this can only
A P : 2 4 :059(260) [0405] in II Cor. 3:6, the only **sacrifice** of satisfaction it has for
A P : 2 4 :059(260) [0405] it has for the sins of others is the **sacrifice** of Christ.
A P : 2 4 :059(260) [0405] It has no **sacrifices** like the Levitical which could be
A P : 2 4 :065(261) [0407] Patristic Teaching on **Sacrifice**
A P : 2 4 :066(261) [0407] Fathers call the Mass a **sacrifice**; but they do not mean
A P : 2 4 :067(261) [0407] said that a eucharistic **sacrifice** does not merit
A P : 2 4 :067(261) [0407] but are eucharistic **sacrifices** when the reconciled endure
A P : 2 4 :067(261) [0407] **Sacrifice** and the Use of the Sacrament
A P : 2 4 :074(262) [0409] There is also a **sacrifice**, since one action can have several
A P : 2 4 :074(263) [0411] Thus the ceremony becomes a **sacrifice** of praise.
A P : 2 4 :075(263) [0411] nature of the sacrament, and the second to the **sacrifice**.
A P : 2 4 :078(263) [0411] that the Mass is called a **sacrifice** that it grants grace *ex*
A P : 2 4 :079(264) [0411] the Mass "liturgy," and this, they say, means "**sacrifice**."
A P : 2 4 :080(264) [0411] It does not really mean a **sacrifice** but a public service.
A P : 2 4 :084(264) [0413] the Mass must be a **sacrifice**; for Paul uses the figure of
A P : 2 4 :088(265) [0413] supplications and bloodless **sacrifices** for all the people."
A P : 2 4 :088(265) [0413] and supplications and bloodless **sacrifices** for the people.
A P : 2 4 :088(265) [0413] It calls even prayers "bloodless **sacrifices**."
A P : 2 4 :089(266) [0415] *operato*, a ceremony is a **sacrifice** that reconciles God and
A P : 2 4 :091(266) [0415] This is the abolition of the daily **sacrifice** in the church.
A P : 2 4 :092(267) [0417] the meaning of neither **sacrifice** nor sacrament nor
A P : 2 4 :097(268) [0417] forgiveness of sins by **sacrifices** *ex opere operato* rather
A P : 2 4 :097(268) [0417] Hence they increased the services and **sacrifices**.
A P : 2 4 :097(268) [0417] worship of Baal; in Judah they even **sacrificed** in groves.
A P : 2 4 :097(268) [0417] priests who perform the **sacrifices** instituted by God with
A P : 2 4 :097(268) [0417] always will, that services and **sacrifices** are propitiations.
A P : 2 4 :097(268) [0417] stand it when only the **sacrifice** of Christ is honored as a
A P : 2 4 :097(268) [0417] faith but give equal honor to other **sacrifices** and services.
A P : 2 4 :098(268) [0417] A false idea about **sacrifices** clung to the wicked priests in
A P : 2 7 :049(277) [0437] rule, or of Abraham to **sacrifice** his son, are not for us to
S 2 : 0 2 :001(293) [0463] for it is held that this **sacrifice** or work of the Mass (even
S 2 : 0 2 :026(297) [0469] say Masses and offer **sacrifices** to them, establish
S 2 : 0 2 :027(297) [0469] say Masses and offer **sacrifices** in your honor, or trust in
T R : 0 0 :071(332) [0525] "I give thee the power to **sacrifice** for the living and the
L C : 0 1 :304(406) [0667] of and forced to **sacrifice** what he cannot spare without
L C : 0 3 :065(429) [0715] will have peace; he must **sacrifice** all he has on earth —
E P : 0 7 :023(484) [0815] 2. The papistic **sacrifice** of the Mass for the sins of the
S D : 0 6 :022(567) [0969] us that our spiritual **sacrifices** are acceptable to God
S D : 0 7 :049(578) [0989] which he had won for us by the **sacrifice** of his body.
S D : 0 7 :050(578) [0989] the many kinds of **sacrifice** in the Old Testament, and
S D : 0 7 :057(579) [0993] who were eating idol-**sacrifices** and participating in pagan
S D : 0 7 :109(588) [1011] the abomination of the **sacrifice** of the Mass for the living

Sacrificer (1), Sacrificers (1)
A P : 2 4 :057(260) [0405] with priests and **sacrificers** who daily peddle their wares in
A P : 2 4 :082(264) [0411] to my need," which surely does not mean a **sacrificer**.

Sacrificial (4)
A P : 1 3 :008(212) [0311] We teach that the **sacrificial** death of Christ on the cross
A P : 2 4 :023(253) [0391] The Latins offered a **sacrificial** victim to placate the wrath
A P : 2 4 :023(253) [0391] that Christ became a **sacrificial** victim or trespass offering
A P : 2 4 :029(255) [0393] It rejects **sacrificial** victims and requires prayer: "Do I eat

Sacrilege (1), Sacrilegious (2)
A P : 2 4 :091(266) [0415] and blood of the Lord for their own **sacrilegious** profit.
A P : 2 4 :091(266) [0415] Some day they will pay the penalty for this **sacrilege**.
A P : 2 8 :026(285) [0451] What evil there is in the **sacrilegious** desecration of the

Sacrosanct (1)
A P : 2 3 :024(243) [0371] synods while they want others to accept it as **sacrosanct**.

Sad (1), Sadden (1), Saddened (1), Sadly (1)
S C : 0 9 :003(355) [0561] do this joyfully, and not **sadly**, for that would be of no
S D : 0 3 :030(544) [0925] also in order to afford **saddened** consciences dependable
S D : 0 7 :044(577) [0987] death for our sin, in this **sad**, last hour of his life, this
S D : 1 0 :016(613) [1057] on the other hand, it will **sadden** and scandalize true

Safe (6), Safely (2), Safest (3), Safety (3)
A P : 1 2 :147(205) [0297] From this we may **safely** conclude that canonical
A P : 1 6 :001(222) [0329] ordinances in which a Christian may **safely** take part.
A P : 2 1 :044(236) [0357] God they should defend the life and **safety** of the innocent.
A P : 2 4 :092(266) [0417] Scriptures, and it is not **safe** to institute services in the
L C : 0 1 :046(370) [0593] yet inevitably he remained **safe** from Saul and became
L C : 0 1 :185(390) [0633] to get the quarrel settled for the **safety** of all concerned.
L C : 0 1 :231(396) [0647] steal and rob openly are **safe** and free, unmolested by
L C : 0 2 :031(414) [0685] from sin to righteousness, and now keeps us **safe** there.
L C : 0 3 :030(424) [0705] must know, that all our **safety** and protection consist in
L C : 0 3 :116(435) [0731] us, we would not be **safe** from him for a single hour.
L C : 0 5 :084(456) [0773] and body, so that you cannot be **safe** from him one hour.
S D : 0 1 :050(517) [0875] however, the best and **safest** procedure is to use and keep
S D : 0 4 :036(557) [0949] exaggerations, it is **safest** to follow the advice of St. Paul
S D : 0 8 :053(601) [1033] But the best, **safest**, and most certain way in this

Safeguards (2)
A P : 1 6 :012(224) [0333] This rule **safeguards** consciences, for it teaches that if
A P : 1 8 :009(226) [0337] This **safeguards** outward discipline, because all men

Safekeeping (1)
S D : 1 1 :046(624) [1079] and put it for **safekeeping** into the almighty hand of our

Sagacious (1)
L C : 0 1 :259(400) [0653] upright but also a wise, **sagacious**, brave, and fearless

Sages (1)
A P : 0 4 :235(140) [0185] All the books of the **sages** are full of these commands of

Sail (1)
L C : 0 4 :082(446) [0751] climb aboard again and **sail** on in it as he had done

Saint (8), Saints (171)
A G : 0 8 :001(033) [0047] of all believers and **saints**, yet because in this life many
A G : 1 7 :005(039) [0051] resurrection of the dead, **saints** and godly men will
A G : 2 0 :003(041) [0053] like rosaries, the cult of **saints**, monasticism, pilgrimages,
A G : 2 1 :000(046) [0057] XXI. The Cult of **Saints**
A G : 2 1 :001(046) [0057] also taught among us that **saints** should be kept in
A G : 2 1 :002(047) [0057] that we are to invoke **saints** or seek help from them.
A G : 2 8 :037(087) [0089] and new venerations of **saints** have been instituted in
A L : 0 7 :001(032) [0047] church is the assembly of **saints** in which the Gospel is
A L : 0 8 :001(033) [0047] the church is the assembly of **saints** and true believers.
A L : 2 0 :003(041) [0053] services in honor of **saints**, rosaries, monasticism, and the
A L : 2 1 :000(046) [0057] XXI. The Cult of **Saints**
A L : 2 1 :001(046) [0057] that the remembrance of **saints** may be commended to us
A L : 2 1 :002(047) [0057] teach us to pray to the **saints** or seek their help, for the
A P : 0 4 :057(114) [0137] of sins by faith, just as the **saints** in the New Testament.
A P : 0 4 :189(133) [0175] pits the witness of the **saints** against the rule of the devil;
A P : 0 4 :198(134) [0175] Yet God exercises his **saints** in different ways and often
A P : 0 4 :198(134) [0175] as is evident in Job, in Christ, and in other **saints**.
A P : 0 4 :203(135) [0177] sees the works of the **saints**, he supposes, in human
A P : 0 4 :203(135) [0177] through these works the **saints** merited grace and the
A P : 0 4 :208(135) [0177] The examples of the **saints** call forth imitation in those
A P : 0 4 :252(143) [0191] the good works of the **saints** are righteous and please God
A P : 0 4 :290(151) [0203] and feeble keeping of the law is rare, even among **saints**.
A P : 0 4 :322(157) [0209] of the works that **saints** perform after justification,
A P : 0 4 :326(157) [0211] even to all the **saints** and servants of God, if God does
A P : 0 4 :328(158) [0211] in the Lord's Prayer the **saints** pray for the forgiveness of
A P : 0 4 :328(158) [0211] for the forgiveness of sins; therefore **saints** have sins, too.
A P : 0 4 :355(161) [0217] There will be distinctions in the glory of the **saints**.
A P : 0 4 :363(162) [0219] This promise the **saints** must know.
A P : 0 7 :001(168) [0227] in which we said the church is the assembly of **saints**.
A P : 0 7 :008(169) [0229] "the communion of **saints**," seems to have been added to
A P : 0 7 :008(169) [0229] namely, the assembly of **saints** who share the association
A P : 0 7 :016(171) [0231] church (that is, with the **saints** among the Old Testament
A P : 0 7 :016(171) [0231] is, precisely speaking, the congregation of the **saints**.
A P : 0 7 :028(173) [0237] sense is the assembly of **saints** who truly believe the
A P : 1 2 :054(189) [0265] For all the **saints** were justified by faith in this promise,
A P : 1 2 :055(189) [0265] These two parts also appear in the lives of the **saints**.
A P : 1 2 :073(192) [0273] know that this is what the **saints** in the church have
A P : 1 2 :151(206) [0299] Furthermore, the **saints** are subject to death and to all the
A P : 1 2 :151(206) [0299] are a discipline by which God exercises the **saints**.
A P : 1 2 :152(206) [0299] present sin because in the **saints** they kill and wipe out
A P : 1 2 :156(207) [0301] have said before that the **saints** suffer penalties which are
A P : 1 2 :159(207) [0301] were killed, and John the Baptist, and other **saints**.
A P : 1 5 :024(218) [0321] are the examples of the **saints**; when men strive to imitate
A P : 1 5 :042(221) [0327] traditions, the worship of the **saints**, and similar trifles.
A P : 1 8 :008(226) [0337] Even for the **saints** it is hard to keep this faith; for the
A P : 2 1 :000(229) [0343] [Article XXI. The Invocation of the **Saints**]
A P : 2 1 :001(229) [0343] because we do not require the invocation of the **saints**.
A P : 2 1 :001(229) [0343] to prove is that the **saints** should be honored and that the
A P : 2 1 :001(229) [0343] honored and that the living **saints** should pray for others.
A P : 2 1 :001(229) [0343] the invocation of the departed **saints** were also necessary.
A P : 2 1 :002(229) [0343] about invoking, but only about honoring, the **saints**.
A P : 2 1 :004(229) [0343] Our Confession approves giving honor to the **saints**.
A P : 2 1 :004(229) [0343] we should also praise the **saints** themselves for using these
A P : 2 1 :009(230) [0345] We also grant that the **saints** in heaven pray for the
A P : 2 1 :010(230) [0345] Even if the **saints** do pray fervently for the church, it does
A P : 2 1 :010(230) [0345] does not teach us to invoke the **saints** or to ask their help.
A P : 2 1 :010(230) [0345] for the invocation of the **saints**; from this it follows that
A P : 2 1 :010(230) [0345] from Scripture, that the **saints** hear the individual's
A P : 2 1 :011(230) [0345] attribute divinity to the **saints**, the power to perceive the
A P : 2 1 :011(230) [0345] this up to honor the **saints** but to defend their religious
A P : 2 1 :012(230) [0345] we cannot affirm that the **saints** are aware of it or, even if
A P : 2 1 :013(230) [0345] prayers mention the **saints**, but they do not invoke them.
A P : 2 1 :014(230) [0345] in the veneration of the **saints**; they even apply the merits
A P : 2 1 :014(230) [0345] apply the merits of the **saints** to others and make the
A P : 2 1 :014(230) [0345] to others and make the **saints** propitiators as well as
A P : 2 1 :014(230) [0345] for it transfers to the **saints** honor belonging to Christ
A P : 2 1 :014(231) [0347] they obviously make the **saints** mediators of redemption.
A P : 2 1 :015(231) [0347] Christ and transfers to the **saints** the trust we should have
A P : 2 1 :015(231) [0347] is more severe and the **saints** more approachable; so they
A P : 2 1 :015(231) [0347] more in the mercy of the **saints** than in the mercy of
A P : 2 1 :015(231) [0347] of Christ and they flee from Christ and turn to the **saints**.
A P : 2 1 :016(231) [0347] they actually make the **saints** not only intercessors but
A P : 2 1 :017(231) [0347] But for the **saints** there is no such promise, and hence
A P : 2 1 :017(231) [0347] be sure that we shall be heard if we invoke the **saints**.
A P : 2 1 :018(231) [0347] produce from Scripture for the invocation of the **saints**?
A P : 2 1 :021(232) [0349] first of all, to invoke the **saints**, though they have neither
A P : 2 1 :021(232) [0349] more in the mercy of the **saints** than in the mercy of
A P : 2 1 :021(232) [0349] commanded us to come to him and not to the **saints**.
A P : 2 1 :022(232) [0349] They tell us, secondly, to trust in the merits of the **saints**.
A P : 2 1 :023(232) [0349] indulgences they claim to apply the merits of the **saints**.
A P : 2 1 :023(232) [0349] refuge in the help of the **saints**, so that we may be saved
A P : 2 1 :023(232) [0349] What is this if not to make the **saints** propitiators?
A P : 2 1 :024(232) [0349] take refuge in the help of the **saints**," as this man says?
A P : 2 1 :025(232) [0349] virgin Mary and of all the **saints** be to thee for the
A P : 2 1 :025(232) [0349] by Christ's merits but also by the merits of other **saints**.
A P : 2 1 :029(233) [0351] in the transfer of the **saints'** merits to us, as though God
A P : 2 1 :029(233) [0351] About the other **saints** it has been said (I Cor. 3:8), "Each
A P : 2 1 :031(233) [0351] in the invocation of the **saints**, though they have neither a
A P : 2 1 :031(233) [0351] apply the merits of the **saints** in the same way as the
A P : 2 1 :031(233) [0351] and thus transfer to the **saints** the honor that belongs to
A P : 2 1 :031(233) [0351] about venerating the **saints** or their practice of praying to
A P : 2 1 :031(233) [0351] by the merits of the blessed Virgin or of the other **saints**.
A P : 2 1 :032(233) [0351] hold to the error that each **saint** has a special sphere of
A P : 2 1 :033(233) [0351] that the invocation of the **saints** could be taught with
A P : 2 1 :034(233) [0353] It seems that when the **saints** were first mentioned, as in
A P : 2 1 :035(234) [0353] the fairy tales about the **saints** which are being taught in
A P : 2 1 :036(234) [0353] The great things that the **saints** have done serve as
A P : 2 1 :036(234) [0353] no one has sought out in the true stories about the **saints**.
A P : 2 1 :036(234) [0353] The **saints** administered public affairs, underwent
A P : 2 1 :038(234) [0355] require the invocation of **saints** and condemn abuses in
A P : 2 1 :038(235) [0355] abuses in the worship of **saints** in order to emphasize the
A P : 2 1 :041(235) [0355] mercenary worship of the **saints**, the confusion in the
A P : 2 3 :027(243) [0371] The **saints** prayed even when they were not carrying on
A P : 2 3 :065(248) [0381] Besides, the **saints** will know the value of moderation in
A P : 2 4 :025(253) [0391] the afflictions of the **saints**, yes, all the good works of the
A P : 2 4 :025(253) [0391] of the saints, yes, all the good works of the **saints**.
A P : 2 4 :043(257) [0399] discuss the worship of **saints**, human satisfactions, and
A P : 2 4 :055(259) [0403] as in the New, the **saints** had to be justified by faith in the
A P : 2 4 :055(259) [0403] of the world, all the **saints** have had to believe that Christ
A P : 2 4 :082(264) [0411] only supplies what the **saints** need but also causes many
A P : 2 7 :009(270) [0423] the wicked services to the **saints**, and the conspiracies
A P : 2 7 :021(272) [0427] Hence the **saints** can use them without sinning, as did
A P : 2 7 :025(273) [0427] accuse all the **saints**, "You shall love the Lord your God
A P : 2 7 :053(278) [0437] there is the worship of **saints** which is guilty of a double
A P : 2 7 :053(278) [0437] Christ's place to the **saints**, and it worships them
S 2 : 0 2 :024(296) [0469] merits of all the **saints** and the entire church.
S 2 : 0 2 :025(297) [0469] The Invocation of **Saints**
S 2 : 0 2 :025(297) [0469] The invocation of **saints** is also one of the abuses of the
S 2 : 0 2 :025(297) [0469] Even if the invocation of **saints** were a precious practice
S 2 : 0 2 :026(297) [0469] also does), and although **saints** on earth, and perhaps also
S 2 : 0 2 :026(297) [0469] should invoke angels and **saints**, pray to them, keep fasts
S 2 : 0 2 :027(297) [0469] As a Christian and a **saint** on earth, you can pray for me,
S 2 : 0 2 :028(297) [0469] from angels and dead **saints**, the honor that remains will
S 2 : 0 2 :028(297) [0469] no longer expected, the **saints** will cease to be molested in
S 3 : 0 2 :003(303) [0479] Hypocrites and false **saints** are produced in this way.
S 3 : 0 3 :002(304) [0479] with one blow destroys both open sinners and false **saints**.
S 3 : 0 3 :003(304) [0481] are manifest sinners or **saints**, you must all become other
S 3 : 0 3 :029(308) [0487] and Pharisees in Christ's time were just such **saints**.
S 3 : 0 3 :032(308) [0487] penitents, and those of you in the latter are false **saints**.
S 3 : 0 3 :041(309) [0491] the Gospel, and yet it is called a heresy by godless **saints**.
T R : 0 0 :047(328) [0517] there is the invocation of **saints** — how many abuses and
T R : 0 0 :053(329) [0519] cruelty in the murder of **saints**, whose blood God will
T R : 0 0 :054(329) [0519] and countless other crimes and for the murder of **saints**.
S C : 0 2 :005(345) [0545] *the communion of* ***saints****, the forgiveness of sins, the*
L C : P R :009(359) [0569] and presumptuous **saints**, for God's sake, to get it into
L C : P R :016(361) [0571] bored, presumptuous **saints** who will not or cannot read
L C : P R :016(361) [0573] All the **saints** know of nothing better or different to
L C : P R :016(361) [0573] end, and all prophets and **saints** have been busy learning
L C : P R :019(361) [0573] have become wiser than God himself and all his **saints**.
L C : S P :013(363) [0577] the communion of **saints**, the forgiveness of sins, the
L C : 0 1 :011(366) [0583] person selected his own **saint** and worshiped and invoked
L C : 0 1 :015(366) [0583] formerly sought from the **saints**, or what you hoped to
L C : 0 1 :021(367) [0585] help and consolation from creatures, **saints**, or devils.
L C : 0 1 :065(373) [0599] and yet Christ, St. Paul, and other **saints** took oaths.
L C : 0 1 :074(375) [0601] to St. Nicholas and other **saints**, but the other practices
L C : 0 1 :091(377) [0607] had the bones of all the **saints** or all the holy and
L C : 0 1 :091(377) [0607] By it all the **saints** themselves have been sanctified.
L C : 0 1 :092(377) [0607] but on account of the Word which makes us all **saints**.
L C : 0 1 :145(385) [0623] such as all who pass for the greatest **saints** do not have.
L C : 0 1 :290(404) [0663] blind world and the false **saints** would recognize them.
L C : 0 1 :312(407) [0671] see, now, how our great **saints** can boast of their spiritual
L C : 0 1 :315(408) [0671] part of those desperate **saints** to dare to find a higher and
L C : 0 1 :315(408) [0671] man, whereas theirs is for the **saints** and the perfect.
L C : 0 1 :333(410) [0677] Let all wise men and **saints** step forward and produce, if
L C : 0 2 :034(415) [0687] *the communion of* ***saints****, the forgiveness of sins, the*
L C : 0 2 :037(415) [0687] the communion of **saints** or Christian church, the
L C : 0 2 :047(416) [0689] church a *communio sanctorum*, "a communion of **saints**."
L C : 0 2 :049(417) [0691] this "communion of **saints**," although no German would
L C : 0 2 :049(417) [0691] to say "a community of **saints**," that is, a community
L C : 0 2 :049(417) [0691] composed only of **saints**, or, still more clearly, "a holy
L C : 0 2 :051(417) [0691] or community of pure **saints** under one head, Christ.
L C : 0 3 :016(422) [0701] to God as those of St. Paul and the holiest of **saints**.
L C : 0 3 :016(422) [0703] on which all the **saints** base their prayer, I, too, base
L C : 0 3 :017(422) [0703] whether we be sinners or **saints**, worthy or unworthy.
L C : 0 4 :010(437) [0735] of much greater value than the work of any man or **saint**.
L C : 0 4 :051(443) [0745] Holy Christian church, the communion of **saints**," etc.
L C : 0 5 :016(448) [0757] As no **saint** on earth, yes, no angel in heaven can
S D : 0 2 :015(523) [0885] all the petitions of the **saints** for divine instruction,
S D : 0 6 :016(566) [0967] Such people are **saints** after the order of Cain.
S D : 0 7 :024(573) [0981] As little as a **saint** on earth, or even an angel in heaven,
S D : 0 7 :033(575) [0983] Judas receive orally as well as St. Peter and all the **saints**.
S D : 0 8 :027(596) [1025] not just like some other **saint** but, in the words of the
S D : 0 8 :040(598) [1029] in his passion and death than any other ordinary **saint**.
S D : 0 8 :052(601) [1033] finite qualities, as in the **saints**, and on the basis of their
S D : 0 8 :065(604) [1039] publicly before all the **saints** in heaven and on earth, and
S D : 0 8 :068(604) [1039] (especially believers and **saints**), he dwells, and since he
S D : 0 8 :072(605) [1041] the Spirit's gifts not by measure, like other **saints**.
S D : 0 8 :073(605) [1041] in the way in which other **saints** know and can do things
S D : 0 8 :077(606) [1043] Peter, Paul, and all the **saints** in heaven would also be

Sainted (2)
P R : P R :008(005) [0009] At a later date our **sainted** predecessors and some of us
P R : P R :018(009) [0015] in the archives of those **sainted** forebears of ours who

Sake (257)
A G : 0 4 :001(030) [0045] God by grace, for Christ's **sake**, through faith, when we
A G : 0 4 :002(030) [0045] for us and that for his **sake** our sin is forgiven and
A G : 0 6 :001(031) [0045] should do them for God's **sake** and not place our trust in
A G : 1 6 :001(037) [0051] ordained by God for the **sake** of good order, and that

Continued ▶

AG : 20 :009(042) [0053] are forgiven for Christ's **sake**, who alone is the mediator
AG : 20 :015(043) [0055] knows that for Christ's **sake** it has a gracious God, as
AG : 23 :016(054) [0063] severity and rigor for the **sake** of human weakness and to
AG : 24 :013(057) [0065] under compulsion for the **sake** of revenues and stipends,
AG : 25 :013(063) [0071] is to be retained for the **sake** of absolution (which is its
AG : 26 :005(064) [0071] faith in Christ that we obtain grace for Christ's **sake**.
AG : 27 :037(077) [0081] us into his favor for the **sake** of Christ, his only Son.
AG : 27 :049(079) [0083] and trust that for Christ's **sake** we have a gracious,
AG : 28 :004(081) [0085] been compelled, for the **sake** of comforting consciences,
AG : 28 :029(085) [0087] to their subjects for the **sake** of peace and to prevent
AG : 28 :055(090) [0091] such ordinances for the **sake** of love and peace, to be
AL : 04 :001(030) [0045] freely justified for Christ's **sake** through faith when they
AL : 05 :003(031) [0045] believe that they are received into favor for Christ's **sake**.
AL : 12 :005(035) [0049] are forgiven for Christ's **sake**, comforts the conscience,
AL : 20 :009(042) [0053] into favor for Christ's **sake**, who alone has been ordained
AL : 20 :015(043) [0055] are sure that for Christ's **sake** they have a gracious God.
AL : 24 :013(057) [0065] any private Masses were held except for the **sake** of gain.
AL : 24 :020(058) [0067] to have been so abused for the **sake** of gain as the Mass.
AL : 26 :004(064) [0071] are forgiven for Christ's **sake** may be exalted far above
AL : 26 :005(064) [0071] believes that for Christ's **sake** we are received into grace.
AL : 27 :037(077) [0081] that they are received by God into favor for Christ's **sake**.
AL : 27 :049(079) [0083] to trust that for Christ's **sake** we have a gracious God, to
AL : 28 :004(081) [0085] been compelled, for the **sake** of instructing consciences, to
AL : 28 :029(085) [0087] to their subjects for the **sake** of maintaining public peace.
AL : 28 :055(090) [0091] such ordinances for the **sake** of love and tranquility and
AP : 04 :001(107) [0121] own merits, but freely for Christ's **sake**, by faith in him.
AP : 04 :005(108) [0121] and eternal life for his **sake**, or when, in the New
AP : 04 :009(108) [0123] to love God and that he wants to do good for God's **sake**.
AP : 04 :009(108) [0123] elicits an act of love to God or does good for God's **sake**.
AP : 04 :018(109) [0125] and believe that for his **sake** they freely receive the
AP : 04 :044(113) [0133] reconciliation for Christ's **sake**, which we do not accept
AP : 04 :051(114) [0135] namely, that for Christ's **sake** and not because of our own
AP : 04 :057(114) [0137] of the Christ, that for his **sake** God intended to forgive
AP : 04 :062(115) [0139] For Christ's **sake** it offers forgiveness of sins and
AP : 04 :062(115) [0139] promise that for his **sake** we have the forgiveness of sins.
AP : 04 :069(116) [0141] and believe that for his **sake** we are accounted righteous?
AP : 04 :080(118) [0143] hearts with trust in the mercy promised for Christ's **sake**.
AP : 04 :081(118) [0143] by trust in the mercy promised for Christ's **sake**.
AP : 04 :081(118) [0145] therefore, for Christ's **sake** we receive the forgiveness of
AP : 04 :083(118) [0145] his name, that is, for his **sake**: therefore, not for the sake
AP : 04 :083(118) [0145] therefore, not for the **sake** of our merits, our contrition,
AP : 04 :084(119) [0145] forgiveness of sins is a thing promised for Christ's **sake**.
AP : 04 :085(119) [0147] of sins for Christ's **sake** only by faith; here they have a
AP : 04 :086(119) [0147] promise that for Christ's **sake** he wishes to be propitious
AP : 04 :087(119) [0147] to us for Christ's **sake** we are justified freely by faith.
AP : 04 :097(121) [0149] righteous for Christ's **sake** when we believe that God is
AP : 04 :101(121) [0151] accomplish what he has promised for Christ's **sake**.
AP : 04 :102(121) [0151] of sins, and of our gracious acceptance for Christ's **sake**.
AP : 04 :114(123) [0155] by this faith for Christ's **sake** before we love and keep the
AP : 04 :117(123) [0155] of sins for Christ's **sake**, and by faith alone are justified,
AP : 04 :120(124) [0155] forgiven freely for Christ's **sake**) must be retained in the
AP : 04 :132(125) [0159] was given so that for his **sake** we might receive the gift of
AP : 04 :139(126) [0161] We know that for Christ's **sake** we have a gracious God
AP : 04 :157(128) [0165] come freely for Christ's **sake**, but for the sake of our love,
AP : 04 :157(128) [0165] Christ's sake, but for the **sake** of our love, nobody will
AP : 04 :158(129) [0165] Justification is reconciliation for Christ's **sake**.
AP : 04 :159(129) [0167] by faith for Christ's **sake**, not for the sake of love or the
AP : 04 :159(129) [0167] Christ's sake, not for the **sake** of love or the keeping of
AP : 04 :160(129) [0167] not please God for its own **sake**, and it is not acceptable
AP : 04 :160(129) [0167] for its own sake, and it is not acceptable for its own **sake**.
AP : 04 :163(129) [0169] always be sure that for his **sake** we have a gracious God in
AP : 04 :163(129) [0169] by faith for Christ's **sake**, according to the statement
AP : 04 :163(129) [0169] we are accounted righteous by faith for the **sake** of Christ.
AP : 04 :166(130) [0169] not please God for its own **sake**, but for the sake of faith
AP : 04 :166(130) [0169] God for its own sake, but for the **sake** of faith in Christ.
AP : 04 :172(130) [0171] our faith that for Christ's **sake** we please God and that
AP : 04 :174(131) [0171] is sure that for Christ's **sake** we have a gracious God.
AP : 04 :179(131) [0171] propitiation, for whose **sake** they are now accounted
AP : 04 :179(131) [0171] you, because for Christ's **sake** we have a firm and sure
AP : 04 :182(132) [0173] reconciliation for Christ's **sake**, and reconciliation or
AP : 04 :186(132) [0173] free promise of the forgiveness of sins for Christ's **sake**.
AP : 04 :195(134) [0175] who believe that their sins are forgiven for Christ's **sake**.
AP : 04 :198(134) [0175] for righteousness' **sake**, for theirs is the kingdom of
AP : 04 :203(135) [0175] his heart that for Christ's **sake** he is freely forgiven and
AP : 04 :212(136) [0179] by faith we are accounted righteous for Christ's **sake**.
AP : 04 :214(136) [0179] accounted righteous before God for Christ's **sake** by faith.
AP : 04 :217(137) [0179] to us for Christ's **sake**, according to the saying
AP : 04 :222(138) [0181] and believe that for his **sake** God is gracious to us.
AP : 04 :230(139) [0183] we believe that for Christ's **sake** God is gracious to us.
AP : 04 :235(140) [0185] put up with many things for the **sake** of mutual peace.
AP : 04 :238(141) [0187] if we believe that for the **sake** of Christ, the propitiator,
AP : 04 :239(141) [0187] because we know that for Christ's **sake** we are forgiven.
AP : 04 :257(144) [0193] promise, that for Christ's **sake** sins are forgiven and that
AP : 04 :260(145) [0193] if we believe that our sins are forgiven for Christ's **sake**.
AP : 04 :270(147) [0197] to us for Christ's **sake** even though we cannot satisfy the
AP : 04 :270(147) [0197] is pleasing to God for the **sake** of Christ, the mediator,
AP : 04 :273(148) [0199] I John 2:12, "Your sins are forgiven for his **sake**."
AP : 04 :281(149) [0201] of the law, that for his **sake** good works please God.
AP : 04 :288(151) [0203] works but that for the **sake** of social tranquillity there
AP : 04 :292(152) [0203] he wishes to forgive and to be reconciled for Christ's **sake**.
AP : 04 :292(152) [0203] and believes that he has a gracious God for Christ's **sake**.
AP : 04 :293(152) [0203] faith that for Christ's **sake** we have a gracious God.
AP : 04 :295(152) [0203] by faith, that for Christ's **sake** the Father is reconciled
AP : 04 :297(153) [0205] and eternal life are assured to us for Christ's **sake**.
AP : 04 :306(154) [0207] And II Cor. 5:21, "For our **sake** he made him to be sin
AP : 04 :308(155) [0207] the law, but for Christ's **sake** this is forgiven us, as Paul
AP : 04 :316(156) [0209] or the fact that for Christ's **sake** we please God by faith.
AP : 04 :320(156) [0209] and eternal life are given us freely for Christ's **sake**.
AP : 04 :331(158) [0211] act; delay not, for thy own **sake**, O my God, because thy
AP : 04 :350(161) [0217] cares for us, forgives us, and hears us for Christ's **sake**.
AP : 04 :356(161) [0217] on us for Christ's **sake** at the same time makes us sons of
AP : 04 :358(162) [0219] access to God for Christ's **sake**, not for our works' sake.
AP : 04 :358(162) [0219] access to God for Christ's sake, not for our works' **sake**.
AP : 04 :360(162) [0219] please God for their own **sake**, not for the sake of Christ,
AP : 04 :360(162) [0219] their own sake, not for the **sake** of Christ, the mediator.
AP : 04 :362(162) [0219] by faith for Christ's **sake** and that good works are
AP : 04 :368(163) [0221] the Gospel offers justification freely for Christ's **sake**.
AP : 04 :377(165) [0223] and the teaching of the promise given for Christ's **sake**.
AP : 04 :379(165) [0223] to us for Christ's **sake**, there is not a syllable in the
AP : 04 :393(167) [0225] own works and devotions, not by faith for Christ's **sake**.
AP : 07 :033(174) [0239] universal rites are observed for the **sake** of tranquility.
AP : 07 :034(175) [0239] to observe them for the **sake** of tranquility or bodily
AP : 07 :043(177) [0243] be celebrated, but for the **sake** of harmony they wanted
AP : 11 :002(180) [0249] to us freely for Christ's **sake** and that we should be sure
AP : 12 :009(183) [0255] it fears God for his own **sake** or is running away from
AP : 12 :029(186) [0259] righteousness for Christ's **sake**, to grant the Holy Spirit
AP : 12 :036(186) [0261] grasps the forgiveness of sins granted for Christ's **sake**.
AP : 12 :036(186) [0261] grasps the forgiveness of sins granted for Christ's **sake**.
AP : 12 :044(187) [0263] Christ means to believe that for his **sake** sins are forgiven.
AP : 12 :045(187) [0263] to believe that for Christ's **sake** the forgiveness of sins has
AP : 12 :064(191) [0269] mediator, and believes the promises given for his **sake**.
AP : 12 :067(191) [0271] of sins by faith for Christ's **sake** and not for the sake of
AP : 12 :067(191) [0271] faith for Christ's sake and not for the **sake** of our works.
AP : 12 :076(193) [0273] and promises the forgiveness of sins freely for his **sake**.
AP : 12 :079(193) [0275] of sins granted for Christ's **sake**, and he teaches us to
AP : 12 :079(194) [0275] the forgiveness of sins by faith, freely for Christ's **sake**.
AP : 12 :080(194) [0275] of sins granted for Christ's **sake**, and to be sure that freely
AP : 12 :080(194) [0275] that freely for Christ's **sake** they have a gracious Father.
AP : 12 :084(194) [0277] of sins for Christ's **sake**, by faith we ought to set against
AP : 12 :088(195) [0277] forgiven freely for Christ's **sake**, not doubting that they
AP : 12 :094(196) [0281] Oh, blessed are we for whose **sake** God swears an oath!
AP : 12 :121(200) [0287] were instituted for the **sake** of church discipline.
AP : 12 :156(207) [0301] God imposes only on them, for the **sake** of example.
AP : 12 :161(208) [0303] did not abolish it, for the **sake** of righteousness, that is, to
AP : 12 :167(208) [0303] established for the **sake** of setting an example; they did
AP : 13 :004(211) [0309] believe that God really forgives us for Christ's **sake**.
AP : 15 :005(215) [0317] that by faith, for Christ's **sake**, we freely receive the
AP : 15 :006(215) [0317] God not because of works but freely for Christ's **sake**.
AP : 15 :011(216) [0317] gracious God for Christ's **sake**, it is an ungodly error to
AP : 15 :012(216) [0317] righteous for his **sake** but must first merit this by other
AP : 15 :012(216) [0317] gracious to us for Christ's **sake**, we dare not add the
AP : 15 :013(216) [0319] instituted them for the **sake** of good order and tranquility
AP : 15 :018(217) [0319] are freely justified before God by faith for Christ's **sake**.
AP : 15 :018(217) [0319] not justified freely for his **sake** but by such rites, and
AP : 15 :020(218) [0321] by faith for Christ's **sake**, not for the sake of these human
AP : 15 :020(218) [0321] for Christ's sake, not for the **sake** of these human rites.
AP : 15 :040(220) [0325] learn or pray but for the **sake** of the rite, as if this work
AP : 16 :005(223) [0331] but also "for the **sake** of conscience" (Rom. 13:5).
AP : 20 :002(227) [0339] is freely given for Christ's **sake**, that not our works but
AP : 20 :007(227) [0339] of sins freely for Christ's **sake** and that our works do not
AP : 20 :008(227) [0341] in the forgiveness of sins freely given for Christ's **sake**.
AP : 20 :010(228) [0341] as it were, that sins are freely forgiven for Christ's **sake**.
AP : 20 :011(228) [0341] not on account of our works but freely for Christ's **sake**.
AP : 21 :020(232) [0349] we are heard for Christ's **sake** and that by his merits we
AP : 21 :044(235) [0357] Emperor Charles, for the **sake** of the glory of Christ,
AP : 23 :021(242) [0369] eunuchs for the **sake** of the kingdom of heaven"
AP : 23 :036(244) [0373] but freely for Christ's **sake** when we believe that for his
AP : 23 :036(244) [0373] when we believe that for his **sake** God is gracious to us.
AP : 23 :039(244) [0375] believing that for Christ's **sake** he obtains the forgiveness
AP : 23 :040(245) [0375] commends virginity for the **sake** of mediation and study.
AP : 23 :040(245) [0375] but he adds, "for the **sake** of the kingdom of heaven"
AP : 23 :049(246) [0377] should be praised "for the **sake** of discipline and the
AP : 23 :071(249) [0383] in change for its own **sake**, but they have greater respect
AP : 24 :003(250) [0385] we keep Latin for the **sake** of those who study and
AP : 24 :012(251) [0387] of Christ; for his **sake** we are forgiven, his merits and
AP : 24 :043(257) [0399] or point out that sins are freely forgiven for Christ's **sake**.
AP : 24 :046(258) [0401] and about the free forgiveness of sins for Christ's **sake**.
AP : 24 :048(258) [0401] that the forgiveness of sins comes freely for Christ's **sake**.
AP : 24 :055(259) [0403] promise of the forgiveness of sins given for Christ's **sake**.
AP : 24 :072(262) [0409] or a celebration for the **sake** of example, the way plays
AP : 24 :090(266) [0415] Supper was instituted for the **sake** of forgiving guilt.
AP : 27 :002(269) [0419] equanimity for Christ's **sake** inasmuch as he had neither
AP : 27 :009(270) [0421] of religion, but actually for the **sake** of appetite or hatred?
AP : 27 :011(270) [0423] given us freely for Christ's **sake**, as we have said at length
AP : 27 :012(270) [0423] everything for Christ's **sake** and try to live more closely
AP : 27 :013(271) [0423] of sins is received freely for Christ's **sake**, through faith.
AP : 27 :019(272) [0425] attain the forgiveness of sins by faith for Christ's **sake**?
AP : 27 :023(272) [0427] teaches that for Christ's **sake** righteousness and eternal
AP : 27 :032(274) [0431] by mercy for Christ's **sake** to those who accept
AP : 27 :043(277) [0435] become monks not for the **sake** of the Gospel but for the
AP : 27 :043(277) [0435] of the Gospel but for the **sake** of food and leisure; instead
AP : 27 :053(278) [0437] Mass by its application to the dead for the **sake** of profit.
AP : 27 :053(278) [0437] This wickedness, too, is used only for the **sake** of profit.
AP : 27 :054(278) [0437] of sins for Christ's **sake**, about the righteousness of faith,
AP : 27 :065(280) [0441] eternal life for us instead of mercy for Christ's **sake**.
AP : 27 :069(280) [0443] all this not only for the **sake** of our opponents, but even
AP : 27 :069(281) [0443] but even more for the **sake** of showing pious hearts why
AP : 27 :070(281) [0443] of sins freely for Christ's **sake**, that for Christ's sake by
AP : 27 :070(281) [0443] sake, that for Christ's **sake** by mercy they would attain
AP : 27 :070(281) [0443] eternal life and not for the **sake** of such services, and that
AP : 28 :007(282) [0445] receive forgiveness of sins freely for Christ's **sake** by faith.
AP : 28 :015(283) [0447] of preserving order in the church, for the **sake** of peace.
AP : 28 :023(284) [0451] of sins for Christ's **sake**, brings enough good to hide all
S1 : PR :010(290) [0457] for a council for our own **sake**, and we have no reason to
S2 : 02 :008(294) [0465] to communicate himself for the **sake** of his own devotion.
S3 : 08 :001(312) [0493] church, especially for the **sake** of timid consciences and
S3 : 08 :001(312) [0493] consciences and for the **sake** of untrained young people
S3 : 10 :001(314) [0497] might be permitted (for the **sake** of love and unity, but
S3 : 13 :001(315) [0499] righteous and holy for the **sake** of Christ, our mediator.
S3 : 13 :002(315) [0499] reckoned as sin or defect for the **sake** of the same Christ.
S3 : 15 :005(317) [0501] this concession for the **sake** of peace and general unity
TR : 00 :044(328) [0517] forgiven freely for Christ's **sake** and that by this faith we
TR : 00 :046(328) [0517] which are nothing but lies devised for the **sake** of gain.
SC : PR :006(338) [0533] beg of you for God's **sake**, my beloved brethren who are
SC : 05 :021(350) [0553] and declare that my sins are forgiven for God's **sake**."
SC : 09 :005(355) [0561] to avoid God's wrath but also for the **sake** of conscience.

Continued ▶

SC : 09 :005(355) [0561] "Be subject for the Lord's **sake** to every human
LC : PR :001(358) [0567] preachers for their bellies' **sake** and had nothing to do
LC : PR :009(359) [0569] saints, for God's **sake**, to get it into their heads that they
LC : 01 :077(375) [0603] This I say plainly for the **sake** of the young, so that it may
LC : 01 :083(376) [0603] keep holy days not for the **sake** of intelligent and well
LC : 01 :083(376) [0603] We keep them, first, for the **sake** of bodily need.
LC : 01 :086(376) [0605] of the Word for the **sake** of the young and the poor
LC : 01 :323(409) [0675] him alone and for his **sake** does all that he asks of us,
LC : 01 :327(409) [0675] to them not on their own account but for God's **sake**.
LC : 03 :068(429) [0717] But for our own **sake** we must pray that his will may be
LC : 03 :073(430) [0719] in this world; only for its **sake** do we need daily bread.
LC : 05 :052(452) [0765] what you ought to do, not for our **sake** but for your own.
LC : 06 :021(459) [0000] willingly and for the **sake** of absolution, let him just
EP : 03 :005(473) [0793] God," and that for Christ's **sake** such faith is reckoned for
EP : 03 :009(474) [0795] as certain that for Christ's **sake**, on the basis of the
EP : 04 :014(477) [0799] Nevertheless, for Christ's **sake** the Lord does not reckon
EP : 10 :003(493) [0829] introduced solely for the **sake** of good order and the
SD : 01 :014(511) [0863] and forgiven before God only for the Lord Christ's **sake**.
SD : 01 :031(513) [0869] nature unless the sin is forgiven for Christ's **sake**.
SD : 01 :045(516) [0873] receives man for Christ's **sake** into his grace but remains
SD : 02 :018(524) [0887] sin (to which for the **sake** of brevity we only refer), that
SD : 02 :054(531) [0903] of sins for Christ's **sake** and comforts itself with the
SD : 03 :011(541) [0919] in him, that solely for the **sake** of his obedience we have
SD : 03 :019(542) [0921] of sins solely for Christ's **sake** and the subsequent
SD : 03 :022(543) [0923] through faith and for the **sake** of Christ's obedience,
SD : 03 :023(543) [0923] who by sheer grace, for the **sake** of the only mediator,
SD : 03 :033(545) [0927] faith alone for the **sake** of the Mediator without the
SD : 03 :039(546) [0929] grace, entirely for the **sake** of Christ's merit, which
SD : 03 :058(550) [0937] and remitted by sheer grace for Christ's **sake** alone.
SD : 03 :067(551) [0937] we direct him for the **sake** of brevity to Dr. Luther's
SD : 04 :008(552) [0941] agree that this is so for the **sake** of the Lord Christ
SD : 04 :008(552) [0941] and that alone for Christ's **sake** — before that person's
SD : 04 :038(557) [0951] with them for Christ's **sake** and he promises to reward
SD : 05 :002(558) [0953] mercy of God for Christ's **sake**, which proclamation
SD : 05 :021(562) [0959] not to punish sins but to forgive them for Christ's **sake**.
SD : 05 :025(563) [0961] accepts them for his **sake** as God's children, and out of
SD : 06 :022(567) [0969] through faith for Christ's **sake** (I Pet. 2:5; Heb. 11:4;
SD : 07 :039(576) [0985] Word of God and for the **sake** of our salvation had flesh
SD : 07 :062(581) [0995] eternal salvation for the **sake** of Jesus Christ, and hold to
SD : 07 :091(586) [1005] shall therefore, for the **sake** of desirable brevity, merely
SD : 07 :128(591) [1015] exposition; for the **sake** of desirable brevity we have not
SD : 08 :035(597) [1027] For the **sake** of a better and simpler presentation it can be
SD : 08 :086(608) [1047] For the **sake** of brevity we here merely go on record as
SD : 10 :001(610) [1053] good intentions for the **sake** of good order and decorum
SD : 10 :019(614) [1059] might be permitted (for the **sake** of love and unity, but
SD : 11 :043(623) [1077] and merit, purely by grace and solely for Christ's **sake**.
SD : 11 :095(632) [1095] truth of God for the **sake** of temporal peace, tranquility,

Sale (2)
AP : 12 :137(203) [0293] monastic orders, the **sale** of Masses, and endless
S2 : 02 :021(296) [0467] (by legal and open **sale**) all Masses, good works, etc. for

Salt (3)
AP : 04 :282(149) [0201] water mixed with **salt** "sanctifies and cleanses the people,"
AP : 27 :006(269) [0421] Christ warns that tasteless **salt** is usually "thrown out and
SD : 02 :020(525) [0889] soul, man is like a pillar of **salt**, like Lot's wife, yes, like a

Salutary (22)
PR : PR :024(013) [0023] anxiously for this **salutary** work of Christian concord and
PR : PR :024(013) [0023] not now — to keep this **salutary** and most necessary effort
PR : PR :024(013) [0023] Christian pleasure in this **salutary**, most necessary, and
PR : PR :026(014) [0025] the supervision of printers, and other **salutary** means.
AG : 20 :015(043) [0055] terrified consciences find it most comforting and **salutary**.
AG : 21 :001(046) [0057] Imperial Majesty may in **salutary** and godly fashion
AP : 12 :002(182) [0253] Gospel, so exceedingly **salutary** and full of consolation.
AP : 12 :003(182) [0253] what is true, godly, **salutary**, and necessary for the
AP : 12 :007(183) [0255] Then the **salutary** power of the keys would be a ministry
AP : 12 :090(195) [0279] teaching is more godly and **salutary** for consciences.
AP : 15 :042(221) [0327] they even attack this most **salutary** part of the Gospel.
LC : 04 :033(440) [0741] worthy to receive the **salutary**, divine water profitably.
LC : 04 :035(441) [0741] works, however, are **salutary** and necessary for salvation,
EP : 11 :013(496) [0835] comfort which this **salutary** doctrine gives us, namely,
SD : 05 :009(559) [0955] it is not sufficient for a **salutary** conversion to God unless
SD : 05 :015(561) [0957] for genuine and **salutary** repentance; the Gospel must also
SD : 07 :061(580) [0995] It is intrinsically useful, **salutary**, and necessary to
SD : 07 :061(581) [0995] the Supper is not only **salutary** but actually pernicious
SD : 10 :009(612) [1055] beneficial, and **salutary** for good order, Christian
SD : 11 :025(620) [1071] exposition and the **salutary** use of the teaching of God's
SD : 11 :043(623) [1077] it is indeed a useful, **salutary**, and comforting doctrine,
SD : 11 :051(625) [1079] this article in a profitable, comforting, and **salutary** way.

Salvation (170)
PR : PR :002(003) [0007] Word that alone brings **salvation** to appear to our
PR : PR :008(005) [0011] Word that alone gives **salvation**, to commit themselves to
PR : PR :008(005) [0011] to it, and for the **salvation** of their souls and their eternal
PR : PR :024(013) [0023] of his that alone brings **salvation**, to the tranquillity and
AG : 15 :002(036) [0049] by the notion that such things are necessary for **salvation**.
AG : 28 :009(082) [0085] is the power of God for **salvation** to everyone who has
AG : 28 :043(088) [0089] God's grace or as if they were necessary for **salvation**.
AG : 28 :056(090) [0091] things are necessary for **salvation** or that it is a sin to
AG : 28 :061(091) [0093] new ceremonies which would be necessary for **salvation**.
AL : 09 :001(033) [0047] Baptism is necessary for **salvation**, that the grace of God
AL : 15 :002(036) [0049] as if observances of this kind were necessary for **salvation**.
AL : 28 :009(082) [0085] is the power of God for **salvation** to everyone who has
AL : 28 :043(088) [0089] appeasing God or as if they were necessary for **salvation**.
AL : 28 :056(090) [0091] they are necessary for **salvation** or by judging that those
AL : 28 :061(091) [0093] new ceremonies which would be necessary for **salvation**.
AP : 04 :067(116) [0139] is the power of God for **salvation** to every one who has
AP : 04 :098(121) [0149] And there is **salvation** in no one else, for there is no other
AP : 04 :098(121) [0151] here means that which is cited as the cause of **salvation**.
AP : 04 :119(123) [0155] which the faithful may receive the sure hope of **salvation**.
AP : 04 :154(128) [0165] or seek from him the forgiveness of sins and **salvation**!
AP : 04 :288(151) [0203] seek righteousness, grace, and **salvation** *ex opere operato*.
AP : 04 :344(160) [0217] mercy and if, prior to **salvation**, there is nothing to
AP : 04 :354(161) [0217] of your faith you obtain the **salvation** of your souls."
AP : 04 :386(166) [0225] we are "guarded for a **salvation** ready to be revealed."
AP : 09 :001(178) [0245] Baptism is necessary for **salvation**; children are to be
AP : 09 :001(178) [0245] not useless but is necessary and efficacious for **salvation**.
AP : 09 :002(178) [0245] that the promise of **salvation** also applies to little
AP : 09 :002(178) [0245] so that the promise of **salvation** might be applied to them
AP : 09 :002(178) [0245] Just as there **salvation** is offered to all, so Baptism is
AP : 09 :002(178) [0245] be baptized because **salvation** is offered with Baptism.
AP : 12 :094(196) [0281] says: "He invites us to **salvation** with an offer and even an
AP : 12 :111(198) [0285] is necessary for **salvation**; this is completely false, as well
AP : 13 :006(212) [0309] require as necessary for **salvation** since they do not have
AP : 13 :011(212) [0311] is the power of God for **salvation** to every one who has
AP : 15 :050(222) [0329] so-called "universal rites" as necessary for **salvation**.
AP : 21 :023(232) [0349] to trust in them for our **salvation**, they are being put on
AP : 23 :040(245) [0375] say that virginity merits **salvation** or the forgiveness of
S2 : 02 :027(297) [0469] sacrifices in your honor, or trust in you for my **salvation**.
S2 : 04 :004(299) [0473] that is needful for **salvation**, this is nothing and all in vain
S3 : 15 :001(316) [0501] or sins or merit **salvation** is unchristian and to be
TR : 00 :002(320) [0503] that it is necessary for **salvation** to believe these things,
TR : 00 :006(320) [0505] that it is necessary to **salvation** to believe all these things.
TR : 00 :036(326) [0515] and that he can attach **salvation** to these impious and
TR : 00 :036(326) [0515] that it is necessary for **salvation** to believe that such
TR : 00 :052(329) [0519] embraced for the glory of God and the **salvation** of souls.
SC : PR :026(341) [0539] It is now a ministry of grace and **salvation**.
SC : 04 :006(349) [0551] devil, and grants eternal **salvation** to all who believe, as
SC : 06 :006(352) [0557] of sins, life, and **salvation** are given to us in the
SC : 06 :006(352) [0557] is forgiveness of sins, there are also life and **salvation**.
LC : 01 :022(367) [0585] help, comfort, and **salvation** in its own works and
LC : 01 :041(370) [0591] blessing, happiness, and **salvation**, or eternal wrath,
LC : 01 :103(379) [0611] God and the benefit and **salvation** of our neighbor and
LC : 01 :157(387) [0627] of joy, happiness, and **salvation**, both here and in
LC : 02 :033(415) [0687] Upon it all our **salvation** and blessedness are based, and
LC : 02 :038(415) [0689] Spirit to offer and apply to us this treasure of **salvation**.
LC : 03 :051(427) [0711] righteousness, life, and **salvation** against sin, death, and
LC : 03 :052(427) [0711] become partakers of **salvation**, so that we may all remain
LC : 03 :060(428) [0715] God's glory and to our **salvation**, in which we appropriate
LC : 04 :027(440) [0739] where God's name is, there must also be life and **salvation**.
LC : 04 :029(440) [0739] in which there is sheer **salvation** and life, not through the
LC : 04 :034(440) [0741] do with the intention of meriting **salvation** through them.
LC : 04 :034(441) [0741] nothing toward **salvation**, and receives nothing.
LC : 04 :035(441) [0741] works are of no use for **salvation**, what becomes of
LC : 04 :035(441) [0741] Yes, it is true that our works are of no use for **salvation**.
LC : 04 :035(441) [0741] and necessary for **salvation**, and they do not exclude but
LC : 04 :036(441) [0741] God, you may receive in the water the promised **salvation**.
LC : 04 :046(442) [0743] perfect holiness and **salvation**, which no other kind of life
EP : RN :005(465) [0777] the laity and the **salvation** of their souls, we subscribe Dr.
EP : RN :005(465) [0777] and which a Christian must know for his **salvation**.
EP : 02 :004(470) [0787] is a "power of God" for **salvation**; likewise, that faith
EP : 03 :009(474) [0795] through faith or the **salvation** of their souls, but they
EP : 04 :002(475) [0797] works are necessary to **salvation**; that it is impossible to
EP : 04 :002(475) [0797] asserted that good works are detrimental to **salvation**.
EP : 04 :007(476) [0799] of the article of man's **salvation** as well as from the article
EP : 04 :007(476) [0799] also David declares that **salvation** pertains only to the
EP : 04 :015(477) [0799] working through faith, preserves faith and **salvation** in us.
EP : 04 :016(477) [0801] works are necessary to **salvation**; likewise, that no one
EP : 04 :017(477) [0801] statement that good works are detrimental to **salvation**.
EP : 07 :002(482) [0809] believers for life and **salvation**, the unbelievers for
EP : 07 :016(484) [0813] them not to life and **salvation** but to their judgment and
EP : 08 :018(489) [0823] the sole foundation of our comfort, life, and **salvation**.
EP : 08 :039(492) [0827] we shall lose Christ altogether along with our **salvation**.
EP : 11 :004(495) [0833] wickedness it must minister to the **salvation** of his elect.
EP : 11 :005(495) [0833] It is a cause of their **salvation**, for he alone brings it
EP : 11 :005(495) [0833] Our **salvation** is so firmly established upon it that the
EP : 11 :009(495) [0833] God has elected me to **salvation** I cannot be damned, do
EP : 12 :030(500) [0843] they dearly love their soul's eternal welfare and **salvation**.
SD : PR :008(505) [0853] who for their eternal **salvation** must as Christians know
SD : 02 :005(521) [0881] our conversion and **salvation**, he is by nature blind and
SD : 02 :009(522) [0883] the promise of eternal **salvation**, they cannot by their own
SD : 02 :014(523) [0885] for the grace of God and eternal **salvation** in their hearts.
SD : 02 :018(524) [0889] peace, and **salvation**, cannot cooperate, and cannot obey,
SD : 02 :018(524) [0889] offers the grace of God and **salvation** through the Gospel.
SD : 02 :020(525) [0889] which concern the **salvation** of his soul, man is like a
SD : 02 :050(531) [0901] to call men to eternal **salvation**, to draw them to himself,
SD : 03 :034(545) [0927] David also says that **salvation** belongs solely to that
SD : 03 :052(548) [0933] without works or that **salvation** cannot be obtained
SD : 03 :053(548) [0933] to Paul's statement that **salvation** belongs to that man to
SD : 03 :053(548) [0933] righteousness and our **salvation** in one and the same way;
SD : 03 :053(548) [0933] adoption and the inheritance of eternal life and **salvation**.
SD : 03 :053(548) [0933] in the article of **salvation** as he does in the article of
SD : 03 :067(551) [0937] God, on which the **salvation** of our souls depends, we
SD : 04 :001(551) [0939] works are necessary to **salvation**," and "It is impossible to
SD : 04 :001(551) [0939] is dead, although such love is not a cause of **salvation**.
SD : 04 :002(551) [0939] necessary — not for **salvation**, however, but for other
SD : 04 :002(551) [0939] for believers the firm and certain promise of **salvation**.
SD : 04 :003(551) [0939] principle "that good works are detrimental to **salvation**."
SD : 04 :015(553) [0943] righteousness, and **salvation** even though he still is and
SD : 04 :022(554) [0945] and mingled with the article of justification and **salvation**.
SD : 04 :022(554) [0945] for the believers' **salvation**, or that it is impossible to be
SD : 04 :022(554) [0945] of justification and **salvation** (that is, they are
SD : 04 :022(554) [0945] of justification and **salvation** and ascribe everything solely
SD : 04 :023(555) [0945] against the pure doctrine of **salvation** by faith alone.
SD : 04 :024(555) [0945] ascribes the bliss of **salvation** solely to the man to whom
SD : 04 :027(555) [0945] have them as something necessary for **salvation**;
SD : 04 :028(555) [0947] works as necessary to **salvation**, we nevertheless do not
SD : 04 :030(555) [0947] good works preserve **salvation** or are necessary to
SD : 04 :030(555) [0947] necessary to preserve faith, righteousness, and **salvation**.
SD : 04 :030(556) [0947] how righteousness and **salvation** are preserved in us so
SD : 04 :031(556) [0947] of righteousness and **salvation**, once it has been received,
SD : 04 :031(556) [0947] faith, the grace of God, righteousness, and **salvation**.
SD : 04 :034(556) [0949] righteousness and **salvation** only at the beginning, and
SD : 04 :034(556) [0949] the righteousness that has been received, and **salvation**.
SD : 04 :034(556) [0949] righteousness and **salvation** may be very certain to us,

Continued ▶

SD : 04 :034(557) [0949] through faith for a **salvation**," and again, "As the
SD : 04 :034(557) [0949] faith, you obtain the **salvation** of your souls" (I Pet. 1:5,
SD : 04 :035(557) [0949] righteousness and **salvation** are not only received but also
SD : 04 :035(557) [0949] good works preserve **salvation**, or that our works either
SD : 04 :037(557) [0949] to be detrimental to **salvation**, we give the following clear
SD : 04 :037(557) [0949] or his assurance of **salvation** on good works in order to
SD : 04 :038(557) [0951] to believers as far as their **salvation** is concerned.
SD : 04 :038(557) [0951] are an indication of **salvation** in believers (Phil. 1:28).
SD : 04 :039(558) [0951] diligence whatever is detrimental to one's **salvation**.
SD : 05 :009(559) [0955] a "contrition that leads to **salvation**" (II Cor. 7:10).
SD : 05 :022(562) [0959] "the power of God for **salvation** to everyone who has
SD : 07 :039(576) [0985] and for the sake of our **salvation** had flesh and blood, so
SD : 07 :061(580) [0995] and necessary to **salvation** for all Christians at all times.
SD : 07 :062(581) [0995] God and eternal **salvation** for the sake of Jesus Christ,
SD : 07 :089(585) [1003] them it does not effect **salvation**), so whether those who
SD : 10 :012(613) [1057] for righteousness and **salvation**, Paul said that he would
SD : 10 :016(613) [1057] his soul's welfare and **salvation**, every Christian is
SD : 11 :004(616) [1063] the eternal election of his children to eternal **salvation**.
SD : 11 :005(617) [1065] God's predestination to **salvation** does not extend over
SD : 11 :006(617) [1065] his divine name and the **salvation** of his elect, and thereby
SD : 11 :007(617) [1065] misfortune, but in me alone is thy **salvation**" (Hos. 13:9).
SD : 11 :008(617) [1065] and foreknows the **salvation** of the elect, but by God's
SD : 11 :008(617) [1065] helps, and furthers our **salvation** and whatever pertains to
SD : 11 :008(617) [1065] Our **salvation** is based on it in such a way that "the gates
SD : 11 :010(618) [1067] his elect to **salvation** 'before the foundations of the world
SD : 11 :010(618) [1067] have been foreknown to **salvation**, it will do me no harm
SD : 11 :011(618) [1067] are not foreknown to **salvation** from eternity everything
SD : 11 :012(618) [1067] and to assure us of our **salvation** (Eph. 1:9, 13, 14;
SD : 11 :014(619) [1069] call, justification, and **salvation**, as Paul treats and
SD : 11 :023(619) [1069] has not only prepared **salvation** in general, but he has also
SD : 11 :023(619) [1069] and elected to **salvation** each and every individual among
SD : 11 :023(619) [1069] to bring them to **salvation** and to help, further,
SD : 11 :024(620) [1069] election of God to adoption and to eternal **salvation**.
SD : 11 :024(620) [1069] election, and ordinance of God to eternal **salvation**.
SD : 11 :025(620) [1071] God's foreknowledge to **salvation**: Since only the elect
SD : 11 :028(620) [1071] our eternal election to **salvation** profitably, we must by
SD : 11 :039(623) [1077] to righteousness and **salvation** outside of Christ
SD : 11 :043(623) [1077] good, God elected us to **salvation** "according to his
SD : 11 :045(624) [1079] righteousness, and **salvation** and so faithfully minded
SD : 11 :046(624) [1079] wanted to insure my **salvation** so firmly and certainly —
SD : 11 :046(624) [1079] — that he ordained my **salvation** in his eternal purpose,
SD : 11 :079(629) [1089] has prepared beforehand for **salvation**" (Rom. 9:22, 23).
SD : 11 :084(630) [1091] not want to grant him **salvation** or because it was God's
SD : 11 :090(631) [1093] of knowing that their **salvation** does not rest in their own
SD : 11 :090(631) [1093] Their **salvation** rests in the gracious election of God,
SD : 12 :039(636) [1103] as dearly as they love their soul's welfare and **salvation**.

Samosata (1)
SD : 08 :016(594) [1021] of Paul, a native of **Samosata** who had become a bishop

Samosatenes (3)
AG : 01 :006(028) [0043] them; also that of the **Samosatenes**, old and new, who
AL : 01 :006(028) [0043] also condemn the **Samosatenes**, old and new, who contend
SD : 08 :015(594) [1019] of Nestorius and the **Samosatenes**, who on the witness of

Sanctification (23)
AP : 04 :086(119) [0147] our righteousness and **sanctification** and redemption"
AP : 04 :306(154) [0207] our righteousness and **sanctification** and redemption."
SC : 02 :005(345) [0545] The Third Article: **Sanctification**
LC : 01 :087(376) [0605] the day needs no **sanctification**, for it was created holy.
LC : 02 :006(411) [0679] redemption; the third, of the Holy Spirit, **sanctification**.
LC : 02 :035(415) [0687] have said, I cannot give a better title than "**Sanctification**."
LC : 02 :037(415) [0687] Holy Spirit effects our **sanctification** through the
LC : 02 :053(417) [0693] creates and increases **sanctification**, causing it daily to
EP : 01 :003(466) [0779] creation, redemption, **sanctification**, and the resurrection
SD : 01 :045(516) [0873] in the article of **sanctification** we have the testimony of
SD : 02 :015(523) [0885] for divine instruction, illumination, and **sanctification**.
SD : 02 :037(528) [0895] and increases **sanctification** so that we grow daily and
SD : 02 :039(528) [0895] deeds and grow in **sanctification**), nevertheless, as
SD : 03 :021(542) [0921] means the **sanctification** or renewal which follows the
SD : 03 :028(544) [0925] although renewal and **sanctification** are a blessing of
SD : 03 :028(544) [0925] because in this life **sanctification** is never wholly pure and
SD : 03 :035(545) [0927] beginning of renewal, **sanctification**, love, virtues, and
SD : 03 :039(546) [0929] That neither renewal, **sanctification**, virtues, nor other
SD : 03 :040(546) [0929] well as between justification and renewal or **sanctification**.
SD : 03 :041(546) [0929] precede faith, nor is **sanctification** prior to justification.
SD : 03 :041(546) [0929] this renewal and **sanctification** the fruits of good works
SD : 03 :041(546) [0929] justification and **sanctification** are separated from each
SD : 03 :048(548) [0933] sins and, as a second element, renewal or **sanctification**.

Sanctifier (2)
LC : 02 :036(415) [0687] Spirit must be called **Sanctifier**, the One who makes holy.
LC : 02 :043(416) [0689] Christ as the Lord, or the Holy Spirit as the **Sanctifier**.

Sanctify (14), Sanctifying (5), Sanctifies (13), Sanctified (21)
AG : 03 :004(030) [0045] the Holy Spirit he may **sanctify**, purify, strengthen, and
AL : 03 :004(030) [0045] over all creatures, and **sanctify** those who believe in him
AL : 24 :026(059) [0067] Hebrews, "We have been **sanctified** through the offering
AL : 24 :027(059) [0067] he has perfected for all time those who are **sanctified**."
AP : 03 :001(107) [0119] to rule, justify, and **sanctify** the believers, etc., according
AP : 04 :189(133) [0175] For in these works he **sanctifies** hearts and suppresses the
AP : 04 :279(149) [0199] wants to be justified, **sanctified**, and governed by God.
AP : 04 :282(149) [0201] water mixed with salt "**sanctifies** and cleanses the people,"
AP : 07 :007(169) [0229] up for it, that he might **sanctify** it, having cleansed it by
AP : 12 :161(208) [0303] and test the righteousness of those who are **sanctified**.
AP : 23 :028(243) [0371] pure because it has been **sanctified** by the Word of God;
AP : 24 :022(253) [0391] that will we have been **sanctified** through the offering of
AP : 24 :034(256) [0395] may be acceptable, **sanctified** by the Holy Spirit," that is,
AP : 24 :036(257) [0397] sprinkling, that is, the **sanctifying** of believers throughout
AP : 24 :036(257) [0397] Peter says (I Pet. 1:2); "**Sanctified** by the Spirit for
AP : 24 :038(257) [0399] proclamation, as we are **sanctified**, put to death, and
SC : 02 :006(345) [0545] me with his gifts, and **sanctified** and preserved me in true
SC : 02 :006(345) [0545] gathers, enlightens, and **sanctifies** the whole Christian
LC : 01 :078(375) [0603] *"You shall **sanctify** the holy day."*
LC : 01 :081(376) [0603] it meant that we should **sanctify** the holy day or day of
LC : 01 :087(376) [0605] asked what "You shall **sanctify** the holy day" means,
LC : 01 :088(377) [0605] How does this **sanctifying** take place?
LC : 01 :090(377) [0607] ringing bells, without **sanctifying** the holy day because
LC : 01 :091(377) [0607] for they are all dead things that can **sanctify** no one.
LC : 01 :091(377) [0607] But God's Word is the treasure that **sanctifies** all things.
LC : 01 :091(377) [0607] By it all the saints themselves have been **sanctified**.
LC : 01 :092(377) [0607] day, and the work are **sanctified** by it, not on account of
LC : 01 :094(378) [0607] of the resting but of the **sanctifying**, so that this day
LC : 01 :095(378) [0607] Word that no holy day is **sanctified** without it, we must
LC : 01 :209(393) [0639] of God's Word, by which it is adorned and **sanctified**.
LC : 02 :007(411) [0679] me; I believe in the Holy Spirit, who **sanctifies** me."
LC : 02 :036(415) [0687] Spirit, that is, he who has **sanctified** and still sanctifies us.
LC : 02 :036(415) [0687] Spirit, that is, he who has sanctified and still **sanctifies** us.
LC : 02 :037(415) [0687] How does this **sanctifying** take place?
LC : 02 :039(415) [0689] Therefore to **sanctify** is nothing else than to bring us to
LC : 02 :064(419) [0695] us for this very purpose, to redeem and **sanctify** us.
LC : 04 :014(438) [0735] God's Word and commandment and **sanctified** by them.
LC : 04 :049(442) [0745] God has **sanctified** many who have been thus baptized
EP : 01 :006(466) [0781] nature as his creation, **sanctifies** it as his creation,
EP : 01 :006(467) [0781] not redeemed it, has not **sanctified** it, will not quicken it
SD : 01 :039(515) [0871] Son he might cleanse it from sin, **sanctify** it, and save it.
SD : 01 :045(516) [0873] sin, purifies him, and **sanctifies** him and that Christ has
SD : 01 :045(516) [0873] of the holy Trinity, is **sanctified** and saved, and other
SD : 02 :038(528) [0895] us into the church, **sanctifies** us therein, and effects in us a
SD : 02 :040(528) [0895] me with his gifts, and **sanctified** and preserved me in true
SD : 02 :040(528) [0895] gathers, enlightens, and **sanctifies** the whole Christian
SD : 02 :042(529) [0897] Spirit, who enlightens, **sanctifies**, and brings us to Christ
SD : 02 :050(531) [0901] beget them anew, and **sanctify** them through this means
SD : 02 :051(531) [0901] "**Sanctify** them in the truth; thy Word is truth.
SD : 03 :023(543) [0923] Spirit, who renews and **sanctifies** them and creates within
SD : 03 :041(546) [0929] Spirit next renews and **sanctifies** him, and from this
SD : 11 :019(619) [1069] 5. That he also would **sanctify** in love all who are thus
SD : 11 :030(621) [1073] and give thanks, are **sanctified** in love, have hope,

Sanction (4), Sanctioned (2), Sanctioning (2)
AP : PR :004(098) [0099] insisted that we **sanction** certain manifest abuses and
AP : 11 :009(182) [0251] But we do not want to **sanction** the torture of the
S2 : 02 :008(294) [0465] and imagination without the **sanction** of God's Word.
LC : 01 :188(390) [0635] should neither use nor **sanction** any means or methods
LC : 01 :206(393) [0639] the married life, **sanctioning** and protecting it by his
LC : 01 :206(393) [0639] He **sanctioned** it above in the fourth commandment, "You
EP : 10 :006(493) [0831] liberty, and the **sanctioning** of public idolatry, as well as
SD : PR :008(505) [0853] have been unanimously **sanctioned** and accepted and are

Sanctity (1)
LC : 01 :214(394) [0641] under the guise of great **sanctity** avoid marriage and

Sanctorum (1)
LC : 02 :047(416) [0689] church a *communio **sanctorum***, "a communion of saints."

Sand (1), Sandals (2)
AP : 22 :008(237) [0359] very well, but they throw **sand** in the eyes of the
AP : 27 :027(274) [0429] receiving another hood or other **sandals** or other girdles."
AP : 27 :069(281) [0443] chants, vestments, **sandals**, cinctures — all these are

Sane (3)
AP : 04 :375(164) [0223] No **sane** man can judge otherwise.
AP : 23 :060(247) [0381] No **sane** man can argue with these cogent facts.
AP : 24 :013(251) [0387] No **sane** person can approve this pharisaic and pagan

Sarah (1)
SC : 09 :007(355) [0563] to your husbands, as **Sarah** obeyed Abraham, calling him

Sarcastic (1)
EP : 07 :041(486) [0817] God all presumptuous, **sarcastic**, and blasphemous

Satan (22)
S2 : 04 :016(301) [0477] Zechariah, "The Lord rebuke you, O **Satan**" (Zech. 3:2).
LC : 03 :087(432) [0723] Besides, **Satan** is at our backs, besieging us on every side
EP : 01 :017(468) [0783] something which **Satan** infused into and mingled with
EP : 01 :025(469) [0785] the distinction between God's work and **Satan**'s work.
EP : 01 :025(469) [0785] **Satan** cannot create a substance; he can only, with God's
SD : 01 :007(510) [0861] Through **Satan**'s scheme, "by one man sin (which is the
SD : 01 :019(511) [0865] and is in the kingdom and under the dominion of **Satan**.
SD : 01 :026(512) [0867] pure, and that afterward **Satan** infuses and blends
SD : 01 :027(512) [0867] nature in such a way that **Satan** created or made
SD : 01 :027(513) [0867] The fact is, that **Satan** misled Adam and Eve through the
SD : 01 :027(513) [0867] and wounding which **Satan** brought about, this loss has so
SD : 01 :041(515) [0871] devil is the author of sin, **Satan** is the creator of our
SD : 01 :041(515) [0871] also necessarily have to be **Satan**'s handiwork or creature
SD : 01 :042(515) [0873] origin the handiwork of **Satan**, who through sin has in
SD : 02 :029(527) [0893] is much too weak for **Satan**, who incites men to sin."
SD : 02 :030(527) [0893] the contrary, it declares that man is the captive of **Satan**.
SD : 03 :029(544) [0925] we may not be diverted (as **Satan** would very much like)
SD : 07 :029(574) [0981] and that there is no end to the rage and fury of **Satan**.
SD : 07 :031(574) [0983] of God I have learned to know a great deal about **Satan**.
SD : 07 :067(582) [0997] invention of which even **Satan** himself would be
SD : 07 :067(582) [0997] the majesty of Christ as "**Satan**'s dung, by which the devil
SD : 11 :083(630) [1091] prepare their hearts for **Satan** (Luke 11:24, 25), and

Satiety (2)
AP : 15 :047(221) [0327] lest we be overcome by **satiety** and become complacent
LC : 01 :099(378) [0609] — that is, indolence or **satiety** — a malignant, pernicious

Satires (1), Satirize (1)
AP : 23 :006(240) [0365] have thought up some subterfuges to **satirize** our position.
AP : 23 :052(246) [0377] In its **satires** Rome still reads and recognizes its own

Satisfaction (84)
AG : 15 :004(037) [0049] earn grace and make **satisfaction** for sin, are useless and
AG : 20 :021(044) [0055] purpose of earning grace and making **satisfaction** for sins.

Continued ▶

AG : 24 :021(058) [0067] has by his death made **satisfaction** only for original sin,
AG : 24 :027(059) [0067] once and by this offering made **satisfaction** for all sin.
AG : 24 :025(059) [0067] should have made **satisfaction** only for original sin and
AG : 26 :001(064) [0071] by men serve to earn grace and make **satisfaction** for sin.
AG : 27 :038(077) [0081] spiritual life makes **satisfaction** for sin and obtains God's
AG : 28 :035(086) [0089] in order to make **satisfaction** for sins and obtain grace,
AG : 28 :053(090) [0091] God's grace or making **satisfaction** for sins, nor in order
AL : 04 :002(030) [0045] of Christ, who by his death made **satisfaction** for our sins.
AL : 15 :003(036) [0049] merit grace, and make **satisfaction** for sins are opposed to
AL : 15 :004(037) [0049] merit grace and make **satisfaction** for sins, are useless and
AL : 20 :021(044) [0055] kind to merit grace and make **satisfaction** for sins.
AL : 24 :021(058) [0067] by his passion made **satisfaction** for original sin and had
AL : 24 :025(058) [0067] was an oblation and **satisfaction** not only for original
AL : 26 :007(065) [0071] of faith; only works of **satisfaction** were proposed, and
AL : 26 :021(067) [0073] merit grace or make **satisfaction** for sins by the
AL : 26 :033(069) [0075] forgiveness of sins or **satisfaction** for sins by means of
AL : 27 :038(077) [0081] observances make **satisfaction** for sins and merit grace
AL : 28 :035(086) [0089] the purpose of making **satisfaction** for sins or meriting
AL : 28 :053(090) [0091] of these we make **satisfaction** for sins, nor that
AP : 04 :040(112) [0131] given for us to make **satisfaction** for the sins of the world
AP : 04 :052(114) [0135] for our sins if our merits make **satisfaction** for them?
AP : 04 :178(131) [0171] placed the death and **satisfaction** of Christ, bestowed
AP : 04 :178(131) [0171] us that because of this **satisfaction** and not because of our
AP : 04 :286(150) [0203] shown all this to the **satisfaction** of pious consciences.
AP : 12 :013(184) [0257] There remains the third step, **satisfaction**.
AP : 12 :060(190) [0269] contrition, confession, and **satisfaction** *ex opere operato.*
AP : 12 :097(197) [0281] Confession and **Satisfaction**
AP : 12 :098(197) [0281] have written nothing about confession and **satisfaction**.
AP : 12 :113(199) [0285] Our word **"satisfaction"** is a relic from this rite of public
AP : 12 :115(199) [0285] obsolete, the word **"satisfaction"** still remains together
AP : 12 :116(199) [0285] ancient exhibitions of **satisfaction** in public penitence
AP : 12 :117(199) [0287] example, in defining **satisfaction** they say that it is done to
AP : 12 :137(203) [0293] which make **satisfaction** for punishment, if not for guilt.
AP : 12 :140(204) [0295] furthermore, is a **satisfaction** not only for guilt but also
AP : 12 :140(204) [0295] to say that Christ's **satisfaction** redeems our guilt but our
AP : 12 :142(204) [0295] he can make **satisfaction** for the sins he commits.
AP : 12 :142(204) [0295] to trust that thereby we make **satisfaction** to God's law.
AP : 12 :143(204) [0297] They attribute **satisfaction** to the mere performance of
AP : 12 :147(205) [0297] The **satisfaction** for eternal death is the death of Christ;
AP : 12 :147(205) [0297] that the works of **satisfaction** are not obligatory works
AP : 12 :150(206) [0299] be so great as to make **satisfaction** unnecessary; thus
AP : 12 :150(206) [0299] is a more genuine punishment than is **satisfaction**.
AP : 12 :154(207) [0301] do they add that we must make **satisfaction** in purgatory?
AP : 12 :165(208) [0303] be transferred to the **satisfaction** and performance of
AP : 12 :167(209) [0305] punishment, or a **satisfaction**, but the cleansing of
AP : 12 :168(209) [0305] Fathers take the word **"satisfaction"** from the public rite
AP : 12 :168(209) [0305] Augustine says, "True **satisfaction** means cutting off the
AP : 12 :173(209) [0305] If works of **satisfaction** are non-obligatory works, why
AP : 12 :175(210) [0307] The term **"satisfaction"** no longer refers to civil discipline
AP : 15 :001(215) [0315] grace, and to make **satisfaction** for sin are contrary to the
AP : 21 :019(231) [0347] be authorized to make **satisfaction** for others and to be
AP : 24 :019(252) [0389] this is a work of **satisfaction** for guilt and punishment
AP : 24 :023(253) [0391] of Christ is a real **satisfaction** or expiation for our sins, as
AP : 24 :023(253) [0391] God and make **satisfaction** for our sins, so that men
AP : 24 :055(259) [0403] be the offering and the **satisfaction** for sin, as Isa. 53:10
AP : 24 :058(260) [0405] to look for some other **satisfaction** that was valid for the
AP : 24 :059(260) [0405] the only sacrifice of **satisfaction** it has for the sins of
AP : 24 :089(266) [0415] that reconciles God and makes **satisfaction** for sins.
AP : 24 :090(266) [0415] of the doctrine of **satisfaction**, which we have refuted
AP : 24 :090(266) [0415] it does not make **satisfaction** for guilt; otherwise, the
AP : 24 :090(266) [0415] the Mass is not a **satisfaction** but a promise and a
AP : 24 :091(266) [0415] transferred to the dead and to **satisfaction** for penalties.
AP : 24 :092(266) [0415] Since the Mass is not a **satisfaction** for either punishment
AP : 24 :093(267) [0417] apply the offering as a **satisfaction** for the dead because it
AP : 24 :093(267) [0417] and do not apply it as a **satisfaction** for penalties.
AP : 27 :011(270) [0423] before God or makes **satisfaction** for sins before God.
S3 : 03 :012(305) [0481] confession, and **satisfaction** — with the added consolation
S3 : 03 :012(305) [0481] confesses, and makes **satisfaction** has merited forgiveness
S3 : 03 :013(305) [0483] Lord God, until I make **satisfaction** for my sins and
S3 : 03 :019(306) [0485] better he would make **satisfaction** for his sins, for such
S3 : 03 :021(306) [0485] **Satisfaction** was even more complicated, for nobody could
S3 : 03 :023(306) [0485] was placed in man's own works of **satisfaction**.
S3 : 03 :023(306) [0485] If the **satisfaction** could have been perfect, full confidence
S3 : 03 :024(307) [0485] But these **satisfaction** was remitted and canceled, first for
S3 : 03 :024(307) [0485] for himself alone the right to remit the entire **satisfaction**.
S3 : 03 :029(308) [0487] What **satisfaction** should they render when they were
S3 : 03 :038(309) [0489] Nor can our **satisfaction** be uncertain, for it consists not
SC : 08 :008(353) [0559] Greed and anxiety about food prevent such **satisfaction**.)
LC : 02 :031(414) [0687] that he might make **satisfaction** for me and pay what I
LC : 03 :097(433) [0725] because I can make **satisfaction** or merit anything by my
SD : 03 :056(549) [0935] nature, could render **satisfaction** to the eternal and
SD : 03 :057(549) [0935] therefore it is a perfect **satisfaction** and reconciliation of

Satisfactions (76)
AG : 04 :001(030) [0045] own merits, works, or **satisfactions**, but that we receive
AG : 12 :010(035) [0049] through faith but through the **satisfactions** made by man.
AG : 25 :005(062) [0069] of sins, with **satisfactions**, with indulgences, with
AL : 12 :010(035) [0049] us to merit grace through **satisfactions** of our own.
AL : 25 :005(062) [0069] In former times **satisfactions** were immoderately extolled,
AL : 26 :001(064) [0071] profitable to merit grace and make **satisfactions** for sins.
AL : 28 :038(087) [0089] we can still see some traces of these in the **satisfactions**.
AP : 12 :013(184) [0257] of the keys and another part is redeemed by **satisfactions**.
AP : 12 :014(184) [0257] They add further that **satisfactions** ought to be works of
AP : 12 :015(184) [0257] buy off purgatory with **satisfactions**, so later on a most
AP : 12 :015(184) [0257] profitable way of buying off **satisfactions** was invented.
AP : 12 :015(184) [0257] as the remission of **satisfactions**, and collect this revenue
AP : 12 :015(184) [0257] They buy off the **satisfactions** of the dead not only by
AP : 12 :016(184) [0257] the whole business of **satisfactions** is endless, and we
AP : 12 :022(185) [0257] to impose certain **satisfactions** upon consciences, to
AP : 12 :022(185) [0257] and to make such **satisfactions** and acts of devotion
AP : 12 :024(185) [0257] 8. Canonical **satisfactions** are necessary to redeem the
AP : 12 :095(196) [0281] of our works, contrition, confession, or **satisfactions**.
AP : 12 :112(198) [0285] without certain **satisfactions**, they made confession to the
AP : 12 :112(198) [0285] priests so that these **satisfactions** might be suited to their
AP : 12 :112(198) [0285] before God but that **satisfactions** could not be prescribed
AP : 12 :115(199) [0285] custom in prescribing certain **satisfactions** in confession.
AP : 12 :115(199) [0285] that are not due; we call them canonical **satisfactions**.
AP : 12 :116(199) [0285] of sins, that canonical **satisfactions** are not necessary by
AP : 12 :116(199) [0287] we have discussed **satisfactions** in particular, lest by their
AP : 12 :118(199) [0287] opponents admit that **satisfactions** do not contribute to
AP : 12 :118(199) [0287] the keys, and the rest must be bought off by **satisfactions**.
AP : 12 :118(200) [0287] forgiven; in that case **satisfactions** would only be
AP : 12 :118(200) [0287] They say that these **satisfactions** avail even when they are
AP : 12 :119(200) [0287] even Peter Lombard speaks this way about **satisfactions**.
AP : 12 :120(200) [0287] saw that there were **satisfactions** in the church, but they
AP : 12 :120(200) [0287] imagined that **satisfactions** were valid not for discipline in
AP : 12 :120(200) [0287] secular improperly, so also in the case of **satisfactions**.
AP : 12 :122(200) [0289] that the abolition of **satisfactions** in the church would be
AP : 12 :123(200) [0289] of purgatory; therefore **satisfactions** buy off the
AP : 12 :131(202) [0291] about canonical **satisfactions** or the opinions of the
AP : 12 :132(202) [0293] those hypocritical **satisfactions** which the scholastics
AP : 12 :133(202) [0293] of Scripture apply in no way to scholastic **satisfactions**.
AP : 12 :133(202) [0293] They suppose that **satisfactions** are works that are not
AP : 12 :134(202) [0293] refuses to assume the **satisfactions** he does not sin but
AP : 12 :134(203) [0293] cannot be applied to **satisfactions** that one may refuse,
AP : 12 :135(203) [0293] Thirdly, it is just such **satisfactions** that indulgences
AP : 12 :135(203) [0293] to apply these passages to canonical **satisfactions**.
AP : 12 :136(203) [0293] of purgatory are **satisfactions**, or rather "satispassions,"
AP : 12 :136(203) [0293] "satispassions," or if **satisfactions** are a redemption from
AP : 12 :138(203) [0293] that canonical **satisfactions** compensate for these
AP : 12 :139(203) [0295] purgatory or canonical **satisfactions** can remit eternal
AP : 12 :146(205) [0297] us the victory if we set our **satisfactions** against death."
AP : 12 :147(205) [0297] that canonical **satisfactions** are not necessary by divine
AP : 12 :148(205) [0299] or price, as our opponents imagine **satisfactions** to be.
AP : 12 :149(205) [0299] think that canonical **satisfactions** are more genuine
AP : 12 :149(205) [0299] to those vain **satisfactions** and not to apply them to the
AP : 12 :154(206) [0299] Canonical **satisfactions**, moreover, do not apply to these
AP : 12 :154(206) [0301] keys remit both the **satisfactions** and the penalties on
AP : 12 :154(206) [0301] penalties on account of which the **satisfactions** are made.
AP : 12 :157(207) [0301] we should not mingle the merit of **satisfactions** with this.
AP : 12 :162(208) [0303] of canonical **satisfactions** does not do away with the
AP : 12 :167(208) [0303] decisions about **satisfactions** were a matter of
AP : 12 :171(209) [0305] described by the canons dealing with **satisfactions**.
AP : 12 :171(209) [0305] one required in the canons dealing with **satisfactions**.
AP : 12 :172(209) [0305] intolerable to abolish **satisfactions** contrary to the clear
AP : 12 :172(209) [0305] that these canonical **satisfactions** or non-obligatory works
AP : 12 :173(209) [0305] works, though in their **satisfactions** they impose
AP : 12 :173(210) [0305] their schools that it is not a sin to reject **satisfactions**.
AP : 12 :173(210) [0305] Gospel compels us to assume these canonical **satisfactions**.
AP : 12 :175(210) [0307] authority can remit **satisfactions** and penalties, this
AP : 12 :178(211) [0309] of offenses, and **satisfactions**, and that these touch neither
AP : 24 :024(253) [0391] By analogy they were **satisfactions** since they gained the
AP : 24 :025(253) [0391] These sacrifices are not **satisfactions** on behalf of those
AP : 24 :043(257) [0399] of saints, human **satisfactions**, and human traditions with
AP : 24 :046(258) [0401] **Satisfactions** and the enumeration of sins were a torture
AP : 24 :091(266) [0415] of guilt and faith to vain ideas of **satisfactions**.
AP : 24 :091(266) [0415] under the pretext of **satisfactions** they have debased the
AP : 27 :009(270) [0421] Are they **satisfactions** for sins?
S3 : 03 :021(306) [0485] to of imposing small **satisfactions** which were easy to
TR : 00 :045(328) [0517] have also invented **satisfactions**, by means of which they

Satisfactorily (2), Satisfactory (1)
AP : 04 :344(160) [0217] To this we must give a **satisfactory** answer.
AP : 12 :005(183) [0253] which the theologians could never explain **satisfactorily**.
AP : 12 :178(211) [0309] and they themselves cannot **satisfactorily** explain them.

Satisfy (21), Satisfied (14), Satisfies (2), Satisfying (1)
AP : 02 :051(106) [0119] This, we believe, will **satisfy** His Imperial Majesty about
AP : 04 :018(109) [0125] fact that the law is never **satisfied**, that reason performs
AP : 04 :034(112) [0129] Content with this, they think they **satisfy** the law of God.
AP : 04 :134(125) [0159] outward and civil works **satisfy** the law of God and that
AP : 04 :146(127) [0163] In this life we cannot **satisfy** the law, because our
AP : 04 :164(129) [0169] be sure that it pleases God, since we never **satisfy** the law?
AP : 04 :166(130) [0169] and the church proclaim that the law cannot be **satisfied**.
AP : 04 :179(131) [0171] them, even though they have not really **satisfied** the law.
AP : 04 :222(138) [0181] of God; that our love **satisfies** the law of God; that by our
AP : 04 :270(147) [0197] which does not **satisfy** the law and therefore flees in
AP : 04 :270(147) [0197] us for Christ's sake even though we cannot **satisfy** the law.
AP : 04 :285(150) [0201] works cannot be sure that its work will **satisfy** God.
AP : 04 :296(152) [0205] In the flesh we never **satisfy** the law.
AP : 04 :308(155) [0207] We do not **satisfy** the law, but for Christ's sake this is
AP : 12 :088(195) [0277] always accuse us because we never **satisfy** the law of God.
AP : 12 :145(205) [0297] outward and civil works **satisfy** God's law; and second,
AP : 12 :169(209) [0305] is false if it does not **satisfy** those whose property we have
AP : 16 :012(224) [0333] contracts will never **satisfy** good consciences unless they
AP : 22 :010(237) [0361] our laity should be **satisfied** with the one part offered by
AP : 22 :010(238) [0361] They say, "They should be **satisfied**."
AP : 22 :011(238) [0361] But why should they be **satisfied**?
AP : 22 :011(238) [0361] "Whether they like it or not, they should be **satisfied**!"
AP : 23 :059(247) [0379] we know that to **satisfy** our opponents we would have to
AP : 27 :025(273) [0427] to believe that they **satisfy** the Ten Commandments in
AP : 27 :025(273) [0429] of a monastic life **satisfies** the Commandments and does
S1 : PR :013(291) [0459] we might just as well be **satisfied** with such a council.
SC : 03 :014(347) [0547] Everything required to **satisfy** our bodily needs, such as
SC : 08 :008(353) [0559] is to be observed that **"satisfying** the desire of every living
LC : SP :006(362) [0575] however, we should be **satisfied** if they learned the three
LC : 01 :004(365) [0581] I am the one who will **satisfy** you and help you out of
LC : 01 :212(394) [0641] allotted portion and be **satisfied** with it — although here,
LC : 03 :058(428) [0713] God even for enough to **satisfy** the belly, let alone expect,
LC : 03 :080(431) [0721] He is not **satisfied** to obstruct and overthrow spiritual
LC : 05 :049(452) [0765] must from time to time **satisfy** and obey this
LC : 06 :016(459) [0000] simply a good work with which we could **satisfy** God.
EP : 05 :005(478) [0803] namely, that Christ has **satisfied** and paid for all guilt and
SD : 03 :014(541) [0919] of Christ when he **satisfied** the law for us and paid for
SD : 03 :057(549) [0935] the human race, since it **satisfied** the eternal and

Satisfiest (1)
SC : 08 :007(353) [0559] openest thy hand; Thou **satisfiest** the desire of every living

Satispassions (1)
AP : 1 2 :136(203) [0293] or rather "**satispassions**," or if satisfactions are a

Saul (6)
AP : 1 2 :008(183) [0255] Why did not **Saul**, Judas, and men like them attain grace
AP : 1 2 :036(186) [0261] contrition of Judas and **Saul** on the one hand and that of
AP : 1 2 :036(186) [0261] contrition of Judas and **Saul** did not avail because it
S3 : 0 3 :007(304) [0481] death and hell, and man must despair like **Saul** and Judas.
LC : 0 1 :045(370) [0593] **Saul** was a great king, chosen by God, and an upright
LC : 0 1 :046(370) [0593] inevitably he remained safe from **Saul** and became king.

Savage (4)
AP : 2 3 :003(239) [0363] country, however **savage** or cruel, would consider.
AP : 2 3 :071(249) [0383] up marriages and to issue **savage** and cruel prohibitions.
TR : 0 0 :049(328) [0519] defends these errors with **savage** cruelty and punishment.
LC : 0 3 :078(431) [0721] and bloodshed, famine, **savage** beasts, wicked men, etc.

Save (25), Saved (107), Saves (19), Saving (8)
AG : 0 6 :003(032) [0047] believes in Christ shall be **saved**, and he shall have
AG : 2 0 :011(042) [0055] by grace you have been **saved** through faith; and this is
AG : 2 6 :027(068) [0073] we believe that we shall be **saved** through the grace of the
AL : 0 6 :003(032) [0047] believes in Christ shall be **saved**, not through works but
AL : 0 9 :003(033) [0047] and declare that children are **saved** without Baptism.
AL : 2 0 :011(042) [0055] by grace you have been **saved** through faith; and this is
AL : 2 6 :027(068) [0073] we believe that we shall be **saved** through the grace of the
AP : 0 4 :054(114) [0137] the holy Fathers often say that we are **saved** by mercy.
AP : 0 4 :056(114) [0137] faith does not justify or **save** because it is a good work in
AP : 0 4 :087(120) [0147] that we are **saved** freely by "the gift of God, not
AP : 0 4 :093(120) [0149] by grace you have been **saved** through faith; and this is
AP : 0 4 :096(121) [0149] world, but that the world might be **saved** through him.
AP : 0 4 :098(121) [0149] heaven given among men by which we must be **saved**."
AP : 0 4 :098(121) [0151] Therefore we are **saved** by trust in the name of Christ,
AP : 0 4 :098(121) [0151] as the cause or price on account of which we are **saved**.
AP : 0 4 :152(127) [0163] words when he adds: "Your faith has **saved** you"
AP : 0 4 :153(127) [0163] Therefore he clearly says, "Your faith has **saved** you."
AP : 0 4 :261(145) [0195] is no other God who can **save** this way" (Dan. 3:29).
AP : 0 4 :278(149) [0199] almsgiving that it is the whole newness of life which **saves**.
AP : 0 4 :330(158) [0211] a trust in mercy; mercy **saves** us, our own merits and
AP : 0 4 :330(158) [0211] mercy saves us, our own merits and efforts do not **save** us.
AP : 0 4 :334(158) [0215] words clearly say that God **saves** through mercy and
AP : 0 4 :338(159) [0215] Faith **saves** because it takes hold of mercy and the
AP : 0 4 :338(159) [0215] the whole church we teach that we are **saved** by mercy.
AP : 0 4 :344(160) [0217] the church's confession that we are **saved** through mercy.
AP : 0 4 :344(160) [0217] will be uncertain if we are **saved** through mercy and if,
AP : 0 4 :344(160) [0217] distinguish those who are **saved** from those who are not."
AP : 0 4 :345(160) [0217] between those who are **saved** and those who are not, we
AP : 0 4 :345(160) [0217] are not, we must hold that we are **saved** through mercy.
AP : 0 4 :345(160) [0217] world, but that the world might be **saved** through him.
AP : 0 4 :347(160) [0217] between those who are **saved** and those who are not.
AP : 0 4 :364(163) [0219] that it is the will of God to help, rescue, and **save** them.
AP : 0 4 :383(166) [0225] justified, and he confesses with his lips and so is **saved**."
AP : 0 4 :384(166) [0225] act of confessing does not **save**, but that it saves only
AP : 0 4 :384(166) [0225] does not save, but that it **saves** only because of faith in
AP : 0 4 :384(166) [0225] Paul says that confession **saves** in order to show what
AP : 0 9 :003(178) [0245] to none, none would be **saved**, and ultimately there would
AP : 1 2 :057(189) [0267] Your faith has **saved** you; go in peace."
AP : 1 2 :166(208) [0303] reconciled to God and **saved** their city from destruction.
AP : 1 5 :006(216) [0317] "By grace you have been **saved** through faith; and this is
AP : 1 8 :006(225) [0335] the faith that God hears, forgives, helps, or **saves** them.
AP : 2 1 :004(229) [0343] mercy, revealing his will to **save** men, and giving teachers
AP : 2 1 :023(232) [0349] saints, so that we may be **saved** by their merits and
AP : 2 1 :029(233) [0351] us or accounted us righteous or **saved** us on this account.
AP : 2 3 :032(243) [0373] he says, "Woman will be **saved** through bearing children."
AP : 2 3 :032(243) [0373] Paul says that woman is **saved** through bearing children.
AP : 2 3 :032(243) [0373] to say that woman is **saved** by the marital functions
AP : 2 3 :032(244) [0373] and a believing woman is **saved** if she serves faithfully in
AP : 2 4 :018(252) [0389] "He who believes and is baptized will be **saved**."
AP : 2 4 :028(254) [0393] the one who justifies and **saves**, because of my Word and
AP : 2 7 :009(270) [0421] Do these merits **save** others when they are transferred to
S1 : PR :006(289) [0457] not, many souls that might have been **saved** are neglected.
S2 : 0 1 :005(292) [0463] among men by which we must be **saved**" (Acts 4:12).
S2 : 0 2 :005(293) [0463] it, and that one can be **saved** in a better way without the
S2 : 0 4 :004(299) [0473] that no Christian can be **saved** unless he is obedient to the
S2 : 0 4 :010(300) [0475] permit Christians to be **saved** except by his own power,
S2 : 0 4 :012(300) [0475] that one must be obedient to him in order to be **saved**.
S3 : 0 8 :007(313) [0495] and is baptized will be **saved**" (Mark 16:16), even if they
S3 : 0 8 :008(313) [0497] that he now had to be **saved** by the present Messiah and
SC : 0 4 :008(349) [0551] and is baptized will be **saved**; but he who does not believe
SC : 0 4 :010(349) [0551] wrote to Titus (3:5-8), "He **saved** us by the washing of
LC : SP :021(364) [0579] and is baptized will be **saved**; but he who does not believe
LC : 0 1 :024(367) [0587] us from evil, he who **saves** and delivers us when any evil
LC : 0 1 :074(374) [0601] monstrous or fearful and exclaim, "Lord God, **save** us!"
LC : 0 1 :189(391) [0635] to prevent, protect, and **save** him from suffering bodily
LC : 0 1 :190(391) [0635] in similar peril and do not **save** him although you know
LC : 0 1 :190(391) [0635] of the service by which his life might have been **saved**.
LC : 0 1 :192(391) [0635] hand to pull him out and **save** him, and yet I did not do
LC : 0 2 :044(416) [0689] teaching us to obtain grace and be **saved** by our works.
LC : 0 4 :005(437) [0733] *and is baptized will be saved; but he who does not believe*
LC : 0 4 :006(437) [0733] that we must be baptized or we shall not be **saved**.
LC : 0 4 :023(439) [0737] above, "He who believes and is baptized shall be **saved**."
LC : 0 4 :024(439) [0737] effect, benefit, fruit, and purpose of Baptism is to **save**.
LC : 0 4 :024(439) [0737] to become a prince, but as the words say, to "be **saved**."
LC : 0 4 :025(439) [0737] To be **saved**, we know, is nothing else than to be delivered
LC : 0 4 :028(440) [0739] assert that faith alone **saves** and that works and external
LC : 0 4 :031(440) [0739] words, "He who believes and is baptized will be **saved**."
LC : 0 4 :033(440) [0741] and is baptized will be **saved**," that is, faith alone makes
LC : 0 4 :043(442) [0743] which swallows up death and **saves** the lives of all men.
LC : 0 4 :044(442) [0743] promise that I shall be **saved** and have eternal life, both in
LC : 0 4 :046(442) [0743] body and soul shall be **saved** and live forever: the soul
EP : 0 1 :006(467) [0781] will not quicken it in the elect, will not glorify it or **save** it.
EP : 0 2 :013(471) [0789] them, justifies them, and **saves** them without means,
EP : 0 3 :001(472) [0791] justified before God and **saved** solely by faith in Christ, so
EP : 0 3 :006(473) [0793] righteous by God the Father, and shall be **saved** eternally.
EP : 0 3 :010(474) [0795] become righteous and are **saved** "alone by faith" in
EP : 0 3 :019(475) [0795] 7. That faith **saves** because by faith there is begun in us
EP : 0 3 :021(475) [0797] justified before God and **saved** both by the righteousness
EP : 0 4 :002(475) [0797] that it is impossible to be **saved** without good works; and
EP : 0 4 :002(475) [0797] and that no one has ever been **saved** without good works.
EP : 0 4 :007(476) [0799] by grace you have been **saved** through faith; and this is
EP : 0 4 :016(477) [0801] that no one has ever been **saved** without good works;
EP : 0 4 :016(477) [0801] that it is impossible to be **saved** without good works.
EP : 1 1 :007(495) [0833] all who are to be eternally **saved** are inscribed and
EP : 1 1 :012(496) [0835] does not mean that God does not desire to **save** everyone.
EP : 1 1 :013(496) [0835] counsel that he would **save** no one except those who
EP : 1 1 :015(496) [0835] without any merit of ours, **saves** us "according to the
EP : 1 1 :019(497) [0837] not want everybody to be **saved**, but that merely by an
EP : 1 1 :019(497) [0837] certain people to damnation so that they cannot be **saved**.
EP : 1 2 :006(498) [0839] use of reason they will be **saved** in this innocence without
EP : 1 2 :022(499) [0841] and creates in them the **saving** knowledge of Christ,
SD : PR :007(502) [0849] righteous and to be **saved** by the works of the law
SD : 0 1 :039(515) [0871] Son he might cleanse it from sin, sanctify it, and **save** it.
SD : 0 1 :045(516) [0873] him and that Christ has **saved** his people from their sins.
SD : 0 1 :045(516) [0873] Trinity, is sanctified and **saved**, and other similar
SD : 0 2 :004(520) [0881] and brings them to the **saving** understanding of Christ.
SD : 0 2 :010(522) [0883] Gospel that we preach to **save** those who believe"
SD : 0 2 :049(530) [0901] men should turn themselves to him and be **saved** forever.
SD : 0 2 :050(530) [0901] the holy and only **saving** Gospel of his eternal Son, our
SD : 0 2 :051(531) [0901] folly of what we preach to **save** those who believe"
SD : 0 2 :051(531) [0901] by which you will be **saved**, you and your household"
SD : 0 2 :052(531) [0901] All who would be **saved** must hear this preaching, for the
SD : 0 2 :080(536) [0911] man to himself, illuminates, justifies, and **saves** him.
SD : 0 3 :004(540) [0917] redeemed us from our sins, justified and **saved** us.
SD : 0 3 :011(541) [0919] and holy by God the Father, and are **saved** forever.
SD : 0 3 :015(541) [0919] holy and righteous, and **saves** us forever on account of
SD : 0 3 :019(542) [0921] when he states, "He **saved** us by the washing of
SD : 0 3 :026(543) [0923] there cannot be genuine **saving** faith in those who live
SD : 0 3 :029(544) [0925] how a person may be justified before God and be **saved**.
SD : 0 3 :036(545) [0927] are justified before God and **saved** "through faith alone."
SD : 0 3 :043(547) [0931] the power to justify and **save**, and what belongs thereto,
SD : 0 3 :052(548) [0933] it is taught that man is **saved** in a different way or by a
SD : 0 3 :052(548) [0933] but that we cannot be **saved** without works or that
SD : 0 4 :001(551) [0939] and "It is impossible to be **saved** without good works,"
SD : 0 4 :001(551) [0939] and "No one has been **saved** without good works," since
SD : 0 4 :002(551) [0939] in which we confess that faith alone justifies and **saves**.
SD : 0 4 :022(554) [0945] that it is impossible to be **saved** without good works,
SD : 0 4 :024(555) [0945] Confession, "We are **saved** without works solely by faith."
SD : 0 4 :030(555) [0947] endures to the end will be **saved** (Matt. 24:13) and "We
SD : 0 4 :037(557) [0949] grace of God and to be **saved** thereby, it is not we, but
SD : 0 5 :019(561) [0957] strictly speaking, teaches about **saving** faith in Christ.
SD : 0 5 :020(561) [0959] and all the punishments of sin, and are **saved** eternally.
SD : 0 5 :025(563) [0961] without any merit of their own, justifies and **saves** them.
SD : 0 7 :123(590) [1013] truthful, living, and **saving** faith, receive only bread and
SD : 1 1 :009(618) [1065] and how many are to be **saved**, who and how many are to
SD : 1 1 :009(618) [1065] muster: This one shall be **saved**, that one shall be
SD : 1 1 :010(618) [1067] I shall and must be **saved** since God's foreknowledge
SD : 1 1 :022(619) [1069] finally, he would eternally **save** and glorify in eternal life
SD : 1 1 :023(619) [1069] the elect who are to be **saved** through Christ, and also
SD : 1 1 :025(620) [1071] the book of life" will be **saved**, how can and should one
SD : 1 1 :029(621) [1073] so that they may be illuminated, converted, and **saved**.
SD : 1 1 :029(621) [1073] (II Cor. 3:8) and a "power of God" to **save** (Rom. 1:16).
SD : 1 1 :033(621) [1073] "Lord, will those who are **saved** be few?" by saying,
SD : 1 1 :040(623) [1077] that he would justify and **save** all who accept Christ
SD : 1 1 :043(623) [1077] that we are justified and **saved** without our works and
SD : 1 1 :048(624) [1079] bring everything to such an issue that we shall be **saved**.
SD : 1 1 :066(627) [1085] that whomever he would **save** he would save through
SD : 1 1 :066(627) [1085] he would save he would **save** through Christ, as Christ
SD : 1 1 :066(627) [1085] if anyone enters by me, he will be **saved**" (John 10:9).
SD : 1 1 :070(627) [1085] no one who wants to be **saved** should burden and torture
SD : 1 1 :070(627) [1085] sin to come to him and find refreshment and be **saved**.
SD : 1 1 :078(629) [1089] damnation is not that God did not want them to be **saved**.
SD : 1 1 :083(630) [1091] should come to the knowledge of the truth and be **saved**.
SD : 1 1 :086(631) [1091] damnation so that he could not and might not be **saved**.
SD : 1 1 :087(631) [1091] of the eternal and **saving** election of the elect children of
SD : 1 1 :087(631) [1093] It sets forth that he **saves** us "according to the purpose"
SD : 1 1 :096(632) [1095] and thus justify and **save** him for ever through the sole
SD : 1 2 :011(634) [1099] innocence they will be **saved** without Baptism, which they
SD : 1 2 :030(635) [1101] Spirit teaches men the **saving** knowledge of Christ,

Saviour (16)
PR : PR :023(012) [0021] advent of our only Redeemer and **Saviour** Jesus Christ.
AG : 2 1 :002(047) [0057] Tim. 2:5), who is the only **saviour**, the only highpriest,
AP : 0 4 :030(111) [0129] so likewise he is the **Saviour** of man's corrupted nature,
S2 : 0 2 :010(294) [0465] considered equal or superior to my **Saviour**, Jesus Christ.
S3 : 0 1 :011(303) [0479] concerning sin and concerning Christ, our **Saviour**.
SC : 0 4 :010(349) [0551] through Jesus Christ our **Saviour**, so that we might be
SD : 0 2 :050(530) [0901] his eternal Son, our only **Saviour** and Redeemer, Jesus
SD : 0 7 :039(576) [0985] just as Jesus Christ, our **Saviour**, was incarnate through
SD : 0 7 :043(576) [0987] It is our Lord and **Saviour** Jesus Christ concerning
SD : 0 7 :048(578) [0989] words of our Lord and **Saviour** Jesus Christ, which in
SD : 0 7 :089(585) [1003] of our almighty God and **Saviour**, Jesus Christ, which
SD : 0 7 :090(585) [1003] the omnipotence of our Lord and **Saviour**, Jesus Christ.
SD : 0 7 :106(588) [1009] true and eternal God, our Lord and **Saviour** Jesus Christ.
SD : 0 8 :040(599) [1029] Christ would be a poor **Saviour** for me, in fact, he himself
SD : 0 8 :040(599) [1029] Saviour for me, in fact, he himself would need a **Saviour**.
SD : 1 1 :046(624) [1079] almighty hand of our **Saviour**, Jesus Christ, out of which

Savor (1)
LC : PR :010(360) [0569] up any incense or other **savor** more potent against the

Saxe (4)
PR : PR :027(014) [0025] Duke Frederick William [of **Saxe**-Altenburg] and
PR : PR :027(014) [0025] Duke John [of **Saxe**-Weimar] the above two through
PR : PR :027(014) [0025] Duke John Casimir [of **Saxe**-Coburg] and
PR : PR :027(014) [0025] Duke John Ernest [of **Saxe**-Eisenach] the above two

Saxons (1)
LC : 0 3 :101(433) [0727] (or, as the ancient **Saxons** called it, *Bekoerunge*) is of

Saxony (8)
PR : PR :013(007) [0013] we, the elector of **Saxony**, etc., with the counsel and
PR : PR :027(014) [0025] August, duke of **Saxony**, elector
AG : 0 0 :007(096) [0095] John, duke of **Saxony**, elector
AG : 0 0 :007(096) [0095] John Frederick, duke of **Saxony**
AL : 0 0 :017(096) [0095] John, duke of **Saxony**, elector
AL : 0 0 :017(096) [0095] John Frederick, duke of **Saxony**
TR : 0 0 :082(000) [0529] Prince, the Elector of **Saxony**, and by the other princes
SD : 0 7 :012(571) [0977] 1536 the theologians of **Saxony** and Upper Germany

Sayings (6)
AP : 0 4 :380(165) [0223] they have taken certain **sayings**, decrees as it were, and
AP : 1 2 :097(196) [0281] the Fathers, they select **sayings** about a part of penitence,
AP : 1 2 :097(197) [0281] do not understand the **sayings** elsewhere about faith, they
AP : 2 4 :095(267) [0417] to life now and saw their **sayings** being twisted to support
LC : 0 1 :303(406) [0667] Hence the **sayings**, "First come, first served," and "Every
EP : 0 7 :025(485) [0815] but that they are dark **sayings** whose meaning must first

Scale (3), Scales (1)
AP : 2 4 :064(261) [0405] The scholastics have **scales** of merit, like the
LC : 0 1 :300(405) [0667] much farther down in the **scale**, where the Seventh
SD : 0 8 :044(599) [1029] we shall sink to the bottom with our **scale**.
SD : 0 8 :044(599) [1029] dead lie in the opposite **scale**, then his side goes down and

Scandal (6), Scandalize (3), Scandalized (1), Scandalous (4), Scandals (7)
PR : PR :004(004) [0007] about destructive and **scandalous** division in churches and
PR : PR :021(010) [0019] misunderstanding and **scandal** on this account will be
PR : PR :024(013) [0021] errors, aggravated **scandals**, dissensions, and
PR : PR :024(013) [0021] pure doctrine, to start **scandalous** controversies at will
PR : PR :026(014) [0025] in order that all kinds of **scandal** might be obviated.
AG : 2 3 :013(053) [0063] occasion for many great and evil vices and much **scandal**.
AG : 2 6 :041(070) [0075] a sin to omit them if this is done without causing **scandal**.
AG : 2 7 :008(072) [0077] this arrangement, what **scandals** and burdened
AL : 2 3 :003(051) [0061] to avoid such open **scandals**, they took wives and taught
AL : 2 3 :018(054) [0063] celibacy causes many **scandals**, adulteries, and other
AL : 2 6 :041(070) [0075] no sin is committed if they are omitted without **scandal**.
AL : 2 7 :008(072) [0077] this arrangement, what **scandals** were created, what
AP : 1 2 :016(184) [0257] Beneath these **scandalous** and demonic doctrines the
AP : 2 3 :006(240) [0365] for it produces endless **scandals**, sins, and the corruption
AP : 2 7 :052(278) [0437] with such dangers and **scandals** going on before their very
TR : 0 0 :058(330) [0521] they are reproached for **scandal**, schism, and discord.
SD : PR :008(502) [0849] the other hand, will be **scandalized**; some will doubt if the
SD : 0 1 :045(516) [0873] we do not want to **scandalize** the uninstructed people
SD : 1 0 :016(613) [1057] hand, it will sadden and **scandalize** true believers and
SD : 1 0 :025(615) [1061] enemies of God's Word, and **scandalize** the weak in faith.
SD : 1 1 :001(616) [1063] has been no public, **scandalous**, and widespread

Scarcely (6)
AG : 2 8 :067(092) [0093] **Scarcely** any of the ancient canons are observed according
AL : 2 8 :067(092) [0093] **Scarcely** any of the canons are observed according to the
LC : 0 1 :042(370) [0591] nor honor, and can **scarcely** even keep alive; meanwhile,
LC : 0 1 :273(401) [0659] into disgrace, from which he could **scarcely** clear himself.
LC : 0 3 :057(428) [0713] we shall receive them and **scarcely** venture to ask for a
LC : 0 3 :109(435) [0729] into my heart that I can **scarcely** stand, for he is an enemy

Scare (1)
AP : 2 8 :008(282) [0445] this thunderbolt does not **scare** our opponents, who

Scarlet (2)
AP : 0 4 :258(144) [0193] though your sins are like **scarlet**, they shall be white as
AP : 1 2 :164(208) [0303] Though your sins are like **scarlet**, they shall be white as

Scatter (1), Scattered (4)
PR : PR :004(003) [0007] bestirred himself to **scatter** his seed of false doctrine and
AP : PR :019(099) [0103] regard his afflicted and **scattered** churches and to restore
AP : 0 7 :010(170) [0229] rather, made up of men **scattered** throughout the world
AP : 0 7 :020(171) [0233] and righteous men **scattered** throughout the world.
TR : 0 0 :016(322) [0509] kingdom of Christ is **scattered** over all the earth and that

Scheme (3)
LC : 0 1 :296(405) [0665] pretext, to covet or **scheme** to despoil his neighbor of
LC : 0 3 :069(429) [0717] exterminate us so that their will and **scheme** may prevail.
SD : 0 1 :007(510) [0861] Through Satan's **scheme**, "by one man sin (which is the

Schism (11), Schismatics (2), Schisms (9)
PR : PR :024(013) [0021] and long-standing **schisms** a Christian explanation and
AG : 2 8 :078(094) [0095] occasion for division and **schism**, which they should in
AL : 2 6 :043(070) [0075] accused the East of **schism**, they were admonished by
AL : 2 8 :078(094) [0095] God that by their obstinacy they offer occasion for **schism**
AP : 0 4 :232(140) [0185] disintegrate into various **schisms** and the hatreds,
AP : 0 4 :232(140) [0185] factions, and heresies that arise from such **schisms**.
AP : 0 7 :049(178) [0245] we should not incite **schisms**, as the Donatists wickedly
AP : 0 7 :050(178) [0245] those who have incited **schisms** because they denied to
AP : 2 3 :059(247) [0379] open to the charge of **schism** because we seem to have
AP : 2 8 :025(285) [0451] give an account for the **schism** that has been provoked.
TR : 0 0 :042(328) [0517] nations and to be called **schismatics** is a serious matter.
TR : 0 0 :058(330) [0521] they are reproached for scandal, **schism**, and discord.
TR : 0 0 :062(330) [0523] over the rest to prevent **schism**, lest several persons, by
TR : 0 0 :072(332) [0525] that give occasion to **schism** and discord, for Paul
LC : 0 2 :051(417) [0691] of gifts, yet is united in love without sect or **schism**.
EP : RN :004(465) [0777] 3. With reference to the **schism** in matters of faith which
SD : PR :007(502) [0849] serious and dangerous **schisms** in the true Evangelical
SD : PR :008(502) [0849] papists, rejoice over the **schisms** which have occurred
SD : 0 3 :006(540) [0917] pure, in beautiful harmony, and without any **schisms**.
SD : 0 7 :029(574) [0981] *Confession:* "I see that **schisms** and errors are increasing
SD : 1 0 :023(615) [1061] nations and to be called **schismatics** is a serious matter.
SD : 1 1 :001(616) [1063] as we can, disunity and **schism** in this article among our

Schlagenhaufen (2)
S3 : 1 5 :005(317) [0501] I, John **Schlagenhaufen**, pastor of the church in Koethen,
TR : 0 0 :082(335) [0529] John **Schlagenhaufen** subscribes with his own hand

Schleusingen (1)
PR : PR :027(015) [0025] Ernest, count and lord of Henneberg [-**Schleusingen**]

Schmiedelfeld (1)
PR : PR :027(015) [0025] Henry, baron of Limpurg [-**Schmiedelfeld**], Semperfrei

Schneeweiss (2)
S3 : 1 5 :005(317) [0501] Simon **Schneeweiss**, pastor of the church in Crailsheim
TR : 0 0 :082(335) [0529] Simon **Schneeweiss**, pastor at Crailsheim

Schnepf (2)
S3 : 1 5 :005(317) [0501] I, Erhard **Schnepf**, preacher in Stuttgart, subscribe
TR : 0 0 :082(334) [0529] I, Erhard **Schnepf**, subscribe

Schoenburg (2)
PR : PR :027(015) [0025] George, baron of **Schoenburg** [-Waldenburg]
PR : PR :027(015) [0025] Wolf, baron of **Schoenburg** [-Penig-Remissa]

Scholars (6)
AP : 1 5 :035(220) [0325] soldiers wear one kind of uniform and **scholars** another.
LC : 0 5 :012(448) [0755] that all the spirits and **scholars** put together have less
SD : 0 1 :054(517) [0877] But when **scholars** use the terms among themselves or in
SD : 0 1 :055(518) [0877] On this basis all **scholars** and intelligent people have
SD : 0 7 :022(573) [0979] all the enthusiasts and **scholars** put together have less
SD : 0 8 :043(599) [1029] to the other nature, all of which **scholars** know right well.

Scholastic (12), Scholastics (36)
PR : PR :021(011) [0019] and subjectively (to use **scholastic** terminology), as if
AP : PR :017(099) [0103] of the monks, canonists, and **scholastic** theologians.
AP : 0 2 :004(101) [0105] Our **scholastic** opponents admit that concupiscence is the
AP : 0 2 :007(101) [0107] done this because the **scholastics** misunderstand the
AP : 0 2 :008(101) [0107] to the law of God, the **scholastics** do not even mention.
AP : 0 2 :010(102) [0107] above all things, as the **scholastics** confidently assert, then
AP : 0 2 :012(102) [0109] The **scholastics** mingled Christian doctrine with
AP : 0 2 :013(102) [0109] Word of God, which the **scholastics** do not often employ
AP : 0 2 :015(102) [0109] Here the **scholastics** quibble about philosophical
AP : 0 2 :023(103) [0111] Even the **scholastic** theologians teach that these things
AP : 0 2 :043(106) [0117] Here the **scholastics** have taken over from philosophy the
AP : 0 2 :043(106) [0117] ideas appear in the **scholastics**, who improperly mingle
AP : 0 2 :046(106) [0117] Although the **scholastics** minimize both sin and its
AP : 0 4 :009(108) [0123] Here the **scholastics** have followed the philosophers.
AP : 0 4 :009(108) [0123] In this way the **scholastics** teach men to merit the
AP : 0 4 :011(108) [0123] in such works, the **scholastics** have declared that by
AP : 0 4 :121(124) [0155] The **scholastics** do not say a word about this faith.
AP : 0 4 :229(139) [0183] the great and learned **scholastics** proclaimed the highest
AP : 0 4 :271(147) [0199] Though the **scholastics** have said nothing at all about
AP : 0 4 :289(151) [0203] handed down by the **scholastic** theologians, teaches that
AP : 0 4 :304(154) [0205] is easy, since even the **scholastics** admit that the will
AP : 0 4 :312(155) [0207] in fact the way they are in idle **scholastic** speculations.
AP : 0 4 :344(160) [0217] some such reason the **scholastics** invented the term "merit
AP : 0 4 :379(165) [0223] for Christ's sake, there is not a syllable in the **scholastics**.
AP : 0 4 :383(165) [0225] The **scholastics** do not teach the righteousness of faith.
AP : 1 1 :002(180) [0249] about works, since the **scholastics** and monks teach
AP : 1 2 :003(183) [0253] the opinions of the **scholastics** and canonists had
AP : 1 2 :016(184) [0257] of penitence as taught by the **scholastics** and canonists.
AP : 1 2 :028(185) [0259] these labyrinths of the **scholastics**, we have given
AP : 1 2 :041(187) [0261] penitence, as even the more learned of the **scholastics** say.
AP : 1 2 :091(196) [0279] of faith, and the **scholastics** add nothing about faith in
AP : 1 2 :117(199) [0287] many statements of the **scholastics**; for example, in
AP : 1 2 :120(200) [0287] The **scholastics** saw that there were satisfactions in the
AP : 1 2 :131(202) [0291] or the opinions of the **scholastics** because these are
AP : 1 2 :132(202) [0293] satisfactions which the **scholastics** imagine avail as a
AP : 1 2 :133(202) [0293] of Scripture apply in no way to **scholastic** satisfactions.
AP : 1 3 :018(213) [0313] the whole crowd of **scholastic** doctors who teach that
AP : 1 3 :023(214) [0313] the Fathers that supports the **scholastics** on this question.
AP : 2 1 :040(235) [0355] the teachings of the **scholastics** and canonists contain
AP : 2 1 :041(235) [0355] ask for limitations upon **scholastic** doctrine because it
AP : 2 1 :041(235) [0355] The earlier **scholastics** are usually closer to Scripture than
AP : 2 1 :041(235) [0355] disputations of the **scholastic** theologians and canonists
AP : 2 4 :013(251) [0387] The monks and **scholastics** have brought this pharisaic
AP : 2 4 :031(255) [0395] shameless fabrications of the monks and **scholastics**.
AP : 2 4 :064(261) [0405] The **scholastics** have scales of merit, like the
S3 : 0 1 :003(302) [0477] What the **scholastic** theologians taught concerning this
S3 : 0 2 :003(303) [0479] was just said above concerning the **scholastic** theologians.
SD : 0 2 :076(536) [0911] error of the papists and **scholastics**, whose doctrine was

School (3), Schools (34)
PR : PR :000(001) [0004] of their Lands, Churches, **Schools**, and Descendants
PR : PR :003(003) [0007] many churches and **schools** committed themselves to this
PR : PR :004(004) [0007] division in churches and **schools** so that he might thereby
PR : PR :004(004) [0007] to discredit us and our **schools** and churches so as to
PR : PR :005(004) [0009] that our churches and **schools** might have been preserved
PR : PR :007(004) [0009] of ourselves and of our churches and **schools**.
PR : PR :009(006) [0011] from our churches, **schools**, doctrine, faith, and
PR : PR :009(006) [0011] now and again introduced into our churches and **schools**.
PR : PR :018(008) [0015] we and the churches and **schools** of our lands have
PR : PR :018(009) [0015] our lands, churches, and **schools** other than in the form in
PR : PR :021(010) [0019] by teachers in the **schools** and the churches): This divine
PR : PR :022(011) [0019] our lands, churches, and **schools** inasmuch as such
PR : PR :022(012) [0019] Word and unite with us and our churches and **schools**.
PR : PR :023(012) [0021] in our lands, territories, **schools**, and churches than that
PR : PR :023(012) [0021] our churches and **schools** first of all to the Holy
PR : PR :024(013) [0023] and peace of Christian **schools** and churches, and to the
PR : PR :026(014) [0025] of churches and **schools**, the supervision of printers, and
AG : 2 7 :015(073) [0077] had conducted **schools** of Holy Scripture and other
AL : 2 6 :015(066) [0073] **Schools** and sermons were so preoccupied with gathering
AL : 2 7 :015(073) [0077] Formerly there had been **schools** of the Holy Scriptures
AP : 0 2 :002(100) [0105] obviously come from the **schools**, and not from the
AP : 0 4 :341(159) [0215] We leave these thorny questions to the **schools**.
AP : 0 4 :381(165) [0223] way, boasting in the **schools** that good works please God
AP : 0 4 :382(165) [0225] In the **schools** they also boast that our good works are
AP : 1 2 :173(210) [0305] fact, they admit in their **schools** that it is not a sin to
AP : 1 8 :003(225) [0335] notions which the **schools** teach with great authority!
AP : 2 7 :005(269) [0421] upon a time they were **schools** of Christian instruction,
AP : 2 7 :055(278) [0439] the way lessons are in **school**, with the purpose of

Continued ▸

LC : SP :005(362) [0575] Christian doctrine than children and beginners at **school**.
LC : 0 1 :055(372) [0595] belong in the hangman's **school**, not ours), but also those
EP : 0 1 :024(469) [0785] In **schools** and learned circles these words can profitably
SD : PR :008(505) [0853] in the churches, the **schools**, and the homes of those
SD : PR :009(505) [0853] The pure churches and **schools** have everywhere
SD : PR :011(506) [0855] that all Evangelical churches and **schools** received them.
SD : 0 1 :056(518) [0877] the theologians in our **schools** and churches, following
SD : 0 1 :059(519) [0879] for our churches and **schools** therefore requires that every
SD : 1 2 :006(633) [1097] into our churches and **schools** in which the almighty God

Schoolmaster (3)
PR : PR :015(007) [0013] minister, and **schoolmaster** in our lands and territories
PR : PR :016(008) [0015] every minister and **schoolmaster** in our lands and
LC : 0 1 :141(384) [0621] child, he calls upon a **schoolmaster** to teach him; if he is

Schwaebisch (1)
PR : PR :027(015) [0027] Mayor and Council of the City of **Schwaebisch**-Hall

Schwarzburg (3)
PR : PR :027(015) [0025] John Guenther, count of **Schwarzburg** [-Sondershausen]
PR : PR :027(015) [0025] William, count of **Schwarzburg** [Frankenhausen]
PR : PR :027(015) [0025] Albert, count of **Schwarzburg** [-Rudolstadt]

Schweinfurt (1)
PR : PR :027(016) [0027] Mayor and Council of the City of **Schweinfurt**

Schwenkfelders (4)
EP : 1 2 :019(499) [0841] Errors of the **Schwenkfelders**
SD : 1 2 :001(632) [1095] the Anabaptists, the **Schwenkfelders**, and the New Arians
SD : 1 2 :027(635) [1101] Erroneous Articles of the **Schwenkfelders**
SD : 1 2 :028(635) [1101] We reject and condemn these errors of the **Schwenkfelders**

Science (1)
AP : 2 3 :038(244) [0373] eloquence, military **science** surpasses agriculture, and

Scoffers (1), Scoffing (1)
SD : 0 7 :123(590) [1015] godless Epicureans and **scoffers** at the Word of God who
SD : 0 7 :127(591) [1015] all presumptuous, **scoffing**, and blasphemous questions

Scold (1), Scolds (1)
AP : 0 4 :224(138) [0181] Paul **scolds** them for this and calls them back to the
SD : 0 2 :021(525) [0889] is useless to threaten, to **scold**, or even to teach and

Scope (3)
AP : 0 4 :262(145) [0195] These words deal with the total **scope** of penitence.
LC : 0 1 :013(366) [0583] understand the nature and **scope** of this commandment.
SD : 1 2 :008(633) [1097] allowed neither room nor **scope**, where the true teachers

Scorn (3)
LC : 0 1 :119(381) [0615] and meanwhile have only **scorn** and trouble for their
LC : 0 3 :044(425) [0709] account the father suffers **scorn** and reproach, so God is
LC : 0 3 :104(434) [0727] His purpose is to make us **scorn** and despise both the

Scorpion (1)
SD : 1 1 :072(628) [1087] serpent; or if he asks for an egg, will give him a **scorpion**?

Scotus (4)
AP : 1 2 :068(192) [0271] reputation, like Duns **Scotus**, Gabriel Biel, and the like in
AP : 1 2 :143(204) [0297] control the flesh but, as **Scotus** says, to pay homage to
AP : 1 2 :148(205) [0299] The saying of **Scotus** may be beautiful, that penitence is
S3 : 0 5 :003(311) [0491] Nor do we agree with **Scotus** and the Franciscans who

Scoundrel (5), Scoundrels (4)
S2 : 0 2 :001(293) [0463] when offered by an evil **scoundrel**) delivers men from
S2 : 0 2 :007(293) [0463] even a work of evil **scoundrels** (as the cannon and all
S2 : 0 4 :003(298) [0471] through a tyrant or **scoundrel**) which contribute to the
S3 : 1 1 :001(314) [0499] tyrannical, and wicked **scoundrels**, and thereby they gave
SC : PR :013(339) [0535] whether he is a believer or, at heart, a **scoundrel** or knave.
LC : 0 1 :192(391) [0635] in any other light than as a murderer and a **scoundrel**?
LC : 0 1 :232(396) [0647] chiefly to knaves and **scoundrels**, though it might be more
LC : 0 1 :262(400) [0655] apostates, even seditious and accursed **scoundrels**.
LC : 0 3 :057(427) [0713] a rogue and a **scoundrel** who had made a mockery of his

Scrape (3), Scraped (1), Scraping (1)
LC : 0 1 :043(370) [0591] care and diligence to **scraping** together great wealth and
LC : 0 1 :242(397) [0649] they have scrimped and **scraped** for a long time, he will
LC : 0 1 :243(397) [0649] How many people **scrape** and scratch day and night and
LC : 0 1 :247(398) [0651] your favor, you skin and **scrape** him right down to the
LC : 0 1 :253(399) [0653] more than you could **scrape** together by perfidy and

Scratch (1)
LC : 0 1 :243(397) [0649] many people scrape and **scratch** day and night and yet

Screams (1)
AP : 2 0 :010(228) [0341] at ease, for Paul fairly **screams**, as it were, that sins are

Scribbling (1)
S3 : 0 8 :006(312) [0495] their chattering and **scribbling**, as if the Spirit could not

Scribes (2)
AL : 0 8 :001(033) [0047] saying of Christ, "The **scribes** and Pharisees sit on Moses'
S3 : 0 3 :029(308) [0487] The **scribes** and Pharisees in Christ's time were just such

Scrimped (1)
LC : 0 1 :242(397) [0649] After they have **scrimped** and scraped for a long time, he

Scriptural (4)
AP : 0 4 :286(150) [0201] They omit the clearest **scriptural** passages on faith, select
AP : 2 4 :089(265) [0413] But for this they have no **scriptural** proof or command.
SD : PR :004(502) [0847] and thoroughly **scriptural** Augsburg Confession, and we
SD : 0 2 :033(527) [0893] "That there is no **scriptural** basis for the position that the

Scripture (123), Scriptures (171)
PR : PR :002(003) [0007] out of the divine, prophetic, and apostolic **Scriptures**.
PR : PR :003(003) [0007] solidly on the divine **Scriptures**, and that is also briefly
PR : PR :023(012) [0021] is based on the Holy **Scriptures** of God and is embodied
PR : PR :023(012) [0021] first of all to the Holy **Scriptures** and the Creeds, and then
PR : PR :024(013) [0021] prophetic, and apostolic **Scriptures** and have been
PR : PR :025(013) [0023] prophetic and apostolic **Scriptures** and is comprehended
AG : PR :008(025) [0039] on the basis of the Holy **Scriptures**, these things are
AG : 2 0 :025(044) [0057] just been indicated, the **Scriptures** speak of faith but do
AG : 2 0 :026(045) [0057] the word "faith" in the **Scriptures** to mean confidence in
AG : 2 1 :002(047) [0057] be proved from the **Scriptures** that we are to invoke saints
AG : 2 1 :003(047) [0057] according to the **Scriptures**, the highest form of divine
AG : 0 0 :001(047) [0059] clearly on the Holy **Scriptures** and is not contrary or
AG : 0 0 :001(048) [0059] without any solid basis of divine command or **Scripture**.
AG : 0 0 :000(048) [0059] is contrary to the Holy **Scriptures** or what is common to
AG : 2 3 :003(051) [0061] especially since the **Scriptures** clearly assert that the estate
AG : 2 3 :014(053) [0063] last times of which the **Scriptures** prophesy, the world is
AG : 2 3 :019(054) [0063] fact that in the Holy **Scriptures** God commanded that
AG : 2 4 :026(058) [0067] first of all, that the **Scriptures** show in many places that
AG : 2 4 :041(061) [0069] and Friday the **Scriptures** were read and expounded in
AG : 2 5 :012(063) [0071] not commanded by the **Scriptures**, but was instituted by
AG : 2 6 :022(067) [0073] Reasons for this shall be cited from the **Scriptures**.
AG : 2 7 :015(073) [0077] schools of Holy **Scripture** and other branches of learning
AG : 2 7 :016(073) [0077] purpose of learning the **Scriptures**, but now it is claimed
AG : 2 8 :028(085) [0087] something contrary to the divine Holy **Scriptures**.
AG : 2 8 :043(088) [0089] clear passages of divine **Scripture** which forbid the
AG : 2 8 :049(089) [0091] why does the divine **Scripture** so frequently forbid the
AG : 2 8 :059(091) [0091] mistaken, for the Holy **Scriptures** have abrogated the
AG : 0 0 :005(095) [0095] that is contrary to Holy **Scripture** or the universal
AG : 0 0 :007(096) [0095] information on the basis of the divine Holy **Scripture**.
AL : 2 0 :026(045) [0057] he teaches that in the **Scriptures** the word "faith" is to be
AL : 2 1 :002(047) [0057] However, the **Scriptures** do not teach us to pray to the
AL : 2 1 :002(047) [0057] intercessor whom the **Scriptures** set before us is Christ.
AL : 0 0 :001(047) [0059] that departs from the **Scriptures** or the catholic church or
AL : 2 2 :010(050) [0061] only in defiance of the **Scriptures** but also in contradiction
AL : 2 4 :024(058) [0067] depart from the Holy **Scriptures** and diminish the glory of
AL : 2 4 :028(059) [0067] The **Scriptures** also teach that we are justified before God
AL : 2 4 :029(059) [0067] But the **Scriptures** do not allow this.
AL : 2 4 :040(061) [0069] church as seen from the **Scriptures** and the Fathers, we
AL : 2 4 :041(061) [0069] in Alexandria, the **Scriptures** are read and the doctors
AL : 2 6 :015(066) [0073] had no time to treat the **Scriptures** and seek for the more
AL : 2 6 :022(067) [0073] Our teachers add testimonies from the **Scriptures**.
AL : 2 7 :015(073) [0077] schools of the Holy **Scriptures** and other branches of
AL : 2 8 :028(085) [0087] anything contrary to the canonical **Scriptures** of God.
AL : 2 8 :035(086) [0089] Besides, it is against **Scripture** to require the observances
AL : 2 8 :049(089) [0091] traditions, why does **Scripture** so often prohibit the
AL : 2 8 :059(091) [0091] The **Scriptures**, not the church, abrogated the Sabbath,
AL : 0 0 :005(095) [0095] that is contrary to **Scripture** or to the church catholic.
AL : 0 0 :017(096) [0095] present ampler information according to the **Scriptures**.
AP : PR :008(098) [0101] they have refuted our Confession from the **Scriptures**.
AP : PR :009(099) [0101] contentions from the **Scriptures**, they have condemned
AP : PR :009(099) [0101] in opposition to the clear **Scripture** of the Holy Spirit.
AP : 0 1 :002(100) [0103] we believe that the Holy **Scriptures** testify to it firmly,
AP : 0 2 :011(102) [0109] But it is of these that the **Scripture** everywhere warns us
AP : 0 2 :016(102) [0109] In the **Scriptures** righteousness contains not merely the
AP : 0 2 :018(102) [0109] This the **Scripture** shows when it says that man was
AP : 0 2 :030(104) [0113] These opinions agree with the **Scriptures**.
AP : 0 2 :032(104) [0113] that is contrary to the **Scripture** or the church catholic,
AP : 0 2 :032(104) [0113] teachings of the **Scriptures** and the Fathers that had been
AP : 0 2 :042(105) [0115] many passages of the **Scripture** contradict them, but the
AP : 0 2 :050(106) [0119] have set forth the Holy **Scripture** and the teachings of the
AP : 0 4 :005(108) [0121] All **Scripture** should be divided into these two chief
AP : 0 4 :006(108) [0121] of the Decalogue, wherever they appear in the **Scriptures**.
AP : 0 4 :029(111) [0129] of ours not only in the **Scriptures**, but also in the Fathers.
AP : 0 4 :054(114) [0137] **Scripture** contains many pleas for mercy, and the holy
AP : 0 4 :072(117) [0141] For **Scripture** speaks both ways.
AP : 0 4 :086(119) [0147] Thus the **Scriptures** testify that we are accounted
AP : 0 4 :102(121) [0151] But the **Scripture** is full of such testimonies.
AP : 0 4 :107(122) [0153] many passages in the **Scriptures** that clearly attribute
AP : 0 4 :113(123) [0155] in the true sense, as the **Scriptures** use the word, is that
AP : 0 4 :117(123) [0155] far, on the basis of the **Scriptures** and arguments derived
AP : 0 4 :117(123) [0155] derived from the **Scriptures**, was to make clear that by
AP : 0 4 :155(128) [0165] act of worship, as the **Scriptures** often do when they
AP : 0 4 :166(130) [0169] All the **Scriptures** and the church proclaim that the law
AP : 0 4 :171(130) [0171] not only the **Scriptures** but also the holy Fathers.
AP : 0 4 :186(132) [0173] that in some places the **Scripture** presents the law, while
AP : 0 4 :188(133) [0173] We must see what the **Scriptures** ascribe to the law and
AP : 0 4 :260(145) [0195] maliciously twist the **Scriptures** to suit the man-made
AP : 0 4 :273(148) [0199] So the **Scriptures** testify in many other places.
AP : 0 4 :284(150) [0201] with the rest of the **Scripture**; for if hearts are clean and
AP : 0 4 :286(150) [0201] maliciously twist the **Scriptures** to fit their own opinions.
AP : 0 4 :286(150) [0203] add human opinions to what the words of **Scripture** say.
AP : 0 4 :304(154) [0205] This is how **Scripture** uses the word "faith," as this
AP : 0 4 :321(157) [0209] of condignity — was made up to evade the **Scriptures**
AP : 0 4 :323(157) [0209] clear testimonies in the **Scriptures** and in the Church
AP : 0 4 :326(157) [0211] **Scripture** often stresses the same thing.
AP : 0 4 :357(162) [0217] do violence not only to **Scripture** but also to the very
AP : 0 4 :365(163) [0219] about good works, the **Scriptures** often include faith, since
AP : 0 4 :371(164) [0221] works are praised in the **Scriptures** must be taken to mean
AP : 0 4 :371(164) [0221] of the heart, since the **Scriptures** do not speak of
AP : 0 4 :374(164) [0221] In this way the **Scriptures** lump together the righteousness
AP : 0 4 :376(164) [0223] such passages of the **Scriptures** in either a philosophical
AP : 0 4 :389(166) [0225] prophetic and apostolic **Scriptures**, with the holy Fathers
AP : 0 4 :392(167) [0225] The **Scriptures**, the holy Fathers, and the judgment of all
AP : 0 4 :393(167) [0225] Moreover, the **Scriptures** predicted that human traditions
AP : 0 7 :023(172) [0235] of faith, abolish the **Scriptures** by his leave, institute
AP : 0 7 :028(173) [0237] In accordance with the **Scriptures**, therefore, we maintain
AP : 0 7 :037(175) [0241] obvious throughout the **Scriptures** and we have assembled
AP : 1 0 :003(179) [0247] this would be completely foreign to the sacred **Scriptures**.
AP : 1 2 :016(184) [0257] and foreign to the Holy **Scriptures** as well as the Church
AP : 1 2 :031(186) [0259] **Scripture** speaks of these terrors, as in Ps. 38:4, 8, "For
AP : 1 2 :044(187) [0265] we must show that **Scripture** makes them the chief parts in
AP : 1 2 :049(188) [0265] passages since there are so many throughout **Scripture**?
AP : 1 2 :052(189) [0265] In this way **Scripture** makes a practice of joining these

Continued ▶

AP : 12 :053(189) [0265] other of these works is spoken of throughout **Scripture**.
AP : 12 :053(189) [0265] continually throughout **Scripture**; first it was given to
AP : 12 :081(194) [0275] and in Gal. 3:22, "The **scripture** consigned all things to
AP : 12 :083(194) [0275] every devout reader of **Scripture**, and we want to avoid
AP : 12 :106(197) [0283] make passages of **Scripture** mean whatever they want
AP : 12 :119(200) [0287] authority either in the **Scriptures** or in the ancient writers
AP : 12 :122(200) [0287] They quote many **Scripture** passages to give the
AP : 12 :122(200) [0287] idea has authority in **Scripture**, though it was unknown in
AP : 12 :131(202) [0291] The **Scripture** passages quoted by our opponents say
AP : 12 :131(202) [0291] and a distortion of the **Scriptures** to suit their opinions.
AP : 12 :133(202) [0293] that these passages of **Scripture** apply in no way to
AP : 12 :133(202) [0293] but in these passages **Scripture** requires works that are
AP : 12 :137(203) [0293] Clearly **Scripture** is speaking about obligatory works,
AP : 12 :138(203) [0293] The **Scripture** passages they quote do not say that
AP : 12 :138(203) [0293] Where does **Scripture** say this?
AP : 12 :139(203) [0295] But nowhere in Holy **Scripture** are we told that only
AP : 12 :142(204) [0295] than it requires, but **Scripture** cries out everywhere that
AP : 12 :157(207) [0301] Where does **Scripture** teach that we can be freed from
AP : 12 :157(207) [0301] we still have troubles, **Scripture** interprets them as the
AP : 12 :158(207) [0301] **Scripture** explains that Job's afflictions were not imposed
AP : 12 :174(210) [0307] But **Scripture** does not teach that only the observance of
AP : 13 :002(211) [0309] ceremonies instituted in **Scripture**, whatever their
AP : 13 :002(211) [0309] provided what is handed down in **Scripture** is preserved.
AP : 15 :004(215) [0315] **Scripture** calls traditions "doctrines of demons"
AP : 16 :011(224) [0333] because it is so out of harmony with the **Scriptures**.
AP : 16 :011(224) [0333] **Scripture** does not command holding property in
AP : 18 :004(225) [0335] without the Holy Spirit, **Scripture** calls the righteousness
AP : 18 :010(226) [0337] not our invention but the clear teaching of the **Scriptures**.
AP : 20 :005(227) [0339] endless passages from **Scripture** and the Fathers, but we
AP : 20 :010(228) [0341] find many passages in **Scripture** to set his mind at ease,
AP : 20 :012(228) [0341] opponents quote many **Scripture** passages to show why
AP : 20 :012(228) [0341] the trick of deducing from **Scripture** whatever suits them.
AP : 21 :009(230) [0345] there is no passage in **Scripture** about the dead praying,
AP : 21 :010(230) [0345] only this much, that **Scripture** does not teach us to invoke
AP : 21 :010(230) [0345] can be shown from **Scripture** for the invocation of the
AP : 21 :010(230) [0345] without proof from **Scripture**, that the saints hear the
AP : 21 :015(231) [0347] even have proof from **Scripture** for calling them
AP : 21 :018(231) [0347] produce from **Scripture** for the invocation of the saints?
AP : 21 :021(232) [0349] promise nor a command nor an example from **Scripture**.
AP : 21 :024(232) [0349] Let him produce one example or precept from **Scripture**.
AP : 21 :031(233) [0351] a Word of God nor an example from **Scripture** for this.
AP : 21 :041(235) [0355] are usually closer to **Scripture** than the more recent ones,
AP : 22 :017(238) [0361] decide, especially when **Scripture** prophesies about
AP : 23 :011(241) [0367] fact in mind, taught by **Scripture** and wisely put by the
AP : 23 :028(243) [0371] permits and approves, as the **Scriptures** abundantly testify
AP : 23 :063(248) [0381] with clear passages of **Scripture** commanding each man to
AP : 24 :003(250) [0385] that men may learn the **Scriptures** and that those who
AP : 24 :014(251) [0387] many passages of **Scripture** in defense of their errors.
AP : 24 :014(251) [0389] explain the passages of **Scripture** which they have
AP : 24 :015(252) [0389] "sacrifice" in either the **Scriptures** or the Fathers and use
AP : 24 :030(255) [0395] But **Scripture** is full of such passages which teach that
AP : 24 :053(259) [0403] The **Scripture** itself adds immediately that Christ is the
AP : 24 :061(260) [0405] also shown that the **Scripture** passages quoted against us
AP : 24 :065(261) [0407] a syllable from the **Scriptures** in support of the fairy tales
AP : 24 :066(261) [0407] we have explained the **Scripture** passages that they quote
AP : 24 :067(261) [0407] what actually agrees with the Fathers and with **Scripture**.
AP : 24 :084(264) [0413] that since the Holy **Scriptures** mention an altar, the Mass
AP : 24 :089(266) [0415] God and the example of **Scripture**, and to apply to the
AP : 24 :092(266) [0417] be proved from the **Scriptures**, and it is not safe to
AP : 24 :092(266) [0417] services in the church without the authority of **Scripture**.
AP : 24 :094(267) [0417] them against the clearest and surest passages of **Scripture**.
AP : 27 :028(274) [0429] stated in the Sacred **Scriptures** that the monastic life
AP : 27 :029(274) [0431] statement of the Sacred **Scriptures** the monastic life merits
AP : 27 :029(274) [0431] Where do the Sacred **Scriptures** talk about monastic life?
AP : 27 :029(274) [0431] is the way these good-for-nothings quote the **Scriptures**.
AP : 27 :029(274) [0431] still cite the authority of **Scripture** and even say that this
AP : 27 :029(274) [0431] say that this decree of theirs is stated in the **Scriptures**.
AP : 27 :040(276) [0433] But this passage of **Scripture** has nothing to do with the
AP : 27 :044(277) [0435] so they quote passages of **Scripture** under false pretenses.
AP : 27 :046(277) [0435] is neither commanded nor advised in the **Scriptures**.
AP : 27 :060(279) [0441] and clear passages of **Scripture**, not against the rule or the
AP : 28 :021(284) [0449] elsewhere (Acts 5:29) **Scripture** commands that we must
AP : 28 :027(285) [0451] have really refuted our Confession with the **Scriptures**.
S2 : 02 :013(295) [0467] cite any passage of the **Scriptures** that would constrain
S2 : 02 :014(295) [0467] the support of the **Scriptures** and whether the dead are to
S2 : 02 :025(297) [0469] nor does it have any precedent in the **Scriptures**.
S2 : 04 :014(301) [0475] from that of the Holy **Scriptures**, or is compared with
S3 : 01 :003(302) [0477] of the revelation in the **Scriptures** (Ps. 51:5, Rom. 5:12ff.,
S3 : 01 :010(303) [0477] be proved from the **Scriptures** that the Holy Spirit and his
S3 : 06 :005(311) [0493] agrees better with the **Scriptures**, as St. Paul himself
S3 : 08 :003(312) [0495] interpret, and twist the **Scriptures** or spoken Word
S3 : 08 :004(312) [0495] is above and contrary to the **Scriptures** or spoken Word.
S3 : 08 :006(312) [0495] not come through the **Scriptures** or the spoken word of
S3 : 08 :006(313) [0495] came upon them without the testimony of the **Scriptures**?
S3 : 12 :003(315) [0499] and above the Holy **Scriptures**, but it consists of the Word
TR : 00 :006(320) [0505] [Testimony of the **Scriptures**]
TR : 00 :042(328) [0517] are manifest, and the **Scriptures** unanimously declare
TR : 00 :082(000) [0529] these agree with Holy **Scripture**, and with the belief of the
SC : PR :018(340) [0537] many examples from the **Scriptures** to show how God
SC : 05 :029(351) [0555] passages of the **Scriptures** with which to comfort and to
SC : 09 :001(354) [0561] *certain passages of the **Scriptures**, selected for various*
SC : 09 :003(354) [0561] and teaching; for the **scripture** says, 'You shall not muzzle
LC : PR :017(361) [0573] Ten Commandments perfectly knows the entire **Scriptures**
LC : PR :018(361) [0573] much less the entire **Scriptures**, yet they pretend to know
LC : PR :018(361) [0573] a brief compend and summary of all the Holy **Scriptures**.
LC : SP :018(363) [0577] everything contained in **Scripture** is comprehended in
LC : SP :022(364) [0579] to know this much about Baptism from the **Scriptures**.
LC : SP :025(364) [0579] will be led into the **Scriptures** so they make progress
LC : 01 :035(369) [0589] records of history, as **Scripture** amply shows and as daily
LC : 01 :134(383) [0619] For, in the **Scriptures**, to have long life means not merely
LC : 01 :142(384) [0621] In the **Scriptures** they are all called fathers because in
LC : 01 :167(388) [0629] many other passages of **Scripture**, and God intends it to
LC : 01 :325(409) [0675] Thus the entire **Scriptures** have proclaimed and presented
LC : 02 :005(411) [0679] contained in the **Scriptures** and belonging to the Creed
LC : 02 :036(415) [0687] are mentioned in the **Scriptures**, such as the spirit of man,
LC : 02 :070(420) [0697] all that they learn in the **Scriptures**, and thus advance and
LC : 03 :011(421) [0701] Therefore we read in the **Scriptures** that he is angry
LC : 04 :012(438) [0735] But the **Scriptures** teach that if we piled together all the
LC : 04 :049(442) [0745] power to interpret the **Scriptures** and to know Christ,
LC : 05 :031(450) [0759] by steadfastly believing the **Scriptures** and the Gospel?
LC : 05 :076(455) [0771] feel the need, therefore, at least believe the **Scriptures**.
LC : 05 :078(455) [0771] sin, at least believe the **Scriptures**, which pronounce this
LC : 05 :079(455) [0771] then take it from the **Scriptures**, which everywhere give
LC : 05 :081(456) [0771] else than what the **Scriptures** call him, a liar and a
LC : 05 :083(456) [0773] yourself, look around a little, cling to the **Scriptures**.
EP : RN :002(465) [0777] names, should not be put on a par with Holy **Scripture**.
EP : RN :002(465) [0777] be subordinated to the **Scriptures** and should be received
EP : RN :005(465) [0777] everything which Holy **Scripture** discusses at greater
EP : RN :007(465) [0779] between the Holy **Scripture** of the Old and New
EP : RN :007(465) [0779] maintained, and Holy **Scripture** remains the only judge,
EP : RN :008(465) [0779] are not judges like Holy **Scripture**, but merely witnesses
EP : RN :008(465) [0779] various times the Holy **Scriptures** were understood by
EP : 03 :007(473) [0793] to the usage of **Scripture** the word "justify" means in this
EP : 05 :006(478) [0803] a single sense in Holy **Scripture**, and this was the original
EP : 05 :011(479) [0805] of Christ and the Holy **Scriptures** are obscured, Christians
EP : 11 :016(497) [0837] devil, since everything in **Scripture**, as St. Paul testifies,
EP : 11 :016(497) [0837] the encouragement of the **Scriptures** we might have hope.
SD : PR :006(505) [0853] clear and irrefutable testimonies from the Holy **Scriptures**
SD : PR :010(506) [0855] of the Holy **Scriptures**, refutations of errors, and
SD : PR :017(507) [0857] certain and solid basis of the holy and divine **Scriptures**.
SD : 01 :008(510) [0861] and believed from the revelation of the **Scriptures**.
SD : 01 :033(514) [0869] According to the Holy **Scriptures** we must and can
SD : 01 :034(514) [0869] in the article of creation **Scripture** testifies not only that
SD : 01 :043(515) [0873] the mighty testimony of **Scripture** that God's Son assumed
SD : 01 :044(516) [0873] Both statements are contrary to the **Scriptures**.
SD : 01 :045(516) [0873] we have the testimony of **Scripture** that God cleanses man
SD : 01 :046(516) [0873] of the resurrection **Scripture** testifies that precisely the
SD : 01 :050(517) [0875] words, as the Holy **Scriptures** and the above-mentioned
SD : 01 :060(519) [0879] Holy **Scripture** alone can lead to a right understanding
SD : 02 :010(522) [0885] In this way **Scripture** calls the natural man simply
SD : 02 :010(522) [0885] Moreover, **Scripture** teaches that the man who is "in sin"
SD : 02 :012(522) [0885] Thus **Scripture** denies to the intellect, heart, and will of
SD : 02 :019(524) [0889] this reason the Holy **Scriptures** compare the heart of
SD : 02 :025(526) [0891] In the third place, Holy **Scriptures** ascribe conversion,
SD : 02 :026(526) [0891] heart to understand the **Scriptures** and to heed the Word,
SD : 02 :026(526) [0891] he opened their minds to understand the **Scriptures**."
SD : 02 :045(530) [0899] contrary to the Holy **Scriptures** of God, the Christian
SD : 02 :060(533) [0905] This the **Scriptures** call the creation of a new heart.
SD : 02 :084(537) [0913] resistance, of which the **Scriptures** say that the desires of
SD : 02 :087(538) [0915] above from clear passages of Holy **Scripture**.
SD : 03 :017(542) [0921] of the word in the Holy **Scriptures** of the Old and the New
SD : 03 :030(544) [0925] and the grace of God, **Scripture** teaches that the
SD : 04 :014(553) [0943] Likewise, Holy **Scripture** itself uses words like "necessity,"
SD : 04 :024(555) [0945] of sound words, like the **Scripture** passage which ascribes
SD : 04 :036(557) [0949] in expounding Holy **Scripture** without in any way
SD : 05 :003(558) [0953] way, both in the Holy **Scripture** of God and by ancient
SD : 05 :007(559) [0953] is not used in a single sense in Holy **Scripture**.
SD : 06 :014(566) [0967] and St. Paul says, "All **Scripture** is inspired by God and
SD : 07 :030(574) [0981] articles through the **Scriptures**, have examined them again
SD : 07 :036(575) [0985] The **Scriptures** do the same thing when they reproduce
SD : 07 :036(575) [0985] Thus the **Scriptures** explain that the divine essence has
SD : 08 :028(596) [1025] maintain without proof from the Holy **Scriptures**.
SD : 08 :041(599) [1029] person in Christ, the **Scriptures** ascribe to the deity,
SD : 08 :050(600) [1031] the testimony of the **Scripture** points in that direction.
SD : 08 :051(600) [1031] The Holy **Scriptures**, and the ancient Fathers on the basis
SD : 08 :051(600) [1031] on the basis of the **Scriptures**, testify mightily that,
SD : 08 :053(601) [1033] life, and wherever the **Scriptures** in this case give us clear,
SD : 08 :054(601) [1033] the majesty which the **Scriptures**, and the ancient Fathers
SD : 08 :054(601) [1033] Fathers on the basis of **Scriptures**, ascribe to the assumed
SD : 08 :055(601) [1033] to the statement of the **Scriptures** these properties have
SD : 08 :057(602) [1035] that whatever the **Scriptures** testify that Christ received in
SD : 08 :058(602) [1035] 2. In the second place, **Scripture** testifies clearly
SD : 08 :059(602) [1035] 3. In the third place, **Scripture** not only speaks in general
SD : 08 :060(602) [1035] According to the **Scriptures** we should and must believe
SD : 08 :061(602) [1035] passages of the Holy **Scriptures**, namely, that such divine
SD : 08 :062(603) [1037] ancient approved councils on the basis of the **Scriptures**.
SD : 08 :064(603) [1037] doctrine on the basis of **Scripture**, that the human nature
SD : 08 :067(604) [1039] the testimonies of the **Scriptures** which speak of the
SD : 08 :077(606) [1043] The **Scriptures** ascribe such presence only to Christ, and
SD : 08 :096(609) [1049] Since the Holy **Scriptures** call Christ a mystery over which
SD : 11 :002(616) [1063] because the Holy **Scriptures** mention this article not only
SD : 11 :003(616) [1063] set forth the correct meaning on the basis of **Scripture**.
SD : 11 :012(618) [1067] foundation: All **Scripture**, inspired by God, should
SD : 11 :012(618) [1067] encouragement of the **Scriptures** we might have hope"
SD : 11 :012(618) [1067] So, too, **Scripture** presents this doctrine in no other way
SD : 11 :024(619) [1069] According to the **Scriptures** all this is included in the
SD : 11 :024(620) [1071] When we follow the **Scriptures** and organize our thinking
SD : 11 :032(621) [1073] In the same vein Holy **Scripture** also assures us that God
SD : 11 :076(628) [1087] correct and true what **Scripture** states, that no one comes
SD : 11 :092(632) [1093] encouragement of the **Scriptures** we might have hope"
SD : 11 :092(632) [1093] interpretation of the **Scriptures** which weakens or even

Scruff (1)
LC : 01 :239(397) [0649] such offenders by the **scruff** of the neck so that others

Scruples (1), Scrupulous (1)
AL : 25 :007(062) [0069] not be burdened with a **scrupulous** enumeration of all
AP : 15 :026(219) [0323] so that many perform them with **scruples** of conscience.

Sea (5)
AP : 27 :046(277) [0435] for throwing a great weight of gold into the **sea**.
LC : 03 :123(436) [0731] doubts is like a wave of the **sea** that is driven and tossed
SD : 08 :027(596) [1025] God but also as man, from **sea** to sea and to the ends of
SD : 08 :027(596) [1025] also as man, from sea to **sea** and to the ends of the earth,
SD : 10 :016(614) [1059] his neck and to be drowned in the depth of the **sea**."

Seal (8), Sealed (1), Seals (6)
PR : PR :027(014) [0025] hereto and ordered our privy **seals** impressed hereon.
AP : 2 4 :049(258) [0401] use of the sacrament as a **seal** and witness of the free
AP : 2 4 :070(262) [0409] is a sort of picture or "**seal**," as Paul calls it (Rom. 4:11),
S3 : 0 3 :028(308) [0487] true, and there are **seals**, letters, and examples to show it.
LC : 0 1 :302(405) [0667] with letters patent and the **seal** of the prince attesting that
LC : 0 3 :097(433) [0725] promise and hast set thy **seal** to it, making it as certain as
LC : 0 4 :009(437) [0733] by virtue of his letters and **seals**, then we ought to regard
EP : 0 7 :029(485) [0815] no more than reminders, **seals**, and pledges to assure us
EP : 1 1 :013(496) [0835] with his oath, and has **sealed** it with his holy sacraments,
EP : 1 2 :023(500) [0841] which the Lord God **seals** the adoption of children and
SD : 0 2 :089(538) [0915] out of it, or wax when a **seal** is impressed into it, for these
SD : 0 7 :044(577) [0987] and all of his blessings, a **seal** of the new covenant, a
SD : 0 7 :053(579) [0991] whereby I establish, **seal**, and confirm with you people
SD : 1 1 :037(622) [1075] which he has attached as a **seal** of the promise and by
SD : 1 2 :031(635) [1101] whereby the Lord God **seals** the adoption of sons and

Search (5)
SC : 0 5 :024(350) [0555] not worry, nor should he **search** for and invent other
LC : 0 1 :028(368) [0587] **Search** and examine your own heart thoroughly and you
LC : 0 1 :043(370) [0591] Reflect on the past, **search** it out, and tell me, When men
LC : 0 1 :332(410) [0677] Commandments, and no one need **search** far for them.
SD : 0 4 :011(553) [0941] blindly tapping around in **search** of faith and good works

Season (1), Seasonable (1), Seasons (3)
AP : 1 5 :020(218) [0321] For different **seasons** and various rites serve as reminders
AP : 1 5 :048(221) [0329] of certain foods and **seasons** contributes nothing to the
AP : 1 6 :006(223) [0331] to the laws of the **seasons** and to the change of winter and
SC : 0 3 :014(347) [0549] good government; **seasonable** weather, peace and health,
SC : 0 8 :007(353) [0559] O Lord, and Thou givest them their food in due **season**.

Seat (10), Seated (4)
PR : PR :018(009) [0015] before the judgment **seat** of our Lord Jesus Christ with
PR : PR :021(010) [0019] of Christ, in that it is **seated** at the right hand of God and
AG : 0 8 :001(033) [0047] "The Pharisees sit on Moses' **seat**" (Matt. 23:2).
AL : 0 8 :001(033) [0047] and Pharisees sit on Moses' **seat**," etc. (Matt. 23:2).
AP : 0 7 :004(169) [0227] Antichrist will "take his **seat** in the temple of God"
S1 : PR :009(290) [0457] day, before the judgment **seat** of Christ, who in their
S1 : 0 1 :000(292) [0461] to heaven; and he is **seated** at the right hand of God, will
TR : 0 0 :039(327) [0515] so that he takes his **seat** in the temple of God,
SC : 0 2 :003(345) [0545] *into heaven, and is* ***seated*** *on the right hand of God, the*
LC : 0 2 :025(413) [0683] *into heaven, and is* ***seated*** *on the right hand of God, the*
LC : 0 3 :103(434) [0727] everyone wants to sit in the chief **seat** and be seen by all.
LC : 0 4 :086(446) [0753] As Christ, the mercy-**seat**, does not recede from us or
SD : 0 7 :029(574) [0981] appear before the judgment **seat** of our Lord Jesus Christ.
SD : 1 2 :040(636) [1103] hearts before the judgment **seat** of Jesus Christ and for

Sebastian (2)
AP : 2 1 :032(233) [0351] Anne grants riches, **Sebastian** wards off pestilence,
LC : 0 1 :011(366) [0583] the plague, he made a vow to St. **Sebastian** or Roch.

Second (98), Secondly (15)
PR : PR :019(009) [0017] As far as the **second** edition of the Augsburg Confession,
PR : PR :019(009) [0017] the words of this same **second** edition and in their open
PR : PR :019(009) [0017] or accepted the **second** edition in any other sense than
AG : 2 4 :028(059) [0067] In the **second** place, St. Paul taught that we obtain grace
AG : 2 6 :008(065) [0071] In the **second** place, such traditions have also obscured
AL : 2 0 :036(046) [0057] do the works of the First or **Second** Commandments.
AL : 2 3 :005(051) [0061] In the **second** place, Christ said, "Not all men can receive
AL : 2 6 :008(065) [0071] In the **second** place, these precepts obscured the
AL : 2 7 :027(075) [0079] In the **second** place, why do our adversaries exaggerate
AP : 0 2 :016(102) [0109] contains not merely the **second** table of the Decalogue,
AP : 0 4 :034(111) [0129] commandments of the **second** table, which contain the
AP : 0 4 :082(118) [0145] **Second**, it is certain that sins are forgiven because of
AP : 0 4 :131(125) [0157] They look at the **second** table and political works; about
AP : 0 4 :204(135) [0177] **Secondly**, they still do not find peace of conscience in
AP : 0 4 :224(138) [0181] God by the works of the **Second** Table, through which we
AP : 0 4 :224(138) [0181] of this happens through the works of the **Second** Table.
AP : 0 4 :231(139) [0183] God to the works of the **Second** Table rather than the
AP : 0 4 :246(142) [0189] **Second**, the context demonstrates that the works spoken
AP : 0 4 :256(144) [0193] **Secondly**, though men can at most do certain outward
AP : 0 4 :267(146) [0197] **Secondly**, because Daniel clearly sets forth a promise, he
AP : 0 4 :290(151) [0203] The **second** contains much that is harmful.
AP : 0 4 :297(152) [0205] God nor love God; and **second**, we are justified by the
AP : 0 4 :319(156) [0209] **Second**, the opponents' teaching leaves consciences in
AP : 0 4 :339(159) [0215] objects of trust in the first are unlike those in the **second**.
AP : 0 4 :339(159) [0215] in our own works; in the **second**, trust is a trust in the
AP : 0 9 :003(178) [0245] **Secondly**, since it is evident that God approves the
AP : 1 2 :001(182) [0253] They condemn the **second** part, in which we say that
AP : 1 2 :001(182) [0253] and they deny that faith is the **second** part of penitence.
AP : 1 2 :035(186) [0261] As the **second** part of our consideration of penitence, we
AP : 1 2 :049(188) [0265] contrition, while the **second** describes how we are revived
AP : 1 2 :050(189) [0265] sentences the first part means contrition, the **second** faith.
AP : 1 2 :057(189) [0267] This was the **second** part of her penance, the faith that
AP : 1 2 :063(191) [0269] **Second**, we suppose our opponents will grant that the
AP : 1 2 :134(202) [0293] **Secondly**, our opponents write that if a penitent refuses to
AP : 1 2 :145(205) [0297] satisfy God's law; and **second**, because they add human
AP : 1 5 :001(215) [0315] completely condemn the **second** part, where we say that
AP : 2 1 :005(229) [0345] The **second** honor is the strengthening of our faith: when
AP : 2 1 :009(230) [0345] dream recorded in the **Second** Book of the Maccabees
AP : 2 1 :019(231) [0347] The **second** qualification in a propitiator is this: His
AP : 2 1 :022(232) [0349] They tell us, **secondly**, to trust in the merits of the saints.
AP : 2 3 :009(240) [0367] ***Second***, because this creation or divine ordinance in man
AP : 2 3 :035(244) [0373] In the **second** place, the proper contrast is between lust
AP : 2 3 :064(248) [0381] The **second** argument of our opponents is that priests
AP : 2 4 :068(261) [0407] In the **second** place, Christ was supposed to be very
AP : 2 4 :075(263) [0411] nature of the sacrament, and the **second** to the sacrifice.
AP : 2 4 :089(266) [0415] name of God in violation of the **Second** Commandment.
AP : 2 7 :021(272) [0427] **Second**, obedience, poverty, and celibacy, provided they
AP : 2 7 :032(274) [0431] In the **second** place, eternal life is given by mercy for
AP : 2 7 :032(274) [0431] by God's indulgence; **secondly**, that you cannot have any
S2 : 0 0 :000(292) [0461] The **second** part treats the articles which pertain to the
S2 : 0 2 :016(295) [0467] The **second** is a consequence of this: evil spirits have
S3 : 0 4 :000(310) [0491] to the whole world; **second**, through Baptism; third,
TR : 0 0 :031(325) [0513] The **second** article is even clearer than the first because
TR : 0 0 :040(327) [0517] **Second**, because he assumes for himself not only the
TR : 0 0 :053(329) [0519] Then, in the **second** place, they should also know how
SC : PR :014(339) [0535] In the **second** place, after the people have become
SC : PR :016(340) [0535] proceed to the **Second** Commandment, and so on.
SC : 0 1 :003(342) [0539] The **Second**
SC : 0 2 :003(345) [0545] The **Second** Article: Redemption
SC : 0 3 :006(346) [0547] The **Second** Petition
SC : 0 4 :005(348) [0551] **Second**
LC : 0 1 :048(371) [0593] The **Second** Commandment
LC : 0 1 :051(371) [0595] "How do you understand the **Second** Commandment?
LC : 0 1 :075(375) [0601] God so that the First and **Second** commandments may
LC : 0 1 :084(376) [0605] **Secondly** and most especially, we keep holy days so that
LC : 0 1 :103(379) [0611] **Secondly**, we should not misuse his holy name in support
LC : 0 1 :112(380) [0613] In the **second** place, notice what a great, good, and holy
LC : 0 1 :189(390) [0635] In the **second** place, this commandment is violated not
LC : 0 1 :211(393) [0641] In the **second** place, remember that it is not only an
LC : 0 1 :326(409) [0675] For example, in the **Second** Commandment we are told to
LC : 0 2 :000(411) [0679] **Second** Part: The Creed
LC : 0 2 :006(411) [0679] explains creation; the **second**, of the Son, redemption; the
LC : 0 2 :024(413) [0683] The **Second** Article
LC : 0 2 :026(413) [0685] we learn to know the **second** person of the Godhead, and
LC : 0 2 :027(414) [0685] do you believe in the **Second** Article, concerning Jesus
LC : 0 3 :005(420) [0699] We were told in the **Second** Commandment, "You shall
LC : 0 3 :008(421) [0699] To pray, as the **Second** Commandment teaches, is to call
LC : 0 3 :015(422) [0701] The **Second** Commandment is given just as much on my
LC : 0 3 :019(423) [0703] In the **second** place, we should be all the more urged and
LC : 0 3 :045(426) [0709] that God demands in the **Second** Commandment: that his
LC : 0 3 :048(426) [0711] The **Second** Petition
LC : 0 3 :053(427) [0711] the Word and faith, and **secondly**, in eternity, it comes
LC : 0 4 :023(439) [0737] In the **second** place, since we now know what Baptism is
LC : 0 4 :081(446) [0751] wrote, "Repentance is the **second** plank on which we
LC : 0 5 :001(447) [0753] so we must deal with the **second** sacrament in the same
LC : 0 5 :064(454) [0769] In the **second** place, a promise is attached to the
LC : 0 6 :010(458) [0000] Similarly the **second** confession, which each Christian
LC : 0 6 :015(459) [0000] The **second** is a work which God does, when he absolves
LC : 0 6 :016(459) [0000] the very necessary **second** part; it was just as if our
EP : 0 2 :001(469) [0785] about man's will and ability in the **second** state.
EP : 0 4 :003(475) [0797] 2. The **second** controversy arose among certain
EP : 0 7 :012(483) [0811] "The **second** ground is: "God's right hand is everywhere.
SD : PR :018(507) [0857] 2. In the **second** place, we reject and condemn all the
SD : 0 1 :007(510) [0861] In the **second** place, it is also a clearly established truth,
SD : 0 1 :043(515) [0873] **Secondly**, in the article of our redemption we have the
SD : 0 2 :017(523) [0887] In the **second** place, the Word of God testifies that in
SD : 0 2 :023(525) [0889] in a similar vein in his **second** book *Against Julian.*
SD : 0 2 :041(529) [0897] in the exposition of the **second** petition of the Lord's
SD : 0 3 :032(544) [0927] of faith and, **second**, also the inchoate righteousness of
SD : 0 3 :048(548) [0933] of sins and, as a **second** element, renewal or
SD : 0 4 :021(554) [0945] **Secondly**, when we teach that good works are necessary
SD : 0 7 :016(572) [0977] "**Secondly**, they hold that it is the institution of this
SD : 0 7 :095(586) [1005] "2. The **second** is that the right hand of God is
SD : 0 7 :100(586) [1005] "2. There is, **secondly**, the incomprehensible, spiritual
SD : 0 7 :101(587) [1007] to him than they are according to the **second** mode.
SD : 0 7 :101(587) [1007] For if according to the **second** mode he can be present in
SD : 0 7 :109(588) [1011] **Secondly**, we also reject and condemn all other papistic
SD : 0 8 :046(600) [1031] In the **second** place, as far as the discharge of Christ's
SD : 0 8 :058(602) [1035] 2. In the **second** place, Scripture testifies clearly
SD : 0 8 :073(605) [1041] to the Godhead is the **second** person in the holy Trinity
SD : 0 8 :085(608) [1045] states: "According to the **second**, temporal, human birth,
SD : 1 1 :027(620) [1071] some at first, some at the **second**, at the third, at the
SD : 1 1 :083(630) [1091] and believe in Christ; **second**, that he would punish those

Secret (20), Secretly (6), Secrets (2)
AP : 1 2 :104(197) [0283] they do not have the command to investigate **secret** sins.
AP : 1 2 :106(197) [0283] "condition" means the **secrets** of conscience and not
AP : 1 2 :112(198) [0285] of penitence, not about this enumeration of **secret** sins.
AP : 2 3 :052(246) [0377] It is no **secret** how harmful this law has been to public
S3 : 0 7 :001(311) [0493] which are subtle and **secret** and which God alone
LC : 0 1 :053(372) [0595] when two persons **secretly** betroth themselves to each
LC : 0 1 :059(372) [0597] We prefer to act in **secret** without anyone's being aware
LC : 0 1 :214(394) [0641] shameless fornication or **secretly** do even worse — things
LC : 0 1 :215(394) [0641] incessant ragings of **secret** passion, which can be avoided
LC : 0 1 :272(401) [0657] In short, what is **secret** should be allowed to remain
LC : 0 1 :272(401) [0657] be allowed to remain **secret**, or at any rate be reproved in
LC : 0 1 :272(401) [0659] or at any rate be reproved in **secret**, as we shall hear.
LC : 0 1 :283(403) [0661] would not sneak about in **secret**, shunning the light of
LC : 0 1 :284(403) [0661] All this refers to **secret** sins.
LC : 0 6 :013(458) [0000] there is also the **secret** confession which takes place
EP : 1 1 :006(495) [0833] this predestination in the **secret** counsel of God, but it is
EP : 1 2 :031(500) [0843] and that we shall neither **secretly** nor publicly say or write
SD : 0 1 :036(514) [0869] when I was being made in **secret**, intricately wrought in
SD : 0 2 :010(522) [0885] been given to know the **secrets** of the kingdom of God"
SD : 0 7 :001(568) [0971] Confession no longer **secretly** but in part openly approved
SD : 0 8 :038(598) [1027] But since **secret** as well as open Sacramentarians hide
SD : 1 0 :011(612) [1055] because of false brethren **secretly** brought in, who slipped
SD : 1 1 :009(617) [1065] to eternal life only in the **secret** and inscrutable counsel of
SD : 1 1 :013(618) [1067] concerning the absolute, **secret**, hidden, and inscrutable
SD : 1 1 :026(620) [1071] to try to explore the **secret** and hidden abyss of divine
SD : 1 1 :070(627) [1085] thoughts concerning the **secret** counsel of God, if he has
SD : 1 1 :086(631) [1091] eternal life, or that in his **secret** counsel God had ordained
SD : 1 2 :008(633) [1097] insinuated themselves **secretly**, after the fashion of these

Sect (5), Sectarians (2), Sects (14)
S2 : 0 4 :007(299) [0473] against the attacks of **sects** and heresies; and suppose that
S2 : 0 4 :008(299) [0473] There would be even more **sects** than before because,
LC : 0 2 :051(417) [0691] of gifts, yet is united in love without **sect** or schism.
LC : 0 3 :047(426) [0709] that the world is full of **sects** and false teachers, all of
LC : 0 4 :002(437) [0733] against heretics and **sectarians** we shall leave to the
LC : 0 4 :007(437) [0733] the world now is full of **sects** who proclaim that Baptism
LC : 0 4 :047(442) [0743] the world through his **sects**, the question of infant
LC : 0 4 :055(443) [0745] So you see that the objection of the **sectarians** is absurd.
EP : RN :004(465) [0777] papacy and against other **sects**, and as the symbol of our

Continued ▶

EP : 1 2 :000(498) [0839] XII. Other Factions and **Sects** Which Have Not
EP : 1 2 :029(500) [0843] This is an entirely new **sect**, unknown in Christendom
SD : PR :005(504) [0851] against the aberrations of the papacy and of other **sects**.
SD : PR :005(504) [0851] the papacy and from other condemned **sects** and heresies.
SD : PR :009(505) [0853] established against the papacy and other **sects**.
SD : PR :018(507) [0857] and condemn all the **sects** and heresies that are rejected in
SD : 0 8 :075(606) [1043] Valens there was a peculiar **sect** among the Arians, called
SD : 0 8 :075(606) [1043] Against this **sect** Gregory the Great also wrote.
SD : 1 2 :000(632) [1095] XII. Other Factions and **Sects** Which Never Accepted the
SD : 1 2 :001(632) [1095] As far as the **sects** and factions are concerned which
SD : 1 2 :007(633) [1097] errors of the aforementioned factions and **sects**.
SD : 1 2 :027(635) [1101] The entire **sect**, however, can be characterized as basically

Secular (20)
AG : 2 6 :010(065) [0071] works were considered **secular** and unspiritual: the works
AG : 2 6 :011(065) [0071] were to be regarded as **secular** and imperfect, while
AL : 2 6 :010(065) [0071] These were regarded as **secular** and imperfect works, far
AP : 0 7 :022(172) [0235] whether ecclesiastical or **secular**, because princes and
AP : 1 1 :008(181) [0251] were enacted between the **secular** and the regular clergy
AP : 1 2 :120(200) [0287] see that this was a discipline, and a **secular** one at that.
AP : 1 2 :120(200) [0287] the spiritual and the **secular** improperly, so also in the
AP : 1 2 :177(210) [0307] But the reservation of cases is a **secular** matter.
AP : 1 5 :035(220) [0325] before God in observing **secular** customs, if soldiers wear
AP : 2 4 :068(262) [0407] But this is a **secular** idea that ignores the chief use of
AP : 2 4 :068(262) [0409] which even profane and **secular** men understand; it does
S 1 : PR :013(290) [0459] of the ecclesiastical and **secular** estates as are contrary to
S 2 : 0 3 :001(298) [0471] who are necessary for **secular** government in cities and
S 2 : 0 4 :001(298) [0471] a human institution (that is, a **secular** government).
S 2 : 0 4 :003(298) [0471] (except what pertains to **secular** government, where God
S 2 : 0 4 :014(301) [0475] is a teaching concerning **secular** transactions and
S 2 : 0 4 :016(301) [0475] the emperor or the **secular** authority, as at Augsburg,
EP : 1 2 :002(498) [0839] or in the body politic and **secular** administration, or in
SD : 0 2 :019(524) [0889] in outward or external **secular** things he cannot have a
SD : 0 2 :020(524) [0889] comments on Ps. 91: "In **secular** and external matters

Secure (12), Secured (2), Securely (3)
PR : PR :008(005) [0009] as far as we might, to **secure** our posterity in the future
AG : 2 8 :041(087) [0089] unless forgiveness is **secured** from the person for whom
AP : 2 4 :013(251) [0387] of guilt and punishment, **secure** whatever they need in
AP : 2 7 :065(280) [0441] forgiveness of sins or to **secure** eternal life for us instead
TR : 0 0 :043(328) [0517] are shamelessly employed to **secure** disgraceful profits.
LC : 0 1 :005(365) [0581] boasts so stubbornly and **securely** that he cares for no
LC : 0 1 :007(365) [0583] money and property feels **secure**, happy, fearless, as if he
LC : 0 1 :010(366) [0583] how presumptuous, **secure**, and proud people become
LC : 0 1 :045(370) [0593] man; but once he was **secure** on his throne and he let his
LC : 0 1 :046(370) [0593] his life nowhere **secure**, yet inevitably he remained safe
LC : 0 1 :206(393) [0639] but here, as I said, he has **secured** it and protected it.
LC : 0 1 :301(405) [0667] them, and they gain such **secure** title to the property as to
LC : 0 3 :070(429) [0717] no matter how proud, **secure**, and powerful they think
LC : 0 3 :109(435) [0729] we shall not go about **securely** and heedlessly as if the
LC : 0 5 :082(456) [0773] reason we go about so **securely** and heedlessly is that we
SD : 0 3 :042(547) [0931] (since many lazy and **secure** Christians delude themselves
SD : 0 5 :009(559) [0955] of sin to indifferent and **secure** hearts, but to the

Security (14)
AP : 0 2 :011(102) [0109] namely, carnal **security**, contempt of God, hate of God,
AP : 0 2 :024(103) [0111] judgment of God in its **security**, or it hates him in its
AP : 1 2 :032(186) [0259] against sin, unknown to men who walk in carnal **security**.
LC : PR :005(359) [0567] and insidious plague of **security** and boredom has
LC : PR :019(361) [0573] against the poisonous infection of such **security** or vanity.
LC : 0 1 :033(369) [0589] lest men live in **security** and commit themselves to luck,
LC : 0 1 :037(369) [0591] from disturbing their **security**, that he is unconcerned or
LC : 0 1 :150(385) [0625] gives us food, house and home, protection and **security**.
LC : 0 2 :015(412) [0681] temporal blessings — good government, peace, **security**.
LC : 0 3 :074(430) [0719] of them or enjoy them in **security** or happiness unless he
LC : 0 3 :104(434) [0727] us into unbelief, false **security**, and stubbornness, or, on
SD : 0 2 :021(525) [0889] continues in his carnal **security** — even knowingly and
SD : 1 1 :010(618) [1065] minds either false **security** and impenitence or anxiety and
SD : 1 1 :012(618) [1067] should minister not to **security** and impenitence but "to

Sed (1)
LC : 0 4 :059(444) [0747] goes, *"Abusus non tollit, **sed** confirmat substantiam,"*

Sedition (1), Seditious (6)
AP : 0 7 :050(178) [0245] We regard as utterly **seditious** those who have incited
AP : 0 9 :002(178) [0245] against the wicked and **seditious** faction of these robbers.
LC : 0 1 :262(400) [0655] heretics, apostates, even **seditious** and accursed
LC : 0 3 :031(424) [0707] their murderous and **seditious** designs by which the devil
LC : 0 3 :080(431) [0721] contention, murder, **sedition**, and war, why he sends
LC : 0 4 :062(444) [0749] Here lurks a sneaky, **seditious** devil who would like to
LC : 0 5 :007(447) [0755] all the babbling of the **seditious** spirits who regard the

Seduces (1), Seductive (1)
PR : PR :022(011) [0019] condemn only false and **seductive** doctrines and their
LC : 0 5 :081(456) [0773] A liar who **seduces** the heart from God's Word and blinds

See (181), Saw (13), Seeing (3), Seen (24), Sees (18) (*See below for the Roman "See"*)
PR : PR :010(006) [0011] these developments, they **saw** clearly that there was no
PR : PR :018(009) [0015] so that everyone may **see** that we were not minded to
PR : PR :026(014) [0025] or new ones arise, we shall **see** to it that they are settled
AG : 2 0 :033(045) [0057] We **see** this in the philosophers who undertook to lead
AG : 2 1 :001(046) [0057] be strengthened when we **see** what grace they received and
AG : 0 0 :002(048) [0059] since this our confession is **seen** to be godly and
AG : 2 3 :025(055) [0065] their lusts, and they should **see** to it that they do not give
AG : 2 5 :010(063) [0069] view of the Fathers can be **seen** in Dist. I, *De*
AG : 2 5 :011(063) [0071] Here it can be clearly **seen** that Chrysostom does not
AG : 2 6 :014(066) [0073] We can **see** in the writings of the summists and canonists
AG : 2 7 :008(072) [0077] past, for they must have **seen** that both boys and girls
AG : 2 7 :008(072) [0077] They must also have **seen** what evils came from this
AL : 2 0 :033(045) [0057] This we may **see** in the philosophers, who, although they
AL : 2 0 :035(046) [0057] Hence it may readily be **seen** that this teaching is not to
AL : 0 0 :001(047) [0059] As can be **seen**, there is nothing here that departs from
AL : 2 4 :040(061) [0069] example of the church as **seen** from the Scriptures and
AL : 2 6 :014(066) [0073] We **see** that the summists and theologians gathered the
AL : 2 6 :022(067) [0073] a tradition which was **seen** to be legalistic and to have a
AL : 2 7 :008(072) [0077] before our time when they **saw** that girls and boys were
AL : 2 7 :008(072) [0077] for their maintenance and **saw** what unfortunately
AL : 2 8 :038(087) [0089] increased, and we can still **see** some traces of these in the
AL : 2 8 :078(094) [0095] do not do this, they must **see** to it how they will answer
AP : PR :002(098) [0099] To **see** what our opponents condemned and to refute
AP : PR :004(098) [0099] they had not even **seen** — and one that was supposed to
AP : PR :014(099) [0101] But recently, when I **saw** the Confutation, I realized it
AP : 0 2 :001(100) [0105] His Imperial Majesty will **see** that the authors of the
AP : 0 2 :008(102) [0107] And they do not **see** the contradiction.
AP : 0 2 :011(102) [0109] Who cannot **see** the foolishness of our opponents'
AP : 0 2 :012(102) [0109] But thereby they failed to **see** the inner uncleanness of
AP : 0 2 :031(104) [0113] reader will easily be able to **see** that when the fear of God
AP : 0 2 :039(105) [0115] And again, "I **see** in my members another law at war with
AP : 0 4 :015(109) [0123] We **see** that there are books in existence which compare
AP : 0 4 :034(112) [0129] Meanwhile they do not **see** the first table, which
AP : 0 4 :036(112) [0131] wrath cannot love him unless it **sees** that he is reconciled.
AP : 0 4 :059(115) [0137] so little of faith when they **see** it praised everywhere as the
AP : 0 4 :087(120) [0147] the ability that the Lord **saw** fit to grant us, we conclude
AP : 0 4 :118(123) [0155] One can easily **see** how necessary it is to understand this
AP : 0 4 :121(124) [0155] faith, our opponents fail to **see** that thereby they destroy
AP : 0 4 :135(125) [0159] Only then do we **see** how far we are from keeping the
AP : 0 4 :188(133) [0173] We must **see** what the Scriptures ascribe to the law and
AP : 0 4 :203(135) [0177] When such a person **sees** the works of the saints, he
AP : 0 4 :207(135) [0177] Here we **see** how vehemently the prophets rebuke the
AP : 0 4 :208(135) [0177] The people of Israel had **seen** the prophets sacrifice on
AP : 0 4 :229(139) [0183] wisdom, they did not **see** the true face of Moses but only
AP : 0 4 :241(141) [0187] of hatred, as we often **see** the greatest tragedies come from
AP : 0 4 :244(141) [0189] they quote the text, "You **see** that a man is justified by
AP : 0 4 :265(146) [0197] admires them; because it **sees** only works and neither
AP : 0 4 :266(146) [0197] We **see** that the Gospel and the promise of Christ are
AP : 0 4 :298(153) [0205] that we are astonished to **see** how furiously our
AP : 0 4 :299(153) [0205] faithful consciences **see** the most complete consolation
AP : 0 4 :303(154) [0205] Sensible people can easily **see** that a faith which believes
AP : 0 4 :310(155) [0207] Father, that everyone who **sees** the Son and believes in
AP : 0 4 :343(160) [0217] Everyone can **see** that this passage condemns trust in our
AP : 0 4 :356(161) [0217] seem to our opponents to be in conflict, let them **see** to it.
AP : 0 4 :358(162) [0219] Who cannot **see** that this is a fallacious conclusion?
AP : 0 4 :394(167) [0225] that reason can **see** is the righteousness of the law,
AP : 0 4 :398(167) [0227] Who does not **see** that this doctrine—that by faith we
AP : 0 7 :009(169) [0229] We **see** the infinite dangers that threaten the church with
AP : 0 7 :029(173) [0237] Nor do we **see** how it could be defined otherwise, since
AP : 0 7 :046(177) [0243] But **see** what religious men our opponents are!
AP : 1 0 :001(179) [0247] with those things that are **seen**, the bread and the wine, to
AP : 1 0 :004(180) [0247] offered with those things that are **seen**, bread and wine.
AP : 1 2 :003(182) [0253] All good men will **see** that especially on this issue we have
AP : 1 2 :003(182) [0253] They will **see** that the writings of our theologians have
AP : 1 2 :032(186) [0259] It **sees** the foulness of sin and is genuinely sorry that it
AP : 1 2 :045(188) [0263] You **see** that here, too, the two parts are combined:
AP : 1 2 :048(188) [0265] seriously, for they neither **see** nor read the sentence of the
AP : 1 2 :052(189) [0265] We cannot **see** how the nature of penitence could be
AP : 1 2 :058(189) [0267] passages godly readers can **see** that we put into penitence
AP : 1 2 :061(190) [0269] from confession, we fail to **see** what value there is in
AP : 1 2 :062(190) [0269] We do not **see** how anyone can be said to receive
AP : 1 2 :087(195) [0277] and from this they will **see** why we said above that men
AP : 1 2 :095(196) [0281] an anxious conscience **sees** that these works are not good
AP : 1 2 :120(200) [0287] The scholastics **saw** that there were satisfactions in the
AP : 1 2 :120(200) [0287] that is, they did not **see** that this was a discipline, and a
AP : 1 2 :125(201) [0289] with your wisdom, to **see** to it that on such important
AP : 1 2 :126(201) [0289] You **see**, Campegius, that these are the last times, in
AP : 1 2 :142(204) [0295] They do not **see** that it requires us to love God "with all
AP : 1 2 :147(205) [0297] They do not **see** how, in the remission of guilt, faith frees
AP : 1 2 :158(207) [0301] terrified consciences **see** only God's punishment and
AP : 1 2 :178(211) [0307] of our opponents, they will **see** that our opponents have
AP : 1 2 :178(211) [0309] They will **see**, too, that our opponents have made up a
AP : 1 4 :002(214) [0315] Let them **see** to it how they will answer to God for
AP : 1 6 :008(223) [0333] Thus they failed to **see** that the Gospel brings eternal
AP : 1 8 :005(225) [0335] is rare among men, as we **see** from the fact that even
AP : 2 0 :006(227) [0339] We **see** that a horrible decree has been drawn up against
AP : 2 0 :006(227) [0339] Now that we **see** in our conscience that our opponents are
AP : 2 0 :012(228) [0341] Now you **see**, dear reader, that our opponents have
AP : 2 1 :002(229) [0343] These asses do not **see** that in the controversy between
AP : 2 1 :005(229) [0345] of our faith: when we **see** Peter forgiven after his denial,
AP : 2 1 :026(232) [0349] Some of us have **seen** a certain monastic theologian,
AP : 2 1 :034(234) [0353] In one monastery we **saw** a statue of the blessed Virgin
AP : 2 1 :036(234) [0353] hear of these things and to **see** some examples of mercy.
AP : 2 1 :041(235) [0355] outset did so because they **saw** that he was freeing human
AP : 2 3 :005(239) [0365] Now we **see** the correctness of Peter's warning
AP : 2 3 :026(243) [0371] reasons, since they **see** that it is not being observed, still
AP : 2 3 :052(246) [0377] or for those whom they **saw** in danger, but none of the
AP : 2 3 :070(249) [0383] Then you will **see** the emptiness of our opponents'
AP : 2 4 :023(253) [0391] an offering for sin, he shall **see** his offspring, he shall
AP : 2 4 :026(254) [0393] We **see** this from the phrase, "Through him let us offer,"
AP : 2 4 :039(257) [0399] *ex opere operato*, we can **see** that their real meaning is
AP : 2 4 :041(257) [0399] Now good men can easily **see** the falsity of the charge
AP : 2 4 :061(260) [0405] Good men in every country can **see** this.
AP : 2 4 :074(262) [0409] a conscience to **see** its liberation from terror, then it really
AP : 2 4 :095(267) [0417] came back to life now and **saw** their sayings being twisted
AP : 2 7 :001(268) [0419] We have **seen** his writings, and from them the nature of
AP : 2 7 :019(272) [0425] passage, you would have **seen** to it that such blasphemy
AP : 2 8 :003(281) [0443] churches, and they do not **see** to it that there is proper
AP : 2 8 :005(281) [0445] But here you should **see** the tears of the sufferers and
AP : 2 8 :005(281) [0445] God undoubtedly **sees** and hears them, and it is to him
AP : 2 8 :018(284) [0449] We do not **see** what possible objection there can be to
S 1 : PR :003(289) [0455] that the pope prefers to **see** all Christendom lost and all
S 1 : PR :010(290) [0457] I should be very happy to **see** a true council assemble in
S 1 : PR :010(290) [0457] dioceses of the papists we **see** so many vacant and
S 3 : 0 3 :018(306) [0483] Here we **see** how blind reason gropes about in matters
S 3 : 0 3 :018(306) [0483] this in the light, we **see** that such contrition is an artificial
S 3 : 0 3 :042(309) [0491] already present, such as I **saw** with my own eyes at the
S 3 : 0 8 :002(312) [0495] I **see** in my members another law," etc. (Rom. 7:23).
TR : 0 0 :014(322) [0509] candidate (as we have **seen** it done among you in the

Continued ▶

TR : 00 :054(329) [0519] of the church and to **see** to it that errors are removed and
TR : 00 :056(329) [0521] license of the pontiffs and **see** to it that the church is not
TR : 00 :076(333) [0527] to godly pastors and **see** to it that it is used properly for
LC : PR :001(358) [0567] For we **see** to our sorrow that many pastors and
LC : 01 :004(365) [0581] The meaning is: "**See** to it that you let me alone be your
LC : 01 :013(366) [0583] To have God, you **see**, does not mean to lay hands upon
LC : 01 :037(369) [0591] shall be impressed and **see** that this is no laughing matter
LC : 01 :042(370) [0591] For the world **sees** that those who trust God and not
LC : 01 :055(372) [0595] **See**, all this is an attempt to embellish yourself with God's
LC : 01 :059(372) [0597] over our disgrace so that no one may **see** it or know it.
LC : 01 :068(373) [0599] This I have **seen** in the case of many who broke their
LC : 01 :074(374) [0601] cross themselves when they **see** or hear anything
LC : 01 :114(380) [0613] In this way, you **see**, we should have had godly children,
LC : 01 :115(381) [0613] works of their own choice: "**See**, this work is well pleasing
LC : 01 :116(381) [0615] difficult works; we shall **see** whether they can produce a
LC : 01 :132(383) [0619] Here you **see** how important God considers this
LC : 01 :137(384) [0621] They **see** their children's children, as we said above, "to
LC : 01 :152(386) [0625] Let us **see**, though, whether you are the man to defy him.
LC : 01 :155(386) [0625] but we are unwilling to **see** that we ourselves are knaves
LC : 01 :171(388) [0629] No one is willing to **see** that this is the command of the
LC : 01 :177(389) [0631] state of things, but we do not **see** that it is our own fault.
LC : 01 :184(390) [0633] When we **see** such people, our hearts in turn rage and we
LC : 01 :187(390) [0633] as a mirror in which to **see** ourselves, so that we may be
LC : 01 :190(391) [0635] If you **see** anyone suffer hunger and do not feed him, you
LC : 01 :190(391) [0635] Likewise, if you **see** anyone condemned to death or in
LC : 01 :192(391) [0635] It is just as if I **saw** someone wearily struggling in deep
LC : 01 :197(392) [0637] Everybody would **see** how the monks mock and mislead
LC : 01 :213(394) [0641] From this you **see** how the papal rabble, priests, monks,
LC : 01 :225(395) [0643] common people so that we may **see** how honest we are.
LC : 01 :236(397) [0647] But **see** what you gain.
LC : 01 :247(398) [0651] you despise and defy this, **see** whom you have brought
LC : 01 :265(401) [0657] publicly, even when he has **seen** a sin committed, unless
LC : 01 :266(401) [0657] I may **see** and hear that my neighbor sins, but to make
LC : 01 :274(401) [0659] So you **see** that we are absolutely forbidden to speak evil
LC : 01 :274(402) [0659] We have **seen** that the Fifth Commandment forbids us to
LC : 01 :276(402) [0659] has done, teach him, if he **saw** the wrongdoing, to go and
LC : 01 :277(402) [0659] the master of the house **sees** a servant failing to do his
LC : 01 :278(402) [0661] heaped up together, and **see** if they can make the boast
LC : 01 :303(405) [0667] Or, **seeing** an opportunity for profit — let us say, when a
LC : 01 :304(406) [0667] this wrong, and it does not **see** that the neighbor is being
LC : 01 :308(406) [0669] but God will not, for he **sees** your wicked heart and the
LC : 01 :312(407) [0671] Let us **see**, now, how our great saints can boast of their
LC : 01 :314(407) [0671] and candles until nothing else can be **seen** or heard.
LC : 01 :316(408) [0671] They fail to **see**, these miserable, blind people, that no
LC : 01 :321(408) [0673] it so that we may **see** why we are constrained and
LC : 01 :329(410) [0677] Thus you **see** how the First Commandment is the chief
LC : 02 :001(411) [0679] In it we have **seen** all that God wishes us to do or not to
LC : 02 :017(412) [0681] us all that we have and **see** before our eyes, but also daily
LC : 02 :020(412) [0683] and recite it, but we neither **see** nor consider what the
LC : 02 :023(413) [0683] Everything we **see**, and every blessing that comes our
LC : 02 :023(413) [0683] so that we may sense and **see** in them his fatherly heart
LC : 02 :024(413) [0683] For here we **see** how the Father has given himself to us,
LC : 02 :026(413) [0685] of the Godhead, and we **see** what we receive from God
LC : 02 :055(418) [0693] have sin, the Holy Spirit **sees** to it that it does not harm
LC : 02 :065(419) [0695] Apart from him we **see** nothing but an angry and terrible
LC : 02 :067(419) [0697] Now you **see** that the Creed is a very different teaching
LC : 02 :069(420) [0697] of God because we **see** that God gives himself completely
LC : 03 :003(420) [0697] has taught us both the way and the words, as we shall **see**.
LC : 03 :022(423) [0703] Thus we **see** how sincerely he is concerned over our
LC : 03 :027(424) [0705] enough, but the trouble is that we do not feel or **see** them.
LC : 03 :029(424) [0705] say because I would like to **see** the people brought again
LC : 03 :045(426) [0709] So you **see** that in this petition we pray for exactly the
LC : 03 :047(426) [0709] **See**, then, what a great need there is for this kind of
LC : 03 :047(426) [0709] Since we **see** that the world is full of sects and false
LC : 03 :055(427) [0713] You **see** that we are praying here not for a crust of bread
LC : 03 :082(431) [0721] Thus, you **see**, God wishes to show us how he cares for us
LC : 03 :083(431) [0721] of time, as indeed we **see** and experience every day.
LC : 03 :102(434) [0727] example of other people and by things we hear and **see**.
LC : 03 :103(434) [0727] everyone wants to sit in the chief seat and be **seen** by all.
LC : 03 :111(435) [0729] Then you will **see** the temptation cease and eventually
LC : 03 :117(436) [0731] Thus you **see** how God wants us to pray to him for
LC : 04 :019(439) [0737] gross, external mask (as we **see** the shell of a nut) but as
LC : 04 :020(439) [0737] mother," I **see** another man, adorned and clothed with the
LC : 04 :026(439) [0739] Here you **see** again how precious and important a thing
LC : 04 :029(440) [0739] the blind are unwilling to **see** that faith must have
LC : 04 :037(441) [0741] Thus you **see** plainly that Baptism is not a work which we
LC : 04 :055(443) [0745] So you **see** that the objection of the sectarians is absurd.
LC : 04 :061(444) [0747] And because they **see** neither faith nor obedience, they
LC : 04 :074(445) [0751] Here you **see** that Baptism, both by its power and by its
LC : 04 :083(446) [0751] Thus we **see** what a great and excellent thing Baptism is,
LC : 05 :013(448) [0755] we shall take our stand and **see** who dares to instruct
LC : 05 :026(449) [0759] a furious enemy; when he **sees** that we resist him and
LC : 05 :040(451) [0761] For we **see** that men are becoming listless and lazy about
LC : 05 :043(451) [0763] may be induced to **see** the reason and the need for
LC : 05 :049(452) [0765] Thus you **see** that we are not granted liberty to despise
LC : 05 :050(452) [0765] your inner life and reflect: "**See** what sort of Christian I
LC : 05 :056(453) [0767] Because nature and reason **see** this, such people refuse to
LC : 05 :079(455) [0771] Again, look about you and **see** whether you are also in
LC : 05 :079(455) [0771] cling to the Gospel, and **see** whether you will not acquire
LC : 05 :082(456) [0773] If you could **see** how many daggers, spears, and arrows
LC : 05 :084(456) [0773] unfortunately, you do not **see**, though God grants his
LC : 06 :024(460) [0000] but just letting everyone **see** how poor and miserable he
LC : 06 :026(460) [0000] that men should look to **see** how full of filthiness you are,
LC : 06 :034(461) [0000] In this way, you **see**, confession would be rightly taught,
EP : 01 :010(467) [0781] and in my flesh I shall **see** God; him I shall **see** for
EP : 01 :010(467) [0781] I shall see God; him I shall see for myself, and mine eyes
SD : PR :010(503) [0849] Christian intelligence can **see** which opinion in the
SD : 02 :010(522) [0883] "**Seeing** they do not see, and hearing they do not hear, nor
SD : 02 :010(522) [0885] "Seeing they do not **see**, and hearing they do not hear,
SD : 02 :017(524) [0889] has regenerated), but I **see** in my members another law at
SD : 02 :021(525) [0889] inasmuch as man does not **see** or recognize the dreadful,
SD : 02 :026(526) [0891] an understanding heart, **seeing** eyes, and hearing ears
SD : 02 :032(527) [0893] From this we **see** clearly that the Apology does not
SD : 02 :064(533) [0905] in my inmost self, but I **see** in my members another law
SD : 02 :085(537) [0913] self, though he also **sees** in his members the law of sin at
SD : 05 :010(560) [0955] so that they do not **see** the law spiritually, or how much it
SD : 05 :016(561) [0957] order that everyone may **see** that we are concealing
SD : 06 :008(565) [0965] Likewise, "I **see** in my members another law at war with
SD : 06 :025(568) [0971] But just as they will **see** God face to face, so through
SD : 07 :029(574) [0981] to his *Great Confession:* "I **see** that schisms and errors are
SD : 07 :103(587) [1009] Who has **seen** the limits of his power?
SD : 11 :004(616) [1063] For the fact that God **sees** and knows everything before it
SD : 11 :004(616) [1063] He **sees** and knows in advance all that is or shall be, all
SD : 11 :006(617) [1065] (*praescientia*) **sees** and knows in advance the evil as well,
SD : 11 :006(617) [1065] To be sure, he **sees** and knows beforehand whatever the
SD : 11 :011(618) [1067] Especially when they **see** their own weakness and the
SD : 11 :058(625) [1081] the case of the one group we are to **see** God's judgment.
SD : 11 :067(627) [1085] Father, that everyone who **sees** the Son and believes in
SD : 11 :072(627) [1085] And in order that we may **see** it through and abide and
SD : 12 :005(633) [1097] everyone to be able to **see** that we were not proposing or

See (6) (*Roman "See"*)
AP : 12 :125(201) [0289] If the Roman **See** thinks it is right for all nations to
AP : 12 :125(201) [0289] might tend to diminish the prestige of the Roman **See**.
S2 : 04 :007(299) [0473] If, I say, the pope and the **see** of Rome were to concede
S3 : 03 :024(307) [0485] Here the holy **see** in Rome came to the aid of the poor
TR : 00 :050(329) [0519] shall judge the supreme **see**, for the judge is judged
LC : 01 :230(396) [0645] of all thieves, the Holy **See** at Rome, and all its retinue,

Seeburg (2)
S3 : 15 :005(317) [0501] Wendal Faber, pastor of **Seeburg** in Mansfeld
TR : 00 :082(335) [0529] Wendal Faber, pastor of **Seeburg** in Mansfeld

Seed (15)
PR : PR :004(003) [0007] himself to scatter his **seed** of false doctrine and discord
AP : 02 :046(106) [0119] woman, and between your **seed** and her seed" (Gen. 3:15).
AP : 02 :046(106) [0119] woman, and between your seed and her **seed**" (Gen. 3:15).
AP : 07 :019(171) [0233] Matt. 13:38 that "the good **seed** means the sons of the
AP : 12 :055(189) [0267] and said there would be a **seed** that would destroy the
AP : 23 :008(240) [0367] "Let the earth put forth vegetation, plants yielding **seed**."
AP : 27 :061(279) [0441] because of the promised **Seed**, through the mercy of God
EP : 01 :021(468) [0785] in us through our sinful **seed** and the source of all other,
SD : 01 :007(510) [0861] and birth out of sinful **seed** from our father and mother.
SD : 01 :028(513) [0867] of our conception the **seed** from which man is formed is
SD : 05 :023(562) [0959] of the woman's **seed**, who would bruise the serpent's
SD : 05 :023(562) [0959] head; likewise, of the **seed** of Abraham, but whom all
SD : 07 :046(577) [0987] concerning the promised **seed**, Christ, who was to be born
SD : 07 :046(577) [0989] promise of the blessed **seed** of Isaac, although this seemed
SD : 07 :046(577) [0989] promises concerning the **seed** of Isaac than he could

Seek (75), Seeking (6), Seeks (15), Sought (18)
AG : 20 :010(042) [0055] grace, despises Christ and **seeks** his own way to God,
AG : 21 :002(047) [0057] that we are to invoke saints or **seek** help from them.
AG : 21 :003(047) [0059] service is sincerely to **seek** and call upon this same Jesus
AG : 26 :014(066) [0073] collate the traditions and **sought** mitigations to relieve
AG : 27 :037(077) [0081] that one is not to **seek** for righteousness in the precepts
AG : 27 :057(080) [0083] from the world and **seeking** a life more pleasing to God
AL : 20 :010(042) [0055] and grace of Christ and **seeks** a way to God without
AL : 20 :037(046) [0057] or bear the cross, but it **seeks** and trusts in man's help.
AL : 21 :002(047) [0057] us to pray to the saints or **seek** their help, for the only
AL : 26 :014(066) [0073] traditions together and **sought** mitigations to relieve
AL : 26 :015(066) [0073] to treat the Scriptures and **seek** for the more profitable
AL : 27 :037(077) [0081] righteousness is not to be **sought** for in observances and
AL : 27 :057(080) [0083] "fleeing from the world" and "**seeking** a holy kind of life."
AP : 02 :024(103) [0111] God or believe in him, it **seeks** and loves carnal things;
AP : 04 :007(108) [0121] the law and by it they **seek** forgiveness of sins and
AP : 04 :013(109) [0123] that men ought to **seek** some righteousness beyond the
AP : 04 :020(110) [0125] waver and doubt and then **seek** to pile up other works to
AP : 04 :030(111) [0129] comes from God, and **seeking** to establish your own, you
AP : 04 :068(116) [0139] have said so far we have **sought** to show the manner of
AP : 04 :154(128) [0163] believing that she should **seek** the forgiveness of sins from
AP : 04 :154(128) [0165] or accept the Messiah or **seek** from him the forgiveness of
AP : 04 :176(131) [0171] to be at peace we must **seek** justification elsewhere.
AP : 04 :178(131) [0171] If, then, we must **seek** justification elsewhere, our love
AP : 04 :180(132) [0171] timid consciences should **seek** reconciliation and
AP : 04 :181(132) [0171] Therefore, if we are to **seek** justification and peace of
AP : 04 :198(134) [0175] own righteousness, but to **seek** the will of God rather than
AP : 04 :229(139) [0183] wisdom looks at the law and **seeks** righteousness in it.
AP : 04 :233(140) [0185] some minor fault and then **seek** after some other kinds of
AP : 04 :258(144) [0193] do evil, learn to do good; **seek** justice, correct oppression;
AP : 04 :267(147) [0197] alone, because it is vain to **seek** remission of punishment
AP : 04 :283(150) [0201] cleanness is to be **sought** in works commanded by God,
AP : 04 :285(150) [0201] because a conscience that **seeks** forgiveness through
AP : 04 :288(151) [0203] not that we should **seek** righteousness through these
AP : 04 :288(151) [0203] Mass, through which they **seek** righteousness, grace, and
AP : 04 :317(156) [0209] in Christ must then **seek** his righteousness elsewhere, he
AP : 04 :318(156) [0209] way it often does, we must **seek** grace through a good
AP : 04 :321(157) [0209] their works and therefore continually **seek** other works.
AP : 04 :392(167) [0225] church have taught us to **seek** forgiveness of sins, grace,
AP : 04 :400(168) [0227] Shall we **seek** it in our own words or in the words of its
AP : 04 :400(168) [0227] I think we should **seek** it in the words of him who is the
AP : 12 :107(198) [0283] by our works, and yet we **seek** mercy because of the
AP : 12 :149(206) [0299] not put on armor and **seek** out the church of St. James or
AP : 12 :151(206) [0299] they may learn to **seek** God's help and to acknowledge
AP : 14 :004(215) [0315] present among those who **seek** to destroy the Word of
AP : 15 :005(215) [0317] through which they **seek** to gain the forgiveness of sins
AP : 15 :018(217) [0319] and works by which it **seeks** to be justified before God,
AP : 21 :018(231) [0347] as an ensign to the peoples; him shall the nations **seek**."
AP : 21 :024(232) [0349] as our intercessor and high priest, why **seek** others?
AP : 21 :028(233) [0351] trusted in her mercy, and **sought** through her to appease
AP : 21 :034(233) [0351] of Christ disappears if we **seek** out other mediators
AP : 21 :036(234) [0353] But these no one has **sought** out in the true stories about
AP : 24 :007(250) [0385] Although St. Francis **sought** to regulate this with the
AP : 24 :027(254) [0393] and truth, for such the Father **seeks** to worship him.
AP : 24 :028(254) [0393] Truly and wholeheartedly **seek** and expect help from me."
AP : 27 :011(270) [0423] Those who **seek** the forgiveness of sins not by faith in

Continued ▶

A P : 2 7 :033(275) [0431] of the divine law, but must **seek** the mercy promised in
A P : 2 7 :036(275) [0433] But our opponents slyly **seek** to give the impression that
A P : 2 7 :037(275) [0433] their calling, ought to **seek** perfection, that is, growth in
S 1 : P R :015(291) [0459] unto Thee and earnestly **seek** Thee according to the grace
S 2 : 0 2 :008(294) [0465] Somebody may **seek** to justify himself by saying that he
S 2 : 0 2 :018(296) [0467] and God's grace were **sought** here, too, for Masses
S 3 : 0 3 :018(306) [0483] which pertain to God, **seeking** consolation in its own
S 3 : 0 3 :033(308) [0489] no, not one; no one understands, no one **seeks** for God.
T R : 0 0 :005(320) [0505] the whole world should **seek** ordination and confirmation
T R : 0 0 :008(321) [0505] just as a child neither **seeks** nor takes pre-eminence for
T R : 0 0 :010(321) [0505] Peter as one from whom confirmation should be **sought**.
T R : 0 0 :010(321) [0507] that he did not desire to **seek** confirmation from Peter,
T R : 0 0 :010(321) [0507] or confirmation was not to be **sought** from Peter alone.
T R : 0 0 :012(322) [0507] should forever have **sought** ordination and confirmation
T R : 0 0 :015(322) [0509] nor confirmation were **sought** from the bishop of Rome
T R : 0 0 :016(322) [0509] in remote places to **seek** ordination from him alone.
T R : 0 0 :016(322) [0509] East today which do not **seek** ordination or confirmation
S C : 0 1 :018(343) [0541] God, and so we should not **seek** by craftiness to gain
L C : 0 1 :004(365) [0581] you let me alone be your God, and never **seek** another."
L C : 0 1 :004(365) [0581] lack, look to me for it and **seek** it from me, and whenever
L C : 0 1 :011(366) [0583] if he feared fire, he **sought** St. Lawrence as his patron; if
L C : 0 1 :012(366) [0583] They neither expect nor **seek** anything from him.
L C : 0 1 :015(366) [0583] "What you formerly **sought** from the saints, or what you
L C : 0 1 :021(367) [0585] pursues other things and **seeks** help and consolation from
L C : 0 1 :022(367) [0585] that conscience which **seeks** help, comfort, and salvation
L C : 0 1 :027(368) [0587] nor are we arrogantly to **seek** other ways and means than
L C : 0 1 :027(368) [0587] our blessings from God but **seeking** them from ourselves.
L C : 0 1 :093(377) [0607] not know God's Word but **seek** holiness in their own
L C : 0 1 :151(386) [0625] What we **seek** and deserve, then, is paid back to us in
L C : 0 1 :252(399) [0651] Anyone whom **seeks** and desires good works will here find
L C : 0 1 :316(408) [0671] Through them we must **seek** and pray for help and
L C : 0 1 :318(408) [0673] to do that you will neither **seek** nor pay attention to any
L C : 0 2 :056(418) [0693] Therefore, all who **seek** to merit holiness through their
L C : 0 2 :063(419) [0695] the whole world has **sought** painstakingly to learn what
L C : 0 3 :011(421) [0701] and assuage his wrath and **seek** grace by their prayers.]
L C : 0 3 :058(428) [0713] as Christ teaches, "**Seek** first the kingdom of God, and all
L C : 0 3 :115(435) [0731] a murderer, he incessantly **seeks** our life and vents his
L C : 0 3 :117(436) [0731] welfare and directs us to **seek** and expect help from no
L C : 0 5 :002(447) [0753] who do not know what they **seek** or why they come.
L C : 0 5 :020(449) [0757] that we know what we should **seek** and obtain there.
L C : 0 5 :030(450) [0759] the Word, otherwise we could never know of it or **seek** it.
L C : 0 5 :078(455) [0771] you have to go to the sacrament and **seek** a remedy.
L C : 0 5 :083(456) [0773] Take others' advice and **seek** their prayers, and never give
L C : 0 6 :013(458) [0000] before a brother, **seeking** his advice, comfort, and
E P : 0 5 :009(479) [0803] and that we should now **seek** all our righteousness in
E P : 0 7 :005(482) [0809] wine of the Holy Supper, **seek** the body and blood of
E P : 0 7 :025(485) [0815] whose meaning must first be **sought** in other passages.
E P : 0 7 :036(485) [0815] the believers should not **seek** the body of Christ in the
E P : 0 7 :036(485) [0815] the bread to heaven and there **seek** the body of Christ.
E P : 1 1 :013(496) [0835] In Christ we should **seek** the eternal election of the
S D : 0 2 :010(522) [0885] "No one understands, no one **seeks** for God.
S D : 0 2 :043(529) [0897] ourselves for righteousness and life or **seek** after it.
S D : 0 3 :055(549) [0935] the principle that we must **seek** our entire righteousness
S D : 0 7 :001(568) [0971] their own consciences **sought** forcibly to adduce and
S D : 0 7 :122(590) [1013] are not directed to **seek** the body of Christ in the bread
S D : 1 1 :039(623) [1077] (Matt. 7:15; 22:12), or **seek** other ways to righteousness
S D : 1 1 :066(627) [1085] of life in whom they are to **seek** the Father's eternal
S D : 1 1 :073(628) [1087] and should diligently **seek** to "confirm their call and
S D : 1 1 :089(631) [1093] when people are taught to **seek** their eternal election in

Seem (16), Seemed (8), Seemly (1), Seems (22)
A G : 2 7 :007(071) [0077] it would have been **seemly** to show more consideration to
A L : 2 3 :017(054) [0063] And it **seems** that the churches will soon be lacking in
A L : 2 4 :020(058) [0067] of divine institution **seems** ever to have been so abused
A L : 2 7 :031(075) [0079] age a person does not **seem** to have sufficient judgment to
A L : 2 7 :034(076) [0079] might be rebuked, yet it **seems** not to follow of necessity
A L : 2 8 :040(087) [0089] written, and the pontiffs **seem** in some measure to have
A L : 2 8 :060(091) [0091] for this purpose, and it **seems** that the church was the
A L : 0 0 :005(095) [0095] been recounted which it **seemed** necessary to say in order
A P : P R :013(099) [0101] If any expression **seems** too strong, let me explain that
A P : 0 4 :035(112) [0131] God corrupts works that **seem** virtuous, for God judges
A P : 0 4 :036(112) [0131] While he terrifies us and **seems** to be casting us into
A P : 0 4 :103(121) [0151] The law would **seem** to be harmful since it has made all
A P : 0 4 :185(132) [0173] the sources, will correct everything that **seems** offensive.
A P : 0 4 :312(155) [0207] of faith and hope **seem** to be confused, since it is hope
A P : 0 4 :344(160) [0217] It **seems** that for some such reason the scholastics
A P : 0 4 :345(160) [0217] Unless it is qualified, this statement **seems** absurd.
A P : 0 4 :356(161) [0217] If these passages **seem** to our opponents to be in conflict,
A P : 0 4 :391(166) [0225] Their authority ought not **seem** so great as to end all
A P : 0 4 :399(168) [0227] father said that no plan **seemed** better to him than to give
A P : 0 7 :008(169) [0229] communion of saints," **seems** to have been added to
A P : 0 7 :029(173) [0237] For the time being this **seemed** enough to defend the
A P : 1 0 :002(179) [0247] And Vulgarius, who **seems** to us to be a sensible writer,
A P : 1 2 :113(199) [0285] There **seem** to have been many reasons for this.
A P : 1 5 :026(219) [0323] ceremonies such tasks **seem** profane, so that many perform
A P : 1 8 :005(225) [0335] even philosophers who **seem** to have wanted this
A P : 2 1 :034(233) [0353] It **seems** that when the saints were first mentioned, as in
A P : 2 1 :034(234) [0353] like a puppet so that it **seemed** to nod Yes or No to the
A P : 2 3 :045(245) [0377] meat or marriage, which **seemed** profane and unclean and
A P : 2 3 :050(246) [0377] than the Encratites, who **seem** to have gone astray
A P : 2 3 :059(247) [0379] of schism because we **seem** to have separated ourselves
A P : 2 4 :023(253) [0391] amid great calamities, it **seemed** to be unusually severe;
A P : 2 4 :028(254) [0393] this declaration, which **seems** to contradict Moses
A P : 2 4 :037(257) [0397] and not for another symbol that **seems** to be a sacrifice.
A P : 2 4 :086(265) [0413] It **seems** that because of such contributions the Mass was
A P : 2 4 :093(267) [0417] Therefore it **seems** that the Greeks offer it only as a
A P : 2 4 :098(268) [0419] And it **seems** that this worship of Baal will endure
A P : 2 7 :002(269) [0419] have already happened, and others **seem** to be pending.
A P : 2 7 :002(269) [0419] for his doctrine, which **seemed** to be injuring his food.
A P : 2 7 :036(275) [0433] It **seems** that wise men were offended by the immoderate
S C : P R :018(340) [0537] or other parts which **seem** to require special attention
L C : 0 1 :117(381) [0615] Even though it **seems** very trivial and contemptible, make
L C : 0 1 :287(403) [0663] parts of the body which **seem** to be weaker are
L C : 0 1 :313(407) [0671] It **seems** to me that we shall have our hands full to keep
L C : 0 1 :325(409) [0675] He **seems** to explain the whole commandment in one
L C : 0 3 :113(435) [0729] The petition **seems** to be speaking of the devil as the sum
S D : 0 7 :046(577) [0989] of Isaac, although this **seemed** impossible to his reason,
S D : 1 0 :009(612) [1055] way, as at any time may **seem** to be most profitable,

Segregate (1)
S D : 0 3 :007(540) [0919] doctrine, we clearly **segregate**, expose, and condemn the

Seize (2), Seized (1), Seizing (1)
A P : 2 4 :091(266) [0415] kind of sorrow must **seize** all the faithful if they ponder
T R : 0 0 :035(326) [0513] Then the popes began to **seize** kingdoms for themselves,
L C : 0 1 :296(405) [0665] commandment prohibits **seizing** or withholding another's
L C : 0 5 :036(450) [0761] a gift and eternal treasure cannot be **seized** with the hand.

Seldom (3)
L C : 0 1 :137(384) [0619] that we behold, for it **seldom** happens that such wicked
L C : 0 1 :160(387) [0627] But they very **seldom** receive it, for the world's way of
L C : 0 1 :258(400) [0653] that men of integrity **seldom** preside in courts of justice.

Select (7), Selected (3), Selecting (1)
A P : 0 4 :007(108) [0121] doctrines our opponents **select** the law and by it they seek
A P : 0 4 :145(127) [0161] **Selecting** love, which is only one of these effects of faith,
A P : 0 4 :286(150) [0201] passages on faith, **select** the passages on works, and even
A P : 1 2 :093(196) [0279] have been in order to **select** and combine their opinions
A P : 1 2 :097(196) [0281] of the Fathers, they **select** sayings about a part of
T R : 0 0 :062(331) [0523] in which an army might **select** a commander for itself, the
S C : 0 9 :001(354) [0561] *of the Scriptures, **selected** for various estates and*
L C : 0 1 :011(366) [0583] and every person **selected** his own saint and worshiped
L C : 0 2 :048(416) [0691] For we who assemble **select** a special place and give the
L C : 0 3 :030(424) [0707] we must carefully **select** the weapons with which
S D : 0 7 :044(577) [0987] Redeemer Jesus Christ, **selected** his words with great

Self (30), Selves (1)
P R : P R :024(013) [0023] welfare of our own **selves** and of the subjects that belong
A G : 2 6 :020(067) [0073] supposed that grace is earned through **self**-chosen works.
A P : 0 7 :035(175) [0241] in promoting rigor of devotion and **self**-abasement."
S 3 : 0 3 :020(306) [0485] rest on his enumeration of sins and on his **self**-abasement.
S C : 0 9 :013(356) [0563] day; whereas she who is **self**-indulgent is dead even while
L C : 0 1 :119(381) [0615] in vain with their **self**-devised works and meanwhile have
L C : 0 1 :256(399) [0653] every man maintain his **self**-respect before his wife,
E P : 0 1 :017(468) [0783] original sin is an essential, **self**-existing something which
E P : 0 6 :004(480) [0807] devotion they undertake **self**-decreed and self-chosen acts
E P : 0 6 :004(480) [0807] undertake self-decreed and **self**-chosen acts of serving
E P : 0 6 :004(480) [0807] necessary lest the Old Adam go his own **self**-willed way.
E P : 1 1 :016(497) [0837] are strengthened in their **self**-will, he is not teaching the
E P : 1 2 :005(498) [0839] on one's own individual **self**-chosen spirituality, which in
S D : 0 1 :054(518) [0877] be a substance (that is, a **self**-subsisting essence) or an
S D : 0 1 :054(518) [0877] accidental thing that is not **self**-subsistent but that
S D : 0 1 :054(518) [0877] but that subsists in another **self**-subsistent essence and can
S D : 0 1 :055(518) [0877] that every substance or **self**-subsisting essence, in as far as
S D : 0 1 :055(518) [0877] is not a part of another **self**-subsisting essence, but is
S D : 0 1 :055(518) [0877] (that is, something **self**-subsistent) but an accident (that
S D : 0 1 :057(518) [0877] accident (that is, either a **self**-subsisting essence or
S D : 0 2 :017(524) [0887] law of God in my inmost **self** (which the Holy Spirit has
S D : 0 2 :063(533) [0905] the law of God according to his inmost **self** (Rom. 7:22).
S D : 0 2 :064(533) [0905] law of God in my inmost **self**, but I see in my members
S D : 0 2 :070(534) [0909] It is, of course, **self**-evident that in true conversion there
S D : 0 2 :085(537) [0913] according to the inmost **self**, though he also sees in his
S D : 0 4 :019(554) [0945] law of God in his inmost **self**, and on the other that in his
S D : 0 6 :018(567) [0967] According to the inmost **self** they delight in the law of
S D : 0 6 :020(567) [0969] Spirit's guidance set up a **self**-elected service of God and
S D : 0 6 :023(568) [0969] according to their inmost **self** they do what is pleasing to
S D : 0 7 :125(591) [1015] who fail to meet their own **self**-devised standard of
S D : 1 2 :010(634) [1097] own peculiar precepts and **self**-chosen spirituality as on a

Selfishness (1)
L C : 0 5 :075(455) [0771] strife, jealousy, anger, **selfishness**, dissension, party spirit,

Selfsame (1)
L C : 0 4 :055(443) [0745] to take it again the **selfsame** hour, as if he had not really

Sell (11), Sellers (1), Selling (2), Sells (1)
A G : 1 6 :002(037) [0051] serve as soldiers, buy and **sell**, take required oaths,
A G : 2 4 :010(057) [0065] of fair, by buying and **selling** it, and by observing it in
A L : 0 0 :002(095) [0095] have been troubled in many ways by indulgence **sellers**.
A P : 0 4 :360(162) [0219] others, as when monks **sell** the merits of their orders to
A P : 1 2 :015(184) [0257] They **sell** indulgences, which they interpret as the
A P : 2 4 :064(261) [0407] They **sell** the Mass as a price for success, to merchants for
A P : 2 7 :024(273) [0427] supererogation, these liberal men then **sell** them to others.
A P : 2 7 :034(275) [0431] works of supererogation and **sell** them to others.
A P : 2 7 :039(276) [0433] They **sell** merits and transfer them to others under the
A P : 2 7 :045(277) [0435] you would be perfect, go, **sell** what you possess and give
S 2 : 0 2 :006(293) [0463] through the buying and **selling** of Masses, it would be
S 2 : 0 2 :024(296) [0469] and by which the pope **sells** the merits of Christ together
S 3 : 0 3 :029(308) [0487] evil deeds and could even **sell** their superfluous
L C : 0 1 :240(397) [0649] his right and privilege to **sell** his goods as dearly as he
L C : 0 1 :303(406) [0667] on to his property, nor yet **sell** it without loss — he hurries

Selnecker (2)
E P : 1 2 :031(501) [0843] Dr. Nicholas **Selnecker** subscribed
S D : 1 2 :040(636) [1103] Dr. Nicholas **Selnecker**, subscribed

Semantic (3)
E P : 0 4 :004(476) [0797] At first this was merely a **semantic** issue.
S D : P R :009(503) [0849] the strife reflects a mere **semantic** problem of little or no
S D : 0 4 :005(551) [0939] ceased to be only a **semantic** problem and became a

Semblance (1)
L C : 0 1 :301(405) [0667] have the least **semblance** of right, so varnishing and

Semi (1)
E P : 0 2 :010(471) [0789] also reject the error of the **Semi**-Pelagians who teach that

Semperfrei (1)
PR : PR :027(015) [0025] Henry, baron of Limpurg [-Schmiedelfeld], **Semperfrei**

Senate (2)
AL : 0 0 :017(096) [0095] **Senate** and magistrate of Nuremberg
AL : 0 0 :017(096) [0095] **Senate** of Reutlingen

Send (7), Sending (1), Sends (3), Sent (27)
PR : PR :013(007) [0013] Afterward it was **sent** to a considerable number of
PR : PR :014(007) [0013] explanation that had been **sent** out might be fortified with
AG : 2 8 :006(081) [0085] For Christ **sent** out the apostles with this command, "As
AG : 2 8 :006(082) [0085] "As the Father has **sent** me, even so I send you.
AG : 2 8 :006(082) [0085] "As the Father has sent me, even so I **send** you.
AL : 0 3 :004(030) [0045] who believe in him by **sending** the Holy Spirit into their
AL : 2 8 :006(082) [0085] For Christ **sent** out the apostles with this command, "As
AL : 2 8 :006(082) [0085] "As the Father has **sent** me, even so I send you.
AL : 2 8 :006(082) [0085] "As the Father has sent me, even so I **send** you.
AP : 0 4 :096(121) [0149] John 3:17, 18, "God **sent** the Son into the world, not to
AP : 0 4 :167(130) [0169] endures patiently enough the afflictions that God **sends**?
AP : 0 4 :345(160) [0217] "God **sent** the Son into the world, not to condemn the
AP : 1 3 :011(212) [0311] and prosper in the thing for which I **sent** it" (Isa. 55:11).
AP : 2 7 :002(269) [0419] the filth of the prison, he **sent** for the guardian to tell him
S 1 : PR :008(290) [0457] doctor here in Wittenberg, **sent** from France, who
S 3 : 0 3 :025(307) [0485] So they **sent** their legates out into all lands until every
TR : 0 0 :008(320) [0505] the apostles should be **sent** forth as equals and exercise
TR : 0 0 :009(321) [0505] to John 20:21 Christ **sent** his disciples out as equals,
TR : 0 0 :009(321) [0505] he said, "As the Father has **sent** me, even so I send you."
TR : 0 0 :009(321) [0505] he said, "As the Father has sent me, even so I **send** you."
TR : 0 0 :009(321) [0505] He **sent** out each one individually, he said, in the same
TR : 0 0 :009(321) [0505] said, in the same way in which he had himself been **sent**.
TR : 0 0 :023(324) [0511] the apostles and that the apostles were **sent** out as equals.
TR : 0 0 :031(325) [0513] also, "As the Father has **sent** me, even so I send you"
TR : 0 0 :031(325) [0513] the Father has sent me, even so I **send** you" (John 20:21).
TR : 0 0 :031(325) [0513] that Christ was not **sent** to wield a sword or possess a
SC : 0 9 :005(355) [0561] or to governors as **sent** by him to punish those who do
LC : SP :020(364) [0579] Christ said farewell to his disciples and **sent** them forth.
LC : 0 1 :136(383) [0619] him to anger, he will **send** upon you both death and the
LC : 0 1 :190(391) [0635] If you **send** a person away naked when you could clothe
LC : 0 1 :270(401) [0657] I might be called a liar and **sent** away in disgrace."
LC : 0 3 :051(426) [0711] Creed, namely, that God **sent** his Son, Christ our Lord,
LC : 0 3 :080(431) [0721] sedition, and war, why he **sends** tempest and hail to
LC : 0 3 :109(435) [0729] likely in this very hour to **send** such a shaft into my heart
EP : 1 0 :006(493) [0831] in consequence what God **sends** us and what he lets the
SD : 0 2 :026(526) [0891] that you believe in him whom he has **sent**" (John 6:29).
SD : 0 5 :011(560) [0955] Christ has obtained and **sent** us the Spirit, and for this
SD : 1 1 :027(620) [1071] the messengers whom he **sent** out, some at first, some at

Sensation (1)
SD : 0 1 :011(510) [0863] from Adam a heart, **sensation**, and mind-set which, in its

Sense (60), Senses (11)
PR : PR :018(009) [0015] Latin copies were afterward found to be identical in **sense**
PR : PR :019(009) [0017] edition in any other **sense** than that of the first Augsburg
AP : 0 2 :003(101) [0105] In this **sense** the Latin definition denies that human
AP : 0 2 :047(106) [0119] tyranny of the devil are, in the precise **sense**, penalties.
AP : 0 4 :112(123) [0155] we mean faith in the true **sense** of the word—since the
AP : 0 4 :113(123) [0155] But faith in the true **sense**, as the Scriptures use the word,
AP : 0 4 :131(125) [0159] law, far beyond the **senses** and understanding of all
AP : 0 4 :235(140) [0185] And so it does not make **sense** when our opponents argue
AP : 0 4 :252(143) [0191] In this **sense** it is said, "The doers of the law will be
AP : 0 7 :010(170) [0229] "the church in the larger **sense** includes both the godly
AP : 0 7 :028(173) [0237] the church in the proper **sense** is the assembly of saints
AP : 1 2 :045(187) [0263] but, in the true **sense**, to believe that for Christ's
AP : 1 2 :046(188) [0263] these terms in a Platonic **sense** as counterfeit changes; but
AP : 1 2 :148(205) [0299] But in a formal **sense** revenge is part of penitence because
AP : 1 2 :153(206) [0299] no longer that sting and **sense** of wrath of which Paul
AP : 1 2 :153(206) [0299] This power of sin, this **sense** of wrath, is a real
AP : 1 2 :153(206) [0299] it is present; without this **sense** of wrath death is actually
AP : 1 3 :003(211) [0309] easily determine which are sacraments in the strict **sense**.
AP : 1 3 :003(211) [0309] sacraments in the strict **sense** since men do not have the
AP : 1 3 :014(213) [0311] which are, in the strict **sense**, "signs of the New
AP : 1 8 :004(225) [0335] about the things that the **senses** can grasp, it also retains a
AP : 2 0 :004(227) [0339] theologians have lost all **sense** of shame if they dare to
AP : 2 1 :040(235) [0355] in their party with a little **sense** would admit that the
SC : 0 2 :002(345) [0543] soul, all my limbs and **senses**, my reason and all the
LC : 0 1 :038(369) [0591] to bring them to their **senses** and cause them to mend
LC : 0 1 :082(376) [0603] to its literal, outward **sense**, this commandment does not
LC : 0 1 :123(382) [0617] and unruly; they have no **sense** of modesty or honor; they
LC : 0 2 :023(413) [0683] things so that we may **sense** and see in them his fatherly
LC : 0 2 :043(416) [0689] Christ is our Lord in the **sense** that he won for us this
LC : 0 4 :030(440) [0739] and grasped by the **senses** and thus brought into the
LC : 0 5 :051(452) [0765] sacrament, men can easily **sense** what sort of Christians
LC : 0 5 :053(453) [0765] that they may come to their **senses** and wake up.
EP : 0 4 :009(476) [0799] 4. In this **sense** the words "necessary," "ought," and
EP : 0 5 :006(478) [0803] is not used in a single **sense** in Holy Scripture, and this
EP : 0 6 :006(481) [0807] In this **sense** the children of God live in the law and walk
EP : 0 7 :007(482) [0811] way than in their literal **sense**, and not as though the
EP : 0 7 :025(484) [0815] or believed in their simple **sense**, as they read, but that
EP : 0 7 :042(486) [0817] we cannot comprehend with our human **sense** or reason.
EP : 0 9 :002(492) [0827] comprehended with our **senses** and reason, but must be
SD : 0 1 :002(508) [0859] corruption thereof, in the **sense** that man lacks the
SD : 0 1 :038(515) [0871] ears, and all my members, my reason and all my **senses**."
SD : 0 1 :051(517) [0875] It is in this latter **sense** that Luther writes that sin and
SD : 0 1 :052(517) [0875] term is applied in a wider **sense** to include the concrete
SD : 0 1 :054(518) [0877] they use them in the **sense** of a perfect dichotomy (that is,
SD : 0 1 :058(519) [0879] or an accident in the right and strict **sense** of the word.
SD : 0 2 :020(525) [0889] mouth nor eyes nor **senses** nor heart, inasmuch as man
SD : 0 2 :061(533) [0905] a mode of acting in the **sense** of a mode of doing
SD : 0 3 :018(542) [0921] and so that in their strict **senses** the two will be
SD : 0 3 :019(542) [0921] is also used in the limited **sense** of the forgiveness of sins
SD : 0 3 :019(542) [0921] In this latter **sense** it is frequently used in the Apology,
SD : 0 3 :020(542) [0921] made alive, has sometimes been used in the same **sense**.
SD : 0 3 :020(542) [0921] The Apology often uses the term in this **sense**.
SD : 0 4 :015(553) [0943] in their strict and Christian **sense**, as some have done.
SD : 0 4 :018(554) [0943] this meaning and in this **sense** it is right to say and teach
SD : 0 4 :020(554) [0945] are free to believers in the **sense** that it lies within their
SD : 0 5 :002(558) [0953] the Gospel in its strict **sense** is a proclamation of the
SD : 0 5 :005(559) [0953] is used in its broad **sense** and apart from the strict
SD : 0 5 :006(559) [0953] "Gospel" is also used in another (that is, in a strict) **sense**.
SD : 0 5 :007(559) [0953] is not used in a single **sense** in Holy Scripture.
SD : 0 6 :016(566) [0967] of the law" in the strict **sense**, because his good works are
SD : 0 7 :038(576) [0985] of Christ in their strict **sense** and as they read, and they
SD : 0 7 :045(577) [0987] obedience in their strict and clear **sense**, just as they read.
SD : 0 7 :049(578) [0989] of his body in a figurative **sense**, or of the virtue of his
SD : 0 7 :092(586) [1005] we shall understand and believe them in the simple **sense**.
SD : 0 7 :104(587) [1009] also show clearly in what **sense** our churches use the word
SD : 0 7 :105(588) [1009] In this **sense**, too, we use the word "spiritual" when we say
SD : 0 7 :113(589) [1011] understood in their strict **sense**, as they read, concerning
SD : 0 7 :113(589) [1011] are to be given a different, new, and strange **sense**.
SD : 0 8 :018(594) [1021] term "mixture" in a good **sense** and with the right
SD : 0 9 :003(610) [1051] With our reason and five **senses** this article cannot be
SD : 1 1 :041(623) [1077] In this **sense** "many are called, but few are chosen," for

Senseless (1)
LC : PR :015(360) [0571] O what mad, **senseless** fools we are!

Sensible (6)
AP : 0 2 :027(103) [0113] ones — at least the more **sensible** among them — teach
AP : 0 4 :303(154) [0205] **Sensible** people can easily see that a faith which believes
AP : 1 0 :002(179) [0247] who seems to us to be a **sensible** writer, says distinctly
S 2 : 0 2 :005(293) [0463] for all godly, Christian, **sensible**, God-fearing people —
S 3 : 0 0 :000(302) [0477] discuss with learned and **sensible** men, or even among
SC : 0 9 :002(354) [0561] only once, temperate, **sensible**, dignified, hospitable, an

Sensitive (1)
LC : 0 5 :084(456) [0773] you may become more **sensitive** to it and more hungry

Sentence (21), Sentenced (1), Sentences (10)
AG : 1 6 :002(037) [0051] decisions and pass **sentence** according to imperial and
AP : 0 2 :046(106) [0117] For there this fearful **sentence** is pronounced, "I will put
AP : 0 4 :065(116) [0139] one commentary on the ***Sentences*** that tells how
AP : 0 4 :105(122) [0153] commentators on the ***Sentences*** with all their magnificent
AP : 0 4 :105(122) [0153] of Paul than this one **sentence** from Ambrose.
AP : 0 4 :280(149) [0201] are, pick out garbled **sentences** to put something over on
AP : 1 2 :005(183) [0253] commentaries on the ***Sentences*** are full of endless
AP : 1 2 :048(188) [0265] neither see nor read the **sentence** of the law written in
AP : 1 2 :048(188) [0265] The **sentence** is understood only amid genuine sorrows
AP : 1 2 :048(188) [0265] is the removal of the **sentence** which declares that we are
AP : 1 2 :048(188) [0265] the substitution of the **sentence** by which we know that
AP : 1 2 :048(188) [0265] This new **sentence** is faith, abolishing the earlier sentence
AP : 1 2 :048(188) [0265] abolishing the earlier **sentence** and restoring peace and
AP : 1 2 :050(189) [0265] In each of these **sentences** the first part means contrition,
AP : 1 2 :068(192) [0271] commentators on the ***Sentences*** who as though by a
AP : 1 2 :070(192) [0271] to the many legions of commentators on the ***Sentences***.
AP : 1 2 :084(194) [0277] opponents twist Paul's **sentences**, for nothing can be said
AP : 1 2 :088(195) [0277] In the ***Sentences*** our opponents ask the same question.
AP : 1 2 :093(196) [0279] have compiled these centos of the **sentences** and decrees.
AP : 1 2 :103(197) [0281] case before pronouncing **sentence**, that is irrelevant
AP : 1 2 :108(198) [0283] thou art justified in thy **sentence** and blameless in thy
AP : 1 2 :151(206) [0299] that we had received the **sentence** of death; but that was
AP : 2 0 :012(228) [0341] say to a man who was **sentenced** to die and then
AP : 2 3 :003(239) [0363] of their marriage, you **sentence** innocent men to cruel
AP : 2 7 :032(274) [0431] things that follow this **sentence**, but at the end Bernard
S 1 : PR :009(290) [0457] I am sure that he will pronounce **sentence** upon them.
SC : 0 9 :014(356) [0563] are summed up in this **sentence**: 'You shall love your
LC : 0 1 :181(389) [0631] own children to judgment and **sentence** them to death.
LC : 0 1 :191(391) [0635] will pass a most terrible **sentence** upon them in the day of
LC : 0 1 :266(401) [0657] If I interfere and pass **sentence** on him, I fall into a
LC : 0 1 :268(401) [0657] kind of verdict and **sentence**, for the harshest verdict a
LC : 0 1 :280(403) [0661] testimony the judge can base his decision and **sentence**.

Separate (28), Separated (26), Separates (2), Separating (1), Separation (1)
AG : 0 0 :001(048) [0059] to reject, avoid, and **separate** from our churches as if our
AP : 0 4 :141(126) [0161] that it is impossible to **separate** faith from love for God,
AP : 0 7 :001(168) [0227] wicked are not to be **separated** from the church since
AP : 0 7 :003(168) [0227] the impression that we **separate** evil men and hypocrites
AP : 0 7 :014(170) [0231] is a spiritual people, **separated** from the heathen not by
AP : 0 7 :014(170) [0231] inasmuch as God had **separated** these physical
AP : 0 7 :019(171) [0233] and says that the true church will be **separated** from it.
AP : 0 7 :019(171) [0233] spiritual people will be **separated** from the physical
AP : 1 2 :009(184) [0255] in fact they are not so **separated** as these clever sophists
AP : 1 2 :061(190) [0269] a subtle distinction **separating** absolution from
AP : 1 2 :061(190) [0269] other hand, they do not **separate** the reception of
AP : 2 3 :027(243) [0371] Testament were to be **separated** from their wives; since
AP : 2 3 :059(247) [0379] we seem to have **separated** ourselves from those who are
AP : 2 4 :035(256) [0397] of them and ought not to be **separated** from them.
S 3 : 1 1 :002(314) [0499] they had the power to **separate** such creatures of God or
TR : 0 0 :062(330) [0523] persons, by gathering **separate** followings around
LC : 0 1 :066(373) [0599] himself intervenes and **separates** right from wrong, good
LC : 0 2 :031(414) [0687] completely divide and **separate** us from the wicked world,
LC : 0 2 :056(418) [0693] of sin have expelled and **separated** themselves from the
LC : 0 4 :016(438) [0735] know that water is water, if such a **separation** is proper?
LC : 0 4 :016(438) [0735] which he does not wish his ordinance to be **separated**?
LC : 0 4 :022(439) [0737] water, must by no means be **separated** from each other.
LC : 0 4 :022(439) [0737] For where the Word is **separated** from the water, the
LC : 0 4 :030(440) [0739] are so foolish as to **separate** faith from the object to which
LC : 0 6 :018(459) [0000] therefore take care to keep the two parts clearly **separate**.
EP : 0 1 :010(467) [0781] except God alone can **separate** the corruption of our
EP : 0 1 :010(467) [0781] sin and completely **separated** and removed from it, as Job
EP : 0 3 :010(474) [0795] holy apostle Paul which **separate** the merit of Christ
EP : 0 7 :001(481) [0807] Confession since they **separated** themselves from the
EP : 1 2 :029(500) [0843] distinct divine essence, **separate** from the other persons of
EP : 1 2 :029(500) [0843] people who are essentially **separate** from one another.
SD : PR :014(506) [0857] from strange voices and **separate** the precious from the
SD : 0 1 :033(514) [0869] itself as two manifestly **separate** things, nevertheless our
SD : 0 3 :041(546) [0929] and sanctification are **separated** from each other in such a

Continued ▶

SD : 04 :012(553) [0941] as impossible to **separate** works from faith as it is to
SD : 04 :012(553) [0941] from faith as it is to **separate** heat and light from fire."
SD : 07 :119(590) [1013] it as heaven and earth are **separated** from each other.
SD : 08 :006(592) [1017] the Son of God is a **separate**, distinct, and complete
SD : 08 :007(592) [1017] will henceforth never be **separated**, blended with each
SD : 08 :015(594) [1019] This would **separate** the two natures from each other and
SD : 08 :016(594) [1021] and human natures are **separated** and distinct from each
SD : 08 :032(597) [1025] and that these are not **separated** from one nature and
SD : 08 :036(598) [1027] nature as something **separate** but to the entire person who
SD : 08 :043(599) [1029] works are divided and **separated**, the person will also
SD : 08 :043(599) [1029] will also have to be **separated**, since all the doing and
SD : 08 :071(605) [1041] received equal majesty, **separated** or divided from the
SD : 08 :073(605) [1041] Spirit, who is never **separated** from the Son), it follows
SD : 08 :082(607) [1045] too, since he is not two **separate** persons but a single
SD : 08 :083(607) [1045] space and place had **separated** the two natures from one
SD : 08 :083(607) [1045] devils had been unable to **separate** and tear them apart.
SD : 08 :084(607) [1045] not let themselves be **separated** and divided from each
SD : 08 :084(608) [1045] one person and never **separates** the assumed humanity
SD : 10 :006(611) [1055] out from them and be **separate** from them, says the Lord"
SD : 11 :047(624) [1079] of God, "who will **separate** us from the love of God in
SD : 11 :049(624) [1079] death nor life, etc. can **separate** us from the love of God
SD : 12 :024(634) [1099] each other, to go their **separate** ways, and to enter into a
SD : 12 :037(636) [1103] person has a distinct essence **separate** from the other two.
SD : 12 :037(636) [1103] distinct and essentially **separate** human persons, have the

Sequence (1)
AP : 07 :040(176) [0241] they also observed other rites and a **sequence** of lessons.

Serene (1)
AG : PR :001(024) [0039] Most **serene**, most mighty, invincible Emperor, most

Series (1)
AP : 04 :361(162) [0219] By such a **series** of arguments the blessings of Christ and

Serious (23), Seriously (11), Seriousness (3)
PR : PR :008(005) [0011] confession the more **seriously** to investigate the truth of
AG : 23 :012(052) [0063] that time there was such **serious** and strong resistance
AG : 28 :002(081) [0083] careless confusion many **serious** wars, tumults, and
AP : 02 :008(101) [0107] do not mention the more **serious** faults of human nature,
AP : 04 :062(115) [0139] terrifies our consciences with real and **serious** fears.
AP : 12 :009(183) [0255] — especially in those **serious**, true, and great terrors
AP : 12 :048(188) [0265] men do not say this **seriously**, for they neither see nor
AP : 16 :004(223) [0331] These ideas **seriously** obscure the Gospel and the spiritual
AP : 22 :007(237) [0359] We do not **seriously** object if someone takes these
AP : 23 :004(239) [0365] we have the most **serious** of reasons, taken from the Word
AP : 23 :005(239) [0365] But they are not **serious** in their defense of celibacy.
AP : 23 :018(242) [0369] are only clowning; they do not mean this **seriously**.
AP : 27 :001(269) [0419] that he was a mild old man, **serious** but not morose.
AP : 27 :056(278) [0439] Therefore there are many **serious** and cogent reasons that
AP : 28 :004(281) [0445] In these very **serious** and difficult controversies the people
S1 : PR :002(288) [0455] ever became so bold as **seriously**, in good faith, and
TR : 00 :042(328) [0517] nations and to be called schismatics is a **serious** matter.
TR : 00 :075(333) [0525] since this is a very **serious** charge, nobody should be
SC : PR :006(338) [0533] the duties of your office **seriously**, that you have pity on
LC : 01 :097(378) [0609] to and admonished but we listen without **serious** concern.
LC : 01 :101(379) [0609] other hand, when we **seriously** ponder the Word, hear it,
LC : 01 :171(388) [0629] necessary it is to devote **serious** attention to the young.
LC : 01 :208(393) [0639] institution and an object of God's **serious** concern.
LC : 01 :322(409) [0673] and esteemed as a **serious** matter to God because he
EP : 11 :018(497) [0837] doctrine that God is not **serious** about wanting all men to
SD : PR :007(502) [0849] This caused **serious** and dangerous schisms in the true
SD : PR :007(502) [0849] would involve **serious** offense for both the unbelievers and
SD : 01 :055(518) [0877] deliberately and **seriously** condemned and rejected the
SD : 01 :062(519) [0879] explained with special **seriousness** and great zeal and
SD : 02 :080(536) [0911] must condemn with all **seriousness** and zeal, and in no
SD : 03 :036(546) [0929] with all diligence and **seriousness** in the treatment of this
SD : 04 :030(555) [0947] This, of course, is a **serious** and important question since
SD : 10 :005(611) [1053] of the papists, or that we are not **seriously** opposed to it.
SD : 10 :015(613) [1057] of the holy apostle so **seriously** commanded the church to
SD : 10 :023(615) [1061] nations and to be called schismatics is a **serious** matter.
SD : 11 :001(616) [1063] the occasion of very **serious** controversies at other places
SD : 11 :094(632) [1095] some have erred and **serious** religious contentions have

Sermon (11), Sermons (22)
AG : 20 :003(041) [0053] when for the most part **sermons** were concerned with
AG : 00 :002(095) [0095] about burials, about **sermons** on special occasions, and
AL : 20 :008(042) [0053] righteousness of faith in **sermons** while only the teaching
AL : 26 :015(066) [0073] Schools and **sermons** were so preoccupied with gathering
AP : 04 :014(109) [0123] of some who, in their **sermons**, laid aside the Gospel and
AP : 04 :190(133) [0175] The dangers, labors, and **sermons** of the apostle Paul,
AP : 04 :261(145) [0195] Thus in Daniel's **sermon** (4:24) faith is required.
AP : 04 :261(145) [0195] Daniel's **sermon** contains two parts.
AP : 04 :284(150) [0201] Moreover, why do they not present the whole **sermon**?
AP : 12 :158(207) [0301] Isaiah teaches in a long **sermon** in his twenty-eighth
AP : 15 :042(220) [0325] many regions where no **sermons** are preached during the
AP : 15 :043(221) [0327] on the other hand, all **sermons** deal with topics like these:
AP : 21 :023(232) [0349] opponents' books and **sermons** there are even greater
AP : 24 :043(257) [0399] In their **sermons** they do not preach the Gospel or
AP : 24 :046(258) [0401] All their books and **sermons** were silent about the
AP : 24 :050(259) [0401] Practical and clear **sermons** hold an audience, but neither
AP : 27 :004(269) [0421] vain they are in their **sermons** and in thinking up new
LC : PR :002(358) [0567] in their titles to be: "**Sermons** That Preach Themselves,"
LC : SP :001(362) [0575] This **sermon** has been undertaken for the instruction of
LC : SP :003(362) [0575] Catechism or children's **sermons** and diligently drilled in
LC : SP :024(364) [0579] will learn and retain this teaching from **sermons** alone.
LC : 01 :099(378) [0609] who, after hearing a **sermon** or two, become sick and
LC : 02 :032(415) [0687] not the brief children's **sermons**, but rather the longer
LC : 02 :032(415) [0687] but rather the longer **sermons** throughout the year,
EP : 01 :023(469) [0785] not be employed in **sermons** delivered to common,
EP : 09 :003(492) [0827] memory taught in his **sermon** preached at Torgau in the
EP : 12 :010(498) [0839] That no one should hear **sermons** or attend services in
SD : PR :007(502) [0849] all of these in their **sermons** and in their writings, though
SD : 01 :054(517) [0877] be spared these terms in **sermons**, since they are not the
SD : 02 :053(531) [0903] can go to church, listen to the **sermon**, or not listen to it.
SD : 07 :076(583) [0999] Chrysostom says in his ***Sermon** on the Passion*: "Christ
SD : 09 :001(610) [1051] Luther directs us in the **sermon** that he held in the castle
SD : 12 :015(634) [1099] not hear or attend on a **sermon** in those temples in which

Serpent (9)
AP : 02 :007(101) [0107] the apple or through the **serpent**'s breath, and whether
AP : 04 :095(121) [0149] "As Moses lifted up the **serpent** in the wilderness, so must
S3 : 08 :005(312) [0495] the old devil and the old **serpent** who made enthusiasts of
LC : 03 :111(435) [0729] For he has a **serpent**'s head; if it finds an opening into
EP : 01 :022(469) [0785] say, "It is the nature of a **serpent** to sting," and, "It is the
SD : 01 :051(517) [0875] the statement, "It is the **serpent**'s nature to bite and
SD : 05 :023(562) [0959] through the deceit of the **serpent** transgressed God's laws,
SD : 05 :023(562) [0959] who would bruise the **serpent**'s head; likewise, of the seed
SD : 11 :072(628) [1087] of a fish give him a **serpent**; or if he asks for an egg, will

Servant (25), Servants (45)
AG : 06 :002(032) [0047] you, say, 'We are unworthy **servants**'" (Luke 17:10).
AG : 09 :007(096) [0095] Your Imperial Majesty's most obedient **servants**:
AL : 06 :001(032) [0047] things, say, 'We are unprofitable **servants**'" (Luke 17:10).
AP : 04 :168(130) [0169] into judgment with thy **servant**; for no man living is
AP : 04 :168(130) [0169] Even this **servant** of God prays God to avert his
AP : 04 :326(157) [0211] into judgment with thy **servant**, for no man living is
AP : 04 :326(157) [0211] even to all the saints and **servants** of God, if God does
AP : 04 :334(158) [0215] is commanded you, say, 'We are unworthy **servants**.'"
AP : 04 :337(159) [0215] believed everything, say, 'We are unworthy **servants**.'"
AP : 04 :337(159) [0215] in the promise confesses that we are unworthy **servants**.
AP : 04 :338(159) [0215] believed everything, say, 'We are unworthy **servants**,'"
AP : 04 :342(159) [0215] to interpret "unworthy **servants**" as meaning that works
AP : 04 :342(160) [0215] "Unworthy **servants**" means "insufficient servants," since
AP : 04 :342(160) [0215] means "insufficient **servants**," since no one fears, loves, or
AP : 12 :078(193) [0275] into judgment with thy **servant**; for no man living is
S1 : PR :015(291) [0459] own, and by thy glorious advent deliver thy **servants**.
S3 : 07 :002(312) [0493] into judgment with thy **servant**, for no man living is
SC : PR :018(340) [0537] and even farmers and **servants**, for many of these are
SC : 01 :020(344) [0543] our neighbor's wife, **servants**, or cattle, but encourage
SC : 03 :014(347) [0549] children, trustworthy **servants**, godly and faithful rulers,
SC : 05 :020(350) [0553] or daughter, a master or **servant**; whether you have been
SC : 05 :023(350) [0553] in training my children, **servants**, and wife to the glory of
SC : 09 :004(355) [0561] sword in vain; he is the **servant** of God to execute his
SC : 09 :010(356) [0563] Laborers and **Servants**, Male and Female
SC : 09 :010(356) [0563] as men-pleasers, but as **servants** of Christ, doing the will
LC : PR :002(358) [0567] shameful gluttons and **servants** of their bellies would
LC : SP :004(362) [0575] his children and **servants** at least once a week and
LC : SP :010(363) [0577] not covet his wife, man-**servant**, maid-servant, cattle, or
LC : SP :010(363) [0577] wife, man-servant, maid-**servant**, cattle, or anything that
LC : SP :017(363) [0577] he should dismiss man-**servants** and maid-servants if they
LC : SP :017(363) [0577] man-servants and maid-**servants** if they do not know
LC : 01 :060(372) [0597] wives and children and **servants**, and troubles of every
LC : 01 :073(374) [0601] and body, wife, children, **servants**, and all that we have —
LC : 01 :083(376) [0603] common people — man-**servants** and maid-servants who
LC : 01 :083(376) [0603] man-servants and maid-**servants** who have attended to
LC : 01 :142(384) [0621] have domestics (man-**servants** and maid-servants) under
LC : 01 :142(384) [0621] (man-servants and maid-**servants**) under him to manage
LC : 01 :143(385) [0621] Therefore man-**servants** and maid-servants should take
LC : 01 :143(385) [0623] man-servants and maid-**servants** should take care not
LC : 01 :145(385) [0623] upon the poor people, a **servant** girl would dance for joy
LC : 01 :151(386) [0625] will turn out badly; **servants**, neighbors, or strangers and
LC : 01 :154(386) [0625] as much wrong from your own wife, children, or **servants**.
LC : 01 :168(388) [0629] of their children, **servants**, subjects, etc., but especially to
LC : 01 :170(388) [0629] and amusement, gave us **servants** merely to put them to
LC : 01 :175(389) [0631] bring up their children and **servants** to be godly.
LC : 01 :225(395) [0643] for example, that a man-**servant** or maid-servant is
LC : 01 :225(395) [0643] a man-servant or maid-**servant** is unfaithful in his or her
LC : 01 :225(395) [0645] carelessness, or malice a **servant** wastes and neglects
LC : 01 :225(395) [0645] and unintentionally — a **servant** can cheat his employer
LC : 01 :225(395) [0645] with a noose, but the **servant** may even become defiant
LC : 01 :226(395) [0645] my good friends, my own **servants**, from whom I expect
LC : 01 :235(397) [0647] Now, you **servants** ought to take care of your master's or
LC : 01 :256(399) [0653] before his wife, children, **servants**, and neighbors.
LC : 01 :277(402) [0659] master of the house sees a **servant** failing to do his duty,
LC : 01 :277(402) [0659] so foolish as to leave the **servant** at home while he went
LC : 01 :292(404) [0663] *not covet his wife, man-**servant**, maid-servant, cattle, or*
LC : 01 :292(404) [0663] *wife, man-servant, maid-**servant**, cattle, or anything that*
LC : 01 :294(404) [0665] Jewish government man-**servants** and maid-servants were
LC : 01 :294(404) [0665] man-servants and maid-**servants** were not free, as now, to
LC : 01 :295(404) [0665] a master to dismiss his **servants** or entice his neighbor's
LC : 01 :296(405) [0665] to him, such as his wife, **servants**, house, fields, meadows,
LC : 01 :306(406) [0669] lure away another's man-**servant** or maid-servant or
LC : 01 :306(406) [0669] man-servant or maid-**servant** or otherwise estrange them
LC : 02 :013(412) [0681] of support, wife and child, **servants**, house and home, etc.
LC : 03 :028(424) [0705] magistrates, neighbors, **servants**; and, as we have said, he
LC : 03 :076(431) [0721] good wife, children, and **servants**; to cause our work,
SD : 02 :085(537) [0913] resists God entirely and is completely the **servant** of sin.
SD : 06 :021(567) [0969] into judgment with thy **servant**; for no man living is
SD : 08 :026(596) [1023] entirely the form of a **servant** (without, however, laying
SD : 08 :051(600) [1031] after the form of the **servant** had been laid aside and after

Serve (54), Served (7), Serves (13), Serving (4)
PR : PR :017(008) [0015] to ourselves the right and **served** notice that we would
AG : PR :013(026) [0041] allow, that may **serve** the cause of Christian unity.
AG : 16 :002(037) [0051] sin occupy civil offices or **serve** as princes and judges,
AG : 16 :002(037) [0051] engage in just wars, **serve** as soldiers, buy and sell, take
AG : 26 :001(064) [0071] been instituted by men **serve** to earn grace and make
AG : 26 :040(069) [0075] and the like) which **serve** to preserve order in the church.
AG : 27 :013(073) [0077] or the like, all of whom **serve** in their appointed calling
AG : 27 :057(080) [0083] understand that one is to **serve** God by observing the
AL : 16 :002(037) [0051] to engage in just wars, to **serve** as soldiers, to make legal
AL : 27 :013(073) [0077] man-made observances, **serve** their calling in accordance
AL : 27 :057(080) [0083] perceive that God is to be **served** by observing the
AP : 04 :168(130) [0169] (Rom. 7:25), "I of myself **serve** the law of God with my
AP : 04 :168(130) [0169] with my mind, but with my flesh I **serve** the law of sin."
AP : 04 :168(130) [0169] Here he openly says that he **serves** the law of sin.

Continued ▶

AP : 07 :033(175) [0239] contain a discipline that **serves** to educate and instruct the
AP : 12 :113(199) [0285] Chastising the lapsed **served** as an example, as the gloss
AP : 12 :144(205) [0297] and so they do not **serve** to placate God's displeasure, as
AP : 12 :153(206) [0299] Death itself **serves** this same purpose: to destroy this
AP : 15 :015(217) [0319] to establish rites that **serve** to merit grace or
AP : 15 :020(218) [0321] seasons and various rites **serve** as reminders for the
AP : 15 :036(220) [0325] them, for this was to **serve** as an example to the Pharisees
AP : 21 :036(234) [0353] that the saints have done **serve** as examples to men in
AP : 22 :004(236) [0359] says, "The priests who **serve** the Eucharist and distribute
AP : 23 :032(244) [0373] woman is saved if she **serves** faithfully in these duties of
AP : 23 :039(244) [0375] Each should **serve** faithfully in what he has been given to
AP : 23 :040(244) [0375] praying, teaching, and **serving** and is not so distracted by
AP : 27 :022(272) [0427] are still some good men **serving** the ministry of the Word
AP : 27 :064(280) [0441] on the widows who **served** the church and were
S1 : PR :001(288) [0455] articles of our faith to **serve** as a basis for possible
S2 : 02 :026(297) [0469] and services for them, **serve** them in still other ways,
S2 : 03 :002(298) [0471] If they are unwilling to **serve** this purpose, it would be
TR : 00 :008(321) [0505] let the greatest among you become as one who **serves**."
SC : 01 :008(343) [0541] them to anger, but honor, **serve**, obey, love, and esteem
SC : 02 :002(345) [0543] of this I am bound to thank, praise, **serve**, and obey him.
SC : 02 :004(345) [0545] him in his kingdom, and **serve** him in everlasting
LC : 01 :042(370) [0591] meanwhile, those who **serve** mammon have power,
LC : 01 :111(380) [0613] body and possessions), **serving** them, helping them, and
LC : 01 :115(381) [0613] If they wish to **serve** God with truly good works, they
LC : 01 :119(381) [0615] It **serves** them right for their devilish perversity in
LC : 01 :147(385) [0623] a person holy; faith alone **serves** him, while our works
LC : 01 :147(385) [0623] faith alone serves him, while our works **serve** the people.
LC : 01 :151(386) [0625] obedient, willing, ready to **serve**, and cheerfully gives
LC : 01 :172(388) [0629] and educating our children to **serve** God and mankind.
LC : 01 :178(389) [0631] This is enough to **serve** as a warning; a more extensive
LC : 01 :208(393) [0639] persons be brought up to **serve** the world, promote
LC : 01 :282(403) [0661] It would **serve** such gossips right to have their sport
LC : 01 :288(404) [0663] doing our utmost to **serve** and help him to promote his
LC : 01 :294(404) [0665] were not free, as now, to **serve** for wages according to
LC : 01 :303(406) [0667] sayings, "First come, first **served**," and "Every man must
LC : 02 :021(413) [0683] ourselves, as if we ourselves were to be feared and **served**.
LC : 02 :022(413) [0683] in duty bound to **serve** and obey him for all these things.
LC : 02 :031(414) [0685] parts of this article simply **serve** to clarify and express
LC : 03 :007(421) [0699] when properly used, may **serve** as an exercise for young
LC : 03 :027(424) [0705] Therefore it may **serve** to remind us and impress upon us
LC : 03 :037(425) [0707] with himself that all that is God's must **serve** for our use.
LC : 03 :090(432) [0723] This should **serve** God's purpose to break our pride and
LC : 05 :009(447) [0755] but not mere bread or wine such as is **served** at the table.
LC : 05 :052(452) [0765] anyone partake of the sacrament to **serve** or please us.
LC : 05 :085(456) [0773] Let this **serve** as an exhortation, then, not only for us who
LC : 05 :087(457) [0773] of the sacrament so that they may **serve** us and be useful.
EP : 06 :004(480) [0807] self-decreed and self-chosen acts of **serving** God.
EP : 10 :011(494) [0831] of the holy Gospel (which **serve** to impair the truth) in
EP : 12 :011(499) [0841] nor should one **serve** them or work for them in any way,
EP : 12 :013(499) [0841] 2. That no Christian can **serve** or function in any civic
SD : 01 :061(519) [0879] The term **serves** only to set forth the distinction between
SD : 02 :064(533) [0907] "So then, I of myself **serve** the law of God with my mind,
SD : 02 :085(537) [0913] the law of his mind he **serves** the law of God, but with his
SD : 02 :085(537) [0913] God, but with his flesh he **serves** the law of sin
SD : 03 :038(546) [0929] office and property is to **serve** as the only and exclusive
SD : 04 :012(553) [0941] do good to everyone, to **serve** everyone, to suffer
SD : 05 :001(558) [0951] brilliant light which **serves** the purpose that the Word of
SD : 06 :001(563) [0963] The law of God **serves** (1) not only to maintain external
SD : 06 :003(564) [0963] true believers learn to **serve** God not according to their
SD : 07 :069(582) [0997] wish that they might **serve** God with a stronger and more
SD : 10 :007(611) [1055] foolish spectacles, which **serve** neither good order,
SD : 10 :028(615) [1061] to their practices, since this **serves** to imperil the truth.
SD : 11 :088(631) [1093] of his call, she was told, 'The elder will **serve** the younger.'
SD : 12 :016(634) [1099] neither may one **serve** them or work for them at all, but

Service (66), Serviceable (1), Services (46)
PR : PR :001(003) [0007] below, tender our due **service**, friendship, gracious
PR : PR :001(003) [0007] humble, and willing **service**, and hereby declare:
PR : PR :023(012) [0021] who are being trained for **service** in the church and for
PR : PR :025(014) [0025] to his station, all affection, **service**, and friendship.
AG : 21 :003(047) [0057] highest form of divine **service** is sincerely to seek and call
AG : 24 :023(058) [0067] faith in Christ and true **service** of God were forgotten.
AG : 24 :041(061) [0069] Alexandria, and all these **services** were held without
AG : 26 :002(064) [0071] if these were a necessary **service** of God by means of
AG : 26 :012(066) [0073] of the opinion that they were a necessary **service** of God.
AG : 26 :021(067) [0073] they should not be made into a necessary **service** of God.
AG : 26 :023(067) [0073] Since he calls them vain **service**, they must not be
AG : 26 :029(068) [0075] nobody is a Christian unless he performs such **services**.
AG : 26 :039(069) [0075] is making a necessary **service** of fasts on prescribed days
AG : 26 :041(070) [0075] such outward forms of **service** do not make us righteous
AG : 27 :036(076) [0081] For all such **service** of God that is chosen and instituted
AG : 27 :037(077) [0081] in the precepts and **services** invented by men but that
AG : 27 :039(077) [0081] vows were an improper and false **service** of God.
AG : 27 :048(078) [0081] be presented with such a **service** of God, invented by men
AG : 27 :048(078) [0081] be taught that such a **service** would make men good and
AG : 27 :049(078) [0083] God and true and proper **service** of God are obscured
AG : 27 :050(079) [0083] True perfection and right **service** of God consist of these
AG : 28 :039(087) [0089] grace there had to be a **service** of God among Christians
AG : 28 :039(087) [0089] like the Levitical **service**, and as if God had commanded
AG : 28 :048(089) [0091] He rejects such **service** of God and says, "Every plant
AG : 28 :050(089) [0091] all proper for the bishops to require such **services** of God.
AG : 28 :052(089) [0091] we do not merit it by **services** of God instituted by men.
AG : 28 :053(090) [0091] these things necessary **services** of God and counting it a
AG : 28 :061(091) [0093] one must have **services** of God like the Levitical or Jewish
AG : 28 :061(091) [0093] the Levitical or Jewish **services** and that Christ
AL : 20 :003(041) [0053] pilgrimages, **services** in honor of saints, rosaries,
AL : 26 :002(064) [0071] exacted these works as a **service** necessary to merit grace
AL : 27 :036(076) [0081] Every **service** of God that is instituted and chosen by men
AL : 27 :037(077) [0081] for in observances and **services** devised by men but that it
AL : 27 :039(077) [0081] taken were wicked **services** and on this account were
AL : 27 :048(078) [0081] to the people a certain **service** invented by men without
AL : 27 :048(078) [0081] of God and to teach that such **service** justifies men.
AL : 27 :049(078) [0083] of God and true **service** of God are obscured when men
AL : 27 :050(079) [0083] True perfection and true **service** of God consist of these
AL : 28 :039(087) [0089] there had to be a **service** among Christians similar to the
AL : 28 :048(089) [0091] He rebukes such **services** and says, "Every plant which my
AL : 28 :050(089) [0091] bishops to institute such **services** or require them as
AL : 28 :053(090) [0091] are bound so as to regard these as necessary **services**.
AL : 28 :061(091) [0093] that there must be a **service** in the church like the
AL : 28 :061(091) [0093] church like the Levitical **service** and that Christ
AP : 04 :057(114) [0137] This **service** and worship is especially praised throughout
AP : 04 :285(150) [0201] invents other works and **services** until it despairs utterly.
AP : 04 :310(155) [0207] Thus the **service** and worship of the Gospel is to receive
AP : 12 :129(202) [0291] for men of discretion will value this **service** highly.
AP : 15 :047(221) [0327] these exercises not as **services** that justify but as restraints
AP : 16 :001(222) [0329] wars, render military **service**, enter into legal contracts,
AP : 16 :007(223) [0331] are court decisions, punishments, wars, military **service**.
AP : 23 :043(245) [0375] are occupied with public **service**, which is often so
AP : 23 :045(245) [0377] these works and **services** instead of using wine or meat or
AP : 23 :049(246) [0377] as lessons for the ignorant and not as **services** that justify.
AP : 24 :034(256) [0395] of "the priestly **service** of the gospel of God, so that
AP : 24 :052(259) [0403] The **services** of the Mass and the rest of the papal order
AP : 24 :062(260) [0405] this the church might have a **service** that reconciles God."
AP : 24 :080(264) [0411] It does not really mean a sacrifice but a public **service**.
AP : 24 :088(265) [0413] but about the whole **service**, about the prayers and
AP : 24 :088(265) [0413] "We offer Thee this reasonable and bloodless **service**."
AP : 24 :088(265) [0413] talking about the whole **service**; and by "reasonable
AP : 24 :088(265) [0413] and by "reasonable **service**" (Rom. 12:1) Paul meant the
AP : 24 :088(265) [0413] Paul meant the **service** of the mind, fear, faith,
AP : 24 :089(265) [0413] to establish such **services** in the church without the
AP : 24 :092(266) [0417] it is not safe to institute **services** in the church without the
AP : 24 :093(267) [0417] Thee this reasonable **service** for those who have departed
AP : 24 :093(267) [0417] And "reasonable **service**" does not mean the host itself
AP : 24 :097(268) [0417] Hence they increased the **services** and sacrifices.
AP : 24 :097(268) [0417] and always will, that **services** and sacrifices are
AP : 24 :097(268) [0417] faith but give equal honor to other sacrifices and **services**.
AP : 24 :098(268) [0417] church of God was there, condemning wicked **services**.
AP : 24 :098(268) [0419] reject those wicked **services** invented against God's
AP : 27 :008(269) [0421] human and "factitious" **services**, as some writers call
AP : 27 :009(269) [0421] Do those **services** merit the forgiveness of sins and
AP : 27 :009(270) [0423] of the Mass, the wicked **services** to the saints, and the
AP : 27 :021(272) [0427] works themselves are **services** that justify or merit eternal
AP : 27 :023(272) [0427] these observances are **services** because of which we are
AP : 27 :023(273) [0427] maintain that these are **services** which God approves as
AP : 27 :024(273) [0427] they teach that these observances are **services** that justify.
AP : 27 :024(273) [0427] they are more perfect **services** than other ways of life,
AP : 27 :026(273) [0429] Hence they are neither justifying **services** nor perfection.
AP : 27 :035(275) [0431] calls traditions "useless **services**," they are not evangelical
AP : 27 :042(276) [0435] from this that it is a **service** to God to commit suicide and
AP : 27 :042(276) [0435] to maintain that it is a **service** to God to leave
AP : 27 :047(277) [0437] therefore merely a human tradition, it is a useless **service**.
AP : 27 :069(281) [0443] cinctures — all these are unprofitable **services** before God.
AP : 27 :070(281) [0443] not for the sake of such **services**, and that God is pleased
AP : 27 :070(281) [0443] God is pleased only with **services** instituted by his Word
S2 : 02 :012(295) [0465] and all the pomp, **services**, and business transactions
S2 : 02 :023(296) [0469] Mass, etc., their use is a good work and a **service** of God.
S2 : 02 :026(297) [0469] churches, altars, and **services** for them, serve them in still
S2 : 03 :002(298) [0471] with their blasphemous **services**, invented by men, which
S2 : 03 :002(298) [0471] the prophets call such **service** of God *aven*, that is,
S2 : 04 :014(301) [0475] and human works and **services** (which are the essence of
TR : 00 :048(328) [0519] most trivial traditions are **services** of God and perfection,
SC : 01 :018(344) [0541] of legal right, but be of **service** and help to him so that he
SC : 09 :010(356) [0563] not in the way of eye-**service**, as men-pleasers, but as
SC : 09 :010(356) [0563] the heart, rendering **service** with a good will as to the
LC : 01 :022(367) [0585] as if God were in our **service** or debt and we were his liege
LC : 01 :064(373) [0599] to use it in the **service** of truth and all that is good — for
LC : 01 :064(373) [0599] calling upon his name in **service** of truth and using it
LC : 01 :114(380) [0613] home in obedience and **service** to their parents, and we
LC : 01 :136(383) [0619] obedience and love and **service**, and he will reward you
LC : 01 :144(385) [0623] pay for the privilege of **service** and be glad to acquire
LC : 01 :174(388) [0631] so that they may be of **service** wherever they are needed.
LC : 01 :190(391) [0635] and robbed him of the **service** by which his life might
LC : 01 :233(396) [0647] especially when he takes remuneration for such **services**.
LC : 01 :235(397) [0647] to do them the favor and **service** of protecting them from
LC : 01 :309(407) [0669] may be profitable and **serviceable** to him, as we wish that
LC : 02 :019(412) [0681] all these things to his **service**, as he has required and
EP : 12 :010(498) [0839] hear sermons or attend **services** in those temples where
SD : 06 :020(567) [0969] set up a self-elected **service** of God and without his Word
SD : 12 :017(634) [1099] Testament era government **service** is not a godly estate.

Servile (1)
AP : 12 :038(187) [0261] anxious heart, whereas in **servile** fear faith does not

Servitude (1)
SD : 01 :013(511) [0863] abandoned to his power, and held captive in his **servitude**.

Session (1)
PR : PR :020(010) [0017] his ascension, and his **session** at the right hand of God's

Set (157), Sets (15), Setting (14)
PR : PR :011(006) [0011] a document in which they **set** forth how the differences
PR : PR :014(007) [0013] the Christian doctrine **set** forth in the explanation that
PR : PR :022(011) [0019] Supper, these have to be **set** forth expressly and distinctly
AG : PR :008(025) [0039] and of our own faith, **setting** forth how and in what
AG : 12 :005(035) [0049] this faith will comfort the heart and again **set** it at rest.
AG : 00 :001(047) [0059] cannot disagree with us in the articles **set** forth above.
AG : 27 :006(071) [0077] even the papal canons might have **set** many of them free.
AG : 28 :002(081) [0083] but have also presumed to **set** up and depose kings and
AG : 28 :013(083) [0085] of the other, should not **set** up and depose kings, should
AG : 28 :052(089) [0091] "For freedom Christ has **set** us free; stand fast, therefore,
AL : 13 :002(035) [0049] the promises that are **set** forth and offered, is added.
AL : 21 :002(047) [0057] intercessor whom the Scriptures **set** before us is Christ.
AL : 00 :003(095) [0095] at issue, being briefly **set** forth, may more readily be
AP : 02 :050(106) [0119] any innovations, but have **set** forth the Holy Scripture
AP : 04 :032(111) [0129] "The mind that is **set** on the flesh is hostile to God;
AP : 04 :033(111) [0129] If the mind that is **set** on the flesh is hostile to God, then

Continued ▶

A P : 0 4 :046(113) [0133] forgiveness of sins, faith **sets** against God's wrath not our
A P : 0 4 :080(118) [0143] Since Christ is **set** forth to be the propitiator, through
A P : 0 4 :080(118) [0143] appease God's wrath by **setting** forth our own works.
A P : 0 4 :081(118) [0145] We cannot **set** our love or our works against the wrath of
A P : 0 4 :082(118) [0145] mercy promised in him and **set** it against the wrath and
A P : 0 4 :106(122) [0153] righteousness of law is **set** forth in the statement that he
A P : 0 4 :137(126) [0161] own strength cannot achieve what they **set** out to do.
A P : 0 4 :146(127) [0163] the judgment of God they **set** a trust in their own works,
A P : 0 4 :195(134) [0175] conscience, for we cannot **set** any works of ours against
A P : 0 4 :212(136) [0179] great work that they can **set** against the wrath and
A P : 0 4 :215(137) [0179] due him, for he has been **set** forth as the propitiator
A P : 0 4 :222(138) [0181] sin and death; that we can **set** our love against the wrath
A P : 0 4 :247(142) [0191] promise of Christ when we **set** it against the terrors of sin
A P : 0 4 :267(146) [0197] because Daniel clearly **sets** forth a promise, he necessarily
A P : 0 4 :270(147) [0197] (Ex. 20:6), **setting** forth the most ample promise of the
A P : 0 4 :291(152) [0203] and that we should **set** him, the mediator and
A P : 0 4 :300(153) [0205] not mention how we must **set** Christ against the wrath of
A P : 0 4 :314(156) [0207] and death since we cannot **set** our love and keeping of the
A P : 0 7 :009(169) [0229] We **set** forth this doctrine for a very necessary reason.
A P : 0 7 :042(177) [0243] of having to observe a **set** time, since they tell them not to
A P : 1 1 :005(181) [0249] But we do not prescribe a **set** time because not everyone
A P : 1 1 :005(181) [0249] ancient canons and the Fathers do not appoint a **set** time.
A P : 1 2 :035(186) [0261] of Christ ought to be **set** forth to consciences — the
A P : 1 2 :060(190) [0267] this personal faith, and we **set** it in opposition to the
A P : 1 2 :078(193) [0275] We cannot **set** them against the wrath and judgment of
A P : 1 2 :084(194) [0277] sake, by faith we ought to **set** against the wrath of God
A P : 1 2 :085(194) [0277] and that we ought to **set** our love and works against the
A P : 1 2 :087(195) [0277] For we must not **set** our love or works against the wrath
A P : 1 2 :091(195) [0279] We have said why we **set** forth contrition and faith as the
A P : 1 2 :108(198) [0283] eternal wrath, and I cannot **set** my righteousness or my
A P : 1 2 :108(198) [0283] Yes, we cannot **set** our merits against Thy judgment, but
A P : 1 2 :130(202) [0291] hear teachers capable of **setting** their consciences at rest.
A P : 1 2 :143(204) [0297] by God's law but have a **set** form derived from human
A P : 1 2 :146(205) [0297] death assails us, we must **set** something else against it.
A P : 1 2 :146(205) [0297] gives us the victory if we **set** our satisfactions against
A P : 1 2 :167(208) [0303] for the sake of **setting** an example; they did not think that
A P : 1 5 :005(215) [0317] on the other hand, **set** up these traditions as another
A P : 1 5 :007(216) [0317] What is this but to **set** up another justifier and mediator
A P : 1 5 :020(218) [0321] they gave the people a **set** time to assemble, because they
A P : 1 5 :038(220) [0325] keep the old traditions **set** up in the church because they
A P : 2 0 :010(228) [0341] passages in Scripture to **set** his mind at ease, for Paul
A P : 2 3 :004(239) [0365] God, while our opponents **set** against them their own
A P : 2 3 :022(242) [0369] and no snares should be **set** for the weak through this
A P : 2 3 :024(243) [0371] the Roman pontiffs have **set** up since the ancient synods
A P : 2 4 :007(250) [0385] long time good men have wanted some limits **set** to them.
A P : 2 4 :014(251) [0389] and to do this we must first **set** down the nature of a
A P : 2 4 :024(253) [0391] Gospel was promised in order to **set** forth a propitiation.
A P : 2 4 :031(255) [0395] rising of the sun to its **setting** my name is great among the
A P : 2 4 :058(260) [0405] We would be **setting** up other mediators besides Christ if
A P : 2 4 :094(267) [0417] more recent theologians, we **set** them against the clearest
A P : 2 4 :099(268) [0419] We have **set** forth such an important issue with the
A P : 2 7 :017(271) [0425] of our works but by **setting** his merits and his propitiation
A P : 2 7 :017(271) [0425] Whoever **sets** his own merits, in addition to Christ's
A P : 2 7 :032(274) [0431] by faith and do not **set** their merits against the judgment
A P : 2 7 :049(277) [0437] This **sets** forth the example of obedience in a calling.
A P : 2 7 :052(278) [0437] the Pharisees for **setting** up traditions contrary to the
A P : 2 7 :062(280) [0441] vastly different purposes are **set** forth for monasticism.
A P : 2 8 :004(281) [0445] evident questions they **set** forth an edict written in blood,
A P : 2 8 :015(283) [0447] with which Christ has **set** you free, and do not submit
A P : 2 8 :016(283) [0449] by time, and they did not **set** them down as though they
A P : 2 8 :021(284) [0449] Clearly it does not **set** down the universal commandment
S 1 : P R :012(290) [0459] twenty diets would not be able to **set** things right again.
S 2 : 0 4 :010(300) [0475] has raised himself over and **set** himself against Christ, for
S 2 : 0 4 :013(300) [0475] He had to **set** himself up as equal to and above Christ and
S 3 : 0 3 :014(305) [0483] priests and monks, that we might **set** ourselves against sin.
S 3 : 0 6 :004(311) [0493] of both as heresy and thus **set** themselves against and
S 3 : 1 4 :001(315) [0501] the first chief article, they must be absolutely **set** aside.
T R : 0 0 :011(321) [0507] more than the Word, nor **set** the authority of Cephas
T R : 0 0 :032(325) [0513] worldly kingdom would be **set** up on the pretext of
T R : 0 0 :034(325) [0513] be that external government which the pope had **set** up.
T R : 0 0 :040(327) [0515] the church and that he has **set** up this kingdom for
T R : 0 0 :059(330) [0521] in the Apology we have **set** forth in general terms what
T R : 0 0 :062(331) [0523] chose one of their number, **set** him in a higher place, and
S C : P R :024(341) [0539] you need to do is clearly to **set** forth the advantage and
S C : 0 5 :023(350) [0553] I have **set** a bad example by my immodest language and
S C : 0 9 :013(356) [0563] and is left all alone, has **set** her hope on God and
L C : 0 1 :017(367) [0585] Everyone has **set** up a god of his own, to which he looked
L C : 0 1 :023(367) [0587] an "apple-god" — and **setting** up ourselves as God?
L C : 0 1 :080(375) [0603] In the Old Testament God **set** apart the seventh day and
L C : 0 1 :082(376) [0603] from all of which we are now **set** free through Christ.
L C : 0 1 :085(376) [0605] do, at least one day in the week must be **set** apart for it.
L C : 0 1 :089(377) [0605] time and leisure, we must **set** apart several hours a week
L C : 0 1 :112(380) [0613] would have been able to **set** his conscience right toward
L C : 0 1 :114(380) [0613] men did not feel obliged to **set** forth God's
L C : 0 1 :116(381) [0615] toward God and are not **set** into opposition to the
L C : 0 1 :125(382) [0617] that God would **set** up a block or a stone which we might
L C : 0 1 :157(386) [0625] this I have been obliged to **set** forth with such a profusion
L C : 0 1 :185(390) [0633] of others, and he has **set** up this commandment as a wall,
L C : 0 1 :221(395) [0643] — which you can joyfully **set** over against all "spiritual
L C : 0 1 :261(400) [0655] Here we have a goal **set** for our jurists: perfect justice and
L C : 0 1 :284(403) [0661] teaching, which is publicly **set** forth in books and shouted
L C : 0 1 :301(405) [0667] lawsuits in which someone **sets** out to gain and squeeze
L C : 0 1 :310(407) [0669] Therefore he **sets** it forth in plain words: "You shall not
L C : 0 2 :001(411) [0679] Creed properly follows, **setting** forth all that we must
L C : 0 2 :002(411) [0679] as we said above, they are **set** on so high a plane that all
L C : 0 3 :072(430) [0719] take a loaf of bread from the oven to **set** on the table.
L C : 0 3 :096(433) [0725] But he has **set** up this condition for our strengthening and
L C : 0 3 :097(433) [0725] given the promise and hast **set** thy seal to it, making it as
L C : 0 3 :119(436) [0731] Thus God has briefly **set** before us all the afflictions that
L C : 0 4 :011(437) [0735] Here the devil **sets** to work to blind us with false
L C : 0 5 :044(451) [0763] that the devil always **sets** himself against this and every
L C : 0 6 :001(457) [0000] We have been **set** free from his coercion and from the
L C : 0 6 :013(458) [0000] some problem or quarrel **sets** us at one another's throats
L C : 0 6 :018(459) [0000] We should **set** little value on our work but exalt and
E P : R N :006(465) [0779] should conform to the standards **set** forth above.
E P : R N :008(465) [0779] expositions of the faith, **setting** forth how at various
E P : 0 1 :007(467) [0781] These points clearly **set** forth the distinction between the
E P : 0 1 :025(469) [0785] This terminology **sets** forth very clearly the distinction
E P : 0 2 :003(470) [0787] Likewise, "The mind that is **set** on the flesh is hostile to
E P : 0 5 :006(478) [0803] and which his apostles also **set** forth (examples of this
E P : 0 7 :003(482) [0809] crass Sacramentarians who **set** forth in clear German
E P : 0 7 :012(483) [0811] Christ, really and truly **set** at this right hand of God
E P : 0 7 :012(483) [0811] but only Mary's Son, is so **set** down at the right hand of
E P : 0 7 :021(484) [0813] to the doctrine **set** forth above and to our simple faith and
E P : 1 0 :006(493) [0829] "For freedom Christ has **set** us free; stand fast therefore,
E P : 1 1 :022(497) [0837] since we have not only **set** forth the pure doctrine but
S D : P R :001(501) [0847] was once more clearly **set** forth on the basis of the Word
S D : P R :003(501) [0847] Christian witness, **setting** forth the faith and the teaching
S D : P R :005(502) [0847] Confession or to **set** up a different and new confession.
S D : P R :006(502) [0847] the Christian doctrine **set** forth in this Confession has
S D : P R :005(504) [0851] the form in which it was **set** down in writing in the year
S D : P R :006(504) [0853] and published in 1531 to **set** forth clearly the true and
S D : P R :007(505) [0853] grounds and reasons are **set** forth at necessary length for
S D : P R :009(505) [0853] of blessed memory clearly **set** forth in his writings on the
S D : P R :016(507) [0857] This agreement we have **set** forth as a certain and public
S D : P R :019(507) [0857] reasons, we wanted to **set** forth and explain our faith and
S D : 0 1 :004(509) [0861] aforementioned writings to **set** forth in short chapters the
S D : 0 1 :011(510) [0863] heart, sensation, and mind-**set** which, in its highest
S D : 0 1 :061(519) [0879] The term serves only to **set** forth the distinction between
S D : 0 2 :001(520) [0881] We shall therefore first of all **set** forth the real issue in
S D : 0 2 :013(523) [0885] For the mind that is **set** on the flesh (the natural man's
S D : 0 2 :017(524) [0887] this text: "The mind that is **set** on the flesh is hostile to
S D : 0 2 :027(526) [0891] opinion as he had **set** it forth in his treatise *Concerning*
S D : 0 2 :048(530) [0901] We shall now **set** forth from the Word of God how man
S D : 0 2 :089(538) [0915] way and after the manner **set** forth and explained above.
S D : 0 2 :090(539) [0915] God, in the manner and degree **set** forth in detail above.
S D : 0 3 :005(540) [0917] otherwise, which will be **set** forth below in the antitheses,
S D : 0 3 :041(546) [0931] This has been **set** forth above.
S D : 0 3 :044(547) [0931] The doctrine has been **set** forth in detail in the previously
S D : 0 3 :066(550) [0937] by faith before God as it is **set** forth, explained, and
S D : 0 4 :018(554) [0943] spirit by those whom the Son of God has **set** free.
S D : 0 5 :023(562) [0959] have continually been **set** forth side by side in the church
S D : 0 5 :026(563) [0961] is thoroughly and mightily **set** forth by St. Paul in II Cor.
S D : 0 6 :010(565) [0965] It is also necessary to **set** forth distinctly what the Gospel
S D : 0 6 :020(567) [0969] the Holy Spirit's guidance **set** up a self-elected service of
S D : 0 7 :002(569) [0973] Yet when we press them to **set** forth their meaning
S D : 0 7 :011(571) [0975] And it is not only **set** forth still more clearly in the
S D : 0 7 :017(572) [0979] correct and true meaning is **set** forth briefly and precisely
S D : 0 7 :042(576) [0985] Thus the position **set** forth above rests on a unique, firm,
S D : 0 7 :076(583) [0999] make of the bread and wine **set** before us the body and
S D : 0 7 :076(583) [0999] is my body,' the elements **set** before us in the Supper are
S D : 0 7 :084(584) [1001] just as St. Paul **sets** the whole action of the breaking of
S D : 0 7 :111(589) [1011] we have intended to **set** forth primarily our confession
S D : 0 7 :111(589) [1011] We shall therefore **set** forth and recite the errors
S D : 0 7 :112(589) [1011] or contrary to the doctrine **set** forth above, based as it is
S D : 0 7 :128(591) [1015] or opposed to the doctrine **set** forth above, well founded
S D : 0 8 :063(603) [1037] To **set** forth correctly the majesty of Christ by way of
S D : 0 8 :070(605) [1041] glory and honor and didst **set** him over the works of thy
S D : 0 8 :088(609) [1047] with the doctrine here **set** forth as contrary to the
S D : 1 0 :011(612) [1055] "For freedom Christ has **set** us free; stand fast therefore,
S D : 1 1 :001(616) [1063] we have determined to **set** forth our explanation of this
S D : 1 1 :002(616) [1063] teaching of this article is **set** forth out of the divine Word
S D : 1 1 :003(616) [1063] misunderstanding, we must **set** forth the correct meaning
S D : 1 1 :006(617) [1065] in such a way that God **sets** a limit and measure for the
S D : 1 1 :058(625) [1081] Paul **sets** a definite limit for us as to how far we should go
S D : 1 1 :086(631) [1091] sole purpose of thereby **setting** forth the righteousness of
S D : 1 1 :087(631) [1091] It **sets** forth that he saves us "according to the purpose"
S D : 1 1 :091(631) [1093] Hence if anyone so **sets** forth this teaching concerning
S D : 1 1 :091(632) [1093] this teaching is not being **set** forth according to the Word
S D : 1 2 :006(633) [1097] We wanted to **set** forth our position so clearly that our

Settle (9), Settled (11), Settlement (3)

P R : P R :011(006) [0011] differences might be **settled** and brought to a conclusion
P R : P R :022(011) [0019] and thorough **settlement** of the controverted articles in
P R : P R :026(014) [0025] see to it that they are **settled** and composed in timely
A G : P R :023(027) [0043] weighed, charitably **settled**, and brought to Christian
A P : 0 4 :241(141) [0187] should be quieted and **settled** by calmness and
A P : 0 7 :034(175) [0239] This must be **settled** in this controversy, and only then
A P : 1 2 :129(202) [0291] issues be examined and **settled** now in order to heal
A P : 2 4 :013(251) [0387] If this were the whole problem, the case would be **settled**.
L C : 0 1 :066(373) [0599] obedience is rendered, and quarrels are **settled**.
L C : 0 1 :185(390) [0633] to get the quarrel **settled** for the safety of all concerned.
L C : 0 6 :013(458) [0000] throats and we cannot **settle** it, and yet we do not find
E P : 0 0 :000(464) [0777] Expounded and **Settled** in Christian Fashion in
E P : 0 8 :004(487) [0819] To explain and to **settle** this controversy according to our
E P : 1 0 :003(493) [0829] 1. To **settle** this controversy we believe, teach, and
E P : 1 1 :022(497) [0837] that have developed receive a basic **settlement**.
S D : 0 0 :000(501) [0845] a Time, Resolved and **Settled** According to the Word of
S D : 0 1 :059(519) [0879] Really to **settle** this offensive and highly detrimental
S D : 0 2 :006(521) [0883] In order to **settle** this controversy in a Christian way
S D : 0 3 :008(540) [0919] the Word of God and to **settle** it by his grace, we affirm
S D : 0 4 :006(552) [0939] to arrive at a complete **settlement**, we shall state our
S D : 0 6 :004(564) [0963] explain and definitively to **settle** this controversy, we
S D : 0 8 :005(592) [1017] Christian creed, and to **settle** it definitely by God's grace,
S D : 1 0 :004(611) [1053] this controversy and to **settle** it definitively by the grace

Seven (9), Seventh (9)

A G : 2 8 :041(087) [0089] a mortal sin to omit the **seven** hours, that some foods
A P : 0 7 :001(168) [0227] have condemned the **seventh** article of our Confession in
A P : 0 7 :030(173) [0237] condemn the part of the **seventh** article in which we said,
A P : 1 3 :001(211) [0309] But they insist that we enumerate **seven** sacraments.
S 3 : 0 3 :022(306) [0485] to the ancient canons, **seven** years of penance were
S 3 : 0 3 :024(307) [0485] and canceled, first for **seven** years in a single case, then
S 3 : 1 2 :002(315) [0499] church, for, thank God, a **seven**-year-old child knows
S C : P R :018(340) [0537] For example, the **Seventh** Commandment, which treats of
S C : 0 1 :013(343) [0541] The **Seventh**

Continued ▶

S C : 0 3 :019(348) [0549] The **Seventh** Petition
L C : P R :003(358) [0567] babbling of the **Seven** Hours, it would be fine if every
L C : 0 1 :080(375) [0603] God set apart the **seventh** day and appointed it for rest
L C : 0 1 :103(379) [0611] Now follow the other **seven**, which relate to our
L C : 0 1 :221(395) [0643] The **Seventh** Commandment
L C : 0 1 :296(405) [0665] Above, the **seventh** commandment prohibits seizing or
L C : 0 1 :300(405) [0667] in the scale, where the **Seventh** Commandment applies,
L C : 0 3 :034(425) [0707] In **seven** successive articles or petitions are comprehended
S D : 1 0 :019(614) [1059] church, for, thank God, a **seven**-year-old child knows

Sever (2), Severed (8)
P R : P R :004(004) [0007] doctrine of God's Word, **sever** the bond of Christian
A G : 2 7 :041(077) [0081] in Gal. 5:4, "You are **severed** from Christ, you who would
A G : 2 7 :042(077) [0081] be justified by vows are **severed** from Christ and have
A L : 2 7 :041(077) [0081] Paul says, "You are **severed** from Christ, you who would
A L : 2 7 :042(077) [0081] be justified by vows are **severed** from Christ and fall away
A P : 0 4 :030(111) [0129] sorrow—'You are **severed** from Christ, you who would be
A P : 1 5 :008(216) [0317] Galatians (5:4), "You are **severed** from Christ, you who
A P : 2 4 :016(252) [0389] like an unskilled cook he **sever** the member at the wrong
A P : 2 7 :011(270) [0423] (Gal. 5:4), "You are **severed** from Christ, you who would
E P : 0 8 :027(490) [0825] and property has been **severed** from God and

Several (24), Severally (1)
P R : P R :000(001) [0004] as the Only Norm, of **Several** Articles about which
A G : P R :002(025) [0039] and beliefs of the **several** parties among us to unite the
A G : 2 2 :005(050) [0061] In **several** places Cyprian mentions that the cup was given
A G : 2 7 :031(075) [0079] **Several** canons and papal regulations annul vows that are
A L : 2 0 :002(041) [0053] kinds of work are pleasing to God in the **several** callings.
A L : 2 2 :005(050) [0061] Cyprian in **several** places testifies that the blood was given
A P : P R :004(098) [0099] supposed to condemn **several** articles where they could
A P : P R :005(098) [0101] They commanded me and **several** others to prepare an
A P : P R :009(099) [0101] they have condemned **several** articles in opposition to the
A P : 0 4 :106(122) [0153] A little later we shall quote **several** other statements.
A P : 0 4 :303(154) [0205] we have said **several** times that we are talking
A P : 1 2 :121(200) [0287] gloss on the canons says **several** times that these
A P : 1 8 :001(224) [0335] on free will, but they add **several** proofs which are hardly
A P : 2 3 :057(247) [0379] are making the law even more unbearable in **several** ways.
A P : 2 4 :074(262) [0409] a sacrifice, since one action can have **several** purposes.
T R : 0 0 :062(330) [0523] to prevent schism, lest **several** persons, by gathering
L C : 0 1 :089(377) [0605] we must set apart **several** hours a week for the young, and
E P : 0 1 :022(469) [0785] to observe that the word "nature" has **several** meanings.
S D : P R :006(502) [0847] did depart from it in **several** important and significant
S D : P R :002(503) [0851] the outbreak of the **several** controversies among the
S D : P R :007(505) [0853] Confession is repeated, **several** articles are further
S D : P R :016(507) [0857] we have collectively and **severally** come to a clear and
S D : 0 2 :044(529) [0897] writings he also takes up **several** disputed points which
S D : 0 3 :001(539) [0917] which has arisen among **several** theologians of the
S D : 0 3 :005(540) [0917] **Several** other controversies concerning this article of

Severe (8), Severely (4), Severest (1), Severity (2)
P R : P R :022(012) [0021] before the solemn and **severe** throne of God's judgment,
A G : 2 3 :016(054) [0063] necessary to relax **severity** and rigor for the sake of
A G : 2 6 :015(066) [0073] such as faith, consolation in **severe** trials, and the like.
A G : 2 7 :008(071) [0077] Such **severity** and rigor displeased many devout people in
A L : 0 0 :002(048) [0059] the canons are not so **severe** as to demand that rites
A L : 2 4 :012(057) [0065] But Paul **severely** threatened those who dealt unworthily
A P : 0 4 :350(161) [0217] No one learns this without many **severe** struggles.
A P : 2 1 :015(231) [0347] that Christ is more **severe** and the saints more
A P : 2 4 :023(253) [0391] it seemed to be unusually **severe**; this they called a
L C : 0 1 :037(369) [0591] and punish them so **severely** that he will not forget his
L C : 0 1 :268(401) [0657] of God, pronouncing the **severest** kind of verdict and
L C : 0 3 :107(434) [0729] have more frequent and **severe** temptations than others.
S D : 0 2 :022(525) [0889] God in his righteous and **severe** judgment cast away
S D : 0 5 :010(560) [0955] it requires of us, or how **severely** it curses and condemns
S D : 1 1 :058(625) [1081] for sin when God so **severely** punishes a land or a people

Sex (8), Sexes (1)
A G : 2 7 :007(071) [0077] to show more consideration to women as the weaker **sex**.
A L : 2 7 :007(071) [0077] consideration should have been given to the weaker **sex**.
A P : 2 3 :007(240) [0365] to be fruitful and that one **sex** should have a proper
A P : 2 3 :007(240) [0365] This love of one **sex** for the other is truly a divine
A P : 2 3 :010(241) [0367] men were born with a **sex** and now they are not, or that
A P : 2 3 :012(241) [0367] the natural desire of one **sex** for the other is an ordinance
A P : 2 3 :012(241) [0367] otherwise, why would both **sexes** have been created?
S 3 : 1 1 :002(314) [0499] or abolish distinctions of **sex** altogether, so little have
S C : 0 9 :006(355) [0561] the woman as the weaker **sex**, since you are joint heirs of

Shadow (5), Shadows (1)
A G : 2 8 :044(088) [0089] These are only a **shadow** of what is to come; but the
A P : 0 7 :015(170) [0231] Gospel brings not the **shadow** of eternal things but the
A P : 0 7 :035(175) [0239] These are only a **shadow** of what is to come; but the
A P : 1 5 :030(219) [0323] These are only a **shadow** of what is to come; but the
A P : 2 4 :036(257) [0397] had pictures or **shadows** of what was to come; thus this
A P : 2 4 :037(257) [0397] as we discern the **shadow** in the Old Testament, so in the

Shaft (1)
L C : 0 3 :109(435) [0729] very hour to send such a **shaft** into my heart that I can

Sham (4), Shams (1)
A G : 2 7 :048(078) [0081] angelic spirituality and **sham** of poverty, humility, and
A P : 2 7 :016(271) [0425] obedience — hypocrisies all, since they are all full of **sham**
A P : 2 7 :017(271) [0425] By this **sham**, to be sure, the monks "pattern their lives
A P : 2 7 :069(281) [0443] the hypocrisy and the **sham** worship of the monks, which
L C : 0 1 :304(406) [0667] this it is clear that all these pretexts and **shams** are false.

Shame (26), Shamed (1), Shameful (14), Shamefully (6), Shameless (4), Shamelessly (3), Shames (1)
A G : 0 0 :000(023) [0037] testimonies before kings, and shall not be put to **shame**."
A L : 2 4 :010(057) [0065] Masses were being **shamefully** profaned and applied to
A P : 0 4 :239(141) [0187] "He who believes in him will not be put to **shame**."
A P : 0 4 :239(141) [0187] does not free us from **shame** when God judges and
A P : 0 4 :253(143) [0193] which our opponents **shamelessly** infer from his words.
A P : 1 2 :065(191) [0271] "He who believes in him will not be put to **shame**."
A P : 1 2 :065(191) [0271] therefore must be put to **shame**, for they trust in their
A P : 2 0 :004(227) [0339] have lost all sense of **shame** if they dare to smuggle such a
A P : 2 0 :011(228) [0341] The **shameful** way in which our opponents have treated
A P : 2 1 :031(233) [0351] "He who believes in him will not be put to **shame**."
A P : 2 3 :001(239) [0363] Empire be disgraced and **shamed** by the marriage of
A P : 2 3 :002(239) [0363] marriage disgraces and **shames** the empire, as if the
A P : 2 3 :052(246) [0377] morals and how productive of vices and **shameful** lusts.
A P : 2 3 :067(248) [0383] So it is a **shameless** lie to say that the marriage of priests
A P : 2 4 :031(255) [0395] nothing about these **shameless** fabrications of the monks
S 1 : P R :003(289) [0455] council and flees from the light in a **shameful** fashion.
S 1 : P R :005(289) [0457] themselves busy by **shamefully** twisting and corrupting
S 1 : P R :007(289) [0457] they slander us so **shamefully** and try by their lies to keep
S 1 : P R :007(289) [0457] and still causes, them and their lies to be put to **shame**.
S 1 : P R :011(290) [0457] because we mock him so **shamefully** with the council.
S 2 : 0 2 :014(295) [0467] make men believe their **shameful**, blasphemous, accursed
T R : 0 0 :043(328) [0517] other abuses they are **shamelessly** employed to secure
T R : 0 0 :054(329) [0519] it would be most **shameful** of them to use their authority
T R : 0 0 :076(333) [0525] themselves and have **shamefully** abused it, there is no
S C : P R :004(338) [0533] Christ that you have so **shamefully** neglected the people
S C : 0 3 :018(348) [0549] and other great and **shameful** sins, but that, although we
L C : P R :002(358) [0567] Such **shameful** gluttons and servants of their bellies would
L C : P R :003(358) [0567] they might feel a little **shame** because, like pigs and dogs,
L C : P R :003(359) [0567] than this rotten, pernicious, **shameful**, carnal liberty.
L C : P R :005(359) [0567] Besides, a **shameful** and insidious plague of security and
L C : 0 1 :056(372) [0597] God's name and using it as a cloak to cover our **shame**.
L C : 0 1 :071(374) [0601] wait to lure us into sin and **shame**, calamity and trouble.
L C : 0 1 :118(381) [0615] they shall blush with **shame** before a little child that has
L C : 0 1 :142(385) [0621] the country) to the great **shame** of us would-be Christians
L C : 0 1 :149(385) [0623] commandment, then take **shame**, misery, and grief for
L C : 0 1 :154(386) [0625] now so full of unfaithfulness, **shame**, misery, and murder?
L C : 0 1 :197(392) [0637] Moreover, they have **shamelessly** boasted and bragged of
L C : 0 1 :202(392) [0639] Inasmuch as there is a **shameful** mess and cesspool of all
L C : 0 1 :214(394) [0641] indulge in open and **shameless** fornication or secretly do
L C : 0 1 :217(394) [0643] prostitution and other **shameful** vices resulting from
L C : 0 1 :262(400) [0655] must undergo the most **shameful** and spiteful persecution
L C : 0 1 :264(400) [0655] to the detestable, **shameful** vice of back-biting or slander
L C : 0 1 :273(401) [0659] him straight to his face and make him blush for **shame**.
L C : 0 3 :039(425) [0709] he may receive from us not **shame** but honor and praise.
L C : 0 3 :042(425) [0709] name as a cloak for their **shame**, by swearing, cursing,
L C : 0 3 :044(425) [0709] Just as it is a **shame** and disgrace to an earthly father to
L C : 0 3 :058(428) [0713] fault lies wholly in that **shameful** unbelief which does not
L C : 0 3 :062(428) [0715] and exposed in all their **shame**, when he himself is driven
L C : 0 3 :105(434) [0727] and weary and to fall back into sin, **shame**, and unbelief.
L C : 0 3 :115(435) [0731] devil's kingdom: poverty, **shame**, death, and, in short, all
L C : 0 3 :118(436) [0731] preserve us from sin and **shame** and from everything else
L C : 0 4 :059(444) [0747] remains no less gold if a harlot wears it in sin and **shame**.
L C : 0 5 :058(453) [0767] Those who are **shameless** and unruly must be told to stay
L C : 0 5 :067(454) [0769] Surely it is a sin and a **shame** that, when he tenderly and
S D : 0 4 :031(556) [0947] lusts without fear and **shame**, resists the Holy Spirit, and

Shape (1)
S 3 : 0 6 :005(311) [0493] only the appearance and **shape** of bread without any

Share (17), Shared (2), Shares (2), Sharing (6)
P R : P R :022(012) [0021] We want absolutely no **share** of the responsibility for this
A P : 0 4 :254(143) [0193] Isa. 58:7, 9, "**Share** your bread with the hungry.
A P : 0 4 :259(144) [0193] Isaiah says (Isa. 58:7) "**Share** your bread with the hungry,
A P : 0 7 :008(169) [0229] assembly of saints who **share** the association of the same
A P : 0 7 :028(173) [0237] with them in this life **share** an association in the outward
S 3 : 0 3 :028(308) [0487] of good works, and so we **shared** our good works with
S C : 0 9 :003(354) [0561] who is taught the word **share** all good things with him
L C : 0 1 :111(380) [0613] and at his side and will **share** with them all he has to the
L C : 0 1 :251(399) [0651] want we are to help, **share**, and lend to both friends and
L C : 0 6 :006(457) [0000] have our permission to **share** and enjoy any part of our
L C : 0 6 :028(460) [0000] yourself and beg me for the privilege of **sharing** in it.
L C : 0 6 :030(460) [0000] to do with him, nor may he have any **share** in the Gospel.
E P : 0 1 :005(466) [0781] therefore the children **share** in flesh and blood, he himself
E P : 0 8 :002(487) [0817] is, in deed and truth) **share** with each other, and how far
E P : 0 8 :002(487) [0817] with each other, and how far does this **sharing** extend?
E P : 0 8 :003(487) [0817] is, in deed and in truth) **shares** in the properties of the
E P : 0 8 :009(488) [0819] exalted and ineffable **sharing** there flows everything
E P : 0 8 :009(488) [0819] this union and **sharing** of the natures by the analogy of
E P : 0 8 :011(488) [0821] is, in deed and in truth) **shared** only the name of God with
E P : 0 8 :018(489) [0823] He denied the genuine **sharing** of the properties of the two
E P : 0 8 :035(491) [0825] but that he does not **share** in the omnipotence of God,
S D : 0 4 :030(555) [0947] (Matt. 24:13) and "We **share** in Christ only if we hold our
S D : 0 4 :034(556) [0949] of grace and our hope of **sharing** the glory of God
S D : 0 8 :067(604) [1039] such a way that it merely **shares** the bare titles and the
S D : 0 8 :067(604) [1039] the human nature has no **share** in the divine majesty.
S D : 0 8 :095(609) [1049] nature in Christ does not **share** in deed and truth the
S D : 1 2 :008(633) [1097] that we have no part or **share** in their errors, be they few

Shareholder (1)
S D : 0 2 :036(528) [0895] Christian church, a **shareholder** and partaker in it of all

Sharp (2), Sharpest (1), Sharply (1)
S 3 : 0 8 :003(312) [0495] who wish to distinguish **sharply** between the letter and the
L C : 0 1 :227(396) [0645] underhanded tricks and **sharp** practices and crafty
L C : 0 1 :299(405) [0665] In short, whoever is **sharpest** and shrewdest in such
S D : P R :015(506) [0857] shall at all times make a **sharp** distinction between

Shed (7), Shedding (4)
A G : 2 3 :023(055) [0063] to maintain such a teaching with the **shedding** of blood.
A L : 2 5 :006(062) [0069] us that our teachers have **shed** light on the doctrine of
A P : 0 4 :103(122) [0151] could escape and by **shedding** his blood canceled the bond
A P : 1 2 :003(182) [0253] of our theologians have **shed** much light on the Gospel
L C : S P :023(364) [0579] in my blood, which is **shed** for you for the forgiveness of
L C : 0 1 :184(390) [0633] rage and we are ready to **shed** blood and take revenge.
S D : 0 7 :044(577) [0987] the new covenant which is **shed** for you for the remission
S D : 0 7 :049(578) [0989] essential blood, which was **shed** for us on the tree of the
S D : 0 7 :050(578) [0991] by adding the words, "given for you, **shed** for you."
S D : 0 7 :062(581) [0995] for us into death and by **shedding** his blood for us (that is
S D : 0 7 :081(584) [1001] us by his death and the **shedding** of his blood and which

Sheep (9)
AP : 0 4 :400(168) [0227] as the Lord says, "My **sheep** hear my voice" (John 10:27).
S 1 : PR :010(290) [0457] speak to them as the true shepherd speaking to his **sheep**.
S 3 : 1 2 :002(315) [0499] holy believers and **sheep** who hear the voice of their
TR : 0 0 :022(323) [0511] Again, "Feed my **sheep**" (John 21:17), and certain other
TR : 0 0 :030(325) [0513] to the passages "Feed my **sheep**" (John 21:17) and "Do
TR : 0 0 :030(325) [0513] bids Peter to pasture the **sheep**, that is, to preach the
SD : 1 0 :019(614) [1059] holy believers and **sheep** who hear the voice of their
SD : 1 1 :008(617) [1065] "No one shall snatch my **sheep** out of my hand"
SD : 1 1 :030(621) [1073] described as follows: "My **sheep** hear my voice, and I

Sheer (18)
AP : 1 2 :123(201) [0289] This is not logic or even sophistry, but **sheer** dishonesty.
AP : 1 3 :018(213) [0313] It is **sheer** Judaism to believe that we are justified by a
AP : 2 8 :002(281) [0443] This is **sheer** slander, for in this article we have been
LC : PR :001(358) [0567] others because of **sheer** laziness and gluttony, behave in
LC : 0 1 :025(368) [0587] which overflows with **sheer** goodness and pours forth all
LC : 0 1 :039(370) [0591] who cling to God alone — **sheer** goodness and blessing,
LC : 0 2 :064(419) [0695] depths of his fatherly heart, his **sheer**, unutterable love.
LC : 0 4 :015(438) [0735] Therefore it is **sheer** wickedness and devilish blasphemy
LC : 0 4 :029(440) [0739] Baptism in which there is **sheer** salvation and life, not
LC : 0 6 :003(457) [0000] Instead, it was made **sheer** anguish and a hellish torture
EP : 0 8 :026(490) [0823] 7. That it is a **sheer** matter of words when we say that the
SD : 0 2 :043(529) [0897] reject and condemn as **sheer** error every doctrine which
SD : 0 3 :009(541) [0919] or subsequent works, by **sheer** grace, solely through the
SD : 0 3 :023(543) [0923] And to those who by **sheer** grace, for the sake of the only
SD : 0 3 :039(546) [0929] the forgiveness of sins by **sheer** grace, entirely for the sake
SD : 0 3 :058(550) [0937] forgiven and remitted by **sheer** grace for Christ's sake
SD : 0 6 :025(568) [0971] completely, and with **sheer** joy, and will rejoice therein
SD : 1 1 :087(631) [1093] of his will through **sheer** mercy in Christ without our

Shell (1)
LC : 0 4 :019(439) [0737] mask (as we see the **shell** of a nut) but as that in which

Shelter (2)
AG : 2 7 :056(080) [0083] and also their civil office, to take **shelter** in a monastery.
LC : 0 1 :148(385) [0623] everything that is good — **shelter** and protection in the

Sheol (3)
AP : 1 2 :031(186) [0259] days I must depart; I am consigned to the gates of **Sheol**.
AP : 1 2 :050(189) [0265] and brings to life; he brings down to **Sheol** and raises up."
SD : 0 6 :012(566) [0967] brings to life, he brings down into **Sheol**, and raises up."

Shepherd (4), Shepherds (2)
S 1 : PR :010(290) [0457] speak to them as the true **shepherd** speaking to his sheep.
S 3 : 1 2 :002(315) [0499] believers and sheep who hear the voice of their **Shepherd**.
SD : PR :014(506) [0855] "Faithful **shepherds**," as Luther states, "must both pasture
SD : 0 8 :047(600) [1031] king, high priest, head, **shepherd**, and so forth, not only
SD : 1 0 :019(614) [1059] and sheep who hear the voice of their **Shepherd**," etc.
SD : 1 2 :006(633) [1097] Jesus Christ has appointed us teachers and **shepherds**.

Shift (1)
LC : 0 1 :303(406) [0667] look out for himself while others **shift** for themselves."

Shines (3)
SD : 0 2 :010(522) [0885] "The light **shines** in the darkness (that is, in the dark,
SD : 0 8 :064(603) [1037] This fullness **shines** forth with all its majesty, power,
SD : 0 8 :066(604) [1039] But it **shines** forth and manifests itself fully, though

Ship (5), Ships (1)
AP : 2 4 :081(264) [0411] tax to pay for the games, **ships**, care of the gymnasium,
TR : 0 0 :067(331) [0523] of two Christians in a **ship**, one of whom baptized the
LC : 0 4 :081(446) [0751] must swim ashore after the **ship** founders" in which we
LC : 0 4 :082(446) [0751] The **ship** does not founder since, as we said, it is God's
LC : 0 4 :082(446) [0751] But it does happen that we slip and fall out of the **ship**.
LC : 0 4 :082(446) [0751] immediately head for the **ship** and cling to it until he can

Shocking (3)
AG : 2 3 :018(054) [0063] and such terrible, **shocking** immorality and abominable
SC : PR :020(340) [0537] very plain to them the **shocking** evils they introduce when
LC : 0 1 :072(374) [0601] Many a terrible and **shocking** calamity would befall us if

Shoddy (1)
SC : 0 1 :014(343) [0541] trade or by dealing in **shoddy** wares, but help him to

Shoemaker (2)
AP : 2 7 :038(275) [0433] in a dream to a certain **shoemaker** in the city of
AP : 2 7 :038(275) [0433] city and came to the **shoemaker** to find out about his

Shop (3), Shopkeepers (1)
SC : PR :018(340) [0537] laborers and **shopkeepers**, and even farmers and servants,
LC : 0 1 :224(395) [0643] at the market, in a grocery **shop**, butcher stall, wine- and
LC : 0 1 :224(395) [0643] and beer-cellar, work-**shop**, and, in short, wherever
LC : 0 2 :060(418) [0695] (flesh), we think no farther than the butcher **shop**.

Short (46), Shortage (2), Shortcomings (1), Shortly (14)
PR : PR :002(003) [0007] Thereupon a **short** confession was compiled out of the
PR : PR :004(003) [0007] German fatherland **shortly** after the Christian death of
AG : PR :001(024) [0039] A **short** time ago Your Imperial Majesty graciously
AG : 2 3 :017(054) [0063] longer, there may be a **shortage** of priests and pastors in
AL : 2 6 :023(067) [0073] **Shortly** afterward Christ says, "Not what goes into the
AP : 0 4 :032(111) [0129] Rom. 3:23 says, "All fall **short** of the glory of God," that
AP : 0 4 :321(157) [0209] In **short**, everything our opponents teach on this question
AP : 1 2 :016(184) [0257] In **short**, the whole business of satisfactions is endless,
AP : 1 6 :001(222) [0329] or contract marriage — in **short**, that lawful civil
AP : 2 4 :027(254) [0393] In **short**, the worship of the New Testament is spiritual; it
S 2 : 0 2 :029(297) [0471] In **short**, we cannot allow but must condemn the Mass,
S 2 : 0 4 :007(299) [0473] In **short**, he cannot do it.
S 3 : 0 1 :002(302) [0477] despair, blindness — in **short**, ignorance or disregard of
S 3 : 0 8 :009(313) [0497] In **short**, enthusiasm clings to Adam and his descendants
SC : 0 5 :023(350) [0555] him, giving him inferior goods and **short** measure."
LC : SP :018(363) [0577] is comprehended in **short**, plain, and simple terms, for the
LC : SP :022(364) [0579] be dealt with similarly, in **short**, simple words according
LC : 0 1 :026(368) [0587] and all authorities — in **short**, all people placed in the
LC : 0 1 :062(373) [0597] swear, conjure, and, in **short**, to practice wickedness of
LC : 0 1 :136(383) [0619] This, in **short**, is the way God will have it: render him
LC : 0 1 :160(387) [0627] In **short**, as St. Paul says, they must be "the refuse of the
LC : 0 1 :195(391) [0637] patience, and, in **short**, love and kindness toward our
LC : 0 1 :205(393) [0639] In **short**, everyone is required both to live chastely
LC : 0 1 :215(394) [0641] In **short**, even though they abstain from the act, yet their
LC : 0 1 :224(395) [0643] and there would be a **shortage** of both hangmen and
LC : 0 1 :224(395) [0643] work-shop, and, in **short**, wherever business is transacted
LC : 0 1 :228(396) [0645] In **short**, thievery is the most common craft and the
LC : 0 1 :231(396) [0647] This, in **short**, is the way of the world.
LC : 0 1 :245(398) [0649] In **short**, however much you steal, depend on it that just
LC : 0 1 :272(401) [0657] In **short**, what is secret should be allowed to remain
LC : 0 1 :299(405) [0665] In **short**, whoever is sharpest and shrewdest in such
LC : 0 2 :019(412) [0681] without ceasing, and, in **short**, to devote all these things
LC : 0 2 :054(417) [0693] the sacraments and, in **short**, the entire Gospel and all the
LC : 0 2 :063(419) [0695] his work exquisitely depicted in very **short** but rich words.
LC : 0 3 :073(430) [0719] we live and move — in **short**, everything that pertains to
LC : 0 3 :081(431) [0721] In **short**, it pains him that anyone receives a morsel of
LC : 0 3 :091(432) [0723] In **short**, unless God constantly forgives, we are lost.
LC : 0 3 :102(434) [0727] against our neighbor — in **short**, into all kinds of evil lusts
LC : 0 3 :103(434) [0727] In **short**, there is in it nothing but hatred and envy,
LC : 0 3 :115(435) [0731] shame, death, and, in **short**, all the tragic misery and
LC : 0 4 :030(440) [0739] In **short**, whatever God effects in us he does through such
LC : 0 4 :039(441) [0743] and ordained; in **short**, it is so full of comfort and grace
LC : 0 4 :042(442) [0743] In **short**, the blessings of Baptism are so boundless that if
LC : 0 4 :050(443) [0745] nor any part of him; in **short**, all this time down to the
LC : 0 4 :057(444) [0747] My neighbor and I — in **short**, all men — may err and
LC : 0 5 :078(455) [0771] In **short**, the less you feel your sins and infirmities, the
LC : 0 6 :030(460) [0000] In **short**, we approve of no coercion.
EP : 0 3 :009(474) [0793] weakness and many **shortcomings** down to their graves,
SD : 0 1 :004(509) [0861] writings to set forth in **short** chapters the true doctrine
SD : 0 2 :017(524) [0887] sin" (Rom. 7:14), and **shortly** thereafter St. Paul says, "I
SD : 0 2 :026(526) [0891] In **short**, every good gift comes from God (James 1:17).
SD : 0 2 :029(527) [0893] And **shortly** afterward the article states that "human
SD : 0 2 :031(527) [0893] And **shortly** thereafter: "Hearts which are without the
SD : 0 2 :033(527) [0893] and to avoid evil," and **shortly** thereafter, "That there is
SD : 0 5 :004(559) [0953] **Shortly** thereafter the chief parts are announced, namely,
SD : 0 5 :006(559) [0953] So it appears **shortly** afterward in the first chapter of St.
SD : 0 7 :021(573) [0979] And **shortly** thereafter: "The Word, I say, is what makes
SD : 0 7 :022(573) [0979] And **shortly** thereafter: "You can strengthen your
SD : 0 7 :033(575) [0983] **Shortly** before his death, in his last confession, he repeated
SD : 0 8 :040(599) [1029] In **short** it is indescribable what the devil attempts with
SD : 0 8 :041(599) [1029] And **shortly** thereafter he states: "If the old witch, Dame
SD : 0 8 :085(608) [1045] *of David*, which he wrote **shortly** before his death, Dr.
SD : 1 0 :022(615) [1061] **Shortly** after: "Since this is the situation, all Christians

Shot (1)
LC : 0 3 :104(434) [0727] which are venomously **shot** into our hearts, not by flesh

Shouted (1)
LC : 0 1 :284(403) [0661] set forth in books and **shouted** throughout the world.

Shoved (1)
LC : 0 2 :043(416) [0689] where faith was entirely **shoved** under the bench and no

Show (105), Showed (3), Showing (10), Shown (24), Shows (61)
AG : 2 0 :002(041) [0053] and other writings as well, **show** that they have given
AG : 2 0 :023(044) [0055] is also given among us to **show** that the faith here spoken
AG : 2 2 :003(049) [0059] if they apply only to priests, Paul **shows** in I Cor. 11:20ff.
AG : 2 3 :002(053) [0063] As his biography **shows**, even one of the popes, Pius II,
AG : 2 3 :026(055) [0065] addition, all the canons **show** great leniency and fairness
AG : 2 4 :026(058) [0067] of all, that the Scriptures **show** in many places that there
AG : 2 5 :011(063) [0069] obey the prophet who says, '**Show** your way to the Lord.'
AG : 2 7 :007(071) [0077] would have been seemly to **show** more consideration to
AL : 2 0 :035(046) [0057] be commended for **showing** how we are enabled to do
AL : 2 3 :026(055) [0065] The canons **show** some consideration toward those who
AL : 2 5 :011(063) [0069] obey the prophet who says, '**Show** your way to the Lord.'
AL : 2 6 :005(064) [0071] traditions in order to **show** that the righteousness of a
AL : 2 6 :038(069) [0075] By this he clearly **shows** that he pommeled his body not
AL : 2 7 :036(076) [0081] offer still another reason to **show** that vows are void.
AL : 2 8 :004(081) [0085] consciences, to **show** the difference between the power of
AL : 2 8 :074(094) [0095] with the passing of time, as the canons themselves **show**.
AP : PR :007(098) [0101] His Imperial Majesty, to **show** him that very weighty
AP : PR :009(098) [0101] It will **show** you what our opponents have judged, as we
AP : PR :012(099) [0101] But our opponents **show** by their actions that they are
AP : 0 2 :002(100) [0105] But to **show** all good men that our teaching on this point
AP : 0 2 :004(101) [0105] Later on we shall **show** at length that our definition
AP : 0 2 :004(101) [0105] First we must **show** why we used these words here.
AP : 0 2 :006(101) [0107] To **show** our disagreement with this evil doctrine, we
AP : 0 2 :014(102) [0109] We wanted to **show** that original sin also involves such
AP : 0 2 :018(102) [0109] This the Scripture **shows** when it says that man was
AP : 0 2 :020(103) [0111] and Col. 3:10 Paul **shows** that the image of God is the
AP : 0 2 :043(106) [0117] to these things, as the Psalms and the prophets **show**.
AP : 0 2 :045(106) [0117] when Luther wanted to **show** the magnitude of original
AP : 0 2 :049(106) [0119] World history itself **shows** the great power of the devil's
AP : 0 4 :050(114) [0135] Paul clearly **shows** that faith does not simply mean
AP : 0 4 :053(114) [0137] excludes our merits and **shows** that the blessing is offered
AP : 0 4 :061(115) [0139] Later we shall **show** that it justifies and what this means,
AP : 0 4 :068(116) [0139] so far we have sought to **show** the manner of regeneration
AP : 0 4 :069(116) [0141] Now we shall **show** that faith justifies.
AP : 0 4 :072(117) [0141] Therefore we want to **show** first that faith alone makes a
AP : 0 4 :074(117) [0143] This we shall clearly **show**.
AP : 0 4 :079(118) [0143] through the law, which **shows** God's wrath against sin.
AP : 0 4 :081(118) [0145] And to **show** how this happens, he adds that through
AP : 0 4 :117(123) [0155] What we have **shown** thus far, on the basis of the
AP : 0 4 :125(124) [0157] impulses are, the prophet **shows** when he says
AP : 0 4 :128(125) [0157] always accuses us, it always **shows** that God is wrathful.
AP : 0 4 :135(125) [0159] taken away, when God **shows** us our uncleanness and the
AP : 0 4 :136(126) [0159] we not only require them but **show** how they can be done.
AP : 0 4 :137(126) [0161] The results **show** that hypocrites who try to keep the law
AP : 0 4 :140(126) [0161] because we are in Christ, as we shall **show** a little later.
AP : 0 4 :154(128) [0163] And the account here **shows** what he calls "love."

Continued ▶

AP : 04 :154(128) [0165] Messiah, though he did **show** him the outward courtesies
AP : 04 :168(130) [0169] Here he **show** that even the godly must pray for the
AP : 04 :189(133) [0175] of Christ, whereby he **shows** his rule before the world.
AP : 04 :192(133) [0175] these works Christ **shows** his victory over the devil, just
AP : 04 :201(134) [0175] and require them, and we **show** many reasons why they
AP : 04 :219(137) [0179] Now that we have **shown** what we believe about love and
AP : 04 :236(140) [0185] to talk so much about love when they never **show** it.
AP : 04 :240(141) [0187] the antithesis clearly **shows** what it means: "Hatred stirs
AP : 04 :246(142) [0189] that follow faith and **show** that it is not dead but living
AP : 04 :249(142) [0191] We have already **shown** often enough what we mean by
AP : 04 :252(143) [0191] that faith produces, as he **shows** when he says of
AP : 04 :254(143) [0193] Dan. 4:27, "Redeem your sins by **showing** mercy."
AP : 04 :261(145) [0195] your iniquities by **showing** mercy to the oppressed," that
AP : 04 :267(146) [0197] but about faith as well, as the narrative in the text **shows**.
AP : 04 :270(147) [0197] Decalogue itself states, "**Showing** steadfast love to
AP : 04 :279(149) [0199] Tobit's statement **shows** that faith is required before
AP : 04 :282(149) [0201] of the whole passage **shows** that it requires faith.
AP : 04 :284(150) [0201] of the whole passage **shows** its agreement with the rest of
AP : 04 :286(150) [0203] We hope we have **shown** all this to the satisfaction of
AP : 04 :291(152) [0203] The Gospel **shows** another way.
AP : 04 :295(152) [0203] accuses us and thus always **shows** us an angry God.
AP : 04 :304(154) [0205] as this statement of Paul **shows**, "Since we are justified by
AP : 04 :350(161) [0217] us to despair when it **shows** our old or new sins or the
AP : 04 :362(162) [0219] We have **shown** above that justification is strictly a gift of
AP : 04 :374(164) [0223] the inexperienced and to **show** that a new life and new
AP : 04 :384(166) [0225] saves in order to **show** what kind of faith obtains eternal
AP : 04 :385(166) [0225] No faith is firm that does not **show** itself in confession.
AP : 04 :387(166) [0225] comfort in all afflictions and **shows** us the work of Christ.
AP : 04 :399(168) [0227] they have hitherto **shown** toward many godly men.
AP : 07 :019(171) [0233] than for them since it **shows** that the true and spiritual
AP : 07 :021(172) [0233] of the holy Fathers **show** that even they sometimes built
AP : 07 :042(176) [0243] the words of this decree **show**, the apostles did not want
AP : 09 :003(178) [0245] of little children is **shown** by the fact that God gives the
AP : 11 :006(181) [0251] They ought rather **show** from divine law that the
AP : 12 :034(186) [0261] when amid such terrors they **show** men only the law?
AP : 12 :036(186) [0261] This faith **shows** the difference between the contrition of
AP : 12 :044(187) [0263] to penitence, we must **show** that Scripture makes them
AP : 12 :045(187) [0263] part he consoles us and **shows** us the forgiveness of sins.
AP : 12 :057(189) [0267] came to Christ in tears, which **showed** her contrition.
AP : 12 :059(190) [0267] add a few proofs to **show** that the forgiveness of sins does
AP : 12 :069(192) [0271] In this they **showed** no judgment, but like petty public
AP : 12 :076(193) [0273] in Christ; for the Gospel **shows** us Christ and promises
AP : 12 :094(196) [0281] death of the wicked, God **shows** that he requires the faith
AP : 12 :160(208) [0303] should be sacrifices, to **show** our obedience but not to pay
AP : 12 :171(209) [0305] that penitence should be **shown** in other ways besides this
AP : 12 :172(209) [0305] As we have already **shown**, the Gospel does not command
AP : 15 :006(215) [0317] We have previously **shown** at length that men are justified
AP : 15 :052(222) [0329] very assembly we have **shown** ample evidence of our
AP : 18 :009(226) [0337] At the same time it **shows** the difference between human
AP : 20 :002(227) [0339] framers of the Confutation have **shown** their true spirit.
AP : 20 :012(228) [0341] Scripture passages to **show** why they have condemned
AP : 21 :004(229) [0343] we should thank God for **showing** examples of his mercy,
AP : 21 :010(230) [0345] nor an example can be **shown** from Scripture for the
AP : 22 :003(236) [0357] but the text clearly **shows** that this was the use of both
AP : 23 :015(241) [0367] opponents demand to be **shown** a command requiring
AP : 23 :019(242) [0369] Christ **shows** that it does require a special gift; therefore,
AP : 23 :024(243) [0371] The pontiffs **show** contempt for the authority of the
AP : 23 :058(247) [0379] Such murders **show** that this law is a doctrine of demons
AP : 23 :068(248) [0383] Such statements **show** our opponents' purpose in writing
AP : 23 :068(249) [0383] this; hence they refuse to **show** us a copy of the
AP : 24 :019(252) [0389] reconciled give thanks or **show** their gratitude for the
AP : 24 :028(254) [0393] you to know me when I **show** mercy and help you, for I
AP : 24 :029(255) [0393] thy promises of willingness to **show** mercy and to help."
AP : 24 :041(257) [0399] Experience **shows** the sort of tyrants who rule the church.
AP : 24 :048(258) [0401] of Christ, and they **show** that the forgiveness of sins
AP : 24 :060(260) [0405] We have **shown** the conflict between the righteousness of
AP : 24 :061(260) [0405] We have also **shown** that the Scripture passages quoted
AP : 24 :070(262) [0409] as Paul calls it (Rom. 4:11), **showing** forth the promise.
AP : 24 :072(262) [0409] the vain celebration of a **show** or a celebration for the
AP : 24 :079(264) [0411] "communion," which **shows** that formerly the Mass was
AP : 24 :080(264) [0411] minister who consecrates **shows** forth the body and blood
AP : 24 :080(264) [0411] a minister who preaches **shows** forth the gospel to the
AP : 24 :081(264) [0411] oration *Leptines* **shows**, it is completely taken up with
AP : 24 :081(264) [0411] on the law of immunity **shows**: "Even though the number
AP : 24 :085(264) [0413] except perhaps to **show** off their knowledge of Hebrew?
AP : 24 :086(265) [0413] The apostolic canons **show** that when they gathered they
AP : 24 :088(265) [0413] an offering; but it clearly **shows** that it is not talking
AP : 24 :099(268) [0419] of the Mass, that we **show** its proper use, and that we
AP : 27 :004(269) [0419] History will **show** how much credence should be given to
AP : 27 :014(271) [0423] to human traditions, as he clearly **shows** in Col. 2:16.
AP : 27 :020(272) [0425] Since we have above **shown** at length the wickedness of
AP : 27 :038(275) [0433] Anthony asked God to **show** him what progress he was
AP : 27 :041(276) [0435] Gospel" (Mark 10:29) to **show** that he is talking not
AP : 27 :058(279) [0439] intended to exercise or **show** faith before men, not to
AP : 27 :069(281) [0443] more for the sake of **showing** pious hearts why they
AP : 28 :008(282) [0445] the imposing of a yoke, **showing** how dangerous this is
AP : 28 :011(283) [0447] will never be able to **show** that bishops have the power to
S1 : PR :003(289) [0455] have previously given) to **show** where I have stood until
S2 : 04 :014(301) [0475] transactions and judgments, as the papal decretals **show**.
S3 : 02 :004(303) [0479] original sin manifest and **show** man to what utter depths
S3 : 03 :028(308) [0487] true, and there are seals, letters, and examples to **show** it.
S3 : 15 :005(317) [0501] by a letter which I have **shown** to these brethren who
TR : 00 :007(320) [0505] of all, therefore, let us **show** from the Gospel that the
TR : 00 :008(321) [0505] The antithesis here **shows** that lordship is disapproved.
TR : 00 :017(323) [0509] This also **shows** that the church did not then acknowledge
TR : 00 :023(324) [0511] These words **show** that the keys were given equally to all
TR : 00 :024(324) [0511] the whole church, as is **shown** by many clear and
TR : 00 :049(329) [0519] much more impudently by the pontiffs, as examples **show**.
SC : PR :018(340) [0537] from the Scriptures to **show** how God punished and
SC : PR :019(340) [0537] They must be **shown** that they are obliged to do so, and
SC : 01 :021(344) [0543] those who hate me, but **showing** steadfast love to
LC : PR :003(358) [0567] In this way they might **show** honor and gratitude to the
LC : PR :020(361) [0573] If they **show** such diligence, then I promise them — and
LC : 01 :029(368) [0589] Consequently, in order to **show** that God will not have
LC : 01 :030(369) [0589] *those who hate me, and* ***showing*** *mercy to many*
LC : 01 :035(369) [0589] as Scripture amply **shows** and as daily experience can
LC : 01 :107(379) [0611] but above all to **show** by our actions, both of heart and
LC : 01 :112(380) [0613] of none better than to **show** all honor and obedience to
LC : 01 :113(380) [0613] by commanding them he **shows** that he is well pleased
LC : 01 :125(382) [0617] should we be happy to **show** them honor and obedience.
LC : 01 :127(382) [0617] duty before the world to **show** gratitude for the kindness
LC : 01 :161(387) [0627] owe it to God to **show** "double honor" to those who
LC : 01 :193(391) [0635] man to suffer harm, but **show** to everyone all kindness
LC : 01 :194(391) [0635] To **show** kindness to our friends is but an ordinary
LC : 01 :197(392) [0637] with a false, hypocritical **show** of holiness, while they
LC : 01 :229(396) [0645] and yet with a great **show** of legality they rob and steal.
LC : 01 :232(396) [0647] commandment is very far-reaching, as we have **shown**.
LC : 01 :246(398) [0651] your arrogance and **show** forgiveness and mercy, as the
LC : 01 :252(399) [0653] the help and kindness we **show** to our neighbor, as King
LC : 01 :310(407) [0669] constantly accuses us and **shows** just how upright we
LC : 01 :313(407) [0671] one neighbor toward another, with no **show** about them.
LC : 01 :319(408) [0673] in order to **show** how much effort God requires us to
LC : 01 :320(408) [0673] *my commandments, I* ***show*** *mercy unto a thousand*
LC : 01 :323(409) [0675] he asks of us, because he **shows** himself a kind father and
LC : 03 :082(431) [0721] you see, God wishes to **show** us how he cares for us in all
LC : 04 :020(439) [0737] crown on his head, which **shows** me how and why I
LC : 04 :026(439) [0739] This **shows** that it is not simple, ordinary water, for
LC : 04 :026(440) [0739] It **shows** also (as we said above) that God's name is in it.
LC : 05 :051(452) [0765] Indeed, since we **show** such an aversion toward the
LC : 06 :025(460) [0000] together in hordes just to **show** what impure and filthy
LC : 06 :029(460) [0000] ought to despise, and you **show** thereby that you can have
EP : 01 :024(469) [0785] and they clearly **show** the distinction between the essence
EP : 11 :013(496) [0835] the Word of God, which **shows** us Christ as the "book of
SD : PR :020(508) [0857] Such a comparison will **show** him clearly that there is no
SD : 01 :040(515) [0871] This article **shows** the difference irrefutably and clearly,
SD : 01 :048(517) [0875] of our Christian faith **show** powerfully and mightily why
SD : 02 :078(536) [0911] But we have **shown** above that such a capacity naturally
SD : 03 :041(546) [0931] intention, but this merely **shows** the order in which one
SD : 05 :010(560) [0955] heaven over all sinners and **shows** how great this wrath is.
SD : 05 :012(560) [0955] is a proclamation that **shows** and gives nothing but grace
SD : 05 :017(561) [0957] immutable will of God, **shows** how man ought to be
SD : 05 :022(562) [0959] all his writings and **showed** in detail that there is a vast
SD : 06 :012(566) [0967] out of it and to **show** and indicate to them in the Ten
SD : 06 :021(567) [0969] way that, as in a mirror, it **shows** and indicates to them
SD : 07 :103(587) [1007] My only purpose was to **show** what crass fools our
SD : 07 :104(587) [1009] words of Dr. Luther also **show** clearly in what sense our
SD : 07 :108(588) [1009] it is instituted in the Word of God, as was **shown** above.
SD : 07 :121(590) [1013] of the Supper, as **shown** above in a previous exposition.
SD : 08 :056(601) [1033] arguments which **show** that this communication is not
SD : 08 :082(607) [1045] And if you could **show** me one place where God is and
SD : 10 :018(614) [1059] and adopted in 1537, **show** that this has consistently been
SD : 11 :033(622) [1075] and eleventh chapters will **show** you how comforting
SD : 11 :059(626) [1081] and some persons God **shows** his own people what all of
SD : 11 :064(626) [1083] The great apostle Paul **shows** us that we cannot and
SD : 11 :064(626) [1083] to the point where he **shows** how much of this mystery
SD : 11 :075(628) [1087] right faith, he will always **show** the same old fatherly
SD : 11 :084(630) [1091] have I let you live to **show** you my power, so that my

Shower (1), Showered (1)
LC : 01 :333(410) [0677] promises that he will **shower** us with all good things and
LC : 02 :024(413) [0683] life, and, further, has **showered** us with inexpressible

Shrewdest (1), Shrewdness (1)
LC : 01 :298(405) [0665] called not rascality but **shrewdness** and business acumen.
LC : 01 :299(405) [0665] whoever is sharpest and **shrewdest** in such affairs gets

Shriek (1)
AP : 23 :024(243) [0371] our opponents **shriek** that the councils have commanded

Shrine (1)
S3 : 08 :004(312) [0495] that "all laws are in the **shrine** of his heart," and he claims

Shrink (1), Shrinkage (1)
AP : 20 :009(227) [0341] is so weighty that we **shrink** from no danger on account
LC : PR :019(361) [0573] Vain imaginations, like new cloth, suffer **shrinkage**!

Shun (5), Shunned (2), Shunning (2)
S1 : PR :003(289) [0455] for those knaves who **shun** the light and flee from the day
S3 : 03 :032(308) [0487] sin really is, to say nothing of repenting and **shunning** sin.
TR : 00 :041(328) [0517] teachers should be **shunned** and execrated as accursed,
LC : 01 :056(372) [0595] is and diligently **shun** and avoid every misuse of the holy
LC : 01 :069(374) [0599] be trained in due time to **shun** falsehood and especially to
LC : 01 :283(403) [0661] not sneak about in secret, **shunning** the light of day.
LC : 01 :284(403) [0661] of it, you can without sin **shun** and avoid the person as
SD : 07 :111(589) [1011] forewarn our readers so they can avoid and **shun** these.
SD : 10 :022(615) [1061] teachers should be **shunned** and execrated as accursed,

Shut (1), Shutting (1)
LC : 01 :013(366) [0583] him, or put him into a purse, or **shut** him up in a chest.
LC : 01 :259(400) [0655] therefore be quite blind, **shutting** his eyes and ears to

Sick (8), Sickness (2)
AG : 02 :002(029) [0043] Moreover, this inborn **sickness** and hereditary sin is truly
AP : 04 :185(132) [0173] ancient poet is true, "Being **sick** in itself, an unjust cause
AP : 21 :036(234) [0353] the power of faith in **sickness** and constantly affirmed
LC : 01 :099(378) [0609] a sermon or two, become **sick** and tired of it and feel that
LC : 01 :111(380) [0613] them when they are old, **sick**, feeble, or poor; all this you
LC : 01 :191(391) [0635] did not clothe me, I was **sick** and in prison and you did
LC : 05 :069(454) [0769] wholesome, just as when a **sick** person willfully eats and
LC : 05 :071(455) [0769] but those who are **sick**," that is, those who labor and are
SD : 02 :010(522) [0885] sin" is not only weak and **sick**, but that he is truly lifeless
SD : 07 :070(582) [0997] well have no need of a physician, but those who are **sick**."

Side (24), Sided (1), Sides (4)
AG : PR :003(025) [0039] or treated by either **side**, to have all of us embrace and
AG : PR :010(025) [0041] in writing on both **sides**, they may be discussed amicably

Continued ▶

AG : 2 5 :001(061) [0069] has not been abolished by the preachers on our **side**.
AG : 2 5 :013(063) [0071] Yet the preachers on our **side** diligently teach that
AP : PR :003(098) [0099] it was clear that our **side** was willing to put up with
AP : 1 2 :068(192) [0271] They have on their **side** some theologians of great
AP : 2 1 :041(235) [0355] Those who **sided** with Luther from the outset did so
AP : 2 4 :010(251) [0387] and not wander off into **side** issues, like wrestlers fighting
AP : 2 4 :010(251) [0387] easy to evaluate the arguments both **sides** have presented.
S 1 : PR :007(289) [0457] keep the people on their **side**, God has constantly
LC : 0 1 :051(371) [0595] men take oaths in court and one **side** lies against the other
LC : 0 1 :111(380) [0613] above himself and at his **side** and will share with them all
LC : 0 3 :031(424) [0707] a few godly men intervened like an iron wall on our **side**?
LC : 0 3 :087(432) [0723] besieging us on every **side** and, as we have heard,
LC : 0 3 :104(434) [0727] baits and badgers us on all **sides**, but especially exerts
LC : 0 3 :105(434) [0727] hunted, and harried on all **sides**, we are constrained to cry
EP : 0 7 :021(484) [0813] On the other **side**, we unanimously reject and condemn
SD : 0 1 :001(508) [0859] One **side** contended that "man's nature and essence are
SD : 0 3 :003(539) [0917] On the other **side** some have held and taught that Christ
SD : 0 3 :007(540) [0917] it is that this article, **side** by side with the true doctrine,
SD : 0 3 :007(540) [0917] is that this article, side by **side** with the true doctrine, we
SD : 0 3 :041(546) [0931] and survive for a while **side** by side with a wicked
SD : 0 3 :041(546) [0931] survive for a while side by **side** with a wicked intention,
SD : 0 5 :015(561) [0957] of them have to be urged **side** by side, but in proper order
SD : 0 5 :015(561) [0957] have to be urged side by **side**, but in proper order and
SD : 0 5 :023(562) [0959] continually been set forth **side** by side in the church of
SD : 0 5 :023(562) [0959] been set forth side by **side** in the church of God with the
SD : 0 8 :044(599) [1029] opposite scale, then his **side** goes down and we go upward
SD : 1 1 :055(625) [1081] and knows exactly how many there will be on either **side**.

Sigh (1), Sighing (1), Sighs (1)
PR : PR :024(013) [0023] high station and low, are **sighing** anxiously for this
AP : 2 7 :002(269) [0419] Then with a **sigh** Hilten omitted all mention of his illness
LC : 0 1 :247(398) [0651] Such a man's **sighs** and cries will be no joking matter.

Sight (29)
AG : 2 6 :005(064) [0071] not become good in God's **sight** by our works but that it
AG : 2 7 :037(077) [0081] and godliness in God's **sight** come from faith and trust
AG : 2 8 :078(094) [0095] will answer for it in God's **sight**, inasmuch as by their
AL : 0 4 :003(030) [0045] God imputes for righteousness in his **sight** (Rom. 3-4).
AL : 2 0 :031(045) [0057] are too weak to do works which are good in God's **sight**.
AP : 0 4 :177(131) [0171] to us, although the **sight** of our impurity thoroughly
AP : 1 6 :012(224) [0333] or of laws, they are legitimate in the **sight** of God as well.
AP : 2 3 :064(248) [0381] virginity is not pure in the **sight** of God, and that because
AP : 2 4 :020(252) [0389] others, we must never lose **sight** of these two types of
AP : 2 4 :021(252) [0391] forgiveness of sins in the **sight** of God, but they did on the
AP : 2 4 :053(259) [0403] forgiveness of sins in the **sight** of God; as we have already
S 3 : 0 3 :001(303) [0479] to God, for no human being will be justified in his **sight**."
LC : 0 1 :093(377) [0607] Word is unholy in the **sight** of God, no matter how
LC : 0 1 :108(380) [0611] we are all equal in the **sight** of God, but among ourselves
LC : 0 1 :111(380) [0613] but with humility and reverence, as in God's **sight**.
LC : 0 1 :115(381) [0613] all other things from **sight** and give first place to this
LC : 0 1 :147(385) [0623] In the **sight** of God it is really faith that makes a person
LC : 0 1 :310(407) [0669] and shows just how upright we really are in God's **sight**.
EP : 1 2 :006(498) [0839] 4. That in the **sight** of God unbaptized children are not
SD : 0 1 :006(509) [0861] This means that in the **sight** of God original sin, like a
SD : 0 1 :012(510) [0863] them that they amount to nothing in the **sight** of God.
SD : 0 1 :019(511) [0865] and truly such a sin in the **sight** of God that apart from
SD : 0 1 :025(512) [0867] Worse than that, in the **sight** of God it can by and of
SD : 0 1 :029(513) [0867] and incorrupt in the **sight** of God, and only the original
SD : 0 1 :060(519) [0879] sin man is in God's **sight** spiritually lifeless and with all
SD : 0 3 :063(550) [0937] indwelling our sins are covered up in the **sight** of God.
SD : 0 4 :008(552) [0941] praiseworthy in the **sight** of the world, and even God will
SD : 0 4 :008(552) [0941] spattered with sins in the **sight** of God), and God regards
SD : 1 1 :074(628) [1087] I am driven far from thy **sight**" (Ps. 31:22), then,

Sigismund (2)
PR : PR :027(015) [0025] Duke **Sigismund** August of Mecklenburg (in Ivernack)
S 3 : 1 5 :005(318) [0501] the Rev. Master **Sigismund** Kirchner

Sign (26), Signed (1), Signing (1), Signs (34)
AG : 1 3 :001(035) [0049] instituted not only to be **signs** by which people might be
AG : 1 3 :001(035) [0049] but that they are **signs** and testimonies of God's will
AL : 1 3 :001(035) [0049] men but especially to be **signs** and testimonies of the will
AP : 0 4 :154(128) [0165] crying, all of which were a **sign** and confession of faith
AP : 0 4 :155(128) [0165] me with faith and with the acts and **signs** of faith.
AP : 0 4 :201(134) [0175] was added to give him a **sign** written in his body by which
AP : 0 4 :210(136) [0179] the church so that as this **sign** reminds us of the promises
AP : 0 4 :275(148) [0199] is that we need external **signs** of this exceedingly great
AP : 0 4 :276(148) [0199] Supper, for example, are **signs** that constantly admonish,
AP : 0 4 :276(148) [0199] them and are glad to have **signs** and testimonies of this
AP : 0 4 :276(148) [0199] they exercise themselves in these **signs** and testimonies.
AP : 1 2 :042(187) [0261] These are **signs** of the new testament, that is, signs of the
AP : 1 2 :042(187) [0261] the new testament, that is, **signs** of the forgiveness of sins.
AP : 1 2 :158(207) [0301] afflictions are not always punishments or **signs** of wrath.
AP : 1 3 :001(211) [0309] imagine, but are rather **signs** and testimonies of God's
AP : 1 3 :003(211) [0309] Hence **signs** instituted without God's command are not
AP : 1 3 :003(211) [0309] command are not sure **signs** of grace, even though they
AP : 1 3 :014(213) [0311] are, in the strict sense, "**signs** of the New Testament,"
AP : 1 3 :017(213) [0313] which in themselves are **signs** to which God has added
AP : 1 3 :019(213) [0313] says that circumcision was a **sign** given to exercise faith.
AP : 1 3 :020(213) [0313] The sacraments are **signs** of the promises.
AP : 2 4 :069(262) [0409] sacraments are not only **signs** among men, but signs of
AP : 2 4 :069(262) [0409] signs among men, but **signs** of God's will toward us; so it
AP : 2 4 :069(262) [0409] is correct to define the New Testament sacraments as **signs**
AP : 2 4 :069(262) [0409] are two parts to a sacrament, the **sign** and the Word.
AP : 2 7 :004(269) [0421] But there are other **signs**, no less sure than oracles, which
AP : 2 7 :006(269) [0421] this way, therefore, the monks are **signing** their own fate.
AP : 2 7 :007(269) [0421] Another **sign** is the fact that sometimes they are
SC : 0 7 :001(352) [0557] when you rise, make the **sign** of the cross and say, "In the
SC : 0 7 :004(353) [0559] when you retire, make the **sign** of the cross and say, "In
LC : PR :008(359) [0569] Well, this, too, is a sure **sign** that they despise both their
LC : PR :010(360) [0571] is the true holy water, the **sign** which routs the devil and
LC : PR :014(360) [0571] our eyes and in our hands as a constant token and **sign**.
LC : 0 1 :182(389) [0631] hand, heart, or word, by **signs** or gestures, or by aiding
LC : 0 2 :055(418) [0693] the Word and through **signs** appointed to comfort and
LC : 0 3 :096(433) [0725] and assurance as a **sign** along with the promise which is in
LC : 0 3 :097(433) [0725] This **sign** is attached to the petition, therefore, that when
LC : 0 3 :098(433) [0725] are appointed as outward **signs**, this sign also can effect to
LC : 0 3 :098(433) [0725] as outward signs, this **sign** also can effect to strengthen
LC : 0 4 :018(438) [0737] a sacrament, that is, a holy, divine thing and **sign**.
LC : 0 4 :063(444) [0749] Baptism merely as an empty **sign**, as the fanatics dream.
LC : 0 4 :064(444) [0749] why God ordained just this **sign** and external observance
LC : 0 4 :072(445) [0751] So the external **sign** has been appointed not only on
LC : 0 4 :073(445) [0751] where faith is lacking, it remains a mere unfruitful **sign**.
LC : 0 5 :022(449) [0757] to me as a sure pledge and **sign** . indeed, as the very gift
LC : 0 5 :077(455) [0771] is all the worse, for it is a **sign** that ours is a leprous flesh
LC : 0 6 :029(460) [0000] And this is a sure **sign** that you also despise the Gospel.
EP : 0 7 :030(485) [0815] solely by the external **signs** of bread and wine and not by
SD : 0 7 :002(569) [0973] Christ are distant from the **signs** by as great an interval as
SD : 0 7 :003(569) [0973] quickened by the visible **signs** in the same way as by the
SD : 0 7 :004(569) [0973] was only an external **sign** whereby one can identify
SD : 0 7 :004(569) [0973] and wine, which are only **signs** of the absent body of
SD : 0 7 :007(570) [0975] as a "symbol" (that is, a **sign** or figure of the body of
SD : 0 7 :012(571) [0977] Luther and other theologians of both parties **signed** them:
SD : 0 7 :050(578) [0989] of other covenant-**signs** and signs of grace or sacraments,
SD : 0 7 :050(578) [0989] other covenant-signs and **signs** of grace or sacraments,
SD : 0 7 :060(580) [0993] and wine, not only against **signs** and symbols and figures
SD : 0 7 :116(589) [1011] Christ, and through these **signs**, as through an external
SD : 0 7 :116(589) [1011] the Supper we receive the external **sign** with our mouth.
SD : 0 7 :116(589) [1013] Christ, distributed to us, but through the external **signs**.
SD : 0 7 :117(590) [1013] of the relation between the **sign** and that which is signified
SD : 0 8 :027(596) [1025] the message by the **signs** that attended it (Mark 16:20).

Signatures (3)
EP : 1 2 :031(501) [0843] of God, subscribed our **signatures** with our own hands.
SD : 1 2 :004(633) [1097] few bare words or our **signatures**, but to present a clear,
SD : 1 2 :040(636) [1103] of God, subscribed our **signatures** with our own hands.

Significant (2), Significantly (1), Signification (2), Signified (4), Signifies (9), Signify (3), Signifying (2)
AG : 0 1 :006(028) [0043] but that the Word **signifies** a physical word or voice and
AL : 0 1 :004(028) [0043] it in this connection, to **signify** not a part or a quality in
AL : 0 1 :006(028) [0043] persons since "Word" **signifies** a spoken word and "Spirit"
AL : 0 1 :006(028) [0043] word and "Spirit" **signifies** a movement which is produced
AL : 2 0 :023(044) [0055] the term "faith" does not **signify** mere knowledge of the
AL : 2 0 :023(044) [0055] and the devil), but it **signifies** faith which believes not
AP : 0 4 :264(146) [0195] It **signifies** that the forgiveness of sins is possible, that
AP : 1 3 :005(212) [0309] of picture of the Word, **signifying** the same thing as the
AP : 2 2 :007(237) [0359] of language, naming one part also **signifies** the other.
AP : 2 4 :021(252) [0389] because of what they **signified** and foreshadowed.
TR : 0 0 :008(321) [0505] midst of the disciples, **signifying** thereby that there was to
TR : 0 0 :032(325) [0513] mocked in royal purple **signified** that the time would
SC : 0 4 :011(349) [0551] What does such baptizing with water **signify**?
SC : 0 4 :012(349) [0551] Answer: It **signifies** that the old Adam in us, together with
LC : 0 1 :207(393) [0639] **Significantly** he established it as the first of all
LC : 0 4 :064(444) [0749] must know what Baptism **signifies** and why God ordained
LC : 0 4 :068(445) [0749] among Christians, **signified** by baptizing with water.
LC : 0 4 :072(445) [0751] of what it confers, but also on account of what it **signifies**.
LC : 0 4 :074(445) [0751] by its power and by its **signification**, comprehends also
LC : 0 4 :078(446) [0751] and the effect and **signification** of Baptism would
SD : PR :006(502) [0847] several important and **significant** articles, either because
SD : PR :016(507) [0857] the chief and most **significant** articles which were in
SD : 0 7 :117(590) [1013] sign and that which is **signified** — in other words, only as

Silence (11), Silenced (1), Silent (8), Silently (1)
AL : 2 0 :005(041) [0053] faith, about which there used to be marvelous **silence**.
AL : 2 0 :008(042) [0053] there has been profound **silence** concerning the
AL : 2 5 :002(061) [0069] which there has been profound **silence** before this time.
AL : 2 7 :027(075) [0079] a vow while they remain **silent** concerning the nature of a
AP : 0 4 :274(148) [0199] Our opponents try to **silence** this proclamation of the
AP : 0 4 :329(158) [0211] Zech. 2:13 says, "Be **silent**, all flesh, before the Lord."
AP : 1 2 :127(201) [0291] How much **silent** indignation is there because you refuse
AP : 1 2 :129(202) [0291] of men and the **silent** desires of all nations; they certainly
AP : 2 4 :009(251) [0387] they adduce are **silenced** by the fact that the Mass does
AP : 2 4 :046(258) [0401] books and sermons were **silent** about the exercise of faith
S 3 : 0 8 :006(312) [0495] yet they do not remain **silent** but fill the world with their
SC : PR :025(341) [0539] negligent if you fail to do your duty and remain **silent**.
LC : 0 1 :273(401) [0659] Then you will **silence** many a one who otherwise would
LC : 0 3 :008(421) [0699] all, so that you may **silence** and repel any thoughts that
LC : 0 3 :010(421) [0699] things so that you may **silence** and repel thoughts which
LC : 0 6 :025(460) [0000] have in the past kept **silence** about this wonderful, rich
EP : 1 2 :001(498) [0839] But lest as a result of our **silence** these errors be attributed
SD : 1 1 :052(625) [1081] which God has remained **silent** and which he has not
SD : 1 1 :064(626) [1083] immediately commands **silence** and cuts off further
SD : 1 2 :006(633) [1097] look on idly or stand by **silently** while something contrary
SD : 1 2 :007(633) [1097] no one as a result of our **silence** attribute to us the

Silly (13)
AP : 1 2 :106(197) [0283] It is **silly** to transfer here the saying of Solomon
AP : 1 2 :137(203) [0293] words in refuting these **silly** arguments of our opponents.
AP : 1 2 :141(204) [0295] sorry to have to list these **silly** opinions of our opponents,
AP : 2 3 :008(240) [0365] opponents reply with the **silly** argument that originally
AP : 2 3 :062(247) [0381] recited and refuted the **silly** counter-arguments of our
AP : 2 4 :084(264) [0413] It is **silly** to argue that since the Holy Scriptures mention
AP : 2 4 :087(265) [0413] It is **silly** for our opponents to raise such quibbles about
AP : 2 7 :014(271) [0425] how much less do these **silly** observances merit the
AP : 2 7 :027(274) [0429] is eternal life, in these **silly** observances of vestments and
AP : 2 7 :042(276) [0435] But it would be **silly** to conclude from this that it is a
AP : 2 7 :042(276) [0435] So it is **silly** to maintain that it is a service to God to leave
S 3 : 1 5 :004(316) [0501] magic tricks which contains **silly** and childish articles,
LC : PR :005(359) [0567] the Catechism as a simple, **silly** teaching which they can

Silver (7)
AP : 1 5 :019(218) [0319] shall honor with gold and **silver**, with precious stones and
AP : 1 5 :021(218) [0321] God "with gold and **silver** and precious stones," believing
AP : 2 4 :034(256) [0395] refine them like gold and **silver**, till they present right
AP : 2 4 :051(259) [0403] describes as worshiping their God with gold and **silver**.

Continued ▶

A P : 2 4 :064(261) [0407] of merit, like the money-changers with gold or **silver**.
S C : 0 2 :004(345) [0545] of the devil, not with **silver** and gold but with his holy and
L C : 0 2 :031(414) [0687] pay what I owed, not with **silver** and gold but with his

Similar (64), Similarity (2), Similarly (21)
A G : P R :009(025) [0039] and estates also submit a **similar** written statement of
A G : 2 3 :013(053) [0063] station have expressed **similar** opinions and the misgiving
A G : 2 6 :001(063) [0071] among foods and **similar** traditions which had been
A G : 2 8 :039(087) [0089] sin to foods, days, and **similar** things and burden
A G : 2 8 :053(089) [0091] about Sunday and other **similar** church ordinances and
A G : 2 8 :057(091) [0091] Easter, Pentecost, and **similar** holy days and usages.
A L : 2 0 :014(043) [0055] Ambrose teaches **similarly** in *De vocatione gentium* and
A L : 2 6 :001(064) [0071] among foods and **similar** human traditions are works
A L : 2 6 :006(065) [0071] by distinctions among foods and **similar** acts of worship.
A L : 2 8 :039(087) [0089] sin to foods, days, and **similar** things and burden the
A L : 2 8 :039(087) [0089] service among Christians **similar** to the Levitical, and as
A L : 2 8 :053(089) [0091] about Sunday and about **similar** rites in our churches?
A L : 2 8 :057(091) [0091] Sunday, Easter, Pentecost, and **similar** festivals and rites.
A P : 0 2 :011(102) [0109] of God, hate of God, and **similar** faults that we are born
A P : 0 4 :055(114) [0137] **Similarly**, at every mention of faith we are also thinking
A P : 0 4 :082(118) [0145] There is a **similar** statement in Heb. 4:14-16, "Since then
A P : 0 4 :103(121) [0151] There are **similar** statements here and there in the holy
A P : 0 4 :122(124) [0157] (Rom. 2:13), and many **similar** passages regarding the law
A P : 0 4 :124(124) [0157] These and **similar** passages assert that we should begin to
A P : 0 4 :155(128) [0165] Later we shall take up **similar** passages, like Luke 11:41,
A P : 0 4 :203(135) [0177] in the delusion that by **similar** works he will merit grace
A P : 0 4 :208(135) [0177] those who hope that by **similar** actions they can obtain
A P : 0 4 :232(139) [0185] **Similarly**, in all families and communities harmony should
A P : 0 4 :259(144) [0193] We must interpret all **similar** passages in the same way.
A P : 0 4 :259(144) [0193] **Similarly**, when Isaiah says (Isa. 58:7) "Share your bread
A P : 0 4 :283(150) [0201] the distinctions of foods, and **similar** pompous acts.
A P : 0 4 :326(158) [0211] **Similarly**, in Ps. 130:3 he says that no one can stand the
A P : 0 7 :021(172) [0233] **Similarly**, why will faith be necessary if sacraments justify
A P : 0 7 :031(174) [0237] For this unity, we say, a **similarity** of human rites,
A P : 0 7 :032(174) [0239] **Similarly**, some churches have excommunicated others
A P : 0 7 :045(177) [0243] Many **similar** instances can be gathered from the histories
A P : 0 7 :045(177) [0243] food, days, clothing, and **similar** matters without divine
A P : 1 2 :014(184) [0257] pilgrimages, rosaries, or **similar** observances that do not
A P : 1 2 :068(192) [0271] about the merits of attrition and works and **similar** ideas.
A P : 1 2 :163(208) [0303] St. James dressed in armor or to perform **similar** works."
A P : 1 2 :167(209) [0305] that distrust of God and **similar** attitudes are destroyed.
A P : 1 2 :170(209) [0305] **Similarly**, Chrysostom says, "In the heart contrition, in
A P : 1 5 :021(218) [0321] and innumerable **similar** observances in the human
A P : 1 5 :042(221) [0327] traditions, the worship of the saints, and **similar** trifles.
A P : 2 1 :037(234) [0355] about rosaries and **similar** ceremonies, or the legends, as
A P : 2 2 :014(238) [0361] danger of spilling and **similar** factors which are not
A P : 2 3 :030(243) [0371] says marriage, food, and **similar** things are "consecrated
A P : 2 3 :054(246) [0379] **Similar** vices have preceded the fall of many other cities,
A P : 2 4 :081(264) [0411] of the gymnasium, and **similar** public responsibilities.
A P : 2 4 :097(268) [0417] the Old Testament had a **similar** notion that they merited
A P : 2 7 :027(274) [0429] in these silly observances of vestments and **similar** trifles.
A P : 2 7 :037(275) [0433] in the love of their neighbor, and **similar** spiritual virtues.
A P : 2 8 :007(282) [0445] depends upon food, drink, clothing, and **similar** matters.
S 1 : P R :013(291) [0459] hats and crosiers, and **similar** nonsense would soon be
S 3 : 0 1 :011(303) [0479] Such and many **similar** notions have resulted from
T R : 0 0 :008(321) [0505] by a parable when, in a **similar** dispute concerning the
T R : 0 0 :033(325) [0513] "Omnes," and other **similar** statements which claim that
T R : 0 0 :075(333) [0525] non-observance of fasts or festivals and **similar** trifles.
L C : S P :022(364) [0579] may be dealt with **similarly**, in short, simple words
L C : 0 1 :190(391) [0635] to death or in **similar** peril and do not save him although
L C : 0 1 :302(405) [0667] **Similarly**, if anyone covets a castle, city, county, or other
L C : 0 1 :326(409) [0675] **Similarly**, this fear, love, and trust should impel us not to
L C : 0 4 :038(441) [0741] **Similarly** the commandment, "You shall honor your
L C : 0 4 :049(442) [0745] **Similarly** by God's grace we have been given the power to
L C : 0 4 :054(443) [0745] **Similarly**, those who partake unworthily of the Lord's
L C : 0 4 :055(443) [0745] **Similarly**, the Sacrament of the Altar is not vitiated if
L C : 0 6 :010(458) [0000] **Similarly** the second confession, which each Christian
E P : 0 2 :008(471) [0789] murder, theft, and **similar** sins under compulsion.
E P : 1 2 :030(500) [0843] All these and **similar** articles, together with their
S D : P R :005(502) [0847] **Similarly** we are determined by the grace of the Almighty
S D : P R :008(502) [0849] **Similarly** at the present time our adversaries, the papists,
S D : 0 1 :025(512) [0865] and reject these and **similar** false doctrines because God's
S D : 0 1 :026(512) [0867] that reason the following and **similar** errors are rejected:
S D : 0 1 :038(515) [0871] **Similarly** we confess in the Large Catechism, "I hold and
S D : 0 1 :045(516) [0873] and saved, and other **similar** expressions with which we
S D : 0 2 :015(523) [0887] We find **similar** prayers in St. Paul's letters (Eph. 1:17,
S D : 0 2 :023(525) [0889] has written in a **similar** vein in his second book *Against*
S D : 0 3 :028(544) [0925] **Similarly**, although renewal and sanctification are a
S D : 0 3 :044(547) [0933] reject the following and **similar** errors as contrary to the
S D : 0 3 :059(550) [0937] the following and all **similar** errors as contrary to the
S D : 0 3 :066(550) [0937] These and all **similar** errors we reject unanimously as
S D : 0 4 :036(557) [0949] teachers used these and **similar** formulas in expounding
S D : 0 5 :004(559) [0953] **Similarly** when Christ after his resurrection commands his
S D : 0 7 :036(575) [0985] him," or "God was in Christ," and **similar** expressions.
S D : 0 7 :117(590) [1013] bread and wine have a **similarity** with the body and blood
S D : 0 8 :010(593) [1019] thirst, frost, heat, and **similar** things are properties of the
S D : 0 8 :062(603) [1037] These and **similar** erroneous doctrines have been justly
S D : 0 8 :086(608) [1047] There are many **similar** testimonies in Dr. Luther's
S D : 1 0 :013(613) [1057] Peter and Barnabas in a **similar** situation yielded to a
S D : 1 1 :058(625) [1081] we should go in these and **similar** questions
S D : 1 2 :027(635) [1101] They hold other **similar** articles.
S D : 1 2 :039(636) [1103] All these and **similar** articles, and whatever attaches to

Simon (2)
S 3 : 1 5 :005(317) [0501] **Simon** Schneeweiss, pastor of the church in Crailsheim
T R : 0 0 :082(335) [0529] **Simon** Schneeweiss, pastor at Crailsheim

Simple (55), Simpler (1), Simplest (2), Simplicity (3), Simply (61)
P R : P R :010(006) [0011] might be provided for **simple** and pious hearts, so that
P R : P R :019(009) [0017] to palm them off on **simple** folk in spite of the fact that
P R : P R :022(011) [0019] go their way in the **simplicity** of their hearts, do not
A G : 2 3 :021(055) [0063] persecute innocent people **simply** because they are
A L : 2 8 :021(084) [0087] doing all this without human power, **simply** by the Word.
A P : 0 2 :001(100) [0105] While we wanted **simply** to describe what original sin
A P : 0 4 :050(114) [0135] shows that faith does not **simply** mean historical
A P : 0 4 :065(116) [0139] What can we say more **simply** and clearly about the
A P : 0 4 :146(127) [0163] Such a trust is **simply** wicked and vain.
A P : 0 4 :186(133) [0173] our opponents **simply** abolish this free promise.
A P : 0 4 :231(139) [0183] about perfection, we shall **simply** present Paul's meaning.
A P : 0 4 :242(141) [0187] have arisen in the church **simply** from the hatred of the
A P : 0 4 :253(143) [0191] These words, spoken so **simply**, contain no error, but our
A P : 0 4 :321(157) [0209] Rather, smug hypocrites **simply** believe that their works
A P : 1 2 :052(189) [0265] of penitence could be presented more clearly and **simply**.
A P : 1 2 :078(193) [0275] contrition and love, is **simply** a doctrine of the law — and
A P : 1 2 :084(194) [0277] nothing can be said so **simply** that some quibbler cannot
A P : 1 2 :149(206) [0299] comes over even the **simplest** people in true penitence?
A P : 1 3 :003(211) [0309] though they may instruct or admonish the **simple** folk.
A P : 1 5 :003(215) [0315] this doctrine, we have an easy and **simple** case.
A P : 1 5 :018(217) [0319] of sins, they are **simply** establishing the kingdom of
A P : 1 5 :050(222) [0329] But our case is plain and **simple** because our opponents
A P : 2 3 :040(245) [0375] Thus Christ does not **simply** commend those who make
A P : 2 3 :056(247) [0379] though it is obviously a matter of **simple** human right.
A P : 2 4 :005(250) [0385] not teach or admonish, **simply** *ex opere operato*, by the
A P : 2 7 :034(275) [0431] of sins or eternal life are **simply** crushing the Gospel
A P : 2 7 :058(279) [0439] but should be regarded **simply** as a matter of
A P : 2 8 :017(283) [0449] This is the **simple** way to interpret traditions.
S 2 : 0 2 :019(296) [0467] They do so **simply** because the devil has possessed the
S C : P R :001(338) [0533] to prepare this brief and **simple** catechism or statement of
S C : 0 5 :024(350) [0555] into torture; he should **simply** mention one or two sins of
S C : 0 5 :029(351) [0555] This is intended **simply** as an ordinary form of confession
L C : P R :002(358) [0567] to them in clear and **simple** form in the many excellent
L C : P R :005(359) [0567] the Catechism as a **simple**, silly teaching which they can
L C : S P :018(363) [0579] in short, plain, and **simple** terms, for the dear fathers or
L C : S P :022(364) [0579] with similarly, in short, **simple** words according to the
L C : S P :026(364) [0579] it is not enough for them **simply** to learn and repeat these
L C : S P :027(364) [0581] but briefly and very **simply**, so that it may penetrate
L C : 0 1 :050(371) [0595] you must learn to grasp **simply** the meaning of this and
L C : 0 1 :052(371) [0595] stand as the plain and **simple** meaning of this
L C : 0 1 :062(373) [0597] very briefly, it is either **simply** to lie and assert under his
L C : 0 1 :105(379) [0611] that he commands us not **simply** to love our parents but
L C : 0 1 :114(380) [0613] not lay it to heart; they **simply** gaped in astonishment at
L C : 0 1 :140(384) [0621] These are plain and **simple** words, and everyone thinks he
L C : 0 1 :152(386) [0625] a reward, we shall be **simply** overwhelmed with our
L C : 0 1 :182(389) [0631] This commandment is **simple** enough.
L C : 0 1 :257(399) [0653] In its first and **simplest** meaning, as the words stand
L C : 0 1 :266(401) [0657] become aware of a sin, **simply** make your ears a tomb and
L C : 0 1 :315(408) [0671] we have said, that this is a **simple** life for the ordinary
L C : 0 1 :324(409) [0675] no other gods," means **simply**, "You shall fear, love, and
L C : 0 1 :327(409) [0675] or omitting to do things **simply** in order to please them.
L C : 0 2 :004(411) [0679] as a first step, for very **simple** persons to learn to
L C : 0 2 :006(411) [0679] make it most clear and **simple** for teaching to children, we
L C : 0 2 :026(413) [0685] to treat it briefly and **simply**, we shall take up one phrase
L C : 0 2 :031(414) [0685] the little word "Lord" **simply** means the same as
L C : 0 2 :031(414) [0685] parts of this article **simply** serve to clarify and express
L C : 0 2 :048(416) [0691] "church," by which **simple** folk understand not a group of
L C : 0 3 :007(421) [0699] children, pupils, and **simple** folk; while it may be called
L C : 0 3 :046(426) [0709] This petition, then, is **simple** and clear as soon as we
L C : 0 3 :051(426) [0711] Answer: **Simply** what we learned in the Creed, namely,
L C : 0 3 :054(427) [0713] All this is **simply** to say: "Dear Father, we pray Thee, give
L C : 0 3 :068(429) [0717] himself have been very **simply** expressed, yet we have
L C : 0 3 :072(430) [0717] It is a brief and **simple** word, but very comprehensive.
L C : 0 3 :084(431) [0721] there now is in the world **simply** on account of false
L C : 0 4 :014(438) [0735] It is not **simply** common water, but water comprehended
L C : 0 4 :017(438) [0737] Therefore it is not **simply** a natural water, but a divine,
L C : 0 4 :024(439) [0737] To put it most **simply**, the power, effect, benefit, fruit,
L C : 0 4 :026(439) [0739] This shows that it is not **simple**, ordinary water, for
L C : 0 4 :048(442) [0743] we reply briefly: Let the **simple** dismiss this question from
L C : 0 4 :051(443) [0745] best and strongest proof for the **simple** and unlearned.
L C : 0 4 :053(443) [0745] said, that Baptism is **simply** water and God's Word in and
L C : 0 4 :065(445) [0749] of Baptism, which is **simply** the slaying of the old Adam
L C : 0 5 :041(451) [0763] of necessity, and that it is enough if they **simply** believe.
L C : 0 5 :044(451) [0763] patience it is not enough **simply** to teach and instruct, but
L C : 0 6 :007(458) [0000] confession to instruct and admonish the **simple** folk.
L C : 0 6 :016(459) [0000] as if our confession were **simply** a good work with which
L C : 0 6 :018(459) [0000] to present to him, but **simply** to accept and receive
L C : 0 6 :025(460) [0000] treasure; they have **simply** driven men together in hordes
L C : 0 6 :032(460) [0000] to go to confession, I am **simply** urging you to be a
E P : 0 1 :022(469) [0785] to conceal their error and to mislead many **simple** people.
E P : 0 1 :023(469) [0785] unlearned people, but **simple** folk should be spared them.
E P : 0 7 :021(484) [0813] forth above and to our **simple** faith and confession about
E P : 0 7 :025(484) [0815] or believed in their **simple** sense, as they read, but that
E P : 0 7 :042(486) [0817] in accord with the **simple** words of Christ's testament, we
E P : 0 8 :019(490) [0823] Word of God and our **simple** Christian Creed the
E P : 0 8 :039(491) [0827] the divine Word and our **simple** Christian faith, we shall
E P : 0 9 :001(492) [0827] how, according to our **simple** Christian Creed, did Christ
E P : 0 9 :003(492) [0827] and teach it in all **simplicity**, as Dr. Luther of blessed
E P : 0 9 :003(492) [0827] and admonishes all Christians to **simplicity** of faith.
E P : 0 9 :004(492) [0827] comprehend in this life but which we **simply** accept.
E P : 1 1 :022(497) [0837] This is a brief and **simple** explanation of the various
E P : 1 1 :022(497) [0837] plain Catechism, every **simple** Christian can understand
S D : P R :008(505) [0853] in a most correct and **simple**, yet sufficiently explicit,
S D : P R :020(508) [0859] but that it is the same **simple**, unchanging, constant
S D : 0 1 :021(511) [0865] that original sin is only a **simple**, insignificant, external
S D : 0 1 :049(517) [0875] Let this suffice as a **simple** exposition of the doctrine and
S D : 0 1 :057(518) [0879] compels us to answer **simply** and roundly that original sin
S D : 0 1 :062(519) [0879] accident is, which did not **simply** sully human nature but
S D : 0 2 :010(522) [0885] calls the natural man **simply** "darkness" in spiritual and
S D : 0 4 :013(553) [0943] explain only the controverted points **simply** and clearly.
S D : 0 7 :045(577) [0987] we must accept them in **simple** faith and due obedience in
S D : 0 7 :046(577) [0989] of God plainly and **simply**, as the words read, and
S D : 0 7 :048(578) [0989] which in themselves are **simple**, clear, manifest, certain,
S D : 0 7 :050(578) [0989] but the most appropriate, **simple**, indubitable, and clear
S D : 0 7 :051(578) [0991] let his disciples keep this **simple** and strict understanding
S D : 0 7 :052(578) [0991] and syllables repeat these **simple**, clear, certain, and
S D : 0 7 :059(580) [0993] unanimously by this **simple** and well-founded explanation
S D : 0 7 :092(586) [1005] to lead us away from the **simple**, explicit, and clear

Continued ▶

SD : 07 :092(586) [1005] we shall understand and believe them in the **simple** sense.
SD : 07 :113(589) [1011] institution are not to be **simply** understood in their strict
SD : 08 :017(594) [1021] has always held in **simple** faith that the divine and human
SD : 08 :035(597) [1027] becomes tangled up and the **simple** reader is easily misled.
SD : 08 :035(598) [1027] the sake of a better and **simpler** presentation it can be
SD : 08 :053(601) [1033] testimony, we shall **simply** believe it and not argue that
SD : 08 :084(607) [1045] They **simply** will not let themselves be separated and
SD : 08 :096(609) [1049] but with the holy apostles **simply** to believe, close the eyes
SD : 09 :001(610) [1051] we let matters rest on the **simple** statement of our
SD : 09 :002(610) [1051] distinct articles, and we **simply** believe that after the
SD : 11 :093(632) [1093] We shall abide by this **simple**, direct, and useful
SD : 11 :093(632) [1095] are contrary to these true, **simple**, and useful expositions.
SD : 12 :006(633) [1097] we abide by the true, **simple**, natural, and proper meaning
SD : 12 :008(633) [1097] and where the poor, **simple** people, who were forced into

Simulated (1)
SD : 03 :042(547) [0931] distinguish it from a **simulated** and dead faith (since many

Simultaneously (12)
AP : 02 :025(103) [0111] about when they **simultaneously** attribute to man a
AP : 13 :005(211) [0309] and the rite God **simultaneously** moves the heart to
SD : 03 :025(543) [0923] to conversion is **simultaneously** also a part of
SD : 03 :032(545) [0927] or introduced **simultaneously** into the article of
SD : 03 :053(548) [0933] through faith we **simultaneously** receive adoption and the
SD : 04 :015(553) [0943] as if there could **simultaneously** be in a single heart both a
SD : 06 :012(566) [0967] way the Holy Spirit **simultaneously** performs both
SD : 07 :103(587) [1007] to make a body be **simultaneously** in many places, even in
SD : 08 :006(592) [1017] in *one* person **simultaneously** true eternal God, born of
SD : 08 :036(598) [1027] entire person who is **simultaneously** God and man
SD : 08 :037(598) [1027] to the person is **simultaneously** the property of both
SD : 11 :028(621) [1071] "He is **simultaneously** one Lord of all, rich toward all who

Sin (694)
PR : PR :005(004) [0009] our own and the ungrateful world's impenitence and **sin**.
AG : 02 :000(029) [0043] II. [Original **Sin**]
AG : 02 :001(029) [0043] to the course of nature are conceived and born in **sin**.
AG : 02 :002(029) [0043] sickness and hereditary **sin** is truly sin and condemns to
AG : 02 :002(029) [0043] and hereditary sin is truly **sin** and condemns to the
AG : 02 :003(029) [0045] who deny that original **sin** is sin, for they hold that
AG : 02 :003(029) [0045] deny that original sin is **sin**, for they hold that natural
AG : 03 :003(030) [0045] not only for original **sin** but also for all other sins and to
AG : 03 :005(030) [0045] protect and defend them against the devil and against **sin**.
AG : 04 :001(030) [0045] obtain forgiveness of **sin** and righteousness before God by
AG : 04 :001(030) [0045] we receive forgiveness of **sin** and become righteous before
AG : 04 :002(030) [0045] us and that for his sake our **sin** is forgiven and
AG : 06 :002(032) [0045] we receive forgiveness of **sin** and righteousness through
AG : 12 :001(034) [0049] among us that those who **sin** after Baptism receive
AG : 12 :001(034) [0049] receive forgiveness of **sin** whenever they come to
AG : 12 :005(034) [0049] or terror, on account of **sin**, and yet at the same time to
AG : 12 :005(034) [0049] absolution (namely, that **sin** has been forgiven and grace
AG : 12 :006(035) [0049] of life and the forsaking of **sin** would then follow, for
AG : 12 :010(035) [0049] teach that forgiveness of **sin** is not obtained through faith
AG : 15 :001(036) [0049] may be observed without **sin** and which contribute to
AG : 15 :004(037) [0049] and make satisfaction for **sin**, are useless and contrary to
AG : 16 :002(037) [0051] Christians may without **sin** occupy civil offices or serve as
AG : 16 :006(038) [0051] commands and laws in all that can be done without **sin**.
AG : 16 :007(038) [0051] cannot be obeyed without **sin**, we must obey God rather
AG : 19 :000(040) [0053] XIX. The Cause of **Sin**
AG : 19 :000(040) [0053] still preserves nature, yet **sin** is caused in all wicked men
AG : 20 :023(044) [0055] we receive grace and forgiveness of **sin** through Christ.
AG : 20 :025(044) [0057] the forgiveness of **sin**, and so they are at enmity with
AG : 20 :028(045) [0057] faith alone that apprehends grace and forgiveness of **sin**.
AG : 24 :021(058) [0067] only for original **sin**, and had instituted the Mass as a
AG : 24 :022(058) [0067] by means of which **sin** was taken away and God was
AG : 24 :026(058) [0067] is no sacrifice for original **sin**, or for any other sin, except
AG : 24 :026(058) [0067] sin, or for any other **sin**, except the one death of Christ.
AG : 24 :027(059) [0067] once and by this offering made satisfaction for all **sin**.
AG : 24 :025(059) [0067] only for original **sin** and not for other sins as well.
AG : 24 :029(059) [0067] the Mass is used to remove **sin** and obtain grace and all
AG : 24 :030(059) [0067] provision for a sacrifice for **sin** — for the sacrifice has
AG : 24 :030(059) [0067] grace and forgiveness of **sin** are promised us by Christ.
AG : 25 :003(062) [0069] Word of God, who forgives **sin**, for it is spoken in God's
AG : 26 :001(064) [0071] by men serve to earn grace and make satisfaction for **sin**.
AG : 26 :002(064) [0071] were observed and a great **sin** committed if they were
AG : 26 :021(067) [0073] cannot be reconciled, and **sin** cannot be atoned for by
AG : 26 :029(068) [0075] of earning forgiveness of **sin** or with the notion that
AG : 26 :033(069) [0075] does not give occasion to **sin**, but not as if he earned
AG : 26 :041(070) [0075] is to say that it is not a **sin** to omit them if this is done
AG : 27 :011(072) [0077] could earn forgiveness of **sin** and justification before
AG : 27 :038(077) [0081] life makes satisfaction for **sin** and obtains God's grace and
AG : 27 :040(077) [0081] teach that an oath should not be an obligation to **sin**.
AG : 27 :053(079) [0083] keep his possessions and engage in business without **sin**.
AG : 28 :039(087) [0089] when they attach **sin** to foods, days, and similar things
AG : 28 :041(087) [0089] example, that it is a mortal **sin** to do manual work on
AG : 28 :041(087) [0089] others), that it is a mortal **sin** to omit the seven hours,
AG : 28 :041(087) [0089] that in a reserved case **sin** is not forgiven unless
AG : 28 :053(090) [0091] of God and counting it a **sin** to omit their observance
AG : 28 :056(090) [0091] for salvation or that it is a **sin** to omit them, even when no
AG : 28 :056(090) [0091] that a woman commits a **sin** if without offense to others
AG : 28 :065(092) [0093] not observe it commit no **sin**, for the apostles did not wish
AG : 28 :069(093) [0093] of regulations which cannot be kept without **sin**.
AG : 28 :075(094) [0095] not to be observed without **sin**, we are bound to follow
AG : 28 :077(094) [0095] and pray that they may not coerce our consciences to **sin**.
AL : 02 :000(029) [0043] II. [Original **Sin**]
AL : 02 :001(029) [0043] who are propagated according to nature are born in **sin**.
AL : 02 :002(029) [0043] or vice of origin is truly **sin**, which even now damns and
AL : 02 :003(029) [0045] that the vice of origin is **sin** and who obscure the glory of
AL : 03 :005(030) [0045] and defend them against the devil and the power of **sin**.
AL : 12 :004(034) [0049] with a knowledge of **sin**, and the other is faith, which is
AL : 12 :008(035) [0049] may attain such perfection in this life that they cannot **sin**.
AL : 15 :001(036) [0049] can be observed without **sin** and which contribute to
AL : 16 :006(038) [0051] when commanded to **sin**, for then they ought to obey God
AL : 19 :000(040) [0053] XIX. The Cause of **Sin**
AL : 19 :000(040) [0053] nature, the cause of **sin** is the will of the wicked, that is,
AL : 24 :013(057) [0065] concerning this **sin**, private Masses were discontinued
AL : 24 :021(058) [0067] satisfaction for original **sin** and had instituted the Mass in
AL : 24 :033(060) [0067] said, "Because I always **sin**, I ought always take the
AL : 26 :033(069) [0075] idleness may tempt him to **sin**, but not in order to merit
AL : 26 :041(070) [0075] before God and that no **sin** is committed if they are
AL : 27 :021(074) [0079] obey this command and institution of God do not **sin**.
AL : 28 :039(087) [0089] of God when they attach **sin** to foods, days, and similar
AL : 28 :041(087) [0089] as this, that it is a mortal **sin** to do manual work on holy
AL : 28 :041(087) [0089] God, that it is a mortal **sin** to omit the canonical hours,
AL : 28 :041(087) [0089] that in a reserved case a **sin** cannot be forgiven except by
AL : 28 :042(088) [0089] Why do they multiply **sin** with such traditions?
AL : 28 :056(090) [0091] offense to others commit a **sin**, any more than one would
AL : 28 :065(092) [0093] not observe it commit no **sin**, for the apostles did not wish
AL : 28 :075(094) [0095] cannot be kept without **sin**, we are bound to follow the
AL : 28 :077(094) [0095] some few observances which cannot be kept without **sin**.
AP : 02 :000(100) [0105] [Article II. Original **Sin**]
AP : 02 :001(100) [0105] Article II, "Original **Sin**," but they criticize our definition
AP : 02 :001(100) [0105] Sin," but they criticize our definition of original **sin**.
AP : 02 :001(100) [0105] to describe what original **sin** includes, they viciously
AP : 02 :002(100) [0105] to the course of nature are conceived and born in **sin**.
AP : 02 :004(101) [0105] is the so-called "material element" of original **sin**.
AP : 02 :005(101) [0107] who claim that original **sin** is not some vice or corruption
AP : 02 :005(101) [0107] death because of original **sin** but, like a child born of a
AP : 02 :007(101) [0107] definition of original **sin** and therefore minimize original
AP : 02 :007(101) [0107] of original sin and therefore minimize original **sin**.
AP : 02 :008(101) [0107] they talk about original **sin**, they do not mention the
AP : 02 :010(102) [0107] confidently assert, then what can original **sin** be?
AP : 02 :014(102) [0109] our definition of original **sin** we also mentioned
AP : 02 :014(102) [0109] to show that original **sin** also involves such faults as
AP : 02 :015(102) [0109] the same thing, "Original **sin** is the lack of original
AP : 02 :023(103) [0111] Thus when the ancient definition says that **sin** is lack of
AP : 02 :024(103) [0111] Augustine's definition that original **sin** is concupiscence.
AP : 02 :026(103) [0111] our definition of original **sin**, therefore, we have correctly
AP : 02 :027(103) [0113] them — teach that original **sin** is truly composed of the
AP : 02 :027(104) [0113] Thomas says: "Original **sin** denotes the privation of
AP : 02 :028(104) [0113] is asked what original **sin** is, it is correct to answer that it
AP : 02 :029(104) [0113] when he says that original **sin** is ignorance in the mind
AP : 02 :032(104) [0113] nothing about original **sin** that is contrary to the
AP : 02 :033(104) [0113] Recognition of original **sin** is a necessity, nor can we
AP : 02 :035(104) [0113] he wrote that original **sin** remains after Baptism, and they
AP : 02 :035(105) [0115] by this statement that original **sin** remains after Baptism.
AP : 02 :035(105) [0115] the guilt of original **sin**, even though concupiscence
AP : 02 :035(105) [0115] remains — or, as they call it, the "material element" of **sin**
AP : 02 :036(105) [0115] same way when he says, "**Sin** is forgiven in Baptism, not
AP : 02 :036(105) [0115] Here he openly attests that **sin** is — that is, remains —
AP : 02 :038(105) [0115] is a penalty and not a **sin**, while Luther contends that it is
AP : 02 :038(105) [0115] and not a sin, while Luther contends that it is a **sin**.
AP : 02 :038(105) [0115] that Augustine defines original **sin** as concupiscence.
AP : 02 :039(105) [0115] me captive to the law of **sin** which dwells in my members"
AP : 02 :040(105) [0115] For they clearly call lust **sin**, by nature worthy of death if
AP : 02 :043(106) [0117] Or they say that nothing is **sin** unless it is voluntary.
AP : 02 :043(106) [0117] it is not right to twist it in order to minimize original **sin**.
AP : 02 :045(106) [0117] the magnitude of original **sin** and of human weakness, he
AP : 02 :045(106) [0117] the remnants of original **sin** in man are not in their nature
AP : 02 :046(106) [0117] scholastics minimize both **sin** and its penalty when they
AP : 02 :046(106) [0117] powers, Genesis describes another penalty for original **sin**.
AP : 02 :047(106) [0119] and concupiscence are **sin** as well as penalty; death, other
AP : 02 :050(106) [0119] given to us to bear both **sin** and penalty and to destroy
AP : 02 :050(106) [0119] the rule of the devil, **sin**, and death; so we cannot know
AP : 02 :051(107) [0119] formal element of original **sin** or the so-called deficiency.
AP : 04 :009(108) [0123] if reason in its sorrow over **sin** elicits an act of love to
AP : 04 :028(111) [0129] of God outside a state of grace do not **sin**.
AP : 04 :034(112) [0129] that God is wrathful at our **sin**, to fear him truly, and to
AP : 04 :035(112) [0131] Therefore men really **sin** even when they do virtuous
AP : 04 :035(112) [0131] "whatever does not proceed from faith is **sin**."
AP : 04 :037(112) [0131] a man guilty of mortal **sin** can love God above all things,
AP : 04 :040(112) [0131] and they are all under **sin** and subject to eternal wrath
AP : 04 :040(112) [0131] law cannot free us from **sin** or justify us, but the promise
AP : 04 :044(113) [0133] But to us, oppressed by **sin** and death, the promise freely
AP : 04 :048(113) [0135] knowledge and teach that it can exist with mortal **sin**.
AP : 04 :048(114) [0135] accounted righteous before God do not live in mortal **sin**.
AP : 04 :062(115) [0139] that all men are under **sin** and are worthy of eternal wrath
AP : 04 :064(116) [0139] cannot exist with mortal **sin**, but whenever it appears it
AP : 04 :075(117) [0143] For we are all under **sin**.
AP : 04 :079(117) [0143] of sins, the terrors of **sin** and of eternal death must be
AP : 04 :079(118) [0143] "The sting of death is **sin**, and the power of sin is law.
AP : 04 :079(118) [0143] "The sting of death is sin, and the power of **sin** is law.
AP : 04 :079(118) [0143] That is, **sin** terrifies consciences; this happens through the
AP : 04 :079(118) [0143] through the law, which shows God's wrath against **sin**.
AP : 04 :084(119) [0145] consigned all things to **sin**, that what was promised to
AP : 04 :084(119) [0145] merit, for he says that all are guilty and consigned to **sin**.
AP : 04 :085(119) [0147] against the terrors of **sin**, against eternal death, and
AP : 04 :103(121) [0151] that is, by the law **sin** is recognized but its guilt is not
AP : 04 :103(122) [0151] he forgave all men the **sin** that none could escape and by
AP : 04 :103(122) [0151] the trespass; but where **sin** increased, grace abounded all
AP : 04 :103(122) [0151] he took away the **sin** of the whole world, as John testified
AP : 04 :103(122) [0151] the Lamb of God, who takes away the **sin** of the world!'
AP : 04 :103(122) [0151] is forgiven, whose **sin** is covered' (Ps. 32:1)."
AP : 04 :109(123) [0153] because they imagine that faith can exist with mortal **sin**.
AP : 04 :115(123) [0155] nor can it exist with mortal **sin**; but it is a work of the
AP : 04 :135(125) [0159] shows us our uncleanness and the greatness of our **sin**.
AP : 04 :142(126) [0161] and looks for forgiveness of sins and deliverance from **sin**.
AP : 04 :144(127) [0161] terrified and fleeing from **sin**, therefore, such a faith does
AP : 04 :144(127) [0161] obey their lusts, nor does it exist together with mortal **sin**.
AP : 04 :148(127) [0163] did not die in vain, conquers the terrors of **sin** and death.
AP : 04 :149(127) [0163] because he thinks that his **sin** is greater and stronger than
AP : 04 :149(127) [0163] grace abounded more than **sin** (Rom. 5:20), that mercy is
AP : 04 :149(127) [0163] sin (Rom. 5:20), that mercy is more powerful than **sin**.
AP : 04 :168(130) [0169] with my mind, but with my flesh I serve the law of **sin**."
AP : 04 :168(130) [0169] Here he openly says that he serves the law of **sin**.

Continued ▶

A P : 0 4 :168(130) [0169] weakness there is always **sin** that could be imputed to us;
A P : 0 4 :179(131) [0171] the punishment of **sin** and becoming a sacrifice for us, the
A P : 0 4 :179(131) [0171] still the remnants of your **sin** do not condemn you,
A P : 0 4 :179(131) [0171] through faith, though **sin** still sticks to your flesh."
A P : 0 4 :214(136) [0179] overcome the terrors of **sin**, but faith alone can overcome
A P : 0 4 :222(138) [0181] conquers the terrors of **sin** and death; that we can set our
A P : 0 4 :238(140) [0187] say that our love conquers **sin** and death; or that in place
A P : 0 4 :244(142) [0189] conquer the terrors of **sin** and death; that good works are
A P : 0 4 :247(142) [0191] Christ when we set it against the terrors of **sin** and death.
A P : 0 4 :257(144) [0193] enough to preach the law, the Word that convicts of **sin**.
A P : 0 4 :262(145) [0195] amid the terrors of **sin**, a human being must have a very
A P : 0 4 :263(146) [0195] they truly believe and by faith conquer **sin** and death.
A P : 0 4 :277(148) [0199] same way, "Alms free from every **sin** and from death."
A P : 0 4 :277(148) [0199] Christ, whose prerogative it is to free from **sin** and death.
A P : 0 4 :278(149) [0199] does not free from **sin** and death *ex opere operato.*
A P : 0 4 :278(149) [0199] for us in the perils of **sin** and death, as we said a little
A P : 0 4 :290(151) [0203] it teaches that our works are a propitiation for **sin**.
A P : 0 4 :290(151) [0203] faith in Christ we overcome the terrors of **sin** and death.
A P : 0 4 :291(152) [0203] and victory over the terrors of **sin** and death.
A P : 0 4 :294(152) [0203] we receive forgiveness of **sin** because of our love but
A P : 0 4 :304(154) [0205] more clearly: The terrors of **sin** and death are not merely
A P : 0 4 :306(154) [0207] sake he made him to be **sin** who knew no sin, so that in
A P : 0 4 :306(154) [0207] him to be sin who knew no **sin**, so that in him we might
A P : 0 4 :314(156) [0207] we overcome the terrors of **sin** and death since we cannot
A P : 0 4 :317(156) [0209] makes Christ "an agent of **sin**" since he does not justify in
A P : 0 4 :327(158) [0211] 'I have made my heart clean, I am pure from my **sin**?"
A P : 0 4 :328(158) [0211] "If we say we have no **sin**, we deceive ourselves, and
A P : 0 4 :352(161) [0217] bodies are dead because of **sin**, your spirits are alive
A P : 0 4 :383(165) [0225] quickening the heart amid the terrors of **sin** and death.
A P : 0 4 :398(167) [0227] we obtain forgiveness of **sin**, conquer the terrors of sin,
A P : 0 4 :398(167) [0227] sin, conquer the terrors of **sin**, and receive peace for our
A P : 0 4 :398(167) [0227] we obtain the forgiveness of **sin**—is most true and certain
A P : 0 7 :039(176) [0241] food, and the like a matter of righteousness or of **sin**.
A P : 1 2 :006(183) [0255] of the keys accomplish if the **sin** is forgiven already?
A P : 1 2 :019(185) [0257] 3. To blot out **sin**, it is enough to detest the sin.
A P : 1 2 :019(185) [0257] 3. To blot out sin, it is enough to detest the **sin**.
A P : 1 2 :029(185) [0259] feels God's wrath against **sin** and is sorry that it has
A P : 1 2 :029(185) [0259] takes place when the Word of God denounces **sin**.
A P : 1 2 :029(185) [0259] the Gospel is to denounce **sin**, to offer the forgiveness of
A P : 1 2 :032(186) [0259] feels God's wrath against **sin**, unknown to men who walk
A P : 1 2 :032(186) [0259] It sees the foulness of **sin** and is genuinely sorry that it
A P : 1 2 :034(186) [0261] faith, but present only the Word that denounces **sin**.
A P : 1 2 :037(187) [0261] life it struggles with **sin** to conquer sin and death.
A P : 1 2 :037(187) [0261] life it struggles with sin to conquer **sin** and death.
A P : 1 2 :040(187) [0261] Word, the keys truly forgive **sin** before him, according to
A P : 1 2 :042(187) [0263] in its struggles against the terrors of **sin** and death.
A P : 1 2 :044(187) [0263] mean contrition, anxiety, and the terrors of **sin** and death.
A P : 1 2 :053(189) [0265] is the law, which reveals, denounces, and condemns **sin**.
A P : 1 2 :055(189) [0267] was rebuked and terrified after his **sin**; this was contrition.
A P : 1 2 :055(189) [0267] of the devil, death, and **sin**! this was the offer of the
A P : 1 2 :055(189) [0267] this punishment does not merit the forgiveness of **sin**.
A P : 1 2 :056(189) [0267] "The Lord has put away your **sin**; you shall not die."
A P : 1 2 :058(190) [0267] in conversion or regeneration and the forgiveness of **sin**.
A P : 1 2 :058(190) [0267] follow regeneration and the forgiveness of **sin**.
A P : 1 2 :072(192) [0271] against despair and against the terrors of **sin** and death.
A P : 1 2 :078(193) [0275] neither love nor works can be a propitiation for **sin**.
A P : 1 2 :081(194) [0275] consigned all things to **sin**, that what was promised to
A P : 1 2 :081(194) [0275] That is, all men are under **sin**, and they cannot be freed in
A P : 1 2 :089(195) [0279] "Whatever does not proceed from faith is **sin**."
A P : 1 2 :107(198) [0283] to the Lord'; then thou didst forgive the guilt of my **sin**."
A P : 1 2 :114(199) [0285] had certain expiations or **sin** by which they supposed they
A P : 1 2 :118(199) [0287] that in the forgiveness of **sin** God remits the guilt, and
A P : 1 2 :118(199) [0287] righteousness to punish **sin**, he commutes the eternal
A P : 1 2 :118(200) [0287] have relapsed into mortal **sin**, as though those who are in
A P : 1 2 :118(200) [0287] those who are in mortal **sin** could placate the divine
A P : 1 2 :132(202) [0293] even when they come from men in mortal **sin**.
A P : 1 2 :134(203) [0293] satisfactions he does not **sin** but will have to pay the
A P : 1 2 :140(204) [0295] to abolish death, even when they are done in mortal **sin**.
A P : 1 2 :143(204) [0297] command: and where they do, it is a **sin** to omit them.
A P : 1 2 :143(204) [0297] for they teach that they avail even for those in mortal **sin**.
A P : 1 2 :150(206) [0299] object that it is in accord with God's justice to punish **sin**.
A P : 1 2 :151(206) [0299] As a rule, these troubles are punishments for **sin**.
A P : 1 2 :152(206) [0299] on account of present **sin** because in the saints they kill
A P : 1 2 :152(206) [0299] body is dead because of **sin**"; that is, it is being killed
A P : 1 2 :152(206) [0299] being killed because of the **sin** still present and remaining
A P : 1 2 :153(206) [0299] "The sting of death is **sin**, and the power of sin is the
A P : 1 2 :153(206) [0299] sting of death is sin, and the power of **sin** is the law."
A P : 1 2 :153(206) [0299] This power of **sin**, this sense of wrath, is a real
A P : 1 2 :157(207) [0301] because of Christ, who is the victor over **sin** and death.
A P : 1 2 :157(207) [0301] mortification of present **sin**, not as a payment for or a
A P : 1 2 :159(207) [0301] for his blindness was not **sin** but "that the works of God
A P : 1 2 :161(208) [0303] that because of his **sin** he would be humiliated by his son,
A P : 1 2 :161(208) [0303] he carry out the threat even when the **sin** was forgiven?
A P : 1 2 :161(208) [0303] The answer is that the **sin** was forgiven so as not to
A P : 1 2 :161(208) [0303] death on man because of **sin**, and even after the
A P : 1 2 :161(208) [0303] after the forgiveness of **sin** he did not abolish it, for the
A P : 1 2 :162(208) [0303] that even those in mortal **sin** can buy off their
A P : 1 2 :165(208) [0303] not, as these men imagine, by works done in mortal **sin**.
A P : 1 2 :168(209) [0305] cutting off the causes of **sin**, that is, mortifying and
A P : 1 2 :168(209) [0305] punishments but to keep the flesh from alluring us to **sin**."
A P : 1 2 :173(210) [0305] their schools that it is not a **sin** to reject satisfactions.
A P : 1 5 :001(215) [0315] can be observed without **sin** and which are conducive to
A P : 1 5 :001(215) [0315] to make satisfaction for **sin** are contrary to the Gospel.
A P : 1 5 :017(217) [0319] "Whatever does not proceed from faith is **sin**."
A P : 1 5 :031(219) [0323] that to put this burden on the church is a great **sin**.
A P : 1 5 :051(222) [0329] which can be kept without **sin** or without great
A P : 1 8 :006(225) [0335] to say that a man does not **sin** if, outside the state of
A P : 1 9 :000(226) [0337] [Article XIX. The Cause of **Sin**]
A P : 1 9 :001(226) [0337] Nevertheless, the cause of **sin** is the will of the devil and
A P : 2 0 :002(227) [0339] that not our works but Christ is the propitiation for **sin**?
A P : 2 0 :008(227) [0341] no sure foundation when **sin** and death terrify them and
A P : 2 1 :005(230) [0345] grace does indeed abound more than **sin** (Rom. 5:20).
A P : 2 4 :021(253) [0391] propitiatory sacrifices for **sin** or burnt offerings for
A P : 2 4 :023(253) [0391] himself an offering for **sin**, he shall see his offspring, he
A P : 2 4 :023(253) [0391] the same word as "**sin**" in Rom. 8:3, "As a sin offering he
A P : 2 4 :023(253) [0391] as "sin" in Rom. 8:3, "As a **sin** offering he condemned
A P : 2 4 :023(253) [0391] sin offering he condemned **sin**," that is, through an
A P : 2 4 :023(253) [0391] he condemned sin," that is, through an offering for **sin**.
A P : 2 4 :031(255) [0395] it merits the forgiveness of **sin** when it is transferred to
A P : 2 4 :034(256) [0397] ceremonial sacrifices for **sin** offered by a Levitical
A P : 2 4 :053(259) [0403] The Levitical sacrifices for **sin** did not merit the
A P : 2 4 :055(259) [0403] and the satisfaction for **sin**, as Isa. 53:10 teaches, "When
A P : 2 4 :055(259) [0403] teaches, "When he makes himself an offering for **sin**."
A P : 2 4 :058(260) [0405] a priest who sacrifices for **sin**, this can only apply to
A P : 2 4 :060(260) [0405] of the terrors of death and **sin** through any work or
A P : 2 4 :076(263) [0411] greatness of our ills, our **sin** and our death; and it gives
A P : 2 4 :089(266) [0415] Then, too, **sin** and death cannot be conquered except by
A P : 2 4 :099(268) [0419] Mass lest they burden themselves with other men's **sin**.
A P : 2 7 :023(273) [0427] "Whatever does not proceed from faith is **sin**."
A P : 2 7 :044(277) [0435] they are guilty of a double **sin** — deceiving men, and
A P : 2 7 :065(280) [0441] idea that they merit forgiveness of **sin** and justification.
A P : 2 7 :068(280) [0443] people who have a mortal **sin**; therefore he says that those
A P : 2 8 :007(282) [0445] and that therefore neither **sin** nor righteousness depends
A P : 2 8 :008(282) [0445] such traditions so that it would be a **sin** to omit them.
A P : 2 8 :008(282) [0445] this is and enlarging on the **sin** of those who burden the
A P : 2 8 :011(283) [0447] consciences so that their omission is judged to be a **sin**.
S 2 : 0 1 :002(292) [0461] of God, who takes away the **sin** of the world" (John 1:29).
S 2 : 0 2 :003(293) [0463] and so it can be omitted without **sin** and danger.
S 2 : 0 2 :005(293) [0463] can be omitted without **sin**, that no one will be damned
S 2 : 0 2 :007(294) [0465] of God and the Son of God who takes away our **sin**."
S 2 : 0 2 :018(296) [0467] way and may omit pilgrimages without **sin** and danger.
S 2 : 0 2 :023(296) [0469] and the forgiveness of **sin** and that, like the Mass, etc.,
S 3 : 0 1 :000(302) [0477] I. **Sin**
S 3 : 0 1 :001(302) [0477] in Rom. 5:12, namely, that **sin** had its origin in one man,
S 3 : 0 1 :001(302) [0477] This is called original **sin**, or the root sin.
S 3 : 0 1 :001(302) [0477] This is called original sin, or the root **sin**.
S 3 : 0 1 :002(302) [0477] The fruits of this **sin** are all the subsequent evil deeds
S 3 : 0 1 :003(302) [0477] This hereditary **sin** is so deep a corruption of nature that
S 3 : 0 1 :009(302) [0477] an evil intention to commit **sin**, for such is the goodness
S 3 : 0 1 :011(303) [0479] and ignorance concerning **sin** and concerning Christ, our
S 3 : 0 1 :011(303) [0479] would be no defect or **sin** in man for which he would
S 3 : 0 2 :001(303) [0479] because of the wickedness which **sin** has worked in man.
S 3 : 0 2 :004(303) [0479] the law is to make original **sin** manifest and show man to
S 3 : 0 3 :001(303) [0479] "The Holy Spirit will convince the world of **sin**."
S 3 : 0 3 :008(304) [0481] As St. Paul says, the law slays through **sin**.
S 3 : 0 3 :008(304) [0481] the dreadful captivity to **sin**, and this comes to us through
S 3 : 0 3 :010(304) [0481] repentance because they did not know what **sin** really is.
S 3 : 0 3 :010(305) [0481] concerning original **sin** but asserted that the natural
S 3 : 0 3 :011(305) [0481] they did not consider **sin**), wicked words, and wicked
S 3 : 0 3 :014(305) [0483] priests and monks, that we might set ourselves against **sin**.
S 3 : 0 3 :015(305) [0483] that when a hidden **sin** was afterwards remembered, it
S 3 : 0 3 :017(305) [0483] repent or be sorry for his **sin** (which might have been
S 3 : 0 3 :017(306) [0483] on the basis of this good work of his, his **sin** was forgiven.
S 3 : 0 3 :018(306) [0483] It did not extinguish the lust for **sin**.
S 3 : 0 3 :021(306) [0485] he was to do for one single **sin**, to say nothing of all his
S 3 : 0 3 :022(306) [0485] years of penance were required for a single mortal **sin**.
S 3 : 0 3 :028(308) [0487] were, as we taught, without **sin** and full of good works,
S 3 : 0 3 :032(308) [0487] neither of you knows what **sin** really is, to say nothing of
S 3 : 0 3 :032(308) [0487] sin really is, to say nothing of repenting and shunning **sin**.
S 3 : 0 3 :035(309) [0489] teaches us to acknowledge **sin** — that is, to acknowledge
S 3 : 0 3 :036(309) [0489] It does not debate what is **sin** and what is not sin, but
S 3 : 0 3 :036(309) [0489] what is sin and what is not **sin**, but lumps everything
S 3 : 0 3 :036(309) [0489] we might imagine to be good enough to pay for our **sin**.
S 3 : 0 3 :038(309) [0489] Lamb of God who takes away the **sin** of the world.
S 3 : 0 3 :042(310) [0491] in faith even if they **sin** afterwards, and such sin will not
S 3 : 0 3 :042(310) [0491] if they sin afterwards, and such **sin** will not harm them.
S 3 : 0 3 :043(310) [0491] possess and feel original **sin** and daily repent and strive
S 3 : 0 3 :043(310) [0491] against it, fall into open **sin** (as David fell into adultery,
S 3 : 0 3 :044(310) [0491] Holy Spirit does not permit **sin** to rule and gain the upper
S 3 : 0 3 :044(310) [0491] hand in such a way that **sin** is committed, but the Holy
S 3 : 0 3 :044(310) [0491] If the **sin** does what it wishes, the Holy Spirit and faith
S 3 : 0 3 :045(310) [0491] says, "No one born of God commits **sin**; he cannot sin."
S 3 : 0 3 :045(310) [0491] says, "No one born of God commits sin; he cannot **sin**."
S 3 : 0 3 :045(310) [0491] "If we say we have no **sin**, we deceive ourselves, and the
S 3 : 0 4 :000(310) [0491] council and help against **sin** in more than one way, for
S 3 : 0 4 :000(310) [0491] by which the forgiveness of **sin** (the peculiar function of
S 3 : 0 5 :002(310) [0491] power which, through the water, washes away **sin**.
S 3 : 0 5 :003(311) [0493] that Baptism washes away **sin** through the assistance of
S 3 : 0 7 :001(311) [0493] that in his flesh he was captive to "the law of **sin**."
S 3 : 0 8 :001(312) [0493] and help against **sin** and a bad conscience, confession and
S 3 : 0 8 :002(312) [0495] not be untruthful if we say, "I am a poor man, full of **sin**.
S 3 : 0 9 :000(314) [0497] in the church until they mend their ways and avoid **sin**.
S 3 : 1 3 :001(315) [0499] Although the **sin** in our flesh has not been completely
S 3 : 1 3 :002(315) [0499] will not be reckoned as **sin** or defect for the sake of the
S 3 : 1 5 :002(316) [0501] say that it is a mortal **sin** to break such precepts of men,
T R : 0 0 :045(328) [0517] the teaching concerning **sin** and have invented a tradition
S C : P R :019(340) [0537] are guilty of damnable **sin** if they do not do so, for by
S C : P R :020(340) [0537] and governing authorities **sin** in this respect is beyond
S C : P R :023(341) [0537] thereby that he has no **sin**, no flesh, no devil, no world,
S C : 0 3 :016(347) [0549] Although we **sin** daily and deserve nothing but
S C : 0 3 :016(347) [0549] and cheerfully do good to those who may **sin** against us.
S C : 0 3 :018(347) [0549] God tempts no one to **sin**, but we pray in this petition
S C : 0 5 :025(350) [0555] you have knowledge of no **sin** at all (which is quite
S C : 0 6 :006(352) [0557] in the words "for you" and "for the forgiveness of **sin**."
S C : 0 7 :002(352) [0557] me this day, too, from all **sin** and evil, that in all my
S C : 0 7 :005(353) [0559] Thee to forgive all my **sin** and the wrong which I have
L C : 0 1 :056(372) [0595] holy name as the greatest **sin** that can be committed
L C : 0 1 :056(372) [0595] deceive is in itself a gross **sin**, but it is greatly aggravated
L C : 0 1 :071(374) [0601] in wait to lure us into **sin** and shame, calamity and
L C : 0 1 :099(378) [0609] This is precisely the **sin** that used to be classed among the
L C : 0 1 :176(389) [0631] You bring upon yourself **sin** and wrath, thus earning hell
L C : 0 1 :216(394) [0641] remain they will inevitably **sin** more and more against
L C : 0 1 :258(399) [0653] is such a government, instances of this **sin** still occur.
L C : 0 1 :262(400) [0655] and the children of God and yet consider this no **sin**.
L C : 0 1 :265(401) [0657] even when he has seen a **sin** committed, unless he has
L C : 0 1 :266(401) [0657] difference between judging **sin** and having knowledge of

Continued ▶

L C : 0 1 :266(401) [0657] between judging sin and having knowledge of **sin**.
L C : 0 1 :266(401) [0657] Knowledge of **sin** does not entail the right to judge it.
L C : 0 1 :266(401) [0657] pass sentence on him, I fall into a greater **sin** than his.
L C : 0 1 :266(401) [0657] you become aware of a **sin**, simply make your ears a tomb
L C : 0 1 :274(402) [0659] and evil, yet he does not **sin** against God's
L C : 0 1 :274(402) [0659] duty it is fail to do so, they **sin** as much as those who take
L C : 0 1 :284(403) [0661] But where the **sin** is so public that the judge and the
L C : 0 1 :284(403) [0661] of it, you can without **sin** shun and avoid the person as
L C : 0 1 :284(403) [0661] Where the **sin** is public, the punishment ought to be
L C : 0 1 :295(404) [0665] considered this no more a **sin** or disgrace than it is now
L C : 0 2 :022(413) [0683] For we **sin** daily with eyes and ears, hands, body and
L C : 0 2 :027(414) [0685] he has redeemed me from **sin**, from the devil, from death,
L C : 0 2 :027(414) [0685] condemned to death and entangled in **sin** and blindness.
L C : 0 2 :028(414) [0685] came and led us into disobedience, **sin**, death, and all evil.
L C : 0 2 :031(414) [0685] from death to life, from **sin** to righteousness, and now
L C : 0 2 :031(414) [0687] and born without **sin**, of the Holy Spirit and the Virgin,
L C : 0 2 :031(414) [0687] might become Lord over **sin**; moreover, he suffered, died,
L C : 0 2 :031(414) [0687] us from the wicked world, the devil, death, **sin**, etc.
L C : 0 2 :054(418) [0693] are encumbered with our flesh we are never without **sin**.
L C : 0 2 :055(418) [0693] Although we have **sin**, the Holy Spirit sees to it that it
L C : 0 2 :055(418) [0693] Christian church, where there is full forgiveness of **sin**.
L C : 0 2 :056(418) [0693] and the forgiveness of **sin** have expelled and separated
L C : 0 2 :058(418) [0693] completely freed from **sin**, death, and all evil, living in
L C : 0 3 :011(421) [0701] were struck down for their **sin** did not return to him and
L C : 0 3 :051(427) [0711] life, and salvation against **sin**, death, and an evil
L C : 0 3 :054(427) [0713] be utterly destroyed and **sin**, death, and hell
L C : 0 3 :086(432) [0723] gift and blessing, nevertheless we are not without **sin**.
L C : 0 3 :088(432) [0723] that he does not forgive **sin** even without and before our
L C : 0 3 :089(432) [0723] and devices, so that we **sin** daily in word and deed, in acts
L C : 0 3 :094(433) [0725] Inasmuch as we **sin** greatly against God everyday and yet
L C : 0 3 :105(434) [0727] and weary and to fall back into **sin**, shame, and unbelief.
L C : 0 3 :118(436) [0731] he will preserve us from **sin** and shame and from
L C : 0 4 :025(439) [0739] than to be delivered from **sin**, death and the devil and to
L C : 0 4 :041(442) [0743] the devil, forgiveness of **sin**, God's grace, the entire
L C : 0 4 :059(444) [0747] remains no less gold if a harlot wears it in **sin** and shame.
L C : 0 4 :077(446) [0751] though we fall from it and **sin**, nevertheless we always
L C : 0 4 :080(446) [0751] which we can no longer use after falling again into **sin**.
L C : 0 4 :083(446) [0751] overcomes and takes away **sin** and daily strengthens the
L C : 0 4 :086(446) [0753] to him even though we **sin**, so all his treasures and gifts
L C : 0 5 :059(453) [0767] man has committed such a **sin** that he has forfeited the
L C : 0 5 :061(453) [0767] pure and without **sin**; on the contrary, we come as poor,
L C : 0 5 :067(454) [0769] Surely it is a **sin** and a shame that, when he tenderly and
L C : 0 5 :071(455) [0769] and are heavy-laden with **sin**, fear of death, and the
L C : 0 5 :077(455) [0771] we are insensitive to our **sin** is all the worse, for it is a sign
L C : 0 5 :078(455) [0771] you are so utterly dead in **sin**, at least believe the
L C : 0 5 :079(455) [0771] you and give you occasion for **sin** and wrong-doing.
L C : 0 6 :001(457) [0000] to make confession on pain of the gravest mortal **sin**.
L C : 0 6 :002(457) [0000] enumeration of all kinds of **sin** that no one was able to
L C : 0 6 :014(458) [0000] is a heart that feels its **sin** and desires consolation, it has
L C : 0 6 :015(458) [0000] and act, when I lament my **sin** and desire comfort and
L C : 0 6 :016(459) [0000] the absolution was not valid and the **sin** was not forgiven.
L C : 0 6 :029(460) [0000] you show thereby that you can have no forgiveness of **sin**.
E P : 0 1 :000(466) [0779] I. Original **Sin**
E P : 0 1 :001(466) [0779] any distinction, original **sin** is man's corrupted nature,
E P : 0 1 :001(466) [0779] the one hand, and original **sin** on the other hand, so that
E P : 0 1 :001(466) [0779] is one thing and original **sin**, which inheres in the
E P : 0 1 :002(466) [0779] man's nature and original **sin**, not only in the beginning
E P : 0 1 :002(466) [0779] pure and holy and without **sin**, but also as we now have
E P : 0 1 :002(466) [0779] our nature and original **sin** is as great as the difference
E P : 0 1 :003(466) [0779] human nature and original **sin** militates against and
E P : 0 1 :005(466) [0781] nature, though without **sin**, and thus took on himself not
E P : 0 1 :005(466) [0781] be made like his brethren in every respect," **sin** excepted.
E P : 0 1 :006(467) [0781] he has not created original **sin**, has not assumed it, has
E P : 0 1 :008(467) [0781] and confess that original **sin** is not a slight corruption of
E P : 0 1 :010(467) [0781] forever, without original **sin** and completely separated
E P : 0 1 :011(467) [0781] the teaching that original **sin** is only a debt which we owe
E P : 0 1 :012(467) [0781] that evil desires are not **sin** but concreated and essential
E P : 0 1 :012(467) [0783] and damage is not truly **sin** on account of which man
E P : 0 1 :014(467) [0783] the teaching that original **sin** is a slight, insignificant spot
E P : 0 1 :015(468) [0783] Furthermore, that original **sin** is only an external
E P : 0 1 :017(468) [0783] error that original **sin** is an essential, self-existing
E P : 0 1 :018(468) [0783] man himself who commits **sin** but something extraneous
E P : 0 1 :018(468) [0783] man but only the original **sin** which is in the nature is
E P : 0 1 :019(468) [0783] the teaching that original **sin** is strictly and without any
E P : 0 1 :019(468) [0783] after the Fall and original **sin**, and that the two cannot be
E P : 0 1 :020(468) [0783] Luther calls original **sin** "nature-sin," "person-sin,"
E P : 0 1 :020(468) [0783] calls original sin "nature-**sin**," "person-sin," "essential sin,"
E P : 0 1 :020(468) [0783] sin "nature-sin," "person-**sin**," "essential sin," not in order
E P : 0 1 :020(468) [0783] "person-sin," "essential **sin**," not in order to identify
E P : 0 1 :020(468) [0783] essence itself with original **sin** but by such terminology to
E P : 0 1 :020(468) [0783] difference between original **sin**, which inheres in human
E P : 0 1 :021(468) [0783] For original **sin** is not a sin which man commits; it
E P : 0 1 :021(468) [0783] For original sin is not a **sin** which man commits; it
E P : 0 1 :021(468) [0785] corrupted through original **sin**, innate in us through our
E P : 0 1 :022(469) [0785] or quality of a man to **sin**," or, "Man's nature is sin."
E P : 0 1 :022(469) [0785] or quality of a man to sin," or, "Man's nature is **sin**."
E P : 0 1 :024(469) [0785] the discussion of original **sin** because they are familiar
E P : 0 2 :003(470) [0787] can man who through **sin** is spiritually dead raise himself
E P : 0 3 :007(473) [0793] in this article "absolve," that is, pronounce free from **sin**.
E P : 0 3 :011(474) [0795] with a wicked intention to **sin** and to act contrary to one's
E P : 0 3 :015(475) [0795] or to be absolved from **sin** and to obtain the forgiveness
E P : 0 3 :017(475) [0795] resulting love, but continues to **sin** against his conscience.
E P : 0 4 :011(477) [0799] keep his faith even if he deliberately were to persist in **sin**.
E P : 0 4 :019(477) [0801] not lost through malicious **sin**, but that the holy ones and
E P : 0 5 :004(478) [0801] which condemns **sin** is and belongs to the proclamation
E P : 0 5 :008(478) [0803] Now as to the disclosure of **sin**, as long as men hear only
E P : 0 5 :008(479) [0803] to learn the true nature of **sin** from the law, and thus they
E P : 0 5 :008(479) [0803] the real nature of their **sin**, and acknowledgment which
E P : 0 6 :001(479) [0805] men to a knowledge of their **sin**, (3) after they are reborn,
E P : 1 1 :004(494) [0833] is not a cause of evil or of **sin** which compels anyone to
E P : 1 1 :019(497) [0837] without regard for their **sin**, God has predestined certain
E P : 1 2 :006(498) [0839] entire doctrine of original **sin** and everything that pertains
S D : 0 1 :000(508) [0859] I. Original **Sin**
S D : 0 1 :001(508) [0859] Confession about what original **sin**, strictly understood, is
S D : 0 1 :001(508) [0859] powers) is original **sin** itself, which has been called
S D : 0 1 :001(508) [0859] has been called "nature-**sin**" or "person-sin" because it is
S D : 0 1 :001(508) [0859] "nature-sin" or "person-**sin**" because it is not a thought, a
S D : 0 1 :001(508) [0859] between man's nature or essence and original **sin**.
S D : 0 1 :002(508) [0859] and taught that original **sin**, strictly speaking, is not
S D : 0 1 :002(508) [0859] maintained that original **sin** is something in man's nature,
S D : 0 1 :002(509) [0859] corruption and this inborn **sin** which inheres in his
S D : 0 1 :002(509) [0859] after the Fall) and original **sin** (which is a work of the
S D : 0 1 :003(509) [0859] concerning original **sin** is not a useless contention about
S D : 0 1 :004(509) [0861] concerning original **sin**, we shall use the aforementioned
S D : 0 1 :005(509) [0861] regard and recognize as **sin** not only the actual
S D : 0 1 :005(509) [0861] consider this as the chief **sin**, the root and fountain of all
S D : 0 1 :005(509) [0861] as the chief sin, the root and fountain of all actual **sin**.
S D : 0 1 :006(509) [0861] Dr. Luther calls this **sin** "nature-sin" or "person-sin" in
S D : 0 1 :006(509) [0861] Luther calls this sin "nature-**sin**" or "person-sin" in order
S D : 0 1 :006(509) [0861] sin "nature-sin" or "person-**sin**" in order to indicate that
S D : 0 1 :006(509) [0861] the sight of God original **sin**, like a spiritual leprosy, has
S D : 0 1 :007(510) [0861] that God is not the creator, author, or cause of **sin**.
S D : 0 1 :007(510) [0861] scheme, "by one man **sin** (which is the work of the devil)
S D : 0 1 :007(510) [0861] this corruption, God does not create and make **sin** in us.
S D : 0 1 :007(510) [0861] the present time, original **sin** is transmitted through our
S D : 0 1 :010(510) [0863] Furthermore, that original **sin** is the complete lack or
S D : 0 1 :010(510) [0863] description of original **sin** denies to unrenewed human
S D : 0 1 :011(510) [0863] 3. That original **sin** in human nature is not only a total
S D : 0 1 :013(511) [0863] and penalty of original **sin** which God imposes upon
S D : 0 1 :013(511) [0863] children and upon original **sin** is death, eternal
S D : 0 1 :014(511) [0863] nature, which original **sin** has perverted and corrupted.
S D : 0 1 :017(511) [0865] and doctrine that original **sin** is only an obligation
S D : 0 1 :018(511) [0865] wicked desires are not **sin** but concreated and essential
S D : 0 1 :019(511) [0865] not really and truly such a **sin** in the sight of God that
S D : 0 1 :021(511) [0865] 5. Or that original **sin** is only a simple, insignificant,
S D : 0 1 :022(512) [0865] 6. Or that original **sin** is not a deprivation or absence of
S D : 0 1 :025(512) [0867] it can by and of itself do nothing but **sin** (Gen. 6:5; 8:21).
S D : 0 1 :026(512) [0867] infuses and blends original **sin** (as something essential)
S D : 0 1 :027(512) [0867] pure, good, and holy, **sin** did not invade their nature in
S D : 0 1 :028(513) [0867] through original **sin**, but in the first moment of our
S D : 0 1 :028(513) [0867] Hence original **sin** is not something which exists
S D : 0 1 :029(513) [0867] Nor are original **sin** and the human nature that has been
S D : 0 1 :029(513) [0867] of God, and only the original **sin** which dwells in it is evil.
S D : 0 1 :030(513) [0867] of his inborn original **sin** but a strange and foreign
S D : 0 1 :030(513) [0867] man's nature, corrupted by **sin**, but only the original sin.
S D : 0 1 :030(513) [0867] man's nature, corrupted by sin, but only the original **sin**.
S D : 0 1 :030(513) [0867] correct doctrine of original **sin**, the whole nature of every
S D : 0 1 :030(513) [0867] and perverted by original **sin** in body and in soul, in all
S D : 0 1 :031(513) [0869] corrupted nature unless the **sin** is forgiven for Christ's
S D : 0 1 :032(514) [0869] far as our nature has been poisoned and corrupted by **sin**.
S D : 0 1 :033(514) [0869] in Luther's words, original **sin**, like a spiritual poison and
S D : 0 1 :033(514) [0869] by itself and original **sin** by itself as two manifestly
S D : 0 1 :033(514) [0869] God (within which original **sin**, by which the nature,
S D : 0 1 :033(514) [0869] not identical with original **sin** (which dwells in man's
S D : 0 1 :033(514) [0869] by God and in which **sin** dwells and (b) original sin itself
S D : 0 1 :033(514) [0869] sin dwells and (b) original **sin** itself which dwells in the
S D : 0 1 :038(514) [0871] unqualifiedly with **sin** itself, for in that case God would
S D : 0 1 :038(514) [0871] sin itself, for in that case God would be the creator of **sin**.
S D : 0 1 :038(515) [0871] miserably corrupted by **sin**, for the dough out of which
S D : 0 1 :039(515) [0871] so miserably corrupted by **sin**, in order that through his
S D : 0 1 :039(515) [0871] Son he might cleanse it from **sin**, sanctify it, and save it.
S D : 0 1 :040(515) [0871] clearly, because original **sin** does not come from God, nor
S D : 0 1 :040(515) [0871] come from God, nor is God the creator or author of **sin**.
S D : 0 1 :040(515) [0871] Neither is original **sin** the creature or handiwork of God;
S D : 0 1 :041(515) [0871] are corrupted by original **sin**) and original sin itself (by
S D : 0 1 :041(515) [0871] original sin) and original **sin** itself (by which our nature is
S D : 0 1 :041(515) [0871] created and made original **sin**, which thus would also
S D : 0 1 :041(515) [0871] the devil is the author of **sin**, Satan is the creator of our
S D : 0 1 :041(515) [0871] nature were unqualifiedly identical with **sin** itself.
S D : 0 1 :042(515) [0873] of Satan, who through **sin** has in this fashion corrupted
S D : 0 1 :043(515) [0873] our nature, though without **sin**, so that in every respect he
S D : 0 1 :043(516) [0873] made like us, his brethren, **sin** alone excepted
S D : 0 1 :043(516) [0873] all its essential attributes — **sin** alone excepted — identical
S D : 0 1 :044(516) [0873] man and original **sin**, it would have to follow that Christ
S D : 0 1 :044(516) [0873] as he did not assume **sin**, or that Christ assumed sin
S D : 0 1 :044(516) [0873] sin, or that Christ assumed **sin** inasmuch as he assumed
S D : 0 1 :044(516) [0873] our nature, but not original **sin**, it is evident that even
S D : 0 1 :044(516) [0873] human nature and original **sin** are not identical with but
S D : 0 1 :045(516) [0873] God cleanses man from **sin**, purifies him, and sanctifies
S D : 0 1 :045(516) [0873] **Sin** thus cannot be identified with man himself, since God
S D : 0 1 :045(516) [0873] grace but remains the enemy of **sin** throughout eternity!
S D : 0 1 :045(516) [0873] to say that original **sin** is baptized in the name of the holy
S D : 0 1 :046(516) [0873] this our flesh, but without **sin**, shall arise, and that in
S D : 0 1 :046(516) [0873] have and keep precisely this soul, although without **sin**.
S D : 0 1 :047(516) [0873] the one hand and original **sin** on the other, then it would
S D : 0 1 :047(516) [0875] we there shall be without **sin**, or else that sin would be
S D : 0 1 :047(516) [0875] be without sin, or else that **sin** would be raised and would
S D : 0 1 :048(516) [0875] when it is said that original **sin** is the very nature of
S D : 0 1 :048(517) [0875] corrupted nature or substance or being and original **sin**.
S D : 0 1 :048(517) [0875] man, which is corrupted by **sin**, and the sin by and
S D : 0 1 :048(517) [0875] corrupted by sin, and the **sin** by and through which man
S D : 0 1 :051(517) [0875] that Luther writes that **sin** and sinning are man's
S D : 0 1 :052(517) [0875] therefore, original **sin** is the deep corruption of our nature
S D : 0 1 :052(517) [0875] the body and soul in which **sin** is and inheres) because
S D : 0 1 :052(517) [0875] inheres) because through **sin** man is corrupted, poisoned,
S D : 0 1 :052(517) [0875] your entire essence is **sin**, that is sinful and unclean."
S D : 0 1 :053(517) [0875] he uses the terms "nature-**sin**," "person-sin," "essential sin"
S D : 0 1 :053(517) [0875] terms "nature-sin," "person-**sin**," "essential sin" to indicate
S D : 0 1 :053(517) [0875] "person-sin," "essential **sin**" to indicate that not only
S D : 0 1 :053(517) [0875] words, and deeds are **sin** but that the entire nature,
S D : 0 1 :053(517) [0877] corrupted though original **sin** to its very foundation.
S D : 0 1 :055(518) [0877] the statement, "Original **sin** is the nature or essence of
S D : 0 1 :056(518) [0877] in this fashion: Original **sin** is not man's nature itself, but
S D : 0 1 :057(518) [0877] were to ask if original **sin** is a substance (that is, a thing
S D : 0 1 :057(518) [0879] and roundly that original **sin** is not a substance but an
S D : 0 1 :058(519) [0879] whether or not original **sin** is a substance or an accident

Continued ▶

SD : 0 1 :060(519) [0879] inquires further, What kind of accident is original **sin**?
SD : 0 1 :060(519) [0879] understanding and give a correct definition of original **sin**.
SD : 0 1 :060(519) [0879] It testifies that original **sin** is an inexpressible impairment
SD : 0 1 :060(519) [0879] so that through original **sin** man is in God's sight
SD : 0 1 :061(519) [0879] any way minimize original **sin** if the term is explained in
SD : 0 1 :061(519) [0879] writes earnestly against a minimizing of original **sin**.
SD : 0 1 :061(519) [0879] the devil's handiwork, the **sin** which inheres in and most
SD : 0 1 :062(519) [0879] "Whether we call original **sin** a quality or a disease,
SD : 0 1 :062(519) [0879] 3, "The venom of original **sin** has poisoned us from the
SD : 0 2 :007(521) [0883] himself," but is a slave of **sin** (John 8:34), the captive of
SD : 0 2 :010(522) [0885] that the man who is "in **sin**" is not only weak and sick,
SD : 0 2 :011(522) [0885] who is spiritually dead, in **sin**, prepare or address himself
SD : 0 2 :011(522) [0885] liberated him from the death of **sin** and made him alive.
SD : 0 2 :015(523) [0887] and the bondage of **sin** and death through his Son, and
SD : 0 2 :017(524) [0887] but also that by original **sin** he is so miserably perverted,
SD : 0 2 :017(524) [0887] but I am carnal, sold under **sin**" (Rom. 7:14), and shortly
SD : 0 2 :017(524) [0887] making me captive to the law of **sin**" (Rom. 7:18, 22, 23).
SD : 0 2 :018(524) [0887] in the article on original **sin** (to which for the sake of
SD : 0 2 :021(525) [0889] cruel wrath of God over **sin** and death but continues in
SD : 0 2 :029(527) [0893] He drives them into many kinds of manifest **sin**.
SD : 0 2 :029(527) [0893] is much too weak for Satan, who incites men to **sin**."
SD : 0 2 :031(527) [0893] them, that he forgives their **sin**, or that he will help them
SD : 0 2 :034(527) [0895] for it contends with the **sin** remaining in the flesh
SD : 0 2 :034(528) [0895] sweeps out the remaining **sin** and operates to make man
SD : 0 2 :043(529) [0897] Outside of Christ death and **sin** are our masters and the
SD : 0 2 :043(529) [0897] the dupes and captives of **sin** and the property of the
SD : 0 2 :059(532) [0905] him from the death of **sin**, illuminates him, and renews
SD : 0 2 :061(533) [0905] conversion man is dead in **sin** (Eph. 2:5); hence there can
SD : 0 2 :064(533) [0905] me captive to the law of **sin** which dwells in my
SD : 0 2 :064(533) [0907] but with my flesh the law of **sin**" (Rom. 7:22, 23, 25).
SD : 0 2 :069(534) [0907] conscience and permit **sin** to rule in themselves and thus
SD : 0 2 :070(535) [0909] the heart learns to know **sin**, to fear the wrath of God, to
SD : 0 2 :070(535) [0909] wrath of God, to turn from **sin**, to understand and accept
SD : 0 2 :072(535) [0909] what a grievous **sin** it is to hinder and resist such
SD : 0 2 :075(536) [0911] obedience earn the forgiveness of **sin** and eternal life.
SD : 0 2 :085(537) [0913] resists God entirely and is completely the servant of **sin**.
SD : 0 2 :085(537) [0913] in his members the law of **sin** at war with the law of his
SD : 0 2 :085(537) [0913] with his flesh he serves the law of **sin** (Rom. 7:22, 23, 25).
SD : 0 3 :014(541) [0919] when he satisfied the law for us and paid for our **sin**.
SD : 0 3 :022(543) [0923] follow in the ways of **sin**, abide and continue therein
SD : 0 3 :023(543) [0923] in this life and because **sin** still dwells in the flesh even in
SD : 0 3 :026(543) [0923] to remain and abide in **sin**, for true contrition precedes
SD : 0 3 :056(549) [0935] by the Holy Spirit without **sin** and had been born and had
SD : 0 3 :057(550) [0935] Son, cleanses us from all **sin**" (I John 1:7), and again,
SD : 0 3 :058(550) [0937] the law for us, bore our **sin**, and in his path to the Father
SD : 0 3 :064(550) [0937] no love follows) but against his conscience remains in **sin**.
SD : 0 4 :008(552) [0941] and God regards them as **sin** and as impure because of
SD : 0 4 :008(552) [0941] does not proceed from faith is **sin**" (Rom. 14:23).
SD : 0 4 :015(553) [0943] to continue and abide in **sin**, which is impossible.
SD : 0 4 :031(556) [0947] been received, through any **sin**, even a wanton and
SD : 0 4 :031(556) [0947] deliberately proceeds to **sin** against his conscience, he can
SD : 0 4 :033(556) [0949] we do not fall from our calling by lapsing again into **sin**.
SD : 0 5 :002(558) [0951] of repentance, which rebukes the greatest **sin**, unbelief.
SD : 0 5 :004(559) [0953] and forgiveness of **sin** should be preached in his name to
SD : 0 5 :009(559) [0955] preach the forgiveness of **sin** to indifferent and secure
SD : 0 5 :010(560) [0955] he really learns to know his **sin**, an insight that Moses
SD : 0 5 :011(560) [0955] the office of the law, must also convince the world of **sin**.
SD : 0 5 :012(560) [0955] that preaches about our **sin** and the wrath of God, no
SD : 0 5 :012(560) [0955] will convince the world of **sin** because they do not believe
SD : 0 5 :012(560) [0955] of God's wrath over **sin** than the passion and death of
SD : 0 5 :013(560) [0957] will convince the world of **sin**' (John 16:8), which cannot
SD : 0 5 :014(560) [0957] of the law, which reveals **sin** and God's wrath, but to this
SD : 0 5 :015(561) [0957] and would have us criticize **sin** and teach contrition and
SD : 0 5 :017(561) [0957] "Everything that rebukes **sin** is and belongs to the law,
SD : 0 5 :017(561) [0957] of which is to condemn **sin** and to lead to a knowledge of
SD : 0 5 :017(561) [0957] sin and to lead to a knowledge of **sin**" (Rom. 3:20; 7:7).
SD : 0 5 :017(561) [0957] of all culpable **sin**, the law reproves unbelief also.
SD : 0 5 :018(561) [0957] the law remains, to rebuke **sin** and to give instruction
SD : 0 5 :020(561) [0959] and all the punishments of **sin**, and are saved eternally.
SD : 0 5 :022(562) [0959] who "was made **sin** though he knew no sin, so that in him
SD : 0 5 :022(562) [0959] sin though he knew no **sin**, so that in him we might
SD : 0 5 :024(562) [0961] to a knowledge of their **sin** and to repentance, but not in
SD : 0 5 :025(563) [0961] men may abuse the grace of God and **sin** against grace.
SD : 0 5 :027(563) [0961] the law is a message that rebukes and condemns **sin**.
SD : 0 6 :001(563) [0963] to a knowledge of their **sin** through the law, (3) but those
SD : 0 6 :008(565) [0965] of my mind and making me captive to the law of **sin**."
SD : 0 6 :012(566) [0967] the Old Adam belongs) of **sin** and of righteousness and of
SD : 0 6 :013(566) [0967] **Sin** is everything that is contrary to the law of God, and
SD : 0 6 :022(567) [0969] still imperfect and impure because of the **sin** in our flesh.
SD : 0 6 :024(568) [0971] miseries, until the flesh of **sin** is put off entirely and man
SD : 0 7 :044(577) [0987] passion and death for our **sin**, in this sad, last hour of his
SD : 0 7 :060(580) [0993] eating and drinking **sin** grievously against the body and
SD : 0 8 :020(595) [1021] that has suffered for the **sin** of the world, but the Son of
SD : 0 8 :025(596) [1023] in his death he conquered **sin**, death, the devil, hell, and
SD : 0 8 :055(601) [1033] his feet, to cleanse from **sin**, and so forth are not created
SD : 0 8 :059(602) [1035] of Jesus his Son cleanses us from all **sin**" (I John 1:7).
SD : 1 0 :016(613) [1057] world for temptations to **sin**," and again, "Whoever
SD : 1 0 :016(613) [1059] ones who believe in me to **sin**, it were better for him to
SD : 1 0 :029(615) [1061] we hold it to be a culpable **sin** when in a period of
SD : 1 1 :010(618) [1067] harm if I live in all kinds of **sin** and vice without
SD : 1 1 :027(620) [1071] the preaching of repentance and forgiveness of **sin**.
SD : 1 1 :028(620) [1071] Christ has taken away the **sin** of the world (John 1:29); he
SD : 1 1 :028(620) [1071] propitiation for the whole world's" **sin** (I John 1:7; 2:2).
SD : 1 1 :033(622) [1073] up the warfare against **sin** as Paul teaches from the first to
SD : 1 1 :039(623) [1077] (Acts 7:51), remain in **sin** without repentance (Luke
SD : 1 1 :058(625) [1081] deserved punishment for the **sin** when God so severely
SD : 1 1 :060(626) [1083] our nature is corrupted by **sin** and is worthy and
SD : 1 1 :061(626) [1083] those who are punished and receive their "wages of **sin**."
SD : 1 1 :070(627) [1085] laden and burdened with **sin** to come to him and find
SD : 1 1 :071(627) [1085] they are to desist from **sin**, repent, believe his promise,
SD : 1 1 :081(629) [1089] the devil and man through **sin**, and in no way from God.
SD : 1 1 :081(629) [1089] God is not the cause of **sin**, nor is he the cause of the
SD : 1 1 :081(629) [1089] of man's damnation is **sin**, for the "wages of sin is death"
SD : 1 1 :081(629) [1089] is sin, for the "wages of **sin** is death" (Rom. 6:23).
SD : 1 1 :081(629) [1089] And as God does not will **sin** and has no pleasure in sin,
SD : 1 1 :081(629) [1089] sin and has no pleasure in **sin**, so he also does not will the
SD : 1 1 :083(630) [1091] that God punishes **sin** with sin, that is, because of their
SD : 1 1 :083(630) [1091] that God punishes sin with **sin**, that is, because of their
SD : 1 1 :085(630) [1091] that Pharaoh continued to **sin** and became the more
SD : 1 1 :085(630) [1091] for his preceding **sin** and his horrible tyranny with which
SD : 1 2 :011(634) [1099] entire teaching of original **sin** and all that pertains

Sins (752)

AG : 0 3 :003(030) [0045] sin but also for all other **sins** and to propitiate God's
AG : 0 6 :003(032) [0047] shall have forgiveness of **sins**, not through works but
AG : 1 1 :001(034) [0047] enumerate all trespasses and **sins**, for this is impossible.
AG : 2 0 :009(042) [0053] when we believe that our **sins** are forgiven for Christ's
AG : 2 0 :021(044) [0055] purpose of earning grace and making satisfaction for **sins**.
AG : 2 0 :032(045) [0057] the devil, who drives poor human beings into many **sins**.
AG : 2 0 :033(045) [0057] this, and instead fell into many great and open **sins**.
AG : 2 1 :004(047) [0059] "If anyone **sins**, we have an advocate with the Father,
AG : 2 4 :021(058) [0067] and had instituted the Mass as a sacrifice for other **sins**.
AG : 2 4 :025(059) [0067] only for original sin and not for other **sins** as well.
AG : 2 4 :034(060) [0067] a sacrifice to remove the **sins** of others, whether living or
AG : 2 5 :004(062) [0069] that through such faith we obtain forgiveness of **sins**.
AG : 2 5 :005(062) [0069] long enumerations of **sins**, with satisfactions, with
AG : 2 5 :007(062) [0069] be compelled to recount **sins** in detail, for this is
AG : 2 5 :008(062) [0069] is so deeply submerged in **sins** that it is unable to perceive
AG : 2 5 :009(063) [0069] to compel people to give a detailed account of their **sins**.
AG : 2 5 :011(063) [0071] prayer, telling him of your **sins** not with your tongue but
AG : 2 5 :011(063) [0071] does not require a detailed enumeration of **sins**.
AG : 2 7 :044(078) [0081] and earned forgiveness of **sins** by their vows and their
AG : 2 8 :005(081) [0085] to forgive and retain **sins**, and to administer and
AG : 2 8 :006(082) [0085] If you forgive the **sins** of any, they are forgiven; if you
AG : 2 8 :006(082) [0085] forgiven; if you retain the **sins** of any, they are retained"
AG : 2 8 :021(084) [0087] preach the Gospel, forgive **sins**, judge doctrine and
AG : 2 8 :035(086) [0089] to make satisfaction for **sins** and obtain grace, for the
AG : 2 8 :042(088) [0089] Why, then, do they multiply **sins** with such requirements?
AG : 2 8 :053(090) [0091] or making satisfaction for **sins**, nor in order to bind men's
AL : 0 3 :003(030) [0045] only for original guilt but also for all actual **sins** of men.
AL : 0 4 :002(030) [0045] into favor and that their **sins** are forgiven on account of
AL : 0 4 :002(030) [0045] of Christ, who by his death made satisfaction for our **sins**.
AL : 0 6 :001(032) [0045] God, for forgiveness of **sins** and justification are
AL : 0 6 :003(032) [0047] alone, and he shall receive forgiveness of **sins** by grace."
AL : 1 1 :001(034) [0047] an enumeration of all **sins** is not necessary, for this is not
AL : 1 2 :001(034) [0049] can receive forgiveness of **sins** whenever they are
AL : 1 2 :005(034) [0049] of absolution, believes that **sins** are forgiven for Christ's
AL : 1 2 :010(035) [0049] not teach that remission of **sins** comes through faith but
AL : 1 3 :003(036) [0049] faith, which believes that **sins** are forgiven, is required in
AL : 1 5 :003(037) [0049] and make satisfaction for **sins** are opposed to the Gospel
AL : 1 5 :004(037) [0049] and make satisfaction for **sins**, are useless and contrary to
AL : 2 0 :009(042) [0053] God or merit forgiveness of **sins** and grace but that we
AL : 2 0 :021(044) [0055] kind to merit grace and make satisfaction for **sins**.
AL : 2 0 :022(044) [0055] grace and forgiveness of **sins** are apprehended by faith in
AL : 2 0 :023(044) [0055] article of the forgiveness of **sins** — that is, that we have
AL : 2 0 :023(044) [0055] righteousness, and forgiveness of **sins** through Christ.
AL : 2 0 :025(044) [0057] article of the forgiveness of **sins**; hence they hate God as
AL : 2 0 :028(045) [0057] by faith that forgiveness of **sins** and grace are
AL : 2 0 :032(045) [0057] who impels men to various **sins**, impious opinions, and
AL : 2 1 :004(047) [0059] "If anyone **sins**, we have an advocate with the Father,"
AL : 2 4 :021(058) [0067] oblation should be made for daily **sins**, mortal and venial.
AL : 2 4 :022(058) [0067] takes away the **sins** of the living and the dead.
AL : 2 4 :025(058) [0067] not only for original guilt but also for others **sins**.
AL : 2 4 :029(059) [0067] if the Mass takes away the **sins** of the living and the dead
AL : 2 5 :004(062) [0069] faith truly obtains and receives the forgiveness of **sins**.
AL : 2 5 :007(062) [0069] that an enumeration of **sins** is not necessary and that
AL : 2 5 :007(062) [0069] enumeration of all **sins** because it is impossible to recount
AL : 2 5 :009(062) [0069] But if no **sins** were forgiven except those which are
AL : 2 5 :009(063) [0069] never find peace, for many **sins** can neither be perceived
AL : 2 5 :011(063) [0071] Therefore, confess your **sins** to God, the true judge, in
AL : 2 5 :011(063) [0071] Tell him of your **sins** not with your tongue but with the
AL : 2 6 :001(064) [0071] profitable to merit grace and make satisfactions for **sins**.
AL : 2 6 :004(064) [0071] faith which believes that **sins** are forgiven for Christ's
AL : 2 6 :021(067) [0073] or make satisfaction for **sins** by the observance of human
AL : 2 6 :033(069) [0075] to merit forgiveness of **sins** or satisfaction for sins by
AL : 2 6 :033(069) [0075] of sins or satisfaction for **sins** by means of such exercises.
AL : 2 6 :038(069) [0075] not to merit forgiveness of **sins** by that discipline but to
AL : 2 7 :011(072) [0077] merited forgiveness of **sins** and justification before God
AL : 2 7 :038(077) [0081] make satisfaction for **sins** and merit grace and
AL : 2 7 :044(078) [0081] and merited forgiveness of **sins** by their vows and
AL : 2 8 :005(081) [0085] Gospel, to remit and retain **sins**, and to administer the
AL : 2 8 :006(082) [0085] If you forgive the **sins** of any, they are forgiven; if you
AL : 2 8 :006(082) [0085] forgiven; if you retain the **sins** of any, they are retained."
AL : 2 8 :021(084) [0087] except to forgive **sins**, to reject doctrine which is contrary
AL : 2 8 :035(086) [0089] of making satisfaction for **sins** or meriting justification,
AL : 2 8 :053(090) [0091] we make satisfaction for **sins**, nor that consciences are
AL : 2 8 :056(090) [0091] would say that a woman **sins** by going out in public with
AP : 0 2 :047(106) [0119] opinions and errors and incites it to all kinds of **sins**.
AP : 0 4 :001(107) [0119] receive the forgiveness of **sins** because of their own
AP : 0 4 :001(107) [0121] receive the forgiveness of **sins** because of their merits, and
AP : 0 4 :001(107) [0121] receive the forgiveness of **sins** by faith and by faith in
AP : 0 4 :003(107) [0121] neither the forgiveness of **sins** nor faith nor grace nor
AP : 0 4 :005(108) [0121] promises forgiveness of **sins**, justification, and eternal life
AP : 0 4 :005(108) [0121] promises forgiveness of **sins**, justification, and eternal
AP : 0 4 :007(108) [0121] and by it they seek forgiveness of **sins** and justification.
AP : 0 4 :009(108) [0123] to merit the forgiveness of **sins** by doing what is within
AP : 0 4 :012(109) [0123] we merit the forgiveness of **sins** by these elicited acts of
AP : 0 4 :015(109) [0123] merit the forgiveness of **sins** rather than receiving it freely
AP : 0 4 :016(109) [0123] we merit forgiveness of **sins** and justification by the works
AP : 0 4 :018(109) [0125] receive the forgiveness of **sins** and reconciliation, but
AP : 0 4 :018(109) [0125] merit the forgiveness of **sins** and are accounted righteous
AP : 0 4 :020(110) [0125] how the forgiveness of **sins** takes place, or how the
AP : 0 4 :020(110) [0125] of the free forgiveness of **sins** and the righteousness of
AP : 0 4 :025(110) [0127] false that by our works we merit the forgiveness of **sins**.
AP : 0 4 :031(111) [0129] cannot free us from our **sins** or merit for us the
AP : 0 4 :031(111) [0129] us from our sins or merit for us the forgiveness of **sins**.

Continued ▶

A P : 0 4 :033(111) [0129] to God, then the flesh **sins** even when it performs outward
A P : 0 4 :036(112) [0131] merit the forgiveness of **sins** by an elicited act of love,
A P : 0 4 :036(112) [0131] God unless faith has first accepted the forgiveness of **sins**.
A P : 0 4 :038(112) [0131] not say that by the law men merit the forgiveness of **sins**.
A P : 0 4 :038(112) [0131] law and by their works they merit the forgiveness of **sins**.
A P : 0 4 :040(112) [0131] of the forgiveness of **sins** and justification was given
A P : 0 4 :040(112) [0131] make satisfaction for the **sins** of the world and has been
A P : 0 4 :041(113) [0133] but offers the forgiveness of **sins** and justification freely.
A P : 0 4 :041(113) [0133] that is, the forgiveness of **sins** is offered freely.
A P : 0 4 :042(113) [0133] If the forgiveness of **sins** depended upon our merits and if
A P : 0 4 :043(113) [0133] promise of forgiveness of **sins** and justification because of
A P : 0 4 :045(113) [0133] a man believes that his **sins** are forgiven because of Christ
A P : 0 4 :045(113) [0133] faith obtains the forgiveness of **sins** and justifies us.
A P : 0 4 :046(113) [0133] the forgiveness of **sins**, faith sets against God's wrath not
A P : 0 4 :048(114) [0135] God's offer promising forgiveness of **sins** and justification.
A P : 0 4 :048(114) [0135] the promised offer of forgiveness of **sins** and justification.
A P : 0 4 :051(114) [0135] to the article of the Creed on the forgiveness of **sins**.
A P : 0 4 :051(114) [0135] the purpose of the history, "the forgiveness of **sins**."
A P : 0 4 :051(114) [0135] own merits the forgiveness of **sins** is bestowed upon us.
A P : 0 4 :052(114) [0135] have to be offered for our **sins** if our merits make
A P : 0 4 :053(114) [0137] because there must be a certain propitiation for our **sins**.
A P : 0 4 :057(114) [0137] the free forgiveness of **sins**, the patriarchs knew the
A P : 0 4 :057(114) [0137] the Christ, that for his sake God intended to forgive **sins**.
A P : 0 4 :057(114) [0137] would be the price for our **sins**, they knew that our works
A P : 0 4 :057(114) [0137] and the forgiveness of **sins** by faith, just as the saints in
A P : 0 4 :058(115) [0137] the psalmist confesses his **sins**, but he does not lay claim
A P : 0 4 :058(115) [0137] the forgiveness of **sins** I am sustained by thy promise.
A P : 0 4 :062(115) [0139] and forgiveness of **sins** should be preached in his name.
A P : 0 4 :062(115) [0139] it offers forgiveness of **sins** and justification, which are
A P : 0 4 :062(115) [0139] promise that for his sake we have the forgiveness of **sins**.
A P : 0 4 :062(115) [0139] receives the forgiveness of **sins**, justifies and quickens us.
A P : 0 4 :070(116) [0141] For the law does not teach the free forgiveness of **sins**.
A P : 0 4 :072(117) [0141] one, that is, that it receives the forgiveness of **sins**.
A P : 0 4 :074(117) [0143] We Obtain the Forgiveness of **Sins** Only by Faith in
A P : 0 4 :075(117) [0143] that the forgiveness of **sins** is supremely necessary in
A P : 0 4 :076(117) [0143] First, forgiveness of **sins** is the same as justification
A P : 0 4 :077(117) [0143] obtain the forgiveness of **sins** only by faith in Christ, not
A P : 0 4 :079(117) [0143] if we know how the forgiveness of **sins** takes place.
A P : 0 4 :079(117) [0143] whether the forgiveness of **sins** and the infusion of grace
A P : 0 4 :079(117) [0143] In the forgiveness of **sins**, the terrors of sin and of eternal
A P : 0 4 :080(118) [0143] obtain the forgiveness of **sins** when we comfort our hearts
A P : 0 4 :081(118) [0143] receive the forgiveness of **sins** when we are comforted by
A P : 0 4 :081(118) [0145] for Christ's sake we receive the forgiveness of **sins**.
A P : 0 4 :082(118) [0145] Second, it is certain that **sins** are forgiven because of
A P : 0 4 :083(118) [0145] in him receives forgiveness of **sins** through his name."
A P : 0 4 :083(118) [0145] receive the forgiveness of **sins**, he says, through his name,
A P : 0 4 :084(119) [0145] Fourth, the forgiveness of **sins** is a thing promised for
A P : 0 4 :084(119) [0145] of the forgiveness of **sins** and justification is a gift, and
A P : 0 4 :085(119) [0147] receive the forgiveness of **sins** for Christ's sake only by
A P : 0 4 :086(119) [0147] receive the forgiveness of **sins** and the Holy Spirit by faith
A P : 0 4 :087(120) [0147] merited the forgiveness of **sins** and justification, there
A P : 0 4 :097(121) [0149] this man forgiveness of **sins** is proclaimed to you, and by
A P : 0 4 :102(121) [0151] of the forgiveness of **sins**, and of our gracious acceptance
A P : 0 4 :110(123) [0153] receives the forgiveness of **sins** on account of love, the
A P : 0 4 :110(123) [0153] of love, the forgiveness of **sins** will always be unsure, for
A P : 0 4 :110(123) [0153] sure that the forgiveness of **sins** has been granted to us.
A P : 0 4 :110(123) [0153] love for the forgiveness of **sins** and justification, they
A P : 0 4 :110(123) [0153] abolish the Gospel of the free forgiveness of **sins**.
A P : 0 4 :110(123) [0153] they believe that the forgiveness of **sins** is received freely.
A P : 0 4 :112(123) [0155] receive the forgiveness of **sins** by trust in this love or on
A P : 0 4 :112(123) [0155] receive the forgiveness of **sins** on account of the other
A P : 0 4 :112(123) [0155] For the forgiveness of **sins** is received by faith alone—and
A P : 0 4 :114(123) [0155] receives the forgiveness of **sins** and reconciles us to God,
A P : 0 4 :116(123) [0155] receives the forgiveness of **sins**, renders us acceptable to
A P : 0 4 :117(123) [0155] receive the forgiveness of **sins** for Christ's sake, and by
A P : 0 4 :119(124) [0155] doubt whether they have received the forgiveness of **sins**.
A P : 0 4 :119(124) [0155] they should doubt about receiving the forgiveness of **sins**?
A P : 0 4 :120(124) [0155] (that is, the promise that **sins** are forgiven freely for
A P : 0 4 :121(124) [0155] of the free forgiveness of **sins** and of the righteousness of
A P : 0 4 :132(125) [0159] gift of the forgiveness of **sins** and the Holy Spirit, to bring
A P : 0 4 :135(125) [0159] of the forgiveness of **sins**, we receive the Holy Spirit, so
A P : 0 4 :141(126) [0161] received the forgiveness of **sins**, we become sure that we
A P : 0 4 :141(126) [0161] because he gave his Son for us and forgave us our **sins**.
A P : 0 4 :142(126) [0161] God's wrath against our **sins** and looks for forgiveness of
A P : 0 4 :142(126) [0161] and looks for forgiveness of **sins** and deliverance from sin.
A P : 0 4 :144(127) [0161] the forgiveness of **sins** for a heart terrified and fleeing
A P : 0 4 :145(127) [0163] receive the forgiveness of **sins** by faith, nor that on
A P : 0 4 :147(127) [0163] receive the forgiveness of **sins** through love or on account
A P : 0 4 :149(127) [0163] somebody doubts that his **sins** are forgiven, he insults
A P : 0 4 :150(127) [0163] obtains the forgiveness of **sins** because he loves, he insults
A P : 0 4 :151(127) [0163] receive the forgiveness of **sins** by other virtues of the law
A P : 0 4 :151(127) [0163] receive the forgiveness of **sins** on account of love, though
A P : 0 4 :152(127) [0163] says in Luke 7:47, "Her **sins**, which are many, are
A P : 0 4 :152(127) [0163] of love the woman had merited the forgiveness of **sins**.
A P : 0 4 :154(128) [0163] that she should seek the forgiveness of **sins** from Christ.
A P : 0 4 :154(128) [0163] for the forgiveness of **sins** from him, she truly
A P : 0 4 :154(128) [0165] she was looking for the forgiveness of **sins** from Christ.
A P : 0 4 :154(128) [0165] or seek from him the forgiveness of **sins** and salvation!
A P : 0 4 :155(128) [0165] way he says here, "Her **sins**, which are many, are
A P : 0 4 :155(128) [0165] accepts the forgiveness of **sins**, though love, confession,
A P : 0 4 :155(128) [0165] earns the forgiveness of **sins** that reconciles us to God.
A P : 0 4 :157(128) [0165] For if the forgiveness of **sins** and reconciliation do not
A P : 0 4 :157(128) [0165] will have the forgiveness of **sins** unless he keeps the whole
A P : 0 4 :158(129) [0165] sure that we receive the forgiveness of **sins** by faith alone.
A P : 0 4 :159(129) [0167] receive the forgiveness of **sins** and reconciliation by faith
A P : 0 4 :168(130) [0169] that even the godly must pray for the forgiveness of **sins**.
A P : 0 4 :169(130) [0169] evil desires in the flesh are **sins**, about which Paul says
A P : 0 4 :182(132) [0173] receive the forgiveness of **sins** and reconciliation for
A P : 0 4 :186(132) [0173] free promise of the forgiveness of **sins** for Christ's sake.
A P : 0 4 :186(132) [0173] receive the forgiveness of **sins** and reconciliation, our
A P : 0 4 :187(133) [0173] If the forgiveness of **sins** were conditional upon our
A P : 0 4 :188(133) [0173] the free forgiveness of **sins** and the reconciliation that
A P : 0 4 :194(133) [0175] for the forgiveness of **sins**, grace, or justification (for we
A P : 0 4 :195(134) [0175] But the forgiveness of **sins** is the same and equal to all, as
A P : 0 4 :195(134) [0175] all who believe that their **sins** are forgiven for Christ's
A P : 0 4 :195(134) [0175] The forgiveness of **sins** and justification are received only
A P : 0 4 :202(134) [0175] to merit the forgiveness of **sins** and grace through this
A P : 0 4 :203(135) [0177] works the saints merited grace and the forgiveness of **sins**.
A P : 0 4 :203(135) [0177] grace and forgiveness of **sins**, appease the wrath of God,
A P : 0 4 :208(135) [0177] to merit grace, righteousness, and the forgiveness of **sins**.
A P : 0 4 :208(135) [0177] grace and forgiveness of **sins** by this deed, but because
A P : 0 4 :211(136) [0179] to merit the forgiveness of **sins**, grace, and righteousness.
A P : 0 4 :213(136) [0179] merit the forgiveness of **sins** and grace and that we are
A P : 0 4 :214(136) [0179] merit the forgiveness of **sins**, grace, and righteousness
A P : 0 4 :222(138) [0181] promised forgiveness of **sins** — Paul is saying none of
A P : 0 4 :238(140) [0187] statement (I Pet. 4:8), "Love covers a multitude of **sins**."
A P : 0 4 :242(141) [0187] speaks not of one's own **sins** but of other people's when it
A P : 0 4 :242(141) [0187] merits the forgiveness of **sins** in relation to God; that in
A P : 0 4 :244(142) [0189] we merit the forgiveness of **sins**; that good works are a
A P : 0 4 :246(142) [0189] good works we merit grace and the forgiveness of **sins**.
A P : 0 4 :246(142) [0189] and accepted and have obtained the forgiveness of **sins**.
A P : 0 4 :246(142) [0189] grace and forgiveness of **sins** by good works and that by
A P : 0 4 :253(143) [0193] merit the forgiveness of **sins**; that works regenerate our
A P : 0 4 :254(143) [0193] Dan. 4:27, "Redeem your **sins** by showing mercy."
A P : 0 4 :255(144) [0193] They do not add that **sins** are forgiven without faith or
A P : 0 4 :257(144) [0193] voice of God, clearly promising the forgiveness of **sins**.
A P : 0 4 :257(144) [0193] that for Christ's sake **sins** are forgiven and that by faith in
A P : 0 4 :257(144) [0193] that by faith in Christ we obtain the forgiveness of **sins**.
A P : 0 4 :258(144) [0193] the Lord: though your **sins** are like scarlet, they shall be
A P : 0 4 :258(144) [0193] merit the forgiveness of **sins** *ex opere operato*, but he
A P : 0 4 :258(144) [0193] he wants the forgiveness of **sins** to be received by faith,
A P : 0 4 :259(144) [0193] merits the forgiveness of **sins** *ex opere operato*, but he
A P : 0 4 :259(144) [0193] he wants the forgiveness of **sins** to be received by faith.
A P : 0 4 :259(145) [0193] he wishes the forgiveness of **sins** to be received by faith.
A P : 0 4 :260(145) [0193] is, that the forgiveness of **sins** is granted to us if we
A P : 0 4 :260(145) [0193] to us if we believe that our **sins** are forgiven for Christ's
A P : 0 4 :260(145) [0195] that by our works we purchase the forgiveness of **sins**.
A P : 0 4 :261(145) [0195] that is, redeem your **sins** by changing your heart and
A P : 0 4 :261(145) [0195] other part Daniel promises the king forgiveness of **sins**.
A P : 0 4 :261(145) [0195] of the forgiveness of **sins** is not the preaching of the law,
A P : 0 4 :262(145) [0195] that the forgiveness of **sins** in the Christ was promised
A P : 0 4 :262(145) [0195] he could not have promised the king forgiveness of **sins**.
A P : 0 4 :262(145) [0195] promise, "Redeem your **sins** by righteousness and your
A P : 0 4 :263(145) [0195] **Sins** are redeemed by penitence, that is, the obligation or
A P : 0 4 :264(146) [0195] less authority that the forgiveness of **sins** is uncertain.
A P : 0 4 :264(146) [0195] Gospel promises the forgiveness of **sins** with certainty.
A P : 0 4 :264(146) [0195] that the forgiveness of **sins** must surely be given by a
A P : 0 4 :264(146) [0195] that the forgiveness of **sins** is possible, that sins can be
A P : 0 4 :264(146) [0195] of sins is possible, that **sins** can be redeemed, that the
A P : 0 4 :265(146) [0197] of these works brings forgiveness of **sins** and justification.
A P : 0 4 :266(146) [0197] had said, "Redeem your **sins** by penitence," our
A P : 0 4 :267(146) [0197] faith, which believes that God freely forgives **sins**.
A P : 0 4 :267(147) [0197] say that by these works we merit the forgiveness of **sins**.
A P : 0 4 :268(147) [0197] first come forgiveness of **sins** and justification without
A P : 0 4 :269(147) [0197] of them a propitiation that merits the forgiveness of **sins**.
A P : 0 4 :272(148) [0199] promises the forgiveness of **sins**, it necessarily requires
A P : 0 4 :272(148) [0199] Only faith accepts the forgiveness of **sins**.
A P : 0 4 :272(148) [0199] of the forgiveness of **sins** is added, depending not on the
A P : 0 4 :273(148) [0199] in him receives forgiveness of **sins** through his name."
A P : 0 4 :273(148) [0199] I John 2:12, "Your **sins** are forgiven for his sake."
A P : 0 4 :274(148) [0199] we obtain forgiveness of **sins** by faith because of Christ
A P : 0 4 :274(148) [0199] such works we merit forgiveness of **sins** or justification.
A P : 0 4 :275(148) [0199] the promise of forgiveness of **sins** with good works.
A P : 0 4 :276(148) [0199] minds to believe more firmly that their **sins** are forgiven.
A P : 0 4 :278(149) [0199] accepts forgiveness of **sins** and overcomes death as it
A P : 0 4 :282(149) [0201] and the gloss says that it cleanses from venial **sins**.
A P : 0 4 :285(150) [0201] merit the forgiveness of **sins**, because a conscience that
A P : 0 4 :285(150) [0201] promised forgiveness of **sins** and righteousness of faith.
A P : 0 4 :286(150) [0201] by our works we merit grace and the forgiveness of **sins**.
A P : 0 4 :290(151) [0203] does not teach that justification is the forgiveness of **sins**.
A P : 0 4 :290(151) [0203] that the forgiveness of **sins** precedes our love, but it
A P : 0 4 :290(151) [0203] an act of love whereby we merit the forgiveness of **sins**.
A P : 0 4 :291(152) [0203] receive the forgiveness of **sins**, reconciliation, and victory
A P : 0 4 :292(152) [0203] accepts the forgiveness of **sins**, justifies, and regenerates.
A P : 0 4 :297(153) [0205] the promise of the forgiveness of **sins** and righteousness.
A P : 0 4 :303(154) [0205] and in the forgiveness of **sins**, a faith that truly and
A P : 0 4 :304(154) [0205] promise offers — reconciliation and forgiveness of **sins**.
A P : 0 4 :310(155) [0207] to receive forgiveness of **sins**, grace, and righteousness.
A P : 0 4 :311(155) [0207] love God unless we have received the forgiveness of **sins**.
A P : 0 4 :312(155) [0207] the present the forgiveness of **sins** that the promise offers.
A P : 0 4 :322(157) [0209] and taught that he **sins** daily, since he is commanded to
A P : 0 4 :322(157) [0209] daily, since he is commanded to pray daily for his **sins**."
A P : 0 4 :326(158) [0211] of God if he observes our **sins**, "If thou, O Lord, shouldst
A P : 0 4 :328(158) [0211] pray for the forgiveness of **sins**; therefore saints have sins,
A P : 0 4 :328(158) [0211] for the forgiveness of sins; therefore saints have **sins**, too.
A P : 0 4 :350(161) [0217] it shows our old or new **sins** or the uncleanness of our
A P : 0 4 :382(165) [0225] faith and believe that our **sins** are blotted out by Christ's
A P : 0 4 :392(167) [0225] us to seek forgiveness of **sins**, grace, and righteousness
A P : 0 4 :395(167) [0225] merited the forgiveness of **sins** by their works, and so they
A P : 0 7 :009(170) [0229] — the forgiveness of **sins**, answer to prayer, and the gift of
A P : 0 7 :021(172) [0233] doctrine that the forgiveness of **sins** is received by faith.
A P : 0 7 :021(172) [0233] merit the forgiveness of **sins** by their love for God before
A P : 0 7 :025(173) [0235] we obtain forgiveness of **sins** through faith in him and
A P : 1 1 :001(180) [0249] and that even though all **sins** cannot be enumerated, one
A P : 1 1 :002(180) [0249] that the forgiveness of **sins** is granted to us freely for
A P : 1 1 :006(181) [0251] to the enumeration of **sins** in confession we teach men in
A P : 1 1 :006(181) [0251] that the enumeration of **sins** is necessary to obtain their
A P : 1 1 :007(181) [0251] of the regulation that requires all **sins** to be confessed.
A P : 1 1 :007(181) [0251] added to it later, including the circumstances of the **sins**.
A P : 1 1 :008(181) [0251] that the enumeration of **sins** is not required by divine
A P : 1 1 :008(181) [0251] namely, that we make confession of all our **sins**.
A P : 1 1 :008(181) [0251] understand most of our **sins**, according to the statement
A P : 1 1 :009(182) [0251] obtains the forgiveness of **sins** there is not a syllable in
A P : 1 1 :009(182) [0251] They only recite lists of **sins**.
A P : 1 1 :009(182) [0253] The greater part deals with **sins** against human traditions,
A P : 1 1 :010(182) [0253] that an enumeration of **sins** was necessary by divine law

Continued ▶

Continued ▶

AP : 24 :092(267) [0417] sacrifice nor sacrament nor forgiveness of **sins** nor faith?
AP : 24 :097(268) [0417] merited the forgiveness of **sins** by sacrifices *ex opere*
AP : 27 :009(270) [0421] services merit the forgiveness of **sins** and justification?
AP : 27 :009(270) [0421] Are they satisfactions for **sins**?
AP : 27 :011(270) [0423] merits the forgiveness of **sins** before God or makes
AP : 27 :011(270) [0423] before God or makes satisfaction for **sins** before God.
AP : 27 :011(270) [0423] that the forgiveness of **sins** is given us freely for Christ's
AP : 27 :011(270) [0423] who seek the forgiveness of **sins** not by faith in Christ,
AP : 27 :013(271) [0423] said that the forgiveness of **sins** is received freely for
AP : 27 :013(271) [0423] receive the forgiveness of **sins** not because of our merits
AP : 27 :014(271) [0423] merit the forgiveness of **sins**, he refuses even more to give
AP : 27 :014(271) [0425] merit the forgiveness of **sins**, how much less do these silly
AP : 27 :014(271) [0425] merit the forgiveness of **sins**, opposed as they are to the
AP : 27 :015(271) [0425] not give the forgiveness of **sins** freely but on account of
AP : 27 :017(271) [0425] place, not by forgiving **sins** on account of our works but
AP : 27 :017(272) [0425] attain to the forgiveness of **sins** because of his own merits
AP : 27 :019(272) [0425] attain to the forgiveness of **sins** by faith for Christ's sake?
AP : 27 :020(272) [0425] attain to the forgiveness of **sins** because of our works, we
AP : 27 :020(272) [0425] we do not merit the forgiveness of **sins** by monastic works
AP : 27 :024(273) [0427] they merit forgiveness of **sins** and justification more than
AP : 27 :031(274) [0431] merit the forgiveness of **sins** but that we receive this freely
AP : 27 :032(274) [0431] have the forgiveness of **sins** except by God's indulgence;
AP : 27 :033(274) [0431] merit the forgiveness of **sins** or eternal life even by the
AP : 27 :033(275) [0431] credit for meriting the forgiveness of **sins** or eternal life.
AP : 27 :034(275) [0431] merits the forgiveness of **sins** or eternal life are simply
AP : 27 :034(275) [0431] the free forgiveness of **sins** and the promised mercy
AP : 27 :035(275) [0431] which the forgiveness of **sins** and eternal life are granted.
AP : 27 :040(276) [0433] because it merits the forgiveness of **sins** and eternal life.
AP : 27 :040(276) [0433] to merit the forgiveness of **sins** or eternal life, he is
AP : 27 :054(278) [0437] the free forgiveness of **sins** for Christ's sake, about the
AP : 27 :055(278) [0439] to merit the forgiveness of **sins** for them and for others.
AP : 27 :058(279) [0439] to merit the forgiveness of **sins** before God or to justify
AP : 27 :058(279) [0439] to merit forgiveness of **sins** and justification, with the
AP : 27 :058(279) [0439] to merit the forgiveness of **sins** but to be an outward
AP : 27 :061(279) [0441] do not merit the forgiveness of **sins** or justification.
AP : 27 :061(279) [0441] would merit forgiveness of **sins** by it, or that this work
AP : 27 :062(280) [0441] and that they merit forgiveness of **sins** and justification.
AP : 27 :065(280) [0441] to merit the forgiveness of **sins** or to secure eternal life for
AP : 27 :069(281) [0443] merit the forgiveness of **sins**; that because of them we are
AP : 27 :070(281) [0443] they had forgiveness of **sins** freely for Christ's sake, that
AP : 28 :007(282) [0445] we receive forgiveness of **sins** freely for Christ's sake by
AP : 28 :008(282) [0445] merited the forgiveness of **sins** or were acts of worship
AP : 28 :009(282) [0445] merit the forgiveness of **sins**; here they also say that
AP : 28 :009(282) [0445] Do they merit forgiveness of **sins**?
AP : 28 :011(283) [0447] to merit forgiveness of **sins** or to be acts of worship that
AP : 28 :021(284) [0449] that they merit forgiveness of **sins** and eternal life.
AP : 28 :023(284) [0451] of the forgiveness of **sins**, that by faith we freely obtain
AP : 28 :023(284) [0451] obtain the forgiveness of **sins** for Christ's sake, brings
S1 : PR :014(291) [0459] But our **sins** oppress us and keep God from being
S2 : 02 :001(293) [0463] delivers men from their **sins**, both here in this life and
S2 : 02 :007(294) [0465] and obtain and merit grace and the forgiveness of **sins**.
S2 : 02 :018(296) [0467] Masses, forgiveness of **sins**, and God's grace were sought
S3 : 02 :001(303) [0479] God first of all to restrain **sins** by threats and fear of
S3 : 03 :005(304) [0481] a preacher of repentance — but for the remission of **sins**.
S3 : 03 :005(304) [0481] and to expect and accept from him the forgiveness of **sins**.
S3 : 03 :006(304) [0481] and the forgiveness of **sins** should be preached in his
S3 : 03 :011(305) [0481] penance only for actual **sins**, such as wicked thoughts to
S3 : 03 :012(305) [0481] merited forgiveness and has paid for his **sins** before God.
S3 : 03 :013(305) [0483] until I make satisfaction for my **sins** and amend my life."
S3 : 03 :014(305) [0483] works to overcome and blot out their **sins** before God.
S3 : 03 :015(305) [0483] nobody could recall all his **sins** (especially those
S3 : 03 :019(306) [0483] give an account of all his **sins** — an impossibility and the
S3 : 03 :019(306) [0483] The **sins** which had been forgotten were pardoned only
S3 : 03 :019(306) [0485] make satisfaction for his **sins**, for such humiliation would
S3 : 03 :020(306) [0485] rest on his enumeration of **sins** and on his
S3 : 03 :021(306) [0485] was to do for one single sin, to say nothing of all his **sins**.
S3 : 03 :028(308) [0487] they were guilty of actual **sins** — that is, of sinful
S3 : 03 :032(308) [0487] need the forgiveness of **sins**, for neither of you knows
S3 : 03 :036(309) [0489] like repentance for actual **sins**, nor is it uncertain like
S3 : 03 :037(309) [0489] sinful embraces all **sins** in his confession without omitting
S3 : 03 :040(309) [0489] life it contends with the **sins** that remain in the flesh.
S3 : 03 :040(309) [0489] of the Holy Spirit which follows the forgiveness of **sins**.
S3 : 03 :040(309) [0489] cleanses and expels the **sins** that remain and enables man
S3 : 03 :042(309) [0491] Spirit or the forgiveness of **sins**, or once they have
S3 : 03 :042(310) [0491] not as long as you believe, for faith blots out all **sins**," etc.
S3 : 03 :042(310) [0491] They add that if anyone **sins** after he has received faith
S3 : 07 :001(311) [0493] Christ to bind and loose **sins**, not only the gross and
S3 : 07 :001(311) [0493] the gross and manifest **sins** but also those which are
S3 : 07 :002(312) [0493] to judge which, how great, and how many our **sins** are.
S3 : 08 :002(312) [0495] the enumeration of **sins** should be left free to everybody
S3 : 11 :001(314) [0499] abominable, and countless **sins**, in which they are still
S3 : 15 :001(316) [0501] effect forgiveness or **sins** or merit salvation is unchristian
TR : 00 :023(324) [0511] it is written, "If you forgive the **sins**," etc. (John 20:23).
TR : 00 :031(325) [0513] proclaim the forgiveness of **sins**, administer the
TR : 00 :044(328) [0517] adherents, who teach that **sins** are forgiven on account of
TR : 00 :044(328) [0517] Nowhere do they teach that **sins** are forgiven freely for
TR : 00 :044(328) [0517] and that by this faith we obtain the remission of **sins**.
TR : 00 :045(328) [0517] the enumeration of **sins** which has produced many errors
TR : 00 :048(328) [0519] righteousness before God and merit forgiveness of **sins**.
TR : 00 :049(328) [0519] To these errors, then, two great **sins** must be added.
TR : 00 :060(330) [0521] preach the Gospel, remit **sins**, administer the sacraments,
SC : PR :020(340) [0537] God will inflict awful punishments on them for these **sins**.
SC : 02 :004(345) [0545] me and freed me from all **sins**, from death, and from the
SC : 02 :005(345) [0545] *of saints, the forgiveness of* ***sins****, the resurrection of the*
SC : 02 :006(345) [0545] abundantly forgives all my **sins**, and the sins of all
SC : 02 :006(345) [0545] all my sins, and the **sins** of all believers, and on the last
SC : 03 :016(347) [0549] may not look upon our **sins**, and on their account deny
SC : 03 :018(348) [0549] other great and shameful **sins**, but that, although we may
SC : 04 :006(348) [0551] It effects forgiveness of **sins**, delivers from death and the
SC : 04 :012(349) [0551] in us, together with all **sins** and evil lusts, should be
SC : 05 :016(349) [0553] One is that we confess our **sins**.
SC : 05 :016(350) [0553] firmly believing that our **sins** are thereby forgiven before
SC : 05 :017(350) [0553] What **sins** should we confess?
SC : 05 :018(350) [0553] are guilty of all manner of **sins**, even those of which we
SC : 05 :018(350) [0553] should confess only those **sins** of which we have
SC : 05 :019(350) [0553] What are such **sins**?
SC : 05 :021(350) [0553] and declare that my **sins** are forgiven for God's sake."
SC : 05 :022(350) [0553] sinner, confess before God that I am guilty of all **sins**.
SC : 05 :024(350) [0555] by such or by greater **sins**, he should not worry, nor
SC : 05 :024(350) [0555] for and invent other **sins**, for this would turn confession
SC : 05 :024(350) [0555] simply mention one or two **sins** of which he is aware.
SC : 05 :028(351) [0555] Christ, I forgive you your **sins** in the name of the Father
SC : 06 :004(351) [0557] which is poured out for many for the forgiveness of **sins**.
SC : 06 :006(352) [0557] words the forgiveness of **sins**, life, and salvation are given
SC : 06 :006(352) [0557] there is forgiveness of **sins**, there are also life and
SC : 06 :008(352) [0557] but the words "for you" and "for the forgiveness of **sins**."
SC : 06 :008(352) [0557] has what they say and declare: the forgiveness of **sins**.
SC : 06 :010(352) [0557] these words: "for you" and "for the forgiveness of **sins**."
LC : SP :013(363) [0577] of saints, the forgiveness of **sins**, the resurrection of the
LC : SP :023(364) [0579] my blood, which is shed for you for the forgiveness of **sins**
LC : 01 :099(378) [0609] classed among the mortal **sins** and was called *acidia* —
LC : 01 :249(398) [0651] may not themselves be charged with other men's **sins**.
LC : 01 :263(400) [0655] It forbids all **sins** of the tongue by which we may injure
LC : 01 :266(401) [0657] and hear that my neighbor **sins**, but to make him the talk
LC : 01 :276(402) [0659] says, "If your brother **sins** against you, go and tell him his
LC : 01 :284(403) [0661] All this refers to secret **sins**.
LC : 01 :285(403) [0663] to cover his neighbor's **sins** and infirmities, to overlook
LC : 02 :034(415) [0687] *of saints, the forgiveness of* ***sins****, the resurrection of the*
LC : 02 :037(415) [0687] church, the forgiveness of **sins**, the resurrection of the
LC : 02 :041(416) [0689] church, the forgiveness of **sins**, the resurrection of the
LC : 02 :054(417) [0693] we have the forgiveness of **sins**, which is granted through
LC : 02 :055(418) [0693] obtain full forgiveness of **sins** through the Word and
LC : 02 :059(418) [0695] means, the Christian church and the forgiveness of **sins**.
LC : 02 :062(419) [0695] faith through the same Word and the forgiveness of **sins**.
LC : 03 :092(432) [0723] to God not to regard our **sins** and punish us as we daily
LC : 03 :092(433) [0725] only come from the knowledge that our **sins** are forgiven.
LC : 03 :104(434) [0727] atheism, blasphemy, and countless other abominable **sins**.
LC : 04 :044(442) [0743] comfort from it when our **sins** or conscience oppress us,
LC : 04 :086(446) [0753] obtained forgiveness of **sins** in Baptism, so forgiveness
LC : 05 :003(447) [0753] *which is poured out for you for the forgiveness of* ***sins****.*
LC : 05 :021(449) [0757] given and poured out *for you* for the forgiveness of **sins**."
LC : 05 :022(449) [0757] through and in which we obtain the forgiveness of **sins**.
LC : 05 :022(449) [0757] has provided for me against my **sins**, death, and all evils.
LC : 05 :028(449) [0759] can bread and wine forgive **sins** or strengthen faith?"
LC : 05 :031(450) [0759] that we cannot have forgiveness of **sins** in the sacrament.
LC : 05 :031(450) [0759] and forgiveness of **sins** was acquired on the cross, yet it
LC : 05 :032(450) [0759] church, the forgiveness of **sins**," are embodied in this
LC : 05 :034(450) [0761] promises forgiveness of **sins**, it cannot be received except
LC : 05 :058(453) [0767] receive the forgiveness of **sins** since they do not desire it
LC : 05 :064(454) [0769] my blood, poured out *for you* for the forgiveness of **sins**."
LC : 05 :070(454) [0769] lips the forgiveness of **sins**, which contains and conveys
LC : 05 :078(455) [0771] the less you feel your **sins** and infirmities, the more reason
LC : 05 :079(455) [0771] do not think that there will be any lack of **sins** and needs.
LC : 06 :004(457) [0000] released from the torture of enumerating all **sins** in detail.
LC : 06 :014(458) [0000] and commanded us to absolve one another from **sins**.
LC : 06 :014(458) [0000] a man God looses and absolves him from his **sins**.
LC : 06 :015(459) [0000] when he absolves me of my **sins** through a word placed in
LC : 06 :032(460) [0000] Christians, free from their **sins**, and happy in their
EP : 01 :020(468) [0783] in human nature, and the other so-called actual **sins**.
EP : 01 :021(468) [0785] source of all other, actual **sins**, such as evil thoughts,
EP : 02 :008(471) [0789] murder, theft, and similar **sins** under compulsion.
EP : 02 :009(471) [0789] law, and thus merit forgiveness of **sins** and eternal life.
EP : 03 :002(473) [0793] indwelling Godhead, the **sins** of all men are esteemed like
EP : 03 :003(473) [0793] for us in the forgiveness of **sins** and eternal life, as it is
EP : 03 :004(473) [0793] that God forgives us our **sins** purely by his grace, without
EP : 03 :006(473) [0793] we have forgiveness of **sins**, are regarded as holy and
EP : 03 :015(475) [0795] obtain the forgiveness of **sins**, but mean to be made
EP : 03 :016(475) [0795] us), and that by such indwelling our **sins** are covered up.
EP : 04 :007(476) [0799] are forgiven, and whose **sins** are covered'" (Rom. 4:6-8).
EP : 04 :019(477) [0801] they fall into adultery and other **sins** and persist in them.
EP : 05 :001(478) [0801] the forgiveness of **sins**, or is it also a preaching of
EP : 05 :005(478) [0803] won for him forgiveness of **sins**, the "righteousness that
EP : 05 :006(478) [0803] both of repentance and of forgiveness of **sins**.
EP : 07 :023(484) [0815] of the Mass for the **sins** of the living and the dead.
EP : 08 :026(490) [0823] Son of God died for the **sins** of the world or that the Son
EP : 11 :011(496) [0835] to acknowledge their **sins**, to believe in Christ, and to
SD : 01 :001(508) [0859] of which, as the root and source, all other **sins** proceed.
SD : 01 :002(509) [0859] inheres in his nature, all actual **sins** flow out of his heart.
SD : 01 :030(513) [0867] man himself who **sins** because of his inborn original sin
SD : 01 :045(516) [0873] him and that Christ has saved his people from their **sins**.
SD : 02 :034(528) [0895] Holy Spirit which follows upon the forgiveness of **sins**.
SD : 02 :050(531) [0901] and knowledge of their **sins** and true faith in the Son of
SD : 02 :051(531) [0901] and the remission of **sins**, "Listen to him" (Matt. 17:5).
SD : 02 :054(531) [0903] man learns to know his **sins** and the wrath of God and
SD : 02 :054(531) [0903] the gracious forgiveness of **sins** in Christ there is kindled
SD : 02 :054(531) [0903] accepts the forgiveness of **sins** for Christ's sake and
SD : 02 :057(532) [0903] and perishes in his **sins**, he can neither comfort himself
SD : 02 :074(535) [0909] and to avoid manifest **sins** and vices; or that the will of
SD : 02 :077(536) [0911] grace, the forgiveness of **sins**, and eternal life, then the
SD : 03 :002(539) [0917] with this righteousness the **sins** of all men are like a drop
SD : 03 :004(540) [0917] redeemed us from our **sins**, justified and saved us.
SD : 03 :004(540) [0917] of faith is forgiveness of **sins**, reconciliation with God,
SD : 03 :009(540) [0919] utterly free from all his **sins**, and from the verdict of well
SD : 03 :011(541) [0919] we have forgiveness of **sins** by grace, are accounted
SD : 03 :015(541) [0919] God forgives us our **sins**, accounts us holy and righteous,
SD : 03 :016(541) [0921] with God, forgiveness of **sins**, the grace of God,
SD : 03 :017(542) [0921] righteous and free from **sins** and from the eternal
SD : 03 :017(542) [0921] punishment of these **sins** on account of the righteousness
SD : 03 :017(542) [0921] (Rom. 8:33), that is, absolves and acquits from **sins**.
SD : 03 :019(542) [0921] both the forgiveness of **sins** solely for Christ's sake and
SD : 03 :019(542) [0921] sense of the forgiveness of **sins** and our adoption as God's
SD : 03 :022(543) [0923] obedience covers all our **sins** which throughout this life
SD : 03 :023(543) [0923] of our works, so that our **sins** are forgiven and covered up
SD : 03 :025(543) [0923] obtain the forgiveness of **sins**, reconciliation with God,
SD : 03 :030(544) [0925] or the forgiveness of **sins**, which is bestowed upon us by
SD : 03 :031(544) [0925] and the forgiveness of **sins** offered to us in the promise of

Continued ▶

SD : 0 3 :039(546) [0929] solely in the forgiveness of **sins** by sheer grace, entirely
SD : 0 3 :043(547) [0931] who have obtained forgiveness of **sins** through Christ.
SD : 0 3 :048(548) [0933] the gracious forgiveness of **sins** and, as a second element,
SD : 0 3 :054(549) [0935] precisely the forgiveness of **sins** and the gracious
SD : 0 3 :056(549) [0935] the eternal and almighty God for the **sins** of all the world.
SD : 0 3 :062(550) [0937] not mean "to absolve from **sins**" and "to receive
SD : 0 3 :062(550) [0937] "to receive forgiveness of **sins**," but to be made really and
SD : 0 3 :063(550) [0937] by such indwelling our **sins** are covered up in the sight of
SD : 0 4 :008(552) [0941] (that is, spattered with **sins** in the sight of God), and God
SD : 0 4 :015(553) [0943] he were to persist in **sins** against conscience or embark
SD : 0 4 :015(553) [0943] deliberately on such **sins** again, which is impious and
SD : 0 5 :002(558) [0951] of God, which reproves all **sins**, including unbelief,
SD : 0 5 :004(559) [0953] namely, repentance and forgiveness of **sins** (Mark 1:4).
SD : 0 5 :005(559) [0953] of both repentance and the forgiveness of **sins**.
SD : 0 5 :005(559) [0953] promises of the forgiveness of **sins** but also the divine law.
SD : 0 5 :008(559) [0953] and forgiveness of **sins** (Luke 24:46) are distinguished
SD : 0 5 :008(559) [0953] truly to recognize one's **sins**, to feel heartily sorry for
SD : 0 5 :012(560) [0955] as yet neither know their **sins** nor are terrified by the
SD : 0 5 :020(561) [0959] obtain the forgiveness of **sins** from God, since man has
SD : 0 5 :020(561) [0959] and paid for all our **sins**, that through him alone we
SD : 0 5 :020(561) [0959] God, obtain forgiveness of **sins** through faith, are freed
SD : 0 5 :021(562) [0959] God wills not to punish **sins** but to forgive them for
SD : 0 5 :025(563) [0961] God forgives them all their **sins** through Christ, accepts
SD : 0 5 :027(563) [0961] both of repentance and of forgiveness of **sins**.
SD : 0 5 :027(563) [0961] promise of forgiveness of **sins** and justification through
SD : 0 6 :006(564) [0965] would be totally free from **sins**, they would require no
SD : 0 6 :007(565) [0965] For although their **sins** are covered up through the
SD : 0 7 :044(577) [0987] covenant which is shed for you for the remission of **sins**."
SD : 0 7 :049(578) [0989] for us on the tree of the cross for the forgiveness of **sins**.
SD : 0 7 :053(579) [0991] and new covenant, namely, the forgiveness of **sins**."
SD : 0 7 :060(580) [0993] manner" (I Cor. 11:27) **sins** not only against the bread and
SD : 0 7 :062(581) [0995] of God, forgiveness of **sins**, righteousness, and everlasting
SD : 0 7 :063(581) [0995] and assurance that their **sins** are truly forgiven, that
SD : 0 7 :068(582) [0997] and sorrow for their **sins**, without true faith, and without
SD : 0 7 :069(582) [0997] of their many and great **sins**, who consider themselves
SD : 0 7 :081(584) [1001] Christ, the forgiveness of **sins**, and all the benefits which
SD : 0 8 :059(602) [1035] Christ but also his blood actually cleanses us from all **sins**
SD : 1 1 :028(620) [1071] and forgiveness of **sins** in his name among all nations."
SD : 1 1 :033(621) [1073] Gospel so that you learn to know your **sins** and his grace.
SD : 1 1 :083(630) [1091] and deliberate **sins** God punishes with obduracy and
SD : 1 1 :089(631) [1093] to a knowledge of their **sins**, and to faith in Christ and

Sinful (23), Sinfully (1), Sinless (1)
AG : 2 7 :054(079) [0083] conclude that it is not **sinful** to take revenge outside of
AP : 0 4 :179(131) [0171] a sacrifice for us, the **sinless** Christ took away the right of
AP : 1 2 :123(200) [0289] wicked sophists who so **sinfully** twist the Word of God to
AP : 1 2 :153(206) [0299] purpose: to destroy this **sinful** flesh so that we may rise
AP : 2 3 :007(240) [0365] We are not talking about **sinful** lust but about so-called
AP : 2 3 :013(241) [0367] we are not talking about **sinful** lust but about the desire
AP : 2 3 :026(243) [0371] marriage were impure and **sinful** or as though celibacy
S3 : 0 3 :028(308) [0487] of actual sins — that is, of **sinful** thoughts, words, and
S3 : 0 3 :036(309) [0489] together and says, "We are wholly and altogether **sinful**."
S3 : 0 3 :037(309) [0489] that he is altogether **sinful** embraces all sins in his
S3 : 0 3 :038(309) [0489] not of the dubious, **sinful** works which we do but of the
S3 : 1 3 :002(315) [0499] Whatever is still **sinful** or imperfect in these works will
LC : 0 1 :293(404) [0665] to teach them that it is **sinful** and forbidden to covet our
EP : 0 1 :021(468) [0785] innate in us through our **sinful** seed and the source of all
EP : 0 5 :003(478) [0801] everything that is **sinful** and contrary to God's will.
SD : 0 1 :006(509) [0861] nevertheless man's nature and person would still be **sinful**.
SD : 0 1 :007(510) [0861] and birth out of **sinful** seed from our father and mother.
SD : 0 1 :018(511) [0865] 2. Again, that the **sinful** wicked desires are not sin but
SD : 0 1 :028(513) [0867] seed from which man is formed is **sinful** and corrupted.
SD : 0 1 :032(513) [0869] God but because we are **sinful** and evil; not because and
SD : 0 1 :039(515) [0871] corrupted, perverted, and **sinful** dough into hell-fire, but
SD : 0 1 :052(517) [0875] through sin man is corrupted, poisoned, and **sinful**.
SD : 0 1 :052(517) [0875] your entire essence is sin, that is **sinful** and unclean."
SD : 0 4 :008(552) [0941] from true faith, they are **sinful** (that is, spattered with sins
SD : 1 0 :015(613) [1057] omission were wrong and **sinful**, the door has been

Sinned (11), Sinning (4)
AG : 1 2 :009(035) [0049] denied absolution to such as had **sinned** after Baptism.
AP : 0 4 :033(111) [0129] God's law, it is certainly **sinning** even when it produces
AP : 0 7 :029(173) [0237] who believed that men **sinned** if they received the
AP : 1 2 :029(185) [0259] God's wrath against sin and is sorry that it has **sinned**.
AP : 1 2 :032(186) [0259] sorry that it has **sinned**; at the same time it flees God's
AP : 1 2 :048(188) [0265] David (II Sam. 12:13), "I have **sinned** against the Lord."
AP : 1 2 :056(189) [0267] he says (II Sam. 12:13), "I have **sinned** against the Lord."
AP : 1 2 :108(198) [0283] "Against thee only have I **sinned**, so that thou art justified
AP : 1 2 :159(207) [0301] disciples asked who had **sinned** in the case of the blind
AP : 2 0 :013(228) [0341] call, that is, lest they fall from their call by **sinning** again.
AP : 2 3 :016(241) [0369] Ever since man **sinned**, natural desire and the lust that
AP : 2 7 :021(272) [0427] can use them without **sinning**, as did Bernard, Francis,
S2 : 0 1 :003(292) [0461] Moreover, "all have **sinned**," and "they are justified by his
S3 : 0 3 :018(306) [0483] but he would rather have **sinned** if he had been free to do
SD : 0 1 :051(517) [0875] writes that sin and **sinning** are man's disposition and

Sinner (18), Sinners (36)
AG : 0 8 :001(033) [0047] and even open **sinners** remain among the godly, the
AP : 0 4 :103(121) [0151] since it has made all men **sinners**, but when the Lord
AP : 0 4 :173(131) [0171] we confess that we are **sinners**; and our righteousness
AP : 0 7 :011(170) [0229] says, "Therefore the **sinner** who has been defiled by any
AP : 1 2 :057(189) [0267] The woman who was a **sinner** came to Christ in tears,
AP : 1 2 :108(198) [0283] is "I confess that I am a **sinner** worthy of eternal wrath,
AP : 1 2 :112(198) [0285] the lapsed or notorious **sinners** were not accepted without
AP : 1 2 :113(199) [0285] lapsed or the notorious **sinners** unless they had given
AP : 2 4 :024(253) [0391] the exclusion of the **sinner** from the commonwealth.
S3 : 0 1 :001(302) [0477] all men were made **sinners** and became subject to death
S3 : 0 3 :002(304) [0479] with one blow destroys both open **sinners** and false saints.
S3 : 0 3 :003(304) [0481] Whether you are manifest **sinners** or saints, you must all
S3 : 0 3 :005(304) [0481] them that they were **sinners** in order that they might know
S3 : 0 3 :015(305) [0483] etc., but meanwhile the **sinner** was commended to the
S3 : 0 3 :018(306) [0483] A poor **sinner** who reflected on his lust or revenge in this
S3 : 0 3 :029(308) [0487] sell their superfluous righteousness to other poor **sinners**?
S3 : 0 9 :000(314) [0497] manifest and impenitent **sinners** from the sacrament and
SC : 0 5 :022(350) [0553] "I, a poor **sinner**, confess before God that I am guilty of
LC : 0 3 :010(421) [0699] prayers because we are **sinners** and have merited nothing
LC : 0 3 :011(421) [0701] even though we are **sinners**; he wishes rather to draw us to
LC : 0 3 :017(422) [0703] person, whether we be **sinners** or saints, worthy or
LC : 0 3 :121(436) [0731] I am only a poor **sinner**," etc.
LC : 0 5 :074(455) [0771] neither feel their infirmities nor admit to being **sinners**.
LC : 0 5 :084(456) [0773] as low as any other poor **sinner** and are much in need of
LC : 0 6 :009(458) [0000] to acknowledge that we are **sinners** and to pray for grace.
EP : 0 3 :001(472) [0791] Confession that we poor **sinners** are justified before God
EP : 0 3 :003(473) [0793] many were made **sinners**, so by *one man's obedience*
EP : 0 5 :008(479) [0803] from heaven" over all **sinners** and men learn how fierce it
EP : 1 1 :008(495) [0833] 7. This Christ calls all **sinners** to himself and promises
EP : 1 2 :006(498) [0839] children are not **sinners** but are righteous and innocent,
EP : 1 2 :009(498) [0839] is not truly Christian if **sinners** are still found in it.
SD : 0 3 :001(539) [0917] through faith reckons to poor **sinners** as righteousness.
SD : 0 3 :009(540) [0919] above, that a poor **sinner** is justified before God (that is,
SD : 0 3 :022(543) [0923] nature, they are still **sinners** and remain sinners until they
SD : 0 3 :022(543) [0923] they are still sinners and remain **sinners** until they die.
SD : 0 3 :036(545) [0927] the justification of poor **sinners** before God they should
SD : 0 3 :054(549) [0935] acceptance of poor **sinners** on account of the obedience
SD : 0 3 :057(549) [0935] many will be made **sinners**, so by one man's obedience
SD : 0 3 :058(550) [0937] in the stead of us poor **sinners**, and thus covered up our
SD : 0 5 :007(559) [0953] there will be joy in heaven over one **sinner** who repents."
SD : 0 5 :009(559) [0955] offers to all penitent **sinners** who have been terrified by
SD : 0 5 :010(560) [0955] from heaven over all **sinners** and shows how great this
SD : 0 5 :010(560) [0955] This directs the **sinner** to the law, and there he really
SD : 0 5 :022(562) [0959] every penitent **sinner** must believe — that is, he must put
SD : 0 5 :023(562) [0959] God's laws, became a **sinner**, corrupted himself and all
SD : 0 8 :087(608) [1047] deity, which to us poor **sinners** is like a consuming fire on
SD : 1 1 :077(629) [1089] Every poor **sinner** must therefore attend on it, hear it with
SD : 1 1 :081(629) [1089] not will the death of a **sinner** and has no pleasure in his
SD : 1 1 :089(631) [1093] not exclude any repentant **sinner** but invites and calls all
SD : 1 1 :089(631) [1093] and heavy-laden **sinners** to repentance, to a knowledge of
SD : 1 1 :091(631) [1093] or when impenitent **sinners** are strengthened in their
SD : 1 1 :096(632) [1095] but will lead the poor **sinner** to true and sincere
SD : 1 2 :011(634) [1099] children are not **sinners** before God but righteous and
SD : 1 2 :014(634) [1099] congregation in the midst of which **sinners** are still found.

Sincere (6), Sincerely (5), Sincerity (1)
AG : 2 1 :003(047) [0059] form of divine service is **sincerely** to seek and call upon
AG : 2 7 :049(079) [0083] hearts, and yet have **sincere** confidence, faith, and trust
AP : 0 4 :245(142) [0189] a pure heart and a good conscience and **sincere** faith."
AP : 1 0 :003(179) [0247] joined to Christ spiritually by true faith and **sincere** love.
LC : 0 1 :157(387) [0627] the Word and will of God and **sincerely** accept it.
LC : 0 3 :022(423) [0703] Thus we see how **sincerely** he is concerned over our
LC : 0 3 :054(427) [0713] that the Gospel may be **sincerely** preached throughout the
SD : PR :012(506) [0855] nor can anyone who **sincerely** adheres to the Augsburg
SD : 1 1 :018(619) [1069] of eternal life all who in **sincere** repentance and true faith
SD : 1 1 :069(627) [1085] (Rom. 10:17) when it is preached in **sincerity** and purity.
SD : 1 1 :095(632) [1095] We have a **sincere** delight in and deep love for true
SD : 1 1 :096(632) [1095] poor sinner to true and **sincere** repentance, raise him up

Sinews (1)
SD : 0 1 :035(514) [0869] and flesh, and knit me together with bones and **sinews**.

Sing (3), Singing (5), Sings (2), Sang (1), Sung (3)
AG : 0 1 :002(056) [0065] places German hymns are **sung** in addition to the Latin
AL : 2 0 :040(046) [0057] and the church **sings**, "Where Thou art not, man
AL : 2 4 :002(056) [0065] here and there among the parts **sung** in Latin.
AL : 2 8 :010(082) [0085] as little as the art of **singing** interferes with civil
AP : 1 5 :040(220) [0325] order to learn; the people **sing**, too, in order to learn or to
AP : 2 4 :004(250) [0385] almost everywhere the people **sang** in their own language.
SC : 0 7 :003(352) [0557] After **singing** a hymn (possibly a hymn on the Ten
LC : PR :010(360) [0571] and words and to speak, **sing**, and meditate on them.
LC : 0 1 :090(377) [0607] daily in the churches, **singing** and ringing bells, without
LC : 0 1 :314(407) [0671] is burning of incense, **singing** and ringing of bells, lighting
LC : 0 3 :007(421) [0699] while it may be called **singing** or reading exercise, it is not
EP : 0 1 :008(467) [0781] It is as the church **sings**, "Through Adam's fall man's
SD : 0 1 :023(512) [0865] way the hymn which we **sing** in our churches describes it,
SD : 0 7 :079(584) [1001] are to be spoken or **sung** distinctly and clearly before the

Single (47)
AG : PR :004(025) [0039] embrace and adhere to a **single**, true religion and live
AG : 2 2 :008(050) [0061] Not a **single** canon can be found which requires the
AL : 2 4 :027(059) [0067] for all," and again, "By a **single** offering he has perfected
AP : 0 4 :280(149) [0201] to judge or reply to a **single** passage without taking the
AP : 0 4 :283(150) [0201] the universal particle to a **single** part: "All things will be
AP : 1 3 :023(214) [0313] No one can produce a **single** word from the Fathers that
AP : 1 5 :027(219) [0323] that do not contain a **single** syllable about Christ or faith
AP : 2 4 :007(250) [0385] should be content with a **single** common daily Mass,
AP : 2 4 :009(251) [0387] This **single** answer refutes all our opponents' objections,
S3 : 0 3 :021(306) [0485] much he was to do for one **single** sin, to say nothing of
S3 : 0 3 :022(306) [0485] years of penance were required for a **single** mortal sin.
S3 : 0 3 :024(307) [0485] first for seven years in a **single** case, then for a hundred,
S3 : 0 3 :030(308) [0487] With a **single** thunderbolt he strikes and destroys both.
S3 : 0 3 :037(309) [0489] his confession without omitting or forgetting a **single** one.
SC : PR :005(338) [0533] Ten Commandments, or a **single** part of the Word of
SC : PR :008(339) [0535] way that we do not alter a **single** syllable or recite the
SC : PR :015(340) [0535] them without changing a **single** syllable, as stated above
LC : PR :018(361) [0573] do not understand a **single** Psalm, much less the entire
LC : 0 1 :056(372) [0597] So from a **single** lie a double one results — indeed,
LC : 0 1 :116(381) [0615] they can produce a **single** work that is greater and nobler
LC : 0 1 :118(381) [0615] could bring before God a **single** work done in accordance
LC : 0 1 :150(385) [0623] a man is father not of a **single** family, but of as many
LC : 0 1 :166(388) [0629] life or raise from the earth a **single** grain of wheat for us.
LC : 0 1 :316(408) [0671] "Of course, I haven't a **single** groschen to pay, but I
LC : 0 2 :048(416) [0691] a church except for the **single** reason that the group of
LC : 0 3 :069(429) [0717] armed with this **single** petition, shall be our bulwark,
LC : 0 3 :116(435) [0731] us, we would not be safe from him for a **single** hour.
LC : 0 4 :034(440) [0741] So this **single** expression, "He who believes," is so potent
LC : 0 5 :047(452) [0765] of the first full moon, without variation of a **single** day.
LC : 0 6 :013(458) [0000] which takes place privately before a **single** brother.

Continued ▶

SINGLENESS 491 SLIGHT

E P : R N :002(465) [0777] Every **single** one of them should be subordinated to the
E P : 0 5 :006(478) [0803] "Gospel" is not used in a **single** sense in Holy Scripture,
E P : 0 7 :014(483) [0811] place, and not only the **single** mode which the
E P : 0 7 :034(485) [0815] present at more than one place at a **single** given time.
E P : 0 8 :005(487) [0819] the Son of man, but a **single** individual is both the Son of
S D : P R :010(506) [0855] was only to have a **single**, universally accepted, certain,
S D : 0 3 :006(540) [0917] declared: "Where this **single** article remains pure,
S D : 0 4 :015(553) [0943] simultaneously be in a **single** heart both a right faith and
S D : 0 5 :007(559) [0953] is not used in a **single** sense in Holy Scripture.
S D : 0 8 :007(592) [1017] that henceforth in this **single** undivided person there are
S D : 0 8 :011(593) [1019] way that they constitute a **single** person in which there are
S D : 0 8 :011(593) [1019] different persons, but one **single** person, in spite of the
S D : 0 8 :034(597) [1027] in such a way that God and man are a **single** person!
S D : 0 8 :066(604) [1039] remains in Christ only a **single** divine omnipotence,
S D : 0 8 :082(607) [1045] since he is not two separate persons but a **single** person.
S D : 0 8 :082(607) [1045] this person is, it is the **single**, indivisible person, and if
S D : 0 8 :084(607) [1045] were present only at one **single** place as a divine and

Singleness (1)
S C : 0 9 :010(356) [0563] and trembling, with **singleness** of heart, as to Christ; not

Singular (4)
P R : P R :013(007) [0013] in good order, by the **singular** grace of the Holy Spirit,
A L : 2 3 :006(052) [0061] alter his creation without a **singular** gift and work of God.
A L : 2 7 :020(074) [0079] marry who are not excepted by a **singular** work of God.
T R : 0 0 :023(324) [0511] is here spoken in the **singular** number ("I will give you the

Sink (3), Sunk (2)
L C : 0 1 :077(375) [0603] the young, so that it may **sink** into their minds, for when
L C : 0 1 :123(382) [0617] punishes them so that they **sink** into all kinds of trouble
L C : 0 1 :157(386) [0627] in which we are so deeply **sunk** and may rightly
L C : 0 5 :084(456) [0773] will perceive that you have **sunk** twice as low as any other
S D : 0 8 :044(599) [1029] a counterbalance, we shall **sink** to the bottom with our

Sired (1)
A P : 2 4 :064(261) [0405] These errors have **sired** endless others, like the one that

Sisters (4)
A G : 2 3 :025(055) [0065] not give their brothers and **sisters** occasion for offense."
A L : 2 3 :025(055) [0065] they should give no offense to their brothers and **sisters**."
L C : 0 1 :105(379) [0611] With respect to brothers, **sisters**, and neighbors in general
L C : 0 1 :275(402) [0659] even brothers and **sisters** and other good friends are

Sit (13), Sits (2), Sitting (3), Sat (1)
A G : 0 3 :004(030) [0045] ascended into heaven and **sits** on the right hand of God,
A G : 0 8 :001(033) [0047] indicated, "The Pharisees **sit** on Moses' seat"
A L : 0 3 :004(030) [0045] he ascended into heaven to **sit** on the right hand of the
A L : 0 8 :001(033) [0047] "The scribes and Pharisees **sit** on Moses' seat," etc.
A L : 1 6 :002(037) [0051] to hold civil office, to **sit** as judges, to decide matters by
A P : 1 2 :126(201) [0289] You, therefore, who should **sit** as though on a
A P : 1 3 :013(213) [0311] They **sit** in a dark corner doing and saying nothing, but
L C : P R :014(360) [0571] his precepts whether **sitting**, walking, standing, lying
L C : P R :017(361) [0573] He is qualified to **sit** in judgment upon all doctrines,
L C : S P :012(363) [0577] ascended into heaven, and **sits** on the right hand of God,
L C : 0 1 :007(365) [0583] fearless, as if he were **sitting** in the midst of paradise.
L C : 0 1 :088(377) [0605] Not when we **sit** behind the stove and refrain from
L C : 0 1 :229(396) [0645] who loot a cash box, they **sit** in office chairs and are
L C : 0 1 :258(399) [0653] or others in authority **sit** in judgment, we always find
L C : 0 3 :103(434) [0727] but everyone wants to **sit** in the chief seat and be seen by
S D : 0 8 :044(599) [1031] But he could never have **sat** in the pan unless he had
S D : 0 8 :096(610) [1049] in Christ been made to **sit** so high at the right hand of the
S D : 0 9 :003(610) [1051] Christ has been made to **sit** at the right hand of the
S D : 1 1 :004(617) [1065] And again, "I know your **sitting** down and your going

Situated (1), Situation (12)
P R : P R :004(003) [0007] how in this anguished **situation** and amid the disruption
A P : 2 3 :006(240) [0365] but in this one the **situation** is so clear that no discussion
S 3 : 0 3 :015(305) [0483] contrition, this was the **situation**: Since nobody could
S 3 : 0 3 :019(306) [0483] As for confession, the **situation** was like this: Everybody
T R : 0 0 :016(322) [0509] world or for churches **situated** in remote places to seek
T R : 0 0 :041(327) [0517] Since this is the **situation**, all Christians ought to beware
L C : 0 1 :219(394) [0643] deed in his particular **situation** (that is, especially in the
L C : 0 1 :275(402) [0659] is no different from the **situation** of the physician who, to
L C : 0 1 :301(405) [0667] This **situation** occurs most frequently in lawsuits in which
L C : 0 3 :002(420) [0697] Mankind is in such a **situation** that no one can keep the
S D : 0 1 :023(512) [0865] matters, or that the **situation** is not the way the hymn
S D : 1 0 :013(613) [1057] Barnabas in a similar **situation** yielded to a certain
S D : 1 0 :022(615) [1061] after: "Since this is the **situation**, all Christians ought to

Six (1), Sixth (8), Sixty (1)
A P : 0 4 :001(107) [0119] In the fourth, fifth, and **sixth** articles, and later in the
A P : 2 3 :051(246) [0377] ***Sixth***, we have many reasons for rejecting the law of
A P : 2 7 :066(280) [0441] as a widow who is under **sixty** years of age" (I Tim. 5:9).
S 2 : 0 2 :024(296) [0469] The **sixth** place belongs to the precious indulgences,
S 3 : 0 3 :026(307) [0487] be so cheap that they were released at **six** pence a head.
S C : 0 1 :011(343) [0541] The **Sixth**
S C : 0 3 :017(347) [0549] The **Sixth** Petition
L C : 0 1 :199(392) [0637] The **Sixth** Commandment
L C : 0 3 :098(433) [0725] The **Sixth** Petition
S D : 1 1 :027(620) [1071] at the third, at the **sixth**, at the ninth, and even at the

Size (1)
S D : 0 7 :099(586) [1005] earth and vacated or occupied space according to his **size**.

Skill (4), Skilled (1)
A P : 2 4 :016(252) [0389] that if he found someone **skilled** in making them he would
L C : 0 4 :043(442) [0743] a physician who had such **skill** that people would not die,
E P : 0 1 :016(468) [0783] for example, the capacity, **skill**, capability, or power to
S D : 0 1 :023(512) [0865] as the faculty, aptitude, **skill**, or ability to initiate and
S D : 0 2 :012(522) [0885] every capacity, aptitude, **skill**, and ability to think

Skin (6), Skins (1)
A P : 0 2 :041(105) [0115] is a neutral thing, like the color of the **skin** or ill health.
L C : 0 1 :227(396) [0645] a trade and deliberately fleeces, **skins**, and torments him.
L C : 0 1 :247(398) [0651] live by your favor, you **skin** and scrape him right down to
L C : 0 4 :020(439) [0737] to their noses, eyes, **skin** and hair, flesh and bones, they
L C : 0 5 :023(449) [0757] our human flesh and blood have not lost their old **skin**.
E P : 0 1 :010(467) [0781] be covered by this my **skin**, and in my flesh I shall see
S D : 0 1 :035(514) [0869] Thou didst clothe me with **skin** and flesh, and knit me

Skinflints (1)
L C : P R :006(359) [0569] there are some louts and **skinflints** who declare that we

Skip (4)
A P : 0 4 :284(150) [0201] about works and **skip** the passages about faith.
A P : 1 2 :107(197) [0283] But let us **skip** over things like this.
A P : 2 8 :026(285) [0451] But let us **skip** over the comparison.
L C : 0 1 :114(380) [0613] were able to ignore it and **skip** lightly over it, and so

Skulks (1)
L C : 0 5 :026(449) [0759] by force, he sneaks and **skulks** about everywhere, trying

Slack (1)
L C : 0 3 :031(424) [0707] if we only persevere diligently and do not become **slack**.

Slander (16), Slandered (2), Slanderers (2), Slanderous (1), Slanderously (4), Slanders (5)
P R : P R :008(005) [0011] from their fabricated **slanders** and defamation of us and
P R : P R :011(006) [0011] the pretext and basis for **slander** that the adversaries were
A L : 0 0 :002(049) [0059] disseminate astonishing **slanders** among the people in
A P : P R :014(099) [0101] written so cleverly and **slanderously** that in some places it
A P : 0 2 :035(105) [0115] Imperial Majesty will recognize an obvious **slander** here.
A P : 0 2 :051(107) [0119] with which our opponents have **slandered** our article.
A P : 0 4 :073(117) [0141] or the sacraments, as our opponents **slanderously** claim.
A P : 0 4 :136(126) [0159] Our opponents **slanderously** claim that we do not require
A P : 0 4 :348(160) [0217] We have refuted this **slander** earlier.
A P : 0 7 :002(168) [0227] that there is no defense against the attacks of **slanderers**.
A P : 0 7 :003(168) [0227] to defend ourselves at any length against this **slander**.
A P : 0 7 :020(171) [0233] republic, as has been **slanderously** alleged, but we teach
A P : 1 2 :124(201) [0289] among good men these **slanders** will not gain any
A P : 1 2 :125(201) [0289] will posterity think about these **slanderous** judgments?
A P : 2 3 :068(249) [0383] the Confutation, lest their fraud and **slander** be exposed.
A P : 2 8 :002(281) [0443] This is sheer **slander**, for in this article we have been
S 1 : P R :007(289) [0457] For although they **slander** us so shamefully and try by
S 3 : 0 6 :004(311) [0493] prohibit, condemn, and **slander** the use of both as heresy
S C : 0 1 :016(343) [0541] our neighbor, nor betray, **slander**, or defame him, but
L C : 0 1 :055(372) [0595] also those who publicly **slander** the truth and God's Word
L C : 0 1 :081(375) [0603] They **slandered** Christ and would not permit him to do
L C : 0 1 :264(400) [0655] vice of back-biting or **slander** by which the devil rides us.
L C : 0 1 :273(401) [0659] tongue who gossips and **slanders** someone, rebuke him
L C : 0 1 :276(402) [0659] not be quick to spread **slander** and gossip about your
L C : 0 1 :284(403) [0661] can be no question of **slander** or injustice or false witness.
L C : 0 3 :042(425) [0709] drunkards, gluttons, jealous persons, and **slanderers**.
L C : 0 3 :103(434) [0727] cursing, reviling, **slander**, arrogance, and pride, along
L C : 0 4 :015(438) [0735] new spirits, in order to **slander** Baptism, ignore God's
S D : P R :002(501) [0847] and raised no end of **slanders** and insinuations against it.
S D : 0 3 :029(544) [0925] the adversaries falsely **slander** and accuse us) but so that

Slaughter (4), Slaughtered (1), Slaughtering (1)
A P : 0 4 :236(140) [0185] They are **slaughtering** priests and other good men if they
A P : 2 3 :003(239) [0363] to cruel punishments, **slaughter** priests whom even the
A P : 2 4 :026(254) [0391] where cattle were **slaughtered**, but with any worship
A P : 2 4 :034(256) [0397] The **slaughter** of animals in the Old Testament
A P : 2 7 :058(279) [0439] as circumcision or the **slaughter** of victims would not be
L C : 0 5 :042(451) [0763] or compelled, lest we institute a new **slaughter** of souls.

Slave (7), Slavery (7)
A G : 2 8 :052(089) [0091] therefore, and do not submit again to a yoke of **slavery**."
A L : 2 8 :052(089) [0091] Galatians, "Do not submit again to a yoke of **slavery**."
A P : 0 2 :005(101) [0107] but, like a child born of a **slave**, is in this condition
A P : 0 2 :048(106) [0119] so we cannot buy our way out of the **slavery** by ourselves.
A P : 1 5 :031(219) [0323] Gal. 5:1 Paul forbids them to "submit again to **slavery**."
A P : 2 8 :015(283) [0447] you free, and do not submit again to a yoke of **slavery**."
S C : 0 9 :010(356) [0563] from the Lord, whether he is a **slave** or free" (Eph. 6:5-8).
E P : 0 4 :012(477) [0799] fear of punishment, like a **slave**, but out of a love of
E P : 0 8 :016(489) [0821] completely the form of a **slave** (not the human nature)
E P : 0 8 :033(491) [0825] he laid aside the form of a **slave**, does not perform all
E P : 1 0 :006(493) [0829] and do not submit again to a yoke of **slavery**" (Gal. 5:11).
S D : 0 2 :007(521) [0883] from himself," but is a **slave** of sin (John 8:34), the
S D : 0 8 :065(604) [1039] now, since the form of a **slave** has been laid aside, it takes
S D : 1 0 :011(612) [1055] and do not submit again to a yoke of **slavery**" (Gal. 5:1).

Slay (1), Slaying (1), Slays (1)
S 2 : 0 4 :014(301) [0475] to God, and to damn, **slay**, and plague all Christians who
S 3 : 0 3 :008(304) [0481] As St. Paul says, the law **slays** through sin.
L C : 0 4 :065(445) [0749] which is simply the **slaying** of the old Adam and the

Sleep (2), Slept (1)
S 3 : 0 3 :028(308) [0487] do, sometimes while we **slept** (as St. Augustine, St.
S C : 0 7 :005(353) [0559] Then quickly lie down and **sleep** in peace.
L C : P R :002(358) [0567] Preach Themselves," "**Sleep** Soundly," "Prepared!" and

Sleight (1)
S D : 0 8 :039(598) [1029] Here Zwingli performs a **sleight**-of-hand trick and

Slender (1)
A P : 2 7 :043(277) [0435] and leisure; instead of a **slender** inheritance they find the

Slight (2), Slightest (3), Slightly (1)
P R : P R :024(013) [0023] We do not have the **slightest** doubt that all pious people
S C : P R :005(338) [0533] yet you do not take the **slightest** interest in teaching the
L C : 0 1 :091(377) [0607] could not help us in the **slightest** degree, for they are all
E P : 0 1 :008(467) [0781] that original sin is not a **slight** corruption of human
E P : 0 1 :014(467) [0783] that original sin is a **slight**, insignificant spot or blemish
S D : 0 2 :076(536) [0911] whose doctrine was **slightly** more subtle and who taught

Slip (5), Slipped (1), Slips (1)
A P : 2 7 :011(270) [0423] how the architects of the Confutation **slip** away here!
L C : 0 1 :067(373) [0599] gain by the false oath will **slip** through his fingers and
L C : 0 1 :303(405) [0667] where one cunningly **slips** something out of another's
L C : 0 3 :111(435) [0729] opening into which it can **slip**, the whole body will
L C : 0 4 :082(446) [0751] But it does happen that we **slip** and fall out of the ship.
S D : 1 0 :011(612) [1055] secretly brought in, who **slipped** in to spy out our freedom
S D : 1 1 :046(624) [1079] of our flesh it could easily **slip** from our fingers, and

Sluggish (1)
L C : P R :004(359) [0567] can we expect if we are **sluggish** and lazy, as we used to

Sly (1), Slyly (1)
A P : 2 7 :036(275) [0433] But our opponents **slyly** seek to give the impression that
L C : 0 1 :298(405) [0665] think up artful dodges and **sly** tricks (better and better

Smalcald (30)
P R : P R :025(014) [0023] followed it, and in the **Smalcald** Articles and the Large
S 1 : 0 0 :027(287) [0453] The **Smalcald** Articles
S 3 : 1 5 :005(317) [0501] on his departure from **Smalcald** directed me orally and by
T R : 0 0 :000(319) [0503] the Theologians Assembled in **Smalcald** in the Year 1537
T R : 0 0 :082(334) [0529] in this assembly in **Smalcald** unanimously declare that in
T R : 0 0 :082(334) [0529] presented to the princes here in this assembly in **Smalcald**.
T R : 0 0 :082(334) [0529] the papacy presented to the princes in **Smalcald**
T R : 0 0 :082(000) [0529] at the Assembly at **Smalcald** in the German language by
T R : 0 0 :082(000) [0529] have now assembled at **Smalcald** I acknowledge that I am
E P : R N :004(465) [0777] the Articles drafted at **Smalcald** in the year 1537, which
E P : 1 2 :030(500) [0843] the Apology, the **Smalcald** Articles, and the Catechisms
S D : P R :007(505) [0853] of theologians at **Smalcald** in 1537 and there approved
S D : P R :011(506) [0855] the Apology, the **Smalcald** Articles, and Luther's Large
S D : 0 1 :008(510) [0861] As the **Smalcald** Articles point out, it is something that
S D : 0 1 :052(517) [0875] of our nature as it is described in the **Smalcald** Articles.
S D : 0 2 :033(527) [0893] The **Smalcald** Articles reject the following errors
S D : 0 2 :034(527) [0893] The **Smalcald** Articles state further: "This repentance
S D : 0 2 :045(530) [0899] its Apology, the **Smalcald** Articles, the Large and Small
S D : 0 5 :014(560) [0957] In the same vein, the **Smalcald** Articles state: "The New
S D : 0 7 :017(572) [0977] all parts of Germany in **Smalcald** to consider what kind
S D : 0 7 :017(572) [0979] Dr. Luther drafted the **Smalcald** Articles, which all the
S D : 0 7 :019(572) [0979] The **Smalcald** Articles state that "the bread and the wine
S D : 0 7 :110(589) [1011] the Apology, the **Smalcald** Articles, and other writings of
S D : 1 0 :018(614) [1059] drawn from the **Smalcald** Articles, which were drafted
S D : 1 0 :019(614) [1059] The **Smalcald** Articles of 1537 declare on this: "We do not
S D : 1 0 :019(614) [1059] Just before this the **Smalcald** Articles declare: "If the
S D : 1 0 :020(614) [1059] of the pope, the **Smalcald** Articles state: "Just as we
S D : 1 0 :021(614) [1059] an appendix to the **Smalcald** Articles and which all the
S D : 1 0 :021(614) [1059] assembled in **Smalcald** subscribed with their own hands,
S D : 1 2 :039(636) [1103] and the Apology, to the **Smalcald** Articles, to Luther's

Small (18), Smaller (3), Smallest (5)
P R : P R :025(014) [0023] Articles and the Large and **Small** Catechism of that highly
A G : 2 7 :048(078) [0081] Now, it is no **small** offense in the Christian church that
A P : 0 4 :141(126) [0161] to separate faith from love for God, be it ever so **small**.
S 1 : P R :007(289) [0457] has made their following **smaller** and smaller and ours
S 1 : P R :007(289) [0457] following smaller and **smaller** and ours ever larger, and
S 2 : 0 4 :015(301) [0475] concede to us even the **smallest** fraction of these articles.
S 3 : 0 3 :021(306) [0485] resorted to of imposing **small** satisfactions which were
S C : 0 0 :000(337) [0531] The **Small** Catechism of Dr. Martin Luther for Ordinary
L C : 0 1 :291(404) [0663] matters, than this **smallest** and weakest of his members,
L C : 0 2 :013(412) [0681] my members great and **small**, all the faculties of my
L C : 0 2 :016(412) [0681] preserve any of them, however **small** and unimportant.
E P : R N :005(465) [0777] we subscribe Dr. Luther's **Small** and Large Catechisms as
S D : P R :008(505) [0853] adherence to Dr. Luther's **Small** and Large Catechisms,
S D : P R :011(506) [0855] and Luther's Large and **Small** Catechisms — in the cited
S D : 0 1 :023(512) [0865] — even though in only a **small**, limited, and poor degree
S D : 0 1 :038(514) [0871] Article of the Creed in the **Small** Catechism we confess, "I
S D : 0 1 :038(515) [0871] my members great and **small**, all the faculties of my
S D : 0 2 :007(521) [0883] or in the tiniest or **smallest** degree, "of himself as coming
S D : 0 2 :040(528) [0895] In Dr. Luther's **Small** Catechism we read: "I believe that
S D : 0 2 :045(530) [0899] Articles, the Large and **Small** Catechisms of Luther, and
S D : 0 2 :077(536) [0911] degree — though only to a **small** extent and in a weak
S D : 0 3 :037(546) [0929] or even only to the **smallest** degree factors in our
S D : 0 7 :010(571) [0975] the same view in the **Small** Catechism in the following
S D : 0 7 :071(582) [0997] of faith, be it greater or **smaller**, but solely in the merits
S D : 0 7 :091(585) [1005] *Stand Firm*, his *Great* and ***Small** Confessions concerning*
S D : 1 1 :096(632) [1095] will not give place to the **smallest** error but will lead the

Smart (1)
A P : 2 1 :035(234) [0353] Some **smart** person painted Christopher in such a way as

Smeared (2)
E P : 0 1 :015(468) [0783] just as garlic juice, **smeared** upon a magnet, impedes but
S D : 0 1 :022(512) [0865] them, just as garlic juice **smeared** on a magnet does not

Smell (2)
L C : P R :020(361) [0573] now they cannot bear to **smell** because they are so bloated
L C : 0 1 :270(401) [0657] Ah, now do you **smell** the roast?

Smiles (1)
L C : 0 1 :036(369) [0589] whether God frowns or **smiles**, boast defiantly of their

Smiting (1), Smitten (1), Smote (1)
A L : 1 2 :004(034) [0049] contrition, that is, terror **smiting** the conscience with a
A P : 0 2 :034(104) [0113] "After I was instructed, I **smote** upon my thigh"
S 3 : 0 3 :018(306) [0483] perchance he was really **smitten** by the law or vainly

Smothered (2)
A L : 2 6 :006(064) [0071] has been almost wholly **smothered** by traditions which
A P : 1 1 :002(180) [0249] of absolution had been **smothered** by teachings about

Smudge (1)
S D : 0 1 :022(512) [0865] be washed off, like a **smudge** of dirt from one's face or

Smug (5), Smuggle (1), Smugness (3)
A P : 0 4 :020(110) [0125] **Smug** hypocrites always believe that they have the merit
A P : 0 4 :021(110) [0127] In **smug** hypocrites, who think that they are keeping the
A P : 0 4 :034(112) [0129] judgment of God in its **smugness**, or in the midst of
A P : 0 4 :135(125) [0159] how our flesh in its **smugness** and indifference does not
A P : 0 4 :248(142) [0191] condemns the idle and **smug** minds who dream they have
A P : 0 4 :321(157) [0209] Rather, **smug** hypocrites simply believe that their works
A P : 1 2 :048(188) [0265] Wicked and **smug** men do not say this seriously, for they
A P : 1 2 :051(189) [0265] not feel God's wrath in their **smugness** spurn consolation.
A P : 2 0 :004(227) [0339] of shame if they dare to **smuggle** such a notion into the

Snares (8)
A G : 2 8 :064(092) [0093] What are such discussions but **snares** of conscience?
A L : 2 7 :008(072) [0077] were created, what **snares** were placed on consciences.
A L : 2 8 :064(092) [0093] What are discussions of this kind but **snares** of conscience
A P : 1 2 :111(198) [0285] What **snares** this requirement of complete confession has
A P : 1 5 :049(221) [0329] experience that traditions are real **snares** for consciences.
A P : 2 3 :022(242) [0369] be left free, and no **snares** should be set for the weak
T R : 0 0 :078(333) [0527] There are also other **snares** of conscience in their laws,
L C : 0 3 :104(434) [0727] These are **snares** and nets; indeed, they are the real

Snatch (3), Snatched (2), Snatches (2)
L C : 0 2 :030(414) [0685] He has **snatched** us, poor lost creatures, from the jaws of
L C : 0 4 :062(444) [0749] devil who would like to **snatch** the crown from the rulers
L C : 0 4 :083(446) [0751] thing Baptism is, which **snatches** us from the jaws of the
L C : 0 6 :032(461) [0000] They **snatch** at the bread just like a hunted hart, burning
S D : 1 1 :008(617) [1065] is written, "No one shall **snatch** my sheep out of my
S D : 1 1 :046(624) [1079] world it could easily be **snatched** and taken from our
S D : 1 1 :076(629) [1089] with a net by which he **snatches** the elect from the maw

Sneak (4), Sneaks (1), Sneaky (1)
L C : 0 1 :226(395) [0645] these are far worse than **sneak**-thieves, against whom we
L C : 0 1 :229(396) [0645] from being picklocks and **sneak**-thieves who loot a cash
L C : 0 1 :231(396) [0647] Meanwhile the little **sneak**-thieves who have committed
L C : 0 1 :283(403) [0661] of truth, you would not **sneak** about in secret, shunning
L C : 0 4 :062(444) [0749] Here lurks a **sneaky**, seditious devil who would like to
L C : 0 5 :026(449) [0759] rout us by force, he **sneaks** and skulks about everywhere,

Snouts (1)
L C : 0 1 :267(401) [0657] roll in the mud and root around in it with their **snouts**.

Snow (4)
A P : 0 4 :258(144) [0193] are like scarlet, they shall be white as **snow**" (Isa. 1:16-18).
A P : 0 4 :327(158) [0211] "If I wash myself with **snow**, and cleanse my hands with
A P : 1 2 :164(208) [0303] your sins are like scarlet, they shall be white as **snow**.
L C : 0 4 :043(442) [0743] how the world would **snow** and rain money upon him!

Soars (1)
S D : 1 1 :063(626) [1083] discussion on this subject **soars** too high and goes beyond

Social (2)
A P : 0 4 :288(151) [0203] but that for the sake of **social** tranquillity there should be
L C : 0 1 :317(408) [0673] men produce a doctrine or **social** order equal to that of

Society (3)
E P : 1 2 :002(498) [0839] politic and secular administration, or in domestic **society**.
E P : 1 2 :016(499) [0841] *Intolerable Errors which Undermine Domestic **Society***
S D : 1 2 :009(633) [1097] the churches or in the body politic or in domestic **society**.

Socrates (2)
A P : 0 4 :015(109) [0123] with the teachings of **Socrates**, Zeno, and others, as
A P : 2 4 :016(252) [0389] In Plato's *Phaedrus*, **Socrates** says that he is very fond of

Sodom (2)
A P : 2 3 :054(246) [0379] flood and the burning of **Sodom** and Gomorrah reveal
S 1 : P R :011(290) [0457] destroy us utterly, like **Sodom** and Gomorrah, because we

Soest (2)
S 3 : 1 5 :005(317) [0501] of Christ which is in **Soest**, subscribe the articles of the
T R : 0 0 :082(335) [0529] Brixius Northanus, minister in **Soest**

Soft (1)
L C : 0 1 :197(392) [0637] that they might live a nice, **soft** life without the cross and

Solace (1)
L C : 0 3 :070(429) [0717] It is our **solace** and boast that the will and purpose of the

Sold (3)
S 3 : 0 3 :028(308) [0487] works with others and **sold** them to others in the belief
S D : 0 2 :017(524) [0887] spiritual; but I am carnal, **sold** under sin" (Rom. 7:14),
S D : 1 1 :004(617) [1063] as it is written, "Are not two sparrows **sold** for a penny?

Soldiers (5)
A G : 1 6 :002(037) [0051] in just wars, serve as **soldiers**, buy and sell, take required
A L : 1 6 :002(037) [0051] in just wars, to serve as **soldiers**, to make legal contracts,
A P : 1 5 :035(220) [0325] secular customs, if **soldiers** wear one kind of uniform and
A P : 2 7 :032(274) [0431] even with ten thousand **soldiers** he cannot stand up
L C : 0 1 :244(398) [0649] or he quarters a troop of **soldiers** upon us; in one hour

Sole (7), Solely (50)
A G : 2 0 :007(042) [0053] than the teaching that we are to rely **solely** on our works.
L C : 0 2 :021(413) [0683] blessings and gifts of God **solely** for its own pride and
L C : 0 4 :009(437) [0733] altars and churches **solely** by virtue of his letters and
L C : 0 4 :057(444) [0747] him on that account, but **solely** on the command of God.
E P : 0 2 :004(470) [0787] it and thus are converted **solely** through the grace and

Continued ▶

EP : 02 :018(472) [0791] changed and renewed ***solely by God's power and***
EP : 02 :019(472) [0791] it by his own powers but **solely** by the grace and
EP : 03 :001(472) [0791] before God and saved **solely** by faith in Christ, so that
EP : 03 :003(473) [0793] is our righteousness **solely** in his obedience which as God
EP : 03 :006(473) [0793] and trust in him, so that **solely** because of his obedience,
EP : 04 :004(476) [0797] to do good works **solely** on the basis of the Gospel.
EP : 05 :007(478) [0803] by the law, directs them **solely** to the merit of Christ, and
EP : 07 :008(482) [0811] but it is to be ascribed **solely** and alone to the almighty
EP : 07 :020(484) [0813] feast is and consists **solely** and alone in the most holy
EP : 07 :030(485) [0815] Holy Supper is effected **solely** by the external signs of
EP : 08 :018(489) [0823] apostles testifies, and the **sole** foundation of our comfort,
EP : 10 :003(493) [0829] have been introduced **solely** for the sake of good order
SD : PR :009(505) [0855] is and should remain the **sole** rule and norm of all
SD : 02 :002(520) [0881] The chief issue is **solely** and alone what the unregenerated
SD : 02 :026(526) [0891] heart, mind, and spirit, is **solely** the work of the Holy
SD : 02 :078(536) [0911] own natural powers but **solely** through the operation of
SD : 02 :087(538) [0915] from spiritual death, is **solely** and alone the work of God,
SD : 02 :090(539) [0915] that conversion to God is **solely** of God the Holy Spirit,
SD : 03 :004(540) [0917] adopted as God's children **solely** on account of the
SD : 03 :009(541) [0919] works, by sheer grace, **solely** through the merit of the
SD : 03 :011(541) [0919] and to trust in him, that **solely** for the sake of his
SD : 03 :019(542) [0921] the forgiveness of sins **solely** for Christ's sake and the
SD : 03 :023(543) [0923] faith before God consists **solely** in the gracious reckoning
SD : 03 :030(544) [0925] faith before God consists **solely** in a gracious
SD : 03 :030(544) [0925] nor in other virtues, but **solely** in Christ and (in him) in
SD : 03 :034(545) [0927] that salvation belongs **solely** to that person to whom God
SD : 03 :036(545) [0929] article of justification listed above) consists **solely** therein.
SD : 03 :038(546) [0929] 2. That faith's **sole** office and property is to serve as the
SD : 03 :039(546) [0929] of faith consists **solely** in the forgiveness of sins by sheer
SD : 03 :039(546) [0929] applied to us, and made our own **solely** through faith.
SD : 03 :043(547) [0931] Faith justifies **solely** for this reason and on this account,
SD : 03 :052(548) [0933] we are indeed justified **solely** through faith without works
SD : 03 :055(549) [0935] our righteousness rests **solely** and alone on the Lord
SD : 03 :055(549) [0935] who as God and man in his **sole**, total, and perfect
SD : 03 :063(550) [0937] That faith does not look **solely** to the obedience of
SD : 04 :022(555) [0945] and ascribe everything **solely** to the grace of God and the
SD : 04 :024(555) [0945] the bliss of salvation **solely** to the man to whom God
SD : 04 :024(555) [0945] Confession, "We are saved without works **solely** by faith."
SD : 05 :006(559) [0953] of repentance but **solely** the preaching of God's grace.
SD : 05 :015(561) [0957] and sorrow not from the law but **solely** from the Gospel.
SD : 05 :022(562) [0959] must put his confidence **solely** on the Lord Jesus Christ,
SD : 07 :071(582) [0997] it greater or smaller, but **solely** in the merits of Christ, of
SD : 07 :089(585) [1003] makes the sacrament, but **solely** the Word and institution
SD : 07 :089(585) [1003] not through our faith, but **solely** through his
SD : 11 :036(622) [1075] and promises it to us **solely** from his Word, through
SD : 11 :043(623) [1077] and merit, purely by grace and **solely** for Christ's sake.
SD : 11 :052(625) [1081] but has kept reserved **solely** to his own wisdom and
SD : 11 :055(625) [1081] or brood over it, but cling **solely** to his revealed Word, to
SD : 11 :075(628) [1087] on our piety or virtue but **solely** on the merit of Christ
SD : 11 :086(631) [1091] Pharaoh's example for the **sole** purpose of thereby setting
SD : 11 :096(632) [1095] him for ever through the **sole** merit of Christ, and so
SD : 12 :010(633) [1097] not depend alone on the **sole** obedience and merit of

Solemn (4), Solemnly (7)
PR : PR :022(012) [0021] of the Lord before the **solemn** and severe throne of God's
AL : 24 :041(061) [0069] are done except for the **solemn** remembrance of the
S1 : PR :014(291) [0459] while we trample his **solemn** commandments underfoot.
LC : PR :014(360) [0571] Deut. 6:7, 8 **solemnly** enjoins that we should always
LC : PR :014(360) [0571] and command this so **solemnly** without good reason.
LC : 01 :057(372) [0597] to this commandment a **solemn** threat: "for the Lord will
LC : 01 :171(388) [0629] divine Majesty, who will **solemnly** call us to account and
LC : 01 :211(393) [0641] necessary one, and it is **solemnly** commanded by God
LC : 03 :006(420) [0699] is as strictly and **solemnly** commanded as all the other
LC : 04 :006(437) [0733] Moreover, it is **solemnly** and strictly commanded that we
SD : 02 :043(529) [0897] *Holy Supper* in which he **solemnly** declares that he will

Soles (1)
SD : 01 :062(519) [0879] has poisoned us from the **soles** of our feet to the crown of

Solid (7), Solidly (3)
PR : PR :003(003) [0007] in it, that is based **solidly** on the divine Scriptures, and
PR : PR :010(006) [0011] might be stopped by **solid** reasoning, and a correct
AG : 00 :001(048) [0059] and do so without any **solid** basis of divine command or
SD : 00 :000(501) [0845] [Part II. **Solid** Declaration]
SD : PR :004(504) [0851] within the Christian church are clearly and **solidly** refuted.
SD : PR :005(504) [0851] the Word of God and **solidly** and well grounded therein.
SD : PR :017(507) [0857] on the certain and **solid** basis of the holy and divine
SD : 07 :106(588) [1009] are so strong and **solid** that they will confirm and fortify
SD : 08 :002(591) [1015] Luther maintained with **solid** arguments the true,
SD : 08 :080(607) [1045] On the basis of this **solid** foundation, Dr. Luther, of

Solomon (3)
AP : 12 :106(197) [0283] here the saying of **Solomon** (Prov. 27:23), "Know well the
AP : 12 :106(197) [0283] **Solomon** is not talking about confession.
LC : 01 :252(399) [0653] our neighbor, as King **Solomon** teaches in Prov. 19:17,

Solutions (1)
AP : 04 :185(132) [0173] and dangerous issues produce many and varied **solutions**.

Solved (2)
AP : 15 :034(220) [0325] the Gordian knot, he **solved** it for good by cutting it with
LC : 01 :065(373) [0599] you have easily **solved** the question that has tormented so

Somebody (10)
AP : 04 :149(127) [0163] If **somebody** doubts that his sins are forgiven, he insults
AP : 04 :150(127) [0163] If **somebody** believes that he obtains the forgiveness of
AP : 07 :034(175) [0239] God, it follows that **somebody** can be righteous and a
AP : 15 :014(216) [0319] If **somebody** wants to institute certain works to merit the
AP : 24 :033(255) [0395] It **somebody** wants to include the ceremony here, we
S2 : 02 :008(294) [0465] **Somebody** may seek to justify himself by saying that he
S3 : 03 :017(305) [0483] And when **somebody** said that he was unable to repent or
LC : 01 :188(390) [0635] For to do evil to **somebody** who desires and does you
LC : 01 :268(401) [0657] pronounce is to declare **somebody** a thief, a murderer, a
LC : 01 :273(401) [0659] if you encounter **somebody** with a worthless tongue who

Somehow (1)
AP : 04 :008(108) [0121] external works that reason can **somehow** perform.

Sometimes (27)
PR : PR :021(011) [0019] as if somewhere or **sometimes** it were being taught that
AG : 23 :016(054) [0063] also state that it is **sometimes** necessary to relax severity
AG : 27 :029(075) [0079] monastic vows, and **sometimes** have been compelled and
AL : 27 :029(075) [0079] are persuaded, and **sometimes** even compelled, to take the
AP : 02 :030(104) [0113] For Paul **sometimes** mentions the deficiency, as in
AP : 04 :152(127) [0163] by which we **sometimes** combine cause and effect in the
AP : 04 :321(157) [0209] distinction — that men **sometimes** acquire the merit of
AP : 04 :321(157) [0209] merit of congruity and **sometimes** the merit of condignity
AP : 04 :365(163) [0219] Just so they **sometimes** offer grace with other rewards, as
AP : 07 :021(172) [0233] of the holy Fathers show that even they **sometimes** built
AP : 12 :093(196) [0279] the Fathers discuss **sometimes** one part, sometimes
AP : 12 :093(196) [0279] sometimes one part, **sometimes** another part of
AP : 23 :043(245) [0375] They know that **sometimes** they must withdraw to have
AP : 24 :023(253) [0391] **Sometimes** they offered up human sacrifices, perhaps
AP : 27 :007(269) [0421] sign is the fact that **sometimes** they are responsible for
S2 : 04 :003(298) [0471] where God **sometimes** permits much good to come to a
S3 : 03 :028(308) [0487] what is its nature to do, **sometimes** while we slept (as St.
TR : 00 :035(326) [0513] and wars, **sometimes** in order to occupy Italian cities and
TR : 00 :035(326) [0513] Italian cities and **sometimes** in order to make the German
TR : 00 :049(329) [0519] councils, as the canons **sometimes** impudently declare —
TR : 00 :075(333) [0525] To be sure, they **sometimes** punished persons involved in
LC : 01 :275(402) [0659] to cure a patient, is **sometimes** compelled to examine and
EP : 01 :022(469) [0785] **Sometimes** the term means man's essence, as when we
EP : 03 :008(474) [0793] **Sometimes**, as in the Apology, the words *regeneratio*
SD : 01 :052(517) [0875] **Sometimes**, however, the term is applied in a wider sense
SD : 03 :018(542) [0921] word "regeneration" is **sometimes** used in place of
SD : 03 :020(542) [0921] being made alive, has **sometimes** been used in the same

Somewhat (3)
AP : 02 :012(102) [0109] we agree is subject to reason and **somewhat** in our power.
AP : 04 :130(125) [0157] Although it is **somewhat** possible to do civil works, that
LC : 02 :012(412) [0681] For the **somewhat** more advanced and the educated,

Somewhere (3)
PR : PR :021(011) [0019] terminology), as if **somewhere** or sometimes it were being
LC : 01 :156(386) [0625] **Somewhere** on earth there must still be some godly
EP : 08 :035(491) [0825] is, a power that lies **somewhere** between God's

Son (145) (*Ref. to Jesus Christ*)
PR : PR :020(010) [0017] the incarnation of God's **Son**, his ascension, and his
AG : 01 :002(027) [0043] God the Father, God the **Son**, God the Holy Spirit.
AG : 03 :000(029) [0045] III. [The **Son** of God]
AG : 03 :001(029) [0045] among us that God the **Son** became man, born of the
AG : 27 :037(077) [0081] us into his favor for the sake of Christ, his only **Son**.
AL : 01 :003(028) [0043] also coeternal: the Father, the **Son**, and the Holy Spirit.
AL : 03 :000(029) [0045] III. [The **Son** of God]
AL : 03 :001(029) [0045] the Word — that is, the **Son** of God — took on man's
AP : 01 :001(100) [0103] of the same divine essence, Father, **Son**, and Holy Spirit.
AP : 04 :031(111) [0129] John 8:36 says, "If the **Son** makes you free, you will be
AP : 04 :095(121) [0149] the wilderness, so must the **Son** of man be lifted up, that
AP : 04 :096(121) [0149] "God sent the **Son** into the world, not to
AP : 04 :139(126) [0161] says, "The reason the **Son** of God appeared was to
AP : 04 :141(126) [0161] that is, because he gave his **Son** for us and forgave us our
AP : 04 :297(153) [0205] believed in the testimony that God has borne to his **Son**.
AP : 04 :297(153) [0205] that God gave us eternal life, and this life is in his **Son**.
AP : 04 :297(153) [0205] He who has the **Son**, has life; he who has not the Son, has
AP : 04 :297(153) [0205] the Son, has life; he who has not the **Son**, has not life."
AP : 04 :297(153) [0205] Christ says, "If the **Son** makes you free, you will be free
AP : 04 :310(155) [0207] that everyone who sees the **Son** and believes in him should
AP : 04 :310(155) [0207] "This is my beloved **Son**, with whom I am well
AP : 04 :345(160) [0217] "God sent the **Son** into the world, not to condemn the
AP : 04 :356(161) [0217] (John 3:36), "He who believes in the **Son** has eternal life."
AP : 04 :366(163) [0221] into the kingdom of God's **Son**," as Paul says (Col. 1:13),
AP : 12 :062(191) [0269] believed in the testimony that God has borne to his **Son**."
AP : 12 :160(208) [0303] for this God has another price, the death of his **Son**.
AP : 21 :018(231) [0347] "That all may honor the **Son**, even as they honor the
S1 : 01 :000(291) [0461] 1. That Father, **Son**, and Holy Spirit, three distinct
S1 : 01 :000(291) [0461] begotten by no one, the **Son** was begotten by the Father,
S1 : 01 :000(291) [0461] the Holy Spirit proceeded from the Father and the **Son**.
S1 : 01 :000(291) [0461] 3. That only the **Son** became man, and neither the Father
S1 : 01 :000(291) [0461] 4. That the **Son** became man in this manner: he was
S2 : 02 :007(294) [0465] the Lamb of God and the **Son** of God who takes away
TR : 00 :025(324) [0511] when he declared Jesus to be the Christ, the **Son** of God.
TR : 00 :028(325) [0511] than "You are the Christ, the **Son** of the living God"?
TR : 00 :029(325) [0513] that he should say, 'You are the **Son** of the living God.'
SC : 02 :003(345) [0545] *in Jesus Christ, his only son, our Lord: who was*
SC : 04 :004(348) [0551] of the Father and of the **Son** and of the Holy Spirit."
SC : 05 :028(351) [0555] name of the Father and of the **Son** and of the Holy Spirit.
SC : 07 :001(352) [0557] name of God, the Father, the **Son**, and the Holy Spirit.
SC : 07 :002(352) [0557] Father, through thy dear **Son** Jesus Christ, that Thou
SC : 07 :004(353) [0559] name of God, the Father, the **Son**, and the Holy Spirit.
SC : 07 :005(353) [0559] Father, through thy dear **Son** Jesus Christ, that Thou
LC : SP :012(363) [0577] in Jesus Christ, his only **Son**, our Lord: who was
LC : SP :021(364) [0579] of the Father and of the **Son** and of the Holy Spirit"
LC : 02 :006(411) [0679] creation; the second, of the **Son**, redemption; the third, of
LC : 02 :007(411) [0679] me; I believe in God the **Son**, who redeemed me; I believe
LC : 02 :024(413) [0683] treasures through his **Son** and the Holy Spirit, as we shall
LC : 02 :025(413) [0683] *in Jesus Christ, his only* ***Son****, our Lord: who was*
LC : 02 :027(414) [0685] that Jesus Christ, true **Son** of God, has become my Lord."
LC : 02 :029(414) [0685] until this only and eternal **Son** of God, in his
LC : 02 :036(415) [0687] is called Creator and the **Son** is called Redeemer, so on
LC : 02 :037(415) [0687] Answer: Just as the **Son** obtains dominion by purchasing
LC : 02 :064(419) [0695] earth, he has given us his **Son** and his Holy Spirit, through
LC : 03 :051(426) [0711] namely, that God sent his **Son**, Christ our Lord, into the
LC : 04 :004(437) [0733] *of the Father and of the* ***Son*** *and of the Holy Spirit."*
EP : 01 :005(466) [0781] Furthermore, the **Son** of God assumed into the unity of
EP : 05 :009(479) [0803] and death of Christ, the **Son** of God, is an earnest and
EP : 06 :002(480) [0805] have been redeemed by the **Son** of God precisely that they

Continued ▶

E P : 0 7 :012(483) [0811] no angel, but only Mary's **Son**, is so set down at the right
E P : 0 8 :005(487) [0819] not two Christs, one the **Son** of God and the other the
E P : 0 8 :005(487) [0819] of God and the other the **Son** of man, but a single
E P : 0 8 :005(487) [0819] individual is both the **Son** of God and the Son of man
E P : 0 8 :005(487) [0819] the Son of God and the **Son** of man (Luke 1:35;
E P : 0 8 :011(488) [0821] could the man, Mary's **son**, truly be called or be God, or
E P : 0 8 :011(488) [0821] be called or be God, or the **Son** of the most high God, if
E P : 0 8 :011(488) [0821] and truly united with the **Son** of God and hence really
E P : 0 8 :012(488) [0821] mere man but the veritable **Son** of God; for this reason
E P : 0 8 :013(488) [0821] and communion with the **Son** of God that it has become
E P : 0 8 :014(488) [0821] 9. Therefore the **Son** of God has truly suffered for us, but
E P : 0 8 :015(488) [0821] teach, and confess that the **Son** of man according to his
E P : 0 8 :015(488) [0821] was personally united with the **Son** of the Most High.
E P : 0 8 :020(490) [0823] one person, but that the **Son** of God is one person and the
E P : 0 8 :020(490) [0823] God is one person and the **Son** of man another, as
E P : 0 8 :026(490) [0823] words when we say that the **Son** of God died for the sins
E P : 0 8 :026(490) [0823] of the world or that the **Son** of man has become almighty.
E P : 0 8 :031(491) [0825] and that in the passion the **Son** of God had no
E P : 0 8 :033(491) [0825] 14. That the **Son** of God who assumed the human nature,
E P : 1 1 :013(496) [0835] who acknowledge his **Son**, Christ, and truly believe on
E P : 1 2 :029(500) [0843] belonging to the Father, **Son**, and Holy Spirit, but as God
E P : 1 2 :029(500) [0843] but as God the Father, **Son**, and Holy Spirit are three
S D : 0 1 :039(515) [0871] that through his beloved **Son** he might cleanse it from sin,
S D : 0 1 :043(515) [0873] of Scripture that God's **Son** assumed our nature, though
S D : 0 1 :044(516) [0873] Since, however, God's **Son** assumed our nature, but not
S D : 0 2 :009(522) [0883] or hear the Gospel of the **Son** of God and the promise of
S D : 0 2 :011(522) [0885] and life, unless the **Son** of God has liberated him from the
S D : 0 2 :014(523) [0885] up everything, what the **Son** of God says remains eternally
S D : 0 2 :015(523) [0887] sin and death through his **Son**, and for having reborne
S D : 0 2 :026(526) [0891] the Father except the **Son** and any one to whom the Son
S D : 0 2 :026(526) [0891] and any one to whom the **Son** chooses to reveal him"
S D : 0 2 :049(530) [0901] world that he gave his only **Son**, that whoever believes on
S D : 0 2 :050(530) [0901] Gospel of his eternal **Son**, our only Saviour and
S D : 0 2 :050(531) [0901] of their sins and true faith in the **Son** of God, Jesus Christ
S D : 0 2 :051(531) [0901] concerning his beloved **Son** and concerning all who in his
S D : 0 3 :002(539) [0917] the true, natural, essential **Son** of God, who through faith
S D : 0 3 :054(548) [0935] that God the Father, **Son**, and Holy Spirit, who is the
S D : 0 3 :054(549) [0935] of God the Father, **Son**, and Holy Spirit, who impels
S D : 0 3 :056(549) [0935] Likewise, if the **Son** of God had not become man, the
S D : 0 3 :057(550) [0935] "the blood of Jesus, his **Son**, cleanses us from all sin"
S D : 0 4 :018(554) [0943] spirit by those whom the **Son** of God has set free.
S D : 0 5 :004(559) [0953] beginning of the Gospel of Jesus Christ, the **Son** of God."
S D : 0 5 :012(560) [0955] sin than the passion and death of Christ, his own **Son**?
S D : 0 5 :020(561) [0959] the Gospel is this, that the **Son** of God, Christ our Lord,
S D : 0 5 :023(562) [0959] likewise, of David's **son**, who should restore the kingdom
S D : 0 6 :002(564) [0963] have been liberated by the **Son** of God, have become his
S D : 0 7 :045(577) [0987] truthful, and almighty **Son** of God, Jesus Christ, our
S D : 0 7 :070(582) [0997] whoever believes on the **Son** of God, be his faith strong or
S D : 0 8 :006(592) [1017] confess that although the **Son** of God is a separate,
S D : 0 8 :007(592) [1017] in time into the unity of the person of the **Son** of God.
S D : 0 8 :011(593) [1019] person of Christ, or the **Son** of God who has assumed
S D : 0 8 :020(595) [1021] sin of the world, but the **Son** of God himself has truly
S D : 0 8 :024(595) [1023] being who is truly the **Son** of the most high God, as the
S D : 0 8 :029(597) [1025] both natures in Christ, the way Jesus, the **son** of Mary, is.
S D : 0 8 :037(598) [1027] Thus, for example, "the **Son** was descended from David
S D : 0 8 :042(599) [1029] and therefore it is correct to say: the **Son** of God suffers.
S D : 0 8 :042(599) [1029] For the **Son** of God truly is crucified for us — that is, this
S D : 0 8 :045(600) [1031] Creed teaches us that the **Son** of God, who was made
S D : 0 8 :058(602) [1035] to Christ because he is the **Son** of Man and inasmuch as
S D : 0 8 :059(602) [1035] terms of the person of the **Son** of Man, but expressly
S D : 0 8 :059(602) [1035] "The blood of Jesus his **Son** cleanses us from all sin"
S D : 0 8 :061(602) [1035] from eternity to the **Son** according to the divine nature so
S D : 0 8 :067(604) [1039] of the divine nature of the **Son** of God, is to be ascribed
S D : 0 8 :067(604) [1039] in the person of the **Son** of Man only according to his
S D : 0 8 :071(605) [1041] nature and essence of the **Son** of God, as when water,
S D : 0 8 :072(605) [1041] to Christ, his beloved **Son**, according to the assumed
S D : 0 8 :073(605) [1041] never separated from the **Son**), it follows that through
S D : 0 8 :073(605) [1041] to the flesh that is personally united with the **Son** of God.
S D : 0 8 :075(606) [1043] who taught that the **Son**, the Father's Word, indeed
S D : 0 8 :082(607) [1045] For if he was the **Son** of God, he had to be in his mother's
S D : 0 8 :085(608) [1047] our calendar Jesus the **son** of Mary is 1543 years old this
S D : 0 8 :085(608) [1047] person this man, Mary's **son**, is and is called the almighty
S D : 0 8 :085(608) [1047] me, Jesus of Nazareth, Mary's **son**, born a human being.
S D : 0 8 :085(608) [1047] says, 'He is designated the **Son** of God in power'
S D : 0 8 :093(609) [1049] alone, with which the **Son** of God had no communion
S D : 0 9 :001(610) [1051] in the Lord Christ, God's **Son**, who died, was buried, and
S D : 1 1 :027(620) [1071] the king invites to his **son**'s wedding he calls through the
S D : 1 1 :028(620) [1071] world" and gave to it his only begotten **Son** (John 3:16).
S D : 1 1 :049(624) [1079] elect to "the image of his **Son**," and that in each case the
S D : 1 1 :065(627) [1083] says, "This is my beloved **Son** with whom I am well
S D : 1 1 :066(627) [1085] Trinity, God the Father, **Son**, and Holy Spirit, directs all
S D : 1 1 :067(627) [1085] Christ, "the only begotten **Son**, who is in the bosom of
S D : 1 1 :067(627) [1085] that everyone who sees the **Son** and believes in him should
S D : 1 1 :076(629) [1087] of either the Father or the **Son** that any one should refuse
S D : 1 2 :037(636) [1103] essence of the Father, **Son**, and Holy Spirit, but that, as
S D : 1 2 :037(636) [1103] distinct persons, Father, **Son**, and Holy Spirit, so also

Son (9) (*Other than Jesus Christ*), Sons (16)
A P : 0 4 :196(134) [0175] Because faith makes us **sons** of God, moreover, it also
A P : 0 4 :196(134) [0175] which makes us **sons** of God and co-heirs with Christ, we
A P : 0 4 :209(135) [0177] The people heard that Abraham had offered up his **son**.
A P : 0 4 :209(135) [0177] And so they put their **sons** to death in order by this cruel
A P : 0 4 :209(136) [0179] did not offer up his **son** with the idea that this work was a
A P : 0 4 :356(161) [0217] at the same time makes us **sons** of God and fellow heirs
A P : 0 7 :016(171) [0231] the devil "is now at work in the **sons** of disobedience."
A P : 0 7 :019(171) [0233] "the good seed means the **sons** of the kingdom, the weeds
A P : 0 7 :019(171) [0233] of the kingdom, the weeds are the **sons** of the evil one."
A P : 1 2 :161(208) [0303] would be humiliated by his **son**, why did he carry out the
A P : 2 2 :010(237) [0359] mention the case of Eli's **sons**; after the loss of the high
A P : 2 2 :010(237) [0361] when they apply the story of Eli's **sons** to the sacrament.
A P : 2 4 :034(256) [0395] "And he will purify the **sons** of Levi and refine them like
A P : 2 4 :034(256) [0395] The offerings of the **sons** of Levi (that is, of those who
A P : 2 7 :049(277) [0437] of Abraham to sacrifice his **son**, are not for us to imitate.
S C : 0 5 :020(350) [0553] are a father or mother, a **son** or daughter, a master or
L C : 0 3 :009(421) [0699] It would be improper for a **son** to say to his father:
S D : 0 2 :063(533) [0905] all who are led by the Spirit of God are **sons** of God."
S D : 0 4 :032(556) [0947] of God is coming upon the **sons** of disobedience"
S D : 0 6 :009(565) [0965] you are illegitimate children and not **sons**" (Heb. 12:8).
S D : 0 7 :046(577) [0987] words about offering up his **son**, because these words
S D : 1 1 :005(617) [1065] us in love to be his **sons** through Jesus Christ" (Eph. 1:4,
S D : 1 1 :072(628) [1087] father among you, if his **son** asks for a fish, will instead
S D : 1 1 :087(631) [1093] us in love to be his **son** through Jesus Christ, according to
S D : 1 2 :031(635) [1101] God seals the adoption of **sons** and works regeneration.

Sonship (1)
S D : 0 3 :032(545) [0927] God and is adopted to **sonship** and the inheritance of

Sondershausen (1)
P R : P R :027(015) [0025] John Guenther, count of Schwarzburg [-**Sondershausen**]

Song (1)
L C : 0 1 :084(376) [0605] God's Word and then praise God with **song** and prayer.

Soon (12), Sooner (3)
A G : 1 9 :000(041) [0053] and of all ungodly men; as **soon** as God withdraws his
A L : 2 3 :017(054) [0063] that the churches will **soon** be lacking in pastors if
A P : 0 4 :270(147) [0197] a man keeps the law as **soon** as he hears that God is
A P : 2 7 :007(269) [0421] Without doubt, God will **soon** avenge these murders.
S 1 : P R :013(291) [0459] crosiers, and similar nonsense would **soon** be forgotten.
S 3 : 0 3 :018(306) [0483] in this fashion would **sooner** have laughed than wept,
S 3 : 0 3 :019(306) [0485] before the priest, the **sooner** and the better he would
L C : 0 1 :134(383) [0619] it is that he will perish **sooner** and never be happy in life.
L C : 0 1 :186(390) [0633] which, if they came true, would **soon** put an end to him.
L C : 0 1 :224(395) [0643] gallows, the world would **soon** be empty, and there would
L C : 0 1 :239(397) [0649] well regulated, such insolence might **soon** be checked.
L C : 0 3 :046(426) [0709] is simple and clear as **soon** as we understand the
S D : 0 2 :065(534) [0907] this it follows that as **soon** as the Holy Spirit has initiated
S D : 1 0 :015(613) [1057] As **soon** as this article is weakened and human
S D : 1 1 :064(626) [1083] revealed Word of God, as **soon** as he comes to the point

Soothing (1)
L C : 0 5 :068(454) [0769] as a pure, wholesome, **soothing** medicine which aids and

Sophist (2), Sophistic (1), Sophistically (2), Sophistries (1), Sophistry (6), Sophists (9)
A G : 0 1 :006(028) [0043] only one person and **sophistically** assert that the other
A P : P R :015(099) [0101] not taken up all their **sophistries**, for this would be an
A P : 0 2 :002(100) [0105] This **sophistry** is easy to refute.
A P : 0 2 :032(104) [0113] been obscured by the **sophistic** arguments of modern
A P : 0 4 :109(123) [0153] they have thought up a piece of **sophistry** to evade them.
A P : 0 4 :283(150) [0201] twist his meaning by **sophistically** transferring the
A P : 0 4 :304(154) [0205] Some **sophist** may quibble here that righteousness is in
A P : 0 4 :336(159) [0215] Look how this childish **sophistry** delights our opponents!
A P : 1 2 :009(184) [0255] they are not so separated as these clever **sophists** imagine.
A P : 1 2 :123(200) [0289] destroy these wicked **sophists** who so sinfully twist the
A P : 1 2 :123(201) [0289] This is not logic or even **sophistry**, but sheer dishonesty.
A P : 1 2 :124(201) [0289] turning over to these **sophists** such an important
A P : 1 2 :124(201) [0289] than in that of the **sophists** who wrote the Confutation.
A P : 2 1 :001(229) [0343] do they expend so much **sophistry**, but all they manage to
A P : 2 7 :068(280) [0443] He talks about faith differently from the **sophists**.
S 3 : 0 3 :009(304) [0481] false repentance of the **sophists** with true repentance so
S 3 : 0 3 :012(305) [0481] Such repentance the **sophists** divided into three parts —
S 3 : 0 3 :012(305) [0483] teaching of penance the **sophists** thus instructed the
S 3 : 0 6 :002(311) [0493] specious learning of the **sophists** and the Council of
S 3 : 0 6 :005(311) [0493] no regard for the subtle **sophistry** of those who teach that
S D : 0 1 :060(519) [0879] no papist, no **sophist**, indeed, no human reason, be it ever

Sorcerer (1), Sorcerers (2), Sorcery (1)
A P : 2 1 :034(234) [0353] magical power, just as **sorcerers** imagine that horoscopes
A P : 2 1 :036(234) [0353] for having been a **sorcerer**; Augustine experienced the
L C : 0 1 :012(366) [0583] lost possessions, etc., as magicians and **sorcerers** do.
L C : 0 5 :075(455) [0771] licentiousness, idolatry, **sorcery**, enmity, strife, jealousy,

Sorely (10)
A L : 2 6 :002(064) [0071] to merit grace and **sorely** terrified the consciences of those
A L : 2 6 :015(066) [0073] affairs, and the consolation of **sorely** tried consciences.
A P : P R :017(099) [0103] articles of Christian doctrine that the church **sorely** needs.
A P : 1 2 :031(186) [0259] My soul also is **sorely** troubled.
A P : 1 2 :049(188) [0265] Lord has chastened me **sorely**, but he has not given me
A P : 1 5 :027(219) [0323] consciences are **sorely** troubled because they cannot keep
S C : 0 5 :029(351) [0555] heavily burdened or who are distressed and **sorely** tried.
L C : 0 3 :086(432) [0723] world among people who **sorely** vex us and give us
L C : 0 5 :027(449) [0759] when our heart feels too **sorely** pressed, this comfort of
S D : 1 1 :059(626) [1083] God's Word and often **sorely** grieve the Holy Spirit.

Sorites (1)
A P : 0 4 :360(162) [0219] out, dear reader, you have not yet heard the whole **sorites**.

Sorrow (14), Sorrowful (2), Sorrowing (3), Sorrows (4)
A G : 1 2 :003(034) [0049] to have contrition and **sorrow**, or terror, on account of
A P : 0 4 :009(108) [0123] that is, if reason in its **sorrow** over sin elicits an act of
A P : 0 4 :030(111) [0129] them with a Christian's **sorrow**—'You are severed from
A P : 1 2 :034(186) [0261] They say that by these **sorrows** and terrors men merit
A P : 1 2 :048(188) [0265] is understood only amid genuine **sorrows** and terrors.
A P : 1 2 :049(188) [0265] "My soul melts away for **sorrow**; strengthen me according
A P : 1 2 :131(202) [0291] True terrors and **sorrows** of the soul do not permit the
A P : 1 2 :148(205) [0299] of the body which follows true **sorrow** in the mind.
A P : 1 2 :149(205) [0299] which David says, "The **sorrows** of death encompassed
A P : 2 4 :091(266) [0415] the bitterest kind of **sorrow** must seize all the faithful if
S 3 : 0 3 :002(304) [0479] *passiva contritio* (true **sorrow** of the heart, suffering, and
S 3 : 0 3 :018(306) [0483] law or vainly vexed with a **sorrowful** spirit by the devil.
S C : 0 3 :020(348) [0549] take us from this world of **sorrow** to himself in heaven.
S C : 0 4 :012(349) [0551] be drowned by daily **sorrow** and repentance and be put to
L C : P R :001(358) [0567] For we see to our **sorrow** that many pastors and
L C : 0 1 :247(398) [0651] who watches over poor, **sorrowful** hearts, and he will not
S D : 0 2 :054(531) [0903] terror, contrition, and **sorrow** in his heart, and through
S D : 0 3 :026(543) [0923] without contrition and **sorrow** and have a wicked

Continued ▶

SD : 0 5 :015(561) [0957] and teach contrition and **sorrow** not from the law but
SD : 0 7 :044(577) [0987] a comfort for all **sorrowing** hearts, and a true bond and
SD : 0 7 :068(582) [0997] true contrition and **sorrow** for their sins, without true
SD : 1 1 :090(631) [1093] This doctrine gives **sorrowing** and tempted people the
SD : 1 1 :091(631) [1093] gracious election that **sorrowing** Christians can find no

Sorry (10)
AP : 1 2 :029(185) [0259] as to when we are **sorry** because we love God and when
AP : 1 2 :029(185) [0259] God's wrath against sin and is **sorry** that it has sinned.
AP : 1 2 :032(186) [0259] of sin and is genuinely **sorry** that it has sinned; at the
AP : 1 2 :091(196) [0279] by a person who is **sorry**, punishing in himself what he is
AP : 1 2 :091(196) [0279] punishing in himself what he is **sorry** for having done."
AP : 1 2 :141(204) [0295] We are very **sorry** to have to list these silly opinions of
AP : 1 2 :169(209) [0305] on stealing is not really **sorry** that he has stolen or
S3 : 0 3 :017(305) [0483] was unable to repent or be **sorry** for his sin (which might
SC : 0 5 :022(350) [0553] For all this I am **sorry** and pray for grace.
SD : 0 5 :008(559) [0953] one's sins, to feel heartily **sorry** for them, and to desist

Sort (31), Sorts (12)
PR : PR :003(003) [0007] over against both the papacy and all **sorts** of factions.
PR : PR :014(007) [0013] Word of God against all **sorts** of perilous
AG : 2 0 :019(043) [0055] their own efforts, and all **sorts** of works were undertaken.
AG : 2 3 :006(052) [0061] upright, and honorable **sort** of conduct has resulted in
AG : 2 4 :010(057) [0065] known, by turning it into a **sort** of fair, by buying and
AG : 2 4 :029(059) [0067] and obtain grace and all **sorts** of benefits from God, not
AG : 2 7 :027(075) [0079] first ascertaining whether a vow is of the proper **sort**?
AL : 2 6 :005(064) [0071] other than works of this **sort**; it is faith which believes
AL : 2 6 :039(069) [0075] foods as if works of this **sort** were necessary acts of
AL : 2 8 :057(091) [0091] Of the same **sort** is the observance of Sunday, Easter,
AL : 0 0 :003(095) [0095] passed over matters of this **sort** so that the chief points at
AP : PR :017(099) [0103] they lay hidden under all **sorts** of dangerous opinions in
AP : 0 4 :015(109) [0123] had come to give some **sort** of laws by which we could
AP : 1 2 :067(192) [0271] hold this faith be put to death with all **sorts** of cruelties.
AP : 1 2 :067(192) [0271] this we can judge what **sort** of church it is that is made up
AP : 1 2 :091(196) [0279] Again, "Penitence is a **sort** of revenge by a person who is
AP : 1 2 :171(209) [0305] was enough for the **sort** of public or formal penitence
AP : 1 3 :005(212) [0309] by the eyes and is a **sort** of picture of the Word, signifying
AP : 1 4 :002(214) [0315] forsake and condemn the **sort** of doctrine we have
AP : 1 5 :025(218) [0321] has deceived men, all **sorts** of troubles follow.
AP : 2 1 :034(234) [0353] they contained some **sort** of magical power, just as
AP : 2 3 :050(246) [0377] seem to have gone astray through some **sort** of religion.
AP : 2 4 :041(257) [0399] Experience shows the **sort** of tyrants who rule the church.
AP : 2 4 :052(259) [0403] priests, it must also have some **sort** of sacrifice for sins.
AP : 2 4 :070(262) [0409] while the ceremony is a **sort** of picture or "seal," as Paul
AP : 2 4 :075(263) [0411] many statements of this **sort** in the Fathers, all of which
AP : 2 4 :090(266) [0415] Now we shall pass over the **sort** of proofs our opponents
AP : 2 4 :090(266) [0415] have for purgatory, the **sort** of penalties they suppose
S2 : 0 2 :026(297) [0469] of need, and attribute all **sorts** of help to them, assigning
S3 : 1 1 :001(314) [0499] they gave occasion for all **sorts** of horrible, abominable,
LC : 0 1 :017(367) [0585] it did not establish and maintain some **sort** of worship.
LC : 0 1 :062(373) [0597] conjure, and, in short, to practice wickedness of any **sort**.
LC : 0 1 :108(380) [0611] there must be this **sort** of inequality and proper
LC : 0 1 :224(395) [0643] of our neighbor in any **sort** of dealing that results in loss
LC : 0 1 :305(406) [0667] That **sort** of thing undoubtedly was quite prevalent in the
LC : 0 2 :017(412) [0681] misfortune, warding off all **sorts** of danger and disaster.
LC : 0 3 :045(426) [0709] uses God's name for any **sort** of wrong profanes and
LC : 0 5 :050(452) [0765] inner life and reflect: "See what **sort** of Christian I am!
LC : 0 5 :051(452) [0765] men can easily sense what **sort** of Christians we were
SD : 0 1 :013(511) [0863] blindness, and drives them headlong into all **sorts** of vice.
SD : 0 4 :029(555) [0947] confession against all **sorts** of corruptions and
SD : 0 8 :019(594) [1021] introduced thereby any **sort** of blending or equalization
SD : 1 1 :009(618) [1065] or that he merely held a **sort** of military muster: This one

Soul (82), Souls (39)
PR : PR :008(006) [0011] for the salvation of their **souls** and their eternal welfare to
PR : PR :022(012) [0021] of the danger to their **souls** and to warn them against it,
AG : 0 0 :001(047) [0059] not wish to put our own **souls** and consciences in grave
AG : 2 7 :026(075) [0079] dispensations be granted for necessities of men's **souls**!
AG : 2 8 :011(082) [0085] power does not protect the **soul**, but with the sword and
AL : 2 8 :011(082) [0085] The state protects not **souls** but bodies and goods from
AL : 2 8 :011(082) [0085] while the Gospel protects **souls** from heresies, the devil,
AP : 0 2 :019(103) [0111] it, Ambrose says, "That **soul** is not in the image of God in
AP : 0 2 :027(104) [0113] this, the inordinate disposition of the parts of the **soul**.
AP : 0 4 :058(115) [0137] quotes the promise: "My **soul** waits for his word, my soul
AP : 0 4 :058(115) [0137] waits for his word, my **soul** hopes in the Lord," that is,
AP : 0 4 :106(122) [0153] under this fear, the **soul** by faith flees to the mercy of
AP : 0 4 :354(161) [0217] of your faith you obtain the salvation of your **souls**."
AP : 0 4 :392(167) [0225] of Christ has remained with some faithful **souls**.
AP : 1 2 :026(185) [0259] keys, through indulgences, **souls** are delivered from
AP : 1 2 :031(186) [0259] My **soul** also is sorely troubled.
AP : 1 2 :049(188) [0265] Ps. 119:28, "My **soul** melts away for sorrow; strengthen
AP : 1 2 :131(202) [0291] terrors and sorrows of the **soul** do not permit the
AP : 1 2 :136(203) [0293] passages command that **souls** should be punished in
AP : 1 2 :167(209) [0305] or a satisfaction, but the cleansing of imperfect **souls**.
AP : 1 2 :175(210) [0307] misinterpreted as a liberation of **souls** from purgatory.
AP : 2 1 :027(232) [0349] church, does she receive **souls** in death, does she
AP : 2 1 :035(234) [0353] Gospel, must be strong of **soul** because they have to
AP : 2 3 :051(246) [0377] approving a burden that has destroyed so many **souls**.
AP : 2 4 :064(261) [0407] it to the dead and free **souls** from purgatorial punishment
AP : 2 4 :077(263) [0411] of sins for them or to free the **souls** of the dead.
AP : 2 4 :089(265) [0413] the ceremony to free the **souls** of the dead, from which
S1 : PR :003(289) [0455] Christendom lost and all **souls** damned rather than suffer
S1 : PR :006(289) [0457] If one does not, many **souls** that might have been saved
S1 : PR :015(291) [0459] us, poor and wretched **souls** who cry unto Thee and
S2 : 0 2 :012(294) [0465] common week, with All **Souls'** Day, and with soul-baths
S2 : 0 2 :012(295) [0465] All Souls' Day, and with **soul**-baths that the Mass was
S2 : 0 2 :012(295) [0465] Christ alone, and not the work of man, can help **souls**.
S2 : 0 2 :014(295) [0467] in Masses which are offered for **souls** in purgatory, etc.
S2 : 0 4 :014(301) [0475] destruction of body and **soul** are characteristic of his
S3 : 0 1 :011(303) [0479] the body and not for the **soul** inasmuch as the soul would
S3 : 0 1 :011(303) [0479] the **soul** inasmuch as the soul would be sound and only
S3 : 0 3 :026(307) [0487] In time **souls** got to be so cheap that they were released at
S3 : 0 3 :027(307) [0487] nobody knew which **soul** was in purgatory, and nobody
TR : 0 0 :040(327) [0517] this life but also the jurisdiction over **souls** after this life.
TR : 0 0 :048(328) [0519] from the glory of God and bring destruction to **souls**.
TR : 0 0 :051(329) [0519] of worship, and countless **souls** are lost generation after
TR : 0 0 :052(329) [0519] embraced for the glory of God and the salvation of **souls**.
SC : 0 2 :002(345) [0543] still sustains my body and **soul**, all my limbs and senses,
SC : 0 3 :020(348) [0549] whether it affect body or **soul**, property or reputation,
SC : 0 7 :002(352) [0557] hands I commend my body and **soul** and all that is mine.
SC : 0 7 :005(353) [0559] hands I commend my body and **soul** and all that is mine.
SC : 0 9 :003(355) [0561] keeping watch over your **souls**, as men who will have to
LC : PR :008(359) [0569] office and the people's **souls**, yes, even God and his
LC : 0 1 :053(372) [0595] himself, swearing by God's name or by his own **soul**.
LC : 0 1 :068(374) [0599] they miserably perished, body, **soul**, and possessions.
LC : 0 1 :073(374) [0601] each day to God — our **soul** and body, wife, children,
LC : 0 1 :128(382) [0617] how many blessings of body and **soul** he bestows upon us.
LC : 0 1 :161(387) [0627] who watch over their **souls** and to treat them well and
LC : 0 1 :188(390) [0635] all people in body and **soul**, especially toward him who
LC : 0 2 :013(412) [0681] sustains my body, **soul**, and life, my members great and
LC : 0 2 :022(413) [0683] and ears, hands, body and **soul**, money and property, and
LC : 0 4 :015(438) [0735] then babble, "How can a handful of water help the **soul**?"
LC : 0 4 :044(442) [0743] be saved and have eternal life, both in **soul** and body."
LC : 0 4 :045(442) [0743] the Word is spoken so that the **soul** may grasp it.
LC : 0 4 :046(442) [0743] one Baptism, body and **soul** shall be saved and live
LC : 0 4 :046(442) [0743] saved and live forever: the **soul** through the Word in
LC : 0 4 :046(442) [0743] it is united with the **soul** and apprehends Baptism in the
LC : 0 4 :046(442) [0743] can adorn our body and **soul** than Baptism, for through
LC : 0 5 :023(449) [0757] called the food of the **soul** since it nourishes and
LC : 0 5 :042(451) [0763] or compelled, lest we institute a new slaughter of **souls**.
LC : 0 5 :068(454) [0769] which aids and quickens us in both **soul** and body.
LC : 0 5 :068(454) [0769] For where the **soul** is healed, the body has benefited also.
LC : 0 5 :084(456) [0773] to trap and destroy you, **soul** and body, so that you
LC : 0 6 :015(459) [0000] my sin and desire comfort and restoration for my **soul**.
LC : 0 6 :017(459) [0000] and bitter, to the manifest harm and destruction of **souls**.
LC : 0 6 :033(461) [0000] for flowing streams, so longs my **soul** for thee, O God."
EP : RN :005(465) [0777] and the salvation of their **souls**, we subscribe Dr. Luther's
EP : 0 1 :001(466) [0779] being (that is, his rational **soul** in its highest form and
EP : 0 1 :001(466) [0779] nature, essence, body, and **soul** on the one hand, and
EP : 0 1 :004(466) [0781] only created the body and **soul** of Adam and Eve before
EP : 0 1 :004(466) [0781] but also our bodies and **souls** after the Fall, even though
EP : 0 1 :008(467) [0781] survived in man's body or **soul**, in his inward or outward
EP : 0 2 :014(471) [0789] especially the rational **soul**, and that in conversion and
EP : 0 2 :014(471) [0789] he creates out of nothing a new essence of the **soul**.
EP : 0 3 :009(474) [0795] or the salvation of their **souls**, but they must regard it as
EP : 0 8 :009(488) [0819] iron and the union of body and **soul** in man.
EP : 0 8 :023(490) [0823] nature with a body and a **soul**, as Marcion imagined.
EP : 0 9 :001(492) [0827] only according to the **soul**, or only according to the deity,
EP : 0 9 :001(492) [0827] or according to body and **soul**, spiritually or corporeally?
EP : 1 2 :030(500) [0843] if they dearly love their **soul's** eternal welfare and
SD : 0 1 :001(508) [0859] (namely, his rational **soul** in its highest degree and
SD : 0 1 :002(508) [0859] (that is, man's body or **soul**), which even after the Fall are
SD : 0 1 :002(508) [0859] man's nature, in his body, **soul**, and all his powers, and
SD : 0 1 :002(509) [0859] is, between his body and **soul**, which are God's handiwork
SD : 0 1 :011(510) [0863] and foremost powers of the **soul** in mind, heart, and will.
SD : 0 1 :028(513) [0867] the proper essence, body, or **soul** of man or man himself.
SD : 0 1 :030(513) [0867] original sin in body and in **soul**, in all its powers from
SD : 0 1 :033(514) [0869] man, our body and **soul** or man himself created by God
SD : 0 1 :038(514) [0871] God is man's creator who creates body and **soul** for him.
SD : 0 1 :038(515) [0871] still sustains my body and **soul**, eyes, ears, and all my
SD : 0 1 :038(515) [0871] sustains my body, **soul**, and life, my members great and
SD : 0 1 :041(515) [0871] essence of our body and **soul** (which are corrupted by
SD : 0 1 :041(515) [0871] our nature, our body and **soul**, which would also
SD : 0 1 :042(515) [0871] that man has a body and **soul**; likewise, that it is God's
SD : 0 1 :046(516) [0873] have and keep precisely this **soul**, although without sin.
SD : 0 1 :047(516) [0873] our corrupted body and **soul** on the one hand and
SD : 0 1 :047(516) [0875] essence of our body and **soul**, we should have another
SD : 0 1 :047(516) [0875] substance or another **soul** since we there shall be without
SD : 0 1 :048(517) [0875] its essence, its body or **soul**, so that there is allegedly no
SD : 0 1 :051(517) [0875] the word "nature" means man's essence, body and **soul**.
SD : 0 1 :052(517) [0875] himself with the body and **soul** in which sin is and
SD : 0 2 :020(525) [0889] the salvation of his **soul**, man is like a pillar of salt, like
SD : 0 2 :081(537) [0911] and especially the rational **soul**, are completely destroyed
SD : 0 2 :081(537) [0911] and a new substance of the **soul** is created out of nothing.
SD : 0 2 :084(537) [0913] flesh wage war against the **soul**, and the law in our
SD : 0 3 :067(551) [0937] which the salvation of our **souls** depends, we direct him
SD : 0 4 :034(557) [0949] you obtain the salvation of your **souls**" (I Pet. 1:5, 9).
SD : 0 7 :048(578) [0989] Christ were spiritual bread or a spiritual food for the **soul**.
SD : 0 7 :115(589) [1011] of Christ with its merit is spiritual food for our **souls**).
SD : 0 8 :018(594) [1021] by analogies of the **soul** and the body and of glowing
SD : 0 8 :019(594) [1021] For the body and **soul**, as well as fire and iron, have a
SD : 0 8 :064(603) [1039] glory, and efficacy, as the **soul** does in the body and fire
SD : 1 0 :016(613) [1057] As he values his **soul's** welfare and salvation, every
SD : 1 0 :020(614) [1059] destruction of body and **soul** are characteristic of his
SD : 1 2 :039(636) [1103] as dearly as they love their **soul's** welfare and salvation.

Sound (18), Sounding (1), Soundly (3)
AP : 0 4 :293(152) [0203] with the Gospel, and any **sound** mind can grasp them.
AP : 1 8 :005(225) [0335] more often than their **sound** judgment, while the devil,
AP : 2 1 :043(235) [0357] have been killed and **sound** doctrine crushed, fanatical
AP : 2 1 :044(236) [0357] happened before, nor crush **sound** doctrine in the church.
AP : 2 1 :044(236) [0357] maintain and propagate **sound** doctrine and to defend
AP : 2 3 :026(243) [0371] they cloak it with pious-**sounding** phrases to give it a
S3 : 0 1 :011(303) [0479] as the soul would be **sound** and only the body would be
LC : PR :002(358) [0567] Themselves," "Sleep **Soundly**," "Prepared!" and
LC : 0 1 :175(389) [0631] We would also have **soundly** instructed citizens, virtuous
LC : 0 3 :076(431) [0721] house, home, and a **sound** body; to cause the grain and
EP : 0 1 :008(467) [0781] a corruption that nothing **sound** or uncorrupted has
EP : 0 2 :016(472) [0791] agree with the form of **sound** doctrine and that
EP : 0 4 :009(476) [0799] contrary to the pattern of **sound** words and terminology.
SD : PR :004(504) [0851] as it was correctly and **soundly** understood was drawn
SD : 0 1 :050(517) [0875] and keep the pattern of **sound** words, as the Holy
SD : 0 2 :086(538) [0913] conform to the form of **sound** doctrine but rather
SD : 0 4 :002(551) [0939] contrary to the form of **sound** doctrine and words which
SD : 0 4 :024(555) [0945] contrary to the pattern of **sound** words, like the Scripture
SD : 0 4 :036(557) [0949] maintain the pattern of **sound** words as well as the true

Continued ▶

SD : 0 7 :007(570) [0975] the way the letters **sound**, but as figurative speech.
SD : 0 7 :100(586) [1007] any space; a musical **sound** or tone passes through air or
SD : 0 8 :061(602) [1035] herein on the basis of **sound** passages of the Holy

Source (15), Sources (4)
AP : 0 4 :004(108) [0121] way of preface so that the **sources** of both kinds of
AP : 0 4 :156(128) [0165] honor of Christ and the **source** of sure and firm
AP : 0 4 :185(132) [0173] taken from the **sources**, will correct everything that seems
AP : 0 4 :306(154) [0207] (I Cor. 1:30), "He is the **source** of your life in Jesus
AP : 0 4 :388(166) [0225] we have pointed out the **sources** of this conflict and have
AP : 1 2 :005(183) [0253] of penitence nor the **source** of the peace of conscience.
AP : 2 1 :020(232) [0349] of merits are therefore the **sources** of trust in mercy.
S3 : 0 3 :019(306) [0483] his sins — an impossibility and the **source** of great torture.
S3 : 0 8 :009(313) [0497] old dragon, and it is the **source**, strength, and power of
LC : 0 1 :074(374) [0601] From the same **source** came the custom of children who
LC : 0 1 :187(390) [0633] to remove the root and **source** of this bitterness toward
LC : 0 1 :329(410) [0677] is the chief **source** and fountainhead from which all the
LC : 0 5 :022(449) [0757] be mine and may be a **source** of blessing to me as a sure
EP : 0 1 :021(468) [0785] our sinful seed and the **source** of all other, actual sins,
EP : 1 1 :004(494) [0833] wrong; the original **source** of this is the devil and man's
SD : 0 1 :001(508) [0859] of which, as the root and **source**, all other sins proceed.
SD : 0 4 :009(552) [0941] alone is the mother and **source** of the truly good and
SD : 0 7 :041(576) [0985] or better from any other **source** than from Dr. Luther's
SD : 1 1 :007(617) [1065] The **source** and cause of evil is not God's foreknowledge

Sovereign (1)
EP : 1 2 :015(499) [0841] feudal homage to his territorial **sovereign** or liege-lord.

Sowing (1), Sows (2)
AP : 0 4 :367(163) [0221] "He who **sows** sparingly will also reap sparingly, he who
AP : 0 4 :367(163) [0221] reap sparingly, he who **sows** bountifully will also reap
EP : 0 2 :006(470) [0787] and effort," our planting, **sowing**, and watering are in vain

Space (8)
SD : 0 7 :099(586) [1005] earth and vacated or occupied **space** according to his size.
SD : 0 7 :099(586) [1005] spirit dreams, for God is not a corporeal **space** or place.
SD : 0 7 :100(586) [1005] occupies nor vacates **space** but penetrates every creature,
SD : 0 7 :100(586) [1007] not occupy or vacate any **space**; a musical sound or tone
SD : 0 7 :100(586) [1007] occupies nor vacates **space**; likewise light and heat go
SD : 0 7 :100(586) [1007] occupying or vacating **space**, and many more like these.
SD : 0 7 :119(590) [1013] by a certain **space** in heaven that he is neither able nor
SD : 0 8 :083(607) [1045] follow from this that **space** and place had separated the

Spain (1)
AP : 1 2 :127(201) [0289] In Germany, England, **Spain**, France, Italy, even in Rome

Spalatin (2)
S3 : 1 5 :005(316) [0501] George **Spalatin**, of Altenburg, subscribed
TR : 0 0 :082(334) [0529] George **Spalatin**, of Altenburg, subscribed

Spare (4), Spared (4)
PR : PR :018(009) [0017] on our adversaries will **spare** us and our churches and
AG : 2 3 :021(055) [0063] all others should be **spared** — although this is done
AP : 2 3 :003(239) [0363] the barbarians reverently **spare**, and banish deserted
LC : 0 1 :172(388) [0629] leadership, we must **spare** no effort, time, and expense in
LC : 0 1 :304(406) [0667] forced to sacrifice what he cannot **spare** without injury.
EP : 0 1 :023(469) [0785] unlearned people, but simple folk should be **spared** them.
EP : 1 0 :005(493) [0829] weak in faith are to be **spared** (I Cor. 8:9-13;
SD : 0 1 :054(517) [0877] ought rightly be **spared** these terms in sermons, since they

Sparingly (2)
AP : 0 4 :367(163) [0221] "He who sows **sparingly** will also reap sparingly, he who
AP : 0 4 :367(163) [0221] sparingly will also reap **sparingly**, he who sows

Spark (4)
SD : 0 2 :007(521) [0883] to his conversion not a **spark** of spiritual powers has
SD : 0 2 :009(521) [0883] intellect still has a dim **spark** of the knowledge that there
SD : 0 2 :014(523) [0885] and discover a little **spark** and a longing for the grace of
SD : 0 2 :054(531) [0903] there is kindled in him a **spark** of faith which accepts the

Sparrows (1)
SD : 1 1 :004(617) [1063] as it is written, "Are not two **sparrows** sold for a penny?

Spatial (2)
EP : 0 7 :014(483) [0811] single mode which the philosophers call *local* or **spatial**."
SD : 0 7 :097(586) [1005] the one which the philosophers call local or **spatial**.

Spattered (1)
SD : 0 4 :008(552) [0941] they are sinful (that is, **spattered** with sins in the sight of

Spawned (2)
AP : 0 4 :391(167) [0225] falsehood, this teaching has **spawned** many errors.
AP : 1 3 :023(214) [0313] in the one using them, has **spawned** in the church.

Speak (70), Speaking (60), Speaks (33), Spoke (9), Spoken (42)
AG : 0 0 :000(023) [0037] Ps 119:46 "I will also **speak** of thy testimonies before
AG : 0 8 :001(033) [0047] church, properly **speaking**, is nothing else than the
AG : 1 2 :003(034) [0049] Properly **speaking**, true repentance is nothing else than to
AG : 1 9 :000(041) [0053] "When the devil lies, he **speaks** according to his own
AG : 2 0 :005(041) [0053] they have also learned to **speak** now of faith, about which
AG : 2 0 :023(044) [0055] show that the faith here **spoken** of is not that possessed
AG : 2 0 :025(044) [0057] indicated, the Scriptures **speak** of faith but do not mean
AG : 2 5 :003(061) [0069] or word of the man who **speaks** it, but it is the Word of
AG : 2 5 :003(062) [0069] who forgives sin, for it is **spoken** in God's stead and by
AG : 2 6 :035(069) [0075] Christ **speaks** of this in Luke 21:34, "Take heed to
AG : 2 7 :060(080) [0083] innovation of his time to **speak** of monastic life as a state
AG : 2 8 :041(087) [0089] reservation of guilt but **speaks** only about the reservation
AG : 2 8 :054(090) [0091] preachers should not all **speak** at once, but one after
AG : 0 0 :005(095) [0095] manifest and evident (to **speak** without boasting) that we
AL : 0 1 :006(028) [0043] since "Word" signifies a **spoken** word and "Spirit"
AL : 0 8 :001(033) [0047] Properly **speaking**, the church is the assembly of saints
AL : 1 2 :003(034) [0049] Properly **speaking**, repentance consists of these two
AL : 1 9 :000(041) [0053] "When the devil lies, he **speaks** according to his own
AL : 2 4 :035(060) [0067] private Masses but **speak** often of the common Mass.
AL : 2 8 :041(087) [0089] the canons themselves **speak** only of reserving
AP : 0 2 :036(105) [0115] Augustine **speaks** the same way when he says, "Sin is
AP : 0 4 :043(113) [0133] The Gospel is, strictly **speaking**, the promise of
AP : 0 4 :053(114) [0135] In **speaking** of justifying faith, therefore, we must
AP : 0 4 :061(115) [0137] think that we are **speaking** of an idle historical
AP : 0 4 :072(117) [0141] For Scripture **speaks** both ways.
AP : 0 4 :099(121) [0151] of which the apostles **speak** is not idle knowledge, but a
AP : 0 4 :124(124) [0157] We are not **speaking** of ceremonies, but of Decalogue, the
AP : 0 4 :142(126) [0161] faith of which we are **speaking**, moreover, has its
AP : 0 4 :221(137) [0181] to other texts that **speak** of faith they always add the
AP : 0 4 :226(138) [0183] passage, however, Paul **speaks** specifically about love to
AP : 0 4 :235(140) [0185] justifies, when Paul is **speaking** of unity and peace in the
AP : 0 4 :242(141) [0187] This text therefore **speaks** not of one's own sins but of
AP : 0 4 :243(141) [0189] reason that the apostles **speak** so often about this duty of
AP : 0 4 :246(142) [0189] that the works **spoken** of here are those that follow faith
AP : 0 4 :253(143) [0191] These words, **spoken** so simply, contain no error, but our
AP : 0 4 :259(145) [0193] Nor does the prophet **speak** of this one work alone, but
AP : 0 4 :262(145) [0195] language Daniel's words **speak** even more clearly about
AP : 0 4 :267(147) [0197] Daniel is not **speaking** about remission of punishment
AP : 0 4 :271(148) [0199] so mad as to deny that absolution is the **spoken** Gospel.
AP : 0 4 :306(154) [0207] righteousness, we must **speak** of righteousness in a
AP : 0 4 :308(155) [0207] We must **speak** technically because of certain carping
AP : 0 4 :310(155) [0207] About this worship Christ **speaks** in John 6:40, "This is
AP : 0 4 :322(157) [0209] **Speaking** of the works that saints perform after
AP : 0 4 :326(157) [0211] his righteousness, he is **speaking** of his cause against the
AP : 0 4 :342(159) [0215] Christ is **speaking** of that worthiness whereby God
AP : 0 4 :345(160) [0217] Properly **speaking**, the Gospel is the command to believe
AP : 0 4 :346(160) [0217] So whenever mercy is **spoken** of, faith in the promise
AP : 0 4 :349(160) [0217] The faith we **speak** of has its existence in penitence.
AP : 0 4 :352(161) [0217] This rebirth is, so to **speak**, the beginning of eternal life,
AP : 0 4 :371(164) [0221] the Scriptures do not **speak** of hypocrisy but of
AP : 0 4 :399(168) [0227] as unworthy of being **spoken** in such an assembly.
AP : 0 7 :006(169) [0229] criticize our description, which **speaks** of living members.
AP : 0 7 :016(171) [0231] of Christ, is, precisely **speaking**, the congregation of the
AP : 0 7 :019(171) [0233] Thus John **speaks** (Matt. 3:12) about the whole Jewish
AP : 0 7 :022(172) [0235] But the church, properly **speaking**, is that which has the
AP : 0 7 :022(172) [0235] they are not, properly **speaking**, the kingdom of Christ.
AP : 0 7 :029(173) [0237] On this issue we have **spoken** out clearly enough in our
AP : 1 1 :001(180) [0249] this whole issue we shall **speak** more fully a little later
AP : 1 2 :012(184) [0255] it is by divine right, they **speak** very coldly about
AP : 1 2 :031(186) [0259] Scripture **speaks** of these terrors, as in Ps. 38:4, 8, "For
AP : 1 2 :039(187) [0261] In **speaking** of faith, therefore, we also include absolution
AP : 1 2 :053(189) [0265] other of these works is **spoken** of throughout Scripture.
AP : 1 2 :094(196) [0281] For Tertullian **speaks** excellently about faith, dwelling
AP : 1 2 :109(198) [0283] But this does not **speak** of the specific confession to be
AP : 1 2 :119(200) [0287] Not even Peter Lombard **speaks** this way about
AP : 1 2 :137(203) [0293] Clearly Scripture is **speaking** about obligatory works,
AP : 1 2 :150(206) [0299] This certainly **speaks** of the most bitter punishments.
AP : 1 2 :176(210) [0307] It is of a spiritual kingdom that Christ is **speaking**.
AP : 1 3 :016(213) [0311] and thus given, so to **speak**, a more exalted position, this
AP : 1 9 :001(226) [0337] "When he lies, he **speaks** according to his own
AP : 2 3 :005(239) [0365] Our opponents will not **speak**, write, or act honestly,
AP : 2 3 :016(241) [0369] Hence Paul **speaks** of marriage as a remedy and
AP : 2 3 :045(245) [0375] therefore they have **spoken** contemptuously about
AP : 2 4 :028(254) [0393] Jer. 7:22, 23, "I did not **speak** to your fathers or command
AP : 2 4 :034(256) [0395] Thus Paul **speaks** in Rom. 15:16 of "the priestly service of
AP : 2 4 :075(263) [0411] The Fathers **speak** of a twofold effect, of the comfort for
AP : 2 4 :075(263) [0411] clearly require faith and **speak** of the appropriation of the
AP : 2 4 :093(267) [0417] But they **speak** not only of offering the body and blood
AP : 2 4 :094(267) [0417] We know that the ancients **spoke** of prayer for the dead.
AP : 2 7 :041(276) [0435] The fact that Christ **speaks** of leaving wife and children
S1 : PR :010(290) [0457] people cannot hear Christ **speak** to them as the true
S1 : PR :010(290) [0457] speak to them as the true shepherd **speaking** to his sheep.
S2 : 0 2 :002(293) [0463] papists, one would **speak** to them in the following friendly
S2 : 0 4 :016(301) [0477] but we ought rather **speak** as the angel spoke to the devil
S2 : 0 4 :016(301) [0477] rather speak as the angel **spoke** to the devil in Zechariah,
S3 : 0 3 :002(304) [0479] of which Jeremiah **speaks**, "Is not my word like a
S3 : 0 4 :000(310) [0491] grace: First, through the **spoken** word, by which the
S3 : 0 8 :003(312) [0495] concern the external, **spoken** Word, we must hold firmly
S3 : 0 8 :003(312) [0495] twist the Scriptures or **spoken** Word according to their
S3 : 0 8 :004(312) [0495] is above and contrary to the Scriptures or **spoken** Word.
S3 : 0 8 :006(312) [0495] the Scriptures or the **spoken** word of the apostles but
S3 : 0 8 :011(313) [0497] burning bush and the **spoken** word, and no prophet,
S3 : 0 8 :013(313) [0497] nor did he leap in his mother's womb until Mary **spoke**.
S3 : 0 8 :013(313) [0497] that when the prophets **spoke**, they did not prophesy by
S3 : 0 8 :013(313) [0497] not have moved them to **speak** while they were still
S3 : 0 8 :013(313) [0497] Peter says, because the Holy Spirit **spoke** through them.
TR : 0 0 :008(320) [0505] disputing when Christ **spoke** of his passion: Who was to
TR : 0 0 :023(324) [0511] And what is here **spoken** in the singular number ("I will
TR : 0 0 :024(324) [0511] arguments, for after **speaking** of the keys in Matt. 18:19,
TR : 0 0 :039(327) [0515] He **speaks** therefore of one who rules in the church and
TR : 0 0 :073(332) [0525] We have **spoken** of ordination, which is the one thing (as
TR : 0 0 :073(332) [0525] Nor is it necessary to **speak** about confirmation or the
SC : 0 1 :016(343) [0541] should apologize for him, **speak** well of him, and
SC : 0 5 :023(350) [0555] injured my neighbor by **speaking** evil of him, over
SC : 0 5 :024(350) [0555] On one occasion I also **spoke** indecently.
LC : PR :010(360) [0571] and words and to **speak**, sing, and meditate on them.
LC : 0 1 :038(369) [0591] They refuse to hear what is preached or **spoken** to them.
LC : 0 1 :041(370) [0591] be careful not to regard this as if it were **spoken** by man.
LC : 0 1 :055(372) [0595] Of this there is no need to **speak** further.
LC : 0 1 :077(375) [0603] we preach to children, we must also **speak** their language.
LC : 0 1 :106(379) [0611] modesty, directed (so to **speak**) toward a majesty hidden
LC : 0 1 :142(385) [0621] Christians who do not **speak** of our rulers in the same
LC : 0 1 :149(385) [0623] God **speaks** to you and demands obedience.
LC : 0 1 :167(388) [0629] commandment in which he **speaks** of father and mother.
LC : 0 1 :184(390) [0633] gives vent to his irritation and envy by **speaking** ill of you.
LC : 0 1 :206(393) [0639] and gives occasion to **speak** of it, let us carefully note,
LC : 0 1 :225(395) [0645] — for I am not **speaking** of what happens inadvertently
LC : 0 1 :258(399) [0653] Instead, they **speak** dishonestly with an eye to gaining
LC : 0 1 :264(400) [0655] tolerate having evil **spoken** of us; we want the golden
LC : 0 1 :264(400) [0655] Yet we cannot bear to hear the best **spoken** of others.
LC : 0 1 :269(401) [0657] God forbids you to **speak** evil about another even

Continued ▶

LC : 01 :270(401) [0657] But you say: "Why shouldn't I **speak** if it is the truth?"
LC : 01 :274(401) [0659] we are absolutely forbidden to **speak** evil of our neighbor.
LC : 01 :285(403) [0661] No one shall **speak** evil of him, whether truly or falsely,
LC : 01 :285(403) [0663] should use his tongue to **speak** only good of everyone, to
LC : 02 :049(417) [0691] To **speak** idiomatically, we ought to say "a community of
LC : 02 :061(419) [0695] on earth, through which he **speaks** and does all his work.
LC : 03 :041(425) [0709] men preach, teach, and **speak** in God's name anything
LC : 03 :044(425) [0709] blessings fail to teach, **speak**, and live as godly and
LC : 03 :113(435) [0729] The petition seems to be **speaking** of the devil as the sum
LC : 04 :001(436) [0733] It remains for us to **speak** of our two sacraments,
LC : 04 :020(439) [0737] In the same way we **speak** about the parental estate and
LC : 04 :030(440) [0739] No matter where he **speaks** — indeed, no matter for what
LC : 04 :030(440) [0739] or by what means he **speaks** — there faith must look and
LC : 04 :045(442) [0743] meanwhile the Word is **spoken** so that the soul may grasp
LC : 05 :013(448) [0755] who dares to instruct Christ and alter what he has **spoken**.
LC : 05 :033(450) [0761] give, for they are not **spoken** or preached to stone and
LC : 05 :065(454) [0769] in the "you" so that he may not **speak** to you in vain.
LC : 05 :076(455) [0771] If St. Paul can **speak** thus of his flesh, let us not pretend
EP : 01 :021(468) [0785] man, no idle word were **spoken**, or no wicked act or deed
EP : 03 :015(474) [0795] righteousness of faith is **spoken** of in the pronouncements
EP : 04 :003(476) [0797] word "necessary" when **speaking** of the new obedience,
EP : 04 :016(477) [0801] we reject and condemn **spoken** and written formulations
EP : 05 :001(477) [0801] the Holy Gospel strictly **speaking** only a preaching of
EP : 05 :003(478) [0801] and confess that, strictly **speaking**, the law is a divine
EP : 05 :005(478) [0801] But the Gospel, strictly **speaking**, is the kind of doctrine
EP : 05 :007(478) [0803] other, as when Moses is **spoken** of as a teacher of the law
EP : 05 :007(478) [0803] reproof but is, strictly **speaking**, precisely a comforting
EP : 05 :010(479) [0803] people, it is not, strictly **speaking**, the preaching of the
EP : 05 :010(479) [0803] And this is the preaching of the Gospel, strictly **speaking**.
EP : 05 :011(479) [0805] that the Gospel, strictly **speaking**, is a proclamation of
EP : 07 :009(483) [0811] omitted, but should be **spoken** publicly, as it is written,
EP : 11 :011(496) [0835] and only then does he **speak** of the mystery of God's
SD : 01 :002(508) [0859] that original sin, strictly **speaking**, is not man's nature,
SD : 01 :006(509) [0861] man were to think no evil, **speak** no evil, or do no evil —
SD : 01 :022(512) [0865] it; or that the spots **spoken** of can easily be washed off,
SD : 01 :033(514) [0869] thing, so, if one wishes to **speak** strictly, one must
SD : 01 :042(515) [0871] man is able to think, to **speak**, to act, and to do anything,
SD : 01 :052(517) [0875] Strictly **speaking**, therefore, original sin is the deep
SD : 01 :056(518) [0877] therefore constantly **speaks** in this fashion: Original sin is
SD : 02 :081(537) [0913] by adding, 'Therefore lay aside lies and **speak** the truth.'
SD : 03 :042(547) [0931] If we **speak** of the manner in which faith justifies, it is St.
SD : 03 :043(547) [0931] declares, James is **speaking** of the good works of those
SD : 03 :054(549) [0935] of faith of which St. Paul **speaks** and which he calls the
SD : 03 :062(550) [0937] prophets and the apostles **speak** of the righteousness of
SD : 05 :002(558) [0951] claimed that, strictly **speaking**, the Gospel is not only a
SD : 05 :002(558) [0951] contended that, strictly **speaking**, the Gospel is not a
SD : 05 :017(561) [0957] have said that, strictly **speaking**, the law is a divine
SD : 05 :019(561) [0957] (which alone, strictly **speaking**, teaches and commands
SD : 05 :019(561) [0957] Gospel alone, strictly **speaking**, teaches about saving faith
SD : 05 :021(562) [0959] of the law strictly **speaking** is, and is called, the Gospel, a
SD : 05 :027(563) [0961] indicates that, strictly **speaking**, the Gospel is the promise
SD : 06 :015(566) [0967] special diligence that in **speaking** of good works that are
SD : 06 :017(566) [0967] These works are, strictly **speaking**, not works of the law
SD : 07 :022(573) [0979] he can correct Christ and change what he has **spoken**.
SD : 07 :023(573) [0979] it must be as Christ's lips **speak** and declare, since he
SD : 07 :043(577) [0987] what and how he must **speak**, and he is able mightily to
SD : 07 :043(577) [0987] and achieve what he **speaks** and promises, as he says,
SD : 07 :047(578) [0989] The Lord who has **spoken** these words is himself infinite
SD : 07 :048(578) [0989] be no doubt that he was **speaking** of true, natural bread
SD : 07 :049(578) [0989] He was not **speaking** of a symbol of his body, or of a
SD : 07 :049(578) [0989] He was **speaking** of his true, essential body, which he
SD : 07 :056(579) [0991] If Paul were **speaking** only of a spiritual participation in
SD : 07 :056(579) [0991] he certainly cannot be **speaking** of a spiritual eating but
SD : 07 :057(579) [0993] certainly could not be **speaking** of a spiritual fellowship
SD : 07 :061(580) [0995] spiritual, of which Christ **speaks** chiefly in John 6:48-58.
SD : 07 :074(583) [0999] be it the merit or the **speaking** of the minister, be it the
SD : 07 :075(583) [0999] of Jesus Christ which he **spoke** in the first institution were
SD : 07 :075(583) [0999] of the same words which Christ **spoke** in the first Supper.
SD : 07 :075(583) [0999] his institution and **speak** his words over the bread and
SD : 07 :075(583) [0999] is still active through the **spoken** words by the virtue of
SD : 07 :076(583) [0999] The words are **spoken** by the mouth of the priest, but by
SD : 07 :076(583) [0999] the words that he **speaks**, 'This is my body,' the elements
SD : 07 :076(583) [0999] and fill the earth,' were **spoken** only once but are ever
SD : 07 :076(583) [0999] so this word was indeed **spoken** only once, but it is
SD : 07 :077(583) [0999] it is not our word or **speaking** but the command and
SD : 07 :078(584) [1001] not because of our **speaking** or of our efficacious word,
SD : 07 :078(584) [1001] which he has told us so to **speak** and to do and has
SD : 07 :078(584) [1001] attached his own command and deed to our **speaking**."
SD : 07 :079(584) [1001] of institution are to be **spoken** or sung distinctly and
SD : 07 :099(586) [1005] and going to the Father **speak** of this mode of presence.
SD : 08 :019(594) [1021] only after a manner of **speaking** and in a strictly verbal
SD : 08 :037(598) [1027] But in this mode of **speaking** it does not follow that
SD : 08 :042(599) [1029] Although, so to **speak**, the one part (namely, the deity)
SD : 08 :059(602) [1035] place, Scripture not only **speaks** in general terms of the
SD : 08 :063(603) [1037] way of contrast, we have **spoken** of a "real exchange" in
SD : 08 :067(604) [1039] of the Scriptures which **speak** of the majesty to which the
SD : 08 :087(608) [1047] he, he, the man who has **spoken** with them, who has
SD : 10 :012(612) [1057] Paul is here **speaking** of circumcision, which at that time
SD : 11 :013(618) [1067] if we wish to think or **speak** correctly and profitably
SD : 11 :024(620) [1069] or omitted when we **speak** of the purpose,
SD : 11 :034(622) [1075] although I **speak** differently in my call to them."
SD : 11 :052(625) [1081] and of which we have **spoken** thus far, there are many
SD : 12 :040(636) [1103] Nor shall we **speak** or write anything, privately or

Spears (1)
LC : 05 :082(456) [0773] see how many daggers, **spears**, and arrows are at every

Special (36)
PR : PR :015(007) [0013] such a plan because **special** circumstances interfered, as
PR : PR :022(012) [0021] charity causes us to have **special** sympathy with them, so
PR : PR :025(014) [0023] Holy Empire and of the **special** treaties into which we
AG : 23 :006(052) [0061] or vows without a **special** gift or grace of God.
AG : 24 :023(058) [0067] merited as much as a **special** Mass held for an individual.
AG : 27 :020(074) [0079] endowed with the gift of virginity by a **special** act of God.
AG : 00 :002(095) [0095] about sermons on **special** occasions, and about countless
AL : 24 :023(058) [0067] is worth as much as a **special** Mass said for individuals,
AP : 12 :057(189) [0267] Nor are **special** punishments always added, but contrition
AP : 12 :156(207) [0301] troubles there is a **special** penalty in purgatory, where the
AP : 21 :032(233) [0351] that each saint has a **special** sphere of activity assigned to
AP : 21 :044(236) [0357] It is your **special** responsibility before God to maintain
AP : 23 :019(242) [0369] possible for everyone, it would not require a **special** gift.
AP : 23 :019(242) [0369] that it does require a **special** gift; therefore, it is not for
AP : 28 :018(284) [0449] something prescribed," about a **special** commandment.
S2 : 02 :026(297) [0469] to each of them a **special** function, as the papists teach
TR : 00 :024(324) [0511] not ascribe to Peter any **special** prerogative, superiority,
TR : 00 :030(325) [0513] that they bestow a **special** authority on Peter, for Christ
TR : 00 :081(334) [0527] so great that they require **special** courts, but these cannot
SC : PR :018(340) [0537] which seem to require **special** attention among the people
LC : 01 :086(376) [0605] The **special** office of this day, therefore, should be the
LC : 01 :105(379) [0611] God has given the **special** distinction, above all estates
LC : 01 :313(407) [0671] pompous, restricted to **special** times, places, rites, and
LC : 02 :048(416) [0691] we who assemble select a **special** place and give the house
LC : 04 :040(441) [0743] It takes **special** understanding to believe this, for it is not
LC : 05 :047(452) [0763] be free, not bound to a **special** time like the Passover,
LC : 05 :047(452) [0765] need, being bound to no **special** place or time" (although
EP : 03 :010(474) [0795] before God, we must give **special** attention to the
SD : PR :001(501) [0847] By the **special** grace and mercy of the Almighty, the
SD : PR :005(504) [0851] 3. By a **special** grace our merciful God has in these last
SD : 01 :062(519) [0879] time he explained with **special** seriousness and great zeal
SD : 06 :015(566) [0967] we must observe with **special** diligence that in speaking of
SD : 07 :054(579) [0991] and earnestly as a **special** and manifest testimony to the
SD : 08 :051(600) [1033] and abiding properties, **special**, high, great, supernatural,
SD : 10 :024(615) [1061] In a **special** opinion Dr. Luther exhaustively instructs the
SD : 12 :002(632) [1095] reason intended to make **special** and detailed mention of

Species (3)
SD : 07 :108(588) [1009] so that only the mere **species** of bread and wine, or their
SD : 07 :108(588) [1009] assert that under the **species** of the bread, which they
SD : 07 :110(588) [1011] that only one **species** is administered to the laity contrary

Specific (4), Specifically (8), Specifications (1), Specified (2)
PR : PR :017(008) [0015] would furnish further **specifications** concerning our
PR : PR :022(011) [0019] the contrary, we mean **specifically** to condemn only false
AG : PR :024(027) [0043] our associates, and it is **specifically** stated, article by
AG : 26 :034(069) [0075] not be limited to certain **specified** days but should be
AG : 26 :039(069) [0075] days and with **specified** foods, for this confuses
AP : 04 :107(122) [0153] justification to faith and **specifically** deny it to works.
AP : 04 :224(138) [0181] which we deal with men and not **specifically** with God.
AP : 04 :226(138) [0183] however, Paul speaks **specifically** about love to our
AP : 12 :109(198) [0283] does not speak of the **specific** confession to be made to
LC : 01 :206(393) [0639] is concerned **specifically** with the estate of marriage and
SD : 01 :050(517) [0875] With **specific** reference to vocabulary and phraseology,
SD : 03 :007(540) [0917] And St. Paul says **specifically** of this doctrine that a little
SD : 08 :028(596) [1025] of God, which is not a **specific** place in heaven, as the
SD : 11 :049(624) [1079] counsel through which **specific** cross and affliction he
SD : 11 :082(630) [1091] of mercy" he says **specifically** that the Lord himself "has

Specious (6)
AP : 23 :064(248) [0381] We have already refuted this very **specious** argument.
S3 : 06 :002(311) [0493] We need not resort to the **specious** learning of the
LC : 01 :296(405) [0665] anyone, even with a **specious** pretext, to covet or scheme
LC : 01 :304(406) [0667] how much he can acquire by such **specious** pretexts?
LC : 03 :062(428) [0715] honored under the most **specious** pretexts of God's name,
SD : 11 :093(632) [1095] and flee all abstruse and **specious** questions and

Specks (1)
S1 : PR :013(291) [0459] stand and dispute about **specks**, we might just as well be

Spectacle (2), Spectacles (3)
AP : 11 :008(181) [0251] What tragic **spectacles** were enacted between the secular
AP : 12 :114(199) [0285] Still these **spectacles** tend to beguile the inexperienced
LC : 05 :042(451) [0763] be treated merely as a **spectacle**, but commanded his
SD : 07 :108(588) [1009] or is carried about as a **spectacle** and for adoration).
SD : 10 :007(611) [1055] are useless and foolish **spectacles**, which serve neither

Speculate (1), Speculation (1), Speculations (7)
AP : 04 :037(112) [0131] how vain these philosophical **speculations** are.
AP : 04 :312(155) [0207] in fact the way they are in idle scholastic **speculations**.
AP : 12 :147(205) [0297] carry on idle **speculations** about the remission of guilt.
SD : 07 :103(587) [1009] unable to do it, but who will believe their **speculations**?"
SD : 07 :103(587) [1009] How will they establish that kind of **speculation**?
SD : 09 :003(610) [1051] with exalted and acute **speculations** about how this
SD : 11 :013(618) [1067] ourselves not to **speculate** concerning the absolute, secret,
SD : 11 :055(625) [1081] it through our own **speculations** but has earnestly warned
SD : 11 :055(625) [1081] on the basis of our **speculations**, to make our own

Speech (7)
PR : PR :021(010) [0019] the kind and manner of **speech** employed with reference
AP : 04 :152(127) [0163] is a familiar figure of **speech**, called synecdoche, by which
LC : 03 :040(425) [0709] on earth may be classified as word or deed, **speech** or act.
EP : 08 :025(490) [0823] a verbalism and figure of **speech** when we say "God is
SD : 07 :002(569) [0971] to the formulas and **speech**-patterns of the Augsburg
SD : 07 :007(570) [0975] the way the letters sound, but as figurative **speech**.
SD : 08 :063(603) [1037] it is all only a mode of **speech**, mere words, titles, and

Spend (4), Spent (1)
AP : 12 :031(186) [0259] I am utterly **spent** and crushed; I groan because of the
AP : 27 :054(278) [0439] But they **spend** their time either on philosophical
S3 : 03 :036(309) [0489] We need not **spend** our time weighing, distinguishing,
LC : 01 :087(377) [0605] account, according as you **spend** the day in doing holy or
LC : 01 :090(377) [0607] Non-Christians can **spend** a day in rest and idleness, too,

Sphere (1)
AP : 21 :032(233) [0351] each saint has a special **sphere** of activity assigned to

Spices (1)
S3 : 15 :005(316) [0501] are blessings of candles, palms, **spices**, oats, cakes, etc.

Spilling (1)
A P : 2 2 :014(238) [0361] refer to the danger of **spilling** and similar factors which

Spires (2)
A G : P R :015(026) [0041] instruction at the diet in **Spires** in 1526, that for reasons
A G : P R :017(026) [0041] at the last diet in **Spires** a year ago, the electors, princes,

Spirit (492) (*Ref. to the Holy Spirit; See below for Christ's spirit, man's spirit*)
P R : P R :013(007) [0013] singular grace of the Holy **Spirit**, everything that pertains
P R : P R :022(012) [0019] the guidance of the Holy **Spirit**, turn to the infallible truth
P R : P R :023(012) [0021] and assistance of the Holy **Spirit** until the glorious advent
P R : P R :024(013) [0021] the grace of the Holy **Spirit**, the most acute and urgent
P R : P R :025(014) [0023] by the grace of the Holy **Spirit** to abide and remain
A G : 0 1 :002(027) [0043] God the Father, God the Son, God the Holy **Spirit**.
A G : 0 1 :006(028) [0043] the Word and the Holy **Spirit**, are not necessarily distinct
A G : 0 1 :006(028) [0043] or voice and that the Holy **Spirit** is a movement induced
A G : 0 2 :002(029) [0043] are not born again through Baptism and the Holy **Spirit**.
A G : 0 3 :004(030) [0045] that through the Holy **Spirit** he may sanctify, purify,
A G : 0 5 :002(031) [0045] means, he gives the Holy **Spirit**, who works faith, when
A G : 0 5 :004(031) [0045] who teach that the Holy **Spirit** comes to us through our
A G : 0 7 :004(032) [0047] is one body and one **Spirit**, just as you were called to the
A G : 1 8 :002(039) [0051] and activity of the Holy **Spirit** man is not capable of
A G : 1 8 :003(039) [0051] accomplished by the Holy **Spirit**, who is given through the
A G : 1 8 :003(039) [0051] man does not receive the gifts of the **Spirit** of God."
A G : 2 0 :029(045) [0057] through faith the Holy **Spirit** is given, the heart is moved
A G : 2 0 :031(045) [0057] when it is without the Holy **Spirit**, the heart is too weak.
A G : 2 0 :034(045) [0057] true faith and the Holy **Spirit** and governs himself by his
A G : 2 8 :006(082) [0085] Receive the Holy **Spirit**.
A G : 2 8 :008(082) [0085] eternal righteousness, the Holy **Spirit**, and eternal life.
A G : 2 8 :031(085) [0087] When the **Spirit** of truth comes, he will guide you into all
A G : 2 8 :049(089) [0091] it possible that the Holy **Spirit** warned against them for
A L : 0 1 :003(028) [0043] also coeternal: the Father, the Son, and the Holy **Spirit**.
A L : 0 1 :006(028) [0043] the Word and the Holy **Spirit** are not distinct persons
A L : 0 1 :006(028) [0043] a spoken word and "**Spirit**" signifies a movement which is
A L : 0 2 :002(029) [0043] are not born again through Baptism and the Holy **Spirit**.
A L : 0 3 :004(030) [0045] him by sending the Holy **Spirit** into their hearts to rule,
A L : 0 5 :002(031) [0045] instruments, the Holy **Spirit** is given, and the Holy Spirit
A L : 0 5 :002(031) [0045] is given, and the Holy **Spirit** produces faith, where and
A L : 0 5 :003(031) [0045] we might receive the promise of the **Spirit** through faith."
A L : 0 5 :004(031) [0045] who think that the Holy **Spirit** comes to men without the
A L : 1 2 :007(035) [0049] can lose the Holy **Spirit**, and also those who contend that
A L : 1 8 :002(039) [0051] power, without the Holy **Spirit**, to attain the
A L : 1 8 :002(039) [0051] perceive the gifts of the **Spirit** of God (I Cor. 2:14); but
A L : 1 8 :003(039) [0051] the heart when the Holy **Spirit** is received through the
A L : 1 8 :008(040) [0053] that without the Holy **Spirit**, by the power of nature
A L : 2 0 :029(045) [0057] through faith the Holy **Spirit** is received, hearts are so
A L : 2 0 :031(045) [0057] For without the Holy **Spirit** man's powers are full of
A L : 2 0 :034(045) [0057] strength alone without faith and without the Holy **Spirit**.
A L : 2 8 :006(082) [0085] Receive the Holy **Spirit**.
A L : 2 8 :008(082) [0085] as eternal righteousness, the Holy **Spirit**, and eternal life.
A L : 2 8 :031(086) [0087] When the **Spirit** of truth comes, he will guide you into all
A L : 2 8 :049(089) [0091] Was it in vain that the Holy **Spirit** warned against these?
A P : P R :009(099) [0101] in opposition to the clear Scripture of the Holy **Spirit**.
A P : 0 1 :001(100) [0103] of the same divine essence, Father, Son, and Holy **Spirit**.
A P : 0 2 :010(102) [0109] need is there for the Holy **Spirit** if human powers by
A P : 0 2 :025(103) [0111] quenched by the Holy **Spirit** and a love for God above all
A P : 0 2 :030(104) [0113] man does not receive the gifts of the **Spirit** of God."
A P : 0 2 :035(105) [0115] also said that the Holy **Spirit**, given in Baptism, begins to
A P : 0 2 :045(106) [0117] Christ to be forgiven and the Holy **Spirit** to be mortified.
A P : 0 4 :009(108) [0123] that without the Holy **Spirit** reason can love God above
A P : 0 4 :031(111) [0129] is born of water and the **Spirit**, one cannot enter the
A P : 0 4 :031(111) [0129] again through the Holy **Spirit**, then the righteousness of
A P : 0 4 :034(112) [0129] But without the Holy **Spirit**, the human heart either
A P : 0 4 :035(112) [0131] things without the Holy **Spirit**; for they do them with a
A P : 0 4 :045(113) [0133] us and brings us the Holy **Spirit**, so that we can finally
A P : 0 4 :063(115) [0139] can our opponents say how the Holy **Spirit** is given.
A P : 0 4 :063(115) [0139] bestow the Holy **Spirit** *ex opere operato* without the
A P : 0 4 :063(115) [0139] as though the gift of the Holy **Spirit** were a minor matter.
A P : 0 4 :064(116) [0139] a new life in our hearts, and is a work of the Holy **Spirit**.
A P : 0 4 :070(116) [0141] cannot keep the law unless we first receive the Holy **Spirit**.
A P : 0 4 :086(119) [0147] the forgiveness of sins and the Holy **Spirit** by faith alone.
A P : 0 4 :099(121) [0151] but a thing that receives the Holy **Spirit** and justifies us.
A P : 0 4 :108(122) [0153] that these words fell from the Holy **Spirit** unawares?
A P : 0 4 :115(123) [0155] it is a work of the Holy **Spirit** that frees us from death,
A P : 0 4 :116(123) [0155] God, and brings the Holy **Spirit**, it should be called "grace
A P : 0 4 :125(124) [0157] faith brings the Holy **Spirit** and produces a new life in our
A P : 0 4 :126(124) [0157] being justified and regenerated, we receive the Holy **Spirit**.
A P : 0 4 :126(124) [0157] it is impossible to keep the law without the Holy **Spirit**.
A P : 0 4 :127(125) [0157] But the **Spirit** is received by faith, according to Paul's
A P : 0 4 :127(125) [0157] we might receive the promise of the **Spirit** through faith."
A P : 0 4 :130(125) [0157] Christ and the Holy **Spirit**, still the impulses of the heart
A P : 0 4 :130(125) [0157] without the Holy **Spirit**; this is evident from what we have
A P : 0 4 :132(125) [0159] of sins and the Holy **Spirit**, to bring forth in us eternal
A P : 0 4 :132(125) [0159] the law unless by faith we have received the Holy **Spirit**.
A P : 0 4 :132(125) [0159] the law can be kept only when the Holy **Spirit** is given.
A P : 0 4 :133(125) [0159] removed except by faith, which receives the Holy **Spirit**.
A P : 0 4 :133(125) [0159] Now, the Lord is the **Spirit**, and where the Spirit of the
A P : 0 4 :133(125) [0159] the Spirit, and where the **Spirit** of the Lord is, there is
A P : 0 4 :135(125) [0159] sins, we receive the Holy **Spirit**, so that we can think
A P : 0 4 :135(126) [0159] and without the Holy **Spirit** we cannot keep the law.
A P : 0 4 :139(126) [0161] we pray that the Holy **Spirit** may govern and defend us, so
A P : 0 4 :139(126) [0161] his promise and the Holy **Spirit**, so that with the help of
A P : 0 4 :143(126) [0161] walk according to the flesh, but according to the **Spirit**."
A P : 0 4 :143(127) [0161] you will die, but if by the **Spirit** you put to death the
A P : 0 4 :146(127) [0163] forth evil desires, though the **Spirit** in us resists them.
A P : 0 4 :147(127) [0163] is the work of the Holy **Spirit** and since it is righteousness
A P : 0 4 :169(130) [0169] of the flesh are against the **Spirit**, and the desires of the
A P : 0 4 :169(130) [0169] Spirit, and the desires of the **Spirit** are against the flesh."
A P : 0 4 :170(130) [0171] The Holy **Spirit** in our hearts battles against such feelings
A P : 0 4 :175(131) [0171] by faith receive the Holy **Spirit** and that their impulses
A P : 0 4 :182(132) [0173] keeping of the law follows with the gift of the Holy **Spirit**.
A P : 0 4 :189(133) [0175] hinders what the Holy **Spirit** motivates, fouling it with its
A P : 0 4 :219(137) [0181] it ever so great, because he will not keep the Holy **Spirit**.
A P : 0 4 :220(137) [0181] urging to bear good fruits lest they lose the Holy **Spirit**.
A P : 0 4 :230(139) [0183] for the help of his Holy **Spirit** to make it clear and
A P : 0 4 :293(152) [0203] quickened by faith in this way, it receives the Holy **Spirit**.
A P : 0 4 :319(156) [0209] The flesh always lusts against the **Spirit** (Gal. 5:17).
A P : 0 4 :349(160) [0217] and receive the Holy **Spirit**, that this new life might have
A P : 0 4 :372(164) [0221] who are led by the **Spirit** of Christ; nor can good works
A P : 0 7 :005(169) [0227] association of faith and of the Holy **Spirit** in men's hearts.
A P : 0 7 :005(169) [0227] and governs by his **Spirit**, as Paul testifies when he says
A P : 0 7 :008(169) [0229] and of the same Holy **spirit**, who renews, consecrates, and
A P : 0 7 :009(170) [0229] of sins, answer to prayer, and the gift of the Holy **Spirit**.
A P : 0 7 :010(170) [0229] Christ, the same Holy **Spirit**, and the same sacraments,
A P : 0 7 :013(170) [0231] and the gift of the Holy **Spirit** but would think of it as
A P : 0 7 :014(170) [0231] but by being God's true people, reborn by the Holy **Spirit**.
A P : 0 7 :015(170) [0231] themselves, the Holy **Spirit** and the righteousness by
A P : 0 7 :016(170) [0231] are the true people who accept this promise of the **Spirit**.
A P : 0 7 :016(171) [0231] are his captives; they are not ruled by the **Spirit** of Christ.
A P : 0 7 :018(171) [0233] What he quickens by his **Spirit** is always the same
A P : 0 7 :022(172) [0235] will always have the Holy **Spirit**, so it also has the warning
A P : 0 7 :022(172) [0235] properly speaking, is that which has the Holy **Spirit**.
A P : 0 7 :028(173) [0237] believe the Gospel of Christ and who have the Holy **Spirit**.
A P : 0 7 :031(174) [0239] they wrought by the Holy **Spirit**, as are chastity, patience,
A P : 0 7 :036(175) [0241] are not works of the Holy **Spirit** (like love of neighbor,
A P : 0 7 :036(175) [0241] but righteousness and peace and joy in the Holy **Spirit**."
A P : 0 9 :003(178) [0245] that God gives the Holy **Spirit** to those who were baptized
A P : 0 9 :003(178) [0245] were useless, the Holy **Spirit** would be given to none, none
A P : 1 2 :007(183) [0255] not of life and of the **Spirit**, but only of wrath and
A P : 1 2 :029(186) [0259] sake, to grant the Holy **Spirit** and eternal life, and to lead
A P : 1 2 :044(187) [0263] When we believe, the Holy **Spirit** quickens our hearts
A P : 1 2 :071(192) [0271] The testimony of the Holy **Spirit** was added to this
A P : 1 2 :071(192) [0271] still saying this, the Holy **Spirit** fell on all who heard the
A P : 1 2 :073(192) [0273] the witness that the Holy **Spirit** brings in your heart,
A P : 1 2 :074(192) [0273] our hearts and the Holy **Spirit** grants them peace.
A P : 1 2 :082(194) [0275] receive the Holy **Spirit** and therefore begin to keep the
A P : 1 2 :152(206) [0299] kill and wipe out lust so that the **Spirit** may renew them.
A P : 1 2 :174(210) [0307] surrendering to the devil or offending the Holy **Spirit**.
A P : 1 3 :013(212) [0311] who dream that the Holy **Spirit** does not come through
A P : 1 8 :002(225) [0335] that without the Holy **Spirit** men can love God and
A P : 1 8 :002(225) [0335] and that without the Holy **Spirit** men can merit grace and
A P : 1 8 :004(225) [0335] its own without the Holy **Spirit**, Scripture calls the
A P : 1 8 :006(225) [0335] Without the Holy **Spirit** human hearts have neither the
A P : 1 8 :007(226) [0337] the human heart cannot perform without the Holy **Spirit**.
A P : 1 8 :009(226) [0337] to the operation of the Holy **Spirit** in the regenerate.
A P : 1 8 :009(226) [0337] the teaching of the Holy **Spirit**; and it points out the need
A P : 1 8 :009(226) [0337] Holy Spirit; and it points out the need for the Holy **Spirit**.
A P : 1 8 :010(226) [0337] of God without the Holy **Spirit** and that the Holy Spirit is
A P : 1 8 :010(226) [0337] Spirit and that the Holy **Spirit** is given to them out of
A P : 2 0 :013(228) [0343] those who lose the Holy **Spirit** and reject penitence; as we
A P : 2 0 :015(229) [0343] we have received the Holy **Spirit** by faith, the keeping of
A P : 2 0 :015(229) [0343] chastity, and other fruits of the **Spirit** gradually increase.
A P : 2 4 :026(254) [0391] refers to the operation of the Holy **Spirit** within us.
A P : 2 4 :034(256) [0395] sanctified by the Holy **Spirit**," that is, so that the Gentiles
A P : 2 4 :036(257) [0397] 1:2); "Sanctified by the **Spirit** for obedience to Jesus
A P : 2 4 :039(257) [0399] of things, for the Holy **Spirit** who puts us to death and
A P : 2 4 :059(260) [0405] is a ministry of the **Spirit**, as Paul teaches in II Cor. 3:6,
A P : 2 4 :059(260) [0405] receive faith and the Holy **Spirit** and be put to death and
A P : 2 4 :059(260) [0405] The ministry of the **Spirit** contradicts any such transfer *ex*
A P : 2 4 :059(260) [0405] the ministry of the **Spirit**, the Holy Spirit works in the
A P : 2 4 :059(260) [0405] ministry of the Spirit, the Holy **Spirit** works in the heart.
A P : 2 4 :070(262) [0409] For the Holy **Spirit** works through the Word and the
A P : 2 7 :013(271) [0423] is a witness, the Holy **Spirit** is a witness, thy whole church
A P : 2 7 :027(274) [0429] changed from glory to glory, as by the **Spirit** of the Lord."
A P : 2 7 :051(278) [0437] of the Holy **Spirit** (I Cor. 7:2), "Because of the temptation
A P : 2 8 :010(282) [0447] Word of God and the Holy **Spirit**, that work eternal life
S 1 : P R :015(291) [0459] hast given us by thy Holy **Spirit**, who with Thee and the
S 1 : 0 1 :000(291) [0461] Father, Son, and Holy **Spirit**, three distinct persons in one
S 1 : 0 1 :000(291) [0461] the Father, and the Holy **Spirit** proceeded from the
S 1 : 0 1 :000(291) [0461] became man, and neither the Father nor the Holy **Spirit**.
S 1 : 0 1 :000(291) [0461] was conceived by the Holy **Spirit**, without the cooperation
S 2 : 0 4 :015(301) [0475] will accomplish his purpose by his **Spirit** and his coming.
S 3 : 0 1 :010(303) [0479] Scriptures that the Holy **Spirit** and his gifts are necessary
S 3 : 0 3 :001(303) [0479] in John 16:8, "The Holy **Spirit** will convince the world of
S 3 : 0 3 :040(309) [0489] with the gift of the Holy **Spirit** which follows the
S 3 : 0 3 :042(309) [0491] they have received the **Spirit** or the forgiveness of sins, or
S 3 : 0 3 :042(310) [0491] has received faith and the **Spirit**, he never really had the
S 3 : 0 3 :042(310) [0491] and the Spirit, he never really had the **Spirit** and faith.
S 3 : 0 3 :043(310) [0491] blasphemy), faith and the **Spirit** have departed from
S 3 : 0 3 :044(310) [0491] is so because the Holy **Spirit** does not permit sin to rule
S 3 : 0 3 :044(310) [0491] committed, but the Holy **Spirit** represses and restrains it
S 3 : 0 3 :044(310) [0491] what it wishes, the Holy **Spirit** and faith are not present,
S 3 : 0 8 :003(312) [0495] that God gives no one his **Spirit** or grace except through
S 3 : 0 8 :003(312) [0495] that they possess the **Spirit** without and before the Word
S 3 : 0 8 :006(312) [0495] and scribbling, as if the **Spirit** could not come through the
S 3 : 0 8 :006(312) [0495] and writing until the **Spirit** himself comes to the people
S 3 : 0 8 :006(313) [0495] since they boast that the **Spirit** came upon them without
S 3 : 0 8 :007(313) [0495] and did not receive the **Spirit** and Baptism until ten years
S 3 : 0 8 :010(313) [0497] is attributed to the **Spirit** apart from such Word and
S 3 : 0 8 :011(313) [0497] or Elisha, received the **Spirit** without the Ten
S 3 : 0 8 :013(313) [0497] were moved by the Holy **Spirit**, yet as holy men of God.
S 3 : 0 8 :013(313) [0497] not holy, and the Holy **Spirit** would not have moved them
S 3 : 0 8 :013(313) [0497] Peter says, because the Holy **Spirit** spoke through them.
S 3 : 1 5 :005(317) [0501] and taught, and by the **Spirit** of Christ I will thus continue
S C : 0 2 :003(345) [0545] *was conceived by the Holy **Spirit**, born of the virgin*
S C : 0 2 :005(345) [0545] *"I believe in the Holy **Spirit**, the holy Christian church,*
S C : 0 2 :006(345) [0545] But the Holy **Spirit** has called me through the Gospel,
S C : 0 3 :008(346) [0547] Father gives us his Holy **Spirit** so that by his grace we
S C : 0 4 :004(348) [0551] of the Father and of the Son and of the Holy **Spirit**."
S C : 0 4 :010(349) [0551] regeneration in the Holy **Spirit**, as St. Paul wrote to Titus
S C : 0 4 :010(349) [0551] and renewal in the Holy **Spirit**, which he poured out upon
S C : 0 5 :028(351) [0555] name of the Father and of the Son and of the Holy **Spirit**.
S C : 0 7 :001(352) [0557] name of God, the Father, the Son, and the Holy **Spirit**.
S C : 0 7 :004(353) [0559] name of God, the Father, the Son, and the Holy **Spirit**.
L C : P R :009(359) [0569] and meditation the Holy **Spirit** is present and bestows
L C : S P :012(363) [0577] was conceived by the Holy **Spirit**, born of the virgin

Continued ▶

L C : S P :013(363) [0577] I believe in the Holy **Spirit**, the holy Christian church, the
L C : S P :021(364) [0579] and of the Son and of the Holy **Spirit**" (Matt. 28:19).
L C : 0 1 :128(383) [0617] and considers this, unless he is led to it by the Holy **Spirit**.
L C : 0 2 :006(411) [0679] redemption; the third, of the Holy **Spirit**, sanctification.
L C : 0 2 :007(411) [0679] me; I believe in the Holy **Spirit**, who sanctifies me."
L C : 0 2 :024(413) [0683] through his Son and the Holy **Spirit**, as we shall hear.
L C : 0 2 :025(413) [0683] *was conceived by the Holy* ***Spirit****, born of the virgin*
L C : 0 2 :031(414) [0687] without sin, of the Holy **Spirit** and the Virgin, that he
L C : 0 2 :034(415) [0687] *"I believe in the Holy* ***Spirit****, the holy Christian Church,*
L C : 0 2 :035(415) [0687] and portrayed the Holy **Spirit** and his office, which is that
L C : 0 2 :035(415) [0687] on the term "Holy **Spirit**," because it is so precise that we
L C : 0 2 :036(415) [0687] But God's **Spirit** alone is called Holy Spirit, that is, he
L C : 0 2 :036(415) [0687] Spirit alone is called Holy **Spirit**, that is, he who has
L C : 0 2 :036(415) [0687] of his work the Holy **Spirit** must be called Sanctifier, the
L C : 0 2 :037(415) [0687] etc., so the Holy **Spirit** effects our sanctification through
L C : 0 2 :038(415) [0689] through the preaching of the Gospel by the Holy **Spirit**.
L C : 0 2 :038(415) [0689] he has given the Holy **Spirit** to offer and apply to us this
L C : 0 2 :040(416) [0689] "I believe in the Holy **Spirit**"? you can answer, "I believe
L C : 0 2 :040(416) [0689] "I believe that the Holy **Spirit** makes me holy, as his name
L C : 0 2 :042(416) [0689] The Holy **Spirit** reveals and preaches that Word, and by it
L C : 0 2 :043(416) [0689] Christ as the Lord, or the Holy **Spirit** as the Sanctifier.
L C : 0 2 :044(416) [0689] There was no Holy **Spirit** present to reveal this truth and
L C : 0 2 :045(416) [0689] preached, there is no Holy **Spirit** to create, call, and
L C : 0 2 :051(417) [0691] together by the Holy **Spirit** in one faith, mind, and
L C : 0 2 :052(417) [0691] brought to it by the Holy **Spirit** and incorporated into it
L C : 0 2 :053(417) [0691] Until the last day the Holy **Spirit** remains with the holy
L C : 0 2 :053(417) [0693] become strong in the faith and in the fruits of the **Spirit**.
L C : 0 2 :054(417) [0693] been wrought by the Holy **Spirit** through God's Word in
L C : 0 2 :055(418) [0693] we have sin, the Holy **Spirit** sees to it that it does not
L C : 0 2 :058(418) [0693] The Holy **Spirit** must continue to work in us through the
L C : 0 2 :059(418) [0693] and work of the Holy **Spirit**, to begin and daily to
L C : 0 2 :061(419) [0695] but the Holy **Spirit** carries on his work unceasingly until
L C : 0 2 :064(419) [0695] us his Son and his Holy **Spirit**, through whom he brings
L C : 0 2 :065(419) [0695] of Christ, had it not been revealed by the Holy **Spirit**.
L C : 0 2 :066(419) [0697] not illuminated and blessed by the gifts of the Holy **Spirit**.
L C : 0 2 :067(420) [0697] the Creed; it must be taught by the Holy **Spirit** alone.
L C : 0 2 :069(420) [0697] creation, Christ all his works, the Holy **Spirit** all his gifts.
L C : 0 3 :051(427) [0711] end he also gave his Holy **Spirit** to teach us this through
L C : 0 3 :052(427) [0711] pray that, led by the Holy **Spirit**, many may come into the
L C : 0 3 :054(427) [0713] the power of the Holy **Spirit**, that the devil's kingdom
L C : 0 3 :061(428) [0715] faith, and for the Holy **Spirit**, that he may govern us who
L C : 0 4 :004(437) [0733] *of the Father and of the Son and of the Holy* ***Spirit****."*
L C : 0 4 :021(439) [0737] be baptized, that the Holy **Spirit** descended visibly, and
L C : 0 4 :041(442) [0743] grace, the entire Christ, and the Holy **Spirit** with his gifts.
L C : 0 4 :049(442) [0745] been thus baptized and has given them the Holy **Spirit**.
L C : 0 4 :049(442) [0745] doctrine and life attest that they have the Holy **Spirit**.
L C : 0 4 :049(442) [0745] know Christ, which is impossible without the Holy **Spirit**.
L C : 0 4 :050(443) [0745] any of them the Holy **Spirit** nor any part of him; in short,
L C : 0 4 :050(443) [0745] the gift of His Holy **Spirit**, as we have perceived in some
L C : 0 4 :050(443) [0745] and wickedness, or give his grace and **Spirit** for such ends.
L C : 0 4 :076(445) [0751] we are given the grace, **Spirit**, and power to suppress the
L C : 0 5 :070(454) [0769] conveys God's grace and **Spirit** with all his gifts,
E P : 0 2 :001(469) [0785] reborn through the Holy **Spirit**, dispose and prepare
E P : 0 2 :002(470) [0787] not receive the gifts of the **Spirit** of God, for they are folly
E P : 0 2 :004(470) [0787] 3. God the Holy **Spirit**, however, does not effect
E P : 0 2 :004(470) [0787] The Holy **Spirit** is present with this Word and opens
E P : 0 2 :004(470) [0787] and power of the Holy **Spirit**, for man's conversion is the
E P : 0 2 :004(470) [0787] Spirit, for man's conversion is the **Spirit**'s work alone.
E P : 0 2 :009(471) [0789] the grace of the Holy **Spirit**, man can convert himself to
E P : 0 2 :010(471) [0789] could not complete it without the grace of the Holy **Spirit**.
E P : 0 2 :011(471) [0789] powers, yet after the Holy **Spirit** has made the beginning
E P : 0 2 :015(471) [0789] resists the Holy **Spirit**, and that the Holy Spirit is given to
E P : 0 2 :015(471) [0789] Spirit, and that the Holy **Spirit** is given to such as resist
E P : 0 2 :017(472) [0791] the attraction of the Holy **Spirit**, God changes stubborn
E P : 0 2 :017(472) [0791] all the works which the Holy **Spirit** performs through us.
E P : 0 2 :018(472) [0791] the will, that is, when the **Spirit** of God through the Word
E P : 0 2 :018(472) [0791] But after the Holy **Spirit** has performed and accomplished
E P : 0 2 :018(472) [0791] means of God the Holy **Spirit**, so that man not only lays
E P : 0 2 :018(472) [0791] cooperates with the Holy **Spirit** in the works that follow.
E P : 0 2 :019(472) [0791] causes, namely, the Holy **Spirit** and the Word of God as
E P : 0 2 :019(472) [0791] Word of God as the Holy **Spirit**'s instrument whereby he
E P : 0 2 :019(472) [0791] solely by the grace and operation of God the Holy **Spirit**.
E P : 0 3 :015(475) [0795] and virtue that the Holy **Spirit** has infused and the works
E P : 0 4 :008(476) [0799] and renewed by the Holy **Spirit**, are obligated to do good
E P : 0 4 :015(477) [0799] works but only the Holy **Spirit**, working through faith,
E P : 0 4 :015(477) [0799] testimonies of the Holy **Spirit**'s presence and indwelling.
E P : 0 4 :019(477) [0801] indwelling of the Holy **Spirit** are not lost through
E P : 0 4 :019(477) [0801] the elect retain the Holy **Spirit** even though they fall into
E P : 0 6 :004(480) [0807] and plagues, to follow the **Spirit** and surrender himself a
E P : 0 6 :005(480) [0807] the law and fruits of the **Spirit** we believe, teach, and
E P : 0 6 :006(480) [0807] 5. Fruits of the **Spirit**, however, are those works which the
E P : 0 6 :006(480) [0807] are those works which the **Spirit** of God, who dwells in
E P : 0 8 :015(488) [0821] was conceived by the Holy **Spirit** in his mother's womb
E P : 1 1 :008(495) [0833] and operation of the Holy **Spirit** and divine assistance for
E P : 1 1 :012(496) [0835] ordinary way for the Holy **Spirit**, so that he cannot work
E P : 1 1 :022(497) [0837] us the grace of his Holy **Spirit** that we may all be of one
E P : 1 2 :004(498) [0839] has more gifts of the Holy **Spirit** than any other holy
E P : 1 2 :022(499) [0841] which God the Holy **Spirit** teaches people and creates in
E P : 1 2 :025(500) [0843] born again through the **Spirit** of God can perfectly keep
E P : 1 2 :028(500) [0843] the Father and the Holy **Spirit**, but is merely adorned
E P : 1 2 :029(500) [0843] Father, Son, and Holy **Spirit**, but as God the Father,
E P : 1 2 :029(500) [0843] Father, Son, and Holy **Spirit** are three distinct persons, so
S D : 0 1 :003(509) [0861] his precious merits, and the Holy **Spirit**'s gracious activity.
S D : 0 1 :014(511) [0863] Likewise, only the Holy **Spirit**'s regeneration and
S D : 0 2 :002(520) [0881] things after the Holy **Spirit** has regenerated him and rules
S D : 0 2 :003(520) [0881] the gift of the Holy **Spirit** man is unable to fulfill the
S D : 0 2 :003(520) [0881] the gift of the Holy **Spirit** he could accomplish nothing
S D : 0 2 :004(520) [0881] man through the Holy **Spirit** without any means or
S D : 0 2 :005(521) [0881] by the power of the Holy **Spirit**, through the Word which
S D : 0 2 :009(522) [0883] and until the Holy **Spirit** enlightens and teaches them they
S D : 0 2 :010(522) [0883] not receive the gifts of the **Spirit** of God, for they are folly
S D : 0 2 :010(522) [0883] not reborn through God's **Spirit**, "walk in the futility of
S D : 0 2 :012(523) [0885] the gifts of the **Spirit** of God (that is, he has no capacity
S D : 0 2 :015(523) [0887] and illuminated us through Baptism and the Holy **Spirit**.
S D : 0 2 :016(523) [0887] God, through the Holy **Spirit** in Baptism, has kindled and
S D : 0 2 :016(523) [0887] that by the same **Spirit** and grace, through daily exercise
S D : 0 2 :017(524) [0887] of the flesh are against the **Spirit**, and these are opposed
S D : 0 2 :017(524) [0887] self (which the Holy **Spirit** has regenerated), but I see in
S D : 0 2 :018(524) [0889] give assent when the Holy **Spirit** offers the grace of God
S D : 0 2 :018(524) [0889] his will unless the Holy **Spirit** illuminates and rules him.
S D : 0 2 :021(525) [0889] preach" until the Holy **Spirit** enlightens, converts, and
S D : 0 2 :022(525) [0889] the gracious and efficacious working of the Holy **Spirit**.
S D : 0 2 :024(525) [0891] and drawn by the Holy **Spirit**, he can do nothing in
S D : 0 2 :024(526) [0891] of God unless the Holy **Spirit** is active in him and kindles
S D : 0 2 :025(526) [0891] operation and the Holy **Spirit**, as the Apology declares.
S D : 0 2 :026(526) [0891] mind, and spirit, is solely the work of the Holy **Spirit**.
S D : 0 2 :026(526) [0891] The Holy **Spirit** is a Spirit "of regeneration and renewal"
S D : 0 2 :026(526) [0891] The Holy Spirit is a **Spirit** "of regeneration and renewal"
S D : 0 2 :026(526) [0891] Jesus is Lord, except by the Holy **Spirit**" (I Cor. 12:3).
S D : 0 2 :029(527) [0893] without faith and the Holy **Spirit** are in the power of the
S D : 0 2 :029(527) [0893] through which the Holy **Spirit** is given, and by pointing
S D : 0 2 :031(527) [0893] are without the Holy **Spirit** are without fear of God,
S D : 0 2 :033(527) [0893] the position that the Holy **Spirit** and his grace are
S D : 0 2 :034(528) [0895] the gift of the Holy **Spirit** which follows upon the
S D : 0 2 :035(528) [0895] to the gift of the Holy **Spirit**, who purifies and daily
S D : 0 2 :036(528) [0895] The Holy **Spirit** has brought me thereto and has
S D : 0 2 :037(528) [0895] the Last Day, the Holy **Spirit** remains with the holy
S D : 0 2 :038(528) [0895] everything to the Holy **Spirit**, namely, that through the
S D : 0 2 :039(528) [0895] and power, but the Holy **Spirit**, as St. Paul says, creates
S D : 0 2 :040(528) [0895] But the Holy **Spirit** has called me through the Gospel,
S D : 0 2 :041(529) [0897] Father gives us his Holy **Spirit** so that by his grace we
S D : 0 2 :042(529) [0897] God must give us his Holy **Spirit**, who enlightens,
S D : 0 2 :046(530) [0899] the work of the Holy **Spirit** and they can do nothing of
S D : 0 2 :047(530) [0901] through his Holy **Spirit** to work these gifts of his within
S D : 0 2 :048(530) [0901] holy sacraments) the Holy **Spirit** wills to be efficacious in
S D : 0 2 :052(531) [0901] God's Word are the Holy **Spirit**'s instrument in, with, and
S D : 0 2 :054(531) [0903] And in this way the Holy **Spirit**, who works all of this, is
S D : 0 2 :055(531) [0903] and operation of the Holy **Spirit**, who through the Word
S D : 0 2 :055(532) [0903] and operation of the Holy **Spirit**, but should be certain
S D : 0 2 :056(532) [0903] judgment on the Holy **Spirit**'s presence, operations, and
S D : 0 2 :056(532) [0903] because the Holy **Spirit**'s activity often is hidden, and
S D : 0 2 :056(532) [0903] and work of the Holy **Spirit**, whereby he assuredly is
S D : 0 2 :058(532) [0903] instruments of the Holy **Spirit** and will not hear, no
S D : 0 2 :058(532) [0903] is done him if the Holy **Spirit** does not illuminate him but
S D : 0 2 :060(533) [0905] who always resist the Holy **Spirit** and oppose and
S D : 0 2 :063(533) [0905] and as long as the Holy **Spirit** motivates him, as St. Paul
S D : 0 2 :063(533) [0905] all who are led by the **Spirit** of God are sons of God."
S D : 0 2 :064(533) [0905] This impulse of the Holy **Spirit** is no coercion or
S D : 0 2 :064(533) [0907] of the flesh are against the **Spirit**, and the desires of the
S D : 0 2 :064(533) [0907] and the desires of the **Spirit** are against the flesh; for these
S D : 0 2 :065(534) [0907] that as soon as the Holy **Spirit** has initiated his work of
S D : 0 2 :065(534) [0907] by the power of the Holy **Spirit**, even though we still do
S D : 0 2 :065(534) [0907] and gifts which the Holy **Spirit** has begun in us in
S D : 0 2 :066(534) [0907] in him through his Holy **Spirit**, guides and leads him, but
S D : 0 2 :066(534) [0907] alongside the Holy **Spirit**, the way two horses draw a
S D : 0 2 :068(534) [0907] only the first fruits of the **Spirit**, and regeneration is not
S D : 0 2 :068(534) [0907] of the flesh against the **Spirit** continues also in the elect
S D : 0 2 :068(534) [0907] the other strong in the **Spirit**, but even the individual
S D : 0 2 :068(534) [0907] moment he is joyful in the **Spirit** and at another moment
S D : 0 2 :069(534) [0907] and thus grieve the Holy **Spirit** within them and lose him,
S D : 0 2 :071(535) [0909] through which the Holy **Spirit** wills to work such
S D : 0 2 :071(535) [0909] so that they are gifts and works of the Holy **Spirit** alone.
S D : 0 2 :072(535) [0909] through which the Holy **Spirit** wills to begin and
S D : 0 2 :072(535) [0909] is to hinder and resist such operations of the Holy **Spirit**.
S D : 0 2 :073(535) [0909] resists the Holy **Spirit**, and if he does nothing at all, but
S D : 0 2 :073(535) [0909] Whether the Holy **Spirit** is given to those who resist him?
S D : 0 2 :075(536) [0911] powers, without the Holy **Spirit**, the free will can convert
S D : 0 2 :076(536) [0911] to complete it, the Holy **Spirit** comes to the aid of the
S D : 0 2 :077(536) [0911] after the Holy **Spirit** has made the beginning and has
S D : 0 2 :077(536) [0911] cooperate with the Holy **Spirit** in the continuation and
S D : 0 2 :078(536) [0911] but solely through the operation of the Holy **Spirit**.
S D : 0 2 :082(537) [0913] resists the Holy **Spirit**, and that the Holy Spirit is given to
S D : 0 2 :082(537) [0913] Spirit, and that the Holy **Spirit** is given to those who
S D : 0 2 :083(537) [0913] clear that when the Holy **Spirit**'s activity produces no
S D : 0 2 :083(537) [0913] change through the Holy **Spirit**'s activity in the intellect,
S D : 0 2 :083(537) [0913] such working of the Holy **Spirit** is able to accept the
S D : 0 2 :083(537) [0913] resist the Holy **Spirit**'s activities and impulses, which take
S D : 0 2 :083(537) [0913] do not receive the Holy **Spirit** but grieve and lose him.
S D : 0 2 :084(537) [0913] of the flesh are against the **Spirit**, and likewise that the
S D : 0 2 :088(538) [0915] the drawing of the Holy **Spirit**, God makes willing people
S D : 0 2 :088(538) [0915] in all the works that the Holy **Spirit** does through us.
S D : 0 2 :089(538) [0915] in conversion the Holy **Spirit** engenders no new impulses
S D : 0 2 :089(538) [0915] and work of the Holy **Spirit** alone, who accomplishes and
S D : 0 2 :090(538) [0915] and heard, the Holy **Spirit**, and man's will) concur.
S D : 0 2 :090(539) [0915] is solely of God the Holy **Spirit**, who is the true craftsman
S D : 0 2 :090(539) [0915] dead, in whom the Holy **Spirit** works conversion and
S D : 0 2 :090(539) [0915] cooperates with the Holy **Spirit** in subsequent good works
S D : 0 3 :010(541) [0919] The Holy **Spirit** offers these treasures to us in the promise
S D : 0 3 :016(541) [0921] offered to us by the Holy **Spirit** through the Gospel and
S D : 0 3 :019(542) [0921] renewal which the Holy **Spirit** works in those who are
S D : 0 3 :019(542) [0921] regeneration and renewing in the Holy **Spirit**" (Titus 3:5).
S D : 0 3 :020(542) [0921] For when the Holy **Spirit** has brought a person to faith
S D : 0 3 :022(543) [0923] that through the Holy **Spirit**'s work we are reborn and
S D : 0 3 :023(543) [0923] there is given the Holy **Spirit**, who renews and sanctifies
S D : 0 3 :028(544) [0925] and a work of the Holy **Spirit**, it does not belong to the
S D : 0 3 :033(545) [0927] afterward when the Holy **Spirit** had renewed and adorned
S D : 0 3 :041(546) [0929] First the Holy **Spirit** kindles faith in us in conversion
S D : 0 3 :041(546) [0929] is justified, the Holy **Spirit** next renews and sanctifies
S D : 0 3 :042(547) [0931] works and the fruits of the **Spirit** do not follow," and the
S D : 0 3 :047(548) [0933] the renewal which the Holy **Spirit** works and is within us.
S D : 0 3 :054(548) [0935] Father, Son, and Holy **Spirit**, who is the eternal and
S D : 0 3 :054(549) [0935] Father, Son, and Holy **Spirit**, who impels them to do
S D : 0 3 :056(549) [0935] conceived by the Holy **Spirit** without sin and had been
S D : 0 3 :062(550) [0937] into them by the Holy **Spirit** and the consequent good
S D : 0 4 :007(552) [0941] through the Holy **Spirit**, or, as St. Paul says, "has been
S D : 0 4 :009(552) [0941] reason St. Paul calls them fruits of faith or of the **Spirit**.

Continued ▶

SD : 0 4 :010(552) [0941] and all our powers, and brings the Holy **Spirit** with it.
SD : 0 4 :012(553) [0941] This the Holy **Spirit** works by faith, and therefore without
SD : 0 4 :031(556) [0947] shame, resists the Holy **Spirit**, and deliberately proceeds
SD : 0 4 :033(556) [0949] you fall away and lose the **Spirit** and his gifts, which you
SD : 0 4 :033(556) [0949] a wicked life, lose the Holy **Spirit**, and reject repentance.'"
SD : 0 4 :038(557) [0951] works which the Holy **Spirit** works in them, and God is
SD : 0 5 :011(560) [0955] Therefore the **Spirit** of Christ must not only comfort but,
SD : 0 5 :011(560) [0955] obtained and sent us the **Spirit**, and for this reason the
SD : 0 5 :012(560) [0955] in John 16:8, 'The Holy **Spirit** will convince the world of
SD : 0 5 :013(560) [0957] "Christ says, 'The Holy **Spirit** will convince the world of
SD : 0 5 :019(561) [0957] Word of God, the Holy **Spirit** through the office of the
SD : 0 5 :022(562) [0959] "a dispensation of righteousness" and "of the **Spirit**."
SD : 0 6 :001(563) [0963] anew through the Holy **Spirit**, who have been converted
SD : 0 6 :002(564) [0963] of God, have become his **Spirit**'s temple, and hence are
SD : 0 6 :002(564) [0963] and impulse of the Holy **Spirit** spontaneously do what
SD : 0 6 :003(564) [0963] motivated by the Holy **Spirit** and hence according to the
SD : 0 6 :003(564) [0963] will of God from a free **spirit**, nevertheless the Holy
SD : 0 6 :003(564) [0963] nevertheless the Holy **Spirit** uses the written law on them
SD : 0 6 :006(564) [0965] through the indwelling **Spirit** in such a way that in their
SD : 0 6 :007(565) [0965] and although the Holy **Spirit** has begun the mortification
SD : 0 6 :008(565) [0965] of the flesh are against the **spirit** and the desires of the
SD : 0 6 :009(565) [0965] on so that they follow the **Spirit** of God, as it is written,
SD : 0 6 :011(565) [0965] It is the Holy **Spirit**, who is not given and received
SD : 0 6 :012(566) [0967] and recalcitrant, the Holy **Spirit** reproves them through
SD : 0 6 :012(566) [0967] In this way the Holy **Spirit** simultaneously performs both
SD : 0 6 :012(566) [0967] written, "When the Holy **Spirit** shall come, he will
SD : 0 6 :014(566) [0967] are rebuked through the **Spirit** of God out of the law.
SD : 0 6 :014(566) [0967] But the same **Spirit** raises them up again and comforts
SD : 0 6 :015(566) [0967] the law and those of the **Spirit**, we must observe with
SD : 0 6 :017(566) [0967] is born anew by the **Spirit** of God and is liberated from
SD : 0 6 :017(566) [0967] driver and is driven by the **Spirit** of Christ), he lives
SD : 0 6 :017(567) [0967] works and fruits of the **Spirit**, or, as St. Paul calls them,
SD : 0 6 :020(567) [0969] the pretext of the Holy **Spirit**'s guidance set up a
SD : 0 6 :023(568) [0969] from the heart by the renewal of the Holy **Spirit**.
SD : 0 6 :025(568) [0971] through God's indwelling **Spirit** they will do his will
SD : 0 7 :005(570) [0973] They say that through the **Spirit** of Christ, which is
SD : 0 7 :005(570) [0973] our bodies, in which the **Spirit** of Christ dwells here upon
SD : 0 7 :011(571) [0975] present, but only the Holy **Spirit**, then when Paul says
SD : 0 7 :028(574) [0981] man foresaw in the **Spirit** that after his death some would
SD : 0 8 :006(592) [1017] the Father and the Holy **Spirit**, yet, when the time had
SD : 0 8 :068(604) [1039] on earth is given, for the **Spirit**, who has all power, has
SD : 0 8 :072(605) [1041] God the Father gave his **Spirit** to Christ, his beloved Son,
SD : 0 8 :072(605) [1041] a way that he received the **Spirit**'s gifts not by measure,
SD : 0 8 :072(605) [1041] The "**Spirit** of wisdom and understanding, of counsel and
SD : 0 8 :072(605) [1041] one essence with the Holy **Spirit**) in such a manner that as
SD : 0 8 :073(605) [1041] things through the Holy **Spirit** who endows them only
SD : 0 8 :073(605) [1041] holy Trinity and the Holy **Spirit** proceeds from him as
SD : 0 8 :073(605) [1041] his and the Father's own **Spirit**, who is never separated
SD : 0 8 :073(605) [1041] the entire fullness of the **Spirit** (as the ancient Fathers say)
SD : 0 8 :074(606) [1043] him without measure the **Spirit** of wisdom and power, so
SD : 1 0 :015(613) [1057] an article which the Holy **Spirit** through the mouth of the
SD : 1 1 :017(619) [1069] active in us by his Holy **Spirit** through the Word when it
SD : 1 1 :029(621) [1073] called is a ministry of the **Spirit** — "which gives the Spirit"
SD : 1 1 :029(621) [1073] Spirit — "which gives the **Spirit**" (II Cor. 3:8) and a
SD : 1 1 :029(621) [1073] And because the Holy **Spirit** wills to be efficacious
SD : 1 1 :031(621) [1073] Thus the **Spirit** of God gives "witness" to the elect "that
SD : 1 1 :033(621) [1073] about it because the Holy **Spirit** gives grace, power, and
SD : 1 1 :039(622) [1075] namely, that the Holy **Spirit** wills to be certainly present
SD : 1 1 :039(623) [1075] resist the Holy **Spirit** (Acts 7:51), remain in sin
SD : 1 1 :040(623) [1077] his counsel that the Holy **Spirit** would call, enlighten, and
SD : 1 1 :040(623) [1077] resist the Holy **Spirit** who wants to work efficaciously in
SD : 1 1 :041(623) [1077] instrument of the Holy **Spirit** which God offers to him
SD : 1 1 :041(623) [1077] call and resists the Holy **Spirit** who wills to be
SD : 1 1 :042(623) [1077] and embitter the Holy **Spirit**, become entangled again in
SD : 1 1 :044(624) [1077] by the power of his Holy **Spirit** through the Word he
SD : 1 1 :059(626) [1083] God's Word and often sorely grieve the Holy **Spirit**.
SD : 1 1 :060(626) [1083] neither his Word, nor his **Spirit**, nor his grace; in fact,
SD : 1 1 :065(627) [1085] And of the Holy **Spirit** Christ says, "He will glorify me"
SD : 1 1 :066(627) [1085] Father, Son, and Holy **Spirit**, directs all men to Christ as
SD : 1 1 :069(627) [1085] come to Christ, the Holy **Spirit** creates true faith through
SD : 1 1 :071(627) [1085] our own powers, the Holy **Spirit** wills to work such
SD : 1 1 :072(628) [1087] Father give the Holy **Spirit** to those who ask him?"
SD : 1 1 :073(628) [1087] Next, since the Holy **Spirit** dwells in the elect who have
SD : 1 1 :073(628) [1087] oppose the urgings of the **Spirit** of God, but should
SD : 1 1 :073(628) [1087] power and might of the **Spirit** within themselves, the less
SD : 1 1 :073(628) [1087] For the **Spirit** testifies to the elect that they are "children
SD : 1 1 :074(628) [1087] whatever of the indwelling **Spirit** of God and say with
SD : 1 1 :075(628) [1087] and through it the Holy **Spirit** wills to effect their
SD : 1 1 :076(629) [1087] by the power of the Holy **Spirit**, but according to his
SD : 1 1 :077(629) [1089] Father because the Holy **Spirit** wills to be present in the
SD : 1 1 :078(629) [1089] and they resisted the Holy **Spirit** who wanted to work
SD : 1 1 :083(630) [1091] and outrage the Holy **Spirit** (Heb. 10:29), and that he
SD : 1 1 :089(631) [1093] promises them the Holy **Spirit** to cleanse and renew them.
SD : 1 1 :092(632) [1093] and hope is contrary to the Holy **Spirit**'s will and intent.
SD : 1 2 :030(635) [1101] whereby God the Holy **Spirit** teaches men the saving
SD : 1 2 :033(635) [1101] born again through the **Spirit** of God is able to keep and
SD : 1 2 :037(636) [1103] Father, Son, and Holy **Spirit**, but that, as there are three
SD : 1 2 :037(636) [1103] Father, Son, and Holy **Spirit**, so also each person has a

Spirit (51) (*Ref. to Christ's spirit or man's spirit*)
AP : 0 4 :087(120) [0147] discussion on *The Spirit and the Letter*, where he says
AP : 0 4 :106(122) [0153] In *The Spirit and the Letter* he says: "The righteousness
AP : 0 4 :254(143) [0193] "Blessed are the poor in **spirit**, for theirs is the kingdom
AP : 0 4 :396(167) [0225] It is easy to evaluate their **spirit**, for in some doctrines
AP : 0 4 :399(168) [0227] One can also judge their **spirit** from the unheard of
AP : 0 7 :033(175) [0239] With a very thankful **spirit** we cherish the useful and
AP : 1 0 :001(179) [0247] of Christ but only in his **spirit** if the Lord's body were not
AP : 2 0 :002(227) [0339] framers of the Confutation have shown their true **spirit**.
AP : 2 4 :026(254) [0391] is a worship in which the **spirit** knows and takes hold of
AP : 2 4 :027(254) [0393] will worship the Father in **spirit** and truth, for such the
AP : 2 4 :027(254) [0393] God is **spirit**, and those who worship him must worship in
AP : 2 4 :027(254) [0393] those who worship him must worship in **spirit** and truth."
AP : 2 4 :027(254) [0393] that worship should be in **spirit**, in faith, and with the
AP : 2 4 :029(255) [0393] to God is a broken **spirit**; a broken and contrite heart, O
S 3 : 0 3 :018(306) [0483] law or vainly vexed with a sorrowful **spirit** by the devil.
S 3 : 0 8 :003(312) [0495] between the letter and the **spirit** without knowing what
S 3 : 0 8 :004(312) [0495] in his churches is **spirit** and law, even when it is above and
LC : 0 1 :101(379) [0609] new pleasure, and a new **spirit** of devotion, and it
LC : 0 1 :187(390) [0633] This **spirit** or revenge clings to every one of us, and it is
LC : 0 1 :188(390) [0635] or malice toward anyone in a **spirit** of anger and hatred.
LC : 0 2 :036(415) [0687] Scriptures, such as the **spirit** of man, heavenly spirits, and
LC : 0 2 :036(415) [0687] as the spirit of man, heavenly spirits, and the evil **spirit**.
LC : 0 5 :075(455) [0771] dissension, party **spirit**, envy, murder, drunkenness,
EP : 0 4 :003(476) [0797] from necessity or coercion but from a spontaneous **spirit**.
EP : 0 4 :010(476) [0799] but from a spontaneous **spirit** because they are "no longer
EP : 0 4 :011(477) [0799] good works from a free **spirit**," should not be understood
EP : 0 4 :012(477) [0799] only to the liberated **spirit** which does good works not
EP : 0 6 :004(480) [0805] have been renewed in the **spirit** of their mind, such
EP : 0 6 :004(480) [0805] has only begun, and in the **spirit** of their mind the
EP : 0 6 :007(481) [0807] and with a willing **spirit**, in so far as he is reborn, does
EP : 0 7 :005(482) [0809] the presence of Christ's **spirit**, or the power of Christ's
EP : 0 8 :036(491) [0825] according to his human **spirit** Christ has certain
EP : 0 8 :038(491) [0825] according to his human **spirit** Christ cannot know what
SD : 0 1 :035(514) [0869] love; and thy care has preserved my **spirit**" (Job 10:8-12).
SD : 0 1 :037(514) [0871] earth as it was, and the **spirit** returns to God who gave it"
SD : 0 2 :026(526) [0891] a new heart, mind, and **spirit**, is solely the work of the
SD : 0 3 :006(540) [0917] pure, it is impossible to repel any error or heretical **spirit**.
SD : 0 4 :003(551) [0939] but flow from a spontaneous **spirit** and a joyful heart.
SD : 0 4 :010(552) [0941] different people in heart, **spirit**, mind, and all our powers,
SD : 0 4 :018(554) [0943] or from a spontaneous **spirit** by those whom the Son of
SD : 0 6 :007(565) [0965] and their renewal in the **spirit** of their minds, nevertheless
SD : 0 6 :008(565) [0965] and the desires of the **spirit** are against the flesh, for these
SD : 0 6 :017(566) [0967] anew, he does everything from a free and merry **spirit**.
SD : 0 6 :018(567) [0967] the conflict between **spirit** and flesh continues in them.
SD : 0 7 :011(571) [0975] a participation not in the body but in the **spirit** of Christ.
SD : 0 7 :055(579) [0991] in the body but in the **spirit**, the virtue, and the benefits
SD : 0 7 :056(579) [0991] the bread but that the **spirit** or faith is participation in the
SD : 0 7 :061(580) [0995] other way than with the **spirit** and faith, in the preaching
SD : 0 7 :099(586) [1005] this mode, as the fanatic **spirit** dreams, for God is not a
SD : 0 7 :104(587) [1009] is established when in **spirit** through faith true believers
SD : 0 7 :126(591) [1015] used, should be adored in **spirit** and in truth in all places

Spirits (17)
AL : 2 8 :045(088) [0089] you died to the elemental **spirits** of the universe, why do
AP : 0 4 :352(161) [0217] dead because of sin, your **spirits** are alive because of
AP : 0 7 :035(175) [0239] you died to the elemental **spirits** of the universe, why do
AP : 2 1 :043(235) [0357] crushed, fanatical **spirits** will arise whom our opponents
S 1 : PR :004(289) [0457] to clothe their venomous **spirits** in the garments of my
S 2 : 0 2 :016(295) [0467] consequence of this: evil **spirits** have introduced the
S 2 : 0 2 :016(295) [0467] knavery of appearing as **spirits** of the departed and, with
LC : 0 2 :036(415) [0687] Many other kinds of **spirits** are mentioned in the
LC : 0 2 :036(415) [0687] as the spirit of man, heavenly **spirits**, and the evil spirit.
LC : 0 2 :044(416) [0689] Men and evil **spirits** there were, teaching us to obtain
LC : 0 4 :015(438) [0735] blasphemy when our new **spirits**, in order to slander
LC : 0 4 :028(440) [0739] Our know-it-alls, the new **spirits**, assert that faith alone
LC : 0 5 :007(447) [0755] babbling of the seditious **spirits** who regard the
LC : 0 5 :012(448) [0755] Still I know that all the **spirits** and scholars put together
LC : 0 5 :028(449) [0759] Here again our clever **spirits** comfort themselves with
SD : 0 2 :022(525) [0889] away forever the wicked **spirits** who fell, he has
SD : 1 2 :008(633) [1097] after the fashion of these **spirits**, into those places and

Spiritu (1)
AG : 2 0 :013(043) [0055] His whole book, *De **spiritu** et litera*, proves this.

Spiritual (143)
AG : 2 6 :009(065) [0071] in this way was said to live a **spiritual** and Christian life.
AG : 2 6 :018(067) [0073] malice or contempt of **spiritual** authority, but dire need
AG : 2 7 :038(077) [0081] that their invented **spiritual** life makes satisfaction for sin
AG : 2 7 :046(078) [0081] people that the invented **spiritual** estate of the orders was
AG : 2 8 :004(081) [0085] the difference between **spiritual** and temporal power,
AG : 2 8 :012(083) [0085] the two authorities, the **spiritual** and the temporal, are
AG : 2 8 :012(083) [0085] or confused, for the **spiritual** power has its commission to
AL : 1 8 :002(039) [0051] of God — that is, **spiritual** righteousness — because
AL : 2 6 :009(065) [0071] title of comprising the **spiritual** life and the perfect life.
AL : 2 6 :038(069) [0075] in subjection and fit for **spiritual** things and for
AP : 0 2 :036(105) [0115] members is forgiven by **spiritual** regeneration, but it
AP : 0 4 :062(115) [0139] For this consolation is a new and **spiritual** life.
AP : 0 4 :125(124) [0157] it must also produce **spiritual** impulses in our hearts.
AP : 0 4 :125(124) [0157] because our hearts have **spiritual** and holy impulses.
AP : 0 4 :136(126) [0159] namely, the inward **spiritual** impulses and the outward
AP : 0 4 :170(130) [0171] and destroy them and to give us new **spiritual** impulses.
AP : 0 4 :194(133) [0175] for other physical and **spiritual** rewards in this life and in
AP : 0 4 :211(136) [0179] of Christ, not because of their own **spiritual** exercises.
AP : 0 4 :351(161) [0217] of our terrors, other **spiritual** impulses increase, such as
AP : 0 4 :353(161) [0217] Here is Christian and **spiritual** perfection, if penitence and
AP : 0 4 :355(161) [0217] merit other bodily and **spiritual** rewards because they
AP : 0 4 :366(163) [0219] both bodily and **spiritual**, in various degrees, according to
AP : 0 7 :014(170) [0231] fact that the church is a **spiritual** people, separated from
AP : 0 7 :019(171) [0233] shows that the true and **spiritual** people will be separated
AP : 0 7 :023(172) [0235] the temporal and the **spiritual** realm, both swords, the
AP : 0 7 :023(172) [0235] realm, both swords, the temporal and the **spiritual**.
AP : 0 7 :031(174) [0237] We are talking about true **spiritual** unity, without which
AP : 0 7 :036(175) [0241] of the heart is a **spiritual** thing that quickens men's
AP : 1 2 :120(200) [0287] they often confused the **spiritual** and the secular
AP : 1 2 :176(210) [0307] It is of a **spiritual** kingdom that Christ is speaking.
AP : 1 5 :025(219) [0321] works as perfect and **spiritual**, they will vastly prefer them
AP : 1 5 :043(221) [0327] of Christ (or the **spiritual** kingdom) and political affairs,
AP : 1 5 :046(221) [0327] This is the **spiritual** exercise of fear and faith.
AP : 1 6 :002(222) [0331] Christ's kingdom is **spiritual**; it is the knowledge of God
AP : 1 6 :004(223) [0331] the Gospel and the **spiritual** kingdom; they are also
AP : 1 6 :007(223) [0331] duty to teach that the **spiritual** kingdom does not change
AP : 1 8 :007(225) [0337] do not ascribe to it the **spiritual** capacity for true fear of
AP : 1 8 :009(226) [0337] civil righteousness and **spiritual** righteousness, attributing
AP : 1 8 :009(226) [0337] righteousness and **spiritual** righteousness, between
AP : 2 4 :026(254) [0391] Pet. 2:5, "A holy priesthood, to offer **spiritual** sacrifices."
AP : 2 4 :026(254) [0391] **Spiritual** sacrifices are contrasted not only with the

Continued ▶

A P : 2 4 :026(254) [0391] *ex opere operato*, for "**spiritual**" refers to the operation of
A P : 2 4 :026(254) [0391] and acceptable to God, which is your **spiritual** worship."
A P : 2 4 :026(254) [0391] "**Spiritual** worship" is a worship in which the spirit knows
A P : 2 4 :027(254) [0393] of the New Testament is **spiritual**; it is the righteousness
A P : 2 4 :028(254) [0393] *opere operato* and teach **spiritual** righteousness and
A P : 2 4 :039(257) [0399] their real meaning is **spiritual** worship and the daily
A P : 2 4 :071(262) [0409] New Testament is the **spiritual** motivation, dying and
A P : 2 7 :037(275) [0433] in the love of their neighbor, and similar **spiritual** virtues.
S 1 : P R :013(291) [0459] and precepts in the **spiritual** and temporal estates, we
S 2 : 0 2 :028(297) [0469] When **spiritual** and physical benefit and help are no
S 3 : 0 5 :002(310) [0491] has joined to the water a **spiritual** power which, through
S 3 : 0 9 :000(314) [0497] punishments with this **spiritual** penalty or
T R : 0 0 :031(325) [0513] gave the apostles only **spiritual** power, that is, the
T R : 0 0 :032(325) [0513] would come after his **spiritual** kingdom was despised
T R : 0 0 :034(325) [0513] of faith and of a **spiritual** kingdom was extinguished.
T R : 0 0 :078(333) [0527] traditions concerning **spiritual** relationship are unjust, and
L C : P R :002(358) [0567] or dogkeepers than **spiritual** guides or pastors.
L C : P R :017(361) [0573] make decisions in both **spiritual** and temporal matters.
L C : 0 1 :054(372) [0595] however, occurs in **spiritual** matters, which pertain to the
L C : 0 1 :093(377) [0607] as are the so-called **spiritual** estates who do not know
L C : 0 1 :112(380) [0613] no need to institute monasticism or "**spiritual** estates."
L C : 0 1 :158(387) [0627] these, there are also **spiritual** fathers — not like those in
L C : 0 1 :158(387) [0627] For the name **spiritual** father belongs only to those who
L C : 0 1 :164(387) [0627] to their temporal and **spiritual** fathers, and for the honor
L C : 0 1 :172(388) [0629] men for both civil and **spiritual** leadership, we must spare
L C : 0 1 :180(389) [0631] now dealt with both the **spiritual** and the civil
L C : 0 1 :184(390) [0633] you even the least good, whether physical or **spiritual**.
L C : 0 1 :197(391) [0637] greatly undermine the "**spiritual** estate" and infringe upon
L C : 0 1 :209(393) [0641] Important as the **spiritual** and civil estates are, these must
L C : 0 1 :221(395) [0643] set over against all "**spiritual** estates" that are chosen
L C : 0 1 :262(400) [0655] when it is applied to **spiritual** jurisdiction or
L C : 0 1 :291(404) [0663] good or greater harm, in **spiritual** or in temporal matters,
L C : 0 1 :312(407) [0671] saints can boast of their **spiritual** orders and the great,
L C : 0 3 :080(431) [0721] obstruct and overthrow **spiritual** order, so that he may
L C : 0 3 :104(434) [0727] where the conscience and **spiritual** matters are at stake.
L C : 0 3 :107(434) [0729] who are concerned with **spiritual** matters (that is, strong
E P : 0 1 :013(467) [0783] and especially that in **spiritual** things its natural powers
E P : 0 1 :014(468) [0783] unimpaired its powers for good even in **spiritual** things.
E P : 0 1 :015(468) [0783] to man's good **spiritual** powers and not the complete
E P : 0 1 :016(468) [0783] good about him even in **spiritual** matters — for example,
E P : 0 1 :016(468) [0783] initiate, to effect, or to cooperate in something **spiritual**.
E P : 0 2 :001(469) [0785] does man possess in **spiritual** matters after the fall of our
E P : 0 2 :002(470) [0787] and confession that in **spiritual** matters man's
E P : 0 2 :002(470) [0787] them" when he is examined concerning **spiritual** things.
E P : 0 2 :003(470) [0787] dead raise himself to **spiritual** life, as it is written, "When
E P : 0 7 :005(482) [0809] To them the word "**spiritual**" means no more than the
S D : 0 1 :002(508) [0859] created, that in **spiritual** matters he is dead to that which
S D : 0 1 :006(509) [0861] God original sin, like a **spiritual** leprosy, has thoroughly
S D : 0 1 :010(510) [0863] acts, to begin and to effect anything in **spiritual** matters."
S D : 0 1 :011(510) [0863] a total lack of good in **spiritual**, divine things, but that at
S D : 0 1 :011(510) [0863] against God, especially in divine and **spiritual** matters.
S D : 0 1 :013(511) [0863] with other bodily, **spiritual**, temporal, and eternal misery,
S D : 0 1 :020(511) [0865] and, especially, that in **spiritual** matters it is good, pure,
S D : 0 1 :021(512) [0865] retains its goodness and powers also in **spiritual** matters.
S D : 0 1 :022(512) [0865] or absence of man's **spiritual** good powers, but only an
S D : 0 1 :023(512) [0865] goodness that belongs to **spiritual** and divine matters, or
S D : 0 1 :023(512) [0865] and effect something in **spiritual** matters or to cooperate
S D : 0 1 :025(512) [0867] do no good thing in **spiritual**, divine matters, not even the
S D : 0 1 :033(514) [0869] words, original sin, like a **spiritual** poison and leprosy,
S D : 0 2 :002(520) [0881] nor what man can do in **spiritual** things after the Holy
S D : 0 2 :007(521) [0883] We believe that in **spiritual** and divine things the intellect,
S D : 0 2 :007(521) [0883] not a spark of **spiritual** powers has remained or exists in
S D : 0 2 :009(522) [0883] to comprehend these **spiritual** things with their reason,
S D : 0 2 :010(522) [0885] man simply "darkness" in **spiritual** and divine things
S D : 0 2 :011(522) [0885] his own power to obtain **spiritual** and heavenly
S D : 0 2 :012(522) [0885] good or right in **spiritual** matters, to understand them, to
S D : 0 2 :012(523) [0885] he has no capacity for **spiritual** things) for they are folly
S D : 0 2 :017(524) [0887] know that the law is **spiritual**; but I am carnal, sold under
S D : 0 2 :020(525) [0889] In **spiritual** and divine things, however, which concern the
S D : 0 2 :024(525) [0891] he can do nothing in **spiritual** things of himself and by his
S D : 0 2 :030(527) [0893] the freedom of the human will in **spiritual** matters.
S D : 0 2 :032(527) [0893] works, we declare that in **spiritual** things our free will and
S D : 0 2 :046(530) [0899] of themselves in these **spiritual** matters, they will refuse to
S D : 0 2 :048(530) [0901] faith, and new **spiritual** power and ability for good in our
S D : 0 2 :062(533) [0905] by which he does anything good in **spiritual** matters.
S D : 0 2 :070(535) [0909] in Christ, to have good **spiritual** thoughts, Christian
S D : 0 2 :077(536) [0911] who maintain that in **spiritual** things man is not wholly
S D : 0 2 :087(538) [0915] of the will from **spiritual** death, is solely and alone the
S D : 0 2 :089(538) [0915] no new impulses and begins no **spiritual** operations in us.
S D : 0 6 :022(567) [0969] teaches us that our **spiritual** sacrifices are acceptable to
S D : 0 7 :018(572) [0979] nothing more than the **spiritual** presence of the body of
S D : 0 7 :048(578) [0989] the body of Christ were **spiritual** bread or a spiritual food
S D : 0 7 :048(578) [0989] Christ were spiritual bread or a **spiritual** food for the soul.
S D : 0 7 :056(579) [0991] were speaking only of a **spiritual** participation in the body
S D : 0 7 :056(579) [0991] cannot be speaking of a **spiritual** eating but of a
S D : 0 7 :057(579) [0993] not be speaking of a **spiritual** fellowship with Christ,
S D : 0 7 :061(580) [0995] The one is **spiritual**, of which Christ speaks chiefly in
S D : 0 7 :061(580) [0995] Without this **spiritual** participation, even the sacramental
S D : 0 7 :062(581) [0995] This **spiritual** eating, however, is precisely faith —
S D : 0 7 :065(581) [0995] eating he ordains the **spiritual** eating, when he said, "Do
S D : 0 7 :088(585) [1003] as referring only to the **spiritual** and internal use of faith
S D : 0 7 :100(586) [1005] the incomprehensible, **spiritual** mode of presence
S D : 0 7 :104(587) [1009] our churches use the word "**spiritual**" in this context.
S D : 0 7 :104(587) [1009] this word "**spiritual**" means precisely that spiritual
S D : 0 7 :104(587) [1009] means precisely that **spiritual** communion which is
S D : 0 7 :104(587) [1009] Christ and become true, **spiritual** members of his body.
S D : 0 7 :105(588) [1009] or we use the word "**spiritual**" in this discussion, we have
S D : 0 7 :105(588) [1009] we have in mind the **spiritual**, supernatural, heavenly
S D : 0 7 :105(588) [1009] too, we use the word "**spiritual**" when we say that the
S D : 0 7 :105(588) [1009] such eating occurs with the mouth, the mode is **spiritual**.
S D : 0 7 :115(589) [1011] of Christ with its merit is **spiritual** food for our souls).
S D : 0 8 :068(604) [1039] were so, since God is a **spiritual** and indivisible essence

Spiritualists (2)
S 3 : 0 8 :003(312) [0495] — that is, from the **spiritualists** who boast that they
S D : 0 7 :091(585) [1005] The **spiritualists** have advanced no new arguments since

Spirituality (4), Spiritualizing (1), Spiritually (25)
A G : 2 7 :013(073) [0077] God's Word and command without invented **spirituality**.
A G : 2 7 :048(078) [0081] this curious angelic **spirituality** and sham of poverty,
A P : 1 0 :003(179) [0247] we are joined to Christ **spiritually** by true faith and
S 3 : 0 8 :005(312) [0495] Word of God to **spiritualizing** and to their own
E P : 0 2 :003(470) [0787] man who through sin is **spiritually** dead raise himself to
E P : 0 5 :008(479) [0803] hands and explains it **spiritually** (Matt. 5:21-48);
E P : 0 7 :004(482) [0809] Supper but assert that this takes place **spiritually** by faith.
E P : 0 7 :015(483) [0811] are received not only **spiritually**, by faith, but also orally
E P : 0 7 :026(485) [0815] we receive the body of Christ only **spiritually** by faith.
E P : 0 9 :001(492) [0827] or according to body and soul, **spiritually** or corporeally?
E P : 1 2 :005(498) [0839] individual self-chosen **spirituality**, which in fact is nothing
S D : 0 1 :060(519) [0879] man is in God's sight **spiritually** lifeless and with all his
S D : 0 2 :010(522) [0883] understand them because they are **spiritually** discerned."
S D : 0 2 :011(522) [0885] little can a man who is **spiritually** dead, in sin, prepare or
S D : 0 2 :090(539) [0915] will of a man who is **spiritually** dead, in whom the Holy
S D : 0 5 :010(559) [0955] hands and explains it **spiritually** (Matt. 5:21ff.; Rom. 7:6,
S D : 0 5 :010(560) [0955] they do not see the law **spiritually**, or how much it
S D : 0 7 :003(569) [0973] but still only **spiritually**, of the body of Christ which is
S D : 0 7 :005(570) [0973] to be received **spiritually** (that is, according to its power,
S D : 0 7 :006(570) [0975] body and blood to eat **spiritually** by faith but not to
S D : 0 7 :008(570) [0975] do they partake **spiritually** by faith also of the body of
S D : 0 7 :059(580) [0993] Supper the body of Christ is received only **spiritually**.
S D : 0 7 :059(580) [0993] means whereby we are **spiritually** united with Christ and
S D : 0 7 :066(581) [0997] is received not only **spiritually** through faith, which
S D : 0 7 :072(582) [0997] the one through faith **spiritually**, the other orally, which
S D : 0 7 :088(585) [1003] Christ takes place only **spiritually** through faith, or that
S D : 0 7 :105(588) [1009] eaten, and drunk **spiritually**, for although such eating
S D : 0 7 :114(589) [1011] is partaken of only **spiritually** through faith and that in
S D : 0 7 :118(590) [1013] only received and partaken of through faith, **spiritually**.
S D : 1 2 :010(634) [1097] and self-chosen **spirituality** as on a kind of new monkery.

Spite (19), Spiteful (3)
P R : P R :009(006) [0011] In **spite** of all this we found, not without distress on our
P R : P R :019(009) [0017] them off on simple folk in **spite** of the fact that this
A G : 2 3 :019(054) [0063] if it were a great crime, in **spite** of that fact that in the
A G : 2 7 :006(071) [0077] compelled to remain, in **spite** of the fact that even the
A G : 2 8 :041(087) [0089] the case is reserved, in **spite** of the fact that canon law
A P : 0 4 :018(109) [0125] This in **spite** of the fact that the law is never satisfied,
A P : 0 4 :163(129) [0169] we have a gracious God in **spite** of our unworthiness.
A P : 0 4 :392(167) [0225] This in **spite** of the fact that prelates and some
A P : 1 1 :009(182) [0251] of the summists, which, in **spite** of everything, would be
A P : 1 2 :060(190) [0269] believes the same, in **spite** of our opponents' cries to the
S 1 : P R :004(289) [0455] are some who are so **spiteful** — not only among our
L C : 0 1 :262(400) [0655] the most shameful and **spiteful** persecution and
L C : 0 3 :032(424) [0707] it shall indeed be done in **spite** of the devil and all the
L C : 0 3 :068(429) [0717] us without hindrance, in **spite** of their fury, so that they
L C : 0 4 :066(445) [0749] us from Adam, irascible, **spiteful**, envious, unchaste,
E P : 0 8 :034(491) [0825] 15. That in **spite** of Christ's express assertion, "All
E P : 1 1 :004(495) [0833] on its duration, so that in **spite** of its intrinsic wickedness
E P : 1 2 :008(498) [0839] nor encourage it, in **spite** of the expressed word of God's
S D : 0 1 :021(512) [0865] in human nature, in **spite** of which and beneath which
S D : 0 1 :061(519) [0879] handiwork, our nature in **spite** of its being corrupted,
S D : 0 7 :105(588) [1009] upon our churches in **spite** of our public and oft-repeated
S D : 0 8 :011(593) [1019] but one single person, in **spite** of the fact that two distinct

Splashed (2)
E P : 0 1 :014(468) [0783] only been sprinkled or **splashed** on externally and that
S D : 0 1 :021(512) [0865] spot or blemish, merely **splashed** on, or a corruption only

Splendid (4), Splendor (3)
A P : 0 7 :007(169) [0229] presented before him in **splendor**, without spot or wrinkle
L C : 0 1 :093(377) [0607] of God, no matter how **splendid** and brilliant it may
L C : 0 1 :314(407) [0671] Aided by great pomp, **splendor**, and magnificent
L C : 0 1 :326(409) [0675] is to illuminate and impart its **splendor** to all the others.
L C : 0 4 :011(438) [0735] It makes a much more **splendid** appearance when a
S D : 0 2 :044(529) [0897] Again, in his **splendid** exposition of Genesis, especially of
S D : 0 3 :067(551) [0937] Luther's beautiful and **splendid** exposition of St. Paul's

Split (1)
E P : 1 2 :002(498) [0839] The Anabaptists have **split** into many factions, some of

Spoil (1), Spoiled (1)
L C : 0 1 :242(397) [0649] them: "Your grain will **spoil** in the garner and your beer
L C : 0 1 :282(403) [0661] right to have their sport **spoiled**, as a warning to others.

Sponsors (2)
S 3 : 1 5 :004(316) [0501] to such ceremonies of **sponsors** who might make gifts,
S C : P R :011(339) [0535] be accepted as **sponsors** in Baptism, or be allowed to

Spontaneity (1), Spontaneous (11), Spontaneously (14)
A L : 2 7 :029(075) [0079] who have taken the vow **spontaneously** and deliberately!
A L : 2 7 :030(075) [0079] make a promise which is not **spontaneous** and deliberate.
L C : 0 1 :219(394) [0643] always follows **spontaneously** without any command.
L C : 0 1 :330(410) [0677] heart, there will arise a **spontaneous** impulse and desire
L C : 0 3 :026(424) [0705] prayer will come **spontaneously**, as it should, and we
E P : 0 4 :003(476) [0797] from necessity or coercion but from a **spontaneous** spirit.
E P : 0 4 :010(476) [0799] of the law but from a **spontaneous** spirit because they are
E P : 0 4 :013(477) [0799] children of God this **spontaneity** is not perfect, but they
E P : 0 6 :006(481) [0807] and do them as **spontaneously** as if they knew of no
S D : 0 2 :064(533) [0905] the converted man **spontaneously** does that which is
S D : 0 2 :075(536) [0911] the heart, and by this **spontaneous** obedience earn the
S D : 0 3 :015(541) [0919] dying, but also in his **spontaneous** subjection to the law in
S D : 0 4 :003(551) [0939] are not necessary but **spontaneous**, since they are not
S D : 0 4 :003(551) [0939] law but flow from a **spontaneous** spirit and a joyful
S D : 0 4 :018(554) [0943] willingly or from a **spontaneous** spirit by those whom the
S D : 0 4 :018(554) [0943] the proposition that good works are **spontaneous**.
S D : 0 6 :002(564) [0963] that just as the sun **spontaneously** completes its regular

Continued ▶

SD : 0 6 :002(564) [0963] of the Holy Spirit **spontaneously** do what God requires
SD : 0 6 :006(565) [0965] and altogether **spontaneously**, without any instruction,
SD : 0 6 :006(565) [0965] once and for all, **spontaneously** and unhindered, without
SD : 0 6 :006(565) [0965] angels render God a completely **spontaneous** obedience.
SD : 0 6 :023(568) [0969] law but willingly and **spontaneously** from the heart by the
SD : 0 6 :025(568) [0971] they will do his will **spontaneously**, without coercion,
SD : 0 8 :064(603) [1037] the assumed nature, **spontaneously** and when and where
SD : 0 8 :066(604) [1039] fully, though always **spontaneously**, *in, with, and*
SD : 0 8 :074(606) [1041] and manifests itself **spontaneously** and with all power in,

Sport (1)
LC : 0 1 :282(403) [0661] gossips right to have their **sport** spoiled, as a warning to

Spot (5), Spots (1)
AP : 0 7 :007(169) [0229] him in splendor, without **spot** or wrinkle or any such
AP : 0 7 :011(170) [0229] has been defiled by any **spot** cannot be called part of the
EP : 0 1 :014(468) [0783] sin is a slight, insignificant **spot** or blemish that has only
EP : 0 1 :015(468) [0783] be removed as readily as a **spot** can be washed from the
SD : 0 1 :021(512) [0865] insignificant, external **spot** or blemish, merely splashed
SD : 0 1 :022(512) [0865] impedes it; or that the **spots** spoken of can easily be

Spouse (2)
SC : 0 3 :014(347) [0547] and property; a pious **spouse** and good children,
LC : 0 1 :223(395) [0643] our own person and our **spouse**, our temporal property is

Spread (8), Spreading (1)
PR : PR :008(005) [0009] adopt, to defend, or to **spread** a different or a new
AL : 1 7 :005(038) [0051] others who are now **spreading** Jewish opinions to the
AP : 0 4 :101(121) [0151] which by the Gospel he has **spread** throughout the world?
AP : 1 2 :053(189) [0265] among the Jews, and **spread** by the apostles throughout
AP : 2 4 :052(259) [0403] priesthood and sacrifices is **spread** before their eyes.
TR : 0 0 :026(324) [0511] priesthood is, but is **spread** abroad through the whole
LC : 0 1 :267(401) [0657] about someone else, they **spread** it into every corner,
LC : 0 1 :276(402) [0659] should not be quick to **spread** slander and gossip about
LC : 0 3 :027(424) [0705] and greater desires and **spread** your cloak wide to receive

Spring (5), Sprung (2)
AL : 0 1 :005(028) [0043] all heresies which have **sprung** up against this article, such
AL : 1 8 :005(040) [0051] I mean the acts which **spring** from the good in nature,
TR : 0 0 :048(328) [0519] many profligate acts have **sprung** from the tradition of
LC : 0 1 :075(375) [0601] good may take root, **spring** up, and bear fruit, and men
LC : 0 1 :311(407) [0671] all good works must **spring**, the true channel through
LC : 0 1 :326(409) [0675] and thanksgiving, which **spring** from that love and trust
LC : 0 6 :033(461) [0000] with eagerness for a fresh **spring**, so I yearn and tremble

Sprinkled (1), Sprinkles (1), Sprinkling (4)
AP : 0 4 :282(149) [0201] sure which — said that **sprinkling** water mixed with salt
AP : 0 4 :283(150) [0201] our own time the daily **sprinkling** with water, the habit of
AP : 2 4 :036(257) [0397] offering symbolizes the **sprinkling**, that is, the sanctifying
AP : 2 4 :036(257) [0397] to Jesus Christ and for **sprinkling** with his blood."
AP : 2 4 :038(257) [0399] alive when the Gospel **sprinkles** us with the blood of
EP : 0 1 :014(468) [0783] that has only been **sprinkled** or splashed on externally

Spun (2)
LC : 0 4 :006(437) [0733] the Lord's Prayer are not **spun** out of any man's
SD : 0 7 :045(577) [0987] or human contradiction, **spun** out of human reason, to

Spurious (1)
TR : 0 0 :071(332) [0525] he may be, just as the writings of Clement are **spurious**.

Spurn (4)
AP : 1 2 :051(189) [0265] not feel God's wrath in their smugness **spurn** consolation.
LC : 0 1 :155(386) [0625] We **spurn** favor and happiness; therefore, it is only fair
LC : 0 5 :053(453) [0765] more callous and cold, and eventually **spurn** it altogether.
SD : 1 1 :040(623) [1077] called through the Word, **spurn** the Word and persistently

Spurred (1)
LC : 0 1 :102(379) [0609] yet everyone should be **spurred** on by the realization that

Spy (1)
SD : 1 0 :011(612) [1055] in, who slipped in to **spy** out our freedom which we have

Squares (2)
AP : 2 4 :080(264) [0411] Thus it **squares** with our position that a minister who
AP : 2 4 :081(264) [0411] Thus the term "liturgy" **squares** well with the ministry.

Squeeze (1)
LC : 0 1 :301(405) [0667] sets out to gain and **squeeze** something out of his

Stable (2)
LC : 0 1 :228(396) [0645] it is nothing but a vast, wide **stable** full of great thieves.
LC : 0 3 :074(430) [0719] unless he gives us a **stable**, peaceful government.

Stage (1)
AP : 2 3 :032(243) [0373] celibacy, they would **stage** a wonderful victory

Stake (2), Stakes (1)
LC : 0 3 :014(422) [0701] But that is to **stake** prayer on luck and to mumble
LC : 0 3 :104(434) [0727] where the conscience and spiritual matters are at **stake**.
LC : 0 4 :017(438) [0735] God himself **stakes** his honor, his power, and his might on

Stall (2)
LC : 0 1 :224(395) [0643] in a grocery shop, butcher **stall**, wine- and beer-cellar,
LC : 0 1 :242(397) [0649] Your cattle will die in the **stall**.

Stamp (1), Stamped (2)
AP : 2 3 :012(241) [0367] because it is an ordinance divinely **stamped** on nature.
LC : 0 3 :075(430) [0719] or if a loaf of bread were **stamped** on coins, to remind
SD : 0 1 :011(510) [0863] an inborn wicked **stamp**, an interior uncleanness of the

Stand (48), Standing (9), Stands (9), Stood (6)
PR : PR :024(013) [0021] dissensions, and long-**standing** schisms a Christian
PR : PR :024(013) [0023] and will allow nothing to **stand** in the way of this cause
AG : 2 3 :012(053) [0063] also broke up the marriages which were of long **standing**.
AG : 2 4 :036(060) [0067] reports how the priest **stood** every day, inviting some to
AG : 2 8 :052(089) [0091] Christ has set us free; **stand** fast, therefore, and do not
AL : 2 4 :036(060) [0067] says that the priest **stands** daily at the altar, inviting some
AP : 0 4 :058(115) [0137] mark iniquities, Lord, who shall **stand**?" (Ps. 130:3).
AP : 0 4 :103(122) [0151] blood canceled the bond that **stood** against us (Col. 2:14).
AP : 0 4 :326(158) [0211] he says that no one can **stand** the judgment of God if he
AP : 0 4 :326(158) [0211] O Lord, shouldst mark iniquities, Lord, who could **stand**?"
AP : 0 4 :329(158) [0211] of the flesh cannot **stand** the judgment of God.
AP : 1 2 :048(188) [0265] cancels the bond which **stood** against us with its legal
AP : 1 2 :084(194) [0277] without which no one can **stand** before the judgment of
AP : 2 0 :004(227) [0339] of the Confutation **stand** if their attention had been called
AP : 2 1 :018(231) [0347] day the root of Jesse shall **stand** as an ensign to the
AP : 2 1 :035(234) [0353] the whole Psalter every day while **standing** on one foot.
AP : 2 3 :070(249) [0383] of God's Word will **stand**, as Isaiah says (40:6), "All flesh
AP : 2 4 :023(253) [0391] Let this **stand** in this issue, then, that the death of Christ
AP : 2 4 :040(257) [0399] refute but supports our **stand** because we require all the
AP : 2 4 :044(258) [0399] temples" and the altars **standing** unadorned, without
AP : 2 4 :097(268) [0417] Carnal men cannot **stand** it when only the sacrifice of
AP : 2 7 :032(274) [0431] soldiers he cannot **stand** up against the Lord who comes
AP : 2 7 :057(279) [0439] many arguments for the **stand** that monastic vows, as
AP : 2 8 :015(283) [0447] when he says (Gal. 5:1), "**Stand** fast in the freedom with
S 1 : PR :003(289) [0455] to show where I have **stood** until now and where, by
S 1 : PR :003(289) [0455] now and where, by God's grace, I will continue to **stand**.
S 1 : PR :013(291) [0459] out gnats, if we let logs **stand** and dispute about specks,
S 2 : 0 4 :001(298) [0471] an overlord but chose to **stand** beside him as Christian
S 2 : 0 4 :016(301) [0475] council we shall not be **standing** before the emperor or
S 2 : 0 4 :016(301) [0475] hearing, but we shall **stand** before the pope and the devil
S 3 : 0 3 :005(304) [0481] might know how they **stood** before God and recognize
S 3 : 1 5 :003(316) [0501] articles on which I must **stand** and on which I will stand,
S 3 : 1 5 :003(316) [0501] stand and on which I will **stand**, God willing, until my
SC : 0 7 :002(352) [0557] Then, kneeling or **standing**, say the Apostles' Creed and
SC : 0 7 :005(353) [0559] Then, kneeling or **standing**, say the Apostles' Creed and
LC : PR :014(360) [0571] whether sitting, walking, **standing**, lying down, or rising,
LC : 0 1 :031(369) [0589] to this one which **stands** at the head of the list because it
LC : 0 1 :046(370) [0593] These words must **stand** and prove to be true since God
LC : 0 1 :052(371) [0595] Let this **stand** as the plain and simple meaning of this
LC : 0 1 :090(377) [0607] of clerics in our day who **stand** daily in the churches,
LC : 0 1 :100(379) [0609] For where the heart **stands** idle and the Word is not
LC : 0 1 :118(381) [0615] wretched people when, **standing** before God and the
LC : 0 1 :142(384) [0621] all who are called masters **stand** in the place of parents
LC : 0 1 :241(397) [0649] We shall **stand** by and let such persons fleece, grab, and
LC : 0 1 :257(399) [0653] meaning, as the words **stand** ("You shall not bear false
LC : 0 1 :280(403) [0661] Then you do not **stand** alone.
LC : 0 1 :314(407) [0671] For when a priest **stands** in a gold-embroidered chasuble
LC : 0 1 :332(410) [0677] looks, and even wherever he goes or wherever he **stands**.
LC : 0 3 :002(420) [0697] and remove all that **stands** in our way and hinders us from
LC : 0 3 :009(421) [0699] But there **stands** the commandment, "You shall and must
LC : 0 3 :030(424) [0707] to arm themselves in order to **stand** against the devil.
LC : 0 3 :087(432) [0723] is not possible always to **stand** firm in such a ceaseless
LC : 0 3 :092(432) [0725] and cheerful conscience to **stand** before him in prayer.
LC : 0 3 :100(433) [0725] yet such is life that one **stands** today and falls tomorrow.
LC : 0 3 :100(433) [0727] we are upright and **stand** before God with a good
LC : 0 3 :109(435) [0729] heart that I can scarcely **stand**, for he is an enemy who
LC : 0 4 :008(437) [0733] external it may be, here **stand** God's Word and command
LC : 0 4 :029(440) [0739] to which it may cling and upon which it may **stand**.
LC : 0 5 :013(448) [0755] Here we shall take our **stand** and see who dares to
LC : 0 5 :064(454) [0769] Here **stand** the gracious and lovely words, "This is my
EP : 0 7 :010(483) [0811] The grounds on which we **stand** in this controversy with
EP : 1 0 :006(493) [0829] Christ has set us free; **stand** fast therefore, and do not
SD : 0 3 :032(545) [0927] can therewith and thereby **stand** before the tribunal of
SD : 0 3 :032(545) [0927] is reckoned to faith can **stand** before God's tribunal.
SD : 0 4 :034(557) [0949] of their unbelief, and you **stand** fast only through faith"
SD : 0 7 :091(585) [1005] *"This Is My Body" Still **Stand** Firm*, his *Great* and *Small*
SD : 0 7 :093(586) [1005] on which we have **stood** consistently from the outbreak
SD : 0 8 :043(599) [1029] If Zwingli's *alloeosis* **stands**, then Christ will have to be
SD : 0 8 :082(607) [1045] Here you must take your **stand** and say that wherever
SD : 0 8 :086(608) [1047] *That These Words Still **Stand** Firm* and in his *Great*
SD : 1 0 :011(612) [1055] Christ has set us free; **stand** fast therefore, and do not
SD : 1 2 :006(633) [1097] propose to look on idly or **stand** by silently while

Standard (2), Standards (3)
AP : 1 5 :033(220) [0325] do not find any sure **standards** by which to free
SC : PR :013(339) [0535] wrong according to the **standards** of those among whom
EP : RN :006(465) [0779] should conform to the **standards** set forth above.
EP : 0 1 :001(466) [0779] *to the aforesaid **Standard** and Comprehensive*
SD : 0 7 :125(591) [1015] their own self-devised **standard** of preparation, may

Standpoint (2)
LC : 0 5 :033(450) [0761] the sacrament from the **standpoint** both of its essence and
SD : 0 7 :050(578) [0989] best qualified from the **standpoint** of wisdom and

Star (2), Stars (3)
AP : 0 4 :024(110) [0127] says, "Neither the evening **star** nor the morning star is
AP : 0 4 :024(110) [0127] star nor the morning **star** is more beautiful than
AP : 0 7 :050(178) [0245] fixed movements of the **stars** are truly ordinances of God
LC : 0 2 :014(412) [0681] of life — sun, moon, and **stars** in the heavens, day and
SD : 0 6 :006(565) [0965] sun, the moon, and all the **stars** of heaven regularly run

Start (4)
PR : PR :024(013) [0021] of pure doctrine, to **start** scandalous controversies at will
AP : 0 4 :071(116) [0141] as though faith were the **start** of justification or a
EP : 1 1 :002(494) [0831] 1. To **start** with, the distinction between the
SD : 0 2 :076(536) [0911] natural powers man can **start** out toward that which is

Starve (1)
LC : 0 1 :190(391) [0635] hunger and do not feed him, you have let him **starve**.

State (60), States (37), Stated (24), Stating (2)
AG : PR :016(026) [0041] that for reasons there **stated** Your Imperial Majesty was
AG : PR :024(027) [0043] and it is specifically **stated**, article by article, in what
AG : 0 3 :006(030) [0045] the living and the dead, as **stated** in the Apostles' Creed.
AG : 1 6 :005(038) [0051] civil authority, the **state**, and marriage but requires that

Continued ▶

AG : 22 :006(050) [0061] St. Jerome also **states** that the priests who administered
AG : 23 :003(051) [0061] some of our priests have entered the married **state**.
AG : 23 :016(054) [0063] The old canons also **state** that it is sometimes necessary to
AG : 23 :020(055) [0063] imperial laws and in all **states** in which there have been
AG : 27 :013(072) [0077] life than by all other **states** of life instituted by God —
AG : 27 :016(073) [0077] In fact, it is called a **state** of perfection and is regarded as
AG : 27 :049(078) [0083] are told that monks alone are in a **state** of perfection.
AG : 27 :051(079) [0083] people, hearing the **state** of celibacy praised above all
AG : 27 :058(080) [0083] That is a good and perfect **state** of life which has God's
AG : 27 :058(080) [0083] hand, that is a dangerous **state** of life which does not have
AG : 27 :060(080) [0083] his time to speak of monastic life as a **state** of perfection.
AL : 16 :004(038) [0051] the heart, but it does not destroy the **state** or the family.
AL : 23 :016(054) [0063] The canons themselves **state** that in later times the old
AL : 23 :020(055) [0063] laws of all well-ordered **states**, even among the heathen,
AL : 27 :016(073) [0077] they assert that it is a **state** of perfection, and they put it
AL : 27 :023(074) [0079] The canons **state** that every vow is subject to the right of
AL : 27 :046(078) [0081] invented observances were a **state** of Christian perfection.
AL : 27 :049(078) [0083] men hear that only monks are in a **state** of perfection.
AL : 27 :056(080) [0083] the administration of the **state**, withdrew into a
AL : 27 :060(080) [0083] in his day to say that monastic life is a **state** of perfection.
AL : 28 :009(082) [0085] has faith," and Ps. 119:50 **states**, "Thy Word gives me
AL : 28 :011(082) [0085] The **state** protects not souls but bodies and goods from
AP : 04 :028(111) [0129] of God outside a **state** of grace do not sin.
AP : 04 :079(117) [0143] It is easy to **state** the minor premise if we know how the
AP : 04 :086(119) [0147] add clear testimonies **stating** that faith is the very
AP : 04 :087(119) [0147] deals with this subject and **states** that when we believe
AP : 04 :133(125) [0159] In II Cor. 3:15-17 he **states** that the veil that covered the
AP : 04 :185(132) [0173] The rule I have just **stated** interprets all the passages they
AP : 04 :191(133) [0175] war and in governing the **state** are holy works, true
AP : 04 :207(135) [0177] observances in the **state**, but they do condemn the wicked
AP : 04 :236(140) [0185] them, they would bring peace to both church and **state**.
AP : 04 :270(147) [0197] of the Decalogue itself **states**, "Showing steadfast love to
AP : 04 :292(152) [0203] As we have already **stated**, we teach that a man is justified
AP : 07 :021(172) [0233] sins by their love for God before entering a **state** of grace.
AP : 12 :042(187) [0263] Lord's Supper clearly **state**, "This is my body which is
AP : 13 :015(213) [0311] then many other **states** or offices might also be called
AP : 15 :044(221) [0327] this description of the **state** of our churches it is evident
AP : 16 :004(223) [0331] called it an evangelical **state** to hold property in common,
AP : 16 :004(223) [0331] spiritual kingdom; they are also dangerous to the **state**.
AP : 16 :005(223) [0331] does not destroy the **state** or the family but rather
AP : 16 :013(224) [0333] and humility far above the **state** and the family, even
AP : 18 :006(225) [0335] does not sin if, outside the **state** of grace, he does the
AP : 20 :001(226) [0337] Article XX they expressly **state** their rejection and
AP : 21 :002(229) [0343] So our opponents **state** a triumph as though the war were
AP : 21 :043(235) [0357] many indications that the **state** of the church does not
AP : 23 :016(241) [0369] marriage is more necessary now than in the **state** of purity.
AP : 23 :069(249) [0383] We have previously **stated** our position in the Jovinian
AP : 24 :011(251) [0387] our Confession we have **stated** our position that the
AP : 24 :014(251) [0387] Though we have already **stated** our case, we must add a
AP : 27 :028(274) [0429] they say: "It has been **stated** in the Sacred Scriptures that
AP : 27 :029(274) [0431] say that this decree of theirs is **stated** in the Scriptures.
AP : 27 :036(275) [0433] but they say that it is a **state** for acquiring perfection.
AP : 27 :036(275) [0433] this correction, that it is a **state** for acquiring perfection.
AP : 27 :037(275) [0433] life will be no more a **state** of perfection than the life of a
AP : 27 :037(275) [0433] These, too, are **states** for acquiring perfection.
AP : 28 :001(281) [0443] that the present article **states** about the immunity of
AP : 28 :003(281) [0443] Meanwhile they neglect the **state** of the churches, and
S1 : PR :008(290) [0457] no government, and no **state** of matrimony, but that all
S1 : PR :014(291) [0459] tasks upon us in church, **state**, and family that we can
S2 : 02 :001(293) [0463] by the Lamb of God alone, as has been **stated** above.
S2 : 03 :001(298) [0471] government in cities and **states**, and also well trained girls
S2 : 04 :008(300) [0473] a complicated and confused **state** of affairs that would be!
S3 : 03 :010(304) [0481] For, as **stated** above, they did not have the right teaching
S3 : 06 :005(311) [0493] as St. Paul himself **states**, "The bread which we break"
S3 : 10 :003(314) [0497] own laws, for their laws **state** that those who are ordained
TR : 00 :014(322) [0507] For Cyprian **states** in his fourth letter to Cornelius:
TR : 00 :019(323) [0509] And in the records he **states** that at the Council of
TR : 00 :050(329) [0519] of the third canon **states**, "No one shall judge the supreme
TR : 00 :063(331) [0523] this, for the power is the same, as I have already **stated**.
TR : 00 :073(332) [0525] the one thing (as Jerome **states**) that distinguishes bishops
TR : 00 :080(334) [0527] the churches, as the rule **states**, "The benefice is given
SC : PR :015(340) [0535] a single syllable, as **stated** above with reference to the
LC : 01 :133(383) [0619] implied, yet in none is it so plainly and explicitly **stated**.
LC : 01 :167(388) [0629] superiors is not explicitly **stated** in the Ten
LC : 01 :177(389) [0631] We all complain about this **state** of things, but we do not
LC : 01 :201(392) [0637] The **state** of virginity was not commended, neither were
LC : 04 :029(440) [0739] as we have sufficiently **stated**, but through its
LC : 05 :001(447) [0753] in the same way, **stating** what it is, what its benefits are,
LC : 05 :075(455) [0771] For persons in such a **state** of mind that they cannot feel
EP : 02 :001(469) [0785] discussed in four different **states**: (1) before the Fall, (2)
EP : 02 :001(469) [0785] about man's will and ability in the second **state**.
EP : 02 :006(470) [0787] Christ also **states**, "Apart from me you can do nothing."
EP : 08 :016(489) [0821] But in the **state** of his humiliation he dispensed with it
EP : 08 :016(489) [0821] to me," and as St. Paul **states**, He ascended "far above all
EP : 08 :039(491) [0827] nature, as though in the **state** of humiliation he had laid
SD : PR :014(506) [0855] shepherds," as Luther **states**, "must both pasture or feed
SD : 01 :006(509) [0861] we are redeemed from this **state** through Christ's merit.
SD : 01 :030(513) [0867] As **stated** in a foregoing thesis when we discussed the
SD : 02 :002(520) [0881] and viewed as being in four distinct and dissimilar **states**.
SD : 02 :002(520) [0881] is not concerning the **state** of man's will before the Fall,
SD : 02 :008(521) [0883] the questions and issues **stated** at the beginning of this
SD : 02 :029(527) [0893] afterward the article **states** that "human reason and
SD : 02 :034(527) [0893] The Smalcald Articles **state** further: "This repentance
SD : 02 :044(529) [0897] On the contrary, he **states** that blind and captive man
SD : 02 :053(531) [0903] externally because, as **stated** above, even after the Fall
SD : 03 :019(542) [0921] discriminately when he **states**, "He saved us by the
SD : 03 :028(544) [0925] of the Epistle to the Galatians Dr. Luther well **states**:
SD : 03 :042(547) [0931] Latin text of the Apology **states**, "James teaches correctly
SD : 04 :006(552) [0939] settlement, we shall **state** our teaching, belief, and
SD : 04 :033(556) [0947] election," the Apology **states** in Article XX: "Peter
SD : 04 :034(556) [0949] grace but also our present **state** of grace and our hope of
SD : 04 :040(558) [0951] this proposition, unqualifiedly **stated**, in our churches.
SD : 05 :012(560) [0955] He **states**: "Everything that preaches about our sin and
SD : 05 :014(560) [0957] the Smalcald Articles **state**: "The New Testament retains
SD : 07 :019(572) [0979] The Smalcald Articles **state** that "the bread and the wine
SD : 07 :077(583) [0999] And Luther **states**: "This his command and institution can
SD : 07 :092(586) [1005] the letters read, but, as **stated** above, we shall understand
SD : 08 :025(596) [1023] ascension but also in the **state** of his humiliation — for
SD : 08 :026(596) [1025] kept it hidden during the **state** of his humiliation and did
SD : 08 :041(599) [1029] And shortly thereafter he **states**: "If the old witch, Dame
SD : 08 :044(599) [1029] Likewise, Dr. Luther **states** in his treatise *Concerning the*
SD : 08 :059(602) [1035] human nature when it **states**, "The blood of Jesus his Son
SD : 08 :064(604) [1039] used in explaining this doctrine, as we **stated** above.
SD : 08 :076(606) [1043] attested when they **stated** that Christ's flesh is a life-giving
SD : 08 :085(608) [1045] his death, Dr. Luther **states**: "According to the second,
SD : 10 :020(614) [1059] the Smalcald Articles **state**: "Just as we cannot adore the
SD : 11 :038(622) [1075] the Augsburg Confession **states** in Article XI, we retain
SD : 11 :042(623) [1077] the devil so that their last **state** will be worse than the
SD : 11 :076(628) [1087] and true what Scripture **states**, that no one comes to

Statement (95), Statements (37)

AG : PR :009(025) [0041] submit a similar written **statement** of their judgments and
AG : 23 :002(053) [0063] man, made this **statement** because of grave misgivings.
AG : 23 :023(055) [0063] These two **statements** fit together well, for it must be a
AG : 24 :035(060) [0067] be proved by St. Paul's **statement** in I Cor. 11:20ff. and
AG : 24 :035(060) [0067] in I Cor. 11:20ff. and by many **statements** of the Fathers.
AG : 26 :044(070) [0075] in faith," and there is a **statement** in Dist. 12 that such
AL : 26 :045(070) [0075] are gathered, and this **statement** is made: "It was not the
AP : 02 :001(100) [0105] and distort a **statement** that has nothing wrong in it.
AP : 02 :035(105) [0115] Luther meant by this **statement** that original sin remains
AP : 02 :043(106) [0117] we do not object to this **statement**, but it is not right to
AP : 04 :082(118) [0145] There is a similar **statement** in Heb. 4:14-16, "Since then
AP : 04 :082(118) [0145] but in Christ, the high priest, this **statement** requires faith.
AP : 04 :088(120) [0149] that Paul made the **statement** "Faith justifies"
AP : 04 :103(121) [0151] There are similar **statements** here and there in the holy
AP : 04 :106(122) [0153] of law is set forth in the **statement** that he who keeps the
AP : 04 :106(122) [0153] A little later we shall quote several other **statements**.
AP : 04 :163(129) [0169] sake, according to the **statement** (Ps. 32:1; Rom. 4:7),
AP : 04 :184(132) [0173] To all their **statements** about the law we answer
AP : 04 :219(137) [0181] law, according to the **statement** (Jer. 31:33), "I will put
AP : 04 :238(140) [0187] Peter they quote this **statement** (I Pet. 4:8), "Love covers
AP : 04 :238(140) [0187] for he connects this **statement** with the commandment of
AP : 04 :240(141) [0187] Furthermore, this **statement** about love is taken from
AP : 04 :241(141) [0187] same thing as Paul's **statement** in Col. 3:13, namely, that
AP : 04 :245(142) [0189] condemn this faith in **statements** and writings, but they
AP : 04 :254(143) [0193] Other **statements** about works are also quoted against us.
AP : 04 :256(144) [0193] works, this universal **statement** must be permitted to
AP : 04 :258(144) [0193] be foolish in such a **statement** to look only at these
AP : 04 :270(147) [0197] In the **statement**, "If you would enter life, keep the
AP : 04 :277(148) [0199] The **statement** in Tob. 4:11 ought to be taken the same
AP : 04 :279(149) [0199] in its entirety, Tobit's **statement** shows that faith is
AP : 04 :304(154) [0205] the word "faith," as this **statement** of Paul shows, "Since
AP : 04 :314(156) [0207] We stress this **statement** so often because it is so clear.
AP : 04 :334(158) [0215] Here Christ's **statement** (Luke 17:10) also applies, "When
AP : 04 :339(159) [0215] unwarranted: from the **statement**, "When you have done
AP : 04 :339(159) [0215] in your works," to the **statement**, "When you have
AP : 04 :339(159) [0215] The two **statements** are not analogous since the causes
AP : 04 :341(159) [0215] twist against faith **statements** made in support of faith.
AP : 04 :345(160) [0217] Unless it is qualified, this **statement** seems absurd.
AP : 04 :353(161) [0217] From these **statements** the fair-minded reader can judge
AP : 04 :383(166) [0225] Therefore they corrupt many other **statements**.
AP : 07 :007(169) [0229] We have repeated this **statement** almost verbatim in our
AP : 07 :028(173) [0237] Christ's **statement** teaches us this in order that we may
AP : 11 :008(181) [0251] sins, according to the **statement** (Ps. 19:12), "Who can
AP : 12 :040(187) [0261] him, according to the **statement** (Luke 10:16), "He who
AP : 12 :059(190) [0267] expressly condemn our **statement** that men obtain the
AP : 12 :068(192) [0271] in addition to patristic **statements** which the decrees
AP : 12 :069(192) [0271] attaches to the **statements** of later theologians who did
AP : 12 :070(192) [0271] to oppose this **statement** of Peter, citing the consensus of
AP : 12 :071(192) [0271] Spirit was added to this **statement** of Peter, for the text
AP : 12 :091(195) [0279] do this because many **statements** about penitence are
AP : 12 :091(196) [0279] These **statements** make no mention of faith, and the
AP : 12 :092(196) [0279] obvious danger in these **statements**, requiring contrition
AP : 12 :096(196) [0281] makes this very clear **statement** about penitence: "We
AP : 12 :097(196) [0281] Thus there are **statements** in the Fathers not only about
AP : 12 :117(199) [0287] support from many **statements** of the scholastics; for
AP : 12 :122(200) [0289] Then they quote certain **statements** from the Fathers and
AP : 12 :122(200) [0289] penitence, following the **statement** of Paul, "He gave
AP : 12 :139(203) [0295] Peter Lombard's **statement** about remitting part of the
AP : 12 :140(204) [0295] Thus the **statement**, "I will be your death," should be
AP : 12 :165(208) [0303] A **statement** that is important and wholesome with regard
AP : 12 :176(210) [0307] loose, according to the **statement** (Matt. 16:19),
AP : 12 :176(210) [0307] according to the **statement** (II Cor. 10:8), "Our authority,
AP : 13 :001(211) [0309] opponents approve the **statement** that the sacraments are
AP : 13 :023(214) [0313] And Paul's **statement** is familiar (Rom. 10:10), "Man
AP : 15 :018(217) [0319] condemns our **statement** in the article on the church that
AP : 15 :031(219) [0323] In the apostolic **statement** in Acts 15:10, "Why do you
AP : 20 :001(226) [0337] condemnation of our **statement** that men do not merit the
AP : 20 :004(227) [0339] have refused to let this **statement** of the Confutation stand
AP : 23 :016(241) [0369] they cannot abolish the **statement**, "It is better to marry
AP : 23 :064(248) [0381] pure, according to the **statement** (Isa. 52:11), "Purify
AP : 23 :064(248) [0381] pure, according to the **statement** (Titus 1:15), "To the
AP : 23 :068(248) [0383] Such **statements** show our opponents' purpose in writing
AP : 24 :001(249) [0383] repeat the prefatory **statement** that we do not abolish the
AP : 24 :009(250) [0387] have collected many **statements** to prove that the Mass is
AP : 24 :075(263) [0411] There are many **statements** of this sort in the Fathers, all
AP : 24 :076(263) [0411] There are also **statements** about thanksgiving, like the
AP : 24 :076(263) [0411] like the beautiful **statement** of Cyprian about the godly
AP : 27 :003(269) [0419] friends found this same **statement** about the decline of the
AP : 27 :004(269) [0421] how much credence should be given to this **statement**.
AP : 27 :011(270) [0423] for us to quote Paul's **statement** from Galatians
AP : 27 :013(271) [0423] Gospel, if it is not the **statement** of the eternal Father
AP : 27 :018(272) [0425] we have quoted Paul's **statement** in support of this, they
AP : 27 :019(272) [0425] rascals have the audacity to call this **statement** wicked.
AP : 27 :023(273) [0427] conflicts with Christ's **statement** (Matt. 15:9), "In vain do
AP : 27 :023(273) [0427] also conflicts with this **statement** (Rom. 14:23):

Continued ▶

A P : 2 7 :029(274) [0431] that according to the **statement** of the Sacred Scriptures
A P : 2 7 :043(276) [0435] life, unless perhaps the **statement** that they will receive a
A P : 2 8 :018(284) [0449] Certainly the **statement**, "He who hears you hears me"
A P : 2 8 :019(284) [0449] Thus these asses take a **statement** that supports our
A P : 2 8 :020(284) [0449] They also quote the **statement** (Heb. 13:17), "Obey your
A P : 2 8 :020(284) [0449] This **statement** requires obedience to the Gospel; it does
A P : 2 8 :020(284) [0449] to obey them by the **statement** (Gal. 1:8), "If anyone
S 2 : 0 2 :014(295) [0467] with them whether **statements** of St. Augustine are to be
T R : 0 0 :025(324) [0511] As to the **statement**, "On this rock I will build my church"
T R : 0 0 :027(324) [0511] and Bede) interpret the **statement** "on this rock" in this
T R : 0 0 :033(325) [0513] and other similar **statements** which claim that the pope is
S C : P R :001(338) [0533] and simple catechism or **statement** of Christian teaching.
L C : 0 4 :082(446) [0751] Therefore the **statement** is incorrect.
E P : 0 2 :015(471) [0789] 8. Likewise when these **statements** are made without
E P : 0 2 :018(472) [0791] 9. Likewise Luther's **statement** that man's will in
E P : 0 4 :011(477) [0799] and confess that the **statement**, "The regenerated do good
E P : 0 4 :017(477) [0801] discipline that bald **statement** that good works are
E P : 0 7 :034(485) [0815] is unable (a dreadful **statement**!) to cause his body to be
E P : 0 7 :041(486) [0817] questions and **statements**, which decency forbids us to
E P : 0 8 :034(491) [0825] to me," and St. Paul's **statement**, "In him dwells the
S D : P R :005(502) [0847] subsequent doctrinal **statements**, to depart from the
S D : P R :009(505) [0853] to further extensive **statements** in his doctrinal and
S D : 0 1 :044(516) [0873] Both **statements** are contrary to the Scriptures.
S D : 0 1 :051(517) [0875] Thus in the **statement**, "God creates man's nature," the
S D : 0 1 :051(517) [0875] But in the **statement**, "It is the serpent's nature to bite and
S D : 0 1 :055(518) [0877] and rejected the **statement**, "Original sin is the nature or
S D : 0 2 :027(526) [0891] by St. Augustine's own **statement**, persuaded him to
S D : 0 2 :030(527) [0893] These **statements** indicate clearly that the Augsburg
S D : 0 2 :043(529) [0897] We shall also include a **statement** from Dr. Luther's
S D : 0 2 :044(529) [0897] how he intended his **statements** to be understood, and
S D : 0 2 :046(530) [0899] As a result of their **statements** many people have become
S D : 0 3 :012(541) [0919] Thus the following **statements** of St. Paul are to be
S D : 0 3 :019(542) [0921] the Apology, where the **statement** is made, "Justification
S D : 0 3 :033(545) [0927] At this point St. Paul's **statement** concerning Abraham is
S D : 0 3 :041(546) [0931] Dr. Luther's excellent **statement** remains true: "There is a
S D : 0 3 :053(548) [0933] opposed to Paul's **statement** that salvation belongs to
S D : 0 4 :024(555) [0945] (Rom. 4:6), or the **statement** in Article VI of the
S D : 0 7 :017(572) [0979] what kind of doctrinal **statement** they should submit to
S D : 0 7 :034(575) [0983] From these **statements** and especially from the exposition
S D : 0 7 :036(575) [0985] and explain the **statement**, "The Word became flesh," with
S D : 0 8 :035(597) [1027] because the **statements** that we make about the person of
S D : 0 8 :054(601) [1033] The **statement** is, of course, correct and true that Christ's
S D : 0 8 :055(601) [1033] Yet according to the **statement** of the Scriptures these
S D : 0 8 :061(602) [1035] accept and repeat the **statements** which the ancient
S D : 0 9 :001(610) [1051] rest on the simple **statement** of our Christian Creed, to
S D : 1 0 :021(614) [1059] we find the following **statement**: "No one should assume
S D : 1 2 :001(632) [1095] adverted in this **statement** of ours (such as the

Station (7), Stations (2)
P R : P R :001(003) [0007] the requirements of his **station** and dignity, under whose
P R : P R :024(013) [0023] Christian persons, of high **station** and low, are sighing
P R : P R :025(014) [0025] according to his **station**, all affection, service, and
A G : 1 6 :005(038) [0051] love and genuine good works in his **station** of life.
A G : 2 3 :013(053) [0063] intelligent people in high **station** have expressed similar
A G : 2 7 :049(079) [0083] our particular calling and **station** in life; and that
A L : 2 0 :002(041) [0053] good purpose about all **stations** and duties of life,
A P : 0 7 :022(172) [0235] as well as those in lesser **stations** have apostasized from
L C : 0 1 :047(371) [0593] Let each person be in his **station** in life according to

Statue (3), Statues (2)
A P : 2 1 :034(234) [0353] one monastery we saw a **statue** of the blessed Virgin
A P : 2 1 :035(234) [0353] marvelous tales about **statues** and pictures do not even
A P : 2 4 :044(258) [0399] altars standing unadorned, without candles or **statues**.
S D : 0 2 :020(525) [0889] or a stone, like a lifeless **statue** which uses neither mouth
S D : 0 2 :089(538) [0915] as a stone does when a **statue** is carved out of it, or wax

Statutes (4)
A P : 1 5 :014(217) [0319] "Do not walk in the **statutes** of your fathers, nor observe
A P : 1 5 :014(217) [0319] your God; walk in my **statutes**, and be careful to observe
A P : 2 7 :030(274) [0431] Ezek. 20:25, "I gave them **statutes** that were not good and
S D : 0 6 :009(565) [0965] was afflicted that I might learn thy **statutes**" (Ps. 119:71).

Stay (6), Stays (1)
P R : P R :020(010) [0017] faith they are to **stay** with the plain words of Christ.
L C : 0 5 :053(453) [0765] own case, that if a person **stays** away from the sacrament,
L C : 0 5 :058(453) [0767] and unruly must be told to **stay** away, for they are not fit
L C : 0 5 :073(455) [0771] purely and worthily, you must **stay** away from it forever.
L C : 0 6 :021(459) [0000] purity of his confession, let him just **stay** away from it.
L C : 0 6 :029(460) [0000] you despise it and proudly **stay** away from confession,
S D : 1 1 :043(623) [1077] If we **stay** with this and hold ourselves thereto, it is indeed

Stead (7)
A G : 2 5 :003(062) [0069] for it is spoken in God's **stead** and by God's command.
A P : 0 7 :028(173) [0237] or the sacraments, they do so in Christ's place and **stead**.
A P : 0 7 :047(177) [0243] ministers act in Christ's **stead** and do not represent their
S D : 0 3 :015(541) [0919] to the law in our **stead** and his keeping of the law in so
S D : 0 3 :030(544) [0925] the law of God in our **stead** and which is reckoned to the
S D : 0 3 :058(550) [0937] birth to his death in the **stead** of us poor sinners, and thus
S D : 1 1 :027(620) [1071] ambassadors in Christ's **stead**, and God is admonishing

Steadfast (8), Steadfastly (6), Steadfastness (4)
A P : 0 1 :002(100) [0103] We **steadfastly** maintain that those who believe otherwise
A P : 0 4 :270(147) [0197] itself states, "Showing **steadfast** love to thousands of
S C : 0 1 :021(344) [0543] hate me, but showing **steadfast** love to thousands of those
S C : 0 3 :011(347) [0547] us and keeps us **steadfast** in his Word and in faith even to
S C : 0 8 :010(354) [0559] for he is good; for his **steadfast** love endures forever.
S C : 0 8 :010(354) [0559] who fear him, in those who hope in his **steadfast** love."
L C : 0 3 :066(429) [0717] that we must remain **steadfast**, suffer patiently whatever
L C : 0 3 :068(429) [0717] and we may remain **steadfast** in the face of all violence
L C : 0 5 :031(450) [0759] it, except by **steadfastly** believing the Scriptures and the
E P : 1 1 :008(495) [0833] and divine assistance for **steadfastness** and eternal life.
E P : 1 1 :016(497) [0837] instruction that by **steadfastness** and by the
S D : P R :013(506) [0855] who remained **steadfastly** in the pure doctrine.
S D : 0 1 :035(514) [0869] has granted me life and **steadfast** love; and thy care has
S D : 0 3 :066(550) [0937] grace we shall remain **steadfastly** and constantly with the
S D : 0 7 :033(575) [0983] one else, remained by it **steadfastly** and defended it
S D : 1 1 :012(618) [1067] but in order that "by **steadfastness**, by the encouragement
S D : 1 1 :092(632) [1093] instruction, that by **steadfastness** and by encouragement
S D : 1 2 :006(633) [1097] God's grace to remain **steadfastly** in our commitment to

Steadily (1), Steady (1)
A P : 2 1 :041(235) [0355] recent ones, so their theology has **steadily** degenerated.
L C : 0 3 :075(430) [0719] we could not have the **steady** blessing of daily bread.

Steal (15), Stealing (7), Steals (2), Stolen (5)
A P : 0 4 :222(137) [0181] It is also necessary not to **steal**.
A P : 0 4 :222(137) [0181] it is necessary not to **steal**, therefore not stealing justifies;
A P : 0 4 :222(137) [0181] to steal, therefore not **stealing** justifies; for justification is
A P : 1 2 :169(209) [0305] Anyone who keeps on **stealing** is not really sorry that he
A P : 1 2 :169(209) [0305] really sorry that he has **stolen** or robbed, for he is still a
A P : 1 2 :169(209) [0305] as it is written (Eph. 4:28), "Let the thief no longer **steal**."
A P : 1 6 :011(224) [0333] command, "You shall not **steal**," the Decalogue
A P : 2 0 :012(228) [0341] that from now on you **steal** no more, and therefore you
A P : 2 7 :046(277) [0435] in the commandment (Ex. 20:15), "You shall not **steal**."
S C : P R :018(340) [0537] which treats of **stealing**, must be emphasized when
S C : 0 1 :013(343) [0541] *"You shall not steal."*
S C : 0 5 :020(350) [0553] and whether you have **stolen**, neglected, or wasted
L C : S P :007(362) [0575] 7. You shall not **steal**.
L C : 0 1 :100(378) [0609] night relaxes his effort to **steal** upon you unawares and to
L C : 0 1 :222(395) [0643] *"You shall not steal."*
L C : 0 1 :224(395) [0643] For to **steal** is nothing else than to acquire another's
L C : 0 1 :224(395) [0643] **Stealing** is a widespread, common vice, but people pay so
L C : 0 1 :224(395) [0643] I have just said, a person **steals** not only when he robs a
L C : 0 1 :229(396) [0645] and yet with a great show of legality they rob and **steal**.
L C : 0 1 :230(396) [0645] which has plundered and **stolen** the treasures of the whole
L C : 0 1 :231(396) [0647] Those who can **steal** and rob openly are safe and free,
L C : 0 1 :243(397) [0649] eyes every day that no **stolen** or ill-gotten possession
L C : 0 1 :245(398) [0649] short, however much you **steal**, depend on it that just as
L C : 0 1 :245(398) [0649] depend on it that just as much will be **stolen** from you.
L C : 0 1 :245(398) [0649] since everyone robs and **steals** from the other, he
L C : 0 1 :246(398) [0651] with those of you who despise, defraud, **steal**, and rob us.
L C : 0 1 :250(398) [0651] Enough has been said concerning the nature of **stealing**.
L C : 0 1 :307(406) [0669] It may not be called **stealing** or fraud, yet it is coveting —
L C : 0 3 :006(420) [0699] as having no other God, not killing, not **stealing**, etc.

Stealthily (1)
L C : 0 1 :099(378) [0609] take us by surprise and **stealthily** take the Word of God

Stench (1)
L C : 0 1 :198(392) [0637] human holiness is only **stench** and filth, and it merits

Step (10), Steps (2)
A G : 2 3 :003(051) [0061] and moved to take this **step** by the great distress of their
A P : 1 2 :006(183) [0255] any one of our opponents **step** forward and tell us when
A P : 1 2 :011(184) [0255] All this happens in the first **step**.
A P : 1 2 :013(184) [0257] There remains the third **step**, satisfaction.
A P : 2 1 :034(234) [0353] From invocation the next **step** was to images.
A P : 2 1 :042(235) [0355] gracious emperor take **steps** to correct the abuses, for
L C : 0 1 :185(390) [0633] God, like a kind father, **steps** in and intervenes to get the
L C : 0 1 :278(402) [0661] all monks and holy orders **step** forth, with all their works
L C : 0 1 :333(410) [0677] Let all wise men and saints **step** forward and produce, if
L C : 0 2 :004(411) [0679] it is sufficient, as a first **step**, for very simple persons to
L C : 0 2 :052(417) [0691] hear God's Word, which is the first **step** in entering it.
L C : 0 5 :063(454) [0767] rely firmly upon itself; otherwise it refuses to take a **step**.

Stephen (3)
S 3 : 1 5 :005(317) [0501] I, **Stephen** Agricola, minister in Hof, subscribe
T R : 0 0 :082(334) [0529] **Stephen** Agricola, minister in Chur, subscribed with his
S D : 0 2 :060(533) [0905] acknowledged truth, as **Stephen** describes the obstinate

Stettin (2)
S 3 : 1 5 :005(317) [0501] Paul Rhode, superintendent of **Stettin**
T R : 0 0 :082(334) [0529] Paul Rhode, preacher in **Stettin**

Stewardship (1)
A P : 2 8 :005(282) [0445] will some day have to give account of your **stewardship**.

Stick (1), Sticks (1)
A P : P R :011(099) [0101] always made it a point to **stick** as closely as possible to
A P : 0 4 :179(131) [0171] through faith, though sin still **sticks** to your flesh."

Stiff (1)
P R : P R :022(011) [0019] doctrines and their **stiff**-necked proponents and

Stilled (3)
A P : 0 4 :224(138) [0181] God; his wrath must be **stilled** and the conscience find
A P : 0 4 :264(146) [0195] debt can be removed, that the wrath of God can be **stilled**.
A P : 0 4 :319(156) [0209] so that they can never be **stilled**; for the law always

Stimulated (1), Stimulates (1), Stimulations (1)
P R : P R :008(005) [0011] been reminded and **stimulated** by this our reiterated and
A P : 0 4 :017(109) [0125] but that this disposition **stimulates** it to do so more
L C : 0 1 :212(393) [0641] inclinations and **stimulations** have their way without let

Sting (4)
A P : 0 4 :079(118) [0143] in I Cor. 15:56, 57: "The **sting** of death is sin, and the
A P : 1 2 :153(206) [0299] there is no longer that **sting** and sense of wrath of which
A P : 1 2 :153(206) [0299] says (I Cor. 15:56), "The **sting** of death is sin, and the
E P : 0 1 :022(469) [0785] the nature of a serpent to **sting**," and, "It is the nature or

Stipends (2)
A G : 2 4 :013(057) [0065] the sake of revenues and **stipends**, were discontinued in
A L : 2 4 :011(057) [0065] only for revenues or **stipends**, and how many celebrate

Stirs (2)
A P : 0 4 :240(141) [0187] what it means: "Hatred **stirs** up strife, but love covers all
L C : 0 3 :063(428) [0715] These he **stirs** up, fanning and feeding the flames, in

Stoic (1), Stoics (1)
EP : 0 2 :008(470) [0787] mad dream of the so-called **Stoic** philosophers and of
SD : 0 2 :074(535) [0909] 1. The absurdity of the **Stoics** and Manichaeans in holding

Stolberg (2)
PR : PR :027(015) [0025] Albert Geroge, count of **Stolberg**
PR : PR :027(015) [0025] Wolf Ernest, count of **Stolberg**

Stone (14), Stones (3)
AP : 0 4 :098(121) [0149] Acts 4:11, 12, "This is the **stone** which was rejected by you
AP : 1 5 :019(218) [0319] with gold and silver, with precious **stones** and costly gifts."
AP : 1 5 :021(218) [0321] and silver and precious **stones**," believing that he is
S3 : 1 5 :004(316) [0501] bells, the baptism of altar **stones**, the invitation to such
LC : 0 1 :125(382) [0617] would set up a block or a **stone** which we might call
LC : 0 5 :033(450) [0761] not spoken or preached to **stone** and wood but to those
LC : 0 5 :065(454) [0769] not preached to wood or **stone** but to you and me;
LC : 0 5 :083(456) [0773] never give up until the **stone** is removed from your heart.
SD : 0 2 :019(524) [0889] man to a hard **stone** which resists rather than yields in
SD : 0 2 :020(525) [0889] wife, yes, like a log or a **stone**, like a lifeless statue which
SD : 0 2 :022(525) [0889] destiny for which only man, no **stone** or log, was created.
SD : 0 2 :024(525) [0891] in anything as a **stone**, a block, or a lump of clay could.
SD : 0 2 :059(532) [0905] case it is correct to say that man is not a **stone** or a block.
SD : 0 2 :059(532) [0905] A **stone** or a block does not resist the person who moves
SD : 0 2 :059(532) [0905] is much worse than a **stone** or block, for he resists the
SD : 0 2 :062(533) [0905] to work in irrational creatures or in a **stone** or block.
SD : 0 2 :089(538) [0915] suffers — though not as a **stone** does when a statue is

Stony (1)
SD : 0 2 :026(526) [0891] God removes the hard, **stony** heart and bestows a new

Stop (9), Stopped (2), Stopping (1), Stops (2)
PR : PR :010(006) [0011] the adversaries might be **stopped** by solid reasoning, and
AP : 0 4 :162(129) [0169] first of all, Christ does not **stop** being the mediator after
AP : 1 4 :005(215) [0315] provided that the bishops **stop** raging against our
AP : 1 8 :005(225) [0335] in the ungodly, never **stops** inciting this feeble nature to
AP : 2 4 :024(253) [0391] of the Gospel they had to **stop**; therefore they were not
S1 : PR :005(289) [0457] But how can I **stop** all the mouths of the devil?
S3 : 0 8 :006(312) [0495] Why do they not **stop** preaching and writing until the
LC : PR :019(361) [0573] Let them never **stop** until they have proved by experience
LC : 0 1 :079(375) [0603] common expression for "**stopping** work" literally means
LC : 0 3 :109(435) [0729] he is an enemy who never **stops** or becomes weary; when
LC : 0 5 :026(449) [0759] of tricks, and does not **stop** until he has finally worn us
EP : 0 2 :004(470) [0787] that men should hear his Word and not **stop** their ears.
EP : 1 1 :008(495) [0833] hear the Word and do not **stop** their ears or despise it.
SD : 0 7 :018(572) [0979] In this way was **stopped** up every subterfuge and

Storm (1)
LC : 0 3 :068(429) [0717] the devil and all his host **storm** and rage furiously against

Story (3), Stories (4)
AP : 2 1 :036(234) [0353] no one has sought out in the true **stories** about the saints.
AP : 2 1 :037(234) [0355] many things that resemble the "true **stories**" of Lucian.
AP : 2 2 :010(237) [0361] when they apply the **story** of Eli's sons to the sacrament.
AP : 2 2 :010(237) [0361] The **story** describes Eli's punishment.
AP : 2 7 :038(275) [0433] of the hermits there are **stories** of Anthony and of others
LC : 0 1 :270(401) [0657] For when you repeat a **story** that you cannot prove, even
EP : 0 3 :006(473) [0793] a mere knowledge of the **stories** about Christ, but the

Stove (1)
LC : 0 1 :088(377) [0605] when we sit behind the **stove** and refrain from external

Straight (3), Straightforward (1)
LC : 0 1 :004(365) [0581] the heart, and these fly **straight** to the one true God and
LC : 0 1 :047(371) [0593] the right path and walk **straight** ahead, using all of God's
LC : 0 1 :273(401) [0659] someone, rebuke him **straight** to his face and make him
SD : 1 0 :013(613) [1057] they had not been **straightforward** about the truth of the

Strain (1), Straining (1)
S1 : PR :013(291) [0459] to swallow camels and **strain** out gnats, if we let logs
LC : 0 1 :299(405) [0665] to suit their purpose, **straining** words and using them for

Strange (10), Stranger (1), Strangers (1)
AP : 0 4 :059(115) [0137] It is **strange** that our opponents make so little of faith
AP : 1 2 :051(189) [0265] wroth, to do his deed — **strange** is his deed! and to work
AP : 2 7 :052(278) [0437] It is indeed **strange** that with such dangers and scandals
S3 : 0 2 :004(303) [0479] God or that he worships **strange** gods — something that
LC : 0 1 :151(386) [0625] servants, neighbors, or **strangers** and tyrants will inflict
LC : 0 1 :191(391) [0635] food or drink, I was a **stranger**, and you did not welcome
SD : PR :014(506) [0855] that they will flee from **strange** voices and separate the
SD : 0 1 :030(513) [0867] inborn original sin but a **strange** and foreign something
SD : 0 5 :011(560) [0955] what the prophet calls "a **strange** deed" (that is, to
SD : 0 7 :092(586) [1005] word and testament to a **strange** meaning different from
SD : 0 7 :113(589) [1011] are to be given a different, new, and **strange** sense.
SD : 1 1 :010(618) [1065] to draw and formulate **strange**, dangerous, and

Strangled (4)
AG : 2 8 :032(086) [0087] the eating of blood and what is **strangled** was forbidden.
AG : 2 8 :065(092) [0093] should abstain from blood and from what is **strangled**.
AL : 2 8 :032(086) [0087] men to abstain from blood and from what is **strangled**.
LC : 0 1 :225(395) [0645] such sums he would be **strangled** with a noose, but the

Strasbourg (1)
TR : 0 0 :082(335) [0529] Paul Fagius, of **Strasbourg**

Straw (4)
LC : 0 1 :156(386) [0625] not have a penny in the house or a **straw** in the field.
LC : 0 3 :081(431) [0721] we would not have a **straw** in the field, a penny in the
LC : 0 4 :008(437) [0733] though to all appearances it may not be worth a **straw**.
LC : 0 4 :012(438) [0735] be as noble and good as if God were to pick up a **straw**.

Straying (1)
PR : PR :006(004) [0009] might be preserved from **straying** from the right course of

Streams (1)
LC : 0 6 :033(461) [0000] a hart longs for flowing **streams**, so longs my soul for

Streets (1)
LC : 0 1 :277(402) [0659] while he went out on the **streets** to complain to his

Strength (31), Strengthen (23), Strengthened (6), Strengthening (8), Strengthens (8)
AG : 0 3 :004(030) [0045] he may sanctify, purify, **strengthen**, and comfort all who
AG : 1 3 :001(035) [0049] the purpose of awakening and **strengthening** our faith.
AG : 1 3 :002(036) [0049] in faith and for the purpose of **strengthening** faith.
AG : 2 0 :034(045) [0057] and governs himself by his own human **strength** alone.
AG : 2 0 :036(046) [0057] nature and human **strength** are much too weak to do
AG : 2 1 :001(046) [0057] that our faith may be **strengthened** when we see what
AG : 2 7 :005(071) [0077] not sufficiently appreciated or understood their **strength**.
AL : 0 2 :003(029) [0045] be justified before God by his own **strength** and reason.
AL : 0 4 :001(030) [0045] before God by their own **strength**, merits, or works but
AL : 2 0 :010(042) [0055] Christ, by human **strength**, although Christ has said of
AL : 2 0 :034(045) [0057] himself by human **strength** alone without faith and
AL : 2 7 :005(071) [0077] in years, they were unable to judge their own **strength**.
AP : 0 4 :023(110) [0127] righteousness by its own **strength**, though it is often
AP : 0 4 :027(111) [0127] too, that by its own **strength** reason can love God above
AP : 0 4 :040(112) [0131] the law by their own **strength**, and they are all under sin
AP : 0 4 :106(122) [0153] by faith, not by his own **strength** nor by the letter of that
AP : 0 4 :137(126) [0161] the law by their own **strength** cannot achieve what they
AP : 0 4 :138(126) [0161] to be able by its own **strength** to resist the devil, who
AP : 0 4 :142(126) [0161] ought to grow and be **strengthened** in these terrors and in
AP : 0 4 :189(133) [0175] rule of the devil; in our weakness he displays his **strength**.
AP : 0 4 :210(136) [0179] remembrance might **strengthen** our faith and we might
AP : 0 4 :389(166) [0225] will find it useful for **strengthening** their faith and for
AP : 1 2 :008(183) [0255] did not believe nor **strengthen** himself with the Gospel
AP : 1 2 :036(186) [0261] This faith **strengthens**, sustains, and quickens the contrite
AP : 1 2 :039(187) [0261] and hearing absolution **strengthens** and consoles the
AP : 1 2 :049(188) [0265] melts away for sorrow; **strengthen** me according to thy
AP : 1 2 :127(201) [0291] because you do not **strengthen** wavering consciences,
AP : 1 6 :013(224) [0333] not weaken but rather **strengthens** the authority of
AP : 2 1 :005(229) [0345] second honor is the **strengthening** of our faith: when we
AP : 2 2 :010(237) [0361] to console and **strengthen** terrified hearts when they
AP : 2 4 :074(262) [0409] Once faith has **strengthened** a conscience to see its
S2 : 0 4 :003(298) [0471] and done on the **strength** of such false, mischievous,
S3 : 0 8 :009(313) [0497] and it is the source, **strength**, and power of all heresy,
TR : 0 0 :059(330) [0521] of the church by so **strengthening** errors and other crimes
SC : 0 2 :006(345) [0545] by my own reason or **strength** I cannot believe in Jesus
SC : 0 3 :011(347) [0547] kingdom, and when he **strengthens** us and keeps us
SC : 0 5 :026(351) [0555] say: "God be merciful to you and **strengthen** your faith.
SC : 0 5 :029(351) [0555] to comfort and to **strengthen** the faith of those whose
SC : 0 8 :010(354) [0559] His delight is not in the **strength** of the horse, nor his
LC : PR :011(360) [0571] and gives us immeasurable **strength**, comfort, and help.
LC : 0 2 :002(411) [0679] may know where and how to obtain **strength** for this task.
LC : 0 2 :003(411) [0679] If we could by our own **strength** keep the Ten
LC : 0 2 :062(419) [0695] increases, and **strengthens** faith through the same Word
LC : 0 3 :051(427) [0711] and to enlighten and **strengthen** us in faith by his power.
LC : 0 3 :058(428) [0713] Therefore we must **strengthen** ourselves against unbelief
LC : 0 3 :077(431) [0721] officials, with wisdom, **strength**, and prosperity to govern
LC : 0 3 :096(433) [0725] this condition for our **strengthening** and assurance as a
LC : 0 3 :098(433) [0725] sign also can effect to **strengthen** and gladden our
LC : 0 3 :106(434) [0727] God gives us power and **strength** to resist, even though
LC : 0 4 :044(442) [0743] aright, we must draw **strength** and comfort from it when
LC : 0 4 :056(444) [0747] of the Altar not on the **strength** of my own faith, but on
LC : 0 4 :056(444) [0747] of my own faith, but on the **strength** of Christ's Word.
LC : 0 4 :083(446) [0751] away sin and daily **strengthens** the new man, always
LC : 0 5 :012(448) [0755] With this Word you can **strengthen** your conscience and
LC : 0 5 :023(449) [0757] the soul since it nourishes and **strengthens** the new man.
LC : 0 5 :024(449) [0759] faith may refresh and **strengthen** itself and not weaken in
LC : 0 5 :027(449) [0759] Supper is given to bring us new **strength** and refreshment.
LC : 0 5 :028(449) [0759] can bread and wine forgive sins or **strengthen** faith?"
LC : 0 5 :072(455) [0769] and receive refreshment, comfort, and **strength**.
LC : 0 6 :004(457) [0000] for the comforting and **strengthening** of our conscience.
LC : 0 6 :013(458) [0000] a brother, seeking his advice, comfort, and **strength**.
EP : 0 7 :019(484) [0813] to comfort them and to **strengthen** their weak faith.
EP : 0 7 :030(485) [0815] the assurance and **strengthening** of our faith in the Holy
EP : 1 1 :016(497) [0837] the impenitent are **strengthened** in their self-will, he is not
SD : 0 2 :016(523) [0887] heavenly gifts in us and **strengthen** us daily until our end.
SD : 0 2 :040(528) [0895] by my own reason or **strength** I cannot believe in Jesus
SD : 0 2 :072(535) [0909] also how he preserves, **strengthens**, and increases these
SD : 0 5 :025(563) [0961] once more comfort and **strengthen** them with the
SD : 0 7 :022(573) [0979] thereafter: "You can **strengthen** your conscience from the
SD : 0 7 :081(584) [1001] is awakened, **strengthened**, and confirmed through his
SD : 1 1 :012(618) [1067] to **strengthen** our faith and to assure us of our salvation
SD : 1 1 :021(619) [1069] 7. That he would also **strengthen** and increase in them the
SD : 1 1 :023(619) [1069] and to help, further, **strengthen**, and preserve them to this
SD : 1 1 :029(621) [1073] through the Word, to **strengthen** us, and to give us power
SD : 1 1 :091(631) [1093] impenitent sinners are **strengthened** in their malice, then
SD : 1 1 :096(632) [1095] him up through faith, **strengthen** him in his new

Stress (1), Stressed (3), Stresses (5)
AP : 0 2 :050(106) [0119] our preachers have **stressed** this in their teaching.
AP : 0 4 :314(156) [0207] We **stress** this statement so often because it is so clear.
AP : 0 4 :326(157) [0211] Scripture often **stresses** the same thing.
AP : 1 6 :007(223) [0331] revenge, and Christ **stresses** this so often lest the apostles
SC : PR :018(340) [0537] Commandment must be **stressed** when instructing
LC : 0 1 :029(368) [0589] should be thoroughly **stressed** and impressed upon young
SD : 0 3 :007(540) [0917] Therefore he **stresses** the exclusive terms, that is, the
SD : 0 3 :007(540) [0917] He **stresses** these terms with such zeal in order to indicate
SD : 0 3 :036(545) [0927] earnestly and diligently **stresses** such exclusive terms (that

Stretch (1)
LC : 0 1 :299(405) [0665] lawyers who twist and **stretch** the law to suit their

Stricken (1)
S3 : 0 2 :004(303) [0479] Thus he is terror-**stricken** and humbled, becomes

Strict (23), Stricter (2), Strictest (1), Strictly (36), Strictness (1)
AG : 2 7 :007(071) [0077] The practice was **stricter** in women's convents than in
AG : 2 7 :009(072) [0077] matter the canons were not **strictly** adhered to.
AP : 0 4 :043(113) [0133] The Gospel is, **strictly** speaking, the promise of

Continued ▶

A P : 0 4 :233(140) [0185] clergy's behavior too **strictly** or despise them because of
A P : 0 4 :362(162) [0219] above that justification is **strictly** a gift of God; it is a
A P : 1 3 :003(211) [0309] easily determine which are sacraments in the **strict** sense.
A P : 1 3 :003(211) [0309] are not sacraments in the **strict** sense since men do not
A P : 1 3 :014(213) [0311] to physical life and not **strictly** to the New Testament.
A P : 1 3 :014(213) [0311] ones which are, in the **strict** sense, "signs of the New
A P : 1 5 :027(219) [0323] interpretations that make them either **stricter** or easier.
A P : 1 5 :028(219) [0323] that comes from this **strict** interpretation of the
A P : 2 3 :055(247) [0379] guard marriage with the **strictest** laws and examples and
A P : 2 8 :003(281) [0445] They demand greater **strictness** in the observance of their
L C : 0 1 :029(368) [0589] taken lightly but will **strictly** watch over it, he has
L C : 0 1 :061(372) [0597] young people should be **strictly** required and trained to
L C : 0 1 :095(378) [0607] that God insists upon a **strict** observance of this
L C : 0 1 :139(384) [0621] it, and besides is so **strict** about punishing those who
L C : 0 1 :169(388) [0629] It is a **strict** commandment and injunction of God, who
L C : 0 1 :322(409) [0673] are to him and how **strictly** he will watch over them,
L C : 0 3 :006(420) [0699] Prayer, therefore, is as **strictly** and solemnly commanded .
L C : 0 3 :018(423) [0703] pray and backed it up with such a **strict** commandment.
L C : 0 4 :006(437) [0733] it is solemnly and **strictly** commanded that we must be
E P : 0 1 :001(466) [0779] in this controversy is if, **strictly** and without any
E P : 0 1 :019(468) [0783] that original sin is **strictly** and without any distinction
E P : 0 5 :001(477) [0801] of the Holy Gospel **strictly** speaking only a preaching of
E P : 0 5 :003(478) [0801] teach, and confess that, **strictly** speaking, the law is a
E P : 0 5 :005(478) [0801] 4. But the Gospel, **strictly** speaking, is the kind of
E P : 0 5 :007(478) [0803] and reproof but is, **strictly** speaking, precisely a
E P : 0 5 :010(479) [0803] terrifies people, it is not, **strictly** speaking, the preaching
E P : 0 5 :010(479) [0803] And this is the preaching of the Gospel, **strictly** speaking.
E P : 0 5 :011(479) [0805] teach that the Gospel, **strictly** speaking, is a proclamation
E P : 0 7 :017(484) [0813] accept him even contrary to their will as a **strict** judge.
S D : 0 1 :001(508) [0859] Confession about what original sin, **strictly** understood, is.
S D : 0 1 :002(508) [0859] taught that original sin, **strictly** speaking, is not man's
S D : 0 1 :033(514) [0869] so, if one wishes to speak **strictly**, one must maintain a
S D : 0 1 :052(517) [0875] **Strictly** speaking, therefore, original sin is the deep
S D : 0 1 :058(519) [0879] or an accident in the right and **strict** sense of the word.
S D : 0 3 :018(542) [0921] to explain the term **strictly** so that the renewal which
S D : 0 3 :018(542) [0921] and so that in their **strict** senses the two will be
S D : 0 4 :015(553) [0943] when they are used in their **strict** and Christian sense, as
S D : 0 5 :002(558) [0951] one party claimed that, **strictly** speaking, the Gospel is
S D : 0 5 :002(558) [0951] and contended that, **strictly** speaking, the Gospel is not a
S D : 0 5 :002(558) [0951] This, they said, is **strictly** a function of the law of God,
S D : 0 5 :002(558) [0953] whereas the Gospel in its **strict** sense is a proclamation of
S D : 0 5 :005(559) [0953] sense and apart from the **strict** distinction of law and
S D : 0 5 :006(559) [0953] "Gospel" is also used in another (that is, in a **strict**) sense.
S D : 0 5 :017(561) [0957] what we have said that, **strictly** speaking, the law is a
S D : 0 5 :019(561) [0957] the Gospel (which alone, **strictly** speaking, teaches and
S D : 0 5 :019(561) [0957] this Gospel alone, **strictly** speaking, teaches about saving
S D : 0 5 :021(562) [0959] transgressors of the law **strictly** speaking is, and is called,
S D : 0 5 :022(562) [0959] to us as righteousness in the **strict** judgment of God.
S D : 0 5 :027(563) [0961] to make of the Gospel, **strictly** so called in distinction
S D : 0 5 :027(563) [0961] also indicates that, **strictly** speaking, the Gospel is the
S D : 0 6 :015(566) [0967] teach and to maintain the **strict** distinction between the
S D : 0 6 :016(566) [0967] "works of the law" in the **strict** sense, because his good
S D : 0 6 :017(566) [0967] These works are, **strictly** speaking, not works of the law
S D : 0 7 :007(570) [0975] "This is my body," not **strictly**, the way the letters sound,
S D : 0 7 :038(576) [0985] words of Christ in their **strict** sense and as they read, and
S D : 0 7 :045(577) [0987] and due obedience in their **strict** and clear sense, just as
S D : 0 7 :048(578) [0989] only in their usual, **strict**, and commonly accepted
S D : 0 7 :051(578) [0991] keep this simple and **strict** understanding and commanded
S D : 0 7 :113(589) [1011] understood in their **strict** sense, as they read, concerning
S D : 0 8 :019(594) [1021] of speaking and in a **strictly** verbal fashion, but in deed

Strife (6)
P R : P R :000(001) [0004] which Disputation and **Strife** Arose after the blessed
A G : 2 6 :016(066) [0073] traditions caused so much **strife** in the church that godly
A P : 0 4 :240(141) [0187] it means: "Hatred stirs up **strife**, but love covers all
L C : 0 3 :074(430) [0719] For where dissension, **strife**, and war prevail, there our
L C : 0 5 :075(455) [0771] idolatry, sorcery, enmity, **strife**, jealousy, anger,
S D : P R :009(503) [0849] past the other, so that the **strife** reflects a mere semantic

Strike (2), Strikes (2)
A P : 1 3 :005(212) [0309] enters through the ears to **strike** the heart, so the rite
S 3 : 0 3 :030(308) [0487] With a single thunderbolt he **strikes** and destroys both.
L C : 0 1 :037(369) [0591] in such matters, he must **strike** and punish them so
S D : 0 1 :013(511) [0863] errors and heresies, **strikes** them with other kinds of

Stripes (2)
S 2 : 0 1 :005(292) [0463] "And with his **stripes** we are healed" (Isa. 53:5).
S D : 0 5 :023(562) [0959] for our iniquities and with whose **stripes** we are healed."

Strive (6), Strives (1), Strove (1)
A P : 1 5 :024(218) [0321] of the saints; when men **strive** to imitate them, they copy
A P : 2 7 :016(271) [0425] pure this is in most of those who **strive** to be continent.
A P : 2 7 :016(271) [0425] And how many of them **strive** to be continent?
S 3 : 0 3 :043(310) [0491] sin and daily repent and **strive** against it, fall into open sin
L C : 0 1 :018(367) [0585] Others who **strove** for riches, happiness, pleasure, and a
L C : 0 3 :064(429) [0715] For this end he **strives** without rest day and night, using
S D : 0 2 :044(529) [0897] of its own to prepare itself and to **strive** for righteousness.
S D : 1 1 :033(621) [1073] be few?" by saying, "**Strive** to enter by the narrow door"

Strong (22), Stronger (7), Strongest (2), Strongly (4)
A G : 2 3 :012(052) [0063] was such serious and **strong** resistance that an archbishop
A G : 2 6 :004(064) [0071] urges them upon us and **strongly** insists that we regard
A G : 2 7 :027(075) [0079] our opponents insist so **strongly** that vows must be kept
A P : P R :013(099) [0101] any expression seems too **strong**, let me explain that my
A P : 0 4 :149(127) [0163] his sin is greater and **stronger** than the death and promise
A P : 0 4 :234(140) [0185] is preserved when the **strong** bear with the weak, when
A P : 0 4 :278(149) [0199] death as it becomes ever **stronger** through such exercise.
A P : 0 4 :309(155) [0207] of God, but he grew **strong** in his faith as he gave glory to
A P : 0 4 :350(160) [0217] so that we become ever **stronger** in the conviction that
A P : 0 4 :364(163) [0219] The **strong** hear the mention of punishments and rewards
A P : 1 6 :009(224) [0333] of the heart, like a deep fear of God and a **strong** faith.
A P : 2 1 :035(234) [0353] the Gospel, must be **strong** of soul because they have to
L C : P R :001(358) [0567] treat the Catechism and **strongly** urge others to do the
L C : 0 1 :125(382) [0617] should be the first and **strongest** reason impelling us to
L C : 0 1 :131(383) [0619] above all this, another **strong** incentive for us to keep this
L C : 0 2 :053(417) [0693] daily to grow and become **strong** in the faith and in the
L C : 0 3 :027(424) [0705] may kindle your heart to **stronger** and greater desires and
L C : 0 3 :107(434) [0729] spiritual matters (that is, **strong** Christians) are tempted
L C : 0 4 :051(443) [0745] This is the best and **strongest** proof for the simple and
L C : 0 4 :056(444) [0747] I may be **strong** or weak; I leave that in God's hands.
L C : 0 4 :068(445) [0749] and continually grows **stronger**, Baptism is not being used
L C : 0 4 :076(446) [0751] old man so that the new may come forth and grow **strong**.
L C : 0 5 :024(449) [0759] not weaken in the struggle but grow continually **stronger**.
L C : 0 5 :040(451) [0763] as if they were such **strong** Christians that they have no
L C : 0 6 :013(458) [0000] ourselves sufficiently **strong** in faith, we may at any time
S D : 0 2 :037(528) [0895] grow daily and become **strong** in faith and in its fruits,
S D : 0 2 :047(530) [0901] them, since they feel no **strong**, ardent faith and cordial
S D : 0 2 :068(534) [0907] being weak and the other **strong** in the Spirit, but even
S D : 0 2 :068(534) [0907] one time ardent in love, **strong** in faith and in hope, and
S D : 0 7 :069(582) [0997] might serve God with a **stronger** and more cheerful faith
S D : 0 7 :070(582) [0997] Son of God, be his faith **strong** or weak, has eternal life
S D : 0 7 :071(582) [0997] Paul, and others who had a cheerful and **strong** faith.
S D : 0 7 :106(588) [1009] These arguments are so **strong** and solid that they will
S D : 0 8 :056(601) [1033] There are three **strong** and irrefutable arguments which
S D : 0 8 :063(603) [1037] They have insisted so **strongly** on this that they will hear

Strongholds (1)
A G : 2 8 :017(083) [0085] power to destroy **strongholds** and every proud obstacle to

Strongbox (1)
L C : 0 1 :224(395) [0643] when he robs a man's **strongbox** or his pocket, but also

Struck (2)
L C : 0 3 :011(421) [0701] because those who were **struck** down for their sin did not
S D : 0 8 :025(596) [1023] when with one word he **struck** his enemies to the ground,

Structures (1)
A P : 0 7 :020(172) [0233] foundation perishing **structures** of stubble, that is,

Struggle (4), Struggles (4), Struggling (2)
A P : 0 2 :036(105) [0115] to work those desires against which the faithful **struggle**."
A P : 0 4 :350(161) [0217] No one learns this without many severe **struggles**.
A P : 1 2 :037(187) [0261] and throughout life it **struggles** with sin to conquer sin
A P : 1 2 :042(187) [0263] may not succumb in its **struggles** against the terrors of sin
A P : 2 0 :008(227) [0341] and life to the heart in its hardest **struggle** against despair.
A P : 2 4 :046(258) [0401] exercise of faith in its **struggle** with despair and about the
A P : 2 4 :051(259) [0403] in faith, and in its **struggles**, they should be classified with
T R : 0 0 :044(328) [0517] (that is, the exercise of faith **struggling** against despair).
L C : 0 1 :192(391) [0635] I saw someone wearily **struggling** in deep water, or fallen
L C : 0 5 :024(449) [0759] and not weaken in the **struggle** but grow continually

Stubble (3)
A P : 0 7 :020(172) [0233] perishing structures of **stubble**, that is, unprofitable
A P : 0 7 :021(172) [0233] **stubble** on the foundation but that this did not overthrow
S D : 0 8 :087(608) [1047] a consuming fire on dry **stubble**, will be with them, but

Stubborn (1), Stubbornly (3), Stubbornness (2)
A P : P R :004(098) [0099] But our opponents **stubbornly** insisted that we sanction
L C : 0 1 :005(365) [0581] of them he boasts so **stubbornly** and securely that he
L C : 0 1 :038(369) [0591] that is, those who persist in their **stubbornness** and pride.
L C : 0 3 :104(434) [0727] false security, and **stubbornness**, or, on the contrary, to
E P : 0 2 :017(472) [0791] Spirit, God changes **stubborn** and unwilling people into
S D : 0 2 :083(537) [0913] All who **stubbornly** and perseveringly resist the Holy

Students (1)
S D : 0 2 :090(538) [0915] The young **students** at our universities have been greatly

Study (11)
A P : 0 4 :211(136) [0179] a certain kind of life for **study** or for other useful
A P : 0 4 :284(150) [0201] A **study** of the whole passage shows its agreement with
A P : 2 3 :040(245) [0375] commends virginity for the sake of mediation and **study**.
A P : 2 4 :003(250) [0385] for the sake of those who **study** and understand it, and we
L C : P R :008(359) [0569] I must still read and **study** the Catechism daily, yet I
L C : P R :016(361) [0571] will not or cannot read and **study** the Catechism daily.
L C : P R :016(361) [0573] we know it all and need not read or **study** it any more?
L C : 0 1 :174(388) [0631] opportunity to learn and **study** so that they may be of
L C : 0 2 :023(413) [0683] reason we ought daily to **study** this article and impress it
L C : 0 4 :041(441) [0743] Christian has enough to **study** and to practice all his life.
S D : 0 2 :016(523) [0887] is our teacher, we cannot **study** and learn anything

Stuff (1)
L C : 0 1 :235(397) [0647] which enables you to **stuff** your craw and your belly.

Stumble (4), Stumbling (3)
A P : 0 4 :029(111) [0129] and therefore also 'the **stumbling**-block of the cross has
A P : 0 7 :019(171) [0233] wicked men so that this **stumbling** block may not offend
L C : 0 3 :086(432) [0723] We still **stumble** daily and transgress because we live in
L C : 0 3 :100(433) [0725] is not accomplished without failures and **stumbling**.
L C : 0 5 :023(449) [0757] we often grow weary and faint, at times even **stumble**.
S D : 1 1 :020(619) [1069] up again when they **stumble**, and comfort and preserve
S D : 1 1 :075(628) [1087] become disobedient and **stumble**, he arranges to recall

Stupid (3), Stupidity (1)
A P : 1 2 :014(184) [0257] and these consist of **stupid** observances like pilgrimages,
A P : 2 7 :053(278) [0437] is mere babbling, as **stupid** as it is wicked, nourishing a
S 3 : 0 1 :003(302) [0477] is therefore nothing but error and **stupidity**, namely,
L C : 0 4 :058(444) [0747] only presumptuous and **stupid** persons draw the

Stuttgart (1)
S 3 : 1 5 :005(317) [0501] I, Erhard Schnepf, preacher in **Stuttgart**, subscribe

Style (2)
A P : 0 7 :034(175) [0239] Thus if the German **style** of dress is not a devotion to God
A P : 0 7 :034(175) [0239] according to the French rather than the German **style**.

Subdue (7), Subdued (1)
AG : 2 6 :037(069) [0075] pommeled his body and **subdued** it, and by this he
AL : 2 6 :037(069) [0075] Paul also said, "I pommel my body and **subdue** it."
AP : 1 5 :046(221) [0327] says (I Cor. 9:27), "I pommel my body and **subdue** it."
AP : 2 3 :018(242) [0369] for continence and to **subdue** their bodies with labors and
LC : 0 1 :195(391) [0637] protect us, so that he may **subdue** our desire for revenge.
LC : 0 4 :077(446) [0751] access to it so that we may again **subdue** the old man.
SD : 0 4 :019(554) [0945] "I pommel my body and **subdue** it" (I Cor. 9:27), and
SD : 0 6 :009(565) [0965] "I pommel my body and **subdue** it, lest after preaching to

Subject (45), Subjected (6), Subjection (8), Subjects (22)
PR : PR :006(004) [0009] be checked and that our **subjects** might be preserved from
PR : PR :024(013) [0023] own selves and of the **subjects** that belong to us, to do
AG : 1 6 :006(038) [0051] are obliged to be **subject** to civil authority and obey its
AG : 2 1 :001(046) [0057] demands the defense and protection of their **subjects**.
AG : 2 8 :029(085) [0087] justice to their **subjects** for the sake of peace and to
AL : 1 8 :001(039) [0051] and for the choice of things **subject** to reason.
AL : 2 6 :038(069) [0075] but to keep his body in **subjection** and fit for spiritual
AL : 2 7 :023(074) [0079] state that every vow is **subject** to the right of a superior.
AL : 2 8 :029(085) [0087] justice to their **subjects** for the sake of maintaining public
AL : 0 0 :017(096) [0095] Your Imperial Majesty's faithful **subjects**:
AP : 0 2 :005(101) [0107] nature, but only the **subjection** to mortality that Adam's
AP : 0 2 :012(102) [0109] which we agree is **subject** to reason and somewhat in our
AP : 0 2 :046(106) [0117] There human nature is **subjected** not only to death and
AP : 0 4 :039(112) [0131] of faith, the **subject** itself will compel us to cite further
AP : 0 4 :040(112) [0131] are all under sin and **subject** to eternal wrath and death.
AP : 0 4 :087(119) [0147] Paul deals with this **subject** and states that when we
AP : 0 4 :103(121) [0151] "But the world was **subjected** to him through the law; for
AP : 0 4 :103(122) [0151] the whole world was **subjected**, he took away the sin of
AP : 0 4 :171(130) [0171] more testimonies on this **subject**, though they are obvious
AP : 0 7 :011(170) [0229] of Christ, nor can he be said to be **subject** to Christ."
AP : 0 7 :023(172) [0235] for as the Father **subjected** everything to him, so now this
AP : 1 0 :004(179) [0247] an argument on this **subject** (his Imperial Majesty does
AP : 1 1 :003(180) [0249] On this **subject** our theologians have written many things
AP : 1 2 :124(201) [0289] numerous, and varied **subjects** in whose learning and faith
AP : 1 2 :151(206) [0299] the saints are **subject** to death and to all the common
AP : 1 2 :172(209) [0305] This is obvious from the **subject**-matter itself.
AP : 1 5 :048(221) [0329] seasons contributes nothing to the **subjection** of the flesh.
AP : 1 5 :049(221) [0329] This **subject** of traditions involves many difficult and
AP : 1 6 :004(223) [0331] extensively on this **subject** because the monks had
AP : 1 6 :006(223) [0331] governments but **subjects** us to them, just as we are
AP : 1 6 :006(223) [0331] as we are necessarily **subjected** to the laws of the seasons
AP : 2 0 :005(227) [0339] Fathers, but we have already said enough on this **subject**.
AP : 2 8 :006(282) [0445] article of the Confessions we included various **subjects**.
AP : 2 8 :006(282) [0445] in order to guide their **subjects** toward the goal of eternal
S1 : PR :010(290) [0457] But let us return to the **subject**.
S1 : PR :012(290) [0459] disobedience of **subjects**, domestics, and laborers,
S2 : 0 2 :007(294) [0463] and all books on the **subject** declare), for by means of the
S2 : 0 4 :004(299) [0473] me your god and are obedient and **subject** to me."
S2 : 0 4 :008(299) [0473] because, inasmuch as **subjection** to such a head would
S3 : 0 1 :001(302) [0477] made sinners and became **subject** to death and the devil.
S3 : 0 1 :011(303) [0479] be sound and only the body would be **subject** to death.
S3 : 1 3 :001(315) [0499] constantly taught on this **subject**, namely, that by faith
TR : 0 0 :035(326) [0513] make the German bishops **subject** to their power and
SC : PR :025(341) [0539] adopt odious laws on the **subject**, it is your own fault if
SC : PR :027(341) [0539] It **subjects** us to greater burdens and labors, dangers and
SC : 0 9 :004(355) [0561] "Let every person be **subject** to the governing authorities.
SC : 0 9 :005(355) [0561] Duties **Subjects** Owe to Governing Authorities
SC : 0 9 :005(355) [0561] "Let every person be **subject** to the governing authorities.
SC : 0 9 :005(355) [0561] Therefore one must be **subject**, not only to avoid God's
SC : 0 9 :005(355) [0561] "Be **subject** for the Lord's sake to every human
SC : 0 9 :012(356) [0563] "You that are younger, be **subject** to the elders.
LC : PR :009(359) [0569] read it and make it the **subject** of meditation and
LC : SP :025(364) [0579] hymns, based on these **subjects**, to supplement and
LC : 0 1 :150(385) [0623] many people as he has inhabitants, citizens, or **subjects**.
LC : 0 1 :168(388) [0629] their children, servants, **subjects**, etc., but especially to
LC : 0 1 :170(388) [0629] or asses, and gave us **subjects** to treat them as we please,
LC : 0 1 :177(389) [0631] we train them, we have unruly and disobedient **subjects**.
LC : 0 2 :018(412) [0681] further discussion of this **subject** belongs in the other two
LC : 0 2 :031(414) [0687] therefore, must be **subject** to him and lie beneath his feet
LC : 0 2 :070(420) [0697] have enough to preach and learn on the **subject** of faith.
LC : 0 3 :062(428) [0715] might, marshaling all his **subjects** and even enlisting the
LC : 0 3 :075(430) [0719] remind both princes and **subjects** that through the office
LC : 0 3 :077(431) [0721] enemies; to grant their **subjects** and the people at large to
LC : 0 4 :003(437) [0733] that is to be said on the **subject**, namely, where the Lord
LC : 0 5 :044(451) [0763] exhortation, so on this **subject** we must be persistent in
LC : 0 6 :006(457) [0000] bring them back into **subjection** and coerce them like the
EP : 1 2 :014(499) [0841] wicked people, and that **subjects** may not call upon the
SD : PR :009(505) [0855] a par with it, but that everything must be **subjected** to it.
SD : 0 1 :012(510) [0863] external things which are **subject** to reason man still
SD : 0 1 :013(511) [0863] so that human nature is **subject** to the devil's dominion,
SD : 0 1 :024(512) [0865] civil affairs which are **subject** to human reason in the
SD : 0 1 :052(517) [0875] the concrete person or **subject** (that is, man himself with
SD : 0 2 :089(538) [0915] Man is, as it were, the **subject** which suffers.
SD : 0 3 :015(541) [0919] also in his spontaneous **subjection** to the law in our stead
SD : 0 5 :020(561) [0959] law, and he is therefore **subject** to the wrath of God, to
SD : 0 7 :108(588) [1009] and wine, or their accidents without a **subject**, remain.
SD : 0 8 :070(605) [1041] thy hands, putting everything in **subjection** under his feet.
SD : 0 8 :070(605) [1041] putting everything in **subjection** to him, he left nothing
SD : 1 0 :014(613) [1057] which accordingly are not **subject** either to a command or
SD : 1 1 :063(626) [1083] in the discussion on this **subject** soars too high and goes
SD : 1 2 :019(634) [1099] may arise, nor may a **subject** call upon the government

Subjectively (1)
PR : PR :021(011) [0019] habitually, and **subjectively** (to use scholastic

Sublime (3)
S1 : 0 1 :000(291) [0461] of the Articles treats the **sublime** articles of the divine
LC : 0 1 :055(372) [0595] worldly affairs or in **sublime** and difficult matters of faith
LC : 0 1 :125(382) [0617] we can do, next to the **sublime** worship of God described

Submerged (1)
AG : 2 5 :008(062) [0069] nature is so deeply **submerged** in sins that it is unable to

Submit (26), Submits (1), Submitted (22), Submitting (3), Submission (2), Submissive (4)
PR : PR :002(003) [0007] It was **submitted** in the German and Latin languages by
PR : PR :004(004) [0009] more compliant in **submitting** to the papal yoke as well as
PR : PR :008(005) [0009] which had been **submitted** to Emperor Charles V in the
PR : PR :009(006) [0011] the true and originally **submitted** Augsburg Confession.
PR : PR :017(008) [0015] the Augsburg Confession as **submitted** in the year 1530.
PR : PR :018(008) [0015] Confession which was **submitted** to Emperor Charles V
PR : PR :018(009) [0015] of ours who themselves **submitted** it to Emperor Charles
PR : PR :018(009) [0015] actual original that was **submitted** to the emperor and
PR : PR :018(009) [0015] that was then **submitted** into our declaration and Book of
PR : PR :019(009) [0017] in the confession **submitted** at Augsburg and that a very
PR : PR :019(009) [0017] that of the first Augsburg Confession as it was **submitted**.
PR : PR :023(012) [0021] one that was previously **submitted** at Augsburg in the
PR : PR :025(013) [0023] Augsburg Confession, **submitted** in the year 1530 to
AG : PR :009(025) [0039] princes, and estates also **submit** a similar written
AG : PR :014(026) [0041] in the confession which we and our associates **submit**.
AG : 2 8 :045(088) [0089] Why do you **submit** to regulations, 'Do not handle, Do
AG : 2 8 :052(089) [0091] therefore, and do not **submit** again to a yoke of slavery."
AL : 2 8 :045(088) [0089] Why do you **submit** to regulations, 'Do not handle, Do
AL : 2 8 :052(089) [0091] the Galatians, "Do not **submit** again to a yoke of
AP : 0 4 :030(111) [0129] your own, you did not **submit** to God's righteousness'
AP : 0 4 :032(111) [0129] to God; it does not **submit** to God's law, indeed it
AP : 0 4 :033(111) [0129] If it cannot **submit** to God's law, it is certainly sinning
AP : 0 4 :125(124) [0157] and praise him, and to **submit** to him in our afflictions.
AP : 0 7 :035(175) [0241] Why do you **submit** to regulations, 'Do not handle, Do
AP : 1 5 :031(219) [0323] Gal. 5:1 Paul forbids them to "**submit** again to slavery."
AP : 2 3 :059(247) [0379] of priests who refuse to **submit**, and the exile of poor
AP : 2 8 :015(283) [0447] set you free, and do not **submit** again to a yoke of
S1 : PR :002(288) [0455] these articles and **submitted** them to our representatives.
S2 : 0 4 :004(299) [0473] obedient to the pope and **submits** to him in all that he
TR : 0 0 :058(330) [0521] evident reasons for not **submitting** to the pope, and these
SC : 0 9 :002(354) [0561] keeping his children **submissive** and respectful in every
SC : 0 9 :003(355) [0561] "Obey your leaders and **submit** to them; for they are
SC : 0 9 :005(355) [0561] "Remind them to be **submissive** to rulers and authorities,
SC : 0 9 :007(355) [0563] "You wives, be **submissive** to your husbands, as Sarah
LC : 0 1 :110(380) [0613] and censoriously, but **submit** to them and hold your
LC : 0 1 :135(383) [0619] father and mother or to **submit** to them, then obey the
LC : 0 1 :327(409) [0675] all in authority, being **submissive** and obedient to them
LC : 0 3 :068(429) [0717] violence and persecution, **submitting** to the will of God.
LC : 0 3 :086(432) [0723] although we obey and **submit** to his will and are
LC : 0 6 :005(457) [0000] under the pope and **submit** to being driven and tormented
EP : 0 2 :003(470) [0787] to God; it does not **submit** to God's law, indeed it
EP : 0 7 :001(481) [0809] when the Augsburg Confession was being **submitted**.
EP : 1 0 :006(493) [0829] therefore, and do not **submit** again to a yoke of slavery"
EP : 1 0 :006(493) [0829] them we did not yield **submission** even for a moment,
SD : PR :003(501) [0847] of God's Word and **submitted** it to Emperor Charles V at
SD : PR :005(504) [0851] in the year 1530 and **submitted** to Emperor Charles V at
SD : PR :006(504) [0853] Confession had been **submitted**, an extensive Apology
SD : PR :020(508) [0859] the Augsburg Confession as it was originally **submitted**.
SD : 0 2 :006(521) [0883] to bring it to an end, we **submit** the following as our
SD : 0 2 :013(523) [0885] to God; it does not **submit** to God's law, indeed it
SD : 0 5 :016(561) [0957] clearly for the Christian reader, we **submit** the following:
SD : 0 7 :001(568) [0971] was drafted and **submitted** to the emperor, the
SD : 0 7 :001(568) [0971] withdrew from it, and **submitted** their own confession.
SD : 0 7 :009(570) [0975] who at the same time **submitted** their own confession at
SD : 0 7 :012(571) [0977] who at Augsburg had **submitted** their own confession
SD : 0 7 :017(572) [0979] doctrinal statement they should **submit** to the council.
SD : 1 0 :011(612) [1055] therefore, and do not **submit** again to a yoke of slavery"
SD : 1 0 :011(612) [1057] whom we did not yield **submission** even for a moment,

Subordinated (2)
LC : 0 1 :116(381) [0615] that these, too, are **subordinated** to obedience toward
EP : RN :002(465) [0777] one of them should be **subordinated** to the Scriptures and

Subscribe (24), Subscribed (37), Subscribes (6), Subscription (1)
PR : PR :008(005) [0009] and again unanimously **subscribed** this Christian
PR : PR :016(008) [0013] approved, and **subscribed** this Book of Concord as the
PR : PR :027(014) [0025] one mind and heart **subscribed** our names hereto and
AL : 0 0 :017(096) [0095] Philip, landgrave of Hesse, **subscribes**
AP : 1 3 :012(212) [0311] to this we must **subscribe** wholeheartedly, for we know
S3 : 1 5 :005(316) [0501] Dr. Martin Luther **subscribed**
S3 : 1 5 :005(316) [0501] Dr. Justus Jonas, rector, **subscribed** with his own hand
S3 : 1 5 :005(316) [0501] Dr. John Bugenhagen, of Pomerania, **subscribed**
S3 : 1 5 :005(316) [0501] Dr. Caspar Creutziger **subscribed**
S3 : 1 5 :005(316) [0501] Nicholas Amsdorf, of Magdeburg, **subscribed**
S3 : 1 5 :005(316) [0501] George Spalatin, of Altenburg, **subscribed**
S3 : 1 5 :005(317) [0501] John Agricola, of Eisleben, **subscribed**
S3 : 1 5 :005(317) [0501] Gabriel Didymus **subscribed**
S3 : 1 5 :005(317) [0501] Duchy of Lueneburg, **subscribe** in my own name and in
S3 : 1 5 :005(317) [0501] I, Stephen Agricola, minister in Hof, **subscribe**
S3 : 1 5 :005(317) [0501] Drach, professor and minister in Marburg, **subscribe**
S3 : 1 5 :005(317) [0501] for the glory of God **subscribe** that I have thus believed
S3 : 1 5 :005(317) [0501] I, Andrew Osiander, minister in Nuremberg, **subscribe**
S3 : 1 5 :005(317) [0501] I, Master Veit Dietrich, minister in Nuremberg, **subscribe**
S3 : 1 5 :005(317) [0501] I, Erhard Schnepf, preacher in Stuttgart, **subscribe**
S3 : 1 5 :005(317) [0501] pastor of the church in Koethen, **subscribe**
S3 : 1 5 :005(317) [0501] of Pomerania, again **subscribe** in the name of Master
S3 : 1 5 :005(317) [0501] I have shown to these brethren who have **subscribed**
S3 : 1 5 :005(317) [0501] I, Dionysius Melander, **subscribe** the Confession, the
S3 : 1 5 :005(317) [0501] Christ which is in Soest, **subscribe** the articles of the
S3 : 1 5 :005(317) [0501] Michael Caelius, preacher in Mansfeld, **subscribe**
S3 : 1 5 :005(317) [0501] Master Peter Geltner, preacher in Frankfurt, **subscribed**
S3 : 1 5 :005(317) [0501] I, John Aepinus, **subscribe**
S3 : 1 5 :005(317) [0501] in Gotha, Thuringia, **subscribe** in my own name and in
S3 : 1 5 :005(318) [0501] the Rev. Andrew Menser (I **Subscribe** with my hand)
S3 : 1 5 :005(318) [0501] And I, Egidius Melcher, have **subscribed** with my hand
TR : 0 0 :082(334) [0529] and Preachers Who **Subscribed** the Confession and
TR : 0 0 :082(334) [0529] Accordingly they **subscribe** their names.
TR : 0 0 :082(334) [0529] of Pomerania, **subscribe** the articles of the Augsburg
TR : 0 0 :082(334) [0529] of the churches in the Duchy of Lueneburg, **subscribe**
TR : 0 0 :082(334) [0529] Nicholas Amsdorf, of Magdeburg, **subscribed**
TR : 0 0 :082(334) [0529] George Spalatin, of Altenburg, **subscribed**

Continued ▶

TR : 0 0 :082(334) [0529] I, Andrew Osiander, **subscribe**
TR : 0 0 :082(334) [0529] Master Veit Dietrich, of Nuremberg, **subscribes**
TR : 0 0 :082(334) [0529] Agricola, minister in Chur, **subscribed** with his own hand
TR : 0 0 :082(334) [0529] John Drach, of Marburg, **subscribed**
TR : 0 0 :082(334) [0529] Conrad Figenbotz **subscribes** to all throughout
TR : 0 0 :082(334) [0529] I, Erhard Schnepf, **subscribe**
TR : 0 0 :082(335) [0529] I, Pomeranus, again **subscribe** in the name of Master
TR : 0 0 :082(335) [0529] Philip Melanchthon **subscribes** with his own hand
TR : 0 0 :082(335) [0529] Anthony Corvinus **subscribes** with his own hand both in
TR : 0 0 :082(335) [0529] John Schlagenhaufen **subscribes** with his own hand
TR : 0 0 :082(335) [0529] David Melander, **subscribed**
TR : 0 0 :082(335) [0529] in Hamburg, **subscribed** with his own hand
TR : 0 0 :082(335) [0529] Fontanus, superintendent of Lower Hesse, **subscribed**
TR : 0 0 :082(335) [0529] Frederick Myconius **subscribed** for himself and for Justus
EP : RN :004(465) [0777] theologians approved by their **subscription** at that time.
EP : RN :005(465) [0777] of their souls, we **subscribe** Dr. Luther's Small and Large
EP : 1 2 :031(501) [0843] and invocation of God, **subscribed** our signatures with
EP : 1 2 :031(501) [0843] Dr. James Andreae **subscribed**
EP : 1 2 :031(501) [0843] Dr. Nicholas Selnecker **subscribed**
EP : 1 2 :031(501) [0843] Dr. Andrew Musculus **subscribed**
EP : 1 2 :031(501) [0843] Dr. Christopher Koerner **subscribed**
SD : PR :004(502) [0847] again whole-heartedly **subscribe** this Christian and
SD : PR :010(506) [0855] Evangelical churches **subscribe** and from which and
SD : PR :011(506) [0855] of that time **subscribed** them, and that all Evangelical
SD : 0 7 :017(572) [0979] the theologians collectively and individually **subscribed**.
SD : 1 0 :021(614) [1059] assembled in Smalcald **subscribed** with their own hands,
SD : 1 2 :040(636) [1103] and invocation of God, **subscribed** our signatures with
SD : 1 2 :040(636) [1103] Dr. James Andreae, **subscribed**
SD : 1 2 :040(636) [1103] Dr. Nicholas Selnecker, **subscribed**
SD : 1 2 :040(636) [1103] Dr. Andrew Musculus, **subscribed**
SD : 1 2 :040(636) [1103] Dr. Christopher Koerner, **subscribed**

Subsequent (12), Subsequently (6)
PR : PR :003(003) [0007] **Subsequently** many churches and schools committed
PR : PR :024(013) [0023] and views will be transmitted to **subsequent** generations.
AG : 2 7 :035(076) [0081] even though some have **subsequently** differed from him.
AL : 2 7 :035(076) [0081] although others have **subsequently** differed from him.
S3 : 0 1 :002(302) [0477] of this sin are all the **subsequent** evil deeds which are
S3 : 0 3 :039(309) [0489] which Christ **subsequently** preaches in the Gospel, and
EP : 0 3 :004(473) [0793] preceding, present, or **subsequent** work, merit, or
SD : PR :005(502) [0847] either in this or in **subsequent** doctrinal statements, to
SD : PR :007(502) [0849] titanic errors and the **subsequent** bitter controversies
SD : 0 1 :028(513) [0867] and is corrupted only **subsequently** through original sin,
SD : 0 2 :090(539) [0915] with the Holy Spirit in **subsequent** good works by doing
SD : 0 3 :009(541) [0919] preceding, present, or **subsequent** works, by sheer grace,
SD : 0 3 :019(542) [0921] Christ's sake and the **subsequent** renewal which the Holy
SD : 0 3 :027(543) [0925] contrition nor the **subsequent** works belong in the article
SD : 0 3 :066(550) [0937] in the Augsburg Confession and its **subsequent** Apology.
SD : 0 4 :033(556) [0949] because of your **subsequent** works but which have come
SD : 0 4 :036(557) [0949] since a controversy **subsequently** arose on this point
SD : 1 1 :083(630) [1091] is, because of their **subsequent** impurity, impenitence, and

Subsist (4), Subsistent (3), Subsisting (4), Subsists (4)
AL : 0 1 :004(028) [0043] or a quality in another but that which **subsists** of itself.
SD : 0 1 :054(518) [0877] (that is, a self-**subsisting** essence) or an accident (that is,
SD : 0 1 :054(518) [0877] thing that is not self-**subsistent** but that subsists in
SD : 0 1 :054(518) [0877] self-subsistent but that **subsists** in another self-subsistent
SD : 0 1 :054(518) [0877] subsists in another self-**subsistent** essence and can be
SD : 0 1 :055(518) [0877] every substance or self-**subsisting** essence, in as far as it is
SD : 0 1 :055(518) [0877] that whatever does not **subsist** by itself and is not a part
SD : 0 1 :055(518) [0877] a part of another self-**subsisting** essence, but is present in
SD : 0 1 :055(518) [0877] (that is, something self-**subsistent**) but an accident (that
SD : 0 1 :057(518) [0877] (that is, either a self-**subsisting** essence or something
SD : 0 1 :057(518) [0877] (that is, a thing that **subsists** by itself and not in another
SD : 0 1 :057(518) [0877] is, a thing that does not **subsist** by itself but is in another
SD : 0 1 :057(518) [0877] thing and cannot exist or **subsist** by itself), then necessity
SD : 0 8 :011(593) [1019] in Christ henceforth **subsists** for itself so as to be or
SD : 0 8 :011(593) [1019] in which there are and **subsist** at the same time both the

Substance (56)
AG : 2 8 :044(088) [0089] of what is to come; but the **substance** belongs to Christ."
AL : 1 8 :008(040) [0053] of God in so far as the **substance** of the acts is concerned.
AP : 0 2 :008(102) [0107] commandments "according to the **substance** of the act."
AP : 0 7 :035(175) [0239] of what is to come; but the **substance** belongs to Christ."
AP : 1 5 :030(219) [0323] of what is to come; but the **substance** belongs to Christ."
AP : 2 4 :039(257) [0399] we should look for the **substance** of things, for the Holy
S3 : 0 6 :005(311) [0493] or lose their natural **substance** and retain only the
LC : 0 1 :065(373) [0599] Here you have the **substance** of the entire commandment
LC : 0 1 :285(403) [0661] we have the sum and **substance** of this commandment: No
LC : 0 2 :026(413) [0685] which contains the **substance** of the article; from it we
LC : 0 2 :046(416) [0689] Let this suffice concerning the **substance** of this article.
LC : 0 2 :051(417) [0691] This is the sum and **substance** of this phrase: I believe
LC : 0 2 :070(420) [0697] they understand the **substance** of it, they may on their
LC : 0 3 :113(435) [0729] in order that the entire **substance** of our prayer may be
LC : 0 4 :017(438) [0735] by virtue of the natural **substance** but because here
LC : 0 4 :018(438) [0737] element or the natural **substance**, it becomes a sacrament,
LC : 0 4 :059(444) [0747] does not destroy the **substance**, but confirms its
EP : 0 1 :001(466) [0779] man's corrupted nature, **substance**, and essence, or indeed
EP : 0 1 :001(466) [0779] the Fall, between man's **substance**, nature, essence, body,
EP : 0 1 :019(468) [0783] corrupted man's **substance**, nature, and essence, so that
EP : 0 1 :021(468) [0783] it inheres in the nature, **substance**, and essence of man in
EP : 0 1 :022(469) [0785] does not mean the **substance** of man but something which
EP : 0 1 :022(469) [0785] but something which inheres in the nature or **substance**.
EP : 0 1 :025(469) [0785] Satan cannot create a **substance**; he can only, with God's
EP : 0 1 :025(469) [0785] corrupt accidentally the **substance** which God has
EP : 0 2 :014(471) [0789] God wholly destroys the **substance** and essence of the Old
EP : 0 7 :022(484) [0813] Holy Supper lose their **substance** and natural essence and
EP : 0 8 :028(490) [0825] the divine nature in its **substance** and essence, or in its
SD : 0 1 :001(508) [0859] the Fall the nature, **substance**, and essence of fallen man,
SD : 0 1 :002(508) [0859] is not man's nature, **substance**, or essence (that is, man's
SD : 0 1 :030(513) [0867] into some other **substance** essentially different from our
SD : 0 1 :036(514) [0869] behold my uniformed **substance**; in thy book were
SD : 0 1 :046(516) [0873] that precisely the **substance** of this our flesh, but without
SD : 0 1 :047(516) [0875] we should have another **substance** or another soul since
SD : 0 1 :048(516) [0875] of corrupted man, its **substance**, its essence, its body or
SD : 0 1 :048(517) [0875] our corrupted nature or **substance** or being and original
SD : 0 1 :048(517) [0875] between the nature or **substance** of man, which is
SD : 0 1 :054(518) [0877] thing must either be a **substance** (that is, a self-subsisting
SD : 0 1 :055(518) [0877] in theology that every **substance** or self-subsisting
SD : 0 1 :055(518) [0877] in as far as it is a **substance**, is either God himself or a
SD : 0 1 :055(518) [0877] thing mutably, is not a **substance** (that is, something
SD : 0 1 :057(518) [0877] existing thing is either a **substance** or an accident (that is,
SD : 0 1 :057(518) [0877] ask if original sin is a **substance** (that is, a thing that
SD : 0 1 :057(518) [0879] that original sin is not a **substance** but an accident.
SD : 0 1 :058(519) [0879] or not original sin is a **substance** or an accident in the
SD : 0 2 :081(537) [0911] in such a way that the **substance** and essence of the Old
SD : 0 2 :081(537) [0911] destroyed and a new **substance** of the soul is created out
SD : 0 2 :081(537) [0911] might think that the **substance** or essence of man must be
SD : 0 7 :035(575) [0983] the untransformed **substance** of the bread and the body
SD : 0 7 :108(588) [1009] completely lose their **substance** and essence and are
SD : 0 7 :108(588) [1009] are converted into the **substance** of the body and blood
SD : 0 7 :108(588) [1009] has lost its natural **substance** and is no longer bread, the
SD : 0 8 :071(605) [1041] do we believe that in its **substance** and essence the human
SD : 0 8 :091(609) [1049] the divine nature in its **substance** and essence or in its
SD : 1 1 :004(617) [1063] beheld my unformed **substance**, in thy book were written
SD : 1 1 :032(621) [1073] fast until the end the **substance** which has been begun" in

Substantia (2)
EP : 0 1 :023(469) [0785] far as the Latin words ***substantia*** and *accidens* are
SD : 0 1 :054(517) [0877] use of the Latin terms ***substantia*** and *accidens*, we

Substantiam (1)
LC : 0 4 :059(444) [0747] *tollit, sed confirmat* ***substantiam***," that is, "Misuse does

Substantially (2), Substantiate (1), Substantiated (1), Substantiates (1)
AP : 0 4 :004(107) [0121] To **substantiate** our Confession and to refute the
AP : 1 0 :001(179) [0247] of Christ are truly and **substantially** present and are truly
AP : 1 0 :004(179) [0247] of Christ are truly and **substantially** present and are truly
LC : 0 1 :272(401) [0657] publicly assert as truth what is not publicly **substantiated**.
SD : 1 1 :043(623) [1077] for it mightily **substantiates** the article that we are

Substitute (2), Substitutes (1)
S3 : 0 3 :016(305) [0483] was reckoned as a **substitute** for contrition when people
LC : 0 2 :035(415) [0687] it is so precise that we can find no **substitute** for it.
SD : 0 8 :039(598) [1029] trick and **substitutes** the human nature for Christ.

Substitution (1)
AP : 1 2 :048(188) [0265] condemned and the **substitution** of the sentence by which

Subterfuge (1), Subterfuges (1)
AP : 2 3 :006(240) [0365] have thought up some **subterfuges** to satirize our
SD : 0 7 :018(572) [0979] was stopped up every **subterfuge** and loop-hole which the

Subtle (11)
AP : 0 4 :105(122) [0153] called "angelic," others "**subtle**," and others "irrefutable"
AP : 0 4 :375(164) [0223] not trying to be overly **subtle** here in distinguishing the
AP : 0 4 :378(165) [0223] not trying to be overly **subtle** when we condemn those
AP : 1 2 :061(190) [0269] If they try to make a **subtle** distinction separating
S3 : 0 6 :005(311) [0493] we have no regard for the **subtle** sophistry of those who
S3 : 0 7 :001(311) [0493] but also those which are **subtle** and secret and which God
LC : 0 1 :023(367) [0587] however, is a little too **subtle** to be understood by young
LC : 0 4 :053(443) [0745] This, perhaps, is a rather **subtle** point, but it is based
EP : 0 7 :004(482) [0809] Others, however, are **subtle** Sacramentarians, the most
SD : 0 2 :076(536) [0911] was slightly more **subtle** and who taught that by his
SD : 0 7 :090(585) [1003] error when some by a **subtle** perversion of this common

Suburban (1)
TR : 0 0 :012(322) [0507] should administer the **suburban** churches, that is, those

Subversive (2)
EP : 0 4 :017(477) [0801] as offensive and as **subversive** of Christian discipline that
EP : 0 6 :008(481) [0807] as dangerous and **subversive** of Christian discipline and

Succeed (6), Succeeded (1)
AL : 2 6 :014(066) [0073] they did not altogether **succeed** in releasing them but
LC : 0 1 :036(369) [0589] But they will not **succeed**.
LC : 0 1 :067(373) [0599] he does will in the end **succeed**; everything he may gain by
LC : 0 1 :247(398) [0651] If you **succeed** and prosper, before all the world you may
LC : 0 2 :063(419) [0695] he thinks and does, yet it has never **succeeded** in the least.
LC : 0 3 :076(431) [0721] may be, to prosper and **succeed**; to grant us faithful
LC : 0 5 :086(456) [0773] who come after us and **succeed** us in our office and work,

Success (2), Successfully (1), Successive (1), Successor (1)
AP : 2 3 :020(242) [0369] tried to control their body but without much **success**.
AP : 2 4 :064(261) [0407] the Mass as a price for **success**, to merchants for good
TR : 0 0 :035(326) [0513] throne is vacant, the pope is the legitimate **successor**."
LC : 0 3 :034(425) [0707] In seven **successive** articles or petitions are comprehended
LC : 0 5 :086(456) [0773] that they in turn may bring up their children **successfully**.

Succinct (1)
SD : PR :004(504) [0851] of the faith . **succinct**, Christian, and based upon the

Succumb (2)
AP : 1 2 :042(187) [0263] so that it may not **succumb** in its struggles against the
SD : 0 2 :003(520) [0881] with these powers but would **succumb** in the conflict.

Sudden (1)
LC : 0 1 :072(374) [0601] by experience that often **sudden**, great calamity was

Sue (1)
AP : 2 1 :018(231) [0347] "The richest of the people will **sue** your favor."

Suffer (51), Suffered (23), Sufferers (1), Suffering (23), Sufferings (5), Suffers (14)
AG : 0 2 :003(029) [0045] thus disparaging the **sufferings** and merit of Christ.
AG : 0 3 :002(029) [0045] man, who was truly born, **suffered**, was crucified, died,
AG : 0 4 :002(030) [0045] we believe that Christ **suffered** for us and that for his sake

Continued ▶

AG : 1 7 :004(038) [0051] condemned men will not **suffer** eternal pain and torment.
AG : 2 0 :023(044) [0055] the history of Christ's **suffering** and his resurrection from
AG : 2 0 :037(046) [0057] God, have patience in **suffering**, love one's neighbor,
AG : 2 6 :031(068) [0075] Christians are obliged to **suffer**, and this is true and real
AL : 0 3 :002(030) [0045] of the virgin Mary, truly **suffered**, was crucified, dead,
AL : 2 6 :031(068) [0075] the cross that Christians are obliged to **suffer** afflictions.
AP : 0 3 :001(107) [0119] that this same Christ **suffered** and died to reconcile the
AP : 0 4 :051(114) [0135] that Christ was born, **suffered**, and was raised unless we
AP : 0 4 :301(153) [0205] so many terrible evils, **sufferings** in this life and the fear
AP : 0 4 :382(165) [0225] our good works are valid by virtue of Christ's **suffering**.
AP : 0 4 :382(165) [0225] us because of Christ's **suffering**, then indeed Christ's
AP : 0 4 :382(165) [0225] suffering, then indeed Christ's **suffering** benefits us.
AP : 0 4 :382(165) [0225] our works are valid by virtue of the **suffering** of Christ.
AP : 1 2 :136(203) [0293] "Be penitent" will mean "**Suffer** the penalties of purgatory
AP : 1 2 :156(207) [0301] said before that the saints **suffer** penalties which are the
AP : 1 2 :156(207) [0301] Some of them **suffer** penalties which God imposes only on
AP : 1 5 :028(219) [0323] How the great Gerson **suffers** as he looks for the degrees
AP : 2 0 :006(227) [0339] bear whatever we have to **suffer** for Christ and the
AP : 2 2 :016(238) [0361] the church, which has **suffered** this injury because it could
AP : 2 4 :030(255) [0395] of the Gospel, **suffering** because of the Gospel, etc.
AP : 2 4 :057(260) [0405] the merit of Christ's **suffering** and the righteousness of
AP : 2 4 :063(261) [0405] the glory of Christ's **suffering** and the righteousness of
AP : 2 4 :074(263) [0409] it really gives thanks for the blessing of Christ's **suffering**.
AP : 2 4 :096(267) [0417] which rob Christ's **suffering** of its glory and utterly
AP : 2 8 :005(281) [0445] see the tears of the **sufferers** and hear the pitiful
S 1 : P R :003(289) [0455] souls damned rather than **suffer** himself and his adherents
S 1 : 0 1 :000(292) [0461] Afterwards he **suffered**, died, was buried, descended to
S 2 : 0 2 :010(294) [0465] in Augsburg: he would **suffer** himself to be torn to pieces
S 2 : 0 2 :010(294) [0465] So by God's help I would **suffer** myself to be burned to
S 2 : 0 4 :007(299) [0473] he would have to **suffer** the overthrow and destruction of
S 2 : 0 4 :014(301) [0475] or God, so we cannot **suffer** his apostle, the pope or
S 3 : 0 3 :002(304) [0479] (true sorrow of the heart, **suffering**, and pain of death).
S 3 : 0 3 :038(309) [0489] which we do but of the **sufferings** and blood of the
S 3 : 1 1 :003(315) [0499] to their abominable celibacy, nor shall we **suffer** it.
SC : 0 2 :003(345) [0545] *born of the virgin Mary, **suffered** under Pontius Pilate,*
SC : 0 2 :004(345) [0545] and with his innocent **sufferings** and death, in order that I
SC : 0 5 :022(350) [0553] neglected to do my duty, and caused him to **suffer** loss.
LC : P R :006(359) [0569] both pastors and preachers to **suffer** distress and hunger.
LC : P R :019(361) [0573] Vain imaginations, like new cloth, **suffer** shrinkage!
LC : S P :012(363) [0577] born of the virgin Mary, **suffered** under Pontius Pilate,
LC : 0 1 :004(365) [0581] me, and whenever you **suffer** misfortune and distress,
LC : 0 1 :042(370) [0591] God and not mammon **suffer** grief and want and are
LC : 0 1 :111(380) [0613] will not allow them to **suffer** want or hunger, but will
LC : 0 1 :154(386) [0625] own household you must **suffer** ten times as much wrong
LC : 0 1 :161(387) [0627] those who do so and will not let them **suffer** want.
LC : 0 1 :162(387) [0627] that their bellies will **suffer**, and therefore they cannot
LC : 0 1 :187(390) [0633] that no one willingly **suffers** injury from another.
LC : 0 1 :187(390) [0633] and prayer commit to him whatever wrong we **suffer**.
LC : 0 1 :189(391) [0635] and save him from **suffering** bodily harm or injury.
LC : 0 1 :190(391) [0635] If you see anyone **suffer** hunger and do not feed him, you
LC : 0 1 :193(391) [0635] should allow no man to **suffer** harm, but show to
LC : 0 1 :197(392) [0637] might live a nice, soft life without the cross and **suffering**.
LC : 0 1 :197(392) [0637] they might not have to **suffer** wrong from anyone or do
LC : 0 1 :215(394) [0641] and evil desires that they **suffer** incessant ragings of secret
LC : 0 1 :234(397) [0647] and a beggar and will **suffer** all kinds of troubles and
LC : 0 1 :237(397) [0647] whom we are obliged to **suffer** such intolerable insolence.
LC : 0 1 :243(398) [0649] a great hoard, they must **suffer** so many troubles and
LC : 0 1 :251(399) [0651] interests, and when he **suffers** want we are to help, share,
LC : 0 1 :258(399) [0653] oppressed, loses his case, and **suffers** punishment.
LC : 0 1 :307(406) [0669] that is his, letting him **suffer** loss while you gratify your
LC : 0 2 :025(413) [0683] *born of the virgin Mary, **suffered** under Pontius Pilate,*
LC : 0 2 :031(414) [0687] over sin; moreover, he **suffered**, died, and was buried that
LC : 0 2 :038(415) [0689] treasure for us by his **sufferings**, death, and resurrection,
LC : 0 3 :029(424) [0705] damage and harm he **suffers** when prayer is in proper
LC : 0 3 :044(425) [0709] on his account the father **suffers** scorn and reproach, so
LC : 0 3 :058(428) [0713] could God allow us to **suffer** want in temporal things
LC : 0 3 :061(428) [0715] these treasures, we must **suffer** an astonishing amount of
LC : 0 3 :066(429) [0717] we must remain steadfast, **suffer** patiently whatever
LC : 0 3 :067(429) [0717] that whatever we must **suffer** on its account, we may
LC : 0 3 :106(434) [0729] We cannot help but **suffer** tribulations, and even be
LC : 0 5 :026(449) [0759] Meanwhile it must **suffer** much opposition.
EP : 0 5 :009(479) [0803] the proclamation of the **suffering** and death of Christ, the
EP : 0 8 :008(487) [0819] and circumscribed, to **suffer**, to die, to ascend and to
EP : 0 8 :013(488) [0821] mere man who for us **suffered**, died, was buried,
EP : 0 8 :014(488) [0821] Son of God has truly **suffered** for us, but according to the
EP : 0 8 :014(488) [0821] his own, so that he could **suffer** and be our high priest for
EP : 0 8 :031(490) [0825] only the mere humanity **suffered** for us and redeemed us,
EP : 0 8 :032(491) [0825] had redeemed us by his **suffering** and death he no longer
EP : 0 9 :001(492) [0827] article belong to Christ's **suffering** or to his glorious
EP : 1 0 :006(493) [0831] confession and **suffer** in consequence what God sends us
SD : 0 1 :062(519) [0879] but that we do not even realize what we are **suffering**."
SD : 0 2 :073(535) [0909] nothing at all, but merely **suffers** what God accomplishes
SD : 0 2 :089(538) [0915] it and that man only **suffers** that which God works in
SD : 0 2 :089(538) [0915] Man is, as it were, the subject which **suffers**.
SD : 0 2 :089(538) [0915] works nothing; he only **suffers** — though not as a stone
SD : 0 3 :015(541) [0919] — as he was obligated to **suffer** and die for his person.
SD : 0 3 :015(541) [0919] consists not only in his **suffering** and dying, but also in
SD : 0 3 :015(541) [0919] which, by doing and **suffering**, in life and in death, Christ
SD : 0 4 :012(553) [0941] to serve everyone, to **suffer** everything for the love of God
SD : 0 5 :004(559) [0953] that the Christ should **suffer** and on the third day rise
SD : 0 8 :010(593) [1019] and circumscribed, to **suffer** and die, to ascend and
SD : 0 8 :010(593) [1019] one place to another, to **suffer** hunger, thirst, frost, heat,
SD : 0 8 :020(595) [1021] (whose property it is to **suffer** and to die) that has suffered
SD : 0 8 :020(595) [1021] and to die) that has **suffered** for the sin of the world, but
SD : 0 8 :020(595) [1021] of God himself has truly **suffered** (although according to
SD : 0 8 :020(595) [1021] although the divine nature can neither **suffer** nor die.
SD : 0 8 :037(598) [1027] death in the flesh" and "**suffered** for us in the flesh"
SD : 0 8 :038(598) [1027] the human nature had **suffered** for us) and since Dr.
SD : 0 8 :039(598) [1029] that the Christ should **suffer** these things and enter into
SD : 0 8 :040(598) [1029] only the human nature **suffered** for me, then Christ would
SD : 0 8 :041(599) [1029] the deity surely cannot **suffer** and die, then you must
SD : 0 8 :042(599) [1029] must say that the person (pointing to Christ) **suffers**, dies.
SD : 0 8 :042(599) [1029] and therefore it is correct to say: the Son of God **suffers**.
SD : 0 8 :042(599) [1029] the deity) does not **suffer**, nevertheless the person who is
SD : 0 8 :042(599) [1029] person who is true God **suffers** in the other part (namely,
SD : 0 8 :043(599) [1029] since all the doing and **suffering** are not ascribed to the
SD : 0 8 :043(599) [1029] the person who does and **suffers** everything, the one thing
SD : 0 8 :045(600) [1031] cited locutions, "God **suffered**," "God died," are merely
SD : 0 8 :045(600) [1031] who was made man, **suffered** for us, died, and redeemed
SD : 0 8 :093(609) [1049] whatever in the passion, **suffered** for us and redeemed us.
SD : 1 0 :020(614) [1059] or God, so we cannot **suffer** his apostle, the pope or
SD : 1 1 :015(619) [1069] his innocent obedience, **suffering**, and death Christ has
SD : 1 1 :080(629) [1089] his will, he would not have needed any long-**suffering**.
SD : 1 2 :009(633) [1097] which cannot be **suffered** or tolerated in the churches or

Suffice (10)
SC : 0 5 :024(350) [0555] Let this **suffice**.
LC : 0 1 :048(371) [0593] Let this **suffice** for the First Commandment.
LC : 0 1 :319(408) [0673] Let this **suffice** concerning the first part, both for
LC : 0 2 :046(416) [0689] Let this **suffice** concerning the substance of this article.
LC : 0 4 :046(442) [0743] Let this **suffice** concerning the nature, benefits, and use of
LC : 0 5 :063(454) [0767] Let this **suffice** for the first point.
SD : 0 1 :049(517) [0875] Let this **suffice** as a simple exposition of the doctrine and
SD : 0 3 :044(547) [0931] Let this **suffice** as a summary exposition of the doctrine
SD : 0 7 :072(582) [0997] Let this **suffice** concerning the true presence and the
SD : 1 1 :094(632) [1095] This will **suffice** concerning the controverted articles

Sufficiency (3), Sufficient (20), Sufficiently (19)
AG : P R :014(026) [0041] will be graciously and **sufficiently** assured from what
AG : 0 7 :002(032) [0047] For it is **sufficient** for the true unity of the Christian
AG : 2 7 :005(071) [0077] young, they had not **sufficiently** appreciated or
AG : 2 7 :031(076) [0079] one does not possess **sufficient** understanding to
AL : 2 7 :031(075) [0079] does not seem to have **sufficient** judgment to make a
AL : 2 8 :062(092) [0093] of faith was not taught with **sufficient** clarity.
AP : 0 4 :029(111) [0129] of free will, is in itself **sufficient** both for discovering how
AP : 1 2 :094(196) [0281] promises ought to be **sufficient** for us, but this promise is
AP : 1 3 :008(212) [0311] Christ on the cross was **sufficient** for the sins of the whole
AP : 1 3 :008(212) [0311] sacrifices as though this were not **sufficient** for our sins.
S 3 : 0 3 :019(306) [0483] when he had made a **sufficiently** complete or a sufficiently
S 3 : 0 3 :019(306) [0483] a sufficiently complete or a **sufficiently** pure confession.
S 3 : 0 8 :006(313) [0495] After all, we have treated them **sufficiently** elsewhere.
TR : 0 0 :042(328) [0517] Consequently our consciences are **sufficiently** excused.
TR : 0 0 :079(333) [0527] cases; there are **sufficiently** numerous and compelling
LC : P R :009(359) [0569] perfectly, or at least **sufficiently**, even though they think
LC : 0 1 :021(367) [0585] good things from him **sufficiently** to trust that he wants to
LC : 0 1 :126(382) [0617] God ought to provide us **sufficient** reason and incentive to
LC : 0 1 :130(383) [0619] teachers can never be **sufficiently** thanked and repaid."
LC : 0 1 :248(398) [0651] We have now given **sufficient** warning and exhortation.
LC : 0 1 :253(399) [0653] Surely he is **sufficient** for your needs and will let you lack
LC : 0 1 :293(404) [0663] since these vices were **sufficiently** forbidden in
LC : 0 1 :314(407) [0671] a precious work that cannot be **sufficiently** extolled.
LC : 0 2 :004(411) [0679] of the Creed, it is **sufficient**, as a first step, for very simple
LC : 0 4 :017(438) [0737] Word which no one can **sufficiently** extol, for it contains
LC : 0 4 :029(440) [0739] the water, as we have **sufficiently** stated, but through its
LC : 0 4 :049(442) [0743] is pleasing to Christ is **sufficiently** proved from his own
LC : 0 6 :013(458) [0000] do not find ourselves **sufficiently** strong in faith, we may
EP : 0 2 :003(470) [0787] we are not of ourselves "**sufficient** to claim anything as
EP : 0 2 :003(470) [0787] as coming from us; our **sufficiency** is from God"
EP : 1 2 :019(499) [0841] difference of faith is **sufficient** ground for married people
SD : P R :008(505) [0853] a most correct and simple, yet **sufficiently** explicit, form.
SD : 0 2 :012(522) [0885] "Not that we are **sufficient** of ourselves to claim anything
SD : 0 2 :012(522) [0885] as coming from us; our **sufficiency** is from God"
SD : 0 2 :026(526) [0891] "All our **sufficiency** is from God" (II Cor. 3:6).
SD : 0 2 :069(534) [0907] again, as we have **sufficiently** reported above on this
SD : 0 2 :088(538) [0915] also been explained in **sufficient** detail above that in
SD : 0 5 :009(559) [0955] the law, but it is not **sufficient** for a salutary conversion to
SD : 0 5 :015(561) [0957] of the law is not **sufficient** for genuine and salutary
SD : 0 7 :029(574) [0981] he did not consider it **sufficiently**,' etc, let me say now as
SD : 0 7 :046(577) [0987] Abraham certainly had **sufficient** ground for a disputation
SD : 1 2 :024(634) [1099] difference in faith is **sufficient** ground for married people

Suggest (2), Suggested (1), Suggesting (1), Suggestion (1), Suggests (4)
AL : 2 8 :056(090) [0091] not be burdened by **suggesting** that they are necessary for
AP : 2 4 :005(250) [0385] one has ever written or **suggested** that men benefit from
S 2 : 0 4 :004(299) [0473] a lion (as the angel in Rev. 10:3 **suggests**), are available.
SC : P R :023(341) [0537] esteem the sacrament **suggests** thereby that he has no sin,
SC : P R :023(341) [0539] On the other hand, he **suggests** that he needs no grace, no
SC : 0 7 :003(352) [0557] your devotion may **suggest**, you should go to your work
LC : 0 5 :075(455) [0771] no better advice than to **suggest** that they put their hands
EP : 1 0 :012(494) [0831] in a way which **suggests** that the community of God does
SD : 1 1 :091(632) [1093] to reason and the **suggestion** of the wicked devil.

Suicide (3)
AG : 2 6 :013(066) [0073] some even committed **suicide**, because they had not heard
AP : 2 7 :042(276) [0435] to God to commit **suicide** and to leave our body without
LC : 0 3 :115(435) [0731] and many he hounds to **suicide** or other dreadful

Suidas (1)
SD : 0 8 :015(594) [1019] who on the witness of **Suidas** and Theodore, the presbyter

Suit (5), Suitable (1), Suited (7), Suits (2)
AG : 2 7 :018(073) [0079] all those who are not **suited** for celibacy have the power,
AL : 2 3 :005(051) [0061] that all men are not **suited** for celibacy because God
AL : 2 3 :007(052) [0061] those who are not **suited** for celibacy ought to marry, for
AL : 2 7 :018(073) [0079] for all who are not **suited** for celibacy to marry, for vows
AP : 0 4 :260(145) [0195] twist the Scriptures to **suit** the man-made theory that by
AP : 1 2 :112(198) [0285] that these satisfactions might be **suited** to their offenses.
AP : 1 2 :123(200) [0289] sinfully twist the Word of God to **suit** their vain dreams!
AP : 1 2 :131(202) [0291] and a distortion of the Scriptures to **suit** their opinions.
AP : 1 6 :006(223) [0331] other teachings that were not **suited** to civil relationships.
AP : 2 0 :012(228) [0341] the trick of deducing from Scripture whatever **suits** them.
AP : 2 3 :014(241) [0367] command, directed to anyone not **suited** for celibacy.
AP : 2 4 :008(250) [0385] So when it **suits** them, they change the institutions of the
AP : 2 4 :096(267) [0417] But we are at **suit** with you for wickedly defending a
S 3 : 1 0 :003(314) [0497] and ought ourselves ordain **suitable** persons to this office.
LC : 0 1 :299(405) [0665] and stretch the law to **suit** their purpose, straining words

Sully (1)
SD : 0 1 :062(519) [0879] is, which did not simply **sully** human nature but corrupted

Sum (13), Sums (1)
AL : 0 0 :001(047) [0059] This is about the **sum** of our teaching.
AP : 1 2 :005(183) [0253] could grasp neither the **sum** of the matter nor the chief
AP : 1 2 :029(185) [0259] For the **sum** of the proclamation of the Gospel is to
AP : 1 2 :124(201) [0289] we covered almost the **sum** total of all Christian doctrine,
AP : 2 4 :045(258) [0401] ideas and could not grasp the **sum** of Christian doctrine.
LC : 0 1 :225(395) [0645] If a thief had taken such **sums** he would be strangled with
LC : 0 1 :250(399) [0651] To **sum** up, as we have done in the previous
LC : 0 1 :285(403) [0661] Now we have the **sum** and substance of this
LC : 0 2 :006(411) [0679] children, we shall briefly **sum** up the entire Creed in three
LC : 0 2 :051(417) [0691] This is the **sum** and substance of this phrase: I believe
LC : 0 3 :113(435) [0729] of the devil as the **sum** of all evil in order that the entire
LC : 0 3 :114(435) [0729] Therefore we **sum** it all up by saying, "Dear Father, help
SD : PR :009(505) [0853] accepted documents as the **sum** and pattern of the
SD : 0 7 :041(576) [0985] whose entire doctrine in **sum** and content was

Summae (1)
AP : 1 1 :009(182) [0251] of constitutions, glosses, **summae**, and penitential letters.

Summarily (1), Summarized (5), Summarizes (5), Summary (23), Summed (2), Summing (1)
PR : PR :003(003) [0007] and that is also briefly **summarized** in the approved
AG : 0 0 :001(047) [0059] This is just about a **summary** of the doctrines that are
AL : 0 0 :006(096) [0095] in them and that a **summary** of the doctrine taught
AP : 0 4 :245(142) [0189] and love in presenting a **summary** of the Christian life
AP : 0 4 :314(156) [0207] It **summarizes** our case very well, and a careful
AP : 1 2 :030(186) [0259] Christ gives this **summary** of the Gospel in the last
AP : 1 2 :178(211) [0307] have expounded here a **summary** of our doctrine on
AP : 2 1 :043(235) [0357] no effort to provide a **summary** of the doctrines of the
AP : 2 8 :001(281) [0443] they conclude with the **summary**: "Everything is false that
SC : 0 3 :020(348) [0549] in this petition, as in a **summary**, that our Father in
SC : 0 9 :014(356) [0563] commandments are **summed** up in this sentence: 'You
LC : PR :018(361) [0573] is a brief compend and **summary** of all the Holy
LC : SP :019(363) [0579] they were, have thus **summed** up the doctrine, life,
LC : 0 1 :064(373) [0599] All this is **summarized** in the command in Ps. 50:15,
LC : 0 1 :182(389) [0631] himself explains and **summarizes** it: We must not kill,
LC : 0 1 :311(407) [0669] Ten Commandments, a **summary** of divine teaching on
LC : 0 2 :031(414) [0685] Let this be the **summary** of this article, that the little word
EP : 0 0 :000(463) [0775] and the Comprehensive **Summary** of our Christian
EP : 0 0 :000(464) [0777] A **Summary** Epitome of the Articles in Controversy
EP : RN :000(464) [0777] The Comprehensive **Summary**, Rule, and Norm
SD : 0 0 :000(501) [0845] Word of God and the **Summary** Formulation of Our
SD : RN :000(503) [0849] The **Summary** Formulation, Basis, Rule, and Norm,
SD : PR :001(503) [0849] within the church is a **summary** formula and pattern,
SD : PR :001(503) [0849] in which the **summarized** doctrine commonly confessed
SD : PR :005(504) [0851] the Word of God, is **summarized** in the articles and
SD : PR :011(506) [0855] — in the cited **summary** of our Christian doctrine is that
SD : 0 1 :008(510) [0861] The Apology **summarizes** the matter under these heads:
SD : 0 1 :015(511) [0863] which we have given in **summary** form, are explained in
SD : 0 1 :049(517) [0875] but are treating only the chief points in **summary** fashion.
SD : 0 2 :008(521) [0883] explanation of and **summary** reply to the questions and
SD : 0 2 :014(523) [0885] **Summing** up everything, what the Son of God says
SD : 0 3 :009(540) [0919] in accord with the **summary** formulation of our Christian
SD : 0 3 :029(544) [0925] For this reason we **summarily** cut off every reference to
SD : 0 3 :036(545) [0927] terms may be **summarized** in the assertion that we are
SD : 0 3 :044(547) [0931] Let this suffice as a **summary** exposition of the doctrine
SD : 0 5 :004(559) [0953] world (Mark 16:15), he **summarizes** his doctrine in a few
SD : 0 5 :004(559) [0953] (Acts 20:24) and **summarizes** it under these heads:

Summer (2)
AP : 1 6 :006(223) [0331] the change of winter and **summer** as ordinances of God.
SD : 0 6 :009(565) [0965] at greater length in the **summer** portion of the Church

Summists (5)
AG : 2 6 :014(066) [0073] in the writings of the **summists** and canonists how
AL : 2 6 :014(066) [0073] We see that the **summists** and theologians gathered the
AP : 0 7 :032(174) [0239] there are many foolish books by the **summists** and others.
AP : 1 1 :007(181) [0251] damage as what the **summists** added to it later, including
AP : 1 1 :009(182) [0251] the torture of the **summists**, which, in spite of everything,

Summoned (5), Summons (8)
AG : PR :001(024) [0039] Majesty graciously **summoned** a diet of the empire to
AG : PR :001(024) [0039] In the **summons** Your Majesty indicated an earnest desire
AG : PR :005(025) [0039] associates, have been **summoned** for these purposes,
AG : PR :006(025) [0039] with the imperial **summons**, Your Imperial Majesty also
AG : PR :011(026) [0041] with Your Imperial Majesty's aforementioned **summons**.
AG : PR :012(026) [0041] Your Imperial Majesty's **summons**, if no amicable and
AG : PR :023(027) [0043] Your Imperial Majesty's **summons**) as we herewith
AG : 0 0 :006(095) [0095] In keeping with the **summons**, we have desired to present
AP : 2 1 :026(232) [0349] monastic theologian, **summoned** to console a dying
S1 : PR :001(288) [0455] that we might be **summoned** to appear before the council
S1 : PR :001(288) [0455] the council or be condemned without being **summoned**.
S2 : 0 4 :016(301) [0475] responded to a gracious **summons** and were given a
LC : 0 5 :067(454) [0769] tenderly and faithfully **summons** and exhorts us to our

Sumptuous (1), Sumptuously (1)
AP : 1 5 :048(221) [0329] are more luxurious and **sumptuous** than others' feasts,
AP : 2 7 :059(279) [0441] than kings' palaces and who live most **sumptuously**.

Sun (5)
AP : 2 4 :031(255) [0395] "From the rising of the **sun** to its setting my name is great
LC : 0 2 :014(412) [0681] and necessities of life — **sun**, moon, and stars in the
LC : 0 5 :056(453) [0767] in contrast to the bright **sun**, or as dung in contrast to
SD : 0 6 :002(564) [0963] are free, so that just as the **sun** spontaneously completes
SD : 0 6 :006(565) [0965] the will of God, just as the **sun**, the moon, and all the

Sunday (13), Sundays (1)
AG : 2 8 :033(086) [0087] Sabbath was changed to **Sunday** — contrary, as they say,
AG : 2 8 :053(089) [0091] we to say, then, about **Sunday** and other similar church
AG : 2 8 :057(091) [0091] is the observance of **Sunday**, Easter, Pentecost, and
AG : 2 8 :058(091) [0091] the appointment of **Sunday** in place of the Sabbath as a
AG : 2 8 :060(091) [0091] church appointed **Sunday** for this purpose, and it was the
AG : 2 8 :063(092) [0093] argue that although **Sunday** must not be kept as of divine
AL : 2 8 :053(089) [0091] are we to think about **Sunday** and about similar rites in
AL : 2 8 :057(091) [0091] sort is the observance of **Sunday**, Easter, Pentecost, and
AP : 2 4 :001(249) [0383] Mass is celebrated every **Sunday** and on other festivals,
AP : 2 4 :006(250) [0385] one public Mass, and this only on **Sundays** and festivals.
LC : 0 1 :085(376) [0605] Since from ancient times **Sunday** has been appointed for
LC : 0 1 :097(378) [0609] used to be thought that **Sunday** had been properly
SD : 0 5 :011(560) [0955] of the Gospel for the Fifth **Sunday** after Trinity.
SD : 0 6 :009(565) [0965] on the Epistle for the Nineteenth **Sunday** after Trinity.

Superabundant (1)
S2 : 0 2 :024(296) [0469] together with the **superabundant** merits of all the saints

Supererogation (9)
AG : 2 7 :061(080) [0083] furnish the works of **supererogation** which we are not
AL : 2 7 :061(080) [0083] precepts, and that monks do works of **supererogation**.
AP : 1 2 :014(184) [0257] ought to be works of **supererogation**, and these consist of
AP : 1 2 :142(204) [0295] is by the works of **supererogation**, he can make
AP : 1 2 :144(205) [0297] call them works of **supererogation**, and they ascribe to
AP : 2 7 :009(270) [0421] Do they have merits of **supererogation**?
AP : 2 7 :024(273) [0427] they have merits of **supererogation**, these liberal men then
AP : 2 7 :034(275) [0431] fabricate works of **supererogation** and sell them to
LC : 0 1 :022(367) [0585] by works of **supererogation**, just as if God were in our

Superfluous (1)
S3 : 0 3 :029(308) [0487] could even sell their **superfluous** righteousness to other

Superintendent (6)
S3 : 1 5 :005(317) [0501] Dr. Urban Rhegius, **superintendent** of the churches in the
S3 : 1 5 :005(317) [0501] Paul Rhode, **superintendent** of Stettin
S3 : 1 5 :005(317) [0501] Gerard Oemcken, **superintendent** of the church in
TR : 0 0 :082(334) [0529] Dr. Urban Rhegius, **superintendent** of the churches in the
TR : 0 0 :082(335) [0529] John Aepinus, **superintendent** in Hamburg, subscribed
TR : 0 0 :082(335) [0529] John Fontanus, **superintendent** of Lower Hesse,

Superior (12), Superiority (11), Superiors (4)
AG : 2 7 :016(073) [0077] and is regarded as far **superior** to the other estates
AL : 2 7 :023(074) [0079] state that every vow is subject to the right of a **superior**.
AP : 0 4 :308(155) [0207] to the edict of a **superior** is obviously a kind of
AP : 1 2 :069(192) [0271] the errors of their **superiors**, without understanding
S2 : 0 2 :010(294) [0465] be considered equal or **superior** to my Saviour, Jesus
S2 : 0 3 :002(298) [0471] men, which claim to be **superior** to the ordinary Christian
S3 : 1 5 :005(316) [0501] concede to him that **superiority** over the bishops which he
TR : 0 0 :008(320) [0505] have lordship or **superiority** among them but that the
TR : 0 0 :010(321) [0505] Peter as his **superior** if Peter had been his superior by
TR : 0 0 :010(321) [0505] his superior if Peter had been his **superior** by divine right.
TR : 0 0 :010(321) [0507] God, that Peter was not **superior** to the other apostles,
TR : 0 0 :011(321) [0507] not attribute to Peter **superiority** or authority over the
TR : 0 0 :011(321) [0507] He is an apostle of **superior** rank.
TR : 0 0 :011(321) [0507] that Peter's authority is **superior** to that of the others and
TR : 0 0 :012(322) [0507] of Rome had his **superiority** by divine right, it would not
TR : 0 0 :015(322) [0509] did not attribute **superiority** and lordship to the bishop of
TR : 0 0 :016(322) [0509] 7. Such **superiority** is impossible, for it is not possible for
TR : 0 0 :016(322) [0509] inasmuch as such **superiority** is impossible and the
TR : 0 0 :017(323) [0509] the primacy or **superiority** of the bishop of Rome.
TR : 0 0 :018(323) [0509] of poverty that makes a bishop **superior** or inferior."
TR : 0 0 :024(324) [0511] to Peter any special prerogative, **superiority**, or power.
TR : 0 0 :027(325) [0511] and not as applying to the person or **superiority** of Peter.
TR : 0 0 :038(326) [0515] possess primacy and **superiority** by divine right,
SC : 0 1 :008(343) [0541] despise our parents and **superiors**, nor provoke them to
LC : 0 1 :141(384) [0621] of obedience due to our **superiors**, persons whose duty it
LC : 0 1 :167(388) [0629] Although the duty of **superiors** is not explicitly stated in
LC : 0 3 :023(423) [0703] So this prayer is far **superior** to all others that we might

Supernatural (11)
AP : 0 4 :303(154) [0205] us, and hears us is a **supernatural** thing, for of itself the
LC : 0 1 :211(393) [0641] has released by a high **supernatural** gift so that they can
EP : 0 7 :015(483) [0811] union in a **supernatural** and heavenly manner.
EP : 0 7 :041(486) [0817] way concerning the **supernatural** and celestial mysteries
EP : 0 7 :042(486) [0817] in a true, though **supernatural**, eating of Christ's body
SD : 0 7 :064(581) [0995] manner, but in a **supernatural**, incomprehensible manner.
SD : 0 7 :105(588) [1009] in mind the spiritual, **supernatural**, heavenly mode
SD : 0 7 :127(591) [1015] way about the **supernatural** and heavenly mysteries of
SD : 0 8 :051(600) [1033] special, high, great, **supernatural**, unsearchable, ineffable,
SD : 0 8 :081(607) [1045] according to the third **supernatural** manner, he is and can
SD : 0 8 :081(607) [1045] manner, but according to the **supernatural**, divine manner.

Superseded (1)
AL : 2 0 :014(043) [0055] works would not be **superseded** by the mercy of God if

Superstition (5), Superstitious (3), Superstitiously (1)
PR : PR :002(003) [0007] to light its way out of papistic **superstition** and darkness.
AP : 1 2 :120(200) [0287] Thus they **superstitiously** imagined that satisfactions were
AP : 2 1 :037(234) [0353] epics and bring only **superstitious** examples of certain
AP : 2 3 :060(247) [0381] with the canons; it is **superstitious** and full of danger;
AP : 2 4 :007(250) [0385] of private Masses; so **superstitious** and so mercenary have
AP : 2 8 :017(284) [0449] place and without **superstition**, in order to avoid
EP : RN :004(465) [0777] worship, idolatry, and **superstition** of the papacy and
SD : 0 4 :015(553) [0943] a dead faith or **superstition**, without repentance and
SD : 1 0 :014(613) [1057] false doctrines, **superstition**, and idolatry and to suppress

Supervising (1), Supervision (1)
PR : PR :026(014) [0025] and schools, the **supervision** of printers, and other
LC : 0 1 :218(394) [0643] have the duty of so **supervising** youth that they will be

Supper (154)
PR : PR :019(009) [0017] concerning the Holy **Supper** as well as other adulterated
PR : PR :020(010) [0017] of the Holy **Supper** into a discussion of the personal union
PR : PR :020(010) [0017] treatment of the Lord's **Supper** to this and only this one
PR : PR :022(011) [0019] concerning the Lord's **Supper**, these have to be set forth
PR : PR :022(012) [0019] against the Holy **Supper** as it is celebrated in our churches
AG : 1 0 :000(034) [0047] X. The Holy **Supper** of Our Lord
AG : 1 0 :001(034) [0047] are really present in the **Supper** of our Lord under the
AL : 1 0 :000(034) [0047] X. Lord's **Supper**
AL : 1 0 :001(034) [0047] are distributed to those who eat in the **Supper** of the Lord

Continued ▶

A L : 2 2 :001(049) [0059] sacrament of the Lord's **Supper** both kinds are given to
A P : 0 4 :210(136) [0179] Thus the Lord's **Supper** was instituted in the church so
A P : 0 4 :276(148) [0199] Baptism and the Lord's **Supper**, for example, are signs
A P : 0 4 :276(148) [0199] Just as the Lord's **Supper** does not justify *ex opere*
A P : 0 7 :046(177) [0243] in the use of the Lord's **Supper**, which certainly was
A P : 0 7 :046(177) [0243] the ordinance of Christ's **Supper**, which is not human but
A P : 1 0 :000(179) [0247] [Article X. The Holy **Supper**]
A P : 1 0 :001(179) [0247] belief that in the Lord's **Supper** the body and blood of
A P : 1 0 :003(179) [0247] teaches that Christ is offered to us bodily in the **Supper**.
A P : 1 0 :004(179) [0247] — that in the Lord's **Supper** the body and blood of Christ
A P : 1 1 :003(180) [0249] absolution and the Lord's **Supper**, many times a year.
A P : 1 2 :042(187) [0263] the words in the Lord's **Supper** clearly state, "This is my
A P : 1 3 :004(211) [0309] are Baptism, the Lord's **Supper**, and absolution (which is
A P : 1 3 :020(213) [0313] that anyone who uses the Lord's **Supper** uses it this way.
A P : 1 5 :040(220) [0325] our circles use the Lord's **Supper**, but only after they have
A P : 2 2 :000(236) [0357] [Article XXII.] The Lord's **Supper** Under Both Kinds
A P : 2 2 :001(236) [0357] both kinds in the Lord's **Supper** is godly and in accord
A P : 2 2 :003(236) [0359] who would use the Lord's **Supper** should use it jointly.
A P : 2 3 :045(245) [0375] wine, even in the Lord's **Supper**; they abstained from the
A P : 2 4 :011(251) [0387] position that the Lord's **Supper** does not grant grace *ex*
A P : 2 4 :033(256) [0395] reception of the Lord's **Supper** itself can be praise or
A P : 2 4 :033(256) [0395] not only about the Lord's **Supper**, and he does not
A P : 2 4 :068(261) [0407] imagine that the Lord's **Supper** was instituted for two
A P : 2 4 :087(265) [0413] not about prayers, but really about the Lord's **Supper**.
A P : 2 4 :089(266) [0415] to the dead the Lord's **Supper** which was instituted for
A P : 2 4 :090(266) [0415] Surely the Lord's **Supper** was instituted for the sake of
A P : 2 4 :094(267) [0417] the transfer of the Lord's **Supper** to the dead *ex opere*
S 3 : 0 6 :001(311) [0493] bread and the wine in the **Supper** are the true body and
S C : P R :005(338) [0533] the cup in the Lord's **Supper** and insist on the observance
S C : 0 6 :004(351) [0555] he took the cup, after **supper**, and when he had given
L C : S P :023(364) [0579] way also the cup, after **supper**, saying, 'This cup is the new
L C : 0 3 :098(433) [0725] Baptism and the Lord's **Supper**, which are appointed as
L C : 0 4 :054(443) [0745] unworthily of the Lord's **Supper** receive the true
L C : 0 5 :003(447) [0753] *he took the cup, after* ***supper****, gave thanks, and gave it to*
L C : 0 5 :004(447) [0753] For the Lord's **Supper** was not invented or devised by any
L C : 0 5 :024(449) [0759] The Lord's **Supper** is given as a daily food and sustenance
L C : 0 5 :027(449) [0759] comfort of the Lord's **Supper** is given to bring us new
L C : 0 5 :031(450) [0759] out for us in the Lord's **Supper** and hence that we cannot
L C : 0 5 :047(452) [0765] "I institute a Passover or **Supper** for you, which you shall
E P : 0 7 :000(481) [0807] VII. The Holy **Supper** of Christ
E P : 0 7 :003(482) [0809] namely, that in the Holy **Supper** only bread and wine are
E P : 0 7 :004(482) [0809] of Christ in the Holy **Supper** but assert that this takes
E P : 0 7 :004(482) [0809] opinion that in the Holy **Supper** nothing but bread and
E P : 0 7 :005(482) [0809] and wine of the Holy **Supper**, seek the body and blood of
E P : 0 7 :005(482) [0809] *Doctrine of the Holy* ***Supper*** *Against the*
E P : 0 7 :006(482) [0809] confess that in the Holy **Supper** the body and blood of
E P : 0 7 :008(482) [0811] of Christ in the Holy **Supper**, but it is to be ascribed solely
E P : 0 7 :009(483) [0811] celebration of the Holy **Supper** the words of Christ's
E P : 0 7 :019(484) [0813] will receive the Holy **Supper** to his condemnation, for
E P : 0 7 :019(484) [0813] for Christ instituted this **Supper** particularly for
E P : 0 7 :021(484) [0813] to our simple faith and confession about Christ's **Supper**:
E P : 0 7 :022(484) [0813] and wine in the Holy **Supper** lose their substance and
E P : 0 7 :027(485) [0815] and wine in the Holy **Supper** are no more than tokens
E P : 0 7 :029(485) [0815] as truly as we eat and drink bread and wine in the **Supper**.
E P : 0 7 :030(485) [0815] of our faith in the Holy **Supper** is effected solely by the
E P : 0 7 :031(485) [0815] 10. That in the Holy **Supper** only the power, operation,
E P : 0 7 :032(485) [0815] still less in all places, where his Holy **Supper** is observed.
E P : 0 7 :033(485) [0815] present in the Holy **Supper**, nor could he have kept such a
E P : 0 7 :035(485) [0815] of the body and blood of Christ in the Holy **Supper**.
E P : 0 7 :036(485) [0815] and wine of the Holy **Supper**, but should lift their eyes
E P : 0 7 :037(485) [0815] 16. That in the Holy **Supper** unbelieving and impenitent
E P : 0 8 :001(486) [0817] controversy on the Holy **Supper** a disagreement has arisen
E P : 0 8 :017(489) [0823] are present in the Holy **Supper**, *not according to the mode*
E P : 1 2 :024(500) [0843] and wine in the Holy **Supper** are not means through and
S D : 0 2 :043(529) [0897] *Concerning the Holy* ***Supper*** in which he solemnly
S D : 0 7 :000(568) [0971] The Holy **Supper**
S D : 0 7 :002(569) [0973] confess that in the Holy **Supper** the body of Christ is truly
S D : 0 7 :002(569) [0973] bread and wine in the **Supper** as the highest heaven is
S D : 0 7 :003(569) [0973] but bread and wine are orally received in the **Supper**.
S D : 0 7 :004(569) [0973] alleged that the Lord's **Supper** was only an external sign
S D : 0 7 :004(569) [0973] is truly present in the **Supper**, namely, according to the
S D : 0 7 :005(570) [0973] of Christ is present in the **Supper**, they still did not
S D : 0 7 :006(570) [0973] Christ is present in his **Supper** truly, essentially, and alive.
S D : 0 7 :007(570) [0975] the words of the **Supper**, "This is my body," not strictly,
S D : 0 7 :008(570) [0975] on earth in the Lord's **Supper**, although invisibly and
S D : 0 7 :009(570) [0975] present in the Holy **Supper** under the forms of bread and
S D : 0 7 :011(571) [0975] confess that in the Lord's **Supper** the body and blood of
S D : 0 7 :011(571) [0975] dwells bodily in the **Supper** through the communication
S D : 0 7 :019(572) [0979] bread and the wine in the **Supper** are the true body and
S D : 0 7 :027(574) [0981] of Christ in the holy **Supper** from God's Word and
S D : 0 7 :033(575) [0983] the Lord's bread in the **Supper** is his true, natural body,
S D : 0 7 :035(575) [0983] (the bread in the Lord's **Supper** "is true body of Christ" or
S D : 0 7 :037(575) [0985] united, so in the Holy **Supper** the two essences, the
S D : 0 7 :040(576) [0985] the formula which Christ employed in the Last **Supper**.
S D : 0 7 :044(577) [0987] After the Last **Supper**, as he was about to begin his bitter
S D : 0 7 :048(578) [0989] of the institution of this **Supper** testify that these words of
S D : 0 7 :048(578) [0989] at table and during **supper**, there can be no doubt that he
S D : 0 7 :054(579) [0991] Christ blessed in the Last **Supper** and not only the bread
S D : 0 7 :057(579) [0993] and broken bread in the **Supper** participate in the body of
S D : 0 7 :059(580) [0993] error that in the Lord's **Supper** the body of Christ is
S D : 0 7 :061(580) [0995] of the Gospel as well as in the Lord's **Supper**.
S D : 0 7 :061(581) [0995] or oral eating in the **Supper** is not only salutary but
S D : 0 7 :063(581) [0995] and wine in the Lord's **Supper** receive and partake of the
S D : 0 7 :064(581) [0995] when at table and during **supper** he handed his disciples
S D : 0 7 :068(582) [0997] unworthy guests at this **Supper** are, namely, those who go
S D : 0 7 :074(583) [0999] presence of the body and blood of Christ in the **Supper**.
S D : 0 7 :075(583) [0999] efficacious in the first **Supper** but they still retain their
S D : 0 7 :075(583) [0999] in all places where the **Supper** is observed according to
S D : 0 7 :075(583) [0999] of the same words which Christ spoke in the first **Supper**.
S D : 0 7 :076(583) [0999] body,' the elements set before us in the **Supper** are blessed.
S D : 0 7 :076(583) [0999] true body and blood are present in the church's **Supper**."
S D : 0 7 :078(583) [1001] command in the Lord's **Supper** and say, 'This is my
S D : 0 7 :083(584) [1001] action of the Lord's **Supper** as Christ ordained it is not
S D : 0 7 :085(584) [1001] concerning the Holy **Supper** and to obviate and eliminate
S D : 0 7 :086(584) [1003] and visible action of the **Supper** as ordained by Christ: the
S D : 0 7 :088(585) [1003] Christ's body in the Holy **Supper** and that therefore the
S D : 0 7 :091(585) [1005] *concerning the Holy* ***Supper****,* and other writings of his.
S D : 0 7 :100(587) [1007] and wine in the Lord's **Supper**, and, as people believe,
S D : 0 7 :105(588) [1009] is present in the Holy **Supper**, not only to work comfort
S D : 0 7 :105(588) [1009] of Christ in the Holy **Supper** are received, eaten, and
S D : 0 7 :106(588) [1009] of Christ in the Holy **Supper** is built upon the truth and
S D : 0 7 :108(588) [1009] and wine in the Holy **Supper** completely lose their
S D : 0 7 :113(589) [1011] blood of Christ in the **Supper**, but through tropes or a
S D : 0 7 :114(589) [1011] blood of Christ in the **Supper**, and the contrary teaching
S D : 0 7 :114(589) [1011] teaching that in the **Supper** the body of Christ is partaken
S D : 0 7 :114(589) [1011] faith and that in the **Supper** our mouth receives only
S D : 0 7 :115(589) [1011] bread and wine in the **Supper** are no more than badges
S D : 0 7 :116(589) [1011] it turns away from the **Supper** and rises above all
S D : 0 7 :116(589) [1011] Christ as truly as in the **Supper** we receive the external
S D : 0 7 :116(589) [1013] of our faith in the **Supper** allegedly take place not through
S D : 0 7 :117(589) [1013] 6. Or that in the **Supper** there is distributed to faith only
S D : 0 7 :119(590) [1013] present with us in the **Supper**, which is celebrated
S D : 0 7 :120(590) [1013] his body and blood in the **Supper** because the nature and
S D : 0 7 :121(590) [1013] of Christ in the Holy **Supper**, whence some omit the
S D : 0 7 :121(590) [1013] words of institution in the administration of the **Supper**.
S D : 0 7 :121(590) [1013] the administration of the **Supper**, as shown above in a
S D : 0 7 :122(590) [1013] bread and wine of the **Supper**, but to look away from the
S D : 0 7 :122(590) [1013] from the bread of the **Supper** and by their faith to look to
S D : 0 7 :123(590) [1013] bread and wine in the **Supper** and not the body and blood
S D : 0 7 :123(590) [1015] in the use of the Holy **Supper** and not the body and the
S D : 0 7 :126(591) [1015] essentially present in the **Supper** when it is rightly used,
S D : 0 7 :127(591) [1015] the supernatural and heavenly mysteries of this **Supper**.
S D : 0 8 :002(591) [1015] Jesus Christ in the Lord's **Supper** on the basis of the
S D : 0 8 :002(592) [1015] heaven and in the Holy **Supper** on earth since such
S D : 0 8 :003(592) [1017] concerning the Holy **Supper**, to which we herewith
S D : 0 8 :004(592) [1017] in the doctrine of the **Supper** of the Lord, did operate with
S D : 0 8 :004(592) [1017] to eliminate from his **Supper** the true, essential presence
S D : 0 8 :021(595) [1021] *concerning the Holy* ***Supper*** against the blasphemous
S D : 0 8 :029(596) [1025] and blood in the Holy **Supper** according to the words of
S D : 0 8 :038(598) [1027] *concerning the Holy* ***Supper*** has written about Zwingli's
S D : 0 8 :079(607) [1045] he instituted his Holy **Supper** that he might be present
S D : 0 8 :081(607) [1045] *concerning the Holy* ***Supper*** he writes about the person of
S D : 0 8 :086(608) [1047] and in his *Great Confession concerning the Holy* ***Supper****.*
S D : 0 8 :086(608) [1047] his covenant in the Holy **Supper** in connection with the
S D : 1 2 :032(635) [1101] and wine in the Holy **Supper** are not means through which

Supplement (1)
L C : S P :025(364) [0579] on these subjects, to **supplement** and confirm their

Supplications (8)
A P : 0 4 :331(158) [0211] we do not present our **supplications** before thee on the
A P : 0 4 :337(159) [0215] we do not present our **supplications** before thee on the
A P : 2 4 :088(265) [0413] Thee entreaties and **supplications** and bloodless sacrifices
A P : 2 4 :088(265) [0413] to offer prayers and **supplications** and bloodless sacrifices
S C : 0 9 :005(355) [0561] "I urge that **supplications**, prayers, intercessions, and
S C : 0 9 :013(356) [0563] God and continues in **supplications** and prayers night and
S C : 0 9 :014(356) [0563] "I urge that **supplications**, prayers, intercessions, and
S D : 1 1 :074(628) [1087] thou didst hear my **supplications** when I cried to thee for

Supply (1), Supplied (2), Supplies (2)
A P : 0 7 :009(169) [0229] the wicked, and Christ **supplies** it with the gifts he has
A P : 2 4 :082(264) [0411] this collection not only **supplies** what the saints need but
S 1 : P R :010(290) [0457] been so enlightened and **supplied** with the pure Word and
L C : 0 1 :208(393) [0639] and, in addition, has **supplied** and endowed it with
S D : 0 3 :035(545) [0927] and impure, in order to **supply** tempted consciences with

Support (56), Supported (9), Supporting (1), Supports (7)
A G : 1 9 :000(041) [0053] as God withdraws his **support**, the will turns away from
A G : 2 6 :010(065) [0071] husband should labor to **support** his wife and children
A G : 2 7 :058(080) [0083] has God's command to **support** it; on the other hand,
A L : 2 0 :012(043) [0055] this whole matter is **supported** by testimonies of the
A L : 2 4 :040(060) [0069] the Mass among us is **supported** by the example of the
A P : 0 4 :011(108) [0123] To **support** and increase trust in such works, the
A P : 0 4 :104(122) [0151] Ambrose, which clearly **support** our position; he denies
A P : 0 4 :341(159) [0215] twist against faith statements made in **support** of faith.
A P : 1 2 :046(188) [0263] which nature could not bear without the **support** of faith.
A P : 1 2 :066(191) [0271] of the church in **support** of our position: "To him all the
A P : 1 2 :117(199) [0287] Such errors received **support** from many statements of
A P : 1 3 :023(214) [0313] from the Fathers that **supports** the scholastics on this
A P : 1 5 :014(217) [0319] God since they do not have **support** in God's Word?
A P : 2 0 :008(227) [0341] This faith gives **support** and life to the heart in its hardest
A P : 2 1 :003(229) [0343] of merits, surely has no **support** among the ancient
A P : 2 1 :042(235) [0357] Instead of **supporting** this most honorable and holy desire
A P : 2 3 :042(245) [0375] If anybody **supports** the law of celibacy in order to
A P : 2 3 :064(248) [0381] They give many quotations to **support** this.
A P : 2 4 :033(256) [0395] therefore he does not refute our position but **supports** it.
A P : 2 4 :034(256) [0395] therefore it does not **support** the notion of ceremonies *ex*
A P : 2 4 :040(257) [0399] does not refute but **supports** our stand because we require
A P : 2 4 :058(260) [0405] whole Epistle to the Hebrews **supports** this interpretation.
A P : 2 4 :061(260) [0405] against us give no **support** to our opponents' wicked idea
A P : 2 4 :065(261) [0407] from the Scriptures in **support** of the fairy tales which
A P : 2 4 :065(261) [0407] nor do they have the **support** of the ancient church and
A P : 2 4 :075(263) [0411] our opponents twist in **support** of their idea that
A P : 2 4 :090(266) [0415] reasons they adduce in **support** of the doctrine of
A P : 2 4 :091(266) [0415] should be careful not to **support** the abuses of our
A P : 2 4 :094(267) [0417] The ancients do not **support** the opponents' idea of the
A P : 2 4 :094(267) [0417] Even though they have **support** at most from Gregory and
A P : 2 4 :095(267) [0417] sayings being twisted to **support** the obvious lies which
A P : 2 4 :096(267) [0417] We do not **support** Aerius either.
A P : 2 7 :009(270) [0421] the monastery to be **supported** at public expense without
A P : 2 7 :009(270) [0423] forced to approve and **support** the abuses of the Mass,
A P : 2 7 :010(270) [0423] arguments and what they adduce to **support** their case.
A P : 2 7 :018(272) [0425] Paul's statement in **support** of this, they have written,
A P : 2 7 :064(280) [0441] the church and were **supported** from public funds, "They
A P : 2 7 :065(280) [0441] this passage does not **support** monastic vows, taken for
A P : 2 7 :067(280) [0441] wanton while being **supported** from public funds and

Continued ▶

A P : 2 8 :019(284) [0449] take a statement that **supports** our position and contains
S 2 : 0 2 :014(295) [0467] they are without the **support** of the Scriptures and
T R : 0 0 :042(328) [0517] with and not to **support** impiety and unjust cruelty.
T R : 0 0 :053(329) [0519] how great a crime it is to **support** unjust cruelty in the
T R : 0 0 :054(329) [0519] and power for the **support** of idolatry and countless other
T R : 0 0 :079(333) [0527] godly teachers but rather **support** the cruelty of the pope;
T R : 0 0 :080(334) [0527] these means for the **support** of ministers, the promotion
L C : 0 1 :051(371) [0595] any way whatsoever to **support** falsehood or wrong of
L C : 0 1 :064(373) [0599] to use the holy name in **support** of falsehood or
L C : 0 1 :066(373) [0599] We are not to swear in **support** of evil (that is, to a
L C : 0 1 :066(373) [0599] or unnecessarily; but in **support** of the good and for the
L C : 0 1 :069(374) [0599] to avoid calling upon God's name in its **support**.
L C : 0 1 :103(379) [0611] misuse his holy name in **support** of lies or any evil
L C : 0 1 :162(387) [0627] they cannot now **support** one good preacher although in
L C : 0 1 :165(387) [0627] it to God how he will **support** you and provide for all
L C : 0 1 :168(388) [0629] provide for the material **support** of their children,
L C : 0 1 :207(393) [0639] beget children, and **support** and bring them up to the
L C : 0 1 :301(405) [0667] them that the law **supports** them, and they gain such
L C : 0 2 :013(412) [0681] drink, clothing, means of **support**, wife and child,
L C : 0 3 :086(432) [0723] to his will and are **supported** by God's gift and blessing,
L C : 0 3 :116(435) [0731] For if God did not **support** us, we would not be safe from
L C : 0 4 :050(443) [0745] in conflict with himself, **support** lies and wickedness, or
S D : P R :008(502) [0849] which of the contending parties they should **support**.
S D : P R :006(505) [0853] and also because it is **supported** with clear and irrefutable
S D : P R :019(507) [0857] might be found or who may have said it or **supported** it.
S D : 0 2 :008(521) [0883] from the Word of God **support** and confirm the foregoing
S D : 0 2 :014(523) [0885] wills to continue to **support** them in their great weakness
S D : 0 2 :086(538) [0913] wills," were introduced to **support** the view that man's
S D : 0 5 :001(558) [0951] for by it Christians can **support** themselves in their
S D : 0 7 :011(571) [0975] Apology, but it is also **supported** there with the words of
S D : 0 7 :119(590) [1013] In **support** of their error, some Sacramentarians have
S D : 1 0 :016(613) [1057] been achieved, will **support** the idolaters in their idolatry,
S D : 1 0 :023(615) [1061] with and not to **support** impiety and unjust cruelty."
S D : 1 1 :012(618) [1067] will in no way cause or **support** either impenitence or

Suppose (36), Supposed (16), Supposes (4), Supposing (2)
A G : 2 6 :020(067) [0073] be understood if it is **supposed** that grace is earned
A L : 2 6 :020(067) [0073] be understood if men **suppose** that they merit grace by
A L : 2 8 :036(086) [0089] is dishonored when we **suppose** that we are justified by
A P : P R :004(098) [0099] — and one that was **supposed** to condemn several articles
A P : 0 4 :020(110) [0125] They never **suppose** that they have the merit of
A P : 0 4 :075(117) [0143] opponents will grant, we **suppose**, that the forgiveness of
A P : 0 4 :081(118) [0143] Our opponents **suppose** that Christ is the mediator and
A P : 0 4 :088(120) [0149] And lest we **suppose** that Paul made the statement "Faith
A P : 0 4 :108(122) [0153] Do they **suppose** that this is repeated so often for no
A P : 0 4 :108(122) [0153] Do they **suppose** that these words fell from the Holy
A P : 0 4 :135(125) [0159] providential care, but **supposes** that men are born and die
A P : 0 4 :162(129) [0169] It is an error to **suppose** that he merely merited "initial
A P : 0 4 :164(129) [0169] who are regenerated are **supposed** later to believe that
A P : 0 4 :203(135) [0177] works of the saints, he **supposes**, in human fashion, that
A P : 0 4 :231(139) [0183] We have no right to **suppose** that Paul would ascribe
A P : 0 4 :244(141) [0189] No other passage is **supposed** to contradict our position
A P : 0 4 :301(153) [0205] If they are **supposed** to believe that they have a gracious
A P : 0 4 :360(162) [0219] They even **suppose** that they have extra merits which they
A P : 0 7 :038(176) [0241] because they are **supposed** to have been handed down by
A P : 1 2 :007(183) [0255] are more careful and **suppose** that the power of the keys
A P : 1 2 :063(191) [0269] Second, we **suppose** our opponents will grant that the
A P : 1 2 :078(193) [0275] Even **supposing** that love and works are present, neither
A P : 1 2 :110(198) [0285] never be at rest if they **suppose** that they cannot obtain
A P : 1 2 :114(199) [0285] or sin by which they **supposed** they were reconciled to
A P : 1 2 :127(201) [0289] You are mistaken if you **suppose** that churches should be
A P : 1 2 :128(201) [0291] of religion if you **suppose** that the doctrinal doubts of
A P : 1 2 :129(202) [0291] members of the hierarchy **suppose** that they can take care
A P : 1 2 :133(202) [0293] They **suppose** that satisfactions are works that are not
A P : 1 2 :140(204) [0295] These are **supposed** to abolish death, even when they are
A P : 1 5 :022(218) [0321] of faith, it naturally **supposes** that such works justify men
A P : 2 1 :015(231) [0347] Men **suppose** that Christ is more severe and the saints
A P : 2 1 :033(233) [0351] Even **supposing** that the invocation of the saints could be
A P : 2 2 :001(236) [0357] human authority, as we **suppose** our opponents admit, all
A P : 2 2 :010(237) [0359] priesthood, they were **supposed** to ask for the one part
A P : 2 4 :026(254) [0391] any worship where men **suppose** they are offering God a
A P : 2 4 :068(261) [0407] First, it was **supposed** to be a mark and witness of
A P : 2 4 :068(262) [0407] place, Christ was **supposed** to be very pleased with a mark
A P : 2 4 :087(265) [0413] *opere operato* and its **supposed** applicability to merit the
A P : 2 4 :090(266) [0415] sort of penalties they **suppose** purgatory has, the reasons
A P : 2 7 :011(270) [0423] vow if the one making it **supposes** that by it he merits the
A P : 2 7 :065(280) [0441] First, even if we **suppose** that Paul is talking here about
S 1 : P R :005(289) [0457] I **suppose** I should reply to everything while I am still
S 2 : 0 2 :013(295) [0465] They **suppose** that we do not understand for what
S 2 : 0 4 :007(299) [0473] **Suppose** that the pope would renounce the claim that he
S 2 : 0 4 :007(299) [0473] or by God's command; **suppose** that it were necessary to
S 2 : 0 4 :007(299) [0473] sects and heresies; and **suppose** that such a head would
S 3 : 0 3 :031(308) [0487] there are others who **suppose**, "We need no repentance."
S C : P R :003(338) [0533] Although the people are **supposed** to be Christian, are
L C : 0 1 :225(395) [0643] **Suppose**, for example, that a man-servant or
L C : 0 1 :225(395) [0645] Or **suppose** that through laziness, carelessness, or malice
L C : 0 3 :014(422) [0701] attention to it, and men **supposed** it was enough if the act
L C : 0 3 :123(436) [0731] For that person must not **suppose** that he will receive
L C : 0 4 :043(442) [0743] **Suppose** there were a physician who had such skill that
L C : 0 5 :055(453) [0765] But **suppose** you say, "What if I feel that I am unfit?"
L C : 0 5 :075(455) [0771] **Suppose** you say, "What shall I do if I cannot feel this
L C : 0 6 :024(460) [0000] **Suppose**, now, that the invitation were changed into a
E P : 0 8 :036(491) [0825] as to how much he is **supposed** to know, and that he does
S D : 0 4 :037(557) [0949] that good works are **supposed** to be detrimental to

Suppress (9), Suppressed (6), Suppresses (1), Suppressing (2), Suppression (1)
A G : 2 8 :037(086) [0089] and righteousness of faith has almost been **suppressed**.
A L : 1 7 :005(039) [0051] of the world, the ungodly being **suppressed** everywhere.
A L : 2 8 :037(086) [0089] of faith has been **suppressed**, for from time to time more
A P : 0 4 :170(130) [0171] such feelings in order to **suppress** and destroy them and to
A P : 0 4 :189(133) [0175] these works he sanctifies hearts and **suppresses** the devil.
A P : 1 2 :141(204) [0295] in the church to **suppress** the knowledge of law and
A P : 1 8 :010(226) [0337] it has been criminally **suppressed** by those who dream
T R : 0 0 :032(325) [0513] after the Gospel was **suppressed**) when another worldly
L C : 0 1 :261(400) [0655] or concealing or **suppressing** anything on account of
L C : 0 3 :047(426) [0711] pure doctrine and try to **suppress** it, as the bishops,
L C : 0 3 :067(429) [0717] would persecute and **suppress** thy holy Word or prevent
L C : 0 3 :069(429) [0717] plot and plan how to **suppress** and exterminate us so that
L C : 0 4 :071(445) [0749] he is not restrained and **suppressed** by the power of
L C : 0 4 :076(446) [0751] Spirit, and power to **suppress** the old man so that the new
L C : 0 4 :084(446) [0753] every day he should be **suppressing** the old man and
S D : 1 0 :003(611) [1053] methods to **suppress** the pure doctrine and gradually to
S D : 1 0 :010(612) [1055] Word of God desire to **suppress** the pure doctrine of the
S D : 1 0 :014(613) [1057] and idolatry and to **suppress** the pure doctrine and
S D : 1 1 :095(632) [1095] to the truth and actually intended for its **suppression**.

Supreme (8), Supremely (1)
A G : 2 3 :006(052) [0061] the creation of God, the **supreme** Majesty, by means of
A P : 0 4 :075(117) [0143] forgiveness of sins is **supremely** necessary in justification.
A P : 0 7 :022(172) [0235] because princes and **supreme** pontiffs as well as those in
A P : 0 7 :023(172) [0235] It is the **supreme** outward monarchy of the whole world
S 2 : 0 2 :001(293) [0463] others, it has been the **supreme** and most precious of the
T R : 0 0 :038(326) [0515] high priest was the **supreme** pontifex by divine right;
T R : 0 0 :050(329) [0519] "No one shall judge the **supreme** see, for the judge is
S C : 0 9 :005(355) [0561] it be to the emperor as **supreme**, or to governors as sent
L C : 0 1 :018(367) [0585] and dominion exalted Jupiter as their **supreme** god.

Surer (2), Surest (2)
P R : P R :020(010) [0017] This is the **surest** and most edifying way as far as the
A P : 0 2 :017(102) [0109] but these gifts as well: a **surer** knowledge of God, fear of
A P : 2 4 :094(267) [0417] against the clearest and **surest** passages of Scripture.
A P : 2 7 :019(272) [0425] But what is **surer** than that men attain the forgiveness of

Surfeited (1)
L C : P R :020(361) [0573] bear to smell because they are so bloated and **surfeited**.

Surpasses (8), Surpassing (1), Surpassingly (2)
A P : 2 3 :038(244) [0373] One gift **surpasses** another.
A P : 2 3 :038(244) [0373] Thus prophecy **surpasses** eloquence, military science
A P : 2 3 :038(244) [0373] military science **surpasses** agriculture, and eloquence
A P : 2 3 :038(244) [0373] agriculture, and eloquence **surpasses** architecture.
A P : 2 3 :038(244) [0373] So also virginity is a gift that **surpasses** marriage.
A P : 2 3 :045(245) [0375] of all animals, thus **surpassing** the Dominican friars, who
A P : 2 3 :046(246) [0377] It **surpasses** the knowledge of Christ by making men
S 3 : 0 4 :000(310) [0491] one way, for God is **surpassingly** rich in his grace: First,
L C : 0 1 :209(393) [0639] others; it precedes and **surpasses** them all, whether those
L C : 0 2 :063(419) [0695] all our wisdom, which **surpasses** all the wisdom,
L C : 0 6 :015(459) [0000] This is the **surpassingly** grand and noble thing that makes

Surplices (1)
S 3 : 1 2 :003(315) [0499] does not consist of **surplices**, tonsures, albs, or other

Surprise (1)
L C : 0 1 :099(378) [0609] that he may take us by **surprise** and stealthily take the

Surrender (6), Surrendering (1), Surrenders (1)
A P : P R :002(098) [0099] many articles that we could not conscientiously **surrender**.
A P : P R :016(099) [0103] But we cannot **surrender** truth that is so clear and
A P : 1 2 :174(210) [0307] but to keep from **surrendering** to the devil or offending
A P : 2 3 :037(244) [0373] outcry will make us **surrender** the truth of the
A P : 2 7 :026(273) [0429] among clothes or foods, nor the **surrender** of property.
S 3 : 0 6 :005(311) [0493] that bread and wine **surrender** or lose their natural
E P : 0 6 :004(480) [0807] to follow the Spirit and **surrender** himself a captive.
S D : 0 8 :071(605) [1041] nature is weakened or **surrenders** to another something

Surreptitious (1), Surreptitiously (2)
E P : 0 7 :001(481) [0809] they endeavored **surreptitiously** to insinuate themselves
S D : P R :006(504) [0853] someone might **surreptitiously** undertake to insinuate into
S D : 1 0 :003(611) [1053] and coercion or by **surreptitious** methods to suppress the

Survive (1), Survived (1)
E P : 0 1 :008(467) [0781] or uncorrupted has **survived** in man's body or soul, in his
S D : 0 3 :041(546) [0929] faith could coexist and **survive** for a while side by side

Suspect (2)
A L : 2 6 :018(067) [0073] or out of hatred for the bishops, as some wrongly **suspect**.
S D : 0 7 :028(574) [0981] would try to make him **suspect** by giving the impression

Suspend (2), Suspended (2)
P R : P R :024(013) [0023] or a table, we ought not **suspend** or postpone its printing
A P : 2 3 :007(240) [0365] of God cannot be **suspended** without an extraordinary
A P : 2 3 :057(247) [0379] that priests be **suspended**; our canonists suspend them all
A P : 2 3 :057(247) [0379] our canonists **suspend** them all right — not from office

Suspicion (2), Suspicious (1)
S D : P R :019(507) [0857] incorrect, dubious, **suspicious**, and condemned doctrine
S D : 0 1 :056(518) [0877] and without incurring **suspicion**, and for that reason
S D : 0 8 :063(603) [1037] direction in order to cast **suspicion** on the pure doctrine.

Sustain (5), Sustained (6), Sustaining (2), Sustains (9)
P R : P R :009(006) [0011] In addition, we **sustained** the further disadvantage that,
A G : 2 1 :001(046) [0057] grace they received and how they were **sustained** by faith.
A P : 0 4 :058(115) [0137] the forgiveness of sins I am **sustained** by thy promise.
A P : 0 4 :119(124) [0155] hour of death, what will **sustain** those who have heard
A P : 0 4 :165(129) [0169] This must **sustain** us in our weakness, and we must firmly
A P : 0 4 :180(132) [0171] and justification, **sustaining** themselves with this promise
A P : 0 4 :320(156) [0209] life, if indeed hope ought to be **sustained** by merits?
A P : 1 2 :032(186) [0259] cannot bear it unless it is **sustained** by the Word of God.
A P : 1 2 :036(186) [0261] This faith strengthens, **sustains**, and quickens the contrite
A P : 1 2 :038(187) [0261] where faith consoles and **sustains** the anxious heart,
A P : 1 2 :038(187) [0261] in servile fear faith does not **sustain** the anxious heart.
A P : 1 2 :046(188) [0263] but as consolation truly **sustaining** a life that flees in
A P : 1 2 :049(189) [0265] This **sustains** and quickens the heart.
A P : 1 2 :056(189) [0267] David and by faith it **sustains**, justifies, and quickens
A P : 1 2 :072(192) [0271] Let them **sustain** themselves with this command of God
S C : 0 2 :002(345) [0543] he has given me and still **sustains** my body and soul, all

Continued ▶

L C : 0 1 :060(372) [0597] is a great mercy that the earth still bears and **sustains** us.
L C : 0 2 :013(412) [0681] has given and constantly **sustains** my body, soul, and life,
L C : 0 2 :019(412) [0681] is daily given and **sustained** by God, it inevitably follows
S D : 0 1 :038(515) [0871] he has given me and still **sustains** my body and soul, eyes,
S D : 0 1 :038(515) [0871] has given and constantly **sustains** my body, soul, and life,
S D : 0 4 :035(557) [0949] either entirely or in part **sustain** and preserve either the

Sustenance (4)
L C : 0 1 :145(385) [0623] for which she receives **sustenance** and wages, she would
L C : 0 1 :164(387) [0627] or two, but long life, **sustenance**, and peace, and
L C : 0 3 :072(430) [0719] provide for us our daily bread and all kinds of **sustenance**.
L C : 0 5 :024(449) [0759] as a daily food and **sustenance** so that our faith may

Swagger (1)
L C : 0 2 :021(413) [0683] act accordingly, and not **swagger** about and brag and

Swallow (1), Swallowed (2), Swallows (1)
S 1 : P R :013(291) [0459] But if we are willing to **swallow** camels and strain out
S 3 : 0 3 :025(307) [0485] The more money they **swallowed**, the wider became their
L C : 0 2 :031(414) [0687] again from the dead, **swallowed** up and devoured death,
L C : 0 4 :043(442) [0743] priceless medicine which **swallows** up death and saves the

Swamped (1)
A P : 2 4 :045(258) [0401] The people were **swamped** by the many different

Swarm (1)
L C : 0 1 :090(377) [0607] and so can the whole **swarm** of clerics in our day who

Swear (8), Swearing (6), Swears (6), Sworn (2)
A G : 2 8 :070(093) [0093] ministry unless he first **swears** an oath that he will not
A L : 1 6 :002(037) [0051] to hold property, to **swear** oaths when required by
A L : 2 8 :070(093) [0093] to the ministry unless he **swears** that he will not teach the
A P : 1 2 :094(196) [0281] By **swearing** that he has no pleasure in the death of the
A P : 1 2 :094(196) [0281] we believe him when he **swears** and are sure that he
A P : 1 2 :094(196) [0281] he denies that God has **sworn** to the truth; a more
A P : 1 2 :094(196) [0281] Oh, blessed are we for whose sake God **swears** an oath!
A P : 1 2 :094(196) [0281] we do not believe the Lord even when he **swears** an oath!"
S 3 : 0 1 :002(302) [0477] — and then also lying, **swearing** by God's name, failure to
S C : 0 1 :004(342) [0539] not use his name to curse, **swear**, practice magic, lie, or
S C : 0 5 :022(350) [0553] I have grumbled and **sworn** at my mistress, etc.
L C : 0 1 :053(372) [0595] person perjures himself, **swearing** by God's name or by
L C : 0 1 :062(373) [0597] that is not so, or to curse, **swear**, conjure, and, in short, to
L C : 0 1 :064(373) [0599] — for example, when we **swear** properly where it is
L C : 0 1 :065(373) [0599] so many teachers: why **swearing** is forbidden in the
L C : 0 1 :066(373) [0599] briefly this: We are not to **swear** in support of evil (that
L C : 0 1 :066(373) [0599] and for the advantage of our neighbor we are to **swear**.
L C : 0 1 :067(373) [0599] If one party in a dispute **swears** falsely, he will not escape
L C : 0 3 :042(425) [0709] for their shame, by **swearing**, cursing, conjuring, etc.
L C : 0 3 :045(426) [0709] not be taken in vain by **swearing**, cursing, deceiving, etc.,
E P : 1 2 :015(499) [0841] That a Christian cannot **swear** an oath with a good
S D : 1 2 :020(634) [1099] with a good conscience **swear** an oath before a court or

Sweat (1)
L C : 0 1 :163(387) [0627] to the devil — and wring **sweat** and blood out of us

Sweeps (1)
S D : 0 2 :034(528) [0895] gift purifies us and daily **sweeps** out the remaining sin and

Swiftly (1)
A G : 2 3 :018(054) [0063] has in many places been **swiftly** punished, as if it were a

Swim (1)
L C : 0 4 :081(446) [0751] plank on which we must **swim** ashore after the ship

Swindlers (1), Swindles (1)
L C : 0 1 :227(396) [0645] Or again, one **swindles** another in a trade and deliberately
L C : 0 1 :229(396) [0645] men are called gentlemen **swindlers** or big operators.

Swine (1), Swineherds (1)
L C : P R :002(358) [0567] would make better **swineherds** or dogkeepers than
L C : 0 1 :096(378) [0607] taverns dead drunk like **swine**, but also by that multitude

Sword (16), Swords (2)
A G : 1 6 :002(037) [0051] punish evildoers with the **sword**, engage in just wars,
A G : 2 8 :001(081) [0083] confused the power of bishops with the temporal **sword**.
A G : 2 8 :004(081) [0085] and temporal power, **sword**, and authority, and they have
A G : 2 8 :011(082) [0085] the soul, but with the **sword** and physical penalties it
A G : 2 8 :019(083) [0087] authority and the **sword**, they possess it not as bishops by
A L : 2 8 :001(081) [0083] the power of the church with the power of the **sword**.
A L : 2 8 :004(081) [0085] and the power of the **sword**, and they have taught that on
A L : 2 8 :011(082) [0085] constrains men with the **sword** and physical penalties,
A L : 2 8 :019(083) [0087] have any power of the **sword**, they have this not as
A P : 0 4 :245(142) [0189] but they also try to wipe it out with **sword** and torture.
A P : 0 7 :023(172) [0235] the spiritual realm, both **swords**, the temporal and the
A P : 1 2 :067(191) [0271] out by force and the **sword**, and that good men who hold
A P : 1 5 :034(220) [0325] knot, he solved it for good by cutting it with his **sword**.
T R : 0 0 :002(320) [0503] right he possesses both **swords**, that is, the authority to
T R : 0 0 :031(325) [0513] them the power of the **sword** or the right to establish,
T R : 0 0 :031(325) [0513] was not sent to wield a **sword** or possess a worldly
S C : 0 9 :004(355) [0561] does not bear the **sword** in vain; he is the servant of God
L C : 0 1 :268(401) [0657] you do not wield the **sword**, you use your venomous

Sybaris (1)
A P : 2 3 :054(246) [0379] the fall of many other cities, like **Sybaris** and Rome.

Syllable (8), Syllables (1)
A P : 0 4 :047(113) [0133] this faith there is not a **syllable** in the teaching of our
A P : 0 4 :379(165) [0223] for Christ's sake, there is not a **syllable** in the scholastics.
A P : 1 1 :009(182) [0251] of sins there is not a **syllable** in this heap of constitutions,
A P : 1 5 :027(219) [0323] do not contain a single **syllable** about Christ or faith in
A P : 2 1 :002(229) [0343] Vigilantius there is not a **syllable** about invoking, but only
A P : 2 4 :065(261) [0407] cannot produce a **syllable** from the Scriptures in support
S C : P R :008(339) [0535] we do not alter a single **syllable** or recite the catechism
S C : P R :015(340) [0535] without changing a single **syllable**, as stated above with
S D : 0 7 :052(578) [0991] with the same words and **syllables** repeat these simple,

Symbol (9), Symbols (13)
P R : P R :003(003) [0007] as the contemporary **symbol** of their faith in the chief
P R : P R :003(003) [0007] in the approved ancient **symbols**, recognizing the doctrine
A P : 2 4 :024(253) [0391] were so called only as **symbols** of a future offering.
A P : 2 4 :037(257) [0397] and not for another **symbol** that seems to be a sacrifice.
A P : 2 4 :068(262) [0407] because banquets are **symbols** of agreement and
L C : 0 4 :073(445) [0751] Baptism is no empty **symbol**, but the effect accompanies
E P : R N :003(465) [0777] church formulated **symbols** (that is, brief and explicit
E P : R N :004(465) [0777] other sects, and as the **symbol** of our time, the first and
E P : R N :008(465) [0779] Other **symbols** and other writings are not judges like Holy
S D : P R :004(502) [0847] a genuinely Christian **symbol** which all true Christians
S D : P R :004(502) [0847] ancient times Christian **symbols** and confessions were
S D : P R :004(502) [0847] themselves to these **symbols** with heart and mouth.
S D : P R :001(503) [0851] the ancient church always had its dependable **symbols**.
S D : P R :002(503) [0851] public and well-known **symbols** or common confessions
S D : P R :005(504) [0851] churches) as our **symbol** in this epoch, not because this
S D : P R :005(504) [0851] This **symbol** distinguishes our reformed churches from
S D : 0 7 :007(570) [0975] "body" is the same as a "**symbol**" (that is, a sign or figure
S D : 0 7 :007(570) [0975] reality is joined to the **symbols** in such a way that Christ's
S D : 0 7 :049(578) [0989] He was nct speaking of a **symbol** of his body, or of a
S D : 0 7 :060(580) [0993] only against signs and **symbols** and figures of the body
S D : 0 7 :116(589) [1011] are nothing more than **symbols** and reminders of the
S D : 1 2 :037(636) [1101] the old, approved **symbols**, the Nicene and Athanasian

Symbolically (1), Symbolize (2), Symbolized (3), Symbolizes (6), Symbolizing (1)
A P : 2 1 :035(234) [0353] in such a way as to **symbolize** that those who would carry
A P : 2 4 :034(256) [0397] in the Old Testament **symbolized** both the death of Christ
A P : 2 4 :036(256) [0397] This analogy **symbolizes** not only the ceremony but the
A P : 2 4 :036(257) [0397] The burning of the lamb **symbolizes** the death of Christ.
A P : 2 4 :036(257) [0397] The drink offering **symbolizes** the sprinkling, that is, the
A P : 2 4 :036(257) [0397] The offering of flour **symbolizes** faith, prayer, and
A P : 2 4 :040(257) [0399] because we require all the actions that it **symbolizes**.
A P : 2 4 :040(257) [0399] imagine that it **symbolizes** the ceremony alone and not
A P : 2 4 :054(259) [0403] before God, but only to **symbolize** the future death of
A P : 2 4 :056(259) [0403] reconciliation — but only **symbolized** the coming sacrifice
A P : 2 4 :068(262) [0407] the form of a meal **symbolizing** the mutual union and
E P : 0 7 :007(482) [0811] as though the bread **symbolized** the absent body and the
S D : 0 7 :008(570) [0975] is sacramentally or **symbolically** united with the bread in

Sympathize (1), Sympathy (1)
P R : P R :022(012) [0021] us to have special **sympathy** with them, so we entertain a
S D : 0 8 :087(608) [1047] and who can therefore **sympathize** with us as with men

Synecdoche (1)
A P : 0 4 :152(127) [0163] figure of speech, called **synecdoche**, by which we

Synergists (1)
S D : 0 2 :077(536) [0911] 4. The teaching of the **synergists**, who maintain that in

Synods (7)
A P : 2 3 :023(242) [0369] the decision of the **synods** but the private judgment of the
A P : 2 3 :024(243) [0371] set up since the ancient **synods** and contrary to their
A P : 2 3 :024(243) [0371] for the authority of the **synods** while they want others to
T R : 0 0 :017(323) [0507] 8. Many ancient **synods** were called and held in which the
T R : 0 0 :055(329) [0521] if the pope should hold **synods**, how can the church be
T R : 0 0 :056(329) [0521] Since decisions of **synods** are decisions of the church and
S D : P R :005(504) [0853] and customary for later **synods** and Christian bishops and

Synonymous (1)
S D : 0 3 :012(541) [0919] and taken as **synonymous**: "We are justified by faith"

Syria (1)
S D : 0 8 :016(594) [1021] a bishop in Antioch in **Syria**, taught godlessly that the

System (2), Systematic (1), Systematically (1), Systems (1)
A P : 0 4 :221(137) [0181] texts in which he **systematically** discusses the mode of
A P : 0 4 :287(150) [0203] The opponents' whole **system** is derived either from
A P : 2 7 :044(277) [0435] as the whole monastic **system** is full of counterfeits, so
L C : 0 4 :002(436) [0733] we shall treat it in a **systematic** way and confine ourselves
L C : 0 5 :070(454) [0769] as a precious antidote against the poison in their **systems**.

Tabernacle (3)
S D : 0 7 :015(572) [0977] aside or reserved in the **tabernacle** or carried about and
S D : 0 7 :108(588) [1009] is locked up in the **tabernacle** or is carried about as a
S D : 1 1 :042(623) [1077] their hearts as a **tabernacle** for the devil so that their last

Table (24)
P R : P R :024(013) [0023] truth under a basket or a **table**, we ought not suspend or
A P : 0 2 :014(102) [0109] transgressing as they do the first **table** of the Decalogue.
A P : 0 2 :016(102) [0109] not merely the second **table** of the Decalogue, but also
A P : 0 4 :034(111) [0129] of the second **table**, which contain the civil righteousness
A P : 0 4 :034(112) [0129] they do not see the first **table**, which commands us to love
A P : 0 4 :035(112) [0129] So it does not obey the first **table**.
A P : 0 4 :131(125) [0157] They look at the second **table** and political works; about
A P : 0 4 :131(125) [0157] works; about the first **table** they care nothing, as though
A P : 0 4 :224(138) [0181] the works of the Second **Table**, through which we deal
A P : 0 4 :224(138) [0181] of this happens through the works of the Second **Table**.
A P : 0 4 :231(139) [0183] to the works of the Second **Table** rather than the First.
A P : 1 8 :007(226) [0337] the real works of the first **table**, which the human heart
S C : 0 8 :006(353) [0559] [Grace at **Table**]
S C : 0 8 :006(353) [0559] *his household to offer blessing and thanksgiving at* ***table***
S C : 0 8 :007(353) [0559] household gather at the **table**, they should reverently fold
S C : 0 9 :001(354) [0561] [IX] **Table** of Duties
L C : 0 3 :072(430) [0719] take a loaf of bread from the oven to set on the **table**.
L C : 0 5 :009(447) [0755] but not mere bread or wine such as is served at the **table**.
L C : 0 5 :035(450) [0761] door, yes, upon everyone's **table**, but it is also your
S D : 0 7 :048(578) [0989] gave this command at **table** and during supper, there can
S D : 0 7 :057(579) [0993] likewise were going to the **table** of the Lord and partaking
S D : 0 7 :060(580) [0993] who come to the Lord's **table** without true repentance and
S D : 0 7 :064(581) [0995] of institution say, when at **table** and during supper he
S D : 0 7 :076(583) [0999] *Passion*: "Christ himself prepares this **table** and blesses it.

Tail (2)
SP : 0 2 :011(294) [0465] Besides, this dragon's **tail** . that is, the Mass . has
SD : 0 7 :067(582) [0997] "two hairs of a horse's **tail** and an invention of which even

Taint (1), Tainted (1)
AL : 2 0 :040(046) [0057] good in deed or thought, Nothing free from **taint** of ill."
SD : 0 1 :012(510) [0863] has so poisoned and **tainted** them that they amount to

Take (180), Taken (63), Takes (76), Taking (7), Took (36)
PR : PR :004(003) [0007] troublesome disturbances **took** place in our beloved
PR : PR :004(004) [0007] adversaries of divine truth **took** occasion to discredit us
PR : PR :008(005) [0009] We **took** up the repeatedly mentioned Augsburg
PR : PR :009(006) [0011] that little account was **taken** by our adversaries of this
PR : PR :010(006) [0011] know what attitude to **take** toward these differences and
PR : PR :011(006) [0011] were looking for could be abolished and **taken** away.
PR : PR :011(006) [0011] Finally they **took** to hand the controverted articles,
PR : PR :021(011) [0019] ancient church put it, it **takes** place on account of the
PR : PR :022(011) [0019] understand the issues, and **take** no pleasure in
PR : PR :024(013) [0023] will, together with us, **take** Christian pleasure in this
AG : PR :012(026) [0041] charitable negotiations **take** place between us, and if no
AG : 1 6 :002(037) [0051] as soldiers, buy and sell, **take** required oaths, possess
AG : 1 8 :005(040) [0051] whether to build a house, **take** a wife, engage in a trade,
AG : 2 3 :003(051) [0061] impelled and moved to **take** this step by the great distress
AG : 2 3 :009(052) [0061] and other clergy have **taken** wives to themselves for these
AG : 2 3 :012(052) [0063] were compelled by force to **take** the vows of celibacy.
AG : 2 3 :014(053) [0063] Majesty will graciously **take** into account that fact that, in
AG : 2 4 :022(058) [0067] means of which sin was **taken** away and God was
AG : 2 4 :030(059) [0067] the sacrifice has already **taken** place — but to awaken our
AG : 2 6 :035(069) [0075] of this in Luke 21:34, "**Take** heed to yourselves lest your
AG : 2 7 :015(073) [0077] so that pastors and bishops were **taken** from monasteries.
AG : 2 7 :029(075) [0079] men or women, who have **taken** monastic vows of
AG : 2 7 :029(075) [0079] they were persuaded to **take** monastic vows, and
AG : 2 7 :032(076) [0079] for it prohibits the **taking** of monastic vows before the
AG : 2 7 :054(079) [0083] it is only a counsel not to **take** revenge, it is natural that
AG : 2 7 :054(079) [0083] that it is not sinful to **take** revenge outside of the exercise
AG : 2 7 :056(080) [0083] and also their civil office, to **take** shelter in a monastery.
AL : 0 3 :001(029) [0045] that is, the Son of God — **took** on man's nature in the
AL : 1 7 :005(039) [0051] of the dead the godly will **take** possession of the kingdom
AL : 2 3 :003(051) [0061] such open scandals, they **took** wives and taught that it
AL : 2 3 :014(053) [0063] weaker, it is also well to **take** precautions against the
AL : 2 4 :019(058) [0067] will not hold him guiltless who **takes** his name in vain."
AL : 2 4 :022(058) [0067] by which its performance **takes** away the sins of the living
AL : 2 4 :029(059) [0067] Now, if the Mass **takes** away the sins of the living and the
AL : 2 4 :033(060) [0067] "Because I always sin, I ought always **take** the medicine."
AL : 2 6 :013(066) [0073] despair, and some even **took** their own lives, because they
AL : 2 6 :018(067) [0073] be looked upon as having **taken** up this matter rashly or
AL : 2 6 :035(069) [0075] So Christ commands, "**Take** heed to yourselves lest your
AL : 2 7 :015(073) [0077] church, and pastors and bishops were **taken** from them.
AL : 2 7 :029(075) [0079] few there are who have **taken** the vow spontaneously and
AL : 2 7 :029(075) [0079] and sometimes even compelled, to **take** the vow.
AL : 2 7 :033(076) [0079] a majority of them **took** vows before they reached such an
AL : 2 7 :039(077) [0081] vows thus customarily **taken** were wicked services and on
AL : 2 7 :040(077) [0081] void, for a wicked vow, **taken** contrary to the commands
AL : 2 7 :054(079) [0083] evangelical counsel not to **take** revenge, and therefore
AL : 2 7 :054(079) [0083] some are not afraid to **take** vengeance in their private life
AL : 2 8 :002(081) [0085] of this world and **take** away the imperial power.
AP : PR :006(098) [0101] reading some of us had **taken** notes on the main points of
AP : PR :015(099) [0101] I have not **taken** up all their sophistries, for this would be
AP : PR :016(099) [0101] We **take** no pleasure in discord, nor are we indifferent to
AP : 0 2 :043(106) [0117] Here the scholastics have **taken** over from philosophy the
AP : 0 4 :012(108) [0123] vicious errors that would **take** a long time to enumerate.
AP : 0 4 :020(110) [0125] the forgiveness of sins **takes** place, or how the judgment
AP : 0 4 :060(115) [0137] and our opponents **take** it away when they despise and
AP : 0 4 :065(116) [0139] on the *Sentences* that tells how regeneration **takes** place.
AP : 0 4 :067(116) [0139] Therefore justification **takes** place through the Word, as
AP : 0 4 :067(116) [0139] For if justification **takes** place only through the Word,
AP : 0 4 :079(117) [0143] if we know how the forgiveness of sins **takes** place.
AP : 0 4 :083(119) [0145] We cannot **take** hold of the name of Christ except by
AP : 0 4 :098(121) [0149] But only faith **takes** hold of the name of Christ.
AP : 0 4 :103(122) [0151] world was subjected, he **took** away the sin of the whole
AP : 0 4 :103(122) [0151] the Lamb of God, who **takes** away the sin of the world!'
AP : 0 4 :135(125) [0159] from us, and this error **taken** away, when God shows us
AP : 0 4 :143(126) [0161] to the flesh, who **take** pleasure in their lusts and obey
AP : 0 4 :154(128) [0163] way, and in this way to worship and **take** hold of him.
AP : 0 4 :155(128) [0165] Later we shall **take** up similar passages, like Luke 11:41,
AP : 0 4 :175(131) [0171] this should not be **taken** to mean only that those
AP : 0 4 :179(131) [0171] for us, the sinless Christ **took** away the right of the law to
AP : 0 4 :185(132) [0173] one or two explanations, **taken** from the sources, will
AP : 0 4 :189(133) [0175] They **take** place in a flesh that is partly unregenerate and
AP : 0 4 :197(134) [0175] but rather that when it **takes** place in the justified it
AP : 0 4 :206(135) [0177] had sacrifices which they **took** over from the patriarchs.
AP : 0 4 :216(137) [0179] with men, and by which we **take** hold of grace and peace
AP : 0 4 :222(138) [0181] are justified only when we **take** hold of Christ, the
AP : 0 4 :227(138) [0183] that virtue justifies which **takes** hold of Christ,
AP : 0 4 :231(139) [0183] Only faith **takes** hold of Christ, the propitiator.
AP : 0 4 :234(140) [0185] clergy, when the bishops **take** into account the weakness
AP : 0 4 :240(141) [0187] statement about love is **taken** from Proverbs (10:12),
AP : 0 4 :245(142) [0189] the faith by which we **take** hold of Christ, the propitiator.
AP : 0 4 :247(142) [0191] said that regeneration **takes** place through the Gospel.
AP : 0 4 :247(142) [0191] For it is only faith that **takes** hold of the promise of
AP : 0 4 :263(145) [0195] promise he forgives those who **take** hold of that promise.
AP : 0 4 :263(145) [0195] They do not **take** hold of it unless they truly believe and
AP : 0 4 :266(146) [0197] We must first **take** hold of the promise so that we may be
AP : 0 4 :270(147) [0197] When faith **takes** hold of Christ, the mediator, the heart
AP : 0 4 :277(148) [0199] in Tob. 4:11 ought to be **taken** the same way, "Alms free
AP : 0 4 :277(148) [0199] be understood so as not to **take** away from the glory of
AP : 0 4 :279(149) [0199] **Taken** in its entirety, Tobit's statement shows that faith is
AP : 0 4 :280(149) [0201] a single passage without **taking** the whole law into
AP : 0 4 :292(152) [0203] preaching of penitence, he **takes** heart and believes that
AP : 0 4 :295(152) [0203] Therefore we must first **take** hold of the promise by faith,
AP : 0 4 :300(153) [0205] blessings our opponents **take** from the church in
AP : 0 4 :308(155) [0207] obedience to the Gospel **takes** hold of Christ, the
AP : 0 4 :324(157) [0209] to add nothing about this faith that **takes** hold of mercy.
AP : 0 4 :324(157) [0211] and that only faith can **take** hold of the promise, so we
AP : 0 4 :324(157) [0211] faith and that only faith can **take** hold of this mercy.
AP : 0 4 :331(158) [0211] So Daniel teaches us to **take** hold of mercy when we
AP : 0 4 :338(159) [0215] Faith saves because it **takes** hold of mercy and the
AP : 0 4 :359(162) [0219] because of the faith that **takes** hold of Christ, the
AP : 0 4 :369(163) [0221] the law, but since it would **take** too long we shall expound
AP : 0 4 :371(164) [0221] in the Scriptures must be **taken** to mean not only outward
AP : 0 4 :378(165) [0223] omitting the faith that **takes** hold of the mediator Christ.
AP : 0 4 :380(165) [0223] ancient writers they have **taken** certain sayings, decrees as
AP : 0 4 :381(165) [0223] should be added, since we **take** hold of God's mercy,
AP : 0 4 :381(165) [0225] please God because of grace; for faith **takes** hold of grace.
AP : 0 7 :004(169) [0227] that Antichrist will "**take** his seat in the temple of God"
AP : 0 7 :010(170) [0229] church catholic" lest we **take** it to mean an outward
AP : 1 0 :002(179) [0247] the Greek Church has **taken** and still takes this position.
AP : 1 0 :002(179) [0247] The Greek Church has taken and still **takes** this position.
AP : 1 2 :006(183) [0255] and tell us when the forgiveness of sins **takes** place.
AP : 1 2 :006(183) [0255] the forgiveness of sins **takes** place in attrition or in
AP : 1 2 :006(183) [0255] If it **takes** place because of contrition, what is the need of
AP : 1 2 :029(185) [0259] This contrition **takes** place when the Word of God
AP : 1 2 :034(186) [0261] **Taken** alone, this is the teaching of the law, not of the
AP : 1 2 :064(191) [0269] finds peace only when it **takes** hold of Christ, the
AP : 1 2 :080(194) [0275] for the contrite by faith to **take** hold of the promise of the
AP : 1 2 :081(194) [0275] in any other way than by **taking** hold through faith of the
AP : 1 2 :087(195) [0277] We must **take** hold of the promise of the forgiveness of
AP : 1 2 :125(201) [0289] of the faith, she should **take** care that men of learning and
AP : 1 2 :126(201) [0289] threats which, unless you **take** care, indicate a change in
AP : 1 2 :129(202) [0291] suppose that they can **take** care of this easily since they
AP : 1 2 :140(204) [0295] be your death," should be **taken** to mean not Christ but
AP : 1 2 :148(205) [0299] because regeneration itself **takes** place by constantly
AP : 1 2 :168(209) [0305] Occasionally the Fathers **take** the word "satisfaction"
AP : 1 2 :169(209) [0305] if it does not satisfy those whose property we have **taken**.
AP : 1 3 :005(211) [0309] the heart to believe and **take** hold of faith, as Paul says
AP : 1 5 :018(217) [0319] They **take** honor away from Christ when they teach that
AP : 1 5 :046(221) [0327] Christ says (Luke 21:34), "**Take** heed to yourselves lest
AP : 1 6 :001(222) [0329] contracts, own property, **take** an oath when the
AP : 1 6 :001(222) [0329] ordinances in which a Christian may safely **take** part.
AP : 2 1 :023(232) [0349] order that we should **take** refuge in the help of the saints,
AP : 2 1 :024(232) [0349] order that we should **take** refuge in the help of the
AP : 2 1 :042(235) [0355] most gracious emperor **take** steps to correct the abuses,
AP : 2 1 :044(236) [0357] They should **take** care to maintain and propagate divine
AP : 2 2 :002(236) [0357] church, why is one kind **taken** away from part of the
AP : 2 2 :007(237) [0359] object if someone **takes** these passages as referring to the
AP : 2 3 :004(239) [0365] most serious of reasons, **taken** from the Word of God,
AP : 2 3 :053(246) [0377] So God **takes** revenge against those who despise his gift
AP : 2 3 :064(248) [0381] of the Lord," must be **taken** to mean purity of the heart
AP : 2 3 :070(249) [0383] persuade the princes to **take** a position contrary to the
AP : 2 4 :013(251) [0387] Yet this notion has **taken** hold among the people and has
AP : 2 4 :022(253) [0391] that the blood of bulls and goats should **take** away sins."
AP : 2 4 :026(254) [0391] the spirit knows and **takes** hold of God, as it does when it
AP : 2 4 :032(255) [0395] This **takes** place through the proclamation of the Gospel,
AP : 2 4 :035(256) [0397] **Taken** together, these are the daily sacrifice of the New
AP : 2 4 :043(258) [0399] want to look more learned **take** up philosophical
AP : 2 4 :068(262) [0407] pleased with a mark that **took** the form of a meal
AP : 2 4 :078(263) [0411] names for the Mass they **take** arguments which do not
AP : 2 4 :081(264) [0411] shows, it is completely **taken** up with public duties and
AP : 2 4 :082(264) [0411] **Taking** this collection not only supplies what the saints
AP : 2 4 :086(265) [0413] Part of this was **taken** to be consecrated, the rest was
AP : 2 7 :009(270) [0421] legitimate that have been **taken** with the pretext of
AP : 2 7 :011(270) [0423] but by monastic works, **take** away from Christ's honor
AP : 2 7 :015(271) [0425] of Moses and that Christ **took** its place, so that he does
AP : 2 7 :017(271) [0425] Christ **takes** Moses' place, not by forgiving sins on
AP : 2 7 :041(276) [0435] wife, and children, even life itself, be **taken** from us.
AP : 2 7 :057(279) [0439] release many who **took** their vows without proper
AP : 2 7 :065(280) [0441] support monastic vows, **taken** for wicked acts of worship
AP : 2 8 :003(281) [0445] on them, as though they **took** pleasure in the destruction
AP : 2 8 :019(284) [0449] Thus these asses **take** a statement that supports our
S 1 : PR :003(289) [0455] and flee from the day **take** such wretched pains to
S 1 : PR :012(290) [0459] in like a deluge and have **taken** on the color of legality.
S 2 : 0 1 :002(292) [0461] "the Lamb of God, who **takes** away the sin of the world"
S 2 : 0 2 :007(294) [0465] of God and the Son of God who **takes** away our sin."
S 2 : 0 4 :002(298) [0471] will nor should nor can **take** upon our consciences.
S 2 : 0 4 :014(301) [0475] of the pope has been **taken** from the imperial, pagan law
S 3 : 0 3 :027(307) [0487] So the pope **took** the money, consoled the people with his
S 3 : 0 3 :038(309) [0489] Lamb of God who **takes** away the sin of the world.
S 3 : 0 5 :003(311) [0493] will, as if the washing **takes** place only through God's will
S 3 : 1 4 :001(315) [0501] Whoever **takes** the vows of monastic life believes that he
TR : 0 0 :008(321) [0505] a child neither seeks nor **takes** pre-eminence for himself.
TR : 0 0 :031(325) [0513] or the right to establish, **take** possession of, or transfer
TR : 0 0 :039(327) [0515] of worship, so that he **takes** his seat in the temple of God,
TR : 0 0 :048(328) [0519] Such errors are not to be **taken** lightly, for they detract
TR : 0 0 :051(329) [0519] judicial process has been **taken** away, the churches are
TR : 0 0 :067(331) [0523] no human authority can **take** it away from the church.
SC : PR :005(338) [0533] laws, yet you do not **take** the slightest interest in teaching
SC : PR :006(338) [0533] and preachers, that you **take** the duties of your office
SC : PR :006(338) [0533] to do better at least **take** this booklet and these forms and
SC : PR :007(338) [0533] place, the preacher should **take** the utmost care to avoid
SC : PR :014(339) [0535] For this purpose, **take** the explanations in this booklet, or
SC : PR :016(340) [0535] for it is not necessary to **take** up all the parts at once.
SC : PR :017(340) [0535] this brief catechism, **take** up a large catechism so that the
SC : PR :019(340) [0537] You should also **take** pains to urge governing authorities
SC : 0 1 :003(342) [0539] *"You shall not **take** the name of the Lord your God in*
SC : 0 3 :020(348) [0549] blessed end and graciously **take** us from this world of
SC : 0 6 :004(351) [0555] when he was betrayed, **took** bread, and when he had
SC : 0 6 :004(351) [0555] to the disciples and said, '**Take**, eat; this is my body which
SC : 0 6 :004(351) [0555] In the same way also he **took** the cup, after supper, and
SC : 0 8 :010(354) [0559] of a man; but the Lord **takes** pleasure in those who fear
LC : PR :004(359) [0567] it is, the common people **take** the Gospel altogether too
LC : PR :002(362) [0575] 2. You shall not **take** the name of God in vain.
LC : SP :023(364) [0579] when he was betrayed **took** bread, gave thanks, and
LC : SP :023(364) [0579] it to his disciples, saying, '**Take** and eat, this is my body,
LC : SP :027(364) [0581] The reason we **take** such care to preach on the Catechism
LC : SP :028(365) [0581] Now we shall **take** up the above-mentioned parts one by
LC : 0 1 :027(368) [0587] should presume to **take** or give anything except as God

Continued ▶

L C : 0 1 :028(368) [0587] Let everyone, then, **take** care to magnify and exalt this
L C : 0 1 :029(368) [0589] have this commandment **taken** lightly but will strictly
L C : 0 1 :029(368) [0589] people so that they may **take** them to heart and
L C : 0 1 :034(369) [0589] He is a God who **takes** vengeance upon men who turn
L C : 0 1 :049(371) [0593] *"You shall not **take** the name of God in vain."*
L C : 0 1 :051(371) [0595] does it mean to misuse or **take** the name of God in vain?"
L C : 0 1 :051(371) [0595] to God's name falsely or **taking** his name upon our lips
L C : 0 1 :051(371) [0595] — for example, where men **take** oaths in court and one
L C : 0 1 :056(372) [0595] Let us **take** to heart how important this commandment is
L C : 0 1 :057(372) [0597] will not hold him guiltless who **takes** his name in vain."
L C : 0 1 :062(373) [0597] understand what it means to **take** God's name in vain.
L C : 0 1 :063(373) [0599] the words, "You shall not **take** the name of God in vain,"
L C : 0 1 :065(373) [0599] and yet Christ, St. Paul, and other saints **took** oaths.
L C : 0 1 :067(373) [0599] Though it may **take** a long time, nothing he does will in
L C : 0 1 :075(375) [0601] Then some good may **take** root, spring up, and bear
L C : 0 1 :077(375) [0603] This kind of training **takes** such root in their hearts that
L C : 0 1 :088(377) [0605] How does this sanctifying **take** place?
L C : 0 1 :094(378) [0607] this, as we have heard, **takes** place only through God's
L C : 0 1 :099(378) [0609] of many so that he may **take** us by surprise and stealthily
L C : 0 1 :099(378) [0609] by surprise and stealthily **take** the Word of God away
L C : 0 1 :121(382) [0615] our eyes and ears and **take** this to heart so that we may
L C : 0 1 :128(382) [0617] forget God, and no one **takes** thought how God feeds,
L C : 0 1 :143(385) [0623] and maid-servants should **take** care not only to obey their
L C : 0 1 :149(385) [0623] let everyone who can **take** advice remember that God is
L C : 0 1 :149(385) [0623] take advice remember that God is not to be **taken** lightly.
L C : 0 1 :149(385) [0623] this commandment, then **take** shame, misery, and grief
L C : 0 1 :157(386) [0627] hope that someone may **take** it to heart, so that we may
L C : 0 1 :180(389) [0631] yet their right to **take** human life is not abrogated.
L C : 0 1 :184(390) [0633] rage and we are ready to shed blood and **take** revenge.
L C : 0 1 :224(395) [0643] a few words, this includes **taking** advantage of our
L C : 0 1 :224(395) [0643] pocket, but also when he **takes** advantage of his neighbor
L C : 0 1 :225(395) [0645] If a thief had **taken** such sums he would be strangled with
L C : 0 1 :227(396) [0645] and bad coins, and **takes** advantage of him by
L C : 0 1 :233(396) [0647] not to harm his neighbor, **take** advantage of him, or
L C : 0 1 :233(396) [0647] especially when he **takes** remuneration for such services.
L C : 0 1 :235(397) [0647] you servants ought to **take** care of your master's or
L C : 0 1 :235(397) [0647] But you go your own way, **take** your wages like a thief,
L C : 0 1 :236(397) [0647] for every penny you have **taken** and for every penny's
L C : 0 1 :239(397) [0649] for example, promptly **took** such offenders by the scruff
L C : 0 1 :239(397) [0649] by the scruff of the neck so that others **took** warning.
L C : 0 1 :242(397) [0649] we shall trust God, who **takes** matters into his own
L C : 0 1 :245(398) [0649] Anyone who robs and **takes** things by violence and
L C : 0 1 :261(400) [0655] plainest meaning, applying to all that **takes** place in court.
L C : 0 1 :270(401) [0657] unless these have first been **take** away from him publicly.
L C : 0 1 :273(401) [0659] and good name are easily **taken** away, but not easily
L C : 0 1 :274(402) [0659] sin as much as those who **take** the law into their own
L C : 0 1 :277(402) [0659] failing to do his duty, he **takes** him to task personally.
L C : 0 1 :279(402) [0661] "If he does not listen, **take** one or two others along with
L C : 0 1 :293(404) [0663] two commandments, **taken** literally, were given
L C : 0 1 :295(404) [0665] by giving her a bill of divorce and to **take** another wife.
L C : 0 1 :295(404) [0665] them that if anyone **took** a fancy to another's wife, he
L C : 0 1 :295(404) [0665] the other's from him so that he might legally **take** her.
L C : 0 1 :302(405) [0667] until the property is **taken** away from the owner and
L C : 0 1 :304(406) [0667] that the neighbor is being **taken** advantage of and forced
L C : 0 1 :305(406) [0667] tricks like this: If a man **took** a fancy to another woman,
L C : 0 1 :305(406) [0669] Gospel that King Herod **took** his brother's wife while the
L C : 0 1 :308(406) [0669] the world an inch, it will **take** a yard, and at length open
L C : 0 1 :325(409) [0675] when he says, "The Lord **takes** pleasure in those who fear
L C : 0 1 :325(409) [0675] as if to say, "The Lord **takes** pleasure in those who have
L C : 0 1 :326(409) [0675] told to fear God and not **take** his name in vain by
L C : 0 1 :330(410) [0677] men consider this and **take** it to heart, there will arise a
L C : 0 2 :026(413) [0685] and simply, we shall **take** up one phrase which contains
L C : 0 2 :030(414) [0685] and their place has been **taken** by Jesus Christ, the Lord
L C : 0 2 :030(414) [0685] He has **taken** us as his own, under his protection, in order
L C : 0 2 :037(415) [0687] How does this sanctifying **take** place?
L C : 0 2 :038(415) [0689] or believe in him and **take** him as our Lord, unless these
L C : 0 3 :005(420) [0699] Commandment, "You shall not **take** God's name in vain."
L C : 0 3 :012(422) [0701] **Take** an illustration from the other commandments.
L C : 0 3 :014(422) [0701] and exhort everyone to **take** these words to heart and in
L C : 0 3 :022(423) [0703] and promise, God **takes** the initiative and puts into our
L C : 0 3 :045(426) [0709] his name should not be **taken** in vain by swearing,
L C : 0 3 :066(429) [0717] whatever befalls us, and let go whatever is **taken** from us.
L C : 0 3 :072(430) [0719] the field, we could never **take** a loaf of bread from the
L C : 0 3 :074(430) [0719] there our daily bread is **taken** away, or at least reduced.
L C : 0 3 :080(431) [0721] purpose and desire it is to **take** away or interfere with all
L C : 0 3 :084(432) [0723] the church, and let them **take** care lest this petition of the
L C : 0 3 :110(435) [0729] only help or comfort is to **take** refuge in the Lord's
L C : 0 4 :002(436) [0733] First we shall **take** up Baptism, through which we are
L C : 0 4 :040(441) [0743] It **takes** special understanding to believe this, for it is not
L C : 0 4 :051(443) [0745] For no one can **take** from us or overthrow this article, "I
L C : 0 4 :055(443) [0745] account of that abuse to **take** it again the selfsame hour,
L C : 0 4 :068(445) [0749] of life does not **take** place but the old man is given free
L C : 0 4 :083(446) [0751] our own, overcomes and **takes** away sin and daily
L C : 0 5 :003(447) [0753] *when he was betrayed **took** bread, gave thanks, broke it,*
L C : 0 5 :003(447) [0753] *to his disciples and said, '**Take**, eat; this is my body, which*
L C : 0 5 :003(447) [0753] *"In the same way also he **took** the cup, after supper, gave*
L C : 0 5 :013(448) [0755] Here we have Christ's word, '**Take**, eat; this is my body.'
L C : 0 5 :013(448) [0755] Here we shall **take** our stand and see who dares to
L C : 0 5 :014(448) [0755] is true, indeed, that if you **take** the Word away from the
L C : 0 5 :017(448) [0757] my body and blood," but, "**Take**, eat and drink, this is my
L C : 0 5 :017(448) [0757] do, what I institute, what I give you and bid you **take**.
L C : 0 5 :033(450) [0761] hear them, those to whom Christ says, "**Take** and eat,"
L C : 0 5 :034(450) [0761] and drink, that you may **take** it as your own and enjoy
L C : 0 5 :035(450) [0761] also your responsibility to **take** it and confidently believe
L C : 0 5 :049(452) [0765] you may just as well **take** the further liberty not to be a
L C : 0 5 :063(454) [0767] rely firmly upon itself; otherwise it refuses to **take** a step.
L C : 0 5 :079(455) [0771] not experienced this, then **take** it from the Scriptures,
L C : 0 5 :083(456) [0773] **Take** others' advice and seek their prayers, and never give
L C : 0 6 :005(457) [0000] whatever they please and **take** advantage of their
L C : 0 6 :009(458) [0000] should and must **take** place incessantly as long as we live.
L C : 0 6 :013(458) [0000] secret confession which **takes** place privately before a
L C : 0 6 :018(459) [0000] We should therefore **take** care to keep the two parts
E P : 0 1 :005(466) [0781] without sin, and thus **took** on himself not alien flesh, but
E P : 0 1 :010(467) [0781] This will **take** place wholly by way of death in the
E P : 0 1 :021(468) [0785] or no wicked act or deed **took** place, nevertheless man's
E P : 0 2 :018(472) [0791] use of the holy sacraments **takes** hold of man's will and
E P : 0 5 :008(479) [0803] Therefore Christ **takes** the law into his own hands and
E P : 0 7 :004(482) [0809] Supper but assert that this **takes** place spiritually by
E P : 0 7 :015(483) [0811] when they direct us to **take**, eat, and drink, all of which
E P : 0 7 :015(483) [0813] and drink, all of which **took** place in the case of the
E P : 0 7 :042(486) [0817] Here we **take** our intellect captive in obedience to Christ,
E P : 0 8 :009(487) [0819] gives anything to or **takes** anything from the other.
E P : 0 8 :038(491) [0827] everywhere today, nor what will yet **take** place in eternity.
E P : 0 9 :004(492) [0827] How this **took** place is something that we should
E P : 1 2 :026(500) [0843] orderly process of excommunication do not **take** place.
S D : P R :003(502) [0847] The adversaries **took** a jaundiced view of this Confession,
S D : P R :005(504) [0851] but because it is **taken** from the Word of God and solidly
S D : 0 1 :002(508) [0859] The other party, however, **took** a contrary view and
S D : 0 2 :012(523) [0885] has it, does not grasp, **take** hold of, or apprehend) the
S D : 0 2 :044(529) [0897] In these writings he also **takes** up several disputed points
S D : 0 2 :055(532) [0903] what man is unable by his own powers to **take** or to give.
S D : 0 2 :070(535) [0909] For if none of these things **takes** place or exists, there is
S D : 0 2 :083(537) [0913] the Word, conversion does not and cannot **take** place.
S D : 0 2 :083(537) [0913] and impulses, which **take** place through the Word, do not
S D : 0 2 :089(538) [0915] not mean that conversion **takes** place without the
S D : 0 3 :012(541) [0919] are to be considered and **taken** as synonymous: "We are
S D : 0 3 :020(542) [0921] a regeneration has indeed **taken** place because he has
S D : 0 3 :037(546) [0929] justification which God **takes** into consideration in this
S D : 0 4 :003(551) [0939] Another party **took** the contrary view that good works
S D : 0 5 :010(559) [0955] Therefore Christ **takes** the law into his hands and
S D : 0 6 :001(564) [0963] veil of Moses has been **taken** away, learn from the law to
S D : 0 6 :020(567) [0969] You shall not add to it nor **take** from it" (Deut. 12:8, 28,
S D : 0 7 :003(569) [0973] the body of Christ not as **taking** place here on earth but
S D : 0 7 :022(573) [0979] Here we have Christ's word, '**Take** eat, this is my body.
S D : 0 7 :023(573) [0979] is true indeed that if you **take** the Word away or look
S D : 0 7 :026(573) [0981] my body and blood,' but, '**Take**, eat and drink, this is my
S D : 0 7 :026(573) [0981] instituting, giving you, and commanding you to **take**.
S D : 0 7 :044(577) [0987] and proffered bread, "**Take**, eat, this is my body which is
S D : 0 7 :084(584) [1001] a Christian assembly we **take** bread and wine, consecrate
S D : 0 7 :088(585) [1003] of the body of Christ **takes** place only spiritually through
S D : 0 7 :089(585) [1003] in his words when he says, "**Take** eat, this is my body."
S D : 0 7 :116(589) [1013] in the Supper allegedly **take** place not through the true
S D : 0 7 :119(590) [1013] in Acts 3:21, "Christ must **take** possession of heaven," to
S D : 0 7 :119(590) [1013] that is, Christ must be so **taken** in or circumscribed or
S D : 0 8 :006(592) [1017] time had fully come, he **took** the human nature into the
S D : 0 8 :021(595) [1023] that one nature must be **taken** and understood for the
S D : 0 8 :028(596) [1025] Yet, this does not **take** place in a mundane way, but as
S D : 0 8 :032(597) [1025] of properties could not **take** place or continue if the
S D : 0 8 :062(603) [1037] or communication did not **take** place through an
S D : 0 8 :063(603) [1037] or exchange that **takes** place in deed and in truth — to
S D : 0 8 :065(604) [1039] has been laid aside, it **takes** place fully, mightily, and
S D : 0 8 :082(607) [1045] Here you must **take** your stand and say that wherever
S D : 0 8 :096(609) [1049] close the eyes of reason, **take** their intellect captive to
S D : 0 9 :002(610) [1051] hell's power, and **took** from the devil all his might.
S D : 0 9 :003(610) [1053] hell nor the devil can **take** us or any believer in Christ
S D : 1 0 :005(611) [1055] and from true religion has **taken** place or will allegedly
S D : 1 1 :014(619) [1069] means that we must always **take** as one unit the entire
S D : 1 1 :028(620) [1071] Christ has **taken** away the sin of the world (John 1:29); he
S D : 1 1 :029(621) [1073] this call of God which **takes** place through the preaching
S D : 1 1 :033(621) [1073] Then **take** up the warfare against sin as Paul teaches from
S D : 1 1 :034(622) [1075] not that in his call, which **takes** place through the Word,
S D : 1 1 :046(624) [1079] easily be snatched and **taken** from our hands — that he
S D : 1 1 :051(625) [1079] ears to hear, let him hear"; and "**Take** heed how ye hear."
S D : 1 1 :053(625) [1081] In our presumption we **take** much greater delight in
S D : 1 2 :034(635) [1101] does not **take** place is not a true Christian congregation.

Tale (1), Tales (4)

A P : 2 1 :035(234) [0353] But all these marvelous **tales** about statues and pictures
A P : 2 1 :035(234) [0353] compare with the fairy **tales** about the saints which are
A P : 2 1 :038(234) [0355] monstrous and ungodly **tales** because they make money.
A P : 2 4 :065(261) [0407] in support of the fairy **tales** which they teach so
L C : P R :011(360) [0571] is not like some empty **tale**, such as the one about

Talk (30), Talking (40), Talks (3)

A P : 0 2 :008(101) [0107] Thus when they **talk** about original sin, they do not
A P : 0 2 :025(103) [0111] not know what they are **talking** about when they
A P : 0 2 :051(107) [0119] frequently do not know what they are **talking** about.
A P : 0 4 :018(109) [0125] Though they **talk** about this disposition, yet without the
A P : 0 4 :019(110) [0125] They do not know what they are **talking** about.
A P : 0 4 :064(116) [0139] But we are **talking** about a faith that is not an idle
A P : 0 4 :066(116) [0139] When they **talk** about the disposition of love, they
A P : 0 4 :087(120) [0147] ceremonies, but Paul is **talking** about the whole law, not
A P : 0 4 :087(120) [0147] But Paul is **talking** about the whole law, as Augustine
A P : 0 4 :216(137) [0179] We are **talking** now about the righteousness by which we
A P : 0 4 :232(139) [0185] So he is **talking** not about personal perfection but about
A P : 0 4 :236(140) [0185] grace for our opponents to **talk** so much about love when
A P : 0 4 :238(140) [0187] Obviously Peter, too, is **talking** here about love to the
A P : 0 4 :246(142) [0189] He is **talking** about the works of the justified, who have
A P : 0 4 :249(142) [0191] We are not **talking** about idle knowledge, such as even
A P : 0 4 :302(154) [0205] not know what they are **talking** about; like the walls of a
A P : 0 4 :303(154) [0205] several times that we are **talking** about faith in Christ and
A P : 0 4 :311(155) [0207] Our opponents **talk** about obedience to the law; they do
A P : 0 4 :311(155) [0207] to the law; they do not **talk** about obedience to the
A P : 0 4 :337(159) [0215] We are not **talking** about a knowledge of history,
A P : 0 4 :365(163) [0219] When they **talk** about good works, the Scriptures often
A P : 0 4 :379(165) [0223] least wrought by the impulse of the love they **talk** about.
A P : 0 7 :019(171) [0233] Christ is **talking** about the outward appearance of the
A P : 0 7 :031(174) [0237] We are **talking** about true spiritual unity, without which
A P : 1 0 :004(180) [0247] We are **talking** about the presence of the living Christ,
A P : 1 2 :060(190) [0267] When our opponents **talk** about faith and say that it
A P : 1 2 :106(197) [0283] Solomon is not **talking** about confession.
A P : 1 2 :112(198) [0285] confession, but they are **talking** about the public rite of
A P : 1 2 :129(202) [0291] We are **talking** about the judgments of men and the silent
A P : 1 2 :132(202) [0291] penitent," he is surely **talking** about total penitence and
A P : 1 2 :132(202) [0291] He is not **talking** about those hypocritical satisfactions
A P : 1 2 :138(203) [0293] Christ is **talking** about the remission of sins when he says

Continued ▶

A P : 1 3 :021(214) [0313] Here we are **talking** about personal faith, which accepts
A P : 1 5 :030(219) [0323] and say that Paul is **talking** only about the law of Moses.
A P : 1 5 :030(219) [0323] perfectly clear that he is **talking** about human traditions.
A P : 1 5 :030(219) [0323] Our opponents do not know what they are **talking** about.
A P : 1 5 :042(221) [0327] opponents do preach, they **talk** about human traditions,
A P : 1 5 :042(221) [0327] ones are now beginning to **talk** about good works, but
A P : 1 8 :004(225) [0335] It can **talk** about God and express its worship of him in
A P : 2 0 :013(228) [0341] Peter is **talking** about the works that follow the
A P : 2 1 :036(234) [0353] examples as these which **talk** about faith or fear in the
A P : 2 2 :007(237) [0359] quote other passages that **talk** about the breaking of the
A P : 2 3 :007(240) [0365] We are not **talking** about sinful lust but about so-called
A P : 2 3 :013(241) [0367] As we said, we are not **talking** about sinful lust but about
A P : 2 3 :032(244) [0373] He is **talking** about the whole class of mothers, and above
A P : 2 3 :067(248) [0383] Fine **talk**!
A P : 2 4 :033(256) [0395] Malachi is **talking** about all the worship of the New
A P : 2 4 :048(258) [0401] God commands, and they **talk** about the value and use of
A P : 2 4 :053(259) [0403] The preceding words **talk** about the Levitical priesthood
A P : 2 4 :066(261) [0407] make clear that they are **talking** about thanksgiving;
A P : 2 4 :068(262) [0409] It **talks** only about the practice of love, which even
A P : 2 4 :068(262) [0409] understand; it does not **talk** about faith, whose true
A P : 2 4 :079(264) [0411] But let us **talk** about the term "liturgy."
A P : 2 4 :088(265) [0413] shows that it is not **talking** about the body and blood of
A P : 2 4 :088(265) [0413] For the canon is **talking** about the whole service; and by
A P : 2 4 :093(267) [0417] benefit the communicants; they do not **talk** about others.
A P : 2 7 :004(269) [0421] other vices, too, which we would rather not **talk** about.
A P : 2 7 :029(274) [0431] Where do the Sacred Scriptures **talk** about monastic life?
A P : 2 7 :041(276) [0435] to show that he is **talking** not about those who do
A P : 2 7 :049(277) [0437] but only for the person with whom Christ is **talking** here.
A P : 2 7 :065(280) [0441] we suppose that Paul is **talking** here about vows, this
A P : 2 7 :068(280) [0443] He **talks** about faith differently from the sophists.
A P : 2 8 :012(283) [0447] But we are **talking** about a bishop according to the
L C : P R :010(359) [0569] with the Word of God, **talk** about it, and meditate on it.
L C : 0 1 :263(400) [0655] court and their lying and malicious **talk** outside of court.
L C : 0 1 :266(401) [0657] sins, but to make him the **talk** of the town is not my
E P : 0 7 :004(482) [0809] harmful kind, who in part **talk** our language very
S D : P R :009(503) [0849] words, with one party **talking** past the other, so that the
S D : 0 2 :024(526) [0891] degree, and can even **talk** about it, as Pharisees and
S D : 0 3 :024(543) [0923] article, since we cannot **talk** in one and the same way
S D : 0 7 :031(574) [0983] out to be a joke or idle **talk**; I am in dead earnest, since
S D : 0 8 :035(597) [1027] kind and mode, and if one **talks** about them without due
S D : 0 8 :044(599) [1031] one person, it is correct to **talk** about God's death when

Tamper (1)
L C : 0 4 :016(438) [0735] But how dare you **tamper** thus with God's ordinance and

Tangled (2)
S D : 0 5 :027(563) [0961] two doctrines would be **tangled** together and made into
S D : 0 8 :035(597) [1027] the doctrine becomes **tangled** up and the simple reader is

Tapers (1)
L C : 0 1 :314(407) [0671] of bells, lighting of **tapers** and candles until nothing else

Tapping (1)
S D : 0 4 :011(553) [0941] a faithless man, blindly **tapping** around in search of faith

Tartars (1)
S 2 : 0 4 :011(300) [0475] Neither the Turks nor the **Tartars**, great as is their enmity

Task (5), Tasks (4)
A P : P R :015(099) [0101] up all their sophistries, for this would be an endless **task**.
A P : 1 5 :025(219) [0323] God commands, like the **tasks** of one's calling, the
A P : 1 5 :026(219) [0323] with these ceremonies such **tasks** seem profane, so that
A P : 2 3 :032(244) [0373] Then he adds a certain **task** of her calling, as performance
A P : 2 3 :032(244) [0373] as performance of the **tasks** of a particular calling should
S 1 : P R :014(291) [0459] God has laid so many **tasks** upon us in church, state, and
L C : 0 1 :117(381) [0615] fitted you to perform a **task** so precious and pleasing to
L C : 0 1 :277(402) [0659] failing to do his duty, he takes him to **task** personally.
L C : 0 2 :002(411) [0679] may know where and how to obtain strength for this **task**.

Taste (5), Tasted (1), Tasteless (1)
A G : 2 8 :045(088) [0089] 'Do not handle, Do not **taste**, Do not touch' (referring to
A L : 2 8 :045(088) [0089] 'Do not handle, Do not **taste**, Do not touch' (referring to
A P : 0 7 :035(175) [0241] 'Do not handle, Do not **taste**, Do not touch' (referring to
A P : 1 2 :146(205) [0297] useless and in this life does not even get a **taste** of death.
A P : 2 7 :006(269) [0421] But Christ warns that **tasteless** salt is usually "thrown out
S D : 0 8 :087(608) [1047] with them, who has **tasted** every tribulation in his
S D : 1 1 :051(624) [1079] men who were invited shall **taste** my banquet"

Tauber (1)
P R : P R :027(015) [0027] Mayor and Council of Rothenburg-on-the-**Tauber**

Taverns (1)
L C : 0 1 :096(378) [0607] Word or lie around in **taverns** dead drunk like swine, but

Tax (1), Taxes (4)
A P : 2 4 :081(264) [0411] "public duties," like the **taxes** collected for equipping a
A P : 2 4 :081(264) [0411] that "liturgy" is a kind of **tax** to pay for the games, ships,
S C : 0 9 :005(355) [0561] same reason you also pay **taxes**, for the authorities are
S C : 0 9 :005(355) [0561] Pay all of them their dues, **taxes** to whom taxes are due,
S C : 0 9 :005(355) [0561] their dues, taxes to whom **taxes** are due, revenue to whom

Teach (325)
P R : P R :022(012) [0019] and as we concordantly **teach** about it on the basis of the
A G : 0 1 :001(027) [0043] We unanimously hold and **teach**, in accordance with the
A G : 0 5 :004(031) [0045] and others who **teach** that the Holy Spirit comes to us
A G : 0 6 :003(032) [0047] The Fathers also **teach** thus, for Ambrose says, "It is
A G : 0 9 :003(033) [0047] the Anabaptists who **teach** that infant Baptism is not
A G : 1 2 :007(035) [0049] here are those who **teach** that persons who have once
A G : 1 2 :010(035) [0049] also are those who **teach** that forgiveness of sin is not
A G : 1 4 :000(036) [0049] nobody should publicly **teach** or preach or administer the
A G : 1 6 :003(037) [0051] are the Anabaptists who **teach** that none of the things
A G : 1 6 :004(037) [0051] condemned are those who **teach** that Christian perfection
A G : 1 6 :004(038) [0051] for the Gospel does not **teach** an outward and temporal
A G : 1 7 :004(038) [0051] are the Anabaptists who **teach** that the devil and
A G : 1 7 :005(039) [0051] an appearance and which **teach** that, before the
A G : 2 0 :006(041) [0053] They do not **teach** now that we become righteous before
A G : 0 1 :003(056) [0065] of all ceremonies is to **teach** the people what they need to
A G : 2 5 :004(062) [0069] We **teach** with great diligence about this command and
A G : 2 5 :004(062) [0069] We also **teach** that God requires us to believe this
A G : 2 5 :007(062) [0069] Concerning confession we **teach** that no one should be
A G : 2 5 :013(063) [0071] on our side diligently **teach** that confession is to be
A G : 2 6 :033(069) [0075] They also **teach** that everybody is under obligation to
A G : 2 6 :045(070) [0075] to institute holy days but to **teach** faith and love."
A G : 2 7 :017(073) [0077] and understand what our teachers **teach** and preach.
A G : 2 7 :040(077) [0081] Even the canons **teach** that an oath should not be an
A G : 2 8 :023(084) [0087] On the other hand, if they **teach**, introduce, or institute
A G : 2 8 :028(085) [0087] if they err or if they **teach** or command something
A G : 2 8 :059(091) [0091] the Sabbath and **teach** that after the revelation of the
A L : 0 1 :001(027) [0043] Our churches **teach** with great unanimity that the decree
A L : 0 2 :001(029) [0043] Our churches also **teach** that since the fall of Adam all
A L : 0 3 :001(029) [0045] Our churches also **teach** that the Word — that is, the Son
A L : 0 4 :001(030) [0045] Our churches also **teach** that men cannot be justified
A L : 0 6 :001(031) [0045] Our churches also **teach** that this faith is bound to bring
A L : 0 7 :001(032) [0047] Our churches also **teach** that one holy church is to
A L : 0 9 :001(033) [0047] Our churches **teach** that Baptism is necessary for
A L : 1 0 :001(034) [0047] Our churches **teach** that the body and blood of Christ are
A L : 1 0 :002(034) [0047] They disapprove of those who **teach** otherwise.
A L : 1 1 :001(034) [0047] Our churches **teach** that private absolution should be
A L : 1 2 :001(034) [0049] Our churches **teach** that those who have fallen after
A L : 1 2 :010(035) [0049] also are those who do not **teach** that remission of sins
A L : 1 3 :001(035) [0049] Our churches **teach** that the sacraments were instituted
A L : 1 3 :003(036) [0049] condemn those who **teach** that the sacraments justify by
A L : 1 3 :003(036) [0049] act and who do not **teach** that faith, which believes that
A L : 1 4 :000(036) [0049] Our churches **teach** that nobody should preach publicly in
A L : 1 5 :001(036) [0049] Our churches **teach** that those rites should be observed
A L : 1 6 :001(037) [0051] Our churches **teach** that lawful civil ordinances are good
A L : 1 7 :001(038) [0051] Our churches also **teach** that at the consummation of the
A L : 1 8 :001(039) [0051] Our churches **teach** that man's will has some liberty for
A L : 1 8 :008(040) [0053] Pelagians and others who **teach** that without the Holy
A L : 1 9 :000(040) [0053] Our churches **teach** that although God creates and
A L : 2 0 :003(041) [0053] Concerning such things preachers used to **teach** little.
A L : 2 0 :006(041) [0053] They **teach** that we are justified not by works only, but
A L : 2 0 :027(045) [0057] Our teachers **teach** in addition that it is necessary to do
A L : 2 1 :001(046) [0057] Our churches **teach** that the remembrance of saints may
A L : 2 1 :002(047) [0057] the Scriptures do not **teach** us to pray to the saints or seek
A L : 2 3 :009(052) [0061] these reasons our priests **teach** that it is lawful for them to
A L : 2 4 :028(059) [0067] The Scriptures also **teach** that we are justified before God
A L : 2 5 :007(062) [0069] confession they **teach** that an enumeration of sins is not
A L : 2 6 :001(063) [0071] but also of those who **teach** in the churches that
A L : 2 6 :033(069) [0075] Besides, they **teach** that every Christian ought so to
A L : 2 7 :018(073) [0077] In the first place, we **teach** concerning those who contract
A L : 2 7 :048(078) [0081] command of God and to **teach** that such service justifies
A L : 2 8 :023(084) [0087] However, when bishops **teach** or ordain anything
A L : 2 8 :070(093) [0093] he swears that he will not **teach** the pure doctrine of the
A P : 0 2 :023(103) [0111] the scholastic theologians **teach** that these things cannot
A P : 0 2 :027(103) [0113] sensible among them — **teach** that original sin is truly
A P : 0 2 :032(104) [0113] So we **teach** nothing about original sin that is contrary to
A P : 0 2 :046(106) [0117] and its penalty when they **teach** that man can obey the
A P : 0 4 :009(108) [0123] Thus they **teach** only the righteousness of reason—that is,
A P : 0 4 :009(108) [0123] In this way the scholastics **teach** men to merit the
A P : 0 4 :021(110) [0127] Thus our opponents **teach** nothing but the righteousness
A P : 0 4 :039(112) [0131] of law or of reason which our opponents **teach**.
A P : 0 4 :043(113) [0133] of faith in Christ, which the law does not **teach**.
A P : 0 4 :048(113) [0135] historical knowledge and **teach** that it can exist with
A P : 0 4 :057(114) [0137] though the law does not **teach** the free forgiveness of sins,
A P : 0 4 :060(115) [0137] and disparage faith and **teach** men to deal with God only
A P : 0 4 :070(116) [0141] For the law does not **teach** the free forgiveness of sins.
A P : 0 4 :120(124) [0155] Whoever fails to **teach** about this faith we are discussing
A P : 0 4 :140(126) [0161] We **teach**, furthermore, not only how the law can be
A P : 0 4 :145(127) [0161] effects of faith, our opponents **teach** that love justifies.
A P : 0 4 :145(127) [0163] From this it is clear that they **teach** only the law.
A P : 0 4 :145(127) [0163] They do not **teach** that we must first receive the
A P : 0 4 :188(133) [0173] the promises, and we **teach** them about the free
A P : 0 4 :194(133) [0175] We **teach** that rewards have been offered and promised to
A P : 0 4 :194(133) [0175] We **teach** that good works are meritorious—not for the
A P : 0 4 :198(134) [0175] Many Psalms **teach** us this as they console us against the
A P : 0 4 :214(136) [0179] We believe and **teach**, therefore, that good works must
A P : 0 4 :215(136) [0179] This is what we believe and **teach**.
A P : 0 4 :221(137) [0181] from justification and **teach** only the righteousness of the
A P : 0 4 :229(139) [0183] because everywhere they **teach** and require the
A P : 0 4 :245(142) [0189] They **teach** that a man is justified by love and works but
A P : 0 4 :274(148) [0199] those passages which **teach** about the law or works.
A P : 0 4 :281(149) [0201] they exclude Christ and **teach** that we merit justification
A P : 0 4 :285(150) [0201] very badly when they **teach** that works merit the
A P : 0 4 :286(150) [0203] They **teach** the law in such a way as to hide the Gospel of
A P : 0 4 :287(150) [0203] They **teach** two modes of justification, one based upon
A P : 0 4 :290(151) [0203] It does not **teach** us to avail ourselves of Christ in our
A P : 0 4 :290(151) [0203] It does not **teach** that justification is the forgiveness of
A P : 0 4 :290(151) [0203] It does not **teach** that the forgiveness of sins precedes our
A P : 0 4 :290(151) [0203] It does not **teach** that by faith in Christ we overcome the
A P : 0 4 :292(152) [0203] we have already stated, we **teach** that a man is justified
A P : 0 4 :299(153) [0205] becomes brighter when we **teach** men to make use of him
A P : 0 4 :313(155) [0207] if indeed we want to **teach** the righteousness of the
A P : 0 4 :313(155) [0207] Those who **teach** that we are justified by love teach the
A P : 0 4 :313(155) [0207] we are justified by love **teach** the righteousness of the
A P : 0 4 :313(155) [0207] of the law, they do not **teach** us to use Christ as the
A P : 0 4 :314(156) [0207] consideration of it will **teach** us much about the whole
A P : 0 4 :318(156) [0209] when our opponents **teach** that good works earn grace by
A P : 0 4 :321(157) [0209] everything our opponents **teach** on this question is full of
A P : 0 4 :324(157) [0209] Our opponents **teach** wrongly when they praise merits in
A P : 0 4 :338(159) [0215] with the whole church we **teach** that we are saved by
A P : 0 4 :353(161) [0217] good works, since we **teach** that this faith arises in
A P : 0 4 :353(161) [0217] than what our opponents **teach** about contemplation or
A P : 0 4 :378(165) [0223] we condemn those who **teach** that we merit eternal life by
A P : 0 4 :381(165) [0223] trust our love when they **teach** that we cannot know
A P : 0 4 :383(165) [0225] The scholastics do not **teach** the righteousness of faith.

Continued ▶

AP : 04 :387(166) [0225] They **teach** a doctrine of justification derived either from
AP : 04 :400(168) [0227] Christ is among those who **teach** the Gospel of Christ,
AP : 07 :020(171) [0233] alleged, but we **teach** that this church actually exists,
AP : 07 :021(172) [0233] error when our opponents **teach** that men merit the
AP : 09 :003(178) [0245] children, the Anabaptists **teach** wickedly when they
AP : 11 :002(180) [0249] scholastics and monks **teach** nothing about faith and free
AP : 11 :006(181) [0251] of sins in confession we **teach** men in such a way as not to
AP : 12 :008(183) [0255] They **teach** that by contrition we merit grace.
AP : 12 :034(186) [0261] What do they **teach** but despair, when amid such terrors
AP : 12 :052(189) [0265] terror and consolation, to **teach** that these are the chief
AP : 12 :075(193) [0273] Besides, they **teach** us to believe that we obtain the
AP : 12 :088(195) [0277] We **teach** that such a certainty of faith is required in the
AP : 12 :118(199) [0287] They **teach** that in the forgiveness of sin God remits the
AP : 12 :143(204) [0297] of these acts, for they **teach** that they avail even for those
AP : 12 :157(207) [0301] Where does Scripture **teach** that we can be freed from
AP : 12 :165(208) [0303] It is wholesome to **teach** that our common evils are
AP : 12 :174(210) [0307] But Scripture does not **teach** that only the observance of
AP : 12 :178(211) [0307] have neglected to **teach** the faith that justifies and
AP : 13 :008(212) [0311] We **teach** that the sacrificial death of Christ on the cross
AP : 13 :013(213) [0311] taught formerly and the Anabaptists **teach** now.
AP : 13 :018(213) [0313] of scholastic doctors who **teach** that unless there is some
AP : 13 :019(213) [0313] Thus we **teach** that in using the sacraments there must be
AP : 14 :004(214) [0315] among those who rightly **teach** the Word of God and
AP : 15 :018(217) [0319] from Christ when they **teach** that we are not justified
AP : 15 :018(217) [0319] and especially when they **teach** that for justification such
AP : 15 :034(220) [0325] They compel us to **teach** that traditions do not justify;
AP : 15 :045(221) [0327] discipline of the flesh we **teach** exactly what we said in the
AP : 15 :052(222) [0329] This is what we **teach**.
AP : 16 :007(223) [0331] them know their duty to **teach** that the spiritual kingdom
AP : 18 :003(225) [0335] notions which the schools **teach** with great authority!
AP : 20 :005(227) [0339] on the other hand, **teach** that God has laid our iniquities
AP : 21 :010(230) [0345] that Scripture does not **teach** us to invoke the saints or to
AP : 21 :031(233) [0351] Our opponents **teach** that we should put our trust in the
AP : 21 :035(234) [0353] that is, those who would **teach** or confess the Gospel,
AP : 21 :044(236) [0357] sound doctrine and to defend those who **teach** it.
AP : 23 :033(244) [0373] These passages **teach** that marriage is a lawful thing.
AP : 24 :005(250) [0385] ceremonies that do not **teach** or admonish, simply *ex*
AP : 24 :028(254) [0393] *ex opere operato* and **teach** spiritual righteousness and
AP : 24 :030(255) [0395] of such passages which **teach** that sacrifices do not
AP : 24 :034(256) [0395] Levi (that is, of those who **teach** in the New Testament)
AP : 24 :043(258) [0399] The better ones **teach** the law and say nothing about the
AP : 24 :048(258) [0401] ministry of the Word, they **teach** the Gospel of the
AP : 24 :065(261) [0407] the fairy tales which they **teach** so authoritatively in the
AP : 24 :095(267) [0413] lies which our opponents **teach** about transfer *ex opere*
AP : 27 :024(273) [0427] Not only do they **teach** that these observances are services
AP : 27 :034(275) [0431] Thus those who **teach** that the monastic life merits the
AP : 27 :055(278) [0439] them in order to **teach** and exhort the hearers, brief and
AP : 28 :014(283) [0447] of God, which he ought to **teach** and according to which
AP : 28 :019(284) [0449] Christ requires them to **teach** in such a way that he might
AP : 28 :021(284) [0449] To the extent that they **teach** wicked things, they should
S1 : PR :004(289) [0455] although they know very well that I **teach** otherwise.
S1 : 01 :000(292) [0461] and the Catechism in common use for children **teach**.
S2 : 01 :005(292) [0463] article rests all that we **teach** and practice against the
S2 : 02 :026(297) [0469] them a special function, as the papists **teach** and practice.
S3 : 01 :004(302) [0477] understanding and a good will, as the philosophers **teach**.
S3 : 03 :010(304) [0481] impossible for them to **teach** correctly about repentance
S3 : 03 :043(310) [0491] necessary to know and to **teach** that when holy people,
S3 : 05 :003(311) [0491] and the Franciscans who **teach** that Baptism washes away
S3 : 06 :005(311) [0493] sophistry of those who **teach** that bread and wine
S3 : 08 :003(312) [0495] and the spirit without knowing what they say or **teach**.
S3 : 10 :002(314) [0497] are unwilling to preach or **teach** or baptize or administer
S3 : 15 :005(317) [0501] Spirit of Christ I will thus continue to believe and **teach**
TR : 00 :031(325) [0513] said, "Go therefore and **teach** them to observe all that I
TR : 00 :038(326) [0515] canons likewise clearly **teach** that a heretical pope is not
TR : 00 :044(328) [0517] and his adherents, who **teach** that sins are forgiven on
TR : 00 :044(328) [0517] Nowhere do they **teach** that sins are forgiven freely for
TR : 00 :072(332) [0525] that bishops who **teach** and defend impious doctrines and
TR : 00 :082(334) [0529] churches they believe and **teach** in conformity with the
TR : 00 :082(000) [0529] and constantly will **teach**, through Jesus Christ, our
SC : PR :006(338) [0533] and that you help me to **teach** the catechism to the
SC : PR :008(339) [0535] We, too, should **teach** these things to the young and
SC : PR :014(339) [0535] become familiar with the text, **teach** them what it means.
SC : 01 :000(342) [0539] *the head of the family shall* ***teach*** *them to his household*
SC : 02 :000(344) [0543] *the head of the family shall* ***teach*** *it to his household*
SC : 03 :000(346) [0545] *the head of the family shall* ***teach*** *it to his household*
SC : 04 :000(348) [0551] *the head of the family shall* ***teach*** *it to his household*
SC : 06 :000(351) [0555] *the head of the family shall* ***teach*** *it to his household*
SC : 07 :000(352) [0557] *head of the family shall* ***teach*** *his household to say*
SC : 08 :006(353) [0559] *head of the family shall* ***teach*** *his household to offer*
LC : PR :002(358) [0567] that they are to **teach** and preach is now available to them
LC : PR :016(361) [0573] himself is not ashamed to **teach** it daily, for he knows of
LC : PR :016(361) [0573] of nothing better to **teach**, and he always keeps on
LC : PR :019(361) [0573] continue to read and **teach**, to learn and meditate and
LC : SP :021(364) [0579] "Go and **teach** all nations, and baptize them in the name
LC : SP :024(364) [0579] we should constantly **teach** and require young people to
LC : 01 :035(369) [0589] amply shows and as daily experience can still **teach** us.
LC : 01 :064(373) [0599] So, also, when we **teach** properly; again, when we call on
LC : 01 :090(377) [0607] nor practice God's Word but **teach** and live contrary to it.
LC : 01 :115(381) [0613] therefore, let us at last **teach** our young people to banish
LC : 01 :141(384) [0621] upon a schoolmaster to **teach** him; if he is too weak, he
LC : 01 :200(392) [0637] They all **teach** us to guard against harming our neighbor
LC : 01 :244(398) [0649] God must punish us and **teach** us morals in a different
LC : 01 :276(402) [0659] or that person has done, **teach** him, if he saw the
LC : 01 :293(404) [0665] two commandments to **teach** them that it is sinful and
LC : 01 :315(408) [0671] better way of life than the Ten Commandments **teach**?
LC : 01 :319(408) [0673] devote to learning how to **teach** and practice the Ten
LC : 01 :330(410) [0677] and necessary always to **teach**, admonish, and remind
LC : 02 :053(417) [0693] it he gathers us, using it to **teach** and preach the Word.
LC : 02 :067(419) [0697] The latter **teach** us what we ought to do; the Creed tells
LC : 03 :006(421) [0699] hypocritical prayers we **teach** that there is no duty or need
LC : 03 :041(425) [0709] when men preach, **teach**, and speak in God's name
LC : 03 :044(425) [0709] manifold blessings fail to **teach**, speak, and live as godly
LC : 03 :051(427) [0711] gave his Holy Spirit to **teach** us this through his holy
LC : 03 :062(428) [0715] He cannot bear to have anyone **teach** or believe rightly.
LC : 04 :004(437) [0733] *into all the world, and* ***teach*** *all nations, baptizing them in*
LC : 04 :012(438) [0735] But the Scriptures **teach** that if we piled together all the
LC : 04 :019(438) [0737] Therefore, we constantly **teach** that the sacraments and
LC : 05 :044(451) [0763] it is not enough simply to **teach** and instruct, but there
LC : 05 :087(456) [0773] and command, to **teach** or have taught to his children the
LC : 06 :028(460) [0000] Thus we **teach** what a wonderful, precious, and
EP : RN :001(464) [0777] 1. We believe, **teach**, and confess that the prophetic and
EP : 01 :002(466) [0779] 1. We believe, **teach**, and confess that there is a distinction
EP : 01 :003(466) [0779] 2. We also believe, **teach**, and confess that we must
EP : 01 :008(467) [0781] other hand, we believe, **teach**, and confess that original
EP : 02 :003(470) [0787] 2. Likewise we believe, **teach**, and confess that man's
EP : 02 :010(471) [0789] the Semi-Pelagians who **teach** that man by virtue of his
EP : 03 :003(473) [0793] recounted, we believe, **teach**, and confess unanimously
EP : 03 :004(473) [0793] 2. Accordingly we believe, **teach**, and confess that our
EP : 03 :005(473) [0793] 3. We believe, **teach**, and confess that faith is the only
EP : 03 :006(473) [0793] 4. We believe, **teach**, and confess that this faith is not a
EP : 03 :007(473) [0793] 5. We believe, **teach**, and confess that according to the
EP : 03 :009(474) [0793] 6. We also believe, **teach**, and confess that, although the
EP : 03 :010(474) [0795] 7. We believe, **teach**, and confess that if we would
EP : 03 :011(474) [0795] 8. We believe, **teach**, and confess that the contrition that
EP : 04 :007(476) [0799] 2. We believe, **teach**, and confess that good works should
EP : 04 :008(476) [0799] 3. We believe, **teach**, and confess further that all men, but
EP : 04 :011(476) [0799] Therefore we also believe, **teach**, and confess that the
EP : 04 :015(477) [0799] 10. We also believe, **teach**, and confess that not our
EP : 04 :016(477) [0801] formulations which **teach** that good works are necessary
EP : 05 :002(478) [0801] 1. We believe, **teach**, and confess that the distinction
EP : 05 :003(478) [0801] 2. We believe, **teach**, and confess that, strictly speaking,
EP : 05 :006(478) [0803] Therefore we believe, **teach**, and confess that when the
EP : 05 :007(478) [0803] Gospel, then we believe, **teach**, and confess that the
EP : 05 :011(479) [0805] detrimental when men **teach** that the Gospel, strictly
EP : 06 :002(480) [0805] 1. We believe, **teach**, and confess that although people
EP : 06 :003(480) [0805] 2. We believe, **teach**, and confess that the preaching of the
EP : 06 :005(480) [0807] of the Spirit we believe, **teach**, and confess that works
EP : 07 :006(482) [0809] 1. We believe, **teach**, and confess that in the Holy Supper
EP : 07 :007(482) [0811] 2. We believe, **teach**, and confess that the words of the
EP : 07 :008(482) [0811] consecration we believe, **teach**, and confess that no man's
EP : 07 :009(482) [0811] the same time we believe, **teach**, and confess with one
EP : 07 :015(483) [0811] 6. We believe, **teach**, and confess that with the bread and
EP : 07 :015(483) [0811] The words of Christ **teach** this clearly when they direct us
EP : 07 :016(483) [0813] 7. We believe, **teach**, and confess that not only the
EP : 07 :018(484) [0813] 8. We believe, **teach**, and confess that there is only one
EP : 07 :019(484) [0813] 9. We believe, **teach**, and confess that no genuine
EP : 07 :020(484) [0813] 10. We believe, **teach**, and confess that the entire
EP : 08 :004(487) [0819] to our Christian faith we **teach**, believe, and confess the
EP : 08 :006(487) [0819] 2. We believe, **teach**, and confess that the divine and the
EP : 08 :009(487) [0819] in one person) we believe, **teach**, and confess that this
EP : 08 :010(488) [0819] 6. Therefore we believe, **teach**, and confess that God is
EP : 08 :012(488) [0821] 7. Therefore we believe, **teach**, and confess that Mary
EP : 08 :013(488) [0821] Therefore we also believe, **teach**, and confess that it was
EP : 08 :015(488) [0821] 10. Therefore we believe, **teach**, and confess that the Son
EP : 08 :017(489) [0823] of our Christian faith as we **teach** this to our children.
EP : 09 :003(492) [0827] article, but believe and **teach** it in all simplicity, as Dr.
EP : 10 :003(493) [0829] controversy we believe, **teach**, and confess unanimously
EP : 10 :004(493) [0829] 2. We believe, **teach**, and confess that the community of
EP : 10 :006(493) [0829] 4. We believe, **teach**, and confess that in time of
EP : 10 :007(493) [0831] 5. We believe, **teach**, and confess that no church should
EP : 12 :002(498) [0839] factions, some of which **teach** many errors, others teach
EP : 12 :002(498) [0839] some of which teach many errors, others **teach** fewer.
EP : 12 :027(500) [0843] of the church cannot **teach** profitably or administer true
SD : PR :014(506) [0855] the adversaries who **teach** otherwise (I Tim. 3:9;
SD : 01 :023(512) [0865] and condemn those who **teach** that, though man's nature
SD : 02 :021(525) [0889] to scold, or even to **teach** and preach" until the Holy
SD : 02 :045(530) [0899] Therefore men **teach** wrongly when they pretend that
SD : 02 :085(537) [0913] and should explain and **teach** the correct opinion in this
SD : 03 :009(540) [0919] before God we believe, **teach**, and confess unanimously,
SD : 03 :022(543) [0923] When we **teach** that through the Holy Spirit's work we
SD : 03 :029(544) [0925] grant that we must **teach** about love and good works too.
SD : 03 :056(549) [0935] Therefore we believe, **teach**, and confess that the total
SD : 04 :018(554) [0943] sense it is right to say and **teach** that truly good works are
SD : 04 :021(554) [0945] Secondly, when we **teach** that good works are necessary
SD : 04 :028(555) [0947] we nevertheless do not **teach** people to put their trust in
SD : 04 :040(558) [0951] and should not tolerate, **teach**, or defend this
SD : 05 :015(561) [0957] have us criticize sin and **teach** contrition and sorrow not
SD : 05 :017(561) [0957] We unanimously believe, **teach**, and confess on the basis
SD : 06 :004(564) [0963] we unanimously believe, **teach**, and confess that, although
SD : 06 :015(566) [0967] all misunderstandings, to **teach** and to maintain the strict
SD : 06 :022(567) [0969] It does not **teach** us how and why the good works of
SD : 07 :014(571) [0977] they maintain and **teach** that with the bread and wine the
SD : 07 :029(574) [0981] were living now, he would **teach** and hold this or that
SD : 07 :051(578) [0991] and commanded them to **teach** all nations to observe all
SD : 07 :066(581) [0995] holy Christian church **teach** unanimously that the body
SD : 07 :108(588) [1009] when they **teach** that the consecrated or blessed bread and
SD : 08 :006(592) [1017] 1. We believe, **teach**, and confess that although the Son
SD : 08 :007(592) [1017] 2. We believe, **teach**, and confess that henceforth in this
SD : 08 :008(593) [1017] We furthermore believe, **teach**, and confess that in their
SD : 08 :009(593) [1017] 4. We also believe, **teach**, and confess that to be
SD : 08 :011(593) [1019] 6. We also believe, **teach**, and confess that after the
SD : 08 :012(593) [1019] We furthermore believe, **teach**, and confess that the
SD : 08 :023(595) [1023] Creed we believe, **teach**, and confess everything that is
SD : 08 :064(603) [1037] We therefore hold and **teach** with the ancient orthodox
SD : 08 :071(605) [1041] do not in any way believe, **teach**, and confess an
SD : 08 :072(605) [1041] But we believe, **teach**, and confess that God the Father
SD : 08 :089(609) [1047] anyone were to believe or **teach** that because of the
SD : 10 :008(611) [1055] We believe, **teach**, and confess that true adiaphora or
SD : 10 :009(612) [1055] We further believe, **teach**, and confess that the
SD : 10 :010(612) [1055] We believe, **teach**, and confess that at a time of
SD : 10 :019(614) [1059] are unwilling to preach or **teach** or baptize or administer
SD : 11 :001(616) [1063] men may know what we **teach**, believe, and confess in
SD : 11 :038(622) [1075] individual absolution and **teach** that it is God's command
SD : 11 :088(631) [1093] and wrong when men **teach** that the cause of our election
SD : 12 :009(633) [1097] They **teach**:
SD : 12 :029(635) [1101] They also **teach** that through the exaltation Christ's flesh

Continued ▶

SD : 12 :035(635) [1101] and pious cannot **teach** profitably nor administer genuine
SD : 12 :036(635) [1101] of the New Arians who **teach** that Christ is not a true,
SD : 12 :037(636) [1103] terminology, and instead **teach** that there is not one
SD : 12 :037(636) [1103] Some **teach** that all three persons in the Trinity, like any
SD : 12 :037(636) [1103] and glory, while others **teach** that the three persons in the

Taught (154)

PR : PR :021(011) [0019] sometimes it were being **taught** that the divine and human
PR : PR :023(012) [0021] doctrine be treated and **taught** in our lands, territories,
AG : PR :008(025) [0039] things are preached, **taught**, communicated, and
AG : 02 :001(029) [0043] It is also **taught** among us that since the fall of Adam all
AG : 03 :001(029) [0045] It is also **taught** among us that God the Son became
AG : 04 :001(030) [0045] It is also **taught** among us that we cannot obtain
AG : 06 :001(031) [0045] It is also **taught** among us that such faith should produce
AG : 07 :001(032) [0047] It is also **taught** among us that one holy Christian church
AG : 09 :001(033) [0047] It is **taught** among us that Baptism is necessary and that
AG : 10 :001(034) [0047] It is **taught** among us that the true body and blood of
AG : 11 :001(034) [0047] It is **taught** among us that private absolution should be
AG : 12 :001(034) [0049] It is **taught** among us that those who sin after Baptism
AG : 13 :001(035) [0049] It is **taught** among us that the sacraments were instituted
AG : 14 :000(036) [0049] It is **taught** among us that nobody should publicly teach
AG : 15 :001(036) [0049] established by men, it is **taught** among us that those
AG : 15 :003(036) [0049] Moreover it is **taught** that all ordinances and traditions
AG : 16 :001(037) [0051] It is **taught** among us that all government in the world
AG : 17 :001(038) [0051] It is also **taught** among us that our Lord Jesus Christ will
AG : 18 :001(039) [0051] It is also **taught** among us that man possesses some
AG : 19 :000(040) [0053] It is **taught** among us that although almighty God has
AG : 20 :003(041) [0053] About these little was **taught** in former times, when for
AG : 20 :027(045) [0057] It is also **taught** among us that good works should and
AG : 21 :001(046) [0057] It is also **taught** among us that saints should be kept in
AG : 00 :001(047) [0059] that are preached and **taught** in our churches for proper
AG : 00 :000(048) [0059] manifest that nothing is **taught** in our churches
AG : 24 :021(058) [0067] according to which it was **taught** that our Lord Christ has
AG : 24 :026(058) [0067] They were **taught**, first of all, that the Scriptures show in
AG : 24 :028(059) [0067] second place, St. Paul **taught** that we obtain grace before
AG : 25 :005(062) [0069] times the preachers who **taught** much about confession
AG : 26 :001(063) [0071] In former times men **taught**, preached, and wrote that
AG : 26 :006(064) [0071] by those who have **taught** that grace is to be earned by
AG : 26 :017(066) [0073] many traditions, and he **taught** in this connection that
AG : 26 :018(066) [0073] Our teachers have not **taught** concerning these matters
AG : 26 :021(067) [0073] It is therefore **taught** that grace cannot be earned, God
AG : 26 :031(068) [0075] They have always **taught** concerning the holy cross that
AG : 27 :018(073) [0077] For one thing, it is **taught** among us with regard to those
AG : 27 :038(077) [0081] that the monks have **taught** and preached that their
AG : 27 :044(078) [0081] deny that the monks have **taught** and preached that they
AG : 27 :048(078) [0081] of God, and should be **taught** that such a service would
AG : 28 :004(081) [0085] authority, and they have **taught** that because of God's
AG : 28 :034(086) [0089] indicated above and as is **taught** by canon law
AG : 28 :062(092) [0093] of faith was no longer **taught** and preached with clarity
AL : 06 :003(032) [0047] The same is also **taught** by the Fathers of the ancient
AL : 07 :001(032) [0047] in which the Gospel is **taught** purely and the sacraments
AL : 20 :002(041) [0053] witness that they have **taught** to good purpose about all
AL : 23 :003(051) [0061] they took wives and **taught** that it was lawful for them to
AL : 24 :003(056) [0065] especially in order that the unlearned may be **taught**.
AL : 25 :002(061) [0069] people are very diligently **taught** concerning faith in
AL : 25 :003(061) [0069] Our people are **taught** to esteem absolution highly
AL : 26 :021(067) [0073] our teachers have **taught** that we cannot merit grace or
AL : 26 :031(068) [0075] for they have always **taught** concerning the cross that
AL : 27 :001(070) [0075] What is **taught** among us concerning monastic vows will
AL : 27 :011(072) [0077] to Baptism, and they **taught** that they merited forgiveness
AL : 27 :038(077) [0081] that the monks have **taught** that their invented
AL : 27 :044(078) [0081] be denied that the monks **taught** that they were justified
AL : 27 :048(078) [0081] ought especially to be **taught** in the church, is obscured
AL : 28 :004(081) [0085] the sword, and they have **taught** that on account of God's
AL : 28 :062(092) [0093] of faith was not **taught** with sufficient clarity.
AL : 28 :077(094) [0095] allow the Gospel to be **taught** purely and that they relax
AL : 00 :006(096) [0095] summary of the doctrine **taught** among us may be
AP : 01 :002(100) [0103] We have always **taught** and defended this doctrine and we
AP : 02 :002(100) [0105] for it says: "It is also **taught** that since the fall of Adam
AP : 02 :012(102) [0109] They **taught** that men are justified before God by
AP : 02 :045(106) [0117] of human weakness, he **taught** that the remnants of
AP : 04 :265(146) [0197] and it cannot be driven out unless we are divinely **taught**.
AP : 04 :299(153) [0205] They are **taught** to believe and to rely on the sure fact
AP : 04 :322(157) [0209] more, he is instructed and **taught** that he sins daily, since
AP : 04 :392(167) [0225] monks in the church have **taught** us to seek forgiveness of
AP : 04 :393(167) [0225] the righteousness of faith **taught** that men were reconciled
AP : 04 :394(167) [0225] some in the world who **taught** only this outward
AP : 04 :395(167) [0225] this opinion and **taught** the righteousness of faith.
AP : 07 :016(171) [0231] they held high positions and they sacrificed and **taught**.
AP : 09 :001(178) [0245] Among us, the Gospel is **taught** purely and diligently.
AP : 12 :003(182) [0253] on this issue we have **taught** what is true, godly, salutary,
AP : 12 :016(184) [0257] doctrine of penitence as **taught** by the scholastics and
AP : 12 :123(200) [0289] Who ever **taught** these asses such logic?
AP : 12 :158(207) [0301] them but they should be **taught** that troubles have other
AP : 13 :013(213) [0311] as the enthusiasts **taught** formerly and the Anabaptists
AP : 13 :018(213) [0313] and wicked notion is **taught** with great authority
AP : 15 :020(218) [0321] or work of Christ but **taught** that we are justified by faith
AP : 21 :033(233) [0351] of the saints could be **taught** with great moderation, the
AP : 21 :035(234) [0353] saints which are being **taught** in public on the highest
AP : 21 :035(234) [0353] Then the foolish monks **taught** the people to call on
AP : 21 :036(234) [0353] in time of great danger, **taught** the Gospel, battled
AP : 23 :011(241) [0367] keep this fact in mind, **taught** by Scripture and wisely put
AP : 27 :002(269) [0419] had neither written nor **taught** anything that threatened
AP : 28 :008(282) [0445] All this is **taught** by that one passage in Acts (15:9),
S3 : 01 :003(302) [0477] scholastic theologians **taught** concerning this article is
S3 : 03 :001(303) [0479] of the law is retained and **taught** by the New Testament.
S3 : 03 :027(307) [0487] for although the pope **taught** the people to rely on and
S3 : 03 :028(308) [0487] of the others were, as we **taught**, without sin and full of
S3 : 10 :003(314) [0497] Accordingly, as we are **taught** by the examples of the
S3 : 13 :001(315) [0499] heretofore constantly **taught** on this subject, namely, that
S3 : 15 :005(317) [0501] thus believed and **taught**, and by the Spirit of Christ I
TR : 00 :008(320) [0505] for this error and **taught** them that no one should have
TR : 00 :008(321) [0505] The same thing is **taught** by a parable when, in a similar
SC : PR :017(340) [0535] place, after you have thus **taught** this brief catechism,
SC : 03 :005(346) [0547] When the Word of God is **taught** clearly and purely and
SC : 05 :015(349) [0553] *How Plain People Are to Be **Taught** to Confess*
SC : 09 :003(354) [0561] "Let him who is **taught** the word share all good things
LC : PR :007(359) [0569] Yet I do as a child who is being **taught** the Catechism.
LC : PR :019(361) [0573] experience that they have **taught** the devil to death and
LC : SP :006(362) [0575] though they were rarely **taught** and treated correctly, so
LC : SP :013(363) [0577] III. The Prayer, or Our Father, Which Christ **Taught**
LC : SP :016(363) [0577] Our children should be **taught** the habit of reciting them
LC : 01 :050(371) [0593] instructed the heart and **taught** faith, so this
LC : 01 :050(371) [0593] As I have **taught** above how to answer the question,
LC : 01 :077(375) [0603] of the divine name and **taught** that its right use consists
LC : 01 :092(377) [0607] time God's Word is **taught**, preached, heard, read, or
LC : 01 :097(378) [0609] one asked about God's Word, and no one **taught** it either.
LC : 01 :108(379) [0611] people must therefore be **taught** to revere their parents as
LC : 01 :114(380) [0613] godly children, properly **taught**, and reared in true
LC : 01 :140(384) [0621] the past was neither heeded nor **taught** under the papacy.
LC : 01 :209(393) [0639] Therefore I have always **taught** that we should not
LC : 01 :333(410) [0677] and works which are **taught** and practiced apart from
LC : 02 :010(412) [0679] This is **taught** here and in the following articles.
LC : 02 :067(420) [0697] the Creed; it must be **taught** by the Holy Spirit alone.
LC : 03 :003(420) [0697] Lord Christ himself has **taught** us both the way and the
LC : 03 :014(422) [0701] Prayer used to be **taught**, in the devil's name, in such a
LC : 03 :026(424) [0705] we shall not need to be **taught** how to prepare for it or
LC : 03 :048(426) [0711] else and his Word **taught** in its purity and cherished and
LC : 04 :001(436) [0733] unfortunately in the past nothing was **taught** about them.
LC : 04 :018(438) [0737] as St. Augustine **taught**, *"Accedat verbum ad elementum*
LC : 05 :041(451) [0763] from it because we have **taught** that no one should go
LC : 05 :087(456) [0773] to teach or have **taught** to his children the things they
LC : 06 :001(457) [0000] we have always **taught** that it should be voluntary and
LC : 06 :003(457) [0000] Worst of all, no one **taught** or understood what
LC : 06 :034(461) [0000] would be rightly **taught**, and such a desire and love for it
EP : 02 :008(471) [0787] and of Manichaeans who **taught** that whatever happens
EP : 02 :009(471) [0789] the crass Pelagians who **taught** that by his own powers,
EP : 07 :022(484) [0813] when it is **taught** in the papacy that the bread and wine in
EP : 08 :018(489) [0823] together in one essence, as Eutyches erroneously **taught**.
EP : 09 :003(492) [0827] of blessed memory **taught** in his sermon preached at
SD : PR :020(508) [0857] between what we **taught** and confessed originally and
SD : 01 :002(508) [0859] took a contrary view and **taught** that original sin, strictly
SD : 02 :003(520) [0881] The one party held and **taught** that, although by his own
SD : 02 :004(520) [0881] modern enthusiasts have **taught** that God converts man
SD : 02 :005(520) [0881] Confession have **taught** and argued that through the fall
SD : 02 :076(536) [0911] more subtle and who **taught** that by his natural powers
SD : 03 :003(539) [0917] side some have held and **taught** that Christ is our
SD : 03 :052(548) [0933] is also an error when it is **taught** that man is saved in a
SD : 04 :029(555) [0947] are not to be **taught**, defended, or condoned but are to be
SD : 05 :022(562) [0959] Gospel and that which is **taught** by and learned from the
SD : 06 :002(564) [0963] This one party **taught** and held that the regenerated do
SD : 06 :003(564) [0963] The other party **taught** that although true believers are
SD : 07 :011(571) [0975] the Greek Church has **taught** the bodily presence of
SD : 07 :042(576) [0987] God and so understood, **taught**, and transmitted by the
SD : 08 :015(594) [1019] the presbyter of Rhaitu, **taught** that the two natures have
SD : 08 :016(594) [1021] in Antioch in Syria, **taught** godlessly that the Lord Christ
SD : 08 :021(595) [1023] of Zwingli, who **taught** that one nature must be taken and
SD : 08 :062(603) [1037] or of their essential properties be **taught** or conceded.
SD : 08 :075(606) [1043] called the Agnoetes, who **taught** that the Son, the
SD : 11 :035(622) [1075] In this way it would be **taught** that God, who is the
SD : 11 :089(631) [1093] when people are **taught** to seek their eternal election in

Teaches (113)

AG : 05 :003(031) [0045] And the Gospel **teaches** that we have a gracious God, not
AG : 20 :013(043) [0055] question thoroughly and **teaches** the same thing, namely,
AG : 20 :025(044) [0057] Heb. 11:1 **teaches** about faith in such a way as to make it
AG : 25 :012(063) [0071] *poenitentia*, Dist. 5, also **teaches** that such confession is
AG : 27 :037(077) [0081] St. Paul also **teaches** everywhere that one is not to seek
AL : 16 :004(038) [0051] The Gospel **teaches** an eternal righteousness of the heart,
AL : 20 :014(043) [0055] Ambrose **teaches** similarly in *De vocatione gentium* and
AL : 20 :016(043) [0055] It is as Paul **teaches** in Rom. 5:1, "Since we are justified
AL : 20 :026(045) [0057] the word "faith" when he **teaches** that in the Scriptures
AL : 27 :037(077) [0081] Paul also **teaches** everywhere that righteousness is not to
AP : 02 :029(104) [0113] Hugo **teaches** the same thing when he says that original
AP : 02 :037(105) [0115] what Luther believes and **teaches**; and since they cannot
AP : 04 :070(116) [0141] denies that faith justifies **teaches** only the law and does
AP : 04 :081(118) [0145] Paul, on the other hand, **teaches** that we have access (that
AP : 04 :102(121) [0151] In some places it **teaches** the law; in others it teaches the
AP : 04 :102(121) [0151] the law; in others it **teaches** the promises of Christ, of the
AP : 04 :106(122) [0153] Here he **teaches** that our hearts are terrified by the law
AP : 04 :139(126) [0161] So the Psalm **teaches** (Ps. 68:18), "He led captivity
AP : 04 :141(126) [0161] So John **teaches** in his first epistle (4:19); "We love," he
AP : 04 :155(128) [0165] but meanwhile he **teaches** that it is faith that properly
AP : 04 :163(129) [0169] Paul clearly **teaches** this when he says (I Cor. 4:4), "I am
AP : 04 :179(131) [0171] Paul **teaches** this when he says in Gal. 3:13, "Christ
AP : 04 :201(134) [0175] Paul **teaches** the same thing about works when he says
AP : 04 :221(137) [0181] one text in which Paul **teaches** about the fruits, and they
AP : 04 :241(141) [0187] It **teaches** exactly the same thing as Paul's statement in
AP : 04 :246(142) [0189] this text that James **teaches** we merit grace and
AP : 04 :247(142) [0191] by the Gospel, he **teaches** that we are regenerated and
AP : 04 :289(151) [0203] scholastic theologians, **teaches** that we are righteous
AP : 04 :290(151) [0203] is obvious because it **teaches** that our works are a
AP : 04 :290(151) [0203] Without any warrant it **teaches** that men come to God
AP : 04 :291(152) [0203] It **teaches** that through him we have access to God
AP : 04 :291(152) [0203] It **teaches** that by faith in Christ we receive the
AP : 04 :294(152) [0203] Paul **teaches** that we are justified not by the law but by
AP : 04 :324(157) [0211] of condignity since it **teaches** nothing about justifying
AP : 04 :331(158) [0211] So Daniel **teaches** us to take hold of mercy when we
AP : 07 :016(171) [0231] devil's kingdom, as Paul **teaches** in Eph. 2:2 when he says
AP : 07 :019(171) [0233] He **teaches** us that the church is hidden under a crowd of
AP : 07 :019(171) [0233] Meanwhile he **teaches** that though these wicked men
AP : 07 :028(173) [0237] Christ's statement **teaches** us this in order that we may
AP : 07 :035(175) [0239] Paul clearly **teaches** this in Colossians (2:16, 17): "Let no
AP : 10 :003(179) [0247] John 15 in Cyril which **teaches** that Christ is offered to us
AP : 12 :043(187) [0263] blessing of Christ, and it **teaches** us to make use of Christ
AP : 12 :061(190) [0269] proved from Paul, who **teaches** in Rom. 4:16 that only

Continued ▶

A P : 1 2 :074(192) [0273] And he **teaches** us how to be sure of the forgiveness of
A P : 1 2 :079(193) [0275] for Christ's sake, and he **teaches** us to accept the
A P : 1 2 :135(203) [0293] as the chapter on "Penitence and Remission" **teaches**.
A P : 1 2 :157(207) [0301] contrary, it constantly **teaches** that we obtain the
A P : 1 2 :158(207) [0301] proper work, as Isaiah **teaches** in a long sermon in his
A P : 1 2 :164(208) [0303] as Isa. 1:16-19 **teaches**: "Cease to do evil, learn to do
A P : 1 3 :010(212) [0311] Epistle to the Hebrews **teaches** clearly enough, we do not
A P : 1 4 :004(215) [0315] butcher anyone who **teaches** what is right and true,
A P : 1 5 :004(215) [0315] Tim. 4:1) when someone **teaches** that religious rites are
A P : 1 5 :005(215) [0317] The Gospel **teaches** that by faith, for Christ's sake, we
A P : 1 5 :006(216) [0317] Gospel, for Paul clearly **teaches** (Eph. 2:8), "By grace you
A P : 1 6 :012(224) [0333] consciences, for it **teaches** that if contacts have the
A P : 2 3 :007(240) [0365] *First*, Gen. 1:28 **teaches** that men were created to be
A P : 2 4 :022(253) [0391] Epistle to the Hebrews **teaches** (10:4), "It is impossible
A P : 2 4 :026(254) [0391] are of this type, as Peter **teaches** in I Pet. 2:5, "A holy
A P : 2 4 :026(254) [0391] Paul **teaches** the same in Rom. 12:1, "Present your bodies
A P : 2 4 :026(254) [0391] Epistle to the Hebrews **teaches** the same (13:15):
A P : 2 4 :027(254) [0393] *ex opere operato*, and it **teaches** that worship should be in
A P : 2 4 :030(255) [0395] the New Testament **teaches** that there should be a new
A P : 2 4 :055(259) [0403] for sin, as Isa. 53:10 **teaches**, "When he makes himself an
A P : 2 4 :059(260) [0405] of the Spirit, as Paul **teaches** in II Cor. 3:6, the only
A P : 2 4 :089(266) [0415] faith in Christ, as Paul **teaches** (Rom. 5:1), "Being
A P : 2 7 :011(270) [0423] to the Gospel, which **teaches** that the forgiveness of sins is
A P : 2 7 :023(272) [0427] of faith, which **teaches** that for Christ's sake
A P : 2 8 :015(283) [0447] This is what Paul **teaches** when he says (Gal. 5:1), "Stand
S 3 : 0 3 :033(308) [0489] St. Paul **teaches** the same thing in Rom. 3:10-12: "None is
S 3 : 0 3 :035(309) [0489] Such repentance **teaches** us to acknowledge sin — that is,
T R : 0 0 :010(321) [0507] he had come to him, he **teaches** that the authority of the
T R : 0 0 :011(321) [0507] on an equality and **teaches** that the church is above the
T R : 0 0 :038(326) [0515] So Paul clearly **teaches**, "If an angel from heaven should
T R : 0 0 :062(330) [0521] Accordingly Jerome **teaches** clearly that in the apostolic
T R : 0 0 :063(331) [0523] Jerome therefore **teaches** that the distinction between the
S C : 0 3 :005(346) [0547] But whoever **teaches** and lives otherwise than as the Word
S C : 0 3 :005(346) [0547] as the Word of God **teaches**, profanes the name of God
S C : 0 9 :003(354) [0561] the word share all good things with him who **teaches**.
L C : 0 1 :083(376) [0603] Nature **teaches** and demands that the common people —
L C : 0 1 :113(380) [0613] Now, he amply **teaches** what we should do if we wish to
L C : 0 1 :186(390) [0633] What this commandment **teaches**, then, is that no one
L C : 0 1 :246(398) [0651] forgiveness and mercy, as the Lord's Prayer **teaches**.
L C : 0 1 :252(399) [0653] as King Solomon **teaches** in Prov. 19:17, "He who is kind
L C : 0 1 :279(402) [0661] Christ **teaches** further: "If he does not listen, take one or
L C : 0 1 :287(403) [0663] Even nature **teaches** the same thing in our own bodies, as
L C : 0 1 :325(409) [0675] David particularly **teaches** it throughout the Psalter, as
L C : 0 2 :001(411) [0679] from God; in brief, it **teaches** us to know him perfectly.
L C : 0 3 :008(421) [0699] Second Commandment **teaches**, is to call upon God in
L C : 0 3 :058(428) [0713] in abundance, as Christ **teaches**, "Seek first the kingdom
L C : 0 3 :096(433) [0725] grace, because he has promised it, as the Gospel **teaches**.
E P : 0 5 :003(478) [0801] a divine doctrine which **teaches** what is right and
E P : 0 5 :005(478) [0801] the kind of doctrine that **teaches** what a man who has not
E P : 1 1 :016(497) [0837] maintain that if anybody **teaches** the doctrine of the
E P : 1 2 :022(499) [0841] God the Holy Spirit **teaches** people and creates in them
E P : 1 2 :029(500) [0843] now, which believes, **teaches**, and confesses that there is
S D : 0 1 :007(510) [0861] Augsburg Confession **teaches**, that God is not the
S D : 0 1 :025(512) [0867] because God's Word **teaches** that man's corrupted nature
S D : 0 2 :009(522) [0883] Spirit enlightens and **teaches** them they consider it all
S D : 0 2 :010(522) [0885] Moreover, Scripture **teaches** that the man who is "in sin"
S D : 0 2 :031(527) [0893] The Apology **teaches** as follows concerning free will: "We
S D : 0 3 :030(544) [0925] grace of God, Scripture **teaches** that the righteousness of
S D : 0 3 :042(547) [0931] Apology states, "James **teaches** correctly when he denies
S D : 0 4 :033(556) [0947] in Article XX: "Peter **teaches** why we should do good
S D : 0 5 :019(561) [0957] alone, strictly speaking, **teaches** and commands faith in
S D : 0 5 :019(561) [0957] alone, strictly speaking, **teaches** about saving faith in
S D : 0 5 :020(561) [0959] is that doctrine which **teaches** what a man should believe
S D : 0 6 :022(567) [0969] But the Gospel **teaches** us that our spiritual sacrifices are
S D : 0 7 :009(570) [0975] on the other hand, **teaches** on the basis of God's Word
S D : 0 7 :060(580) [0993] But St. Paul **teaches** expressly that not only godly, pious,
S D : 0 8 :045(600) [1031] plain Christian Creed **teaches** us that the Son of God,
S D : 1 1 :033(622) [1073] against sin as Paul **teaches** from the first to the eighth
S D : 1 1 :050(624) [1079] At the same time it **teaches** us what the true church is,
S D : 1 2 :030(635) [1101] God the Holy Spirit **teaches** men the saving knowledge of

Teaching (254), Teachings (27)

P R : P R :005(004) [0009] been preserved in the **teaching** of God's Word and in
P R : P R :005(004) [0009] insinuated perverted **teachings** into the churches in which
P R : P R :019(009) [0017] well as other adulterated **teaching** under the words of this
P R : P R :019(009) [0017] false and adulterated **teaching** that might be concealed
P R : P R :022(011) [0019] inasmuch as such **teachings** are contrary to the expressed
P R : P R :023(012) [0021] therein, so that the pure **teaching** and confession of the
A G : P R :008(025) [0039] pastors' and preachers' **teaching** and of our own faith,
A G : 1 5 :003(037) [0049] to the Gospel and the **teaching** about faith in Christ.
A G : 1 8 :004(039) [0051] may be evident that this **teaching** is no novelty, the clear
A G : 2 0 :007(042) [0053] This **teaching** may offer a little more comfort than the
A G : 2 0 :007(042) [0053] more comfort than the **teaching** that we are to rely solely
A G : 2 0 :008(042) [0053] Since the **teaching** about faith, which is the chief article in
A G : 2 0 :009(042) [0053] We begin by **teaching** that our works cannot reconcile us
A G : 2 0 :011(042) [0055] This **teaching** about faith is plainly and clearly treated by
A G : 2 0 :015(043) [0055] Although this **teaching** is held in great contempt among
A G : 2 0 :035(046) [0057] Consequently this **teaching** concerning faith is not to be
A G : 2 0 :035(046) [0057] rather to be praised for **teaching** that good works are to
A G : 0 0 :001(047) [0059] and posterity any other **teaching** than that which agrees
A G : 0 0 :001(047) [0059] Since this **teaching** is grounded clearly on the Holy
A G : 0 0 :001(047) [0059] (in so far as the latter's **teaching** is reflected in the
A G : 0 0 :001(048) [0059] our churches as if our **teaching** were heretical, act in an
A G : 2 3 :022(055) [0063] apostle Paul calls the **teaching** that forbids marriage a
A G : 2 3 :023(055) [0063] as to maintain such a **teaching** with the shedding of
A G : 0 1 :007(056) [0065] about other false **teachings** concerning the sacrament.
A G : 2 4 :029(059) [0067] contrary to this **teaching** is the misuse of the Mass by
A G : 2 6 :004(064) [0071] grace of Christ and the **teaching** concerning faith are
A G : 2 6 :006(064) [0071] This **teaching** has been almost completely extinguished by
A G : 2 6 :015(066) [0073] all wholesome Christian **teachings** about more important
A G : 2 6 :020(067) [0073] Gospel demands that the **teaching** about faith should and
A G : 2 6 :020(067) [0073] in the church, but this **teaching** cannot be understood if it
A G : 2 6 :022(067) [0073] do they worship me, **teaching** as doctrines the precepts of
A G : 2 7 :036(076) [0081] do they worship me, **teaching** as doctrines the precepts of
A G : 2 8 :008(082) [0085] and exercised only by **teaching** and preaching the Word
A G : 2 8 :037(086) [0089] beyond calculation while **teaching** concerning faith and
A G : 2 8 :051(089) [0091] necessary to preserve the **teaching** of Christian liberty in
A G : 0 0 :005(095) [0095] any new and godless **teaching** from creeping into our
A G : 0 0 :006(095) [0095] of our confession and the **teaching** of our preachers.
A L : 0 5 :001(031) [0045] faith, the ministry of **teaching** the Gospel and
A L : 0 7 :002(032) [0047] to agree concerning the **teaching** of the Gospel and the
A L : 1 5 :003(037) [0049] are opposed to the Gospel and the **teaching** about faith.
A L : 2 0 :007(041) [0053] This **teaching** is more tolerable than the former one, and
A L : 2 0 :007(042) [0053] it can afford more consolation than their old **teaching**.
A L : 2 0 :008(042) [0053] Inasmuch, then, as the **teaching** about faith which ought
A L : 2 0 :008(042) [0053] ought to be the chief **teaching** in the church, has so long
A L : 2 0 :008(042) [0053] sermons while only the **teaching** about works has been
A L : 2 0 :009(042) [0053] We begin by **teaching** that our works cannot reconcile
A L : 2 0 :011(042) [0055] This **teaching** concerning faith is everywhere treated in
A L : 2 0 :015(043) [0055] Although this **teaching** is despised by inexperienced men,
A L : 2 0 :017(043) [0055] This whole **teaching** is to be referred to that conflict of
A L : 2 0 :018(043) [0055] have bad judgment concerning this **teaching**.
A L : 2 0 :022(044) [0055] of and to restore this **teaching** concerning faith in Christ
A L : 2 0 :035(046) [0057] readily be seen that this **teaching** is not to be charged with
A L : 0 0 :001(047) [0059] This is about the sum of our **teaching**.
A L : 0 0 :004(049) [0059] that the forms of **teaching** and of ceremonies observed
A L : 2 6 :006(064) [0071] This **teaching** of Paul has been almost wholly smothered
A L : 2 6 :015(066) [0073] for the more profitable **teachings** concerning faith, the
A L : 2 6 :016(066) [0073] to devote their attention to a better kind of **teaching**.
A L : 2 6 :020(067) [0073] in the church on the **teaching** concerning grace and the
A L : 2 7 :017(073) [0077] in order that our **teaching** on this topic may better be
A L : 2 8 :008(082) [0085] is exercised only by **teaching** or preaching the Gospel and
A L : 2 8 :037(086) [0089] calculation, while the **teaching** concerning faith and the
A P : P R :018(099) [0103] points our Confession's **teaching** is better than that which
A P : 0 1 :001(100) [0103] asserts our faith and **teaching** that there is one undivided
A P : 0 2 :002(100) [0105] all good men that our **teaching** on this point is not
A P : 0 2 :032(104) [0113] to light important **teachings** of the Scriptures and the
A P : 0 2 :050(106) [0119] our preachers have stressed this in their **teaching**.
A P : 0 2 :050(106) [0119] the Holy Scripture and the **teachings** of the holy Fathers.
A P : 0 4 :001(107) [0119] they condemn us for **teaching** that men do not receive the
A P : 0 4 :012(109) [0123] is there between philosophy and the **teaching** of Christ?
A P : 0 4 :013(109) [0123] people ridicule us for **teaching** that men ought to seek
A P : 0 4 :015(109) [0123] which compare certain **teachings** of Christ with the
A P : 0 4 :015(109) [0123] of Christ with the **teachings** of Socrates, Zeno, and
A P : 0 4 :016(109) [0123] So if we accept this **teaching** of the opponents that we
A P : 0 4 :020(110) [0125] they hear, beyond the **teaching** of the law, the Gospel of
A P : 0 4 :022(110) [0127] has given laws, learning, **teaching**, governments, and
A P : 0 4 :047(113) [0133] there is not a syllable in the **teaching** of our opponents.
A P : 0 4 :047(113) [0133] our opponents for **teaching** the righteousness of the law
A P : 0 4 :081(118) [0145] completely and do away with the whole **teaching** of faith?
A P : 0 4 :188(133) [0173] Later we add the **teaching** of the law.
A P : 0 4 :208(135) [0177] but because they were **teaching** in these places and thus
A P : 0 4 :230(139) [0183] know how repulsive this **teaching** is to the judgment of
A P : 0 4 :230(139) [0183] and law and that the **teaching** of the law about love is
A P : 0 4 :245(142) [0189] How much better is James's **teaching**!
A P : 0 4 :260(145) [0195] We must always keep this important **teaching** in view.
A P : 0 4 :266(146) [0197] the very opposite of the **teaching** of grace and faith, while
A P : 0 4 :267(146) [0197] penitence he is **teaching** not only about works but about
A P : 0 4 :269(147) [0197] The **teaching** of the law is certainly not intended to
A P : 0 4 :274(148) [0199] It is true that in **teaching** penitence works are required,
A P : 0 4 :277(149) [0199] that without Christ the **teaching** of the law has no value.
A P : 0 4 :287(150) [0203] reason or from the **teaching** of the law rather than the
A P : 0 4 :299(153) [0205] In this **teaching**, faithful consciences see the most
A P : 0 4 :300(153) [0205] Our opponents' **teaching** does not mention how we must
A P : 0 4 :302(154) [0205] How confused and unclear their **teaching** is!
A P : 0 4 :303(154) [0205] easily understand our **teaching** and that it will bring godly
A P : 0 4 :314(156) [0207] to refute the opponents' **teaching** that we come to God by
A P : 0 4 :316(156) [0209] we reject our opponents' **teaching** on the merit of
A P : 0 4 :319(156) [0209] Second, the opponents' **teaching** leaves consciences in
A P : 0 4 :325(157) [0211] no one think that we are **teaching** anything new in this
A P : 0 4 :353(161) [0217] can understand this **teaching** better than what our
A P : 0 4 :377(165) [0223] This **teaching** about the righteousness of faith dare not be
A P : 0 4 :377(165) [0223] justification is nothing more than the **teaching** of the law.
A P : 0 4 :377(165) [0223] to the Gospel and the **teaching** of the promise given for
A P : 0 4 :389(166) [0225] their faith and for **teaching** and comforting their
A P : 0 4 :391(167) [0225] obvious falsehood, this **teaching** has spawned many
A P : 0 4 :393(167) [0225] traditions and the **teaching** of works would obscure the
A P : 0 4 :396(167) [0225] by the crowd of adversaries who condemn our **teaching**.
A P : 0 7 :005(169) [0227] outward marks, the pure **teaching** of the Gospel and the
A P : 0 7 :007(169) [0229] the church this way, **teaching** us to believe that there is a
A P : 0 7 :008(169) [0229] of the same Gospel or **teaching** and of the same Holy
A P : 0 7 :020(171) [0233] add its marks, the pure **teaching** of the Gospel and the
A P : 0 7 :030(173) [0237] to agree concerning the **teaching** of the Gospel and the
A P : 1 1 :001(180) [0249] later when we explain our whole **teaching** on penitence.
A P : 1 1 :002(180) [0249] consciences have received consolation from our **teaching**.
A P : 1 1 :002(180) [0249] This **teaching** has encouraged many devout minds, and in
A P : 1 1 :002(180) [0249] had been smothered by **teachings** about works, since the
A P : 1 1 :010(182) [0253] This **teaching** has driven many devout minds to hopeless
A P : 1 1 :010(182) [0253] In our opponents' **teaching** on penitence there are other
A P : 1 2 :010(184) [0255] Our opponents' whole **teaching** on the questions we have
A P : 1 2 :016(184) [0257] The following **teachings** are clearly false and foreign to
A P : 1 2 :034(186) [0261] Taken alone, this is the **teaching** of the law, not of the
A P : 1 2 :067(191) [0271] they condemn this **teaching** that we obtain the forgiveness
A P : 1 2 :067(191) [0271] and demand that this **teaching** be wiped out by force and
A P : 1 2 :075(193) [0273] This is nothing but the **teaching** of the law, the
A P : 1 2 :085(194) [0277] This is a **teaching** of the law and not of the Gospel, to
A P : 1 2 :090(195) [0279] and decide whether our **teaching** or our opponents'
A P : 1 2 :090(195) [0279] or our opponents' **teaching** is more godly and salutary for
A P : 1 2 :098(197) [0281] of preserving the true **teaching** about contrition and
A P : 1 2 :172(209) [0305] satisfactions contrary to the clear **teaching** of the Gospel.
A P : 1 2 :173(209) [0305] works, why cite the clear **teaching** of the Gospel?
A P : 1 2 :173(210) [0305] they say that the clear **teaching** of the Gospel compels us
A P : 1 2 :174(210) [0307] of the Gospel, the **teaching** of the Gospel, obedience to
A P : 1 2 :178(211) [0307] men will compare our **teaching** with the complicated
A P : 1 3 :002(211) [0309] if, for purposes of **teaching**, the enumeration varies,
A P : 1 4 :003(214) [0315] those who persecute this **teaching**, for we know that our

Continued ▶

AP : 1 5 :006(215) [0317] This is definitely the **teaching** of the Gospel, for Paul
AP : 1 5 :034(220) [0325] example the apostles compel us to oppose this **teaching**.
AP : 1 5 :050(222) [0329] condemn us for **teaching** that human traditions do not
AP : 1 5 :051(222) [0329] more hostile to the true **teaching** of the Gospel because of
AP : 1 6 :006(223) [0331] redress and by other **teachings** that were not suited to
AP : 1 8 :009(226) [0337] between philosophical **teaching** and the teaching of the
AP : 1 8 :009(226) [0337] teaching and the **teaching** of the Holy Spirit; and it points
AP : 1 8 :010(226) [0337] not our invention but the clear **teaching** of the Scriptures.
AP : 2 1 :040(235) [0355] distinguish between their **teachings** and obvious abuses.
AP : 2 1 :040(235) [0355] would admit that the **teachings** of the scholastics and
AP : 2 1 :041(235) [0355] and canonists and was **teaching** things profitable for
AP : 2 1 :043(235) [0357] with their godless **teachings** and overthrow the whole
AP : 2 3 :040(244) [0375] more time for praying, **teaching**, and serving and is not so
AP : 2 3 :040(245) [0375] that is, to make room for hearing or **teaching** the Gospel.
AP : 2 4 :048(258) [0401] This **teaching** really consoles consciences.
AP : 2 4 :048(258) [0401] They add to it the **teaching** of the good works which God
AP : 2 4 :050(259) [0401] the clergy have ever understood our opponents' **teaching**.
AP : 2 4 :051(259) [0401] practical, and clear **teaching**, the godly use of the
AP : 2 4 :057(260) [0405] of faith, it corrupts the **teaching** of both the Old and the
AP : 2 4 :065(261) [0407] Patristic **Teaching** on Sacrifice
AP : 2 7 :001(268) [0419] them the nature of his **teaching** can be well understood.
AP : 2 7 :013(271) [0423] witness: this is truly the **teaching** of the Gospel that we
AP : 2 7 :021(272) [0427] to have more leisure for **teaching** and other pious duties,
AP : 2 7 :055(278) [0439] with the purpose of **teaching** the listeners and, in the
AP : 2 7 :055(278) [0439] and, in the process of **teaching**, prompting some of them
AP : 2 7 :062(280) [0441] to remind them of the **teaching** of faith and immortality
AP : 2 8 :007(282) [0445] we must keep this **teaching**, that we receive forgiveness of
AP : 2 8 :007(282) [0445] We must also keep the **teaching** that human traditions are
AP : 2 8 :019(284) [0449] kind of comfort and **teaching**, and they misapply it to
AP : 2 8 :022(284) [0451] which have arisen under the pretext of our **teaching**.
S 1 : PR :004(289) [0455] they dare to cite my writings and **teachings** against me.
S 2 : 0 2 :002(293) [0463] do they worship me, **teaching** as doctrines the precepts of
S 2 : 0 4 :014(301) [0475] When the **teaching** of the pope is distinguished from that
S 2 : 0 4 :014(301) [0475] that, at its best, the **teaching** of the pope has been taken
S 2 : 0 4 :014(301) [0475] pagan law and is a **teaching** concerning secular
S 2 : 0 4 :014(301) [0475] In keeping with such **teaching**, instructions are given
S 3 : 0 1 :011(303) [0479] If such **teachings** were true, Christ would have died in
S 3 : 0 3 :010(305) [0481] did not have the right **teaching** concerning original sin
S 3 : 0 3 :012(305) [0483] In their **teaching** of penance the sophists thus instructed
S 3 : 0 3 :041(309) [0491] It is a **teaching** from heaven, revealed in the Gospel, and
S 3 : 1 5 :001(316) [0501] do they worship me, **teaching** as doctrines the precepts of
TR : 0 0 :045(328) [0517] They have obscured the **teaching** concerning sin and have
TR : 0 0 :048(328) [0519] what darkness has the **teaching** about vows covered the
TR : 0 0 :048(328) [0519] have utterly extinguished the **teaching** concerning faith.
TR : 0 0 :051(329) [0519] able to remove impious **teachings** and impious forms of
TR : 0 0 :052(329) [0519] and that the true **teaching** must be embraced for the glory
SC : PR :001(338) [0533] and simple catechism or statement of Christian **teaching**.
SC : PR :002(338) [0533] whatever of Christian **teaching**, and unfortunately many
SC : PR :002(338) [0533] pastors are quite incompetent and unfitted for **teaching**.
SC : PR :005(338) [0533] the slightest interest in **teaching** the people the Lord's
SC : PR :008(339) [0533] to use the same form in **teaching** the Lord's Prayer, the
SC : PR :009(339) [0535] But when you are **teaching** the young, adhere to a fixed
SC : PR :010(339) [0535] Begin by **teaching** them the Ten Commandments, the
SC : 0 9 :003(354) [0561] labor in preaching and **teaching**; for the scripture says,
LC : PR :001(358) [0567] and despise both their office and this **teaching** itself.
LC : PR :005(359) [0567] as a simple, silly **teaching** which they can absorb and
LC : PR :016(361) [0573] and he always keeps on **teaching** this one thing without
LC : PR :016(361) [0573] in one hour what God himself cannot finish **teaching**!
LC : PR :016(361) [0573] Actually, he is busy **teaching** it from the beginning of the
LC : SP :024(364) [0579] will learn and retain this **teaching** from sermons alone.
LC : 0 1 :069(374) [0601] unbridled men whom no **teaching** or punishment can
LC : 0 1 :113(380) [0613] than God, there can also be no better **teaching** than his.
LC : 0 1 :172(388) [0629] time, and expense in **teaching** and educating our children
LC : 0 1 :197(392) [0637] For in this **teaching** the ordinary Christian life would be
LC : 0 1 :263(400) [0655] with their corrupt **teaching** and blasphemy, to false
LC : 0 1 :284(403) [0661] censure the pope and his **teaching**, which is publicly set
LC : 0 1 :311(407) [0669] a summary of divine **teaching** on what we are to do to
LC : 0 1 :333(411) [0677] them above all other **teachings** as the greatest treasure
LC : 0 2 :006(411) [0679] most clear and simple for **teaching** to children, we shall
LC : 0 2 :044(416) [0689] evil spirits there were, **teaching** us to obtain grace and be
LC : 0 2 :067(419) [0697] Creed is a very different **teaching** from the Ten
LC : 0 2 :070(420) [0697] more, relating these **teachings** of the Catechism all that
LC : 0 3 :039(425) [0709] is: When both our **teaching** and our life are godly and
LC : 0 4 :001(436) [0733] the three chief parts of our common Christian **teaching**.
LC : 0 5 :086(456) [0773] these and other **teachings** unless we train the people who
LC : 0 6 :021(459) [0000] For our **teaching**, as I have said, is this: If anybody does
EP : 0 0 :000(463) [0775] the Comprehensive Summary of our Christian **Teaching**
EP : RN :003(465) [0777] reject all heresies and **teachings** which have been
EP : RN :008(465) [0779] and how contrary **teachings** were rejected and
EP : 0 1 :010(467) [0781] *Rejection of the Contrary False* ***Teaching***
EP : 0 1 :011(467) [0781] reject and condemn the **teaching** that original sin is only a
EP : 0 1 :012(467) [0781] 2. Likewise the **teaching** that evil desires are not sin but
EP : 0 1 :012(467) [0783] of human nature, or the **teaching** that the cited defect and
EP : 0 1 :014(467) [0783] 4. Likewise the **teaching** that original sin is a slight,
EP : 0 1 :019(468) [0783] a Manichaean error the **teaching** that original sin is
EP : 0 2 :001(470) [0787] *The Pure* ***Teaching*** *concerning this Article on the Basis of*
EP : 0 2 :002(470) [0787] It is our **teaching**, faith, and confession that in spiritual
EP : 0 2 :011(471) [0789] 4. Likewise the **teaching** that while before his conversion
EP : 0 3 :001(473) [0791] mutually contradictory **teachings** have invaded some
EP : 0 4 :019(477) [0801] reject and condemn the **teaching** that faith and the
EP : 0 5 :006(478) [0803] personally in his **teaching** ministry and which his apostles
EP : 0 5 :011(479) [0805] is again changed into a **teaching** of the law, the merit of
EP : 0 6 :001(480) [0805] *The Correct Christian* ***Teaching*** *in this Controversy*
EP : 0 6 :008(481) [0807] true piety the erroneous **teaching** that the law is not to be
EP : 0 7 :015(483) [0813] also been the unanimous **teaching** of the leading Church
EP : 0 7 :025(484) [0815] 4. The **teaching** that the words of Christ's testament are
EP : 0 7 :042(486) [0817] in order to make our **teaching** obnoxious to their hearers.
EP : 0 8 :003(487) [0819] *The Pure* ***Teaching*** *of the Christian Church concerning*
EP : 1 0 :003(493) [0829] do they worship me, **teaching** as doctrines the precepts of
EP : 1 0 :008(494) [0831] and contrary to God's Word the following **teachings**:
EP : 1 1 :016(497) [0837] their self-will, he is not **teaching** the doctrine according to
EP : 1 1 :022(497) [0837] been discussing and **teaching** in mutually contradictory
SD : PR :001(501) [0847] of the Almighty, the **teaching** concerning the chief articles
SD : PR :003(501) [0847] forth the faith and the **teaching** of the Evangelical
SD : PR :003(504) [0851] which all teachers and **teachings** are to be judged and
SD : 0 2 :006(521) [0883] the following as our **teaching**, belief, and confession:
SD : 0 2 :009(521) [0883] a God, as well as of the **teaching** of the law
SD : 0 2 :029(527) [0893] reason we begin our **teaching** with faith, through which
SD : 0 2 :067(534) [0907] according to the **teaching** of St. Paul, "all who have been
SD : 0 2 :077(536) [0911] 4. The **teaching** of the synergists, who maintain that in
SD : 0 2 :079(536) [0911] Likewise we reject the **teachings** of the papists and the
SD : 0 3 :008(540) [0919] his grace, we affirm our **teaching**, belief, and confession
SD : 0 3 :059(550) [0937] to the Word of God, the **teaching** of the prophets and
SD : 0 4 :006(552) [0939] we shall state our **teaching**, belief, and confession.
SD : 0 5 :004(558) [0953] by it the entire **teaching** of Christ, our Lord, which in his
SD : 0 5 :004(559) [0953] Paul calls his entire **teaching** "Gospel" (Acts 20:24) and
SD : 0 5 :027(563) [0961] more make the Gospel a **teaching** of law, as happened in
SD : 0 5 :027(563) [0961] as referring to the entire **teaching**, a usage that we find
SD : 0 6 :009(565) [0965] life not only the daily **teaching** and admonition, warning
SD : 0 6 :014(566) [0967] inspired by God and profitable for **teaching**, for reproof."
SD : 0 6 :020(567) [0969] furthermore, require the **teaching** of the law so that they
SD : 0 6 :021(567) [0969] furthermore, require the **teaching** of the law in connection
SD : 0 7 :001(569) [0971] full agreement with the **teaching** of the Sacramentarians
SD : 0 7 :008(570) [0975] But the **teaching** that the body of Christ is essentially
SD : 0 7 :114(589) [1011] and the contrary **teaching** that in the Supper the body of
SD : 0 7 :115(589) [1011] 3. Likewise, the **teaching** that bread and wine in the
SD : 0 7 :119(590) [1013] 8. Likewise, the **teaching** that because of his bodily
SD : 0 7 :125(591) [1015] 14. Likewise, the **teaching** that even true believers who
SD : 0 7 :126(591) [1015] 15. Likewise, the **teaching** that the elements (the visible
SD : 0 8 :004(592) [1017] load down Dr. Luther's **teaching**, as well as that of those
SD : 0 8 :005(592) [1017] grace, our unanimous **teaching**, belief, and confession are
SD : 1 0 :008(612) [1055] do they worship me, **teaching** for doctrines the precepts
SD : 1 1 :002(616) [1063] If the **teaching** of this article is set forth out of the divine
SD : 1 1 :003(616) [1063] not by-pass or reject a **teaching** of the divine Word
SD : 1 1 :003(616) [1063] total and content of the **teaching** on this article consists
SD : 1 1 :012(618) [1067] or the right use of the **teaching** of God's eternal
SD : 1 1 :024(619) [1069] all this is included in the **teaching** of the eternal election
SD : 1 1 :025(620) [1071] the salutary use of the **teaching** of God's foreknowledge to
SD : 1 1 :025(620) [1071] can and should comfort themselves with this **teaching**?
SD : 1 1 :051(625) [1079] it is possible to use the **teaching** in this article in a
SD : 1 1 :071(627) [1085] According to Christ's **teaching** they are to desist from sin,
SD : 1 1 :087(631) [1091] This **teaching** and explanation of the eternal and saving
SD : 1 1 :091(631) [1093] anyone so sets forth this **teaching** concerning God's
SD : 1 1 :091(631) [1093] clearly evident that this **teaching** is not being set forth
SD : 1 2 :009(633) [1097] erroneous and heretical **teaching** of the Anabaptists which
SD : 1 2 :011(634) [1099] and reject the entire **teaching** of original sin and all that
SD : 1 2 :040(636) [1103] and none other, is our **teaching**, belief, and confession in

Teacher (9), Teachers (76)

PR : PR :005(004) [0009] it happened that false **teachers** insinuated perverted
PR : PR :005(004) [0009] of God, so such false **teachers** were also inflicted on our
PR : PR :013(007) [0013] for the promotion of concord among Christian **teachers**.
PR : PR :021(010) [0019] been used univocally by **teachers** in the schools and the
PR : PR :021(011) [0019] On the contrary, as the **teachers** of the ancient church put
AG : 2 0 :001(041) [0053] Our **teachers** have been falsely accused of forbidding good
AG : 2 6 :018(066) [0073] Our **teachers** have not taught concerning these matters
AG : 2 6 :030(068) [0075] Although our **teachers** are, like Jovinian, accused of
AG : 2 7 :017(073) [0077] and understand what our **teachers** teach and preach.
AG : 2 7 :036(076) [0081] monastic vows, our **teachers** offer still more reasons why
AG : 2 8 :004(081) [0085] On this account our **teachers** have been compelled, for
AG : 2 8 :005(081) [0085] Our **teachers** assert that according to the Gospel the
AG : 2 8 :018(083) [0085] Thus our **teachers** distinguish the two authorities and the
AG : 2 8 :034(086) [0087] this question our **teachers** assert that bishops do not have
AG : 2 8 :053(090) [0091] To this our **teachers** reply that bishops or pastors may
AL : 2 0 :008(042) [0053] in the church), our **teachers** have instructed our churches
AL : 2 0 :027(045) [0057] Our **teachers** teach in addition that it is necessary to do
AL : 0 0 :001(047) [0059] who insist that our **teachers** are to be regarded as heretics
AL : 2 4 :024(058) [0067] these opinions our **teachers** have warned that they depart
AL : 2 5 :006(062) [0069] concede to us that our **teachers** have shed light on the
AL : 2 6 :018(066) [0073] Our **teachers**, therefore, must not be looked upon as
AL : 2 6 :021(067) [0073] Accordingly our **teachers** have taught that we cannot
AL : 2 6 :022(067) [0073] Our **teachers** add testimonies from the Scriptures.
AL : 2 6 :030(068) [0075] charge that our **teachers**, like Jovinian, forbid discipline
AL : 2 6 :030(068) [0075] in the writings of our **teachers**, for they have always
AL : 2 7 :036(076) [0081] from their vows, our **teachers** offer still another reason to
AL : 2 8 :004(081) [0085] Accordingly our **teachers** have been compelled, for the
AL : 2 8 :005(081) [0085] Our **teachers** hold that according to the Gospel the power
AL : 2 8 :018(083) [0085] In this way our **teachers** distinguish the functions of the
AL : 2 8 :034(086) [0087] this question our **teachers** assert, as has been pointed out
AL : 2 8 :053(090) [0091] To this our **teachers** reply that it is lawful for bishops or
AP : 0 4 :072(117) [0141] grammar produces the **teachers** of all the arts since it
AP : 0 4 :190(133) [0175] Augustine, and other **teachers** of the church are holy
AP : 0 4 :224(138) [0181] as Paul indicates, they began to dislike good **teachers**.
AP : 0 4 :394(167) [0225] of faith, and such **teachers** there will always be.
AP : 0 7 :022(172) [0235] warning that there will be ungodly **teachers** and wolves.
AP : 0 7 :022(172) [0235] wolves and ungodly **teachers** may run rampant in the
AP : 0 7 :048(177) [0243] should forsake wicked **teachers** because they no longer
AP : 1 2 :130(202) [0291] issues but do not hear **teachers** capable of setting their
AP : 2 1 :004(229) [0343] to save men, and giving **teachers** and other gifts to the
TR : 0 0 :026(324) [0511] God gives his gifts, apostles, prophets, pastors, **teachers**.
TR : 0 0 :041(328) [0517] that ungodly **teachers** should be shunned and execrated
TR : 0 0 :067(331) [0523] enumerates pastors and **teachers** among the gifts
TR : 0 0 :079(333) [0527] and do not ordain godly **teachers** but rather support the
SC : PR :007(339) [0533] are easily confused if a **teacher** employs one form now
SC : 0 9 :002(354) [0561] hospitable, an apt **teacher**, no drunkard, not violent but
SC : 0 9 :003(354) [0561] Duties Christians Owe Their **Teachers** and Pastors
LC : 0 1 :065(373) [0599] has tormented so many **teachers**: why swearing is
LC : 0 1 :113(380) [0613] is no greater or better **teacher** to be found than God,
LC : 0 1 :130(383) [0619] said, "God, parents, and **teachers** can never be sufficiently
LC : 0 3 :047(426) [0709] is full of sects and false **teachers**, all of whom wear the
EP : RN :001(464) [0777] which all doctrines and **teachers** alike must be appraised
EP : RN :002(464) [0777] of ancient and modern **teachers**, whatever their names,
EP : RN :003(465) [0777] their lifetime — false **teachers** and heretics invaded the
EP : 0 2 :016(472) [0789] ancient and modern **teachers** have used expressions such
EP : 0 5 :007(478) [0803] Moses is spoken of as a **teacher** of the law in contrast to
EP : 0 7 :001(481) [0807] The Zwinglian **teachers** cannot be numbered among the

Continued ▶

SD : PR :004(502) [0847] broke out, and orthodox **teachers** and hearers pledged
SD : PR :003(504) [0851] according to which all **teachers** and teachings are to be
SD : PR :005(504) [0853] Christian bishops and **teachers** to appeal and confess
SD : 0 1 :043(516) [0873] all the ancient orthodox **teachers** held that according to
SD : 0 1 :055(518) [0877] with all dependable **teachers**, deliberately and seriously
SD : 0 1 :056(518) [0877] by any other dependable **teacher** of our pure Evangelical
SD : 0 1 :057(518) [0877] of the church's **teachers**, and never questioned by any
SD : 0 2 :005(520) [0881] of these parties the pure **teachers** of the Augsburg
SD : 0 2 :016(523) [0887] Unless God himself is our **teacher**, we cannot study and
SD : 0 3 :004(539) [0917] both parties the other **teachers** of the Augsburg
SD : 0 4 :036(557) [0949] not a few orthodox **teachers** used these and similar
SD : 0 7 :034(575) [0983] Dr. Luther, as the chief **teacher** of the Augsburg
SD : 0 7 :037(575) [0985] Many prominent ancient **teachers**, like Justin, Cyprian,
SD : 0 7 :041(576) [0985] as the most eminent **teacher** of the churches which adhere
SD : 0 7 :043(576) [0987] whom, as our unique **teacher**, the earnest command has
SD : 0 7 :058(580) [0993] Luther and other pure **teachers** of the Augsburg
SD : 0 7 :060(580) [0995] Christian fathers and **teachers** of the church have
SD : 0 7 :066(581) [0995] all the ancient Christian **teachers** and the entire holy
SD : 0 7 :073(583) [0999] dissension among some **teachers** of the Augsburg
SD : 0 8 :018(594) [1021] communion, the ancient **teachers** of the church, both
SD : 0 8 :022(595) [1023] this reason the ancient **teachers** of the church have
SD : 0 8 :025(596) [1023] years old, among the **teachers**, again in the garden when
SD : 0 9 :001(610) [1051] as among the ancient **teachers** of the Christian church.
SD : 1 0 :018(614) [1059] confession of the chief **teachers** of the Augsburg
SD : 1 0 :022(615) [1061] that ungodly **teachers** should be shunned and execrated
SD : 1 2 :003(633) [1095] our churches and their **teachers** there are not two
SD : 1 2 :006(633) [1097] Jesus Christ has appointed us **teachers** and shepherds.
SD : 1 2 :008(633) [1097] scope, where the true **teachers** and confessors of the

Tear (4), Tearing (4), Tears (2)
AG : 2 8 :026(084) [0087] has given me for building up and not for **tearing** down."
AG : 2 8 :042(088) [0089] was given for building up and not for **tearing** down.
AL : 2 8 :026(084) [0087] the authority for building up and not for **tearing** down."
AL : 2 8 :042(088) [0089] was given for building up and not for **tearing** down?
AP : 1 2 :057(189) [0267] a sinner came to Christ in **tears**, which showed her
AP : 2 8 :005(281) [0445] here you should see the **tears** of the sufferers and hear the
S 2 : 0 3 :002(298) [0471] better to abandon them or **tear** them down rather than
LC : 0 3 :104(434) [0727] and the works of God, to **tear** us away from faith, hope,
LC : 0 4 :016(438) [0735] with God's ordinance and **tear** from it the precious
SD : 0 8 :083(607) [1045] devils had been unable to separate and **tear** them apart.

Technically (1)
AP : 0 4 :308(155) [0207] We must speak **technically** because of certain carping

Teeth (2)
AG : 2 7 :045(078) [0081] of casting them into their **teeth**, how many items could be
EP : 0 7 :042(486) [0817] Christ's flesh with one's **teeth** and digested it like other

Tell (21), Telling (5), Tells (4), Told (19)
AG : 2 5 :011(063) [0071] judge, in your prayer, **telling** him of your sins not with
AG : 2 7 :049(078) [0083] obscured when people are **told** that monks alone are in a
AL : 2 5 :004(062) [0069] terrified consciences, are **told** that God requires faith to
AL : 2 5 :011(063) [0071] **Tell** him of your sins not with your tongue but with the
AL : 2 7 :054(079) [0083] private life since they are **told** that this is prohibited by a
AP : 0 4 :061(115) [0137] knowledge, we must **tell** how faith comes into being.
AP : 0 4 :065(116) [0139] on the *Sentences* that **tells** how regeneration takes place.
AP : 0 4 :067(116) [0139] But we have other more **telling** arguments.
AP : 0 7 :042(177) [0243] a set time, since they **tell** them not to be bothered even if
AP : 0 7 :044(177) [0243] consciences, since they **tell** him not to be bothered even if
AP : 1 2 :006(183) [0255] step forward and **tell** us when the forgiveness of sins takes
AP : 1 2 :106(197) [0283] the head of a household, **telling** him to pay diligent
AP : 1 2 :139(203) [0295] in Holy Scripture are we **told** that only non-obligatory
AP : 2 1 :021(232) [0349] Our opponents **tell** us, first of all, to invoke the saints,
AP : 2 1 :022(232) [0349] They **tell** us, secondly, to trust in the merits of the saints.
AP : 2 4 :016(252) [0389] He **tells** the person making the distinctions to cut the
AP : 2 7 :002(269) [0419] prison, he sent for the guardian to **tell** him of his illness.
AP : 2 7 :019(272) [0425] doubt that if you had been **told** about this passage, you
AP : 2 8 :021(284) [0449] passage (Matt. 23:3), "Observe whatever they **tell** you."
S 2 : 0 2 :005(293) [0463] "Let the people be **told** openly that the Mass, as
S 3 : 0 2 :004(303) [0479] So the law must **tell** him that he neither has nor cares for
S 3 : 0 3 :019(306) [0485] his own works, and he was **told** that the more completely
SC : PR :011(339) [0535] receive your instructions, **tell** them that they deny Christ
SC : PR :020(340) [0537] notaries, etc., and **tell** them that God will inflict awful
SC : PR :020(340) [0537] governing authorities sin in this respect is beyond **telling**.
SC : PR :022(341) [0537] This can be done by **telling** them: It is to be feared that
SC : PR :024(341) [0539] to come, let them be, and **tell** them that those who do not
SC : 0 1 :016(343) [0541] God, and so we should not **tell** lies about our neighbor,
SC : 0 5 :022(350) [0553] for here and there I have not done what I was **told**.
SC : 0 6 :006(352) [0557] Answer: We are **told** in the words "for you" and "for the
LC : 0 1 :043(370) [0591] the past, search it out, and **tell** me, When men have
LC : 0 1 :100(378) [0609] Let me **tell** you this.
LC : 0 1 :231(396) [0647] But the latter should be **told** that in the eyes of God they
LC : 0 1 :276(402) [0659] sins against you, go and **tell** him his fault, between you
LC : 0 1 :277(402) [0661] to his neighbors, he would no doubt be **told**: "You fool!
LC : 0 1 :277(402) [0661] Why don't you **tell** him yourself?"
LC : 0 1 :314(407) [0671] faithfully does what she is **told**, that is regarded as
LC : 0 1 :326(409) [0675] Commandment we are **told** to fear God and not take his
LC : 0 2 :067(419) [0697] we ought to do; the Creed **tells** us what God does for us
LC : 0 3 :005(420) [0699] We were **told** in the Second Commandment, "You shall
LC : 0 5 :035(450) [0761] confidently believe that it is just as the words **tell** you.
LC : 0 5 :058(453) [0767] and unruly must be **told** to stay away, for they are not fit
LC : 0 6 :016(459) [0000] complete detail, we were **told** that the absolution was not
SD : 0 6 :011(565) [0965] The law indeed **tells** us that it is God's will and command
SD : 0 7 :078(584) [1001] command in which he has **told** us so to speak and to do
SD : 0 8 :075(606) [1043] The histories **tell** us that during the time of Emperor
SD : 1 1 :051(624) [1079] themselves" (Luke 7:30); "I **tell** you, none of those men
SD : 1 1 :065(627) [1085] and recall everything to you that I have **told** you.
SD : 1 1 :088(631) [1093] because of his call, she was **told**, 'The elder will serve the

Temper (1)
AG : 2 8 :074(093) [0093] to be so gracious as to **temper** these regulations inasmuch

Temperance (1), Temperances (1), Temperate (1), Tempered (1)
AP : 2 3 :048(246) [0377] We do not disparage **temperances** or continence; we have
SC : 0 5 :020(350) [0553] unfaithful, lazy, ill-**tempered**, or quarrelsome; whether
SC : 0 9 :002(354) [0561] married only once, **temperate**, sensible, dignified,
SD : 1 1 :073(628) [1087] all godliness, modesty, **temperance**, patience, and

Tempest (2)
LC : 0 3 :078(431) [0721] and our livelihood, from **tempest**, hail, fire, and flood;
LC : 0 3 :080(431) [0721] and war, why he sends **tempest** and hail to destroy crops

Temple (4), Temples (4)
AP : 0 7 :004(169) [0227] will "take his seat in the **temple** of God" (II Thess. 2:4),
AP : 2 4 :044(258) [0399] "the desolation of the **temples**" and the altars standing
TR : 0 0 :039(327) [0515] he takes his seat in the **temple** of God, proclaiming
EP : 1 2 :010(498) [0839] attend services in those **temples** where formerly papistic
SD : 0 3 :054(549) [0935] since all Christians are **temples** of God the Father, Son,
SD : 0 6 :002(564) [0963] have become his Spirit's **temple**, and hence are free, so
SD : 1 1 :073(628) [1087] faith as he dwells in his **temple**, and is not idle in them
SD : 1 2 :015(634) [1099] on a sermon in those **temples** in which the papistic Mass

Temporal (53)
PR : PR :024(013) [0023] we bear, over against the **temporal** and eternal welfare of
PR : PR :024(013) [0023] and the common welfare, both eternal and **temporal**.
AG : 1 6 :004(038) [0051] teach an outward and **temporal** but an inward and
AG : 2 7 :026(075) [0079] for the maintenance of **temporal** interests, how much
AG : 2 8 :001(081) [0083] confused the power of bishops with the **temporal** sword.
AG : 2 8 :004(081) [0085] between spiritual and **temporal** power, sword, and
AG : 2 8 :010(082) [0085] interfere at all with government or **temporal** authority.
AG : 2 8 :011(082) [0085] **Temporal** authority is concerned with matters altogether
AG : 2 8 :011(082) [0085] **Temporal** power does not protect the soul, but with the
AG : 2 8 :012(083) [0085] the spiritual and the **temporal**, are not to be mingled or
AG : 2 8 :013(083) [0085] kings, should not annul **temporal** laws or undermine
AG : 2 8 :013(083) [0085] make or prescribe to the **temporal** power laws concerning
AG : 2 8 :019(083) [0087] where bishops possess **temporal** authority and the sword,
AG : 2 8 :019(083) [0087] and kings for the **temporal** administration of their lands.
AP : 0 2 :008(101) [0107] despairing of his grace, trusting in **temporal** things, etc.
AP : 0 4 :128(125) [0157] is overwhelming us with **temporal** and eternal calamities?
AP : 0 4 :170(130) [0169] God and trusts in **temporal** things; in trouble it looks to
AP : 0 7 :023(172) [0235] power in both the **temporal** and the spiritual realm, both
AP : 0 7 :023(172) [0235] realm, both swords, the **temporal** and the spiritual.
AP : 1 2 :007(183) [0255] but only changes eternal punishments into **temporal** ones.
AP : 1 2 :022(185) [0257] to commute eternal to **temporal** punishments, to impose
AP : 1 2 :118(199) [0287] the eternal punishment to a **temporal** punishment.
AP : 1 2 :118(199) [0287] further that part of this **temporal** punishment is forgiven
AP : 1 2 :155(207) [0301] of sins there must be **temporal** punishments
S 1 : PR :012(290) [0459] there are countless **temporal** matters that need reform.
S 1 : PR :013(291) [0459] in the spiritual and **temporal** estates, we would find
S 2 : 0 1 :005(292) [0461] and earth and things **temporal** should be destroyed.
S 3 : 1 0 :002(314) [0497] They are **temporal** lords and princes who are unwilling to
TR : 0 0 :077(333) [0527] By divine right **temporal** magistrates are compelled to
LC : PR :017(361) [0573] make decisions in both spiritual and **temporal** matters.
LC : 0 1 :024(367) [0587] protection, peace, and all **temporal** and eternal blessings.
LC : 0 1 :047(371) [0593] of an inn, food, and bed (only for his **temporal** need).
LC : 0 1 :164(387) [0627] they contribute to their **temporal** and spiritual fathers,
LC : 0 1 :223(395) [0643] and our spouse, our **temporal** property is dearest to us.
LC : 0 1 :255(399) [0653] or husband, and our **temporal** property, we have one
LC : 0 1 :291(404) [0663] harm, in spiritual or in **temporal** matters, than this
LC : 0 2 :015(412) [0681] he gives all physical and **temporal** blessings — good
LC : 0 2 :026(413) [0685] God over and above the **temporal** goods mentioned
LC : 0 3 :055(427) [0713] a crust of bread or for a **temporal**, perishable blessing,
LC : 0 3 :058(428) [0713] us to suffer want in **temporal** things when he promises
LC : 0 5 :006(447) [0755] No, all **temporal** things remain as God has created and
SD : 0 1 :013(511) [0863] other bodily, spiritual, **temporal**, and eternal misery, the
SD : 0 1 :024(512) [0865] concerning the external, **temporal**, and civil affairs which
SD : 0 2 :002(520) [0881] things affecting this **temporal** life, nor what man can do in
SD : 0 2 :011(522) [0885] himself to regain **temporal** life, so little can a man who is
SD : 0 4 :008(552) [0941] will reward them with **temporal** blessings in this world,
SD : 0 5 :017(561) [0957] with God's wrath and **temporal** and eternal punishment.
SD : 0 5 :020(561) [0959] of God, to death, to **temporal** miseries, and to the
SD : 0 7 :068(582) [0997] with judgment (that is, **temporal** and eternal
SD : 0 8 :085(608) [1045] to the second, **temporal**, human birth, the eternal power
SD : 0 8 :085(608) [1045] also given to him — in a **temporal** way, however, and not
SD : 1 0 :019(614) [1059] They are **temporal** lords and princes who are unwilling to
SD : 1 1 :095(632) [1095] of God for the sake of **temporal** peace, tranquility, and

Tempt (2), Temptation (22), Temptations (12), Tempted (8), Tempts (3)
AG : 2 3 :004(051) [0061] says, "Because of the **temptation** to immorality, each man
AG : 2 7 :019(074) [0079] reads, "Because of the **temptation** to immorality, each
AL : 2 3 :004(051) [0061] says, "Because of the **temptation** to immorality each man
AL : 2 6 :033(069) [0075] plenty nor idleness may **tempt** him to sin, but not in
AP : 0 4 :167(130) [0169] Who is not **tempted** by lust?
AP : 0 4 :350(160) [0217] good works as well as **temptations** and dangers, so that
AP : 0 4 :350(161) [0217] our aroused conscience **tempts** us to despair when it
AP : 1 2 :042(187) [0261] in many ways, amid **temptations**, through the
AP : 1 2 :151(206) [0299] them so that in their **temptations** they may learn to seek
AP : 2 0 :008(227) [0341] them and the devil **tempts** them to despair unless they
AP : 2 3 :014(241) [0367] "Because of the **temptation** to immorality, each man
AP : 2 3 :017(241) [0369] "Because of the **temptation** of immorality, each man
AP : 2 3 :063(248) [0381] wife because of the **temptation** to immorality (I Cor. 7:2)
AP : 2 7 :051(278) [0437] "Because of the **temptation** to immorality, each man
SC : PR :027(341) [0539] labors, dangers and **temptations**, with little reward or
SC : 0 3 :017(347) [0549] *"And lead us not into **temptation**."*
SC : 0 3 :018(347) [0549] Answer: God **tempts** no one to sin, but we pray in this
SC : 0 3 :018(348) [0549] although we may be so **tempted**, we may finally prevail
LC : SP :014(363) [0577] and lead us not into **temptation**, but deliver us from evil.
LC : 0 3 :099(433) [0725] *"And lead us not into **temptation**."*
LC : 0 3 :100(433) [0727] not allow us to fall and yield to trials and **temptations**.
LC : 0 3 :101(433) [0727] **Temptation** (or, as the ancient Saxons called it,
LC : 0 3 :105(434) [0727] grievous perils and **temptations** which every Christian
LC : 0 3 :105(434) [0727] it is impossible to overcome even the least **temptation**.
LC : 0 3 :106(434) [0727] is "leading us not into **temptation**" when God gives us
LC : 0 3 :106(434) [0727] For no one can escape **temptations** and allurements as
LC : 0 3 :107(434) [0729] To feel **temptation**, therefore, is quite a different thing
LC : 0 3 :107(434) [0729] have more frequent and severe **temptations** than others.

Continued ▶

LC : 03 :107(434) [0729] Youths, for example, are **tempted** chiefly by the flesh;
LC : 03 :107(434) [0729] by the flesh; older people are **tempted** by the world.
LC : 03 :107(434) [0729] (that is, strong Christians) are **tempted** by the devil.
LC : 03 :108(434) [0729] by the mere feeling of **temptation** as long as it is contrary
LC : 03 :108(435) [0729] If we did not feel it, it could not be called a **temptation**.
LC : 03 :110(435) [0729] me to pray; let me not fall because of **temptation**."
LC : 03 :111(435) [0729] Then you will see the **temptation** cease and eventually
LC : 05 :023(449) [0757] many hindrances and **temptations** of the devil and the
LC : 05 :055(453) [0765] Answer: This also is my **temptation**, especially inherited
EP : 11 :013(496) [0835] in our greatest **temptations** and thus extinguish the
SD : 03 :035(545) [0927] in order to supply **tempted** consciences with abiding
SD : 04 :023(555) [0945] propositions deprive **tempted** and troubled consciences of
SD : 05 :001(558) [0951] in their greatest **temptations** against the terrors of the
SD : 07 :062(581) [0995] Christ, and hold to it in all difficulty and **temptation**.
SD : 10 :016(613) [1057] "Woe to the world for **temptations** to sin," and again,
SD : 11 :020(619) [1069] comfort and preserve them in tribulation and **temptation**.
SD : 11 :070(627) [1085] adversary is accustomed to **tempt** and vex pious hearts.
SD : 11 :074(628) [1087] fall into such grave **temptation** that they feel that they are
SD : 11 :090(631) [1093] gives sorrowing and **tempted** people the permanently

Ten (59), Tenth (4)
AG : 20 :002(041) [0053] Their writings on the **Ten** Commandments, and other
AG : 28 :033(086) [0087] — contrary, as they say, to the **Ten** Commandments.
AG : 28 :033(086) [0087] from and altered part of the **Ten** Commandments.
AL : 20 :002(041) [0053] Their publications on the **Ten** Commandments and others
AL : 28 :033(086) [0087] for it dispensed from one of the **Ten** Commandments!
AP : 07 :019(171) [0233] is like a net (Matt. 13:47) or like **ten** virgins (Matt. 25:1).
AP : 10 :001(179) [0247] They approve the **tenth** article, where we confess our
AP : 24 :015(251) [0389] For the last **ten** years our opponents have been publishing
AP : 27 :025(273) [0427] believe that they satisfy the **Ten** Commandments in such a
AP : 27 :032(274) [0431] discover that even with **ten** thousand soldiers he cannot
S1 : PR :012(290) [0459] to such an extent that **ten** councils and twenty diets would
S3 : 01 :002(302) [0477] which are forbidden in the **Ten** Commandments, such as
S3 : 08 :007(313) [0495] not receive the Spirit and Baptism until **ten** years later.
S3 : 08 :011(313) [0497] received the Spirit without the **Ten** Commandments.
SC : PR :003(338) [0533] Prayer, the Creed, or the **Ten** Commandments, they live
SC : PR :005(338) [0533] Prayer, the Creed, the **Ten** Commandments, or a single
SC : PR :007(339) [0533] text and wording of the **Ten** Commandments, the Creed,
SC : PR :008(339) [0535] Lord's Prayer, the Creed, and the **Ten** Commandments.
SC : PR :010(339) [0535] Begin by teaching them the **Ten** Commandments, the
SC : 01 :000(342) [0539] [I] The **Ten** Commandments *in the plain form in which*
SC : 01 :019(344) [0543] The **Tenth**
SC : 05 :020(350) [0553] in the light of the **Ten** Commandments: whether you are a
SC : 07 :003(352) [0557] (possibly a hymn on the **Ten** Commandments) or
LC : PR :007(359) [0569] word the Lord's Prayer, the **Ten** Commandments, the
LC : PR :017(361) [0573] anyone who knows the **Ten** Commandments perfectly
LC : SP :006(362) [0575] I. The **Ten** Commandments of God
LC : 01 :000(365) [0581] [First Part: The **Ten** Commandments]
LC : 01 :089(377) [0605] deal especially with the **Ten** Commandments, the Creed,
LC : 01 :151(386) [0625] a gulden by his unfaithfulness, he will lose **ten** elsewhere.
LC : 01 :154(386) [0625] household you must suffer **ten** times as much wrong from
LC : 01 :162(387) [0627] preacher although in the past they filled **ten** fat paunches.
LC : 01 :167(388) [0629] not explicitly stated in the **Ten** Commandments, it is
LC : 01 :226(395) [0645] One would **ten** times rather lose the money from one's
LC : 01 :291(404) [0663] The Ninth and **Tenth** Commandments
LC : 01 :310(407) [0669] Conclusion of the **Ten** Commandments
LC : 01 :311(407) [0669] Here, then, we have the **Ten** Commandments, a summary
LC : 01 :311(407) [0671] Apart from these **Ten** Commandments no deed, no
LC : 01 :315(408) [0671] and better way of life than the **Ten** Commandments teach?
LC : 01 :316(408) [0671] much as to keep one of the **Ten** Commandments as it
LC : 01 :316(408) [0671] single groschen to pay, but I promise to pay **ten** gulden."
LC : 01 :317(408) [0673] order equal to that of the **Ten** Commandments, for they
LC : 01 :319(408) [0673] how to teach and practice the **Ten** Commandments.
LC : 01 :321(408) [0673] and compelled to keep these **Ten** Commandments.
LC : 01 :331(410) [0677] men to write the **Ten** Commandments on every wall and
LC : 01 :332(410) [0677] enough to practice the **Ten** Commandments, and no one
LC : 01 :333(410) [0677] again how highly these **Ten** Commandments are to be
LC : 02 :002(411) [0679] to help us do what the **Ten** Commandments require of us.
LC : 02 :003(411) [0679] our own strength keep the **Ten** Commandments as they
LC : 02 :010(411) [0679] Since the **Ten** Commandments have explained that we are
LC : 02 :019(412) [0681] he has required and enjoined in the **Ten** Commandments.
LC : 02 :067(419) [0697] is a very different teaching from the **Ten** Commandments.
LC : 02 :067(419) [0697] The **Ten** Commandments, moreover, are inscribed in the
LC : 02 :068(420) [0697] Therefore the **Ten** Commandments do not by themselves
LC : 02 :069(420) [0697] power, to help us keep the **Ten** Commandments: the
LC : 03 :002(420) [0697] that no one can keep the **Ten** Commandments perfectly,
LC : 03 :002(420) [0697] faith and obedience to the **Ten** Commandments and
LC : 04 :006(437) [0733] truly as I can say that the **Ten** Commandments, the
LC : 05 :005(447) [0755] Therefore, just as the **Ten** Commandments, the Lord's
LC : 05 :085(456) [0773] may more easily instill the **Ten** Commandments, the
SD : 02 :015(523) [0887] David asks God more than **ten** times to give him
SD : 06 :012(566) [0967] and indicate to them in the **Ten** Commandments what the
SD : 06 :021(567) [0969] before them precisely the **Ten** Commandments
SD : 11 :033(622) [1075] in tribulation, the ninth, **tenth**, and eleventh chapters will

Tenaciously (2)
AP : 07 :042(176) [0241] certain nations held **tenaciously** to the custom of using
S2 : 02 :002(293) [0463] "Why do you cling so **tenaciously** to your Masses?

Tend (2), Tends (3)
AP : 12 :114(199) [0285] Still these spectacles **tend** to beguile the inexperienced
AP : 12 :125(201) [0289] now or in the future might **tend** to diminish the prestige
LC : 01 :288(404) [0663] we should prevent everything that **tends** to his disgrace.
LC : 01 :314(407) [0671] But when a poor girl **tends** a little child, or faithfully does
SD : 04 :035(557) [0949] and anything else that **tends** toward the same opinion,

Tender (2), Tenderly (1)
PR : PR :001(003) [0007] who are named below, **tender** our due service, friendship,
LC : 05 :067(454) [0769] a shame that, when he **tenderly** and faithfully summons
SD : 02 :026(526) [0891] and bestows a new and **tender** heart of flesh that we may

Tensions (1)
SD : 07 :106(588) [1009] and fortify our faith in all **tensions** concerning this article.

Term (47), Termed (1), Terms (37)
AG : 01 :004(028) [0043] the Fathers employed the **term** in this connection, not as
AL : 01 :004(028) [0043] And the **term** "person" is used, as the ancient Fathers
AL : 20 :023(044) [0055] admonished that here the **term** "faith" does not signify
AL : 26 :042(070) [0075] Such liberty in human **terms** was not unknown to the
AP : PR :002(098) [0099] have obtained it only on **terms** so risky that we could not
AP : 02 :003(101) [0105] When we use the **term** "concupiscence," we do not mean
AP : 02 :029(104) [0113] He includes these things in the **term** "ignorance."
AP : 04 :073(117) [0141] the other exclusive **terms** from Paul, too, like "freely,"
AP : 04 :073(117) [0141] "it is a gift," etc., for these **terms** are also exclusive.
AP : 04 :337(159) [0215] opponents are deceived with regard to the **term** "faith."
AP : 04 :344(160) [0217] the scholastics invented the **term** "merit of condignity."
AP : 04 :358(162) [0219] We hear the **term** "reward": therefore we need neither
AP : 04 :359(162) [0219] We are not arguing about the **term** "reward."
AP : 04 :362(162) [0219] forward an empty quibble about the **term** "reward."
AP : 04 :362(162) [0219] then we will not argue much about the **term** "reward."
AP : 04 :369(163) [0221] We might say more on the **term** "reward," based on the
AP : 07 :029(173) [0237] church, properly so called, is **termed** the body of Christ.
AP : 12 :046(188) [0263] not to understand these **terms** in a Platonic sense as
AP : 12 :149(205) [0299] distortion to apply the **term** "punishments" to those vain
AP : 12 :175(210) [0307] The **term** "satisfaction" no longer refers to civil discipline
AP : 24 :014(251) [0389] we purposely avoided this **term** because of its ambiguity.
AP : 24 :015(251) [0389] They find the **term** "sacrifice" in either the Scriptures or
AP : 24 :034(256) [0397] always apply the **term** "sacrifice" only to the ceremony.
AP : 24 :076(263) [0411] From this **term** "eucharist" arose in the church.
AP : 24 :077(263) [0411] The **Term** "Mass"
AP : 24 :079(264) [0411] they not mention the old **term** "communion," which
AP : 24 :079(264) [0411] But let us talk about the **term** "liturgy."
AP : 24 :081(264) [0411] Thus the **term** "liturgy" squares well with the ministry.
AP : 24 :085(264) [0413] is derived from *mizbeach*, the Hebrew **term** for altar.
AP : 24 :085(264) [0413] the etymology when the **term** occurs in Deut. 16:10,
AP : 24 :086(265) [0413] practice they also kept the **term** "Mass" as the name for
AP : 24 :087(265) [0413] offering, what does that **term** have to do with these
S3 : 03 :016(305) [0483] neither of these **terms**, and to this day they are as far from
TR : 00 :059(330) [0521] have set forth in general **terms** what we have to say about
LC : SP :018(363) [0579] short, plain, and simple **terms**, for the dear fathers or
LC : 02 :035(415) [0687] must concentrate on the **term** "Holy Spirit," because it is
LC : 02 :048(416) [0691] are accustomed to the **term** *Kirche*, "church," by which
LC : 02 :060(418) [0695] The **term** "resurrection of the flesh," however, is not well
LC : 04 :017(438) [0737] — praise it in any other **terms** you can — all by virtue of
EP : 01 :022(469) [0785] Sometimes the **term** means man's essence, as when we
EP : 01 :023(469) [0785] they are not biblical **terms** and, besides, they are unknown
EP : 03 :008(474) [0793] though otherwise these **terms** refer to the renovation of
EP : 03 :010(474) [0795] to the "exclusive **terms**," that is, to those words of the
EP : 04 :007(476) [0799] Apostle affirms in clear **terms**, "So also David declares
EP : 11 :022(497) [0837] discussing and teaching in mutually contradictory **terms**.
SD : PR :009(505) [0853] necessary and Christian **terms** and manner in which he
SD : 01 :051(517) [0875] distinctly all equivocal **terms**, that is, words and formulas
SD : 01 :051(517) [0875] to bite and poison," the **term** "nature" means — as it often
SD : 01 :052(517) [0875] Sometimes, however, the **term** is applied in a wider sense
SD : 01 :053(517) [0875] explains that he uses the **terms** "nature-sin," "person-sin,"
SD : 01 :054(517) [0877] the use of the Latin **terms** *substantia* and *accidens*, we
SD : 01 :054(517) [0877] rightly be spared these **terms** in sermons, since they are
SD : 01 :054(517) [0877] But when scholars use the **terms** among themselves or in
SD : 01 :054(518) [0877] division without a middle **term**), so that every existing
SD : 01 :061(519) [0879] Thus the **term** "accident" does not in any way minimize
SD : 01 :061(519) [0879] minimize original sin if the **term** is explained in harmony
SD : 01 :061(519) [0879] The **term** serves only to set forth the distinction between
SD : 01 :062(519) [0879] Luther used both the **term** "accident" and the term
SD : 01 :062(519) [0879] term "accident" and the **term** "quality" when treating this
SD : 03 :007(540) [0917] he stresses the exclusive **terms**, that is, the terms by which
SD : 03 :007(540) [0917] terms, that is, the **terms** by which all human works are
SD : 03 :007(540) [0917] He stresses these **terms** with such zeal in order to indicate
SD : 03 :018(542) [0921] is necessary to explain the **term** strictly so that the
SD : 03 :019(542) [0921] just as St. Paul uses the **terms** discriminately when he
SD : 03 :020(542) [0921] Likewise the **term** "vivification," that is, being made alive,
SD : 03 :020(542) [0921] The Apology often uses the **term** in this sense.
SD : 03 :021(542) [0921] as Dr. Luther used the **term** in his book *On the Councils*
SD : 03 :036(545) [0927] stresses such exclusive **terms** (that is, terms that exclude
SD : 03 :036(545) [0927] exclusive terms (that is, **terms** that exclude works from
SD : 03 :036(545) [0927] all of which exclusive **terms** may be summarized in the
SD : 03 :036(545) [0929] of the exclusive **terms** in the article of justification (that
SD : 03 :036(545) [0929] (that is, of the **terms** in the article of justification listed
SD : 03 :043(547) [0931] and that the exclusive **terms** which St. Paul employs, such
SD : 03 :053(548) [0933] uses and urges exclusive **terms** (that is, terms that wholly
SD : 03 :053(548) [0933] exclusive terms (that is, **terms** that wholly exclude works
SD : 04 :022(554) [0945] the doctrine of exclusive **terms** in the articles of
SD : 05 :004(558) [0953] Here the **term** includes both the exposition of the law and
SD : 07 :117(589) [1013] Accordingly the **term** "sacramental union" is to be
SD : 07 :117(589) [1013] is to be understood in **terms** of the relation between the
SD : 08 :018(594) [1021] have often used the **term** "mixture" in a good sense and
SD : 08 :059(602) [1035] not only speaks in general **terms** of the person of the Son
SD : 08 :063(603) [1037] have never understood the **term** "real exchange" — a
SD : 08 :063(603) [1037] We have used this **term** merely in opposition to a "verbal
SD : 11 :001(616) [1063] Nor have our theologians always used the same **terms**.
SD : 11 :080(629) [1089] says in unmistakable **terms** that God "endured the vessels

Terminology (12)
PR : PR :021(011) [0019] (to use scholastic **terminology**), as if somewhere or
AP : 13 :017(213) [0313] of sacraments or the **terminology**, so long as those things
EP : 01 :020(468) [0783] sin but by such **terminology** to indicate the difference
EP : 01 :025(469) [0785] This **terminology** sets forth very clearly the distinction
EP : 04 :009(476) [0799] contrary to the pattern of sound words and **terminology**.
EP : 07 :004(482) [0809] under this plausible **terminology** they really retain the
SD : PR :016(507) [0857] to insure that familiar **terminology** may not hide and
SD : 01 :056(518) [0877] of logic, used the same **terminology** freely and without
SD : 03 :036(545) [0927] This **terminology** does not exclude works, however, as
SD : 07 :002(569) [0971] endeavor to employ **terminology** which is as close as
SD : 08 :063(603) [1037] twisted our words and **terminology** in this direction in
SD : 12 :037(636) [1103] both as to content and **terminology**, and instead teach

Terminus (1)
AP : 12 :063(191) [0269] or its goal — the "**terminus** to which," as they call it.

Terrible (19), Terribly (4)
A G : 2 3 :006(052) [0061] It is well known what **terrible** torment and frightful
A G : 2 3 :018(054) [0063] much adultery, and such **terrible**, shocking immorality
A G : 2 4 :012(057) [0065] were reminded of the **terrible** responsibility which should
A P : 0 4 :128(125) [0157] while it knows that in his **terrible** wrath he is
A P : 0 4 :301(153) [0205] human nature so many **terrible** evils, sufferings in this life
A P : 1 2 :008(183) [0255] them attain grace even though they were **terribly** contrite?
A P : 1 2 :034(186) [0261] when they feel the **terrible** and indescribable wrath of
A P : 1 2 :123(201) [0289] may demand that such **terrible** heretics, who reject
A P : 2 1 :028(233) [0351] not a propitiator but only a **terrible** judge and avenger.
A P : 2 7 :027(274) [0429] It is **terrible** to read and hear such pharisaical and even
L C : 0 1 :029(368) [0589] has attached to it, first, a **terrible** threat and, then, a
L C : 0 1 :039(370) [0591] **Terrible** as these threats are, much mightier is the comfort
L C : 0 1 :072(374) [0601] Many a **terrible** and shocking calamity would befall us if
L C : 0 1 :077(375) [0603] richly reward it, even as he will **terribly** punish its misuse.
L C : 0 1 :177(389) [0631] is disregarded, God **terribly** punishes the world; hence
L C : 0 1 :191(391) [0635] He will pass a most **terrible** sentence upon them in the
L C : 0 1 :322(409) [0673] over them, fearfully and **terribly** punishing all who
L C : 0 2 :065(419) [0695] from him we see nothing but an angry and **terrible** Judge.
E P : 1 1 :021(497) [0837] are all blasphemous and **terrible** errors, for they rob
S D : 0 1 :013(511) [0863] men of the world with **terrible** errors and heresies, strikes
S D : 0 1 :014(511) [0863] damage is so great and **terrible** that in baptized believers
S D : 0 5 :012(560) [0955] there a more earnest and **terrible** revelation and preaching
S D : 0 7 :067(582) [0997] These expressions are so **terrible** that a pious Christian

Terrify (9), Terrifying (1), Terrified (34), Terrifies (10), Terror (13), Terrors (54)
A G : 1 2 :003(034) [0049] contrition and sorrow, or **terror**, on account of sin, and
A G : 2 0 :015(043) [0055] that weak and **terrified** consciences find it most
A G : 0 1 :007(056) [0065] as a comfort for **terrified** consciences) in order that the
A G : 2 5 :004(062) [0069] comforting and necessary it is for **terrified** consciences.
A G : 2 5 :013(063) [0071] for the consolation of **terrified** consciences, and also for
A L : 1 2 :004(034) [0049] one is contrition, that is, **terror** smiting the conscience
A L : 1 2 :005(035) [0049] sake, comforts the conscience, and delivers it from **terror**.
A L : 2 0 :017(043) [0055] to that conflict of the **terrified** conscience, nor can it be
A L : 2 0 :026(045) [0057] as confidence which consoles and lifts up **terrified** hearts.
A L : 2 5 :004(062) [0069] consolation it brings to **terrified** consciences, are told that
A L : 2 6 :002(064) [0071] merit grace and sorely **terrified** the consciences of those
A P : 0 2 :024(103) [0111] of God in its security, or it hates him in its **terror**.
A P : 0 4 :020(110) [0125] of God and the **terrors** of conscience drive out our trust in
A P : 0 4 :020(110) [0125] But **terrified** consciences waver and doubt and then seek
A P : 0 4 :036(112) [0131] While he **terrifies** us and seems to be casting us into
A P : 0 4 :038(112) [0131] For the law always accuses and **terrifies** consciences.
A P : 0 4 :038(112) [0131] because a conscience **terrified** by the law flees before
A P : 0 4 :045(113) [0133] In penitence and the **terrors** of conscience it consoles and
A P : 0 4 :062(115) [0139] preaching of penitence **terrifies** our consciences with real
A P : 0 4 :079(117) [0143] forgiveness of sins, the **terrors** of sin and of eternal death
A P : 0 4 :079(118) [0143] That is, sin **terrifies** consciences; this happens through the
A P : 0 4 :085(119) [0147] consolation against the **terrors** of sin, against eternal
A P : 0 4 :106(122) [0153] that our hearts are **terrified** by the law but receive
A P : 0 4 :115(123) [0155] us from death, comforting and quickening **terrified** minds.
A P : 0 4 :142(126) [0161] is, it is conceived in the **terrors** of a conscience that feels
A P : 0 4 :142(126) [0161] be strengthened in these **terrors** and in other afflictions.
A P : 0 4 :144(127) [0161] of sins for a heart **terrified** and fleeing from sin,
A P : 0 4 :148(127) [0163] did not die in vain, conquers the **terrors** of sin and death.
A P : 0 4 :195(134) [0175] This is evident in **terrors** of conscience, for we cannot set
A P : 0 4 :204(135) [0177] these works, but in real **terror** they pile up works and
A P : 0 4 :214(136) [0179] cannot overcome the **terrors** of sin, but faith alone can
A P : 0 4 :222(138) [0181] that love conquers the **terrors** of sin and death; that we
A P : 0 4 :244(142) [0189] good works conquer the **terrors** of sin and death; that
A P : 0 4 :247(142) [0191] Christ when we set it against the **terrors** of sin and death.
A P : 0 4 :249(143) [0191] a faith that resists the **terrors** of conscience and
A P : 0 4 :249(143) [0191] conscience and encourages and consoles **terrified** hearts.
A P : 0 4 :257(144) [0193] works wrath; it only accuses; it only **terrifies** consciences.
A P : 0 4 :262(145) [0195] Especially amid the **terrors** of sin, a human being must
A P : 0 4 :270(147) [0197] law and therefore flees in **terror** before the judgment and
A P : 0 4 :271(148) [0199] be received by faith, to cheer the **terrified** conscience.
A P : 0 4 :275(148) [0199] great promise, since a **terrified** conscience needs manifold
A P : 0 4 :276(148) [0199] cheer, and confirm **terrified** minds to believe more firmly
A P : 0 4 :288(151) [0203] forms of worship to get rid of the **terrors** of conscience.
A P : 0 4 :288(151) [0203] to counteract the **terrors** of conscience and the wrath of
A P : 0 4 :290(151) [0203] faith in Christ we overcome the **terrors** of sin and death.
A P : 0 4 :291(152) [0203] and victory over the **terrors** of sin and death.
A P : 0 4 :292(152) [0203] with his conscience **terrified** by the preaching of
A P : 0 4 :301(153) [0205] When will it love God amid these doubts and **terrors**?
A P : 0 4 :304(154) [0205] still more clearly: The **terrors** of sin and death are not
A P : 0 4 :314(155) [0207] faith we overcome the **terrors** of sin and death since we
A P : 0 4 :318(156) [0209] when our conscience **terrifies** us after justification, the
A P : 0 4 :321(157) [0209] them righteous, whereas **terrified** consciences are
A P : 0 4 :351(161) [0217] in the midst of our **terrors**, other spiritual impulses
A P : 0 4 :383(165) [0225] quickening the heart amid the **terrors** of sin and death.
A P : 0 4 :398(167) [0227] of sin, conquer the **terrors** of sin, and receive peace for
A P : 1 1 :007(181) [0251] These **terrors** made no impression on wild and profane
A P : 1 2 :009(183) [0255] When can a **terrified** conscience judge whether it fears
A P : 1 2 :009(183) [0255] serious, true, and great **terrors** described in the Psalms
A P : 1 2 :029(185) [0259] contrition is the genuine **terror** of a conscience that feels
A P : 1 2 :031(186) [0259] Scripture speaks of these **terrors**, as in Ps. 38:4, 8, "For
A P : 1 2 :032(186) [0259] In these **terrors** the conscience feels God's wrath against
A P : 1 2 :034(186) [0261] For the law only accuses and **terrifies** the conscience.
A P : 1 2 :034(186) [0261] In these **terrors** our opponents say nothing about faith,
A P : 1 2 :034(186) [0261] by these sorrows and **terrors** men merit grace if they love
A P : 1 2 :034(186) [0261] love God amid such real **terrors** when they feel the
A P : 1 2 :034(186) [0261] despair, when amid such **terrors** they show men only the
A P : 1 2 :035(186) [0261] Christ, that amid these **terrors** the Gospel of Christ ought
A P : 1 2 :042(187) [0263] in its struggles against the **terrors** of sin and death.
A P : 1 2 :044(187) [0263] mean contrition, anxiety, and the **terrors** of sin and death.
A P : 1 2 :046(188) [0263] means genuine **terrors**, like those of the dying, which
A P : 1 2 :048(188) [0265] is understood only amid genuine sorrows and **terrors**.
A P : 1 2 :051(189) [0265] it God's alien work to **terrify** because God's own proper
A P : 1 2 :051(189) [0265] But he **terrifies**, he says, to make room for consolation
A P : 1 2 :052(189) [0265] of joining these two, **terror** and consolation, to teach that
A P : 1 2 :053(189) [0265] works of God in men, to **terrify** and to justify and quicken
A P : 1 2 :053(189) [0265] in men, to terrify and to justify and quicken the **terrified**.
A P : 1 2 :055(189) [0267] Adam was rebuked and **terrified** after his sin; this was
A P : 1 2 :056(189) [0267] by Nathan, and in his **terror** he says (II Sam. 12:13), "I
A P : 1 2 :060(190) [0269] This faith follows on our **terrors**, overcoming them and
A P : 1 2 :060(190) [0269] for it frees us from our **terrors** and brings forth peace,
A P : 1 2 :064(191) [0269] For a **terrified** conscience cannot pit our works or our
A P : 1 2 :072(192) [0271] against despair and against the **terrors** of sin and death.
A P : 1 2 :131(202) [0291] True **terrors** and sorrows of the soul do not permit the
A P : 1 2 :148(205) [0299] and revenge, that is, contrition and true **terrors**.
A P : 1 2 :149(205) [0299] genuine punishments than are real **terrors** in the heart.
A P : 1 2 :149(205) [0299] apply them to the fearful **terrors** of conscience of which
A P : 1 2 :150(206) [0299] it when amid the **terrors** of contrition he reveals his
A P : 1 2 :153(206) [0299] his faith has overcome its **terrors**, there is no longer that
A P : 1 2 :156(207) [0301] of God, like contrition or **terrors** of conscience, as well as
A P : 1 2 :158(207) [0301] in the midst of troubles **terrified** consciences see only
A P : 1 8 :008(226) [0337] comes into being when **terrified** hearts hear the Gospel
A P : 2 0 :006(227) [0339] we can easily ignore the **terrors** of the world and bravely
A P : 2 0 :008(227) [0341] when sin and death **terrify** them and the devil tempts them
A P : 2 0 :009(228) [0341] our opponents use their **terrors**, tortures, and
A P : 2 0 :010(228) [0341] it, when would a **terrified** conscience find a work that it
A P : 2 2 :010(237) [0361] console and strengthen **terrified** hearts when they believe
A P : 2 4 :012(251) [0387] of faith to conquer the **terrors** of sins and death and to
A P : 2 4 :060(260) [0405] and no conquest of the **terrors** of death and sin through
A P : 2 4 :071(262) [0409] when faith gives life to **terrified** hearts, is the worship of
A P : 2 4 :073(262) [0409] is to make clear that **terrified** consciences are the ones
A P : 2 4 :074(263) [0409] to see its liberation from **terror**, then it really gives thanks
S 3 : 0 2 :004(303) [0479] Thus he is **terror**-stricken and humbled, becomes
S 3 : 0 3 :002(304) [0479] He drives all together into **terror** and despair.
S C : 0 9 :007(355) [0563] if you do right and let nothing **terrify** you" (I Pet. 3:1, 6).
L C : 0 1 :322(408) [0673] promise, not only to **terrify** and warn us but also to
L C : 0 2 :022(413) [0683] article would humble and **terrify** us all if we believed it.
E P : 0 5 :007(478) [0803] which does not reprove or **terrify** but comforts
E P : 0 5 :009(479) [0803] God, is an earnest and **terrifying** preaching and
E P : 0 5 :010(479) [0803] God's wrath and **terrifies** people, it is not, strictly
S D : 0 2 :054(531) [0903] and experiences genuine **terror**, contrition, and sorrow in
S D : 0 2 :068(534) [0907] moment fearful and **terrified**, at one time ardent in love,
S D : 0 5 :001(558) [0951] their greatest temptations against the **terrors** of the law.
S D : 0 5 :009(559) [0955] sinners who have been **terrified** by the proclamation of
S D : 0 5 :009(559) [0955] that contrition or the **terrors** of the law may not end in
S D : 0 5 :012(560) [0955] know their sins nor are **terrified** by the wrath of God, as
S D : 0 5 :012(560) [0955] the wrath of God and **terrifies** man, it is not yet the
S D : 0 5 :012(560) [0957] ordained and given us to **terrify** or to condemn us, but to
S D : 0 5 :012(560) [0957] and lift upright those who are **terrified** and disconsolate."
S D : 0 5 :024(562) [0961] law and its threats will **terrify** the hearts of the
S D : 0 5 :027(563) [0961] in the Gospel against the **terrors** of the law and reopen
S D : 0 7 :069(582) [0997] faith, who are heartily **terrified** because of their many and

Territorial (1), Territories (5)
P R : P R :006(004) [0009] into our lands and **territories** and which are insinuating
P R : P R :015(007) [0013] in our lands and **territories** and have had them reminded
P R : P R :016(008) [0015] minister and schoolmaster in our lands and **territories**.
P R : P R :023(012) [0021] taught in our lands, **territories**, schools, and churches
A G : P R :008(025) [0039] our lands, principalities, dominions, cities and **territories**.
E P : 1 2 :015(499) [0841] feudal homage to his **territorial** sovereign or liege-lord.

Tertullian (2)
A P : 1 2 :094(196) [0281] For **Tertullian** speaks excellently about faith, dwelling
A P : 1 2 :094(196) [0281] This is what **Tertullian** says: "He invites us to salvation

Test (3), Tested (2)
A P : 1 2 :120(200) [0287] as an example and to **test** those who wanted to be
A P : 1 2 :161(208) [0303] humiliation his piety might be exercised and **tested**.
A P : 1 2 :161(208) [0303] that is, to exercise and **test** the righteousness of those who
L C : 0 1 :318(408) [0673] upon them and **test** yourself thoroughly, do your very
S D : 1 1 :033(622) [1075] eighth chapter you are **tested** under the cross and in

Testament (96), Testaments (5)
P R : P R :020(010) [0017] namely, the words of institution of Christ's **testament**.
P R : P R :020(010) [0017] of the words of the **testament** of Christ and decry and
P R : P R :022(012) [0019] teach about it on the basis of the words of his **testament**.
A G : 2 8 :061(091) [0093] ceremonies of the New **Testament**, and of the change of
A P : 0 4 :005(108) [0121] or when, in the New **Testament**, the Christ who came
A P : 0 4 :057(115) [0137] of sins by faith, just as the saints in the New **Testament**.
A P : 0 4 :207(135) [0177] The people of the Old **Testament** imitated these sacrifices
A P : 0 7 :014(170) [0231] be between the church and the Old **Testament** people?
A P : 0 7 :014(170) [0231] church from the Old **Testament** people by the fact that the
A P : 0 7 :014(170) [0231] Among the Old **Testament** people, those born according
A P : 0 7 :016(171) [0231] saints among the Old **Testament** people), for they held
A P : 0 7 :040(176) [0241] to observe certain Old **Testament** customs, which the
A P : 1 2 :042(187) [0261] are signs of the new **testament**, that is, signs of the
A P : 1 2 :042(187) [0263] This cup is the new **testament**" (Luke 22:19, 20).
A P : 1 3 :004(211) [0309] promise of grace, which is the heart of the New **Testament**
A P : 1 3 :009(212) [0311] people, as in the Old **Testament**, but they are called to
A P : 1 3 :014(213) [0311] not in the New **Testament** but in the very beginning, at the
A P : 1 3 :014(213) [0311] to physical life and not strictly to the New **Testament**.
A P : 1 3 :014(213) [0311] sense, "signs of the New **Testament**," testimonies of grace
A P : 1 3 :020(213) [0313] a sacrament of the New **Testament**, as Christ clearly says
A P : 1 3 :020(213) [0313] promised in the New **Testament**, is being offered to him.
A P : 1 5 :032(219) [0323] True, in the Old **Testament** ceremonies were necessary for
A P : 2 2 :002(236) [0357] changed, especially since he himself calls it his **testament**?
A P : 2 2 :002(236) [0357] illegal to annul a man's **testament**, it is much more illegal
A P : 2 3 :027(243) [0371] the priests of the Old **Testament** were to be separated from
A P : 2 3 :027(243) [0371] the priests of the New **Testament** must pray continually,
A P : 2 3 :064(248) [0381] purity laws of the Old **Testament** do not apply here
A P : 2 4 :021(252) [0389] The Old **Testament** called certain sacrifices propitiatory
A P : 2 4 :023(253) [0391] In the Old **Testament** this meant that a victim was to come
A P : 2 4 :026(254) [0391] sacrifices of the New **Testament** are of this type, as Peter
A P : 2 4 :027(254) [0393] the worship of the New **Testament** is spiritual; it is the
A P : 2 4 :028(254) [0393] The Old **Testament** prophets also condemn the popular
A P : 2 4 :030(255) [0395] worship, the New **Testament** teaches that there should be
A P : 2 4 :033(256) [0395] the worship of the New **Testament**, not only about the
A P : 2 4 :034(256) [0395] who teach in the New **Testament**) are the proclamation of
A P : 2 4 :034(256) [0397] of animals in the Old **Testament** symbolized both the
A P : 2 4 :034(256) [0397] The New **Testament** requires sacrifices of the heart, not
A P : 2 4 :035(256) [0397] sacrifice in the Old **Testament**, so the Mass ought to be

Continued ▶

A P : 2 4 :035(256) [0397] Mass ought to be the daily sacrifice of the New **Testament**.
A P : 2 4 :035(256) [0397] sacrifice of the New **Testament**; the ceremony was
A P : 2 4 :036(257) [0397] The Old **Testament** had pictures or shadows of what was
A P : 2 4 :036(257) [0397] Christ and the whole worship of the New **Testament**.
A P : 2 4 :037(257) [0397] the shadow in the Old **Testament**, so in the New we should
A P : 2 4 :039(257) [0399] heart, for in the New **Testament** we should look for the
A P : 2 4 :052(259) [0403] that since the New **Testament** has priests and high priests,
A P : 2 4 :052(259) [0403] the pomp of the Old **Testament** priesthood and sacrifices
A P : 2 4 :052(259) [0403] or sacrifice for sins, just as the Old **Testament** did.
A P : 2 4 :055(259) [0403] In the Old **Testament** as in the New, the saints had to be
A P : 2 4 :056(259) [0403] The Old **Testament** sacrifices, therefore, did not merit
A P : 2 4 :056(260) [0405] sacrifice left in the New **Testament** except the one sacrifice
A P : 2 4 :057(260) [0405] be sacrifices in the New **Testament** besides the death of
A P : 2 4 :057(260) [0405] the Old and the New **Testament**, and it replaces Christ as
A P : 2 4 :058(260) [0405] therefore, that the New **Testament** must have a priest who
A P : 2 4 :059(260) [0405] priesthood of the New **Testament** is a ministry of the
A P : 2 4 :069(262) [0409] is correct to define the New **Testaments** as signs of grace.
A P : 2 4 :069(262) [0409] In the New **Testament**, the Word is the added promise of
A P : 2 4 :069(262) [0409] The promise of the New **Testament** is the promise of the
A P : 2 4 :069(262) [0409] is the cup of the new **testament** with my blood, which is
A P : 2 4 :071(262) [0409] the worship of the New **Testament**, because what matters
A P : 2 4 :071(262) [0409] what matters in the New **Testament** is the spiritual
A P : 2 4 :097(268) [0417] people in the Old **Testament** had a similar notion that they
A P : 2 7 :058(279) [0439] us the example of the Nazarites from the Old **Testament**.
A P : 2 7 :058(279) [0439] exercise like the other ceremonies of the Old **Testament**.
A P : 2 7 :058(279) [0439] be said about other vows described in the Old **Testament**.
S 3 : 0 3 :001(303) [0479] of the law is retained and taught by the New **Testament**.
S 3 : 0 3 :004(304) [0481] of the law the New **Testament** immediately adds the
T R : 0 0 :026(324) [0511] the ministry of the New **Testament** is not bound to places
L C : P R :003(358) [0567] Prayer Book, the New **Testament**, or something else from
L C : S P :023(364) [0579] This cup is the new **testament** in my blood, which is shed
L C : 0 1 :080(375) [0603] In the Old **Testament** God set apart the seventh day and
L C : 0 1 :082(376) [0603] ordinances of the Old **Testament** connected with
L C : 0 1 :306(406) [0669] another, for in the New **Testament** married people are
L C : 0 1 :331(410) [0677] reason that the Old **Testament** commands men to write
L C : 0 5 :003(447) [0753] *This cup is the new **testament** in my blood, which is*
E P : R N :001(464) [0777] of the Old and New **Testaments** are the only rule and
E P : R N :007(465) [0779] of the Old and New **Testaments** and all other writings is
E P : 0 7 :007(482) [0811] that the words of the **testament** of Christ are to be
E P : 0 7 :024(484) [0815] clear Word of Christ's **testament**, so that they are
E P : 0 7 :025(484) [0815] the words of Christ's **testament** are not to be understood
E P : 0 7 :035(485) [0815] words of Christ's **testament**, effect and cause this presence
E P : 0 7 :042(486) [0817] words of Christ's **testament**, we hold and believe in a
E P : 0 8 :017(489) [0823] as the words of Christ's **testament** declare, *"This is, is, is*
E P : 0 8 :039(491) [0827] the words of Christ's **testament**, but it opens a way for the
E P : 1 2 :012(499) [0841] is not a God-pleasing estate in the New **Testament**.
E P : 1 2 :016(499) [0841] 5. That in the New **Testament** the government cannot with
S D : P R :003(503) [0851] of the Old and New **Testaments** as the pure and clear
S D : 0 3 :017(542) [0921] the Holy Scriptures of the Old and the New **Testaments**.
S D : 0 4 :017(554) [0943] the people of the New **Testament** are to be a people who
S D : 0 5 :004(558) [0953] on earth and in the New **Testament** he ordered to be
S D : 0 5 :011(560) [0955] Thus, even in the New **Testament**, he must perform what
S D : 0 5 :014(560) [0957] Articles state: "The New **Testament** retains and performs
S D : 0 5 :024(562) [0961] the ministry of the New **Testament** the proclamation of
S D : 0 7 :037(575) [0985] to the words of Christ's **testament**, "This is my body."
S D : 0 7 :038(576) [0985] is, the words of Christ's **testament**), "This is my body," we
S D : 0 7 :050(578) [0989] of his last will and **testament** and of his abiding covenant
S D : 0 7 :050(578) [0989] kinds of sacrifice in the Old **Testament**, and holy Baptism.
S D : 0 7 :053(579) [0991] with you people this my **testament** and new covenant,
S D : 0 7 :081(584) [1001] he gives to us in his **testament**) is awakened,
S D : 0 7 :085(584) [1001] and perversion of this **testament**, the following useful rule
S D : 0 7 :092(586) [1005] of Christ's word and **testament** to a strange meaning
S D : 1 2 :017(634) [1099] 8. That in the New **Testament** era government service is

Testified (10), Testifies (38), Testify (21)

P R : P R :008(005) [0009] This we did that we might **testify** and declare to our most
P R : P R :016(008) [0013] thanks to almighty God **testified** that of their own volition
P R : P R :022(012) [0021] this reason we desire to **testify** before the face of almighty
A G : 2 8 :074(094) [0095] disuse and are not obligatory, as papal law itself **testifies**.
A L : 0 6 :001(032) [0047] as Christ himself also **testifies**, "When you have done all
A L : 2 2 :005(050) [0061] Cyprian in several places **testifies** that the blood was given
A L : 2 2 :006(050) [0061] The same is **testified** by Jerome, who said, "The priests
A L : 2 2 :009(050) [0061] approved, as the canons **testify** (Dist. 3, chap. "Veritate"
A L : 2 4 :041(061) [0069] as the Tripartite History **testifies** in Book 9, "Again, in
A L : 2 5 :007(062) [0069] So the Psalm **testifies**, "Who can discern his errors?"
A L : 2 5 :010(063) [0069] The ancient writers also **testify** that such an enumeration
A L : 2 7 :060(080) [0083] perfection and **testified** that it was a novelty in his day to
A P : P R :015(099) [0101] the main arguments, to **testify** to all nations that we hold
A P : P R :018(099) [0103] Many good men have **testified** publicly and thanked God
A P : 0 1 :002(100) [0103] that the Holy Scriptures **testify** to it firmly, surely, and
A P : 0 2 :003(101) [0105] This passage **testifies** that in those who are born
A P : 0 4 :086(119) [0147] Thus the Scriptures **testify** that we are accounted
A P : 0 4 :103(122) [0151] whole world, as John **testified** when he said (John 1:29),
A P : 0 4 :201(134) [0175] and through his witness **testify** to his faith before others
A P : 0 4 :273(148) [0199] So the Scriptures **testify** in many other places.
A P : 0 4 :350(161) [0217] in which experience **testifies** how difficult a thing faith is.
A P : 0 7 :005(169) [0227] by his Spirit, as Paul **testifies** when he says
A P : 0 7 :022(172) [0235] So Lyra **testifies** when he says: "The church is not made
A P : 0 7 :028(173) [0237] church's call, as Christ **testifies** (Luke 10:16), "He who
A P : 1 2 :174(210) [0305] We have **testified** often enough that penitence ought to
A P : 1 6 :013(224) [0333] and in business have **testified** how they were helped after
A P : 2 3 :020(242) [0369] Gerson **testifies** that many good men have tried to
A P : 2 3 :028(243) [0371] and approves, as the Scriptures abundantly **testify**.
A P : 2 4 :096(267) [0417] Epiphanius **testifies** that Aerius believed that prayers for
A P : 2 7 :001(268) [0419] Those who knew him **testify** that he was a mild old man,
A P : 2 8 :002(281) [0443] Besides we have often **testified** that we do not criticize
A P : 2 8 :011(283) [0447] The Gospel clearly **testifies** that traditions should not be
S 3 : 0 3 :040(309) [0489] As St. Paul **testifies** in Rom. 7:23, he wars with the law in
T R : 0 0 :010(321) [0507] Since Paul clearly **testifies** that he did not desire to seek
T R : 0 0 :014(322) [0507] in the Latin churches, as Cyprian and Augustine **testify**.
T R : 0 0 :067(331) [0523] It is as Paul **testifies** to the Ephesians when he says,
T R : 0 0 :068(331) [0523] of Christ apply which **testify** that the keys were given to
T R : 0 0 :082(000) [0529] For I **testify** in this my own handwriting that I thus hold,
L C : 0 1 :212(394) [0641] as everyone's observation and experience **testify**.
L C : 0 1 :284(403) [0661] himself, and you may **testify** publicly concerning him.
L C : 0 1 :305(406) [0669] posed as an honorable, upright man, as St. Mark **testifies**.
L C : 0 3 :020(423) [0703] For by his Word God **testifies** that our prayer is heartily
E P : 0 8 :016(489) [0821] his hands, as he himself **testifies**, "All authority in heaven
E P : 0 8 :018(489) [0823] mystery, as the apostles **testifies**, and the sole foundation
E P : 1 1 :010(495) [0833] alone, which clearly **testifies** that "God has consigned all
E P : 1 1 :016(497) [0837] in Scripture, as St. Paul **testifies**, was written for our
S D : 0 1 :034(514) [0869] of creation Scripture **testifies** not only that God created
S D : 0 1 :046(516) [0873] resurrection Scripture **testifies** that precisely the substance
S D : 0 1 :060(519) [0879] It **testifies** that original sin is an inexpressible impairment
S D : 0 2 :017(523) [0887] place, the Word of God **testifies** that in divine matters the
S D : 0 5 :010(560) [0955] For Paul **testifies** that although "Moses is read," the veil
S D : 0 7 :016(572) [0977] For it was instituted to **testify** that those who truly repent
S D : 0 7 :048(578) [0989] institution of this Supper **testify** that these words of our
S D : 0 8 :024(595) [1023] truly the Son of the most high God, as the angel **testifies**.
S D : 0 8 :026(596) [1025] womb, but, as the apostle **testifies**, he laid it aside, and as
S D : 0 8 :027(596) [1025] and as the apostles **testify** that he worked with them
S D : 0 8 :030(597) [1025] joy in looking into it, as St. Peter **testifies** (I Pet. 1:12).
S D : 0 8 :034(597) [1027] Since St. Peter **testifies** with clear words that even we, in
S D : 0 8 :051(600) [1031] basis of the Scriptures, **testify** mightily that, because the
S D : 0 8 :057(602) [1035] whatever the Scriptures **testify** that Christ received in
S D : 0 8 :058(602) [1035] second place, Scripture **testifies** clearly (John 5:21, 27;
S D : 1 0 :014(613) [1057] so that, as the apostle **testifies**, the truth of the Gospel
S D : 1 1 :027(620) [1071] St. Paul **testified** to the same effect when he wrote, "We
S D : 1 1 :069(627) [1085] Word, as the apostle **testifies**, "Faith comes from the
S D : 1 1 :070(627) [1085] to eternal life, and who **testifies** to all men without
S D : 1 1 :073(628) [1087] For the Spirit **testifies** to the elect that they are "children
S D : 1 1 :082(630) [1089] And St. Paul **testifies** with clear words that God's power
S D : 1 1 :092(632) [1093] For the apostle **testifies** that "Whatever was written in
S D : 1 2 :040(636) [1103] we wish to have **testified** that the present explanation of

Testimonies (30), Testimony (35)

P R : P R :027(014) [0025] In **testimony** whereof we have with one mind and heart
A G : 0 0 :000(023) [0037] will also speak of thy **testimonies** before kings, and shall
A G : 1 3 :001(035) [0049] that they are signs and **testimonies** of God's will toward
A L : 1 3 :001(035) [0049] to be signs and **testimonies** of the will of God toward us,
A L : 2 0 :012(043) [0055] whole matter is supported by **testimonies** of the Fathers.
A L : 2 6 :022(067) [0073] Our teachers add **testimonies** from the Scriptures.
A L : 2 8 :043(088) [0089] Yet there are clear **testimonies** which prohibit the making
A P : 0 4 :063(115) [0139] can grasp it, and it has the **testimony** of the church.
A P : 0 4 :086(119) [0147] therefore add clear **testimonies** stating that faith is the
A P : 0 4 :102(121) [0151] But the Scripture is full of such **testimonies**.
A P : 0 4 :171(130) [0171] we shall assemble more **testimonies** on this subject,
A P : 0 4 :184(132) [0173] are commended because of faith as its fruit or **testimony**.
A P : 0 4 :189(133) [0175] our faith, to give **testimony**, and to render thanks.
A P : 0 4 :276(148) [0199] glad to have signs and **testimonies** of this great promise.
A P : 0 4 :276(148) [0199] they exercise themselves in these signs and **testimonies**.
A P : 0 4 :297(153) [0205] has not believed in the **testimony** that God has borne to
A P : 0 4 :297(153) [0205] And this is the **testimony**, that God gave us eternal life,
A P : 0 4 :323(157) [0209] and has many clear **testimonies** in the Scriptures and in
A P : 0 4 :400(168) [0227] Fathers, and contrary to the **testimony** of pious minds.
A P : 1 2 :062(191) [0269] has not believed in the **testimony** that God has borne to
A P : 1 2 :071(192) [0271] The **testimony** of the Holy Spirit was added to this
A P : 1 2 :073(192) [0273] same thing; nor are **testimonies** of the Fathers lacking.
A P : 1 3 :001(211) [0309] are rather signs and **testimonies** of God's will toward us,
A P : 1 3 :014(213) [0311] the New Testament," **testimonies** of grace and the
A P : 1 3 :020(214) [0313] and believe that the **testimonies** are not false but as
A P : 1 4 :001(214) [0315] we have given frequent **testimony** in the assembly to our
A P : 1 5 :017(217) [0319] without the Word and **testimony** of God, and Paul says
A P : 1 5 :017(217) [0319] these rites have no **testimony** in the Word of God, the
A P : 2 2 :004(236) [0359] Toledo gives the same **testimony**, and it would not be
A P : 2 2 :004(236) [0359] not be hard to collect a great multitude of **testimonies**.
A P : 2 8 :018(284) [0449] It is a **testimony** given to the apostles so that we may
S 1 : P R :003(289) [0455] after me may have my **testimony** and confession (in
S 3 : 0 8 :006(313) [0495] came upon them without the **testimony** of the Scriptures?
T R : 0 0 :006(320) [0505] [**Testimony** of the Scriptures]
T R : 0 0 :011(321) [0507] **Testimony** from History
L C : 0 1 :120(381) [0615] a sure text and a divine **testimony** that God has
L C : 0 1 :280(403) [0661] one and on whose **testimony** the judge can base his
L C : 0 3 :023(423) [0703] for it has the excellent **testimony** that God loves to hear
L C : 0 5 :079(455) [0771] which everywhere give this **testimony** about the world.
E P : 0 4 :015(477) [0799] The good works are **testimonies** of the Holy Spirit's
E P : 1 2 :031(500) [0843] In **testimony** that this is the doctrine, faith and confession
S D : P R :006(505) [0853] clear and irrefutable **testimonies** from the Holy Scriptures
S D : P R :016(507) [0857] as a certain and public **testimony**, not only to our
S D : 0 1 :043(515) [0873] we have the mighty **testimony** of Scripture that God's Son
S D : 0 1 :045(516) [0873] we have the **testimony** of Scripture that God cleanses man
S D : 0 1 :057(518) [0877] demonstrated by the **testimonies** of the church's teachers,
S D : 0 2 :028(527) [0893] mentioned, as the following **testimonies** will indicate.
S D : 0 2 :042(529) [0897] These **testimonies** indicate clearly that we cannot by our
S D : 0 2 :042(529) [0897] These **testimonies** make no mention whatever of our will
S D : 0 7 :001(569) [0971] refrain from giving **testimony** to the divine truth by
S D : 0 7 :054(579) [0991] a special and manifest **testimony** to the true and essential
S D : 0 7 :059(580) [0993] explanation of the noble **testimony** in I Cor. 10:16.
S D : 0 7 :066(581) [0997] Since these **testimonies** are too long to list here, in the
S D : 0 7 :105(588) [1009] of our public and oft-repeated **testimony** to the contrary.
S D : 0 7 :110(589) [1011] Word of God and the **testimony** of the ancient church.
S D : 0 8 :018(594) [1021] We could adduce many **testimonies** on this point from the
S D : 0 8 :050(600) [1031] even though the **testimony** of the Scripture points in that
S D : 0 8 :053(601) [1033] give us clear, certain **testimony**, we shall simply believe it
S D : 0 8 :059(602) [1035] Many other noble **testimonies** of the ancient orthodox
S D : 0 8 :067(604) [1039] do not understand the **testimonies** of the Scriptures which
S D : 0 8 :077(606) [1043] not understand these **testimonies** to mean that only the
S D : 0 8 :086(608) [1047] There are many similar **testimonies** in Dr. Luther's
S D : 1 0 :018(614) [1059] The following **testimonies** drawn from the Smalcald
S D : 1 1 :050(624) [1079] also gives a glorious **testimony** that the church of God
S D : 1 1 :065(627) [1083] according to St. Paul's **testimony** we have been elected in

Text (38), Texts (8)

A L : 2 7 :020(074) [0079] This is according to the **text** in Gen. 2:18, "It is not good
A L : 2 8 :022(084) [0087] bishops according to the **text**, "He who hears you hears
A P : 0 2 :002(100) [0105] them first to look at the German **text** of the Confession.

Continued ▶

AP : 0 4 :122(124) [0157] urge against us the **texts**, "If you would enter life, keep
AP : 0 4 :218(137) [0179] Now we shall answer the **texts** that our opponents quote
AP : 0 4 :219(137) [0179] In this **text** Paul requires love.
AP : 0 4 :220(137) [0181] But in this **text** Paul is not discussing the mode of
AP : 0 4 :221(137) [0181] They quote this one **text** in which Paul teaches about the
AP : 0 4 :221(137) [0181] they omit the many other **texts** in which he systematically
AP : 0 4 :221(137) [0181] Besides, to other **texts** that speak of faith they always add
AP : 0 4 :222(137) [0181] anything more from this **text** than that love is necessary.
AP : 0 4 :224(138) [0181] Our opponents twist many **texts** because they read their
AP : 0 4 :224(138) [0181] of deriving the meaning from the **texts** themselves.
AP : 0 4 :224(138) [0181] There is no problem in this **text** if we remove the
AP : 0 4 :235(140) [0185] Ambrose interprets the **text** this way: "Just as a building
AP : 0 4 :242(141) [0187] This **text** therefore speaks not of one's own sins but of
AP : 0 4 :244(141) [0189] James they quote the **text**, "You see that a man is justified
AP : 0 4 :245(142) [0189] we must note that this **text** is more against our opponents
AP : 0 4 :246(142) [0189] to argue from this **text** that James teaches we merit grace
AP : 0 4 :259(145) [0193] of all of penitence, as the **text** indicates; but at the same
AP : 0 4 :264(146) [0195] the interpretation of this **text**, though the promise is
AP : 0 4 :264(146) [0195] The **text** does not say this, but rather requires faith.
AP : 0 4 :267(146) [0197] but about faith as well, as the narrative in the **text** shows.
AP : 0 4 :268(147) [0197] of punishment, this **text** proves nothing against us,
AP : 0 7 :042(176) [0243] The **text** of the decree is preserved in Epiphanius: "Do
AP : 1 1 :007(181) [0251] The **text** by itself has not done as much damage as what
AP : 1 2 :071(192) [0271] statement of Peter, for the **text** says (Acts 10:44), "While
AP : 2 1 :031(233) [0351] we believe in him, as the **text** says (Rom. 9:33), "He who
AP : 2 2 :003(236) [0357] he was delivering, but the **text** clearly shows that this was
AP : 2 4 :069(262) [0409] forgiveness of sins, as the **text** says, "This is my body,
AP : 2 7 :048(277) [0437] but they do violence to the **text** when they quote it in a
TR : 0 0 :023(324) [0511] as is apparent from the **text** itself, for Christ did not
TR : 0 0 :082(000) [0529] John Brentz, Minister of Hall (Triglotta **text** only)].
SC : PR :007(339) [0533] or variations in the **text** and wording of the Ten
SC : PR :007(339) [0533] instructed on the basis of a uniform, fixed **text** and form.
SC : PR :010(339) [0535] Prayer, etc., following the **text** word for word so that the
SC : PR :014(339) [0535] become familiar with the **text**, teach them what it means.
SC : PR :015(340) [0535] single syllable, as stated above with reference to the **text**.
LC : SP :020(364) [0579] of Christ, according to the **texts** of Matthew and Mark at
LC : SP :022(364) [0579] in short, simple words according to the **text** of St. Paul.
LC : 0 1 :120(381) [0615] Hence you have a sure **text** and a divine testimony that
LC : 0 1 :319(408) [0673] we must repeat the **text** which we have already treated
LC : 0 5 :045(451) [0763] first place, we have a clear **text** in the words of Christ,
SD : 0 2 :017(524) [0887] St. Paul explains this **text**: "The mind that is set on the
SD : 0 3 :042(547) [0931] not follow," and the Latin **text** of the Apology states,
SD : 0 8 :043(599) [1029] Zwingli applies all the **texts** concerning the passion only

Thall (1)
S 3 : 1 5 :005(318) [0501] the Rev. John **Thall**

Thank (16), Thanked (3), Thankful (1), Thanks (26), Thanksgiving (21), Thanksgivings (5)
PR : PR :016(008) [0013] gladly and with heartfelt **thanks** to almighty God testified
AP : PR :018(099) [0103] testified publicly and **thanked** God for this great blessing,
AP : 0 4 :079(118) [0143] But **thanks** be to God, who gives us the victory through
AP : 0 4 :125(124) [0157] expect help from him, to **thank** and praise him, and to
AP : 0 4 :141(126) [0161] we call upon him, give **thanks** to him, fear and love him.
AP : 0 4 :189(133) [0175] our faith, to give testimony, and to render **thanks**.
AP : 0 7 :033(175) [0239] With a very **thankful** spirit we cherish the useful and
AP : 1 2 :146(205) [0297] Paul says (1 Cor. 15:57), "**Thanks** be to God, who gives us
AP : 1 2 :174(210) [0307] — prayer, **thanksgiving**, the confession of the Gospel, the
AP : 2 1 :004(229) [0343] The first is **thanksgiving**: we should thank God for
AP : 2 1 :004(229) [0343] thanksgiving: we should **thank** God for showing
AP : 2 4 :019(252) [0389] have been reconciled give **thanks** or show their gratitude
AP : 2 4 :021(253) [0391] the drink offerings, the **thank** offering, the first fruits, and
AP : 2 4 :025(253) [0391] Gospel, faith, prayer, **thanksgiving**, confession, the
AP : 2 4 :026(254) [0393] praises, that is, prayer, **thanksgiving**, confession, and the
AP : 2 4 :029(255) [0393] to thee sacrifices of **thanksgiving** and call on the name of
AP : 2 4 :029(255) [0393] Prayer is called a sacrifice of **thanksgiving**.
AP : 2 4 :030(255) [0395] this is faith, prayer, **thanksgiving**, confession, and
AP : 2 4 :032(255) [0395] call upon God, they give **thanks** to God, they bear
AP : 2 4 :033(256) [0395] itself can be praise or **thanksgiving**, but it does not justify
AP : 2 4 :035(256) [0397] of the Gospel, faith, prayer, and **thanksgiving**.
AP : 2 4 :036(257) [0397] symbolizes faith, prayer, and **thanksgiving** in the heart.
AP : 2 4 :038(257) [0399] also be an offering in **thanksgiving**, confession, and
AP : 2 4 :066(261) [0407] they are talking about **thanksgiving**; hence they call it
AP : 2 4 :074(263) [0409] then it really gives **thanks** for the blessing of Christ's
AP : 2 4 :075(263) [0411] the conscience and of **thanksgiving** or praise; the first of
AP : 2 4 :076(263) [0411] also statements about **thanksgiving**, like the beautiful
AP : 2 4 :076(263) [0411] is forgiven, and it gives **thanks** to the Giver of such a
AP : 2 4 :076(263) [0411] of our ills, our sin and our death; and it gives **thanks**.
AP : 2 4 :077(263) [0411] The ceremony is not a **thanksgiving** that can be
AP : 2 4 :082(264) [0411] but also causes many to **thank** God more abundantly.
AP : 2 4 :087(265) [0413] because prayers, **thanksgivings**, and the whole worship
AP : 2 4 :088(265) [0413] the whole service, about the prayers and **thanksgivings**.
AP : 2 4 :088(265) [0413] fear, faith, prayer, **thanksgiving**, and the like, in
AP : 2 4 :093(267) [0417] offer it only as a **thanksgiving** and do not apply it as a
AP : 2 4 :093(267) [0417] parts of the Mass, namely, prayers and **thanksgivings**.
S 2 : 0 2 :027(297) [0469] ways in which I can honor, love, and **thank** you in Christ.
S 3 : 1 2 :002(315) [0499] name of the church, for, **thank** God, a seven-year-old
SC : PR :027(341) [0539] To him be praise and **thanks** forever, through Christ, our
SC : 0 1 :004(342) [0539] upon him, pray to him, praise him, and give him **thanks**.
SC : 0 2 :002(345) [0543] all of this I am bound to **thank**, praise, serve, and obey
SC : 0 3 :013(347) [0547] enable us to receive our daily bread with **thanksgiving**.
SC : 0 6 :004(351) [0555] and when he had given **thanks**, he broke it, and gave it to
SC : 0 6 :004(351) [0555] and when he had given **thanks** he gave it to them, saying,
SC : 0 7 :002(352) [0557] "I give Thee **thanks**, heavenly Father, through thy dear
SC : 0 7 :005(353) [0559] "I give Thee **thanks**, heavenly Father, through thy dear
SC : 0 8 :006(353) [0559] *his household to offer blessing and **thanksgiving** at table*
SC : 0 8 :010(353) [0559] [**Thanksgiving** after Eating]
SC : 0 8 :010(354) [0559] "O give **thanks** to the Lord, for he is good; for his
SC : 0 8 :011(354) [0559] "We give Thee **thanks**, Lord God, our Father, for all thy
SC : 0 9 :005(355) [0561] intercessions, and **thanksgivings** be made for all men, for
SC : 0 9 :014(356) [0563] intercessions, and **thanksgivings** be made for all men"
LC : SP :023(364) [0579] took bread, gave **thanks**, and broke it and gave it to his
LC : 0 1 :027(368) [0587] as God's gifts and **thank** him for them, as this
LC : 0 1 :064(373) [0599] of need, or praise and **thank** him in time of prosperity,
LC : 0 1 :073(374) [0601] grace and returning **thanks** at meals and saying other
LC : 0 1 :074(374) [0601] "God be praised and **thanked**!" "This God has bestowed
LC : 0 1 :117(381) [0615] rejoice heartily and **thank** God that he has chosen and
LC : 0 1 :130(383) [0619] teachers can never be sufficiently **thanked** and repaid."
LC : 0 1 :145(385) [0623] for joy and praise and **thank** God; and with her careful
LC : 0 1 :166(387) [0629] we lift our hands in joyful **thanks** to God for giving us
LC : 0 1 :244(398) [0649] and then by way of **thanks** they burn and ravage house
LC : 0 1 :326(409) [0675] in prayer, praise, and **thanksgiving**, which spring from
LC : 0 2 :019(412) [0681] bound to love, praise, and **thank** him without ceasing,
LC : 0 2 :021(413) [0683] once turning to God to **thank** him or acknowledge him as
LC : 0 5 :003(447) [0753] *took bread, gave **thanks**, broke it, and gave it to his*
LC : 0 5 :003(447) [0753] *cup, after supper, gave **thanks**, and gave it to them,*
LC : 0 6 :035(461) [0000] our hands in praise and **thanks** to God that we have
SD : PR :003(502) [0847] of this Confession, but, **thank** God, it has remained
SD : 0 2 :015(523) [0887] all things we should **thank** God from our hearts for
SD : 1 0 :019(614) [1059] name of the church, for, **thank** God, a seven-year-old
SD : 1 1 :030(621) [1073] on Christ, pray and give **thanks**, are sanctified in love,

Thee (39)
AP : 0 4 :058(115) [0137] He adds, "There is forgiveness with **thee**" (v. 4).
AP : 0 4 :168(130) [0169] thy servant; for no man living is righteous before **thee**."
AP : 0 4 :168(130) [0169] let every one who is godly offer prayer to **thee**" (Ps. 32:6).
AP : 0 4 :326(157) [0211] thy servant, for no man living is righteous before **thee**."
AP : 0 4 :331(158) [0211] our supplications before **thee** on the ground of our
AP : 0 4 :337(159) [0215] our supplications before **thee** on the ground of our
AP : 1 2 :078(193) [0275] thy servant; for no man living is righteous before **thee**."
AP : 1 2 :108(198) [0283] (Ps. 51:4), "Against **thee** only have I sinned, so that thou
AP : 1 2 :108(198) [0283] Therefore I declare **Thee** to be justified in condemning
AP : 1 2 :108(198) [0283] I declare **Thee** to be blameless when hypocrites judge Thee
AP : 1 2 :108(198) [0283] when hypocrites judge **Thee** to be unrighteous in
AP : 2 1 :025(232) [0349] and of all the saints be to **thee** for the forgiveness of sins."
AP : 2 4 :029(255) [0393] Ps. 116:17, "I will offer to **thee** sacrifices of thanksgiving
AP : 2 4 :088(265) [0413] us worthy to come to offer **Thee** entreaties and
AP : 2 4 :088(265) [0413] a little later: "We offer **Thee** this reasonable and bloodless
AP : 2 4 :093(267) [0417] they add, "Yet we offer **Thee** this reasonable service for
AP : 2 7 :013(271) [0423] because of our merits but because of **Thee**, through faith.
S 1 : PR :015(291) [0459] They will have nothing to do with **Thee**.
S 1 : PR :015(291) [0459] souls who cry unto **Thee** and earnestly seek Thee
S 1 : PR :015(291) [0459] Thee and earnestly seek **Thee** according to the grace which
S 1 : PR :015(291) [0459] thy Holy Spirit, who with **Thee** and the Father liveth and
S 3 : 0 7 :002(312) [0493] living is righteous before **thee**" (Ps. 143:2), and Paul also
TR : 0 0 :071(332) [0525] added the words, "I give **thee** the power to sacrifice for
SC : 0 7 :002(352) [0557] "I give **Thee** thanks, heavenly Father, through thy dear
SC : 0 7 :002(352) [0557] I beseech **Thee** to keep me this day, too, from all sin and
SC : 0 7 :002(352) [0557] in all my thoughts, words, and deeds I may please **Thee**.
SC : 0 7 :005(353) [0559] "I give **Thee** thanks, heavenly Father, through thy dear
SC : 0 7 :005(353) [0559] I beseech **Thee** to forgive all my sin and the wrong which
SC : 0 8 :007(353) [0559] "The eyes of all look to **Thee**, O Lord, and Thou givest
SC : 0 8 :011(354) [0559] "We give **Thee** thanks, Lord God, our Father, for all thy
LC : 0 1 :118(381) [0615] "Now I know that this work is well pleasing to **Thee**!"
LC : 0 3 :021(423) [0703] him and say, "I come to **Thee**, dear Father, and pray not
LC : 0 3 :054(427) [0713] "Dear Father, we pray **Thee**, give us thy Word, that the
LC : 0 3 :097(433) [0725] "Dear Father, I come to **Thee** praying for forgiveness, not
LC : 0 6 :033(461) [0000] for flowing streams, so longs my soul for **thee**, O God."
SD : 0 1 :036(514) [0869] David says: "I will praise **thee**, for I am wonderfully
SD : 0 1 :036(514) [0869] was not hidden from **thee** when I was being made in
SD : 0 6 :021(567) [0969] for no man living is righteous before **thee**" (Ps. 143:2).
SD : 1 1 :074(628) [1087] my supplications when I cried to **thee** for help" (Ps. 31:23).

Theft (6)
AL : 1 8 :009(040) [0053] can keep the hands from **theft** and murder), yet it cannot
AP : 1 8 :004(225) [0335] choose to keep the hands from murder, adultery, or **theft**.
S 3 : 0 1 :002(302) [0477] to parents, murder, unchastity, **theft**, deceit, etc.
LC : 0 1 :226(395) [0645] dares to give them a hard look or accuse them of **theft**.
LC : 0 1 :293(404) [0663] referring to unchastity or **theft**, since these vices were
EP : 0 2 :008(471) [0789] robbery, murder, **theft**, and similar sins under

Theme (1)
AP : 2 4 :054(259) [0403] epistle is devoted to the **theme** that the ancient priesthood

Theodore (2), Theodoret (1)
SD : 0 8 :015(594) [1019] witness of Suidas and **Theodore**, the presbyter of Rhaitu,
SD : 0 8 :016(594) [1019] **Theodore** the Presbyter wrote: "A contemporary of the
SD : 0 8 :022(595) [1023] Gregory of Nyssa, in **Theodoret**; John Damascene, Book

Theologian (3), Theologians (101)
PR : PR :000(001) [0004] Confession and of their **Theologians**, Together with an
PR : PR :009(006) [0011] neither we nor our **theologians** knew which version was
PR : PR :010(006) [0011] irenic, and learned **theologians** noted these developments,
PR : PR :011(006) [0011] At first the said **theologians** clearly and correctly
PR : PR :013(007) [0013] and learned **theologians** at Torgau in the year 1576 for
PR : PR :013(007) [0013] they and their chief **theologians** peruse it with particular
PR : PR :015(007) [0013] to each and every **theologian**, minister, and schoolmaster
PR : PR :016(008) [0015] only of a few of our **theologians** but generally of each and
PR : PR :020(010) [0017] though a number of **theologians**, like Luther himself,
PR : PR :020(010) [0017] natures in Christ, our **theologians** clearly assert in the
PR : PR :020(010) [0017] on this basis, **theologians** are not to argue from some
PR : PR :021(010) [0019] God and is exalted, our **theologians** declare in clear and
PR : PR :022(012) [0019] devolves upon the **theologians** and ministers duly to
AL : 2 6 :014(066) [0073] that the summists and **theologians** gathered the traditions
AL : 2 6 :016(066) [0073] and certain other **theologians** greatly lamented that they
AP : PR :001(098) [0099] a number of **theologians** and monks prepared a
AP : PR :013(099) [0101] my quarrel is with the **theologians** and monks who wrote
AP : PR :017(099) [0103] of the monks, canonists, and scholastic **theologians**.
AP : 0 2 :023(103) [0111] Even the scholastic **theologians** teach that these things
AP : 0 2 :027(103) [0111] Not the ancient **theologians** alone, but even the more
AP : 0 2 :032(104) [0113] by the sophistic arguments of modern **theologians**.
AP : 0 2 :032(104) [0113] Modern **theologians** have evidently not paid attention to
AP : 0 4 :131(125) [0157] But our opponents are fine **theologians**!
AP : 0 4 :289(151) [0203] down by the scholastic **theologians**, teaches that we are
AP : 0 4 :390(166) [0225] or bishops or some **theologians** or monks advance.
AP : 0 4 :390(166) [0225] also obvious that the **theologians** have mingled more than
AP : 0 4 :392(167) [0225] that prelates and some **theologians** and monks in the

Continued ▶

A P : 1 1 :003(180) [0249] On this subject our **theologians** have written many things
A P : 1 2 :003(182) [0253] the writings of our **theologians** have shed much light on
A P : 1 2 :004(183) [0253] of all classes, even the **theologians**, admit that before
A P : 1 2 :005(183) [0253] questions which the **theologians** could never explain
A P : 1 2 :068(192) [0271] on their side some **theologians** of great reputation, like
A P : 1 2 :069(192) [0271] the statements of later **theologians** who did not produce
A P : 1 2 :110(198) [0285] many of the most generally accepted **theologians**.
A P : 1 6 :002(222) [0329] The writings of our **theologians** have profitably illumined
A P : 1 6 :004(223) [0331] Our **theologians** have written extensively on this subject
A P : 1 6 :013(224) [0333] Our **theologians** have explained this whole matter of
A P : 2 0 :003(227) [0339] There have indeed been **theologians** who held that after
A P : 2 0 :004(227) [0339] These **theologians** have lost all sense of shame if they dare
A P : 2 1 :016(231) [0347] people but discuss only the views of the **theologians**.
A P : 2 1 :026(232) [0349] seen a certain monastic **theologian**, summoned to console
A P : 2 1 :032(233) [0351] Even the **theologians** hold to the error that each saint has
A P : 2 1 :038(234) [0355] Bishops, **theologians**, and monks applaud these
A P : 2 1 :041(235) [0355] have heard excellent **theologians** ask for limitations upon
A P : 2 1 :041(235) [0355] of the scholastic **theologians** and canonists and was
A P : 2 2 :011(238) [0361] reason; but whatever the **theologians** say, let that be law!
A P : 2 4 :017(252) [0389] The **theologians** make a proper distinction between
A P : 2 4 :094(267) [0417] and the more recent **theologians**, we set them against the
S 3 : 0 1 :003(302) [0477] What the scholastic **theologians** taught concerning this
S 3 : 0 2 :003(303) [0479] was just said above concerning the scholastic **theologians**.
S 3 : 0 3 :041(309) [0491] which the pope, the **theologians**, the jurists, and all men
T R : 0 0 :000(319) [0503] Compiled by the **Theologians** Assembled in Smalcald in
T R : 0 0 :022(323) [0511] in the books of our **theologians**, and all the details cannot
E P : 0 0 :000(463) [0775] among Some of the **Theologians** Adhering to this
E P : 0 0 :000(464) [0777] Controversy among the **theologians** of the Augsburg
E P : R N :004(465) [0777] which the leading **theologians** approved by their
E P : 0 4 :002(475) [0797] division among some **theologians** was occasioned when
E P : 0 4 :003(475) [0797] arose among certain **theologians** concerning the use of the
E P : 0 6 :001(480) [0805] that a controversy has arisen among a few **theologians**.
E P : 0 7 :001(481) [0807] numbered among the **theologians** identified with the
E P : 0 8 :001(486) [0817] between the authentic **theologians** of the Augsburg
E P : 0 8 :001(486) [0817] misled some other **theologians** also) concerning the
E P : 0 9 :001(492) [0827] a dispute among some **theologians** of the Augsburg
E P : 1 0 :001(492) [0829] been a division among **theologians** of the Augsburg
E P : 1 1 :001(494) [0831] developed among the **theologians** of the Augsburg
E P : 1 1 :022(497) [0837] which for a time the **theologians** of the Augsburg
S D : 0 0 :000(501) [0845] Among Some **Theologians** for a Time, Resolved and
S D : P R :006(502) [0847] be denied that some **theologians** did depart from it in
S D : P R :005(504) [0851] was prepared by our **theologians** but because it is taken
S D : P R :007(505) [0853] the great assembly of **theologians** at Smalcald in 1537 and
S D : P R :011(506) [0855] and most illustrious **theologians** of that time subscribed
S D : P R :012(506) [0855] arose among the **theologians** of the Augsburg
S D : P R :019(507) [0857] among some of the **theologians** of the Augsburg
S D : P R :019(507) [0857] the writings of certain **theologians**, lest anyone be misled
S D : P R :019(507) [0857] by the high regard in which these **theologians** were held.
S D : 0 1 :001(508) [0859] among a number of **theologians** of the Augsburg
S D : 0 1 :056(518) [0877] this controversy, the **theologians** in our schools and
S D : 0 2 :001(519) [0881] the papists and our **theologians** but also among a number
S D : 0 2 :001(520) [0881] among a number of **theologians** of the Augsburg
S D : 0 2 :002(520) [0881] argued by some of the **theologians** of the churches of the
S D : 0 2 :045(530) [0899] other writings of this eminent and enlightened **theologian**.
S D : 0 3 :001(539) [0917] arisen among several **theologians** of the Augsburg
S D : 0 3 :055(549) [0935] in our churches the **theologians** of the Augsburg
S D : 0 4 :001(551) [0939] arisen among the **theologians** of the Augsburg
S D : 0 4 :003(551) [0939] A few **theologians** also maintained that good works are
S D : 0 5 :002(558) [0951] among some **theologians** of the Augsburg Confession.
S D : 0 5 :003(558) [0953] Scripture of God and by ancient and modern **theologians**.
S D : 0 6 :001(564) [0963] has arisen among a few **theologians** concerning this third
S D : 0 7 :001(568) [0971] controversy among the **theologians** of the Augsburg
S D : 0 7 :001(568) [0971] years a number of **theologians** and others who professed
S D : 0 7 :012(571) [0977] In 1536 the **theologians** of Saxony and Upper Germany
S D : 0 7 :012(571) [0977] Luther and other **theologians** of both parties signed
S D : 0 7 :017(572) [0977] year the leading **theologians** who were committed to the
S D : 0 7 :017(572) [0979] Articles, which all the **theologians** collectively and
S D : 0 7 :038(576) [0985] as Dr. Luther and our **theologians** call it in the
S D : 0 8 :001(591) [1015] likewise arisen among **theologians** of the Augsburg
S D : 0 8 :004(592) [1017] after his death a few **theologians** of the Augsburg
S D : 0 9 :001(610) [1051] among some of our **theologians** just as among the ancient
S D : 1 0 :001(610) [1053] among some **theologians** of the Augsburg Confession
S D : 1 0 :021(614) [1059] and which all the **theologians** assembled in Smalcald
S D : 1 1 :001(616) [1063] dissension among the **theologians** of the Augsburg
S D : 1 1 :001(616) [1063] Nor have our **theologians** always used the same terms.
S D : 1 1 :094(632) [1095] been disputed among **theologians** of the Augsburg
S D : 1 2 :004(633) [1097] controversy among the **theologians** of the Augsburg

Theological (2)

A P : 2 3 :006(240) [0365] call for some **theological** discussion, but in this one the
S D : 0 4 :005(551) [0939] a vehemently argued **theological** controversy when some

Theology (3)

A P : 2 1 :026(232) [0349] a dying doctor of **theology**, do nothing but urge this
A P : 2 1 :041(235) [0355] recent ones, so their **theology** has steadily degenerated.
S D : 0 1 :055(518) [0877] irrefutable axioms in **theology** that every substance or

Theory (7), Theories (3)

A P : 0 4 :260(145) [0195] to suit the man-made **theory** that by our works we
A P : 0 4 :264(146) [0195] to them the human **theory** that forgiveness depends upon
A P : 1 2 :119(200) [0287] This whole **theory** is a recent fiction, without authority
A P : 1 6 :010(224) [0333] they have praised the **theory** that the Gospel requires us
A P : 1 6 :013(224) [0333] were helped after the **theories** of the monks had troubled
A P : 1 6 :013(224) [0333] by foolish monastic **theories** which put a hypocritical
A P : 2 1 :003(229) [0343] The **theory** of invocation, together with the theories our
A P : 2 1 :003(229) [0343] together with the **theories** our opponents now hold about
A P : 2 4 :077(263) [0411] The **theory** that a ceremony can benefit either the
A P : 2 4 :088(265) [0413] the like, in opposition to a **theory** of *ex opere operato*.

Thesis (2), Theses (11)

E P : 0 1 :001(466) [0779] Affirmative **Theses**
E P : 0 2 :001(470) [0787] Affirmative **Theses**
E P : 0 3 :002(473) [0793] Affirmative **Theses**
E P : 0 4 :004(476) [0797] Affirmative **Theses**
E P : 0 5 :001(478) [0801] Affirmative **Theses**
E P : 0 6 :001(480) [0805] Affirmative **Theses**
E P : 0 7 :005(482) [0809] Affirmative **Theses**
E P : 0 8 :003(487) [0819] Affirmative **Theses**
E P : 1 0 :002(493) [0829] Affirmative **Theses**
S D : P R :019(507) [0857] and distinctly in these **theses** and antitheses, opposing the
S D : 0 1 :004(509) [0861] the true doctrine and its opposite in **theses** and antitheses.
S D : 0 1 :030(513) [0867] As stated in a foregoing **thesis** when we discussed the
S D : 0 1 :049(517) [0875] the contrary doctrine, the **thesis** and antithesis, as far as

Thief (7), Thievery (2), Thieves (9)

A P : 1 2 :169(209) [0305] or robbed, for he is still a **thief** and a robber as long as he
A P : 1 2 :169(209) [0305] as it is written (Eph. 4:28), "Let the **thief** no longer steal."
S C : P R :018(340) [0537] for many of these are guilty of dishonesty and **thievery**.
L C : 0 1 :224(395) [0643] If all who are **thieves**, though they are unwilling to admit
L C : 0 1 :225(395) [0645] If a **thief** had taken such sums he would be strangled with
L C : 0 1 :225(395) [0645] defiant and insolent and dare anyone to call him a **thief**!
L C : 0 1 :226(395) [0645] are far worse than sneak-**thieves**, against whom we can
L C : 0 1 :228(396) [0645] In short, **thievery** is the most common craft and the
L C : 0 1 :228(396) [0645] it is nothing but a vast, wide stable full of great **thieves**.
L C : 0 1 :229(396) [0645] picklocks and sneak-**thieves** who loot a cash box, they sit
L C : 0 1 :230(396) [0645] here about various petty **thieves** in order to launch an
L C : 0 1 :230(396) [0645] the great, powerful arch-**thieves** who consort with lords
L C : 0 1 :230(396) [0645] and chief protector of all **thieves**, the Holy See at Rome,
L C : 0 1 :231(396) [0647] Meanwhile the little sneak-**thieves** who have committed
L C : 0 1 :231(396) [0647] God they are the greatest **thieves**, and that he will punish
L C : 0 1 :235(397) [0647] take your wages like a **thief**, and even expect to be revered
L C : 0 1 :245(398) [0649] the other, he punishes one **thief** by means of another.
L C : 0 1 :268(401) [0657] is to declare somebody a **thief**, a murderer, a traitor, etc.

Thigh (1)

A P : 0 2 :034(104) [0113] I was instructed, I smote upon my **thigh**" (Jer. 31:19).

Thine (3)

S 1 : P R :015(291) [0459] assemble a council of **thine** own, and by thy glorious
L C : S P :014(363) [0577] For **thine** is the kingdom and the power and the glory,
S D : 1 1 :004(617) [1063] Again, "**Thine** eyes beheld my unformed substance, in thy

Think (90), Thinking (9), Thinks (9), Thought (41), Thoughts (35)

A G : 0 5 :004(031) [0045] our own preparations, **thoughts**, and works without the
A G : 0 0 :001(047) [0059] of the Fathers), we **think** that our opponents cannot
A G : 2 4 :029(059) [0067] of the Mass by those who **think** that grace is obtained
A G : 2 7 :055(079) [0083] Still others **think** that it is not right at all for Christians,
A G : 0 0 :004(095) [0095] It must not be **thought** that anything has been said or
A L : 0 5 :004(031) [0045] and others who **think** that the Holy Spirit comes to men
A L : 0 8 :003(033) [0047] church and who have **thought** the ministry of evil men to
A L : 1 7 :004(038) [0051] the Anabaptists who **think** that there will be an end to the
A L : 2 0 :040(046) [0057] Nothing good in deed or **thought**, Nothing free from
A L : 2 6 :002(064) [0071] That the world **thought** so is evident from the fact that
A L : 2 6 :007(065) [0071] the whole of repentance was **thought** to consist of these.
A L : 2 6 :008(065) [0071] Christianity was **thought** to consist wholly in the
A L : 2 6 :021(067) [0073] of this kind are not to be **thought** of as necessary acts of
A L : 2 8 :037(087) [0089] authors of these things **thought** that they would merit
A L : 2 8 :053(089) [0091] What, then, are we to **think** about Sunday and about
A P : 0 2 :051(107) [0119] We have **thought** it worthwhile rather to list, in the usual
A P : 0 4 :021(110) [0127] In smug hypocrites, who **think** that they are keeping the
A P : 0 4 :034(112) [0129] Content with this, they **think** they satisfy the law of God.
A P : 0 4 :055(114) [0137] of faith we are also **thinking** of its object, the promised
A P : 0 4 :061(115) [0137] First of all, lest anyone **think** that we are speaking of an
A P : 0 4 :064(116) [0139] a faith that is not an idle **thought**, but frees us from
A P : 0 4 :071(116) [0141] faith justifies, some may **think** this refers to the
A P : 0 4 :109(122) [0153] But they have **thought** up a piece of sophistry to evade
A P : 0 4 :112(123) [0155] We are not to **think** from this that we receive the
A P : 0 4 :124(124) [0157] the law that deals with the **thoughts** of the heart.
A P : 0 4 :134(125) [0159] that is, hypocrites **think** that outward and civil works
A P : 0 4 :135(125) [0159] Holy Spirit, so that we can **think** rightly about God, fear
A P : 0 4 :145(127) [0163] They **think** this is on account of our love, though they do
A P : 0 4 :149(127) [0163] insults Christ because he **thinks** that his sin is greater and
A P : 0 4 :154(128) [0163] Truly to believe means to **think** of Christ in this way, and
A P : 0 4 :159(129) [0167] are mistaken when they **think** that we are justified by the
A P : 0 4 :165(129) [0169] If anyone **thinks** that he is righteous and acceptable
A P : 0 4 :208(135) [0177] at rest, they kept **thinking** up new works beyond God's
A P : 0 4 :266(146) [0197] to express this same **thought**, and our opponents
A P : 0 4 :271(147) [0199] of penitence, yet we **think** that none of our opponents is
A P : 0 4 :282(149) [0201] the Pharisees for **thinking** that they are cleansed before
A P : 0 4 :288(151) [0203] of the heart, reason **thinks** that it pleases God if it does
A P : 0 4 :288(151) [0203] Later on men **thought** up monastic orders, which
A P : 0 4 :304(154) [0205] death are not merely **thoughts** in the intellect but are also
A P : 0 4 :325(157) [0211] Let no one **think** that we are teaching anything new in
A P : 0 4 :357(161) [0217] also omit the central **thought** of the discussion; they pick
A P : 0 4 :384(166) [0225] Here we **think** that our opponents will grant that the
A P : 0 4 :400(168) [0227] I **think** we should seek it in the words of him who is the
A P : 0 7 :013(170) [0231] the Holy Spirit but would **think** of it as only the outward
A P : 0 7 :027(173) [0235] care anything for the Gospel or **think** it worth reading?
A P : 0 7 :032(174) [0239] Some have **thought** that human traditions are devotions
A P : 1 0 :003(179) [0247] Does he **think** perhaps that we do not know the power of
A P : 1 2 :087(195) [0277] We **think** this is clear enough for devout consciences, and
A P : 1 2 :114(199) [0285] the inexperienced into **thinking** that by these works they
A P : 1 2 :116(199) [0287] be obscured or people **think** that because of these works
A P : 1 2 :125(201) [0289] If the Roman See **thinks** it is right for all nations to
A P : 1 2 :125(201) [0289] What will posterity **think** about these slanderous
A P : 1 2 :127(201) [0289] itself — how many do you **think** there are in these places
A P : 1 2 :145(205) [0297] ways: first, because they **think** that outward and civil
A P : 1 2 :149(205) [0299] are badly mistaken if they **think** that canonical
A P : 1 2 :167(208) [0303] an example; they did not **think** that this discipline was
A P : 1 3 :002(211) [0309] We do not **think** it makes much difference if, for
A P : 1 5 :003(215) [0315] We did not **think** that they would actually condemn the
A P : 1 5 :008(216) [0317] observance of the law you **think** you deserve to be
A P : 1 5 :010(216) [0317] because they were **thought** of as works meriting
A P : 1 6 :007(223) [0331] so often lest the apostles **think** that they should usurp the
A P : 2 0 :010(228) [0341] find a work that it **thought** adequate to placate the wrath
A P : 2 1 :011(230) [0345] power to perceive the unspoken **thought** of our minds.

Continued ▶

A P : 2 1 :011(230) [0345] They have not **thought** this up to honor the saints but to
A P : 2 1 :032(233) [0351] The Romans **thought** that Juno granted riches, Febris
A P : 2 1 :034(234) [0353] Men venerated these and **thought** they contained some
A P : 2 3 :005(239) [0365] their authority, which they **think** celibacy enhances.
A P : 2 3 :006(240) [0365] our opponents have **thought** up some subterfuges to
A P : 2 3 :010(241) [0367] than this foolishness, **thought** up in order to circumvent
A P : 2 3 :045(245) [0377] They **thought** they would merit grace by performing these
A P : 2 4 :013(251) [0387] work of these Masses they **think** they can placate God's
A P : 2 4 :028(254) [0393] How are we to **think** the Jews accepted this declaration,
A P : 2 4 :052(259) [0403] deceives them, and they **think** that we should have some
A P : 2 4 :086(265) [0413] unless some one prefers to **think** it was called that
A P : 2 7 :004(269) [0421] in their sermons and in **thinking** up new ways of making
A P : 2 7 :008(269) [0421] We **think** that here and there in the monasteries there are
A P : 2 7 :015(271) [0425] the works of other laws that have now been **thought** up.
A P : 2 7 :025(273) [0429] liars"; that is, they do not **think** correctly about God, they
A P : 2 7 :058(279) [0439] compare monasticism, **thought** up without a Word of
S 1 : P R :006(289) [0457] I often **think** of the good Gerson, who doubted whether
S 3 : 0 3 :003(304) [0481] great, wise, mighty, and holy you may **think** yourselves.
S 3 : 0 3 :011(305) [0481] sins, such as wicked **thoughts** to which they consented
S 3 : 0 3 :022(306) [0485] Some **thought** that they would never get out of purgatory
S 3 : 0 3 :028(308) [0487] were some who did not **think** they were guilty of actual
S 3 : 0 3 :028(308) [0487] actual sins — that is, of sinful **thoughts**, words, and deeds.
S 3 : 0 3 :028(308) [0487] fought against evil **thoughts** by fasting, vigils, prayers,
S 3 : 0 3 :029(308) [0487] to repent of when they did not consent to evil **thoughts**?
S 3 : 0 3 :030(308) [0487] hand there are some who **think**, "We have already done
S 3 : 0 3 :032(308) [0489] And you hypocrites who **think** you do not need to
S 3 : 0 3 :036(309) [0489] pin our hope on anything that we are, **think**, say, or do.
T R : 0 0 :034(325) [0513] righteousness was **thought** to be that external
S C : 0 7 :002(352) [0557] and evil, that in all my **thoughts**, words, and deeds I may
L C : P R :008(359) [0569] their ABC's, which they **think** they have outgrown long
L C : P R :009(359) [0569] and truly such learned and great doctors as they **think**.
L C : P R :009(359) [0569] even though they **think** they know them ever so well.
L C : P R :010(359) [0569] the flesh, and all evil **thoughts** as to occupy oneself with
L C : P R :011(360) [0571] you obtain from it is to rout the devil and evil **thoughts**.
L C : P R :015(360) [0571] our weapons and armor, too lazy to give them a **thought**!
L C : P R :016(361) [0573] Most marvelous fellows, to **think** we can finish learning in
L C : 0 1 :005(365) [0581] Many a person **thinks** he has God and everything he
L C : 0 1 :025(368) [0587] This, I **think**, is why we Germans from ancient times have
L C : 0 1 :033(369) [0589] to luck, like brutes who **think** that it makes no great
L C : 0 1 :036(369) [0589] have perished who **thought** themselves to be so high and
L C : 0 1 :097(378) [0609] It used to be **thought** that Sunday had been properly
L C : 0 1 :100(379) [0609] unbelief and wicked **thoughts** against all these
L C : 0 1 :108(379) [0611] Therefore, we are not to **think** of their persons, whatever
L C : 0 1 :128(382) [0617] God, and no one takes **thought** how God feeds, guards,
L C : 0 1 :140(384) [0621] words, and everyone **thinks** he already knows them well.
L C : 0 1 :152(386) [0625] How difficult do you **think** it will be for him to pay you
L C : 0 1 :154(386) [0625] Why, do you **think**, is the world now so full of
L C : 0 1 :172(388) [0629] We must not **think** only of amassing money and property
L C : 0 1 :176(389) [0631] **Think** what deadly harm you do when you are negligent
L C : 0 1 :195(391) [0637] wants to remind us to **think** back to the First
L C : 0 1 :215(394) [0641] so full of unchaste **thoughts** and evil desires that they
L C : 0 1 :219(394) [0643] only to live chastely in **thought**, word, and deed in his
L C : 0 1 :278(402) [0661] Do you **think** it is an insignificant thing to gain a
L C : 0 1 :287(403) [0663] of the body which we **think** less honorable we invest with
L C : 0 1 :293(404) [0663] They **thought** they were keeping the commandments when
L C : 0 1 :298(405) [0665] We **think** up artful dodges and sly tricks (better and
L C : 0 1 :315(408) [0671] Just **think**, is it not a devilish presumption on the part of
L C : 0 2 :005(411) [0679] Of course, if all the **thoughts** contained in the Scriptures
L C : 0 2 :060(418) [0695] word *Fleisch* (flesh), we **think** no farther than the butcher
L C : 0 2 :063(419) [0695] what God is and what he **thinks** and does, yet it has never
L C : 0 3 :006(421) [0699] Let no one **think** that it makes no difference whether I
L C : 0 3 :008(421) [0699] silence and repel any **thoughts** that would prevent or
L C : 0 3 :010(421) [0699] may silence and repel **thoughts** which would prevent or
L C : 0 3 :010(421) [0699] always flees from God, **thinking** that he neither wants nor
L C : 0 3 :011(421) [0699] Against such **thoughts**, I say, we should respect this
L C : 0 3 :013(422) [0701] We should **think**, "On my account this prayer would
L C : 0 3 :015(422) [0701] and deterred by such **thoughts** as these: "I am not holy
L C : 0 3 :015(422) [0701] Away with such **thoughts**!
L C : 0 3 :025(423) [0705] night; not one of them **thinks** of asking for the least
L C : 0 3 :025(423) [0705] They only **thought**, at best, of doing a good work as a
L C : 0 3 :031(424) [0707] What do you **think** has accomplished such great results in
L C : 0 3 :064(429) [0715] This is his only purpose, his desire and **thought**.
L C : 0 3 :065(429) [0715] Let nobody **think** that he will have peace; he must
L C : 0 3 :070(429) [0717] how proud, secure, and powerful they **think** they are.
L C : 0 3 :072(430) [0719] enlarge and extend your **thoughts** to include not only the
L C : 0 3 :088(432) [0723] but forgiveness, before we prayed or even **thought** of it.
L C : 0 3 :091(432) [0723] Let no one **think** that he will ever in this life reach the
L C : 0 3 :095(433) [0725] If you do not forgive, do not **think** that God forgives you.
L C : 0 3 :097(433) [0725] may recall the promise and **think**, "Dear Father, I come
L C : 0 3 :111(435) [0729] yourself by your own **thoughts** and counsels, you will
L C : 0 4 :020(439) [0737] and say, "Why should I **think** more of this person than of
L C : 0 4 :021(439) [0737] Do you **think** it was a jest that the heavens opened when
L C : 0 4 :043(442) [0743] Just **think** how the world would snow and rain money
L C : 0 4 :055(443) [0747] How dare we **think** that God's Word and ordinance
L C : 0 5 :006(447) [0755] Do you **think** God cares so much about our faith and
L C : 0 5 :079(455) [0771] are in the world, do not **think** that there will be any lack
E P : 0 1 :021(468) [0783] a way that even if no evil **thought** would ever arise in the
E P : 0 1 :021(468) [0785] actual sins, such as evil **thoughts**, words, and deeds, as it
E P : 0 1 :021(469) [0785] of the heart come evil **thoughts**," etc, and "The
E P : 0 7 :005(482) [0809] should ascend with the **thoughts** of our faith and there,
E P : 1 1 :009(495) [0833] to despair and waken dangerous **thoughts** in their hearts.
E P : 1 2 :008(498) [0839] the Anabaptists neither **think** highly of infant Baptism
S D : P R :009(503) [0849] are not, as some may **think**, mere misunderstandings or
S D : 0 1 :001(508) [0859] because it is not a **thought**, a word, or a deed but the very
S D : 0 1 :006(509) [0861] though a man were to **think** no evil, speak no evil, or do
S D : 0 1 :025(512) [0867] thing (such as, for example, producing a good **thought**).
S D : 0 1 :042(515) [0871] work that man is able to **think**, to speak, to act, and to do
S D : 0 1 :042(515) [0873] is corrupted, that our **thoughts**, words, and deeds are
S D : 0 1 :053(517) [0875] indicate that not only **thoughts**, words, and deeds are sin
S D : 0 2 :012(522) [0885] skill, and ability to **think** anything good or right in
S D : 0 2 :043(529) [0897] of the devil to do and to **think** what pleases them and
S D : 0 2 :044(529) [0897] of itself does not once **think** to turn to the holy Gospel
S D : 0 2 :044(529) [0897] Chapter 26, he repeats and explicates the same **thought**.
S D : 0 2 :070(535) [0909] to have good spiritual **thoughts**, Christian intentions, and
S D : 0 2 :081(537) [0911] "Lest anyone might **think** that the substance or essence of
S D : 0 3 :042(547) [0931] delude themselves into **thinking** that they have faith when
S D : 0 3 :058(550) [0937] in our nature, in its **thoughts**, words, and deeds, so that
S D : 0 5 :017(561) [0957] disposed in his nature, **thoughts**, words, and deeds in
S D : 0 5 :020(561) [0959] it, his corrupted nature, **thoughts**, words, and deeds war
S D : 0 7 :022(573) [0979] anyone in the eye who **thinks** that he can correct Christ
S D : 0 7 :103(587) [1009] enthusiasts may indeed **think** that God is unable to do it,
S D : 1 1 :011(618) [1067] And such **thoughts** may well come to pious hearts, too,
S D : 1 1 :011(618) [1067] fell away again, they may **think**, "If you are not
S D : 1 1 :012(618) [1067] false imagining and **thoughts** with the following clear,
S D : 1 1 :013(618) [1067] Hence if we wish to **think** or speak correctly and
S D : 1 1 :024(620) [1071] and organize our **thinking** about this article in this light,
S D : 1 1 :034(622) [1075] in my heart I am not **thinking** of all, but only of a certain
S D : 1 1 :035(622) [1075] they say one thing and **think** and intend something
S D : 1 1 :052(625) [1081] we to follow our own **thoughts** in this matter and draw
S D : 1 1 :070(627) [1085] and torture himself with **thoughts** concerning the secret
S D : 1 1 :070(627) [1085] With such **thoughts** the troublesome adversary is

Third (60), Thirdly (6)

A G : 0 3 :004(030) [0045] rose from the dead on the **third** day, ascended into
A G : 1 8 :004(039) [0051] are here quoted from the **third** book of his
A G : 2 4 :030(059) [0067] In the **third** place, the holy sacrament was not instituted
A G : 2 6 :012(065) [0071] In the **third** place, such traditions have turned out to be a
A L : 0 3 :004(030) [0045] descended into hell, and on the **third** day truly rose again.
A L : 2 6 :012(065) [0071] In the **third** place, traditions brought great dangers to
A P : 0 3 :001(107) [0119] opponents approve our **third** article, in which we confess
A P : 0 4 :083(118) [0145] **Third**, in Acts 10:43, Peter says, "To him all the prophets
A P : 0 4 :204(135) [0177] **Thirdly**, such people never attain the knowledge of God,
A P : 0 4 :247(142) [0191] **Third**, James has just said that regeneration takes place
A P : 0 4 :321(156) [0209] **Third**, how will the conscience know when a work has
A P : 1 2 :013(184) [0257] There remains the **third** step, satisfaction.
A P : 1 2 :028(185) [0259] whole life and character a **third** part, we shall not object.
A P : 1 2 :075(193) [0273] **Third**, our opponents say that sins are forgiven in this
A P : 1 2 :135(203) [0293] **Thirdly**, it is just such satisfactions that indulgences remit,
A P : 2 1 :006(230) [0345] The **third** honor is the imitation, first of their faith and
A P : 2 3 :014(241) [0367] ***Third***, Paul says (I Cor. 7:2), "Because of the temptation
A P : 2 3 :067(248) [0383] Their **third** argument is horrible: the marriage of priests is
A P : 2 7 :051(277) [0437] **Third**, in monastic vows chastity is promised.
S 2 : 0 2 :018(296) [0467] The **third** are pilgrimages.
S 3 : 0 4 :000(310) [0491] second, through Baptism; **third**, through the holy
T R : 0 0 :038(326) [0515] On the **third** article this must be added: Even if the bishop
T R : 0 0 :040(327) [0517] **Third**, because the pope is unwilling to be judged by the
T R : 0 0 :050(329) [0519] The ninth question of the **third** canon states, "No one
S C : P R :017(340) [0535] In the **third** place, after you have thus taught this brief
S C : 0 1 :005(342) [0541] The **Third**
S C : 0 1 :021(344) [0543] upon the children to the **third** and the fourth generation
S C : 0 2 :003(345) [0545] *he descended into hell, the* ***third*** *day he rose from the*
S C : 0 2 :005(345) [0545] The **Third** Article: Sanctification
S C : 0 3 :009(347) [0547] The **Third** Petition
S C : 0 4 :009(349) [0551] **Third**
L C : S P :012(363) [0577] he descended into hell, the **third** day he rose from the
L C : 0 1 :030(368) [0589] *upon the children to the* ***third*** *and fourth generation of*
L C : 0 1 :043(370) [0593] their wealth, nor has it ever lasted to the **third** generation.
L C : 0 1 :077(375) [0603] The **Third** Commandment
L C : 0 1 :103(379) [0611] **Thirdly**, on holy days or days of rest we should diligently
L C : 0 1 :137(384) [0621] as we said above, "to the **third** and fourth generation."
L C : 0 1 :263(400) [0655] The **third** aspect of this commandment concerns us all.
L C : 0 1 :320(408) [0673] *upon the children to the* ***third*** *and fourth generation of*
L C : 0 2 :006(411) [0679] the Son, redemption; the **third**, of the Holy Spirit,
L C : 0 2 :025(413) [0683] *he descended into hell, the* ***third*** *day he rose from the*
L C : 0 2 :033(415) [0687] The **Third** Article
L C : 0 3 :000(420) [0697] **Third** Part: The Lord's Prayer
L C : 0 3 :001(420) [0697] Now follows the **third** part, how we are to pray.
L C : 0 3 :058(428) [0715] The **Third** Petition
L C : 0 4 :032(440) [0739] In the **third** place, having learned the great benefit and
L C : 0 4 :074(445) [0751] comprehends also the **third** sacrament, formerly called
E P : 0 6 :000(479) [0805] VI. The **Third** Function of the Law
E P : 0 6 :001(480) [0805] It is concerning the **third** function of the law that a
E P : 0 7 :013(483) [0811] "The **third** ground is that God's Word is not false nor
S D : P R :019(507) [0857] 3. In the **third** place, since within the past twenty-five
S D : 0 1 :008(510) [0861] **Thirdly**, reason does not know and understand the true
S D : 0 1 :045(516) [0873] **Thirdly**, in the article of sanctification we have the
S D : 0 2 :025(526) [0891] In the **third** place, Holy Scriptures ascribe conversion,
S D : 0 3 :001(539) [0917] The **third** controversy which has arisen among several
S D : 0 4 :030(555) [0947] In the **third** place, a disputation has arisen as to whether
S D : 0 5 :004(559) [0953] should suffer and on the **third** day rise from the dead, and
S D : 0 6 :000(563) [0963] VI. The **Third** Function of the Law
S D : 0 6 :001(564) [0963] concerning this **third** and last function of the law.
S D : 0 7 :096(586) [1005] "3. The **third** is that the Word of God is not false or
S D : 0 7 :101(587) [1007] "3. **Thirdly**, since he is one person with God, the divine,
S D : 0 7 :101(587) [1007] according to this exalted **third** mode, where they cannot
S D : 0 8 :048(600) [1031] matter when, in the **third** place, the question being treated
S D : 0 8 :059(602) [1035] 3. In the **third** place, Scripture not only speaks in general
S D : 0 8 :081(607) [1045] that according to the **third** supernatural manner, he is and
S D : 1 1 :027(620) [1071] some at the second, at the **third**, at the sixth, at the ninth,

Thirst (9), Thirsty (2)

A P : 2 4 :075(263) [0411] not hunger, and he who believes in me shall never **thirst**.'"
L C : P R :020(361) [0573] Only then, hungry and **thirsty**, will they truly relish what
L C : 0 1 :191(391) [0635] say: "I was hungry and **thirsty** and you gave me no food
L C : 0 1 :191(391) [0635] to die of hunger, **thirst**, and cold, to be torn to pieces by
L C : 0 5 :041(451) [0763] go unless he feels a hunger and **thirst** impelling him to it.
L C : 0 5 :075(455) [0771] need or experience hunger and **thirst** for the sacrament?"
L C : 0 6 :032(461) [0000] their conscience, already have the true hunger and **thirst**.
L C : 0 6 :032(461) [0000] burning with heat and **thirst**, as Ps. 42:2 says, "As a hart
E P : 0 8 :008(487) [0819] place, to endure hunger, **thirst**, cold, heat, and the like,
S D : 0 8 :010(593) [1019] another, to suffer hunger, **thirst**, frost, heat, and similar
S D : 1 1 :030(621) [1073] nevertheless hunger and **thirst** after righteousness

Thirty (3)

A P : 2 7 :001(268) [0419] **Thirty** years ago, in the Thuringian town of Eisenach,
L C : 0 1 :225(395) [0645] cheat his employer out of **thirty** or forty gulden or more a
L C : 0 1 :236(397) [0647] you have done you will have to pay back **thirty**-fold.

Thomas (7)
A P : 0 2 :027(104) [0113] Thus **Thomas** says: "Original sin denotes the privation of
A P : 1 5 :024(218) [0321] be rites which justify, as **Thomas** writes, "Fasting avails to
A P : 1 5 :024(218) [0321] This is what **Thomas** says.
A P : 2 4 :062(260) [0405] reject the error of **Thomas** when he writes, "The body of
A P : 2 7 :020(272) [0427] blasphemy when **Thomas** says that a monastic profession
S 3 : 0 5 :002(310) [0491] we do not agree with **Thomas** and the Dominicans who
S 3 : 1 4 :001(316) [0501] the authority of their St. **Thomas**, such people boast that

Thorns (1), Thorny (1)
A P : 0 4 :341(159) [0215] We leave these **thorny** questions to the schools.
T R : 0 0 :032(325) [0513] was crowned with **thorns** and that he was led forth to be

Thorough (5), Thoroughly (24)
P R : P R :007(004) [0009] and should discuss in a **thorough** and friendly way
P R : P R :018(008) [0015] may be clearly and **thoroughly** informed and possess
P R : P R :022(011) [0019] in this explanation and **thorough** settlement of the
P R : P R :024(013) [0021] explanation must be **thoroughly** grounded in God's Word
A G : 2 0 :013(043) [0055] discusses this question **thoroughly** and teaches the same
A P : 0 4 :177(131) [0171] the sight of our impurity **thoroughly** frightens us.
S 3 : 0 1 :011(303) [0479] They are **thoroughly** pagan doctrines, and we cannot
T R : 0 0 :014(322) [0507] of the people who are **thoroughly** acquainted with the life
L C : S P :003(362) [0575] people should be **thoroughly** instructed in the various
L C : 0 1 :028(368) [0587] your own heart **thoroughly** and you will find whether or
L C : 0 1 :029(368) [0589] These should be **thoroughly** stressed and impressed upon
L C : 0 1 :120(382) [0615] no one believes this; so **thoroughly** has the devil
L C : 0 1 :140(384) [0621] I say that it may be **thoroughly** impressed upon the young
L C : 0 1 :196(391) [0637] If this could be **thoroughly** impressed on people's minds,
L C : 0 1 :318(408) [0673] them and test yourself **thoroughly**, do your very best, and
L C : 0 5 :007(447) [0755] for thus we can **thoroughly** refute all the babbling of the
E P : 0 0 :000(463) [0775] A **Thorough**, Pure, Correct, and Final Restatement and
S D : P R :004(502) [0847] this Christian and **thoroughly** scriptural Augsburg
S D : P R :014(506) [0855] and to maintain a **thorough**, lasting, and God-pleasing
S D : 0 1 :006(509) [0861] a spiritual leprosy, has **thoroughly** and entirely poisoned
S D : 0 2 :017(524) [0887] and nature he is **thoroughly** wicked, opposed and hostile
S D : 0 2 :073(535) [0909] On the basis of this **thorough** presentation of the entire
S D : 0 2 :085(537) [0913] opinion in this matter **thoroughly**, clearly, and
S D : 0 2 :087(538) [0915] to God alone, as was **thoroughly** demonstrated above
S D : 0 5 :026(563) [0961] law and the Gospel is **thoroughly** and mightily set forth
S D : 0 6 :009(565) [0965] Dr. Luther **thoroughly** explains this at greater length in
S D : 0 7 :091(585) [1005] and the like have been **thoroughly**, extensively, and
S D : 0 8 :021(595) [1021] has explained this **thoroughly** in his *Great Confession*
S D : 0 8 :053(601) [1033] know better and more **thoroughly** than the Lord Christ

Thou (39)
A L : 2 0 :040(046) [0057] the church sings, "Where **Thou** art not, man hath naught,
A P : 0 4 :058(115) [0137] here; for example, "If **thou**, O Lord, shouldst mark
A P : 0 4 :058(115) [0137] the Lord," that is, because **thou** has promised the
A P : 0 4 :326(158) [0211] if he observes our sins, "If **thou**, O Lord, shouldst mark
A P : 0 4 :327(158) [0211] my hands with lye, yet **thou** wilt plunge me into a pit."
A P : 1 2 :031(186) [0259] But **thou**, O Lord — how long?"
A P : 1 2 :107(197) [0283] to the Lord'; then **thou** didst forgive the guilt of my sin."
A P : 1 2 :108(198) [0283] only have I sinned, so that **thou** art justified in thy
A P : 1 2 :108(198) [0283] we shall be justified when **Thou** dost justify us and
A P : 1 2 :150(206) [0299] measure; not in thy anger, lest **thou** bring me to nothing."
A P : 2 1 :008(230) [0345] of hosts, how long wilt **thou** have no mercy on
A P : 2 4 :029(255) [0393] "Sacrifice and offering **thou** dost not desire; but thou hast
A P : 2 4 :029(255) [0393] thou dost not desire; but **thou** hast given me an open
A P : 2 4 :029(255) [0393] That is, "**Thou** has offered me thy Word to hear, and dost
A P : 2 4 :029(255) [0393] Ps. 51:16, 17 says, "**Thou** hast no delight in burnt offering.
A P : 2 4 :029(255) [0393] broken and contrite heart, O God, **thou** wilt not despise."
A P : 2 7 :013(271) [0423] O Christ, how long wilt **Thou** bear these insults with
A P : 2 7 :013(271) [0423] the eternal Father which **Thou** who are in the bosom of
S 1 : P R :015(291) [0459] to the grace which **Thou** hast given us by thy Holy Spirit,
S C : 0 7 :002(352) [0557] Son Jesus Christ, that **Thou** hast protected me through
S C : 0 7 :005(353) [0559] Son Jesus Christ, that **Thou** hast this day graciously
S C : 0 8 :007(353) [0559] to Thee, O Lord, and **Thou** givest them their food in due
S C : 0 8 :007(353) [0559] **Thou** openest thy hand; Thou satisfiest the desire of every
S C : 0 8 :007(353) [0559] Thou openest thy hand; **Thou** satisfiest the desire of every
S C : 0 8 :009(353) [0559] of thy bountiful goodness **Thou** hast bestowed on us,
L C : 0 3 :097(433) [0725] by my works, but because **Thou** hast given the promise
L C : 0 3 :110(435) [0729] your heart, "Dear Father, **Thou** hast commanded me to
L C : 0 5 :062(454) [0767] of thy Word, because **Thou** hast commanded it and I
S D : 0 1 :035(514) [0869] made me together round about, and **thou** dost destroy me?
S D : 0 1 :035(514) [0869] Remember that **thou** hast made me of clay, and wilt thou
S D : 0 1 :035(514) [0869] made me of clay, and wilt **thou** turn me to dust again?
S D : 0 1 :035(514) [0869] Didst **thou** not pour me out like milk and curdle me like
S D : 0 1 :035(514) [0869] **Thou** didst clothe me with skin and flesh, and knit me
S D : 0 1 :035(514) [0869] **Thou** has granted me life and steadfast love; and thy care
S D : 0 1 :036(514) [0869] **Thou** knowest me right well; my frame was not hidden
S D : 0 8 :070(605) [1041] (Col. 2:9); likewise, "**Thou** has crowned him with glory
S D : 1 1 :007(617) [1065] as it is written, "Israel, **thou** hast plunged thyself into
S D : 1 1 :007(617) [1065] Likewise, "**Thou** art not a God who delights in
S D : 1 1 :074(628) [1087] in the next words, "But **thou** didst hear my supplications

Though (250)
P R : P R :020(010) [0017] Furthermore, even **though** a number of theologians, like
A G : 2 7 :007(071) [0077] than in those of men, **though** it would have been seemly
A G : 2 7 :035(076) [0081] Christian church, even **though** some have subsequently
A G : 2 8 :071(093) [0093] their honor and dignity (**though** it is incumbent on the
A L : 2 7 :006(071) [0077] compelled to remain, **though** some could have been freed
A P : P R :011(099) [0101] same thing here, even **though** I could lead our
A P : 0 2 :035(105) [0115] guilt of original sin, even **though** concupiscence remains
A P : 0 2 :036(105) [0115] sin is — that is, remains — even **though** it is not imputed.
A P : 0 2 :040(105) [0115] death if it is not forgiven, **though** it is not imputed to
A P : 0 2 :042(105) [0115] Even **though** complete unanimity may be impossible, no
A P : 0 4 :015(109) [0123] Zeno, and others, as **though** Christ had come to give
A P : 0 4 :018(109) [0125] **Though** they talk about this disposition, yet without the
A P : 0 4 :023(110) [0127] by its own strength, **though** it is often overwhelmed by its
A P : 0 4 :057(114) [0137] Even **though** the law does not teach the free forgiveness
A P : 0 4 :063(115) [0139] in the recipient, as **though** the gift of the Holy Spirit were
A P : 0 4 :071(116) [0141] to the beginning, as **though** faith were the start of
A P : 0 4 :072(117) [0141] prepares for them, even **though** it is his own art that
A P : 0 4 :073(117) [0141] some people, even **though** Paul says (Rom. 3:28), "We
A P : 0 4 :074(117) [0143] they are not excluded as **though** they did not follow, but
A P : 0 4 :077(117) [0143] because of love or works, **though** love does follow faith.
A P : 0 4 :081(118) [0143] Instead, as **though** Christ were completely buried, they
A P : 0 4 :084(119) [0145] and be guaranteed," as **though** he were to say, "If it
A P : 0 4 :131(125) [0157] they care nothing, as **though** it were irrelevant, or at best
A P : 0 4 :145(127) [0163] on account of our love, **though** they do not and cannot
A P : 0 4 :146(127) [0163] claim to keep the law, **though** this glory properly belongs
A P : 0 4 :146(127) [0163] brings forth evil desires, **though** the Spirit in us resists
A P : 0 4 :149(127) [0163] and promise of Christ, **though** Paul says that grace
A P : 0 4 :151(127) [0163] government, etc.), even **though** these virtues must follow.
A P : 0 4 :151(127) [0163] of sins on account of love, **though** it, too, must follow.
A P : 0 4 :154(128) [0165] him as the Messiah, **though** he did show him the outward
A P : 0 4 :155(128) [0165] the forgiveness of sins, **though** love, confession, and other
A P : 0 4 :171(130) [0171] on this subject, **though** they are obvious throughout not
A P : 0 4 :179(131) [0171] or condemn them, even **though** they have not really
A P : 0 4 :179(131) [0171] It is as **though** he were saying, "Though you are still far
A P : 0 4 :179(131) [0171] though he were saying, "**Though** you are still far away
A P : 0 4 :179(131) [0171] through faith, **though** sin still sticks to your flesh."
A P : 0 4 :182(132) [0173] received by faith alone, **though** the keeping of the law
A P : 0 4 :224(138) [0181] Even **though** these are necessary, it would be a foolish
A P : 0 4 :231(139) [0183] **Though** we could give many answers about perfection, we
A P : 0 4 :242(141) [0187] Even **though** these offenses occur, love covers them up,
A P : 0 4 :244(142) [0189] into James's mind, **though** our opponents uphold it under
A P : 0 4 :256(144) [0193] Secondly, **though** men can at most do certain outward
A P : 0 4 :258(144) [0193] together, says the Lord: **though** your sins are like scarlet,
A P : 0 4 :264(146) [0195] of this text, **though** the promise is involved even in the
A P : 0 4 :270(147) [0197] us for Christ's sake even **though** we cannot satisfy the
A P : 0 4 :270(147) [0199] the mediator, even **though** its incipient keeping of the law
A P : 0 4 :271(147) [0199] **Though** the scholastics have said nothing at all about faith
A P : 0 4 :293(152) [0203] Even **though** they are a long way from the perfection of
A P : 0 4 :294(152) [0203] faith rather than to love, **though** love follows faith since
A P : 0 4 :300(153) [0205] the wrath of God, as **though** we could overcome the
A P : 0 4 :318(156) [0209] merit of condignity, as **though** when our conscience
A P : 0 4 :332(158) [0211] and ask for grace as **though** they had earned it, then they
A P : 0 4 :335(159) [0215] that if we are unworthy **though** we have done everything,
A P : 0 4 :335(159) [0215] that we are unworthy **though** we have believed
A P : 0 4 :336(159) [0215] **Though** these absurdities do not deserve a refutation, we
A P : 0 4 :338(159) [0215] promise of grace, even **though** our works are worthless.
A P : 0 4 :342(160) [0215] his grace upon us, **though** it is out of place here to discuss
A P : 0 4 :366(163) [0219] have often declared, that **though** justification and eternal
A P : 0 4 :367(163) [0221] but to justification, **though** the Gospel offers justification
A P : 0 4 :381(165) [0223] by which we love God, as **though** the ancients meant to
A P : 0 7 :019(171) [0233] Meanwhile he teaches that **though** these wicked men
A P : 0 7 :022(172) [0235] **Though** wolves and ungodly teachers may run rampant in
A P : 0 7 :032(174) [0239] God in so many ways, as **though** these observances were
A P : 0 7 :034(175) [0239] church of Christ even **though** they dress according to the
A P : 1 1 :001(180) [0249] annually, and that even **though** all sins cannot be
A P : 1 2 :008(183) [0255] them attain grace even **though** they were terribly contrite?
A P : 1 2 :063(191) [0269] But it is very sure, **though** all the gates of hell
A P : 1 2 :068(192) [0271] on the *Sentences* who as **though** by a conspiracy defend
A P : 1 2 :085(194) [0277] to God through Christ, **though** Christ says (John 15:5),
A P : 1 2 :118(199) [0287] to the remission of guilt, **though** they imagine that they
A P : 1 2 :118(200) [0287] into mortal sin, as **though** those who are in mortal sin
A P : 1 2 :122(200) [0287] authority in Scripture, **though** it was unknown in the time
A P : 1 2 :126(201) [0289] who should sit as **though** on a watchtower to guide
A P : 1 2 :128(202) [0291] against those who, **though** they ought to be healing
A P : 1 2 :142(204) [0295] For **though** we can do external works that God's law
A P : 1 2 :157(207) [0301] And **though** we still have troubles, Scripture interprets
A P : 1 2 :164(208) [0303] **Though** your sins are like scarlet, they shall be white as
A P : 1 2 :173(209) [0305] with obligatory works, **though** in their satisfactions they
A P : 1 3 :003(211) [0309] sure signs of grace, even **though** they may instruct or
A P : 1 3 :007(212) [0311] reference to sacrifice, as **though** the new covenant needed
A P : 1 3 :008(212) [0311] additional sacrifices as **though** this were not sufficient for
A P : 1 3 :020(214) [0313] not false but as certain as **though** God, by a new miracle,
A P : 1 4 :004(215) [0315] what is right and true, **though** the canons themselves are
A P : 1 5 :012(216) [0317] in this connection that **though** we do not merit the
A P : 1 5 :024(218) [0321] **Though** their purpose is to restrain the flesh, reason
A P : 1 5 :031(219) [0323] power to institute rites as **though** they justified or were
A P : 1 5 :041(220) [0325] of the children at all, **though** even the canons give
A P : 1 6 :006(223) [0331] Nazianzus, and others, **though** they are very easy to
A P : 1 6 :009(224) [0333] **Though** they were wealthy and held high positions,
A P : 1 6 :013(224) [0333] and the family, even **though** these have God's command
A P : 2 1 :001(229) [0343] They present this as **though** on this account the
A P : 2 1 :002(229) [0343] state a triumph as **though** the war were already over.
A P : 2 1 :014(230) [0347] Even **though** they distinguish between mediators of
A P : 2 1 :019(231) [0347] accounted righteous as **though** the merits were our own.
A P : 2 1 :019(231) [0347] freed by the merit of another as **though** it were his own.
A P : 2 1 :019(231) [0347] trust in Christ's merits as **though** we had merits of our
A P : 2 1 :021(232) [0349] all, to invoke the saints, **though** they have neither God's
A P : 2 1 :021(232) [0349] in the mercy of Christ, **though** Christ commanded us to
A P : 2 1 :022(232) [0349] same way as Christ's, as **though** we were accounted
A P : 2 1 :027(232) [0349] Even **though** she is worthy of the highest honors, she
A P : 2 1 :028(233) [0351] her to appease Christ, as **though** he were not a
A P : 2 1 :029(233) [0351] saints' merits to us, as **though** God were reconciled to us
A P : 2 1 :031(233) [0351] invocation of the saints, **though** they have neither a Word
A P : 2 1 :035(234) [0353] call on Christopher, as **though** there had really been such
A P : 2 1 :039(235) [0355] the obvious offenses, as **though** they intended, by forcing
A P : 2 2 :013(238) [0361] with our opponents, even **though** otherwise we might
A P : 2 3 :015(241) [0367] priests should marry — as **though** priests were not human
A P : 2 3 :023(242) [0369] have been contracted, **though** they remove those from the
A P : 2 3 :026(243) [0371] because it is pure, as **though** marriage were impure and
A P : 2 3 :026(243) [0371] impure and sinful or as **though** celibacy merited
A P : 2 3 :027(243) [0371] celibacy on priests, **though** in this very analogy marriage
A P : 2 3 :045(245) [0377] pleasing to God, even **though** it was not completely
A P : 2 3 :056(247) [0379] adamant and inexorable, **though** it is obviously a matter
A P : 2 3 :063(248) [0381] of perpetual celibacy, **though** it conflicts with clear
A P : 2 4 :004(250) [0385] **Though** German hymns have varied in frequency, yet
A P : 2 4 :006(250) [0385] The monasteries have public, **though** daily, Mass.
A P : 2 4 :014(251) [0387] **Though** we have already stated our case, we must add a
A P : 2 4 :014(251) [0389] to say about sacrifice, **though** in our Confession we
A P : 2 4 :034(256) [0397] and things like that, **though** it was for these that the
A P : 2 4 :053(259) [0403] **Though** the main proofs for our position are in the Epistle

Continued ▶

A P : 2 4 :064(261) [0407] of the sacrament, **though** without faith the Mass does not
A P : 2 4 :081(264) [0411] immunity shows: "Even **though** the number of children
A P : 2 4 :087(265) [0413] For even **though** the Mass is called an offering, what does
A P : 2 4 :094(267) [0417] Even **though** they have support at most from Gregory and
A P : 2 7 :005(269) [0421] **Though** once upon a time they were schools of Christian
A P : 2 7 :016(271) [0425] brag about obedience **though** no class of men has greater
A P : 2 7 :018(272) [0425] **Though** we have quoted Paul's statement in support of
A P : 2 7 :029(274) [0431] **Though** everyone knows that monasticism is a recent
A P : 2 7 :059(279) [0441] **Though** they were poor in everything, the Rechabites were
A P : 2 7 :059(279) [0441] Rechabites were married; **though** our monks abound in
A P : 2 8 :003(281) [0445] burdens on them, as **though** they took pleasure in the
A P : 2 8 :008(282) [0445] apart from the Gospel as **though** they merited the
A P : 2 8 :012(283) [0447] according to the Gospel, **though** they may well be bishops
A P : 2 8 :015(283) [0447] ensnare consciences as **though** they were commanding
A P : 2 8 :016(283) [0449] did not set them down as **though** they could not be
L C : P R :009(359) [0569] at least sufficiently, even **though** they think they know
L C : P R :009(359) [0569] Catechism were perfect (**though** that is impossible in this
L C : P R :016(361) [0573] or different to learn, **though** they cannot learn it to
L C : S P :006(362) [0575] from ancient times, **though** they were rarely taught and
L C : 0 1 :053(371) [0595] God's name is abused, **though** it is impossible to
L C : 0 1 :067(373) [0599] **Though** it may take a long time, nothing he does will in
L C : 0 1 :091(377) [0607] **Though** we had the bones of all the saints or all the holy
L C : 0 1 :100(378) [0609] Even **though** you know the Word perfectly and have
L C : 0 1 :117(381) [0615] Even **though** it seems very trivial and contemptible, make
L C : 0 1 :120(381) [0615] all the Carthusians, even **though** they kill themselves with
L C : 0 1 :152(386) [0625] Let us see, **though**, whether you are the man to defy him.
L C : 0 1 :186(390) [0633] Many persons, **though** they may not actually commit
L C : 0 1 :189(390) [0635] good to his neighbor, or, **though** he has the opportunity
L C : 0 1 :204(392) [0639] you fail to do this (**though** you could prevent a wrong) or
L C : 0 1 :215(394) [0641] In short, even **though** they abstain from the act, yet their
L C : 0 1 :224(395) [0643] If all who are thieves, **though** they are unwilling to admit
L C : 0 1 :232(396) [0647] knaves and scoundrels, **though** it might be more fitting if
L C : 0 1 :234(397) [0647] **Though** he pursues his defiant and arrogant course for a
L C : 0 1 :243(397) [0649] **Though** they gather a great hoard, they must suffer so
L C : 0 1 :264(400) [0655] Evil **though** we are, we cannot tolerate having evil spoken
L C : 0 1 :268(401) [0657] For **though** you do not wield the sword, you use your
L C : 0 1 :269(401) [0657] evil about another even **though**, to your certain
L C : 0 1 :296(405) [0665] correctly (**though** they also have a broader and higher
L C : 0 1 :296(405) [0665] your neighbor, even **though** in the eyes of the world you
L C : 0 1 :307(406) [0669] gratify your greed, even **though** in the eyes of the world
L C : 0 1 :310(407) [0669] hearts to be pure, even **though** as long as we live here we
L C : 0 1 :328(410) [0675] in that order, even **though** you have the opportunity and
L C : 0 2 :066(419) [0697] and hypocrites, even **though** they believe in and worship
L C : 0 3 :002(420) [0697] perfectly, even **though** he has begun to believe.
L C : 0 3 :010(421) [0699] deter us from praying, as **though** it made no great
L C : 0 3 :010(421) [0699] if we do not pray, or as **though** prayer were commanded
L C : 0 3 :011(421) [0701] or drive us away, even **though** we are sinners; he wishes
L C : 0 3 :068(429) [0717] be done and prevail even **though** the devil and all his host
L C : 0 3 :100(433) [0727] Therefore, even **though** at present we are upright and
L C : 0 3 :106(434) [0727] strength to resist, even **though** the tribulation is not
L C : 0 3 :107(434) [0729] We must all feel it, **though** not all to the same degree;
L C : 0 4 :008(437) [0733] most precious thing, even **though** to all appearances it
L C : 0 4 :037(441) [0741] they cry out against us as **though** we preach against faith.
L C : 0 4 :038(441) [0741] would be enough, even **though** Baptism is an entirely
L C : 0 4 :043(442) [0743] would not die, or even **though** they died would afterward
L C : 0 4 :045(442) [0743] has water poured over it, **though** it cannot receive
L C : 0 4 :053(443) [0745] the water, Baptism is valid, even **though** faith be lacking.
L C : 0 4 :054(443) [0745] Even **though** a Jew should today come deceitfully and
L C : 0 4 :054(443) [0745] with God's Word, even **though** he failed to receive it
L C : 0 4 :054(443) [0745] the true sacrament even **though** they do not believe.
L C : 0 4 :077(446) [0751] Even **though** we fall from it and sin, nevertheless we
L C : 0 4 :086(446) [0753] us to return to him even **though** we sin, so all his
L C : 0 5 :016(448) [0757] Our conclusion is: Even **though** a knave should receive or
L C : 0 5 :059(453) [0767] absent themselves, even **though** in other respects they are
L C : 0 5 :077(455) [0771] flesh which feels nothing **though** the disease rages and
L C : 0 5 :084(456) [0773] you do not see, **though** God grants his grace that you may
L C : 0 6 :003(457) [0000] to make confession even **though** nothing was more
E P : 0 1 :004(466) [0781] souls after the Fall, even **though** they are corrupted, and
E P : 0 1 :005(466) [0781] this same human nature, **though** without sin, and thus
E P : 0 2 :011(471) [0789] to add something (**though** it be little and feeble) to help,
E P : 0 2 :019(472) [0791] should hear this Word, **though** he cannot give it credence
E P : 0 3 :008(474) [0793] the same thing, even **though** otherwise these terms refer to
E P : 0 3 :017(475) [0795] and remain in a person **though** he does not truly repent
E P : 0 4 :011(477) [0799] not be understood as **though** it were left to the
E P : 0 4 :019(477) [0801] the Holy Spirit even **though** they fall into adultery and
E P : 0 7 :007(482) [0811] literal sense, and not as **though** the bread symbolized the
E P : 0 7 :042(486) [0817] of the body of Christ as **though** one rent Christ's flesh
E P : 0 7 :042(486) [0817] and believe in a true, **though** supernatural, eating of
E P : 0 8 :031(491) [0825] human nature in fact, as **though** it did not concern him at
E P : 0 8 :037(491) [0825] of God and all his works, **though** it is written that in him
E P : 0 8 :039(491) [0827] to the divine nature, as **though** in the state of humiliation
S D : P R :007(502) [0849] and in their writings, **though** they knew that these titanic
S D : 0 1 :006(509) [0861] to indicate that even **though** a man were to think no evil,
S D : 0 1 :023(512) [0865] those who teach that, **though** man's nature has been
S D : 0 1 :023(512) [0865] that is good — even **though** in only a small, limited, and
S D : 0 1 :043(515) [0873] Son assumed our nature, **though** without sin, so that in
S D : 0 1 :053(517) [0877] man is wholly corrupted **though** original sin to its very
S D : 0 2 :003(520) [0881] and give his assent to it, **though** weakly, but that without
S D : 0 2 :032(527) [0893] Therefore, **though** we grant that it lies within our power
S D : 0 2 :065(534) [0907] of the Holy Spirit, even **though** we still do so in great
S D : 0 2 :066(534) [0907] were to be understood as **though** the converted man
S D : 0 2 :067(534) [0907] to it and accept it, even **though** it be in great weakness.
S D : 0 2 :069(534) [0907] not be baptized again, **though** they must certainly be
S D : 0 2 :077(536) [0911] and to some degree — **though** only to a small extent and
S D : 0 2 :085(537) [0913] to the inmost self, **though** he also sees in his members the
S D : 0 2 :089(538) [0915] he only suffers — **though** not as a stone does when a
S D : 0 3 :022(543) [0923] on the cross for us, even **though**, on account of their
S D : 0 3 :036(545) [0927] works, however, as **though** there could well be true faith
S D : 0 3 :036(545) [0927] without contrition, or as **though** good works should,
S D : 0 3 :036(545) [0927] unquestioned fruits, or as **though** believers must or dare
S D : 0 3 :041(546) [0929] understood, however, as **though** justification and
S D : 0 3 :041(546) [0929] other in such a way as **though** on occasion true faith
S D : 0 3 :052(548) [0933] justified before God, as **though** we are indeed justified
S D : 0 3 :056(549) [0935] For even **though** Christ had been conceived by the Holy
S D : 0 4 :008(552) [0941] acceptable to God, even **though** they are still impure and
S D : 0 4 :015(553) [0943] and salvation even **though** he still is and continues to be a
S D : 0 4 :015(553) [0943] fruits appear, yes, even **though** he were to persist in sins
S D : 0 4 :031(556) [0947] works; and that even **though** a Christian follows his evil
S D : 0 5 :022(562) [0959] who "was made sin **though** he knew no sin, so that in him
S D : 0 6 :005(564) [0963] without qualification, as **though** the righteous should live
S D : 0 6 :018(567) [0967] Thus **though** they are never without the law, they are not
S D : 0 6 :022(567) [0969] are pleasing to God, even **though** in this life they are still
S D : 0 6 :023(568) [0969] **Though** their good works are still imperfect and impure,
S D : 0 7 :024(573) [0979] conclusion is that even **though** a rascal receives or gives
S D : 0 7 :024(573) [0981] alter or change the sacrament, even **though** it is misused.
S D : 0 7 :032(574) [0983] in the bread and wine, **though** the priests who distribute
S D : 0 7 :038(576) [0985] action of the sacrament, **though** the union of the body
S D : 0 7 :038(576) [0985] to indicate that, even **though** they also use these different
S D : 0 7 :048(578) [0989] in the word "bread," as **though** the body of Christ were
S D : 0 7 :102(587) [1007] Since this is true, even **though** unknown to us, we should
S D : 0 8 :036(598) [1027] therefore any property, **though** it belongs only to one of
S D : 0 8 :050(600) [1031] natural properties, even **though** the testimony of the
S D : 0 8 :066(604) [1039] and manifests itself fully, **though** always spontaneously,
S D : 0 8 :083(607) [1045] divided the person, even **though** death and all the devils
S D : 1 0 :005(611) [1053] the Word of God, even **though** they go under the name
S D : 1 0 :015(613) [1057] as necessary and as **though** their omission were wrong
S D : 1 1 :006(617) [1065] but not in such a way as **though** it were God's gracious
S D : 1 1 :009(617) [1065] counsel of God, as **though** it comprised no more and that
S D : 1 1 :010(618) [1067] is in vain, even **though** I were to hold to the Word,
S D : 1 1 :011(618) [1067] pious hearts, too, even **though** by the grace of God they
S D : 1 1 :030(621) [1073] **Though** this is still very weak in them, they nevertheless

Thousand (13), Thousandfold (1), Thousands (5)

A P : 0 4 :270(147) [0197] steadfast love to **thousands** of those who love me and
A P : 2 0 :014(228) [0343] was condemned a **thousand** years ago, in the days of
A P : 2 7 :032(274) [0431] that even with ten **thousand** soldiers he cannot stand up
A P : 2 7 :032(274) [0431] the Lord who comes at him with twenty **thousand**."
S 2 : 0 2 :025(297) [0469] not), we have everything a **thousandfold** better in Christ.
S C : 0 1 :021(344) [0543] steadfast love to **thousands** of those who love me and
L C : P R :012(360) [0571] The devil is called the master of a **thousand** arts.
L C : P R :012(360) [0571] destroys this master of a **thousand** arts with all his wiles
L C : P R :012(360) [0571] indeed, be master of more than a hundred **thousand** arts.
L C : P R :013(360) [0571] attacks and ambushes of the devil with his **thousand** arts.
L C : 0 1 :030(369) [0589] *mercy to many **thousands** of those who love me and keep*
L C : 0 1 :033(369) [0589] extend to many **thousands**, lest men live in security and
L C : 0 1 :039(370) [0591] for their children to a **thousand** and even many
L C : 0 1 :039(370) [0591] to a thousand and even many **thousands** of generations.
L C : 0 1 :320(408) [0673] *I show mercy unto a **thousand** generations."*
L C : 0 5 :012(448) [0755] declare: "Let a hundred **thousand** devils, with all the
S D : 0 2 :021(525) [0889] and thereby runs into a **thousand** dangers and finally into
S D : 0 4 :012(553) [0941] grace, so certain that it would die a **thousand** times for it.
S D : 0 7 :022(573) [0979] declare, 'Let a hundred **thousand** devils and all the

Thrasonian (1)

A P : 2 2 :011(238) [0361] We recognize these **Thrasonian** voices, and if we wanted

Thread (1)

L C : 0 1 :047(371) [0593] uses his needle, awl, and **thread** (for work, eventually to

Threat (10), Threaten (3), Threatened (3), Threatening (5), Threatens (2), Threats (9)

A L : 2 4 :012(057) [0065] But Paul severely **threatened** those who dealt unworthily
A P : 0 4 :035(112) [0131] God and to doubt his Word with its **threats** and promises.
A P : 0 4 :200(134) [0175] wrath of God is revealed, **threatening** all the impenitent.
A P : 0 7 :009(169) [0229] the infinite dangers that **threaten** the church with ruin.
A P : 1 2 :126(201) [0289] There are many **threats** which, unless you take care,
A P : 1 2 :161(208) [0303] he says: "If God had **threatened** that because of his sin he
A P : 1 2 :161(208) [0303] why did he carry out the **threat** even when the sin was
A P : 1 2 :161(208) [0303] life, but the lesson of the **threat** followed so that especially
A P : 2 7 :002(269) [0419] taught anything that **threatened** the monastic estate but
A P : 2 7 :004(269) [0421] sure than oracles, which **threaten** a change in the
A P : 2 8 :004(281) [0445] edict written in blood, **threatening** men with horrible
S 3 : 0 2 :001(303) [0479] of all to restrain sins by **threats** and fear of punishment
S C : 0 1 :022(344) [0543] Answer: God **threatens** to punish all who transgress these
S C : 0 9 :011(356) [0563] to them, and forbear **threatening**, knowing that he who is
L C : 0 1 :029(368) [0589] to it, first, a terrible **threat** and, then, a beautiful,
L C : 0 1 :039(370) [0591] Terrible as these **threats** are, much mightier is the
L C : 0 1 :057(372) [0597] commandment a solemn **threat**: "for the Lord will not
L C : 0 1 :069(374) [0599] by means of warning and **threat**, restraint and
L C : 0 1 :322(408) [0673] contain both a wrathful **threat** and a friendly promise,
L C : 0 1 :333(410) [0677] and enjoins under **threat** of his greatest wrath and
E P : 0 6 :004(480) [0807] by the admonitions and **threats** of the law, but also by its
E P : 0 6 :005(480) [0807] coercion of punishments and the **threat** of God's wrath.
E P : 0 6 :006(481) [0807] as if they knew of no command, **threat**, or reward.
E P : 0 6 :007(481) [0807] is reborn, does what no **threat** of the law could ever have
S D : 0 2 :021(525) [0889] It is useless to **threaten**, to scold, or even to teach and
S D : 0 4 :032(556) [0947] immutable, and divine **threats** and earnest punishments
S D : 0 5 :017(561) [0957] acceptable to God, and **threatens** the transgressors of the
S D : 0 5 :024(562) [0961] of the law and its **threats** will terrify the hearts of the
S D : 0 6 :009(565) [0965] warning and **threatening** of the law, but frequently the
S D : 0 6 :019(567) [0969] into obedience by the **threats** of the law (I Cor. 9:27;
S D : 0 6 :024(568) [0969] urging, and **threatening** of the law, but frequently also
S D : 0 6 :024(568) [0971] of the law or its **threats** and punishments, just as he will

Three (59), Threefold (2)

P R : P R :025(013) [0023] is comprehended in the **three** Creeds as well as in the
A G : 0 1 :002(027) [0043] God, and that there are **three** persons in this one divine
A G : 0 1 :003(027) [0043] All **three** are one divine essence, eternal, without division,
A L : 0 1 :001(027) [0043] and concerning the **three** persons is true and should be
A L : 0 1 :003(027) [0043] Yet there are **three** persons, of the same essence and
A P : 0 1 :001(100) [0103] that there are nevertheless **three** distinct and coeternal
A P : 0 4 :053(114) [0137] must remember that these **three** elements always belong
A P : 2 1 :004(229) [0343] This honor is **threefold**.
A P : 2 4 :008(250) [0385] was celebrated **three** times a week, and that this practice
A P : 2 4 :036(257) [0397] Num. 28:4ff. lists **three** parts of this daily sacrifice, the
S 1 : 0 1 :000(291) [0461] Son, and Holy Spirit, **three** distinct persons in one divine
S 2 : 0 4 :007(299) [0473] to the popes when it deposed **three** and elected a fourth.

Continued ▶

S 3 : 0 3 :012(305) [0481] the sophists divided into **three** parts — contrition,
S 3 : 0 4 :000(310) [0491] Matt. 18:20, "Where two or **three** are gathered," etc.
T R : 0 0 :004(320) [0503] These **three** articles we acknowledge and hold to be false,
T R : 0 0 :024(324) [0511] Christ said, "If two or **three** of you agree on earth," etc.
T R : 0 0 :040(327) [0515] pope arrogates to himself a **threefold** divine authority.
T R : 0 0 :068(331) [0523] "Where two or **three** are gathered in my name, there am I
S C : P R :022(341) [0537] the sacrament at least **three** or four times a year despises
L C : P R :009(359) [0569] Matt. 18:20, "Where two or **three** are gathered in my
L C : S P :006(362) [0575] if they learned the **three** parts which have been heritage
L C : S P :018(363) [0577] he refuses to learn these **three** parts in which everything
L C : S P :020(364) [0579] When these **three** parts are understood, we ought also to
L C : 0 1 :103(379) [0611] we have learned the first **three** commandments, which are
L C : 0 1 :158(387) [0627] Thus we have **three** kinds of fathers presented in this
L C : 0 1 :279(403) [0661] be confirmed by the evidence of two or **three** witnesses."
L C : 0 2 :006(411) [0679] up the entire Creed in **three** articles, according to the
L C : 0 2 :006(411) [0679] articles, according to the **three** persons of the Godhead, to
L C : 0 2 :007(411) [0679] God and one faith, but **three** persons, and therefore three
L C : 0 2 :007(411) [0679] three persons, and therefore **three** articles or confessions.
L C : 0 2 :012(412) [0681] the educated, however, all **three** articles can be treated
L C : 0 2 :064(419) [0695] In these **three** articles God himself has revealed and
L C : 0 3 :068(429) [0717] Observe that in these **three** petitions interests which
L C : 0 3 :101(433) [0727] it, *Bekoerunge*) is of **three** kinds: of the flesh, the world,
L C : 0 4 :001(436) [0733] now finished with the **three** chief parts of our common
L C : 0 4 :038(441) [0741] we have considered the **three** things that must be known
L C : 0 5 :001(447) [0753] Holy Baptism under **three** headings, so we must deal with
L C : 0 5 :040(451) [0763] let a year, or two, **three**, or more years go by without
L C : 0 6 :004(457) [0000] These **three** things have now been removed and made
E P : 0 6 :001(479) [0805] has been given to men for **three** reasons: (1) to maintain
E P : 1 2 :029(500) [0843] Son, and Holy Spirit are **three** distinct persons, so each
E P : 1 2 :029(500) [0843] maintain that each of the **three** has the same power,
E P : 1 2 :029(500) [0843] and glory, just like any **three** individual people who are
E P : 1 2 :029(500) [0843] Others maintain that the **three** are unequal in essence and
E P : 1 2 :030(500) [0843] to the Word of God, the **three** Creeds, the Augsburg
S D : P R :004(504) [0851] pledge allegiance to the **three** general Creeds, the
S D : 0 2 :057(532) [0903] that, where two or **three** are gathered together in his
S D : 0 2 :090(538) [0915] by the doctrine of the **three** efficient causes of
S D : 0 2 :090(538) [0915] manner in which these **three** (the Word of God preached
S D : 0 4 :037(557) [0951] who declares no less than **three** times in Phil. 3:7ff. that
S D : 0 7 :052(578) [0991] Therefore also all **three** evangelists, Matthew (26:26),
S D : 0 7 :098(586) [1005] one body of Christ has **three** different modes, or all three
S D : 0 7 :098(586) [1005] different modes, or all **three** modes, of being at any given
S D : 0 8 :035(598) [1027] it can be comprehended under **three** main points.
S D : 0 8 :056(601) [1033] There are **three** strong and irrefutable arguments which
S D : 0 8 :076(606) [1043] truthfully, "Where two or **three** are gathered in my name,
S D : 1 2 :037(636) [1103] but that, as there are **three** distinct persons, Father, Son,
S D : 1 2 :037(636) [1103] Some teach that all **three** persons in the Trinity, like any
S D : 1 2 :037(636) [1103] in the Trinity, like any **three** distinct and essentially
S D : 1 2 :037(636) [1103] while others teach that the **three** persons in the Trinity are
S D : 1 2 :039(636) [1103] the Word of God, to the **three** Creeds, to the Augsburg

Threshing (1)
A P : 0 7 :001(168) [0227] the church to a **threshing** floor on which chaff and wheat

Thrives (1)
L C : 0 1 :243(397) [0649] every day that no stolen or ill-gotten possession **thrives**.

Throats (1)
L C : 0 6 :013(458) [0000] sets us at one another's **throats** and we cannot settle it,

Throne (3)
P R : P R :022(012) [0021] the solemn and severe **throne** of God's judgment, and
T R : 0 0 :035(326) [0513] "When the imperial **throne** is vacant, the pope is the
L C : 0 1 :045(370) [0593] once he was secure on his **throne** and he let his heart

Throw (1), Throwing (1), Thrown (5), Throws (1)
A P : 2 2 :008(237) [0359] this very well, but they **throw** sand in the eyes of the
A P : 2 7 :001(268) [0419] He was **thrown** into prison by his order because he had
A P : 2 7 :006(269) [0421] tasteless salt is usually "**thrown** out and trodden under
A P : 2 7 :046(277) [0435] praise Aristippus for **throwing** a great weight of gold into
L C : 0 1 :197(392) [0637] holiness, while they have **thrown** this and the other
L C : 0 5 :055(453) [0767] timid that everyone was **thrown** into consternation,
S D : 0 6 :020(567) [0969] so that they will not be **thrown** back on their own
S D : 0 8 :044(599) [1029] God is in the balance and **throws** in weight as a

Thrust (3)
A G : 2 7 :008(072) [0077] both boys and girls were **thrust** into monasteries to
A L : 2 7 :008(072) [0077] that girls and boys were **thrust** into monasteries for their
A P : 1 2 :122(200) [0287] that they dared to **thrust** upon his Imperial Majesty.

Thunderbolt (3)
A P : 2 8 :008(282) [0445] But this **thunderbolt** does not scare our opponents, who
S 3 : 0 3 :002(304) [0479] This, then, is the **thunderbolt** by means of which God
S 3 : 0 3 :030(308) [0487] With a single **thunderbolt** he strikes and destroys both.

Thuringia (2), Thuringian (1)
P R : P R :008(005) [0009] and some of us gathered at Naumburg, in **Thuringia**.
A P : 2 7 :001(268) [0419] Thirty years ago, in the **Thuringian** town of Eisenach,
S 3 : 1 5 :005(317) [0501] of the church in Gotha, **Thuringia**, subscribe in my own

Thwart (1), Thwarted (1)
L C : 0 1 :260(400) [0655] allow these rights to be **thwarted** or distorted but should
L C : 0 3 :061(428) [0715] venture to hinder and **thwart** the fulfillment of the first

Thy (74), Thyself (2)
A G : 0 0 :000(023) [0037] "I will also speak of **thy** testimonies before kings,
A L : 2 8 :009(082) [0085] has faith," and Ps. 119:50 states, "**Thy** Word gives me life."
A P : 0 4 :058(115) [0137] the forgiveness of sins I am sustained by **thy** promise.
A P : 0 4 :168(130) [0169] not into judgment with **thy** servant; for no man living is
A P : 0 4 :326(157) [0211] not into judgment with **thy** servant, for no man living is
A P : 0 4 :331(158) [0211] our righteousness, but on the ground of **thy** great mercy.
A P : 0 4 :331(158) [0211] heed and act; delay not, for **thy** own sake, O my God,
A P : 0 4 :331(158) [0211] sake, O my God, because **thy** city and thy people are
A P : 0 4 :331(158) [0211] God, because thy city and **thy** people are called by thy
A P : 0 4 :331(158) [0211] because thy city and thy people are called by **thy** name."
A P : 1 2 :049(188) [0265] away for sorrow; strengthen me according to **thy** word!"
A P : 1 2 :078(193) [0275] not into judgment with **thy** servant; for no man living is
A P : 1 2 :108(198) [0283] justified in they sentence and blameless in **thy** judgment."
A P : 1 2 :108(198) [0283] set my righteousness or my merits against **Thy** wrath.
A P : 1 2 :108(198) [0283] set our merits against **Thy** judgment, but we shall be
A P : 1 2 :108(198) [0283] justify us and account us righteous through **Thy** mercy."
A P : 1 2 :150(206) [0299] "O Lord, rebuke me not in **thy** anger"; and Jer. 10:24,
A P : 1 2 :150(206) [0299] but in just measure; not in **thy** anger, lest thou bring me
A P : 1 2 :151(206) [0299] in which they cry out is **thy** chastening upon them"
A P : 2 4 :029(255) [0393] is, "Thou has offered me **thy** Word to hear, and dost
A P : 2 4 :029(255) [0393] me to believe it and **thy** promises of willingness to show
A P : 2 7 :013(271) [0423] these insults with which our enemies attack **thy** Gospel!
A P : 2 7 :013(271) [0423] But **thy** death is a witness, thy resurrection is a witness,
A P : 2 7 :013(271) [0423] But thy death is a witness, **thy** resurrection is a witness,
A P : 2 7 :013(271) [0423] Holy Spirit is a witness, **thy** whole church is a witness:
S 1 : P R :015(291) [0459] of thine own, and by **thy** glorious advent deliver thy
S 1 : P R :015(291) [0459] own, and by thy glorious advent deliver **thy** servants.
S 1 : P R :015(291) [0459] Thou hast given us by **thy** Holy Spirit, who with Thee
S 3 : 0 7 :002(312) [0493] not into judgment with **thy** servant, for no man living is
S C : 0 3 :003(346) [0547] *"Hallowed be **thy** name."*
S C : 0 3 :006(346) [0547] *"**Thy** kingdom come."*
S C : 0 3 :009(347) [0547] *"**Thy** will be done, on earth as it is in heaven."*
S C : 0 7 :002(352) [0557] heavenly Father, through **thy** dear Son Jesus Christ, that
S C : 0 7 :002(352) [0557] Into **thy** hands I command my body and soul and all that
S C : 0 7 :002(352) [0557] Let **thy** holy angel have charge of me, that the wicked one
S C : 0 7 :005(353) [0559] heavenly Father, through **thy** dear Son Jesus Christ, that
S C : 0 7 :005(353) [0559] Into **thy** hands I commend my body and soul and all that
S C : 0 7 :005(353) [0559] Let **thy** holy angels have charge of me, that the wicked
S C : 0 8 :007(353) [0559] Thou openest **thy** hand; Thou satisfiest the desire of every
S C : 0 8 :009(353) [0559] these they gifts which of **thy** bountiful goodness Thou
S C : 0 8 :011(354) [0559] God, our Father, for all **thy** benefits, through Jesus
L C : S P :014(363) [0577] Our Father who art in heaven, hallowed be **thy** name.
L C : S P :014(363) [0577] **Thy** kingdom come, thy will be done, on earth as it is in
L C : S P :014(363) [0577] Thy kingdom come, **thy** will be done, on earth as it is in
L C : 0 3 :021(423) [0703] my own worthiness, but at **thy** commandment and
L C : 0 3 :032(424) [0707] prays, "Dear Father, **thy** will be done," God replies from
L C : 0 3 :035(425) [0707] *"Hallowed be **thy** name."*
L C : 0 3 :036(425) [0707] Father, grant that **thy** name alone may be holy."
L C : 0 3 :049(426) [0711] *"**Thy** kingdom come."*
L C : 0 3 :054(427) [0713] we pray Thee, give us **thy** Word, that the Gospel may be
L C : 0 3 :054(427) [0713] So we pray that **thy** kingdom may prevail among us
L C : 0 3 :059(428) [0715] *"**Thy** will be done on earth, as it is in heaven."*
L C : 0 3 :067(429) [0717] to pray without ceasing: "**Thy** will be done, dear Father,
L C : 0 3 :067(429) [0717] persecute and suppress **thy** holy Word or prevent thy
L C : 0 3 :067(429) [0717] thy holy Word or prevent **thy** kingdom from coming; and
L C : 0 3 :097(433) [0725] the promise and hast set **thy** seal to it, making it as certain
L C : 0 3 :097(433) [0725] it as certain as an absolution pronounced by **thyself**."
L C : 0 4 :056(444) [0747] On this I build, that it is **thy** Word and command."
L C : 0 5 :062(454) [0767] of mine, but on account of **thy** Word, because Thou hast
L C : 0 5 :062(454) [0767] it and I want to be **thy** disciple, no matter how
E P : R N :001(464) [0777] is written in Ps. 119:105, "**Thy** word is a lamp to my feet
E P : 0 1 :004(466) [0781] as it is written, "**Thy** hands fashioned and made me, all
S D : 0 1 :035(514) [0869] Job says: "**Thy** hands fashioned and made me together
S D : 0 1 :035(514) [0869] life and steadfast love; and **thy** care has preserved my
S D : 0 1 :036(514) [0869] Wonderful are **thy** works!
S D : 0 1 :036(514) [0869] **Thy** eyes behold my uniformed substance; in thy book
S D : 0 1 :036(514) [0869] my uniformed substance; in **thy** book were written, every
S D : 0 2 :051(531) [0901] "Sanctify them in the truth; **thy** Word is truth.
S D : 0 6 :009(565) [0965] was afflicted that I might learn **thy** statutes" (Ps. 119:71).
S D : 0 6 :021(567) [0969] "I will run in the way of **thy** commandments"
S D : 0 6 :021(567) [0969] not into judgment with **thy** servant; for no man living is
S D : 0 8 :070(605) [1041] set him over the works of **thy** hands, putting everything in
S D : 1 1 :004(617) [1063] my unformed substance, in **thy** book were written every
S D : 1 1 :007(617) [1065] thou hast plunged **thyself** into misfortune, but in me
S D : 1 1 :007(617) [1065] misfortune, but in me alone is **thy** salvation" (Hos. 13:9).
S D : 1 1 :074(628) [1087] I am driven far from **thy** sight" (Ps. 31:22), then,

Tied (2), Ties (1)
A P : 0 7 :005(169) [0227] an association of outward **ties** and rites like other civic
A P : 0 7 :031(174) [0237] faith is not a righteousness **tied** to certain traditions, as
A P : 0 7 :031(174) [0237] of the law was **tied** to the Mosaic ceremonies, because

Till (1)
A P : 2 4 :034(256) [0395] them like gold and silver, **till** they present right offerings

Timber (1)
S D : 0 2 :019(524) [0889] touch, or to an unhewn **timber**, or to a wild, unbroken

Time (201), Times (88)
P R : P R :002(003) [0007] In these last **times** of this transitory world almighty God
P R : P R :017(008) [0015] by any one or if at any **time** it might become necessary to
P R : P R :018(008) [0015] lands have hitherto at all **times** adhered and appealed to,
A G : P R :001(024) [0039] A short **time** ago Your Imperial Majesty graciously
A G : P R :022(027) [0043] We have at various **times** made our protestations and
A G : 1 2 :005(034) [0049] of sin, and yet at the same **time** to believe the Gospel and
A G : 2 0 :003(041) [0053] was taught in former **times**, when for the most part
A G : 2 0 :005(041) [0053] about which they did not preach at all in former **times**.
A G : 2 0 :019(043) [0055] In former **times** this comfort was not heard in preaching,
A G : 2 1 :003(047) [0059] call upon this same Jesus Christ in every **time** of need.
A G : 2 2 :004(050) [0061] in the church for a long **time**, as can be demonstrated from
A G : 2 2 :005(050) [0061] mentions that the cup was given to laymen in his **time**.
A G : 2 3 :010(052) [0061] deacons to marry in the Christian church of former **times**.
A G : 2 3 :012(052) [0063] At that **time** there was such serious and strong resistance
A G : 2 3 :012(053) [0063] that the pope at the **time** not only forbade future
A G : 2 3 :014(053) [0063] fact that, in these last **times** of which the Scriptures
A G : 2 3 :021(055) [0063] Only in our **time** does one begin to persecute innocent
A G : 2 4 :010(057) [0065] Before our **time**, however, the Mass came to be misused
A G : 2 4 :010(057) [0065] by learned and devout men even before our **time**.
A G : 2 4 :021(058) [0067] At the same **time** the abominable error was condemned
A G : 2 4 :034(060) [0067] On holy days, and at other **times** when communicants are
A G : 2 4 :040(061) [0069] the church from ancient **times**, and since no conspicuous
A G : 2 4 :041(061) [0069] In **times** past, even in large churches where there were

Continued ▶

AG : 25 :002(061) [0069] At the same **time** the people are carefully instructed
AG : 25 :005(062) [0069] In former **times** the preachers who taught much about
AG : 25 :006(062) [0069] a more fitting fashion than had been done for a long **time**.
AG : 26 :001(063) [0071] In former **times** men taught, preached, and wrote that
AG : 26 :016(066) [0073] learned people before our **time** have also complained that
AG : 26 :041(070) [0075] At the same **time**, however, the people are instructed that
AG : 26 :043(070) [0075] East they kept Easter at a **time** different from that in
AG : 27 :016(073) [0077] In former **times** people gathered and adopted monastic
AG : 27 :060(080) [0083] In former **times** Gerson censured the error of the monks
AG : 27 :060(080) [0083] was an innovation of his **time** to speak of monastic life as
AG : 28 :001(081) [0083] been written in former **times** about the power of bishops,
AG : 28 :065(092) [0093] but forbade such eating for a **time** to avoid offense.
AG : 28 :072(093) [0093] in the church in former **times** and which were introduced
AG : 28 :073(093) [0093] introducing them, but they are not adapted to our **times**.
AG : 28 :074(094) [0093] have with the passing of **time** fallen into disuse and are
AL : 00 :001(048) [0059] by the fault of the **times** although contrary to the intent
AL : 22 :004(050) [0061] This usage continued in the church for a long **time**.
AL : 22 :008(050) [0061] only a custom of quite recent **times** that holds otherwise.
AL : 23 :016(054) [0063] state that in later **times** the old rigor should be relaxed
AL : 23 :026(056) [0065] and as a rule vows used to be so made in former **times**.
AL : 24 :010(057) [0065] is evident that for a long **time** there has been open and
AL : 24 :014(057) [0065] had corrected them in **time**, there would now have been
AL : 24 :027(059) [0067] he has perfected for all **time** those who are sanctified."
AL : 24 :035(060) [0067] the church, for before the **time** of Gregory the ancients do
AL : 24 :041(061) [0069] In former **times**, even in churches most frequented, Mass
AL : 25 :002(061) [0069] which there has been profound silence before this **time**.
AL : 25 :005(062) [0069] In former **times** satisfactions were immoderately extolled,
AL : 26 :015(066) [0073] that they have had no **time** to treat the Scriptures and
AL : 26 :034(069) [0075] to be encouraged at all **times**, and not merely on a few
AL : 26 :041(069) [0075] At the same **time** men are warned that such observances
AL : 26 :043(070) [0075] was kept in the East at a **time** different from that in
AL : 27 :002(071) [0077] In Augustine's **time** they were voluntary associations.
AL : 27 :008(072) [0077] many good men before our **time** when they saw that girls
AL : 27 :010(072) [0077] to those monks in former **times** who had a little more
AL : 27 :026(075) [0079] monastery, and there is no want of examples in our **time**.
AL : 27 :049(079) [0083] fear God and at the same **time** to have great faith and to
AL : 27 :060(080) [0083] Before our **times** Gerson rebuked the error of the monks
AL : 28 :001(081) [0083] In former **times** there has been great controversy about
AL : 28 :037(086) [0089] been suppressed, for from **time** to time more holy days
AL : 28 :037(086) [0089] for from time to **time** more holy days were appointed,
AL : 28 :065(092) [0093] but forbade such eating for a **time** to avoid offense.
AL : 28 :073(093) [0093] were introduced, but they are not adapted to later **times**.
AL : 28 :074(094) [0095] with the passing of **time**, as the canons themselves show.
AP : 04 :012(108) [0123] vicious errors that would take a long **time** to enumerate.
AP : 04 :200(134) [0175] At the same **time** the doctrine of penitence is preached to
AP : 04 :211(136) [0179] At the same **time** they believed that through faith they
AP : 04 :258(144) [0193] At the same **time** he wants the forgiveness of sins to be
AP : 04 :259(144) [0193] At the same **time** he wants the forgiveness of sins to be
AP : 04 :259(145) [0193] indicates; but at the same **time** he wishes the forgiveness
AP : 04 :283(150) [0201] those days, or in our own **time** the daily sprinkling with
AP : 04 :303(154) [0205] we have said several **times** that we are talking
AP : 04 :356(161) [0217] Christ's sake at the same **time** makes us sons of God and
AP : 07 :029(173) [0237] For the **time** being this seemed enough to defend the
AP : 07 :042(176) [0241] celebrated Easter at one **time** and others at another, but
AP : 07 :042(176) [0241] falls at a different **time** from the Jewish Passover.
AP : 07 :042(176) [0241] held tenaciously to the custom of using the Jewish **time**.
AP : 07 :042(176) [0243] do not correctly compute the **time** in celebrating Easter.
AP : 07 :042(176) [0243] do, celebrate it at the same **time** with them; even if they
AP : 07 :042(177) [0243] of having to observe a set **time**, since they tell them not to
AP : 07 :043(177) [0243] not intend it to refer to the **time** when Easter should be
AP : 11 :003(180) [0249] With regard to the **time**, it is certain that most people in
AP : 11 :003(180) [0249] absolution and the Lord's Supper, many **times** a year.
AP : 11 :005(181) [0249] we do not prescribe a set **time** because not everyone is
AP : 11 :005(181) [0249] not everyone is ready in the same way at the same **time**.
AP : 11 :005(181) [0249] rushed in at the same **time**, the people could not be heard
AP : 11 :005(181) [0249] ancient canons and the Fathers do not appoint a set **time**.
AP : 12 :032(186) [0259] it has sinned; at the same **time** it flees God's horrible
AP : 12 :107(197) [0283] mention confession from **time** to time; for example
AP : 12 :107(197) [0283] confession from time to **time**; for example (Ps. 32:5), "I
AP : 12 :121(200) [0287] on the canons says several **times** that these observances
AP : 12 :122(200) [0287] though it was unknown in the **time** of Peter Lombard.
AP : 12 :126(201) [0289] that these are the last **times**, in which Christ predicted
AP : 12 :126(201) [0289] affairs, ought in such **times** to exercise unusual wisdom
AP : 12 :151(206) [0299] says (I Pet. 4:17), "For the **time** has come for judgment to
AP : 15 :020(218) [0321] they gave the people a set **time** to assemble, because they
AP : 15 :028(219) [0323] Yet at the same **time** he deplores the danger to
AP : 15 :032(219) [0323] Testament ceremonies were necessary for the **time** being.
AP : 15 :047(221) [0327] we must be diligent at all **times** because God commands
AP : 15 :047(221) [0327] diligent at all times because God commands it at all **times**.
AP : 16 :002(222) [0331] At the same **time** it lets us make outward use of the
AP : 18 :009(226) [0337] At the same **time** it shows the difference between human
AP : 21 :034(234) [0353] horoscopes carved at a particular **time** contain power.
AP : 21 :036(234) [0353] dangers, helped kings in **time** of great danger, taught the
AP : 23 :023(242) [0369] In those **times** such a dismissal was an act of kindness.
AP : 23 :040(244) [0375] but because it gives more **time** for praying, teaching, and
AP : 23 :043(245) [0375] At the same **time** good men will know how to use
AP : 23 :052(246) [0377] this burden for a long **time**, either for themselves or for
AP : 23 :053(246) [0379] reasons for changing it, especially in these last **times**.
AP : 23 :054(247) [0379] given us a picture of the **times** that will precede the end of
AP : 23 :055(247) [0379] In a **time** like this it was appropriate to guard marriage
AP : 23 :067(248) [0383] In Jovinian's **time** the world still did not know the law of
AP : 23 :067(248) [0383] or that the church condemned marriage at that **time**.
AP : 24 :007(250) [0385] they been that for a long **time** good men have wanted
AP : 24 :008(250) [0385] was celebrated three **times** a week, and that this practice
AP : 24 :081(264) [0411] used it this way in the **time** of the Romans, as the rescript
AP : 27 :005(269) [0421] Though once upon a **time** they were schools of Christian
AP : 27 :049(277) [0437] themselves vary with **times** and persons; but the example
AP : 27 :054(278) [0439] But they spend their **time** either on philosophical
AP : 28 :016(283) [0449] that were changed by **time**, and they did not set them
AP : 28 :026(285) [0451] For the **time** being we have made this reply to the
S1 : PR :013(291) [0459] we would find enough **time** to reform the regulations
S2 : 02 :026(297) [0469] regard them as helpers in **time** of need, and attribute all
S2 : 03 :001(297) [0471] which in former **times** had been founded with good
S2 : 04 :001(298) [0471] as the ancient councils and the **time** of Cyprian prove.
S2 : 04 :004(299) [0473] been under the pope and are not at the present **time**.
S3 : 03 :019(306) [0485] At the same **time** his attention was directed to his own
S3 : 03 :026(307) [0487] In **time** souls got to be so cheap that they were released at
S3 : 03 :029(308) [0487] and Pharisees in Christ's **time** were just such saints.
S3 : 03 :036(309) [0489] We need not spend our **time** weighing, distinguishing,
S3 : 03 :042(309) [0491] with my own eyes at the **time** of the uprising) who hold
S3 : 08 :006(313) [0495] There is no **time** to dispute further about these matters.
TR : 00 :011(321) [0507] At that **time**, however, they reasoned thus: "Cephas
TR : 00 :021(323) [0509] when there had for a long **time** been disputes between the
TR : 00 :032(325) [0513] purple signified that the **time** would come after his
TR : 00 :062(331) [0523] in Alexandria, from the **time** of Mark the Evangelist to
TR : 00 :062(331) [0523] Mark the Evangelist to the **time** of Bishops Heracles and
TR : 00 :070(332) [0525] to this, for there was a **time** when the people elected
SC : PR :007(339) [0533] In this way all the **time** and labor will be lost.
SC : PR :016(340) [0535] allow yourself ample **time**, for it is not necessary to take
SC : PR :016(340) [0535] They can be presented one at a **time**.
SC : PR :021(340) [0537] made concerning it, and no **time** or place should be
SC : PR :022(341) [0537] at least three or four **times** a year despises the sacrament
SC : 01 :004(342) [0539] or deceive, but in every **time** of need call upon him, pray
SC : 03 :008(346) [0547] live a godly life, both here in **time** and hereafter forever.
SC : 09 :012(356) [0563] hand of God, that in due **time** he may exalt you"
LC : PR :007(359) [0569] and whenever else I have **time**, I read and recite word for
LC : PR :012(360) [0571] **Time** and paper would fail me if I were to recount all the
LC : PR :020(361) [0573] Then in due **time** they themselves will make the noble
LC : SP :001(362) [0575] Hence from ancient **times** it has been called in Greek, a
LC : SP :005(362) [0575] I well remember the **time** when there were old people who
LC : SP :006(362) [0575] Christendom from ancient **times**, though they were rarely
LC : SP :026(364) [0579] especially at the **time** designated for the Catechism, so
LC : 01 :002(365) [0581] good and in which we find refuge in every **time** of need.
LC : 01 :011(366) [0583] saint and worshiped and invoked him in **time** of need.
LC : 01 :025(368) [0587] we Germans from ancient **times** have called God by a
LC : 01 :040(370) [0591] we desire all good things in **time** and eternity, this ought
LC : 01 :046(371) [0593] which indeed endures for a **time** but in the end is
LC : 01 :063(373) [0599] in vain," God at the same **time** gives us to understand
LC : 01 :064(373) [0599] we call on his name in **time** of need, or praise and thank
LC : 01 :064(373) [0599] need, or praise and thank him in **time** of prosperity, etc.
LC : 01 :067(373) [0599] Though it may take a long **time**, nothing he does will in
LC : 01 :069(374) [0599] children be trained in due **time** to shun falsehood and
LC : 01 :081(375) [0603] In **time**, however, the Jews interpreted this
LC : 01 :082(376) [0603] customs, persons, **times**, and places, from all of which we
LC : 01 :084(376) [0605] so that people may have **time** and opportunity, which
LC : 01 :085(376) [0605] restricted to a particular **time**, as it was among the Jews,
LC : 01 :085(376) [0605] Since from ancient **times** Sunday has been appointed for
LC : 01 :089(377) [0605] do not have this much **time** and leisure, we must set apart
LC : 01 :092(377) [0607] At whatever **time** God's Word is taught, preached, heard,
LC : 01 :094(378) [0607] Places, **times**, persons, and the entire outward order of
LC : 01 :095(378) [0607] to hear and learn it, especially at the **times** appointed.
LC : 01 :129(383) [0619] he would have perished a hundred **times** in his own filth.
LC : 01 :142(384) [0621] So from ancient **times** the Romans and other peoples
LC : 01 :154(386) [0625] you must suffer ten **times** as much wrong from your own
LC : 01 :172(388) [0629] we must spare no effort, **time**, and expense in teaching
LC : 01 :181(389) [0631] place of parents; in early **times**, as we read in Moses,
LC : 01 :217(394) [0641] Thus it may in due **time** regain its proper honor, and
LC : 01 :226(395) [0645] One would ten **times** rather lose the money from one's
LC : 01 :234(397) [0647] arrogant course for a long **time**, still he will remain a
LC : 01 :242(397) [0649] and scraped for a long **time**, he will pronounce this kind
LC : 01 :253(399) [0653] you can enjoy a hundred **times** more than you could
LC : 01 :305(406) [0667] was also the case in ancient **times** with respect to wives.
LC : 01 :305(406) [0667] was quite prevalent in the **time** of the law, for we read
LC : 01 :313(407) [0671] restricted to special **times**, places, rites, and ceremonies,
LC : 01 :317(408) [0673] It will be a long **time** before men produce a doctrine or
LC : 01 :333(410) [0677] while at the same **time** he adds such glorious promises
LC : 02 :032(415) [0687] the year, especially at the **times** appointed for dealing at
LC : 02 :047(416) [0691] In early **times** the latter phrase was missing, and it is
LC : 02 :057(418) [0693] daily, we await the **time** when our flesh will be put to
LC : 03 :053(427) [0711] first, it comes here, in **time**, through the Word and faith,
LC : 03 :073(430) [0719] life itself cannot be maintained for any length of **time**.
LC : 03 :083(431) [0721] or last for any length of **time**, as indeed we see and
LC : 03 :098(433) [0725] and practice every hour, keeping it with us at all **times**.
LC : 03 :109(435) [0729] from us but shall at all **times** expect his blows and parry
LC : 03 :110(435) [0729] At such **times** your only help or comfort is to take refuge
LC : 04 :050(443) [0745] of him; in short, all this **time** down to the present day no
LC : 04 :055(443) [0747] he had not really received the sacrament the first **time**.
LC : 04 :078(446) [0751] in water a hundred **times**, it would nevertheless be only
LC : 04 :084(446) [0753] as the daily garment which he is to wear all the **time**.
LC : 05 :023(449) [0757] we often grow weary and faint, at **times** even stumble.
LC : 05 :027(449) [0759] For such **times**, when our heart feels too sorely pressed,
LC : 05 :042(451) [0763] over a long period of **time** are not to be considered
LC : 05 :047(452) [0763] not bound to a special **time** like the Passover, which the
LC : 05 :047(452) [0765] to no special place or **time**" (although the pope afterward
LC : 05 :049(452) [0765] him, lets a long period of **time** elapse without ever
LC : 05 :049(452) [0765] Christian, you must from **time** to time satisfy and obey
LC : 05 :049(452) [0765] you must from time to **time** satisfy and obey this
LC : 05 :057(453) [0767] are, to work toward the **time** when nothing will prick
LC : 06 :013(458) [0000] in faith, we may at any **time** and as often as we wish lay
EP : 00 :000(463) [0775] on Which for Some **Time** There Has Been Disagreement
EP : RN :002(465) [0777] and apostles was preserved in post-apostolic **times**.
EP : RN :003(465) [0777] 2. Immediately after the **time** of the apostles — in fact,
EP : RN :004(465) [0777] which has occurred in our **times**, we regard, as the
EP : RN :004(465) [0777] and as the symbol of our **time**, the first and unaltered
EP : RN :004(465) [0777] theologians approved by their subscription at that **time**.
EP : RN :008(465) [0779] forth how at various **times** the Holy Scriptures were
EP : 01 :022(469) [0785] At other **times** the word means the good or bad quality
EP : 04 :018(477) [0801] Especially in these last **times**, it is just as necessary to
EP : 05 :008(479) [0803] learn from it for the first **time** the real nature of their sin,
EP : 05 :009(479) [0803] now know for the first **time** what great things God
EP : 07 :009(482) [0811] 4. But at the same **time** we believe, teach, and confess
EP : 07 :032(485) [0815] at one and the same **time** in may places, still less in all
EP : 07 :034(485) [0815] present at more than one place at a single given **time**.
EP : 08 :030(490) [0825] to be present at the same **time** at more than one place,
EP : 10 :002(492) [0829] question has been, In **times** of persecution, when a
EP : 10 :006(493) [0829] teach, and confess that in **time** of persecution, when a

Continued ▶

EP : 1 0 :011(494) [0831] 3. That in a **time** of persecution and when a public
EP : 1 1 :022(497) [0837] articles which for a **time** the theologians of the Augsburg
SD : 0 0 :000(501) [0845] Some Theologians for a **Time**, Resolved and Settled
SD : PR :003(501) [0847] At that **time** a number of Christian electors, princes, and
SD : PR :004(502) [0847] of God, just as in ancient **times** Christian symbols and
SD : PR :008(502) [0849] Similarly at the present **time** our adversaries, the papists,
SD : PR :002(503) [0851] which have at all **times** and in all places been accepted in
SD : PR :004(504) [0851] 2. Since in ancient **times** the true Christian doctrine as it
SD : PR :004(504) [0851] heresies which at that **time** had arisen within the Christian
SD : PR :011(506) [0855] theologians of that **time** subscribed them, and that all
SD : PR :015(506) [0857] that we shall at all **times** make a sharp distinction between
SD : PR :016(507) [0857] significant articles which were in controversy at this **time**.
SD : 0 1 :007(510) [0861] and makes at the present **time**, original sin is transmitted
SD : 0 1 :011(510) [0863] but that at the same **time** it replaces the lost image of God
SD : 0 1 :062(519) [0879] But at the **time** he explained with special seriousness and
SD : 0 2 :015(523) [0887] asks God more than ten **times** to give him understanding
SD : 0 2 :068(534) [0907] and terrified, at one **time** ardent in love, strong in faith
SD : 0 2 :068(534) [0907] in faith and in hope, and at another **time** cold and weak.
SD : 0 3 :029(544) [0925] But it must be done at the **time** and place where it is
SD : 0 3 :041(546) [0931] And yet faith is at no **time** ever alone."
SD : 0 3 :058(550) [0937] of the person who is God and man at the same **time**.
SD : 0 4 :004(551) [0939] obedient to God, but at **times** it implies the coercion with
SD : 0 4 :005(551) [0939] In the course of **time**, however, the issue ceased to be only
SD : 0 4 :012(553) [0941] grace, so certain that it would die a thousand **times** for it.
SD : 0 4 :029(555) [0947] and as issues which in **times** of persecution, when it was
SD : 0 4 :037(557) [0951] declares no less than three **times** in Phil. 3:7ff. that good
SD : 0 5 :002(558) [0951] grace but also at the same **time** a proclamation of
SD : 0 5 :012(560) [0955] At the same **time** it is true and right that the apostles and
SD : 0 7 :009(570) [0975] who at the same **time** submitted their own confession at
SD : 0 7 :029(574) [0981] with the passage of **time**, and that there is no end to the
SD : 0 7 :032(574) [0983] as the enemies of the sacrament do at the present **time**.
SD : 0 7 :035(575) [0983] body of Christ"), we at **times** also use the formulas "
SD : 0 7 :061(580) [0995] and necessary to salvation for all Christians at all **times**.
SD : 0 7 :099(586) [1005] manifest at the proper **time** by the blessed God"
SD : 0 8 :002(591) [1015] were present at the same **time** in heaven and in the Holy
SD : 0 8 :006(592) [1017] Holy Spirit, yet, when the **time** had fully come, he took
SD : 0 8 :007(592) [1017] which was assumed in **time** into the unity of the person of
SD : 0 8 :009(593) [1017] be everywhere at the same **time** naturally (that is,
SD : 0 8 :011(593) [1019] and subsist at the same **time** both the divine and the
SD : 0 8 :026(596) [1025] and did not use it at all **times**, but only when he wanted
SD : 0 8 :057(602) [1035] that Christ received in **time** he received not according to
SD : 0 8 :057(602) [1035] the person received this in **time** according to the assumed
SD : 0 8 :065(604) [1039] During the **time** of the humiliation the divine majesty was
SD : 0 8 :068(604) [1039] with and about him at all **times**, it could be said with
SD : 0 8 :075(606) [1043] tell us that during the **time** of Emperor Valens there was a
SD : 0 8 :085(608) [1047] man I received it in **time** according to the humanity and
SD : 1 0 :009(612) [1055] every place and at every **time** has the right, authority, and
SD : 1 0 :009(612) [1055] appropriate way, as at any **time** may seem to be most
SD : 1 0 :010(612) [1055] and confess that at a **time** of confession, as when enemies
SD : 1 0 :012(612) [1057] which at that **time** was a matter of indifference and which
SD : 1 0 :013(613) [1057] the weak as far as foods, **times**, and days were concerned
SD : 1 0 :015(613) [1057] At the same **time** this concerns the article of Christian
SD : 1 0 :030(616) [1061] or more ceremonies at any **time** and place, according to
SD : 1 1 :043(623) [1077] Before the creation of **time**, "before the foundation of the
SD : 1 1 :048(624) [1079] the glorious comfort, in **times** of trial and affliction, that
SD : 1 1 :050(624) [1079] At the same **time** it teaches us what the true church is,
SD : 1 1 :056(625) [1081] for each person the **time** and hour of his call and
SD : 1 1 :056(625) [1081] Word, while we leave the **time** and hour to God
SD : 1 1 :078(629) [1089] with the Pharisees and their party at the **time** of Christ.
SD : 1 2 :008(633) [1097] and especially at those **times** where the pure Word of the

Timely (2)
PR : PR :026(014) [0025] settled and composed in **timely** fashion before they
LC : 0 1 :137(384) [0619] that such wicked people die a natural and **timely** death.

Timid (7)
AP : 0 4 :021(110) [0127] **Timid** consciences, on the other hand, they drive to
AP : 0 4 :180(132) [0171] In this promise **timid** consciences should seek
AP : 2 4 :049(258) [0401] and as an admonition to **timid** consciences really to trust
S3 : 0 8 :001(312) [0493] especially for the sake of **timid** consciences and for the
LC : 0 4 :042(442) [0743] are so boundless that if **timid** nature considers them, it
LC : 0 5 :055(453) [0767] of this we became so **timid** that everyone was thrown into
SD : 0 7 :069(582) [0997] the other hand, are those **timid**, perturbed Christians,

Tiniest (2)
SD : 0 2 :007(521) [0883] or half-way or in the **tiniest** or smallest degree, "of
SD : 0 2 :025(526) [0891] one-half or the least and **tiniest** part, but altogether and

Tire (1), Tired (1)
S3 : 1 5 :005(316) [0501] to their god and to themselves until they **tire** of them.
LC : 0 1 :099(378) [0609] or two, become sick and **tired** of it and feel that they know

Titanic (1)
SD : PR :007(502) [0849] they knew that these **titanic** errors and the subsequent

Tithes (3)
AG : 2 8 :029(085) [0087] matrimonial cases and in **tithes**), they have these by virtue
AL : 2 8 :029(085) [0087] pertaining to matrimony, **tithes**, etc.), bishops have this
AP : 2 4 :021(253) [0391] the thank offering, the first fruits, and the **tithes**.

Title (8), Titles (7)
AG : 2 6 :011(065) [0071] to be given the glamorous **title** of alone being holy and
AL : 2 6 :009(065) [0071] themselves the glamorous **title** of comprising the spiritual
AP : 0 4 :105(122) [0153] with all their magnificent **titles** — for some are called
AP : 1 2 :144(205) [0297] up these works with fancy **titles**; they call them works of
AP : 2 7 :026(273) [0429] under the cover of these **titles**, they are "doctrines of
LC : PR :002(358) [0567] manuals claimed in their **titles** to be: "Sermons That
LC : 0 1 :150(385) [0625] they bear this name and **title** with all honor as their chief
LC : 0 1 :158(387) [0627] papacy who applied this **title** to themselves but performed
LC : 0 1 :301(405) [0667] and they gain such secure **title** to the property as to put it
LC : 0 2 :035(415) [0687] said, I cannot give a better **title** than "Sanctification."
EP : 0 8 :024(490) [0823] personal union achieves only common names and **titles**.
SD : 0 3 :039(546) [0929] any kind of pretense, **title**, or name are they to be mingled
SD : 0 8 :063(603) [1037] all only a mode of speech, mere words, **titles**, and names.
SD : 0 8 :067(604) [1039] it merely shares the bare **titles** and the names in words
SD : 0 8 :095(609) [1049] but has only the bare **title** and name in common with it.

Today (9)
AG : PR :007(025) [0039] present our case in German and Latin **today** (Friday).
AP : 2 4 :006(250) [0385] Even **today**, Greek parishes have no private Masses but
TR : 0 0 :016(322) [0509] many churches in the East **today** which do not seek
LC : 0 1 :069(374) [0599] is evident that the world **today** is more wicked than it has
LC : 0 3 :100(433) [0725] yet such is life that one stands **today** and falls tomorrow.
LC : 0 4 :049(442) [0745] Even **today** there are not a few whose doctrine and life
LC : 0 4 :054(443) [0745] Even though a Jew should **today** come deceitfully and
EP : 0 8 :038(491) [0827] is happening everywhere **today**, nor what will yet take
SD : 0 1 :007(510) [0861] And even **today**, in this corruption, God does not create

Together (89)
PR : PR :000(001) [0004] of their Theologians, **Together** with an Appended
PR : PR :013(007) [0013] diligence, they brought **together** in good order, by the
PR : PR :021(011) [0019] and human natures, **together** with their respective
PR : PR :021(011) [0019] properties, are mixed **together** and the human nature
PR : PR :024(013) [0023] concord will, **together** with us, take Christian pleasure in
AG : PR :004(025) [0039] true religion and live **together** in unity and in one
AG : PR :005(025) [0039] for these purposes, **together** with other electors, princes,
AG : PR :018(026) [0041] imperial government (**together** with the absent electors,
AG : 2 3 :023(055) [0063] These two statements fit **together** well, for it must be a
AL : 2 4 :005(056) [0065] to receive the sacrament **together**, in so far as they are fit
AL : 2 6 :014(066) [0073] gathered the traditions **together** and sought mitigations to
AL : 2 7 :016(073) [0077] Formerly people came **together** in monasteries to learn.
AP : 0 4 :053(114) [0137] elements always belong **together**: the promise itself, the
AP : 0 4 :144(127) [0161] obey their lusts, nor does it exist **together** with mortal sin.
AP : 0 4 :235(140) [0185] perfect or whole when all its parts fit **together** properly."
AP : 0 4 :258(144) [0193] Come now, let us reason **together**, says the Lord: though
AP : 0 4 :278(149) [0199] consider faith and fruits **together**, so here we say in
AP : 0 4 :353(161) [0217] if penitence and faith amid penitence grow **together**.
AP : 0 4 :374(164) [0221] way the Scriptures lump **together** the righteousness of the
AP : 0 7 :001(168) [0227] and wheat are heaped **together** (Matt. 3:12) and Christ
AP : 1 2 :115(199) [0285] still remains **together** with a remnant of the custom in
AP : 1 5 :027(219) [0323] but only the traditions **together** with interpretations that
AP : 2 1 :003(229) [0343] theory of invocation, **together** with the theories our
AP : 2 3 :016(241) [0369] that inflames it come **together**; therefore marriage is more
AP : 2 3 :023(242) [0371] "What God has joined **together**, let no man put asunder."
AP : 2 3 :029(243) [0371] he says in Matt. 19:6, "What God has joined **together**."
AP : 2 4 :035(256) [0397] Taken **together**, these are the daily sacrifice of the New
AP : 2 4 :098(268) [0419] of Baal will endure **together** with the papal realm until
AP : 2 8 :023(284) [0451] all the offenses are put **together**, still the one doctrine of
S2 : 0 2 :024(296) [0469] sells the merits of Christ **together** with the superabundant
S2 : 0 4 :007(299) [0473] whole rule and estate, **together** with all his rights and
S2 : 0 4 :009(300) [0473] and diligently joined **together** in unity of doctrine, faith,
S2 : 0 4 :009(300) [0475] governed the churches **together** and in common.
S3 : 0 3 :002(304) [0479] He drives all **together** into terror and despair.
S3 : 0 3 :033(308) [0489] All have turned aside, **together** they have gone wrong."
S3 : 0 3 :036(309) [0489] but lumps everything **together** and says, "We are wholly
S3 : 1 1 :002(315) [0499] God or forbid them to live **together** honestly in marriage.
SC : 0 2 :002(345) [0543] faculties of my mind, **together** with food and clothing,
SC : 0 4 :012(349) [0551] the old Adam in us, **together** with all sins and evil lusts,
LC : 0 1 :003(365) [0581] For these two belong **together**, faith and God.
LC : 0 1 :043(370) [0591] diligence to scraping **together** great wealth and money,
LC : 0 1 :091(377) [0607] vestments gathered **together** in one heap, they could not
LC : 0 1 :219(394) [0643] husband and wife live **together** in love and harmony,
LC : 0 1 :253(399) [0653] than you could scrape **together** by perfidy and injustice.
LC : 0 1 :278(402) [0661] their works heaped up **together**, and see if they can make
LC : 0 1 :326(409) [0675] the end to the beginning and holds everything **together**.
LC : 0 1 :329(410) [0677] that end and beginning are all linked and bound **together**.
LC : 0 2 :005(411) [0679] the Creed were gathered **together**, there would be many
LC : 0 2 :051(417) [0691] It is called **together** by the Holy Spirit in one faith, mind,
LC : 0 2 :062(419) [0695] he has not yet gathered **together** all his Christian people,
LC : 0 3 :025(423) [0705] all the churches **together**, with all their clergy, they would
LC : 0 3 :052(427) [0711] that we may all remain **together** eternally in this kingdom
LC : 0 3 :077(431) [0721] people at large to live **together** in obedience, peace, and
LC : 0 4 :012(438) [0735] teach that if we piled **together** all the works of all the
LC : 0 4 :046(442) [0743] the water and the Word **together** constitute one Baptism,
LC : 0 4 :054(443) [0745] there would be water **together** with God's Word, even
LC : 0 5 :012(448) [0755] spirits and scholars put **together** have less wisdom than
LC : 0 6 :025(460) [0000] have simply driven men **together** in hordes just to show
EP : RN :004(465) [0777] Diet in the year 1530, **together** with the Apology thereof
EP : 0 2 :003(470) [0787] our trespasses, he made us alive **together** with Christ."
EP : 0 8 :002(487) [0817] and human natures, **together** with their properties, *really*
EP : 0 8 :009(487) [0819] two boards are glued **together** and neither gives anything
EP : 0 8 :018(489) [0823] and their properties **together** in one essence, as Eutyches
EP : 1 2 :030(500) [0843] and similar articles, **together** with their erroneous
SD : PR :001(503) [0851] religion is drawn **together** out of the Word of God.
SD : PR :004(504) [0851] understood was drawn **together** out of God's Word in
SD : 0 1 :010(510) [0863] and righteousness, **together** with a disability and
SD : 0 1 :013(511) [0863] eternal damnation, **together** with other bodily, spiritual,
SD : 0 1 :035(514) [0869] fashioned and made me **together** round about, and thou
SD : 0 1 :035(514) [0869] and flesh, and knit me **together** with bones and sinews.
SD : 0 2 :010(522) [0885] All have turned aside, **together** they have gone wrong; no
SD : 0 2 :057(532) [0903] or three are gathered **together** in his name and occupy
SD : 0 2 :058(532) [0903] gathered your children **together** as a hen gathers her
SD : 0 2 :066(534) [0907] reminds us, "Working **together** with him, then, we entreat
SD : 0 2 :066(534) [0907] horses draw a wagon **together**, such a view could by no
SD : 0 3 :020(542) [0921] he made us alive **together** with Christ" (Eph. 2:5).
SD : 0 5 :015(561) [0957] doctrines are always **together**, and both of them have to
SD : 0 5 :027(563) [0961] may not be mingled **together** and confused so that what
SD : 0 5 :027(563) [0961] would be tangled **together** and made into one doctrine.
SD : 0 7 :018(572) [0979] that the body of Christ, **together** with all his benefits, is
SD : 0 7 :022(573) [0979] and scholars put **together** have less wisdom than the
SD : 0 7 :033(575) [0983] them all as belonging **together** (that is, as
SD : 0 7 :037(575) [0985] of Christ, are present **together** here on earth in the
SD : 0 7 :062(581) [0995] true God and man, **together** with all the benefits that he
SD : 0 8 :014(594) [1019] like two boards glued **together**, so that in deed and truth
SD : 0 8 :060(602) [1035] they are not blended **together** or the one is changed into
SD : 0 8 :070(604) [1039] while it is true that God, **together** with the whole fullness

Continued ▶

SD : 1 1 :041(623) [1077] I have gathered you **together** and you would not!"
SD : 1 1 :049(624) [1079] should and must "work **together** for good" since they are

Toil (1)
LC : 0 1 :043(370) [0591] wasted their effort and **toil** or, if they have amassed great

Token (2), Tokens (1)
LC : PR :014(360) [0571] our eyes and in our hands as a constant **token** and sign.
EP : 0 7 :027(485) [0815] Supper are no more than **tokens** whereby Christians
EP : 0 7 :041(486) [0817] 20. By the same **token** we commend to the righteous

Toledo (1)
AP : 2 2 :004(236) [0359] The Council of **Toledo** gives the same testimony, and it

Tolerable (3), Tolerate (9), Tolerated (13)
PR : PR :022(011) [0019] by any means intend to **tolerate** in our lands, churches,
AL : 2 0 :007(041) [0053] This teaching is more **tolerable** than the former one, and
AL : 2 4 :018(058) [0067] the Mass as have been **tolerated** in the church for many
AP : 1 1 :009(182) [0251] would be more **tolerable** if they had added one word on
AP : 2 1 :038(234) [0355] And they refuse to **tolerate** us because we do not require
AP : 2 1 :043(235) [0357] They do not **tolerate** capable clergy in the churches.
AP : 2 7 :055(278) [0439] like — which could be **tolerated** if they were used as
S2 : 0 2 :021(296) [0469] Therefore, it is under no circumstances to be **tolerated**.
S2 : 0 2 :024(296) [0469] These are not to be **tolerated**.
S3 : 0 1 :011(303) [0479] pagan doctrines, and we cannot **tolerate** them.
S3 : 1 5 :004(316) [0501] mockery of holy Baptism which should not be **tolerated**.
LC : SP :018(363) [0577] should a person be **tolerated** if he is so rude and
LC : 0 1 :047(371) [0593] and realize that God will **tolerate** no presumption and no
LC : 0 1 :201(392) [0637] prostitution and lewdness **tolerated** as they are now.
LC : 0 1 :264(400) [0655] we are, we cannot **tolerate** having evil spoken of us; we
EP : 1 1 :021(497) [0837] Hence they should not be **tolerated** in God's church.
EP : 1 2 :002(498) [0839] of a kind that cannot be **tolerated** either in the church, or
EP : 1 2 :002(498) [0839] *Errors which Cannot be **Tolerated** in the Church*
SD : PR :009(503) [0849] erring party cannot be **tolerated** in the church of God,
SD : 0 2 :080(536) [0911] and zeal, and in no wise **tolerate** in the church of God,
SD : 0 4 :002(551) [0939] should not be **tolerated** in the church, lest the merit of
SD : 0 4 :040(558) [0951] cannot and should not **tolerate**, teach, or defend this
SD : 0 7 :046(577) [0987] or if it was to receive a **tolerable** and loose interpretation.
SD : 1 0 :010(612) [1055] nor should we **tolerate** the imposition of such ceremonies
SD : 1 2 :009(633) [1097] cannot be suffered or **tolerated** in the churches or in the

Tollit (1)
LC : 0 4 :059(444) [0747] saying goes, "*Abusus non **tollit**, sed confirmat*

Tomb (1)
LC : 0 1 :266(401) [0657] simply make your ears a **tomb** and bury it until you are

Tomes (1)
AP : 1 5 :027(219) [0323] There are huge **tomes**, even whole libraries, that do not

Tomfoolery (1)
S1 : PR :013(291) [0459] that their trifling and **tomfoolery** with albs, great

Tomorrow (1)
LC : 0 3 :100(433) [0727] yet such is life that one stands today and falls **tomorrow**.

Tone (1)
SD : 0 7 :100(586) [1007] space; a musical sound or **tone** passes through air or

Tongue (18), Tongues (2)
AG : 2 5 :011(063) [0071] of your sins not with your **tongue** but in your conscience."
AL : 2 5 :011(063) [0071] your sins not with your **tongue** but with the memory of
S1 : PR :006(289) [0457] venomous and malicious **tongues** and thus destroying the
LC : 0 1 :050(371) [0593] directs the lips and the **tongue** into the right relation to
LC : 0 1 :110(380) [0613] to them and hold your **tongue**, even if they go too far.
LC : 0 1 :188(390) [0633] we should not use our **tongue** to advocate or advise
LC : 0 1 :263(400) [0655] It forbids all sins of the **tongue** by which we may injure
LC : 0 1 :263(400) [0655] False witness is clearly a work of the **tongue**.
LC : 0 1 :263(400) [0655] Whatever is done with the **tongue** against a neighbor,
LC : 0 1 :268(401) [0657] you use your venomous **tongue** to the disgrace and harm
LC : 0 1 :270(401) [0657] before the proper authorities, then hold your **tongue**.
LC : 0 1 :273(401) [0659] with a worthless **tongue** who gossips and slanders
LC : 0 1 :276(402) [0659] precept for governing the **tongue** which ought to be
LC : 0 1 :276(402) [0659] reprove the man personally, otherwise to hold his **tongue**.
LC : 0 1 :285(403) [0661] harm his neighbor, whether friend or foe, with his **tongue**.
LC : 0 1 :285(403) [0663] A person should use his **tongue** to speak only good of
LC : 0 1 :289(404) [0663] against the poisonous **tongues** of those who are busy
LC : 0 1 :291(404) [0663] this smallest and weakest of his members, the **tongue**.
LC : 0 2 :048(416) [0691] In our mother **tongue** therefore it ought to be called "a
LC : 0 3 :036(425) [0707] In our mother **tongue** we would say, "Heavenly Father,

Tonsures (3)
S1 : PR :013(291) [0459] with albs, great **tonsures**, broad cinctures, bishops' and
S1 : PR :013(291) [0459] concerning fasts, vestments, **tonsures**, and chasubles.
S3 : 1 2 :003(315) [0499] not consist of surplices, **tonsures**, albs, or other

Toothache (1)
LC : 0 1 :011(366) [0583] If anyone had a **toothache**, he fasted to the honor of St.

Topic (2), Topics (2)
AL : 2 7 :017(073) [0077] that our teaching on this **topic** may better be understood.
AP : 1 5 :043(221) [0327] all sermons deal with **topics** like these: penitence, the fear
AP : 2 7 :052(278) [0437] On this whole **topic** we have said enough earlier.
SC : PR :009(339) [0535] and to discuss these **topics** from different angles and in

Torgau (3)
PR : PR :013(007) [0013] learned theologians at **Torgau** in the year 1576 for the
EP : 0 9 :003(492) [0827] his sermon preached at **Torgau** in the year 1533, where he
SD : 0 9 :001(610) [1051] he held in the castle at **Torgau** in the year 1533, "I believe

Torment (4), Tormented (7), Torments (1)
AG : 1 7 :004(038) [0051] condemned men will not suffer eternal pain and **torment**.
AG : 2 3 :006(052) [0061] well known what terrible **torment** and frightful
AG : 2 5 :005(062) [0069] matters but only **tormented** consciences without long
AL : 1 7 :003(038) [0051] and devils he will condemn to be **tormented** without end.
AL : 2 6 :011(065) [0071] This error greatly **tormented** the consciences of devout
AP : 0 4 :285(150) [0201] It is always **tormented** and constantly invents other works
AP : 1 7 :001(224) [0335] the ungodly to endless **torment** with the devil.
TR : 0 0 :074(332) [0525] other evil desires, have **tormented** men and
LC : 0 1 :065(373) [0599] the question that has **tormented** so many teachers: why
LC : 0 1 :227(396) [0645] a trade and deliberately fleeces, skins, and **torments** him.
LC : 0 6 :005(457) [0000] to being driven and **tormented** to confess, fast, etc., more
LC : 0 6 :034(461) [0000] We shall let the papists **torment** and torture themselves

Torn (5)
S2 : 0 2 :010(294) [0465] would suffer himself to be **torn** to pieces before he would
LC : 0 1 :016(366) [0585] in him, nor let itself be **torn** from him, but for him should
LC : 0 1 :191(391) [0635] thirst, and cold, to be **torn** to pieces by wild beasts, to rot
LC : 0 3 :060(428) [0715] things and never allow ourselves to be **torn** from them.
LC : 0 5 :032(450) [0761] we allow this treasure to be **torn** out of the sacrament?

Torture (14), Tortured (3), Tortures (3), Torturing (1)
AP : 0 4 :245(142) [0189] but they also try to wipe it out with sword and **torture**.
AP : 1 1 :007(181) [0251] What great **tortures** for the most pious minds!
AP : 1 1 :009(182) [0251] not want to sanction the **torture** of the summists, which,
AP : 1 2 :011(184) [0255] And to **torture** godly minds still more, they imagine that
AP : 1 5 :049(221) [0329] they bring exquisite **torture** to a conscience that has
AP : 2 0 :009(228) [0341] use their terrors, **tortures**, and punishments to try to drive
AP : 2 1 :035(234) [0353] In the midst of her **tortures**, Barbara asks for a reward —
AP : 2 3 :070(249) [0383] breaking up marriages and **torturing** and killing priests.
AP : 2 4 :046(258) [0401] the enumeration of sins were a **torture** for consciences.
AP : 2 8 :004(281) [0445] of alleviating such minds **tortured** by doubt, they call to
S3 : 0 3 :019(306) [0483] his sins — an impossibility and the source of great **torture**.
S3 : 0 3 :020(306) [0485] the place to recount the **torture**, rascality, and idolatry
SC : 0 5 :024(350) [0555] turn confession into **torture**; he should simply mention
LC : 0 1 :119(381) [0615] foot that they must **torture** themselves in vain with their
LC : 0 5 :055(453) [0765] under the pope when we **tortured** ourselves to become so
LC : 0 6 :002(457) [0000] so greatly burdened and **tortured** consciences with the
LC : 0 6 :003(457) [0000] anguish and a hellish **torture** since people had to make
LC : 0 6 :004(457) [0000] we are released from the **torture** of enumerating all sins in
LC : 0 6 :034(461) [0000] the papists torment and **torture** themselves and other
SD : 0 6 :005(564) [0963] with God, nor may it **torture** the regenerated with its
SD : 1 1 :070(627) [1085] saved should burden and **torture** himself with thoughts

Toss (1), Tossed (2)
AP : 1 2 :089(195) [0279] Constantly **tossed** about in such doubt, they never
LC : PR :005(359) [0567] After reading it once they **toss** the book into a corner as
LC : 0 3 :123(436) [0731] a wave of the sea that is driven and **tossed** by the wind.

Total (15), Totally (6)
AP : 0 2 :043(106) [0117] over from philosophy the **totally** foreign idea that because
AP : 0 4 :222(137) [0181] the approval of a particular act but of the **total** person.
AP : 0 4 :262(145) [0195] These words deal with the **total** scope of penitence.
AP : 1 2 :112(198) [0285] All of this is **totally** different from the enumeration we
AP : 1 2 :124(201) [0289] we covered almost the sum **total** of all Christian doctrine,
AP : 1 2 :132(202) [0291] he is surely talking about **total** penitence and total
AP : 1 2 :132(202) [0291] about total penitence and **total** newness of life and fruits.
AP : 1 2 :170(209) [0305] to be not a fraud but an improvement of the **total** life.
AP : 2 3 :064(248) [0381] be taken to mean purity of the heart and **total** penitence.
SD : 0 1 :011(510) [0863] nature is not only a **total** lack of good in spiritual, divine
SD : 0 1 :030(513) [0867] human nature has been **totally** destroyed, or has been
SD : 0 1 :033(514) [0869] the nature, essence, or **total** man is corrupted, dwells) are
SD : 0 2 :017(523) [0887] man is not only **totally** turned away from God, but is also
SD : 0 3 :009(541) [0919] through the merit of the **total** obedience, the bitter
SD : 0 3 :055(549) [0935] God and man in his sole, **total**, and perfect obedience is
SD : 0 3 :056(549) [0935] and confess that the **total** obedience of Christ's total
SD : 0 3 :056(549) [0935] total obedience of Christ's **total** person, which he
SD : 0 6 :006(564) [0965] its powers they would be **totally** free from sins, they
SD : 0 8 :011(593) [1019] nature belong to the **total** person of Christ; and that
SD : 1 1 :003(616) [1063] Accordingly, the net **total** and content of the teaching on
SD : 1 1 :036(622) [1075] undermine and **totally** destroy for us the necessary and

Touch (6), Touched (1)
AG : 2 8 :045(088) [0089] Do not taste, Do not **touch**' (referring to things which all
AL : 2 8 :045(088) [0089] Do not taste, Do not **touch**' (referring to things which all
AP : 0 7 :035(175) [0241] Do not taste, Do not **touch**' (referring to things which all
AP : 1 2 :178(211) [0309] and that these **touch** neither earth nor heaven and they
AP : 2 4 :003(250) [0385] those who have been **touched** by the Word may receive
SD : 0 2 :019(524) [0889] in any way to human **touch**, or to an unhewn timber, or
SD : 0 7 :101(587) [1007] way that they do not feel, **touch**, measure, or comprehend

Touchstone (1)
EP : RN :007(465) [0779] to which as the only **touchstone** all doctrines should and

Town (3)
AP : 2 7 :001(268) [0419] ago, in the Thuringian **town** of Eisenach, there was a
TR : 0 0 :062(330) [0523] presbyters in every **town**," and points out that these
LC : 0 1 :266(401) [0657] but to make him the talk of the **town** is not my business.

Traced (1), Traces (1)
AL : 2 8 :038(087) [0089] and we can still see some **traces** of these in the
SD : 0 7 :030(574) [0981] I have most diligently **traced** all these articles through the

Tract (2)
TR : 0 0 :082(000) [0529] revered preceptor, and the **tract** concerning the Papacy
SD : 0 8 :085(608) [1045] In his **tract** *Concerning the Last Words of David*, which

Trade (6), Trades (2), Trading (1)
AG : 1 8 :005(040) [0053] take a wife, engage in a **trade**, or do whatever else may be
S1 : PR :012(290) [0459] extortion in every **trade** and on the part of peasants —
SC : 0 1 :014(343) [0541] possession by dishonest **trade** or by dealing in shoddy
LC : 0 1 :083(376) [0603] to their work and **trades** the whole week long — should
LC : 0 1 :094(378) [0607] Other **trades** and occupations are not properly called holy
LC : 0 1 :227(396) [0645] one swindles another in a **trade** and deliberately fleeces,
LC : 0 1 :249(398) [0651] order in all areas of **trade** and commerce in order that the
LC : 0 3 :023(423) [0703] This we should not **trade** for all the riches in the world.
LC : 0 3 :084(431) [0723] usury in public business, **trading**, and labor on the part of

Tradition (14), Traditional (5), Traditions (148)
AG : PR :001(024) [0039] to the Turk, that **traditional** foe of ours and of the
AG : 1 5 :003(036) [0049] that all ordinances and **traditions** instituted by men for
AG : 1 5 :004(037) [0049] vows and other **traditions** concerning distinction of
AG : 0 0 :002(048) [0059] are concerned chiefly with various **traditions** and abuses.
AG : 0 0 :002(048) [0059] among us in regard to **traditions**, although we hope to
AG : 0 0 :002(048) [0059] why we have changed certain **traditions** and abuses.
AG : 2 6 :001(063) [0071] foods and similar **traditions** which had been instituted by
AG : 2 6 :005(064) [0071] and against human **tradition** so that we should learn that
AG : 2 6 :008(065) [0071] the second place, such **traditions** have also obscured the
AG : 2 6 :008(065) [0071] of God, for these **traditions** were exalted far above God's
AG : 2 6 :011(065) [0071] and imperfect, while **traditions** were to be given the
AG : 2 6 :011(065) [0071] was no end or limit to the making of such **traditions**.
AG : 2 6 :012(065) [0071] In the third place, such **traditions** have turned out to be a
AG : 2 6 :012(065) [0071] possible to keep all the **traditions**, and yet the people were
AG : 2 6 :014(066) [0073] undertook to collate the **traditions** and sought
AG : 2 6 :016(066) [0073] complained that such **traditions** caused so much strife in
AG : 2 6 :017(066) [0073] burdened with so many **traditions**, and he taught in this
AG : 2 6 :019(067) [0073] which have arisen from a wrong estimation of **tradition**.
AG : 2 6 :021(067) [0073] be atoned for by observing the said human **traditions**.
AG : 2 6 :022(067) [0073] the customary **traditions**, and he adds, "In vain do they
AG : 2 6 :040(069) [0075] many ceremonies and **traditions** (such as the liturgy of the
AL : 0 7 :003(032) [0047] necessary that human **traditions** or rites and ceremonies,
AL : 1 5 :003(036) [0049] that human **traditions** which are instituted to propitiate
AL : 1 5 :004(037) [0049] Wherefore vows and **traditions** about foods and days,
AL : 2 6 :001(064) [0071] and similar human **traditions** are works which are
AL : 2 6 :003(064) [0071] this opinion concerning **traditions** much harm has
AL : 2 6 :005(064) [0071] the law and human **traditions** in order to show that the
AL : 2 6 :006(064) [0071] wholly smothered by **traditions** which have produced the
AL : 2 6 :008(065) [0071] commands of God, for **traditions** were exalted far above
AL : 2 6 :012(065) [0071] In the third place, **traditions** brought great dangers to
AL : 2 6 :012(065) [0071] impossible to keep all **traditions**, and yet men judged
AL : 2 6 :013(066) [0073] they could not keep the **traditions** and, meanwhile, they
AL : 2 6 :014(066) [0073] gathered the **traditions** together and sought mitigations to
AL : 2 6 :015(066) [0073] with gathering **traditions** that they have had no time to
AL : 2 6 :016(066) [0073] these bickerings about **traditions** that they were unable to
AL : 2 6 :019(067) [0073] which had arisen from misunderstanding of **traditions**.
AL : 2 6 :021(067) [0073] for sins by the observance of human **traditions**.
AL : 2 6 :022(067) [0073] observing the customary **tradition**, a tradition which was
AL : 2 6 :022(067) [0073] customary tradition, a **tradition** which was seen to be
AL : 2 6 :039(069) [0075] not fasting in itself, but **traditions** which with peril to
AL : 2 6 :040(069) [0075] Many **traditions** are nevertheless kept among us (such as
AL : 2 8 :035(086) [0089] the observances of **traditions** for the purpose of making
AL : 2 8 :037(086) [0089] a result of this notion **traditions** have multiplied in the
AL : 2 8 :039(087) [0089] Again, the authors of **traditions** act contrary to the
AL : 2 8 :042(088) [0089] right to impose such **traditions** on the churches and thus
AL : 2 8 :042(088) [0089] Why do they multiply sin with such **traditions**?
AL : 2 8 :043(088) [0089] prohibit the making of **traditions** for the purpose of
AL : 2 8 :047(088) [0089] those who require **traditions**, "Let them alone; they are
AL : 2 8 :049(089) [0091] consciences with such **traditions**, why does Scripture so
AL : 2 8 :049(089) [0091] does Scripture so often prohibit the making of **traditions**?
AL : 2 8 :064(092) [0093] they try to mitigate the **traditions**, moderation can never
AL : 2 8 :067(093) [0093] from day to day even among those who favor **traditions**.
AL : 2 8 :069(093) [0093] on the observance of **traditions** which cannot be kept with
AL : 2 8 :074(094) [0093] as many human **traditions** have been changed with the
AP : PR :011(099) [0101] as closely as possible to **traditional** doctrinal formulas in
AP : 0 2 :004(101) [0105] length that our definition agrees with the **traditional** one.
AP : 0 4 :236(140) [0185] so bitterly on certain **traditions** which have no value for
AP : 0 4 :283(150) [0201] by God, not in human **traditions** like the ablutions in
AP : 0 4 :393(167) [0225] predicted that human **traditions** and the teaching of
AP : 0 7 :010(170) [0229] whether they have the same human **traditions** or not.
AP : 0 7 :030(174) [0237] necessary that human **traditions** or rites and ceremonies,
AP : 0 7 :031(174) [0237] tied to certain **traditions**, as the righteousness of the law
AP : 0 7 :031(174) [0237] this quickening human **traditions**, whether universal or
AP : 0 7 :032(174) [0239] foolish opinions about **traditions** have crept into the
AP : 0 7 :032(174) [0239] thought that human **traditions** are devotions necessary
AP : 0 7 :032(174) [0239] others because of such **traditions** as the observance of
AP : 0 7 :034(175) [0239] observance of human **traditions** is an act of worship
AP : 0 7 :034(175) [0239] of the church that human **traditions** be alike everywhere.
AP : 0 7 :034(175) [0239] If human **traditions** are not acts of worship necessary for
AP : 0 7 :034(175) [0239] if he does not observe **traditions** that have been
AP : 0 7 :036(175) [0241] is evident that human **traditions** do not quicken the
AP : 0 7 :037(175) [0241] whether human **traditions** are acts of devotion necessary
AP : 0 7 :038(175) [0241] say that universal **traditions** should be observed because
AP : 1 1 :008(181) [0251] it, like other human **traditions**, is not an act of worship
AP : 1 1 :009(182) [0253] with sins against human **traditions**, which is the height of
AP : 1 2 :011(184) [0255] of sins, most of them against human **traditions**!
AP : 1 2 :143(204) [0297] derived from human **tradition**, such works belong to the
AP : 1 2 :143(204) [0297] belong to the human **traditions** of which Christ says
AP : 1 2 :145(205) [0297] they add human **traditions**, whose works they rank above
AP : 1 2 :147(205) [0297] but works of human **tradition**, which Christ calls useless
AP : 1 2 :162(208) [0303] performance of human **traditions** which they say avails *ex*
AP : 1 2 :165(208) [0303] to the satisfaction and performance of human **traditions**.
AP : 1 2 :174(210) [0307] observance of certain **traditions** and the penalties of
AP : 1 5 :000(215) [0315] [Article XV.] Human **Traditions** in the Church
AP : 1 5 :001(215) [0315] we say that human **traditions** instituted to appease God,
AP : 1 5 :002(215) [0315] we have discussed **traditions** at length in Article XXVI of
AP : 1 5 :003(215) [0315] opponents to defend human **traditions** on other grounds.
AP : 1 5 :003(215) [0315] of sins by the observance of human **traditions**.
AP : 1 5 :004(215) [0315] Scripture calls **traditions** "doctrines of demons"
AP : 1 5 :005(215) [0317] other hand, set up these **traditions** as another mediator
AP : 1 5 :009(216) [0317] gracious because of the **traditions** and not because of
AP : 1 5 :010(216) [0317] difference between our **traditions** and the ceremonies of
AP : 1 5 :010(216) [0317] of Moses as well as **traditions** because they were thought
AP : 1 5 :010(216) [0317] of the law and of the **traditions**, he therefore contends
AP : 1 5 :012(216) [0317] justified do merit grace by observing these **traditions**.
AP : 1 5 :013(216) [0319] did not institute any **traditions** for the purpose of
AP : 1 5 :020(218) [0321] had rites and **traditions**, they did not regard them as
AP : 1 5 :021(218) [0321] the same reasons we also believe in keeping **traditions**.
AP : 1 5 :021(218) [0321] maintain that **traditions** have another purpose, namely, to
AP : 1 5 :021(218) [0321] innumerable similar observances in the human **traditions**.
AP : 1 5 :022(218) [0321] Paul writes that **traditions** "have an appearance of
AP : 1 5 :027(219) [0323] calling, but only the **traditions** together with
AP : 1 5 :028(219) [0323] comes from this strict interpretation of the **traditions**.
AP : 1 5 :030(219) [0323] law of Moses and the **traditions** of men, so that our
AP : 1 5 :030(219) [0323] perfectly clear that he is talking about human **traditions**.
AP : 1 5 :030(219) [0323] justify, how much less do the **traditions** of men justify?
AP : 1 5 :032(220) [0323] of the law or **traditions** be regarded as necessary.
AP : 1 5 :033(220) [0325] for loopholes in the **traditions** to ease their consciences,
AP : 1 5 :034(220) [0325] compel us to teach that **traditions** do not justify; that they
AP : 1 5 :034(220) [0325] to create or accept **traditions** with the idea that they merit
AP : 1 5 :036(220) [0325] The apostles violated **traditions**, and Christ excused
AP : 1 5 :037(220) [0325] drop certain useless **traditions**, they have excuse enough
AP : 1 5 :037(220) [0325] For such an idea of **traditions** is wicked.
AP : 1 5 :038(220) [0325] We gladly keep the old **traditions** set up in the church
AP : 1 5 :042(221) [0327] they talk about human **traditions**, the worship of the
AP : 1 5 :049(221) [0329] This subject of **traditions** involves many difficult and
AP : 1 5 :049(221) [0329] actual experience that **traditions** are real snares for
AP : 1 5 :050(222) [0329] teaching that human **traditions** do not merit the
AP : 2 4 :001(249) [0385] We keep **traditional** liturgical forms, such as the order of
AP : 2 4 :023(253) [0391] from their misinterpretation of the patriarchal **tradition**.
AP : 2 4 :043(257) [0399] and human **traditions** with the claim that these justify
AP : 2 4 :045(258) [0401] by the many different **traditions** and ideas and could not
AP : 2 7 :014(271) [0423] this credit to human **traditions**, as he clearly shows in
AP : 2 7 :020(272) [0427] madness to put a human **tradition**, which has neither a
AP : 2 7 :026(273) [0429] These are human **traditions**, about all of which it has been
AP : 2 7 :027(273) [0429] evangelical perfection is to be found in human **traditions**.
AP : 2 7 :033(275) [0431] mere human **traditions**, deserve the credit for meriting the
AP : 2 7 :035(275) [0431] penance, and human **traditions**, it is quite clear that
AP : 2 7 :035(275) [0431] And since Christ calls **traditions** "useless services," they
AP : 2 7 :039(276) [0433] perfection to human **traditions** if they say that monks
AP : 2 7 :047(277) [0437] therefore merely a human **tradition**, it is a useless service.
AP : 2 7 :052(278) [0437] should defend their **traditions**, contrary to the clear
AP : 2 7 :052(278) [0437] Pharisees for setting up **traditions** contrary to the
AP : 2 7 :054(278) [0439] or on ceremonial **traditions** that obscure Christ.
AP : 2 8 :003(281) [0445] in the observance of their **traditions** than of the Gospel.
AP : 2 8 :007(282) [0445] teaching that human **traditions** are useless acts of
AP : 2 8 :008(282) [0445] have no right to create **traditions** apart from the Gospel
AP : 2 8 :008(282) [0445] consciences with such **traditions** so that it would be a sin
AP : 2 8 :008(282) [0445] vigorously defend their **traditions** and wicked notions.
AP : 2 8 :009(282) [0445] we maintained that **traditions** do not merit the
AP : 2 8 :009(282) [0445] here they also say that **traditions** are conducive to eternal
AP : 2 8 :010(282) [0447] Paul denies that **traditions** avail for eternal righteousness
AP : 2 8 :010(282) [0447] opponents explain how **traditions** are conducive to
AP : 2 8 :011(283) [0447] clearly testifies that **traditions** should not be imposed on
AP : 2 8 :015(283) [0447] for them to create **traditions**, namely, that they must not
AP : 2 8 :017(283) [0449] This is the simple way to interpret **traditions**.
AP : 2 8 :018(284) [0449] is not referring to **traditions** but is rather directed against
AP : 2 8 :018(284) [0449] to traditions but is rather directed against **traditions**.
AP : 2 8 :019(284) [0449] who hears you hears me" cannot be applied to **traditions**.
AP : 2 8 :019(284) [0449] his voice, His Word to be heard, not human **traditions**.
AP : 2 8 :020(284) [0449] Bishops must not create **traditions** contrary to the
AP : 2 8 :020(284) [0449] nor interpret their **traditions** in a manner contrary to the
AP : 2 8 :021(284) [0449] things: that human **traditions** are the worship of God;
S 3 : 1 5 :000(316) [0501] XV. Human **Traditions**
S 3 : 1 5 :001(316) [0501] the papists that human **traditions** effect forgiveness or
TR : 0 0 :011(321) [0507] burden the church with **traditions**, nor let anybody's
TR : 0 0 :014(322) [0507] according to divine **tradition** and apostolic usage, what is
TR : 0 0 :015(322) [0509] this custom a divine **tradition** and an apostolic usage, and
TR : 0 0 :045(328) [0517] sin and have invented a **tradition** concerning the
TR : 0 0 :048(328) [0519] profligate acts have sprung from the **tradition** of celibacy!
TR : 0 0 :048(328) [0519] from Christ to human **traditions** and have utterly
TR : 0 0 :048(328) [0519] that the most trivial **traditions** are services of God and
TR : 0 0 :078(333) [0527] For the **traditions** concerning spiritual relationship are
TR : 0 0 :078(333) [0527] and equally unjust is the **tradition** which forbids an
SD : PR :005(504) [0853] ancient church it was **traditional** and customary for later
SD : 0 4 :007(552) [0941] are based on human **traditions**; that truly good works are
SD : 1 0 :021(614) [1061] burden the church with **traditions**, nor let anybody's

Traffic (3)
AP : 2 1 :011(230) [0345] up to honor the saints but to defend their religious **traffic**.
S 2 : 0 2 :014(295) [0467] blasphemous, accursed **traffic** in Masses which are offered
S 2 : 0 2 :014(295) [0467] they have abolished their **traffic** in purgatorial Masses

Tragic (2), Tragedies (2)
AP : 0 4 :241(141) [0187] we often see the greatest **tragedies** come from the most
AP : 0 7 :027(173) [0237] the rest as mythology, like the **tragedies** of the poets.
AP : 1 1 :008(181) [0251] What **tragic** spectacles were enacted between the secular
LC : 0 3 :115(435) [0731] and, in short, all the **tragic** misery and heartache of which

Train (3), Trained (8), Training (5), Trains (1)
PR : PR :023(012) [0021] men who are being **trained** for service in the church and
AP : 2 7 :021(272) [0427] Paul says (I Tim. 4:8), "Bodily **training** is of little value."
S 2 : 0 3 :001(298) [0471] and states, and also well **trained** girls to become mothers,
SC : PR :020(340) [0537] refuse their aid in the **training** of children to become
SC : 0 5 :023(350) [0553] have not been faithful in **training** my children, servants,
LC : SP :006(362) [0575] and old, may be well-**trained** in them and familiar with
LC : 0 1 :061(373) [0597] be strictly required and **trained** to hold this as well as the
LC : 0 1 :069(374) [0599] punishment, children be **trained** in due time to shun
LC : 0 1 :074(374) [0601] Children used to be **trained** to fast and pray to St.
LC : 0 1 :076(375) [0603] so long as they can be **trained** with kind and pleasant
LC : 0 1 :077(375) [0603] This kind of **training** takes such root in their hearts that
LC : 0 1 :124(382) [0617] do very much; one fool **trains** another, and as they have
LC : 0 1 :173(388) [0629] with the command that we **train** and govern them
LC : 0 1 :175(388) [0631] so that men might be **trained** who would be a benefit to
LC : 0 1 :177(389) [0631] Because of the way we **train** them, we have unruly and
LC : 0 5 :085(456) [0773] With such **training** we may more easily instill the Ten
LC : 0 5 :086(456) [0773] other teachings unless we **train** the people who come after

Traitor (1)
LC : 0 1 :268(401) [0657] is to declare somebody a thief, a murderer, a **traitor**, etc.

Tramp (1), Trample (4), Trampling (1)
S 1 : PR :014(291) [0459] our mummeries while we **trample** his solemn
LC : 0 1 :119(381) [0615] devilish perversity in **trampling** God's commandment
LC : 0 1 :234(397) [0647] still he will remain a **tramp** and a beggar and will suffer

Continued ▶

LC : 03 :030(424) [0707] forces arrayed against us, trying to **trample** us under foot.
LC : 04 :062(444) [0749] from the rulers and **trample** it under foot and would, in
LC : 05 :080(456) [0771] You will not entirely **trample** him under foot because our

Tranquil (1), Tranquility (6), Tranquillity (5)
PR : PR :024(013) [0023] brings salvation, to the **tranquillity** and peace of Christian
AL : 28 :055(090) [0091] the sake of love and **tranquility** and that they keep them;
AP : 04 :091(120) [0149] is, our consciences are **tranquil** and joyful before God,
AP : 04 :232(139) [0185] not possible to preserve **tranquility** unless men cover and
AP : 04 :243(141) [0189] of domestic **tranquillity**, which cannot endure unless
AP : 04 :288(151) [0203] for the sake of social **tranquillity** there should be some
AP : 07 :033(174) [0239] universal rites are observed for the sake of **tranquility**.
AP : 07 :034(175) [0239] observe them for the sake of **tranquility** or bodily profit.
AP : 15 :001(215) [0315] which are conducive to **tranquillity** and good order in the
AP : 15 :013(216) [0319] for the sake of good order and **tranquility** in the church.
AP : 15 :038(220) [0325] are useful and promote **tranquillity**, and we interpret them
SD : 11 :095(632) [1095] of temporal peace, **tranquility**, and outward harmony.

Transacted (1), Transaction (1), Transactions (3)
S2 : 02 :012(295) [0465] services, and business **transactions** associated with it are
S2 : 04 :003(298) [0471] are purely diabolical **transactions** and deeds (except what
S2 : 04 :014(301) [0475] concerning secular **transactions** and judgments, as the
LC : 01 :224(395) [0643] wherever business is **transacted** and money is exchanged
LC : 01 :233(396) [0647] him by any faithless or underhanded business **transaction**.

Transcends (4)
SD : 07 :101(587) [1007] as far as God **transcends** them, and you must posit it
SD : 07 :102(587) [1007] we do not know; it **transcends** nature and reason, even
SD : 08 :004(592) [1017] person of Christ that **transcends** or contravenes its
SD : 08 :050(600) [1031] nature in Christ which **transcends** or contravenes its

Transfer (24), Transference (1), Transferred (23), Transferring (2), Transfers (3)
AL : 27 :044(078) [0081] claimed that they could **transfer** their works to others.
AL : 28 :002(081) [0083] also have undertaken to **transfer** kingdoms of this world
AL : 28 :013(083) [0085] the other's function, nor **transfer** the kingdoms of the
AP : 04 :283(150) [0201] by sophistically **transferring** the universal particle to a
AP : 04 :302(154) [0205] It **transfers** Christ's glory to human works; it leads
AP : 04 :317(156) [0209] what else is this but a **transfer** of Christ's glory to our
AP : 04 :360(162) [0219] who merit them can **transfer** these merits to others."
AP : 04 :361(162) [0219] "sacraments" of this **transfer**, as when a monk's hood is
AP : 04 :366(163) [0221] First they have been "**transferred** into the kingdom of
AP : 07 :023(172) [0235] him, so now this right has been **transferred** to the pope.
AP : 07 :027(173) [0235] Nor should that be **transferred** to the popes which is the
AP : 12 :069(192) [0271] from earlier ones and **transferred** these opinions from one
AP : 12 :078(193) [0275] should the honor of Christ be **transferred** to our works.
AP : 12 :106(197) [0283] It is silly to **transfer** here the saying of Solomon
AP : 12 :165(208) [0303] by God should not be **transferred** to the satisfaction and
AP : 21 :014(230) [0345] intolerable, for it **transfers** to the saints honor belonging
AP : 21 :015(231) [0347] the work of Christ and **transfers** to the saints the trust we
AP : 21 :029(233) [0351] we dare not trust in the **transfer** of the saints' merits to
AP : 21 :031(233) [0351] merits of Christ and thus **transfer** to the saints the honor
AP : 24 :025(253) [0391] them, nor can they be **transferred** to merit the forgiveness
AP : 24 :031(255) [0395] the forgiveness of sin when it is **transferred** to others.
AP : 24 :033(256) [0395] the forgiveness of sins when it is **transferred** to others.
AP : 24 :042(257) [0399] that this work can be **transferred** to someone else to merit
AP : 24 :059(260) [0405] which could be **transferred** to others *ex opere operato;*
AP : 24 :059(260) [0405] the Spirit contradicts any such **transfer** *ex opere operato.*
AP : 24 :059(260) [0405] does not happen by the **transfer** of one man's work to
AP : 24 :063(261) [0405] for those to whom it is **transferred**, even for wicked
AP : 24 :064(261) [0405] are valid when they are **transferred** to many just as when
AP : 24 :064(261) [0405] to many just as when they are **transferred** to one.
AP : 24 :064(261) [0407] Finally, they even **transfer** it to the dead and free souls
AP : 24 :066(261) [0407] and of punishment for those to whom it is **transferred**.
AP : 24 :075(263) [0411] *operato* and can be **transferred** to others; but the Fathers
AP : 24 :075(263) [0411] of the appropriation of the comfort, not of any **transfer**.
AP : 24 :077(263) [0411] that can be **transferred** to others *ex opere operato* to
AP : 24 :078(263) [0411] the forgiveness of sins for those to whom it is **transferred**.
AP : 24 :091(266) [0415] Mass has largely been **transferred** to the dead and to
AP : 24 :091(266) [0415] of tyrants who **transferred** the blessed promises of the
AP : 24 :092(266) [0417] faith, it follows that it is useless to **transfer** it to the dead.
AP : 24 :092(266) [0417] Clearly this **transference** to the dead cannot be proved
AP : 24 :094(267) [0417] but rather we reject the **transfer** of the Lord's Supper to
AP : 24 :094(267) [0417] the opponents' idea of the **transfer** *ex opere operato.*
AP : 24 :095(267) [0417] opponents teach about **transfer** *ex opere operato,* they
AP : 27 :009(270) [0421] merits save others when they are **transferred** to them?
AP : 27 :034(275) [0431] in Christ and are **transferring** to their own foolish
AP : 27 :039(276) [0433] They sell merits and **transfer** them to others under the
S1 : PR :001(288) [0455] Afterwards he **transferred** the council from Mantua, and
S2 : 02 :021(296) [0467] obligated themselves to **transfer** (by legal and open sale)
TR : 00 :002(320) [0503] that is, the authority to bestow and **transfer** kingdoms.
TR : 00 :012(322) [0507] any right from him and **transfer** it to the bishop of
TR : 00 :031(325) [0513] take possession of, or **transfer** the kingdoms of the world.
TR : 00 :035(326) [0513] for themselves, **transfer** kingdoms, and harass the kings
TR : 00 :036(326) [0515] be censured that he can **transfer** the keys of a worldly
TR : 00 :048(328) [0519] Thus they have **transferred** merit from Christ to human

Transform (2), Transformation (3), Transformed (7), Transforming (1), Transforms (1)
AG : 24 :022(058) [0067] This **transformed** the Mass into a sacrifice for the living
AG : 28 :061(091) [0093] discussions of the **transformation** of the law, of the
AP : 12 :106(197) [0283] By a marvelous **transformation**, our opponents make
LC : 05 :016(448) [0757] no angel in heaven can **transform** bread and wine into
SD : 01 :030(513) [0867] destroyed, or has been **transformed** into some other
SD : 03 :020(542) [0921] place because he has **transformed** a child of wrath into a
SD : 04 :010(552) [0941] divine work in us that **transforms** us and begets us anew
SD : 07 :036(575) [0985] essence has not been **transformed** into the human nature
SD : 08 :062(603) [1037] and is now either **transformed** into the God-head or by
SD : 08 :066(604) [1039] without any **transformation** of the natural properties of
SD : 08 :071(605) [1041] be denied and completely **transformed** into the Godhead.
SD : 08 :089(609) [1047] blended with the divine or has been **transformed** into it.
SD : 08 :092(609) [1049] Without **transforming** or destroying his true human
SD : 11 :082(630) [1089] and operation can **transform** the vessels of dishonor into

Transfusion (1)
SD : 08 :063(603) [1037] natural exchange or **transfusion** which would blend the

Transgress (7), Transgressed (2), Transgressing (1), Transgression (5), Transgressions (2), Transgressors (2)
AP : 02 :014(102) [0109] in human nature, **transgressing** as they do the first table
AP : 04 :076(117) [0143] Ps. 32:1, "Blessed is he whose **transgression** is forgiven."
AP : 04 :103(122) [0151] 'blessed is he whose **transgression** is forgiven, whose sin is
AP : 04 :163(129) [0169] Rom. 4:7), "Blessed is he whose **transgression** is forgiven."
AP : 12 :107(197) [0283] 'I will confess my **transgressions** to the Lord'; then thou
AP : 24 :023(253) [0391] here (*'asam*) means a victim sacrificed for **transgression**.
S3 : 03 :039(309) [0489] the law (as Christ says in John 7:19) but all **transgress** it.
SC : 01 :022(344) [0543] to punish all who **transgress** these commandments.
LC : 01 :061(373) [0597] Whenever they **transgress**, we must be after them at once
LC : 01 :139(384) [0621] is so strict about punishing those who **transgress** it.
LC : 01 :182(389) [0631] upon those who **transgress** this and the other
LC : 01 :322(409) [0673] all who despise and **transgress** his commandments; and
LC : 03 :086(432) [0723] still stumble daily and **transgress** because we live in the
SD : 01 :005(509) [0861] not only the actual **transgression** of God's
SD : 05 :017(561) [0957] God, and threatens the **transgressors** of the law with
SD : 05 :020(561) [0959] law of God and has **transgressed** it, his corrupted nature,
SD : 05 :021(562) [0959] and grace of God to **transgressors** of the law strictly
SD : 05 :023(562) [0959] deceit of the serpent **transgressed** God's laws, became a
SD : 05 :023(562) [0959] was wounded for our **transgressions** and bruised for our

Transitory (1)
PR : PR :002(003) [0007] these last times of this **transitory** world almighty God in

Translate (2), Translated (2), Translation (1)
AP : 24 :088(265) [0413] is a misinterpretation to **translate** this as "reasonable
LC : 02 :047(416) [0691] was missing, and it is unintelligible in our **translation**.
LC : 02 :049(417) [0691] should not be **translated** "communion" but "community."
SD : 03 :020(542) [0921] of God and thus has **translated** him from death into life,
SD : 07 :067(582) [0997] a pious Christian should be ashamed to **translate** them.

Transmit (1), Transmitted (6)
PR : PR :014(007) [0013] of the truth might be **transmitted** to our posterity as well.
PR : PR :024(013) [0023] and views will be **transmitted** to subsequent generations.
AP : 07 :040(176) [0241] instruction they might **transmit** to posterity the memory
AP : 07 :041(176) [0241] But if they were **transmitted** as something necessary for
SD : 01 :007(510) [0861] time, original sin is **transmitted** through our carnal
SD : 01 :038(515) [0871] in Adam and is **transmitted** to us in this condition.
SD : 07 :042(576) [0987] taught, and **transmitted** by the holy evangelists and

Transmuted (1)
EP : 07 :022(484) [0813] a way that they are **transmuted** into the body of Christ

Transubstantiation (5)
S3 : 06 :005(311) [0493] As for **transubstantiation**, we have no regard for the
EP : 07 :022(484) [0813] 1. The papistic **transubstantiation**, when it is taught in the
SD : 07 :014(571) [0977] they deny a **transubstantiation** (that is, an essential
SD : 07 :035(575) [0983] reject the papistic **transubstantiation** and to indicate the
SD : 07 :108(588) [1009] First, papistic **transubstantiation**, when they teach that

Trap (1)
LC : 05 :084(456) [0773] you and lies in wait to **trap** and destroy you, soul and

Traveler (1)
LC : 01 :047(371) [0593] lay them aside) or as a **traveler** avails himself of an inn,

Treachery (1)
S1 : PR :002(289) [0455] without deception or **treachery** to hold a truly free

Treading (1)
SC : 09 :003(354) [0561] muzzle an ox when it is **treading** out the grain,' and 'The

Treasure (40), Treasured (1), Treasures (12), Treasury (2)
S3 : 03 :025(307) [0485] the discovery and digging up of the **treasures** of the earth.
LC : PR :002(358) [0567] "Sleep Soundly," "Prepared!" and "**Treasury**."
LC : 01 :043(370) [0591] have amassed great **treasures**, that these have turned to
LC : 01 :091(377) [0607] But God's Word is the **treasure** that sanctifies all things.
LC : 01 :109(380) [0611] and prize them as the most precious **treasure** on earth.
LC : 01 :117(381) [0615] that jewel and holy **treasure**, the Word and
LC : 01 :122(382) [0617] themselves of this **treasure** and joy of conscience and lay
LC : 01 :145(385) [0623] wages, she would gain a **treasure** such as all who pass for
LC : 01 :150(386) [0625] them as the most precious **treasure** and jewel on earth.
LC : 01 :230(396) [0645] and stolen the **treasures** of the whole world and holds
LC : 01 :255(399) [0653] we have one more **treasure** which is indispensable to us,
LC : 01 :333(411) [0677] other teachings as the greatest **treasure** God has given us.
LC : 02 :024(413) [0683] is an excellent knowledge, but an even greater **treasure**.
LC : 02 :024(413) [0683] inexpressible eternal **treasures** through his Son and the
LC : 02 :038(415) [0689] acquired and won the **treasure** for us by his sufferings,
LC : 02 :038(415) [0689] In order that this **treasure** might not be buried but put to
LC : 02 :038(415) [0689] Spirit to offer and apply to us this **treasure** of salvation.
LC : 02 :043(416) [0689] that he won for us this **treasure** without our works and
LC : 03 :038(425) [0707] it as the greatest **treasure** and most sacred thing we have,
LC : 03 :048(426) [0711] his Word taught in its purity and cherished and **treasured**.
LC : 03 :055(427) [0713] for an eternal, priceless **treasure** and everything that God
LC : 03 :060(428) [0715] in which we appropriate God with all his **treasures**.
LC : 03 :061(428) [0715] we try to hold fast these **treasures**, we must suffer an
LC : 04 :016(438) [0735] God's name, and this is a **treasure** greater and nobler than
LC : 04 :026(439) [0739] being, for in it we obtain such an inexpressible **treasure**.
LC : 04 :029(440) [0739] it to us so that we may grasp the **treasure** it contains?
LC : 04 :034(440) [0741] no use, although in itself it is an infinite, divine **treasure**.
LC : 04 :037(441) [0741] which we do but is a **treasure** which God gives us and
LC : 04 :037(441) [0741] cross is not a work but a **treasure** comprehended and
LC : 04 :040(441) [0743] this, for it is not the **treasure** that is lacking; rather, what
LC : 04 :086(446) [0753] even though we sin, so all his **treasures** and gifts remain.
LC : 05 :022(449) [0757] we receive there a great **treasure**, through and in which
LC : 05 :028(449) [0759] no other, we say, are the **treasure** through which
LC : 05 :029(449) [0759] This **treasure** is conveyed and communicated to us in no
LC : 05 :029(449) [0759] blood and that these are yours as your **treasure** and gift.
LC : 05 :030(449) [0759] Yet, however great the **treasure** may be in itself, it must
LC : 05 :032(450) [0761] should we allow this **treasure** to be torn out of the
LC : 05 :035(450) [0761] The **treasure** is opened and placed at everyone's door,

Continued ▶

LC : 05 :036(450) [0761] Since this **treasure** is fully offered in the words, it can be
LC : 05 :036(450) [0761] Such a gift and eternal **treasure** cannot be seized with the
LC : 05 :037(451) [0761] faith of the heart which discerns and desires this **treasure**.
LC : 05 :039(451) [0761] entreaty that so great a **treasure**, which is daily
LC : 05 :066(454) [0769] he offers us all the **treasure** he brought from heaven for
LC : 06 :007(458) [0000] precious and comforting **treasure** which the Gospel
LC : 06 :020(459) [0000] faithful advice to go and obtain this precious **treasure**.
LC : 06 :022(459) [0000] as a great and wonderful **treasure** to be accepted with all
LC : 06 :025(460) [0000] and this indescribable **treasure**; they have simply driven
LC : 06 :034(461) [0000] who ignore such a **treasure** and bar themselves from it.
EP : 08 :037(491) [0825] in him are hid "all the **treasures** of wisdom and
EP : 12 :017(499) [0841] is in conscience bound to put it into a common **treasury**.
SD : 03 :010(541) [0919] Holy Spirit offers these **treasures** to us in the promise of
SD : 03 :039(546) [0929] of Christ's merit, which **treasures** are offered to us in the
SD : 07 :069(582) [0997] unworthy of this noble **treasure** and the benefits of Christ
SD : 08 :068(604) [1039] likewise are hid all **treasures** of wisdom and knowledge,
SD : 08 :074(606) [1043] In this way all the **treasures** of wisdom are hid in him, all

Treat (16), Treated (23), Treating (4), Treats (5)
PR : PR :023(012) [0021] that no other doctrine be **treated** and taught in our lands,
AG : PR :003(025) [0039] rightly interpreted or **treated** by either side, to have all of
AG : 20 :011(042) [0055] is plainly and clearly **treated** by Paul in many passages,
AG : 25 :006(062) [0069] have written about and **treated** of true Christian
AL : 20 :008(042) [0053] about works has been **treated** in the church), our teachers
AL : 20 :011(042) [0055] faith is everywhere **treated** in Paul, as in Eph. 2:8, "For by
AL : 20 :022(044) [0055] was very great need to **treat** of and to restore this teaching
AL : 25 :006(062) [0069] doctrine of repentance and have **treated** it with great care.
AL : 26 :007(065) [0071] In **treating** of repentance no mention was made of faith;
AL : 26 :015(066) [0073] they have had no time to **treat** the Scriptures and seek for
AP : 20 :011(228) [0341] our opponents have **treated** this issue has compelled us to
S1 : 01 :000(291) [0461] first part of the Articles **treats** the sublime articles of the
S1 : 01 :000(292) [0461] it is not necessary to **treat** them at greater length.
S2 : 00 :000(292) [0461] The second part **treats** the articles which pertain to the
S3 : 00 :000(302) [0477] The following articles **treat** matters which we may discuss
S3 : 08 :006(313) [0495] After all, we have **treated** them sufficiently elsewhere.
TR : 00 :022(323) [0511] controversy has been **treated** fully and accurately in the
SC : PR :017(340) [0537] as you will find all of this **treated** at length in the many
SC : PR :018(340) [0537] Commandment, which **treats** of stealing, must be
SC : PR :021(340) [0537] to receive the sacrament and they **treat** it with contempt.
SC : PR :025(341) [0539] own fault if the people **treat** the sacrament with
LC : PR :001(358) [0567] that we constantly **treat** the Catechism and strongly urge
LC : SP :006(362) [0575] were rarely taught and **treated** correctly, so that all who
LC : 01 :142(385) [0621] way, or at least do not **treat** and honor them as such.
LC : 01 :154(386) [0625] another person comes along and **treats** you likewise.
LC : 01 :161(387) [0627] over their souls and to **treat** them well and make
LC : 01 :167(388) [0629] office, how they should **treat** those committed to their
LC : 01 :170(388) [0629] and gave us subjects to **treat** them as we please, as if it
LC : 01 :246(398) [0649] God's commandment and must not be **treated** as a joke.
LC : 01 :287(403) [0663] our unpresentable parts are **treated** with greater modesty."
LC : 01 :319(408) [0673] which we have already **treated** above in connection with
LC : 02 :012(412) [0681] all three articles can be **treated** more fully and divided
LC : 02 :026(413) [0685] but in order to **treat** it briefly and simply, we shall take up
LC : 03 :018(422) [0703] have this commandment **treated** as a jest but will be angry
LC : 03 :034(425) [0707] Now we shall **treat** the Lord's Prayer very briefly and
LC : 04 :002(436) [0733] understood, we shall **treat** it in a systematic way and
LC : 05 :001(447) [0753] As we **treated** Holy Baptism under three headings, so we
LC : 05 :006(447) [0755] and ordered them, regardless of how we **treat** them.
LC : 05 :033(450) [0761] So far we have **treated** the sacrament from the standpoint
LC : 05 :042(451) [0763] did not institute it to be **treated** merely as a spectacle, but
EP : 11 :001(494) [0831] when it is correctly **treated**, we have included an
SD : 01 :049(517) [0875] it here at length but are **treating** only the chief points in
SD : 01 :050(517) [0875] above-mentioned books use them in **treating** this article.
SD : 01 :062(519) [0879] "accident" and the term "quality" when **treating** this issue.
SD : 08 :035(597) [1027] the two natures be **treated** and explained with due
SD : 08 :048(600) [1031] place, the question being **treated** in the discussion is this:
SD : 10 :024(615) [1061] of God on how we are to **treat** ceremonies in general and
SD : 11 :014(619) [1069] and salvation, as Paul **treats** and explains this article

Treatment (5)
PR : PR :020(010) [0017] are to be directed in the **treatment** of the Lord's Supper to
AP : 04 :271(147) [0199] all about faith in their **treatment** of the doctrine of
SD : 03 :029(544) [0925] cannot admit any **treatment** or discussion of works.
SD : 03 :036(545) [0927] so that in the **treatment** of the justification of poor
SD : 03 :036(546) [0929] diligence and seriousness in the **treatment** of this article:

Treaties (1)
PR : PR :025(014) [0023] Empire and of the special **treaties** into which we have

Treatise (6)
TR : 00 :000(319) [0503] **Treatise** on the Power and Primacy of the Pope
EP : 08 :018(489) [0823] as Luther explains it in his **treatise** *On the Councils.*
SD : 02 :027(526) [0891] he had set it forth in his **treatise** *Concerning*
SD : 07 :029(574) [0981] to do, I desire with this **treatise** to confess my faith before
SD : 08 :044(599) [1029] Dr. Luther states in his **treatise** *Concerning the Councils*
SD : 10 :021(614) [1059] In the **Treatise** on the Power and Primacy of the Pope,

Tree (6), Trees (1)
AP : 18 :006(225) [0335] are ungodly; for "a bad **tree** cannot bear good fruit"
AP : 23 :057(247) [0379] suspend them all right — not from office but from **trees**!
EP : 04 :006(476) [0797] works, like fruits of a good **tree**, certainly and indubitably
SD : 02 :032(527) [0893] An evil **tree** cannot bear good fruit, and without faith no
SD : 04 :008(552) [0941] A bad **tree** cannot bear good fruit, and "Whatsoever does
SD : 04 :015(553) [0943] to be a barren, unfruitful **tree** since no good fruits
SD : 07 :049(578) [0989] was shed for us on the **tree** of the cross for the forgiveness

Tremble (2), Trembles (1), Trembling (1)
SC : 09 :010(356) [0563] masters, with fear and **trembling**, with singleness of
LC : 06 :033(461) [0000] That is, as a hart **trembles** with eagerness for a fresh
LC : 06 :033(461) [0000] spring, so I yearn and **tremble** for God's Word,
SD : 11 :075(628) [1087] fatherly heart to all who **tremble** at his Word and

Trent (1)
SD : 04 :035(557) [0949] decree of the Council of **Trent** and anything else that

Trespass (5), Trespassed (1), Trespasses (9)
AG : 11 :001(034) [0047] to enumerate all **trespasses** and sins, for this is
AP : 04 :103(122) [0151] came in, to increase the **trespass**; but where sin increased,
AP : 04 :272(148) [0199] you forgive men their **trespasses**, your heavenly Father
AP : 04 :273(148) [0199] through his blood, the forgiveness of our **trespasses**."
AP : 24 :021(253) [0391] sacrifices for sin or burnt offerings for **trespasses**.
AP : 24 :023(253) [0391] to be unusually severe; this they called a **trespass** offering.
AP : 24 :023(253) [0391] a sacrificial victim or **trespass** offering to reconcile God
S2 : 01 :001(292) [0461] put to death for our **trespasses** and raised again for our
S3 : 02 :005(303) [0479] and Rom. 5:20, "Law came in to increase the **trespass**."
LC : 01 :205(393) [0639] husband or wife guarded and protected from any **trespass**.
LC : 01 :307(406) [0669] no one, you have **trespassed** on your neighbor's rights.
LC : 03 :096(433) [0725] you forgive men their **trespasses**, your heavenly Father
EP : 02 :003(470) [0787] were dead through our **trespasses**, he made us alive
SD : 03 :020(542) [0921] were dead through our **trespasses**, he made us alive
SD : 05 :022(562) [0959] was put to death for our **trespasses** and raised for our

Trial (6), Trials (2)
AG : 26 :015(066) [0073] such as faith, consolation in severe **trials**, and the like.
AG : 26 :027(068) [0073] says, "Why do you make **trial** of God by putting a yoke
AL : 26 :027(068) [0073] says, "Why do you make **trial** of God by putting a yoke
AP : 07 :025(173) [0235] pope for which no one has ever been brought to **trial**.
AP : 15 :031(219) [0323] "Why do you make a **trial** of God by putting a yoke,"
AP : 28 :008(282) [0445] "Why do you make a **trial** of God?" they say (Acts 15:10).
LC : 03 :100(433) [0727] not allow us to fall and yield to **trials** and temptations.
SD : 11 :048(624) [1079] comfort, in times of **trial** and affliction, that in his

Tribulation (5), Tribulations (1)
LC : 03 :106(434) [0727] resist, even though the **tribulation** is not removed or
LC : 03 :106(434) [0729] cannot help but suffer **tribulations**, and even be entangled
SD : 08 :087(608) [1047] who has tasted every **tribulation** in his assumed human
SD : 11 :020(619) [1069] comfort and preserve them in **tribulation** and temptation.
SD : 11 :033(622) [1075] under the cross and in **tribulation**, the ninth, tenth, and
SD : 11 :049(624) [1079] that neither "**tribulation** nor anguish, neither death nor

Tribunal (2), Tribunals (2)
AP : 23 :068(249) [0383] and convicted by many previous **tribunals** of the church.
AP : 23 :068(249) [0383] So they often misquote these **tribunals** of the church.
SD : 03 :032(545) [0927] therewith and thereby stand before the **tribunal** of God.
SD : 03 :032(545) [0927] is reckoned to faith can stand before God's **tribunal**.

Tribute (1)
S2 : 04 :011(300) [0475] and they receive bodily **tribute** and obedience from

Trick (3), Trickery (1), Tricks (8)
AP : 12 :123(201) [0289] With such **tricks** they try to alienate men's minds and fan
AP : 12 :131(202) [0291] Therefore this is merely a **trick** and a distortion of the
AP : 20 :012(228) [0341] for they have learned the **trick** of deducing from Scripture
AP : 27 :057(279) [0439] they were deceived by the **tricks** of the monks or because
S3 : 15 :004(316) [0501] the pope's bag of magic **tricks** which contains silly and
LC : 01 :227(396) [0645] of him by underhanded **tricks** and sharp practices and
LC : 01 :298(405) [0665] up artful dodges and sly **tricks** (better and better ones are
LC : 01 :305(406) [0667] They knew **tricks** like this: If a man took a fancy to
LC : 01 :306(406) [0669] that someone may by **trickery** entice a rich bride away
LC : 03 :064(429) [0715] night, using all the arts, **tricks**, ways, and means that he
LC : 05 :026(449) [0759] trying all kinds of **tricks**, and does not stop until he has
SD : 08 :039(598) [1029] performs a sleight-of-hand **trick** and substitutes the

Trifle (1), Trifles (8), Trifling (3)
AP : 04 :241(141) [0187] greatest tragedies come from the most **trifling** offenses.
AP : 15 :042(221) [0327] traditions, the worship of the saints, and similar **trifles**.
AP : 24 :044(258) [0399] They call these **trifles** the ornament of the churches.
AP : 24 :087(265) [0413] But let us pass over these **trifles**.
AP : 27 :027(274) [0429] in these silly observances of vestments and similar **trifles**.
AP : 27 :039(276) [0433] and obey the rule in **trifles** like clothing and food.
AP : 28 :019(284) [0449] they misapply it to these **trifles**, distinction of foods and
S1 : PR :013(291) [0459] would be so full that their **trifling** and tomfoolery with
S2 : 02 :009(294) [0465] own private need and thus **trifle** with it according to his
TR : 00 :058(330) [0521] errors of the pope are manifest, and they are not **trifling**.
TR : 00 :075(333) [0525] non-observance of fasts or festivals and similar **trifles**.
LC : 01 :330(410) [0677] These are not **trifles** of men but the commandments of

Trinitarians (4)
EP : 12 :028(500) [0843] Error of the Anti-**Trinitarians**
SD : 12 :001(632) [1095] New Arians and Anti-**Trinitarians** whose errors all the
SD : 12 :036(636) [1101] Erroneous Articles of the New Anti-**Trinitarians**
SD : 12 :037(636) [1101] 1. Some Anti-**Trinitarians** reject and condemn the old,

Trinity (12)
EP : 08 :018(489) [0823] Next to the holy **Trinity** this is the highest mystery, as the
EP : 12 :021(499) [0841] flesh of Christ belongs to the essence of the holy **Trinity**.
SD : 01 :045(516) [0873] in the name of the holy **Trinity**, is sanctified and saved,
SD : 05 :011(560) [0955] of the Gospel for the Fifth Sunday after **Trinity**.
SD : 06 :009(565) [0965] on the Epistle for the Nineteenth Sunday after **Trinity**.
SD : 08 :022(595) [1023] *Epictetus;* Hilary, *On the Trinity,* Book IX; Basil and
SD : 08 :033(597) [1027] to the article of the holy **Trinity**, the greatest mystery in
SD : 08 :073(605) [1041] second person in the holy **Trinity** and the Holy Spirit
SD : 11 :066(627) [1085] Thus the entire holy **Trinity**, God the Father, Son, and
SD : 12 :029(635) [1101] Christ's flesh belongs to the essence of the holy **Trinity**.
SD : 12 :037(636) [1103] all three persons in the **Trinity**, like any three distinct and
SD : 12 :037(636) [1103] the three persons in the **Trinity** are unequal in their

Trip (2), Tripartite (4)
AG : 24 :041(061) [0069] for according to the **Tripartite** History, Book 9, on
AG : 26 :045(070) [0075] Moreover, the **Tripartite** History, Book 9, gathers many
AL : 24 :041(061) [0069] held every day; as the **Tripartite** History testifies in Book
AL : 26 :045(070) [0075] In the **Tripartite** History, Book 9, many examples of
AP : 12 :144(205) [0297] variety, with one making a **trip** in armor and another
SD : 06 :014(566) [0967] therefore, as Christians **trip**, they are rebuked through the

Triumph (2)
AP : 21 :002(229) [0343] So our opponents state a **triumph** as though the war were
EP : 09 :001(492) [0827] Christ's suffering or to his glorious victory and **triumph**?

Trivial (6)
AP : 02 :051(107) [0119] about the childish and **trivial** quibbling with which our
AP : 20 :006(227) [0339] more if we were arguing about dubious or **trivial** matters.
TR : 00 :048(328) [0519] pretended that the most **trivial** traditions are services of
LC : PR :001(358) [0567] It is not for **trivial** reasons that we constantly treat the
LC : 01 :074(374) [0601] good fortune, however **trivial**, he may say, "God be
LC : 01 :117(381) [0615] Even though it seems very **trivial** and contemptible, make

Trodden (1)
AP : 27 :006(269) [0421] usually "thrown out and **trodden** under foot"

Troop (1)
LC : 01 :244(398) [0649] another, or he quarters a **troop** of soldiers upon us; in

Tropes (1)
SD : 07 :113(589) [1011] the Supper, but through **tropes** or a figurative

Trouble (23), Troubled (15), Troubles (23), Troublesome (2)
PR : PR :004(003) [0007] perilous events and **troublesome** disturbances took place
AG : 27 :052(079) [0083] their consciences are **troubled** because they are married.
AL : 24 :016(057) [0067] to complain about the **troubles** of the church, although
AL : 27 :052(079) [0083] engage in their married life with a **troubled** conscience.
AL : 27 :053(079) [0083] therefore they have a **troubled** conscience when they keep
AL : 00 :002(095) [0095] Parishes have been **troubled** in many ways by indulgence
AP : 02 :042(106) [0117] does not deliver us from **trouble** right away; fretting
AP : 04 :059(115) [0137] upon me in the day of **trouble**; I will deliver you, and you
AP : 04 :170(130) [0169] in temporal things; in **trouble** it looks to men for help; it
AP : 04 :244(141) [0189] of James will cause no **trouble** if our opponents do not
AP : 04 :268(147) [0197] "Call upon me in the day of **trouble**" (Ps. 50:15).
AP : 04 :396(167) [0225] let not pious minds be **troubled** by the crowd of
AP : 11 :002(180) [0249] of the keys that many **troubled** consciences have received
AP : 12 :031(186) [0259] languishing; O Lord, heal me, for my bones are **troubled**.
AP : 12 :031(186) [0259] My soul also is sorely **troubled**.
AP : 12 :046(188) [0263] of sins" because in these **troubles** our natural lust is
AP : 12 :151(206) [0299] and to all the common **troubles**, as Peter says
AP : 12 :151(206) [0299] As a rule, these **troubles** are punishments for sin.
AP : 12 :151(206) [0299] (Isa. 26:16); that is, **troubles** are a discipline by which God
AP : 12 :152(206) [0299] So **troubles** are inflicted on account of present sin
AP : 12 :154(206) [0301] remove these common **troubles**; but if this is what they
AP : 12 :156(207) [0301] terrors of conscience, as well as other common **troubles**.
AP : 12 :156(207) [0301] and above our common **troubles** there is a special penalty
AP : 12 :157(207) [0301] of certain penalties over and above our common **troubles**?
AP : 12 :157(207) [0301] And though we still have **troubles**, Scripture interprets
AP : 12 :158(207) [0301] When in the midst of **troubles** terrified consciences see
AP : 12 :158(207) [0301] should be taught that **troubles** have other and more
AP : 12 :160(207) [0301] Therefore **troubles** are not always penalties for certain
AP : 13 :020(214) [0313] by faith, comfort his **troubled** conscience, and believe
AP : 13 :022(214) [0313] of the sacrament comforts devout and **troubled** minds.
AP : 15 :025(218) [0321] has deceived men, all sorts of **troubles** follow.
AP : 15 :027(219) [0323] consciences are sorely **troubled** because they cannot keep
AP : 15 :045(221) [0327] that the cross and the **troubles** with which God disciplines
AP : 16 :013(224) [0333] of the monks had **troubled** them and put them in doubt
AP : 21 :036(234) [0353] public affairs, underwent **troubles** and dangers, helped
AP : 21 :043(235) [0357] They will **trouble** the church with their godless teachings
AP : 23 :047(246) [0377] consciences being very **troubled** about the legitimacy of
AP : 24 :029(255) [0393] upon me in the day of **trouble**; I will deliver you, and you
S1 : PR :003(289) [0455] be, and are not a little **troubled** on this account, for they
SC : 05 :018(350) [0553] sins of which we have knowledge and which **trouble** us.
LC : PR :003(358) [0567] so many burdens and **troubles**, and they might feel a little
LC : 01 :019(367) [0585] The **trouble** is that their trust is false and wrong, for it is
LC : 01 :042(370) [0591] The **trouble** is that the world does not believe this at all,
LC : 01 :060(372) [0597] and children and servants, and **troubles** of every kind.
LC : 01 :064(373) [0599] upon me in the day of **trouble**: I will deliver you and you
LC : 01 :071(374) [0601] wait to lure us into sin and shame, calamity and **trouble**.
LC : 01 :119(381) [0615] meanwhile have only scorn and **trouble** for their reward.
LC : 01 :123(382) [0617] so that they sink into all kinds of **trouble** and misery.
LC : 01 :148(385) [0623] you will have all kinds of **trouble** and misfortune.
LC : 01 :170(388) [0629] The **trouble** is that no one perceives or heeds this.
LC : 01 :234(397) [0647] and will suffer all kinds of **troubles** and misfortunes.
LC : 01 :243(398) [0649] must suffer so many **troubles** and misfortunes that they
LC : 03 :019(423) [0703] upon me in the day of **trouble**, and I will deliver you,"
LC : 03 :027(424) [0705] needs enough, but the **trouble** is that we do not feel or see
LC : 03 :084(431) [0721] How much **trouble** there now is in the world simply on
LC : 03 :100(433) [0725] heard enough about the **trouble** and effort required to
LC : 05 :015(448) [0757] of questions which now **trouble** men — for example,
SD : 02 :031(527) [0893] he will help them in their **troubles**; therefore they are
SD : 04 :023(555) [0945] deprive tempted and **troubled** consciences of the
SD : 07 :024(573) [0979] of questions which now **trouble** people — for example,
SD : 08 :087(608) [1047] to be with us in all our **troubles** also according to that
SD : 11 :010(618) [1067] As a result they **trouble** themselves with burdensome
SD : 11 :070(627) [1085] With such thoughts the **troublesome** adversary is

True (378)
PR : PR :009(006) [0011] which version was the **true** and originally submitted
AG : PR :004(025) [0039] and adhere to a single, **true** religion and live together in
AG : PR :010(025) [0041] we may be united in one, **true** religion, even as we are all
AG : 02 :001(029) [0043] unable by nature to have **true** fear of God and true faith
AG : 02 :001(029) [0043] by nature to have true fear of God and **true** faith in God.
AG : 03 :002(029) [0045] that there is one Christ, **true** God and true man, who was
AG : 03 :002(029) [0045] one Christ, true God and **true** man, who was truly born,
AG : 07 :002(032) [0047] For it is sufficient for the **true** unity of the Christian
AG : 07 :003(032) [0047] It is not necessary for the **true** unity of the Christian
AG : 10 :001(034) [0047] taught among us that the **true** body and blood of Christ
AG : 12 :003(034) [0049] Properly speaking, **true** repentance is nothing else than to
AG : 16 :004(037) [0051] Actually, **true** perfection consists alone of proper fear of
AG : 16 :005(038) [0051] that all these be kept as **true** orders of God and that
AG : 20 :002(041) [0053] instructions concerning **true** Christian estates and works.
AG : 20 :023(044) [0055] dead, but we mean such **true** faith as believes that we
AG : 20 :034(045) [0057] when a man is without **true** faith and the Holy Spirit and
AG : 24 :023(058) [0067] faith in Christ and **true** service of God were forgotten.
AG : 25 :006(062) [0069] about and treated of **true** Christian repentance in a more
AG : 25 :011(063) [0071] to the Lord God, the **true** judge, in your prayer, telling
AG : 26 :032(068) [0075] to suffer, and this is **true** and real rather than invented
AG : 27 :002(071) [0077] Later, when **true** discipline and doctrine had become
AG : 27 :049(078) [0083] commands of God and **true** and proper service of God
AG : 27 :050(079) [0083] **True** perfection and right service of God consist of these
AL : 01 :001(027) [0043] the three persons is **true** and should be believed without
AL : 03 :002(029) [0045] of his person, one Christ, **true** God and true man, who
AL : 03 :002(029) [0045] one Christ, true God and **true** man, who was born of the
AL : 07 :002(032) [0047] For the **true** unity of the church it is enough to agree
AL : 08 :001(033) [0047] the church is the assembly of saints and **true** believers.
AL : 25 :011(063) [0071] confess your sins to God, the **true** judge, in your prayer.
AL : 26 :032(068) [0075] be crucified with Christ is **true** and real, rather than
AL : 27 :049(078) [0083] commands of God and **true** service of God are obscured
AL : 27 :050(079) [0083] **True** perfection and true service of God consist of these
AL : 27 :050(079) [0083] True perfection and **true** service of God consist of these
AP : 02 :002(100) [0105] unable by nature to have **true** fear of God or true faith in
AP : 02 :002(100) [0105] by nature to have true fear of God or **true** faith in God."
AP : 02 :003(101) [0105] and cannot produce **true** fear and trust in God.
AP : 04 :008(108) [0121] the reach of reason, like **true** fear of God, true love of
AP : 04 :008(108) [0121] like true fear of God, **true** love of God, true prayer to
AP : 04 :008(108) [0121] of God, true love of God, **true** prayer to God, true
AP : 04 :008(108) [0121] God, true prayer to God, **true** conviction that God hears
AP : 04 :046(113) [0133] This faith is the **true** knowledge of Christ, it uses his
AP : 04 :112(123) [0155] we mean faith in the **true** sense of the word—since the
AP : 04 :113(123) [0155] But faith in the **true** sense, as the Scriptures use the word,
AP : 04 :185(132) [0173] word of the ancient poet is **true**, "Being sick in itself, an
AP : 04 :190(133) [0175] church are holy works, **true** sacrifices acceptable to God,
AP : 04 :191(133) [0175] the state are holy works, **true** sacrifices, battles of God to
AP : 04 :228(139) [0183] blessings from him; this he declares to be **true** worship.
AP : 04 :229(139) [0183] they did not see the **true** face of Moses but only his veiled
AP : 04 :274(148) [0199] It is **true** that in teaching penitence works are required,
AP : 04 :351(161) [0217] that is, we acquire the **true** knowledge of God, enabling
AP : 04 :398(167) [0227] forgiveness of sin—is most **true** and certain and
AP : 07 :002(168) [0227] The saying is certainly **true** that there is no defense
AP : 07 :012(170) [0231] indeed associated with the **true** church as far as outward
AP : 07 :014(170) [0231] rites but by being God's **true** people, reborn by the Holy
AP : 07 :016(170) [0231] only those are the **true** people who accept this promise of
AP : 07 :019(171) [0233] nation and says that the **true** church will be separated
AP : 07 :019(171) [0233] since it shows that the **true** and spiritual people will be
AP : 07 :019(171) [0233] marks, still they are not the **true** kingdom of Christ and
AP : 07 :020(171) [0233] actually exists, made up of **true** believers and righteous
AP : 07 :020(171) [0233] (I Cor. 3:12), that is, the **true** knowledge of Christ and
AP : 07 :022(172) [0235] persons in whom there is **true** knowledge and the
AP : 07 :027(173) [0235] is the prerogative of the **true** church: that they are pillars
AP : 07 :030(173) [0237] in which we said, "For the **true** unity of the church it is
AP : 07 :031(174) [0237] We are talking about **true** spiritual unity, without which
AP : 07 :033(174) [0239] so we believe that the **true** unity of the church is not
AP : 07 :034(175) [0239] it is necessary for the **true** unity of the church that human
AP : 10 :003(179) [0247] joined to Christ spiritually by **true** faith and sincere love.
AP : 12 :003(182) [0253] doctrine of the Gospel, the **true** knowledge of Christ, and
AP : 12 :003(182) [0253] true knowledge of Christ, and the **true** worship of God.
AP : 12 :003(182) [0253] we have taught what is **true**, godly, salutary, and
AP : 12 :009(183) [0255] especially in those serious, **true**, and great terrors
AP : 12 :039(187) [0261] through absolution, which is the **true** voice of the Gospel.
AP : 12 :045(187) [0263] (James 2:19), but, in the **true** sense, to believe that for
AP : 12 :089(195) [0279] life is without God and without the **true** worship of God.
AP : 12 :098(197) [0281] of preserving the **true** teaching about contrition and
AP : 12 :130(202) [0291] We know that it is **true**, godly, and beneficial to godly
AP : 12 :131(202) [0291] There can be no **true** conversion or contrition where
AP : 12 :131(202) [0291] **True** terrors and sorrows of the soul do not permit the
AP : 12 :131(202) [0291] of the body in lusts, and **true** faith is not ungrateful to
AP : 12 :139(203) [0295] and that good fruits like **true** fasting, prayer, and charity
AP : 12 :143(204) [0295] **True** prayer, charity, and fasting have God's command:
AP : 12 :148(205) [0299] Certainly **true** punishment and revenge, that is, contrition
AP : 12 :148(205) [0299] and revenge, that is, contrition and **true** terrors.
AP : 12 :148(205) [0299] of the body which follows **true** sorrow in the mind.
AP : 12 :149(206) [0299] comes over even the simplest people in **true** penitence?
AP : 12 :165(208) [0303] by our penitence and its **true** fruits, good works done from
AP : 12 :168(209) [0305] So Augustine says, "**True** satisfaction means cutting off
AP : 14 :003(214) [0315] we know that our confession is **true**, godly, and catholic.
AP : 14 :004(215) [0315] teaches what is right and **true**, though the canons
AP : 15 :018(217) [0319] on the church that for the **true** unity of the church it is
AP : 15 :032(219) [0323] **True**, in the Old Testament ceremonies were necessary for
AP : 15 :051(222) [0329] become more hostile to the **true** teaching of the Gospel
AP : 18 :007(225) [0337] the spiritual capacity for **true** fear of God, true faith in
AP : 18 :007(225) [0337] for true fear of God, **true** faith in God, true knowledge
AP : 18 :007(225) [0337] of God, true faith in God, **true** knowledge and trust that
AP : 20 :002(227) [0339] framers of the Confutation have shown their **true** spirit.
AP : 21 :036(234) [0353] no one has sought out in the **true** stories about the saints.
AP : 21 :037(234) [0355] many things that resemble the "**true** stories" of Lucian.
AP : 23 :022(242) [0369] We, too, commend **true** continence, but now we are
AP : 24 :027(254) [0393] in John 4:23, 24, "The **true** worshipers will worship the
AP : 24 :029(255) [0393] indicating that other sacrifices are not **true** and right.
AP : 24 :068(262) [0409] not talk about faith, whose **true** meaning very few
AP : 27 :013(271) [0423] If this is not the **true** voice of the Gospel, if it is not the
AP : 27 :013(271) [0423] revealed to the world — then the charge against us is **true**.
AP : 27 :050(277) [0437] for each of us with **true** faith to obey his own calling.
AP : 27 :054(278) [0437] of faith, about **true** penitence, about works that have the
S1 : PR :010(290) [0457] be very happy to see a **true** council assemble in order that
S1 : PR :010(290) [0457] callings of life, and with **true** works, that we do not ask
S1 : PR :010(290) [0457] Christ speak to them as the **true** shepherd speaking to his
S3 : 01 :011(303) [0479] If such teachings were **true**, Christ would have died in
S3 : 03 :002(304) [0479] but *passiva contritio* (**true** sorrow of the heart, suffering,
S3 : 03 :003(304) [0481] This is what the beginning of **true** repentance is like.
S3 : 03 :009(304) [0481] of the sophists with **true** repentance so that both may be
S3 : 03 :028(308) [0487] This is certainly **true**, and there are seals, letters, and
S3 : 03 :030(308) [0487] St. John, the preacher of **true** repentance, intervenes.
S3 : 03 :045(310) [0491] Yet it is also **true**, as the same St. John writes, "If we say
S3 : 06 :001(311) [0493] wine in the Supper are the **true** body and blood of Christ
S3 : 06 :003(311) [0493] Even if it were **true** that as much is included under one
S3 : 10 :001(314) [0497] If the bishops were **true** bishops and were concerned
S3 : 10 :001(314) [0497] However, they neither are nor wish to be **true** bishops.
S3 : 12 :003(315) [0499] but it consists of the Word of God and **true** faith.
S3 : 13 :003(315) [0499] good works do not follow, our faith is false and not **true**.
TR : 00 :044(328) [0517] consolation, and abolish **true** worship (that is, the

Continued ▶

TR : 0 0 :052(329) [0519] be rejected and that the **true** teaching must be embraced
TR : 0 0 :056(330) [0521] he evades and obstructs **true** understanding and true
TR : 0 0 :056(330) [0521] true understanding and **true** judgment on the part of the
TR : 0 0 :067(331) [0523] Where the **true** church is, therefore, the right of electing
TR : 0 0 :069(331) [0525] These words apply to the **true** church which, since it
TR : 0 0 :082(000) [0529] and with the belief of the **true** and genuine catholic
SC : 0 2 :002(345) [0543] This is most certainly **true**.
SC : 0 2 :004(345) [0545] I believe that Jesus Christ, **true** God, begotten of the
SC : 0 2 :004(345) [0545] from eternity, and also **true** man, born of the virgin
SC : 0 2 :004(345) [0545] This is most certainly **true**.
SC : 0 2 :006(345) [0545] and preserved me in **true** faith, just as he calls, gathers,
SC : 0 2 :006(345) [0545] it in union with Jesus Christ in the one **true** faith.
SC : 0 2 :006(345) [0545] This is most certainly **true**.
SC : 0 3 :014(347) [0549] health, order and honor; **true** friends, faithful neighbors,
SC : 0 6 :002(351) [0555] by Christ himself, it is the **true** body and blood of our
LC : PR :010(360) [0571] This, indeed, is the **true** holy water, the sign which routs
LC : 0 1 :003(365) [0581] faith and trust are right, then your God is the **true** God.
LC : 0 1 :003(365) [0581] trust is false and wrong, then you have not the **true** God.
LC : 0 1 :004(365) [0581] therefore, is to require **true** faith and confidence of the
LC : 0 1 :004(365) [0581] fly straight to the one **true** God and cling to him alone.
LC : 0 1 :010(366) [0583] in them, he also has a god, but not the one, **true** God.
LC : 0 1 :012(366) [0583] fix their heart and trust elsewhere than in the **true** God.
LC : 0 1 :016(366) [0585] Behold, here you have the **true** honor and the true
LC : 0 1 :016(366) [0585] the true honor and the **true** worship which please God
LC : 0 1 :028(368) [0587] Then you have the one **true** God.
LC : 0 1 :042(370) [0591] they neither lie nor deceive but will yet prove to be **true**.
LC : 0 1 :046(370) [0593] must stand and prove to be **true** since God cannot lie or
LC : 0 1 :070(374) [0601] and experiences, for **true** honor to God's name consists of
LC : 0 1 :091(377) [0607] The Word of God is the **true** holy thing above all holy
LC : 0 1 :114(380) [0613] taught, and reared in **true** blessedness; they would have
LC : 0 1 :148(385) [0623] You are a **true** nobleman if you are upright and obedient.
LC : 0 1 :186(390) [0633] head, which, if they came **true**, would soon put an end to
LC : 0 1 :195(391) [0637] encourage and urge us to **true**, noble, exalted deeds, such
LC : 0 1 :198(392) [0637] God's Word which are the **true**, holy, and divine works in
LC : 0 1 :207(393) [0639] not for lewdness but to be **true** to each other, be fruitful,
LC : 0 1 :258(399) [0653] we always find that, **true** to the usual course of the world,
LC : 0 1 :270(401) [0657] you cannot prove, even if it is **true**, you appear as a liar.
LC : 0 1 :311(407) [0669] They are the **true** fountain from which all good works
LC : 0 1 :311(407) [0671] works must spring, the **true** channel through which all
LC : 0 1 :324(409) [0675] "You shall fear, love, and trust me as your one **true** God."
LC : 0 2 :022(413) [0683] This is especially **true** of those who even fight against the
LC : 0 2 :027(414) [0685] believe that Jesus Christ, **true** Son of God, has become
LC : 0 2 :066(419) [0697] and worship only the one, **true** God, nevertheless do not
LC : 0 3 :007(421) [0699] It is quite **true** that the kind of babbling and bellowing
LC : 0 3 :026(423) [0705] But where there is **true** prayer there must be earnestness.
LC : 0 3 :120(436) [0731] Where such faith is wanting, there can be no **true** prayer.
LC : 0 4 :028(440) [0739] We answer: It is **true**, nothing that is in us does it but
LC : 0 4 :035(441) [0741] you may answer: Yes, it is **true** that our works are of no
LC : 0 4 :042(442) [0743] them, it may well doubt whether they could all be **true**.
LC : 0 4 :054(443) [0745] Lord's Supper receive the **true** sacrament even though
LC : 0 4 :058(444) [0747] that where there is no **true** faith, there also can be no true
LC : 0 4 :058(444) [0747] there is no true faith, there also can be no **true** Baptism.
LC : 0 4 :060(444) [0747] were baptized and he, moreover, did not have **true** faith.
LC : 0 5 :008(447) [0755] Answer: It is the **true** body and blood of the Lord Christ
LC : 0 5 :014(448) [0755] It is **true**, indeed, that if you take the Word away from
LC : 0 5 :016(448) [0757] or administer it, it is the **true** sacrament (that is, Christ's
LC : 0 5 :023(449) [0757] While it is **true** that through Baptism we are first born
LC : 0 5 :035(450) [0761] and believes that they are **true** has what the words
LC : 0 5 :042(451) [0763] Now it is **true**, we repeat, that no one should under any
LC : 0 5 :043(451) [0763] Indeed, **true** Christians who cherish and honor the
LC : 0 5 :047(452) [0763] I answer: That is **true**, but it does not say that we should
LC : 0 5 :053(453) [0765] It is certainly **true**, as I have found in my own experience,
LC : 0 5 :069(454) [0769] Of course, it is **true** that those who despise the sacrament
LC : 0 6 :011(458) [0000] For it is **true**, as the proverb says, "If one man is upright,
LC : 0 6 :032(461) [0000] their conscience, already have the **true** hunger and thirst.
EP : RN :003(465) [0777] of the orthodox and **true** church, namely, the Apostles'
EP : 0 3 :011(474) [0795] been justified by faith, a **true** living faith becomes "active
EP : 0 5 :008(479) [0803] result they fail to learn the **true** nature of sin from the
EP : 0 5 :011(479) [0805] are robbed of their **true** comfort, and the doors are again
EP : 0 6 :008(481) [0807] of Christian discipline and **true** piety the erroneous
EP : 0 7 :002(481) [0809] Holy Communion are the **true** body and blood of our
EP : 0 7 :004(482) [0809] and claim to believe a **true** presence of the true, essential,
EP : 0 7 :004(482) [0809] a true presence of the **true**, essential, and living body and
EP : 0 7 :011(483) [0811] faith: Jesus Christ is **true**, essential, natural, complete
EP : 0 7 :016(484) [0813] unbelievers receive the **true** body and blood of Christ; but
EP : 0 7 :038(486) [0817] does not consist only in **true** faith in Christ, but also
EP : 0 7 :042(486) [0817] we hold and believe in a **true**, though supernatural, eating
EP : 0 8 :010(488) [0819] did not have a real and **true** communion with each other.
EP : 0 8 :017(489) [0823] for him to impart to us his **true** body and blood which are
EP : 0 8 :017(489) [0823] Capernaitic although it is **true** and essential, as the words
EP : 0 8 :022(490) [0823] 3. That Christ is not **true**, natural, and eternal God, as
EP : 0 8 :023(490) [0823] That Christ did not have a **true** human nature with a
EP : 0 8 :029(490) [0825] (something that is not **true** of the divine nature either).
EP : 1 0 :002(493) [0829] *The Correct, **True** Doctrine and Confession about this*
EP : 1 1 :001(494) [0831] *Pure and **True** Doctrine concerning this Article*
EP : 1 2 :004(498) [0839] 2. That Christ is not **true** God but that he only has more
EP : 1 2 :026(500) [0843] 7. That it is no **true** Christian congregation in which
EP : 1 2 :027(500) [0843] profitably or administer **true** and genuine sacraments
EP : 1 2 :028(500) [0843] That Christ is not a **true**, essential, natural God, of one
EP : 1 2 :031(500) [0843] by it, we have advisedly, in **true** fear and invocation of
SD : PR :004(502) [0847] Christian symbol which all **true** Christians ought to
SD : PR :006(502) [0847] they failed to grasp their **true** meaning or because they did
SD : PR :007(502) [0849] dangerous schisms in the **true** Evangelical churches, just
SD : PR :007(502) [0849] others even denied that Christ was eternal and **true** God.
SD : PR :003(504) [0851] of Israel, which is the only **true** norm according to which
SD : PR :004(504) [0851] Since in ancient times the **true** Christian doctrine as it
SD : PR :006(504) [0853] to set forth clearly the **true** and genuine meaning of the
SD : PR :008(505) [0853] the difference between **true** and false doctrine, we declare
SD : PR :014(506) [0855] not only to present the **true** and wholesome doctrine
SD : PR :016(507) [0857] It is **true** that the Christian reader who really delights in
SD : PR :016(507) [0857] accept as correct and **true** in each of the controverted
SD : PR :019(507) [0857] antitheses, opposing the **true** doctrine to the false
SD : 0 1 :004(509) [0861] of God and to preserve the **true** and correct doctrine
SD : 0 1 :004(509) [0861] forth in short chapters the **true** doctrine and its opposite
SD : 0 1 :008(510) [0861] know and understand the **true** nature of this inherited
SD : 0 1 :012(510) [0863] **True**, in natural and external things which are subject to
SD : 0 1 :038(515) [0871] It is of course **true** that this creature and handiwork of
SD : 0 1 :057(518) [0877] Since it is irrefutably **true**, attested and demonstrated by
SD : 0 2 :008(521) [0883] It is **true** that they are contrary to proud reason and
SD : 0 2 :014(523) [0885] God says remains eternally **true**, "Apart from me you can
SD : 0 2 :014(523) [0885] what St. Paul says is also **true**, "For God is at work in
SD : 0 2 :014(523) [0885] kindled this beginning of **true** godliness in their heart,
SD : 0 2 :014(523) [0885] and to help them to remain in **true** faith until their end.
SD : 0 2 :016(523) [0887] wrought a beginning of **true** knowledge of God and faith,
SD : 0 2 :040(528) [0895] and preserved me in **true** faith, just as he calls, gathers,
SD : 0 2 :040(528) [0895] it in union with Jesus Christ in the one **true** faith."
SD : 0 2 :042(529) [0897] and brings us to Christ in **true** faith and keeps us with
SD : 0 2 :048(530) [0901] us by giving and working **true** repentance, faith, and new
SD : 0 2 :050(531) [0901] works in the hearts of men **true** repentance and
SD : 0 2 :050(531) [0901] of their sins and **true** faith in the Son of God, Jesus
SD : 0 2 :055(531) [0903] On the one hand, it is **true** that both the preacher's
SD : 0 2 :059(532) [0905] And it is equally **true** that prior to his conversion man is
SD : 0 2 :060(532) [0905] It is **true** that God does not coerce anyone to piety, for
SD : 0 2 :070(534) [0909] course, self-evident that in **true** conversion there must be
SD : 0 2 :070(535) [0909] things takes place or exists, there is no **true** conversion.
SD : 0 2 :090(539) [0915] the Holy Spirit, who is the **true** craftsman who alone
SD : 0 3 :002(539) [0917] Christ himself as the **true**, natural, essential Son of God,
SD : 0 3 :004(540) [0917] by pure grace to all **true** believers as righteousness, and
SD : 0 3 :007(540) [0919] side by side with the **true** doctrine, we clearly segregate,
SD : 0 3 :026(543) [0923] and abide in sin, for **true** contrition precedes and genuine
SD : 0 3 :026(543) [0923] and genuine faith exists only in or with **true** repentance.
SD : 0 3 :027(543) [0923] a fruit which certainly and necessarily follows **true** faith.
SD : 0 3 :036(545) [0927] though there could well be **true** faith without contrition,
SD : 0 3 :036(545) [0927] must, and dare not follow **true** faith as certain and
SD : 0 3 :041(546) [0929] way as though on occasion **true** faith could coexist and
SD : 0 3 :041(546) [0931] statement remains **true**: "There is a beautiful agreement
SD : 0 3 :042(547) [0931] or in the case of others, a **true** living faith and distinguish
SD : 0 3 :042(547) [0931] when they do not have **true** faith), the Apology gives the
SD : 0 3 :054(548) [0935] On the one hand, it is **true** indeed that God the Father,
SD : 0 3 :056(549) [0935] but had not been **true**, eternal God, the obedience and
SD : 0 3 :064(550) [0937] in a person who has no **true** repentance (and upon which
SD : 0 4 :001(551) [0939] works are required of **true** believers as fruits of faith and
SD : 0 4 :008(552) [0941] they do not flow from **true** faith, they are sinful (that is,
SD : 0 4 :015(553) [0943] could have and retain **true** faith, righteousness, and
SD : 0 4 :032(556) [0947] justified by faith these **true**, immutable, and divine threats
SD : 0 4 :036(557) [0949] sound words as well as the **true** doctrine itself
SD : 0 5 :012(560) [0955] At the same time it is **true** and right that the apostles and
SD : 0 5 :018(561) [0957] But it is also **true** that the Gospel illustrates and explains
SD : 0 5 :018(561) [0957] doctrine; nevertheless the **true** function of the law
SD : 0 5 :027(563) [0961] with all diligence the **true** and proper distinction between
SD : 0 5 :027(563) [0961] thus rob Christians of the **true** comfort which they have in
SD : 0 6 :003(564) [0963] party taught that although **true** believers are indeed
SD : 0 6 :003(564) [0963] them, and thereby even **true** believers learn to serve God
SD : 0 6 :005(564) [0963] It is **true** that the law is not laid down for the just, as St.
SD : 0 6 :026(568) [0971] to Christian discipline and **true** godliness, the erroneous
SD : 0 6 :026(568) [0971] urged upon Christians and **true** believers but only upon
SD : 0 7 :001(569) [0971] and from repeating the **true** intention and the right
SD : 0 7 :002(569) [0973] unanimously that the **true**, essential body and blood of
SD : 0 7 :006(570) [0973] divine nature and is not **true** of his body and blood, which
SD : 0 7 :006(570) [0973] wine Christ gives us his **true** body and blood to eat
SD : 0 7 :009(570) [0975] of God's Word "that the **true** body and blood of Christ
SD : 0 7 :010(571) [0975] by Christ himself, is the **true** body and blood of our Lord
SD : 0 7 :016(572) [0977] they receive it without **true** repentance and without faith.
SD : 0 7 :017(572) [0979] In these the correct and **true** meaning is set forth briefly
SD : 0 7 :019(572) [0979] wine in the Supper are the **true** body and blood of Jesus
SD : 0 7 :020(573) [0979] Answer: It is the **true** body and blood of Christ in and
SD : 0 7 :023(573) [0979] It is **true** indeed that if you take the Word away or look
SD : 0 7 :024(573) [0979] the sacrament, it is the **true** sacrament (that is, Christ's
SD : 0 7 :027(574) [0981] which establishes the **true** presence of the body and blood
SD : 0 7 :033(575) [0983] who understood the **true** intention of the Augsburg
SD : 0 7 :033(575) [0983] bread in the Supper is his **true**, natural body, which the
SD : 0 7 :035(575) [0983] in the Lord's Supper "is **true** body of Christ" or "a
SD : 0 7 :037(575) [0985] the natural bread and the **true** natural body of Christ, are
SD : 0 7 :039(576) [0985] Word and prayer is the **true** flesh and blood of the Lord
SD : 0 7 :041(576) [0985] Charles V, therefore the **true** meaning and intention of
SD : 0 7 :044(577) [0987] all sorrowing hearts, and a **true** bond and union of
SD : 0 7 :048(578) [0989] that he was speaking of **true**, natural bread and natural
SD : 0 7 :049(578) [0989] He was speaking of his **true**, essential body, which he
SD : 0 7 :049(578) [0989] death for us, and of his **true**, essential blood, which was
SD : 0 7 :054(579) [0991] manifest testimony to the **true** and essential presence and
SD : 0 7 :054(579) [0991] receive and partake of the **true** body and blood of Christ.
SD : 0 7 :060(580) [0993] Christians receive the **true** body and blood of Christ
SD : 0 7 :060(580) [0993] the Lord's table without **true** repentance and conversion
SD : 0 7 :062(581) [0995] of God, in which Christ, **true** God and man, together with
SD : 0 7 :063(581) [0995] receive and partake of the **true**, essential body and blood
SD : 0 7 :064(581) [0995] wine, which he called his **true** body and blood, and said
SD : 0 7 :068(582) [0997] to this sacrament without **true** contrition and sorrow for
SD : 0 7 :068(582) [0997] for their sins, without **true** faith, and without a good
SD : 0 7 :069(582) [0997] **True** and worthy communicants, on the other hand, are
SD : 0 7 :072(582) [0997] this suffice concerning the **true** presence and the twofold
SD : 0 7 :074(583) [0999] can effect the **true** presence of the body and blood of
SD : 0 7 :076(583) [0999] it brings about that his **true** body and blood are present in
SD : 0 7 :085(584) [1001] To maintain this **true** Christian doctrine concerning the
SD : 0 7 :088(585) [1003] faith in order to deny the **true**, essential presence and the
SD : 0 7 :089(585) [1003] Gospel is and remains the **true** Gospel even when godless
SD : 0 7 :094(586) [1005] Christ is essential, natural, **true**, complete God and man
SD : 0 7 :102(587) [1007] Since this is **true**, even though unknown to us, we should
SD : 0 7 :104(587) [1009] in spirit through faith **true** believers are incorporated into
SD : 0 7 :104(587) [1009] into Christ and become **true**, spiritual members of his
SD : 0 7 :106(588) [1009] this article concerning the **true** presence of the body and
SD : 0 7 :106(588) [1009] and omnipotence of the **true** and eternal God, our Lord
SD : 0 7 :111(589) [1011] concerning the **true** presence of the body and blood of
SD : 0 7 :113(589) [1011] they read, concerning the **true** essential presence of the
SD : 0 7 :116(589) [1013] take place not through the **true** present body and blood
SD : 0 7 :120(590) [1013] been able to achieve the **true**, essential presence of his
SD : 0 7 :124(591) [1015] does not consist in **true** faith alone but also in man's own

Continued ▶

SD : 07 :125(591) [1015] the teaching that even **true** believers who have and retain
SD : 07 :125(591) [1015] who have and retain a **true**, genuine, living faith, but who
SD : 07 :126(591) [1015] will deny Christ himself, **true** God and man, who is truly
SD : 08 :002(591) [1015] with solid arguments the **true**, essential presence of the
SD : 08 :002(591) [1015] of Christ could not be a **true** and genuine human body if
SD : 08 :004(592) [1017] from his Supper the **true**, essential presence of the body
SD : 08 :006(592) [1017] has been from all eternity **true**, essential, and perfect God
SD : 08 :006(592) [1017] person simultaneously **true** eternal God, born of the
SD : 08 :006(592) [1017] from eternity, and also a **true** man, born of the most
SD : 08 :017(594) [1021] such a way that they have **true** communion with each
SD : 08 :020(595) [1021] without which such a **true** communion of the natures is
SD : 08 :031(597) [1025] of properties (that is, of a **true** communication of the
SD : 08 :032(597) [1025] Since it is **true** that each nature retains its essential
SD : 08 :041(599) [1029] answer and say: That is **true**, but since the divinity and
SD : 08 :042(599) [1029] the person who is **true** God suffers in the other part
SD : 08 :044(599) [1029] that this way: If it is not **true** that God died for us, but
SD : 08 :054(601) [1033] is, of course, correct and **true** that Christ's human nature
SD : 08 :070(604) [1039] For while it is **true** that God, together with the whole
SD : 08 :077(606) [1043] If that were **true**, Peter, Paul, and all the saints in heaven
SD : 08 :085(608) [1047] because he is one person with the deity and is **true** God.
SD : 08 :092(609) [1049] or destroying his **true** human nature, Christ's
SD : 10 :005(611) [1053] and are given a different color from their **true** one.
SD : 10 :005(611) [1055] of the Gospel and from **true** religion has taken place or
SD : 10 :007(611) [1055] decorum in the church, **true** adiaphora or things
SD : 10 :008(611) [1055] teach, and confess that **true** adiaphora or things
SD : 10 :010(612) [1055] deeds and actions, the **true** doctrine and all that pertains
SD : 10 :016(613) [1057] will sadden and scandalize **true** believers and weaken them
SD : 10 :019(614) [1059] "If the bishops were **true** bishops and were concerned
SD : 10 :019(614) [1059] However, they neither are nor wish to be **true** bishops.
SD : 11 :012(618) [1067] beyond all doubt that the **true** understanding or the right
SD : 11 :013(619) [1067] who is the genuine and **true** "book of life" as it is revealed
SD : 11 :017(619) [1069] would convert hearts to **true** repentance, and would
SD : 11 :017(619) [1069] repentance, and would enlighten them in the **true** faith.
SD : 11 :018(619) [1069] all who in sincere repentance and **true** faith accept Christ.
SD : 11 :040(623) [1077] who accept Christ through **true** faith, so he has also
SD : 11 :050(624) [1079] time it teaches us what the **true** church is, lest we be
SD : 11 :069(627) [1085] the Holy Spirit creates **true** faith through the hearing of
SD : 11 :075(628) [1087] If they return to him in **true** repentance through a right
SD : 11 :076(628) [1087] It is indeed correct and **true** what Scripture states, that no
SD : 11 :093(632) [1095] which are contrary to these **true**, simple, and useful
SD : 11 :095(632) [1095] up any falsification of **true** doctrine or any publicly
SD : 11 :095(632) [1095] in and deep love for **true** harmony and are cordially
SD : 11 :096(632) [1095] will lead the poor sinner to **true** and sincere repentance,
SD : 12 :006(633) [1097] questions we abide by the **true**, simple, natural, and
SD : 12 :008(633) [1097] room nor scope, where the **true** teachers and confessors
SD : 12 :029(635) [1101] place, that no one has a **true** knowledge of Christ, the
SD : 12 :034(635) [1101] does not take place is not a **true** Christian congregation.
SD : 12 :035(635) [1101] profitably nor administer genuine and **true** sacraments.
SD : 12 :036(635) [1101] teach that Christ is not a **true**, essential, and natural God,

Truly (171)
AG : 01 :002(027) [0043] is called and which is **truly** God, and that there are three
AG : 02 :002(029) [0043] and hereditary sin is **truly** sin and condemns to the
AG : 03 :002(029) [0045] and true man, who was **truly** born, suffered, was
AG : 03 :004(030) [0045] also descended into hell, **truly** rose from the dead on the
AG : 20 :024(044) [0055] he has a gracious God, **truly** knows God, calls upon him,
AL : 02 :002(029) [0043] disease or vice of origin is **truly** sin, which even now
AL : 03 :002(030) [0045] born of the virgin Mary, **truly** suffered, was crucified,
AL : 03 :004(030) [0045] descended into hell, and on the third day **truly** rose again.
AL : 10 :001(034) [0047] and blood of Christ are **truly** present and are distributed
AL : 20 :024(044) [0055] to him through Christ **truly** knows God, knows that God
AL : 24 :031(059) [0067] and realize that they are **truly** offered to us; and it is not
AL : 25 :004(062) [0069] are assured that such faith **truly** obtains and receives the
AP : 02 :027(104) [0113] — teach that original sin is **truly** composed of the defects
AP : 04 :018(109) [0125] neither fears God nor **truly** believes that he cares.
AP : 04 :019(110) [0125] have him doubt whether the disposition is **truly** present.
AP : 04 :027(111) [0127] things and keep his law, **truly** fear him, truly believe that
AP : 04 :027(111) [0127] his law, truly fear him, **truly** believe that he hears prayer,
AP : 04 :034(112) [0129] at our sin, to fear him **truly**, and to be sure that he hears
AP : 04 :045(113) [0133] obey God's law, love him, **truly** fear him, be sure that he
AP : 04 :072(117) [0141] Christ by faith itself we are **truly** accounted righteous or
AP : 04 :101(121) [0151] blessings is rightly and **truly** to believe in Christ, to
AP : 04 :135(125) [0159] does not fear God or **truly** believe in his providential
AP : 04 :154(128) [0163] of sins from him, she **truly** acknowledged him as the
AP : 04 :154(128) [0163] **Truly** to believe means to think of Christ in this way, and
AP : 04 :154(128) [0165] without reason that this **truly** powerful example moved
AP : 04 :155(128) [0165] much," that is, because she **truly** worshiped me with faith
AP : 04 :261(145) [0195] of the law, but a **truly** prophetic and evangelical voice
AP : 04 :263(146) [0195] take hold of it unless they **truly** believe and by faith
AP : 04 :285(150) [0201] This is what Paul really and **truly** means.
AP : 04 :289(151) [0203] **Truly** the law says, "You shall love the Lord your God"
AP : 04 :303(154) [0205] of sins, a faith that **truly** and wholeheartedly accepts the
AP : 04 :308(155) [0207] carping critics: faith is **truly** righteousness because it is
AP : 04 :351(161) [0217] of God, enabling us **truly** to fear him and to trust that he
AP : 04 :386(166) [0225] the promise of grace, **truly** enlivens the fearful mind, and
AP : 07 :016(171) [0231] Thus the church, which is **truly** the kingdom of Christ, is,
AP : 07 :017(171) [0231] If the church, which is **truly** the kingdom of Christ, is
AP : 07 :028(173) [0237] assembly of saints who **truly** believe the Gospel of Christ
AP : 07 :050(178) [0245] movements of the stars are **truly** ordinances of God and
AP : 10 :001(179) [0247] and blood of Christ are **truly** and substantially present
AP : 10 :001(179) [0247] present and are **truly** offered with those things that are
AP : 10 :001(179) [0247] only in his spirit if the Lord's body were not **truly** present.
AP : 10 :002(179) [0247] is not merely a figure but is **truly** changed into flesh."
AP : 10 :003(179) [0247] this way and that we are **truly** branches, deriving life from
AP : 10 :004(179) [0247] and blood of Christ are **truly** and substantially present
AP : 10 :004(179) [0247] present and are **truly** offered with those things that are
AP : 11 :002(180) [0249] be sure that by this faith we are **truly** reconciled to God.
AP : 12 :009(183) [0255] certainly experienced by those who are **truly** converted?
AP : 12 :027(185) [0259] be reserved in the case of someone who is **truly** converted.
AP : 12 :040(187) [0261] Because God **truly** quickens through the Word, the keys
AP : 12 :040(187) [0261] the Word, the keys **truly** forgive sin before him, according
AP : 12 :046(188) [0263] but as consolation **truly** sustaining a life that flees in
AP : 12 :077(193) [0275] **Truly**, we insult Christ and abrogate the Gospel if we
AP : 12 :084(194) [0277] is what Paul really and **truly** means; we know that this
AP : 12 :163(208) [0303] "If we judged ourselves **truly**, we should not be judged" by
AP : 12 :177(210) [0307] of guilt before God in the case of the **truly** converted.
AP : 13 :016(213) [0311] not prayer, which can most **truly** be called a sacrament?
AP : 21 :036(234) [0353] It is **truly** worthwhile to hear of these things and to see
AP : 23 :007(240) [0365] love of one sex for the other is **truly** a divine ordinance.
AP : 23 :017(242) [0369] his own wife," binds all those who are not **truly** continent.
AP : 23 :035(244) [0373] or Jacob than in many others who are **truly** continent.
AP : 24 :028(254) [0393] **Truly** and wholeheartedly seek and expect help from me."
AP : 24 :038(257) [0399] of the faith which **truly** believes that by the death of
AP : 24 :098(268) [0419] Meanwhile all those who **truly** believe the Gospel should
AP : 27 :013(271) [0423] church is a witness: this is **truly** the teaching of the
S1 : PR :002(289) [0455] or treachery to hold a **truly** free council, as indeed the
S3 : 03 :027(307) [0487] of those in purgatory had **truly** repented and properly
S3 : 03 :040(309) [0489] remain and enables man to become **truly** pure and holy.
S3 : 09 :000(314) [0497] the lesser (that is, the **truly** Christian) excommunication
SC : 03 :002(346) [0545] us to believe that he is **truly** our Father and we are truly
SC : 03 :002(346) [0545] our Father and we are **truly** his children in order that we
SC : 06 :010(352) [0557] discipline, but he is **truly** worthy and well prepared who
SC : 06 :010(352) [0557] for the words "for you" require **truly** believing hearts.
LC : PR :009(359) [0569] they are not really and **truly** such learned and great
LC : PR :020(361) [0573] and thirsty, will they **truly** relish what now they cannot
LC : 01 :019(367) [0585] apart from whom there is **truly** no god in heaven or on
LC : 01 :066(373) [0599] This is a **truly** good work by which God is praised, truth
LC : 01 :090(377) [0605] Wherever this practice is in force, a holy day is **truly** kept.
LC : 01 :107(379) [0611] to honor, we must **truly** regard as high and great.
LC : 01 :113(380) [0613] do if we wish to perform **truly** good works, and by
LC : 01 :115(381) [0613] wish to serve God with **truly** good works, they must do
LC : 01 :144(385) [0623] consciences and know how to do **truly** golden works.
LC : 01 :285(403) [0661] speak evil of him, whether **truly** or falsely, unless it is
LC : 04 :006(437) [0733] As **truly** as I can say that the Ten Commandments, the
LC : 04 :010(437) [0735] by men's hands, it is nevertheless **truly** God's own act.
LC : 04 :069(445) [0749] as the proverb says very **truly**, "Evil unchecked becomes
LC : 05 :014(448) [0757] in virtue of them they are **truly** the body and blood of
LC : 05 :016(448) [0757] body and blood) just as **truly** as when one uses it most
EP : 01 :005(466) [0781] and according to our flesh has **truly** become our brother.
EP : 01 :012(467) [0783] defect and damage is not **truly** sin on account of which
EP : 03 :001(472) [0791] He is **truly** God and man since in him the divine and
EP : 03 :009(474) [0793] genuinely believing and **truly** regenerated persons retain
EP : 03 :017(475) [0795] person though he does not **truly** repent and gives no
EP : 06 :002(480) [0805] and whom God has **truly** converted are freed through
EP : 06 :003(480) [0805] are genuinely believing, **truly** converted, regenerated, and
EP : 07 :002(481) [0809] of our Lord Jesus Christ **truly** and essentially present if
EP : 07 :006(482) [0809] and blood of Christ are **truly** and essentially present and
EP : 07 :006(482) [0809] essentially present and are **truly** distributed and received
EP : 07 :007(482) [0811] union they are **truly** the body and blood of Christ.
EP : 07 :012(483) [0811] Christ, really and **truly** set at this right hand of God
EP : 07 :029(485) [0815] and blood of Christ as **truly** as we eat and drink bread
EP : 07 :030(485) [0815] and wine and not by the **truly** present body and blood of
EP : 08 :009(487) [0819] is the highest communion which God **truly** has with man.
EP : 08 :011(488) [0821] the man, Mary's son, **truly** be called or be God, or the son
EP : 08 :011(488) [0821] were not personally and **truly** united with the Son of God
EP : 08 :012(488) [0821] she is rightly called, and **truly** is, the mother of God.
EP : 08 :014(488) [0821] the Son of God has **truly** suffered for us, but according to
EP : 08 :016(489) [0821] with it and could therefore **truly** increase in age, wisdom,
EP : 11 :013(496) [0835] acknowledge his Son, Christ, and **truly** believe on him.
EP : 12 :009(498) [0839] That a congregation is not **truly** Christian if sinners are
EP : 12 :025(500) [0843] 6. That a Christian who is **truly** born again through the
EP : 12 :027(500) [0843] unless he is himself **truly** reborn, righteous, and pious.
EP : 12 :029(500) [0843] and that only the Father is rightly and **truly** God.
SD : 01 :019(511) [0865] are not really and **truly** such a sin in the sight of God that
SD : 02 :003(520) [0881] of God, to trust God **truly**, to fear and to love him, man
SD : 02 :010(522) [0885] and sick, but that he is **truly** lifeless and "dead" (Eph. 2:1,
SD : 02 :013(523) [0885] Much less will he be able **truly** to believe the Gospel, give
SD : 02 :023(525) [0889] to God and become **truly** free, a condition for which it
SD : 02 :034(528) [0895] sin and operates to make man **truly** pure and holy."
SD : 02 :046(530) [0899] feel and to perceive that God has **truly** converted them.
SD : 02 :067(534) [0907] (Gal. 3:27), are thus **truly** born again, and now have a
SD : 02 :068(534) [0907] the Spirit continues also in the elect and **truly** reborn.
SD : 03 :062(550) [0937] but to be made really and **truly** righteous on account of
SD : 04 :007(552) [0939] works; that only those are **truly** good works which God
SD : 04 :007(552) [0941] on human traditions; that **truly** good works are not done
SD : 04 :009(552) [0941] mother and source of the **truly** good and God-pleasing
SD : 04 :018(554) [0943] right to say and teach that **truly** good works are to be
SD : 05 :008(559) [0953] means nothing more than **truly** to recognize one's sins, to
SD : 06 :004(564) [0963] and confess that, although **truly** believing Christians,
SD : 06 :009(565) [0965] the desires of the flesh the **truly** believing, elect, and
SD : 07 :002(569) [0973] Supper the body of Christ is **truly** received by believers.
SD : 07 :003(569) [0973] and receives and partakes **truly** and essentially, but still
SD : 07 :004(569) [0973] that the Lord Christ is **truly** present in the Supper,
SD : 07 :006(570) [0973] Christ is present in his Supper **truly**, essentially, and alive.
SD : 07 :009(571) [0975] into heaven it is not **truly** and essentially present here on
SD : 07 :011(571) [0975] and blood of Christ are **truly** and essentially present and
SD : 07 :011(571) [0975] essentially present and are **truly** offered with the visible
SD : 07 :011(571) [0975] body of Christ were not **truly** present, but only the Holy
SD : 07 :014(571) [0977] and blood of Christ are **truly** and essentially present,
SD : 07 :016(572) [0977] and blood of Christ are **truly** distributed to the
SD : 07 :016(572) [0977] to the unworthy, too, and that they **truly** receive it.
SD : 07 :016(572) [0977] to testify that those who **truly** repent and comfort
SD : 07 :023(573) [0979] with the words it is **truly** the body and blood of Christ.
SD : 07 :032(574) [0983] and blood of Christ are **truly** eaten and drunk in the
SD : 07 :054(579) [0991] bread and drink the cup **truly** receive and partake of the
SD : 07 :055(579) [0991] body of Christ were not **truly** and essentially present and
SD : 07 :063(581) [0995] that their sins are **truly** forgiven, that Christ dwells and is
SD : 07 :075(583) [0999] and blood of Christ are **truly** present, distributed, and
SD : 07 :116(589) [1011] and blood of Christ as **truly** as in the Supper we receive
SD : 07 :119(590) [1013] able nor willing to be **truly** and essentially present with us
SD : 07 :126(591) [1015] true God and man, who is **truly** and essentially present in
SD : 08 :020(595) [1021] Son of God himself has **truly** suffered (although
SD : 08 :020(595) [1021] plain Christian Creed, has **truly** died, although the divine
SD : 08 :024(595) [1023] but a human being who is **truly** the Son of the most high
SD : 08 :024(595) [1023] Therefore she is **truly** the mother of God and yet
SD : 08 :027(596) [1025] all heavens that he might **truly** fill all things, he is

Continued ▶

SD : 0 8 :029(596) [1025] power he can be and is **truly** present with his body and
SD : 0 8 :032(597) [1027] of natures in the person of Christ did not **truly** exist.
SD : 0 8 :042(599) [1029] But this person is **truly** God, and therefore it is correct to
SD : 0 8 :042(599) [1029] For the Son of God **truly** is crucified for us — that is, this
SD : 0 8 :074(606) [1043] union, he really and **truly** has received all knowledge and
SD : 0 8 :076(606) [1043] example, that his flesh is **truly** a life-giving food and his
SD : 0 8 :076(606) [1043] food and his blood **truly** a quickening beverage, as the
SD : 1 0 :005(611) [1053] Nor do we include among **truly** free adiaphora or things
SD : 1 1 :015(619) [1069] Christ the human race has **truly** been redeemed and
SD : 1 1 :038(622) [1075] of absolution we are as **truly** reconciled with God as if we
SD : 1 1 :039(623) [1077] (Luke 14:18, 24), do not **truly** believe in Christ
SD : 1 2 :014(634) [1099] 5. That that is no **truly** Christian assembly or
SD : 1 2 :026(635) [1099] 17. That Christ is not **truly** and essentially God but only
SD : 1 2 :033(635) [1101] 5. That a Christian who is **truly** born again through the
SD : 1 2 :035(635) [1101] church who is himself not **truly** renewed, righteous, and
SD : 1 2 :038(636) [1103] 2. That only the Father is genuinely and **truly** God.

Trumpery (2)

S 2 : 0 2 :005(293) [0463] openly that the Mass, as **trumpery**, can be omitted
S 2 : 0 2 :021(296) [0469] only is this mere human **trumpery**, utterly unnecessary

Trust (140), Trusted (2), Trusting (1), Trusts (13)

AG : 0 6 :001(032) [0045] sake and not place our **trust** in them as if thereby to merit
AG : 2 7 :037(077) [0081] sight come from faith and **trust** when we believe that God
AG : 2 7 :049(079) [0083] confidence, faith, and **trust** that for Christ's sake we have
AL : 0 2 :001(029) [0043] fear of God, are without **trust** in God, and are
AL : 1 8 :009(040) [0053] such as fear of God, **trust** in God, patience, etc.]
AL : 2 0 :010(042) [0055] Consequently whoever **trusts** that he merits grace by
AL : 2 0 :027(045) [0057] works, not that we should **trust** to merit grace by them
AL : 2 0 :037(046) [0057] or bear the cross, but it seeks and **trusts** in man's help.
AL : 2 0 :038(046) [0057] when there is no faith and **trust** in God, all manner of
AL : 2 7 :049(079) [0083] to have great faith and to **trust** that for Christ's sake we
AP : PR :016(099) [0103] We **trust** that God approves our faithfulness, and we
AP : 0 2 :003(101) [0105] not only of actual fear and **trust** in God but also of the
AP : 0 2 :003(101) [0105] and cannot produce true fear and **trust** in God.
AP : 0 2 :003(101) [0105] to produce the fear and **trust** of God, and it denies that
AP : 0 2 :008(101) [0107] him, lacking fear and **trust** in him, hating his judgment
AP : 0 2 :008(101) [0107] despairing of his grace, **trusting** in temporal things, etc.
AP : 0 2 :014(102) [0109] denied to man's natural powers the fear and **trust** of God.
AP : 0 2 :014(102) [0109] of the fear of God and of **trust** in him, inability to love
AP : 0 2 :017(102) [0109] of God, fear of God, **trust** in God, or at least the
AP : 0 2 :018(103) [0111] the knowledge of God, fear of God, and **trust** in God?
AP : 0 2 :023(103) [0111] he has knowledge of God, **trust** in God, fear and love of
AP : 0 2 :023(103) [0111] gifts knowledge of God, fear of God, and **trust** in God.
AP : 0 2 :023(103) [0111] man not only fear and **trust** of God but also the gifts and
AP : 0 2 :026(103) [0111] elements: lack of ability to **trust**, fear, or love God; and
AP : 0 2 :026(103) [0111] righteousness in which it **trusts** while it despises God).
AP : 0 2 :033(104) [0113] of itself the heart is lacking in love, fear, and **trust** in God.
AP : 0 2 :044(106) [0117] prevailed, feeding a **trust** in human powers and obscuring
AP : 0 4 :011(108) [0123] To support and increase **trust** in such works, the
AP : 0 4 :020(110) [0125] and the terrors of conscience drive out our **trust** in works.
AP : 0 4 :020(110) [0125] because men naturally **trust** their own righteousness.
AP : 0 4 :021(110) [0127] presumption, a vain **trust** in works and a contempt for
AP : 0 4 :038(112) [0131] therefore, for men to **trust** that by the law and by their
AP : 0 4 :044(113) [0133] This faith brings to God a **trust** not in our own merits,
AP : 0 4 :058(115) [0137] Here he comforts himself with his **trust** in God's mercy.
AP : 0 4 :069(116) [0141] But to believe means to **trust** in Christ's merits, that
AP : 0 4 :074(117) [0143] they did not follow, but **trust** in the merit of love or
AP : 0 4 :079(118) [0143] comfort ourselves by firm **trust** in the mercy promised
AP : 0 4 :080(118) [0143] comfort our hearts with **trust** in the mercy promised for
AP : 0 4 :081(118) [0143] when we are comforted by **trust** in the mercy promised
AP : 0 4 :082(118) [0145] us draw near to God with **trust** not in our merits but in
AP : 0 4 :089(120) [0149] who does not work but **trusts** in him who justifies the
AP : 0 4 :098(121) [0151] Therefore we are saved by **trust** in the name of Christ,
AP : 0 4 :098(121) [0151] the name of Christ is to **trust** in the name of Christ as the
AP : 0 4 :110(123) [0153] opponents require us to **trust** in our own love for the
AP : 0 4 :112(123) [0155] the forgiveness of sins by **trust** in this love or on account
AP : 0 4 :146(127) [0163] of God they set a **trust** in their own works, for they say
AP : 0 4 :146(127) [0163] Such a **trust** is simply wicked and vain.
AP : 0 4 :150(127) [0163] he will discover that this **trust** in his own righteousness
AP : 0 4 :156(128) [0165] we should put our **trust** in Christ or in our own works.
AP : 0 4 :157(128) [0165] we shall learn that this **trust** was vain and our consciences
AP : 0 4 :161(129) [0167] We must not **trust** that we are accounted righteous before
AP : 0 4 :170(130) [0169] flesh distrusts God and **trusts** in temporal things; in
AP : 0 4 :198(134) [0175] Thus they learn not to **trust** in their own righteousness,
AP : 0 4 :304(154) [0205] in the intellect but also **trust** in the will, that is, to desire
AP : 0 4 :330(158) [0211] lying vanities"; that is, all **trust** is vain except a trust in
AP : 0 4 :330(158) [0211] all trust is vain except a **trust** in mercy; mercy saves us,
AP : 0 4 :331(158) [0211] when we pray, that is, to **trust** the mercy of God and not
AP : 0 4 :337(159) [0215] however, but about **trust** in God's promise and in his
AP : 0 4 :337(159) [0215] This **trust** in the promise confesses that we are unworthy
AP : 0 4 :339(159) [0215] done everything, do not **trust** in your works," to the
AP : 0 4 :339(159) [0215] believed everything, do not **trust** in the divine promise."
AP : 0 4 :339(159) [0215] the causes and objects of **trust** in the first are unlike those
AP : 0 4 :339(159) [0215] In the first, **trust** is a trust in our own works; in the
AP : 0 4 :339(159) [0215] In the first, trust is a **trust** in our own works; in the
AP : 0 4 :339(159) [0215] own works; in the second, **trust** is a trust in the divine
AP : 0 4 :339(159) [0215] works; in the second, trust is a **trust** in the divine promise.
AP : 0 4 :339(159) [0215] Christ condemns **trust** in our own works; he does not
AP : 0 4 :339(159) [0215] our own works; he does not condemn **trust** in his promise.
AP : 0 4 :341(159) [0215] We should **trust** the promise of grace, not our own
AP : 0 4 :342(160) [0215] since no one fears, loves, or **trusts** God as he ought.
AP : 0 4 :343(160) [0217] see that this passage condemns **trust** in our own works.
AP : 0 4 :351(161) [0217] us truly to fear him and to **trust** that he cares for us and
AP : 0 4 :381(165) [0223] that they advise us to **trust** our love when they teach that
AP : 0 4 :397(167) [0227] namely, "We ought to **trust** that we have been absolved,
AP : 1 2 :060(190) [0267] the opinion that bids us **trust** not in the promise of Christ
AP : 1 2 :065(191) [0271] be put to shame, for they **trust** in their own works and
AP : 1 2 :075(193) [0273] is this but to place our **trust** in our own works rather than
AP : 1 2 :076(193) [0273] to the Gospel, away from **trust** in their own works to
AP : 1 2 :076(193) [0273] in their own works to **trust** in the promise and in Christ;
AP : 1 2 :076(193) [0273] This promise bids us **trust** that because of Christ we are
AP : 1 2 :078(193) [0275] and love, and should **trust** their contrition and love, is
AP : 1 2 :087(195) [0277] the wrath of God or **trust** in our love or works, but only
AP : 1 2 :142(204) [0295] it is vain and wicked to **trust** that thereby we make
AP : 1 5 :025(218) [0321] is obscured and replaced by a vain **trust** in such works.
AP : 1 8 :006(225) [0335] the fear of God nor **trust** in God nor the faith that God
AP : 1 8 :007(226) [0337] God, true knowledge and **trust** that God considers, hears,
AP : 2 1 :015(231) [0347] transfers to the saints the **trust** we should have in Christ's
AP : 2 1 :015(231) [0347] approachable; so they **trust** more in the mercy of the
AP : 2 1 :019(231) [0347] righteous by our **trust** in Christ's merits as though we had
AP : 2 1 :020(232) [0349] of merits are therefore the sources of **trust** in mercy.
AP : 2 1 :020(232) [0349] Such **trust** in God's promise and Christ's merits must be
AP : 2 1 :021(232) [0349] Yet they would have us **trust** more in the mercy of the
AP : 2 1 :022(232) [0349] They tell us, secondly, to **trust** in the merits of the saints.
AP : 2 1 :023(232) [0349] If we are to **trust** in them for our salvation, they are being
AP : 2 1 :028(233) [0351] Men have invoked her, **trusted** in her mercy, and sought
AP : 2 1 :029(233) [0351] maintain that we dare not **trust** in the transfer of the
AP : 2 1 :031(233) [0351] that we should put our **trust** in the invocation of the
AP : 2 1 :031(233) [0351] that we must put our **trust** in the intercession of Christ
AP : 2 1 :034(233) [0351] other mediators besides Christ and put our **trust** in them.
AP : 2 1 :041(235) [0355] abuses of the Mass, the **trust** in monastic observances, the
AP : 2 3 :048(246) [0377] we deny that one should **trust** in certain observances for
AP : 2 4 :026(254) [0391] takes hold of God, as it does when it fears and **trusts** him.
AP : 2 4 :029(255) [0393] "Offer right sacrifices, and put your **trust** in the Lord."
AP : 2 4 :029(255) [0393] He commands us to **trust** and says that this is a right
AP : 2 4 :049(258) [0401] consciences really to **trust** and believe that their sins are
AP : 2 7 :027(273) [0429] in the fear of God, in **trust** in the mercy promised in
AP : 2 7 :034(275) [0431] their own foolish observances the **trust** that is due Christ.
AP : 2 7 :046(277) [0435] but in the absence of greed and of **trust** in riches.
S 2 : 0 2 :027(297) [0469] sacrifices in your honor, or **trust** in you for my salvation.
S 3 : 0 3 :027(307) [0487] the people to rely on and **trust** in such indulgences, he
SC : 0 1 :002(342) [0539] We should fear, love, and **trust** in God above all things.
SC : 0 1 :022(344) [0543] should therefore love him, **trust** in him, and cheerfully do
LC : 0 1 :002(365) [0581] god is nothing else than to **trust** and believe him with our
LC : 0 1 :002(365) [0581] As I have often said, the **trust** and faith of the heart alone
LC : 0 1 :003(365) [0581] If your faith and **trust** are right, then your God is the true
LC : 0 1 :003(365) [0581] On the other hand, if your **trust** is false and wrong, then
LC : 0 1 :005(365) [0581] and property; in them he **trusts** and of them he boasts so
LC : 0 1 :010(366) [0583] family, and honor, and **trusts** in them, he also has a god,
LC : 0 1 :010(366) [0583] to have something in which the heart **trusts** completely.
LC : 0 1 :012(366) [0583] these fix their heart and **trust** elsewhere than in the true
LC : 0 1 :018(367) [0585] the heathen who put their **trust** in power and dominion
LC : 0 1 :018(367) [0585] therefore, to have a god means to **trust** and believe.
LC : 0 1 :019(367) [0585] The trouble is that their **trust** is false and wrong, for it is
LC : 0 1 :021(367) [0585] from him sufficiently to **trust** that he wants to help, nor
LC : 0 1 :024(367) [0587] commandment: We are to **trust** in God alone and turn to
LC : 0 1 :032(369) [0589] he is to those who **trust** and believe him alone with their
LC : 0 1 :036(369) [0589] along with all they have **trusted** in, just as all others have
LC : 0 1 :042(370) [0591] world sees that those who **trust** God and not mammon
LC : 0 1 :047(371) [0593] no presumption and no **trust** in any other object; he
LC : 0 1 :047(371) [0593] demand of us than a hearty **trust** in him for all blessings.
LC : 0 1 :058(372) [0597] just as there are few who **trust** in God with their whole
LC : 0 1 :103(379) [0611] First, we should **trust**, fear, and love him with our whole
LC : 0 1 :242(397) [0649] But we shall **trust** God, who takes matters into his own
LC : 0 1 :270(401) [0657] If you do not **trust** yourself to make your charges before
LC : 0 1 :306(406) [0669] Such examples, I **trust**, will not be found among us,
LC : 0 1 :323(409) [0673] wrath; and, conversely, **trusts** him alone and for his sake
LC : 0 1 :324(409) [0675] "You shall fear, love, and **trust** me as your one true God."
LC : 0 1 :325(409) [0675] these two things, fear of God and **trust** in God.
LC : 0 1 :326(409) [0675] spring from that love and **trust** which the First
LC : 0 1 :326(409) [0675] this fear, love, and **trust** should impel us not to despise
LC : 0 3 :089(432) [0723] a nature that it does not **trust** and believe God and is
EP : 0 3 :006(473) [0793] as our redeemer and **trust** in him, so that solely because
EP : 0 3 :017(475) [0795] 5. That faith is a kind of **trust** in the obedience of Christ
SD : 0 2 :003(520) [0881] commandment of God, to **trust** God truly, to fear and to
SD : 0 2 :031(527) [0893] God, without faith, do not **trust** or believe that God will
SD : 0 3 :011(541) [0919] Word of the Gospel and to **trust** in him, that solely for
SD : 0 3 :030(544) [0925] before God faith **trusts** neither in contrition nor in love
SD : 0 3 :034(545) [0927] who does not work, but **trusts** him who justifies the
SD : 0 3 :037(546) [0929] worthiness, glory, and **trust** in any of our works, so that
SD : 0 3 :064(550) [0937] faith is such a kind of **trust** in the obedience of Christ
SD : 0 4 :012(553) [0941] Faith is a vital, deliberate **trust** in God's grace, so certain
SD : 0 4 :023(555) [0945] confirm presumptuous **trust** in one's own righteousness
SD : 0 4 :028(555) [0947] teach people to put their **trust** in their work (in his
SD : 0 7 :062(581) [0995] indomitably, with certain **trust** and confidence, on this
SD : 0 7 :106(588) [1009] heart to rely on and **trust** in them with absolute certainty.
SD : 1 1 :071(627) [1085] believe his promise, and **trust** in him completely and

Trustworthy (3)

PR : PR :013(007) [0013] number of prominent, **trustworthy**, experienced, and
SC : 0 3 :014(347) [0549] and good children, **trustworthy** servants, godly and
SD : 0 7 :050(578) [0989] no more faithful or **trustworthy** interpreter of the words

Truth (125), Truths (1)

PR : PR :004(004) [0007] the adversaries of divine **truth** took occasion to discredit
PR : PR :006(004) [0009] the right course of divine **truth** which they had once
PR : PR :008(005) [0009] witness of the unalterable **truth** of the divine Word, in
PR : PR :008(005) [0009] and abide loyally by the **truth** once recognized and
PR : PR :008(005) [0011] to investigate the **truth** of the divine Word that alone
PR : PR :010(006) [0011] false doctrine, and clearly to confess the divine **truth**.
PR : PR :011(006) [0011] without violation of divine **truth**, and in this way the
PR : PR :014(007) [0013] a pure declaration of the **truth** might be transmitted to
PR : PR :022(011) [0019] who do not blaspheme the **truth** of the divine Word, and
PR : PR :022(012) [0019] turn to the infallible **truth** of the divine Word and unite
PR : PR :024(013) [0023] to put the light of divine **truth** under a basket or a table,
PR : PR :024(013) [0023] an upright love for divine **truth** and for Christian,
PR : PR :025(013) [0023] from the divine **truth** that our pious forebears and we
AG : PR :002(025) [0039] on one Christian **truth**, to put aside whatever may not
AG : PR :011(026) [0041] done according to divine **truth** we invoke almighty God in
AG : 0 0 :001(047) [0059] agrees with the pure Word of God and Christian **truth**.
AG : 2 8 :025(084) [0087] do anything against the **truth**, but only for the truth."
AG : 2 8 :025(084) [0087] do anything against the truth, but only for the **truth**."
AG : 2 8 :031(085) [0087] When the Spirit of **truth** comes, he will guide you into all
AG : 2 8 :031(085) [0087] Spirit of truth comes, he will guide you into all the **truth**."

Continued ▶

AG : 2 8 :046(088) [0089] myths or to commands of men who reject the **truth**.
AG : 2 8 :078(094) [0095] and schism, which they should in **truth** help to prevent.
AL : 2 0 :010(042) [0055] "I am the way, and the **truth**, and the life" (John 14:6).
AL : 0 0 :005(049) [0059] The **truth** cannot be gathered from common rumors or
AL : 2 8 :025(084) [0087] do anything against the **truth**, but only for the truth"
AL : 2 8 :025(084) [0087] the truth, but only for the **truth**" (II Cor. 13:8), and also,
AL : 2 8 :031(086) [0087] When the Spirit of **truth** comes, he will guide you into all
AL : 2 8 :031(086) [0087] Spirit of truth comes, he will guide you into all the **truth**."
AL : 2 8 :046(088) [0089] myths or to commands of men who reject the **truth**."
AP : P R :012(099) [0101] that they are after neither **truth** no harmony, but our
AP : P R :016(099) [0103] But we cannot surrender **truth** that is so clear and
AP : 0 2 :020(103) [0111] of God is the knowledge of God, righteousness, and **truth**.
AP : 0 2 :051(107) [0119] to reply in defense of the **truth**, for in this case our
AP : 0 4 :247(142) [0191] us forth by the word of **truth** that we should be a kind of
AP : 0 4 :328(158) [0211] no sin, we deceive ourselves, and the **truth** is not in us."
AP : 0 4 :396(167) [0225] they have condemned a **truth** so manifest and clear that
AP : 0 4 :400(168) [0227] words of him who is the **truth** and who knows his body
AP : 0 7 :020(171) [0233] called "the pillar of **truth**" (I Tim. 3:15), for it retains the
AP : 0 7 :022(172) [0235] is true knowledge and the confession of faith and **truth**."
AP : 0 7 :027(173) [0235] that they are pillars of the **truth** and that they do not err.
AP : 1 2 :090(195) [0279] they condemn the open **truth**, it is not right for us to
AP : 1 2 :094(196) [0281] God has sworn to the **truth**; a more horrible blasphemy
AP : 2 0 :006(227) [0339] condemning the obvious **truth** — truth which the church
AP : 2 0 :006(227) [0339] the obvious truth — **truth** which the church must defend
AP : 2 3 :006(240) [0365] In the face of the clear **truth** which we have advanced,
AP : 2 3 :037(244) [0373] will make us surrender the **truth** of the righteousness of
AP : 2 3 :059(247) [0379] our opponents we would have to reject the clear **truth**.
AP : 2 4 :027(254) [0393] the Father in spirit and **truth**, for such the Father seeks to
AP : 2 4 :027(254) [0393] those who worship him must worship in spirit and **truth**."
AP : 2 7 :056(278) [0439] are forced to agree with the persecutors of the **truth**.
AP : 2 8 :024(285) [0451] we will not forsake the **truth** which the church needs, nor
AP : 2 8 :025(285) [0451] condemned the clear **truth**, and are now most cruelly
S 1 : P R :009(290) [0457] foreign peoples as if they were the unadulterated **truth**!
S 3 : 0 3 :045(310) [0491] no sin, we deceive ourselves, and the **truth** is not in us."
S 3 : 1 5 :001(316) [0501] written in Titus 1:14, "They are men who reject the **truth**."
LC : 0 1 :055(372) [0595] who publicly slander the **truth** and God's Word and
LC : 0 1 :064(373) [0599] to use it in the service of **truth** and all that is good — for
LC : 0 1 :064(373) [0599] upon his name in service of **truth** and using it devoutly.
LC : 0 1 :066(373) [0599] by which God is praised, **truth** and justice are
LC : 0 1 :145(385) [0623] If this **truth** could be impressed upon the poor people, a
LC : 0 1 :262(400) [0655] and persecute the **truth** and the children of God and yet
LC : 0 1 :270(401) [0657] But you say: "Why shouldn't I speak if it is the **truth**?"
LC : 0 1 :272(401) [0657] should publicly assert as **truth** what is not publicly
LC : 0 1 :283(403) [0661] or from the love of **truth**, you would not sneak about in
LC : 0 2 :044(416) [0689] Spirit present to reveal this **truth** and have it preached.
LC : 0 5 :029(449) [0759] Here you have both **truths**, that it is Christ's body and
EP : 0 8 :002(487) [0817] (that is, in deed and **truth**) share with each other, and how
EP : 0 8 :003(487) [0817] (that is, in deed and in **truth**) shares in the properties of
EP : 0 8 :003(487) [0819] (that is, in deed and in **truth**) has nothing in common with
EP : 0 8 :011(488) [0821] (that is, in deed and in **truth**) shared only the name of
EP : 0 8 :015(488) [0821] (that is, in deed and in **truth**) exalted to the right hand of
EP : 1 0 :006(493) [0829] for a moment, that the **truth** of the Gospel might be
EP : 1 0 :006(493) [0829] which has to do with the **truth** of the Gospel, Christian
EP : 1 0 :011(494) [0831] (which serve to impair the **truth**) in such indifferent
SD : P R :010(503) [0849] concerned about the **truth** may know how to guard and
SD : P R :005(504) [0851] days brought to light the **truth** of his Word amid the
SD : P R :012(506) [0855] gladly admit and accept them as witnesses to the **truth**.
SD : P R :013(506) [0855] Word of God as the eternal **truth**, so we introduce and
SD : P R :013(506) [0855] writings as a witness to the **truth** and as exhibiting the
SD : P R :015(507) [0857] error must be refuted in order to preserve the **truth**).
SD : P R :016(507) [0857] who really delights in the **truth** of God's Word will find in
SD : P R :016(507) [0857] to insure that the **truth** may be established the most
SD : P R :019(507) [0857] the foundation of divine **truth** might be made apparent in
SD : P R :020(508) [0859] but that it is the same simple, unchanging, constant **truth**.
SD : 0 1 :005(509) [0861] place, it is an established **truth** that Christians must
SD : 0 1 :007(510) [0861] also a clearly established **truth**, as Article XIX of the
SD : 0 1 :010(510) [0863] was originally created in **truth**, holiness, and
SD : 0 1 :030(513) [0867] affecting the goodness, **truth**, holiness, and righteousness
SD : 0 2 :009(522) [0883] it, understand it, or believe and accept it as the **truth**.
SD : 0 2 :013(523) [0885] the Gospel, give his assent to it, and accept it as **truth**.
SD : 0 2 :027(527) [0891] in the preaching of the **truth** reveals his will; but to assent
SD : 0 2 :051(531) [0901] "Sanctify them in the **truth**; thy Word is truth.
SD : 0 2 :051(531) [0901] "Sanctify them in the truth; thy Word is **truth**.
SD : 0 2 :060(533) [0905] against acknowledged **truth**, as Stephen describes the
SD : 0 2 :066(534) [0907] means be conceded without detriment to the divine **truth**.
SD : 0 2 :081(537) [0913] by adding, 'Therefore lay aside lies and speak the **truth**.'
SD : 0 7 :001(569) [0971] testimony to the divine **truth** by means of our confession
SD : 0 7 :034(575) [0983] person who loves **truth** and peace can understand beyond
SD : 0 7 :042(576) [0985] and indubitable rock of **truth** in the words of institution
SD : 0 7 :043(576) [0987] but himself the eternal **truth** and wisdom and the
SD : 0 7 :047(578) [0989] infinite Wisdom and **Truth** and can certainly accomplish
SD : 0 7 :106(588) [1009] Supper is built upon the **truth** and omnipotence of the
SD : 0 7 :126(591) [1015] be adored in spirit and in **truth** in all places but especially
SD : 0 8 :014(594) [1019] so that in deed and **truth** the two natures allegedly have
SD : 0 8 :019(594) [1021] and in a strictly verbal fashion, but in deed and in **truth**.
SD : 0 8 :023(595) [1023] did not exist in deed and **truth**, all of this would be
SD : 0 8 :028(596) [1025] humanity in deed and in **truth** without any blending or
SD : 0 8 :031(597) [1025] but also in deed and **truth** have communion between each
SD : 0 8 :042(599) [1029] within the bounds of **truth**, for you must say that the
SD : 0 8 :063(603) [1037] takes place in deed and in **truth** — to describe any
SD : 0 8 :063(603) [1037] occurred in deed and in **truth** but without any blending
SD : 0 8 :067(604) [1039] while in deed and in **truth** the human nature has no share
SD : 0 8 :068(604) [1039] could be said with equal **truth** that in all creatures in
SD : 0 8 :076(606) [1043] each other in deed and **truth** in the person of Christ,
SD : 0 8 :095(609) [1049] not share in deed and **truth** the divine power, might,
SD : 1 0 :003(611) [1053] prejudice to the divine **truth**, even as far as things
SD : 1 0 :011(612) [1057] for a moment, that the **truth** of the gospel might be
SD : 1 0 :012(613) [1057] for a moment, so that the **truth** of the Gospel might be
SD : 1 0 :013(613) [1057] straightforward about the **truth** of the Gospel (Gal. 2:14).
SD : 1 0 :014(613) [1057] as the apostle testifies, the **truth** of the Gospel might be
SD : 1 0 :028(615) [1061] to their practices, since this serves to imperil the **truth**.
SD : 1 1 :035(622) [1075] that God, who is the eternal **Truth**, contradicts himself.
SD : 1 1 :083(630) [1091] should come to the knowledge of the **truth** and be saved.
SD : 1 1 :095(632) [1095] eternal and unchangeable **truth** of God for the sake of
SD : 1 1 :095(632) [1095] would be contrary to the **truth** and actually intended for
SD : 1 1 :096(632) [1095] anything from the divine **truth** of the holy Gospel, that

Truthful (7), Truthfully (3), Truthfulness (2)
AP : 1 2 :174(210) [0307] and fornication, **truthfulness** — not to buy off eternal
AP : 1 5 :039(220) [0325] We can **truthfully** claim that in our churches the public
SD : 0 7 :043(576) [0987] an angel; he is not only **truthful**, wise, and mighty, but
SD : 0 7 :044(577) [0987] last hour of his life, this **truthful** and almighty Lord, our
SD : 0 7 :045(577) [0987] words of the eternal, **truthful**, and almighty Son of God,
SD : 0 7 :046(577) [0989] gave God the honor of **truthfulness** and concluded and
SD : 0 7 :052(578) [0991] clear, certain, and **truthful** words of Christ, "This is my
SD : 0 7 :075(583) [0999] For the **truthful** and almighty words of Jesus Christ
SD : 0 7 :089(585) [1003] nonetheless remains **truthful** in his words when he says,
SD : 0 7 :123(590) [1013] but do not have a right, **truthful**, living, and saving faith,
SD : 0 8 :076(606) [1043] and on earth can say **truthfully**, "Where two or three are
SD : 0 8 :082(607) [1045] and I could at once say **truthfully**, 'Here is God who is

Try (28), Trying (7), Tried (10), Tries (1)
PR : P R :017(008) [0015] concord, and some even **tried** to appeal to them for the
PR : P R :019(009) [0017] and in public print have **tried** to palm them off on simple
AL : 2 0 :033(045) [0057] who, although they **tried** to live honest lives, were not
AL : 0 0 :003(049) [0059] and now they are **trying** by the same method to increase
AL : 2 6 :015(066) [0073] affairs, and the consolation of sorely **tried** consciences.
AL : 2 8 :064(092) [0093] Although they **try** to mitigate the traditions, moderation
AP : 0 4 :008(108) [0121] and all afflictions, lest we **try** to flee these things or turn
AP : 0 4 :106(122) [0153] faith, and that before we **try** to keep the law we should
AP : 0 4 :137(126) [0161] show that hypocrites who **try** to keep the law by their own
AP : 0 4 :245(142) [0189] and writings, but they also **try** to wipe it out with sword
AP : 0 4 :274(148) [0199] Our opponents **try** to silence this proclamation of the
AP : 0 4 :300(153) [0205] in condemning and **trying** to destroy the doctrine of
AP : 0 4 :375(164) [0223] We are not **trying** to be overly subtle here in
AP : 0 4 :378(165) [0223] We are not **trying** to be overly subtle when we condemn
AP : 1 1 :001(180) [0249] one should diligently **try** to recall them and to enumerate
AP : 1 2 :061(190) [0269] If they **try** to make a subtle distinction separating
AP : 1 2 :123(201) [0289] With such tricks they **try** to alienate men's minds and fan
AP : 1 6 :003(223) [0331] It was mad of Carlstadt to **try** to impose on us the
AP : 2 0 :009(228) [0341] and punishments to **try** to drive you away from the
AP : 2 2 :006(236) [0359] our opponents do not even **try** to explain to the church
AP : 2 3 :005(240) [0365] is in danger and they are **trying** to fortify it with a wicked
AP : 2 3 :020(242) [0369] that many good men have **tried** to control their body but
AP : 2 3 :042(245) [0375] required circumcision and **tried** to impose the law of
AP : 2 3 :068(249) [0383] that our cause had been **tried** and convicted by many
AP : 2 4 :096(267) [0417] comparing them with our position they **try** to crush us.
AP : 2 7 :012(270) [0423] for Christ's sake and **try** to live more closely according to
AP : 2 7 :017(271) [0425] wrath of God; whoever **tries** to attain to the forgiveness
AP : 2 7 :039(276) [0433] itself they say that monks **try** to pattern their lives more
S 1 : P R :004(289) [0457] They **try** to clothe their venomous spirits in the garments
S 1 : P R :007(289) [0457] us so shamefully and **try** by their lies to keep the people
S 1 : P R :014(291) [0459] do not repent and we even **try** to justify all our
S 2 : 0 2 :007(294) [0463] by means of the Mass men **try** to reconcile themselves and
S 3 : 0 3 :028(308) [0487] and hard beds and **tried** earnestly and mightily to be
SC : 0 5 :029(351) [0555] heavily burdened or who are distressed and sorely **tried**.
LC : P R :019(361) [0573] and preachers, not to **try** to be doctors prematurely and
LC : 0 1 :072(374) [0601] I have **tried** it myself and learned by experience that often
LC : 0 3 :030(424) [0707] forces arrayed against us, **trying** to trample us under
LC : 0 3 :047(426) [0711] and pure doctrine and **try** to suppress it, as the bishops,
LC : 0 3 :061(428) [0715] If we **try** to hold fast these treasures, we must suffer an
LC : 0 5 :026(449) [0759] skulks about everywhere, **trying** all kinds of tricks, and
LC : 0 5 :083(456) [0773] **Try** this, therefore, and practice it well.
LC : 0 5 :086(456) [0773] For it is clearly useless to **try** to change old people.
SD : 0 7 :028(574) [0981] after his death some would **try** to make him suspect by
SD : 0 7 :103(587) [1007] For who wants to **try** to prove that God is unable to do
SD : 1 1 :026(620) [1071] we permit ourselves to **try** to explore the secret and
SD : 1 1 :064(626) [1083] we cannot and should not **try** to explore and explain

Tumult (1), Tumults (3)
AG : 2 8 :002(081) [0083] many serious wars, **tumults**, and uprisings have resulted
AL : 2 8 :002(081) [0083] great wars and **tumults** have resulted, while the pontiffs,
AP : 0 4 :236(140) [0185] These **tumults** would die down if our opponents did not
AP : 1 2 :031(186) [0259] and crushed; I groan because of the **tumult** of my heart."

Turk (3), Turks (4)
AG : P R :001(024) [0039] matters pertaining to the **Turk**, that traditional foe of ours
AG : 2 1 :001(046) [0057] in making war on the **Turk**, for both are incumbents of a
AL : 2 1 :001(046) [0057] in waging war to drive the **Turk** out of his country, for
S 2 : 0 4 :011(300) [0475] Neither the **Turks** nor the Tartars, great as is their enmity
LC : 0 2 :066(419) [0697] church, whether heathen, **Turks**, Jews, or false Christians
LC : 0 3 :077(431) [0721] to be victorious over the **Turks** and all our enemies; to
LC : 0 4 :020(439) [0737] bones, they look no different from **Turks** and heathen.

Turmoil (1)
AP : 0 4 :304(154) [0205] but are also a horrible **turmoil** in the will as it flees God's

Turn (36), Turned (14), Turning (5), Turns (6)
PR : P R :021(010) [0019] **Turning** to the kind and manner of speech employed with
PR : P R :022(012) [0019] of the Holy Spirit, **turn** to the infallible truth of the divine
AG : P R :023(027) [0043] and we shall not be **turned** aside from our position by
AG : 1 9 :000(041) [0053] his support, the will **turns** away from God to evil.
AG : 2 4 :010(057) [0065] as is well known, by **turning** it into a sort of fair, by
AG : 2 6 :012(065) [0071] such traditions have **turned** out to be a grievous burden to
AL : 1 9 :000(041) [0053] the will of the wicked **turns** away from God, as Christ
AP : 0 4 :008(108) [0121] try to flee these things or **turn** away when God imposes
AP : 0 4 :133(125) [0159] minds; but when a man **turns** to the Lord the veil is
AP : 0 4 :266(146) [0197] The mind must be **turned** from such fleshly opinions to
AP : 0 4 :296(152) [0205] from Moses, we must **turn** our eyes to Christ, and believe
AP : 1 2 :094(196) [0281] wicked, but that the wicked **turn** from his way and live."
AP : 1 2 :124(201) [0289] of such defenders and men **turning** over to these sophists such
AP : 1 9 :001(226) [0337] of the devil and of men **turning** away from God, as Christ
AP : 2 1 :015(231) [0347] of Christ and they flee from Christ and **turn** to the saints.
S 1 : P R :009(290) [0457] are capable of conversion and **turn** them to repentance!
S 2 : 0 2 :019(296) [0467] multitudes of people may **turn** aside from Christ to their
S 3 : 0 3 :033(308) [0489] All have **turned** aside, together they have gone wrong."

Continued ▶

SC : PR :011(339) [0535] contrary, they should be **turned** over to the pope and his
SC : 0 5 :024(350) [0555] other sins, for this would **turn** confession into torture; he
LC : 0 1 :015(366) [0583] He wishes to **turn** us away from everything else, and draw
LC : 0 1 :015(366) [0585] mammon or anything else, **turn** to me for all this; look
LC : 0 1 :024(367) [0587] to trust in God alone and **turn** to him, expecting from him
LC : 0 1 :034(369) [0589] vengeance upon men who **turn** away from him, and his
LC : 0 1 :043(370) [0593] treasures, that these have **turned** to dust and vanished.
LC : 0 1 :057(372) [0597] will permit the heart that **turns** away from him to go
LC : 0 1 :059(372) [0597] have to be dragged in to **turn** the villainy into
LC : 0 1 :151(386) [0625] or his children will **turn** out badly; servants, neighbors, or
LC : 0 1 :184(390) [0633] such people, our hearts in **turn** rage and we are ready to
LC : 0 1 :240(397) [0649] will overtake those who **turn** the free public market into a
LC : 0 1 :247(398) [0651] bone, and you arrogantly **turn** him away whom you
LC : 0 2 :021(413) [0683] and never once **turning** to God to thank him or
LC : 0 3 :011(421) [0701] this commandment and **turn** to God so that we may not
LC : 0 3 :084(432) [0723] this petition of the Lord's Prayer be **turned** against them.
LC : 0 3 :089(432) [0723] is necessary constantly to **turn** to this petition for the
LC : 0 4 :063(444) [0749] not allow ourselves to be **turned** aside from the Word,
LC : 0 5 :048(452) [0765] perverted it and **turned** it back into a Jewish feast).
LC : 0 5 :075(455) [0771] then for your own good **turn** to St. Paul's Epistle to the
LC : 0 5 :086(456) [0773] and work, so that they in **turn** may bring up their children
EP : 0 2 :003(470) [0787] will is not only **turned** away from God, but has also
SD : 0 1 :002(508) [0859] that which is good and is **turned** to everything evil, and
SD : 0 1 :035(514) [0869] made me of clay, and wilt thou **turn** me to dust again?
SD : 0 2 :010(522) [0885] All have **turned** aside, together they have gone wrong; no
SD : 0 2 :017(523) [0887] man is not only totally **turned** away from God, but is also
SD : 0 2 :017(523) [0887] from God, but is also **turned** and perverted against God
SD : 0 2 :030(527) [0893] man by his own powers **turn** to the Gospel or to Christ?
SD : 0 2 :044(529) [0897] does not once think to **turn** to the holy Gospel and to
SD : 0 2 :049(530) [0901] but that all men should **turn** themselves to him and be
SD : 0 2 :049(530) [0901] but that the wicked **turn** from his way and live"
SD : 0 2 :070(535) [0909] fear the wrath of God, to **turn** from sin, to understand
SD : 0 5 :010(560) [0955] "When a man **turns** to the Lord, the veil is removed"
SD : 0 7 :042(576) [0987] and apostles, and by their disciples and hearers in **turn**.
SD : 0 7 :045(577) [0987] out of human reason, to **turn** us away from these words,
SD : 0 7 :116(589) [1011] that our faith, when it **turns** away from the Supper and
SD : 1 1 :028(621) [1071] perish, but that all should **turn** to repentance"
SD : 1 1 :032(621) [1073] it, if we ourselves do not **turn** away from him but "hold
SD : 1 1 :042(623) [1077] is that they willfully **turn** away from the holy
SD : 1 1 :068(627) [1085] own word Christ will not **turn** them away, "Him who
SD : 1 1 :081(630) [1089] but that the wicked **turn** from his way and live"
SD : 1 1 :083(630) [1091] those who deliberately **turn** away from the holy
SD : 1 1 :084(630) [1091] wicked, but that the wicked **turn** from his way and live."

Twelfth (1), Twelve (2)

AP : 1 2 :001(182) [0253] In the **twelfth** article they approve the first part, where we
LC : 0 2 :005(411) [0679] place, the Creed used to be divided into **twelve** articles.
SD : 0 8 :025(596) [1023] again when he was **twelve** years old, among the teachers,

Twentieth (1), Twenty (4)

AP : 0 4 :001(107) [0119] articles, and later in the **twentieth**, they condemn us for
AP : 1 2 :158(207) [0301] teaches in a long sermon in his **twenty**-eighth chapter.
AP : 2 7 :032(274) [0431] the Lord who comes at him with **twenty** thousand."
S 1 : PR :012(290) [0459] that ten councils and **twenty** diets would not be able to
SD : PR :019(507) [0857] since within the past **twenty**-five years a number of

Twice (1)

LC : 0 5 :084(456) [0773] that you have sunk **twice** as low as any other poor sinner

Twist (19), Twisted (5), Twisting (3)

AP : 0 2 :037(105) [0115] refute the principle, they **twist** his words in order by this
AP : 0 2 :043(106) [0117] but it is not right to **twist** it in order to minimize original
AP : 0 4 :224(138) [0181] Our opponents **twist** many texts because they read their
AP : 0 4 :253(143) [0191] error, but our opponents **twist** them by reading into them
AP : 0 4 :260(145) [0195] Gospel, and maliciously **twist** the Scriptures to suit the
AP : 0 4 :266(146) [0197] opponents immediately **twist** his words to mean the very
AP : 0 4 :274(148) [0199] of the Gospel by **twisting** those passages which teach
AP : 0 4 :283(150) [0201] Our opponents **twist** his meaning by sophistically
AP : 0 4 :286(150) [0201] Our opponents maliciously **twist** the Scriptures to fit their
AP : 0 4 :288(151) [0203] the canonists have **twisted** ecclesiastical regulations.
AP : 0 4 :341(159) [0215] As usual, our opponents **twist** against faith statements
AP : 0 4 :380(165) [0223] and these they quote in a **twisted** way, boasting in the
AP : 0 7 :029(173) [0237] opponents still continue to **twist** it, we shall not mind
AP : 1 2 :084(194) [0277] minds if our opponents **twist** Paul's sentences, for nothing
AP : 1 2 :123(200) [0289] sophists who so sinfully **twist** the Word of God to suit
AP : 2 4 :014(251) [0387] way our opponents have **twisted** many passages of
AP : 2 4 :053(259) [0403] Hebrews, our opponents **twist** passages from this very
AP : 2 4 :075(263) [0411] of which our opponents **twist** in support of their idea that
AP : 2 4 :095(267) [0417] saw their sayings being **twisted** to support the obvious lies
AP : 2 7 :010(270) [0423] to hear how they **twist** our arguments and what they
AP : 2 7 :043(276) [0435] that they wickedly **twist** the saying of Christ in applying
S 1 : PR :005(289) [0457] busy by shamefully **twisting** and corrupting my every
S 3 : 0 8 :003(312) [0495] judge, interpret, and **twist** the Scriptures or spoken Word
LC : 0 1 :289(404) [0663] misconstruing and **twisting** things in the worst way.
LC : 0 1 :299(405) [0665] by jurists and lawyers who **twist** and stretch the law to
SD : 0 7 :031(574) [0983] If he can **twist** and pervert the Word of God, what will he
SD : 0 8 :063(603) [1037] maliciously and wickedly **twisted** our words and

Two (148)

PR : PR :020(010) [0017] the personal union of the **two** natures in Christ, our
PR : PR :027(014) [0025] [of Saxe-Weimar] the above **two** through their guardian.
PR : PR :027(014) [0025] Saxe-Eisenach] the above **two** through their guardians.
PR : PR :027(015) [0025] [in Ivernack] the above **two** through their guardians.
PR : PR :027(015) [0025] [-Hachberg] the above **two** through their guardians.
AG : 0 1 :005(028) [0043] who assert that there are **two** gods, one good and one
AG : 0 1 :006(028) [0043] assert that the other **two**, the Word and the Holy Spirit,
AG : 0 3 :002(029) [0045] virgin Mary, and that the **two** natures, divine and
AG : 2 3 :023(055) [0063] These **two** statements fit together well, for it must be a
AG : 2 8 :004(081) [0085] with all reverence as the **two** highest gifts of God on
AG : 2 8 :012(083) [0085] Therefore, the **two** authorities, the spiritual and the
AG : 2 8 :018(083) [0085] teachers distinguish the **two** authorities and the functions
AG : 2 8 :018(083) [0085] and the functions of the **two** powers, directing that both
AL : 0 1 :005(028) [0043] Manichaeans, who posited **two** principles, one good and
AL : 0 3 :002(029) [0045] So there are **two** natures, divine and human, inseparably
AL : 1 2 :003(034) [0049] consists of these **two** parts: one is contrition, that is,
AL : 2 8 :018(083) [0085] the functions of the **two** powers, and they command that
AP : 0 3 :001(107) [0119] we confess that there are **two** natures in Christ, namely,
AP : 0 4 :005(108) [0121] be divided into these **two** chief doctrines, the law and the
AP : 0 4 :007(108) [0121] Of these **two** doctrines our opponents select the law and
AP : 0 4 :185(132) [0173] and sure issues, one or **two** explanations, taken from the
AP : 0 4 :255(144) [0193] They contain **two** elements.
AP : 0 4 :256(144) [0193] of the law there are **two** things we must always keep in
AP : 0 4 :261(145) [0195] Daniel's sermon contains **two** parts.
AP : 0 4 :275(148) [0199] follow reconciliation — but he does so for **two** reasons.
AP : 0 4 :287(150) [0203] They teach **two** modes of justification, one based upon
AP : 0 4 :297(152) [0205] There are **two** basic facts: First we are not justified by the
AP : 0 4 :321(157) [0209] work does not distinguish between the **two** kinds of merit.
AP : 0 4 :339(159) [0215] The **two** statements are not analogous since the causes
AP : 1 2 :009(183) [0255] distinction between these **two** motives is possible, but in
AP : 1 2 :028(185) [0259] we have given penitence **two** parts, namely, contrition and
AP : 1 2 :044(187) [0263] us for assigning these **two** parts to penitence, we must
AP : 1 2 :044(187) [0263] There are **two** parts here.
AP : 1 2 :045(187) [0263] There are, then, **two** chief parts here, contrition and
AP : 1 2 :045(188) [0263] You see that here, too, the **two** parts are combined:
AP : 1 2 :046(188) [0263] almost always names these **two** parts, mortifying and
AP : 1 2 :046(188) [0263] These are **two** parts here.
AP : 1 2 :047(188) [0263] There are therefore **two** parts here, contrition and faith.
AP : 1 2 :048(188) [0265] Here, too, there are **two** parts, the bond and the
AP : 1 2 :052(189) [0265] a practice of joining these **two**, terror and consolation, to
AP : 1 2 :053(189) [0265] These are the **two** chief works of God in men, to terrify
AP : 1 2 :055(189) [0265] These **two** parts also appear in the lives of the saints.
AP : 1 2 :058(190) [0267] We have put in these **two** parts in order to emphasize the
AP : 1 2 :091(195) [0279] forth contrition and faith as the **two** parts of penitence.
AP : 1 2 :098(197) [0281] contrition and faith, the **two** parts of penitence we have
AP : 1 2 :145(205) [0297] obscure the law of God in **two** ways: first, because they
AP : 2 1 :017(231) [0347] **Two** qualifications must be present if one is to be a
AP : 2 4 :019(252) [0389] There are **two**, and only two, basic types of sacrifice.
AP : 2 4 :019(252) [0389] There are two, and only **two**, basic types of sacrifice.
AP : 2 4 :020(252) [0389] never lose sight of these **two** types of sacrifice and be very
AP : 2 4 :068(261) [0407] that the Lord's Supper was instituted for **two** reasons.
AP : 2 4 :069(262) [0409] There are **two** parts to a sacrament, the sign and the
AP : 2 7 :041(276) [0435] There are **two** kinds of leaving.
S 3 : 0 4 :000(310) [0491] Matt. 18:20, "Where **two** or three are gathered," etc.
TR : 0 0 :024(324) [0511] Matt. 18:19, Christ said, "If **two** or three of you agree on
TR : 0 0 :049(328) [0519] To these errors, then, **two** great sins must be added.
TR : 0 0 :067(331) [0523] which Augustine relates of **two** Christians in a ship, one
TR : 0 0 :068(331) [0523] individuals: "Where **two** or three are gathered in my
SC : 0 5 :016(349) [0553] Answer: Confession consists of **two** parts.
SC : 0 5 :024(350) [0555] simply mention one or **two** sins of which he is aware.
LC : PR :003(358) [0567] instead, at least a page or **two** from the Catechism, the
LC : PR :009(359) [0569] in Matt. 18:20, "Where **two** or three are gathered in my
LC : 0 1 :003(365) [0581] For these **two** belong together, faith and God.
LC : 0 1 :053(372) [0595] in marriage matters when **two** persons secretly betroth
LC : 0 1 :099(378) [0609] after hearing a sermon or **two**, become sick and tired of it
LC : 0 1 :164(387) [0627] and money for a year or **two**, but long life, sustenance,
LC : 0 1 :230(396) [0645] daily plunder not only a city or **two**, but all Germany.
LC : 0 1 :279(402) [0661] does not listen, take one or **two** others along with you,
LC : 0 1 :279(403) [0661] be confirmed by the evidence of **two** or three witnesses."
LC : 0 1 :293(404) [0663] These **two** commandments, taken literally, were given
LC : 0 1 :293(404) [0665] God therefore added these **two** commandments to teach
LC : 0 1 :325(409) [0675] emphasizing these **two** things, fear of God and trust in
LC : 0 2 :018(412) [0681] belongs in the other **two** parts of this article, where we
LC : 0 2 :059(418) [0695] on earth through these **two** means, the Christian church
LC : 0 2 :059(418) [0695] us in it by means of the last **two** parts of this article.
LC : 0 3 :053(427) [0711] kingdom comes to us in **two** ways: first, it comes here, in
LC : 0 3 :060(428) [0715] These **two** points embrace all that pertains to God's glory
LC : 0 3 :060(428) [0715] we keep firm hold of these **two** things and never allow
LC : 0 3 :061(428) [0715] hinder and thwart the fulfillment of the first **two** petitions.
LC : 0 3 :069(429) [0717] One or **two** Christians, armed with this single petition,
LC : 0 3 :073(430) [0719] For where these **two** relations are interfered with and
LC : 0 4 :001(436) [0733] for us to speak of our **two** sacraments, instituted by
LC : 0 4 :022(439) [0737] you again that these **two**, the Word and the water, must
LC : 0 4 :045(442) [0743] is the reason why these **two** things are done in Baptism:
LC : 0 4 :065(444) [0749] These **two** parts, being dipped under the water and
LC : 0 5 :040(451) [0763] authority, let a year, or **two**, three, or more years go by
LC : 0 6 :008(458) [0000] discussing here there are **two** other kinds, which have an
LC : 0 6 :008(458) [0000] These **two** kinds are expressed in the Lord's Prayer when
LC : 0 6 :014(458) [0000] like the other **two** but is left to everyone to use whenever
LC : 0 6 :015(458) [0000] as I have often said, that confession consists of **two** parts.
LC : 0 6 :018(459) [0000] therefore take care to keep the **two** parts clearly separate.
EP : 0 1 :019(468) [0783] original sin, and that the **two** cannot be differentiated in
EP : 0 2 :019(472) [0791] conversion there are only **two** efficient causes, namely,
EP : 0 3 :001(473) [0791] **Two** false and mutually contradictory teachings have
EP : 0 3 :003(473) [0793] 1. In opposition to these **two** errors just recounted, we
EP : 0 4 :001(475) [0797] 1. **Two** controversies have arisen in some churches
EP : 0 7 :003(482) [0809] first of all, that there are **two** kinds of Sacramentarians.
EP : 0 8 :001(486) [0817] the person of Christ, the **two** natures in Christ, and their
EP : 0 8 :003(487) [0817] a way that neither of the **two** *really* (that is, in deed and in
EP : 0 8 :005(487) [0819] a way that there are not **two** Christs, one the Son of God
EP : 0 8 :009(487) [0819] personal union), as when **two** boards are glued together
EP : 0 8 :018(489) [0823] of the properties of the **two** natures in Christ and thus he
SD : 0 1 :033(514) [0869] and original sin by itself as **two** manifestly separate
SD : 0 1 :033(514) [0869] discuss, and believe these **two** as distinct from each other.
SD : 0 1 :051(517) [0875] and formulas that have **two** or more accepted meanings in
SD : 0 2 :057(532) [0903] has promised that, where **two** or three are gathered
SD : 0 2 :066(534) [0907] the Holy Spirit, the way **two** horses draw a wagon
SD : 0 3 :018(542) [0921] in their strict senses the **two** will be differentiated from
SD : 0 3 :032(545) [0927] But these **two** dare not be confused with one another or
SD : 0 3 :048(548) [0933] because God consists of **two** pieces or parts, namely, the
SD : 0 5 :001(558) [0951] lest we confuse the **two** doctrines and change the Gospel
SD : 0 5 :023(562) [0959] of the world these **two** proclamations have continually
SD : 0 5 :024(562) [0961] and confess that these **two** doctrines must be urged
SD : 0 5 :027(563) [0961] between them by which the **two** doctrines would be
SD : 0 7 :014(571) [0977] of Irenaeus, that there are **two** things in this sacrament,
SD : 0 7 :037(575) [0985] For as in Christ **two** distinct and untransformed natures
SD : 0 7 :037(575) [0985] so in the Holy Supper the **two** essences, the natural bread

Continued ▶

SD : 0 7 :038(576) [0985] union, like that of the **two** natures in Christ, but a
SD : 0 7 :067(582) [0997] the part of the unworthy "**two** hairs of a horse's tail and
SD : 0 7 :123(590) [1015] There are only **two** kinds of guests at this heavenly meal,
SD : 0 8 :006(592) [1017] manner that there are now **two** persons or two Christs,
SD : 0 8 :006(592) [1017] are now two persons or **two** Christs, but in such a way
SD : 0 8 :007(592) [1017] undivided person there are **two** distinct natures: the
SD : 0 8 :007(592) [1017] These **two** natures in the person of Christ will henceforth
SD : 0 8 :008(593) [1017] nature and essence the **two** natures referred to remain
SD : 0 8 :011(593) [1019] person, but that the **two** natures are united in such a way
SD : 0 8 :011(593) [1019] Therefore Christ is not **two** different persons, but one
SD : 0 8 :011(593) [1019] in spite of the fact that **two** distinct natures, each with its
SD : 0 8 :014(594) [1019] united with each other like **two** boards glued together, so
SD : 0 8 :014(594) [1019] that in deed and truth the **two** natures allegedly have no
SD : 0 8 :015(594) [1019] of Rhaitu, taught that the **two** natures have no
SD : 0 8 :015(594) [1019] This would separate the **two** natures from each other and
SD : 0 8 :015(594) [1019] each other and thus make **two** Christs, so that Christ is
SD : 0 8 :028(596) [1025] or equalization of the **two** natures in their essence and
SD : 0 8 :035(597) [1027] of properties between the **two** natures be treated and
SD : 0 8 :036(598) [1027] first place, since in Christ **two** distinct natures are and
SD : 0 8 :043(599) [1029] then Christ will have to be **two** persons, one a divine and
SD : 0 8 :066(604) [1039] glowing iron there are not **two** powers of illumination and
SD : 0 8 :076(606) [1043] beverage, as the **two** hundred fathers of the Council of
SD : 0 8 :076(606) [1043] can say truthfully, "Where **two** or three are gathered in
SD : 0 8 :082(607) [1045] there, too, since he is not **two** separate persons but a
SD : 0 8 :083(607) [1045] place had separated the **two** natures from one another
SD : 1 0 :005(611) [1053] that intention) that these **two** opposing religions have
SD : 1 0 :008(612) [1055] distinguish between the **two**, as it is written, "In vain do
SD : 1 1 :004(617) [1063] as it is written, "Are not **two** sparrows sold for a penny?
SD : 1 2 :003(633) [1095] teachers there are not **two** preachers who are agreed in
SD : 1 2 :029(635) [1101] eternal Word, so that the **two** natures of Christ have but
SD : 1 2 :037(636) [1103] person has a distinct essence separate from the other **two**.

Twofold (7)
AP : 0 4 :282(149) [0201] false cleansing he puts a **twofold** cleanness, one internal
AP : 2 4 :075(263) [0411] The Fathers speak of a **twofold** effect, of the comfort for
TR : 0 0 :051(329) [0519] the pope exercises a **twofold** tyranny: he defends his
LC : 0 6 :012(458) [0000] in the Lord's Prayer a **twofold** absolution: our debts both
SD : 0 5 :003(558) [0953] meaning but is used in a **twofold** way, both in the Holy
SD : 0 7 :061(580) [0995] There is therefore a **twofold** eating of the flesh of Christ.
SD : 0 7 :072(582) [0997] true presence and the **twofold** participation in the body

Type (6), Types (7)
AP : 0 4 :010(108) [0123] and increased many **types** of worship in the church, like
AP : 0 4 :017(109) [0125] the disposition and those after it are of the same **type**.
AP : 0 4 :395(167) [0225] of the people of Israel is a **type** of what was to happen in
AP : 2 0 :005(227) [0339] inclined to mention here the **type** of works they require.
AP : 2 4 :015(252) [0389] Sacrifice, Its Nature and **Types**
AP : 2 4 :016(252) [0389] as our enumeration of the **types** of sacrifice will make
AP : 2 4 :019(252) [0389] There are two, and only two, basic **types** of sacrifice.
AP : 2 4 :019(252) [0389] The other **type** is the eucharistic sacrifice; this does not
AP : 2 4 :020(252) [0389] lose sight of these two **types** of sacrifice and be very
AP : 2 4 :026(254) [0391] New Testament are of this **type**, as Peter teaches in
AP : 2 4 :068(261) [0407] just as a certain **type** of hood is the mark of a particular
EP : 0 7 :028(485) [0815] only figures, images, and **types** of the far-distant body and
SD : 0 7 :115(589) [1011] only figures, parables, and **types** of the far-distant body

Tyrant (5), Tyrants (7), Tyrannical (2), Tyrannically (4), Tyranny (14)
AP : 0 2 :047(106) [0119] physical ills, and the **tyranny** of the devil are, in the
AP : 2 2 :011(238) [0361] This is the way a **tyrant** would act.
AP : 2 2 :011(238) [0361] Like some **tyrant** in a play, he commands, "Whether they
AP : 2 3 :025(243) [0371] to this new pontifical **tyranny**, and with good reason:
AP : 2 4 :041(257) [0399] Experience shows the sort of **tyrants** who rule the church.
AP : 2 4 :091(266) [0415] It is the kingdom of **tyrants** who transferred the blessed
AP : 2 7 :041(276) [0435] when a government or a **tyranny** forces us to leave or to
AP : 2 8 :014(283) [0447] not have the power of a **tyrant** to act without a definite
S 1 : PR :003(289) [0455] a little and allow limitations to be placed on his **tyranny**.
S 2 : 0 4 :003(298) [0471] to a people through a **tyrant** or scoundrel) which
S 3 : 1 1 :001(314) [0499] acted like antichristian, **tyrannical**, and wicked
TR : 0 0 :004(320) [0503] to be false, impious, **tyrannical**, and injurious to the
TR : 0 0 :036(326) [0515] but he even exalted himself **tyrannically** over all kings.
TR : 0 0 :051(329) [0519] pope exercises a twofold **tyranny**: he defends his errors by
TR : 0 0 :052(329) [0519] enormous errors of the pope's kingdom and his **tyranny**.
TR : 0 0 :055(329) [0521] and curses to defend his **tyranny** and wickedness without
TR : 0 0 :072(332) [0525] it is the wickedness and **tyranny** of the bishops that give
TR : 0 0 :074(332) [0525] This the bishops have **tyrannically** reserved for
TR : 0 0 :074(332) [0525] What **tyranny** it is for civil officers to have the power to
TR : 0 0 :076(333) [0525] the bishops have **tyrannically** reserved this jurisdiction for
TR : 0 0 :079(333) [0527] from the pastors and **tyrannically** exercise it alone; and
SC : PR :021(340) [0357] are freed from the **tyranny** of the pope, they are unwilling
LC : 0 1 :151(386) [0625] or strangers and **tyrants** will inflict injury, injustice, and
LC : 0 1 :168(388) [0629] want to have knaves or **tyrants** in this office and
LC : 0 2 :030(414) [0685] Those **tyrants** and jailers now have been routed, and their
LC : 0 3 :047(426) [0711] it, as the bishops, **tyrants**, fanatics, and others do.
LC : 0 3 :069(429) [0717] that the devil, bishops, **tyrants**, and heretics can do
LC : 0 6 :001(457) [0000] it should be voluntary and purged of the pope's **tyranny**.
LC : 0 6 :006(457) [0000] back into subjection and coerce them like the **tyrant** he is.
LC : 0 6 :021(459) [0000] we abolish the pope's **tyranny**, commandments, and
SD : 0 1 :013(511) [0863] and eternal misery, the **tyranny** and dominion of the
SD : 1 1 :085(630) [1091] sin and his horrible **tyranny** with which he oppressed the

Ulm (1)
PR : PR :027(015) [0027] Mayor and Council of the City of **Ulm**.

Ulric (2)
S 3 : 1 5 :005(317) [0501] Conrad Oettinger, preacher of Duke **Ulric** of Pforzheim
TR : 0 0 :082(335) [0529] of Pforzheim, preacher of **Ulric**, duke of Wuerttemberg

Ulrich (1)
PR : PR :027(015) [0025] **Ulrich**, duke of Mecklenburg [-Guestrow]

Ultimate (1), Ultimately (11)
AP : 0 4 :204(135) [0177] they pile up works and **ultimately** despair because they
AP : 0 9 :003(178) [0245] would be saved, and **ultimately** there would be no
AP : 1 3 :016(213) [0311] **Ultimately**, if we should list as sacraments all the things
S 1 : PR :005(289) [0457] I shall let the devil — or **ultimately** the wrath of God —
S 2 : 0 4 :008(299) [0473] be despised and would **ultimately** be without any
LC : 0 1 :035(369) [0589] so that all who persist in it must **ultimately** perish.
LC : 0 5 :041(451) [0763] quite barbarous, and **ultimately** despise both the
SD : PR :008(502) [0849] disagreements will **ultimately** lead to the ruin of the pure
SD : PR :007(505) [0853] (or wherever it would **ultimately** be held) as an
SD : 0 1 :030(513) [0867] to end, down to the **ultimate** part involving and affecting
SD : 0 1 :062(519) [0879] a quality or a disease, **ultimately** the worst damage is that
SD : 1 0 :015(613) [1057] opened to idolatry, and **ultimately** the commandments of

Ulysses (1)
AP : 2 4 :072(262) [0409] way plays celebrate the memory of Hercules or **Ulysses**.

Un (1)
SD : 1 0 :019(614) [1059] without pretense, humbug, and **un**-Christian ostentation.

Unabashedly (1)
LC : 0 1 :055(372) [0595] disgrace God's name **unabashedly** (these belong in the

Unable (23)
AG : 0 2 :001(029) [0043] mothers' wombs and are **unable** by nature to have true
AG : 2 3 :025(055) [0065] that women who were **unable** to keep their vows of
AG : 2 3 :025(055) [0065] "If they are unwilling or **unable** to keep their chastity, it is
AG : 2 5 :008(062) [0069] in sins that it is **unable** to perceive or know them all, and
AG : 2 7 :057(080) [0083] They were **unable** to understand that one is to serve God
AL : 2 3 :025(055) [0065] "If they are unwilling or **unable** to persevere, it is better
AL : 2 6 :016(066) [0073] traditions that they were **unable** to devote their attention
AL : 2 7 :005(071) [0077] in years, they were **unable** to judge their own strength.
AP : 0 2 :002(100) [0105] mothers' wombs and are **unable** by nature to have true
AP : 2 1 :043(235) [0357] will arise whom our opponents will be **unable** to restrain.
AP : 2 7 :003(269) [0419] He will destroy you, and you will be **unable** to resist him."
S 3 : 0 3 :017(305) [0483] said that he was **unable** to repent or be sorry for his sin
LC : 0 1 :141(384) [0621] Where a father is **unable** by himself to bring up his child,
LC : 0 5 :081(456) [0773] blinds it, making you **unable** to feel your needs or come
EP : 0 7 :034(485) [0815] all his omnipotence, is **unable** (a dreadful statement!) to
SD : 0 2 :003(520) [0881] of the Holy Spirit man is **unable** to fulfill the
SD : 0 2 :055(532) [0903] and gives what man is **unable** by his own powers to take
SD : 0 2 :089(538) [0915] by his natural powers is **unable** to do anything and
SD : 0 7 :103(587) [1007] Christ although they are **unable** to prove that even this
SD : 0 7 :103(587) [1009] who wants to try to prove that God is **unable** to do that?
SD : 0 7 :103(587) [1009] indeed think that God is **unable** to do it, but who will
SD : 0 8 :083(607) [1045] all the devils had been **unable** to separate and tear them
SD : 1 1 :071(627) [1085] And since we are **unable** to do this by our own powers,

Unabolished (1)
SD : 0 8 :008(593) [1017] remain unmingled and **unabolished**, so that each retains

Unadorned (1)
AP : 2 4 :044(258) [0399] and the altars standing **unadorned**, without candles or

Unadulterated (3)
PR : PR :002(003) [0007] pure, unalloyed, and **unadulterated** light of his holy
PR : PR :005(004) [0009] had planted the pure, **unadulterated** Word of God, so
S 1 : PR :009(290) [0457] foreign peoples as if they were the **unadulterated** truth!

Unalloyed (2)
PR : PR :002(003) [0007] has permitted the pure, **unalloyed**, and unadulterated
SD : 0 2 :055(532) [0903] is preached, pure and **unalloyed** according to God's

Unalterable (2)
PR : PR :008(005) [0009] is on the witness of the **unalterable** truth of the divine
PR : PR :018(008) [0015] pure, infallible, and **unalterable** Word of God, to that

Unaltered (2)
EP : RN :004(465) [0777] our time, the first and **unaltered** Augsburg Confession,
SD : PR :005(504) [0851] adherence to the first, **unaltered** Augsburg Confession (in

Unanimity (3)
PR : PR :017(008) [0015] have reached Christian **unanimity** and agreement among
AL : 0 1 :001(027) [0043] teach with great **unanimity** that the decree of the Council
AP : 0 2 :042(105) [0115] Even though complete **unanimity** may be impossible, no

Unanimous (15), Unanimously (28)
PR : PR :000(001) [0004] Reiterated, and **Unanimous** Confession of the Doctrine
PR : PR :000(001) [0004] for Publication by the **Unanimous** Agreement and Order
PR : PR :003(003) [0007] in a Christian and **unanimous** interpretation thereof.
PR : PR :008(005) [0009] year 1530, and again **unanimously** subscribed this
PR : PR :016(008) [0015] called and also is the **unanimous** and concordant
PR : PR :025(014) [0023] to abide and remain **unanimously** in this confession of
AG : 0 1 :001(027) [0043] We **unanimously** hold and teach, in accordance with the
AP : 0 4 :323(157) [0209] Fathers, who declare **unanimously** that even if we have
S 1 : PR :002(288) [0455] latter accepted them, **unanimously** adopted them as their
TR : 0 0 :042(328) [0517] and the Scriptures **unanimously** declare these errors to be
TR : 0 0 :082(334) [0529] assembly in Smalcald **unanimously** declare that in their
EP : RN :003(465) [0777] were accepted as the **unanimous**, catholic, Christian faith
EP : RN :004(465) [0777] we regard, as the **unanimous** consensus and exposition of
EP : RN :006(465) [0779] as opposed to the **unanimous** declaration of our faith.
EP : 0 3 :001(472) [0791] It is the **unanimous** confession of our churches according
EP : 0 3 :003(473) [0793] teach, and confess **unanimously** that Christ is our
EP : 0 7 :015(483) [0813] This has also been the **unanimous** teaching of the leading
EP : 0 7 :021(484) [0813] On the other side, we **unanimously** reject and condemn
EP : 0 9 :002(492) [0827] Therefore it is our **unanimous** opinion that we should not
EP : 1 0 :003(493) [0829] teach, and confess **unanimously** that the ceremonies or
SD : PR :001(503) [0849] formula and pattern, **unanimously** approved, in which the
SD : PR :002(503) [0851] were everywhere and **unanimously** faithful to the pure
SD : PR :006(504) [0853] We therefore **unanimously** pledge our adherence to this
SD : PR :008(505) [0853] we declare our **unanimous** adherence to Dr. Luther's
SD : PR :008(505) [0853] since they have been **unanimously** sanctioned and
SD : PR :013(506) [0855] and as exhibiting the **unanimous** and correct
SD : 0 3 :004(539) [0917] Confession held **unanimously** that Christ is our
SD : 0 3 :009(540) [0919] teach, and confess **unanimously**, in accord with the
SD : 0 3 :059(550) [0937] Accordingly we **unanimously** reject and condemn, in

Continued ▶

SD : 0 3 :066(550) [0937] errors we reject **unanimously** as contrary to the clear
SD : 0 5 :017(561) [0957] We **unanimously** believe, teach, and confess on the basis
SD : 0 6 :004(564) [0963] this controversy, we **unanimously** believe, teach, and
SD : 0 7 :002(569) [0973] they all declare **unanimously** that the true, essential body
SD : 0 7 :052(578) [0991] (I Cor. 11:25), **unanimously** and with the same words and
SD : 0 7 :059(580) [0993] We shall abide **unanimously** by this simple and
SD : 0 7 :060(580) [0995] of the church have **unanimously** understood and
SD : 0 7 :066(581) [0995] Christian church teach **unanimously** that the body of
SD : 0 7 :074(583) [0999] fraternal and **unanimous** agreement among ourselves: No
SD : 0 8 :005(592) [1017] by God's grace, our **unanimous** teaching, belief, and
SD : 0 8 :057(602) [1035] the first place, it is a **unanimously** accepted rule of the
SD : 0 8 :088(609) [1047] Therefore we **unanimously** reject and condemn with
SD : 1 2 :002(632) [1095] Confession have **unanimously** condemned), we had not
SD : 1 2 :004(633) [1097] not only to declare our **unanimous** opinion with a few

Unattacked (1)
PR : PR :020(010) [0017] When they remain **unattacked** on this basis, theologians

Unavenged (1)
LC : 0 1 :247(398) [0651] sorrowful hearts, and he will not leave them **unavenged**.

Unavoidable (1)
LC : 0 1 :086(376) [0605] so narrow as to forbid incidental and **unavoidable** work.

Unaware (1), Unawares (2)
AP : 0 4 :108(122) [0153] that these words fell from the Holy Spirit **unawares**?
LC : 0 1 :100(378) [0609] effort to steal upon you **unawares** and to kindle in your
LC : 0 3 :027(424) [0705] wants, not because he is **unaware** of them, but in order

Unbaptized (3)
EP : 1 2 :006(498) [0839] in the sight of God **unbaptized** children are not sinners
SD : 0 2 :067(534) [0907] baptized people and **unbaptized** people because,
SD : 1 2 :011(634) [1099] 2. That **unbaptized** children are not sinners before God

Unbearable (2)
AP : 2 3 :057(247) [0379] are making the law even more **unbearable** in several ways.
S3 : 0 3 :025(307) [0485] eager to be delivered from the heavy, **unbearable** burden.

Unbecoming (2)
AG : 2 3 :003(051) [0061] In order to avoid such **unbecoming** offense, adultery, and
AG : 2 8 :055(090) [0091] may be no disorder or **unbecoming** conduct in the

Unbelief (25)
AP : 0 2 :029(104) [0113] an ignorance of God, **unbelief**, distrust, contempt, and
AP : 1 2 :151(206) [0299] help and to acknowledge the **unbelief** in their hearts.
S3 : 0 1 :002(302) [0477] Commandments, such as **unbelief**, false belief, idolatry,
S3 : 0 3 :032(308) [0487] All of you are full of **unbelief**, blindness, and ignorance
SC : 0 3 :018(347) [0549] us or mislead us into **unbelief**, despair, and other great
LC : 0 1 :100(378) [0609] to kindle in your heart **unbelief** and wicked thoughts
LC : 0 3 :058(428) [0713] wholly in that shameful **unbelief** which does not look to
LC : 0 3 :058(428) [0713] ourselves against **unbelief** and let the kingdom of God be
LC : 0 3 :104(434) [0727] love, to draw us into **unbelief**, false security, and
LC : 0 3 :105(434) [0727] and weary and to fall back into sin, shame, and **unbelief**.
LC : 0 5 :017(448) [0757] false because of an individual's unworthiness or **unbelief**.
EP : 0 5 :001(478) [0801] reproof that condemns **unbelief**, since unbelief is
EP : 0 5 :001(478) [0801] unbelief, since **unbelief** is condemned not in the law but
SD : 0 2 :058(532) [0903] in the darkness of his **unbelief** and be lost, as it is written,
SD : 0 4 :034(556) [0949] off because of their **unbelief**, and you stand fast only
SD : 0 5 :002(558) [0951] of repentance, which rebukes the greatest sin, **unbelief**.
SD : 0 5 :002(558) [0951] all sins, including **unbelief**, whereas the Gospel in its
SD : 0 5 :002(558) [0953] to Christ that their **unbelief**, in which they formerly had
SD : 0 5 :017(561) [0957] Since **unbelief** is a root and fountainhead of all culpable
SD : 0 5 :017(561) [0957] of all culpable sin, the law reproves **unbelief** also.
SD : 0 5 :019(561) [0957] which the law rebukes **unbelief**, when a person does not
SD : 0 5 :019(561) [0957] of the law rebukes the **unbelief** involved in men's failure
SD : 0 7 :025(573) [0981] rendered false because an individual's person or **unbelief**.
SD : 0 7 :032(574) [0983] rest on man's faith or **unbelief** but on the Word and
SD : 0 7 :089(585) [1003] of the minister or the **unbelief** of him who receives the

Unbelievable (1)
LC : 0 3 :062(428) [0715] It is **unbelievable** how the devil opposes and obstructs

Unbeliever (1), Unbelievers (14), Unbelieving (9)
AP : 0 4 :154(128) [0165] the Pharisee, this wise and honest but **unbelieving** man.
AP : 1 3 :020(214) [0313] good would such miracles or promises do an **unbeliever**?
AP : 2 3 :031(243) [0371] he says, "The **unbelieving** husband is consecrated
S3 : 0 8 :008(313) [0495] with the hardened, **unbelieving** Jews, but he knew that he
TR : 0 0 :041(328) [0517] not be mismated with **unbelievers**, for what fellowship
LC : 0 4 :066(445) [0749] lazy, proud, yes, and **unbelieving**; he is beset with all vices
EP : 0 6 :003(480) [0805] applied not only to **unbelievers** and the impenitent but
EP : 0 6 :008(481) [0807] but only upon **unbelievers**, non-Christians, and the
EP : 0 7 :002(481) [0809] or godless, believers or **unbelievers**, the believers for life
EP : 0 7 :002(482) [0809] for life and salvation, the **unbelievers** for judgment?
EP : 0 7 :016(484) [0813] the unworthy and the **unbelievers** receive the true body
EP : 0 7 :037(485) [0815] in the Holy Supper **unbelieving** and impenitent Christians
EP : 1 0 :006(493) [0829] not be mismated with **unbelievers**, for what fellowship
SD : PR :007(502) [0849] offense for both the **unbelievers** and the weak believers.
SD : 0 4 :008(552) [0941] discipline and which **unbelievers** and the unconverted are
SD : 0 6 :026(568) [0971] believers but only upon **unbelievers**, non-Christians, and
SD : 0 7 :027(574) [0981] communicants but also to the **unbelieving** and unworthy.
SD : 0 7 :063(581) [0995] is efficacious in them; **unbelievers** receive it orally, too,
SD : 0 7 :066(581) [0997] and this by unworthy, **unbelieving**, false, and wicked
SD : 0 7 :088(585) [1003] the unworthy and **unbelieving** hypocrites do not receive
SD : 0 7 :105(588) [1009] in believers but also to wreak judgment on **unbelievers**.
SD : 0 7 :123(590) [1013] reject the doctrine that **unbelieving**, unrepentant, and
SD : 1 0 :006(611) [1055] must be heeded: "Do not be mismated with **unbelievers**.
SD : 1 0 :022(615) [1061] not be mismated with **unbelievers**, for what fellowship

Unblended (2)
SD : 0 8 :011(593) [1019] essence and properties, are found **unblended** in him.
SD : 0 8 :036(598) [1027] remain unchanged and **unblended** in their natural essence

Unbridled (1)
LC : 0 1 :069(374) [0601] faith — only perverse, **unbridled** men whom no teaching

Unbroken (2)
AP : 0 4 :232(139) [0185] that love is a bond and **unbroken** chain linking the many
SD : 0 2 :019(524) [0889] timber, or to a wild, **unbroken** animal — not that man

Unceasingly (1)
LC : 0 2 :061(419) [0695] Spirit carries on his work **unceasingly** until the last day.

Uncertain (20), Uncertainly (1), Uncertainty (2)
PR : PR :009(006) [0011] religion as if we were so **uncertain** of our faith and of the
PR : PR :018(009) [0017] pretense that we are **uncertain** of our faith and for that
PR : PR :024(013) [0023] and nothing beyond **uncertain** opinions and dubious,
AG : 2 7 :053(079) [0083] are perfect, he is **uncertain** whether he can keep his
AP : 0 4 :084(119) [0145] the promise would be **uncertain** and useless inasmuch as
AP : 0 4 :264(146) [0195] less authority that the forgiveness of sins is **uncertain**.
AP : 0 4 :321(157) [0209] terrified consciences are **uncertain** about all their works
AP : 0 4 :344(160) [0217] may say, "Hope will be **uncertain** if we are saved through
AP : 0 4 :345(160) [0217] a right or debt is certain, while mercy is **uncertain**.
AP : 1 2 :062(190) [0269] it maintains that God's promises are **uncertain** and inane.
AP : 1 2 :088(195) [0277] our opponents leave consciences wavering and **uncertain**.
AP : 2 1 :013(230) [0345] us to adopt something **uncertain**, for prayer without faith
S2 : 0 2 :008(294) [0465] commune by himself is **uncertain** and unnecessary, and he
S2 : 0 2 :018(296) [0467] these unnecessary, **uncertain**, harmful will-o'-the-wisps of
S2 : 0 2 :019(296) [0467] abortive, **uncertain**, and even harmful thing.
S3 : 0 3 :027(307) [0487] he again introduced **uncertainty** when he declared in his
S3 : 0 3 :027(307) [0487] as we have heard above, are **uncertain** and hypocritical.
S3 : 0 3 :027(308) [0487] once again directed attention to **uncertain** human works.
S3 : 0 3 :036(309) [0489] repentance for actual sins, nor is it **uncertain** like that.
S3 : 0 3 :036(309) [0489] account there is no **uncertainty** in such repentance, for
S3 : 0 3 :037(309) [0489] cannot be false, **uncertain**, or partial, for a person who
S3 : 0 3 :038(309) [0489] can our satisfaction be **uncertain**, for it consists not of the
LC : 0 3 :020(423) [0703] that we may not despise or disdain it or pray **uncertainly**.

Unchallenged (1)
SD : PR :006(502) [0847] remained practically **unchallenged** — except for the

Unchangeable (3)
AP : 2 3 :009(240) [0367] since natural right is **unchangeable**, the right to contract
EP : 0 6 :007(481) [0807] and the same law, namely, the **unchangeable** will of God.
SD : 1 1 :095(632) [1095] of the eternal and **unchangeable** truth of God for the sake

Unchanged (1), Unchanging (3)
AP : 0 4 :011(108) [0123] necessity of **unchanging** order, not of compulsion—God
SC : PR :009(339) [0535] adhere to a fixed and **unchanging** form and method.
SD : PR :020(508) [0859] but that it is the same simple, **unchanging**, constant truth.
SD : 0 8 :036(598) [1027] natures are and remain **unchanged** and unblended in their

Unchaste (4), Unchastity (8)
AG : 2 3 :015(054) [0063] marriage to aid human infirmity and prevent **unchastity**.
S3 : 0 1 :002(302) [0477] to parents, murder, **unchastity**, theft, deceit, etc.
LC : 0 1 :201(392) [0637] was the most common form of **unchastity** among them.
LC : 0 1 :202(392) [0639] applies to every form of **unchastity**, however it is called.
LC : 0 1 :202(392) [0639] afford no occasion, aid, or encouragement to **unchastity**.
LC : 0 1 :212(394) [0641] easier for man to avoid **unchastity** in some measure, God
LC : 0 1 :215(394) [0641] hearts remain so full of **unchaste** thoughts and evil desires
LC : 0 1 :216(394) [0641] to forsake their **unchaste** existence and enter the married
LC : 0 1 :293(404) [0663] them as referring to **unchastity** or theft, since these vices
LC : 0 3 :102(434) [0727] and lures us daily into **unchastity**, laziness, gluttony and
LC : 0 4 :066(445) [0749] spiteful, envious, **unchaste**, greedy, lazy, proud, yes, and
LC : 0 4 :070(445) [0749] vice, becomes vicious and **unchaste** as he grows.

Unchecked (2)
LC : 0 4 :069(445) [0749] says very truly, "Evil **unchecked** becomes worse and
LC : 0 4 :071(445) [0749] man therefore follows **unchecked** the inclinations of his

Unchristian (9)
AG : 0 0 :000(049) [0059] we have not acted in an **unchristian** and frivolous manner
AG : 2 3 :018(054) [0063] so much frightful and **unchristian** offense, so much
AG : 2 4 :040(061) [0069] not in fairness be condemned as heretical or **unchristian**.
S3 : 1 0 :001(314) [0497] without pretense, humbug, and **unchristian** ostentation.
S3 : 1 5 :001(316) [0501] or merit salvation is **unchristian** and to be condemned.
LC : 0 5 :069(454) [0769] sacrament and lead **unchristian** lives receive it to their
SD : PR :008(502) [0849] among us, in the **unchristian** but futile hope that these
SD : 0 1 :045(516) [0873] Hence it is **unchristian** and abominable to say that
SD : 0 2 :046(530) [0899] Epicureans have in an **unchristian** fashion misused the

Uncircumcision (1)
AP : 0 4 :111(123) [0155] circumcision nor **uncircumcision** is of any avail, but faith

Unclean (3), Uncleanness (8)
AP : 0 2 :012(102) [0109] they failed to see the inner **uncleanness** of human nature.
AP : 0 4 :135(125) [0159] God shows us our **uncleanness** and the greatness of our
AP : 0 4 :288(151) [0203] Being blind to the **uncleanness** of the heart, reason thinks
AP : 0 4 :350(161) [0217] our old or new sins or the **uncleanness** of our nature!
AP : 0 4 :381(165) [0223] love, which we know by experience is weak and **unclean**.
AP : 2 3 :041(245) [0375] the Levitical laws about **uncleanness** do not apply to us.
AP : 2 3 :041(245) [0375] to these laws was **uncleanness**; now it is not, for Paul says
AP : 2 3 :045(245) [0377] seemed profane and **unclean** and hardly pleasing to God,
LC : 0 2 :057(418) [0693] be buried with all its **uncleanness**, and will come forth
SD : 0 1 :011(510) [0863] stamp, an interior **uncleanness** of the heart and evil
SD : 0 1 :052(517) [0875] your entire essence is sin, that is sinful and **unclean**."

Unclear (2)
AP : 0 4 :302(154) [0205] How confused and **unclear** their teaching is!
AP : 1 2 :073(192) [0273] in words that are not **unclear** at all: "You must believe,

Uncoerced (1)
AG : 2 7 :027(075) [0079] what is possible and voluntary and must be **uncoerced**.

Uncommanded (1)
S2 : 0 2 :019(296) [0467] it is an unnecessary, **uncommanded**, abortive, uncertain,

Uncommon (2)
LC : 0 1 :306(406) [0669] But it is not **uncommon** among us for a person to lure
LC : 0 6 :005(457) [0000] us, and we grasp with **uncommon** ease whatever in the

Unconcealed (1)
PR : PR :004(003) [0007] knowledge, patent and **unconcealed**, what very perilous

Unconcerned (1)
LC : 0 1 :037(369) [0591] security, that he is **unconcerned** or uninterested in such

Unconverted (5)
AP : 1 2 :138(203) [0295] penalties but to retaining the sins of the **unconverted**.
SD : 0 2 :090(539) [0915] The **unconverted** man's intellect and will are only that
SD : 0 4 :008(552) [0941] unbelievers and the **unconverted** are also able and require
SD : 0 5 :012(560) [0957] is Moses and the law pronounced upon the **unconverted**.
SD : 0 6 :019(567) [0969] coercion, just as the **unconverted** are driven and coerced

Uncorrupted (6)
AP : 2 3 :007(240) [0365] the desire which was meant to be in **uncorrupted** nature.
S3 : 0 1 :004(302) [0477] remained whole and **uncorrupted**, and that man by
S3 : 0 3 :010(305) [0481] remained whole and **uncorrupted**, that reason is capable
EP : 0 1 :008(467) [0781] that nothing sound or **uncorrupted** has survived in man's
EP : 0 1 :013(467) [0783] that man's nature is **uncorrupted** even after the Fall, and
SD : 0 1 :062(519) [0879] deeply that nothing in it remained pure and **uncorrupted**.

Uncovered (2)
AG : 2 8 :056(090) [0091] offense to others she goes out with **uncovered** head.
AL : 2 8 :056(090) [0091] in public with her head **uncovered**, provided no offense is

Unction (1)
AP : 1 3 :006(212) [0309] and extreme **unction** are rites received from the Fathers

Undaunted (1)
AP : 2 7 :052(278) [0437] They are also **undaunted** by the voice of Christ

Undecided (1)
S2 : 0 2 :013(295) [0467] He leaves it **undecided** whether or not there is a purgatory

Underfoot (1)
S1 : PR :014(291) [0459] while we trample his solemn commandments **underfoot**.

Undergo (3), Undergoing (1)
AP : 0 4 :179(131) [0171] all men, but by **undergoing** the punishment of sin and
AP : 1 2 :149(206) [0299] of St. Peter rather than **undergo** the unspeakable power
AP : 2 1 :035(234) [0353] strong of soul because they have to **undergo** great danger.
LC : 0 1 :262(400) [0655] the Word of God must **undergo** the most shameful and

Underhanded (4)
TR : 0 0 :078(333) [0527] all clandestine and **underhanded** betrothals in violation
LC : 0 1 :227(396) [0645] advantage of him by **underhanded** tricks and sharp
LC : 0 1 :233(396) [0647] him by any faithless or **underhanded** business transaction.
LC : 0 1 :307(406) [0669] To do so is dark and **underhanded** wickedness, and, as we

Undermine (6), Undermined (1), Undermines (1)
AG : 2 8 :013(083) [0085] annul temporal laws or **undermine** obedience to
AP : 1 4 :005(215) [0315] charge that we have **undermined** the authority of the
S2 : 0 2 :025(297) [0469] first, chief article and **undermines** knowledge of Christ.
SC : PR :019(340) [0537] by such neglect they **undermine** and lay waste both the
LC : 0 1 :197(391) [0637] It would too greatly **undermine** the "spiritual estate" and
EP : 1 2 :016(499) [0841] *Intolerable Errors which **Undermine** Domestic Society*
SD : 1 0 :010(612) [1055] adversaries in order to **undermine** the genuine worship of
SD : 1 1 :036(622) [1075] would also completely **undermine** and totally destroy for

Underneath (1)
EP : 0 1 :014(468) [0783] on externally and that **underneath** man's nature has

Undersigned (2)
PR : PR :000(001) [0004] and Faith of the **undersigned** Electors, Princes, and
AG : PR :005(025) [0039] Inasmuch as we, the **undersigned** elector and princes and

Understand (99), Understandable (1), Understanding (58), Understands (7), Understood (87)
PR : PR :004(004) [0009] consciences from an **understanding** of pure evangelical
PR : PR :009(006) [0011] of ours was again **understood** and interpreted in such a
PR : PR :019(009) [0017] inasmuch as we never **understood** or accepted the second
PR : PR :020(010) [0019] that our ingenuous **understanding** of the words of Christ
PR : PR :022(011) [0019] of their hearts, do not **understand** the issues, and take no
PR : PR :023(012) [0021] its Apology, correctly **understood**, and that no doctrine
AG : PR :002(025) [0039] and charitably to hear, **understand**, and weigh the
AG : PR :019(026) [0041] a good, Christian **understanding**, Your Imperial Majesty
AG : 0 1 :004(028) [0043] word "person" is to be **understood** as the Fathers
AG : 0 7 :002(032) [0047] with a pure **understanding** of it and that the sacraments
AG : 1 8 :004(039) [0051] for all have a natural, innate **understanding** and reason.
AG : 2 0 :026(045) [0057] us that we would **understand** the word "faith" in the
AG : 2 4 :025(059) [0067] that everyone will **understand** that this error is not
AG : 2 5 :008(062) [0069] heart is desperately corrupt; who can **understand** it?"
AG : 2 6 :020(067) [0073] teaching cannot be **understood** if it is supposed that grace
AG : 2 7 :005(071) [0077] not sufficiently appreciated or **understood** their strength.
AG : 2 7 :010(072) [0077] monks with even a little **understanding** were displeased.
AG : 2 7 :017(073) [0077] may better grasp and **understand** what our teachers teach
AG : 2 7 :029(075) [0079] they came to a right **understanding** they were persuaded
AG : 2 7 :031(076) [0079] not possess sufficient **understanding** to determine or
AG : 2 7 :057(080) [0083] They were unable to **understand** that one is to serve God
AG : 2 8 :064(092) [0093] as long as there is no **understanding** of the righteousness
AG : 2 8 :074(093) [0093] regulations were adopted from want of **understanding**.
AL : 2 0 :017(043) [0055] nor can it be **understood** apart from that conflict.
AL : 2 0 :026(045) [0057] word "faith" is to be **understood** not as knowledge, such
AL : 2 3 :023(055) [0063] This can be readily **understood** now that the prohibition
AL : 2 4 :004(056) [0065] should be used which is **understood** by the people.
AL : 2 6 :020(067) [0073] and this cannot be **understood** if men suppose that they
AL : 2 7 :001(071) [0075] vows will be better **understood** if it is recalled what the
AL : 2 7 :010(072) [0077] in former times who had a little more **understanding**.
AL : 2 7 :017(073) [0077] that our teaching on this topic may better be **understood**.
AL : 2 8 :064(092) [0093] where there is no **understanding** of the righteousness of
AL : 0 0 :003(095) [0095] being briefly set forth, may more readily be **understood**.
AL : 0 0 :005(095) [0095] in order that it may be **understood** that nothing has been
AP : 0 2 :015(102) [0109] Properly **understood**, the old definition says exactly the
AP : 0 4 :002(107) [0121] when it is properly **understood**, it illumines and magnifies
AP : 0 4 :003(107) [0121] For since they **understand** neither the forgiveness of sins
AP : 0 4 :007(108) [0121] reason naturally **understands** the law since it has the same
AP : 0 4 :017(109) [0125] grace," which they **understand** as a disposition inclining
AP : 0 4 :018(109) [0125] man can neither have nor **understand** the love of God.
AP : 0 4 :033(111) [0129] do not need an acute **understanding** but only attentive
AP : 0 4 :034(111) [0129] contain the civil righteousness that reason **understands**.
AP : 0 4 :057(114) [0137] As they **understood** that the Christ would be the price for
AP : 0 4 :078(117) [0143] justification being **understood** as making an unrighteous
AP : 0 4 :084(119) [0145] Experienced consciences can readily **understand** this.
AP : 0 4 :105(122) [0153] contribute less to an **understanding** of Paul than this one
AP : 0 4 :110(123) [0153] can neither render nor **understand** this love unless they
AP : 0 4 :118(123) [0155] how necessary it is to **understand** this faith, for through it
AP : 0 4 :131(125) [0159] the senses and **understanding** of all creatures: "You shall
AP : 0 4 :165(130) [0169] It is hard to **understand** how a man can do away with
AP : 0 4 :221(137) [0181] that they should be **understood** in reference to "faith
AP : 0 4 :224(138) [0181] on their own, for they **understand** neither what
AP : 0 4 :237(140) [0187] they have no more **understanding** than the walls that fling
AP : 0 4 :265(146) [0197] neither looks at nor **understands** faith, it dreams that the
AP : 0 4 :268(147) [0197] If our opponents **understand** Daniel as referring only to
AP : 0 4 :272(148) [0199] penitence we should **understand** that faith is required, not
AP : 0 4 :277(148) [0199] is how it ought to be **understood** so as not to take away
AP : 0 4 :288(151) [0203] works, it can be **understood** and, to some extent, its
AP : 0 4 :288(151) [0203] They did not **understand** why the Fathers had enacted
AP : 0 4 :291(152) [0203] on this will easily **understand** that we are justified neither
AP : 0 4 :297(153) [0205] on all this will easily **understand** that justification must
AP : 0 4 :302(154) [0205] they echo the word "love" without **understanding** it.
AP : 0 4 :303(154) [0205] pious minds will easily **understand** our teaching and that
AP : 0 4 :313(155) [0207] of faith will be clearly **understood**, as well as the reasons
AP : 0 4 :316(156) [0209] From this it is **understandable** why we reject our
AP : 0 4 :353(161) [0217] The devout can **understand** this teaching better than what
AP : 0 4 :373(164) [0221] to his works," we must **understand** not merely outward
AP : 0 4 :377(165) [0223] of Christ cannot be **understood**, and what is left of the
AP : 0 4 :381(165) [0223] If they **understood** it this way, they would be correct
AP : 0 4 :387(166) [0225] Christians need to **understand** this faith, for it brings the
AP : 0 4 :394(167) [0225] righteousness of the law, **understood** as civic uprightness.
AP : 0 7 :013(170) [0231] We must **understand** what it is that chiefly makes us
AP : 0 7 :013(170) [0231] then men would not **understand** that the kingdom of
AP : 0 7 :031(174) [0237] We do not quite **understand** what our opponents mean.
AP : 1 0 :003(179) [0247] to the habit which we **understand** as love, but also by a
AP : 1 1 :008(181) [0251] neither remember nor **understand** most of our sins,
AP : 1 2 :016(184) [0257] All good men will **understand**, therefore, that good and
AP : 1 2 :024(185) [0257] This is how uninformed people **understand** it.
AP : 1 2 :043(187) [0263] This **understanding** of penitence is plain and clear, it adds
AP : 1 2 :046(188) [0263] raised — we are not to **understand** these terms in a
AP : 1 2 :046(188) [0263] should not be **understood** as a Platonic figment but as
AP : 1 2 :048(188) [0265] The sentence is **understood** only amid genuine sorrows
AP : 1 2 :058(190) [0267] It is easier to **understand** the faith proclaimed by the
AP : 1 2 :059(190) [0267] and which we believe all Christians must **understand**.
AP : 1 2 :064(191) [0269] faith in Christ do not **understand** what the forgiveness of
AP : 1 2 :069(192) [0271] the errors of their superiors, without **understanding** them.
AP : 1 2 :083(194) [0275] in order to make our case more easily **understood**.
AP : 1 2 :097(196) [0281] since our opponents **understand** neither the nature of
AP : 1 2 :097(197) [0281] Since they do not **understand** the sayings elsewhere about
AP : 1 2 :101(197) [0281] private absolution **understand** neither the forgiveness of
AP : 1 2 :118(199) [0287] We cannot **understand** which punishments are partly
AP : 1 5 :022(218) [0321] human reason does not **understand** the righteousness of
AP : 1 6 :013(224) [0333] outside our group may **understand** that our doctrine does
AP : 2 3 :035(244) [0373] lust and purity **understood** as the purity of the heart and
AP : 2 3 :070(249) [0383] arguments and **understand** that in the judgment of God
AP : 2 4 :002(249) [0385] from hearing a Mass that he does not **understand**.
AP : 2 4 :002(250) [0385] act of worship even where there is no **understanding**.
AP : 2 4 :003(250) [0385] of those who study and **understand** it, and we insert
AP : 2 4 :005(250) [0385] lessons they do not **understand**, or from ceremonies that
AP : 2 4 :014(251) [0389] described the current **understanding** of sacrifice among
AP : 2 4 :016(252) [0389] can be explained or **understood** in a discussion, and that
AP : 2 4 :023(253) [0391] We can **understand** the meaning of the word more readily
AP : 2 4 :035(256) [0397] for the Mass to be **understood** as a daily sacrifice,
AP : 2 4 :043(258) [0399] questions, which neither they nor the people **understand**.
AP : 2 4 :046(258) [0401] the people has ever **understood** our opponents' doctrine
AP : 2 4 :050(259) [0401] the clergy have ever **understood** our opponents' teaching.
AP : 2 4 :068(262) [0409] and secular men **understand**; it does not talk about faith,
AP : 2 4 :068(262) [0409] about faith, whose true meaning very few **understand**.
AP : 2 4 :088(265) [0413] Properly **understood**, this is not offensive.
AP : 2 4 :092(267) [0417] our opponents who **understand** the meaning of neither
AP : 2 4 :097(268) [0417] For they do not **understand** the righteousness of faith but
AP : 2 4 :099(268) [0419] to let all good men **understand** that we most zealously
AP : 2 7 :001(268) [0419] them the nature of his teaching can be well **understood**.
AP : 2 7 :038(276) [0433] Thus Anthony came to **understand** that justification was
S1 : PR :010(290) [0457] sacraments, with an **understanding** of the various callings
S2 : 0 2 :013(295) [0465] that we do not **understand** for what purpose and to what
S3 : 0 1 :003(302) [0477] a corruption of nature that reason cannot **understand** it.
S3 : 0 1 :004(302) [0477] possesses a right **understanding** and a good will, as the
S3 : 0 3 :009(304) [0481] true repentance so that both may be better **understood**.
S3 : 0 3 :010(305) [0481] is capable of right **understanding** and the will is capable
S3 : 0 3 :016(305) [0483] They **understood** neither of these terms, and to this day
S3 : 0 3 :033(308) [0489] no, not one; no one **understands**, no one seeks for God.
S3 : 0 3 :041(309) [0491] theologians, the jurists, and all men **understand** nothing.
TR : 0 0 :005(320) [0503] our assertion may be **understood**, we must at the outset
TR : 0 0 :056(330) [0521] and obstructs true **understanding** and true judgment on
SC : PR :008(339) [0533] This was well **understood** by our good fathers, who were
SC : PR :016(340) [0535] have a proper **understanding** of the First Commandment,
SC : PR :017(340) [0535] the people may have a richer and fuller **understanding**.
SC : PR :021(340) [0537] but with this **understanding**: No one is to be compelled to
LC : PR :018(361) [0573] fellows do not **understand** a single Psalm, much less the
LC : SP :005(362) [0575] more and have a fuller **understanding** of all Christian
LC : SP :020(364) [0579] these three parts are **understood**, we ought also to know
LC : 0 1 :001(365) [0581] What does this mean, and how is it to be **understood**?
LC : 0 1 :005(365) [0581] so that it may be **understood** and remembered, by citing
LC : 0 1 :013(366) [0583] Thus you can easily **understand** the nature and scope of
LC : 0 1 :023(367) [0587] is a little too subtle to be **understood** by young pupils.
LC : 0 1 :051(371) [0595] asked, "How do you **understand** the Second
LC : 0 1 :062(373) [0597] Now you **understand** what it means to take God's name in
LC : 0 1 :063(373) [0599] same time gives us to **understand** that we are to use his

Continued ▶

LC : 01 :065(373) [0599] If it is so **understood**, you have easily solved the question
LC : 01 :101(379) [0609] always awakens new **understanding**, new pleasure, and a
LC : 01 :157(386) [0627] sunk and may rightly **understand** the Word and will of
LC : 01 :200(392) [0637] are easily **understood** from the preceding one.
LC : 02 :004(411) [0679] simple persons to learn to **understand** the Creed itself.
LC : 02 :013(412) [0681] mind, my reason and **understanding**, and so forth; my
LC : 02 :033(415) [0687] depends on the proper **understanding** of this article.
LC : 02 :043(416) [0689] and does not awaken **understanding** in the heart, all is
LC : 02 :048(416) [0691] by which simple folk **understand** not a group of people
LC : 02 :049(417) [0691] some among us, who **understand** neither Latin nor
LC : 02 :049(417) [0691] no German would use or **understand** such an expression.
LC : 02 :050(417) [0691] the expression may be **understood**; it has become so
LC : 02 :051(417) [0691] by the Holy Spirit in one faith, mind, and **understanding**.
LC : 02 :060(418) [0695] importance, as long as the words are rightly **understood**.
LC : 02 :063(419) [0695] all the wisdom, **understanding**, and reason of men.
LC : 02 :070(420) [0697] After they **understand** the substance of it, they may on
LC : 02 :070(420) [0697] and thus advance and grow richer in **understanding**.
LC : 03 :046(426) [0709] and clear as soon as we **understand** the language, namely,
LC : 04 :002(436) [0733] that it may be readily **understood**, we shall treat it in a
LC : 04 :014(438) [0735] Now you can **understand** how to answer properly the
LC : 04 :023(439) [0737] Nor can we **understand** this better than from the words
LC : 04 :040(441) [0743] It takes special **understanding** to believe this, for it is not
LC : 05 :042(451) [0763] Nevertheless, let it be **understood** that people who abstain
LC : 05 :085(456) [0773] up in Christian doctrine and a right **understanding** of it.
LC : 06 :003(457) [0000] of all, no one taught or **understood** what confession is
LC : 06 :005(457) [0000] We quickly **understand** whatever benefits us, and we
EP : RN :007(465) [0779] should and must be **understood** and judged as good or
EP : RN :008(465) [0779] Holy Scriptures were **understood** by contemporaries in
EP : 02 :002(470) [0787] matters man's **understanding** and reason are blind and
EP : 02 :002(470) [0787] are blind and that he **understands** nothing by his own
EP : 02 :002(470) [0787] and he is not able to **understand** them" when he is
EP : 02 :018(472) [0791] nothing at all) must be **understood** as referring to the
EP : 04 :010(476) [0799] "necessary" are to be **understood** as involving not
EP : 04 :011(477) [0799] spirit," should not be **understood** as though it were left to
EP : 04 :012(477) [0799] however, should be **understood** exactly as our Lord and
EP : 07 :007(482) [0811] of Christ are to be **understood** in no other way than in
EP : 07 :025(484) [0815] are not to be **understood** or believed in their simple
EP : 10 :002(493) [0829] and thus come to an **understanding** with them in such
EP : 10 :011(494) [0831] to or come to an **understanding** with the enemies of the
EP : 11 :022(497) [0837] simple Christian can **understand** what is right and what is
EP : 12 :020(499) [0841] do not have a right **understanding** of Christ as the
SD : PR :004(504) [0851] correctly and soundly **understood** was drawn together
SD : PR :007(505) [0853] to come to an **understanding** with the pope about these
SD : PR :013(506) [0855] and correct **understanding** of our predecessors who
SD : 01 :001(508) [0859] Confession about what original sin, strictly **understood**, is.
SD : 01 :003(509) [0861] declares) we are led to **understand** better and to magnify
SD : 01 :008(510) [0861] does not know and **understand** the true nature of this
SD : 01 :038(515) [0871] faculties of my mind, my reason and **understanding**," etc.
SD : 01 :060(519) [0879] can lead to a right **understanding** and give a correct
SD : 02 :004(520) [0881] and brings them to the saving **understanding** of Christ.
SD : 02 :005(521) [0881] does not and cannot **understand** the Word of God when
SD : 02 :007(521) [0883] powers in any way **understand**, believe, accept, imagine,
SD : 02 :009(522) [0883] this, comprehend it, **understand** it, or believe and accept
SD : 02 :009(522) [0883] reason, the less they **understand** or believe, and until the
SD : 02 :010(522) [0883] and he is not able to **understand** them because they are
SD : 02 :010(522) [0883] are darkened in their **understanding**, alienated from the
SD : 02 :010(522) [0885] and hearing they do not hear, nor do they **understand**.
SD : 02 :010(522) [0885] "No one **understands**, no one seeks for God.
SD : 02 :012(522) [0885] in spiritual matters, to **understand** them, to begin them, to
SD : 02 :012(523) [0885] him, and he is not able to **understand** them" (I Cor. 2:14).
SD : 02 :013(523) [0885] (the natural man's **understanding**) "is hostile to God; it
SD : 02 :015(523) [0887] ten times to give him **understanding** so that he might
SD : 02 :026(526) [0891] and the heart to **understand** the Scriptures and to heed
SD : 02 :026(526) [0891] he opened their minds to **understand** the Scriptures."
SD : 02 :026(526) [0891] God gives an **understanding** heart, seeing eyes, and
SD : 02 :044(529) [0897] his statements to be **understood**, and defends them
SD : 02 :059(532) [0905] moves it, neither does it **understand** or perceive what is
SD : 02 :066(534) [0907] This is to be **understood** in no other way than that the
SD : 02 :066(534) [0907] But if this were to be **understood** as though the converted
SD : 02 :070(535) [0909] to turn from sin, to **understand** and accept the promise of
SD : 02 :089(538) [0915] the contrary, it is his **understanding** that man of himself
SD : 03 :006(540) [0917] comfort or rightly **understand** the riches of the grace of
SD : 03 :036(545) [0929] And the right **understanding** of the exclusive terms in the
SD : 03 :041(546) [0929] This is not to be **understood**, however, as though
SD : 04 :016(554) [0943] context, it is not to be **understood** as implying
SD : 05 :001(558) [0951] and apostles may be explained and **understood** correctly.
SD : 05 :004(558) [0953] in such a way that we **understand** by it the entire teaching
SD : 05 :007(559) [0953] the word is used and **understood** as the entire conversion
SD : 05 :022(562) [0959] although they neither **understood** nor honored him
SD : 05 :027(563) [0961] when it is generally **understood** as referring to the entire
SD : 06 :005(564) [0963] But this dare not be **understood** without qualification, as
SD : 07 :001(569) [0971] and the right **understanding** of the words of Christ and of
SD : 07 :003(569) [0973] Therefore they **understand** this presence of the body of
SD : 07 :005(570) [0973] they still did not **understand** and explain it except as
SD : 07 :006(570) [0973] However, they **understand** that this is so only according
SD : 07 :007(570) [0975] They **understand** the words of the Supper, "This is my
SD : 07 :027(574) [0981] that it is to be **understood** not only with reference to
SD : 07 :033(575) [0983] Dr. Luther, who **understood** the true intention of the
SD : 07 :034(575) [0983] truth and peace can **understand** beyond all doubt what
SD : 07 :038(576) [0985] (that is, it is not to be **understood** as a figurative, flowery
SD : 07 :042(576) [0987] Word of God and so **understood**, taught, and transmitted
SD : 07 :046(577) [0987] command was to be **understood** literally or if it was to
SD : 07 :046(577) [0989] So Abraham **understood** and believed the words and
SD : 07 :048(578) [0989] can and should be **understood** only in their usual, strict,
SD : 07 :050(578) [0989] himself, who best **understands** his words and heart and
SD : 07 :051(578) [0991] this simple and strict **understanding** and commanded them
SD : 07 :060(580) [0995] have unanimously **understood** and explained this passage
SD : 07 :064(581) [0995] command can only be **understood** as referring precisely to
SD : 07 :092(586) [1005] explicit, and clear **understanding** of Christ's word and
SD : 07 :092(586) [1005] stated above, we shall **understand** and believe them in the
SD : 07 :113(589) [1011] are not to be simply **understood** in their strict sense, as
SD : 07 :117(589) [1013] union" is to be **understood** in terms of the relation
SD : 08 :014(594) [1019] union is not to be **understood**, as some have incorrectly
SD : 08 :021(595) [1023] one nature must be taken and **understood** for the other.
SD : 08 :038(598) [1027] they nevertheless **understand** by that only the one nature
SD : 08 :056(601) [1033] of words but is to be **understood** of the person not only
SD : 08 :063(603) [1037] We have never **understood** the term "real exchange" — a
SD : 08 :067(604) [1039] Hence we do not **understand** the testimonies of the
SD : 08 :072(605) [1041] of wisdom and **understanding**, of counsel and might and
SD : 08 :077(606) [1043] We do not **understand** these testimonies to mean that
SD : 11 :012(618) [1067] doubt that the true **understanding** or the right use of the
SD : 11 :024(620) [1069] It should be **understood** as included therein and never be
SD : 11 :095(632) [1095] and foes may clearly **understand** that we have no

Undertake (8), Undertaken (7), Undertaking (1), Undertook (5)
PR : PR :012(006) [0013] about this Christian **undertaking** reached some of us, we
PR : PR :015(007) [0013] to date been able to **undertake** such a plan because
PR : PR :023(012) [0021] purposed, and **undertaken**, and we desire once more to
AG : 18 :007(040) [0053] choice man can also **undertake** evil, as when he wills to
AG : 20 :019(043) [0055] their own efforts, and all sorts of works were **undertaken**.
AG : 20 :033(045) [0057] the philosophers who **undertook** to lead honorable and
AG : 26 :014(066) [0073] been confused, for they **undertook** to collate the
AG : 28 :064(092) [0093] For although they **undertake** to lighten and mitigate
AL : 28 :002(081) [0083] but also have **undertaken** to transfer kingdoms of this
AP : PR :010(099) [0101] Originally we **undertook** the Apology in consultation with
AP : 04 :288(151) [0203] human victims and **undertook** many other painful works
AP : 15 :047(221) [0327] We should **undertake** these exercises not as services that
AP : 27 :038(276) [0433] was not to be attributed to the way he had **undertaken**.
AP : 27 :055(278) [0439] If they **undertook** them in order to teach and exhort the
AP : 27 :058(279) [0439] But those men did not **undertake** their vows with the
S2 : 04 :003(298) [0471] that the pope has **undertaken** and done on the strength of
LC : SP :001(362) [0575] This sermon has been **undertaken** for the instruction of
LC : 03 :025(423) [0705] None of them has ever **undertaken** to pray out of
EP : 06 :004(480) [0807] human devotion they **undertake** self-decreed and
SD : PR :006(504) [0853] might surreptitiously **undertake** to insinuate into the
SD : 02 :012(522) [0885] them, to will them, to **undertake** them, to do them, to

Underwent (1)
AP : 21 :036(234) [0353] public affairs, **underwent** troubles and dangers, helped

Undivided (5)
AP : 01 :001(100) [0103] that there is one **undivided** divine essence, and that there
EP : 07 :011(483) [0811] God and man in one person, inseparable and **undivided**.
SD : 03 :015(541) [0919] God and man in one **undivided** person, he was as little
SD : 07 :094(586) [1005] God and man in one person, **undivided** and inseparable.
SD : 08 :007(592) [1017] henceforth in this single **undivided** person there are two

Undoing (1)
LC : 01 :236(397) [0647] let you acquire to your **undoing** — there will come a day

Undoubtedly (10)
AL : 00 :004(049) [0059] Imperial Majesty will **undoubtedly** discover that the
AP : PR :017(099) [0103] For we have **undoubtedly** brought into view many
AP : 02 :041(105) [0115] This is **undoubtedly** what the Fathers believe.
AP : 04 :199(134) [0175] Such praise **undoubtedly** moves the faithful to good
AP : 11 :003(180) [0249] they are but honest, will **undoubtedly** approve and praise.
AP : 12 :010(184) [0255] They will **undoubtedly** confess that our opponents'
AP : 27 :032(274) [0431] carefully, he will **undoubtedly** discover that even with ten
AP : 28 :005(281) [0445] God **undoubtedly** sees and hears them, and it is to him
TR : 00 :053(329) [0519] of saints, whose blood God will **undoubtedly** avenge.
LC : 01 :305(406) [0667] That sort of thing **undoubtedly** was quite prevalent in the

Undress (1)
AG : 18 :005(040) [0051] whether to dress or **undress**, whether to build a house,

Undue (2)
AG : 00 :001(095) [0095] to avoid prolixity and **undue** length we have indicated
AL : 00 :001(095) [0095] be mentioned, to avoid **undue** length we have discussed

Uneducated (2)
AP : 04 :154(128) [0165] What a disgrace that an **uneducated** woman should
LC : SP :001(362) [0575] for the instruction of children and **uneducated** people.

Unenthusiastic (1)
SD : 04 :019(554) [0945] not only unwilling or **unenthusiastic** but actually wars

Unequal (2)
EP : 12 :029(500) [0843] that the three are **unequal** in essence and properties and
SD : 12 :037(636) [1103] in the Trinity are **unequal** in their essence and properties.

Unequivocal (2), Unequivocally (1)
EP : 10 :006(493) [0831] we should witness an **unequivocal** confession and suffer in
SD : PR :003(501) [0847] they gave a clear and **unequivocal** Christian witness,
SD : PR :019(507) [0857] faith and confession **unequivocally**, clearly, and distinctly

Unexpected (1)
LC : 01 :074(374) [0601] if anyone meets with **unexpected** good fortune, however

Unfailing (1)
SD : 11 :012(618) [1067] clear, certain, and **unfailing** foundation: All Scripture,

Unfair (1)
LC : 04 :037(441) [0741] Therefore they are **unfair** when they cry out against us as

Unfaithful (3), Unfaithfulness (3)
SC : 05 :020(350) [0553] have been disobedient, **unfaithful**, lazy, ill-tempered, or
SC : 05 :022(350) [0553] maidservant, etc., I am **unfaithful** to my master, for here
LC : 01 :151(386) [0625] a gulden by his **unfaithfulness**, he will lose ten elsewhere.
LC : 01 :154(386) [0625] world now so full of **unfaithfulness**, shame, misery, and
LC : 01 :155(386) [0625] and complain of **unfaithfulness**, violence, and injustice;
LC : 01 :225(395) [0643] or maid-servant is **unfaithful** in his or her domestic duty

Unfamiliar (1)
SD : 01 :054(518) [0877] these words are not **unfamiliar**, as did Eusebius,

Unfathomable (1)
LC : 02 :029(414) [0685] Son of God, in his **unfathomable** goodness, had mercy on

Unfit (1), Unfitted (1)
SC : PR :002(338) [0533] pastors are quite incompetent and **unfitted** for teaching.
LC : 0 5 :055(453) [0765] But suppose you say, "What if I feel that I am **unfit**?"

Unformed (2)
SD : 0 1 :036(514) [0869] Thy eyes behold my **unformed** substance; in thy book
SD : 1 1 :004(617) [1063] "Thine eyes beheld my **unformed** substance, in thy book

Unfortunate (1), Unfortunately (10)
AL : 2 7 :008(072) [0077] and saw what **unfortunately** resulted from this
AP : 1 4 :002(214) [0315] of cruelty, they kill the **unfortunate** and innocent men.
SC : PR :002(338) [0533] teaching, and **unfortunately** many pastors are quite
LC : 0 1 :058(372) [0597] **Unfortunately** it is now a common calamity all over the
LC : 0 1 :214(394) [0641] evil to mention, as **unfortunately** has been only too well
LC : 0 4 :001(436) [0733] a Christian, although **unfortunately** in the past nothing
LC : 0 4 :056(443) [0747] indeed was right, but **unfortunately** I did not receive it
LC : 0 5 :084(456) [0773] This misery, **unfortunately**, you do not see, though God
LC : 0 6 :005(457) [0000] **Unfortunately**, men have learned in only too well; they do
SD : 0 7 :001(568) [0971] **Unfortunately**, however, in later years a number of
SD : 1 2 :008(633) [1097] beliefs of the papacy, **unfortunately** accepted in their

Unfounded (2)
PR : PR :009(006) [0011] By this **unfounded** allegation many pious hearts were
AG : 0 0 :002(048) [0059] then, there is nothing **unfounded** or defective in the

Unfrocked (1)
AP : 2 2 :008(237) [0359] that they had been **unfrocked** and were no longer

Unfruitful (3)
LC : 0 4 :073(445) [0751] where faith is lacking, it remains a mere **unfruitful** sign.
LC : 0 5 :030(449) [0759] body can never be an **unfruitful**, vain thing, impotent and
SD : 0 4 :015(553) [0943] to be a barren, **unfruitful** tree since no good fruits

Ungodliness (3), Ungodly (39)
AG : 1 7 :003(038) [0051] elect but to condemn **ungodly** men and the devil to hell
AG : 1 9 :000(041) [0053] of the devil and of all **ungodly** men; as soon as God
AG : 2 0 :023(044) [0055] by the devil and the **ungodly**, who also believe the history
AG : 2 0 :025(044) [0057] For the devil and the **ungodly** do not believe this article
AG : 2 0 :025(044) [0057] it such knowledge as the devil and **ungodly** men possess.
AG : 2 7 :040(077) [0081] are not binding, for an **ungodly** vow, made contrary to
AG : 2 8 :021(084) [0087] Christian community the **ungodly** whose wicked conduct
AL : 1 7 :003(038) [0051] life and endless joy, but **ungodly** men and devils he will
AL : 1 7 :005(039) [0051] of the world, the **ungodly** being suppressed everywhere.
AL : 1 9 :000(041) [0053] will of the wicked, that is, of the devil and **ungodly** men.
AL : 2 0 :023(044) [0055] history (such as is in the **ungodly** and the devil), but it
AL : 2 0 :025(044) [0057] heathen, for devils and **ungodly** men are not able to
AL : 2 0 :026(045) [0057] such as is in the **ungodly**, but as confidence which
AL : 2 0 :031(045) [0057] man's powers are full of **ungodly** affections and are too
AL : 0 0 :004(049) [0059] so intolerable as those **ungodly** and malicious men
AL : 2 4 :032(059) [0067] for the Jews and the **ungodly** can also remember this.
AL : 2 8 :021(084) [0087] fellowship of the church **ungodly** persons whose
AL : 0 0 :005(095) [0097] into our churches of any new and **ungodly** doctrines.
AP : 0 4 :089(120) [0149] in him who justifies the **ungodly**, his faith is reckoned as
AP : 0 4 :258(144) [0193] do evil," as he denounces **ungodly** hearts and requires
AP : 0 4 :290(151) [0203] The **ungodliness** of the first is obvious because it teaches
AP : 0 4 :300(153) [0205] beware, therefore, of yielding to their **ungodly** counsels.
AP : 0 4 :396(167) [0227] and clear that their **ungodliness** comes out into the open.
AP : 0 7 :009(169) [0229] is an infinite number of **ungodly** within the church who
AP : 0 7 :022(172) [0235] warning that there will be **ungodly** teachers and wolves.
AP : 0 7 :022(172) [0235] Though wolves and **ungodly** teachers may run rampant in
AP : 0 9 :003(178) [0245] godly minds against the **ungodly** and fanatical opinions
AP : 1 3 :018(213) [0313] Yet this **ungodly** and wicked notion is taught with great
AP : 1 5 :011(216) [0317] for Christ's sake, it is an **ungodly** error to maintain that
AP : 1 7 :001(224) [0335] but condemning the **ungodly** to endless torment with the
AP : 1 8 :005(225) [0335] is at work in the **ungodly**, never stops inciting this
AP : 1 8 :006(225) [0335] Therefore they are **ungodly**; for "a bad tree cannot bear
AP : 1 8 :008(226) [0337] is hard to keep this faith; for the **ungodly** it is impossible.
AP : 2 1 :038(234) [0355] these monstrous and **ungodly** tales because they make
AP : 2 3 :034(244) [0373] virginity is impure in the **ungodly**, therefore, so marriage
S3 : 0 3 :001(303) [0479] heaven against all **ungodliness** and wickedness of men."
TR : 0 0 :041(328) [0517] also commanded that **ungodly** teachers should be
SD : 0 3 :034(545) [0927] him who justifies the **ungodly**, his faith is reckoned as
SD : 0 6 :005(564) [0963] the just, as St. Paul says (I Tim. 1:9), but for the **ungodly**.
SD : 1 0 :022(615) [1061] also commanded that **ungodly** teachers should be
SD : 1 1 :005(617) [1065] both the godly and the **ungodly**, but only over the
SD : 1 1 :006(617) [1065] of his elect, and thereby the **ungodly** are confounded.

Ungrateful (3)
PR : PR :005(004) [0009] of our own and the **ungrateful** world's impenitence and
AP : 1 2 :131(202) [0291] and true faith is not **ungrateful** to God or contemptuous
LC : 0 3 :047(426) [0711] Word of God but are **ungrateful** for it and fail to live

Unhappiness (1)
LC : 0 1 :155(386) [0625] that we have nothing but **unhappiness** without mercy.

Unheard (2)
AP : 0 4 :399(168) [0227] their spirit from the **unheard** of cruelty which, as
AP : 1 4 :002(214) [0315] or else, in their **unheard** of cruelty, they kill the

Unhewn (1)
SD : 0 2 :019(524) [0889] human touch, or to an **unhewn** timber, or to a wild,

Unhindered (2)
SD : 0 6 :006(565) [0965] all, spontaneously and **unhindered**, without any
SD : 0 6 :025(568) [0971] without coercion, **unhindered**, perfectly, completely, and

Unholy (5)
S3 : 0 8 :013(313) [0497] have moved them to speak while they were still **unholy**.
LC : 0 1 :087(377) [0605] So it becomes holy or **unholy** on your account, according
LC : 0 1 :087(377) [0605] as you spend the day in doing holy or **unholy** things.
LC : 0 1 :093(377) [0607] from God's Word is **unholy** in the sight of God, no
LC : 0 3 :045(426) [0709] profaned, thus rendering **unholy** by misuse that which is

Uniform (3)
AP : 0 7 :046(177) [0243] They require **uniform** human ceremonies for the unity of
AP : 1 5 :035(220) [0325] soldiers wear one kind of **uniform** and scholars another.
SC : PR :007(339) [0533] instructed on the basis of a **uniform**, fixed text and form.

Uniformity (2), Uniformly (1)
AG : 0 7 :003(032) [0047] by men, should be observed **uniformly** in all places.
AG : 2 6 :043(070) [0075] was not necessary to maintain **uniformity** in such customs.
AP : 0 7 :045(177) [0243] regard as necessary a **uniformity** of observances in food,

Unimpaired (3)
AP : 0 2 :008(101) [0107] to human nature **unimpaired** power to love God above
LC : 0 5 :005(447) [0755] sacrament remain **unimpaired** and inviolate even if we use
EP : 0 1 :014(468) [0783] nature has retained **unimpaired** its powers for good even

Unimportant (2)
LC : 0 1 :098(378) [0609] Do not regard it as an optional or **unimportant** matter.
LC : 0 2 :016(412) [0681] preserve any of them, however small and **unimportant**.

Unimpregnable (1)
SD : PR :003(502) [0847] has remained unrefuted and **unimpregnable** until this day.

Uninformed (1)
AP : 1 2 :024(185) [0257] This is how **uninformed** people understand it.

Uninitiated (6)
AP : 0 7 :032(174) [0239] From this the **uninitiated** have concluded that there can
AP : 1 2 :123(201) [0289] us so that when the **uninitiated** hear this they will
AP : 1 2 :123(201) [0289] hatred, so that the **uninitiated** may demand that such
AP : 1 2 :173(209) [0305] this is intended to put something over on the **uninitiated**.
AP : 2 1 :016(231) [0347] As to the rest even the **uninitiated** can pass judgment.
AP : 2 2 :008(237) [0359] sand in the eyes of the **uninitiated**, who when they hear

Uninstructed (2)
SD : 0 1 :045(516) [0873] want to scandalize the **uninstructed** people although they
SD : 0 1 :054(517) [0877] the assemblies of the **uninstructed** ought rightly be spared

Unintelligible (1)
LC : 0 2 :047(416) [0691] was missing, and it is **unintelligible** in our translation.

Unintentionally (1)
LC : 0 1 :225(395) [0645] inadvertently and **unintentionally** — a servant can cheat

Uninterested (1)
LC : 0 1 :037(369) [0591] he is unconcerned or **uninterested** in such matters, he

Union (62)
PR : PR :020(010) [0017] discussion of the personal **union** of the two natures in
PR : PR :021(011) [0019] outside the personal **union**, or in such a way that even in
PR : PR :021(011) [0019] that even in the personal **union** it is alleged to have this
PR : PR :021(011) [0019] account of the personal **union**, which is an inscrutable
AP : 2 3 :009(240) [0367] and correctly that the **union** of man and woman is by
AP : 2 3 :011(241) [0367] put by the jurists: The **union** of man and woman is by
AP : 2 3 :029(243) [0371] calls marriage a divine **union** when he says in Matt. 19:6,
AP : 2 4 :068(262) [0407] symbolizing the mutual **union** and friendship among
SC : 0 2 :006(345) [0545] earth and preserves it in **union** with Jesus Christ in the
EP : 0 7 :007(482) [0811] of the sacramental **union** they are truly the body and
EP : 0 7 :015(483) [0811] of the sacramental **union** in a supernatural and heavenly
EP : 0 8 :002(487) [0817] been, Because of personal **union** in the person of Christ,
EP : 0 8 :003(487) [0819] boldly that the "personal **union** makes merely the names
EP : 0 8 :009(487) [0819] confess that this personal **union** is not a combination or
EP : 0 8 :009(487) [0819] account of the personal **union**), as when two boards are
EP : 0 8 :009(488) [0819] Out of this personal **union** and the resultant exalted and
EP : 0 8 :009(488) [0819] have illustrated this **union** and sharing of the natures by
EP : 0 8 :009(488) [0819] iron and the **union** of body and soul in man.
EP : 0 8 :013(488) [0821] a profound and ineffable **union** and communion with the
EP : 0 8 :016(488) [0821] According to the personal **union** he always possessed this
EP : 0 8 :024(490) [0823] 5. That personal **union** achieves only common names and
SD : 0 2 :040(528) [0895] earth and preserves it in **union** with Jesus Christ in the
SD : 0 7 :014(572) [0977] that through sacramental **union** the bread is the body of
SD : 0 7 :018(572) [0979] and that the sacramental **union** is intended to mean
SD : 0 7 :035(575) [0983] indicate the sacramental **union** between the
SD : 0 7 :037(575) [0985] have cited the personal **union** as an analogy to the words
SD : 0 7 :038(576) [0985] sacrament, though the **union** of the body and blood of
SD : 0 7 :038(576) [0985] wine is not a personal **union**, like that of the two natures
SD : 0 7 :038(576) [0985] Christ, but a sacramental **union**, as Dr. Luther and our
SD : 0 7 :044(577) [0987] and a true bond and **union** of Christians with Christ their
SD : 0 7 :050(578) [0989] his abiding covenant and **union**, he uses no flowery
SD : 0 7 :117(589) [1013] the term "sacramental **union**" is to be understood in terms
SD : 0 8 :012(593) [1019] through the personal **union** with the deity and afterward
SD : 0 8 :014(594) [1019] 9. But this personal **union** is not to be understood, as
SD : 0 8 :018(594) [1021] account of this personal **union** and communion, the
SD : 0 8 :018(594) [1021] illustrated the personal **union** and communion by
SD : 0 8 :019(595) [1021] But the **union** of the divine and human natures in the
SD : 0 8 :019(595) [1021] For the communion and **union** between the divine and
SD : 0 8 :019(595) [1021] since on account of this **union** and communion God is
SD : 0 8 :020(595) [1021] account of this personal **union**, without which such a true
SD : 0 8 :022(595) [1023] words, "communion" and "**union**," in expounding this
SD : 0 8 :023(595) [1023] Because of this personal **union** and communion of the
SD : 0 8 :023(595) [1023] If the personal **union** and communion of the natures in
SD : 0 8 :024(595) [1023] account of this personal **union** and communion of the
SD : 0 8 :029(597) [1025] and in the personal **union** of both natures in Christ, the
SD : 0 8 :030(597) [1025] and in this personal **union** they have such an
SD : 0 8 :031(597) [1025] explained the personal **union** (that is, the fact that the
SD : 0 8 :032(597) [1025] continue if the personal **union** or communion of natures
SD : 0 8 :033(597) [1027] on earth is the personal **union**, as Paul says, "Great
SD : 0 8 :041(599) [1029] because of this personal **union**, all that happens to the
SD : 0 8 :048(600) [1031] natures in the personal **union** have nothing else and
SD : 0 8 :050(600) [1031] that even in the personal **union** with the deity the human
SD : 0 8 :051(601) [1033] through the personal **union**, glorification, and exaltation.
SD : 0 8 :053(601) [1033] through the personal **union**, glorification, or exaltation
SD : 0 8 :064(603) [1037] manner of the personal **union**, that is, because the

Continued ▶

SD : 0 8 :066(604) [1039] account and through this **union** the glowing iron has the
SD : 0 8 :070(605) [1041] is because of the personal **union** that Christ says, also
SD : 0 8 :073(605) [1041] that through personal **union** the entire fullness of the
SD : 0 8 :074(606) [1043] man, through the personal **union**, he really and truly has
SD : 0 8 :076(606) [1043] Because of this personal **union** and the resultant
SD : 0 8 :076(606) [1043] essence outside of this **union**, cannot intrinsically be or
SD : 0 8 :089(609) [1047] because of the personal **union** the human nature has

Unique (5)
LC : 0 2 :042(416) [0689] the first place, he has a **unique** community in the world.
EP : 1 2 :005(498) [0839] not consist wholly in the **unique** merit of Christ, but in
SD : 0 3 :030(544) [0925] pure grace because of the **unique** merit of Christ, the
SD : 0 7 :042(576) [0985] set forth above rests on a **unique**, firm, immovable, and
SD : 0 7 :043(576) [0987] concerning whom, as our **unique** teacher, the earnest

Unit (1)
SD : 1 1 :014(619) [1069] we must always take as one **unit** the entire doctrine of

Unite (2), United (32)
PR : PR :022(012) [0019] of the divine Word and **unite** with us and our churches
AG : PR :002(025) [0039] parties among us to **unite** the same in agreement on one
AG : PR :010(025) [0041] and we may be **united** in one, true religion, even as we are
AG : 0 3 :002(029) [0045] are so inseparably **united** in one person that there is one
LC : 0 2 :051(417) [0691] a variety of gifts, yet is **united** in love without sect or
LC : 0 4 :046(442) [0743] the body because it is **united** with the soul and
EP : 0 3 :001(472) [0791] natures are personally **united** to one another (Jer. 23:6;
EP : 0 8 :003(487) [0817] natures are personally **united** in such a way that neither
EP : 0 8 :005(487) [0819] natures are personally **united** in Christ in such a way that
EP : 0 8 :009(487) [0819] 5. Since both natures are **united** personally (that is, in one
EP : 0 8 :011(488) [0821] not personally and truly **united** with the Son of God and
EP : 0 8 :015(488) [0821] nature was personally **united** with the Son of the Most
SD : 0 7 :005(570) [0973] here upon earth, are **united** with the body of Christ,
SD : 0 7 :008(570) [0975] or symbolically **united** with the bread in such a way that
SD : 0 7 :014(571) [0977] other way permanently **united** with it apart from the use
SD : 0 7 :036(575) [0985] that both untransformed natures are personally **united**.
SD : 0 7 :037(575) [0985] natures are indivisibly **united**, so in the Holy Supper the
SD : 0 7 :059(580) [0993] whereby believers are **united** with Christ, just as the Word
SD : 0 7 :059(580) [0993] whereby we are spiritually **united** with Christ and are
SD : 0 8 :011(593) [1019] that the two natures are **united** in such a way that they
SD : 0 8 :013(594) [1019] when the divine and human nature were personally **united**.
SD : 0 8 :014(594) [1019] and the human, are **united** with each other like two
SD : 0 8 :017(594) [1021] the person of Christ are **united** in such a way that they
SD : 0 8 :025(596) [1023] had not been personally **united** with the divine nature and
SD : 0 8 :029(597) [1025] since no human being is **united** in this manner with the
SD : 0 8 :030(597) [1025] natures are personally **united** in such a way that in Christ
SD : 0 8 :031(597) [1025] and human natures are **united** with each other in such a
SD : 0 8 :044(599) [1031] since God and man are **united** in one person, it is correct
SD : 0 8 :051(600) [1031] in Christ is personally **united** with the divine nature in
SD : 0 8 :060(602) [1035] both natures in Christ are **united** in such a way that they
SD : 0 8 :066(604) [1039] fire — but since the fire is **united** with the iron, it
SD : 0 8 :070(604) [1041] nor is he personally **united** with them as in the case of
SD : 0 8 :073(605) [1041] to the flesh that is personally **united** with the Son of God.
SD : 0 8 :085(608) [1047] and the humanity were **united** in one person this man,

Unity (37)
AG : PR :004(025) [0039] and live together in **unity** and in one fellowship and
AG : PR :010(025) [0041] practical and equitable ways as may restore **unity**.
AG : PR :013(026) [0041] allow, that may serve the cause of Christian **unity**.
AG : 0 7 :002(032) [0047] it is sufficient for the true **unity** of the Christian church
AG : 0 7 :003(032) [0047] not necessary for the true **unity** of the Christian church
AG : 0 0 :001(048) [0059] contrary to all Christian **unity** and love, and do so
AG : 2 6 :044(070) [0075] fasting does not destroy **unity** in faith," and there is a
AG : 2 6 :044(070) [0075] is not in conflict with the **unity** of Christendom.
AG : 2 8 :071(093) [0093] should restore peace and **unity** at the expense of their
AG : 2 8 :074(094) [0093] changes do not destroy the **unity** of Christian churches.
AL : 0 1 :001(027) [0043] of Nicaea concerning the **unity** of the divine essence and
AL : 0 3 :002(029) [0045] conjoined in the **unity** of his person, one Christ, true God
AL : 0 7 :002(032) [0047] For the true **unity** of the church it is enough to agree
AL : 2 6 :044(070) [0075] fasting does not destroy **unity** in faith," and Pope Gregory
AL : 2 6 :044(070) [0075] such diversity does not violate the **unity** of the church.
AL : 2 8 :074(093) [0093] does not impair the **unity** of the church inasmuch as
AP : 0 3 :001(107) [0119] human nature into the **unity** of his person; that this same
AP : 0 4 :235(140) [0185] when Paul is speaking of **unity** and peace in the church.
AP : 0 7 :030(173) [0237] we said, "For the true **unity** of the church it is enough to
AP : 0 7 :031(174) [0237] about true spiritual **unity**, without which there can be no
AP : 0 7 :031(174) [0237] For this **unity**, we say, a similarity of human rites,
AP : 0 7 :033(174) [0239] night does not harm the **unity** of the church, so we believe
AP : 0 7 :033(174) [0239] so we believe that the true **unity** of the church is not
AP : 0 7 :034(175) [0239] it is necessary for the true **unity** of the church that human
AP : 0 7 :045(177) [0243] human observances does not harm the **unity** of the faith.
AP : 0 7 :046(177) [0243] human ceremonies for the **unity** of the church while they
AP : 1 5 :018(217) [0319] church that for the true **unity** of the church it is not
S 2 : 0 4 :007(299) [0473] adhere, in order that the **unity** of Christendom might
S 2 : 0 4 :009(300) [0473] joined together in **unity** of doctrine, faith, sacraments,
S 3 : 1 0 :001(314) [0497] (for the sake of love and **unity**, but not of necessity) to
S 3 : 1 5 :005(317) [0501] sake of peace and general **unity** among the Christians who
LC : 0 2 :054(417) [0693] God's Word in the **unity** of the Christian church, yet
EP : 0 1 :005(466) [0781] of God assumed into the **unity** of his person this same
EP : 0 8 :014(488) [0821] which he assumed into the **unity** of his divine person and
SD : 0 8 :006(592) [1017] human nature into the **unity** of his person, not in such a
SD : 0 8 :007(592) [1017] assumed in time into the **unity** of the person of the Son
SD : 1 0 :019(614) [1059] (for the sake of love and **unity**, but not of necessity) to

Universal (29), Universally (2)
PR : PR :003(003) [0007] consensus which the **universal** and orthodox church of
AG : 0 0 :001(047) [0059] opposed to that of the **universal** Christian church, or even
AG : 2 8 :072(093) [0093] contrary to the custom of the **universal** Christian church.
AG : 0 0 :005(095) [0095] to Holy Scripture or the **universal** Christian church.
AP : 0 4 :256(144) [0193] outward works, this **universal** statement must be
AP : 0 4 :283(149) [0201] Our opponents misinterpret the **universal** particle "all."
AP : 0 4 :283(150) [0201] transferring the **universal** particle to a single part: "All
AP : 0 7 :030(174) [0237] article, but if we mean "**universal** rites" they disapprove
AP : 0 7 :031(174) [0237] of human rites, whether **universal** or particular, is not
AP : 0 7 :031(174) [0237] traditions, whether **universal** or particular, contribute
AP : 0 7 :033(174) [0239] we like it when **universal** rites are observed for the sake
AP : 0 7 :038(175) [0241] Our opponents say that **universal** traditions should be
AP : 0 7 :046(177) [0243] which certainly was previously a **universal** ordinance.
AP : 0 7 :046(177) [0243] But if **universal** ordinances are necessary, why do they
AP : 1 2 :003(182) [0253] salutary, and necessary for the **universal** church of Christ.
AP : 1 2 :066(191) [0271] be interpreted as the consensus of the **universal** church.
AP : 1 2 :155(207) [0301] they construct the **universal** rule that for the forgiveness
AP : 1 2 :156(207) [0301] it does not follow as a **universal** rule that over and above
AP : 1 5 :050(222) [0329] they require so-called "**universal** rites" as necessary for
AP : 2 0 :009(228) [0341] which this article of ours offers to the **universal** church.
AP : 2 1 :009(230) [0345] prayed for the church **universal** while they were on earth.
AP : 2 3 :019(242) [0369] wants the rest to use the **universal** law of nature which he
AP : 2 7 :049(277) [0437] and persons; but the example of obedience is **universal**.
AP : 2 8 :021(284) [0449] it does not set down the **universal** commandment that we
TR : 0 0 :005(320) [0503] that the pope is the **universal** bishop or, as they put it, the
TR : 0 0 :019(323) [0509] objected to having himself designated as **universal** bishop.
LC : 0 1 :210(393) [0641] estate, but the most **universal** and the noblest, pervading
LC : 0 1 :258(400) [0653] It is the **universal** misfortune of the world that men of
LC : 0 6 :011(458) [0000] However, besides our **universal** guilt there is also a
SD : PR :010(506) [0855] only to have a single, **universally** accepted, certain, and
SD : PR :011(506) [0855] as the common and **universally** accepted belief of our

Universe (4)
AL : 2 8 :045(088) [0089] elemental spirits of the **universe**, why do you live as if you
AP : 0 7 :035(175) [0239] elemental spirits of the **universe**, why do you live as if you
AP : 0 7 :050(178) [0245] For as this **universe** and the fixed movements of the stars
AP : 2 3 :008(240) [0367] yearly the fields are clothed as long as this **universe** exists.

Universities (1)
SD : 0 2 :090(538) [0915] young students at our **universities** have been greatly

Univocally (1)
PR : PR :021(010) [0019] has not been used **univocally** by teachers in the schools

Unjust (21), Unjustly (4)
AG : 2 2 :010(050) [0061] and also contrary to the ancient canons, is **unjust**.
AG : 0 1 :001(056) [0065] We are **unjustly** accused of having abolished the Mass.
AG : 2 4 :025(059) [0067] will understand that this error is not **unjustly** condemned.
AL : 2 8 :072(093) [0093] ask only that they relax **unjust** burdens which are new
AP : 0 4 :185(132) [0173] "Being sick in itself, an **unjust** cause needs wise remedies."
AP : 1 2 :169(209) [0305] a robber as long as he **unjustly** holds on to another man's
AP : 1 4 :005(215) [0315] our protest against the **unjust** cruelty of the bishops, we
AP : 2 3 :051(246) [0377] even if the law were not **unjust**, it is dangerous to public
AP : 2 3 :059(247) [0379] in the defense of this **unjust** law, the dissolution of
TR : 0 0 :035(326) [0513] of Germany, with **unjust** excommunications and wars,
TR : 0 0 :041(327) [0517] doctrines, blasphemies, and **unjust** cruelties of the pope.
TR : 0 0 :042(328) [0517] with and not to support impiety and **unjust** cruelty.
TR : 0 0 :053(329) [0519] a crime it is to support **unjust** cruelty in the murder of
TR : 0 0 :058(330) [0521] flee from idolatry, impious doctrines, and **unjust** cruelty.
TR : 0 0 :078(333) [0527] they have framed certain **unjust** laws concerning marriage
TR : 0 0 :078(333) [0527] spiritual relationship are **unjust**, and equally unjust is the
TR : 0 0 :078(333) [0527] are unjust, and equally **unjust** is the tradition which
TR : 0 0 :078(333) [0527] **Unjust**, too, is the law that in general approves all
TR : 0 0 :078(333) [0527] law concerning the celibacy of priests is likewise **unjust**.
TR : 0 0 :078(333) [0527] out that there are many **unjust** papal laws on
TR : 0 0 :079(333) [0527] finally, they observe **unjust** laws in matrimonial cases;
LC : 0 1 :224(395) [0643] else than to acquire another's property by **unjust** means.
SD : 0 7 :067(581) [0997] these it is evident how **unjustly** and poisonously the
SD : 1 0 :022(615) [1061] doctrines, blasphemies, and **unjust** cruelties of the pope.
SD : 1 0 :023(615) [1061] with and not to support impiety and **unjust** cruelty."

Unkind (1)
AG : 0 0 :001(048) [0059] were heretical, act in an **unkind** and hasty fashion,

Unknown (8)
AL : 2 6 :042(070) [0075] human terms was not **unknown** to the Fathers, for Easter
AL : 2 7 :028(075) [0079] Yet it is not **unknown** to what an extent perpetual
AP : 1 2 :032(186) [0259] God's wrath against sin, **unknown** to men who walk in
AP : 1 2 :122(200) [0287] Scripture, though it was **unknown** in the time of Peter
EP : 0 1 :023(469) [0785] and, besides, they are **unknown** to the common man.
EP : 1 2 :029(500) [0843] is an entirely new sect, **unknown** in Christendom until
SD : 0 7 :102(587) [1007] is true, even though **unknown** to us, we should not give
SD : 0 8 :075(606) [1043] assumed human nature many things are **unknown** to him.

Unlawful (1)
AP : 0 7 :041(176) [0241] of divine right, it was **unlawful** for men to assume the

Unlearned (5)
AL : 2 4 :003(056) [0065] especially in order that the **unlearned** may be taught.
AP : 1 1 :006(181) [0251] to accustom the **unlearned** to enumerate certain things so
SC : PR :008(339) [0535] to the young and **unlearned** in such a way that we do not
LC : 0 4 :051(443) [0745] best and strongest proof for the simple and **unlearned**.
EP : 0 1 :023(469) [0785] delivered to common, **unlearned** people, but simple folk

Unlearning (1)
AL : 2 0 :004(041) [0053] things, they are now **unlearning** them and do not preach

Unless (85)
AG : PR :023(027) [0043] following negotiations (**unless** the matters in dissension
AG : 2 6 :029(068) [0075] nobody is a Christian **unless** he performs such services.
AG : 2 8 :041(087) [0089] case sin is not forgiven **unless** forgiveness is secured from
AG : 2 8 :068(093) [0093] or help to consciences **unless** this mitigation is practiced,
AG : 2 8 :070(093) [0093] no one to the ministry **unless** he first swears an oath that
AL : 1 4 :000(036) [0049] or administer the sacraments **unless** he is regularly called.
AL : 2 4 :006(056) [0065] for none are admitted **unless** they are first heard and
AL : 2 8 :068(093) [0093] to counsel consciences **unless** this mitigation is practiced,
AL : 2 8 :070(093) [0093] no one to the ministry **unless** he swears that he will not
AP : 0 2 :033(104) [0113] of the grace of Christ **unless** we acknowledge our faults.
AP : 0 2 :033(104) [0113] hypocrisy before God **unless** we acknowledge that of
AP : 0 2 :043(106) [0117] Or they say that nothing is sin **unless** it is voluntary.
AP : 0 2 :050(106) [0119] we cannot know his blessings **unless** we recognize our evil.
AP : 0 4 :020(110) [0125] headlong into despair, **unless** they hear, beyond the

Continued ▶

A P : 0 4 :031(111) [0129] in John 3:5 it is written, "**Unless** one is born of water and
A P : 0 4 :036(112) [0131] is impossible to love God **unless** faith has first accepted
A P : 0 4 :036(112) [0131] wrath cannot love him **unless** it sees that he is reconciled.
A P : 0 4 :051(114) [0135] suffered, and was raised **unless** we add this article, the
A P : 0 4 :070(116) [0141] we cannot keep the law **unless** we first receive the Holy
A P : 0 4 :110(123) [0153] fact, we do not love at all **unless** our hearts are sure that
A P : 0 4 :110(123) [0153] nor understand this love **unless** they believe that the
A P : 0 4 :132(125) [0159] correctly keep the law **unless** by faith we have received
A P : 0 4 :157(128) [0165] the forgiveness of sins **unless** he keeps the whole law,
A P : 0 4 :232(139) [0185] to preserve tranquility **unless** men cover and forgive
A P : 0 4 :243(141) [0189] which cannot endure **unless** pastors and churches
A P : 0 4 :256(144) [0193] we cannot keep the law **unless** we have been reborn by
A P : 0 4 :257(144) [0193] cannot find peace **unless** they hear the voice of God,
A P : 0 4 :263(146) [0195] do not take hold of it **unless** they truly believe and by
A P : 0 4 :265(146) [0197] and it cannot be driven out **unless** we are divinely taught.
A P : 0 4 :267(147) [0197] remission of punishment **unless** the heart first receives
A P : 0 4 :298(153) [0205] bring against this proof **unless** he wants utterly to abolish
A P : 0 4 :310(155) [0207] offer anything to God **unless** we have first been reconciled
A P : 0 4 :311(155) [0207] we cannot obey the law **unless** we have been reborn
A P : 0 4 :311(155) [0207] and we cannot love God **unless** we have received the
A P : 0 4 :345(160) [0217] **Unless** it is qualified, this statement seems absurd.
A P : 0 4 :368(163) [0221] would not please God **unless** we had been accepted
A P : 1 2 :032(186) [0259] nature cannot bear it **unless** it is sustained by the Word
A P : 1 2 :062(190) [0269] can be said to receive absolution **unless** he believes it.
A P : 1 2 :088(195) [0277] nor consciences quieted **unless** we know it is God's
A P : 1 2 :113(199) [0285] or the notorious sinners **unless** they had given public
A P : 1 2 :118(199) [0287] by the power of the keys, **unless** they say that part of the
A P : 1 2 :126(201) [0289] are many threats which, **unless** you take care, indicate a
A P : 1 3 :018(213) [0313] doctors who teach that **unless** there is some obstacle, the
A P : 1 3 :020(213) [0313] A promise is useless **unless** faith accepts it.
A P : 1 4 :001(214) [0315] and the sacraments in the church **unless** he is duly called.
A P : 1 6 :012(224) [0333] satisfy good consciences **unless** they keep the rule in
A P : 2 0 :008(227) [0341] tempts them to despair **unless** they know that they must
A P : 2 4 :056(259) [0403] not merit reconciliation — **unless** by analogy, since they
A P : 2 4 :070(262) [0409] As the promise is useless **unless** faith accepts it, so the
A P : 2 4 :086(265) [0413] *agape* in some places, **unless** some one prefers to think it
A P : 2 7 :032(274) [0431] have any good work at all **unless** he has given this, too;
A P : 2 7 :043(276) [0435] it to monastic life, **unless** perhaps the statement that they
A P : 2 8 :004(281) [0445] with horrible punishments **unless** they act in clear
S 2 : 0 4 :004(299) [0473] no Christian can be saved **unless** he is obedient to the
S 2 : 0 4 :004(299) [0473] is nothing and all in vain **unless** you consider me your god
S 3 : 0 3 :018(306) [0483] have laughed than wept, **unless** perchance he was really
L C : 0 1 :094(378) [0607] properly called holy work **unless** the doer himself is first
L C : 0 1 :128(383) [0617] and considers this, **unless** he is led to it by the Holy
L C : 0 1 :265(401) [0657] has seen a sin committed, **unless** he has been authorized
L C : 0 1 :270(401) [0657] his honor and good name **unless** these have first been
L C : 0 1 :285(403) [0661] whether truly or falsely, **unless** it is done with proper
L C : 0 2 :038(415) [0689] take him as our Lord, **unless** these were first offered to us
L C : 0 3 :074(430) [0719] in security or happiness **unless** he gives us a stable,
L C : 0 3 :091(432) [0723] In short, **unless** God constantly forgives, we are lost.
L C : 0 4 :033(440) [0741] they cannot be received **unless** we believe them
L C : 0 5 :041(451) [0763] that no one should go **unless** he feels a hunger and thirst
L C : 0 5 :059(453) [0767] As St. Hilary has said, "**Unless** a man has committed such
L C : 0 5 :086(456) [0773] these and other teachings **unless** we train the people who
E P : 0 2 :006(470) [0787] and watering are in vain **unless** he "gives the growth."
E P : 0 3 :023(475) [0797] righteousness and that **unless** they are present a person
E P : 0 8 :039(491) [0827] Hence, **unless** we refute these errors on the firm basis of
E P : 1 2 :027(500) [0843] and genuine sacraments **unless** he is himself truly reborn,
S D : 0 1 :006(509) [0861] death, and of damnation **unless** we are redeemed from
S D : 0 1 :031(513) [0869] entire corrupted nature **unless** the sin is forgiven for
S D : 0 2 :011(522) [0885] righteousness and life, **unless** the Son of God has
S D : 0 2 :016(523) [0887] **Unless** God himself is our teacher, we cannot study and
S D : 0 2 :018(524) [0889] resists God and his will **unless** the Holy Spirit illuminates
S D : 0 2 :024(526) [0891] hostile to the will of God **unless** the Holy Spirit is active
S D : 0 2 :026(526) [0891] one can come to Christ **unless** the Father draws him
S D : 0 5 :007(559) [0953] of man, as in Luke 13:5, "**Unless** you repent you will all
S D : 0 5 :009(559) [0955] conversion to God **unless** there is added faith in Christ,
S D : 0 7 :032(574) [0983] and ordinance of God — **unless** they first change God's
S D : 0 8 :044(599) [1029] must know that **unless** God is in the balance and throws
S D : 0 8 :044(599) [1031] never have sat in the pan **unless** he had become a man
S D : 1 1 :076(628) [1087] that no one comes to Christ **unless** the Father draw him.

Unlike (1), Unlikely (1)
A P : 0 4 :339(159) [0215] objects of trust in the first are **unlike** those in the second.
S C : 0 5 :025(350) [0555] sin at all (which is quite **unlikely**), you should mention

Unlimited (2)
A P : 0 7 :023(172) [0235] pontiff must have **unlimited** power beyond question or
A P : 2 8 :018(284) [0449] a "commandment with **unlimited** authority," but rather a

Unmanageable (1)
S D : 0 6 :024(568) [0969] Old Adam, like an **unmanageable** and recalcitrant

Unmarried (2)
A P : 2 3 :040(245) [0375] says (I Cor. 7:32), "The **unmarried** man is anxious about
A P : 2 7 :039(276) [0433] not have property, are **unmarried**, and obey the rule in

Unmerited (2)
S D : 1 1 :060(626) [1083] praise God's pure and **unmerited** grace toward the
S D : 1 1 :061(626) [1083] God commends his pure and **unmerited** grace and mercy.

Unmingled (1)
S D : 0 8 :008(593) [1017] referred to remain **unmingled** and unabolished, so that

Unmistakable (2), Unmistakably (1)
L C : 0 1 :188(390) [0633] then, to impress it **unmistakably** upon the common
S D : 1 1 :080(629) [1089] The apostle says in **unmistakable** terms that God
S D : 1 2 :004(633) [1097] a clear, lucid, and **unmistakable** exposition of all the

Unmolested (1)
L C : 0 1 :231(396) [0647] are safe and free, **unmolested** by anyone, even claiming

Unmoved (1)
A P : 0 4 :107(122) [0153] that our opponents are **unmoved** by the many passages in

Unnatural (2)
A P : 2 3 :002(239) [0363] public disgrace and the **unnatural** lusts of the holy fathers
A P : 2 3 :063(248) [0381] in the results, the many **unnatural** lusts and the many

Unnecessarily (1), Unnecessary (22)
A G : 2 4 :040(061) [0069] Mass except that other **unnecessary** Masses which were
A P : 0 4 :223(138) [0181] the Gospel, if Christ is **unnecessary** and by our love we
A P : 0 4 :231(139) [0183] men perfect, Christ, the propitiator, will be **unnecessary**.
A P : 0 4 :348(160) [0217] that good works are **unnecessary** if they do not merit
A P : 1 2 :150(206) [0299] as to make satisfaction **unnecessary**; thus contrition is a
A P : 2 1 :007(230) [0345] even if it were not dangerous, is certainly **unnecessary**.
A P : 2 4 :083(264) [0411] But further proofs are **unnecessary** since anyone who
S 2 : 0 2 :003(293) [0463] "2. The Mass is **unnecessary**, and so it can be omitted
S 2 : 0 2 :004(293) [0463] woe on account of an **unnecessary** and fictitious matter
S 2 : 0 2 :006(293) [0463] abuses when it is so **unnecessary**, useless, and dangerous
S 2 : 0 2 :008(294) [0465] is uncertain and **unnecessary**, and he does not know what
S 2 : 0 2 :018(296) [0467] etc. and pursue these **unnecessary**, uncertain, harmful
S 2 : 0 2 :019(296) [0467] Besides, it is an **unnecessary**, uncommanded, abortive,
S 2 : 0 2 :021(296) [0469] trumpery, utterly **unnecessary** and without command, but
S 2 : 0 2 :022(296) [0469] They are utterly **unnecessary** and useless.
S 2 : 0 2 :024(296) [0469] Not only are they **unnecessary** and without
S 2 : 0 3 :002(298) [0471] this is without commandment, **unnecessary**, and useless.
S 2 : 0 4 :005(299) [0473] it is not commanded, it is **unnecessary**, and it is useless.
L C : 0 1 :066(373) [0599] is, to a falsehood) or **unnecessarily**; but in support of the
L C : 0 1 :085(376) [0605] no one will create disorder by **unnecessary** innovation.
L C : 0 1 :197(392) [0637] regarding them as **unnecessary**, as if they were not
E P : 0 9 :003(492) [0827] manner, eliminates all **unnecessary** questions, and
S D : 1 1 :002(616) [1063] considered useless and **unnecessary**, still less offensive and

Unpleasant (1)
A P : P R :003(098) [0099] with anything, however **unpleasant**, that did not violate

Unprecedented (1)
A G : 2 4 :025(059) [0067] It is an **unprecedented** novelty in church doctrine that

Unprejudiced (1)
A P : 0 2 :003(101) [0105] explanation should be enough for any **unprejudiced** man.

Unprepared (1)
S C : 0 6 :010(352) [0557] them, is unworthy and **unprepared**, for the words "for

Unpresentable (1)
L C : 0 1 :287(403) [0663] honor; and our **unpresentable** parts are treated with

Unprofitable (7)
A L : 0 6 :001(032) [0047] things, say, 'We are **unprofitable** servants'" (Luke 17:10).
A L : 0 8 :003(033) [0047] ministry of evil men to be **unprofitable** and without effect.
A L : 2 0 :004(041) [0053] not preach about such **unprofitable** works as much as
A L : 2 6 :023(067) [0073] So he does not require an **unprofitable** act of worship.
A P : 0 7 :020(172) [0233] structures of stubble, that is, **unprofitable** opinions.
A P : 2 7 :069(281) [0443] cinctures — all these are **unprofitable** services before God.
S D : P R :015(507) [0857] between needless and **unprofitable** contentions (which,

Unpunished (3)
L C : 0 1 :057(372) [0597] no one shall a violation be condoned or left **unpunished**.
L C : 0 1 :057(372) [0597] away from him to go **unpunished**, so little will he permit
L C : 0 1 :274(402) [0659] in such a way that evil shall not go **unpunished**.

Unqualifiedly (3)
S D : 0 1 :038(514) [0871] cannot be identified **unqualifiedly** with sin itself, for in
S D : 0 1 :041(515) [0871] corrupted nature were **unqualifiedly** identical with sin
S D : 0 4 :040(558) [0951] this proposition, **unqualifiedly** stated, in our churches.

Unquestionably (1), Unquestioned (2), Unquestioning (1)
A P : 1 2 :134(203) [0293] these passages are **unquestionably** commandments
L C : 0 3 :120(436) [0731] nothing else than an **unquestioning** affirmation of faith on
S D : 0 1 :055(518) [0877] It is one of the **unquestioned** and irrefutable axioms in
S D : 0 3 :036(545) [0927] faith as certain and **unquestioned** fruits, or as though

Unreal (1)
S 3 : 0 3 :039(309) [0489] this is constructed on an **unreal** and rotten foundation

Unreasonable (1)
A G : 2 8 :072(093) [0093] bishops relax certain **unreasonable** burdens which did not

Unrefuted (1)
S D : P R :003(502) [0847] God, it has remained **unrefuted** and unimpregnable until

Unregenerate (1), Unregenerated (10)
A P : 0 4 :189(133) [0175] a flesh that is partly **unregenerate** and hinders what the
E P : 0 2 :003(470) [0787] confess that man's **unregenerated** will is not only turned
E P : 0 6 :007(481) [0807] for regenerated and **unregenerated** people the law is and
E P : 0 6 :007(481) [0807] with man, for the **unregenerated** man — just like the
S D : 0 2 :002(520) [0881] and alone what the **unregenerated** man's intellect and will
S D : 0 2 :007(521) [0883] heart, and will of **unregenerated** man cannot by any
S D : 0 2 :017(523) [0887] and will of a natural, **unregenerated** man is not only
S D : 0 2 :019(524) [0889] compare the heart of **unregenerated** man to a hard stone
S D : 0 2 :045(530) [0899] when they pretend that **unregenerated** man still has
S D : 0 2 :085(537) [0913] Hence the **unregenerated** man resists God entirely and is
S D : 0 2 :090(538) [0915] efficient causes of **unregenerated** man's conversion to

Unrelated (1)
A P : 0 7 :032(174) [0239] of discipline, completely **unrelated** to the righteousness of

Unreliable (1)
L C : 0 1 :226(395) [0645] people and yet are careless and **unreliable** in their work.

Unremoved (1)
S D : 0 5 :010(560) [0955] over his face" remains **unremoved**, so that they do not see

Unrenewed (2)
A P : 0 2 :031(104) [0113] but an abiding deficiency in an **unrenewed** human nature.
S D : 0 1 :010(510) [0863] of original sin denies to **unrenewed** human nature the

Unrepentant (4)
EP : 07 :017(484) [0813] his judgment on **unrepentant** guests as he is to work life
SD : 05 :024(562) [0961] the hearts of the **unrepentant** and bring them to a
SD : 06 :026(568) [0971] upon unbelievers, non-Christians, and the **unrepentant**.
SD : 07 :123(590) [1013] that unbelieving, **unrepentant**, and wicked Christians,

Unrighteous (6), Unrighteousness (3)
AP : 04 :072(117) [0141] means to make **unrighteous** men righteous or to
AP : 04 :072(117) [0141] man out of an **unrighteous** one, that is, that it receives the
AP : 04 :078(117) [0143] as making an **unrighteous** man righteous or effecting his
AP : 04 :117(123) [0155] that is, out of **unrighteous** we are made righteous and
AP : 04 :373(164) [0221] works but the entire righteousness or **unrighteousness**.
AP : 12 :108(198) [0283] judge Thee to be **unrighteous** in punishing them or
SD : 03 :004(540) [0917] from all their **unrighteousness** because of this obedience.
SD : 03 :022(543) [0923] regeneration no **unrighteousness** in essence and life
SD : 04 :032(556) [0947] you not know that the **unrighteous** will not inherit the

Unruly (6)
LC : SP :018(363) [0577] **unruly** that he refuses to learn these three parts in which
LC : 01 :123(382) [0617] altogether wayward and **unruly**; they have no sense of
LC : 01 :177(389) [0631] we train them, we have **unruly** and disobedient subjects.
LC : 03 :044(425) [0709] father to have a bad, **unruly** child who antagonizes him in
LC : 05 :058(453) [0767] who are shameless and **unruly** must be told to stay away,
EP : 06 :001(479) [0805] discipline against **unruly** and disobedient men, (2) to lead

Unscriptural (1)
AP : 04 :213(136) [0179] maintain these wicked and **unscriptural** ideas about works

Unsearchable (2)
SD : 08 :051(600) [1033] great, supernatural, **unsearchable**, ineffable, heavenly
SD : 11 :064(626) [1083] How **unsearchable** are his judgements and how

Unskilled (1)
AP : 24 :016(252) [0389] at the joint, lest like an **unskilled** cook he sever the

Unspeakable (4)
AP : 12 :149(206) [0299] than undergo the **unspeakable** power of the grief that
S2 : 02 :006(293) [0463] such countless and **unspeakable** abuses have arisen
S2 : 02 :016(295) [0467] departed and, with **unspeakable** lies and cunning, of
EP : 01 :009(467) [0781] This damage is so **unspeakable** that it may not be

Unspiritual (7)
AG : 26 :010(065) [0071] considered secular and **unspiritual**: the works which
AP : 02 :030(104) [0113] as in I Cor. 2:14, "The **unspiritual** man does not receive
AP : 04 :022(110) [0127] to restrain the **unspiritual**, and to preserve it he has given
AP : 04 :146(127) [0163] the law, because our **unspiritual** nature continually brings
EP : 02 :002(470) [0787] in I Cor. 2:14, "The **unspiritual** man does not receive the
SD : 02 :010(522) [0883] in I Cor. 2:14, "The **unspiritual** man does not receive the
SD : 02 :012(522) [0885] "The **unspiritual** man does not receive (or, as the Greek

Unspoken (1)
AP : 21 :011(230) [0345] power to perceive the **unspoken** thought of our minds.

Unsuited (1)
LC : 01 :211(393) [0641] — some who are **unsuited** for married life and others

Unsure (5)
AP : 04 :110(123) [0153] of sins will always be **unsure**, for we never love as much
AP : 04 :187(133) [0173] it would be completely **unsure** and the promise would be
AP : 04 :285(150) [0201] Thus the promise would be vain and **unsure**.
AP : 04 :346(160) [0217] then it would really be **unsure** since works cannot still the
AP : 12 :095(196) [0281] it immediately becomes **unsure** because an anxious

Unthinkable (1)
SD : 08 :020(595) [1021] of the natures is **unthinkable** and impossible, it is not only

Untie (1)
AP : 15 :034(220) [0325] When Alexander could not **untie** the Gordian knot, he

Untrained (1)
S3 : 08 :001(312) [0493] and for the sake of **untrained** young people who need to

Untransformed (3)
SD : 07 :035(575) [0983] union between the **untransformed** substance of the bread
SD : 07 :036(575) [0985] nature but that both **untransformed** natures are
SD : 07 :037(575) [0985] two distinct and **untransformed** natures are indivisibly

Untried (1)
AG : 20 :015(043) [0055] great contempt among **untried** people, yet it is a matter

Untruthful (1)
S3 : 08 :002(312) [0495] flesh we shall not be **untruthful** if we say, "I am a poor

Unusual (3), Unusually (1)
AP : 12 :126(201) [0289] in such times to exercise **unusual** wisdom and diligence.
AP : 24 :023(253) [0391] it seemed to be **unusually** severe; this they called a
LC : 01 :313(407) [0671] They are not **unusual** and pompous, restricted to special
SD : 07 :038(576) [0985] predication, but with an **unusual** one (that is, it is not to

Unutterable (1)
LC : 02 :064(419) [0695] depths of his fatherly heart, his sheer, **unutterable** love.

Unveiled (1)
SD : 08 :087(608) [1047] that not only his **unveiled** deity, which to us poor sinners

Unwarranted (2), Unwarrantedly (1)
PR : PR :018(008) [0015] to be led astray by the **unwarranted** calumny of our
AP : 04 :339(159) [0215] from analogy is **unwarranted**: from the statement, "When
SD : PR :002(501) [0847] it violently (although **unwarrantedly**), and raised no end

Unwary (1)
AP : 23 :045(245) [0375] the Encratites captured the imagination of the **unwary**.

Unwilled (1), Unwilling (27), Unwillingly (1), Unwillingness (1)
AG : 23 :025(055) [0065] letter, "If they are **unwilling** or unable to keep their
AG : 28 :078(094) [0095] If they are **unwilling** to do this and ignore our petition,
AL : 12 :009(035) [0049] Novatians who were **unwilling** to absolve those who had
AL : 23 :025(055) [0065] are these: "If they are **unwilling** or unable to persevere, it
AP : 15 :040(220) [0325] Among our opponents, **unwilling** celebrants and hirelings
AP : 27 :009(270) [0421] been extorted from the **unwilling**, or from those who are
S2 : 03 :002(298) [0471] If they are **unwilling** to serve this purpose, it would be
S2 : 04 :012(300) [0475] This we are **unwilling** to do even if we have to die for it in
S3 : 02 :002(303) [0479] what they are **unwilling** to do, are made worse thereby.
S3 : 10 :002(314) [0497] and princes who are **unwilling** to preach or teach or
S3 : 11 :003(315) [0499] We are therefore **unwilling** to consent to their abominable
TR : 00 :040(327) [0517] because the pope is **unwilling** to be judged by the church
TR : 00 :040(327) [0517] Such **unwillingness** to be judged by the church or by
TR : 00 :066(331) [0523] of the Gospel and are **unwilling** to administer ordination,
SC : PR :021(340) [0537] of the pope, they are **unwilling** to receive the sacrament
LC : SP :017(363) [0577] do not know these things and are **unwilling** to learn them.
LC : 01 :022(367) [0585] and of them it boasts, **unwilling** to receive anything as a
LC : 01 :135(383) [0619] If you are **unwilling** to obey father and mother or to
LC : 01 :155(386) [0625] injustice; but we are **unwilling** to see that we ourselves are
LC : 01 :224(395) [0643] thieves, though they are **unwilling** to admit it, were
LC : 01 :235(397) [0647] and mistresses and **unwilling** to do them the favor and
LC : 04 :029(440) [0739] leaders of the blind are **unwilling** to see that faith must
EP : 02 :015(471) [0789] willing people out of **unwilling** people and dwells in the
EP : 02 :017(472) [0791] changes stubborn and **unwilling** people into willing
EP : 06 :007(481) [0807] of him by the law under coercion and **unwillingly**.
SD : 02 :088(538) [0915] out of resisting and **unwilling** people, and that after such
SD : 04 :017(554) [0943] something that is really **unwilled** by him or even contrary
SD : 04 :019(554) [0945] law which is not only **unwilling** or unenthusiastic but
SD : 04 :019(554) [0945] Concerning this **unwilling** and recalcitrant flesh, Paul
SD : 10 :019(614) [1059] and princes who are **unwilling** to preach or teach or

Unworthily (4), Unworthiness (6), Unworthy (49)
AG : 06 :002(032) [0047] you, say, 'We are **unworthy** servants'" (Luke 17:10).
AG : 24 :012(057) [0065] uses the sacrament **unworthily** is guilty of the body and
AL : 24 :012(057) [0065] those who dealt **unworthily** with the Eucharist when he
AL : 24 :012(057) [0065] cup of the Lord in an **unworthy** manner will be guilty of
AL : 27 :055(079) [0083] and all civil offices are **unworthy** of Christians and in
AP : 04 :163(129) [0169] we have a gracious God in spite of our **unworthiness**.
AP : 04 :334(158) [0215] is commanded you, say, 'We are **unworthy** servants.'"
AP : 04 :335(159) [0215] argue that if we are **unworthy** though we have done
AP : 04 :335(159) [0215] must we say that we are **unworthy** though we have
AP : 04 :337(159) [0215] believed everything, say, 'We are **unworthy** servants.'"
AP : 04 :337(159) [0215] in the promise confesses that we are **unworthy** servants.
AP : 04 :338(159) [0215] believed everything, say, 'We are **unworthy** servants,'"
AP : 04 :342(159) [0215] quibble to interpret "**unworthy** servants" as meaning that
AP : 04 :342(160) [0215] "**Unworthy** servants" means "insufficient servants," since
AP : 04 :347(160) [0217] the worthy and the **unworthy** because eternal life is
AP : 04 :399(168) [0227] this expression as **unworthy** of being spoken in such an
AP : 07 :028(173) [0237] are administered by **unworthy** men, this does not rob them
AP : 07 :028(173) [0237] we may not be offended by the **unworthiness** of ministers.
AP : 07 :029(173) [0237] the sacraments from **unworthy** men in the church.
AP : 11 :005(181) [0251] those who receive in an **unworthy** manner receive
AP : 24 :081(264) [0411] "He will say that some **unworthy** men have found an
AP : 27 :028(274) [0429] Now listen to the **unworthy** verdict our judges have
SC : 06 :010(352) [0557] or doubts them, is **unworthy** and unprepared, for the
LC : 03 :017(422) [0703] whether we be sinners or saints, worthy or **unworthy**.
LC : 03 :057(427) [0713] command and was **unworthy** to come into his presence.
LC : 04 :054(443) [0745] those who partake **unworthily** of the Lord's Supper
LC : 05 :005(447) [0755] and inviolate even if we use and handle it **unworthily**.
LC : 05 :017(448) [0757] false because of an individual's **unworthiness** or unbelief.
LC : 05 :018(448) [0757] matter whether you are **unworthy** or worthy, you here
LC : 05 :056(453) [0767] begin to contrast our **unworthiness** with this great and
LC : 05 :061(453) [0767] poor, miserable men, precisely because we are **unworthy**.
LC : 05 :074(455) [0771] Therefore they alone are **unworthy** who neither feel their
LC : 06 :005(457) [0000] pigs, as I have said, are **unworthy** to appear in the
EP : 07 :002(481) [0809] be they worthy or **unworthy**, godly or godless, believers
EP : 07 :016(483) [0813] are worthy but also the **unworthy** and the unbelievers
EP : 07 :018(484) [0813] is only one kind of **unworthy** guest, namely, those who do
EP : 07 :018(484) [0813] The **unworthy** use of the holy sacrament increases,
SD : 07 :016(572) [0977] on the worthiness or **unworthiness** of the minister who
SD : 07 :016(572) [0977] as St. Paul says, the **unworthy** receive the sacrament too.
SD : 07 :016(572) [0977] truly distributed to the **unworthy**, too, and that they truly
SD : 07 :026(573) [0981] you are worthy or **unworthy**, you here have his body and
SD : 07 :027(574) [0981] communicants but also to the unbelieving and **unworthy**.
SD : 07 :060(580) [0993] sacrament, but also the **unworthy** and godless hypocrites,
SD : 07 :060(580) [0993] God, and who by their **unworthy** eating and drinking sin
SD : 07 :060(580) [0993] cup of the Lord in an **unworthy** manner" (I Cor. 11:27)
SD : 07 :066(581) [0997] also orally, and this by **unworthy**, unbelieving, false, and
SD : 07 :067(582) [0997] on the part of the **unworthy** "two hairs of a horse's tail
SD : 07 :068(582) [0997] great diligence who the **unworthy** guests at this Supper
SD : 07 :068(582) [0997] life and who by their **unworthy** oral eating of the body of
SD : 07 :069(582) [0997] who consider themselves **unworthy** of this noble treasure
SD : 07 :072(582) [0997] happens in the case of both the worthy and the **unworthy**.
SD : 07 :088(585) [1003] earth both the worthy and the **unworthy** alike participate.
SD : 07 :088(585) [1003] This implies that for the **unworthy** it is no sacrament, and
SD : 07 :088(585) [1003] and that therefore the **unworthy** and unbelieving
SD : 07 :089(585) [1003] the worthiness or **unworthiness** of the minister or the
SD : 07 :123(590) [1015] at this heavenly meal, the worthy and the **unworthy**.
SD : 07 :123(590) [1015] a distinction among the **unworthy** which alleges that
SD : 07 :125(591) [1015] this sacrament for judgment, just as **unworthy** guests.
SD : 11 :060(626) [1083] us and make ourselves **unworthy** of eternal life

Upbraiding (2)
AP : 04 :282(149) [0201] Christ is **upbraiding** the Pharisees for thinking that they
AP : 27 :052(278) [0437] by the voice of Christ **upbraiding** the Pharisees for setting

Uphold (2), Upholds (2)
AP : 04 :123(124) [0157] says that faith does not overthrow but **upholds** the law.
AP : 04 :132(125) [0159] does not overthrow but **upholds** the law (Rom. 3:31)
AP : 04 :244(142) [0189] though our opponents **uphold** it under the pretext that
AP : 20 :015(229) [0343] says (Rom. 3:31), but **uphold** it; for when we have

Upper (3)
AG : 0 0 :005(095) [0095] into our churches and gaining the **upper** hand in them.
S 3 : 0 3 :044(310) [0491] sin to rule and gain the **upper** hand in such a way that sin
SD : 0 7 :012(571) [0977] of Saxony and **Upper** Germany drafted the following

Upright (18), Uprightness (1)
PR : PR :024(013) [0023] people who have an **upright** love for divine truth and for
AG : 2 3 :006(052) [0061] of life, what Christian, **upright**, and honorable sort of
AP : 0 4 :394(167) [0225] righteousness of the law, understood as civic **uprightness**.
LC : PR :002(358) [0567] However, they are not so **upright** and honest as to buy
LC : 0 1 :045(370) [0593] chosen by God, and an **upright** man; but once he was
LC : 0 1 :148(385) [0623] You are a true nobleman if you are **upright** and obedient.
LC : 0 1 :246(398) [0651] The **upright**, meanwhile, will not want, and you will hurt
LC : 0 1 :259(400) [0653] of integrity, and not only **upright** but also a wise,
LC : 0 1 :259(400) [0653] be fearless; more than that, he should be an **upright** man.
LC : 0 1 :298(405) [0665] Yet we all pretend to be **upright**.
LC : 0 1 :300(405) [0665] but precisely to the most **upright** — to people who wish to
LC : 0 1 :305(406) [0669] posed as an honorable, **upright** man, as St. Mark
LC : 0 1 :310(407) [0669] us and shows just how **upright** we really are in God's
LC : 0 2 :068(420) [0697] pure grace and makes us **upright** and pleasing to God.
LC : 0 3 :075(430) [0719] coat-of-arms of every **upright** prince were emblazoned
LC : 0 3 :100(433) [0727] though at present we are **upright** and stand before God
LC : 0 5 :074(455) [0771] "If you are pure and **upright**, you have no need of me and
LC : 0 6 :011(458) [0000] says, "If one man is **upright**, so are they all"; no one does
SD : 0 5 :012(560) [0957] but to comfort and lift **upright** those who are terrified and

Uprising (3), Uprisings (1)
AG : 2 3 :012(053) [0063] almost killed during an **uprising** of the entire body of
AG : 2 8 :002(081) [0083] wars, tumults, and **uprisings** have resulted because the
AL : 2 3 :012(053) [0063] was almost killed by the enraged priests in an **uprising**.
S 3 : 0 3 :042(309) [0491] eyes at the time of the **uprising**) who hold that once they

Uprooted (1)
LC : 0 2 :050(417) [0691] that it cannot well be **uprooted**, and it would be next to

Upward (1)
SD : 0 8 :044(599) [1029] goes down and we go **upward** like a light and empty pan.

Urban (3)
PR : PR :019(009) [0017] or of [John] Brenz, **Urban** Rhegius, [John Bugenhagen]
S 3 : 1 5 :005(317) [0501] I, Dr. **Urban** Rhegius, superintendent of the churches in
TR : 0 0 :082(334) [0529] I also, Dr. **Urban** Rhegius, superintendent of the churches

Urge (21), Urged (17), Urges (5), Urging (3), Urgings (1)
AG : PR :016(026) [0041] faith but would diligently **urge** it upon the pope to call a
AG : 2 6 :004(064) [0071] yet the Gospel earnestly **urges** them upon us and strongly
AG : 2 7 :020(074) [0079] God's command that **urges**, drives, and compels us to do
AG : 2 8 :033(086) [0087] No case is appealed to and **urged** so insistently as the
AG : 2 8 :047(088) [0089] concerning those who **urge** human ordinances on people,
AL : 2 0 :003(041) [0053] Instead, they **urged** childish and needless works, such as
AP : 0 4 :122(124) [0157] Here our opponents **urge** against us the texts, "If you
AP : 0 4 :220(137) [0181] being justified, needed **urging** to bear good fruits lest they
AP : 0 4 :258(144) [0193] Thus the prophet **urges** penitence and adds a promise.
AP : 0 4 :276(148) [0199] in good works, which thus **urge** us to believe more firmly.
AP : 0 4 :370(163) [0221] Our opponents **urge** that good works properly merit
AP : 2 1 :026(232) [0349] theology, do nothing but **urge** this prayer upon the dying
AP : 2 3 :001(239) [0363] law, but they even **urge** the emperor and the princes not
S 1 : PR :009(290) [0457] who in their writings have **urged** such big lies upon the
SC : PR :019(340) [0537] should also take pains to **urge** governing authorities and
SC : 0 9 :005(355) [0561] "I **urge** that supplications, prayers, intercessions, and
SC : 0 9 :014(356) [0563] "I **urge** that supplications, prayers, intercessions, and
LC : PR :001(358) [0567] the Catechism and strongly **urge** others to do the same.
LC : 0 1 :069(374) [0599] Therefore I advise and **urge**, as I have before, that by
LC : 0 1 :070(374) [0601] should be constantly **urged** and encouraged to honor
LC : 0 1 :195(391) [0637] he wants to encourage and **urge** us to true, noble, exalted
LC : 0 3 :019(423) [0703] we should be all the more **urged** and encouraged to pray
LC : 0 5 :043(451) [0763] will of their own accord **urge** and impel themselves to
LC : 0 5 :052(452) [0765] All we are doing is to **urge** you to do what you ought to
LC : 0 6 :022(459) [0000] We **urge** you, however, to confess and express your
LC : 0 6 :028(460) [0000] confession is, and we **urge** that such a precious blessing
LC : 0 6 :032(460) [0000] Therefore, when I **urge** you to go to confession, I am
LC : 0 6 :032(460) [0000] to confession, I am simply **urging** you to be a Christian.
EP : 0 6 :001(480) [0805] or not the law is to be **urged** upon reborn Christians.
EP : 0 6 :008(481) [0807] that the law is not to be **urged**, in the manner and
SD : 0 3 :036(546) [0929] same points should be **urged** with all diligence and
SD : 0 3 :053(548) [0933] this reason Paul uses and **urges** exclusive terms (that is,
SD : 0 4 :015(553) [0943] rightly be used and **urged** to criticize and reject a
SD : 0 4 :040(558) [0951] to be admonished and **urged** to apply themselves to good
SD : 0 5 :005(559) [0953] and expounded and **urged** not only the gracious promises
SD : 0 5 :015(561) [0957] both of them have to be **urged** side by side, but in proper
SD : 0 5 :022(562) [0959] Dr. Luther very diligently **urged** this distinction in nearly
SD : 0 5 :024(562) [0961] two doctrines must be **urged** constantly and diligently in
SD : 0 5 :027(563) [0961] other, it is necessary to **urge** and to maintain with all
SD : 0 6 :002(564) [0963] doctrine in any way be **urged** on the basis of the law,
SD : 0 6 :004(564) [0963] eyes and continually to **urge** it upon them with diligence.
SD : 0 6 :024(568) [0969] instruction, admonition, **urging**, and threatening of the
SD : 0 6 :026(568) [0971] above is not to be **urged** upon Christians and true
SD : 0 7 :085(584) [1003] and should be profitably **urged** and retained in the church
SD : 1 1 :012(618) [1067] repent (II Tim. 3:16), to **urge** us to godliness
SD : 1 1 :073(628) [1087] is not idle in them but **urges** them to obey the
SD : 1 1 :073(628) [1087] idle, still less oppose the **urgings** of the Spirit of God, but

Urgent (3), Urgently (5)
PR : PR :024(013) [0021] Spirit, the most acute and **urgent** necessity demands that
AG : 2 6 :002(064) [0071] and were ardently and **urgently** promoted, as if these were
TR : 0 0 :058(330) [0521] to the pope, and these **urgent** reasons are a comfort to the
LC : 0 1 :220(394) [0643] This is why St. Paul so **urgently** admonishes husbands
LC : 0 1 :232(396) [0647] may be continually and **urgently** kept before their eyes.
LC : 0 1 :269(401) [0657] All the more **urgent** is the prohibition if you are not sure
LC : 0 3 :012(422) [0701] the fact that prayer is so **urgently** commanded, we ought
LC : 0 3 :014(422) [0701] We therefore **urgently** beg and exhort everyone to take

Usage (13), Usages (8)
AG : 1 5 :000(036) [0049] XV. Church **Usages**
AG : 1 5 :001(036) [0049] With regard to church **usages** that have been established
AG : 1 5 :001(036) [0049] among us that those **usages** are to be observed which may
AG : 2 2 :004(050) [0061] This **usage** continued in the church for a long time, as can
AG : 2 6 :045(070) [0075] of dissimilar church **usages** and adds the profitable
AG : 2 8 :057(091) [0091] Easter, Pentecost, and similar holy days and **usages**.
AL : 2 2 :001(049) [0059] to laymen because this **usage** has the command of the
AL : 2 2 :004(050) [0061] This **usage** continued in the church for a long time.
AL : 2 8 :068(093) [0093] to consciences even if the **usage** of men changes in such
AP : 0 4 :357(162) [0217] to Scripture but also to the very **usage** of the language.
AP : 2 1 :024(232) [0349] this "order" from the **usage** at royal courts, where friends
AP : 2 2 :007(237) [0359] given; for by the ordinary **usage** of language, naming one
TR : 0 0 :014(322) [0507] tradition and apostolic **usage**, what is observed by us and
TR : 0 0 :015(322) [0509] and an apostolic **usage**, and he asserts that it was
LC : 0 2 :050(417) [0691] become so established in **usage** that it cannot well be
EP : 0 3 :007(473) [0793] that according to the **usage** of Scripture the word "justify"
EP : 1 0 :000(492) [0829] X. Church **Usages**, Called Adiaphora or Indifferent
EP : 1 0 :001(492) [0829] ceremonies or church **usages** which are neither
EP : 1 0 :003(493) [0829] the ceremonies or church **usages** which are neither
SD : 0 3 :017(542) [0921] And this is the usual **usage** and meaning of the word in
SD : 0 5 :027(563) [0961] to the entire teaching, a **usage** that we find occasionally in

Use (197), Used (93), Uses (33), Using (17)
PR : PR :021(010) [0019] "abstract" has not been **used** univocally by teachers in the
PR : PR :021(011) [0019] and subjectively (to **use** scholastic terminology), as if
AG : 1 3 :000(035) [0049] XIII. The **Use** of the Sacraments
AG : 1 3 :002(036) [0049] faith, and they are rightly **used** when they are received in
AG : 2 2 :008(050) [0061] Cardinal Cusanus mentions when the **use** was approved.
AG : 0 1 :007(056) [0065] and how it is to be **used** (namely, as a comfort for
AG : 2 4 :012(057) [0065] (namely, that whoever **uses** the sacrament unworthily is
AG : 2 4 :024(058) [0067] might know how the sacrament is to be **used** rightly.
AG : 2 4 :029(059) [0067] known that the Mass is **used** to remove sin and obtain
AG : 2 4 :030(059) [0067] requires faith, and without faith it is **used** in vain.
AG : 2 4 :035(060) [0067] among us in its proper **use**, the use which was formerly
AG : 2 4 :035(060) [0067] us in its proper use, the **use** which was formerly observed
AG : 2 8 :002(081) [0083] reserved cases and violent **use** of the ban, but have also
AG : 2 8 :008(082) [0085] of keys or of bishops is **used** and exercised only by
AG : 2 8 :010(082) [0085] bestows eternal gifts and is **used** and exercised only
AG : 2 8 :045(088) [0089] which all perish as they are **used**), according to human
AL : 0 1 :004(028) [0043] And the term "person" is **used**, as the ancient Fathers
AL : 0 8 :001(033) [0047] believers, it is allowable to **use** the sacraments even when
AL : 0 8 :003(033) [0047] of evil men may be **used** in the church and who have
AL : 1 3 :000(035) [0049] XIII. The **Use** of the Sacraments
AL : 1 3 :001(035) [0049] to awaken and confirm faith in those who **use** them.
AL : 1 3 :002(035) [0049] sacraments should be so **used** that faith, which believes
AL : 1 3 :003(036) [0049] are forgiven, is required in the **use** of the sacraments.]
AL : 2 0 :003(041) [0053] Concerning such things preachers **used** to teach little.
AL : 2 0 :005(041) [0053] faith, about which there **used** to be marvelous silence.
AL : 2 0 :019(043) [0055] Consciences **used** to be plagued by the doctrine of works
AL : 2 2 :003(050) [0059] it appears that a whole congregation **used** both kinds.
AL : 2 2 :011(050) [0061] if any people preferred to **use** both kinds in the
AL : 2 3 :026(056) [0065] age, and as a rule vows **used** to be so made in former
AL : 2 4 :004(056) [0065] a language should be **used** which is understood by the
AL : 2 4 :007(056) [0065] concerning the value and **use** of the sacrament and the
AL : 2 4 :008(057) [0065] pleases God, and such **use** of the sacrament nourishes
AL : 2 4 :030(059) [0067] on the part of those who **use** the sacrament should
AL : 2 4 :033(060) [0067] the Mass is to be **used** to this end, that the sacrament is
AL : 2 8 :045(088) [0089] which all perish as they are **used**), according to human
AP : 0 2 :003(101) [0105] When we **use** the term "concupiscence," we do not mean
AP : 0 2 :004(101) [0105] First we must show why we **used** these words here.
AP : 0 4 :012(109) [0123] of sins by these elicited acts of ours, of what **use** is Christ?
AP : 0 4 :018(109) [0125] Christ; men should not **use** him as mediator and believe
AP : 0 4 :033(111) [0129] only attentive listening—to **use** the words that Augustine
AP : 0 4 :033(111) [0129] the words that Augustine **uses** in discussing this matter.
AP : 0 4 :046(113) [0133] knowledge of Christ, it **uses** his blessings, it regenerates
AP : 0 4 :069(116) [0141] the mediator if we do not **use** him as mediator in our
AP : 0 4 :081(118) [0143] would not have us make **use** of him now as our mediator.
AP : 0 4 :113(123) [0155] sense, as the Scriptures **use** the word, is that which
AP : 0 4 :154(128) [0163] Moreover, Christ **used** the word "love" not toward the
AP : 0 4 :203(135) [0175] they are put to a different **use** by anyone who cannot
AP : 0 4 :266(146) [0197] He **uses** other words to express this same thought, and
AP : 0 4 :291(152) [0203] It compels us to make **use** of Christ in justification.
AP : 0 4 :299(153) [0205] we teach men to make **use** of him as mediator and
AP : 0 4 :304(154) [0205] This is how Scripture **uses** the word "faith," as this
AP : 0 4 :305(154) [0205] In this passage "justify" is **used** in a judicial way to mean
AP : 0 4 :313(155) [0207] they do not teach us to **use** Christ as the mediator in
AP : 0 7 :003(169) [0227] we may legitimately **use** sacraments that are administered
AP : 0 7 :021(172) [0233] *operato*, without a good attitude in the one **using** them?
AP : 0 7 :032(174) [0239] as the observance of Easter, the **use** of icons, and the like.
AP : 0 7 :035(175) [0241] which all perish as they are **used**), according to human
AP : 0 7 :036(175) [0241] do not pertain to the heart and "perish as they are **used**."
AP : 0 7 :042(176) [0241] held tenaciously to the custom of **using** the Jewish time.
AP : 0 7 :046(177) [0243] ordinance of Christ in the **use** of the Lord's Supper, which
AP : 0 7 :050(178) [0245] for Christians to **use** civil ordinances just as it is
AP : 0 7 :050(178) [0245] it is legitimate for them to **use** the air, light, food, and
AP : 1 1 :003(180) [0249] people in our churches **use** the sacraments, absolution and
AP : 1 1 :003(180) [0249] such a way as to invite them to **use** the sacraments often.
AP : 1 1 :005(181) [0251] not force those who are not ready to **use** the sacraments.
AP : 1 2 :042(187) [0261] proclamation of the Gospel and the **use** of the sacraments.
AP : 1 2 :043(187) [0263] and it teaches us to make **use** of Christ as our mediator
AP : 1 2 :124(201) [0289] to his dignity in making **use** of such defenders and turning
AP : 1 2 :168(209) [0305] from the public rite and **use** it to denote the real
AP : 1 3 :000(211) [0309] [Article XIII.] The Number and **Use** of the Sacraments
AP : 1 3 :002(211) [0309] the Fathers did not always **use** the same enumeration.
AP : 1 3 :018(213) [0313] much more necessary to know how to **use** the sacraments.
AP : 1 3 :018(213) [0313] without a good disposition in the one **using** them.
AP : 1 3 :019(213) [0313] Thus we teach that in **using** the sacraments there must be
AP : 1 3 :020(213) [0313] When they are **used**, therefore, there must be faith, so
AP : 1 3 :020(213) [0313] faith, so that anyone who **uses** the Lord's Supper uses it
AP : 1 3 :020(213) [0313] that anyone who uses the Lord's Supper **uses** it this way.
AP : 1 3 :022(214) [0313] Such **use** of the sacrament comforts devout and troubled
AP : 1 3 :023(214) [0313] disposition in the one **using** them, has spawned in the
AP : 1 5 :008(216) [0317] God, then Christ is of no **use** to you, for why does anyone

Continued ▶

AP : 15 :030(219) [0323] that our opponents cannot **use** their customary evasion
AP : 15 :040(220) [0325] Day many in our circles **use** the Lord's Supper, but only
AP : 15 :051(222) [0329] in these matters should be **used** moderately, lest the weak
AP : 16 :002(222) [0331] it lets us make outward **use** of the legitimate political
AP : 16 :002(222) [0331] live, just as it lets us make **use** of medicine or
AP : 16 :012(224) [0333] may legitimately make **use** of civil ordinances and laws.
AP : 18 :007(226) [0337] man," that is, the man who **uses** only his natural powers,
AP : 20 :009(228) [0341] when our opponents **use** their terrors, tortures, and
AP : 21 :004(229) [0343] the saints themselves for **using** these gifts, just as Christ
AP : 21 :024(232) [0349] royal courts, where friends must be **used** as intercessors.
AP : 21 :025(232) [0349] this form of absolution is **used**: "The passion of our Lord
AP : 22 :001(236) [0357] can be no doubt that the **use** of both kinds in the Lord's
AP : 22 :001(236) [0357] admit, all of the church **uses** the sacrament, not only the
AP : 22 :002(236) [0357] take away from part of the church and its **use** prohibited?
AP : 22 :003(236) [0357] the text clearly shows that this was the **use** of both kinds.
AP : 22 :003(236) [0359] said that those who would **use** the Lord's Supper should
AP : 22 :003(236) [0359] who would use the Lord's Supper should **use** it jointly.
AP : 22 :008(237) [0359] But this was not the **use** of only one kind.
AP : 22 :008(237) [0359] priests were commanded to **use** lay communion, this
AP : 22 :010(237) [0361] They say this indicates the **use** of one kind, and they add,
AP : 22 :012(238) [0361] and rage against good men who **use** the entire sacrament?
AP : 22 :015(238) [0361] if we grant the freedom to **use** one kind or both, how can
AP : 22 :016(238) [0361] violently persecute anyone that **uses** the entire sacrament.
AP : 23 :001(239) [0363] our opponents not only **use** the wicked and false pretext
AP : 23 :005(239) [0365] practice chastity, but they **use** religion as a pretext to
AP : 23 :019(242) [0369] God wants the rest to **use** the universal law of nature
AP : 23 :019(242) [0369] wants men to be chaste by **using** the remedy he offers,
AP : 23 :019(242) [0369] as he wants to nourish our life by **using** food and drink.
AP : 23 :030(243) [0371] that is, by faith which **uses** it gratefully as a gift of God.
AP : 23 :031(243) [0371] his wife"; that is, the **use** of marriage is permissible and
AP : 23 :031(243) [0373] faith in Christ just as the **use** of food, etc. is permissible.
AP : 23 :043(245) [0375] men will know how to **use** marriage moderately,
AP : 23 :044(245) [0375] the verse, "The boy who is **used** to being lazy hates those
AP : 23 :045(245) [0377] and services instead of **using** wine or meat or marriage,
AP : 23 :046(246) [0377] commands and gifts, which he wants us to **use** devoutly.
AP : 23 :050(246) [0377] They **use** religion as a pretext to put something over on
AP : 23 :050(246) [0377] These Epicureans purposely **use** religion as a pretext.
AP : 23 :053(246) [0379] weaker, so that we ought to **use** the remedies God has
AP : 23 :058(247) [0379] a murderer (John 8:44), he **uses** these murders to defend
AP : 24 :002(249) [0385] a long harangue about the **use** of Latin in the Mass, our
AP : 24 :015(252) [0389] or the Fathers and **use** it out of context, attaching their
AP : 24 :023(253) [0391] The word he **uses** here (*'asam*) means a victim sacrificed
AP : 24 :048(258) [0401] and they talk about the value and **use** of the sacraments.
AP : 24 :049(258) [0401] If the **use** of the sacrament were the daily sacrifice, we
AP : 24 :049(258) [0401] in their churches mercenary priests **use** the sacrament.
AP : 24 :049(258) [0401] In our churches the **use** is more frequent and more
AP : 24 :049(258) [0401] It is the people who **use** it, and this only when they have
AP : 24 :049(258) [0401] about the proper **use** of the sacrament as a seal and
AP : 24 :049(258) [0401] the Gospel and the proper **use** of the sacraments, we still
AP : 24 :051(259) [0401] clear teaching, the godly **use** of the sacraments, ardent
AP : 24 :063(261) [0405] *opere operato* on one who **uses** it, or that it merits the
AP : 24 :067(261) [0407] we shall say about the **use** of the sacrament what actually
AP : 24 :067(261) [0407] Sacrifice and the **Use** of the Sacrament
AP : 24 :068(262) [0409] idea that ignores the chief **use** of what God has instituted.
AP : 24 :071(262) [0409] This **use** of the sacrament, when faith gives life to terrified
AP : 24 :071(262) [0409] For such **use** Christ instituted it, as he commanded
AP : 24 :073(262) [0409] The principal **use** of the sacrament is to make clear that
AP : 24 :073(262) [0409] are the ones worthy of it, and how they ought to **use** it.
AP : 24 :074(263) [0409] It **uses** the ceremony itself as praise to God, as a
AP : 24 :081(264) [0411] It is an old word, ordinarily **used** in public law.
AP : 24 :081(264) [0411] They **used** it this way in the time of the Romans, as the
AP : 24 :082(264) [0411] In II Cor. 9:12 Paul **uses** this word for a collection.
AP : 24 :083(264) [0413] everywhere of their **use** of "liturgy" to mean public duties
AP : 24 :084(264) [0413] be a sacrifice; for Paul **uses** the figure of an altar only for
AP : 24 :091(266) [0415] of the Gospel, a corruption of the **use** of the sacraments.
AP : 24 :096(267) [0417] They often **use** this dodge.
AP : 24 :099(268) [0419] that we show its proper **use**, and that we have most valid
AP : 27 :010(270) [0423] we have produced; these are the very words they **used**.
AP : 27 :021(272) [0427] Hence the saints can **use** them without sinning, as did
AP : 27 :021(272) [0427] They **used** them for their physical advantage, to have
AP : 27 :053(278) [0437] This wickedness, too, is **used** only for the sake of profit.
AP : 27 :055(278) [0439] be tolerated if they were **used** as exercises, the way
AP : 27 :067(280) [0441] He **uses** "faith" this way in the same chapter (I Tim. 5:8),
AP : 28 :007(282) [0445] Christ wanted to leave their **use** free when he said
AP : 28 :010(282) [0447] and the like are things which perish as they are **used**.
AP : 28 :016(283) [0447] Therefore the **use** of such ordinances ought to be left
S1 : PR :010(290) [0457] pure Word and the right **use** of the sacraments, with an
S1 : PR :014(291) [0459] What is the **use** of adopting a multitude of decrees and
S1 : 01 :000(292) [0461] and the Catechism in common **use** for children teach.
S2 : 02 :009(294) [0465] is in order) for anyone to **use** the sacrament, which is the
S2 : 02 :012(295) [0465] that the Mass was **used** almost exclusively for the dead
S2 : 02 :014(295) [0467] But our papists make **use** of such human opinions to
S2 : 02 :023(296) [0469] like the Mass, etc., their **use** is a good work and a service
S2 : 02 :029(297) [0471] institution of Christ and may **use** and receive it in faith.
S2 : 04 :006(299) [0473] The papacy is of no **use** to the church because it exercises
S3 : 06 :004(311) [0493] condemn, and slander the **use** of both as heresy and thus
TR : 00 :054(329) [0519] most shameful of them to **use** their authority and power
TR : 00 :076(333) [0527] and see to it that it is **used** properly for the reformation
SC : PR :007(339) [0533] one form, adhere to it, and **use** it repeatedly year after
SC : PR :008(339) [0533] who were accustomed to **use** the same form in teaching
SC : 01 :004(342) [0539] God, and so we should not **use** his name to curse, swear,
SC : 04 :002(348) [0551] water, but it is water **used** according to God's command
LC : PR :001(358) [0567] land all their days, as they **used** to do under the papacy.
LC : PR :004(359) [0567] are sluggish and lazy, as we **used** to be under the papacy?
LC : PR :013(360) [0571] daily bread; we also must **use** it daily against the daily,
LC : 01 :011(366) [0583] Again, consider what we **used** to do in our blindness
LC : 01 :047(371) [0593] and walk straight ahead, **using** all of God's gifts exactly
LC : 01 :047(371) [0593] gifts exactly as a cobbler **uses** his needle, awl, and thread
LC : 01 :056(372) [0597] invoking God's name and **using** it as a cloak to cover our
LC : 01 :057(372) [0597] will he permit his name to be **used** to gloss over a lie.
LC : 01 :058(372) [0597] there are few who do not **use** the name of God for lies and
LC : 01 :063(373) [0597] you must also know how to **use** the name of God aright.
LC : 01 :063(373) [0599] understand that we are to **use** his name properly, for it
LC : 01 :063(373) [0599] revealed and given to us precisely for our **use** and benefit.
LC : 01 :064(373) [0599] we are forbidden here to **use** the holy name in support of
LC : 01 :064(373) [0599] that we are commanded to **use** it in the service of truth
LC : 01 :064(373) [0599] upon his name in service of truth and **using** it devoutly.
LC : 01 :074(374) [0601] Children **used** to be trained to fast and pray to St.
LC : 01 :077(375) [0603] and taught that its right **use** consists not only of words
LC : 01 :077(375) [0603] well pleased with the right **use** of his name and will as
LC : 01 :097(378) [0609] It **used** to be thought that Sunday had been properly
LC : 01 :099(378) [0609] is precisely the sin that **used** to be classed among the
LC : 01 :101(379) [0609] Word, hear it, and put it to **use**, such is its power that it
LC : 01 :103(379) [0611] purpose whatsoever, but **use** it for the praise of God and
LC : 01 :188(390) [0633] deed; next, we should not **use** our tongue to advocate or
LC : 01 :188(390) [0635] again, we should neither **use** nor sanction any means or
LC : 01 :268(401) [0657] not wield the sword, you **use** your venomous tongue to
LC : 01 :285(403) [0663] A person should **use** his tongue to speak only good of
LC : 01 :299(405) [0665] straining words and **using** them for pretexts, without
LC : 01 :326(409) [0675] and wickedness, but to **use** his name properly by calling
LC : 02 :005(411) [0679] the first place, the Creed **used** to be divided into twelve
LC : 02 :023(413) [0683] to God and a desire to **use** all these blessings to his glory
LC : 02 :038(415) [0689] not be buried but put to **use** and enjoyed, God has caused
LC : 02 :049(417) [0691] no German would **use** or understand such an expression.
LC : 02 :053(417) [0693] Through it he gathers us, **using** it to teach and preach the
LC : 03 :007(421) [0699] and bellowing that **used** to pass for prayers in the church
LC : 03 :007(421) [0699] repetition, when properly **used**, may serve as an exercise
LC : 03 :008(421) [0699] the name of God is glorified and **used** to good purpose.
LC : 03 :009(421) [0699] to say to his father: "What is the **use** of being obedient?
LC : 03 :014(422) [0701] Prayer **used** to be taught, in the devil's name, in such a
LC : 03 :022(423) [0703] and puts into our mouths the very words we are to **use**.
LC : 03 :029(424) [0705] damage and harm he suffers when prayer is in proper **use**.
LC : 03 :037(425) [0707] Answer: Yes, in itself it is holy, but not our **use** of it.
LC : 03 :037(425) [0707] with himself that all that is God's must serve for our **use**.
LC : 03 :041(425) [0709] is false and deceptive, **using** his name to cloak lies and
LC : 03 :045(426) [0709] deceiving, etc., but **used** rightly to the praise and glory of
LC : 03 :045(426) [0709] Whoever **uses** God's name for any sort of wrong profanes
LC : 03 :049(426) [0711] prevent the world from **using** his glory and name to cloak
LC : 03 :064(429) [0715] rest day and night, **using** all the arts, tricks, ways, and
LC : 03 :098(433) [0725] instituted for us to **use** and practice every hour, keeping it
LC : 04 :007(437) [0733] an external thing and that external things are of no **use**.
LC : 04 :009(437) [0733] If people **used** to consider it a great thing when the pope
LC : 04 :034(440) [0741] faith Baptism is of no **use**, although in itself it is an
LC : 04 :035(441) [0741] say that works are of no **use** for salvation, what becomes
LC : 04 :035(441) [0741] Yes, it is true that our works are of no **use** for salvation.
LC : 04 :044(442) [0743] To appreciate and **use** Baptism aright, we must draw
LC : 04 :046(442) [0743] the nature, benefits, and **use** of Baptism as answering the
LC : 04 :053(443) [0745] if it is wrongly received or **used**, for it is bound not to our
LC : 04 :055(443) [0747] should be wrong and invalid because we **use** it wrongly?
LC : 04 :068(445) [0749] This is the right **use** of Baptism among Christians,
LC : 04 :068(445) [0749] grows stronger, Baptism is not being **used** but resisted.
LC : 04 :080(446) [0751] which we can no longer **use** after falling again into sin.
LC : 04 :082(446) [0751] Baptism of its value, making it of no further **use** to us.
LC : 05 :005(447) [0755] and inviolate even if we **use** and handle it unworthily.
LC : 05 :016(448) [0757] blood) just as truly as when one **uses** it most worthily.
LC : 05 :070(454) [0769] help, should regard and **use** the sacrament as a precious
LC : 06 :004(457) [0000] of knowing how to **use** confession beneficially for the
LC : 06 :014(458) [0000] two but is left to everyone to **use** whenever he needs it.
LC : 06 :026(460) [0000] miserable, then go and make **use** of the healing medicine.
EP : 02 :013(471) [0789] God's Word and without the **use** of the holy sacraments.
EP : 02 :016(472) [0789] and modern teachers have **used** expressions such as, "God
EP : 02 :018(472) [0791] been heard or through the **use** of the holy sacraments
EP : 03 :008(474) [0793] (making alive) are **used** in place of justification, and then
EP : 03 :010(474) [0795] Thus the holy apostle Paul **uses** such expressions as *"by*
EP : 04 :003(476) [0797] theologians concerning the **use** of the words "necessary"
EP : 04 :003(476) [0797] that we should not **use** the word "necessary" when
EP : 05 :006(478) [0803] The word "Gospel" is not **used** in a single sense in Holy
EP : 07 :002(481) [0809] orally by all those who **use** the sacrament, be they worthy
EP : 07 :018(484) [0813] The unworthy **use** of the holy sacrament increases,
EP : 08 :016(489) [0821] was established in the full **use**, revelation, and
EP : 10 :007(493) [0831] as well as in the right **use** of the holy sacraments,
EP : 11 :021(497) [0837] in the holy Gospel and in the **use** of the holy sacraments.
EP : 12 :006(498) [0839] they have not achieved the **use** of reason they will be
EP : 12 :007(498) [0839] they have achieved the **use** of reason and can confess
EP : 12 :014(499) [0841] his conscience, may **use** an office of the government
EP : 12 :014(499) [0841] upon the government to **use** the power that it possesses
SD : PR :002(503) [0851] and which were kept and **used** during that period when
SD : PR :008(505) [0853] and accepted and are **used** publicly in the churches, the
SD : PR :010(506) [0855] are to be accepted and **used** as helpful expositions and
SD : 01 :004(509) [0861] original sin, we shall **use** the aforementioned writings to
SD : 01 :050(517) [0875] and safest procedure is to **use** and keep the pattern of
SD : 01 :050(517) [0875] above-mentioned books **use** them in treating this article.
SD : 01 :051(517) [0875] have two or more accepted meanings in common **use**.
SD : 01 :053(517) [0875] himself explains that he **uses** the terms "nature-sin,"
SD : 01 :054(517) [0877] Concerning the **use** of the Latin terms *substantia* and
SD : 01 :054(517) [0877] But when scholars **use** the terms among themselves or in
SD : 01 :054(518) [0877] against heretics, they **use** them in the sense of a perfect
SD : 01 :054(518) [0877] This dichotomy was also **used** by Cyril and Basil.
SD : 01 :056(518) [0877] the rules of logic, **used** the same terminology freely and
SD : 01 :062(519) [0879] In this fashion Luther **used** both the term "accident" and
SD : 02 :020(525) [0889] like a lifeless statue which **uses** neither mouth nor eyes
SD : 02 :037(528) [0895] he heals us and which he **uses** to proclaim and propagate
SD : 02 :048(530) [0901] how we are to relate ourselves to and **use** these means.
SD : 02 :050(531) [0901] sacraments (when they are **used** according to his Word).
SD : 02 :080(536) [0911] Word and without the **use** of the holy sacraments, God
SD : 02 :082(537) [0913] formulas if they are **used** without explanation: that man's
SD : 02 :090(539) [0915] these things, for which he **uses** the preaching and the
SD : 03 :018(542) [0921] is sometimes **used** in place of "justification," it is necessary
SD : 03 :019(542) [0921] The word "regeneration" is **used**, in the first place, to
SD : 03 :019(542) [0921] But this word is also **used** in the limited sense of the
SD : 03 :019(542) [0921] latter sense it is frequently **used** in the Apology, where the
SD : 03 :019(542) [0921] just as St. Paul **uses** the terms discriminately when he
SD : 03 :020(542) [0921] made alive, has sometimes been **used** in the same sense.
SD : 03 :020(542) [0921] The Apology often **uses** the term in this sense.
SD : 03 :021(542) [0921] of faith, as Dr. Luther **used** the term in his book *On the*
SD : 03 :053(548) [0933] For this reason Paul **uses** and urges exclusive terms (that

Continued ▶

SD : 0 4 :002(551) [0939] words which have been **used** by the papists, now as well
SD : 0 4 :014(553) [0943] Holy Scripture itself **uses** words like "necessity,"
SD : 0 4 :015(553) [0943] formulas when they are **used** in their strict and Christian
SD : 0 4 :015(553) [0943] They should rightly be **used** and urged to criticize and
SD : 0 4 :016(554) [0943] the word "necessary" is **used** in this context, it is not to be
SD : 0 4 :017(554) [0943] I Pet. 5:2, "necessity" is **used** with reference to that which
SD : 0 4 :023(555) [0945] by the papists and **used** to their own advantage against
SD : 0 4 :036(557) [0949] a few orthodox teachers **used** these and similar formulas
SD : 0 5 :003(558) [0953] the same meaning but is **used** in a twofold way, both in
SD : 0 5 :004(558) [0953] the one case the word is **used** in such a way that we
SD : 0 5 :005(559) [0953] when the word "Gospel" is **used** in its broad sense and
SD : 0 5 :006(559) [0953] the word "Gospel" is also **used** in another (that is, in a
SD : 0 5 :007(559) [0953] word "repentance" is not **used** in a single sense in Holy
SD : 0 5 :007(559) [0953] of Holy Writ the word is **used** and understood as the
SD : 0 6 :003(564) [0963] the Holy Spirit **uses** the written law on them to instruct
SD : 0 7 :014(571) [0977] with it apart from the **use** of the sacrament, they grant
SD : 0 7 :015(572) [0977] is present apart from the **use**, as when the bread is laid
SD : 0 7 :035(575) [0983] Christ"), we at times also **use** the formulas "*under* the
SD : 0 7 :038(576) [0985] even though they also **use** these different formulas, "in the
SD : 0 7 :050(578) [0989] covenant and union, he **uses** no flowery language but the
SD : 0 7 :073(583) [0999] that there is no sacrament apart from the instituted **use**.
SD : 0 7 :075(583) [0999] and where his words are **used**, and the body and blood of
SD : 0 7 :082(584) [1001] or blessed in this holy **use**, so that therewith the body and
SD : 0 7 :085(584) [1001] a sacrament apart from the **use** instituted by Christ, or
SD : 0 7 :086(584) [1003] In this context "**use**" or "action" does not primarily mean
SD : 0 7 :087(585) [1003] Apart from this **use** it is not to be deemed a sacrament, as
SD : 0 7 :087(585) [1003] or Baptism if it should be **used** to consecrate bells, or to
SD : 0 7 :088(585) [1003] the spiritual and internal **use** of faith in order to deny the
SD : 0 7 :100(586) [1007] To **use** some imperfect illustrations, my vision penetrates
SD : 0 7 :104(587) [1009] in what sense our churches **use** the word "spiritual" in this
SD : 0 7 :105(588) [1009] But when Dr. Luther or we **use** the word "spiritual" in
SD : 0 7 :105(588) [1009] In this sense, too, we **use** the word "spiritual" when we say
SD : 0 7 :108(588) [1009] and the ordained **use** for which it is instituted in the Word
SD : 0 7 :123(590) [1015] only bread and wine in the **use** of the Holy Supper and
SD : 0 7 :126(591) [1015] Supper when it is rightly **used**, should be adored in spirit
SD : 0 8 :004(592) [1017] Lord, did operate with and **use** the same basic arguments
SD : 0 8 :018(594) [1021] of Chalcedon, have often **used** the term "mixture" in a
SD : 0 8 :026(596) [1023] the complete exercise and **use** of the divine majesty
SD : 0 8 :026(596) [1025] his humiliation and did not **use** it at all times, but only
SD : 0 8 :063(603) [1037] We have **used** this term merely in opposition to a "verbal
SD : 0 8 :064(604) [1039] the entire ancient church **used** in explaining this doctrine,
SD : 0 8 :094(609) [1049] Word and in the right **use** of the holy sacraments Christ
SD : 1 0 :014(613) [1057] prohibition, requiring us to **use** them or to discontinue
SD : 1 0 :030(615) [1061] does not have the liberty to **use** one or more ceremonies
SD : 1 0 :031(616) [1063] in Christian liberty one **uses** fewer or more of them, as
SD : 1 0 :031(616) [1063] agreed concerning the right **use** of the holy sacraments,
SD : 1 1 :001(616) [1063] Nor have our theologians always **used** the same terms.
SD : 1 1 :012(618) [1067] understanding or the right **use** of the teaching of God's
SD : 1 1 :021(619) [1069] in the grace of God, and **use** faithfully the gifts they have
SD : 1 1 :025(620) [1071] exposition and the salutary **use** of the teaching of God's
SD : 1 1 :051(625) [1079] Thus it is possible to **use** the teaching in this article in a
SD : 1 1 :082(630) [1089] he will be a vessel for noble **use**, consecrated and useful to
SD : 1 2 :012(634) [1099] they have achieved the **use** of reason and are able to make
SD : 1 2 :019(634) [1099] an inviolate conscience **use** an office of the government

Useful (29), Usefully (1), Usefulness (1), Useless (42), Uselessness (1)
PR : PR :014(007) [0013] Christian, necessary, and **useful** memoranda on the way
PR : PR :024(013) [0023] to do everything that is **useful** and profitable to the
AG : 1 5 :004(037) [0049] satisfaction for sin, are **useless** and contrary to the
AG : 2 0 :003(041) [0053] with childish and **useless** works like rosaries, the cult of
AG : 2 0 :004(041) [0053] no longer praise these **useless** works so highly as they
AG : 2 7 :062(080) [0083] all these things are false, **useless**, and invented, monastic
AL : 1 5 :004(037) [0049] satisfaction for sin, are **useless** and contrary to the
AL : 1 8 :005(040) [0053] will to learn various **useful** arts, or will to do whatever
AL : 2 5 :013(063) [0071] and because it is otherwise **useful** to consciences.
AL : 2 7 :062(080) [0083] since they are false and **useless**, make vows null and void.
AP : 0 4 :042(113) [0133] and if reconciliation were by the law, it would be **useless**.
AP : 0 4 :042(113) [0133] we never keep, it would follow that the promise is **useless**.
AP : 0 4 :084(119) [0145] would be uncertain and **useless** inasmuch as we could
AP : 0 4 :211(136) [0179] certain kind of life for study or for other **useful** exercises.
AP : 0 4 :389(166) [0225] that good men will find it **useful** for strengthening their
AP : 0 7 :033(175) [0239] spirit we cherish the **useful** and ancient ordinances,
AP : 0 9 :001(178) [0245] Baptism of children is not **useless** but is necessary and
AP : 0 9 :002(178) [0245] also their assertion that the Baptism of children is **useless**.
AP : 0 9 :003(178) [0245] For if this Baptism were **useless**, the Holy Spirit would be
AP : 1 2 :029(185) [0259] from contrition those **useless** and endless discussions as to
AP : 1 2 :079(194) [0275] which would certainly be **useless** if we were justified by
AP : 1 2 :110(198) [0285] that some examination is **useful** to instruct men better,
AP : 1 2 :144(205) [0297] Christ calls these **useless** acts of worship, and so they do
AP : 1 2 :146(205) [0297] death because it is **useless** and in this life does not even
AP : 1 2 :147(205) [0297] tradition, which Christ calls **useless** acts of worship.
AP : 1 3 :006(212) [0311] Hence it is **useful** to distinguish these from the earlier
AP : 1 3 :020(213) [0313] A promise is **useless** unless faith accepts it.
AP : 1 4 :001(214) [0315] Fathers had good and **useful** reasons for instituting
AP : 1 5 :018(217) [0319] justification such rites are not only **useful** but necessary.
AP : 1 5 :020(218) [0321] did not regard them as **useful** or necessary for
AP : 1 5 :036(220) [0325] to the Pharisees of the **uselessness** of these acts of
AP : 1 5 :037(220) [0325] our people drop certain **useless** traditions, they have
AP : 1 5 :038(220) [0325] church because they are **useful** and promote tranquillity,
AP : 2 1 :036(234) [0353] It would be **useful** to recall such examples as these which
AP : 2 4 :070(262) [0409] As the promise is **useless** unless faith accepts it, so the
AP : 2 4 :070(262) [0409] it, so the ceremony is **useless** without the faith which
AP : 2 4 :092(266) [0417] faith, it follows that it is **useless** to transfer it to the dead.
AP : 2 4 :096(267) [0417] Aerius believed that prayers for the dead were **useless**.
AP : 2 7 :035(275) [0431] Christ calls traditions "**useless** services," they are not
AP : 2 7 :047(277) [0437] therefore merely a human tradition, it is a **useless** service.
AP : 2 7 :055(278) [0439] lessons would be more **useful** than these endless
AP : 2 8 :006(282) [0445] to create laws which are **useful** for attaining eternal life.
AP : 2 8 :007(282) [0445] human traditions are **useless** acts of worship, and that
S 2 : 0 2 :006(293) [0463] when it is so unnecessary, **useless**, and dangerous and
S 2 : 0 2 :006(293) [0463] is more necessary, more **useful**, and more certain without
S 2 : 0 2 :022(296) [0469] They are utterly unnecessary and **useless**.
S 2 : 0 3 :002(298) [0471] this is without commandment, unnecessary, and **useless**.
S 2 : 0 4 :005(299) [0473] it is not commanded, it is unnecessary, and it is **useless**.
LC : PR :003(358) [0567] they are free from the **useless**, bothersome babbling of the
LC : 0 1 :071(374) [0601] This is a blessed and **useful** habit, and very effective
LC : 0 1 :176(389) [0631] and fail to bring up your children to **usefulness** and piety.
LC : 0 1 :330(410) [0677] It is **useful** and necessary always to teach, admonish, and
LC : 0 3 :033(424) [0707] do denounce the utterly **useless** howling and growling, as
LC : 0 4 :008(437) [0733] What God instituted and commands cannot be **useless**.
LC : 0 5 :030(449) [0759] never be an unfruitful, vain thing, impotent and **useless**.
LC : 0 5 :086(456) [0773] For it is clearly **useless** to try to change old people.
LC : 0 5 :087(457) [0773] of the sacrament so that they may serve us and be **useful**.
LC : 0 6 :003(457) [0000] what confession is and how **useful** and comforting it is.
LC : 0 6 :017(459) [0000] was not only made **useless** to us but it also became
SD : PR :010(506) [0855] mean that other good, **useful**, and pure books, such as
SD : 0 1 :003(509) [0859] original sin is not a **useless** contention about words.
SD : 0 2 :021(525) [0889] It is **useless** to threaten, to scold, or even to teach and
SD : 0 3 :042(546) [0931] distinction explains **usefully** and well the various disputed
SD : 0 4 :036(557) [0949] would eliminate much **useless** wrangling and preserve the
SD : 0 4 :037(557) [0951] good works not only are **useless** and an impediment to
SD : 0 7 :061(580) [0995] It is intrinsically **useful**, salutary, and necessary to
SD : 0 7 :085(584) [1001] testament, the following **useful** rule and norm has been
SD : 0 7 :088(585) [1003] maliciously pervert this **useful** and necessary rule and
SD : 1 0 :007(611) [1055] Neither are **useless** and foolish spectacles, which serve
SD : 1 1 :002(616) [1063] nor should be considered **useless** and unnecessary, still
SD : 1 1 :043(623) [1077] thereto, it is indeed a **useful**, salutary, and comforting
SD : 1 1 :082(630) [1089] use, consecrated and **useful** to the master of the house,
SD : 1 1 :093(632) [1093] by this simple, direct, and **useful** exposition which is
SD : 1 1 :093(632) [1095] are contrary to these true, simple, and **useful** expositions.

Usual (7), Usually (3)
AP : 0 2 :051(107) [0119] rather to list, in the **usual** familiar phrases, the opinions
AP : 0 4 :224(138) [0181] As **usual**, their zeal was very fervent in the beginning.
AP : 0 4 :341(159) [0215] As **usual**, our opponents twist against faith statements
AP : 1 2 :046(188) [0263] Thus what we **usually** call contrition Paul calls "putting
AP : 2 1 :041(235) [0355] The earlier scholastics are **usually** closer to Scripture than
AP : 2 3 :050(246) [0377] for they know that chastity is not the **usual** thing.
AP : 2 7 :006(269) [0421] warns that tasteless salt is **usually** "thrown out and
LC : 0 1 :258(399) [0653] find that, true to the **usual** course of the world, men are
SD : 0 3 :017(542) [0921] And this is the **usual** usage and meaning of the word in
SD : 0 7 :048(578) [0989] understood only in their **usual**, strict, and commonly

Usurp (2), Usurped (2), Usurping (1)
AP : 1 6 :007(223) [0331] think that they should **usurp** the government from
AP : 2 4 :041(257) [0399] pretext of religion they **usurp** the kingdom of the world,
S 2 : 0 4 :003(298) [0471] blasphemous, **usurped** authority have been and still are
TR : 0 0 :036(326) [0515] So the pope not only **usurped** dominion contrary to the
LC : 0 1 :268(401) [0657] This is nothing else than **usurping** the judgment and

Usury (2)
S 1 : PR :012(290) [0459] **Usury** and avarice have burst in like a deluge and have
LC : 0 3 :084(431) [0723] of daily exploitation and **usury** in public business,

Utmost (4)
SC : PR :007(338) [0533] preacher should take the **utmost** care to avoid changes or
LC : PR :004(359) [0567] too lightly, and even our **utmost** exertions accomplish
LC : 0 1 :031(369) [0589] list because it is of the **utmost** importance for a man to
LC : 0 1 :288(404) [0663] our neighbor, doing our **utmost** to serve and help him to

Utriusque (3)
AP : 1 1 :001(180) [0249] the regulation *Omnis* ***utriusque*** should be observed, that
AP : 1 1 :006(181) [0251] us the regulation *Omnis* ***utriusque;*** we are aware of it.
AP : 1 1 :008(181) [0251] the regulation *Omnis* ***utriusque***, for we judge that it, like

Utter (3), Uttered (1)
AP : 2 3 :002(239) [0363] things these men do with **utter** abandon cannot even be
S 3 : 0 2 :004(303) [0479] and show man to what **utter** depths his nature has fallen
LC : 0 1 :071(374) [0601] long remain when it is **uttered** and invoked from the
SD : 1 1 :054(625) [1081] right well and with **utter** certainty, and that he still

Utterly (27)
AG : 2 3 :013(053) [0063] civil law, but was also **utterly** opposed and contrary to
AL : 2 7 :009(072) [0077] authority of the canons was **utterly** ignored and despised.
AP : 0 4 :021(110) [0127] And at last they despair **utterly**.
AP : 0 4 :131(125) [0159] They **utterly** overlook that eternal law, far beyond the
AP : 0 4 :153(128) [0163] that this is faith, he **utterly** misunderstands the nature of
AP : 0 4 :191(133) [0175] of God might not perish **utterly** from the earth.
AP : 0 4 :285(150) [0201] invents other works and services until it despairs **utterly**.
AP : 0 4 :298(153) [0205] proof unless he wants **utterly** to abolish Christ and the
AP : 0 4 :320(156) [0209] God"; we ought to be **utterly** sure that righteousness and
AP : 0 7 :050(178) [0245] We regard as **utterly** seditious those who have incited
AP : 1 2 :031(186) [0259] I am **utterly** spent and crushed; I groan because of the
AP : 2 4 :096(268) [0417] suffering of its glory and **utterly** destroy the doctrine of
S 1 : PR :011(290) [0457] Germany and destroy us **utterly**, like Sodom and
S 2 : 0 2 :021(296) [0469] mere human trumpery, **utterly** unnecessary and without
S 2 : 0 2 :022(296) [0469] They are **utterly** unnecessary and useless.
S 3 : 0 3 :035(309) [0489] that we are all **utterly** lost, that from head to foot there is
TR : 0 0 :048(328) [0519] traditions and have **utterly** extinguished the teaching
LC : 0 1 :034(369) [0589] the fourth generation, until they are **utterly** exterminated.
LC : 0 1 :112(380) [0613] Alas, it is **utterly** despised and brushed aside, and no one
LC : 0 3 :033(424) [0707] but we do denounce the **utterly** useless howling and
LC : 0 3 :054(427) [0713] devil's kingdom shall be **utterly** destroyed and sin, death,
LC : 0 3 :068(429) [0717] against it in their attempt **utterly** to exterminate the
LC : 0 5 :078(455) [0771] said, even if you are so **utterly** dead in sin, at least believe
EP : 0 1 :006(467) [0781] contrary, in the resurrection it will be **utterly** destroyed.
SD : 0 3 :009(540) [0919] is absolved and declared **utterly** free from all his sins, and
SD : 0 3 :029(544) [0925] a way as if we thereby **utterly** rejected works and love (as
SD : 0 5 :010(559) [0955] law by external works, or drives man **utterly** to despair.

Vacant (2)
S 1 : PR :010(290) [0457] papists we see so many **vacant** and desolate parishes
TR : 0 0 :035(326) [0513] the imperial throne is **vacant**, the pope is the legitimate

Vacate (1), Vacated (1), Vacates (2), Vacating (1)
SD : 0 7 :099(586) [1005] bodily on earth and **vacated** or occupied space according

Continued ▸

SD : 07 :100(586) [1005] he neither occupies nor **vacates** space but penetrates every
SD : 07 :100(586) [1007] and does not occupy or **vacate** any space; a musical sound
SD : 07 :100(586) [1007] and neither occupies nor **vacates** space; likewise light and
SD : 07 :100(586) [1007] without occupying or **vacating** space, and many more like

Vain (69), Vainly (2)
AG : 24 :030(059) [0067] requires faith, and without faith it is used in **vain**.
AG : 26 :022(067) [0073] and he adds, "In **vain** do they worship me, teaching as
AG : 26 :023(067) [0073] Since he calls them **vain** service, they must not be
AG : 27 :036(076) [0081] says in Matt. 15:9, "In **vain** do they worship me, teaching
AL : 24 :019(058) [0067] will not hold him guiltless who takes his name in **vain**."
AL : 26 :022(067) [0073] the law, and he says, "In **vain** do they worship me with
AL : 27 :036(076) [0081] wicked, for Christ says, "In **vain** do they worship me with
AL : 28 :049(089) [0091] Was it in **vain** that the Holy Spirit warned against these?
AP : 04 :021(110) [0127] arouse presumption, a **vain** trust in works and a
AP : 04 :037(112) [0131] experiences how **vain** these philosophical speculations
AP : 04 :146(127) [0163] Such a trust is simply wicked and **vain**.
AP : 04 :148(127) [0163] Christ did not die in **vain**, conquers the terrors of sin and
AP : 04 :157(128) [0165] learn that this trust was **vain** and our consciences will
AP : 04 :267(147) [0197] alone, because it is **vain** to seek remission of punishment
AP : 04 :285(150) [0201] Thus the promise would be **vain** and unsure.
AP : 04 :291(151) [0203] But the Gospel was not given to the world in **vain**.
AP : 04 :291(152) [0203] promised, revealed, born, crucified, and raised in **vain**.
AP : 04 :297(153) [0205] crucified, and raised in **vain**; the promise of grace in
AP : 04 :297(153) [0205] in Christ was not given in **vain**, either, before the law and
AP : 04 :330(158) [0211] that is, all trust is **vain** except a trust in mercy; mercy
AP : 04 :382(165) [0225] of faith is omitted, it is **vain** to say that our works are
AP : 12 :123(200) [0289] sinfully twist the Word of God to suit their **vain** dreams!
AP : 12 :140(204) [0295] has commanded but the **vain** works that men have
AP : 12 :142(204) [0295] law does not require, it is **vain** and wicked to trust that
AP : 12 :143(204) [0297] says (Matt. 15:9), "In **vain** do they worship me with the
AP : 12 :149(205) [0299] "punishments" to those **vain** satisfactions and not to apply
AP : 15 :005(215) [0317] says (Matt. 15:9), "In **vain** do they worship me with the
AP : 15 :025(218) [0321] is obscured and replaced by a **vain** trust in such works.
AP : 23 :004(239) [0365] set against them their own foolish and **vain** opinions.
AP : 24 :072(262) [0409] of Christ is not the **vain** celebration of a show or a
AP : 24 :091(266) [0415] of guilt and faith to **vain** ideas of satisfactions.
AP : 27 :004(269) [0421] men are; and how **vain** they are in their sermons and in
AP : 27 :023(273) [0427] (Matt. 15:9), "In **vain** do they worship me with the
AP : 27 :041(276) [0435] which we have chosen are "**vain** worship" (Matt. 15:9).
AP : 27 :069(281) [0443] he says (Matt. 15:9), "In **vain** do they worship me with
S1 : PR :012(290) [0459] dress, gluttony, gambling, **vain** display, all manner of vice
S2 : 02 :002(293) [0463] for Christ says, "In **vain** do they worship me, teaching as
S2 : 04 :004(299) [0473] this is nothing and all in **vain** unless you consider me
S3 : 01 :011(303) [0479] Christ would have died in **vain**, for there would be no
S3 : 03 :018(306) [0483] smitten by the law or **vainly** vexed with a sorrowful spirit
S3 : 15 :001(316) [0501] As Christ says, "In **vain** do they worship me, teaching as
SC : 01 :003(342) [0539] *shall not take the name of the Lord your God in* ***vain***."
SC : 09 :004(355) [0561] does not bear the sword in **vain**; he is the servant of God
LC : PR :019(361) [0573] **Vain** imaginations, like new cloth, suffer shrinkage!
LC : SP :002(362) [0575] 2. You shall not take the name of God in **vain**.
LC : 01 :049(371) [0593] *"You shall not take the name of God in* ***vain***."
LC : 01 :051(371) [0595] take the name of God in **vain**?" you should answer
LC : 01 :057(372) [0597] will not hold him guiltless who takes his name in **vain**."
LC : 01 :062(373) [0597] understand what it means to take God's name in **vain**.
LC : 01 :063(373) [0599] take the name of God in **vain**," God at the same time
LC : 01 :119(381) [0615] must torture themselves in **vain** with their self-devised
LC : 01 :326(409) [0675] and not take his name in **vain** by cursing, lying,
LC : 02 :038(415) [0689] no one knew of it, it would have been all in **vain**, all lost.
LC : 03 :005(420) [0699] Commandment, "You shall not take God's name in **vain**."
LC : 03 :033(424) [0707] distinguish between **vain** babbling and praying for
LC : 03 :045(426) [0709] should not be taken in **vain** by swearing, cursing,
LC : 03 :124(436) [0731] that we do not pray in **vain** and that we must not in any
LC : 05 :030(449) [0759] can never be an unfruitful, **vain** thing, impotent and
LC : 05 :035(450) [0761] blessing be offered to him in **vain** and refuses to enjoy it.
LC : 05 :065(454) [0769] in the "you" so that he may not speak to you in **vain**.
EP : 02 :006(470) [0787] and watering are in **vain** unless he "gives the growth."
EP : 10 :003(493) [0829] "In **vain** do they worship me, teaching as doctrines the
EP : 11 :009(495) [0833] I do is of no avail; everything is in **vain** in that case."
SD : 02 :021(525) [0889] All pleas, all appeals, all admonitions are in **vain**.
SD : 02 :055(531) [0903] and willing would be in **vain**, and no conversion would
SD : 02 :066(534) [0907] we entreat you not to accept the grace of God in **vain**."
SD : 02 :072(535) [0909] this grace of God in **vain** but to exercise ourselves in
SD : 07 :097(586) [1005] only, as the enthusiasts **vainly** imagine, the one which the
SD : 10 :008(612) [1055] two, as it is written, "In **vain** do they worship me,
SD : 11 :010(618) [1067] then everything is in **vain**, even though I were to hold to
SD : 11 :011(618) [1067] to salvation from eternity everything is in **vain**."

Valens (1)
SD : 08 :075(606) [1043] the time of Emperor **Valens** there was a peculiar sect

Valentine (1)
AP : 21 :032(233) [0351] wards off pestilence, **Valentine** heals epilepsy, and George

Valentinians (2)
AG : 01 :005(028) [0043] evil; also that of the **Valentinians**, Arians, Eunomians,
AL : 01 :005(028) [0043] and also those of the **Valentinians**, Arians, Eunomians,

Valiantly (1)
AP : 28 :003(281) [0443] Our opponents **valiantly** defend their own position and

Valid (21), Validity (2)
AL : 27 :023(074) [0079] much less are those vows **valid** which are made contrary
AP : 04 :382(165) [0225] that our good works are **valid** by virtue of Christ's
AP : 04 :382(165) [0225] to say that our works are **valid** by virtue of the suffering
AP : 07 :032(174) [0239] For good and **valid** reasons, these vary according to the
AP : 12 :021(185) [0257] power of the keys has **validity** for the forgiveness of sins
AP : 12 :120(200) [0287] that satisfactions were **valid** not for discipline in the
AP : 22 :006(237) [0359] have given the church a **valid** explanation to instruct
AP : 24 :026(254) [0393] These are **valid**, not *ex opere operato* but because of
AP : 24 :027(254) [0393] that the sacrifices are **valid** *ex opere operato*, and it
AP : 24 :056(260) [0405] sacrifice of Christ can be **valid** for the sins of others, and
AP : 24 :057(260) [0405] the death of Christ that are **valid** for the sins of others.
AP : 24 :058(260) [0405] other satisfaction that was **valid** for the sins of others and
AP : 24 :064(261) [0405] the one that Masses are **valid** when they are transferred to
AP : 24 :099(268) [0419] and that we have most **valid** reasons for disagreeing with
TR : 00 :026(324) [0511] Nor is this ministry **valid** because of any individual's
TR : 00 :065(331) [0523] by a pastor in his own church is **valid** by divine right.
LC : 04 :053(443) [0745] the water, Baptism is **valid**, even though faith be lacking.
LC : 04 :054(443) [0745] we should have to admit that his Baptism was **valid**.
LC : 04 :055(443) [0745] their Baptism would be **valid** and no one should rebaptize
LC : 04 :060(444) [0747] Baptism always remains **valid** and retains its integrity,
LC : 06 :016(459) [0000] the absolution was not **valid** and the sin was not
SD : 07 :016(572) [0977] by Christ, that makes it **valid** in Christendom, and that it
SD : 07 :075(583) [0999] but they still retain their **validity** and efficacious power in

Value (26), Valued (1), Values (1)
AL : 20 :014(043) [0055] would become of little **value** and the preeminence of
AL : 24 :007(056) [0065] concerning the **value** and use of the sacrament and the
AP : 04 :172(131) [0171] works in themselves do not have the **value** to please God.
AP : 04 :236(140) [0185] traditions which have no **value** for piety and most of
AP : 04 :277(149) [0199] that without Christ the teaching of the law has no **value**.
AP : 12 :061(190) [0269] we fail to see what **value** there is in confession without
AP : 12 :129(202) [0291] for men of discretion will **value** this service highly.
AP : 15 :035(220) [0325] so without claiming any **value** before God for them, just
AP : 15 :035(220) [0325] them, just as there is no **value** before God in observing
AP : 16 :013(224) [0333] of magistrates and the **value** of civil ordinances generally.
AP : 23 :065(248) [0381] the saints will know the **value** of moderation in marital
AP : 23 :069(249) [0383] on the relative **value** of marriage and celibacy.
AP : 24 :048(258) [0401] and they talk about the **value** and use of the sacraments.
AP : 27 :021(272) [0427] Paul says (I Tim. 4:8), "Bodily training is of little **value**."
S2 : 02 :006(293) [0463] even if it actually possessed some **value** in and of itself.
S3 : 03 :023(306) [0485] neither faith nor Christ would have been of any **value**.
S3 : 08 :002(312) [0495] be highly esteemed and **valued**, like all other functions of
LC : 01 :333(411) [0677] we should prize and **value** them above all other teachings
LC : 03 :033(424) [0707] may learn above all to **value** prayer as a great and
LC : 04 :010(437) [0735] that it is of much greater **value** than the work of any man
LC : 04 :058(444) [0747] the thing that he misuses has no existence or no **value**?
LC : 04 :059(444) [0747] has been wrongly received, it has existence and **value**.
LC : 04 :082(446) [0751] deprives Baptism of its **value**, making it of no further use
LC : 05 :005(447) [0755] retain their nature and **value** even if we never keep, pray,
LC : 05 :032(450) [0761] the sacrament are of no **value** just as little as they dare say
LC : 05 :032(450) [0761] or Word of God apart from the sacrament is of no **value**.
LC : 06 :018(459) [0000] We should set little **value** on our work but exalt and
SD : 10 :016(613) [1057] As he **values** his soul's welfare and salvation, every

Vanished (2)
LC : 01 :043(370) [0593] treasures, that these have turned to dust and **vanished**.
LC : 01 :072(374) [0601] was averted and **vanished** in the very moment I called

Vanity (4), Vanities (2)
AP : 04 :330(158) [0211] mercy observe lying **vanities**"; that is, all trust is vain
AP : 11 :009(182) [0253] against human traditions, which is the height of **vanity**.
AP : 27 :025(273) [0427] All this is full of pharisaical **vanity**.
S2 : 03 :002(298) [0471] the prophets call such service of God *aven*, that is, **vanity**.
LC : PR :019(361) [0573] against the poisonous infection of such security or **vanity**.
LC : 01 :121(382) [0615] the pure Word of God to the lying **vanities** of the devil.

Variation (2), Variations (1)
SC : PR :007(339) [0533] to avoid changes or **variations** in the text and wording of
LC : 05 :047(452) [0765] of the first full moon, without **variation** of a single day.
SD : 08 :049(600) [1031] Since there is no **variation** with God (James 1:17),

Variety (6)
AP : 12 :144(205) [0297] of these there is a great **variety**, with one making a trip in
AP : 15 :021(218) [0321] that he is reconciled by a **variety** of vestments,
AP : 24 :094(267) [0417] There is also great **variety** among the Fathers.
TR : 00 :081(334) [0527] The **variety** and number of matrimonial disputes are so
SC : PR :009(339) [0535] angles and in such a **variety** of ways as you may be
LC : 02 :051(417) [0691] It possesses a **variety** of gifts, yet is united in love without

Varnishing (1)
LC : 01 :301(405) [0667] semblance of right, so **varnishing** and garnishing them

Vary (3), Varying (1), Varied (3), Varies (1), Various (32)
PR : PR :007(004) [0009] and friendly way **various** matters which our adversaries
AG : PR :022(027) [0043] We have at **various** times made our protestations and
AG : 00 :002(048) [0059] are concerned chiefly with **various** traditions and abuses.
AG : 26 :040(069) [0075] liturgy of the Mass and **various** canticles, festivals, and
AG : 28 :001(081) [0083] Many and **various** things have been written in former
AG : 28 :029(085) [0087] bishops may have in **various** matters (for example, in
AL : 18 :005(040) [0053] keep cattle, will to learn **various** useful arts, or will to do
AL : 20 :032(045) [0057] devil, who impels men to **various** sins, impious opinions,
AL : 26 :032(068) [0075] To be harassed by **various** afflictions and to be crucified
AP : 04 :185(132) [0173] and dangerous issues produce many and **varied** solutions.
AP : 04 :232(140) [0185] church disintegrate into **various** schisms and the hatreds,
AP : 04 :366(163) [0219] bodily and spiritual, in **various** degrees, according to
AP : 07 :032(174) [0239] and valid reasons, these **vary** according to the
AP : 12 :124(201) [0289] numerous, and **varied** subjects in whose learning and faith
AP : 13 :002(211) [0309] the enumeration **varies**, provided what is handed down in
AP : 14 :001(214) [0315] the church polity and **various** ranks of the ecclesiastical
AP : 15 :020(218) [0321] For different seasons and **various** rites serve as reminders
AP : 16 :007(223) [0331] Now the **various** kinds of public redress are court
AP : 18 :005(225) [0335] never stops inciting this feeble nature to **various** offenses.
AP : 24 :004(250) [0385] German hymns have **varied** in frequency, yet almost
AP : 24 :016(252) [0389] and mutilate the **various** members of the concept
AP : 27 :038(275) [0433] and of others which put **various** ways of life on the same
AP : 27 :049(277) [0437] Since callings **vary**, this calling is not for everyone, but
AP : 27 :049(277) [0437] of business themselves **vary** with times and persons; but
AP : 28 :006(282) [0445] article of the Confessions we included **various** subjects.
S1 : PR :010(290) [0457] an understanding of the **various** callings of life, and with
SC : 09 :001(354) [0561] *Scriptures, selected for* ***various*** *estates and conditions of*
LC : PR :016(361) [0573] this one thing without **varying** it with anything new or
LC : SP :003(362) [0575] instructed in the **various** parts of the Catechism or
LC : 01 :141(384) [0621] more to be said about the **various** kinds of obedience due
LC : 01 :230(396) [0645] keep quiet here about **various** petty thieves in order to

Continued ▶

L C : 0 2 :046(416) [0689] But since **various** points in it are not quite clear to the
E P : R N :008(465) [0779] setting forth how at **various** times the Holy Scriptures
E P : 0 7 :014(483) [0811] that God has and knows **various** modes of being at a
E P : 1 1 :022(497) [0837] explanation of the **various** articles which for a time the
S D : P R :012(506) [0855] none of the parties in the **various** controversies can or
S D : 0 3 :042(546) [0931] usefully and well the **various** disputed issues which the
S D : 0 7 :097(586) [1005] that God has and knows **various** ways to be present at a
S D : 0 7 :113(589) [1011] views, no matter how manifold and **various** they may be.
S D : 1 1 :085(630) [1091] of Israel by many, **various**, and most inhuman devices

Vast (2), Vastly (3)
A P : 1 5 :025(219) [0321] and spiritual, they will **vastly** prefer them to the works
A P : 2 4 :045(258) [0399] Daniel describes a **vastly** different desolation, ignorance
A P : 2 7 :062(280) [0441] But **vastly** different purposes are set forth for
L C : 0 1 :228(396) [0645] it is nothing but a **vast**, wide stable full of great thieves.
S D : 0 5 :022(562) [0959] in detail that there is a **vast** difference between the

Veer (1)
S D : P R :020(508) [0859] as our adversaries charge, **veer** from one doctrine to

Vegetation (1)
A P : 2 3 :008(240) [0367] "Let the earth put forth **vegetation**, plants yielding seed."

Vehemently (2)
A P : 0 4 :207(135) [0177] Here we see how **vehemently** the prophets rebuke the
S D : 0 4 :005(551) [0939] problem and became a **vehemently** argued theological

Veil (14), Veiled (2)
A P : 0 4 :021(110) [0127] they look as the Jews did at the **veiled** face of Moses.
A P : 0 4 :133(125) [0159] 3:15-17 he states that the **veil** that covered the face of
A P : 0 4 :133(125) [0159] whenever Moses is read a **veil** lies over their minds; but
A P : 0 4 :133(125) [0159] but when a man turns to the Lord the **veil** is removed.
A P : 0 4 :134(125) [0159] By the "**veil**" Paul means human opinion about the entire
A P : 0 4 :135(125) [0159] But this **veil** is removed from us, and this error taken
A P : 0 4 :229(139) [0183] of Moses but only his **veiled** face, just as the Pharisees,
A P : 1 2 :078(193) [0275] as the Jews looked at Moses' face covered by a **veil**.
L C : 0 1 :285(403) [0663] them, and to cloak and **veil** them with his own honor.
L C : 0 1 :287(403) [0663] eyes, even the whole body, must help cover and **veil** them.
L C : 0 1 :288(404) [0663] one another, we should **veil** whatever blemishes and
E P : 0 5 :008(478) [0803] nothing about Christ, the **veil** of Moses covers their eyes,
E P : 0 5 :009(479) [0803] into the law, after the **veil** of Moses has been removed for
S D : 0 5 :010(560) [0955] "Moses is read," the **veil** which "he put over his face"
S D : 0 5 :010(560) [0955] man turns to the Lord, the **veil** is removed"
S D : 0 6 :001(563) [0963] Lord and from whom the **veil** of Moses has been taken

Vein (5)
A P : 0 4 :106(122) [0153] writes many things in the same **vein** against the Pelagians.
S D : 0 2 :023(525) [0889] has written in a similar **vein** in his second book *Against*
S D : 0 3 :006(540) [0917] In the same **vein** Dr. Luther declared: "Where this single
S D : 0 5 :014(560) [0957] In the same **vein**, the Smalcald Articles state: "The New
S D : 1 1 :032(621) [1073] In the same **vein** Holy Scripture also assures us that God

Veit (2)
S 3 : 1 5 :005(317) [0501] I, Master **Veit** Dietrich, minister in Nuremberg, subscribe
T R : 0 0 :082(334) [0529] Master **Veit** Dietrich, of Nuremberg, subscribes

Venerable (2), Venerated (2), Venerating (1), Veneration (1), Venerations (1)
A G : 2 8 :037(087) [0089] ceremonies and new **venerations** of saints have been
A P : 2 1 :014(230) [0345] invocation in the **veneration** of the saints; they even apply
A P : 2 1 :031(233) [0351] either their ideas about **venerating** the saints or their
A P : 2 1 :034(234) [0353] Men **venerated** these and thought they contained some
L C : 0 1 :018(367) [0585] and a life of ease **venerated** Hercules, Mercury, Venus, or
S D : 0 7 :044(577) [0987] instituting this most **venerable** sacrament, which was to
S D : 0 7 :070(582) [0997] This most **venerable** sacrament was instituted and

Vengeance (4)
A L : 2 7 :054(079) [0083] are not afraid to take **vengeance** in their private life since
L C : 0 1 :034(369) [0589] He is a God who takes **vengeance** upon men who turn
L C : 0 3 :086(432) [0723] give us occasion for impatience, wrath, **vengeance**, etc.
L C : 0 3 :103(434) [0727] and injustice, perfidy, **vengeance**, cursing, reviling,

Venial (4)
A L : 2 4 :021(058) [0067] oblation should be made for daily sins, mortal and **venial**.
A P : 0 4 :282(149) [0201] and the gloss says that it cleanses from **venial** sins.
A P : 1 2 :167(209) [0305] So Augustine says that **venial** sins are consumed, that is,
A P : 2 4 :009(251) [0387] others the forgiveness of **venial** or mortal sins, of guilt, or

Venom (1), Venomous (3), Venomously (1)
S 1 : P R :004(289) [0457] They try to clothe their **venomous** spirits in the garments
S 1 : P R :006(289) [0457] by wagging countless **venomous** and malicious tongues
L C : 0 1 :268(401) [0657] sword, you use your **venomous** tongue to the disgrace and
L C : 0 3 :104(434) [0727] darts" which are **venomously** shot into our hearts, not by
S D : 0 1 :062(519) [0879] again on Gen. 3, "The **venom** of original sin has poisoned

Vent (1), Vents (2)
L C : 0 1 :184(390) [0633] fortune than he, gives **vent** to his irritation and envy by
L C : 0 1 :330(410) [0677] great earnestness, who **vents** his wrath upon those who
L C : 0 3 :115(435) [0731] seeks our life and **vents** his anger by causing accidents and

Venture (3), Ventured (1), Ventures (1)
A P : 2 4 :042(257) [0399] which they put on in public as a money-making **venture**.
L C : 0 1 :268(401) [0657] Whoever therefore **ventures** to accuse his neighbor of
L C : 0 3 :057(428) [0713] them and scarcely **venture** to ask for a morsel of bread.
L C : 0 3 :061(428) [0715] assaults from all who **venture** to hinder and thwart the
S D : 0 8 :004(592) [1017] the Sacramentarians **ventured** to eliminate from his

Venus (1)
L C : 0 1 :018(367) [0585] Hercules, Mercury, **Venus**, or others, while pregnant

Veracious (1)
P R : P R :020(010) [0017] He is almighty and **veracious**, and hence he is able to

Verb (1), Verbal (2)
A P : 2 4 :083(264) [0413] public goods; thus the **verb** means to care for or to
S D : 0 8 :019(594) [1021] speaking and in a strictly **verbal** fashion, but in deed and
S D : 0 8 :063(603) [1037] merely in opposition to a "**verbal** exchange," the doctrine

Verbalism (1)
E P : 0 8 :025(490) [0823] 6. That it is only a **verbalism** and figure of speech when

Verbatim (2)
A P : 0 7 :007(169) [0229] this statement almost **verbatim** in our Confession.
L C : S P :026(364) [0579] for them simply to learn and repeat these parts **verbatim**.

Verbum (2)
L C : 0 4 :018(438) [0737] taught, *"Accedat **verbum** ad elementum et fit*
L C : 0 5 :010(448) [0755] It is said, *"Accedat **verbum** ad elementum et fit*

Verden (1)
P R : P R :027(014) [0025] of Luebeck, administrator of the diocese of **Verden**.

Verdict (6), Verdicts (1)
A P : 1 6 :001(222) [0329] public office, render **verdicts** according to imperial or
A P : 2 7 :017(272) [0425] This is the **verdict** of Paul.
A P : 2 7 :028(274) [0429] listen to the unworthy **verdict** our judges have rendered in
L C : 0 1 :268(401) [0657] the severest kind of **verdict** and sentence, for the harshest
L C : 0 1 :268(401) [0657] sentence, for the harshest **verdict** a judge can pronounce
S D : 0 1 :027(513) [0867] by God's judgment and **verdict** man lost the concreated
S D : 0 3 :009(540) [0919] all his sins, and from the **verdict** of well deserved

Veritable (1)
E P : 0 8 :012(488) [0821] mere man but the **veritable** Son of God; for this reason

Veritate (1)
A L : 2 2 :009(050) [0061] testify (Dist. 3, chap. "**Veritate**" and the following

Vermin (1)
S 2 : 0 2 :011(294) [0465] brought forth a brood of **vermin** and the poison of

Versa (3)
L C : 0 1 :031(369) [0589] head is right, the whole life must be right, and vice **versa**.
S D : 0 8 :039(598) [1027] to the humanity, or vice **versa** — for example, 'Was it not
S D : 0 8 :041(599) [1029] union, all that happens to the humanity, and vice **versa**.

Verse (2)
A P : 2 3 :044(245) [0375] We all know the **verse**, "The boy who is used to being lazy
L C : 0 1 :325(409) [0675] commandment in one **verse**, as if to say, "The Lord takes

Version (2)
P R : P R :009(006) [0011] theologians knew which **version** was the true and
S D : P R :007(505) [0853] We follow the **version** as it was initially prepared and

Very (152)
P R : P R :004(003) [0007] and unconcealed, what **very** perilous events and
P R : P R :007(004) [0009] been interpreting to the **very** great disadvantage of
P R : P R :018(009) [0015] was afterward collated **very** diligently by well-certified
P R : P R :019(009) [0017] at Augsburg and that a **very** different doctrine by far can
P R : P R :024(013) [0023] Therefore, just as from the **very** beginning of this
A G : 2 3 :016(054) [0063] would certainly be both Christian and **very** necessary.
A G : 2 7 :030(075) [0079] that it belongs to the **very** nature and character of a vow
A G : 2 8 :058(091) [0091] a necessary institution are **very** much mistaken, for the
A G : 0 0 :005(095) [0095] order that it may be made **very** clear that we have
A L : 2 0 :022(044) [0055] Hence there was **very** great need to treat of and to restore
A L : 2 4 :010(057) [0065] there has been open and **very** grievous complaint by all
A L : 2 4 :018(058) [0067] for many centuries by the **very** men who were able to
A L : 2 5 :002(061) [0069] The people are **very** diligently taught concerning faith in
A P : P R :007(098) [0101] Majesty, to show him that **very** weighty reasons prevented
A P : 0 2 :001(100) [0105] Here at the **very** outset His Imperial Majesty will see that
A P : 0 2 :021(103) [0111] righteousness is the **very** likeness of God which he put
A P : 0 4 :036(112) [0131] Finally, it was **very** foolish of our opponents to write that
A P : 0 4 :072(117) [0141] For beginnings are **very** important; or, as the common
A P : 0 4 :086(119) [0147] stating that faith is the **very** righteousness by which we
A P : 0 4 :172(130) [0171] Augustine says **very** clearly, "All the commandments of
A P : 0 4 :224(138) [0181] As usual, their zeal was **very** fervent in the beginning.
A P : 0 4 :236(140) [0185] All this does not fit **very** well with their praises of love; if
A P : 0 4 :262(145) [0195] human being must have a **very** definite Word of God to
A P : 0 4 :265(146) [0197] In human eyes, works are **very** impressive.
A P : 0 4 :266(146) [0197] his words to mean the **very** opposite of the teaching of
A P : 0 4 :285(150) [0203] counsel pious consciences **very** badly when they teach
A P : 0 4 :290(151) [0203] Then it imagines that this **very** keeping of the law without
A P : 0 4 :297(153) [0205] and outside the law from the **very** beginning of the world.
A P : 0 4 :301(153) [0205] opponents admit, or surely they feel that it is **very** weak.
A P : 0 4 :314(156) [0207] It summarizes our case **very** well, and a careful
A P : 0 4 :321(157) [0209] This **very** distinction — that men sometimes acquire the
A P : 0 4 :337(159) [0215] works are worthless is the **very** voice of faith, as is
A P : 0 4 :348(160) [0217] We are justified for this **very** purpose, that, being
A P : 0 4 :353(161) [0217] reader can judge that we **very** definitely require good
A P : 0 4 :357(162) [0217] to Scripture but also to the **very** usage of the language.
A P : 0 4 :397(167) [0227] of Leo X has condemned a **very** necessary doctrine that
A P : 0 4 :398(167) [0227] Now in this **very** gathering the authors of the Confutation
A P : 0 7 :009(169) [0229] We set forth this doctrine for a **very** necessary reason.
A P : 0 7 :033(174) [0239] With a **very** thankful spirit we cherish the useful and
A P : 1 0 :002(179) [0247] may be changed and become the **very** body of Christ.
A P : 1 1 :002(180) [0249] of God — yes, the **very** voice of the Gospel — that we
A P : 1 2 :002(182) [0253] This is the **very** voice of the Gospel, that by faith we
A P : 1 2 :004(183) [0253] writings the doctrine of penitence was **very** confused.
A P : 1 2 :010(184) [0255] opponents' discussions are **very** confused and intricate.
A P : 1 2 :012(184) [0255] by divine right, they speak **very** coldly about absolution,
A P : 1 2 :059(190) [0267] and the doctrine of justification are **very** closely related.
A P : 1 2 :063(191) [0269] But it is **very** sure, though all the gates of hell
A P : 1 2 :090(195) [0279] with our opponents, we would **very** gladly keep quiet.
A P : 1 2 :096(196) [0281] Ambrose makes this **very** clear statement about
A P : 1 2 :141(204) [0295] We are **very** sorry to have to list these silly opinions of
A P : 1 3 :014(213) [0311] New Testament but in the **very** beginning, at the creation
A P : 1 5 :019(217) [0319] of human rites will be the **very** form and constitution of
A P : 1 5 :022(218) [0321] This good order is **very** becoming in the church and is

Continued ▶

AP : 1 5 :041(220) [0325] youth publicly, a custom that produces **very** good results.
AP : 1 5 :052(222) [0329] In this **very** assembly we have shown ample evidence of
AP : 1 6 :006(223) [0331] These questions were **very** disturbing to Origen,
AP : 1 6 :006(223) [0331] others, though they are **very** easy to answer if we keep
AP : 1 8 :010(226) [0337] more recently William of Paris has discussed it **very** well.
AP : 2 1 :004(229) [0343] we should extol them **very** highly; we should also praise
AP : 2 1 :043(235) [0357] the state of the church does not concern them **very** much.
AP : 2 1 :043(235) [0357] of the church, which we are **very** anxious to maintain.
AP : 2 2 :008(237) [0359] Our opponents know this **very** well, but they throw sand
AP : 2 3 :006(240) [0365] law and conflicts with the **very** decrees of councils.
AP : 2 3 :027(243) [0371] on priests, though in this **very** analogy marriage is
AP : 2 3 :047(246) [0377] of godly consciences being **very** troubled about the
AP : 2 3 :064(248) [0381] We have already refuted this **very** specious argument.
AP : 2 4 :016(252) [0389] Socrates says that he is **very** fond of distinctions because
AP : 2 4 :020(252) [0389] types of sacrifice and be **very** careful not to confuse them.
AP : 2 4 :052(259) [0403] This is a **very** convincing argument for the ignorant,
AP : 2 4 :053(259) [0403] twist passages from this **very** epistle against us — like this
AP : 2 4 :068(262) [0407] Christ was supposed to be **very** pleased with a mark that
AP : 2 4 :068(262) [0409] about faith, whose true meaning **very** few understand.
AP : 2 4 :092(266) [0417] There is no need here of a **very** lengthy discussion.
AP : 2 7 :010(270) [0423] we have produced; these are the **very** words they used.
AP : 2 7 :032(274) [0431] As Bernard also says **very** powerfully, "First of all, you
AP : 2 7 :046(277) [0435] Thus David was poor in a **very** rich kingdom.
AP : 2 7 :052(278) [0437] going on before their **very** eyes, our opponents should
AP : 2 8 :004(281) [0445] In these **very** serious and difficult controversies the people
S 1 : P R :004(289) [0455] although they know **very** well that I teach otherwise.
S 1 : P R :009(290) [0457] and judge of us all, knows **very** well that they lie and have
S 1 : P R :010(290) [0457] I should be **very** happy to see a true council assemble in
S 2 : 0 4 :005(299) [0473] Christian church can exist **very** well without such a head,
S 2 : 0 4 :008(299) [0473] command, he would **very** easily and quickly be despised
TR : 0 0 :008(320) [0505] For this was the **very** question the disciples were disputing
TR : 0 0 :075(333) [0525] Besides, since this is a **very** serious charge, nobody should
SC : P R :020(340) [0537] Make **very** plain to them the shocking evils they
SC : 0 9 :003(355) [0561] you, and to esteem them **very** highly in love because of
SC : 0 9 :005(355) [0561] are ministers of God, attending to this **very** thing.
LC : P R :001(358) [0567] pastors and preachers are **very** negligent in this respect
LC : S P :027(364) [0581] manner but briefly and **very** simply, so that it may
LC : 0 1 :009(365) [0583] **Very** few there are who are cheerful, who do not fret and
LC : 0 1 :055(372) [0595] blasphemers, not only the **very** crass ones who are well
LC : 0 1 :062(373) [0597] To repeat **very** briefly, it is either simply to lie and assert
LC : 0 1 :071(374) [0601] and useful habit, and **very** effective against the devil, who
LC : 0 1 :072(374) [0601] and vanished in the **very** moment I called upon God.
LC : 0 1 :107(379) [0611] body, that we respect them **very** highly and that next to
LC : 0 1 :107(379) [0611] and that next to God we give them the **very** highest place.
LC : 0 1 :117(381) [0615] Even though it seems **very** trivial and contemptible, make
LC : 0 1 :121(382) [0615] I repeat, I should be **very** glad if we were to open our eyes
LC : 0 1 :124(382) [0617] can parents, as a rule, do **very** much; one fool trains
LC : 0 1 :129(383) [0617] The perversity of the world God knows **very** well.
LC : 0 1 :160(387) [0627] But they **very** seldom receive it, for the world's way of
LC : 0 1 :171(388) [0629] nor is it recognized how **very** necessary it is to devote
LC : 0 1 :232(396) [0647] This commandment is **very** far-reaching, as we have
LC : 0 1 :243(397) [0649] the evidence before our **very** eyes every day that no stolen
LC : 0 1 :318(408) [0673] thoroughly, do your **very** best, and you will surely find so
LC : 0 2 :004(411) [0679] as a first step, for **very** simple persons to learn to
LC : 0 2 :024(413) [0683] Such, **very** briefly, is the meaning of this article.
LC : 0 2 :026(413) [0685] This article is **very** rich and far-reaching, but in order to
LC : 0 2 :063(419) [0695] his work exquisitely depicted in **very** short but rich words.
LC : 0 2 :064(419) [0695] He created us for this **very** purpose, to redeem and
LC : 0 2 :067(419) [0697] you see that the Creed is a **very** different teaching from
LC : 0 3 :004(420) [0699] Prayer part by part, it is **very** necessary to exhort and
LC : 0 3 :015(422) [0701] The **very** commandment that applied to St. Paul applies
LC : 0 3 :022(423) [0703] and puts into our mouths the **very** words we are to use.
LC : 0 3 :034(425) [0707] we shall treat the Lord's Prayer **very** briefly and clearly.
LC : 0 3 :057(427) [0713] Imagine a **very** rich and mighty emperor who bade a poor
LC : 0 3 :068(429) [0717] God himself have been **very** simply expressed, yet we
LC : 0 3 :072(430) [0719] It is a brief and simple word, but **very** comprehensive.
LC : 0 3 :076(431) [0719] Let us outline **very** briefly how comprehensively this
LC : 0 3 :109(435) [0729] the devil is likely in this **very** hour to send such a shaft
LC : 0 4 :017(438) [0735] then: Baptism is a **very** different thing from all other
LC : 0 4 :069(445) [0749] It is as the proverb says **very** truly, "Evil unchecked
LC : 0 5 :022(449) [0757] and sign — indeed, as the **very** gift he has provided for me
LC : 0 5 :032(450) [0761] confess that these are the **very** words which we hear
LC : 0 5 :047(452) [0763] Indeed, the **very** words, "as often as you do it," imply that
LC : 0 5 :071(455) [0769] your neck and which is the **very** reason for this command
LC : 0 6 :016(459) [0000] noticed nor preached the **very** necessary second part; it
EP : 0 1 :025(469) [0785] This terminology sets forth **very** clearly the distinction
EP : 0 7 :001(481) [0807] from the latter at the **very** outset when the Augsburg
EP : 0 7 :004(482) [0809] in part talk our language **very** plausibly and claim to
SD : P R :007(502) [0849] just as during the **very** lifetime of the holy apostles
SD : 0 1 :001(508) [0859] a word, or a deed but the **very** nature itself out of which,
SD : 0 1 :048(516) [0875] said that original sin is the **very** nature of corrupted man,
SD : 0 1 :053(517) [0877] corrupted though original sin to its **very** foundation.
SD : 0 2 :014(523) [0885] appealing passage is of **very** great comfort to all devout
SD : 0 2 :020(525) [0889] of the body, man is indeed **very** clever, intelligent, and
SD : 0 3 :007(540) [0917] in order to indicate how **very** important it is that this
SD : 0 3 :029(544) [0925] diverted (as Satan would **very** much like) from the main
SD : 0 3 :029(544) [0925] condemn works, since the **very** nature of this article
SD : 0 4 :003(551) [0939] In this controversy a **very** few asserted the provocative
SD : 0 4 :034(556) [0949] and salvation may be **very** certain to us, Paul ascribes to
SD : 0 5 :022(562) [0959] Dr. Luther **very** diligently urged this distinction in nearly
SD : 0 7 :043(576) [0987] He knows **very** well what and how he must speak, and he
SD : 0 7 :093(586) [1005] Sacramentarians at the **very** beginning in the following
SD : 0 7 :101(587) [1007] he is one person with God, **very** far beyond creatures, as
SD : 1 1 :001(616) [1063] become the occasion of **very** serious controversies at
SD : 1 1 :004(616) [1063] At the **very** outset we must carefully note the difference
SD : 1 1 :030(621) [1073] Though this is still **very** weak in them, they nevertheless
SD : 1 1 :079(629) [1089] Hence Paul **very** carefully distinguishes between the work
SD : 1 2 :006(633) [1097] position so clearly that our **very** adversaries would have
SD : 1 2 :013(634) [1099] not esteem infant Baptism **very** highly and do not

Vessel (5), Vessels (14)
AP : 2 3 :043(245) [0375] each one to possess his **vessel** in holiness (I Thess. 4:4).
AP : 2 3 :064(248) [0381] "Purify yourselves, you who bear the **vessels** of the Lord."
AP : 2 3 :064(248) [0381] you who bear the **vessels** of the Lord," must be taken to
AP : 2 3 :065(248) [0381] Paul calls possessing one's **vessel** in holiness
AP : 2 3 :066(248) [0381] you who bear the **vessels** of the Lord," requires impure
AP : 2 4 :051(259) [0401] Candles, golden **vessels**, and ornaments like that are
SD : 1 1 :060(626) [1083] pure and unmerited grace toward the "**vessels** of mercy."
SD : 1 1 :079(629) [1089] God, who alone prepares **vessels** of honor, and the work
SD : 1 1 :079(629) [1089] and not of God, has made himself a **vessel** of dishonor.
SD : 1 1 :079(629) [1089] with much patience the **vessels** of wrath fitted for
SD : 1 1 :079(629) [1089] riches of his glory in the **vessels** of mercy, which he has
SD : 1 1 :080(629) [1089] that God "endured the **vessels** of wrath with much
SD : 1 1 :080(629) [1089] He does not say that God made them **vessels** of wrath.
SD : 1 1 :082(630) [1089] can transform the **vessels** of dishonor into vessels of
SD : 1 1 :082(630) [1089] vessels of dishonor into **vessels** of honor when he writes,
SD : 1 1 :082(630) [1089] ignoble, then he will be a **vessel** for noble use, consecrated
SD : 1 1 :082(630) [1091] have been impure and therefore a **vessel** of dishonor.
SD : 1 1 :082(630) [1091] Concerning "the **vessels** of mercy" he says specifically that
SD : 1 1 :082(630) [1091] who have prepared themselves to be **vessels** of damnation.

Vestments (9)
AG : 2 6 :006(064) [0071] prescribed fasts, distinctions among foods, **vestments**, etc.
AL : 2 6 :008(065) [0071] of certain holy days, rites, fasts, and **vestments**.
AP : 1 5 :021(218) [0321] by a variety of **vestments**, ornaments, and innumerable
AP : 2 4 :001(249) [0385] such as the order of the lessons, prayers, **vestments**, etc.
AP : 2 7 :027(274) [0429] in these silly observances of **vestments** and similar trifles.
AP : 2 7 :069(281) [0443] foods, lessons, chants, **vestments**, sandals, cinctures — all
S 1 : P R :013(291) [0459] concerning fasts, **vestments**, tonsures, and chasubles.
S 2 : 0 4 :014(301) [0475] ceremonies of churches, **vestments**, food, personnel, and
LC : 0 1 :091(377) [0607] holy and consecrated **vestments** gathered together in one

Vex (2), Vexation (1), Vexed (1), Vexes (1)
S 3 : 0 3 :018(306) [0483] by the law or vainly **vexed** with a sorrowful spirit by the
LC : 0 1 :125(382) [0617] and all the angels, that it **vexes** all devils, and, besides,
LC : 0 1 :225(395) [0645] neglects things to the **vexation** and annoyance of his
LC : 0 3 :086(432) [0723] among people who sorely **vex** us and give us occasion for
SD : 1 1 :070(627) [1085] adversary is accustomed to tempt and **vex** pious hearts.

Vicar (2), Vicars (2)
AP : 2 1 :044(236) [0357] Gospel of Christ, and as **vicars** of God they should defend
S 2 : 0 2 :021(296) [0467] monasteries, chapters, and **vicars** have obligated
TR : 0 0 :002(320) [0503] bishop of Rome calls himself the **vicar** of Christ on earth.
TR : 0 0 :008(320) [0505] leader and, as it were, the **vicar** of Christ after his

Vice (19), Vices (13)
AG : 2 3 :001(051) [0061] and who went so far as to engage in abominable **vices**.
AG : 2 3 :013(053) [0063] occasion for many great and evil **vices** and much scandal.
AG : 2 3 :014(054) [0063] disgraceful lewdness and **vice** to prevail in German lands.
AG : 2 3 :018(054) [0063] and abominable **vice** that even some honest men among
AG : 2 3 :018(054) [0063] have complained that such **vices** among the clergy would,
AL : 0 2 :002(029) [0043] And this disease or **vice** of origin is truly sin, which even
AL : 0 2 :003(029) [0045] others who deny that the **vice** of origin is sin and who
AL : 2 3 :014(053) [0063] against the introduction into Germany of more **vices**.
AP : 0 2 :005(101) [0107] original sin is not some **vice** or corruption in human
AP : 0 2 :049(106) [0119] In others, even grosser **vices** appear.
AP : 2 3 :052(246) [0377] morals and how productive of **vices** and shameful lusts.
AP : 2 3 :054(246) [0379] Sodom and Gomorrah reveal God's wrath at human **vice**.
AP : 2 3 :054(246) [0379] Similar **vices** have preceded the fall of many other cities,
AP : 2 7 :004(269) [0421] There are other **vices**, too, which we would rather not talk
S 1 : P R :012(290) [0459] vain display, all manner of **vice** and wickedness,
LC : 0 1 :031(369) [0589] head is right, the whole life must be right, and **vice** versa.
LC : 0 1 :202(392) [0639] cesspool of all kinds of **vice** and lewdness among us, this
LC : 0 1 :217(394) [0643] and other shameful **vices** resulting from contempt of
LC : 0 1 :224(395) [0643] is a widespread, common **vice**, but people pay so little
LC : 0 1 :264(400) [0655] the detestable, shameful **vice** of back-biting or slander by
LC : 0 1 :264(400) [0655] It is a common **vice** of human nature that everyone would
LC : 0 1 :265(400) [0655] To avoid this **vice**, therefore, we should note that nobody
LC : 0 1 :293(404) [0663] or theft, since these **vices** were sufficiently forbidden in
LC : 0 4 :066(445) [0749] he is beset with all **vices** and by nature has nothing good
LC : 0 4 :070(445) [0749] **Vice** thus grows and increases in him from his youth up.
LC : 0 4 :070(445) [0749] who has no particular **vice**, becomes vicious and unchaste
LC : 0 4 :070(445) [0749] full manhood, the real **vices** become more and more
SD : 0 1 :013(511) [0863] blindness, and drives them headlong into all sorts of **vice**.
SD : 0 2 :074(535) [0909] to avoid manifest sins and **vices**; or that the will of man is
SD : 0 8 :039(598) [1027] to the humanity, or **vice** versa — for example, 'Was it not
SD : 0 8 :041(599) [1029] union, all that happens to the humanity, and **vice** versa.
SD : 1 1 :010(618) [1067] live in all kinds of sin and **vice** without repentance,

Viceroy (2)
AG : P R :018(026) [0041] Your Imperial Majesty's **viceroy** (His Royal Majesty of
AG : P R :018(026) [0041] Your Imperial Majesty's **viceroy**, administrators, and

Vicious (5), Viciously (1)
AP : 0 2 :001(100) [0105] sin includes, they **viciously** misinterpret and distort a
AP : 0 2 :024(103) [0111] both the defect and the **vicious** disposition that follows.
AP : 0 4 :012(108) [0123] of view there are many **vicious** errors that would take a
AP : 1 2 :003(183) [0253] and have corrected many **vicious** errors which through
AP : 1 2 :007(183) [0255] This is also a **vicious** error.
LC : 0 4 :070(445) [0749] particular vice, becomes **vicious** and unchaste as he

Victim (8), Victims (4)
AP : 0 4 :288(151) [0203] sacrificed human **victims** and undertook many other
AP : 2 3 :070(249) [0383] of the many innocent **victims** of their rage will also cry
AP : 2 4 :023(253) [0391] uses here (*'asam*) means a **victim** sacrificed for
AP : 2 4 :023(253) [0391] this meant that a **victim** was to come to reconcile God
AP : 2 4 :023(253) [0391] Latins offered a sacrificial **victim** to placate the wrath of
AP : 2 4 :023(253) [0391] had heard that a human **victim** was going to placate God
AP : 2 4 :023(253) [0391] Christ became a sacrificial **victim** or trespass offering to
AP : 2 4 :029(255) [0393] It rejects sacrificial **victims** and requires prayer: "Do I eat
AP : 2 4 :088(265) [0413] this as "reasonable **victim**" and apply it to the body of
AP : 2 7 :058(279) [0439] or the slaughter of **victims** would not be an act of worship
LC : 0 1 :151(386) [0625] Or he will fall **victim** to the hangman, or perish through
LC : 0 1 :303(405) [0667] another's hand so that the **victim** is helpless to prevent it.

Victor (1), Victorious (1), Victory (11)
AP : 0 4 :079(118) [0143] to God, who gives us the **victory** through our Lord Jesus

Continued ▶

AP : 04 :192(133) [0175] works Christ shows his **victory** over the devil, just as the
AP : 04 :218(137) [0179] Here they celebrate a great **victory**.
AP : 04 :291(152) [0203] sins, reconciliation, and **victory** over the terrors of sin and
AP : 12 :146(205) [0297] to God, who gives us the **victory** through our Lord Jesus
AP : 12 :146(205) [0297] say, "Who gives us the **victory** if we set our satisfactions
AP : 12 :157(207) [0301] because of Christ, who is the **victor** over sin and death.
AP : 23 :032(243) [0373] they would stage a wonderful **victory** celebration.
S2 : 01 :005(292) [0463] the devil, and all our adversaries will gain the **victory**.
SC : 03 :018(348) [0549] so tempted, we may finally prevail and gain the **victory**.
LC : 03 :077(431) [0721] govern well and to be **victorious** over the Turks and all
LC : 04 :041(441) [0743] promises and brings — **victory** over death and the devil,
EP : 09 :001(492) [0827] Christ's suffering or to his glorious **victory** and triumph?

View (36), Viewed (1), Viewpoint (1), Views (9)
PR : PR :012(007) [0013] earnestness and zeal in **view** of the office that we bear and
PR : PR :024(013) [0023] imaginations and **views** will be transmitted to subsequent
AG : 08 :003(033) [0047] and all others who hold contrary **views** are condemned.
AG : 25 :010(063) [0069] That this was also the **view** of the Fathers can be seen in
AP : PR :004(098) [0099] to the opponents' point of **view** with a clear conscience?
AP : PR :017(099) [0103] undoubtedly brought into **view** many articles of Christian
AP : 02 :012(102) [0109] with philosophical **views** about the perfection of nature
AP : 02 :034(104) [0113] all liars," that is, they do not have the right **view** of God.
AP : 02 :036(105) [0115] This **view** pleased later generations so much that they
AP : 04 :010(108) [0123] Because this **view** naturally flatters men, it has produced
AP : 04 :010(108) [0123] that form of worship or devotion with this **view** in mind.
AP : 04 :012(108) [0123] In this point of **view** there are many vicious errors that
AP : 04 :180(132) [0171] or our works: this promise we must always keep in **view**.
AP : 04 :231(139) [0185] excluded, and hence this **view** is far removed from his
AP : 04 :260(145) [0195] We must always keep this important teaching in **view**.
AP : 04 :271(147) [0199] In this way we must **view** the preaching of penitence.
AP : 11 :008(181) [0251] The same **viewpoint** was approved by Panormitanus and
AP : 15 :010(216) [0317] From this point of **view** there is no difference between
AP : 16 :008(223) [0333] from their erroneous **view** that the Gospel is something
AP : 21 :016(231) [0347] people but discuss only the **views** of the theologians.
LC : 01 :130(383) [0619] He who **views** the matter in this light will, without
LC : 01 :209(393) [0639] the false clergy do, but **view** it in the light of God's Word,
LC : 04 :081(446) [0751] is responsible for this **view**, for he wrote, "Repentance is
LC : 05 :014(448) [0755] away from the elements or **view** them apart from the
EP : 01 :003(466) [0779] diligently, because the **view** that admits no distinction
EP : 01 :015(468) [0783] of the magnet; likewise the **view** that this blemish may be
EP : 08 :003(487) [0819] for the opposite **view** against the Sacramentarians.
EP : 12 :006(498) [0839] Baptism (which according to this **view** they do not need).
SD : PR :003(502) [0847] took a jaundiced **view** of this Confession, but, thank
SD : PR :006(504) [0853] Confession, with a **view** both to presenting the doctrines
SD : 01 :002(508) [0859] however, took a contrary **view** and taught that original
SD : 02 :002(520) [0881] will can be found and **viewed** as being in four distinct and
SD : 02 :045(530) [0899] Such erroneous **views** are contrary to the Holy Scriptures
SD : 02 :066(534) [0907] a wagon together, such a **view** could by no means be
SD : 02 :086(538) [0913] introduced to support the **view** that man's naturally free
SD : 03 :037(546) [0929] we might or should not **view** our works as either the
SD : 04 :003(551) [0939] party took the contrary **view** that good works are
SD : 04 :020(554) [0945] and condemn as false the **view** that good works are free to
SD : 07 :010(571) [0975] clearly presents the same **view** in the Small Catechism in
SD : 07 :103(587) [1007] to prove that even this mode is contrary to our **view**.
SD : 07 :113(589) [1011] mutually contradictory **views**, no matter how manifold
SD : 07 :128(591) [1015] and rejected erroneous **views** have been criticized and
SD : 07 :128(591) [1015] opinions or erroneous **views** there may be can easily be
SD : 10 :026(615) [1061] condemn as wrongful the **view** that the commandments
SD : 11 :009(617) [1065] we are not to **view** this eternal election or divine ordering
SD : 11 :010(618) [1065] Such a **view**, however, leads many to draw and formulate
SD : 12 :040(636) [1103] In **view** of this we have advisedly, in the fear and

Vigilant (2)
LC : 01 :299(405) [0665] law, for as the saying has it, "The law favors the **vigilant**."
LC : 03 :061(428) [0715] but also for defenders, protectors, and **vigilant** guardians.

Vigilantius (3)
AP : 21 :002(229) [0343] controversy with **Vigilantius** and say, "On this field of
AP : 21 :002(229) [0343] Jerome conquered **Vigilantius** eleven hundred years ago."
AP : 21 :002(229) [0343] between Jerome and **Vigilantius** there is not a syllable

Vigils (4)
S2 : 02 :012(294) [0465] with requiem Masses, with **vigils**, with the weekly,
S2 : 02 :016(295) [0467] of demanding Masses, **vigils**, pilgrimages, and other
S3 : 03 :026(307) [0487] by instituting Masses and **vigils** for the dead and
S3 : 03 :028(308) [0487] evil thoughts by fasting, **vigils**, prayers, Masses, coarse

Vigorously (2)
AP : 28 :008(282) [0445] our opponents, who **vigorously** defend their traditions
SD : PR :007(502) [0849] were compelled **vigorously** to denounce all of these in

Vile (3)
LC : 03 :063(428) [0715] For our flesh is in itself **vile** and inclined to evil, even
LC : 03 :105(434) [0727] long as we remain in this **vile** life in which we are
SD : PR :014(506) [0857] the precious from the **vile**" (John 10:12-16, 27; Jer.

Villainy (1)
LC : 01 :059(372) [0597] be dragged in to turn the **villainy** into righteousness and

Vine (2)
AP : 10 :003(179) [0247] doubted that Christ is a **vine** in this way and that we are
AP : 12 :085(194) [0277] do nothing," and "I am the **vine**, you are the branches."

Violate (5), Violated (5), Violating (2), Violation (6)
PR : PR :011(006) [0011] to a conclusion without **violation** of divine truth, and in
AL : 26 :044(070) [0075] such diversity does not **violate** the unity of the church.
AL : 27 :034(076) [0079] Finally, although the **violation** of vows might be
AL : 27 :034(076) [0081] marriages of persons who **violated** them ought to be
AP : PR :003(098) [0099] however unpleasant, that did not **violate** our consciences.
AP : 14 :004(215) [0315] themselves are gentler with those who **violate** them.
AP : 15 :036(220) [0325] The apostles **violated** traditions, and Christ excused
AP : 24 :089(266) [0415] of the name of God in **violation** of the Second
AP : 27 :064(280) [0441] incur condemnation for having **violated** their first faith."
TR : 00 :078(333) [0527] betrothals in **violation** of the right of parents.
LC : 01 :057(372) [0597] that in no one shall a **violation** be condoned or left
LC : 01 :096(378) [0607] this commandment is **violated** not only by those who
LC : 01 :189(390) [0635] this commandment is **violated** not only when a person
EP : 10 :010(494) [0831] as necessary things, in **violation** of the Christian liberty
EP : 12 :014(499) [0841] no Christian, without **violating** his conscience, may use an
SD : 08 :024(595) [1023] he was born of a virgin without **violating** her virginity.
SD : 10 :025(615) [1061] the wrath of God, **violate** love, confirm the enemies of
SD : 11 :096(632) [1095] such harmony as will not **violate** God's honor, that will

Violence (13), Violent (6), Violently (4)
AG : 00 :000(049) [0059] been introduced with **violence**), we are obliged by our
AG : 28 :002(081) [0083] with reserved cases and **violent** use of the ban, but have
AL : 28 :002(081) [0083] reservation of cases and **violent** excommunications but
AP : 04 :236(140) [0185] up to even by those who most **violently** defend them.
AP : 04 :357(162) [0217] in their explanation do **violence** not only to Scripture but
AP : 21 :044(236) [0357] you not to agree to the **violent** counsels of our opponents
AP : 22 :016(238) [0361] excommunicate and **violently** persecute anyone that uses
AP : 24 :043(258) [0399] wickedness of some of this, they **violently** defend it.
AP : 27 :048(277) [0437] Yes, he does, but they do **violence** to the text when they
S2 : 02 :001(293) [0463] it runs into direct and **violent** conflict with this
TR : 00 :031(325) [0513] excommunicate the godless without physical **violence**.
SC : 09 :002(354) [0561] no drunkard, not **violent** but gentle, not quarrelsome, and
LC : 01 :151(386) [0625] will inflict injury, injustice, and **violence** upon him.
LC : 01 :155(386) [0625] of unfaithfulness, **violence**, and injustice; but we are
LC : 01 :185(390) [0633] the wickedness and **violence** of others, and he has set up
LC : 01 :245(398) [0649] robs and takes things by **violence** and dishonesty must
LC : 01 :308(406) [0669] a yard, and at length open injustice and **violence** follow.
LC : 01 :328(410) [0675] no harm, injury, or **violence**, nor in any way molest him,
LC : 03 :068(429) [0717] in the face of all **violence** and persecution, submitting to
LC : 03 :094(433) [0725] who does us harm, **violence**, and injustice, bears malice
LC : 03 :103(434) [0727] hatred and envy, enmity, **violence** and injustice, perfidy,
SD : PR :002(501) [0847] institutions, attacked it **violently** (although
SD : 07 :060(580) [0995] actually and in deed laid **violent** hands upon the body of

Vipers (1)
S3 : 03 :032(308) [0489] to repent, you brood of **vipers**, who has given you any

Virgin (21), Virginity (17), Virgins (3)
AG : 03 :001(029) [0045] became man, born of the **virgin** Mary, and that the two
AG : 27 :020(074) [0079] endowed with the gift of **virginity** by a special act of God.
AL : 03 :001(029) [0045] on man's nature in the womb of the blessed **virgin** Mary.
AL : 03 :002(030) [0045] man, who was born of the **virgin** Mary, truly suffered,
AP : 07 :019(171) [0233] is like a net (Matt. 13:47) or like ten **virgins** (Matt. 25:1).
AP : 21 :025(232) [0349] merits of the most blessed **virgin** Mary and of all the
AP : 21 :028(232) [0351] estimation the blessed **Virgin** has completely replaced
AP : 21 :030(233) [0351] Hilary says of the foolish **virgins**: "Since the foolish
AP : 21 :030(233) [0351] virgins: "Since the foolish **virgins** could not go out with
AP : 21 :031(233) [0351] by the merits of the blessed **Virgin** or of the other saints.
AP : 21 :034(234) [0353] a statue of the blessed **Virgin** which was manipulated like
AP : 23 :020(242) [0369] correctly observes, "**Virginity** is something that can only
AP : 23 :034(244) [0373] As **virginity** is impure in the ungodly, therefore, so
AP : 23 :036(244) [0373] Neither by **virginity** nor by marriage are we justified, but
AP : 23 :037(244) [0373] marriage on the same level with **virginity**, as Jovinian did.
AP : 23 :038(244) [0373] We do not put marriage on the same level with **virginity**.
AP : 23 :038(244) [0373] So also **virginity** is a gift that surpasses marriage.
AP : 23 :039(244) [0375] makes an architect, so the **virgin** does not merit
AP : 23 :039(244) [0375] not merit justification by **virginity** any more than the
AP : 23 :040(244) [0375] nor Paul commends **virginity** because it justifies but
AP : 23 :040(245) [0375] He commends **virginity** for the sake of mediation and
AP : 23 :040(245) [0375] He does not say that **virginity** merits salvation or the
AP : 23 :064(248) [0381] said that without faith **virginity** is not pure in the sight of
AP : 23 :069(249) [0383] do not put marriage and **virginity** on the same level, but
AP : 23 :069(249) [0383] same level, but neither **virginity** nor marriage merits
AP : 27 :027(273) [0429] **Virginity** is recommended — but to those who have the
AP : 27 :053(278) [0437] the rosary of the blessed **Virgin**, which is mere babbling,
S1 : 01 :000(292) [0461] of man, and was born of the pure, holy, and **virgin** Mary.
SC : 02 :003(345) [0545] *Holy Spirit, born of the* ***virgin*** *Mary, suffered under*
SC : 02 :004(345) [0545] true man, born of the **virgin** Mary, is my Lord, who has
LC : SP :012(363) [0577] Holy Spirit, born of the **virgin** Mary, suffered under
LC : 01 :201(392) [0637] The state of **virginity** was not commended, neither were
LC : 02 :025(413) [0683] *Holy Spirit, born of the* ***virgin*** *Mary, suffered under*
LC : 02 :031(414) [0687] of the Holy Spirit and the **Virgin**, that he might become
EP : 12 :003(498) [0839] body and blood from the **virgin** Mary, but brought them
SD : 08 :006(592) [1017] born of the most blessed **virgin** Mary, as it is written, "Of
SD : 08 :024(595) [1023] Mary, the most blessed **virgin**, did not conceive a mere,
SD : 08 :024(595) [1023] in that he was born of a **virgin** without violating her
SD : 08 :024(595) [1023] he was born of a virgin without violating her **virginity**.
SD : 08 :024(595) [1023] she is truly the mother of God and yet remained a **virgin**.
SD : 12 :025(635) [1099] flesh and blood from the **virgin** Mary but brought it

Virtue (36), Virtues (18), Virtuous (5)
AG : 28 :029(085) [0087] and in tithes), they have these by **virtue** of human right.
AP : 04 :035(112) [0131] sin even when they do **virtuous** things without the Holy
AP : 04 :035(112) [0131] works that seem **virtuous**, for God judges the heart.
AP : 04 :151(127) [0163] of sins by other **virtues** of the law or on account of them
AP : 04 :151(127) [0163] government, etc.), even though these **virtues** must follow.
AP : 04 :181(132) [0171] not justify; still they are **virtues**, in keeping with the
AP : 04 :225(138) [0183] that the greatest and the main **virtue** should justify.
AP : 04 :226(138) [0183] neighbor is the greatest **virtue** because the great
AP : 04 :226(138) [0183] The greatest **virtue**, they say, justifies.
AP : 04 :227(138) [0183] not justify, neither does the greatest **virtue** of the law.
AP : 04 :227(138) [0183] But that **virtue** justifies which takes hold of Christ,
AP : 04 :227(139) [0183] This **virtue** is faith.
AP : 04 :243(141) [0189] This **virtue** is necessary for the preservation of domestic
AP : 04 :382(165) [0225] our good works are valid by **virtue** of Christ's suffering.
AP : 04 :382(165) [0225] our works are valid by **virtue** of the suffering of Christ.
AP : 21 :006(230) [0345] and then of their other **virtues**, which each should imitate
AP : 27 :037(275) [0433] in the love of their neighbor, and similar spiritual **virtues**.
LC : 01 :059(372) [0597] we all have this beautiful **virtue** that whenever we commit
LC : 01 :175(389) [0631] instructed citizens, **virtuous** and home-loving wives who
LC : 01 :194(391) [0635] but an ordinary heathen **virtue**, as Christ says in Matthew
LC : 01 :208(393) [0639] God, godly living, and all **virtues**, and fight against

Continued ▶

LC : 0 1 :266(401) [0657] to administer punishment by **virtue** of your office.
LC : 0 1 :274(402) [0659] By **virtue** of his office he does not do his neighbor good
LC : 0 1 :289(404) [0663] a particularly fine, noble **virtue** always to put the best
LC : 0 1 :300(405) [0667] as honest and **virtuous** because they have not offended
LC : 0 1 :313(407) [0671] chastity, kindness, etc., and all that these **virtues** involve.
LC : 0 2 :048(416) [0691] and give the house its name by **virtue** of the assembly.
LC : 0 4 :009(437) [0733] and churches solely by **virtue** of his letters and seals, then
LC : 0 4 :017(438) [0735] all other water, not by **virtue** of the natural substance but
LC : 0 4 :017(438) [0737] terms you can — all by **virtue** of the Word, which is a
LC : 0 5 :014(448) [0755] and necessary, then in **virtue** of them they are truly the
LC : 0 5 :018(448) [0757] body and blood by **virtue** of these words which are
EP : 0 2 :010(471) [0789] who teach that man by **virtue** of his own powers could
EP : 0 3 :015(475) [0795] account of the love and **virtue** that the Holy Spirit has
EP : 0 3 :022(475) [0797] and by the confession of the lips, along with other **virtues**.
EP : 0 7 :020(484) [0813] not at all in our own **virtues** or in our internal and
EP : 1 2 :008(498) [0839] the children of God by **virtue** of their birth from Christian
SD : 0 2 :024(526) [0891] and other God-pleasing **virtues** and obedience in him.
SD : 0 2 :026(526) [0891] and free will are able to lead an outwardly **virtuous** life.
SD : 0 2 :071(535) [0909] and other God-pleasing **virtues** in us, so that they are
SD : 0 3 :013(541) [0919] and so God-pleasing a **virtue**, but because it lays hold on
SD : 0 3 :030(544) [0925] nor in love nor in other **virtues**, but solely in Christ and
SD : 0 3 :031(544) [0925] nor love nor any other **virtue** the means and instrument
SD : 0 3 :035(545) [0927] sanctification, love, **virtues**, and good works, these should
SD : 0 3 :038(546) [0929] we must exclude love and every other **virtue** or work.
SD : 0 3 :039(546) [0929] renewal, sanctification, **virtues**, nor other good works are
SD : 0 3 :051(548) [0933] we make with our mouth, and through other **virtues**.
SD : 0 3 :055(549) [0935] human merits, works, **virtues**, and worthiness and that
SD : 0 3 :062(550) [0937] account of the love and **virtues** which are poured into
SD : 0 7 :026(573) [0981] his body and blood by **virtue** of these words which are
SD : 0 7 :049(578) [0989] figurative sense, or of the **virtue** of his body and the
SD : 0 7 :055(579) [0991] only according to its **virtue** and operation, then the bread
SD : 0 7 :055(579) [0991] body but in the spirit, the **virtue**, and the benefits of
SD : 0 7 :075(583) [0999] and received by the **virtue** and potency of the same words
SD : 0 7 :075(583) [0999] the spoken words by the **virtue** of the first institution,
SD : 0 7 :117(589) [1013] to faith only the **virtue**, operation, and merit of the
SD : 0 8 :085(608) [1047] everlasting God, who by **virtue** of the exchange of
SD : 1 1 :073(628) [1087] in all Christian **virtues**, in all godliness, modesty,
SD : 1 1 :075(628) [1087] not rest on our piety or **virtue** but solely on the merit of

Visible (8), Visibly (2)
AG : 0 1 :003(028) [0043] creator and preserver of all things **visible** and invisible.
AL : 0 1 :002(027) [0043] maker and preserver of all things, **visible** and invisible.
AP : 0 4 :189(133) [0175] Gospel among men, he **visibly** pits the witness of the
AP : 1 3 :005(212) [0309] called the sacrament "the **visible** Word," for the rite is
LC : 0 4 :021(439) [0737] Holy Spirit descended **visibly**, and that the divine glory
EP : 0 7 :040(486) [0817] 19. That the external **visible** elements of bread and wine
SD : 0 7 :003(569) [0973] and quickened by the **visible** signs in the same way as by
SD : 0 7 :011(571) [0975] are truly offered with the **visible** elements, the bread and
SD : 0 7 :086(584) [1003] the entire external and **visible** action of the Supper as
SD : 0 7 :126(591) [1015] that the elements (the **visible** forms of the blessed bread

Vision (1)
SD : 0 7 :100(586) [1007] illustrations, my **vision** penetrates air, light, or water and

Visit (2), Visitation (1), Visitations (1), Visiting (3), Visitor (1), Visits (1)
PR : PR :026(014) [0025] through diligent **visitation** of churches and schools, the
AG : 1 8 :005(040) [0051] or not to eat or drink or **visit** a friend, whether to dress or
AP : 0 4 :027(111) [0127] him in death and in his other **visitations**, and not covet.
AP : 0 4 :301(153) [0205] judgment of God, who **visits** on human nature so many
SC : PR :001(338) [0533] when I was a **visitor** constrained me to prepare this brief
SC : 0 1 :021(344) [0543] God am a jealous God, **visiting** the iniquity of the fathers
LC : 0 1 :030(368) [0589] *God, mighty and jealous,* ***visiting*** *the iniquity of the*
LC : 0 1 :191(391) [0635] me, I was sick and in prison and you did not **visit** me."
LC : 0 1 :320(408) [0673] *God, am a jealous God,* ***visiting*** *the iniquity of the fathers*

Vital (1)
SD : 0 4 :012(553) [0941] Faith is a **vital**, deliberate trust in God's grace, so certain

Vitiated (1)
LC : 0 4 :055(443) [0745] of the Altar is not **vitiated** if someone approaches it with

Vivificatio (1)
EP : 0 3 :008(474) [0793] (rebirth) and ***vivificatio*** (making alive) are used in place of

Vivification (1)
SD : 0 3 :020(542) [0921] Likewise the term "**vivification**," that is, being made alive,

Vocabulary (2)
SD : 0 1 :050(517) [0875] specific reference to **vocabulary** and phraseology,
SD : 0 1 :054(517) [0877] since they are not the common man's **vocabulary**.

Vocation (2)
S3 : 1 0 :000(314) [0497] X. Ordination and **Vocation**
TR : 0 0 :024(324) [0511] the church especially possesses the right of **vocation**.

Vocatione (2)
AL : 2 0 :014(043) [0055] teaches similarly in *De* ***vocatione*** *gentium* and elsewhere,
AL : 2 0 :014(043) [0055] elsewhere, for in his *De* ***vocatione*** *gentium* he says:

Voice (29), Voices (2)
AG : 0 1 :006(028) [0043] a physical word or **voice** and that the Holy Spirit is a
AG : 2 5 :003(061) [0069] It is not the **voice** or word of the man who speaks it, but
AG : 2 5 :004(062) [0069] much as if we heard God's **voice** from heaven, that we
AL : 2 5 :003(062) [0069] highly because it is the **voice** of God and is pronounced
AL : 2 5 :004(062) [0069] absolution as God's own **voice** heard from heaven, and
AP : 0 4 :257(144) [0193] peace unless they hear the **voice** of God, clearly promising
AP : 0 4 :261(145) [0195] prophetic and evangelical **voice** which Daniel surely
AP : 0 4 :337(159) [0215] are worthless is the very **voice** of faith, as is evident from
AP : 0 4 :400(168) [0227] as the Lord says, "My sheep hear my **voice**" (John 10:27).
AP : 1 1 :002(180) [0249] of God — yes, the very **voice** of the Gospel — that we
AP : 1 2 :002(182) [0253] This is the very **voice** of the Gospel, that by faith we
AP : 1 2 :002(182) [0253] This **voice** of the Gospel these writers of the Confutation
AP : 1 2 :002(182) [0253] We cannot condemn the **voice** of the Gospel, so
AP : 1 2 :039(187) [0261] through absolution, which is the true **voice** of the Gospel.
AP : 1 2 :040(187) [0261] we must believe the **voice** of the one absolving no less
AP : 1 2 :040(187) [0261] less than we would believe a **voice** coming from heaven.
AP : 1 2 :048(188) [0265] condemning us; it is the **voice** that says with David
AP : 1 2 :056(189) [0267] This **voice** encourages David and by faith it sustains,
AP : 1 2 :105(197) [0283] absolution, which is the **voice** of the Gospel forgiving sins
AP : 1 2 :107(198) [0283] from the heart and not just from the **voice**, as in a play.
AP : 2 2 :011(238) [0361] these Thrasonian **voices**, and if we wanted to answer them
AP : 2 4 :028(254) [0393] I gave them, 'Obey my **voice**, and I will be your God.'"
AP : 2 7 :013(271) [0423] If this is not the true **voice** of the Gospel, if it is not the
AP : 2 7 :052(278) [0437] are also undaunted by the **voice** of Christ upbraiding the
AP : 2 8 :019(284) [0449] Therefore he wants his **voice**, His Word to be heard, not
S3 : 1 2 :002(315) [0499] believers and sheep who hear the **voice** of their Shepherd.
SD : PR :014(506) [0855] will flee from strange **voices** and separate the precious
SD : 1 0 :019(614) [1059] and sheep who hear the **voice** of their Shepherd," etc.
SD : 1 1 :030(621) [1073] "My sheep hear my **voice**, and I know them, and they
SD : 1 1 :038(622) [1075] God as if we had heard a **voice** from heaven," as the
SD : 1 1 :085(630) [1091] inhuman devices contrary to the **voice** of his conscience.

Void (7)
AG : 2 7 :036(076) [0081] still more reasons why monastic vows are null and **void**.
AG : 2 7 :040(077) [0081] vow, made contrary to God's command, is null and **void**.
AG : 2 7 :062(080) [0083] useless, and invented, monastic vows are null and **void**.
AL : 2 7 :036(076) [0081] offer still another reason to show that vows are **void**.
AL : 2 7 :039(077) [0081] and on this account were **void**, for a wicked vow, taken
AL : 2 7 :062(080) [0083] since they are false and useless, make vows null and **void**.
AP : 0 4 :042(113) [0133] are to be the heirs, faith is null and the promise is **void**."

Volition (2)
PR : PR :016(008) [0013] that of their own **volition** and with due consideration they
SD : 0 2 :059(532) [0905] in divine things or a **volition** that wills what is good and

Volumes (1)
AL : 2 0 :013(043) [0055] In many **volumes** Augustine defends grace and the

Voluntarily (1), Voluntary (10)
AG : 2 7 :002(071) [0077] In the days of St. Augustine monastic life was **voluntary**.
AG : 2 7 :027(075) [0079] what is possible and **voluntary** and must be uncoerced.
AG : 2 7 :030(075) [0079] a vow that it should be **voluntary** and should be assumed
AL : 2 7 :002(071) [0077] In Augustine's time they were **voluntary** associations.
AL : 2 7 :027(075) [0079] vow, which ought to be **voluntary** and chosen freely and
AP : 0 2 :043(106) [0117] Or they say that nothing is sin unless it is **voluntary**.
AP : 1 5 :046(221) [0327] on by the cross, a **voluntary** kind of exercise is also
AP : 2 3 :020(242) [0369] not commanded; it is **voluntary** rather than obligatory."
S2 : 0 4 :001(298) [0471] themselves to him **voluntarily** or through a human
LC : 0 6 :001(457) [0000] taught that it should be **voluntary** and purged of the
LC : 0 6 :004(457) [0000] removed and made **voluntary** so that we may confess

Voluptuously (1)
AP : 2 3 :044(245) [0375] where they can live **voluptuously**, cannot even keep this

Votes (1)
TR : 0 0 :014(322) [0509] in order that by the **votes** of all the brethren and by the

Vow (27), Vows (99)
AG : 1 5 :004(037) [0049] Accordingly monastic **vows** and other traditions
AG : 2 3 :006(052) [0061] of human resolutions or **vows** without a special gift or
AG : 2 3 :008(052) [0061] be altered by any human **vows** or laws, our priests and
AG : 2 3 :012(052) [0063] were compelled by force to take the **vows** of celibacy.
AG : 2 3 :018(054) [0063] were married and that the **vow** of celibacy has been the
AG : 2 3 :024(055) [0065] of God, neither can any **vow** alter a command of God.
AG : 2 3 :025(055) [0065] were unable to keep their **vows** of chastity should marry.
AG : 2 3 :026(055) [0065] those who have made **vows** in their youth — and most of
AG : 2 7 :000(070) [0075] XXVII. Monastic **Vows**
AG : 2 7 :001(070) [0075] In discussing monastic **vows** it is necessary to begin by
AG : 2 7 :002(071) [0077] corrupted, monastic **vows** were invented, and the attempt
AG : 2 7 :002(071) [0077] by means of these **vows** as if in a well-conceived prison.
AG : 2 7 :003(071) [0077] In addition to monastic **vows** many other requirements
AG : 2 7 :010(072) [0077] Besides, monastic **vows** gained such a reputation, as is
AG : 2 7 :011(072) [0077] was claimed that monastic **vows** were equal to Baptism,
AG : 2 7 :013(072) [0077] kept, and so monastic **vows** were praised more highly
AG : 2 7 :018(073) [0079] authority to marry, for **vows** cannot nullify God's order
AG : 2 7 :022(074) [0079] how much one extols the **vow** and the obligation, no
AG : 2 7 :023(074) [0079] Learned men say that a **vow** made contrary to papal
AG : 2 7 :024(074) [0079] of the obligation of a **vow**, the popes could not have
AG : 2 7 :027(075) [0079] insist so strongly that **vows** must be kept without first
AG : 2 7 :027(075) [0079] first ascertaining whether a **vow** is of the proper sort?
AG : 2 7 :027(075) [0079] For a **vow** must involve what is possible and voluntary
AG : 2 7 :029(075) [0079] who have taken monastic **vows** of themselves, willingly,
AG : 2 7 :029(075) [0079] to take monastic **vows**, and sometimes have been
AG : 2 7 :030(075) [0079] about the obligation of **vows** inasmuch as it is generally
AG : 2 7 :030(075) [0079] nature and character of a **vow** that it should be voluntary
AG : 2 7 :031(075) [0079] papal regulations annul **vows** that are made under the age
AG : 2 7 :032(076) [0079] the taking of monastic **vows** before the eighteenth year.
AG : 2 7 :034(076) [0079] the breaking of monastic **vows** might be censured, it
AG : 2 7 :036(076) [0081] many from monastic **vows**, our teachers offer still more
AG : 2 7 :036(076) [0081] still more reasons why monastic **vows** are null and void.
AG : 2 7 :039(077) [0081] this that the customary **vows** were an improper and false
AG : 2 7 :040(077) [0081] binding, for an ungodly **vow**, made contrary to God's
AG : 2 7 :042(077) [0081] who would be justified by **vows** are severed from Christ
AG : 2 7 :043(077) [0081] and bestow this honor upon their **vows** and monastic life.
AG : 2 7 :044(078) [0081] of sins by their **vows** and their monastic life and
AG : 2 7 :061(080) [0083] associated with monastic **vows**: that they justify and
AG : 2 7 :062(080) [0083] useless, and invented, monastic **vows** are null and void.
AL : 1 5 :004(037) [0049] Wherefore **vows** and traditions about foods and days,
AL : 2 3 :008(052) [0061] for no law of man and no **vow** can nullify a
AL : 2 3 :024(055) [0065] law can nullify a command of God, so no **vow** can do so.
AL : 2 3 :026(056) [0065] those who have made **vows** before attaining a proper age,
AL : 2 3 :026(056) [0065] proper age, and as a rule **vows** used to be so made in
AL : 2 7 :000(070) [0075] XXVII. Monastic **Vows**
AL : 2 7 :001(070) [0075] us concerning monastic **vows** will be better understood if
AL : 2 7 :002(071) [0077] discipline fell into decay, **vows** were added for the
AL : 2 7 :003(071) [0077] observances were gradually added in addition to **vows**.

Continued ▶

A L : 2 7 :010(072) [0077] was added the fact that **vows** had such a reputation that
A L : 2 7 :011(072) [0077] They said that **vows** were equal to Baptism, and they
A L : 2 7 :018(073) [0079] for celibacy to marry, for **vows** can not nullify the
A L : 2 7 :022(074) [0079] the obligation of a **vow** as much as one pleases, it cannot
A L : 2 7 :022(074) [0079] be brought about that a **vow** abrogates the command of
A L : 2 7 :023(074) [0079] canons state that every **vow** is subject to the right of a
A L : 2 7 :023(074) [0079] How much less are those **vows** valid which are made
A L : 2 7 :024(074) [0079] If the obligation of **vows** could not be changed for any
A L : 2 7 :025(075) [0079] we read that they often granted dispensation from **vows**.
A L : 2 7 :027(075) [0079] obligation or effect of a **vow** while they remain silent
A L : 2 7 :027(075) [0079] concerning the nature of a **vow**, which ought to be
A L : 2 7 :029(075) [0079] are who have taken the **vow** spontaneously and
A L : 2 7 :029(075) [0079] and sometimes even compelled, to take the **vow**.
A L : 2 7 :030(075) [0079] contrary to the nature of a **vow** to make a promise which
A L : 2 7 :031(075) [0079] Many canons annul **vows** made before the age of fifteen
A L : 2 7 :032(076) [0079] and forbids making a **vow** before the eighteenth year.
A L : 2 7 :033(076) [0079] a majority of them took **vows** before they reached such an
A L : 2 7 :034(076) [0079] although the violation of **vows** might be rebuked, yet it
A L : 2 7 :036(076) [0081] frees many from their **vows**, our teachers offer still
A L : 2 7 :036(076) [0081] offer still another reason to show that **vows** are void.
A L : 2 7 :039(077) [0081] therefore, that the **vows** thus customarily taken were
A L : 2 7 :040(077) [0081] were void, for a wicked **vow**, taken contrary to the
A L : 2 7 :040(077) [0081] As the canon says, no **vow** ought to bind men to iniquity.
A L : 2 7 :042(077) [0081] who would be justified by **vows** are severed from Christ
A L : 2 7 :043(077) [0081] justification to their **vows** ascribe to their own works
A L : 2 7 :044(078) [0081] merited forgiveness of sins by their **vows** and observances.
A L : 2 7 :061(080) [0083] which are associated with **vows**: that they justify, that
A L : 2 7 :062(080) [0083] since they are false and useless, make **vows** null and void.
A P : 0 4 :010(108) [0123] the church, like monastic **vows** and the abuses of the
A P : 0 4 :212(136) [0179] up new devotions, new **vows**, and new monastic orders
A P : 1 5 :052(222) [0329] issue when we discuss **vows** and ecclesiastical authority.
A P : 2 1 :023(232) [0349] so that we may be saved by their merits and **vows**."
A P : 2 3 :007(240) [0365] neither regulations nor **vows** can abolish the right to
A P : 2 3 :008(240) [0367] of the earth, so neither **vows** nor human regulations can
A P : 2 3 :016(241) [0369] regulations, and **vows** cannot abolish either nature or
A P : 2 7 :000(268) [0419] [Article XXVII.] Monastic **Vows**
A P : 2 7 :009(269) [0421] defending, not the question whether **vows** should be kept.
A P : 2 7 :009(269) [0421] maintain that legitimate **vows** should be kept, but we are
A P : 2 7 :009(270) [0421] Are **vows** made with these notions in mind legitimate?
A P : 2 7 :009(270) [0421] Are **vows** legitimate that have been taken with the pretext
A P : 2 7 :009(270) [0421] Are **vows** really vows if they have been extorted from the
A P : 2 7 :009(270) [0421] Are vows really **vows** if they have been extorted from the
A P : 2 7 :009(270) [0421] Are **vows** legitimate if they openly point to an evil end,
A P : 2 7 :010(270) [0423] we said much about such **vows**, which even the papal
A P : 2 7 :010(270) [0423] his book called *Monastic* ***Vows***, we want to be interpreted
A P : 2 7 :011(270) [0423] is not a legitimate **vow** if the one making it supposes that
A P : 2 7 :035(275) [0431] quite clear that monastic **vows** are not a price for which
A P : 2 7 :051(277) [0437] Third, in monastic **vows** chastity is promised.
A P : 2 7 :051(278) [0437] law of nature in men cannot be repealed by **vows** or laws.
A P : 2 7 :051(278) [0437] Nor can any **vows** or any laws abolish the commandment
A P : 2 7 :051(278) [0437] Therefore such a **vow** is not lawful for anybody whose
A P : 2 7 :057(279) [0439] many who took their **vows** without proper judgment
A P : 2 7 :057(279) [0439] even the canons maintain that such **vows** are really vows.
A P : 2 7 :057(279) [0439] even the canons maintain that such vows are really **vows**.
A P : 2 7 :057(279) [0439] the stand that monastic **vows**, as made until now, are not
A P : 2 7 :057(279) [0439] made until now, are not **vows**, and that therefore it is
A P : 2 7 :058(279) [0439] did not undertake their **vows** with the opinions which, as
A P : 2 7 :058(279) [0439] as we have said, we condemn in the **vows** of the monks.
A P : 2 7 :058(279) [0439] can be said about other **vows** described in the Old
A P : 2 7 :065(280) [0441] Paul is talking here about **vows**, this passage does not
A P : 2 7 :065(280) [0441] does not support monastic **vows**, taken for wicked acts of
A P : 2 7 :065(280) [0441] Therefore the **vows** of the widows, if any, must have been
A P : 2 7 :065(280) [0441] if any, must have been different from monastic **vows**.
A P : 2 7 :066(280) [0441] this passage to **vows**, they must also misapply the other
A P : 2 7 :066(280) [0441] Thus **vows** made before that age must be invalid.
A P : 2 7 :067(280) [0441] of fact, the church did not yet know about these **vows**.
A P : 2 7 :067(280) [0441] calls "first faith" — not a monastic **vows**, but Christianity.
A P : 2 7 :069(281) [0443] Hence the **vows** themselves and the observance of foods,
S 3 : 1 4 :000(315) [0501] XIV. Monastic **Vows**
S 3 : 1 4 :001(315) [0501] Since monastic **vows** are in direct conflict with the first
S 3 : 1 4 :001(315) [0501] Whoever takes the **vows** of monastic life believes that he
S 3 : 1 4 :001(316) [0501] people boast that a monastic **vow** is equal to Baptism.
T R : 0 0 :048(328) [0519] darkness has the teaching about **vows** covered the Gospel!
T R : 0 0 :048(328) [0519] they have feigned that **vows** produce righteousness before
L C : 0 1 :011(366) [0583] the plague, he made a **vow** to St. Sebastian or Roch.
L C : 0 1 :213(394) [0641] marriage, and boast and **vow** that they will maintain
L C : 0 1 :216(394) [0641] Therefore all **vows** of chastity apart from marriage are
L C : 0 1 :216(394) [0641] deceived by their monastic **vows** are even commanded to

Vulgar (1)
L C : 0 3 :006(421) [0699] whether I pray or not, as **vulgar** people do who say in

Vulgarius (1)
A P : 1 0 :002(179) [0247] And **Vulgarius**, who seems to us to be a sensible writer,

Wage (2), Wages (11), Waging (2)
A L : 2 1 :001(046) [0057] the example of David in **waging** war to drive the Turk
A P : 0 4 :089(120) [0149] "To one who works, his **wages** are not reckoned as a gift
A P : 0 4 :191(133) [0175] David's labors in **waging** war and in governing the state
A P : 0 4 :194(133) [0175] "Each shall receive his **wages** according to his labor."
A P : 0 4 :366(163) [0221] "Each shall receive his **wages** according to his labor."
A P : 2 1 :029(233) [0351] "Each shall receive his **wages** according to his labor"; that
A P : 2 4 :041(257) [0399] They **wage** war like the kings of the world, and they have
S C : 0 9 :003(354) [0561] provide, for the laborer deserves his **wages**" (Luke 10:7).
S C : 0 9 :003(354) [0561] and 'The laborer deserves his **wages**'" (I Tim. 5:17, 18).
L C : 0 1 :145(385) [0623] receives sustenance and **wages**, she would gain a treasure
L C : 0 1 :235(397) [0647] your own way, take your **wages** like a thief, and even
L C : 0 1 :294(404) [0665] free, as now, to serve for **wages** according to their own
S D : 0 2 :084(537) [0913] the passions of the flesh **wage** war against the soul, and
S D : 1 1 :061(626) [1083] those who are punished and receive their "**wages** of sin."
S D : 1 1 :081(629) [1089] damnation is sin, for the "**wages** of sin is death"

Wagging (1)
S 1 : P R :006(289) [0457] pervert everything by **wagging** countless venomous and

Wagon (1)
S D : 0 2 :066(534) [0907] way two horses draw a **wagon** together, such a view could

Wait (9), Waiting (1), Waits (1)
A L : 2 4 :039(060) [0069] Communion that one **wait** for another in order that there
A P : 0 4 :058(115) [0137] the promise: "My soul **waits** for his word, my soul hopes
A P : 1 3 :013(213) [0311] saying nothing, but only **waiting** for illumination, as the
L C : 0 1 :071(374) [0601] is ever around us, lying in **wait** to lure us into sin and
L C : 0 2 :062(419) [0695] We now **wait** in faith for this to be accomplished through
L C : 0 5 :056(453) [0767] go to the sacrament and **wait** until they become prepared,
L C : 0 5 :073(455) [0771] If you **wait** until you are rid of your burden in order to
L C : 0 5 :084(456) [0773] besieges you and lies in **wait** to trap and destroy you,
S D : 0 2 :046(530) [0899] wholly to resist God or **wait** until God forcibly converts
S D : 0 2 :046(530) [0899] the sacraments but will **wait** until God pours his gifts into
S D : 1 1 :076(629) [1087] of his Word and should **wait** for the Father to draw him

Wake (1), Waken (1)
L C : 0 5 :053(453) [0765] that they may come to their senses and **wake** up.
E P : 1 1 :009(495) [0833] drive men to despair and **waken** dangerous thoughts in

Waldenburg (1)
P R : P R :027(015) [0025] George, baron of Schoenburg [-**Waldenburg**]

Walk (19), Walked (1), Walking (3)
A P : 0 4 :143(126) [0161] Christ Jesus, who do not **walk** according to the flesh, but
A P : 0 4 :348(160) [0217] justified, but those who **walk** according to the flesh can
A P : 1 2 :032(186) [0259] against sin, unknown to men who **walk** in carnal security.
A P : 1 5 :014(217) [0319] it is written, "Do not **walk** in the statutes of your
A P : 1 5 :014(217) [0319] I the Lord am your God; **walk** in my statutes, and be
A P : 1 5 :042(221) [0327] people rightly despise and **walk** out on them after the
S C : 0 4 :014(349) [0553] glory of the Father, we too might **walk** in newness of life."
L C : P R :014(360) [0571] precepts whether sitting, **walking**, standing, lying down,
L C : 0 1 :047(371) [0593] be on the right path and **walk** straight ahead, using all of
L C : 0 4 :075(445) [0751] therefore, you are **walking** in Baptism, which not only
E P : 0 6 :006(481) [0807] of God live in the law and **walk** according to the law of
S D : 0 2 :010(522) [0883] through God's Spirit, "**walk** in the futility of their minds;
S D : 0 2 :026(526) [0891] heart of flesh that we may **walk** in his commandments
S D : 0 2 :039(528) [0895] beforehand, that we should **walk** in them" (Eph. 2:10).
S D : 0 4 :007(552) [0939] command that believers **walk** in good works; that only
S D : 0 6 :001(564) [0963] away, learn from the law to live and **walk** in the law.
S D : 0 6 :002(564) [0963] good works they should **walk**) from the law; nor should
S D : 0 6 :011(565) [0965] command that we should **walk** in the new life, but it does
S D : 0 6 :012(566) [0967] has prepared beforehand, they should **walk** (Eph. 2:10).
S D : 0 6 :018(567) [0969] in the law, they live and **walk** in the law of the Lord, and
S D : 0 7 :099(586) [1005] of presence, as when he **walked** bodily on earth and
S D : 1 0 :018(614) [1059] and we who are **walking** in their footsteps intend by the
S D : 1 2 :010(634) [1097] and in our own piety, in which we **walk** before God.

Wall (6), Walls (2)
A P : 0 4 :237(140) [0187] more understanding than the **walls** that fling back an echo
A P : 0 4 :302(154) [0205] are talking about; like the **walls** of a house, they echo the
L C : 0 1 :185(390) [0633] up this commandment as a **wall**, fortress, and refuge
L C : 0 1 :331(410) [0677] Commandments on every **wall** and corner, and even on
L C : 0 3 :031(424) [0707] a few godly men intervened like an iron **wall** on our side?
E P : 0 1 :015(468) [0783] spot can be washed from the face or color from the **wall**.
S D : 0 1 :022(512) [0865] a smudge of dirt from one's face or paint from the **wall**.
S D : 0 7 :100(586) [1007] or water or a board and a **wall** and neither occupies nor

Wander (1)
A P : 2 4 :010(251) [0387] point at issue and not **wander** off into side issues, like

Want (85), Wanted (28), Wanting (3), Wants (48)
P R : P R :017(008) [0015] our minds and hearts to **want** to introduce, palliate, or
P R : P R :019(009) [0017] Nor do we **want** to have rejected or condemned any other
P R : P R :022(012) [0021] We **want** absolutely no share of the responsibility for this
P R : P R :024(013) [0021] individuals, who do not **want** to be bound to any certain
A G : 2 8 :074(093) [0093] regulations were adopted from **want** of understanding.
A L : 2 7 :005(071) [0077] although they were not **wanting** in years, they were
A L : 2 7 :026(075) [0079] monastery, and there is no **want** of examples in our time.
A P : 0 2 :001(100) [0105] While we **wanted** simply to describe what original sin
A P : 0 2 :014(102) [0109] We **wanted** to show that original sin also involves such
A P : 0 2 :045(106) [0117] So when Luther **wanted** to show the magnitude of
A P : 0 4 :009(108) [0123] he can imagine that he **wants** to love God and that he
A P : 0 4 :009(108) [0123] to love God and that he **wants** to do good for God's sake.
A P : 0 4 :022(110) [0127] For God **wants** this civil discipline to restrain the
A P : 0 4 :048(114) [0135] to have faith means to **want** and to accept the promised
A P : 0 4 :049(114) [0135] It is by faith that God **wants** to be worshiped, namely,
A P : 0 4 :060(115) [0137] This is how God **wants** to be known and worshiped, that
A P : 0 4 :069(116) [0141] that because of him God **wants** to be reconciled to us.
A P : 0 4 :072(117) [0141] Therefore we **want** to show first that faith alone makes a
A P : 0 4 :152(127) [0163] Now Christ did not **want** to say that by her works of love
A P : 0 4 :168(130) [0169] "I do not do the good I **want**, but the evil I do not want is
A P : 0 4 :168(130) [0169] the good I want, but the evil I do not **want** is what I do."
A P : 0 4 :228(139) [0183] God **wants** us to believe him and to accept blessings from
A P : 0 4 :258(144) [0193] At the same time he **wants** the forgiveness of sins to be
A P : 0 4 :259(144) [0193] At the same time he **wants** the forgiveness of sins to be
A P : 0 4 :261(145) [0195] voice which Daniel surely **wanted** to be received by faith.
A P : 0 4 :266(146) [0197] while Daniel most emphatically **wants** to include faith.
A P : 0 4 :279(149) [0199] of his mercy and which **wants** to be justified, sanctified,
A P : 0 4 :298(153) [0205] this proof unless he **wants** utterly to abolish Christ and
A P : 0 4 :312(155) [0207] If someone **wants** a distinction anyway, we say that the
A P : 0 4 :313(155) [0207] by faith, if indeed we **want** to teach the righteousness of
A P : 0 4 :317(156) [0209] If we **want** to please God because of our works and not
A P : 0 4 :339(159) [0215] He does not **want** us to despair of God's grace and
A P : 0 7 :038(176) [0241] Apostolic rites they **want** to keep, apostolic doctrine they
A P : 0 7 :038(176) [0241] want to keep, apostolic doctrine they do not **want** to keep.
A P : 0 7 :039(176) [0241] They did not **want** us to believe that we are justified by
A P : 0 7 :039(176) [0241] They did not **want** to impose such a burden on
A P : 0 7 :042(176) [0243] show, the apostles did not **want** to impose an ordinance
A P : 0 7 :042(176) [0243] judge that the apostles **wanted** to disabuse the people of
A P : 0 7 :043(177) [0243] sake of harmony they **wanted** others to follow the
A P : 1 1 :008(181) [0251] We do not **want** to impose on our people's consciences

Continued ▶

A P : 1 1 :009(182) [0251] But we do not **want** to sanction the torture of the
A P : 1 2 :028(185) [0259] If someone **wants** to call fruits worthy of penitence
A P : 1 2 :083(194) [0275] of Scripture, and we **want** to avoid being lengthy in order
A P : 1 2 :086(194) [0277] They **want** to be justified by the law and to offer our
A P : 1 2 :094(196) [0281] When God says, 'As I live,' he **wants** to be believed.
A P : 1 2 :106(197) [0283] of Scripture mean whatever they **want** them to mean.
A P : 1 2 :106(197) [0283] But if anybody **wants** by analogy to apply the
A P : 1 2 :113(199) [0285] The holy Fathers did not **want** to accept the lapsed or the
A P : 1 2 :120(200) [0287] and to test those who **wanted** to be accepted into the
A P : 1 3 :014(213) [0311] If anybody therefore **wants** to call it a sacrament, he
A P : 1 4 :005(215) [0315] Furthermore, we **want** at this point to declare our
A P : 1 5 :009(216) [0317] Christ as the mediator; he **wants** to be gracious to us
A P : 1 5 :014(216) [0319] If somebody **wants** to institute certain works to merit the
A P : 1 8 :005(225) [0335] who seem to have **wanted** this righteousness did not
A P : 2 1 :024(232) [0349] intercessor, he does not **want** appeals to be addressed to
A P : 2 1 :027(232) [0349] honors, she does not **want** to be put on the same level as
A P : 2 1 :044(236) [0357] which we know you **want** to extol and advance, we
A P : 2 2 :010(237) [0361] Do they also **want** to say that the laity has been kept from
A P : 2 2 :011(238) [0361] voices, and if we **wanted** to answer them we would have
A P : 2 2 :013(238) [0361] otherwise we might **want** to maintain their practice.
A P : 2 3 :019(242) [0369] God **wants** the rest to use the universal law of nature
A P : 2 3 :019(242) [0369] instituted, for he does not **want** us to despise his
A P : 2 3 :019(242) [0369] He **wants** men to be chaste by using the remedy he offers,
A P : 2 3 :019(242) [0369] he offers, just as he **wants** to nourish our life by using
A P : 2 3 :024(243) [0371] of the synods while they **want** others to accept it as
A P : 2 3 :043(245) [0375] prayer, but Paul does not **want** this to be perpetual
A P : 2 3 :046(246) [0377] commands and gifts, which he **wants** us to use devoutly.
A P : 2 3 :061(247) [0381] marriage on anyone who **wants** to remain continent, as
A P : 2 4 :003(250) [0385] We do not **want** to belabor this point, but we leave it up
A P : 2 4 :007(250) [0385] long time good men have **wanted** some limits set to them.
A P : 2 4 :010(251) [0387] We **want** to remind our readers of the real issue.
A P : 2 4 :015(252) [0389] ideas to it as if it meant whatever they **want** it to mean.
A P : 2 4 :023(253) [0391] know that God does not **want** our own righteousness but
A P : 2 4 :028(254) [0393] and that this is the way I **want** you to know me when I
A P : 2 4 :028(254) [0393] Believe that I **want** to be God, the one who justifies and
A P : 2 4 :033(255) [0395] It somebody **wants** to include the ceremony here, we
A P : 2 4 :043(258) [0399] The preachers who **want** to look more learned take up
A P : 2 4 :099(268) [0419] We **want** all good men to be warned not to help our
A P : 2 7 :002(269) [0419] We do not **want** to recite them here lest we give the
A P : 2 7 :010(270) [0423] called *Monastic Vows*, we **want** to be interpreted here as
A P : 2 7 :062(280) [0441] their father apparently **wanted** to distinguish them by
A P : 2 7 :062(280) [0441] By these marks he **wanted** to remind them of the teaching
A P : 2 8 :004(281) [0445] the people desperately **want** instruction in order to have a
A P : 2 8 :007(282) [0445] Christ **wanted** to leave their use free when he said
A P : 2 8 :018(284) [0449] For Christ **wants** to assure us, as was necessary, that the
A P : 2 8 :019(284) [0449] Therefore he **wants** his voice, His Word to be heard, not
S 3 : 0 3 :017(305) [0483] the devil himself would **want** to say No?) it was accounted
T R : 0 0 :018(323) [0509] "If it is authority that you **want**, the world is greater than
L C : 0 1 :021(367) [0585] to trust that he **wants** to help, nor does it believe that
L C : 0 1 :028(368) [0587] especially in distress and **want**, and renounces and
L C : 0 1 :042(370) [0591] mammon suffer grief and **want** and are opposed and
L C : 0 1 :077(375) [0603] We **want** them to know that God is well pleased with the
L C : 0 1 :087(377) [0605] But God **wants** it to be holy to you.
L C : 0 1 :111(380) [0613] not allow them to suffer **want** or hunger, but will place
L C : 0 1 :161(387) [0627] those who do so and will not let them suffer **want**.
L C : 0 1 :165(387) [0627] how he will support you and provide for all your **wants**.
L C : 0 1 :168(388) [0629] God does not **want** to have knaves or tyrants in this office
L C : 0 1 :172(388) [0629] If we **want** qualified and capable men for both civil and
L C : 0 1 :187(390) [0633] He **wants** us to keep this commandment ever before our
L C : 0 1 :191(391) [0635] by wild beasts, to rot in prison or perish from **want**."
L C : 0 1 :195(391) [0637] God's Word by which he **wants** to encourage and urge us
L C : 0 1 :195(391) [0637] He always **wants** to remind us to think back to the First
L C : 0 1 :205(393) [0639] God by his commandment **wants** every husband or wife
L C : 0 1 :223(395) [0643] This, too, God **wants** to have protected.
L C : 0 1 :246(398) [0651] meanwhile, will not **want**, and you will hurt yourself
L C : 0 1 :251(399) [0651] and when he suffers **want** we are to help, share, and lend
L C : 0 1 :253(399) [0653] for your needs and will let you lack or **want** for nothing.
L C : 0 1 :264(400) [0655] evil spoken of us; we **want** the golden compliments of the
L C : 0 1 :310(407) [0669] Above all, he **wants** our hearts to be pure, even though as
L C : 0 1 :327(409) [0675] Rather, ask what God **wants** of you and what he will
L C : 0 3 :008(421) [0699] obligation to pray if we **want** to be Christians, just as it is
L C : 0 3 :010(421) [0699] thinking that he neither **wants** nor cares for our prayers
L C : 0 3 :024(423) [0705] A person who **wants** to pray must present a petition,
L C : 0 3 :027(424) [0705] express your needs and **wants**, not because he is unaware
L C : 0 3 :029(424) [0705] This is just what the devil **wants** and works for with all
L C : 0 3 :058(428) [0713] God allow us to suffer **want** in temporal things when he
L C : 0 3 :103(434) [0727] be the least, but everyone **wants** to sit in the chief seat and
L C : 0 3 :117(436) [0731] Thus you see how God **wants** us to pray to him for
L C : 0 3 :120(436) [0731] Where such faith is **wanting**, there can be no true prayer.
L C : 0 5 :049(452) [0765] If you **want** such liberty, you may just as well take the
L C : 0 5 :058(453) [0767] since they do not desire it and do not **want** to be good.
L C : 0 5 :062(454) [0767] hast commanded it and I **want** to be thy disciple, no
L C : 0 5 :079(455) [0771] Just begin to act as if you **want** to become good and cling
L C : 0 6 :018(459) [0000] We should not act as if we **wanted** to perform a
L C : 0 6 :032(460) [0000] Those who really **want** to be good Christians, free from
E P : 1 1 :010(495) [0833] and that he does not **want** anyone to perish (Ezek. 33:11;
E P : 1 1 :017(497) [0837] that God does not **want** all men to come to repentance
E P : 1 1 :018(497) [0837] God is not serious about **wanting** all men to come to him
E P : 1 1 :019(497) [0837] that God does not **want** everybody to be saved, but that
S D : P R :007(502) [0849] Some **wanted** to become righteous and to be saved by the
S D : P R :019(507) [0857] for other reasons, we **wanted** to set forth and explain our
S D : P R :020(508) [0859] On the contrary, we **want** to be found faithful to the
S D : 0 1 :045(516) [0873] with which we do not **want** to scandalize the uninstructed
S D : 0 2 :009(522) [0883] and diligently they **want** to comprehend these spiritual
S D : 0 2 :045(530) [0899] still has enough powers to **want** to accept the Gospel and
S D : 0 4 :017(554) [0943] Such works of pretense God does not **want**.
S D : 0 4 :020(554) [0945] free option if they may or **want** to do or not do them or
S D : 0 6 :008(565) [0965] "I do not do the good I **want**, but the evil I do not want is
S D : 0 6 :008(565) [0965] the good I want, but the evil I do not **want** is what I do."
S D : 0 7 :030(574) [0983] light thereof, and have **wanted** to defend all of them as
S D : 0 7 :075(583) [0999] of the first institution, which he **wants** to be repeated.
S D : 0 7 :103(587) [1007] For I do not **want** to deny in any way that God's power is
S D : 0 7 :103(587) [1007] For who **wants** to try to prove that God is unable to do
S D : 0 7 :128(591) [1015] brevity we have not **wanted** to repeat them at this point.
S D : 0 8 :025(596) [1023] to his good pleasure, when and how he **wanted** to.
S D : 0 8 :026(596) [1025] did not use it at all times, but only when he **wanted** to.
S D : 0 8 :040(598) [1029] after whom I would not **want** to be called a Christian,
S D : 0 8 :050(600) [1031] Christ is concerned, some **wanted** to contend that even in
S D : 1 0 :013(613) [1057] to false apostles who **wanted** to impose such things on
S D : 1 1 :028(620) [1071] Hence if we **want** to consider our eternal election to
S D : 1 1 :040(623) [1077] resist the Holy Spirit who **wants** to work efficaciously in
S D : 1 1 :042(623) [1077] is not that God does not **want** to impart the grace of
S D : 1 1 :046(624) [1079] Furthermore, God **wanted** to insure my salvation so
S D : 1 1 :070(627) [1085] Therefore no one who **wants** to be saved should burden
S D : 1 1 :070(627) [1085] distinction that God **wants** all men who are laden and
S D : 1 1 :078(629) [1089] damnation is not that God did not **want** them to be saved.
S D : 1 1 :078(629) [1089] the Holy Spirit who **wanted** to work within them, as was
S D : 1 1 :081(629) [1089] Since God does not **want** any man to be damned, how
S D : 1 1 :084(630) [1091] because God did not **want** to grant him salvation or
S D : 1 1 :086(631) [1091] and in no way does he **want** us to infer that God had not
S D : 1 1 :086(631) [1091] infer that God had not **wanted** to grant Pharaoh or any
S D : 1 2 :005(633) [1097] We **wanted** everyone to be able to see that we were not
S D : 1 2 :005(633) [1097] mere pretense but that we **wanted** to help matters
S D : 1 2 :006(633) [1097] We **wanted** to set forth our position so clearly that our

Wanton (3), Wantonly (1), Wantonness (2)
A P : 2 7 :067(280) [0441] but because they became **wanton** while being supported
A P : 2 7 :068(280) [0443] way he says that the **wanton** women had rejected the
S 1 : P R :012(290) [0459] **Wantonness**, lewdness, extravagance in dress, gluttony,
L C : 0 1 :232(396) [0647] be restrained in their **wantonness** and that the wrath of
L C : 0 3 :084(431) [0723] the part of those who **wantonly** oppress the poor and
S D : 0 4 :031(556) [0947] through any sin, even a **wanton** and deliberate one, or

War (21), Warfare (5), Wars (11)
A G : 1 6 :002(037) [0051] the sword, engage in just **wars**, serve as soldiers, buy and
A G : 2 1 :001(046) [0057] of David in making **war** on the Turk, for both are
A G : 2 8 :002(081) [0083] confusion many serious **wars**, tumults, and uprisings have
A G : 2 8 :017(083) [0085] "The weapons of our **warfare** are not worldly but have
A L : 1 6 :002(037) [0051] to engage in just **wars**, to serve as soldiers, to make legal
A L : 2 1 :001(046) [0057] of David in waging **war** to drive the Turk out of his
A L : 2 8 :002(081) [0083] From this confusion great **wars** and tumults have
A L : 2 8 :017(083) [0085] "The weapons of our **warfare** are not worldly but have
A P : 0 2 :039(105) [0115] my members another law at **war** with the law of my mind
A P : 0 4 :191(133) [0175] David's labors in waging **war** and in governing the state
A P : 0 4 :241(141) [0187] have brought on civil **war** if either had yielded the least
A P : 1 6 :001(222) [0329] engage in just **wars**, render military service, enter into
A P : 1 6 :007(223) [0331] are court decisions, punishments, **wars**, military service.
A P : 2 1 :002(229) [0343] state a triumph as though the **war** were already over.
A P : 2 4 :041(257) [0399] They wage **war** like the kings of the world, and they have
S 3 : 0 3 :040(309) [0489] testifies in Rom. 7:23, he **wars** with the law in his
T R : 0 0 :031(325) [0513] "The weapons of our **warfare** are not worldly," etc.
T R : 0 0 :035(326) [0513] excommunications and **wars**, sometimes in order to
L C : 0 1 :060(372) [0597] what we deserve: plague, **war**, famine, fire, flood,
L C : 0 1 :151(386) [0625] or perish through **war**, pestilence, or famine, or his
L C : 0 3 :074(430) [0719] dissension, strife, and **war** prevail, there our daily bread is
L C : 0 3 :078(431) [0721] and cattle-plague; from **war** and bloodshed, famine,
L C : 0 3 :080(431) [0721] murder, sedition, and **war**, why he sends tempest and hail
E P : 0 6 :004(480) [0805] believers are in a constant **war** against their flesh (that is,
S D : 0 2 :017(524) [0887] my members another law at **war** with the law of my mind
S D : 0 2 :018(524) [0887] other regenerated persons **wars** against the law of God
S D : 0 2 :034(528) [0895] says in Rom. 7:23, that he **wars** with the law in his
S D : 0 2 :064(533) [0905] my members another law at **war** with the law of my mind
S D : 0 2 :068(534) [0907] in us, the conflict and **warfare** of the flesh against the
S D : 0 2 :084(537) [0913] passions of the flesh wage **war** against the soul, and the
S D : 0 2 :084(537) [0913] law in our members is at **war** with the law of our mind.
S D : 0 2 :085(537) [0913] members the law of sin at **war** with the law of his mind.
S D : 0 4 :019(554) [0945] but actually **wars** against the law of his mind.
S D : 0 5 :020(561) [0959] words, and deeds **war** against the law, and he is therefore
S D : 0 6 :008(565) [0965] my members another law at **war** with the law of my mind
S D : 0 6 :018(567) [0967] law in their members is at **war** against the law of their
S D : 1 1 :033(622) [1073] Then take up the **warfare** against sin as Paul teaches from

Warded (1), Warding (1)
A P : 2 1 :032(233) [0351] granted riches, Febris **warded** off fever, and Castor and
L C : 0 2 :017(412) [0681] evil and misfortune, **warding** off all sorts of danger and

Wards (1)
A P : 2 1 :032(233) [0351] grants riches, Sebastian **wards** off pestilence, Valentine

Wares (2)
A P : 2 4 :057(260) [0405] sacrificers who daily peddle their **wares** in the churches.
S C : 0 1 :014(343) [0541] or by dealing in shoddy **wares**, but help him to improve

Warmed (2)
L C : 0 2 :023(413) [0683] Thus our hearts will be **warmed** and kindled with
L C : 0 5 :054(453) [0765] more will our heart be **warmed** and kindled, and it will

Warn (7), Warned (10), Warning (11), Warnings (2), Warns (5)
P R : P R :008(005) [0009] Word, in order thereby to **warn** and, as far as we might,
P R : P R :022(011) [0019] Besides, pious people should be **warned** against them.
P R : P R :022(012) [0021] to their souls and to **warn** them against it, lest one blind
A G : 2 8 :049(089) [0091] that the Holy Spirit **warned** against them for nothing?
A L : 2 4 :024(058) [0067] our teachers have **warned** that they depart from the Holy
A L : 2 6 :019(067) [0073] There was great need to **warn** the churches of these errors
A L : 2 6 :041(070) [0075] At the same time men are **warned** that such observances
A L : 2 8 :049(089) [0091] Was it in vain that the Holy Spirit **warned** against these?
A P : 0 2 :011(102) [0109] the Scripture everywhere **warns** us and of these that the
A P : 0 4 :275(148) [0199] of necessity, and so he **warns** that penitence is
A P : 0 7 :022(172) [0235] Spirit, so it also has the **warning** that there will be
A P : 0 7 :049(178) [0245] Christ has also **warned** us in his parables on the church
A P : 1 2 :106(197) [0283] other people's alone, but **warning** him not to be so
A P : 1 2 :113(199) [0285] as the gloss on the decree **warns**, and admitting notorious
A P : 2 3 :005(239) [0365] correctness of Peter's **warning** (II Pet. 2:1) that false
A P : 2 4 :099(268) [0419] want all good men to be **warned** not to help our
A P : 2 7 :006(269) [0421] But Christ **warns** that tasteless salt is usually "thrown out
T R : 0 0 :054(329) [0519] O kings, be wise; be **warned**, O rulers of the earth"

Continued ▶

LC : PR :014(360) [0571] So he wishes to **warn**, equip, and protect us against them
LC : 0 1 :069(374) [0599] before, that by means of **warning** and threat, restraint and
LC : 0 1 :178(389) [0631] is enough to serve as a **warning**; a more extensive
LC : 0 1 :239(397) [0649] by the scruff of the neck so that others took **warning**.
LC : 0 1 :248(398) [0651] We have now given sufficient **warning** and exhortation.
LC : 0 1 :274(402) [0659] that office, and as he **warns** in the Fifth Commandment,
LC : 0 1 :282(403) [0661] right to have their sport spoiled, as a **warning** to others.
LC : 0 1 :322(408) [0673] not only to terrify and **warn** us but also to attract and
LC : 0 6 :030(460) [0000] to hear and heed the **warning** of our preaching, we shall
EP : 0 4 :018(477) [0801] toward God, as it is to **warn** against mingling good works
SD : 0 6 :009(565) [0965] and admonition, **warning** and threatening of the law, but
SD : 0 7 :001(569) [0971] also, and faithfully to **warn** our hearers and other pious
SD : 0 7 :057(579) [0993] discouraging them and **warning** them against receiving
SD : 0 7 :057(579) [0993] could misuse and against which no one should be **warned**.
SD : 1 1 :051(624) [1079] mighty admonitions and **warnings**, among others: They
SD : 1 1 :055(625) [1081] but has earnestly **warned** against it (Rom. 11:33),
SD : 1 1 :085(630) [1091] all the admonitions and **warnings**, God withdrew his hand

Warrant (3)
AP : 0 4 :253(143) [0193] They do not **warrant** any of these conclusions: that works
AP : 0 4 :290(151) [0203] Without any **warrant** it teaches that men come to God
LC : 0 3 :047(426) [0711] name as a cloak and **warrant** for their devilish doctrine,

Wash (1), Washed (4), Washes (2), Washing (7), Washings (1)
AP : 0 4 :103(122) [0151] has it as a gift because he was justified after being **washed**.
AP : 0 4 :282(149) [0201] cleansed before God and justified by frequent **washings**.
AP : 0 4 :327(158) [0211] my works"; vv. 30-31, "If I **wash** myself with snow, and
AP : 0 7 :007(169) [0229] having cleansed it by the **washing** of water with the word,
S3 : 0 5 :001(310) [0491] or as Paul says, "the **washing** of water with the word"; or,
S3 : 0 5 :002(310) [0491] power which, through the water, **washes** away sin.
S3 : 0 5 :003(311) [0493] who teach that Baptism **washes** away sin through the
S3 : 0 5 :003(311) [0493] the divine will, as if the **washing** takes place only through
SC : 0 4 :010(349) [0551] water of life and a **washing** of regeneration in the Holy
SC : 0 4 :010(349) [0551] "He saved us by the **washing** of regeneration and renewal
LC : 0 4 :027(440) [0739] power to become the "**washing** of regeneration," as St.
EP : 0 1 :015(468) [0783] readily as a spot can be **washed** from the face or color
SD : 0 1 :022(512) [0865] spoken of can easily be **washed** off, like a smudge of dirt
SD : 0 3 :019(542) [0921] "He saved us by the **washing** of regeneration and
SD : 0 7 :016(572) [0977] into Christ, and are **washed** by the blood of Christ."

Waste (3), Wasted (2), Wastes (1)
AP : 1 2 :137(203) [0293] We hate to **waste** any more words in refuting these silly
SC : PR :019(340) [0537] they undermine and lay **waste** both the kingdom of God
SC : 0 5 :020(350) [0553] have stolen, neglected, or **wasted** anything, or done other
LC : PR :012(360) [0571] Why should I **waste** words?
LC : 0 1 :043(370) [0591] will find that they have **wasted** their effort and toil or, if
LC : 0 1 :225(395) [0645] or malice a servant **wastes** and neglects things to the

Watch (4), Watches (2), Watchful (1)
SC : 0 9 :003(355) [0561] for they are keeping **watch** over your souls, as men who
LC : 0 1 :029(368) [0589] lightly but will strictly **watch** over it, he has attached to
LC : 0 1 :161(387) [0627] honor" to those who **watch** over their souls and to treat
LC : 0 1 :247(398) [0651] will reach God, who **watches** over poor, sorrowful hearts,
LC : 0 1 :322(409) [0673] and how strictly he will **watch** over them, fearfully and
LC : 0 1 :330(410) [0677] the most high God, who **watches** over them with great
LC : 0 4 :063(444) [0749] We must therefore be **watchful** and well armed and not

Watchtower (1)
AP : 1 2 :126(201) [0289] sit as though on a **watchtower** to guide religious affairs,

Water (76), Watering (2)
AP : 0 4 :031(111) [0129] "Unless one is born of **water** and the Spirit, one cannot
AP : 0 4 :282(149) [0201] — said that sprinkling **water** mixed with salt "sanctifies
AP : 0 4 :283(150) [0201] the daily sprinkling with **water**, the habit of the monks,
AP : 0 7 :007(169) [0229] it by the washing of **water** with the word, that the church
S3 : 0 5 :001(310) [0491] than the Word of God in **water**, commanded by the
S3 : 0 5 :001(310) [0491] Paul says, "the washing of **water** with the word"; or,
S3 : 0 5 :002(310) [0491] God has joined to the **water** a spiritual power which,
S3 : 0 5 :002(310) [0491] power which, through the **water**, washes away sin.
S3 : 0 5 :003(311) [0493] God's will and not at all through the Word and the **water**.
SC : 0 4 :002(348) [0551] Baptism is not merely **water**, but it is water used
SC : 0 4 :002(348) [0551] not merely water, but it is **water** used according to God's
SC : 0 4 :009(349) [0551] How can **water** produce such great effects?
SC : 0 4 :010(349) [0551] Answer: It is not the **water** that produces these effects,
SC : 0 4 :010(349) [0551] God connected with the **water**, and our faith which relies
SC : 0 4 :010(349) [0551] relies on the Word of God connected with the **water**.
SC : 0 4 :010(349) [0551] the Word of God the **water** is merely water and no
SC : 0 4 :010(349) [0551] Word of God the water is merely **water** and no Baptism.
SC : 0 4 :010(349) [0551] that is, a gracious **water** of life and a washing of
SC : 0 4 :011(349) [0551] What does such baptizing with **water** signify?
LC : PR :010(360) [0571] indeed, is the true holy **water**, the sign which routs the
LC : 0 1 :118(381) [0615] lives they are not worthy to offer him a cup of **water**?
LC : 0 1 :192(391) [0635] wearily struggling in deep **water**, or fallen into a fire, and
LC : 0 2 :014(412) [0681] day and night, air, fire, **water**, the earth and all that it
LC : 0 4 :014(438) [0735] It is not simply common **water**, but water comprehended
LC : 0 4 :014(438) [0735] common water, but **water** comprehended in God's Word
LC : 0 4 :014(438) [0735] nothing else than a divine **water**, not that the water in
LC : 0 4 :014(438) [0735] divine water, not that the **water** in itself is nobler than
LC : 0 4 :014(438) [0735] itself is nobler than other **water** but that God's Word and
LC : 0 4 :015(438) [0735] consider nothing but the **water** drawn from the well, and
LC : 0 4 :015(438) [0735] then babble, "How can a handful of **water** help the soul?"
LC : 0 4 :016(438) [0735] Who does not know that **water** is water, if such a
LC : 0 4 :016(438) [0735] not know that water is **water**, if such a separation is
LC : 0 4 :016(438) [0735] For the nucleus in the **water** is God's Word or
LC : 0 4 :017(438) [0735] thing from all other **water**, not by virtue of the natural
LC : 0 4 :017(438) [0737] it is not simply a natural **water**, but a divine, heavenly,
LC : 0 4 :017(438) [0737] holy, and blessed **water** — praise it in any other terms you
LC : 0 4 :022(439) [0737] two, the Word and the **water**, must by no means be
LC : 0 4 :022(439) [0737] is separated from the **water**, the water is no different from
LC : 0 4 :022(439) [0737] from the water, the **water** is no different from that which
LC : 0 4 :026(439) [0739] it is not simple, ordinary **water**, for ordinary water could
LC : 0 4 :026(440) [0739] water, for ordinary **water** could not have such an effect.
LC : 0 4 :027(440) [0739] fruitful, and gracious **water**, for through the Word
LC : 0 4 :029(440) [0739] Thus faith clings to the **water** and believes it to be Baptism
LC : 0 4 :029(440) [0739] and life, not through the **water**, as we have sufficiently
LC : 0 4 :031(440) [0739] to Baptism, that is, the **water** comprehended in God's
LC : 0 4 :033(440) [0741] worthy to receive the salutary, divine **water** profitably.
LC : 0 4 :033(440) [0741] which accompany the **water**, they cannot be received
LC : 0 4 :036(441) [0741] Just by allowing the **water** to be poured over you, you do
LC : 0 4 :036(441) [0741] God, you may receive in the **water** the promised salvation.
LC : 0 4 :045(442) [0743] in Baptism: the body has **water** poured over it, though it
LC : 0 4 :045(442) [0743] receive anything but the **water**, and meanwhile the Word
LC : 0 4 :046(442) [0743] Since the **water** and the Word together constitute one
LC : 0 4 :053(443) [0745] that Baptism is simply **water** and God's Word in and with
LC : 0 4 :053(443) [0745] Word accompanies the **water**, Baptism is valid, even
LC : 0 4 :054(443) [0745] For there would be **water** together with God's Word, even
LC : 0 4 :061(444) [0747] regard Baptism only as **water** in the brook or in the pot,
LC : 0 4 :065(444) [0749] in being dipped into the **water**, which covers us
LC : 0 4 :065(444) [0749] being dipped under the **water** and emerging from it,
LC : 0 4 :068(445) [0749] among Christians, signified by baptizing with **water**.
LC : 0 4 :078(446) [0751] But we need not again have the **water** poured over us.
LC : 0 4 :078(446) [0751] if we were immersed in **water** a hundred times, it would
LC : 0 5 :009(447) [0755] that it is not mere **water**, so we say here that the
EP : 0 2 :006(470) [0787] planting, sowing, and **watering** are in vain unless he
EP : 0 3 :002(473) [0793] esteemed like a drop of **water** over against the immense
EP : 1 2 :023(500) [0841] 4. That the **water** of Baptism is not a means through
SD : 0 1 :026(512) [0867] into man's nature, as when poison is blended with **water**.
SD : 0 2 :055(531) [0903] preacher's planting and **watering** and the hearer's running
SD : 0 3 :002(539) [0917] all men are like a drop of **water** compared to the mighty
SD : 0 7 :004(569) [0973] When this did not hold **water**, they confessed that the
SD : 0 7 :087(585) [1003] just as the baptismal **water** is no sacrament or Baptism if
SD : 0 7 :100(586) [1007] penetrates air, light, or **water** and does not occupy or
SD : 0 7 :100(586) [1007] passes through air or **water** or a board and a wall and
SD : 0 7 :100(586) [1007] and heat go through air, **water**, glass, or crystal and exist
SD : 0 8 :019(594) [1021] is made out of honey and **water** and ceases to be
SD : 0 8 :019(595) [1021] be distinguishably either **water** or honey but is a blended
SD : 0 8 :032(597) [1025] the other nature, the way **water** is poured from one
SD : 0 8 :071(605) [1041] the Son of God, as when **water**, wine, or oil is poured
SD : 1 2 :031(635) [1101] 3. That the **water** of Baptism is not a means whereby the

Wave (1)
LC : 0 3 :123(436) [0731] he who doubts is like a **wave** of the sea that is driven and

Waver (2), Wavering (2)
AP : 0 4 :020(110) [0125] But terrified consciences **waver** and doubt and then seek
AP : 0 4 :309(155) [0207] "No distrust made him **waver** concerning the promise of
AP : 1 2 :088(195) [0277] our opponents leave consciences **wavering** and uncertain.
AP : 1 2 :127(201) [0291] you do not strengthen **wavering** consciences, because you

Wax (1)
SD : 0 2 :089(538) [0915] is carved out of it, or **wax** when a seal is impressed into

Way (384), Ways (43)
PR : PR :002(003) [0007] nation, and to light its **way** out of papistic superstition
PR : PR :004(004) [0007] and agreement, and in this **way** hold back and perceptibly
PR : PR :007(004) [0009] in a thorough and friendly **way** various matters which our
PR : PR :008(005) [0009] else that it was in no **way** our disposition and intention to
PR : PR :008(006) [0011] persist in it in a Christian **way** without any further
PR : PR :009(006) [0011] and interpreted in such a **way** by adherents of erroneous
PR : PR :010(006) [0011] that there was no better **way** to counteract the
PR : PR :010(006) [0011] In this **way** the mouths of the adversaries might be
PR : PR :011(006) [0011] of divine truth, and in this **way** the pretext and basis for
PR : PR :011(006) [0011] that had occurred were to be decided in a Christian **way**.
PR : PR :014(007) [0013] useful memoranda on the **way** in which the Christian
PR : PR :020(010) [0017] surest and most edifying **way** as far as the common
PR : PR :021(011) [0019] union, or in such a **way** that even in the personal union it
PR : PR :022(011) [0019] These people go their **way** in the simplicity of their
PR : PR :022(012) [0021] that it is in no **way** our disposition and purpose to give
PR : PR :024(012) [0021] Since this is the **way** things are, and since we are certain
PR : PR :024(013) [0021] doctrine and so that the **way** may not be left free and
PR : PR :024(013) [0023] nothing to stand in the **way** of this cause and the
PR : PR :025(013) [0023] or to depart in any **way** at all, either in content or
AG : PR :010(025) [0041] practical and equitable **ways** as may restore unity.
AG : PR :020(026) [0041] and to allow no hindrance to be put in the **way**.
AG : 2 0 :010(042) [0055] Christ and seeks his own **way** to God, contrary to the
AG : 2 0 :025(044) [0057] about faith in such a **way** as to make it clear that faith is
AG : 2 3 :014(054) [0063] matters in a better or wiser **way** than God himself, who
AG : 2 4 :010(057) [0065] to be misused in many **ways**, as is well known, by turning
AG : 2 5 :011(063) [0069] obey the prophet who says, 'Show your **way** to the Lord.'
AG : 2 6 :009(065) [0071] observed festivals in this **way**, prayed in this way, fasted
AG : 2 6 :009(065) [0071] in this way, prayed in this **way**, fasted in this way, and
AG : 2 6 :009(065) [0071] in this way, fasted in this **way**, and dressed in this way
AG : 2 6 :009(065) [0071] way, and dressed in this **way** was said to live a spiritual
AG : 2 7 :042(077) [0081] In the same **way**, those who would be justified by vows
AG : 2 8 :008(082) [0085] In this **way** are imparted no bodily but eternal things and
AG : 2 8 :055(090) [0091] the regulations in such a **way** that one does not give
AG : 2 8 :077(094) [0095] not our intention to find **ways** of reducing the bishops'
AL : 2 0 :010(042) [0055] grace of Christ and seeks a **way** to God without Christ, by
AL : 2 0 :010(042) [0055] said of himself, "I am the **way**, and the truth, and the life"
AL : 2 0 :026(045) [0057] his readers in this **way** concerning the word "faith" when
AL : 2 5 :011(063) [0069] obey the prophet who says, 'Show your **way** to the Lord.'
AL : 2 8 :018(083) [0085] In this **way** our teachers distinguish the functions of the
AL : 0 0 :002(095) [0095] have been troubled in many **ways** by indulgence sellers.
AP : 0 2 :003(101) [0105] that anyone born in this **way** has concupiscence and
AP : 0 2 :007(101) [0107] body; in their awkward **way** they ask whether it came
AP : 0 2 :036(105) [0115] Augustine speaks the same **way** when he says, "Sin is
AP : 0 2 :048(106) [0119] help, so we cannot buy our **way** out of the slavery by
AP : 0 4 :004(108) [0121] have to say a few things by **way** of preface so that the
AP : 0 4 :009(108) [0123] In this **way** the scholastics teach men to merit the
AP : 0 4 :070(116) [0141] In the same **way**, if we must defend the proposition, "The
AP : 0 4 :072(117) [0141] For Scripture speaks both **ways**.
AP : 0 4 :075(117) [0143] Therefore we argue this **way**:
AP : 0 4 :081(118) [0143] In this **way** we are reconciled to the Father and receive
AP : 0 4 :154(128) [0163] This is the highest **way** of worshiping Christ.
AP : 0 4 :154(128) [0163] to think of Christ in this **way**, and in this way to worship
AP : 0 4 :154(128) [0163] in this way, and in this **way** to worship and take hold of

Continued ▶

AP : 04 :155(128) [0165] In this **way**, therefore, he praises her entire act of
AP : 04 :155(128) [0165] In the same **way** he says here, "Her sins, which are many,
AP : 04 :188(133) [0173] praise works in such a **way** as not to remove the free
AP : 04 :192(133) [0175] We feel the same **way** about every work done in the most
AP : 04 :198(134) [0175] his saints in different **ways** and often puts off the rewards
AP : 04 :203(134) [0175] Good works ought to follow faith in this **way**.
AP : 04 :212(136) [0179] The world judges this **way** about all works, that they are a
AP : 04 :232(139) [0185] In the same **way** Paul commands that there be love in the
AP : 04 :235(140) [0185] interprets the text this **way**: "Just as a building is said to
AP : 04 :252(143) [0191] righteous in a forensic **way**, just as in the passage
AP : 04 :259(144) [0193] We must interpret all similar passages in the same **way**.
AP : 04 :260(145) [0195] In this **way** we can oppose those who reject Christ,
AP : 04 :261(145) [0195] is no other God who can save this **way**" (Dan. 3:29).
AP : 04 :263(146) [0195] Reborn in this **way**, they bring forth fruits worthy of
AP : 04 :269(147) [0197] interpret the law in such a **way** that they attribute Christ's
AP : 04 :271(147) [0199] In this **way** we must view the preaching of penitence.
AP : 04 :277(148) [0199] ought to be taken the same **way**, "Alms free from every
AP : 04 :279(149) [0199] God always, and ask him to direct your **ways**" (4:19).
AP : 04 :286(150) [0203] teach the law in such a **way** as to hide the Gospel of
AP : 04 :288(151) [0203] In this **way** they have also distorted the sacraments,
AP : 04 :291(152) [0203] The Gospel shows another **way**.
AP : 04 :293(152) [0203] quickened by faith in this **way**, it receives the Holy Spirit.
AP : 04 :293(152) [0203] though they are a long **way** from the perfection of the
AP : 04 :305(154) [0205] is used in a judicial **way** to mean "to absolve a guilty man
AP : 04 :306(154) [0207] in a different **way** here from the philosophical or judicial
AP : 04 :312(155) [0207] be divided in fact the **way** they are in idle scholastic
AP : 04 :318(156) [0209] us after justification, the **way** it often does, we must seek
AP : 04 :324(157) [0209] praise merits in such a **way** as to add nothing about this
AP : 04 :364(163) [0219] and rewards in one **way**, and the weak in another; for the
AP : 04 :374(164) [0221] In this **way** the Scriptures lump together the
AP : 04 :380(165) [0223] they quote in a twisted **way**, boasting in the schools that
AP : 04 :381(165) [0223] If they understood it this **way**, they would be correct
AP : 04 :393(167) [0225] would obscure the righteousness of faith in this **way**.
AP : 07 :007(169) [0229] the church in the same **way** in Eph. 5:25-27, saying that it
AP : 07 :007(169) [0229] defines the church this **way**, teaching us to believe that
AP : 07 :025(172) [0235] we defined the church that **way**, we would probably have
AP : 07 :032(174) [0239] worship God in so many **ways**, as though these
AP : 07 :032(174) [0239] vary according to the circumstances, one **way** or another.
AP : 07 :041(176) [0241] why did the bishops later change them in so many **ways**?
AP : 07 :043(177) [0243] He interprets it the same **way** that we do; for the apostles
AP : 09 :003(178) [0245] gives the Holy Spirit to those who were baptized this **way**.
AP : 10 :003(179) [0247] that Christ is a vine in this **way** and that we are truly
AP : 11 :003(180) [0249] of the sacraments in such a **way** as to invite them to use
AP : 11 :005(181) [0249] not everyone is ready in the same **way** at the same time.
AP : 11 :006(181) [0251] we teach men in such a **way** as not to ensnare their
AP : 12 :002(182) [0253] and therefore we can in no **way** agree to the confutation.
AP : 12 :004(183) [0253] of our position, we must say something by **way** of preface.
AP : 12 :015(184) [0257] later on a most profitable **way** of buying off satisfactions
AP : 12 :042(187) [0261] is nourished in many **ways**, amid temptations, through
AP : 12 :052(189) [0265] In this **way** Scripture makes a practice of joining these
AP : 12 :074(192) [0273] we believe in a general **way** that sins are forgiven by
AP : 12 :075(193) [0273] sins are forgiven in this **way**: Because a person who has
AP : 12 :077(193) [0275] of the law or in any other **way** except by faith in Christ.
AP : 12 :081(194) [0275] be freed in any other **way** than by taking hold through
AP : 12 :094(196) [0281] wicked, but that the wicked turn from his **way** and live."
AP : 12 :096(196) [0281] be pardoned, in such a **way** that we hope for pardon from
AP : 12 :119(200) [0287] even Peter Lombard speaks this **way** about satisfactions.
AP : 12 :133(202) [0293] of Scripture apply in no **way** to scholastic satisfactions.
AP : 12 :136(203) [0293] these passages will have to be interpreted in a new **way**.
AP : 12 :142(204) [0295] can keep the law in such a **way** as to do even more than it
AP : 12 :145(205) [0297] In this **way** they obscure the law of God in two ways:
AP : 12 :145(205) [0297] the law of God in two **ways**: first, because they think that
AP : 12 :171(209) [0305] should be shown in other **ways** besides this formal one
AP : 13 :012(212) [0311] is interpreted this **way**, we shall not object either to
AP : 13 :020(213) [0313] that anyone who uses the Lord's Supper uses it this **way**.
AP : 13 :021(214) [0313] a faith which believes in a general **way** that God exists.
AP : 15 :038(220) [0325] them in an evangelical **way**, excluding the opinion which
AP : 20 :011(228) [0341] The shameful **way** in which our opponents have treated
AP : 21 :022(232) [0349] to others in the same **way** as Christ's, as though we were
AP : 21 :031(233) [0351] of the saints in the same **way** as the merits of Christ and
AP : 21 :034(233) [0353] ancient prayers, this was not done in a reprehensible **way**.
AP : 21 :035(234) [0353] Christopher in such a **way** as to symbolize that those who
AP : 21 :043(235) [0357] This **way** of doing things helps neither their position nor
AP : 21 :044(236) [0357] to find other honorable **ways** of establishing harmony —
AP : 21 :044(236) [0357] of establishing harmony — **ways** that will not burden
AP : 22 :011(238) [0361] This is the **way** a tyrant would act.
AP : 23 :047(246) [0377] this evil is the exaggerated **way** the monks have praised
AP : 23 :057(247) [0379] are making the law even more unbearable in several **ways**.
AP : 23 :068(249) [0383] They decided that the best **way** to arouse the ignorant
AP : 24 :010(251) [0387] In the same **way** our opponents should be forced to
AP : 24 :014(251) [0387] a few things because of the **way** our opponents have
AP : 24 :018(252) [0389] By **way** of contrast, a sacrifice is a ceremony or act which
AP : 24 :028(254) [0393] God and that this is the **way** I want you to know me when
AP : 24 :033(256) [0395] In the same **way**, the reception of the Lord's Supper itself
AP : 24 :063(261) [0405] wicked people, if they do not put an obstacle in its **way**.
AP : 24 :072(262) [0409] the sake of example, the **way** plays celebrate the memory
AP : 24 :081(264) [0411] They used it this **way** in the time of the Romans, as the
AP : 27 :004(269) [0421] sermons and in thinking up new **ways** of making money.
AP : 27 :006(269) [0421] When they act this **way**, therefore, the monks are signing
AP : 27 :009(270) [0421] own minds about their **way** of life, whom parents or
AP : 27 :024(273) [0427] perfect services than other **ways** of life, that is, that they
AP : 27 :025(273) [0427] Commandments in such a **way** that there are merits left
AP : 27 :029(274) [0431] That is the **way** our opponents argue their case; that is the
AP : 27 :029(274) [0431] argue their case; that is the **way** these good-for-nothings
AP : 27 :038(275) [0433] of others which put various **ways** of life on the same level.
AP : 27 :038(275) [0433] he was making in his **way** of life, God pointed in a dream
AP : 27 :038(276) [0433] was not to be attributed to the **way** he had undertaken.
AP : 27 :047(277) [0437] to praise it the **way** the *Extravagant* does, saying that
AP : 27 :047(277) [0437] God is meritorious and holy and the **way** of perfection.
AP : 27 :055(278) [0439] were used as exercises, the **way** lessons are in school, with
AP : 27 :056(278) [0439] reasons that release good men from this **way** of life.
AP : 27 :057(279) [0439] it is proper to abandon a **way** of life so full of hypocrisy
AP : 27 :061(279) [0441] they did not observe their **way** of life out of the belief
AP : 27 :067(280) [0441] He uses "faith" this **way** in the same chapter (I Tim. 5:8),
AP : 27 :068(280) [0443] In the same **way** he says that the wanton women had
AP : 27 :070(281) [0443] men who followed this **way** of life must have come to
AP : 28 :004(281) [0445] want instruction in order to have a sure **way** to go.
AP : 28 :017(283) [0449] This is the simple **way** to interpret traditions.
AP : 28 :018(284) [0449] This is the **way** many great and learned men in the church
AP : 28 :019(284) [0449] them to teach in such a **way** that he might be heard,
S2 : 02 :004(293) [0463] sacrament can be had in another and more blessed **way**?
S2 : 02 :005(293) [0463] that one can be saved in a better **way** without the Mass.
S2 : 02 :018(296) [0467] and grace in a better **way** and may omit pilgrimages
S2 : 02 :026(297) [0469] serve them in still other **ways**, regard them as helpers in
S2 : 02 :027(297) [0469] There are other **ways** in which I can honor, love, and
S2 : 04 :007(299) [0473] This is just the **way** in which the Council of Constance
S2 : 04 :007(299) [0473] he could, Christendom would not be helped in any **way**.
S3 : 02 :003(303) [0479] Hypocrites and false saints are produced in this **way**.
S3 : 03 :005(304) [0481] In this **way** they were to be prepared to receive grace from
S3 : 03 :008(304) [0481] and forgiveness in more **ways** than one, for with God
S3 : 03 :016(305) [0483] (which I might call half-**way** or partially repentant).
S3 : 03 :023(307) [0485] had done penance in this **way** for a hundred years, one
S3 : 03 :026(307) [0485] the popes forced their **way** into purgatory, first by
S3 : 03 :044(310) [0491] the upper hand in such a **way** that sin is committed, but
S3 : 04 :000(310) [0491] sin in more than one **way**, for God is surpassingly rich in
S3 : 09 :000(314) [0497] in the church until they mend their **ways** and avoid sin.
TR : 00 :009(321) [0505] he said, in the same **way** in which he had himself been
TR : 00 :023(324) [0511] we shall respond briefly by **way** of interpretation.
TR : 00 :027(325) [0511] "on this rock" in this **way** and not as applying to the
TR : 00 :040(327) [0515] pope conflicts in many **ways** with the Gospel, and the
TR : 00 :062(331) [0523] Moreover, in the same **way** in which an army might select
SC : PR :007(339) [0533] In this **way** all the time and labor will be lost.
SC : PR :008(339) [0535] and unlearned in such a **way** that we do not alter a single
SC : PR :009(339) [0535] and in such a variety of **ways** as you may be capable of.
SC : 06 :004(351) [0555] In the same **way** also he took the cup, after supper, and
SC : 09 :002(354) [0561] his children submissive and respectful in every **way**.
SC : 09 :005(355) [0561] life, godly and respectful in every **way**" (I Tim. 2:1-2).
SC : 09 :010(356) [0563] as to Christ; not in the **way** of eye-service, as
LC : PR :003(358) [0567] In this **way** they might show honor and gratitude to the
LC : SP :023(364) [0579] "In the same **way** also the cup, after supper, saying, 'This
LC : 01 :009(366) [0583] clings and cleaves to our nature all the **way** to the grave.
LC : 01 :027(368) [0587] Therefore, this **way** of receiving good through God's
LC : 01 :027(368) [0587] arrogantly to seek other **ways** and means than God has
LC : 01 :038(369) [0591] cause them to mend their **ways** before punishment
LC : 01 :051(371) [0595] upon the Lord God in any **way** whatsoever to support
LC : 01 :053(371) [0595] when and in how many **ways** God's name is abused,
LC : 01 :076(375) [0601] This would be the right **way** to bring up children, so long
LC : 01 :085(376) [0605] In this **way** a common order will prevail and no one will
LC : 01 :099(378) [0609] In the same **way** those conceited fellows should be
LC : 01 :102(379) [0609] the realization that in this **way** the devil is cast out and
LC : 01 :108(379) [0611] of their honor because of their **ways** or their failings.
LC : 01 :114(380) [0613] In this **way**, you see, we should have had godly children,
LC : 01 :123(382) [0617] That is the **way** things go in the world now, as everyone
LC : 01 :123(382) [0617] one another behind their backs in any **way** they can.
LC : 01 :136(383) [0619] This, in short, is the **way** God will have it: render him
LC : 01 :142(385) [0621] of our rulers in the same **way**, or at least do not treat and
LC : 01 :160(387) [0627] receive it, for the world's **way** of honoring them is to
LC : 01 :176(389) [0631] thus earning hell by the **way** you have reared your own
LC : 01 :177(389) [0631] Because of the **way** we train them, we have unruly and
LC : 01 :190(391) [0635] him although you know **ways** and means to do so, you
LC : 01 :200(392) [0637] us to guard against harming our neighbor in any **way**.
LC : 01 :212(393) [0641] Where nature has its **way**, as God implanted it, it is not
LC : 01 :212(393) [0641] stimulations have their **way** without let or hindrance, as
LC : 01 :219(394) [0643] This is one of the chief **ways** to make chastity attractive
LC : 01 :226(395) [0645] and never know enough **ways** to overcharge people and
LC : 01 :231(396) [0647] This, in short, is the **way** of the world.
LC : 01 :235(397) [0647] But you go your own **way**, take your wages like a thief,
LC : 01 :240(397) [0649] willful, conceited, arrogant **way**, as if it were his right and
LC : 01 :244(398) [0649] must punish us and teach us morals in a different **way**.
LC : 01 :244(398) [0649] last penny, and then by **way** of thanks they burn and
LC : 01 :248(398) [0651] this may go his own **way** until he learns it by experience.
LC : 01 :250(399) [0651] any injury or wrong in any **way** imaginable, whether by
LC : 01 :274(402) [0659] commandment in such a **way** that evil shall not go
LC : 01 :276(402) [0659] But the right **way** to deal with this matter would be to
LC : 01 :289(404) [0663] misconstruing and twisting things in the worst **way**.
LC : 01 :305(406) [0667] by any of a number of **ways**, to make her husband
LC : 01 :315(408) [0671] to find a higher and better **way** of life than the Ten
LC : 01 :328(410) [0675] or violence, nor in any **way** molest him, either in his
LC : 01 :331(410) [0677] memory, and practice them in all our works and **ways**.
LC : 02 :010(412) [0679] or describe him in such a **way** as to make him known?"
LC : 02 :021(413) [0683] This is the **way** the wretched, perverse world acts,
LC : 02 :023(413) [0683] every blessing that comes our **way**, should remind us of it.
LC : 03 :002(420) [0697] all that stands in our **way** and hinders us from fulfilling
LC : 03 :003(420) [0697] has taught us both the **way** and the words, as we shall
LC : 03 :014(422) [0701] the devil's name, in such a **way** that no one paid any
LC : 03 :039(425) [0709] it is our duty in every **way** to behave as good children so
LC : 03 :053(427) [0711] comes to us in two **ways**: first, it comes here, in time,
LC : 03 :064(429) [0715] using all the arts, tricks, **ways**, and means that he can
LC : 03 :121(436) [0731] when people pay in such a **way** that they dare not
LC : 03 :124(436) [0731] vain and that we must not in any **way** despise our prayers.
LC : 04 :002(436) [0733] treat it in a systematic **way** and confine ourselves to that
LC : 04 :020(439) [0737] In the same **way** we speak about the parental estate and
LC : 04 :046(442) [0743] the soul and apprehends Baptism in the only **way** it can.
LC : 04 :055(443) [0747] blaspheme and desecrate the sacrament in the worst **way**.
LC : 05 :001(447) [0753] sacrament in the same **way**, stating what it is, what its
LC : 05 :003(447) [0753] *"In the same* **way** *also he took the cup, after supper, gave*
LC : 05 :029(449) [0759] to us in no other **way** than through the words, "given and
LC : 05 :031(450) [0759] come to us in any other **way** than through the Word.
LC : 05 :063(454) [0767] would like to act in such a **way** that it may rest and rely
LC : 06 :025(460) [0000] In the same **way** the pope's preachers have in the past
LC : 06 :027(460) [0000] and do not come of their own accord, we let go their **way**.
LC : 06 :034(461) [0000] In this **way**, you see, confession would be rightly taught,
EP : RN :000(464) [0777] Should Be Explained and Decided in a Christian **Way**
EP : RN :002(465) [0777] be received in no other **way** and no further than as
EP : RN :007(465) [0779] In this **way** the distinction between the Holy Scripture of
EP : 01 :010(467) [0781] will take place wholly by **way** of death in the

Continued ▶

E P : 0 1 :021(468) [0783] essence of man in such a **way** that even if no evil thought
E P : 0 3 :023(475) [0797] good works, in such a **way** that good works are necessary
E P : 0 4 :009(476) [0799] and in a Christian **way** applied to the regenerated and are
E P : 0 4 :009(476) [0799] regenerated and are in no **way** contrary to the pattern of
E P : 0 6 :002(480) [0805] In the same **way** our first parents even before the Fall did
E P : 0 6 :004(480) [0807] constantly to light their **way** lest in their merely human
E P : 0 6 :004(480) [0807] necessary lest the Old Adam go his own self-willed **way**.
E P : 0 7 :005(482) [0809] present in any manner or **way**, since in their opinion it is
E P : 0 7 :007(482) [0811] be understood in no other **way** than in their literal sense,
E P : 0 7 :022(484) [0813] thus annihilated, in such a **way** that they are transmuted
E P : 0 7 :032(485) [0815] in heaven that it can in no **way** be present at one and the
E P : 0 7 :041(486) [0817] Capernaitic, and abhorrent **way** concerning the
E P : 0 7 :042(486) [0817] this mystery in no other **way** than by faith and as it is
E P : 0 8 :003(487) [0817] personally united in such a **way** that neither of the two
E P : 0 8 :005(487) [0819] united in Christ in such a **way** that there are not two
E P : 0 8 :016(489) [0821] into his glory in such a **way** that now not only as God,
E P : 0 8 :039(491) [0827] testament, but it opens a **way** for the accursed Arian
E P : 1 0 :012(494) [0831] things are abolished in a **way** which suggests that the
E P : 1 1 :012(496) [0835] and thus bar the ordinary **way** for the Holy Spirit, so that
E P : 1 1 :016(497) [0837] to eternal life in such a **way** that disconsolate Christians
E P : 1 1 :016(497) [0837] and despair, or in such a **way** that the impenitent are
E P : 1 1 :022(497) [0837] In this **way** the offensive controversies that have
E P : 1 2 :011(499) [0841] or work for them in any **way**, but flee and avoid them as
E P : 1 2 :019(499) [0841] another, each go his own **way**, and marry someone else
E P : 1 2 :021(499) [0841] divine properties in such a **way** that Christ as man is fully
S D : R N :000(503) [0849] writings in such a **way** that anybody with Christian
S D : P R :010(503) [0849] Are to Be Explained and Decided in a Christian **Way**
S D : P R :002(503) [0851] In the same **way** we have from our hearts and with our
S D : P R :009(505) [0855] he expressly asserts by **way** of distinction that the Word
S D : 0 1 :016(511) [0865] this doctrine in such a **way** that we fall neither into
S D : 0 1 :023(512) [0865] the situation is not the **way** the hymn which we sing in
S D : 0 1 :027(512) [0867] their nature in such a **way** that Satan created or made
S D : 0 1 :027(513) [0867] and born in the natural **way** from a father and a mother,
S D : 0 1 :029(513) [0867] from each other in such a **way** that man's nature is
S D : 0 1 :030(513) [0867] being born in the natural **way** from a father and a mother
S D : 0 1 :056(518) [0877] In the same **way**, prior to this controversy, the
S D : 0 1 :061(519) [0879] "accident" does not in any **way** minimize original sin if
S D : 0 2 :006(521) [0883] controversy in a Christian **way** according to the Word of
S D : 0 2 :007(521) [0883] or natural powers in any **way** understand, believe, accept,
S D : 0 2 :007(521) [0883] either altogether or half-**way** or in the tiniest or smallest
S D : 0 2 :010(522) [0885] In this **way** Scripture calls the natural man simply
S D : 0 2 :019(524) [0889] rather than yields in any **way** to human touch, or to an
S D : 0 2 :023(525) [0889] for this freedom in such a **way** that by divine grace it can
S D : 0 2 :025(526) [0891] and completion in no **way** to the human powers of the
S D : 0 2 :030(527) [0893] Confession does not in any **way** recognize the freedom of
S D : 0 2 :049(530) [0901] that the wicked turn from his **way** and live" (Ezek. 33:11).
S D : 0 2 :050(531) [0901] means and in no other **way** — namely, through his holy
S D : 0 2 :054(531) [0903] And in this **way** the Holy Spirit, who works all of this, is
S D : 0 2 :060(533) [0905] and draws him in such a **way** that man's darkened reason
S D : 0 2 :066(534) [0907] be understood in no other **way** than that the converted
S D : 0 2 :066(534) [0907] the Holy Spirit, the **way** two horses draw a wagon
S D : 0 2 :071(535) [0909] our doctrine answers this **way**: Man's natural powers
S D : 0 2 :071(535) [0909] anything or help in any **way** (I Cor. 2:4-12);
S D : 0 2 :077(536) [0911] small extent and in a weak **way** — help and cooperate and
S D : 0 2 :081(537) [0911] and a new man in such a **way** that the substance and
S D : 0 2 :083(537) [0913] and heart, when man in no **way** believes the promise and
S D : 0 2 :085(537) [0913] In this **way** one can and should explain and teach the
S D : 0 2 :089(538) [0915] behaves in a purely passive **way** in his conversion (that is,
S D : 0 2 :089(538) [0915] and cannot assist in any **way** toward his conversion, and
S D : 0 2 :089(538) [0915] with it, but in the **way** and after the manner set forth and
S D : 0 3 :002(539) [0917] what is right, and is in this **way** their righteousness), and
S D : 0 3 :008(540) [0919] controversy in a Christian **way** according to the Word of
S D : 0 3 :022(543) [0923] or should follow in the **ways** of sin, abide and continue
S D : 0 3 :024(543) [0923] talk in one and the same **way** about conversion and
S D : 0 3 :029(544) [0925] love — not in such a **way** as if we thereby utterly rejected
S D : 0 3 :040(546) [0929] In this **way**, too, the proper order between faith and good
S D : 0 3 :041(546) [0929] from each other in such a **way** as though on occasion true
S D : 0 3 :049(548) [0933] before God, in such a **way**, however, that they are not the
S D : 0 3 :052(548) [0933] man is saved in a different **way** or by a different thing
S D : 0 3 :053(548) [0933] in one and the same **way**; in fact, that when we are
S D : 0 3 :055(549) [0935] consider carefully in what **way** Christ is called our
S D : 0 3 :067(551) [0937] more as necessary by **way** of a detailed explanation of
S D : 0 4 :006(552) [0939] in a Christian **way** and according to the Word of God,
S D : 0 4 :023(555) [0945] are dangerous in many **ways**, confirm presumptuous trust
S D : 0 4 :036(557) [0949] Scripture without in any **way** intending to confirm the
S D : 0 4 :039(558) [0951] a wicked, wild, complacent, and Epicurean **way** of life.
S D : 0 5 :003(558) [0953] but is used in a twofold **way**, both in the Holy Scripture
S D : 0 5 :004(558) [0953] the word is used in such a **way** that we understand by it
S D : 0 5 :019(561) [0957] This is the **way** in which the law rebukes unbelief, when a
S D : 0 5 :024(563) [0961] but not in such a **way** that they become despondent and
S D : 0 6 :002(564) [0963] should this doctrine in any **way** they be urged on the basis of
S D : 0 6 :006(564) [0965] indwelling Spirit in such a **way** that in their nature and
S D : 0 6 :012(566) [0967] In this **way** the Holy Spirit simultaneously performs both
S D : 0 6 :021(567) [0969] works for faith in such a **way** that, as in a mirror, it
S D : 0 6 :021(567) [0969] says, "I will run in the **way** of thy commandments"
S D : 0 7 :003(569) [0973] visible signs in the same **way** as by the preached Word,
S D : 0 7 :007(570) [0975] my body," not strictly, the **way** the letters sound, but as
S D : 0 7 :007(570) [0975] to the symbols in such a **way** that Christ's body is even
S D : 0 7 :008(570) [0975] with the bread in such a **way** that as certainly as believing
S D : 0 7 :014(571) [0977] or are in some other **way** permanently united with it
S D : 0 7 :017(572) [0979] agree in the most exact **way** with the words of Christ.
S D : 0 7 :018(572) [0979] In this **way** was stopped up every subterfuge and
S D : 0 7 :018(572) [0979] bread in precisely the same **way** as with the Word of the
S D : 0 7 :032(574) [0983] following: "In the same **way** I also say and confess that in
S D : 0 7 :046(577) [0989] that God had many more **ways** and means of fulfilling the
S D : 0 7 :047(578) [0989] In the same **way** we are to believe in all humility and
S D : 0 7 :058(580) [0993] agree in the best possible **way** with the words of Christ by
S D : 0 7 :060(580) [0995] understood and explained this passage in this **way**.
S D : 0 7 :061(580) [0995] This occurs, in no other **way** than with the spirit and
S D : 0 7 :085(584) [1003] This rule dare not in any **way** be rejected, but it can and
S D : 0 7 :092(586) [1005] meaning different from the **way** the letters read, but, as
S D : 0 7 :097(586) [1005] has and knows various **ways** to be present at a certain
S D : 0 7 :101(587) [1007] with creatures in such a **way** that they do not feel, touch,
S D : 0 7 :103(587) [1007] do not want to deny in any **way** that God's power is able
S D : 0 7 :117(589) [1013] of Christ, and that in this **way** we partake of his absent
S D : 0 7 :119(590) [1013] or in heaven that he in no **way** can or wills to be with us
S D : 0 7 :127(591) [1015] fleshly, Capernaitic **way** about the supernatural and
S D : 0 8 :005(592) [1017] controversy in a Christian **way** according to the Word of
S D : 0 8 :006(592) [1017] two Christs, but in such a **way** that Christ Jesus is
S D : 0 8 :011(593) [1019] are united in such a **way** that they constitute a single
S D : 0 8 :017(594) [1021] Christ are united in such a **way** that they have true
S D : 0 8 :025(596) [1023] another man but in such a **way** that by and in his death
S D : 0 8 :028(596) [1025] take place in a mundane **way**, but as Dr. Luther explains,
S D : 0 8 :029(597) [1025] both natures in Christ, the **way** Jesus, the son of Mary,
S D : 0 8 :030(597) [1025] personally united in such a **way** that in Christ the whole
S D : 0 8 :031(597) [1025] with each other in such a **way** that they not only have
S D : 0 8 :032(597) [1025] into the other nature, the **way** water is poured from one
S D : 0 8 :034(597) [1027] bodily" (Col. 2:9) in such a **way** that God and man are a
S D : 0 8 :038(598) [1027] be forearmed in the best possible **way** against this error.
S D : 0 8 :044(599) [1029] I mean that this **way**: If it is not true that God died for
S D : 0 8 :053(601) [1033] safest, and most certain **way** in this controversy is to
S D : 0 8 :060(602) [1035] Christ are united in such a **way** that they are not blended
S D : 0 8 :060(602) [1035] properties in such a **way** that the properties of the one
S D : 0 8 :061(602) [1035] human nature in the same **way** in which the Father
S D : 0 8 :061(603) [1037] in the flesh of Christ the **way** it is in his divine nature,
S D : 0 8 :062(603) [1037] human nature in such a **way** that the humanity of Christ
S D : 0 8 :062(603) [1037] essence, nor in such a **way** that the human nature in
S D : 0 8 :062(603) [1037] Godhead, nor in such a **way** that the natural, essential
S D : 0 8 :062(603) [1037] For in no **way** should any conversion, blending, or
S D : 0 8 :063(603) [1037] the majesty of Christ by **way** of contrast, we have spoken
S D : 0 8 :066(604) [1039] through the iron in such a **way** that on that account and
S D : 0 8 :067(604) [1039] nature only in such a **way** that it merely shares the bare
S D : 0 8 :069(604) [1039] In this **way** no distinction would be made between Christ
S D : 0 8 :071(605) [1041] We do not in any **way** believe, teach, and confess an
S D : 0 8 :071(605) [1041] of God in such a **way** that it would become an
S D : 0 8 :072(605) [1041] or the Anointed) in such a **way** that he received the
S D : 0 8 :073(605) [1041] only certain things in the **way** in which other saints know
S D : 0 8 :074(606) [1043] In this **way** all the treasures of wisdom are hid in him, all
S D : 0 8 :077(606) [1043] this presence of Christ in no **way** involves his humanity.
S D : 0 8 :085(608) [1045] to him — in a temporal **way**, however, and not from
S D : 0 8 :090(609) [1047] present in the same **way** as the Deity, as an infinite
S D : 0 8 :094(609) [1049] involve his assumed human nature in any **way** whatever.
S D : 0 8 :096(610) [1049] In this **way** they will be certain to find abiding comfort in
S D : 1 0 :009(612) [1055] orderly and appropriate **way**, as at any time may seem to
S D : 1 0 :030(615) [1061] are abolished in such a **way** as to give the impression that
S D : 1 1 :003(616) [1063] In the same **way**, one must not by-pass or reject a
S D : 1 1 :006(617) [1065] as well, but not in such a **way** as though it were God's
S D : 1 1 :006(617) [1065] operates in such a **way** that God sets a limit and measure
S D : 1 1 :006(617) [1065] everything in such a **way** that it must redound to the glory
S D : 1 1 :008(617) [1065] is based on it in such a **way** that "the gates of Hades" are
S D : 1 1 :012(618) [1067] foreknowledge will in no **way** cause or support either
S D : 1 1 :012(618) [1067] this doctrine in no other **way** than to direct us thereby to
S D : 1 1 :020(619) [1069] guide and lead them in his **ways**, raise them up again
S D : 1 1 :029(621) [1073] God reveals his will in this **way**, and that in those whom
S D : 1 1 :033(621) [1073] Luther puts it this **way**: "Follow the order in the Epistle to
S D : 1 1 :035(622) [1075] In this **way** it would be taught that God, who is the
S D : 1 1 :039(623) [1077] or seek other **ways** to righteousness and salvation
S D : 1 1 :042(623) [1077] In the same **way** many "receive the Word with joy," but
S D : 1 1 :051(625) [1079] this article in a profitable, comforting, and salutary **way**.
S D : 1 1 :064(626) [1083] are his judgements and how inscrutable his **ways**!
S D : 1 1 :077(629) [1089] with diligence, and in no **way** doubt the drawing of the
S D : 1 1 :081(629) [1089] the devil and man through sin, and in no **way** from God.
S D : 1 1 :081(630) [1089] the wicked turn from his **way** and live" (Ezek. 18:23;
S D : 1 1 :084(630) [1091] wicked, but that the wicked turn from his **way** and live."
S D : 1 1 :086(631) [1091] of his Word, and in no **way** does he want us to infer that
S D : 1 2 :024(634) [1099] other, to go their separate **ways**, and to enter into a new
S D : 1 2 :029(635) [1101] divine properties in such a **way** that in might, in power, in
S D : 1 2 :029(635) [1101] and in glory he is in every **way** equal in grade and rank of

Wayward (3)

L C : 0 1 :060(372) [0597] war, famine, fire, flood, **wayward** wives and children and
L C : 0 1 :123(382) [0617] and old are altogether **wayward** and unruly; they have no
L C : 0 1 :248(398) [0651] and not follow the old, **wayward** crowd, but may keep

Weak (45), Weaken (5), Weakened (4), Weakens (1), Weaker (7), Weakest (2), Weakly (1)

A G : 2 0 :015(043) [0055] matter of experience that **weak** and terrified consciences
A G : 2 0 :031(045) [0057] when it is without the Holy Spirit, the heart is too **weak**.
A G : 2 0 :036(046) [0057] strength are much too **weak** to do good works, call upon
A G : 2 3 :014(053) [0063] worse and men are becoming **weaker** and more infirm.
A G : 2 7 :007(071) [0077] to show more consideration to women as the **weaker** sex.
A L : 2 0 :031(045) [0057] affections and are too **weak** to do works which are good
A L : 2 3 :014(053) [0063] man's nature is becoming **weaker**, it is also well to take
A L : 2 7 :007(071) [0077] consideration should have been given to the **weaker** sex.
A P : 0 4 :138(126) [0161] human nature is far too **weak** to be able by its own
A P : 0 4 :160(129) [0167] is indeed righteousness; but in us it is **weak** and impure.
A P : 0 4 :234(140) [0185] the strong bear with the **weak**, when the people put the
A P : 0 4 :290(151) [0203] life, although even a **weak** and feeble keeping of the law
A P : 0 4 :301(153) [0205] opponents admit, or surely they feel that it is very **weak**.
A P : 0 4 :364(163) [0219] in one way, and the **weak** in another; for the weak work
A P : 0 4 :364(163) [0219] weak in another; for the **weak** work for their own
A P : 0 4 :381(165) [0223] love, which we know by experience is **weak** and unclean.
A P : 0 7 :020(171) [0233] there are also many **weak** people in it who build on this
A P : 1 5 :051(222) [0329] used moderately, lest the **weak** be offended and become
A P : 1 6 :013(224) [0333] our doctrine does not **weaken** but rather strengthens the
A P : 2 3 :022(242) [0369] snares should be set for the **weak** through this regulation.
A P : 2 3 :053(246) [0379] older and progressively **weaker**, so that we ought to use
S C : 0 9 :006(355) [0561] on the woman as the **weaker** sex, since you are joint heirs
L C : 0 1 :141(384) [0621] to teach him; if he is too **weak**, he enlists the help of his
L C : 0 1 :287(403) [0663] body which seem to be **weaker** are indispensable, and
L C : 0 1 :287(403) [0663] But the **weakest** members, of which we are ashamed, we
L C : 0 1 :291(404) [0663] than this smallest and **weakest** of his members, the
L C : 0 2 :002(411) [0679] all human ability is far too feeble and **weak** to keep them.
L C : 0 3 :030(424) [0707] We are far too **weak** to cope with the devil and all his
L C : 0 4 :056(444) [0747] I may be strong or **weak**; I leave that in God's hands.
L C : 0 5 :024(449) [0759] strengthen itself and not **weaken** in the struggle but grow
L C : 0 5 :043(451) [0763] common people and the **weak**, who also would like to be

Continued ▶

LC : 0 5 :059(453) [0767] even though in other respects they are **weak** and frail.
EP : 0 2 :011(471) [0789] man is indeed too **weak** by his free will to make a
EP : 0 7 :019(484) [0813] believer, no matter how **weak** he may be, as long as he
EP : 0 7 :019(484) [0813] for Christians who are **weak** in faith but repentant, to
EP : 0 7 :019(484) [0813] to comfort them and to strengthen their **weak** faith.
EP : 1 0 :005(493) [0829] and particularly the **weak** in faith are to be spared
EP : 1 0 :006(493) [0831] as well as preventing offense to the **weak** in faith.
EP : 1 1 :013(496) [0835] evil foe in an attempt to **weaken** for us or to rob us
SD : PR :007(502) [0849] offense for both the unbelievers and the **weak** believers.
SD : PR :008(502) [0849] The **weak** in faith, on the other hand, will be scandalized;
SD : 0 1 :012(510) [0863] ability, although greatly **weakened** since the inherited
SD : 0 1 :023(512) [0865] nature has been greatly **weakened** and corrupted through
SD : 0 2 :003(520) [0881] his assent to it, though **weakly**, but that without the gift
SD : 0 2 :010(522) [0885] who is "in sin" is not only **weak** and sick, but that he is
SD : 0 2 :017(524) [0887] that man is not only **weak**, impotent, incapable, and dead
SD : 0 2 :029(527) [0893] Christ is much too **weak** for Satan, who incites men to
SD : 0 2 :068(534) [0907] Christians, one being **weak** and the other strong in the
SD : 0 2 :068(534) [0907] in faith and in hope, and at another time cold and **weak**.
SD : 0 2 :076(536) [0911] since man is too **weak** to complete it, the Holy Spirit
SD : 0 2 :077(536) [0911] a result, his free will is too **weak** to make a beginning and
SD : 0 2 :077(536) [0911] to a small extent and in a **weak** way — help and cooperate
SD : 0 4 :039(557) [0951] and offensive, might **weaken** discipline and decency, and
SD : 0 7 :069(582) [0997] perturbed Christians, **weak** in faith, who are heartily
SD : 0 7 :070(582) [0997] "As for a man who is **weak** in faith, welcome him, for
SD : 0 7 :070(582) [0997] God, be his faith strong or **weak**, has eternal life
SD : 0 7 :071(582) [0997] the distressed father of **weak** faith (Mark 9:24) partook no
SD : 0 8 :071(605) [1041] the divine nature is **weakened** or surrenders to another
SD : 1 0 :009(612) [1055] give in and yield to the **weak** in faith in such external
SD : 1 0 :013(613) [1057] yielded and gave in to the **weak** as far as foods, times, and
SD : 1 0 :015(613) [1057] As soon as this article is **weakened** and human
SD : 1 0 :016(613) [1057] scandalize true believers and **weaken** them in their faith.
SD : 1 0 :025(615) [1061] enemies of God's Word, and scandalize the **weak** in faith.
SD : 1 1 :030(621) [1073] Though this is still very **weak** in them, they nevertheless
SD : 1 1 :092(632) [1093] of the Scriptures which **weakens** or even removes this

Weakness (35)
AG : 2 3 :016(054) [0063] for the sake of human **weakness** and to prevent and avoid
AL : 2 3 :016(054) [0063] on account of man's **weakness**, and it is devoutly to be
AL : 2 7 :032(076) [0079] concession to human **weakness**, adds a few years and
AP : 0 2 :024(103) [0111] Since nature in its **weakness** cannot fear and love God or
AP : 0 2 :045(106) [0117] sin and of human **weakness**, he taught that the remnants
AP : 0 4 :023(110) [0127] by its natural **weakness** and by the devil, who drives it to
AP : 0 4 :106(122) [0153] that by recognizing his **weakness** one may attain to it,
AP : 0 4 :165(129) [0169] must sustain us in our **weakness**, and we must firmly
AP : 0 4 :168(130) [0169] Therefore in our present **weakness** there is always sin that
AP : 0 4 :189(133) [0175] rule of the devil; in our **weakness** he displays his strength.
AP : 0 4 :233(140) [0185] on the people or have no regard for their **weakness**.
AP : 0 4 :234(140) [0185] the bishops take into account the **weakness** of the people.
AP : 1 2 :142(204) [0295] in condescension to our **weakness** God has fixed a certain
AP : 1 2 :160(207) [0301] of God might be made more manifest in our **weakness**.
AP : 1 2 :160(207) [0303] power of God is made perfect in **weakness**" (II Cor. 12:9).
AP : 2 7 :009(270) [0421] evil end, either because **weakness** prevents their
AP : 2 7 :051(278) [0437] many fail in their continence because of **weakness**.
AP : 2 7 :051(278) [0437] for anybody whose **weakness** causes him to defile himself
LC : 0 3 :067(429) [0717] not yield or fall away through **weakness** or indolence."
LC : 0 5 :070(454) [0769] But those who feel their **weakness**, who are anxious to be
LC : 0 5 :072(455) [0769] and feel your **weakness**, go joyfully to the sacrament and
EP : 0 3 :009(474) [0793] persons retain much **weakness** and many shortcomings
EP : 0 4 :013(477) [0799] encumbered with much **weakness**, as St. Paul complains
EP : 0 4 :014(477) [0799] does not reckon this **weakness** against his elect, as it is
SD : 0 2 :014(523) [0885] them in their great **weakness** and to help them to remain
SD : 0 2 :047(530) [0901] obedience but only **weakness** and anxiety and misery.
SD : 0 2 :056(532) [0903] under cover of great **weakness**, we should be certain,
SD : 0 2 :065(534) [0907] Holy Spirit, even though we still do so in great **weakness**.
SD : 0 2 :067(534) [0907] to it and accept it, even though it be in great **weakness**.
SD : 0 7 :069(582) [0997] and who perceive their **weakness** in faith, deplore it, and
SD : 0 7 :070(582) [0997] "The power of God is made perfect in **weakness**."
SD : 0 7 :071(582) [0997] does not consist in the **weakness** or certainty of faith, be
SD : 1 1 :011(618) [1067] when they see their own **weakness** and the example of
SD : 1 1 :020(619) [1069] them in their great **weakness** against the devil, the world,
SD : 1 1 :046(624) [1079] — for due to the **weakness** and wickedness of our flesh it

Weal (1)
AP : 2 3 :049(246) [0377] and the common **weal**" (that is, for the discipline of the

Wealth (7), Wealthy (1)
AP : 0 2 :042(106) [0117] people; yielding to anger, desire, ambition, **wealth**, etc.
AP : 1 6 :009(224) [0333] Though they were **wealthy** and held high positions,
AP : 2 8 :003(281) [0443] opponents valiantly defend their own position and **wealth**.
LC : 0 1 :009(366) [0583] This desire for **wealth** clings and cleaves to our nature all
LC : 0 1 :042(370) [0591] power, prestige, honor, **wealth**, and every comfort in the
LC : 0 1 :043(370) [0591] scraping together great **wealth** and money, what have
LC : 0 1 :043(370) [0593] found happiness in their **wealth**, nor has it ever lasted to
LC : 0 1 :184(390) [0633] and estate or greater **wealth** and good fortune than he,

Weapons (5)
AG : 2 8 :017(083) [0085] in II Cor. 10:4, 5, "The **weapons** of our warfare are not
AL : 2 8 :017(083) [0085] in II Cor. 10:4, 5, "The **weapons** of our warfare are not
TR : 0 0 :031(325) [0513] and again, "The **weapons** of our warfare are not
LC : PR :015(360) [0571] and yet we despise our **weapons** and armor, too lazy to
LC : 0 3 :030(424) [0707] must carefully select the **weapons** with which Christians

Wear (3), Wearing (1), Wears (1)
AG : 2 7 :050(079) [0083] not of mendicancy or **wearing** a black or gray cowl, etc.
AP : 1 5 :035(220) [0325] customs, if soldiers **wear** one kind of uniform and
LC : 0 3 :047(426) [0711] teachers, all of whom **wear** the holy name as a cloak and
LC : 0 4 :059(444) [0747] remains no less gold if a harlot **wears** it in sin and shame.
LC : 0 4 :084(446) [0753] as the daily garment which he is to **wear** all the time.

Wearily (1), Weary (3)
LC : 0 1 :192(391) [0635] just as if I saw someone **wearily** struggling in deep water,
LC : 0 3 :105(434) [0727] us to become faint and **weary** and to fall back into sin,
LC : 0 3 :109(435) [0729] never stops or becomes **weary**; when one attack ceases,
LC : 0 5 :023(449) [0757] world that we often grow **weary** and faint, at times even

Weather (1)
SC : 0 3 :014(347) [0549] government; seasonable **weather**, peace and health, order

Wedding (3)
SD : 0 8 :025(596) [1023] — for example, at the **wedding** in Cana of Galilee, again
SD : 1 1 :027(620) [1071] king invites to his son's **wedding** he calls through the
SD : 1 1 :041(623) [1077] despise the Word and refuse to come to the **wedding**.

Wednesday (3)
AG : PR :007(025) [0039] it was decided last **Wednesday** that, in keeping with Your
AG : 2 4 :041(061) [0069] History, Book 9, on **Wednesday** and Friday the Scriptures
AL : 2 4 :041(061) [0069] expound them on **Wednesday** and Friday, and all things

Weeds (1)
AP : 0 7 :019(171) [0233] sons of the kingdom, the **weeds** are the sons of the evil

Week (7), Weekly (1)
AP : 2 4 :008(250) [0385] celebrated three times a **week**, and that this practice came
S2 : 0 2 :012(294) [0465] with vigils, with the **weekly**, monthly, and yearly
S2 : 0 2 :012(294) [0465] with the common **week**, with All Souls' Day, and with
LC : SP :004(362) [0575] servants at least once a **week** and ascertain what they
LC : 0 1 :083(376) [0603] work and trades the whole **week** long — should retire for
LC : 0 1 :085(376) [0605] do, at least one day in the **week** must be set apart for it.
LC : 0 1 :089(377) [0605] set apart several hours a **week** for the young, and at least
LC : 0 5 :056(453) [0767] prepared, until one **week** passes into another and one half

Weigh (2), Weighed (5), Weighing (1), Weight (4), Weightier (2), Weights (1), Weighty (7)
AG : PR :002(025) [0039] to hear, understand, and **weigh** the judgments, opinions,
AG : PR :022(027) [0043] concerning these most **weighty** matters, and have done so
AG : PR :023(027) [0043] finally heard, amicably **weighed**, charitably settled, and
AG : 2 3 :002(053) [0063] important, better, and **weightier** reasons for permitting
AG : 2 6 :035(069) [0075] lest your hearts be **weighed** down with dissipation," and
AG : 0 0 :001(095) [0095] The others can readily be **weighed** in the light of these.
AL : 2 3 :002(051) [0061] that there are now far **weightier** reasons why this right
AL : 2 6 :005(064) [0071] lays the greatest **weight** on this article and puts aside the
AL : 2 6 :035(069) [0075] lest your hearts be **weighed** down with dissipation," and
AP : PR :007(098) [0101] to show him that very **weighty** reasons prevented us from
AP : 0 7 :032(174) [0239] We certainly had **weighty** reasons for presenting this
AP : 1 2 :031(186) [0259] gone over my head; they **weigh** like a burden too heavy
AP : 1 5 :046(221) [0327] lest your hearts be **weighed** down with dissipation," and
AP : 2 0 :009(227) [0341] This issue is so **weighty** that we shrink from no danger on
AP : 2 3 :062(247) [0381] shall briefly review their **weighty** arguments in defense of
AP : 2 7 :046(277) [0435] for throwing a great **weight** of gold into the sea.
S3 : 0 3 :036(309) [0489] need not spend our time **weighing**, distinguishing,
TR : 0 0 :058(330) [0521] all the godly have **weighty**, compelling, and evident
SC : PR :018(340) [0537] Lay the greatest **weight** on those commandments or other
LC : 0 1 :227(396) [0645] measures, dishonest **weights**, and bad coins, and takes
SD : PR :009(503) [0849] controversies deal with **weighty** and important matters,
SD : 0 8 :044(599) [1029] balance and throws in **weight** as a counterbalance, we

Weimar (1)
PR : PR :027(014) [0025] Duke John [of Saxe-**Weimar**] the above two through

Weitmann (1)
S3 : 1 5 :005(318) [0501] the Rev. Melchior **Weitmann**

Welcome (2), Welcomed (1)
LC : 0 1 :191(391) [0635] and you did not **welcome** me, I was naked and you did
SD : 0 7 :070(582) [0997] who is weak in faith, **welcome** him, for God has
SD : 0 7 :070(582) [0997] welcome him, for God has **welcomed** him" (Rom. 14:1, 3).

Welfare (11)
PR : PR :008(006) [0011] souls and their eternal **welfare** to abide by it and persist in
PR : PR :024(013) [0023] the temporal and eternal **welfare** of our own selves and of
PR : PR :024(013) [0023] glory and the common **welfare**, both eternal and
TR : 0 0 :059(330) [0521] of God, and hinder the **welfare** of the church by so
LC : 0 1 :132(383) [0619] intended for our greatest **welfare**, to lead us to a quiet,
LC : 0 3 :117(436) [0731] that affects our bodily **welfare** and directs us to seek and
EP : 1 0 :001(492) [0829] in the interest of good order and the general **welfare**.
EP : 1 0 :003(493) [0829] order and the general **welfare**, are in and for themselves
EP : 1 2 :030(500) [0843] they dearly love their soul's eternal **welfare** and salvation.
SD : 1 0 :016(613) [1057] As he values his soul's **welfare** and salvation, every
SD : 1 2 :039(636) [1103] as dearly as they love their soul's **welfare** and salvation.

Wendal (2)
S3 : 1 5 :005(317) [0501] **Wendal** Faber, pastor of Seeburg in Mansfeld
TR : 0 0 :082(335) [0529] **Wendal** Faber, pastor of Seeburg in Mansfeld

Wept (1)
S3 : 0 3 :018(306) [0483] sooner have laughed than **wept**, unless perchance he was

West (2)
TR : 0 0 :012(322) [0507] is, those that were in the Roman provinces in the **West**.
TR : 0 0 :014(322) [0507] was also observed in the **West** and in the Latin churches,

Wheat (2)
AP : 0 7 :001(168) [0227] floor on which chaff and **wheat** are heaped together
LC : 0 1 :166(388) [0629] life or raise from the earth a single grain of **wheat** for us.

Wheel (1)
LC : 0 1 :137(384) [0619] or broken on the **wheel** if not because of disobedience?

Whim (1), Whims (1)
AP : 0 4 :222(138) [0181] only our opponents should not add their own **whims** to it.
LC : 0 1 :169(388) [0629] the parental office is a matter of your pleasure and **whim**.

Whisper (1)
LC : 0 1 :276(402) [0659] if someone should **whisper** to you what this or that person

White (2), Whitewash (1)
AP : 0 4 :258(144) [0193] are like scarlet, they shall be **white** as snow" (Isa. 1:16-18).
AP : 1 2 :164(208) [0303] your sins are like scarlet, they shall be **white** as snow.
SD : 1 1 :095(632) [1095] by far are we minded to **whitewash** or cover up any

Whither (1)

E P : 0 7 :005(482) [0809] highest heaven above, **whither** we should ascend with the

Whitsuntide (1)

S 1 : P R :001(288) [0455] a council to meet in Mantua last year, in **Whitsuntide**.

Whole (172)

P R : P R :022(012) [0021] of almighty God and the **whole** of Christendom that it is
P R : P R :027(016) [0027] The **whole** administration of the City of Hildesheim
A G : 1 8 :002(039) [0051] believing in God with his **whole** heart, or of expelling
A G : 1 8 :004(039) [0051] as loving God with their **whole** heart or fearing him), for
A G : 2 0 :013(043) [0055] His **whole** book, *De spiritu et litera*, proves this.
A G : 2 2 :003(050) [0059] that the **whole** assembly of the congregation in Corinth
A G : 2 3 :016(054) [0063] be of disadvantage to the Christian church as a **whole**?
A G : 2 4 :029(059) [0067] himself but also for the **whole** world and for others, both
A G : 2 7 :031(076) [0079] determine or arrange the order of one's **whole** future life.
A G : 2 7 :049(079) [0083] God honestly with our **whole** hearts, and yet have sincere
A G : 2 8 :034(086) [0089] canon law throughout the **whole** of the ninth Distinction.
A L : 2 0 :012(043) [0055] of Paul, this **whole** matter is supported by testimonies of
A L : 2 0 :017(043) [0055] This **whole** teaching is to be referred to that conflict of
A L : 0 0 :002(047) [0059] The **whole** dissension is concerned with a certain few
A L : 2 2 :003(050) [0059] which it appears that a **whole** congregation used both
A L : 2 6 :007(065) [0071] were proposed, and the **whole** of repentance was thought
A L : 2 8 :007(082) [0085] said, "Go and preach the gospel to the **whole** creation."
A L : 2 8 :034(086) [0089] The canons concede this throughout the **whole** of Dist. 9.
A P : 0 2 :042(105) [0115] of the Scripture contradict them, but the **whole** church.
A P : 0 4 :020(110) [0125] But this **whole** business is the invention of idle men who
A P : 0 4 :081(118) [0145] completely and do away with the **whole** teaching of faith?
A P : 0 4 :087(119) [0147] the basic issue of the **whole** discussion: "We hold that
A P : 0 4 :087(120) [0147] Paul is talking about the **whole** law, not only about
A P : 0 4 :087(120) [0147] Paul is talking about the **whole** law, as Augustine
A P : 0 4 :103(122) [0151] For after the **whole** world was subjected, he took away
A P : 0 4 :103(122) [0151] took away the sin of the **whole** world, as John testified
A P : 0 4 :154(128) [0163] Christ contrasted the **whole** act of reverence of the
A P : 0 4 :155(128) [0165] He includes the **whole** act of worship; but meanwhile he
A P : 0 4 :157(128) [0165] of sins unless he keeps the **whole** law, because the law
A P : 0 4 :218(137) [0179] Before the **whole** church, they say, Paul asserts that faith
A P : 0 4 :235(140) [0185] is said to be perfect or **whole** when all its parts fit
A P : 0 4 :278(149) [0199] almsgiving that it is the **whole** newness of life which
A P : 0 4 :280(149) [0201] single passage without taking the **whole** law into account.
A P : 0 4 :282(149) [0201] An examination of the **whole** passage shows that it
A P : 0 4 :284(150) [0201] A study of the **whole** passage shows its agreement with
A P : 0 4 :284(150) [0201] Moreover, why do they not present the **whole** sermon?
A P : 0 4 :287(150) [0203] The opponents' **whole** system is derived either from
A P : 0 4 :314(156) [0207] teach us much about the **whole** issue and bring
A P : 0 4 :322(157) [0209] Fourth, the **whole** church confesses that eternal life
A P : 0 4 :338(159) [0215] worthless, and with the **whole** church we teach that we
A P : 0 4 :360(162) [0219] out, dear reader, you have not yet heard the **whole** sorites.
A P : 0 4 :389(166) [0225] many others, and with the **whole** church of Christ, which
A P : 0 7 :005(169) [0227] the fullness," that is, the **whole** congregation "of him who
A P : 0 7 :019(171) [0233] (Matt. 3:12) about the **whole** Jewish nation and says that
A P : 0 7 :023(172) [0235] outward monarchy of the **whole** world in which the
A P : 0 7 :023(172) [0235] pope must be lord of the **whole** world, of all the
A P : 0 7 :046(177) [0243] But on this **whole** controversy we shall have a few things
A P : 1 0 :004(179) [0247] doctrine received in the **whole** church — that in the Lord's
A P : 1 1 :001(180) [0249] On this **whole** issue we shall speak more fully a little later
A P : 1 1 :001(180) [0249] later when we explain our **whole** teaching on penitence.
A P : 1 1 :002(180) [0249] Previously the **whole** power of absolution had been
A P : 1 1 :007(181) [0251] The **whole** church throughout Europe knows how
A P : 1 2 :010(184) [0255] Our opponents' **whole** teaching on the questions we have
A P : 1 2 :016(184) [0257] In short, the **whole** business of satisfactions is endless,
A P : 1 2 :028(185) [0259] an improvement of the **whole** life and character a third
A P : 1 2 :089(195) [0277] So their **whole** life is without God and without the true
A P : 1 2 :119(200) [0287] This **whole** theory is a recent fiction, without authority
A P : 1 2 :137(203) [0293] works, about the **whole** newness of life, and not about
A P : 1 2 :163(208) [0303] word "judge" refers to the **whole** process of penitence and
A P : 1 2 :164(208) [0303] The **whole** process of penitence — contrition, faith, and
A P : 1 2 :165(208) [0303] with regard to the **whole** process of penitence and
A P : 1 2 :166(208) [0303] penitence — we mean the **whole** process of penitence —
A P : 1 3 :008(212) [0311] for the sins of the **whole** world and that there is no need
A P : 1 3 :018(213) [0313] Here we condemn the **whole** crowd of scholastic doctors
A P : 1 5 :027(219) [0323] are huge tomes, even **whole** libraries, that do not contain
A P : 1 5 :042(221) [0325] are preached during the **whole** year, except in Lent.
A P : 1 5 :052(222) [0329] more to say about this **whole** issue when we discuss vows
A P : 1 6 :002(222) [0329] profitably illumined this **whole** question of the distinction
A P : 1 6 :013(224) [0333] have explained this **whole** matter of political affairs so
A P : 2 0 :011(228) [0341] our proofs in our earlier discussion of this **whole** issue.
A P : 2 1 :034(233) [0351] As I have said earlier, our **whole** knowledge of Christ
A P : 2 1 :035(234) [0353] Another one recited the **whole** Psalter every day while
A P : 2 1 :043(235) [0357] and overthrow the **whole** organization of the church,
A P : 2 2 :004(236) [0359] the entire sacrament was instituted for the **whole** church.
A P : 2 3 :005(240) [0365] or act honestly, frankly, or openly in this **whole** business.
A P : 2 3 :032(244) [0373] He is talking about the **whole** class of mothers, and above
A P : 2 3 :060(247) [0381] and full of danger; finally, the **whole** thing is a fraud.
A P : 2 4 :013(251) [0387] If this were the **whole** problem, the case would be settled.
A P : 2 4 :023(253) [0391] was going to placate God for the **whole** human race.
A P : 2 4 :035(256) [0397] provided this means the **whole** Mass, the ceremony and
A P : 2 4 :036(257) [0397] depicted Christ and the **whole** worship of the New
A P : 2 4 :058(260) [0405] The **whole** Epistle to the Hebrews supports this
A P : 2 4 :067(261) [0407] But to make the **whole** matter as clear as possible, we
A P : 2 4 :087(265) [0413] thanksgivings, and the **whole** worship are offered there.
A P : 2 4 :088(265) [0413] particular, but about the **whole** service, about the prayers
A P : 2 4 :088(265) [0413] is talking about the **whole** service; and by "reasonable
A P : 2 4 :092(266) [0417] ever arises, we shall discuss this **whole** issue more fully.
A P : 2 7 :010(270) [0423] Luther discussed this **whole** issue carefully and fully in his
A P : 2 7 :013(271) [0423] Spirit is a witness, thy **whole** church is a witness: this is
A P : 2 7 :038(275) [0433] in a few words for the **whole** city and then paid attention
A P : 2 7 :044(277) [0435] But as the **whole** monastic system is full of counterfeits,
A P : 2 7 :052(278) [0437] On this **whole** topic we have said enough earlier.
A P : 2 7 :055(278) [0439] we shall not discuss their **whole** ceremonial worship —
A P : 2 7 :056(278) [0439] Thus the **whole** monastic life is full of hypocrisy and false
S 2 : 0 4 :007(299) [0473] and destruction of his **whole** rule and estate, together with
S 2 : 0 4 :013(300) [0475] the lord of the church, and finally of the **whole** world.
S 3 : 0 1 :004(302) [0477] of man have remained **whole** and uncorrupted, and that
S 3 : 0 3 :001(303) [0479] in Rom. 3:19, 20, "The **whole** world may be held
S 3 : 0 3 :010(305) [0481] of man have remained **whole** and uncorrupted, that
S 3 : 0 3 :015(305) [0483] during the course of a **whole** year), the following loophole
S 3 : 0 4 :000(310) [0491] Gospel) is preached to the **whole** world; second, through
S 3 : 0 6 :003(311) [0493] in one form is not the **whole** order and institution as it
S 3 : 1 3 :002(315) [0499] The **whole** man, in respect both of his person and of his
T R : 0 0 :005(320) [0505] pastors throughout the **whole** world should seek
T R : 0 0 :020(323) [0509] can the pope be over the **whole** church by divine right
T R : 0 0 :022(323) [0511] Since this **whole** controversy has been treated fully and
T R : 0 0 :024(324) [0511] individual but to the **whole** church, as is shown by many
T R : 0 0 :026(324) [0511] abroad through the **whole** world and exists wherever God
T R : 0 0 :040(327) [0517] above the decisions of councils and the **whole** church.
S C : 0 2 :006(345) [0545] and sanctifies the **whole** Christian church on earth and
S C : 0 8 :007(353) [0559] When children and the **whole** household gather at the
L C : P R :018(361) [0573] What is the **whole** Psalter but meditations and exercises
L C : S P :024(364) [0579] Thus we have, in all, five parts covering the **whole** of
L C : 0 1 :002(365) [0581] else than to trust and believe him with our **whole** heart.
L C : 0 1 :006(365) [0583] and possessions — on which he fixes his **whole** heart.
L C : 0 1 :013(366) [0583] It requires that man's **whole** heart and confidence be
L C : 0 1 :031(369) [0589] the head is right, the **whole** life must be right, and vice
L C : 0 1 :032(369) [0589] who trust and believe him alone with their **whole** heart.
L C : 0 1 :058(372) [0597] as there are few who trust in God with their **whole** heart.
L C : 0 1 :059(372) [0597] as to boast before the **whole** world of the wickedness he
L C : 0 1 :083(376) [0603] their work and trades the **whole** week long — should retire
L C : 0 1 :089(377) [0605] and at least a day for the **whole** community, when we can
L C : 0 1 :089(377) [0605] Thus we may regulate our **whole** life and being according
L C : 0 1 :090(377) [0607] too, and so can the **whole** swarm of clerics in our day who
L C : 0 1 :103(379) [0611] and love him with our **whole** heart all the days of our
L C : 0 1 :107(379) [0611] For anyone whom we are **whole**-heartedly to honor, we
L C : 0 1 :118(381) [0615] before God and the **whole** world, they shall blush with
L C : 0 1 :118(381) [0615] with the merits of their **whole** lives they are not worthy to
L C : 0 1 :166(388) [0629] combined efforts of the **whole** world cannot add an hour
L C : 0 1 :202(392) [0639] heart, your lips, and your **whole** body are to be chaste
L C : 0 1 :219(394) [0643] cherishing each other **whole**-heartedly and with perfect
L C : 0 1 :230(396) [0645] stolen the treasures of the **whole** world and holds them to
L C : 0 1 :238(397) [0649] neither prosper nor gain anything their **whole** life long.
L C : 0 1 :264(400) [0655] us; we want the golden compliments of the **whole** world.
L C : 0 1 :284(403) [0661] that the judge and the **whole** world are aware of it, you
L C : 0 1 :287(403) [0663] hands and eyes, even the **whole** body, must help cover
L C : 0 1 :311(407) [0669] what we are to do to make our **whole** life pleasing to God.
L C : 0 1 :314(407) [0671] remains on his knees a **whole** day in church, this is
L C : 0 1 :321(408) [0673] and all of them as a **whole** ought to be referred and
L C : 0 1 :325(409) [0675] He seems to explain the **whole** commandment in one
L C : 0 2 :021(413) [0683] if we believed it with our **whole** heart, we would also act
L C : 0 2 :063(419) [0695] Although the **whole** world has sought painstakingly to
L C : 0 3 :025(423) [0705] that they never prayed **whole**-heartedly for so much as a
L C : 0 3 :048(426) [0711] If you pray the petition **whole**-heartedly, you can be sure
L C : 0 3 :072(430) [0719] the broad fields and the **whole** land which produce and
L C : 0 3 :080(431) [0721] enemy, the devil, whose **whole** purpose and desire it is to
L C : 0 3 :111(435) [0729] into which it can slip, the **whole** body will irresistibly
L C : 0 3 :121(436) [0731] a way that they dare not **whole**-heartedly add "yes" and
L C : 0 4 :033(440) [0741] be received unless we believe them **whole**-heartedly.
L C : 0 4 :065(445) [0749] of which actions must continue in us our **whole** life long.
L C : 0 5 :019(449) [0757] upon these words rest our **whole** argument, protection,
L C : 0 5 :032(450) [0759] Now, the **whole** Gospel and the article of the Creed, "I
L C : 0 5 :032(450) [0761] as they dare say that the **whole** Gospel or Word of God
L C : 0 6 :009(458) [0000] Indeed, the **whole** Lord's Prayer is nothing else than such
E P : 0 2 :009(471) [0789] God, believe the Gospel, **whole**-heartedly obey God's
E P : 0 2 :011(471) [0789] himself to God, and **whole**-heartedly obey God's law by
E P : 0 8 :034(491) [0825] "In him dwells the **whole** fullness of deity bodily"
S D : P R :004(502) [0847] Herewith we again **whole**-heartedly subscribe this
S D : 0 1 :030(513) [0867] of original sin, the **whole** nature of every human being
S D : 0 1 :033(514) [0869] and corrupted man's **whole** nature that within the
S D : 0 2 :040(528) [0895] and sanctifies the **whole** Christian church on earth and
S D : 0 3 :007(540) [0917] this doctrine that a little leaven ferments the **whole** lump.
S D : 0 7 :026(573) [0981] on these words rest our **whole** argument, protection, and
S D : 0 7 :036(575) [0985] in us," or "In Christ the **whole** fullness of the deity dwells
S D : 0 7 :084(584) [1001] which comprehends the **whole** action or administration
S D : 0 7 :084(584) [1001] just as St. Paul sets the **whole** action of the breaking of
S D : 0 8 :030(597) [1025] a way that in Christ the **whole** fullness of deity dwells
S D : 0 8 :034(597) [1027] says that "in Christ the **whole** fullness of the deity dwells
S D : 0 8 :070(604) [1039] God, together with the **whole** fullness of deity which he
S D : 0 8 :070(605) [1041] "In him dwells the **whole** fullness of deity bodily"
S D : 1 1 :028(620) [1071] "the propitiation for the **whole** world's" sin (I John 1:7;
S D : 1 2 :003(633) [1095] and proclaim to the **whole** world that among our

Wholeheartedly (3), Wholesome (10)

A G : 2 6 :015(066) [0073] that they neglected all **wholesome** Christian teachings
A P : 0 4 :303(154) [0205] it will bring godly and **wholesome** consolation to
A P : 0 4 :303(154) [0205] a faith that truly and **wholeheartedly** accepts the promise
A P : 1 2 :165(208) [0303] that is important and **wholesome** with regard to the
A P : 1 2 :165(208) [0303] It is **wholesome** to teach that our common evils are
A P : 1 2 :178(211) [0307] that it is godly and **wholesome** for the minds of the
A P : 1 3 :012(212) [0311] we must subscribe **wholeheartedly**, for we know that God
A P : 2 4 :028(254) [0393] Truly and **wholeheartedly** seek and expect help from me."
L C : 0 5 :068(454) [0769] flee, but as a pure, **wholesome**, soothing medicine which
L C : 0 5 :069(454) [0769] nothing can be good or **wholesome**, just as when a sick
S D : P R :014(506) [0855] to present the true and **wholesome** doctrine correctly, but
S D : 0 2 :059(532) [0905] or a volition that wills what is good and **wholesome**).
S D : 0 2 :061(533) [0905] doing something good and **wholesome** in divine matters.

Wholly (22)

A L : 2 6 :006(064) [0071] of Paul has been almost **wholly** smothered by traditions
A L : 2 6 :008(065) [0071] was thought to consist **wholly** in the observance of certain
S 3 : 0 3 :036(309) [0489] together and says, "We are **wholly** and altogether sinful."
L C : 0 3 :058(428) [0713] The fault lies **wholly** in that shameful unbelief which does
L C : 0 3 :100(433) [0725] and have been **wholly** absolved, yet such is life that one
E P : 0 1 :010(467) [0781] This will take place **wholly** by way of death in the
E P : 0 1 :013(467) [0783] things its natural powers remained **wholly** good and pure.
E P : 0 2 :014(471) [0789] and rebirth God **wholly** destroys the substance and
E P : 0 5 :001(478) [0801] not in the law but **wholly** through the Gospel?
E P : 0 8 :034(491) [0825] to the human nature, is **wholly** incapable of omnipotence

Continued ▶

E P : 0 9 :003(492) [0827] explains this article in a **wholly** Christian manner,
E P : 1 2 :005(498) [0839] God does not consist **wholly** in the unique merit of
S D : P R :002(501) [0847] as a new doctrine and as **wholly** contrary to the Word of
S D : 0 1 :001(508) [0859] nature and essence are **wholly** corrupt as a result of the
S D : 0 1 :023(512) [0865] nature and being are **wholly** corrupted, "but that human
S D : 0 1 :053(517) [0877] and essence of man is **wholly** corrupted though original
S D : 0 2 :046(530) [0899] they will continue **wholly** to resist God or wait until God
S D : 0 2 :077(536) [0911] things man is not **wholly** dead toward that which is good,
S D : 0 2 :083(537) [0913] by God for grace, but **wholly** resists the Word, conversion
S D : 0 3 :028(544) [0925] sanctification is never **wholly** pure and perfect on account
S D : 0 3 :053(548) [0933] terms (that is, terms that **wholly** exclude works and our
S D : 0 8 :038(598) [1027] only the one nature and **wholly** eliminate the other

Whoredom (1)

S 3 : 0 3 :017(305) [0483] let us say, in **whoredom**, revenge, or the like), such a

Why (126)

P R : P R :022(011) [0019] also many other reasons **why** condemnations cannot by
A G : 0 0 :002(048) [0059] firm grounds and reasons **why** we have changed certain
A G : 0 1 :007(056) [0065] the holy sacrament, **why** it was instituted, and how it is to
A G : 2 6 :027(068) [0073] Acts 15:10, II Peter says, "**Why** do you make trial of God
A G : 2 7 :027(075) [0079] **Why**, then, do our opponents insist so strongly that vows
A G : 2 7 :036(076) [0081] offer still more reasons **why** monastic vows are null and
A G : 2 8 :042(088) [0089] **Why**, then, do they multiply sins with such requirements?
A G : 2 8 :045(088) [0089] regulations of the world, **why** do you live as if you still
A G : 2 8 :045(088) [0089] **Why** do you submit to regulations, 'Do not handle, Do
A G : 2 8 :049(089) [0091] thus ensnare consciences, **why** does the divine Scripture
A G : 2 8 :049(089) [0091] **Why** does it call them doctrines of the devil?
A L : 2 3 :002(051) [0061] there were some reasons **why** priests were forbidden to
A L : 2 3 :002(051) [0061] now far weightier reasons **why** this right should be
A L : 2 6 :027(068) [0073] Acts 15:10, II Peter says, "**Why** do you make trial of God
A L : 2 7 :027(075) [0079] In the second place, **why** do our adversaries exaggerate
A L : 2 8 :042(088) [0089] **Why** do they multiply sin with such traditions?
A L : 2 8 :045(088) [0089] spirits of the universe, **why** do you live as if you still
A L : 2 8 :045(088) [0089] **Why** do you submit to regulations, 'Do not handle, Do
A L : 2 8 :049(089) [0091] with such traditions, **why** does Scripture so often prohibit
A L : 2 8 :049(089) [0091] **Why** does it call them doctrines of demons?
A P : P R :005(098) [0101] to His Imperial Majesty **why** we could not accept the
A P : 0 2 :004(101) [0105] First we must show **why** we used these words here.
A P : 0 2 :014(102) [0109] This was **why** in our definition of original sin we also
A P : 0 4 :030(111) [0129] **Why** then may I not myself exclaim, too—yes, I will
A P : 0 4 :043(113) [0133] Otherwise, **why** would a promise be necessary?
A P : 0 4 :050(114) [0135] (Rom. 4:16): "That is **why** it depends on faith, in order
A P : 0 4 :052(114) [0135] For **why** did Christ have to be offered for our sins if our
A P : 0 4 :084(119) [0145] Paul says, "That is **why** it depends on faith, in order
A P : 0 4 :147(127) [0163] is the keeping of the law, **why** do we deny that it justifies?
A P : 0 4 :201(134) [0175] and we show many reasons **why** they should be done.
A P : 0 4 :257(144) [0193] law were enough by itself, **why** would Christ and the
A P : 0 4 :273(148) [0199] **Why** recite passages?
A P : 0 4 :284(150) [0201] Moreover, **why** do they not present the whole sermon?
A P : 0 4 :288(151) [0203] They did not understand **why** the Fathers had enacted
A P : 0 4 :294(152) [0203] article it is clear **why** we ascribe justification to faith
A P : 0 4 :316(156) [0209] this it is understandable **why** we reject our opponents'
A P : 0 4 :381(165) [0223] **Why** not expound here God's grace and mercy toward us?
A P : 0 4 :382(165) [0225] But **why** not say something about faith?
A P : 0 7 :003(168) [0227] That is **why** we added the eighth article, to avoid the
A P : 0 7 :006(169) [0229] We wonder **why** they criticize our description, which
A P : 0 7 :017(171) [0231] But **why** belabor the obvious?
A P : 0 7 :021(172) [0233] Similarly, **why** will faith be necessary if sacraments justify
A P : 0 7 :035(175) [0239] spirits of the universe, **why** do you live as if you still
A P : 0 7 :035(175) [0241] **Why** do you submit to regulations, 'Do not handle, Do
A P : 0 7 :041(176) [0241] necessary for justification, **why** did the bishops later
A P : 0 7 :045(177) [0243] But **why** discuss it?
A P : 0 7 :046(177) [0243] ordinances are necessary, **why** do they change the
A P : 1 2 :008(183) [0255] **Why** did not Saul, Judas, and men like them attain grace
A P : 1 2 :081(194) [0275] in Rom. 4:16, "That is **why** it depends on faith, in order
A P : 1 2 :087(195) [0277] and from this they will see **why** we said above that men
A P : 1 2 :091(195) [0279] We have said **why** we set forth contrition and faith as the
A P : 1 2 :154(207) [0301] if this is what they mean, **why** do they add that we must
A P : 1 2 :161(208) [0303] be humiliated by his son, **why** did he carry out the threat
A P : 1 2 :173(209) [0305] are non-obligatory works, **why** cite the clear teaching of
A P : 1 3 :016(213) [0311] added to them, then **why** not prayer, which can most
A P : 1 5 :008(216) [0317] is of no use to you, for **why** does anyone need Christ if he
A P : 1 5 :015(217) [0319] grace or righteousness, **why** did not the heathen and
A P : 1 5 :031(219) [0323] statement in Acts 15:10, "**Why** do you make a trial of God
A P : 2 0 :012(228) [0341] Scripture passages to show **why** they have condemned
A P : 2 1 :024(232) [0349] as our intercessor and high priest, **why** seek others?
A P : 2 1 :033(233) [0351] **Why** should it be defended if it has no command or proof
A P : 2 2 :002(236) [0357] it for all of the church, **why** is one kind taken away from
A P : 2 2 :002(236) [0357] **Why** is Christ's ordinance changed, especially since he
A P : 2 2 :006(237) [0359] to explain to the church **why** one part of the sacrament
A P : 2 2 :009(237) [0359] Among the reasons **why** both kinds are not given,
A P : 2 2 :011(238) [0361] But **why** should they be satisfied?
A P : 2 2 :013(238) [0361] there is no mystery as to **why** they defend this distinction
A P : 2 3 :012(241) [0367] it is a right; otherwise, **why** would both sexes have been
A P : 2 3 :018(242) [0369] **Why** do they not apply these magnificent commandments
A P : 2 3 :040(245) [0375] This is **why** Paul says (I Cor. 7:32), "The unmarried man
A P : 2 3 :053(246) [0377] good demanded it, **why** was not the same done to this
A P : 2 3 :060(247) [0379] We have explained **why** we cannot conscientiously agree
A P : 2 4 :079(264) [0411] **Why** do they not mention the old term "communion,"
A P : 2 4 :085(264) [0413] **Why** such a far-fetched etymology, except perhaps to
A P : 2 4 :085(264) [0413] **Why** go so far afield for the etymology when the term
A P : 2 4 :092(267) [0417] **Why** should we wrangle with our opponents who
A P : 2 7 :055(278) [0439] That is **why** they multiply these ceremonies.
A P : 2 7 :069(281) [0443] of showing pious hearts **why** they should reject the
A P : 2 8 :008(282) [0445] "**Why** do you make a trial of God?" they say (Acts 15:10).
S 1 : P R :004(289) [0455] **Why** do I say this?
S 1 : P R :004(289) [0455] **Why** should I complain?
S 2 : 0 2 :002(293) [0463] "**Why** do you cling so tenaciously to your Masses?
S 2 : 0 2 :004(293) [0463] **Why**, then, do you drive the world into wretchedness and
S 2 : 0 2 :018(296) [0467] **Why** do they neglect their own parishes, the Word of
S 3 : 0 8 :006(312) [0495] **Why** do they not stop preaching and writing until the
T R : 0 0 :062(330) [0521] quotes from Titus, "This is **why** I left you in Crete, that
T R : 0 0 :078(333) [0527] there is additional reason **why** other courts should be
T R : 0 0 :079(333) [0527] and compelling reasons **why** the churches should not
L C : P R :012(360) [0571] **Why** should I waste words?
L C : 0 1 :025(368) [0587] This, I think, is **why** we Germans from ancient times have
L C : 0 1 :065(373) [0599] so many teachers: **why** swearing is forbidden in the
L C : 0 1 :137(384) [0619] **Why** do we have so many criminals who must daily be
L C : 0 1 :154(386) [0625] **Why**, do you think, is the world now so full of
L C : 0 1 :197(392) [0637] This is **why** they fled to the monasteries, so that they
L C : 0 1 :220(394) [0643] This is **why** St. Paul so urgently admonishes husbands
L C : 0 1 :270(401) [0657] But you say: "**Why** shouldn't I speak if it is the truth?"
L C : 0 1 :270(401) [0657] I reply: "**Why** don't you bring it before the regular judge?"
L C : 0 1 :277(402) [0661] **Why** don't you tell him yourself?"
L C : 0 1 :314(407) [0671] Otherwise, **why** should monks and nuns go into cloisters?
L C : 0 1 :321(408) [0673] it so that we may see **why** we are constrained and
L C : 0 3 :006(421) [0699] people do who say in their delusion: "**Why** should I pray?
L C : 0 3 :080(431) [0721] This is **why** he causes so much contention, murder,
L C : 0 3 :080(431) [0721] murder, sedition, and war, **why** he sends tempest and hail
L C : 0 3 :080(431) [0721] to destroy crops and cattle, **why** he poisons the air, etc.
L C : 0 3 :121(436) [0731] remain in doubt, saying, "**Why** should I be so bold as to
L C : 0 4 :012(438) [0735] **Why**?
L C : 0 4 :020(439) [0737] might come and say, "**Why** should I think more of this
L C : 0 4 :020(439) [0737] which shows me how and **why** I should honor this
L C : 0 4 :045(442) [0743] This is the reason **why** these two things are done in
L C : 0 4 :057(444) [0747] **Why**?
L C : 0 4 :064(444) [0749] what Baptism signifies and **why** God ordained just this
L C : 0 5 :002(447) [0753] who do not know what they seek or **why** they come.
L C : 0 5 :022(449) [0757] **Why**?
L C : 0 5 :032(450) [0759] **Why**, then, should we allow this treasure to be torn out of
L C : 0 5 :034(450) [0761] *you,*" as if he said, "This is **why** I give it and bid you eat
L C : 0 5 :068(454) [0769] **Why**, then, do we act as if the sacrament were a poison
S D : P R :011(506) [0855] The reason **why** we have embodied the writings above
S D : 0 1 :009(510) [0861] damage is the reason **why** all of us, because of the
S D : 0 1 :048(517) [0875] powerfully and mightily **why** we must maintain a
S D : 0 2 :026(526) [0891] If then you received it, **why** do you boast as if it were not
S D : 0 4 :008(552) [0941] among us as to how and **why** the good works of believers
S D : 0 4 :021(554) [0945] we must also explain **why** and for what causes they are
S D : 0 4 :033(556) [0947] Article XX: "Peter teaches **why** we should do good
S D : 0 6 :022(567) [0969] does not teach us how and **why** the good works of
S D : 1 1 :034(622) [1075] The reason **why** "many are called and few are chosen" is
S D : 1 1 :078(629) [1089] The reason **why** all who hear the Word do not come to

Wicked (157), Wickedly (8), Wickedness (28)

A G : 0 8 :001(033) [0047] who administer them are **wicked** men, for as Christ
A G : 1 9 :000(040) [0053] yet sin is caused in all **wicked** men and despisers of God
A G : 2 8 :021(084) [0087] the ungodly whose **wicked** conduct is manifest.
A L : 1 9 :000(040) [0053] of sin is the will of the **wicked**, that is, of the devil and
A L : 1 9 :000(041) [0053] by God, the will of the **wicked** turns away from God, as
A L : 2 7 :036(076) [0081] the command of God is **wicked**, for Christ says, "In vain
A L : 2 7 :039(077) [0081] customarily taken were **wicked** services and on this
A L : 2 7 :040(077) [0081] account were void, for a **wicked** vow, taken contrary to
A L : 2 8 :021(084) [0087] ungodly persons whose **wickedness** is known, doing all
A P : 0 2 :047(106) [0119] devil, who deludes it with **wicked** opinions and errors and
A P : 0 2 :049(106) [0119] Blasphemy and **wicked** doctrines fill the world, and by
A P : 0 4 :035(112) [0131] for they do them with a **wicked** heart, and (Rom. 14:23)
A P : 0 4 :065(116) [0139] the conversion of the **wicked** or the manner of
A P : 0 4 :146(127) [0163] Such a trust is simply **wicked** and vain.
A P : 0 4 :150(127) [0163] this trust in his own righteousness was **wicked** and empty.
A P : 0 4 :167(130) [0169] complain because the **wicked** have better luck than the
A P : 0 4 :167(130) [0169] the devout, because the **wicked** persecute the devout?
A P : 0 4 :198(134) [0175] the good fortune of the **wicked**, like Psalm 37:1, "Be not
A P : 0 4 :200(134) [0175] is preached to the **wicked**, whose works are evil, and the
A P : 0 4 :204(135) [0177] We condemn this **wicked** idea about works.
A P : 0 4 :206(135) [0177] This **wicked** idea about works has always clung to the
A P : 0 4 :207(135) [0177] but they do condemn the **wicked** belief of those who did
A P : 0 4 :213(136) [0179] maintain these **wicked** and unscriptural ideas about
A P : 0 4 :244(142) [0189] falsely add their **wicked** opinions that by good works we
A P : 0 4 :252(143) [0191] does not mean that a **wicked** man is made righteous but
A P : 0 4 :253(143) [0193] them by reading into them their own **wicked** opinions.
A P : 0 4 :303(154) [0205] quibble that many **wicked** people and demons also believe
A P : 0 4 :303(154) [0205] Therefore neither **wicked** people nor demons can have the
A P : 0 4 :337(159) [0215] of history that the **wicked** and demons also have
A P : 0 4 :400(168) [0227] among those who defend **wicked** opinions against the
A P : 0 7 :001(168) [0227] dissertation, that the **wicked** are not to be separated from
A P : 0 7 :005(169) [0227] also admit, that the **wicked** are dead members of the
A P : 0 7 :007(169) [0229] Certainly the **wicked** are not a holy church!
A P : 0 7 :009(169) [0229] great multitude of the **wicked**, and Christ supplies it with
A P : 0 7 :010(170) [0229] both the godly and the **wicked**," and that the wicked are
A P : 0 7 :010(170) [0229] the wicked," and that the **wicked** are part of the church
A P : 0 7 :013(170) [0231] both the good and the **wicked**, then men would not
A P : 0 7 :014(170) [0231] these promises even the **wicked** among them were called
A P : 0 7 :016(170) [0231] moreover, that the **wicked** are in the power of the devil
A P : 0 7 :016(171) [0231] The **wicked** are ruled by the devil and are his captives;
A P : 0 7 :017(171) [0231] follows that since the **wicked** belong to the kingdom of
A P : 0 7 :018(171) [0233] come does not make the **wicked** the kingdom of Christ.
A P : 0 7 :019(171) [0233] hidden under a crowd of **wicked** men so that this
A P : 0 7 :019(171) [0233] are efficacious even when **wicked** men administer them.
A P : 0 7 :019(171) [0233] that though these **wicked** men participate in the outward
A P : 0 7 :021(172) [0233] It is also an open and **wicked** error when our opponents
A P : 0 7 :025(173) [0235] many extravagant and **wicked** writings about the power
A P : 0 7 :029(173) [0237] It is clear that the **wicked** belong to the kingdom and
A P : 0 7 :048(177) [0243] We should forsake **wicked** teachers because they no
A P : 0 7 :049(178) [0245] should not incite schisms, as the Donatists **wickedly** did.
A P : 0 9 :002(178) [0245] God's Word against the **wicked** and seditious faction of
A P : 0 9 :003(178) [0245] the Anabaptists teach **wickedly** when they condemn the
A P : 1 1 :004(180) [0249] The openly **wicked** and the despisers of the sacraments
A P : 1 2 :006(183) [0255] labor still more and **wickedly** minimize the power of the
A P : 1 2 :044(187) [0263] chief parts in the penitence or conversion of the **wicked**.
A P : 1 2 :048(188) [0265] **Wicked** and smug men do not say this seriously, for they
A P : 1 2 :060(190) [0267] God exists, that punishments hang over the **wicked**, etc.
A P : 1 2 :094(196) [0281] in the death of the **wicked**, but that the wicked turn from
A P : 1 2 :094(196) [0281] the wicked, but that the **wicked** turn from his way and
A P : 1 2 :094(196) [0281] in the death of the **wicked**, God shows that he requires
A P : 1 2 :100(197) [0281] It would therefore be **wicked** to remove private absolution

Continued ▶

A P : 1 2 :123(200) [0289] May God destroy these **wicked** sophists who so sinfully
A P : 1 2 :135(203) [0293] So it is clearly a **wicked** distortion to apply these passages
A P : 1 2 :142(204) [0295] not require, it is vain and **wicked** to trust that thereby we
A P : 1 3 :018(213) [0313] Yet this ungodly and **wicked** notion is taught with great
A P : 1 5 :037(220) [0325] For such an idea of traditions is **wicked**.
A P : 2 0 :009(227) [0341] "Do not yield to the **wicked**, but go on still more boldly,"
A P : 2 3 :001(239) [0363] not only use the **wicked** and false pretext of divine
A P : 2 3 :005(240) [0365] are trying to fortify it with a **wicked** pretense of godliness.
A P : 2 3 :060(247) [0381] domination, for which religion is just a **wicked** pretext.
A P : 2 3 :070(249) [0383] like these they defend a **wicked** and immoral law.
A P : 2 4 :043(258) [0399] Despite the obvious **wickedness** of some of this, they
A P : 2 4 :047(258) [0401] and introduced much **wicked** worship into the churches.
A P : 2 4 :061(260) [0405] to our opponents' **wicked** idea that the Mass justifies *ex*
A P : 2 4 :063(261) [0405] it is transferred, even for **wicked** people, if they do not
A P : 2 4 :063(261) [0405] These are the **wicked** and recent fictions of the ignorant
A P : 2 4 :096(267) [0417] are at suit with you for **wickedly** defending a heresy that
A P : 2 4 :096(267) [0417] punishment even for the **wicked** to whom it is applied, if
A P : 2 4 :096(267) [0417] We reject these **wicked** errors which rob Christ's suffering
A P : 2 4 :097(268) [0417] The **wicked** people in the Old Testament had a similar
A P : 2 4 :097(268) [0417] instituted by God with this **wicked** notion in mind.
A P : 2 4 :098(268) [0417] sacrifices clung to the **wicked** priests in Judah, and in
A P : 2 4 :098(268) [0417] church of God was there, condemning **wicked** services.
A P : 2 4 :098(268) [0417] the forgiveness of guilt and punishment for the **wicked**.
A P : 2 4 :098(268) [0419] should reject those **wicked** services invented against God's
A P : 2 7 :009(270) [0423] abuses of the Mass, the **wicked** services to the saints, and
A P : 2 7 :012(271) [0423] has here been charged against monasticism is **wicked**."
A P : 2 7 :016(271) [0425] By this **wicked** and fanatical notion they bury the blessing
A P : 2 7 :018(272) [0425] has been charged against monasticism here is **wicked**."
A P : 2 7 :019(272) [0425] rascals have the audacity to call this statement **wicked**.
A P : 2 7 :020(272) [0425] shown at length the **wickedness** of the opinion that we
A P : 2 7 :022(272) [0427] Word who follow these observances without **wicked** ideas.
A P : 2 7 :024(273) [0427] To this they add many other false and **wicked** ideas.
A P : 2 7 :025(273) [0427] It is the height of **wickedness** to believe that they satisfy
A P : 2 7 :027(273) [0429] However, it is a most **wicked** error to believe that
A P : 2 7 :034(275) [0431] mercy themselves, they **wickedly** fabricate works of
A P : 2 7 :043(276) [0435] therefore, that they **wickedly** twist the saying of Christ in
A P : 2 7 :053(278) [0437] are released by such **wicked** ceremonies as the desecration
A P : 2 7 :053(278) [0437] Christ's place to the saints, and it worships them **wickedly**.
A P : 2 7 :053(278) [0437] as stupid as it is **wicked**, nourishing a false confidence.
A P : 2 7 :053(278) [0437] This **wickedness**, too, is used only for the sake of profit.
A P : 2 7 :062(280) [0441] they fall back into the **wickedness** of their countrymen.
A P : 2 7 :065(280) [0441] monastic vows, taken for **wicked** acts of worship and with
A P : 2 8 :008(282) [0445] vigorously defend their traditions and **wicked** notions.
A P : 2 8 :021(284) [0449] extent that they teach **wicked** things, they should not be
A P : 2 8 :021(284) [0449] But these are **wicked** things: that human traditions are the
S 1 : P R :012(290) [0459] all manner of vice and **wickedness**, disobedience of
S 3 : 0 2 :001(303) [0479] failed because of the **wickedness** which sin has worked in
S 3 : 0 2 :002(303) [0479] These are the rude and **wicked** people who do evil
S 3 : 0 3 :001(303) [0479] all ungodliness and **wickedness** of men." and in
S 3 : 0 3 :011(305) [0481] for actual sins, such as **wicked** thoughts to which they
S 3 : 0 3 :011(305) [0481] did not consider sin), **wicked** words, and wicked works
S 3 : 0 3 :011(305) [0481] sin), wicked words, and **wicked** works which man with
S 3 : 0 3 :039(309) [0489] no good work but only **wicked** works are there and
S 3 : 0 6 :001(311) [0493] received not only by godly but also by **wicked** Christians.
S 3 : 1 1 :001(314) [0499] tyrannical, and **wicked** scoundrels, and thereby they gave
T R : 0 0 :055(329) [0521] defend his tyranny and **wickedness** without any regard
T R : 0 0 :072(332) [0525] And it is the **wickedness** and tyranny of the bishops that
T R : 0 0 :082(334) [0527] that there would be **wicked** bishops in the future who
S C : 0 3 :013(347) [0547] daily bread, even to the **wicked**, without our prayer, but
S C : 0 7 :002(352) [0557] charge of me, that the **wicked** one may have no power
S C : 0 7 :005(353) [0559] charge of me, that the **wicked** one may have no power
L C : 0 1 :017(367) [0585] never been a people so **wicked** that it did not establish
L C : 0 1 :058(372) [0597] lies and all kinds of **wickedness**, just as there are few who
L C : 0 1 :059(372) [0597] the whole world of the **wickedness** he has committed.
L C : 0 1 :062(373) [0597] conjure, and, in short, to practice **wickedness** of any sort.
L C : 0 1 :064(373) [0599] of falsehood or **wickedness**, it follows, conversely that we
L C : 0 1 :069(374) [0599] the world today is more **wicked** than it has ever been.
L C : 0 1 :100(379) [0609] your heart unbelief and **wicked** thoughts against all these
L C : 0 1 :137(384) [0619] happens that such **wicked** people die a natural and timely
L C : 0 1 :138(384) [0621] hand, it is written of the **wicked** in Ps. 109:13, "May his
L C : 0 1 :185(390) [0633] and protected from the **wickedness** and violence of
L C : 0 1 :208(393) [0639] and all virtues, and fight against **wickedness** and the devil.
L C : 0 1 :280(403) [0661] procedure for restraining and reforming a **wicked** person.
L C : 0 1 :300(405) [0665] the world considers **wicked** rogues, but precisely to the
L C : 0 1 :307(406) [0669] dark and underhanded **wickedness**, and, as we say, it is
L C : 0 1 :308(406) [0669] will not, for he sees your **wicked** heart and the
L C : 0 1 :326(409) [0675] of corruption and **wickedness**, but to use his name
L C : 0 2 :031(414) [0687] and separate us from the **wicked** world, the devil, death,
L C : 0 3 :010(421) [0699] by nature so desperately **wicked** that it always flees from
L C : 0 3 :042(425) [0709] by an openly evil life and **wicked** works, when those who
L C : 0 3 :049(426) [0711] to cloak its lies and **wickedness**, but would rather keep
L C : 0 3 :063(428) [0715] The world, too, is perverse and **wicked**.
L C : 0 3 :078(431) [0721] and bloodshed, famine, savage beasts, **wicked** men, etc.
L C : 0 3 :083(431) [0721] bountifully, even for **wicked** men and rogues, yet he
L C : 0 3 :113(435) [0729] or keep us from the Evil One, or the **Wicked** One."
L C : 0 4 :015(438) [0735] Therefore it is sheer **wickedness** and devilish blasphemy
L C : 0 4 :050(443) [0745] support lies and **wickedness**, or give his grace and Spirit
L C : 0 5 :015(448) [0757] example, whether even a **wicked** priest can administer the
L C : 0 5 :082(456) [0773] we are in the flesh, in this **wicked** world, or under the
L C : 0 6 :018(459) [0000] dare not come and say how good or how **wicked** you are.
E P : 0 1 :021(468) [0785] word were spoken, or no **wicked** act or deed took place,
E P : 0 3 :007(473) [0793] "He who justifies the **wicked** and he who condemns the
E P : 0 3 :011(474) [0795] and co-persist with a **wicked** intention to sin and to act
E P : 1 1 :004(495) [0833] of this is the devil and man's **wicked** and perverse will.
E P : 1 1 :004(495) [0833] in spite of its intrinsic **wickedness** it must minister to the
E P : 1 1 :012(496) [0835] lie in God or his election, but in their own **wickedness**.
E P : 1 2 :014(499) [0841] the government against **wicked** people, and that subjects
S D : 0 1 :011(510) [0863] God in man with a deep, **wicked**, abominable,
S D : 0 1 :011(510) [0863] man inherits an inborn **wicked** stamp, an interior
S D : 0 1 :018(511) [0865] 2. Again, that the sinful **wicked** desires are not sin but
S D : 0 2 :017(524) [0887] nature he is thoroughly **wicked**, opposed and hostile to
S D : 0 2 :017(524) [0887] deceitful and desperately **wicked**," that is, is so perverted
S D : 0 2 :018(524) [0889] contrary, because of the **wicked** and obstinate disposition
S D : 0 2 :022(525) [0889] cast away forever the **wicked** spirits who fell, he has
S D : 0 2 :046(530) [0899] the impotence and the **wickedness** of our natural free
S D : 0 2 :049(530) [0901] in the death of the **wicked**, but that the wicked turn from
S D : 0 2 :049(530) [0901] the wicked, but that the **wicked** turn from his way and
S D : 0 2 :074(536) [0909] coerced into doing such **wicked** acts as lechery, robbery,
S D : 0 3 :017(542) [0921] "He who justifies the **wicked** and he who condemns the
S D : 0 3 :026(543) [0923] and sorrow and have a **wicked** intention to remain and
S D : 0 3 :041(546) [0931] while side by side with a **wicked** intention, but this merely
S D : 0 4 :015(553) [0943] both a right faith and a **wicked** intention to continue and
S D : 0 4 :031(556) [0947] one, or through **wicked** works; and that even though a
S D : 0 4 :033(556) [0949] in those who lead a **wicked** life, lose the Holy Spirit, and
S D : 0 4 :039(557) [0951] introduce and confirm a **wicked**, wild, complacent, and
S D : 0 7 :019(572) [0979] not only by godly but also by **wicked** Christians."
S D : 0 7 :024(573) [0979] example, whether even a **wicked** priest can administer and
S D : 0 7 :066(581) [0997] unbelieving, false, and **wicked** Christians as well as by the
S D : 0 7 :123(590) [1013] unrepentant, and **wicked** Christians, who only bear the
S D : 0 8 :063(603) [1037] have maliciously and **wickedly** twisted our words and
S D : 1 1 :006(617) [1065] the perverse and **wicked** will of the devil and of men will
S D : 1 1 :006(617) [1065] But even in **wicked** acts and works God's foreknowledge
S D : 1 1 :007(617) [1065] it), but rather the **wicked** and perverse will of the devil
S D : 1 1 :007(617) [1065] art not a God who delights in **wickedness**" (Ps. 5:4).
S D : 1 1 :035(622) [1075] punishes men for such **wickedness** when they say one
S D : 1 1 :046(624) [1079] to the weakness and **wickedness** of our flesh it could
S D : 1 1 :081(629) [1089] in the death of the **wicked**, but that the wicked turn from
S D : 1 1 :081(629) [1089] the wicked, but that the **wicked** turn from his way and
S D : 1 1 :084(630) [1091] in the death of the **wicked**, but that the wicked turn from
S D : 1 1 :084(630) [1091] the wicked, but that the **wicked** turn from his way and
S D : 1 1 :091(632) [1093] to reason and the suggestion of the **wicked** devil.
S D : 1 2 :019(634) [1099] the government against **wicked** persons as occasion may

Wide (3), Widely (1), Wider (2), Widespread (3)
P R : P R :002(003) [0007] in all of Christendom throughout the **wide** world.
P R : P R :026(014) [0025] become dangerously **widespread** in order that all kinds of
A L : 2 4 :011(057) [0065] is also well known how **widely** this abuse extends in all
S 3 : 0 3 :025(307) [0485] money they swallowed, the **wider** became their maws.
L C : 0 1 :224(395) [0643] Stealing is a **widespread**, common vice, but people pay so
L C : 0 1 :228(396) [0645] it is nothing but a vast, **wide** stable full of great thieves.
L C : 0 3 :027(424) [0705] and spread your cloak **wide** to receive many things.
S D : 0 1 :052(517) [0875] the term is applied in a **wider** sense to include the
S D : 1 1 :001(616) [1063] public, scandalous, and **widespread** dissension among the

Widow (3), Widows (4)
A P : 0 4 :258(144) [0193] oppression; defend the fatherless, plead for the **widow**.
A P : 2 7 :064(280) [0441] I Tim. 5:11, 12 on the **widows** who served the church and
A P : 2 7 :065(280) [0441] the vows of the **widows**, if any, must have been different
A P : 2 7 :066(280) [0441] anyone "be enrolled as a **widow** who is under sixty years
A P : 2 7 :067(280) [0441] Paul condemns the **widows**, not because they were getting
S C : 0 9 :013(356) [0563] **Widows**
S C : 0 9 :013(356) [0563] "She who is a real **widow**, and is left all alone, has set her

Wield (2)
T R : 0 0 :031(325) [0513] Christ was not sent to **wield** a sword or possess a worldly
L C : 0 1 :268(401) [0657] For though you do not **wield** the sword, you use your

Wife (52), Wives (14)
A G : 1 6 :004(037) [0051] of house and home, **wife** and child, and the renunciation
A G : 1 8 :005(040) [0051] to build a house, take a **wife**, engage in a trade, or do
A G : 2 3 :004(051) [0061] man should have his own **wife**" (I Cor. 7:2), and again,
A G : 2 3 :009(052) [0061] other clergy have taken **wives** to themselves for these and
A G : 2 6 :010(065) [0071] labor to support his **wife** and children and bring them up
A G : 2 6 :010(065) [0071] in the fear of God, that a **wife** should bear children and
A G : 2 7 :019(074) [0079] man should have his own **wife** and each woman her own
A G : 2 7 :056(080) [0083] of men who forsook **wife** and child, and also their civil
A L : 2 3 :003(051) [0061] open scandals, they took **wives** and taught that it was
A L : 2 3 :004(051) [0061] man should have his own **wife**" (I Cor. 7:2), and again,
A L : 2 3 :009(052) [0061] our priests teach that it is lawful for them to have **wives**.
A L : 2 7 :019(074) [0079] "Because of fornication let every man have his own **wife**."
A P : 2 3 :003(239) [0363] spare, and banish deserted **wives** and orphaned children.
A P : 2 3 :014(241) [0367] to immorality, each man should have his own **wife**."
A P : 2 3 :017(242) [0369] man should have his own **wife**," binds all those who are
A P : 2 3 :027(243) [0371] be separated from their **wives**; since the priests of the New
A P : 2 3 :031(243) [0371] is consecrated through his **wife**"; that is, the use of
A P : 2 3 :063(248) [0381] each man to have his own **wife** because of the temptation
A P : 2 7 :040(276) [0433] say that leaving parents or **wife** or brothers is a work we
A P : 2 7 :040(276) [0433] his parents or his **wife** in order by this act to merit the
A P : 2 7 :041(276) [0435] Christ speaks of leaving **wife** and children makes it even
A P : 2 7 :041(276) [0435] the command of God forbids deserting **wife** and children.
A P : 2 7 :041(276) [0435] the injury, to let property, **wife**, and children, even life
A P : 2 7 :041(276) [0435] those who do injury to **wife** and children but about those
A P : 2 7 :042(276) [0435] leave possessions, friends, **wife**, and children without the
A P : 2 7 :051(278) [0437] to immorality, each man should have his own **wife**."
S 2 : 0 2 :018(296) [0467] Word of God, their **wives** and children, etc. and pursue
S C : 0 1 :012(343) [0541] each one loving and honoring his **wife** or her husband.
S C : 0 1 :019(344) [0543] *not covet your neighbor's* ***wife****, or his manservant, or his*
S C : 0 1 :020(344) [0543] entice away our neighbor's **wife**, servants, or cattle, but
S C : 0 5 :023(350) [0553] my children, servants, and **wife** to the glory of God.
S C : 0 9 :006(355) [0561] considerately with your **wives**, bestowing honor on the
S C : 0 9 :006(355) [0561] "Husbands, love your **wives**, and do not be harsh with
S C : 0 9 :007(355) [0563] **Wives**
S C : 0 9 :007(355) [0563] "You **wives**, be submissive to your husbands, as Sarah
L C : S P :010(363) [0577] 10. You shall not covet his **wife**, man-servant,
L C : 0 1 :060(372) [0597] fire, flood, wayward **wives** and children and servants, and
L C : 0 1 :073(374) [0601] God — our soul and body, **wife**, children, servants, and
L C : 0 1 :134(383) [0619] to long life — health, **wife** and child, livelihood, peace,
L C : 0 1 :154(386) [0625] as much wrong from your own **wife**, children, or servants.
L C : 0 1 :175(389) [0631] virtuous and home-loving **wives** who would faithfully
L C : 0 1 :200(392) [0637] dearest to him, namely, his **wife**, who is one flesh and
L C : 0 1 :200(392) [0637] it is explicitly forbidden here to dishonor his **wife**.
L C : 0 1 :205(393) [0639] wants every husband or **wife** guarded and protected from
L C : 0 1 :219(394) [0643] to love and cherish the **wife** or husband whom God has
L C : 0 1 :219(394) [0643] essential that husband and **wife** live together in love and
L C : 0 1 :220(394) [0643] admonishes husbands and **wives** to love and honor each
L C : 0 1 :244(398) [0649] house and home and outrage and kill **wife** and children.

Continued ▶

LC : 01 :255(399) [0653] Besides our own body, our **wife** or husband, and our
LC : 01 :256(399) [0653] his self-respect before his **wife**, children, servants, and
LC : 01 :292(404) [0663] *"You shall not covet his **wife**, man-servant, maid-servant,*
LC : 01 :293(404) [0665] to covet our neighbor's **wife** or property, or to have any
LC : 01 :295(404) [0665] had power to dismiss his **wife** publicly by giving her a bill
LC : 01 :295(404) [0665] by giving her a bill of divorce and to take another **wife**.
LC : 01 :295(404) [0665] took a fancy to another's **wife**, he might on any flimsy
LC : 01 :295(404) [0665] excuse dismiss his own **wife** and estrange the other's from
LC : 01 :296(405) [0665] belongs to him, such as his **wife**, servants, house, fields,
LC : 01 :305(406) [0667] was also the case in ancient times with respect to **wives**.
LC : 01 :305(406) [0669] Herod took his brother's **wife** while the latter was still
LC : 01 :328(410) [0675] either in his person, his **wife**, his property, his honor or
LC : 02 :013(412) [0681] means of support, **wife** and child, servants, house and
LC : 03 :065(429) [0717] honor, house and home, **wife** and children, body and life.
LC : 03 :076(431) [0721] and preserve to us a good **wife**, children, and servants; to
SD : 02 :020(525) [0889] a pillar of salt, like Lot's **wife**, yes, like a log or a stone,
SD : 11 :075(628) [1087] "If a man divorces his **wife** and she goes from him and
SD : 11 :075(628) [1087] becomes another man's **wife**, may he receive her again?

Wild (4)
AP : 11 :007(181) [0251] terrors made no impression on **wild** and profane men.
LC : 01 :191(391) [0635] to be torn to pieces by **wild** beasts, to rot in prison or
SD : 02 :019(524) [0889] an unhewn timber, or to a **wild**, unbroken animal — not
SD : 04 :039(558) [0951] and confirm a wicked, **wild**, complacent, and Epicurean

Wildenfels (1)
PR : PR :027(015) [0025] Anarck Frederick, baron of **Wildenfels**

Wilderness (1)
AP : 04 :095(121) [0149] up the serpent in the **wilderness**, so must the Son of man

Wiles (1)
LC : PR :012(360) [0571] master of a thousand arts with all his **wiles** and might?

Will (296) (Intent, purpose, desire)
PR : PR :001(003) [0007] and favorably inclined **will**, as well as our most
PR : PR :018(009) [0015] now on our adversaries **will** spare us and our churches
PR : PR :020(010) [0017] (although against the **will** of the former) from a
PR : PR :024(013) [0021] controversies at **will** and to introduce and defend
AG : 13 :001(035) [0049] and testimonies of God's **will** toward us for the purpose
AG : 18 :000(039) [0051] XVIII. Freedom of the **Will**
AG : 18 :001(039) [0051] measure of freedom of the **will** which enables him to live
AG : 18 :004(039) [0051] words of Augustine on free **will** are here quoted from the
AG : 18 :004(039) [0051] that all men have a free **will**, for all have a natural, innate
AG : 19 :000(041) [0053] wicked men and despisers of God by the perverted **will**.
AG : 19 :000(041) [0053] This is the **will** of the devil and of all ungodly men; as
AG : 19 :000(041) [0053] withdraws his support, the **will** turns away from God to
AG : 20 :027(045) [0057] earn grace but that we may do God's **will** and glorify him.
AG : 28 :076(094) [0095] had power to coerce the churches according to their **will**.
AL : 06 :001(031) [0045] do so because it is God's **will** and not because we rely on
AL : 13 :001(035) [0049] and testimonies of the **will** of God toward us, intended to
AL : 18 :000(039) [0051] XVIII. Free **Will**
AL : 18 :001(039) [0051] churches teach that man's **will** has some liberty for the
AL : 18 :004(039) [0051] that all men have a free **will** which enables them to make
AL : 18 :005(040) [0051] good in nature, that is, to **will** to labor in the field, will to
AL : 18 :005(040) [0051] will to labor in the field, **will** to eat and drink, will to
AL : 18 :005(040) [0051] field, will to eat and drink, **will** to have a friend, will to
AL : 18 :005(040) [0051] will to have a friend, **will** to clothe oneself, will to build a
AL : 18 :005(040) [0051] will to clothe oneself, **will** to build a house, will to marry,
AL : 18 :005(040) [0051] will to build a house, **will** to marry, will to keep cattle,
AL : 18 :005(040) [0051] a house, will to marry, **will** to keep cattle, will to learn
AL : 18 :005(040) [0051] marry, will to keep cattle, **will** to learn various useful
AL : 18 :005(040) [0053] various useful arts, or **will** to do whatever good pertains
AL : 18 :007(040) [0053] I mean such things as to **will** to worship an idol, will to
AL : 18 :007(040) [0053] as to will to worship an idol, **will** to commit murder," etc.
AL : 19 :000(040) [0053] the cause of sin is the **will** of the wicked, that is, of the
AL : 19 :000(041) [0053] If not aided by God, the **will** of the wicked turns away
AL : 20 :027(045) [0057] to merit grace by them but because it is the **will** of God.
AL : 20 :030(045) [0057] "Faith is the mother of the good **will** and the right deed."
AL : 28 :029(085) [0087] bound, even against their **will**, to administer justice to
AP : 02 :012(102) [0109] more than was proper to free **will** and to "elicited acts."
AP : 04 :017(109) [0125] that the acts of the **will** before the disposition and those
AP : 04 :017(109) [0125] They imagine that the **will** can love God, but that this
AP : 04 :029(111) [0129] with the help of free **will**, is in itself sufficient both for
AP : 04 :094(120) [0149] not of blood nor of the **will** of the flesh nor of the will of
AP : 04 :094(120) [0149] of the will of the flesh nor of the **will** of man, but of God."
AP : 04 :139(126) [0161] and err, nor be driven to do anything against God's **will**.
AP : 04 :170(130) [0171] help; it even defies God's **will** and runs away from
AP : 04 :198(134) [0175] but to seek the **will** of God rather than the rewards, as is
AP : 04 :247(142) [0191] (James 1:18), "Of his own **will** he brought us forth by the
AP : 04 :262(145) [0195] to learn to know God's **will**, namely, that he is no longer
AP : 04 :304(154) [0205] that righteousness is in the **will** and thus cannot be
AP : 04 :304(154) [0205] scholastics admit that the **will** commands the intellect to
AP : 04 :304(154) [0205] a horrible turmoil in the **will** as it flees God's judgment;
AP : 04 :304(154) [0205] but also trust in the **will**, that is, to desire and to accept
AP : 04 :306(154) [0207] own righteousness, which certainly resides in the **will**.
AP : 04 :310(155) [0207] in John 6:40, "This is the **will** of my Father, that everyone
AP : 04 :322(157) [0209] says in *Grace and Free **Will***, "God leads us to eternal life,
AP : 04 :364(163) [0219] should know that it is the **will** of God to help, rescue, and
AP : 12 :160(207) [0303] It is the **will** of God that our bodies should be sacrifices,
AP : 13 :001(211) [0309] and testimonies of God's **will** toward us, through which
AP : 13 :020(214) [0313] God, by a new miracle, promised his **will** to forgive.
AP : 15 :014(217) [0319] he inform men of God's **will** without the command and
AP : 15 :017(217) [0319] affirm nothing about the **will** of God without the Word
AP : 15 :045(221) [0327] we must obey God's **will**, as Paul says (Rom. 12:1),
AP : 18 :000(224) [0335] [Article XVIII. Free **Will**]
AP : 18 :001(224) [0335] Article XVIII on free **will**, but they add several proofs
AP : 18 :001(225) [0335] much be conceded to free **will**, as in Pelagianism, or all
AP : 18 :004(225) [0335] We are not denying freedom to the human **will**.
AP : 18 :004(225) [0335] The human **will** has freedom to choose among the works
AP : 18 :007(225) [0337] we concede to free **will** the liberty and ability to do the
AP : 18 :008(226) [0337] hearts believe about God's **will**, whether they really
AP : 18 :009(226) [0337] the former to the free **will** and the latter to the operation
AP : 19 :001(226) [0337] the cause of sin is the **will** of the devil and of men turning
AP : 21 :004(229) [0343] of his mercy, revealing his **will** to save men, and giving
AP : 23 :071(249) [0383] certainly contrary to God's **will** and Word to break up
AP : 24 :022(253) [0391] later it says about the **will** of Christ (v. 10), "By that will
AP : 24 :022(253) [0391] of Christ (v. 10), "By that **will** we have been sanctified
AP : 24 :069(262) [0409] men, but signs of God's **will** toward us; so it is correct to
AP : 24 :072(262) [0409] we should acknowledge the **will** and mercy of God.
AP : 28 :024(285) [0451] Luther not only our good **will** but that of many who are
AP : 28 :024(285) [0451] "The former good **will** ceases, and mortals are forgetful,"
S2 : 02 :005(293) [0463] fabricated and invented without God's Word and **will**?
S2 : 02 :028(297) [0469] the honor that remains **will** do no harm and will quickly
S3 : 01 :004(302) [0477] understanding and a good **will**, as the philosophers teach.
S3 : 01 :005(302) [0477] Again, that man has a free **will**, either to do good and
S3 : 03 :010(305) [0481] understanding and the **will** is capable of acting
S3 : 03 :010(305) [0481] who does as much as he can according to his free **will**.
S3 : 03 :011(305) [0481] which man with his free **will** might well have avoided.
S3 : 03 :032(308) [0487] unbelief, blindness, and ignorance of God and God's **will**.
S3 : 05 :003(311) [0493] the assistance of the divine **will**, as if the washing takes
S3 : 05 :003(311) [0493] place only through God's **will** and not at all through the
TR : 00 :055(329) [0521] be decreed contrary to his **will** and grants nobody the
SC : 03 :009(347) [0547] *"Thy **will** be done, on earth as it is in heaven."*
SC : 03 :010(347) [0547] the good and gracious **will** of God is done without our
SC : 03 :011(347) [0547] This is his good and gracious **will**.
SC : 09 :010(356) [0563] of Christ, doing the **will** of God from the heart, rendering
SC : 09 :010(356) [0563] service with a good **will** as to the Lord and not to men,
LC : SP :014(363) [0577] Thy kingdom come, thy **will** be done, on earth as it is in
LC : 01 :108(379) [0611] they are, but of the **will** of God, who has created and
LC : 01 :116(381) [0615] If God's Word and **will** are placed first and observed,
LC : 01 :116(381) [0615] more important than the **will** and word of our parents,
LC : 01 :126(382) [0617] This **will** and pleasure of God ought to provide us
LC : 01 :157(387) [0627] understand the Word and **will** of God and sincerely
LC : 01 :164(387) [0627] keep their eyes on God's **will** and commandment,
LC : 01 :173(388) [0629] them according to his **will**; otherwise God would have no
LC : 01 :187(390) [0633] we may be attentive to his **will** and with hearty confidence
LC : 01 :307(406) [0669] away from him against his **will**, and begrudging what God
LC : 01 :323(409) [0673] all that is contrary to his **will**, lest he be moved to wrath;
LC : 01 :330(410) [0677] a spontaneous impulse and desire gladly to do God's **will**.
LC : 02 :010(411) [0679] of God the Father, his nature, his **will**, and his work.
LC : 02 :063(419) [0695] entire essence of God, his **will**, and his work exquisitely
LC : 03 :032(424) [0707] prays, "Dear Father, thy **will** be done," God replies from
LC : 03 :059(428) [0715] *"Thy **will** be done on earth, as it is in heaven."*
LC : 03 :061(428) [0715] devil — we must also pray that God's **will** may be done.
LC : 03 :067(429) [0717] pray without ceasing: "Thy **will** be done, dear Father, and
LC : 03 :067(429) [0717] dear Father, and not the **will** of the devil or of our
LC : 03 :068(429) [0717] our prayer, so must his **will** be done and prevail even
LC : 03 :068(429) [0717] sake we must pray that his **will** may be done among us
LC : 03 :068(429) [0717] violence and persecution, submitting to the **will** of God.
LC : 03 :069(429) [0717] exterminate us so that their **will** and scheme may prevail.
LC : 03 :070(429) [0717] solace and boast that the **will** and purpose of the devil
LC : 03 :070(429) [0717] For if their **will** were not broken and frustrated, the
LC : 03 :086(432) [0723] we obey and submit to his **will** and are supported by
LC : 03 :108(435) [0729] as it is contrary to our **will** and we would prefer to be rid
LC : 03 :113(435) [0729] glory, God's kingdom and **will**, our daily bread, a good
LC : 03 :118(436) [0731] in us, his kingdom come among us, and his **will** be done.
EP : 02 :000(469) [0785] II. Free **Will**
EP : 02 :001(469) [0785] The **will** of man may be discussed in four different states:
EP : 02 :001(469) [0785] exclusively about man's **will** and ability in the second
EP : 02 :003(470) [0787] that man's unregenerated **will** is not only turned away
EP : 02 :004(470) [0787] It is God's **will** that men should hear his Word and not
EP : 02 :006(470) [0787] Without his grace our "**will** and effort," our planting,
EP : 02 :006(470) [0787] he denies all power to free **will** and ascribes everything to
EP : 02 :011(471) [0789] too weak by his free **will** to make a beginning, convert
EP : 02 :011(471) [0789] offered his grace, man's **will** is forthwith able by its own
EP : 02 :015(471) [0789] explanation that man's **will** before, in, and after
EP : 02 :016(472) [0789] who is willing," or, "Man's **will** is not idle in conversion,
EP : 02 :016(472) [0791] the role of natural free **will** in conversion contrary to the
EP : 02 :017(472) [0791] of repentance, the reborn **will** of man is not idle but
EP : 02 :018(472) [0791] statement that man's **will** in conversion behaves
EP : 02 :018(472) [0791] new movements within the **will**, that is, when the Spirit of
EP : 02 :018(472) [0791] takes hold of man's **will** and works the new birth and
EP : 02 :018(472) [0791] accomplished this and the **will** of man has been changed
EP : 02 :018(472) [0791] *and activity*, man's new **will** becomes an instrument and
EP : 03 :003(473) [0793] *man's obedience* many **will** be made righteous" (Rom.
EP : 05 :003(478) [0801] everything that is sinful and contrary to God's **will**.
EP : 06 :004(480) [0807] in people's intellect, **will**, and all their powers, it is
EP : 06 :004(480) [0807] be coerced against his own **will** not only by the
EP : 06 :007(481) [0807] and the same law, namely, the unchangeable **will** of God.
EP : 07 :017(484) [0813] accept him even contrary to their **will** as a strict judge.
EP : 11 :004(495) [0833] of this is the devil and man's wicked and perverse **will**.
EP : 11 :008(495) [0833] in his Word, and it is his **will** that they hear the Word and
EP : 11 :011(495) [0835] himself with the revealed **will** of God and observes the
EP : 11 :014(496) [0835] to live according to the **will** of God and "to confirm our
EP : 11 :015(496) [0835] of ours, saves us "according to the purpose" of his **will**.
EP : 11 :016(497) [0837] strengthened in their self-**will**, he is not teaching the
EP : 11 :016(497) [0837] according to the Word and **will** of God, but in accord
EP : 11 :019(497) [0837] counsel, purpose, and **will**, without regard for their sin,
EP : 12 :021(499) [0841] divine essence, property, **will**, and glory and that the flesh
SD : 01 :011(510) [0863] and foremost powers of the soul in mind, heart, and **will**.
SD : 02 :000(519) [0881] II. Free **Will** or Human Powers
SD : 02 :001(519) [0881] concerning free **will**, not only between the papists and our
SD : 02 :002(520) [0881] Man with his free **will** can be found and viewed as being
SD : 02 :002(520) [0881] the state of man's **will** before the Fall, nor what man after
SD : 02 :002(520) [0881] him, nor what man's free **will** is going to be like after he
SD : 02 :002(520) [0881] man's intellect and **will** can do in his conversion and
SD : 02 :007(521) [0883] the intellect, heart, and **will** of unregenerated man cannot
SD : 02 :007(521) [0883] believe, accept, imagine, **will**, begin, accomplish, do,
SD : 02 :007(521) [0883] and nature the natural free **will** is mighty and active only
SD : 02 :012(522) [0885] to the intellect, heart, and **will** of the natural man every
SD : 02 :012(522) [0885] them, to begin them, to **will** them, to undertake them, to
SD : 02 :014(523) [0885] is at work in you, both to **will** and to work for his good
SD : 02 :017(523) [0887] the intellect, heart, and **will** of a natural, unregenerated
SD : 02 :017(524) [0887] which is displeasing to God and contrary to his **will**.
SD : 02 :018(524) [0887] the natural or carnal free **will** of St. Paul and other

Continued ▶

SD : 0 2 :018(524) [0887] their regeneration, the **will** of man prior to his conversion
SD : 0 2 :018(524) [0887] obstinately opposed and hostile to God's law and **will**.
SD : 0 2 :018(524) [0887] we only refer), that the free **will** by its own natural
SD : 0 2 :018(524) [0889] resists God and his **will** unless the Holy Spirit illuminates
SD : 0 2 :023(525) [0889] the Fathers defend free **will**, they affirm a capacity for
SD : 0 2 :024(526) [0891] resistant and hostile to the **will** of God unless the Holy
SD : 0 2 :025(526) [0891] powers of the natural free **will**, be it entirely or one-half
SD : 0 2 :026(526) [0891] extent reason and free **will** are able to lead an outwardly
SD : 0 2 :026(526) [0891] is at work in you, both to **will** and to work" (Phil. 2:13).
SD : 0 2 :027(527) [0891] of the truth reveals his **will**; but to assent to this Gospel
SD : 0 2 :027(527) [0893] power to believe and to **will**, but that it is God's work to
SD : 0 2 :027(527) [0893] to achieve something to those who believe and **will**."
SD : 0 2 :030(527) [0893] the freedom of the human **will** in spiritual matters.
SD : 0 2 :031(527) [0893] as follows concerning free **will**: "We also declare that to a
SD : 0 2 :031(527) [0893] also declare that to a certain extent reason has a free **will**.
SD : 0 2 :031(527) [0893] can be comprehended by reason we have a free **will**."
SD : 0 2 :032(527) [0893] in spiritual things our free **will** and reason can do
SD : 0 2 :032(527) [0893] does not ascribe to man's **will** any ability either to initiate
SD : 0 2 :033(527) [0893] errors concerning free **will**: "That man has a free will to
SD : 0 2 :033(527) [0893] will: "That man has a free **will** to do good and to avoid
SD : 0 2 :035(528) [0895] nothing at all about our **will**, nor do they say that even in
SD : 0 2 :035(528) [0895] even in the regenerated the **will** can do something of
SD : 0 2 :038(528) [0895] whatever of our free **will** or of our contribution, but
SD : 0 2 :039(528) [0895] we do this not of our own **will** and power, but the Holy
SD : 0 2 :042(529) [0897] make no mention whatever of our **will** and cooperation.
SD : 0 2 :043(529) [0897] which glorifies our free **will**, as directly and diametrically
SD : 0 2 :044(529) [0897] memory, grants our free **will** no power of its own to
SD : 0 2 :044(529) [0897] performs only the devil's **will** and what is contrary to the
SD : 0 2 :044(529) [0897] cooperation on the part of our **will** in man's conversion.
SD : 0 2 :044(529) [0897] book *The Bondage of the* ***Will***, in which he writes
SD : 0 2 :044(529) [0897] concerning the enslaved **will** of man against Erasmus and
SD : 0 2 :045(530) [0899] it, and that thus the human **will** cooperates in conversion.
SD : 0 2 :046(530) [0899] of our natural free **will**, as well as the doctrine that our
SD : 0 2 :046(530) [0899] wait until God forcibly converts them against their **will**.
SD : 0 2 :049(530) [0901] It is not God's **will** that anyone should be damned but
SD : 0 2 :050(531) [0901] And it is God's **will** to call men to eternal salvation, to
SD : 0 2 :052(531) [0901] to God, and to work in them both to **will** and to achieve.
SD : 0 2 :053(531) [0903] has something of a free **will** in these external matters, so
SD : 0 2 :055(532) [0903] to God's command and **will**, and when the people
SD : 0 2 :059(532) [0905] a man does who with his **will** resists the Lord God until
SD : 0 2 :059(532) [0905] with an intellect and **will** (not, however, an intellect in
SD : 0 2 :059(532) [0905] he resists the Word and **will** of God until God raises him
SD : 0 2 :060(533) [0905] one and his resisting **will** becomes an obedient will.
SD : 0 2 :060(533) [0905] one and his resisting will becomes an obedient **will**.
SD : 0 2 :063(533) [0905] enlightened, and his **will** is renewed, then he wills that
SD : 0 2 :067(534) [0907] and now have a liberated **will** — that is, as Christ says,
SD : 0 2 :070(535) [0909] emotions in the intellect, **will**, and heart, so that the heart
SD : 0 2 :073(535) [0909] the entire doctrine of free **will** it is possible to decide the
SD : 0 2 :073(535) [0909] forcibly compels a man to be converted against his **will**?
SD : 0 2 :074(535) [0909] in external works man's **will** has no freedom or power
SD : 0 2 :074(536) [0909] sins and vices; or that the **will** of man is coerced into
SD : 0 2 :075(536) [0911] the Holy Spirit, the free **will** can convert itself to God,
SD : 0 2 :077(536) [0911] As a result, his free **will** is too weak to make a beginning
SD : 0 2 :077(536) [0911] eternal life, then the free **will** by its own natural powers
SD : 0 2 :082(537) [0913] explanation: that man's **will** before, in, and after
SD : 0 2 :083(537) [0913] the good in the intellect, **will**, and heart, when man in no
SD : 0 2 :083(537) [0913] activity in the intellect, **will**, and heart of man whereby
SD : 0 2 :086(537) [0913] The formulas, "Man's **will** is not idle in conversion but
SD : 0 2 :086(538) [0913] that man's naturally free **will** cooperates in his
SD : 0 2 :087(538) [0913] of our corrupted **will**, which is nothing else but a
SD : 0 2 :087(538) [0915] but a resurrection of the **will** from spiritual death, is
SD : 0 2 :088(538) [0915] conversion man's reborn **will** is not idle in the daily
SD : 0 2 :089(538) [0915] through the Word in the intellect, **will**, and heart of man.
SD : 0 2 :089(538) [0915] is going on or perceive or **will** anything in connection with
SD : 0 2 :090(538) [0915] and heard, the Holy Spirit, and man's **will**) concur.
SD : 0 2 :090(539) [0915] man's intellect and **will** are only that which is to be
SD : 0 2 :090(539) [0915] they are the intellect and **will** of a man who is spiritually
SD : 0 2 :090(539) [0915] Toward this work the **will** of the person who is to be
SD : 0 4 :007(552) [0939] points: That it is God's **will**, ordinance, and command
SD : 0 4 :014(553) [0943] because of God's ordinance, commandment, and **will**
SD : 0 4 :016(554) [0943] order of God's immutable **will**, whose debtors we are, as
SD : 0 4 :017(554) [0943] from a person against his **will**, by coercion or otherwise,
SD : 0 4 :017(554) [0943] that is really unwilled by him or even contrary to his **will**.
SD : 0 4 :017(554) [0943] (Ps. 110:3), who bring free-**will** offerings (Ps. 54:6), not
SD : 0 4 :038(557) [0951] It is God's **will** and express command that believers
SD : 0 5 :017(561) [0957] and immutable **will** of God, shows how man ought to be
SD : 0 6 :003(564) [0963] to the inner man do the **will** of God from a free spirit,
SD : 0 6 :003(564) [0963] in accord with God's external and immutable **will**.
SD : 0 6 :004(564) [0963] is a mirror in which the **will** of God and what is pleasing
SD : 0 6 :006(565) [0965] to do according to the **will** of God, just as the sun, the
SD : 0 6 :011(565) [0965] tells us that it is God's **will** and command that we should
SD : 0 6 :012(566) [0967] what the acceptable **will** of God is (Rom. 12:2) and in
SD : 0 6 :015(566) [0967] namely, the immutable **will** of God according to which
SD : 0 6 :016(566) [0967] about living according to the law and the **will** of God.
SD : 0 6 :017(566) [0967] to the immutable **will** of God as it is comprehended in the
SD : 0 6 :019(567) [0969] does everything against his **will** and by coercion, just as
SD : 0 6 :025(568) [0971] Spirit they **will** do his **will** spontaneously, without
SD : 0 7 :050(578) [0989] the institution of his last **will** and testament and of his
SD : 1 1 :004(617) [1063] to the ground without your Father's **will**" (Matt. 10:29).
SD : 1 1 :006(617) [1065] though it were God's gracious **will** that it should happen.
SD : 1 1 :006(617) [1065] the perverse and wicked **will** of the devil and of men will
SD : 1 1 :006(617) [1065] wicked will of the devil and of men **will** attempt and do.
SD : 1 1 :006(617) [1065] the evil which he does not **will** — how far it is to go, how
SD : 1 1 :007(617) [1065] the wicked and perverse **will** of the devil and of men, as it
SD : 1 1 :008(617) [1065] but by God's gracious **will** and pleasure in Christ Jesus it
SD : 1 1 :014(619) [1069] of God's purpose, counsel, **will**, and ordinance concerning
SD : 1 1 :026(620) [1071] Instead we must heed the revealed **will** of God.
SD : 1 1 :026(620) [1071] to us the mystery of his **will**" and has brought it forth
SD : 1 1 :028(621) [1071] "This is the **will** of the Father, that all who believe on
SD : 1 1 :029(621) [1073] that God reveals his **will** in this way, and that in those
SD : 1 1 :029(621) [1073] and ability, it is God's **will** that we should accept the
SD : 1 1 :033(621) [1073] with this revealed **will** of God, follow it, and be diligent
SD : 1 1 :034(622) [1075] For it is my **will** that the majority of those whom I call
SD : 1 1 :036(622) [1075] and to determine God's **will** toward us and what assures
SD : 1 1 :038(622) [1075] could not determine God's **will** toward us from the call
SD : 1 1 :041(623) [1077] but man's own perverse **will**, which rejects or perverts the
SD : 1 1 :044(623) [1077] the powers of our natural **will**, for in his counsel God has
SD : 1 1 :067(627) [1085] proclaimed the Father's **will** and thereby our eternal
SD : 1 1 :067(627) [1085] when he says, "This is the **will** of my Father, that
SD : 1 1 :075(628) [1087] of Christ and the gracious **will** of the Father, who cannot
SD : 1 1 :075(628) [1087] himself because he is changeless in his **will** and essence.
SD : 1 1 :076(629) [1087] It is not the **will** of either the Father or the Son that any
SD : 1 1 :080(629) [1089] If that had been his **will**, he would not have needed any
SD : 1 1 :081(629) [1089] And as God does not **will** sin and has no pleasure in sin,
SD : 1 1 :081(629) [1089] in sin, so he also does not **will** the death of a sinner and
SD : 1 1 :081(629) [1089] He does not **will** that "any should perish, but that all
SD : 1 1 :083(630) [1091] never been God's gracious **will** that such people should
SD : 1 1 :083(630) [1091] God's revealed **will** involves both items: First, that he
SD : 1 1 :085(630) [1091] Word proclaimed and his **will** revealed to Pharaoh, and
SD : 1 1 :087(631) [1093] to the purpose" of his **will** through sheer mercy in Christ
SD : 1 1 :087(631) [1093] to the purpose of his **will**, and to the praise of his glorious
SD : 1 1 :091(632) [1093] according to the Word and **will** of God but according to
SD : 1 1 :092(632) [1093] and hope is contrary to the Holy Spirit's **will** and intent.
SD : 1 1 :093(632) [1095] in God's revealed **will**, we shall avoid and flee all abstruse
SD : 1 2 :029(635) [1101] kind of essence, property, **will**, and glory and so that

Will-o'-the-wisps (1)

S2 : 0 2 :018(296) [0467] uncertain, harmful **will-o'-the-wisps** of the devil?

Willed (2), Willful (2), Willfully (4), Willing (29), Willingly (10), Willingness (4), Wills (28)

PR : PR :001(003) [0007] respectful, humble, and **willing** service, and hereby
AG : 1 8 :007(040) [0053] undertake evil, as when he **wills** to kneel before an idol,
AG : 2 7 :029(075) [0079] vows of themselves, **willingly**, and after due
AL : 0 0 :017(096) [0095] we are ready, God **willing**, to present ampler information
AP : PR :003(098) [0099] clear that our side was **willing** to put up with anything,
AP : 0 4 :027(111) [0127] that he hears prayer, **willingly** obey him in death and in
AP : 0 7 :033(174) [0239] So in our churches we **willingly** observe the order of the
AP : 1 2 :091(195) [0279] We were all the more **willing** to do this because many
AP : 1 2 :164(208) [0303] If you are **willing** and obedient, you shall eat the good of
AP : 1 4 :005(215) [0315] point to declare our **willingness** to keep the ecclesiastical
AP : 1 4 :005(215) [0315] This **willingness** will be our defense, both before God and
AP : 1 5 :052(222) [0329] a person evidence of our **willingness** to observe adiaphora
AP : 2 1 :017(231) [0347] to assure us that God is **willing** to have mercy and to
AP : 2 4 :029(255) [0393] it and thy promises of **willingness** to show mercy and to
AP : 2 4 :035(256) [0397] We are perfectly **willing** for the Mass to be understood as
S1 : PR :001(288) [0455] and in how far we were **willing** and able to yield to the
S1 : PR :013(291) [0459] But if we are **willing** to swallow camels and strain out
S3 : 1 5 :003(316) [0501] and on which I will stand, God **willing**, until my death.
LC : 0 1 :034(369) [0589] Therefore he **wills** to be feared and not to be despised.
LC : 0 1 :069(374) [0601] punishment upon such **willful** contempt of this
LC : 0 1 :144(385) [0623] They ought even to be **willing** to pay for the privilege of
LC : 0 1 :151(386) [0625] He who is obedient, **willing**, ready to serve, and cheerfully
LC : 0 1 :166(387) [0629] We ought to be **willing** to run to the ends of the world to
LC : 0 1 :171(388) [0629] No one is **willing** to see that this is the command of the
LC : 0 1 :187(390) [0633] knowledge that no one **willingly** suffers injury from
LC : 0 1 :234(397) [0647] A person who **willfully** disregards this commandment
LC : 0 1 :240(397) [0649] the market in his own **willful**, conceited, arrogant way, as
LC : 0 1 :246(398) [0649] Whoever is **willing** to learn a lesson, let him know that
LC : 0 1 :309(407) [0669] occasion for it; we are **willingly** to leave him what is his,
LC : 0 3 :025(423) [0705] as a payment to God, not **willing** to receive anything from
LC : 0 3 :103(434) [0727] No one is **willing** to be the least, but everyone wants to sit
LC : 0 5 :069(454) [0769] as when a sick person **willfully** eats and drinks what is
LC : 0 6 :021(459) [0000] not go to confession **willingly** and for the sake of
LC : 0 6 :025(460) [0000] Who could thus go to confession **willingly**?
EP : 0 2 :003(470) [0787] God, so that he desires and **wills** only that which is evil
EP : 0 2 :015(471) [0789] conversion God makes **willing** people out of unwilling
EP : 0 2 :015(471) [0789] out of unwilling people and dwells in the **willing** ones.
EP : 0 2 :016(472) [0789] draws the person who is **willing**," or, "Man's will is not
EP : 0 2 :017(472) [0791] and unwilling people into **willing** people, and that after
EP : 0 6 :004(480) [0807] necessary lest the Old Adam go his own self-**willed** way.
EP : 0 6 :007(481) [0807] any coercion and with a **willing** spirit, in so far as he is
EP : 1 1 :012(496) [0835] Word of God at all but **willfully** despise it, harden their
SD : 0 2 :014(523) [0885] godliness in their heart, **wills** to continue to support them
SD : 0 2 :021(525) [0889] — even knowingly and **willingly** — and thereby runs into
SD : 0 2 :022(525) [0889] fell, he has nevertheless **willed**, out of particular and pure
SD : 0 2 :039(528) [0895] Paul says, creates such **willing** and doing (Phil. 2:13), just
SD : 0 2 :048(530) [0901] the Holy Spirit **wills** to be efficacious in us by giving and
SD : 0 2 :052(531) [0901] and through which he **wills** to act efficaciously, to
SD : 0 2 :055(531) [0903] the hearer's running and **willing** would be in vain, and no
SD : 0 2 :057(532) [0903] holy sacraments, earnestly **wills** that we hear it, and has
SD : 0 2 :059(532) [0905] things or a volition that **wills** what is good and
SD : 0 2 :060(533) [0905] draws the person whom he **wills** to convert, and draws
SD : 0 2 :063(533) [0905] his will is renewed, then he **wills** that which is good, in so
SD : 0 2 :071(535) [0909] which the Holy Spirit **wills** to work such conversion and
SD : 0 2 :072(535) [0909] which the Holy Spirit **wills** to begin and accomplish all
SD : 0 2 :086(537) [0913] he draws the person who **wills**," were introduced to
SD : 0 2 :088(538) [0915] Holy Spirit, God makes **willing** people out of resisting
SD : 0 4 :012(553) [0941] any coercion a man is **willing** and desirous to do good to
SD : 0 4 :018(554) [0943] works are to be done **willingly** or from a spontaneous
SD : 0 4 :019(554) [0945] that he is **willing** and delights in the law of God
SD : 0 4 :038(557) [0951] in them, and God is **willing** to be pleased with them for
SD : 0 5 :021(562) [0959] joyful message that God **wills** not to punish sins but to
SD : 0 6 :023(568) [0969] coercion of the law but **willingly** and spontaneously from
SD : 0 7 :099(586) [1005] mode of presence when he **wills** to do so, as he did after
SD : 0 7 :100(586) [1007] space but penetrates every creature, wherever he **wills**.
SD : 0 7 :119(590) [1013] he is neither able nor **willing** to be truly and essentially
SD : 0 7 :119(590) [1013] that he in no way can or **wills** to be with us on earth with
SD : 0 8 :064(603) [1037] nature, spontaneously and when and where he **wills**.
SD : 0 8 :078(607) [1043] and is present wherever he **wills**, and in particular that he
SD : 0 8 :087(608) [1047] men and his brethren, he **wills** to be with us in all our
SD : 1 1 :023(619) [1069] manner just recounted he **wills** by his grace, gifts, and
SD : 1 1 :029(621) [1073] because the Holy Spirit **wills** to be efficacious through the
SD : 1 1 :039(622) [1075] that the Holy Spirit **wills** to be certainly present with and
SD : 1 1 :041(623) [1077] the Holy Spirit who **wills** to be efficaciously active
SD : 1 1 :042(623) [1077] The reason is that they **willfully** turn away from the holy
SD : 1 1 :068(627) [1085] The Father **wills** that all men should hear this

Continued ▶

SD : 1 1 :071(627) [1085] powers, the Holy Spirit **wills** to work such repentance and
SD : 1 1 :075(628) [1087] through it the Holy Spirit **wills** to effect their conversion
SD : 1 1 :077(629) [1089] because the Holy Spirit **wills** to be present in the Word

William (4)
PR : PR :027(014) [0025] Duke Frederick **William** [of Saxe-Altenburg] and
PR : PR :027(014) [0025] **William** the Younger, duke of Brunswick and Lueneburg
PR : PR :027(015) [0025] **William**, count of Schwarzburg [Frankenhausen]
AP : 1 8 :010(226) [0337] it too, and more recently **William** of Paris has discussed it

Wilt (5)
AP : 0 4 :327(158) [0211] my hands with lye, yet thou **wilt** plunge me into a pit."
AP : 2 1 :008(230) [0345] Lord of hosts, how long **wilt** thou have no mercy on
AP : 2 4 :029(255) [0393] broken and contrite heart, O God, thou **wilt** not despise."
AP : 2 7 :013(271) [0423] O Christ, how long **wilt** Thou bear these insults with
SD : 0 1 :035(514) [0869] hast made me of clay, and **wilt** thou turn me to dust

Wimpfen (1)
PR : PR :027(016) [0027] Mayor and Council of the City of **Wimpfen**

Win (2)
LC : 0 1 :121(382) [0615] and children would **win** their parents' hearts completely.
LC : 0 2 :031(414) [0685] paid and risked in order to **win** us and bring us under his

Wind (2), Winds (1)
LC : 0 1 :197(392) [0637] commandments to the **winds**, regarding them as
LC : 0 3 :123(436) [0731] a wave of the sea that is driven and tossed by the **wind**.
EP : 1 1 :012(496) [0835] Word, they cast it to the **wind** and pay no attention to it.

Wine (87)
AG : 1 0 :001(034) [0047] the form of bread and **wine** and are there distributed and
AP : 1 0 :001(179) [0247] seen, the bread and the **wine**, to those who receive the
AP : 1 0 :004(180) [0247] offered with those things that are seen, bread and **wine**.
AP : 2 3 :045(245) [0375] They abstained from **wine**, even in the Lord's Supper;
AP : 2 3 :045(245) [0377] services instead of using **wine** or meat or marriage, which
AP : 2 4 :086(265) [0413] they gathered they brought bread, **wine**, and other things.
AP : 2 7 :059(279) [0439] neither had any possessions nor drank any **wine**.
S 3 : 0 6 :001(311) [0493] that the bread and the **wine** in the Supper are the true
S 3 : 0 6 :005(311) [0493] who teach that bread and **wine** surrender or lose their
SC : 0 6 :002(351) [0555] under the bread and **wine**, given to us Christians to eat
LC : 0 1 :224(395) [0643] shop, butcher stall, **wine**- and beer-cellar, work-shop,
LC : 0 3 :025(423) [0705] prayed whole-heartedly for so much as a drop of **wine**.
LC : 0 5 :008(447) [0755] and under the bread and **wine** which we Christians are
LC : 0 5 :009(447) [0755] sacrament is bread and **wine**, but not mere bread or wine
LC : 0 5 :009(447) [0755] but not mere bread or **wine** such as is served at the table.
LC : 0 5 :009(447) [0755] It is bread and **wine** comprehended in God's Word and
LC : 0 5 :010(448) [0755] it from mere bread and **wine** and constitutes it a
LC : 0 5 :012(448) [0755] say, 'How can bread and **wine** be Christ's body and
LC : 0 5 :014(448) [0755] Word, you have nothing but ordinary bread and **wine**.
LC : 0 5 :016(448) [0757] can transform bread and **wine** into Christ's body and
LC : 0 5 :018(448) [0757] these words which are coupled with the bread and **wine**."
LC : 0 5 :028(449) [0759] "How can bread and **wine** forgive sins or strengthen
LC : 0 5 :028(449) [0759] claim this of bread and **wine** — since in itself bread is
LC : 0 5 :028(449) [0759] — but of that bread and **wine** which are Christ's body and
EP : 0 1 :017(468) [0783] with human nature, as when poison and **wine** are mixed.
EP : 0 7 :002(481) [0809] with the bread and the **wine** and if they are received orally
EP : 0 7 :003(482) [0809] Supper only bread and **wine** are present, distributed, and
EP : 0 7 :004(482) [0809] nothing but bread and **wine** are present and received with
EP : 0 7 :005(482) [0809] but not in the bread and **wine** of the Holy Supper, seek
EP : 0 7 :006(482) [0809] truly distributed and received with the bread and **wine**.
EP : 0 7 :007(482) [0811] the absent body and the **wine** the absent blood of Christ,
EP : 0 7 :015(483) [0811] that with the bread and **wine** the body and blood of
EP : 0 7 :022(484) [0813] papacy that the bread and **wine** in the Holy Supper lose
EP : 0 7 :026(485) [0815] we receive only bread and **wine** and that we receive the
EP : 0 7 :027(485) [0815] 6. That bread and **wine** in the Holy Supper are no more
EP : 0 7 :028(485) [0815] 7. That the bread and **wine** are only figures, images, and
EP : 0 7 :029(485) [0815] 8. That the bread and **wine** are no more than reminders,
EP : 0 7 :029(485) [0815] truly as we eat and drink bread and **wine** in the Supper.
EP : 0 7 :030(485) [0815] signs of bread and **wine** and not by the truly present body
EP : 0 7 :036(485) [0815] of Christ in the bread and **wine** of the Holy Supper, but
EP : 0 7 :037(486) [0815] the body and blood of Christ, but only bread and **wine**.
EP : 0 7 :040(486) [0817] elements of bread and **wine** in the holy sacrament should
EP : 1 2 :024(500) [0843] 5. That bread and **wine** in the Holy Supper are not means
SD : 0 7 :002(569) [0973] the blessed bread and **wine** in the Supper as the highest
SD : 0 7 :003(569) [0973] For just as the bread and **wine** are here on earth and not
SD : 0 7 :003(569) [0973] nothing but bread and **wine** are orally received in the
SD : 0 7 :004(569) [0973] more than mere bread and **wine**, which are only signs of
SD : 0 7 :006(570) [0973] that with the bread and **wine** Christ gives us his true body
SD : 0 7 :009(570) [0975] the forms of bread and **wine** and that they are distributed
SD : 0 7 :010(571) [0975] under the bread and **wine**, given to us Christians to eat
SD : 0 7 :011(571) [0975] the bread and the **wine**, to those who receive the
SD : 0 7 :014(571) [0977] that with the bread and **wine** the body and blood of
SD : 0 7 :014(571) [0977] change of the bread and **wine** into the body and blood of
SD : 0 7 :019(572) [0979] that "the bread and the **wine** in the Supper are the true
SD : 0 7 :020(573) [0979] and under the bread and **wine** which Christ's word
SD : 0 7 :021(573) [0979] it is not mere bread and **wine** but is and is called Christ's
SD : 0 7 :022(573) [0979] ask, How can bread and **wine** be the body and blood of
SD : 0 7 :023(573) [0979] you then have nothing but ordinary bread and **wine**.
SD : 0 7 :024(573) [0981] can change bread and **wine** into the body and blood of
SD : 0 7 :026(573) [0981] of these words which are added to the bread and **wine**.'
SD : 0 7 :032(574) [0983] drunk in the bread and **wine**, though the priests who
SD : 0 7 :032(575) [0983] have only bread and **wine**, for they do not also have the
SD : 0 7 :038(576) [0985] Christ with the bread and **wine** is not a personal union,
SD : 0 7 :044(577) [0987] concerning the cup or the **wine**, "This is my blood of the
SD : 0 7 :048(578) [0989] natural bread and natural **wine** as well as of oral eating
SD : 0 7 :060(580) [0993] only against the bread and **wine**, not only against signs
SD : 0 7 :063(581) [0995] the blessed bread and **wine** in the Lord's Supper receive
SD : 0 7 :064(581) [0995] natural bread and natural **wine**, which he called his true
SD : 0 7 :076(583) [0999] make of the bread and **wine** set before us the body and
SD : 0 7 :077(583) [0999] ordinary bread and **wine** but his body and blood, as his
SD : 0 7 :077(583) [0999] bread the body and the **wine** the blood that are daily
SD : 0 7 :082(584) [1001] the elements of bread and **wine** are hallowed or blessed in
SD : 0 7 :084(584) [1001] we take bread and **wine**, consecrate it, distribute it,
SD : 0 7 :086(585) [1003] of the blessed bread and **wine**, the body and blood of
SD : 0 7 :100(586) [1007] doors, in the bread and **wine** in the Lord's Supper, and,
SD : 0 7 :108(588) [1009] or blessed bread and **wine** in the Holy Supper completely
SD : 0 7 :108(588) [1009] mere species of bread and **wine**, or their accidents
SD : 0 7 :114(589) [1011] in the Supper our mouth receives only bread and **wine**.
SD : 0 7 :115(589) [1011] teaching that bread and **wine** in the Supper are no more
SD : 0 7 :115(589) [1011] just as bread and **wine** are external food for our body, so
SD : 0 7 :117(590) [1013] words, only as bread and **wine** have a similarity with the
SD : 0 7 :122(590) [1013] of Christ in the bread and **wine** of the Supper, but to look
SD : 0 7 :123(590) [1013] receive only bread and **wine** in the Supper and not the
SD : 0 7 :123(590) [1015] receive only bread and **wine** in the use of the Holy
SD : 0 7 :126(591) [1015] forms of the blessed bread and **wine**) are to be adored.
SD : 0 8 :071(605) [1041] of God, as when water, **wine**, or oil is poured from one
SD : 1 2 :032(635) [1101] 4. That the bread and **wine** in the Holy Supper are not

Wings (1)
SD : 0 2 :058(532) [0905] her brood under her **wings**, and you would not!"

Wink (1)
LC : 0 1 :204(392) [0639] could prevent a wrong) or **wink** at it as if it were no

Winter (1)
AP : 1 6 :006(223) [0331] and to the change of **winter** and summer as ordinances of

Wipe (2), Wiped (1)
AP : 0 4 :245(142) [0189] but they also try to **wipe** it out with sword and torture.
AP : 1 2 :067(191) [0271] that this teaching be **wiped** out by force and the sword,
AP : 1 2 :152(206) [0299] in the saints they kill and **wipe** out lust so that the Spirit

Wisdom (54)
AG : 0 1 :003(028) [0043] end, of infinite power, **wisdom**, and goodness, one
AG : 2 8 :045(088) [0089] These have an appearance of **wisdom**."
AL : 0 1 :002(027) [0043] of infinite power, **wisdom**, and goodness, the maker and
AL : 2 8 :045(088) [0089] These have an appearance of **wisdom**."
AP : 0 2 :018(102) [0111] else is this than that a **wisdom** and righteousness was
AP : 0 2 :026(103) [0111] the body but also carnal **wisdom** and righteousness in
AP : 0 4 :032(111) [0129] that is, they lack the **wisdom** and righteousness of God
AP : 0 4 :086(119) [0147] "God made Christ our **wisdom**, our righteousness and
AP : 0 4 :229(139) [0183] Human **wisdom** looks at the law and seeks righteousness
AP : 0 4 :229(139) [0183] Deceived by human **wisdom**, they did not see the true
AP : 0 4 :230(139) [0183] about love is more plausible; for this is human **wisdom**.
AP : 0 4 :306(154) [0207] whom God made our **wisdom**, our righteousness and
AP : 0 7 :035(175) [0241] indeed an appearance of **wisdom** in promoting rigor of
AP : 1 2 :125(201) [0289] in keeping with your **wisdom**, to see to it that on such
AP : 1 2 :126(201) [0289] in such times to exercise unusual **wisdom** and diligence.
AP : 1 5 :022(218) [0321] "have an appearance of **wisdom**," and indeed they have.
AP : 1 5 :024(218) [0321] by the appearance of **wisdom** and righteousness in such
AP : 1 5 :025(218) [0321] Once this appearance of **wisdom** and righteousness has
AP : 1 5 :029(219) [0323] deceptive appearance of **wisdom** and righteousness in
LC : S P :019(363) [0579] up the doctrine, life, **wisdom**, and learning which
LC : 0 1 :010(366) [0583] boasts of great learning, **wisdom**, power, prestige, family,
LC : 0 1 :113(380) [0613] it embodies his highest **wisdom**, then I shall never
LC : 0 2 :030(414) [0685] us by his righteousness, **wisdom**, power, life, and
LC : 0 2 :063(419) [0695] In them consists all our **wisdom**, which surpasses all the
LC : 0 2 :063(419) [0695] which surpasses all the **wisdom**, understanding, and
LC : 0 2 :067(420) [0697] No human **wisdom** can comprehend the Creed; it must be
LC : 0 3 :077(431) [0721] and officials, with **wisdom**, strength, and prosperity to
LC : 0 5 :012(448) [0755] put together have less **wisdom** than the divine Majesty
LC : 0 5 :028(449) [0759] their great learning and **wisdom**, bellowing and
LC : 0 5 :061(453) [0767] that it is the highest **wisdom** to realize that this sacrament
EP : 0 8 :016(489) [0821] truly increase in age, **wisdom**, and favor with God and
EP : 0 8 :037(491) [0825] hid "all the treasures of **wisdom** and knowledge,
EP : 1 2 :029(500) [0843] has the same power, **wisdom**, majesty, and glory, just like
SD : 0 2 :008(521) [0883] we also know that "the **wisdom** of this perverse world is
SD : 0 2 :010(522) [0883] Again, "Since, in the **wisdom** of God, the world did not
SD : 0 2 :010(522) [0883] know God through its **wisdom**, it pleased God through
SD : 0 2 :051(531) [0901] "For since, in the **wisdom** of God, the world did not know
SD : 0 2 :051(531) [0901] not know God through **wisdom**, it pleased God through
SD : 0 7 :022(573) [0979] put together have less **wisdom** than the divine Majesty
SD : 0 7 :043(576) [0987] the eternal truth and **wisdom** and the almighty God
SD : 0 7 :046(577) [0989] God's omnipotence and **wisdom**, knowing that God had
SD : 0 7 :047(578) [0989] words is himself infinite **Wisdom** and Truth and can
SD : 0 7 :050(578) [0989] from the standpoint of **wisdom** and intelligence to explain
SD : 0 8 :068(604) [1039] are hid all treasures of **wisdom** and knowledge, and to
SD : 0 8 :072(605) [1041] The "Spirit of **wisdom** and understanding, of counsel and
SD : 0 8 :074(606) [1043] measure the Spirit of **wisdom** and power, so that as a
SD : 0 8 :074(606) [1043] way all the treasures of **wisdom** are hid in him, all
SD : 0 8 :092(609) [1049] Christ's omnipotence and **wisdom** can readily provide
SD : 0 8 :095(609) [1049] the divine power, might, **wisdom**, majesty, and glory, but
SD : 1 1 :052(625) [1081] kept reserved solely to his own **wisdom** and knowledge.
SD : 1 1 :055(625) [1081] this mystery to his own **wisdom** and not revealed
SD : 1 1 :064(626) [1083] for his own hidden **wisdom**, Paul immediately commands
SD : 1 1 :064(626) [1083] depth of the riches and **wisdom** and knowledge of God!
SD : 1 2 :037(636) [1103] have the same power, **wisdom**, majesty, and glory, while

Wise (17), Wisely (4), Wiser (5)
AG : 2 3 :014(054) [0063] matters in a better or **wiser** way than God himself, who
AP : 0 2 :031(104) [0113] The **wise** reader will easily be able to see that when the
AP : 0 2 :043(106) [0117] It is no **wiser** to say that nature is not evil.
AP : 0 2 :049(106) [0119] enthralled those who are **wise** and righteous in the eyes of
AP : 0 4 :154(128) [0165] to chide the Pharisee, this **wise** and honest but
AP : 0 4 :185(132) [0173] "Being sick in itself, an unjust cause needs **wise** remedies."
AP : 0 7 :044(177) [0243] The apostles **wisely** admonished the reader neither to
AP : 1 2 :010(184) [0255] Here we appeal to the judgment of all good and **wise** men.
AP : 1 2 :129(202) [0291] As a **wise** man you can easily imagine what will happen if
AP : 2 1 :030(233) [0351] extinguished, they begged the **wise** ones to lend them oil.
AP : 2 3 :009(240) [0367] the jurists have said **wisely** and correctly that the union of
AP : 2 3 :011(241) [0367] taught by Scripture and **wisely** put by the jurists: The
AP : 2 7 :036(275) [0433] It seems that **wise** men were offended by the immoderate
S 3 : 0 3 :003(304) [0481] and no matter how great, **wise**, mighty, and holy you may
TR : 0 0 :030(325) [0513] (John 21:15), it in no **wise** follows that they bestow a
TR : 0 0 :054(329) [0519] therefore, O kings, be **wise**; be warned, O rulers of the
SC : PR :019(340) [0537] and parents to rule **wisely** and educate their children.

Continued ▶

LC : PR :016(361) [0571] consider themselves much **wiser** than God himself, and
LC : PR :016(361) [0573] than God himself, and **wiser** than all his holy angels,
LC : PR :019(361) [0573] death and have become **wiser** than God himself and all
LC : 0 1 :130(383) [0619] The **wise** men of old were right when they said, "God,
LC : 0 1 :259(400) [0653] not only upright but also a **wise**, sagacious, brave, and
LC : 0 1 :333(410) [0677] out the challenge: Let all **wise** men and saints step
SD : 0 1 :013(511) [0863] many influential and **wise** men of the world with terrible
SD : 0 2 :080(536) [0911] and zeal, and in no **wise** tolerate in the church of God,
SD : 0 7 :043(576) [0987] he is not only truthful, **wise**, and mighty, but himself the

Wish (40), Wished (6), Wishes (33), Wishing (3)
AG : PR :007(025) [0039] with Your Majesty's **wish**, we should present our case in
AG : 0 0 :001(047) [0059] Certainly we would not **wish** to put our own souls and
AG : 0 0 :001(047) [0059] or Word, nor should we **wish** to bequeath to our children
AG : 2 7 :045(078) [0081] are now ashamed of and **wish** had never occurred!
AG : 2 8 :033(086) [0087] Sabbath, for thereby they **wish** to maintain that the
AG : 2 8 :065(092) [0093] for the apostles did not **wish** to burden consciences with
AL : 2 5 :011(063) [0069] before others, but I **wish** you to obey the prophet who
AL : 2 8 :065(092) [0093] for the apostles did not **wish** to burden consciences with
AP : 0 4 :086(119) [0147] that for Christ's sake he **wishes** to be propitious to
AP : 0 4 :180(131) [0171] because of Christ, God **wishes** to be favorably disposed to
AP : 0 4 :259(145) [0193] but at the same time he **wishes** the forgiveness of sins to
AP : 0 4 :292(152) [0203] the assurance that he **wishes** to forgive and to be
AP : 0 4 :312(155) [0207] that if it is faith that **wishes** for what the promise offers,
AP : 0 4 :365(163) [0219] include faith, since they **wish** to include the righteousness
AP : 0 7 :023(172) [0235] from any laws, divine, canonical, or civil, as he **wishes**.
AP : 0 7 :040(176) [0241] To determine the apostles' **wish** and intention, therefore,
AP : 1 2 :129(202) [0291] can open heaven for themselves whenever they **wish**.
AP : 2 4 :001(249) [0385] is offered to those who **wish** for it after they have been
S2 : 0 2 :008(294) [0465] himself by saying that he **wishes** to communicate himself
S2 : 0 4 :002(298) [0471] Those who **wish** to do so had better not count on us!
S2 : 0 4 :013(300) [0475] is a consequence of his **wishing** to be the head of the
S3 : 0 3 :017(305) [0483] was asked if he did not **wish** or desire to be repentant.
S3 : 0 3 :027(307) [0487] in his bulls, "Whoever **wishes** to benefit from the
S3 : 0 3 :028(308) [0487] others like myself who **wished** to be monks and priests in
S3 : 0 3 :044(310) [0491] and restrains it so that it does not do what it **wishes**.
S3 : 0 3 :044(310) [0491] If the sin does what it **wishes**, the Holy Spirit and faith
S3 : 0 8 :003(312) [0495] still do it in our day who **wish** to distinguish sharply
S3 : 0 8 :011(313) [0497] For even to Moses God **wished** to appear first through
S3 : 1 0 :001(314) [0497] However, they neither are nor **wish** to be true bishops.
S3 : 1 5 :003(316) [0501] If anybody **wishes** to make some concessions, let him do
S3 : 1 5 :005(316) [0501] We do not **wish** to have anything to do with them.
TR : 0 0 :006(320) [0505] He **wishes** his articles, his decrees, and his laws to be
TR : 0 0 :022(324) [0511] refer to those writings and **wish** them to be regarded as
TR : 0 0 :040(327) [0517] by God, and he **wishes** to have his own doctrine and
SC : PR :022(341) [0537] Surely he **wishes** that this be done and not that it be
LC : PR :008(359) [0569] yet I cannot master it as I **wish**, but must remain a child
LC : PR :014(360) [0571] So he **wishes** to warn, equip, and protect us against them
LC : SP :006(362) [0575] correctly, so that all who **wish** to be Christians in fact as
LC : 0 1 :015(366) [0583] He **wishes** to turn us away from everything else, and draw
LC : 0 1 :015(366) [0585] upon me as the one who **wishes** to help you and to lavish
LC : 0 1 :113(380) [0613] what we should do if we **wish** to perform truly good
LC : 0 1 :115(381) [0613] If they **wish** to serve God with truly good works, they
LC : 0 1 :125(382) [0617] and mother, we should **wish**, on account of the
LC : 0 1 :154(386) [0625] It is because everyone **wishes** to be his own master, be
LC : 0 1 :185(390) [0633] Briefly, he **wishes** to have all people defended, delivered,
LC : 0 1 :187(390) [0633] Therefore God **wishes** to remove the root and source of
LC : 0 1 :188(390) [0635] soul, especially toward him who **wishes** or does you evil.
LC : 0 1 :195(391) [0637] he is our God; that is, he **wishes** to help and protect us, so
LC : 0 1 :207(393) [0639] Therefore he also **wishes** us to honor, maintain, and
LC : 0 1 :286(403) [0663] neighbor, "Whatever you **wish** that men would do to you,
LC : 0 1 :300(405) [0665] upright — to people who **wish** to be commended as
LC : 0 1 :304(406) [0667] Yet no one **wishes** this to happen to himself.
LC : 0 1 :307(406) [0669] learn that God does not **wish** you to deprive your
LC : 0 1 :309(407) [0669] and serviceable to him, as we **wish** that he would do to us.
LC : 0 2 :001(411) [0679] we have seen all that God **wishes** us to do or not to do.
LC : 0 2 :049(417) [0691] by which someone **wished** to explain what the Christian
LC : 0 3 :011(421) [0701] we are sinners; he **wishes** rather to draw us to himself so
LC : 0 3 :027(424) [0705] God therefore **wishes** you to lament and express your
LC : 0 3 :082(431) [0721] Thus, you see, God **wishes** to show us how he cares for us
LC : 0 3 :083(431) [0721] men and rogues, yet he **wishes** us to pray for them so we
LC : 0 4 :016(438) [0735] from which he does not **wish** his ordinance to be
LC : 0 4 :048(442) [0743] But if you **wish** to answer, then say:
LC : 0 4 :085(446) [0753] If we **wish** to be Christians, we must practice the work
LC : 0 5 :002(447) [0753] So everyone who **wishes** to be a Christian and go to the
LC : 0 5 :004(447) [0753] We have no **wish** on this occasion to quarrel and dispute
LC : 0 5 :047(452) [0763] are added because Christ **wishes** the sacrament to be free,
LC : 0 5 :049(452) [0765] But if you **wish** to be a Christian, you must from time to
LC : 0 6 :006(457) [0000] would happen if you **wished** to enjoy the Gospel's
LC : 0 6 :013(458) [0000] time and as often as we **wish** lay our complaint before a
LC : 0 6 :022(459) [0000] a work but to hear what God **wishes** to say to you.
EP : 0 7 :001(481) [0809] and therefore we have **wished** to report as far as necessary
EP : 1 2 :001(498) [0839] be attributed to us, we **wish** here at the end merely to
SD : PR :009(505) [0853] We also **wish** to be regarded as appealing to further
SD : 0 1 :033(514) [0869] the same thing, so, if one **wishes** to speak strictly, one
SD : 0 7 :038(576) [0985] Thereby they **wished** to indicate that, even though they
SD : 0 7 :069(582) [0997] deplore it, and heartily **wish** that they might serve God
SD : 0 7 :103(587) [1007] "I do not **wish** to have denied by the foregoing that God
SD : 1 0 :019(614) [1059] However, they neither are nor **wish** to be true bishops.
SD : 1 1 :013(618) [1067] Hence if we **wish** to think or speak correctly and
SD : 1 1 :028(621) [1071] "The Lord is not **wishing** that any should perish, but that
SD : 1 1 :084(630) [1091] For God "is not **wishing** that any should perish," nor has
SD : 1 2 :040(636) [1103] and our posterity, we **wish** to have testified that the

Wisps (1)
S2 : 0 2 :018(296) [0467] uncertain, harmful will-o'-the-**wisps** of the devil?

Wit (1)
SD : PR :016(507) [0857] and abiding answer in the controverted issues, to **wit**:

Witch (1)
SD : 0 8 :041(599) [1029] he states: "If the old **witch**, Dame Reason, the

Withdraw (3), Withdrawal (1), Withdrawn (1), Withdraws (2), Withdrew (3)
AG : 1 9 :000(041) [0053] men; as soon as God **withdraws** his support, the will
AL : 2 7 :056(080) [0083] administration of the state, **withdrew** into a monastery.
AP : 2 3 :043(245) [0375] sometimes they must **withdraw** to have opportunity for
S2 : 0 2 :028(297) [0469] idolatrous honor is **withdrawn** from angels and dead
TR : 0 0 :012(322) [0507] for the council to **withdraw** any right from him and
LC : 0 3 :083(431) [0721] When he **withdraws** his hand, nothing can prosper or last
SD : 0 2 :066(534) [0907] him, but if God should **withdraw** his gracious hand man
SD : 0 7 :001(568) [0971] Augsburg Confession, **withdrew** from it, and submitted
SD : 0 7 :091(585) [1005] Christ, concerning his **withdrawal** from this world, and
SD : 1 1 :085(630) [1091] and warnings, God **withdrew** his hand from him, and so

Withers (1)
AP : 0 4 :329(158) [0211] The grass **withers**, the flower fades, when the breath of

Withheld (2), Withhold (3), Withholding (6)
AP : 2 2 :006(237) [0359] church why one part of the sacrament has been **withheld**.
AP : 2 2 :012(238) [0361] exonerate those who **withhold** a part of the sacrament
AP : 2 2 :013(238) [0361] If they **withhold** it to make a distinction of orders, this in
AP : 2 2 :015(238) [0361] how can they make the **withholding** of one kind
AP : 2 2 :016(238) [0361] the legitimacy of **withholding** both kinds in the sacrament
SC : PR :005(338) [0533] You **withhold** the cup in the Lord's Supper and insist on
LC : 0 1 :190(391) [0635] or deed, for you have **withheld** your love from him and
LC : 0 1 :250(399) [0651] whether by damaging, **withholding**, or interfering with his
LC : 0 1 :296(405) [0665] prohibits seizing or **withholding** another's possessions to
LC : 0 2 :026(413) [0685] has completely given himself to us, **withholding** nothing.
EP : 0 7 :024(484) [0815] to the laity and the **withholding** of the cup from them,

Within (37)
AG : 2 7 :028(075) [0079] perpetual chastity lies **within** human power and ability,
AP : 0 4 :009(108) [0123] of sins by doing what is **within** them, that is, if reason in
AP : 0 4 :219(137) [0181] (Jer. 31:33), "I will put my law **within** their hearts."
AP : 0 7 :009(169) [0229] number of ungodly **within** the church who oppress it.
AP : 2 4 :026(254) [0391] refers to the operation of the Holy Spirit **within** us.
LC : 0 1 :106(379) [0611] (so to speak) toward a majesty hidden **within** them.
LC : 0 1 :117(381) [0615] because it has its place **within** that jewel and holy
LC : 0 5 :076(455) [0771] that nothing good dwells **within** me, that is, in my flesh."
EP : 0 1 :018(468) [0783] extraneous and alien **within** man, and that therefore not
EP : 0 2 :018(472) [0791] kindling new movements **within** the will, that is, when the
EP : 0 3 :016(475) [0795] as it dwells and works **within** us), and that by such
EP : 1 1 :020(497) [0837] but that there is also **within** us a cause of God's election,
SD : PR :001(503) [0849] and permanent concord **within** the church is a summary
SD : PR :004(504) [0851] at that time had arisen **within** the Christian church are
SD : PR :014(506) [0855] God-pleasing concord **within** the church, it is essential
SD : PR :019(507) [0857] In the third place, since **within** the past twenty-five years
SD : 0 1 :028(513) [0867] exists independently **within** or apart from man's
SD : 0 1 :030(513) [0867] and foreign something **within** man, so that God by his law
SD : 0 1 :033(514) [0869] man's whole nature that **within** the corrupted nature we
SD : 0 1 :033(514) [0869] himself created by God (**within** which original sin, by
SD : 0 2 :017(524) [0887] that nothing good dwells **within** me, that is, in my flesh,
SD : 0 2 :027(527) [0893] is our own work and lies **within** our own power."
SD : 0 2 :027(527) [0893] when I said that it lies **within** our power to believe and to
SD : 0 2 :032(527) [0893] we grant that it lies **within** our power to perform such
SD : 0 2 :047(530) [0901] to work these gifts of his **within** them, since they feel no
SD : 0 2 :069(534) [0907] grieve the Holy Spirit **within** them and lose him, they
SD : 0 2 :077(536) [0911] the continuation and preservation of this work **within** us.
SD : 0 3 :023(543) [0923] them and creates **within** them love toward God and their
SD : 0 3 :047(548) [0933] the renewal which the Holy Spirit works and is **within** us.
SD : 0 3 :063(550) [0937] as it dwells and works **within** us, and that by such
SD : 0 4 :020(554) [0945] in the sense that it lies **within** their free option if they may
SD : 0 6 :008(565) [0965] writes, "I know that nothing good dwells **within** me."
SD : 0 8 :042(599) [1029] And this is likewise **within** the bounds of truth, for you
SD : 1 1 :073(628) [1087] and might of the Spirit **within** themselves, the less they
SD : 1 1 :074(628) [1087] of what they experience **within** themselves, they should
SD : 1 1 :078(629) [1089] who wanted to work **within** them, as was the case with
SD : 1 1 :088(631) [1093] but that there is also **within** us a cause of God's election

Without (512)
PR : PR :003(003) [0007] and appealed to it **without** either controversy or doubt in
PR : PR :008(006) [0011] in it in a Christian way **without** any further disputation
PR : PR :009(006) [0011] of all this we found, not **without** distress on our part, that
PR : PR :011(006) [0011] brought to a conclusion **without** violation of divine truth,
PR : PR :013(007) [0013] and communicate to us **without** reserve their considered
PR : PR :022(012) [0021] Payment for it will **without** doubt be required of the
AG : PR :005(025) [0039] command and can say **without** boasting that we were
AG : 0 1 :003(027) [0043] divine essence, eternal, **without** division, without end, of
AG : 0 1 :003(027) [0043] without division, **without** end, of infinite power, wisdom,
AG : 0 5 :004(031) [0045] thoughts, and works **without** the external word of the
AG : 0 6 :003(032) [0047] through works but through faith alone, **without** merit."
AG : 1 4 :000(036) [0049] the sacraments in the church **without** a regular call.
AG : 1 5 :001(036) [0049] which may be observed **without** sin and which contribute
AG : 1 6 :002(037) [0051] and that Christians may **without** sin occupy civil offices
AG : 1 6 :006(038) [0051] commands and laws in all that can be done **without** sin.
AG : 1 6 :007(038) [0051] cannot be obeyed **without** sin, we must obey God rather
AG : 1 8 :002(039) [0051] But **without** the grace, help, and activity of the Holy
AG : 1 8 :006(040) [0053] None of these is or exists **without** God, but all things are
AG : 2 0 :022(044) [0055] of God is appropriated **without** merits, through faith
AG : 2 0 :024(044) [0057] calls upon him, and is not, like the heathen, **without** God.
AG : 2 0 :031(045) [0057] Before that, when it is **without** the Holy Spirit, the heart
AG : 2 0 :034(045) [0057] happens when a man is **without** true faith and the Holy
AG : 2 0 :036(046) [0057] For **without** faith and without Christ human nature and
AG : 2 0 :036(046) [0057] For without faith and **without** Christ human nature and
AG : 2 0 :038(046) [0057] works cannot be done **without** the help of Christ, as he
AG : 0 0 :001(048) [0059] and love, and do so **without** any solid basis of divine
AG : 2 3 :006(052) [0061] resolutions or vows **without** a special gift or grace of
AG : 0 1 :009(056) [0065] **Without** boasting, it is manifest that the Mass is observed
AG : 2 4 :024(058) [0067] Demanded **without** doubt by the necessity of such
AG : 2 4 :030(059) [0067] requires faith, and **without** faith it is used in vain.
AG : 2 4 :041(061) [0069] Alexandria, and all these services were held **without** Mass.
AG : 2 5 :005(062) [0069] tormented consciences **without** long enumerations of
AG : 2 6 :041(070) [0075] they are to be observed **without** burdening consciences,
AG : 2 6 :041(070) [0075] a sin to omit them if this is done **without** causing scandal.

Continued ▶

A G : 2 7 :013(073) [0077] God's Word and command **without** invented spirituality.
A G : 2 7 :017(073) [0077] All this is mentioned, **without** misrepresentation, in order
A G : 2 7 :027(075) [0079] that vows must be kept **without** first ascertaining whether
A G : 2 7 :036(076) [0081] and God's grace **without** the command and authority of
A G : 2 7 :048(078) [0081] of God, invented by men **without** the command of God,
A G : 2 7 :053(079) [0083] keep his possessions and engage in business **without** sin.
A G : 2 8 :052(089) [0091] through faith in Christ **without** our merits; we do not
A G : 2 8 :053(090) [0091] their observance even when this is done **without** offense.
A G : 2 8 :056(090) [0091] woman commits a sin if **without** offense to others she
A G : 2 8 :069(093) [0093] of regulations which cannot be kept **without** sin.
A G : 2 8 :075(094) [0095] are not to be observed **without** sin, we are bound to follow
A G : 0 0 :005(095) [0095] and evident (to speak **without** boasting) that we have
A L : 0 1 :001(027) [0043] is true and should be believed **without** any doubting.
A L : 0 2 :001(029) [0043] That is to say, they are **without** fear of God, are without
A L : 0 2 :001(029) [0043] without fear of God, are **without** trust in God, and are
A L : 0 5 :004(031) [0045] Holy Spirit comes to men **without** the external Word,
A L : 0 8 :003(033) [0047] ministry of evil men to be unprofitable and **without** effect.
A L : 0 9 :003(033) [0047] and declare that children are saved **without** Baptism.
A L : 1 5 :001(036) [0049] which can be observed **without** sin and which contribute
A L : 1 7 :003(038) [0051] and devils he will condemn to be tormented **without** end.
A L : 1 8 :002(039) [0051] does not have the power, **without** the Holy Spirit, to
A L : 1 8 :004(039) [0051] does not enable them, **without** God, to begin or (much
A L : 1 8 :006(040) [0053] None of these exists **without** the providence of God;
A L : 1 8 :008(040) [0053] others who teach that **without** the Holy Spirit, by the
A L : 2 0 :010(042) [0055] and seeks a way to God **without** Christ, by human
A L : 2 0 :025(044) [0057] He is not **without** God, as are the heathen, for devils and
A L : 2 0 :031(045) [0057] For **without** the Holy Spirit man's powers are full of
A L : 2 0 :034(045) [0057] by human strength alone **without** faith and without the
A L : 2 0 :034(045) [0057] strength alone without faith and **without** the Holy Spirit.
A L : 2 0 :036(046) [0057] For **without** faith human nature cannot possibly do the
A L : 2 0 :037(046) [0057] **Without** faith it does not call upon God, expect anything
A L : 0 0 :002(047) [0059] have crept into the churches **without** proper authority.
A L : 2 3 :006(052) [0061] to alter his creation **without** a singular gift and work of
A L : 2 6 :010(065) [0071] to callings were **without** honor — for example, that a
A L : 2 6 :029(068) [0075] righteousness cannot exist **without** such acts of worship.
A L : 2 6 :041(070) [0075] no sin is committed if they are omitted **without** scandal.
A L : 2 7 :013(073) [0077] and the like who, **without** man-made observances, serve
A L : 2 7 :017(073) [0077] rehearsed these things **without** odious exaggeration in
A L : 2 7 :036(076) [0081] justification and grace **without** the command of God is
A L : 2 7 :048(078) [0081] service invented by men **without** the command of God
A L : 2 8 :021(084) [0087] is known, doing all this **without** human power, simply by
A L : 2 8 :055(090) [0091] churches may be done in order and **without** confusion.
A L : 2 8 :056(090) [0091] those who omit them **without** offense to others commit a
A L : 2 8 :068(093) [0093] that canons are kept **without** holding them to be
A L : 2 8 :075(094) [0095] which cannot be kept **without** sin, we are bound to follow
A L : 2 8 :077(094) [0095] some few observances which cannot be kept **without** sin.
A P : P R :002(098) [0099] would produce the document **without** hesitation.
A P : 0 2 :001(100) [0105] They say that being **without** the fear of God and faith is
A P : 0 2 :005(101) [0107] bear because of his guilt, **without** any evil of their own.
A P : 0 2 :023(103) [0111] cannot be produced **without** certain gifts and help of
A P : 0 2 :048(106) [0119] cannot be conquered **without** Christ's help, so we cannot
A P : 0 4 :009(108) [0123] works—and maintain that **without** the Holy Spirit reason
A P : 0 4 :018(109) [0125] this disposition, yet **without** the righteousness of faith
A P : 0 4 :034(112) [0129] But **without** the Holy Spirit, the human heart either
A P : 0 4 :035(112) [0131] they do virtuous things **without** the Holy Spirit; for they
A P : 0 4 :063(115) [0139] Spirit *ex opere operato* **without** the proper attitude in the
A P : 0 4 :089(120) [0149] would not be accounted for righteousness **without** works.
A P : 0 4 :126(124) [0157] to keep the law **without** Christ; it is impossible to keep
A P : 0 4 :126(124) [0157] it is impossible to keep the law **without** the Holy Spirit.
A P : 0 4 :130(125) [0157] works of the law, **without** Christ and the Holy Spirit, still
A P : 0 4 :130(125) [0157] law, are impossible **without** the Holy Spirit; this is
A P : 0 4 :135(126) [0159] From this it is clear that **without** Christ and without the
A P : 0 4 :135(126) [0159] that without Christ and **without** the Holy Spirit we
A P : 0 4 :154(128) [0165] It was not **without** reason that this truly powerful
A P : 0 4 :167(130) [0169] **Without** this, the law always accuses us.
A P : 0 4 :184(132) [0173] the law cannot be kept **without** Christ, and that if civil
A P : 0 4 :184(132) [0173] if civil works are done **without** Christ they do not please
A P : 0 4 :211(136) [0179] but only their behavior **without** their faith in order by
A P : 0 4 :214(136) [0179] because of our works **without** Christ, the mediator.
A P : 0 4 :222(138) [0181] have access to God even **without** Christ, the propitiator;
A P : 0 4 :222(138) [0181] even to be dreamed **without** Christ, the propitiator.
A P : 0 4 :223(138) [0181] and can have access to God **without** him as propitiator.
A P : 0 4 :238(141) [0187] or that love is righteousness **without** Christ, the mediator.
A P : 0 4 :243(141) [0189] It is not **without** reason that the apostles speak so often
A P : 0 4 :246(142) [0189] we have access to God **without** Christ, the propitiator.
A P : 0 4 :250(143) [0191] in denying that we are justified by a faith **without** works.
A P : 0 4 :253(143) [0193] that works please God **without** Christ, the propitiator;
A P : 0 4 :255(144) [0193] that sins are forgiven **without** faith or that these works
A P : 0 4 :256(144) [0193] entire law (Heb. 11:6), "**Without** faith it is impossible to
A P : 0 4 :268(147) [0197] come forgiveness of sins and justification **without** works.
A P : 0 4 :269(147) [0197] that the law is not kept **without** Christ—as he himself has
A P : 0 4 :269(147) [0197] (John 15:5)—and that "**without** faith it is impossible to
A P : 0 4 :269(147) [0197] they do not please him **without** Christ, the propitiator.
A P : 0 4 :269(147) [0197] (Rom. 5:2), not by works **without** Christ, the mediator.
A P : 0 4 :270(147) [0197] keep the commandments or please God **without** Christ.
A P : 0 4 :270(147) [0197] But **without** Christ this law is not kept.
A P : 0 4 :276(148) [0199] justify *ex opere operato* **without** faith, so almsgiving does
A P : 0 4 :276(148) [0199] does not justify *ex opere operato* **without** faith.
A P : 0 4 :277(148) [0199] back to the rule that **without** Christ the teaching of the
A P : 0 4 :280(149) [0201] reply to a single passage **without** taking the whole law
A P : 0 4 :290(151) [0203] **Without** any warrant it teaches that men come to God
A P : 0 4 :290(151) [0203] very keeping of the law **with[out]** Christ, the propitiator, is
A P : 0 4 :294(152) [0203] We cannot come to God **without** Christ, the mediator;
A P : 0 4 :302(154) [0205] they echo the word "love" **without** understanding it.
A P : 0 4 :303(154) [0205] This does not come **without** a great battle in the human
A P : 0 4 :314(156) [0207] God by love and merits **without** Christ, the mediator,
A P : 0 4 :315(156) [0207] It is also clear that **without** the help of Christ we cannot
A P : 0 4 :316(156) [0209] and earns eternal life **without** needing Christ, the
A P : 0 4 :319(156) [0209] because of Christ, how will it have peace **without** faith?
A P : 0 4 :321(157) [0209] to doubt and to work **without** faith until despair ensues.
A P : 0 4 :322(157) [0209] praiseworthy, if it is to be judged **without** mercy."
A P : 0 4 :333(158) [0211] name," he says, because **without** the high priest we
A P : 0 4 :350(161) [0217] No one learns this **without** many severe struggles.
A P : 0 4 :350(161) [0217] is not erased **without** a great conflict in which experience
A P : 0 4 :357(162) [0219] of grace and eternal life **without** needing mercy or the
A P : 0 4 :372(164) [0221] good works please God **without** the mediator Christ and
A P : 0 4 :372(164) [0221] according to Heb. 11:6, "**Without** faith it is impossible to
A P : 0 4 :377(165) [0223] in the church of Christ; **without** it the work of Christ
A P : 0 4 :388(166) [0225] the law cannot be kept **without** Christ, and that we are
A P : 0 7 :007(169) [0229] before him in splendor, **without** spot or wrinkle or any
A P : 0 7 :007(169) [0229] such thing, that it might be holy and **without** blemish."
A P : 0 7 :021(172) [0233] justify *ex opere operato,* **without** a good attitude in the
A P : 0 7 :031(174) [0237] true spiritual unity, **without** which there can be no faith in
A P : 0 7 :032(174) [0239] of the heart before God **without** these observances.
A P : 0 7 :045(177) [0243] clothing, and similar matters **without** divine command.
A P : 1 2 :012(184) [0257] grace *ex opere operato,* **without** a right attitude in the
A P : 1 2 :025(185) [0259] grace *ex opere operato,* **without** the proper attitude in the
A P : 1 2 :025(185) [0259] attitude in the recipient, that is, **without** faith in Christ.
A P : 1 2 :037(186) [0261] For the law is not kept **without** Christ, according to the
A P : 1 2 :046(188) [0263] with a circumcision made **without** hands, by putting off
A P : 1 2 :046(188) [0263] which nature could not bear **without** the support of faith.
A P : 1 2 :061(190) [0269] see what value there is in confession **without** absolution.
A P : 1 2 :064(191) [0269] the heart can find peace **without** faith in Christ do not
A P : 1 2 :069(192) [0271] the errors of their superiors, **without** understanding them.
A P : 1 2 :084(194) [0277] a firm consolation **without** which no one can stand before
A P : 1 2 :086(194) [0277] contends that we cannot keep the law **without** Christ.
A P : 1 2 :089(195) [0279] So their whole life is **without** God and without the true
A P : 1 2 :089(195) [0279] life is without God and **without** the true worship of God.
A P : 1 2 :110(198) [0285] the forgiveness of sins **without** enumerating all their sins.
A P : 1 2 :112(198) [0285] were not accepted **without** certain satisfactions, they
A P : 1 2 :112(198) [0285] confession was not that **without** it there could be no
A P : 1 2 :112(198) [0285] could not be prescribed **without** knowing the character of
A P : 1 2 :119(200) [0287] is a recent fiction, **without** authority either in the
A P : 1 2 :153(206) [0299] as long as it is present; **without** this sense of wrath death
A P : 1 2 :175(210) [0307] obsolete, and that **without** objection from the bishops,
A P : 1 3 :003(211) [0309] Hence signs instituted **without** God's command are not
A P : 1 3 :018(213) [0313] grace *ex opere operato,* **without** a good disposition in the
A P : 1 3 :018(213) [0313] justified by a ceremony **without** a good disposition in our
A P : 1 3 :018(213) [0313] a good disposition in our heart, that is, **without** faith.
A P : 1 3 :023(214) [0313] *ex opere operato* **without** a good disposition in the one
A P : 1 5 :001(215) [0315] which can be observed **without** sin and which are
A P : 1 5 :014(217) [0319] men of God's will **without** the command and Word of
A P : 1 5 :014(217) [0319] of additional ceremonies **without** his command?
A P : 1 5 :017(217) [0319] rites established by men **without** God's command can
A P : 1 5 :017(217) [0319] nothing about the will of God **without** the Word of God?
A P : 1 5 :017(217) [0319] cannot maintain this **without** the Word and testimony of
A P : 1 5 :024(218) [0321] copy their outward behavior **without** copying their faith.
A P : 1 5 :035(220) [0325] them, let him do so **without** claiming any value before
A P : 1 5 :051(222) [0329] in the accustomed rites **without** good reason, and to
A P : 1 5 :051(222) [0329] kept which can be kept **without** sin or without great
A P : 1 5 :051(222) [0329] can be kept without sin or **without** great disadvantage.
A P : 1 5 :052(222) [0329] possible public harmony, **without** offense to consciences,
A P : 1 6 :001(222) [0329] Our opponents approve Article XVI **without** exception.
A P : 1 7 :001(224) [0335] Our opponents accept Article XVII **without** exception.
A P : 1 8 :002(225) [0335] since both believe that **without** the Holy Spirit men can
A P : 1 8 :002(225) [0335] commandments and that **without** the Holy Spirit men can
A P : 1 8 :004(225) [0335] can achieve on its own **without** the Holy Spirit, Scripture
A P : 1 8 :006(225) [0335] **Without** the Holy Spirit human hearts have neither the
A P : 1 8 :006(225) [0335] fruit" (Matt. 7:18) and "**without** faith it is impossible to
A P : 1 8 :007(226) [0337] the human heart cannot perform **without** the Holy Spirit.
A P : 1 8 :010(226) [0337] can obey the law of God **without** the Holy Spirit and that
A P : 2 1 :010(230) [0345] How do we know, **without** proof from Scripture, that the
A P : 2 1 :013(230) [0345] uncertain, for prayer **without** faith is not prayer.
A P : 2 1 :035(234) [0353] one who calls upon her should die **without** the Eucharist.
A P : 2 3 :002(239) [0363] abandon cannot even be mentioned **without** blushing.
A P : 2 3 :007(240) [0365] cannot be suspended **without** an extraordinary work of
A P : 2 3 :008(240) [0367] the nature of man **without** an extraordinary act of God.
A P : 2 3 :020(242) [0369] tried to control their body but **without** much success.
A P : 2 3 :064(248) [0381] We have said that **without** faith virginity is not pure in
A P : 2 4 :016(252) [0389] of distinctions because **without** them nothing can be
A P : 2 4 :041(257) [0399] the world, and they rule **without** regard for religion and
A P : 2 4 :044(258) [0399] altars standing unadorned, **without** candles or statues.
A P : 2 4 :064(261) [0407] of the sacrament, though **without** faith the Mass does not
A P : 2 4 :070(262) [0409] the ceremony is useless **without** the faith which really
A P : 2 4 :077(263) [0411] worshiper or anyone else **without** faith conflicts with the
A P : 2 4 :087(265) [0413] provide an advantage *ex opere operato* **without** faith.
A P : 2 4 :089(265) [0413] services in the church **without** the command of God and
A P : 2 4 :089(266) [0415] Gospel to maintain that **without** faith, *ex opere operato,* a
A P : 2 4 :092(266) [0415] *ex opere operato* and **without** faith, it follows that it is
A P : 2 4 :092(266) [0417] services in the church **without** the authority of Scripture.
A P : 2 4 :099(268) [0419] and now we have replied **without** casting any reproach.
A P : 2 7 :007(269) [0421] **Without** doubt, God will soon avenge these murders.
A P : 2 7 :009(270) [0421] at public expense **without** the loss of their private
A P : 2 7 :021(272) [0427] the saints can use them **without** sinning, as did Bernard,
A P : 2 7 :022(272) [0427] Word who follow these observances **without** wicked ideas.
A P : 2 7 :041(276) [0435] One happens **without** a call, without a command of God;
A P : 2 7 :041(276) [0435] happens without a call, **without** a command of God; this
A P : 2 7 :042(276) [0435] and to leave our body **without** the command of God.
A P : 2 7 :042(276) [0435] friends, wife, and children **without** the command of God.
A P : 2 7 :057(279) [0439] who took their vows **without** proper judgment because
A P : 2 7 :058(279) [0439] monasticism, thought up **without** a Word of God as an
A P : 2 8 :014(283) [0447] power of a tyrant to act **without** a definite law, nor that
A P : 2 8 :017(284) [0449] them in their place and **without** superstition, in order to
S 1 : P R :001(288) [0455] the council or be condemned **without** being summoned.
S 1 : P R :002(288) [0455] in good faith, and **without** deception or treachery to hold
S 1 : 0 1 :000(291) [0461] by the Holy Spirit, **without** the cooperation of man, and
S 2 : 0 2 :003(293) [0463] and so it can be omitted **without** sin and danger.
S 2 : 0 2 :005(293) [0463] can be omitted **without** sin, that no one will be damned
S 2 : 0 2 :005(293) [0463] that one can be saved in a better way **without** the Mass.
S 2 : 0 2 :005(293) [0463] fabricated and invented **without** God's Word and will?
S 2 : 0 2 :006(293) [0463] would be prudent to do **without** the Mass for no other
S 2 : 0 2 :006(293) [0463] more useful, and more certain **without** the Mass.
S 2 : 0 2 :008(294) [0465] opinion and imagination **without** the sanction of God's
S 2 : 0 2 :014(295) [0467] accepted when they are **without** the support of the
S 2 : 0 2 :018(296) [0467] way and may omit pilgrimages **without** sin and danger.
S 2 : 0 2 :021(296) [0469] utterly unnecessary and **without** command, but it is

Continued ▶

S 2 : 0 2 :024(296) [0469] are they unnecessary and **without** commandment, but
S 2 : 0 2 :024(296) [0469] by grace, through faith, **without** our work or pennies.
S 2 : 0 2 :024(296) [0469] They are offered to us **without** our money or merit, not
S 2 : 0 3 :002(298) [0471] inventions, all this is **without** commandment,
S 2 : 0 4 :004(299) [0473] that the holy church was **without** a pope for more that
S 2 : 0 4 :005(299) [0473] can exist very well **without** such a head, and it would
S 2 : 0 4 :006(299) [0473] the church must continue to exist **without** the pope.
S 2 : 0 4 :008(299) [0473] and would ultimately be **without** any adherents at all.
S 2 : 0 4 :014(301) [0475] fantasies, and follies **without** so much as a mention of
S 3 : 0 1 :002(302) [0477] belief, idolatry, being **without** the fear of God,
S 3 : 0 2 :004(303) [0479] not have believed before **without** a knowledge of the law.
S 3 : 0 3 :007(304) [0481] exercises its office alone, **without** the addition of the
S 3 : 0 3 :018(306) [0483] to its own inventions, **without** being able to consider
S 3 : 0 3 :018(306) [0483] by man's own powers **without** faith and without
S 3 : 0 3 :018(306) [0483] powers without faith and **without** knowledge of Christ.
S 3 : 0 3 :028(308) [0487] were, as we taught, **without** sin and full of good works,
S 3 : 0 3 :032(308) [0487] No man can be just before God **without** him.
S 3 : 0 3 :037(309) [0489] all sins in his confession **without** omitting or forgetting a
S 3 : 0 6 :005(311) [0493] and shape of bread **without** any longer being real bread,
S 3 : 0 8 :003(312) [0495] they possess the Spirit **without** and before the Word and
S 3 : 0 8 :003(312) [0495] the letter and the spirit **without** knowing what they say or
S 3 : 0 8 :006(312) [0495] comes to the people **without** and before their writings
S 3 : 0 8 :006(313) [0495] Spirit came upon them **without** the testimony of the
S 3 : 0 8 :011(313) [0497] received the Spirit **without** the Ten Commandments.
S 3 : 0 8 :012(313) [0497] was not conceived **without** the preceding word of
S 3 : 0 8 :013(313) [0497] But **without** the external Word they were not holy, and
S 3 : 1 0 :001(314) [0497] this could be done **without** pretense, humbug, and
S 3 : 1 0 :003(314) [0497] was originally governed **without** bishops by priests and
S 3 : 1 5 :005(316) [0501] Such frauds, which are **without** number, we commend for
T R : 0 0 :009(321) [0505] disciples out as equals, **without** discrimination, when he
T R : 0 0 :010(321) [0505] he at once preached the Gospel **without** consulting Peter.
T R : 0 0 :031(325) [0513] excommunicate the godless **without** physical violence.
T R : 0 0 :055(329) [0521] tyranny and wickedness **without** any regard for the Word
T R : 0 0 :074(332) [0525] and excommunicated them **without** due process of law.
T R : 0 0 :074(332) [0525] power to ban men arbitrarily **without** due process of law!
T R : 0 0 :075(333) [0525] nobody should be condemned **without** due process of law.
T R : 0 0 :081(334) [0527] cannot be established **without** the endowments of the
S C : P R :015(340) [0535] and adhere to them **without** changing a single syllable, as
S C : P R :022(341) [0537] of their own accord and **without** any law, the people will
S C : P R :024(341) [0539] of their own accord and **without** compulsion on your
S C : 0 2 :002(345) [0543] goodness and mercy, **without** any merit or worthiness on
S C : 0 3 :007(346) [0547] of God comes of itself, **without** our prayer, but we pray in
S C : 0 3 :010(347) [0547] will of God is done **without** our prayer, but we pray in
S C : 0 3 :013(347) [0547] even to the wicked, **without** our prayer, but we pray in
S C : 0 4 :010(349) [0551] For **without** the Word of God the water is merely water
L C : P R :006(359) [0569] declare that we can do **without** pastors and preachers
L C : P R :014(360) [0571] and command this so solemnly **without** good reason.
L C : P R :016(361) [0573] teaching this one thing **without** varying it with anything
L C : S P :026(364) [0581] thus the preaching will not be **without** benefit and fruit.
L C : 0 1 :059(372) [0597] We prefer to act in secret **without** anyone's being aware
L C : 0 1 :090(377) [0607] and ringing bells, **without** sanctifying the holy day
L C : 0 1 :095(378) [0607] no holy day is sanctified **without** it, we must realize that
L C : 0 1 :097(378) [0609] to and admonished but we listen **without** serious concern.
L C : 0 1 :101(379) [0609] use, such is its power that it never departs **without** fruit.
L C : 0 1 :114(380) [0613] we have devised **without** ever asking God's approval.
L C : 0 1 :120(381) [0615] with fasting and pray on their knees **without** ceasing"?
L C : 0 1 :130(383) [0619] matter in this light will, **without** compulsion, give all
L C : 0 1 :134(383) [0619] good government, etc., **without** which this life can neither
L C : 0 1 :155(386) [0625] that we have nothing but unhappiness **without** mercy.
L C : 0 1 :173(388) [0629] and make them rich **without** our help, as indeed he does
L C : 0 1 :197(392) [0637] might live a nice, soft life **without** the cross and suffering.
L C : 0 1 :212(393) [0641] have their way **without** let or hindrance, as everyone's
L C : 0 1 :219(394) [0643] always follows spontaneously **without** any command.
L C : 0 1 :221(395) [0643] estates" that are chosen **without** God's Word and
L C : 0 1 :240(397) [0649] goods as dearly as he pleases **without** a word of criticism.
L C : 0 1 :274(402) [0659] the law into their own hands **without** such a commission.
L C : 0 1 :284(403) [0661] are aware of it, you can **without** sin shun and avoid the
L C : 0 1 :296(405) [0665] could do it honorably, **without** accusation or blame for
L C : 0 1 :299(405) [0665] using them for pretexts, **without** regard for equity or for
L C : 0 1 :303(406) [0667] property, nor yet sell it **without** loss — he hurries and
L C : 0 1 :304(406) [0667] forced to sacrifice what he cannot spare **without** injury.
L C : 0 1 :331(410) [0677] Therefore it is not **without** reason that the Old Testament
L C : 0 2 :017(412) [0681] pure love and goodness, **without** our merit, as a kind
L C : 0 2 :019(412) [0681] praise, and thank him **without** ceasing, and, in short, to
L C : 0 2 :031(414) [0687] man, conceived and born **without** sin, of the Holy Spirit
L C : 0 2 :043(416) [0689] won for us this treasure **without** our works and merits
L C : 0 2 :051(417) [0691] of gifts, yet is united in love **without** sect or schism.
L C : 0 2 :054(418) [0693] are encumbered with our flesh we are never **without** sin.
L C : 0 2 :070(420) [0697] for the common people **without** overburdening them.
L C : 0 3 :024(423) [0705] ought to drive and impel us to pray **without** ceasing.
L C : 0 3 :050(426) [0711] kingdom comes of itself **without** our prayer and yet we
L C : 0 3 :058(428) [0713] belly, let alone expect, **without** doubting, eternal blessings
L C : 0 3 :064(429) [0715] For this end he strives **without** rest day and night, using
L C : 0 3 :067(429) [0717] every other case to pray **without** ceasing: "Thy will be
L C : 0 3 :068(429) [0717] otherwise must be done **without** us may also be done in
L C : 0 3 :068(429) [0717] must come even **without** our prayer, so must his will be
L C : 0 3 :068(429) [0717] may be done among us **without** hindrance, in spite of
L C : 0 3 :075(430) [0719] and peace and that **without** them we could not have the
L C : 0 3 :086(432) [0723] gift and blessing, nevertheless we are not **without** sin.
L C : 0 3 :088(432) [0723] does not forgive sin even **without** and before our prayer;
L C : 0 3 :100(433) [0725] is not accomplished **without** failures and stumbling.
L C : 0 4 :001(436) [0733] in them because **without** these no one can be a Christian,
L C : 0 4 :034(440) [0741] **Without** faith Baptism is of no use, although in itself it is
L C : 0 4 :035(441) [0741] rather demand faith, for **without** faith they could not be
L C : 0 4 :037(441) [0741] as so necessary that **without** it nothing can be received or
L C : 0 4 :049(442) [0745] know Christ, which is impossible **without** the Holy Spirit.
L C : 0 5 :004(447) [0755] was instituted by Christ **without** man's counsel or
L C : 0 5 :040(451) [0763] or more years go by **without** receiving the sacrament, as
L C : 0 5 :047(452) [0765] of the first full moon, **without** variation of a single day.
L C : 0 5 :049(452) [0765] period of time elapse **without** ever desiring the
L C : 0 5 :051(452) [0765] men's commandments, **without** joy and love and even
L C : 0 5 :051(452) [0765] joy and love and even **without** regard for Christ's
L C : 0 5 :061(453) [0767] to confession pure and **without** sin; on the contrary, we
L C : 0 6 :004(457) [0000] so that we may confess **without** coercion or fear, and we
E P : 0 1 :001(466) [0779] is if, strictly and **without** any distinction, original sin is
E P : 0 1 :002(466) [0779] man pure and holy and **without** sin, but also as we now
E P : 0 1 :005(466) [0781] human nature, though **without** sin, and thus took on
E P : 0 1 :010(467) [0781] arise and live forever, **without** original sin and completely
E P : 0 1 :011(467) [0781] else's wrongdoing, **without** any kind of corruption of our
E P : 0 1 :019(468) [0783] sin is strictly and **without** any distinction corrupted man's
E P : 0 1 :020(468) [0783] not in order to identify **without** any distinction man's
E P : 0 2 :004(470) [0787] not effect conversion **without** means; he employs to this
E P : 0 2 :006(470) [0787] **Without** his grace our "will and effort," our planting,
E P : 0 2 :009(471) [0789] that by his own powers, **without** the grace of the Holy
E P : 0 2 :010(471) [0789] could not complete it **without** the grace of the Holy
E P : 0 2 :013(471) [0789] them, and saves them **without** means, without the hearing
E P : 0 2 :013(471) [0789] them without means, **without** the hearing of God's Word
E P : 0 2 :013(471) [0789] of God's Word and **without** the use of the holy
E P : 0 2 :015(471) [0789] statements are made **without** explanation that man's will
E P : 0 3 :004(473) [0793] sins purely by his grace, **without** any preceding, present,
E P : 0 3 :010(474) [0795] as *"by grace,"* "**without** merit," "without the law,"
E P : 0 3 :010(474) [0795] *grace,"* "without merit," "**without** the law," "without
E P : 0 3 :010(474) [0795] "without the law," "**without** works," "not by works," etc.
E P : 0 3 :020(475) [0797] incomplete and imperfect **without** such love and renewal.
E P : 0 3 :023(475) [0797] faith does not justify **without** good works, in such a way
E P : 0 4 :002(475) [0797] impossible to be saved **without** good works; and that no
E P : 0 4 :002(475) [0797] and that no one has ever been saved **without** good works.
E P : 0 4 :016(477) [0801] one has ever been saved **without** good works; likewise,
E P : 0 4 :016(477) [0801] that it is impossible to be saved **without** good works.
E P : 0 5 :005(478) [0803] and paid for all guilt and **without** man's merit has
E P : 0 6 :002(480) [0805] are not on that account **without** the law; on the contrary,
E P : 0 6 :002(480) [0805] the Fall did not live **without** the law, for the law of God
E P : 0 6 :007(481) [0807] But the believer **without** any coercion and with a willing
E P : 0 7 :042(486) [0817] we herewith condemn **without** any qualification the
E P : 1 1 :013(496) [0835] of pure grace in Christ **without** any merit of our own, and
E P : 1 1 :015(496) [0835] out of pure grace alone, **without** any merit of ours, saves
E P : 1 1 :019(497) [0837] purpose, and will, **without** regard for their sin, God has
E P : 1 2 :006(498) [0839] saved in this innocence **without** Baptism (which according
E P : 1 2 :008(498) [0839] 6. That **without** and prior to Baptism the children of
E P : 1 2 :014(499) [0841] arises no Christian, **without** violating his conscience, may
S D : 0 1 :017(511) [0865] someone else's action **without** any corruption of our own
S D : 0 1 :043(515) [0873] our nature, though **without** sin, so that in every respect he
S D : 0 1 :046(516) [0873] of this our flesh, but **without** sin, shall arise, and that in
S D : 0 1 :046(516) [0873] have and keep precisely this soul, although **without** sin.
S D : 0 1 :047(516) [0875] since we there shall be **without** sin, or else that sin would
S D : 0 1 :054(518) [0877] (that is, a division **without** a middle term), so that every
S D : 0 1 :056(518) [0877] terminology freely and **without** incurring suspicion, and
S D : 0 1 :056(518) [0877] and for that reason **without** ever being corrected either by
S D : 0 2 :003(520) [0881] by his own powers and **without** the gift of the Holy Spirit
S D : 0 2 :003(520) [0881] though weakly, but that **without** the gift of the Holy
S D : 0 2 :004(520) [0881] through the Holy Spirit **without** any means or created
S D : 0 2 :004(520) [0881] instruments (that is, **without** the external preaching and
S D : 0 2 :005(521) [0881] purely out of grace and **without** any cooperation on his
S D : 0 2 :019(524) [0889] he is converted to God **without** hearing and meditating
S D : 0 2 :029(527) [0893] outside of Christ and **without** faith and the Holy Spirit
S D : 0 2 :029(527) [0893] reason and power **without** Christ is much too weak for
S D : 0 2 :031(527) [0893] "Hearts which are **without** the Holy Spirit are without
S D : 0 2 :031(527) [0893] the Holy Spirit are **without** fear of God, without faith, do
S D : 0 2 :031(527) [0893] are without fear of God, **without** faith, do not trust or
S D : 0 2 :031(527) [0893] them in their troubles; therefore they are **without** God.
S D : 0 2 :032(527) [0893] bear good fruit, and **without** faith no one can please
S D : 0 2 :044(529) [0897] **Without** this our heart of itself does not once think to turn
S D : 0 2 :046(530) [0899] them out of heaven, **without** means, and they are able
S D : 0 2 :066(534) [0907] no means be conceded **without** detriment to the divine
S D : 0 2 :075(536) [0911] his own natural powers, **without** the Holy Spirit, the free
S D : 0 2 :080(536) [0911] who imagine that **without** means, without hearing the
S D : 0 2 :080(536) [0911] that without means, **without** hearing the divine Word and
S D : 0 2 :080(536) [0911] the divine Word and **without** the use of the holy
S D : 0 2 :082(537) [0913] if they are used **without** explanation: that man's will
S D : 0 2 :089(538) [0915] conversion takes place **without** the preaching and the
S D : 0 3 :006(540) [0917] Christian doctrine," "**without** which no poor conscience
S D : 0 3 :006(540) [0917] pure, in beautiful harmony, and **without** any schisms.
S D : 0 3 :007(540) [0917] are excluded, such as "**without** the law," "without works,"
S D : 0 3 :007(540) [0917] as "without the law," "**without** works," "by grace alone."
S D : 0 3 :009(540) [0919] an heir of eternal life) **without** any merit or worthiness on
S D : 0 3 :009(541) [0919] on our part, and **without** any preceding, present, or
S D : 0 3 :022(543) [0923] and continue therein **without** repentance, conversion, and
S D : 0 3 :023(543) [0923] through faith alone, **without** any work or merit, are
S D : 0 3 :023(543) [0923] righteousness to us, **without** the addition of our works, so
S D : 0 3 :026(543) [0923] faith in those who live **without** contrition and sorrow and
S D : 0 3 :033(545) [0927] the sake of the Mediator **without** the addition of his own
S D : 0 3 :034(545) [0927] God reckons righteousness **without** the addition of works.
S D : 0 3 :036(545) [0927] by faith) as "**without** works," "without the law," "freely,"
S D : 0 3 :036(545) [0927] as "without works," "**without** the law," "freely," "not of
S D : 0 3 :036(545) [0927] could well be true faith **without** contrition, or as though
S D : 0 3 :041(546) [0931] faith alone which apprehends the blessing **without** works.
S D : 0 3 :042(547) [0931] that faith alone justifies **without** works when, as we have
S D : 0 3 :042(547) [0931] by such a faith as is **without** works, which is a dead
S D : 0 3 :043(547) [0931] Faith cannot justify **without** works; or, faith justifies or
S D : 0 3 :043(547) [0931] justification, as a cause **without** which a person cannot be
S D : 0 3 :049(548) [0933] incomplete or imperfect **without** such love and renewal.
S D : 0 3 :052(548) [0933] solely through faith **without** works but that we cannot be
S D : 0 3 :052(548) [0933] that we cannot be saved **without** works or that salvation
S D : 0 3 :052(548) [0933] or that salvation cannot be obtained **without** works.
S D : 0 3 :053(548) [0933] God reckons righteousness **without** works (Rom. 4:6).
S D : 0 3 :053(548) [0933] such as "by grace" and "**without** works") just as
S D : 0 3 :056(549) [0935] by the Holy Spirit **without** sin and had been born and had
S D : 0 3 :056(549) [0935] the human nature alone, **without** the divine nature, could
S D : 0 3 :056(549) [0935] Likewise, the deity alone, **without** the humanity, could
S D : 0 4 :001(551) [0939] impossible to be saved **without** good works," and "No one
S D : 0 4 :001(551) [0939] "No one has been saved **without** good works," since good
S D : 0 4 :001(551) [0939] of faith and since faith **without** love is dead, although
S D : 0 4 :011(553) [0941] of faith and good works **without** knowing what either
S D : 0 4 :012(553) [0941] by faith, and therefore **without** any coercion a man is
S D : 0 4 :015(553) [0943] faith or superstition, **without** repentance and without
S D : 0 4 :015(553) [0943] without repentance and **without** good works, as if there

Continued ▶

SD : 0 4 :022(554) [0945] impossible to be saved **without** good works, since such
SD : 0 4 :024(555) [0945] Confession, "We are saved **without** works solely by faith."
SD : 0 4 :031(556) [0947] follows his evil lusts **without** fear and shame, resists the
SD : 0 4 :033(556) [0947] works can be instilled **without** darkening the doctrine of
SD : 0 4 :036(557) [0949] Holy Scripture **without** in any way intending to confirm
SD : 0 4 :038(557) [0951] that one may say **without** any qualifications that good
SD : 0 4 :039(557) [0951] because when asserted **without** explanation it is false and
SD : 0 5 :001(558) [0951] is preached purely and **without** admixture, for by it
SD : 0 5 :010(559) [0955] preaching of the law **without** Christ either produces
SD : 0 5 :013(560) [0957] which cannot be done **without** the explanation of the
SD : 0 5 :025(563) [0961] and out of pure grace, **without** any merit of their own,
SD : 0 6 :002(564) [0963] its regular course **without** any outside impulse, they, too,
SD : 0 6 :005(564) [0963] dare not be understood **without** qualification, as though
SD : 0 6 :005(564) [0963] as though the righteous should live **without** the law.
SD : 0 6 :006(565) [0965] spontaneously, **without** any instruction, admonition,
SD : 0 6 :006(565) [0965] and unhindered, **without** any admonition, exhortation,
SD : 0 6 :009(565) [0965] again, "If you are left **without** discipline in which all have
SD : 0 6 :018(567) [0969] though they are never **without** the law, they are not under
SD : 0 6 :020(567) [0969] service of God and **without** his Word and command, as it
SD : 0 6 :025(568) [0971] his will spontaneously, **without** coercion, unhindered,
SD : 0 7 :016(572) [0977] since they receive it **without** true repentance and without
SD : 0 7 :016(572) [0977] they receive it without true repentance and **without** faith.
SD : 0 7 :023(573) [0979] look upon the elements **without** the Word, you then have
SD : 0 7 :047(578) [0989] Creator and Redeemer, **without** any doubts or arguments
SD : 0 7 :052(578) [0991] and proffered bread **without** any interpretation and
SD : 0 7 :060(580) [0993] come to the Lord's table **without** true repentance and
SD : 0 7 :061(580) [0995] **Without** this spiritual participation, even the sacramental
SD : 0 7 :068(582) [0997] who go to this sacrament **without** true contrition and
SD : 0 7 :068(582) [0997] sorrow for their sins, **without** true faith, and without a
SD : 0 7 :068(582) [0997] without true faith, and **without** a good intention to
SD : 0 7 :100(586) [1007] or crystal and exist **without** occupying or vacating space,
SD : 0 7 :108(588) [1009] and wine, or their accidents **without** a subject, remain.
SD : 0 8 :011(593) [1019] of Christ; and that **without** his humanity no less than
SD : 0 8 :011(593) [1019] humanity no less than **without** his deity the person of
SD : 0 8 :019(595) [1021] man and man is God but **without** thereby blending the
SD : 0 8 :020(595) [1021] of this personal union, **without** which such a true
SD : 0 8 :024(595) [1023] he was born of a virgin **without** violating her virginity.
SD : 0 8 :026(596) [1023] the form of a servant (**without**, however, laying aside the
SD : 0 8 :028(596) [1025] maintain **without** proof from the Holy Scriptures.
SD : 0 8 :028(596) [1025] in deed and in truth **without** any blending or equalization
SD : 0 8 :031(597) [1025] between each other **without** any blending or equalization
SD : 0 8 :035(597) [1027] if one talks about them **without** due discrimination, the
SD : 0 8 :052(601) [1033] should be capable or incapable **without** being destroyed.
SD : 0 8 :053(601) [1033] and above its natural properties **without** being destroyed.
SD : 0 8 :063(603) [1037] in deed and in truth but **without** any blending of the
SD : 0 8 :066(604) [1039] and combustion **without** any transformation of the
SD : 0 8 :071(605) [1041] something that belongs to it **without** keeping it for itself.
SD : 0 8 :074(606) [1043] poured out upon him **without** measure the Spirit of
SD : 0 8 :084(607) [1045] isolated God and a divine person **without** the humanity.
SD : 0 8 :092(609) [1049] **Without** transforming or destroying his true human
SD : 1 0 :003(611) [1053] a clear conscience and **without** prejudice to the divine
SD : 1 0 :009(612) [1055] as long as it does so **without** frivolity and offense but in
SD : 1 0 :019(614) [1059] this could be done **without** pretense, humbug, and
SD : 1 1 :004(617) [1063] will fall to the ground **without** your Father's will"
SD : 1 1 :010(618) [1067] all kinds of sin and vice **without** repentance, despise Word
SD : 1 1 :027(620) [1071] Now, God does not call **without** means but through the
SD : 1 1 :039(623) [1077] remain in sin **without** repentance (Luke 14:18, 24),
SD : 1 1 :043(623) [1077] are justified and saved **without** our works and merit,
SD : 1 1 :056(625) [1081] **Without** doubt God also knows and has determined for
SD : 1 1 :059(626) [1083] God's goodness to us **without** and contrary to our
SD : 1 1 :070(627) [1085] who testifies to all men **without** distinction that God
SD : 1 1 :076(628) [1087] Father will not do this **without** means, and he has
SD : 1 1 :076(629) [1087] the Father to draw him **without** Word and sacraments.
SD : 1 1 :087(631) [1093] sheer mercy in Christ **without** our merit and good works,
SD : 1 2 :011(634) [1099] they will be saved **without** Baptism, which they do not
SD : 1 2 :013(634) [1099] and children of God even **without** and prior to Baptism.

Withstand (1)
LC : 0 1 :036(369) [0589] mammon and believe that they can **withstand** his wrath.

Witness (38), Witnessed (3), Witnesses (7), Witnessing (1)
PR : PR :008(005) [0009] based as it is on the **witness** of the unalterable truth of the
PR : PR :023(012) [0021] once more to have **witnessed** publicly before God and all
AG : PR :023(027) [0043] summons) as we herewith publicly **witness** and assert.
AL : 2 0 :002(041) [0053] of like import bear **witness** that they have taught to good
AP : 0 4 :083(118) [0145] him all the prophets bear **witness** that every one who
AP : 0 4 :189(133) [0175] men, he visibly pits the **witness** of the saints against the
AP : 0 4 :201(134) [0175] in faith, and through his **witness** testify to his faith before
AP : 0 4 :273(148) [0199] him all the prophets bear **witness** that every one who
AP : 1 2 :065(191) [0271] him all the prophets bear **witness** that every one who
AP : 1 2 :066(191) [0271] him all the prophets bear **witness** that every one who
AP : 1 2 :073(192) [0273] This is the **witness** that the Holy Spirit brings in your
AP : 2 0 :002(227) [0339] him all the prophets bear **witness** that every one who
AP : 2 4 :049(258) [0401] sacrament as a seal and **witness** of the free forgiveness of
AP : 2 4 :068(261) [0407] to be a mark and **witness** of profession, just as a certain
AP : 2 4 :074(263) [0411] of its gratitude, and a **witness** of its high esteem for God's
AP : 2 7 :013(271) [0423] But thy death is a **witness**, thy resurrection is a witness,
AP : 2 7 :013(271) [0423] thy resurrection is a **witness**, the Holy Spirit is a witness,
AP : 2 7 :013(271) [0423] the Holy Spirit is a **witness**, thy whole church is a
AP : 2 7 :013(271) [0423] thy whole church is a **witness**: this is truly the teaching of
TR : 0 0 :063(331) [0523] The fact itself bears **witness** to this, for the power is the
TR : 0 0 :070(332) [0525] of the church also bears **witness** to this, for there was a
SC : 0 1 :015(343) [0541] *"You shall not bear false* **witness** *against your neighbor."*
LC : SP :008(362) [0575] 8. You shall not bear false **witness** against your neighbor.
LC : 0 1 :035(369) [0589] This he has **witnessed** in all the records of history, as
LC : 0 1 :254(399) [0653] *"You shall not bear false* **witness** *against your neighbor."*
LC : 0 1 :257(399) [0653] shall not bear false **witness**"), this commandment pertains
LC : 0 1 :257(399) [0653] and maligned by false **witnesses** and consequently
LC : 0 1 :259(400) [0653] Likewise, a **witness** should be fearless; more than that, he
LC : 0 1 :260(400) [0655] whether he be judge or **witness**, let the consequences be
LC : 0 1 :262(400) [0655] too, everyone bears false **witness** against his neighbor.
LC : 0 1 :263(400) [0655] False **witness** is clearly a work of the tongue.
LC : 0 1 :263(400) [0655] to false judges and **witnesses** with their corrupt behavior
LC : 0 1 :271(401) [0657] then, that cannot be adequately proved is false **witness**.
LC : 0 1 :275(402) [0659] evil, to prefer charges, to attest, examine, and **witness**.
LC : 0 1 :279(403) [0661] be confirmed by the evidence of two or three **witnesses**."
LC : 0 1 :280(403) [0661] You have **witnesses** with you through whom you can
LC : 0 1 :281(403) [0661] you are called upon to **witness**, you will probably deny
LC : 0 1 :284(403) [0661] can be no question of slander or injustice or false **witness**.
LC : 0 3 :031(424) [0707] they would have **witnessed** a far different drama: the
EP : RN :002(465) [0777] and no further than as **witnesses** to the fashion in which
EP : RN :008(465) [0779] Scripture, but merely **witnesses** and expositions of the
EP : 0 7 :042(486) [0817] this doctrine, against the **witness** of their own consciences
EP : 1 0 :006(493) [0831] to make, but we should **witness** an unequivocal confession
SD : PR :003(501) [0847] unequivocal Christian **witness**, setting forth the faith and
SD : PR :012(506) [0855] gladly admit and accept them as **witnesses** to the truth.
SD : PR :013(506) [0855] cite these writings as a **witness** to the truth and as
SD : 0 8 :015(594) [1019] Samosatenes, who on the **witness** of Suidas and
SD : 1 1 :031(621) [1073] the Spirit of God gives "**witness**" to the elect "that they
SD : 1 2 :008(633) [1097] able to refrain from **witnessing** publicly before all

Wittenberg (3)
S 1 : PR :008(290) [0457] was a doctor here in **Wittenberg**, sent from France, who
TR : 0 0 :082(000) [0529] Sacrament, made at **Wittenberg** with Dr. Bucer and
SD : 0 7 :012(571) [0977] Christian agreement in **Wittenberg**, and Dr. Martin

Woe (7)
AP : 0 4 :322(157) [0209] the *Confessions* he says, "**Woe** to the life of men, however
S 1 : PR :009(290) [0457] the rest, wretchedness and **woe** will be their lot forever.
S 2 : 0 2 :004(293) [0463] into wretchedness and **woe** on account of an unnecessary
SC : PR :005(338) [0533] **Woe** to you forever!
LC : 0 1 :041(370) [0591] and salvation, or eternal wrath, misery, and **woe**.
SD : 0 3 :017(542) [0921] "**Woe** to those who acquit the godless for a bribe, and
SD : 1 0 :016(613) [1057] both, as it is written, "**Woe** to the world for temptations to

Wolf (3)
PR : PR :027(014) [0025] **Wolf**, duke of Brunswick [-Grubenhagen] and
PR : PR :027(015) [0025] **Wolf** Ernest, count of Stolberg
PR : PR :027(015) [0025] **Wolf**, baron of Schoenburg [-Penig-Remissa]

Wolves (3)
AP : 0 7 :022(172) [0235] warning that there will be ungodly teachers and **wolves**.
AP : 0 7 :022(172) [0235] Though **wolves** and ungodly teachers may run rampant in
SD : PR :014(506) [0855] lambs and guard against **wolves** so that they will flee from

Wolfart (1)
TR : 0 0 :082(335) [0529] Boniface **Wolfart**, minister of the Word in the church in

Wolfenbuettel (2)
PR : PR :027(014) [0025] duke of Brunswick [-**Wolfenbuettel**] and Lueneburg
PR : PR :027(014) [0025] duke of Brunswick [-**Wolfenbuettel**] and Lueneburg

Wolfgang (3)
AG : 0 0 :007(096) [0095] **Wolfgang**, prince of Anhalt
AL : 0 0 :017(096) [0095] **Wolfgang**, prince of Anhalt
S 3 : 1 5 :005(318) [0501] the Rev. **Wolfgang** Kiswetter

Woman (26), Women (15)
AG : 2 3 :025(055) [0065] offered the counsel that **women** who were unable to keep
AG : 2 7 :007(071) [0077] practice was stricter in **women**'s convents than in those of
AG : 2 7 :007(071) [0077] to show more consideration to **women** as the weaker sex.
AG : 2 7 :019(074) [0079] have his own wife and each **woman** her own husband."
AG : 2 7 :029(075) [0079] are few, whether men or **women**, who have taken
AG : 2 8 :054(090) [0091] in I Cor. 11:5 that **women** should cover their heads in the
AG : 2 8 :056(090) [0091] no one would say that a **woman** commits a sin if without
AL : 2 3 :025(055) [0065] Cyprian advised that **women** who did not keep the
AL : 2 7 :007(071) [0077] the case in convents of **women** more than in those of
AL : 2 8 :054(090) [0091] So Paul ordained that **women** should cover their heads in
AL : 2 8 :056(090) [0091] one would say that a **woman** sins by going out in public
AP : 0 2 :046(106) [0119] between you and the **woman**, and between your seed and
AP : 0 4 :152(127) [0163] by her works of love the **woman** had merited the
AP : 0 4 :154(128) [0163] The **woman** came, believing that she should seek the
AP : 0 4 :154(128) [0163] "love" not toward the **woman** but against the Pharisee,
AP : 0 4 :154(128) [0165] act of reverence of the Pharisee with that of the **woman**.
AP : 0 4 :154(128) [0165] He points to the **woman** and praises her reverence, her
AP : 0 4 :154(128) [0165] and reproves him with the example of the **woman**.
AP : 0 4 :154(128) [0165] that an uneducated **woman** should believe God, while a
AP : 0 9 :002(178) [0245] is offered to all — men, **women**, children, and infants.
AP : 1 2 :057(189) [0267] The **woman** who was a sinner came to Christ in tears,
AP : 2 3 :009(240) [0367] that the union of man and **woman** is by natural right.
AP : 2 3 :011(241) [0367] jurists: The union of man and **woman** is by natural right.
AP : 2 3 :025(243) [0371] of Antichrist's kingdom to despise **women** (11:37).
AP : 2 3 :032(243) [0373] In I Tim. 2:15 he says, "**Woman** will be saved through
AP : 2 3 :032(243) [0373] Paul says that **woman** is saved through bearing children.
AP : 2 3 :032(243) [0373] bestow than to say that **woman** is saved by the marital
AP : 2 3 :032(244) [0373] the faith by which a **woman** accepts the forgiveness of
AP : 2 3 :032(244) [0373] So a **woman**'s duties please God because of faith, and a
AP : 2 3 :032(244) [0373] of faith, and a believing **woman** is saved if she serves
AP : 2 3 :059(247) [0379] and the exile of poor **women** and orphaned children.
AP : 2 7 :068(280) [0443] way he says that the wanton **women** had rejected the faith.
S 2 : 0 3 :001(297) [0471] learned men and decent **women** should be restored to
S 3 : 1 1 :002(314) [0499] us or to them to make a **woman** out of a man or a man
S 3 : 1 1 :002(314) [0499] a man or a man out of a **woman** or abolish distinctions
SC : 0 9 :006(355) [0561] bestowing honor on the **woman** as the weaker sex, since
LC : 0 1 :018(367) [0585] or others, while pregnant **women** worshiped Diana or
LC : 0 1 :207(393) [0639] and he created man and **woman** differently (as is evident)
LC : 0 1 :211(393) [0641] that in general men and **women** in all conditions, who
LC : 0 1 :305(406) [0667] took a fancy to another **woman**, he managed, either
SD : 0 5 :023(562) [0959] the proclamation of the **woman**'s seed, who would bruise

Womb (8), Wombs (2)
AG : 0 2 :001(029) [0043] from their mothers' **wombs** and are unable by nature to
AL : 0 3 :001(029) [0045] on man's nature in the **womb** of the blessed virgin Mary.
AP : 0 2 :002(100) [0105] from their mothers' **wombs** and are unable by nature to
S 3 : 0 8 :013(313) [0497] nor did he leap in his mother's **womb** until Mary spoke.
EP : 0 8 :015(488) [0821] Spirit in his mother's **womb** and his human nature was

Continued ▶

SD : 0 8 :013(594) [1019] conceived in his mother's **womb** and became man and
SD : 0 8 :024(595) [1023] even in his mother's **womb** in that he was born of a virgin
SD : 0 8 :026(596) [1023] even in his mother's **womb**, but, as the apostle testifies, he
SD : 0 8 :082(607) [1045] his conception in his mother's **womb** proves conclusively.
SD : 0 8 :082(607) [1045] had to be in his mother's **womb** naturally and personally

Won (8)
LC : 0 2 :030(414) [0685] from the jaws of hell, **won** us, made us free, and restored
LC : 0 2 :038(415) [0689] Christ has acquired and **won** the treasure for us by his
LC : 0 2 :043(416) [0689] Lord in the sense that he **won** for us this treasure without
LC : 0 2 :054(417) [0693] God's grace has been **won** by Christ, and holiness has
EP : 0 3 :003(473) [0737] Thereby he **won** for us in the forgiveness of sins and
EP : 0 5 :005(478) [0803] merit has obtained and **won** for him forgiveness of sins,
SD : 0 7 :049(578) [0989] the benefits which he had **won** for us by the sacrifice of
SD : 0 7 :081(584) [1001] benefits which Christ has **won** for us by his death and the

Wonder (5), Wonderful (10), Wonderfully (1), Wonders (1)
AP : 0 4 :167(130) [0169] Who does not often **wonder** whether history is governed
AP : 0 4 :332(158) [0211] We **wonder** what our opponents do when they pray, if
AP : 0 7 :006(169) [0229] We **wonder** why they criticize our description, which
AP : 1 2 :006(183) [0255] They **wonder** whether the forgiveness of sins takes place
AP : 2 3 :032(243) [0373] they would stage a **wonderful** victory celebration.
AP : 2 4 :072(262) [0409] "He has caused his **wonderful** works to be
LC : 0 1 :145(385) [0623] Is it not a **wonderful** thing to be able to boast to yourself,
LC : 0 1 :252(399) [0653] lavishes upon them a **wonderful** blessing: We shall be
LC : 0 4 :021(439) [0737] and deeds and has confirmed it by **wonders** from heaven.
LC : 0 6 :015(459) [0000] that makes confession so **wonderful** and comforting.
LC : 0 6 :022(459) [0000] it as a great and **wonderful** treasure to be accepted with
LC : 0 6 :025(460) [0000] kept silence about this **wonderful**, rich alms and this
LC : 0 6 :028(460) [0000] Thus we teach what a **wonderful**, precious, and
SD : 0 1 :036(514) [0869] David says: "I will praise thee, for I am **wonderfully** made.
SD : 0 1 :036(514) [0869] **Wonderful** are thy works!
SD : 0 2 :047(530) [0901] anxiety and doubt, and **wonder** if God has really elected
SD : 0 2 :050(530) [0901] eternal law and the **wonderful** counsel concerning our

Wood (2)
LC : 0 5 :033(450) [0761] or preached to stone and **wood** but to those who hear
LC : 0 5 :065(454) [0769] said, are not preached to **wood** or stone but to you and

Word (755)
PR : PR :000(001) [0004] Firmly Founded on the **Word** of God as the Only Norm,
PR : PR :002(003) [0007] his holy Gospel and of the **Word** that alone brings
PR : PR :004(004) [0007] pure doctrine of God's **Word**, sever the bond of Christian
PR : PR :004(004) [0009] embracing other errors that militate against God's **Word**.
PR : PR :005(004) [0009] in the teaching of God's **Word** and in agreeable Christian
PR : PR :005(004) [0009] in harmony with God's **Word**, as they were while Dr.
PR : PR :005(004) [0009] the pure, unadulterated **Word** of God, so such false
PR : PR :008(005) [0009] truth of the divine **Word**, in order thereby to warn and, as
PR : PR :008(005) [0009] that is impure, false, and contrary to the **Word** of God.
PR : PR :008(005) [0011] the truth of the divine **Word** that alone gives salvation, to
PR : PR :010(006) [0011] on the basis of God's **Word**, carefully and accurately to
PR : PR :011(006) [0011] writings based on God's **Word**, how the aforementioned
PR : PR :014(007) [0013] might be fortified with the **Word** of God against all sorts
PR : PR :016(008) [0013] first of all to the **Word** of God and then to the Augsburg
PR : PR :018(008) [0015] infallible, and unalterable **Word** of God, to that Augsburg
PR : PR :020(010) [0017] what he has ordained and promised in his **Word**.
PR : PR :021(010) [0019] removed inasmuch as the **word** "abstract" has not been
PR : PR :022(011) [0019] the truth of the divine **Word**, and far less do we mean
PR : PR :022(011) [0019] contrary to the expressed **Word** of God and cannot
PR : PR :022(012) [0019] truth of the divine **Word** and unite with us and our
PR : PR :024(013) [0021] grounded in God's **Word** so that pure doctrine can be
PR : PR :024(013) [0023] the propagation of that **Word** of his that alone brings
AG : 0 1 :004(028) [0043] The **word** "person" is to be understood as the Fathers
AG : 0 1 :006(028) [0043] that the other two, the **Word** and the Holy Spirit, are not
AG : 0 1 :006(028) [0043] persons but that the **Word** signifies a physical word or
AG : 0 1 :006(028) [0043] Word signifies a physical **word** or voice and that the Holy
AG : 0 5 :004(031) [0045] and works without the external **word** of the Gospel.
AG : 0 7 :002(032) [0047] be administered in accordance with the divine **Word**.
AG : 1 8 :003(039) [0051] who is given through the **Word** of God, for Paul says in
AG : 2 0 :026(045) [0057] we would understand the **word** "faith" in the Scriptures to
AG : 0 0 :001(047) [0059] by misusing his name or **Word**, nor should we wish to
AG : 0 0 :001(047) [0059] which agrees with the pure **Word** of God and Christian
AG : 2 3 :008(052) [0061] Since God's **Word** and command cannot be altered by any
AG : 2 3 :018(054) [0063] may marry is based on God's **Word** and command.
AG : 2 5 :002(061) [0069] the consolation of the **Word** of absolution so that they
AG : 2 5 :003(061) [0069] It is not the voice or **word** of the man who speaks it, but
AG : 2 5 :003(061) [0069] who speaks it, but it is the **Word** of God, who forgives
AG : 2 5 :005(062) [0069] never mentioned a **word** concerning these necessary
AG : 2 7 :001(071) [0077] contrary not only to the **Word** of God but also to papal
AG : 2 7 :013(073) [0077] calling according to God's **Word** and command without
AG : 2 8 :008(082) [0085] and preaching the **Word** of God and by administering the
AG : 2 8 :021(084) [0087] be done not by human power but by God's **Word** alone.
AG : 2 8 :035(086) [0089] to God's command and **Word** to make laws out of
AL : 0 1 :006(028) [0043] impiously argue that the **Word** and the Holy Spirit are
AL : 0 1 :006(028) [0043] not distinct persons since "**Word**" signifies a spoken word
AL : 0 1 :006(028) [0043] "Word" signifies a spoken **word** and "Spirit" signifies a
AL : 0 3 :001(029) [0045] also teach that the **Word** — that is, the Son of God —
AL : 0 5 :002(031) [0045] For through the **Word** and the sacraments, as through
AL : 0 5 :004(031) [0045] men without the external **Word**, through their own
AL : 0 8 :002(033) [0047] the sacraments and the **Word** are effectual by reason of
AL : 1 8 :003(039) [0051] heart when the Holy Spirit is received through the **Word**.
AL : 2 0 :026(045) [0057] this way concerning the **word** "faith" when he teaches
AL : 2 0 :026(045) [0057] that in the Scriptures the **word** "faith" is to be understood
AL : 2 8 :009(082) [0085] the ministry of the **Word** and sacraments, for Paul says,
AL : 2 8 :009(082) [0085] has faith," and Ps. 119:50 states, "Thy **Word** gives me life."
AL : 2 8 :010(082) [0085] the ministry of the **Word**, it interferes with civil
AL : 2 8 :021(084) [0087] the ministry of the **Word** and sacraments) except to
AL : 2 8 :021(084) [0087] doing all this without human power, simply by the **Word**.
AP : 0 2 :013(102) [0109] adjudged except from the **Word** of God, which the
AP : 0 2 :026(103) [0111] ends contrary to the **Word** of God (that is, not only the
AP : 0 2 :042(105) [0117] wrath, his grace, and his **Word**; anger at his judgments;
AP : 0 3 :001(107) [0119] Christ, namely, that the **Word** assumed the human nature
AP : 0 4 :035(112) [0131] God and to doubt his **Word** with its threats and promises.
AP : 0 4 :058(115) [0137] "My soul waits for his **word**, my soul hopes in the Lord,"
AP : 0 4 :066(116) [0139] they deny that it is received through the **Word**.
AP : 0 4 :067(116) [0139] deal with God or grasp him except through the **Word**.
AP : 0 4 :067(116) [0139] takes place through the **Word**, as Paul says (Rom. 1:16),
AP : 0 4 :067(116) [0139] place only through the **Word**, and the Word is received
AP : 0 4 :067(116) [0139] the Word, and the **Word** is received only by faith, then it
AP : 0 4 :073(117) [0141] claim of merit, not the **Word** or the sacraments, as our
AP : 0 4 :073(117) [0141] faith is conceived by the **Word**, and we give the highest
AP : 0 4 :073(117) [0143] and we give the highest praise to the ministry of the **Word**
AP : 0 4 :112(123) [0155] in the true sense of the **word**—since the promise can be
AP : 0 4 :113(123) [0155] as the Scriptures use the **word**, is that which accepts the
AP : 0 4 :121(124) [0155] The scholastics do not say a **word** about this faith.
AP : 0 4 :127(125) [0157] faith, according to Paul's **word** (Gal. 3:14), "That we
AP : 0 4 :153(128) [0163] which grasps God's free mercy because of God's **Word**.
AP : 0 4 :154(128) [0163] Moreover, Christ used the **word** "love" not toward the
AP : 0 4 :185(132) [0173] For the **word** of the ancient poet is true, "Being sick in
AP : 0 4 :191(133) [0175] people who had God's **Word** against the devil, that the
AP : 0 4 :193(133) [0175] Let us add a **word** here about reward and merit.
AP : 0 4 :235(140) [0185] argue on the basis of the **word** "perfection" that love
AP : 0 4 :247(142) [0191] he brought us forth by the **word** of truth that we should
AP : 0 4 :257(144) [0193] enough to preach the law, the **Word** that convicts of sin.
AP : 0 4 :262(145) [0195] must have a very definite **Word** of God to learn to know
AP : 0 4 :264(146) [0195] the promise is involved even in the **word** "redeem."
AP : 0 4 :266(146) [0197] be turned from such fleshly opinions to the **Word** of God.
AP : 0 4 :293(152) [0203] the law, love God and his **Word**, obey God in the midst of
AP : 0 4 :302(154) [0205] of a house, they echo the **word** "love" without
AP : 0 4 :304(154) [0205] will commands the intellect to assent to the **Word** of God.
AP : 0 4 :304(154) [0205] is how Scripture uses the **word** "faith," as this statement
AP : 0 4 :326(158) [0211] the persecutors of God's **Word**, not of his personal purity.
AP : 0 4 :346(160) [0217] hope, for it rests on the **Word** and commandment of God.
AP : 0 4 :357(161) [0217] But they are not fair judges, for they omit the **word** "gift."
AP : 0 4 :357(161) [0217] central thought of the discussion; they pick out the **word**
AP : 0 4 :360(162) [0219] when they hear this one **word** "reward": "It is called a
AP : 0 4 :397(167) [0227] but because of the **word** of Christ, 'Whatever you bind,'
AP : 0 7 :003(169) [0227] church's marks — that is, **Word**, confession, and
AP : 0 7 :007(169) [0229] added the outward marks, the **Word** and the sacraments.
AP : 0 7 :007(169) [0229] washing of water with the **word**, that the church might be
AP : 0 7 :019(171) [0233] we may know that the **Word** and the sacraments are
AP : 0 7 :028(173) [0237] When they offer the **Word** of Christ or the sacraments,
AP : 0 7 :036(175) [0241] believe (like the divinely instituted **Word** and sacraments).
AP : 0 7 :047(177) [0243] persons, according to the **word** (Luke 10:16), "He who
AP : 0 9 :002(178) [0245] have been armed by God's **Word** against the wicked and
AP : 0 9 :002(178) [0245] where there is neither **Word** nor sacrament, because
AP : 0 9 :002(178) [0245] because Christ regenerates through **Word** and sacrament.
AP : 1 1 :009(182) [0251] if they had added one **word** on faith, which consoles and
AP : 1 2 :029(185) [0259] takes place when the **Word** of God denounces sin.
AP : 1 2 :032(186) [0259] cannot bear it unless it is sustained by the **Word** of God.
AP : 1 2 :034(186) [0261] about faith, but present only the **Word** that denounces sin
AP : 1 2 :040(187) [0261] quickens through the **Word**, the keys truly forgive sin
AP : 1 2 :044(187) [0263] Spirit quickens our hearts through the **Word** of Christ.
AP : 1 2 :047(188) [0265] quickens, according to the **word** (Hab. 2:4), "The
AP : 1 2 :049(188) [0265] away for sorrow; strengthen me according to thy **word**!"
AP : 1 2 :049(188) [0265] in contrition by the **Word** of God which offers us grace.
AP : 1 2 :071(192) [0271] this, the Holy Spirit fell on all who heard the **word**."
AP : 1 2 :075(193) [0273] rather than in God's **Word** and the promise of Christ?
AP : 1 2 :099(197) [0281] of absolution, which is the **Word** of God that the power
AP : 1 2 :106(197) [0283] the fear of God or faith or his concern for God's **Word**.
AP : 1 2 :113(199) [0285] Our **word** "satisfaction" is a relic from this rite of public
AP : 1 2 :115(199) [0285] has become obsolete, the **word** "satisfaction" still remains
AP : 1 2 :123(200) [0289] who so sinfully twist the **Word** of God to suit their vain
AP : 1 2 :123(201) [0289] They quote the **word**, "Be penitent," against us so that
AP : 1 2 :131(202) [0291] In a **word**, there is no penitence inwardly which does not
AP : 1 2 :133(202) [0293] For this **word** of Christ is a word of command, "Be
AP : 1 2 :133(202) [0293] this word of Christ is a **word** of command, "Be penitent."
AP : 1 2 :163(208) [0303] by the Lord; but the **word** "judge" refers to the whole
AP : 1 2 :168(209) [0305] the Fathers take the **word** "satisfaction" from the public
AP : 1 3 :005(211) [0309] Through the **Word** and the rite God simultaneously
AP : 1 3 :005(212) [0309] As the **Word** enters through the ears to strike the heart, so
AP : 1 3 :005(212) [0309] The **Word** and the rite have the same effect, as Augustine
AP : 1 3 :005(212) [0309] the sacrament "the visible **Word**," for the rite is received
AP : 1 3 :005(212) [0309] is a sort of picture of the **Word**, signifying the same thing
AP : 1 3 :005(212) [0309] of the Word, signifying the same thing as the **Word**.
AP : 1 3 :007(212) [0311] to the ministry of the **Word** or the administration of the
AP : 1 3 :011(212) [0311] to the ministry of the **Word**, we have no obligation to
AP : 1 3 :011(212) [0311] The ministry of the **Word** has God's command and
AP : 1 3 :011(212) [0311] (Rom. 1:16), again, "My **word** that goes forth from my
AP : 1 3 :013(212) [0311] extol the ministry of the **Word** with every possible kind of
AP : 1 3 :013(212) [0311] not come through the **Word** but because of their own
AP : 1 3 :023(214) [0313] one can produce a single **word** from the Fathers that
AP : 1 4 :001(214) [0315] allowed to administer the **Word** and the sacraments in the
AP : 1 4 :004(214) [0315] who rightly teach the **Word** of God and rightly administer
AP : 1 4 :004(215) [0315] who seek to destroy the **Word** of God with their edicts,
AP : 1 5 :014(217) [0319] please God since they do not have support in God's **Word**?
AP : 1 5 :014(217) [0319] of God's will without the command and **Word** of God?
AP : 1 5 :017(217) [0319] nothing about the will of God without the **Word** of God?
AP : 1 5 :017(217) [0319] maintain this without the **Word** and testimony of God,
AP : 1 5 :017(217) [0319] have no testimony in the **Word** of God, the conscience
AP : 1 5 :029(219) [0323] rites, let us therefore arm ourselves with the **Word** of God.
AP : 2 1 :012(230) [0345] be proved from the **Word** of God, we cannot affirm that
AP : 2 1 :017(231) [0347] place, there must be a **Word** of God to assure us that God
AP : 2 1 :031(233) [0351] they have neither a **Word** of God nor an example from
AP : 2 1 :033(233) [0351] if it has no command or proof in the **Word** of God?
AP : 2 3 :004(239) [0365] of reasons, taken from the **Word** of God, while our
AP : 2 3 :008(240) [0365] The **Word** of God did not form the nature of men to be
AP : 2 3 :008(240) [0367] Just so this **Word** makes the earth fruitful (Gen. 1:11),
AP : 2 3 :028(243) [0371] has been sanctified by the **Word** of God; that is, it is
AP : 2 3 :028(243) [0371] it is something which the **Word** of God permits and
AP : 2 3 :030(243) [0371] are "consecrated by the **word** of God and prayer"
AP : 2 3 :030(243) [0371] (I Tim. 4:5): by the **Word** which assures the conscience
AP : 2 3 :033(244) [0373] are pure since they are approved by the **Word** of God.
AP : 2 3 :034(244) [0373] is pure in the godly, through the **Word** of God and faith.
AP : 2 3 :070(249) [0383] no perversion of God's **Word** will stand, as Isaiah says
AP : 2 3 :071(249) [0383] to God's will and **Word** to break up marriages and to

Continued ▶

AP : 2 3 :071(249) [0383] greater respect for the **Word** of God than for anything
AP : 2 4 :003(250) [0385] have been touched by the **Word** may receive faith and fear
AP : 2 4 :023(253) [0391] The **word** he uses here (*'asam*) means a victim sacrificed
AP : 2 4 :023(253) [0391] Paul interprets the same **word** as "sin" in Rom. 8:3, "As a
AP : 2 4 :023(253) [0391] the meaning of the **word** more readily if we look at the
AP : 2 4 :028(254) [0393] and saves, because of my **Word** and promise, not because
AP : 2 4 :029(255) [0393] "Thou has offered me thy **Word** to hear, and dost require
AP : 2 4 :033(256) [0395] of praise we include the proclamation of the **Word**.
AP : 2 4 :048(258) [0401] to the ministry of the **Word**, they teach the Gospel of the
AP : 2 4 :069(262) [0409] There are two parts to a sacrament, the sign and the **Word**
AP : 2 4 :069(262) [0409] the New Testament, the **Word** is the added promise of
AP : 2 4 :070(262) [0409] Therefore the **Word** offers the forgiveness of sins, while
AP : 2 4 :070(262) [0409] As the **Word** was given to arouse this faith, so the
AP : 2 4 :070(262) [0409] Holy Spirit works through the **Word** and the sacraments.
AP : 2 4 :080(264) [0411] of God," that is, of the **Word** and sacraments; and
AP : 2 4 :081(264) [0411] It is an old **word**, ordinarily used in public law.
AP : 2 4 :082(264) [0411] In II Cor. 9:12 Paul uses this **word** for a collection.
AP : 2 7 :022(272) [0427] the ministry of the **Word** who follow these observances
AP : 2 7 :023(273) [0427] when they have no proof for this from the **Word** of God?
AP : 2 7 :046(277) [0435] approved by the **Word** of God in the commandment
AP : 2 7 :058(279) [0439] thought up without a **Word** of God as an act of worship
AP : 2 7 :058(279) [0439] Nazarites, which had a **Word** of God and was not meant
AP : 2 7 :070(281) [0443] with services instituted by his **Word** and done in faith.
AP : 2 8 :010(282) [0447] But it is eternal things, the **Word** of God and the Holy
AP : 2 8 :013(283) [0447] the order, namely, the ministry of **Word** and sacraments.
AP : 2 8 :014(283) [0447] command, a definite **Word** of God, which he ought to
AP : 2 8 :014(283) [0447] They have the **Word**, they have the command about when
AP : 2 8 :014(283) [0447] contrary to that **Word** which they have received from
AP : 2 8 :018(284) [0449] on the basis of another's **Word** rather than on the basis of
AP : 2 8 :018(284) [0449] as was necessary, that the **Word** is efficacious when it is
AP : 2 8 :018(284) [0449] that we should not look for another **word** from heaven.
AP : 2 8 :019(284) [0449] he wants his voice, His **Word** to be heard, not human
S 1 : PR :005(289) [0457] twisting and corrupting my every **word** and letter?
S 1 : PR :010(290) [0457] supplied with the pure **Word** and the right use of the
S 2 : 0 2 :005(293) [0463] was fabricated and invented without God's **Word** and will?
S 2 : 0 2 :008(294) [0465] and imagination without the sanction of God's **Word**.
S 2 : 0 2 :015(295) [0467] This means that the **Word** of God shall establish articles
S 2 : 0 2 :018(296) [0467] their own parishes, the **Word** of God, their wives and
S 2 : 0 2 :024(296) [0469] power of the pope but by the preaching of God's **Word**.
S 2 : 0 4 :001(298) [0471] or according to God's **Word**, for this position belongs
S 3 : 0 1 :002(302) [0477] God, neglect of God's **Word**, disobedience to parents,
S 3 : 0 3 :002(304) [0479] speaks, "Is not my **word** like a hammer which breaks the
S 3 : 0 3 :008(304) [0481] comes to us through the **Word**, the sacraments, and the
S 3 : 0 4 :000(310) [0491] First, through the spoken **word**, by which the forgiveness
S 3 : 0 5 :001(310) [0491] is nothing else than the **Word** of God in water,
S 3 : 0 5 :001(310) [0491] washing of water with the **word**"; or, again, as Augustine
S 3 : 0 5 :001(310) [0491] as Augustine puts it, "The **Word** is added to the element
S 3 : 0 5 :002(310) [0491] who forget the **Word** (God's institution) and say that God
S 3 : 0 5 :003(311) [0493] God's will and not at all through the **Word** and the water.
S 3 : 0 8 :003(312) [0495] the external, spoken **Word**, we must hold firmly to the
S 3 : 0 8 :003(312) [0495] through or with the external **Word** which comes before.
S 3 : 0 8 :003(312) [0495] without and before the **Word** and who therefore judge,
S 3 : 0 8 :003(312) [0495] the Scriptures or spoken **Word** according to their
S 3 : 0 8 :004(312) [0495] is above and contrary to the Scriptures or spoken **Word**.
S 3 : 0 8 :005(312) [0495] them from the external **Word** of God to spiritualizing and
S 3 : 0 8 :006(312) [0495] day condemn the external **Word**, yet they do not remain
S 3 : 0 8 :006(312) [0495] Scriptures or the spoken **word** of the apostles but must
S 3 : 0 8 :007(313) [0495] to their faith through the external **Word** which preceded.
S 3 : 0 8 :008(313) [0495] and been justified if the **Word** and his hearing of it had
S 3 : 0 8 :010(313) [0497] with us except through his external **Word** and sacrament.
S 3 : 0 8 :010(313) [0497] Spirit apart from such **Word** and sacrament is of the
S 3 : 0 8 :011(313) [0497] bush and the spoken **word**, and no prophet, whether
S 3 : 0 8 :012(313) [0497] without the preceding **word** of Gabriel, nor did he leap in
S 3 : 0 8 :013(313) [0497] But without the external **Word** they were not holy, and
S 3 : 1 2 :003(315) [0499] but it consists of the **Word** of God and true faith.
TR : 0 0 :010(321) [0507] ministry depends on the **Word** of God, that Peter was not
TR : 0 0 :011(321) [0507] count for more than the **Word**, nor set the authority of
TR : 0 0 :026(324) [0511] authority but because of the **Word** given by Christ.
TR : 0 0 :030(325) [0513] that is, to preach the **Word** or govern the church with the
TR : 0 0 :030(325) [0513] to preach the Word or govern the church with the **Word**.
TR : 0 0 :055(329) [0521] and wickedness without any regard for the **Word** of God?
TR : 0 0 :056(330) [0521] judgments and decisions according to the **Word** of God.
TR : 0 0 :082(335) [0529] Wolfart, minister of the **Word** in the church in Augsburg
SC : PR :005(338) [0533] Ten Commandments, or a single part of the **Word** of God.
SC : PR :006(338) [0533] read them to the people **word** for word in this manner:
SC : PR :006(338) [0533] read them to the people word for **word** in this manner:
SC : PR :010(339) [0535] etc., following the text **word** for word so that the young
SC : PR :010(339) [0535] the text word for **word** so that the young may repeat
SC : 0 1 :006(342) [0541] we should not despise his **Word** and the preaching of the
SC : 0 1 :012(343) [0541] a chaste and pure life in **word** and deed, each one loving
SC : 0 3 :005(346) [0547] Answer: When the **Word** of God is taught clearly and
SC : 0 3 :005(346) [0547] otherwise than as the **Word** of God teaches, profanes the
SC : 0 3 :008(346) [0547] we may believe his holy **Word** and live a godly life, both
SC : 0 3 :011(347) [0547] keeps us steadfast in his **Word** and in faith even to the
SC : 0 4 :002(348) [0551] to God's command and connected with God's **Word**.
SC : 0 4 :003(348) [0551] What is this **Word** of God?
SC : 0 4 :006(349) [0551] to all who believe, as the **Word** and promise of God
SC : 0 4 :007(349) [0551] What is this **Word** and promise of God?
SC : 0 4 :010(349) [0551] these effects, but the **Word** of God connected with the
SC : 0 4 :010(349) [0551] faith which relies on the **Word** of God connected with the
SC : 0 4 :010(349) [0551] For without the **Word** of God the water is merely water
SC : 0 4 :010(349) [0551] when connected with the **Word** of God it is a Baptism,
SC : 0 5 :020(350) [0553] have harmed anyone by **word** or deed; and whether you
SC : 0 5 :022(350) [0553] I have also been immodest in **word** and deed.
SC : 0 9 :003(354) [0561] him who is taught the **word** share all good things with him
LC : PR :007(359) [0569] time, I read and recite **word** for word the Lord's Prayer,
LC : PR :007(359) [0569] I read and recite word for **word** the Lord's Prayer, the
LC : PR :008(359) [0569] office and the people's souls, yes, even God and his **Word**.
LC : PR :010(359) [0569] occupy oneself with the **Word** of God, talk about it, and
LC : PR :011(360) [0571] For he cannot bear to hear God's **Word**.
LC : PR :011(360) [0571] God's **Word** is not like some empty tale, such as the one
LC : PR :012(360) [0571] to recount all the blessings that flow from God's **Word**.
LC : PR :012(360) [0571] then, shall we call God's **Word**, which routs and destroys
LC : PR :013(360) [0571] only do we need God's **Word** daily as we need our daily
LC : SP :015(363) [0577] We should learn to repeat them **word** for word.
LC : SP :015(363) [0577] We should learn to repeat them word for **word**.
LC : SP :024(364) [0579] teach and require young people to recite **word** for word.
LC : SP :024(364) [0579] teach and require young people to recite word for **word**.
LC : 0 1 :025(368) [0587] a name derived from the **word** "good" because he is an
LC : 0 1 :042(370) [0591] this at all, and does not recognize it as God's **Word**.
LC : 0 1 :054(372) [0595] arise and peddle their lying nonsense as the **Word** of God.
LC : 0 1 :055(372) [0595] the truth and God's **Word** and consign it to the devil.
LC : 0 1 :079(375) [0603] Our **word** "holy day" or "holiday" is so called from the
LC : 0 1 :079(375) [0603] called from the Hebrew **word** "Sabbath," which properly
LC : 0 1 :084(376) [0605] to hear and discuss God's **Word** and then praise God with
LC : 0 1 :086(376) [0605] should devote their observance to learning God's **Word**.
LC : 0 1 :086(376) [0605] be the ministry of the **Word** for the sake of the young and
LC : 0 1 :088(377) [0605] ourselves with God's **Word** and exercise ourselves in it.
LC : 0 1 :089(377) [0605] ourselves daily with God's **Word** and carry it in our hearts
LC : 0 1 :089(377) [0605] our whole life and being according to God's **Word**.
LC : 0 1 :090(377) [0607] preach nor practice God's **Word** but teach and live
LC : 0 1 :091(377) [0607] The **Word** of God is the true holy thing above all holy
LC : 0 1 :091(377) [0607] But God's **Word** is the treasure that sanctifies all things.
LC : 0 1 :092(377) [0607] At whatever time God's **Word** is taught, preached, heard,
LC : 0 1 :092(377) [0607] but on account of the **Word** which makes us all saints.
LC : 0 1 :092(377) [0607] must be guided by God's **Word** if they are to be
LC : 0 1 :093(377) [0607] done apart from God's **Word** is unholy in the sight of
LC : 0 1 :093(377) [0607] who do not know God's **Word** but seek holiness in their
LC : 0 1 :094(378) [0607] as we have heard, takes place only through God's **Word**.
LC : 0 1 :094(378) [0607] in order that God's **Word** may exert its power publicly.
LC : 0 1 :095(378) [0607] much depends on God's **Word** that no holy day is
LC : 0 1 :095(378) [0607] punish all who despise his **Word** and refuse to hear and
LC : 0 1 :096(378) [0607] neglect to hear God's **Word** or lie around in taverns dead
LC : 0 1 :096(378) [0609] others who listen to God's **Word** as they would to any
LC : 0 1 :096(378) [0609] as little knowledge of the **Word** at the end of the year as
LC : 0 1 :097(378) [0609] no one asked about God's **Word**, and no one taught it
LC : 0 1 :097(378) [0609] Now that we have God's **Word**, we still fail to remove the
LC : 0 1 :098(378) [0609] only about hearing the **Word** but also about learning and
LC : 0 1 :098(378) [0609] how you have heard and learned and honored his **Word**.
LC : 0 1 :099(378) [0609] and stealthily take the **Word** of God away from us.
LC : 0 1 :100(378) [0609] though you know the **Word** perfectly and have already
LC : 0 1 :100(379) [0609] continually keep God's **Word** in your heart, on your lips,
LC : 0 1 :100(379) [0609] heart stands idle and the **Word** is not heard, the devil
LC : 0 1 :101(379) [0609] we seriously ponder the **Word**, hear it, and put it to use,
LC : 0 1 :102(379) [0609] or need drove us to the **Word**, yet everyone should be
LC : 0 1 :103(379) [0611] devote ourselves to God's **Word** so that all our conduct
LC : 0 1 :112(380) [0613] as God's command or as a holy, divine **word** and precept.
LC : 0 1 :116(381) [0615] If God's **Word** and will are placed first and observed,
LC : 0 1 :116(381) [0615] than the will and **word** of our parents, provided that
LC : 0 1 :117(381) [0615] and holy treasure, the **Word** and commandment of God.
LC : 0 1 :120(382) [0615] the other things he has commanded not a **word**.
LC : 0 1 :121(382) [0615] led astray from the pure **Word** of God to the lying vanities
LC : 0 1 :152(386) [0625] But God's **Word** and commandment are despised, as if
LC : 0 1 :157(387) [0627] may rightly understand the **Word** and will of God and
LC : 0 1 :157(387) [0627] From God's **Word** we could learn how to obtain an
LC : 0 1 :158(387) [0627] to those who govern and guide us by the **Word** of God.
LC : 0 1 :163(387) [0627] God deprive us of his **Word** and his blessings and once
LC : 0 1 :166(388) [0629] and disdains this is not worthy to hear a **word** from God.
LC : 0 1 :182(389) [0631] either by hand, heart, or **word**, by signs or gestures, or by
LC : 0 1 :190(391) [0635] contribute to his death by **word** or deed, for you have
LC : 0 1 :195(391) [0637] Here again we have God's **Word** by which he wants to
LC : 0 1 :198(392) [0637] commanded by God's **Word** which are the true, holy, and
LC : 0 1 :209(393) [0639] it in the light of God's **Word**, by which it is adorned and
LC : 0 1 :219(394) [0643] live chastely in thought, **word**, and deed in his particular
LC : 0 1 :221(395) [0643] that are chosen without God's **Word** and commandment.
LC : 0 1 :240(397) [0649] goods as dearly as he pleases without a **word** of criticism.
LC : 0 1 :249(398) [0651] is only to instruct and reprove by means of God's **Word**.
LC : 0 1 :262(400) [0655] Moreover, the **Word** of God must undergo the most
LC : 0 1 :279(402) [0661] along with you, that every **word** may be confirmed by the
LC : 0 1 :289(404) [0663] especially to the precious **Word** of God and its preachers.
LC : 0 1 :324(409) [0675] This **word**, "You shall have no other gods," means
LC : 0 1 :326(409) [0675] us not to despise his **Word**, but learn it, hear it gladly,
LC : 0 2 :016(412) [0681] All this is comprehended in the **word** "Creator."
LC : 0 2 :022(413) [0683] true of those who even fight against the **Word** of God.
LC : 0 2 :031(414) [0685] this article, that the little **word** "Lord" simply means the
LC : 0 2 :038(415) [0689] God has caused the **Word** to be published and
LC : 0 2 :042(416) [0689] and bears every Christian through the **Word** of God.
LC : 0 2 :042(416) [0689] reveals and preaches that **Word**, and by it he illumines
LC : 0 2 :043(416) [0689] he does not cause the **Word** to be preached and does not
LC : 0 2 :047(416) [0691] The **word** *ecclesia* properly means an assembly.
LC : 0 2 :048(416) [0691] Thus the **word** "church" *(Kirche)* really means nothing
LC : 0 2 :048(416) [0691] not of German but of Greek origin, like the **word** *ecclesia*.
LC : 0 2 :048(416) [0691] In that language the **word** is *kyria*, and in Latin *curia*.
LC : 0 2 :049(417) [0691] Likewise the **word** *communio*, which is appended, should
LC : 0 2 :050(417) [0691] uprooted, and it would be next to heresy to alter a **word**.
LC : 0 2 :052(417) [0691] heard and still hear God's **Word**, which is the first step in
LC : 0 2 :053(417) [0693] it he gathers us, using it to teach and preach the **Word**.
LC : 0 2 :054(417) [0693] Holy Spirit through God's **Word** in the unity of the
LC : 0 2 :055(418) [0693] of sins through the **Word** and through signs appointed to
LC : 0 2 :058(418) [0693] to work in us through the **Word**, daily granting
LC : 0 2 :060(418) [0695] we Germans hear the **word** *Fleisch* (flesh), we think no
LC : 0 2 :062(419) [0695] community through the **Word**, and imparts, increases,
LC : 0 2 :062(419) [0695] faith through the same **Word** and the forgiveness of sins.
LC : 0 2 :062(419) [0695] wait in faith for this to be accomplished through the **Word**
LC : 0 3 :016(422) [0701] but on account of his **Word** and the obedience accorded
LC : 0 3 :020(423) [0703] For by his **Word** God testifies that our prayer is heartily
LC : 0 3 :040(425) [0709] on earth may be classified as **word** or deed, speech or act.
LC : 0 3 :044(425) [0709] who antagonizes him in **word** and deed with the result
LC : 0 3 :046(426) [0709] our idiom "to praise, extol, and honor" in **word** and deed.
LC : 0 3 :047(426) [0711] ourselves who have the **Word** of God but are ungrateful
LC : 0 3 :048(426) [0711] everything else and his **Word** taught in its purity and
LC : 0 3 :051(427) [0711] us this through his holy **Word** and to enlighten and
LC : 0 3 :052(427) [0711] be praised through his holy **Word** and our Christian lives.
LC : 0 3 :053(427) [0711] here, in time, through the **Word** and faith, and secondly,
LC : 0 3 :054(427) [0713] we pray Thee, give us thy **Word**, that the Gospel may be
LC : 0 3 :054(427) [0713] among us through the **Word** and the power of the Holy

Continued ▶

LC : 03 :063(428) [0715] evil, even when we have accepted and believe God's **Word**.
LC : 03 :065(429) [0715] For where God's **Word** is preached, accepted or believed,
LC : 03 :067(429) [0717] and suppress thy holy **Word** or prevent thy kingdom from
LC : 03 :072(430) [0717] It is a brief and simple **word**, but very comprehensive.
LC : 03 :081(431) [0721] those of us who have the **Word** of God and would like to
LC : 03 :086(432) [0723] Although we have God's **Word** and believe, although we
LC : 03 :089(432) [0723] so that we sin daily in **word** and deed, in acts of
LC : 03 :103(434) [0727] world, which assails us by **word** and deed and drives us to
LC : 03 :104(434) [0727] and despise both the **Word** and the works of God, to tear
LC : 03 :120(436) [0731] This **word** is nothing else than an unquestioning
LC : 04 :008(437) [0733] may be, here stand God's **Word** and command which have
LC : 04 :014(438) [0735] comprehended in God's **Word** and commandment and
LC : 04 :014(438) [0735] water but that God's **Word** and commandment are added
LC : 04 :015(438) [0735] Baptism, ignore God's **Word** and ordinance, consider
LC : 04 :016(438) [0735] in the water is God's **Word** or commandment and God's
LC : 04 :017(438) [0737] can — all by virtue of the **Word**, which is a heavenly, holy
LC : 04 :017(438) [0737] which is a heavenly, holy **Word** which no one can
LC : 04 :018(438) [0737] From the **Word** it derives its nature as a sacrament, as St.
LC : 04 :018(438) [0737] This means that when the **Word** is added to the element
LC : 04 :019(439) [0737] of a nut) but as that in which God's **Word** is enclosed.
LC : 04 :021(439) [0737] Baptism on account of the **Word**, since God himself has
LC : 04 :022(439) [0737] again that these two, the **Word** and the water, must by no
LC : 04 :022(439) [0737] For where the **Word** is separated from the water, the
LC : 04 :022(439) [0737] But when the **Word** is present according to God's
LC : 04 :026(440) [0739] But the **Word** has.
LC : 04 :027(440) [0739] water, for through the **Word** Baptism receives the power
LC : 04 :029(440) [0739] incorporation with God's **Word** and ordinance and the
LC : 04 :029(440) [0739] who has implanted his **Word** in this external ordinance
LC : 04 :031(440) [0739] Baptism rejects God's **Word**, faith, and Christ, who
LC : 04 :037(441) [0741] and offered to us in the **Word** and received by faith.
LC : 04 :045(442) [0743] water, and meanwhile the **Word** is spoken so that the soul
LC : 04 :046(442) [0743] Since the water and the **Word** together constitute one
LC : 04 :046(442) [0743] the soul through the **Word** in which it believes, the body
LC : 04 :053(443) [0745] depends upon the **Word** and commandment of God.
LC : 04 :053(443) [0745] is simply water and God's **Word** in and with each other;
LC : 04 :053(443) [0745] other; that is, when the **Word** accompanies the water,
LC : 04 :053(443) [0745] or used, for it is bound not to our faith but to the **Word**.
LC : 04 :054(443) [0745] water together with God's **Word**, even though he failed to
LC : 04 :055(443) [0747] dare we think that God's **Word** and ordinance should be
LC : 04 :056(444) [0747] On this I build, that it is thy **Word** and command."
LC : 04 :056(444) [0747] of my own faith, but on the strength of Christ's **Word**.
LC : 04 :057(444) [0747] men — may err and deceive, but God's **Word** cannot err.
LC : 04 :060(444) [0747] For God's ordinance and **Word** cannot be changed or
LC : 04 :061(444) [0747] that they do not discern God's **Word** and commandment.
LC : 04 :063(444) [0749] be turned aside from the **Word**, regarding Baptism merely
LC : 05 :004(447) [0753] namely, God's **Word** and ordinance or command, which
LC : 05 :007(447) [0755] contrary to the **Word** of God, as human performances.
LC : 05 :008(447) [0755] are commanded by Christ's **word** to eat and drink.
LC : 05 :009(447) [0755] wine comprehended in God's **Word** and connected with it.
LC : 05 :010(448) [0755] It is the **Word**, I maintain, which distinguishes it from
LC : 05 :010(448) [0755] that is, "When the **Word** is joined to the external element,
LC : 05 :010(448) [0755] The **Word** must make the element a sacrament; otherwise
LC : 05 :011(448) [0755] Now, this is not the **word** and ordinance of a prince or
LC : 05 :012(448) [0755] With this **Word** you can strengthen your conscience and
LC : 05 :013(448) [0755] Here we have Christ's **word**, 'Take, eat; this is my body.'
LC : 05 :014(448) [0755] that if you take the **Word** away from the elements or view
LC : 05 :014(448) [0755] view them apart from the **Word**, you have nothing but
LC : 05 :016(448) [0757] founded on the holiness of men but on the **Word** of God.
LC : 05 :017(448) [0757] For the **Word** by which it was constituted a sacrament is
LC : 05 :030(450) [0759] be comprehended in the **Word** and offered to us through
LC : 05 :030(450) [0759] offered to us through the **Word**, otherwise we could never
LC : 05 :031(450) [0759] come to us in any other way than through the **Word**.
LC : 05 :031(450) [0759] if it were not proclaimed by preaching, by the oral **Word**?
LC : 05 :032(450) [0759] in this sacrament and offered to us through the **Word**.
LC : 05 :032(450) [0761] that the whole Gospel or **Word** of God apart from the
LC : 05 :034(450) [0761] he himself demands in the **Word** when he says, "Given *for*
LC : 05 :041(451) [0763] despise both the sacrament and the **Word** of God.
LC : 05 :062(454) [0767] but on account of thy **Word**, because Thou hast
LC : 05 :081(456) [0773] the heart from God's **Word** and blinds it, making you
LC : 05 :086(456) [0773] Thus the **Word** of God and the Christian church will be
LC : 06 :014(458) [0000] when it hears in God's **Word** that through a man God
LC : 06 :015(459) [0000] me of my sins through a **word** placed in the mouth of a
LC : 06 :018(459) [0000] value on our work but exalt and magnify God's **Word**.
LC : 06 :022(459) [0000] The **Word** or absolution, I say, is what you should
LC : 06 :033(461) [0000] and tremble for God's **Word**, absolution, the sacrament,
EP : 00 :000(463) [0775] under the Guidance of the **Word** of God and the
EP : 00 :000(464) [0777] in Conformity with God's **Word** in the Recapitulation
EP : RN :001(464) [0777] in Ps. 119:105, "Thy **word** is a lamp to my feet and a light
EP : 01 :009(467) [0781] by a rational process, but only from God's **Word**.
EP : 01 :021(468) [0783] of corrupted man, no idle **word** were spoken, or no
EP : 01 :022(469) [0785] to observe that the **word** "nature" has several meanings.
EP : 01 :022(469) [0785] At other times the **word** means the good or bad quality
EP : 01 :022(469) [0785] Here the **word** "nature" does not mean the substance of
EP : 02 :001(469) [0785] of God offered in the **Word** and the holy sacraments?
EP : 02 :001(470) [0787] *concerning this Article on the Basis of God's Word*
EP : 02 :004(470) [0787] and the hearing of God's **Word**, as it is written that the
EP : 02 :004(470) [0787] comes from the hearing of God's **Word** (Rom. 10:17).
EP : 02 :004(470) [0787] will that men should hear his **Word** and not stop their ears
EP : 02 :004(470) [0787] Spirit is present with this **Word** and opens hearts so that,
EP : 02 :007(470) [0787] errors as being contrary to the norm of the **Word** of God:
EP : 02 :011(471) [0789] the preaching of the **Word** and in it has offered his grace,
EP : 02 :013(471) [0789] the hearing of God's **Word** and without the use of the holy
EP : 02 :018(472) [0791] Spirit of God through the **Word** that has been heard or
EP : 02 :019(472) [0791] the Holy Spirit and the **Word** of God as the Holy Spirit's
EP : 02 :019(472) [0791] Man should hear this **Word**, though he cannot give it
EP : 03 :001(472) [0791] churches according to the **Word** of God and the content
EP : 03 :006(473) [0793] of God by which in the **Word** of the Gospel we recognize
EP : 03 :007(473) [0793] the usage of Scripture the **word** "justify" means in this
EP : 03 :009(474) [0795] of the promises and the **Word** of the holy Gospel, they
EP : 04 :003(476) [0797] we should not use the **word** "necessary" when speaking of
EP : 04 :003(476) [0797] held with reference to the **word** "necessary" that the new
EP : 05 :001(478) [0801] *The Pure Doctrine of God's Word*
EP : 05 :002(478) [0801] St. Paul's admonition, the **Word** of God may be divided
EP : 05 :006(478) [0803] 5. The **word** "Gospel" is not used in a single sense in Holy
EP : 05 :006(478) [0803] and confess that when the **word** "Gospel" means the
EP : 07 :005(482) [0809] To them the **word** "spiritual" means no more than the
EP : 07 :013(483) [0811] ground is that God's **Word** is not false nor does it lie.
EP : 07 :024(484) [0815] contrary to the clear **Word** of Christ's testament, so that
EP : 07 :042(486) [0817] other way than by faith and as it is revealed in the **Word**.
EP : 08 :019(490) [0823] as contrary to the **Word** of God and our simple Christian
EP : 08 :032(491) [0825] with us on earth in the **Word**, in the sacraments, and in
EP : 08 :039(491) [0827] firm basis of the divine **Word** and our simple Christian
EP : 10 :001(492) [0829] nor forbidden in the **Word** of God but have been
EP : 10 :003(493) [0829] nor forbidden in the **Word** of God, but which have been
EP : 10 :008(494) [0831] false and contrary to God's **Word** the following teachings:
EP : 11 :006(495) [0833] is to be looked for in his **Word**, where he has revealed it.
EP : 11 :007(495) [0833] 6. The **Word** of God, however, leads us to Christ, who is
EP : 11 :008(495) [0833] he offers himself in his **Word**, and it is his will that they
EP : 11 :008(495) [0833] his will that they hear the **Word** and do not stop their ears
EP : 11 :012(496) [0835] men either do not hear the **Word** of God at all but
EP : 11 :012(496) [0835] or, if they do hear the **Word**, they cast it to the wind and
EP : 11 :013(496) [0835] far as it is revealed in the **Word** of God, which shows us
EP : 11 :014(496) [0835] to abide by the revealed **Word** which cannot and will not
EP : 11 :016(497) [0837] doctrine according to the **Word** and will of God, but in
EP : 11 :022(497) [0837] under the guidance of the **Word** of God and the plain
EP : 12 :008(498) [0839] in spite of the expressed **word** of God's promise which
EP : 12 :011(499) [0841] way, but flee and avoid them as perverters of God's **Word**.
EP : 12 :021(499) [0841] to the Father and to the **Word** as far as might, power,
EP : 12 :022(499) [0841] of the church — the **Word** preached and heard — is not a
EP : 12 :030(500) [0843] and contrary to the **Word** of God, the three Creeds, the
SD : 00 :000(501) [0845] Settled According to the **Word** of God and the Summary
SD : PR :001(501) [0847] forth on the basis of the **Word** of God and purified by Dr.
SD : PR :002(501) [0847] as wholly contrary to the **Word** of God and Christian
SD : PR :003(501) [0847] reformed according to the **Word** of God, ordered the
SD : PR :003(501) [0847] on the basis of God's **Word** and submitted it to Emperor
SD : PR :004(502) [0847] to accept next to the **Word** of God, just as in ancient
SD : PR :010(503) [0849] on the basis of God's **Word** and of approved writings in
SD : PR :010(503) [0849] issues agrees with the **Word** of God and the Christian
SD : RN :000(503) [0849] in Conformity with the **Word** of God and Errors Are to
SD : PR :001(503) [0851] religion is drawn together out of the **Word** of God.
SD : PR :002(503) [0851] the pure doctrine of the **Word** of God as Dr. Luther of
SD : PR :004(504) [0851] together out of God's **Word** in brief articles or chapters
SD : PR :004(504) [0851] and based upon the **Word** of God — in which all those
SD : PR :005(504) [0851] to light the truth of his **Word** amid the abominable
SD : PR :005(504) [0851] and conformed to the **Word** of God, is summarized in the
SD : PR :005(504) [0851] it is taken from the **Word** of God and solidly and well
SD : PR :007(505) [0853] on the basis of God's **Word**, and in addition the grounds
SD : PR :008(505) [0853] on the basis of God's **Word** for ordinary laymen in a most
SD : PR :009(505) [0853] on the basis of God's **Word** and conclusively established
SD : PR :009(505) [0855] way of distinction that the **Word** of God is and should
SD : PR :010(506) [0855] it is drawn from the **Word** of God, all other writings are
SD : PR :013(506) [0855] base our position on the **Word** of God as the eternal
SD : PR :016(507) [0857] in the truth of God's **Word** will find in the previously
SD : PR :016(507) [0857] writings of God's **Word**, and what he should reject, flee,
SD : 01 :001(508) [0859] it is not a thought, a **word**, or a deed but the very nature
SD : 01 :003(509) [0859] and according to the **Word** of God and is purged of all
SD : 01 :004(509) [0861] and according to the **Word** of God and to preserve the
SD : 01 :025(512) [0867] doctrines because God's **Word** teaches that man's
SD : 01 :051(517) [0875] creates man's nature," the **word** "nature" means man's
SD : 01 :058(519) [0879] or an accident in the right and strict sense of the **word**.
SD : 01 :061(519) [0879] in harmony with the **Word** of God, just as Dr. Luther in
SD : 02 :002(520) [0881] after the Fall, when the **Word** of God is preached and the
SD : 02 :004(520) [0881] and hearing of the **Word** of God) and brings them to the
SD : 02 :005(521) [0881] cannot understand the **Word** of God when it is preached,
SD : 02 :005(521) [0881] Holy Spirit, through the **Word** which is preached and
SD : 02 :006(521) [0883] way according to the **Word** of God, and by God's grace to
SD : 02 :008(521) [0883] reasons from the **Word** of God support and confirm the
SD : 02 :008(521) [0883] that it is only from the **Word** of God that judgments on
SD : 02 :012(522) [0885] "My **Word** finds no place in you" (John 8:37).
SD : 02 :012(523) [0885] receive (or, as the Greek **word** actually has it, does not
SD : 02 :015(523) [0887] and meditating on the **Word** of God, but were written in
SD : 02 :016(523) [0887] exercise in reading his **Word** and putting it into practice,
SD : 02 :017(523) [0887] In the second place, the **Word** of God testifies that in
SD : 02 :019(524) [0889] meditating upon the divine **Word**, or that in outward or
SD : 02 :026(526) [0891] Scriptures and to heed the **Word**, as we read in Luke
SD : 02 :028(527) [0893] is founded upon the **Word** of God and accords with the
SD : 02 :036(528) [0895] this, that I have heard the **Word** of God and still hear it,
SD : 02 :037(528) [0895] and propagate his **Word**, whereby he initiates and
SD : 02 :041(529) [0897] grace we may believe his holy **Word** and live a godly life."
SD : 02 :046(530) [0899] to heed, hear, or read the **Word** and the sacraments but
SD : 02 :048(530) [0901] now set forth from the **Word** of God how man is
SD : 02 :048(530) [0901] means (namely, the oral **Word** and the holy sacraments)
SD : 02 :050(531) [0901] namely, through his holy **Word** (when one hears it
SD : 02 :050(531) [0901] sacraments (when they are used according to his **Word**).
SD : 02 :051(531) [0901] "Sanctify them in the truth; thy **Word** is truth.
SD : 02 :051(531) [0901] are to believe in me through their **Word**" (John 17:17, 20).
SD : 02 :052(531) [0901] and the hearing of God's **Word** are the Holy Spirit's
SD : 02 :053(531) [0903] can hear and read this **Word** externally because, as stated
SD : 02 :054(531) [0903] and the hearing of his **Word**) God is active, breaks our
SD : 02 :055(531) [0903] Spirit, who through the **Word** preached and heard
SD : 02 :055(532) [0903] so that men believe this **Word** and give their assent to it.
SD : 02 :055(532) [0903] be certain that, when the **Word** of God is preached, pure
SD : 02 :056(532) [0903] his promise, that the **Word** which is heard and preached
SD : 02 :057(532) [0903] hear preaching or read the **Word** of God, but despises the
SD : 02 :057(532) [0903] of God, but despises the **Word** and the community of
SD : 02 :057(532) [0903] his grace to all men in the **Word** and the holy sacraments,
SD : 02 :057(532) [0903] themselves with his holy **Word**, he is in the midst of them.
SD : 02 :059(532) [0905] or block, for he resists the **Word** and will of God until
SD : 02 :065(534) [0907] renewal in us through the **Word** and the holy sacraments,
SD : 02 :067(534) [0907] they not only hear the **Word** of God but also are able to
SD : 02 :071(535) [0909] the preaching of his **Word** and our meditation upon it
SD : 02 :080(536) [0911] without hearing the divine **Word** and without the use of
SD : 02 :083(537) [0913] but wholly resists the **Word**, conversion does not and
SD : 02 :083(537) [0913] take place through the **Word**, do not receive the Holy
SD : 02 :089(538) [0915] the hearing of the divine **Word**, nor did he mean that in
SD : 02 :089(538) [0915] and might through the **Word** in the intellect, will, and

Continued ▶

SD : 02 :090(538) [0915] in which these three (the **Word** of God preached and
SD : 02 :090(539) [0915] the hearing of his holy **Word** as his ordinary means and
SD : 03 :008(540) [0919] way according to the **Word** of God and to settle it by his
SD : 03 :011(541) [0919] as our redeemer in the **Word** of the Gospel and to trust in
SD : 03 :017(541) [0921] Accordingly the **word** "justify" here means to declare
SD : 03 :017(542) [0921] usage and meaning of the **word** in the Holy Scriptures of
SD : 03 :018(542) [0921] Since the **word** "regeneration" is sometimes used in place
SD : 03 :019(542) [0921] The **word** "regeneration" is used, in the first place, to
SD : 03 :019(542) [0921] But this **word** is also used in the limited sense of the
SD : 03 :021(542) [0921] Frequently the **word** "regeneration" means the
SD : 03 :059(550) [0937] errors as contrary to the **Word** of God, the teaching of the
SD : 03 :066(550) [0937] as contrary to the clear **Word** of God, and by God's grace
SD : 03 :066(550) [0937] demonstrated from God's **Word** in the Augsburg
SD : 04 :004(551) [0939] "necessary" and "free," especially the **word** "necessary."
SD : 04 :004(551) [0939] This **word** may refer to the immutable order which
SD : 04 :006(552) [0939] way and according to the **Word** of God, and by God's
SD : 04 :007(552) [0941] and commands in his **Word**, and not those that an
SD : 04 :016(554) [0943] namely, that when the **word** "necessary" is used in this
SD : 04 :035(557) [0949] it is evident from the **Word** of God that faith is the proper
SD : 04 :037(557) [0951] contrary to the express **Word** of God, is being placed
SD : 05 :001(558) [0951] the purpose that the **Word** of God may be rightly divided
SD : 05 :003(558) [0953] by the fact that the little **word** "Gospel" does not always
SD : 05 :004(558) [0953] In the one case the **word** is used in such a way that we
SD : 05 :005(559) [0953] And when the **word** "Gospel" is used in its broad sense
SD : 05 :005(559) [0953] it is correct to define the **word** as the proclamation of
SD : 05 :006(559) [0953] In addition, however, the **word** "Gospel" is also used in
SD : 05 :007(559) [0953] Again, the little **word** "repentance" is not used in a single
SD : 05 :007(559) [0953] passages of Holy Writ the **word** is used and understood
SD : 05 :019(561) [0957] unbelief, when a person does not believe the **Word** of God
SD : 05 :019(561) [0957] faith in Christ) is the **Word** of God, the Holy Spirit
SD : 06 :003(564) [0963] to his written law and **Word**, which is a certain rule and
SD : 06 :015(566) [0967] are not good works — the **word** "law" here has but one
SD : 06 :020(567) [0969] of God and without his **Word** and command, as it is
SD : 07 :001(569) [0971] contrary to the holy **Word** of God and to the Augsburg
SD : 07 :003(569) [0973] way as by the preached **Word**, lifts itself up and ascends
SD : 07 :007(570) [0975] They interpret the **word** "is" sacramentally or in a
SD : 07 :009(570) [0975] on the basis of God's **Word** "that the true body and blood
SD : 07 :018(572) [0979] the same way as with the **Word** of the Gospel, and that
SD : 07 :020(572) [0979] at greater length from the **Word** of God in the Large
SD : 07 :020(573) [0979] and wine which Christ's **word** commands us Christians to
SD : 07 :021(573) [0979] shortly thereafter: "The **Word**, I say, is what makes this
SD : 07 :022(573) [0979] your conscience from the **Word** of God and declare, 'Let
SD : 07 :022(573) [0979] Here we have Christ's **word**, 'Take eat, this is my body.
SD : 07 :023(573) [0979] that if you take the **Word** away or look upon the elements
SD : 07 :023(573) [0979] the elements without the **Word**, you then have nothing
SD : 07 :024(573) [0981] not based on the holiness of men but on the **Word** of God
SD : 07 :025(573) [0981] The **Word** by which it has been instituted and has become
SD : 07 :027(574) [0981] holy Supper from God's **Word** and confirms that it is to
SD : 07 :031(574) [0983] can twist and pervert the **Word** of God, what will he not
SD : 07 :032(574) [0983] or unbelief but on the **Word** and ordinance of God —
SD : 07 :032(574) [0983] they first change God's **Word** and ordinance and
SD : 07 :032(575) [0983] they do not also have the **Word** and instituted ordinance
SD : 07 :036(575) [0985] the statement, "The **Word** became flesh," with such
SD : 07 :036(575) [0985] phrases as, "The **Word** dwelt in us," or "In Christ the
SD : 07 :039(576) [0985] was incarnate through the **Word** of God and for the sake
SD : 07 :039(576) [0985] by him through the **Word** and prayer is the true flesh and
SD : 07 :042(576) [0987] recorded in the holy **Word** of God and so understood,
SD : 07 :048(578) [0989] change in meaning) in the **word** "bread," as though the
SD : 07 :049(578) [0989] (that is, a change in meaning) in the **word** "body."
SD : 07 :059(580) [0993] with Christ, just as the **Word** of the Gospel, when it is laid
SD : 07 :062(581) [0995] to ourselves the **Word** of God, in which Christ, true God
SD : 07 :074(583) [0999] ourselves: No man's **word** or work, be it the merit or the
SD : 07 :074(583) [0999] power of God and the **Word**, institution, and ordinance of
SD : 07 :076(583) [0999] grow and multiply, so this **word** was indeed spoken only
SD : 07 :077(583) [0999] Thus it is not our **word** or speaking but the command and
SD : 07 :078(584) [1001] or of our efficacious **word**, but because of his command
SD : 07 :081(584) [1001] strengthened, and confirmed through his **Word**.
SD : 07 :089(585) [1003] sacrament, but solely the **Word** and institution of our
SD : 07 :091(585) [1005] on the basis of God's **Word** by Dr. Luther in his
SD : 07 :092(586) [1005] understanding of Christ's **word** and testament to a
SD : 07 :096(586) [1005] "3. The third is that the **Word** of God is not false or
SD : 07 :104(587) [1009] our churches use the **word** "spiritual" in this context.
SD : 07 :104(587) [1009] the Sacramentarians this **word** "spiritual" means precisely
SD : 07 :105(588) [1009] Dr. Luther or we use the **word** "spiritual" in this
SD : 07 :105(588) [1009] this sense, too, we use the **word** "spiritual" when we say
SD : 07 :107(588) [1009] doctrine, based as it is on the **Word** of God:
SD : 07 :108(588) [1009] which it is instituted in the **Word** of God, as was shown
SD : 07 :110(589) [1011] of ours on the basis of the **Word** of God and the testimony
SD : 07 :112(589) [1011] set forth above, based as it is on the **Word** of God.
SD : 07 :121(590) [1013] which ascribes to the **word** and work of the priest the
SD : 07 :123(590) [1015] and scoffers at the **Word** of God who are in the external
SD : 07 :128(591) [1015] set forth above, well founded as it is in God's **Word**.
SD : 08 :004(592) [1017] being in harmony with the **Word** of God, with accusations
SD : 08 :005(592) [1017] way according to the **Word** of God and in accordance
SD : 08 :015(594) [1019] one person and God the **Word** who dwells in Christ is
SD : 08 :016(594) [1021] a mere man in whom the **Word** of God dwelled just as in
SD : 08 :016(594) [1021] individual and God the **Word** who dwells in him another."
SD : 08 :025(596) [1023] the garden when with one **word** he struck his enemies to
SD : 08 :029(597) [1025] covenant, to which he has directed us through his **Word**.
SD : 08 :051(600) [1031] on the basis of God's **Word** that this opinion is erroneous
SD : 08 :053(601) [1033] In his **Word** he has revealed to us as much as we need to
SD : 08 :075(606) [1043] that the Son, the Father's **Word**, indeed knows all things,
SD : 08 :092(609) [1049] his presence in his **Word**, as in the Holy Communion.
SD : 08 :094(609) [1049] that in the preached **Word** and in the right use of the holy
SD : 08 :096(609) [1049] being contrary to the pure **Word** of God, the writings of
SD : 09 :003(610) [1051] We must only believe and cling to the **Word**.
SD : 10 :001(610) [1053] nor forbidden in the **Word** of God but which have been
SD : 10 :005(611) [1053] basically contrary to the **Word** of God, even though they
SD : 10 :010(612) [1055] as when enemies of the **Word** of God desire to suppress
SD : 10 :010(612) [1055] the ministers of the **Word** as the leaders of the community
SD : 10 :010(612) [1055] and all that pertains to it, according to the **Word** of God.
SD : 10 :021(614) [1061] authority count for more than the **Word** of God."
SD : 10 :025(615) [1061] the enemies of God's **Word**, and scandalize the weak in
SD : 11 :002(616) [1063] set forth out of the divine **Word** and according to the
SD : 11 :003(616) [1063] a teaching of the divine **Word** because some people misuse
SD : 11 :010(618) [1067] repentance, despise **Word** and sacraments, and do not
SD : 11 :010(618) [1067] I were to hold to the **Word**, repent, believe, etc., since I
SD : 11 :012(618) [1067] everything in the **Word** of God is written down for us, not
SD : 11 :012(618) [1067] to direct us thereby to the **Word** (Eph. 1:13, 14;
SD : 11 :013(619) [1069] "book of life" as it is revealed to us through the **Word**.
SD : 11 :016(619) [1069] and distributed to us through his **Word** and sacraments.
SD : 11 :017(619) [1069] Holy Spirit through the **Word** when it is preached, heard,
SD : 11 :021(619) [1069] end, if they cling to God's **Word**, pray diligently, persevere
SD : 11 :027(620) [1071] means but through the **Word**, as indeed he has
SD : 11 :029(621) [1073] the preaching of the **Word** as a deception, but should
SD : 11 :029(621) [1073] active through the **Word** so that they may be illuminated,
SD : 11 :029(621) [1073] For the **Word** through which we are called is a ministry of
SD : 11 :029(621) [1073] be efficacious through the **Word**, to strengthen us, and to
SD : 11 :029(621) [1073] will that we should accept the **Word**, believe and obey it.
SD : 11 :033(621) [1073] and ability through the **Word** by which he has called us.
SD : 11 :034(622) [1075] takes place through the **Word**, God intended to say:
SD : 11 :034(622) [1075] I do indeed through the **Word** call all of you, to whom I
SD : 11 :034(622) [1075] you, to whom I give my **Word**, into my kingdom, but
SD : 11 :034(622) [1075] whom I call through the **Word** are not to be illuminated
SD : 11 :036(622) [1075] it to us solely from his **Word**, through which he deals with
SD : 11 :038(622) [1075] that when we believe the **word** of absolution we are as
SD : 11 :038(622) [1075] comes to us through the **Word** and through the
SD : 11 :039(622) [1075] and active through the **Word** when it is proclaimed,
SD : 11 :039(622) [1075] elect who despise God's **Word** and who reject, blaspheme,
SD : 11 :040(623) [1077] the elect through the **Word** and that he would justify and
SD : 11 :040(623) [1077] are called through the **Word**, spurn the Word and
SD : 11 :040(623) [1077] the Word, spurn the **Word** and persistently resist the Holy
SD : 11 :040(623) [1077] wants to work efficaciously in them through the **Word**.
SD : 11 :041(623) [1077] for few accept the **Word** and obey it; the majority despise
SD : 11 :041(623) [1077] the majority despise the **Word** and refuse to come to the
SD : 11 :041(623) [1077] for such contempt of the **Word** is not God's
SD : 11 :041(623) [1077] active through the **Word**, as Christ says, "How often
SD : 11 :042(623) [1077] many "receive the **Word** with joy," but after that "they
SD : 11 :043(623) [1077] revealed the mystery of foreknowledge to us in his **Word**.
SD : 11 :044(624) [1077] Holy Spirit through the **Word** he would create and effect
SD : 11 :052(625) [1081] expressly revealed in his **Word** and what he has not
SD : 11 :052(625) [1081] but we are to adhere exclusively to the revealed **Word**.
SD : 11 :053(625) [1081] of the question which God has revealed to us in his **Word**.
SD : 11 :055(625) [1081] concerning it in the **Word**, still less has commanded us to
SD : 11 :055(625) [1081] cling solely to his revealed **Word**, to which he directs us.
SD : 11 :056(625) [1081] constantly with the **Word**, while we leave the time and
SD : 11 :057(625) [1081] observe that God gives his **Word** at one place and not at
SD : 11 :058(626) [1081] people for contempt of his **Word** that the punishment
SD : 11 :059(626) [1081] over against God's **Word** and often sorely grieve the Holy
SD : 11 :059(626) [1083] he gives and preserves his **Word** and whom he does not
SD : 11 :060(626) [1083] God owes us neither his **Word**, nor his Spirit, nor his
SD : 11 :061(626) [1083] gives and preserves his **Word**, whereby he enlightens,
SD : 11 :064(626) [1083] the basis of the revealed **Word** of God, as soon as he
SD : 11 :064(626) [1083] and beyond what he has revealed to us in his **Word**.
SD : 11 :065(627) [1083] through the proclaimed **Word** when the Father says, "This
SD : 11 :068(627) [1085] and according to his own **word** Christ will not turn them
SD : 11 :069(627) [1085] the hearing of God's **Word**, as the apostle testifies, "Faith
SD : 11 :069(627) [1085] from the hearing of God's **Word**" (Rom. 10:17) when it is
SD : 11 :071(627) [1085] and faith in us through the **Word** and the sacraments.
SD : 11 :072(628) [1087] We have his **word**, "What father among you, if his son
SD : 11 :075(628) [1087] to repentance through the **Word**, and through it the Holy
SD : 11 :075(628) [1087] all who tremble at his **Word** and cordially return to
SD : 11 :076(628) [1087] and he has ordained **Word** and sacraments as the ordinary
SD : 11 :076(629) [1087] the preaching of his **Word** and should wait for the Father
SD : 11 :076(629) [1087] the Father to draw him without **Word** and sacraments.
SD : 11 :076(629) [1089] hearing of his holy, divine **Word**, as with a net by which
SD : 11 :077(629) [1089] wills to be present in the **Word** and to be efficacious with
SD : 11 :078(629) [1089] why all who hear the **Word** do not come to faith and
SD : 11 :078(629) [1089] because they heard the **Word** of God not to learn but only
SD : 11 :085(630) [1091] God arranged to have his **Word** proclaimed and his will
SD : 11 :086(631) [1091] and despisers of his **Word**, and in no way does he want us
SD : 11 :091(632) [1093] set forth according to the **Word** and will of God but
SD : 12 :008(633) [1097] times where the pure **Word** of the holy Gospel was
SD : 12 :016(634) [1099] and avoid them as people who pervert the **Word** of God.
SD : 12 :029(635) [1101] Father and the eternal **Word**, so that the two natures of
SD : 12 :030(635) [1101] ministry of the church, the **Word** proclaimed and heard, is
SD : 12 :039(636) [1103] heretical, contrary to the **Word** of God, to the three

Words (322)

PR : PR :019(009) [0017] teaching under the **words** of this same second edition and
PR : PR :020(010) [0017] foundation, namely, the **words** of institution of Christ's
PR : PR :020(010) [0017] faith they are to stay with the plain **words** of Christ.
PR : PR :020(010) [0017] and interpretation of the **words** of the testament of Christ
PR : PR :020(010) [0019] understanding of the **words** of Christ as described above
PR : PR :021(010) [0019] in clear and candid **words** (so that all misunderstanding
PR : PR :022(012) [0019] teach about it on the basis of the **words** of his testament.
AG : 18 :004(039) [0051] is no novelty, the clear **words** of Augustine on free will
AG : 22 :002(049) [0059] commands with clear **words** that all should drink of it.
AG : 22 :003(049) [0059] one might question these **words** and interpret them as if
AG : 24 :038(060) [0067] for the **words** of the Nicene canon read, "After the priests
AG : 25 :011(063) [0069] *poenitentia*, where these **words** of Chrysostom are
AG : 27 :020(074) [0079] appears from God's own **words** in Gen. 2:18, "It is not
AL : 18 :004(039) [0051] these things in so many **words**: "We concede that all men
AL : 23 :025(055) [0065] His **words** in the first book of his letters, Epistle XI, are
AL : 24 :037(060) [0067] Lord from him, for the **words** of the Nicene canon read,
AL : 26 :017(066) [0073] are to be regarded as things indifferent, for these are his **words**.
AP : 02 :004(101) [0105] First we must show why we used these **words** here.
AP : 02 :037(105) [0115] principle, they twist his **words** in order by this device to
AP : 04 :033(111) [0129] These **words** are so clear that they do not need an acute
AP : 04 :033(111) [0129] listening—to use the **words** that Augustine uses in
AP : 04 :104(122) [0151] These are the **words** of Ambrose, which clearly support
AP : 04 :108(122) [0153] they suppose that these **words** fell from the Holy Spirit
AP : 04 :152(127) [0163] But he interprets his own **words** when he adds: "Your
AP : 04 :244(141) [0189] The **words** of James will cause no trouble if our
AP : 04 :252(143) [0191] As these **words**, "the doers of the law will be justified,"
AP : 04 :252(143) [0191] the same about James's **words**, "A man is justified by

Continued ▶

Continued ▶

Wordiness (1), Wording (1)

Work (250)

Continued ▶

LC : 01 :079(375) [0603] expression for “stopping **work**” literally means “observing
LC : 01 :080(375) [0603] were to abstain from hard **work** and to rest, so that both
LC : 01 :083(376) [0603] who have attended to their **work** and trades the whole
LC : 01 :086(376) [0605] so narrow as to forbid incidental and unavoidable **work**.
LC : 01 :088(377) [0605] and refrain from external **work**, or deck ourselves with
LC : 01 :092(377) [0607] person, the day, and the **work** are sanctified by it, not on
LC : 01 :092(377) [0607] on account of the external **work** but on account of the
LC : 01 :092(377) [0607] that all our life and **work** must be guided by God’s Word
LC : 01 :093(377) [0607] any conduct or **work** done apart from God’s Word is
LC : 01 :094(378) [0607] so that this day should have its own particular holy **work**.
LC : 01 :094(378) [0607] not properly called holy **work** unless the doer himself is
LC : 01 :094(378) [0607] But here a **work** must be performed by which the doer
LC : 01 :102(379) [0609] more pleased than by any **work** of hypocrisy, however
LC : 01 :112(380) [0613] a great, good, and holy **work** is here assigned to children.
LC : 01 :115(381) [0615] own choice: “See, this **work** is well pleasing to my God in
LC : 01 :116(381) [0615] they can produce a single **work** that is greater and nobler
LC : 01 :118(381) [0615] bring before God a single **work** done in accordance with
LC : 01 :118(381) [0615] “Now I know that this **work** is well pleasing to Thee!”
LC : 01 :120(381) [0615] with joy when it can go to **work** and do what is
LC : 01 :125(382) [0617] that it is the greatest **work** that we can do, next to the
LC : 01 :140(384) [0621] precious and acceptable a **work** he does when he observes
LC : 01 :145(385) [0623] God; and with her careful **work**, for which she receives
LC : 01 :170(388) [0629] merely to put them to **work** like cows or asses, and gave
LC : 01 :221(395) [0643] another precious good **work** — indeed, many and great
LC : 01 :224(395) [0643] wine- and beer-cellar, **work**-shop, and, in short, wherever
LC : 01 :226(395) [0645] people and yet are careless and unreliable in their **work**.
LC : 01 :263(400) [0655] False witness is clearly a **work** of the tongue.
LC : 01 :278(402) [0661] Then you have done a great and excellent **work**.
LC : 01 :314(407) [0671] is considered a precious **work** that cannot be sufficiently
LC : 01 :333(410) [0677] produce, if they can, any **work** like that which God in
LC : 02 :010(411) [0679] of God the Father, his nature, his will, and his **work**.
LC : 02 :036(415) [0687] so on account of his **work** the Holy Spirit must be called
LC : 02 :038(415) [0689] The **work** is finished and completed, Christ has acquired
LC : 02 :038(415) [0689] But if the **work** remained hidden and no one knew of it,
LC : 02 :058(418) [0693] Spirit must continue to **work** in us through the Word,
LC : 02 :059(418) [0693] then, is the office and **work** of the Holy Spirit, to begin
LC : 02 :061(419) [0695] Holy Spirit carries on his **work** unceasingly until the last
LC : 02 :061(419) [0695] on earth, through which he speaks and does all his **work**.
LC : 02 :062(419) [0695] Then when his **work** has been finished and we abide in it,
LC : 02 :063(419) [0695] of God, his will, and his **work** exquisitely depicted in very
LC : 03 :013(422) [0701] always reflect: “This is a **work** of obedience, and what I
LC : 03 :025(423) [0705] at best, of doing a good **work** as a payment to God, not
LC : 03 :054(427) [0713] it may be received by faith and may **work** and live in us.
LC : 03 :076(431) [0721] and servants; to cause our **work**, craft, or occupation,
LC : 03 :102(434) [0727] our necks; he goes to **work** and lures us daily into
LC : 04 :010(437) [0735] of much greater value than the **work** of any man or saint.
LC : 04 :010(437) [0735] For what **work** can man do that is greater than God’s
LC : 04 :010(437) [0735] what work can man do that is greater than God’s **work**?
LC : 04 :011(437) [0735] Here the devil sets to **work** to blind us with false
LC : 04 :011(437) [0735] and lead us away from God’s **work** to our own.
LC : 04 :035(441) [0741] “If Baptism is itself a **work**, and you say that works are of
LC : 04 :035(441) [0741] however, is not our **work** but God’s (for, as was said, you
LC : 04 :037(441) [0741] that Baptism is not a **work** which we do but is a treasure
LC : 04 :037(441) [0741] upon the cross is not a **work** but a treasure comprehended
LC : 04 :046(442) [0743] no other kind of life and no **work** on earth can acquire.
LC : 04 :049(442) [0745] to Christ is sufficiently proved from his own **work**.
LC : 04 :062(444) [0749] pervert and nullify all God’s **work** and ordinances.
LC : 04 :080(446) [0751] only in the light of a **work** performed once for all.
LC : 04 :082(446) [0751] as we said, it is God’s ordinance and not a **work** of ours.
LC : 04 :085(446) [0753] we must practice the **work** that makes us Christians.
LC : 05 :031(450) [0759] Although the **work** was accomplished and forgiveness of
LC : 05 :052(452) [0765] be forced by men either to faith or to any good **work**.
LC : 05 :057(453) [0767] good and pure you are, to **work** toward the time when
LC : 05 :086(456) [0773] us in our office and **work**, so that they in turn may bring
LC : 06 :015(458) [0000] The first is my **work** and act, when I lament my sin and
LC : 06 :015(459) [0000] The second is a **work** which God does, when he absolves
LC : 06 :016(459) [0000] all the emphasis on our **work** alone, and we were only
LC : 06 :016(459) [0000] were simply a good **work** with which we could satisfy
LC : 06 :018(459) [0000] set little value on our **work** but exalt and magnify God’s
LC : 06 :018(459) [0000] to perform a magnificent **work** to present to him, but
LC : 06 :022(459) [0000] purpose of performing a **work** but to hear what God
EP : 01 :002(466) [0779] the difference between God’s **work** and the devil’s work.
EP : 01 :002(466) [0779] the difference between God’s work and the devil’s **work**.
EP : 01 :025(469) [0785] the distinction between God’s **work** and Satan’s work.
EP : 01 :025(469) [0785] the distinction between God’s work and Satan’s **work**.
EP : 02 :004(470) [0787] Spirit, for man’s conversion is the Spirit’s **work** alone.
EP : 03 :004(473) [0793] present, or subsequent **work**, merit, or worthiness, and
EP : 05 :010(479) [0803] therefore it is an “alien **work**” of Christ by which he
EP : 07 :008(482) [0811] and confess that no man’s **work** nor the recitation of the
EP : 07 :017(484) [0813] guests as he is to **work** life and consolation in the hearts
EP : 11 :012(496) [0835] Spirit, so that he cannot **work** in them; or, if they do hear
EP : 12 :011(499) [0841] should one serve them or **work** for them in any way, but
SD : 01 :002(509) [0859] original sin (which is a **work** of the devil by which man’s
SD : 01 :003(509) [0861] carefully distinguish his **work** and creation in man from
SD : 01 :003(509) [0861] in man from the devil’s **work**, the corruption of human
SD : 01 :007(510) [0861] one man sin (which is the **work** of the devil) entered into
SD : 01 :032(513) [0869] nature and essence are the **work**, the product, and the
SD : 01 :040(515) [0871] handiwork of God; on the contrary, it is the devil’s **work**.
SD : 01 :042(515) [0871] in man from the devil’s **work**, we declare that it is by
SD : 01 :042(515) [0871] likewise, that it is God’s **work** that man is able to think, to
SD : 02 :014(523) [0885] also true, “For God is at **work** in you, both to will and to
SD : 02 :014(523) [0885] you, both to will and to **work** for his good pleasure”
SD : 02 :026(526) [0891] mind, and spirit, is solely the **work** of the Holy Spirit.
SD : 02 :026(526) [0891] “For God is at **work** in you, both to will and to work”
SD : 02 :026(526) [0891] is at work in you, both to will and to **work**” (Phil. 2:13).
SD : 02 :026(526) [0891] “This is the **work** of God, that you believe in him whom
SD : 02 :027(527) [0893] it is preached is our own **work** and lies within our own
SD : 02 :027(527) [0893] will, but that it is God’s **work** to give the ability to
SD : 02 :039(528) [0895] as the apostle ascribes this **work** alone to God when he
SD : 02 :046(530) [0899] are exclusively the **work** of God and not of our own
SD : 02 :046(530) [0899] is altogether the **work** of the Holy Spirit and they can do
SD : 02 :047(530) [0901] his Holy Spirit to **work** these gifts of his within them,
SD : 02 :052(531) [0901] men to God, and to **work** in them both to will and to
SD : 02 :056(532) [0903] preached is an office and **work** of the Holy Spirit,
SD : 02 :062(533) [0905] another mode of action to **work** in irrational creatures or
SD : 02 :065(534) [0907] Spirit has initiated his **work** of regeneration and renewal
SD : 02 :071(535) [0909] the Holy Spirit wills to **work** such conversion and
SD : 02 :076(536) [0911] to the aid of the good **work** which man began by his
SD : 02 :077(536) [0911] the continuation and preservation of this **work** within us.
SD : 02 :087(538) [0915] is solely and alone the **work** of God, just as the bodily
SD : 02 :089(538) [0915] gift, endowment, and **work** of the Holy Spirit alone, who
SD : 02 :090(539) [0915] Toward this **work** the will of the person who is to be
SD : 02 :090(539) [0915] nothing, but only lets God **work** in him, until he is
SD : 03 :013(541) [0919] because it is so good a **work** and so God-pleasing a
SD : 03 :022(543) [0923] through the Holy Spirit’s **work** we are reborn and
SD : 03 :023(543) [0923] faith alone, without any **work** or merit, are justified
SD : 03 :028(544) [0925] the mediator, and a **work** of the Holy Spirit, it does not
SD : 03 :034(545) [0927] “To one who does not **work**, but trusts him who justifies
SD : 03 :038(546) [0929] we must exclude love and every other virtue or **work**.
SD : 04 :010(552) [0941] Romans, “Faith is a divine **work** in us that transforms us
SD : 04 :028(555) [0947] to put their trust in their **work** (in his *Commentary on*
SD : 05 :011(560) [0955] until he comes to his own **work** (that is, to comfort and to
SD : 07 :074(583) [0999] No man’s word or **work**, be it the merit or the speaking
SD : 07 :105(588) [1009] Holy Supper, not only to **work** comfort and life in
SD : 07 :121(590) [1013] ascribes to the word and **work** of the priest the power
SD : 08 :059(602) [1035] in this passage that in the **work** or matter of our
SD : 08 :079(607) [1045] with us, dwell in us, **work** and be mighty in us according
SD : 10 :019(614) [1059] or discharge any office or **work** in the church.
SD : 11 :021(619) [1069] increase in them the good **work** which he has begun, and
SD : 11 :032(621) [1073] “he has begun the good **work** in us” he will also continue
SD : 11 :040(623) [1077] Holy Spirit who wants to **work** efficaciously in them
SD : 11 :042(623) [1077] to those in whom he has “begun the good **work**.”
SD : 11 :049(624) [1079] should and must “**work** together for good” since they are
SD : 11 :071(627) [1085] the Holy Spirit wills to **work** such repentance and faith in
SD : 11 :078(629) [1089] Holy Spirit who wanted to **work** within them, as was the
SD : 11 :079(629) [1089] distinguishes between the **work** of God, who alone
SD : 11 :079(629) [1089] vessels of honor, and the **work** of the devil and of man,
SD : 11 :082(630) [1089] of the house, ready for any good **work**” (II Tim. 2:21).
SD : 12 :016(634) [1099] may one serve them or **work** for them at all, but one is to

Works (833)

AG : 04 :001(030) [0045] God by our own merits, **works**, or satisfactions, but that
AG : 05 :002(031) [0045] the Holy Spirit, who **works** faith, when and where he
AG : 05 :004(031) [0045] thoughts, and **works** without the external word of the
AG : 06 :001(031) [0045] good fruits and goods **works** and that we must do all such
AG : 06 :001(031) [0045] we must do all such good **works** as God has commanded,
AG : 06 :003(032) [0047] of sins, not through **works** but through faith alone,
AG : 16 :005(038) [0051] love and genuine good **works** in his station of life.
AG : 20 :000(041) [0053] XX. Faith and Good **Works**
AG : 20 :001(041) [0053] have been falsely accused of forbidding good **works**.
AG : 20 :002(041) [0053] instructions concerning true Christian estates and **works**.
AG : 20 :003(041) [0053] with childish and useless **works** like rosaries, the cult of
AG : 20 :004(041) [0053] praise these useless **works** so highly as they once did, and
AG : 20 :006(041) [0053] before God by our **works** alone, but they add faith in
AG : 20 :006(042) [0053] and say that faith and **works** make us righteous before
AG : 20 :007(042) [0053] than the teaching that we are to rely solely on our **works**.
AG : 20 :008(042) [0053] admit) while nothing but **works** was preached
AG : 20 :009(042) [0053] by teaching that our **works** cannot reconcile us with God
AG : 20 :010(042) [0055] he can accomplish this by **works**, or that he can merit
AG : 20 :011(042) [0055] of God — not because of **works**, lest any man should
AG : 20 :013(043) [0055] God through faith in Christ and not through **works**.
AG : 20 :015(043) [0055] to rest and peace through **works**, but only through faith,
AG : 20 :019(043) [0055] their own efforts, and all sorts of **works** were undertaken.
AG : 20 :021(044) [0055] Others devised other **works** for the purpose of earning
AG : 20 :027(045) [0057] among us that good **works** should and must be done, not
AG : 20 :029(045) [0057] Spirit is given, the heart is moved to do good **works**.
AG : 20 :035(046) [0057] of forbidding good **works** but is rather to be praised for
AG : 20 :035(046) [0057] for teaching that good **works** are to be done and for
AG : 20 :036(046) [0057] too weak to do good **works**, call upon God, have patience
AG : 20 :038(046) [0057] Such great and genuine **works** cannot be done without
AG : 21 :001(046) [0057] Moreover, their good **works** are to be an example for us,
AG : 24 :028(059) [0067] grace before God through faith and not through **works**.
AG : 26 :004(064) [0071] that faith in Christ is to be esteemed far above all **works**.
AG : 26 :005(064) [0071] in God’s sight by our **works** but that it is only through
AG : 26 :010(065) [0071] other necessary good **works** were considered secular and
AG : 26 :010(065) [0071] and unspiritual: the **works** which everybody is obliged to
AG : 26 :011(065) [0071] Such **works**, commanded by God, were to be regarded as
AG : 26 :011(065) [0071] glamorous title of alone being holy and perfect **works**.
AG : 26 :020(067) [0073] supposed that grace is earned through self-chosen **works**.
AG : 26 :029(068) [0075] institute or practice such **works** for the purpose of earning
AG : 26 :033(069) [0075] to sin, but not as if he earned grace by such **works**.
AG : 27 :044(078) [0081] namely, that they could apply their good **works** to others.
AG : 27 :047(078) [0081] this is exaltation of **works** as a means of attaining
AG : 27 :049(079) [0083] meanwhile we do good **works** for others and diligently
AG : 27 :061(080) [0083] and that they furnish the **works** of supererogation which
AG : 28 :037(087) [0089] in order that by such **works** grace and everything good
AL : 04 :001(030) [0045] own strength, merits, or **works** but are freely justified for
AL : 05 :004(031) [0045] Word, through their own preparations and **works**.
AL : 06 :001(031) [0045] it is necessary to do the good **works** commanded by God.
AL : 06 :001(032) [0045] because we rely on such **works** to merit justification
AL : 06 :003(032) [0047] be saved, not through **works** but through faith alone, and
AL : 12 :006(035) [0049] Then good **works**, which are the fruits of repentance, are
AL : 16 :001(037) [0051] civil ordinances are good **works** of God and that it is
AL : 18 :009(040) [0053] to perform the outward **works** (for it can keep the hands
AL : 20 :000(041) [0053] XX. Faith and Good **Works**
AL : 20 :001(041) [0053] churches are falsely accused of forbidding good **works**.
AL : 20 :003(041) [0053] childish and needless **works**, such as particular holy days,
AL : 20 :004(041) [0053] about such unprofitable **works** as much as formerly.
AL : 20 :006(041) [0053] we are justified not by **works** only, but conjoining faith
AL : 20 :006(041) [0053] but conjoining faith with **works** they say that we are
AL : 20 :006(041) [0053] works they say that we are justified by faith and **works**.
AL : 20 :008(042) [0053] only the teaching about **works** has been treated in the
AL : 20 :009(042) [0053] by teaching that our **works** cannot reconcile God or merit
AL : 20 :010(042) [0055] that he merits grace by **works** despises the merit and
AL : 20 :011(042) [0055] through faith; and this is not because of **works**,” etc.
AL : 20 :013(043) [0055] and the righteousness of faith against the merits of **works**.

Continued ▶

Continued ▶

A P : 0 4 :267(146) [0197] teaching not only about **works** but about faith as well, as
A P : 0 4 :267(146) [0197] Although he mentions **works** in connection with
A P : 0 4 :267(147) [0197] does not say that by these **works** we merit the forgiveness
A P : 0 4 :268(147) [0197] come forgiveness of sins and justification without **works**.
A P : 0 4 :268(147) [0197] by our prayers and good **works**, indeed by our complete
A P : 0 4 :269(147) [0197] Whenever good **works** are praised and the law preached,
A P : 0 4 :269(147) [0197] attribute Christ's glory to **works** and make of them a
A P : 0 4 :269(147) [0197] It follows, therefore, that **works** are praised for pleasing
A P : 0 4 :269(147) [0197] Father (Rom. 5:2), not by **works** without Christ, the
A P : 0 4 :272(148) [0199] not only demands new **works** but also promises the
A P : 0 4 :272(148) [0199] is required, not merely **works**, as in Matt. 6:14, "If you
A P : 0 4 :274(148) [0199] by faith because of Christ and not because of our **works**.
A P : 0 4 :274(148) [0199] those passages which teach about the law or **works**.
A P : 0 4 :274(148) [0199] in teaching penitence **works** are required, since a new life
A P : 0 4 :274(148) [0199] maintain that by such **works** we merit forgiveness of sins
A P : 0 4 :275(148) [0199] the promise of forgiveness of sins with good **works**.
A P : 0 4 :275(148) [0199] does not mean that good **works** are a propitiation — for
A P : 0 4 :276(148) [0199] and pictured in good **works**, which thus urge us to believe
A P : 0 4 :281(149) [0201] of the law, that for his sake good **works** please God.
A P : 0 4 :281(149) [0201] teach that we merit justification by the **works** of the law.
A P : 0 4 :283(150) [0201] is to be sought in **works** commanded by God, not in
A P : 0 4 :284(150) [0201] is added (that is, all the **works** of love), then men are
A P : 0 4 :284(150) [0201] many parts, some of which command faith, others **works**.
A P : 0 4 :284(150) [0201] out the commands about **works** and skip the passages
A P : 0 4 :285(150) [0201] when they teach that **works** merit the forgiveness of sins,
A P : 0 4 :285(150) [0201] seeks forgiveness through **works** cannot be sure that its
A P : 0 4 :285(150) [0201] constantly invents other **works** and services until it
A P : 0 4 :285(150) [0201] not depend upon our **works** because we could never be
A P : 0 4 :285(150) [0201] He concludes that not **works** but faith accepts the
A P : 0 4 :286(150) [0201] justify and that by our **works** we merit grace and the
A P : 0 4 :286(150) [0201] select the passages on **works**, and even distort these.
A P : 0 4 :288(151) [0203] men merit grace by good **works** — first by the merit of
A P : 0 4 :288(151) [0203] many other painful **works** to appease the wrath of God.
A P : 0 4 :288(151) [0203] with outward **works**, it can be understood and, to some
A P : 0 4 :288(151) [0203] through these **works** but that for the sake of social
A P : 0 4 :290(151) [0203] it teaches that our **works** are a propitiation for sin.
A P : 0 4 :293(152) [0203] of the law, these **works** please God on account of the
A P : 0 4 :302(154) [0205] Christ's glory to human **works**; it leads consciences into
A P : 0 4 :308(155) [0207] Our good **works** or obedience to the law can be pleasing
A P : 0 4 :316(156) [0209] They imagine that good **works**, done with the help of a
A P : 0 4 :317(156) [0209] God because of our **works** and not because of Christ,
A P : 0 4 :317(156) [0209] of Christ's glory to our **works**, a destruction of his glory
A P : 0 4 :318(156) [0209] teach that good **works** earn grace by the merit of
A P : 0 4 :319(156) [0209] stilled; for the law always accuses us, even in good **works**.
A P : 0 4 :321(157) [0209] simply believe that their **works** are worth enough to
A P : 0 4 :321(157) [0209] uncertain about all their **works** and therefore continually
A P : 0 4 :321(157) [0209] their works and therefore continually seek other **works**.
A P : 0 4 :322(157) [0209] Speaking of the **works** that saints perform after
A P : 0 4 :323(157) [0209] that even if we have good **works** we need mercy in them.
A P : 0 4 :325(157) [0211] the doctrine that we need mercy even in our good **works**.
A P : 0 4 :327(158) [0211] Job 9:28, "I feared all my **works**"; vv. 30-31, "If I wash
A P : 0 4 :332(158) [0211] they have love and good **works**, and ask for grace as
A P : 0 4 :334(159) [0215] as a payment which he owes to us for our good **works**.
A P : 0 4 :335(159) [0215] Then they add that **works** are worthless to God, but that
A P : 0 4 :337(159) [0215] this confession that our **works** are worthless is the very
A P : 0 4 :338(159) [0215] promise of grace, even though our **works** are worthless.
A P : 0 4 :338(159) [0215] For our **works** are worthless, and with the whole church
A P : 0 4 :339(159) [0215] do not trust in your **works**," to the statement, "When you
A P : 0 4 :339(159) [0215] trust is a trust in our own **works**; in the second, trust is a
A P : 0 4 :339(159) [0215] trust in our own **works**; he does not condemn trust in his
A P : 0 4 :339(159) [0215] He denounces our **works** as worthless, but he does not
A P : 0 4 :342(159) [0215] servants" as meaning that **works** are worthless to God but
A P : 0 4 :343(160) [0217] see that this passage condemns trust in our own **works**.
A P : 0 4 :346(160) [0217] our hope were to rest on **works**, then it would really be
A P : 0 4 :346(160) [0217] really be unsure since **works** cannot still the conscience,
A P : 0 4 :348(160) [0217] raise the cry that good **works** are unnecessary if they do
A P : 0 4 :348(160) [0217] Of course, good **works** are necessary.
A P : 0 4 :348(160) [0217] we might begin to do good **works** and obey God's law.
A P : 0 4 :349(160) [0217] new life might have new **works** and new impulses, the
A P : 0 4 :350(160) [0217] become firmer amid good **works** as well as temptations
A P : 0 4 :353(161) [0217] definitely require good **works**, since we teach that this
A P : 0 4 :355(161) [0217] Afterwards **works** merit other bodily and spiritual
A P : 0 4 :356(161) [0217] merited by the merit of condignity through good **works**.
A P : 0 4 :357(162) [0217] they argue that our **works** ought to be counted so
A P : 0 4 :358(162) [0219] access to God for Christ's sake, not for our **works**' sake.
A P : 0 4 :359(162) [0219] the issue whether good **works** of themselves are worthy of
A P : 0 4 :360(162) [0219] opponents attribute to **works** a worthiness of grace and
A P : 0 4 :360(162) [0219] therefore we have **works** that are precious enough to earn
A P : 0 4 :360(162) [0219] earn a reward; therefore **works** please God for their own
A P : 0 4 :362(162) [0219] sake and that good **works** are pleasing to God because of
A P : 0 4 :365(163) [0219] they talk about good **works**, the Scriptures often include
A P : 0 4 :366(163) [0219] belong to faith, still good **works** merit other rewards, both
A P : 0 4 :366(163) [0221] reward is offered and owed, not gratis but for our **works**.
A P : 0 4 :367(163) [0221] **Works** and afflictions merit not justification but other
A P : 0 4 :367(163) [0221] as in these passages a reward is offered for **works**.
A P : 0 4 :370(163) [0221] opponents urge that good **works** properly merit eternal
A P : 0 4 :370(164) [0221] man according to his **works**"; and v. 10, "Glory and
A P : 0 4 :371(164) [0221] all others like them where **works** are praised in the
A P : 0 4 :371(164) [0221] mean not only outward **works** but also the faith of the
A P : 0 4 :372(164) [0221] Whenever law and **works** are mentioned, we must know
A P : 0 4 :372(164) [0221] said earlier, all passages on **works** can be interpreted.
A P : 0 4 :372(164) [0221] eternal life is granted to **works**, it is granted to the
A P : 0 4 :372(164) [0221] None can do good **works** except the justified, who are led
A P : 0 4 :372(164) [0221] of Christ; nor can good **works** please God without the
A P : 0 4 :373(164) [0221] man according to his **works**," we must understand not
A P : 0 4 :373(164) [0221] not merely outward **works** but the entire righteousness or
A P : 0 4 :376(164) [0223] passages they reason that **works** merit grace by the merit
A P : 0 4 :376(165) [0223] our **works** but because of Christ, and that through his
A P : 0 4 :378(165) [0223] we merit eternal life by **works**, omitting the faith that
A P : 0 4 :379(165) [0223] righteous because of our **works**, either done by the reason
A P : 0 4 :381(165) [0223] in the schools that good **works** please God because of
A P : 0 4 :381(165) [0223] in grace and that good **works** please God because of virtue of
A P : 0 4 :382(165) [0225] also boast that our good **works** are valid by virtue of
A P : 0 4 :382(165) [0225] it is vain to say that our **works** are valid by virtue of the
A P : 0 4 :385(166) [0225] Thus other good **works** please God because of faith, as
A P : 0 4 :388(166) [0225] a passage on love or **works** is quoted, that the law cannot
A P : 0 4 :392(167) [0225] through our **works** and new devotions, obscuring the
A P : 0 4 :393(167) [0225] and the teaching of **works** would obscure the
A P : 0 4 :393(167) [0225] and justified by their own **works** and devotions, not by
A P : 0 4 :393(167) [0225] men judge that God ought to be appeased by **works**.
A P : 0 4 :395(167) [0225] of sins by their **works**, and so they multiplied sacrifices
A P : 0 7 :031(174) [0239] of God, the love of our neighbor, and the **works** of love.
A P : 0 7 :036(175) [0241] quicken the heart, are not **works** of the Holy Spirit (like
A P : 1 1 :002(180) [0249] by teachings about **works**, since the scholastics and
A P : 1 2 :014(184) [0257] satisfactions ought to be **works** of supererogation, and
A P : 1 2 :017(185) [0257] we merit grace by good **works** done apart from grace.
A P : 1 2 :053(189) [0265] These are the two chief **works** of God in men, to terrify
A P : 1 2 :053(189) [0265] One or the other of these **works** is spoken of throughout
A P : 1 2 :064(191) [0269] conscience cannot pit our **works** or our love against the
A P : 1 2 :065(191) [0271] they trust in their own **works** and not in Christ to receive
A P : 1 2 :065(191) [0271] him and not because of any merits or **works** of our own.
A P : 1 2 :067(191) [0271] faith for Christ's sake and not for the sake of our **works**.
A P : 1 2 :068(192) [0271] about the merits of attrition and **works** and similar ideas.
A P : 1 2 :072(192) [0271] forgiven because of Christ, not because of our **works**.
A P : 1 2 :075(193) [0273] only the law and our **works** because the law demands
A P : 1 2 :075(193) [0273] our trust in our own **works** rather than in God's Word
A P : 1 2 :076(193) [0273] from trust in their own **works** to trust in the promise and
A P : 1 2 :076(193) [0275] sins not because of these **works** but because of Christ, the
A P : 1 2 :078(193) [0275] supposing that love and **works** are present, neither love
A P : 1 2 :078(193) [0275] present, neither love nor **works** can be a propitiation for
A P : 1 2 :078(193) [0275] should the honor of Christ be transferred to our **works**.
A P : 1 2 :084(194) [0277] the wrath of God not our **works** but Christ, the mediator.
A P : 1 2 :085(194) [0277] merit it by our love and **works**, and that we ought to set
A P : 1 2 :085(194) [0277] ought to set our love and **works** against the wrath of
A P : 1 2 :086(194) [0277] the law and to offer our **works** to God before being
A P : 1 2 :087(195) [0277] must not set our love or **works** against the wrath of God
A P : 1 2 :087(195) [0277] or trust in our love or **works**, but only in Christ, the
A P : 1 2 :092(196) [0279] contrition or good **works** and making no mention of
A P : 1 2 :095(196) [0281] not because of our **works**, contrition, confession, or
A P : 1 2 :095(196) [0281] For if faith relies on these **works**, it immediately becomes
A P : 1 2 :095(196) [0281] conscience sees that these **works** are not good enough.
A P : 1 2 :097(196) [0281] not only about contrition and **works**, but also about faith.
A P : 1 2 :097(197) [0281] select sayings about a part of penitence, namely **works**.
A P : 1 2 :107(198) [0283] be placated by our **works**, and yet we seek mercy because
A P : 1 2 :114(199) [0285] by such practices or such **works** men merit the
A P : 1 2 :114(199) [0285] thinking that by these **works** they merit the forgiveness of
A P : 1 2 :115(199) [0285] They define these as **works** that are not due; we call them
A P : 1 2 :116(199) [0287] Christ, not because of our **works**, either preceding or
A P : 1 2 :116(199) [0287] that because of these **works** they obtain the forgiveness of
A P : 1 2 :131(202) [0291] come good fruits and good **works** in every phase of life.
A P : 1 2 :133(202) [0293] that satisfactions are **works** that are not obligatory, but in
A P : 1 2 :133(202) [0293] passages Scripture requires **works** that are obligatory.
A P : 1 2 :137(203) [0293] about obligatory **works**, about the whole newness of life,
A P : 1 2 :137(203) [0293] about observances and **works** that are not obligatory such
A P : 1 2 :138(203) [0293] say that non-obligatory **works** compensate for eternal
A P : 1 2 :139(203) [0295] that only non-obligatory **works** like the punishments of
A P : 1 2 :140(204) [0295] mean not Christ but our **works** — and not even works
A P : 1 2 :140(204) [0295] our works — and not even **works** that God has
A P : 1 2 :140(204) [0295] commanded but the vain **works** that men have devised.
A P : 1 2 :142(204) [0295] above this, that is by the **works** of supererogation, he can
A P : 1 2 :142(204) [0295] we can do external **works** that God's law does not
A P : 1 2 :143(204) [0297] human tradition, such **works** belong to the human
A P : 1 2 :144(204) [0297] Some **works**, like pilgrimages, depart even further from
A P : 1 2 :144(205) [0297] Still they dress up these **works** with fancy titles; they call
A P : 1 2 :144(205) [0297] titles; they call them **works** of supererogation, and they
A P : 1 2 :145(205) [0297] they rank them above the **works** of God's
A P : 1 2 :145(205) [0297] that outward and civil **works** satisfy God's law; and
A P : 1 2 :145(205) [0297] human traditions, whose **works** they rank above the
A P : 1 2 :145(205) [0297] whose works they rank above the **works** of the law.
A P : 1 2 :146(205) [0297] This payment of **works** does not atone for eternal death
A P : 1 2 :147(205) [0297] opponents admit that the **works** of satisfaction are not
A P : 1 2 :147(205) [0297] are not obligatory **works** but works of human tradition,
A P : 1 2 :147(205) [0297] not obligatory works but **works** of human tradition,
A P : 1 2 :159(207) [0301] was not sin but "that the **works** of God might be made
A P : 1 2 :160(207) [0301] certain past deeds, but **works** of God, intended for our
A P : 1 2 :163(208) [0303] and the fruits that are due, not to "non-obligatory **works**."
A P : 1 2 :163(208) [0303] St. James dressed in armor or to perform similar **works**."
A P : 1 2 :165(208) [0303] penitence and obligatory **works** commanded by God
A P : 1 2 :165(208) [0303] and its true fruits, good **works** done from faith, but not,
A P : 1 2 :165(208) [0303] not, as these men imagine, by **works** done in mortal sin.
A P : 1 2 :170(209) [0305] Good **works** ought to follow penitence, and penitence
A P : 1 2 :172(209) [0305] or non-obligatory **works** be done to compensate for
A P : 1 2 :173(209) [0305] If **works** of satisfaction are non-obligatory works, why
A P : 1 2 :173(209) [0305] are non-obligatory **works**, why cite the clear teaching of
A P : 1 2 :173(209) [0305] off punishment by such **works**, then they would certainly
A P : 1 2 :173(209) [0305] dealing with obligatory **works**, though in their
A P : 1 2 :173(209) [0305] in their satisfactions they impose non-obligatory **works**.
A P : 1 5 :006(215) [0317] God not because of **works** but freely for Christ's sake.
A P : 1 5 :010(216) [0317] they were thought of as **works** meriting righteousness
A P : 1 5 :010(216) [0317] not because of our **works** but freely because of Christ,
A P : 1 5 :014(216) [0319] wants to institute certain **works** to merit the forgiveness
A P : 1 5 :014(216) [0319] will he know that these **works** please God since they do
A P : 1 5 :018(217) [0319] Mohammed has rites and **works** by which it seeks to be
A P : 1 5 :022(218) [0321] supposes that such **works** justify men and reconcile God.
A P : 1 5 :024(218) [0321] appearance of wisdom and righteousness in such **works**.
A P : 1 5 :025(218) [0321] is obscured and replaced by a vain trust in such **works**.
A P : 1 5 :025(219) [0321] when men regard these **works** as perfect and spiritual,
A P : 1 5 :025(219) [0323] vastly prefer them to the **works** that God commands, like
A P : 1 5 :027(219) [0323] faith in him or the good **works** to be performed in one's
A P : 1 5 :042(221) [0327] to talk about good **works**, but they say nothing about the
A P : 1 5 :043(221) [0327] of children, chastity, and all the **works** of love.
A P : 1 8 :002(225) [0335] grace and justification by **works** that reason produces on
A P : 1 8 :004(225) [0335] to choose among the **works** and things which reason by
A P : 1 8 :004(225) [0335] achieve civil righteousness or the righteousness of **works**.
A P : 1 8 :004(225) [0335] God and express its worship of him in outward **works**.
A P : 1 8 :006(225) [0335] of grace, he does the **works** prescribed in the

Continued ▶

Continued ▶

SD : 0 3 :029(544) [0925] should also do good **works** and love, but how a person
SD : 0 3 :029(544) [0925] and not through the **works** of the law or through love —
SD : 0 3 :029(544) [0925] we thereby utterly rejected **works** and love (as the
SD : 0 3 :029(544) [0925] we reject and condemn **works**, since the very nature of
SD : 0 3 :029(544) [0925] cannot admit any treatment or discussion of **works**.
SD : 0 3 :029(544) [0925] to the law and the **works** of the law in this conjunction."
SD : 0 3 :032(545) [0927] righteousness of the new obedience or of good **works**.
SD : 0 3 :032(545) [0927] he has done many good **works** and leads the best kind of
SD : 0 3 :033(545) [0927] the addition of his own **works**, not only when he was first
SD : 0 3 :033(545) [0927] and had no good **works**, but also afterward when the
SD : 0 3 :033(545) [0927] many resplendent good **works** (Rom. 4:3; Gen. 15:6;
SD : 0 3 :034(545) [0927] God reckons righteousness without the addition of **works**.
SD : 0 3 :035(545) [0927] love, virtues, and good **works**, these should and must not
SD : 0 3 :036(545) [0927] is, terms that exclude **works** from the article of
SD : 0 3 :036(545) [0927] by faith) as "without **works**," "without the law," "freely,"
SD : 0 3 :036(545) [0927] the law," "freely," "not of **works**," all of which exclusive
SD : 0 3 :036(545) [0927] does not exclude **works**, however, as though there could
SD : 0 3 :036(545) [0927] or as though good **works** should, must, and dare not
SD : 0 3 :036(545) [0927] The point is that good **works** are excluded from the
SD : 0 3 :037(546) [0929] justification all our own **works**, merit, worthiness, glory,
SD : 0 3 :037(546) [0929] and trust in any of our **works**, so that we might or should
SD : 0 3 :037(546) [0929] or should not view our **works** as either the cause or the
SD : 0 3 :039(546) [0929] virtues, nor other good **works** are our righteousness
SD : 0 3 :040(546) [0929] between faith and good **works** is bound to be maintained
SD : 0 3 :041(546) [0929] For good **works** do not precede faith, nor is sanctification
SD : 0 3 :041(546) [0929] and sanctification the fruits of good **works** will follow.
SD : 0 3 :041(546) [0931] between faith and good **works**; nevertheless, it is faith
SD : 0 3 :041(546) [0931] faith alone which apprehends the blessing without **works**.
SD : 0 3 :042(547) [0931] alone justifies without **works** when, as we have said
SD : 0 3 :042(547) [0931] where all kinds of good **works** and the fruits of the Spirit
SD : 0 3 :042(547) [0931] by such a faith as is without **works**, which is a dead faith."
SD : 0 3 :043(547) [0931] is speaking of the good **works** of those who are already
SD : 0 3 :043(547) [0931] cannot justify without **works**; or, faith justifies or makes
SD : 0 3 :043(547) [0931] or, the presence of good **works** along with faith is
SD : 0 3 :043(547) [0931] or, the presence of good **works** is necessary in the article
SD : 0 3 :043(547) [0931] such as "apart from **works**," do not exclude works from
SD : 0 3 :043(547) [0931] works," do not exclude **works** from the article of
SD : 0 3 :045(547) [0933] That our love or our good **works** are a meritorious basis
SD : 0 3 :046(548) [0933] 2. That by good **works** man must make himself worthy
SD : 0 3 :047(548) [0933] the renewal which the Holy Spirit **works** and is within us.
SD : 0 3 :052(548) [0933] through faith without **works** but that we cannot be saved
SD : 0 3 :052(548) [0933] cannot be saved without **works** or that salvation cannot
SD : 0 3 :052(548) [0933] or that salvation cannot be obtained without **works**.
SD : 0 3 :053(548) [0933] God reckons righteousness without **works** (Rom. 4:6).
SD : 0 3 :053(548) [0933] that wholly exclude **works** and our own merit, such as "by
SD : 0 3 :053(548) [0933] "by grace" and "without **works**") just as emphatically in
SD : 0 3 :055(549) [0935] all other human merits, **works**, virtues, and worthiness
SD : 0 3 :062(550) [0937] them by the Holy Spirit and the consequent good **works**.
SD : 0 3 :063(550) [0937] in so far as it dwells and **works** within us, and that by
SD : 0 4 :000(551) [0939] IV. Good **Works**
SD : 0 4 :001(551) [0939] concerning good **works** has likewise arisen among the
SD : 0 4 :001(551) [0939] and formulas as "Good **works** are necessary to salvation,"
SD : 0 4 :001(551) [0939] to be saved without good **works**," and "No one has been
SD : 0 4 :001(551) [0939] been saved without good **works**," since good works are
SD : 0 4 :001(551) [0939] good works," since good **works** are required of true
SD : 0 4 :002(551) [0939] on the contrary that good **works** are indeed necessary —
SD : 0 4 :003(551) [0939] or principle "that good **works** are detrimental to
SD : 0 4 :003(551) [0939] maintained that good **works** are not necessary but
SD : 0 4 :003(551) [0939] took the contrary view that good **works** are necessary.
SD : 0 4 :004(551) [0939] with which the law forces men to do good **works**.
SD : 0 4 :007(552) [0939] believers walk in good **works**; that only those are truly
SD : 0 4 :007(552) [0939] only those are truly good **works** which God himself
SD : 0 4 :007(552) [0941] that truly good **works** are not done by a person's own
SD : 0 4 :007(552) [0941] says, "has been created in Christ Jesus for good **works**."
SD : 0 4 :008(552) [0941] to how and why the good **works** of believers are pleasing
SD : 0 4 :008(552) [0941] For **works** which belong to the maintenance of outward
SD : 0 4 :008(552) [0941] Christ's sake — before that person's **works** are pleasing.
SD : 0 4 :009(552) [0941] good and God-pleasing **works** that God will reward both
SD : 0 4 :011(553) [0941] faith does not ask if good **works** are to be done, but
SD : 0 4 :011(553) [0941] not perform such good **works** is a faithless man, blindly
SD : 0 4 :011(553) [0941] search of faith and good **works** without knowing what
SD : 0 4 :011(553) [0941] what either faith or good **works** are, and in the meantime
SD : 0 4 :011(553) [0941] and jabbers a great deal about faith and good **works**.
SD : 0 4 :012(553) [0941] This the Holy Spirit **works** by faith, and therefore
SD : 0 4 :012(553) [0941] as impossible to separate **works** from faith as it is to
SD : 0 4 :014(553) [0943] question whether good **works** are necessary or free, both
SD : 0 4 :014(553) [0943] like these: "Good **works** are necessary"; again, "It is
SD : 0 4 :014(553) [0943] is necessary to do good **works** because they necessarily
SD : 0 4 :014(553) [0943] must of necessity do good **works** that God has
SD : 0 4 :015(553) [0943] and without good **works**, as if there could simultaneously
SD : 0 4 :017(554) [0943] Such **works** of pretense God does not want.
SD : 0 4 :018(554) [0943] and teach that truly good **works** are to be done willingly
SD : 0 4 :018(554) [0943] the proposition that good **works** are spontaneous.
SD : 0 4 :021(554) [0945] when we teach that good **works** are necessary we must
SD : 0 4 :022(554) [0945] be extremely careful that **works** are not drawn into and
SD : 0 4 :022(554) [0945] propositions that good **works** are necessary for the
SD : 0 4 :022(554) [0945] to be saved without good **works**, since such propositions
SD : 0 4 :022(554) [0945] words which exclude our **works** and merit completely
SD : 0 4 :023(555) [0945] in one's own good **works**, and are adopted by the papists
SD : 0 4 :024(555) [0945] righteousness apart from **works** (Rom. 4:6), or the
SD : 0 4 :024(555) [0945] Confession, "We are saved without **works** solely by faith."
SD : 0 4 :027(555) [0945] faith in the merit of our **works**, but we must nevertheless
SD : 0 4 :028(555) [0947] although we require good **works** as necessary to
SD : 0 4 :030(555) [0947] arisen as to whether good **works** preserve salvation or are
SD : 0 4 :031(556) [0947] one, or through wicked **works**; and that even though a
SD : 0 4 :033(556) [0947] exhortation to do good **works** can be instilled without
SD : 0 4 :033(556) [0947] why we should do good **works**, namely, that we confirm
SD : 0 4 :033(556) [0949] He says: 'Do good **works** so that you remain in your
SD : 0 4 :033(556) [0949] of your subsequent **works** but which have come to you by
SD : 0 4 :034(556) [0949] delegates this function to **works**, as if works should
SD : 0 4 :034(556) [0949] function to works, as if **works** should henceforth preserve
SD : 0 4 :035(557) [0949] namely, that our good **works** preserve salvation, or that
SD : 0 4 :035(557) [0949] salvation, or that our **works** either entirely or in part
SD : 0 4 :037(557) [0949] proposition that good **works** are supposed to be
SD : 0 4 :037(557) [0949] If anyone draws good **works** into the article of
SD : 0 4 :037(557) [0949] of salvation on good **works** in order to merit the grace of
SD : 0 4 :037(557) [0951] in Phil. 3:7ff. that good **works** not only are useless and an
SD : 0 4 :037(557) [0951] lies not with the good **works** themselves, but with the
SD : 0 4 :037(557) [0951] express Word of God, is being placed upon good **works**.
SD : 0 4 :038(557) [0951] qualifications that good **works** are detrimental to
SD : 0 4 :038(557) [0951] For when good **works** are done on account of right
SD : 0 4 :038(557) [0951] believers should do good **works** which the Holy Spirit
SD : 0 4 :038(557) [0951] which the Holy Spirit **works** in them, and God is willing
SD : 0 4 :040(558) [0951] to be deterred from good **works**, but are most diligently
SD : 0 4 :040(558) [0951] apply themselves to good **works**, we cannot and should
SD : 0 5 :010(559) [0955] fulfill the law by external **works**, or drives man utterly to
SD : 0 5 :018(561) [0957] to rebuke sin and to give instruction about good **works**.
SD : 0 6 :002(564) [0963] (that is, in what good **works** they should walk) from the
SD : 0 6 :010(565) [0965] Gospel does, creates, and **works** in connection with the
SD : 0 6 :010(565) [0965] matter, as far as the good **works** of believers are
SD : 0 6 :012(566) [0967] and in what good **works**, which God has prepared
SD : 0 6 :015(566) [0967] distinction between the **works** of the law and those of the
SD : 0 6 :015(566) [0967] that in speaking of good **works** that are in accord with
SD : 0 6 :015(566) [0967] they are not good **works** — the word "law" here has but
SD : 0 6 :016(566) [0967] The distinction between **works** is due to the difference in
SD : 0 6 :016(566) [0967] to the law, and does its **works** merely because they are
SD : 0 6 :016(566) [0967] St. Paul calls the **works** of such a man "works of the law"
SD : 0 6 :016(566) [0967] the works of such a man "**works** of the law" in the strict
SD : 0 6 :016(566) [0967] sense, because his good **works** are extorted by the law,
SD : 0 6 :017(566) [0967] These **works** are, strictly speaking, not works of the law
SD : 0 6 :017(566) [0967] are, strictly speaking, not **works** of the law but works and
SD : 0 6 :017(566) [0967] not works of the law but **works** and fruits of the Spirit,
SD : 0 6 :021(567) [0969] with their good **works**, because otherwise they can easily
SD : 0 6 :021(567) [0969] easily imagine that their **works** and life are perfectly pure
SD : 0 6 :021(567) [0969] of God prescribes good **works** for faith in such a way
SD : 0 6 :021(567) [0969] that in this life our good **works** are imperfect and impure,
SD : 0 6 :021(567) [0969] born anew to do good **works**, he holds up before them
SD : 0 6 :021(567) [0969] from the law that his **works** are still imperfect and impure
SD : 0 6 :022(567) [0969] us how and why the good **works** of believers are pleasing
SD : 0 6 :023(568) [0969] Though their good **works** are still imperfect and impure,
SD : 0 8 :043(599) [1029] But if the **works** are divided and separated, the person
SD : 0 8 :070(605) [1041] and didst set him over the **works** of thy hands, putting
SD : 1 0 :012(613) [1057] false doctrine that the **works** of the law are necessary for
SD : 1 1 :006(617) [1065] even in wicked acts and **works** God's foreknowledge
SD : 1 1 :007(617) [1065] God neither creates nor **works** evil, nor does he help it
SD : 1 1 :043(623) [1077] and saved without our **works** and merit, purely by grace
SD : 1 1 :087(631) [1093] our merit and good **works**, as it is written, "He destined
SD : 1 1 :088(631) [1093] continue, not because of **works** but because of his call,
SD : 1 2 :030(635) [1101] repentance, and faith or **works** new obedience in them.
SD : 1 2 :031(635) [1101] God seals the adoption of sons and **works** regeneration.

Worked (3), Workers (1), Working (10)

AP : 0 4 :111(123) [0155] is of any avail, but faith **working** through love"
AP : 0 4 :250(143) [0191] raised with him through faith in the **working** of God."
AP : 1 2 :046(188) [0263] with him through faith in the **working** of God"
AP : 2 4 :013(251) [0387] pagan notion about the **working** of the Mass *ex opere*
AP : 2 8 :016(283) [0449] writings, in which they **worked** hard to free the church
S3 : 0 2 :001(303) [0479] because of the wickedness which sin has **worked** in man.
S3 : 1 5 :005(318) [0501] the names of my other co-**workers** in the Gospel, namely:
EP : 0 4 :015(477) [0799] but only the Holy Spirit, **working** through faith,
SD : 0 2 :022(525) [0889] the gracious and efficacious **working** of the Holy Spirit.
SD : 0 2 :048(530) [0901] in us by giving and **working** true repentance, faith, and
SD : 0 2 :066(534) [0907] earnestly reminds us, "**Working** together with him, then,
SD : 0 2 :083(537) [0913] man through such **working** of the Holy Spirit is able to
SD : 0 8 :027(596) [1025] apostles testify that he **worked** with them everywhere and
SD : 1 1 :023(619) [1069] grace, gifts, and effective **working** to bring them to

Workmanship (1), Workmen (1)

LC : 0 1 :226(395) [0645] must be said of artisans, **workmen**, and day-laborers who
SD : 0 2 :039(528) [0895] he says, "We are his **workmanship**, created in Christ

World (227)

PR : PR :002(003) [0007] times of this transitory **world** almighty God in his
PR : PR :002(003) [0007] in all of Christendom throughout the wide **world**.
PR : PR :005(004) [0009] our own and the ungrateful **world**'s impenitence and sin.
AG : 1 6 :001(037) [0051] all government in the **world** and all established rule and
AG : 2 3 :001(051) [0061] complaint throughout the **world** concerning the flagrant
AG : 2 3 :014(053) [0063] Scriptures prophesy, the **world** is growing worse and men
AG : 2 4 :029(059) [0067] but also for the whole **world** and for others, both living
AG : 2 7 :057(080) [0083] said, is fleeing from the **world** and seeking a life more
AG : 2 8 :014(083) [0085] kingship is not of this **world**," and again, "Who made me
AG : 2 8 :045(088) [0089] to the regulations of the **world**, why do you live as if you
AG : 2 8 :045(088) [0089] why do you live as if you still belonged to the **world**?
AL : 1 7 :001(038) [0051] the consummation of the **world** Christ will appear for
AL : 1 7 :005(039) [0051] of the kingdom of the **world**, the ungodly being
AL : 2 3 :014(053) [0063] Inasmuch as the **world** is growing old and man's nature is
AL : 2 4 :018(058) [0067] Perhaps the **world** is being punished for such long
AL : 2 4 :020(058) [0067] Since the beginning of the **world** nothing of divine
AL : 2 6 :002(064) [0071] That the **world** thought so is evident from the fact that
AL : 2 7 :057(080) [0083] this "fleeing from the **world**" and "seeking a holy kind of
AL : 2 8 :002(081) [0085] transfer kingdoms of this **world** and take away the
AL : 2 8 :013(083) [0085] the kingdoms of the **world**, nor abrogate the laws of civil
AL : 2 8 :014(083) [0085] kingdom is not of this **world**," and again, "Who made me
AL : 2 8 :045(088) [0089] why do you live as if you still belonged to the **world**?
AP : 0 2 :049(106) [0119] **World** history itself shows the great power of the devil's
AP : 0 2 :049(106) [0119] wicked doctrines fill the **world**, and by these bonds the
AP : 0 2 :049(106) [0119] those who are wise and righteous in the eyes of the **world**.
AP : 0 4 :040(112) [0131] for the sins of the **world** and has been appointed as the
AP : 0 4 :096(121) [0149] sent the Son into the **world**, not to condemn the world,
AP : 0 4 :096(121) [0149] not to condemn the **world**, but that the world might be
AP : 0 4 :096(121) [0149] the world, but that the **world** might be saved through
AP : 0 4 :101(121) [0151] which by the Gospel he has spread throughout the **world**?
AP : 0 4 :103(121) [0151] Ambrose says: "But the **world** was subjected to him
AP : 0 4 :103(122) [0151] For after the whole **world** was subjected, he took away
AP : 0 4 :103(122) [0151] away the sin of the whole **world**, as John testified when
AP : 0 4 :103(122) [0151] the Lamb of God, who takes away the sin of the **world**!'

Continued ▶

A P : 0 4 :189(133) [0175] of Christ, whereby he shows his rule before the **world**.
A P : 0 4 :206(135) [0177] wicked idea about works has always clung to the **world**.
A P : 0 4 :212(136) [0179] The **world** judges this way about all works, that they are a
A P : 0 4 :291(151) [0203] But the Gospel was not given to the **world** in vain.
A P : 0 4 :297(153) [0205] and outside the law from the very beginning of the **world**.
A P : 0 4 :345(160) [0217] sent the Son into the **world**, not to condemn the world,
A P : 0 4 :345(160) [0217] not to condemn the **world**, but that the world might be
A P : 0 4 :345(160) [0217] the world, but that the **world** might be saved through
A P : 0 4 :394(167) [0225] always been some in the **world** who taught only this
A P : 0 7 :010(170) [0229] scattered throughout the **world** who agree on the Gospel
A P : 0 7 :019(171) [0233] The field, he says, is the **world**, not the church.
A P : 0 7 :020(171) [0233] and righteous men scattered throughout the **world**.
A P : 0 7 :023(172) [0235] monarchy of the whole **world** in which the Roman
A P : 0 7 :023(172) [0235] must be lord of the whole **world**, of all the kingdoms of
A P : 0 7 :023(172) [0235] of all the kingdoms of the **world**, and of all public and
A P : 0 7 :035(175) [0241] why do you live as if you still belonged to the **world**?
A P : 1 2 :053(189) [0265] Jews, and spread by the apostles throughout the **world**.
A P : 1 2 :073(192) [0273] church have believed since the beginning of the **world**.
A P : 1 2 :125(201) [0289] How will the **world** evaluate the Confutation — if it is
A P : 1 3 :008(212) [0311] for the sins of the whole **world** and that there is no need
A P : 1 7 :001(224) [0335] the consummation of the **world** Christ will appear and
A P : 2 0 :006(227) [0339] ignore the terrors of the **world** and bravely bear whatever
A P : 2 2 :010(237) [0361] given for the life of the **world**, is their food and that they
A P : 2 3 :067(248) [0383] In Jovinian's time the **world** still did not know the law of
A P : 2 4 :022(253) [0391] sacrifice in the **world**, the death of Christ, as the Epistle to
A P : 2 4 :036(257) [0397] believers throughout the **world** with the blood of the
A P : 2 4 :041(257) [0399] usurp the kingdom of the **world**, and they rule without
A P : 2 4 :041(257) [0399] war like the kings of the **world**, and they have instituted
A P : 2 4 :055(259) [0403] Since the beginning of the **world**, all the saints have had
A P : 2 4 :097(268) [0417] this notion clings to the **world**, and always will, that
A P : 2 7 :013(271) [0423] hast revealed to the **world** — then the charge against us is
S 2 : 0 1 :002(292) [0461] of God, who takes away the sin of the **world**" (John 1:29).
S 2 : 0 1 :005(292) [0463] and practice against the pope, the devil, and the **world**.
S 2 : 0 2 :004(293) [0463] then, do you drive the **world** into wretchedness and woe
S 2 : 0 4 :013(300) [0475] the lord of the church, and finally of the whole **world**.
S 3 : 0 3 :001(303) [0479] Rom. 3:19, 20, "The whole **world** may be held
S 3 : 0 3 :001(303) [0479] "The Holy Spirit will convince the **world** of sin."
S 3 : 0 3 :038(309) [0489] Lamb of God who takes away the sin of the **world**.
S 3 : 0 4 :000(310) [0491] is preached to the whole **world**; second, through Baptism;
S 3 : 0 8 :006(312) [0495] remain silent but fill the **world** with their chattering and
S 3 : 0 8 :009(313) [0497] descendants from the beginning to the end of the **world**.
T R : 0 0 :005(320) [0505] throughout the whole **world** should seek ordination and
T R : 0 0 :015(322) [0509] in the greater part of the **world**, whether in Greek or
T R : 0 0 :016(322) [0509] of all the churches in the **world** or for churches situated in
T R : 0 0 :016(323) [0509] in the greater part of the **world** never recognized or acted
T R : 0 0 :018(323) [0509] that you want, the **world** is greater than the city.
T R : 0 0 :026(324) [0511] abroad through the whole **world** and exists wherever God
T R : 0 0 :031(325) [0513] take possession of, or transfer the kingdoms of the **world**.
T R : 0 0 :031(325) [0513] he said, "My kingship is not of this **world**" (John 18:36).
T R : 0 0 :033(325) [0513] lord of the kingdoms of the **world** are false and impious.
S C : P R :019(340) [0537] and the kingdom of the **world** and are the worst enemies
S C : P R :023(341) [0537] has no sin, no flesh, no devil, no **world**, no death, no hell.
S C : P R :027(341) [0539] with little reward or gratitude from the **world**.
S C : 0 3 :011(347) [0547] of the devil, of the **world**, and of our flesh which would
S C : 0 3 :018(347) [0549] us that the devil, the **world**, and our flesh may not deceive
S C : 0 3 :020(348) [0549] take us from this **world** of sorrow to himself in heaven.
L C : P R :010(359) [0569] against the devil, the **world**, the flesh, and all evil
L C : P R :016(361) [0573] from the beginning of the **world** to the end, and all
L C : P R :017(361) [0573] estates, persons, laws, and everything else in the **world**.
L C : 0 1 :017(366) [0585] can easily judge how the **world** practices nothing but false
L C : 0 1 :022(367) [0585] practiced up to now, and it is still prevalent in the **world**.
L C : 0 1 :042(370) [0591] The trouble is that the **world** does not believe this at all,
L C : 0 1 :042(370) [0591] For the **world** sees that those who trust God and not
L C : 0 1 :042(370) [0591] honor, wealth, and every comfort in the eyes of the **world**.
L C : 0 1 :046(370) [0593] it to the devil and the **world** to deceive you with their
L C : 0 1 :058(372) [0597] calamity all over the **world** that there are few who do not
L C : 0 1 :059(372) [0597] to boast before the whole **world** of the wickedness he has
L C : 0 1 :060(372) [0597] This is the common course of the **world**.
L C : 0 1 :069(374) [0599] It is evident that the **world** today is more wicked than it
L C : 0 1 :118(381) [0615] before God and the whole **world**, they shall blush with
L C : 0 1 :120(382) [0615] miserable blindness of the **world** that no one believes
L C : 0 1 :123(382) [0617] the way things go in the **world** now, as everyone
L C : 0 1 :127(382) [0617] it is our duty before the **world** to show gratitude for the
L C : 0 1 :128(382) [0617] the devil rules in the **world**; children forget their parents,
L C : 0 1 :129(383) [0617] The perversity of the **world** God knows very well.
L C : 0 1 :154(386) [0625] Why, do you think, is the **world** now so full of
L C : 0 1 :160(387) [0627] seldom receive it, for the **world's** way of honoring them is
L C : 0 1 :160(387) [0627] must be "the refuse of the **world**, and every man's
L C : 0 1 :166(387) [0629] be willing to run to the ends of the **world** to obtain them.
L C : 0 1 :166(388) [0629] efforts of the whole **world** cannot add an hour to our life
L C : 0 1 :177(389) [0631] God terribly punishes the **world**; hence there is no longer
L C : 0 1 :183(389) [0631] as God well knows, the **world** is evil and this life is full of
L C : 0 1 :192(391) [0635] I appear before all the **world** in any other light than as a
L C : 0 1 :197(392) [0637] mock and mislead the **world** with a false, hypocritical
L C : 0 1 :208(393) [0639] it with everything in the **world** in order that this estate
L C : 0 1 :208(393) [0639] brought up to serve the **world**, promote knowledge of
L C : 0 1 :209(393) [0639] marriage, as the blind **world** and the false clergy do, but
L C : 0 1 :210(393) [0641] and even extending throughout all the **world**.
L C : 0 1 :224(395) [0643] on the gallows, the **world** would soon be empty, and there
L C : 0 1 :230(396) [0645] the treasures of the whole **world** and holds them to this
L C : 0 1 :231(396) [0647] This, in short, is the way of the **world**.
L C : 0 1 :247(398) [0651] heavy for you and all the **world** to bear, for they will
L C : 0 1 :247(398) [0651] prosper, before all the **world** you may call God and me
L C : 0 1 :258(399) [0653] to the usual course of the **world**, men are loathe to offend
L C : 0 1 :258(400) [0653] misfortune of the **world** that men of integrity seldom
L C : 0 1 :262(400) [0655] must endure having the **world** call them heretics,
L C : 0 1 :262(400) [0655] this pass; it is the blind **world's** nature to condemn and
L C : 0 1 :264(400) [0655] us; we want the golden compliments of the whole **world**.
L C : 0 1 :284(403) [0661] the judge and the whole **world** are aware of it, you can
L C : 0 1 :284(403) [0661] set forth in books and shouted throughout the **world**.
L C : 0 1 :290(404) [0663] blessings, if only the blind **world** and the false saints
L C : 0 1 :296(405) [0665] though in the eyes of the **world** you could do it
L C : 0 1 :300(405) [0665] not to those whom the **world** considers wicked rogues,
L C : 0 1 :304(406) [0667] The **world** does not consider this wrong, and it does not
L C : 0 1 :307(406) [0669] though in the eyes of the **world** you might honorably
L C : 0 1 :308(406) [0669] sees your wicked heart and the deceitfulness of the **world**.
L C : 0 1 :308(406) [0669] If you give the **world** an inch, it will take a yard, and at
L C : 0 1 :311(407) [0671] how great or precious it may be in the eyes of the **world**.
L C : 0 1 :313(407) [0671] are not important or impressive in the eyes of the **world**.
L C : 0 2 :021(413) [0683] the wretched, perverse **world** acts, drowned in its
L C : 0 2 :031(414) [0687] us from the wicked **world**, the devil, death, sin, etc.
L C : 0 2 :042(416) [0689] the first place, he has a unique community in the **world**.
L C : 0 2 :062(419) [0695] in it, having died to the **world** and all evil, he will finally
L C : 0 2 :063(419) [0695] Although the whole **world** has sought painstakingly to
L C : 0 3 :002(420) [0697] the devil, along with the **world** and our flesh, resists our
L C : 0 3 :023(423) [0703] This we should not trade for all the riches in the **world**.
L C : 0 3 :032(424) [0707] indeed be done in spite of the devil and all the **world**."
L C : 0 3 :038(425) [0709] may also be kept holy on earth by us and all the **world**.
L C : 0 3 :047(426) [0709] Since we see that the **world** is full of sects and false
L C : 0 3 :049(426) [0711] God would prevent the **world** from using his glory and
L C : 0 3 :051(426) [0711] Christ our Lord, into the **world** to redeem and deliver us
L C : 0 3 :052(427) [0711] people and advance with power throughout the **world**.
L C : 0 3 :054(427) [0713] preached throughout the **world** and that it may be
L C : 0 3 :062(428) [0715] and even enlisting the **world** and our own flesh as his
L C : 0 3 :063(428) [0715] The **world**, too, is perverse and wicked.
L C : 0 3 :065(429) [0715] with all his angels and the **world** as our enemies and must
L C : 0 3 :073(430) [0719] to our entire life in this **world**; only for its sake do we
L C : 0 3 :084(431) [0721] there now is in the **world** simply on account of false
L C : 0 3 :086(432) [0723] because we live in the **world** among people who sorely vex
L C : 0 3 :101(433) [0727] is of three kinds: of the flesh, the **world**, and the devil.
L C : 0 3 :103(434) [0727] Next comes the **world**, which assails us by word and deed
L C : 0 3 :107(434) [0729] by the flesh; older people are tempted by the **world**.
L C : 0 4 :004(437) [0733] *"Go into all the **world**, and teach all nations, baptizing*
L C : 0 4 :007(437) [0733] and battles because the **world** now is full of sects who
L C : 0 4 :043(442) [0743] Just think how the **world** would snow and rain money
L C : 0 4 :047(442) [0743] the devil confuses the **world** through his sects, the
L C : 0 4 :050(443) [0745] abide until the end of the **world**, our adversaries must
L C : 0 5 :023(449) [0757] of the devil and the **world** that we often grow weary and
L C : 0 5 :079(455) [0771] about you and see whether you are also in the **world**.
L C : 0 5 :079(455) [0771] If you are in the **world**, do not think that there will be any
L C : 0 5 :079(455) [0771] which everywhere give this testimony about the **world**.
L C : 0 5 :080(456) [0771] Besides the flesh and the **world**, you will surely have the
L C : 0 5 :082(456) [0773] the flesh, in this wicked **world**, or under the kingdom of
E P : 0 6 :004(480) [0805] regeneration and renewal is incomplete in this **world**.
E P : 0 8 :026(490) [0823] died for the sins of the **world** or that the Son of man has
E P : 0 9 :004(492) [0827] postpone until the other **world**, where there will be
E P : 1 1 :007(495) [0833] us in him before the foundation of the **world**" (Eph. 1:4).
S D : 0 1 :007(510) [0861] the devil) entered into the **world**" (Rom. 5:12;
S D : 0 1 :013(511) [0863] and wise men of the **world** with terrible errors and
S D : 0 2 :008(521) [0883] wisdom of this perverse **world** is folly with God" and that
S D : 0 2 :010(522) [0883] the wisdom of God, the **world** did not know God through
S D : 0 2 :010(522) [0885] (that is, in the dark, blind **world** which neither knows nor
S D : 0 2 :049(530) [0901] "For God so loved the **world** that he gave his only Son,
S D : 0 2 :051(531) [0901] the wisdom of God, the **world** did not know God through
S D : 0 3 :056(549) [0935] the eternal and almighty God for the sins of all the **world**.
S D : 0 4 :008(552) [0941] in the sight of the **world**, and even God will reward them
S D : 0 4 :008(552) [0941] temporal blessings in this **world**, but since they do not
S D : 0 4 :009(552) [0941] that God will reward both in this and in the next **world**.
S D : 0 5 :004(559) [0953] the Gospel in all the **world** (Mark 16:15), he summarizes
S D : 0 5 :011(560) [0955] the office of the law, must also convince the **world** of sin.
S D : 0 5 :012(560) [0955] Spirit will convince the **world** of sin because they do not
S D : 0 5 :013(560) [0957] Spirit will convince the **world** of sin' (John 16:8), which
S D : 0 5 :023(562) [0959] Since the beginning of the **world** these two proclamations
S D : 0 5 :024(562) [0961] God until the end of the **world**, but with the due
S D : 0 6 :012(566) [0967] he will convince the **world** (to which the Old Adam
S D : 0 7 :029(574) [0981] my faith before God and all the **world**, point by point.
S D : 0 7 :029(574) [0981] faith to depart from this **world** and to appear before the
S D : 0 7 :044(577) [0987] until the end of the **world** and which was to be an abiding
S D : 0 7 :077(583) [0999] until the end of the **world**, make the bread the body and
S D : 0 7 :091(585) [1005] withdrawal from this **world**, and the like have been
S D : 0 7 :099(586) [1005] Christ's leaving the **world** and going to the Father speak
S D : 0 8 :020(595) [1021] suffered for the sin of the **world**, but the Son of God
S D : 1 0 :016(613) [1057] it is written, "Woe to the **world** for temptations to sin,"
S D : 1 1 :005(617) [1065] the foundation of the **world** was laid," as St. Paul says,
S D : 1 1 :010(618) [1067] the foundations of the **world** were laid' (Eph. 1:4) and
S D : 1 1 :020(619) [1069] against the devil, the **world**, and the flesh, guide and lead
S D : 1 1 :028(620) [1071] For God "loved the **world**" and gave to it his only
S D : 1 1 :028(620) [1071] taken away the sin of the **world** (John 1:29); he has given
S D : 1 1 :028(620) [1071] flesh "for the life of the **world**" (John 6:51); his blood is
S D : 1 1 :028(620) [1071] propitiation for the whole **world's**" sin (I John 1:7; 2:2).
S D : 1 1 :042(623) [1077] again in the filth of the **world**, and decorate their hearts
S D : 1 1 :043(623) [1077] the foundation of the **world** was laid" (Eph. 1:4), before
S D : 1 1 :044(624) [1077] and decreed before the **world** began that by the power of
S D : 1 1 :045(624) [1079] the foundation of the **world** was laid" he held counsel and
S D : 1 1 :046(624) [1079] power of the devil and the **world** it could easily be
S D : 1 1 :048(624) [1079] The foundation of the **world** God has determined and
S D : 1 1 :049(624) [1079] points out that before the **world** began God ordained in
S D : 1 1 :054(625) [1081] no doubt that before the **world** began God foresaw right
S D : 1 1 :065(627) [1083] the foundation of the **world** was laid" (Eph. 1:4), as it is
S D : 1 1 :067(627) [1085] and again, "God so loved the **world**," etc. (John 3:16).
S D : 1 1 :083(630) [1091] again in the filth of this **world** (II Pet. 2:20), prepare their
S D : 1 1 :088(631) [1093] the foundation of the **world** was laid") God elected us in
S D : 1 2 :003(633) [1095] proclaim to the whole **world** that among our churches

Worldly (10)

A G : 1 7 :005(039) [0051] godly men will possess a **worldly** kingdom and annihilate
A G : 2 8 :013(083) [0085] to the temporal power laws concerning **worldly** matters.
A G : 2 8 :017(083) [0085] of our warfare are not **worldly** but have divine power to
A L : 2 8 :017(083) [0085] of our warfare are not **worldly** but have divine power to
T R : 0 0 :031(325) [0513] a sword or possess a **worldly** kingdom, for he said, "My
T R : 0 0 :031(325) [0513] of our warfare are not **worldly**," etc. (II Cor. 10:4).
T R : 0 0 :032(325) [0513] when another **worldly** kingdom would be set up on the
T R : 0 0 :036(326) [0515] transfer the keys of a **worldly** kingdom by the authority
L C : 0 1 :053(371) [0595] occurs most obviously in **worldly** business and in matters
L C : 0 1 :055(372) [0595] whether in ordinary **worldly** affairs or in sublime and

Worn (1)

L C : 0 5 :026(449) [0759] stop until he has finally **worn** us out so that we either

Worry (1), Worries (1)
S C : 0 5 :024(350) [0555] sins, he should not **worry**, nor should he search for and
L C : 0 1 :303(406) [0667] loss — he hurries and **worries** him until he acquires a half

Worse (16)
A G : 2 3 :014(053) [0063] the world is growing **worse** and men are becoming
A G : 2 3 :014(054) [0063] marriage may not cause **worse** and more disgraceful
A P : 1 2 :128(201) [0291] many good men to whom such doubt is **worse** than death.
A P : 2 1 :034(234) [0353] with abuses that were enormous and **worse** than pagan.
S 3 : 0 2 :002(303) [0479] what they are unwilling to do, are made **worse** thereby.
L C : 0 1 :214(394) [0641] or secretly do even **worse** — things too evil to mention, as
L C : 0 1 :226(395) [0645] All these are far **worse** than sneak-thieves, against whom
L C : 0 3 :111(435) [0729] will only make the matter **worse** and give the devil a
L C : 0 4 :069(445) [0749] are outside of Christ can only grow **worse** day by day.
L C : 0 4 :069(445) [0749] very truly, "Evil unchecked becomes **worse** and worse."
L C : 0 4 :069(445) [0749] very truly, "Evil unchecked becomes worse and **worse**."
L C : 0 5 :077(455) [0771] to our sin is all the **worse**, for it is a sign that ours is a
S D : 0 1 :025(512) [0867] **Worse** than that, in the sight of God it can by and of itself
S D : 0 2 :024(526) [0891] In this respect he is **worse** than a block because he is
S D : 0 2 :059(532) [0905] in this respect is much **worse** than a stone or block, for he
S D : 1 1 :042(623) [1077] their last state will be **worse** than the first (II Pet. 2:10;

Worship (155), Worshiped (6), Worshiper (1), Worshipers (2), Worshiping (3), Worships (2)
A G : 2 6 :022(067) [0073] he adds, "In vain do they **worship** me, teaching as
A G : 2 7 :036(076) [0081] "In vain do they **worship** me, teaching as doctrines
A G : 2 8 :002(081) [0083] new forms of **worship** and burdened consciences with
A L : 1 8 :007(040) [0053] such things as to will to **worship** an idol, will to commit
A L : 2 1 :003(047) [0057] Such **worship** Christ especially approves, namely, that in
A L : 0 0 :006(049) [0059] of dignity in public **worship** and the cultivation of
A L : 2 4 :006(056) [0065] and devotion of public **worship**, for none are admitted
A L : 2 4 :008(056) [0065] Such **worship** pleases God, and such use of the sacrament
A L : 2 6 :004(064) [0071] far above works and above all other acts of **worship**.
A L : 2 6 :006(065) [0071] by distinctions among foods and similar acts of **worship**.
A L : 2 6 :012(065) [0073] judged these observances to be necessary acts of **worship**.
A L : 2 6 :021(067) [0073] are not to be thought of as necessary acts of **worship**.
A L : 2 6 :022(067) [0073] he says, "In vain do they **worship** me with the precepts of
A L : 2 6 :023(067) [0073] So he does not require an unprofitable act of **worship**.
A L : 2 6 :029(068) [0075] righteousness cannot exist without such acts of **worship**.
A L : 2 6 :039(069) [0075] as if works of this sort were necessary acts of **worship**.
A L : 2 7 :036(076) [0081] says, "In vain do they **worship** me with the precepts of
A L : 2 8 :002(081) [0083] instituted new forms of **worship** and burdened
A L : 2 8 :052(089) [0091] certain observances or acts of **worship** instituted by men.
A P : 0 4 :010(108) [0123] increased many types of **worship** in the church, like
A P : 0 4 :010(108) [0123] up this or that form of **worship** or devotion with this view
A P : 0 4 :049(114) [0135] Faith is that **worship** which receives God's offered
A P : 0 4 :049(114) [0135] of the law is that **worship** which offers God our own
A P : 0 4 :049(114) [0135] that God wants to be **worshiped**, namely, that we receive
A P : 0 4 :057(114) [0137] This service and **worship** is especially praised throughout
A P : 0 4 :059(115) [0137] as the foremost kind of **worship**, as in Ps. 50:15: "Call
A P : 0 4 :060(115) [0137] wants to be known and **worshiped**, that we accept his
A P : 0 4 :083(118) [0145] merits, our contrition, attrition, love, **worship**, or works.
A P : 0 4 :131(125) [0159] or at best they require only outward acts of **worship**.
A P : 0 4 :154(128) [0163] This is the highest way of **worshiping** Christ.
A P : 0 4 :154(128) [0163] way, and in this way to **worship** and take hold of him.
A P : 0 4 :155(128) [0165] praises her entire act of **worship**, as the Scriptures often
A P : 0 4 :155(128) [0165] is, because she truly **worshiped** me with faith and with the
A P : 0 4 :155(128) [0165] the whole act of **worship**; but meanwhile he teaches that
A P : 0 4 :228(139) [0183] offered promise, is no less an act of **worship** than is love.
A P : 0 4 :228(139) [0183] blessings from him; this he declares to be true **worship**.
A P : 0 4 :288(151) [0203] they add other forms of **worship** to get rid of the terrors
A P : 0 4 :310(155) [0207] Thus the service and **worship** of the Gospel is to receive
A P : 0 4 :310(155) [0207] from God, while the **worship** of the law is to offer and
A P : 0 4 :310(155) [0207] doctrine that the highest **worship** in the Gospel is the
A P : 0 4 :310(155) [0207] About this **worship** Christ speaks in John 6:40, "This is
A P : 0 7 :032(174) [0239] that they had come to **worship** God in so many ways, as
A P : 0 7 :032(174) [0239] to the righteousness of the heart or the **worship** of God.
A P : 0 7 :034(175) [0239] traditions is an act of **worship** necessary for righteousness
A P : 0 7 :034(175) [0239] are not acts of **worship** necessary for righteousness before
A P : 1 1 :008(181) [0251] is not an act of **worship** necessary for justification.
A P : 1 2 :003(182) [0253] true knowledge of Christ, and the true **worship** of God.
A P : 1 2 :089(195) [0279] life is without God and without the true **worship** of God.
A P : 1 2 :143(204) [0297] "In vain do they **worship** me with the precepts of
A P : 1 2 :143(204) [0297] are performed as acts of **worship** which *ex opere operato*
A P : 1 2 :144(205) [0297] calls these useless acts of **worship**, and so they do not
A P : 1 2 :147(205) [0297] tradition, which Christ calls useless acts of **worship**.
A P : 1 2 :176(210) [0307] or to institute forms of **worship**; they only have the
A P : 1 5 :005(215) [0317] "In vain do they **worship** me with the precepts of
A P : 1 5 :017(217) [0319] What if God does not approve these acts of **worship**?
A P : 1 5 :018(217) [0319] is a new kind of **worship** of God, devised by human
A P : 1 5 :019(218) [0321] says that a god will be **worshiped** whom the fathers did
A P : 1 5 :036(220) [0325] the Pharisees of the uselessness of these acts of **worship**.
A P : 1 5 :040(220) [0325] this work were an act of **worship** or at least worth some
A P : 1 5 :040(220) [0325] the people sing, too, in order to learn or to **worship**.
A P : 1 5 :042(221) [0327] But the chief **worship** of God is the preaching of the
A P : 1 5 :042(221) [0327] human traditions, the **worship** of the saints, and similar
A P : 1 8 :004(225) [0335] God and express its **worship** of him in outward works.
A P : 2 1 :038(235) [0355] condemn abuses in the **worship** of saints in order to
A P : 2 1 :041(235) [0355] the mercenary **worship** of the saints, the confusion in the
A P : 2 3 :046(246) [0377] Paul condemns such "**worship** of angels" in Colossians
A P : 2 4 :002(250) [0385] is a beneficial act of **worship** even where there is no
A P : 2 4 :026(254) [0391] and acceptable to God, which is your spiritual **worship**."
A P : 2 4 :026(254) [0391] "Spiritual **worship**" is a worship in which the spirit knows
A P : 2 4 :026(254) [0391] "Spiritual worship" is a **worship** in which the spirit knows
A P : 2 4 :026(254) [0391] not only with Levitical **worship**, where cattle were
A P : 2 4 :026(254) [0391] but with any **worship** where men suppose they are
A P : 2 4 :027(254) [0393] In short, the **worship** of the New Testament is spiritual; it
A P : 2 4 :027(254) [0393] Thus it abrogates Levitical **worship**.
A P : 2 4 :027(254) [0393] "The true **worshipers** will worship the Father in
A P : 2 4 :027(254) [0393] true worshipers will **worship** the Father in spirit and
A P : 2 4 :027(254) [0393] and truth, for such the Father seeks to **worship** him.
A P : 2 4 :027(254) [0393] is spirit, and those who **worship** him must worship in
A P : 2 4 :027(254) [0393] those who worship him must **worship** in spirit and truth."
A P : 2 4 :027(254) [0393] and it teaches that **worship** should be in spirit, in faith,
A P : 2 4 :028(254) [0393] the popular notion of **worship** *ex opere operato* and teach
A P : 2 4 :028(254) [0393] God, namely, that such **worship** pleased him *ex opere*
A P : 2 4 :029(255) [0393] calling upon God is really **worshiping** and honoring him.
A P : 2 4 :030(255) [0395] abrogation of Levitical **worship**, the New Testament
A P : 2 4 :033(256) [0395] is talking about all the **worship** of the New Testament,
A P : 2 4 :033(256) [0395] For he requires the **worship** of the heart, by which the
A P : 2 4 :036(257) [0397] Christ and the whole **worship** of the New Testament.
A P : 2 4 :039(257) [0399] real meaning is spiritual **worship** and the daily sacrifice of
A P : 2 4 :041(257) [0399] and they have instituted new **worship** in the church.
A P : 2 4 :043(257) [0399] Instead, they discuss the **worship** of saints, human
A P : 2 4 :047(258) [0401] and introduced much wicked **worship** into the churches.
A P : 2 4 :051(259) [0403] opponents center their **worship** in such things rather than
A P : 2 4 :051(259) [0403] describes as **worshiping** their God with gold and
A P : 2 4 :071(262) [0409] to terrified hearts, is the **worship** of the New Testament,
A P : 2 4 :077(263) [0411] can benefit either the **worshiper** or anyone else without
A P : 2 4 :087(265) [0413] thanksgivings, and the whole **worship** are offered there.
A P : 2 4 :097(268) [0417] they introduced the **worship** of Baal; in Judah they even
A P : 2 4 :097(268) [0417] not only against the **worshipers** of Baal but also against
A P : 2 4 :098(268) [0417] Judah, and in Israel the **worship** of Baal continued; yet
A P : 2 4 :098(268) [0417] in the papal realm the **worship** of Baal clings — namely,
A P : 2 4 :098(268) [0419] And it seems that this **worship** of Baal will endure
A P : 2 4 :099(268) [0419] the prophet Elijah in condemning the **worship** of Baal.
A P : 2 7 :023(273) [0427] "In vain do they **worship** me with the precepts of
A P : 2 7 :034(275) [0431] Instead of Christ they **worship** their own cowls and their
A P : 2 7 :041(276) [0435] which we have chosen are "vain **worship**" (Matt. 15:9).
A P : 2 7 :053(278) [0437] Then there is the **worship** of saints which is guilty of a
A P : 2 7 :053(278) [0437] Christ's place to the saints, and it **worships** them wickedly.
A P : 2 7 :055(278) [0439] their whole ceremonial **worship** — lessons, chants, and the
A P : 2 7 :055(278) [0439] these ceremonies are the **worship** of God to merit the
A P : 2 7 :058(279) [0439] would not be an act of **worship** now, so the ritual of the
A P : 2 7 :058(279) [0439] be proposed as an act of **worship** but should be regarded
A P : 2 7 :058(279) [0439] Word of God as an act of **worship** to merit forgiveness of
A P : 2 7 :061(279) [0441] work was itself an act of **worship** that justified, or that
A P : 2 7 :062(280) [0441] monasticism are acts of **worship** and that they merit
A P : 2 7 :065(280) [0441] taken for wicked acts of **worship** and with the idea that
A P : 2 7 :065(280) [0441] loudly condemns all **worship**, all laws, all works, if they
A P : 2 7 :069(281) [0443] hypocrisy and the sham **worship** of the monks, which
A P : 2 7 :069(281) [0443] "In vain do they **worship** me with the precepts of
A P : 2 8 :007(282) [0445] are useless acts of **worship**, and that therefore neither sin
A P : 2 8 :008(282) [0445] of sins or were acts of **worship** that pleased God as
A P : 2 8 :009(282) [0445] Are they acts of **worship** which please God as
A P : 2 8 :011(283) [0447] of sins or to be acts of **worship** that please God as
A P : 2 8 :011(283) [0447] bishops have the power to institute such acts of **worship**.
A P : 2 8 :014(283) [0447] may institute new acts of **worship**, for worship does not
A P : 2 8 :014(283) [0447] new acts of worship, for **worship** does not belong to their
A P : 2 8 :015(283) [0447] not be necessary acts of **worship** but a means of
A P : 2 8 :015(283) [0447] though they were commanding necessary acts of **worship**.
A P : 2 8 :016(283) [0447] that they be not regarded as necessary acts of **worship**.
A P : 2 8 :016(283) [0449] the idea that human rites are necessary acts of **worship**.
A P : 2 8 :017(283) [0449] are not necessary acts of **worship**, and yet we should
A P : 2 8 :021(284) [0449] human traditions are the **worship** of God; that they are
A P : 2 8 :021(284) [0449] are necessary acts of **worship**; that they merit forgiveness
S 2 : 0 2 :002(293) [0463] says, 'In vain do they **worship** me, teaching as doctrines
S 3 : 0 2 :004(303) [0479] cares for God or that he **worships** strange gods —
S 3 : 1 5 :001(316) [0501] says, "In vain do they **worship** me, teaching as doctrines
T R : 0 0 :006(320) [0505] make laws concerning **worship**, concerning changes in the
T R : 0 0 :038(326) [0515] defend godless forms of **worship**, idolatry, and doctrines
T R : 0 0 :039(327) [0515] and godless forms of **worship**, and it is plain that the
T R : 0 0 :039(327) [0515] god or object of **worship**, so that he takes his seat in the
T R : 0 0 :040(327) [0515] of Christ and the **worship** instituted by God, and he
T R : 0 0 :040(327) [0517] to have his own doctrine and **worship** observed as divine.
T R : 0 0 :044(328) [0517] and abolish true **worship** (that is, the exercise of faith
T R : 0 0 :051(329) [0519] and impious forms of **worship**, and countless souls are
T R : 0 0 :057(330) [0521] impious forms of **worship** and doctrines which are in
T R : 0 0 :059(330) [0521] doctrines and forms of **worship** defile themselves with
T R : 0 0 :072(332) [0525] and impious forms of **worship** should be regarded as
T R : 0 0 :079(333) [0527] and impious forms of **worship** and do not ordain godly
L C : 0 1 :011(366) [0583] his own saint and **worshiped** and invoked him in time of
L C : 0 1 :016(366) [0585] true honor and the true **worship** which please God and
L C : 0 1 :017(366) [0585] world practices nothing but false **worship** and idolatry.
L C : 0 1 :017(367) [0585] it did not establish and maintain some sort of **worship**.
L C : 0 1 :018(367) [0585] while pregnant women **worshiped** Diana or Lucina, and
L C : 0 1 :022(367) [0585] There is, moreover, another false **worship**.
L C : 0 1 :035(369) [0589] he overthrows all false **worship** so that all who persist in
L C : 0 1 :084(376) [0605] to participate in public **worship**, that is, that they may
L C : 0 1 :085(376) [0605] Actually, there should be **worship** daily; however, since
L C : 0 1 :094(378) [0607] entire outward order of **worship** are therefore instituted
L C : 0 1 :125(382) [0617] do, next to the sublime **worship** of God described in the
L C : 0 2 :066(419) [0697] they believe in and **worship** only the one, true God,
E P : R N :004(465) [0777] against the false **worship**, idolatry, and superstition of the
E P : 1 0 :003(493) [0829] and for themselves no divine **worship** or even a part of it.
E P : 1 0 :003(493) [0829] "In vain do they **worship** me, teaching as doctrines the
E P : 1 0 :009(494) [0831] regarded as in themselves divine **worship** or a part of it.
S D : 0 7 :057(579) [0993] in pagan devil-**worship** and who likewise were going to
S D : 1 0 :008(612) [1055] in and of themselves no **worship** of God or even a part of
S D : 1 0 :008(612) [1055] written, "In vain do they **worship** me, teaching for
S D : 1 0 :010(612) [1055] undermine the genuine **worship** of God and to introduce
S D : 1 0 :015(613) [1057] and be put as divine **worship** not only on a par with
S D : 1 0 :026(615) [1061] as of themselves **worship** of God or a part thereof.

Worst (10)
S 2 : 0 2 :019(296) [0467] own merits and (what is **worst** of all) become idolaters.
S 2 : 0 2 :023(296) [0469] **Worst** of all, however, is the claim that relics effect
S C : P R :019(340) [0537] of the world and are the **worst** enemies of God and man.
L C : 0 1 :187(390) [0633] to let our enemies rave and rage and do their **worst**.
L C : 0 1 :289(404) [0663] misconstruing and twisting things in the **worst** way.
L C : 0 3 :041(425) [0709] acceptable; this is the **worst** profanation and dishonor of
L C : 0 3 :069(429) [0717] all rage and do their **worst**, let them plot and plan how to
L C : 0 4 :055(443) [0747] blaspheme and desecrate the sacrament in the **worst** way.
L C : 0 6 :003(457) [0000] **Worst** of all, no one taught or understood what confession
S D : 0 1 :062(519) [0879] a disease, ultimately the **worst** damage is that we shall

Worth (10), Worthily (4), Worthiness (21), Worthless (12), Worthy (50)

A L : 2 4 :023(058) [0067] said for many people is **worth** as much as a special Mass
A P : 0 2 :040(105) [0115] call lust sin, by nature **worthy** of death if it is not
A P : 0 4 :062(115) [0139] men are under sin and are **worthy** of eternal wrath and
A P : 0 4 :086(119) [0147] not because it is a work **worthy** in itself, but because it
A P : 0 4 :263(146) [0195] they bring forth fruits **worthy** of penitence, as John the
A P : 0 4 :289(151) [0203] obedience to the law is **worthy** of grace and eternal life.
A P : 0 4 :290(151) [0203] is a righteousness **worthy** of grace and eternal life,
A P : 0 4 :316(156) [0209] of love, are a **worthy** righteousness that pleases God of
A P : 0 4 :320(156) [0209] it find that it will count **worthy** of eternal life, if indeed
A P : 0 4 :321(157) [0209] that their works are **worth** enough to account them
A P : 0 4 :332(158) [0211] declare that they are **worthy** because they have love and
A P : 0 4 :335(159) [0215] they add that works are **worthless** to God, but that to us
A P : 0 4 :335(159) [0215] to God, but that to us they are **worth** something.
A P : 0 4 :337(159) [0215] argument that faith is **worthless** would be correct when
A P : 0 4 :337(159) [0215] that our works are **worthless** is the very voice of faith, as
A P : 0 4 :338(159) [0215] promise of grace, even though our works are **worthless**.
A P : 0 4 :338(159) [0215] For our works are **worthless**, and with the whole church
A P : 0 4 :339(159) [0215] denounces our works as **worthless**, but he does not
A P : 0 4 :342(159) [0215] meaning that works are **worthless** to God but worth
A P : 0 4 :342(159) [0215] that works are worthless to God but **worth** something to
A P : 0 4 :342(159) [0215] is speaking of that **worthiness** whereby God obligates
A P : 0 4 :342(160) [0215] out of place here to discuss what is **worthy** or worthless.
A P : 0 4 :342(160) [0215] out of place here to discuss what is worthy or **worthless**.
A P : 0 4 :347(160) [0217] difference between the **worthy** and the unworthy because
A P : 0 4 :357(162) [0219] that therefore they are **worthy** of grace and eternal life
A P : 0 4 :359(162) [0219] works of themselves are **worthy** of grace and eternal life
A P : 0 4 :360(162) [0219] attribute to works a **worthiness** of grace and eternal life.
A P : 0 4 :375(164) [0223] but in themselves are not **worthy** of grace and eternal life.
A P : 0 4 :376(164) [0223] they are righteousness that they are **worthy** of eternal life.
A P : 0 7 :027(173) [0235] care anything for the Gospel or think it **worth** reading?
A P : 1 1 :003(180) [0249] the people about the **worth** and fruits of the sacraments in
A P : 1 2 :028(185) [0259] wants to call fruits **worthy** of penitence (Matt. 3:8) and an
A P : 1 2 :058(190) [0267] **Worthy** fruits as well as punishments follow regeneration
A P : 1 2 :068(192) [0271] is a great crowd of **worthless** commentators on the
A P : 1 2 :106(197) [0283] surely is a neat one, **worthy** of these men who despise
A P : 1 2 :108(198) [0283] that I am a sinner **worthy** of eternal wrath, and I cannot
A P : 1 5 :040(220) [0325] were an act of worship or at least **worth** some reward.
A P : 2 1 :027(232) [0349] Even though she is **worthy** of the highest honors, she
A P : 2 4 :073(262) [0409] consciences are the ones **worthy** of it, and how they
A P : 2 4 :088(265) [0413] it says: "And make us **worthy** to come to offer Thee
A P : 2 4 :088(265) [0413] that we might be made **worthy** to offer prayers and
T R : 0 0 :044(328) [0517] sins are forgiven on account of the **worth** of our work.
S C : 0 2 :002(345) [0543] and mercy, without any merit or **worthiness** on my part.
S C : 0 6 :009(352) [0557] Who, then, receives this sacrament **worthily**?
S C : 0 6 :010(352) [0557] discipline, but he is truly **worthy** and well prepared who
S C : 0 9 :003(354) [0561] rule well be considered **worthy** of double honor,
L C : 0 1 :025(368) [0587] a name more elegant and **worthy** than any found in other
L C : 0 1 :117(381) [0615] not on account of your **worthiness** but because it has its
L C : 0 1 :118(381) [0615] whole lives they are not **worthy** to offer him a cup of
L C : 0 1 :166(388) [0629] and disdains this is not **worthy** to hear a word from God.
L C : 0 1 :273(401) [0659] somebody with a **worthless** tongue who gossips and
L C : 0 3 :013(422) [0701] not because of my **worthiness**, but because of the
L C : 0 3 :014(422) [0701] Such a prayer is **worthless**.
L C : 0 3 :015(422) [0701] am not holy enough or **worthy** enough; if I were as godly
L C : 0 3 :017(422) [0703] whether we be sinners or saints, **worthy** or unworthy.
L C : 0 3 :021(423) [0703] or because of my own **worthiness**, but at thy
L C : 0 3 :075(430) [0719] Rulers are **worthy** of all honor, and we should render
L C : 0 3 :122(436) [0731] their own works and **worthiness**, so that they despise God
L C : 0 4 :008(437) [0733] though to all appearances it may not be **worth** a straw.
L C : 0 4 :012(438) [0735] to the person, from whom they must derive their **worth**.
L C : 0 4 :013(438) [0735] like the works which we do, regards it as **worthless**.
L C : 0 4 :033(440) [0741] alone makes the person **worthy** to receive the salutary,
L C : 0 5 :016(448) [0757] blood) just as truly as when one uses it most **worthily**.
L C : 0 5 :017(448) [0757] you believe, or if you are **worthy**, you receive my body
L C : 0 5 :018(448) [0757] you are unworthy or **worthy**, you here have Christ's body
L C : 0 5 :036(450) [0761] of a Christian for receiving this sacrament **worthily**.
L C : 0 5 :055(453) [0767] into consternation, saying, "Alas, I am not **worthy**!"
L C : 0 5 :061(453) [0767] this sacrament does not depend upon our **worthiness**.
L C : 0 5 :061(453) [0767] baptized because we are **worthy** and holy, nor do we
L C : 0 5 :062(454) [0767] "I would really like to be **worthy**, but I come not on
L C : 0 5 :062(454) [0767] not on account of any **worthiness** of mine, but on
L C : 0 5 :062(454) [0767] thy disciple, no matter how insignificant my **worthiness**."
L C : 0 5 :073(455) [0771] sacrament purely and **worthily**, you must stay away from
E P : 0 3 :004(473) [0793] work, merit, or **worthiness**, and reckons to us the
E P : 0 7 :002(481) [0809] the sacrament, be they **worthy** or unworthy, godly or
E P : 0 7 :016(483) [0813] and those who are **worthy** but also the unworthy and the
E P : 0 7 :017(484) [0813] consolation in the hearts of believing and **worthy** guests.
E P : 0 7 :020(484) [0813] confess that the entire **worthiness** of the guests at this
E P : 0 7 :020(484) [0813] **Worthiness** consists not at all in our own virtues or in our
E P : 0 7 :038(486) [0817] 17. That the **worthiness** of the guests at this heavenly
S D : 0 3 :009(541) [0919] without any merit or **worthiness** on our part, and without
S D : 0 3 :037(546) [0929] our own works, merit, **worthiness**, glory, and trust in any
S D : 0 3 :046(548) [0933] man must make himself **worthy** and fit to have the merit
S D : 0 3 :055(549) [0935] works, virtues, and **worthiness** and that our righteousness
S D : 0 7 :016(572) [0977] does not depend on the **worthiness** or unworthiness of the
S D : 0 7 :024(573) [0981] one does so in the most **worthy** manner, for the
S D : 0 7 :026(573) [0981] 'If you believe and are **worthy**, you have my body and
S D : 0 7 :026(573) [0981] to say, 'Whether you are **worthy** or unworthy, you here
S D : 0 7 :027(574) [0981] to believers and **worthy** communicants but also to the
S D : 0 7 :069(582) [0997] True and **worthy** communicants, on the other hand, are
S D : 0 7 :071(582) [0997] And **worthiness** does not consist in the weakness or
S D : 0 7 :072(582) [0997] happens in the case of both the **worthy** and the unworthy.
S D : 0 7 :088(585) [1003] here on earth both the **worthy** and the unworthy alike
S D : 0 7 :089(585) [1003] impotent by either the **worthiness** or unworthiness of the
S D : 0 7 :123(590) [1015] at this heavenly meal, the **worthy** and the unworthy.
S D : 0 7 :124(591) [1015] reject the doctrine that **worthiness** does not consist in true
S D : 1 1 :060(626) [1083] corrupted by sin and is **worthy** and deserving of God's

Worthwhile (4)

A P : 0 2 :051(107) [0119] We have thought it **worthwhile** rather to list, in the usual
A P : 2 0 :012(228) [0341] our article, and it is **worthwhile** to examine some of
A P : 2 1 :036(234) [0353] It is truly **worthwhile** to hear of these things and to see
A P : 2 7 :010(270) [0423] It is **worthwhile** to hear how they twist our arguments and

Wounded (2), Wounding (1), Wounds (1)

L C : 0 3 :102(434) [0727] All this often **wounds** and inflames even an innocent
S D : 0 1 :027(513) [0867] this corruption and **wounding** which Satan brought
S D : 0 2 :077(536) [0911] is good, but only grievously **wounded** and half-dead.
S D : 0 5 :023(562) [0959] the nations, "who was **wounded** for our transgressions

Woven (1)

S D : 0 3 :036(545) [0929] God they should not be drawn, **woven**, or mingled in.

Wrangle (2), Wrangling (1)

A P : 2 4 :092(267) [0417] Why should we **wrangle** with our opponents who
L C : 0 1 :301(405) [0667] example, when people **wrangle** and wrestle over a large
S D : 0 4 :036(557) [0949] eliminate much useless **wrangling** and preserve the church

Wrath (132), Wrathful (6), Wroth (1)

A G : 0 2 :002(029) [0043] condemns to the eternal **wrath** of God all those who are
A G : 0 3 :003(030) [0045] but also for all other sins and to propitiate God's **wrath**.
A G : 2 3 :018(054) [0063] abomination and prevalence, arouse the **wrath** of God.
A P : 0 2 :042(105) [0117] — doubt about God's **wrath**, his grace, and his Word;
A P : 0 4 :009(108) [0123] he does not feel God's **wrath** or judgment, he can imagine
A P : 0 4 :034(112) [0129] to be sure that God is **wrathful** at our sin, to fear him
A P : 0 4 :036(112) [0131] men who are under eternal **wrath** merit the forgiveness of
A P : 0 4 :036(112) [0131] that really feels God's **wrath** cannot love him unless it
A P : 0 4 :036(112) [0131] bring itself to love a **wrathful**, judging, punishing God.
A P : 0 4 :037(112) [0131] themselves do not feel the **wrath** or judgment of God.
A P : 0 4 :038(112) [0131] Paul says (Rom. 4:15), "The law brings **wrath**."
A P : 0 4 :040(112) [0131] are all under sin and subject to eternal **wrath** and death.
A P : 0 4 :046(113) [0133] faith sets against God's **wrath** not our merits of love, but
A P : 0 4 :062(115) [0139] are under sin and are worthy of eternal **wrath** and death.
A P : 0 4 :079(118) [0143] through the law, which shows God's **wrath** against sin.
A P : 0 4 :080(118) [0143] we cannot appease God's **wrath** by setting forth our own
A P : 0 4 :081(118) [0145] set our love or our works against the **wrath** of God.
A P : 0 4 :082(118) [0145] in him and set it against the **wrath** and judgment of God.
A P : 0 4 :128(125) [0157] knows that in his terrible **wrath** he is overwhelming us
A P : 0 4 :128(125) [0157] always accuses us, it always shows that God is **wrathful**.
A P : 0 4 :142(126) [0161] that feels God's **wrath** against our sins and looks for
A P : 0 4 :195(134) [0175] works of ours against the **wrath** of God, as Paul clearly
A P : 0 4 :200(134) [0175] works are evil, and the **wrath** of God is revealed,
A P : 0 4 :203(135) [0177] of sins, appease the **wrath** of God, and achieve
A P : 0 4 :204(135) [0177] The law always accuses them and brings forth **wrath**.
A P : 0 4 :207(135) [0177] that through these works they placated the **wrath** of God.
A P : 0 4 :209(136) [0177] this cruel and painful deed to placate the **wrath** of God.
A P : 0 4 :212(136) [0179] that they can set against the **wrath** and judgment of God.
A P : 0 4 :214(136) [0179] pit our works against the **wrath** and judgment of God.
A P : 0 4 :214(136) [0179] mediator, can be pitted against God's **wrath** and judgment
A P : 0 4 :222(138) [0181] set our love against the **wrath** and judgment of God; that
A P : 0 4 :224(138) [0181] business is with God; his **wrath** must be stilled and the
A P : 0 4 :257(144) [0193] For the law works **wrath**; it only accuses; it only terrifies
A P : 0 4 :260(145) [0193] because the law works **wrath** and continually accuses.
A P : 0 4 :264(146) [0195] debt can be removed, that the **wrath** of God can be stilled.
A P : 0 4 :270(147) [0197] of the law, "for the law brings **wrath**" (Rom. 4:15).
A P : 0 4 :288(151) [0203] many other painful works to appease the **wrath** of God.
A P : 0 4 :288(151) [0203] the terrors of conscience and the **wrath** of God.
A P : 0 4 :291(152) [0203] the mediator and propitiator, against the **wrath** of God.
A P : 0 4 :300(153) [0205] must set Christ against the **wrath** of God, as though we
A P : 0 4 :300(153) [0205] we could overcome the **wrath** of God with our love or
A P : 0 4 :301(153) [0205] evils, sufferings in this life and the fear of eternal **wrath**.
A P : 0 4 :312(155) [0207] as we feel that he is **wrathful** against us, human nature
A P : 0 4 :312(155) [0207] against us, human nature flees his **wrath** and judgment.
A P : 0 4 :314(156) [0207] our love and keeping of the law against the **wrath** of God.
A P : 0 4 :365(163) [0219] of punishments the **wrath** of God is displayed, and hence
A P : 1 2 :007(183) [0255] life and of the Spirit, but only of **wrath** and punishment.
A P : 1 2 :029(185) [0259] that feels God's **wrath** against sin and is sorry that it has
A P : 1 2 :032(186) [0259] conscience feels God's **wrath** against sin, unknown to men
A P : 1 2 :032(186) [0259] it flees God's horrible **wrath**, for human nature cannot
A P : 1 2 :034(186) [0261] they feel the terrible and indescribable **wrath** of God?
A P : 1 2 :051(189) [0265] "The Lord will be **wroth**, to do his deed — strange
A P : 1 2 :051(189) [0265] that do not feel God's **wrath** in their smugness spurn
A P : 1 2 :064(191) [0269] or our love against the **wrath** of God, but it finds peace
A P : 1 2 :078(193) [0275] set them against the **wrath** and judgment of God,
A P : 1 2 :084(194) [0277] ought to set against the **wrath** of God not our works but
A P : 1 2 :085(194) [0277] ought to set our love and works against the **wrath** of God.
A P : 1 2 :087(195) [0277] love or works against the **wrath** of God or trust in our
A P : 1 2 :088(195) [0277] As Paul says (Rom. 4:15), "The law brings **wrath**."
A P : 1 2 :107(198) [0283] contrition; feeling God's **wrath**, we confess that he is
A P : 1 2 :107(198) [0283] confess that he is justly **wrathful** and cannot be placated
A P : 1 2 :108(198) [0283] a sinner worthy of eternal **wrath**, and I cannot set my
A P : 1 2 :108(198) [0283] set my righteousness or my merits against Thy **wrath**.
A P : 1 2 :146(205) [0297] overcomes death, just as it overcomes the **wrath** of God.
A P : 1 2 :147(205) [0297] frees the heart from the **wrath** of God and eternal death.
A P : 1 2 :150(206) [0299] when amid the terrors of contrition he reveals his **wrath**.
A P : 1 2 :153(206) [0299] that sting and sense of **wrath** of which Paul says
A P : 1 2 :153(206) [0299] power of sin, this sense of **wrath**, is a real punishment as
A P : 1 2 :153(206) [0299] without this sense of **wrath** death is actually no
A P : 1 2 :158(207) [0301] afflictions are not always punishments or signs of **wrath**.
A P : 1 2 :158(207) [0301] God's punishment and **wrath**, they should not feel that
A P : 1 5 :005(215) [0317] the forgiveness of sins and appease the **wrath** of God.
A P : 2 0 :010(228) [0341] that it thought adequate to placate the **wrath** of God?
A P : 2 3 :054(246) [0379] Sodom and Gomorrah reveal God's **wrath** at human vice.
A P : 2 4 :013(251) [0387] they can placate God's **wrath**, gain the remission of guilt
A P : 2 4 :019(252) [0389] God or placates his **wrath** or merits the forgiveness of
A P : 2 4 :023(253) [0391] victim to placate the **wrath** of God when, amid great
A P : 2 7 :017(271) [0425] propitiation against the **wrath** of God for us so that we
A P : 2 7 :017(271) [0425] propitiation, against the **wrath** of God; whoever tries to
S 1 : P R :005(289) [0457] devil — or ultimately the **wrath** of God — answer them as
S 3 : 0 2 :005(303) [0479] "The law brings **wrath**," and Rom. 5:20, "Law came
S 3 : 0 3 :001(303) [0479] says in Rom. 1:18, "The **wrath** of God is revealed from
S 3 : 0 3 :032(308) [0489] any assurance that you will escape the **wrath** to come?"
S C : 0 1 :022(344) [0543] should therefore fear his **wrath** and not disobey these
S C : 0 9 :004(355) [0561] of God to execute his **wrath** on the wrongdoer"
S C : 0 9 :005(355) [0561] not only to avoid God's **wrath** but also for the sake of
L C : 0 1 :016(366) [0585] under penalty of eternal **wrath**, namely, that the heart

Continued ▶

LC : 0 1 :032(369) [0589] His **wrath** does not abate until the fourth generation.
LC : 0 1 :036(369) [0589] mammon and believe that they can withstand his **wrath**.
LC : 0 1 :038(369) [0591] and foolish that they justly merit the **wrath** they receive.
LC : 0 1 :041(370) [0591] and salvation, or eternal **wrath**, misery, and woe.
LC : 0 1 :069(374) [0601] All this is God's **wrath** and punishment upon such willful
LC : 0 1 :148(385) [0623] will have nothing but the **wrath** and displeasure of God;
LC : 0 1 :176(389) [0631] upon yourself sin and **wrath**, thus earning hell by the way
LC : 0 1 :198(392) [0637] and filth, and it merits nothing but **wrath** and damnation.
LC : 0 1 :232(396) [0647] wantonness and that the **wrath** of God may be
LC : 0 1 :234(397) [0647] but he will not escape God's **wrath** and punishment.
LC : 0 1 :248(398) [0651] commandment, lest his **wrath** and punishment come upon
LC : 0 1 :253(399) [0653] this blessing will find **wrath** and misfortune enough.
LC : 0 1 :322(408) [0673] words contain both a **wrathful** threat and a friendly
LC : 0 1 :323(409) [0673] will, lest he be moved to **wrath**; and, conversely, trusts him
LC : 0 1 :330(410) [0677] who vents his **wrath** upon those who despise them, and,
LC : 0 1 :333(410) [0677] threat of his greatest **wrath** and punishment, while at the
LC : 0 2 :028(414) [0685] We lay under God's **wrath** and displeasure, doomed to
LC : 0 2 :066(419) [0697] they remain in eternal **wrath** and damnation, for they do
LC : 0 2 :068(420) [0697] us Christians, for God's **wrath** and displeasure still remain
LC : 0 3 :009(421) [0699] and obligation [on pain of God's **wrath** and displeasure].
LC : 0 3 :010(421) [0699] we are sinners and have merited nothing but **wrath**.
LC : 0 3 :011(421) [0701] to him and assuage his **wrath** and seek grace by their
LC : 0 3 :086(432) [0723] give us occasion for impatience, **wrath**, vengeance, etc.
LC : 0 3 :089(432) [0723] restless; it fears God's **wrath** and displeasure, and so it
EP : 0 1 :012(467) [0783] of which man outside of Christ is a child of **wrath**.
EP : 0 5 :008(479) [0803] Then "God's **wrath** is revealed from heaven" over all
EP : 0 5 :009(479) [0803] advertisement of God's **wrath** which really directs people
EP : 0 5 :010(479) [0803] Christ — proclaims God's **wrath** and terrifies people, it is
EP : 0 6 :005(480) [0807] coercion of punishments and the threat of God's **wrath**.
SD : 0 1 :006(509) [0861] "by nature the children of **wrath**," of death, and of
SD : 0 1 :009(510) [0861] and are children of **wrath** by nature, as St. Paul says
SD : 0 1 :019(511) [0865] is necessarily a child of **wrath** and of damnation and is in
SD : 0 1 :062(519) [0879] only endure God's eternal **wrath** and death but that we do
SD : 0 2 :021(525) [0889] the dreadful, cruel **wrath** of God over sin and death but
SD : 0 2 :054(531) [0903] to know his sins and the **wrath** of God and experiences
SD : 0 2 :070(535) [0909] to know sin, to fear the **wrath** of God, to turn from sin, to
SD : 0 3 :020(542) [0921] transformed a child of **wrath** into a child of God and thus
SD : 0 4 :032(556) [0947] "On account of these the **wrath** of God is coming upon
SD : 0 5 :010(560) [0955] thus he reveals his **wrath** from heaven over all sinners
SD : 0 5 :010(560) [0955] heaven over all sinners and shows how great this **wrath** is.
SD : 0 5 :012(560) [0955] about our sin and the **wrath** of God, no matter how or
SD : 0 5 :012(560) [0955] nor are terrified by the **wrath** of God, as he says in John
SD : 0 5 :012(560) [0955] and preaching of God's **wrath** over sin than the passion
SD : 0 5 :012(560) [0955] as all this proclaims the **wrath** of God and terrifies man,
SD : 0 5 :014(560) [0957] reveals sin and God's **wrath**, but to this office it
SD : 0 5 :017(561) [0957] of the law with God's **wrath** and temporal and eternal
SD : 0 5 :020(561) [0959] is therefore subject to the **wrath** of God, to death, to
SD : 1 0 :025(615) [1061] they do not provoke the **wrath** of God, violate love,
SD : 1 1 :060(626) [1083] and deserving of God's **wrath** and damnation, God owes
SD : 1 1 :079(629) [1089] patience the vessels of **wrath** fitted for damnation in
SD : 1 1 :080(629) [1089] God "endured the vessels of **wrath** with much patience."
SD : 1 1 :080(629) [1089] He does not say that God made them vessels of **wrath**.

Wreak (1)
SD : 0 7 :105(588) [1009] in believers but also to **wreak** judgment on unbelievers.

Wrecked (1)
LC : 0 1 :036(369) [0589] know it they will be **wrecked**, along with all they have

Wreath (2)
LC : 0 1 :326(409) [0675] clasp or the hoop of a **wreath** that binds the end to the
LC : 0 3 :075(430) [0719] instead of a lion or a **wreath** of rue, or if a loaf of bread

Wrest (1), Wrested (1), Wrestle (1), Wrestlers (1), Wrests (1)
AP : 2 4 :010(251) [0387] off into side issues, like **wrestlers** fighting for their
TR : 0 0 :049(328) [0519] The other is that the pope **wrests** judgment from the
TR : 0 0 :079(333) [0527] in addition, they have **wrested** jurisdiction from the
LC : 0 1 :022(367) [0585] its own works and presumes to **wrest** heaven from God.
LC : 0 1 :301(405) [0667] when people wrangle and **wrestle** over a large

Wretched (6), Wretchedness (4)
AG : 2 5 :008(062) [0069] Our **wretched** human nature is so deeply submerged in
S 1 : PR :003(289) [0455] from the day take such **wretched** pains to postpone and
S 1 : PR :009(290) [0457] As for the rest, **wretchedness** and woe will be their lot
S 1 : PR :015(291) [0459] But help us, poor and **wretched** souls who cry unto Thee
S 2 : 0 2 :004(293) [0463] drive the world into **wretchedness** and woe on account of
SC : PR :002(338) [0533] Good God, what **wretchedness** I beheld!
LC : 0 1 :118(381) [0615] become of these poor **wretched** people when, standing
LC : 0 1 :247(398) [0651] aid, he will go away **wretched** and dejected, and because
LC : 0 2 :021(413) [0683] This is the way the **wretched**, perverse world acts,
LC : 0 2 :029(414) [0685] on our misery and **wretchedness** and came from heaven to

Wring (2), Wrung (3)
AP : 2 4 :044(258) [0399] our opponents **wring** their hands over "the desolation of
LC : 0 1 :163(387) [0627] lead us to the devil — and **wring** sweat and blood out of
EP : 0 5 :008(479) [0803] which Moses could never have **wrung** from them.
EP : 0 6 :007(481) [0807] no threat of the law could ever have **wrung** from him.
SD : 0 5 :010(560) [0955] an insight that Moses could never have **wrung** out of him.

Wrinkle (1)
AP : 0 7 :007(169) [0229] without spot or **wrinkle** or any such thing, that it might

Writ (1)
SD : 0 5 :007(559) [0953] In some passages of Holy **Writ** the word is used and

Write (13), Writes (30), Writing (11), Wrote (22)
PR : PR :013(007) [0013] and criticisms reduced to **writing**, and communicate to us
AG : PR :006(025) [0039] estates should commit to **writing** and present, in German
AG : PR :010(025) [0041] us may be presented in **writing** on both sides, they may be
AG : 2 3 :025(055) [0065] He **wrote** in his eleventh letter, "If they are unwilling or
AG : 2 6 :001(063) [0071] men taught, preached, and **wrote** that distinctions among
AG : 2 6 :013(066) [0073] Gerson **writes** that many fell into despair on this account,
AG : 2 8 :016(083) [0085] Paul also **wrote** in Phil. 3:20, "Our commonwealth is in
AG : 2 8 :024(084) [0087] St. Paul also **writes** in Gal. 1:8, "Even if we, or an angel
AG : 2 8 :028(085) [0087] St. Augustine also **writes** in his reply to the letters of
AG : 2 8 :052(089) [0091] justification, as St. Paul **writes** in Gal. 5:1, "For freedom
AL : 2 3 :002(051) [0061] Platina **writes** to this effect.
AL : 2 6 :013(066) [0073] Gerson **writes** that many fell into despair, and some even
AL : 2 8 :016(083) [0085] Paul also **wrote** in Phil. 3:20, "Our commonwealth is in
AP : PR :013(099) [0101] and monks who **wrote** the Confutation, not with the
AP : 0 2 :028(104) [0113] Bonaventure **writes**: "When the question is asked what
AP : 0 2 :035(104) [0113] out at Luther because he **wrote** that original sin remains
AP : 0 4 :014(109) [0123] proper, for Aristotle **wrote** so well on natural ethics that
AP : 0 4 :036(112) [0131] of our opponents to **write** that men who are under
AP : 0 4 :087(120) [0147] have been wrong in **writing** to the Ephesians (2:8) that we
AP : 0 4 :106(122) [0153] Augustine **writes** many things in the same vein against the
AP : 0 4 :173(131) [0171] the Pelagians, Jerome **writes**, "We are righteous,
AP : 0 4 :179(131) [0171] He **writes** to the same effect in Col. 2:10, "You have come
AP : 0 4 :210(136) [0179] in those for whom it is offered, as Gabriel Biel **writes**.
AP : 0 4 :220(137) [0181] He is **writing** to people who, upon being justified, needed
AP : 0 4 :236(140) [0185] They are **writing** laws in blood and are asking the
AP : 0 4 :236(140) [0185] not for others, as the poet **writes**, "I forgive myself, says
AP : 1 2 :124(201) [0289] than in that of the sophists who **wrote** the Confutation.
AP : 1 2 :125(201) [0289] issues they did not **write** anything that now or in the
AP : 1 2 :134(202) [0293] Secondly, our opponents **write** that if a penitent refuses to
AP : 1 2 :171(209) [0305] Furthermore, the Fathers **wrote** that once in a lifetime
AP : 1 5 :022(218) [0321] In Col. 2:23 Paul **writes** that traditions "have an
AP : 1 5 :024(218) [0321] which justify, as Thomas **writes**, "Fasting avails to destroy
AP : 2 3 :005(239) [0365] opponents will not speak, **write**, or act honestly, frankly,
AP : 2 3 :068(248) [0383] show our opponents' purpose in **writing** the Confutation.
AP : 2 4 :008(250) [0385] Epiphanius **writes** that in Asia Minor there were no daily
AP : 2 4 :062(260) [0405] error of Thomas when he **writes**, "The body of the Lord,
AP : 2 7 :059(279) [0439] who, as Jeremiah **writes** (35:6), neither had any
S 1 : PR :004(289) [0455] I am still **writing**, preaching, and lecturing every day.
S 1 : PR :005(289) [0457] pay attention to what I **write** and who keep themselves
S 2 : 0 2 :013(295) [0465] and to what end the authors **wrote** these passages.
S 2 : 0 2 :013(295) [0467] St. Augustine does not **write** that there is a purgatory,
S 2 : 0 4 :009(300) [0473] So St. Jerome **writes** that the priests of Alexandria
S 3 : 0 3 :045(310) [0491] as the same St. John **writes**, "If we say we have no sin, we
S 3 : 0 8 :006(312) [0495] not stop preaching and **writing** until the Spirit himself
S 3 : 1 0 :003(314) [0497] St. Jerome, too, **wrote** concerning the church in
TR : 0 0 :019(323) [0509] 10. When **writing** to the patriarch of Alexandria, Gregory
TR : 0 0 :041(328) [0517] as accursed, and he **wrote** in II Cor. 6:14, "Do not be
SC : 0 4 :010(349) [0551] Holy Spirit, as St. Paul **wrote** to Titus (3:5-8), "He saved
SC : 0 4 :014(349) [0553] In Romans 6:4, St. Paul **wrote**, "We were buried
SC : 0 6 :004(351) [0555] Luke, and also St. Paul, **write** thus: "Our Lord Jesus
LC : 0 1 :331(410) [0677] commands men to **write** the Ten Commandments on
LC : 0 4 :081(446) [0751] for this view, for he **wrote**, "Repentance is the second
EP : 0 5 :006(478) [0803] then it is correct to say or **write** that the Gospel is a
EP : 1 0 :006(493) [0829] as the apostle Paul **writes**, "For freedom Christ has set us
EP : 1 2 :031(500) [0843] nor publicly say or **write** anything contrary to it but
SD : PR :005(504) [0851] which it was set down in **writing** in the year 1530 and
SD : 0 1 :051(517) [0875] latter sense that Luther **writes** that sin and sinning are
SD : 0 1 :061(519) [0879] of Genesis 3 likewise **writes** earnestly against a minimizing
SD : 0 1 :062(519) [0879] exposition of Ps. 90:12 he **wrote**, "Whether we call
SD : 0 2 :036(528) [0895] Catechism Dr. Luther **writes**: "I am also a part and
SD : 0 2 :044(529) [0897] *of the Will*, in which he **writes** concerning the enslaved
SD : 0 4 :010(552) [0941] For, as Luther **writes** in his Preface to the Epistle of St.
SD : 0 6 :008(565) [0965] this the apostle **writes**, "I know that nothing good dwells
SD : 0 7 :020(572) [0979] Catechism, where he **writes** as follows: "What is the
SD : 0 7 :033(575) [0983] with great fervor and **wrote** as follows: "I reckon them all
SD : 0 7 :059(580) [0993] They **write** as follows: "The bread is participation in the
SD : 0 8 :016(594) [1019] Theodore the Presbyter **wrote**: "A contemporary of the
SD : 0 8 :017(594) [1021] one essence but, as Dr. Luther **writes**, into one person.
SD : 0 8 :045(600) [1031] wrongly put to say or to **write** that the cited locutions,
SD : 0 8 :075(606) [1043] Against this sect Gregory the Great also **wrote**.
SD : 0 8 :081(607) [1045] *the Holy Supper* he **writes** about the person of Christ:
SD : 0 8 :085(608) [1045] *Words of David*, which he **wrote** shortly before his death,
SD : 1 0 :022(615) [1061] as accursed, and he **wrote** in II Cor. 6:14, 'Do not be
SD : 1 1 :027(620) [1071] the same effect when he **wrote**, "We are ambassadors in
SD : 1 1 :082(630) [1089] vessels of honor when he **writes**, "If any one purifies
SD : 1 2 :040(636) [1103] Nor shall we speak or **write** anything, privately or

Written (111)
PR : PR :013(007) [0013] and also the just cited **written** agreement composed with
AG : PR :009(025) [0041] also submit a similar **written** statement of their judgments
AG : PR :017(026) [0041] Again, by means of a **written** instruction at the last diet in
AG : 2 4 :027(059) [0067] For it is **written** in the Epistle to the Hebrews that Christ
AG : 2 5 :006(062) [0069] that we have **written** about and treated of true Christian
AG : 2 8 :001(081) [0083] various things have been **written** in former times about
AG : 2 8 :039(087) [0089] apostles and bishops to institute it, as some have **written**.
AL : 2 4 :019(058) [0067] For in the Decalogue it is **written**, "The Lord will not
AL : 2 4 :026(058) [0067] So it is **written** in the Epistle to the Hebrews, "We have
AL : 2 6 :024(067) [0073] It is also **written** in Rom. 14:17, "The kingdom of God is
AL : 2 8 :040(087) [0089] For thus some have **written**, and the pontiffs seem in
AL : 2 8 :052(089) [0091] for justification, as it is **written** in the Epistle to the
AP : PR :013(099) [0101] Now, I have **written** as moderately as I could.
AP : PR :014(099) [0101] I realized it was **written** so cleverly and slanderously that
AP : 0 2 :035(105) [0115] He has always **written** that Baptism removes the guilt of
AP : 0 4 :007(108) [0121] it has the same judgment naturally **written** in the mind.
AP : 0 4 :031(111) [0129] And in John 3:5 it is **written**, "Unless one is born of water
AP : 0 4 :123(124) [0157] It is **written** in the prophet (Jer. 31:33), "I will put my law
AP : 0 4 :201(134) [0175] added to give him a sign **written** in his body by which he
AP : 0 4 :263(145) [0195] those who are penitent, as is **written** in Ezek. 18:21, 22.
AP : 0 4 :276(148) [0199] This same promise is **written** and pictured in good works,
AP : 0 4 :356(161) [0217] (Luke 6:23) it is **written**, "Your reward is great in
AP : 0 4 :399(168) [0227] than to give an answer **written** in blood to our Confession
AP : 0 4 :399(168) [0227] answer written in blood to our Confession **written** in ink.
AP : 1 1 :003(180) [0249] our theologians have **written** many things which our
AP : 1 2 :048(188) [0265] nor read the sentence of the law **written** in their hearts.
AP : 1 2 :062(190) [0269] So it is **written** in I John 5:10, "He who does not believe
AP : 1 2 :096(196) [0281] faith just as faith obtains it from the **written** agreement."
AP : 1 2 :098(197) [0281] and thus far have **written** nothing about confession and
AP : 1 2 :169(209) [0305] is necessary, as it is **written** (Eph. 4:28), "Let the thief no
AP : 1 5 :014(217) [0319] In Ezek. 20:18, 19, it is **written**, "Do not walk in the
AP : 1 6 :004(223) [0331] Our theologians have **written** extensively on this subject

Continued ▶

AP : 24 :005(250) [0385] No one has ever **written** or suggested that men benefit
AP : 27 :002(269) [0419] as he had neither **written** nor taught anything that
AP : 27 :003(269) [0419] same number of years **written** down by him in the
AP : 27 :018(272) [0425] of this, they have **written**, "What has been charged
AP : 27 :038(275) [0433] It is **written** that when Anthony asked God to show him
AP : 28 :004(281) [0445] they set forth an edict **written** in blood, threatening men
S1 : 00 :000(287) [0453] **Written** by Dr. Martin Luther in the year 1537
S2 : 02 :013(295) [0465] Fathers who are said to have **written** about purgatory.
S3 : 07 :001(311) [0493] So it is **written**, "Who can discern his errors?" (Ps. 19:12).
S3 : 07 :002(312) [0493] As it is **written**, "Enter not into judgment with thy
S3 : 13 :003(315) [0499] and mercy, but, as it is **written**, "Let him who boasts,
S3 : 15 :001(316) [0501] (Matt. 15:9), and it is **written** in Titus 1:14, "They are men
TR : 00 :023(324) [0511] In John, too, it is **written**, "If you forgive the sins," etc.
TR : 00 :035(326) [0513] Indeed, it is even **written** in the Clementines, "When the
TR : 00 :038(326) [0515] And it is **written** in Acts, "We must obey God rather than
TR : 00 :082(000) [0529] also read the articles **written** at the Assembly at Smalcald
SC : PR :017(340) [0537] at length in the many books **written** for this purpose.
SC : 04 :013(349) [0553] Where is this **written**?
SC : 06 :003(351) [0555] Where is this **written**?
LC : 01 :138(384) [0621] On the other hand, it is **written** of the wicked in
LC : 01 :332(410) [0677] dealings, as if they were **written** everywhere he looks, and
EP : RN :001(464) [0777] and judged, as it is **written** in Ps. 119:105, "Thy word is a
EP : 01 :004(466) [0781] as his handiwork, as it is **written**, "Thy hands fashioned
EP : 01 :021(468) [0785] words, and deeds, as it is **written**, "Out of the heart come
EP : 02 :002(470) [0787] his own powers, as it is **written** in I Cor. 2:14, "The
EP : 02 :003(470) [0787] opposed to God, as it is **written**, "The imagination of
EP : 02 :003(470) [0787] to spiritual life, as it is **written**, "When we were dead
EP : 02 :004(470) [0787] of God's Word, as it is **written** that the Gospel is a
EP : 03 :003(473) [0793] and eternal life, as it is **written**, "For as by one man's
EP : 04 :014(477) [0799] against his elect, as it is **written**, "There is therefore now
EP : 04 :016(477) [0801] condemn spoken and **written** formulations which teach
EP : 06 :002(480) [0805] for the law of God was **written** into their hearts when they
EP : 07 :009(483) [0811] spoken publicly, as it is **written**, "the cup of blessing
EP : 07 :015(483) [0813] of the apostles, since it is **written**, "And they all drank of
EP : 07 :018(484) [0813] Of such it is **written**, "He who does not believe is
EP : 08 :014(488) [0821] with God, as it is **written** in I Cor. 2:8, They have
EP : 08 :037(491) [0825] all his works, though it is **written** that in him are hid "all
EP : 11 :003(494) [0833] they happen, as it is **written**, "There is a God in heaven
EP : 11 :007(495) [0833] and elected, as it is **written**, "He chose us in him before
EP : 11 :013(496) [0835] this book for us, as it is **written**, "Those he predestined,
EP : 11 :016(497) [0837] as St. Paul testifies, was **written** for our instruction that
SD : PR :001(503) [0851] such books as had been **written**, approved, and accepted
SD : 01 :036(514) [0869] in thy book were **written**, every one of them, the days
SD : 02 :015(523) [0887] and impotence were not **written** so that we might become
SD : 02 :015(523) [0887] Word of God, but were **written** in order that above all
SD : 02 :023(525) [0889] Augustine has **written** in a similar vein in his second book
SD : 02 :058(532) [0903] and be lost, as it is **written**, "How often would I have
SD : 03 :020(542) [0921] death into life, as it is **written**, "When we were dead
SD : 03 :057(549) [0935] reckons to faith, as it is **written**, "For as by one man's
SD : 05 :004(559) [0953] heavenly Father, as it is **written** in Mark 1:1, "The
SD : 05 :004(559) [0953] a few words, "Thus it is **written**, that the Christ should
SD : 06 :003(564) [0963] the Holy Spirit uses the **written** law on them to instruct
SD : 06 :003(564) [0963] but according to his **written** law and Word, which is a
SD : 06 :004(564) [0963] law of the Lord, as it is **written**, "Blessed is the man
SD : 06 :005(564) [0963] For the law of God is **written** on their hearts, just as the
SD : 06 :009(565) [0965] the Spirit of God, as it is **written**, "It is good for me that I
SD : 06 :012(566) [0967] also to rebuke, as it is **written**, "When the Holy Spirit
SD : 06 :020(567) [0969] and command, as it is **written**, "You shall not do every
SD : 08 :006(592) [1017] virgin Mary, as it is **written**, "Of their race, according to
SD : 08 :038(598) [1027] *the Holy Supper* has **written** about Zwingli's *alloeosis*, we
SD : 08 :080(607) [1045] of blessed memory, has **written** about the majesty of
SD : 10 :008(612) [1055] between the two, as it is **written**, "In vain do they worship
SD : 10 :011(612) [1055] It is **written**, "For freedom Christ has set us free; stand
SD : 10 :016(613) [1057] to avoid both, as it is **written**, "Woe to the world for
SD : 11 :004(617) [1063] present to God, as it is **written**, "Are not two sparrows
SD : 11 :004(617) [1063] in thy book were **written** every one of them, the days that
SD : 11 :007(617) [1065] devil and of men, as it is **written**, "Israel, thou hast
SD : 11 :008(617) [1065] it (Matt. 16:18), as it is **written**, "No one shall snatch my
SD : 11 :012(618) [1067] in the Word of God is **written** down for us, not for the
SD : 11 :025(620) [1071] elect "whose names are **written** in the book of life" will be
SD : 11 :062(626) [1083] on the right path, as it is **written**, "O Israel, it is your own
SD : 11 :065(627) [1083] laid" (Eph. 1:4), as it is **written**, "He has loved us in the
SD : 11 :075(628) [1087] return to him, as it is **written**, "If a man divorces his wife
SD : 11 :079(629) [1089] It is **written**, "God endured with much patience the
SD : 11 :081(629) [1089] It is **written** in Ezekiel, "As I live, says the Lord God, I
SD : 11 :087(631) [1093] and good works, as it is **written**, "He destined us in love
SD : 11 :088(631) [1093] As it is **written**, 'Jacob I loved, but Esau I hated'"
SD : 11 :092(632) [1093] that "Whatever was **written** in former days was written
SD : 11 :092(632) [1093] in former days was **written** for our instruction, that by

Writer (3), Writers (14)
AL : 00 :001(047) [0059] far as the ancient church is known to us from its **writers**.
AL : 25 :010(063) [0069] The ancient **writers** also testify that such an enumeration
AP : 04 :065(116) [0139] such a great crowd of **writers**, let them produce one
AP : 04 :100(121) [0151] Here the **writer** says first that men are righteous by the
AP : 04 :356(161) [0217] says, as do many later **writers**, "God crowns his gifts in
AP : 04 :380(165) [0223] From ancient **writers** they have taken certain sayings,
AP : 10 :002(179) [0247] to us to be a sensible **writer**, says distinctly that "the bread
AP : 12 :002(182) [0253] voice of the Gospel these **writers** of the Confutation
AP : 12 :112(198) [0285] The church **writers** do mention confession, but they are
AP : 12 :119(200) [0287] in the Scriptures or in the ancient **writers** of the church.
AP : 12 :172(209) [0305] The **writers** of the Confutation say it is intolerable to
AP : 16 :008(223) [0331] the judgment of many **writers** in these matters has been is
AP : 20 :002(227) [0339] with those damnable **writers** of the Confutation who so
AP : 22 :016(238) [0361] but we do blame the **writers** who defend the legitimacy of
AP : 27 :008(269) [0421] services, as some **writers** call them, and who do not
TR : 00 :071(332) [0525] he is a late and fictitious **writer**, whoever he may be, just
TR : 00 :071(332) [0525] Still more recent **writers** added the words, "I give thee the

Writings (74)
PR : PR :011(006) [0011] one another, in extensive **writings** based on God's Word,
PR : PR :019(009) [0017] edition and in their open **writings** and in public print have
PR : PR :019(009) [0017] any other profitable **writings** of Master Philip
AG : 20 :002(041) [0053] Their **writings** on the Ten Commandments, and other
AG : 20 :002(041) [0053] and other **writings** as well, show that they have given
AG : 00 :001(047) [0059] is reflected in the **writings** of the Fathers), we think that
AG : 22 :004(050) [0061] from history and from **writings** of the Fathers.
AG : 23 :010(052) [0061] history and from the **writings** of the Fathers that it was
AG : 26 :014(066) [0073] We can see in the **writings** of the summists and canonists
AG : 26 :030(068) [0075] and discipline, their **writings** reveal something quite
AL : 26 :030(068) [0075] may be perceived in the **writings** of our teachers, for they
AP : PR :017(099) [0103] opinions in the **writings** of the monks, canonists, and
AP : PR :018(099) [0103] which appears everywhere in our opponents' **writings**.
AP : 04 :245(142) [0189] faith in statements and **writings**, but they also try to wipe
AP : 07 :021(172) [0233] The **writings** of the holy Fathers show that even they
AP : 07 :025(173) [0235] extravagant and wicked **writings** about the power of the
AP : 07 :039(176) [0241] rites just as the apostles themselves did in their **writings**.
AP : 07 :040(176) [0241] we must consult their **writings**, not merely their example.
AP : 12 :003(182) [0253] They will see that the **writings** of our theologians have
AP : 12 :004(183) [0253] that before Luther's **writings** the doctrine of penitence
AP : 12 :073(192) [0273] of the prophets; the **writings** of the apostles attest that
AP : 16 :002(222) [0329] The **writings** of our theologians have profitably illumined
AP : 27 :001(268) [0419] We have seen his **writings**, and from them the nature of
AP : 28 :016(283) [0449] not contradict their own **writings**, in which they worked
S1 : PR :004(289) [0455] that they dare to cite my **writings** and teachings against
S1 : PR :006(289) [0457] doubted whether one ought to make good **writings** public.
S1 : PR :009(290) [0457] of Christ, who in their **writings** have urged such big lies
S3 : 08 :006(312) [0495] but must come through their own **writings** and words.
S3 : 08 :006(313) [0495] without and before their **writings** since they boast that the
TR : 00 :022(324) [0511] more, we refer to those **writings** and wish them to be
TR : 00 :071(332) [0525] he may be, just as the **writings** of Clement are spurious.
EP : RN :001(464) [0777] prophetic and apostolic **writings** of the Old and New
EP : RN :002(464) [0777] Other **writings** of ancient and modern teachers, whatever
EP : RN :007(465) [0779] Testaments and all other **writings** is maintained, and Holy
EP : RN :008(465) [0779] Other symbols and other **writings** are not judges like Holy
SD : PR :007(502) [0849] sermons and in their **writings**, though they knew that
SD : PR :010(503) [0849] Word and of approved **writings** in such a way that
SD : PR :001(503) [0851] not on mere private **writings**, but on such books as had
SD : PR :003(503) [0851] prophetic and apostolic **writings** of the Old and New
SD : PR :009(505) [0853] clearly set forth in his **writings** on the basis of God's
SD : PR :009(505) [0853] doctrinal and polemical **writings**, but in the necessary and
SD : PR :009(505) [0855] that no human being's **writings** dare be put on a par with
SD : PR :010(506) [0855] Word of God, all other **writings** are to be approved and
SD : PR :011(506) [0855] we have embodied the **writings** above listed — the
SD : PR :013(506) [0855] articles from these **writings**, for just as we base our
SD : PR :013(506) [0855] introduce and cite these **writings** as a witness to the truth
SD : PR :016(507) [0857] previously mentioned **writings** what he should accept as
SD : PR :016(507) [0857] prophetic and apostolic **writings** of God's Word, and
SD : PR :019(507) [0857] here and there in the **writings** of certain theologians, lest
SD : PR :020(507) [0857] position with the aforementioned doctrinal **writings**.
SD : 01 :004(509) [0861] use the aforementioned **writings** to set forth in short
SD : 01 :045(516) [0873] they are found in the **writings** of the modern
SD : 01 :055(518) [0877] Thus in many of his **writings** against the Manichaeans,
SD : 02 :028(527) [0893] Confession and the other **writings** before mentioned, as
SD : 02 :044(529) [0897] In these **writings** he also takes up several disputed points
SD : 02 :044(529) [0897] hereby appeal to these **writings** and refer others to them.
SD : 02 :045(530) [0899] of Luther, and other **writings** of this eminent and
SD : 03 :044(547) [0931] set forth in detail in the previously mentioned **writings**.
SD : 04 :026(555) [0945] 2. In his **writings** against the papists at many places;
SD : 04 :027(555) [0945] 3. In his **writings** against the Anabaptists, who advanced
SD : 05 :001(558) [0951] rightly divided and the **writings** of the holy prophets and
SD : 05 :022(562) [0959] in nearly all his **writings** and showed in detail that there is
SD : 07 :029(574) [0981] to me or misuse my **writings** to confirm their error, as the
SD : 07 :041(576) [0985] than from Dr. Luther's doctrinal and polemical **writings**.
SD : 07 :066(581) [0997] direct the Christian reader to our more extensive **writings**.
SD : 07 :091(585) [1005] Luther in his polemical **writings**, *Against the Heavenly*
SD : 07 :091(585) [1005] *concerning the Holy Supper*, and other **writings** of his.
SD : 07 :091(586) [1005] Christian reader to these **writings** and desire to have them
SD : 07 :110(589) [1011] Articles, and other **writings** of ours on the basis of the
SD : 08 :003(592) [1017] doctrinal and polemical **writings** concerning the Holy
SD : 08 :018(594) [1021] and have frequently quoted them in our **writings**.
SD : 08 :086(608) [1047] in Dr. Luther's **writings**, especially in the book *That*
SD : 08 :088(609) [1047] prophetic and apostolic **writings**, the orthodox Creeds,
SD : 08 :096(609) [1049] pure Word of God, the **writings** of the holy prophets and

Wrong (40), Wronged (1)
AG : 26 :019(067) [0073] which have arisen from a **wrong** estimation of tradition.
AG : 27 :055(079) [0083] for Christians, even in the government, to avenge **wrong**.
AP : 02 :001(100) [0105] and distort a statement that has nothing **wrong** in it.
AP : 02 :003(101) [0105] What is **wrong** with this?
AP : 04 :087(120) [0147] Then he would have been **wrong** in writing to the
AP : 23 :071(249) [0383] if the priests had done **wrong** in marrying, it is certainly
AP : 24 :016(252) [0389] unskilled cook he sever the member at the **wrong** place.
S3 : 03 :033(308) [0489] All have turned aside, together they have gone **wrong**."
SC : PR :013(339) [0535] between right and **wrong** according to the standards of
SC : 07 :005(353) [0559] to forgive all my sin and the **wrong** which I have done.
SC : 09 :005(355) [0561] to punish those who do **wrong** and to praise those who do
LC : 01 :003(365) [0581] if your trust is false and **wrong**, then you have not the
LC : 01 :019(367) [0585] their trust is false and **wrong**, for it is not founded upon
LC : 01 :028(368) [0587] it flee not to him but from him when things go **wrong**?
LC : 01 :051(371) [0595] whatsoever to support falsehood or **wrong** of any kind."
LC : 01 :059(372) [0597] whenever we commit a **wrong** we like to cover and gloss
LC : 01 :066(373) [0599] and separates right from **wrong**, good from evil.
LC : 01 :154(386) [0625] suffer ten times as much **wrong** from your own wife,
LC : 01 :187(390) [0633] and prayer commit to him whatever **wrong** we suffer.
LC : 01 :197(392) [0637] might not have to suffer **wrong** from anyone or do
LC : 01 :204(392) [0639] you could prevent a **wrong**) or wink at it as if it were no
LC : 01 :213(394) [0641] common people with lying words and **wrong** impressions.
LC : 01 :250(399) [0651] neighbor any injury or **wrong** in any way imaginable,
LC : 01 :304(406) [0667] does not consider this **wrong**, and it does not see that the
LC : 01 :307(406) [0669] may act as if you have **wronged** no one, you have
LC : 03 :045(426) [0709] name for any sort of **wrong** profanes and desecrates this
LC : 04 :055(443) [0747] and ordinance should be **wrong** and invalid because we
LC : 05 :079(455) [0771] enemies who harm, **wrong**, and injure you and give you
LC : 05 :079(455) [0771] you and give you occasion for sin and **wrong**-doing.
EP : RN :007(465) [0779] be understood and judged as good or evil, right or **wrong**.

Continued ▶

EP : 11 :004(494) [0833] anyone to do something **wrong**; the original source of this
EP : 11 :022(497) [0837] what is right and what is **wrong**, since we have not only
EP : 12 :030(500) [0843] we reject and condemn as **wrong**, false, heretical, and
SD : PR :016(507) [0857] what he should reject, flee, and avoid as false and **wrong**.
SD : 02 :010(522) [0885] together they have gone **wrong**; no one does good, not
SD : 03 :053(548) [0933] This is **wrong** because it is diametrically opposed to
SD : 04 :015(553) [0943] It is **wrong**, therefore, to criticize and reject the cited
SD : 05 :027(563) [0961] therefore dangerous and **wrong** to make of the Gospel,
SD : 10 :015(613) [1057] their omission were **wrong** and sinful, the door has been
SD : 11 :088(631) [1093] It is therefore false and **wrong** when men teach that the
SD : 12 :008(633) [1097] all these errors as **wrong**, heretical, and contrary to our

Wrongdoer (1), Wrongdoers (1), Wrongdoing (2), Wrongful (3)
AP : 04 :255(144) [0193] which condemns **wrongdoers** and commands that they do
SC : 09 :004(355) [0561] to execute his wrath on the **wrongdoer**" (Rom. 13:1-4).
LC : 01 :276(402) [0659] him, if he saw the **wrongdoing**, to go and reprove the man
EP : 01 :011(467) [0781] of someone else's **wrongdoing**, without any kind of
SD : 10 :026(615) [1061] reject and condemn as **wrongful** the view that the
SD : 10 :027(615) [1061] reject and condemn as **wrongful** they procedure whereby
SD : 10 :028(615) [1061] reject and condemn as **wrongful** the opinion of those who

Wrongly (8), Wrongs (2)
AG : 00 :001(094) [0095] many more abuses and **wrongs**, to avoid prolixity and
AL : 26 :018(067) [0073] or out of hatred for the bishops, as some **wrongly** suspect.
AL : 28 :003(081) [0085] These **wrongs** have long since been rebuked in the church
AP : 04 :324(157) [0209] Our opponents teach **wrongly** when they praise merits in
LC : 01 :327(409) [0675] or fear father or mother **wrongly**, doing or omitting to do
LC : 04 :053(443) [0745] invalid even if it is **wrongly** received or used, for it is
LC : 04 :055(443) [0747] should be wrong and invalid because we use it **wrongly**?
LC : 04 :059(444) [0747] Baptism has been **wrongly** received, it has existence and
SD : 02 :045(530) [0899] Therefore men teach **wrongly** when the pretend that
SD : 08 :045(600) [1031] it is evident that it is **wrongly** put to say or to write that

Wrought (6)
AL : 18 :003(039) [0051] but this righteousness is **wrought** in the heart when the
AP : 04 :379(165) [0223] by the reason or at least **wrought** by the impulse of the
AP : 07 :031(174) [0239] nothing; nor are they **wrought** by the Holy Spirit, as are
LC : 02 :054(417) [0693] and holiness has been **wrought** by the Holy Spirit through
SD : 01 :036(514) [0869] in secret, intricately **wrought** in the depths of the earth.
SD : 02 :016(523) [0887] has kindled and **wrought** a beginning of true knowledge

Wuerttemberg (3)
PR : PR :027(015) [0025] Louis, duke of **Wuerttemberg**
PR : PR :027(015) [0025] Frederick, count of **Wuerttemberg** and Montbeliard
TR : 00 :082(335) [0529] of Pforzheim, preacher of Ulric, duke of **Wuerttemberg**

Wycliffe (1)
AP : 16 :011(224) [0333] **Wycliffe** was obviously out of his mind in claiming that

Wycliffites (1)
AP : 07 :029(173) [0237] the Donatists and the **Wycliffites**, who believed that men

Yard (1)
LC : 01 :308(406) [0669] an inch, it will take a **yard**, and at length open injustice

Ye (1)
SD : 11 :051(625) [1079] ears to hear, let him hear"; and "Take heed how **ye** hear."

Year (49), Yearly (2), Years (30)
PR : PR :002(003) [0007] Diet of Augsburg in the **year** 1530, presented in the
PR : PR :007(004) [0009] of the electors in the **year** 1558) that we should assemble
PR : PR :008(005) [0009] at Augsburg in the **year** 1530, and again unanimously
PR : PR :008(005) [0011] at Augsburg in the **year** 1530, in the confidence and hope
PR : PR :013(007) [0013] at Torgau in the **year** 1576 for the promotion of concord
PR : PR :017(008) [0015] the Augsburg Confession as submitted in the **year** 1530.
PR : PR :018(008) [0015] in Augsburg in the **year** 1530, which has been available in
PR : PR :018(009) [0015] at Augsburg in the **year** 1530 by the electors, princes, and
PR : PR :018(009) [0017] make a new confession almost every **year** or every month.
PR : PR :023(012) [0021] at Augsburg in the **year** 1530 to Emperor Charles V, of
PR : PR :025(013) [0023] submitted in the **year** 1530 to Emperor Charles V, of
AG : PR :017(026) [0041] at the last diet in Spires a **year** ago, the electors, princes,
AG : 00 :000(049) [0059] having crept in over the **years** and others of them having
AG : 23 :012(052) [0063] It was only four hundred **years** ago that the priests in
AG : 27 :031(075) [0079] annul vows that are made under the age of fifteen **years**.
AG : 27 :032(076) [0079] canon concedes still more **years** to human frailty, for it
AG : 27 :032(076) [0079] the taking of monastic vows before the eighteenth **year**.
AL : 23 :012(052) [0063] not until four hundred **years** ago were priests in Germany
AL : 27 :005(071) [0077] they were not wanting in **years**, they were unable to judge
AL : 27 :032(076) [0079] weakness, adds a few **years** and forbids making a vow
AL : 27 :032(076) [0079] and forbids making a vow before the eighteenth **year**.
AP : 11 :003(180) [0249] absolution and the Lord's Supper, many times a **year**.
AP : 15 :042(221) [0325] are preached during the whole **year**, except in Lent.
AP : 20 :014(228) [0343] condemned a thousand **years** ago, in the days of
AP : 21 :002(229) [0343] Jerome conquered Vigilantius eleven hundred **years** ago."
AP : 23 :008(240) [0367] only at the beginning, but **yearly** the fields are clothed as
AP : 24 :015(251) [0389] For the last ten **years** our opponents have been publishing
AP : 27 :001(268) [0419] Thirty **years** ago, in the Thuringian town of Eisenach,
AP : 27 :003(269) [0419] one will come," he said, "in the **year** of our Lord 1516.
AP : 27 :003(269) [0419] and this same number of **years** written down by him in
AP : 27 :066(280) [0441] as a widow who is under sixty **years** of age" (I Tim. 5:9).
S1 : 00 :000(287) [0453] Written by Dr. Martin Luther in the **year** 1537
S1 : PR :001(288) [0455] a council to meet in Mantua last **year**, in Whitsuntide.
S2 : 02 :012(294) [0465] the weekly, monthly, and **yearly** celebrations of requiems,
S2 : 04 :004(299) [0473] more that five hundred **years** at the least and that the
S3 : 03 :015(305) [0483] the course of a whole **year**), the following loophole was
S3 : 03 :022(306) [0485] the ancient canons, seven **years** of penance were required
S3 : 03 :023(307) [0485] in this way for a hundred **years**, one would still not have
S3 : 03 :024(307) [0485] canceled, first for seven **years** in a single case, then for a
S3 : 03 :024(307) [0485] grant them for a hundred **years**, another for a hundred
S3 : 03 :025(307) [0485] pope invented the jubilee **year** and attached it to Rome.
S3 : 03 :025(307) [0485] went further and quickly multiplied the jubilee **years**.
S3 : 03 :026(307) [0487] indulgences for the dead through bulls and jubilee **years**.
S3 : 03 :027(307) [0487] the indulgence or jubilee **year** must be contrite, make
S3 : 08 :007(313) [0495] not receive the Spirit and Baptism until ten **years** later.
S3 : 12 :002(315) [0499] for, thank God, a seven-**year**-old child knows what the
TR : 00 :000(319) [0503] the Theologians Assembled in Smalcald in the **Year** 1537
SC : PR :007(339) [0533] form, adhere to it, and use it repeatedly **year** after year.
SC : PR :007(339) [0533] form, adhere to it, and use it repeatedly year after **year**.
SC : PR :008(339) [0535] or recite the catechism differently from **year** to year.
SC : PR :008(339) [0535] or recite the catechism differently from year to **year**.
SC : PR :022(341) [0537] least three or four times a **year** despises the sacrament and
LC : 01 :096(378) [0609] of the Word at the end of the **year** as at the beginning.
LC : 01 :164(387) [0627] clothing, and money for a **year** or two, but long life,
LC : 01 :182(389) [0631] We hear it explained every **year** in the Gospel, Matthew
LC : 01 :225(395) [0645] his employer out of thirty or forty gulden or more a **year**.
LC : 02 :032(415) [0687] sermons throughout the **year**, especially at the times
LC : 04 :070(445) [0749] If a **year** ago a man was proud and greedy, this year he is
LC : 04 :070(445) [0749] man was proud and greedy, this **year** he is much more so.
LC : 05 :040(451) [0763] and authority, let a **year**, or two, three, or more years go
LC : 05 :040(451) [0763] or two, three, or more **years** go by without receiving the
LC : 05 :047(452) [0763] obliged to eat only once a **year**, precisely on the evening
LC : 05 :047(452) [0765] on this one evening of the **year**, but frequently, whenever
LC : 05 :056(453) [0767] passes into another and one half **year** into yet another.
LC : 05 :085(456) [0773] grown and advanced in **years**, but also for the young
EP : RN :004(465) [0777] the great Diet in the **year** 1530, together with the Apology
EP : RN :004(465) [0777] drafted at Smalcald in the **year** 1537, which the leading
EP : 09 :003(492) [0827] preached at Torgau in the **year** 1533, where he explains
SD : PR :005(504) [0851] set down in writing in the **year** 1530 and submitted to
SD : PR :019(507) [0857] within the past twenty-five **years** a number of divisions
SD : 02 :002(520) [0881] of the Augsburg Confession for quite a few **years**.
SD : 02 :073(535) [0909] a considerable number of **years** have been agitated in the
SD : 07 :001(568) [0971] however, in later **years** a number of theologians and
SD : 07 :017(572) [0977] In the following **year** the leading theologians who were
SD : 07 :018(572) [0979] adopted in the previous **year**, to their own advantage,
SD : 08 :025(596) [1023] again when he was twelve **years** old, among the teachers,
SD : 08 :085(608) [1047] Jesus the son of Mary is 1543 **years** old this year.
SD : 08 :085(608) [1047] Jesus the son of Mary is 1543 years old this **year**.
SD : 09 :001(610) [1051] the castle at Torgau in the **year** 1533, "I believe in the
SD : 10 :019(614) [1059] for, thank God, a seven-**year**-old child knows what the
SD : 11 :094(632) [1095] Confession for many **years** and in which some have erred

Yearn (1)
LC : 06 :033(461) [0000] for a fresh spring, so I **yearn** and tremble for God's

Yes (37)
AP : 04 :030(111) [0129] I not myself exclaim, too—**yes**, I will exclaim and chide
AP : 04 :133(125) [0159] For this is what he says: "**Yes**, to this day whenever Moses
AP : 04 :178(131) [0171] above our purity—**yes**, far above the law itself—should
AP : 11 :002(180) [0249] is the command of God — **yes**, the very voice of the
AP : 12 :108(198) [0283] **Yes**, we cannot set our merits against Thy judgment, but
AP : 21 :034(234) [0353] so that it seemed to nod **Yes** or No to the petitioners.
AP : 24 :025(253) [0391] afflictions of the saints, **yes**, all the good works of the
AP : 27 :048(277) [0437] **Yes**, he does, but they do violence to the text when they
AP : 27 :059(279) [0439] **Yes**, indeed, the example of the Rechabites is a beautiful
S3 : 03 :017(305) [0483] If he said **Yes** (for who but the devil himself would want
SC : 03 :021(348) [0549] "Amen, amen" means "**Yes**, yes, it shall be so."
SC : 03 :021(348) [0549] "Amen, amen" means "Yes, **yes**, it shall be so."
SC : 05 :027(351) [0555] Answer: "**Yes**, I do."
LC : PR :007(359) [0569] a doctor and a preacher — **yes**, and as learned and
LC : PR :008(359) [0569] office and the people's souls, **yes**, even God and his Word.
LC : 01 :230(396) [0645] **Yes**, we might well keep quiet here about various petty
LC : 01 :242(397) [0649] **Yes**, where you have cheated and defrauded anyone out
LC : 03 :032(424) [0707] God replies from on high, "**Yes**, dear child, it shall indeed
LC : 03 :037(425) [0707] Answer: **Yes**, in itself it is holy, but not our use of it.
LC : 03 :084(431) [0721] account of false coinage, **yes**, on account of daily
LC : 03 :121(436) [0731] not whole-heartedly add "**yes**" and conclude with
LC : 04 :020(439) [0737] chain about his neck, **yes**, the crown on his head, which
LC : 04 :030(440) [0739] **Yes**, it must be external so that it can be perceived and
LC : 04 :035(441) [0741] To this you may answer: **Yes**, it is true that our works are
LC : 04 :066(445) [0749] greedy, lazy, proud, **yes**, and unbelieving; he is beset with
LC : 05 :016(448) [0757] As no saint on earth, **yes**, no angel in heaven can
LC : 05 :035(450) [0761] placed at everyone's door, **yes**, upon everyone's table, but
LC : 05 :076(455) [0771] **Yes**, and St. Paul concludes in Rom. 7:18, "For I know
LC : 06 :021(459) [0000] **Yes**, and if anybody goes about relying on the purity of
EP : 06 :001(480) [0805] One party said **Yes**, the other says No.
EP : 07 :002(482) [0809] The Sacramentarians say No; we say **Yes**.
EP : 10 :002(493) [0829] One party said **Yes** to this, the other party said No.
SD : 02 :020(525) [0889] of salt, like Lot's wife, **yes**, like a log or a stone, like a
SD : 04 :015(553) [0943] no good fruits appear, **yes**, even though he were to persist
SD : 07 :003(569) [0973] which is there in heaven, **yes**, of Christ himself and all his
SD : 10 :010(612) [1055] entire community of God, **yes**, every individual Christian,
SD : 11 :090(631) [1093] and Eve did in paradise — **yes**, would be losing it every

Yield (23), Yielded (3), Yielding (5), Yields (2)
AP : 02 :042(106) [0117] than good people; **yielding** to anger, desire, ambition,
AP : 04 :241(141) [0187] on civil war if either had **yielded** the least bit to the other.
AP : 04 :242(141) [0187] covers them up, forgives, **yields**, and does not go to the
AP : 04 :280(149) [0201] own context, they often **yield** their own interpretation.
AP : 04 :300(153) [0205] men beware, therefore, of **yielding** to their ungodly
AP : 12 :122(200) [0289] penitence" (Matt. 3:8); "**Yield** your members to
AP : 12 :132(202) [0291] he says (Rom. 6:19), "**Yield** your members to
AP : 12 :134(203) [0293] that befits penitence," **Yield** your members to
AP : 20 :009(227) [0341] "Do not **yield** to the wicked, but go on still more boldly,"
AP : 23 :008(240) [0367] "Let the earth put forth vegetation, plants **yielding** seed."
S1 : 00 :000(287) [0453] to indicate what we could or could not accept or **yield**.
S1 : PR :001(288) [0455] were willing and able to **yield** to the papists and, on the
S2 : 02 :010(294) [0465] it would not be possible for them to **yield** on this article.
S3 : 03 :025(307) [0485] When this began to **yield** money and the bull market
LC : 03 :067(429) [0717] our poor flesh may not **yield** or fall away through
LC : 03 :076(431) [0721] of the field to grow and **yield** richly; to help us manage
LC : 03 :100(433) [0727] not allow us to fall and **yield** to trials and temptations.
LC : 03 :107(434) [0729] quite a different thing from consenting and **yielding** to it.
LC : 05 :026(449) [0759] renounce our faith or **yield** hand and foot and become
EP : 10 :002(493) [0829] an inviolate conscience **yield** to their pressure and
EP : 10 :006(493) [0829] of us, we dare not **yield** to the enemies in such indifferent
EP : 10 :006(493) [0829] "To them we did not **yield** submission even for a

Continued ▶

SD : 0 2 :019(524) [0889] which resists rather than **yields** in any way to human
SD : 1 0 :009(612) [1055] conscience give in and **yield** to the weak in faith in such
SD : 1 0 :010(612) [1055] such a case we should not **yield** to adversaries even in
SD : 1 0 :011(612) [1057] to whom we did not **yield** submission even for a moment,
SD : 1 0 :012(613) [1057] said that he would not **yield**, not even for a moment, so
SD : 1 0 :013(613) [1057] Thus Paul **yielded** and gave in to the weak as far as
SD : 1 0 :013(613) [1057] But he would not **yield** to false apostles who wanted to
SD : 1 0 :013(613) [1057] in a similar situation **yielded** to a certain extent, Paul
SD : 1 0 :016(613) [1057] Hence **yielding** or conforming in external things, where
SD : 1 0 :028(615) [1061] of persecution we may **yield** to enemies of the holy
SD : 1 1 :095(632) [1095] no authority to do so) to **yield** anything of the eternal and

Yoke (12)
PR : PR :004(004) [0009] in submitting to the papal **yoke** as well as in embracing
AG : 2 6 :027(068) [0073] trial of God by putting a **yoke** upon the neck of the
AG : 2 8 :042(088) [0089] St. Peter forbids putting a **yoke** on the neck of the
AG : 2 8 :052(089) [0091] therefore, and do not submit again to a **yoke** of slavery."
AL : 2 6 :027(068) [0073] trial of God by putting a **yoke** upon the neck of the
AL : 2 8 :042(088) [0089] Peter forbids putting a **yoke** on the disciples and Paul
AL : 2 8 :052(089) [0091] Galatians, "Do not submit again to a **yoke** of slavery."
AP : 1 5 :031(219) [0323] a trial of God by putting a **yoke**," etc., Peter charges that
AP : 2 8 :008(282) [0445] forbid the imposing of a **yoke**, showing how dangerous
AP : 2 8 :015(283) [0447] you free, and do not submit again to a **yoke** of slavery."
EP : 1 0 :006(493) [0829] and do not submit again to a **yoke** of slavery" (Gal. 5:1).
SD : 1 0 :011(612) [1055] and do not submit again to a **yoke** of slavery" (Gal. 5:1).

Yonder (3)
S 2 : 0 2 :001(293) [0463] both here in this life and **yonder** in purgatory, although in
SD : 0 1 :014(511) [0863] in this life, not to be completed until the life **yonder**.
SD : 0 8 :065(604) [1039] and on earth, and in **yonder** life we shall behold his glory

Young (38), Younger (6)
PR : PR :023(012) [0021] particularly that the **young** men who are being trained for
PR : PR :027(014) [0025] Henry the **Younger**, duke of Brunswick [-Wolfenbuettel]
PR : PR :027(014) [0025] William the **Younger**, duke of Brunswick and Lueneburg
PR : PR :027(015) [0025] Peter Ernest the **Younger**, count of Mansfeld [-Eisleben]
AG : 2 3 :026(056) [0065] into their estates ignorantly when they were **young**.
AG : 2 7 :005(071) [0077] they were not too **young**, they had not sufficiently
AP : 2 7 :050(277) [0437] been perfection for this **young** man to believe and obey
AP : 2 7 :067(280) [0441] (he commands the **younger** ones to marry, v. 14), but
S 3 : 0 8 :001(312) [0493] for the sake of untrained **young** people who need to be
SC : PR :006(338) [0533] catechism to the people, especially those who are **young**.
SC : PR :007(339) [0533] **Young** and inexperienced people must be instructed on
SC : PR :008(339) [0535] teach these things to the **young** and unlearned in such a
SC : PR :009(339) [0535] when you are teaching the **young**, adhere to a fixed and
SC : PR :010(339) [0535] word for word so that the **young** may repeat these things
SC : 0 8 :010(354) [0559] the beasts their food, and to the **young** ravens which cry.
SC : 0 9 :012(356) [0563] **Young** Persons in General
SC : 0 9 :012(356) [0563] "You that are **younger**, be subject to the elders.
LC : SP :003(362) [0575] For this reason **young** people should be thoroughly
LC : SP :006(362) [0575] as well as in name, both **young** and old, may be
LC : SP :024(364) [0579] teach and require **young** people to recite word for word.
LC : SP :026(364) [0579] The **young** people should also attend preaching, especially
LC : 0 1 :023(367) [0587] is a little too subtle to be understood by **young** pupils.
LC : 0 1 :029(368) [0589] and impressed upon **young** people so that they may take
LC : 0 1 :061(372) [0597] all things, therefore, our **young** people should be strictly
LC : 0 1 :077(375) [0603] plainly for the sake of the **young**, so that it may sink into
LC : 0 1 :086(376) [0605] Word for the sake of the **young** and the poor common
LC : 0 1 :089(377) [0605] hours a week for the **young**, and at least a day for the
LC : 0 1 :108(379) [0611] **Young** people must therefore be taught to revere their
LC : 0 1 :115(381) [0613] let us at last teach our **young** people to banish all other
LC : 0 1 :123(382) [0617] But **young** and old are altogether wayward and unruly;
LC : 0 1 :140(384) [0621] impressed upon the **young** people, for no one will believe
LC : 0 1 :171(388) [0629] necessary it is to devote serious attention to the **young**.
LC : 0 1 :217(394) [0641] things in order that our **young** people may be led to
LC : 0 1 :248(398) [0651] to be impressed upon the **young** people so that they may
LC : 0 1 :321(408) [0673] should keep it before the **young** and insist that they learn
LC : 0 1 :330(410) [0677] admonish, and remind **young** people of all this so that
LC : 0 2 :011(412) [0681] If you were to ask a **young** child, "My boy, what kind of
LC : 0 2 :012(412) [0681] But for **young** pupils it is enough to indicate the most
LC : 0 3 :007(421) [0699] serve as an exercise for **young** children, pupils, and simple
LC : 0 4 :070(445) [0749] A **young** child, who has no particular vice, becomes
LC : 0 5 :085(456) [0773] in years, but also for the **young** people who ought to be
LC : 0 5 :085(456) [0773] Lord's Prayer into the **young** so that they will receive them
SD : 0 2 :090(538) [0915] The **young** students at our universities have been greatly
SD : 1 1 :088(631) [1093] of his call, she was told, 'The elder will serve the **younger**.'

Youth (12), Youths (2)
AG : 2 3 :026(055) [0065] have made vows in their **youth** — and most of the priests
AP : 1 5 :041(220) [0325] instruct and examine the **youth** publicly, a custom that
LC : SP :025(364) [0579] Thus our **youth** will be led into the Scriptures so they
LC : SP :027(364) [0581] is to impress it upon our **youth**, not in a lofty and learned
LC : 0 1 :075(375) [0601] we may bring up our **youth** in the fear and honor of God
LC : 0 1 :201(392) [0637] **Youths** were married at the earliest age possible.
LC : 0 1 :218(394) [0643] the duty of so supervising **youth** that they will be brought
LC : 0 3 :028(424) [0705] form the habit from his **youth** up to pray daily for all his
LC : 0 3 :107(434) [0729] **Youths**, for example, are tempted chiefly by the flesh;
LC : 0 4 :070(445) [0749] Vice thus grows and increases in him from his **youth** up.
LC : 0 5 :085(456) [0773] practice them from their **youth**, and become accustomed
EP : 0 1 :021(469) [0785] "The imagination of man's heart is evil from his **youth**."
EP : 0 2 :003(470) [0787] "The imagination of man's heart is evil from his **youth**."
SD : 0 2 :017(524) [0887] of man's heart is evil from his **youth**" (Gen. 8:21).

Zeal (7), Zealous (3), Zealously (4)
PR : PR :012(007) [0013] Christian earnestness and **zeal** in view of the office that
PR : PR :013(007) [0013] earnestness and Christian **zeal**, consider it in all its
AP : 0 4 :208(135) [0177] the people began **zealously** to copy this action in order
AP : 0 4 :224(138) [0181] As usual, their **zeal** was very fervent in the beginning."
AP : 1 2 :122(200) [0289] a people of his own who are **zealous** for good deeds."
AP : 2 0 :012(228) [0341] quote (II Pet. 1:10), "Be **zealous** to confirm your call."
AP : 2 2 :013(238) [0361] as to why they defend this distinction so **zealously**.
AP : 2 4 :099(268) [0419] that we most **zealously** preserve the dignity of the Mass,
SD : 0 1 :062(519) [0879] seriousness and great **zeal** and impressed on everyone how
SD : 0 2 :009(522) [0883] the contrary, the more **zealously** and diligently they want
SD : 0 2 :080(536) [0911] with all seriousness and **zeal**, and in no wise tolerate in
SD : 0 3 :007(540) [0917] these terms with such **zeal** in order to indicate how very
SD : 0 4 :033(556) [0947] Pet. 1:10, "Be the more **zealous** to confirm your call and
SD : 0 7 :040(576) [0985] Luther defended with great **zeal** and earnestness the

Zeno (1)
AP : 0 4 :015(109) [0123] the teachings of Socrates, **Zeno**, and others, as though

Zephaniah (1)
AP : 2 2 :004(236) [0359] In his commentary on **Zephaniah**, Jerome says, "The

Zwingli (6), Zwinglian (1), Zwinglians (1)
EP : 0 7 :001(481) [0807] The **Zwinglian** teachers cannot be numbered among the
SD : 0 8 :002(591) [1015] words of institution, the **Zwinglians** countered by saying
SD : 0 8 :021(595) [1023] blasphemous *alloeosis* of **Zwingli**, who taught that one
SD : 0 8 :038(598) [1027] *Supper* has written about **Zwingli's** *alloeosis*, we shall here
SD : 0 8 :039(598) [1027] "**Zwingli** calls that an *alloeosis* when something is said
SD : 0 8 :039(598) [1029] Here **Zwingli** performs a sleight-of-hand trick and
SD : 0 8 :043(599) [1029] If **Zwingli's** *alloeosis* stands, then Christ will have to be
SD : 0 8 :043(599) [1029] a human person, since **Zwingli** applies all the texts

**Words Not Indexed with
Word Frequency in Parentheses**

a (2916)
about (509)
above (183)
according (361)
aforementioned (19)
aforesaid (1)
after (186)
afterward (19)
afterwards (16)
again (191)
against (340)
all (1397)
almost (23)
along (18)
alongside (2)
already (43)
also (641)
although (145)
am (80)
amid (19)
among (231)
an (443)
and (11775)
another (151)
any (300)
anybody (30)
anyhow (1)
anyone (94)
anything (108)
anyway (2)
anywhere (3)
are (2423)
as (2464)
at (462)
be (2199)
became (27)
because (663)
become (139)
becomes (31)
becoming (8)
been (483)
before (379)
beforehand (5)
being (133)
below (5)
beneath (5)
besides (57)
better (72)
between (110)
beyond (26)
both (210)
but (1896)
by (1834)
can (630)
cannot (332)
come (173)
could (199)
did (215)
do (970)
does (598)
doing (39)
done (124)
either (99)
else (93)
elsewhere (26)
et (4)
etc (147)
even (494)

ever (57)
every (193)
everybody (19)
everyday (4)
everyone (82)
everything (144)
everywhere (52)
ex (68)
for (2634)
from (1232)
had (265)
has (917)
hast (13)
hath (1)
have (1686)
having (33)
he (1861)
her (40)
here (292)
him (636)
himself (249)
his (1557)
however (151)
if (877)
in (5758)
inasmuch (38)
into (332)
is (4990)
it (3213)
its (260)
itself (128)
later (60)
let (225)
lets (10)
like (240)
likewise (111)
many (345)
matt (120)
matter (105)
matters (96)
may (476)
me (256)
more (349)
moreover (49)
most (175)
much (154)
must (547)
my (269)
namely (109)
never (114)
nevertheless (78)
no (775)
none (38)
nonetheless (2)
nor (339)
not (3115)
now (242)
o (28)
of (9774)
often (87)
on (1068)
once (61)
one (775)
only (726)
or (1842)
other (590)
others (197)
otherwise (55)
ought (138)
our (1982)
ours (23)

ourselves (92)
out (210)
over (131)
own (404)
said (227)
same (252)
say (343)
saying (55)
says (461)
shall (324)
she (29)
should (754)
shouldn (1)
shouldst (2)
since (378)
so (940)
some (239)
someone (39)
something (95)
still (156)
substances (1)
such (697)
sure (73)
surely (34)
than (322)
that (5495)
the (17594)
their (911)
theirs (9)
them (934)
themselves (170)
then (273)
there (538)
thereafter (8)
thereby (58)
therefore (567)
therefrom (2)
therein (15)
thereof (5)
thereto (8)
thereunder (1)
thereupon (5)
therewith (6)
these (816)
they (2293)
thing (106)
things (304)
this (2803)
those (489)
through (631)
throughout (36)
thus (277)
to (7515)
too (134)
toward (78)
under (164)
until (84)
unto (8)
up (195)
upon (209)
us (1223)
was (603)
we (3218)
well (194)
were (536)
what (670)
whatever (89)
whatsoever (6)
when (778)
whence (8)
whenever (26)

where (162)
whereas (7)
whereby (30)
wherefore (11)
wherefrom (1)
whereof (1)
wherever (28)
whether (125)
which (1488)
while (73)
who (1255)
whoever (43)
whom (117)
whomever (2)
whose (46)
with (1440)
would (473)
yet (150)
you (956)
your (311)
yours (6)
yourself (29)
yourselves (11)

**BIBLICAL REFERENCES TO
THE BOOK OF CONCORD
(Including those found in footnotes
to the Tappert edition.)**

Genesis
1:11 – A P : 2 3 : 008(240) [0367]
1:27 – A G : 2 3 : 005(052) [0061]
    – A P : 0 2 : 018(102) [0109]
1:28 – A L : 2 3 : 005(052) [0061]
    – A P : 2 3 : 007(240) [0365]
    – S D : 0 7 : 076(583) [0999]
2:3 – L C : 0 1 : 080(375) [0603]
2:16 – E P : 0 6 : 002(480) [0805]
2:18 – A G : 2 7 : 020(074) [0079]
    – A L : 2 7 : 020(074) [0079]
2:24 – L C : 0 1 : 200(392) [0637]
3 – S D : 0 1 : 061(519) [0879]
  – S D : 0 1 : 062(519) [0879]
3:3 – E P : 0 6 : 002(480) [0805]
3:6ff – S 3 : 0 1 : 003(302) [0477]
3:15 – A P : 0 2 : 046(106) [0119]
    – S D : 0 5 : 023(562) [0959]
4:10 – A P : 2 3 : 070(249) [0383]
6:5 – E P : 0 1 : 021(469) [0785]
   – S D : 0 1 : 025(512) [0867]
8:21 – E P : 0 1 : 021(469) [0785]
    – E P : 0 2 : 003(470) [0787]
    – S D : 0 1 : 025(512) [0867]
    – S D : 0 2 : 017(524) [0887]
15:6 – S D : 0 3 : 033(545) [0927]
17:4-8 – E P : 1 2 : 008(498) [0839]
      – S D : 1 2 : 013(634) [1099]
17:19-21 – E P : 1 2 : 008(498) [0839]
        – S D : 1 2 : 013(634) [1099]
22 – A P : 0 4 : 209(135) [0177]
  – S D : 0 4 : 028(555) [0947]
22:18 – S D : 0 5 : 023(562) [0959]
25:23 – S D : 1 1 : 088(631) [1093]
26 – S D : 0 2 : 044(529) [0897]
28:14 – S D : 0 5 : 023(562) [0959]

Exodus
3:2 – S 3 : 0 8 : 011(313) [0497]
3:4 – S 3 : 0 8 : 011(313) [0497]
9:16 – S D : 1 1 : 084(630) [1091]
20:2-17 – S C : 0 1 : 001(342) [0539]
      – L C : S P : 010(363) [0577]
20:5 – L C : 0 1 : 030(369) [0589]
20:6 – A P : 0 4 : 270(147) [0197]
20:7 – A L : 2 4 : 019(058) [0067]
20:12 – A P : 0 4 : 367(163) [0221]
     – A P : 2 7 : 061(280) [0441]
20:15 – A P : 2 7 : 046(277) [0435]
20:17 – A P : 2 7 : 025(273) [0427]
32:6 – A P : 2 4 : 020(252) [0389]
33:20 – S 3 : 0 1 : 003(302) [0477]
34:30-35 – A P : 0 4 : 021(110) [0127]

Leviticus
1-7 – A P : 2 4 : 021(253) [0391]
19:18 – A P : 0 4 : 289(151) [0203]
20:2ff – A P : 0 4 : 209(136) [0177]
23:5 – L C : 0 5 : 047(452) [0765]

Numbers
6:2 – A P : 2 7 : 058(279) [0439]
14:18 – A P : 0 4 : 329(158) [0211]
28:4ff – A P : 2 4 : 036(257) [0397]

Deuteronomy
4:24 – A P : 0 4 : 329(158) [0211]
5:6-21 – S C : 0 1 : 001(342) [0539]
     – L C : S P : 010(363) [0577]
6:5 0 4 : 131(125) [0159]
   – A P : 0 4 : 289(151) [0203]
   – A P : 1 2 : 142(204) [0295]
   – A P : 2 7 : 025(273) [0427]
6:7, 8 – L C : P R : 014(360) [0571]
6:8f – L C : 0 1 : 331(410) [0677]
11:20 – L C : 0 1 : 331(410) [0677]
12:8 – S D : 0 6 : 020(567) [0969]
12:28 – S D : 0 6 : 020(567) [0969]
12:32 – S D : 0 6 : 020(567) [0969]
16:10 – A P : 2 4 : 085(265) [0413]
21:18-20 – L C : 0 1 : 181(389) [0631]
23:21, 22 – A P : 2 7 : 058(279) [0439]
24:1 – L C : 0 1 : 295(404) [0665]
29:4 – S D : 0 2 : 026(526) [0891]

30:6 – S D : 0 2 : 026(526) [0891]
32:6 – E P : 0 1 : 004(466) [0781]
    – S D : 0 1 : 034(514) [0869]
    – S D : 0 1 : 034(514) [0869]

**Joshua
Judges
Ruth
1 Samuel**
2:6 – A P : 1 2 : 050(189) [0265]
   – S D : 0 6 : 012(566) [0967]
2:36 – A P : 2 2 : 010(237) [0359]
9:12, 13 – A P : 0 4 : 208(135) [0177]
10 – L C : 0 1 : 045(370) [0593]
15 – L C : 0 1 : 045(370) [0593]
16 – L C : 0 1 : 045(370) [0593]
16:14 – L C : 0 2 : 036(415) [0687]
16:23 – L C : 0 2 : 036(415) [0687]
18-31 – L C : 0 1 : 045(370) [0593]
28:20 – S 3 : 0 3 : 007(304) [0481]
31:4 – S 3 : 0 3 : 007(304) [0481]

2 Samuel
1-2 – L C : 0 1 : 046(370) [0593]
4 – L C : 0 1 : 045(370) [0593]
6:17 – A P : 2 4 : 020(252) [0389]
11 – S 3 : 0 3 : 043(310) [0491]
12:13 – A P : 1 2 : 048(188) [0265]
     – A P : 1 2 : 056(189) [0267]
12:14 – A P : 1 2 : 056(189) [0267]
22:5 – A P : 1 2 : 149(206) [0299]

1 Kings
12:28ff – A P : 1 5 : 015(217) [0319]
18:17-46 – A P : 2 4 : 099(268) [0419]
18:20ff – A P : 0 4 : 208(135) [0177]

2 Kings
23:10 – A P : 0 4 : 209(136) [0177]

**1 Chronicles
2 Chronicles
Ezra
Nehemiah
Esther
Job**
9:28 – A P : 0 4 : 327(158) [0211]
9:30-31 – A P : 0 4 : 327(158) [0211]
10:8 – E P : 0 1 : 004(466) [0781]
10:8-12 – S D : 0 1 : 035(514) [0869]
19:26, 27 – E P : 0 1 : 010(467) [0781]

Psalms
1:1, 2 – S D : 0 6 : 004(564) [0963]
1:2 – L C : P R : 010(360) [0569]
2:10 – T R : 0 0 : 054(329) [0519]
4:5 – A P : 2 4 : 029(255) [0393]
5:4 – S D : 1 1 : 007(617) [1065]
5:10, 11 – S D : 1 1 : 035(622) [1075]
6:1 – A P : 1 2 : 150(206) [0299]
6:2, 3 – A P : 1 2 : 031(186) [0259]
7:8 – A P : 0 4 : 326(158) [0211]
8:6 – S D : 0 8 : 027(596) [1025]
12:3, 4 – S D : 1 1 : 035(622) [1075]
19:12 – A G : 1 1 : 002(034) [0047]
     – A L : 1 1 : 002(034) [0047]
     – A G : 2 5 : 008(062) [0069]
     – A P : 1 1 : 008(181) [0251]
     – S 3 : 0 7 : 001(311) [0493]
25 – S D : 0 2 : 081(537) [0911]
31:22 – S D : 1 1 : 074(628) [1087]
31:23 – S D : 1 1 : 074(628) [1087]
32:1 – A P : 0 4 : 076(117) [0143]
    – A P : 0 4 : 103(122) [0151]
    – A P : 0 4 : 163(129) [0169]
32:2 – A P : 0 4 : 168(130) [0169]
32:5 – A P : 1 2 : 107(197) [0283]
32:6 – A P : 0 4 : 168(130) [0169]
37:1 – A P : 0 4 : 198(134) [0175]
37:5 – A G : 2 5 : 011(063) [0069]
38:4 – A P : 1 2 : 031(186) [0259]
38:8 – A P : 1 2 : 031(186) [0259]
40:6 – A P : 2 4 : 029(255) [0393]
42:2 – L C : 0 6 : 033(461) [0000]
45:12, 13 – A P : 2 1 : 018(231) [0347]
50:8 – A P : 0 4 : 207(135) [0177]
50:13 – A P : 2 4 : 029(255) [0393]
50:15 – A P : 0 4 : 059(115) [0137]

    – A P : 0 4 : 268(147) [0197]
    – A P : 2 4 : 029(255) [0393]
    – L C : 0 1 : 064(373) [0599]
    – L C : 0 3 : 019(423) [0703]
51:3 – S D : 0 1 : 051(517) [0875]
51:4 – A P : 1 2 : 108(198) [0283]
51:5 – S 3 : 0 1 : 003(302) [0477]
51:12 – S D : 0 2 : 026(526) [0891]
51:16, 17 – A P : 2 4 : 029(255) [0393]
54:6 – S D : 0 4 : 017(554) [0943]
68:18 – A P : 0 4 : 139(126) [0161]
72:11 – A P : 2 1 : 018(231) [0347]
72:15 – A P : 2 1 : 018(231) [0347]
73:22 – S D : 0 2 : 019(524) [0889]
82:6 – A P : 2 1 : 044(236) [0357]
90 – S D : 0 2 : 020(524) [0889]
90:12 – S D : 0 1 : 062(519) [0879]
93:1 – S D : 0 8 : 027(596) [1025]
95:8 – E P : 0 2 : 004(470) [0787]
100:3 – E P : 0 1 : 004(466) [0781]
106:1 – S C : 0 8 : 010(354) [0559]
109:13 – L C : 0 1 : 138(384) [0621]
110:1 – S D : 0 5 : 023(562) [0959]
110:3 – S D : 0 2 : 064(533) [0905]
     – S D : 0 4 : 017(554) [0943]
111:4, 5 – A P : 2 4 : 072(262) [0409]
116:11 – A P : 0 2 : 034(104) [0113]
      – A P : 2 7 : 025(273) [0429]
116:17 – A P : 2 4 : 029(255) [0393]
118:18 – A P : 1 2 : 049(188) [0265]
119 – S D : 0 2 : 015(523) [0887]
119:1 – E P : 0 6 : 002(480) [0805]
     – E P : 0 6 : 004(480) [0807]
     – S D : 0 6 : 004(564) [0963]
119:18, 19 – S D : 0 2 : 015(523) [0887]
119:26, 27 – S D : 0 2 : 015(523) [0887]
119:28 – A P : 1 2 : 049(188) [0265]
119:32 – S D : 0 6 : 021(567) [0969]
119:33, 34 – S D : 0 2 : 015(523) [0887]
119:35 – S D : 0 6 : 004(564) [0963]
119:46 – A G : 0 0 : 027(023) [0037]
119:47 – S D : 0 6 : 004(564) [0963]
119:50 – A L : 2 8 : 009(082) [0085]
119:66 – S D : 0 2 : 015(523) [0887]
119:70 – S D : 0 6 : 004(564) [0963]
119:71 – S D : 0 6 : 009(565) [0965]
119:97 – S D : 0 6 : 004(564) [0963]
119:105 – E P : R N : 001(464) [0777]
119:124, 125 – S D : 0 2 : 015(523) [0887]
119:135 – S D : 0 2 : 015(523) [0887]
119:144 – S D : 0 2 : 015(523) [0887]
119:169 – S D : 0 2 : 015(523) [0887]
130:3 – A P : 0 4 : 326(158) [0211]
130:3, 4 – A P : 0 4 : 058(115) [0137]
130:7 – S 3 : 0 3 : 008(304) [0481]
136:26 – S C : 0 8 : 010(354) [0559]
139:14 – E P : 0 1 : 004(466) [0781]
139:14-16 – S D : 0 1 : 036(514) [0869]
139:16 – S D : 1 1 : 004(617) [1065]
143:2 – A P : 0 4 : 168(130) [0169]
     – A P : 0 4 : 326(157) [0211]
     – A P : 1 2 : 078(193) [0275]
     – S 3 : 0 7 : 002(312) [0493]
     – S D : 0 6 : 021(567) [0969]
145:15, 16 – S C : 0 8 : 007(353) [0559]
147:9-11 – S C : 0 8 : 010(354) [0559]
147:11 – L C : 0 1 : 325(409) [0675]

Proverbs
10:12 – A P : 0 4 : 240(141) [0187]
17:15 – E P : 0 3 : 007(474) [0793]
     – S D : 0 3 : 017(542) [0921]
19:17 – L C : 0 1 : 252(399) [0653]
20:9 – A P : 0 4 : 327(158) [0211]
27:23 – A P : 1 2 : 106(197) [0283]

Ecclesiastes
12:1 – E P : 0 1 : 004(466) [0781]
12:7 – S D : 0 1 : 037(514) [0871]

**Song of Solomon
Isaiah**
1:13 – S 2 : 0 3 : 002(298) [0471]
1:16-18 – A P : 0 4 : 258(144) [0193]
1:16-19 – A P : 1 2 : 164(208) [0303]
5:22 – S D : 0 3 : 017(542) [0921]
11:2 – S D : 0 8 : 072(605) [1041]
11:10 – A P : 2 1 : 018(231) [0347]

Continued ▶

Continued ▶

Matthew, *Continued*
— T R : 0 0 : 023(324) [0511]
— T R : 0 0 : 040(327) [0515]
17:5 — A P : 0 4 : 310(155) [0207]
— S D : 0 2 : 051(531) [0901]
— S D : 0 7 : 043(576) [0987]
18:6 — S D : 1 0 : 016(614) [1059]
18:7 — S D : 1 0 : 016(613) [1057]
18:15 — L C : 0 1 : 276(402) [0659]
— L C : 0 1 : 278(402) [0661]
18:15-19 — L C : 0 6 : 014(458) [0000]
18:16 — L C : 0 1 : 279(403) [0661]
18:17 — A P : 1 1 : 004(181) [0249]
— T R : 0 0 : 024(324) [0511]
18:18 — A P : 1 2 : 138(203) [0293]
— S 3 : 0 7 : 001(311) [0493]
— T R : 0 0 : 023(324) [0511]
18:19 — T R : 0 0 : 024(324) [0511]
18:19, 20 — T R : 0 0 : 024(324) [0511]
18:20 — S 3 : 0 4 : 000(310) [0491]
— T R : 0 0 : 068(331) [0523]
— L C : P R : 009(359) [0569]
— S D : 0 2 : 057(532) [0903]
— S D : 0 8 : 076(606) [1043]
19:3-9 — L C : 0 1 : 306(406) [0669]
19:6 — A P : 2 3 : 023(242) [0371]
— A P : 2 3 : 029(243) [0371]
— A P : 2 3 : 063(248) [0381]
19:11 — A G : 2 3 : 005(051) [0061]
— A L : 2 3 : 005(051) [0061]
— A P : 2 3 : 016(241) [0369]
19:12 — A P : 2 3 : 021(242) [0369]
— A P : 2 3 : 040(245) [0375]
19:14 — S 3 : 0 5 : 004(311) [0493]
19:17 — A P : 0 4 : 122(124) [0157]
— A P : 0 4 : 123(124) [0157]
— A P : 0 4 : 270(147) [0197]
19:21 — A P : 2 7 : 045(277) [0435]
19:29 — A P : 2 7 : 028(274) [0429]
— A P : 2 7 : 040(276) [0433]
20:1-16 — S D : 1 1 : 027(620) [1071]
20:2-14 — S D : 1 1 : 014(619) [1069]
20:16 — E P : 1 1 : 012(496) [0835]
— S D : 1 1 : 034(622) [1075]
— S D : 1 1 : 041(623) [1077]
22:2-14 — S D : 1 1 : 027(620) [1071]
22:5 — S D : 1 1 : 041(623) [1077]
22:5, 6 — S D : 1 1 : 039(622) [1075]
22:12 — S D : 1 1 : 039(623) [1077]
22:14 — S D : 1 1 : 034(622) [1075]
— S D : 1 1 : 041(623) [1077]
— S D : 1 1 : 051(624) [1079]
22:21 — S C : 0 9 : 005(355) [0561]
2227 — A P : 0 4 : 226(138) [0183]
23:2 — A G : 0 8 : 001(033) [0047]
— A L : 0 8 : 001(033) [0047]
23:3 — A P : 2 8 : 021(284) [0449]
23:5 — L C : 0 1 : 331(410) [0677]
23:14 — L C : 0 3 : 033(425) [0707]
23:24 — S 1 : P R : 013(291) [0459]
23:26ff — S D : 1 1 : 078(629) [1089]
23:37 — S D : 0 2 : 058(532) [0905]
— S D : 1 1 : 041(623) [1077]
24:5 — S 3 : 1 4 : 001(315) [0501]
24:13 — S D : 0 4 : 030(555) [0947]
25:1 — A P : 0 7 : 019(171) [0233]
25:21 — A P : 2 1 : 004(229) [0345]
25:23 — A P : 2 1 : 004(229) [0345]
25:35 — A P : 0 4 : 370(164) [0221]
— A P : 0 4 : 373(164) [0221]
25:41 — L C : 0 3 : 065(429) [0715]
25:42, 43 — L C : 0 1 : 191(391) [0635]
26:26 — S D : 0 7 : 035(575) [0983]
— S D : 0 7 : 044(577) [0987]
— S D : 0 7 : 052(578) [0991]
26:26-28 — S C : 0 6 : 004(351) [0557]
— L C : 0 5 : 003(447) [0753]
26:27 — A G : 2 2 : 001(049) [0059]
— A L : 2 2 : 001(049) [0059]
26:28 — A P : 2 4 : 069(262) [0409]
— S D : 0 7 : 044(577) [0987]
— S D : 0 7 : 053(579) [0991]
26:63f — L C : 0 1 : 065(373) [0599]
27:3-5 — S 3 : 0 3 : 007(304) [0481]
28:18 — E P : 0 8 : 016(489) [0821]
— E P : 0 8 : 034(491) [0825]
— E P : 0 8 : 039(491) [0827]
— S D : 0 7 : 043(577) [0987]
— S D : 0 8 : 055(601) [1033]
— S D : 0 8 : 070(604) [1039]
— S D : 0 8 : 070(605) [1041]
— S D : 0 8 : 074(606) [1043]
— S D : 0 8 : 085(608) [1047]
28:19 — A P : 0 9 : 002(178) [0245]
— S C : 0 4 : 004(348) [0551]
— L C : S P : 021(364) [0579]
— L C : 0 4 : 003(437) [0733]
28:19, 20 — T R : 0 0 : 031(325) [0513]
28:20 — S D : 0 8 : 076(606) [1043]

Mark
1:1 — S D : 0 5 : 004(559) [0953]
1:4 — S D : 0 5 : 004(559) [0953]
1:15 — A P : 1 2 : 045(187) [0263]
— S 3 : 0 3 : 004(304) [0481]
— E P : 0 5 : 006(478) [0803]
— S D : 0 5 : 006(559) [0953]
— S D : 0 5 : 008(559) [0953]
— S D : 1 1 : 067(627) [1085]
2:23ff — L C : 0 1 : 081(375) [0603]
3 — L C : 0 1 : 082(376) [0603]
5:34 — S C : 0 5 : 028(351) [0555]
6:17ff — L C : 0 1 : 305(406) [0669]
9:24 — S D : 0 7 : 071(582) [0997]
9:29 — A G : 2 6 : 036(069) [0075]
10:2-12 — L C : 0 1 : 306(406) [0669]
10:29 — A P : 2 7 : 041(276) [0435]
10:42, 43 — T R : 0 0 : 036(326) [0515]
14:22 — S D : 0 7 : 035(575) [0983]
— S D : 0 7 : 052(578) [0991]
14:22-24 — S C : 0 6 : 004(351) [0557]
— L C : 0 5 : 003(447) [0753]
14:23 — E P : 0 7 : 015(483) [0813]
14:24 — S D : 0 7 : 044(577) [0987]
— S D : 0 7 : 053(579) [0991]
16:15 — A L : 2 8 : 007(082) [0085]
— S D : 0 5 : 004(559) [0953]
— S D : 1 1 : 028(621) [1073]
16:16 — A P : 2 4 : 018(252) [0389]
— S 3 : 0 8 : 007(313) [0495]
— S C : 0 4 : 008(349) [0551]
— L C : S P : 021(364) [0579]
— L C : 0 4 : 004(437) [0733]
— L C : 0 4 : 023(439) [0737]
— S D : 1 1 : 039(623) [1077]
16:20 — S D : 0 8 : 027(596) [1025]

Luke
1:13-42 — S 3 : 0 8 : 013(313) [0497]
1:35 — E P : 0 8 : 005(487) [0819]
241-52 — S D : 0 8 : 025(596) [1023]
3:22 — S D : 0 7 : 043(576) [0987]
— S D : 1 1 : 065(627) [1083]
4:18 — S D : 0 5 : 009(559) [0955]
61ff — L C : 0 1 : 081(375) [0603]
6:23 — A P : 0 4 : 356(161) [0217]
6:37 — A P : 0 4 : 254(143) [0193]
— A P : 0 4 : 259(144) [0193]
— L C : 0 3 : 096(433) [0725]
7:30 — S D : 1 1 : 051(624) [1079]
7:37ff — A P : 1 2 : 057(189) [0267]
7:47 — A P : 0 4 : 152(127) [0163]
7:48 — A P : 1 2 : 057(189) [0267]
7:50 — A P : 0 4 : 152(127) [0163]
— A P : 1 2 : 057(189) [0267]
— S C : 0 5 : 028(351) [0555]
8:8 — S D : 1 1 : 051(625) [1079]
8:13 — S D : 1 1 : 042(623) [1077]
8:18 — S D : 1 1 : 051(625) [1079]
8:48 — S C : 0 5 : 028(351) [0555]
10:7 — S C : 0 9 : 003(354) [0561]
10:16 — A G : 2 8 : 022(084) [0087]
— A P : 0 7 : 028(173) [0237]
— A P : 0 7 : 047(177) [0243]
— A P : 1 2 : 040(187) [0261]
— A P : 2 8 : 018(284) [0449]
11:2-4 — L C : S P : 014(363) [0577]
11:11-13 — S D : 1 1 : 072(628) [1087]
11:24, 25 — S D : 1 1 : 042(623) [1077]
— S D : 1 1 : 083(630) [1091]
11:39ff — S D : 1 1 : 078(629) [1089]
11:41 — A P : 0 4 : 155(128) [0165]
— A P : 0 4 : 281(149) [0201]
11:49 — E P : 1 1 : 012(496) [0835]
11:52 — E P : 1 1 : 012(496) [0835]
12:14 — A G : 2 8 : 015(083) [0085]
13:5 — S D : 0 5 : 007(559) [0953]
13:10ff — L C : 0 1 : 081(375) [0603]
13:23, 24 — S D : 1 1 : 033(621) [1073]
14:1ff — L C : 0 1 : 081(375) [0603]
14:18 — S D : 1 1 : 039(623) [1077]
14:18-20 — S D : 1 1 : 041(623) [1077]
14:24 — S D : 1 1 : 039(623) [1077]
— S D : 1 1 : 051(624) [1079]
15:7 — S D : 0 5 : 007(559) [0953]
16:18 — L C : 0 1 : 306(406) [0669]
17:10 — A G : 0 6 : 002(032) [0047]
— A L : 0 6 : 002(032) [0047]
— A P : 0 4 : 334(158) [0215]
18:1 — L C : 0 3 : 004(420) [0699]
18:11 — A P : 0 4 : 332(158) [0211]
21:33 — S D : 0 7 : 043(577) [0987]
21:34 — A G : 2 6 : 035(069) [0075]
— A P : 1 5 : 046(221) [0327]
21:36 — L C : 0 3 : 004(420) [0699]
22:19 — A P : 2 4 : 069(262) [0409]
— S D : 0 7 : 035(575) [0983]
— S D : 0 7 : 044(577) [0987]
— S D : 0 7 : 052(578) [0991]
22:19, 20 — A P : 1 2 : 042(187) [0263]
— S C : 0 6 : 004(351) [0557]
22:19f — L C : 0 5 : 003(447) [0753]
22:20 — S D : 0 7 : 044(577) [0987]
— S D : 0 7 : 053(579) [0991]
22:24-27 — T R : 0 0 : 007(320) [0505]
24:26 — S D : 0 8 : 039(598) [1029]
24:35 — A P : 2 2 : 007(237) [0359]
24:45 — S D : 0 2 : 026(526) [0891]
24:46 — S D : 0 5 : 008(559) [0953]
24:46,47 — S D : 0 5 : 004(559) [0953]
24:47 — A P : 0 4 : 062(115) [0139]
— A P : 1 2 : 030(186) [0259]
— A P : 1 2 : 122(200) [0289]
— S 3 : 0 3 : 006(304) [0481]
— S D : 1 1 : 027(620) [1071]
— S D : 1 1 : 028(620) [1071]
— S D : 1 1 : 028(621) [1073]

John
1:3 — S D : 0 8 : 055(601) [1033]
1:5 — S D : 0 2 : 010(522) [0885]
— S D : 0 2 : 012(522) [0885]
1:10 — S D : 0 8 : 055(601) [1033]
1:12, 13 — A P : 0 4 : 094(120) [0149]
1:14 — L C : 0 2 : 060(418) [0695]
— S D : 0 7 : 036(575) [0985]
— S D : 0 7 : 036(575) [0985]
1:16 — S 3 : 0 3 : 032(308) [0487]
1:18 — S D : 1 1 : 067(627) [1085]
1:29 — A P : 0 4 : 103(122) [0151]
— S 2 : 0 1 : 002(292) [0461]
— S 2 : 0 2 : 007(294) [0465]
— S 3 : 0 3 : 038(309) [0489]
— S D : 1 1 : 028(620) [1071]
2:1-11 — S D : 0 8 : 025(596) [1023]
3:5 — A P : 0 4 : 031(111) [0129]
3:14, 15 — A P : 0 4 : 095(121) [0149]
3:16 — S D : 0 2 : 049(530) [0901]
— S D : 0 7 : 070(582) [0997]
— S D : 1 1 : 028(620) [1071]
— S D : 1 1 : 067(627) [1085]
3:17, 18 — A P : 0 4 : 096(121) [0149]
— A P : 0 4 : 345(160) [0217]
3:18 — E P : 0 7 : 018(484) [0813]
3:31 — S D : 0 8 : 055(601) [1033]
3:35 — S D : 0 8 : 055(601) [1033]
3:36 — A P : 0 4 : 356(161) [0217]
4:23, 24 — A P : 2 4 : 027(254) [0393]
5:9ff — L C : 0 1 : 081(375) [0603]
5:21 — S D : 0 8 : 055(601) [1033]
— S D : 0 8 : 058(602) [1035]
5:23 — A P : 2 1 : 018(231) [0347]
5:27 — S D : 0 8 : 055(601) [1033]
— S D : 0 8 : 058(602) [1035]
5:29 — A P : 0 4 : 370(164) [0221]
6:26 — E P : 0 7 : 015(483) [0811]
6:29 — S D : 0 2 : 026(526) [0891]
6:35 — A P : 2 4 : 075(263) [0411]
6:37 — S D : 1 1 : 068(627) [1085]
6:39 — S D : 0 8 : 055(601) [1033]
— S D : 0 8 : 058(602) [1035]
6:40 — A P : 0 4 : 310(155) [0207]
— S D : 0 8 : 055(601) [1033]
— S D : 0 8 : 058(602) [1035]
— S D : 1 1 : 028(621) [1073]
— S D : 1 1 : 067(627) [1085]
6:44 — S D : 0 2 : 026(526) [0891]
— S D : 1 1 : 076(628) [1087]

Continued ►

John, *Continued*		
6:48-58	— S D : 0 7 : 061(580) [0995]	
	— S D : 0 8 : 059(602) [1035]	
6:51	— S D : 1 1 : 028(620) [1071]	
6:52	— E P : 0 7 : 015(483) [0811]	
6:52-65	— S D : 0 7 : 064(581) [0995]	
719	— S 3 : 0 3 : 039(309) [0489]	
7:22ff	— L C : 0 1 : 081(375) [0603]	
7:39	— S D : 0 8 : 085(608) [1047]	
7:48	— S D : 1 1 : 078(629) [1089]	
8:13	— S D : 1 1 : 078(629) [1089]	
8:34	— S D : 0 2 : 007(521) [0883]	
8:36	— A P : 0 4 : 031(111) [0129]	
8:36	— A P : 0 4 : 297(153) [0205]	
	— S D : 0 2 : 067(534) [0907]	
8:37	— S D : 0 2 : 012(522) [0885]	
8:44	— A L : 1 9 : 000(041) [0053]	
	— A G : 2 3 : 023(055) [0063]	
	— A P : 0 7 : 016(171) [0231]	
	— A P : 1 9 : 001(226) [0337]	
	— A P : 2 3 : 058(247) [0379]	
	— L C : 0 3 : 115(435) [0731]	
	— L C : 0 5 : 081(456) [0773]	
9:3	— A P : 1 2 : 159(207) [0301]	
9:14ff	— L C : 0 1 : 081(375) [0603]	
9:16	— S D : 1 1 : 078(629) [1089]	
9:41	— S D : 1 1 : 078(629) [1089]	
10:3	— S 3 : 1 2 : 002(315) [0499]	
10:9	— S D : 1 1 : 066(627) [1085]	
10:12-16	— S D : P R : 014(506) [0857]	
:27	— A P : 0 4 : 400(168) [0227]	
	— S D : P R : 014(506) [0857]	
10:27, 28	— S D : 1 1 : 030(621) [1073]	
10:27-30	— S D : 1 1 : 012(618) [1067]	
10:28	— E P : 1 1 : 005(495) [0833]	
	— S D : 1 1 : 008(617) [1065]	
	— S D : 1 1 : 046(624) [1079]	
	— S D : 1 1 : 090(631) [1093]	
12:42	— S D : 1 1 : 078(629) [1089]	
13:3	— E P : 0 8 : 016(489) [0821]	
	— S D : 0 8 : 055(601) [1033]	
	— S D : 0 8 : 070(605) [1041]	
14:6	— A L : 2 0 : 010(042) [0055]	
	— S D : 1 1 : 066(627) [1085]	
15:3, 4	— S D : 1 1 : 012(618) [1067]	
15:5	— A L : 2 0 : 039(046) [0057]	
	— A P : 0 4 : 256(144) [0193]	
	— A P : 0 4 : 266(146) [0197]	
	— A·P : 0 4 : 269(147) [0197]	
	— A P : 0 4 : 315(156) [0207]	
	— A P : 0 4 : 372(164) [0221]	
	— A P : 1 2 : 085(194) [0277]	
	— E P : 0 2 : 006(470) [0787]	
	— S D : 0 2 : 014(523) [0885]	
	— S D : 0 2 : 026(526) [0891]	
15:10	— S D : 1 1 : 012(618) [1067]	
15:12	— S D : 0 4 : 014(553) [0943]	
	— S D : 1 1 : 012(618) [1067]	
15:16, 17	— S D : 1 1 : 012(618) [1067]	
16:7	— S D : 0 5 : 011(560) [0955]	
16:8	— S 3 : 0 3 : 001(303) [0479]	
	— S D : 0 5 : 012(560) [0955]	
	— S D : 0 5 : 013(560) [0957]	
	— S D : 0 6 : 012(566) [0967]	
16:12, 13	— A G : 2 8 : 031(085) [0087]	
16:14	— S D : 1 1 : 065(627) [1085]	
16:23	— A P : 0 4 : 333(158) [0211]	
	— A P : 2 1 : 017(231) [0347]	
17:10	— S D : 0 8 : 085(608) [1047]	
17:17	— S D : 0 2 : 051(531) [0901]	
17:20	— S D : 0 2 : 051(531) [0901]	
17:24	— S D : 0 8 : 065(604) [1039]	
18:6	— S D : 0 2 : 025(596) [1023]	
18:36	— A G : 2 8 : 014(083) [0085]	
	— T R : 0 0 : 031(325) [0513]	
20:21	— T R : 0 0 : 009(321) [0505]	
	— T R : 0 0 : 031(325) [0513]	
20:21-23	— A G : 2 8 : 006(082) [0085]	
20:23	— T R : 0 0 : 023(324) [0511]	
21:15	— T R : 0 0 : 030(325) [0513]	
21:17	— T R : 0 0 : 022(323) [0511]	
	— T R : 0 0 : 030(325) [0513]	
Acts		
1:7	— S D : 1 1 : 056(625) [1081]	
2:38	— A P : 1 2 : 122(200) [0289]	
2:42	— A P : 2 2 : 007(237) [0359]	
2:46	— A P : 2 2 : 007(237) [0359]	
3:21	— S D : 0 7 : 119(590) [1013]	
4:11, 12	— A P : 0 4 : 098(121) [0149]	
4:12	— S 2 : 0 1 : 005(292) [0463]	
5:29	— A G : 1 6 : 007(038) [0051]	
	— A L : 1 6 : 007(038) [0051]	
	— A G : 2 8 : 075(094) [0095]	
	— A P : 2 8 : 021(284) [0449]	
	— A P : 2 8 : 025(285) [0451]	
	— T R : 0 0 : 038(326) [0515]	
	— S D : 0 4 : 014(553) [0943]	
5:51	— S D : 0 2 : 026(526) [0891]	
7:51	— S D : 0 2 : 060(533) [0905]	
	— S D : 1 1 : 039(623) [1077]	
10:1ff	— S 3 : 0 8 : 008(313) [0495]	
10:2	— S 3 : 0 8 : 008(313) [0495]	
10:22	— S 3 : 0 8 : 008(313) [0495]	
10:38	— S D : 0 7 : 036(575) [0985]	
10:43	— A P : 0 4 : 083(118) [0145]	
	— A P : 0 4 : 273(148) [0199]	
	— A P : 1 2 : 065(191) [0271]	
	— A P : 2 0 : 002(227) [0339]	
10:44	— A P : 1 2 : 071(192) [0271]	
11:14	— S D : 0 2 : 051(531) [0901]	
13:1, 2	— A P : 2 4 : 078(263) [0411]	
13:38, 39	— A P : 0 4 : 097(121) [0149]	
13:40f	— S D : 1 1 : 039(622) [1075]	
13:46	— S D : 1 1 : 039(622) [1075]	
	— S D : 1 1 : 060(626) [1083]	
13:48	— S D : 1 1 : 008(617) [1065]	
15	— A P : 2 3 : 042(245) [0375]	
15:1-5	— S D : P R : 007(502) [0849]	
15:9	— A P : 0 4 : 099(121) [0151]	
	— A P : 0 4 : 284(150) [0201]	
	— A P : 2 8 : 008(282) [0445]	
	— S 3 : 1 3 : 001(315) [0499]	
15:10	— A G : 2 8 : 042(088) [0089]	
	— A P : 1 5 : 031(219) [0323]	
	— A P : 2 8 : 008(282) [0445]	
	— S D : P R : 007(502) [0849]	
15:10, 11	— A G : 2 6 : 027(068) [0073]	
	— A L : 2 6 : 027(068) [0073]	
15:20	— A G : 2 8 : 032(085) [0087]	
15:23-29	— A G : 2 6 : 006(092) [0093]	
15:24	— S D : P R : 007(502) [0849]	
15:29	— A G : 2 8 : 032(085) [0087]	
16:3	— S D : 1 0 : 009(612) [1055]	
16:14	— E P : 0 2 : 004(470) [0787]	
	— S D : 0 2 : 026(526) [0891]	
17:25, 26	— S D : 0 1 : 034(514) [0869]	
17:25-28	— E P : 0 1 : 004(466) [0781]	
17:28	— S D : 0 1 : 042(515) [0873]	
17:30	— S 3 : 0 3 : 034(308) [0489]	
19:12	— L C : 0 2 : 036(415) [0687]	
19:15	— L C : 0 2 : 036(415) [0687]	
19:39f	— L C : 0 2 : 048(417) [0691]	
20:7	— A P : 2 2 : 007(237) [0359]	
20:21	— S D : 0 5 : 008(559) [0953]	
20:24	— E P : 0 5 : 006(478) [0803]	
	— S D : 0 5 : 004(559) [0953]	
20:28	— E P : 0 8 : 014(488) [0821]	
21:26	— S D : 1 0 : 009(612) [1055]	
26:18	— S D : 0 2 : 010(522) [0885]	
Romans		
1:3	— S D : 0 8 : 037(598) [1027]	
1:4	— S D : 0 8 : 085(608) [1047]	
1:16	— A G : 2 8 : 009(082) [0085]	
	— A P : 0 4 : 067(116) [0139]	
	— A P : 0 4 : 230(139) [0183]	
	— A P : 1 3 : 011(212) [0311]	
	— L C : P R : 011(360) [0571]	
	— E P : 0 2 : 004(470) [0787]	
	— S D : 0 5 : 022(562) [0959]	
	— S D : 1 1 : 029(621) [1073]	
1:17	— E P : 0 5 : 005(478) [0803]	
	— S D : 0 3 : 020(542) [0921]	
	— S D : 0 3 : 054(549) [0935]	
	— S D : 1 1 : 015(619) [1069]	
1:18	— S 3 : 0 3 : 001(303) [0479]	
	— E P : 0 5 : 008(479) [0803]	
1:19-21	— S D : 0 2 : 009(521) [0883]	
1:21	— S D : 0 5 : 022(562) [0959]	
1:22	— S D : 0 3 : 002(539) [0917]	
1:28	— S D : 0 2 : 009(521) [0883]	
1:32	— S D : 0 2 : 009(521) [0883]	
2:6	— A P : 0 4 : 370(164) [0221]	
2:10	— A P : 0 4 : 370(164) [0221]	
2:13	— A P : 0 4 : 122(124) [0157]	
	— A P : 0 4 : 252(143) [0191]	
2:15	— L C : 0 2 : 067(419) [0697]	
	— S D : 0 6 : 016(566) [0967]	
3-4	— A L : 0 4 : 003(030) [0045]	
3:5	— S D : 0 3 : 054(549) [0935]	
3:10-12	— S 3 : 0 3 : 033(308) [0489]	
3:11-12	— S D : 0 2 : 010(522) [0885]	
3:12	— S D : 0 2 : 012(522) [0885]	
3:19, 20	— S 3 : 0 3 : 001(303) [0479]	
3:20	— S D : 0 5 : 017(561) [0957]	
	— S D : 0 6 : 016(566) [0967]	
3:20, 21	— E P : 0 3 : 010(474) [0795]	
3:21	— A P : 0 4 : 041(113) [0133]	
3:21-26	— A G : 0 4 : 003(030) [0045]	
3:22	— S D : 0 3 : 054(549) [0935]	
	— S D : 1 1 : 028(621) [1071]	
3:23	— A P : 0 4 : 032(111) [0129]	
3:23-25	— S 2 : 0 1 : 003(292) [0461]	
3:24	— A P : 0 4 : 073(117) [0141]	
	— A P : 2 0 : 010(228) [0341]	
	— E P : 0 3 : 010(474) [0795]	
3:25	— A P : 0 4 : 082(118) [0145]	
	— A P : 0 4 : 382(165) [0225]	
	— A P : 1 2 : 063(191) [0269]	
	— L C : 0 4 : 086(446) [0753]	
	— S D : 0 3 : 054(549) [0935]	
3:26	— S 2 : 0 1 : 004(292) [0461]	
3:28	— A P : 0 4 : 073(117) [0141]	
	— A P : 0 4 : 087(120) [0147]	
	— S 2 : 0 1 : 004(292) [0461]	
	— E P : 0 3 : 010(474) [0795]	
	— S D : 0 3 : 012(541) [0919]	
	— S D : 0 3 : 027(543) [0925]	
	— S D : 0 3 : 043(547) [0931]	
3:31	— A P : 0 4 : 123(124) [0157]	
	— A P : 0 4 : 132(125) [0159]	
	— A P : 0 4 : 175(131) [0171]	
	— A P : 2 0 : 015(229) [0343]	
4	— A P : 0 4 : 088(120) [0149]	
4:1	— S D : 0 3 : 033(545) [0927]	
4:1-6	— A P : 0 4 : 087(120) [0147]	
4:3	— A P : 0 4 : 293(152) [0203]	
	— S D : 0 3 : 033(545) [0927]	
4:4, 5	— A P : 0 4 : 089(120) [0149]	
4:5	— A G : 0 4 : 003(030) [0045]	
	— A P : 0 4 : 293(152) [0203]	
	— A P : 0 4 : 307(154) [0207]	
	— E P : 0 3 : 005(473) [0793]	
	— S D : 0 3 : 012(541) [0919]	
4:5, 6	— S D : 0 3 : 034(545) [0927]	
4:5ff	— A P : 0 4 : 285(150) [0201]	
4:6	— S D : 0 3 : 053(548) [0933]	
	— S D : 0 4 : 024(555) [0945]	
4:6-8	— E P : 0 4 : 007(476) [0799]	
	— S D : 0 3 : 023(543) [0923]	
4:7	— A P : 0 4 : 163(129) [0169]	
4:9	— A P : 0 4 : 090(120) [0149]	
	— A P : 1 3 : 019(213) [0313]	
4:9-22	— A P : 0 4 : 201(134) [0175]	
4:11	— A P : 2 4 : 070(262) [0409]	
4:13	— A P : 0 4 : 292(152) [0203]	
4:14	— A P : 0 4 : 042(113) [0133]	
4:15	— A P : 0 4 : 038(112) [0131]	
	— A P : 0 4 : 270(147) [0197]	
	— A P : 1 2 : 088(195) [0277]	
	— S 3 : 0 2 : 005(303) [0479]	
4:16	— A P : 0 4 : 050(114) [0135]	
	— A P : 0 4 : 084(119) [0145]	
	— A P : 0 4 : 084(119) [0145]	
	— A P : 1 2 : 061(190) [0269]	
	— A P : 1 2 : 081(194) [0275]	
	— A P : 2 0 : 010(228) [0341]	
4:18	— A P : 0 4 : 320(156) [0209]	
4:20	— A P : 0 4 : 309(155) [0207]	
4:25	— S 2 : 0 1 : 001(292) [0461]	
	— S D : 0 5 : 022(562) [0959]	
5:1	— A G : 2 0 : 016(043) [0055]	
	— A L : 2 0 : 016(043) [0055]	
	— A P : 0 4 : 091(120) [0149]	
	— A P : 0 4 : 195(134) [0175]	
	— A P : 0 4 : 217(137) [0179]	
	— A P : 0 4 : 304(154) [0205]	
	— A P : 0 4 : 320(156) [0209]	
	— A P : 1 2 : 036(186) [0261]	
	— A P : 2 4 : 012(251) [0387]	
	— A P : 2 4 : 060(260) [0405]	
	— A P : 2 4 : 089(266) [0415]	
5:2	— A P : 0 4 : 081(118) [0143]	
	— A P : 0 4 : 256(144) [0193]	
	— A P : 0 4 : 269(147) [0197]	
	— A P : 0 4 : 291(152) [0203]	

Continued ►

Romans, *Continued*

	— A P : 0 4 : 297(153) [0205]
	— A P : 0 4 : 314(156) [0207]
	— A P : 1 2 : 037(186) [0261]
	— A P : 1 2 : 063(191) [0269]
	— S D : 0 4 : 034(556) [0949]
5:12	— S 3 : 0 1 : 001(302) [0477]
	— S D : 0 1 : 007(510) [0861]
	— S D : 0 1 : 009(510) [0861]
5:12ff	— S 3 : 0 1 : 003(302) [0477]
5:18	— S D : 0 3 : 012(541) [0919]
5:19	— E P : 0 3 : 003(473) [0793]
	— S D : 0 3 : 057(550) [0935]
5:20	— A P : 0 4 : 103(122) [0151]
5:20	— A P : 0 4 : 149(127) [0163]
	— A P : 2 1 : 005(230) [0345]
	— S 3 : 0 2 : 005(303) [0479]
6:4	— S C : 0 4 : 014(349) [0553]
6:7	— S D : 0 4 : 017(554) [0943]
6:9	— A P : 1 0 : 004(180) [0247]
6:12	— E P : 0 6 : 004(480) [0807]
6:14	— E P : 0 4 : 010(476) [0799]
	— S D : 0 6 : 017(567) [0967]
6:19	— A P : 1 2 : 122(200) [0289]
	— A P : 1 2 : 132(202) [0291]
6:23	— A P : 0 4 : 356(161) [0217]
	— S D : 1 1 : 081(629) [1089]
7:5	— A P : 0 2 : 030(104) [0113]
7:6	— E P : 0 4 : 010(476) [0799]
	— S D : 0 5 : 010(559) [0955]
7:7	— A P : 0 2 : 039(105) [0115]
	— A P : 0 4 : 087(120) [0147]
	— S D : 0 5 : 017(561) [0957]
7:10	— S 3 : 0 3 : 007(304) [0481]
7:14	— E P : 0 5 : 008(479) [0803]
	— S D : 0 2 : 017(524) [0887]
	— S D : 0 6 : 008(565) [0965]
7:14-25	— E P : 0 4 : 013(477) [0799]
7:18	— L C : 0 5 : 076(455) [0771]
	— S D : 0 2 : 017(524) [0887]
	— S D : 0 6 : 008(565) [0965]
7:18, 19	— S D : 0 6 : 019(567) [0969]
	— S D : 0 6 : 021(567) [0969]
7:19	— A P : 0 4 : 168(130) [0169]
	— S D : 0 6 : 008(565) [0965]
7:21	— E P : 0 6 : 004(480) [0805]
7:22, 23	— S D : 0 2 : 017(524) [0887]
	— S D : 0 2 : 064(533) [0907]
	— S D : 0 2 : 085(537) [0913]
	— S D : 0 4 : 019(554) [0945]
7:23	— A P : 0 2 : 039(105) [0115]
	— S 3 : 0 3 : 040(309) [0489]
	— S 3 : 0 7 : 001(311) [0493]
	— S 3 : 0 8 : 002(312) [0495]
	— E P : 0 6 : 004(480) [0805]
	— E P : 0 6 : 006(481) [0807]
	— S D : 0 2 : 034(528) [0895]
	— S D : 0 2 : 084(537) [0913]
	— S D : 0 6 : 008(565) [0965]
	— S D : 0 6 : 018(567) [0967]
7:25	— A P : 0 4 : 168(130) [0169]
	— S D : 0 2 : 064(533) [0907]
	— S D : 0 2 : 085(537) [0913]
8:1	— A P : 0 4 : 143(126) [0161]
	— A P : 0 4 : 308(155) [0207]
	— E P : 0 4 : 014(477) [0799]
	— E P : 0 6 : 006(481) [0807]
8:2	— S D : 0 6 : 017(567) [0967]
8:3	— A P : 2 4 : 023(253) [0391]
8:7	— E P : 0 2 : 003(470) [0787]
	— S D : 0 2 : 013(523) [0885]
	— S D : 0 2 : 017(524) [0887]
8:7, 8	— A P : 0 4 : 032(111) [0129]
8:10	— A P : 0 4 : 352(161) [0217]
	— A P : 1 2 : 152(206) [0299]
8:12, 13	— A P : 0 4 : 143(126) [0161]
8:13	— S D : 0 4 : 019(554) [0945]
	— S D : 0 4 : 032(556) [0947]
8:14	— E P : 0 4 : 010(476) [0799]
	— E P : 0 6 : 006(481) [0807]
	— S D : 0 2 : 063(533) [0905]
8:15	— E P : 0 4 : 012(477) [0799]
8:16	— S D : 1 1 : 073(628) [1087]
8:16-26	— S D : 1 1 : 031(621) [1073]
8:17	— A P : 0 4 : 354(161) [0217]
	— A P : 0 4 : 356(161) [0217]
	— A P : 0 4 : 366(163) [0221]
8:25	— S D : 1 1 : 030(621) [1073]
8:28, 29	— S D : 1 1 : 049(624) [1079]
8:28ff	— S D : 1 1 : 014(619) [1069]

8:29, 30	— S D : 1 1 : 027(620) [1071]
8:30	— A P : 0 4 : 196(134) [0175]
	— A P : 0 4 : 362(162) [0219]
	— E P : 1 1 : 013(496) [0835]
8:33	— E P : 0 3 : 007(474) [0793]
	— S D : 0 3 : 017(542) [0921]
8:34	— A G : 2 1 : 002(047) [0057]
	— A P : 0 4 : 165(129) [0169]
8:35	— S D : 1 1 : 047(624) [1079]
	— S D : 1 1 : 049(624) [1079]
8:38, 39	— S D : 1 1 : 049(624) [1079]
9:5	— E P : 0 8 : 005(487) [0819]
	— S D : 0 8 : 006(592) [1017]
9:8ff	— S D : 1 1 : 050(624) [1079]
9:11	— S D : 1 1 : 010(618) [1067]
	— S D : 1 1 : 043(623) [1077]
	— S D : 1 1 : 088(631) [1093]
9:11-13	— S D : 1 1 : 088(631) [1093]
9:14ff	— S D : 1 1 : 058(625) [1081]
9:16	— E P : 0 2 : 006(470) [0787]
9:17	— S D : 1 1 : 084(630) [1091]
9:19	— S D : 1 1 : 010(618) [1067]
9:20	— S D : 1 1 : 063(626) [1083]
9:22, 23	— S D : 1 1 : 079(629) [1089]
9:23	— S D : 1 1 : 060(626) [1083]
	— S D : 1 1 : 082(630) [1091]
9:31	— S D : 1 1 : 039(623) [1077]
9:33	— A P : 2 1 : 031(233) [0351]
10:3	— A P : 0 4 : 030(111) [0129]
10:4	— A P : 0 4 : 030(111) [0129]
	— A P : 0 4 : 372(164) [0221]
	— S D : 0 5 : 024(563) [0961]
10:10	— A P : 0 4 : 092(120) [0149]
	— A P : 0 4 : 383(166) [0225]
	— A P : 1 3 : 023(214) [0313]
10:12	— S D : 1 1 : 028(621) [1071]
10:17	— A P : 0 4 : 067(116) [0139]
	— A P : 1 2 : 039(187) [0261]
	— A P : 1 3 : 005(211) [0309]
	— E P : 0 2 : 004(470) [0787]
	— S D : 0 2 : 051(531) [0901]
	— S D : 1 1 : 069(627) [1085]
11:5	— S D : 1 1 : 060(626) [1083]
11:6	— A P : 0 4 : 041(113) [0133]
	— E P : 0 3 : 010(474) [0795]
11:20	— S D : 0 4 : 034(557) [0949]
11:22ff	— S D : 1 1 : 058(625) [1081]
11:32	— E P : 1 1 : 010(495) [0833]
	— S D : 1 1 : 028(621) [1071]
11:33	— S D : 1 1 : 055(625) [1081]
11:33, 34	— S D : 1 1 : 064(626) [1083]
12:1	— A P : 1 2 : 132(202) [0291]
	— A P : 1 5 : 045(221) [0327]
	— A P : 2 4 : 026(254) [0391]
	— A P : 2 4 : 088(265) [0413]
12:2	— S D : 0 6 : 012(566) [0967]
12:5	— A P : 1 0 : 003(179) [0247]
12:6-8	— S 2 : 0 4 : 009(300) [0473]
12:7, 8	— E P : 0 6 : 004(480) [0807]
12:12	— L C : 0 3 : 004(420) [0699]
12:19	— A P : 1 6 : 007(223) [0331]
13:1	— S C : 0 9 : 005(355) [0561]
13:1-4	— S C : 0 9 : 004(355) [0561]
13:1ff	— A P : 1 6 : 007(223) [0331]
13:5	— A P : 1 6 : 005(223) [0331]
13:5, 6	— S D : 0 4 : 014(553) [0943]
13:5-7	— S C : 0 9 : 005(355) [0561]
13:9	— S C : 0 9 : 014(356) [0563]
	— S D : 0 4 : 014(553) [0943]
	— S D : 0 6 : 021(567) [0969]
14	— S D : 1 0 : 009(612) [1055]
14:1	— S D : 0 7 : 070(582) [0997]
14:3	— S D : 0 7 : 070(582) [0997]
14:6	— S D : 1 0 : 013(613) [1057]
14:13ff	— E P : 1 0 : 005(493) [0829]
14:17	— A G : 2 6 : 024(067) [0073]
	— A L : 2 6 : 024(067) [0073]
	— A P : 0 7 : 036(175) [0241]
	— A P : 2 7 : 027(273) [0429]
	— A P : 2 8 : 007(282) [0445]
14:23	— A P : 0 4 : 035(112) [0131]
	— A P : 1 2 : 089(195) [0279]
	— A P : 1 5 : 017(217) [0319]
	— A P : 2 7 : 023(273) [0427]
	— S D : 0 4 : 008(552) [0941]
15:4	— S D : 1 1 : 012(618) [1067]
	— S D : 1 1 : 092(632) [1093]
15:16	— A P : 2 4 : 034(256) [0395]

1 Corinthians

1:2	— L C : 0 2 : 048(417) [0691]
1:8	— S D : 1 1 : 032(621) [1073]
1:9	— L C : 0 2 : 052(417) [0691]
1:21	— S D : 0 2 : 010(522) [0883]
	— S D : 0 2 : 051(531) [0901]
	— S D : 1 1 : 012(618) [1067]
1:30	— A P : 0 4 : 086(119) [0147]
	— A P : 0 4 : 306(154) [0207]
	— E P : 0 3 : 001(472) [0791]
	— S D : 0 5 : 022(562) [0959]
1:30, 31	— S D : 1 1 : 012(618) [1067]
1:31	— S 3 : 1 3 : 003(315) [0499]
2:4-12	— S D : 0 2 : 071(535) [0909]
2:8	— E P : 0 8 : 014(488) [0821]
2:11	— L C : 0 2 : 036(415) [0687]
2:14	— A G : 1 8 : 003(039) [0051]
	— A L : 1 8 : 002(039) [0051]
	— A P : 0 2 : 030(104) [0113]
	— A P : 1 8 : 007(226) [0337]
	— E P : 0 2 : 002(470) [0787]
	— S D : 0 2 : 010(522) [0883]
	— S D : 0 2 : 012(523) [0885]
3:4-8	— T R : 0 0 : 011(321) [0507]
3:7	— E P : 0 2 : 006(470) [0787]
3:8	— A P : 0 4 : 194(133) [0175]
	— A P : 0 4 : 366(163) [0219]
	— A P : 2 1 : 029(233) [0351]
3:9	— S D : 0 2 : 066(534) [0907]
3:12	— A P : 0 7 : 020(171) [0233]
3:16	— S D : 0 2 : 066(534) [0907]
3:19	— S D : 0 2 : 008(521) [0883]
3:21, 22	— T R : 0 0 : 011(321) [0507]
3:23	— A P : 0 4 : 230(139) [0183]
4:1	— A P : 2 4 : 080(264) [0411]
4:4	— A P : 0 4 : 163(129) [0169]
	— S 3 : 0 7 : 003(312) [0493]
	— S D : 0 6 : 021(567) [0969]
4:7	— S D : 0 2 : 026(526) [0891]
4:13	— A P : 2 4 : 023(253) [0391]
	— L C : 0 1 : 160(387) [0627]
4:15	— L C : 0 1 : 159(387) [0627]
5:6	— S D : 0 3 : 007(540) [0917]
	— S D : 0 3 : 007(540) [0917]
6:9	— S D : 0 4 : 032(556) [0947]
7:2	— A G : 2 3 : 004(051) [0061]
	— A L : 2 3 : 004(051) [0061]
	— A G : 2 7 : 019(073) [0079]
	— A P : 2 3 : 014(241) [0367]
	— A P : 2 3 : 063(248) [0381]
	— A P : 2 7 : 051(278) [0437]
7:5	— A P : 2 3 : 043(245) [0375]
7:9	— A G : 2 3 : 004(051) [0061]
	— A L : 2 3 : 004(051) [0061]
	— A P : 2 3 : 016(241) [0369]
7:10f	— L C : 0 1 : 306(406) [0669]
7:14	— A P : 2 3 : 031(243) [0371]
7:18, 19	— S D : 1 0 : 002(611) [1053]
	— S D : 1 0 : 012(612) [1057]
7:32	— A P : 2 3 : 040(245) [0375]
8:8	— A P : 2 7 : 026(273) [0429]
8:9-13	— E P : 1 0 : 005(493) [0829]
9:9	— S D : 0 4 : 014(553) [0943]
9:10	— S D : 1 0 : 009(612) [1055]
9:14	— S C : 0 9 : 003(354) [0561]
9:16	— E P : 0 2 : 006(470) [0787]
9:27	— A G : 2 6 : 037(069) [0075]
	— A P : 1 5 : 046(221) [0327]
	— E P : 0 6 : 004(480) [0807]
	— S D : 0 4 : 019(554) [0945]
	— S D : 0 6 : 009(565) [0965]
	— S D : 0 6 : 019(567) [0969]
10:16	— A P : 1 0 : 001(179) [0247]
	— S 3 : 0 6 : 005(311) [0493]
	— E P : 0 7 : 009(483) [0811]
	— E P : 0 7 : 015(483) [0813]
	— S D : 0 7 : 011(571) [0975]
	— S D : 0 7 : 035(575) [0983]
	— S D : 0 7 : 054(579) [0991]
	— S D : 0 7 : 059(580) [0993]
	— S D : 0 7 : 082(584) [1001]
	— S D : 0 7 : 084(584) [1001]
10:17	— A P : 1 0 : 003(179) [0247]
10:18-33	— S D : 0 7 : 057(579) [0993]
11:5	— A G : 2 8 : 054(090) [0091]
11:20ff	— A G : 2 2 : 003(049) [0059]
	— A L : 2 2 : 003(049) [0059]
	— A G : 2 4 : 035(060) [0067]

Continued ▶

1 Corinthians, *Continued*

11:23, 24	— A P : 2 2 : 003(236) [0357]
11:23-25	— S C : 0 6 : 004(351) [0557]
	— L C : S P : 023(364) [0579]
	— L C : 0 5 : 003(447) [0753]
	— E P : 0 7 : 009(483) [0811]
11:24	— A P : 2 4 : 071(262) [0409]
	— S D : 0 7 : 007(570) [0975]
	— S D : 0 7 : 035(575) [0983]
11:25	— A L : 2 4 : 030(059) [0067]
	— A P : 1 3 : 020(213) [0313]
	— S C : P R : 022(341) [0537]
	— S D : 0 7 : 052(578) [0991]
	— S D : 0 7 : 053(579) [0991]
11:26	— A P : 0 4 : 210(136) [0179]
	— A P : 2 4 : 035(256) [0397]
11:27	— A G : 2 4 : 012(057) [0065]
	— A P : 2 4 : 091(266) [0415]
	— E P : 0 7 : 018(484) [0813]
	— S D : 0 7 : 060(580) [0993]
11:28	— S 3 : 0 6 : 005(311) [0493]
11:29	— A P : 1 1 : 005(181) [0251]
	— E P : 0 7 : 018(484) [0813]
11:31	— A P : 0 4 : 268(147) [0197]
	— A P : 1 2 : 163(208) [0303]
11:33	— A L : 2 4 : 039(060) [0069]
12:3	— S D : 0 2 : 026(526) [0891]
12:4	— S 2 : 0 4 : 009(300) [0473]
12:8-10	— S 2 : 0 4 : 009(300) [0473]
12:22, 23	— L C : 0 1 : 287(403) [0663]
13:2	— A P : 0 4 : 123(124) [0157]
	— A P : 0 4 : 218(137) [0179]
13:13	— A P : 0 4 : 225(138) [0183]
14:2	— A L : 2 4 : 004(056) [0065]
14:9	— A L : 2 4 : 004(056) [0065]
14:19	— A P : 2 4 : 002(249) [0385]
14:30	— A G : 2 8 : 054(090) [0091]
14:40	— A P : 1 5 : 020(218) [0321]
15:12	— S D : P R : 007(502) [0849]
15:20	— S D : 0 2 : 066(534) [0907]
15:27	— S D : 0 8 : 055(601) [1033]
	— S D : 0 8 : 070(605) [1041]
15:56	— A P : 1 2 : 153(206) [0299]
15:56, 57	— A P : 0 4 : 079(118) [0143]
15:57	— A P : 1 2 : 146(205) [0297]
16:1	— A P : 0 4 : 192(133) [0175]

2 Corinthians

1:9	— A P : 1 2 : 151(206) [0299]
1:23	— L C : 0 1 : 065(373) [0599]
1:24	— T R : 0 0 : 031(325) [0513]
2:14ff	— S D : 0 2 : 056(532) [0903]
3:4-12	— S D : 0 2 : 071(535) [0909]
3:5	— E P : 0 2 : 003(470) [0787]
	— S D : 0 2 : 012(522) [0885]
3:6	— A P : 2 4 : 059(260) [0405]
	— S D : 0 2 : 026(526) [0891]
	— S D : 0 5 : 022(562) [0959]
3:7-9	— S D : 0 5 : 026(563) [0961]
3:8	— S D : 0 5 : 022(562) [0959]
	— S D : 1 1 : 029(621) [1073]
3:9	— S D : 0 5 : 022(562) [0959]
	— S D : 0 5 : 022(562) [0959]
3:12	— A P : 0 4 : 229(139) [0183]
3:13	— A P : 0 4 : 021(110) [0127]
	— A P : 1 2 : 078(193) [0275]
3:13-15	— S D : 0 5 : 010(560) [0955]
3:13-16	— E P : 0 5 : 008(478) [0803]
3:15	— S D : 0 2 : 007(521) [0883]
3:15-17	— A P : 0 4 : 133(125) [0159]
3:18	— A P : 0 4 : 351(161) [0217]
	— A P : 2 7 : 027(273) [0429]
5:2, 3	— A P : 0 4 : 352(161) [0217]
5:17	— S D : 0 2 : 026(526) [0891]
5:19	— S D : 0 7 : 036(575) [0985]
5:20	— A P : 2 4 : 080(264) [0411]
	— S D : 1 1 : 027(620) [1071]
5:21	— A P : 0 4 : 306(154) [0207]
	— E P : 0 3 : 001(472) [0791]
	— E P : 0 5 : 005(478) [0803]
	— S D : 0 3 : 054(549) [0935]
	— S D : 0 5 : 022(562) [0959]
	— S D : 1 1 : 015(619) [1069]
6:1	— S D : 0 2 : 066(534) [0907]
6:14	— T R : 0 0 : 041(328) [0517]
	— E P : 1 0 : 006(493) [0829]
	— S D : 1 0 : 006(611) [1055]
	— S D : 1 0 : 022(615) [1061]
6:17	— S D : 1 0 : 006(611) [1055]

7:10	— S D : 0 5 : 009(559) [0955]
9:6	— A P : 0 4 : 367(163) [0221]
9:7	— S D : 0 4 : 017(554) [0943]
	— S D : 0 4 : 017(554) [0943]
	— S D : 0 4 : 017(554) [0943]
9:12	— A P : 2 4 : 082(264) [0411]
10:4	— T R : 0 0 : 031(325) [0513]
10:4, 5	— A G : 2 8 : 017(083) [0085]
	— A L : 2 8 : 017(083) [0085]
10:8	— A G : 2 8 : 042(088) [0089]
	— A P : 1 2 : 176(210) [0307]
12:9	— A P : 1 2 : 160(207) [0303]
	— S D : 0 7 : 070(582) [0997]
13:8	— A G : 2 8 : 025(084) [0087]
	— A L : 2 8 : 025(084) [0087]
13:10	— A G : 2 8 : 026(084) [0087]

Galatians

1:2	— L C : 0 2 : 048(417) [0691]
1:7-9	— T R : 0 0 : 072(332) [0525]
1:8	— A G : 2 8 : 024(084) [0087]
	— A L : 2 8 : 024(084) [0087]
	— A P : 2 8 : 020(284) [0449]
	— S 2 : 0 2 : 015(295) [0467]
	— T R : 0 0 : 038(326) [0515]
	— E P : R N : 001(464) [0777]
1:9	— A P : 0 7 : 048(177) [0245]
1:20	— L C : 0 1 : 065(373) [0599]
2:2	— T R : 0 0 : 010(321) [0505]
2:3	— S D : 1 0 : 012(611) [1053]
2:4, 5	— S D : 1 0 : 011(612) [1057]
2:5	— E P : 1 0 : 006(493) [0829]
	— S D : 1 0 : 012(613) [1057]
	— S D : 1 0 : 014(613) [1057]
2:6	— T R : 0 0 : 010(321) [0505]
	— T R : 0 0 : 010(321) [0505]
2:14	— S D : 1 0 : 013(613) [1057]
2:16	— A P : 0 4 : 093(120) [0149]
	— E P : 0 3 : 010(474) [0795]
	— S D : 0 6 : 016(566) [0967]
2:17	— A P : 0 4 : 317(156) [0209]
	— A P : 1 5 : 012(216) [0317]
2:19	— A P : 1 2 : 033(186) [0259]
2:21	— A P : 0 4 : 029(111) [0129]
3:2	— S D : 0 6 : 011(566) [0965]
	— S D : 0 6 : 016(566) [0967]
3:10	— S D : 0 6 : 016(566) [0967]
3:13	— A P : 0 4 : 179(131) [0171]
3:14	— A L : 0 5 : 003(031) [0045]
	— A P : 0 4 : 127(125) [0157]
	— S D : 0 6 : 011(566) [0965]
3:15	— A P : 1 5 : 012(216) [0317]
3:18	— A P : 0 4 : 084(119) [0145]
3:22	— A P : 0 4 : 084(119) [0145]
	— A P : 1 2 : 081(194) [0275]
3:24	— A P : 0 4 : 022(110) [0127]
	— S D : 0 5 : 024(563) [0961]
3:27	— S D : 0 2 : 067(534) [0907]
4:9	— A P : 0 4 : 393(167) [0225]
5:1	— A G : 2 8 : 052(089) [0091]
	— A P : 1 5 : 031(219) [0323]
	— A P : 2 8 : 015(283) [0447]
	— E P : 1 0 : 006(493) [0829]
	— S D : 1 0 : 011(612) [1055]
5:4	— A G : 2 7 : 041(077) [0081]
	— A P : 0 4 : 030(111) [0129]
	— A P : 1 5 : 008(216) [0317]
	— A P : 2 7 : 011(270) [0423]
	— A P : 2 7 : 012(271) [0423]
5:6	— A P : 0 4 : 111(123) [0155]
	— E P : 0 3 : 011(474) [0795]
5:7	— A P : 0 4 : 393(167) [0225]
5:9	— S D : 0 3 : 007(540) [0917]
5:11	— A P : 0 4 : 029(111) [0129]
5:17	— A P : 0 4 : 169(130) [0169]
	— A P : 0 4 : 319(156) [0209]
	— E P : 0 4 : 013(477) [0799]
	— E P : 0 6 : 004(480) [0805]
	— S D : 0 2 : 017(524) [0887]
	— S D : 0 2 : 064(533) [0907]
	— S D : 0 2 : 084(537) [0913]
	— S D : 0 6 : 008(565) [0965]
5:19, 20	— L C : 0 5 : 075(455) [0771]
5:21	— S D : 0 4 : 032(556) [0947]
5:22	— S D : 0 4 : 009(552) [0941]
5:24	— S D : 0 4 : 019(554) [0945]
6:6, 7	— S C : 0 9 : 003(354) [0561]
6:14	— E P : 0 6 : 004(480) [0807]
6:15	— S D : 0 2 : 026(526) [0891]
6:15	— S D : 0 2 : 026(526) [0891]

Ephesians

1:4	— E P : 1 1 : 007(495) [0833]
	— S D : 1 1 : 010(618) [1067]
	— S D : 1 1 : 019(619) [1069]
	— S D : 1 1 : 043(623) [1077]
	— S D : 1 1 : 045(624) [1079]
	— S D : 1 1 : 065(627) [1083]
	— S D : 1 1 : 088(631) [1093]
1:4, 5	— S D : 1 1 : 005(617) [1065]
1:4ff	— S D : 1 1 : 014(619) [1069]
1:5, 6	— S D : 1 1 : 087(631) [1093]
1:6	— S D : 1 1 : 065(627) [1083]
1:7	— A P : 0 4 : 273(148) [0199]
1:9	— S D : 1 1 : 012(618) [1067]
1:9, 10	— S D : 1 1 : 026(620) [1071]
1:11	— E P : 1 1 : 015(496) [0835]
1:11	— S D : 1 1 : 030(621) [1073]
1:13	— S D : 1 1 : 030(621) [1073]
1:13, 14	— S D : 1 1 : 012(618) [1067]
	— S D : 1 1 : 012(618) [1067]
1:15ff	— S D : 1 1 : 012(618) [1067]
1:17, 18	— S D : 0 2 : 015(523) [0887]
1:21	— S D : 0 8 : 012(593) [1019]
	— S D : 0 8 : 051(601) [1033]
1:22	— S 2 : 0 4 : 009(300) [0473]
	— S D : 0 8 : 055(601) [1033]
1:22,23	— A P : 0 7 : 005(169) [0227]
2:1	— S D : 0 2 : 010(522) [0885]
2:2	— A P : 0 7 : 016(171) [0231]
	— A P : 1 8 : 005(225) [0335]
	— S D : 0 2 : 007(521) [0883]
2:3	— S D : 0 1 : 006(509) [0861]
2:5	— E P : 0 2 : 003(470) [0787]
	— S D : 0 2 : 010(522) [0885]
	— S D : 0 2 : 061(533) [0905]
	— S D : 0 3 : 020(542) [0921]
2:8	— A L : 2 0 : 011(042) [0055]
	— A P : 0 4 : 087(120) [0147]
	— A P : 0 4 : 093(120) [0149]
	— A P : 1 5 : 006(216) [0317]
	— S D : 0 2 : 026(526) [0891]
2:8, 9	— A G : 2 0 : 011(042) [0055]
	— A P : 0 4 : 073(117) [0141]
2:8-9	— E P : 0 4 : 007(476) [0799]
2:9	— E P : 0 3 : 010(474) [0795]
2:10	— S D : 0 2 : 026(526) [0891]
	— S D : 0 2 : 039(528) [0895]
	— S D : 0 4 : 007(552) [0941]
	— S D : 0 6 : 012(566) [0967]
4:4, 5	— A G : 0 7 : 004(032) [0047]
4:5, 6	— A L : 0 7 : 004(032) [0047]
4:8	— T R : 0 0 : 067(331) [0523]
4:10	— E P : 0 8 : 016(489) [0821]
	— S D : 0 8 : 027(596) [1025]
4:11, 12	— T R : 0 0 : 067(331) [0523]
4:15	— S 2 : 0 4 : 009(300) [0473]
4:17, 18	— S D : 0 2 : 010(522) [0883]
4:28	— A P : 1 2 : 169(209) [0305]
5:3-11	— S D : 1 1 : 042(623) [1077]
5:5	— S D : 0 4 : 032(556) [0947]
5:8	— S D : 0 2 : 010(522) [0885]
5:9	— A P : 0 2 : 020(103) [0111]
	— S D : 0 4 : 009(552) [0941]
5:18	— S D : 1 1 : 042(623) [1077]
5:22	— L C : 0 1 : 220(395) [0643]
5:25	— S 2 : 0 4 : 009(300) [0473]
	— L C : 0 1 : 220(395) [0643]
5:25-27	— A P : 0 7 : 005(169) [0229]
5:26	S 3 : 0 5 : 001(310) [0491]
5:30	— S D : 0 8 : 078(607) [1045]
6:1-3	— S C : 0 9 : 009(356) [0563]
6:2, 3	— A P : 0 4 : 197(134) [0175]
	— L C : 0 1 : 133(383) [0619]
6:4	— S C : 0 9 : 008(356) [0563]
6:5-8	— S C : 0 9 : 010(356) [0563]
6:9	— S C : 0 9 : 011(356) [0563]
6:11	— L C : P R : 014(360) [0571]
6:16	— L C : P R : 014(360) [0571]
	— L C : 0 3 : 104(434) [0727]

Philippians

1:6	— S D : 1 1 : 042(623) [1077]
1:6ff	— S D : 1 1 : 032(621) [1073]
1:9, 10	— S D : 0 2 : 015(523) [0887]
1:28	— S D : 0 4 : 038(557) [0951]
1:29	— S D : 0 2 : 026(526) [0891]
2:7	— E P : 0 8 : 016(489) [0821]
	— S D : 0 8 : 026(596) [1025]

Continued ▶

Philippians, *Continued*

2:13	— S D : 0 2 : 014(523) [0885]
	— S D : 0 2 : 026(526) [0891]
	— S D : 0 2 : 039(528) [0895]
2:25	— A P : 2 4 : 082(264) [0411]
3:7ff	— S D : 0 4 : 037(557) [0951]
3:9	— S D : 0 3 : 017(542) [0921]
3:20	— A G : 2 8 : 016(083) [0085]
	— A L : 2 8 : 016(083) [0085]
4:3	— E P : 1 1 : 007(495) [0833]
	— S D : 1 1 : 013(619) [1067]
	— S D : 1 1 : 025(620) [1071]

Colossians

1	— S D : P R : 007(502) [0849]
1:9	— S D : 0 2 : 015(523) [0887]
1:11	— S D : 0 2 : 015(523) [0887]
1:13	— A P : 0 4 : 366(163) [0221]
1:18	— S 2 : 0 4 : 009(300) [0473]
1:22	— S D : 0 4 : 034(557) [0949]
1:27	— S D : 0 8 : 096(609) [1049]
2	— S D : P R : 007(502) [0849]
2:3	— E P : 0 8 : 037(491) [0825]
	— S D : 0 8 : 074(606) [1043]
2:8	— A P : 0 4 : 393(167) [0225]
2:9	— E P : 0 8 : 034(491) [0825]
	— S D : 0 7 : 036(575) [0985]
	— S D : 0 8 : 030(597) [1025]
	— S D : 0 8 : 034(597) [1027]
	— S D : 0 8 : 064(603) [1037]
	— S D : 0 8 : 070(605) [1041]
2:10	— A P : 0 4 : 179(131) [0171]
2:11	— A P : 1 2 : 046(188) [0263]
2:12	— A P : 0 4 : 250(143) [0191]
	— A P : 1 2 : 046(188) [0263]
2:13	— S D : 0 2 : 010(522) [0885]
2:14	— A P : 0 4 : 103(122) [0151]
	— A P : 0 4 : 350(161) [0217]
	— A P : 1 2 : 048(188) [0265]
2:16	— A G : 2 6 : 025(067) [0073]
	— A L : 2 6 : 025(067) [0073]
	— A G : 2 8 : 044(088) [0089]
	— A L : 2 8 : 044(088) [0089]
	— A P : 2 7 : 014(271) [0423]
	— S D : 1 0 : 013(613) [1057]
2:16, 17	— A P : 0 4 : 393(167) [0225]
	— A P : 0 7 : 035(175) [0239]
	— A P : 1 5 : 030(219) [0323]
2:16f	— L C : 0 1 : 082(376) [0603]
2:17	— A P : 2 4 : 036(257) [0397]
2:18	— A P : 2 3 : 046(246) [0377]
2:20, 21	— A L : 2 6 : 025(068) [0073]
2:20-23	— A G : 2 8 : 045(088) [0089]
	— A P : 0 7 : 035(175) [0239]
	— A P : 2 8 : 010(282) [0447]
2:23	— A P : 1 5 : 022(218) [0321]
3:4	— S D : 0 7 : 099(586) [1005]
3:6	— S D : 0 4 : 032(556) [0947]
3:10	— A P : 0 2 : 020(103) [0111]
	— A P : 0 4 : 351(161) [0217]
3:13	— A P : 0 4 : 241(141) [0187]
3:14	— A P : 0 4 : 231(139) [0183]
3:18f	— L C : 0 1 : 220(395) [0643]
3:19	— S C : 0 9 : 006(355) [0561]
3:21	— S C : 0 9 : 008(356) [0563]
4:2	— L C : 0 3 : 004(420) [0699]

1 Thessalonians

4:4	— A P : 2 3 : 043(245) [0375]
	— A P : 2 3 : 065(248) [0381]
5:12, 13	— S C : 0 9 : 003(355) [0561]
5:17	— L C : 0 3 : 004(420) [0699]

2 Thessalonians

2:3, 4	— T R : 0 0 : 039(327) [0515]
2:4	— A P : 0 7 : 004(169) [0227]
	— S 2 : 0 4 : 011(300) [0475]
2:8	— S 2 : 0 4 : 015(301) [0475]
2:13-15	— S D : 1 1 : 012(618) [1067]
2:16, 17	— A P : 2 1 : 018(231) [0347]

1 Timothy

1:5	— A P : 0 4 : 245(142) [0189]
1:9	— A P : 0 4 : 022(110) [0127]
	— S D : 0 6 : 005(564) [0963]
2:1	— S C : 0 9 : 014(356) [0563]
	— L C : 0 3 : 004(420) [0699]
2:1, 2	— S C : 0 9 : 005(355) [0561]
2:5	— A G : 2 1 : 002(047) [0057]
	— S D : P R : 007(502) [0849]

2:6	— E P : 1 1 : 010(495) [0833]
2:15	— A P : 2 3 : 032(243) [0373]
3:2	— A G : 2 3 : 011(052) [0063]
	— A L : 2 3 : 011(052) [0063]
3:2-6	— S C : 0 9 : 002(354) [0561]
3:9	— S D : P R : 014(506) [0855]
3:15	— A P : 0 7 : 020(171) [0233]
	— A P : 0 7 : 027(173) [0235]
3:16	— E P : 0 8 : 018(489) [0823]
	— S D : 0 8 : 033(597) [1027]
4:1	— A G : 2 3 : 022(055) [0063]
	— A G : 2 6 : 029(068) [0075]
	— A L : 2 6 : 029(068) [0075]
	— A G : 2 8 : 049(089) [0091]
	— A P : 0 7 : 040(176) [0241]
	— A P : 1 5 : 004(215) [0315]
4:1	— A P : 2 3 : 063(248) [0381]
	— A P : 2 7 : 026(273) [0429]
	— T R : 0 0 : 042(328) [0517]
4:1-3	— A P : 2 3 : 058(247) [0379]
	— S 3 : 1 1 : 003(315) [0499]
4:2, 3	— A P : 0 4 : 393(167) [0225]
4:3	— A G : 2 3 : 022(055) [0063]
	— A L : 2 3 : 022(055) [0063]
	— A G : 2 6 : 029(068) [0075]
	— A L : 2 6 : 029(068) [0075]
4:5	— A P : 2 3 : 030(243) [0371]
4:8	— A P : 2 7 : 021(272) [0427]
5:5, 6	— S C : 0 9 : 013(356) [0563]
5:8	— A P : 2 7 : 067(280) [0441]
5:9	— A P : 2 7 : 066(280) [0441]
5:11, 12	— A P : 2 7 : 064(280) [0441]
5:14	— A P : 2 7 : 067(280) [0441]
5:17	— L C : 0 1 : 161(387) [0627]
5:17,18	— S C : 0 9 : 003(354) [0561]
6:15	— S D : 0 7 : 099(586) [1005]

2 Timothy

1:9	— S D : 1 1 : 043(623) [1077]
	— S D : 1 1 : 045(624) [1079]
1:9-11	— S D : 1 1 : 012(620) [1071]
1:13	— S D : 0 4 : 036(557) [0949]
2:15	— A P : 0 4 : 188(133) [0173]
	— E P : 0 5 : 002(478) [0801]
	— S D : 0 5 : 001(558) [0951]
2:19	— S D : 1 1 : 090(631) [1093]
2:21	— S D : 1 1 : 082(630) [1089]
2:24	— S D : P R : 014(506) [0855]
2:25	— S D : 0 2 : 026(526) [0891]
2:26	— S D : 0 2 : 007(521) [0883]
3:16	— S D : P R : 014(506) [0855]
	— S D : 0 6 : 014(566) [0967]
	— S D : 1 1 : 012(618) [1067]
	— S D : 1 1 : 012(618) [1067]
4:3, 4	— P R : P R : 005(004) [0009]
4:8	— A P : 0 4 : 363(162) [0219]

Titus

1:5-7	— T R : 0 0 : 062(330) [0523]
1:9	— S D : P R : 014(506) [0855]
1:14	— A G : 2 8 : 046(088) [0089]
	— A L : 2 8 : 046(088) [0089]
	— S 3 : 1 5 : 001(316) [0501]
1:15	— A P : 2 3 : 034(244) [0373]
	— A P : 2 3 : 041(245) [0375]
	— A P : 2 3 : 064(248) [0381]
2:14	— A P : 1 2 : 122(200) [0289]
3	— S D : 0 2 : 020(524) [0889]
3:1	— S C : 0 9 : 005(355) [0561]
3:5	— L C : 0 4 : 027(440) [0739]
	— E P : 0 3 : 010(474) [0795]
	— S D : 0 3 : 019(542) [0921]
3:5, 6	— S D : 0 2 : 026(526) [0891]
3:5-8	— S C : 0 4 : 010(349) [0551]
3:10	— T R : 0 0 : 041(328) [0517]

Philemon

14	— S D : 0 4 : 017(554) [0943]

Hebrews

1:3	— S D : 0 8 : 074(606) [1043]
2:7, 8	— S D : 0 8 : 070(605) [1041]
2:8	— S D : 0 8 : 055(601) [1033]
2:14-17	— E P : 0 1 : 005(466) [0781]
2:17	— S D : 0 1 : 043(516) [0873]
3:14	— S D : 0 4 : 030(555) [0947]
	— S D : 1 1 : 032(621) [1073]
4:2	— S D : 1 1 : 039(623) [1075]
4:7	— S D : 1 1 : 039(623) [1075]
4:14-16	— A P : 0 4 : 082(118) [0145]

4:16	— L C : 0 4 : 086(446) [0753]
5:1	— A P : 2 4 : 052(259) [0403]
	— A P : 2 4 : 053(259) [0403]
7-9	— A P : 1 3 : 010(212) [0311]
9:28	— A G : 2 4 : 027(059) [0067]
10:4	— A P : 2 4 : 022(253) [0391]
10:5-16	— A P : 2 4 : 020(252) [0389]
10:10	— A G : 2 4 : 027(059) [0067]
	— A P : 2 4 : 022(253) [0391]
10:14	— A G : 2 4 : 027(059) [0067]
10:26	— S D : 1 1 : 042(623) [1077]
10:29	— S D : 1 1 : 083(630) [1091]
11:1	— A G : 2 0 : 025(044) [0057]
	— A P : 0 4 : 312(155) [0207]
11:4	— A P : 0 4 : 202(134) [0175]
	— S D : 0 6 : 022(567) [0969]
11:6	— A P : 0 4 : 256(144) [0193]
	— A P : 0 4 : 269(147) [0197]
	— A P : 0 4 : 372(164) [0221]
	— A P : 1 8 : 006(225) [0335]
11:8	— S D : 0 3 : 033(545) [0927]
12:8	— S D : 0 6 : 009(565) [0965]
12:25	— E P : 1 1 : 012(496) [0835]
13:15	— A P : 2 4 : 026(254) [0391]
	— S D : 0 6 : 022(567) [0969]
13:17	— A P : 2 8 : 020(284) [0449]
	— S C : 0 9 : 003(355) [0561]
13:21	— E P : 0 6 : 004(480) [0807]

James

1:6	— L C : 0 3 : 004(420) [0699]
1:6, 7	— L C : 0 3 : 123(436) [0731]
1:17	— S D : 0 2 : 026(526) [0891]
	— S D : 0 8 : 049(600) [1031]
1:18	— A P : 0 4 : 247(142) [0191]
2:19	— A G : 2 0 : 023(044) [0055]
	— A P : 0 4 : 303(154) [0205]
	— A P : 0 4 : 337(159) [0215]
	— A P : 1 2 : 045(187) [0263]
2:22	— A P : 0 4 : 252(143) [0191]
2:24	— A P : 0 4 : 244(141) [0189]
	— S D : 0 3 : 042(546) [0931]
3:5	— L C : 0 1 : 291(404) [0663]
5:13	— L C : 0 3 : 004(420) [0699]
5:16	— A P : 1 2 : 109(198) [0283]

1 Peter

1:2	— A P : 2 4 : 036(257) [0397]
1:5	— A P : 0 4 : 386(166) [0225]
	— S D : 0 4 : 034(557) [0949]
1:9	— A P : 0 4 : 354(161) [0217]
	— S D : 0 4 : 034(557) [0949]
1:12	— S D : 0 8 : 030(597) [1025]
2:4, 5	— A P : 0 4 : 239(141) [0187]
2:5	— A P : 2 4 : 026(254) [0391]
	— S D : 0 6 : 022(567) [0969]
2:6	— A P : 0 4 : 239(141) [0187]
	— A P : 1 2 : 065(191) [0271]
2:9	— T R : 0 0 : 069(331) [0523]
2:11	— S D : 0 2 : 084(537) [0913]
2:13, 14	— S C : 0 9 : 005(355) [0561]
3:1	— S C : 0 9 : 007(355) [0563]
3:6	— S C : 0 9 : 007(355) [0563]
3:7	— S C : 0 9 : 006(355) [0561]
3:18	— S D : 0 8 : 037(598) [1027]
4:1	— S D : 0 8 : 037(598) [1027]
4:8	— A P : 0 4 : 238(140) [0187]
	— A P : 0 4 : 238(140) [0187]
	— L C : 0 3 : 004(420) [0699]
4:17	— A P : 1 2 : 151(206) [0299]
5:1	— T R : 0 0 : 062(330) [0523]
5:2	— A G : 2 8 : 076(094) [0095]
	— S D : 0 4 : 017(554) [0943]
5:3	— T R : 0 0 : 011(321) [0507]
5:5, 6	— S C : 0 9 : 012(356) [0563]

2 Peter

1:4	— S D : 0 8 : 034(597) [1027]
1:10	— A P : 2 0 : 012(228) [0341]
	— E P : 1 1 : 014(496) [0835]
	— S D : 0 4 : 033(556) [0947]
1:21	— S 3 : 0 8 : 013(313) [0497]
2:1	— P R : P R : 005(004) [0009]
	— A P : 2 3 : 005(239) [0365]
2:1-10	— S D : P R : 007(502) [0849]
2:2ff	— E P : 1 1 : 012(496) [0835]
2:10	— S D : 1 1 : 042(623) [1077]
	— S D : 1 1 : 073(628) [1087]

Continued ▶

2 Peter, *Continued*

2:20	— S D : 1 1 :	083(630) [1091]
3:9	— S D : 1 1 :	028(621) [1071]
	— S D : 1 1 :	032(621) [1073]
	— S D : 1 1 :	081(629) [1089]
	— S D : 1 1 :	084(630) [1091]

1 John

1:7	— S D : 0 3 :	057(550) [0935]
	— S D : 0 8 :	059(602) [1035]
	— S D : 1 1 :	028(620) [1071]
1:8	— A P : 0 4 :	328(158) [0211]
	— S 3 : 0 3 :	045(310) [0491]
2:1	— A G : 2 1 :	004(047) [0059]
	— A L : 2 1 :	004(047) [0059]
2:2	— E P : 1 1 :	010(495) [0833]
	— S D : 1 1 :	028(620) [1071]
2:12	— A P : 0 4 :	273(148) [0199]
3:8	— A P : 0 4 :	139(126) [0161]
	— S D : 0 1 :	007(510) [0861]
3:9	— S 3 : 0 3 :	045(310) [0491]
3:14	— S D : 0 3 :	027(543) [0923]
4:1	— P R : P R :	005(004) [0009]
4:11	— S D : 0 4 :	014(553) [0943]
4:19	— A P : 0 4 :	141(126) [0161]
5:10	— A P : 1 2 :	062(190) [0269]
	— A P : 1 2 :	088(195) [0277]
5:10-12	— A P : 0 4 :	297(153) [0205]
5:18	— S 3 : 0 3 :	045(310) [0491]

2 John

1	— T R : 0 0 :	062(330) [0523]

3 John

	— T R : 0 0 :	062(330) [0523]

Jude

4-8	— S D : P R :	007(502) [0849]
20	— L C : 0 3 :	004(420) [0699]

Revelation

3:5	— E P : 1 1 :	007(495) [0833]
	— S D : 1 1 :	013(619) [1067]
4:11	— S D : 0 1 :	034(514) [0869]
10:1	— S 3 : 0 3 :	030(308) [0487]
10:3	— S 2 : 0 4 :	004(299) [0473]
20:15	— E P : 1 1 :	007(495) [0833]
	— S D : 1 1 :	013(619) [1067]
	— S D : 1 1 :	025(620) [1071]